W9-BDR-479

The World Book Dictionary

Clarence L. Barnhart, *Editor in Chief*

Robert K. Barnhart, *Managing Editor*

Prepared in Cooperation with Field Enterprises Educational Corporation

Publishers of THE WORLD BOOK ENCYCLOPEDIA

William H. Nault, *Editorial Director*

Robert O. Zeleny, *Executive Editor*

Donald H. Ludgin, *Associate Editor*

L-Z

Volume Two

A THORNDIKE-BARNHART DICTIONARY *Published Exclusively for*

FIELD ENTERPRISES EDUCATIONAL CORPORATION

Chicago London Rome Sydney Toronto

1971 Edition

The World Book Dictionary

Printed in the United States of America
ISBN 0-7166-0271-7
Library of Congress Catalog Card Number 78-130801

Contents

Volume One: A-K

Volume Two: L-Z

Complete Pronunciation Key

The pronunciation of each word is shown just following the word, in this way: **ab·bre·vi·ate** (ə brē′vē āt). The symbols within parentheses are pronounced as in the words in the key below.

Diacritical marks appear above some of the vowel symbols listed below. Here are their names, and the vowels with which they appear:

circumflex (sėr′kəm fleks)—the mark over the ô, as in order.

dieresis (dī er′ə sis)—two dots over the ä, as in father, or the ü, as in rule.

macron (mā′kron)—the long mark over the ā, as in age; the ē, as in equal; the ī, as in ice; and the ō, as in open.

single dot—over the ė in the ėr, as in term, and over the u̇, as in full.

tilde (til′də)—the curved mark over the ã, as in care.

These diacritics have arbitrary values and do not necessarily correspond to their values elsewhere.

The stress mark ′ is placed after a syllable with primary or strong accent, as in the pronunciation of *abbreviate,* the example above. The stress mark ′ after a syllable shows a secondary or lighter accent, as in **ab·bre·vi·a·tion** (ə brē′vē a′shən).

Some words, taken from foreign languages, are spoken with sounds that otherwise do not occur in English. Symbols for these sounds are given at the end of the table below as "Foreign Sounds."

a	hat, cap	j	jam, enjoy	u	cup, butter
ā	age, face	k	kind, seek	u̇	full, put
ã	care, air	l	land, coal	ü	rule, move
ä	father, far	m	me, am		
		n	no, in	v	very, save
b	bad, rob	ng	long, bring	w	will, woman
ch	child, much			y	young, yet
d	did, red	o	hot, rock	z	zero, breeze
		ō	open, go	zh	measure, seizure
e	let, best	ô	order, all		
ē	equal, see	oi	oil, voice	ə	represents:
ėr	term, learn	ou	house, out		a in about
					e in taken
f	fat, if	p	paper, cup		i in pencil
g	go, bag	r	run, try		o in lemon
h	he, how	s	say, yes		u in circus
		sh	she, rush		
		t	tell, it		
i	it, pin	th	thin, both		
ī	ice, five	ᴛʜ	then, smooth		

Foreign Sounds

Y	as in French *du.* Pronounce ē with the lips rounded as for English ü in *rule.*
œ	as in French *peu.* Pronounce ā with the lips rounded as for ō.
N	as in French *bon.* The N is not pronounced, but shows that the vowel before it is nasal.
H	as in German *ach.* Pronounce k without closing the breath passage.
ȧ	as in French *ami.* The quality of this vowel is midway between the a of *hat* and the ä of *far,* but closer to the former.

Etymology Key

The origin of a word is its etymology. This dictionary includes etymologies under main entries. The etymologies are placed at the end of the definition of the entry. Etymologies are enclosed in square brackets.

ba·zoo·ka . . . [American English < name of a trombome-like instrument invented and named by comedian Bob Burns]

Two symbols are used in describing etymologies: < means "derived from; taken from."

ca·jole . . . [< French *cajoler*] . . . .

+ means "and."

clyp·e·i·form . . . [< Latin *clypeus* round shield + English *-form*]

Roman 100's A.D. — Greek 600's B.C. — Phoenician 1000's B.C. — Semitic 1500's B.C. — Egyptian 3000's B.C.

Ll Ll *Ll* *Ll*

L or **l** (el), *n., pl.* **L's** or **Ls, l's** or **ls. 1.** the 12th letter of the English alphabet. **2.** any sound represented by the letter. **3.** the Roman numeral symbol for 50. In the ancient Roman notation, L with a stroke above represented 50,000. **4.** the twelfth, or more usually eleventh, of a series (either I or J being omitted).

L[1] (el), *n., pl.* **L's.** a thing shaped like the letter L, as an extension to a building at right angles with the main part or a joint connecting two pipes at right angles.

L[2] (el), *n.* an elevated railroad: *The Third Avenue "L" gave up the ghost last Thursday, in its seventy-seventh year, leaving no descendants* (New Yorker). Also, **el.** [short for *elevated*]

L- or **l-,** *combining form.* levo- (left-handed) in configuration: *l-glyceraldehyde = levo-glyceraldehyde.* [< *l*(evo-)]

l., an abbreviation for the following:
1. book (Latin, *liber*).
2. lake.
3. land.
4. latitude.
5. law.
6. leaf.
7. league.
8. left.
9. length.
10. *pl.* **ll.** line.
11. link.
12. lira or liras; lire (Italian money).
13. liter.
14. locus.
15. lodge (of a fraternal order).
16. low.

L (no period), an abbreviation or symbol for the following:
1. *Electricity.* coefficient of self-inductance.
2. Large (especially of garment sizes).
3. Latin.
4. *British.* learner.
5. Lebanese (as in £L, the Lebanese pound).
6. *Physics.* length.
7. Libra (constellation).
8. pound (Latin, *libra*).
9. *Geodetics.* longitude.
10. luminosity (of stellar bodies).

L., an abbreviation for the following:
1. book (Latin, *liber*).
2. Lady.
3. Lake.
4. Latin.
5. latitude.
6. law.
7. league.
8. left (in stage directions).
9. length.
10. Liberal (Party).
11. Licentiate.
12. line.
13. link.
14. *Botany.* Linnaeus.
15. lira or liras; lire (Italian money).
16. lodge (of a fraternal order).
17. London.
18. Low: *LG = Low German.*

£., pound or pounds sterling (in British Commonwealth money).

la[1] (lä), *n. Music.* the sixth tone of the diatonic scale. [< Latin *labii.* See GAMUT.]

la[2] (lä, lô), *interj. Archaic.* an exclamation of surprise. [variant of *lo*]

la[3] (lȧ), *French.* the (feminine singular definite article).

La (no period), lanthanum (chemical element).

La., Louisiana.

L.A., an abbreviation for the following:
1. Legislative Assembly.
2. Library Association.
3. Local Authority.
4. Los Angeles.

laa·ger (lä′gər), *n., v.,* **-gered, -ger·ing.** —*n.* a camp or encampment, especially (among the South African Boers) a camp in the open country protected by a circle of wagons: *Captain Mansell, with the native police force, has been obliged to go into laager at Ekowe for safety* (The Standard). —*v.t., v.i.* to arrange or encamp in a laager: *The waggons were not 'laagered' or drawn up so close as to make it difficult to force the camp* (Daily News). Also, **lager.** [< Afrikaans *laager,* probably < German *Lager*]

lab (lab), *n. Informal.* laboratory.

lab., 1. a. labor. **b.** laborer. **2.** laboratory.

Lab., 1. Labrador. **2.** *British.* **a.** Labour (Party). **b.** Labourite.

LAB (no periods), low-altitude bombing.

La·ban (lā′bən), *n.* (in the Bible) the father of Leah and Rachel, the wives of Jacob. Genesis 29: 13-29.

La·ban·o·ta·tion (lä′bə nō tā′shən, lā′-), *n. Trademark.* a method of noting and recording dance movements and arrangements. [< Rudolf von *Laban,* a Hungarian-German teacher of the dance, who devised and wrote about the method in 1938]

La·ban system (lä′bən, lā′bən), Labanotation.

lab·a·rum (lab′ər əm), *n., pl.* **-a·rums, -a·ra** (-ər ə). **1.** the military banner of Constantine the Great after his conversion and of later Christian emperors of Rome, bearing Christian symbols. **2.** (in the Roman Catholic Church) a banner or standard borne in ecclesiastical processions. **3.** any symbolic banner or standard. [< Late Latin *labarum* imperial banner < Latin, a military banner < Greek *lábaron*]

lab·ba (lab′ə), *n.* the paca. [< a native name]

lab·da·num (lab′də nəm), *n.* a soft, dark-colored gum resin that exudes from various rockroses, much used in perfumery, cosmetics, and formerly in medicines. Also, **ladanum.** [alteration of Latin *lādanum* (influenced by Greek *lábda,* variant of *lámbda* L) < Greek *lḗdanon* gum from the *lēdon* mastic]

lab·e·fac·tion (lab′ə fak′shən), *n.* a shaking; weakening; overthrow; downfall. [< Late Latin *labefactiō, -ōnis* < Latin *labefacere* shake, loosen < *labāre* to totter + *facere* make]

la·bel (lā′bəl), *n., v.,* **-beled, -bel·ing** or (*especially British*) **-belled, -bel·ling.** —*n.* **1.** a slip of paper, cardboard, metal, or other material attached to anything and marked to show what or whose it is, or where it is to go: *Can you read the label on the box?* **2.** a short phrase used to describe some person, thing, or idea: *In winter, Chicago deserves its label of "the Windy City."* **3.** a narrow strip of material attached to a document to carry the seal. **4.** *U.S. Informal.* a company producing phonograph records: *A new label, Washington Records, has made a noteworthy initial release* (Better Listening). **5.** *Architecture.* a dripstone or other molding across the top of a door or window, especially one that also extends downward at the sides. **6.** a narrow band or strip of linen, cloth, etc., as a fillet, ribbon, or tassel, or one of the strips that hang down from a bishop's miter: *a knit night-cap . . . With two long labels button'd to his chin* (Bishop Joseph Hall). **7.** *Heraldry.* a narrow band with pendants, used especially to distinguish the oldest son during his father's life.
—*v.t.* **1.** to put or write a label on: *The bottle is labeled "Poison."* **2.** to put in a class; call; name: *to label a man a liar.* **3.** to infuse or treat (a substance) with a radioactive chemical or isotope so that its course or activity can be noted.
[< Old French *label;* origin uncertain]
—**Syn.** *v.t.* **2.** designate, tag.

la·bel·er (lā′bə lər), *n.* a person or thing that affixes labels to anything.

la·bel·late (lə bel′āt), *adj.* labiate; lipped. [< Latin *labellum* + English *-ate*[1]]

la belle dame sans mer·ci (lȧ bel dȧm′ säɴ mer sē′), *French.* the fair lady without mercy.

la belle é·poque (lȧ bel′ ā pôk′), *French.* **1.** the period at the turn of the century: *The Ashenden series . . . are still unusually good spy stories, but now they seem overdressed, in the manner of la belle époque* (Saturday Night). **2.** (literally) the beautiful epoch.

la belle France (lȧ bel′ fräɴs′), *French.* the beautiful France; fair France.

la·bel·ler (lā′bə lər), *n. Especially British.* labeler.

la·bel·loid (lə bel′oid), *adj.* shaped like a lip or labellum.

la·bel·lum (lə bel′əm), *n.,pl.* **-bel·la** (-bel′ə). *Botany.* a part of the perianth of flowers, as the middle petal of an orchid, usually different in shape and color from the other two, and suggesting a lip. [< Latin *labellum* (diminutive) < *labium* lip]

la·bi·a (lā′bē ə), *n.* the plural of **labium.**

la·bi·al (lā′bē əl), *adj.* **1.** of the lips: . . . *the labial melody with which the Typee girls carry on an ordinary conversation* (Herman Melville). **2.** having to do with or like a labium. **3.** *Phonetics.* made by closing, nearly closing, or rounding the lips. **4.** *Music.* having tones produced by the impact of an air current on the edge of a lip, as a flute or an organ flue pipe.
—*n.* **1.** *Phonetics.* a labial sound. *B, p,* and *m* are labials. **2.** *Music.* a flue pipe, as distinguished from a reed pipe.
[< Medieval Latin *labialis* < Latin *labium* lip]

la·bi·al·ism (lā′bē ə liz′əm), *n. Phonetics.* a tendency to labialize sounds; labial pronunciation.

la·bi·al·i·za·tion (lā′bē ə lə zā′shən), *n.* conversion to a labial.

la·bi·al·ize (lā′bē ə līz), *v.t.,* **-ized, -iz·ing.** *Phonetics.* **1.** to give a labial character to (a sound). **2.** to round (a vowel).

la·bi·al·ly (lā′bē ə lē), *adv.* by means of the lips.

labia ma·jo·ra (mə jôr′ə, -jōr′-), *Anatomy.* the outer folds at the opening of the vulva. [< Latin *labia,* plural of *labium* lip, and *majora,* neuter plural of *major* greater]

labia mi·no·ra (mi nôr′ə, -nōr′-), *Anatomy.* the inner folds at the opening of the vulva. [< Latin *minora,* neuter plural of *minor* lesser]

la·bi·ate (lā′bē āt, -it), *adj.* **1.** having one or more liplike parts. **2.** *Botany.* belonging to the mint family. —*n.* a labiate plant. [< New Latin *labiatus* < Latin *labium* lip]

Labiate Corolla

la·bi·at·ed (lā′bē ā′tid), *adj.* labiate.

la·bile (lā′bəl), *adj.* **1.** changing easily; plastic; adaptable. **2.** apt to lapse or change; unstable: *a labile chemical compound, a labile fund.* **3.** (of electrodes used in medical diagnosis) moving over the part treated. [< Latin *lābilis* < *lābī* to slip, lapse]

la·bil·i·ty (lə bil′ə tē), *n., pl.* **-ties.** instability of form or character.

la·bi·li·za·tion (lā′bə lə zā′shən), *n.* a making or being unstable.

la·bi·lize (lā′bə līz), *v.t.,* **-lized, -liz·ing.** to make unstable.

labio-, *combining form.* made with the lips and —: *Labiodental = made with the lips and teeth.* [< Latin *labium* lip]

la·bi·o·den·tal (lā′bē ō den′təl), *Phonetics.* —*adj.* made with the lower lip and the upper teeth; made with the lips and teeth. —*n.* a sound made in this way. *F* and *v* are labiodentals.

la·bi·o·na·sal (lā′bē ō nā′zəl), *Phonetics.* —*adj.* made with the lips, but with the breath stream passing out through the nose. —*n.* a sound made in this way. *M* is a labionasal.

la·bi·o·ve·lar (lā′bē ō vē′lər), *Phonetics.* —*adj.* made with rounded lips and with the back of the tongue toward or against the soft palate. —*n.* a sound made in this way. *W* is a labiovelar.

la·bi·um (lā′bē əm), *n., pl.* **-bi·a. 1.** a lip or liplike part. **2.** *Botany.* a portion of the corolla of certain flowers, especially the lower part, shaped to suggest a lip. **3.** *Zoology.* the organ that constitutes the lower lip of an insect, derived from the second pair of maxillae. **4.** the inner margin of the opening of a gastropod's shell. [< Latin *labium* lip]

lab·lab (lab′lab), *n.* **1.** a vine of the pea family, with edible seeds, native to India but widely cultivated in other warm countries. 2. any of various related species. [< Arabic *lablāb*]

la·bor (lā′bər), *n.* **1.** work; toil: *Labor disgraces no man* (Ulysses S. Grant). **2.** a piece of work; task: *Our life is but a little holding, lent to do a mighty labour* (George Meredith). **3. a.** work done by skilled and unskilled workers who are not clerks, managers, professional workers, or owners. **b.** *Economics.* the work of human beings that produces goods or services. *Land, labor,* and *capital* are the three principal factors of production. *Labor is prior to, and independent of, capital* (Abraham Lincoln). **4.** skilled and unskilled workers as a group: *Labor's function is to join with capital and management in the common enterprise of meeting the needs of the universal consumer* (Emory S. Bogardus). *Labor in general favors a seven-hour day.* **5.** childbirth: *She was in labor for two hours.*
—*v.i.* **1.** to work hard; exert one's powers of body or mind, especially to gain a livelihood; toil. **2.** to move slowly and heavily: *The ship labored in the high waves.* **3.** to be long and drawn out; be elaborate. **4.** to be in childbirth. —*v.t.* **1.** to elaborate with effort or in detail: *The speaker labored the point so that we lost interest.* **2. a.** to work (a mine). **b.** *Archaic.* to till; cultivate. **3.** *Archaic.* to work or strive to bring about or achieve.
labor under, to be burdened, troubled, or distressed by; suffer from the shortcoming of: *to labor under a mistake or handicap.*
—*adj.* of or having to do with labor: *a labor shortage, labor leaders.*
[< Old French *labour,* learned borrowing from Latin *labor, -ōris* toil, pain]
—**Syn.** *n.* **1.** exertion, effort. See **work. 5.** travail, parturition.

la·bo·ra·re est o·ra·re (lab′ə rãr′ē est ō rãr′ē), *Latin.* **1.** work is prayer. **2.** (literally) to work is to pray.

lab·o·ra·to·ri·al (lab′ər ə tôr′ē əl, -tōr′-; lab′rə-), *adj.* having to do with the laboratory. —**lab′o·ra·to′ri·al·ly,** *adv.*

lab·o·ra·to·ri·an (lab′ər ə tôr′ē ən, -tōr′-; lab′rə-), *n.* a chemist who works in a laboratory. —*adj.* laboratorial.

lab·o·ra·to·ry (lab′ər ə tôr′ē, -tōr′-; lab′rə-), *n., pl.* **-ries,** *adj.* —*n.* **1.** a place where scientific work is done; a room or building fitted with apparatus for conducting scientific investigations, experiments, tests, etc.: *a chemical laboratory.* **2.** a place equipped for manufacturing chemicals, medicines, explosives, etc. **3.** any place, not a classroom or library, equipped for systematic study: *a language laboratory.*
—*adj.* used or performed in, or having to do with a laboratory: *Automation is overtaking even the highly trained medical laboratory technician* (Science News Letter).
[< Medieval Latin *laboratorium* < Latin *labōrāre* to work < *labor, -ōris* work, toil]

laboratory animal, any animal commonly used for experiments in a laboratory, such as guinea pigs and mice: *A laboratory animal, such as a rabbit . . ., reacts to any protein from a source outside its body in the same way it does to invading disease germs* (Fred W. Emerson).

labor camp, (in totalitarian countries) a concentration camp for political prisoners and common criminals sentenced to hard labor.

Labor Day, the first Monday in September, a legal holiday throughout the United States, Puerto Rico, and Canada in honor of labor and laborers.

la·bored (lā′bərd), *adj.* done with effort; forced; not easy or natural: *labored speech, labored cordiality.* —**la′bored·ly,** *adv.* —**la′bored·ness,** *n.*
—**Syn.** laborious, studied, constrained, stiff. See **elaborate.**

la·bor·er (lā′bər ər), *n.* **1.** a worker. **2.** a person who does work requiring strength rather than skill or training.

labor exchange, an employment office, especially in Great Britain, that helps to find jobs and makes job-payment benefits.

labor force, 1. the work force of a country. The labor force of the United States comprises all the employable people 14 years old or over. **2.** any work force.

la·bor·ing (lā′bər ing), *adj.* **1.** that labors. **2.** engaged in manual or mechanical labor: *the laboring class.* **3.** struggling, as under difficulty, emotion, etc.: *an occasional sigh from the laboring heart of the Captain* (Longfellow). **4.** rolling or pitching, as a ship. —**la′bor·ing·ly,** *adv.*

la·bo·ri·ous (lə bôr′ē əs, -bōr′-), *adj.* **1.** requiring much work; requiring hard work: *Climbing a mountain is laborious.* **2.** hard-working; industrious: *Bees and ants are laborious insects.* **3.** showing signs of effort; not easy: *laborious excuses.* [< Latin *labōriōsus* < *labor, -ōris* labor] —**la·bo′ri·ous·ly,** *adv.* —**la·bo′ri·ous·ness,** *n.*
—**Syn. 1.** toilsome, arduous, onerous, wearisome, fatiguing. **2.** diligent, assiduous, careful.

La·bor·ism (lā′bə riz əm), *n.* **1.** the principles or tenets of a Labor Party, especially the British Labour Party. **2.** adherence to them.

La·bor·ist (lā′bər ist), *n.* **1.** a supporter of Laborism, especially British Laborism. **2.** a Laborite.

la·bor·is·tic (lā′bə ris′tik), *adj.* of, having to do with, or tending to favor labor: *The production of wealth is almost wholly capitalistic; the distribution of wealth is largely laboristic* (Wall Street Journal).

la·bor·ite (lā′bə rīt), *n.* a person who supports the interests of workers.

La·bor·ite (lā′bə rīt), *n.* a member of a Labor Party.

la·bor·less (lā′bər lis), *adj.* free from labor; doing or requiring no labor.

labor market, the supply of labor in relation to the demand for it, especially in a particular area.

labor of love, any work done with eager willingness, either from fondness for the work itself or from affection for the person for whom it is done.

la·bor om·ni·a vin·cit (lā′bôr om′nē ə vin′sit), *Latin.* work conquers all things (the motto of the state of Oklahoma).

labor organization, any group of workers legally empowered to deal with employers on labor disputes, grievances, or conditions of employment.

labor pains, 1. the pains of childbirth. **2.** the difficulties encountered at the beginning of an endeavor or enterprise: *the labor pains of starting a new book.*

Labor Party, any political party organized to protect and promote the interests of workers.

labor relations, the study or practice of improving relations between labor and management.

la·bor-sav·ing (lā′bər sā′ving), *adj.* that takes the place of or lessens labor: *The neat labor-saving cook-stove had as yet no being* (Harriet Beecher Stowe).

labor skate, *U.S. Slang.* a labor unionist: *These were no local cops picking up a labor skate for disturbing the peace* (Newsweek).

la·bor·some (lā′bər səm), *adj.* **1.** laborious or toilsome. **2.** *Obsolete.* industrious. —**la′bor·some·ly,** *adv.*

labor turnover, 1. the number of new workers hired by an employer in place of workers who have left their jobs. **2.** the proportion of new workers hired (per year, month, etc.) in place of others to the average number of workers an employer has working for him: *In many industries men are "hired and fired" freely, and a labor turnover of 100 per cent in a year has been known to occur* (Emory S. Bogardus).

labor union, an association of workers to protect and promote their interests, and for dealing collectively with employers; union.

labor unionist, a member of a labor union: *Labor unionists believe in collective bargaining* (Emory S. Bogardus).

la·bour (lā′bər), *n., v.i., v.t. Especially British.* labor. —**la′boured,** *adj.* —**la′bour·er,** *n.* —**la′bour·ing,** *adj.*

La·bour·ite (lā′bə rīt), *n.* a member of the British Labour Party: *A large majority of the Labourites in Parliament disapproved. Abbr.:* Lab.

Labour Party, one of the two major British political parties, which claims especially to protect and advance the interests of working people. It was founded by the trade unions late in the 1800's but has attracted much middle-class and intellectual support.

Lab·ra·dor (lab′rə dôr), *n.* Labrador retriever.

Labrador blue, a very dark blue color.

Labrador Current, a cold current of water that rises in the Arctic Ocean and flows along the coast of Labrador past Newfoundland, where it meets the Gulf Stream.

Labrador duck, a large sea duck, the male of which was black with white head and markings. It formerly lived along the northern Atlantic coast of North America, but has been extinct since the 1870's.

lab·ra·dor·es·cence (lab′rə dô res′əns), *n.* the brilliant play of colors exhibited by labradorite.

Lab·ra·dor·i·an (lab′rə dôr′ē ən), *adj.* of or having to do with the peninsula of Labrador, in northeastern North America between Hudson Bay and the Atlantic. —*n.* a native of Labrador.

lab·ra·dor·ite (lab′rə dôr īt, lab′rə dôr′-), *n.* a mineral, a kind of feldspar, that shows a brilliant variety of color when turned in the light, and is used as an ornamental stone. [< *Labrador,* where it is found + *-ite*[1]]

lab·ra·dor·it·ic (lab′rə dô rit′ik), *adj.* of or like labradorite.

Labrador retriever, any of a breed of hunting dogs of medium size used as a retriever on land or water. It has a thick, water-resistant coat and is black, chocolate, or yellow in color. The breed originated in Newfoundland.

Labrador Retriever (21 to 24½ in. high at the shoulder)

labrador tea, 1. any of a group of low, evergreen shrubs of the heath family, growing in bogs and swamps of arctic and subarctic regions. **2.** tea made with the leaves of a plant of this group.

la·bral (lā′brəl, lab′rəl), *adj.* of a labrum or liplike part.

la·bret (lā′bret), *n.* an ornament, often merely a piece of wood, stone, bone, or shell, stuck into or through the lip, worn by certain primitive peoples.
[< *labr*(um) + *-et*]

lab·roid (lab′roid), *adj.* of, belonging to, or having the characteristics, especially the spiny fins and thick lips, of the family of fishes comprising the wrasses. —*n.* any fish belonging to this family.
[< New Latin *Labroidea* the family name < *Labrus* the typical genus < Latin *labrum* lip; see LABRUM]

la·brum (lā′brəm, lab′rəm), *n., pl.* **la·bra** (lā′brə, lab′rə). **1.** a lip or liplike part. **2.** *Zoology.* **a.** the part forming the upper border of the mouth in arthropods. **b.** the outer margin of the opening of a gastropod shell. **3.** labrum glenoidale. [< Latin *labrum* lip, related to *labium* labium]

labrum gle·noi·da·le (glē′noi dā′lē), a ring of cartilage surrounding a bony socket and increasing the depth of the socket. [< New Latin *labrum glenoidale* glenoid lip]

la·bur·num (lə bėr′nəm), *n.* any of a group of small, poisonous, Old World trees or shrubs of the pea family, much cultivated for their profuse, hanging clusters of bright-yellow flowers, as the golden chain: *Laburnum, rich In streaming gold* (William Cowper). [< Latin *laburnum*]

lab·ware (lab′wãr′), *n.* utensils of glass, porcelain, metal, etc., that are used in a laboratory: *Like all Pyrex labware, these coils are corrosion resistant* (Scientific American). [< *lab* + *ware*]

Lab·y·rinth (lab′ə rinth), *n. Greek Mythology.* the maze built by Daedalus for King Minos of Crete to imprison the Minotaur. [< Latin *labyrinthus* < Greek *labýrinthos*]

lab·y·rinth (lab′ə rinth), *n.* **1.** a place through which it is hard to find one's way; place consisting of a number of connecting passages; maze, as in a park or garden. **2.** a confusing, complicated arrangement, as of streets or buildings: *He was dragged into a labyrinth of dark narrow courts* (Dickens). **3.** a confusing, complicated state of affairs: *No one could soar into a more intricate*

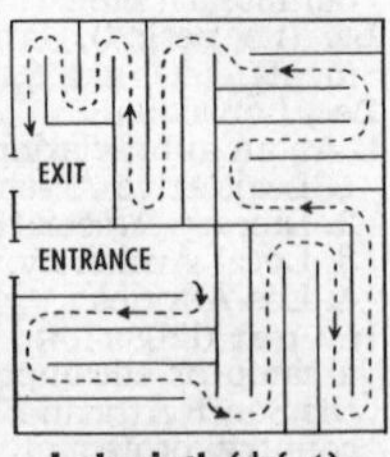

Labyrinth (def. 1)

labyrinth of phraseology (Anthony Trollope). **4.** *Anatomy.* the inner ear. [< *Labyrinth*] —**lab′y·rinth·like′**, *adj.* —**Syn. 3.** intricacy, complexity.

lab·y·rin·thal (lab′ə rin′thəl), *adj.* labyrinthine.

labyrinth fish, any of a group of brightly colored tropical fishes having a cavity above the gills for storing air.

lab·y·rin·thi·an (lab′ə rin′thē ən), *adj.* labyrinthine.

lab·y·rin·thic (lab′ə rin′thik), *adj.* labyrinthine. —**lab′y·rin′thi·cal·ly,** *adv.*

lab·y·rin·thi·cal (lab′ə rin′thə kəl), *adj.* labyrinthine.

lab·y·rin·thine (lab′ə rin′thin, -thēn), *adj.* **1.** of or forming a labyrinth: *labyrinthine passages.* **2.** intricate; confusing; complicated: . . . *down the labyrinthine ways Of my own mind* (Francis Thompson). —**Syn. 2.** involved, inextricable.

lab·y·rin·thi·tis (lab′ə rin thī′tis), *n.* inflammation of the inner ear.

lab·y·rin·tho·don (lab′ə rin′thə don), *n.* a labyrinthodont.

lab·y·rin·tho·dont (lab′ə rin′thə dont), *adj.* **1.** having teeth with a labyrinthlike internal structure. **2.** belonging or having to do with a family of large, sometimes huge, extinct amphibians, characterized by such a tooth structure. —*n.* a labyrinthodont amphibian: *Some primitive fossil labyrinthodonts probably were ancestral to the oldest reptiles and so to all higher land vertebrates* (Tracy I. Storer). [< Greek *labýrinthos* + *odoús, odóntos* tooth]

lac[1] (lak), *n.* a resinous substance excreted on various trees in southern Asia by scale insects. Lac is used in making sealing wax, varnish, red dye, etc. [< Hindustani *lākh* < Sanskrit *lākṣā*. Related to LACQUER.]

lac[2] (lak), *n., adj.* lakh.

LAC (no periods), *British.* leading aircraftsman.

lac·cate (lak′āt), *adj.* having the appearance of being lacquered: *laccate leaves.*

lac·co·lite (lak′ə līt), *n.* a large mass of igneous rock that has spread on rising from below, causing the overlying strata to bulge upward in a domelike formation. [< Greek *lákkos* storage pit, reservoir, pond + English *-lite*]

lac·co·lith (lak′ə lith), *n.* laccolite.

lac·co·lit·ic (lak′ə lit′ik), *adj.* of or having to do with a laccolite or laccolites: *a laccolitic mountain.*

lac dye, a scarlet dye prepared from lac.

lace (lās), *n., v.,* **laced, lac·ing.** —*n.* **1.** an open weaving or net of fine thread in an ornamental pattern. **2.** a cord, string, leather strip, etc., for pulling or holding together: *These shoes need new laces.* **3.** gold or silver braid used for trimming: *Some uniforms have lace on them.* **4.** a dash of brandy, whiskey, etc., added to coffee, tea, etc.
—*v.t.* **1.** to trim with lace. **2. a.** to put laces through; pull or hold together with a lace or laces. **b.** to squeeze the waist of (a person) by drawing the laces of a corset tight. **3.** to adorn or trim with narrow braid: *His uniform was laced with gold.* **4. a.** to interlace; intertwine. **b.** to mix; blend (with): . . . *found that sawdust laced with oatmeal makes a much better soil for mushroom farming* (Scientific American). **5.** to mark with streaks; streak: *a white petunia laced with purple. A waterfall of foam, lacing the black rocks with a thousand snowy streams* (Charles Kingsley). **6.** *Informal.* to lash; beat; thrash. **7.** to add a dash of brandy, whiskey, etc., to (a beverage, especially coffee): *Let's go drink a dish of laced coffee, and talk of the times* (William Wycherley). **8.** to spread a network over or through: *If any nation were to begin lacing the earth's waters with . . . bombs . . .* (New Yorker). —*v.i.* **1.** to be laced: *These shoes lace easily.* **2.** to squeeze in the waist by a tight corset.

lace into, *Informal.* **a.** to attack: *One of the two quarreling boys suddenly laced into the other, knocking him down.* **b.** to criticize severely: *He* [*Secretary of State Dulles*] *laced into the Reds, though . . . naming no country specifically* (Newsweek).
[< Old French *laz,* and *las* < Latin *laqueus* noose. Doublet of LASSO.] —**lace′like′,** *adj.* —**lac′er,** *n.*
—**Syn.** *v.t.* **2. b.** compress. **7.** flavor.

lace·bark (lās′bärk′), *n.* lacewood.

lace·bug (lās′bug′), *n.* a sucking insect with lacelike markings on the body and wings that attacks broadleaf evergreens: *Lacebugs reach full growth in June and then have wings with a lacework pattern of veins.*

lace-cur·tain (lās′kėr′tən), *adj.* **1.** fancy; pretentious: *Maybe if I describe the game in another, less lace-curtain, way it will be easier to see* (Scientific American). **2.** proper; genteel: *He is a man with a strong middle-class provincial, even, lace-curtain . . . background* (Harper's). **3.** middle class as opposed to working class.

lace-cur·tained (lās′kėr′tənd), *adj.* furnished with lace curtains: *Another was a large, lace-curtained sleeping room* (New Yorker).

Lac·e·dae·mo·ni·an (las′ə di mō′nē ən), *adj., n.* Spartan.

lace fern, a small fern having the underside of the frond covered with matted wool.

lace·flow·er (lās′flou′ər), *n.* **1.** a small, delicate blue flower of an Australian plant of the parsley family. **2.** the plant.

lace glass, Venetian glass with lacelike designs.

lace·leaf (lās′lēf′), *n., pl.* **-leaves.** latticeleaf.

lace·less (lās′lis), *adj.* without laces: *laceless boots.*

lace paper, paper cut or stamped in imitation of lace.

lace pillow, a round or oval board with a stuffed covering, held on the knees to support the fabric when making pillow lace.

lace plant, latticeleaf.

lac·er·a·bil·i·ty (las′ər ə bil′ə tē), *n.* a being lacerable.

lac·er·a·ble (las′ər ə bəl), *adj.* that can be lacerated.

lac·er·ate (*v.* las′ə rāt; *adj.* las′ə rāt, -ər it), *v.,* **-at·ed, -at·ing,** *adj.* —*v.t.* **1. a.** to tear roughly; mangle: *The bear's claws lacerated the hunter's flesh.* **b.** to tear to pieces; tear up. **2.** to wound; hurt (the feelings, etc.): *Sharp words lacerate a person's feelings.*
—*adj.* **1.** deeply or irregularly indented as if torn: *lacerate leaves.* **2.** torn; jagged.
[< Latin *lacerāre* (with English *-ate*[1]) < *lacer* mangled]
—**Syn.** *v.t.* **1. a.** rend, wound. **2.** harrow, afflict.

lac·er·at·ed (las′ə rā′tid), *adj.* mangled; torn; hurt: *a lacerated arm, a lacerated mind.*

lac·er·a·tion (las′ə rā′shən), *n.* **1.** the act or process of lacerating. **2.** a rough tear; mangled place; wound. —**Syn. 1.** mangling. **2.** mutilation.

lac·er·a·tive (las′ə rā′tiv), *adj.* having the power to lacerate or tear; tearing.

lac·er·a·tor (las′ə rā tər), *n.* a person or thing that lacerates.

La·cer·ta (lə sėr′tə), *n., genitive* **La·cer·tae.** a northern constellation near Pegasus. [< Latin *lacerta* lizard]

La·cer·tae (lə sėr′tē), *n.* genitive of **Lacerta.**

la·cer·tian (lə sėr′shən), *adj., n.* lacertilian.

la·cer·tid (lə sėr′tid), *n.* a lizard.

lac·er·til·i·an (las′ər til′ē ən), *adj.* **1.** of or belonging to the suborder of reptiles that comprises the lizards and lizardlike animals, including the geckos, chameleons, skinks, etc. **2.** lizardlike. —*n.* a lizard or lizardlike reptile. [< New Latin *Lacertilia* the suborder name (< Latin *lacerta* lizard) + English *-an*]

la·cer·tine (lə sėr′tin), *adj.* **1.** lacertilian. **2.** (of decorative work) consisting of intertwined or curving lizardlike forms. [< Latin *lacerta* lizard + English *-ine*[1]]

lac·er·y (lā′sər ē), *n., pl.* **-er·ies.** lacelike work.

lace·wing (lās′wing′), *n.* any of the common small neuropteran insects that have four lacelike wings.

lace·wood (lās′wu̇d′), *n.* the fibrous bark of the currajong tree of Australia.

lace·work (lās′wėrk′), *n.* **1.** lace. **2.** openwork like lace. **3.** a network: . . . *a $3 million lacework of pipes, tubing and furnaces is taking shape* (Wall Street Journal).

lach·e·na·li·a (lash′ə nā′lē ə), *n.* any of a genus of South African plants of the lily family, bearing yellow, bell-shaped flowers. [< New Latin *Lachenalia* the genus name < *Lachenal,* a Swiss botanist of the 1800's]

lach·es (lach′iz), *n., pl.* **lach·es.** **1.** *Law.* failure to do a thing at the right time; delay in asserting a right, claiming a privilege, or applying for redress. **2.** inexcusable negligence: *His conduct had shown laches which others . . . were free from* (George Eliot). [< Anglo-French *lachesse,* Old French *laschesse* < *lasche* negligent < Latin *laxus,* loose, lax]

Lach·e·sis (lak′ə sis), *n. Greek Mythology.* one of the three Fates. Lachesis measures off the thread of human life. [< Latin *Lachesis* < Greek *Láchesis*]

lach·ry·ma Chris·ti (lak′rə mə kris′tē), *pl.* **lach·ry·mae Chris·ti** (lak′rə mē kris′tē). lacryma Christi.

lach·ry·mal (lak′rə məl), *adj.* **1.** of tears; producing tears: *Mostly a salt solution, lachrymal fluid also contains substances that fight bacteria, and proteins that help make the eye immune to infection.* **2.** for tears: *Collecting the drops of public sorrow into his volume, as into a lachrymal vase* (Washington Irving). **3.** *Anatomy.* of, having to do with, or situated near the glands (lachrymal glands) that secrete tears, or the ducts leading from them.
—*n.* a lachrymatory. Also, **lacrimal, lacrymal.**
lachrymals, tears: *Something else I said . . . made her laugh in the midst of her lachrymals* (Samuel Richardson).
[< Medieval Latin *lachrymalis* < Latin *lacrima* tear[1]]

lach·ry·ma·tion (lak′rə mā′shən), *n.* the shedding of tears.

lach·ry·ma·tor (lak′rə mā′tər), *n.* a substance that makes the eyes water, such as tear gas. Also, **lacrimator.**

lach·ry·ma·to·ry (lak′rə mə tôr′ē, -tōr′-), *adj., n., pl.* **-ries.** —*adj.* **1.** of tears; producing tears. **2.** for tears. —*n.* a small vase with a narrow neck found in ancient Roman tombs and once believed to be used to hold the tears of mourning friends: *no . . . lachrymatories, or tear-bottles* (Sir Thomas Browne). Also, **lacrimatory, lacrymatory.**

lach·ry·mist (lak′rə mist), *n.* one who is addicted to tears; weeper.

lach·ry·mose (lak′rə mōs), *adj.* **1.** given to shedding tears; tearful. **2.** suggestive or tending to cause tears; mournful: *lachrymose poetry.* Also, **lacrymose.** [< Latin *lacrimōsus* < *lacrima* tear[1]] —**lach′ry·mose·ly,** *adv.*
—**Syn. 1.** weeping. **2.** maudlin, melancholy.

lach·ry·mos·i·ty (lak′rə mos′ə tē), *n.* tearfulness.

lach·ry·mous (lak′rə məs), *adj.* lachrymose.

lac·i·ly (lā′sə lē), *adv.* in a lacy way or manner.

lac·i·ness (lā′sē nis), *n.* a being lacy.

lac·ing (lā′sing), *n.* **1.** a cord, string, etc., for pulling or holding something together: *Many shoes have lacings to hold them on the feet.* **2.** gold or silver braid used for trimming. **3.** *Informal.* a lashing; beating; thrashing. **4.** streaked coloration, as of flowers or plumage.

la·cin·i·a (lə sin′ē ə), *n.* **1.** a slash in a leaf, petal, etc. **2.** the apex of an insect's maxilla. [< New Latin *lacinia;* see LACINIATE]

la·cin·i·ate (lə sin′ē āt, -it), *adj.* **1.** *Botany.* cut into deep and narrow irregular lobes; slashed; jagged. **2.** *Anatomy.* shaped or formed like a fringe, as a ligament. [< New Latin *lacinia* a slashed lobe of a petal (< Latin, small piece < *lacer* mangled) + English *-ate*[1]]

Laciniate Leaf

la·cin·i·at·ed (lə sin′ē ā′tid), *adj.* laciniate.

la·cin·i·a·tion (lə sin′ē ā′shən), *n.* a lobe or projecting segment; laciniate formation.

la·cin·i·ose (lə sin′ē ōs), *adj.* laciniate.

lac insect, the scale insect which secretes lac.

la·cis (lā′səs), *n.* lacework. [< French *lacis*]

lack (lak), *v.t.* **1.** to have not enough; need: *A desert lacks water.* **2.** to be without; have no: *A homeless person lacks a home. Guinea pigs lack tails.* —*v.i.* **1.** to be absent or missing, as something requisite or desirable: *Here lacks but your mother for to say amen* (Shakespeare). **2. a.** to be short (of). **b.** *Obsolete.* to be in want or need: *He that giveth unto the poor shall not lack* (Proverbs 28:27). [< noun]
—*n.* **1.** shortage; not having enough: *That lack of energy that distinguishes the occupants of almshouses* (Hawthorne). *Let his lack of years be no impediment* (Shakespeare). **2.**

the fact or condition of being without: *Lack of a fire made him cold.* **3.** something needed: *If you are cold, your lack is heat.*
for lack of, **a.** because of too little: *I sold the business for lack of capital.* **b.** for want of; being without: *He . . . slew some of them with his fist for lack of another weapon* (John Playford).
[origin uncertain. Compare Middle Dutch *lac,* Middle Low German *lak.*]
—**Syn.** *v.t.* **1, 2. Lack, want, need** mean to be without something. **Lack** means to be completely without or without enough of something, good or bad: *A coward lacks courage.* **Want** means to lack something worth having, desired, or, especially, necessary for completeness: *That dress wants a belt.* **Need** means to lack something required for a purpose or that cannot be done without: *He does not have the tools he needs. She needs more sleep.* -*n.* **1.** deficiency, deficit, dearth, paucity, scarcity.
lack·a·dai·si·cal (lak′ə dā′zə kəl), *adj.* **1.** listless; languid; dreamy: *On the subject of color, almost all dealers find buyer interest lackadaisical* (Wall Street Journal). **2.** weakly sentimental: *Mrs. Leyburn, poor lackadaisical thing! is no good whatever* (Mrs. Humphry Ward). [< *lackadaisy,* variant of *lackaday* + *-ic* + *-al*[1]] —**lack′a·dai′si·cal·ly,** *adv.* —**lack′a·dai′si·cal·ness,** *n.* —**Syn. 1.** spiritless, lethargic.
lack·a·dai·sy (lak′ə dā′zē), *interj.* lackaday.
lack·a·day (lak′ə dā′), *interj.* an exclamation of sorrow or regret; alas. [variant of *alackaday!*]
lack·er (lak′ər), *n., v.* lacquer. —**lack′er·er,** *n.*
lack·ey (lak′ē), *n., pl.* **-eys,** *v.,* **-eyed, -ey·ing.** —*n.* **1.** a male servant; footman: *I saw a gay gilt chariot . . . the coachman with a new cockade, and the lackeys with insolence and plenty in their countenances* (Sir Richard Steele). **2.** a slavish follower; toady.
—*v.t.* **1.** to wait on: *A thousand liveried angels lacky her* (Milton). **2.** to be slavish to. —*v.i. Obsolete.* to act or serve as a lackey, especially as a running footman.
[< Middle French *laquais* < Spanish *lacayo* foot soldier, perhaps < Arabic *al-qā'id* chief, captain (usually a Moor who occupies a lesser post because he was captured by Christians). Compare ALCAIDE.]
—**Syn.** *n.* **1.** flunky. **2.** sycophant.
lackey moth, a bombycid moth whose caterpillars have bright-colored, striped coats resembling a lackey's uniform.
lack·ing (lak′ing), *adj.* **1.** not having enough; deficient: *A weak person is lacking in strength.* **2.** absent; not here: *Water is lacking because the pipe is broken.* —*prep.* without; not having: *Lacking anything better, use what you have.*
lack·land (lak′land′), *adj.* without land; landless. —*n.* a person who has no land.
lack·lus·ter (lak′lus′tər), *adj.* **1.** not shining or bright; dull; drab: *A small, lackluster, political meeting in front of City Hall* (New York Times). **2.** pallid; leaden: *lackluster visages* (Washington Irving). —*n. Rare.* the absence of luster or brightness.
lack·lus·tre (lak′lus′tər), *adj., n. Especially British.* lackluster: *looking on it with lack-lustre eye* (Shakespeare).
lack·wit (lak′wit′), *n. Informal.* a stupid person.
lac·moid (lak′moid), *n.* a coal-tar color used in dyeing. [< *lacm*(us) + *-oid*]
lac·mus (lak′məs), *n.* litmus. [< Dutch *lakmoes* < *lak* lac[1] + *moes* pulp]
La·co·ni·an (lə kō′nē ən), *adj.* having to do with Laconia, an ancient country in southern Greece, or its inhabitants; Spartan or Lacedaemonian. —*n.* an inhabitant of Laconia.
la·con·ic (lə kon′ik), *adj.* using few words; brief in speech or expression; concise: *Boccalini . . . indicts a laconic writer for speaking that in three words which he might have said in two* (Sir Richard Steele). [< Latin *Lacōnicus* < Greek *Lakōnikós* Spartan < *Lákōn* a Spartan (because Spartans were noted for brevity in speech)] —**Syn.** short, condensed, terse, succinct, pithy, sententious.
la·con·i·cal·ly (lə kon′ə klē), *adv.* in few words; briefly; concisely: *Following regulations, he recorded the report, laconically marking it "Unconfirmed"* (New Yorker).
la·con·i·cism (lə kon′ə siz əm), *n.* laconism.
la·con·i·cum (lə kon′ə kəm), *n.* (in ancient Rome) the sweating room of a bath. [< Latin *Laconicum,* neuter of *Lacōnicus* (because it was first used by the Spartans); see LACONIC]
lac·o·nism (lak′ə niz əm), *n.* **1.** laconic brevity. **2.** a laconic speech or expression. [< Greek *lakōnismós* < *lakōnízein* to imitate Lacedaemonians, especially in speech < *Lákōn;* see LACONIC]
lac·quer (lak′ər), *n.* **1.** a varnish consisting of a solution of pale shellac dissolved in alcohol, or some other solvent, sometimes tinged with coloring matters, and used for coating metals, wood, etc. **2.** any of various kinds of varnish made from the resin of the varnish tree. It takes a hard, high polish and is used for coating articles of wood or other materials. **3.** wooden articles coated with such varnish. **4.** *Obsolete.* lac[1].
—*v.t.* **1.** to coat with or as with lacquer. **2.** *Slang.* to polish; make more presentable: *. . . the Actors Studio, an organization dedicated to lacquering up-and-coming performers* (New York Times).
[< Middle French *lacre* < Portuguese, sealing wax < *lacca* lac < Arabic *lakk* < Persian *lak* lac gum. Related to LAKE[2], SHELLAC.] —**lac′quer·er,** *n.*
lacquer tree, varnish tree.
lac·quer·ware (lak′ər wãr′), *n.* wooden articles coated with lacquer.
lac·quer·work (lak′ər wėrk′), *n.* **1.** lacquerware. **2.** the making of lacquerware.
lac·quey (lak′ē), *n., pl.* **-queys,** *v.,* **-queyed, -quey·ing.** lackey.
lac·ri·mal or **lac·ry·mal** (lak′rə məl), *adj., n.* lachrymal.
lac·ri·ma·tor (lak′rə mā′tər), *n.* lachrymator.
lac·ri·ma·to·ry or **lac·ry·ma·to·ry** (lak′rə mə tôr′ē, -tōr′-), *adj., n., pl.* **-ries.** lachrymatory.
la·crosse (lə krôs′, -kros′), *n.* a game that originated among the Canadian Indians, played with a ball and long-handled sticks with webbed baskets by two teams of 10 players each. The players try to send the ball into a goal. [American English < Canadian French *la crosse* (originally) hooked stick, cross]

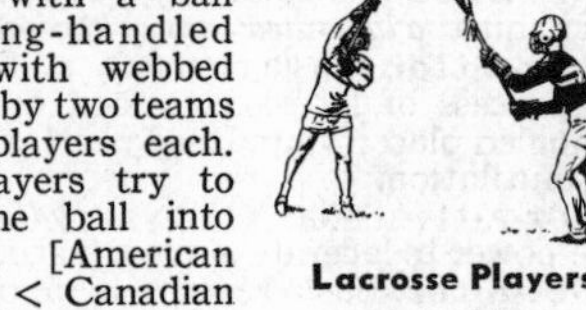
Lacrosse Players

lac·ry·ma Chris·ti (lak′rə mə kris′tē), *pl.* **lac·ry·mae Chris·ti** (lak′rə mē kris′tē). a strong, sweet red wine of southern Italy. [< New Latin *lacryma Christi* (literally) tears of Christ]
lac·ry·mose (lak′rə mōs), *adj.* lachrymose.
lact-, *combining form.* the form of **lacto-** before vowels, as in *lactase.*
lac·ta·gogue (lak′tə gôg, -gog), *adj., n.* galactagogue. [< *lact-* + Greek *-agōgos* a leading]
lact·al·bu·min (lak′tal byü′min), *n.* the albumin found in milk. [< *lact-* + *albumin*]
lac·tam (lak′tam), *n. Chemistry.* any of a group of compounds containing the NH·CO group. It is a cyclic anhydride of an amino acid, produced by the elimination of water from the amino ($-NH_2$) and carboxyl (-COOH) radicals. [< *lact*(one) + *am*(ino acid)]
lac·ta·rene (lak′tə rēn), *n.* a preparation of the casein of milk, used as a color fixative in printing calico. [< Latin *lactārius* having to do with milk (< *lac, lactis* milk) + English *-ene*]
lac·ta·rine (lak′tə rin, -rēn), *n.* lactarene.
lac·ta·ry (lak′tər ē), *adj., n., pl.* **-ries.** —*adj.* of or having to do with milk. —*n.* a house used as a dairy. [< Latin *lactārius* < *lac, lactis* milk]
lac·tase (lak′tās), *n. Biochemistry.* an enzyme capable of hydrolyzing lactose into glucose and galactose. [< *lact*(ose) + *-ase*]
lac·tate[1] (lak′tāt), *n. Chemistry.* any salt of lactic acid. [< *lact*(ic acid) + *-ate*[2]]
lac·tate[2] (lak′tāt), *v.,* **-tat·ed, -tat·ing.** —*v.i.* **1.** to secrete milk. **2.** to give suck. —*v.t.* to convert into milk; cause to resemble milk. [< Latin *lactāre* (with English *-ate*[1]) to suckle]
lac·ta·tion (lak tā′shən), *n.* **1.** the formation or secretion of milk. **2.** the time during which a mother gives milk. **3.** the act of suckling a baby. [< Latin *lactāre* to suckle + English *-ation*]
lac·ta·tion·al (lak tā′shə nəl), *adj.* of or having to do with lactation. —**lac·ta′tion·al·ly,** *adv.*
lac·te·al (lak′tē əl), *adj.* **1.** of or like milk; milky. **2.** carrying chyle, a milky liquid formed from digested food: *lacteal vessels.* —*n.* any of the tiny lymphatic vessels that carry chyle from the small intestine to be mixed with the blood in the thoracic duct. [< Latin *lacteus* (< *lac, lactis* milk) + English *-al*[1]] —**lac′te·al·ly,** *adv.*
lac·te·ous (lak′tē əs), *adj.* milky. —**lac′te·ous·ly,** *adv.*
lac·tes·cence (lak tes′əns), *n.* **1.** a milky appearance; milkiness. **2.** an abundant flow of sap from a plant when wounded. The sap is commonly white, but sometimes red or yellow.
lac·tes·cen·cy (lak tes′ən sē), *n.* lactescence.
lac·tes·cent (lak tes′ənt), *adj.* **1.** becoming or being milky; having a milky appearance. **2.** producing or secreting milk. **3.** (of plants and insects) producing a milky fluid. [< Latin *lactēscēns, -entis,* present participle of *lactēscere* become milky, be able to give milk < *lactēre* have milk or juice; suckle < *lac, lactis* milk]
lac·tic (lak′tik), *adj.* of milk; from milk, especially sour milk. [< Latin *lac, lactis* milk + English *-ic*]
lactic acid, a colorless, odorless, syrupy acid, formed in sour milk, the fermentation of vegetable juices, etc. *Formula:* $C_3H_6O_3$
lactic dehydrogenase, an enzyme produced in animal tissue that oxidizes lactic acid and is released in increased amounts by cancerous cells. *Abbr.:* LDH
lac·tide (lak′tīd), *n. Chemistry.* **1.** a compound formed by heating lactic acid, and regarded as an anhydride of that acid. **2.** any of a class of similar compounds. [< *lact*(ic acid) + *-ide*]
lac·tif·er·ous (lak tif′ər əs), *adj.* **1.** (of animals or their organs) secreting or conveying milk or a milky fluid. **2.** (of plants and their organs) yielding a milky juice. [< Latin *lactifer* producing milk or juice (< *lac, lactis* milk + *ferre* to bear) + English *-ous*] —**lac·tif′er·ous·ness,** *n.*
lac·tif·ic (lak tif′ik), *adj.* producing milk.
lac·tiv·o·rous (lak tiv′ər əs), *adj.* devouring milk.
lacto-, *combining form.* milk: *Lactoprotein = any protein found in milk.* Also, **lact-** before vowels. [< Latin *lac, lactis*]
lac·to·ba·cil·lus (lak′tō bə sil′əs), *n., pl.* **-cil·li** (-sil′ī). any of a genus of bacteria that ferments sugar with the production of lactic acid. [< New Latin *Lactobacillus* < Latin *lac, lactis* milk + Late Latin *bacillus* bacillus]
lac·to·duct (lak′tō dukt′), *n.* a plastic pipeline conveying milk from high mountain pastures to villages, especially in Switzerland.
lac·to·fla·vin (lak′tō flā′vin), *n. Biochemistry.* riboflavin.
lac·to·gen·e·sis (lak′tə jen′ə sis), *n.* the power of initiating milk secretion.
lac·to·gen·ic (lak′tə jen′ik), *adj.* that stimulates the secretion and flow of milk: *lactogenic hormones, lactogenic action.*
lac·to·glo·bu·lin (lak′tō glob′yə lin), *n.* the globulin found in milk.
lac·tom·e·ter (lak tom′ə tər), *n.* an instrument for testing the purity or richness of milk. [< *lacto-* + *-meter*]
lac·tone (lak′tōn), *n. Chemistry.* any of a group of cyclic anhydrides produced by the loss of a molecule of water from the hydroxyl (-OH) and carboxyl (-COOH) radicals of hydroxy acids. [< *lact-* + *-one*]
lac·ton·ic (lak ton′ik), *adj.* of or having to do with lactone.
lac·to·phos·phate (lak′tə fos′fāt), *n.* a lactate and a phosphate in combination.
lac·to·prene (lak′tə prēn), *n.* a synthetic rubber with high resistance to oils and heat, made from acrylate and acrylonitrile. [< *lacto-* + (iso)*prene*]
lac·to·pro·te·id (lak′tə prō′tē id), *n.* lactoprotein.
lac·to·pro·tein (lak′tə prō′tēn, -tē in), *n.* any protein found in milk.
lac·to·scope (lak′tə skōp), *n.* an instrument for testing the purity or richness of milk by its resistance to the passage of light. [< *lacto-* + *-scope*]
lac·tose (lak′tōs), *n. Chemistry.* a crystalline sugar, present in milk; milk sugar. It is usually obtained by evaporating whey and

converting it into hard, white crystals. Lactose is an isomer of common table sugar. *Formula:* $C_{12}H_{22}O_{11}\cdot H_2O$ [< French *lactose* < Latin *lac, lactis* milk + French *-ose* -ose]

lac·to·veg·e·tar·i·an (lak′tō vej′ə tãr′ē ən), *adj.* (of a diet) consisting of milk and vegetables.

la·cu·na (lə kyü′nə), *n., pl.* **-nas, -nae** (-nē). **1.** an empty space; gap; blank, especially in a manuscript, inscription, or the like: *There were several lacunas in her letter where words had been erased.* **2.** a tiny cavity or depression in bones, tissues, or cells, supposed to contain nucleated cells. [< Latin *lacūna* hole, pit < *lacus, -ūs* cistern, lake. Doublet of LAGOON.] —**Syn. 1.** hiatus.

la·cu·nal (lə kyü′nəl), *adj.* **1.** of or having to do with a lacuna. **2.** having lacunas.

la·cu·nar (lə kyü′nər), *n., pl.* **la·cu·nars, lac·u·nar·i·a** (lak′yů nãr′ē ə), *adj.* —*n.* **1.** *Architecture.* a ceiling formed of sunken compartments. **2.** one of the compartments; a sunken panel. —*adj.* lacunal.

Lacunar (def. 1)
Pantheon, Rome

lac·u·nar·y (lak′yů ner′ē, lə kyü′nər-), *adj.* lacunal.

la·cune (lə kyün′), *n.* lacuna.

la·cu·nose (lə kyü′nōs), *adj.* having lacunas; pitted; furrowed.

lac·u·nos·i·ty (lak′yü nos′ə tē), *n.* lacunose quality.

la·cu·nu·lose (lə kyü′nyə lōs), *adj.* minutely lacunose.

la·cus·tri·an (lə kus′trē ən), *adj.* lacustrine. —*n.* a lake dweller.

la·cus·trine (lə kus′trin), *adj.* **1.** of lakes. **2.** living or growing in lakes, as various animals and plants. **3.** *Geology.* of or having to do with strata that originated by deposition at the bottom of a lake. [ultimately < Latin *lacus, -ūs* lake; receptacle (on analogy of *paluster, -tris* marshy; palustrine) + English *-ine*[1]]

lac·y (lā′sē), *adj.,* **lac·i·er, lac·i·est. 1.** of lace. **2.** like lace; having an open delicate pattern.

lacy glass, glass pressed with designs of a lacy appearance, made especially in the United States in the early 1800's.

lad (lad), *n.* **1.** a boy; young man. **2.** *Informal.* a man: *How now, old lad?* (Shakespeare). [Middle English *ladde* boy, youth; earlier, serving man; origin uncertain] —**Syn. 1.** youth, stripling, youngster. **2.** fellow, chap.

la·dang (lä′däng), *n.* an Indonesian system of cultivation similar to the Burmese taungya and the Central American milpa. [< Malay *ladang*]

lad·a·num (lad′ə nəm), *n.* labdanum.

lad·der (lad′ər), *n.* **1.** a set of rungs or steps fastened to two side pieces, for use in climbing. **2.** a means of climbing higher: *Hard work is a ladder to success.* **3.** a series of steps to enable fish to ascend a fall or dam by a succession of leaps; fish ladder. **4.** anything resembling or suggesting a ladder: *This company has an elaborate promotion ladder. The mathematician has reached the highest rung on the ladder of human thought* (Havelock Ellis). **5.** *British.* a run in a knitted garment.
—*v.i., v.t. British.* (of knitted garments, especially stockings) to develop ladders as the result of the breaking of a thread.
[Old English *hlǣder*] —**lad′der·less,** *adj.* —**lad′der·like′,** *adj.*

lad·der-back chair (lad′ər bak′), a chair having a back formed by horizontal pieces of wood between two upright pieces, suggesting a ladder.

lad·der-backed (lad′ər bakt′), *adj.* having a back suggesting or resembling the rungs of a ladder: *a ladder-backed armchair.*

ladder-backed woodpecker, *U.S.* a North American woodpecker having the upper parts barred with black and white.

lad·dered (lad′ərd), *adj.* **1.** provided with a ladder or ladders. **2.** in regular, even sequence, resembling the steps or rungs of a ladder: *See, from the laddered shelves Shakespeare and Swift themselves speak straightly down* (Atlantic).

lad·der·proof (lad′ər prüf′), *adj. British.* (of knitted fabrics) resistant to runs.

ladder stitch, an embroidery stitch made with crossbars between ridges of raised work.

ladder truck, a fire engine equipped with extension ladders, fire hooks, etc.

lad·der·y (lad′ə rē), *adj.* resembling a ladder.

lad·die (lad′ē), *n. Scottish.* **1.** a young boy. **2.** a man.

lad·dish (lad′ish), *adj.* like a lad; boyish; juvenile. —**lad′dish·ness,** *n.*

lade (lād), *v.,* **lad·ed, lad·en** or **lad·ed, lad·ing.** —*v.t.* **1. a.** to put a burden on; load. **b.** to put cargo on board (a ship): *lading and unlading the tall barks* (Tennyson). **2.** to take up or remove (liquid) with a ladle, scoop, or the like; dip: *Like one that . . . chides the sea . . . saying he'll lade it dry* (Shakespeare). —*v.i.* **1.** to take on a load or cargo. **2.** to take up with a ladle, scoop, etc.; bail. [Old English *hladan.* Related to LAST[4].] —**Syn.** *v.t.* **1. a.** burden, oppress. **2.** scoop.

lad·en[1] (lā′dən), *adj.* loaded, burdened, or weighed down: *The laden boughs for you alone shall bear* (John Dryden). —*v.* a past participle of **lade:** *The camels were laden with bundles of silk and rice.*

lad·en[2] (lā′dən), *v.t.* to lade; load.

lad·hood (lad′hůd), *n.* the condition of being a lad.

la-di-da (lä′dē dä′), *adj., n., v.* **-daed, -da·ing,** *interj. Slang.* —*adj.* languidly genteel in speech or manner; affected; pretentious: *What can old Pratt be thinking of, publishing a la-di-da book about men's clothes?* (New Yorker).
—*n.* a person who affects gentility; fop.
—*v.i.* to act in an affectedly genteel manner; be snobbish or pretentious.
—*interj.* an exclamation in ridicule of fancy, snobbish, or pretentious speech, manners, etc.

la-di-dah (lä′dē dä′), *adj., n., v.,* **-dahed, -dah·ing,** *interj.* la-di-da.

La·dies Auxiliary (lā′dēz), *U.S.* a women's organization subsidiary to a men's club or similar group.

ladies chain, a square-dancing figure or call in which the women join hands as they cross over to the men.

ladies' day, *U.S.* a day on which a special privilege, as reduced theater prices or free admission to a sporting event, is given to women.

Ladies from Hell, a nickname, said to have originated with the Germans, applied to the kilted Scottish troops during World War I.

ladies' man, lady's man.

ladies' room, *U.S.* a public lavatory for women.

ladies' tresses, lady's-tresses.

la·di·fy (lā′dē fī), *v.,* **-fied, -fy·ing.** ladyfy.

La·din (lə dēn′), *n.* **1.** a Rhaeto-Romanic dialect spoken in parts of Switzerland and Tyrol, closely related to Romansh. **2.** any Rhaeto-Romanic dialect, as Romansh. **3.** one of the people of Switzerland and Tyrol who speak Ladin. [< Rhaeto-Romanic *ladino* < Latin *Latīnus* Latin]

lad·ing (lā′ding), *n.* **1.** the act of loading: *The lading took three full days.* **2.** load; freight; cargo: *bill of lading.*

La·di·no (lə dē′nō), *n., pl.* **-nos. 1.** the ancient Spanish or Castilian language. **2.** a Spanish dialect spoken in Turkey and elsewhere by descendants of Spanish and Portuguese Jews. **3.** (in Spanish America) a Spanish-speaking halfbreed; mestizo. **4.** Ladino clover. [< Spanish *Ladino* (literally) Latin < Latin *Latīnus* Latin]

Ladino clover, a variety of giant clover valuable as a forage crop.

la·dle (lā′dəl), *n., v.,* **-dled, -dling.** —*n.* a large cup-shaped spoon with a long handle, for dipping out liquids. —*v.t.* **1.** to dip out. **2.** to carry in a ladle. [Old English *hlǣdel* < *hladan* lade] —**la′dler,** *n.*

la·dle·ful (lā′dəl fůl), *n., pl.* **-fuls.** the amount that a ladle holds.

la dol·ce vi·ta (lä dōl′chā vē′tä), *Italian.* the sweet life; dolce vita: *Existentialism . . . presents an escape from the morass of conformity, la dolce vita, boredom* (Harper's).

la don·na è mo·bi·le (lä dôn′nä e mô′bē lā), *Italian.* the woman is fickle.

la·drone (lə drōn′), *n.* (in Spain or Spanish America) a robber; highwayman. [< Spanish *ladrón* < Latin *latrō, -ōnis* bandit; (originally) hired servant. Doublet of LATRON.]

la·dron·ism (lə drō′niz əm), *n.* (in the Philippine Islands) organized resistance among the native population to law or authority.

la·dy (lā′dē), *n., pl.* **-dies,** *adj.* —*n.* **1.** a well-bred woman; woman of high social position: *Here lies a lady of beauty and high degree* (John Crowe Ransom). **2.** a noblewoman; woman who has the title of Lady. **3.** any woman: *Which came out of the opened door—the lady or the tiger?* (Frank R. Stockton). **4.** a woman who has the rights or authority of a lord; mistress of a household. **5.** a woman whom a man loves or is devoted to: *My lady sweet, arise!* (Shakespeare). **6.** a wife: *By a former marriage, Mr. Henry Dashwood had one son; by his present lady, three daughters* (Jane Austen). **7.** the bony structure in a lobster's stomach that grinds its food.

lady of the house, the woman who is head of the household: *The salesman asked to speak to the lady of the house.*
—*adj.* **1.** woman; female: *a lady farmer.* **2.** of, having to do with, or befitting a lady; ladylike.
[Old English *hlǣfdīge* (literally) loaf-kneader. Related to LORD.]
—**Syn.** *n.* **1.** gentlewoman. See **female. 5.** sweetheart. **6.** spouse.

➔ **Lady** is often used in everyday speech to refer to any woman, no matter what her social position or background (*lady cab driver, lady clerk*). In many cases *woman,* as in *cleaning woman,* might be more appropriate, though *saleslady* and *landlady* are well established.

La·dy (lā′dē), *n., pl.* **-dies.** (in Great Britain) a title given to women of certain rank, as: **a.** a marchioness, countess, viscountess, or baroness. **b.** the daughter of a duke, marquis, or earl. **c.** the wife of a man with a courtesy title of Lord. **d.** the wife of a baronet or other knight.

Our Lady, the Virgin Mary: *Low on her knees herself she cast, Before Our Lady murmur'd she* (Tennyson).

Lady Am·herst's pheasant (am′ərsts), a brightly colored pheasant, native to parts of China and Tibet. [< *Lady Amherst,* a British noblewoman of the 1800's]

lady apple, a small, delicate, red, or red and yellow, variety of apple, valued chiefly for its waxy-looking ornamental appearance.

Lady Baltimore cake, a white cake of three layers, having a flavored icing which contains chopped figs, nuts, and raisins.

lady beetle, ladybug.

la·dy·bird (lā′dē bėrd′), *n.* ladybug. [< earlier genitive case of (Our) *Lady* + *bird*]

ladybird beetle, a ladybug.

Lady Bountiful, a kind and gracious, usually well-to-do, woman. [< *Lady Bountiful,* a character in George Farquhar's play *The Beaux' Stratagem*]

la·dy·bug (lā′dē bug′), *n.* any of various small, convex beetles, often bright red or yellow, with black or colored spots. Many ladybugs are highly beneficial to fruit and other crops, feeding on aphids and scale insects.

Ladybug
(Line shows actual length.)

lady chair, a kind of seat for a third person, formed by two persons holding each other's hands crossed.

Lady Chapel or **chapel,** a chapel dedicated to the Virgin Mary, generally placed behind the high altar in a cathedral or large church.

lady crab, any of various crabs, especially a species common on the Atlantic Coast of the United States.

lady cracker, a small firecracker.

Lady Day, 1. March 25, the day when the angel Gabriel told Mary that she would be the mother of Jesus; Annunciation Day. **2.** (formerly) any festival day honoring the Virgin Mary.

lady fern, a fern similar to the spleenwort but having curved spore cases.

la·dy·fin·ger (lā′dē fing′gər), *n.* a small sponge cake shaped somewhat like a finger: *'Ladyfingers' . . . suggestive of . . . soft dalliance with pastry, ices, and sparkling Moselle* (Mark Twain). Also, **lady's-finger.** [variant of earlier *ladies' fingers*]

la·dy·fish (lā′dē fish′), *n., pl.* **-fish·es** or (*collectively*) **-fish.** any of various small marine game fishes found in the tropical regions of the Atlantic and Pacific Oceans.

lady friend, 1. a woman friend or companion. **2.** a man's sweetheart; girl friend.

la·dy·fy (lā′dē fī), *v.t.,* **-fied, -fy·ing.** to make a lady of; give the title "Lady" to. Also, **ladify.**

la·dy·hood (lā′dē hu̇d), *n.* **1.** the condition or character of a lady. **2.** ladies collectively.

lady in waiting, *pl.* **ladies in waiting.** a lady who is an attendant of a queen or princess.

la·dy·ish (lā′dē ish), *adj.* like a lady; having a ladylike quality or character. —**la′dy·ish·ly,** *adv.* —**la′dy·ish·ness,** *n.*

la·dy-kill·er (lā′dē kil′ər), *n. Slang.* a man supposed to be dangerously fascinating to women: *I believe your regular lady-killer . . . becomes a very quiet animal by being occasionally jilted* (Charles J. Lever).

la·dy-kill·ing (lā′dē kil′ing), *Slang.* —*n.* the acts or arts of a lady-killer. —*adj.* of or having to do with a lady-killer.

la·dy·kin (lā′dē kin), *n.* a little lady.

la·dy·less (lā′dē lis), *adj.* without a lady or ladies; unaccompanied by a lady.

la·dy·like (lā′dē līk′), *adj.* **1.** like a lady: *a ladylike young woman.* **2. a.** suitable for a lady: *ladylike manners.* **b.** effeminate: *fops at all corners, ladylike in mien* (William Cowper). —**la′dy·like′ness,** *n.* —**Syn. 1.** refined, well-bred.

la·dy·love (lā′dē luv′), *n.* a woman who is loved by a man; sweetheart: *With favour in his crest, or glove, Memorial of his ladylove* (Scott).

lady luck, chance; good fortune: *. . . the large gambling casinos where adventurers have wooed lady luck for generations* (New York Times).

lady mayoress, *British.* the wife of a lord mayor.

lady of the bedchamber, *British.* a personal attendant upon the queen, not a servant.

Lady of the Snows, Our, Canada: *'For we be also a people,' Said our Lady of the Snows* (Rudyard Kipling).

lady's bedstraw, bedstraw, a small plant with clusters of white flowers, and fragrant stems and leaves.

lady's delight, the common pansy; wild pansy.

la·dy's-ear·drop (lā′dēz ir′drop′), *n.* any of various plants with drooping racemes or flowers that suggest eardrops, as the fuchsia.

la·dy's-fin·ger (lā′dēz fing′gər), *n.* ladyfinger.

lady's glove, the foxglove.

la·dy·ship (lā′dē ship), *n.* the rank or position of a lady.

La·dy·ship (lā′dē ship), *n. British.* a title used in speaking to or of a woman having the rank of Lady: *"Your Ladyship," "her Ladyship."*

la·dy-slip·per (lā′dē slip′ər), *n.* lady's-slipper.

lady's maid, a woman servant whose special duty it is to attend a lady in dressing.

lady's man, a man who is devoted to the society of women and is assiduous in paying them small attentions. Also, **ladies' man.**

la·dy's-man·tle (lā′dēz man′təl), *n.* an Old-World, perennial herb of the rose family, formerly used in medicine as an astringent.

la·dy-smock (lā′dē smok′), *n.* lady's-smock.

la·dy's-slip·per (lā′dēz slip′ər), *n.* **1.** any of various terrestrial wild orchids of temperate regions, whose flowers have a pouch-shaped lip that looks somewhat like a slipper; moccasin flower. **2.** any of various allied plants bearing similar flowers, especially a tropical species cultivated in greenhouses.

la·dy's-smock (lā′dēz smok′), *n.* cuckooflower, a plant with white or purple flowers.

la·dy's-thumb (lā′dēz thum′), *n.* a common smartweed whose oblong spike suggests a thumb.

la·dy's-trac·es (lā′dēz trā′siz), *n.* lady's-tresses.

la·dy's-tress·es (lā′dēz tres′iz), *n.* **1.** any of various low terrestrial orchids, bearing spikes of small, spirally arranged flowers. **2.** *British Dialect.* a kind of grass. Also, **ladies' tresses.**

Laën·nec's cirrhosis (lā neks′), cirrhosis of the liver. [< René T.H. *Laënnec,* 1781-1826, a French physician]

La·er·tes (lā ėr′tēz), *n.* **1.** *Greek Legend.* the father of Odysseus. **2.** the son of Polonius and brother of Ophelia in Shakespeare's play *Hamlet.*

Laes·try·go·ni·an (les′trə gō′nē ən), *n.* one of a mythical race of cannibal giants who were encountered by Odysseus (Ulysses), the principal character in Homer's *Odyssey,* in his wanderings, and by whom many of his companions were slain. Also, **Lestrigonian.**

Lae·ta·re Sunday (lē tãr′ē), (in the Roman Catholic Church) the fourth and middle Sunday in Lent, named after the beginning of the introit for the day, "Laetare Jerusalem," taken from Isaiah 66:10. [< Latin *laetāre* be joyful!]

laevo-, *combining form.* a variant of **levo-,** as in *laevogyrate.*

lae·vo·glu·cose (lē′vō glü′kōs), *n.* levoglucose.

lae·vo·gy·rate (lē′vō jī′rāt), *adj.* levorotatory.

lae·vo·gy·rous (lē′vō jī′rəs), *adj.* levorotatory.

lae·vo·ro·ta·tion (lē′vō rō tā′shən), *n.* levorotation.

lae·vo·ro·ta·to·ry (lē′vō rō′tə tôr′ē, -tōr′-), *adj.* levorotatory.

la·fa·yette (laf′ē et′, lä′fē-), *n.* **1.** a small sciaenoid, edible fish of the eastern coast of the United States. **2.** an oval-shaped fish with a deeply split tail and unelevated fins, abundant along the Eastern American coast. [American English < Marquis de *Lafayette,* 1757-1834, a French general who aided the American Revolution]

l'af·faire (lä fer′), *n. French.* the affair, especially in reference to some sensational event or legal case, as one involving political scandal or intrigue (often followed by the name of a major figure involved, as *l'affaire Dreyfus*).

La Fleche (lä flesh′) any of a breed of poultry with a long body, solid black plumage, and white ear lobes. It was developed in France.

LAFTA (no periods) or **L.A.F.T.A.,** Latin American Free Trade Association.

lag[1] (lag), *v.,* **lagged, lag·ging,** *n., adj.* —*v.i.* **1.** to move too slowly; fall behind: *The child lagged because he was tired.* **2.** (in marbles) to cast one's taw toward a line on the ground to fix the order of shooting. **3.** *Billiards.* to string. —*v.t.* **1.** *Physics.* (of an electric current) to fall behind (the voltage) in speed of response to alternations. **2.** *Economic Statistics.* to follow changes in another variable by a regular interval: *Changes in employment tend to lag changes in wholesale prices.*

—*n.* **1.** a lagging: *a long lag in forwarding mail to us.* **2. a.** the amount by which a person or thing lags: *There was a month's lag between order and delivery.* **b.** *Physics.* the retardation, or amount of retardation, in any current or movement. **3.** the last or hindmost one (in a race, game, sequence of any kind): *What makes my ram the lag of all the flock?* (Alexander Pope).

—*adj.* **1.** behindhand; late. **2.** tardy; slow: *An' faith! thou's neither lag nor lame* (Robert Burns). **3.** last; hindmost: *The lag end of my life* (Shakespeare).

[origin unknown]

—**Syn.** *v.i.* **1.** dawdle, delay, tarry. See **linger.**

lag[2] (lag), *v.,* **lagged, lag·ging,** *n. Slang.* —*v.t.* **1.** to transport as a convict; send to penal servitude. **2.** to arrest.

—*n.* **1.** a convict. **2.** a term of transportation or penal servitude.

[origin unknown]

lag[3] (lag), *n., v.,* **lagged, lag·ging.** —*n.* **1.** one of the staves or strips that support the cylindrical surfaces of a wooden drum, the casing of a boiler, or the cylinder of a carding machine. **2.** a barrel stave.

—*v.t.* **1.** to cover with lags or laggings. **2.** to cover a boiler or steam pipe with insulating material.

[apparently < Scandinavian (compare Old Icelandic *lögg* barrel rim, Swedish *lagg* stave)]

lag·an (lag′ən), *n. Law.* goods or wreckage sunk in the sea, but attached to a buoy in order that they may be recovered. Also, **lagend, ligan.** [< Old French *lagan,* perhaps < Scandinavian (compare Old Icelandic *lagnir,* plural of *lögn* net laid in the sea)]

la·gar (lä gär′), *n., pl.* **-gar·es** (-gär′ās). *Portuguese.* a wine press.

Lag Ba'O·mer (läg bō′mər), a Jewish holiday, the 18th of Iyar, when the restrictions on certain activities in force between Passover and Pentecost are lifted. [< Hebrew *lag* thirty-third day + *bə* in + *'Omer* the 49 days from Passover to Pentecost]

lag bolt, lag screw.

lag·end (lag′ənd), *n.* lagan.

la·ger[1] (lä′gər), *n.* a beer with a light body that is slowly fermented at a low temperature and stored from six weeks to six months before being used. —*v.t.* to ferment and store (beer) to make it a lager: *Lagering permits the beer to mature, with the result that both taste and aroma become decidedly mellower* (Scientific American). [American English, short for *lager beer,* half-translation of German *Lagerbier* < *Lager* storehouse + *Bier* beer]

la·ger[2] (lä′gər), *n., v.* laager.

lager beer, lager, a beer with a light body.

lag fault, *Geology.* a fault caused by one layer of rock being moved more slowly than another.

lag·gard (lag′ərd), *n.* a person who moves too slowly or falls behind; backward person: *a laggard in love, and a dastard in war* (Scott). —*adj.* slow; falling behind; backward: *Then mend the horses' laggard pace* (Rudyard Kipling). —**lag′gard·ly,** *adv.* —**lag′gard·ness,** *n.* —**Syn.** *n.* loiterer, lingerer, dawdler. -*adj.* sluggish, dilatory.

lag·gen (lag′ən), *n. Scottish.* laggin.

lag·ger[1] (lag′ər), *n.* a person who lags; laggard.

lag·ger[2] (lag′ər), *n. Slang.* a convict; lag.

lag·gin (lag′in), *n. Scottish.* the inner angle of a wooden dish, between the sides and the bottom. [< Scandinavian (compare Old Icelandic *lögg*)]

lag·ging (lag′ing), *n.* **1.** a lag for a boiler or steam pipes. **2.** the act of lagging a boiler or steam pipes. **3.** *Architecture.* the narrow cross strips in the centering of an arch.

lag line, (in marble games) the line drawn on the ground toward which the players lag.

la·gniappe or **la·gnappe** (lan yap′, lan′yap), *n. U.S. Dialect.* **1.** something given to a customer with a purchase; an extra attraction; prize; bonus: *Dealers have competed fiercely for customers. Some, for example, proposed vacation trips as lagniappe for coy buyers* (Atlantic). **2.** a tip. [American English < Haitian Creole *lagniappe* < American Spanish *la ñapa,* or *la yapa* the gift < Quechua *yapa* something given into the bargain, an extra]

lag·o·morph (lag′ə môrf), *n.* any of an order of mammals consisting of the rabbits and hares and the pikas. They are similar to rodents, but have two pairs of upper incisor teeth, the second pair, just behind the first, being smaller. [< New Latin *Lagomorpha* < Greek *lagṓs* hare < *morphḗ* form, shape]

lag·o·mor·phic (lag′ə môr′fik), *adj.* having the form or structure of a lagomorph.

la·goon (lə gün′), *n.* **1.** a pond or small lake connected with a larger body of water. **2.** an area of shallow salt or brackish water separated from the sea by low sandbanks. **3.** the water within a ring-shaped coral island (atoll). Also, **lagune.** [< French *lagune* (< Italian) or < Italian *laguna* < Latin *lacūna* pond, hole. Doublet of LACUNA.]

la·goon·al (la gü′nəl), *adj.* of or having to do with a lagoon: *Like beaches, lagoonal deposits are only exceptionally preserved among the older rocks* (Gilluly, Waters, and Woodford).

La·grang·i·an (lə grān′jē ən), *adj.* of or having to do with Joseph Louis Lagrange, 1736-1813, French mathematician and astronomer.

lag screw, a wood screw having a square bolt head; lag bolt.

Lag Screw

Lag·thing or **Lag·ting** (läg′ting), *n.* the upper house of the national legislature (Storting) of Norway. [< Norwegian *Lagthing* < *lag* law + *thing* assembly, parliament]

La·gu·na (lə gü′nə), *n., pl.* **-na** or **-nas.** a member of a tribe of North American Indians living in New Mexico.

la·gune (lə gün′), *n.* lagoon.

la·ic (lā′ik), *adj.* lay; secular. —*n.* a layman. [< Latin *lāicus* < Greek *lāikós* < *lāós* people. Doublet of LAY[3].] —**la′i·cal·ly,** *adv.*

la·i·cal (lā′ə kəl), *adj.* laic.

la·i·cism (lā′ə siz əm), *n.* **1.** the removal of religious influence, especially from political affairs; secularization. **2. a.** the power or influence of the laity, especially in politics.

b. the support of such power or influence: *"The illustrious academician," L'Osservatore Romano warned, "seems to have forgotten how many times, in France and elsewhere, charity has been violated and justice offended in the name of laicism"* (Newsweek).

la·i·cist (lā′ə sist), *n.* a person who supports laicism.

la·ic·i·ty (lā is′ə tē), *n., pl.* **-ties.** the principles of the laity; rule or influence of the laity.

la·i·ci·za·tion (lā′ə sə zā′shən), *n.* a removal from clerical rank, influence, or control.

la·i·cize (lā′ə sīz), *v.t.,* **-cized, -ciz·ing.** to secularize; deprive of clerical character.

laid (lād), *v.* the past tense and past participle of **lay**[1]: *He laid down the heavy bundle. And I laid me down with a will* (Robert Louis Stevenson).
—*adj.* marked with close parallel lines as watermarks.

laid paper, paper with a ribbed or lined appearance, from the watermark made by raised parallel wires in the mold.

laigh (lāH), *Scottish.* —*adj.* **1.** near the ground; not elevated. **2.** not loud.
—*adv.* **1.** in a low position; to a low point. **2.** in a low tone.
—*n.* **1.** a hollow. **2.** low-lying ground.
[variant of *low*[1]]

lain (lān), *v.* the past participle of **lie**[2]: *The snow has lain on the ground for a week without melting.*

lair[1] (lãr), *n.* **1.** the den or resting place of a wild animal: *to rouse the lion from his lair.* **2.** a place to lie in; bed; couch: *Rising . . . he summoned his companions from their warm lairs* (James Fenimore Cooper). **3.** *British.* a pen or shelter for cattle.
—*v.i.* to go to or rest in a lair.
—*v.t.* **1.** to place in a lair. **2.** to serve as a lair for.
[Old English *leger* act or place of lying down, related to *licgan* to lie[2]]
—**Syn.** *n.* **1.** shelter, retreat.

lair[2] (lãr), *v.i.* to stick or sink in a mire or bog.
[< Scandinavian (compare Old Icelandic *leir* clay, mud)]

lair[3] (lãr), *n. Scottish.* lore; learning. [variant of *lore*]

lair·age (lãr′ij), *n. British.* **1.** the placing of cattle in lairs. **2.** the space or a place for lairing cattle.

laird (lãrd), *n. Scottish.* the owner of land (in ancient times limited to those who held grants immediately from the king). [variant of *lord*]

laird·ly (lãrd′lē), *adj.* having the rank or quality of lairds.

laird·ship (lãrd′ship), *n.* **1.** the condition or dignity of a laird. **2.** lairds as a whole. **3.** the estate of a laird.

lais·ser-al·ler (le sā′á lā′), *n. French.* lack of restraint; ease.

lais·sez faire or **lais·ser faire** (les′ā fãr′), **1.** the principle of letting people do as they please: *If . . . Western institutions and ideals are to continue to seem relevant to Asia, the Western governments must substitute policy for laisser faire and they must do it soon* (Atlantic). **2.** the absence of regulation and interference by a government in trade, business, industry, etc.: *The economic strains that have appeared prove that the Conservative party's policy of lifting economic controls, of laissez faire, does not work and that worse things are in the offing* (New York Times).
[< French *laissez faire* allow to do (as one pleases)]

lais·sez-faire or **lais·ser-faire** (les′ā-fãr′), *adj.* of or based on laissez faire; not interfering: *A less satisfactory manifestation of the laissez-faire outlook is the states' attitude toward graft and politics* (Harper's).

lais·sez pas·ser or **lais·ser pas·ser** (le sā′ pä sā′), a permit; pass: *When they travelled out of Egypt, if they did, they obtained simple laissez passers as stateless persons* (New Yorker). [< French *laissez passer* allow to pass]

laith (lāth), *adj. Scottish.* loath.

la·i·ty (lā′ə tē), *n., pl.* **-ties.** the people as distinguished from the clergy or from a professional class; laymen: *Doctors use many words that the laity do not understand. The laity nowadays take a pride in speaking evil of the clergy* (Charles Kingsley).

La·ius (lā′əs), *n. Greek Legend.* the king of Thebes and husband of Jocasta. He was killed by their son Oedipus.

lake[1] (lāk), *n.* **1.** a large body of water entirely or nearly surrounded by land: *Lakes differ from ponds chiefly in size, but this carries with it profound changes in all the principal factors of environment—light, temperature, and dissolved gases, with their effect upon nutrition* (A. Franklin Shull). **2.** a wide place in a river. **3.** a pool of liquid, as of oil, tar, etc. [partly Old English *lacu* < Latin *lacus, -ūs* pond, tank, lake; partly < Old French *lac,* learned borrowing < Latin *lacus, -ūs*]

lake[2] (lāk), *n., v.,* **laked, lak·ing.** **1.** a deep-red or purplish-red coloring matter, obtained from lac or cochineal. **2.** any of various colored compounds, insoluble in water, formed by combining animal, vegetable, or coal tar coloring matter with metallic oxides: *madder lake.*
—*v.t.* to make (blood) lake-colored through the diffusion of the hemoglobin in the plasma.
—*v.i.* (of blood) to become lake-colored by this means.
[variant of *lac*[1]. Related to LACQUER, SHELLAC.]

lake basin, 1. a depression for a lake. **2.** the area drained by the streams that empty into a lake.

Lake District or **Country,** a region of beautiful mountains and lakes in northwestern England, including parts of Cumberland, Lancashire, and Westmorland counties, and associated with William Wordsworth, Samuel Taylor Coleridge, Robert Southey, and other English poets.

lake dweller, a person who lived in a house built on piles over a lake, in prehistoric times.

lake dwelling, a house built on piles over a lake in prehistoric times.

lake·front (lāk′frunt′), *n.* the area fronting on a lake: . . . *a great exposition and convention hall on the Chicago lakefront* (Wall Street Journal).

lake·head (lāk′hed′), *n.* the upstream side of a lake.

lake herring, cisco, a whitefish of the Great Lakes area.

lake·land terrier (lāk′lənd), any of a breed of terriers with a narrow body, long head, and beard, weighing 15 to 17 pounds. It was developed in England for hunting the fox and otter.

lake·let (lāk′lit), *n.* a small lake.

lake·like (lāk′līk′), *adj.* resembling a lake: *lakelike glisten of desert sands.*

La·ken·vel·der (lä′kən vel′dər), *n.* any of a breed of poultry with black-and-white plumage and white-shelled eggs. It was developed in Germany.

Lake poets, William Wordsworth, Samuel Taylor Coleridge, Robert Southey, and other English poets who lived in the Lake District.

lak·er (lā′kər), *n.* **1.** a person accustomed to living, working, or sailing on a lake. **2.** a fish living in or taken from a lake, especially a lake trout. **3.** a ship or freighter on a lake, especially the Great Lakes: *Giant lakers, previously land-locked on the Great Lakes, can now navigate right down to the Gulf of St. Lawrence* (Maclean's). **4.** one of the Lake poets: *The Lakers all . . . first despised, and then patronised Walter Scott* (Edward Fitzgerald).

lake salmon, 1. lake trout. **2.** landlocked salmon.

Lake School, the Lake poets of England and their followers.

lake·shore (lāk′shôr′), *n.* lakeside.

lake·side (lāk′sīd′), *n.* the margin or shore of a lake: *the once beautiful shore pimpled with lakeside cottages.*

lake trout, a large, dark trout with gray or yellowish spots, found in cold lakes of Canada and northern United States; namaycush. It may weigh up to 100 pounds when full-grown.

lake·ward (lāk′wərd), *adv., adj.* toward the lake: *Most of the cottages are on the lakeward side of the hill.*

lakh (lak), *n.* in India: **1.** a unit of 100,000, especially a unit of money equivalent to 100,000 rupees. **2.** any large number; great amount.
—*adj.* 100,000. Also, **lac.**
[< Hindustani *lākh* < Sanskrit *lakṣha* 100,000]

la·kin (lā′kin), *n. Obsolete.* ladykin (only in *by our lakin,* a form of *by Our Lady*). [< *la*(dy)*kin*]

La·ko·ta (lə kō′tə), *n., pl.* **-ta** or **-tas.** Dakota: *The Sioux called themselves Dakota or Lakota, meaning allies* (John C. Ewers).

Lak·shmi (luk′shmē), *n.* the Hindu goddess of prosperity and light, wife of Vishnu.

lak·y[1] (lā′kē), *adj.* of or like a lake; lakelike: *By . . . flanking towers, and laky flood, Guarded . . . she stood* (Scott). [< *lak*(e)[1] + *-y*[1]]

lak·y[2] (lā′kē), *adj.* of or like the color of lake; purplish-red. [< *lak*(e)[2] + *-y*[1]]

la·lang (lä′läng), *n.* a long, coarse East Indian grass. [< Malay *lalang*]

La·lique glass (lə lēk′), an ornamental glass decorated in relief with figures or flowers. [< René *Lalique,* 1860-1945, a French designer of glassware and jewelry]

lall (lal), *v.i.* **1.** to speak childishly. **2.** to pronounce the *r*-sound like *l.* [< Latin *lallāre* sing a lullaby]

Lal·lan (lal′ən), *adj., n. Scottish.* Lowland. [variant of *Lowland*]

Lal·lans (lal′ənz), *n.* the lowland Scottish dialect; Lowlands: *Mr. Maurice Lindsay, . . . is a solid intelligent Scottish poet who writes partly in English, partly in Lallans* (Observer).

lal·la·tion (la lā′shən), *n.* the pronunciation of *r* like *l,* as in *velly* for *very.* [< Latin *lallāre* sing a lullaby + English *-ation*]

lal·ly·gag (lal′ē gag), *v.i.,* **-gagged, -gag·ging.** *U.S. Slang.* to while away time idly. Also, **lollygag.**

lam[1] (lam), *v.t., v.i.,* **lammed, lam·ming.** *Informal.* to beat soundly; thrash; whack: *I bet you I'll lam Sid for that. I'll learn him!* (Mark Twain). [probably < Scandinavian (compare Old Icelandic *lemja* thrash)]

lam[2] (lam), *n., v.,* **lammed, lam·ming.** *Slang.*
—*n.* a hurried escape, as from the scene of a crime.
on the lam, a. escaping: *When he [a bear] is on the lam, he can make good time through thickets almost impenetrable to dogs* (Newsweek). **b.** in hiding: *As Rocky tells it, by the time he was old enough for school, he was on the lam from the truant officer* (Time).
take it on the lam, to flee hurriedly; escape: *The heat was on and Antony took it on the lam* (Punch).
—*v.i.* to escape, especially from an officer of the law; run away; flee.
[origin uncertain, perhaps < *lam*[1]]

lam., laminated.

Lam., 1. Lamentations (book of the Old Testament). **2.** *Botany.* Lamarck.

la·ma (lä′mə), *n.* **1.** a monk of the northern Buddhist sect of Tibet and Mongolia. **2.** an ecclesiastic of high rank in Tibetan and Mongolian Buddhism. [< Tibetan *blama*]

La·ma·ism (lä′mə iz əm), *n.* the religious system of the lamas in Mongolia and in Tibet. It is a form of Buddhism adopted from the cult of Siva and from native shamanistic practices, possessing a widespread monastic system and a hierarchical organization headed by the Dalai Lama.

La·ma·ist (lä′mə ist), *n.* a believer in Lamaism. —*adj.* Lamaistic.

La·ma·is·tic (lä′mə is′tik), *adj.* **1.** characteristic of a Lamaist. **2.** of or having to do with Lamaism.

La Man·cha (lä män′chä), a region and former province in central Spain, celebrated in literature through Cervantes' *Don Quixote.*

La·man·ite (lā′mə nīt), *n.* (in the Book of Mormon) one of the ancient Hebrew ancestors of the American Indians. [< *Laman,* son of Lehi, a Hebrew prophet who supposedly led a group of people to America in the 600's B.C. + *-ite*[1]]

La·marck·i·an (lə mär′kē ən), *adj.* of the French biologist Lamarck or his theory. —*n.* a person who supports Lamarckism.

La·marck·i·an·ism (lə mär′kē ə niz əm), *n.* Lamarckism.

La·marck·ism (lə mär′kiz əm), *n.* the theory of evolution proposed and held by Jean de Lamarck, 1790-1869, which maintains that characteristics acquired by parents tend to be inherited by their descendants.

la·ma·ser·y (lä′mə ser′ē), *n., pl.* **-ser·ies.** a monastery of lamas in Mongolia and in Tibet. [< French *lamaserie,* apparently < *lama* lama + Persian *serāi,* or *sarāi* inn. Compare CARAVANSARY.]

lamb (lam), *n.* **1.** a young sheep: *Mary had a little lamb.* **2.** meat from a lamb: *roast lamb.* **3.** lambskin. **4.** a young, dear, or innocent person: *The widow she cried over me and called me a poor lost lamb* (Mark Twain). **5.** *Slang.* **a.** a person who is easily cheated. **b.** an inexperienced speculator. **6.** *Informal.* Persian lamb.

Lamb (def. 1)

like a lamb, a. meekly: *He accepted his defeat like a lamb.* **b.** easily fooled: *He was like a lamb in the hands of the swindlers and they fleeced him of all his savings.*

the Lamb, Jesus Christ. John 1:29, 36. *So shows my soul before the Lamb, My spirit before Thee* (Tennyson).

—*v.i.* to give birth to a lamb or lambs. —*v.t.* to attend (ewes) which are lambing. [Old English *lamb*] —**lamb′like′,** *adj.*

lam·bast (lam bast′), *v.t. Slang and Dialect.* lambaste.

lam·baste (lam bāst′), *v.t.,* **-bast·ed, -bast·ing.** *Slang and Dialect.* **1.** to beat; thrash: *The Queen and husband Philip spent the night at Government House, watched the traditional . . . drummers lambasting their three-foot drums with ferocious, stout-filled glee* (Time). **2.** to scold roughly; denounce violently; condemn: *Apparently the American people expect that in a campaign the two contending parties will lambaste each other unmercifully* (Wall Street Journal). **3.** *Nautical.* to beat with the end of a rope. [perhaps < *lam*[1] + *baste*[3]] —**Syn. 2.** excoriate, revile, score.

lamb·da (lam′də), *n.* the 11th letter of the Greek alphabet (Λ, λ). [< Greek *lámbda*]

lamb·da·cism (lam′də siz əm), *n.* **1.** lallation. **2.** a too frequent use of words containing the letter *l* in speaking or writing. [< Latin *lambdacismus* < Greek *lambdakismós* < *lámbda* lambda]

lambda particle, a heavy elementary particle, a form of hyperon, having a neutral charge and decaying very rapidly.

lamb·doid (lam′doid), *adj.* **1.** shaped like the Greek capital lambda (Λ). **2.** *Anatomy.* of or noting the suture between the occipital bone and the parietal bones of the skull. [< Middle French *lambdoïde* < Medieval Latin *lambdoides* < Greek *lambdoeidḗs* (medical sense) < *lámbda* lambda + *eîdos* shape]

lamb·doi·dal (lam doi′dəl), *adj.* lambdoid.

lamb dysentery, a highly fatal, contagious, ulcerative enteritis of young lambs.

lam·ben·cy (lam′bən sē), *n., pl.* **-cies. 1.** a lambent quality or condition. **2.** an instance or occurrence of this: *In the picture, these colors were all different, all smudgy and gray, and the point of this, said Mr. Fowler, was to accent the lambencies of the hair* (New Yorker).

lam·bent (lam′bənt), *adj.* **1.** moving lightly over a surface: *a lambent flame.* **2.** playing lightly and brilliantly over a subject: *a lambent wit.* **3.** softly bright: *lambent eyes. Moonlight is lambent.* [< Latin *lambēns, -entis,* present participle of *lambere* to lick] —**lam′bent·ly,** *adv.* —**Syn. 1.** flickering. **2.** playful, lively. **3.** shimmery.

lam·bert (lam′bərt), *n.* the unit of brightness, equivalent to the brightness of a perfectly diffused surface that emits or reflects one lumen per square centimeter. [< Johann H. *Lambert,* 1728-1777, a German physicist]

lambert conformal projection or **lambert projection,** a map projection in which the meridians are drawn on the surface of a cone and the parallels are spaced mathematically to conform to the actual shape of the features represented. [< Johann H. *Lambert*]

Lam·beth Conference (lam′bəth), a meeting of bishops of the Anglican Communion held to discuss church policy about once every ten years in London.

Lambeth Palace, the London residence of the Archbishop of Canterbury.

Lambeth walk, a ballroom song and dance popular, especially in England, in the late 1930's.

lamb·kill (lam′kil′), *n. U.S.* the sheep laurel.

lamb·kin (lam′kin), *n.* **1.** a little lamb; young lamb. **2.** a young or dear person.

lamb·like (lam′līk′), *adj.* like a lamb; gentle; humble; meek: *What a lamblike Insurrection!* (Thomas Carlyle).

lamb·ling (lam′ling), *n.* a lambkin.

Lamb of God, Jesus Christ. John 1:29 and 36.

lam·boys (lam′boiz), *n.* a skirt of armor, usually steel, which hung from the waist to the knees. It was used chiefly in the 1400's and 1500's. [origin uncertain]

lam·bre·quin (lam′brə kin, -bər-), *n.* **1.** *U.S.* a drapery covering the top of a window or door, or hanging from a shelf. **2.** a scarf worn in medieval times as a covering over a helmet to protect it from heat, dampness, etc. [< Middle French *lambrequin* < Dutch *lamperkÿn* < *lamper* veil + *-kin* -kin]

lamb·skin (lam′skin′), *n.* **1.** the skin of a lamb, especially with the wool on it: *a heavy coat lined with lambskin.* **2.** leather made from the skin of a lamb. **3.** parchment made from this skin.

lambs-quar·ter (lamz′kwôr′tər), *n.,* or **lamb's quarter,** a weed of the goosefoot family which is sometimes cultivated and used as a potherb and in salad.

lambs·wool (lamz′wu̇l′), *n.* **1.** a light, soft wool yarn spun from the first shearing of a lamb less than a year old. **2.** hot ale mixed with the pulp of roasted apples and sweetened and spiced: *Lay a crab in the fire to roast for lambswool* (George Peele). —*adj.* made from lambswool: *lambswool blankets, a lambswool shawl.*

lamb·y (lam′ē), *adj.,* **lamb·i·er, lamb·i·est. 1.** lamblike. **2.** woolly like a lamb.

lame[1] (lām), *adj.,* **lam·er, lam·est,** *v.,* **lamed, lam·ing.** —*adj.* **1.** not able to walk properly; having an injured leg or foot; crippled. **2.** stiff and sore: *His arm is lame from playing ball.* **3.** poor; weak; unsatisfactory: *Sleeping too long is a lame excuse for being late. Santa Croce and the dome of St. Peter's are lame copies after a divine model* (Emerson). **4.** *Archaic.* crippled or impaired in any way; unable to move; infirm.

—*v.t.* to make lame; cripple: *The accident lamed him for life.* —*v.i.* to become lame; go lame.

[Old English *lama*] —**lame′ness,** *n.*

—**Syn.** *adj.* **1.** disabled, halt, limping, game. **3.** imperfect, defective, inconclusive, unconvincing, feeble.

lame[2] (lām), *n.* **1.** one of numerous thin, small, steel plates laid in an overlapping pattern in making pieces of flexible armor. **2.** *Obsolete.* a thin piece of any substance; lamina. [< Old French *lame* < Latin *lāmina,* and *lāmna.* Doublet of LAMINA.]

la·mé (la mā′, lä-), *n.* a rich fabric knitted or woven wholly or partly of metal, especially gold or silver, threads. [< French *lamé* a fabric, type of thread; (literally) laminated < Old French *lame* metal leaf]

lame-brain (lām′brān′), *n. Informal.* a stupid person: *Only lame-brains and weak sisters resort to handouts* (Wall Street Journal).

lame-brained (lām′brānd′), *adj. Informal.* not bright; foolish; stupid.

la·med (lä′med), *n.* the twelfth letter of the Hebrew alphabet. [< Hebrew *lamedh*]

lame duck, 1. *U.S.* **a.** any elective officeholder, especially a Congressman, who has been defeated for reëlection and is serving the last part of his term. **b.** a President of the United States who is serving a second term in office and cannot be reelected: *President Eisenhower became the first lame-duck President in history after the election of 1956.* **2.** a disabled or helpless person or thing: *They started out in convoy, but they had some engine trouble—and you know the rule of the road nowadays: no waiting for lame ducks* (Graham Greene). **3.** *Stock-Exchange Slang.* a person who cannot meet his financial engagements. —**lame′-duck′,** *adj.*

Lame Duck Amendment, the 20th Amendment to the United States Constitution, which moved forward the opening of a new Congress to January 3 and the inauguration of a new President to January 20, thus providing the earlier assumption of office by newly elected persons.

la·mel·la (lə mel′ə), *n., pl.* **-mel·las, -mel·lae** (-mel′ē). **1.** any structure in the shape of a thin plate, scale, or layer, especially of flesh or bone. **2.** one of the thin scales or plates composing some shells, as in bivalve mollusks. **3.** *Botany.* **a.** one of the gills (thin radiating plates) forming the spore-bearing layer of a mushroom. **b.** one of the erect scales appended to the corolla of some flowers. **c.** (in mosses) an erect sheet of cells on the midrib of a leaf. [< Latin *lāmella* (diminutive) < *lāmina* thin plate, lamina]

la·mel·lar (lə mel′ər, lam′ə lər), *adj.* having, consisting of, or arranged in lamellas. —**la·mel′lar·ly,** *adv.*

lam·el·late (lam′ə lāt, -lit; lə mel′āt, -it), *adj.* **1.** having, composed of, or arranged in lamellas or thin plates or scales; lamellar; lamellose. **2.** consisting of a flat plate or leaf. **3.** platelike or leaflike; flat. **4.** (of insect antennae) ending in a flattened sheetlike segment; lamellicorn. —**lam′el·late·ly,** *adv.*

lam·el·lat·ed (lam′ə lā′tid), *adj.* lamellate.

lam·el·la·tion (lam′ə lā′shən), *n.* lamellate arrangement or structure.

la·mel·li·branch (lə mel′ə brangk), *n.* any of a class of mollusks, including the oysters, clams, scallops, etc., characterized by thin, platelike gills and a bilaterally symmetrical, headless body that is compressed and enclosed in a mantle secreted by a bivalve shell whose parts are connected by a hinge. [< New Latin *Lamellibranchia* the family name < Latin *lāmella* lamella + Greek *bránchia* gills, branchia]

la·mel·li·bran·chi·ate (lə mel′ə brang′kē āt, -it), *adj.* belonging to the lamellibranchs. —*n.* a lamellibranch.

la·mel·li·corn (lə mel′ə kôrn), *adj.* **1.** of or belonging to a group of beetles having antennae ending in flattened segments, as the dung beetles, chafers, and Japanese beetles. **2.** (of antennae) ending in flattened segments; lamellate. —*n.* a cockchafer, dung beetle, scarab, or other beetle whose antennae end in flat plates. [< New Latin *Lamellicornes* the group name < Latin *lāmella* lamella + *cornū, -ūs* horn]

la·mel·li·form (lə mel′ə fôrm), *adj.* having the shape or structure of a lamella or thin plate.

la·mel·li·ros·tral (lə mel′ə ros′trəl), *adj.* (of waterfowl) having a series of lamellas inside the bill adapted for sieving food from water, as in the ducks, geese, and swans. [< New Latin *Lamellirostres* the family name (< Latin *lāmella* lamella + *rōstrum* beak, rostrum) + English *-al*[1]]

la·mel·li·ros·trate (lə mel′ə ros′trāt), *adj.* lamellirostral.

la·mel·lose (lə mel′ōs, lam′ə lōs), *adj.* lamellate.

lame·ly (lām′lē), *adv.* **1.** in a lame manner; with a limp; haltingly. **2.** imperfectly; defectively; poorly: *We left . . . with the main purpose of my visit but lamely accomplished* (Mark Twain).

la·ment (lə ment′), *v.t.* **1.** to express grief for; mourn for: *to lament the dead.* **2.** to regret: *We lamented his absence. I lamented my own folly . . . in attempting a second voyage* (Daniel Defoe). —*v.i.* **1.** to express grief; mourn; weep: *Why does she lament?* **2.** to show great sorrow or regret; repine.

—*n.* **1.** an expression of grief; wail: *Good grandsire, leave these bitter deep laments* (Shakespeare). **2.** a poem, song, or tune that expresses grief; elegy; dirge: *Soon as the dire lament was play'd, It waked the lurking ambuscade* (Scott). **3.** a regret. **4.** *Poetic.* the act of lamenting; lamentation.

[< Latin *lāmentārī* < *lāmentum* a wailing, related to *lātrāre* to bark, cry] —**la·ment′er,** *n.* —**la·ment′ing·ly,** *adv.*

—**Syn.** *v.t.* **1.** bewail, deplore. —*v.i.* **1.** grieve, wail.

lam·en·ta·ble (lam′ən tə bəl, lə men′-), *adj.* **1.** to be regretted or pitied: *a lamentable accident, a lamentable failure. It was a lamentable day when our dog died.* **2.** *Archaic.* sorrowful; mournful: *a lamentable voice.* —**Syn. 1.** pitiable, deplorable.

lam·en·ta·bly (lam′ən tə blē, lə men′-), *adv.* mournfully; pitifully.

lam·en·ta·tion (lam′ən tā′shən), *n.* **1.** loud grief; cries of sorrow; mourning; wailing. **2.** a lament; wail: *She tried to forget, but she could not. Her lamentations continued with a strange abundance, a strange persistency* (Lytton Strachey).

Lam·en·ta·tions (lam′ən tā′shənz), *n.pl.* a book of the Old Testament, said to have been written by Jeremiah. By Christians it is customarily placed among the prophetic books, following Jeremiah, but in the Hebrew Bible it is classed among the sacred writings (Hagiographa) rather than among the Prophets (Nebiim). *Abbr.:* Lam.

la·ment·ed (lə men′tid), *adj.* **1.** mourned for, as one who is dead: *his excellent, learned, and ever lamented friend the late Mr. Yorke* (Edmund Burke). **2.** regretted; deplored.

la·me·ter (lā′mə tər), *n. Scottish and Northern English.* a lame person; cripple: *You have now, no doubt, friends who will . . . not suffer you to devote yourself to a blind lameter like me* (Charlotte Brontë). Also, **lamiter.** [ultimately < *lame*[1]]

la·mi·a (lā′mē ə), *n., pl.* **-mi·as, -mi·ae** (-mē ē). **1.** *Greek and Roman Mythology.* a fabulous monster having the head and breasts of a woman and the body of a serpent, said to lure away children, especially the newborn, to suck their blood. **2.** a witch; female demon. [< Latin *lamia* sorceress, a blood-sucking witch < Greek *lámia* flesh-eating monster]

la·mi·a·ceous (lā′mē ā′shəs), *adj.* belonging to the mint family. [< New Latin *Lamium* the typical genus (< Latin *lāmium* a barren nettle) + English *-aceous*]

lam·i·na (lam′ə nə), *n., pl.* **-nae** (-nē), **-nas. 1.** a thin plate, scale, layer, or flake (of metal, etc.). **2.** the flat, wide part of a leaf. **3.** *Anatomy.* a thin layer of bone, membrane, etc. [< Latin *lāmina* thin piece of metal or wood; plate, leaf, layer. Doublet of LAME[2].]

lam·i·na·ble (lam′ə nə bəl), *adj.* that can be formed into thin plates or layers.

lam·i·nal (lam′ə nəl), *adj.* laminar.

lam·i·nar (lam′ə nər), *adj.* **1.** having, consisting of, or arranged in thin layers, plates, or scales. **2.** smooth; streamlined; not turbulent: *The flow of oil for lubrication in bearings is laminar.*

laminar flow, a smooth, steady flow of air over or about an airfoil or other body, as opposed to turbulent flow.

lam·i·nar·i·a·ceous (lam′ə nãr′ē ā′shəs), *adj.* belonging to a group of brown algae that includes the large kelps. [< New Latin *Laminaria* the genus name (< Latin *lāmina* thin plate) + English *-aceous*]

lam·i·nar·in (lam′ə nãr′in), *n.* a sulfated form of starch derived from seaweed, which serves as an anticoagulant. [< New Latin *Laminaria* the genus name + English *-in*]

lam·i·nate (*v.* lam′ə nāt; *adj., n.* lam′ə-nāt, -nit), *v.,* **-nat·ed, -nat·ing,** *adj., n.* —*v.t.* **1.** to split into thin layers or leaves. **2.** to make by putting layer on layer. **3.** to beat or roll (metal) into a thin plate. **4.** to cover with thin plates. —*v.i.* to separate or split into thin layers or leaves.
—*adj.* laminated; laminar.
—*n.* a laminated plastic.
[< Latin *lāmina* lamina + English *-ate*[1]]

lam·i·nat·ed (lam′ə nā′tid), *adj.* **1.** consisting of, arranged in, or furnished with laminae. **2.** formed or manufactured in a succession of layers of material, as some metallic objects, plywood, or plastics.

lam·i·na·tion (lam′ə nā′shən), *n.* **1.** a laminating. **2.** a being laminated. **3.** a laminated structure; arrangement in thin layers. **4.** a thin layer.

lam·i·na·tive (lam′ə nā′tiv), *adj.* of a laminated texture.

lam·i·na·tor (lam′ə nā′tər), *n.* a device which protects documents by laminating them between sheets of transparent plastic.

lam·i·nec·to·my (lam′ə nek′tə mē), *n., pl.* **-mies.** surgical removal of the posterior arch of a vertebra.

lam·i·ni·tis (lam′ə nī′tis), *n.* inflammation of the sensitive laminar structures of a horse's foot; founder. [< New Latin *laminitis* < *lamina* lamina + *-itis* -itis]

lam·i·nose (lam′ə nōs), *adj.* consisting of or having the form of laminae.

lam·i·nous (lam′ə nəs), *adj.* laminose.

lam·is·ter (lam′ə stər), *n. Slang.* a person who is escaping or hiding from the law; escaped convict; fugitive: *The Irish law was already so well publicized . . . that every major British lamister had long since flown the coop* (Time). Also, **lamster.** [< *lam*[2] + *-ster*]

la·mi·ter (lā′mə tər), *n.* lameter.

Lam·mas (lam′əs), *n.,* or **Lammas Day, 1.** (in the Roman Catholic Church) August 1, a religious feast commemorating the imprisonment and miraculous escape of Saint Peter. Acts 12:4-10. **2.** August 1, the day of a harvest festival formerly held in England. [Old English *hlāfmæsse* < *hlāf* bread, loaf + *mæsse* mass (because of the consecration of loaves of the year's first grain)]

Lam·mas·tide (lam′əs tīd′), *n.* the season around August 1 (Lammas): *How long is it now To Lammastide?* (Shakespeare). [< *Lammas* + *tide*[1] festival time]

lam·mer·gei·er or **lam·mer·gey·er** (lam′ər gī′ər), *n.* the largest European bird of prey, with a wingspread of 9 to 10 feet, inhabiting lofty mountains in southern Europe, Asia, and northern Africa; ossifrage; bearded vulture. [< German *Lämmergeier* < *Lämmer,* plural of *Lamm* lamb + *Geier* vulture]

lam·mer·geir (lam′ər gīr), *n.* lammergeier.

La·mo·na (lə mō′nə), *n.* any of an American breed of poultry with white plumage and white-shelled eggs.

lamp (lamp), *n.* **1. a.** a thing that gives light, or sometimes heat, as by means of electricity, gas or oil, including vessels that burn oil through a wick for illumination. **b.** a torch or flashlight. **2.** something that suggests the light of a lamp: *reason, that heav'n-lighted lamp in man* (Edward Young). **3.** *Slang.* an eye. **4.** one of the heavenly bodies, as the sun, the moon, a star, or a meteor: *that glorious lamp of heaven, the sun* (Robert Herrick).
smell of the lamp, to suggest long hours of hard work late at night; be stuffy or pedantic: *Hardly any poet smells of the lamp less disagreeably than Spenser* (George E. B. Saintsbury).
[< Old French *lampe* < Latin *lampas, -adis* < Greek *lampás, -ados* < *lámpein* to shine]

lam·pads (lam′padz), *n.pl. Poetic.* the seven "lamps of fire" burning before the throne of God. Revelation 4:5. [< Greek *lampás, -ados* lamp]

lam·pas[1] (lam′pəs), *n.* an inflammation of the mucous membrane covering the hard palate of the mouth in the horse. [< Old French *lampas*]

lam·pas[2] (lam′pəs), *n.* a kind of flowered silk fabric, originally imported from China and usually made into shawls or kerchiefs. [< French *lampas*]

lamp·black (lamp′blak′), *n.* a fine black soot consisting of almost pure carbon that is deposited when oil, gas, etc., burns incompletely. Lampblack is used as a coloring matter in paint, ink, cement, etc. —*v.t.* to paint, smear, or coat with lampblack: *A . . . scoundrel who knows no pleasure beyond . . . lampblacking signs* (Thomas Brown).

lam·per eel (lam′pər), **1.** a lamprey. **2.** an eelpout.

lam·pers (lam′pərz), *n.* lampas, inflammation of the mucous membrane of the hard palate of a horse.

lamp holder, *Especially British.* a socket for an electric-light bulb.

lamp·house (lamp′hous′), *n.* an enclosure for a source of light, as in a lantern: *This new carbon in its proper lamphouse gives twice as much light as any . . . unit previously available* (William F. Kelley).

lam·pi·on (lam′pē ən), *n.* a simple small lamp, often of colored glass, used for illumination. [< French *lampion* < Italian *lampione* street or carriage light (augmentative) < *lampa,* probably < Old French *lampe* lamp]

lamp·light (lamp′līt′), *n.* **1.** the light from a lamp. **2.** the time of evening when lamps are lit.

lamp·light·er (lamp′lī′tər), *n.* **1.** a person who lights street lamps. **2.** *U.S.* (formerly) a torch, twisted paper, etc., used to light lamps.

lamp oil, 1. oil used for burning in a lamp. **2.** *U.S.* kerosene.

lam·poon (lam pün′), *n.* a piece of writing, a speech, remark, etc., that attacks and ridicules a person in a malicious or abusive way: *Many popular nursery rhymes probably originated as lampoons on famous people.* —*v.t.* to attack in a lampoon; ridicule; poke fun at: *The timbre of his voice and his facial contour are just right for the pompous creature he was lampooning* (Wall Street Journal). [< earlier French *lampon* drinking song < *lampons* let us drink (a refrain of a drinking song) < slang *lamper* to drink] —**lampoon′er,** *n.* —**Syn.** *n.* satire, pasquinade.

lam·poon·er·y (lam pü′nər ē), *n., pl.* **-eries. 1.** the practice of writing lampoons: *Lichty wants to stay near the newsroom he knows because he likes to keep his lampoonery of everyday situations tied firmly to the news* (Time). **2.** lampooning quality or spirit.

lam·poon·ist (lam pü′nist), *n.* a person who writes or makes lampoons.

lamp·post (lamp′pōst′), *n.* a post used to support a street lamp.

lam·prey (lam′prē), *n., pl.* **-preys.** any of the marine and fresh-water vertebrate animals having a body like an eel, gill slits like a fish, no jaws, and a large round mouth. Lampreys are found throughout the world, are parasitic, and attach themselves to fishes with their mouths, sucking the body fluids. [< Old French *lampreie* < Medieval Latin *lampreda,* uncertain relationship to Late Latin *lampetra* < Latin *lambere* to lick + *petra* rock. Doublet of LIMPET.]

Sea Lamprey (to 3 ft. long)

lam·pri·cide (lam′prə sīd), *n.* a chemical that kills the larvae of lampreys.

lamp shade, a shade over a lamp to soften or direct the light.

lamp shell, a brachiopod: . . . *the term "lamp shell" applies to the resemblance of a valve of the concave shell to an old Roman oil lamp* (Tracy I. Storer).

lam·siek·te (läm′sēk′tə), *n.* lamziekte.

lam·ster (lam′stər), *n.* lamister.

lam·ziek·te (läm′zēk′tə), *n.* a paralytic disease of cattle in South Africa. It is a form of botulism. [< Afrikaans *lamziekte* < Dutch *lam* lame + *ziekte* disease]

la·nai (lä nī′), *n., pl.* **-nais.** *Hawaiian.* a porch or veranda.

la·nate (lā′nāt), *adj. Botany, Entomology.* having a woolly covering or surface; lanose. [< Latin *lānātus* < *lāna* wool]

Lan·cas·ter (lang′kə stər), *n.* the English royal house, descended from John of Gaunt, Duke of Lancaster, that reigned from 1399 to 1461. The three kings of this house were Henry IV, Henry V, and Henry VI.

Lan·cas·te·ri·an (lang′kə stir′ē ən), *adj.* of or having to do with the English educator Joseph Lancaster, or the system of instruction used by him, in which the younger pupils were taught by the more advanced pupils, who were called monitors.

Lan·cas·tri·an (lang kas′trē ən), *adj.* of or having to do with the English royal house of Lancaster. —*n.* **1.** (in English history) a supporter or member of the house of Lancaster, especially in opposition to the Yorkists in the Wars of the Roses, in which the Lancastrian symbol was a red rose. **2.** a native of Lancashire, county in England.

lance[1] (lans, läns), *n., v.,* **lanced, lanc·ing.** —*n.* **1. a.** a long wooden spear with a sharp, pointed iron or steel head, formerly carried by knights, cavalry troops, etc. **b.** any instrument like a soldier's lance, as for spearing fish, killing a whale, etc. **c.** a lancet. **2.** a soldier, especially a mounted soldier, armed with a lance; lancer: *The count, at the head of an hundred lances, was gone toward the frontiers of Brabant* (Scott). **3.** a metal pipe for supplying oxygen under pressure, used to cut or pierce metal or to oxidize molten iron. [< Old French *lance* < Latin *lancea* light Spanish spear]
—*v.t.* **1.** to pierce with or as with a lance: *They lanced his flesh with knives* (John Bunyan). **2.** to cut open with a lancet: *The dentist lanced the gum so that the new tooth could come through.* —*v.i.* to dart, rush, or bound away.
[< Old French *lancier* < Late Latin *lanceāre* < Latin *lancea.* Doublet of LAUNCH[2].]
—**Syn.** *v.t.* **1.** cut, gash, slit.

Lance[1] (def. 1a)

lance[2] (lans, läns), *n.* launce.

lance corporal, (in the British army) a private acting temporarily as a corporal without increase of pay. [formed after earlier *lancepesade* < Middle French *lancepessade* < Italian *lancia spezzata* broken lance]

lance knight, *Obsolete.* a lansquenet. [< German *Lanzknecht* (< *Lanze* lance), alteration of *Landsknecht* < *Land(e)s* the land's + *Knecht* servant]

lance·let (lans′lit, läns′-), *n.* any of various small, limbless, often translucent, fishlike marine animals, among the lowest of existing vertebrates, found in the sand under shallow waters; amphioxus. Lancelets have a thin body, pointed at both ends and no skull. [earlier, a lancet < *lance* + *-let*]

lance·like (lans′līk′), *adj.* shaped like a lance: *Strange that so gigantic a tree [the sequoia] should put out such paltry lancelike leaves* (New Yorker).

Lan·ce·lot (lan′sə lət, -lot; län′-), *n.* the bravest of King Arthur's knights of the Round Table, lover of Queen Guinevere and father of Sir Galahad.

lan·ce·o·late (lan′sē ə lāt, -lit), *adj.* shaped like the head of a lance; tapering from a rounded base toward the apex; narrow and tapering more sharply to one end than the other. [< Latin *lanceolātus* < *lanceola* (diminutive) < *lancea* lance]

Lanceolate Leaves

lan·ce·o·lat·ed (lan′sē ə lā′tid), *adj.* lanceolate.

lanc·er (lan′sər, län′-), *n.* a member of a light cavalry unit armed with lances (now applied to certain regiments of the British Army officially called Lancers): *the Bengal Lancers.*

lance rest, a support attached to a breastplate, on which the butt of a lance rested when raised in an attack.

lanc·ers or **lan·ciers** (lan′sərz, län′-), *n. pl.* **1.** a form of square dance or quadrille popular in the 1800's, having figures imitating military drill. **2.** the music for it.

lance sergeant, *British Army.* a corporal appointed to act temporarily as a sergeant without increase of pay.

lan·cet (lan′sit, län′-), *n.* **1.** a small, sharp-pointed surgical knife, usually having two sharp edges. Doctors use lancets for opening boils, abscesses, etc. **2.** *Architecture.* a lancet arch or lancet window. [< Old French *lancette* (diminutive) < *lance* lance < Latin *lancea*]

lancet arch, *Architecture.* a narrow, sharply pointed arch.

lan·cet·ed (lan′sə tid, län′-), *adj. Architecture.* having a lancet arch or lancet window.

lancet fish, any of various large, fierce marine fishes having an elongated body, long sharp teeth, and a very long, high dorsal fin.

lancet window, *Architecture.* a high, narrow window with a lancet arch at the top but not divided by tracery.

Lancet Window

lance·wood (lans′wu̇d′, läns′-), *n.* **1.** a tough, straight-grained, springy wood used for fishing rods, carriage shafts, cabinetwork, etc. **2.** any of various American trees that yield this wood.

lan·ci·form (lan′sə fôrm), *adj.* spear-shaped; pointed; lanceolate.

lan·ci·nate (lan′sə nāt), *v.t.,* **-nat·ed, -nat·ing.** to pierce; tear. [< Latin *lancināre* (with English *-ate*[1]) destroy, tear to pieces, related to *lacerāre* lacerate]

lan·ci·nat·ing (lan′sə nā′ting), *adj.* piercing; shooting (used especially of pains, as in cancer).

lan·ci·na·tion (lan′sə nā′shən), *n.* **1.** a sharp, shooting pain. **2.** *Obsolete.* laceration; wounding.

land (land), *n.* **1.** the solid part of the earth's surface: *dry land.* **2.** ground or soil, especially as having particular use or characteristics: *This is good land for a garden.* **3. a.** landed property; real estate, as a piece of ground and everything permanently attached to it. **b.** any interest that a person has in land. **c.** *Economics.* anything furnished by nature without the help of man, as soil, mineral deposits, water, wildlife. *Land, labor,* and *capital* are the three principal factors of production. **4. a.** a country; region: *the land of Egypt, the land of the midnight sun, mountainous land. Soldiers are citizens of death's grey land* (Siegfried Sassoon). **b.** the people of a country; nation: *He made songs for all the land* (Shelley). **5.** one of the strips into which a field is divided by plowing. **6.** one of the smooth, raised surfaces between the grooves in the bore of a rifle or rifled weapon.

how the land lies, what the state of affairs is: *Uncle Charles's eyes had discovered how the land lay as regarded Rose and himself* (Mary Bridgman).

lands, a. territorial possessions: *Their lands had been divided by Cromwell among his followers* (Macaulay). **b.** (in South Africa) those parts of a farm on which crops are cultivated: *There are, too, the 'lands' where the mealies and the corn are planted* (Beatrice M. Hicks).

make land, to discover or see land as the ship approaches a shore: *We were at sea a full week before we finally made land.*

—*v.i.* **1.** to come to land or something solid like land: *The ship landed at the pier. After its engine caught fire the plane landed at an emergency field.* **2.** to go ashore: *The passengers landed.* **3.** to arrive: *The thief landed in jail.* —*v.t.* **1. a.** to put on land; set ashore; set on something solid like land: *The ship landed its passengers. The pilot landed the airplane at Seattle.* **b.** to set down from a vehicle: *His hansom landed him at the door of a great mansion* (Mrs. Humphry Ward). **2.** to cause to arrive in any place, position, or condition: *A combination of circumstances landed him in bankruptcy.* **3.** *Slang.* to get (a blow) home: *I landed one on his chin.* **4.** *Informal.* to catch; get: *to land a job, to land a contract.*

[Old English *land*]

—**Syn.** *n.* **2.** earth.

Land (länt), *n., pl.* **Län·der** or **Laen·der** (len′dər), *German.* a state; province.

land agent, 1. a manager of a property and its land. **2.** a real estate agent.

land·am·man or **land·am·mann** (länt′-äm′än), *n.* the title of the chief magistrate in some of the Swiss cantons. [< Swiss German *Landamman* < *Land* land + *Amman* < German *Amtmann* < *Amt* office + *Mann* man]

lan·dau (lan′dô, -dou), *n.* **1.** a four-wheeled carriage with two inside seats facing each other and a top made in two parts that can be folded back. **2.** an automobile with a similar top. [< *Landau,* a town in Germany, where it was first made]

Landau (def. 1)

lan·dau·let or **lan·dau·lette** (lan′dô-let′), *n.* **1.** a landau with only one seat: *The mistress of a very pretty landaulette* (Jane Austen). **2.** an automobile with a single seat and a folding top. [< *landau* + *-let*]

land bank, 1. a bank that grants long-term loans on real property in return for mortgages, as a Federal Land Bank loan to a farmer. **2.** *British.* (formerly) a banking institution that issued notes on the security of real property.

land-based (land′bāst′), *adj.* having its origin or base of operations on land rather than water: *One service officer has drawn up figures to show that carrier-based aviation is fifteen times as expensive as land-based aviation* (Newsweek).

land·bound (land′bound′), *adj.* bound or limited to the land: *In total nuclear warfare, what can a landbound army do?* (Newsweek).

land breeze, a breeze blowing from the land toward the sea: *The land breeze is usually less developed than the sea breeze; it is shallower, has less speed, and extends only 5 or 6 miles over the sea* (Thomas A. Blair).

land bridge, a neck of land connecting two land masses: *Australia may have been settled earlier, when a land bridge still joined that continent to South-East Asia* (Punch).

land crab, any of various large terrestrial adult crabs of the West Indies.

land·drost (land′drōst′, lan′-), *n.* (formerly, in South Africa) a magistrate in charge of a district: *He gave his landdrost the power to seize and prosecute all criminals.* [< Afrikaans *landdrost* < Dutch < *land* land + *drost* steward]

lande (land; *French* läNd), *n.* an uncultivated or unfertile plain covered with heath, broom, ferns, etc., as in southwestern France. [< French *lande*]

land·ed (lan′did), *adj.* **1.** owning land: *landed nobles.* **2.** consisting of land: *Landed property is real estate.*

land·er (lan′dər), *n.* **1.** a person who makes a landing. **2.** a person who settles on land.

land·fall (land′fôl′), *n.* **1.** an approach to land from the sea or air; landing. **2.** a sighting of land. **3.** the land sighted or reached.

land·fast (land′fast′), *adj.* attached to land: *A million years ago the island was either landfast or near the shore.*

land·fill (land′fil), *n.* **1.** a place where rubbish is deposited and covered with earth: *Refuse from Brooklyn and Manhattan . . . is dumped in a landfill* (New York Times). **2.** this system of rubbish disposal.

land·form (land′fôrm′), *n.* the physical characteristics of land; irregularities of land: *Major landforms may be classified on the basis of two characteristics, land relief and surface configuration* (White and Renner).

land grabber, a person who acquires land from another by treachery, force, or other means contrary to the spirit of the law.

land grant, a grant of land; gift of land by the government for colleges, railroads, roads, etc. Land grant colleges or universities are institutions that receive federal aid in land or money under the Morrill Acts of 1862 and 1890, which permitted each state to use public lands to support at least one agricultural or industrial college.

land·gra·vate (land′grā vāt), *n.* landgraviate.

land·grave (land′grāv′), *n.* **1.** a German count in the Middle Ages having authority over a considerable territory or over other counts. **2.** the title of certain German princes. [ultimately < Middle High German *lantgrāve* < *lant* land + *grāve* count]

land·gra·vi·ate (land grā′vē āt, -it), *n.* the office, jurisdiction, authority, or territory of a landgrave.

land·gra·vine (land′grə vēn), *n.* **1.** the wife of a landgrave. **2.** a woman holding a position in her own right equal to that of a landgrave. [< Dutch *landgravin*]

land·hold·er (land′hōl′dər), *n.* a person who owns or occupies land.

land·hold·ing (land′hōl′ding), *adj.* that owns or occupies land: *a landholding corporation.* —*n.* an owning or occupying of land.

land·ing (lan′ding), *n.* **1.** a coming to land or something solid like land: *the landing of the Pilgrims at Plymouth. While in 1936 there were 5 million take-offs and landings at the nation's airports, there are now 65 million, and 115 million are forecast for 1975* (Atlantic). **2.** a place where persons or goods are landed from a ship, helicopter, etc.; landing place: *the steamboat landing.* **3.** the catching of fish, especially in large amounts by commercial methods: *Halibut landings of 37 million pounds were down six million from the 1954 catch* (Wall Street Journal). **4. a.** a platform between flights of stairs. **b.** the floor at the head or foot of a staircase. **5.** (in lumbering) a place where logs are gathered before being transported to a sawmill. —**Syn. 1.** debarkation, disembarkation. **2.** port, wharf.

landing barge, a small boat that carries men or supplies to land from a ship.

landing circle, a circular course for airplanes to follow around on an airfield before landing.

landing craft, any of various kinds of boats or ships used for landing troops or equipment on a shore, especially during an assault. Landing craft usually have a front that opens or drops to form a ramp.

landing field, a field large enough and smooth enough for airplanes to land and take off safely.

landing gear, wheels, pontoons, etc., under an aircraft. When on land or water an aircraft rests on its landing gear. See **undercarriage** for picture.

landing light, 1. any of the lights on an aircraft used to see when landing at night. **2.** any of the lights or systems of lights on the ground used to light up a runway or guide an aircraft to a runway.

landing mat, a 12-by-3-foot mat of meshed steel that can be joined to others to form a smooth landing surface for aircraft on rough or unprepared ground.

landing net, a small net to take fish from the water after they are caught.

landing party, 1. a group of soldiers who make a landing, especially in advance of a main invasion force. **2.** any group of people who make a landing in advance of others.

landing place, 1. a place to land people or goods. **2.** a landing of a staircase.

landing stage, a floating platform used for loading and unloading people and goods.

landing strip, a long, narrow runway for airplanes to take off and land.

landing system, a system of controls which regulates or assists in the landing of an aircraft: *A jet bomber was safely landed by a ground-based, automatic landing system using radar to track the plane and radio to transmit flight path correction signals to the airplane's auto-pilot* (Science News Letter).

Night Visual Landing System
If pilot is descending correctly, he sees red and white lights. If approach is too low, he sees all lights red; too high, he sees all lights white.

land·la·dy (land′lā′dē), *n., pl.* **-dies. 1.** a woman who owns buildings or land that she rents to others. **2.** the mistress of an inn, lodging house, or boarding house.

land·less (land′lis), *adj.* without land; owning no land. —**land′less·ness,** *n.*

land·like (land′līk′), *adj.* like or characteristic of land: *The sea bottom has landlike hills and valleys carved by some earlier terrestrial streams.*

land·line (land′līn′), *n.* a communication cable that runs on or under the land.

land·locked (land′lokt′), *adj.* **1.** shut in, or nearly shut in, by land: *a landlocked harbor.* **2.** living in waters shut off from the sea: *landlocked salmon.*

land·lop·er (land′lō′pər), *n. Especially Scottish.* **1.** a vagabond. **2.** *Obsolete.* a renegade. [< Dutch *landlooper* < *land* land + *loopen* to run]

land·lord (land′lôrd′), *n.* **1.** a person who owns buildings or land that he rents to others: *absentee landlords.* **2.** the keeper of an inn, lodging house, or boarding house. —**Syn. 2.** host, innkeeper.

land·lord·ism (land′lôr′diz əm), *n.* **1.** the methods or practices of landlords; system of renting from landlords: . . . *agriculture with low productivity hampered still by the relics of landlordism* . . . (Wall Street Journal). **2.** the principle of the supremacy of the landlord class.

land·lord·ly (land′lôrd′lē), *adj.* belonging or proper to a landlord.

land·lord·ship (land′lôrd′ship), *n.* the position or function of a landlord.

land·loup·er (land′lou′pər, -lü′-), *n. Especially Scottish.* landloper.

land·lub·ber (land′lub′ər), *n.* a person not used to being on ships: *The sailors called the landsmen landlubbers in scorn.* [< *land* + *lubber*]

land·lub·ber·ly (land′lub′ər lē), *adj.* confined to or used on land rather than the sea: *landlubberly phrases, landlubberly sports.*

land·lub·bing (land′lub′ing), *adj.* living or staying on the land; not seafaring. —*n.* life or activity on land.

land·man (land′mən), *n., pl.* **-men.** *Rare.* landsman.

land·mark (land′märk′), *n.* **1.** something familiar or easily seen, and often used as a guide: *The courthouse tower is a well-known landmark to everyone in Oakville. He did not lose his way in the forest because the mountain served as a landmark.* **2.** an important fact or event; a happening that stands out above others: *The printing press, the telegraph, the telephone, and the radio are landmarks in the progress of communications.* **3.** a stone or other object that marks the boundary of a piece of land: *Thou shalt not remove thy neighbour's landmark* (Deuteronomy 19:14).
—*adj. U.S.* (of a legal or judicial ruling) serving as a guide in future cases; setting a precedent: *a landmark Supreme Court decision.*
—*v.t.* to mark or indicate by or as by a landmark.

land mass, 1. a large, unbroken area of land; continent: *Antarctica is the earth's coldest land mass.* **2.** a large area of land connected both geographically and politically: *The Soviet Union and its satellites form a land mass extending from eastern Europe through most of Asia.*

land measure, a system of square measure for the area of land.

land mine, a container filled with an explosive charge placed on the ground or lightly covered. It is usually set off by the weight of vehicles or troops passing over it or by magnetic contact.

land·oc·ra·cy (land ok′rə sē), *n.* a ruling or dominating landed class in a country. [< *land* + (arist)*ocracy*]

land·o·crat (land′ə krat), *n.* a member of a landocracy.

Land of Beulah, the land of rest and happiness just this side of the river of death in John Bunyan's *Pilgrim's Progress.*

Land of Enchantment, a nickname for New Mexico.

land office, a government office that takes care of the business connected with public lands, and records sales, transfers, etc.

land-of·fice business (land′ôf′is, -of′-), *U.S. Informal.* exceedingly active or rapid business.

Land of Lincoln, a nickname for Illinois.

land of nod, sleep.

Land of Opportunity, a nickname for Arkansas.

Land of Promise, (in the Bible) the country promised by God to Abraham and his descendants; Canaan. Genesis 15:18, 17:8.

land of promise, a country or place that affords the expectation of a better lot.

land of the leal, the abode of the blessed after death; heaven.

land otter, river otter.

land·own·er (land′ō′nər), *n.* a person who owns land.

land·own·er·ship (land′ō′nər ship), *n.* the state of being a landowner.

land·own·ing (land′ō′ning), *adj.* holding or possessing landed estates: *the landowning class.* —*n.* the condition of being a landowner.

land patent, *Law.* a deed that gives a private citizen possession of public land.

land·plane (land′plān′), *n.* an airplane that cannot take off from or land on water.

land plaster, gypsum ground to a powder for use as a fertilizer.

land-poor (land′pu̇r′), *adj.* **1.** owning much land but needing ready money. **2.** poor because of taxes, etc., on one's land. **3.** lacking land.

land power, 1. military strength in land forces. **2.** a nation that maintains large and effective land forces.

Land·race (land′rās′), *adj.* of or designating a breed of large, white hogs introduced from Scandinavia into Great Britain.

land rail, the corn crake, a type of wading bird.

land reform, 1. the redistribution of large land holdings in a way that will benefit more people than before and promote a more equalized system of ownership. **2.** any social or economic measure that will benefit farmers.

Land Rover, *Trademark.* an English motor vehicle resembling a jeep but of heavier construction.

lands (landz), *n.pl.* See under **land,** *n.*

land·scape (land′skāp), *n., v.,* **-scaped, -scap·ing.** —*n.* **1.** a view of scenery on land: *The two hills with the valley formed a beautiful landscape.* **2. a.** a painting showing a land scene. **b.** such paintings as a group: *The art gallery will open a landscape exhibit tomorrow.* **3.** panorama; scene; view: *The landscape of international politics is now very different from what it was* (Listener).
—*v.t.* to make (land) more pleasant to look at by arranging trees, shrubs, flowers, etc.: *The park is landscaped.* —*v.i.* to be a landscape gardener.
[< Dutch *landschap* < *land* land + *-schap* -ship] —**land′scap′er,** *n.*
—**Syn.** *n.* **1.** prospect. **3.** vista.

landscape architect, a person whose business is planning and redesigning landscape.

landscape architecture, the planning and redesigning of landscape, as in a city park or along a highway.

landscape gardener, a person whose business is landscape gardening.

landscape gardening, the art of arranging trees, shrubs, flowers, etc., to give a pleasing appearance to grounds, parks, etc.

land·scap·ist (land′skā pist), *n.* **1.** a painter of landscapes: *Though Europe has produced a host of great landscapists, from Claude Lorrain to Paul Cézanne, the West's best could have learned much from the Chinese* (Time). **2.** a landscape architect or gardener: *In the skillful hands of the Belgian landscapists, the grounds were transformed into a wonderland of light and verdure* (Atlantic).

land shark, *U.S.* a land grabber.

land·ship (land′ship), *n.* **1.** a ship erected and kept on land for training purposes. **2.** a wagon or other vehicle used for transportation on land.

land·side (land′sīd′), *n.* the flat side of a plow, which is turned toward the unplowed land.

land·skip (land′skip), *n. Archaic.* landscape.

lands·leit (länts′līt′), *n.pl. Yiddish.* one's fellow countrymen; fellow townsmen.

land·slide (land′slīd′), *n., v.,* **-slid, -slid·ing.** —*n.* **1.** a sliding down of a mass of soil or rock on a steep slope. **2.** the mass that slides down. **3.** an overwhelming majority of votes for one political party or candidate.
—*v.i.* to win an election by a landslide: *Brown . . . landslid over Knowland in the state's 1958 gubernatorial race* (Time).
[American English < *land* + *slide*]

land·slip (land′slip′), *n. British.* landslide (defs. 1 and 2).

Lands·mål (läns′môl′), *n.* the more recent of the two varieties of standard, literary Norwegian (contrasted with *Riksmål*). It incorporates various native dialects. [< Norwegian *Landsmål* < *lands,* genitive of *land* land + *mål* language, speech]

lands·man (landz′mən), *n., pl.* **-men. 1.** a person who lives or works on land. **2.** *Nautical.* **a.** an inexperienced seaman, below an ordinary seaman in rating. **b.** (formerly) a sailor on his first voyage. **3.** *Rare.* a fellow countryman: *Stand by me, countryman . . . for the love of Scotland and St. Andrew! I am innocent—I am your own native landsman* (Scott).

land·spout (land′spout′), *n.* a funnel-shaped cloud resembling a waterspout but occurring on land, produced by any of certain severe whirling storms of small extent.

Lands·raad (läns′rôd′), *n.* the legislative council of Greenland. [< Danish *Landsraad* < *lands,* genitive of *land* land + *raad* council]

Lands·ting or **Lands·thing** (läns′ting′), *n.* the upper house of the Danish legislature. [< Danish *Landsting* < *lands,* genitive of *land* land + *ting* assembly]

Land·sturm (länt′shtu̇rm′), *n.* in Germany, Switzerland, etc.: **1.** a general levy in time of war. **2.** the force that consists of all men liable to call for military service and not already in the army, navy, or Landwehr. [< German *Landsturm* < *Land* land + *Sturm* storm, military assault]

lands·wom·an (landz′wu̇m′ən), *n., pl.* **-wom·en.** a woman who lives or works on land.

Land·tag (länt′täk′), *n., pl.* **-ta·ge** (-tä′gə). a diet, or lawmaking body, of a German state. [< German *Landtag* (literally) land-day < *Land* land + *Tag* day, assembly]

land·tied (land′tīd′), *adj.* joined to the mainland or to other land by the growth of reefs or sand-spits, as islands.

land·ward (land′wərd), *adv.* toward the land. —*adj.* lying or situated toward the land.

land·wards (land′wərdz), *adv.* landward.

Land·wehr (länt′vār′), *n.* (in Germany, Austria, etc.) that part of the organized military forces of the nation consisting of men who have been trained in regular units for a required period of time and who are required to serve only in time of war. [< German *Landwehr* < *Land* land + *Wehr* defense]

land wind, a wind blowing from the land toward the sea.

lane[1] (lān), *n.* **1.** a narrow way between hedges, walls, or fences; narrow country road: *A parish all of fields, high hedges, and deep-rutted lanes* (George Eliot). **2. a.** any narrow way: *The six generals walked down a lane formed by two lines of soldiers and sailors.* **b.** a lengthwise division of a highway marked for a single line of traffic: *Center lane for left turn only* (highway sign). *Many four-lane highways cross the country.* **3.** an alley between buildings. **4.** a course or route used by ships or aircraft going in the same direction. **5.** one of the narrow alleys on a track, marked by chalked lines, especially one in which a runner must stay during sprint or hurdle races. [Old English *lane*] —**Syn. 1.** passage. **2. a.** path.

lane[2] (lān), *adj. Scottish.* lone.

lane·way (lān′wā′), *n.* **1.** the path or pavement of a lane. **2.** a lane: *One storekeeper cautiously followed a robber to a laneway three blocks away and watched him mount a motorcycle* (Maclean's).

lang (lang, läng), *adj., adv., n. Scottish.* long[1].

lang., language.

lan·ga·ha (läng gä′hä), *n.* a snake of Madagascar, having the snout prolonged into a sharply flexible tip. [< the Malagasy name]

Lang·er·hans islands (läng′ər häns), the islets of Langerhans.

Lang·lauf (läng′louf′), *n. German.* the act or sport of skiing across country.

Lang·läu·fer (läng′loi′fər), *n., pl.* **Lang·läu·fer.** *German.* a person who skis across country.

lang·ley (lang′lē), *n.* a unit of illumination used to measure heat, such as the temperature of a star. It is equal to 1 small calorie per square centimeter. [< Samuel P. *Langley,* 1834-1906, an American astronomer and physicist]

Lan·go·bard (lang′gə bärd), *n.* a Lombard.

Lan·go·bar·di·an (lang′gō bär′dē ən), *n.* the Germanic language of the Lombards.

Lan·go·bar·dic (lang′gə bär′dik), *adj.* Lombardic. —*n.* Langobardian.

lan·gouste (läN güst′), *n. French.* a lobster or crawfish.

lan·grage or **lan·gridge** (lang′grij), *n.* a kind of scattering shot of nails, bolts, etc., fastened together or enclosed in a case, formerly used in naval warfare for damaging sails and rigging. [origin unknown]

lan·grel (lang′grəl), *n. Obsolete.* langrage.

Lang·shan (lang′shan), *n.* any of an Asian breed of large, white-skinned poultry that produces very dark-brown eggs. [< *Langshan,* a locality near Shanghai, China]

lang syne, or **lang·syne** (lang′sīn′, -zīn′), *Scottish.* —*adv.* long since; long ago: . . . *this south-east corner of Scotland, full of memories of men on the march and battles fought lang syne* (London Times). —*n.* a time long ago, especially in the phrase *auld lang syne.* [< Scottish *lang* long + *syne* since]

lan·guage (lang′gwij), *n.* **1. a.** human speech, spoken or written: *Language is the basis of man's uniqueness, and the essence of his culture* (Scientific American). **b.** the power or capacity of speech: *Oh that those lips had language* (William Cowper). **2. a.** the speech of one nation or race; tongue: *the French language.* **b.** any means of expressing thoughts or feelings: *sign language, the language of reason. A dog's language is made up of barks, whines, growls, and tail-waggings.* **3. a.** a form, style, or kind of language; manner of expression: *bad or strong language, Shakespeare's language.* **b.** wording; words: *the simple but unforgettable language of the Gettysburg Address.* **c.** the terms of a science, art, profession, etc., or of a class of persons: *the language of chemistry. There is one language for the pulpit and another for on board ship* (Frederick Marryat). **4.** the study of language or languages; linguistics. **5.** a set of assumptions or attitudes, often held by a group: *He just doesn't speak my language. Abbr.:* lang. [< Old French *langage* < *langue* tongue, language < Latin *lingua*]

—**Syn. 2. a. Language, dialect, idiom** mean the form and pattern of speech of a particular group of people. **Language** applies to the speech of a whole nation or people: *The people of Brazil speak the Portuguese language.* **Dialect** applies to the speech of one locality or group: *The dialect of the English language spoken in Boston sounds strange to a Westerner.* **Idiom** applies to a particular language's characteristic manner of using words and putting them together in phrases and sentences: *The use of prepositions is a striking feature of English idiom.* **3. a.** diction, parlance. **3. c.** phraseology, vocabulary.

language arts, *U.S.* training in reading, writing, and speaking, as distinguished from training in literary appreciation and scholarship.

lan·guaged (lan′gwijd), *adj.* having or versed in a language or languages: *many-languaged nations.*

lan·guage·less (lang′gwij lis), *adj.* without language or speech.

language of flowers, a method of expressing sentiments by means of flowers.

langue d'oc (läNg′ dôk′), *French.* the dialect spoken in southern France (Provence) in the Middle Ages. It became modern Provençal.

langue d'o·ïl (läNg′ dô ēl′), *French.* the dialect spoken in northern France in the Middle Ages. It became modern French.

lan·guet or **lan·guette** (lang′gwet), *n.* **1.** anything shaped like a little tongue. **2.** *Music.* a flat plate or tongue fastened opposite the mouth of an organ flue pipe. **3.** a tongue-shaped part of any of various implements, as a narrow blade projecting at the edge of a type of spade. [< Middle French *languette* (diminutive) < Old French *langue* tongue < Latin *lingua*]

lan·guid (lang′gwid), *adj.* **1.** without energy; drooping; weak; weary: *A hot, sticky day makes a person feel languid.* **2.** without interest or enthusiasm; indifferent: *He was too languid to go anywhere or do anything* (Charles Reade). **3.** not brisk or lively; sluggish; dull: *languid competition.* **4.** without force or effectiveness: *a languid narrative, a languid style.* [< Latin *languidus* < *languēre* be faint, related to *laxus* lax] —**lan′guid·ly,** *adv.* —**lan′guid·ness,** *n.* —**Syn. 1.** feeble, fatigued, exhausted, faint, inert. **2.** apathetic, listless, spiritless.

lan·guish (lang′gwish), *v.i.* **1.** to become weak or weary; lose energy; droop: *The flowers languished from lack of water.* **2.** to suffer under any unfavorable conditions: *He languished in prison for twenty years.* **3.** to grow dull, slack, or less intense: *His vigilance never languished.* **4.** to long; pine (for): *She languished for home.* **5.** to assume a soft, tender look for effect: *When a visitor comes in, she smiles and languishes, you'd think that butter wouldn't melt in her mouth* (Thackeray).

—*n.* **1.** the act or state of languishing: *One desperate grief cures with another's languish* (Shakespeare). **2.** a tender look or glance: *the warm, dark languish of her eyes* (John Greenleaf Whittier).

[< Old French *languiss-,* stem of *languir* < Vulgar Latin *languīre,* for Latin *languēre* be weary] —**lan′guish·er,** *n.* —**Syn.** *v.i.* **1.** wither, fade. **3.** dwindle.

lan·guish·ing (lang′gwi shing), *adj.* **1.** drooping; pining; longing. **2.** failing to excite interest. **3.** tender; sentimental; loving: *languishing glances.* **4.** lasting; lingering. —**lan′guish·ing·ly,** *adv.* —**Syn. 1.** languid, faint, languorous. **2.** lethargic, spiritless.

lan·guish·ment (lang′gwish mənt), *n.* **1.** a languishing: *Yet do I sometimes feel a languishment For skies Italian* (Keats). **2.** a drooping, pining condition. **3.** a languishing look or manner.

lan·guor (lang′gər), *n.* **1.** lack of energy; weakness; weariness: *A long illness causes languor.* **2.** lack of interest or enthusiasm; indifference: *Languor is not in your heart* (Matthew Arnold). **3.** softness or tenderness of mood. **4.** quietness; stillness: *the languor of a summer afternoon.* **5.** lack of activity; sluggishness: *The languor of Rome—its weary pavements, its little life* (Hawthorne). [< Old French *languor,* or *langour* < Latin *languor* < *languēre* be weary] —**Syn. 1.** feebleness, fatigue. **2.** apathy.

lan·guor·ous (lang′gər əs), *adj.* **1.** languid. **2.** causing languor: *languorous fragrance.* —**lan′guor·ous·ly,** *adv.* —**lan′guor·ous·ness,** *n.*

lan·gur (lung gůr′), *n.* any of various large, long-tailed, slender monkeys that live in trees in southern Asia, as the entellus. [< Hindustani *laṅgūr* < Sanskrit *lāṅgūlin* having a long tail < *lāṅgūla* tail]

lan·iard (lan′yərd), *n.* lanyard.

la·ni·ar·y (lā′nē er′ē, lan′ē-), *adj.* (of teeth) fitted for tearing, as the canine teeth. [< Latin *laniārius* having to do with a butcher < *lanius* a butcher < *laniāre* to tear]

la·ni·ate (lā′nē āt, lan′ē-), *v.t.,* **-at·ed, -at·ing.** to tear apart; rend. [< Latin *laniāre* (with English *-ate*[1]) to tear]

la·nif·er·ous (lə nif′ər əs), *adj.* wool-bearing; woolly. [< Latin *lānifer* (< *lāna* wool + *ferre* to bear) + English *-ous*]

la·nig·er·ous (lə nij′ər əs), *adj.* laniferous.

Lan·i·tal (lan′ə tal), *n. Trademark.* a synthetic fiber resembling wool, originally made in Italy from casein. [< Latin *lāna* wool + English *-it*(e)[1] + *-al*[1]]

lank (langk), *adj.* **1. a.** long and thin; slender; lean: *a lank boy.* **b.** long and limp, as grass. **2.** straight and flat; not curly or wavy: *lank locks of hair.* [Old English *hlanc*] —**lank′ly,** *adv.* —**lank′ness,** *n.* —**Syn. 1. a.** skinny, lanky, gaunt.

lank·i·ly (lang′kə lē), *adv.* in a lanky condition or form.

lank·i·ness (lang′kē nis), *n.* lanky state or form.

lank·y (lang′kē), *adj.,* **lank·i·er, lank·i·est.** awkwardly long and thin; tall and ungraceful: *Last of the Manchu dynasty, the lanky, bespectacled Py-yu was Emperor of China at 3* (Newsweek).

lan·ner (lan′ər), *n.* **1.** a falcon found in southern Europe, North Africa, and southern Asia. **2.** *Falconry.* a female lanner. [< Old French *lanier,* probably < Vulgar Latin *lanarius,* variant of Latin *laniārius* a type of falcon < *laniāre* tear flesh]

lan·ner·et (lan′ə ret), *n. Falconry.* a male lanner, smaller than the female. [< Middle French *laneret* (diminutive) < *lanier* lanner + *-et* -et]

lan·o·lin (lan′ə lin), *n.* a yellowish substance consisting of fat or grease obtained from wool, purified and mixed with water; wool fat. It is used in cosmetics, ointments, shoe polish, leather dressing, etc. [< Latin *lāna* wool + English *-ol*[2] + *-in*]

lan·o·line (lan′ə lin, -lēn), *n.* lanolin.

lan·o·lize (lan′ə līz), *v.t.,* **-lized, -liz·ing.** to treat with lanolin: *A woman parts with a modest fortune to be lanolized, moisturized, and petal-fresh* (Punch).

la·nose (lā′nōs), *adj.* woolly; lanate.

lans·downe (lanz′doun), *n.* a fine, soft fabric of silk and wool, used for dresses.

Lan·sing strain (lan′sing), one of three known types of virus causing polio. The other two are the Brunhilde and Leon strains. [< *Lansing,* a city in Michigan, home of a victim of the disease]

lans·que·net (lans′kə net), *n.* **1.** a mercenary foot soldier, commonly armed with a pike or lance, formerly employed in the German and other Continental armies in the 1600's and 1700's. **2.** a card game in which the players bet against the banker. [< Middle French *lansquenet* < German *Landsknecht;* see LANCE KNIGHT]

lan·ta·na (lan tā′nə, -tä′-), *n.* any of a group of tropical or subtropical, chiefly American plants of the verbena family, noted for their bright flowers: *Lantana in glowing shades of orange, yellow or rose* . . . (New York Times). [< New Latin *Lantana* the genus name]

lan·ter·loo (lan′tər lü), *n. Obsolete.* loo, a card game. [< French *lanturelu* (originally) a refrain in a song]

lan·tern (lan′tərn), *n.* **1.** a case to protect a light from wind, rain, etc. It has sides of glass or some other material through which the light can shine. **2. a.** the room at the top of a lighthouse where the light is. **b.** *Obsolete.* a lighthouse. **3. a.** an upright structure on a roof or dome for letting in light and air or for decoration. **b.** a louver on a roof. **4.** a magic lantern. **5.** a street lamp used in the French Revolution as a gallows. **6.** a lantern pinion. [< Old French *lanterne* < Latin *lanterna* (with ending patterned on *lūcerna* lamp) < Greek *lamptḗr* torch < *lámpein* to shine]

Lantern (def. 3a)

lantern fish, any of various fishes, chiefly deep-sea, having luminescent organs or glands.

lantern fly, any of certain homopterous tropical insects having a long head, and formerly thought to produce light in the dark; plant hopper.

lan·tern-jawed (lan′tərn jôd′), *adj.* having long thin jaws and hollow cheeks: . . . *a powerful, lantern-jawed lad, tall for a middleweight and in magnificent condition* (New Yorker).

lantern jaws, long, thin jaws, giving a hollow appearance to the cheeks.

lantern pinion or **wheel,** a kind of gear, used especially in clocks, having a circular top and bottom connected along the circumferences by staves inserted at equal distances, serving as teeth; trundle.

lantern slide, 1. a small thin sheet of glass with a picture on it that is shown on a screen by a projector. **2.** a magic lantern projector.

lan·tha·nide (lan′thə nīd, -nid), *n.* any of the rare-earth elements. [< *lanthanum* (first of the rare-earth elements) + *-ide*]

lanthanide series, the rare-earth elements: *Cerium is the first of the lanthanide series of the periodic table, so-called because they follow lanthanum in the table* (Science News Letter).

lan·tha·non (lan′thə non), *n.* lanthanide.

lan·tha·num (lan′thə nəm), *n.* one of the most common of the rare-earth elements, belonging to the cerium metals. Lanthanum is found in certain rare minerals such as monazite, cerite, and samarskite. *Symbol:* La; *at. wt.:* (C^{12}) 138.91 or (O^{16}) 138.92; *at. no.:* 57; *valence:* 3. [< New Latin *lanthanum* < Greek *lanthánein* lie hidden]

lant·horn (lant′hôrn, lan′tərn), *n. Archaic.* lantern.

la·nu·gi·nose (lə nü′jə nōs, -nyü′-), *adj.* lanuginous.

la·nu·gi·nous (lə nü′jə nəs, -nyü′-), *adj.* **1.** covered with lanugo or soft, downy hairs. **2.** like down; downy. [< Latin *lānūginōsus* < *lānūgo, -inis* down, lanugo]

la·nu·go (lə nü′gō, -nyü′-), *n. Biology.* a growth of fine soft hair, as on the surface of a leaf or fruit, on the body of an insect, or on the skin of a newborn child.

lan·yard (lan′yərd), *n.* **1. a.** a short rope or cord used on ships to fasten rigging, especially upper rigging, by a tarred rope passed through deadeyes. **b.** Also, **knife lanyard.** a cord on which to hang a knife, whistle, etc.: *Aboard ship he carried his crutch by a lanyard round his neck* (Robert Louis Stevenson). **c.** a knife lanyard ornamented or braided in rich colors and worn as part of a uniform. **2.** a cord with a small hook at one end, used in firing certain kinds of cannon. Also, **laniard.** [< French *lanière* thong < Old French *lasniere* < *lasne;* spelling perhaps influenced by English *halyard*]

La·o (lä′ō), *n., pl.* **La·o** or **La·os,** *adj.* —*n.* **1.** a Laotian. **2.** the Thai language spoken by Laotians. —*adj.* Laotian.

La·oc·o·ön (lā ok′ō on), *n. Greek Legend.* a priest of Apollo at Troy who warned the Trojans against the wooden horse, and who was killed together with his two sons, by two serpents sent from the sea by Athena.

La·o·da·mi·a (lā′ə də mī′ə), *n. Greek Legend.* **1.** the wife of Protesilaus, with whom she voluntarily died. **2.** the mother of Sarpedon.

La·od·i·ce·an (lā od′ə sē′ən), *n.* **1.** a lukewarm or indifferent Christian. Revelation 3:15-16. **2.** a lukewarm or indifferent person. —*adj.* **1.** of or having to do with Laodicea, an ancient city of Phrygia in Asia Minor, or its inhabitants. **2.** (in the Bible) lukewarm in religion. Revelation 3:15-16. **3.** indifferent.

La·om·e·don (lā om′ə don), *n. Greek Legend.* the founder of Troy and father of Priam.

La·o·tian (lā ō′shən, lä-), *adj.* of or having to do with Laos, a country in southeastern Asia, in Indo-China. —*n.* a native or inhabitant of Laos.

lap[1] (lap), *n.* **1.** the front part from the waist to the knees of a person sitting down, with the clothing that covers it: *Mother holds the baby on her lap.* **2.** the place where anything rests or is cared for: *the lap of the gods, the lap of luxury. Here rests his head upon the lap of earth* (Thomas Gray). **3.** a hollow place thought of as resembling a lap: *The city of Malaga lies in the lap of a fertile valley, surrounded by mountains* (Washington Irving). **4. a.** a loosely hanging edge of clothing; flap. **b.** the front part of a skirt held up to catch or hold something. **5.** a long rolled sheet of raw cotton cleaned and ready for carding. [Old English *læppa*]

lap[2] (lap), *v.,* **lapped, lap·ping,** *n.* —*v.t.* **1. a.** to lay together, one thing partly over or beside another: *to lap shingles on a roof.* **b.** to put together by overlapping, as a lap joint. **2. a.** to wind or wrap (around); fold (over or about): *He lapped the blanket around him.* **b.** to wrap up (in); enwrap: *He lapped himself in a warm blanket.* **3.** to envelop or surround as with a soothing or stupefying effect: *She was content to be lapped unthinking in this existence* (New Yorker). *For peace her soul was yearning, And now peace laps her round* (Matthew Arnold). **4.** to enfold as in one's lap; nurse; fondle. **5.** to get a lap or more ahead of (other racers) in a race. **6.** to cut or polish (gems or metal) with a lap. —*v.i.* **1.** to lie upon, so as to cover partially or project over; overlap: *Shingles on a roof lap.* **2.** to project into or beyond something. **3.** to extend out beyond a limit: *The reign of Queen Elizabeth (from 1558 to 1603) lapped over into the 1600's.* **4.** to be wound or wrapped around something; be folded.
—*n.* **1.** a lapping over. **2.** the amount of lapping over. **3.** the part that laps over. **4. a.** one time around a race track: *the first lap of the race. Sunday night at 10:00 o'clock, when the checkered flag drops, the car that has covered the most laps will take the grand prize* (Time). **b.** a part of any course traveled: *The last lap of our all-day hike was the toughest.* **5.** a rotating disk of soft metal or wood to hold polishing powder for cutting and polishing gems or metal. [< *lap*[1]]

lap[3] (lap), *v.,* **lapped, lap·ping,** *n.* —*v.t.* **1.** to drink by lifting up with the tongue: *Cats and dogs lap up water.* **2.** to move or strike gently against with a lapping sound: *I . . . hear the water . . . Lapping the steps beneath my feet* (Longfellow). —*v.i.* **1.** to move or beat gently with a lapping; splash gently: *Little waves lapped against the boat.* **2.** *Obsolete.* to take up liquid with the tongue.

lap up, *Informal.* **a.** to believe, especially something untrue: *The children lapped up the old logger's tall tales.* **b.** to drink or eat with great pleasure: *He lapped up the delicious dinner.*
—*n.* **1.** the act of lapping: *With one lap of the tongue the bear finished the honey.* **2.** a sound of lapping: *the lazy whish and lap of the ocean* (Amelia Barr). **3.** the amount lapped; lick; taste. **4.** something that is lapped. **5. a.** liquid food for dogs. **b.** *Slang and Dialect.* any weak beverage or thin liquid food. **c.** *Slang.* liquor in general; drink.
[Old English *lapian*]

lap[4] (lap), *v. Scottish.* a past tense of **leap.**

Lap., Lapland.

lap·a·rec·to·my (lap′ə rek′tə mē), *n., pl.* **-mies.** the surgical removal of a portion of the intestine at the side. [< Greek *lapárā* flank + *ektomḗ* a cutting out]

lap·a·ro·cele (lap′ər ə sēl), *n. Medicine.* hernia in the lumbar regions. [< Greek *lapárā* flank + *kḗlē* tumor]

lap·a·rot·o·my (lap′ə rot′ə mē), *n., pl.* **-mies.** the operation of making an incision into the abdominal wall, especially through the flank. [< Greek *lapárā* flank + *-tomiā* a cutting]

lap·board (lap′bôrd′, -bōrd′), *n.* a thin flat board held on the lap and used as a table.

lap dissolve, (in motion pictures and television) the simultaneous fading out of one scene and fading in of another.

lap dog, a small pet dog.

la·pel (lə pel′), *n.* the part of the front of a coat folded back just below the collar on either side. [diminutive form of *lap*[1]]

lap·ful (lap′fu̇l), *n., pl.* **-fuls.** as much as a lap can hold.

lap·i·dar·i·an (lap′ə dãr′ē ən), *adj.* lapidary.

lap·i·dar·y (lap′ə der′ē), *n., pl.* **-dar·ies,** *adj.* —*n.* **1.** a person who cuts, polishes, or engraves precious stones. **2.** a book about gems.
—*adj.* **1.** having to do with cutting or engraving precious stones. **2.** engraved on stone: *In lapidary inscriptions a man is not upon oath* (Samuel Johnson). **3.** characteristic of stone inscriptions; monumental; stately; grandiose: *lapidary language.*
[< Late Latin *lapidārius* working with stone < *lapis, -idis* stone]

lap·i·date (lap′ə dāt), *v.t.,* **-dat·ed, -dat·ing.** **1.** to throw stones at; pelt with stones. **2.** to stone to death. [< Latin *lapidāre* (with English *-ate*[1]) < *lapis, -idis* a stone]

lap·i·da·tion (lap′ə dā′shən), *n.* **1.** the act of throwing stones at a person. **2.** punishment or execution by stoning..

lap·i·dic·o·lous (lap′ə dik′ə ləs), *adj.* (of beetles and other insects) living under or among stones.

la·pid·i·fi·ca·tion (lə pid′ə fə kā′shən), *n.* a turning into stone; petrification.

la·pid·i·fy (lə pid′ə fī), *v.,* **-fied, -fy·ing.** —*v.t.* to make or turn into stone. —*v.i.* to become stone. [< French *lapidifier* < Latin *lapis, -idis* stone + French *-fier* -fy]

la·pil·li (lə pil′ī), *n. pl., sing.* **-pil·lus** (-pil′əs). small stones or pebbles, now especially the fragments of stone ejected from volcanoes. [< Italian *lapilli,* plural < Latin *lapillus* (diminutive) < *lapis, -idis* stone]

lap·in (lap′in; *French* lȧ paɴ′), *n.* **1.** a rabbit. **2.** rabbit fur. [< French *lapin*]

la·pis (lā′pis, lap′is), *n., pl.* **lap·i·des** (lap′ə dēz). *Latin.* a stone (used in phrases, especially in the names of minerals and gems).

lap·is laz·u·li (lap′is laz′yə lī, -lē), **1.** an azure-blue, opaque, semiprecious stone containing sodium, aluminum, sulfur, and silicon in a mixture of minerals. It is used chiefly for an ornament and sometimes for preparing the pigment ultramarine. *Formula:* $Na_5Al_3Si_3O_{12}S$ **2.** azure blue, the color of this stone: *The sun was gold in a sky of lapis lazuli.* [< Medieval Latin *lapis lazuli* < Latin *lapis* stone + Medieval Latin *lazuli,* genitive of *lazulum* lapis lazuli < Arabic *lāzuward* < Persian *lājward.* Compare AZURE.]

Lap·ith (lap′ith), *n., pl.* **Lap·i·thae, Lap·iths.** one of the Lapithae.

Lap·i·thae (lap′ə thē), *n.pl. Greek Mythology.* a people of Thessaly who defeated the centaurs when, at a bridal feast, they tried to carry off the women of the Lapithae.

lap joint, a joint connecting parts of a heavy beam, formed by overlapping the ends of two timbers and bolting, riveting, or strapping them together.

lap-joint (lap′joint′), *v.t.* to make a lap joint on; overlap.

La·plac·i·an or **La·plac·e·an** (lä′plas′ē ən), *adj.* of or having to do with Pierre de Laplace, 1749-1827, French astronomer and mathematician.

Lap·land·er (lap′lan dər), *n.* a Lapp (def.1).

Lap·land longspur (lap′land′), a variety of longspur with a black throat in the spring plumage, that nests in the arctic and flies south to the United States during winter.

lap money, (in auto racing) money given to the racer who leads the field at the end of a lap or laps.

Lapp (lap), *n.* **1.** a member of a group having certain Mongoloid features that lives in Lapland, a region in northern Norway, Sweden, Finland, and northwestern Soviet Union. The Lapps are small and have short, broad heads. *The Lapps of northerly Scandinavia were formerly classed outright as Mongoloids, but they show perhaps as many Alpine as East Asiatic traits* (Alfred L. Kroeber). **2.** the Finno-Ugric language of the Lapps. [probably < Swedish *Lapp*]

lap·per[1] (lap′ər), *n.* one who laps, or takes up (liquid) with the tongue. [< *lap*[3] + *-er*[1]]

lap·per[2] (lap′ər), *n.* a person who laps or folds (linen, etc.). [< *lap*[2] + *-er*[1]]

lap·per[3] (lap′ər, läp′-), *v.i., v.t., n. Scottish.* lopper (curd).

lap·pet (lap′it), *n.* **1.** a small flap or fold, as of a garment or a woman's headdress. **2.** a loose fold of flesh or membrane. **3.** the lobe of the ear. **4.** a bird's wattle. [< *lap*[1] + *-et*]

lap·pet·ed (lap′ə tid), *adj.* having a lappet or lappets.

lappet moth, a bombycid moth of the eastern United States whose larva has small lobes along its body and feeds on the leaves of many trees, as the apple, oak, and maple.

Lapp·ish (lap′ish), *adj.* of or having to do with the Lapps or their language. —*n.* the language of the Lapps.

lap robe, a blanket, fur robe, etc., used to keep the lap and legs warm when riding in an automobile, carriage, etc.

laps·a·ble (lap′sə bəl), *adj.* that can lapse.

lapse (laps), *n., v.,* **lapsed, laps·ing.** —*n.* **1.** a slight mistake or error; slip of the tongue, pen, or memory. **2.** a slipping or falling away from what is right: *The long strife with evil which began With the first lapse of new-created man* (John Greenleaf Whittier). **3. a.** a slipping back; sinking down; slipping into a lower condition: *a lapse into savage ways.* **b.** a falling or passing into any state: *a lapse into silence.* **4.** a slipping by; gliding along; passing away: *A minute is a short lapse of time. Sunny Plaines, And liquid Lapse of murmuring Streams* (Milton). **5.** the ending of a right or privilege because it was not renewed, not used, or otherwise neglected. **6.** *Meteorology.* a decrease of temperature of the atmosphere with increase of altitude. **7.** a falling into disuse or ruin. **8.** an apostatizing from the faith; a falling into heresy.
—*v.i.* **1.** to make a slight mistake or error. **2.** to slip or fall away from what is right: *Little boys sometimes lapse from good behavior.* **3. a.** to slip back; sink down: *The house lapsed into ruin.* **b.** to fall or pass into any specified state: *to lapse into silence.* **4.** to slip by; pass away: *The boy's interest soon lapsed. I saw the river lapsing slowly onward*

(Hawthorne). **5.** (of a right or privilege) to end because it was not renewed, not used, or otherwise neglected: *If a legal claim is not enforced, it lapses after a certain number of years. He did not pay his insurance premium within the thirty days after it was due, and so his life insurance policy lapsed.* **6.** to apostatize; forsake one's faith: *a lapsed Christian.*
[< Latin *lāpsus, -ūs* a fall < *lābī* to slip, fall] —**laps′er,** *n.* —**Syn.** *n.* **1.** slip, fault, indiscretion, misstep.

lapse rate, the rate of decrease of temperature of the atmosphere with increase in altitude.

laps·i·ble (lap′sə bəl), *adj.* lapsable.

lap·stone (lap′stōn′), *n.* a stone held in the lap by shoemakers, to beat leather on.

lap·strake (lap′strāk), *adj., n.* lapstreak.

lap·streak (lap′strēk), *adj.* (of a boat) constructed with each successive board or plate overlapping the one below it; clinker-built. —*n.* a boat that is clinker-built.

lap·sus (lap′səs), *n. Latin.* a slip or mistake.

lapsus ca·la·mi (kal′ə mī), *Latin.* a slip of the pen.

lapsus lin·guae (ling′gwē), *Latin.* a slip of the tongue.

lapsus me·mo·ri·ae (me môr′ē ē, -mōr′-), *Latin.* a slip of the memory.

La·pu·ta (lə pyü′tə), *n.* the flying island in Jonathan Swift's *Gulliver's Travels,* inhabited by philosophers addicted to visionary and absurd projects.

La·pu·tan (lə pyü′tən), *adj.* **1.** of or having to do with Laputa. **2.** unpractical; visionary. —*n.* **1.** an inhabitant of Laputa. **2.** a visionary.

lap-weld (lap′weld′), *v.t.* to weld with overlapping edges.

lap·wing (lap′wing′), *n.* a plover of Europe, Asia, and northern Africa having a crested head, a slow, irregular flight, and a peculiar wailing cry; pewit; weep. [alteration of Old English *hlēapewince* < *hlēapan* to leap + *-wince* tottering (related to WINK); spelling influenced by English *lap*^{2} and *wing*]

lar (lär), *n., pl.* **lar·es** or **lars.** *Latin.* a household god.

lar·board (lär′bərd, -bôrd, -bōrd), *n.* the side of a ship to the left of a person looking from the stern toward the bow; port. —*adj.* on this side of a ship. —*adv. Obsolete.* to larboard (used as a command). [Middle English *ladeborde* (originally) the loading side; influenced by English *starboard*]
➔ In modern nautical use, **larboard** has been replaced by *port.*

lar·ce·ner (lär′sə nər), *n.* a person who commits larceny.

lar·ce·nist (lär′sə nist), *n.* larcener.

lar·ce·nous (lär′sə nəs), *adj.* **1.** of or like larceny; characterized by larceny: *the larcenous and burglarious world* (Sydney Smith). **2.** guilty of larceny; thievish: *the larcenous habits of jackdaws.* —**lar′ce·nous·ly,** *adv.*

lar·ce·ny (lär′sə nē), *n., pl.* **-nies. 1.** the unlawful taking, carrying away, and using of the personal property of another person without his consent. The distinction between grand larceny and petit larceny, based on the value of the property stolen, still exists in some states of the United States but was abolished in England in 1827. **2.** theft. [< Anglo-French *larcin,* Old French *larrecin* (< Latin *latrōcinium* robbery < *latrō, -ōnis* bandit) + English *-y*^{3}] —**Syn. 1.** robbery, thievery.

larch (lärch), *n.* **1.** any of a group of trees of the pine family, with small, woody cones, and needles that fall off in the autumn. **2.** its strong, tough wood. [< German *Lärche,* ultimately < Latin *larix, -icis*]

Branch of Larch (def. 1)

lard (lärd), *n.* the fat of pigs, hogs, etc., especially the internal fat of the abdomen, melted down and made clear. It is used in cooking: *fritters of flour fried in bear's lard* (Washington Irving).
—*v.t.* **1.** to insert strips of bacon or salt pork in, or lay them on top of (meat) before cooking it. **2.** to give variety to; enrich; embellish: *The mayor larded his speech with jokes and stories. The facts ... are still generally unknown, and they have become larded with myths and barroom fantasy* (Newsweek). **3.** to put lard on or in; smear with lard; grease: *Lard the pan well. Falstaff sweats to death, and Lards the lean earth as he walks along* (Shakespeare). **4.** *Obsolete.* fatten.
[< Old French *lard* bacon fat < Latin *lārdum*] —**lard′like′,** *adj.*
—**Syn.** *v.t.* **2.** garnish, interlard.

lar·da·ceous (lär dā′shəs), *adj.* **1.** of the nature of or like lard. **2.** *Pathology.* of or having to do with a form of degeneration in which a protein substance (amyloid) is deposited in the tissues, especially those of the abdominal organs.

lar·der (lär′dər), *n.* **1.** a place where food is kept; pantry. **2.** a stock of food: *The hunters' larder included flour, bacon, and what they shot or caught.* [< Old French *lardier* < Medieval Latin *lardarium* < Latin *lārdum* lard]

larder beetle, a kind of small beetle whose larvae are very destructive to stored meat, cheese, stuffed animals in museums, etc. The larvae of the larder beetle are covered with whitish-brown hairs.

lar·don (lär′dən), *n.* a narrow strip of bacon fat or salt pork fat inserted in meat in larding. [< Middle French *lardon* < Old French *lard* lard]

lar·doon (lär dün′), *n.* lardon.

lard·y (lär′dē), *adj.,* **lard·i·er, lard·i·est. 1.** full of, containing, or like lard: *Her face was wide and flat and lardy white* (New Yorker). **2.** plump; fat.

lard·y-dard·y (lär′dē där′dē), *adj. Especially British Slang.* languidly genteel or foppish; affected: *The lardy-dardy swells are present* (Punch).

lar·es (lãr′ēz), *n., pl. of* **lar.** *Latin.* the household gods of the ancient Romans; the guardian spirits of the house.

lares and penates, 1. the household gods of the ancient Romans, the lares protecting the home from outside damage, the penates protecting the interior. **2.** the cherished possessions of a household. [< Latin *larēs,* plural of *lār,* household god; *penātes,* plural, related to *penus* sanctuary]

lar·ga·men·te (lär′gä men′tā), *adv. Music.* broadly (used as a direction). [< Italian *largamente* < *largo* largo]

lar·gan·do (lär gän′dō), *adv., adj. Italian.* allargando.

large (lärj), *adj.,* **larg·er, larg·est,** *n., adv.* —*adj.* **1.** of great size, amount, or number; big: *America is a large country. Ten thousand dollars is a large sum of money. Large crowds come to see our team play.* **2.** of great scope or range; extensive; broad: *a man of large experience, large sympathies.* **3. a.** on a great scale: *a large employer of labor.* **b.** grand or pompous: *to talk in a large way.* **4.** *Nautical.* (of the wind) blowing in a favorable direction; fair. **5.** *Rare.* extended or lengthy, as speech or writing. **6.** *Archaic.* abundant, copious, or ample: *We have yet large day; for scarce the sun Hath finish'd half his journey* (Milton). **7.** *Obsolete.* liberal; generous; lavish: *The poor King Reignier whose large style Agrees not with the leanness of his purse* (Shakespeare). **8.** *Obsolete.* of speech, actions, etc.: **a.** lax; free; unrestrained. **b.** licentious; improper; gross.
—*n.* **at large, a.** at liberty; free: *The escaped prisoner is still at large.* **b.** in detail; fully: *I ... told him the story at large* (Daniel Defoe). **c.** as a whole; altogether: *The people at large want peace.* **d.** representing the whole of a state or district, not merely one division of it: *a congressman at large.*
in large or **in the large,** on a big scale: *I have made trial of this method, both in small and in large* (John Smeaton).
—*adv.* **1.** *Nautical.* with the wind blowing from a favorable direction: *to sail large, to go large.* **2.** *Obsolete.* amply; abundantly; liberally; unrestrainedly.
[< Old French *large* < Latin *lārgus* copious] —**large′ness,** *n.*
—**Syn.** *adj.* **1.** huge, great, vast, enormous, immense, gigantic. See **great.**

large calorie, the quantity of heat necessary to raise the temperature of a kilogram of water one degree centigrade.

Large Cloud, the larger of two Magellanic clouds, located in the constellation Dorado.

large cranberry, a variety of cranberry growing in eastern North America that has berries up to 3/4 inch in diameter.

large-hand·ed (lärj′han′did), *adj.* **1.** having large hands. **2.** bountiful; generous.

large-heart·ed (lärj′här′tid), *adj.* generous; liberal. —**large′-heart′ed·ness,** *n.*

large intestine, the lower part of the intestines, between the small intestine and the anus, consisting of the caecum, colon, and rectum. See picture under **liver**^{1}.

large·ish (lär′jish), *adj.* rather large; largish: *It is a decorative Tudor house ... and now has a largeish lounge* (Times Educational Supplement).

large·ly (lärj′lē), *adv.* **1.** in great quantity; much: *When Simon and his sons had drunk largely* (I Maccabees 16:16). **2.** to a great extent; mainly: *Success depends largely on working hard. The region consists largely of desert.*

large-mind·ed (lärj′mīn′did), *adj.* having or showing liberal views; tolerant. —**large′-mind′ed·ness,** *n.*

large·mouth (lärj′mouth′), *n.* largemouth bass.

largemouth bass, a North American fresh-water game fish that has a dark-green or almost black color and reaches a weight of over 20 pounds; black bass: *Contrary to popular belief, the largemouth and smallmouth bass are not true bass at all but belong to the sunfish* (Science News Letter). See picture under **fin.**

large-mouthed black bass (lärj′mouᴛʜd′, -moutht′), largemouth bass.

larg·en (lär′jən), *v.i.* to become larger. —*v.t.* to make larger; enlarge.

large-scale (lärj′skāl′), *adj.* **1.** wide; extensive; involving many persons or things: *Chiang Kai-shek could not hope to effect a large-scale landing on the strongly guarded coast of China without massive American sea and air support* (Wall Street Journal). **2.** made or drawn to a large scale: *... a large-scale, cloth-backed map of France with hand-written annotations* (London Times).

lar·gess or **lar·gesse** (lär′jis), *n.* **1.** a generous giving: *shower'd largess of delight* (Tennyson). **2.** a generous gift or gifts: *Largess in the form of research reactors is only one aspect of the use of nuclear science as an instrument of foreign policy* (Bulletin of Atomic Scientists). [< Old French *largesse* < *large* large]

Large White, any of a breed of large, white hogs developed in Great Britain.

lar·ghet·to (lär get′ō), *adj., adv., n., pl.* **-tos.** *Music.* —*adj.* rather slow; not so slow as largo, but usually slower than andante. —*adv.* in larghetto tempo. —*n.* a passage or piece of music in rather slow time. [< Italian *larghetto* (diminutive) < *largo* largo]

larg·ish (lär′jish), *adj.* rather large.

lar·go (lär′gō), *adj., adv., n., pl.* **-gos.** *Music.* —*adj.* slow and dignified; solemn; stately. —*adv.* in largo tempo. —*n.* a slow, stately passage or piece of music. [< Italian *largo* < Latin *lārgus* large]

lar·i·at (lar′ē ət), *n. U.S.* **1.** a long rope with a running noose at one end, used by cowboys in catching cattle, horses, etc.; lasso. **2.** a rope used for fastening horses, mules, etc., to a stake while they are grazing. [American English < Spanish *la reata* the rope; *reata* < Spanish *re-* again (< Latin *re-*) + *atar* to tie < Latin *aptāre* adjust, adapt. Compare RIATA.]

lar·ine (lar′in, lãr′īn), *adj.* **1.** of or belonging to the family of birds that comprises the gulls. **2.** of or like a gull. [< New Latin *Larinae* the subfamily name < *Lari* the order name < Latin *larus* sea mew < Greek *láros* sea mew, gull]

la·rith·mic (lə riᴛʜ′mik), *adj.* of or having to do with larithmics.

la·rith·mics (lə riᴛʜ′miks), *n.* the science dealing with population in its quantitative aspects. [< Greek *lāós* people + *arithmós* number + English *-ics*]

lark^{1} (lärk), *n.* **1.** any of numerous songbirds of Europe, Asia, America, and North Africa, with brown feathers and long hind claws. One kind, the skylark, sings while soaring in the air. **2.** a meadow lark, titlark, or any of several similar songbirds of other families. [Old English *lāwerce*]

Horned Lark^{1} **(def. 1)**
(7½ in. long)

lark^{2} (lärk), *Informal.* —*n.* a merry adventure; frolic; prank: *When you're well*

enough to go out for a ride—what larks! (Dickens).
—*v.i.* **1.** to have fun; play pranks; frolic. **2.** to ride in a frolicsome manner; ride across country. —*v.t.* **1.** to make fun of; tease. **2.** to ride (a horse) across country. **3.** to clear (a fence) with a flying leap. [origin uncertain] —**lark′er,** *n.*

lark bunting, a finch of the plains and prairies of western North America, the male of which is black with a white patch on the wing in its summer plumage.

lark-heel (lärk′hēl′), *n.* a long, projecting heel, occurring especially in Negroes. [because of the long rear claw of a *lark*[1]]

lark·ish (lär′kish), *adj.* larky: . . . *a small band of novelists led by the larkish and irreverent Kingsley Amis* (Atlantic). —**lark′·ish·ness,** *n.*

lark·some (lärk′səm), *adj.* larky: . . . *a late and larksome diner coming in during grace* (Horace Sutton).

lark sparrow, a sparrow of central North America with a fan-shaped tail, chestnut markings on the head, and a white breast with a single spot in the center.

lark·spur (lärk′spėr), *n.* **1.** any of various plants of the crowfoot family, whose flowers have a curved, petallike upper sepal shaped like a spur. Most larkspurs have clusters of blue flowers on tall stalks. **2.** the blue color characteristic of the larkspur: *larkspur, a pastel blue slightly inclining to the mauve* (London Daily Express). [earlier *larkes spur* < genitive of *lark*[1] + *spur*]

lark·y (lär′kē), *adj.,* **lark·i·er, lark·i·est.** *Informal.* carefree; frolicsome; gay: . . . *those oppressed with the weight of wealth as well as those larky with the lack of it* (New York Times).

lar·moy·ant (lär moi′ənt), *adj.* tearful; lachrymose. [< French *larmoyant,* present participle of *larmoyer* be tearful < *larme* tear[1]]

lar·nax (lär′naks), *n., pl.* **-na·kes** (-nə kēz). a box or coffer, especially a boxlike receptacle of clay or terra cotta, often painted, found in early Greek or Mycenaean tombs. [< Greek *lárnax, -akos*]

lar·oid (lar′oid), *adj.* **1.** belonging to the family of birds that includes the gulls. **2.** gull-like. [< New Latin *Lari* (see LARINE) + English *-oid*]

lar·ri·gan (lar′ə gən), *n.* a kind of moccasin shoe or boot of highly oiled leather worn by lumbermen. [American English; origin unknown]

lar·ri·kin (lar′ə kin), *Especially Australian.* —*n.* a street rowdy; hoodlum; hooligan. —*adj.* rough; rowdy; disorderly. [origin uncertain]

lar·ri·kin·ism (lar′ə kə niz′əm), *n. Especially Australian.* rowdy behavior; hooliganism.

lar·rup (lar′əp), *v.,* **-ruped, -rup·ing,** *n. Informal.* —*v.t.* to beat; thrash: *I . . . was larruped with the rope* (Dickens). —*n.* a blow. [origin uncertain. Compare Dutch *larpen* thrash, box the ears.] —**lar′rup·er,** *n.*

lar·um (lar′əm, lär′-), *n. Archaic.* an alarm; alarum. [short for *alarum*]

lar·va (lär′və), *n., pl.* **-vae** (-vē). **1.** the early form of an insect from the time it leaves the egg until it becomes a pupa. Larvae sometimes have short legs but lack compound eyes. Wings, when present in the adult, develop internally during the larval stage. A caterpillar is the larva of a butterfly or moth. A grub is the larva of a beetle. Maggots are the larvae of flies. **2.** an immature form of certain animals that is different in structure from the adult form and must undergo a change or metamorphosis to become like the parent. A tadpole is the larva of a frog or toad. [earlier, a ghost, specter < Latin *lārva* ghost, mask]

lar·vae (lär′vē), *n.* plural of **larva.**

lar·val (lär′vəl), *adj.* **1. a.** of or having to do with larvae. **b.** characteristic of larvae. **c.** in the form of a larva. **2.** *Medicine.* (of a disease) latent; undeveloped.

lar·vi·cid·al (lär′və sī′dəl), *adj.* of or having to do with killing larvae.

lar·vi·cide (lär′və sīd), *n., v.,* **-cid·ed, -cid·ing.** —*n.* a preparation which kills larvae (of mosquitoes, etc.). —*v.t.* to apply a larvicide to: . . . *the larviciding of breeding places with DDT* (Scientific American). [< *larva* + *-cide*[1]]

lar·vip·a·rous (lär vip′ər əs), *adj.* (of certain insects) giving birth to young that have already passed from the egg to the larval stage. [< *larva* + Latin *parere* to give birth + English *-ous*]

laryng-, *combining form.* the form of **laryngo-** before vowels, as in *laryngitis.*

la·ryn·gal (lə ring′gəl), *Phonetics.* —*adj.* produced in the larynx. The Scottish pronunciation of *t* in *bottle* is laryngal. (The same sound occurs in certain pronunciations of American English). —*n.* a laryngal sound. [< New Latin *larynx, laryngis* larynx + English *-al*[2]]

la·ryn·ge·al (lə rin′jē əl), *adj.* **1.** of or having to do with the larynx. **2.** in the larynx. —*n.* **1.** a laryngeal nerve or artery. **2.** a laryngeal sound. [< New Latin *laryngeus* (< *larynx* larynx) + English *-al*[1]]

lar·yn·gec·to·mee (lar′ən jek′tə mē′), *n.* a person whose larynx has been removed.

lar·yn·gec·to·my (lar′ən jek′tə mē), *n., pl.* **-mies.** the removal of the larynx.

la·ryn·ges (lə rin′jēz), *n.* a plural of **larynx.**

lar·yn·git·ic (lar′ən jit′ik), *adj.* of or like laryngitis. —*n.* a person who has laryngitis.

lar·yn·gi·tis (lar′ən jī′tis), *n.* inflammation of the larynx, resulting in a sore throat and hoarseness. [< New Latin *laryngitis* < *larynx* larynx + *-itis* inflammation]

laryngo-, *combining form.* **1.** larynx: *Laryngoscopy = examination of the larynx.* **2.** larynx and ——: *Laryngopharyngeal = having to do with the larynx and the pharynx.* Also, **laryng-** before vowels. [< Greek *lárynx, lár yngos* upper windpipe]

la·ryn·go·log·i·cal (lə ring′gə loj′ə kəl), *adj.* of or having to do with laryngology.

lar·yn·gol·o·gist (lar′ing gol′ə jist), *n.* a specialist in laryngology.

lar·yn·gol·o·gy (lar′ing gol′ə jē), *n.* the branch of medicine dealing with the larynx and the treatment of its diseases.

la·ryn·go·pha·ryn·ge·al (lə ring′gō fə-rin′jē əl), *adj.* of or having to do with both the larynx and the pharynx.

la·ryn·go·phone (lə ring′gə fōn), *n.* a sound-transmitting apparatus having a receiver which is applied to the throat instead of the ear to receive the speech sounds directly from the vibration of the larynx.

la·ryn·go·scope (lə ring′gə skōp), *n.* an instrument with mirrors for examining the larynx.

la·ryn·go·scop·ic (lə ring′gə skop′ik), *adj.* having to do with a laryngoscope or laryngoscopy.

la·ryn·go·scop·i·cal (lə ring′gə skop′ə-kəl), *adj.* laryngoscopic.

lar·yn·gos·co·pist (lar′ing gos′kə pist), *n.* a person skilled in the use of the laryngoscope.

lar·yn·gos·co·py (lar′ing gos′kə pē), *n., pl.* **-pies.** examination of the larynx; the use of the laryngoscope.

lar·yn·got·o·my (lar′ing got′ə mē), *n., pl.* **-mies.** surgical incision into the larynx.

la·ryn·go·tra·che·i·tis (lə ring′gō trā′kē-ī′tis), *n.* **1.** inflammation of the larynx and trachea. **2.** a viral, infectious respiratory disease of domestic fowl.

lar·ynx (lar′ingks), *n., pl.* **la·ryn·ges** (lə rin′-jēz) or **lar·ynx·es.** **1.** the cavity at the upper end of the human windpipe, containing the vocal cords and acting as an organ of voice. See picture under **pharynx.** **2.** a similar organ in other mammals, or the corresponding structure in other animals. **3.** (in birds) either of two cavities, one at the top and one at the bottom of the windpipe. The syrinx or bottom cavity is the true organ of sound. [< New Latin *larynx* < Greek *lárynx, láryngos* the upper windpipe]

la·sa·gna or **la·sa·gne** (lə zän′yə), *n., pl.* **la·sa·gna.** **1.** an Italian dish consisting of chopped meat, cheese, and tomato sauce, cooked with layers of wide, flat noodles. **2.** a wide, flat noodle. [< Italian *lasagna* < Latin *lasanum* cooking pot < Greek *lásanon* utensil]

las·car (las′kər), *n.* a native sailor of India and Pakistan. [probably Anglo-Indian < Portuguese *laschar,* probably < Hindustani *lashkarī* soldier < *lashkar* army, camp < Persian *laskar*]

las·civ·i·ous (lə siv′ē əs), *adj.* **1.** feeling lust. **2.** showing lust; lewd; wanton. **3.** causing lust or wantonness: *He capers nimbly in a lady's chamber To the lascivious pleasing of a lute* (Shakespeare). [< Late Latin *lascīviōsus* < Latin *lascīvia* playfulness < *lascīvus* playful] —**las·civ′i·ous·ly,** *adv.* —**las·civ′i·ous·ness,** *n.*

lase (lāz), *v.i.,* **lased, las·ing.** *Electronics.* (of a laser) to generate coherent light. [back formation < *laser*]

la·ser (lā′zər), *Electronics.* —*n.* a device which generates and amplifies light waves of a pure color in a narrow and extremely intense beam of light: *A . . . ruby laser . . . generates energy so intense that it can bore an inch hole in . . . sapphire in a thousandth of a second* (Science News Letter). —*v.i.* to act as a laser; lase. [< *l*(ight) *a*(mplification by) *s*(timulated) *e*(mission of) *r*(adiation)]

lash[1] (lash), *n.* **1.** the part of a whip that is not the handle and is usually flexible: *Every time the clown cracked his whip, the lash curled around his own waist.* **2.** a stroke or blow with a whip, thong, etc.: *I gave my horse a lash that sounded through the forest* (Ann Radcliffe). **3.** a sudden, swift movement: *the lash of an animal's tail.* **4.** anything that hurts as a blow from a whip does: *Lest they should fall under the lash of the penal laws* (Alexander Pope). *How smart a lash that speech doth give my conscience* (Shakespeare). **5.** a hair on the edge of an eyelid; eyelash.
—*v.t.* **1.** to beat or drive with a whip, etc.: *Yuba Bill . . . madly lashed his horses forward* (Bret Harte). **2.** to wave or beat back and forth: *The lion lashed his tail. The wind lashes the sails.* **3.** to attack severely in words; hurt severely: *He does not fail to lash the schoolmen directly* (Henry Hallam).
—*v.i.* **1.** to make strokes with a lash or whip: *The youthful charioteers . . . Stoop to the reins, and lash with all their force* (John Dryden). **2.** (of water, tears, etc.) to rush violently; pour: *The rain was still lashing down furiously* (Annie Thomas).
lash out, a. to hit; attack; strike: *The bigger boy wanted to stop fighting, but the smaller one continued to lash out.* **b.** to attack severely in words; scold vigorously: *In his latest article he lashes out at modern historians.* **c.** to break forth into violent action, excess, or extravagance: *Yet could not the Duke . . . sometimes forbear lashing out into very free expressions* (Charles Cotton).
[Middle English *lasshe;* origin uncertain] —**Syn.** *v.t.* **1.** flog, scourge. **3.** castigate, rebuke, berate, scold.

lash[2] (lash), *v.t.* to tie or fasten with a rope, cord, or the like; secure: *to lash a person to the mast, to lash spars together to form a raft. The satellite countries are lashed to Russia.* [< Old French *lachier,* variant of *lacier* < *laz, lache* a lace] —**Syn.** bind.

-lashed, *combining form.* having —— (eye)-lashes: *Long-lashed = having long (eye)-lashes.*

lash·er (lash′ər), *n.* **1.** a person or thing that lashes with a whip or with words. **2.** *British Dialect.* the water that lashes or rushes over an opening in a weir, or the pool formed by it.

lash·ing[1] (lash′ing), *n.* **1.** the act of a person or thing that lashes. **2.** a beating or flogging. **3.** a severe attack in words; sharp scolding.
lashings, abundance; great plenty: *Cigars in loads, whiskey in lashings* (Scott).
[< *lash*[1] + *-ing*[1]]

lash·ing[2] (lash′ing), *n. Especially Nautical.* **1.** the act of tying or fastening any movable thing with a rope, cord, etc. **2.** the rope, cord, etc., used in tying or fastening. [< *lash*[2] + *-ing*[1]]

lash·less (lash′lis), *adj.* without lashes or eyelashes.

lash rope, *U.S.* a rope used for lashing a pack on a horse or vehicle.

lash-up (lash′up′), *n.* anything put together hastily or offhand; an improvisation; makeshift: *This machine was somewhat of a lash-up of available equipment built on the chassis of a trailer fire-pump* (New Scientist).

lass (las), *n.* **1.** a girl; young woman: *A bonnie lass, I will confess, Is pleasant to the ee* (Robert Burns). **2.** a sweetheart: *It was a lover and his lass* (Shakespeare). **3.** *Scottish.* a maidservant. [origin uncertain]

las·sie (las′ē), *n. Especially Scottish.* **1.** a young lass or girl: *My love she's but a lassie yet* (Robert Burns). **2.** a sweetheart.

las·si·tude (las′ə tüd, -tyüd), *n.* lack of energy; weakness; weariness: *His anger had evaporated; he felt nothing but utter lassitude* (John Galsworthy). [< Latin *lassitūdō* < *lassus* tired] —**Syn.** languor, fatigue.

las·so (las′ō, -ü; la sü′), *n., pl.* **-sos** or **-soes,** *v.,* **-soed, -so·ing.** —*n.* a long rope with a running noose at one end; lariat. A cowboy's lasso, used especially for catching steers and horses, is often made of untanned hide and is from 10 to 30 yards in length. —*v.t.* to catch with a lasso.
[American English < Spanish *lazo* < Latin *laqueus* noose. Doublet of LACE.] —**las′so·er,** *n.*

lasso cell, *Zoology.* a nematocyst.

las·sock (las′ək), *n. Scottish.* a little lass. [< *lass* + *-ock,* a diminutive suffix]

last[1] (last, läst), *adj.* **1. a.** coming after all others; being at the end; final: *the last page of a book. This is the last day of May.* **b.** coming after all others in importance or estimation; lowest: *The last of all nations now, though once the first* (William Cowper). **2.** latest; most recent: *last Wednesday, last Christmas. I saw him last week.* **3.** that remains; being the only remaining: *He spent his last dollar. In a desperate last stand against eviction from a doomed apartment house, a building superintendent . . . barricaded himself in his basement apartment* (Time). **4.** most unlikely; least suitable: *That is the last thing one would expect.* **5.** very great; utmost; extreme: *a paper of the last importance, to the last degree.* **6.** final and conclusive: *to say the last word on a subject.*
—*adv.* **1.** after all the others; at the end; finally: *He arrived last. Love thyself last* (Shakespeare). **2.** on the latest or most recent occasion: *When did you last see him?*
—*n.* **1.** the person or thing that is last: *the last in the row. I speak of this last with some hesitation.* **2. a.** the last part; end: *You have not heard the last of this.* **b.** the end of life; death: *Be faithful to the last.*
at last or **at long last,** at the end; after a long time; finally: *His Temper being jovial, he at last got over it* (Sir Richard Steele).
breathe or **gasp one's last,** to die: *On his Cross breathing his painful last* (Thomas Ken).
see the last of, not to see again: *I'm glad to see the last of this unfriendly place.*
[Old English *latost,* or *lætest,* superlative of *læt* late]
—**Syn.** *adj.* **1. Last, final, ultimate** mean coming after all others. **Last** applies to that which comes after all others in a series or succession. **Final** emphasizes the definite end of the series: *The last day of school each year is the final one for graduating seniors.* **Ultimate** emphasizes the last that can ever be reached or found: *The ultimate cause of some diseases is unknown.* **6.** definite.
➔ **Last, latest.** *Last* refers to the final item of a series; *latest,* to the most recent in time of a series that may or may not be continued: *the scholar's latest (we hope it won't be his last) biography.*
➔ See **first** for another usage note.

last[2] (last, läst), *v.i.* **1.** to go on; hold out; continue to be; endure: *The storm lasted three days.* **2.** to continue in good condition, force, etc.: *I hope these shoes last a year.* **3.** to be enough (for): *Our money must last for a while.*
last out, to go or come through safely; survive: *The Puritans lasted out their first winter in New England and began to plant in the spring.*
—*n.* power of holding on or out; staying power: *Few have the last to continue long against adversity.*
[Old English *lǣstan* accomplish, carry out, related to *lāst* track, last[3]]
—**Syn.** *v.i.* **1. Last, continue, endure** mean to go on for a long time. **Last** suggests holding out in good condition or full strength and for an unusually long time: *Those flowers lasted for two weeks.* **Continue** suggests going on and on without an end, usually without a break: *The heavy snow continued all week.* **Endure** implies holding out in spite of adversity or severe trials: *They shall perish, but thou shalt endure* (Psalms 102:26).

last[3] (last, läst), *n.* a block shaped like a foot, used in manufacturing or repairing shoes and boots.
stick to one's last, to pay attention to one's own work; mind one's own business: *The cabdriver told the passenger to stick to her last and stop the backseat driving.*
—*v.t.* to form (shoes and boots) on a last.
[Old English *lǣste* < *lāst* track]

last[4] (last, läst), *n.* a unit of weight or cubic measure, often equal to 4,000 pounds but varying in different localities and for different produce. [Old English *hlæst* a load]

last-ditch (last′dich′, läst′-), *adj.* **1.** of or serving as a last line of defense; used as a last resort: *a last-ditch weapon, a last-ditch stand.* **2.** refusing to give in: *The barricades remain in place, with a few new ones which were erected yesterday by last-ditch supporters* (Manchester Guardian).

last-ditch·er (last′dich′ər, läst′-), *n.* a person who resists to the last extremity.

last·er (las′tər, läs′-), *n.* **1.** a person who fits the parts of boots or shoes to lasts. **2.** a tool used in stretching leather on a last.

Las·tex (las′teks), *n. Trademark.* an elastic yarn made from fibers of cotton, rayon, silk, etc., wrapped around a thread of fine rubber. It is woven or knitted into undergarments, bathing suits, etc.

Last Frontier, a nickname for Alaska.

last in, first out, LIFO.

last·ing (las′ting, läs′-), *adj.* that lasts a long time; that lasts; that will last; permanent; durable: *a lasting color. A just and lasting peace* (Abraham Lincoln). —*n.* **1.** staying power. **2.** everlasting, a plant whose flowers keep their shape and color when dried. —**last′ing·ly,** *adv.* —**last′ing·ness,** *n.*
—**Syn.** *adj.* **Lasting, enduring, permanent** mean existing or continuing for a long time or forever. **Lasting** emphasizes going on and on indefinitely, long past what would be normal or expected: *The experience had a lasting effect on him.* **Enduring** emphasizes the idea of being able to withstand the attacks of time and circumstance: *All the world hoped for enduring peace.* **Permanent** emphasizes staying in the same state or position, without changing or being likely to change: *What is your permanent address?*
—**Ant.** *adj.* ephemeral, transient, transitory, fleeting.

Last Judgment, 1. God's final judgment of all mankind at the end of the world. **2.** the day of this judging; the Day of Judgment; judgment day.

last·ly (last′lē, läst′-), *adv.* in the last place; in conclusion; finally: *Sixth and lastly, they have belied a lady* (Shakespeare).

last-min·ute (last′min′it), *adj.* at the latest possible time; just before it is too late: *Department stores were crowded with last-minute shoppers* (New York Times).

last offices, prayers for a dead person.

last quarter, 1. the period between the second half moon and the new moon. **2.** the phase of the moon represented by the half moon after full moon.

last resort, an attempt to solve a problem beyond which no further attempts are possible: *You stated in your editorial "Last Resorts First" . . . that the President acted hastily and used a last resort first in dealing with the Little Rock situation* (Wall Street Journal).

last rites, a priest's administration of Holy Communion and the saying of prayers for a dying or dead person; extreme unction.

last sleep, death.

last straw, the last of a series of troublesome things that finally causes a collapse, outburst, etc.: *John had been calm through all the day's troubles, but missing the bus was the last straw, and he grew hot with anger.*

Last Supper, the supper of Jesus and His disciples on the evening before He was betrayed and crucified. Matthew 26:20-29. According to the Bible the sacrament of the Eucharist was instituted at the Last Supper. I Corinthians 11:24-25.

last word, 1. the last thing said. **2.** *Informal.* the latest thing; most up-to-date style: *Every one thought that . . . you were as safe on the last word in liners as in your own bedroom* (A.S.M. Hutchinson). **3.** *Informal.* a thing that cannot be improved.

lat[1] (lät), *n., pl.* **lats** or **la·tu. 1.** a former unit of money in Latvia. **2.** a Latvian coin, worth about 20 cents. [< Latvian *lats* < *Latvija* Latvia]

lat[2] (lät), *n.* (in India) an isolated pillar or column, especially one of a class of Buddhist pillars.

lat., latitude.

Lat., Latin.

lat·a·ki·a or **Lat·a·ki·a** (lat′ə kē′ə), *n.* a fine, highly aromatic variety of tobacco: *Enveloped in fragrant clouds of Latakia* (Thackeray). [< *Latakia,* a seaport in Syria, near which the tobacco is grown]

la·ta·ni·a (lə tā′nē ə), *n.* any of a group of fan palms native to the Mascarene Islands and much cultivated in greenhouses. [< New Latin *Latania* the genus name < *latanier* the native name]

latch (lach), *n.* a catch for fastening a door, gate, or window, often one not needing a key. It consists of a movable piece of metal or wood that fits into a notch, opening, etc.
on the latch, not locked, but fastened only by a latch: *They found the door on the latch* (Dickens). [< verb]
—*v.t., v.i.* to fasten or secure with a latch.
latch on to, *Informal.* to get as one's own; catch and hold: *She has, in fact, a habit of latching on to men, and she can be extremely tough about relinquishing them* (Wolcott Gibbs). [Old English *læccan* to grasp]

latch·et (lach′it), *n. Archaic.* a strap or lace for fastening a shoe or sandal: *There cometh one . . . the latchet of whose shoes I am not worthy to stoop down and unloose* (Mark 1:7). [< Old French *lachet,* dialectal variant of *lacet* (diminutive) < *laz,* or *las* lace]

latch·key (lach′kē′), *n.* a key used to draw back or unfasten the latch of a door.

latchkey child, *U.S.* a child left at home unattended while both parents are working.

latch·string (lach′string′), *n.* a string passed through a hole in a door, for raising a latch from the outside.
the latchstring is out, visitors are welcome: *The latchstring is always out at the pastor's house.*

late (lāt), *adj.,* **lat·er** or **lat·ter, lat·est** or **last,** *adv.,* **lat·er, lat·est** or **last.** —*adj.* **1.** happening, coming, etc., after the usual or proper time: *We had a late dinner last night.* **2.** happening, coming, etc., at an advanced age: *success late in life.* **3.** that has recently happened, been performed, etc.; recent: *the late war. The late storm did much damage. He has been abroad a great deal of late years.* **4.** recently dead or gone out of office: *The late Mr. Lee was a good neighbor. Mr. Truman, the late President, is still working actively.*
of late, a short time ago; recently; lately: *The practice has been losing ground of late.*
—*adv.* **1.** after the usual or proper time: *He worked late. Better three hours too soon than a minute too late* (Shakespeare). **2.** at a time nearing the end of: *It rained late in the afternoon. I was up very late last night* (Dickens). **3.** in recent times; recently: *Those climes where I have late been staying* (Byron). **4.** recently but no longer: *John Smith, late of Boston.*
[Old English *læt*] —**late′ness,** *n.*
—**Syn.** *adj.* **1. Late, tardy** mean happening or coming after the usual or proper time. **Late** applies whether the delay is avoidable or not: *Because his car broke down, he was late for school.* **Tardy** applies particularly when the delay is due to mere carelessness: *He was tardy again this morning.*
➔ See **first** and **last**[1] for usage notes.

late blight, a very widespread, destructive fungous disease of potatoes, tomatoes, and celery, characterized by brown discoloration of the plant.

late·com·er (lāt′kum′ər), *n.* a person, group, etc., that has arrived late or recently.

lat·ed (lā′tid), *adj. Poetic.* belated: *Now spurs the lated traveller apace To gain the timely inn* (Shakespeare).

la·teen (la tēn′), *adj.* having a lateen sail. Also, **latteen.** [< French *voile latine* (literally) Latin sail (because of its use in the Mediterranean)]

la·teen-rigged (la tēn′rigd′), *adj.* having a lateen sail.

lateen sail, a triangular sail held up by a long yard on a short mast. It was introduced into the Mediterranean by the Arabs.

Lateen Sails on Mediterranean xebec

Late Greek, the Greek language from about 300 to 700 A.D.

Late Latin, the Latin language from about 300 to 700 A.D.

late·ly (lāt′lē), *adv.* **1.** a short time ago; recently: *They visited Boston lately.* **2.** of late and still in the same condition: *He has not been looking well lately.*

lat·en (lā′tən), *v.i., v.t.* to become or make late. [< *lat*(e) + *-en*[1]]

la·ten·cy (lā′tən sē), *n.* latent condition or quality.

latency period, *Psychoanalysis.* a period between early childhood and puberty when heterosexual drives are apparently inactive or sublimated.

la·ten·si·fi·ca·tion (lā'tən sə fə kā'shən), *n. Photography.* the intensification of a latent image after exposure by means of a chemical solution or vapor or with actinic light.

la·tent (lā'tənt), *adj.* **1.** present but not active; hidden; concealed: *latent hostility, latent ability, latent powers.* **2.** (of infection) present in an undeveloped stage only; not yet manifest: *a test to reveal latent tuberculosis.* **3.** *Botany.* dormant or undeveloped, as buds that are not externally visible until stimulated to grow: *The power of a grain of wheat to grow into a plant remains latent if the wheat is not planted.* **4.** *Psychology.* forming part of the mental content or personality but not apparent in overt acts.
—*n.* a fingerprint not readily visible to the eye: *The police had to take many . . . latents which were found at the scene of the crime* (Erle Stanley Gardner).
[< Latin *latēns, -entis,* present participle of *latēre* lie hidden] —**la'tent·ly,** *adv.*
—**Syn.** *adj.* **1. Latent, potential** mean existing as a possibility or fact, but not showing itself plainly. **Latent** means actually existing as a fact, but lying hidden, not active or plainly to be seen at the present time: *An exertion of a latent genius* (Edmund Burke). **Potential** means existing as a possibility and capable of coming into actual existence or activity if nothing happens to stop development: *That boy has great potential ability in science.*

latent heat, *Physics.* the heat required to change a solid to a liquid or a vapor, or to change a liquid to a vapor, without a change of temperature.

latent image, an image produced on the chemical emulsion of photographic film by the effect of light, visible only when the film has been developed.

latent period, 1. *Medicine.* incubation period; the period that elapses between the original infection and the time when a disease can be diagnosed. **2.** *Physiology.* the time elapsing between a stimulus and the response to it.

lat·er (lā'tər), *adj.* **1.** the comparative of **late. 2.** more late; more recent: *the later border songs of his own country* (R. H. Hutton).
—*adv.* **1.** late in a greater degree: *to stay later than usual.* **2.** at a later time or period; subsequently; afterward: *It can be done later.*
later on, afterward.

-later, *combining form.* one who worships ———; one who is devoted to ———: *Idolater = one who worships idols.* [< Greek *-latrēs.* Related to Greek *latreiā*; see LATRIA]

lat·er·ad (lat'ər ad), *adv. Anatomy.* toward the side. [< Latin *latus, -eris* side + *ad* to]

lat·er·al (lat'ər əl), *adj.* **1.** of the side; at the side; from the side; toward the side: *the river and its lateral streams* (Thomas Huxley). *A lateral branch of a family is a branch not in the direct line of descent.* **2.** *Phonetics.* articulated so that the breath passes out on one or both sides of the tongue, as in pronouncing the English *l.*
—*n.* **1.** a lateral part or outgrowth. **2.** *Phonetics.* a lateral sound, such as *l.* **3.** *Mining.* **a.** a drift other than the main drift. **b.** a connecting tunnel between main haulage ways. **4.** (in football) a lateral pass.
[< Latin *laterālis* < *latus, -eris* side]

lateral chain, *Chemistry.* a side chain.

lat·er·al·i·ty (lat'ə ral'ə tē), *n., pl.* **-ties. 1.** the quality of having distinct sides. **2.** the preference of one side to the other: *Crossed laterality* [*is*] *a condition in which the dominant hand and eye are on opposite sides* (London Times).

lat·er·al·ize (lat'ər ə līz), *v.t.,* **-ized, -iz·ing.** to make lateral.

lateral line, the row of connected pores on the sides of fishes by which they detect change in water pressure or current. Similar organs are present in the aquatic larvae of amphibians.

lat·er·al·ly (lat'ər ə lē), *adv.* **1.** in a lateral direction; at the side; sideways. **2.** from a lateral branch.

lateral pass, a throwing of a football from one player to another in a direction almost parallel with the goal line.

Lat·er·an (lat'ər ən), *adj.* of or having to do with one of the five general church councils held in the official church of the Pope, Church of Saint John Lateran, in Rome. [< Latin *Laterānus* < (*Plautii*) *Laterānī,* a Roman family, who owned a palace on the site]

lat·er·ite (lat'ə rīt), *n.* a reddish soil rich in iron or aluminum and formed under tropical conditions by the decomposition of rock, common in parts of India, southwestern Asia, Africa, and elsewhere. [< Latin *later, -eris* brick, tile + English *-ite*[1]]

lat·er·it·ic (lat'ə rit'ik), *adj.* containing laterite; having the characteristics of laterite: *lateritic soil, lateritic ore.*

lat·er·i·tious (lat'ə rish'əs), *adj.* **1.** having to do with or resembling bricks. **2.** of the red color characteristic of bricks. [< Latin *laterītius* < *later, -eris* brick]

lat·er·i·za·tion (lat'ər ə zā'shən), *n.* the process by which laterite is formed.

la·tes·cence (lā tes'əns), *n.* latescent condition or quality.

la·tes·cent (lā tes'ənt), *adj.* becoming latent, hidden, or obscure. [< Latin *latēscēns, -entis,* present participle of *latēscere* hide oneself < *latēre* conceal]

lat·est (lā'tist), *adj.* **1.** the superlative of **late. 2.** most late; most recent. **3.** *Archaic* or *Poetic.* last; final.
at the latest, no later than (the time specified): *I'll see you next week at the latest.*
the latest, *Informal.* the most up-to-date thing; the newest style, design, etc.: *The latest the dear girls hereabouts are singing, . . . is, "Will he love you as today?"* (Kansas Times and Star).
➔ See **last**[1] for a usage note.

la·tex (lā'teks), *n., pl.* **lat·i·ces** or **la·tex·es,** *v.* —*n.* a milky fluid found in certain plants and trees, such as milkweeds, poppies, and plants yielding rubber. Some kinds of latex coagulate on exposure to the air and are the source of rubber, chicle, and other products. —*v.t.* to add latex to: *. . . latexed sisal pads* (Wall Street Journal). [< Latin *latex, -icis* liquid]

lath (lath, läth), *n., pl.* **laths** (la*TH*z, laths, lä*TH*z, läths), *v.* —*n.* **1.** one of the thin, narrow strips of wood placed over the framework of a wall, ceiling, roof, etc., used to form a support for plaster or to make a lattice. **2.** a wire cloth or sheet metal with holes in it, used in place of laths. **3.** a lining or support made of laths. The walls of a frame house are usually built with lath and plaster. **4.** any thin, narrow, flat piece of wood.
—*v.t.* to cover or line (a wall, ceiling, etc.) with laths.
[Middle English *lathe,* apparently < a variant of Old English *lætt*]

lathe (lā*TH*), *n., v.* **lathed, lath·ing.** —*n.* **1.** a machine for holding articles of wood, metal, etc., and turning them against a cutting tool used to shape them. **2.** potter's wheel. **3.** the movable swing frame in a loom, consisting of the shuttles, reed, picking apparatus, etc.

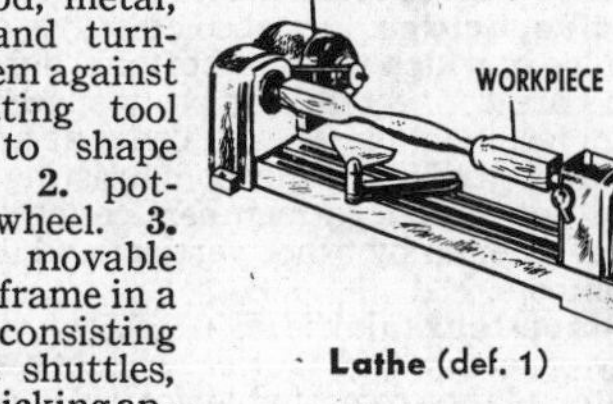

Lathe (def. 1)

—*v.t.* to shape or cut (wood, metal, etc.) on a lathe.
[earlier, scaffolding; origin uncertain; perhaps < Scandinavian (compare Old Icelandic *hlathi* pile, stack)]

lath·er[1] (la*TH*'ər), *n.* **1.** foam made from soap and water. **2.** foam formed in sweating.
in or **into a lather,** *Slang.* in or into a state of great agitation or excitement: *Trade unionists having worked themselves into a lather about it, it was natural for the leader of the Labour Party . . . to relieve their anxiety* (London Times).
[< Old English *lēathor*]
—*v.t.* **1.** to put lather on: *He lathers his face before shaving.* **2.** *Informal.* to beat; thrash. —*v.i.* **1.** to form a lather: *This soap lathers well.* **2.** to become covered with foam formed in sweating: *The horse lathered from his hard gallop.*
[Middle English *latheren,* alteration of Old English *lēthran* cover with lather] —**lath'er·er,** *n.*
—**Syn.** *n.* **1.** suds. **2.** froth.

lath·er[2] (lath'ər, läth'-), *n.* a workman who puts laths on walls, ceilings, etc.

lath·er·y (la*TH*'ər ē), *adj.* consisting of or covered with lather.

lath house, a building for growing plants, made of a frame covered with lath on the top and often the sides, to protect plants from too much sunlight and wind or rain.

la·thi (lä'tē), *n.* (in India) an iron bar inside a bamboo stick, now used by police and soldiers. [< Hindi *lāthī*]

lath·ing (lath'ing, läth'-), *n.* **1.** work consisting of laths; laths collectively. **2.** the work of putting laths on walls, ceilings, etc.

lath·work (lath'wėrk', läth'-), *n.* lathing.

lath·y (lath'ē, läth'-), *adj.,* **lath·i·er, lath·i·est.** long and slender, like a lath: *a lathy young man.*

lath·y·rism (lath'ə riz əm), *n.* a condition in animals and man caused by eating certain plants of the pea family, such as the lupine or vetch. It is characterized by convulsive movements, and sometimes paraplegia, especially in the legs. [< New Latin *Lathyrus* the typical genus, that causes it + English *-ism*]

lat·i·ces (lat'ə sēz), *n.* a plural of **latex.**

lat·i·cif·er·ous (lat'ə sif'ər əs), *adj. Botany.* producing latex. [< Latin *latex, -icis* a liquid + English *-ferous*]

lat·i·fo·li·ate (lat'ə fō'lē āt, -it), *adj. Botany.* having broad leaves. [< New Latin *latifoliatus* < Latin *lātus* broad + *folium* leaf]

lat·i·fo·li·ous (lat'ə fō'lē əs), *adj.* latifoliate.

lat·i·fun·di·um (lat'ə fun'dē əm), *n., pl.* **-di·a** (-dē ə). (in Roman history) a large estate.

lat·i·go (lat'ə gō), *n., pl.* **-gos** or **-goes.** a strong leather strap attached to a saddle, for tightening and fastening the cinch, used in the western United States and Latin America. [American English < Spanish *látigo*]

Lat·in (lat'ən), *n.* **1. a.** the language of the ancient Romans, considered classical in the form acquired during the 200's and 100's B.C. **b.** any of the varieties of Latin, especially written Latin, as Late Latin, Medieval Latin, New Latin, or Vulgar Latin. **2.** a member of any of the peoples whose languages came from Latin: *The Italians, French, Spanish, Portuguese, and Romanians are Latins.* **3.** a native or inhabitant of Latium or of ancient Rome. **4.** a Roman Catholic. **5.** a Latin American.
—*adj.* **1.** of Latin; in Latin: *Latin poetry, Latin grammar, a Latin scholar.* **2.** of the Latin peoples. **3.** of Latium or its people; ancient Roman. **4.** Roman Catholic. **5.** Latin-American. *Abbr.:* Lat.
[< Latin *Latīnus* of Latium, an ancient country in Italy that included Rome]

Latin America, South America, Central America, Mexico, and most of the West Indies.

Lat·in-A·mer·i·can (lat'ən ə mer'ə kən), *adj.* of or having to do with Latin America.

Latin American, a native or inhabitant of Latin America.

Lat·in·ate (lat'ə nāt), *adj.* of, having to do with, or coming from Latin.

Latin Church, that part of the Catholic Church that follows the Latin Rite.

Latin cross, a cross whose upright is crossed above its center by a shorter, horizontal bar. See the diagram of **cross.**

Lat·in·esque (lat'ə nesk'), *adj.* resembling Latin; having a Latin character.

La·tin·ic (la tin'ik), *adj.* **1.** of or having to do with the Latin nations, ancient or modern. **2.** largely Latin: *the prevalent Latinic character of the vocabulary* (J.A.H. Murray).

Lat·in·ism (lat'ə niz əm), *n.* **1.** a Latin idiom or expression. **2.** conformity, especially in literary style, to Latin models.

Lat·in·ist (lat'ə nist), *n.* a person with much knowledge of the Latin language; Latin scholar.

Lat·in·is·tic (lat'ə nis'tik), *adj.* of or having to do with Latinism.

La·tin·i·ty (lə tin'ə tē), *n.* the use of Latin idioms or expressions.

Lat·in·i·za·tion or **lat·in·i·za·tion** (lat'ə nə zā'shən), *n.* **1.** a translating into Latin. **2.** a making Latin or like Latin.

Lat·in·ize or **lat·in·ize** (lat'ə nīz), *v.,* **-ized, -iz·ing.** —*v.t.* **1.** to translate into Latin. **2.** to make Latin in form or character. **3.** to cause to conform to the ideas, customs, etc., of the Latins or the Latin Church. —*v.i.* to use Latin forms, idioms, etc.

La·ti·no (lä tē′nō), *adj., n., pl.* **-nos.** *—adj., n.* Latin-American.

La·ti·no si·ne Flex·i·o·ne (lə ti′nō si′nē flek′sē ō′nē), Interlingua.

Latin Quarter, the Bohemian section of Paris, south of the Seine River; Left Bank.

Latin Rite, church ceremonies as used in the Diocese of Rome.

Latin school, *U.S.* a school, especially a private school, in which Latin is emphasized.

Latin square, a square divided into a number of cells containing Latin letters so arranged that a letter appears only once in each row and column. It is used especially in statistics to order various elements so as to control variability.

lat·ish (lā′tish), *adj., adv.* rather late: *He is in his latish seventies now . . . though no one would guess it to look at him* (H.F. Ellis).

lat·i·tude (lat′ə tüd, -tyüd), *n.* **1.** distance north or south of the equator, measured in degrees. **2.** room to act; freedom from narrow rules; scope: *The President had given Mr. Dulles wide latitude to decide whether the foreign ministers should meet first or meet concurrently* (New York Times). **3.** *Astronomy.* **a.** celestial latitude. **b.** galactic latitude. **4.** *Photography.* the range between the shortest and the longest exposures that produce good negatives on a given film. **5.** transverse dimension; extent as measured from side to side; width of a surface, as opposed to length. *Abbr.:* lat.

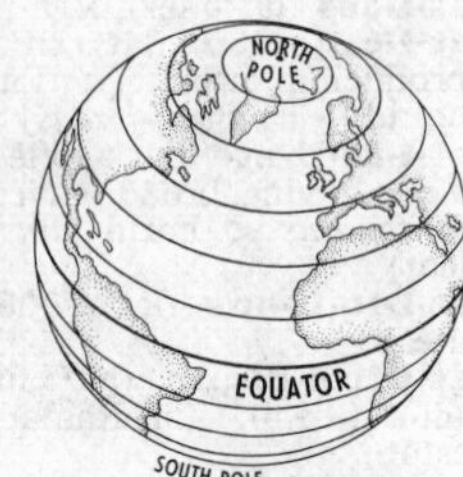

Circles of Latitude (def. 1)

latitudes, a place or region of a certain latitude: *Polar bears live in the cold latitudes.*
[< Latin *lātitūdō, -inis* < *lātus* wide]
—**Syn. 2.** range, play, expanse, amplitude.

lat·i·tu·di·nal (lat′ə tü′də nəl, -tyü′-), *adj.* of or relating to latitude. —**lat′i·tu′di·nal·ly,** *adv.*

lat·i·tu·di·nar·i·an (lat′ə tü′də nãr′ē ən, -tyü′-), *adj.* allowing others their own beliefs; not insisting on strict adherence to established principles, especially in religious views: *His opinions respecting ecclesiastical polity and modes of worship were latitudinarian* (Macaulay). *—n.* a person who cares little about creeds, forms of worship, or methods of church government. —**Syn.** *adj.* broad, liberal, tolerant.

Lat·i·tu·di·nar·i·an (lat′ə tü′də nãr′ē ən, -tyü′-), *n.* **1.** (in the Church of England) one of a school of Episcopal divines who, in the 1600's, strove to unite the dissenters with the Episcopal church by insisting on those doctrines which were held in common by both. They maintained the wisdom of the episcopal form of government and ritual, but denied their divine origin and authority. *Dr. Wilkins, my friend, the Bishop of Chester, is a mighty rising man, as being a Latitudinarian* (Samuel Pepys). **2.** (in later times) a person who cares little about doctrines and forms.

lat·i·tu·di·nar·i·an·ism (lat′ə tü′də nãr′ē ə niz′əm, -tyü′-), *n.* the opinions, principles, or practices of Latitudinarians.

lat·i·tu·di·nous (lat′ə tü′də nəs, -tyü′-), *adj.* of or characterized by latitude.

lat·ke (lät′ke), *n., pl.* **-kes.** *Yiddish.* a pota-to pancake.

La·to·na (lə tō′nə), *n. Roman Mythology.* the mother of Apollo and Diana, identified with the Greek Leto.

la·tri·a (lə trī′ə), *n.* (in the Roman Catholic Church) the supreme worship that can be paid to God alone. [< Late Latin *latrīa* < Greek *latreíā* service (to God) < *latreúein* serve (with prayer)]

la·trine (lə trēn′), *n.* a toilet, especially in a camp, factory, barracks, etc.; privy. [< Middle French *latrines,* plural, learned borrowing from Latin *lātrīna,* earlier *lavātrīna* (originally) washbasin, washroom < *lavāre* to wash]

la·tron (lā′trən), *n. Obsolete.* a robber, brigand, or plunderer. [< Latin *latrō, -ōnis.* Doublet of LADRONE.]

-latry, *combining form.* worship of ———; devotion to ———: *Mariolatry = devotion to the Virgin Mary.* [< Greek *-latreia* < *latreiā;* see LATRIA]

lat·teen (la tēn′), *adj.* lateen.

lat·ten (lat′ən), *n.* **1.** an alloy identical with or closely resembling brass, often hammered into thin sheets, formerly much used for church utensils. **2. a.** tin plate. **b.** any metal made in thin sheets. [< Middle French *laton, laiton,* Old French *leiton* < Arabic *lāṭūn* copper < dialectal Turkish *altan* gold]

lat·ter (lat′ər), *adj.* **1.** the second of two: *Canada and the United States are in North America; the former lies north of the latter.* **2.** more recent; nearer the end; later: *the latter days of life. Friday comes in the latter part of the week.* **3.** *Obsolete.* last: *and in his bosom spend my latter gasp* (Shakespeare). [Old English *lætra* later; (originally) slower, comparative of *læt* late]

lat·ter-day (lat′ər dā′), *adj.* belonging to recent times; modern: *latter-day problems, latter-day poets.*

latter days, *Archaic.* last days.

Latter-day Saint, a Mormon.

latter end, 1. the concluding part: *the latter end of May.* **2.** the end of life; death.

Latter Lammas, a day that will never arrive because there is no second Lammas in the year.

lat·ter·ly (lat′ər lē), *adv.* of late; lately; recently.

lat·ter·most (lat′ər mōst, -məst), *adj.* last; latest.

Latter Prophets, 1. the prophetic books of the Old Testament; the Major and Minor Prophets. **2.** the prophets who are believed to have written these books.

lat·tice (lat′is), *n., v.,* **-ticed, -tic·ing.** *—n.* **1.** a structure of crossed wooden or metal strips with open spaces between them: *a cool porch with a vine-covered lattice.* **2.** a window, gate, etc., having a lattice. **3.** the geometrical pattern of molecules, atoms, or ions in a crystal. **4.** a structure in a nuclear reactor, containing fissionable and non-fissionable materials in a regular geometrical pattern: *By suitable choice of the lattice the production of plutonium can be given an optimum value* (M. L. Oliphant). **5.** *Obsolete.* a window of latticework (usually painted red) or a pattern on the shutter imitating this, formerly a common mark of an ale-house or inn.
—v.t. **1.** to form into a lattice; make like a lattice. **2.** to furnish with a lattice: *Each window was latticed with iron wire on the outside* (Jonathan Swift).
[< Old French *lattis* < *latte* lath < Germanic (compare Old High German *latta*)] —**lat′tice·like′,** *adj.*

lattice beam or **frame,** lattice girder.

lattice bridge, an obsolete type of truss bridge in which top and bottom chord members are connected by closely spaced members fastened across each other at an angle.

lattice girder, a girder consisting of top and bottom chord members connected and strengthened by other vertical and diagonal members.

lat·tice·leaf (lat′is lēf′), *n., pl.* **-leaves.** any of certain Old World monocotyledonous water plants remarkable for their skeleton leaves, which lack cellular tissue between the veins; laceleaf.

lat·tice·work (lat′is wėrk′), *n.* **1.** lattice. **2.** lattices: *Many old New Orleans houses are decorated with wrought-iron latticework.*

lat·tic·ing (lat′ə sing), *n.* **1.** the act or process of making or providing with a lattice or latticework. **2.** latticework.

la·tu (lä′tü), *n.* lats; a plural of **lat.**

Latv., Latvia.

Lat·vi·an (lat′vē ən), *adj.* of or having to do with Latvia or its people. *—n.* **1.** a native or inhabitant of Latvia. **2.** the language of Latvia; Lettish: *Lithuanian and Latvian are the only two languages of any social importance in the Baltic branch* (H.A. Gleason, Jr.).

laud (lôd), *v.t.* to sing or speak the praises of; praise: *aspirations which are lauded up to the skies* (Charles Kingsley). [< Latin *laudāre* < *laus, laudis* praise]
—n. **1.** praise; high commendation: *All glory, laud, and honor to Thee, Redeemer King* (John Mason Neale). **2.** a song or hymn of praise.

lauds or **Lauds, a.** a morning church service with psalms of praise to God: *To make this the matter of my daily lauds* (Henry Hammond). **b.** (in Roman Catholic use) a prescribed devotional service for priests and religious, forming, with matins, the first of the seven canonical hours: *The bell of lauds began to ring, And friars in the chancel 'gan to sing* (Chaucer).
[< Old French *laude,* learned borrowing from Latin *laus, laudis* praise] —**laud′er,** *n.*
—**Syn.** *v.t.* commend, extol, exalt, eulogize.

laud·a·bil·i·ty (lô′də bil′ə tē), *n.* praiseworthiness.

laud·a·ble (lô′də bəl), *adj.* **1.** worthy of praise; commendable: *His attempts were laudable but unsuccessful.* **2.** *Medicine, Rare.* (of secretions, especially pus) healthy; sound. —**laud′a·ble·ness,** *n.* —**Syn. 1.** praiseworthy, meritorious, creditable.

laud·a·bly (lô′də blē), *adv.* in a laudable manner.

lau·dan·o·sine (lô dan′ō sēn, -sin), *n.* a toxic, crystalline alkaloid occurring in opium. *Formula:* $C_{21}H_{27}NO_4$

lau·da·num (lô′də nəm), *n.* **1.** a solution of 10 per cent opium in alcohol and water, used to lessen pain; opium tincture. **2.** (formerly) any of various preparations in which opium was the main ingredient. [< New Latin *laudanum,* alteration (perhaps by Paracelsus) of Latin *lādanum;* see LABDANUM]

lau·da·tion (lô dā′shən), *n.* **1.** the act of praising: *his very liberal laudation of himself* (Dickens). **2.** an instance of this, as a laudatory inscription. **3.** the condition of being praised.

laud·a·tive (lô′də tiv), *adj.* laudatory. *—n. Obsolete.* a laudative expression or discourse; eulogy; panegyric.

lau·da·tor (lô dā′tər), *n.* a person who praises.

lau·da·tor tem·po·ris ac·ti (lô dā′tər tem′pər is ak′tī), *Latin.* a praiser of time past: *No laudator temporis acti. On the contrary: How we progress in everything!* (New Yorker).

laud·a·to·ry (lô′də tôr′ ē, -tōr′-), *adj.* expressing praise.

Laud·i·an (lô′dē ən), *adj.* of, having to do with, or favoring the tenets and practices of Archbishop William Laud (1573-1645) of Canterbury, noted for his persecution of dissenters and nonconformists. *—n.* a follower of Laud or Laudianism.

Laud·i·an·ism (lô′dē ə niz′əm), *n.* the principles and practices of Archbishop William Laud and his followers.

lauds or **Lauds** (lôdz), *n.pl.* See under **laud,** *n.*

laugh (laf, läf), *v.i.* **1.** to make the sounds and movements of the face and body that show mirth, amusement, scorn, etc.: *We all laughed at that television show.* **2.** to suggest the feeling of joy; be lively: *The wood fire . . . laughs broadly through the room* (Hawthorne). **3.** to utter a cry or sound like the laughing of a human being, as some birds do. *—v.t.* **1.** to express with laughter: *to laugh a reply.* **2.** to drive, put, bring, etc., by or with laughing.

laugh at, to make fun of: *Though Pope laughed at the advice, we might fancy that he took it to heart* (Leslie Stephen).

laugh off or away, to pass off or dismiss with a laugh; get out of by laughing: *to laugh off criticism, to laugh away a mistake.*
—n. **1.** the act or sound of laughing. **2.** a characteristic manner of laughing: *. . . gladden this vale of sorrows with a wholesome laugh* (Oliver Wendell Holmes). [Old English *hliehhan*] —**laugh′er,** *n.* —**Syn.** *v.i.* **1.** chuckle, chortle, giggle.

laugh·a·ble (laf′ə bəl, läf′-), *adj.* such as to cause laughter; amusing: *a laughable error.* —**laugh′a·ble·ness,** *n.*
—**Syn.** comical, humorous. See **funny.**

laugh·a·bly (laf′ə blē, läf′-), *adv.* in a laughable manner; so as to excite laughter: *The clowns were laughably engaged in a pie-throwing scene.*

laugh·ing (laf′ing, läf′-), *adj.* **1.** that laughs or seems to laugh: *a laughing child, the laughing brook.* **2.** accompanied by laughter: *a laughing reply.*
—n. the act of one who laughs; laughter: *The clown's laughing brought smiles to children's faces.*

laughing death, a disease which attacks the nervous system, usually causing death. It is common in parts of New Guinea and is marked by involuntary laughter.

laughing gas, nitrous oxide, a colorless

gas that, when inhaled, usually produces exhilaration, followed by insensibility to pain. It is used as an anesthetic, especially in dentistry. *Formula:* N_2O

laughing gull, a small gull of temperate and tropical America that has a cry like laughing: *Identify the laughing gull by his coal-black head that looks as if he had dunked it in a big inkwell, his gray back, dark wing-tips and squared white tail feathers* (New York Times).

laughing jackass, a large bird of Australia and New Guinea, a kind of kingfisher, with a harsh cackling voice; kookaburra.

laugh·ing·ly (laf′ing lē, läf′-), *adv.* in a laughing or merry way; with laughter.

laugh·ing·stock (laf′ing stok′, läf′-), *n.* an object of ridicule; person or thing that is made fun of.

laugh·ter (laf′tər, läf′-), *n.* **1. a.** the action of laughing: *Of all the countless folk who have lived . . . not one is known . . . as having died of laughter* (Max Beerbohm). **b.** (occasionally) a manner of laughing: *There was embarrassed laughter at the vulgar jokes.* **2.** the sound of laughing: *Unextinguish'd laughter shakes the skies* (Alexander Pope). **3.** *Especially Poetic.* a subject or matter for laughter: *Hath Cassius lived To be but mirth and laughter to his Brutus?* (Shakespeare). [Old English *hleahtor*]

laugh·ter·ful (laf′tər fəl, läf′-), *adj.* full of or given to laughter; mirthful.

laugh·ter·less (laf′tər lis, läf′-), *adj.* without laughter.

laugh track, pre-recorded laughter dubbed in on the sound track of a filmed television show to enliven the comedy.

laugh·y (laf′ē, läf′-), *adj.* inclined to laugh.

lau ha·la (lou hä′lə), *n. Hawaiian.* the leaf of the pandanus tree, used in weaving.

lau·lau (lou′lou), *n. Hawaiian.* a dish of chopped taro leaves, meat, and fish wrapped in ti palm leaves and steamed.

launce (lans, läns), *n.* a sand launce. Also, **lance.**

launch[1] (lônch, länch), *n.* **1.** the largest boat carried by a warship. **2.** a more or less open motorboat, used for pleasure trips, carrying passengers to and from larger boats off shore, etc. [< Spanish and Portuguese *lancha*, apparently < Malay *lanchār-an* < *lanchār* quick, agile; spelling influenced by *launch*[2]]

launch[2] (lônch, länch), *v.t.* **1.** to cause to slide into the water; set afloat: *A new ship is launched from the supports on which it was built. Was this the face that launched a thousand ships?* (Christopher Marlowe). **2.** to push out or put forth on the water or into the air: *to launch a plane from an aircraft carrier, to launch a satellite in a rocket.* **3.** to start; set going; set out: *He had formed his new government in an atmosphere full of the promise of change, of new enterprises launched, of fresh young blood reaching power* (Time). **4.** to throw; hurl; send out: *An angry person launches threats against his enemies. A bow launches arrows.*
—*v.i.* **1.** to push forth or out from land; put to sea: *We launched for the main coast of Africa* (Daniel Defoe). **2.** to start; set out: *He used the money to launch into a new business.* **3.** to burst; plunge.

launch out, to begin; start: *The small man . . is . . . slow to launch out into expense, when things are going well* (Augustus Jessopp).
—*n.* **1.** the movement of a boat or ship from the land into the water, especially the sliding of a new ship from its platform. **2.** the act of setting a rocket or missile into motion: . . . *the historic launch of an Atlas by a Strategic Air Command crew* (Scientific American).
[< Old North French *lanchier*, Old French *lancier.* Doublet of LANCE[1], verb.]
—**Syn.** *v.t.* **3.** begin, initiate.

launch·a·ble (lôn′chə bəl, län′-), *adj.* that can be launched: *a launchable project. . . . a launchable nuclear stage for a rocket* (Ralph E. Lapp).

launch complex, the entire physical arrangement at a rocket or missile launching site, including the launching pad, gantry, fueling devices, communications equipment, blockhouse, etc.

launch·er (lôn′chər, län′-), *n.* **1.** a person who launches. **2.** *Military.* **a.** Also, **grenade launcher.** a device attached to a rifle that launches a special grenade when the rifle is fired. **b.** a rocket launcher.

launch·ing pad (lôn′ching, län′-), the raised level surface on which a rocket or missile is prepared for launching and from which it is shot into the air: *Launching pads must withstand high temperatures and high-velocity exhaust blasts. The nuclear-powered missile-carrying submarine . . . may well be the most nearly invulnerable launching pad* (Harper's).

Launching Pad and blockhouse for U.S. Air Force Atlas with space capsule

launching platform, **1.** a launching pad. **2.** a launching site.

launching site, **1.** the place at which a rocket or missile is launched. **2.** a launch complex.

launch pad, a launching pad.

launch point, a launching site.

launch stand, a launch complex.

launch window, the conjunction of time and planetary position in a condition that permits successful launching of a spacecraft.

laun·der (lôn′dər, län′-), *v.t.* to wash and iron (linens, clothes, etc.): *Many homes have machines to launder clothes.* —*v.i.* **1.** (of a fabric) to be able to wash; stand washing: *This fabric does not launder very well; it tends to shrink.* **2.** to wash and iron clothes, etc.: *Many housewives launder on Monday.*
—*n.* **1.** a trough for water, either cut in the earth or formed of wood or other material. **2.** (in ore dressing) a passage for conveying intermediate products or residues that are suspended in water.
[Middle English *lander* one who washes, earlier *lavender* < Old French *lavandier* < Vulgar Latin *lavandārius* < Latin *lavanda* (things) to be washed < *lavāre* to wash] —**laun′der·er,** *n.*

laun·der·a·bil·i·ty (lôn′dər ə bil′ə tē, län′-), *n.* the quality of being launderable.

laun·der·a·ble (lôn′dər ə bəl, län′-), *adj.* that can be laundered without damage.

laun·der·ette (lôn′də ret′, län′-), *n.* laundromat.

laun·dress (lôn′dris, län′-), *n.* a woman whose work is washing and ironing linens, clothes, etc.

laun·dro·mat (lôn′drə mat, län′-), *n.* **1.** a self-service laundry consisting of coin-operated washing machines and dryers. **2.** a laundry in which washing and drying machines are operated by workers who charge for the laundry by the pound.

laun·dry (lôn′drē, län′-), *n., pl.* **-dries. 1.** a room or building where linens, clothes, etc., are washed and ironed. **2.** articles (linens, clothes, etc.) washed or to be washed. **3.** the washing and ironing of clothes.

laun·dry·man (lôn′drē mən, län′-), *n., pl.* **-men. 1.** a man who works in a laundry. **2.** a man who collects and delivers laundry.

laun·dry·wom·an (lôn′drē wům′ən, län′-), *n., pl.* **-wom·en.** a laundress.

Laun·fal (lôn′fəl, län′-), *n.* **Sir,** a knight of the Round Table.

lau·ra (lôr′ə), *n., pl.* **lau·ras, lau·rae** (lôr′ē). (among the early Christians in Palestine, Egypt, etc.) a form of monastic community occupying a row or group of detached cells under the authority of a superior. [< Greek *laúrā* lane, passage, alley]

lau·ra·ceous (lô rā′shəs), *adj.* belonging to the laurel family of plants. [< New Latin *Lauraceae* the family name < Latin *laurus* laurel tree]

lau·re·ate (*adj., n.* lôr′ē it; *v.* lôr′ē āt), *adj., n., v.,* **-at·ed, -at·ing.** —*adj.* **1.** crowned with a laurel wreath as a mark of honor. **2.** honored or distinguished, especially as a poet. **3.** consisting of laurel, as a crown or wreath.
—*n.* **1.** a poet laureate. **2.** a person who is honored or receives a prize for outstanding achievement in a particular field: *a Nobel prize laureate.* **3.** a person who praises enthusiastically; panegyrist: *a laureate of Victorian England.*
—*v.t.* **1.** to appoint as poet laureate. **2.** to crown with laurel in token of honor.
[< Latin *laureātus* < *laurea* laurel tree < *laurus* laurel tree]

lau·re·ate·ship (lôr′ē it ship), *n.* **1.** the position of poet laureate. **2.** the time during which a poet is poet laureate.

lau·re·a·tion (lôr′ē ā′shən), *n.* **1.** the act of crowning with laurel. **2.** the conferring of a university degree; graduation. **3.** the appointment of a poet laureate.

lau·rel (lôr′əl, lor′-), *n., v.,* **-reled, -rel·ing** or (*especially British*) **-relled, -rel·ling.** —*n.* **1.** any of a group of shrubs or trees of the laurel family, as a small evergreen tree of the Mediterranean region, with smooth, shiny leaves and a profusion of dark-purple berries; bay tree; sweet bay. **2.** the leaves of this small evergreen tree. The ancient Greeks and Romans crowned victors with wreaths of laurel. **3.** any of various trees or shrubs having evergreen leaves like those of the laurel tree, as the mountain laurel, sheep laurel, and the great rhododendron. The flower of the mountain laurel is the state flower of Connecticut.

laurels, a. honor; fame: *No other fame can be compared with that of Jesus . . . All other laurels wither before his* (William E. Channing). **b.** victory: *They neither pant for laurels, nor delight in blood* (Samuel Johnson).

look to one's laurels, to guard one's reputation or record from rivals: *The fair widow would be wise to look to her laurels* (J.H. Riddell).

rest on one's laurels, to be satisfied with the honors or achievements one has already attained: *All this does not mean that we can afford to rest on our laurels* (Punch).
—*v.t.* to wreathe with laurel; adorn with or as with laurel.
[< Old French *lorier* and *laurier* laurel tree < *lor* laurel < Latin *laurus* laurel tree]

lau·reled (lôr′əld, lor′-), *adj.* **1.** crowned with a laurel wreath. **2.** honored.

laurel family, a group of dicotyledonous trees or shrubs, found chiefly in warm regions, where they are evergreen. Many of the plants of this family are aromatic and are used for seasoning. The family includes the laurel, cinnamon, sassafras, avocado, camphor tree, and greenheart.

lau·relled (lôr′əld, lor′-), *adj. Especially British.* laureled.

Lau·ren·tian (lô ren′shən), *adj.* **1.** of or having to do with the Canadian upland region extending from Labrador past Hudson Bay and north to the Arctic. **2.** of or having to do with the Laurentian Mountains in eastern Canada. **3.** of or having to do with the St. Lawrence River and the regions through which it flows. **4.** *Geology.* of or having to do with certain granites intrusive in the oldest pre-Cambrian rocks of southern Canada. [< *Laurentius,* Latin form of Lawrence + *-ian*]

lau·ric acid (lôr′ik, lor′-), a fatty acid found in coconut oil and palm oil, used in the manufacture of soap. *Formula:* $C_{12}H_{24}O_2$

lau·rus·tine (lôr′ə stin), *n.* laurustinus.

lau·rus·ti·nus or **lau·res·ti·nus** (lôr′ə stī′nəs), *n.* an evergreen shrub of the honeysuckle family, of the Mediterranean region, having clusters of white or pink flowers that bloom in winter in mild regions. [< New Latin *laurus tinus* < Latin *laurus* laurel tree, and *tīnus* a kind of plant]

laus De·o (lôs dē′ō, lous dā′ō), *Latin.* praise (be) to God.

lau·wine (lä vē′nə; *Anglicized* lô′win), *n.* Lawine.

lav., lavatory.

la·va (lä′və, lav′ə), *n.* **1.** the molten rock flowing from a volcano or fissure in the earth. **2.** the rock formed by the cooling of this molten rock. Some lavas are hard and glassy; others are light and porous. [< Italian *lava* lava flow < *lavare* to wash < Latin *lavāre*]

lava bed, a layer or surface of lava.

la·va·bo (lə vā′bō), *n., pl.* **-boes. 1.** Also, **Lavabo.** in the Roman Catholic Church: **a.** the ritual washing of the celebrant's hands after the Offertory and before beginning the consecration of the elements in the Mass. **b.** the passage recited with this ceremony (Psalm 25:6-12 in the Douay Version). **c.** the basin used for the washing. **d.** the small towel used to wipe the celebrant's hands. **2. a.** (in many monasteries of the Middle Ages) a trough, or the room in which the trough stood, for washing before religious exercises or meals. **b.** *Rare.* a washstand. **3.** a small ornamental basin hung on the wall of a hall or living room and sometimes used for holding plants. [< Latin *lavābo* I shall wash (from the first word of the verses said with the ritual)]

lava field, a large area of cooled lava.

lava flow, 1. the flow of lava from a volcano or fissure. **2.** the site of a former lava flow.

lav·age (lav′ij; *French.* lȧ vȧzh′), *n., v.,* **-aged, -ag·ing.** —*n.* **1.** a laving or washing. **2.** *Medicine.* **a.** a washing out of the stomach, intestines, or other organs. **b.** a cleansing by means of injection, as of a saline solution. —*v.t. Medicine.* to wash out or cleanse (a wound, organ, etc.). [< Middle French *lavage* < *laver* to wash < Latin *lavāre*]

la·va-la·va (lä′vä lä′vä), *n.* a garment of printed calico, worn as a loincloth or waistcloth by the natives of Samoa and Tonga. [< a Samoan word]

lav·a·liere, lav·a·lier, or **lav·al·lière** (lav′ə lir′), *n.* an ornament hanging from a small chain, worn by women around the neck. [< French *lavallière* < (the *Duchesse de*) *La Vallière,* 1644-1710, a mistress of Louis XIV of France]

lav·a·ret (lav′ə ret), *n.* a whitefish that lives in the sea and swims up various European and Asiatic rivers each year. Forms that are landlocked in various European lakes show widely differing characteristics, often being classified in different species. [< French *lavaret*]

la·va·tion (la vā′shən), *n.* **1.** the process of washing. **2.** water for washing. [< Latin *lavātiō, -ōnis* < *lavāre* to wash]

la·va·tion·al (la vā′shə nəl), *adj.* having to do with lavation.

lav·a·to·ri·al (lav′ə tôr′ē əl, -tōr′-), *adj.* of or having to do with washing; lavational.

lav·a·to·ry (lav′ə tôr′ē, -tōr′-), *n., pl.* **-ries.** **1.** a room where a person can wash his hands and face. **2.** a bowl or basin to wash in. **3.** a bathroom; toilet. **4.** *Ecclesiastical.* the ritual washing of the celebrant's hands during Communion service just before the consecration of the elements (the lavabo) and (formerly) after the cleansing of the vessels following the communion. **5.** *Rare.* a laundry. [< Latin *lavātōrium* < *lavāre* to wash. Doublet of LAVER[1].]

lave[1] (lāv), *v.,* **laved, lav·ing.** *Poetic.* —*v.t.* **1.** to wash; bathe: *basins and ewers to lave her dainty hands* (Shakespeare). **2.** to wash or flow against: *The stream laves its banks.* **3.** to pour or throw out, as water; ladle out. —*v.i.* to bathe. [Old English *lafian,* ultimately < Latin *lavāre*]

lave[2] (lāv), *n. Scottish.* what is left; the remainder; the rest. [Old English *lāf*]

la·veer (lə vir′), *v.i. Poetic.* to sail into the wind; tack. [< Dutch *laveeren* < Middle French *loveer* < *lof* windward, probably < Dutch *loef.* Compare LUFF.]

lav·en·der (lav′ən dər), *n.* **1.** a pale purple. **2. a.** any of various plants of the mint family, especially a small shrub native to the Mediterranean region, having spikes of small, fragrant, pale-purple flowers, yielding an oil (lavender oil or oil of lavender) much used in perfumes and in medicine. **b.** its dried flowers, leaves, and stalks placed among linens, clothes, etc., to perfume or preserve them from moths: *a chest full of lavender and old lace.*
—*adj.* pale-purple.
—*v.t.* to perfume with lavender; put lavender among (linen).
[< Anglo-French *lavendre* < Medieval Latin *lavendula,* also *livendula;* origin uncertain]

Lavender (def. 2a)

lavender water, a toilet water or perfume made with oil of lavender.

la·ver[1] (lā′vər), *n.* **1.** (in the Bible) the large brazen vessel, standing on a pedestal, for the ablutions of the Hebrew priests and the washing of the sacrifices, mentioned in the descriptions of the tabernacle and Solomon's Temple. **2. a.** *Ecclesiastical.* the water used in baptizing or the font containing it. **b.** any spiritually cleansing agency. **3.** *Archaic.* **a.** a bowl or basin to wash in. **b.** any bowl or pan for water; a water jug, usually of metal. [< Old French *laveoir,* Old North French *lavur* < Latin *lavātōrium.* Doublet of LAVATORY.]

la·ver[2] (lā′vər), *n.* **1.** any of various edible, red, marine algae that are widely distributed in the world. **2.** such seaweed prepared as food. [< Latin *laver*]

la·ver·bread (lā′vər bred′), *n.* a food made from dried seaweed and prepared like bread, eaten in parts of England and Wales.

lav·er·ock (lav′ər ək, lāv′rək), *n. Scottish.* a lark: *Now laverocks wake the merry morn* (Robert Burns). Also, **lavrock.** [Middle English *laverokke,* Old English *lāwerce*]

La·vin·i·a (lə vin′ē ə), *n. Roman Legend.* the wife of Aeneas.

lav·ish (lav′ish), *adj.* **1.** very free or too free in giving or spending; prodigal: *A very rich person can be lavish with money. Thank the lavish hand that gives world beauty to our eyes* (Julia Ward Howe). **2.** very abundant; more than enough; given or spent too freely: *lavish gifts. The lavish, full-skirted velvet gown of the Renaissance period was rich and made with a fabric such as silk or fine cotton* (Bernice G. Chambers). *The lavish gold of her loose hair* (Lowell). —*v.t.* to give or spend very freely or too freely; pour out wastefully: *It is a mistake to lavish kindness on ungrateful people. Upon the interior decorations Albert and Victoria lavished all their care* (Lytton Strachey). [< Middle French *lavasse* < Old Provençal *lavaci* < Latin *lavātiō;* see LAVATION] —**lav′ish·er,** *n.* —**lav′ish·ly,** *adv.* —**lav′ish·ness,** *n.* —**Syn.** *adj.* **1.** extravagant. **2.** See **profuse.**

lav·ish·ment (lav′ish mənt), *n.* the act of lavishing.

la·vol·ta (lə vol′tə), *n.* an old-time dance, in vogue in the 1500's and later. [< Italian *la* the + *volta* turn]

lav·rock (lav′rək), *n.* laverock.

law[1] (lô), *n.* **1.** the body of rules recognized by a state or a community as binding on its members: *English law is different from French law. The Venetian Law cannot impugn you as you do proceed* (Shakespeare). *The very slowness of the law, its massive impersonality, its insistence upon proceeding according to settled and ancient rules—all this tends to cool and bank the fires of passion and violence and replace them with order and reason* (Robert Traver). **2.** one of these rules: *The law against speeding motorists varies widely in different states. The laws of a game tell how to play it.* **3.** the controlling influence of these rules, or the condition of society brought about by their observance: *to maintain law and order.* **4.** law as a system: *a court of law.* **5.** the department of knowledge or study concerned with these rules; jurisprudence: *He was design'd to the study of the law* (John Dryden). **6.** the body of such rules concerned with a particular subject or derived from a particular source: *commercial law, criminal law, civil law.* **7. a.** the legal profession: *to enter the law.* **b.** *Slang.* a person hired to enforce the law; policeman or detective: *When they heard the sirens one thief said, "Let's scram; here comes the law."* **8.** legal action: *to have recourse to the law.* **9.** any act passed upon by the highest legislative body of a State or nation: *a congressional law.* **10.** any rule or principle that must be obeyed: *the laws of hospitality, a law of grammar.* **11.** a statement of a relation or sequence of phenomena invariable under the same conditions: *the law of gravitation, laws of motion, Mendel's Law.* **12.** a mathematical rule or relationship on which the construction of a curve, a series, etc., depends. **13.** *Theology.* **a.** a divine rule or commandment. **b.** the collective body of precepts held to be received from God: *the Mosaic law.* **c.** Often, **Law.** a system or order based on divine dispensation. **14.** *Sports.* a handicap: *I trust your Grace will treat me as a beast of chase . . . and allow me fair law?* (Scott).

go to law, to appeal to law courts; take legal action: *Dare any of you, having a matter against another, go to law before the unjust?* (I Corinthians 6:1).

lay down the law, a. to give orders that must be obeyed: *There is no official ministry view on chastity . . . to lay down the law on this subject* (New York Times). **b.** to give a scolding: *The teacher laid down the law to the boys who had caused the disturbance.*

read law, to study to be a lawyer: *He's reading law at Harvard.*

take the law into one's own hands, to protect one's rights or punish a crime without appealing to law courts: *The new marshal arrested the vigilantes who had taken the law into their own hands.*

—*v.i. Informal.* to go to law; bring a lawsuit: *Your husband's . . . given to lawing, they say* (George Eliot). —*v.t. Dialect or Informal.* to bring a lawsuit against; sue: *One sends me a challenge; another laws me; but I shall keep them all off* (Horatio Nelson). —*adj.* of or having to do with the law, lawyers, or legal proceedings; defined by law. [Old English *lagu* < Scandinavian (compare Old Icelandic *lög* laws)]

—**Syn.** *n.* **2, 9. Law, statute** mean a rule or regulation recognized by a state or community as governing the action or procedure of its members. **Law** is the general word applying to any such rule or regulation, written or unwritten, laid down by the highest authority, passed by action of a lawmaking body such as Congress, a State legislature, or a city council, or recognized as custom and enforced by the courts. **Statute** applies to a formally written law passed by a legislative body.

law[2] (lô), *adj., adv. Obsolete.* low[1].

Law (lô), *n.* **the, 1.** the books of the Old Testament that contain the Mosaic law. **2. a.** the Old Testament, as containing the Mosaic law. **b.** the part of the Bible setting this forth, especially the Pentateuch. **c.** the Pentateuch; Torah, especially one of the three recognized divisions of the Hebrew Scripture.

law-a·bid·ing (lô′ə bī′ding), *adj.* obedient to the law; peaceful and orderly: *law-abiding man.* —**law′-a·bid′ing·ness,** *n.*

law·book (lô′bu̇k′), *n.* a book relating to law, or containing laws or reports of cases.

law·break·er (lô′brā′kər), *n.* a person who breaks the law.

law·break·ing (lô′brā′king), *n.* a breaking of the law. —*adj.* breaking the law: *a law-breaking offense.*

law clerk, an assistant to a judge or lawyer: *Taking a job as a law clerk in Chicago . . . he saved enough money to start his own law office* (Wall Street Journal).

law court, a place where justice is administered; court of law.

law day, a day appointed for the discharge of a bond: *A person who borrows money with a mortgage promises to repay it by law day.*

Law Day, *U.S.* May 1, celebrated to emphasize the importance of law in American life.

law French, a corrupt form of Norman French in legal use in England from the time of William the Conqueror to that of Edward III or later, and still surviving in some phrases and expressions.

law·ful (lô′fəl), *adj.* **1.** according to law; done as the law directs: *a lawful arrest.* **2.** allowed by law; rightful: *lawful demands.* —**law′ful·ly,** *adv.* —**law′ful·ness,** *n.*

—**Syn. 1, 2. Lawful, legal, legitimate** mean according to law. **Lawful** means in agreement with or not against the laws of the state or community, the laws of a church, or moral law: *To some people gambling is never lawful although it may be legal in some places.* **Legal** means authorized by or according to the actual terms of the legislative acts and other laws of a state or community enforced by the courts: *Divorce is legal in the United States.* **Legitimate** means rightful according to law, recognized authority, or established standards: *Sickness is a legitimate reason for a child's being absent from school.*

law·giv·er (lô′giv′ər), *n.* a person who prepares and puts into effect a system of laws for a people; legislator; lawmaker.

law-hand (lô′hand′), *n.* (in former times) the style of handwriting customarily used in legal documents: *an immense desert of law-hand and parchments* (Dickens).

La·wi·ne (lä vē′nə; *Anglicized* lô′win), *n., pl.* **-nen** (-nən). *German.* an avalanche. Also, **lauwine.**

law·ing (lô′ing), *n. Scottish.* a bill at a tavern. [< obsolete *law* legal charge, share of expense + *-ing*[1]]

lawk (lôk), *n., interj.* an exclamation expressing wonder or surprise: *Lawk help me* (Thomas Hood). [probably alteration of *Lord*]

law·less (lô′lis), *adj.* **1.** paying no attention to the law; breaking the law: *to lead a lawless life.* **2.** hard to control; unruly: *Her lawless hair was caught in a net* (Bret Harte). **3.** having no laws: *a lawless wilderness.* —**law′less·ly,** *adv.* —**law′less·ness,** *n.* —**Syn. 2.** uncontrolled, ungovernable.

law lord, one of the members of the House of Lords qualified to take part in its judicial proceedings.

law·mak·er (lô′mā′kər), *n.* a person who helps to make laws; member of a legislature, congress, or parliament; legislator; lawgiver.
law·mak·ing (lô′mā′king), *adj.* that makes laws; legislative. —*n.* a making the laws; legislation.
law·man (lô′mən), *n., pl.* **-men.** a law enforcement officer.
law merchant, *pl.* **laws merchant. 1.** the body of principles and rules for the regulation of commerce, drawn chiefly from the customs of merchants; mercantile law. **2.** (formerly) the customs that governed legal cases originating in trade or commerce.
lawn[1] (lôn), *n.* **1.** land covered with grass kept closely cut, especially near or around a house. **2.** *Archaic.* an open space between woods; glade. —*v.t.* to turn (land) into lawn: *The grounds are beautifully lawned* (Cape Times). [< Old French *launde,* also *lande* wooded ground, heath, moor < Celtic (compare Breton *lann,* Irish *laun*)]
lawn[2] (lôn), *n.* **1.** a thin, sheer linen or cotton cloth, resembling cambric: *A saint in crape is twice a saint in lawn* (Alexander Pope). **2.** lawn sleeves. [apparently < *Laon,* a city in France, long a center of linen manufacture]
lawn bowling, the game of bowls.
lawn chair, a chair for use outdoors.
lawn mower, a machine with revolving blades for cutting the grass on a lawn.
lawn sleeves, 1. the sleeves of lawn characterizing the dress of an Anglican bishop. **2. a.** the position of a bishop. **b.** a bishop or bishops.
lawn tennis, a game in which a ball is hit back and forth with a racket over a low net. It is played on an open court, sometimes of grass. The game of tennis, as commonly played today, is lawn tennis.
lawn·y[1] (lô′nē), *adj.* like a lawn; level and covered with smooth turf: *lawny slopes* (George W. Curtis). [< *lawn*[1] + *-y*[1]]
lawn·y[2] (lô′nē), *adj.* made of or like the cloth lawn. [< *lawn*[2] + *-y*[1]]
law of contradiction, *Logic.* the law that states that a thing cannot be and not be at the same time or that no statement can be both true and false.
law of Moses, the first five books of the Old Testament (Genesis, Exodus, Leviticus, Numbers, and Deuteronomy); Pentateuch; Torah.
law of nations, 1. international law. **2.** (in ancient Roman use) the rules common to the law of all nations.
law of the Medes and Persians, a law that cannot be changed; something unalterable (with allusion to Daniel 6:12).
law·ren·ci·um (lô ren′sē əm), *n.* a radioactive, artificial chemical element of the actinide series produced by bombarding californium with boron ions. *Symbol:* Lw; *at.wt.:* (C^{12}) 257 or (O^{16}) 257; *at.no.:* 103; *half life:* 8 seconds. [< New Latin *Lawrencium* < Ernest Orlando *Lawrence,* 1901-1958, an American physicist]
Law·ren·tian (lô ren′shən), *adj.* of, having to do with, or characteristic of the English novelist and poet D.H. Lawrence, 1885-1930, or his writings.
Laws of Manu, Code of Manu; the most important legal code of Hinduism.
law·suit (lô′süt′), *n.* a case in a law court; application to a court for justice.
law·yer (lô′yər), *n.* **1.** a person whose profession is giving advice about the laws or acting for others in a law court. **2.** (in the New Testament) a scribe; expounder of the Mosaic law. Luke 10:25. **3.** a burbot (fish). **4.** *Australian Dialect.* a long bramble. [< *law*[1] + *-yer,* variant of *-ier*]
➔ **Lawyer** is a general term for members of the legal profession, as attorneys, barristers, counselors, solicitors, advocates, etc.
law·yer·ing (lô′yər ing), *n.* the state or condition of being a lawyer: *John W. Davis ... left Wall Street in 1924 to become the Democratic candidate for President; he lost and went back to lawyering* (Time).
law·yer·ism (lô′yə riz əm), *n.* the influence, or principles of lawyers.
law·yer·like (lô′yər līk′), *adj.* of or resembling a lawyer or lawyers.
law·yer·ly (lô′yər lē), *adj.* of lawyers; lawyerlike.
lax (laks), *adj.* **1.** not firm or tight; loose; slack: *a lax cord.* **2.** not strict; careless: *lax discipline. Don't let yourself become lax about the schedule you have set for doing your homework. The search had to have all the appearances of formality—neither too lax nor too thorough* (Graham Greene). **3.** loose in morals: *Richard* [*Cromwell*] *was known to be lax and godless in his conduct* (John Richard Green). **4.** not precise or exact; vague: *in a lax way of speaking* (Joseph Butler). **5.** (of tissue, stone, soils, etc.) loose in texture; loosely cohering or compacted. **6.** *Botany.* loose or open; not compact, as some panicles. **7.** *Phonetics.* pronounced with the muscles of the articulating organs relatively relaxed; wide: *lax vowels.* **8. a.** (of the bowels) acting easily; loose. **b.** *Obsolete.* (of a person) having the bowels unduly relaxed. [< Latin *laxus* loose] —**lax′ly,** *adv.* —**lax′ness,** *n.* —**Syn. 1.** relaxed, flabby. **2.** negligent, remiss.
lax·a·tion (lak sā′shən), *n.* **1.** a loosening or relaxing. **2.** a being loosened or relaxed. **3.** a mild purgative; laxative. [< Latin *laxātiō, -ōnis* < *laxāre* loosen < *laxus* loose, lax]
lax·a·tive (lak′sə tiv), *n.* a medicine that makes the bowels move.
—*adj.* **1.** making the bowels move; mildly purgative. **2.** having the property of relaxing. **3.** *Obsolete.* unable to contain one's speech or emotions: *Fellowes of practis'd and most laxative tongues* (Ben Jonson).
[< Latin *laxātīvus* loosening < *laxāre* loosen; see LAXATION] —**lax′a·tive·ly,** *adv.* —**lax′a·tive·ness,** *n.*
lax·i·ty (lak′sə tē), *n.* **1.** lax condition or quality: *moral laxity. The newspapers accused local police of laxity in dealing with gamblers.* **2.** slackness or want of tension (in the muscular or nervous fibers, etc.). **3.** looseness (of the bowels, etc.). [< Middle French *laxité,* learned borrowing from Latin *laxitās* < *laxus* loose]
lay[1] (lā), *v.,* **laid, lay·ing,** *n.* —*v.t.* **1.** to bring down; beat down: *A storm laid the crops low.* **2.** to put down; keep down: *Lay your hat on the table. A shower has laid the dust.* **3.** to make quiet; make disappear: *to lay a ghost. These fears ought now to be laid.* **4.** to smooth down; press: *to lay the nap on cloth.* **5. a.** to place in a lying-down position or a position of rest: *Lay the baby down gently. When, in the evening of her life, the doctors told her that she must return to Europe, she just laid herself down and died* (Observer). **b.** to bury: *He was laid in a quiet churchyard.* **6.** to place, set, or cause to be in a particular situation or condition: *to lay a trap, to lay a table for dinner. She lays great emphasis on good manners. That author lays the scenes for most of his stories in faraway places. The horse laid his ears back.* **7.** to place in proper position or in orderly fashion: *to lay bricks, to lay the keel of a new liner. The President will lay the foundation stone.* **8.** to devise; arrange: *We have laid our plans for dealing with that situation.* **9.** to put down as a bet; wager: *I lay five dollars that he will not come.* **10.** to impose (something) as a burden, obligation, penalty, etc.: *to lay a tax on tea. They laid an embargo on arms shipments.* **11.** to bring forward; place before; present: *to lay claim to an estate. I hope you have no objection to laying your case before the uncle* (Oliver Goldsmith). **12.** to bring forward as an accusation or charge; impute; attribute: *The theft was laid to him. This was laid to her overweening pride.* **13.** (of a hen) to produce (an egg or eggs): *He makes as much fuss as a hen who has laid an egg.* **14.** to bring down (a stick) on a person; deal (blows). **15.** to twist yarn or strands together to form (a strand, rope, etc.). —*v.i.* **1.** to produce eggs: *Hens begin laying about December.* **2.** to wager; bet: *I lay I'll keep drier on my own shanks* (M. E. Carter). **3.** to aim vigorous blows (at, on): *Lay on, Macduff, And damn'd be him that first cries "Hold, enough!"* (Shakespeare). **4.** to apply oneself vigorously: *The men laid to their oars.* **5.** *Substandard.* to lie: *They found him laying on his back.* **6.** *Dialect.* to plan; intend: *... he has laid to arrest me I hear* (Ben Jonson). **7.** *Nautical.* to stop and place oneself in a specified position; take up one's post: *to lay at anchor.*
lay about, a. to hit out on all sides: *They laid about them with their staves* (Benjamin Disraeli). **b.** to exert oneself greatly: *He lays about him on all hands where there is any the least project of gain* (Earl of Essex).
lay aside, away, or **by, a.** to put away for future use; save: *Lay aside that book for me.* **b.** to put away from one's person, from consideration, etc.; put to one side: *Lay by all nicety and prolixious blushes* (Shakespeare).
lay down, a. to declare; state: *The association laid down an advancement agreement signed last October which the union now wants changed* (London Times). **b.** to give; sacrifice: *To waste thy life in arms or lay it down In causeless feuds* (William Cowper). **c.** *Slang.* to quit; resign: *Leahy accused the Irish gridders of laying down and, in effect, dubbed them the "Unfighting Irish"* (Tuscaloosa News). **d.** to store away for future use: *"His first duty is to his family" and is fulfilled ... by laying down vintages* (Robert Louis Stevenson). **e.** to bet: *What shall we lay down? What shall we stake?* (Claudius Hollyband).
lay for, *Informal.* to lie in wait for: *I think a part of my mind has been vulgarly laying for this next bit* (J.D. Salinger).
lay hold of, on, or **upon, a.** to seize; grasp: *For Herod has laid hold on John, and bound him, and put him in prison ...* (Matthew 14:3). **b.** to avail oneself of: *Lady Dysert laid hold on his absence in Scotland to make a breach between them* (Gilbert Burnet).
lay in, to put aside for the future; provide; save: *The trappers laid in a good supply of food for the winter.*
lay into, a. to beat; thrash: *She would lay into Master John with her stick* (George R. Sims). **b.** *Slang.* to scold: *... laying into a politician who was preparing to do something popular which he knew in his heart was wrong* (Economist).
lay off, a. to put aside: *He laid off his winter coat.* **b.** *Slang.* to stop for a time; stop; desist: *ordering local Reds to lay off the subversion* (Newsweek). **c.** to put out of work, especially temporarily: *A hundred men were laid off yesterday because of the strike.* **d.** to mark off: *The surveyor laid off the boundaries of the lot.*
lay on, a. to apply: *Gold leaf is laid on with white of egg.* **b.** to supply: *Water and electricity are laid on in the district.* **c.** to strike; inflict: *I will lay on for Tusculum and lay thou on for Rome* (Macaulay). **d.** to utter (flattery), especially in a fulsome manner: *Well said, that was laid on with a trowel* (Shakespeare).
lay oneself or **one open,** to expose oneself or another (to): *He lays himself open to ridicule by his many boasts.*
lay oneself out, *Informal.* to make a big effort; take great pains: *He laid himself out to be agreeable.*
lay open, a. to make bare; expose: *They ... laid open to him the whole scheme ... and inquired whether they ... could lawfully engage in it* (Washington Irving). **b.** to make an opening in; wound: *With a swift stroke of his sword, he laid open his attacker.*
lay out, a. to spread out: *Refreshments were laid out in an adjoining room* (H.T. Ellis). **b.** to prepare (a dead body) for burial: *They reverently laid out the corpse* (Elizabeth Gaskell). **c.** to arrange; plan: *The roads had been laid out but were not completed* (J. Bacon). **d.** *Slang.* to spend: *He laid out all his gains in purchasing land* (Macaulay). **e.** *Slang.* to knock unconscious; put out of the fight: *Never were so many demagogues laid out in one day* (Nation).
lay over, *Slang.* to be better than; surpass; excel: *They've a street up there in "Roaring," that would lay over any street in Red Dog* (Bret Harte).
lay to, a. to put blame on; accuse of: *She laid her failure to indifference.* **b.** *Nautical.* to head into the wind and stand still: [*He*] *was obliged to lay to until daylight, as the weather was thick* (Robert M. Ballantyne).
lay up, a. to put away for future use; save: *Lay not up for yourselves treasures upon earth* (Matthew 6:19). **b.** to cause to stay in bed or indoors because of illness or injury: *The skier is laid up with a broken leg.* **c.** to put (a ship) out of service for repairs, cleaning, etc.: *The Peloponnesians ... laid up their fleet for the rest of the winter* (Connop Thirlwall). **d.** to put (a ship) out of service by decommissioning: *The Navy laid up many of its outdated battleships after World War II.* **e.** to make (a rope, cable, etc.) by weaving or braiding the separate strands together: *When you have laid it up to within ten inches of the end, lay both strands up together* (H. Stuart).
—*n.* **1.** the way or position in which anything is laid or lies: *The lay of the ground hindered my view of the sea* (Alexander Kinglake). **2.** the amount and direction of the twist given to the strands or other components of a rope. **3.** a share of the profits or of the catch of a whaling or fishing vessel:

All hands, including the captain, received certain shares of the profits called lays (Herman Melville). **4.** *U.S. Dialect.* terms of purchase. **5.** *Slang.* a line of business; field of operations; occupation; job: *He's not to be found on his old lay* (Dickens).
[Middle English *leyen*, Old English *lecgan*, related to *licgan* lie]
—**Syn.** *v.t.* **1.** level. **2.** suppress, quash, quell. **3.** allay. **5. a.** deposit. **8.** design. **12.** ascribe. *-n.* **1.** arrangement.

➔ **lay, lie.** In the English of the uneducated and sometimes in the spoken or written English of the educated the work of these two verbs is generally done by one (*lay, lay* or *laid, laid*): *there let him lay* (Byron). In modern standard writing and most educated speech, they are kept distinct: *lie* (to recline, intransitive), *lay, lain; lay* (to place, transitive), *laid, laid.* You *lie* down for a rest or *lie* down on the job. A farm *lies* in a valley. You *lay* a floor, *lay* a book on the table, *lay* a bet, *lay* out clothes.

lay[2] (lā), *v.* the past tense of **lie**[2]: *After a long walk I lay down for a rest.*

lay[3] (lā), *adj.* **1.** of ordinary people; not of the clergy: *A lay sermon is one preached by a person who is not a clergyman.* **2.** of ordinary people; not of lawyers, doctors, or those learned in the profession in question: *a lay magistrate. The lay mind understands little of the causes of diseases.* [< Old French *lai* < Latin *lāicus.* Doublet of LAIC.] —**Syn. 1.** laic, secular.

lay[4] (lā), *n.* **1.** a short lyric or narrative poem, especially one intended to be sung; poem: *The only way to please a minstrel was to listen . . . to the lays which he liked best to sing* (Scott). **2.** a song; tune. **3.** *Poetic.* the song of a bird: *The blackbird whistles his lay.* [< Old French *lai*, perhaps < Celtic (compare Irish *laid* poem, chant)]

lay·a·bout (lā′ə bout′), *n. British.* a habitually idle person; loafer: *I seem to be giving the impression that all teenagers are work-hating layabouts, but that wouldn't be right* (Punch).

lay·a·way (lā′ə wā′), *n.* **1.** a vat for tanning hides. **2.** the liquid in such vats. —*adj.* of or having to do with a layaway plan.

layaway plan, a method of purchase in which the consumer makes a number of part payments in advance of delivery, and the seller lays away or stores the article until full payment is made.

lay·back (lā′bak′), *n.* **1.** the backward slant of the body in rowing: *Hiram Conibear . . . developer of the upright stroke with short layback that became the trademark of West Coast crews* (Time). **2.** the characteristic backward slant of a bulldog's nose.

lay brother, a man who has taken the vows and habit of a religious order, but is employed chiefly in manual labor and is exempt from the studies and special religious services of the other members.

lay-by (lā′bī′), *n. British.* **1.** an area off the main highway, where vehicles may stop for repairs without interfering with traffic: *"Lay-by 100 yards ahead," says a sign; this means you will find a safety island into which you can turn for emergency repairs* (Holiday). **2.** a similar stopping place for barges on a river or canal.

lay day, *Commerce.* **1.** any one of the total of days specified by a charter party or contract as allowed for loading or unloading a vessel without extra charge. **2.** each day allowed a ship to stay in port.

lay·er (lā′ər), *n.* **1. a.** a person or thing that lays: *a bricklayer.* **b.** (of a hen) a producer of eggs. **2.** one thickness or fold: *the layer of clothing next to the skin, a layer of clay between two layers of sand. A cake is often made of two or more layers put together.* **3.** *Horticulture.* **a.** a branch of a plant bent down and partly covered with earth so that it will take root while still attached to the parent stock and form a new plant. **b.** a plant propagated by layering.
—*v.i.* to spread by layers. —*v.t.* to form (new plants) by layers: *to layer strawberry runners, to layer carnations.*

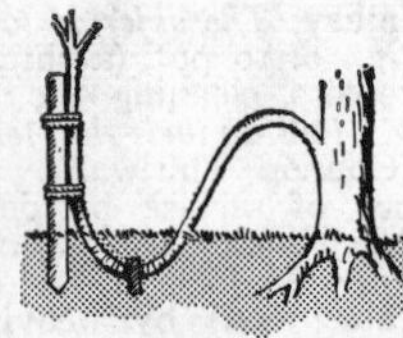
Layer (def. 3a)

lay·er·age (lā′ər ij), *n. Horticulture.* a method of forming new plants by placing a shoot or twig of a plant in the ground so that it will take root while still attached to the parent stock; layering.

layer cake, a cake made in layers put together with filling and often covered with frosting.

lay·ered (lā′ərd), *adj.* arranged in or having layers: *layered rocks.*

lay·er·ing (lā′ər ing), *n.* layerage.

lay·ette (lā et′), *n.* a set of clothes, bedding, etc., for a newborn baby. [< French *layette* < Middle French, a chest of drawers < *laie* chest]

lay figure, 1. a jointed model of the human body. Lay figures are used by artists and in shop windows. **2.** an unimportant person; puppet. **3.** a character in fiction destitute of the attributes of reality. [for earlier *layman* < Dutch *leeman* < *lede* limb + *man* man]

lay·ing on of hands (lā′ing), the act of placing a hand on a person's head or shoulder in order to bless or transmit grace to him, as practiced by the clergy of some Christian churches. It is traditionally performed in administering baptism, confirmation, ordination, or extreme unction.

lay·man (lā′mən), *n., pl.* **-men.** a person outside any particular profession, especially one not belonging to the clergy: *It is hard for a layman to understand technical articles in medical journals.* [< *lay*[3] + *man*]

lay·man·ship (lā′mən ship), *n.* the condition of being a layman: *His laymanship grated on their clericalism* (Athenaeum).

lay·off (lā′ôf′, -of′), *n.* **1.** a dismissing of workmen temporarily: *The majority of those affected will be seasoned employes whose layoff dates will be advanced from one to two months as compared with last year* (Wall Street Journal). **2.** a time during which workmen are out of work. **3.** a period of little or no activity in business, etc.; off-season for professional athletes.

lay of the land, 1. the way in which the land lies. **2.** the condition of things; state of affairs: *Spies were sent to find out the lay of the land.*

lay·out (lā′out′), *n.* **1.** the act of laying out. **2.** an arrangement; plan: *This map shows the layout of the camp.* **3.** a plan or design for an advertisement, book, etc.: *Typography and layout are beautiful* (Harper's). **4.** something laid or spread out; display. **5.** an outfit; supply; set.

lay·o·ver (lā′ō′vər), *n.U.S.* a stopping for a time in a place, especially as an interruption of a trip: *After a twenty-minute layover in Moscow, my wife and I flew on together to Leningrad* (New Yorker).

lay reader, 1. (in the Church of England) a layman appointed by the bishop to read from the Book of Common Prayer and otherwise assist at services. **2.** an assistant to a schoolteacher, who reads compositions and helps in marking papers.

lay sister, a woman who occupies a position in a female religious order corresponding to that of a lay brother.

lay-up (lā′up′), *n.* **1.** *Nautical.* **a.** the laying up or storage of a ship for repair, cleaning, etc., especially of small boats during the winter. **b.** the laying up of a ship while it is out of service: *Some newly-built vessels have gone into immediate lay-up as a result of the depressed shipping market* (Wall Street Journal). **2.** *Basketball.* a shot close under the basket.

lay·wom·an (lā′wům′ən), *n., pl.* **-wom·en.** a woman outside religious orders, the clergy, or a profession, especially the law or medicine.

la·zar (laz′ər, lā′zər), *n. Archaic.* **1.** a leper. **2.** a poor, sick person. [< Medieval Latin *lazarus* a leper < Late Latin *Lazarus*, the beggar in Luke 16:20]

laz·a·ret or **laz·a·rette** (laz′ə ret′), *n.* lazaretto.

laz·a·ret·to (laz′ə ret′ō), *n., pl.* **-tos. 1.** a hospital for people having contagious or loathsome diseases; pesthouse. **2.** a building or ship used for quarantine purposes. **3.** a place in some merchant ships near the stern in which supplies are kept. [< Italian *lazzaretto*, blend of *lazzaro* lazar, and the name of a hospital (*Santa Maria di*) *Nazaret* (St. Mary of) Nazareth]

lazar house, leper house.

Laz·a·rus (laz′ər əs), *n.* **1.** in the Bible: **a.** the brother of Mary and Martha, whom Jesus raised from the dead. John 11:1-44. **b.** a beggar in the parable who suffered on earth but went to heaven. Luke 16:19-25. **2.** any diseased beggar, especially a leper.

laze (lāz), *v.,* **lazed, laz·ing.** —*v.i.* to be lazy or idle. —*v.t.* to pass (time) lazily (away): *to laze away the summer.* [back formation < *lazy*]

la·zi·ly (lā′zə lē), *adv.* in a lazy manner.

la·zi·ness (lā′zē nis), *n.* a dislike of work; unwillingness to work or be active; being lazy.
—**Syn.** indolence, sloth, sluggishness.

laz·u·li (laz′yə lī, -lē), *n.* lapis lazuli.

lazuli bunting, a finch of western North America, the male of which has a greenish-blue head and back, chestnut chest, and blackish wings.

laz·u·lite (laz′yə līt), *n.* a mineral, hydrous phosphate of aluminum, magnesium, and iron, often found in blue crystals. *Formula:* $(FeMg)Al_2P_2O_8(OH)_2$ [< Medieval Latin *lazulum* lapis lazuli + English *-ite*[1]]

laz·u·rite (laz′yə rīt), *n.* lapis lazuli, a mineral. [< Medieval Latin *lazur* azure + English *-ite*[1]]

la·zy (lā′zē), *adj.,* **-zi·er, -zi·est,** *v.,* **-zied, -zy·ing.** —*adj.* **1.** not willing to work or be active: *All . . . combine to drive The lazy drones from the laborious hive* (John Dryden). **2.** characterized by, suggestive of, or conducive to idleness: *a lazy mood, a lazy yawn, a lazy summer day.* **3.** moving slowly; not very active: *a lazy wind, a lazy stream.* **4.** of or having to do with a brand of livestock that lies on its side instead of upright: *the lazy J brand* (⌙).
—*v.t., v.i.* to laze: *So we would put in the day, lazying around, listening to the stillness* (Mark Twain).
[origin uncertain. Compare Middle Low German *lasich* weak, feeble, tired.]
—**Syn.** *adj.* **1.** indolent, slothful. **3.** sluggish.

la·zy·bones (lā′zē bōnz′), *n. Informal.* a very lazy person.

la·zy·boots (lā′zē büts′), *n. Informal.* a lazybones.

lazy dog, *Slang.* a fragmentation bomb: *U.S. planes are dropping lazy dogs, which explode in the air and spray the ground with small, razor-sharp projectiles* (Time).

la·zy·ish (lā′zē ish), *adj.* somewhat lazy.

lazy Susan, a large revolving tray containing foods arranged in individual compartments, which is revolved in order to make the different kinds of food easily accessible for serving.

lazy tongs, 1. a device for picking things up, consisting of a series of pairs of crossing pieces, each pair pivoted like scissors and connected with the next pair at the ends. **2.** a similar arrangement of crossing pieces used for other purposes.

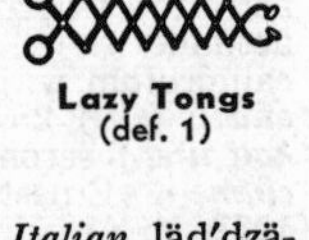
Lazy Tongs (def. 1)

laz·za·ro·ne (laz′ə rō′nā; *Italian* läd′dzä-rō′nā), *n., pl.* **-ni** (-nē; *Italian* -nē). one of a class of very poor persons in Naples, who frequent the streets and live by doing odd jobs or by begging. [< Italian *lazzarone* (augmentative) < *lazzaro* lazar]

lb., pound or pounds.

L.B., *U.S.* Bachelor of Letters (Latin, *Litterarum Baccalaureus*).

lb. ap., pound (apothecary's).

L-bar (el′bär′), *n.* a metal bar or beam shaped like an L.

lb. av., pound (avoirdupois).

L-beam (el′bēm′), *n.* an L-bar.

LBJ, Lyndon Baines Johnson.

lbr., labor.

lbs., pounds.

lb. t., pound (troy).

l.b.w. or **L.B.W.,** leg before wicket.

l.c., lc., or **lc** (no periods), lower case; in small letters, not capital letters.

l.c., 1. left center. **2.** letter of credit. **3.** in the place cited (Latin, *loco citato*).

LC (no periods), **1.** landing craft. **2.** letter of credit.

L.C., 1. *U.S.* Library of Congress. **2.** *British.* Lord Chamberlain. **3.** *British.* Lord Chancellor. **4.** Lower Canada.

L.C.C. or **LCC** (no periods), London County Council.

l.c.d. or **L.C.D.,** lowest common denominator; least common denominator.

LCI (no periods), landing craft infantry.

lcl., local.

L.C.L. or **l.c.l.,** less than carload lot.

L clearance, *U.S.* clearance of atomic information classified as confidential but not secret: *an L-clearance permit.*
l.c.m. or **L.C.M.,** lowest common multiple; least common multiple.
LCM (no periods), landing craft medium.
l.c.t., local civil time.
LCT (no periods), landing craft tank.
L.C.T., local civil time.
LCVP (no periods), landing craft vehicle and personnel.
ld., **1.** land. **2.** limited.
Ld., **1.** limited. **2.** lord.
LD (no periods), **1.** lactic dehydrogenase. **2.** lethal dose. **3.** Low Dutch.
L.D. or **LD.,** Low Dutch.
LDH (no periods), lactic dehydrogenase.
L. Div., Licentiate in Divinity.
Ldp., **1.** Ladyship. **2.** Lordship.
ldr., leader.
L.D.S., **1.** Latter-Day Saints. **2.** Licentiate in Dental Surgery.
-le, *suffix.* **1.** small (diminutive), as in *icicle, kettle.*
2. again and again (frequentative), as in *crackle, sparkle.*
[definition 1, Old English *-el;* definition 2, Middle English *-elen,* Old English *-lian*]
le., lease.
l.e., *Football.* left end.
LE (no periods), **1.** labor exchange. **2.** *Football.* left end.
lea[1] (lē), *n.* a grassy field; meadow; pasture: *The linnet sings wildly across the green lea* (K. T. Hinkson). [Old English *lēah*]
lea[2] (lē), *n.* a measure of yarn of varying quantity, usually equal to 80 yards for wool, 120 yards for cotton and silk, and 300 yards for linen. [perhaps back formation < *leas,* variant of *leash* in sense of "certain quantity of thread"]
lea[3] (lē), *Dialect.* —*adj.* (of land) fallow or untilled. —*n.* fallow or untilled land, usually under grass. [apparently Old English *lǣge-,* as in *lǣghrycg* lea rig]
LEA (no periods), Local Education Authority.
lea., **1.** league. **2.** leather.
leach[1] (lēch), *v.t.* **1.** to run (water or some other liquid) through slowly, as water through wood ashes; filter. **2.** to dissolve out soluble parts from (ashes, ores, etc.) by running water through slowly: *Wood ashes are leached for potash.* **3.** to dissolve out by running water through slowly: *to leach sugar from beets.* —*v.i.* **1.** to lose soluble parts when water passes through. **2.** (of soil, ashes, etc.) to be subjected to the action of percolating water.
—*n. Dialect.* a perforated container for use in leaching.
[apparently Old English *leccan* to wet] —**leach′er,** *n.*
leach[2] (lēch), *n.* leech[2].
Leach's petrel (lēch′əz), a stormy petrel of the northern Atlantic with a forked tail.
leach·y (lē′chē), *adj.,* **leach·i·er, leach·i·est.** that allows water to percolate through.
lead[1] (lēd), *v.,* **led, lead·ing,** *n., adj.* —*v.t.* **1. a.** to guide; show the way by going along with or in front of: *The Star led the three Wise Men to Bethlehem.* **b.** to serve to guide: *His cries for help led us to him.* **2.** to conduct by a hand, rope, etc.: *to lead a horse to water.* **3.** to act as the guide for: *Admiral Byrd led the expedition to his old camp at Little America in Antarctica.* **4.** to be a way or means of bringing something to a particular condition or result: *Lack of understanding and a willingness to compromise led the country to the point of civil war.* **5.** to conduct or bring (water, steam, a rope, a wire, etc.) in a particular channel or course; convey. **6.** to pass or spend (life, time, etc.) in some special way: *He leads a quiet life in the country. Do lead your own life and let ours alone* (Robert Browning). **7.** to give (passage) to; be a path for: *This broad road leads most of the traffic into the city.* **8.** to guide or direct in action, policy, opinion, etc.; influence; persuade: *Such actions lead us to distrust him.* **9.** to go or be at the head of; direct the advance of: *The elephants led the parade. The captain led his men over the unfamiliar terrain.* **10.** to go or be first; have first place; be at the top of: *She leads the class in spelling.* **11.** to be chief of; command; direct: *A general leads an army. The Archbishop is leading the movement. He leads the community orchestra. A woman led the singing.* **12.** to begin or open: *She led the dance. He will lead the program.* **13.** (in card playing) to begin with a trick or round by playing (a card or suit named): *He ought in any case to lead trumps.* **14.** to discharge a firearm at (a moving target), making allowance for the distance it will advance before the shot reaches it; aim in front of: *A flying bird may require to be led several feet.* **15.** *Boxing.* to direct (a blow) at an opponent. **16.** *Archaic.* to take or bring: *We led them away prisoners.*
—*v.i.* **1.** to act as guide; show the way: *Lead, I will follow.* **2.** to provide a way to a certain condition; be a means of proceeding to or effecting a certain result: *Hard work leads to success. The frequent outbreaks led to civil war.* **3.** to form a channel or route: *The drain led into a common sewer. All roads lead to Rome.* **4.** to afford passage or way: *Broad steps lead down into the garden.* **5.** to be led; submit to being led: *This horse leads easily.* **6.** to be chief; direct; act as leader: *And when we think we lead, we are most led* (Byron). **7.** to go first; have the first place: *In arithmetic he is way down in the class, but in spelling he leads.* **8.** to take the leading part; start a dance, begin or open a discussion, etc. **9.** to make the first play at cards. **10.** *Boxing.* to deal one's opponent a blow; take the offensive.
lead off, to begin; start: *He led off with his companion in a sort of quickstep* (Harper's).
lead up to, to prepare the way for: *The harlequinade . . . is led up to by a tasteful transformation scene* (Saturday Review).
—*n.* **1.** guidance; direction; example; precedence: *Many countries in the western world followed the lead of the United States after World War II. Recent work . . . using radio-isotope techniques . . . is giving a new lead on the selective action of weedkillers* (New Scientist). **2.** the first or foremost place; place of a leader; position in advance: *He always takes the lead when we plan to do anything.* **3.** the extent of advance; amount that one is ahead: *He had a lead of 3 yards in the race.* **4.** something that leads; a path, channel, watercourse, etc. **5.** in theatrical use: **a.** the principal part in a play. **b.** the person who plays it. **6.** a string, strap, etc., for leading a dog or other animal; leash: *He had his dog on a lead.* **7.** a guiding indication: *He was not sure where to look for the information, but the librarian gave him several good leads.* **8.** in card playing: **a.** the right of playing first: *It is your lead this time.* **b.** the card or suit so played: *You should usually return your partner's lead.* **9. a.** the opening paragraph in a newspaper or magazine article, usually summarizing the information in the body of the article: *Once the lead is outlined, the rest of a news story can be quickly written.* **b.** the main front-page story in a newspaper. **10. a.** an insulated conductor conveying electricity. **b.** a lead-in. **11.** *Boxing.* a taking of the offensive; a blow directed at an opponent. **12.** *Mining.* **a.** a lode: *the silver leads of the large mines.* **b.** a deposit of gold-bearing gravel along the course of an old river. **13.** an open channel through an ice field: *The explorers found a lead which would get them to open water.* **14.** *Nautical.* the proper course for a rope, especially in a ship's running rigging: *The lead of each rope was fixed in Harvey's mind* (Rudyard Kipling). **15. a.** the aiming of a firearm, etc., in advance of a moving target. **b.** the distance allowed in so aiming.
—*adj.* **1.** that leads or is used for leading; leading: *the lead violin, a horse on a lead rein.* **2.** guided by a lead: *a lead horse.*
[Old English *lǣdan*]
—**Syn.** *v.t.* **1. a, b.** conduct. See **guide. 8.** induce, entice. **11.** head, manage, control.
➤ **lead, led.** *Lead* and *led* show the confusion that English suffers because of representing one sound by different symbols. *Lead* (lēd), the present tense of the verb, gives no trouble; but *led,* the past tense, is often incorrectly spelled with *ea* by analogy with *read* (rēd), *read* (red), or by confusion with the noun *lead* (led): *Please lead the horse away. The culprit was led into the office.*
lead[2] (led), *n.* **1.** a heavy, easily melted, metallic chemical element of a dull, pale bluish-gray color. It is used to make pipes and machinery, as a solder, in alloys, etc. *Symbol:* Pb; *at. wt.:* (C^{12}) 207.19 or (O^{16}) 207.21; *at. no.:* 82; *valence:* 2,4. **2.** something made of lead or one of its alloys. **3.** a weight, usually 7 to 14 pounds, on a marked line used to find out the depth of water; plummet. **4.** bullets; shot: *a hail of lead.* **5.** a long, thin piece of graphite as used in pencils. **6. a.** a thin metal strip, less than type-high, for widening the space between lines in printing. **b.** these strips collectively. **7. a.** graphite; black lead. **b.** white lead.
leads, a. strips of lead used to cover roofs; leading: *The tempest crackles on the leads* (Tennyson). **b.** a lead roof: *A cat . . . whom she used to meet in the evenings, upon the leads of the house* (C. Johnston). **c.** frames of lead in which panes of glass are set, as in stained-glass windows; leading: *It gives the effect of weakness to see large pieces of glass leaded with narrow leads* (F. Miller).
—*adj.* made of lead; consisting of lead.
—*v.t.* **1.** to insert leads between the lines of (print). **2.** to cover, frame, or weight with lead. **3.** to mix or impregnate with lead or a compound containing lead: *to lead gasoline.* **4.** to line or glaze (pottery) with glaze containing lead.
[Old English *lēad*] —**lead′less,** *adj.*
lead·a·ble (lē′də bəl), *adj.* that may be led; apt to be led: *It is no easy task to lead the Labour Party. They are not a very leadable lot* (Punch).
lead acetate (led), a colorless or white, poisonous, crystalline compound used as a reagent, in dyeing, etc.; sugar of lead. *Formula:* $C_4H_{12}O_7Pb$
lead arsenate (led), a poisonous white, crystalline substance used as an insecticide. *Formula:* $Pb_3(AsO_4)_2$
lead-col·ored (led′kul′ərd), *adj.* having the color of lead; of a dull grayish color: *lead-colored clouds.*
lead·ed (led′id), *adj.* (of printed matter) having extra space between the lines, due to the insertion of leads between the lines of type.
lead·en (led′ən), *adj.* **1.** made of lead: *a leaden coffin.* **2.** heavy; hard to lift or move: *leaden arms tired from working.* **3.** oppressive; burdensome: *leaden air.* **4.** dull; gloomy. **5.** of a dull, cold, pale color; dull or bluish-gray: *. . . a dull morning, with leaden skies and a steady downpour of rain* (New Yorker). **6.** of little value.
—*v.t.* to make leaden: *The death of President John Fitzgerald Kennedy leadens the heart with sadness* (Atlanta Constitution).
—**lead′en·ly,** *adv.* —**lead′en·ness,** *n.*
—**Syn.** *adj.* **2.** inert.
lead·en-foot·ed (led′ən fu̇t′id), *adj.* moving or passing slowly, as if with leaden feet: *leaden-footed hours* (Edgar Allan Poe). *The . . . forwards were almost sterile of ideas and their defence was leaden-footed and slow* (London Times).
lead·er (lē′dər), *n.* **1.** a person, animal, or thing that leads: *an orchestra leader, the leader of a discussion. Brigham Young was the leader of the Mormons. Albert Einstein was a leader in the field of mathematics. Lewis and Clark were leaders of an expedition across America to the Pacific Coast.* **2.** a person who is well fitted to lead: *That boy is a born leader.* **3.** a horse harnessed at the front of a team: *The whips cracked, the leaders capered, and . . . away we rattled* (Charles J. Lever). **4.** an important or leading article or editorial in a newspaper: *Give me a man who can write a leader* (Benjamin Disraeli). *In 1944, he wrote a blistering leader demanding that the British Government cease toadying to Washington* (Newsweek). **5.** in angling: **a.** a short length of nylon or plastic cord or wire attaching the lure to a fish line. **b.** a net placed so as to cause fish to swim into a weir, pound, etc. **6.** a pipe carrying water, oil, etc., especially water from a roof gutter to the ground. **7.** an article offered at a low price to attract customers: *a loss leader.* **8.** the concertmaster of an orchestra or vocal group. **9.** *Nautical.* a fair-lead.
leaders, a row of dots or dashes to guide the eye across a printed page: *There are also two or three em leaders, the number of dots being multiplied according to their length* (American Encyclopedia of Printing).
lead·er·ette (lē′də ret′), *n. British.* a short leader or editorial paragraph, as in a newspaper. [< *leader* + *-ette*]
lead·er-gear (lē′dər gir′), *n.* a device for guiding ships over a fixed course, consisting essentially of an insulated cable laid on the bottom of the sea, through which an alternating electric current passes. The navigator is able to tell the position of the cable and to follow it by means of delicate instruments installed on the ship. This de-

vice was used especially for guidance through minefields during World War I. Also, **leading-gear.**

lead·er·less (lē′dər lis), *adj.* without a leader; without direction: *A leaderless mob soon disintegrates.*

lead·er·ly (lē′dər lē), *adj.* having the character of a leader.

lead·ers (lē′dərz), *n.pl.* See under **leader,** *n.*

lead·er·ship (lē′dər ship), *n.* **1.** the position, function, or guidance of a leader. **2.** the ability to lead. —**Syn. 1.** direction.

lead·er-writ·er (lē′dər rī′tər), *n. British.* a person who writes newspaper leaders or editorials; editorialist.

lead glass (led), a type of glass, especially crystal, made with lead.

lead-in (lēd′in′), *n.* **1.** the wire leading from one apparatus or conductor to another, as the wire connecting the street power lines with a house. See picture under **incandescent lamp** or **bulb. 2.** the part of a radio antenna that connects with the transmitter or receiver. **3.** a leading into; introduction: *She delivered a lead-in to a filmed commercial* (Newsweek).
—*adj.* (of an electrical conductor) leading in: *a lead-in wire.*

lead·ing[1] (lē′ding), *n.* **1.** the act of a person or thing that leads; guidance; direction. **2.** (in Quaker use) a spiritual indication of the proper course of action: *a leading from above, a something given* (Wordsworth). [< *lead*[1] + *-ing*[1]]
—*adj.* **1.** guiding; directing: *He developed a series of demolition raids on the Hejaz railway . . . and took the leading hand himself in many of them* (London Times). **2.** most important; chief; principal: *the leading lady in a play, the town's leading citizen.* **3.** that has the front place; that goes first: *the leading end of a pipe.*
[< *lead*[1] + *-ing*[2]]
—**Syn.** *adj.* **2.** main, foremost.

lead·ing[2] (led′ing), *n.* **1.** a covering or frame of lead strips, especially for window glass or roofing. **2.** *Printing.* **a.** the metal strips for widening the space between lines of type. **b.** the space provided by these strips.

lead·ing article (lē′ding), an important editorial or article in a newspaper; leader.

lead·ing edge (lē′ding), *Aeronautics.* the forward edge of an airfoil or propeller blade. See picture under **aileron.**

lead·ing-gear (lē′ding gir′), *n.* leader-gear.

lead·ing mark (lē′ding), any object used as a guide in bringing a ship in or out of port.

lead·ing motive (lē′ding), leitmotif.

lead·ing question (lē′ding), a question so worded that it suggests the answer desired.

lead·ing strings (lē′ding), **1.** strings for supporting a child when learning to walk. **2.** close guidance; too close guidance: *A boy of eighteen should not be kept in leading strings by his mother.*

lead·ing tone (lē′ding), *Music.* the seventh tone of the scale, one half step below the tonic, having a melodic tendency up toward the tonic or keynote; subtonic.

lead-in wire (lēd′in′), *Radio.* a lead-in.

lead line (led), *Nautical.* a sounding line.

lead monoxide (led), litharge.

lead nitrate (led), a poisonous metal salt used in medicine, as a fixative in dyeing textiles, and in the manufacture of lead salts, matches, etc. *Formula:* $Pb(NO_3)_2$

lead·off (lēd′ôf′, -of′), *n.* **1.** an act of beginning or starting something: *The chairman was responsible for the leadoff of the campaign.* **2.** *Baseball.* the first player to come to bat in any inning or half inning. —*adj.* that begins or leads off: *a leadoff witness, a leadoff batter.*

lead oxide (led), any compound of lead and oxygen, such as litharge.

lead pencil (led), pencil having a graphite lead mixed with pipe clay, usually enclosed in wood; ordinary pencil.

lead-pipe cinch (led′pīp′), *U.S. Informal.* **1.** an absolutely certain thing: *"It's still not a lead-pipe cinch that he'll run," confesses one G.O.P. leader* (Wall Street Journal). **2.** an easy thing to do: *Sounds like a headache, but —thanks to xerography—it's turned into a lead-pipe cinch* (Wall Street Journal).

lead·plant (led′plant′, -plänt′), *n.* a shrubby North American plant of the pea family with spikes of blue flowers, supposed to indicate the presence of deposits of lead beneath it.

lead poisoning (led), **1.** a condition characterized by abdominal pain, paralysis, and convulsions, and caused by the introduction of lead into the system; plumbism. **2.** *U.S. Slang.* death or injury from a gunshot or bullets.

leads (ledz), *n.pl.* See under **lead**[2], *n.*

leads·man (ledz′mən), *n., pl.* **-men.** the man who heaves the lead in taking soundings and calls the depths: *The . . . cries of the leadsman announced that there were no more than three feet of water under her keel* (Joseph Conrad).

lead time (lēd), the time that elapses, as the time between the start of or request for a thing and its completion or delivery: *First there comes lead time for planning and engineering* (Bulletin of Atomic Scientists). *. . . the Russians have cut the lead time that it takes a new plane to progress from the blueprint stage to production* (Drew Pearson). *The average lead time for steel-sheet deliveries last week was down to 30 days* (Time). *Lead time for training has always been a limiting factor in developing and employing new weapon systems.* (A. W. Stephens).

lead-time (lēd′tīm′), *adj.* of or requiring lead time: *lead-time financing, long lead-time weapons.*

lead·wort (led′wėrt′), *n.* any of a group of herbs of warm regions, usually with blue, white, or reddish-purple flowers; plumbago.

lead·y (led′ē), *adj.,* **lead·i·er, lead·i·est.** like lead; leaden.

leaf (lēf), *n., pl.* **leaves,** *v.* —*n.* **1. a.** one of the thin, usually flat, green parts that grow on the stem of a tree or other plant. Leaves are essential organs of most plants and use the carbon dioxide of the air or water in which they live and the light from the sun to carry on photosynthesis. Some plants are grown primarily for their leaves, as ornamental trees and shrubs, tobacco and tea plants, forage grasses, etc. **b.** all the leaves of a plant or tree: *the fall of the leaf.* **2.** a petal of a flower: *a rose leaf.* **3.** a sheet of paper. Each side of a leaf is called a page: *a leaf of a book.* **4.** a very thin sheet of metal, etc.: *gold leaf.* **5.** a flat movable piece in the top of a table: *We put two extra leaves in the table for the party.* **6.** the sliding, hinged, or movable part of a door, shutter, etc. **7.** one of the strips of a leaf spring. **8.** a layer of leaf fat.

Leaves (def. 1a)

in leaf, covered with leaves or foliage: *a sycamore tree in leaf.*

take a leaf from one's book, to follow one's example; copy one's conduct: *The Third Estate, taking a leaf from the book of the English House of Commons, then declared that it alone represented the nation* (H.G. Wells).

turn over a new leaf, to try to do or be better in the future; start all over again: *I will turn over a new leaf, and write to you* (Thomas Hughes).
—*v.i.* to put forth leaves: *Along the seashore, trees and shrubs will leaf earlier than inland* (Science News Letter). *There it stood . . . leafing out hopefully in April* (Oliver Wendell Holmes).
—*v.t.* to turn the pages of (a book, magazine, etc.).
[Old English *lēaf*] —**leaf′like′,** *adj.*

leaf·age (lē′fij), *n.* leaves; foliage: *I looked . . . through a frame of leafage, clustering round the high lattice* (Charlotte Brontë).

leaf beetle, any of a large group of small, round, brilliantly colored beetles that feed on the leaves of potatoes, etc.

leaf blister, a disease of the oak caused by a fungus and marked by the blistering and curling of its leaves.

leaf bud, a bud producing a stem with leaves only.

leaf curl, 1. a disease of fruit trees in which the leaves become curled: *Peach leaf curl must be throttled before buds swell* (New York Times). **2.** early blight. **3.** leaf roll of potatoes.

leaf·cut·ter (lēf′kut′ər), *n.* **1.** any of various, largely tropical, American ants that subsist entirely on small mushrooms which they raise underground on a mulch of cut leaves; umbrella ant. **2.** any of a genus of bees that cut oval or round disks from leaves, usually of the rose, to use in preparing their nests.

leaf-cut·ting ant (lēf′kut′ing), leafcutter (def. 1).

leafed (lēft), *adj.* having a leaf or leaves; leaved.

leaf·en (lē′fən), *adj.* consisting or made of leaves.

leaf·er·y (lē′fər ē, lēf′rē), *n., pl.* **-er·ies.** leafage: *. . . the matured and almost arid leafery of summer* (John Wilson).

leaf fat, fat in an animal, especially fat surrounding the kidneys of a hog.

leaf hopper, or **leaf·hop·per** (lēf′hop′ər), *n.* any of various small leaping homopteran insects which feed on plant juices.

leaf·i·ness (lē′fē nis), *n.* leafy condition.

leaf insect, any of various insects native to the East Indies, Australia, etc., remarkable for their resemblance in color and form to the green leaves on which they feed.

leaf lard, lard of the best quality, made from the fat around the kidneys of a hog.

leaf·less (lēf′lis), *adj.* having no leaves. —**leaf′less·ness,** *n.*

leaf·let (lēf′lit), *n.* **1.** a small or young leaf. **2.** *Botany.* one of the separate blades or divisions of a compound leaf. **3.** a small, flat or folded sheet of printed matter, or several sheets folded together; circular: *advertising leaflets.*
—**Syn. 3.** flier, handbill.

leaf miner, any of various insects which, in the larval stage, live and feed between the top and bottom surfaces of a leaf.

leaf mold, 1. the partially decomposed leaves which form a surface layer in wooded areas. **2.** a mold which attacks foliage.

leaf mosaic, an arrangement of the leaves on a tree, bush, or vine in which petiole length and position enable each leaf to receive the maximum amount of sunlight.

leaf-nosed bat (lēf′nōzd′), any of a group of tropical bats with a leaflike projection of skin extending upward from the nose.

leaf roll, a stunting disease of potatoes in which the margins of the leaves roll upwards, caused by a virus.

leaf roller, any of various small moths whose larvae roll up leaves to make nests, as a brown and gold moth that is a common apple pest in northern United States.

leaf spot, 1. any of various plant diseases caused by fungi or bacteria which create discolorations on leaves. **2.** the blemish on leaf surfaces caused by leaf spot.

leaf spring, a spring, as for an automobile, made of layers of curved metal strips.

leaf·stalk (lēf′stôk′), *n.* a stalk by which a leaf is attached to a stem; petiole.

leaf·y (lē′fē), *adj.,* **leaf·i·er, leaf·i·est. 1.** having many leaves; covered with leaves, especially broad leaves: *the leafy woods* (Longfellow). **2.** made or consisting of leaves. **3.** resembling a leaf; laminate.

league[1] (lēg), *n., v.,* **leagued, lea·guing.** —*n.* **1.** an association of persons, parties, or countries formed to help one another. **2.** the persons, parties, or countries associated in a league; confederacy. **3.** an association of sports clubs or teams, as in baseball. **4.** any covenant or compact; alliance: *link'd in happy nuptial league* (Milton).

in league with, having a compact with; allied with: *Look you, villains, this fellow is in league with you* (Charles Kingsley).

in one's league, *Informal.* in the same category or class with one: *[The] quartet is competent, but hardly in his league* (Time).

out of one's league, *Informal.* in a more advanced class or category than one's own: *Moon shots and ICBMs are . . . clearly out of Canada's scientific and industrial league* (Maclean's).
—*v.i., v.t.* to associate in a league; form a league.
[< Old French *ligue* < Italian *liga,* variant of *lega* < *legare* to bind < Latin *ligāre*]
—**Syn.** *n.* **1.** union, federation, society. *-v.i., v.t.* unite, confederate.

league[2] (lēg), *n.* **1.** a unit of linear measure, usually about 3 miles. **2.** a unit of square measure for land. [< Late Latin *leuga,* later *leuca* < a Celtic word]

League (lēg), *n.* the League of Nations.

League of Nations, an association of many countries (originally forty-one), formed in 1920, under the terms of the Treaty of Versailles at the end of World War I, to promote peace and cooperation between nations. It was dissolved on April 18, 1946, and the United Nations assumed some of its functions.

League of Women Voters, a nonpartisan women's political organization founded in 1920.

lea·guer[1] (lē′gər), *Archaic.* —*v.t.* to besiege; beleaguer: *Two mighty hosts a leaguer'd town embrace* (Alexander Pope). [< noun] —*n.* **1.** a military siege. **2.** the camp of a besieging army. [< Dutch *leger* camp; spelling perhaps influenced by *league*[1]]

lea·guer[2] (lē′gər), *n.* a member of a league.

lea·guer[3] (lē′gər), *n.* (in South Africa) a large cask of wine: *The production, approximately 500 leaguers of excellent wines year by year from the farm's own vineyard . . . has been well maintained* (Cape Times). [apparently < Dutch *ligger* cask]

Le·ah (lē′ə), *n.* (in the Bible) Jacob's first wife, Rachel's older sister, and a daughter of Laban. She was the mother of Reuben, Simeon, Levi, Judah, Issachar, and Zebulun. Genesis 29:16.

leak (lēk), *n.* **1.** a hole or crack not meant to be there that lets something in or out: *a leak in the roof, a leak in a paper bag that lets the sugar run out.* **2.** the act of leaking; leakage: *a leak of water, a leak of information.* **3.** a means of escape, loss, etc.: *a leak in the treasury.* **4.** the escape itself. **5.** *Electricity.* **a.** an escape of current from a conductor, especially as a result of poor insulation. **b.** the point where such escape occurs.

spring a leak, to crack or separate and begin to let water through or in; develop a leak: *One of our pipes sprung a leak and flooded the cellar.*

—*v.i.* **1. a.** to go in or out through a hole or crack not meant to be there: *The gas leaked out of the pipe.* **b.** to go in or out through ways suggesting a hole or crack: *Spies leaked into the city.* **2.** to let something in which is meant to stay where it is: *My boat leaks and lets water in.* **3.** to become known gradually: *The secret leaked out.* **4.** to pass (away) by gradual waste: *The natural resources of our country are leaking away through misuse.*

—*v.t.* **1.** to let (something) pass in or out: *That pipe leaks gas.* **2.** *Informal.* to make known: *Tempers flared after he leaked a staff memorandum on improper activities* (Atlantic).

[probably < Middle Dutch *leken*] —**leak′er,** *n.*

—**Syn.** *n.* **1.** fissure, breach.

leak·age (lē′kij), *n.* **1.** the act of leaking; a going in or out through a leak. **2.** something that leaks in or out: *the privilege of battening on . . . the leakage of the tap-room* (Washington Irving). **3.** the amount of leaking. **4.** *Commerce.* an allowance for waste of fluid by leakage. **5.** *Electricity.* a leak. **6.** *Informal.* a disclosure: *Sometimes leakages of secret information come out in newspaper stories accidentally.*

leakage current, *Electricity.* a current, usually weak, which escapes through or along the surface of an insulator in normal use or when the insulator is defective.

leak·i·ness (lē′kē nis), *n.* leaky condition: *Leakiness in the roof caused a damp attic.*

leak·proof (lēk′prüf′), *adj.* that will not leak; free of leaks: *a leakproof flashlight battery, a leakproof hull.*

leak·y (lē′kē), *adj.*, **leak·i·er, leak·i·est. 1.** having a leak or leaks; full of leaks: *The ship was leaky and very much disabled* (Daniel Defoe). **2.** talking too much; blabbing. **3.** forgetful.

leal (lēl), *adj. Archaic or Scottish.* loyal; faithful; honest; true: *Yea, by the honour of the Table Round, I will be leal to thee and work thy work* (Tennyson). [< Old French *leial* < Latin *lēgālis* legal < *lēx, lēgis* law. Doublet of LEGAL, LOYAL.] —**leal′ly,** *adv.*

le·al·ty (lē′əl tē), *n., pl.* **-ties.** *Archaic.* loyalty.

lean[1] (lēn), *v.*, **leaned** or (*especially British*) **leant** (lent), **lean·ing,** *n.* —*v.i.* **1.** to bend or incline in a particular direction; stand slanting, not upright: *A small tree leans over in the wind.* **2.** to rest the body against something for support: *Lean against me.* **3.** to depend; rely: *to lean on a friend's advice.* **4.** to incline or tend in thought, affection, or conduct; bend or turn a little (toward): *to lean toward mercy or a belief. E'en his failings lean'd to virtue's side* (Oliver Goldsmith). **5.** *Obsolete.* to incline (to) for support. —*v.t.* **1.** to set or put in a leaning position; prop: *Lean the ladder against the wall until I am ready for it.* **2.** to cause to bend or incline.

lean over backward. See under **backward.**

—*n.* the act or state of leaning; inclination: *the cracked veranda with a tipsy lean* (John Greenleaf Whittier).

on the lean, inclining; sloping: *Leaden coffins piled thirty feet high, and all on the lean from their own immense weight* (Peter Cunningham).

[Old English *hleonian*]

—**Syn.** *v.i.* **1.** slant, slope.

lean[2] (lēn), *adj.* **1. a.** with little or no fat; not plump; thin: *a lean face, lean cattle. Yond Cassius has a lean and hungry look* (Shakespeare). **b.** containing little or no fat: *lean meat.* **2.** producing little; poor or meager in quantity or quality; scant; mean: *a lean harvest, a lean diet, a lean year for business.* **3.** (of fuels) low in concentration or ability to produce energy: *Rich gas is cheaper to produce than lean gas—gas of low calorific value* (New Scientist).

—*n.* meat having little fat: *Jack Sprat could eat no fat; his wife could eat no lean* (nursery rhyme).

[Old English *hlǣne*] —**lean′ly,** *adv.* —**lean′ness,** *n.*

—**Syn.** *adj.* **1.a.** spare, skinny, gaunt. See **thin. 2.** meager, barren. —**Ant.** *adj.* **1.a.** fat. **2.** bountiful, plentiful.

Le·an·der (lē an′dər), *n. Greek Legend.* a lover who swam the Hellespont nightly to visit his sweetheart, Hero, until he was drowned.

lean·er (lē′nər), *n.* **1.** a person or thing that leans: *There is more fishing lore here (not to mention lyricism) than half the leaners along Bridlington Pier ever dreamed of* (Manchester Guardian Weekly). **2.** a pitched horseshoe or quoit that comes to rest with one side leaning against the stake or peg: *A leaner . . . gets a point only if no other shoe touches the stake* (Walter H. Gregg).

lean·ing (lē′ning), *n.* **1.** inclination; tendency: *political leanings. His leaning was more toward books than baseball.* **2.** the act of a person or thing that leans; reclining; bending. —**Syn. 1.** proneness, bias, bent, penchant.

leant (lent), *v. Especially British.* leaned; a past tense and a past participle of **lean**[1].

lean-to (lēn′tü′), *n., pl.* **-tos,** *adj.* —*n.* **1.** a small building attached to another, toward which its supports or roof slants. **2.** a crude shelter built against a tree or post. It is usually open on one side. *When the rain started, the Boy Scouts hastily put up a lean-to with ponchos.*

Lean-to (def. 1)

—*adj.* having supports pitched against or leaning on an adjoining wall or building: *a lean-to roof.*

leap (lēp), *n., v.*, **leaped** or **leapt** (lept, lēpt), **leap·ing.** —*n.* **1.** a jump or spring; bound: *He went over the fence with a single leap.* **2.** something to be jumped over or from: *Lover's Leap.* **3.** the distance covered by a jump.

a leap in the dark, a thing done without knowing what its results will be; hazardous undertaking; blind venture: *No doubt . . . a great experiment, and "taking a leap in the dark"* (Earl Derby).

by leaps and bounds, very fast and very much; swiftly: *The insurrection spread by leaps and bounds. Anhydrous ammonia and ammonium nitrate mixtures have increased by leaps and bounds as a supplementary application to most crops* (E.F. Degering).

[Old English *hlӯp*]

—*v.i.* **1.** to jump; spring: *That frog leaps very high. He leaped up the stone steps by two at a time* (George Eliot). **2.** to fly, shoot, or flash quickly: *The sword leaps from the scabbard. Water, flame, or light leaps up.* **3.** to beat vigorously, as the heart: *My heart leaps up when I behold A rainbow in the sky* (Wordsworth). **4.** to pass, come, rise, etc., as if with a leap or bound: *A suspicion leaped to his brain* (Bret Harte). —*v.t.* **1.** to jump over: *He leaped the wall. The mind leaps an interval of time.* **2.** to cause to leap: *They leaped their horses—over a trench where they could, into it . . . when they could not* (Thomas De Quincey).

[Old English *hlēapan* jump] —**leap′er,** *n.*

—**Syn.** *v.i.* **1.** See **jump.** *-v.t.* **1.** vault.

leap·a·ble (lē′pə bəl), *adj.* that can be leaped: *Some parts of the precipitous sides approach within leapable distance* (A.S. Alexander).

leap·frog (lēp′frog′, -frôg′), *n., v.*, **-frogged, -frog·ging.** —*n.* **1.** a game in which one player jumps over another who is bending over. **2.** *Military.* a method of advancing against an enemy in which the most forward unit provides protective fire while the rear unit moves past it.

—*v.i., v.t.* **1.** to leap or jump as in the game of leapfrog. **2.** (of military units in an attack) to go in advance of each other by turns as boys do when playing leapfrog. **3.** to skip over; side-step; avoid: *The kind of New England summer we elders are accustomed to will leapfrog northern Vermont and New Hampshire* (Harper's).

leapt (lept, lēpt), *v.* leaped; a past tense and a past participle of **leap.**

leap year, 1. a year having 366 days, the extra day being February 29. A year is a leap year if its number can be divided exactly by four, except years at the end of a century, which must be exactly divisible by 400: *The years 1960 and 2000 are leap years; 1900 and 1959 are not.* **2.** a year in any calendar in which there are added days or months.

lear[1] (lir), *n. Scottish.* instruction; learning. [< obsolete *lere* to teach, Old English *lǣran*]

lear[2] (lir), *adj.* leer; empty. [variant of *leer*[2]]

lea rig (lē, lā), *Dialect.* a ridge left in a grass at the end of a plowed field. [Old English *lǣghrycg*]

learn (lėrn), *v.*, **learned** or **learnt** (lėrnt), **learn·ing.** —*v.t.* **1.** to gain knowledge of (a subject) or skill in (an art, trade, etc.) by study, instruction, or experience: *to learn French. She is learning history and geography.* **2.** to acquire (knowledge, skills, habits, etc.) by study or experience. **3.** to memorize: *to learn a poem by heart, to learn a song.* **4.** to find out; become acquainted with or informed of; come to know: *He learned the details of the train wreck. He learned that 1/4+1/4=1/2.* **5.** *Substandard.* to teach: *After supper she got out her book and learned me about Moses and the Bulrushers* (Mark Twain). —*v.i.* **1.** to acquire knowledge of a subject or matter; receive instruction: *He learns easily but some children learn slowly.* **2.** to become informed; hear: *to learn of an occurrence.* [Old English *leornian*]

➔ **learn, teach.** Substandard English often uses *learn* in the sense of *teach: He learned me to play baseball.* Educated usage keeps the distinction: *I learned to play baseball from him. He taught me to play baseball.*

learn·a·ble (lėr′nə bəl), *adj.* that can be learned.

learn·ed (lėr′nid), *adj.* having, showing, or requiring much knowledge gained by study; scholarly; erudite: *a learned professor, learned pursuits.* —**learn′ed·ly,** *adv.* —**learn′ed·ness,** *n.* —**Syn.** educated.

learned borrowing, 1. the process of borrowing a classical word into a modern Romance language directly, with slight phonetic alteration. **2.** a word borrowed in this way.

learn·er (lėr′nər), *n.* **1.** a person who is learning. **2.** a beginner. —**Syn. 1.** pupil. **2.** novice, neophyte, tyro.

learn·ing (lėr′ning), *n.* **1.** the gaining of knowledge or skill. **2.** the possession of knowledge gained by study; scholarship: *men of learning. A pride there is of rank . . . A pride of learning* (Thomas Hood). **3.** knowledge: *A little learning is a dangerous thing* (Alexander Pope). **4.** *Psychology.* the relatively permanent modification of responses as a result of experience. —**Syn. 2.** education, erudition.

learnt (lėrnt), *v.* learned; a past tense and a past participle of **learn.**

lear·y (lir′ē), *adj.*, **lear·i·er, lear·i·est.** leery[1].

leas·a·ble (lē′sə bəl), *adj.* that can be leased.

lease (lēs), *n., v.*, **leased, leas·ing.** —*n.* **1.** a contract, usually in the form of a written agreement, giving the right to use property for a certain length of time, usually by paying rent: *We are to meet the landlord on Monday to sign the lease for our new apartment.* **2.** the length of time for which such an agreement is made. **3.** the act of giving such a right. **4.** the property held by a lease. **5.** an allotted period or term, especially of life: *a short lease on life.*

a new lease on or **of life,** a chance to live longer, better, or happier: *She was going to have a new lease of life with better health* (Jane Welsh Carlyle).

[< Anglo-French *les* < *lesser;* see the verb]

—*v.t.* **1.** to give a lease on: *The Clarks live on the second floor of their house and lease the first floor.* **2.** to take a lease on: *We have*

leased an apartment for one year. —*v.i.* to be leased.
[< Anglo-French *lesser* let, let go < Latin *laxāre* loosen < *laxus* loose] —**leas'er,** *n.*
—**Syn.** *n.* **2.** tenure.

lease·back (lēs'bak'), *n.* sale and leaseback. —*adj.* of or having to do with sale and leaseback: *Pension funds . . . have concentrated on "leaseback" transactions* (Wall Street Journal).

lease·hold (lēs'hōld'), *n.* **1.** a holding by a lease. **2.** real estate held by a lease. —*adj.* held by lease.

lease·hold·er (lēs'hōl'dər), *n.* a person holding property by a lease.

lease-lend (lēs'lend'), *n., v.t.,* **-lent, -lend·ing,** *adj. Especially British.* lend-lease.

lease-pur·chase (lēs'pėr'chis), *adj.* of or having to do with the lease-purchase program: *the lease-purchase law.*

lease-purchase program, a United States Government program under which money is borrowed from private lenders to finance construction of Federal buildings. The Government takes title to the buildings when the debt is eliminated.

leash (lēsh), *n.* **1.** a strap, chain, etc., for holding a dog or other animal in check: *Dogs must be walked on a leash in the city.* **2.** (in hunting, etc.) a group of three; a brace and a half; three hounds, foxes, hares, etc. **3.** (in hawking) the thong or string which is attached to the jesses to secure the hawk.
hold or **have in leash,** to have control over; keep in bondage: *Thy low voice . . . would . . . hold passion in . . . leash* (Tennyson).
strain at the leash, to be very restless or impatient: *With mankind straining at the leash to reach the moon . . .* (Manchester Guardian Weekly).
—*v.t.* to fasten or hold in with a leash; control: *A French poodle leashed to a French-looking woman* (New Yorker).
[Middle English *leese* < Old French *laisse,* and *lesse* < Latin *laxa,* feminine of *laxus* loose]

leas·ing (lē'zing), *n. Scottish.* **1.** lying; falsehood. **2.** a lie; a falsehood: *Thou shalt destroy them that speak leasing* (Psalms 5:6). [Old English *lēasung* < *lēasian* to lie < *lēas* false]

least (lēst), *adj.* **1.** less than any other; smallest; slightest: *The least bit of dirt in a watch may make it stop. A dime is a little money; five cents is less; one cent is least.* **2.** *Archaic.* lowest in power or position; meanest: *He that is least among you all, the same shall be great* (Luke 9:48).
—*n.* the smallest thing, amount, or degree: *The least you can do is to thank him.*
at least or **at the least, a.** at the lowest estimate: *Yesterday was very hot; the temperature must have been 95 degrees at the least.* **b.** at any rate; in any case: *At least we'll die with harness on our back* (Shakespeare).
not in the least, not at all: *a thing not in the least likely.*
to say the least, at the lowest estimate; at least: *I find many of the standards the referees use, to say the least, curious* (Maclean's).
—*adv.* to the least extent, amount, or degree: *He liked that book least of all.*
[Old English *lǣst* and *lǣsest,* superlative of *lӯtel* small, little]
—**Syn.** *adj.* **1.** minimal. -*n.* minimum.

least bittern, a small wading bird of temperate America with brownish-yellow body and black back and crown. It is the smallest of the herons.

least common denominator, the least common multiple of the denominators of a group of fractions: *30 is the least common denominator of 2/3, 4/5, and 1/6.*

least common multiple, the smallest quantity that contains two or more given quantities without a remainder: *12 is the least common multiple of 3 and 4 and 6.* *Abbr.:* l.c.m.

least flycatcher, a small flycatcher of Canada and northern United States, usually seen about farms, open woods, etc.; chebec.

least sandpiper, a small brownish sandpiper of eastern North America.

least squares, *Statistics.* a method of determining the trend of a group of data when that trend can be represented on a graph by a straight line.

least tern, a small, gray and white American tern, about 9 inches long, that has yellow legs and bill in the summer; fairy bird.

least·ways (lēst'wāz'), *adv. Informal.* leastwise.

least weasel, a small, brown and white weasel of northern regions of the world that turns all white in the winter. It is the smallest living carnivorous animal, weighing from 1 to 2½ ounces.

least·wise (lēst'wīz'), *adv. Informal.* at least; at any rate: *It was a sign that his money would come to light again, or leastwise that the robber would be made to answer for it* (George Eliot).

leat (lēt), *n. British Dialect.* an artificial, open watercourse, especially one on which a mill is located. [Old English *gelæt* conduit]

leath·er (leᴛʜ'ər), *n.* **1.** a material made from the skin of animals by removing the hair and flesh, and then tanning it: *Shoes are made of leather.* **2.** an article made of leather. **3.** the loose hanging part of a dog's ear.
—*adj.* **1.** made of leather: *leather gloves.* **2.** like leather; leathery.
—*v.t.* **1.** to furnish or cover with leather; use leather on. **2.** *Informal.* to beat with a strap, etc.; thrash: *I'd like to leather 'im black and blue* (Tennyson).
[Old English *lether*]

leath·er·back (leᴛʜ'ər bak'), *n.* a large sea turtle of tropical waters, sometimes over 1,000 pounds and possibly a ton in weight, having a flexible, leathery shell studded with small bony plates.

leath·er·board (leᴛʜ'ər bôrd', -bōrd'), *n.* an imitation leather made of leather scraps, paper, etc., pressed together, used especially in shoemaking.

leath·er·cloth (leᴛʜ'ər klôth', -kloth'), *n.* cloth coated on one side with a waterproof varnish.

leath·er·coat (leᴛʜ'ər kōt'), *n.* a russet apple.

leath·er·craft (leᴛʜ'ər kraft', -kräft'), *n.* **1.** things made out of leather. **2.** the art of making things out of leather: *These imported shoes are a beautiful example of hand leathercraft.*

leath·er·ette (leᴛʜ'ə ret'), *n.* **1.** imitation leather. **2. Leatherette.** a trademark for this.

leath·er·head·ed (leᴛʜ'ər hed'id), *adj.* thick-headed; stupid.

leath·er·i·ness (leᴛʜ'ər ē nis), *n.* leathery quality.

leath·er·jack·et (leᴛʜ'ər jak'it), *n. British.* the larva of a crane fly: *Leatherjackets . . . have damaged the barley crop* (London Times).

leath·er-lunged (leᴛʜ'ər lungd'), *adj. Informal.* having powerful lungs; speaking or able to speak very loudly or at great length: *A leather-lunged instructor* [*was*] *teaching an assault bayonet course* (Time).

leath·ern (leᴛʜ'ərn), *adj.* **1.** made of leather: *a leathern belt* (Hawthorne). **2.** like leather; leathery: *the weak-eyed bat . . . flits by on leathern wing* (William Collins). [Old English *letheren* < *lether* leather]

leath·er·neck (leᴛʜ'ər nek'), *n. Slang.* a United States marine.

Leath·er·oid (leᴛʜ'ə roid), *n. Trademark.* imitation leather made of paper treated with chemicals. [< *leather* + *-oid*]

Leath·er·stock·ing or **leath·er·stock·ing** (leᴛʜ'ər stok'ing), *n.* a North American frontiersman: *His limbs were guarded with long leggings of the same material as the moccasins, which gartering over the knees of his tarnished buck-skin breeches, had obtained for him, among the settlers, the nickname of Leatherstocking* (James Fenimore Cooper).

leath·er·wood (leᴛʜ'ər wu̇d'), *n.* **1.** any of a group of shrubs with strong, flexible branches, especially a species grown in eastern North America for ornament, having yellow flowers and a very tough bark; wicopy. **2.** shrub of southeastern United States cultivated for its fragrant white flowers and the autumn colors of its foliage.

leath·er·work (leᴛʜ'ər wėrk'), *n.* **1.** things made out of leather. **2.** a making things out of leather.

leath·er·work·er (leᴛʜ'ər wėr'kər), *n.* a person who makes things out of leather.

leath·er·y (leᴛʜ'ər ē), *adj.* like leather; tough: *A huge grin spread across the old man's leathery face* (Time).

leathery turtle, the leatherback: *The leathery turtle* [*is*] *the largest of all recent chelonians* (Hans Gadow).

leav·a·ble (lē'və bəl), *adj.* that can be left: *The affairs of the "Liberal" were just then in a particularly leavable state* (H.G. Wells).

leave[1] (lēv), *v.,* **left, leav·ing.** —*v.t.* **1.** to go away from; depart from: *He left the house. He left the room suddenly.* **2. a.** to go away from permanently; stop living in, belonging to, or working at or for: *to leave the country, to leave a club, to leave a job.* **b.** to abandon; forsake: *He has left his home and friends and gone to sea.* **3.** to go without taking; let remain: *I left a book on the table. And take from seventy springs a score, It only leaves me fifty more* (A. E. Housman). *Business and ambition take up men's thoughts too much to leave room for philosophy* (Sir Richard Steele). **4.** to go away and let remain in a particular condition: *to leave a thing unsaid or undone, to leave a window open. The story left him unmoved. Being now on that part of his life which I am obliged to leave almost a blank* (Samuel Taylor Coleridge). **5.** to give (to family, friends, charity, etc.) when one dies; let remain; bequeath: *He left a large fortune to his two sons.* **6.** to give to be kept; deposit; give: *I left my suitcase in the station while I walked around the town. He left word that he would soon be home* (Dickens). **7.** to let (a person, etc.) alone to do something; let be: *Leave me to settle the matter. The potatoes must be left to boil for half an hour.* **8.** to let remain for someone to do: *Leave the matter to me. I left the cooking to my sister.* **9.** not to attend to: *I left my homework until tomorrow. Nothing in the Revolution . . . was left to accident* (Edmund Burke). **10.** *Archaic.* to stop; leave off.
—*v.i.* **1.** to go away; depart: *I do not leave for Europe until tomorrow.* **2.** *Obsolete.* to cease; desist; stop: *He . . . began at the eldest, and left at the youngest* (Genesis 44:12).
leave alone, a. to leave to oneself or itself: *He's busy at his desk—you'd better leave him alone.* **b.** to leave undisturbed; keep from interfering with: *Left alone, injured or inflamed skin has remarkable recuperative powers* (Newsweek). **c.** to keep from (doing, using, mentioning, etc.): *Very well, I'll leave that alone and move on to another topic* (Holiday).
leave in, (in bridge) to permit the bid of (one's partner) to stand: *Having poor support for my partner's trumps, I left in his bid of three diamonds.*
leave off, a. to stop; interrupt, or discontinue: *Take up the lesson where I left off. He left off smoking.* **b.** *Archaic.* to give up; forsake: *He would send her sufficient to enable her to leave off her shop* (Daniel Defoe).
leave out, to fail to do, say, or put in; omit: *She left out two words when she read the sentence.*
[Old English *lǣfan*]
—**Syn.** *v.t.* **1, 2.** depart, relinquish. -*v.t., v.i.* **1.** See **go.**
➤ See **let**[1] for usage note.

leave[2] (lēv), *n.* **1.** permission; consent: *They gave him leave to go. I desired leave of this prince to see the curiosities of the island* (Jonathan Swift). **2. a.** permission to be absent from duty. **b.** the length of time this lasts. **3.** an act of parting; farewell.
on leave, absent from or off duty with permission: *He was going on leave, after some years of service, to see his kindred at Remiremont* (Charles Reade).
take leave of, to say good-by to: *The young lord took his leave of us* (Daniel Defoe).
[Old English *lēaf*]

leave[3] (lēv), *v.i.,* **leaved, leav·ing.** to put forth leaves; leaf: *Trees leave in the spring.*
be leaved out, *U.S.* to be filled with leaves: *The poplars were leaved out* (Popular Science Monthly).
[Middle English *levien,* variant of *leaf,* verb]

leave·a·ble (lē'və bəl), *adj.* that can be left: *leaveable possessions.*

leaved (lēvd), *adj.* **1.** having leaves or foliage; in leaf. **2.** having leaves or foliage (of a specified number or kind).

leav·en (lev'ən), *n.* **1.** any substance, such as yeast, that will cause fermentation and raise dough. **2.** a small amount of fermenting dough kept for this purpose. **3.** an influence that, spreading silently and strongly, changes conditions or opinions: *The leaven of reform was working.* **4.** a tempering or modifying element; a tinge or admixture: *to mix a leaven of charity in*

one's judgments. He had a leaven of the old man in him which showed that he was his true-born son (Washington Irving). **5.** character; sort: *two men of the same leaven.*
—*v.t.* **1.** to raise with or as with a leaven; make (dough) light: *Know ye not that a little leaven leaveneth the whole lump?* (I Corinthians 5:6). **2.** to spread through and transform. **3.** to blend or temper with some modifying element.
[< Old French *levain* < Latin *levāmen* a lifting < *levāre* to raise < *levis* light[2]]
—**Syn.** *v.t.* **2.** permeate, pervade.

leav·en·ing (lev′ə ning), *n.* **1.** something that leavens; leaven. **2.** the act of causing to ferment by leaven.

leave of absence, 1. permission to be absent from duty. **2.** the length of time that absence from duty is permitted.

leav·er (lē′vər), *n.* **1.** a person or thing that leaves. **2.** *British.* a student who leaves school, usually to seek employment.

leaves (lēvz), *n.* plural of **leaf.**

leave-tak·ing (lēv′tā′king), *n.* the act of taking leave; saying good-by.

leav·ings (lē′vingz), *n.pl.* leftovers; remnants; residue: *The leavings of the meal were given to the dog.*
—**Syn.** remains, residuum.

Lea·vis·ite (lē′və sīt), *n.* a student or follower of the English critic F.R. Leavis: *Mr. Mellers [is] a Leavisite, and as a result music is always firmly viewed against its moral and social background* (Observer).
—*adj.* of or having to do with F.R. Leavis, his works, or his literary and social theories.

leav·y (lē′vē), *adj.,* **leav·i·er, leav·i·est.** leafy: *the leavy beech* (Tennyson).

Leb·a·nese (leb′ə nēz′, -nēs′), *adj., n., pl.* **-nese.** —*adj.* of or having to do with Lebanon or its inhabitants. —*n.* a native or inhabitant of Lebanon: *The Lebanese . . . have dissociated themselves entirely from the action of the Syrian congress* (Glasgow Herald).

Le·bens·raum or **le·bens·raum** (lā′bəns roum′), *n.* **1.** (in Nazi theory) the additional territory that a nation must control in order to expand economically. **2.** additional room that is needed, as to function or be less densely populated. **3.** freedom of action. [< German *Lebensraum* (literally) living space]

Le·ber·wurst (lā′bər vůrst′), *n. German.* liverwurst.

le·bes (lē′bēz), *n.* (in Ancient Greece) a basinlike or bowllike vessel, commonly of metal, with a rounded base. [< Greek *lébēs* kettle, cauldron]

Leb·ku·chen (lāp′kü′Hən), *n., pl.* **-chen.** *German.* a kind of spice cake often made with honey and bits of fruit, traditionally prepared around Christmastide.

le·cha·te·lier·ite (lə shä′tə lir′īt), *n.* the amorphous form of silica produced by the heat of lightning or meteoric impact. [< Henry Louis *Le Chatelier,* 1850-1936, a French chemist + *-ite*[1]]

lech·er (lech′ər), *n.* a man who indulges in lechery. [< Old French *lecheor* licker < *lechier* to lick, ultimately < Germanic (compare Old High German *lĕchōn*)]

lech·er·ous (lech′ər əs, lech′rəs), *adj.* lewd; lustful. —**lech′er·ous·ly,** *adv.* —**lech′er·ous·ness,** *n.* —**Syn.** lascivious, libidinous.

Lech·er wires (leH′ər), *Electronics.* parallel wires used to measure the wave length of currents having high frequencies, as those produced by radio waves. [< Ernst *Lecher,* 1856-1926, a German physicist]

lech·er·y (lech′ər ē, lech′rē), *n.* habitual indulgence of lust; lewdness.

le·chón a·sa·do (lā chōn′ ä sä′ᴛʜō), *Spanish.* roast young or suckling pig, a popular dish in Caribbean countries.

lech·we (lēch′wē), *n.,* or **lechwe antelope,** an African antelope related to the waterbuck that frequents swamps or other wet places. [probably < Sesuto *letsa* antelope]

lec·i·thin (les′ə thin), *n. Biochemistry.* any of a group of nitrogenous fatty substances containing phosphorus, distributed throughout the body but found especially in nerve cells and brain tissue. Lecithins are obtained especially from egg yolk, soybeans, and corn for use as chemical agents, and as ingredients in cosmetics, food, paints, etc. [< Greek *lékithos* egg yolk + English *-in*]

Le·conte's sparrow (lə konts′), a striped, yellowish-brown sparrow of the prairie marshes of central North America.

lect., lecture.

lec·tern (lek′tərn), *n.* **1.** a reading desk in a church, especially the desk from which the lessons are read at daily prayer. **2.** a reading desk or stand. [Middle English *lectryne,* alteration of earlier *lettorne* < Old French *lettrun,* learned borrowing from Medieval Latin *lectrum* < Latin *legere* read]

Gothic Lectern (def. 1)

lec·tion (lek′shən), *n.* **1.** a reading of a text found in a particular copy or edition. **2.** a portion of a sacred writing appointed to be read in church, usually at a given time of year; lesson. [< Latin *lēctiō, -ōnis* < *legere* read. Doublet of LESSON.]

lec·tion·ar·y (lek′shə ner′ē), *n., pl.* **-ar·ies. 1.** a book containing lessons or portions of Scripture appointed to be read at divine service. **2.** a list of passages appointed to be read at divine service.

lec·tor (lek′tər, -tôr), *n.* **1.** a person in minor orders who reads passages in a church service. **2.** a university reader or lecturer (chiefly in Scandinavia and Germany). [< Latin *lēctor* < *legere* read]

lec·tor·ate (lek′tər it), *n.* the office of lector.

lec·tor·ship (lek′tər ship), *n.* the office of lector; lectorate: *It is hereby expressly stated that the lectorship cannot be held for life* (Westminster Gazette).

lec·tress (lek′tris), *n.* a female reader.

lec·trice (lek′tris), *n.* a woman employed to read aloud. [< French *lĕctrice,* learned borrowing from Latin *lectrix,* feminine of *lēctor* reader, lector]

lec·ture (lek′chər), *n., v.,* **-tured, -tur·ing.** —*n.* **1. a.** a speech; planned talk on a chosen subject, usually for the purpose of instruction: *I can spare the college bell, And the learned lecture well* (Ralph Waldo Emerson). **b.** such a speech or talk written down or printed: *Two lectures . . . appear in appendixes* (New Yorker). **2.** a scolding: *My mother gives me a lecture when I come home late for supper.*
—*v.i.* to give a lecture or lectures. —*v.t.* **1.** to instruct or entertain by a lecture. **2.** to scold; reprove: *Those whom he had lectured withdrew full of resentment* (Thomas Babbington Macaulay).
[< Late Latin *lēctūra* < *legere* read] —**Syn.** *v.t.* **2.** admonish, rebuke, reprimand.

lec·tur·er (lek′chər ər), *n.* **1.** a person who gives a lecture or lectures. **2.** a person in a college or university who gives lectures or performs other academic duties but does not have the rank or title of professor. **3.** *British.* a teaching position in a university, ranking below professor and reader.

lec·ture·ship (lek′chər ship), *n.* the office of lecturer.

lec·tur·ess (lek′chər is), *n.* a woman lecturer.

lec·y·thus (les′ə thəs), *n., pl.* **-thi** (-thī). (in Ancient Greece) a tall, slender, narrow-necked vase with a handle, for holding oil, unguents, etc. Also, **lekythos.** [< Greek *lēkythos*]

Attic Lecythus

led[1] (led), *v.* past tense and past participle of **lead**[1]: *The policeman led the child across the street. That blind man is led by his dog.*
➔ See **lead**[1] for usage note.

led[2] (led), *adj.* under leading or control. [< *led*[1]]

L. Ed., Lawyer's edition (U.S. Supreme Court Reports).

Le·da (lē′də), *n. Greek Mythology.* the wife of Tyndareus of Sparta, the mother by him of Clytemnestra. Zeus visited Leda in the form of a swan, and she was the mother by him of Castor and Pollux and Helen of Troy.

led captain (led), a hanger-on; henchman; parasite: *Mr. Wagg . . . a led captain of my Lord Steyne* (Thackeray).

Le·der·ho·sen (lā′dər hō′zən), *n.pl. German.* Tyrolean leather breeches, often colorfully embroidered, and worn with suspenders.

Lederhosen

ledge (lej), *n.* **1.** a narrow shelf: *a window ledge.* **2. a.** a shelf or ridge of rock: *He climbed up the side of the chasm to gain the ledge above* (Frederick Marryat). **b.** such a ridge of rocks beneath the surface of the sea: *the Maldives, a famous ledge of islands* (Daniel Defoe). **3.** a layer or mass of metal-bearing rock. [Middle English *legge* crossbar on a door, perhaps < *leggen* lay[1], or perhaps Old English *lecg* some part of a short sword] —**ledge′less,** *adj.*

ledg·er (lej′ər), *n.* **1. a.** a book of accounts in which a business keeps a record of all money transactions. **b.** (in bookkeeping and accounting) the book of final entry, where a complete record of all assets, liabilities, and proprietorship items are kept. It shows the changes that occur in these items during the month as a result of business operations carried on, by means of debits and credits. **2.** a flat stone slab covering a grave. **3.** a horizontal member of a scaffold, attached to the uprights and supporting the putlogs. **4.** ledger bait or tackle.
—*v.i.* to fish with a ledger.
—*adj. Obsolete.* **1.** remaining in a place; resident; permanent; stationary. **2.** lying or resting in a place.
[probably Middle English *leggen* lay[1]. Compare Dutch *ligger, legger* ledger.]

ledger bait, bait for fishing fixed so that it stays in one place, usually on the bottom.

ledger board, the horizontal board which forms the top of a fence, balustrade, etc., often serving as a handrail or guard.

ledger line, 1. *Music.* a line added above or below the staff for notes that are too high or too low to be put on the staff. **2.** (in angling) ledger tackle. Also, **leger line.**

Ledger Lines (def. 1) (L)

ledger paper, writing paper of the kind used in ledgers.

ledger tackle, fishing tackle, a line, etc., arranged to keep bait in one place.

ledg·y (lej′ē), *adj.,* **ledg·i·er, ledg·i·est. 1.** having many ledges: *Several of the fields are ledgy in places, and if you wander into the woods, you come on old stone walls made of tons and tons of rock* (New Yorker). **2.** consisting of a ledge or ledges.

lee[1] (lē), *n.* **1.** protection; shelter. **2.** the side or part sheltered from the wind: *Beneath the Castle's sheltering lee, They staid their course in quiet sea* (Scott). **3.** the side away from the wind. **4.** *Nautical.* the direction toward which the wind is blowing.
—*adj.* **1.** sheltered from the wind: *the lee side of a ship.* **2.** on the side away from the wind. **3.** *Nautical.* in the direction toward which the wind is blowing.
[Old English *hlēo* shelter]

lee[2] (lē), *n. Obsolete.* sediment; dregs. See **lees.** [< Old French *lie;* see LEES]

lee·an·gle (lē′ang′gəl), *n.* a heavy club with a bent and pointed end, used by Australian aborigines. [< an Australian native word]

lee·board (lē′bôrd′, -bōrd′), *n.* a large, flat board lowered vertically into the water on the lee side of a sailboat to keep the boat from drifting sideways.

leech[1] (lēch), *n.* **1.** any of various annelid worms having terminal suckers and living on land, in salt water, and especially in fresh-water ponds and streams. Doctors formerly used the common blood-sucking leech to draw blood from sick people. *One day a customer with a black eye . . . asked for a couple of leeches* (New Yorker). **2.** a person who tries persistently to get what he can out of others without doing anything to earn it: *The spendthrift, and the leech that sucks him* (William Cowper). **3.** *Archaic.* a doctor: *Thither came The King's own leech to look into his hurt* (Tennyson). **4.** an instrument to draw blood for medical purposes.
—*v.t. Archaic.* to bleed with leeches for medical purposes; to doctor.
[Old English *lǣce* physician; Old English *lǣce* leech, may be the same word]

leech[2] (lēch), *n.* any edge of a sail not fastened to a rope or spar. Also, **leach.** [Middle English *lyche.* Compare Swedish *lik* bolt rope.]

leech·craft (lēch′kraft′, -kräft′), *n. Archaic.* the art of the leech or physician; medical science, skill, or treatment: *Abbot Jerome, whose leechcraft is famous* (Scott). [Old English *lǣcecræft* < *lǣce* physician + *cræft* craft]

leech·dom (lēch′dəm), *n. Archaic.* a medicine; medicinal remedy. [Old English *lǣcedōm* < *lǣce* physician + *-dōm* -dom]

leek (lēk), *n.* **1.** a vegetable of the amaryllis family somewhat like an onion, but with larger leaves, a smaller bulb shaped like a cylinder, and a milder flavor. It is the national emblem of Wales. **2.** any of several related vegetables. [Old English *lēac.* Compare GARLIC.]

Leek (def. 1)

leek-green (lēk′grēn′), *adj.* of the dull, bluish-green color of the leek.

leer[1] (lir), *n.* a sly, sidelong look; evil glance: *She gives the leer of invitation* (Shakespeare). *Damn with faint praise, assent with civil leer* (Alexander Pope). [< verb] —*v.i.* to give a sly, sidelong look; glance evilly. [perhaps < *leer*[3]] —**leer′ing·ly,** *adv.*

leer[2] (lir), *adj. Dialect.* **1.** empty; unburdened. **2.** hungry. Also, **lear, leery.** [compare Old English *lǣrnes* emptiness]

leer[3] (lir), *n. Obsolete.* **1.** the cheek. **2.** the face. **3.** looks; personal appearance; complexion. [Old English *hlēor* cheek]

leer·i·ly (lir′ə lē), *adv. Informal.* in a leery manner.

leer·i·ness (lir′ē nis), *n. Informal.* the quality of being leery; wariness; caution.

leer·y[1] (lir′ē), *adj.,* **leer·i·er, leer·i·est.** *Informal.* **1.** sly; wide-awake; knowing: *You're a very leery cove, by the look of you* (Arthur Conan Doyle). **2.** wary; doubtful; suspicious: *We are leery of his advice. A . . . new crevasse detector . . . sniffs electronically for hidden chasms . . . So far, however, . . . explorers have been leery of staking their lives on it* (Newsweek). Also, **leary.**

leer·y[2] (lir′ē), *adj.* leer; empty.

lees (lēz), *n. pl.* **1.** the most worthless part of anything; dregs: *I will drink Life to the lees* (Tennyson). **2.** the sediment deposited in the container by wine and some other liquids. [< Old French *lias,* plural of *lie,* probably < Late Latin (Gaul) *lia,* perhaps < a Celtic word]

lee shore, the shore toward which the wind is blowing, especially in relation to a ship.

leet (lēt), *n. English History.* **1.** a court held annually or semiannually in certain manors; court-leet. **2.** its jurisdiction. **3.** the day on which it met. [< Anglo-French *lete;* origin uncertain]

lee tide, a tide running in the direction toward which the wind blows.

lee·ward (lē′wərd; *Nautical* lü′ərd), *adj., adv.* **1.** on the side away from the wind; lee. **2.** in the direction toward which the wind is blowing. —*n.* the side, part, or area away from the wind; lee.

lee wave, *Meteorology.* a stationary atmospheric wave, formed on the lee or downwind sides of mountains and often marked by the presence of an apparently motionless cloud.

lee·way (lē′wā′), *n.* **1.** the side movement or drift of a ship or aircraft from its heading to leeward, out of its course. **2.** extra space at the side; time, money, etc., more than is needed; margin of safety: *If you take $10 more than you think you will need on a trip, you are allowing yourself a leeway of $10.* **3.** convenient room or scope for action: *leeway in planning.*

leeze me (lēz′ mē), *Scottish.* an expression of lively satisfaction; I am pleased with. [short for *lief is me* dear is to me; see LIEF]

left[1] (left), *adj.* **1. a.** belonging to the side of the less used hand (in most people); having to do with the side of anything that is turned west when the main side is turned north: *A person who usually uses his right hand has a slightly larger right hand than left hand. John lost his left shoe while wading through the brook.* **b.** on this side when viewed from in front; having this relation to the front of any object: *the left wing of an army.* **2.** situated nearer the observer's or speaker's left hand than his right: *Take a left turn at the next light.*
—*adv.* on, to, or toward the left side: *to turn left.*
—*n.* **1.** the left side or hand: *He sat at my left.* **2.** what is on the left side. **3.** Often, **Left.** *Politics.* the part of a lawmaking body consisting of the more liberal or radical groups. In some European legislative assemblies this group sits on the left side of the chamber as seen by the presiding officer. **4.** *Sports.* a blow struck with the left hand. [Middle English *left,* variant of *lift, luft,* Old English *lyft* weak]

left[2] (left), *v.* past tense and past participle of **leave**[1]: *He left his hat in the hall.*
be left, to remain: *If you do not make haste to return, there will be little left to greet you, of me, or mine* (Charles Lamb).
get left, *Slang.* **a.** to be left behind or outdone, as in a contest or rivalry: *The horse got left at the post.* **b.** to be disappointed in one's attempts or expectations: *He got left twice, but made the team on his third try.*

Left Bank, 1. the Bohemian section of Paris, on the left bank of the Seine river: *The Left Bank was then full of Americans in temporary exile whooping it up in ways often far from candid* (Sean O'Faolain). **2.** of, having to do with, or characteristic of this section: *A bourgeois young man . . . gets involved with the Left Bank beatniks* (Punch).

left bower, (in certain card games) the jack that has the same color as the jack of trumps.

left-cen·ter (left′sen′tər), *adj.* of or belonging to the liberal or radical segment of a political party or group of the center: *The Communists and . . . left-center forces joined to vote* (Time). —*n.* a left-center party, group, or position: *An apparent swing to the left—mainly the left-center—took place* (New York Times).

left face, (in military drill) a 90-degree turn to the left, made by pivoting on the left heel.

left-face (left′fās′), *v.i.,* **-faced, -fac·ing.** to make a left face.

left field, *Baseball.* the section of the outfield behind third base. *Abbr.:* lf.
out in left field, *U.S. Slang.* wrong; mistaken; out of order: *His argument is way out in left field.*

left fielder, the baseball player whose position is in left field.

left-foot·ed (left′fu̇t′id), *adj.* **1.** using the left foot more easily and readily than the right. **2.** awkward; clumsy: *Vietnam is no place for . . . the left-footed recruit* (Time). —**left′foot′ed·ness,** *n.*

left half, the halfback usually on the left side of the field before the kickoff in football and soccer.

left-hand (left′hand′), *adj.* **1.** on or to the left. **2.** of, for, or with the left hand; left-handed.

left-hand·ed (left′han′did), *adj.* **1.** using the left hand more easily and readily than the right. **2.** done with the left hand. **3.** made to be used by or placed on the left hand. **4.** turning from right to left: *a left-handed screw.* **5.** awkward; clumsy: *It seems to me as if murder and massacre were but a very left-handed way of producing civilization and love* (William Godwin). **6.** ambiguous; doubtful; insincere: *a left-handed compliment.* **7.** (in scientific and technical use) characterized by a direction or rotation to the left; producing such a rotation in the plane of a polarized ray. **8.** (of a blow) delivered with the left hand. **9.** morganatic (from the custom at German morganatic weddings of the bridegroom's giving the bride his left hand rather than his right).
—*adv.* toward the left; with the left hand. —**left′-hand′ed·ly,** *adv.* —**left′-hand′ed·ness,** *n.*

left-handed marriage, a morganatic marriage. See **left-handed** (*adj.* def. 9).

left-hand·er (left′han′dər), *n.* **1.** a left-handed person: *The left-hander has a long way to travel before he catches up with the right-handed majority* (New York Times). **2.** in baseball, a left-handed pitcher; southpaw. **3.** in cricket, a left-handed bowler. **4.** a blow with the left hand.

left·ish (lef′tish), *adj.* favoring or tending to favor the political left: *He accused Kefauver of being "leftish," and a one-worlder* (Time). —**left′ish·ly,** *adv.*

left·ism or **Left·ism** (lef′tiz əm), *n.* adherence or tendency to adhere to liberal or radical views in politics: *Leftism seems everywhere in a majority . . . but nowhere is it in effective control* (H.G. Wells).

left·ist or **Left·ist** (lef′tist), *n.* **1.** a person who has liberal or radical ideas. **2.** a member of a liberal or radical organization.
—*adj. Informal.* having liberal or radical ideas.

left-lug·gage office (left′lug′ij), *British.* a place where baggage may be left and called for later; checkroom.

left-of-cen·ter (left′əv sen′tər), *adj.* occupying a position on the left side of those in the center; holding a leftist view in politics; left-wing: *a left-of-center candidate.*

left·o·ver (left′ō′vər), *n.* a thing that is left: *Scraps of food from a meal are leftovers.* —*adj.* remaining over; that is left: *leftover models, leftover parts. I did carry a handful of leftover flowers around* (R.M. Stuart).

left·ward (left′wərd), *adj., adv.* on or toward the left.

left·wards (left′wərdz), *adv.* leftward: *In education . . . the Liberals have moved leftwards of their original position* (Manchester Guardian Weekly).

left wing, 1. Often, **Left Wing.** the liberal or radical members, especially of a political party. **2.** persons or parties holding liberal or radical views. —**left′-wing′,** *adj.*

left-wing·er (left′wing′ər), *n.* a left-wing member of a political party or a supporter of left-wing political views.

left-wing·ism (left′wing′iz əm), *n.* the doctrines or practices of left-wingers: *The Bill of Rights . . . smacked of the most extreme left-wingism at the time* (Atlanta Constitution).

left·y (lef′tē), *n., pl.* **left·ies.** *Slang.* a left-handed person.

leg (leg), *n., v.,* **legged, leg·ging.** —*n.* **1.** one of the limbs on which men and animals support themselves and walk: *Dogs stand on their four legs. A man uses his two legs in walking and running.* **2.** the part of a garment that covers a leg: *The legs of your trousers are wrinkled.* **3.** anything shaped or used like a leg, as a support that is much longer than it is wide: *a table leg. One leg of a compass holds the pencil. A rainbow, therefore . . . plunges one of its legs down to the river* (Thomas Jefferson). **4.** one of the distinct portions or stages of any course: *the last leg of a trip. A runner fell in the first leg of the relay and his team lost the race.* **5.** a side of a triangle that is not the base or hypotenuse. **6.** *Nautical.* **a.** the course or run made on one tack by a sailing vessel. **b.** each of the straight courses or parts of a sailing race from point to point. **7.** *Cricket.* **a.** that part of the field to the left of and behind a right-handed batsman as he faces the bowler. **b.** the fielder placed there. **8.** *Archaic.* an obeisance made by drawing back one leg and bending the other; scrape: *He is one that cannot make a good leg* (Longfellow).
a leg up, a. assistance in climbing or getting over an obstacle, as mounting a horse: *The wall is very low, Sir, and your servant will give you a leg up* (Dickens). **b.** encouragement; support: *He might see fit to change his mind . . . if the Government would at last give a leg up to the languishing . . . bill, for which he has long and devotedly battled* (New Yorker). **c.** an advantage: *The consensus in the labor field is that 60-year-old Caption Bradley has a "leg up" on his rival* (New York Times).
get on one's hind legs, to go into a rage: *"Don't get on your hind legs," returned Betty composedly* (London Daily News).
have not a leg to stand on, *Informal.* to have no defense or reason: *When he is through adding up his last column of figures, the . . . notion of a coup d'état pulled off by big city bondholders hasn't a leg to stand on* (Wall Street Journal).
legs, timbers used to support a ship upright when dried out: *The yacht fell over, breaking her legs under her.*
on one's last legs, about to fail, collapse, die, etc.; at the end of one's resources: *After the suppression of the revolutionary movement the Second Republic was on its last legs* (Manchester Guardian Weekly).
pull one's leg, *Informal.* to fool, trick, or make fun of one: *"When you write your piece," she giggled, "I won't mind if you pull my leg —just a little"* (Maclean's).
shake a leg, *Slang.* **a.** hurry up!: *You'd better shake a leg or we'll miss our bus.* **b.** to dance: *The bandleader urged the couples to get up and shake a leg.*
stretch one's legs, to take a walk; get

exercise by walking: *The passengers got off the bus to stretch their legs after the long ride.* —*v.i. Informal.* to walk; run: *We could not get a ride, so we had to leg it.*
[< Scandinavian (compare Old Icelandic *leggr*)]

leg., **1.** legal. **2.** legate. **3.** *Music.* legato. **4.** legislative. **5.** legislature.

leg·a·cy (leg′ə sē), *n., pl.* **-cies.** **1.** *Law.* money or other property left to a person by will; bequest. **2.** something that has been handed down from an ancestor or predecessor: *Books are the legacies that a great genius leaves to mankind* (Joseph Addison). [< Anglo-French *legacie* bequest, Old French, legateship, legate's office < Medieval Latin *legatia* < Latin *lēgātum* bequest < *lēgāre* bequeath]
—**Syn. 1.** inheritance. **2.** heritage.

le·gal (lē′gəl), *adj.* **1.** of law: *legal knowledge.* **2.** of lawyers: *legal advice.* **3.** according to law; lawful: *a legal guardian, legal incapacity.* **4.** valid in or recognized by law rather than equity. **5. a.** of Mosaic law. **b.** based on Mosaic law. **c.** having to do with salvation by good works rather than free grace.
—*n.* a legal notice.
legals, securities in which savings banks, trustees, etc., under legal regulation may invest as authorized by law: *the purchase of legals by investors.*
[< Middle French *légal*, learned borrowing from Latin *lēgal*, *lēgālis* < *lēx*, *lēgis* law. Doublet of LEAL, LOYAL.]
—**Syn.** *adj.* **3.** See **lawful.**

legal aid society, an organization of citizens offering legal services at no cost for those who cannot afford to hire a lawyer.

legal cap, *U.S.* writing paper in double sheets of 14 x 8½ inches, used by lawyers.

le·gal·ese (lē′gə lēz′, -lēs′), *n. Informal.* legal jargon.

legal fiction, fiction (def. 5).

legal holiday, a day set by law or statute as exempt from normal labor or business activities and celebrated annually to commemorate an event or honor a person.

le·gal·ise (lē′gə līz), *v.t.,* **-ised, -is·ing.** *Especially British.* legalize.

le·gal·ism (lē′gə liz əm), *n.* **1.** strict adherence to law or prescription. **2.** legal matters, problems, complications, etc.: ... *heavily occupied with civil rights legalisms during his two-year tenure* ... (Time). **3.** *Theology.* the doctrine of salvation by good works; adherence to the Mosaic law rather than the Gospel.

le·gal·ist (lē′gə list), *n.* **1.** a person who adheres strictly to laws or rules. **2.** an expert in law; a person who views things from a legal standpoint. **3.** *Theology.* a supporter of legalism.

le·gal·is·tic (lē′gə lis′tik), *adj.* adhering strictly to law or prescription: *A sizable parcel of National Forest timberland in Oregon is now being cut over by a private company, under the legalistic guise of complying with federal mineral laws* (Harper's). —**le′gal·is′ti·cal·ly,** *adv.*

le·gal·i·ty (li gal′ə tē), *n., pl.* **-ties. 1.** accordance with law; lawfulness: *They raised a question about the legality of the appointment* (New York Times). **2.** attachment to or observance of law or rule. **3.** *Theology.* reliance on good works for salvation, rather than on free grace.
—**Syn. 1.** legitimacy.

le·gal·i·za·tion (lē′gə lə zā′shən), *n.* the act of legalizing.

le·gal·ize (lē′gə līz), *v.t.,* **-ized, -iz·ing.** to make legal; authorize by law; sanction: *Communist ... politicians [in Venezuela], banned by a Supreme Court ruling from a place on the ballot, are having no luck in shopping for a deal with any of the legalized parties* (Wall Street Journal). —**Syn.** legitimize.

le·gal·ly (lē′gə lē), *adv.* **1.** in a legal manner. **2.** according to law: *legally responsible.*

legal reserve, (in banking) the amount of cash or certain other liquid assets which by law must be held in reserve against deposits.

le·gals (lē′gəlz), *n.pl.* See under **legal,** *n.*

legal separation, the living apart of a husband and wife according to an order of a court or judge.

le·gal-size (lē′gəl sīz′), *adj.* (of a page, folder, etc.) having a size suitable for legal documents, usually up to 14 inches long.

le·gal-sized (lē′gəl sīzd′), *adj.* legal-size.

legal tender, money that must, by law, be accepted in payment of debts.

leg·a·tar·y (leg′ə ter′ē), *adj., n., pl.* **-tar·ies.** —*adj.* of or having to do with a bequest or legacy. —*n.* a legatee.
[< Latin *lēgātārius* < *lēgātum* bequest < *lēgāre* bequeath]

leg·ate (leg′it), *n.* **1.** a representative of the Pope: *The Lord Cardinal Pole, sent here as legate From our most Holy Father Julius, Pope* (Tennyson). **2.** an ambassador; representative; messenger: *the legates from Utrecht* (John L. Motley). **3.** in ancient Rome: **a.** an assistant or deputy to a general or to the governor of a province. **b.** (under the empire) the governor of a province. [< Old French *legat*, learned borrowing from Latin *lēgātus* (originally) provided with a contract < *lēgāre* bequeath < *lēx*, *lēgis* contract]

leg·a·tee (leg′ə tē′), *n.* a person to whom a legacy is left. —**Syn.** heir.

leg·ate·ship (leg′it ship), *n.* the dignity and office of a legate.

leg·a·tine (leg′ə tin, -tīn), *adj.* **1.** of or having to do with a legate. **2.** having the authority of a legate.

le·ga·tion (li gā′shən), *n.* **1.** a diplomatic representative of a country and his staff of assistants. A legation ranks next below an embassy and is now usually headed by a minister. **2.** the official residence, offices, etc., of such a representative in a foreign country. **3.** the office, position, or dignity of a legate. **4.** the act of sending a deputy or representative, especially a papal legate. **5.** the fact of his being sent. **6.** the object for which an ambassador or legate is sent; his mission or commission. [< Old French *legation*, learned borrowing from Latin *lēgātiō*, *-ōnis* < *lēgāre* to dispatch (with a commission) < *lēx*, *lēgis* law]

le·ga·tion·ar·y (li gā′shə ner′ē), *adj.* **1.** of or having to do with a legation. **2.** qualified or ready to go on a legation.

le·ga·to (li gä′tō), *adj., adv., n., pl.* **-tos.** *Music.* —*adj., adv.* smooth and connected; without breaks between successive tones: *He has a beautiful legato line on which he places his words without yielding to the common Italian temptation to elide consonants* (London Times). —*n.* a legato performance or style: ... *a smooth method of production which affords her a legato like satin* ... (London Times). [< Italian *legato* bound < Latin *ligātus*, past participle of *ligāre* to bind]

le·ga·tor (li gā′tər, leg′ə tôr′), *n.* a person who leaves something by will; testator.

leg·a·to·ri·al (leg′ə tôr′ē əl, -tōr′-), *adj.* of or having to do with a legator or testator.

leg bail, flight from custody or arrest (a humorous use).
give leg bail, to run away.

leg before, leg before wicket.

leg before wicket, (in cricket) the action of stopping a ball that would have hit the wicket with the leg or other part of the batsman's body, except the hand. It usually results in an out.

leg break, (in cricket) a ball pitched on or breaking from the side of the field that lies in a line with the batsman.

leg bye, (in cricket) a run made on a ball touching any part of the batsman's body except his hand.

leg·end (lej′ənd), *n.* **1.** a story coming down from the past, which many people have believed: *The stories about King Arthur and his knights of the Round Table are legends, not history. Listen to this Indian Legend, To this Song of Hiawatha* (Longfellow). **2.** such stories as a group; the legends of certain peoples: *a hero of Irish legend, a spot rich in legend.* **3.** an inscription on a coin or medal: *Read the legend on a five-cent piece.* **4.** words accompanying a picture or diagram, usually explaining something about it; caption: *The legend underneath the picture identified the man as General Custer.* **5.** in the Middle Ages: **a.** a story of the life of a saint. **b.** a collection of saints' lives or inspirational stories. [< Old French *legende*, learned borrowing from Medieval Latin *legenda* (things) to be read < Latin, neuter plural gerundive of *legere* read]
—**Syn. 1.** saga. **2.** folklore. **3.** motto.

➔ **legend, myth.** *Legend* applies particularly to a story associated with some period in the history of a people or nation, often containing an element of fact but sometimes wholly untrue. Legends are intended to glorify a hero, saint, object, etc., and tell marvelous deeds he or it supposedly performed. *Myth* applies particularly to a story connected with the religion of a primitive civilization. Myths are told about gods or superhuman beings and are invented to explain beliefs or rituals or something in nature.

leg·end·ar·i·ly (lej′ən der′ə lē), *adv.* in a legendary manner.

leg·end·ar·y (lej′ən der′ē), *adj., n., pl.* **-ar·ies.** —*adj.* **1.** of a legend or legends; like a legend; not historical: *Robin Hood is a legendary person. His legendary song ... Of ancient deeds so long forgot* (Scott). **2.** celebrated or described in legend: *a legendary hero or event.* **3.** relating legends: *a legendary writer.* —*n.* a collection of legends, especially of lives of saints.

leg·end·ry (lej′ən drē), *n., pl.* **-ries.** legends collectively.

leg·er (lej′ər), *n., v.i., adj. Obsolete.* ledger.

leg·er·de·main (lej′ər də mān′), *n.* **1.** sleight of hand; conjuring tricks; jugglery: *A common trick of legerdemain is to take rabbits from an apparently empty hat.* **2.** trickery; deception; hocus-pocus: *In a remarkable bit of legerdemain, he transferred his popular film personality to his singing style* (Time). *There is a certain Knack or Legerdemain in argument* (Anthony Ashley Cooper). **3.** *Obsolete.* an artful trick; a juggle. [< Middle French *léger de main* quick of hand < Vulgar Latin *leviārius* (< Latin *levis* light), Latin *dē* of, and *mānus* hand] —**Syn. 1.** prestidigitation.

leg·er·de·main·ist (lej′ər də mā′nist), *n.* a person who practices legerdemain; juggler; trickster.

le·ger·i·ty (lə jer′ə tē), *n.* lightness; nimbleness: *He sprang to the road beneath. ... Alighting with the legerity of a cat, he ... was off, like a streak of lightning* (New Yorker). [< Middle French *légèreté* < *léger* quick (see LEGERDEMAIN) + *-eté* -ity]

leger line, ledger line.

le·ges (lē′jēz), *n. Latin.* plural of **lex.**

-legged, *combining form.* having — legs: *Long-legged = having long legs. Two-legged = having two legs.*

leg·ging (leg′ing), *n.* one of a pair of leggings.

leg·gings (leg′ingz), *n.pl.* extra outer coverings of cloth or leather for the legs, for use out of doors. —**Syn.** puttees.

leg·gy (leg′ē), *adj.,* **-gi·er, -gi·est. 1.** having long legs: *a leggy, gun-totin' singer at the Dirty Shame saloon* (Time). **2.** having awkwardly long legs: *Slapper's long-tailed leggy mare* (Thackeray). **3.** long-stemmed (often said of plants that have grown too tall and thin from being crowded, etc.): *The white meeting-house, and the row of youthful and leggy trees before it* (Oliver Wendell Holmes).

leg hit, *Cricket.* a hit to leg.

leg·horn (leg′hôrn, -ərn), *n.* **1.** a hat made of fine, flat, yellow braided straw or an imitation of it. **2.** this straw, made from cut and bleached green wheat. [< *Leghorn*, a seaport in Italy]

Leg·horn (leg′hôrn, -ərn), *n.* any of a breed of rather small, white, brown, black, buff, or silver poultry with yellow skin. They originated in Italy. [see *leghorn*]

leg·i·bil·i·ty (lej′ə bil′ə tē), *n.* legible condition or quality; clearness of print or writing: ... *words emblazoned in all the legibility of gilt letters* ... (Dickens).

leg·i·ble (lej′ə bəl), *adj.* **1.** easy to read; plain and clear: *Her handwriting is both beautiful and legible.* **2.** that can be read: *the trouble legible in my countenance* (Charles Lamb). [< Late Latin *legibilis* < Latin *legere* read] —**leg′i·ble·ness,** *n.* —**Syn. 1.** distinct. **2.** readable.

leg·i·bly (lej′ə blē), *adv.* clearly; readably: *The next time you make a list, please write more legibly.*

le·gion (lē′jən), *n.* **1.** a body of soldiers; army: *Nor knew great Hector how his legions yield* (Alexander Pope). **2.** a body of soldiers in the ancient Roman army consisting of 3,000 to 6,000 foot soldiers and 300 to 700 cavalrymen. **3.** a great many; very large number: *a legion of difficulties, a legion of supporters. Legions of grasshoppers destroyed the crops.* **4.** a host of angels or spirits: *My name is Legion: for we are many* (Mark 5:9). [< Old French *legion*, learned borrowing from Latin *legiō*, *-ōnis* < *legere* choose] —**Syn. 3.** multitude.

Le·gion (lē′jən), *n.* **1.** the American Legion. **2.** the French Foreign Legion.

le·gion·ar·y (lē′jə ner′ē), *adj., n., pl.* **-ar·ies.** —*adj.* **1.** of or belonging to a legion. **2.** organized as or formed of a legion or legions. —*n.* **1.** a soldier of a legion; legionnaire. **2.** *British.* a member of the British Legion (a veterans' organization).

legionary ant, an army ant of North and South America.

le·gioned (lē′jənd), *adj.* arrayed in legions.

le·gion·naire (lē′jə när′), *n.* **1.** a member of the American Legion or any other group using the title of Legion. **2.** a soldier of a legion. [< French *légionnaire* < Old French *legion* legion]

Legion of Honor, an honorary society founded by Napoleon in 1802. Membership is given as a reward for great services to France.

Legion of Merit, *U.S.* a military award conferred by the President on Americans and people of allied nations, for exceptional services.

leg iron, a shackle or fetter for the leg.

Legis., Legislature.

leg·is·late (lej′is lāt), *v.,* **-lat·ed, -lat·ing.** —*v.i.* to make laws: *Congress legislates for the United States.* —*v.t.* to force by legislation; bring about by legislation: *The council legislated him out of office.* [apparently back formation < *legislator*]

leg·is·la·tion (lej′is lā′shən), *n.* **1.** the making of laws: *Congress has the power of legislation.* **2.** the laws made: *Legislation due to come up at this session will deal with enormously important problems involving national security, farm income, tax rates . . . and immigration policies* (Newsweek). —**Syn. 1.** lawmaking.

leg·is·la·tive (lej′is lā′tiv), *adj.* **1.** having to do with making laws: *legislative reforms.* **2.** having the duty and power of making laws: *Congress is a legislative body.* **3.** ordered by law; enacted by legislation: *a legislative decree. Legislative approval is necessary before a corporation can come into existence in New York State* (New York Times). **4.** suitable to a legislature: *a legislative hall.*
—*n.* the branch of government which makes laws. —**leg′is·la′tive·ly,** *adv.*

legislative assembly, the lower branch of the legislature in some States of the United States.

Legislative Assembly, (in Canada) the popularly elected legislature of a province (except the province of Quebec).

legislative council, a committee of members from both houses that advises some State legislatures of the United States on all matters of law.

Legislative Council, (in Canada) the upper house of the legislature of Quebec. The other Canadian provinces do not have two Houses and are governed by the Legislative Assembly.

leg·is·la·tor (lej′is lā′tər), *n.* a person who makes laws; member of a group that makes laws; lawmaker: *Senators and representatives are legislators.* [< Latin (originally) *lēgis lātor* proposer of a law < *lēx, lēgis* law + *lātus,* past participle of *ferre* bring, bear]

leg·is·la·to·ri·al (lej′is lə tôr′ē əl, -tōr′-), *adj.* **1.** of or having to do with a legislator or legislature. **2.** functioning as a legislator or legislature. —**leg′is·la·to′ri·al·ly,** *adv.*

leg·is·la·tor·ship (lej′is lā′tər ship), *n.* the office or function of a legislator.

leg·is·la·tress (lej′is lā′tris), *n.* a woman legislator.

leg·is·la·trix (lej′is lā′triks), *n.* legislatress.

leg·is·la·ture (lej′is lā′chər), *n.* a group of persons that has the duty and power of making laws for a State or country: *Each State of the United States has a legislature.*

le·gist (lē′jist), *n.* an expert in law. [< Old French *legiste,* learned borrowing from Medieval Latin *legista* < Latin *lēx, lēgis* law]

le·git (lə jit′), *Slang.* —*n.* (in the theater) legitimate drama; the legitimate theater. —*adj.* legitimate: *Is it legit to draw two cards at once? Many of them spoke bravely about going into "something legit, perhaps next year"* (Sidney Katz). *I'm a legit playwright* (Saturday Review).

leg·i·tim (lej′ə tim), *n. Civil and Scots Law.* the portion of the estate of a deceased person to which his children are legally entitled. [< Old French *legitime,* learned borrowing from Latin *lēgitimus* lawful < *lēx, lēgis* law]

le·git·i·ma·cy (lə jit′ə mə sē), *n.* **1.** the fact of being legitimate. **2.** the condition of being recognized as lawful or proper: *I never hear an American citizen speak of the legitimacy of princes without indignation or pity* (Niles Weekly Register).

le·git·i·mate (*adj.* lə jit′ə mit; *v.* lə jit′ə māt), *adj., v.,* **-mat·ed, -mat·ing.** —*adj.* **1.** rightful; lawful; allowed: *Sickness is a legitimate reason for a child's being absent from school.* **2.** conforming to accepted standards; normal; regular. **3.** born of parents who are married. A legitimate child is entitled to full filial rights. **4.** resting on, or ruling by, the principle of hereditary right: *the legitimate title to a throne, a legitimate sovereign.* **5.** logical: *a legitimate conclusion.* **6.** *Obsolete.* genuine; real.
—*v.t.* **1.** to make or declare lawful. **2.** to affirm or show to be legitimate; authorize or justify by word or example: *Necessity legitimates my advice; for it is the only way to save our lives* (Daniel Defoe).
[< Medieval Latin *legitimatus,* past participle of *legitimare* < Latin *lēgitimus* lawful < *lēx, lēgis* law] —**le·git′i·mate·ly,** *adv.* —**le·git′i·mate·ness,** *n.*
—**Syn.** *adj.* **1.** See **lawful.**

legitimate drama, 1. the body of plays of recognized merit. **2.** legitimate theater.

legitimate stage, legitimate theater.

legitimate theater, drama acted on the stage as opposed to motion pictures, vaudeville, etc.

le·git·i·ma·tion (lə jit′ə mā′shən), *n.* the act or process of legitimating.

le·git·i·ma·tize (lə jit′ə mə tīz), *v.t.,* **-tized, -tiz·ing.** to legitimate.

le·git·i·mism (lə jit′ə miz əm), *n.* the principles or views of legitimists; support of legitimate authority, especially of a claim to a throne based on direct descent.

le·git·i·mist (lə jit′ə mist), *n.* **1.** a supporter of legitimate authority, especially of claims to rule based on direct descent. **2.** Also, **Legitimist.** (In Europe in the 1800's), a member of any of various monarchist or reactionary groups, as the supporters of Metternich in Austria, or of the Bourbons, Hapsburgs, etc.: *The legitimists opposed him because they were loyal to the descendants of Charles X* (André Maurois). —*adj.* of or having to do with legitimists; expressing the views of legitimists.

le·git·i·mis·tic (lə jit′ə mis′tik), *adj.* favoring the opinions of the legitimists.

le·git·i·mi·za·tion (lə jit′ə mə zā′shən), *n.* legitimation.

le·git·i·mize (lə jit′ə mīz), *v.t.,* **-mized, -miz·ing.** to make or declare to be legitimate. *The notary's stamp legitimized the deed.*

leg·len (leg′lən), *n. Scottish.* a milk pail. [perhaps variant of *laggin*]

leg·less (leg′lis), *adj.* having no legs; without legs. —**leg′less·ness,** *n.*

leg·let (leg′lit), *n.* **1.** a little leg. **2.** an ornamental ring or band for the leg.

leg·man (leg′man′), *n., pl.* **-men. 1.** a newspaper reporter who gathers information by going to the scene of the news: *Where editors once sent legmen out chasing ambulances . . . some of them are sending their best men out to dig up the background to the news* (Maclean's). **2.** a person who delivers messages, gathers information, or does other legwork: *He was an older attorney's legman* (Time).

leg-of-mut·ton (leg′əv mut′ən), *adj.* having the shape of a leg of mutton; wide at one end and narrow at the other: *a leg-of-mutton sleeve.*

Leg-of-mutton Sleeve, worn about 1895

leg-of-mutton sail, a triangular sail having its head at the masthead, and not set on a gaff or yard.

leg-o'-mut·ton (leg′ə-mut′ən), *adj.* leg-of-mutton.

le·gong or **Le·gong** (le′gông), *n.* a classical Balinese dance which tells a story. The dance is performed by two small girls. [< Balinese *légong*]

leg-pull (leg′pu̇l′), *n. Informal.* an act of fooling, tricking, or ridiculing; hoax; practical joke: *He found it hard to persuade them that his call for help was not another leg-pull* (New Scientist).

leg-pull·er (leg′pu̇l′ər), *n. Informal.* a person who fools, tricks, or makes fun of one.

leg-pull·ing (leg′pu̇l′ing), *n. Informal.* the act or practice of fooling, tricking, or ridiculing.

Le·gree (li grē′), *n.* **Simon,** any harsh, cruel, or demanding employer, superior officer, etc.; taskmaster: *The top sergeant was a regular Simon Legree.* [< Simon Legree, a cruel and brutal slave overseer in Harriet Beecher Stowe's *Uncle Tom's Cabin*]

leg·room (leg′rüm′, -ru̇m′), *n.* enough space to extend one's legs when seated, especially in an automobile, airplane, or the like: *The middle person in the front or back seat will have full legroom* (Time).

legs (legz), *n.pl.* See under **leg,** *n.*

leg stump, *Cricket.* the stump nearest the batsman.

le·guan (lə gwän′), *n.* iguana. [perhaps < French *l'iguane* the iguana]

leg·ume (leg′yüm, li gyüm′), *n.* **1.** a plant having a number of seeds in a pod, such as beans or peas. Many legumes can absorb nitrogen from the air. **2. a.** the seed pod of such a plant. **b.** the fruit or edible portion of such a pod: *A peanut is really a legume, not a nut.* **3.** *Botany.* a dry, several-seeded fruit, characteristic of plants of the pea family. It is formed of a single carpel, which is dehiscent by both sutures and so divides into two valves, the seeds being borne at the inner or ventral suture only.
legumes, vegetables used for food: *The dry edible fruit and other species of food, which we call by the general name of legumes* (Benjamin Jowett).
[< Middle French *légume,* learned borrowing from Latin *legūmen*]

le·gu·min (li gyü′min), *n. Biochemistry.* a globulin found in leguminous seeds. [< *legum*(e) + *-in*]

le·gu·mi·nous (li gyü′mə nəs), *adj.* **1.** of or bearing legumes. **2.** of the pea family.

leg-up (leg′up′), *n. Informal.* help; assistance: *Other sections of the shipping industry . . . are not scheduled to receive any . . . financial leg-up from the government* (New Yorker). *They expect me to give them a leg-up* (Robert Graves).

leg·work (leg′wėrk′), *n.,* or **leg work,** work which involves much moving about or traveling, usually in pursuit of information; the work of a legman: *Government agencies revealed they were spending around $10 million annually to assist the Washington press corps with its legwork* (Newsweek).

lehr (lir), *n.* an oven used for annealing glass. [origin uncertain]

le·hu·a (lā hü′ä), *n.* a hardwood tree of the myrtle family, found in Hawaii, Samoa, and other Pacific islands, having clusters of bright-red flowers. [< Hawaiian *lehua*]

lei[1] (lā), *n., pl.* **leis.** a wreath of flowers, leaves, etc., worn as an ornament around the neck or on the head: *He came ashore to a rousing welcome, complete with . . . hula dancers, a lei of red carnations . . .* (Time). [< Hawaiian *lei*]

Lei[1]

lei[2] (lā), *n.* plural of **leu.**

Leib·nitz·i·an (līp nit′sē ən), *adj.* of or having to do with the philosophy and works of Gottfried Wilhelm von Leibnitz: *My views in this book are very far from being Leibnitzian, but the problems with which I am concerned are most certainly Leibnitzian* (Norbert Wiener).

Leices·ter (les′tər), *n.* any of a breed of long-wooled sheep, originally of Leicestershire, England.

lei·o·my·o·ma (lī′ō mī ō′mə), *n., pl.* **-mas, -ma·ta** (-mə tə). a benign tumor composed of smooth muscle fiber. [< Greek *leîos* smooth + English *myoma*]

leish·man·i·a·sis (lēsh′mə nī′ə sis), *n., pl.* **-ses** (sēz). a disease most common in tropical areas, causing lesions and sores of the skin and mucous membranes. It is caused by a protozoan in the blood stream, and a more serious form, kala-azar, attacks internal organs. [< William B. *Leishman,* 1865-1926, a British army surgeon, who described it + *-iasis*]

leis·ter (lēs′tər), *n.* a rod with three or more prongs on the end, used for spearing fish. —*v.t.* to spear (fish) with such a rod. [< Scandinavian (compare Danish *lyster,* Old Icelandic *ljōstr* < *ljōsta* strike)] —**leis′ter·er,** *n.*

lei·sur·a·ble (lē′zhər ə bəl, lezh′ər-), *adj.* leisurely; deliberate.

lei·sur·a·bly (lē′zhər ə blē, lezh′ər-), *adv.* leisurely; deliberately.

lei·sure (lē′zhər, lezh′ər), *n.* **1.** time free from required work when a person may rest, amuse himself, and do the things he likes to do: *A busy man hasn't much leisure to read. 'Zounds! how has he the leisure to be sick In such a justling time?* (Shakespeare). **2.** the state of having time free: *a gentleman of leisure.*
at leisure, a. free; not busy: *to be at leisure to see a caller.* **b.** without hurry; taking plenty of time: *to proceed at leisure.*
at one's leisure, when one has leisure; at one's convenience: *Let me hear from you at your leisure.*
—*adj.* **1.** free; not busy: *leisure hours. A whole leisure Saturday afternoon was before him* (Longfellow). **2.** leisured: *the leisure class.*
[< Old French *leisir,* noun use of infinitive < Latin *licēre* be allowed; influenced by English *measure*]

lei·sured (lē′zhərd, lezh′ərd), *adj.* **1.** having ample leisure: *the leisured class of society.* **2.** leisurely: *He walked at a leisured pace.*

lei·sure·ful (lē′zhər fəl, lezh′ər-), *adj.* leisurely.

lei·sure·li·ness (lē′zhər lē nis, lezh′ər-), *n.* the quality or condition of being leisurely: *a leisureliness of pace* (New Yorker).

lei·sure·ly (lē′zhər lē, lezh′ər-), *adj., adv.* proceeding without hurry; taking plenty of time; deliberate: *to stroll leisurely through the park. He has written a slow-paced, leisurely, rambling, and discursive novel* (New York Times). —**Syn.** *adj.* See **slow.**

lei·sure-time (lē′zhər tīm′, lezh′ər-), *adj.* of, for, or during the time remaining after work: *leisure-time activities.*

lei·sure·wear (lē′zhər wãr′, lezh′ər-), *n.* casual clothes for leisure-time wear.

leit·mo·tif or **leit·mo·tiv** (līt′mō tēf′), *n.* **1.** a short passage in a musical composition, associated throughout the work with a certain person, situation, or idea. Richard Wagner first used the leitmotif in his operas. **2.** any recurrent theme or motif: *This is the leitmotif of the three novels, the stories of three tormented men* (Scientific American). [< German *Leitmotiv* (literally) leading motive]

lek (lek), *n.* the monetary unit of Albania, worth about 2 cents. [< Albanian *lek*]

lek·y·thos (lek′ə thos), *n., pl.* **-thoi** (-thoi). lecythus.

LEM (no periods), Lunar Excursion Module (a module designed to separate from a spacecraft near the lunar surface).

lem·an (lem′ən, lē′mən), *n. Archaic.* **1.** a lover; sweetheart: *He ... offered kingdoms unto her in view, To be his Leman and his Lady true* (Edmund Spenser). **2.** an unlawful lover or mistress. [Middle English *leofman* < Old English *lēof* dear + *man* person]

lem·ma[1] (lem′ə), *n., pl.* **lem·mas, lem·ma·ta** (lem′ə tə). **1.** *Mathematics.* a subsidiary or auxiliary proposition to be used in the proof of a main proposition. **2.** an argument, theme, subject, or gloss. [< Greek *lêmma, -atos* < *lēm-,* perfect stem of *lambánein* to take]

lem·ma[2] (lem′ə), *n. Botany.* the lower bract of the pair enclosing the flower in a spikelet of grass. [< Greek *lémma* < *lépein* to peel]

lem·ming (lem′ing), *n.* any of several small, mouselike arctic rodents having a short tail and furry feet. At periodic intervals some species undertake mass migrations which end when great numbers fling themselves into the sea, swim a short distance, and usually drown. [< Norwegian *lemming*]

Norwegian Lemming (about 5 in. long)

lem·na·ceous (lem nā′shəs), *adj.* belonging to the same family of plants as the duckweed. [< New Latin *Lemna* the duckweed genus (< Greek *lémna* a water plant) + English *-aceous*]

Lem·ni·an (lem′nē ən), *adj.* of or having to do with the island of Lemnos, in the northern Aegean Sea. —*n.* a native or inhabitant of Lemnos.

Lemnian earth or **bole,** a soft, astringent, clayey substance found on the island of Lemnos, and formerly much used for medicinal purposes; terra sigillata; sphragide.

lem·nis·cus (lem nis′kəs), *n., pl.* **-nis·ci** (-nis′ī). *Anatomy.* a band of nerve fibers in the mesencephalon. [< New Latin *lemniscus* < Latin *lēmniscus* a hanging ribbon < Greek *lēmnískos*]

lem·on (lem′ən), *n.* **1.** a sour, light-yellow citrus fruit of the rue family, growing in warm climates. The juice, used chiefly for flavoring and making beverages, yields citric acid; the rind yields oil or essence of lemons, used in cookery and perfumery. **2.** the thorny tree that bears this fruit. **3.** a clear pale-yellow color, like that of the rind of a ripe lemon. **4.** *Slang.* something disagreeable, unpleasant, or worthless: *A car, fan, refrigerator, or other manufactured product that does not work very well most of the time is sometimes referred to as a lemon.*
—*adj.* **1.** clear pale-yellow; lemon-colored. **2.** flavored with lemon.
[< Old French *limon* < Arabic *līmūn* < Persian] —**lem′on·like′,** *adj.*

Lemon Branch (def. 1)

lem·on·ade (lem′ə nād′), *n.* a drink made of lemon juice, sugar, and water. [< French *limonade* < Old French *limon;* see LEMON]

lemon balm, 1. an herb of the mint family whose leaves have a flavor like that of lemon. **2.** the leaves of this herb, used for seasoning.

lem·on·col·or (lem′ən kul′ər), *n.* a clear, pale, yellow color.

lem·on·col·ored (lem′ən kul′ərd), *adj.* having a lemon-color.

lemon drop, a small, hard candy made of sugar and flavored with lemon.

lemon geranium, a common garden geranium, whose leaves have a lemonlike odor.

lemon grass, a cultivated perennial grass, the source of an essential oil, lemon grass oil, used in perfumes, flavorings, etc., for its strong scent of fresh lemon.

lem·on·ish (lem′ə nish), *adj.* resembling the color or taste of lemon.

lemon oil, an essential oil obtained from the rind of lemons.

lemon shark, a common, yellowish shark of warm, shallow waters on the Atlantic coasts of North and South America.

lemon sole, any of various soles or flatfishes used for food, especially a small variety of European sole.

lemon squash, *British.* lemonade made with carbonated water.

lemon verbena, a small South American garden shrub of the verbena family, whose long, slender leaves have a lemonlike odor.

lem·on·wood (lem′ən wůd′), *n.* **1. a.** a tropical American tree of the madder family with hard, strong wood. **b.** its wood, used especially for making bows. **2.** an evergreen shrub or tree of South Africa, belonging to the madder family, sometimes growing to a height of 20 to 30 feet and having a hard, tough wood. **3.** the tarata tree of New Zealand.

lem·on·y (lem′ə nē), *adj.* lemonlike, as in taste or smell: *lemony iced tea* (New Yorker).

lem·pi·ra (lem pē′rä), *n.* the monetary unit or gold coin of Honduras, worth about 50 cents. [< American Spanish *lempira* < *Lempira,* a department in Honduras, named for a native chief]

le·mur (lē′mər), *n.* any of certain small mammals somewhat like a monkey, but having a foxlike face and woolly fur. Lemurs live in trees, mainly in Madagascar, and hunt at night. They are probably similar to an ancestor of the primates. [< New Latin *lemures,* plural < Latin *lemurēs* specters, ghosts (because of their appearance and nocturnal habits)]

Ruffed Lemur (including tail, about 4 ft. long)

lem·u·res (lem′yə rēz), *n.pl. Roman Mythology.* the spirits of the departed; nocturnal spirits. [< Latin *lemurēs;* see LEMUR]

Le·mur·i·a (li myůr′ē ə), *n.* a legendary lost continent supposed to have sunk beneath the Indian Ocean. [because it was supposed to be where lemurs originated]

lem·u·rine (lem′yə rīn, -yər in), *adj., n.* lemuroid.

lem·u·roid (lem′yə roid), *adj.* of or like the lemurs. —*n.* a lemur.

Len·a·pe (len′ə pē; lə nä′pē), *n., pl.* **-pe** or **-pes.** Delaware (defs. 1a, b).

Le·nard rays (lā′närt), cathode rays which have passed through the window of a Lenard tube. [< Philipp von *Lenard,* 1862-1947, a German physicist]

Lenard tube, a special form of vacuum tube containing a diaphragm or window of aluminum through which cathode rays pass to the outside.

lend (lend), *v.,* **lent, lend·ing,** *n.* —*v.t.* **1.** to let another have or use for a time: *Will you lend me your bicycle for an hour?* **2.** to give the use of (money) for a fixed or specified amount of payment: *Banks lend money and charge interest.* **3.** to give for a time; give: *A becoming dress lends charm to a girl. The Salvation Army is quick to lend aid in time of disaster.* —*v.i.* to make a loan or loans: *A person who borrows should be willing to lend.*
lend itself or **oneself to,** to help or be suitable for: *to lend oneself to the schemes of others. This subject lends itself admirably to dramatic treatment.*
—*n. Informal.* a loan: *He got the lend of my best suit of clothes* (John Galt).
[Middle English *lenen,* Old English *lǣnan* < *lǣn* loan; the *-d* is < *lende,* the Middle English past tense, influenced by *rend, send*] —**lend′er,** *n.*
—**Syn.** *v.t.* **3.** bestow, impart, afford, grant.
➔ See **loan** for usage note.

lend·a·ble (len′də bəl), *adj.* that can be loaned; available for loan: *When lendable funds are plentiful, banks often relax enforcement of compensating balance rules* (Wall Street Journal).

lend·ing (len′ding), *n.* **1.** the act of a person or thing that lends. **2.** something borrowed, or not one's own.

lending library, a public library that permits books to be borrowed.

lend-lease (lend′lēs′), *n., v.,* **-leased, -leasing,** *adj.* —*n.* a policy of making a loan to an allied country of certain equipment in which the lender is superior, and of receiving some service or material in return. The United States used this policy in World War II to bolster the strength of its allies. —*v.t.* to send as a loan under such a policy. —*adj.* of or having to do with such a policy.

Lend-Lease Act, an act passed on March 11, 1941, enabling the President of the United States to give material aid to any nation whose defense he felt vital to United States security.

le·nes (lē′nēz), *n.* plural of **lenis.**

length (lengkth, length), *n.* **1.** how long a thing is; a thing's measurement from end to end; the longest way a thing can be measured: *the length of a rope. The carp ... will grow to a very great bigness and length* (Izaak Walton). **2.** the distance a thing extends: *an arm's length. The length of a race is the distance run. I might ... have gone the length of a ... street* (Daniel Defoe). **3.** an extent in time: *the length of an hour, the length of a visit, a speech, or a book.* **4.** a long stretch or extent: *Large lengths of seas and shores Between my father and my mother lay* (Shakespeare). **5.** a piece or portion of given length: *a length of rope, a dress length of silk.* **6.** the distance from end to end of a boat, horse, etc., as a unit of measurement in racing: *The gray horse finished the race two lengths ahead of the brown one.* **7.** the quality or fact of being long: *Such customs have their force, only from length of time* (Thomas Hobbes). **8.** *Prosody.* the force with which a syllable or vowel is spoken, or the way it is pronounced. **9.** *Phonetics.* **a.** duration of sounds; quantity. **b.** vowel distinction, as between ā and a.
at full length, with the body fully stretched out flat: *The snake lay at full length on the rock, sunning itself.*
at length, a. at last; finally: *They ... pressed for admittance ... which at length was granted them* (George Washington). **b.** with all the details; in full: *to describe something at length.*

go (to) any length or **lengths,** to do everything possible: *I will go to any length to help you. He would go . . . any lengths for his party* (Benjamin Disraeli).
keep at arm's length. See under **arm**[1].
measure one's length, to fall, be thrown, or lie flat on the ground: *He lost his balance and measured his length upon the ground* (Dickens).
[Old English *length* < *lang* long[1]]
➤ The pronunciations (lenth) and (strenth) for **length** and **strength** occur both in America and in Great Britain, but are rare in educated use. Spellings reflecting this type of pronunciation are found as early as the 1300's; in the 1800's it was sometimes described as largely peculiar to Irish and Scottish speech.

length·en (lengk′thən, leng′-), *v.t.* to make longer: *A tailor can lengthen your trousers.* —*v.i.* to become or grow longer: *the shadows lengthening as the vapours rise* (John Dryden). *A child's legs lengthen a great deal between 5 and 10 years old.* —**length′en·er,** *n.*
—**Syn.** *v.t., v.i.* **Lengthen, extend, prolong** mean to make or become longer. **Lengthen** means to make or become longer in space or time: *There is no way to lengthen a day.* **Extend** means to stretch out beyond the present point or limits: *We had to extend the table for Thanksgiving.* **Prolong** means to lengthen in time beyond a normal, proper, or desirable limit: *She prolonged her visit.*

length·i·ly (lengk′thə lē, leng′-), *adv.* in a lengthy manner: *The formal findings of the . . . Commission against him were lengthily published* (Harper's). [American English < *length* + *-ly*[1]]

length·i·ness (lengk′thē nis, leng′-), *n.* the quality of being lengthy.

length·ways (lengkth′wāz′, length′-), *adv., adj.* lengthwise.

length·wise (lengkth′wīz′, length′-), *adv.* in the direction of the length: *He cut the cloth lengthwise.* —*adj.* following the direction of the length; longitudinal.

length·y (lengk′thē, leng′-), *adj.,* **length·i·er, length·i·est. 1. a.** having unusually great length; long. **b.** (of speeches, a speaker, a writer, etc.) too long; longwinded; tedious: *His explanation was clear but lengthy, and his listeners lost interest.* **2.** very tall (a humorous use). **3.** (in technical use, of some animals) long in the body. [American English < *length* + *-y*[1]] —**Syn. 1. b.** prolix.

len·ience (lēn′yəns, lē′nē əns), *n.* mildness; leniency.

len·ien·cy (lēn′yən sē, lē′nē ən-), *n.* mildness; gentleness; mercy: *When you have gone too far to recede, do not sue to me for leniency* (Dickens). —**Syn.** indulgence, tolerance.

len·ient (lēn′yənt, lē′nē ənt), *adj.* **1.** mild; gentle; tolerant; merciful: *a lenient ruler. My father was always very strict about my being on time for meals, but my mother was more lenient.* **2.** *Archaic.* softening, soothing, or relaxing: *Old Time . . . upon these wounds hath laid His lenient touches* (Wordsworth). [< Latin *lēniēns, -entis,* present participle of *lēnīre* soften < *lēnis* mild] —**len′ient·ly,** *adv.* —**Syn. 1.** compassionate, forbearing, indulgent. **2.** emollient.

len·i·fy (len′ə fī), *v.t.,* **-fied, -fy·ing.** *Rare.* to soften, soothe, or mitigate: *to lenify the pain* (John Dryden). [< Latin *lēnis* soft, mild + English *-fy*]

Len·i-Len·a·pe (len′ē len′ə pē, -lə nä′pē), *n., pl.* **-pe** or **-pes.** Lenape.

Len·in·ism (len′i niz əm), *n.* the political and economic principles of V. I. Lenin, adaptations of Marxist theory. Leninism stresses the belief that, although communism is historically inevitable as Marx thought, it must be guided by a well-disciplined core of "professional revolutionaries." [< Vladimir I. *Lenin* (born Ulyanov), 1870-1924, a Russian revolutionary leader, and chief founder of the Soviet Union + English *-ism*]

Len·in·ist (len′i nist), *n.* a believer in or supporter of Leninism. —*adj.* believing in or supporting Leninism: *Tossed into discard was the Leninist tenet that while capitalism exists, wars are an inevitability* (Newsweek).

Len·in·ite (len′i nīt), *n., adj.* Leninist.

le·nis (lē′nis), *adj., n., pl.* **le·nes** (lē′nēz). *Phonetics.* —*adj.* articulated with relatively little muscular tension and force. In English, *b, d, v, z* are generally lenis in comparison with *p, t, f,* and *s,* which are fortis. —*n.* a lenis consonant. [earlier *lene* < Latin *lēnis* smooth, soft]

le·ni·tion (li nish′ən), *n. Phonetics.* the gradual lessening of the force with which a consonant is articulated, sometimes leading to change or loss. [< German *Lenition* < Latin *lēnīre* soften]

len·i·tive (len′ə tiv), *adj.* **1.** softening; mitigating. **2.** (of medicines, etc.) tending to relieve; soothing: *Aspirin is a lenitive medicine.* **3.** mildly laxative.
—*n.* **1.** anything that soothes or softens; palliative. **2.** a soothing medicine or application: *Tranquilizers are lenitives.* **3.** a mild laxative.
[< Medieval Latin *lenitivus* < Latin *lēnīre* to soften]

len·i·ty (len′ə tē), *n., pl.* **-ties. 1.** mildness; gentleness; mercifulness: *His Majesty gave many marks of his great lenity, often . . . endeavouring to extenuate your crimes* (Jonathan Swift). **2.** an instance of this. [< Middle French *lénité,* learned borrowing from Latin *lēnitās* < *lēnis* mild] —**Syn. 1.** leniency.

Len·ni-Len·a·pe (len′ē len′ə pē, -lə nä′pē), *n., pl.* **-pe** or **-pes.** Lenape.

le·no (lē′nō), *n.* **1.** a textile weave in which the warp threads alone intersect and are bound in position by the weft threads. **2.** an open-weave cotton gauze used for caps, veils, curtains, etc. [perhaps alteration of French *linon*]

lens (lenz), *n., pl.* **lens·es. 1.** a piece of glass, or something like glass, that brings closer together or sends wider apart the rays of light passing through it. The lens of a camera forms images; the lenses of a telescope make things look larger and nearer. **2.** a combination of two or more of these pieces, especially as used in a camera. **3.** *Anatomy.* a clear, oval structure in the eye directly behind the iris, that directs light rays upon the retina. See picture under **accommodation. 4.** a device to focus radiations other than those of light. **5.** *Geology.* a layer of uniform sedimentary material that becomes progressively thinner along its edges. [< Latin *lēns, lentis* lentil (which has a biconvex shape)]

Lenses (def. 1)
From left to right: convexo-concave, concavo-convex, convexo-convex, convex surface opposite a plane, concavo-concave, concave surface opposite a plane

lensed (lenzd), *adj.* having a lens or lenses.

lens hood, *Photography.* any of various tube-shaped devices with blackened surfaces, attached to a lens to keep stray light from striking it.

lens·less (lenz′ləs), *adj.* having no lens or lenses.

lens·man (lenz′mən), *n., pl.* **-men.** *Informal.* a photographer: *One of the nation's top amateur lensmen* (Newsweek).

lent (lent), *v.* the past tense and past participle of **lend:** *I lent you my pencils. He had lent me his eraser.*

Lent (lent), *n.* **1.** the solemn Christian religious season from Ash Wednesday to Easter, forty weekdays kept as a time for fasting and repenting of sins; Quadragesima. **2.** *Obsolete.* (in the Middle Ages) any season of religious fasting. [Old English *lencten* spring < *lang* long[1] (probably because of its lengthening days)]

len·ta·men·te (len′tə men′tā), *adv. Music.* slowly (used as a direction). [< Italian *lentamente* < *lento* lento]

len·tan·do (len tän′dō), *adj. Music.* becoming slower (used as a direction). Also, **slentando.** [< Italian *lentando* (literally) present participle of *lentare* slow down, ultimately < Latin *lentus* slow]

Lent·en or **lent·en** (len′tən), *adj.* **1.** of Lent; during Lent; suitable for Lent. **2.** such as may be used in Lent; meager; plain; dismal or somber. [Old English *lencten;* see LENT]

Lenten rose, a perennial herb of the crowfoot family, native to Asia Minor, with showy green to purple flowers that bloom before spring.

len·ti·cel (len′tə sel′), *n. Botany.* a usually lens-shaped body of cells formed in the corky layer of bark, which serves as a pore for the exchange of gases between the plant and the atmosphere. [< French *lenticelle,* or New Latin *lenticella* (diminutive) < Latin *lēns, lentis* lentil (because of its shape)]

len·ti·cel·late (len′tə sel′āt), *adj.* producing lenticels.

len·tic·u·lar (len tik′yə lər), *adj.* **1.** of or having to do with a lens, especially that of the eye. **2.** having the form of a double-convex lens, as some seeds; convexo-convex; biconvex. **3.** resembling a lentil or double-convex lens in size or form. [< Latin *lenticulāris* < Latin *lenticula* (diminutive) < *lēns, lentis* lentil] —**len·tic′u·lar·ly,** *adv.*

lenticular nucleus, *Anatomy.* the lower gray nucleus in the corpus striatum at the base of the brain.

len·ti·cule (len′tə kyül), *n.* one of a large number of cylindrical embossings on black-and-white film that act as lenses to reproduce color images under certain kinds of projection, especially for television. [< Latin *lenticula;* see LENTICULAR]

len·ti·form (len′tə fôrm), *adj.* lenticular.

len·tig·i·nose (len tij′ə nōs), *adj.* lentiginous.

len·tig·i·nous (len tij′ə nəs), *adj. Medicine.* freckled.

len·ti·go (len tī′gō), *n., pl.* **-tig·i·nes** (-tij′ə nēz). *Medicine.* **1.** a freckle. **2.** a freckly condition. [< Latin *lentīgo, -inis* freckle, round red spot < *lēns, lentis* lentil]

len·til (len′təl), *n.* **1.** an annual plant of the pea family, whose pods contain two seeds shaped like double-convex lenses, growing mostly in southern Europe, Egypt, and Asia. **2.** the seed of this plant. Lentils are eaten like peas or in a soup. [< Old French *lentille* < Vulgar Latin *lentīcula* < Latin *lenticula* (diminutive) < *lēns, lentis* lentil]

len·tis·cus (len tis′kəs), *n., pl.* **-tis·cus·es, -tis·ci** (-tis′ī). the mastic tree. [< Latin *lentiscus*]

len·tisk (len′tisk), *n.* lentiscus.

len·tis·si·mo (len tis′ə mō), *Music.* —*adj.* very slow (used as a direction). —*adv.* very slowly. [< Italian *lentissimo,* superlative of *lento* lento]

len·ti·tude (len′tə tüd, -tyüd), *n.* slowness; sluggishness. [< Latin *lentitūdo* slowness < *lentus* slow]

len·to (len′tō), *Music.* —*adj.* slow (used as a direction). —*adv.* slowly. [< Italian *lento* slow < Latin *lentus* slow, lasting, flexible]

len·toid (len′toid), *adj.* lens-shaped. [< Latin *lēns, lentis* (see LENS) + English *-oid*]

l'en·voi or **l'en·voy** (len′voi, len voi′), *n.* **1.** a short, concluding stanza, usually of a ballade. **2.** a postscript to a prose work, giving a moral, dedication, etc. [< Middle French *l'envoi* < *le* the + *envoi* a sending]

Lenz's law (len′zəz, lent′səz), *Physics.* the law that an induced electric current creates a magnetic field that opposes the action of the force that produces the current. [< Heinrich F.E. *Lenz,* a German physicist]

Le·o (lē′ō), *n., genitive* (*def. 1*) **Le·o·nis. 1.** a northern constellation between Cancer and Virgo, originally thought of as arranged in the shape of a lion. **2.** the fifth sign of the zodiac. The sun enters Leo July 23. *Symbol:* ♌. [< Latin *Leō, -ōnis* (literally) the lion < Greek *léōn, léontos*]

Leo Minor, *genitive* **Le·o·nis Mi·no·ris.** a northern constellation south of Ursa Major.

Le·o·nar·desque (lē′ə när desk′), *adj.* in or resembling the style of Leonardo da Vinci.

le·o·ne (lē ō′nē), *n.* **1.** a unit of money in Sierra Leone, worth about $1.40. **2.** a coin equal to one leone.

Le·o·nid (lē′ə nid), *n., pl.* **Le·o·nids, Le·on·i·des** (li on′ə dēz). one of a shower of meteors formerly occurring about November 14. The Leonids, no longer seen, seemed to come from the constellation Leo.

le·o·nine (lē′ə nīn), *adj.* of a lion; like a lion: *The dog's tawny color and heavy coat gave him an almost leonine appearance.* [< Latin *leōnīnus* < *leō, -ōnis* lion; see LEO]

Le·o·nine (lē′ə nīn), *adj.* of or having to do with some person named Leo, Leonius, or Leoninus.

leonine partnership, a partnership in which one partner has all the profits and none of the losses.

Le·o·nines (lē′ə nīnz), *n.pl.* Leonine verse.

Leonine verse, a kind of Latin verse consisting of hexameters or alternate hexameters and pentameters, in which the last word of the line rhymes with the word immediately preceding the middle caesura.

Le·o·nis (lē ō′nis), *n.* genitive of **Leo** (the constellation).

Leonis Mi·no·ris (mi nôr′is, -nōr′-), genitive of **Leo Minor.**

Le·on strain (lē′on), one of the three known types of virus causing polio. The other two are the Brunhilde and Lansing strains. [< *Leon,* the name of a young victim of the disease]

le·on·ti·a·sis (lē′on tī′ə sis), *n., pl.* **-ses** (-sēz). *Medicine.* a form of leprosy in which the face becomes bloated and wrinkled, thus appearing more or less leonine. [< Greek *léōn, léontos* lion + English *-iasis*]

leop·ard (lep′ərd), *n.* **1.** a large, fierce feline mammal of Africa and Asia that has a dull-yellowish skin spotted with black. **2.** any of various animals related to the leopard, as the jaguar or American leopard, the cheetah or hunting leopard, and the ounce or snow leopard. **3.** the fur of any of these leopards. **4.** (in heraldry) a lion shown walking with the dexter front paw raised and looking directly at the spectator, as in the royal arms of England.

Leopard (def. 1) (including tail, about 8 ft. long)

the leopard cannot change its spots, it is impossible to change inborn traits or inveterate habits (in allusion to Jeremiah 13:23): *[They] have maintained in effect that the leopard cannot change its spots and that the new Germany was really no different from the old* (New York Times).

[< Old French *leupart, lebard,* learned borrowing from Late Latin *leopardus* < Greek *leópardos* < *léōn* lion + *párdos* leopard, pard[2]]

leopard cat, 1. a wild, spotted cat of India and the Malay Archipelago. **2.** ocelot.

leop·ard·ess (lep′ər dis), *n.* a female leopard.

leopard frog, a spotted frog common in North America and found as far south as Panama.

leopard man, an African fanatic or ritual murderer who mutilates his victim as if by a leopard's claws.

leop·ard's-bane (lep′ərdz bān′), *n.* a composite herb with yellow flowers; doronicum.

leopard seal, sea leopard.

leop·ard·skin (lep′ərd skin′), *n.* **1.** the pelt of a leopard. **2.** leather made from the skin of a leopard.

le·o·tard (lē′ə tärd), *n.* **1.** a tight-fitting, one-piece garment, with or without sleeves, worn by dancers, acrobats, etc. **2.** Also, **leotards.** tights. [< French *léotard* < Jules *Léotard,* a French aerialist of the 1800's]

Lep·cha (lep′chə), *n., pl.* **-cha** or **-chas.** one of an aboriginal people of Mongoloid extraction living in the Himalayan border states.

lep·er (lep′ər), *n.* a person who has leprosy. [Middle English *lepre* leprosy < Old French, learned borrowing from Late Latin *leprae,* plural < Latin *lepra* < Greek *lépra* < *lépein* to peel, scale off]

leper house, a hospital or asylum for lepers; lazar house.

le·pid·o·lite (lə pid′ə līt, lep′ə də-), *n.* a mineral, a variety of mica containing lithium, commonly occurring in lilac, rose-colored, or grayish-white scaly masses. [< Greek *lepís, -ídos* scale[1] + English *-lite*]

lep·i·dop·ter (lep′ə dop′tər), *n.* a lepidopterous insect.

lep·i·dop·ter·al (lep′ə dop′tər əl), *adj.* lepidopterous.

lep·i·dop·ter·an (lep′ə dop′tər ən), *adj.* lepidopterous. —*n.* a lepidopterous insect.

lep·i·dop·ter·id (lep′ə dop′tər id), *n.* a lepidopterous insect. —*adj.* lepidopterous.

lep·i·dop·ter·ist (lep′ə dop′tər ist), *n.* an expert on, or collector of, moths and butterflies.

lep·i·dop·ter·o·log·i·cal (lep′ə dop′tər ə-loj′ə kəl), *adj.* of or having to do with the scientific study or collection of moths and butterflies: *The varicolored butterflies all had their lepidopterological names on the program* (New Yorker). —**lep′i·dop′ter·o·log′i·cal·ly,** *adv.*

lep·i·dop·ter·ol·o·gy (lep′ə dop′tə rol′ə-jē), *n.* the scientific study of moths and butterflies.

lep·i·dop·ter·on (lep′ə dop′tər on), *n., pl.* **-ter·a** (-tər ə). lepidopter.

lep·i·dop·ter·ous (lep′ə dop′tər əs), *adj.* belonging to the large group of insects including butterflies and moths. The larvae are wormlike; the adults have four broad wings more or less covered with small scales, and a proboscis for sucking. [< New Latin *Lepidoptera* the order name (< Greek *lepís, -ídos* a scale[1] + *pterón* wing, feather) + English *-ous*]

lep·i·do·si·ren (lep′ə dō sī′rən), *n.* any of various eellike lung fishes of South American swamps. [< Greek *lepís, -ídos* a scale[1] + English *siren*]

lep·i·dote (lep′ə dōt), *adj. Botany.* covered with scurfy scales; leprose. [< New Latin *lepidotus* < Greek *lepidōtós* < *lepís, -ídos* a scale[1] < *lépein* to peel]

lep·o·rid (lep′ər id), *n.* any of the group of mammals which consists of the rabbits and hares. [< New Latin *Leporidae* the family name < Latin *lepus, -oris* hare]

lep·o·rine (lep′ə rīn, -ər in), *adj.* of or like a hare. [< Latin *leporīnus* < *lepus, -oris* hare]

Lep·o·ris (lep′ər is), *n.* genitive of **Lepus.**

lep·ra (lep′rə), *n. Medicine.* leprosy. [< Greek *lépra;* see LEPER]

lep·re·chaun (lep′rə kôn), *n. Irish Legend.* a sprite or goblin resembling a little old man, who can be made to reveal buried treasure if he is caught: *But now all the leprechauns and all the four-leafed clover could not stop the destruction wrought by the English* (London Times). [< Irish *lupracan*]

lep·roid (lep′roid), *adj.* resembling leprosy.

lep·rol·o·gist (lep rol′ə jist), *n.* an expert in leprous diseases.

lep·rol·o·gy (lep rol′ə jē), *n.* the scientific study of leprosy.

lep·rom·a·tous (lep rom′ə təs), *adj.* of or like a leprous sore.

lep·ro·sar·i·um (lep′rə sãr′ē əm), *n., pl.* **-sar·i·ums, -sar·i·a** (-sãr′ē ə). **1.** a hospital or institution for the care and treatment of lepers: *The Salvation Army maintains shelters for men, women, and children, hospitals, military canteens, leprosaria, and schools* (New York Times). **2.** a leper colony. [< Medieval Latin *leprosarium* < Late Latin *leprōsus;* see LEPROUS]

lep·rose (lep′rōs), *adj. Botany.* having a scaly or scurfy appearance, as certain lichens in which the thallus adheres to trees or stones like a scurf; lepidote. [< Late Latin *leprōsus* < Latin *lepra;* see LEPER]

lep·ro·ser·y (lep′rə ser′ē), *n., pl.* **-ser·ies.** leprosarium.

lep·ro·sy (lep′rə sē), *n., pl.* **-sies. 1.** a chronic, mildly infectious, bacterial disease, characterized by ulcers and white, scaly scabs; Hansen's disease. Leprosy attacks the nerves, causing weakening and wasting of muscles, and may lead to tuberculosis or other diseases. **2.** a wasting or decadent condition, as of the mind or spirit: . . . *the moral leprosy of the world we live in* (Emanuel Litvinoff). [perhaps < *leprous,* or perhaps noun use of Medieval Latin *leprosius,* for Late Latin *leprōsus* leprous]

lep·rous (lep′rəs), *adj.* **1.** having leprosy: *a leprous person.* **2.** of or like leprosy: *white, leprous scales.* **3.** scaly or scurfy: *One old leprous screen of faded Indian leather* (Dickens). **4.** causing leprosy. **5.** *Botany.* leprose. [< Old French *leprous,* learned borrowing from Late Latin *leprōsus* < Latin *lepra* leprosy; see LEPER] —**lep′rous·ly,** *adv.* —**lep′rous·ness,** *n.*

lep·to·dac·tyl (lep′tə dak′təl), *adj.* (of a bird) having slender toes. [< Greek *leptós* thin + *dáktylos* toe]

lep·to·dac·ty·lous (lep′tə dak′tə ləs), *adj.* leptodactyl.

lep·ton (lep′ton), *n., pl.* **-ta** (-tə). **1.** any of a class of light elementary particles that includes the neutrino, antineutrino, electron, positron, and mu-mesons. **2.** the smallest modern Greek coin, worth 1/100 of a drachma. [< Greek *leptón* (*nómisma*) small (coin), neuter of *leptós* thin, small]

lep·to·phyl·lous (lep′tə fil′əs), *adj.* slender-leaved. [< Greek *leptós* thin + *phýllon* leaf + English *-ous*]

lep·tor·rhine (lep′tər in), *adj. Anthropology.* having a long, narrow nose. [< Greek *leptós* thin + *rhīs, rhīnós* nose]

lep·to·some (lep′tə sōm), *n.* a person having a tall and spare build; an ectomorph. —*adj.* tall and spare; asthenic; ectomorphic: *A strain in the living population of East Africa . . . is most characterized by great attenuation: enormous stature, spindly legs, leptosome proportions, and delicate lines throughout* (Alfred L. Kroeber). [< Greek *leptós* thin + *sôma* body]

lep·to·spi·ro·sis (lep′tō spī rō′sis), *n.* an often fatal disease of livestock, dogs, rats, etc., that can be transmitted to man. It is caused by a spirochete and takes the form of a fever and, usually, infectious jaundice. [< New Latin *Leptospira* a genus of spirochetes that cause the disease (< Greek *leptós* thin + *speîra* coil) + English- *osis*]

lep·tus (lep′təs), *n., pl.* **-tus·es, -ti** (-tī). any of certain mites during the first larval stage when they have six legs. [< New Latin *Leptus* the genus name < Greek *leptós* thin, small]

Le·pus (lē′pəs), *n., genitive* **Lep·o·ris.** a southern constellation south of Orion. [< Latin *Lepus, -oris* (originally) hare]

Ler·nae·an (lėr nē′ən), *adj. Greek Mythology.* of Lake Lerna and the marshy district near Argos, Greece, the abode of the Hydra.

le roi est mort, vive le roi! (lə rwȧ′ e môr′ vēv′ lə rwȧ′), *French.* the king is dead, long live the king!

le roi le veut (lə rwȧ′ lə vœ′), *French.* the king wills it.

Les·bi·an (lez′bē ən), *n.* **1.** a homosexual woman. **2.** a native or inhabitant of the island of Lesbos.

—*adj.* **1.** having to do with homosexuality in women. **2.** of or having to do with the island of Lesbos. **3.** erotic.

[< *Lesbos* + *-ian* (because of the reputed homosexuality of the inhabitants there)]

Les·bi·an·ism (lez′bē ə niz′əm), *n.* homosexual relations between women.

lèse-ma·jes·té (lez′mȧ zhes tā′), *n. French.* lese-majesty.

lese-maj·es·ty (lēz′maj′ə stē), *n.,* or **lese majesty,** any crime or offense against the sovereign power in a state; treason. [< Middle French *lèse-majesté,* learned borrowing from Latin (*crīmen*) *laesae majestātis* (crime) of insulted sovereignty; *laesa,* feminine past participle of *laedere* to damage; *majestās* majesty]

le·sion (lē′zhən), *n.* **1.** an injury; hurt. **2.** *Medicine.* a diseased condition often causing a change in the structure of an organ or tissue. [< Latin *laesiō, -ōnis* injury < *laedere* to strike, damage]

L. ès L., *French.* Licencié ès Lettres (Licentiate in Letters).

Le·so·tho (lə sō′tō, -thō), *adj., n., pl.* **-thos.** —*adj.* of or having to do with Lesotho (the former Basutoland), its people, or their language. —*n.* a native or inhabitant of Lesotho.

les·pe·de·za (les′pə dē′zə), *n.* any of a group of plants of the pea family grown for forage and ornament, as the Japan clover. [< New Latin *Lespedeza* the genus name < *Lespedez,* a former Spanish governor of Florida]

less (les), *adj., comparative of* **little. 1.** not so much; not so well; smaller: *less noise, of less width. Eat less meat. I owe him little Duty and less Love* (Shakespeare). *Never be thy shadow less* (John Greenleaf Whittier). **2.** lower in age, rank, or importance: *no less a person than the President.*

—*n.* a smaller amount or quantity: *I could do no less. He refused to take less than $5.*

none the less, nevertheless: *Though Michelet's way was as alien as possible from their ways, his work remained valid none the less* (Edmund Wilson).

the less, a. something smaller (of two things compared): *Thou . . . wouldst . . . teach me how To name the bigger light, and how the less, That burn by day and night* (Shakespeare). **b.** he who is or they who are less, especially less important: *The less is blessed of the better* (Hebrews 7:7).

—*adv.* to a smaller extent or degree: *less talked of, less known, less important.*

—*prep.* lacking; without; minus: *five less two, a coat less one sleeve, a year less two days.*

[Old English *lǣssa,* adjective; *lǣs,* adverb]

➤ See **fewer** for another usage note.

-less, *suffix.* **1.** without; that has no ____: *Homeless = without a home.*

2. that does not: *Ceaseless = that does not cease.*

3. that cannot be ____ed: *Countless = that cannot be counted.*

[Old English *-lēas* < *lēas* free from, without]

➤ **-less** is freely added to almost any noun and many verbs to form adjectives with the above meanings.

L. ès Sc., *French.* Licencié ès Sciences (Licentiate in Sciences).

les·see (le sē′), *n.* a person to whom a lease is granted; a tenant under a lease.

les·see·ship (le sē′ship), *n.* the condition or position of a lessee.

less·en (les′ən), *v.i.* to grow less or apparently less; diminish: *The fever lessened during the night.* —*v.t.* **1.** to make less, especially in size; decrease; shrink. **2.** to represent as less; minimize; belittle: *to lessen the achievements of a rival.*

less·ened (les′ənd), *adj.* diminished.

less·en·ing (les′ə ning), *n.* the act or process of making or becoming less. —*adj.* **1.** growing less; diminishing. **2.** *Obsolete.* minimizing; belittling; disparaging.

less·er (les′ər), *adj.* **1.** the less important of two: *Both laziness and lying are wrong, but the first is clearly the lesser of the two evils.* **2.** smaller; less: *I have seen the cuckoo chased by lesser fowl* (Tennyson).

Lesser Bear, the northern constellation Ursa Minor.

lesser celandine, celandine (def. 2).

Lesser Dog, the northern constellation Canis Minor.

lesser doxology, the Christian prayer of praise beginning *Gloria Patri* (Glory be to the Father).

Lesser Lion, the northern constellation Leo Minor.

lesser multangular, a bone of the human wrist at the base of the forefinger in the distal row of carpal bones.

lesser omentum, a fold of the peritoneum between the stomach and the liver.

lesser panda, a slender, reddish-brown mammal of the Himalayas, related to and resembling the raccoon; panda.

lesser yellowlegs, a shore bird which breeds in Canada and Alaska, similar in appearance to the greater yellowlegs.

less·ness (les′nis), *n.* inferiority.

les·son (les′ən), *n.* **1.** something to be learned, taught, or studied: *Children study many different lessons in school.* **2.** a unit of learning or teaching; what is to be studied or practiced at one time: *to give a music lesson, to prepare a French lesson. Tomorrow we take the tenth lesson.* **3.** an instructive experience or example, serving to encourage or warn: *The accident taught me a lesson: always look before you leap. On my heart Deeply hath sunk the lesson thou has given* (William Cullen Bryant). **4.** a selection from the Bible or other sacred writing read as part of a church service. **5.** a rebuke; punishment; lecture: *The judge read the speeding driver a stiff lesson.*
—*v.t.* **1.** to give a lesson or lessons to; instruct; teach: *Well hast thou lesson'd us; this shall we do* (Shakespeare). **2.** to rebuke; admonish.
[< Old French *leçon* < Latin *lēctiō, -ōnis* a reading < *legere* read. Doublet of LECTION.]
—**Syn.** *n.* **5.** reprimand, admonition. *-v.t.* **2.** discipline.

les·sor (les′ôr, le sôr′), *n.* a person who grants a lease; a person who leases property to another.

lest (lest), *conj.* **1.** that —— not; for fear that; in order that —— not: *Be careful lest you fall from that tree.* **2.** that: *I was afraid lest he should come too late to save us.* [Old English (*thȳ*) *lǣs the* (literally) whereby less that]

Les·tri·go·ni·an (les′trə gō′nē ən), *n.* Laestrygonian.

le style, c'est l'homme (lə stēl′, se lôm′), *French.* the style is the man (shows what he really is).

let[1] (let), *v.*, **let, let·ting,** *n.* —*v.t.* **1.** to allow; permit: *Let the dog have a bone. She plumes her feathers, and lets grow her wings* (Milton). **2.** to allow to pass, go, or come: *to let a person on board a ship.* **3.** to allow to run out; allow (something) to escape: *Doctors used to let blood from people to lessen a fever.* **4. a.** to rent; hire out: *to let a boat by the hour, to let rooms to college students.* **b.** to assign or give out (a job) by contract for performance: *to let work to a contractor. In connection with the letting of private contracts for demolition of the Third Avenue Elevated Line . . .* (New York Times). **5.** *Let* is used as an auxiliary verb in giving suggestions or giving commands, etc.: *"Let's go home" means "I suggest that we go home." Let every man do his duty.* **6.** to suppose; assume: *Let the two lines be parallel.* **7.** *Obsolete.* to quit; abandon; forsake.
—*v.i.* to be rented or hired out: *That house lets for $80 a month.*
let alone, a. not to bother; not meddle with: *He is gentle as a lamb, if only he is let alone* (H. Rider Haggard). **b.** not to mention: *It would have been a hot day for July, let alone early April.*
let be. See under **be.**
let down, a. to lower: *He let the box down from the roof.* **b.** to slow up: *As her first enthusiasm wore off, she began to let down.* **c.** to disappoint: *Losing the job was bad enough, but even worse was the feeling that I had let my family down.* **d.** to humiliate: *Nothing in the world lets down a character more than that wrong turn* (Lord Chesterfield).
let go. See under **go**[1], *v.*
let in, to permit to enter; admit: *Let in some fresh air. I was let in at the back gate of a lovely house* (Sir Richard Steele).
let in for, to open the way to; cause (trouble, unpleasantness, etc.): *He let his friends in for a lot of questioning when he left town so suddenly.*
let in on, to share a confidence, secret, etc., with: *Once a strong voice in favor of tightly guarding U.S. scientific secrets, physicist Edward Teller . . . now thinks everyone should be let in on most classified information* (Time).
let know, to tell; inform: *Let me know when you arrive.*
let loose, to set free; release; let go: . . . *like so many bedlamites and demoniacs let loose* (Washington Irving). *He was let loose among the woods as soon as he was able to ride on horseback* (Joseph Addison).
let off, a. to allow to go free; excuse from punishment, service, etc.: *I will let Clavering off from that bargain* (Thackeray). **b.** to fire; explode: *On 1 August the Americans let off a hydrogen bomb* (New Scientist). **c.** to discharge; allow to get off: *This train stops to let off passengers on signal.*
let on, *Informal.* **a.** to allow to be known; reveal one's knowledge of: *The kids know too, but they never let on* (Time). *I was more taken aback . . . than I cared to let on* (Scott). **b.** to pretend; make believe: *He let on that he did not see me.*
let out, a. to permit to go out or escape; set free; release: *They oughtn't to have let you out of hospital so soon* (Graham Greene). **b.** to make larger or longer: *This skirt ought to be let out.* **c.** to rent: *We let out two rooms on the top floor.* **d.** *Informal.* to dismiss or be dismissed: *When does your class let out?* **e.** to make known; disclose; divulge: *to let out a secret.*
let up, *Informal.* to stop or pause: *We can go out when the storm lets up.*
let well enough alone, to be satisfied with existing conditions and not try to make them better or different: *He is the kind of worker who cannot leave well enough alone but must do each job perfectly.*
—*n. British.* a letting for hire or rent: *The sign said "House For Let."*
[Old English *lǣtan*]
➔ **let, leave.** A common substandard idiom is the use of *leave* where formal and informal English use *let.* Both idioms are shown in the following sentence by a writer who was obviously making a transition between the two levels: *By the time I got to high school, I was cured of the practice of leaving* [substandard] *notebooks go, but I fell immediately into the habit of letting* [general] *homework slide. Letting* should be used in the sentence above instead of *leaving.*

let[2] (let), *v.*, **let·ted** or **let, let·ting,** *n.* —*v.t. Archaic.* to stand in the way of; prevent; hinder; obstruct: *Mine ancient wound is hardly whole, And lets me from the saddle* (Tennyson). —*n.* **1. a.** *Archaic.* prevention; hindrance; stoppage; obstruction. **b.** something that hinders; an impediment: *That I may know the let, why gentle Peace Should not expel these inconveniences* (Shakespeare). **2.** an interference with the ball in tennis and similar games. The ball or point must be played over again.
without let or hindrance, with nothing to prevent, hinder, or obstruct: *He may hunt for his own amusement, without let or hindrance, throughout the year until September* (Atlantic).
[Old English *lettan* hinder < *lǣt* late]

-let, *suffix.* **1.** little, as in *booklet, hamlet, streamlet.*
2. thing worn as a band on, as in *anklet, armlet, wristlet.*
3. other meanings, as in *couplet, gauntlet, ringlet.*
[< Old French *-elet* < *-el* (< Latin *-ellus,* diminutive suffix, or < Latin *-ale* -al[1]) + *-et* -et]

l'é·tat, c'est moi (lā tá′ se mwá′), *French.* the state, it is I; I am the state (attributed to Louis XIV of France).

letch (lech), *n.* a yen; yearning; desire: *He develops a letch for an attractive Circassian lady* (New Yorker). [origin uncertain, perhaps a back formation from *lecher*]

let·down (let′doun′), *n.* **1.** a slowing up: *Middle age often brings a letdown in vitality. The talked about letdown in copper buying has not yet appeared* (Wall Street Journal). **2.** *Informal.* a disappointment: *Losing the contest was a big letdown for John.* **3.** humiliation. **4.** the approach of an aircraft toward a landing.
—*adj.* characterized by depression or dejection: *a letdown sensation.*

le·thal (lē′thəl), *adj.* causing death; deadly; mortal: *lethal weapons, a lethal dose of a drug.* —*n.* a lethal thing, especially a lethal factor or gene. [< Latin *lēthālis* < *lētum* death] —**le′thal·ly,** *adv.* —**Syn.** *adj.* fatal.

lethal chamber, 1. a chamber in which animals are put painlessly to death, as with deadly gases. **2.** the death chamber, as used in legal executions of criminals by means of gas.

lethal factor or **gene,** *Biology.* any gene, either dominant or recessive, which results in the premature death of the organism bearing it.

le·thal·i·ty (li thal′ə tē), *n.* the quality of being lethal; ability to cause death; deadliness: *Such an attack . . . could envelop an entire nation in lethality* (Saturday Review). *Means may be found to increase or decrease the lethality of the rays* (Science News Letter).

le·thar·gic (lə thär′jik), *adj.* **1.** unnaturally drowsy; sluggish; dull: *A hot, humid day makes most people feel lethargic.* **2.** producing lethargy. —**le·thar′gi·cal·ly,** *adv.* —**Syn. 1.** apathetic.

le·thar·gi·cal (lə thär′jə kəl), *adj.* lethargic.

lethargic encephalitis, a form of inflammation of the brain caused by a virus and characterized by extreme drowsiness or lethargy, sometimes followed by stupor or paralysis; sleeping sickness.

leth·ar·gize (leth′ər jīz), *v.t.*, **-gized, -giz·ing.** to affect with lethargy.

leth·ar·gy (leth′ər jē), *n., pl.* **-gies. 1.** drowsy dullness; lack of energy; sluggish inactivity: *to rouse the nation from its lethargy, to sink into the lethargy of indifference.* **2.** *Medicine.* a condition characterized by an unnatural drowsiness or prolonged sleep. [< Late Latin *lēthargia* < Greek *lēthargiā* < *lēthargos* forgetful < *lēthē* forgetfulness (see LETHE) + *argós* undone, unmade < *an* not + *érgon* work]
—**Syn. 1.** torpor, apathy, stupor.

Le·the (lē′thē), *n.* **1.** *Greek Mythology.* a river in Hades. Drinking its water caused forgetfulness of the past. **2.** forgetfulness; oblivion: *Till that the conquering wine hath steeped our sense In soft and delicate Lethe* (Shakespeare). [< Latin *Lēthē* < Greek *lēthē* oblivion < *lanthanésthai* escape notice, forget]

Le·the·an (li thē′ən), *adj.* **1.** having to do with Lethe or its water. **2.** causing forgetfulness: *daily labour's dull, Lethaean spring* (Matthew Arnold).

le·thif·er·ous (li thif′ər əs), *adj.* that causes or results in death; deadly: *lethiferous diseases.* [< Latin *lethifer* (< *lētum* death + *ferre* to carry, bring) + English *-ous*]

let·kiss (let′kis′), *n.* a kind of polka in which the partners kiss lightly at certain intervals

Le·to (lē′tō), *n. Greek Mythology.* the mother of Apollo and Artemis by Zeus. The Romans called her Latona.

let-off (let′ôf′, -of′), *n.* a letting off; release; exemption: *A light let-off that will be for the murderer* (Punch).

l'é·toile du nord (lā twál′ dʏ nôr′), *French.* the star of the north (Minnesota state motto).

let-out (let′out′), *n. British.* a means of escape or release, especially from a commitment; loophole: *This terminology gives a useful let-out in the event of a conflict* (Manchester Guardian Weekly).

le tout en·sem·ble (lə tü täɴ säɴ′blə), *French.* everything considered together.

let's (lets), let us.

Lett (let), *n.* **1.** a member of a group of people living in Latvia, Lithuania, Estonia, and Germany, related to the Lithuanians. **2.** their language; Lettish.

let·ta·ble (let′ə bəl), *adj.* that can be let or leased: *lettable floor space* (London Times).

let·ter[1] (let′ər), *n.* **1.** a mark or sign (on paper, etc.) that stands for any one of the sounds that make up words: *There are 26 letters in our alphabet.* **2.** a written or printed message: *Put a stamp on that letter. I'd teach them to . . . write their own letters, and read letters that are written to them* (Harriet Beecher Stowe). **3.** the exact wording; actual terms, as of a statement: *He kept the letter of the law but not the spirit.* **4.** *Printing.* **a.** a bit of metal type bearing a letter; a type. **b.** types; type. **c.** a particular style of type. **5.** the initial of a school, college, or other institution made of cloth and given to members of a team as an athletic trophy: *He is a 3-letter man; he has letters in football, basketball, and track.* **6.** a size of paper. **7.** an official document granting some right or privilege: *a letter of attorney.*

letters, a. literature; belles-lettres: *He has devoted his life to philosophy and letters. "The Revival of Letters" was the old term for the Renaissance.* **b.** knowledge of literature; literary culture: *Deign on the passing world to turn thine eyes, And pause awhile from letters to be wise* (Samuel Johnson). **c.** the profession of an author: *Letters kept pace with art* (William H. Prescott).

to the letter, just as one has been told; very exactly: *I carried out your orders to the letter.*

—*v.t.* **1.** to mark with letters: *Letter your answers from A through H.* **2.** to inscribe (something) in letters: *He lettered the notice very carefully.* —*v.i.* to make letters (on).

[< Old French *lettre* < Latin *littera*] —**let′ter·er,** *n.*

—**Syn.** *n.* **2. Letter, epistle** mean a written message. **Letter,** the general word, applies to any written, typed, or printed message, either personal, business, or official: *Please mail this letter for me.* **Epistle,** chiefly literary, applies to a long letter written in formal or elegant language, intended to teach or advise: *This year we are studying the epistles of some famous poets. The Epistles of the New Testament are Saint Paul's letters of advice to newly founded Christian churches.*

let·ter[2] (let′ər), *n.* a person who lets, especially a person who rents something. [< *let*[1] + *-er*[1]]

letter board, *Printing.* a board to arrange type on.

letter book, a book in which letters are filed, or in which copies of letters are kept for reference.

letter box, 1. a box in which letters are mailed or delivered; mailbox. **2.** a box in which letters are kept.

letter carrier, a person who collects or delivers mail; mailman; postman.

letter contract, a letter of intent: *The Air Force stressed that these three companies have actually been working "for a number of years" under preliminary letter contracts* (Wall Street Journal).

let·tered (let′ərd), *adj.* **1.** marked with letters. **2.** able to read and write; educated; literate: *lettered coxcombs without good breeding* (Sir Richard Steele). **3.** knowing literature; having literary culture; learned.

let·ter·gram (let′ər gram), *n.* a long telegram sent at a low rate because it is subject to the priority of regular telegrams; day letter or night letter. [< *letter* + (tele)*gram*]

let·ter·head (let′ər hed′), *n.* **1.** words printed at the top of a sheet of paper, usually a name and address. **2.** a sheet or sheets of paper printed with such a heading.

let·ter·head·ing (let′ər hed′ing), *n.* letterhead: *. . . letterheadings and other business stationery* (London Times).

let·ter·ing (let′ər ing), *n.* **1.** letters drawn, painted, stamped, etc. **2.** a marking with letters; making letters.

let·ter·less (let′ər lis), *adj.* **1.** without letters. **2.** unacquainted with letters or literature; illiterate.

let·ter·man (let′ər man′), *n., pl.* **-men.** an athlete who has won his letter in a sport.

letter of advice, a letter notifying the person addressed that: **a.** a consignment of goods has been made to him, or giving other specific information concerning a commercial shipment. **b.** a bill (of exchange) has been issued against him.

letter of credence, letters of credence.

letter of credit, 1. a document issued by a bank, allowing the person named in it to draw money up to a certain amount from other specified banks. **2.** a document issued by a banker, etc., at one place, authorizing the person to whom it is addressed to draw money up to a certain amount upon the issuer at another place, and promising to be responsible for the credit so extended.

letter of intent, a letter in which the signer declares his intention to buy, produce, deliver, etc., issued in advance of a formal contract: *Boeing has sold 134 [jet planes] to 11 airlines, either on firm contract or letter of intent* (Time).

letter of marque, letters of marque.

let·ter-per·fect (let′ər pėr′fikt), *adj.* **1.** knowing one's part or lesson perfectly: *to practice until one is letter-perfect.* **2.** correct in every detail: *letter-perfect copies.*

letter post, *British.* first-class matter.

let·ter·press (let′ər pres′), *n.* **1.** printed words, as distinguished from illustrations, etc.; print. **2.** printing from type, or from relief plates, as distinguished from offset, lithography, etc., or photogravure, and the like; relief printing.

letter press, a machine for making copies of letters.

let·ters (let′ərz), *n.pl.* See under **letter**[1], *n.*

letters credential, letters of credence.

letters of administration, *Law.* an instrument issued by a court or government official, giving an administrator of a dead person's estate authority to act.

letters of credence, a document accrediting a diplomatic agent to the government to which he is assigned.

letters of marque or **letters of marque and reprisal,** an official document giving a person permission from a government to capture the merchant ships of an enemy.

letters patent, an official document giving a person authority from a government to do some act or to have some right, as the exclusive rights to an invention.

letters testamentary, *Law.* an instrument issued by a court or government official giving an executor of a will authority to act.

let·ter·wood (let′ər wu̇d′), *n.* **1.** a South American tree with a beautifully mottled hard wood. **2.** the wood itself.

let·ter-writ·er (let′ər rī′tər), *n.* a person who writes letters as a profession or avocation: *. . . that inveterate letter-writer Saint Paul* (Manchester Guardian Weekly).

Let·tic (let′ik), *adj.* **1.** of, having to do with, or related to the Letts; Lettish. **2.** of or denoting the group of Indo-European languages that includes Lettish, Lithuanian, and Old Prussian; Baltic.

—*n.* **1.** the Lettish language. **2.** the Baltic division of Indo-European languages.

let·ting (let′ing), *n. Especially British.* a rental: *Any visitor can rent a room . . . and this summer the lettings will probably reach 50,000 guest-nights* (London Times).

Let·tish (let′ish), *adj.* of or having to do with the Letts or their language. —*n.* the Baltic language of the Letts.

let·tre de ca·chet (let′rə də kä shā′), *French.* **1.** a letter under the seal of the King of France, especially one ordering someone to be sent to prison or exile. **2.** an informer's letter.

let·tre de change (let′rə də shäNzh′), *French.* a bill of exchange.

let·tre de cré·ance (let′rə də krā äNs′), *French.* a letter of credit.

let·tuce (let′is), *n.* **1.** the large, crisp, green leaves of a garden plant of the composite family, much used in salad. **2.** the plant itself. There are many types of lettuce, including loose-leaf lettuce, and head varieties. **3.** any of various plants resembling lettuce. **4.** *Slang.* paper money: *It takes a lot of lettuce these days just to bring home the bacon* (Maclean's). [< Old French *laitues*, plural of *laitue* < Latin *lactūca* lettuce < *lac, lactis* milk (because of the milky juice of the plant)]

let·up (let′up′), *n. Informal.* a stop; pause: *There is going to be no letup in the kinds of pressure now going on until something is done* (New York Times). [American English < *let up*, verb phrase]

le·u (le′ü), *n., pl.* **lei** (lā). the monetary unit of Romania, worth about 16⅔ cents. Also, **ley.** [< Romanian *leu* (literally) lion < Latin *leō, -ōnis*]

leuc-, *combining form.* the form of **leuco-** before vowels, as in *leucine.* Also, **leuk-.**

leu·ce·mi·a (lü sē′mē ə, -sēm′yə), *n.* leukemia.

leu·cin (lü′sin), *n.* leucine.

leu·cine (lü′sēn, -sin), *n. Biochemistry.* a white, crystalline amino acid produced in several ways, especially by the digestion of proteins by the pancreatic enzymes. *Formula:* $C_6H_{13}NO_2$ [< *leuc-* + *-ine*[2]]

leu·cite (lü′sīt), *n.* a white or grayish mineral, a silicate of potassium and aluminum, found in certain volcanic rocks. *Formula:* $KAlSi_2O_6$ [< obsolete German *Leucit* < Greek *leukós* white + German *-it* -ite[1]]

leu·cit·ic (lü sit′ik), *adj.* of or like leucite.

leu·co (lü′kō), *adj. Chemistry.* of or designating a colorless or slightly colored substance formed by the reduction of a dye. It can be reconverted into the dye by the action of oxidizing agents: *a leuco base.* [< *leuco-*]

leuco-, *combining form.* white; without color: *Leucocyte = a white corpuscle or blood cell.* Also, **leuko-.** [< Greek *leukós*]

leu·co·ci·din (lü kō′sə din, lü′kə sī′-), *n.* a substance produced by staphylococci and certain other bacteria, that destroys white blood cells. [< *leuco-* + *-cide*[1] + *-in*]

leu·co·cyte (lü′kə sīt), *n.* one of the tiny, colorless cells in the blood that has a nucleus and destroys disease germs; white blood cell; white corpuscle. Normal blood contains five recognized types, the neutrophil, eosinophil, basophil, lymphocyte, and monocyte. Also, **leukocyte.**

leu·co·cy·thae·mi·a or **leu·co·cy·the·mi·a** (lü′kō sī thē′mē ə), *n.* leukemia. [< *leuco-* + Greek *kýtos* -cyte + *haîma* blood]

leu·co·cyt·ic (lü′kə sit′ik), *adj.* **1.** of or having to do with leucocytes. **2.** characterized by an excess of leucocytes.

leu·co·cy·to·sis (lü′kō sī tō′sis), *n.* an increase in the number of leucocytes or white blood cells. [< New Latin *leucocytosis* < English *leucocyte* + *-osis*]

leu·co·cy·tot·ic (lü′kō sī tot′ik), *adj.* of, having to do with, or characterized by leucocytosis.

leu·co·cy·to·zo·on infection (lü′kə sī′tə zō′on), a blood disease of domestic and wild birds, caused by an infection with a parasitic protozoan. [< *leucocyte* + Greek *zôion* small animal]

leu·co·der·ma (lü′kə dėr′mə), *n.* unnatural whiteness or white patches in the skin due to a deficiency of pigment. [< *leuco-* + Greek *dérma* skin]

leu·co·der·mic (lü′kə dėr′mik), *adj.* of or like leucoderma.

leu·co·ma (lü kō′mə), *n.* a white opacity in the cornea of the eye, caused by inflammation, a wound, etc. [< Greek *leúkōma* < *leukós* white]

leu·co·ma·ine (lü kō′mə ēn, -in), *n. Biochemistry.* any of a group of poisonous basic substances normally formed in living animal tissue as metabolic products.

leu·co·me·lan·ic (lü′kō mə lan′ik), *adj.* leucomelanous.

leu·co·mel·a·nous (lü′kō mel′ə nəs), *adj.* having a fair complexion and dark hair. [< *leuco-* + Greek *mélās, mélanos* (with English *-ous*) black, dark]

leu·co·pe·ni·a (lü′kə pē′nē ə), *n.* an abnormal decrease in the number of leucocytes or white blood corpuscles. [< *leuco-* + Greek *peniā* poverty]

leu·co·plast (lü′kə plast), *n. Botany.* one of the colorless bodies found mostly in underground plant storage cells and functioning in the formation of starch. [< *leuco-* + Greek *plastós* something molded]

leu·co·plas·tid (lü′kə plas′tid), *n.* leucoplast.

leu·co·poi·e·sis (lü′kō poi ē′sis), *n.* the production of leucocytes or white blood corpuscles. [< *leuco-* + Greek *poiēsis* production]

leu·cor·rhe·a or **leu·cor·rhoe·a** (lü′kə rē′ə), *n.* a whitish discharge of mucus or pus from the female genital organs. [< New Latin *leucorrhea* < Greek *leukós* white + *rhoiā* flux < *rheîn* to flow]

leu·co·sis (lü kō′sis), *n., pl.* **-ses** (-sēz). **1.** a virus disease of poultry, often characterized by paralysis, swelling of the liver and spleen, poor bone formation, blindness, or leukemia. **2.** leukemia. [< New Latin *leucosis* < Greek *leúkōsis* < *leukós* white]

leu·co·stic·te (lü′kə stik′tē), *n.* any of the rosy finches of western North America. [< New Latin *Leucosticte* the genus name < Greek *leukós* white + *stiktós* pricked]

leu·cot·o·mize (lü kot′ə mīz), *v.t.*, **-mized, -miz·ing.** to lobotomize.

leu·cot·o·my (lü kot′ə mē), *n., pl.* **-mies.** lobotomy. [< New Latin *leucotomia* < *leuco-* lobe of the brain (< Greek *leukós* white) + *-tomia* a cutting < Greek *-tomiā*]

leud (lüd), *n., pl.* **leuds, leu·des** (lü′dēz). a vassal in the Frankish kingdoms during the Middle Ages. [< Medieval Latin *leudes* < Old High German *liudi*]

leuk-, *combining form.* the form of **leuko-** before vowels.

leu·ke·mi·a or **leu·kae·mi·a** (lü kē′mē ə, -kēm′yə), *n.* a cancerous, usually fatal, disease characterized by a large excess of leucocytes or white blood cells in the blood. In some types there is an enlargement of the spleen, the lymph nodes, and other organs. Also, **leucemia.** [< New Latin *leukemia* < Greek *leukós* white + *haîma* blood]

leu·ke·mic or **leu·kae·mic** (lü kē′mik), *adj.* of, having to do with, or characteristic of leukemia: *In leukemia small doses of radiation administered to the whole body can kill many of the leukemic cells and relieve the distress of the disease* (Scientific American). —*n.* a person having leukemia: *Nineteen of the 24 leukaemics were positive, one was doubtful, and four were negative* (New Scientist).

leu·ke·mo·gen·ic (lü kē′mə jen′ik), *adj.* causing leukemia.

leu·ke·moid (lü kē′moid), *adj.* like leukemia; having symptoms resembling leukemia: *a leukemoid disease.* [< *leukem*(ia) + *-oid*]

leuko-, *combining form.* leuco-.

leu·ko·ci·din (lü kō′sə din, lü′kə sī′-), *n.* leucocidin.

leu·ko·cyte (lü′kə sīt), *n.* leucocyte.

leu·ko·cy·to·sis (lü′kō sī tō′sis), *n.* leucocytosis.

leu·ko·cy·tot·ic (lü′kō sī tot′ik), *adj.* leucocytotic.

leu·ko·der·ma (lü′kə dėr′mə), *n.* leucoderma.

leu·ko·ma (lü kō′mə), *n.* leucoma.

leu·ko·pe·ni·a (lü′kə pē′nē ə), *n.* leucopenia.

leu·ko·pla·ki·a (lü′kə plā′kē ə), *n.* a condition of the mouth and throat marked by the presence of small white nodules or patches, that may become malignant. [< New Latin *leukoplakia* < Greek *leukós* white + *pláx, plakós* something flat]

leu·ko·pla·sia (lü′kə plā′zhə, -zhē ə), *n.* leukoplakia.

leu·kor·rhe·a (lü′kə rē′ə), *n.* leucorrhea.

leu·ko·sis (lü kō′sis), *n., pl.* **-ses** (-sēz). leucosis: *It's unknown whether the leukosis virus, if contained in a measles vaccine, could be dangerous to man* (Wall Street Journal).

lev (lef), *n., pl.* **le·va** (le′və). the gold monetary unit of Bulgaria, worth about 85½ cents. [< Bulgarian *lev,* variant of *lŭv* lion < Old Slavic *lĭvŭ,* ultimately < Greek *léōn* lion]

lev-, *combining form.* the form of **levo-** before vowels, as in *levarterenol.*

Lev., Leviticus (book of the Old Testament).

Lev·a·car (lev′ə kär), *n. Trademark.* a kind of hovercraft designed for surface transit at speeds of 200 miles per hour or more: *The Levacar . . . travels on a thin film of air . . . guided by twin rails* (Stacy V. Jones). [< Latin *levāre* to lift, raise + English *car*]

Le·val·loi·si·an (lə val wä′zē ən), *adj. Anthropology.* of, having to do with, or characteristic of an early period in man's culture characterized by a new method of making stone tools and weapons by flaking. [< *Levallois*-Perret, a town in France, where these relics were found + *-ian*]

lev·an (lev′ən), *n.* a naturally occurring polysaccharide of fructose, found in the leaves of various grasses. *Formula:* $(C_6H_{10}O_5)_n$ [< Latin *laevus* left[1] (because of its levorotatory properties)]

Le·vant (lə vant′), *n.* **1.** the countries on the Mediterranean Sea, east of Italy. **2.** *Obsolete.* the East; Orient. [< Middle French *levant,* present participle of (*se*) *lever* rise < Latin *levāre* < *levis* light[2] (from its position relative to the rising sun)]

le·vant[1] (lə vant′), *n.* **1.** Levant morocco. **2.** a Levanter. [< *Levant*]

le·vant[2] (lə vant′), *v.i.* to run away or abscond, especially to avoid paying debts. [perhaps < Spanish *levantar* get up, raise < *levar* to lift < Latin *levāre*]

Levant dollar, an Austrian silver dollar used in trade, bearing the image of Maria Theresa, first issued in Austria and still made for circulation in the Near East.

Le·vant·er or **le·vant·er**[1] (lə van′tər), *n.* a strong and raw easterly wind on the Mediterranean, associated especially with the Strait of Gibraltar and with the channel between Spain and Morocco: *A regular Levanter had now come on and the vessel pitched and tossed* (George Borrow).

le·van·ter[2] (lə van′tər), *n.* a person who levants.

le·van·tine (lə van′tən; lev′ən tīn, -tēn), *n.* a sturdy, twilled silk cloth. [< French *levantine*]

Le·van·tine (lə van′tən; lev′ən tīn, -tēn), *adj.* of or having to do with the Levant. —*n.* **1.** a native or inhabitant of the Levant. **2.** a ship of the Levant.

Levant morocco, a large-grained morocco of finest quality, used in bookbinding.

Levant wormseed, an Asiatic shrub of the composite family cultivated in the western United States and in Russia. Its dried flower heads are a source of santonin and limonene.

lev·ar·ter·en·ol (lev′är tir′ə nol), *n.* levorotatory norepinephrine, a crystalline compound found in the adrenal glands and synthesized for use in medicine as a vasoconstrictor. [< *lev-* + *arterenol*]

le·va·tor (lə vā′tər, -tôr), *n., pl.* **le·va·to·res** (lev′ə tôr′ēz, -tōr′-). **1.** a surgical instrument used to raise a depressed part of the skull. **2.** a muscle that raises some part of the body, such as the one that opens the eye. [< Late Latin *levātor* a "lifter," thief < Latin *levāre* to raise < *levis* light[2]]

lev·ee[1] (lev′ē), *n., v.,* **lev·eed, lev·ee·ing.** —*n.* **1.** *U.S.* a bank built to keep a river from overflowing: *There are levees along the lower Mississippi River.* **2.** a raised bank along a river, occurring naturally as the result of deposits left during successive floods. **3.** a landing place for boats, such as a quay or pier. **4.** a ridge around a piece of irrigated land.

—*v.t. U.S.* to provide with a levee or levees: *An act to authorize the leveeing of Blue River, in Shelby County* (Indiana Senate Journal).

[American English < French *levée* < *lever* to raise < Latin *levāre* to raise < *levis* light[2]]

—**Syn. 1.** embankment.

lev·ee[2] or **lev·ée** (lev′ē, le vē′), *n.* **1.** a reception: *French kings used to hold levees in the morning while they were getting up and dressing.* **2.** (in Great Britain and Ireland) an assembly held in the early afternoon by the sovereign or his representative, for men only: *I think an English gentleman never appears to such disadvantage as at the levee of a minister* (Tobias Smollett). **3.** *U.S.* one of the President's receptions. [< French *levé* (or *lever,* noun use of infinitive) < *lever* to raise; see LEVEE[1]]

lev·el (lev′əl), *adj., n., v.,* **-eled, -el·ing** or (*especially British*) **-elled, -el·ling,** *adv.* —*adj.* **1.** having the same height everywhere; flat; even: *a level floor, a level field.* **2.** lying in a plane parallel to the plane of the horizon; horizontal: *a level stretch of railroad.* **3.** lying in or reaching the same horizontal plane; of equal height: *The table is level with the edge of the window.* **4.** of equal importance, rank, etc.: *Those five students are about level in ability. Young boys and girls are level now with men* (Shakespeare). **5.** even; uniform; steady: *a calm and level tone, level colors.* **6.** well-balanced; sensible: *a level head.* **7.** *Physics.* lying in such a surface that no work is gained or lost in the transportation of a particle from one point of it to any other; equipotential.

one's level best. See under **best,** *n.*

[< noun]

—*n.* **1. a.** something that is level; level or flat surface, tract of land, etc.: *The vessel light along the level glides* (Alexander Pope). *The lake overflowed its banks, and all the level of the valley was covered with the inundation* (Samuel Johnson). *In the far distance, across the vast level, something . . . is moving this way* (George W. Cable). **b.** one of the horizontal sections within a building: *Local trains leave on the lower level of this station. The modern house on that hillside has three levels.* **2.** an instrument for showing whether a surface is level, as a carpenter's level or a surveyor's level. **3.** the measuring of differences in height with such an instrument. **4.** level position or condition: *a river whose course is more upon a level* (Jonathan Swift). **5.** height: *The flood rose to a level of 60 feet. To the level of his ear Leaning with parted lips, some words she spake* (Keats). **6. a.** position or standard from a social, moral, or intellectual point of view: *To degrade human kind to a level with brute beasts* (George Berkeley). *His work is not up to a professional level.* **b.** the standard amount of something; normal quantity or quality: *. . . getting blood samples from people with advanced malnutrition, to determine serum-protein and cholesterol levels at three stages . . .* (New Yorker). **7.** a horizontal passage in a mine: *Water trapped the men working the face on the 1200-foot level. The explosion occurred on the third level near the working face.*

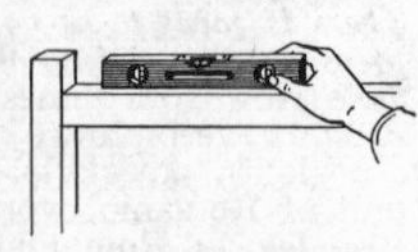

Level (def. 2)

find or **seek one's level,** to arrive at the natural or proper level: *Water seeks its own level.*

on the level, *Informal.* in a fair, straightforward manner; honest; legitimate: *In 1957 members became worried about the scheme, but she thought it was on the level and told them so* (Cape Times).

—*v.t.* **1.** to make level; put on the same level: *to level freshly poured concrete.* **2.** to bring to a level: *They leveled the tennis court by rolling it.* **3.** to lay low; bring (something) to the level of the ground: *The tornado leveled every house in the valley.* **4.** to raise and hold level for shooting, etc.; aim: *to guard all the passes to his valley with the point of his levelled spear* (Herman Melville). **5.** to aim or direct (words, intentions, glances, etc.): *This fellow's writings . . . are levelled at the clergy* (Henry Fielding). *Others were levelling their looks at her* (Byron). **6.** to remove or reduce (differences, etc.); make uniform: *The mercantile spirit levels all distinctions* (Charles Lamb). *The colors must be leveled before they can be used.* **7.** (in surveying) to find the relative heights of different points in (land). —*v.i.* **1.** to aim with a weapon: *They level: a volley, a smoke and the clearing of smoke* (Robert Browning). **2.** to bring things or persons to a common level: *Your levellers wish to level down as far as themselves; but they cannot bear levelling up to themselves* (Samuel Johnson). **3.** to direct one's words, attention, etc.: *The author . . . levels at Nero* (Richard Brinsley Sheridan). **4.** (in surveying) to make measurements of levels.

level off, a. to come to an equilibrium; even off; steady; come to the end of a rise or decline in something: *The money-supply situation hasn't eased up any recently, so that's just one more force working toward a leveling off in capital spending* (Newsweek). **b.** *Aeronautics.* to return to a horizontal position in flight, as in landing or after a climb or dive: *The plane leveled off.*

level out, to level off: *The effects of the "credit squeeze" would now appear to be levelling out, but it is impossible to forecast the future* (London Times).

level with, *Slang.* to be honest with; tell the truth: *She was tempted to squirm out of it, but instead she leveled with him and felt better for it.*

—*adv. Archaic.* in a level manner; directly: *It shall as level to your judgement pierce as day does to your eye* (Shakespeare).

[< Old French *livel* < Vulgar Latin *lībellum* < Latin *lībella* (diminutive) < *lībra* a balance, scale] —**lev′el·ness,** *n.*

—**Syn.** *adj.* **1. Level, even, smooth** mean flat or having a flat surface. **Level** means not sloping and having no noticeably high or low places on the surface: *We built our house on level ground.* **Even** means having a uniformly flat, but not necessarily level, surface with no irregular places: *The top of that card table is not even.* **Smooth** means perfectly even, without a trace of roughness to be seen or felt: *We sandpapered the shelves until they were smooth.* —**Ant.** *adj.* **1.** uneven, rough.

level crossing, *British.* a grade crossing: *Her car stalled on a level crossing toward which a freight engine slowly shunted* (Maclean's).

lev•el•er (lev′ə lər), *n.* **1.** a person or thing that levels: *It has been said that Death is the great leveler.* **2.** a person who would abolish all social and other distinctions and bring all people to a common level. **3.** a surveyor who uses a surveyor's level.

lev•el-head•ed (lev′əl hed′id), *adj.* having good common sense or good judgment; sensible: *This is a level-headed and practical book* (Scientific American). [American English < earlier *level head* + *-ed*²] —**lev′el-head′ed•ly,** *adv.* —**lev′el-head′ed•ness,** *n.* —**Syn.** judicious.

lev•el•ing (lev′ə ling), *n.* **1.** the act of one who or that which levels. **2.** (in surveying) the process or art of finding the relative elevation of points on the earth's surface, as with a surveyor's level and leveling staff, or of determining horizontal lines, grades, etc., by such a method. —*adj.* that levels; especially, bringing all to a common level, or abolishing social or other distinctions: *Some leveling circumstance that puts down the overbearing, the strong, the rich, the fortunate, substantially on the same ground with all others* (Emerson).

leveling rod or **staff,** a graduated rod or staff used with a level to determine heights in surveying.

lev•el•ler (lev′ə lər), *n. Especially British.* leveler.

Lev•el•ler (lev′ə lər), *n. Historical.* a member of a political party which arose in the army of the Long Parliament about 1647 with the aim of leveling all ranks and establishing equality in titles and estates: *The tradition of British radicalism . . ., ever since the Levellers among Cromwell's soldiers talked at Putney in 1647, has striven to transform the privileges of the few into the rights of the citizen* (Harold S. Wilson).

lev•el•ly (lev′əl lē, -ə lē), *adv.* **1.** in a level manner or position; on a level. **2.** in an unemotional manner: *He eyed his accuser levelly for a moment before replying.*

lev•er (lev′ər, lē′vər), *n.* **1. a.** a bar for raising or moving a weight at one end by pushing down at the other end. It must be supported at a point in between, called a fulcrum. **b.** a bar working on the same principle as the lever, used to control machinery, as the throttle of a locomotive or the gearshift lever in an automobile. **2.** any bar working on an axis for support, such as a crowbar, handspike, etc., used to pry. **3.** a means of control; regulating mechanism: *They believed that they had discovered the levers by which to regulate the processes of human society* (Edmund Wilson). —*v.t.* to move, lift, push, etc., with a lever: *It was partly buried in the sand and they were trying to lever it up with rusty iron bars, found on the beach* (London Times). —*v.i.* to use a lever.
[< Old French *leveor* < *lever* to raise < Latin *levāre* < *levis* light²]

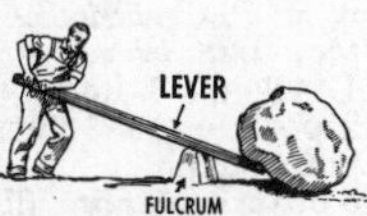

Lever (def. 1a)

lev•er•age (lev′ər ij, lē′vər-; lev′rij), *n.* **1.** the action of a lever. **2.** the advantage or power gained by using a lever. **3.** increased power of action.

lev•er•et (lev′ər it), *n.* a young hare, especially one in its first year. [< Old French *levrete* (diminutive) < *levre* < Latin *lepus, -oris* hare]

Le•vi (lē′vī), *n.* **1.** (in the Bible) a son of Jacob and ancestor of the Levites. Genesis 29:34. **2.** the tribe that claimed to be descended from him, from which the priests and the Levites were drawn.

lev•i•a•ble (lev′ē ə bəl), *adj.* **1.** that can be levied. **2.** liable or subject to a levy.

le•vi•a•than (lə vī′ə thən), *n.* **1.** (in the Bible and Canaanite mythology) a huge sea monster. It was originally defeated in combat with God but will break forth again at Doomsday when He will finally defeat it. Isaiah 27:1. **2.** a huge ship: *the oak leviathans* (Byron). **3.** any great and powerful person or thing: *The indispensable state remains always a leviathan to be watched with suspicion* (Canada Month). —*adj.* huge; monstrous: *a leviathan hall, a leviathan industry.*
[< Late Latin *leviathan* < Hebrew *liwyāthān* dragon, crocodile]

Le•vi•a•than (lə vī′ə thən), *n.* a political and philosophical treatise by Thomas Hobbes, published in 1651, in support of the absolute power of the sovereign authority, and denying that man is social naturally.

leviathan canvas, a coarse canvas of open texture: *You can get this leviathan canvas in many shades of different colors* (Lady's Realm).

lev•i•er (lev′ē ər), *n.* a person who levies.

lev•i•ga•ble (lev′ə gə bəl), *adj.* that can be levigated.

lev•i•gate (lev′ə gāt), *v.,* **-gat•ed, -gat•ing,** *adj.* —*v.t.* **1.** to make into a fine powder by rubbing or grinding: *to levigate mortar.* **2.** to mix into a smooth paste. **3.** *Chemistry.* to mix so as to make homogeneous. **4.** *Obsolete.* to make smooth; polish. —*adj.* smooth, as if polished.
[< Latin *lēvigāre* (with English *-ate*¹) < *lēvis* smooth + *agere* do, make]

lev•i•ga•tion (lev′ə gā′shən), *n.* the act or process of levigating.

lev•in (lev′in), *n. Archaic.* lightning: *the flashing Levin* (Edmund Spenser); *the lurid levin* (Longfellow). [Middle English *levene;* origin unknown]

lev•i•rate (lev′ər it, -ə rāt; lē′vər it, -ə rāt), *n.* (in the Bible) a custom among many patrilineal societies, including the ancient Jews and other Semitic peoples, of binding the brother or nearest patrilineal kinsman of a dead man under certain circumstances to cohabit with his widow, in order to beget children who will be designated legally begotten offspring of the deceased. Deuteronomy 25:5-10. [< Latin *lēvir* brother-in-law + English *-ate*³]

lev•i•rat•ic (lev′ə rat′ik, lē′və-), *adj.* having to do with or according to the levirate.

lev•i•rat•i•cal (lev′ə rat′ə kəl, lē′və-), *adj.* leviratic.

Le•vi's (lē′vīz), *n., pl.* **1.** *Trademark.* tight-fitting, heavy blue denim trousers reinforced at strain points with copper rivets or extra stitching. **2. levis.** blue jeans: *She was wearing levis and a baggy sweater* (Commentary). [American English < *Levi* Strauss and Company, an American manufacturer]

Levit., Leviticus (book of the Old Testament).

lev•i•tate (lev′ə tāt), *v.,* **-tat•ed, -tat•ing.** —*v.i.* to rise or float in the air. —*v.t.* to cause to rise or float in the air: *The magician appeared to levitate a large chair without touching it.* [< Latin *levitās, -ātis* lightness, levity + English *-ate*¹; patterned on English *gravitate*]

lev•i•ta•tion (lev′ə tā′shən), *n.* **1.** a levitating. **2.** the act or process of rising, or raising (a body), from the ground by spiritualistic means: *He claimed to have seen Hindu fakirs perform unbelievable feats of levitation.*

lev•i•ta•tion•al (lev′ə tā′shə nəl), *adj.* of or having to do with levitation.

lev•i•ta•tive (lev′ə tā′tiv), *adj.* that can levitate.

lev•i•ta•tor (lev′ə tā′tər), *n.* a person who believes in the supposed spiritualistic phenomena of levitation, or professes to be able to exercise them.

Le•vite (lē′vīt), *n.* a member of the tribe of Levi, from which assistants to the Jewish priests were chosen. Numbers 18:2,6. [< Latin *levita,* or *levītēs* < Greek *Leuītēs* < Hebrew *Lewi* Levi]

Le•vit•ic (lə vit′ik), *adj.* Levitical.

Le•vit•i•cal (lə vit′ə kəl), *adj.* **1.** of or having to do with the Levites. **2.** of or having to do with Leviticus or the law contained in it. —**Le•vit′i•cal•ly,** *adv.*

Levitical degrees, degrees of kindred within which persons were forbidden to marry. Leviticus 18:6-18.

Levitical law, the part of the Mosaic law regulating Jewish worship and ritual.

Le•vit•i•cus (lə vit′ə kəs), *n.* the third book of the Old Testament, containing the laws for the priests and Levites and the ritual for Jewish rites and ceremonies. *Abbr.:* Lev. [< Late Latin *Levīticus* (*liber*) (The Book) of the Levites < Greek *Leuitikós* < *Leuītēs* Levite]

lev•i•ty (lev′ə tē), *n., pl.* **-ties.** **1.** lightness of mind, character, or behavior; lack of proper seriousness or earnestness: *Our graver business Frowns at this levity* (Shakespeare). *Nothing like a little judicious levity* (Robert Louis Stevenson). **2.** instability; fickleness; inconstancy. **3.** lightness in weight: *. . . ingenious contrivances to facilitate motion, and unite levity with strength* (Samuel Johnson). [< Latin *levitās* < *levis* light²] —**Syn. 1.** flippancy, frivolity.

lev•o (lev′ō), *adj. Chemistry.* turning or turned to the left; levorotatory: *Dextro and levo . . . testosterone molecules are . . . each a mirror image of the other* (Science News Letter). [< Latin *laevus* left]

levo-, *combining form.* **1.** toward the left: *Levorotatory = rotatory toward the left.* **2.** levorotatory: *Levoglucose = levorotatory glucose.* Also, **lev-** before vowels. Also, **laevo-.** [< Latin *laevus* left]

le•vo•glu•cose (lē′vō glü′kōs), *n.* a form of glucose, levorotatory to polarized light.

le•vo•gy•rate (lē′vō jī′rāt), *adj.* levorotatory.

le•vo•gy•rous (lē′vō jī′rəs), *adj.* levorotatory.

le•vo•ro•ta•tion (lē′vō rō tā′shən), *n.* **1.** rotation toward the left. **2.** *Chemistry, Physics.* rotation of the plane of polarization of light to the left when the observer is looking toward the source of light. Also, **laevorotation.**

le•vo•ro•ta•to•ry (lē′vō rō′tə tôr′ē, -tōr′-), *adj.* **1.** turning or causing to turn toward the left. **2.** *Chemistry, Physics.* turning the plane of polarization of light to the left, as certain crystals (contrasted with *dextrorotatory*). Also, **laevorotatory.**

lev•u•lin (lev′yə lin), *n.* a substance resembling dextrin, obtained from the roots of certain composite plants. It forms levulose on hydrolysis. *Formula:* $(C_6H_{10}O_5)_n$ [< *levul*(ose) + *-in*]

lev•u•lin•ic acid (lev′yə lin′ik), an acid obtained chiefly by treating sugar with hydrochloric acid, used in the manufacture of plastics, nylon, etc. *Formula:* $C_5H_8O_3$

lev•u•lose (lev′yə lōs), *n.* a form of sugar in honey, fruits, etc.; fruit sugar; fructose. It is levorotatory to polarized light. *Formula:* $C_6H_{12}O_6$ [< *lev-* *-ul*(e) + *-ose*]

lev•y (lev′ē), *v.,* **lev•ied, lev•y•ing,** *n., pl.* **lev•ies.** —*v.t.* **1.** to order to be paid: *The government levies taxes to pay its expenses.* **2.** to collect (men) for an army: *to levy troops in time of war.* **3.** to seize by law for unpaid debts. —*v.i.* **1.** to make a levy. **2.** to seize property by law for unpaid debts: *They levied on his property for unpaid rent.*
levy war on or **against,** to make war on; start a war against: *Treason against the United States shall consist only in levying war against them* (Constitution of the United States). [< noun]
—*n.* **1.** money collected by authority or force. **2.** men collected for an army. **3.** a levying.
[< Middle French *levée* < *lever* to raise; see LEVEE¹]
—**Syn.** *v.t.* **1.** assess. **2.** conscript. -*n.* **1.** tax.

levy en masse, a collecting of civilian men of a country to bear arms and resist invasion. [partial translation of French *levée en masse;* see LEVY. Compare EN MASSE.]

lev•y•ist (lev′ē ist), *n.* a person who advocates the confiscation of capital.

lewd (lüd), *adj.* **1.** not decent; obscene; lustful: *lewd stories, a lewd song.* **2.** *Obsolete.* **a.** unlearned; ignorant. **b.** base; vile; wicked. **c.** worthless; unprincipled. [Old English *lǣwede* unlearned; (originally) laic] —**lewd′ly,** *adv.* —**lewd′ness,** *n.* —**Syn. 1.** lascivious, lecherous.

lew•is (lü′is), *n.* a wedge or tenon fitted into a dovetail recess or mortise in a block of stone, and having a hoisting ring for lifting the stone. [perhaps < the name *Lewis*]

lew•is•i•a (lü is′ē ə), *n.* any of a group of perennial evergreen herbs of the purslane family, native to western North America. It is widely planted in rock gardens for its narrow, woolly leaves and handsome rose-colored flowers that open only in sunshine. One kind is called *bitterroot.* [< New Latin *Lewisia* the genus name < Meriwether *Lewis,* 1774–1809, an American explorer]

Lew•is•i•an (lü is′ē ən), *adj.* of or having to do with the oldest rocks in Scotland, consisting chiefly of gneisses similar to the Laurentian types of North America, or the geologic period when they were formed, occurring at the beginning of the Archeozoic era. [< the island of *Lewis,* in the Hebrides]

lew•is•ite (lü′ə sīt), *n.* a colorless liquid with an odor like geraniums, that causes extreme injury to the skin and lungs, used in warfare as a poison gas. *Formula:* $C_2H_2AsCl_3$ [< W. Lee *Lewis,* 1878-1943, an American chemist + *-ite*¹]

Lew•is machine gun (lü′is), a light machine gun with a circular magazine, in which the bolt is worked by compressed gas. [< Colonel Isaac N. *Lewis,* 1858-1931, United States Army, who invented it]

lew·is·son (lü′ə sən), *n.* lewis.

Lew·is's woodpecker (lü′is əz), a woodpecker of western North America with greenish-black back and tail, crimson forehead, face, and throat, and light-red chest. [< Meriwether *Lewis,* 1774-1809, an American explorer]

lex (leks), *n., pl.* **le·ges** (lē′jēz). *Latin.* law, especially in reference to a legislative measure enacted by the assembly of the whole Roman people.

lex., lexicon.

Lex·an (lek′san), *n. Trademark.* a polycarbonate plastic resin with characteristics of high impact strength and heat resistance.

lex fo·ri (leks′ fôr′ī, fōr′-), *Latin.* the law of the jurisdiction where an action is pending.

lex·ic (lek′sik), *adj.* lexical.

lex·i·cal (lek′sə kəl), *adj.* **1.** of or having to do with the words or vocabulary of a language, author, etc. **2.** having to do with or like a lexicon or dictionary. [< Greek *lexikós* of words + English *-al*[1]] —**lex′i·cal·ly,** *adv.*

lexical meaning, *Linguistics.* the meaning common to the linguistic forms belonging to a paradigm, as distinguished from grammatical meaning. The words *am, are,* and *is* all have the lexical meaning of "be," although the grammatical meanings are different (person, tense, mood).

lexicog., **1.** lexicographer. **2.** lexicographical. **3.** lexicography.

lex·i·cog·ra·pher (lek′sə kog′rə fər), *n.* a writer or maker of a dictionary: *His new dictionary is the result of thirty years of that faithful drudgery which is the lot of every true lexicographer* (New Scientist). [< Greek *lexikográphos* < *lexikón* wordbook, lexicon + *gráphein* to write]

lex·i·co·graph·ic (lek′sə kə graf′ik), *adj.* lexicographical.

lex·i·co·graph·i·cal (lek′sə kə graf′ə kəl), *adj.* of or having to do with lexicography. —**lex′i·co·graph′i·cal·ly,** *adv.*

lex·i·cog·ra·phist (lek′sə kog′rə fist), *n.* a lexicographer.

lex·i·cog·ra·phy (lek′sə kog′rə fē), *n.* the writing or making of dictionaries.

lex·i·col·o·gist (lek′sə kol′ə jist), *n.* a person who is skilled in lexicology.

lex·i·col·o·gy (lek′sə kol′ə jē), *n.* the study of the form, history, and meaning of words.

lex·i·con (lek′sə kən, -kon), *n.* **1.** a dictionary, especially of Greek, Latin, or Hebrew. **2.** the vocabulary belonging to a certain subject, group, or activity: *In the lexicon of youth . . . there is no such word As —fail!* (Edward Bulwer-Lytton). **3.** *Linguistics.* the total stock of morphemes in a given language. [< Greek *lexikón (biblíon)* wordbook, neuter of *lexikós* of words < *léxis* word < *leg-,* stem of *légein* say] —**Syn. 1.** wordbook.

lex·i·co·sta·tis·tics (lek′sə kō stə tis′tiks), *n. Linguistics.* a method of dating languages, or the separation of related languages, by making statistical comparisons of their basic vocabularies; glottochronology.

lex·i·graph·ic (lek′sə graf′ik), *adj.* having to do with or characterized by lexigraphy. —**lex′i·graph′i·cal·ly,** *adv.*

lex·i·graph·i·cal (lek′sə graf′ə kəl), *adj.* lexigraphic.

lex·ig·ra·phy (lek sig′rə fē), *n.* a system of writing, such as the Chinese, in which each character represents a word; word writing.

lex lo·ci (leks lō′sī), *Latin.* the law of the place where an event occurred.

lex non scrip·ta (leks non skrip′tə), *Latin.* unwritten law.

Lex Sa·li·ca (leks sal′ə kə), *Latin.* the Salic law.

lex scrip·ta (leks skrip′tə), *Latin.* written law; statutory law.

lex ta·li·o·nis (leks tal′ē ō′nis), *Latin.* the law of retaliation ("an eye for an eye, a tooth for a tooth").

ley[1] (lē, lā), *n.* a meadow; pasture; lea: . . . *a system of farming where crops and grass leys alternate in rotation round the farm . . .* (New Scientist). [variant of *lea*[1]]

ley[2] (lā), *n.* leu.

ley de fu·ga (lā ᴛʜā fü′gä), *Spanish.* the right of the authorities to kill a fugitive prisoner, sometimes used in Spanish America in killing a prisoner released especially for this purpose.

Ley·den jar (lī′dən), a device for accumulating frictional electricity, consisting essentially of a glass jar lined inside and outside, for most of its height, with tin foil. [earlier *Leyden phial,* translation of Dutch *Leidsche flesch* < *Leiden,* Holland]

METAL ROD
INSULATOR
GLASS BOTTLE
METAL FOIL INSIDE AND OUT SEPARATED BY GLASS
CHAIN
CHAIN TO GROUND

Leyden Jar

leze-maj·es·ty (lēz′maj′ə stē), *n.,* or **leze majesty,** lese-majesty.

lf., **1.** *Baseball.* **a.** left field. **b.** left fielder. **2.** lightface (type).

LF (no periods), **L.F.,** or **l.f.,** low frequency.

l.f.b., *Soccer and Field Hockey.* left fullback.

lg., long.

l.g., **1.** *Football.* left guard. **2.** lifeguard.

LG (no periods), **L.G.,** or **LG.,** Low German.

lge., large.

LGk. or **L.GK.,** Late Greek.

lgr., larger.

lgth., length.

l.h., left hand.

LH (no periods), luteinizing hormone (the pituitary hormone which fosters the development of a corpus luteum).

L.H.A., Lord High Admiral.

Lha·sa ap·so (lä′sə ap′sō), a small dog with a heavy, usually light-brown, coat and much hair over the eyes. It is native to Tibet, where for 800 years it was trained as a watchdog. [< *Lhasa,* the capital of Tibet + Tibetan *apso (seng kye)* sentinel (lion dog)]

l.h.b., *Football.* left halfback.

L.H.C., Lord High Chancellor.

L.H.D., Doctor of the Humanities (Latin, *Litterarum Humaniorum Doctor*).

L-head engine (el′hed′), a type of internal-combustion engine having cylinders with both valves on one side.

L.H.T., Lord High Treasurer.

li (lē), *n., pl.* **li.** a Chinese unit of linear measure, equal to about one third of a mile. [< Chinese *li*]

Li (no period), lithium (chemical element).

L.I., Long Island.

li·a·bil·i·ty (lī′ə bil′ə tē), *n., pl.* **-ties. 1.** the state of being susceptible: *liability to disease.* **2.** the state of being under obligation: *liability for a debt.* **3.** a thing to one's disadvantage: *Poor handwriting is a liability in getting a job as a clerk.*

liabilities, the debts or other financial obligations of a business, for money, goods, services, etc., received: *A business with more liabilities than assets is bound to fail.*

—**Syn. 1.** susceptibility. **3.** handicap, impediment.

liability insurance, insurance taken out against injury, damage, or loss to others: *Liability insurance will pay the bill if your car pushes over a pedestrian. It won't pay for damage to your own car* (Wall Street Journal).

li·a·ble (lī′ə bəl, lī′bəl), *adj.* **1.** likely; unpleasantly likely: *Glass is liable to break. One is liable to slip on ice.* **2.** in danger of having, doing, etc.: *We are all liable to diseases.* **3.** bound by law to pay; responsible: *The Post Office Department is not liable for damage to a parcel sent by mail unless it is insured.* **4.** under obligation; subject: *Citizens are liable to jury duty.* [< Old French *lier* bind (< Latin *ligāre*) + English *-able*] —**li′a·ble·ness,** *n.* —**Syn. 1.** apt. **3.** accountable, answerable. —**Ant. 2.** immune. **3.** exempt.

➔ See **likely** for usage note.

li·aise (lē az′), *v.i.,* **-aised, -ais·ing.** to form a liaison; make a connection: *Throughout this period I liaised with, and fought alongside, no fewer than three companies of the Kenya regiment* (Manchester Guardian). [back formation < *liaison*]

li·ai·son (lē′ā zon′; lē ā′zon, lē′ə-), *n.* **1. a.** the connection between parts of an army, branches of a service, etc., to secure proper cooperation: *His job was to maintain liaison between the regular army and the company building the tanks.* **b.** any other system of connection between groups of people to secure cooperation, such as a system of product maintenance between a customer and a manufacturer, or a sales force and an engineering department. **2.** an unlawful intimacy between a man and a woman. **3.** (in speaking French) joining a usually silent final consonant to a following word that begins with a vowel or mute *h.* **4.** a thickening, as of beaten eggs, for sauces, soups, etc. [< Old French *liaison* < Latin *ligātiō, -ōnis* < *ligāre* to bind]

liaison officer, a military officer whose duty is to secure proper cooperation between parts of an army or between allied armies.

li·a·na (lē ä′nə, -an′ə), *n.* a general name for a climbing or twining plant: *Giant lianas wind around the trunks and climb from tree to tree in jungles.* [alteration of French *liane,* earlier *liorne,* alteration of *viorne* < Latin *vīburnum* the wayfaring-tree]

li·ane (lē än′), *n.* liana.

liang (lyäng), *n., pl.* **liang.** a Chinese unit of weight, equal to a hectogram. 16 liang equal 1 catty. [< Mandarin *liang*]

li·a·nous (lē ä′nəs), *adj.* vinelike.

li·ar (lī′ər), *n.* a person who tells lies; person who says what is not true: *He's . . . an infinite and endless liar, an hourly promise-breaker* (Shakespeare). —**Syn.** prevaricator.

liard (lyȧr), *n.* a small copper coin formerly used in France, worth one fourth of a sou. [< French *liard,* apparently < a proper name]

li·as (lī′əs), *n.* a compact blue limestone rock. [< Old French *liois,* or *liais,* probably < *lias,* plural of *lie* lee[2] (because of its darkish color)]

Li·as (lī′əs), *n. Geology.* **1.** the earliest epoch of the European Jurassic system, characterized by clayey rocks with fossils. **2.** the rocks of this epoch. [< *lias*]

Li·as·sic (lī as′ik), *adj. Geology.* of or having to do with the Lias.

lib., **1.** book (Latin, *liber*). **2.** librarian. **3.** library.

Lib., **1.** Liberal. **2.** Liberia.

li·ba·tion (lī bā′shən), *n.* **1.** a pouring out of wine, water, etc., as an offering to a god. **2.** the wine, water, etc., offered in this way: *The goblet then she took . . . Sprinkling the first libations on the ground* (John Dryden). **3.** liquid poured out to be drunk; a potation. [< Latin *lībātiō, -ōnis* < *lībāre* pour out]

li·ba·tion·ar·y (lī bā′shə ner′ē), *adj.* libatory: *Mme. Popea scattered scraps of stuff about her room, in a kind of libationary joy* (W.J. Locke).

li·ba·to·ry (lī′bə tôr′ē, -tōr′-), *adj.* having to do with libation.

lib·bets (li′bits), *n.pl. British Dialect.* rags; shreds. [origin uncertain]

Lib. Cong., *U.S.* Library of Congress.

li·bec·cio (lē bet′chō), *n. Italian.* the southwest wind.

li·bel (lī′bəl), *n., v.,* **-beled, -bel·ing** or *(especially British)* **-belled, -bel·ling.** —*n.* **1.** a written or printed statement, picture, etc., tending to damage a person's reputation or hold him up to public ridicule or disgrace. **2.** the crime of writing or printing a libel. **3.** any false or damaging statement or implication about a person: *His conversation is a perpetual libel on all his acquaintance* (Richard Brinsley Sheridan). **4.** (in admiralty, ecclesiastical, and Scottish law) a formal written declaration of the allegations of a plaintiff and the grounds for his suit.

—*v.t.* **1.** to write or print a libel about. **2.** to make false or damaging statements about. **3.** to institute suit against by means of a libel, as in an admiralty court.

[Middle English *libel* a formal written statement, little book < Old French *libel,* or *libelle,* learned borrowing from Latin *libellus* (diminutive) < *liber* book]

—**Syn.** *n.* **1.** calumny. **3.** slander, vilification. *-v.t.* **2.** malign.

➔ See **slander** for usage note.

li·bel·ant (lī′bə lənt), *n. Law.* a person who institutes a suit by means of a libel.

li·bel·ee (lī′bə lē′), *n.* a person against whom a libel instituting a suit has been filed.

li·bel·er (lī′bə lər), *n.* a person who libels another.

li·bel·ist (lī′bə list), *n.* a libeler.

li·bel·ous (lī′bə ləs), *adj.* **1.** containing injurious statements or other libel about a person; like a libel. **2.** making injurious statements or other libel about a person on purpose. —**li′bel·ous·ly,** *adv.*

li·ber (lī′bər), *n. Botany.* the inner bark of exogens; phloem. [< Latin *liber* book; bark[1]]

lib·er·al (lib′ər əl, lib′rəl), *adj.* **1. a.** generous: *a liberal donation. The bearers . . . are persons to whom you cannot be too liberal* (Dickens). *Wisely liberal of his money for comfort and pleasure* (John Ruskin). **b.** plentiful; abundant: *He put in a liberal supply of coal for the winter.* **2. a.** tolerant; not narrow in one's views and ideas; broad-minded: *a liberal thinker, liberal theology.* **b.** not strict; not rigorous: *a liberal interpretation of a rule.* **3.** favoring progress and reforms: *a liberal political program.* **4.** giving the general thought; not a word-for-word rendering; broad and sympathetic as opposed to literal and pedantic: *a liberal translation.* **5.** *Obsolete.* **a.** free from restraint; free in speech or action. **b.** licentious.

—*n.* a person who holds liberal ideas.

[< Old French *liberal,* learned borrowing from Latin *līberālis* befitting free men < *līber* free] —**lib′er·al·ly,** *adv.* —**lib′er·al·ness,** *n.*

—**Syn.** *adj.* **1. a.** bountiful. **b.** ample, large.

Lib·er·al (lib′ər əl, lib′rəl), *adj.* of or having to do with a political party, especially the Liberal Party of Great Britain, favorable to progress and reforms. —*n.* a member of a Liberal Party.

liberal arts, subjects studied for their cultural value rather than for immediate practical use: *Literature, languages, history, and philosophy are some of the liberal arts.* [translation of Latin *artēs līberālēs* the arts befitting *līberī* free men]

liberal education, 1. education for culture rather than as a preparation for a business or profession: *A liberal education develops the mind broadly.* **2.** wide education or experience: *The son of a banker, he had received a liberal education in finance.*

lib·er·al·ise (lib′ər ə līz, lib′rə-), *v.t., v.i.,* **-ised, -is·ing.** *Especially British.* liberalize.

lib·er·al·ism (lib′ər ə liz′əm, lib′rə liz-), *n.* **1.** liberal principles and ideas; belief in progress and reforms. **2.** Also, **Liberalism.** the principles and practices of liberal parties, especially of the Liberal Party in Great Britain. **3.** *Theology.* a recent movement in Protestantism stressing the ethical nature of religion rather than its authoritarian and formal aspects. It emphasizes the freedom of the mind to satisfy its own spiritual needs.

lib·er·al·ist (lib′ər ə list, lib′rə-), *n.* a person who holds liberal principles and ideas; believer in progress and reforms.

lib·er·al·is·tic (lib′ər ə lis′tik, lib′rə-), *adj.* of or characterized by liberalism.

lib·er·al·i·ty (lib′ə ral′ə tē), *n., pl.* **-ties. 1.** generosity; generous act or behavior: *His liberality knew no bottom but an empty purse* (Thomas Fuller). **2.** a gift. **3.** a tolerant and progressive nature; broad-mindedness: *Where look for liberality, if men of science are illiberal to their brethren?* (Edward Bulwer-Lytton). —**Syn. 1.** munificence, bounty. **2.** largess.

lib·er·al·i·za·tion (lib′ər ə lə zā′shən, lib′rə-), *n.* **1.** the act of liberalizing. **2.** liberalized state.

lib·er·al·ize (lib′ər ə līz, lib′rə-), *v.t., v.i.,* **-ized, -iz·ing.** to make or become liberal; remove restrictions from: *Liberalizing of unemployment compensation and pensions will come gradually* (Atlantic). *French and Italian economic and political representatives reached tentative agreement to liberalize trade* (Wall Street Journal). —**lib′er·al·iz′er,** *n.*

Liberal Party, 1. a political party that favors progress and reforms. **2.** a political party in Great Britain formed about 1830.

lib·er·ate (lib′ə rāt), *v.t.,* **-at·ed, -at·ing. 1.** to set free; free: *Allied troops moved in swiftly to liberate the occupied towns.* **2.** *Chemistry.* to set free from combination. [< Latin *līberāre* (with English *-ate*[1]) < *līber* free]

—**Syn. 1.** release, emancipate.

lib·er·a·tion (lib′ə rā′shən), *n.* **1.** a setting free: *As the troops withdrew, the entire city celebrated the liberation.* **2.** a being set free.

lib·er·a·tive (lib′ə rā′tiv), *adj.* that liberates or favors liberation.

lib·er·a·tor (lib′ə rā′tər), *n.* a person or thing that liberates; deliverer.

lib·er·a·to·ry (lib′ə rə tôr′ē, -tōr′-), *adj.* liberative.

lib·er·a·tress (lib′ə rā′tris), *n.* a woman liberator.

Li·be·ri·an (lī bir′ē ən), *adj.* of or having to do with Liberia or its people. —*n.* a native or inhabitant of Liberia.

Li·ber·man·ism (lē′bər mə niz′əm), *n.* the economic theories and ideas of the Soviet economist, Yevsei Grigorievich Liberman, born 1897, stressing the role of profit motive and individual incentive in increasing production.

lib·er·tar·i·an (lib′ər tãr′ē ən), *n.* **1.** a person who advocates liberty, especially in thought or conduct: *Mencken was first and foremost a libertarian. That explains his unceasing warfare against censorship and prohibition* (Newsweek). **2.** a person who maintains the doctrine of the freedom of the will. —*adj.* **1.** of or having to do with liberty or with the doctrine of free will: *It is the modern libertarian idea that a man is accountable only to himself for what he thinks and what he says* (New Yorker). **2.** advocating the doctrine of free will.

lib·er·tar·i·an·ism (lib′ər tãr′ē ə niz′əm), *n.* the principles or doctrines of libertarians.

li·ber·té, é·ga·li·té, fra·ter·ni·té (lē ber tā′ ā gȧ lē tā′ frȧ ter nē tā′), *French.* liberty, equality, fraternity.

li·ber·ti·cid·al (li bėr′tə sī′dəl), *adj.* liberticide[1].

li·ber·ti·cide[1] (li bėr′tə sīd), *n.* a destroyer of liberty. —*adj.* destructive of liberty.

li·ber·ti·cide[2] (li bėr′tə sīd), *n.* the destruction of liberty.

lib·er·tin·age (lib′ər tə nij), *n.* libertinism.

lib·er·tine (lib′ər tēn), *n.* **1.** a person without moral restraints; man who does not respect women. **2.** a person or thing that goes its own way; one not restricted or confined: *When he speaks, The air, a charter'd libertine, is still* (Shakespeare). **3.** a person who holds free or loose opinions about religion; free-thinker. **4.** a freedman in ancient Rome.

—*adj.* **1.** without moral restraints; dissolute; licentious. **2.** free or unrestrained: *He is free and libertine, Pouring of his power the wine To every age, to every race* (Emerson). **3.** free-thinking opinions about religion.

[< Latin *lībertīnus* freedman < *lībertus* made free < *līber* free]

—**Syn.** *n.* **1.** rake, debauchee.

lib·er·tin·ism (lib′ər tē niz′əm, -tə-), *n.* **1.** libertine practices or habits of life. **2.** libertine views in religious matters.

lib·er·ty (lib′ər tē), *n., pl.* **-ties. 1.** freedom: *Lincoln granted liberty to slaves. The American colonies won their liberty. A university should be a place of light, of liberty, and of learning* (Benjamin Disraeli). **2.** the right or power to do as one pleases; power or opportunity to do something: *liberty of speech or action.* **3. a.** leave granted to a sailor to go ashore: *His liberty's stopped for getting drunk* (Frederick Marryat). **b.** permission; consent; leave: *You have my full liberty to publish them* (Henry Fielding). **4.** the right of being in, using, etc.: *We give our dog the liberty of the yard. They allowed him the liberty of the town* (Daniel Defoe). **5.** a privilege or right granted by a government. **6.** too great freedom; setting aside rules and manners: *The novelist allowed himself liberties of fact that no historian could assume.* **7.** *Philosophy.* (of the will) the condition of being free from the control of fate or necessity.

at liberty, a. free: *to set prisoners at liberty.* **b.** allowed; permitted: *You are at liberty to make any choice you please. She is at liberty to be married to whom she will* (I Corinthians 7:39). **c.** not busy: *The principal will see us as soon as he is at liberty.*

take liberty or **liberties, a.** to be unduly or improperly familiar: *The poor man had taken liberty with a wench* (Daniel Defoe). **b.** to act or speak freely, especially beyond the bounds of decorum: *He was repeatedly provoked into striking those who had taken liberties with him* (Macaulay).

[< Old French *liberte,* learned borrowing from Latin *lībertās* < *līber* free]

—**Syn. 1.** emancipation. See **freedom.**

Liberty Bell, *U.S.* a bell in Independence Hall in Philadelphia, regarded as a symbol of liberty. It was rung July 8, 1776, to announce the adoption of the Declaration of Independence by the Continental Congress.

Liberty Bell

Liberty Bond, *U.S.* a government bond issued during World War I to help finance the cost of the war.

liberty cap, a kind of cap worn as a symbol of liberty. In Roman times emancipated slaves were given a cone-shaped cap, and it was adopted as a symbol of liberty during the French Revolution.

liberty horse, a horse trained to perform in a circus without a rider.

liberty pole, a tall pole with the liberty cap or other symbol of liberty on it, used as a flagstaff.

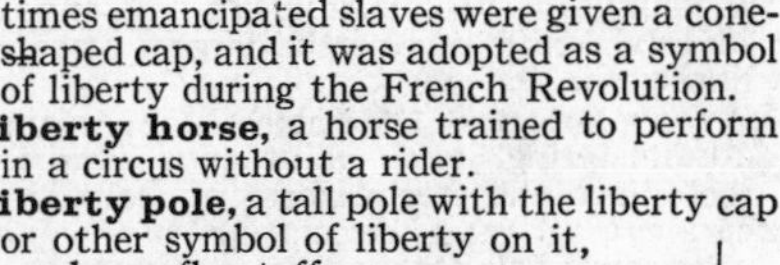
Liberty Pole

Liberty Ship, a cargo ship of about 10,000 gross tons, built in large numbers, mostly in prefabricated sections, by the United States during World War II.

li·be·rum ve·to (lib′ə rəm vē′tō), the power of a single member of a legislature to veto a proposed law: *. . . it could lead to legislative paralysis, like the notorious "liberum veto" by means of which a single deputy could stop the proceedings in the old Polish parliament* (Wall Street Journal). [< Latin *līberum,* accusative of *līber* free, unrestricted + English *veto*]

li·bid·i·nal (lə bid′ə nəl), *adj.* of or having to do with the libido: *libidinal energy* (Time). —**li·bid′i·nal·ly,** *adv.*

li·bid·i·nous (lə bid′ə nəs), *adj.* lustful; lecherous; lewd: *Bare arms were long considered indecent and even in the libidinous court of Charles II, the upper arm was prudently covered* (Newsweek). [< Latin *libīdinōsus* < *libīdō, -inis;* see LIBIDO] —**li·bid′i·nous·ly,** *adv.* —**li·bid′i·nous·ness,** *n.*

li·bi·do (lə bē′dō), *n.* **1.** sexual desire or instinct. **2.** instincts generally; vital impulse; force motivating mental life: *Libido . . . is now very commonly, though not invariably, used to mean the . . . vital impetus of the individual* (F.G.H. Coster). [< Latin *libīdō, -inis* desire < *libēre* be pleasing]

Lib-Lab (lib′lab′), *adj. British.* of, having to do with, or involving both the Liberal Party and the Labour Party: *We have rejected timorous and defeatist proposals for a Lib-Lab alliance* (Manchester Guardian Weekly).

Lib.-Lab., Liberal-Labor (British politics of the early 1900's).

li·bra[1] (lī′brə), *n., pl.* **-brae** (-brē). the ancient Roman pound, equal to about 7/10 of a pound avoirdupois. [< Latin *lībra* balance; a weight]

li·bra[2] (lē′brä), *n., pl.* **-bras** (-bräs). a former Peruvian monetary unit or gold coin replaced by the sol. [< American Spanish *libra* pound < Latin *lībra* balance; a weight]

Li·bra (lī′brə), *n., genitive (def. 1)* **Li·brae. 1.** a southern constellation between Virgo and Scorpio, that was thought of as arranged in the shape of a pair of scales. **2.** the seventh sign of the zodiac. The sun enters Libra about September 23. *Symbol:* ♎. [< Latin *Lībra* (originally) balance]

Li·brae (lī′brē), *n.* genitive of **Libra** (the constellation).

li·brar·i·an (lī brãr′ē ən), *n.* **1.** a person in charge of a library or part of a library. **2.** a person trained for work in a library.

li·brar·i·an·ship (lī brãr′ē ən ship), *n.* **1.** the profession, authority, and duties of a librarian. **2.** the management of a library.

li·brar·y (lī′brer ē, -brər-), *n., pl.* **li·brar·ies. 1. a.** a collection of books: *Those two girls have libraries all their own. Good as it is to inherit a library, it is better to collect one* (Augustine Birrell). **b.** a room or building where a collection of books, periodicals, manuscripts, etc., is kept: *A public library that lends books to members for a certain time is called a lending, circulating, or free library. Reference books may be read only in the reference library.* **2.** a rental library. **3. a.** any classified group of objects, collected and arranged for use or study: *a library of classical records, a film library, a stamp library.* **b.** any room or building where such a collection is kept: *There are a hundred and fifty species of barnacle on file in the library . . .* (New Yorker). **4.** a series of books similar in some respect and issued by the same publisher: *The Complete Home Library of Classics.*

[< Latin *librārium* a chest for books < *liber* book; (originally) bark[1]]

library card, a card entitling the holder to borrow books from a circulating library.

Library of Congress, *U.S.* a library in Washington, D.C., established by Congress in 1800. It is one of the largest research libraries in the world.

library science, the science of organizing, administering, and maintaining libraries, including the techniques of collecting, cataloguing, and circulating books and other materials for reading or reference.

li·brate (lī′brāt), *v.i.*, **-brat·ed, -brat·ing.** **1.** to move from side to side or up and down; sway; oscillate. **2.** to be balanced or poised, as a bird. [< Latin *lībrāre* (with English *-ate*[1]) to weigh, balance < *lībra* a balance]

li·bra·tion (lī brā′shən), *n.* **1.** the act of librating; swaying to and fro. **2.** a being balanced; equipoise; balance. **3.** *Astronomy.* a real or apparent oscillatory motion.

libration of the moon, *Astronomy.* an apparent irregularity of the moon's rotation, whereby those parts very near the border of the lunar disk become alternately visible and invisible.

li·bra·to·ry (lī′brə tôr′ē, -tōr′-), *adj.* librating; oscillatory.

li·bret·tist (lə bret′ist), *n.* the writer of a libretto.

li·bret·to (lə bret′ō), *n., pl.* **-tos, -ti** (-tē). **1.** the words of an opera or other long musical composition. **2.** a book containing the words. [< Italian *libretto* (diminutive) < *libro* book < Latin *liber, librī*]

li·bri·form (lī′brə fôrm), *adj. Botany.* having the form of or resembling liber or bast; elongated, thick-walled, and woody, as certain cells. [< Latin *liber, librī* book; bark[1] + English *-form*]

Lib·y·an (lib′ē ən), *adj.* of or having to do with Libya or its people. —*n.* **1.** a native or inhabitant of Libya. **2.** ancient or modern Berber, or the group of Hamitic languages to which Berber belongs.

lice (līs), *n.* plural of **louse.**

li·cence (lī′səns), *n., v.t.,* **-cenced, -cenc·ing.** license.

li·cen·cee (lī′sən sē′), *n.* licensee.

li·cens·a·ble (lī′sən sə bəl), *adj.* that can be licensed; eligible for a license: *Oversize vehicles are barred from the highways in Oregon and are not licensable* (Wall Street Journal).

li·cense (lī′səns), *n., v.,* **-censed, -cens·ing.** —*n.* **1.** permission given by law to do something: *a license to drive an automobile. The man passed the tests and has a license to be a plumber.* **2.** a paper, card, plate, etc., showing such permission: *The policeman asked the reckless driver for his license.* **3.** the fact or condition of being permitted to do something: *The farmer gave us license to use his road and to fish in his brook.* **4.** freedom of action, speech, thought, etc., that is permitted or conceded: *Poetic license is the freedom from rules that is permitted in poetry and art. He ... had obtained for himself a sort of license for the tongue* (James F. Cooper). **5.** too much liberty; disregard of what is right and proper; abuse of liberty: *License they mean when they cry liberty* (Milton). **6.** formal permission; authorization: *His majesty ... was pleased to give me his license to depart* (Jonathan Swift). —*v.t.* **1.** to give a license to; permit by law: *A doctor is licensed to practice medicine.* **2.** to give permission to do something; allow freedom of action to: *They were licensed to make bold with any of his things* (John Bunyan).
[< Old French *licence,* learned borrowing from Latin *licentia* < *licēre* be allowed]

li·censed (lī′sənst), *adj.* **1.** having a license: *a licensed driver.* **2.** permitted by license: *[They] have installed licensed games of poker* (New York Times). **3.** privileged; recognized; tolerated: *Imagination is a licensed trespasser* (George Eliot).

li·cen·see (lī′sən sē′), *n.* a person to whom a license is given.

li·cense·less (lī′səns lis), *adj.* without a license.

license plate, a metal plate on an automobile, truck, or other vehicle, bearing numbers and letters that identify the vehicle.

li·cens·er or **li·cen·sor** (lī′sən sər), *n. Law.* a person who is authorized to grant licenses.

li·cen·sure (lī′sən shůr), *n.* a licensing, especially to practice a profession.

li·cen·ti·ate (lī sen′shē it, -āt), *n.* **1.** a person who has a license or permit to practice an art or profession: *An attorney is a licentiate in law.* **2.** a person who holds a certain degree between that of bachelor and that of doctor in certain European universities. [< Medieval Latin *licentiatus,* ultimately < Latin *licentia* license < *licēre* be allowed]

li·cen·ti·ate·ship (lī sen′shē it ship, -āt-), *n.* the rank or status of a licentiate.

li·cen·tious (lī sen′shəs), *adj.* **1.** disregarding commonly accepted rules or principles. **2.** not restrained by law or morality; lawless; immoral. **3.** not restrained in sex activities; lewd. [< Latin *licentiōsus* < *licentia;* see LICENSE] **—li·cen′tious·ly,** *adv.* **—li·cen′tious·ness,** *n.* —**Syn. 3.** lustful, lascivious, sensual, wanton.

lich (lich), *n. Archaic.* a dead body; corpse. Also, **lych.** [Old English *līc*]

li·chee (lē′chē), *n.* litchi.

li·chen (lī′kən), *n.* **1.** any of a large group of plants that look somewhat like moss and grow in patches on trees, rocks, etc. A lichen consists of a fungus and an alga growing together so that they look like one plant. The alga provides the food, and the fungus provides the water and protection. **2.** a skin disease characterized by itching and reddish pimples in a small area. —*v.t.* to cover with lichens: *weathered, lichened grave-stones* (New Yorker). [< Latin *līchēn* < Greek *leichēn, -ēnos* (originally) what eats around itself < *leichein* lick]

Common Foliose Lichen (def. 1)

li·chen·a·ceous (lī′kə nā′shəs), *adj.* belonging to the lichens; lichenlike.

li·chen·in (lī′kə nin), *n.* a white gelatinous carbohydrate, a polysaccharide, obtained from Iceland moss and other lichens. *Formula:* $C_6H_{10}O_5$ [< *lichen* + *-in*]

li·chen·ize (lī′kə nīz), *v.t.,* **-ized, -iz·ing.** **1.** to unite (a fungus) with an alga so as to form a lichen: *The lichenized fungi ... have never been found in nature independent of their algae* (Scientific American). **2.** to cover with lichens: *... the weathered and lichenized surfaces of the sandstone* (Roderick Murchison).

li·chen·oid (lī′kə noid), *adj.* like a lichen: *lichenoid eczema.*

li·chen·ol·o·gist (lī′kə nol′ə jist), *n.* an expert in lichenology.

li·chen·ol·o·gy (lī′kə nol′ə jē), *n.* the branch of botany dealing with lichens.

li·chen·ose (lī′kə nōs), *adj.* lichenous.

li·chen·ous (lī′kə nəs), *adj.* of, like, or covered with lichens.

lich gate (lich), a roofed gate to a churchyard, under which a bier was set down to await the coming of the clergyman: *This patient couple walked ... under the lich gate, past the dark yew that shadowed the peaceful graves* (Henry Kingsley). Also, **lych gate.** [< *lich* corpse + *gate*]

Lich Gate

li·chi (lē′chē), *n., pl.* **-chis.** litchi.

licht (liHt), *n., adj., v.t., v.i. Scottish.* light.

licht·ly (liHt′lē), *adv. Scottish.* lightly.

lic·it (lis′it), *adj.* lawful; permitted. [< Latin *licitus* < *licēre* be allowed] **—lic′it·ly,** *adv.* **—lic′it·ness,** *n.* —**Syn.** legitimate, legal.

lick (lik), *v.t.* **1.** to pass the tongue over: *to lick a stamp. He licked the ice cream cone.* **2.** to lap up with the tongue: *Cats and dogs lick water to drink it.* **3.** to make or bring by using the tongue: *The cat licked the plate clean.* **4.** to pass about or play over like a tongue: *The flames were licking the roof.* **5.** *Informal.* to beat; thrash: *to lick the dickens out of a boy.* **6.** *Informal.* to defeat in a fight, etc.; overcome: *I could lick you with one hand tied behind me, if I wanted to* (Mark Twain). *The washing machine filter ... licked a rust problem* (Scientific American).
—*n.* **1.** a stroke of the tongue over something. **2.** a place where natural salt is found and where animals go to lick it up: *shot down like deer standing at a lick* (James F. Cooper). **3.** *Informal.* a blow: *He gave his horse a few gentle licks with his hand. That rascal of a boy gave me a devil of a lick on the shoulder* (Frederick Marryat). **4.** a small quantity; as much as may be had by licking: *Flamingo ... was so badly upset ... that he couldn't run a lick* (New Yorker). **5.** *Informal.* a brief stroke of activity or effort: *to take a lick at a piece of work.* **6.** *Informal.* speed: *to go at full lick.* **7.** *Slang.* an improvised part, derived from the main melody, played at the beginning of a jazz composition.

lick and a promise, *Informal.* slight or hasty work as if with a promise of doing better later: *I wash the dishes, give the house a "lick and promise," except on Friday morning, when I clean into every nook and cranny* (Christian Science Monitor).
[Old English *liccian*] **—lick′er,** *n.*

lick·er·ish (lik′ər ish), *adj.* **1.** fond of choice food. **2.** greedy. **3.** lecherous; lustful. **4.** *Obsolete.* tempting; choice; dainty. Also, **liquorish.**
[alteration of Middle English *lickerous* < an Anglo-French equivalent of Old French *lecheros* lecherous, greedy < *lecheor;* see LECHER] **—lick′er·ish·ly,** *adv.* **—lick′er·ish·ness,** *n.*

lick·e·ty-split (lik′ə tē split′), *adv., adj. U.S. Slang.* at full speed; headlong; rapid; rapidly: *... the lickety-split growth of trailer parks across the land* (Wall Street Journal).

lick·ing (lik′ing), *n.* **1.** the act of a person or thing that licks. **2.** *Informal.* a beating; thrashing: *The bigger boy gave Billy quite a licking.*

lick·spit (lik′spit′), *n.* lickspittle.

lick·spit·tle (lik′spit′əl), *n.* a contemptible flatterer; parasite: *... a parcel of sneaks, a set of lickspittles* (Thackeray).

lic·o·rice (lik′ər is, lik′ris; -ər ish, -rish), *n.* **1.** a sweet, black gummy extract obtained from the roots of a European and Asiatic plant, used as a flavoring. **2.** the perennial plant of the pea family that yields this. It has pinnate leaves and bluish pealike flowers in spikes. **3.** its root. **4.** candy flavored with this extract. **5.** any of various plants whose roots resemble or are used as substitutes for licorice. Also, **liquorice, liquorish.** [< Anglo-French *lycorys* < Late Latin *liquirītia* < Latin *glycyrrhīza* < Greek *glykyrrhīzā* < *glykýs* sweet + *rhīzā* root]

lic·tor (lik′tər), *n.* one of the group of attendants on a public official in ancient Rome who punished offenders at the official's orders. [< Latin *līctor,* related to *ligāre* to bind (from the fasces he carried)]

lid (lid), *n.* **1.** a movable cover; top: *the lid of a box, the lid of a pot or stove.* **2.** a cover of skin that is moved in opening and shutting the eye; eyelid: *She was alone again in the darkness behind her lids ...* (Graham Greene). **3.** *Slang.* a hat; cap. **4.** *Informal.* a restraint; check; curb: *to put the lid on gambling. A protest against the secrecy lid was made by Governor Harriman ...* (New York Times). **5.** *Botany.* **a.** the upper section of a pyxidium which separates transversely. **b.** (in mosses) the coverlike part on the theca. **6.** *U.S. Slang.* a one-ounce package of marijuana.

blow or **flip one's lid,** *U.S. Slang.* to get very angry or excited: *I showed up with my hair all straggly and no makeup on and Hillyer took a look at me and blew his lid* (New Yorker). *All over, people are flipping their lids and offering explanations* (Wall Street Journal).

blow, lift, or **take the lid off,** *U.S. Slang.* to expose (illegal or secret activities or those engaging in such activities): *The ensuing investigation achieved nationwide notoriety as the "Summerdale Police Scandal" and blew the lid off the Chicago Police Department* (O.W. Wilson).
[Old English *hlid*]

li·dar (lī′där), *n.* a radar that uses laser light beams instead of radio waves: *Meteorological lidar [is] a laser "radar" system using high-power pulses of coherent light to portray cloud patterns and atmospheric aberrations* (New Scientist). [< *li*(ght) (ra)*dar*]

lid·ded (lid′id), *adj.* having a lid; covered with or as if with a lid.

-lidded, *combining form.* having —— (eye)-lids: *Heavy-lidded = having heavy (eye)lids.*

lid·less (lid′lis), *adj.* **1.** having no lid. **2.** having no eyelids. **3.** *Poetic.* watchful: *An eye like mine, A lidless watcher of the public weal* (Tennyson).

li·do (lē′dō), *n.* a fashionable resort: *On beaches, mountains, roads, cruising liners and lidos you will find cricket-lovers ...* (Punch). [< the *Lido,* a fashionable resort at Venice < Italian *lido* shore < Latin *lītus, -oris*]

lie[1] (lī), *n., v.,* **lied, ly·ing.** —*n.* **1.** a false statement known to be false by the person who makes it: *A lie which is half a truth is ever the blackest of lies* (Tennyson). **2.** something intended to give a false impression: *My life was all a lie* (William Godwin). **3.** a false statement: *Women love the lie that saves their pride, but never an unflattering truth* (Gertrude Atherton).
give the lie to, a. to call a liar; accuse of lying: *to give each other the lie in a tavern brawl* (Robert Louis Stevenson). **b.** to show to be false; belie: *His actions gave the lie to his statement.*
[Old English *lyge*]
—*v.i.* **1.** to tell lies: *A faithful witness will not lie* (Proverbs 14:5). **2.** to make a false statement. **3.** to convey a false impression: *The sun, who never lies, Foretells the change of weather in the skies* (John Dryden). —*v.t.* to get, bring, put, etc., by lying: *to lie oneself out of a difficulty.*
[Old English *lēogan*]
—**Syn.** *n.* **1. Lie, falsehood, fib** mean an untruthful statement. **Lie** applies to an untruthful statement deliberately made with the knowledge that it is untruthful and with the purpose of deceiving, sometimes of hurting, others: *Saying his friend stole the money was a lie.* **Falsehood** means an untruthful statement made for a purpose, but can apply to one made when the truth would be undesirable or impossible: *Since he did not want to hurt his sister's feelings, he told a falsehood and said he didn't know.* **Fib** means a lie or excusable falsehood about something unimportant: *Many children tell fibs.*

lie[2] (lī), *v.,* **lay, lain, ly·ing,** *n.* —*v.i.* **1.** to have one's body in a flat position along the ground or other surface: *to lie on the grass, to lie in bed.* **2.** to assume such a position: *to lie down on a couch. From off the wold I came, and lay Upon the freshly-flower'd slope* (Tennyson). **3.** to be in a horizontal or flat position: *The book was lying on the table.* **4.** to be kept or stay in a given position, state, etc.: *to lie idle, to lie hidden, to lie unused, to lie asleep.* **5. a.** to be; be placed: *The ship is lying at anchor. Many pioneers wanted land that lay along a river. At Wakefield, six miles off, lay three thousand of the enemy* (Lord Fairfax). *Our course lay along the valley of the Rhone* (Thomas Carlyle). **b.** to exist; be; have its place; belong: *The cure for ignorance lies in education. What a future lies before him!* **6.** to be in the grave; be buried: *His body lies in Plymouth.* **7.** (of the wind) to remain in a specified quarter. **8.** *Archaic.* to spend the night; lodge: *He lay that night at the deanery* (Macaulay). **9.** *Law.* (of an action, charge, etc.) to be sustainable or admissible.
lie back, a. to lean backwards against some support: *I shipped the oars and lay back thinking* (Samuel R. Crockett). **b.** to hold back; keep from exerting oneself: *Landy ran through his carefully planned routine. He lay back, just off the pace* (Time).
lie by, a. to keep quiet; remain inactive; rest: *I must go below, and lie by for a day or two* (Richard Henry Dana). **b.** to remain unused; be laid up in store: *I had ... pillows lying by of no use* (Jane Carlyle).
lie in, to be confined in childbirth: *Five hungry children, and a wife lying in of a sixth* (Henry Fielding).
lie off, (of a ship, etc.) to stay not far from the shore or some other craft: *Intending to lie off at Ramsey for contraband rum* (Hall Caine).
lie over, a. to be left waiting until a later time: *That matter can just as well lie over until fall.* **b.** to suspend traveling; stop: *We arrived there too late for the morning cars. We had, therefore, to lie over a day* (John R. Bartlett).
lie to, (of a ship, etc.) to come almost to a stop, facing the wind: *About ten o'clock we got under way, but lay to for breakfast* (Annie Brassey).
lie up, a. to go into or remain in retreat; remain inactive: *A small herd are shown leaving one of the pools of mud in which they lie up during the day* (New Scientist). **b.** (of a ship) to go into dock: *There they [ships] must lie up, or be three or four years in their return from a place which may be sailed in six weeks* (William Dampier).
lie with, to be up to; be the province of: *It lies now with Turkey to take the initiative* (Manchester Examiner).
take lying down, to yield to; not to stand up to: *That was an insult he just couldn't take lying down, and he demanded an apology.*
—*n.* **1.** manner, position, or direction in which something lies: *I was able from this position to get a very good idea of the general lie of the Italian eastern front* (H.G. Wells). **2.** the state, position, or aspect (of affairs, etc.). **3.** the place where an animal is accustomed to lie or lurk. **4.** *Golf.* the position of the ball after a drive, in regard to obstacles on the ground or accessibility to the green: *His ball landed in an unplayable lie. His second drive landed in the same woods* (New York Times).
[Middle English *lien,* Old English *licgan*]
—**Syn.** *v.i.* **1.** recline, repose.
➔ See **lay** for usage note.

lie-a·bed (lī′ə bed′), *n.* a person who lies late in bed; late riser; sluggard: *What has made a lark of such a lie-abed?* (Richard Blackmore).

Lieb·frau·milch (lēp′frou milH′), *n. German.* a light-colored dry Rhine wine.

lied[1] (līd), *v.* the past tense and past participle of **lie**[1]: *That boy lied about his work. He has lied before.*

lied[2] (lēd; *German* lēt), *n., pl.* **lie·der** (lē′dər). a song or ballad, especially one of the German songs of Franz Schubert or Robert Schumann or one of similar character. [< German *Lied*]

lie·der·kranz (lē′dər kränts′), *n.* **1.** a smooth cheese resembling Camembert in texture but with a stronger flavor and odor. **2. Liederkranz.** *Trademark.* a name for this cheese. **3.** Also, **Liederkranz. a.** a German male singing society; Liedertafel. **b.** a collection of songs. [American English < German *Liederkranz* garland of songs]

Lie·der·ta·fel (lē′dər tä′fəl), *n. German.* a singing society.

lie detector, a device that records the physical reactions of an emotion felt by a person when asked questions. It is used especially in crime detection to determine whether a person is lying or telling the truth.

lief (lēf), *adv.* willingly: *I would as lief go hungry as eat that nasty mess.* —*adj. Obsolete.* **1.** beloved; dear; precious: *I charge thee, quickly go again, as thou are lief and dear* (Tennyson). **2.** willing; glad: *He up arose, however lief or loth, And swore to him true fealtie for aye* (Edmund Spenser). Also, **lieve.** [Old English *lēof* dear]

lief·ly (lēf′lē), *adv.* gladly; willingly.

liege (lēj), *n.* the relation between a lord and his vassals in the Middle Ages: **a.** a lord having a right to the homage and loyal service from his vassals; liege lord: *The young knight knelt and swore loyalty to his liege.* **b.** a vassal obliged to give homage and loyal service to his lord; liegeman.
—*adj.* **1.** having a right to the homage and loyal service of vassals. **2.** obliged to give homage and loyal service to a lord: *every liege subject* (Scott). **3.** of or having to do with the relationship between vassal and lord. **4. a.** *Rare.* loyal; faithful. **b.** *Obsolete.* entitled and bound to mutual fidelity.
[< Old French *liege,* or *lige* < Frankish (compare Old High German *ledig*)]

liege lord, a feudal lord.

liege·man (lēj′mən), *n., pl.* **-men. 1.** a vassal. **2.** a faithful follower: *sworn liegemen of the Cross* (John Keble).

lien (lēn), *n.* a legal right on the property of another for payment of a debt: *The garage owner has a lien upon my automobile until I pay his bill.* [< Old French *lien* < Latin *ligāmen* bond < *ligāre* bind]

li·e·nal (lī ē′nəl), *adj.* of or having to do with the spleen; splenic. [< Latin *liēn* the spleen + English *-al*[1]]

li·en·ic (lī en′ik), *adj.* lienal.

li·e·ni·tis (lī′ə nī′tis), *n. Medicine.* inflammation of the spleen; splenitis. [< Latin *liēn* the spleen + English *-itis*]

lien·or (lē′nər, -nôr), *n. Law.* a person who holds a lien.

li·en·ter·ic (lī′ən ter′ik), *adj.* relating, having to do with, or affected with lientery.

li·en·ter·y (lī′ən ter′ē), *n. Medicine.* a form of diarrhea in which the food is discharged partially or wholly undigested. [< Middle French *lienterie* < Medieval Latin *lienteria* < Greek *leienteriā* < *leîos* slippery, smooth + *éntera* the bowels]

lie of the land, 1. the way in which the land is laid out. **2.** the condition in which things are. See also **lay.**

li·er (lī′ər), *n.* a person who lies (down, etc.).

li·erne (lē ėrn′), *n. Architecture.* a minor rib used as a tie between main vaulting ribs and not springing from the impost of the vault. [< French *lierne*]

lieu (lü), *n.* place; stead.
in lieu of, in place of; instead of: *He was jailed ... and is being held in lieu of $30,000 in property bonds* (New York Times).
[< Old French *lieu* < Latin *locus*]

Lieut., Lieutenant.

lieu·ten·an·cy (lü ten′ən sē; *in general British usage, except in the navy,* lef ten′ən sē), *n., pl.* **-cies.** the rank, commission, or authority of a lieutenant.

lieu·ten·ant (lü ten′ənt; *in general British usage, except in the navy* lef ten′ənt), *n.* **1.** a person who acts in the place of someone above him in authority: *The scoutmaster used the two older boys as his lieutenants.* **2.** a commissioned officer ranking next below a captain. **3.** *U.S.* a commissioned naval officer ranking next below a lieutenant commander and next above a lieutenant junior grade. **4.** a police or fire department officer, usually ranking next below a captain and next above a sergeant. *Abbr.:* Lt. [< Middle French *lieutenant* substitute, (literally) place-holder < *lieu,* or *luef* a place (< Latin *locus*) + *tenant,* present participle of *tenir* to hold < Latin *tenēre*]

lieutenant colonel, a commissioned officer in the army, air force, or Marine Corps ranking next below a colonel and next above a major. *Abbr.:* Lt. Col.

lieutenant commander, a commissioned naval officer ranking next below a commander and next above a lieutenant. *Abbr.:* Lt. Comdr.

lieutenant general, a commissioned officer in the army, air force, or Marine Corps ranking next below a general and next above a major general. *Abbr.:* Lt. Gen.

lieutenant governor, 1. *U.S.* an officer next in rank to the governor of a State. In case of the governor's absence, resignation, or death, the lieutenant governor takes his place. **2.** *British.* an official who acts in place of the governor general in a district or province. *Abbr.:* Lt. Gov.

lieutenant junior grade, a commissioned naval officer ranking next below a lieutenant and next above an ensign. *Abbr.:* Lt. jg.

lieu·ten·ant·ship (lü ten′ənt ship; *in general British usage, except in the navy,* lef-ten′ənt ship), *n.* lieutenancy.

lieve (lēv), *adv., adj.,* **liev·er, liev·est.** lief.

life (līf), *n., pl.* **lives** (līvz), *adj.* —*n.* **1. a.** living; being alive; quality that people, animals, and plants have and that rocks, dirt, and metals lack. Life is shown by growing and producing: *A stone is without life. Life is seen in organized bodies only, and it is in living bodies only that organization is seen* (Ronald Knox). **b.** a state, existence, or principle of existence conceived as belonging to the soul, especially in Biblical and religious use: *the spiritual life, eternal life.* **2. a.** the time of being alive; existence of an individual: *a day of one's life, a short life, food enough to sustain life.* **3.** the time of existence or action of inanimate things: *a machine's life, a lease's life. The life of the Roman Empire was long.* **4.** a living being; person: *Five lives were lost.* **5.** living beings considered together: *The desert island had almost no animal or vegetable life.* **6.** a way of living: *a dull life, a blameless life.* **7.** an account of a person's life: *Several lives of Lincoln have been written.* **8.** spirit; vigor: *Put more life into your work.* **9.** a source of activity or liveliness: *Definiteness is the life of preaching* (Cardinal Newman). **10.** existence in the world of affairs or society: *young men on the threshold of life.* **11.** the living form or model, especially as represented in art. **12. Life.** (in the belief of Christian Scientists) God.
(as) big or **large as life, a.** just as in life and so not lacking in detail; in reality: *There half-way down was my own name, in print, large as life* (Graham Greene). **b.** in person: *There he stood, as large as life.*
bring to life, a. to revive; restore to consciousness: *The prompt use of artificial respiration can often bring to life a victim of drowning.* **b.** cause to live; give life to: *His novels bring to life the Victorian age.*
come to life, a. to be revived; be restored to consciousness: *A drooping plant comes to life in water.* **b.** to be or become vivid: *There are moments when this lethargic and mannered*

story threatens to come to life (Orville Prescott).
for dear life, to save one's life: *to run for dear life. The gripping spectacle unfolded of Swallow driving the master to the limit of his powers and making him hang on for dear life at the end of the third game* (London Times).
for life, during the rest of one's life: *sentenced to hard labor for life.*
for the life of me, *Informal.* if my life depended on it: *I can't for the life of me see why you do it.*
from life, using a living model: *This was painted from life, not from a photograph.*
not on your life, *Informal.* not at all; on no account: *The congressman was asked if there had been any gambling during the trip. "Not on your life," he said* (New York Evening Post).
see life, to get experience, especially of the exciting features of human activities: *Does a man want . . . to see life in metropolitan boulevards and continental spas?* (Edward Garrett).
take (a) life, to kill (someone): *He was sentenced to death for taking a life.*
take one's life in one's hands, a. to take the risk of causing one's own death: *The man who sails far from land during the hurricane season is taking his life in his hands.* **b.** to take any serious risk: *A Republican is taking his life in his hands if he enters the primary in Wisconsin* (Barry Goldwater).
take one's (own) life, to kill oneself: *In a moment of deep dejection she thought of taking her own life.*
to the life, like the model; exactly; perfectly: *The portrait is my uncle to the life.*
true to life, true to reality; as in real life: *Though many of Shakespeare's plays are not historically accurate, most of his characters are true to life.*
—*adj.* **1.** for a lifetime: *a life member, a life sentence.* **2.** having to do with life: *Botany is a life science.* **3.** affecting the life of an individual: *a life decision.* **4.** painted, etc., from life: *A life portrait is a painting for which the subject has actually sat.*
[Old English *līf*]
—**Syn.** *n.* **1a.** being, existence. **7.** biography. **8.** animation, liveliness, vivacity.

life adjustment, *U.S.* an educational theory and program stressing adjustment to society through a system of progressive education.

life-and-death (līf′ən deth′), *adj.* involving life and death; crucial; decisive; critical: [*The majority decision*] *has made the dream of Federal bureaucracy come true by granting it, for the first time, the life-and-death power of dispensation of water rights long administered by state law* (William O. Douglas).

life assurance, *British.* life insurance.

life belt, a life preserver made like a belt.

life•blood (līf′blud′), *n.* **1.** the blood necessary to life: *Fear at my heart, as at a cup, My lifeblood seem'd to sip* (Samuel Taylor Coleridge). **2.** a source of strength and energy; the vital part or vitalizing influence: *Field work is the lifeblood of anthropology. But opportunities for investment . . . are economic lifeblood* (Harper's).

Life Belt for water skiing

life•boat (līf′bōt′), *n.* **1.** a strong, specially built boat kept on shore and used for rescuing people from the water. **2.** a boat carried on davits on a ship for use by the passengers in an emergency.

Lifeboat (def. 2) being lowered on davits

life•boat•man (līf′bōt′mən), *n., pl.* **-men.** a member of a lifeboat's crew: *The ship flew a distress flag . . . and Torbay lifeboatmen went alongside in a small launch* (London Times).

life buoy, a life preserver; something to keep a person afloat until rescued. It is often ring-shaped or made into a jacket.

life company, a life insurance company.

life craft, a lifeboat.

life cycle, *Biology.* the successive stages of development that a living thing passes through from a particular stage in one generation to the same stage in the next.

life•ev•er•last•ing (līf′ev′ər las′ting, -läs′-), *n.* any of certain species of everlasting and cudweed, especially a fragrant herb common in the eastern United States.

life expectancy, the average number of remaining years that a person at a given age can expect to live.

life force, vital energy: *Jung . . . holds that primal libido, or life force, is composed of both sexual and nonsexual energy* (Time).

life•ful (līf′fəl), *adj. Rare.* **1.** full of life; animated. **2.** life-giving.

life•giv•er (līf′giv′ər), *n.* a person or thing that gives life.

life-giv•ing (līf′giv′ing), *adj.* giving life; vivifying.

life•guard (līf′gärd′), *n. U.S.* a person employed to help in case of accident or danger to swimmers or bathers at a bathing beach, swimming pool, etc. [American English < *life* + *guard*]

Life Guards, two British cavalry regiments used to guard the King and Queen of England.

life history, 1. *Biology.* the successive stages of development of an organism from its inception to death. **2.** *Sociology.* a record, based on personal documents or interviews, of an individual's most important experiences in life. **3.** a biography.

life insurance, 1. a system by which a person pays a small sum regularly to have a large sum paid to his family or heirs at his death. **2.** the sum paid by the insurance company at death. **3.** the payments made to the insurance company. **4.** a combination of life insurance and endowment insurance.

life jacket, a sleeveless jacket which is filled with a light material, such as cork or kapok, or with compressed air, and is worn as a life preserver.

life•less (līf′lis), *adj.* **1.** without life: *a lifeless planet, a lifeless stone.* **2.** dead: *lifeless bodies on the battlefield.* **3.** dull: *a lifeless performance.* **4.** (of food) containing no nourishment. —**life′less•ly,** *adv.* —**life′less•ness,** *n.*
—**Syn. 1.** inanimate. **2.** See **dead. 3.** sluggish, torpid.

life•like (līf′līk′), *adj.* like life; looking as if alive; like the real thing: *a lifelike picture, a lifelike description.* —**life′like′ness,** *n.*

life line, 1. a rope for saving life, such as one thrown to a person in the water or a line fired across a ship to haul aboard a breeches buoy. **2.** a line across a deck or passageway of a ship to grab to prevent falling or being washed overboard. **3.** a diver's signaling line. **4.** anything that maintains or helps to maintain something that cannot exist by itself, as a remote military position, etc.

life•long (līf′lông′, -long′), *adj.* lasting all one's life: *a lifelong commitment.*

life•man (līf′mən), *n., pl.* **-men.** *Informal.* a person who practices lifemanship.

life•man•ship (līf′mən ship), *n. Informal.* the skill or act of making others feel inferior so as to gain an advantage. [(coined by Stephen Potter, born 1900, an English author) < *life* + *man* + *-ship*]

life mask, a likeness made from a cast taken from the face of a living person.

Life Master, *U.S.* a player of contract bridge who earns 300 points or more in the national tournaments.

life net, a strong net or sheet of canvas, used to catch people jumping from burning buildings. [American English < *life* + *net*]

life of Ri•ley (rī′lē), *U.S. Slang.* a carefree, easy life, often with a degree of luxury.

life peer, a British peer whose title is only for his lifetime and is not hereditary.

life peerage, the rank of a life peer: *It would always be open to him to have a life peerage, of course, but a fourteenth earl probably looks on a life baron much as a regimental sergeant major looks on an acting lance corporal* (Manchester Guardian Weekly).

life preserver, 1. a wide belt, jacket, circular tube, etc., usually made of cloth filled with kapok or cork, to keep a person afloat in the water; something to keep a person afloat until rescued. **2.** *British.* a short stick with a heavy head or a blackjack used for self-defense.

lif•er (lī′fər), *n. Slang.* a convict in prison for life.

life raft, any raft for saving life in a shipwreck or the wreck of an aircraft at sea.

life•sav•er (līf′sā′vər), *n.* **1. a.** a person who saves people from drowning. **b.** a circular tube, usually made of cork or kapok, used as a life preserver. **2.** a lifeguard. **3.** *Informal.* a person or thing that saves someone from trouble, discomfort, embarrassment, etc.

life•sav•ing (līf′sā′ving), *adj.* **1.** saving people's lives; keeping people from drowning: *a lifesaving service.* **2.** designed or used to save people's lives: *a lifesaving apparatus.* —*n.* the act of saving people's lives.

life sciences, botany, zoology, biochemistry, biophysics, microbiology, and other sciences dealing with living matter (distinguished from *physical sciences*).

life sentence, a decree by a judge or court condemning a person to be imprisoned for the rest of his life.

life-size (līf′sīz′), *adj.* of the same size as the living thing: *a life-size portrait.*

life-sized (līf′sīzd′), *adj.* life-size: *In the chapel . . . is an Adoration of the Magi, a square of 21 feet containing about thirty life-sized figures* (W.M. Rossetti).

life space, *Psychology.* all of those forces acting upon a person that determine his behavior.

life span, 1. a. the length of time that it is possible for a member of a given animal or plant species to live: *Modern medicine has increased man's life span.* **b.** the length of time that such a member lives. **2.** the actual or potential duration of existence of anything: *The average life span of Governments in the Fourth Republic is just over six months* (New York Times).

life style, a person's or group's characteristic manner of living; one's style of life: *The tastes, ideas, cultural preferences and life styles preferred by many Jews are coming to be shared by non-Jews* (Time).

life table, (in insurance and biology) a mortality table: *A life table shows how many individuals may be expected to live up to certain ages.*

life tenure, a position, office, etc., held for life: *The organization of the orchestra was basically a cooperative one, consisting of active members with life tenure* (Atlantic).

life•time (līf′tīm′), *n.* **1.** the time of being alive; time over which a life lasts: *My grandfather has seen many changes during his lifetime.* **2.** the length of time anything lasts, is enforced, or is useful: *the lifetime of an electronic system. It is permitted for the lifetime of the contract to import free of duty* (New York Times).
—*adj.* for life; during one's life: *a lifetime friend, a lifetime investment.*

life vest, life jacket.

life•way (līf′wā′), *n.* way of life: *. . . the virtually extinct lifeways of people from the New World arctic* (New Scientist). *We may reasonably anticipate . . . a world in which only a minority of people are farmers and . . . these will share in the lifeways of the city* (Beals and Hoijer).

life•work (līf′wėrk′), *n.* work that takes or lasts a whole lifetime; main work in life.
—**Syn.** career.

life zone, a region that supports or is capable of supporting life: *During the growth of the last continental ice sheet . . . the climatic belts and the life zones were gradually pressed southward in front of the ice . . .* (New Yorker).

LIFO (lī′fō), *n.* last in, first out (a method of valuing inventory which assumes items in stock are those purchased earliest and values them at prices charged in earliest orders).

lift[1] (lift), *v.t.* **1.** to raise into a higher position; take up; pick up; raise: *to lift a chair. He lifted his eyes from his work.* **2.** to hold up; display on high: *The mountain lifts its head above the clouds. As through a night of storm some tall Strong lighthouse lifts its steady flame* (John Greenleaf Whittier). **3.** to raise in rank, condition, estimation, spirits, etc.; elevate; exalt: *to lift a person out of squalor. Battle-fields where thousands bleed To lift one hero into fame* (Longfellow). **4.** to send up loudly: *to lift a cry, one's voice, etc.* **5.** to bring above the horizon by approaching, as at sea. **6.** *Informal.* **a.** to pick or take up; steal: *to lift things from a store.* **b.** to plagiarize: *to lift lines from another play.* **7.** to tighten the skin and erase the wrinkles of (a person's face) through surgery: *She decided to have her face lifted, hoping that it would make her look younger.* **8.** *U.S.* to pay off: *to lift a mortgage.* **9.** to take up out of the ground, as crops, treasure, etc. **10.** *Dialect.* to take up or collect (rents or moneys due). **11.** to pick up or loft (a ball) with a golf club.

—*v.i.* **1.** to rise: *The big liner rolled and lifted* (Rudyard Kipling). **2.** to rise and go; go away: *the darkness lifts.* **3.** to yield to an effort to raise something; go up: *This window will not lift.* **4.** to pull or tug upward: *to lift at a heavy box.* **5.** to rise to view above the horizon: *the island peaks lifted above the horizon.*

—*n.* **1.** an elevating influence or effect: *without one thrill of inspiration, or one lift above the dust of earth* (Harriet Beecher Stowe). **2.** the act of lifting, raising, or rising: *the lift of a hand, a lift of the fog.* **3.** the distance through which a thing is lifted or moved: *It required a lift of three feet to get the piano in.* **4.** an act of helping; helping hand; assistance: *Give me a lift with this job.* **5.** a ride in a vehicle given to a traveler on foot; free ride: *Can I give you a lift to town?* **6.** *British.* an elevator. **7.** one of the layers of leather in the heel of a shoe or boot. **8.** a rise in state, condition, etc.; promotion; advancement: *a lift of one's fortunes.* **9.** elevated carriage (of the head, neck, eyes, etc.): *a haughty lift of the chin.* **10.** a rise of ground. **11.** the quantity or weight that can be lifted at one time: *A lift of fifty pounds was all the boy could manage.* **12.** a cable or rope with seats or attachments for holding on to raise a skier to the top of a slope: *Ski slopes for all, lifts, well-marked trails* (Atlantic). **13. a.** *Aeronautics.* the force exerted on an airfoil by a flow of air over and around it acting perpendicular to the direction of flight. See picture under **airfoil. b.** the upward tendency of an airship or balloon caused by the gas it contains. **14.** the ore mined in one operation. **15.** *Nautical.* a rope connecting an end of a yard with a masthead and serving to raise, support, square, or trim the yard. **16.** the catch of fish brought up in the raising of a net.

[< Scandinavian (compare Old Icelandic *lypta* raise < *lopt* air, sky, loft)]

—**Syn.** *v.t.* **1.** See **raise.**

lift[2] (lift), *n. Especially Scottish or Poetic.* the sky; upper regions. [Old English *lyft*]

lift·a·ble (lif′tə bəl), *adj.* that can be lifted.

lift·age (lif′tij), *n.* amount or capability of lifting: *the lock liftage of a canal.*

lift·boy (lift′boi′), *n. British.* an elevator operator.

lift bridge, a kind of drawbridge of which part may be lifted to permit the passage of boats.

lift·er (lif′tər), *n.* **1.** a person or thing that lifts. **2.** a thing used for lifting.

lift·man (lift′mən), *n., pl.* **-men.** *British.* an elevator operator.

lift-off (lift′ôf′, -of′), *n.* the firing or launching of a rocket.

lift-on-lift-off (lift′on′ lift′ôf′; -ôn′, -of′), *adj.* (of a boat) transporting freight in sealed truck trailers requiring no additional stowage of cargo.

lift pump, any pump that lifts a liquid without forcing it out under pressure.

lift-slab (lift′slab′), *adj.* of or having to do with preformed concrete slabs of flooring, etc., lifted into place by hydraulic jacks, especially in the construction of tall buildings.

lift truck, a fork-lift truck.

lig·a·ment (lig′ə mənt), *n.* **1.** a band of strong, flexible, white tissue that connects bones or holds parts of the body in place: *to strain a ligament.* **2.** a tie; bond: *By such slight ligaments are we bound to prosperity or ruin* (Mary W. Shelley). **3.** *Obsolete.* a band; bandage; ligature. [< Latin *ligāmentum* < *ligāre* bind]

lig·a·men·tal (lig′ə men′təl), *adj.* ligamentous.

lig·a·men·ta·ry (lig′ə men′tər ē), *adj.* ligamentous.

lig·a·men·tous (lig′ə men′təs), *adj.* having to do with, of the nature of, or forming a ligament.

lig·a·men·tum (lig′ə men′təm), *n., pl.* **-ta** (-tə). *Latin.* ligament.

li·gan (lī′gən), *n.* lagan.

lig·and (lig′ənd), *n. Chemistry.* an ion, molecule, etc., that forms complex compounds (chelates) by establishing a coordinate bond with the ion of a metal. [< Latin *ligāndum,* neuter gerundive of *ligāre* bind]

lig·ase (lig′ās), *n.* an enzyme that joins nucleic acid molecules, used in the synthesis of DNA. [< Latin *ligāre* bind + English *-ase*]

li·gate (lī′gāt), *v.t.,* **-gat·ed, -gat·ing.** to tie up; bind: *to ligate a bleeding artery.* [< Latin *ligāre* (with English *-ate*[1]) bind]

li·ga·tion (lī gā′shən), *n.* **1.** the act of ligating, especially in surgery. **2.** the condition of being bound. **3.** something used in binding, as a ligature. **4.** place of tying.

lig·a·tite (lig′ə tīt), *n.* a defective ligament.

lig·a·ture (lig′ə chůr, -chər), *n., v.,* **-tured, -tur·ing.** —*n.* **1.** anything used to bind or tie up; bandage, cord, etc.; tie. **2.** *Surgery.* a thread, string, etc., used to tie up a bleeding artery or vein. **3.** the act of binding or tying up. **4.** *Music.* **a.** a slur or a group of notes connected by a slur, showing a succession of notes sung to one syllable or in one breath, or played with one stroke of the bow. **b.** a tie; bind. **c.** (in some medieval music) one of various compound note forms designed to indicate groups of two or more tones which were to be sung to a single syllable. **5.** *Printing.* **a.** two or three letters joined in printing. *Æ* and *ffl* are ligatures. **b.** a mark connecting two letters.

Ligature (def. 4a)

—*v.t.* to bind or connect with a ligature.

[< Late Latin *ligātūra* < Latin *ligāre* bind]

li·geance (lī′jəns, lē′-), *n. Law.* **1.** obedience of a subject to his sovereign, a citizen to his government, etc. **2.** the territories subject to a sovereign. [< Old French *ligeance* < *lige;* see LIEGE]

li·ger (lī′gər), *n.* a hybrid animal, the offspring of a lion and a tigress. See **tiglon.** [< *li*(on) + (ti)*ger*]

light[1] (līt), *n., adj., v.,* **light·ed** or **lit, light·ing.** —*n.* **1.** that by which we see; form of radiant energy that acts on the retina of the eye. Light is now generally believed to consist of electromagnetic waves that travel at about 186,282 miles per second. **2.** anything that gives light, as the sun, a lamp, or a burning candle: *the Sandy Hook light. We saw the lights of the city. In the house light after light went out* (Tennyson). **3.** supply of light: *the light of day. A tall building cuts off our light.* **4.** brightness; clearness; illumination; particular case of this: *The light of a standard candle at the distance of one foot is used as a unit of illumination. A good light is needed for reading if eye-strain is to be avoided.* **5.** a bright part: *The Italian masters universally make the horizon the chief light of their picture* (John Ruskin). *When the ripe colours soften and unite, And sweetly melt into just shade and light* (Alexander Pope). **6.** daytime: *the light of day.* **7.** dawn; daybreak: *The workman gets up before light.* **8.** a window or other means of letting in light: *a mullioned window of three lights.* **9.** a thing with which to start something burning, as a match: *He wanted a light for his cigar.* **10.** knowledge; information; illumination of mind: *the men . . . of light and leading in England* (Edmund Burke). *We need more light on this subject. God is light* (I John 1:5). **11.** public knowledge; open view. **12.** aspect in which a thing is viewed: *He put the matter in the right light. We have to interpret his words in a modern light* (Graham Greene). **13.** a gleam or sparkle in the eye, expressing lively feeling: *He has the light of battle in his eyes.* **14.** a shining figure; model; example: *George Washington is one of the lights of history.* **15.** favor; approval: *the light of his countenance.* **16.** *Archaic.* the power of sight; vision: *His ministers with point of piercing sword put out my light for ever* (R. W. Dixon).

bring to light, to reveal; expose: *The reformer brought to light graft in the city government.*

by or **according to one's (own) lights,** following one's own ideas, intelligence, and conscience in the best way that one knows: *In communities like Hull, Mass., the citizens do what they can by their own lights* (Newsweek).

come to light, to be revealed or exposed: *When his prison record came to light, he lost his job.*

hide one's light under a bushel, to shy from the display of one's own talent; hide one's skills; be too modest: *With typical modesty they have hidden their light under a bushel, refusing to brag even to their own people* (New York Times).

in the light of, a. by considering: *We would judge in the light of all the circumstances as to whether or not the situation was out of hand* (Wall Street Journal). **b.** from the standpoint of: *He views progress in the light of scientific achievement.*

see the light (of day), a. to be born: *The helpless infant sees the light* (David Hume). **b.** to be made public: *Had not the doctrines offended France, they had long since seen the light* (William Petty). **c.** to get the right idea: *He had the gardener tell Alexandra . . . that he had finally seen the light and invited her to a New Year's Party* (Edmund Wilson).

shed, throw, or **cast light on,** to explain; make clear: *The space age has cast new light on natural radiation initially in the discovery of the Van Allen belts and more recently in plans for the U.S. moon journey* (Harper's).

stand in one's own light, to oppose one's own interest; frustrate one's purpose: *Even from the first You stood in your own light and darken'd mine* (Tennyson).

strike a light, to make a light: *We had implements to strike a light* (Washington Irving).

—*adj.* **1.** having light: *the lightest room in the house.* **2.** bright; clear: *It is as light as day.* **3.** pale in color; whitish: *light hair, light blue, the light green of larch trees in the spring.*

—*v.t.* **1.** to set fire to; kindle; ignite: *She lighted the candles.* **2.** to cause to give light: *She lighted the lamp.* **3.** to give light to; provide with light: *The room is lighted by six windows.* **4.** to make lively; brighten: *Her face was lighted by a smile. His style is lighted up with flashes of wit.* **5.** to show (a person) the way by means of a light: *Here is a candle to light you to bed.* —*v.i.* **1.** to take fire; become ignited: *Matches light when you scratch them.* **2.** to become bright; be lighted up: *The sky lights up at sunset.* **3.** to become bright with animation, eagerness, or happiness: *Her face lit up with satisfaction.*

[Old English *lēoht,* noun, and adjective]

—**Syn.** *n.* **4.** radiance, luminosity.

➤ **lighted, lit.** Both forms are in good use as the past tense and past participle of *light. Lighted* is the more common form of the attributive adjective: *She carried a lighted lamp.* The predicate adjective is either *lighted* or *lit: The room was well lighted* (or *lit*).

light[2] (līt), *adj.* **1.** easy to carry; not heavy: *a light load.* **2.** of little weight for its size; of low specific gravity: *a light metal. Feathers are light.* **3. a.** of less than usual or normal weight: *Many men wear light suits in summer.* **b.** below the standard or legal weight: *light coin.* **4.** less than usual in amount, force, etc.: *a light sleep, a light rain, a light meal.* **5.** easy to do or bear; not hard or severe: *light punishment, a light task, light taxes. The service will be light and easy* (Benjamin Franklin). **6.** not looking heavy; graceful; delicate: *a light bridge, light carving.* **7.** moving easily; nimble: *a light step.* **8.** happy; gay; cheerfully careless: *a light laugh, light spirits.* **9.** not serious enough; fickle: *a light mind, light of purpose.* **10.** aiming to entertain; not serious: *light reading, light opera.* **11.** not important: *light losses.* **12.** careless in morals; wanton; unchaste: *a light woman.* **13.** not dense: *a light fog.* **14.** porous; sandy: *a light soil.* **15. a.** containing little alcohol: *a light wine.* **b.** that has risen properly; not soggy: *light dough.* **16.** built small and without much weight; adapted for light loads and for swift movement: *a light truck.* **17. a.** carrying a small or comparatively small load. **b.** (of a vessel) with little or no cargo. **18.** having a velocity of 7 miles per hour or less (on the Beaufort scale, force 1 and 2). **19.** *Military.* **a.** lightly armed or equipped: *light cavalry, in light marching order.* **b.** of small size, caliber, or capacity: *light weapons.* **20.** (of a vowel or syllable) not stressed or accented.

make light of, to treat as of little importance: *Making light of what ought to be serious . . .* (Jane Austen).
—*adv.* in a light manner; lightly.
[Old English *lēoht, līht*]
—**Syn.** *adj.* **7.** agile, active. **8.** buoyant. **11.** slight, trivial, unimportant.

light[3] (līt), *v.i.*, **light·ed** or **lit, light·ing. 1.** to come down to the ground; alight: *He lighted from his horse.* **2.** to come down from flight: *On the treetops a crested peacock lit* (Tennyson). **3.** to come by chance: *His eye lighted upon a coin in the road.* **4.** to fall suddenly: *The blow lit on his head.*
light into, *Slang.* **a.** to attack; scold: *Then he lit into Congress for its "passion for economy regardless of the consequences"* (Newsweek). **b.** *Obsolete.* to come by chance; be brought or drawn: *When the Hierarchy of England shall light into the hands of busy and audacious men . . . much mischief is like to ensue* (Milton).
light out, *Slang.* to leave suddenly; go away quickly: *And so when I couldn't stand it no longer, I lit out* (Mark Twain).
[Old English *līhtan* < *līht* light[2]]

light air, *Meteorology.* a condition in which the wind has a velocity of 1-3 miles per hour (on the Beaufort scale, force 1).

light-armed (līt′ärmd′), *adj.* equipped with light weapons.

light·boat (līt′bōt′), *n.* a lightship.

light bomber, a bomber having a gross weight, including bomb load, of less than 100,000 pounds.

light breeze, *Meteorology.* a condition in which the wind has a velocity of 4-7 miles per hour (on the Beaufort scale, force 2).

light bulb, an incandescent lamp: *Three pennies keep a large electric light bulb burning all night* (Atlantic).

light-col·ored (līt′kul′ərd), *adj.* light in color; not dark: *The little boy's light-colored pants were soiled with grass stains.*

light curve, the plotted curve which shows the variations in magnitude of a star's light at different times.

light due or **duty,** a toll on ships to maintain lighthouses and lightships.

light·en[1] (līt′tən), *v.i.* **1.** to grow light; become brighter: *The sky lightens before the dawn.* **2.** to brighten: *Her face lightened.* **3.** to flash with lightning: *It thundered and lightened outside.* —*v.t.* **1.** to make light; give light to: *The city had no need of the sun . . . for the glory of God did lighten it* (Revelation 21:23). **2.** to brighten (the face, eyes, etc.). **3.** to flash like lightning: *Now she lightens scorn At him that mars her plan* (Tennyson). **4.** *Archaic.* to enlighten or illuminate spiritually: *Now the Lord lighten thee! Thou art a great fool* (Shakespeare). [Middle English *lighten* < *light*[1]] —**light′en·er,** *n.*

light·en[2] (lī′tən), *v.t.* **1.** to reduce the load of (a ship, etc.): *I was lightened of my purse, in which was almost every farthing I had* (Washington Irving). **2.** to make less of a burden: *to lighten taxes.* **3.** to make more cheerful: *The good news lightened our hearts.* —*v.i.* **1.** to have the load reduced. **2.** to become less of a burden: *Their luggage . . . lightened every day* (Daniel Defoe). **3.** to become more cheerful: *Their spirits lightened as summer vacation drew near.*
[Middle English *lighten* < *light*[2]] —**light′en·er,** *n.*
—**Syn.** *v.t.* **2.** alleviate, mitigate.

light·en·ing hole (lī′tə ning), a hole cut in a beam or structure to lighten it.

light·er[1] (lī′tər), *n.* **1.** a thing used to set something else on fire, as the various devices for lighting cigarettes. **2.** a person who lights or kindles. [< *light*[1], verb + *-er*[1]]

light·er[2] (lī′tər), *n.* a flat-bottomed barge used for loading and unloading, usually offshore. —*v.t.* to carry (goods) in a flat-bottomed barge: *All day long the surfboats move back and forth between the shore and the freighters at anchor, lightering cargo* (New Yorker). [< *light*[3] (in earlier sense of "unload"), or perhaps < Dutch *lichter*]

light·er·age (lī′tər ij), *n.* **1.** the loading, unloading, or carrying of goods in a lighter. **2.** the charge for this.

light·er·man (lī′tər man′, -mən), *n., pl.* **-men. 1.** a person who works on or manages a flat-bottomed barge. **2.** a flat-bottomed barge; lighter.

light·er-than-air (lī′tər ᴛʜən ãr′), *adj.* **1.** having less weight than the air, as gas-filled balloons or airships. **2.** of or having to do with balloons or airships.

light·face (līt′fās′), *n.* printing type that has thin, light lines. *Abbr.:* lf. —*adj.* lightfaced.

light·faced (līt′fāst′), *adj.* (of type) having thin, light lines.

light-fin·gered (līt′fing′gərd), *adj.* **1.** skillful at picking pockets; thievish. **2.** having light and nimble fingers. —**light′-fin′gered·ness,** *n.*

light-foot (līt′fu̇t′), *adj. Poetic.* light-footed: *light-foot Iris* (Tennyson).

light-foot·ed (līt′fu̇t′id), *adj.* stepping lightly; active; nimble. —**light′-foot′ed·ly,** *adv.* —**light′-foot′ed·ness,** *n.*

light·ful (līt′fəl), *adj.* full of light; bright. —**light′ful·ness,** *n.*

light-hand·ed (līt′hand′id), *adj.* **1.** having a light hand or touch; dexterous. **2.** having little in the hand. **3.** short-handed, as a factory. —**light′-hand′ed·ness,** *n.*

light·head (līt′hed′), *n.* a light-headed person.

light-head·ed (līt′hed′id), *adj.* **1.** dizzy: *A second glass of wine made him light-headed.* **2.** out of one's head; delirious: *The sick man was light-headed from fever.* **3.** frivolous; empty-headed; flighty: *That frivolous, light-headed girl thinks of nothing but parties and clothes.* —**light′-head′ed·ly,** *adv.* —**light′-head′ed·ness,** *n.* —**Syn. 3.** changeable, fickle.

light-heart·ed (līt′här′tid), *adj.* carefree; cheerful; gay: *light-hearted lads, a light-hearted laugh.* —**light′-heart′ed·ly,** *adv.* —**light′-heart′ed·ness,** *n.*

light heavyweight, a boxer or wrestler who weighs between 161 and 175 pounds.

light-heeled (līt′hēld′), *adj.* light-footed; nimble: *The villain is much lighter-heel'd than I: I follow'd fast but faster he did fly* (Shakespeare).

light horse, cavalry that carries light weapons and equipment.

light-horse·man (līt′hôrs′mən), *n., pl.* **-men.** a cavalryman who carries light weapons and equipment.

light·house (līt′hous′), *n.* a tower or framework with a bright light that usually revolves or flashes as it shines far over the water. It is often located at a dangerous place to warn and guide ships.

Lighthouse

light·house·man (līt′hous man′, -hous′mən), *n., pl.* **-men.** a keeper of a lighthouse.

light infantry, infantry that carries light arms and equipment.

light·ing (lī′ting), *n.* **1.** a giving of light; providing with light: *The lighting in the library is inadequate.* **2.** the way in which lights are arranged: *Indirect lighting is used in many modern homes.* **3.** a starting to burn; kindling; ignition. **4.** the way the light falls in a picture: *The photographer was careless in the lighting and the picture had many shadows.*

lighting rehearsal, a rehearsal of changes in lighting in a theatrical or television performance.

light·ish (lī′tish), *adj.* rather light, as in color.

light·less (līt′lis), *adj.* without light: *His undetected offence of riding a lightless bicycle after dark* (London Daily Chronicle). —**light′less·ness,** *n.*

light·ly (līt′lē), *adv., v.,* **-lied, -ly·ing.** —*adv.* **1.** with little weight, force, etc.; gently; superficially: *The seagull rested lightly on the waves. Cares rested lightly on the little girl.* **2.** to a small degree or extent; to no great amount: *lightly clad.* **3.** in an airy way: *flags floating lightly.* **4.** quickly; easily; nimbly: *to jump lightly aside.* **5.** cheerfully or with cheerful unconcern: *to take bad news lightly.* **6.** indifferently; slightingly: *to speak lightly of a person.* **7.** thoughtlessly; carelessly: *to behave lightly, an offer not lightly to be refused. These are opinions that I have not lightly formed, or that I can lightly quit* (Edmund Burke). **8. a.** *Archaic.* readily: *Credulous people believe lightly whatever they hear* (Lord Chesterfield). **b.** *Obsolete.* immediately; at once. **9.** *Obsolete.* not chastely. —*v.t. Especially Scottish.* to make light of; despise; disparage.

light meson, a meson resulting from the decay of heavy mesons, having a rest mass or weight about 273 times that of an electron; L-meson.

light meter, 1. an instrument to measure light, as the photoelectric exposure meter. **2.** a device to measure and record the amount of electricity used.

light-mind·ed (līt′mīn′did), *adj.* empty-headed; thoughtless; frivolous. —**light′-mind′ed·ly,** *adv.* —**light′-mind′ed·ness,** *n.*

light·ness[1] (līt′nis), *n.* **1.** brightness; clearness. **2.** paleness; light color; whitishness. **3.** amount of light: *The lightness of the sky showed that the rain was really over.* [Old English *līhtnes* < *lēoht* light[1]]

light·ness[2] (līt′nis), *n.* **1.** a being light; not being heavy: *The lightness of this load is a relief after the heavy one I was carrying.* **2.** not being hard or severe. **3.** gracefulness; delicacy. **4.** agility; nimbleness; swiftness: *lightness of step.* **5.** being gay or cheerful: *lightness of spirits.* **6.** lack of proper seriousness; fickleness; frivolity. **7.** *Obsolete.* wantonness; lewdness; incontinence. [< *light*[2] + *-ness*]

light·ning (līt′ning), *n.* **1.** a discharge or flash of electricity in the sky. The sound that it makes is thunder. **2.** a flash of light: *The great brand Made lightnings in the splendour of the moon* (Tennyson). —*adj.* quick as lightning; very rapid: *Scores often came in lightning succession* (Wall Street Journal). [Middle English *lightening* < *lighten*[1] + *-ing*[1]]

lightning arrester, a device to protect electrical apparatus from damage by lightning by carrying to the ground the excess voltage produced by lightning discharges.

lightning ball, St. Elmo's fire.

lightning bug, *U.S.* a firefly.

lightning chess, a game of chess in which the players receive only about ten seconds for each move.

lightning rod, a metal rod fixed on a building or ship to conduct lightning into the earth or water.

light-o'-love (līt′ə luv′), *n.* **1.** a woman capricious or inconstant in love; coquette. **2.** a wanton; harlot.

light pen, a photosensitive device shaped like a large fountain pen, used to send messages to a computer in response to light impulses displayed by the computer on a cathode-ray tube.

light quantum, *Physics.* a photon.

light railway, 1. a railroad with light equipment. **2.** a narrow-gauge railway.

lights (līts), *n.pl.* the lungs of sheep, pigs, etc., used as food. [< *light*[2] (from their lack of weight). Compare LUNG.]

light·ship (līt′ship′), *n.* a ship with a bright light that shines far over the water, anchored at a dangerous place to warn and guide ships where it is impractical to build a lighthouse or beacon.

Lightship

light·skirts (līt′skėrts′), *n.* a light or wanton woman.

light·some[1] (līt′səm), *adj.* **1.** lively; nimble; quick: *lightsome feet.* **2.** happy; gay; cheerful. **3.** flighty; frivolous. [< *light*[2] + *-some*[1]] —**light′some·ly,** *adv.* —**light′some·ness,** *n.*

light·some[2] (līt′səm), *adj.* **1.** radiant with light; light-giving; luminous. **2.** well-lighted; bright; illuminated. [< *light*[1] + *-some*[1]] —**light′some·ness,** *n.*

lights-out (līts′out′), *n.* a signal at which lights must be put out.

light-struck (līt′struk′), *adj.* (of photographic film, plates, prints, etc.) injured or fogged by unintentional exposure to light.

light trap, a device for trapping insects by means of a mercury vapor lamp or other light source that attracts insects.

light·weight (līt′wāt′), *n.* **1.** a person, animal, or thing of less than average weight. **2.** a boxer or wrestler who weighs between 126 and 135 pounds. **3.** *Informal.* a person who has little intelligence or importance.
—*adj.* **1.** light in weight: *The hat . . . is made of lightweight leather* (London Daily Chronicle). **2.** unimportant; insignificant: *They were written [as] lightweight affairs with humorous entertainment as their object* (New Yorker).

light·well (līt′wel′), *n.* a narrow space or shaft admitting light within or between buildings: *The new proposal . . . requires that one room of each apartment face on a street or a rear yard, instead of a lightwell* (San Francisco Chronicle).

light·wood (līt′wu̇d′), *n.* (in the southern United States) a dry wood, especially very resinous pine wood, used in lighting a fire.

light-year (līt′yir′), *n.* **1.** the distance that light travels in one year; about 6,000,000,000,000 miles. **2. a.** a very great distance; immeasurably far: *Orthodoxy is still light-years away from any union with Rome* (Time). **b.** a very long time; aeon: *That was 1962—light-years ago in political time* (New Yorker).

lign·al·oes (lĭn′al′ōz, lig nal′-), *n.pl.* **1.** aloes wood. **2.** the bitter drug aloes. [< Late Latin *lignum aloēs* wood of the aloe]

lig·ne·ous (lig′nē əs), *adj.* of or like wood; woody. [< Latin *ligneus* (with English *-ous*) < *lignum* wood]

lig·nic·o·lous (lig nik′ə ləs), *adj.* **1.** living or growing on wood, as fungi. **2.** living in wood, as shipworms. [< Latin *lignum* wood + *colere* to inhabit + English *-ous*]

lig·ni·fi·ca·tion (lig′nə fə kā′shən), *n.* **1.** the act of lignifying. **2.** the state of being lignified.

lig·ni·form (lig′nə fôrm), *adj.* having the form of wood; resembling wood, as a variety of asbestos. [< Latin *lignum* wood + English *-form*]

lig·ni·fy (lig′nə fī), *v.*, **-fied, -fy·ing.** —*v.t.* to change into wood. —*v.i.* to become wood, as cells whose walls have been thickened and indurated by the deposit of lignin. [< Latin *lignum* wood + English *-fy*]

lig·nin (lig′nin), *n. Botany.* an organic substance which, together with cellulose, forms the essential part of woody tissue, making the greater part of the weight of dry wood. [< Latin *lignum* wood + English *-in*]

lig·nite (lig′nīt), *n.* a dark-brown kind of coal in which the texture of the wood can be seen; brown coal; wood coal. [< French *lignite* < Latin *lignum* wood + French *-ite* -ite[1]]

lig·nit·ic (lig nit′ik), *adj.* **1.** of or having to do with lignite. **2.** containing lignite.

lig·ni·tif·er·ous (lig′nə tif′ər əs), *adj.* bearing or containing lignite.

lig·ni·tize (lig′nə tīz), *v.t.*, **-tized, -tiz·ing.** to convert into lignite.

lig·ni·toid (lig′nə toid), *adj.* like lignite.

lig·niv·o·rous (lig niv′ər əs), *adj.* eating wood, as the larvae of many insects. [< Latin *lignum* wood + *vorāre* devour + English *-ous*]

lig·no·cel·lu·lose (lig′nə sel′yə lōs), *n. Botany.* lignin combined with cellulose, forming an essential constituent of woody tissue, as in jute fiber.

lig·nose (lig′nōs), *n.* **1.** one of the constituents of lignin. **2.** an explosive consisting of wood pulp saturated with nitroglycerin. [< Latin *lignōsus* < *lignum* wood]

lig·num vi·tae (lig′nəm vī′tē), **1.** an extremely heavy and hard wood used for making pulleys, rulers, etc. **2.** the guaiacum tree of tropical America from which it comes. **3.** any of several other trees having similar wood. [< New Latin *lignum vitae* (literally) wood of life]

lig·ro·in or **lig·ro·ine** (lig′rō in), *n. Chemistry.* a volatile, inflammable liquid mixture of hydrocarbons obtained by the fractional distillation of petroleum, used as a solvent; petroleum ether. [origin unknown]

lig·u·la (lig′yə lə), *n.*, *pl.* **-lae** (-lē), **-las. 1.** *Zoology.* the terminal or dorsal part of the labium of an insect. **2.** ligule. [< Latin *ligula* strap, tonguelike part, variant of *lingula* (diminutive) < *lingua* tongue]

lig·u·lar (lig′yə lər), *adj.* of or like a ligula.

lig·u·late (lig′yə lit, -lāt), *adj.* **1.** having a ligule or ligules. **2.** *Botany.* strap-shaped.

lig·u·lat·ed (lig′yə lā′tid), *adj.* ligulate.

lig·ule (lig′yül), *n. Botany.* any of several strap-shaped organs or parts, as the flattened corolla in the ray florets of composites or the projection from the top of the leaf sheath in many grasses. [< Latin *ligula;* see LIGULA]

lig·ure (lig′yu̇r), *n.* (in the Bible) an unidentified precious stone in the breastplate of the high priest, thought to be the jacinth. Exodus 28:19. [< Late Latin *ligurius* < Greek *ligŷrion* (diminutive) < *ligyros* a kind of precious stone]

Li·gu·ri·an (li gyu̇r′ē ən), *adj.* of Liguria, a district in northwest Italy, or its people. —*n.* a native or inhabitant of Liguria.

lik·a·bil·i·ty (lī′kə bil′ə tē), *n.* the quality or condition of being likable: *The actor sacrifices his pose, but keeps his likability* (New York Times).

lik·a·ble (lī′kə bəl), *adj.* having qualities that win good will or friendship; popular; pleasing. —**lik′a·ble·ness,** *n.*

like[1] (līk), *adj., Poetic.* **lik·er, lik·est,** *prep., adv., n., conj., v.,* **liked, lik·ing.** —*adj.* **1.** similar; similar to; resembling something or each other: *Our house is like theirs. John's uncle promised him $10 if he could earn a like sum. Like events will follow like actions* (Thomas Hobbes). *A critic like you is one who fights the good fight, contending with stupidity* (Robert Louis Stevenson). *It was very like and very laughable, but hardly caricatured* (Hawthorne). **2.** such as one might expect of; characteristic of: *Isn't that just like a boy? It would be like his impudence . . . to dare to think of such a thing* (Dickens). **3.** giving promise or indication of: *It looks like rain.* **4.** in the right state or frame of mind for: *I feel like working.* **5.** *Archaic.* likely; probable: *The king is sick and like to die. 'Tis like that they will know us* (Shakespeare). **6.** *Dialect.* about: *He seemed like to choke.*

had like, *Dialect.* came near; was about: *He had like to have been killed.*

nothing like, not nearly: *I have had nothing like a bad fall lately* (G. Gambado).

something like, about; almost: *The soldiers of the Guard . . . killed something like a thousand people* (Edmund Wilson).

—*prep.* **1.** similar; similar to; resembling something or each other: *Mary is like her sister. She can sing like a bird.* **2.** characteristic of: *His jaw closed like a steel trap.* **3.** in the right state or frame of mind for: *On Mondays I always feel like going fishing.* **4.** in like manner with; similarly to: *She works like a beaver.*

—*adv.* **1.** *Informal.* probably: *Like enough it will rain.* **2.** in like manner: *Like as a father pitieth his children, so the Lord pitieth them that fear him* (Psalms 103:13). **3.** similarly to: *He works hard like his father.* **4.** *Archaic.* to a like extent or degree: *The enterprise . . . Shall be to you, as us, like glorious* (Shakespeare). **5.** *Dialect.* as it were; so to speak: *They say she was out of her mind like for six weeks or more* (Thackeray).

like crazy. See under **crazy.**

—*n.* **1.** a person or thing like another; match; counterpart or equal: *We shall not see his like again.* **2.** something of similar nature.

and the like, a. and so forth: *He studied music, painting, and the like.* **b.** and other like things: *We went to the zoo and saw tigers, lions, bears, and the like.*

the like(s) of, such a person or thing as: *Are there no harems still left in Stamboul for the likes of thee to sweep and clean?* (George Du Maurier).

—*conj. Informal.* **1.** in the same way as; as: *Unfortunately few have observed like you have done* (Charles Darwin). **2.** as if: *He acted like he was afraid. Drive it like you hate it, it's cheaper than psychiatry* (New York Times).

—*v.t. Obsolete.* to compare. —*v.i. Dialect.* to come near: *He liked to have choked.*

[Middle English *liche,* Old English *gelīc*]

➔ **like, as.** In written English *as* and *as if* (not *like*) introduce clauses: *He writes as* (not *like*) *he used to when he was a child. Act as if* (not *like*) *you were accustomed to being here.* In spoken or informal English *like* is often used in clauses of comparison: *The little boy talks like he were a baby to get attention.* Although historically both *like* and *as* are justified, custom has made *as* the preferred form in introducing clauses in written English.

like[2] (līk), *v.,* **liked, lik·ing,** *n.* —*v.t.* **1.** to be pleased with; be satisfied with; find agreeable or congenial: *to like a place, to like a person. He shall dwell . . . where it liketh him best* (Deuteronomy 23:16). **2.** to wish for; wish to have: *I should like more time.* —*v.i.* **1.** to feel inclined; wish: *Boys like to play. Come whenever you like.* **2.** *Archaic.* to please; be pleasing; suit a person: *They . . . looking liked, and liking loved* (Scott).

—*n.* **likes,** liking; preference: *Mother knows all of Dad's likes and dislikes.*

[Old English *līcian* to please. Related to LIKE[1].] —**lik′er,** *n.*

➔ **Like, love** are not interchangeable. *Like* means to find pleasure or satisfaction in something or someone, or to have friendly feelings for a person, but does not suggest strong feelings or emotion: *I like books. Boys like to play. Love* emphasizes strong feelings and deep attachment, and is used to express the emotion of love: *She loves her mother. He loves music* (suggests deep attachment).

-like, *suffix.* **1.** like: *Wolflike = like a wolf.* **2.** like that of; characteristic of: *Childlike = like that of a child.* **3.** suited to; fit or proper for: *Businesslike = suited to business.*

[< *like*[1], adjective]

➔ **-like** is a living suffix, freely used to form adjectives of nouns and sometimes to form adverbs of adjectives. Words ending in *-like* are usually not hyphenated unless three *l's* come together: *springlike, fall-like.*

like·a·bil·i·ty (lī′kə bil′ə tē), *n.* likability.

like·a·ble (lī′kə bəl), *adj.* likable. —**like′a·ble·ness,** *n.*

like·li·hood (līk′lē hu̇d), *n.* **1.** the quality or fact of being likely or probable; probability. **2.** a probability or chance of something: *Is there any great likelihood of rain this afternoon?* **3.** *Obsolete.* an indication; sign: *Many likelihoods informed me of this before* (Shakespeare).

like·li·ness (līk′lē nis), *n.* the condition or quality of being likely.

like·ly (līk′lē), *adj.,* **-li·er, -li·est,** *adv.* —*adj.* **1.** probable: *One likely result of this heavy rain is the rising of the river.* **2.** to be expected: *It is likely to be hot in August.* **3.** suitable: *Is this a likely place to fish?* **4.** giving promise of success or excellence; promising: *a likely boy.*

—*adv.* probably; in all probability: *I shall very likely be at home all day.*

[< Scandinavian (compare Old Icelandic *līkligr*)]

➔ **Likely, apt, liable** indicate possibility but not in the same way. *Likely* implies probability: *It is likely to rain tonight. Apt* implies natural or habitual tendency: *Children are apt to be noisy at play. Liable* implies risk or danger: *Because he doesn't study, he is liable to fail.*

like-mind·ed (līk′mīn′did), *adj.* **1.** in agreement or accord. **2.** that thinks along the same lines: *And the Presidential nominee . . . should resign his nomination . . . if he does not get the like-minded Vice Presidential running-mate he wants* (New York Times). —**like′-mind′ed·ly,** *adv.* —**like′-mind′ed·ness,** *n.*

lik·en (lī′kən), *v.t.* to represent as like; compare: *The kingdom of heaven is likened unto a man which sowed good seed in his field* (Matthew 13:24).

like·ness (līk′nis), *n.* **1.** a resembling; a being alike: *a boy's likeness to his father.* **2.** something that is like; copy; picture: *to have one's likeness painted.* **3.** appearance; shape: *to assume the likeness of a swan.* —**Syn. 2.** counterpart, image, portrait.

likes (līks), *n.pl.* See under **like**[2], *n.*

like·wake (līk′wāk′), *n. Archaic.* a watch kept at night over a dead body. [Old English *līc* corpse + *wake*[1]]

like·wise (līk′wīz′), *adv.* **1.** the same; similarly: *Watch what I do. Now you do likewise.* **2.** also; as well; moreover; too: *Mary must go home now, and Nell likewise.*

li·kin (lē′kēn′), *n.* a Chinese provincial duty on goods in transit. [< Mandarin *li-chin* < *li* a small coin + *chin* money]

lik·ing (lī′king), *n.* **1.** preference; fondness; kindly feeling: *a liking for apples. Friendships begin with liking* (George Eliot). **2.** taste; pleasure: *food to your liking. James Binnie had found the Continental life pretty much to his liking* (Thackeray). [Old English *līcung* < *līcian* to please, like[2]]

lik·ker (lik′ər), *n. U.S. Dialect.* liquor: *corn likker.*

li·lac (lī′lək, -lak, -läk), *n.* **1.** any of various shrubs of the olive family, especially a common garden plant with clusters of tiny, fragrant, pale pinkish-purple or white flowers. Its blossom is the floral emblem of New Hampshire. **2.** the cluster of flowers. **3.** a pale pinkish purple.

—*adj.* pale pinkish-purple: *She wore a lilac gown.*

[< obsolete French *lilac* < Spanish < Arabic *līlak* < Persian, variant of *nīlak* bluish < *nīl* indigo. Compare ANIL.]

Branch of Common Lilac

li·la·ceous (lī lā′shəs), *adj.* of or resembling the pinkish-purple of most lilacs.

lil·i·a·ceous (lil′ē ā′shəs), *adj.* **1.** of or characteristic of lilies. **2.** belonging to the lily family. [< Late Latin *līliāceus* (with English *-ous*) lilylike < Latin *līlium* lily]

lil·ied (lil′ēd), *adj.* **1.** resembling a lily in fairness of complexion; white. **2.** covered with or full of lilies.

Lil·ith (lil′ith, lī′lith), *n.* **1.** *Semitic Mythology.* a female demon who consorts with men in their dreams. In later legend she was a vampire who dwelt in deserted places and preyed on children. **2.** (in Jewish folklore) Adam's first wife, before Eve was created.

lil·li·bul·le·ro (lil′ē bə lir′ō), *n.* **1.** a part of the refrain of a song ridiculing the Irish Catholics, written in England during the Revolution of 1688. **2.** the song itself. **3.** its tune.

Lil·li·put (lil′ə put, -pət), *n.* an imaginary island described in Jonathan Swift's *Gulliver's Travels* (1726). Its tiny people are represented as being about six inches tall.

Lil·li·pu·tian (lil′ə pyü′shən), *adj.* **1.** of or suitable for Lilliput or its inhabitants. **2.** very small; tiny; petty: *A four-inch fort, with crenellated walls and a ramp, concealing ten Lilliputian soldiers in its base* (New Yorker).
—*n.* **1.** an inhabitant of Lilliput. **2.** a person of little size, character, or mind; a very small person.

li·lo (lī′lō), *n., pl.* **-los.** *British.* an air mattress: *He loaded these onto an inflated rubber lilo which he dragged into the sea, [and] got on board himself* (Manchester Guardian Weekly). [alteration of *lie low*]

lilt (lilt), *v.t., v.i.* to sing or play (a tune) in a light, tripping manner: *She tripped merrily on, lilting a tune to supply the lack of conversation* (Emily Brontë).
—*n.* **1.** a lively song or tune with a swing. **2.** rhythmical cadence or swing: *The lines go with a lilt* (Robert Louis Stevenson). **3.** a springing action; a lively, springing step or movement.
[Middle English *lulten, lylten;* origin uncertain] —**lilt′ing·ly,** *adv.*

lil·y (lil′ē), *n., pl.* **lil·ies,** *adj.* —*n.* **1.** any of a group of plants of the lily family that grow from a bulb. Its flowers are usually large, bellshaped, and beautiful, and are often divided into six parts. **2.** the flower of any of these plants: *The lily is a symbol of whiteness or purity.* **3.** the bulb. **4.** any of various related or similar plants, such as the calla lily, day lily, and water lily, etc. **5.** *Heraldry.* the fleur-de-lis.

Tiger Lily (def. 1) (2 to 4 ft. high)

gild the lily, to ornament or overstate something that is already good or pleasing: *Apparently acknowledging that Mr. Ford had made his point, Commissioner Ploscowe soon cut off the questioning, saying "I don't know why you're gilding the lily"* (New York Times).
—*adj.* **1.** like a lily; white; pale; pure; lovely; delicate: *Elaine, the lily maid of Astolat* (Tennyson). **2.** pallid; colorless; bloodless.
[Old English *lilie* < Latin *līlium*] —**lil′y-like′,** *adj.*

lily family, a group of herbs, shrubs, and trees, that usually have flowers with six parts, grow from fleshy rootstocks or bulbs, and have stemless leaves. Lilies, tulips, hyacinths, trilliums, asparagus, smilax, and aloes are monocotyledonous and belong to the lily family.

lil·y-fin·gered (lil′ē fing′gərd), *adj.* having white or delicate fingers; lilyhanded: *Can't have no lily-fingered boys workin' for me* (Harriet Beecher Stowe).

lil·y-hand·ed (lil′ē han′did), *adj.* having white or delicate hands: *no little lily-handed baronet he* (Tennyson).

lily iron, a harpoon with a detachable head used in killing swordfish.

lil·y-liv·ered (lil′ē liv′ərd), *adj.* cowardly: *thou lily-livered boy* (Shakespeare).

lily of the valley, *pl.* **lilies of the valley.** a plant of the lily family, having tiny, fragrant, bell-shaped, white flowers arranged up and down a single stem. See **raceme** for picture.

lily pad, *U.S.* the broad, flat floating leaf of a water lily: *Huge moccasin darting away beneath the dense reeds and lily pads of the swamp* (Knickerbocker Magazine).

lil·y-white (lil′ē hwīt′), *adj.* **1.** clean; free of stigma: . . . *there was no justification for the "war" that was going on . . . "It should end," he declared, "Neither one is lily-white"* (New York Times). **2.** pure white; white as a lily: *And, as with my lily-white hands I knock up an extra wing in which to house them* . . . (Punch). —**lil′y-white′ness,** *n.*

Lil·y-white (lil′ē hwīt′), *n.* a member of a faction of Republicans in the southern United States seeking to exclude Negroes from political affairs. —*adj.* of or having to do with the Lily-whites.

lim., limit.

li·ma (lī′mə), *n.* any of various bivalve mollusks with an obliquely oval shell, that are able to swim by rapidly opening and closing the valves of the shell. [< New Latin *Lima* the genus name < Latin *līma* a file]

Li·ma (lī′mə), *n. U.S.* a code name for the letter *l,* used in transmitting radio messages.

Lima bean, **1.** a broad, flat bean used for food. **2.** the plant that it grows on. [< *Lima,* the capital of Peru]

lim·a·cine (lim′ə sīn, -sin; lī′mə-), *adj.* **1.** of, having to do with, or belonging to the family of mollusks comprising the slugs. **2.** resembling the slugs. [< New Latin *Limacinae* a sub-family of snails < Latin *līmāx, -ācis* snail, slug < Greek *leímāx, -akos*]

limb[1] (lim), *n.* **1.** a leg, arm, or wing. **2.** a large branch of a tree. **3.** a part that projects, as a section of a building: *the four limbs of a cross.* **4.** a person or thing thought of as a branch or offshoot: *Television is a limb of the electronics industry* (Punch). **5.** a mischievous child; scamp: *I always hated young uns, and this ere's a perfect little limb* (Harriet Beecher Stowe). **6.** a member or clause of a sentence. **7.** a spur of a mountain range. **8.** one of the pieces of a gun lock.
go out on a limb, *Informal.* to risk one's own safety and comfort; expose oneself to attack, criticism, etc.: *He went out on a limb for his wayward brother by recommending him to a friend for a job. The candidate went out on a limb on the budget issue.*
limb from limb, completely apart: *They pulled down . . . their houses, and pulled them . . . limb from limb* (Daniel Defoe).
—*v.t.* to pull limb from limb; dismember.
[Old English *lim*]
—**Syn.** *n.* **2.** See **branch. 3.** arm, shoot.

limb[2] (lim), *n.* **1.** the edge or boundary of a surface, especially: **a.** the graduated edge of a quadrant or similar instrument. **b.** the edge of the disk of a heavenly body: *the sun's lower limb was just free of the hill* (Thomas Hardy). **2.** *Botany.* the expanded flat part of a structure, as the upper part of a gamopetalous corolla or the blade of a leaf. **3.** *Archery.* either part of a bow above or below the grip or handle. [< Latin *limbus* border, edge, fringe. Doublet of LIMBO, LIMBUS.]

lim·ba (lim′bə), *n.* **1.** afara. **2.** the wood of the afara: *Limba [is] a light honey-coloured hardwood from Africa* (London Times). [< a native word]

Lim·ba (lim′bə), *n., pl.* **-ba** or **-bas. 1.** a member of a people living in northern Sierra Leone. **2.** the language of this people, belonging to the Niger-Congo group.

lim·bate (lim′bāt), *adj. Biology.* having a border; bordered, as a flower having an edging of a different color from the rest. [< Late Latin *limbātus* bordered, edged < Latin *limbus* edge, limbus]

-limbed, *combining form.* having ___limbs: *Straight-limbed = having straight limbs.*

lim·ber[1] (lim′bər), *adj.* **1.** bending or moving easily; flexible: *Willow is a limber wood. A piano player should have limber fingers.* **2.** yielding readily to strain or influence: *You put me off with limber vows* (Shakespeare).
—*v.t.* to make limber. —*v.i.* to become limber: *Tom is stiff when he begins to skate, but limbers up easily.*
[perhaps < *limb*[1]] —**lim′ber·ly,** *adv.* —**lim′ber·ness,** *n.*
—**Syn.** *adj.* **1.** supple, nimble, pliant, lithe. See **flexible.**

lim·ber[2] (lim′bər), *n.* the detachable front part of the carriage of a horse-drawn field gun. —*v.t., v.i.* to attach the limber (to) in preparing to move. [alteration of Middle English *lymour,* or *limmer,* perhaps < Middle French *limonière* wagon with shafts < Old French *limon* shaft]

lim·ber·neck (lim′bər nek′), *n.* botulism of domestic poultry.

lim·bers (lim′bərz), *n.pl.* holes or channels through which water may pass to the pump well of a ship. [perhaps < French *lumière* hole; (literally) light]

lim·bic (lim′bik), *adj.* of or having the character of a limbus or border; bordering; marginal.

limbic lobe, *Anatomy.* either of two lobes of the brain, one in each hemisphere.

limb·less (lim′lis), *adj.* having no limbs; deprived of a limb or limbs.

limb·meal (lim′mēl′), *adv. Archaic.* limb from limb: *to tear her limbmeal.*

lim·bo (lim′bō), *n.* **1.** Often, **Limbo.** (in Roman Catholic theology) a place on the border of hell for unbaptized infants, the righteous who died before the coming of Christ, and others who have not received His grace while living, but do not deserve the punishment of willful or impenitent sinners. **2.** a place for people and things forgotten, cast aside, or out of date: *Vast tracts of land will go into a kind of limbo which may or may not mean permanent socialization* (Wall Street Journal). *The belief that the earth is flat belongs to the limbo of outworn ideas.* **3.** prison; jail; confinement: *I should be better satisfied if you were in limbo, with a rope about your neck, and a comfortable bird's-eye prospect to the gallows* (William Godwin). **4.** a West Indian calypso dance in which each participant dances his way under a rod held up horizontally, bending backward to avoid touching the rod as it is progressively lowered: *And when the limbo dancers perform their dazzling gyrations and move their incredibly supple bodies under the low, flaming pole, you will gasp with admiration and excitement* (New Yorker). [< Latin *(in) limbō* (on) the edge, ablative of *limbus.* Doublet of LIMB[2], LIMBUS.]

limb of the law, a policeman, lawyer, or judge.

Lim·burg·er (lim′bėr gər), *n.* a soft cheese having a strong smell. [< German *Limburger* < *Limbourg,* a province in Belgium]

lim·bus (lim′bəs), *n., pl.* **-bi** (-bī). **1.** a border or edge differentiated by color or formation, as in some flowers and shells. **2.** a place on the border of hell; limbo. [< Latin *limbus* border, edge (in Medieval Latin, limbo). Doublet of LIMB[2], LIMBO.]

lime[1] (līm), *n., v.,* **limed, lim·ing.** —*n.* **1. a.** a white substance obtained by burning limestone, shells, bones, etc.; calcium oxide; quicklime. Lime is strongly alkaline and is used in making mortar, cement, glass, etc., in tanning, and on fields to improve the soil. *Formula:* CaO **b.** any of various other compounds containing calcium that are used for soil improvement. **2.** *Poetic.* birdlime.
—*v.t.* **1.** to put lime on: *He drained the land and limed it.* **2.** to smear (branches, twigs, etc.) with birdlime. **3.** to catch (birds) with or as with birdlime. **4.** to entangle; ensnare: *O limed soul, that struggling to be free, Art more engaged!* (Shakespeare). **5.** to cement: *I will not ruinate my father's house, Who gave his blood to lime the stones together* (Shakespeare).
[Old English *līm*]

lime[2] (līm), *n.* **1.** a greenish-yellow citrus fruit much like a lemon, but smaller and sourer. Its juice is used as a flavoring and in medicine. **2.** the tree that it grows on, a small tropical tree of the rue family native to Asia. [< French *lime* < Spanish *lima* < Arabic *līma,* back formation of *līmūn* (< Persian), with *-ūn* taken as an ending. Compare LEMON.]

lime[3] (līm), *n.* a linden tree, often used for shade. [variant of earlier *line,* Old English *lind* linden]

lime·ade (līm′ād′), *n.* a drink made of lime juice, sugar, and water.

lime·burn·er (līm′bėr′nər), *n.* a person who makes lime by burning or calcining limestone, etc.

Lime·house (līm′hous′), *n.* a section of the East End of London, on the northern bank of the Thames, in which most of the Chinese residents of the city used to live. Various writers of fiction have made the section a byword for crime and violence.

lime juice, the juice of limes, used in flavoring beverages, etc., and once used by seamen, arctic explorers, etc., to prevent scurvy.

lime·juic·er (līm′jü′sər), *n. Slang.* a British sailor or ship.

lime·kiln (līm′kil′, -kiln′), *n.* a furnace for making lime by burning limestone, shells, etc.

lime·light (līm′līt′), *n., v.,* **-light·ed** or **-lit, -light·ing.** —*n.* **1.** a strong light thrown upon the stage of a theater to light up certain persons or objects and draw attention to them. **2.** the center or glare of public attention and interest: *Some people are never happy unless they are in the limelight showing off. German bonds took the limelight in the foreign land market* (London Times). **3.** a fixture that produces a strong stage light by burning calcium. **4.** the part of a stage thus lighted, usually the center.
—*v.t.* to illuminate by or as if by limelight; make the center of attention: *Louis MacNiece was a poet's poet. He never sought the easy limelit road to a mass audience* (London Times).

li·men (lī′men), *n. Psychology, Physiology.* a threshold, especially of perception. [< Latin *līmen, -inis* threshold]

lim·er·ick (lim′ər ik, lim′rik), *n.* a kind of humorous verse of five lines. *Example:*
"There was a young lady from Lynn
Who was so exceedingly thin
That when she essayed
To drink lemonade
She slid down the straw and fell in."
A limerick has a rhyme scheme with lines 1, 2, and 5 having three feet, and 3 and 4 having two feet. [apparently from a song that mentioned *Limerick*, Ireland]

li·mes (lī′mēz), *n., pl.* **lim·i·tes.** (in Roman history) a boundary. [< Latin *līmes, -itis* boundary]

Li·mes (lī′mēz), *n.* **1.** *pl.* **Lim·i·tes.** one of the lines of fortifications protecting parts of the Roman Empire. **2.** the Siegfried Line.

lime·stone (līm′stōn′), *n.* a rock consisting mostly of calcium carbonate, used for building and for making lime. Marble is a kind of crystalline limestone: *The rear of City Hall is now sheathed with the same hard Alabama limestone as the front and sides* (New Yorker).

lime tree, 1. any linden tree (used more commonly in Europe than America). **2.** a tupelo or sour gum, found in the southern United States. **3.** a tree that bears limes.

lime twig, 1. a twig smeared with birdlime for catching birds. **2.** anything used to ensnare: *Catch fools with lime twigs dipt with pardons* (Thomas Dekker).

lime·wash (līm′wosh′, -wôsh′), *n.* a mixture of lime and water, used for coating walls, etc. —*v.t.* to whitewash with such a mixture.

lime·wa·ter (līm′wô′tər, -wot′ər), *n.* **1.** a solution of slaked lime in water. It is used to counteract an acid condition. **2.** water that contains naturally a large amount of either calcium carbonate or calcium sulfate.

lim·ey[1] (lī′mē), *n., pl.* **-eys,** *adj. Slang.* —*n.* **1.** any Englishman, especially a sailor or soldier. **2.** an English ship. —*adj.* English: *Naples was the first port this limey ship made* (New Yorker). [American English < *limejuicer* < the use of *lime juice* on British vessels to control scurvy]

lim·ey[2] (lī′mē), *adj.* limy[1].

li·mic·o·line (lī mik′ə līn, -lin), *adj.* of or having to do with certain shore birds or wading birds, as the plovers, snipes, and sandpipers. [< Late Latin *līmicola* a dweller in mud (< *līmus* mud + *colere* inhabit) + English *-ine*[1]]

li·mic·o·lous (lī mik′ə ləs), *adj.* living in mud. [< Late Latin *līmicola* (see LIMICOLINE) + English *-ous*]

lim·i·nal (lim′ə nəl, lī′mə-), *adj.* **1.** *Psychology, Physiology.* of or having to do with a limen or threshold, especially of perception. **2.** *Rare.* of or having to do with the threshold or initial stage of a process. [< Latin *līmen, -inis* threshold; limen + English *-al*[1]]

lim·i·nar·y (lim′ə ner′ē), *adj.* preliminary.

lim·i·ness (lī′mē nis), *n.* limy quality.

lim·it (lim′it), *n.* **1.** the farthest edge or boundary; where something ends or must end; final point as to extent, amount, procedure, etc.: *the limit of vision. Laws put a limit on the authority of policemen, judges, and other officials. Keep within the limits of the school grounds.* **2.** *Mathematics.* a value toward which terms of a sequence, values of a function, etc., approach indefinitely near. **3.** (in betting games) the agreed maximum amount of any bet or raise. **4.** *Obsolete.* the tract or region defined by a boundary.
limits, a. bounds: *As things stand now, Michaels is a healthy man, within limits* (Newsweek). **b.** territories or regions: *At length into the limits of the north They came* (Milton).
the limit, *Slang.* as much as, or more than, one can stand: *You naughty little boy, you are really the limit!*
—*v.t.* **1.** to set a limit to; restrict: *We must limit the expense to $10. Her food was limited to bread and water.* **2.** *Law.* to assign definitely: *to limit an estate over to someone.* [< Middle French *limite,* learned borrowing from Latin *līmes, -itis* boundary]
—**Syn.** *n.* **1.** border, bound. *-v.t.* **1.** restrain, check.

lim·it·a·ble (lim′ə tə bəl), *adj.* that can be limited. —**lim′it·a·ble·ness,** *n.*

lim·it·al (lim′ə təl), *adj.* of or having to do with a limit or boundary.

lim·i·tar·y (lim′ə ter′ē), *adj.* **1.** subject to limits; limited. **2.** of, having to do with, or serving as a limit. **3.** of, having to do with, or situated on a boundary.

lim·i·ta·tion (lim′ə tā′shən), *n.* **1.** a limiting: *the limitation of armaments.* **2.** limited condition: *The import limitation has been reduced to $100 per person.* **3.** a thing that limits; limiting rule or circumstance; restriction: *His hunting suffered from two limitations, a cheap gun and poor eyesight. This was a severe limitation upon some of the historians* (London Times). **4.** a period of time set by law, after which a claim cannot be enforced. —**Syn. 3.** hindrance, handicap.

lim·i·ta·tive (lim′ə tā′tiv), *adj.* limiting; restrictive.

lim·it·ed (lim′ə tid), *adj.* **1.** kept within limits; restricted: *a limited space, limited resources.* **2.** traveling fast and making only a few stops: *This limited train has only sleeping cars, and makes very few stops.* **3.** with legal responsibility only to a limited or restricted extent, usually the nominal stock or shares insofar as it is not yet paid up: *a limited liability. Abbr.:* Ltd. **4.** *English Law.* assigned by a conveyance, settlement, etc.: *Property is limited to a person for life, in tail, etc.*
—*n. U.S.* a train, bus, etc., that travels fast and makes only a few stops. —**lim′it·ed·ly,** *adv.* —**lim′it·ed·ness,** *n.*
—**Syn.** *adj.* **1.** circumscribed, confined.

lim·it·ed-ac·cess (lim′ə tid ak′ses), *adj.* (of highways) having access roads at relatively few points.

limited company, a corporation in which the liability of stockholders is limited to a specified amount.

limited edition, a special edition of a book printed in a limited number of copies. A limited edition is often printed and bound differently, if there is a popular edition.

limited monarchy, a monarchy in which the ruler's powers are limited by the laws of the nation; constitutional monarchy.

limited payment insurance, life insurance for which the insured pays a higher premium for a fixed number of years, after which the policy is fully paid.

limited policy, an insurance policy that covers only a limited number of risks or contingencies.

limited war, a war confined to a limited area, usually of strategic importance: ... *the ability to fight either an all-out or a limited war* (Vernon D. Tate).

lim·it·er (lim′ə tər), *n.* **1.** a person or thing that limits. **2.** *Physics.* a transducer.

lim·i·tes (lim′ə tēz), *n.* plural of **limes.**

Lim·i·tes (lim′ə tēz), *n.* plural of **Limes.**

lim·it·ing (lim′ə ting), *adj.* **1.** that limits. **2.** (of an adjective, etc.) serving to restrict the meaning of the word modified.

lim·it·less (lim′it lis), *adj.* without limits; boundless; infinite: *the limitless expanse of space, limitless ambition. American scientists are hard at work seeking to harness the limitless energy of the H-bomb for peaceful production of power* (Wall Street Journal). —**lim′it·less·ly,** *adv.* —**lim′it·less·ness,** *n.*
—**Syn.** illimitable, unlimited.

lim·its (lim′its), *n.pl.* See under **limit,** *n.*

lim·mer (lim′ər), *n. Scottish.* **1. a.** a worthless woman; strumpet. **b.** a minx: *Grizzel, ye limmer, gang to the door* (Scott). **2.** *Obsolete.* a rogue; scoundrel. [origin uncertain]

limn (lim), *v.t.,* **limned, lim·ning. 1.** to paint (a picture). **2.** to portray in words: *Beatrice was a reticent woman and had too much taste to bare all these grubby secret details, but she limned a general picture for him* (New Yorker). **3.** to illuminate (a manuscript). [Middle English *lymnen,* variant of *luminen* < Old French *luminer;* see LUMINE]

lim·ner (lim′nər, lim′ər), *n.* a person who limns.

lim·net·ic (lim net′ik), *adj.* **1.** inhabiting the open water of lakes, as various animals and plants. **2.** having to do with life or organisms in the open water of lakes.

lim·no·graph (lim′nə graf, -gräf), *n.* an apparatus for measuring and recording the variations of level in a body of water, especially a lake; recording limnometer.

lim·no·log·i·cal (lim′nə loj′ə kəl), *adj.* of or having to do with limnology: *Austrian scientists suggested, in 1956, the formation of a committee for international cooperation in the limnological study of the Danube* (New Scientist).

lim·nol·o·gist (lim nol′ə jist), *n.* a student or expert in limnology.

lim·nol·o·gy (lim nol′ə jē), *n.* the study of fresh-water bodies of inland waters, as lakes and ponds, especially with reference to their physical and biological features. [< Greek *límnē* lake, marsh + English *-logy*]

lim·nom·e·ter (lim nom′ə tər), *n.* an apparatus for measuring small variations of level in a body of water, especially a lake.

Li·moges (li mōzh′), *n.* porcelain made at Limoges, a city in central France.

lim·o·nene (lim′ə nēn), *n.* a terpene having an odor like that of lemons. Limonene is found in three optically different forms, the dextrorotatory one occurring in the essential oils of lemon, orange, etc. *Formula:* $C_{10}H_{16}$ [< New Latin *limonum* lemon + English *-ene*]

li·mo·ni·ad (lī mō′nē ad), *n. Greek and Roman Mythology.* a meadow nymph. [< Late Latin *Līmōniades,* plural < Greek *leimōniádes* < *leimōn* meadow]

li·mo·nite (lī′mə nīt), *n.* a mineral, varying in color from dark brown to yellow, used as an iron ore and yellow pigment; hydrous ferric oxide. *Formula:* $2Fe_2O_3.3H_2O$ [< German *Limonit* < Greek *leimōn* meadow]

li·mo·nit·ic (lī′mə nit′ik), *adj.* consisting of or resembling limonite.

lim·ou·sine (lim′ə zēn′, lim′ə zēn), *n.* a usually closed automobile seating from three to five passengers, with a driver's seat separated from the passengers by a partition. [< French *limousine* < *Limousin,* a former province in France]

limp[1] (limp), *n.* a lame step or walk. [< verb] —*v.i.* **1.** to walk with a limp. **2.** to proceed slowly and with difficulty. [origin uncertain. Compare Old English *lemphealt* lame] —**limp′er,** *n.* —**limp′ing·ly,** *adv.*
—**Syn.** *v.i.* **1.** hobble.

limp[2] (limp), *adj.* **1.** not at all stiff; lacking stiffness; ready to bend or droop: *limp flowers, a limp body.* **2.** lacking firmness, force, energy, or the like: *I am so tired I feel as limp as a rag.* [origin uncertain. Compare Icelandic *lempinn* pliable, gentle] —**limp′ly,** *adv.* —**limp′ness,** *n.*
—**Syn. 1, 2. Limp, flabby** mean lacking firmness, both literally and figuratively. **Limp** suggests a lack of stiffness or, figuratively, of firmness and strength: *Hot weather always makes me feel limp.* **Flabby** suggests a lack of hardness or, figuratively, of forcefulness and vigor: *She is so fat her flesh is flabby.* —**Ant. 1.** stiff. **2.** firm.

lim·pet (lim′pit), *n.* a small shellfish that sticks tightly to rocks, used for bait and sometimes for food. It is a marine gastropod having a tent-shaped shell: *He ... stuck like a limpet to a rock* (Scott). [Old English *lempedu* (perhaps with diminutive *-t*) < Medieval Latin *lampreda.* Doublet of LAMPREY.]

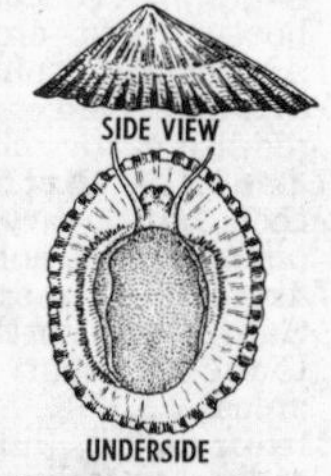

European Limpet

lim·pid (lim′pid), *adj.* clear; transparent: *a spring of limpid water, limpid eyes.* [< Latin *limpidus*] —**lim′pid·ly,** *adv.* —**lim′pid·ness,** *n.* —**Syn.** pellucid.

lim·pid·i·ty (lim pid′ə tē), *n.* limpid quality or condition. —**Syn.** clearness, transparence.

limp·kin (limp′kin), *n.* a brown wading bird of tropical America, related to the cranes and rails, but being the only living member of its family; courlan. [American English < *limp*[1], verb + *-kin* (because of its halting gait)]

limp·sy (limp′sē), *adj. Dialect.* limp.

lim·u·loid (lim′yə loid), *adj.* of, having to do with, or resembling the king crabs. —*n.* a king crab. [< *limul*(us) + *-oid*]

lim·u·lus (lim′yə ləs), *n., pl.* **-li** (-lī). a king crab or horseshoe crab. [< New Latin *Limulus* the genus name < Latin *līmulus* a bit askance (diminutive) < *līmus* askew]

lim·y[1] (lī′mē), *adj.,* **lim·i·er, lim·i·est. 1.** of, containing, or resembling lime. **2.** smeared with birdlime. Also, **limey.**

lim·y[2] (lī′mē), *n., pl.* **lim·ies.** *Slang.* a lime-juicer.

lin., **1.** lineal. **2.** linear.

lin·a·ble (lī′nə bəl), *adj.* ranged in a straight line. Also, **lineable.**

lin·ac (lin′ak), *n.* a linear accelerator. [< *lin*(ear) *ac*(celerator)]

li·na·ceous (lī nā′shəs), *adj.* belonging to a family of herbs and shrubs typified by the flax. [< Latin *līnum* flax (< Greek *línon*) + English *-aceous*]

lin·age (lī′nij), *n.* **1.** alignment. **2. a.** quantity of printed or written matter estimated in number of lines: *Advertising space is usually figured in linage.* **b.** the charge or rate of charge for a line. Also, **lineage.**

lin·al·o·öl (li nal′ō ōl, -ol; lin′ə lül′), *n. Chemistry.* an unsaturated, open-chain, liquid alcohol, related to the terpenes, occurring in various essential oils and used in perfumes. *Formula:* $C_{10}H_{18}O$ [< Spanish *lináloe* (< *lignáloe* < Late Latin *lignum aloēs* wood of aloe) + English *-ol*[1]]

lin·a·ma·rin (lin′ə mãr′in), *n.* a glucoside present in flax that helps to protect it against wilt. *Formula:* $C_{10}H_{17}NO_6$ [< Latin *līnum* flax + *amārus* bitter + English *-in*]

lin·a·ma·rine (lin′ə mãr′ēn, -in), *n.* linamarin.

li·nar·i·a (lī nãr′ē ə), *n.* any of a group of plants of the figwort family; toadflax. [< New Latin *Linaria* < Latin *līnum* flax]

linch·pin (linch′pin′), *n.* **1.** a pin inserted through a hole in the end of an axle to keep the wheel on. **2.** that which keeps something from falling; a critical point: *Sir Brian showed how the small station of Kohima in the Burma Campaign suddenly became the linchpin in the defense of India* (Listener). Also, **lynchpin.** [alteration of Middle English *linspin* < Old English *lynis* linchpin + Middle English *pin* pin]

Linchpin (def. 1)

Lin·coln (ling′kən), *n.* any of a breed of long-wooled sheep, originating in Lincolnshire, England.

Lin·coln·esque (ling′kə nesk′), *adj.* like or characteristic of Abraham Lincoln: *a Lincolnesque quality of mercy.*

Lin·coln·i·an (ling kō′nē ən), *adj.* of, having to do with, or characteristic of Abraham Lincoln: *The Republicans might be tempted to abandon the last vestiges of their Lincolnian heritage and to fight the election on a frankly reactionary ticket* (Manchester Guardian Weekly).

Lin·coln·i·a·na (ling kō′nē ä′nə, -an′ə, -ā′nə), *n.pl.* a collection of objects, documents, books, facts, etc., about or belonging to Abraham Lincoln.

Lincoln Red, any of a British breed of reddish cattle related to the shorthorn.

Lincoln's Birthday, *U.S.* February 12, the anniversary of Abraham Lincoln's birthday, not normally a legal holiday.

Lincoln's sparrow, a striped sparrow of Canada and northern United States, similar to the song sparrow, living in boggy, brushy areas.

lin·crus·ta (lin krus′tə), *n.* a wall or ceiling covering made like linoleum. [< *Lincrusta* Walton, a trademark for this covering < *lin*(oleum) + Latin *crusta* crust]

linc·tus (lingk′təs), *n.* a cough syrup or similar liquid to soothe the throat. [< Latin *linctus* a licking < *lingere* to lick]

lin·dane (lin′dān), *n.* a benzene compound used as an insecticide in place of DDT. *Formula:* $C_6H_6Cl_6$

Lind·bergh Law (lind′bėrg), *U.S.* a law which makes kidnaping a federal crime if the victim is taken across a state line. [< Charles A. *Lindbergh,* born 1902, whose son was kidnapped in 1932]

lin·den (lin′dən), *n.* any of various shade trees with heart-shaped leaves and clusters of small, fragrant, greenish-yellow flowers, as the basswood of eastern North America and a common European species; lime tree. [Old English *linden,* adjective < *lind* linden, lime[3]]

linden looper, a measuring worm that eats the leaves of trees, especially the linden: *Cankerworms, linden loopers, and the gypsy moth are expected again to invade the East, defoliating many acres of forests* (Science News Letter).

Linde process (lind), a method of liquefying gases in which the gas is first cooled by contact with another liquefied gas and then freely expanded. [< Carl von *Linde,* 1842-1934, a German engineer, who developed it]

Lin·dy (lin′dē), *n., pl.* **-dies,** *v.* **-died, -dy·ing.** —*n.* a kind of jitterbug, especially popular in the 1930's and 1940's. —*v.i.* to dance the Lindy. [< Charles A. *Lindbergh,* born 1902, an American aviator (because of the fame attached to his flying exploits)]

Lin·dy-hop (lin′dē hop′), *v.i.,* **-hopped, -hop·ping.** to Lindy.

Lindy Hop or **hop,** the Lindy.

line[1] (līn), *n., v.,* **lined, lin·ing.** —*n.* **1.** a piece of rope, cord, or wire: *a clothes line, a fish line.* **2.** a cord for measuring, making level or straight, etc. **3.** a cord with a hook for catching fish. **4.** a long narrow mark: *Draw two lines along the margin.* **5.** anything like such a mark: *the lines in a rock, the lines in your face.* **6.** a straight line: *The lower edges of the two pictures are about on a line.* **7.** *Mathematics.* the path or track a point may be imagined to leave as it moves. It is considered to have length but no breadth or thickness. **8.** the use of lines in drawing: *a picture in line, clearness of line in an artist's work.* **9.** an edge; limit; boundary: *the line between Texas and Mexico.* **10.** a row of persons or things: *a line of chairs.* **11.** a row of words on a page or in a column: *a column of 40 lines.* **12.** a short letter; note: *Drop me a line.* **13.** a connected set or series of persons or things following one another in time: *The Stuarts were a line of English kings.* **14.** family or lineage: *of noble line.* **15.** course; track; direction; route: *the line of march of an army.* **16.** a course of action, conduct, or thought: *a line of policy, the Communist party line. The State Department denied today any aggressive intent ... saying that was an old propaganda line* (New York Times). *I shall proceed on these lines till further notice. ... he took an unpopular line in advocating peace negotiations* (Edmund Wilson). **17.** the front row of trenches or other defenses: *a line extending along a five-mile front, the Siegfried Line.* **18.** troops or ships arranged abreast. **19.** the arrangement of an army or fleet for battle. **20. a.** wires connecting points or stations in a telegraph system, telephone system, radar warning operation, or the like. **b.** the system itself. **21.** any rope, wire, pipe, hose, etc., running from one point to another: *a steam line, to tie up a boat with the forward line.* **22.** a single track of railroad. **23. a.** one branch of a system of transportation: *the main line of a railroad.* **b.** a whole system of transportation or conveyance: *the Grand Trunk Line.* **24.** a branch of business; kind of activity: *the dry-goods line. This kind of writing is not much in my line* (Thackeray). **25.** a kind or branch of goods: *a good line of hardware.* **26.** a single verse of poetry. **27. a.** talk, usually intended to deceive or confuse: *She fell for the playboy's line and eloped with him. The burglar tried to hand the police a line, but two witnesses saw him break into the house.* **b.** a joke, remark, etc., used frequently by a person, often by an entertainer, for identification. **28.** *Music.* one of the horizontal lines that make a staff in music. **29.** *Football.* the players along the scrimmage line at the start of a play: *a seven-man line T-formation.* **30.** 1/12 of an inch. **31.** *Bowling.* a complete game of ten frames. **32.** *Television.* a single scanning line. **33.** a circle of the terrestrial or celestial sphere: *the equinoctial line. Abbr.:* l.

all along the line, at every point; everywhere: *... has therefore been compelled to lower its sights all along the line* (New Yorker).

down the line, the whole way; as far as possible; to the end: *Castro is now willing to go down the line with the Russians* (Time). *Many Democrats ... have promised to fight him down the line on these* [*proposals*] (New York Times).

draw a or **the line,** to set a limit: *Feathers and flowers are different things. You must draw a line somewhere, and I draw it at feathers* (Scribner's). *They know how to draw the line between private and public feeling* (London Examiner).

get or **have a line on,** *Informal.* to get or have information about: *The "economic diagnosticians" have been busy ... studying the consumer ... to get a line both on what is happening and what may happen* (Petroleum and Chemical Transporter).

hold the line, to prevent or resist successfully a threatened change, such as an increase in prices: *Space officials, for the first time in six years, plan to hold the line or even trim budget requests for new funds* (Wall Street Journal).

in line, a. in alignment; in a row: *The children are all in line.* **b.** in agreement: *This is in line with their thinking.* **c.** ready: *in line for action.* **d.** in order; in succession: *next in line.*

in line with, in agreement with: *The lifting of the discount rate was in line with the Treasury's policy of keeping short-term rates generally high enough to discourage such investment funds from going abroad* (Wall Street Journal).

into line, into a position of agreement or conformity: *It would have the merit of bringing legal theory into line with political reality* (Listener).

lay or **put on the line,** *U.S. Slang.* **a.** to produce or present fully, without suppressing anything: *Next time a full-scale hearing will be laid on the line* (New York Times). **b.** to speak frankly; say openly: *An art instructor laid it on the line: "Children don't have prejudices"* (Time).

lines, a. outline; contour: *a car of fine lines.* **b.** a plan of construction: *two books written on the same lines.* **c.** a double row (front and rear rank) of soldiers: *The lines of infantry are being disbanded.* **d.** words that an actor speaks in a play: *to forget one's lines.* **e.** one's lot in life: *The lines are fallen unto me in pleasant places* (Psalms 16:6). **f.** *U.S.* reins: *He held the lines tightly.* **g.** poetry; verses: *Lines forty thousand, cantos twenty-five* (Byron). **h.** *Informal.* a marriage certificate: *"How should a child like you know that the marriage was irregular?" "Because I had no lines'" cries Caroline* (Thackeray). **i.** a system of curves and straight lines used by naval architects to trace the outline of the shape of a ship: *Her extravagant poop ..., and her lines like a cocked hat reversed* (Charles Reade).

on a line, even; level: *The walk is on a line with the road.*

on the line, a. in between; neither one thing nor the other: *Politically, he is on the line, choosing to avoid both the right and the left.* **b.** approximately on a level with the eye: *a painting hung on the line.* **c.** *Slang.* at once; readily: *Paying on the line is cheaper than on credit.*

out of line, a. in disagreement; not in harmony: *For some time it has been felt that the share capital of the Company was out of line with the capital employed in the business* (London Times). **b.** behaving improperly: *The new boy was impertinent and almost always out of line.*

read between the lines, to discover a meaning or implication not stated outright in something: *They do not say as much to their secret selves; but you can read between the lines these words—"What a weariness it is!"* (Charles H. Spurgeon).

the line, a. (1) the equator: *The sun crosses the line at the equinoxes. We were in the latitude of 12 degrees 35 minutes south of the line* (Daniel Defoe). (2) a circle of the terrestrial or celestial sphere: *... motion of the star in the line* (W.H. Marshall). **b.** the regular army or navy; the soldiers or ships that do all the fighting: *to serve in the line, go into the line.* **c.** the group of officers in charge of such forces: *The combatant officers in the navy are called officers of the line* (Thomas A. Wilhelm).

toe the line or **mark, a.** to stand with the tips of the toes touching a certain line, mark, etc., as before a race, contest, etc.: *The chief mate . . . marked a line on the deck, brought the two boys up to it, making them toe the mark* (Richard H. Dana, Jr.). **b.** to conform to a certain standard, as of duty, conduct, etc.: *The other satellite Communist leaders . . . are all toeing the line and employing terror to extinguish opposition* (Newsweek). *—v.t.* **1.** to mark with lines on paper, etc.: *to line a column in red and one in green, to line out a picture.* **2.** to cover with lines: *a face lined with age.* **3.** to arrange in a line; bring into a line or row; align: *Line your shoes along the edge of the shelf.* **4.** to arrange a line along; form a line along: *to line a frontier with soldiers. Cars lined the road for a mile. The rebels . . . lined the hedges leading to the town* (Macaulay). **5.** to measure or test with a line. **6.** *Baseball.* to hit (a liner): *Wilson . . . capped a four-run outburst in the sixth . . . by lining the ball over the 365-foot marker* (New York Times). *—v.i.* **1.** to form a line; take a position in a line; range. **2.** *Baseball.* to line out: *The batter lined to the first baseman.*

line out, a. (1) *Baseball.* to hit a liner which is caught: *Mantle lined out to the shortstop.* (2) *Rugby.* to put the ball in play by a line-out: *The forward must always be ready to line out and face his man.* **b.** to draw lines on boards, metal, or other material to indicate the general outline for cutting: *It . . . must be lined out into oblong squares* (Patrick Browne). **c.** to transplant (seedlings) from the seed bed to rows in the forest or nursery: *The tomato plants were lined out neatly.* **d.** to read or sing out (a hymn, etc.) a line or two at a time for repetition in singing: *The preacher was lining out a hymn. He lined out two lines, everybody sung it . . . and so on* (Mark Twain).

line up, a. to form a line; form into a line: *The horses lined up for the start of the race.* **b.** to make available or accessible: *The theater agent lined up backers for the new show.*

[fusion of Old English *līne* line, rope, and Middle English *ligne* line < Old French; both ultimately < Latin *līnea* line; linen thread < *līnum* flax]

—Syn. *n.* **4.** stroke, scratch, streak, dash. **10.** rank. **15.** way.

line[2] (lin), *v.,* **lined, lin·ing,** *n. —v.t.* **1.** to put a layer inside of; cover the inner side of with something: *to line a coat with sheepskin, to line a fireplace with brick, to line a book to reinforce it. . . . a great library all lined with books* (Robert Louis Stevenson). **2.** to fill: *to line one's pockets with money.* **3.** to serve as a lining for.

—n. the long parallel fibers of flax, used in making fine linen.

[Old English *līn* flax, linen thread or cloth]

line·a·ble (lī′nə bəl), *adj.* linable.

lin·e·age[1] (lin′ē ij), *n.* **1.** descent in a direct line from an ancestor . . . *he was of the house and lineage of David* (Luke 2:4). **2.** a family; race: *The Lords of Douglas . . . are second to no lineage in Scotland in the antiquity of their descent* (Scott). **3.** the descendants through exclusively male or exclusively female links of a specified ancestor, as by patrilineage or matrilineage. [alteration (influenced by *line*[1]) of Middle English *lynage* < Old French *lignage* < *ligne* line[1] < Latin *līnea*] **—Syn. 1.** ancestry. **2.** stock, extraction.

line·age[2] (lī′nij), *n.* linage.

lin·e·al (lin′ē əl), *adj.* **1.** in the direct line of descent: *A grandson is a lineal descendant of his grandfather.* **2.** having to do with such descent; hereditary: *lineal right.* **3.** of or like a line; linear. [< Late Latin *līneālis* < Latin *līnea* line[1]] **—Syn. 2.** ancestral.

lin·e·al·ly (lin′ē ə lē), *adv.* in the direct line of descent: *A grandson is descended lineally from his grandfather.*

lin·e·a·ment (lin′ē ə mənt), *n.* **1.** a part or feature of a face with attention to its outline: *He was pensively tracing in my countenance the early lineaments of my mother* (Washington Irving). **2.** a part or feature; distinctive characteristic: *The style of Denman is more lofty, and impressed with stronger lineaments of sincerity* (John Galt). **3.** an outline: *lineaments of its subject* (Scientific American). [< Latin *līneāmentum* < *līneāre* reduce to a line < *līnea* line[1]]

lin·e·ar (lin′ē ər), *adj.* **1.** of a line or lines. **2.** made of lines; making use of lines: *linear design.* **3.** in a line or lines: *a linear series.* **4.** of length: *linear measure.* **5.** like a line; long and narrow: *A pine tree has linear leaves.* **6.** proportional: *There is a linear relationship between the size of a star and its luminosity.* [< Latin *līneāris* < *līnea* line[1]] **—lin′e·ar·ly,** *adv.*

Linear A, an ancient language used on Crete from about 1800–1500 B.C., found on clay tablets. The writing is derived from a cuneiform Arcadian script written in a syllabary form.

linear accelerator, *Electronics.* a device for accelerating charged particles in a straight line through a vacuum tube or series of tubes by means of impulses from electric fields.

Linear B, an ancient language used on Crete and found on clay tablets especially at Mycenae. It is an archaic Greek written in a syllabary form.

Linear B
Some signs used in Linear B script

linear equation, *Mathematics.* an equation whose terms involving variables are of the first degree.

lin·e·ar·i·ty (lin′ē ar′ə tē), *n.* linear state or form.

lin·e·ar·i·za·tion (lin′ē ər ə zā′shən), *n.* the act or process of linearizing.

lin·e·ar·ize (lin′ē ə rīz), *v.t.,* **-ized, -iz·ing.** to represent in linear form, or by means of lines.

linear measure, 1. measure of length. **2.** a system for measuring length.

12 inches = 1 foot
3 feet = 1 yard
5½ yards = 1 rod
40 rods = 1 furlong
8 furlongs (1,760 yards or 5,280 feet) = 1 mile
3 miles = 1 league

linear perspective, the branch of perspective that is concerned with the apparent form, magnitude, and position of visual objects.

linear programming, a method of solving operational problems by stating a number of variables simultaneously in the form of linear equations and calculating the optimal solution within the given limitations.

lin·e·ate (lin′ē it, -āt), *adj.* marked with lines, especially longitudinal and more or less parallel lines. [< Latin *līneātus,* past participle of *līneāre* reduce to a line < *līnea* line[1]]

lin·e·at·ed (lin′ē ā′tid), *adj.* lineate.

lin·e·a·tion (lin′ē ā′shən), *n.* **1.** the act or process of drawing lines or marking with lines. **2.** a division into lines. **3.** a line; outline. **4.** a marking or line on a surface, as of the skin. **5.** an arrangement or group of lines.

line·back·er (līn′bak′ər), *n. American Football.* a defensive player whose position is directly behind the line.

line-breed (līn′brēd′), *v.t.,* **-bred, -breed·ing.** to breed within one line or strain of stock.

line breeding, breeding within one line or strain of stock in order to develop certain favorable characteristics.

line·cast·ing (līn′kas′ting, -käs′-), *n.* the act or process of casting lines of printing type in one piece, as with a Linotype. *—adj.* designed for casting lines of type in one piece: *a linecasting machine.*

line drawing, a drawing done with a pen, pencil, etc., completely in lines, with little or no shading or tonal effects and often made especially to be engraved for an illustration.

line drive, a baseball hit so that it travels nearly parallel to the ground.

line engraving, 1. *Fine Arts.* lines cut in a plate or block with a tool, as distinguished from etching, mezzotint, etc. **2.** *Printing.* photoengraved work in line or flat areas, as distinguished from half-tone. **3.** a plate, etc., so engraved. **4.** the impression or print made from it.

line graph, a graph in which points representing quantities are plotted and then connected by a series of short straight lines, usually forming a jagged or smooth curve.

line·less (līn′lis), *adj.* without lines.

line·man (līn′mən), *n., pl.* **-men. 1.** a man who sets up or repairs telegraph, telephone, or electric wires. **2.** *Football.* a center, guard, tackle, or end; player in the line: *The entire cadet backfield and three linemen played sixty minutes* (New York Times). **3.** a man who inspects railroad tracks. **4.** a man who carries the line in surveying.

lin·en (lin′ən), *n.* **1.** cloth, thread, or yarn made from flax fiber. **2.** articles made of linen or some substitute. Tablecloths, napkins, sheets, towels, shirts, and collars may be called linen even when they are made of some substitute. **3.** Also, **linen paper.** writing paper of very fine quality. It was formerly paper made from linen rags.

wash one's dirty linen in public, to mention publicly one's quarrels or difficulties: *I never saw a company wash its dirty linen in public this way* (Wall Street Journal).

—adj. **1.** made of linen, as a garment. **2.** made of flax, as thread or fabrics.

[Old English *linnen, līnen,* adjective < *līn* flax, linen thread or cloth]

lin·en·fold (lin′ən fōld′), *adj.* of, having to do with, or forming a linen scroll: *a linenfold carving. The walls are lined with linenfold panelling* (Manchester Guardian Weekly). *—n.* a linen scroll.

linen scroll or **pattern,** *Architecture.* a form of decorative ornament suggesting the convolutions of rolled or folded linen, used to fill panels, especially during the Tudor period in England.

lin·en·y (lin′ə nē), *adj.* similar to linen: . . . *a lineny texture* (Sunday Times).

line of ap·si·des (ap′sə dēz), the straight line that joins the two points in the elliptical orbit of a planetary body.

line of battle, soldiers or ships in battle formation: . . . *Cochrane sighted three merchantmen who turned out to be French line-of-battle ships* (Wall Street Journal).

line of beauty, *Art.* some kind of curved or wavy line held to be beautiful in itself and considered a necessary element of beauty of form. It is differently represented by different persons, but commonly (as by William Hogarth) as a curve resembling a slender, elongated letter S.

line of credit, the quantity of credit granted by a store to one of its customers.

line of duty, duty or service, especially military duty.

in the line of duty, while performing one's duty, especially in military service: *He said that guards injured in the line of duty got sick pay of $1.50 an hour and medical treatments at Headquarters* (New York Times).

line officer, a commissioned officer in the army or navy commanding a combat unit or force.

line of fire, the path of a bullet, shell, etc.

line of force, *Physics.* a line in a field of electric or magnetic force that indicates the direction in which the force is acting.

line of position, the charted course on which an aircraft or ship is traveling, as determined by visual sightings, as of a railroad, or by radio or celestial means. When an intersecting line is obtained, the exact position of the craft can be determined.

line of scrimmage, scrimmage line.

line of sight, 1. the straight line from the eye to the object it is looking at, as a target in shooting or bombing, etc. **2.** the straight line of the beam from a radar antenna. **—line′-of-sight′,** *adj.*

line of succession, 1. descent; lineage. **2.** the order in which persons succeed one another: *The Speaker of the House stands third in the line of succession to the Presidency.*

line of vision, a straight line from the fovea of the retina to the point on which vision is fixed.

lin·e·o·late (lin′ē ə lāt), *adj. Biology.* marked with minute lines; finely lineate. [< Latin *līneola* (diminutive) < *līnea* line[1]; + English *-ate*[1]]

lin·e·o·lat·ed (lin′ē ə lā′tid), *adj.* lineolate.

line·out (līn′out′), *n. Rugby.* the putting of the ball in play from the sideline.

lin·er[1] (lī′nər), *n.* **1.** a ship or airplane belonging to a transportation system: *During the First World War Kendall commanded HMS Calgarian, a luxury liner serving as a cruiser* (Maclean's). **2. a.** a person who makes lines, as a person who keeps the lines in football. **b.** a device for marking lines or stripes. **3.** *Baseball.* a baseball hit so that it travels nearly parallel to the ground: *Reese followed with a liner high off the left field wall for a double* (New York Times).

lin·er[2] (lī′nər), *n.* **1.** a person who lines or fits a lining to anything. **2.** something that serves as a lining: **a.** an inside cylinder, or a vessel placed inside another. **b.** a thin slip of metal, etc., placed between two parts to adjust them; shim. **3.** a short passage usually on the cover of a phonograph record giving information about the record.

lin·er·board (lī′nər bôrd, -bōrd), *n.* a paper product, the principal material used in making corrugated boxes: *The company has also brought into production white and colored linerboards* (Wall Street Journal).

liner notes, the text on a phonograph record cover.

liner train, *British.* an express train for carrying freight between terminals near industrial centers: *The liner trains were designed by Dr. Beeching to win back freight traffic from the roads to the railways* (Manchester Guardian Weekly).

lines (līnz), *n., pl.* See under **line,** *n.*

lines·man (līnz′mən), *n., pl.* **-men. 1.** a telephone, telegraph, or electric company lineman. **2.** (in lawn tennis, football, etc.) a person who watches the lines that mark out the field, court, etc., and assists the umpire. **3.** one of the forwards, center, guard, tackle, or end, in football.

line spectrum, a spectrum produced by a luminous gas or vapor in which distinct lines characteristic of an element are emitted by its atoms.

line squall, *Meteorology.* a thunderstorm or severe local storm appearing along a cold front.

line-up or **line·up** (līn′up′), *n.* **1.** a formation of persons or things into a line or file. A police line-up is the arrangement of a group of individuals for identification. **2.** the arrangement of the players in football, baseball, etc., before a play begins. **3.** any alignment of persons or groups for a common purpose: *With the present lineup, the balance of power in the commission has shifted from conservative to progressive* (New York Times).

ling[1] (ling), *n., pl.* **lings** or (*collectively*) **ling. 1.** any of a number of marine fish of the North Atlantic, related to the cod, and having an elongated body, largely used for food, either salted or split and dried. **2.** the fresh-water burbot of Europe and North America. **3.** any of several other fishes. [Middle English *lenge,* perhaps < earlier Dutch *lenghe,* or *linghe*]

ling[2] (ling), *n.* any of various heaths, especially the common heather. [< Scandinavian (compare Old Icelandic *lyng*)]

-ling, *suffix.* **1.** little; unimportant: *Duckling = a little duck.* **2.** one that is ——: *Underling = one that is under.* **3.** one belonging to or concerned with: *Earthling = one belonging to the earth.* [Old English *-ling*]

Ling[2]
Common heather or heath (½ to 3 ft. tall)

ling., linguistics.

Lin·ga·la (ling gäl′ə), *n.* a lingua franca much used in the Congo, consisting of Swahili and several Congo dialects: *Congolese players in red shorts, with electric guitars, were singing in a made-up tongue called Lingala* (Punch).

ling cod, cultus; a food fish of the North American Pacific coast.

lin·ger (ling′gər), *v.i.* **1.** to stay on; go slowly, as if unwilling to leave: *Daylight lingers long in the summertime.* **2.** to be slow or late in doing or beginning anything; hesitate; delay; dawdle: *By no remonstrance . . . could he prevail upon his allies to be early in the field . . . Everyone of them lingered, and wondered why the rest were lingering* (Macaulay). **3.** to continue alive, in spite of weakness, sickness, or other adverse conditions: *I would not have thee linger in thy pain* (Shakespeare). *—v.t.* to draw out, prolong, or protract by lingering: *How slow This old moon wanes! She lingers my desires* (Shakespeare).

linger away, to waste (time) by lingering: *Better to rush at once to shades below Than linger life away, and nourish woe* (Alexander Pope).

linger on, to continue to linger; live although near death: *He lingered on in a comatose state.*

[Middle English *lengeren* (frequentative) < *lengen* delay, Old English *lengan* < *lang* long[1]] **—lin′ger·er,** *n.* **—lin′ger·ing·ly,** *adv.*

—**Syn.** *v.i.* **1, 2. Linger, loiter, lag** mean to delay in starting or along the way. **Linger** emphasizes delay in starting, and suggests reluctance to leave: *She lingered long after the others had left.* **Loiter** emphasizes delay along the way, and suggests moving slowly and aimlessly: *Mary loitered downtown, looking into all the shopwindows.* **Lag** means to fall behind others or in one's work, and suggests failing to keep up the necessary speed or pace: *The child lagged because he was tired.*

lin·ge·rie (läṅ′zhə rē′, län′jə rā′), *n.* **1.** women's underwear. **2.** linen articles. [< Middle French *lingerie* linen articles < Old French *linge* linen < Latin *līneus,* adjective < *līnum* flax]

lin·go (ling′gō), *n., pl.* **-goes.** *Used humorously or in contempt.* **1.** language, especially foreign speech or language. **2.** any speech regarded as outlandish or queer, as the jargon of some special group: *Writers about baseball use a strange lingo. Well, well, I shall understand your lingo one of these days, cousin; in the meanwhile I must answer in plain English* (William Congreve). [< Provençal *lengo* < Latin *lingua* language, tongue; influenced by *lingua franca*]

lin·goe (ling′gō), *n., pl.* **-goes.** a metal weight hanging from the bottom of each cord of a Jacquard loom. [apparently < French *lingot* ingot]

lin·gon·ber·ry (ling′gən ber′ē), *n., pl.* **-ries. 1.** a low shrub of the heath family growing in the northern parts of North America, Asia, and Europe; cowberry. **2.** its berry, similar to, and used in place of, the common cranberry. [< Swedish *lingon* lingonberry + English *berry*]

lin·gua (ling′gwə), *n., pl.* **-guae** (-gwē). a tongue or tonguelike organ, as the ligula of some insects and the proboscis of butterflies and moths. [< Latin *lingua* tongue]

lin·gua fran·ca (ling′gwə frang′kə), **1.** a hybrid language, consisting largely of Italian, used by the Latin races in dealing with Arabs, Turks, Greeks, etc.: *A . . . voice . . . pronounced these words . . . in the lingua franca, mutually understood by Christians and Saracens* (Scott). **2.** any hybrid language similarly used, as any jargon. **3.** any language used internationally as a trade or communications medium: *During the whole 500 years . . . of the Abbasid Caliphate's existence, Arabic was the lingua franca of the whole area extending from Soviet Central Asia to Spain and Portugal inclusive* (Arnold Toynbee). [< Italian *lingua franca* (literally) Frankish language]

Lin·gua Ge·ral (ling′gwə zhə räl′), a language based on Tupi-Guarani and widely spoken in the Amazon region of Brazil. [< Portuguese *lingua* language, *geral* general]

lin·gual (ling′gwəl), *adj.* **1.** of the tongue: *a lingual nerve, a lingual defect.* **2.** *Phonetics.* formed with the aid of the tongue, particularly the tip, as *t* and *d.* **3.** having to do with language or languages.
—n. Phonetics. a lingual sound.
[< Medieval Latin *lingualis* < Latin *lingua* tongue] **—lin′gual·ly,** *adv.*

lin·gui·form (ling′gwə fôrm), *adj.* tongue-shaped; lingulate; ligulate.

lin·guine (ling gwēn′), *n.* a kind of pasta, long and thin like spaghetti, but hollow. [< Italian *linguine* (diminutive) < *lingua* tongue]

lin·guist (ling′gwist), *n.* **1.** a person who studies the history and structure of language: *The linguist collects and records utterances, and by comparing these one with another abstracts the way or modes of speaking which, as we have said, constitute the language of the speech community* (Beals and Hoijer). **2.** a person skilled in a number of languages besides his own; polyglot; multilingual. [< Latin *lingua* tongue, language + English *-ist*]

lin·guis·tic (ling gwis′tik), *adj.* having to do with language or the study of languages: *. . . others, accepting the basic premises of the linguist, differ among themselves in the use and presentation of linguistic findings* (Harold B. Allen). **—lin·guis′ti·cal·ly,** *adv.*

lin·guis·ti·cal (ling gwis′tə kəl), *adj.* linguistic.

linguistic atlas, a book, usually of maps, describing dialect features and their boundaries; dialect atlas.

linguistic family, a linguistic stock.

linguistic form, any meaningful unit of speech, such as a sentence, phrase, word, or morpheme.

linguistic geography, the study of the geographical distribution of dialect features; dialect geography.

lin·guis·ti·cian (ling′gwə stish′ən), *n.* linguist (def. 1).

lin·guis·tics (ling gwis′tiks), *n.* the science of language; comparative study of language structures (descriptive or structural linguistics) and the study of the history and historical relationship of languages and linguistic forms (historical or comparative linguistics).

linguistic stock, 1. a group of related languages together with the parent language from which they are derived. **2.** all the people that speak languages of such a related group.

lin·gu·late (ling′gyə lāt), *adj.* tongue-shaped; ligulate; linguiform. [< Latin *lingulātus* < *lingula* (diminutive) < *lingua* tongue]

ling·y (ling′ē), *adj.* abounding in or covered with ling (heather).

lin·i·ment (lin′ə mənt), *n.* a soothing liquid for rubbing on the skin to relieve soreness, sprains, bruises, etc. [< Late Latin *linīmentum* < Latin *linere* anoint, smear] —**Syn.** embrocation.

li·nin (lī′nin), *n.* **1.** *Chemistry.* a crystallizable bitter principle obtained from a European species of flax, used as a purgative. *Formula:* $C_{22}H_{22}O_9$ **2.** *Biology.* a substance now considered to be an artificial product of fixation, but formerly thought to be the achromatic substance composing the network that encloses the granules of chromatin in the nucleus of a cell. [< Latin *līnum* flax + English *-in*]

lin·ing (lī′ning), *n.* **1.** a layer of material covering the inner surface of something: *the lining of a coat, the lining of a stove.* **2.** the material reinforcing the back of a book. **3.** contents, as of the pocket or purse: *the lining of his coffers shall make coats To deck our soldiers* (Shakespeare). **4.** the act of providing with a lining: *Lining a coat is a difficult matter for an inexperienced seamstress.* **5.** concrete or steel applied to the interior of shafts and tunnels for smoothness and strength.

link[1] (lingk), *n.* **1.** one ring or loop of a chain: *The tractor pulled the log with a chain that had very heavy links.* **2. a.** anything that joins as a link joins: *I had severed the link between myself and my former condition* (Frederick Marryat). *Labour thus helped to create a link of friendship between the rising peoples* (London Times). **b.** a part or parts so joined: *links of sausage.* **3.** a fact or thought that connects others: *a link in a chain of evidence.* **4.** one link of a surveyor's chain, used as a measure of length; 7.92 inches. **5.** a rod, bar, or similar piece connected at its ends to two parts of a machine and transmitting motion from one to the other. **6.** *Electricity.* the part of a fuse that melts when too strong a current goes through it. **7.** *Chemistry.* a bond.
—v.t. to join as a link does; connect: *to link arms. Your fortunes and his are linked together* (Charles Kingsley). *—v.i.* to be coupled, joined, or connected.
—adj. arranged in or connected by links; *link sausages.* [apparently < Scandinavian (compare Swedish *länk*)]

link[2] (lingk), *n.* a torch, especially one made of tow and pitch.

link[3] (lingk), *v.i. Scottish.* to move nimbly; pass quickly along; trip. [compare Norwegian *linka* to give a toss, bend]

link·age (ling′kij), *n.* **1.** a linking. **2.** a being linked. **3.** an arrangement or system of links. **4.** *Biology.* the association of two or more genes or their characteristics on the same chromosome so that they are transmitted together. **5.** any of various devices consisting of a number of bars linked or pivoted together, used to produce a desired motion in a machine part, for tracing lines, etc. **6.** *Electricity.* the product of the magnetic flux going through a coil and the number of turns in the coil. It serves as a measure of the voltage that can be induced in the coil.

linkage group, *Biology.* a group of genes or hereditary characteristics that are transmitted together.

link belt, *Machinery.* a belt composed of a series of detachable links, used to transmit motion.

link belting, **1.** material for making link belts. **2.** link belts.
link block, (in a steam engine) the block actuated by the link motion and giving motion to a valve stem.
link·boy (lingk′boi′), *n.* a boy who used to be employed to carry a link or torch to light the way for a person along the streets.
linked (lingkt), *adj.* **1.** connected by or like links. **2.** *Biology.* exhibiting linkage.
link·ing r (ling′king), *Phonetics.* (in dialects in which *r* is not pronounced in final and pre-consonantal position) the final *r*-sound preserved before a word with an initial vowel, as in *far off* with a linking *r* (contrasted with *far* with no *r* sound).
linking verb, a verb, with little or no meaning of its own, that connects a subject with a predicate noun or adjective. *Be* and *seem* are the most common linking verbs.
link·man (lingk′mən), *n., pl.* **-men.** a man formerly employed to carry a link or torch to light the way for a person along the street.
link mechanism, link motion.
link motion, **1.** a valve gear in a steam engine for controlling (including reversing) the valve motion, consisting of a series of links connecting the eccentrics to the link block that operates the valve. **2.** any system of links that connects, and regulates the motion of, two parts, one of which drives the other.
links (lingks), *n.pl.* **1.** a golf course. **2.** *Scottish.* **a.** comparatively level or gently rolling sandy ground near the seashore, covered with turf, coarse grass, etc. **b.** the windings of a stream. **c.** the ground lying along such windings. [Old English *hlinc* rising ground]
➔ **Links** is used as either singular or plural: *Do you know of a links where we can play tomorrow? The Sunnyview Links are always crowded.*
links·man (lingks′mən), *n., pl.* **-men.** a golf player; golfer.
links·wom·an (lingks′wu̇m′ən), *n., pl.* **-wom·en.** a woman golfer.
Link trainer, *Trademark. Aeronautics.* a ground training device in which flight conditions are simulated.
link-up (lingk′up′), *n.* connection; affiliation; tie.
link·work (lingk′wėrk′), *n.* **1.** work composed of or arranged in links. **2.** a mechanism using links to transmit motion.
linn (lin), *n. Especially Scottish.* **1.** a waterfall. **2.** a pool, especially one beneath a waterfall. **3. a.** a precipice. **b.** a steep ravine. [perhaps fusion of Old English *hlynn* torrent, and Gaelic *linne* pool]
Lin·ne·an or **Lin·nae·an** (li nē′ən), *adj.* **1.** of Carolus Linnaeus (1707-1778). The Linnean system of naming animals uses two words, the first for the genus and the second for the species. **2.** of the earlier system of plant classification introduced by Linnaeus, dividing plants into 24 classes.
lin·net (lin′it), *n.* **1.** a small songbird of Europe, Asia, and Africa, having brown or gray plumage, the color changing at different ages. **2.** any of certain allied birds, as the pine siskin or pine linnet, of North America. [perhaps Old English *linetwigle,* or *līnete* < *līn* flax, ultimately < Latin *līnum* (flaxseed forms much of the bird's diet)]

European Linnet (def. 1—about 6 in. long)

li·no (lī′nō), *n., pl.* **-nos.** *Informal.* **1.** linoleum. **2. a.** a linotype. **b.** a linotypist.
li·no·cut (lī′nə kut′), *n.* **1.** a design cut in relief on a block of linoleum. **2.** a print obtained from this.
Li·no·film (lī′nə film), *n. Trademark.* a machine which sets type photographically, consisting chiefly of a keyboard unit which produces a copy on perforated tape and a photographic unit into which the tape is automatically fed to be put on film.
lin·o·le·ic acid (lin′ə lē′ik, lə nō′lē-), an unsaturated acid essential to the human diet, found as a glyceride in linseed and other oils, and used as a drying agent in paint and varnish. *Formula:* $C_{18}H_{32}O_2$
lin·o·le·nic acid (lin′ə lē′nik, -len′ik), an unsaturated fatty acid important to the human diet, found as a glyceride in linseed and other oils: *Linolenic acid inhibits thrombosis* (Observer). *Formula:* $C_{18}H_{30}O_2$
li·no·le·um (lə nō′lē əm), *n.* **1.** a floor covering made by putting a hard surface of ground cork mixed with oxidized linseed oil on a canvas or burlap back. **2.** any similar floor covering. **3.** linseed oil oxidized until hard. [< Latin *līnum* flax + *oleum* oil]
lin·on (lin′on; *French* lē nôN′), *n.* lawn, a linen or cotton fabric. [< French *linon*]
li·no·type (lī′nə tīp), *n., v.,* **-typed, -typ·ing.** —*n.* **1.** a typesetting machine that is operated like a typewriter and that casts each line of type in one piece. **2. Linotype.** *Trademark.* a name for a machine of this kind. —*v.t.* to set with a linotype. [American English (originally) *line o'type* line of type]
li·no·typ·er (lī′nə tī′pər), *n.* **1.** a linotypist. **2.** a linotype.
li·no·typ·ist (lī′nə tī′pist), *n.* a person who operates a linotype.
lin·sang (lin′sang), *n.* any of various catlike, carnivorous mammals of the East Indies, having a very long tail and retractile claws. [< Javanese *linsang*]
lin·seed (lin′sēd′), *n.* the seed of flax. [Old English *līnsǣd* flaxseed]
linseed oil, the yellowish oil pressed from linseed, used in making paints, printing inks, and linoleum.
lin·sey (lin′zē), *n., pl.* **-seys.** linsey-woolsey.
lin·sey-wool·sey (lin′zē wu̇l′zē), *n., pl.* **-wool·seys.** **1.** a strong, coarse fabric made of linen and wool or of cotton and wool. **2.** any poor or incongruous mixture. [Middle English *linsey* a linen fabric (< *lin-,* Old English *līn* linen) + English *wool,* with a rhyming ending]
lin·stock (lin′stok), *n.* a stick with a forked end, formerly used to hold a fuse or match in firing a cannon. [alteration of Dutch *lontstok* < *lont* match (originally made of tow) + *stock* stock, stick]
lint (lint), *n.* **1.** a soft down or fleecy material obtained by scraping linen. Lint was formerly used on wounds to keep out air and dirt. **2.** tiny bits of thread or fluff of any material. **3.** *Scottish.* the flax plant. [Middle English *linnet,* probably ultimately Old English *līn* flax, or < Latin *līnum*] —**lint′less,** *adj.*
lin·tel (lin′təl), *n.* a horizontal beam or stone above a door, window, etc., to support the structure above it. [< Old French *lintel* threshold, ultimately < Latin *līmes, -itis* limit]

LINTEL
SILL
Lintel

lint·er (lin′tər), *n. U.S.* a machine for stripping off the short cotton fibers remaining on the cotton seed after ginning. **linters,** the cotton fibers so removed: *Linters may be used for cotton batting, the manufacture of rayon, and the making of paper and guncotton.*
lint·head (lint′hed′), *n. Southern U.S.* **1.** a worker in a cotton mill. **2.** a poor white.
lint·ie (lin′tē), *n. Scottish.* the linnet.
lint·white (lint′hwīt′), *n. Especially Scottish.* the linnet.
lint·y (lin′tē), *adj.,* **lint·i·er, lint·i·est.** **1.** covered with or full of lint. **2.** like lint.
li·num (lī′nəm), *n.* any of the genus of dicotyledonous herbs that includes flax, especially the ornamental species. [< Latin *linum* flax]
Li·nus (lī′nəs), *n.* **1.** *Greek Mythology.* a son of Apollo who became a skillful musician and taught Orpheus. **2.** Also, **Linus song.** a lamentation sung in ancient times for the fruits of nature dying with the end of summer.
lin·y (lī′nē), *adj.,* **lin·i·er, lin·i·est.** **1.** full of or marked with lines. **2.** linelike.
li·on (lī′ən), *n.* **1.** a large, strong, tawny, carnivorous mammal of the cat family, found in Africa and southern Asia. The male has a full, flowing mane of coarse hair. **2.** a very brave or strong person. **3.** a famous person; celebrity. **4. a.** the lion as the national emblem of Great Britain. **b.** the British nation itself.

African Lion (def. 1) (about 3 ft. high at the shoulder)

beard the lion in his den, to defy a person in his home, office, etc.: *And dar'st thou then to beard the lion in his den, the Douglas in his hall?* (Scott).
put one's head in the lion's mouth. See under **head,** *n.*
twist the lion's tail, to say or do something intended to excite the resentment of some government or other authority, especially the government or people of Great Britain: *Encroachment on that land would twist the lion's tail.*
[< Old French *lion* < Latin *leō, -ōnis* < Greek *léōn, léontos*] —**li′on·like′,** *adj.*
Li·on (lī′ən), *n.* **1.** a constellation and the fifth sign of the zodiac; Leo. **2.** a member of a local organization of the International Association of Lions Clubs, founded in 1917 for community service. [< *lion*]
li·on·ess (lī′ə nis), *n.* a female lion.
li·on·et (lī′ə net), *n.* a little or young lion.
li·on·heart (lī′ən härt′), *n.* a person of great courage.
Li·on·heart (lī′ən härt′), *n.* Richard I of England.
li·on-heart·ed (lī′ən här′tid), *adj.* brave; courageous. —**Syn.** dauntless, valiant.
li·on·ise (lī′ə nīz), *v.t.,* **-ised, -is·ing.** *Especially British.* lionize.
li·on·ism (lī′ə niz əm), *n.* **1.** the practice of lionizing. **2.** the condition of being lionized.
li·on·i·za·tion (lī′ə nə zā′shən), *n.* the act or process of lionizing.
li·on·ize (lī′ə nīz), *v.t.,* **-ized, -iz·ing.** **1.** to treat (a person) as very important: *Never, never have I been so lionized! I assure you, I was cock of the walk* (Henry James). **2.** to visit the sights of (a place); visit or go over (a place of interest). —**li′on·iz′er,** *n.* —**Syn. 1.** adulate, glorify.
lion's provider, **1.** the jackal. **2.** a person who provides for another's requirements or meanly serves his purposes.
lion's share, the biggest or best part: *The liberal publications have the major influence [and] get the lion's share of attention* (New York Times). *He took care of the lion's share of the Institution's growing correspondence* (New Yorker).
lion's tooth, the dandelion.
li·ot·ri·chous (lī ot′rə kəs), *adj.* having smooth hair. [< Greek *leîos* smooth + *thríx, trichós* hair + English *-ous*]
lip (lip), *n., adj., v.,* **lipped, lip·ping.** —*n.* **1.** either of the two fleshy movable edges of the mouth, especially in man and some other animals. **2.** a folding or bent-out edge of any opening: *the lip of a bell or a pitcher, the lip of a crater, one of the lips of a wound.* **3.** *Music.* **a.** the mouthpiece of a musical instrument. **b.** the manner of shaping the mouth to play a wind instrument. **c.** the edges above and below the mouth of a flue pipe of an organ. **4.** *Slang.* impudent talk: *"Don't you give me none o' your lip," says he* (Mark Twain). **5.** *Botany.* **a.** either of the two parts of a labiate corolla or calyx, the upper lip being closest to the axis of the inflorescence and the lower lip farthest away from the axis. See picture under **bilabiate. b.** (in an orchid) the labellum. **6.** *Zoology.* a labium. **7.** an edge of the opening of a gastropod shell. **8.** the spiral blade on the end of an auger.
curl one's lip, to raise the upper lip as an expression of contempt or scorn: *He always curled his lip in pronouncing the name of an enemy.*
hang on the lips of, to listen to with great attentiveness and admiration: *The audience hung on the lips of the orator.*
keep a stiff upper lip, a. to be brave or firm; show no fear or discouragement: *What's the use o' boohooin'? . . . Keep a stiff upper lip; no bones broke* (John Neal). **b.** to be very reserved; show no feeling: *The British male is popularly supposed to keep a stiff upper lip and shun all displays of emotion whatever the cause* (Punch).
lips, a. the mouth: *Her lips formed a perfect bow.* **b.** the lips as organs of speech: *His lips are very mild and meek* (Tennyson).
smack one's lips, a. to open the lips with a sharp sound, especially as a sign of pleasure: *He smacked his lips over the wine.* **b.** to express enjoyment or pleasurable anticipation over something: *TWA has been smacking its lips over the prospect of a $145 million windfall* (Time).

—*adj.* **1.** not heartfelt or deep, but just on the surface: *lip worship.* **2.** of a lip or lips. **3.** *Phonetics.* formed or produced by the lips; labial.

—*v.t.* **1.** to touch with the lips: *after the final adjustment of the mouthpiece, lipping the instrument* (Samuel Lover). **2.** to pronounce with the lips only; murmur softly: *I heard my name Most fondly lipp'd* (Keats). **3.** *Poetic.* to kiss: *A hand that kings Have lipp'd, and trembled kissing* (Shakespeare). **4.** to hit a golf ball so that it touches but does not drop in (the hole).

—*v.i.* to use the lips in playing a wind instrument.

[Old English *lippa*] —**lip′like′,** *adj.*

—**Syn.** *adj.* **1.** superficial, insincere.

lip·a·roid (lip′ə roid), *adj. Rare.* lipoid; fatty. [< Greek *liparós* shiny, greasy]

li·pase (lī′pās, lip′ās), *n.* an enzyme occurring in the pancreatic and gastric juices, certain seeds, etc., that can change fats into fatty acids, glycerin, and sugar. [< Greek *lípos* fat, noun + English *-ase*]

li·pec·to·my (li pek′tə mē), *n., pl.* **-mies.** surgical removal of fat, as in cases of obesity. [< Greek *lípos* fat + *ektomē* a cutting out]

li·pe·mi·a (li pē′mē ə), *n.* the presence of an excessive quantity of fat in the blood: *Lipemia . . . has been induced in animals by . . . diets extremely high in fats and cholesterol* (Herbert Ratcliffe). [< New Latin *lipemia* < Greek *lípos* fat + *haîma* blood]

lip·id (lip′id, lī′pid), *n.* any of a group of compounds including the fats, oils, waxes, and sterols. They are characterized by an oily feeling, solubility in fat solvents such as chloroform, benzene, or ether, and insolubility in water. [< Greek *lípos* fat, noun + English *-id*(e)]

lip·ide (lip′īd, -id; lī′pīd, -pid), *n.* lipid.

li·pin (lī′pin, lip′in), *n.* lipid.

Lip·iz·zan (lip′ə zän), *n.* a Lipizzaner.

Lip·iz·za·ner (lip′ə zä′nər), *n.* a horse bred in Europe since the 1500's for use in the Spanish Riding School, in Austria. Lipizzaners are born with dark coats that turn white after three to seven years. *The famous Lipizzaner horses do their marvellous exhibition of dressage* (New Yorker).

lip·less (lip′lis), *adj.* having no lips.

lip·o·ca·ic (lip′ə kā′ik), *n.* a substance found in the pancreas that is thought to regulate the assimilation of fat by the liver. [< Greek *lípos* fat, noun + *kaíein* to burn + English *-ic*]

lip·o·chrome (lip′ə krōm), *n.* any of a group of fat-soluble pigments, such as the carotenoids, occurring in animals and plants. They produce the bright red or yellow plumage of birds. [< Greek *lípos* fat, noun + *chrôma* color]

lip·o·gen·e·sis (lip′ə jen′ə sis), *n.* the formation of fat in the body. [< Greek *lípos* fat + English *genesis*]

lip·o·gen·ic (lip′ə jen′ik), *adj.* tending to produce fat: *The average German consumes more starches and other lipogenic substances . . .* (Time).

lip·o·gram (lip′ə gram, lī′pə-), *n.* a writing from which all words containing a particular letter or letters are omitted. [< Greek *lip-*, stem of *leípein* to be wanting + English *-gram*]

lip·o·gram·mat·ic (lip′ə grə mat′ik, lī′pə-), *adj.* **1.** having to do with the writing of lipograms. **2.** of the nature of a lipogram.

lip·o·gram·ma·tism (lip′ə gram′ə tiz əm, lī′pə-), *n.* the writing of lipograms.

lip·o·gram·ma·tist (lip′ə gram′ə tist, lī′pə-), *n.* a person who writes lipograms.

li·po·ic acid (li pō′ik), thioctic acid.

lip·oid (lip′oid, lī′poid), *Biochemistry.* —*adj.* like fat or oil. —*n.* any of a group of nitrogenous fatlike substances, as the lecithins. [< Greek *lípos* fat, noun + English *-oid*]

lip·oid·o·sis (lip′oi dō′sis, lī′poi-), *n.* the abnormal deposition of fat in some part of the body.

li·pol·y·sis (li pol′ə sis), *n. Chemistry.* the breakdown or dissolution of a fat, as by the action of lipase.

lip·o·lyt·ic (lip′ə lit′ik), *adj.* of, having to do with, or of the nature of lipolysis.

li·po·ma (li pō′mə), *n., pl.* **-mas, -ma·ta** (-mə tə). a tumor, usually benign and painless, composed of fat cells. [< New Latin *lipoma* < Greek *lípos* fat, noun]

li·pom·a·tous (li pom′ə təs), *adj.* having to do with or of the nature of a lipoma.

lip·o·pro·tein (lip′ə prō′tēn, -tē in), *n. Biochemistry.* any of a class of proteins, one of the components of which is a lipid.

lip·o·trop·ic (lip′ə trop′ik), *adj. Biochemistry.* having an affinity for lipids.

li·pot·ro·pin (li pot′rə pin), *n.* a pituitary hormone that stimulates the conversion of stored solid fats into liquid form for use by the body. [< *lipotrop*(ic) + *-in*]

lipped (lipt), *adj.* **1.** having a lip or lips. **2.** *Botany.* labiate.

-lipped, *combining form.* having —— lips: *Thin-lipped = having thin lips.*

lip·pen (lip′ən), *Scottish and British Dialect.* —*v.i.* to confide; rely; trust. —*v.t.* to expect with confidence. [origin uncertain]

lip·per (lip′ər), *n. Nautical.* a slightly rough or rippling sea.

Lip·pi·zan (lip′ə zän), *n.* Lipizzaner.

Lip·pi·za·ner (lip′ə zä′nər), *n.* Lipizzaner: *The Lippizaner stallions of the Spanish school of Vienna . . . have mastered the balletlike movements of haute école* (Harper's).

lip·py (lip′ē), *adj.* **1.** *Informal.* having a large or protruding lip or lips: *Miss Dee is as wide-eyed and lippy as ever* (New York Times). **2.** *Slang.* impertinent: *Out with all the officials who are lippy . . . with the Little Man* (Maclean's).

lip-read (lip′rēd′), *v.i., v.t.,* **-read, -read·ing.** to understand speech by watching the movements of the speaker's lips.

lip reader, a person who lip-reads.

lip reading, the understanding of speech by watching the movements of the speaker's lips.

lips (lips), *n.pl.* See under **lip,** *n.*

lip service, service with the lip or words only; insincere profession of devotion or good will: *His Budget Message . . . pays lip service to government economy . . . and ends with scores of recommendations for increased spending* (Newsweek). *The Conservatives have realized that they must pay at least lip service to Labour's policy* (London Times).

lip·stick (lip′stik′), *n.* a small stick of a rouge, etc., used for coloring the lips.

lip sync, 1. synchronization of action being performed, photographed, or televised with sound previously recorded: *Pantomiming to a record . . . is a convenient ruse known as "lip sync" (lip synchronization), and is used by virtually all rock'n'rollers when they appear on TV* (Time). **2.** synchronization of a voice with lip movements filmed previously, as in the preparation of a dubbed, native-language version of a foreign film.

liq., 1. liquid. **2.** liquor.

li·quate (lī′kwāt), *v.t.,* **-quat·ed, -quat·ing. 1.** to liquefy. **2.** to separate (a metal) in a liquid state from impurities or from other less fusible metals in a solid form by heating. **3.** to heat (a metal) to produce such separation. [< Latin *liquāre* (with English *-ate*[1]) melt, related to *liquor* liquor]

li·qua·tion (lī kwā′shən), *n.* **1.** the process of liquating. **2.** the separation of metals by fusion.

liq·ue·fa·cient (lik′wə fā′shənt), *n.* something that serves to liquefy.

liq·ue·fac·tion (lik′wə fak′shən), *n.* **1.** the process of changing into a liquid, especially of changing a gas by the application of pressure and cooling. **2.** liquefied condition.

liq·ue·fac·tive (lik′wə fak′tiv), *adj.* causing liquefaction.

liq·ue·fi·a·ble (lik′wə fī′ə bəl), *adj.* that can be liquefied.

liq·ue·fi·ca·tion (lik′wə fə kā′shən), *n.* liquefaction.

liq·ue·fied petroleum gas (lik′wə fīd), bottled gas; LP-gas: *The gas companies may also remove lighter hydrocarbons, such as propane and butane, from natural gas. These gas fuels are sometimes called liquefied petroleum gases* (Harlan W. Nelson). *Abbr.:* LPG (no periods).

liq·ue·fi·er (lik′wə fī′ər), *n.* **1.** a person or thing that liquefies. **2.** an apparatus for the liquefaction of gases.

liq·ue·fy (lik′wə fī), *v.t., v.i.,* **-fied, -fy·ing.** to change into a liquid; make or become liquid: *Liquefied air is extremely cold.* [< Middle French *liquéfier*, learned borrowing from Latin *liquefacere* < *liquēre* be fluid + *facere* make]

li·ques·cence (li kwes′əns), *n.* liquescent condition.

li·ques·cen·cy (li kwes′ən sē), *n.* liquescence.

li·ques·cent (li kwes′ənt), *adj.* **1.** becoming liquid. **2.** apt to become liquid. [< Latin *liquēscēns, -entis*, present participle of *liquēscere* begin to be(come) liquid < *liquēre* be(come) liquid]

li·queur (li kėr′, -kyůr′), *n.* a strong, sweet, highly flavored alcoholic liquor. —*v.t.* to treat or flavor with liqueur. [< French *liqueur* < Old French *licour* liquid. Doublet of LIQUOR.]

liqueur glass, a very small drinking glass used for liqueurs.

liq·uid (lik′wid), *n.* **1.** a substance that is neither a solid nor a gas; substance that flows freely like water. Liquids and gases are classed together as fluids. **2.** *Phonetics.* the sound of *l* or *r;* liquid consonant.

—*adj.* **1.** in the form of a liquid; melted; composed of molecules that move freely over each other so that a mass has the shape of its container to the point it fills but does not tend to separate as a gas does: *butter heated until it is liquid. Many shampoos are made of liquid soap.* **2.** clear and bright like water. **3.** clear and smooth-flowing in sound: *the liquid notes of a bird. Italian is the most liquid . . . language that can possibly be imagined* (David Hume). **4.** easily turned into cash: *liquid assets. United States bonds are a liquid investment.* **5.** *Phonetics.* **a.** having oral vowel-like resonance, as *l* and *r.* **b.** (of consonants, especially *l* or *n*, as in Spanish) palatalized.

[< Latin *liquidus* < *liquēre* to be(come) fluid] —**liq′uid·ly,** *adv.* —**liq′uid·ness,** *n.*

—**Syn.** *n.* **1. Liquid, fluid** mean a substance that flows. **Liquid** applies to a substance that is neither a solid nor a gas, and flows freely like water: *Milk and oil are liquids; oxygen is not.* **Fluid** applies to anything that flows in any way, either a liquid or a gas: *Milk, water, and oxygen are fluids.*

liquid air, the intensely cold, transparent liquid formed when air is very greatly compressed and then cooled. It is used mainly as a source of nitrogen and oxygen, and for refrigerating in the laboratory when low temperatures are required.

liq·uid·am·bar (lik′wid am′bər, -bär), *n.* **1.** any of a small group of trees related to the witch hazel, especially the sweet gum tree of North America, that in warm regions exudes a gum used in the preparation of chewing gum and in medicine, and a species of Asia Minor that yields the balsam known as liquid storax. **2.** Also, **liquid amber.** the resinous gum that exudes from the bark of the sweet gum. [< New Latin *Liquidambar* the genus name < Latin *liquidus* liquid + Medieval Latin *ambar* amber]

liq·ui·date (lik′wə dāt), *v.,* **-dat·ed, -dat·ing.** —*v.t.* **1.** to pay (a debt): *to liquidate a mortgage.* **2.** to settle the accounts of (a business, etc.); clear up the affairs of (a bankrupt). **3.** to get rid of (an undesirable person or thing): *The French Revolution liquidated the nobility.* **4.** to convert into cash. **5.** *Law.* to determine and apportion by agreement or litigation the amount of (indebtedness or damages). **6.** to kill ruthlessly; exterminate. —*v.i.* to liquidate debts, etc.; go into liquidation. [< Late Latin *liquidāre* (with English *-ate*[1]) < Latin *liquidus* liquid]

liq·ui·da·tion (lik′wə dā′shən), *n.* **1.** the act of liquidating a company's assets or the like. **2.** the state or condition of being liquidated: *to go into liquidation.* **3.** the elimination of an undesirable person, idea, etc.: *He advocated the gradual liquidation of the German standing army* (Edmund Wilson).

liq·ui·da·tor (lik′wə dā′tər), *n.* a person who liquidates, especially one appointed, as by a court, to conduct the liquidation of a company.

liquid crystal, a liquid having optical properties characteristic of crystals, but not of ordinary liquids.

liq·uid-drop model (lik′wid drop′), a device used to explain nuclear reactions. The behavior of an electrically charged drop of liquid is used as a model.

liquid fire, a flaming oil or chemical usually hurled from flame throwers, used against fortified emplacements, tanks, insect-infested brush, etc.

liq·uid-fu·eled (lik′wid fyü′əld), *adj.* (of a rocket or missile) powered by a liquid fuel.

liquid helium, the intensely cold, transparent liquid formed when helium is greatly compressed and then cooled: *The system is cooled to 4°Kelvin by liquid helium* (New Scientist).

liquid hydrogen, the intensely cold, transparent liquid formed when hydrogen is greatly compressed and then cooled. It is used as a refrigerant and a rocket fuel.

li·quid·i·ty (li kwid′ə tē), *n.* liquid condition or quality.

liq·uid·ize (lik′wə dīz), *v.t.*, **-ized, -iz·ing.** to make liquid: *The graphite is liquidized and held in suspension in the pencil* (Wall Street Journal). —**liq′uid·iz′er,** *n.*

liquid measure, 1. the measurement of liquids. **2.** a system for measuring liquids.

4 ounces = 1 gill
4 gills = 1 pint = 28.875 cubic inches
2 pints = 1 quart = 57.75 cubic inches
4 quarts = 1 gallon = 231 cubic inches
31½ gallons = 1 barrel = 7276.5 cubic inches
2 barrels (63 gallons) = 1 hogshead = 14,553 cubic inches

liquid oxygen, the intensely cold, transparent liquid formed when pure oxygen is produced, often by liquefying air by expansion and then boiling off the nitrogen. It is used as a rocket fuel.

liquid petrolatum, mineral oil.

liquid propellant, a liquid fuel used in a rocket engine. It contains its own oxygen or combines with oxygen usually released from a separate tank.

liquid rocket, a rocket which uses a liquid propellant.

liquid storax, storax (def. 4).

liq·uor (lik′ər), *n.* **1.** an alcoholic drink, especially brandy, whiskey, gin, or rum. **2.** any of various liquids: **a.** the liquid in which foods are packaged, canned, or cooked: *Pickles are put up in a salty liquor.* **b.** *Pharmaceutics.* a solution of medicinal substances in water: *liquor ammoniae.* **c.** a liquid or a prepared solution used in many industrial processes.

in liquor, in a state of intoxication; drunk: *I smoke like a furnace—I'm always in liquor, A ruffian—a bully—a sot* (W.S.Gilbert).

—*v.t.* **1.** (in various industrial arts) to steep in or soak with a liquor. **2.** to dress (leather, boots, or shoes) with oil or grease. **3.** *Slang.* to supply with liquor to drink; ply with liquor: *Many of the men came back liquored up, and started scrapping on the way* (New Yorker). **4.** *Rare.* to cover or smear with a liquor, especially to lubricate with grease or oil. —*v.i. Slang.* to drink alcoholic liquor: *They . . . liquored at the bar, and played . . . euchre* (Macmillan's Magazine).

[< Old French *licour* liquid, learned borrowing from Latin *liquor* liquid, liquidity < *liquēre* to be(come) fluid. Doublet of LIQUEUR.]

—**Syn.** *n.* **1.** spirits.

liq·uored (lik′ərd), *adj. Slang.* intoxicated.

liq·uo·rice (lik′ər is, lik′ris; -ər ish, -rish), *n.* licorice.

liq·uor·ish[1] (lik′ər ish), *n. Dialect.* licorice.

liq·uor·ish[2] (lik′ər ish), *adj.* lickerish.

li·ra (lir′ə), *n., pl.* **li·re** (lir′ā), **li·ras,** or (for definition 3) **li·rot** (lē′rōt). **1. a.** a unit of money in Italy, formerly worth 19⅓ cents, now worth about ⅙ of a cent. **b.** a coin worth a lira. **2.** a unit of money or gold coin in Turkey, worth 100 kurus or about 11 cents; Turkish pound. **3.** a unit of money in Israel, worth 100 agorot or about 33 cents; the Israeli pound. [< Italian *lira* < Latin *lībra* pound (the weight); balance, scales]

lir·i·o·den·dron (lir′ē ə den′drən), *n., pl.* **-dra** (-drə). any of a small group of trees of the magnolia family, especially the tulip tree of North America. [< New Latin *Liriodendron* the typical genus < Greek *leírion* lily + *déndron* tree]

lir·i·pipe (lir′ə pīp), *n.* **1.** the long tail of a graduate's hood in early academic costume. **2.** a hood. [< Medieval Latin *liripipium,* or *leropipium* tippet, shoe-lace; origin uncertain]

lir·i·poop (lir′ə püp), *n.* liripipe.

lis (lis), *n., pl.* **li·tes.** *Law.* litigation; lawsuit: *The local inquiry provided for in this statute was an inquiry into the nature and extent of the objection. There was no issue or lis* (London Times). [< Latin *līs;* see LITIGATE]

lisle (līl), *n.* **1.** a fine, hard-twisted, strong, linen or cotton thread, used for making stockings, gloves, shirts, etc. **2.** a fabric or garment knit or woven of this thread. —*adj.* made of lisle: *lisle stockings.* [< French *Lisle,* earlier spelling of *Lille,* a town in France, where this cloth was originally made]

lisp (lisp), *v.i.* **1.** to use the sound of *th* in *thin* and *then* instead of the sound of *s* or the sound of *z* in speaking: *She lisped and said "Thing a thong" for "Sing a song."* **2.** to speak falteringly or imperfectly: *I lisped in numbers, for the numbers came* (Alexander Pope). —*v.t.* **1.** to pronounce with a lisp. **2.** to pronounce imperfectly, as in a simple, childlike way.

—*n.* the act, habit, or sound of lisping: *He spoke with a lisp.*

[Old English *-wlispian* < *wlisp* lisping] —**lisp′er,** *n.*

lis pen·dens (lis pen′denz), *Latin, Law.* **1.** a lawsuit that is pending. **2.** the jurisdiction or control of a court over property involved in litigation while a suit is pending.

lis·som (lis′əm), *adj.* lissome. —**lis′som·ness,** *n.*

lis·some (lis′əm), *adj.* **1.** lithe; limber; supple; bending easily: *a daughter of our meadows . . . straight, but as lissome as a hazel wand* (Tennyson). **2.** nimble; active. [variant of *lithesome* < *lithe*] —**lis′some·ly,** *adv.* —**lis′some·ness,** *n.* —**Syn. 1.** lithesome.

lis·sot·ri·chous (li sot′rə kəs), *adj. Anthropology.* having smooth hair. [< Greek *lissós* smooth + *thríx, trichós* hair + English *-ous*]

list[1] (list), *n.* **1.** a series of names, numbers, words, etc.; catalogue or roll usually consisting of a column or series of names, figures, words, or the like: *a shopping list. Edward took a list of the contents* (Frederick Marryat). **2.** all the stocks, etc., that have been officially entered and may be traded on a stock exchange.

—*v.t.* **1.** to make a list of; enter in a list: *I shall list my errands on a card. A dictionary lists words in alphabetical order.* **2.** to enroll (soldiers); enlist. **3.** to enter (a stock, etc.) on the list of those traded on an exchange. —*v.i.* to have one's name entered upon the list of a military body; enlist: *lads . . . that had listed to be soldiers* (John Galt).

[< French *liste,* ultimately < Germanic (compare Old High German *līsta* strip border, English *list*[2])]

—**Syn.** *n.* **1. List, catalogue, roll** mean a series of names or items. **List** is the general word applying to a series of names, figures, etc.: *This is the list of the people who are going to the picnic.* **Catalogue** applies to a complete list arranged alphabetically or according to some other system, often with short descriptions of the items: *Has the new mail-order catalogue come?* **Roll** applies to a list of the names of all members of a group: *His name is on the honor roll.*

list[2] (list), *n.* **1.** the edge of cloth where the material is a little different. **2.** a cheap fabric made out of such edges. **3.** any strip of fabric. **4.** a stripe of color: *Gartered with a red and blue list* (Shakespeare). **5.** one of the divisions of a head of hair or of a beard. **6.** *U.S.* a strip of ground, especially one of the ridges or furrows made by a lister. **7.** *Architecture.* a square molding; fillet. **8.** a narrow strip of wood cut from the edge of a plank, especially sapwood. **9.** *Obsolete.* **a.** a border, hem, or bordering strip (of anything). **b.** a limit; bound; boundary. **c.** an encircling palisade; railed or staked enclosure.

—*adj.* made of list: *a list carpet; her quiet tread muffled in a list slipper* (Charlotte Brontë).

—*v.t.* **1.** to put list around the edges of; border or edge. **2.** to cover an object with list. **3.** to cut a narrow strip from the edge of (a plank, etc.); shape (a block, etc.) by chopping. **4.** *U.S. Dialect.* to prepare (land), especially for a crop of corn or cotton, with a lister or by making alternate strips and beds.

[Old English *līste*] —**Syn.** *n.* **1.** selvage.

list[3] (list), *n.* a tipping to one side, as caused by unequal distribution of weight, especially of a ship; tilt. —*v.i.* to tip to one side, as a ship; careen; heel; tilt: *The sinking ship had listed so far that it was difficult to launch the lifeboats.* —*v.t.* to cause a tipping or list in (a ship): *The shifting cargo had listed the storm-tossed freighter.* [perhaps extended use of *list*[4], noun]

list[4] (list), *Archaic.* —*v.t.* to be pleasing to; please: *Me lists not to speak. When it listeth him to call them to an account* (Sir Walter Raleigh). —*v.i.* to like; wish: *The enemy plundered where they listed.* —*n.* appetite; desire; longing; inclination: *I had little list or leisure to write* (Thomas Fuller). [Old English *lystan* < *lust* pleasure]

list[5] (list), *Archaic and Poetic.* —*v.i.* to listen: *Go forth, under the open sky, and list to Nature's teachings* (William Cullen Bryant). *List, list; I hear Some far off halloo break the silent air* (Milton). —*v.t.* to listen to; hear: *Elves, list your names* (Shakespeare). [Old English *hlystan,* related to *hlyst* hearing. Compare LISTEN.]

list·a·ble (lis′tə bəl), *adj.* that can be listed or entered in a list.

list·ed (lis′tid), *adj.* **1.** set down or entered in a list. **2.** (of securities) entered in or admitted to the regular list of securities which may be traded on a stock exchange.

list·ee (lis tē′), *n.* a person who is listed in a directory, registry, etc.

lis·tel (lis′təl), *n. Architecture.* a narrow list or fillet. [< French *listel* < Italian *listello* (diminutive) < *lista* border < a Germanic word. Compare LIST[1].]

lis·ten (lis′ən), *v.i.* **1.** to try to hear; attend closely for the purpose of hearing: *The mother listens for her baby's cry. I like to listen to music.* **2.** to give heed (to advice, temptation, etc.); pay attention: *Ye who listen with credulity to the whispers of fancy . . .* (Samuel Johnson). —*v.t. Archaic and Poetic.* to hear attentively; pay attention to (a person speaking or what is said).

listen in, a. to listen to others talking on a telephone: *If you want to hear what she is saying, listen in on the extension.* **b.** to listen to the radio: *They listened in every night at seven.*

—*n.* the act of listening.

[Old English *hlysnan.* Compare LIST[5].]

—**lis′ten·er,** *n.* —**Syn.** *v.i.* **1.** See **hear.**

lis·ten·a·bil·i·ty (lis′ə nə bil′ə tē, lis′nə-), *n.* listenable quality or condition.

lis·ten·a·ble (lis′ə nə bəl, lis′nə-), *adj.* pleasant to listen to; worth listening to: *. . . the more listenable current melodies* (Harper's).

lis·ten·er·ship (lis′ə nər ship, lis′nər-), *n.* the number of people who listen (to a radio program, record, etc.): *From bitter experience, all broadcasters know that a routine political speech by a routine politician has a low-low rating in listenership* (Time).

lis·ten·ing post (lis′ə ning, lis′ning), **1.** any position that serves as a center of information or communication, especially on foreign political and economic trends: *. . . Germany is one of the best listening posts for what goes on in Russia* (New York Times). **2.** *Military.* a position in front of a defensive position, encampment, etc., for detecting and warning of enemy movement.

list·er[1] (lis′tər), *n.* a plow with a double moldboard, used especially in corn and beet culture, that throws the dirt to both sides of the furrow. Some kinds plant and cover seeds at the same time. [American English < *list*[2], verb + *-er*[1]]

list·er[2] (lis′tər), *n.* one who makes out a list.

lis·te·ri·o·sis (lis tir′ē ō′sis), *n.* circling disease. [< New Latin *Listeria* genus name of the organism that causes the disease (< Joseph *Lister,* 1827-1912, an English physician) + English *-osis*]

Lis·ter·ism (lis′tə riz əm), *n.* the system of antiseptic surgery originated by Joseph Lister.

Lis·ter·ize (lis′tə rīz), *v.t.,* **-ized, -iz·ing.** to treat according to Listerism.

list·less (list′lis), *adj.* seeming too tired to care about anything; not interested in things; not caring to be active: *a listless mood, listless movements.* [< *list*[4], noun + *-less*] —**list′less·ly,** *adv.* —**list′less·ness,** *n.* —**Syn.** indifferent, languid.

list price, a price given in a catalogue or list. Discounts are figured from it.

lists (lists), *n.pl.* **1. a.** a place where knights fought in tournaments or tilts. **b.** the barriers enclosing such a field. **2.** any place or scene of combat or contest.

enter the lists, to join in a contest; take part in a fight, argument, etc.: *The Royal Society . . . contained few individuals capable of . . . entering the lists against his . . . assailants* (David Brewster).

[blend of *list*[2], and Old French *lice,* or *lisse* place of combat < a Germanic word]

Liszt·i·an (lis′tē ən), *adj.* of or characteristic of the Hungarian composer and pianist Franz Liszt: *. . . a Lisztian exercise in orchestral mastery, abounding in startling harmonies* [*and*] *unexpected melodic turns* (Atlantic).

lit[1] (lit), *v.* lighted; a past tense and a past participle of **light**[1] and **light**[3]**:** *She lit the lamp. His eye lit upon a sentence.*

➤ Both **lighted** and **lit** are in good use as the past tense and past participle. *Lit*, however, is rarely employed as a participial adjective before a substantive: *a lighted candle* rather than *a lit candle*.

lit[2] (lit), *n.* the unit of money in Lithuania, formerly equal to 10 cents. [< Lithuanian *litas*]

lit., **1.** liter. **2. a.** literal. **b.** literally. **3.** literary. **4.** literature.

lit·a·neu·ti·cal (lit′ə nü′tə kəl, -nyü′-), *adj.* of the nature of a litany. [< Greek *litaneutikós* (< *litaneúein* to pray)]

lit·a·ny (lit′ə nē), *n., pl.* **-nies. 1. a.** an arranged prayer consisting of a series of supplications said by the minister or priest, and responses said by the people. **b.** Often, **Litany.** a prayer in similar form, the "general supplication" appointed for use in the Book of Common Prayer. **2.** a repeated series: *a litany of curses.* [< Old French *letanie*, and *litanie*, learned borrowings from Late Latin *litanīa* < Greek *litaneíā* litany; an entreating < *litê* prayer, entreaty < *lítesthai* entreat, pray, beg]

li·tas (lē′täs), *n., pl.* **-tai** (-tī), **-tu.** the former unit of money or gold coin in Lithuania, worth about 10 cents. Also, **lit.** [< Lithuanian *litas*]

Lit. B., Bachelor of Letters (Latin, *Litterarum Baccalaureus*).

li·tchi (lē′chē), *n., pl.* **-tchis. 1.** a nut-shaped fruit with a thin, hard, rough, red skin. Inside the shell is a sweet, white, edible, jellylike pulp with a single brown seed. **2.** the Chinese tree of the soapberry family it grows on, now cultivated in warm regions throughout the world. Also, **lichee, lichi.** [< Cantonese *laichi*]

litchi nut, the litchi fruit when dried. It is of a brownish or black color and is edible.

Lit. D., Doctor of Letters (Latin, *Litterarum Doctor*).

lit de jus·tice (lē′ də zhys tēs′), *French.* **1.** the seat ("bed of justice") of kings of France during a session of the French Parliament. **2.** one of the sessions, during which the monarch approved or disapproved action by the French Parliament or issued decrees.

-lite, *combining form.* stone, stony: *Aerolite = a meteorite made of stone.* [< French *-lite*, earlier *-lithe* < Greek *líthos* a stone]

li·ter (lē′tər), *n.* the common measure of capacity in France, Germany, and other countries that use the metric system. One liter equals 1.0567 quarts U.S. liquid measure, or .908 quart U.S. dry measure. *Abbr.:* l. Also, *especially British,* **litre.** [< French *litre* < *litron*, an obsolete measure of capacity < Medieval Latin *litra* < Greek *lītrā* pound (of 12 ounces)]

lit·er·a·cy (lit′ər ə sē), *n.* the ability to read and write; quality or state of being literate.

literacy test, a test to determine whether a person's ability to read and write meets voting or other requirements: *By 1917, a literacy test had been required for adult immigrants and virtually all Asians were excluded* (New York Times).

lit·er·al (lit′ər əl), *adj.* **1.** following the exact words of the original: *a literal translation.* **2.** taking words in their usual meaning, without exaggeration or imagination; matter-of-fact: *the literal meaning of a word, a literal type of mind, a literal interpretation of the Bible stories.* **3.** true to fact; not exaggerated: *a literal account.* **4.** of letters of the alphabet; expressed by letters. [< Late Latin *litterālis* of the characters (of the alphabet) < Latin *littera* letter] —**lit′er·al·ness,** *n.* —**Syn. 1.** verbatim. **2.** prosaic.

lit·er·al·ism (lit′ər ə liz′əm), *n.* **1.** a keeping to the literal meaning in translation or interpretation. **2.** *Fine Arts.* the faithfully unaltered representation or interpretation of objects without any idealization.

lit·er·al·ist (lit′ər ə list), *n.* **1.** a person who adheres to the exact literal meaning. **2.** a person who represents or portrays without idealizing. —**Syn. 2.** realist.

lit·er·al·is·tic (lit′ər ə lis′tik), *adj.* **1.** having to do with or characteristic of a literalist. **2.** belonging to or having the character of literalism.

lit·er·al·i·ty (lit′ə ral′ə tē), *n., pl.* **-ties. 1.** the quality or fact of being literal. **2.** an instance of this. **3.** *Obsolete.* a literal meaning.

lit·er·al·i·za·tion (lit′ər ə lə zā′shən), *n.* the act of literalizing.

lit·er·al·ize (lit′ər ə līz), *v.t.,* **-ized, -iz·ing.** to make literal; represent or accept as literal. —**lit′er·al·iz′er,** *n.*

lit·er·al·ly (lit′ər ə lē), *adv.* **1.** word for word: *to translate literally. Abbr.:* lit. **2. a.** in a literal sense; without exaggeration: *Is this literally true? I am literally penniless.* **b.** actually: *He is literally coining money with his new business.*

lit·er·ar·i·ly (lit′ə rer′ə lē), *adv.* in a literary manner or respect: *With all the time left over when he stops going to unnecessary lectures and spending unnecessary hours in the university library, the literarily inclined student is likely to find the bookshops a constant joy* (London Times).

lit·er·ar·i·ness (lit′ə rer′ē nis), *n.* the quality of being literary.

lit·er·ar·y (lit′ə rer′ē), *adj.* **1.** having to do with literature: *literary annals.* **2.** knowing much about literature: *a literary authority.* **3.** engaged in literature as a profession: *some gentlemen of the literary fraternity* (Thackeray).

Literary Club, a London club founded in 1764 by Sir Joshua Reynolds, Samuel Johnson, and others.

lit·er·ate (lit′ər it), *adj.* **1.** able to read and write. **2.** acquainted with literature; educated; literary.
—*n.* **1.** a person who can read and write. **2.** an educated person.
[< Latin *litterātus* < *littera* letter (in the plural, literature, learning)]
—**Syn.** *adj.* **2.** lettered.

lit·e·ra·ti (lit′ə rä′tē, -rā′tī), *n., pl. of* **literatus.** men of letters; scholarly or literary people: *the enlightened literati, who turn over the pages of history* (Washington Irving). *After the death of Columbus in 1506, the Spanish literati mourned him as a victim of Castilian ingratitude* (Newsweek). [< Latin *litterātī*, plural of *litterātus*, (literally) lettered; see LITERATE]

lit·e·ra·tim (lit′ə rā′tim), *adv.* letter for letter; exactly as written: *to reproduce a text literatim.* Also, **litteratim.** [< Medieval Latin *litteratim* < Latin *littera* letter]

lit·er·a·tor (lit′ə rā′tər), *n.* a literary man; littérateur: *Literators trudging up to knock At Fame's exalted temple-door* (Robert Browning).

lit·er·a·ture (lit′ər ə chůr, -chər; lit′rə-), *n.* **1.** the writings of a period or of a country, especially those kept alive by their beauty of style or thought: *the literature of Greece. Shakespeare is a great name in English literature. The particular concern of the literature of the last two centuries has been with the self in its standing quarrel with culture* (Newsweek). **2.** all the books and articles on a subject: *the literature of stamp collecting.* **3.** the profession of a writer; literary production: *Never pursue literature as a trade* (Samuel Taylor Coleridge). **4.** the study of literature: *I shall take literature and mathematics this spring. Hoagland spent some time as a cagehand with the circus, when he was not studying literature at Harvard* (Newsweek). **5.** *Informal.* printed matter of any kind. **6.** *Rare.* acquaintance with the world of letters or books; literary culture: *another person of infinite literature* (John Selden).
[< Middle French *literature* teaching of letters; writing < Latin *litterātūra* writing < *littera* letter (in the plural, literature, learning)]
—**Syn. 1.** belles-lettres.

lit·e·ra·tus (lit′ə rä′təs, -rā′-), *n., pl.* **-ti.** a man of learning or scholarship.

li·tes (lī′tēz), *n.* plural of **lis.**

lith (lith), *n. Archaic.* **1.** a limb. **2.** a joint. [Old English *lith*]

lith-, *combining form.* the form of **litho-** before vowels, as in *lithiasis.*

Lith., **1.** lithograph. **2.** lithography.

Lith., **1.** Lithuania. **2.** Lithuanian.

li·thae·mi·a (li thē′mē ə), *n.* lithemia.

li·thae·mic (li thē′mik), *adj.* lithemic.

lith·arge (lith′ärj, li thärj′), *n.* **1.** a yellow or reddish oxide of lead, used in making glass, glazes for pottery, and driers for paints and varnishes; lead monoxide. *Formula:* PbO **2.** (sometimes) any form of lead monoxide, as massicot, which is produced with less heat than litharge. [< Old French *litarge*, also *litargire* < Latin *lithargyrus* < Greek *lithárgyros* < *líthos* stone + *árgyros* silver]

lithe (līᴛʜ), *adj.* bending easily; supple: *to be lithe of body, lithe limbs, a lithe willow.* [Old English *līthe* soft, mild] —**lithe′ly,** *adv.* —**lithe′ness,** *n.* —**Syn.** flexible, limber, pliant, lithesome, lissome, willowy.

li·the·mi·a (li thē′mē ə), *n. Medicine.* an excessive amount of uric acid in the blood. [< New Latin *lithaemia* < Greek *líthos* stone + *haîma* blood]

li·the·mic (li thē′mik), *adj.* of, having to do with, or affected with lithemia.

lith·er (liᴛʜ′ər), *adj.* **1.** *British Dialect and Scottish.* lazy; sluggish; spiritless. **2.** *British Dialect.* active or nimble. **3.** *Archaic.* pliant; supple: *the lither sky* (Shakespeare). **4.** *Obsolete.* **a.** bad or wicked. **b.** poor, sorry, or worthless. **c.** withered. [Old English *lȳthre* bad]

lith·er·ly (liᴛʜ′ər lē), *adj. Obsolete.* **1.** bad; mischievous. **2.** lazy.

lithe·some (līᴛʜ′səm), *adj.* lithe.

lith·i·a (lith′ē ə), *n.* a white oxide of lithium, soluble in water, and forming an acid and caustic solution. *Formula:* Li_2O [< New Latin *lithia*, alteration (after *soda*, etc.) of earlier *lithion* < Greek *líthos* stone (because of its mineral origin)]

li·thi·a·sis (li thī′ə sis), *n. Medicine.* the formation of calculi or stony concretions in the body, especially in the gall bladder and urinary tract.

lithia water, a mineral water, natural or artificial, containing lithium salts.

lith·ic[1] (lith′ik), *adj.* **1.** consisting of stone or rock. **2.** *Medicine.* of or having to do with stone or stony concretions formed within the body, especially in the bladder. [< Greek *lithikós* < *líthos* stone]

lith·ic[2] (lith′ik), *adj. Chemistry.* of, having to do with, or consisting of lithium. [< *lith*(ium) + *-ic*]

lithic acid, uric acid.

lith·i·fi·ca·tion (lith′ə fə kā′shən), *n.* the process by which rocks are formed.

lith·i·fy (lith′ə fī), *v.t.,* **-fied, -fy·ing.** to change into rock.

lith·i·um (lith′ē əm), *n.* a soft silver-white metallic chemical element similar to sodium. Lithium is the lightest known metal and occurs in small quantities in various minerals: *Lithium's use in lubricants, ceramics, and chemical processes is growing* (Wall Street Journal). *Symbol:* Li; *at.wt.:* (C^{12}) 6.939 or (O^{16}) 6.94; *at.no.:* 3; *valence:* 1. [< New Latin *lithium* < *lithia* lithia < Greek *líthos* stone]

lithium chloride, a crystalline salt soluble in water or alcohol, used especially as a dehumidifier in air conditioning and as a flux in soldering and welding. *Formula:* LiCl

lithium fluoride, a white powder used in ceramics, as a flux in soldering and welding, and, in the form of synthetic crystals, in the construction of devices for detecting and measuring radiation. *Formula:* LiF

lith·o (lith′ō), *adj., n., pl.* **lith·os.** —*adj.* lithographic: *litho printing.* —*n.* lithograph.

litho-, *combining form.* stone or stones: *Lithomancy = divination by means of stones. Lithology = the science of stones.* Also, **lith-** before vowels. [< Greek *litho-* < *líthos* stone]

litho. or **lithog.,** **1.** lithograph. **2.** lithography.

li·tho·did (li thō′did), *n.* any of various crabs with a triangular carapace and the fifth pair of legs much reduced. [< New Latin *Lithodidae* the family name < Greek *lithṓdēs* stonelike < *líthos* stone + *eîdos* form]

Lithodid
Agassiz's deep sea spider crab

lith·o·fa·cies (lith′ə fā′shiz), *n.* a record of the rock strata and deposition of a given area.

lith·o·graph (lith′ə graf, -gräf), *n.* a picture, print, etc., made from a flat, specially prepared stone or metal plate. —*v.t.* to print from a stone or plate.

li·thog·ra·pher (li thog′rə fər), *n.* a person who lithographs or practices lithography.

lith·o·graph·ic (lith′ə graf′ik), *adj.* **1.** of a lithograph. **2.** made by lithography. —**lith′o·graph′i·cal·ly,** *adv.*

lith·o·graph·i·cal (lith′ə graf′ə kəl), *adj.* lithographic.

li·thog·ra·phy (li thog′rə fē), *n.* the art or process of making lithographs.

lith·oid (lith′oid), *adj.* of the nature or structure of stone. [< Greek *lithoeidēs* < *líthos* stone + *eîdos* form]

li·thoi·dal (li thoi′dəl), *adj.* lithoid.

lith·o·log·ic (lith′ə loj′ik), *adj.* **1.** of or having to do with lithology. **2.** concerning the nature or composition of stone; petrographic.

lith·o·log·i·cal (lith′ə loj′ə kəl), *adj.* lithologic.

li·thol·o·gist (li thol′ə jist), *n.* an expert in lithology.

li·thol·o·gy (li thol′ə jē), *n.* **1.** the science of rocks and their composition. **2.** the branch of medicine dealing with calculi in the human body.

lith·o·man·cy (lith′ə man′sē), *n.* divination by means of stones. [< *litho-* + Greek *manteíā* divination]

lith·o·marge (lith′ə märj), *n.* any of several kinds of soft, claylike minerals, including kaolin. [< New Latin *lithomarga* < Greek *líthos* stone + Latin *marga* marl]

lith·o·ne·phri·tis (lith′ō ni frī′tis), *n.* inflammation of the kidney due to the presence of calculi.

li·thoph·a·gous (li thof′ə gəs), *adj.* **1.** swallowing gravel, as some birds do. **2.** penetrating stone, as certain mollusks do. [< *litho-* + Greek *phageîn* to eat + English *-ous*]

lith·o·phile (lith′ə fīl), *adj. Geology.* having an affinity for the stony material of the earth's crust: *Lithophile . . . elements . . . tend to associate with silicate and oxide material* (Scientific American).

li·thoph·i·lous (li thof′ə ləs), *adj.* **1.** *Botany.* growing on rocks. **2.** *Entomology.* living in stony places.

lith·o·phyl or **lith·o·phyll** (lith′ə fil), *n.* a fossil of a leaf, or a stone containing one. [< Greek *líthos* stone + *phýllon* leaf]

lith·o·phyte (lith′ə fīt), *n. Botany.* a plant that grows among stone or rock. [< *litho-* + Greek *phytón* plant]

lith·o·pone (lith′ə pōn), *n.* a dry, white pigment or paint, made from zinc instead of white lead. [< *litho-*, perhaps + Latin *ponere* to put, place]

lith·o·sphere (lith′ə sfir), *n.* the land areas of the earth, from its surface to the center of the earth.

lith·o·tom·ic (lith′ə tom′ik), *adj.* of, having to do with, or performed by lithotomy.

lith·o·tom·i·cal (lith′ə tom′ə kəl), *adj.* lithotomic.

li·thot·o·mist (li thot′ə mist), *n.* **1.** a person who practices lithotomy. **2.** a person who cuts inscriptions on stone.

li·thot·o·my (li thot′ə mē), *n., pl.* **-mies.** the surgical removal of stones from the bladder. [< Late Latin *lithotomia* < Greek *lithotomíā* < *líthos* stone + *témnein* to cut]

lith·o·trip·sy (lith′ə trip′sē), *n., pl.* **-sies.** lithotrity.

lith·o·trite (lith′ə trīt), *n.* a surgical instrument used to perform lithotrity.

li·thot·ri·tist (li thot′rə tist), *n.* a person who practices lithotrity.

li·thot·ri·ty (li thot′rə tē), *n., pl.* **-ties.** the surgical operation of crushing stones in the bladder into pieces small enough to pass out. [< French *lithotriteur* lithotrite (ultimately < Greek *líthos* stone + *thrýptein* crush small) + English *-y*[3]]

Lith·u·a·ni·an (lith′ů ā′nē ən), *adj.* belonging or relating to Lithuania, its people, or their language. —*n.* **1.** a native or inhabitant of Lithuania. **2.** the Baltic language of Lithuania.

lith·y (lī′ᴛʜē, liᴛʜ′ē), *adj. Archaic.* flexible; supple; lithe. [Old English *lithig*]

lit·i·ga·ble (lit′ə gə bəl), *adj.* that can be made the subject of a suit in a law court.

lit·i·gant (lit′ə gənt), *n.* a person engaged in a lawsuit. —*adj.* **1.** engaging in a lawsuit. **2.** inclined to go to law. [< Latin *lītigāns, -antis,* present participle of *lītigāre* litigate]

lit·i·gate (lit′ə gāt), *v.,* **-gat·ed, -gat·ing.** —*v.i.* to engage in a lawsuit. —*v.t.* to contest in a lawsuit. [< Latin *lītigāre* (with English *-ate*[1]) < *līs, lītis* lawsuit + *agere* drive, conduct]

lit·i·ga·tion (lit′ə gā′shən), *n.* **1.** a carrying on a lawsuit. **2.** a going to law. **3.** a lawsuit or legal proceeding: *Title litigation scared off the drillers until a recent court decision awarded the mineral rights to the government* (Time). **4.** *Rare.* disputation.

lit·i·ga·tor (lit′ə gā′tər), *n.* a person who litigates.

li·ti·gious (lə tij′əs), *adj.* **1.** having the habit of going to law: *They [Hindus] are very litigious . . . They will persevere in a lawsuit until they are ruined* (Mountstuart Elphinstone). **2.** offering material for a lawsuit; that can be disputed in a court of law. **3.** of lawsuits. [< Latin *lītigiōsus* < *lītigium* dispute < *lītigāre;* see LITIGATE] —**li·ti′gious·ly,** *adv.* —**li·ti′gious·ness,** *n.* —**Syn. 2.** litigable.

lit·mus (lit′məs), *n.* a blue coloring matter obtained from various lichens. [perhaps < Dutch *lakmoes,* Middle Dutch *leecmoes;* perhaps later influenced by obsolete *lit* color, dye]

litmus paper, unsized paper treated with litmus. It turns red when put into an acid and remains blue when put into an alkali, and is used as an indicator of the ion concentration in solutions.

lit·o·ral (lit′ər əl), *adj., n.* littoral.

li·to·tes (lī′tə tēz, lit′ə-), *n.* a figure of speech that makes an assertion by denying its opposite. *Example:* "This was no small storm" means that the storm was quite violent. [< Greek *lītótēs* < *lītós* small, plain, simple]

li·tre (lē′tər), *n. Especially British.* liter.

Litt.B., Bachelor of Letters (Latin, *Litterarum Baccalaureus*).

Litt.D., Doctor of Literature; Doctor of Letters (Latin, *Litterarum Doctor*).

lit·ten (lit′ən), *adj. Poetic.* lighted: *And travellers now within that valley, Through red-litten windows, see vast forms* (Edgar Allan Poe).

lit·ter (lit′ər), *n.* **1.** scattered rubbish; things scattered about or left in disorder: *The kitchen was covered with the litter of dressmakers preparing for the wedding* (Hall Caine). **2.** disorder; untidiness: *She was ashamed to be seen in such a pickle . . . her house was in such a litter* (Henry Fielding). **3.** the young animals produced at one time: *a litter of puppies.* **4.** straw, hay, etc., used as bedding for animals, or for other purposes, as the protection of plants. **5.** a stretcher for carrying a sick or wounded person. **6.** a framework to be carried on men's shoulders or by beasts of burden, with a couch usually enclosed by curtains: *I have sent a message . . . saying that thou wast a little feeble and would need a litter* (Rudyard Kipling).

Litter (def. 6)

—*v.t.* **1.** to leave (odds and ends) lying around; scatter (things) about: *He littered the Sunday paper all over the floor.* **2.** to make disordered or untidy: *He littered his room with books and papers.* **3.** to give birth to (young animals). **4. a.** to make a bed for (an animal) with straw, hay, etc. **b.** to cover with litter: *The floor of the stable had just been littered with fresh straw.* —*v.i.* (of an animal) to bring forth a litter of young. [< Anglo-French *litere,* Old French *litiere,* learned borrowing from Medieval Latin *lectaria, literia,* for Latin *lectīca* litter; sedan < *lectus* bed, couch]

—**Syn.** *n.* **1.** trash, debris. **6.** palanquin. -*v.t.* **1.** strew. **2.** disarrange.

lit·te·rae hu·ma·ni·o·res (lit′ə rē hyü-man′ē ō′rēz), *Latin.* the field of humanities.

lit·té·ra·teur or **lit·te·ra·teur** (lit′ər ə-tėr′), *n.* a literary man; writer or critic of literature. [< French *littérateur,* learned borrowing from Latin *lītterator* < *littera* letter]

lit·te·ra·tim (lit′ə rā′tim), *adv.* literatim.

lit·te·ra·trice (lit′ər ə trēs′), *n.* a literary woman; writer of literary works. [< French *littératrice,* feminine of *littérateur* litterateur]

lit·ter·bug (lit′ər bug′), *n. U.S.* a person who throws down trash along a highway, sidewalk, in a park, etc.: *At Yellowstone, the cost of cleaning up after the litterbugs runs to $400 a day* (Newsweek).

litter mate, an animal born and raised in the same litter as another or others: *If the meat runs lean and heavy . . . then the farmer knows litter mates of the tested hogs are good bets for parenthood* (Wall Street Journal).

lit·ter·y (lit′ər ē), *adj.* consisting of litter; covered with litter; untidy.

lit·tle (lit′əl), *adj.,* **less** or **less·er, least;** or **lit·tler, lit·tlest;** *adv.,* **less, least;** *n.* —*adj.* **1.** not great or big; small: *A grain of sand is little. She was called tall and gawky by some . . . of her own sex, who prefer littler women* (Thackeray). **2.** not much: **a.** small in number: *a little army. In the realm of mere letters, Voltaire is one of the little band of great monarchs* (Christopher Morley). **b.** small in amount: *little money.* **c.** small in degree: *little hope. He has but little ability.* **d.** small in importance or interest; trifling; trivial: *Every little discontent appears to him to portend a revolution* (Macaulay). **3.** short; brief: *Wait a little while and I'll go a little way with you.* **4.** mean; narrow-minded: *little thoughts.*

—*adv.* **1.** in a small amount or degree; slightly: *a little-known author. A zeal little tempered by humanity* (Macaulay). *They live in a little-known town. Little-known metals are now coming into use* (Science News Letter). **2.** not at all: *a coward is little liked. He little knows what will happen.*

—*n.* **1.** a small amount, quantity, or degree: *Add a little. He knows very little about the subject.* **2.** a short time or distance: *Move a little to the left. For a little follow, and do me service* (Shakespeare). **3.** a small thing; trifle: *When a man's being shaved, what a little will make him laugh* (Douglas Jerrold).

in little, on a small scale; in miniature: *to paint in little. A miniature of loveliness, all grace summ'd up . . . in little* (Tennyson).

little by little, by a small amount at a time; slowly; gradually: *Weak and dead for hunger, I went little by little up the street* (David Rowland).

make little of, to treat or represent as of little importance: *They made little of the incident.*

not a little, a great deal; extremely; much; very: *We are not a little hungry, I can tell you* (Frederick Marryat).

think little of, a. to not value much; consider as unimportant or worthless: *The critic thought little of the painting.* **b.** to not hesitate about: *He thought little of commuting to Washington.*

[Old English *lȳtel*] —**lit′tle·ness,** *n.*

—**Syn.** *adj.* **1, 2. Little, small, diminutive** mean not large or great. **Little,** the general term, applies to size, quantity, extent, duration, degree, importance, etc.: *He is a funny little boy.* **Small** applies particularly to size, number, or measure: *He is small for his age.* **Diminutive** applies particularly to size and suggests it is less than normal: *Cinderella's feet were diminutive.*

➔ **Littler** and **littlest** are usually restricted to familiar or affectionate use: *the sweetest, littlest baby in the world.*

➔ See **less** for another usage note.

Little Assembly, *Informal.* the interim committee of the United Nations General Assembly.

little auk, dovekie; a small auk of the Arctic regions.

Little Bear, the Constellation Ursa Minor.

little blue heron, a dark blue, medium-sized heron of the southeastern United States that is snowy white in its immature stage.

Little Corporal, a popular nickname of Napoleon I.

Little Dipper, the group of seven bright stars in the constellation Ursa Minor (the Little Bear) shaped like a dipper with the North Star at the end of the dipper's handle. See picture under **Dipper.**

Little Dog, the northern constellation Canis Minor.

lit·tle-ease (lit′əl ēz′), *n.* a narrow place of confinement, such as the stocks or pillory or a very small dungeon: *The walls of . . . the little-ease were so low, and so contrived, that the wretched inmate could neither stand, walk, sit, nor lie at full length within them* (William H. Ainsworth). [< *Little Ease,* a dungeon in the Tower of London]

Lit·tle-end·i·an or **lit·tle-end·i·an** (lit′-əl en′dē ən), *n.* **1.** a member of the orthodox religious party in Lilliput (in Jonathan Swift's *Gulliver's Travels*) who maintained, in opposition to the Big-endians, that eggs should be broken at the little end. **2.** a disputer about trifles.

Little Englander, an opponent of the territorial enlargement of the British Empire, especially in the 1800's.

Little Eng·land·ism (ing′glən diz əm), the policies or views of Little Englanders:

To me it is . . . a curiously heartless piece of Little Englandism to refuse help to a recently independent Commonwealth partner for whom we were so long responsible (Manchester Guardian Weekly).

Little Europe, the European countries of the Common Market.

little fellow, *U.S. Informal.* an average person having no great political or economic influence; a small businessman or investor.

little finger, the finger farthest from the thumb; smallest finger.

Little Fox, the northern constellation Vulpecula.

little go, *British Informal.* the first examination for the degree of B.A. at Cambridge University; Previous Examination.

little grebe, a dabchick.

little gull, a very small, white and grayish European gull living along the New England coast and around the Great Lakes.

Little Horse, the northern constellation Equuleus.

little hours, (in the Roman Catholic Church) the canonical hours of prime, tierce, sext, and nones, and sometimes vespers and complin.

Little It·a·ly (it′ə lē), *pl.* **-lys** or **-lies.** *U.S.* the section of a city where Italians live.

Little League, 1. a group of baseball clubs for boys twelve years old and under. **2.** one of these clubs.

Little Leaguer, a member of a Little League club.

little magazine or **review,** a small magazine devoted to printing experimental writing, etc.

little man, *U.S.* little fellow: *He is essentially a little man who has had bigness thrust upon him* (Saturday Review).

lit·tle·neck (lit′əl nek′), *n.,* or **littleneck clam, 1.** a young quahog, larger than a cherry stone, usually eaten raw. **2.** any of certain similar clams. [< *Little Neck,* Long Island, New York]

little Neddy, *British Slang.* a committee affiliated with Neddy (NEDC) that deals with the development of a particular sector of the national economy: *So far there are nine "little Neddies." Some 18 other industries are to be approached* (London Times).

little office, (in the Roman Catholic Church) a service honoring the Virgin Mary, similar to the daily prescribed office, but shorter.

Little Parliament, the Parliament with only 140 members, convened by Oliver Cromwell in 1653.

little people, fairies.

Little Rho·dy (rō′dē), a nickname for Rhode Island.

Little Russian, 1. a Ukrainian or Ruthenian. **2.** the Ukrainian or Ruthenian language.

little slam, *Bridge.* a hand in which one side takes all the tricks but one; small slam.

little theatre, 1. a small theater, especially one that produces experimental plays. **2.** the plays produced in such a theater.

lit·to·ral (lit′ər əl), *adj.* **1.** of a shore. **2.** on or near the shore, especially living near the shore. *—n.* a region along the shore: *the Mediterranean littoral of France.* Also, **litoral.** [< Latin *lītorālis* < *lītus* shore]

li·tu (lē′tü), *n.* a plural of **litas.**

li·tur·gic (lə tėr′jik), *adj.* liturgical.

li·tur·gi·cal (lə tėr′jə kəl), *adj.* **1.** of liturgies. **2.** used in liturgics. **3.** of or having to do with the Communion service. [< Late Latin *litūrgicus* (< Greek *leitourgikós* < *leitourgíā* liturgy) + English *-al*[1]] —**li·tur′gi·cal·ly,** *adv.*

li·tur·gics (lə tėr′jiks), *n.* **1.** the branch of theology dealing with the conduct of public worship. **2.** the study of liturgies.

li·tur·gi·ol·o·gist (lə tėr′jē ol′ə jist), *n.* a specialist in the study of liturgies.

li·tur·gi·ol·o·gy (lə tėr′jē ol′ə jē), *n.* the science or study of liturgies.

lit·ur·gist (lit′ər jist), *n.* **1. a.** an expert on liturgies. **b.** a compiler of a liturgy or liturgies. **2.** a person who uses, or favors the use of, a liturgy.

lit·ur·gy (lit′ər jē), *n., pl.* **-gies. 1. a.** a form of public worship. Different churches use different liturgies. **b.** a collection of such forms. **2.** a Communion, especially in the Greek Church. **the liturgy** or **Liturgy, a.** (in the Episcopal Church) the Book of Common Prayer: *It was Sunday . . . and I happened to be reading the Liturgy* (George Borrow). **b.** (in the Greek Church) Communion: *They use the Liturgy of Saint Chrysostome* (Ephraim Pagitt).
[< Late Latin *lītūrgia* < Greek *leitourgíā,* ultimately < *lāós* people + *érgon* work]
—**Syn. 1. a.** ritual.

liv·a·bil·i·ty (liv′ə bil′ə tē), *n.* **1.** Also, **liveability.** the condition of being fit to live in; livable state. **2.** the ability of poultry to survive various conditions and diseases.

liv·a·ble (liv′ə bəl), *adj.* **1.** fit to live in: *a livable house.* **2.** easy to live with: *a livable person.* **3.** worth living; endurable. Also, **liveable.** —**liv′a·ble·ness,** *n.* —**Syn. 1.** habitable. **2.** companionable, sociable.

live[1] (liv), *v.,* **lived** (livd), **liv·ing.** *—v.i.* **1.** to have life; be alive; exist: *All creatures have an equal right to live.* **2.** to remain alive; last; endure: *if I live till May.* **3.** to keep up life: *to live by one's wits. She and her mother now had nothing to live on but a small government pension* (Edmund Wilson). **4.** to feed or subsist: *The Chinese live largely on rice. Lions live upon other animals.* **5.** to pass life in a particular manner: *to live virtuously, live in peace, live extravagantly.* **6.** to dwell; reside: *to live in the country or in an apartment. Here lived I, but now live here no more* (Shakespeare). **7.** to have a rich and full life: *To-morrow do thy worst, for I have liv'd to-day* (John Dryden). **8.** to remain in existence, especially in the memory: *Eliza's glory lives in Spenser's song* (Matthew Prior). **9.** to remain afloat or exist through danger, as a ship: *It blew so hard . . . that I could not suppose their boat could live, or that they ever reached to their own coast* (Daniel Defoe). *—v.t.* **1.** to pass (life): *to live a life of ease. And each half lives a hundred different lives* (Matthew Arnold). **2.** to carry out or show in life: *to live one's ideals, to live one's religion. He . . . lived himself the truth he taught* (John Greenleaf Whittier).
live down, a. to live in such a worthy manner that some fault or sin of the past is overlooked or forgotten: *How long do you think it will take in New York society for a girl with sixty thousand dollars a year to live anything down?* (Archibald C. Gunter). **b.** to outlive (a fashion, custom, or the like): *It is very probable that your cousin will live down his fancy* (H. Rider Haggard).
live in, to dwell in the house where one works as a servant: *The domestics in that house live in.*
live it up, *U.S. Slang.* to enjoy life to the full: *Life is short. Live it up. See all you can. Hear all you can and go all you can* (New York Times).
live out, a. to stay alive through; last through: *He was not expected to live out the night.* **b.** to dwell away from the house where one works as a servant: *Their maid lives out.*
live up to, to act according to; do (what is expected or promised): *It can be so much easier to make a reputation than live up to one* (London Times).
live with, *Informal.* to accept without protest; resign to; put up with: *The employers will have "to live with the new pacts"* (Wall Street Journal).
[Old English *lifian,* or *libban*]
—**Syn.** *v.i.* **6.** sojourn, lodge, abide.

live[2] (līv), *adj.* **1.** having life; alive: *a live dog. I brought two live plants in flower pots* (Jane Carlyle). **2.** burning or glowing: *live coals, a live quarrel.* **3.** full of energy or activity: *a live person.* **4. a.** not recorded on tape or film: *a live television show. Lacking live opera, try a good phonograph record* (Newsweek). **b.** performed by living persons or animals; taken from nature: *a live film about safety.* **5. a.** *Informal.* up-to-date: *live ideas.* **b.** cheerful; gay: *a live party.* **6.** *Especially U.S.* of present interest or importance: *a live question.* **7.** moving or imparting motion: *live wheels, a live axle.* **8.** still in use or to be used; still having power: *live steam, live printing type.* **9.** carrying an electric current: *a live wire.* **10. a.** loaded or unexploded: *a live cartridge.* **b.** not yet lit: *a live match.* **11.** in the native state; not mined or quarried: *live metal, live rocks.* **12.** bright; vivid: *a live color.* **13.** of or belonging to a living being: *All the live murmur of a summer's day* (Matthew Arnold). **14.** living, or containing a living organism, but not able to cause infection: *The live virus polio vaccine may soon make its debut* (Science News Letter).
—adv. with the actual performance or event shown; as it takes place: *The race will be telecast live on a national hook-up* (New York Times).
[variant of *alive*] —**live′ness,** *n.*

live·a·bil·i·ty (liv′ə bil′ə tē), *n.* livability.

live·a·ble (liv′ə bəl), *adj.* livable. —**live′a·ble·ness,** *n.*

live-ac·tion (līv′ak′shən), *adj.* filmed directly from nature or from a performance by living actors: *Walt Disney's latest live-action film is a natural for youngsters and sympathetic grownups* (Newsweek).

live-and-let-live (liv′ən let′liv′), *adj.* not interfering; tolerant: *The H-bomb made imperative a live-and-let-live understanding between the Soviet Union and the West* (Bulletin of Atomic Scientists).

live center (līv), a revolving center or point that holds the work on the spindle of a lathe or on some other machine tool.

-lived (līvd), *combining form.* having a ——life: *Long-lived = having a long life.*

live-for·ev·er (liv′fər ev′ər), *n.* either of two garden plants of the orpine family, widespread in Europe and Asia and naturalized in North America.

live-in (liv′in′), *adj.* living in the place where one works: *The going price for a live-in maid (if one can be found) runs to $35 a week, plus room and board* (Wall Street Journal).

live·li·hood (līv′lē hu̇d), *n.* a means of keeping alive; support: *to write for a livelihood.* [Old English *līflād* < *līf* life + *lād* (see LOAD); influenced by obsolete *livelihood* liveliness] —**Syn.** See **living.**

live·li·ly (līv′lə lē), *adv.* in a lively manner; briskly; vigorously.

live·li·ness (līv′lē nis), *n.* vigor; activity; vividness; gaiety.

live load (līv), **1.** the load that a bridge, floor, or other structure must support in addition to its own weight, as the load of vehicles, people, furniture, etc. **2.** a temporary moving load on a structure.

live·long (liv′lông′, -long′), *adj.* **1.** whole length of; whole; entire: *She is busy the livelong day.* **2.** *Obsolete.* lasting: *Thou . . . Hast built thyself a livelong monument* (Milton). [alteration (taken as < *live,* verb) of Middle English *lefe longe* lief long[1]]

live·ly (līv′lē), *adj.,* **-li·er, -li·est,** *adv., n., pl.* **-lies.** *—adj.* **1.** full of life; active; vigorous; spirited: *A good night's sleep made us all lively again.* **2.** exciting: *We had a lively time during the hurricane.* **3.** bright; vivid: *lively colors.* **4.** full of cheer; gay: *a lively conversation.* **5.** bounding back quickly: *a lively baseball.* **6.** (of air) fresh; invigorating. **7.** lifelike, as an image, picture, etc. **8.** (of a ship) riding the waves buoyantly but with plenty of motion. **9.** brisk or sparkling, as liquors.
—adv. in a lively manner; briskly; nimbly; vigorously.
—n. a lively fellow (used of sailors).
[Old English *līflīc* living]
—**Syn.** *adj.* **1.** brisk, energetic, animated, vivacious. **4.** blithe, buoyant.

liv·en (lī′vən), *v.t.* to make more lively; put life into; cheer up: *A brisk discussion livened the dull conversation.* *—v.i.* to become more lively; brighten: *His hopes livened at the prospect of success.* —**liv′en·er,** *n.*

live oak (līv), **1.** an evergreen oak of the southern United States, having heavy, hard, strong, durable wood, grown as a shade tree; encina. **2.** its wood, formerly used in shipbuilding, etc. **3.** any of various other evergreen oaks.

liv·er[1] (liv′ər), *n.* **1. a.** a large, reddish-brown organ in vertebrate animals that secretes bile, converts sugars into glycogen that it stores, and helps in the absorption of food. A person's liver was once thought to be the source of his emotions. **b.** a large gland in some invertebrates that secretes into the digestive tract. **2.** the liver of an animal used as food. [Old English *lifer*]

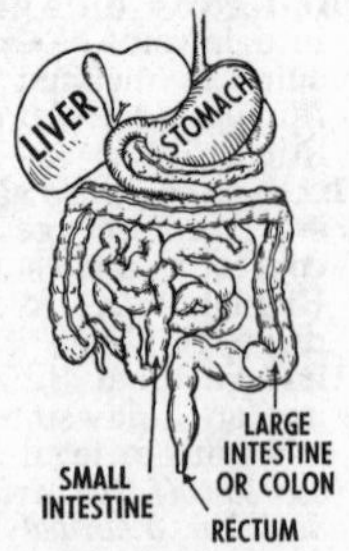

LIVER
STOMACH
LARGE INTESTINE OR COLON
SMALL INTESTINE
RECTUM

Liver[1] **(def. 1a) of a human being**

liv·er[2] (liv′ər), *n.* **1.** a person who lives: *a long liver, evil livers.* **2.** *Especially U.S.* an inhabitant; dweller: *a liver in the country.* [< *liv*(e)[1] + *-er*[1]]

liver color, a dark, reddish-brown color.
liv·er-col·ored (liv′ər kul′ərd), *adj.* of the color of liver, as a certain variety of old Chinese porcelain and its imitations.
-livered, *combining form.* **1.** having a ——liver or livers: *Fat-livered codfish = codfish that have fat livers.* **2.** having the characteristics (formerly attributed to a state of the liver) of: *Lily-livered = having the characteristics of a lily (cowardly).*
liver extract, an extract made from the liver of mammals, used to increase the red corpuscles or blood cells in treating anemia.
liver fluke, any of certain leaf-shaped flukes infesting the liver of various mammals.
liv·er·ied (liv′ər id, liv′rid), *adj.* clothed in a livery, as servants.
liv·er·ish (liv′ər ish), *adj. Informal.* having the symptoms attributed to a disordered liver, especially a disagreeable disposition; testy; cross.
liv·er·leaf (liv′ər lēf′), *n.* any of a group of herbs of the crowfoot family, with delicate white to purple flowers; hepatica.
Liv·er·pud·li·an (liv′ər pud′lē ən), *adj.* of or belonging to Liverpool, a seaport in western England.
—*n.* a native or inhabitant of Liverpool: *Owen's screenplay has captured and probably improved on the Liverpudlians' natural irreverence* (Maclean's).
[< *Liver*(pool) + *puddle* (humorous substitute for *pool*) + *-ian*]
liv·er·wort (liv′ər wėrt′), *n.* any of various plants that grow mostly on damp ground, the trunks of trees, etc. Liverworts are somewhat like mosses and comprise a class of bryophytes.
[< *liver*[1] + *wort,* translation of Medieval Latin *hepatica* hepatica (because of the shape of some of its parts)]
liv·er·wurst (liv′ər wėrst′, -wůrst′), *n.* a sausage consisting largely of liver. [American English, half-translation of German *Leberwurst* liver sausage]
liv·er·y (liv′ər ē, liv′rē), *n., pl.* **-er·ies. 1.** any special uniform provided for the servants of a household, or adopted by any group or profession: *A nurse's livery is often white.* **2.** any characteristic dress, garb, or outward appearance: *trees in summer livery.* **3.** the feeding, stabling, and care of horses for pay; the hiring out of horses and carriages. **4.** the keeping of cars, boats, bicycles, etc., for hire. **5.** *U.S.* a livery stable. **6.** *Law.* the delivery of legal possession of property. **7.** *Obsolete.* liveried retainers or servants as a group. **8.** *Obsolete.* **a.** the dispensing of food, provisions, or clothing to retainers or servants. **b.** the food or provisions so dispensed. **c.** an allowance of provender for horses.
[Middle English *livere* servants' rations < Old French *livree,* past participle of *livrer* dispense < Latin *līberāre* liberate < *līber* free]
livery company, one of the London City companies or guilds which had formerly a distinctive costume for special occasions.
liv·er·y·man (liv′ər ē mən, liv′rē-), *n., pl.* **-men. 1.** a person who works in or keeps a livery stable. **2.** a person wearing livery. **3.** *British.* a freeman who was a member of a guild or livery company of London and entitled to wear its livery.
livery stable, a stable engaged in the livery business.
lives (līvz), *n.* plural of **life.**
live·stock (līv′stok′), *n.* farm animals. Cows, horses, sheep, poultry, and pigs are livestock.
live weight (līv), the weight of an animal while living.
live wire (līv), **1.** a wire having a connection to a source of electricity, especially such a wire in which an electric current is flowing. **2.** *Informal.* an energetic, wide-awake person: *Weaver had earned something of a reputation for himself as a live wire* (New Yorker).
liv·id (liv′id), *adj.* **1. a.** having a dull-bluish or grayish color: *a livid sea, the livid face of a dead man.* **b.** very pale; grayish-white: *livid with rage.* **2.** discolored by a bruise; black-and-blue: *The livid marks of blows on his arm.*
[< Latin *līvidus* < *līvēre* be bluish] —**liv′id·ly,** *adv.* —**liv′id·ness,** *n.*
—**Syn. 1. b.** ashen, ashy.
li·vid·i·ty (li vid′ə tē), *n.* the condition of being livid; discoloration.
liv·ing (liv′ing), *adj.* **1.** having life; being alive: *a living plant.* **2.** full of life; vigorous; strong; active: *a living faith; the living question of the hour* (Oliver Wendell Holmes). **3.** in actual existence; still in use: *a living language.* **4.** true to life; vivid; lifelike: *a living picture, a picture which is the living image of a person.* **5.** of life; for living in: *The tramp had poor living conditions. My living expenses had been considerably larger than my total receipts* (Atlantic). **6.** sufficient to live on: *a living wage.* **7.** of or having to do with human beings: *within living memory.* **8.** burning; flaming; live: *living coals.* **9.** refreshing, as water: . . . *they have forsaken me the fountain of living waters* (Jeremiah 2:13).
—*n.* **1.** the act or condition of one that lives: *the pleasures of living in the country.* **2.** the means of obtaining what is needed to support life; livelihood: *What does he do for a living? He earns his living as a grocer.* **3.** manner of life: *Plain living and high thinking are no more* (Wordsworth). *Under Socrates . . . philosophy became little else than the doctrine of right living* (Herbert Spencer). **4.** position in the church with the income attached; benefice. **5.** *Obsolete.* property in general, especially a landed estate. —**liv′ing·ly,** *adv.* —**liv′ing·ness,** *n.*
—**Syn.** *adj.* **2.** lively. –*n.* **2. Living, livelihood, support** mean a person's means of providing shelter, food, etc., for himself. **Living,** the general word, applies to what he earns and how he does so: *He always had to work hard for his living.* **Livelihood** applies particularly to the kind of work he does: *Mowing lawns is his only livelihood.* **Support** applies particularly to what he must spend: *A family usually depends on the father for their support.*
living death, a state of misery not deserving the name of life: *Hopelessness makes the future a living death.*
living fossil, a plant or animal that is one of the last living species of a group or family which was once very common.
living picture, a tableau vivant.
living quarters, a place to live: *I ducked down the companion ladder where I had seen the captain go, and found myself in his living quarters* (Harper's).
living room, a room for general family use; sitting room.
living wage, sufficient pay to buy the necessities of life.
li·vre (lē′vər), *n.* an old French silver coin or money of account. [< Old French *livre* < Latin *lībra* pound (weight), scale, balance]
li·wa (lē′wə), *n.* one of the administrative districts or provinces into which Iraq is divided. [< Arabic *liwā*]
lix·iv·i·ate (lik siv′ē āt), *v.t.,* **-at·ed, -at·ing. 1.** to impregnate with lixivium or lye. **2.** to subject to lixiviation. [< *lixivi*(um) + *-ate*[1]]
lix·iv·i·a·tion (lik siv′ē ā′shən), *n.* the separating of a soluble substance from one that is insoluble by the percolation of water, as alkaline salts from wood ashes.
lix·iv·i·um (lik siv′ē əm), *n., pl.* **-i·ums, -i·a** (-ē ə). water impregnated with salts extracted by lixiviation, as lye from wood ashes. [< Late Latin *lixīvium,* variant of Latin *lixīvia* < *lixīvius* or *lixīvus* made into lye < *lixa* lye-ashes]
liz·ard (liz′ərd), *n.* **1.** any of a large group of reptiles with dry scaly skin. Lizards are small and have long bodies with four legs and a long tail, as the chameleons, horned toads, and glass snakes. Some lizards without limbs look much like snakes, but have movable eyelids. **2.** any of certain similar reptiles, especially of large size, as the crocodiles, dinosaurs, etc. **3.** *Slang.* an idler or lounger in places of social enjoyment: *a parlor lizard.* [< Old French *lesard,* or *laisarde,* feminine < Latin *lacertus,* or *lacerta*] —**liz′ard·like′,** *adj.*

European Green Lizard (def. 1—to 16 in. long)

lizard fish, any of various large-mouthed fishes with lizardlike heads, especially a species of the Atlantic Ocean.
liz·ard's-tail (liz′ərdz tāl′), *n.* a perennial herb having taillike spikes of small white flowers, growing in wet areas of the eastern and southern United States.
LL (no periods), **L.L.,** or **LL., 1.** Late Latin. **2.** Low Latin.
ll., lines.
lla·ma (lä′mə), *n., pl.* **-mas** or (*especially collectively*) **-ma. 1.** a South American cud-chewing, wooly-haired mammal somewhat like a camel but smaller and without a hump. Llamas are used as beasts of burden in Peru and other countries of the Andes. **2.** the wool of the llama or a fabric made from this: *Her [the Lady Mayoress's] petticoat was of llama and gold* (Tuer and Fagan). [< Spanish *llama* < Quechua (Peru)]

Llama (def. 1) (about 4 to 5 ft. high at the shoulder)

lla·ne·ro (lyä nā′rō, yä-), *n. Spanish.* a plainsman.
lla·no (lä′nō), *n., pl.* **-nos.** *Southwestern U.S.* a broad treeless plain. [American English < Spanish *llano* < Latin *plānus* level]
LL.B., Bachelor of Laws (Latin, *Legum Baccalaureus*).
LL.D., Doctor of Laws (Latin, *Legum Doctor*).
LL.M., Master of Laws (Latin, *Legum Magister*).
Lloyd's (loidz), *n.* an association of businessmen in London dealing in many kinds of insurance, especially marine insurance. Lloyd's is unique in that the risks are borne by the individual underwriters rather than by the corporation.
Lloyd's Register, a publication containing the age, tonnage, classification, etc., of merchant ships and yachts, and other shipping information, published by a nonprofit society allied to Lloyd's, that establishes standards of shipping construction.
Llyr (lir), *n. Celtic Mythology.* the personification of the sea and father of Bran.
lm., lumen.
LM (no periods), Lunar Module. Also, **LEM.**
L.M., 1. Licentiate in Medicine. **2.** Licentiate in Midwifery.
L-mes·on (el′mes′on, -mē′son), *n.* a light meson.
lmn., lineman.
l.m.t., local mean time.
ln., 1. liaison. **2.** loan.
Ln (no period), lanthanide.
lo (lō), *interj.* look! see! behold!
lo and behold, look and see (used as an expression of great surprise): *And then—lo and behold—it was there all the time* (J.B. Priestley). [Old English *lā*]
Lo (lō), *n. Humorous.* a North American Indian. [< "*Lo,* the poor Indian! whose untutor'd mind Sees God in clouds," from Alexander Pope's *Essay on Man; lo* here is the interjection]
loach (lōch), *n., pl.* **loach·es** or (*collectively*) **loach.** any of various small European freshwater fishes related to the minnows. [< Old French *loche*]
load (lōd), *n.* **1.** what one is carrying; burden: *The cart has a load of hay.* **2.** the quantity that can be or usually is carried; such quantity taken as a unit of measure or weight: *Send us four loads of sand.* **3.** something that weighs down, oppresses, or impedes: *a load of debt, a load of anxiety, a load of guilt. A medical student carries a very heavy load of work through school.* **4.** *Mechanics.* the weight or force supported by a structure or part. **5. a.** the external resistance overcome by an engine, dynamo, or the like, under a given condition, measured by the power required. **b.** the total amount of power supplied by a dynamo, generator, or other source of electricity in a given time. **6.** one charge of powder and shot for a gun. **7.** *Slang.* enough liquor to make one drunk.
get a load of, *U.S. Slang.* take note of; notice; observe: *When the boss gets a load of that [fancy car] parked next to his own heap, he fires the hero on the spot* (Time).
loads, *Informal.* **a.** a great quantity or number: *loads of money, loads of people.* **b.** very much: *I like you loads.*
—*v.t.* **1.** to place on or in something for conveyance: *to load grain.* **2.** to put a load in or on: *to load a car, ship, horse, basket, etc.* **3.** to burden; oppress: *to load the stomach with sweets, to load the mind with worries.* **4. a.** to add weight to: *to load dice. Silk was*

formerly loaded with chemicals which made it appear heavier and of better quality than it really was. **b.** to add to the weight of: *to load a thin wine to give it greater body.* **5.** to supply amply or in excess: *They loaded her with compliments on her singing.* **6.** to put a charge in (a gun). **7.** to increase (an insurance premium) by adding an extra charge as a provision against contingencies. —*v.i.* **1.** to take on a load or cargo: *The ship loaded in five days.* **2.** to provide a gun with a charge, bullet, shell, etc.
[Old English *lād* way, course, carrying, related to *lǣdan* lead[1]; influenced in meaning by *lade.* Doublet of LODE.]
—**Syn.** *n.* **1,3. Load, burden** mean what one is carrying. **Load,** the general word, applies literally to whatever is carried by a person or animal or in a vehicle, boat, or plane, and figuratively to something that weighs heavily on the mind or spirit: *That is a heavy load of groceries. That's a load off my mind.* **Burden** means something borne, and now, except in a few phrases, is used only figuratively, applying to sorrow, care, duty, or work: *She had too heavy a burden and became sick.*

load displacement, the displacement of a ship carrying a full load.

load·ed (lōʹdid), *adj.* **1.** carrying a load: *a loaded barge. The loaded apple trees in the orchard* (John Ruskin). **2.** with a charge in it. **3.** weighted, especially with lead or the like: *a loaded stick or whip.* **4.** *U.S. Slang.* drunk. **5.** *U.S. Slang.* having plenty of money; rich: *This money will make me a millionaire. I'll be loaded* (New Yorker). **6.** *U.S. Informal.* full of meaning and implications: *a loaded question.*

load·er (lōʹdər), *n.* **1.** a person who loads. **2.** a loading machine.

load factor, 1. *Electricity.* the ratio of the average to the maximum load of production or consumption. **2.** *Aviation.* the ratio of the average number of seats occupied to the maximum seating capacity.

load·ing (lōʹding), *n.* **1.** the act of a person or thing that loads: *Freight-car loadings continue to slack off* (Newsweek). **2.** *Electricity.* the introduction of additional inductances, as to a telephone circuit or an antenna. **3.** (in insurance) an addition to the net premium, derived from statistics, to provide for expenses, fluctuations in the death rate, and other contingencies. **4.** the weight imposed on a given supporting component, expressed by dividing the gross weight of an airplane by factors of flight, as engine power (power loading), wing span (span loading), or wing area (wing loading).

loading coil, a coil introduced into an electric circuit to increase its inductance.

load line, a line painted amidships on the side of a ship that marks the water line under a full load.

load·mas·ter (lōdʹmasʹtər, -mäsʹ-), *n.* a person in charge of an aircrew loading and unloading an aircraft.

loads (lōdz), *n.pl.* See under **load,** *n.*

load·star (lōdʹstärʹ), *n.* lodestar.

load·stone (lōdʹstōnʹ), *n.* **1.** a stone that attracts iron as a magnet does. It is a kind of magnetite. **2.** something that attracts: *Gold was the loadstone that drew men to Alaska.* Also, **lodestone.** [< earlier *load* or *lode* way, course + *stone*]

loaf[1] (lōf), *n., pl.* **loaves. 1.** bread shaped and baked as one piece: *The loaf came apart easily from the loaves it was baked with.* **2.** a rather large cake, often baked in the shape of a loaf of bread. **3.** anything like a loaf in shape, especially food shaped like a loaf of bread, as meat mixed with bread crumbs, eggs, etc.: *meat loaf, veal loaf.* **4.** a cone-shaped mass of sugar. **5.** *Dialect.* bread. **6.** *Slang.* head; brains.
half a loaf, *Informal.* half of something desired or deserved: *Urban Negroes . . . tend to regard the housing provisions in the rights bill as less than half a loaf* (New York Times).
[Old English *hlāf* loaf, bread]

loaf[2] (lōf), *v.i.* to spend time idly; do nothing: *I can loaf all day Saturday.* —*v.t.* to idle (away): *I haven't loafed my life away* (William Dean Howells). [American English; origin uncertain]

loaf·er (lōʹfər), *n.* **1.** a person who loafs; idler. **2.** a shoe resembling a moccasin, but with sole and heel stitched to the upper.

loaf sugar, 1. a cone-shaped mass of sugar. **2.** sugar in lumps.

loam (lōm), *n.* **1.** rich, fertile earth; earth in which much humus is mixed with clay and sand. **2.** a mixture of clay, sand, and straw used to make molds for large metal castings, and also to plaster walls, stop up holes, etc. **3.** *Archaic.* earth; ground; soil. —*v.t.* to cover or fill with loam. [Old English *lām* clayey earth. Related to LIME[1].]

loam·i·ness (lōmʹē nis), *n.* loamy quality or condition.

loam·less (lōmʹlis), *adj.* without loam; not mixed with loam.

loam·y (lōʹmē), *adj.,* **loam·i·er, loam·i·est.** of or like loam.

loan[1] (lōn), *n.* **1.** the act of lending. **2.** money lent. **3.** anything lent. **4.** a loan word.
—*v.t.* to make a loan of; lend (money, etc.).
—*v.i.* to make a loan.
[< Scandinavian (compare Old Icelandic *lān*)] —**loanʹer,** *n.*
➤ **loan, lend.** In standard British English *loan* is a noun and *lend* a verb. But in American English *loan* and *lend* are verbs, and *loan* is both a verb and a noun: *I loaned (or lent) him my tuxedo. He asked me for a loan of five dollars.*

loan[2] (lōn), *n. Scottish.* **1.** a lane; by-road. **2.** an open, uncultivated piece of ground near a farmhouse or village, on which cows are milked. [Middle English *lone,* variant of *lane* lane]

loan·a·ble (lōʹnə bəl), *adj.* that can be loaned; available for loaning, as capital: *Insurance companies and other savings institutions also were pressed for loanable funds* (Wall Street Journal).

loan office, 1. *U.S. Historical.* an office for receiving subscriptions to a government loan, as those established during the American Revolutionary War. **2.** a pawnshop.

loan shark, *U.S. Informal.* a person who lends money at an extremely high or unlawful rate of interest.

loan-shark·ing (lōnʹshärʹking), *n. U.S. Informal.* the practice of a loan shark: *The rich and elusive racketeers . . . specialize in gambling, narcotics, loan-sharking, and murder-for-profit* (Harper's).

loan translation, an expression that is a literal translation of a foreign expression, as *marriage of convenience* from French *mariage de convenance.*

loan word, a word borrowed from another language, especially a foreign word that has been Anglicized. *Examples:* khaki, intelligentsia. [translation of German *Lehnwort*]

loath (lōth), *adj.* **1.** unwilling; reluctant: *The little girl was loath to leave her mother. I'm loath to think you'd speak false to me* (George Eliot). *And though we are loath to admit it, there has been much to learn from the way others see us* (Wall Street Journal). **2.** *Obsolete.* repulsive; hateful; loathsome.
nothing loath, willing; willingly: *He pulled out a chair beside his desk and Greta sat down in it, nothing loath* (Michael Strange).
—*n. Obsolete.* loathing. Also, **loth.**
[Old English *lāth* hostile]
—**Syn.** *adj.* **1.** See **reluctant.**

loathe (lōᴛʜ), *v.t.,* **loathed, loath·ing.** to feel strong dislike and disgust for; abhor; hate: *We loathe rotten food or a nasty smell. He knew the model boy very well though—and loathed him* (Mark Twain). [Old English *lāthian* to hate < *lāth* hostile, loath] —**loathʹer,** *n.* —**Syn.** abominate, detest.

loath·ful (lōᴛʜʹfəl), *adj.* that is an object of loathing or disgust; hateful; loathsome.

loath·ing (lōʹᴛʜing), *n.* a strong dislike and disgust; intense aversion: *They looked upon the Creature with a loathing undisguised;—It wasn't Disinfected and it wasn't Sterilized* (Arthur Guiterman). —*adj.* that feels an intense aversion. —**loathʹing·ly,** *adv.* —**Syn.** *n.* antipathy, repugnance.

loath·li·ness (lōᴛʜʹlē nis), *n.* the quality of being loathly; loathsomeness.

loath·ly[1] (lōᴛʜʹlē), *adj.* loathsome: *a loathly toad* (James Thomson). [Old English *lāthlīc* < *lāth* hostile]

loath·ly[2] (lōthʹlē, lōᴛʜʹ-), *adv.* unwillingly; reluctantly. Also, **lothly.** [Old English *lāthlīce* < *lāth* hostile]

loath·ness (lōthʹnis), *n.* reluctance; disinclination.

loath·some (lōᴛʜʹsəm), *adj.* disgusting; making one feel sick: *a loathsome smell. Some of the details are loathsome.* Also, **lothsome.** —**loathʹsome·ly,** *adv.* —**loathʹsome·ness,** *n.* —**Syn.** abominable, detestable, repulsive, nauseating, odious.

loaves (lōvz), *n.* the plural of **loaf**[1].

lob[1] (lob), *n., v.,* **lobbed, lob·bing.** —*n.* **1.** a tennis ball hit high to the back of the opponent's court. **2.** a slow underhand throw in cricket. [< verb]
—*v.t.* **1.** to hit (a tennis ball) high to the back of an opponent's court. **2.** to throw (artillery shell, rock, etc.) in a high arc: *mainland shore batteries occasionally lob shells at Quemoy* (New York Times). **3.** to throw (a cricket ball) with a slow underhand movement. **4.** to throw heavily or clumsily. —*v.i.* **1.** to hit a lob in tennis. **2.** to move heavily or clumsily.
[Middle English *lobben.* Probably related to LUBBER.]

lob[2] (lob), *n.* a lugworm.

lob[3] (lob), *n. Dialect.* a country bumpkin; lout. [compare Danish *lobbes* clown, bumpkin]

lo·bar (lōʹbər), *adj.* of, having to do with, or affecting a lobe or lobes: *lobar pneumonia.*

lo·bate (lōʹbāt), *adj.* **1.** having a lobe or lobes. **2.** having the form of a lobe: *The liver is lobate.* **3.** (in birds) of or having to do with a foot that is adapted for paddling by having lobes or flaps along the sides of the toes, as in the coot. [< New Latin *lobatus* < Late Latin *lobus* < Greek *lobós*] —**loʹbate·ly,** *adv.*

Lobate (def. 3) foot of a coot

lo·bat·ed (lōʹbā tid), *adj.* lobate.

lo·ba·tion (lō bāʹshən), *n.* **1.** lobate formation or state. **2.** a lobe.

lob·ber (lobʹər), *n.* a person who lobs.

lob·by (lobʹē), *n., pl.* **-bies,** *v.,* **-bied, -by·ing.** —*n.* **1.** an entrance hall; passageway connected with one or more rooms in a building: *the lobby of a theater. A hotel lobby usually has chairs and couches to sit on.* **2.** (in the House of Commons, and other houses of legislature) a large entrance hall or room, open to the public and chiefly serving for interviews between members and persons not belonging to the House. **3.** a person or group that tries to influence legislators; body of lobbyists: *The governor conceded the legislative proposals probably will be strongly opposed by business interests. An aide said business lobbies had indicated almost "uniform resistance"* (Wall Street Journal).
—*v.i.* to try to influence legislators in their votes: *The jewelry industry has been lobbying against a low tariff on watches.* —*v.t.* **1.** to get or try to get (a bill) passed by lobbying: *The group tried to lobby the bill through.* **2.** to influence (legislators) in their votes: *Aircraft workers might decide to lobby their M.P.s within the next two or three weeks* (London Times).
[< Medieval Latin *lobium, lobia* covered walk < Germanic (compare Old High German *louba* hall, roof). Doublet of LODGE, LOGE, LOGGIA.]
—**Syn.** *n.* **1.** foyer.

lob·by·ism (lobʹē iz əm), *n.* the system or practice of lobbying.

lob·by·ist (lobʹē ist), *n.* a person who tries to influence legislators in their votes, or executives in their administration of laws, especially a member of a group (lobby) having special interests or favoring particular legislation: *Among the principal lobbyists for this clause at that time were the oil, textile, and coal industries* (London Times).

lobe (lōb), *n.* a rounded projecting part, as of a leaf, the lungs, the brain, a gland, or the ear. [< Middle French *lobe,* learned borrowing from Late Latin *lobus* < Greek *lobós*]

lo·bec·to·my (lō bekʹtə mē), *n., pl.* **-mies.** the removal of a lobe of the lung.

lobed (lōbd), *adj.* having a lobe or lobes.

lobe·fin (lōbʹfinʹ), *n.,* or **lobe-fin fish,** a crossopterygian.

lobe·less (lōbʹlis), *adj.* having no lobes.

lo·bel·ia (lō bēlʹyə), *n.* any of various widely distributed plants of the lobelia family, both wild and cultivated, with small blue, red, yellow, purple, or white flowers. [< New Latin *Lobelia* < Matthias de *Lobel,* 1538-1616, a Flemish botanist]

Lobed Oak Leaf

lo·be·li·a·ceous (lō bēʹlē āʹ-

shəs), *adj.* belonging to the lobelia family of plants.

lobelia family, a group of widely distributed, mainly herbaceous, dicotyledonous plants often grown for their showy flowers. The family includes the cardinal flower and Indian tobacco.

lo·be·line (lō′bə lēn), *n.* a poisonous alkaloid obtained from a variety of lobelia, used as a respiratory stimulant and smoking deterrent. *Formula:* $C_{22}H_{27}NO_2$

lob·lol·ly (lob′lol′ē), *n., pl.* **-lies. 1. a.** a long-leaved pine tree with a thick bark, that grows in swampy soils in the southern United States: *Skinny pines, including a kind rather pleasantly known as the loblolly, grew thick as weeds over some 35 million acres* (Time). **b.** its coarse, inferior wood. **2.** *U.S.* thick mud; swamp. **3.** *Dialect.* thick gruel or other liquid food. [American English; apparently special use as "mud, bog" of British English, thick gruel or stew, perhaps < dialectal *lob* bubble up + *lolly* broth, stew]

loblolly bay, an ornamental, white-flowered shrub or small tree of the southern United States. The loblolly bay belongs to the tea family.

loblolly boy, *Obsolete.* the assistant of a ship's surgeon. [probably < *loblolly* thick gruel or stew]

lo·bo (lō′bō), *n., pl.* **-bos.** the timber wolf; gray wolf. [American English < Spanish *lobo* < Latin *lupus*]

lo·bo·la (lō′bə lə), *n.* (in South Africa) a dowry paid by a native for his bride. [< Zulu *lobola*]

lo·bot·o·mize (lō bot′ə mīz), *v.t., v.i.,* **-mized, -miz·ing.** to perform a lobotomy (on).

lo·bot·o·my (lō bot′ə mē), *n., pl.* **-mies.** surgical incision into a lobe of the brain, especially to cut nerve fibers in the treatment of certain mental disorders. [< *lobe* + Greek *-tomiā* a cutting]

lob·scouse (lob′skous′), *n.* a stew of meat, vegetables, hardtack, etc., formerly eaten by sailors. [variant of *lob's couse;* origin uncertain. Compare *loblolly* gruel, *lob* boil with lumps (like porridge).]

Lob's pound (lobz), **1.** *British Dialect.* jail or prison: *Crowdero whom in irons bound, Thou basely threw'st into Lob's pound* (Samuel Butler). **2.** any situation of embarrassment or difficulty. [perhaps < *lob*³ clown, bumpkin]

lob·ster (lob′stər), *n.* **1.** any of various large, edible, marine crustaceans, with two big claws in front and eight legs. **2.** any of various related crustaceans that lack an enlarged pair of claws, as the spiny lobsters. **3.** *Historical.* a British soldier; redcoat. **4. a.** *Slang.* a gullible, foolish, or stupid person. **b.** a red-faced person. [Old English *loppestre,* probably alteration of Latin *lōcusta* locust, lobster]

Maine Lobster (def. 1—about 1 to 2 ft. long)

lob·ster·back (lob′stər bak′), *n. Historical.* a redcoat; lobster: *British lobsterbacks burned the original Capitol in 1814* (Time).

lob·ster·ing (lob′stər ing), *n.* the process or business of catching lobsters.

lob·ster·man (lob′stər mən), *n., pl.* **-men.** a man who catches lobsters for a living or for sport.

lobster New·burg (nü′bėrg, -nyü′), a hot dish of lobster meat cut in chunks, prepared with cheese sauce and sherry.

lobster pot, a trap for lobsters.

lobster shift, *U.S. Informal.* graveyard shift: *I was assigned the lobster shift, from midnight until eight in the morning* (New Yorker).

lobster ther·mi·dor (thėr′mə dôr), a dish of boiled lobster cut up in cream sauce, often with mushrooms and sherry, baked with a covering of grated cheese in a lobster shell.

lob·u·lar (lob′yə lər), *adj.* **1.** having the form of a lobule or small lobe. **2.** of or having to do with lobules: *a lobular vein.*

lob·u·late (lob′yə lit), *adj.* lobulated.

lob·u·lat·ed (lob′yə lā′tid), *adj.* consisting of or separated into lobules: *lobulated kidneys.*

lob·ule (lob′yül), *n.* **1.** a small lobe. **2.** a part of a lobe. [< New Latin *lobulus* < Late Latin *lobus;* see LOBE]

lob·u·lous (lob′yə ləs), *adj.* lobate.

lob·worm (lob′wėrm′), *n.* a lugworm.

loc., local.

lo·cal¹ (lō′kəl), *adj.* **1.** of place: *New Jersey is a local name.* **2.** having to do with a certain place or places: *the local doctor, local news, local self-government. A local thing called Christianity* (Thomas Hardy). **3.** of just one part of the body; affecting a particular organ of the body: *a local pain, local disease, local application of a remedy.* **4.** making all or almost all stops: *a local train.* **5.** of or concerned with position in space: *The poet's pen . . . gives to airy nothing A local habitation and a name* (Shakespeare). —*n.* **1.** a train, bus, etc., that makes all, or almost all, stops. **2.** a local inhabitant. **3.** a branch or chapter of a labor union, fraternity, etc.: *The local would not agree with the national decision to strike.* **4.** a newspaper item of interest to a particular area: *As a young reporter, he covered the locals.* **5.** *British.* a local tavern; pub. [< Latin *locālis* < *locus* place]

lo·cal² (lō kal′), *n.* locale.

local action, 1. the electrical action set up between different parts of a plate of conducting material when it is immersed in an electrolyte. **2.** a legal action which must be brought in the particular locality where the cause of action arose, such as an action to recover lands.

local anesthesia, anesthesia that causes a loss of feeling in a given area of the body but does not cause unconsciousness. It is used especially during minor operations, dental work, etc.

local color, 1. customs, peculiarities, etc., of a certain place or period, used in stories and plays to make them seem more real: *. . . he . . . found plenty of local color in the little Puritan metropolis* (Henry James). **2.** the color that is natural to each object or part of a picture independently of the general color scheme or the distribution of light and shade.

lo·cale (lō kal′), *n.* a place, especially with reference to events or circumstances connected with it: *The locale of "Don Quixote" is Spain in the 1600's. Author Bowles brings the Moroccan locale to life with meticulous realism* (Time). [< French *local,* noun use of adjective, local, learned borrowing from Latin *locālis*]

local government, 1. a. the administration of local affairs in a town, city, etc., by its own people. **b.** *U.S.* any type of government at less than state level. **2.** a group elected for any such administration.

lo·cal·ise (lō′kə līz), *v.t.,* **-ised, -is·ing.** *Especially British.* localize.

lo·cal·ism (lō′kə liz əm), *n.* **1.** a local expression, custom, etc.: *To be sure, some of the varieties of speech are mere localisms* (Scientific American). **2.** sectionalism. **3.** attachment to a certain place.

➔ A **localism** is a word or expression in regular use in a certain region but not in other regions in which the same language is used.

lo·cal·ist (lō′kə list), *n.* a person who is greatly or unduly concerned with local conditions or affairs; sectionalist.

lo·cal·ite (lō′kə līt), *n.* a local inhabitant; local.

lo·cal·i·tis (lō′kə lī′tis), *n. Slang.* overemphasis on narrow or local issues, views, etc.; provincialism.

lo·cal·i·ty (lō kal′ə tē), *n., pl.* **-ties. 1.** place; region; one place and the places near it: *the locality of a mineral, the locality of a crime. A sense of locality enables a person to find his way.* **2.** *Phrenology.* the faculty of recognizing and remembering places and locations. —**Syn. 1.** section, vicinity.

lo·cal·iz·a·ble (lō′kə lī′zə bəl), *adj.* that can be localized.

lo·cal·i·za·tion (lō′kə lə zā′shən), *n.* **1.** the act of localizing. **2.** the state of being localized.

lo·cal·ize (lō′kə līz), *v.t.,* **-ized, -iz·ing.** to fix in, assign, or limit to a particular place or locality; make local: *The infection seemed to be localized in the foot.* —**Syn.** place.

lo·cal·iz·er (lō′kə lī′zər), *n.* **1.** a person or thing that localizes. **2.** a radio beacon to indicate the center of the runway in an instrument landing system.

lo·cal·ly (lō′kə lē), *adv.* **1.** in a local manner or respect; with regard to place: *to be far separated locally.* **2.** in a particular place or particular places; not everywhere; not widely: *Outbreaks of the disease occurred locally.* **3.** in respect to position in space.

local mean time, local time.

local metamorphism, contact metamorphism.

local option, the right of choice exercised by a minor political division, such as a county or city, especially as to whether the sale of liquor shall be permitted within its limits.

local time, time measured from the instant of passing of the mean sun over the particular meridian of a place. *Abbr.:* l.t.

lo·cat·a·ble (lō kā′tə bəl), *adj.* that can be located.

lo·cate (lō′kāt, lō kāt′), *v.,* **-cat·ed, -cat·ing.** —*v.t.* **1.** *Especially U.S.* to establish in a place; settle: *He located his new store on Main Street.* **2.** to find out the exact position of: *The scouts tried to locate the enemy's camp.* **3.** to state or show the position of: *to locate Boston on the map.* **4.** *Especially U.S.* **a.** to fix the site, path, or alignment of: *to locate a building, to locate a highway or railroad.* **b.** to establish the boundaries or rights of: *to locate a claim.* —*v.i. Especially U.S.* to establish oneself in a place: *Early settlers located near water.*

be located, to be situated: *Albany is located on the Hudson.*

[< Latin *locāre* (with English *-ate*¹) < *locus* place] —**lo′cat·er,** *n.*

lo·ca·tion (lō kā′shən), *n.* **1.** the act of locating: *The scouts disputed about the location of the camp.* **2.** a being located. **3.** position; place: *a house in a fine location, a location for a mill.* **4.** *U.S.* a plot of ground marked out by boundaries, as a mining claim; lot. **5.** a place outside a studio, used in making all or part of a motion picture: *The company is on location.* **6.** (in South Africa) the quarters set apart for natives. **7.** (in Australia) a farm or station. **8.** *Civil and Scots Law.* the act of letting or leasing for hire, or a contract by which a thing or person is hired. **9.** a minor civil division in New Hampshire. **10.** a position in the memory of a digital computer storing one word or unit of meaning. —**Syn. 3.** locality. See **place.**

lo·ca·tion·al (lō kā′shə nəl), *adj.* of or having to do with location: *New England is at a locational disadvantage in reaching the rapidly expanding markets of the southeast and the southwest* (Atlantic). —**lo·ca′tion·al·ly,** *adv.*

loc·a·tive (lok′ə tiv), *Grammar.* —*adj.* indicating place. —*n.* **1.** a case used to indicate place in which. **2.** a word in this case, as Latin *domi,* "at home." [< New Latin *locativus* < Latin *locāre;* see LOCATE]

lo·ca·tor (lō′kā tər, lō kā′-), *n.* **1.** *U.S.* a person who marks the boundaries of or takes possession of land or a mining claim. **2.** a person who locates the alignment of roads, railroads, etc. **3.** a radiolocator. [American English < *locate* + *-er*¹]

loc. cit., in the place cited (Latin, *loco citato*).

loch (lok, loH), *n. Scottish.* **1.** a lake: *Loch Lomond.* **2.** an arm of the sea partly shut in by land; bay. [< Scottish Gaelic *loch*]

loch·an (loH′ən), *n. Scottish.* a small loch or lake. [< Scottish Gaelic *lochan,* diminutive of *loch*]

lo·chi·a (lō′kē ə, lok′ē-), *n.pl.* the discharge of fluid from the vagina after childbirth. [< New Latin *lochia* < Greek *lóchia,* neuter plural of *lóchios* < *lóchos* childbirth]

lo·chi·al (lō′kē əl, lok′ē-), *adj.* of or having to do with the lochia.

Loch·in·var (lok′ən vär′), *n.* the hero in a poem by Sir Walter Scott, who boldly carries off his sweetheart just as she is about to be married to another man.

lo·ci (lō′sī), *n.* the plural of **locus.**

lock¹ (lok), *n.* **1.** a means of fastening doors, boxes, etc., consisting of a bolt, usually needing a key of special shape to open it: *But what can Miss Emily want with a box . . . without any locks?* (Walter de la Mare). See picture under **padlock. 2.** an enclosed part of a canal, dock, etc., in which the level

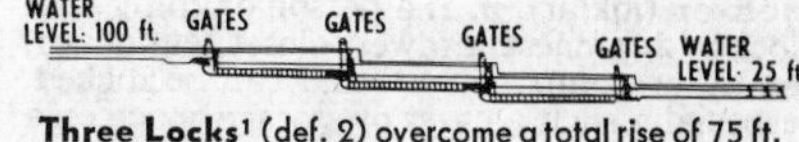

Three Locks¹ (def. 2) overcome a total rise of 75 ft.

of the water can be changed by letting water in or out to raise or lower ships. **3. a.** the part of a gun by means of which the charge is fired; gunlock. **b.** a safety on a gun. **4.** a device to keep a wheel from turning. A lock is used when a vehicle is going downhill: *For a car of this size the lock is excellent* (London Times). **5.** an airtight chamber admitting to a compartment in which there is compressed air. **6.** a locking together; interlocking. **7.** a kind of hold in wrestling. See picture under **hammer lock.**

lock, stock, and barrel, *Informal.* completely; entirely: *It is thus the only foreign city in the world run lock, stock, and barrel by the U.S. Navy* (Time).

under lock and key, locked up; in a place that is locked: *Under lock and key, in the ... store room* (H. Stuart).

—*v.t.* **1.** to fasten with a lock. **2.** to shut (something in or out or up): *to lock someone in a closet, to lock a building up for the night. Where'er she lie, Locked up from mortal eye* (Richard Crashaw). **3.** to hold fast: *The ship was locked in ice. The secret was locked in her heart.* **4.** to join, fit, jam, or link together: *The girls locked arms.* **5.** to make or set fast; fasten. **6.** to fasten (a wheel) to keep from turning. **7.** *Printing.* to fasten (type, blocks, etc., in a chase) for printing or plating. **8. a.** to embrace closely: *Lock'd in each other's arms we stood* (Matthew Arnold). **b.** to grapple in combat: *one glance ... showed me Hands and his companion locked together in deadly wrestle* (Robert Louis Stevenson). **9.** to move (a ship) by means of a lock. **10.** to furnish (a river, canal, etc.) with locks. **11.** to shut off (a portion of a river, canal, etc.) by means of a lock. **12.** to invest (capital) in something that is not easily convertible into money.

—*v.i.* **1.** to be locked; be capable of being locked: *The door will not lock with his key.* **2.** to become fixed or set fast; to become locked: *This gear has locked. Two cars locked together in passing.* **3.** to go or pass by means of a lock. **4.** to provide locks for the passage of vessels.

lock on, a. (of a radar) to fix upon and automatically follow a moving object: *The radar locked on the missile and tracked it until it landed in the desert.* **b.** to aim missiles, shells, etc., at (a target), as by radar: *The 1,500-mph Nike, a target-seeking missile that "locks on" the radar image of a plane* ... (World Book Encyclopedia Annual).

lock out, to refuse to give work to workers until they accept the employer's terms: *Large funds are subscribed, out of which labourers on strike or locked out are supported* (James E. Rogers).

[Old English *loc*]

lock[2] (lok), *n.* **1.** a curl of hair of the head: *Like the white lock of Whistler* (G.K. Chesterton). **2.** a portion of wool, flax, cotton, etc.

locks, the hair of the head: *curly locks.* [Old English *locc*]

—**Syn. 1.** ringlet.

lock·a·ble (lok′ə bəl), *adj.* that can be locked; provided with a lock: *a lockable glove compartment.*

lock·age (lok′ij), *n.* **1.** the construction, use, or operation of locks in canals or streams. **2.** the passing of ships through a lock or series of locks. **3. a.** the walls, gates, etc., forming a lock or locks. **b.** a system of locks or the locks in such a system. **4.** the amount of elevation and descent effected by a lock or locks. **5.** a toll paid for passage through a lock or locks.

lock-box (lok′boks′), *n.* **1.** a box with a lock. **2.** a coin-operated public locker.

Lock·e·an (lok′ē ən), *adj.* of, having to do with, or characteristic of the English philosopher John Locke: *He dismisses ... Lockean representative government as irrelevant to the problems of large-scale industrial societies* (New Yorker).

Lock·e·an·ism (lok′ē ə niz′əm), *n.* the philosophical doctrines of John Locke or his followers: *It is here that Berkeley passes from Lockeanism to Platonism* (Macmillan's Magazine).

lock·er (lok′ər), *n.* **1.** a person or thing that locks. **2.** a chest, drawer, closet, cupboard, or other compartment that can be locked, especially such a chest or storage space on a ship to keep equipment or supplies. **3.** a refrigerated compartment for storing frozen foods.

locker room, 1. a room with lockers for storage: *the locker room of a frozen-food plant.* **2.** a room with lockers near a gymnasium, in a clubhouse, etc., for dressing, storing sports equipment, etc.: *After football practice he was always down in the locker room* (New Yorker).

lock·et (lok′it), *n.* a small, ornamental, often hinged, case of gold, silver, etc., for holding a picture of someone or a lock of hair. It is usually worn around the neck on a necklace. [< Old French *locquet* latch (diminutive) < Old French *loc* < Germanic (compare Old Low German *lok* lock)]

lock·fast (lok′fast′, -fäst′), *adj. Especially Scottish.* fastened or secured by a lock: *All the lockfast places had been broken open in quest of the chart* (Robert Louis Stevenson).

lock·jaw (lok′jô′), *n.* a form of blood poisoning in which the jaws become firmly closed; tetanus.

lock·keep·er (lok′kē′pər), *n.* the supervisor of a lock: *A lockkeeper hauled Mr. Dawber out with a lifebelt* (London Times).

lock·less (lok′lis), *adj.* having no lock or locks: *Convention and pride hold many a man in a lockless prison.*

lock·mas·ter (lok′mas′tər), *n.* a person who operates a lock: *The lockmaster in his control station closes the lower gates by pressing a button* (Alexander Laing).

lock·nut (lok′nut′), *n.* **1.** a nut that can be screwed down on another to keep it securely in place. **2.** a nut that locks in place when tightly screwed.

lock·out (lok′out′), *n.* a refusal to give work to workers until they accept the employer's terms: *The lockout was ordered yesterday evening, following a clash between a section of workers and some representatives of the management* (Times of India).

locks (loks), *n.pl.* See under **lock**[2].

lock·smith (lok′smith′), *n.* a man who makes or repairs locks and keys.

lock·smith·er·y (lok′smith′ər ē), *n., pl.* **-er·ies.** the work or craft of a locksmith.

lock step, a way of marching in step very close together, with the legs of each man nearly touching those of the men in front and back.

lock stitch, a sewing-machine stitch in which two threads are fastened together at short intervals.

lock·up (lok′up′), *n.* **1.** the act of locking up. **2.** the state of being locked up. **3. a.** a house or room for the temporary detention of offenders. **b.** a jail.

lock washer, any of various types of steel washers placed under a nut to keep it from working loose.

lo·co[1] (lō′kō), *n., pl.* **-cos,** *v.,* **-coed, -co·ing,** *adj. U.S.* —*n.* **1.** locoweed. **2.** a disease caused by eating this weed; loco disease.

—*v.t.* **1.** to poison with locoweed. **2.** *Slang.* to make insane.

—*adj. Slang.* crazy.

[American English < Spanish *loco* insane; locoweed, perhaps < Italian *locco* fool < *alocco* owl < Latin *ulucus* < *ululāre* howl]

lo·co[2] (lō′kō), *British Informal.* —*n.* a locomotive. —*adj.* of or having to do with locomotives: *loco engineering.*

lo·co ci·ta·to (lō′kō sī tā′tō), *Latin.* in the place cited or passage quoted previously. *Abbr.:* loc. cit.

loco disease, a disease in horses, cattle, and sheep, affecting the brain, caused by eating locoweed; loco.

lo·co·fo·co (lō′kō fō′kō), *n. Obsolete.* a type of friction match. [perhaps < *loco-* (misunderstood as meaning "self-"), as in *locomotive* + *foco*, rhyming alternation < Italian *fuoco* fire]

Lo·co·fo·co (lō′kō fō′kō), *n. U.S.* a member of the independent or radical section of the Democratic Party (about 1835) which opposed monopolies and advocated hard money, election by direct popular vote, direct taxes, and free trade. [< the use of *locofoco* matches as emergency lighting at one of their meetings]

lo·co·man (lō′kō mən), *n., pl.* **-men.** *British Informal.* a railroad worker.

lo·co·mo·bile (lō′kə mə bēl′; -mō′bəl, -bēl), *adj.* able to move from place to place under its own power; self-propelled. [< Latin *locō* (see LOCOMOTION) + *mobilis* mobile]

lo·co·mo·tion (lō′kə mō′shən), *n.* the act or power of moving from place to place. Walking, swimming, and flying are common forms of locomotion: *I have no taste whatever for locomotion, by earth, air, or sea* (Jane W. Carlyle). [< Latin *locō* from a place, ablative of *locus* + English *motion*]

lo·co·mo·tive (lō′kə mō′tiv), *n.* **1.** a railroad engine. **2.** any engine that goes from place to place on its own power. **3.** *U.S. Slang.* a group cheer that imitates a railroad engine by starting up slowly and gradually gathering speed.

—*adj.* **1.** moving from place to place; having the power of locomotion: *locomotive bacteria.* **2.** having to do with the power to move from place to place: *In these locomotive days one is too apt to forget one's neighbours* (Sir Arthur Helps). —**lo′co·mo′tive·ly,** *adv.* —**lo′co·mo′tive·ness,** *n.*

lo·co·mo·tor (lō′kə mō′tər), *n.* a person, animal, or thing that is capable of locomotion. —*adj.* of or having to do with locomotion.

locomotor ataxia, a degenerative disease of the spinal cord marked by loss of control over walking and certain other voluntary movements, and severe pains in the internal organs; tabes dorsalis. It is often associated with syphilis.

lo·co·mo·to·ry (lō′kə mō′tər ē), *adj.* having to do with or having locomotive power: *But because they can swim, paddle, walk, jump and climb trees, it is surprising that their locomotory specializations have not been studied in detail before* (New Scientist).

lo·co·weed (lō′kō wēd′), *n., pl.* **-weeds** or (collectively) **-weed.** a plant of the western United States that affects the brain of horses, sheep, and other grazing animals that eat it. Locoweed comprises various herbs of the pea family.

Lo·cri·an (lō′krē ən), *adj.* of or having to do with Locris, a city in Greece. —*n.* an inhabitant of Locris.

Lo·crine (lō′krīn), *n.* a mythical king of England, father of Sabrina.

loc·u·lar (lok′yə lər), *adj.* having one or more locules (used chiefly in compounds, as *bilocular, trilocular*).

loc·u·late (lok′yə lāt, -lit), *adj.* having locules.

loc·u·lat·ed (lok′yə lā′tid), *adj.* loculate.

loc·ule (lok′yül), *n.* a small cavity or cell in animal or plant tissue, separated from another locule by a septum, as a compartment in an ovary, fruit, or anther. [< Latin *loculus* chest, compartment; (literally) small place (diminutive) < *locus* place, locus]

loc·u·li·cid·al (lok′yə lə sī′dəl), *adj. Botany.* splitting lengthwise through the back or dorsal suture of each loculus or carpel of a capsule, as in the seed pod of the iris. [< Latin *loculus* loculus + *caedere* to cut + English *-al*[1]]

loc·u·lose (lok′yə lōs), *adj.* divided into loculi or cells.

loc·u·lous (lok′yə ləs), *adj.* loculose.

loc·u·lus (lok′yə ləs), *n., pl.* **-li** (-lī). a locule.

lo·cum (lō′kəm), *n. Informal.* locum tenens.

locum te·nen·cy (tē′nən sē). **1.** the office of employment of a locum tenens. **2.** the holding of a place by temporary substitution.

locum te·nens (tē′nənz), *pl.* **locum te·nen·tes** (tə nen′tēz). a person temporarily holding the place or office of another; deputy; substitute: *There's this locum tenens I was going to take up in the North* (A.S.M. Hutchinson). [< Medieval Latin *locum tenens* < Latin *locum*, accusative of *locus* place, and *tenēns*, present participle of *tenēre* to hold. Compare LIEUTENANT.]

lo·cus (lō′kəs), *n., pl.* **-ci. 1.** the place in which something is situated; locality. **2.** *Mathematics.* a curve, surface, or other figure that contains all the points, and only those points, that satisfy a given condition: *The locus of a point 1 ft. distant from a given point is the surface of a sphere having a radius of 1 ft.* **3.** *Genetics.* the position of a gene on a chromosome. **4.** a shortened form for various Latin phrases, especially *locus classicus.* [< Latin *locus* place]

lo·cus clas·si·cus (lō′kəs klas′ə kəs), *pl.* **lo·ci clas·si·ci** (lō′sī klas′ə sī). *Latin.* a classical passage, usually cited for illustration or explanation of a particular word or subject.

lo·cus si·gil·li (lō′kəs si jil′ī), *pl.* **lo·ci si·gil·li** (lō′sī si jil′ī). *Latin.* the place of the seal (on official papers, etc.). *Abbr.:* L.S.

lo·cus stan·di (lō′kəs stan′dī), *pl.* **lo·ci stan·di** (lō′sī stan′dī). *Latin.* place of standing; a right of place in court; the right to appear and be heard before a tribunal.

lo·cust (lō′kəst), *n.* **1.** any of various grasshoppers with short antennae, certain kinds of which migrate in great swarms, destroying crops. **2.** a cicada. **3. a.** any of a group of American trees of the pea family, with small, rounded pinnate leaves and clusters of sweet-smelling white or rose-colored flowers. **b.** its hard wood that resists decay. **4.** any of several other leguminous trees, as the carob and the honey locust. [< Latin *lōcusta* locust, crab, lobster]

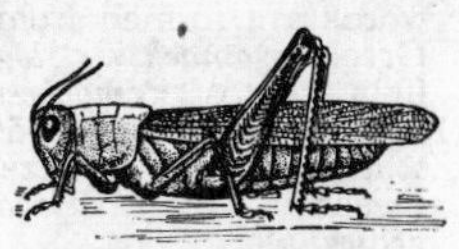

Lesser Migratory Locust (def. 1—1¼ to 3 in. long)

lo·cus·ta (lō kus′tə), *n., pl.* **-tae** (-tē). *Botany.* the inflorescence or spikelet of grasses. [< New Latin *locusta* < Latin *lōcusta* locust (supposedly from the shape)]

locust bean, the fruit of the carob.

lo·cu·tion (lō kyü′shən), *n.* **1.** style of speech; manner of expression: *to be accustomed to the rustic locution.* **2.** a form of expression or phraseology: *unfamiliar locutions, foreign locutions.* **3.** *Obsolete.* speech as the expression of thought; discourse. [< Latin *locūtiō, -ōnis* < *loquī* speak] —**Syn. 2.** idiom.

loc·u·to·ry (lok′yə tôr′ē, -tōr′-), *n.,pl.* **-ries.** a room or place in a monastery set apart for conversation. [< Medieval Latin *locutorium* < Latin *locūtor* one who speaks < *loquī* speak]

lode (lōd), *n.* **1. a.** a vein of metal ore: *The miners struck a rich lode of copper.* **b.** any mineral deposit filling a fissure in the rock. **2.** *British.* a watercourse; aqueduct, channel, or open drain. [Old English *lād* course, way, carrying. Doublet of LOAD.]

lo·den (lō′dən), *n.* **1.** a waterproof woolen cloth with a thick pile. **2.** a garment, especially an overcoat, made of loden. [< German *Loden* < Old High German *lodo*]

lode·star (lōd′stär′), *n.* **1.** a star that shows the way. **2.** the polestar; North Star. **3.** a guiding principle; center of attraction. Also, **loadstar.** [< *lode,* and *load* + *star*]

lode·stone (lōd′stōn′), *n.* loadstone.

lodge (loj), *n., v.,* **lodged, lodg·ing** —*n.* **1. a.** a place to live in. **b.** a small or temporary house, as used during the hunting season or in summer: *a hunting lodge in the Berkshires.* **c.** a cottage on an estate or the like, as for a caretaker, gardener, etc.: *The porter of my father's lodge* (Emily Dickinson). **2. a.** one of the branches of a secret society. **b.** the place where it meets. **3.** the den of an animal, especially the large structure built near or in the water by beavers. **4.** *U.S.* **a.** a wigwam, tepee, or other dwelling of a North American Indian. **b.** the number of Indians living in one dwelling. **5.** the residence of the head of a college at Cambridge University, England, or the Vice Chancellor's residence at certain other schools.

—*v.t.* **1.** to provide with a place to live in or sleep in for a time: *the chief man . . . received us, and lodged us three days courteously* (Acts 28:7). **2.** to rent a room or rooms to. **3.** to put or send into a place: *The marksman lodged a bullet in the center of the target.* **4.** to put for safekeeping: *to lodge money in a bank. I lay all night in the cave where I had lodged my provisions* (Jonathan Swift). **5.** to lay before some authority: *We lodged a complaint with the mayor.* **6.** to put (power, authority, etc.) in a person or thing: *The authority to arrest criminals is lodged with the police.* **7.** to lay flat, as crops by rain or wind. **8.** to search out the lair of (a deer). —*v.i.* **1.** to live in a place for a time: *to lodge at a motel.* **2.** to live in a rented room in another's house: *We are merely lodging at present.* **3.** to get caught or stay in a place without falling or going farther: *The kite lodged in the top of a tree.*

[< Old French *loge* arbor, covered walk < Germanic (compare Old High German *louba* hall, roof). Doublet of LOBBY, LOGE, LOGGIA.]

—**Syn.** *v.t.* **6.** vest. –*v.i.* **1.** dwell, reside.

lodge·a·ble (loj′ə bəl), *adj.* suitable for lodging or dwelling in: *The house is old-fashioned and irregular, but lodgeable and commodious* (Tobias Smollet).

lodge·ment (loj′mənt), *n. Especially British.* lodgment.

lodge·pole pine (loj′pōl′), **1.** a tall pine tree of western North America with yellow-green needles in clusters of two, used for poles, railroad ties, in insulation board, etc. **2.** its wood.

lodg·er (loj′ər), *n.* **1.** a person who lives in a rented room in another's house: *I'm now no more than a mere lodger in my own house* (Oliver Goldsmith). **2.** *Archaic.* **a.** a person who stays in a place; occupant; inhabitant: *Queer Street's full of lodgers just now* (Dickens). **b.** a person who sleeps or passes the night in a place.

lodg·ing (loj′ing), *n.* **1.** a place to live in for a time: *a lodging for the night.* **2.** *Obsolete.* a dwelling; abode.

lodgings, a rented room or rooms in a house, not in a hotel: *Life in lodgings, at the best of times, is not a peculiarly exhilarating state of existence* (J.H. Riddell).

—**Syn. 1.** accommodation.

lodging house, a house in which rooms are rented, not a hotel.

lodg·ment (loj′mənt), *n.* **1.** the act of lodging. **2.** a being lodged: *the lodgment of a claim against a company.* **3.** something lodged or deposited: *a lodgment of earth on a ledge of rock.* **4.** *Military.* **a.** a position gained; foothold. **b.** an entrenchment built temporarily on a position gained from the enemy. **5.** *Law.* the action of depositing (a sum of money, securities, etc.). **6.** a lodging place; lodging house; lodgings.

lod·i·cule (lod′ə kyül), *n. Botany.* one of the small scales in the flowers of most grasses, close to the base of the ovary. [< Latin *lōdīcula* (diminutive) < *lōdix, -īcis* coverlet, blanket]

lo·ess (lō′is, lœs), *n.* a fine, yellowish-brown loam deposited by the wind. It consists of tiny mineral particles, picked up by the wind from deserts and former glaciated areas, and brought to the places where they are now found, as the central United States. [< German *Löss,* apparently < Swiss German *lösen* pour out of a vessel]

lo·ess·i·al (lō es′ē əl), *adj.* of or having to do with loess: *loessial soil, loessial plains.*

loft (lôft, loft), *n.* **1.** an attic. **2.** the room under the roof of a barn: *This loft is full of hay.* **3.** a gallery in a church or hall: *an organ or choir loft.* **4.** *U.S.* an upper floor of a business building or warehouse. **5.** *Golf.* **a.** the backward slope of the face of a club. **b.** a stroke that drives a golf ball upward. **c.** the act of driving a golf ball upward. **6. a.** a pigeon house. **b.** a flock of pigeons.

—LOFT

Loft (def. 5a)

—*v.t.* **1. a.** to hit (a golf ball) high up, especially to clear an obstacle. **b.** to slant back the face of (a golf club). **2.** to keep (pigeons) in a loft or flock. **3.** *Obsolete.* **a.** to build (a building) with a loft or upper story. **b.** to store (goods) in a loft. —*v.i.* to hit a golf ball high up.

[Old English *loft* sky, upper region < Scandinavian (compare Old Icelandic *lopt* air, sky; loft, upper room)]

—**Syn.** *n.* **1.** garret.

loft-bomb·ing (lôft′bom′ing, loft′-), *n.* a method of releasing bombs while the bomber is rising almost vertically, causing the bomb to travel through a long arc and explode after the plane is safely out of range; over the shoulder bombing.

loft·er (lôf′tər, lof′-), *n.* a lofting iron.

loft·i·ly (lôf′tə lē, lof′-), *adv.* in a lofty manner.

loft·i·ness (lôf′tē nis, lof′-), *n.* the state or quality of being lofty.

loft·ing iron (lôf′ting, lof′-), an iron golf club used to make the ball rise over an obstacle.

loft·y (lôf′tē, lof′-), *adj.,* **loft·i·er, loft·i·est.** **1.** very high; towering: *lofty mountains.* **2.** exalted; dignified; grand: *lofty aims.* **3.** proud; haughty; overweening: *He had a lofty contempt for others.* —**Syn. 1.** tall. See **high. 2.** sublime, stately. **3.** arrogant.

log (lôg, log), *n., v.,* **logged, log·ging,** *adj.* —*n.* **1. a.** a length of wood just as it comes from the tree. **b.** a thing or person that is heavy, helpless, or inert: *I must have slept like a log* (Robert Louis Stevenson). **2. a.** the daily record of a ship's voyage; logbook. **b.** a similar record of an airplane trip. **c.** a record of the operation or performance of an engine, etc. **3.** a float for measuring the speed of a ship, as a chip log or patent log. **sleep like a log,** to sleep soundly and heavily: *Exhausted by the day's activities, he slept like a log.*

—*v.i.* to cut down trees, cut them into logs, and get them out of the forest. —*v.t.* **1.** to cut (trees) into logs; cut down and trim (trees). **2.** to cut down trees on (land). **3. a.** to enter in the log of a ship or airplane. **b.** to enter name and offense of (a sailor) in a ship's log. **4.** to travel (a distance), especially as indicated by the rate of speed registered by a log: *One plane logged 150 hours in the sky between July 31 and August 15* (Wall Street Journal).

—*adj.* made of logs: *a log house.*

[Middle English *logge;* origin uncertain]

Log (lôg, log), *n.* **King,** (in Aesop's fables) the log that was made king of the frogs by Jupiter, often alluded to as the type of inertness in rulers.

log (no period) or **log.,** logarithm.

lo·gan·ber·ry (lō′gən ber′ē), *n., pl.* **-ries. 1.** a large, purplish-red fruit of a bramble developed in California, from a cross between a blackberry and a red raspberry. **2.** the plant itself. [American English < J.H. *Logan,* 1841-1928, an American jurist and horticulturist, who developed it + *berry*]

lo·ga·ni·a·ceous (lō gā′nē ā′shəs), *adj.* belonging to a family of tropical and subtropical dicotyledonous plants that includes the nux vomica, buddleia, and gelsemium. [< New Latin *Loganiaceae* the family name (< James *Logan,* an Irish botanist of the 1700's) + English *-ous*]

log·an stone (lôg′ən, log′-), a rock so balanced on its base that it rocks to and fro readily, as under pressure of the hand or of the wind; rocking stone. [perhaps imitative. Compare earlier *log* to rock to and fro.]

log·a·oe·dic (log′ə ē′dik), *adj.* of poetry: **1.** composed of meter combining dactyls and trochees, or anapests and iambs, producing a movement somewhat suggestive of prose. **2.** composed of any mixture of meters. —*n.* a logaoedic verse. [< Late Latin *logaoedicus* < Greek *logaoidikós* between prose and poetry < *lógos* speech (< *légein* speak) + *aoidē* song < *aeídein* sing]

log·a·rithm (lôg′ə riᴛʜ əm, log′-), *n. Mathematics.* **1.** the exponent of the power to which a fixed number (usually 10) must be raised in order to produce a given number. If the fixed number is 10, the logarithm of 1,000 is then 3; the logarithm of 10,000 is 4; the logarithm of 100,000 is 5. *Abbr.:* log (no period). **2.** one of a system of such exponents used to shorten calculations in mathematics. [< New Latin *logarithmus* < Greek *lógos* proportion, calculation; word (< *légein* speak, select words) + *arithmós* a number]

log·a·rith·mic (lôg′ə riᴛʜ′mik, log′-), *adj.* of or having to do with a logarithm or logarithms. —**log′a·rith′mi·cal·ly,** *adv.*

log·a·rith·mi·cal (lôg′ə riᴛʜ′mə kəl, log′-), *adj.* logarithmic.

log·book (lôg′bu̇k′, log′-), *n.* **1.** a book in which a daily record of a ship's voyage is kept. **2.** a book for records of an airplane's trip. **3.** a journal of travel.

log chip, the thin piece of wood of a chip log. Also, **log ship.**

loge (lōzh), *n.* **1.** a box in a theater or opera house. **2.** a booth or stall, as at a fair. [< French *loge* < Old French. Doublet of LODGE, LOBBY, LOGGIA.]

log·gan stone (lôg′ən, log′-), logan stone.

logged (lôgd, logd), *adj.* **1.** cut into logs, as trees. **2.** cleared, as land by the cutting of timber. **3.** inert or unwieldy, like a log. **4.** water-logged, as a vessel. **5.** stagnant, as water.

log·ger[1] (lôg′ər, log′-), *n.* **1.** a person whose work is logging; lumberjack: *Rains and late snows have kept loggers out of the woods* (Wall Street Journal). **2.** a machine for loading or hauling logs, as a donkey engine attached to a boom or a tractor to drag logs from the forest. **3.** an electronic device that automatically records or logs physical processes and events. [< *log* + *-er*[1]]

log·ger[2] (lôg′ər, log′-), *adj. Dialect.* thick, heavy, or stupid. [perhaps back formation < *loggerhead*]

log·ger·head (lôg′ər hed′, log′-), *n.* **1.** a stupid person; blockhead. **2.** Also, **loggerhead turtle.** any of various large-headed, carnivorous marine turtles of the tropical Atlantic and Pacific oceans. **3.** an iron instrument with a long handle and a ball or bulb at the end, used, when heated in the fire, for melting pitch and for heating

liquids. **4.** an upright piece near the stern of a whaleboat, around which the harpoon line is passed. **5.** Also, **loggerhead shrike.** a bluish-gray shrike of eastern North America, with a white breast, black-and-white wings and tail, and two black bars on the side of the head meeting at the forehead.
at loggerheads, disputing; at enmity: *The politicians and the generals were at loggerheads over the advisability of ever starting the business* (London Times).
[< *logger,* variant of *log* + *head*]
loggerhead sponge, a very large sponge found in and to the south of Florida: . . . *big, brown loggerhead sponges, two or three feet high* (New Yorker).
log·gia (loj′ə, loj′ē ə; lôj′-; *Italian* lôd′jä), *n., pl.* **log·gias,** *Italian,* **log·gie** (lôd′jā). a gallery or arcade open to the air on at least one side. [< Italian *loggia* < Old French *loge.* Doublet of LODGE, LOGE, LOBBY.] —**Syn.** piazza.

Loggia of the Ospedale Maggiore, Milan

log·ging (lôg′ing, log′-), *n.* the work of cutting down trees, cutting them into logs, and moving the logs from the forest. [American English]
log·gy (lôg′ē, log′-), *adj.,* **-gi·er, -gi·est.** *Especially British Dialect.* **1.** thick. **2.** heavy; sluggish: *He woke with a loggy head.*
log·i·a (log′ē ə), *n.pl., sing.* **-i·on. 1.** the sayings or maxims attributed to a religious teacher or sage. **2.** Often, **Logia.** the sayings of Jesus, especially those contained in collections supposed to have been among the sources of the present Gospels or those in the Agrapha, attributed to Jesus but not in the Bible. [< Greek *lógia,* plural of *lógion* oracle < *lógos* word]
log·ic (loj′ik), *n.* **1.** the branch of philosophy dealing with forms and processes of thinking, especially those of inference and scientific method: **a.** the science of proof: *Logic is not the science of Belief, but the science of Proof, or Evidence* (John Stuart Mill). **b.** the science of reasoning: *The Grape that can with Logic absolute The Two-and-Seventy jarring Sects confute* (Edward FitzGerald). *Logic, or the science of the general principles of good and bad reasoning* (Adam Smith). **2. a.** a particular system or theory of logic: *The metaphysical logic of Hegel, the empirical logic of Mill, the formal logic of Kant* (Robert Adamson). **b.** the science of reasoning as applied to some particular branch of knowledge or study: *The logic of taste, if I may be allowed the expression* (Edmund Burke). **3.** a book on logic. **4. a.** the use of argument; reasoning: *Vociferated logic kills me quite* (William Cowper). *She could not cope with Lancelot's quaint logic* (Charles Kingsley). **b.** a means of convincing or proving: *the logic of war. The logic of events proved him wrong.* **5.** reason; sound sense.
chop logic, to exchange logical arguments and terms; bandy logic; argue: *A man must not presume to use his reason, unless he has studied the categories, and can chop logic* (Tobias Smollett).
—*adj.* of or having to do with logical operations in a computer: *logic circuits, a logic element.*
[< Late Latin *logicē* < Greek *logikḗ* (*téchnē*) reasoning (art) < *lógos* word, idea < *légein* speak, select words]
log·i·cal (loj′ə kəl), *adj.* **1.** having to do with logic; according to the principles of logic: *logical reasoning. The scientific quest is grounded in reason and logical inference from known facts* (John E. Owen). **2.** reasonably expected; reasonable: *War was the logical consequence of these conditions.* **3.** reasoning correctly or capable of reasoning correctly: *a logical man, a clear and logical mind.* —**log′i·cal·ly,** *adv.* —**log′i·cal·ness,** *n.* —**Syn. 2.** consistent. **3.** rational, sound.
log·i·cal·i·ty (loj′ə kal′ə tē), *n.* the quality of being logical; logicalness.
logical operations, the nonarithmetical operations in a computer, such as comparing, selecting, making references, matching, sorting, etc.
logical positivism, a philosophical school influenced by positivism and symbolic logic, that accepts as meaningful only the analytic propositions of logic and mathematics and propositions that can be verified by empirical procedures.
logical positivist, a person who maintains the doctrines of logical positivism: *Carnap, a prominent logical positivist, holds that "philosophy is nothing but the logic of science"* (Scientific American).
lo·gi·cian (lō jish′ən), *n.* a person skilled in logic.
log·i·on (log′ē on), *n.* singular of **logia.**
lo·gis·tic (lō jis′tik), *adj.* **1.** of or having to do with logistics. **2.** logarithmic. **3.** sexagesimal. [< Medieval Latin *logisticus* < Greek *logistikós,* ultimately < *lógos* reckoning, reason] —**lo·gis′ti·cal·ly,** *adv.*
lo·gis·ti·cal (lō jis′tə kəl), *adj.* logistic.
lo·gis·ti·cian (lō′jə stish′ən), *n.* an expert in logistics.
lo·gis·tics (lō jis′tiks), *n.* **1. a.** the art of planning and carrying out military movement, evacuation, and supply. **b.** the planning and carrying out of any complex or large-scale operation, activity, etc.: *The logistics were staggering, and in fact, the trip was postponed several times before we finally got all the artists organized and together* (New Yorker). **2.** the art of arithmetical calculation. [< French *logistique* (with English *-ics*) < Old French *logis* lodgement or *loger* to lodge; probably influenced by Old French *logistique* < Medieval Latin *logisticus;* see LOGISTIC]
log·jam (lôg′jam′, log′-), *n., v.,* **-jammed, -jam·ming.** —*n.* **1.** a blocking of the downstream movement of logs, causing a jumbled overcrowding of the timber in the river. **2.** a deadlock; delay; standstill: *The Yugoslavs might break the logjam that has stalled formal talks* (Wall Street Journal). **3.** a jamming; mass; congestion: *Yesterday's appointments and prospective appointments represented in part a break in a logjam of unfilled positions* (New York Times).
—*v.t., v.i.* **1.** to crowd or block by crowding: *On the day of the sale customers logjammed the aisles of the store.* **2.** to delay, obstruct, or block by confusion or overloading.
log·like (lôg′līk′, log′-), *adj.* like a log in shape or use.
log line, the line attached to the float for measuring the speed of a ship.
log·o (lôg′ō, log′ō), *n., pl.* **log·os.** logotype: *Now seven out of ten shows have logos and lettering designed by the advertising agencies* (New Yorker).
log·o·dae·da·ly (lôg′ə dē′də lē, -ded′ə-; log′-), *n.* verbal legerdemain; a playing with words, as by passing from one meaning of them to another. [ultimately < Greek *lógos* word + *daídalos* skillfully wrought]
log·o·gram (lôg′ə gram, log′-), *n.* a single character or a combination of characters regarded as a unit, representing a whole word, as in shorthand. [< Greek *lógos* word + English *-gram*]
log·o·gram·mat·ic (lôg′ə grə mat′ik, log′-), *adj.* having to do with logograms.
log·o·graph (lôg′ə graf, -gräf; log′-), *n.* a logogram.
log·o·graph·ic (lôg′ə graf′ik, log′-), *adj.* **1.** of or having to do with logography. **2.** consisting of characters or signs each representing a single word.
log·o·graph·i·cal (lôg′ə graf′ə kəl, log′-), *adj.* logographic.
lo·gog·ra·phy (lō gog′rə fē), *n.* **1.** *Printing.* the use of logotypes. **2.** a former method of longhand reporting, in which several reporters each took down a few words in succession. **3.** a system of writing that uses logographs. [< Greek *logographía* < *logográphos* speech-writer < *lógos* word, speech + *gráphein* write]
log·o·griph (lôg′ə grif, log′-), *n.* **1.** an anagram, or a puzzle involving anagrams. **2.** a puzzle in which a hidden word must be guessed from other words formed from its letters, these words often being themselves discovered by indirect clues, verse, or the like, as in a charade. [< Greek *lógos* word + *grîphos* riddle]
log·o·mach·ic (lôg′ə mak′ik, log′-), *adj.* of, having to do with, or given to logomachy.
lo·gom·a·chist (lō gom′ə kist), *n.* a person who contends about words; person who disputes about verbal subtleties.
lo·gom·a·chy (lō gom′ə kē), *n., pl.* **-chies. 1.** contention about words or in words only. **2.** a game, similar to anagrams, in which words are formed from single letters. [< Greek *logomachíā* < *lógos* word + *máchē* a fight, contest < *máchesthai* to fight]
log·o·pe·dics (lôg′ə pē′diks, log′-), *n.* the study, analysis, and treatment of defective speech. [< Greek *lógos* word + (ortho)*pedics*]
log·or·rhe·a (lôg′ə rē′ə, log′-), *n.* **1.** excessive volubility accompanying some forms of insanity. **2.** the habit of talking too much. [< Greek *lógos* word + *rheîn* to flow]
Log·os (log′os), *n.* **1.** *Theology.* Jesus, the Word of God; the second person of the Trinity; the revelation of God to men. John 1:1-18. **2.** Also, **logos.** *Philosophy.* mind or reason as a universal principle. [< Greek *lógos* word, discourse; (active principles of) reason < *légein* say, select words]
log·o·thete (lôg′ə thēt, log′-), *n.* **1.** one of the administrative officials of the Byzantine Empire, especially the Great Logothete, who was, in effect, prime minister or chancellor of the empire. **2.** (in the Greek Church) the chancellor or keeper of the seal of the Patriarch of Constantinople. [< Medieval Latin *logetheta* < Greek *logothétēs* one who audits accounts < *lógos* word; account + *the-,* stem of *tithénai* to set (down)]
log·o·type (lôg′ə tīp, log′-), *n.* **1.** *Printing.* a single type on which two or more letters are cast (but not connected), to facilitate the printing of combinations frequently used, as *Co.* **2.** a trademark or other figure frequently associated with an enterprise: *KLM changed the sloping diagonal lines of its trademark, or logotype, to horizontal ones because they gave a greater feeling of security* (Listener). [< Greek *lógos* word + English *type*]
log·o·typ·y (lôg′ə tī′pē, log′-), *n.* logography.
log pond, a pond of water next to a sawmill, in which logs are stored before entering the mill.
log reel, the reel by which a float for measuring the speed of a ship is unwound.
log·roll (lôg′rōl′, log′-), *Informal.* —*v.t.* to get (a bill) passed by logrolling. —*v.i.* to take part in logrolling. [American English; perhaps back formation < *logrolling*] —**log′roll′er,** *n.*
log·roll·ing (lôg′rō′ling, log′-), *n.* *Especially U.S.* **1.** a giving of political aid in return for a like favor, especially in order to pass legislation: *Our logrolling, our stumps and their politics . . . are yet unsung* (Emerson). **2. a.** the act of rolling floating logs, especially by treading on them, often engaged in by lumberjacks as a sport. **b.** a gathering at which lumberjacks roll logs, either to move them to a required place or for sport. [American English; earlier, a gathering of neighbors to help someone clear land < *log* + *rolling*]
log ship, log chip.
log·way (lôg′wā′, log′-), *n.* a gangway for logs.
log·wood (lôg′wu̇d′, log′-), *n.* **1.** the heavy, hard, brownish-red wood of a tropical American tree of the pea family, used in dyeing. **2.** the tree itself.
lo·gy (lō′gē), *adj.,* **-gi·er, -gi·est.** *U.S.* heavy; sluggish; dull. Also, **loggy.** [Compare Dutch *log* heavy, dull] —**Syn.** lethargic.
-logy, *combining form.* **1.** account, doctrine, or science of: *Biology = the science of life.* **2.** speaking; discussion, as in *tautology, eulogy.* **3.** special meanings, as in *analogy, tetralogy, anthology.*
[< Greek *-logíā,* sometimes < *lógos* a discourse, but mainly < *lógos* one treating of < *légein* speak (of), recount]
Lo·har (lō′här), *n., pl.* **-har** or **-hars.** a member of a nomadic caste of Hindus typically employed as craftsmen in metal or wood: *You will not travel far in north India without seeing an encampment of Lohars, [their] distinctive black bullock carts . . . seemingly plated with iron* (London Times). [< Hindi *lohār*]
Lo·hen·grin (lō′ən grin), *n.* **1.** *German Legend.* the son of Parsifal, a knight of the Holy Grail. **2.** the title and hero of an opera by Richard Wagner, produced in 1850.
loi-ca·dre (lwä′kä′drə), *n.* a law providing a framework for the gradual establishment of home rule in a territory, protectorate, etc., that is striving for self-government, especially in the French Community. [< French *loi-cadre* (literally) law framework]

loin (loin), *n.* a piece of meat from the front and upper part of a hindquarter of beef, lamb, pork, etc., without the flank.
gird (up) one's loins, to get ready for action: *They girded up their loins for the fray.*
loins, a. the part of the body between the ribs and the hipbone. The loins are on both sides of the backbone: *loins of pork.* **b.** the part of the body that should be clothed, regarded as the seat of physical strength and generative power: *Kings shall come out of thy loins* (Genesis 35:11).
[< Old French *loigne* < Vulgar Latin *lumbea* < Latin *lumbus*]

loin·cloth (loin′klôth′, -kloth′), *n.* a piece of cloth worn around the hips and between the thighs by natives of warm countries.

loi·ter (loi′tər), *v.i.* **1.** to linger idly; stop and play along the way: *to loiter along the street, looking into all the shop windows.* **2.** to waste time in or about a place. *—v.t.* to spend (time) idly: *to loiter the hours away.* [< Dutch *leuteren* be loose, erratic; shake, totter] **—loi′ter·ing·ly,** *adv.* **—Syn.** *v.i.* **1.** delay, tarry, lag, dawdle. See **linger.**

loi·ter·er (loi′tər ər), *n.* a person who lingers idly or delays on his way.

Lo·ki (lō′kē), *n.* the Norse god of destruction and mischief, the brother of Odin. He was imprisoned until earth's last battle, when he and Heimdall were to kill each other.

Lok Sab·ha (lôk sub′hä), the lower house of the parliament of India.

loll (lol), *v.i.* **1.** to recline or lean in a lazy manner: *to loll on a sofa.* **2.** to hang loosely or droop; dangle: *babies with their little round heads lolling forward* (George Eliot). *A dog's tongue lolls out in hot weather. —v.t.* to allow to hang or droop: *A dog lolls out his tongue.*
—n. **1.** a lolling. **2.** a person or thing that lolls.
[Middle English *lollen.* Compare Dutch *lollen* loll.] **—loll′er,** *n.*

Lol·lard (lol′ərd), *n.* one of the followers of John Wycliffe's religious teachings from the late 1300's to the early 1500's. The Lollards advocated certain religious, political, and economic reforms, and were persecuted as heretics. [< Middle Dutch *lollaerd* mumbler < *lollen* mumble]

lol·li·pop or **lol·ly·pop** (lol′ē pop), *n.* a piece of hard candy, usually on the end of a small stick. [origin uncertain]

lol·lop (lol′əp), *v.i.,* **-loped, -lop·ing.** *Informal.* **1.** to lounge or sprawl; lounge indolently. **2.** to bob up and down; go with clumsy movements. [< *loll* + *-op,* as in *wallop*]

lol·ly (lol′ē), *n., pl.* **-lies. 1.** *British.* a lollipop: *He was carrying his skates and eating a lolly* (Punch). **2.** *British Slang.* money: *New settlers admitted that they were after the lolly* (Punch).

lol·ly·gag (lol′ē gag), *v.i.,* **-gagged, -gag·ging.** *U.S. Slang.* to while away time idly.

Lom·bard (lom′bärd, -bərd; lum′-), *n.* **1.** a member of a Germanic tribe which in the 500's A.D. conquered the part of Northern Italy since known as Lombardy. **2.** a native or inhabitant of Lombardy. **3.** *Obsolete.* **a.** a native of Lombardy engaged as a banker, moneychanger, or pawnbroker. **b.** any person carrying on any of these businesses.
—adj. of or having to do with the Lombards or Lombardy; Lombardic.
[< Old French *lombard* < Italian *lombardo* < Late Latin *Langobardus* < Germanic elements meaning "long beard"]

Lom·bar·dic (lom bär′dik), *adj.* Lombard.

Lombard Street, the London money market or financiers. [< *Lombard* Street, London, famous as a financial center]

Lom·bard·y poplar (lom′bər dē, lum′-), a tall, slender poplar with branches that curve upward. It is often planted along roads and drives.

Lom·bro·sian school (lom brō′zhən), a school of criminology advocating the theories and methods of Cesare Lombroso, who believed in the existence of a criminal type.

lo·ment (lō′ment), *n. Botany.* a leguminous fruit which is contracted in the spaces between the seeds, breaking up when mature into one-seeded segments, as in the tick trefoil. [Middle English *lomente* bean meal < Latin *lōmentum;* see LOMENTUM]

lo·men·ta·ceous (lō′mən tā′shəs), *adj. Botany.* **1.** of or like a loment. **2.** bearing loments.

lo·men·tum (lō men′təm), *n., pl.* **-ta** (-tə). *Botany.* a loment. [< Latin *lōmentum* bean meal; a cleansing mixture made of it < a stem related to *-luere,* and *lavāre* to wash]

lo·mi salmon (lō′mē), a Hawaiian dish of salmon kneaded with the fingers, mixed with onions, and seasoned. [< Hawaiian *lomi* knead, mash]

lon., longitude.

Lon·don broil (lun′dən), broiled flank steak cut into thin diagonal slices.

London clay, a bluish clay composing the principal Eocene formation in southeastern England, especially at and near London: *London clay . . . was laid down in the sea some 60 million years ago* (New Scientist).

Lon·don·er (lun′də nər), *n.* a native or inhabitant of London, England.

London plane tree, a large shade tree that is a cross between a buttonwood and another species of plane tree. It is commonly grown along city streets because of its resistance to air pollution and drought.

London smoke, a dark, dull gray color.

lone (lōn), *adj.* **1.** alone; solitary: *The lone traveler was glad to reach home. The explorer was the lone survivor of his expedition to the North Pole.* **2.** lonesome; lonely: *The lone nights are the worst.* **3.** single or widowed (a humorous use): *a poor lone woman* (Shakespeare). **4. a.** standing apart; isolated: *a lone house.* **b.** *Poetic.* (of places) lonely; unfrequented: *Bokhara and lone Khiva in the waste* (Matthew Arnold). [variant of *alone*]

lone·li·ly (lōn′lə lē), *adv.* in a lonely manner.

lone·li·ness (lōn′lē nis), *n.* the state or the feeling of being lonely.

lone·ly (lōn′lē), *adj.,* **-li·er, -li·est. 1.** feeling oneself alone and longing for company or friends; lonesome: *She was lonely when among strangers. Now a lonely man Wifeless and heirless* (Tennyson). **2.** without many people; desolate: *a lonely spot, a lonely road, lonely seas.* **3. a.** alone; isolated: *a lonely tree.* **b.** unaccompanied; solitary: *I go alone, Like to a lonely dragon, that his fen Makes fear'd and talk'd of more than seen* (Shakespeare). **—Syn. 2.** secluded.

lonely hearts, unmarried middle-aged persons who seek to meet eligible members of the opposite sex by consulting matchmakers, joining special clubs, or advertising in newspaper personal columns: *In a bouncy, daffy romantic . . . musical, matchmaker Carol Channing juggles lonely hearts and sassily wangles one for herself* (Time).

lone·ness (lōn′nis), *n.* loneliness.

lon·er (lō′nər), *n. Informal.* **1.** a person who is or prefers to be alone: *He is a loner, but his world is filled with friends* (Time). **2.** an independent person: *a political loner.*

lone·some (lōn′səm), *adj.,* **-som·er, -som·est. 1.** feeling lonely or forlorn. **2.** making one feel lonely: *a lonesome journey.* **3.** unfrequented; desolate: *a lonesome road.* **4.** solitary: *One lonesome pine stood in the yard.* **—lone′some·ly,** *adv.* **—lone′some·ness,** *n.*

Lone Star State, a nickname for Texas (from the single star in its coat of arms).

lone wolf, 1. *Informal.* **a.** a person who works or prefers to work alone: *More than most of today's scientists, she is a lone wolf investigator, living for the excitement of finding things out* (Atlantic). **b.** a person who remains to himself, especially in opinions: *He is obviously not an individualist or a lone wolf* (New Scientist). **2.** a wolf that lives and hunts alone.

long[1] (lông, long), *adj.,* **long·er, long·est,** *adv., n. —adj.* **1. a.** measuring much, or more than usual, from end to end in space or time: *a long distance, a long board, a long speech, a long list. An inch is short; a mile is long. A year is a long time. Like all lank men, my long friend had an appetite of his own* (Herman Melville). **b.** continuing too long; lengthy; tedious: *long hours of waiting.* **c.** beyond the normal extension in space, duration, quantity, etc.: *a long dozen, a long ton.* **2.** having a specified length in space or time or in a series: *five feet long, two hours long, a speech five pages long.* **3.** extending to a great distance in space or time; far-reaching: *a long memory, a long look ahead.* **4.** involving considerable risk, liability to error, etc.: *a long chance.* **5.** *Phonetics.* (of vowels) taking a comparatively long time to speak: *In American English "e" is usually longer in "pen" than in "pet".* **6.** *Prosody.* (of syllables) occupying a longer time to speak. **7. a.** well supplied (with some commodity): *long in salt.* **b.** depending on a rise in prices for profit. **8.** *Especially Law.* (of a date) distant; remote.
long on, well furnished or highly endowed with: *. . . prancing about in an English comedy that is long on eccentricity and short on wit* (New Yorker). *Most advertising today is long on the big promise* (Harper's).
—adv. **1.** throughout the whole length of: *all night long.* **2.** for a long time: *a reform long advocated. I can't stay long.* **3.** at a point of time far distant from the time indicated: *long since. It happened long before you were born.*
as or **so long as,** provided that: *As long as that's the case, we'll go.*
—n. **1.** a long time: *for long.* **2.** a long sound. **3.** *Prosody.* a long syllable. **4.** a person who buys or holds more goods or stock than he needs, generally depending on a rise in prices for profit. **5.** a size of garment for men who are taller than average.
before long, soon; in a short time: *Summer will come before long.*
the long and the short of it, the sum total (of something); substance; upshot: *The long and the short of it . . . is that you must pay me this money* (Walter Besant).
[Old English *lang*]
—Syn. *adj.* **1. a, b.** extended, prolonged.

long[2] (lông, long), *v.i.* to have a strong desire; wish very much: *He longed for his mother. I long'd so heartily then and there, To give him the grasp of fellowship* (Tennyson). [Old English *langian* < *lang* long[1]] **—Syn.** yearn, crave.

long[3] (lông, long), *adj. Dialect.* along.

long[4] (lông, long), *v.i.* **1.** *Archaic.* to be fitting; be appropriate to: *. . . such feast as 'longed unto a mighty king* (William Morris). **2.** *Obsolete.* to be the property or rightful possession; belong. [short for Old English *gelang* at hand, dependent on]

long., longitude.

long-a·go (lông′ə gō′, long′-), *adj.* that has long gone by; that belongs to the distant past: *Hiroshima today is obsessed by that long-ago mushroom cloud* (Time). *—n.* the distant past or its events: *Time is always apt to paint the long-ago in fresh colours* (Augustus Hare).

lon·gan (long′gən), *n.* **1.** a Chinese evergreen tree of the soapberry family, related to the litchi and bearing a similar but smaller and less palatable fruit. **2.** its fruit. Also, **lungan.** [< Cantonese *lung-ngan* (literally) dragon's eye]

lon·ga·nim·i·ty (long′gə nim′ə tē), *n.* long-suffering; forbearance or patience, as under provocation. [< Latin *longanimitās* < *longanimus* patient < *longus* long + *animus* mind]

lon·gan·i·mous (long gan′ə məs), *adj.* long-suffering; patient.

long·beard (lông′bird′, long′-), *n.* **1.** a man with a long beard. **2.** a bellarmine. **3.** Florida moss.

long-billed curlew (lông′bild′, long′-), a curlew of western North America, about two feet long, with a short, rounded tail, and very long, decurved bill.

long-billed marsh wren, a wren of eastern and central North America with a long, slightly curved bill, that nests among reeds and cattail marshes.

long bit, *U.S. Dialect.* 15 cents.

long·boat (lông′bōt′, long′-), *n.* the largest and strongest boat carried by a sailing ship: *The Captain called in at one or two ports, and sent in his longboat for provisions* (Jonathan Swift).

long·bow (lông′bō′, long′-), *n.* a large bow drawn by hand, for shooting a long, feathered arrow.
draw or **pull the longbow,** *Informal.* to tell exaggerated stories: *At speaking truth perhaps they are less clever, But draw the longbow better now than ever* (Byron).

long·case clock (lông′kās′, long′-), *British.* a grandfather clock: *. . . thirty-hour longcase clocks for cottage use* (Listener).

long-chain (lông′chān′, long′-), *adj.* consisting of or denoting molecules containing a long chain of atoms: *The nucleic acids (known as DNA and RNA) [are] long-chain molecules* (Scientific American).

long clam, the soft-shell or soft clam.

long·cloth (lông′klôth′, long′kloth′), *n.* a kind of fine, soft, cotton cloth, often used for underwear.

long-day plant (lông′dā′, long′-), a plant that flowers only when exposed to light for a relatively long period of time each day.

long-dis·tance (lông′dis′təns, long′-), *adj.* **1.** of or having to do with telephone service to another town, city, etc. **2.** for or over great distances: *a long-distance moving van.*
—*n. U.S.* the exchange or operator that takes care of long-distance calls.
[American English < phrase *long distance telephone*]

long division, a method of dividing numbers in which each step of the division is written out. It is used to divide large numbers.

long dog, lurcher (def. 2): . . . *the carefully crossbred "long dog" of gypsies and small-time poachers* (London Times).

long dozen, thirteen.

long-drawn (lông′drôn′, long′-), *adj.* lasting a long time; prolonged to great length: *a long-drawn tale, a long-drawn scream.*

long-drawn-out (lông′drôn′out′, long′-), *adj.* long-drawn: *a long-drawn-out battle. It is a long-drawn-out affair, done in three episodes* (New Yorker).

longe (lunj), *n., v.,* **longed, longe·ing.** lunge².

long-eared (lông′ird′, long′-), *adj.* **1.** having long ears or earlike parts. **2.** asinine.

long-eared owl, a crow-sized owl with long ear tufts, found in woodlands of temperate North America.

lon·ge·ron (lon′jər ən; *French* lôɴzh rôɴ′), *n.* one of the main longitudinal stays or metal girders in the fuselage, nacelle, etc., of an airplane. It is heavier than a stringer. [< French *longéron*]

lon·ge·val (lon jē′vəl), *adj.* living to a great age; long-lived. [< Latin *longaevus* long-lived + English *-al*¹]

lon·gev·i·ty (lon jev′ə tē), *n.* **1.** long life: *a medicine that shall preserve him . . . until the utmost term of patriarchal longevity* (Hawthorne). **2.** length or duration of life: *the average longevity of human beings.* [< Latin *longaevitās* < *longaevus* long-lived < *longus* long + *aevum* age]

lon·ge·vous (lon jē′vəs), *adj.* longeval. [< Latin *longaevus* (with English *-ous*)]

long-gone (lông′gôn′, long′-; -gon′), *adj. U.S. Informal.* long since vanished or passed away: *For a magazine spread there is a suggested scene of plantation life, with the long-gone cotton aristocracy drinking whiskey on a magnificent porch* (New Yorker).

long green, *U.S. Slang.* paper money.

long·hair (lông′hãr′, long′-), *n. Slang.* **1.** a person who enjoys, performs, or composes classical music: *The Mutual radio network has a scheme for attracting longhairs: a chain of classical-music stations to extend from Virginia to Maine* (Time). **2.** an intellectual: *Such current terms as "longhair" and "egghead," he felt, were contributing factors to the U.S.'s inability to obtain good teachers and scientists* (Newsweek).

longhair cat, a breed of domestic cat that is a crossbreed of a Persian cat and an Angora cat.

long-haired (lông′hãrd′, long′-), *adj.* **1.** having long hair: *The long-haired animals come from tropical Africa* (Science News Letter). **2.** *Slang.* **a.** intellectual: . . . *long-haired idealists* (New Yorker). *Industry and business were not concerned with these preoccupations of the long-haired scientist* (Science News Letter). **b.** enjoying, performing, or composing classical music.

long·hand (lông′hand′, long′-), *n.* ordinary handwriting, not shorthand or typewriting: *We were always a week or two behind when we worked by longhand* (Wall Street Journal).

long haul, 1. the transportation of goods over relatively great distances: *long haul truckers.* **2.** any difficult activity extending over a long period of time: *We have a long haul in front of us, and not just a short spurt* (London Times).
for or **over the long haul,** *Informal.* in the long run: *But executives are almost unanimous in contending that over the long haul it's better business* . . . (Wall Street Journal).

long·head (lông′hed′, long′-), *n.* **1.** a person having a long head; dolichocephalic person. **2.** a head whose breadth is less than four-fifths of its length.

long head, shrewdness; foresight; farsightedness: *He has a long head on most matters.*

long-head·ed (lông′hed′id, long′-), *adj.* **1.** having a long head; dolichocephalic. **2.** shrewd; far-sighted: *a long-headed deal; long-headed customers* (Dickens). *That's a short-handed way of expressing a long-headed idea* (Newsweek). —**long′-head′ed·ness,** *n.*

long-hop (lông′hop′, long′-), *n. Cricket.* a ball that hits the ground, bounces, and then travels some distance before reaching the batsman or wicketkeeper.

long·horn (lông′hôrn′, long′-), *n.* any of a breed of cattle that have very long horns and were raised for beef; Texas longhorn. They were formerly common in the southwestern United States and Mexico.

Longhorn Cow

long-horned beetle (lông′hôrnd′, long′-), any of a group of wood-boring beetles with extremely long, heavy antennae, injurious to trees, shrubs, wooden lawn furniture, etc.

long-horned grasshopper, any of a group of grasshoppers with antennae as long as the body, including the katydid and others that cause heavy damage to crops.

long horse, a side horse having one end curved upwards for vaulting.

long house, a large communal dwelling of the Iroquois and certain other American Indians, and various tribal societies in South East Asia, Borneo, New Guinea, and elsewhere.

long hundredweight, the British hundredweight, equal to 112 pounds.

lon·gi·cau·dal (lon′jə kô′dəl), *adj.* having a long tail. [< Latin *longus* long + *cauda* tail + English *-al*¹]

lon·gi·cau·date (lon′jə kô′dāt), *adj.* longicaudal.

lon·gi·corn (lon′jə kôrn), *adj.* **1.** having long antennae. **2.** of or belonging to a family of beetles that often have very long antennae. —*n.* a longicorn beetle; long-horned beetle. [< Latin *longus* long + *cornū* horn]

long·ies (lông′ēz, long′-), *n.pl.* **1.** long underwear. **2.** long winter pants for boys.

long·ing (lông′ing, long′-), *n.* earnest desire: *a longing for home; the restless, unsatisfied longing* (Longfellow). —*adj.* having or showing earnest desire: *a child's longing look at a window full of toys.* —**long′ing·ly,** *adv.*
—**Syn.** *n.* craving, yearning, pining. See **desire.**

lon·gin·qui·ty (lon jing′kwə tē), *n.* **1.** great length, extent, or duration. **2.** distance or remoteness. [< Latin *longinquitās* < *longinquus* distant < *longus* long]

lon·gi·pen·nate (lon′jə pen′āt), *adj.* having long wings. [< Latin *longus* long + English *pennate*]

long iron, a golf club with a steel head inclined at a relatively small angle to its long shaft, suitable for low, long-distance shots.

lon·gi·ros·tral (lon′jə ros′trəl), *adj.* having a long beak or bill. [< Latin *longus* long + *rostrum* beak + English *-al*¹]

lon·gi·ros·trate (lon′jə ros′trāt), *adj.* longirostral.

long·ish (lông′ish, long′-), *adj.* somewhat long.

Long Island duck disease, an acute, usually fatal, virus disease of young ducklings. [< *Long Island duck*(ling), a variety of duckling]

lon·gi·tude (lon′jə tüd, -tyüd), *n.* **1. a.** distance east or west on the earth's surface, measured in degrees from a certain meridian (line from the North to the South Pole). Usually the meridian through Greenwich, England, is used. **b.** *Astronomy.* celestial longitude or galactic longitude. *Abbr.:* long. **2.** *Humorous.* length: *a rusty sword of immense longitude* (Hawthorne). [< Latin *longitūdō, -inis* length < *longus* long]

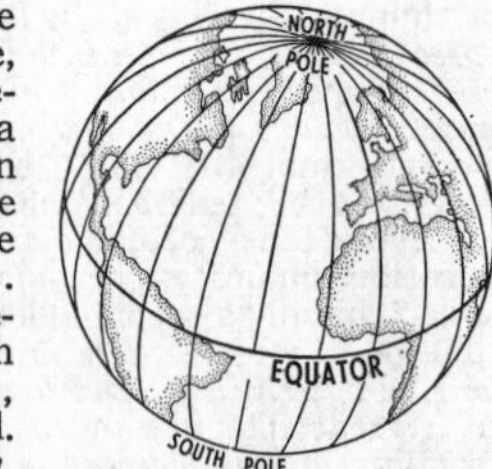

Circles of Longitude (def. 1a)

lon·gi·tu·di·nal (lon′jə tü′də nəl, -tyü′-), *adj.* **1.** of length; in length: *longitudinal measurements.* **2.** running lengthwise: *Our flag has longitudinal stripes.* **3.** of longitude: *The longitudinal difference between New York and San Francisco is about 50 degrees.*

lon·gi·tu·di·nal·ly (lon′jə tü′də nə lē, -tyü′-), *adv.* **1.** lengthwise. **2.** according to longitude.

long johns (jonz), *U.S. Slang.* long, warm underwear: *Everyone wore long johns, ate porridge and preserves, and kids were so lovingly bundled up they couldn't move* (Maclean's).

long jump, a broad jump.

long·leaf pine, or **long·leaf** (lông′lēf′, long′-), *n.* **1.** a pine tree of the southeastern United States, with very long needles; Georgia pine. It is an important source of tar, pitch, turpentine, and resin, and its hard, durable, reddish wood is much used in shipbuilding and construction. **2.** its wood.

long-leg·ged (lông′leg′id, long′-), *adj.* having long legs.

long·legs (lông′legz′, long′-), *n.* **1.** a long-legged person or animal. **2.** a daddy-longlegs.

long-lin·ing (lông′lī′ning, long′-), *n.* a form of fishing using a very long fish line with many baited hooks.

long-lived (lông′līvd′, -livd′; long′-), *adj.* living or lasting a long time: *long-lived legends. Strontium-90 is a long-lived element* (Science News Letter). —**long′-lived′ness,** *n.*

long lumber, *U.S.* lumber used in construction.

long·ly (lông′lē, long′-), *adv.* at or to a great or considerable length.

long measure, linear measure.

long moss, Florida moss.

long·ness (lông′nis, long′-), *n.* length.

long·nose gar (lông′nōz′, long′-), a North American gar with extremely long jaws, used in preying upon other fish.

Lon·go·bard (long′gə bärd), *n., adj.* Lombard.

Lon·go·bar·di (long′gə bär′dī), *n.pl.* Lombards.

Lon·go·bar·dic (long′gə bär′dik), *adj.* Lombard; Lombardic.

Long Parliament, the English Parliament that assembled in 1640, was expelled by Cromwell in 1653, reassembled in 1659, and was dissolved in 1660.

long-pe·ri·od variable (lông′ pir′ē əd, long′-), a variable star whose period from one peak of brightness to the next is over 100 days.

long pig, a human body (from the words used by cannibals of the South Seas).

long·play (lông′plā′, long′-), *n.* a long-playing record; LP.

long-play·er (lông′plā′ər, long′-), *n.* **1.** a long-playing record. **2.** a phonograph that plays long-playing records.

long-play·ing record (lông′plā′ing, long′-), a phonograph record to be played at 33⅓ revolutions per minute. A long-playing record 12 inches in diameter provides about 25 minutes of sound on each side.

long primer, a size of printing type (10 point).

This sentence is set in long primer.

long-pull (lông′pu̇l′, long′-), *adj. Informal.* long-term; long-range: *long-pull prospects, long-pull buying.*

long-range (lông′rānj′, long′-), *adj.* **1. a.** looking ahead; prospective; future: *long-range plans. In the decade since World War II the U.S. has found itself assuming, . . . partly as a matter of long-range policy, responsibility for aid to peoples all around the globe* . . . (Scientific American). **b.** of or for a long period; long-term: *long-range effects, long-range returns, a long-range trend toward inflation.* **2.** having a long range; covering a great distance: *long-range airliners, a long-range ballistic missile.*

long-run (lông′run′, long′-), *adj.* **1.** happening or continuing over a long period of time; occurring after a long period of time: *long-run developments, a long-run play, a long-run objective. My Fair Lady passed its 143rd week . . . on Broadway to set a new sell-out record for long-run shows* (Time). **2.** maturing over a long period of time: *long-run securities.*

long·shanks (lông′shangks′, long′-), *n.* **1.** a long-legged person. **2.** a stilt (bird).

long·shore (lông′shôr′, long′-; -shōr′), *adj.* **1.** existing, found, or employed along the shore: *longshore fisheries, longshore laborers.* **2.** of or having to do with the waterfront or with longshoremen: *a longshore union. The recent longshore dispute . . . resulted in what was regarded by unionists as a favorable contract* (Wall Street Journal). [< *alongshore*]

long·shore·man (lông′shôr′mən, long′-; -shōr′-), *n., pl.* **-men.** a man whose work is loading and unloading ships; stevedore.

long·shor·ing (lông′shôr′ing, long′-; -shōr′-), *n.* the work of loading and unloading ships: *Longshoring ... remains a high hazard industry* (New York Times).

long shot, *Informal.* **1.** an attempt at something difficult. **2.** a venture, racehorse, etc., unlikely to succeed but rewarding if it should: *to bet on a long shot. I made the first test very simple, because the whole idea seemed a long shot* (Scientific American).
not by a long shot, not at all: *This one is not as good as the other by a long shot. He couldn't count on making it—not by a long shot* (New Yorker).

long·sight·ed (lông′sī′tid, long′-), *adj.* **1.** seeing distant things more clearly than near ones; far-sighted. **2.** having foresight; wise: *Her long-sighted notion of a society not solely based on war and agriculture ...* (Manchester Guardian). —**long′-sight′ed·ness,** *n.*

long·some (lông′səm, long′-), *adj. Archaic.* long; lengthy; tedious: *the way there was a little longsome* (Robert Louis Stevenson).

long·spur (lông′spėr′, long′-), *n.* any of certain finches having long hind claws, found in northern climates, as the Lapland longspur.

long-stand·ing (lông′stan′ding, long′-), *adj.* having lasted for a long time: *a long-standing feud, a long-standing friendship.*

long-sta·ple (lông′stā′pəl, long′-), *n.* long-staple cotton.

long-staple cotton, cotton with fibers averaging more than 1⅛ inches in length.

long stop, *Cricket.* a fielder who stands behind the wicketkeeper to stop balls that pass him.

long-suf·fer·ance (lông′suf′ər əns, long′-), *n. Archaic.* long-suffering.

long-suf·fer·ing (lông′suf′ər ing, -suf′ring; long′-), *adj.* enduring trouble, pain, or injury long and patiently: *Various were the excesses committed by the insubordinate troops ... upon the long-suffering inhabitants* (John L. Motley). —*n.* long and patient endurance of trouble, pain, or injury: *Put on therefore, as the elect of God ... humbleness of mind, meekness, long-suffering* (Colossians 3:12).

long suit, 1. (in card games) the suit in which one has most cards. **2.** a strong point: *Patience is his long suit. Frankly, I discount the wisdom of the elder generation unless it comes from their long suit —experience* (Harper's).

long sweetening, *U.S. Dialect.* molasses.

long-tailed jaeger (lông′tāld′), a bird, a jaeger of arctic regions with a long forked tail.

long-tailed tit, a common titmouse with plumage of black, white, and pink, found in parts of Europe, Africa, and Asia.

long-term (lông′tėrm′, long′-), *adj.* of or for a long period of time: *a long-term loan.*

long-term bond or **note,** a bond or note that will not be redeemed for two years or more.

long-term·er (lông′tėr′mər, long′-), *n.* a person who is serving a long prison term: *... the peculiar snobbery of the penitentiary in which the long-termers, or lags, have social precedence over the young or first-term offenders* (Time).

long-time (lông′tīm′, long′-), *adj.* **1.** for a long time: *a long-time companion, a long-time Democrat.* **2.** lasting a long time: *a long-time feud.*

long-tom (lông′tom′, long′-), *n.* (in Australia) a needlefish (def. 1).

long tom, a cradle for washing gold.

Long Tom, 1. any large cannon having a long range. **2.** a large, long-range gun carried on the deck of small warships.

long ton, the British ton, 2,240 pounds.

long-tongued (lông′tungd′, long′-), *adj.* **1.** having a long tongue. **2.** talking much or too much: *a long-tongued babbling gossip* (Shakespeare).

lon·gueur (lông gėr′), *n.* a long or tedious passage in a book, play, piece of music, etc. [< French *longueur* length]

long vacation, *British.* the long summer vacation observed in law courts and universities.

long-waist·ed (lông′wās′tid, long′-), *adj.* comparatively long from neck to waistline: *a long-waisted dress, a long-waisted girl.*

long·wall (lông′wôl′, long′-), *adj.* of or designating a system of mining in which the whole seam of coal, ore, etc., is removed and nothing is left to support the roof except the shaft pillars.

long wave, a radio wave having a wave length above 545 or 600 meters.

long-wave (lông′wāv′, long′-), *adj.* of, for, or by means of long waves.

long·ways (lông′wāz′, long′-), *adv.* in the direction of the length; lengthwise.

long-wind·ed (lông′win′did, long′-), *adj.* **1.** capable of long effort without getting out of breath: *A long-distance runner must be long-winded. These horses are ... remarkably stout and long-winded* (Washington Irving). **2.** talking or writing at great lengths; tiresome: *a long-winded speaker, a long-winded sermon.* —**long′-wind′ed·ly,** *adv.* —**long′-wind′ed·ness,** *n.*

long·wise (lông′wīz′, long′-), *adv.* lengthwise; longways.

long·yi (long′yē), *n.* a sarong worn in Burma. [< a Burmese word]

loo[1] (lü), *n., pl.* **loos,** *v.,* **looed** (lüd), **loo·ing.** —*n.* **1.** a card game in which players who fail to take a trick pay forfeits into a pool. **2.** the forfeit paid. **3.** an instance of being looed.
—*v.t.* to cause to pay into a pool after failing to take a trick at loo.
[short for *lanterloo* < French *lanturelu,* a word in an old refrain]

loo[2] (lü), *n. Scottish.* love.

loo[3] (lü), *n., pl.* **loos.** *British Informal.* toilet; bathroom. [origin uncertain]

loo·by (lü′bē), *n., pl.* **-bies.** *British.* a lazy, hulking fellow; lout. [compare LOB[3]]

loof[1] (lüf), *n. Scottish.* the palm of the hand. [< Scandinavian (compare Old Icelandic *lōfe*)]

loof[2] (lüf), *n., v.* luff.

loo·fah (lü′fə), *n.* **1.** any of a group of tropical plants of the gourd family. **2.** the fruit of such a plant, containing a mass of coarse, strong fibers. **3.** these dried fibers, used as a sponge. [< Arabic *lūfah*]

look (lůk), *v.i.* **1. a.** to direct the eyes; try to see; see: *He looked this way. Look at the pictures. I looked, and, lo, a Lamb stood on the mount Sion* (Revelation 14:1). *It's all his imagining. I've never looked at another man* ... (John Strange). **b.** to glance or gaze in a certain way: *to look questioningly or kindly at a person. ... Looking at one another like cat and dog* (Henry Kingsley). **2.** to search: *I looked through the drawer for my keys.* **3.** to pay attention; examine: *You must look at all the facts.* **4.** to show how one feels by one's appearance; seem; appear: *She looks pale. Flowers look pretty. It looks as if it might rain.* **5.** to have a view; face: *The house looks upon a garden. These windows look to the north.* **6.** to tend; point; indicate: *The facts look to this decision.* **7.** to expect; anticipate. —*v.t.* **1.** to direct a look at: *to look one in the eyes.* **2.** to express or suggest by looks: *He said nothing but looked his disappointment. The old lady ... looked carving-knives at the ... delinquent* (Dickens). **3.** to affect by looking in a certain way: *to look down insubordination.* **4.** to appear equal to: *He doesn't look his age.* **5.** *British and Scottish.* to view; inspect; examine.

look after, a. to attend to; take care of: *Of course they looked after her on the boat* (Graham Greene). *The investor should look after his own interests* (Law Times). **b.** to follow (a departing person or thing) with the eye: *Every man at his tent door ... looked after Moses, until he was gone into the tabernacle* (Exodus 33:8).

look alive, hurry up! be quick!: *Look alive! Keep moving!*

look back, to think about the past; recollect: *An era in its history has ended. It may be worthwhile at this moment to look back and try to see what has happened* (Edmund Wilson).

look down on, to despise; scorn: *The miser looked down on all beggars.*

look for, to expect; anticipate: *to look for a coming Messiah.*

look forward to, to expect with pleasure; be eager for: *The children are looking forward to the picnic.*

look in, to make a short visit: *I just wanted to tell him he'd be welcome to look in* (Graham Greene).

look into, to examine; inspect; investigate: *The management is looking into the situation.*

look on, a. to watch without taking part: *He himself was largely forced to look on* (Edmund Wilson). **b.** to regard; consider: *Although the experiments ... have been looked on with interest ...* (Observer).

look oneself, to seem like oneself; seem well: *But what's the matter, George? ... you don't look yourself* (Dickens).

look out, to be careful; watch out: *Look out for cars as you cross the street.*

look over, to examine; inspect: *The policeman looked over my license.*

look to, a. to attend to; take care of: *A man who has the affairs of such a great bank as ours to look to, must be up with the lark* (Thackeray). **b.** to turn to for help: *And—what is so remarkable—this army all now looked to Lenin in exile* (Edmund Wilson). **c.** to look forward to; expect: *I too had been looking to hear from you* (Robert Southey).

look up, a. to search for; refer to: *to look up a word in a dictionary.* **b.** *Informal.* to call on; visit: *You'd better look him up at his hotel* (Harper's). *So do look me up ... and you will be most welcome* (London Illustrated News). **c.** *Informal.* to get better; improve: *Moneyman Bevan also reported that Pennsy's earnings were looking up* (Time).

look up to, to respect; admire: *The Whig members ... looked up to him as their leader* (Macaulay). *Sweden looks up to British agriculture as the model for imitation* (Journal of the Royal Agricultural Society).

—*n.* **1.** the act of looking; glance of the eyes: *a mother's loving look at her baby.* **2.** a search; examination: *Take a quick look around the house before you leave.* **3.** appearance; aspect: *a kind look. A deserted house has a desolate look.*

looks, personal appearance: *Good looks means a good appearance. His looks are against him.*

[Old English *lōcian*]

—**Syn.** *v.i.* **1. a.** gaze, stare, observe, glance.

➤ **look.** When used as a verb of complete meaning (use the eyes, gaze), *look* is modified by an adverb: *look searchingly, look sharp.* As a linking verb, equivalent to *appear, look* is followed by an adjective which modifies the subject: *He looks well, or healthy, or tired.*

look-a·like (lůk′ə līk′), *U.S. Informal.* —*n.* one of a pair or a set that look just alike: *Pre-engineered metal buildings were rather plain look-alikes* (Wall Street Journal). —*adj.* looking just alike; very similar: *They wore look-alike silks* (Time).

look·er (lůk′ər), *n.* **1.** a person who looks. **2.** *U.S. Slang.* a person who is good-looking.

look·er-on (lůk′ər on′, -ôn′), *n., pl.* **lookers-on.** a person who watches without taking part; spectator; onlooker.

look-in (lůk′in′), *n.* **1.** a glance in; hasty look. **2.** a brief visit. **3.** *Slang.* a chance of success, as in a horse race. **4.** *Slang.* a chance to participate, as in some venture.

look·ing glass (lůk′ing), **1.** a mirror. **2.** the glass used in mirrors.

look·out (lůk′out′), *n.* **1.** a careful watch for someone to come or for something to happen: *Keep a sharp lookout for mother. Be on the lookout for a signal.* **2.** a person or group that keeps such a watch: *There was nothing to do but steer the ship, and relieve the lookouts at the mast-heads* (Herman Melville). **3.** a place from which to watch, such as a tower or a crow's-nest. **4.** what is seen ahead; outlook; prospect: *See those clouds! A poor lookout for our picnic.* **5.** *Informal.* a thing to be cared for or worried about: *Never you mind what I took her for, that's my lookout* (Dickens).

look-o·ver (lůk′ō′vər), *n. Informal.* an inspection or evaluation.

looks (lůks), *n.pl.* See under **look,** *n.*

look-say method (lůk′sā′), word method: *The so-called "look-say" method ... postpones the alphabet to the second or third grade* (John Chamberlain).

look-see (lůk′sē′), *n. Slang.* a quick look; a search.

loom[1] (lüm), *n.* **1.** a machine for weaving yarn or thread into cloth by interlacing the warp and the woof threads: *Weave no more silks, ye Lyons looms* (Julia Ward Howe). **2.** the art, process, or business of weaving: *a splendid silk of foreign loom* (Tennyson).

Loom[1] (def. 1)
(18th century)

3. the part of an oar between the blade and the handle or the part between the oarlock and the hand. —*v.t.* to weave on a loom. [Middle English *lome,* Old English *gelōma* implement]

loom[2] (lüm), *v.i.* **1.** to appear dimly or vaguely: *A large iceberg loomed through the thick, gray fog.* **2.** to appear in a vague, unusually large, or threatening shape: *War loomed ahead. Little things loom large to an anxious mind.*

—*n.* **1.** an indistinct appearance or outline of a thing seen vaguely at a distance or through a fog. **2.** the reflection on the clouds when the light from a lighthouse is below the horizon.

[origin uncertain. Compare dialectal Swedish *loma* to move slowly.]

loom[3] (lüm), *n.* **1.** a loon (bird). **2.** a guillemot. [< Scandinavian (compare Old Icelandic *lōmr*)]

L.O.O.M., Loyal Order of Moose.

loom·age (lü′mij), *n.* fabric woven on looms.

loom·er·y (lü′mər ē), *n., pl.* **-er·ies.** a breeding place of loons or guillemots. [< *loom*[3]]

loon[1] (lün), *n.* any of various large, web-footed diving birds that have a loud cry and live in the northern hemisphere. It is the only living group of its order. *Visitors to . . . the United States will probably never forget the cry of the loon sounding . . . like the hysterical laughter of a lunatic* (A.M. Winchester). [alteration of *loom*[3]]

Common Loon[1] or great northern diver (about 32 in. long)

loon[2] (lün), *n.* **1.** a worthless or stupid person: *thou cream-faced loon* (Shakespeare). **2.** *Scottish.* a boor; lout: *The lairds are as bad as the loons* (Scott). **3.** *Scottish.* a boy; lad. **4.** *Scottish.* a worthless or loose woman. **5.** *Archaic.* a man of low birth or condition. Also, **loun, lown.** [origin uncertain]

loon·ey (lü′nē), *adj.,* **loon·i·er, loon·i·est,** *n., pl.* **loon·ies.** loony.

loon·i·ness (lü′nē nis), *n. Slang.* a being loony or crazy.

loon·y (lü′nē), *adj.,* **loon·i·er, loon·i·est,** *n., pl.* **loon·ies.** *Slang.* —*adj.* crazy; foolish; silly. —*n.* a crazy person; lunatic. Also, **luny.** [variant of earlier *luny* < *lunatic;* probably influenced by *loon*[2]]

loony bin, *Slang.* an insane asylum.

loop[1] (lüp), *n.* **1.** the shape of a curved string, ribbon, bent wire, etc., that crosses itself: *He wound the garden hose in loops and hung it up.* **2.** a thing, bend, course, or motion shaped like a loop. In writing, *b* and *g* and *h* and *l* have loops. *The road makes a wide loop around the lake. Write a more distinct current hand . . . open the loops of your l's* (Scott). **3.** a fastening or ornament formed of cord, etc., bent and crossed. **4.** a complete vertical turn or revolution, especially one made by an airplane. **5.** a ring or curved piece of metal, etc., used for the insertion of something or as a handle. **6.** *Physics.* the portion of a vibrating string, column of air in an organ pipe, etc., between two nodes; antinode. **7.** *Electricity.* **a.** a complete or closed electric circuit. **b.** hysteresis loop. **8.** (in electronic computers or computing systems) **a.** the repetition of instructions in a program **b.** the carrying out of instructions for a fixed number of times. **9.** *U.S. Slang. Sports.* a league: *The teams involved are engaged in a tussle for fourth place in the loop* (New York Times). **10.** an intrauterine contraceptive device.

knock for a loop, *U.S. Slang.* **a.** to knock out: *Ray Robinson knocked Fullmer for a loop in their championship bout.* **b.** to put something out of operation; diminish; make ineffectual: *His testimony confirmed the Chambers story in an essential matter and knocked the Hiss claims for a loop* (Saturday Review). **c.** to impress strongly; overwhelm: *He would have knocked the girls at Bradley for a loop* (Harper's).

loop the loop, to turn over and over; make a loop in the air: *The kite looped the loop in a sudden gust of wind.*

—*v.t.* **1.** to make a loop of. **2.** to make loops in. **3.** to fasten with a loop. **4.** to encircle with a loop. **5.** to cause (an airplane) to fly in a loop or loops. **6.** *Electricity.* to join (conductors) so as to form a loop. —*v.i.* **1.** to form a loop or loops. **2.** to move by forming loops in crawling: *The currant worms went looping and devouring from twig to twig* (Atlantic Monthly). **3.** to perform a loop, as an airplane.

[Middle English *loupe,* perhaps < Celtic (compare Gaelic *lùb* bend)]

loop[2] (lüp), *n. Archaic.* an opening in a wall; loophole: *Stop all sight-holes, every loop* (Shakespeare). [Middle English *loupe,* perhaps < Middle Dutch *lūpen* to peer, watch]

loop[3] (lüp), *n.* a ball-shaped, pasty mass of iron before it is made into a bloom; ball. —*v.i.* to form such a mass. [< French *loupe*]

loop aerial or **antenna,** an aerial or antenna made of several turns of wire looped around a frame, used instead of an outdoor aerial or antenna.

looped (lüpt), *adj. Slang.* drunk.

loop·er (lü′pər), *n.* **1.** a person or thing that loops or forms loops. **2.** a measuring worm. **3.** the part that carries the thread in a sewing machine.

loop·hole (lüp′hōl′), *n., v.,* **-holed, -hol·ing.** —*n.* **1.** a small opening in a wall to shoot through, look through, or let in air and light: *. . . barred with care All the windows, and doors, and loopholes there* (Robert Southey). **2.** a means of escape: *The clever lawyer found a loophole in the law to save his client even though he was guilty. The bill has been watered down somewhat by amendments providing loopholes and escape clauses in favor of special interests* (New York Times). —*v.t.* to provide with loopholes: *a stout loghouse . . . loopholed for musketry on every side* (Robert Louis Stevenson).

loop knot, 1. a single knot tied in a doubled cord, so as to leave a loop beyond the knot; overhand loop. **2.** *Obsolete.* a reef knot.

loop stitch, 1. a blanket stitch. **2.** a fancy stitch consisting of loops.

loop·worm (lüp′wėrm′), *n.* a looper or measuring worm.

loop·y (lü′pē), *adj.,* **loop·i·er, loop·i·est. 1.** full of loops. **2.** *Scottish.* crafty; deceitful. **3.** *Slang.* crazy; intoxicated.

loose (lüs), *adj.,* **loos·er, loos·est,** *v.,* **loosed, loos·ing,** *adv., n.* —*adj.* **1.** not fastened: *a loose thread.* **2.** not tight: *loose clothing, loose reins.* **3.** not firmly set or fastened in: *a loose tooth, loose planks on a bridge.* **4.** not bound together: *loose papers.* **5.** not put in a box, can, etc.: *loose coffee.* **6.** not shut in or up; free: *The dog has been loose all night.* **7.** not pressed close together; having spaces between the parts; open: *cloth with a loose weave.* **8.** not strict, close, or exact: *a loose account of the accident, a loose translation from another language, loose thinking. His loose grammar was the fruit of careless habit, not ignorance* (Mark Twain). **9.** moving too freely; not retentive: *a loose tongue; a good deal of loose information* (Thomas Carlyle). *A kind of men so loose of soul, That in their sleeps will mutter their affairs* (Shakespeare). **10.** careless about morals or conduct: *a loose character. The loose political morality of Fox presented a remarkable contrast to the ostentatious purity of Pitt* (Macaulay). **11.** *Informal.* not tense; relaxed. **12.** *Informal.* not employed; not appropriated: *loose hours, loose funds.* **13.** (of a chemical element) free; uncombined.

—*v.t.* **1.** to set free; let go: *They . . . found the colt tied . . . and they loose him* (Mark 11:4). **2.** to shoot (an arrow, gun, etc.): *The attacking Indians loosed a volley of arrows against the fort.* [*The*] *Agriculture Secretary loosed a blast at Congressional critics of his farm program* (Wall Street Journal). **3.** to make loose; untie; unfasten: *to loose a knot.* **4.** to make less tight; relax; slacken: *The coxswain loosed his grip upon the shrouds* (Robert Louis Stevenson).

—*v.i.* **1.** to become loose. **2.** to shoot an arrow, gun, etc.

—*adv.* in a loose manner; loosely: *Our manners set more loose upon us* (Joseph Addison).

let loose. See under **let**[1].

—*n.* **give a loose** or **loose to,** to give freedom or full vent to: *Give a loose to your fancy, indulge your imagination . . .* (Jane Austen). *He would not give loose to passion* (George Eliot).

in the loose, *British.* in open formation or play, as in rugby: *In the loose, however, the Scottish forwards were yards quicker about the field . . .* (Sunday Times).

on the loose, a. *Informal.* free; without restraint: *The puppy is out on the loose.* **b.** *Slang.* on a spree: *The visitors are on the loose in the town.*

[Middle English *los* < Scandinavian (compare Old Icelandic *lauss*)] —**loose′ly,** *adv.* —**loose′ness,** *n.*

—**Syn.** *adj.* **1.** unbound, unfastened, untied. **8.** vague, indefinite, careless. **10.** wanton, immoral.

loose-box (lüs′boks′), *n. British.* box stall.

loose-cou·pler (lüs′kup′lər), *n.* a coupler or transformer in which the primary coil and the secondary coil are associated without close inductive relation, as by being well separated from each other.

loose ends, bits of unfinished business: *She added that the loose ends left were disturbing and she thought the whole inquiry procedure unsatisfactory* (London Times).

loose-joint·ed (lüs′join′tid), *adj.* **1.** having loose joints; loosely built. **2.** able to move very freely: *a tall, shambling, loose-jointed man* (Harriet Beecher Stowe).

loose-leaf (lüs′lēf′), *adj.* having pages or sheets that can be taken out and replaced: *a loose-leaf notebook.*

loos·en (lü′sən), *v.t.* to make loose or looser; untie; unfasten: *What liberty A loosened spirit brings* (Emily Dickinson). —*v.i.* to become loose or looser. [< *loose,* adjective + *-en*[1]] —**loos′en·er,** *n.*

loos·er (lü′sər), *n.* a person or thing that looses.

loose sentence, a sentence which is grammatically complete and makes sense before its end.

loose·strife (lüs′strīf′), *n.* **1.** any of a group of herbs of the loosestrife family characterized by a cylindrical calyx tube and a capsule included within the calyx, as the purple loosestrife. **2.** any of various erect or creeping herbs of the primrose family, as a common species bearing clusters of yellow flowers, the moneywort. [< *loose,* verb + *strife,* translation of Latin *lysimachia* < Greek *lysimácheios* < *Lysímachos,* the supposed discoverer]

loosestrife family, a group of dicotyledonous herbs, shrubs, and trees most common in tropical America, and including some species often grown as ornamentals, such as the crape myrtle, henna, and purple loosestrife.

loose-tongued (lüs′tungd′), *adj.* talking too freely; blabbing: *He knew how loose-tongued is calumny* (Charles Reade).

loot[1] (lüt), *n.* **1.** spoils; plunder; booty: *loot taken by soldiers from a captured town, burglar's loot.* **2.** *Slang.* money or other capital: *That's a lot of loot to spend for a record player!*

—*v.t.* **1.** to plunder; rob: *Before he left he looted the till.* **2.** to carry off as loot. —*v.i.* to take booty; pillage.

[Anglo-Indian < Hindustani *lūṭ* < Sanskrit *loptram* < *lupati* breaks, plunders] —**loot′er,** *n.*

—**Syn.** *n.* **1.** See **plunder.** -*v.t.* **1.,** *v.i.* sack, rifle.

loot[2] (lüt), *v. Scottish.* past tense of **let**[1].

lop[1] (lop), *v.,* **lopped, lop·ping,** *n.* —*v.t.* **1.** to cut off; cut: *to lop the dead branches from a tree, to lop off the legs of a table. . . . they had lopped off the sentimentality and fantasy which had surrounded the practical perceptions of the utopians* (Edmund Wilson). **2.** to cut branches, twigs, etc., from; trim. **3.** to remove parts as if by cutting: *Expunge the whole or lop the excrescent parts* (Alexander Pope).

—*n.* **1.** the smaller branches and twigs of trees. **2.** a part or parts lopped off.

[Middle English *loppen;* origin uncertain]

lop[2] (lop), *v.,* **lopped, lop·ping,** *adj.* —*v.i.* **1.** to hang loosely or limply; droop: *The sleeping man's hand lopped over the arm of the chair.* **2.** to flop: *She . . . cried about it, she did, and lopped round, as if she'd lost every friend she had* (Harriet Beecher Stowe). —*v.t.* to let hang or droop.

—*adj.* hanging loosely; drooping.

[compare LOB[1]]

lope (lōp), *v.,* **loped, lop·ing,** *n.* —*v.i., v.t.* to run with a long, easy stride, as a horse: *I loped my cayuse full tilt by Mr. Snake* (Owen Wister). —*n.* a long, easy stride: *Now and then a Shawanee passed us, riding his little shaggy pony at a "lope"* (Francis Parkman).

[Middle English *lopen* < Scandinavian (compare Old Icelandic *hlaupa* to leap, run)] —**lop'er,** *n.*

lop-eared (lop'ird'), *adj.* having ears that hang loosely or droop: *a lop-eared rabbit.*

lo·pho·branch (lō'fə brangk, lof'ə-), *adj.* of or belonging to an order of teleost marine fishes having tuftlike gills, including the sea horses and pipefishes. —*n.* a lophobranch fish. [< New Latin *Lophobranchii* the former order name < Greek *lóphos* crest, tuft + *bránchia* gills]

lo·pho·bran·chi·ate (lō'fə brang'kē āt, -it; lof'ə-), *adj., n.* lophobranch.

lo·pho·phore (lō'fə fôr, -fōr; lof'ə-), *n.* a structure having rows of ciliated tentacles, used to set up currents which carry tiny particles of food into the mouth, as in brachiopods, bryozoans, and certain other animals. [< Greek *lóphos* crest + English *-phore*]

lop·o·lith (lop'ə lith), *n.* a large intrusive mass of molten rock that has cooled and hardened, characterized by a basin-shaped upper and lower surface (contrasted with *batholith*). [< Greek *lopós* bent backward, convex + *líthos* stone]

lop·per[1] (lop'ər), *n.* a person who lops (trees, etc.). [< *lop*[1] + *-er*[1]]

lop·per[2] (lop'ər), *Scottish.* —*v.i., v.t.* to curdle, as milk. —*n.* **1.** something curdled, such as milk, blood, etc. **2.** partly melted snow; slush. Also, **lapper.** [perhaps < Scandinavian (compare Old Iceland *hloup* coagulation)]

lop·py (lop'ē), *adj.* hanging loosely; drooping; limp.

lop·sid·ed (lop'sī'did), *adj.* larger or heavier on one side than the other; leaning to one side; unevenly balanced: *a lopsided load, a lopsided score; ... the lopsided economy of Malta, so largely dependent on the dockyard* (London Times). —**lop'sid'ed·ly,** *adv.* —**lop'sid'ed·ness,** *n.*

loq., he, she, or it speaks (Latin, *loquitur*).

lo·qua·cious (lō kwā'shəs), *adj.* **1.** talking much; fond of talking: *Jack became loquacious on his favourite topic* (Frederick Marryat). **2.** making sounds as of much talking: *loquacious birds or frogs, loquacious water.* [< Latin *loquāx, -ācis* (with English *-ous*) talkative < *loquī* speak, talk] —**lo·qua'cious·ly,** *adv.* —**lo·qua'cious·ness,** *n.* —**Syn. 1.** See **talkative.**

lo·quac·i·ty (lō kwas'ə tē), *n.* inclination to talk a great deal; talkativeness: *The only limit to his loquacity was his strength* (Henry T. Buckle). *The songs ... help to compensate for the loquacity* (New Yorker). [< Latin *loquācitās* < *loquāx, -ācis* talkative < < *loquī* to talk]
—**Syn.** garrulity, volubility.

lo·quat (lō'kwot, -kwat), *n.* **1.** a small evergreen tree of the rose family, with small, orange-yellow, edible, plumlike fruit, native to China and Japan but grown in North America since the 1700's. **2.** its rather tart fruit. [< Cantonese *lo-kwat* (literally) rush orange]

lo·qui·tur (lok'wə tər), *v.i. Latin.* he, she, or it speaks (often used as a stage direction).

Lo·rac (lôr'ak, lōr'-), *n. Trademark.* a navigational device used to locate a site or marker, as in offshore oil exploration. [< *lo*(ng) *r*(ange) *ac*(curacy)]

lo·ran (lôr'an, lōr'-), *n.* a system of radio navigation by which an airplane or ship can determine its geographical position by utilizing low-frequency signals sent out from two or more fixed radio stations. It is effective up to about 800 miles during the day and 1,600 miles at night: *The new knowledge of the Gulf Stream was due in great part to the use of loran* (Science News Letter).
[< *lo*(ng) *ra*(nge) *n*(avigation)]

lo·ran·tha·ceous (lôr'an thā'shəs, lōr'-), *adj.* belonging to a family of largely tropical, parasitic plants typified by the mistletoe. [< New Latin *Loranthaceae* the mistletoe family (< *Loranthus* the typical genus < Latin *lōrum* strap + Greek *ánthos* flower) + English *-ous*]

lor·cha (lôr'chə), *n.* a light Chinese sailing ship built somewhat like a European model, but rigged like a junk. [< Portuguese *lorcha*]

lord (lôrd), *n.* **1.** a person or animal that has the power; owner, ruler, or master: *Lions and elephants are lords of the jungle.* **2.** a feudal superior; owner of a manor. **3.** (in Great Britain) a man of rank; peer of the realm; person entitled by courtesy to the title of Lord. **4.** *Archaic.* a husband: *Ye lords of ladies intellectual ... have they not henpeck'd you all?* (Byron). **5.** *Astrology.* the planet that has a dominant influence over an event, period, region, etc.
—*v.i.* to behave like a lord; rule; domineer: *I am not one to be lorded over by a man no better than myself* (Richard Blackmore).
—*v.t.* to raise to the rank of lord; ennoble.
lord it over, domineer over: *He was the oldest and lorded it over the rest of us.*
[Old English *hlāford* < *hlāf* loaf + *weard* keeper, ward. Compare LADY.]

Lord (lôrd), *n.* **1.** God: *Know ye that the Lord he is God: it is he that hath made us, and not we ourselves* (Psalms 100:3). **2.** Jesus Christ: *Unto you is born this day ... a Savior, which is Christ the Lord* (Luke 2:11). **3.** in Great Britain: **a.** a titled nobleman or peer of the realm belonging to the House of Lords, the upper of the two branches of the British Parliament. **b.** a title used in speaking to or of noblemen of certain ranks: *Lord Tennyson. The son of a duke or marquis is called a Lord.* **c.** a title given by courtesy to men holding certain positions: *A bishop is called a Lord. Although clothed in impressive robes and addressed as "My Lord," the judge is still a human being* (Maclean's).
the Lords, the House of Lords; the upper house of the British Parliament: *In the Lords, there were but 12 to 106* (Horace Walpole).

Lord Chamberlain, the official in charge of the royal household of Great Britain.

Lord Chancellor or **Lord High Chancellor,** (in Great Britain) the highest judicial official, who ranks above all peers except royal princes and the Archbishop of Canterbury. He is Keeper of the Great Seal and chairman of the House of Lords. In theory he presides over the chancery division of the High Court of Justice, though in practice he rarely sits there. He recommends or advises on the appointment of most judges. His office, unlike that of other judges, is political and changes with the government.

Lord Chief Justice, (in Great Britain) the officer who presides over the King's Bench division of the High Court of Justice and, usually, over the Court of Criminal Appeal. Formerly, the Courts of King's Bench and Common Pleas each had its own Chief Justice, the Chief Justice of the King's Bench sometimes being referred to as the Lord Chief Justice.

Lord High Admiral, (formerly) a high officer at the head of Great Britain's naval administration.

Lord High Treasurer, (formerly) a high officer of the British Crown who was in charge of the government's revenue.

lord·ing (lôr'ding), *n.* **1.** a lordling. **2.** *Archaic.* a lord or master (used as a form of address).

Lord in Waiting, a nobleman holding an office in attendance on a British sovereign: *Lord Airlie ... was Lord in Waiting to King George V* (London Times).

lord·less (lôrd'lis), *adj.* having no lord; without a master or ruler.

Lord Lieutenancy, the position or office of a Lord Lieutenant.

Lord Lieutenant, *pl.* **Lords Lieutenant.** *British.* **1.** a county official who controls the appointment of justices of the peace. **2.** the former English viceroy of Ireland.

lord·li·ly (lôrd'lə lē), *adv.* in a lordly manner.

lord·li·ness (lôrd'lē nis), *n.* **1.** the state of being lordly; high station. **2.** lordly pride; haughtiness.

lord·ling (lôrd'ling), *n.* a little or unimportant lord.

lord·ly (lôrd'lē), *adj.,* **-li·er, -li·est,** *adv.* —*adj.* **1.** like a lord; suitable for a lord; grand; magnificent: *He saw at a distance the lordly Hudson, far, far below him* (Washington Irving). **2.** haughty; insolent; scornful: *His lordly airs annoyed his country cousins.* **3.** of or having to do with a lord or lords; consisting of lords: *a lordly gathering.*
—*adv.* in a lordly manner.
—**Syn.** *adj.* **1.** noble, aristocratic. **2.** arrogant, proud, overbearing.

Lord Mayor, the title of the mayors of London and some other large English cities.

Lord of Hosts, God; Jehovah as Lord of the heavenly hosts and as director of the armies of Israel or as God over all mankind.

Lord of Misrule, Abbot of Misrule.

lor·do·sis (lôr dō'sis), *n., pl.* **-ses** (-sēz). **1.** a forward curvature of the spine. **2.** any abnormal curvature of the bones, especially one associated with tetanus or rabies. [< Greek *lórdōsis* < *lordós* bent backward]

lor·dot·ic (lôr dot'ik), *adj.* having to do with or affected with lordosis.

Lord Privy Seal, the official, usually a member of the British cabinet, who is Keeper of the Privy Seal.

Lord Protector, the title used by Oliver Cromwell as head of the English government, 1653-1658, and his son Richard, 1658-1659.

Lord Provost, the chief magistrate of a Scottish burgh, equal to a mayor.

Lords (lôrdz), *n.pl.* **the.** See under **Lord.**

lords-and-la·dies (lôrdz'ən lā'dēz), *n.* a common European arum; wake-robin.

Lord's Anointed, the Messiah or Christ.

Lord's Day, Sunday (in Christian nations).

lord·ship (lôrd'ship), *n.* **1.** the rank or position of a lord. **2.** Often, **Lordship.** *British.* the title used in speaking to or of a lord: *Your Lordship, his Lordship.* **3.** rule; authority; ownership: *His lordship over these lands is not questioned. They which are accounted to rule over the Gentiles exercise lordship over them* (Mark 10:42). **4.** the land or domain of a lord: *From many a lordship forth they rode* (William Morris).

Lord's Prayer, (in the Bible) a prayer given by Jesus to His disciples. It begins "Our Father Who art in Heaven." Matthew 6:9-13; Luke 11:2-4.

lords spiritual or **Lords Spiritual,** *British.* the bishops and archbishops in the House of Lords.

Lord's Supper, 1. Jesus' last supper with His disciples before his crucifixion. **2.** the church service in memory of this; Holy Communion.

Lord's Table, the altar on which the elements of the Eucharist are placed; Communion table.

lords temporal or **Lords Temporal,** *British.* the members of the House of Lords other than bishops and archbishops; lay peers.

Lord Steward, the official in charge of the finances of the royal household of Great Britain.

Lord·y (lôr'dē), *interj.* an exclamation of surprise or wonder: *Lordy, but it was hot!* (E.S. Field).

lore (lôr, lōr), *n.* **1.** the facts and stories about a certain subject: *fairy lore, bird lore, Irish lore.* **2.** learning; knowledge: *cobwebs of scholastic lore* (John Greenleaf Whittier); *... many a quaint and curious volume of forgotten lore* (Edgar Allan Poe). **3.** *Archaic.* teaching or something taught: *The subtle fiend his lore Soon learn'd* (Milton). **4.** *Archaic.* advice; counsel. [Old English *lār.* Related to LEARN.]

Lor·e·lei (lôr'ə lī, lor'-), *n. German Legend.* a siren of the Rhine whose beauty and singing distracted sailors and caused them to wreck their ships: *The voices from the East echoed hauntingly, like the lure of the legendary Lorelei* (Newsweek). Also, **Lurlei.**

lores (lôrz, lōrz), *n.pl.* the space between the eye and the bill of birds or the corresponding space in fishes and reptiles. [earlier, strap, thong < Latin *lōrum*]

lo·rette (lô ret'), *n.* (in France) a courtesan of the more elegant or pretentious kind. [< French *lorette*]

lor·gnette (lôr nyet'), *n.* **1.** eyeglasses mounted on a handle to hold in the hand. **2.** an opera glass. [< French *lorgnette* < *lorgner* look sidelong at, to eye < Old French *lorgne* squinting]

Lorgnette (def. 1)

lor·gnon (lôr nyôN'), *n.* **1.** an eyeglass or a pair of eyeglasses, especially a pince-nez. **2.** an opera glass. [< French *lorgnon* earlier, eyeglass, opera glasses < *lorgner;* see LORGNETTE]

lo·ri·ca (lō rī'kə, lō-), *n., pl.* **-cae** (-sē). **1.** *Zoology.* **a.** a hard, thickened body wall, as of a rotifer. **b.** a protective case or sheath, as of a protozoan. **2.** a leather cuirass or corselet worn by the ancient Romans. [< Latin *lōrīca* leather cuirass < *lōrum* strap, thong]

lor·i·cate (lôr'ə kāt, lor'-), *adj. Zoology.* having a lorica.

lor·i·cat·ed (lôr′ə kā′tid, lor′-), *adj.* loricate.

lor·i·keet (lôr′ə kēt, lor′-; lôr′ə kēt′, lor′-), *n.* any of various small parrots, a kind of lory having a brushlike tongue: *Lories, which include the lorikeets, are among the most beautiful parrots* (World Book Encyclopedia). [< *lory* + (para)*keet*]

lo·ris (lôr′is, lōr′-), *n., pl.* **-ris. 1.** either of two small, slow-moving nocturnal lemurs of southern Asia, the slender loris and slow loris. They have very large eyes and no tail, and live mostly in trees. **2.** a larger lemur of India and Malaya. [< French *loris*, perhaps < Dutch *loeris* booby]

lorn (lôrn), *adj. Archaic.* **1.** forsaken; forlorn: *Lorn stream, whose sullen tide no sedge-crown'd sisters now attend* (William Collins). *I am a lone lorn creetur'* (Dickens). **2.** lost; ruined: *If thou readest, thou art lorn! Better hadst thou ne'er been born* (Scott). [Middle English *lorn*, Old English *-loren*, past participle of *-lēosan* lose. Related to FORLORN.]

Lor·raine cross (lə rān′; *French* lô ren′), a cross having two horizontal arms, the upper shorter than the lower. See picture under **Free French.** [< *Lorraine*, a region in France]

lor·ry (lôr′ē, lor′-), *n., pl.* **-ries,** *v.,* **-ried, -ry·ing.** —*n.* **1.** *British.* an automobile truck; motor lorry: *At least once . . . a week they must take down their large machines, pack them on lorries, drive to the next fairground and put them up again* (Economist). **2.** a long flat wagon with or without sides. **3.** a car or other vehicle running on rails, as in a mine.

Lorry (def. 2)

—*v.t.* to transport in a lorry: *In Northern Rhodesia there is no such protection and the smaller game is being lorried out to safety* (Sunday Times).

[compare dialectal *lurry* to pull, lug]

lor·ry·load (lôr′ē lōd, lor′-), *n. British.* as much or as many as a lorry can hold: *An occasional lorryload of helmeted troops or sailors in the streets of Karachi make for tension* (London Times).

lo·ry (lôr′ē, lōr′-), *n., pl.* **-ries.** any of various small, bright-colored parrots with a bristled tongue adapted to their diet of nectar, and found in Australia and nearby islands. [earlier, *lourey* < Malay *luri*]

los·a·ble (lü′zə bəl), *adj.* that can be lost.

Los An·ge·le·no (lôs an′jə lē′nō, los), a native or inhabitant of Los Angeles; Angeleno.

lose (lüz), *v.,* **lost, los·ing.** —*v.t.* **1.** to not have any longer; have taken away from one by accident, carelessness, parting, death, etc.: *to lose a finger, to lose a dollar, to lose a friend, to lose one's life.* **2.** to be unable to find: *to lose a book, to lose an address.* **3.** to fail to keep, preserve, or maintain; cease to have: *to lose patience, to lose all fear, to lose one's mind.* **4.** to fail to follow with eye, hearing, mind, etc.: *to lose words here and there in a speech.* **5.** to fail to have, get, catch, etc.: *to lose a sale, to lose a train.* **6.** to fail to win: *to lose the prize, to lose a bet or game.* **7.** to bring to destruction; ruin: *The ship and its crew were lost.* **8.** to spend or let go by without any result; waste: *to lose an opportunity, to lose time waiting. The hint was not lost on him.* **9.** to cause the loss of: *Delay lost the battle.* **10.** to cause to lose: *That one act lost him his job.* **11.** to leave far behind in a race, pursuit, etc.: *The sly fox lost the dogs.*

—*v.i.* **1.** to be defeated: *Our team lost. The battle's loss may profit those who lose* (Shelley). **2. a.** to suffer loss: *to lose on a contract. Thus, by gaining abroad, he lost at home* (John Dryden). **b.** to be or become worse off in money, numbers, etc.: *The army lost heavily in yesterday's battle. The gambler lost heavily at poker.*

lose oneself, a. to let oneself go astray; become bewildered: *He finally lost himself in the maze of income tax figures.* **b.** to become absorbed or engrossed: *He seemed to lose himself in thought* (Joseph Conrad). *As I pace the darkened chamber and lose myself in melancholy musings* (Washington Irving).

lose out, *U.S.* to fail; be unsuccessful: *He lost out in the election.*

[Old English *losian* be lost < *los* destruction, loss]

lo·sel (lō′zəl, lü′-; loz′əl), *Archaic.* —*n.* a worthless person; profligate; scoundrel. —*adj.* good-for-nothing; worthless: *those losel scouts* (Washington Irving). [Middle English *losel*, apparently alteration of Old English *-losen*, alternate past participle of *-lēosan* lose. Compare LORN.] —**Syn.** *n.* rake, ragamuffin.

los·er (lü′zər), *n.* **1.** a person who loses something. **2.** a person, horse, etc., that is beaten in a race, game, or battle. **3.** *U.S. Informal.* a person who habitually loses or fails.

los·ing (lü′zing), *adj.* that cannot win or be won: *You are playing a losing game if you are not careful crossing streets.*

—*n.* **losings,** losses, especially in gambling. —**los′ing·ly,** *adv.*

loss (lôs, los), *n.* **1. a.** a losing: *The loss of health is more serious than the loss of money.* **b.** being lost: *Thou hast . . . quitted all to save A world from utter loss* (Milton). **2.** a person or thing lost: *The death of the statesman was a great loss to his country.* **3.** the amount lost. **4.** harm or disadvantage caused by losing something: *Our losses by the fire amounted to $10,000.* **5.** a defeat: *Our team had two losses and one tie out of ten games played.* **6.** *Military.* the losing of soldiers by death, capture, or wounding. **7.** *Insurance.* the occurrence of death, property damage, or other contingency against which a person is insured, under circumstances that make the insurer liable under the contract. **8.** *Electricity.* the reduction in power, measured by the difference between the power input and power output, in an electric circuit, device, system, etc., corresponding to the transformation of electric energy into heat.

at a loss, a. uncertain; puzzled; in difficulty: *at a loss how to proceed.* **b.** embarrassed for want of something: *at a loss for words, for information, etc.*

at a loss to, unable to: *at a loss to understand, imagine, explain, etc.*

losses, a. the number of soldiers dead, wounded, or captured: *The losses in that war were great.* **b.** *Accounting.* the excess of money spent or invested over money gained in any business transaction, manufacturing operation, etc.: *The losses put them in the red.* **c.** *Accounting.* the ratio of monetary loss to the amount of capital invested, especially for a fiscal year or other stated period of time: *The firm reported losses in excess of a million.*

[Old English *los*]

loss leader, *Commerce.* an article of trade sold below cost to attract customers: *Retailers are meeting the new competition with such old weapons as special loss leaders, or with price reductions* (Time).

loss ratio, *Insurance.* the ratio of the amounts paid out to insured parties to the value of the premiums received during a given period.

lost (lôst, lost), *v.* a past tense and past participle of **lose:** *I lost my new pen. I had already lost my ruler.*

—*adj.* **1.** no longer possessed or retained: *lost friends.* **2.** no longer to be found; missing: *lost articles.* **3.** attended with defeat; not won: *a lost prize, a lost battle.* **4.** not used to good purpose; wasted: *lost time.* **5.** having gone astray: *a lost child.* **6.** destroyed or ruined: *a lost soul, a lost cause.* **7.** bewildered: *a lost expression.*

be lost on or **upon,** to have no effect on; fail to influence: *Your kindness is not lost upon me* (Harriet Martineau).

lost in, a. so taken up with (it) that one fails to notice anything else; completely absorbed or interested in: *lost in contemplation.* **b.** hidden or obscured in: *outlines lost in the fog.* **c.** merged in or obscured by (something else): *a ball lost in the sun. Her small contribution was lost in the grand total.*

lost to, a. no longer possible or open to: *The opportunity was lost to him.* **b.** no longer belonging to: *He realized that she was lost to him.* **c.** insensible to: *The deserting soldier was lost to all sense of duty to his country.*

—**lost′ness,** *n.*

—**Syn.** *adj.* **2.** astray.

lost cause, a cause that is defeated already or sure to be defeated: *. . . the idealized heroic Lost Cause of the Confederacy* (New York Times).

Lost Generation, the young people, especially writers and artists, who emerged from World War I (1914-1918) disillusioned and without roots.

Lost Pleiad, *Greek Mythology.* one of the seven daughters of Atlas, transformed by the gods into the faintest star of the Pleiades. One account says that Electra is the Lost Pleiad because she withdrew in order not to witness the fall of Troy. Another account says that Merope is the dim star, thus displaying her shame for having loved Sisyphus, a mortal.

lost sheep, a person who has strayed from the right sort of conduct or religious belief. [< the parable of the "Lost Sheep" in Matthew 18:11-14]

lost tribes, the Hebrew tribes inhabiting the northern kingdom of Israel, who were taken into captivity by Sargon of Assyria in 721 B.C. and are believed never to have returned to their tribal lands.

lost-wax (lôst′waks′, lost′-), *adj.* cire-perdue: *. . . long curved tubes intricately cast by the "lost-wax" process* (New Scientist).

lot (lot), *n., v.,* **lot·ted, lot·ting,** *adv.* —*n.* **1.** an object used to decide something by chance, such as bits of paper, wood, etc. **2.** such a method of deciding: *to divide property by lot. It was settled by lot.* **3.** the choice made in this way: *The lot fell to me.* **4.** what a person gets by lot; person's share or portion: *This then was the lot of the tribe . . . of Judah . . . even to the border of Edom* (Joshua 15:1). **5.** a person's destiny; fate; fortune: *a happy lot. A policeman's lot is not a happy one!* (W. S. Gilbert). *We will submit to whatever lot a wise Providence may send us* (Hawthorne). **6.** a plot or portion of land: *His house is between two empty lots.* **7.** a place where motion pictures are made, including the buildings and sets used in making pictures. **8.** a distinct portion or parcel of anything: *Some of the bread in that last lot was moldy. He divided the fruit into ten lots.* **9.** a number of persons or things considered as a group; a collection; set: *a fine lot of boys. This lot of oranges was not as good as the last.* **10.** *Informal.* a great many; a good deal: *a lot of books. I have a lot of marbles.* **11.** *Informal.* a person of a certain kind: *He is a bad lot.*

cast or **draw lots,** to use lots to decide something: *We drew lots to decide who should be captain.*

cast or **throw in one's lot with,** to share the fate of; become a partner with: *I intended to go along with this good man, and to cast in my lot with him* (John Bunyan).

lots, *Informal.* **a.** a great many; a good deal: *lots of time, lots of money.* **b.** very much: *I like you lots.*

the lot, *Especially British.* everyone or everything; all: *Painting, wallpapering, carpeting, roof-tiling—the lot* (Punch).

—*v.t.* **1.** to divide into lots, as land. **2.** to assign to someone as his share or portion, or as his lot or destiny: *Who . . . were lotted their shares in a quarrel not theirs* (Thomas Hardy). **3.** to cast lots for; divide, apportion, or distribute by lot. —*v.i.* to cast lots.

—*adv.* a great deal; much: *I feel a lot better.*

[Old English *hlot*]

—**Syn.** *n.* **4.** allotment, part, parcel. **5.** doom.

➔ **lots, lots of.** Formal English avoids using *lots* and *lots of* in the sense of a considerable quantity or number. Informal: *He tried lots of different shots, but lost.* Formal: *He tried a variety of* (or *a great many different*) *shots, but lost.*

Lot (lot), *n.* (in the Bible) a righteous man, the nephew of Abraham, who was allowed to escape from Sodom with his wife before God destroyed it, provided they did not look back. His wife disobeyed the angels' orders, looked back, and was changed into a pillar of salt. Genesis 19:1-26.

lo·ta or **lo·tah** (lō′tə), *n.* a round water pot, usually of polished brass, used in India, the East Indies, etc. [< Hindi *loṭa*]

lote (lōt), *n. Archaic.* lotus.

loth (lōth), *adj., n.* loath.

Lo·thar·i·o (lō thãr′ē ō), *n., pl.* **-i·os.** a man who makes love to many women; gay deceiver; libertine. [< *Lothario*, a character in Nicholas Rowe's *The Fair Penitent*]

—**Syn.** rake.

loth·ly (lōth′lē, lōᴛʜ′-), *adv.* loathly[2].

loth·some (lōᴛʜ′səm), *adj.* loathsome.

lo·ti·form (lō′tə fôrm), *adj.* shaped like or resembling a lotus, especially in form. [< *lotus* + *-form*]

lo·tion (lō′shən), *n.* **1.** a liquid containing medicine or a cosmetic, used on the skin to soothe, heal, cleanse, or perfume: *Among* *products that can now be packaged in ... squeeze bottles are ... complexion lotions* (Newsweek). **2.** *Obsolete.* the act of washing (the body); ablution. —*v.t.* to put lotion on: *Lotion your hands anytime* (New Yorker). [< Latin *lōtiō, -ōnis* a washing, ultimately < *lavāre* to wash]

lo·to (lō′tō), *n.* lotto.

Lo·toph·a·gi (lō tof′ə jī), *n.pl. Greek Mythology.* lotus-eaters. [< Latin *Lōtophagi* < Greek *Lōtophágoi* < *lōtós* lotus + *phageîn* eat]

lo·tos (lō′təs), *n.* lotus.

lo·tos-eat·er (lō′təs ē′tər), *n.* lotus-eater.

lots (lots), *n.pl.* See under **lot,** *n.*

lot·ter·y (lot′ər ē), *n., pl.* **-ter·ies. 1.** a scheme for distributing prizes by lot or chance. In a lottery a large number of tickets are sold, some of which draw prizes. **2.** something like this: *They thought themselves unfortunate in the lottery of life* (Tobias Smollett). **3.** *Obsolete.* **a.** chance. **b.** the issue of events as determined by chance. [< Italian *lotteria* < *lotto;* see LOTTO]

lottery wheel, the wheel used for shuffling the numbers on lottery tickets.

lot·to (lot′ō), *n.* a game played by drawing numbered disks from a bag or box and covering the corresponding numbers on cards. The first player to complete a blank row is the winner. Also, **loto.** [< Italian *lotto* lot, ultimately < Germanic. Compare *lot.*]

lo·tus (lō′təs), *n.* **1.** any of various water plants of the water-lily family having large, often floating leaves, and showy flowers, commonly represented in the decorative art of the Hindus and the Egyptians: **a.** one of two African water lilies, a white-flowered species and a blue-flowered species. **b.** a perennial plant with large, fragrant rose or pink flowers; sacred lotus of India. **2.** any of various shrubby plants of the pea family, bearing red, pink, or white flowers, as the bird's-foot trefoil. **3. a.** a plant whose fruit was supposed by the ancient Greeks to cause a dreamy and contented forgetfulness in those who ate it, and make them lose all desire to return home. **b.** the fruit itself. **4.** *Architecture.* an ornament representing the Egyptian water lily. Also, **lotos.** [< Latin *lōtus* < Greek *lōtós*]

lo·tus-eat·er (lō′təs ē′tər), *n.* **1.** a person who leads a life of dreamy, indolent ease. **2.** a person who lived on the fruit of the lotus, and became content and indolent, having no desire to return home. Also, **lotos-eater.**

lo·tus·land (lō′təs land′), *n.* **1.** a land of idleness and delight: *Oxford, that lotusland, saps the willpower, the power of action* (New Yorker). **2.** the land of the lotus-eaters.

lotus tree, 1. a kind of jujube of northern Africa and southern Europe, supposed by many to have produced the lotus fruit in Greek myth. **2.** a nettle tree of Europe, also associated with this myth.

louche (lüsh), *adj.* oblique; not straightforward; sinister; shady: *... a bank hold-up by three louche gentlemen who arrive by train on this most fatal Saturday* (London Times). [< French *louche,* ultimately < Latin *luscus* having one eye]

loud (loud), *adj.* **1.** making a noise; not quiet or soft: *a loud bang, a loud voice.* **2.** noisy; resounding: *loud music, a loud place to study. When all is gay With lamps, and loud With sport and song* (Tennyson). **3.** clamorous; insistent: *to be loud in demands.* **4.** *Informal.* showy; flashy, especially in dress or manner: *loud clothes.* **5.** *Informal.* obtrusive; somewhat vulgar: *a loud person.* —*adv.* in a loud manner; with a loud noise or voice; aloud: *He called long and loud.* [Old English *hlūd*] —**loud′ness,** *n.*

—**Syn.** *adj.* **1, 2. Loud, noisy** mean making much or intense sound. **Loud** suggests strength or intensity of sound, but not necessarily disagreeableness: *The speaker's voice was loud, clear, and pleasing.* **Noisy** always suggests disagreeable loudness and sometimes implies that it is constant or habitual: *The people next door are noisy.* **2.** deafening.

loud·en (lou′dən), *v.i.* to become or grow loud or louder. —*v.t.* to make loud or louder.

loud·hail·er (loud′hā′lər), *n. Especially British.* a loudspeaker: *The Rev. James Bevels ... used a police loudhailer to address the crowds* (London Times).

loud·ish (lou′dish), *adj.* somewhat loud: *A super-plump guest in a loudish cape and an oversize Homburg hat stands at the desk* (Alexander Woollcott).

loud·ly (loud′lē), *adv.* **1.** with much noise. **2.** in a loud voice: *He spoke so loudly it startled everyone.*

loud·mouth (loud′mouth′), *n. Slang.* a loud-mouthed person, especially one who is boastful or disparaging.

loud·mouthed (loud′mouᴛʜd′, -moutht′), *adj.* talking loudly; irritatingly or offensively noisy: *Yet, though his loudmouthed tabloids spiel sex, crime, and the workingman's cause ...* (Time). —**Syn.** vociferous, blatant, clamorous.

loud·speak·er (loud′spē′kər), *n.* a device for amplifying the sound of a person's voice, music, etc., especially in a radio or phonograph: *Horn type loudspeakers ... for all parts of the audio range ...* (Roy J. Hoopes).

loud·speak·ing (loud′spē′king), *adj.* **1.** acting as a loudspeaker; amplifying the sound of the voice, music, etc.: *a loudspeaking device.* **2.** having to do with a loudspeaker: *loudspeaking results.* —*n.* the act or function of a loudspeaker in amplifying sound.

lough (loʜ), *n. Anglo-Irish.* **1.** a lake. **2.** an arm of the sea. **3.** *Obsolete.* any body of water. [Middle English *lough.* Compare LOCH.]

lou·is (lü′ē), *n., pl.* **lou·is** (lü′ēz). a louis d'or.

lou·is d'or (lü′ē dôr′), **1.** a French gold coin issued 1640-1795, worth from about $4 to about $4.60 at various times. **2.** a later French gold coin, worth 20 francs. [< French *louis d'or* (literally) gold louis; *louis* < proper name of several French kings]

Lou·is heel (lü′ē), a curved heel on a woman's shoe about 1½ inches high and flared at the base. [< King *Louis* XV of France]

Lou·i·si·an·a heron (lu̇ ē′zē an′ə, lü′i-), a grayish-purple heron with a white throat and breast, common in the southern United States and south to Brazil.

Lou·i·si·an·an (lu̇ ē′zē an′ən, lü′i-), *adj., n.* Louisianian.

Louisiana Purchase, an extensive region that the United States bought from France in 1803. It extended over about 530,000,000 acres from the Mississippi River to the Rocky Mountains and from Canada to the Gulf of Mexico.

Louisiana tanager, a tanager of western North America; western tanager.

Louisiana water thrush, a brownish warbler with a striped breast, found in wooded areas of North America, especially along small streams.

Lou·i·si·an·i·an (lu̇ ē′zē an′ē ən, lü′i-), *adj.* of or having to do with Louisiana, a Southern state of the United States. —*n.* a native or inhabitant of Louisiana.

Louis Qua·torze (kȧ tôrz′), the French title of Louis XIV of France, used to designate the styles in architecture, furniture, decorative art, etc., characteristic of his reign (1643-1715) or of approximately that period.

Louis Quatorze Wardrobe

Louis Quinze (kaɴz), the French title of Louis XV of France, used to designate the styles in architecture, furniture, decorative art, etc., characteristic of his reign (1715-1774) or of approximately that period: *Mary McCarthy, sitting serenely in a Louis Quinze chair ...* (Saturday Review). See also **sofa** for picture.

Louis Seize (sez), the French title of Louis XVI of France, used to designate the styles in architecture, furniture, decorative art, etc., characteristic of his reign (1774-1792) or of approximately that period.

Louis Quinze Sconce

Louis Treize (trez), the French title of Louis XIII of France, used to designate the styles in architecture, furniture, decorative art, etc., characteristic of his reign (1610-1643) or of approximately that period.

lou·koum (lü küm′), *n., pl.* **-kou·mi** (-kü′mē). fig paste. [< Turkish *lokum*]

loun (lün), *n.* loon[2].

loun·der (loun′dər), *Especially Scottish.* —*n.* a heavy or violent blow. —*v.t.* to beat with heavy blows; thrash. [perhaps imitative]

lounge (lounj), *v.,* **lounged, loung·ing,** *n.* —*v.i.* **1.** to stand, stroll, sit, or lie at ease and lazily; loll: *He has lounged long enough in that old chair* (Hawthorne). **2.** to pass time indolently; idle at one's ease. —*v.t.* to pass (time, etc.) away with lounging.

—*n.* **1.** a sofa, couch, or other article of furniture, used for reclining. **2.** a comfortable and informal room in which one can lounge, smoke, and be at ease. **3.** an act or state of lounging: *We went for a lounge in the park after dinner.* **4.** a lounging gait or manner of reclining: *tall, raw-boned Kentuckians ... with the easy lounge peculiar to the race* (Harriet Beecher Stowe).

[origin uncertain; perhaps < Old French *longis* drowsy laggard] —**loung′er,** *n.*

lounge car, a special railroad passenger car equipped with lounge seats, sofas, bar, etc.

lounge lizard, *U.S. Slang.* a lady's man: *Lounge lizard ... is what they call him, and from their tone it is utterly derogatory* (Western Mail).

lounge suit, *British.* a business suit: *I felt quite out of place wearing a lounge suit in Tiflis* (Punch).

lounge·wear (lounj′wãr′), *n.* leisurewear for lounging indoors.

loung·ing·ly (loun′jing lē), *adv.* in a lounging attitude or manner.

loup[1] (loup, lōp, lüp), *n., v.i., v.t. Scottish.* leap: *The horses gave a sudden loup* (John Galt). [variant of *leap*]

loup[2] (lü), *n.* a light mask or half mask of silk or velvet, worn by women. [< French *loup* (literally) wolf < Latin *lupus*]

loup-cer·vier (lü′ser vyā′), *n., pl.* **loup-cer·viers** (lü′ser vyā′). the Canada lynx. [< French *loup-cervier* < Latin *lupus cervārius* lynx that hunts stags < *lupus* wolf, *cervus* stag]

loupe (lüp), *n.* a small eyepiece fitted with a powerful magnifying lens, used by jewelers, watchmakers, etc.: *Finally, Mr. Cohen took out a loupe, a diamond man's magnifying glass, and studied the stone ...* (New Yorker). [< French *loupe*]

loup-ga·rou (lü′gə rü′), *n., pl.* **loups-ga·rous** (lü′gə rü′). a werewolf; lycanthrope. [< Old French *loup-garou* < *loup* wolf (see LOUP[2]) + *garou,* earlier *garoul* werewolf < Germanic (compare Middle High German *wërwolf*)]

loup·ing ill (lou′ping), an acute, infectious nervous and paralytic disease of sheep, caused by a tick-borne virus and characterized by involuntary leaping; trembles.

lour (lour), *v.i., n.* lower[2].

lour·ing (lour′ing), *adj.* lowering. —**lour′ing·ly,** *adv.*

lour·y (lour′ē), *adj.* lowery.

louse (lous), *n., pl.* **lice,** *v.,* **loused, lous·ing.** —*n.* **1.** a small, wingless insect that has a flat body and sucks blood, infesting the hair or skin of people and animals, causing great irritation, as the body louse and the crab louse: *a louse in the locks of literature* (Tennyson). **2.** any of various other insects that are parasitic on animals or plants, as the bee louse and the plant louse or aphid. **3.** any of certain other superficially similar arthropods, as book lice and wood lice. **4.** a mean, contemptible person. —*v.t.* **louse up.** *Slang.* to spoil; get (something) all confused or in a mess: *to louse up a song, joke, or deal.* [Old English *lūs*]

Head Louse (def. 1—Line shows actual length.)

louse·ber·ry (lous′ber′ē, -bər-), *n., pl.* **-ries.** a spindle tree common in Europe, whose powdered berries were reputed to destroy lice.

louse·wort (lous′wėrt′), *n.* any of a large group of herbaceous plants of the figwort family, formerly believed to breed lice in sheep and other livestock that feed on them; wood betony.

lous·i·ly (lou′zə lē), *adv. Slang.* in a lousy manner; filthily; meanly; scurvily.
lous·i·ness (lou′zē nis), *n.* **1.** the condition of being lousy. **2.** *Slang.* meanness; vileness.
lous·y (lou′zē), *adj.*, **lous·i·er, lous·i·est. 1.** infested with lice. **2.** *Slang.* **a.** bad; poor; of low quality: *The thing about bridge is that nobody can play it well. It's so hard that everybody's lousy at it* (New Yorker). **b.** dirty; disgusting; mean. **3.** *Slang.* well supplied: *lousy with money.*
lout[1] (lout), *n.* an awkward, stupid, and often ill-mannered, fellow; bumpkin; boor: *Grimes is a rough rustic lout* (William Godwin). —*v.t. Obsolete.* to treat with contempt; mock. [probably < *lout*[2]. Compare Old Icelandic *lūtr* bent down, stooping, *lūta* to stoop.]
lout[2] (lout), *Archaic.* —*v.i.* **1.** to bend; bow; make obeisance: *He fair the knight saluted, louting low* (Edmund Spenser). **2.** to stoop. —*v.t.* to bow (the head). [Old English *lūtan*]
lout·ish (lou′tish), *adj.* awkward and stupid; boorish. —**lout′ish·ly,** *adv.* —**lout′ish·ness,** *n.*
lou·troph·o·ros (lü trof′ər əs), *n., pl.* **-o·roi** (-ər oi). (in ancient Greece) a tall, long-necked vase for carrying water for a bath, especially for a ceremonial nuptial bath. It was often placed upon the tomb of a young person who died unmarried. [< Greek *loutrophóros*]
lou·ver (lü′vər), *n.* **1.** a window or other opening covered with louver boards. **2.** a ventilating slit, especially for the escape of heat, as one in the hood of an automobile or the bulkhead of a ship. **3.** a turret or lantern constructed on a roof, as in medieval architecture, to supply ventilation or light or allow smoke to escape. **4.** a louver board: *Movable suspended louvers of brown paper control the light for whatever canvas Braque is working on* (New Yorker). [< Old French *lover* < Germanic (compare Old High German *louba* upper roof)]
lou·ver-board·ing (lü′vər bôr′ding, -bōr′-), *n.* louver boards.
louver boards, horizontal strips of wood or other material set slanting in a window or other opening, so as to keep out rain but provide ventilation and light.

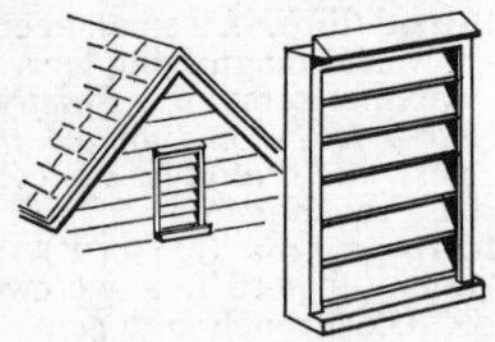

Louver Boards
Left, set in gable; right, detail

lou·vered (lü′vərd), *adj.* **1.** provided with louvers. **2.** arranged like louvers.
louver fence, a fence made of louver boards, providing privacy and ventilation.
lou·vre (lü′vər), *n. British.* louver.
lov·a·bil·i·ty (luv′ə bil′ə tē), *n.* the quality of being lovable. Also, **loveability.**
lov·a·ble (luv′ə bəl), *adj.* deserving love; endearing: *She was a most lovable person, always kind and thoughtful.* Also, **loveable.** —**lov′a·ble·ness,** *n.* —**Syn.** likeable, winning, pleasing, amiable.
lov·a·bly (luv′ə blē), *adv.* in a lovable manner. Also, **loveably.**
lov·age (luv′ij), *n.* a perennial herb of the parsley family, native to southern Europe, grown in herb gardens for its aromatic seeds and leaves. [Middle English *loveache*, alteration of Old French *luvesche*, or *levesche* < Late Latin *levisticum*, apparently alteration of Latin *ligusticum* of Liguria]
lov·at (luv′ət), *n.* a brownish-green color mixture often blended with other colors in fabrics. [< *Lovat*, a Scottish proper name]
love (luv), *n., v.,* **loved, lov·ing.** —*n.* **1.** strong or passionate affection for a person of the opposite sex: *But we loved with a love that was more than love* (Edgar Allan Poe). **2.** an instance of such feeling; being in love: *I suppose, the Colonel was crossed in his first love* (Jonathan Swift). **3.** this feeling as a subject for books or as a personified influence: *There is no love. The whole plot is political* (Macaulay). *I bow before thine altar, Love* (Tobias Smollett). **4.** a loved one, especially a sweetheart: *Live with me and be my love* (Christopher Marlowe). *The young May moon is beaming, love* (Thomas Moore). **5.** fond or tender feeling; warm liking; affection; attachment: *love of one's family, for a friend, etc.* **6.** strong liking: *a love of books, a love of freedom.* **7.** *Informal.* something charming or delightful: *What a love of a bracelet! The garden is quite a love* (Jane Austen). **8.** the kindly feeling or benevolence of God for His creatures, or the reverent devotion due from them to God, or the kindly affection they should have for each other: *Ye have not the love of God in you* (John 5:42). **9.** no score for a player or side in tennis and certain other games.
fall in love, to begin to love; come to feel love: *The young couple fell in love at first sight.*
for love, a. for nothing; without pay: *He did the work for love.* **b.** for pleasure; not for money: *They played the game for love.* **c.** by reason of love; out of affection: *It is commonly a weak man who marries for love* (Samuel Johnson).
for love or money, a. on any terms: *He would not do the work for love or money.* **b.** at any price; by any means: *... Anglo-Saxon texts not elsewhere to be had for love or money* (Francis A. March).
for the love of, for the sake of; because of: *He did it for the love of his country. For the love of God, peace* (Shakespeare).
in love, feeling love: *Mary is in love and wants to get married.*
in love with, a. feeling love for: *Romeo was in love with Juliet.* **b.** very fond of; enamored of: *He is in love with his profession.*
make love, to do as lovers do; pay amorous attention (to); woo: *Demetrius ... made love to Nedar's daughter* (Shakespeare).
no love lost between, a. no love lacking, as between persons who love each other: *We grumble a little now and then ... But there's no love lost between us* (Oliver Goldsmith). **b.** dislike between persons: *There was no love lost between the two ladies* (Thackeray).
[Old English *lufu*]
—*v.t.* **1.** to be in love with; feel love for: *And I will love thee still, my dear, Till a' the seas gang dry* (Robert Burns). **2.** to like very much; take great pleasure in: *He loves music. Most children love ice cream. All that hate contentions, and love quietness, and virtue, and angling* (Izaak Walton). **3.** to be very fond of; hold dear: *to love a friend, one's country, etc. She loves her mother.* **4.** to embrace affectionately. —*v.i.* **1.** to be in love; fall in love: *One that loved not wisely, but too well* (Shakespeare). **2.** to have affection: *He can hate but cannot love.*
[Old English *lufian*]
—**Syn.** *n.* **5. Love, affection** mean a feeling of warm liking and tender attachment. **Love** emphasizes strength, depth, sincerity, and warmth of feeling, suggesting also tenderness, as for a child or parent; devotion and loyalty, as to friends or family; reverence, as for God; passion, as for man or woman, or belief, etc.: *Every person needs to give and receive love.* **Affection** applies to a less strong feeling, suggesting tenderness and warm fondness: *I like my teacher, but feel no affection for her.*
➔ See **like** for usage note.
Love (luv), *n.* **1.** the god or goddess of love: **a.** Venus. **b.** Cupid or Eros. **2.** (in the belief of Christian Scientists) God.
love·a·bil·i·ty (luv′ə bil′ə tē), *n.* lovability.
love·a·ble (luv′ə bəl), *adj.* lovable. —**love′a·ble·ness,** *n.*
love·a·bly (luv′ə blē), *adv.* lovably.
love affair, 1. a particular experience of being in love; amour. **2.** an affinity between two persons, groups, etc.: *... the love affair between the Administration and Pakistan worries many people in Britain* (Harper's).
love apple, an old name for the tomato.
love·bird (luv′bėrd′), *n.* **1.** any of certain small tropical parrots of the Old World that show great affection for their mates. **2.** *Informal.* a person in love.
love child, an illegitimate child.
love feast, 1. a meal eaten together by the early Christians as a symbol of brotherly love, apparently originally in connection with the Eucharistic celebration. **2.** a religious ceremony imitating this. **3.** any banquet or other gathering to promote good feeling: *There will be a great Democratic love feast in which a thousand Democratic editors will take part* (Charleston News and Courier).
love game, a game won in tennis or certain other sports without any score having been made by the opponent.
love-in-a-mist (luv′in ə mist′), *n.* a garden plant of the crowfoot family, native to southern Europe, having feathery leaves and pale-blue flowers; fennelflower.
love-in-i·dle·ness (luv′in ī′dəl nis), *n.* the wild pansy.
love knot, an ornamental knot or bow of ribbon as a token of love.
love·less (luv′lis), *adj.* **1.** not loving: *a loveless heart.* **2.** not loved; unloved: *a loveless child.* —**love′less·ly,** *adv.* —**love′less·ness,** *n.*
love letter, a letter expressing love for another.
love-lies-bleed·ing (luv′līz blē′ding), *n.* any of various garden plants of the amaranth family, having long, crimson spikes of flowers that often droop on the ground.
love·light (luv′līt′), *n.* a gleam or sparkle in the eye, expressing love: *They stare at each other, and suddenly the lovelight shines in their eyes* (Atlantic).
love·li·ly (luv′lə lē), *adv.* in a lovely manner.
love·li·ness (luv′lē nis), *n.* beauty.
love·lock (luv′lok′), *n.* **1.** any conspicuous lock of hair, especially a curl worn on the forehead. **2.** a long, flowing lock dressed separately from the rest of the hair, worn by courtiers in the time of Elizabeth I and James I.
love·lorn (luv′lôrn′), *adj.* suffering because of love for another; forsaken by the person whom one loves. —**love′lorn′ness,** *n.*
love·ly (luv′lē), *adj.*, **-li·er, -li·est,** *n., pl.* **-lies.** —*adj.* **1.** beautiful in mind or character; lovable; beautiful: *She is one of the loveliest girls we know.* **2.** *Informal.* delightful; very pleasing: *It's ... very kind of you, Jack to offer me this lovely holiday* (George Bernard Shaw). **3.** *Obsolete.* loving; affectionate.
—*n. Informal.* a pretty girl: *Two local lovelies whom he and his friend had met in the afternoon, arrived at the pier* (Harper's).
—**Syn.** *adj.* **1.** See **beautiful.**
love-mak·ing (luv′mā′king), *n.* amorous attentions or caresses; courtship.
love match, a marriage for love, not for money or social position.
love-nest (luv′nest′), *n.* a place where lovers dwell or keep a tryst: *By now he'd decided to become an architect so that he could design our love-nest himself* (Punch).
love potion, a potion intended to induce love; philter.
lov·er (luv′ər), *n.* **1.** a person who loves. **2.** a man who is in love with a woman. **3.** a person who loves illicitly; paramour. **4.** a person having a strong liking: *a lover of music, a lover of books.*
lovers, a man and a woman who are in love with each other: *Hero and Leander were famous lovers.*
—**lov′er·like′,** *adj.*
—**Syn. 2.** suitor, admirer, beau.
lov·er·li·ness (luv′ər lē nis), *n.* a loverly state or condition.
lov·er·ly (luv′ər lē), *adj.* like a lover: *loverly attentions.* —*adv.* in the manner of a lover.
love seat, a seat or small sofa for two persons.
love set, a set won without the opponent's winning a game in tennis and certain other games.
love·sick (luv′sik′), *adj.* languishing because of love. —**love′sick′ness,** *n.*
love·some (luv′səm), *adj. Archaic.* **1.** lovable. **2.** lovely; beautiful: *One praised her ankles ... One her dark hair and lovesome mien* (Tennyson). **3.** loving; friendly. **4.** amorous. —**love′some·ness,** *n.*
love vine, the dodder.
Love wave, a seismic wave that travels across the earth's surface in a horizontal motion: *... long-period Love waves are excited by underground explosions* (Bulletin of Atomic Scientists). [< A.E.H. *Love*, 1863-1940, an English mathematician, who discovered it]
love·y-dove·y (luv′ē duv′ē), *Informal.* —*n.* darling: *We will love one another as much as we can, lovey-dovey* (London Daily Chronicle). —*adj.* weakly sentimental; namby-pamby: *Skipping entirely the lovey-dovey stuff about Blanche Ingram, I'd keep up the curdle in my blood with Chapter XX* (Punch). [< *love* + *-y*[1] + *dove*[1] + *-y*[1]]
lov·ing (luv′ing), *adj.* feeling or showing love; affectionate; fond: *loving hearts, loving glances.* —**lov′ing·ly,** *adv.* —**lov′ing·ness,** *n.*
loving cup, 1. a large cup with handles, passed around for all to drink from, as at the

close of a banquet: *Tonight the loving cup we'll drain* (Henry Newbolt). **2.** such a cup awarded as a trophy.

lov·ing-kind·ness (luv′ing kīnd′nis), *n.* kindness coming from love; affectionate tenderness and consideration: *How excellent is thy loving-kindness, O God!* (Psalms 36:7). —**Syn.** kindliness, benevolence.

low[1] (lō), *adj.* **1.** not high or tall; short: *low walls, a low hedge.* **2.** rising but slightly from a surface or background: *low relief.* **3. a.** of less than ordinary height, depth, or quantity: *The well is getting low. The dry summer made all the streams too low for fishing. Our supplies were low.* **b.** (of a dress or garment) cut low; low-necked: *I'm sorry you've come in such low dresses* (Anthony Trollope). **4.** in a low place; near the ground, floor, or other base; not high: *a low shelf.* **5.** lying or being below the general level, as the regions of a country lying near the sea: *low ground.* **6.** small in amount, degree, force, value, etc.: *a low price, a low diet of few calories.* **7.** not loud; soft: *a low whisper.* **8.** inferior in civilization, organization, etc.; not advanced: *Bacteria are low organisms.* **9.** lacking in dignity or elevation: *low thoughts.* **10.** of humble rank: *She had a rather low position as a kitchen maid. One law for gentlemen, another for low people* (Jeremy Bentham). **11.** affording little strength; weak; feeble: *a low state of health. The master seemed extremely low . . . and lay much of the time insensible* (Robert Louis Stevenson). **12.** unfavorable; poor: *I have a low opinion of his abilities.* **13.** depressed or dejected: *low spirits. I am low and dejected at times* (Edmund Burke). **14.** mean or base; coarse; vulgar; degraded: *low company. A person hears some low talk in saloons.* **15.** near the horizon: *the low evening sun.* **16.** near the equator: *low latitudes.* **17.** prostrate or dead: *And wilt thou weep when I am low?* (Byron). **18.** deep: *a low bow.* **19.** not high in the musical scale: *a low pitch, a low note.* **20.** (of speech sounds) pronounced with the tongue far from the palate. The *a* in *fat* and the *o* in *got* are low vowels. **21.** relatively recent: *His dating of the burial seems too low considering the primitive character of the pottery.* **22.** that gives the greatest force and the least speed, as a gear in which the ratio of the drive shaft to that of the crankshaft is smallest. **23.** (in the Church of England) maintaining Low-Church practices.

—*adv.* **1.** near the ground, floor, or base: *to fly low. Party fights are won by aiming low* (Oliver W. Holmes). *The spotted pack, with tails high mounted, ears hung low* (William Cowper). **2.** in, at, or to a low portion, point, degree, condition, price, etc.: *Supplies are running low.* **3. a.** softly; quietly; not loudly: *Lucia, speak low, he is retired to rest* (Joseph Addison). **b.** at a low pitch on the musical scale. **4.** meanly; humbly: *You value yourself too low.* **5.** near the horizon: *The sun sank low.* **6.** near the equator. **7.** lately; at a comparatively recent date.

lay low, a. to knock down: *The boxer laid low his opponent.* **b.** to kill: *The enemy was laid low.*

lie low, *Informal.* to stay hidden; keep still: *After the third robbery, the thieves decided to lie low for a time. I shall lie low and pretend to know nothing about it. Brer Fox, he lay low* (Joel Chandler Harris).

—*n.* **1.** that which is low, or something or someone in a low position: *We take the rough with the smooth, the low with the high. The poor and the low have their way of expressing the last facts of philosophy as well as you* (Emerson). *From the light, flutey high notes, where sopranos often lose character, to rich, viola-like lows* (Time). **2.** an arrangement of the gears used for the lowest speed and greatest force, as in an automobile and similar machines. **3.** *Meteorology.* an area of comparatively low barometric pressure: *These highs and lows are shown on weather maps.* **4. a.** the lowest trump card in certain games. **b.** (in sports and games) the lowest score, number, etc., or the player who makes it. **5.** the lowest point reached in output, prices, business transactions, etc.; a minimum: *Many stocks fell to new lows after the news was received.*

[< Scandinavian (compare Old Icelandic *lāgr*)] —**low′ness,** *n.*

—**Syn.** *adj.* **6.** moderate. **10.** obscure, lowly. **12.** disapproving, disparaging. **14.** See **base**[2].

low[2] (lō), *v.i., v.t.* to make the sound of a cow; moo: *The lowing herd winds slowly o'er the lea* (Thomas Gray). —*n.* the sound a cow makes; mooing. [Old English *hlōwan*]

low[3] (lō), *Especially Scottish.* —*n.* **1.** a flame; blaze. **2.** a lantern, torch, or candle. —*v.i.* to flame, blaze, or glow. Also, **lowe.** [< Scandinavian (compare Old Icelandic *loge*)]

low[4] (lō), *n. Archaic.* a hill, especially a round or conical one; mound. [Old English *hlāw*]

low-ar·e·a storm (lō′ãr′ē ə), *Meteorology.* a cyclone (so called from the region of low barometric pressure at its center).

low blow, a foul blow; unfair treatment.

low·born (lō′bôrn′), *adj.* of humble birth. —**Syn.** plebeian.

low·boy (lō′boi′), *n. U.S.* a low chest of drawers, usually having legs.

Lowboy

low·bred (lō′bred′), *adj.* coarse; vulgar: *a lowbred fellow, lowbred manners.*

low·brow (lō′brou′), *Informal.* —*n.* a person lacking in appreciation of intellectual or artistic things: *Ben . . . said this powerful play was too powerful for a bunch of lowbrows like us* (H.L. Wilson). —*adj.* **1.** being a lowbrow; incapable of culture. **2.** fit for lowbrows: *Generalizations about the proportion of support for highbrow and lowbrow activity in any community must of course be carefully checked* (Harper's).

low-browed (lō′broud′), *adj.* **1.** having a low forehead. **2.** *Informal.* lowbrow: *Never in all those years have I heard Prescott described in such a low-browed, uninformed manner as in your Washington Report* (Atlantic).

low·brow·ism (lō′brou′iz əm), *n. Informal.* the condition of being lowbrow; intellectual inferiority: *But what is irritating is the broad, obvious lowbrowism of the treatment of a theme that demands . . . a more subtle approach* (Punch).

Low-Church (lō′chėrch′), *adj.* laying little stress on church authority and ceremonies; more like other Protestant denominations and less like the Roman Catholic Church (used of a party in the Episcopalian Church and Church of England).

Low Church, a party maintaining Low-Church practices.

Low-Church·man (lō′chėrch′mən), *n., pl.* **-men.** an Anglican favoring Low-Church practices.

low comedy, broadly humorous comedy, using characters of a less polite or refined type than drawing-room comedy; slapstick.

low-cost (lō′kôst, -kost), *adj.* inexpensive.

low-coun·try (lō′kun′trē), *adj.* of the Low Countries; having to do with Netherlands, Belgium, and Luxemburg.

low-cut (lō′kut′), *adj.* **1.** cut low: *a low-cut neckline.* **2.** low-necked: *low-cut dresses.*

low-down[1] (lō′doun′), *adj. Especially U.S. Informal.* **1.** low; mean; contemptible: *a low-down neighborhood.* **2.** earthy: *Delightful low-down musical about Broadway's floating crap games . . .* (Time). [American English; in earlier British English, previous, low in space]

low-down[2] (lō′doun′), *n. Slang.* the actual facts or truth. [American English; origin uncertain]

low-drag (lō′drag′), *adj.* having or creating little resistance to the atmosphere while in flight: *A new, low-drag wing will be incorporated to increase the speed* (Wall Street Journal).

lowe (lō), *n., v.i.,* **lowed, low·ing.** low[3].

low-end (lō′end′), *adj.* at the lower end of the price range: *The demand for low-end wool suits continues strong* (New York Times).

low·er[1] (lō′ər), *v.t.* **1.** to let down or haul down: *We lower the flag at night.* **2.** to make lower: *to lower the water in a canal, to lower the volume of a radio, to lower the price of a car, to lower the steam pressure in a boiler. The fan soon lowered the temperature of the room.* **3.** *Music.* to depress in pitch. **4.** to bring down in rank, station, or estimation; degrade; dishonor. —*v.i.* to become lower; sink: *The sun lowered slowly.* [< adjective] —*adj., adv.* comparative of **low:** *Prices were lower last year than this.* [< *low*[1] + *-er*[3]] —**Syn.** *v.t.* **2.** decrease, diminish. —*v.i.* descend, fall.

low·er[2] (lou′ər), *v.i.* **1.** to look dark and threatening: *Dark lowers the tempest overhead* (Longfellow). **2.** to look angry or sullen; frown; scowl.

—*n.* **1.** a dark and threatening look; gloominess. **2.** a frown; scowl. Also, **lour.** [Middle English *louren*]

—**Syn.** *v.i.* **1.** menace. **2.** glower.

lower bound, *Mathematics.* a number less than or equal to a given function.

Lower Carboniferous, *Geology.* the name outside of North America for the Mississippian period of Carboniferous time.

lower case, *Printing.* **1.** small letters, not capital. *Abbr.:* l.c. **2.** the frame or frames in which small letters are kept for hand setting.

low·er-case (lō′ər kās′), *adj., v.,* **-cased, -cas·ing.** *Printing.* —*adj.* **1.** in small letters, not capitals. **2.** kept in or having to do with the lower case.

—*v.t.* to print in small letters.

low·er-class (lō′ər klas′, -kläs′), *adj.* of or having to do with an inferior class or the lower classes of society.

lower classes, the classes of society having low status, comprising unskilled and farm laborers, people on relief, and (sometimes) the working class.

low·er·class·man (lō′ər klas′mən, -kläs′-), *n., pl.* **-men.** a freshman or sophomore in a college, university, high school, etc.; underclassman.

Lower Cretaceous, the earlier of two divisions of the Cretaceous period in North America, characterized by the slow advance of sea water across areas of Texas and central United States.

lower criticism, the critical physical study of a text, especially of the Bible, having in view the correction of copyists' errors, omissions, and additions, and other corruptions which have crept into the text since it was first written; textual criticism.

low·ered (lō′ərd), *adj.* **1.** made lower. **2.** *Phonetics.* pronounced with tongue lower in the mouth than it normally is for the vowel in question.

Lower House or **lower house,** the more representative branch of a legislature that has two branches, as the House of Representatives in the United States Congress. The members of a Lower House are usually elected by popular vote or represent the nation as a whole; those in a nominative chamber or an Upper House, as the Senate of the United States, are elected to represent the states of a federation, etc.

low·er·ing (lou′ər ing), *adj.* **1.** dark and threatening; gloomy: *a gloomy and lowering day* (Francis Parkman). **2.** frowning; scowling; angry-looking. Also, **louring.** —**low′er·ing·ly,** *adv.*

lower mast, the lowest section of a mainmast, on which the mainsail is carried. See **masthead** for picture.

low·er·most (lō′ər mōst), *adj.* lowest.

lower regions, hell; Hades.

Lower Silurian, Ordovician, the second period of the Paleozoic era.

lower transit, *Astronomy.* the passage of a heavenly body across the part of the meridian that lies below the pole.

lower world, 1. the abode of the dead; hell; Hades. **2.** the earth.

low·er·y (lou′ər ē), *adj.* dull; gloomy; threatening. Also, **loury.**

low·est common denominator (lō′ist), **1.** *Mathematics.* the least common denominator. **2.** that which most fully expresses the feelings or opinions of a large number of persons or a group in general.

lowest common multiple, least common multiple.

Lowes·toft (lōs′toft, -təft), *n.* a kind of china. [< *Lowestoft,* a seaport in Suffolk, England]

low explosive, an explosive used as a propellant for the shell in a gun, etc., rather than to destroy by its own force.

low-fat (lō′fat′), *adj.* containing little or no edible fats: *a low-fat diet.*

low-fre·quen·cy (lō′frē′kwən sē), *adj.* of or having to do with a frequency ranging from 30 to 300 kilocycles per second: *low-frequency radio receivers, low-frequency sound waves.* *Abbr.:* LF (no periods).

low gear, the gear that gives the greatest force and the least speed, especially in an automobile; low.

Low German, **1.** the Germanic speech of the Low Countries (Dutch, Flemish, etc.) and especially of northern Germany. **2.** Plattdeutsch.

low-grade (lō′grād′), *adj.* of poor quality; inferior: *low-grade ores.*

low hurdles, a race in which the runners jump over hurdles 2½ feet high, usually over a distance of 220 yards.

low-key (lō′kē′), *adj.* understated; played down: *To take account of French feelings, the British are reported to be willing to settle for a very low-key communiqué that would not present the nuclear force as a great new development of NATO* (New York Times).

low-keyed (lō′kēd′), *adj.* low-key: *It is ... full of funny, low-keyed idiocy of cocktail parties* (Harper's).

low·land (lō′lənd), *n.* land that is lower and flatter than the neighboring country. —*adj.* of or in the lowlands: *a lowland farm.*

Low·land (lō′lənd), *n.* a low, flat region in southern and eastern Scotland.
Lowlands, the Lowland (Scottish) dialect: *The Scottish word for Lowlands is Lallans.*
—*adj.* of, belonging to, or characteristic of the Lowlands of Scotland.

low·land·er (lō′lən dər), *n.* an inhabitant of the low or level portion of a country or district.

Low·land·er (lō′lən dər), *n.* a native of the Lowlands of Scotland.

Low Latin, Latin as spoken in the post-Classical period.

low-lev·el (lō′lev′əl), *adj.* **1.** having or occurring at a low level of altitude: *low-level explosions, low-level flights, a low-level bridge.* **2.** low in content; containing a relatively small amount of something: *Much of this refuse from fission is low-level and short-lived ...* (Newsweek). *Mice were given low-level doses of streptomycin ...* (Science News Letter). **3.** at the lowest level of authority, rank, quality, etc.: *a low-level official.* **4.** soft; hard to hear: *The recording is low-level, faint, and poor in definition* (New York Times).

low·life (lō′līf′), *n., pl.* **-lifes,** *adj.* —*n. Slang.* **1.** a vicious, degenerate, or vile person; a criminal: *... a scattering of lowlifes whose crimes include an attempted kidnaping* (New Yorker). **2.** immoral people or environment: *The salacious, raucously funny bestiary of Roman lowlife* (Time).
—*adj.* **1.** characteristic of a lowlife; immoral; degenerate: *The guys are a lowlife lot who peddle dope, steal, and double-cross each other* (New Yorker). **2.** unrefined; cheap; crude; mean: *The bands that played jazz were considered lowlife and vulgar* (Saturday Review).

low-lif·er (lō′lī′fər), *n. Slang.* a lowlife or degenerate person.

low·li·head (lō′lē hed), *n. Archaic.* humility; lowliness: *The stately flower ... Of perfect wifehood and pure lowlihead* (Tennyson).

low·li·ly (lō′lə lē), *adv.* in a lowly manner; humbly.

low·li·ness (lō′lē nis), *n.* humbleness of feeling or behavior; humble station in life.

low-lived (lō′līvd′), *adj. Informal.* belonging in or characteristic of a low order of life or society; vulgar; mean: *low-lived manners. A low-lived Yankee, who had never known a gentleman in his life* (Francis Hopkinson Smith).

low·ly (lō′lē), *adj.,* **-li·er, -li·est,** *adv.* —*adj.* **1.** low in rank, station, position, or development: *a lowly corporal, a lowly occupation, the lowly protozoan.* **2.** modest in feeling, behavior, or condition; humble; meek: *He held a lowly opinion of himself. I am meek and lowly in heart* (Matthew 11:29).
—*adv.* humbly; meekly.
—**Syn.** *adj.* **1.** inferior. **2.** unassuming. See **humble.**

low-ly·ing (lō′lī′ing), *adj.* **1.** lying below the normal level or elevation: *Within a few hours the low-lying island city was overrun by the raging waters of the Gulf of Mexico* (New Yorker). **2.** lying close to the ground: *low-lying foothills.*

Low Mass, (in the Roman Catholic Church) a simplified form of High Mass, conducted by one priest assisted by altar boys. Low Mass is usually read, not sung.

low-mind·ed (lō′mīn′did), *adj.* mean; vulgar. —**low′-mind′ed·ly,** *adv.* —**low′-mind′ed·ness,** *n.*

lown[1] (loun), *Scottish.* —*adj., n.* calm; quiet: *the night was lown and peaceful* (John Galt). —*v.i., v.t.* to calm; lull. [< Scandinavian (compare Icelandic *lygn,* Swedish *lugn*)]

lown[2] (lün), *n.* loon[2].

low-necked (lō′nekt′), *adj.* (of a dress, etc.) cut low so as to show the neck, part of the bosom, and shoulders or back. —**Syn.** décolleté.

low-pitched (lō′picht′), *adj.* **1. a.** of low tone or sound; deep. **b.** little elevated: *poor and low-pitched desires* (Milton). **2.** having little slope, as a roof. **3.** having little height between floor and ceiling.

low-pres·sure (lō′presh′ər), *adj.* **1.** having or using less than the usual pressure: *During the seasons in question the coastal low-pressure troughs were farther west than usual* (Scientific American). **2.** easygoing; that does not arouse or annoy: *His books are quiet, low-pressure, and frequently on the edge of becoming pedestrian* (New Yorker).

low relief, sculpture in which the figures stand out only slightly from the background; bas-relief. See picture under **bas-relief.**

low-rise (lō′rīz′), *adj.* having few stories; not high-rise: *low-rise housing developments, a low-rise building without elevators.*

lows (lōz), *adj., adv., v.t., v.i. Obsolete.* loose.

lowse (*adj., adv.* lōs; *v.* lōz), *adj., adv., v.t., v.i.,* **lowsed, lows·ing.** *Obsolete.* loose.

low-slung (lō′slung′), *adj.* built low; standing close to the ground: *It was a low-slung contraption which looked as if it had been built of bed slats* (Atlantic).

low speed, low gear.

low-spir·it·ed (lō′spir′ə tid), *adj.* sad; depressed; dejected. —**low′-spir′it·ed·ly,** *adv.* —**low′-spir′it·ed·ness,** *n.* —**Syn.** dispirited, morose.

low spirits, a condition of little energy or joy; sadness; depression; dejection.

Low Sunday, the Sunday after Easter.

low-ten·sion (lō′ten′shən), *adj.* **1.** (of an electrical device, circuit, etc.) having, or for use at, a low voltage, usually of fewer than 750 volts. **2.** (of a winding of a transformer) to be used at a low voltage.

low-test (lō′test′), *adj.* (of gasoline, etc.) having a relatively high boiling point.

low tide, 1. the lowest level of the tide. **2.** the time when the tide is lowest. **3.** the lowest point of anything.

Low·veld or **low·veld** (lō′velt′), *n.* a fertile plateau in the northern Transvaal of South Africa: *The cloudlets gradually dissolved ... leaving exposed to view hundreds of miles of lowveld* (Napier Davitt). [< *low*[1] + Afrikaans *veld* veld]

low-vol·a·tile (lō′vol′ə təl), *adj.* (of coal) containing only a small percentage of volatile matter: *The low-volatile coal is nearly smokeless and is used as a home fuel* (Wall Street Journal).

low-volt·age (lō′vōl′tij), *adj.* (of an electrical system) designed to operate at a voltage of fewer than 750 volts.

low water, 1. the lowest level of water, as in a channel. **2.** low tide.

low-wa·ter mark (lō′wô′tər, -wot′ər), **1.** the mark showing low water. **2.** the lowest point: *The low-water mark in the Tories' fortunes was reached at the county council elections* (Economist).

low wine, wine of low percentage of alcohol. The first wines produced in the distillation process are low wines.

low-yield (lō′yēld′), *adj.* yielding little, as of radioactivity.

lox[1] (loks), *n.* a kind of smoked salmon. [< Yiddish *laks* < Middle High German *lacs* salmon]

lox[2] or **LOX** (loks), *n.* liquid oxygen: *Liquid oxygen used at steel mills and in chemical processing is the same famous LOX found near many missile launching sites* (Science News Letter). [< *l*(iquid) *ox*(ygen)]

lox·o·drom·ic (lok′sə drom′ik), *adj.* having to do with sailing obliquely across meridians on a rhumb line. [< Greek *loxós* oblique + *drómos* a course + English *-ic*]

lox·o·drom·i·cal (lok′sə drom′ə kəl), *adj.* loxodromic.

loxodromic curve or **line,** a line on the surface of a sphere cutting all meridians at the same angle, as that formed by the path of a ship whose course is constantly directed to the same point of the compass in a direction oblique to the equator.

lox·o·drom·ics (lok′sə drom′iks), *n.* the art of sailing obliquely across meridians on a rhumb line.

lox·od·ro·my (lok sod′rə mē), *n.* loxodromics.

loy·al (loi′əl), *adj.* **1.** true and faithful to love, promise, duty, or other obligations: *loyal conduct or sentiments, loyal devotion. I will remain The loyal'st husband that did e'er plight troth* (Shakespeare). **2.** faithful to one's king, government, or country: *a loyal subject or citizen.* **3.** *Obsolete.* legal; legitimate. [< Middle French *loyal,* Old French *loial,* and *leial* < Latin *lēgālis* legal < *lēx, lēgis* law. Doublet of LEAL, LEGAL.] —**loy′al·ly,** *adv.* —**Syn. 1.** constant. See **faithful.** —**Ant. 1.** disloyal, faithless.

loy·al·ism (loi′ə liz əm), *n.* the principles or actions of loyalists; adherence to the king or the existing government.

loy·al·ist (loi′ə list), *n.* a person who supports his king or the existing government, especially in time of revolt.

Loy·al·ist (loi′ə list), *n.* **1.** an American colonist who opposed independence for the American colonies at the time of the American Revolutionary War; Tory. **2.** a person loyal to the Republic during the civil war in Spain from 1936 to 1939. **3.** (in Canada) a United Empire Loyalist.

loy·al·ty (loi′əl tē), *n., pl.* **-ties.** loyal feeling or behavior; faithfulness: *Loyalty, like love, cannot be forced. In its essence loyalty is love for a person, a group, a cause. ... group loyalty cannot be obtained by force, but group disloyalty can be restrained by force* (Emory S. Bogardus).
—**Syn.** fidelity, constancy.

loyalty oath, an oath pledging loyalty to a government or constitution: *Each has been required to swear a loyalty oath with this ominous clause: "If I betray this oath, I agree to suffer the punishment of a traitor"* (Newsweek).

loz·enge (loz′inj), *n.* **1.** a design or figure shaped like this: ◊. **2.** a small tablet of medicine or piece of candy: *Cough drops are sometimes called lozenges.* [< Old French *losenge,* ultimately < Late Latin *lausa* slab]

loz·enged (loz′injd), *adj.* **1.** having the shape of a lozenge: *the lozenged panes of a very small latticed window* (Charlotte Brontë). **2.** divided into or ornamented with figures in the shape of lozenges, especially of alternate colors.

Lozenged Molding (def. 2)

LP (no periods), **1.** a long-playing phonograph record: *All five LP versions of the Concerto for Orchestra are excellent* (Atlantic). **2.** *Trademark.* a name for a phonograph record of this type.

LPG (no periods), liquefied petroleum gas.

LP-gas (el′pē′gas′), *n.* liquefied petroleum gas.

L plate, *Especially British.* a plate affixed to the vehicle of a person learning to drive.

L.P.O. or **LPO** (no periods), London Philharmonic Orchestra.

L.P.S., Lord Privy Seal.

lr., lira.

LR (no periods), long range.

L.S., an abbreviation for the following:
1. *British.* Leading Seaman.
2. Licentiate in Surgery.
3. the place of the seal (Latin, *locus sigilli*).

L.S.D. or **l.s.d.,** pounds, shillings, and pence (Latin, *librae, solidi, denarii*).

LSD (no periods), **1.** landing ship, dock. **2.** lysergic acid diethylamide: *LSD ... is a chemical that produces hallucinations and delusions in healthy persons like those in mental sickness* (Science News Letter).

L.S.E. or **LSE** (no periods), London School of Economics.

LSM (no periods), landing ship, medium.

L.S.O. or **LSO** (no periods), London Symphony Orchestra.

L.S.S., Lifesaving Service.

l.s.t., local standard time.

LST (no periods), landing ship, tank.

l.t., an abbreviation for the following:
1. lawn tennis.
2. left tackle (in football).
3. local time.
4. long ton.
5. low tension.

Lt., lieutenant.

L.T.A., Lawn Tennis Association.

Lt. Col., lieutenant colonel.

Lt. Comdr., lieutenant commander.

Ltd. or **ltd.,** *Especially British.* limited.

Lt. Gen., lieutenant general.

Lt. Gov., lieutenant governor.

LtH (no periods), luteotrophin.

lthr., leather.

ltr., letter.

Lu (no period), lutetium (chemical element).
lu·au (lü′ou), *n.* a feast, especially in Hawaii, generally held outdoors, with roast pig as the main dish: *An Hawaiian luau, the island feast featuring suckling pig roasted in a pit will be catered for large groups by the newly formed party division* (New York Times). [< Hawaiian *lū'au*]
lub., lubricate.
lub·bard (lub′ərd), *Archaic.* —*n.* a lubber. —*adj.* lubberly; loutish. [alteration of *lubber*]
lub·ber (lub′ər), *n.* **1.** a big, clumsy, stupid fellow; lout: *the rude tricks of an overgrown lubber* (William Godwin). **2.** an inexperienced or clumsy sailor: *He swore woundily at the lieutenant, and called him ... swab and lubber* (Tobias Smollett).
—*adj.* loutish; clumsy; stupid; coarse.
[Middle English *lober.* Compare dialectal Swedish *lubber* fat, lazy fellow.] —**Syn.** *n.* **1.** dolt, bumpkin.
lub·ber·land (lub′ər land′), *n.* any land or place of delightful idleness.
Lub·ber·land (lub′ər land′), *n.* an imaginary land, the paradise of lazy lubbers.
lub·ber·li·ness (lub′ər lē nis), *n.* the state or condition of being lubberly; clumsiness.
lub·ber·ly (lub′ər lē), *adj.* **1.** loutish; clumsy; stupid. **2.** awkward in the work of a sailor: *Such was Rope Yarn; of all land-lubbers the most lubberly and most miserable* (Herman Melville). —*adv.* in a lubberly manner; clumsily. —**Syn.** *adj.* **1.** bungling, gawky.
lubber's hole, an opening in the platform or top at the head of a lower mast, through which an inexperienced sailor may pass, while an expert seaman goes around the outside.
lubber's line, mark, or **point,** *Nautical.* a vertical line on the forward inner surface of a compass bowl in line with the bow, which indicates the direction in which the ship's head is swinging, to assist the helmsman in keeping course at sea.
lube (lüb), *n.*, or **lube oil,** heavy petroleum oil used to lubricate machinery: *Cleaning and relubricating with a thinner lube is called for* (Roy Hoopes). [short for *lubricating oil*]
lu·bra (lü′brə), *n. Australian.* a female aborigine; gin.
lu·bric (lü′brik), *adj. Archaic.* smooth and slippery: *This lubric and adult'rate age* (John Dryden). [< Latin *lūbricus* slippery]
lu·bri·cal (lü′brə kəl), *adj. Archaic.* lubric.
lu·bri·cant (lü′brə kənt), *n.* oil, grease, etc., for putting on parts of machines that slide or move against one another, to make them smooth and slippery so that they will work easily: *We cannot eliminate internal friction, but we do reduce it to a controllable degree by the use of friction reducing lubricants* (Automotive Encyclopedia). —*adj.* lubricating.
lu·bri·cate (lü′brə kāt), *v.t.*, **-cat·ed, -cat·ing.** **1.** to make (machinery) smooth and easy to work by putting on oil, grease, etc. **2.** to make slippery or smooth; expedite: *Dinner lubricates business* (Lord Stowell). [< Latin *lūbricāre* (with English *-ate*[1]) < *lūbricus* slippery]
lu·bri·ca·tion (lü′brə kā′shən), *n.* **1.** a lubricating or oiling. **2.** a being lubricated or oiled.
lu·bri·ca·tion·al (lü′brə kā′shə nəl), *adj.* of or having to do with lubrication: *An automatic lubricational oil pump is fitted at the end of the camshaft* (Westminster Gazette).
lu·bri·ca·tive (lü′brə kā′tiv), *adj.* having the property of lubricating.
lu·bri·ca·tor (lü′brə kā′tər), *n.* **1.** a person or thing that lubricates. **2.** a device for oiling machinery. **3.** a lubricating substance; lubricant.
lu·bri·cious (lü brish′əs), *adj.* lubricous.
lu·bric·i·ty (lü bris′ə tē), *n.*, *pl.* **-ties.** **1.** slipperiness; oily smoothness: *this ... lubricity of all objects, which lets them slip through our fingers then when we clutch hardest* (Emerson). **2.** shiftiness; unsteadiness. **3.** lasciviousness; lewdness; wantonness. [< Late Latin *lūbricitās* < Latin *lūbricus* slippery] —**Syn.** **2.** instability, elusiveness.
lu·bri·cous (lü′brə kəs), *adj.* **1.** slippery; smooth; slimy; oily. **2.** shifty; unstable; elusive. **3.** wanton; lewd. [< Latin *lūbricus* (with English *-ous*)]
lu·bri·fy (lü′brə fī), *v.t.*, **-fied, -fy·ing.** to make slippery or smooth; lubricate.
Lu·ca·lox (lü′kə loks), *n. Trademark.* a synthetic alumina ceramic of excellent clarity, similar to the ruby and sapphire.
Lu·ca·ni·an (lü kā′nē ən), *n.* an inhabitant of Lucania, an ancient region in southern Italy: *The fierce Lucanians swept down and conquered the Greeks around 400 B.C.* (Time). —*adj.* of or having to do with Lucania or its people.
lu·carne (lü kärn′), *n.* an opening in a roof, such as a skylight or dormer window. [< Old French *lucane*, perhaps < a Germanic word]
luce (lüs), *n.* a pike (fish), especially when fully grown. [< Old French *lus, luis* < Late Latin *lūcius*]
lu·cen·cy (lü′sən sē), *n.* brilliance; luminosity.
lu·cent (lü′sənt), *adj. Archaic.* **1.** shining; bright; luminous: *the sun's lucent orb* (Milton). **2.** letting the light through; clear. [< Latin *lūcēns, -entis,* present participle of *lūcēre* to shine] —**lu′cent·ly,** *adv.*
lu·cern (lü sėrn′), *n.* lucerne.
lu·cerne (lü sėrn′), *n. Especially British.* alfalfa. [< French *luzerne,* or *lucerne* < Provençal *luzerno,* ultimately < Latin *lūx, lūcis* light[1], related to *lūcēre* to shine (because of the shiny appearance of the grains)]
lu·ces (lü′sēz), *n.* luxes; a plural of **lux.**
Lu·chu·an (lü chü′ən), *n.* a native or inhabitant of the Ryukyu Islands.
lu·cid (lü′sid), *adj.* **1.** easy to follow or understand: *a lucid explanation. The tangled weights and measures of old France gave place to the simple and lucid decimal system* (H.G. Wells). **2.** bright; shining. **3.** sane; rational: *An insane person sometimes has lucid intervals.* **4.** transparent; clear: *a lucid stream.* [< Latin *lūcidus* < *lūx, lūcis* light[1], related to *lūcēre* to shine] —**lu′cid·ly,** *adv.* —**lu′cid·ness,** *n.* —**Syn.** **1.** plain. **2.** luminous. **4.** pellucid, limpid.
lu·cid·i·ty (lü sid′ə tē), *n.* clearness, especially of thought, expression, perception, etc.; lucid quality or condition: *The lucidity and accuracy of French had, both in style and in thought, served him well* (New Yorker).
Lu·ci·fer (lü′sə fər), *n.* **1.** the chief rebel angel who was cast out of heaven; Satan; the Devil: *When he falls, he falls like Lucifer, Never to hope again* (Shakespeare). *Lucifer ... brighter once amid the host Of angels, than that star the stars among* (Milton). **2.** *Poetic.* the planet Venus when it is the morning star. [< Latin *lūcifer* the morning star, (literally) light-bringing < *lūx, lūcis* light[1] + *ferre* bring]
lu·ci·fer (lü′sə fər), *n.*, or **lucifer match,** a match that lights by friction. [< *Lucifer*]
lu·cif·er·ase (lü sif′ə rās), *n. Biochemistry.* an enzyme found in the cells of luminescent organisms, which acts on luciferin to produce luminosity.
Lu·ci·fer·i·an[1] (lü′sə fir′ē ən), *adj.* like Lucifer; evil; diabolic: *His Luciferian will to power raged in tiny Dublin like a demon in a bottle* (Time). [< *Lucifer* + *-ian*]
Lu·ci·fer·i·an[2] (lü′sə fir′ē ən), *adj.* of or having to do with a sect of the 300's A.D. which broke from the Christian church because of its leniency toward Arians who repented of their heresy. —*n.* an adherent of this sect. [< *Lucifer,* bishop of Cagliari, who founded the sect + *-ian*]
lu·cif·er·in (lü sif′ər in), *n. Biochemistry.* a protein found in the cells of luminescent organisms, as fireflies, which, when acted on by luciferase, undergoes oxidation producing heatless light.
lu·cif·er·ous (lü sif′ər əs), *adj.* **1.** bringing illumination or insight; illuminating. **2.** that brings, conveys, or emits light.
lu·cif·ic (lü sif′ik), *adj.* producing light. [< Late Latin *lūcificus* < Latin *lūx, lūcis* light[1]]
lu·cif·u·gous (lü sif′yə gəs), *adj.* shunning the light, as bats, cockroaches, etc. [< Latin *lūcifugus* (with English *-ous*) < *lūx, lūcis* light[1] + *fugere* to flee]
Lu·ci·na (lü sī′nə), *n. Roman Mythology.* the goddess of childbirth, identified with Juno or sometimes Diana.
Lu·cite (lü′sīt), *n. Trademark.* a clear plastic compound used for airplane windows, ornaments, etc.: *He has devised the tools for brain surgery out of methyl methacrylate (Lucite), a transparent, light plastic* (Science News Letter). [< Latin *lūx, lūcis* light[1], related to *lūcēre* to shine + English *-ite*[1]]
lu·ci·vee (lü′sə vē), *n. U.S. Dialect and Canada.* the Canada lynx. [apparently < French *loup cervier* < Latin *lupus cervārius;* see LOUP-CERVIER]
luck (luk), *n.* **1.** that which seems to happen or come to one by chance; fortune; chance: *Luck favored me, and I won. There is no luck in literary reputation* (Emerson). **2.** good luck: *to wish one luck, to have luck in fishing. She gave me a penny for luck. She had the luck to win first prize.* **3.** some object on which good fortune is supposed to depend.
down on one's luck, *Informal.* having bad luck; unlucky: *He would not hesitate to give money to anyone down on his luck* (London Times).
in luck, having good luck; fortunate; lucky: *I am in luck today; I found a dollar.*
out of luck, having bad luck; unlucky: *In the big storm, the fishermen were out of luck.*
push one's luck, *Informal.* to carry one's advantage too far: *Would you, I asked, pushing my luck, admit His Imperial Majesty Haile Selassie, Emperor of Ethiopia?* (Punch).
try one's luck, to see what one can do: *He tried his luck at various jobs until he found one that suited him.*
worse luck, unfortunately: *Worse luck, it rained.*
—*v.i., v.t. Informal.* to come by sheerest chance or luck: *I will admit that a number of them have lucked in on me while I was backing good, sensible 30-1 shots, but I have never let that affect my basic thinking about horse racing* (New Yorker).
[< Middle Dutch *gheluc,* earlier *luk* or Middle Low German *gelucke*]
—**Syn.** *n.* **2.** success.
luck·ie (luk′ē), *n.* lucky[2].
luck·i·ly (luk′ə lē), *adv.* by good luck.
luck·i·ness (luk′ē nis), *n.* the quality or condition of being lucky; fortunateness.
luck·less (luk′lis), *adj.* having or bringing bad luck; unlucky; unfortunate. —**luck′less·ly,** *adv.* —**luck′less·ness,** *n.*
luck penny, *British.* **1.** a penny or other coin kept or given to bring good luck. **2.** a small sum given back for luck by the seller to the purchaser in a business transaction.
luck·y[1] (luk′ē), *adj.*, **luck·i·er, luck·i·est.** having or bringing good luck: *a person's lucky star, a lucky trade, a lucky meeting.* —**Syn.** happy. See **fortunate.**
luck·y[2] (luk′ē), *n.*, *pl.* **luck·ies.** *Scottish.* **1.** a familiar name for an elderly woman, especially a grandmother. **2.** a woman of any age; a wife, mistress, etc. [perhaps < *lucky*[1]]
lucky dip, *British.* a grab bag: *The BBC's thriller series is something of a lucky dip* (Punch).
lu·cra·tive (lü′krə tiv), *adj.* bringing in money; profitable: *a lucrative profession, a lucrative investment.* [< Latin *lucrātīvus* < *lūcrārī* to gain < *lucrum* gain] —**lu′cra·tive·ly,** *adv.* —**lu′cra·tive·ness,** *n.* —**Syn.** gainful, remunerative.
lu·cre (lü′kər), *n.* money considered as a bad influence or degrading; gain viewed as a low motive for action: *not greedy of filthy lucre* (I Timothy 3:3). [< Latin *lucrum* gain] —**Syn.** pelf, mammon.
Lu·cre·tian (lü krē′shən), *adj.* having to do with Lucretius (about 94–about 55 B.C.), the Roman poet and Epicurean philosopher, or with his philosophical doctrines, set forth in a didactic poem, *De Rerum Natura* (*On the Nature of Things*).
lu·cu·brate (lü′kyə brāt), *v.i.*, **-brat·ed, -brat·ing.** **1.** to work by artificial light. **2.** to produce lucubrations; discourse learnedly in writing. [< Latin *lūcubrāre* (with English *-ate*[1]) work at night, related to *lūcēre* to shine]
lu·cu·bra·tion (lü′kyə brā′shən), *n.* **1.** study carried on late at night: *the well-earned harvest of ... many a midnight lucubration* (Edward Gibbon). **2.** laborious study: *Absolute measure, which always inspired the lucubrations of the Greeks, was never popular in Greek trade* (Atlantic). **3.** a learned or carefully written production, especially one that is labored and dull.
lu·cu·bra·tor (lü′kyə brā′tər), *n.* **1.** a person who studies late at night. **2.** a person who produces lucubrations.
lu·cule (lü′kyül), *n. Astronomy.* any of certain small luminous spots on the sun's surface. [< French *lucule* < Medieval Latin *lucula* (diminutive) < Latin *lūx, lūcis* light[1]]
lu·cu·lent (lü′kyə lənt), *adj.* **1.** (of evidence, arguments, or explanations) clear; convincing; lucid. **2.** full of light; bright; luminous. [< Latin *lūculentus* < *lūx, lūcis* light[1]] —**lu′cu·lent·ly,** *adv.*

Lu·cul·lan (lü kul′ən), *adj.* Lucullian: *The last time that we visited him he produced, alone, a Lucullan tea* (London Times).

Lu·cul·li·an (lü kul′ē ən), *adj.* rich; magnificent; luxurious: *a Lucullian feast.* [< *Lucullus,* about 110-57 B.C., a Roman general famous for wealth and luxury + English *-ian*]

lu·cu·mo (lü′kyə mō), *n., pl.* **lu·cu·mos, lu·cu·mo·nes** (lü′kyə mō′nēz). a prince or ruling noble with priestly functions among the ancient Etruscans. [< Latin *Lucumō*]

lu·cu·mo·ny (lü′kyə mō′nē), *n., pl.* **-nies.** the district or state under the rule of a lucumo. [< French *lucumonie* < Latin *Lucumō* lucumo]

lu·cus a non lu·cen·do (lü′kəs ā non lü sen′dō), *Latin.* **1.** a grove, so called from not being light. **2.** an absurd derivation; illogical reasoning.

Lu·cy Ston·er (lü′sē stō′nər), a woman who believes in keeping and using her maiden name after marriage: *Whoever thought a Lucy Stoner would be so girlishly sensitive as Jane Grant about being called a "newshen"?* (Time). [< *Lucy Stone,* 1818–1893, an American woman suffragist]

Lu·cy's warbler (lü′sēz), a gray and white warbler with chestnut on the crown and base of tail, found in the southwestern United States and Mexico.

lud (lud), *n., interj.* a shortened or vulgar form of *lord: Lud, this news . . . puts me all in a flutter* (Oliver Goldsmith).

Lud·dism (lud′iz əm), *n.* the principles and practices of the Luddites.

Lud·dite (lud′īt), *n.* a member of any of the organized bands of workmen in England (1811–16) who set about destroying manufacturing equipment because they believed that it lessened employment. —*adj.* of or having to do with the Luddites: *Luddite riots.* [perhaps < Ned *Lud,* a weak-minded person, who destroyed equipment in a Leicestershire village about 1779 + *-ite*[1]]

lu·di·crous (lü′də krəs), *adj.* amusingly absurd; ridiculous: *the ludicrous acts of a clown.* [< Latin *lūdicrus* (with English *-ous*) < *lūdus* sport] —**lu′di·crous·ly,** *adv.* —**lu′di·crous·ness,** *n.* —**Syn.** laughable, droll, comical.

lu·do (lü′dō), *n. Especially British.* a game resembling pachisi, played with dice and counters on a special board. [< Latin *lūdo* I play]

lud·wig·i·a (lud wij′ē ə), *n.* any of a group of small herbs of the evening-primrose family, found in swamps, etc., of temperate and warm regions. [< New Latin *Ludwigia* the genus name < Christian G. *Ludwig,* 1709–1773, professor of Botany at Leipzig, Germany]

lu·es (lü′ēz), *n.* syphilis. [< Latin *luēs, luis* plague < *luere* loosen, decompose]

lu·et·ic (lü et′ik), *adj.* having to do with lues; affected with lues; syphilitic. [< Latin *luēs* plague; patterned on *herpetic*]

lu·e·tin (lü′ə tin), *n. Medicine.* a preparation made from the dead microorganisms of syphilis, used in diagnostic tests for syphilis. [< *luet*(ic) + *-in*]

luff (luf), *v.i.* to turn the bow of a ship toward the wind; sail into the wind: *Now, my hearty, luff* (Robert Louis Stevenson). [< noun]
—*n.* **1.** the act of turning the bow of a ship toward the wind. **2.** the forward edge of a fore-and-aft sail. **3.** the fullest and broadest part of a ship's bow. Also, **loof.**
[Middle English *lof,* perhaps < Dutch *loef*]

luf·fa (luf′ə), *n.* loofah.

Luft·brück·e (lůft′bryk′ə), *n. German.* **1.** the airlift to feed and supply West Berlin in 1948–49: *A towering abstract sculpture . . . was put up in 1950, to commemorate the Luftbrücke, or airlift, with which the West had broken the Russian blockade of Berlin the year before* (New Yorker). **2.** (literally) an air bridge.

Luft·waf·fe (lůft′väf′ə), *n. German.* the German air force, especially under the Nazis in World War II.

lug[1] (lug), *v.,* **lugged, lug·ging,** *n.* —*v.t.* **1.** to pull along or carry with effort; drag: *The children lugged home a big Christmas tree.* **2.** to introduce irrelevantly or without appropriateness: *He always had to lug in some reference to his ancestors.* **3.** (of a ship) to carry (sail) beyond the limit of safety in a strong wind. —*v.i.* **1.** to pull; tug. **2.** (in a horse race) to veer or bear toward the rail: *Mark-Ye-Well, who was ridden by Arcaro, lugged toward the rails and got himself boxed in* (New Yorker).
—*n.* **1.** the act of pulling or carrying something heavy; a rough pull. **2.** *U.S. Informal.* something heavy to be carried, dragged, etc. [perhaps < Scandinavian (compare Swedish *lugga* pull by the hair)]

lug[2] (lug), *n.* **1.** a projecting part used to hold or grip something, as a handle on a pitcher, bowl, etc., or a leather loop on the side of the harness saddle in which the shaft rests. **2.** *Scottish.* the ear. **3.** *Slang.* a clumsy or stupid person. [origin uncertain. Compare Swedish *lugg* forelock.]

lug[3] (lug), *n.* a lugsail. [short for *lugsail;* origin uncertain]

lug[4] (lug), *n.* a lugworm.

Lu·gan·da (lü gan′də), *n.* the language of the Baganda, a tribe that inhabits Buganda, a province of Uganda.

luge (lüzh), *n.* a small coasting sled steered by short iron-pointed sticks, used especially in Switzerland. [< French *luge* < Swiss dialect (Grisons)]

lu·ger[1] or **Lu·ger** (lü′gər), *n.* a popular pistol made in Germany: *We both carried Lugers, which were more fashionable with American troops than American weapons* (New Yorker). [< George *Luger,* a German engineer of the late 1800's]

lug·gage (lug′ij), *n.* **1.** baggage, especially of a traveler or passenger; suitcases and the like: *I left my servant at the railway looking after the luggage* (Dickens). **2.** *British.* the baggage of an army. [< *lug*[1] + *-age*]

lug·gage·less (lug′ij lis), *adj.* without luggage.

luggage van, *British.* a baggage car.

lug·ger[1] (lug′ər), *n.* a boat rigged with lugsails: *In 1952 there were 130 luggers working out of Australian ports* (New York Times). [perhaps < *lug*[3] + *-er*[1]. Compare Dutch *logger.*]

Lugger

lug·ger[2] (lug′ər), *n.* a person who lugs or pulls with effort, especially one who stacks or carries things or loads and unloads trucks, etc., as on a dock or in a warehouse. [< *lug*[1] + *-er*[1]]

lug·gie (lug′ē, lůg′-; lü′gē), *n. Scottish.* a small wooden vessel with a lug (handle).

lug·sail (lug′sāl′; *Nautical* lug′səl), *n.* a four-cornered sail held by a hoisting yard that slants across the mast at one third of its length. [perhaps < *lug*[1] or *lug*[2] + *sail*]

lu·gu·bri·ous (lü gü′brē əs, -gyü′-), *adj.* sad; mournful; sorrowful: *A dog set up a long, lugubrious howl* (Mark Twain). [< Latin *lūgubris* (with English *-ous*) < *lūgēre* mourn] —**lu·gu′bri·ous·ly,** *adv.* —**lu·gu′bri·ous·ness,** *n.* —**Syn.** dismal, doleful, melancholy.

lug·worm (lug′wėrm′,) *n.* a kind of worm that burrows in sand along the seashore; lobworm. Lugworms are large marine polychaete worms having a reduced head and a row of gills in pairs along the back. They are largely used for bait. *Like the earthworm, its counterpart on land, the lugworm passes quantities of soil through its body* (New Yorker). [< *lug*[4] lugworm (compare Dutch *log* slow, heavy) + *worm*]

luke (lük), *adj.* lukewarm; tepid: *Let me have nine penn'orth o' brandy and water luke* (Dickens).

Luke (lük), *n.* **1.** (in the Bible) a physician who was the companion of the Apostle Paul and is traditionally believed to have written the third Gospel and the Acts of the Apostles. **2.** the third book of the New Testament, telling the story of the life of Christ. It is one of the Synoptic Gospels.

luke·warm (lük′wôrm′), *adj.* **1.** neither hot nor cold; moderately warm. **2.** showing little enthusiasm; half-hearted: *a lukewarm supporter, lukewarm obedience.* [perhaps < Middle Dutch *leuk* tepid + English *warm*] —**luke′warm′ly,** *adv.* —**luke′warm′ness,** *n.* —**Syn. 1.** tepid. **2.** indifferent, unconcerned.

luke·warmth (lük′wôrmth′), *n.* lukewarmness.

Lu·ki·ko (lü kē′kō), *n.* the native council or parliament of Buganda, a province of Uganda: *The Colonial Office in London stated yesterday that "encouraging decisions" appeared to have been made by the Lukiko over the matter of negotiations for the return of the exiled Kabaka of Buganda* (London Times). [< a Luganda word]

lu·lab (lü′läb), *n., pl.* **lu·labs, lu·la·bim** (lü lä bēm′). *Judaism.* a green palm branch, with attached boughs of myrtle and willow, used together with the ethrog during the Sukkoth morning services. [< Hebrew *lūlābh*]

lu·lav (lü′lôv, -ləv), *n., pl.* **lu·lavs, lu·la·vim** (lü lô′vim, -lô vēm′). lulab.

lull (lul), *v.t.* **1.** to soothe with sounds or caresses; hush to sleep: *The mother lulled the crying baby.* **2.** to quiet; make peaceful or tranquil: *to lull one's suspicions. The captain lulled our fears.* —*v.i.* to become calm or more nearly calm: *The wind lulled.*
—*n.* **1.** a period of less noise or violence; brief calm: *We ran home during a lull in the storm.* **2.** something which lulls; a lulling sound, etc.: *the lull of falling waters.*
[Middle English *lullen,* probably imitative. Compare Swedish *lulla* lull to sleep, Dutch *lullen.*] —**lull′er,** *n.*
—**Syn.** *n.* **1.** respite.

lul·la·by (lul′ə bī), *n., pl.* **-bies,** *v.,* **-bied, -by·ing.** —*n.* **1.** a song for singing to a child in a cradle; soft song to put a baby to sleep; cradlesong. **2.** any song which soothes to rest: *The bees have hummed their noontide lullaby* (Samuel Rogers). **3.** *Obsolete.* farewell; good night.
—*v.t.* to soothe with a lullaby; sing to sleep.
[< earlier *lulla* < *lull*]

lu·lu[1] (lü′lü), *n. U.S. Slang.* an unusual thing; striking person: *They've just one gap left to fill from last February's floods, but it's a lulu—more than 30 feet deep and over 400 feet long* (Wall Street Journal).

lu·lu[2] (lü′lü), *n. U.S. Slang.* an allowance paid to a legislator in lieu of expenses, which he does not have to itemize: *. . . the redistribution of three committee "plums" in the Senate that carry "lulus"* (New York Times). [reduplication of *lieu*]

lum (lum, lům), *n. Scottish.* a chimney. [origin uncertain]

lu·ma·chel·la (lü′mə kel′ə), *n.* a compact limestone or marble containing fossil shells, which are often iridescent, displaying a variety of brilliant colors. [< Italian *lumachella* (diminutive) < *lumaca* snail]

lum·ba·go (lum bā′gō), *n., pl.* **-gos.** a pain in the muscles of the small of the back and in the loins. It is an acute or chronic disorder often caused by a slipping of the cartilage disk between adjacent vertebrae. [< Late Latin *lumbāgō* < Latin *lumbus* loin]

lum·bar (lum′bər), *adj.* of the loin or loins: *the lumbar region.* —*n.* a lumbar vertebra, artery, nerve, etc. [< New Latin *lumbaris* < Latin *lumbus* loin]

lum·ber[1] (lum′bər), *n.* **1.** *U.S. and Canada.* timber, logs, beams, boards, etc., roughly cut and prepared for use: *The huge quantities of lumber sold annually in the United States come principally from . . . the Southeast and the Pacific Northwest* (World Book Encyclopedia). **2.** household articles no longer in use; old furniture, etc., that takes up room. **3.** useless material: *The bookful blockhead, ignorantly read, With loads of learned lumber in his head* (Alexander Pope).
—*v.i. U.S.* to cut and prepare lumber.
—*v.t.* **1.** to obtain lumber from (land). **2.** to fill up or obstruct by taking space that is wanted for something else: *Empty bottles lumbered the bottom of every closet* (Washington Irving). *Do not lumber up my shelf with your collection of stones and insects.* **3.** to heap together in disorder.
[originally, useless goods, perhaps early variant of *lombard* pawnshop]

lum·ber[2] (lum′bər), *v.i.* **1.** to move along heavily and noisily; roll along with difficulty: *to lumber along like an elephant. The old stagecoach lumbered down the road.* **2.** *Obsolete.* to rumble; make a rumbling noise. —*n.* a rumbling noise. [Middle English *lomeren;* origin uncertain. Compare dialectal Swedish *loma* walk heavily.]

lum·ber·er (lum′bər ər), *n.* a lumberjack.

lum·ber·ing[1] (lum′bər ing, -bring), *n.* the act or business of cutting and preparing timber for use. [< *lumber*[1] + *-ing*[1]]

lum·ber·ing[2] (lum′bər ing, -bring), *adj.* **1.** ponderous in movement; inconveniently bulky: *Air coach passengers on various lines now ride a variety of planes, ranging from lumbering 220-mile-an-hour DC-4's to a sprinkling of Super Constellations* (Wall Street Journal). **2.** *Obsolete.* rumbling. [< *lumber*[2] + *-ing*[2]] —**lum′ber·ing·ly,** *adv.*

lum·ber·jack (lum′bər jak′), *n.* a man whose work is cutting down trees and getting out logs: *Among the hopeful immigrants are four lumberjacks, their wallets bulging after seven hard years in Alaska* (Punch). —*v.i.* to do the work of a lumberjack: *Have hunted crocodiles, panned gold, sailed Pacific, lumberjacked, lectured, broken horses* (London Times).

lumber jacket, a short, straight jacket of heavy wool, leather, etc., worn especially by men and boys outdoors.

lum·ber·ly (lum′bər lē), *adj.* clumsy; lumbering.

lum·ber·man (lum′bər mən), *n., pl.* **-men.** **1.** a lumberjack; logger. **2.** a man whose work is cutting and preparing timber for use. **3.** a man whose business is buying and selling timber or lumber.

lumber mill, a sawmill.

lumber port, a porthole or opening in the bow or stern of a vessel, for use in loading and unloading lumber.

lumber room, a room for lumber, or articles not in use.

lum·ber·yard (lum′bər yärd′), *n. U.S. and Canada.* a place where lumber and building supplies are stored and sold.

lum·bri·cal (lum′brə kəl), *n.* any of four small muscles in either the hand or the foot that help move the fingers or toes. —*adj.* of or having to do with these muscles. [< New Latin *lumbricalis* < Latin *lumbrīcus* (parasitic) worm, earthworm]

lum·bri·ca·lis (lum′brə kā′lis), *n., pl.* **-les** (-lēz). lumbrical.

lum·bri·cid (lum′brə sid), *adj.* lumbricoid.

lum·bri·coid (lum′brə koid), *adj.* **1.** like an earthworm. **2.** of a kind of roundworm common as an intestinal parasite in man. [< New Latin *lumbricoides* the roundworm species < Latin *lumbrīcus;* see LUMBRICAL]

lu·men (lü′mən), *n., pl.* **-mi·na** (-mə nə), **-mens.** **1.** *Physics.* a unit of light, equivalent to the amount of light given out per second, per unit solid angle by a point source of one international candle radiating equally in all directions. It is the unit of luminous flux: *Electric lights today are usually compared by lumens instead of by candle power* (World Book Encyclopedia). **2.** *Anatomy.* the space within a tubular organ, as a blood vessel: *These were then diluted with physiological saline and were injected directly into the lumen of the gizzard of groups of 3-day old white Leghorn chicks* (Science). **3.** *Botany.* the central cavity or space within the wall of a cell. [< Latin *lūmen, -inis* light; opening in a tube]

Lu·mi·con (lü′mə kon), *n. Trademark.* a device that greatly amplifies light without distorting the image.

lu·mi·naire (lü′mə nãr′), *n.* a lighting unit complete with all the necessary parts and accessories such as reflector, socket, etc. [< French *luminaire* < Late Latin *lūminarium;* see LUMINARY]

lu·mi·nal (lü′mə nəl), *adj.* of or belonging to a lumen (defs. 2,3). [< Latin *lūmen, -inis* light[1] + English *-al*[1]]

Lu·mi·nal (lü′mə nəl, -nal), *n. Trademark.* phenobarbital.

lu·mi·nance (lü′mə nəns), *n.* the intensity of light in relation to the area of its source; luminosity: *The sensitivity of the eye to differences in luminance decreases as the luminance increases* (New Scientist).

lu·mi·nant (lü′mə nənt), *adj.* illuminating; luminous. —*n.* an illuminating agent; illuminant.

lu·mi·nar·ist (lü′mə nər ist), *n.* a painter who treats light effectively, or whose color is luminous; luminist.

lu·mi·nar·y (lü′mə ner′ē), *n., pl.* **-nar·ies,** *adj.* —*n.* **1.** the sun, moon, or other light-giving body: *If the earth's orbit were perfectly circular, the earth's movement around the great central luminary would be uniform* (H.J. Bernhard). **2.** a famous person. **3.** an artificial light.
—*adj.* having to do with light.
[< Late Latin *lūminarium* light, lamp < Latin *lūmen, -inis* light[1]]
—**Syn.** *n.* **2.** celebrity, notable.

lu·mine (lü′mən), *v.t.,* **-mined, -min·ing.** *Obsolete.* to light up; illumine. [< Old French *luminer,* learned borrowing from Latin *lūmināre* < *lūmen, -inis* light[1]]

lu·mi·nesce (lü′mə nes′), *v.i.,* **-nesced, -nesc·ing.** to exhibit luminescence: *Green plants were found to luminesce like fireflies, although on a small scale* (Science News Letter).

lu·mi·nes·cence (lü′mə nes′əns), *n.* an emission of light occurring at a temperature below that of incandescent bodies. Luminescence includes phosphorescence and fluorescence, and may result from biological or chemical processes: *The intensity of the luminescence that some rocks give off when heated is an indication of their geologic age* (Science News Letter).

lu·mi·nes·cent (lü′mə nes′ənt), *adj.* **1.** giving out light without being much heated. **2.** having to do with luminescence. [< Latin *lūmen, -inis* light[1] + English *-escent*]

lu·mi·nif·er·ous (lü′mə nif′ər əs), *adj.* producing or transmitting light: *The firefly is a luminiferous insect.* [< Latin *lūmen, -inis* light[1] + English *-ferous*]

lu·mi·nist (lü′mə nist), *n.* a luminarist.

lu·mi·nom·e·ter (lü′mə nom′ə tər), *n.* an instrument for measuring the intensity of illumination.

lu·mi·nos·i·ty (lü′mə nos′ə tē), *n., pl.* **-ties.** **1.** luminous quality or condition. **2.** something luminous; a luminous point or area. **3.** the amount of energy in the form of light emitted by the sun or a star.

lu·mi·nous (lü′mə nəs), *adj.* **1. a.** shining by its own light, as the sun and stars or certain animals and plants that emit light. **b.** emitting a certain amount of light, regardless of its distance: *Many stars are more luminous than the sun.* **2.** full of light; shining; bright: *a luminous sunset.* **3.** easily understood; clear; enlightening: *Goethe's wide and luminous view* (Matthew Arnold); *luminous eloquence* (Macaulay). *The whole performance was luminous and moving* (New York Times). **4.** (of a room) well lighted: *The church of Ashbourne . . . is one of the . . . most luminous that I have seen* (James Boswell). [< Latin *lūminōsus* < *lūmen, -inis* light[1]] —**lu′mi·nous·ly,** *adv.* —**lu′mi·nous·ness,** *n.* —**Syn.** **2.** glowing, effulgent, refulgent. **3.** perspicuous, lucid.

luminous energy, light.

luminous flux, the rate at which light (luminous energy) is transmitted. Its unit is the lumen: *Radiant flux, evaluated with respect to its capacity to evoke the sensation of brightness, is called luminous flux* (Sears and Zemansky).

luminous intensity, a measure of the strength of a source of light, equivalent to the luminous flux given out per unit solid angle in a given direction.

lum·me (lum′ē), *interj. British Slang.* an exclamation of surprise: *Lumme, they're going to charge for going over the bridge* (London Times). [altered pronunciation of (God) *love me*]

lum·mox (lum′əks), *n. Informal.* an awkward, stupid person: *A thoughtful weighing of all aspects would surely convince them that the big lummoxes get their money's worth out of the silliest purchase* (Saturday Evening Post). [origin uncertain, apparently related to dialectal *lummock* move heavily]

lump[1] (lump), *n.* **1.** a solid mass of no particular shape: *a lump of coal; a great lump of beeswax . . . which weighed above half a hundred weight* (Daniel Defoe). **2.** a swelling; bump: *There is a lump on my head where I bumped it.* **3.** a lot; mass; heap: *Colonel Harding owed him a lump of money* (Richard Blackmore). **4.** *Informal.* a stupid person. **5.** *Informal.* a big, sturdy person: *a brave lump of a boy* (Samuel Lover). *When we were lumps of lads* (Hall Caine). **6.** *Obsolete.* a collection; clump; cluster.

a lump in one's throat, a feeling of pity, sorrow, or other emotion that makes one unable, or as if unable, to swallow: *The sad story gave her a lump in her throat.*

in the lump, in the mass; as a whole: *He praises or dispraises in the lump* (Joseph Addison).

lumps, *U.S. Slang.* a beating; punishment: *The Sooners had . . . regularly taken their lumps from the likes of Texas (7-40)* (Time).
—*v.t.* **1.** to make lumps of, on, or in. **2.** to put together; deal with in a mass or as a whole: *to lump all of one's effort in a single project. We will lump all our expenses.*
—*v.i.* **1.** to form into a lump or lumps: *The cornstarch lumped because we cooked it too fast. The low-humidity atmosphere keeps the sugar from lumping* (Wall Street Journal). **2.** to move heavily. **3.** to rise in a lump or lumps. **4.** to act as a lumper or longshoreman.
—*adj.* **1.** in lumps; in a lump: *lump coal, lump sugar.* **2.** including a number of items: *a lump sum to pay all expenses.*
[Middle English *lumpe.* Compare earlier Dutch *lompe* mass, chunk, piece.]

lump[2] (lump), *v.t. Informal.* to put up with; endure: *If you don't like what I am doing, you can lump it.* [American English; origin uncertain]

lum·pen (lum′pən), *adj.* of, belonging to, or characteristic of the lumpenproletariat: *a lumpen intellectual.*

lum·pen·pro·le·tar·i·at (lum′pən prō′lə-tãr′ē ət), *n.* the section of the proletariat that lacks class-consciousness: *These are not the real working class. These are the lumpenproletariat, tainted by petty-bourgeois ideology* (New Yorker). [< German *Lumpenproletariat* < *Lumpen*(volk) rabble (< *Lump* ragamuffin < *Lumpen* rag) + *Proletariat* proletariat]

lump·er (lum′pər), *n.* **1.** a laborer employed to load and unload ships; longshoreman. **2.** a person who lumps things together or deals with things in the lump or mass.

lump·fish (lump′fish′), *n., pl.* **-fish·es** or (*collectively*) **-fish.** a clumsy, spiny-finned fish of the northern Atlantic, with a high, ridged back and a sucker on the belly formed by the ventral fins; lumpsucker.

lump-head (lump′hed′), *n. Informal.* a thick-headed person; blockhead.

lump·i·ly (lum′pə lē), *adv.* in a lumpy manner; in lumps.

lump·i·ness (lum′pē′nis), *n.* a being lumpy.

lump·ing·ly (lum′ping lē), *adv.* heavily; clumsily.

lump·ish (lum′pish), *adj.* **1.** like a lump; heavy and clumsy: *The six-story blocks of flats are lumpish, with ponderously silly little balconies* (Wall Street Journal). **2.** heavy and dull; stupid; stolid: *She expects to be paid off . . . for her lumpish efforts in behalf of the party* (Harper's). **3.** *Obsolete.* low-spirited. —**lump′ish·ly,** *adv.* —**lump′ish·ness,** *n.* —**Syn.** **1.** unwieldy. **2.** lumbering.

lumps (lumps), *n.pl.* See under **lump**[1], *n.*

lump·suck·er (lump′suk′ər), *n.* a lumpfish.

lump sum, an amount of money paid all at one time, especially when it represents the total cost of a purchase or service.

lump·y (lum′pē), *adj.,* **lump·i·er, lump·i·est.** **1.** full of lumps: *lumpy gravy, lumpy sugar.* **2.** covered with lumps: *lumpy ground.* **3.** heavy and clumsy: *a lumpy animal.* **4.** rough; choppy. —**Syn.** **3.** lumpish.

lumpy jaw, actinomycosis, a disease of the jaws in cattle and hogs.

Lu·mumb·ist (lə mum′bist), *n.* a follower of Patrice Lumumba, 1925-1961, first prime minister of the Congo (the former Belgian Congo), or of his policies. —*adj.* of or having to do with Lumumbists.

lu·na (lü′nə), *n.* **1.** (in heraldry) argent, in the blazonry of sovereign princes. **2.** *Obsolete.* silver. [< Latin *lūna* moon (because of the silvery light)]

Lu·na (lü′nə), *n.* **1.** the Roman goddess of the moon. **2.** the moon.

lu·na·cy (lü′nə sē), *n., pl.* **-cies.** **1.** insanity, especially intermittent insanity, formerly supposed to be brought about by the changes of the moon: *In one of these fits of lunacy or distraction . . . I fell down, and struck my face* (Daniel Defoe). **2.** extreme folly: *It is lunacy to cross the Atlantic in a rowboat.*

luna moth or **Luna moth,** a large North American moth having light-green wings with a crescent-shaped spot on each wing and a long tail on each hind wing.

lu·nar (lü′nər), *adj.* **1.** of the moon: *lunar mountains.* **2.** like the moon. **3.** of or containing silver. **4.** pale or pallid: *Even the lustre of Partridge [in "Tom Jones"] is pallid and lunar beside the noontide glory of Micawber* (Algernon Charles Swinburne). [< Latin *lūnāris* < *lūna* moon]

lunar caustic, fused silver nitrate, prepared in sticks for use in cauterizing. *Formula:* $AgNO_3$

lunar cycle, the Metonic cycle.

lunar day, the time it takes the moon to make one rotation on its axis: *Tidal rhythms are related to the lunar day of 24 hours, 50 minutes* (Science News Letter).

lunar eclipse, the total or partial cutting off of the light of the full moon by the earth's shadow. It occurs when the sun, earth, and moon are in, or almost in, a straight line. See picture under **eclipse.**

lu·nar·i·an (lü nãr′ē ən), *n.* **1.** a student of lunar phenomena. **2.** a supposed inhabitant of the moon.

lu·nar·i·um (lü nãr′ē əm), *n.* an instrument representing the phases and motions of the moon. [< New Latin *lunarium* < Latin *lūnāris* lunar]

Lunar Module or **Lunar Excursion Module,** a self-contained unit that is part of a spacecraft, designed to function as an exploratory landing vehicle on the moon. *Abbrev.:* LM or LEM

lunar month, the interval between one new moon and the next, about 29½ days: *During the lunar month, the moon travels eastwardly on the celestial sphere* (H.J. Bernhard).

lunar probe, 1. the launching of a space vehicle which passes near the moon and records information about it. **2.** the space vehicle thus launched.

lunar rainbow, moonbow.

lu·na·ry[1] (lü′nər ē), *adj.* lunar.

lu·na·ry[2] (lü′nər ē), *n., pl.* **-ries. 1.** honesty, a European garden herb of the mustard family. **2.** moonwort (def. 1). [< Medieval Latin *lunaria* < Latin *lūna* moon]

lunar year, a period of 12 lunar months, about 354⅓ days.

lu·nate (lü′nāt), *adj.* **1.** crescent-shaped; luniform. **2.** *Anatomy.* of a crescent-shaped bone of the human wrist, in the proximal row of carpal bones. *—n.* the lunate bone. [< Latin *lūnātus*, past participle of *lūnāre* to bend into a crescent < *lūna* moon] **—lu′nate·ly,** *adv.*

lu·nat·ed (lü′nā tid), *adj.* lunate.

lu·na·tic (lü′nə tik), *n.* **1.** an insane person. **2.** an extremely foolish person.
—adj. **1.** insane. **2.** for insane people: *a lunatic asylum.* **3.** extremely foolish; idiotic: *a lunatic policy.*
[< Late Latin *lūnāticus* < Latin *lūna* moon]

lu·nat·i·cal (lü nat′ə kəl), *adj.* lunatic.

lu·nat·i·cal·ly (lü nat′ə klē), *adv.* in a lunatic manner; insanely.

lunatic fringe, *Informal.* those whose zeal in some cause, movement, or ism goes beyond reasonable limits: *the lunatic fringe in all reform movements* (Theodore Roosevelt).

lu·na·tion (lü nā′shən), *n.* the time from one new moon to the next, about 29½ days; lunar month.

lunch (lunch), *n.* **1.** a light meal between breakfast and dinner, or breakfast and supper. **2.** a light meal. **3.** food for a lunch. **4.** *Scottish.* a thick piece; lump: *An' cheese an' bread . . . Was dealt about in lunches* (Robert Burns).
—v.i. to eat lunch: *She . . . made excursions to New York with them, and lunched in fashionable restaurants* (Winston Churchill).
—v.t. Informal. to provide lunch for.
[short for *luncheon*] **—lunch′er,** *n.*

lunch counter, a long table or counter, as in a restaurant, at which persons sit on stools or stand while eating.

lunch·eon (lun′chən), *n.* **1.** lunch. **2.** a formal lunch: *a luncheon of the ladies' auxiliary at the church.* **3.** *Scottish.* a thick piece or lump of food: *Little Benjie . . . was cramming a huge luncheon of pie crust into his mouth* (Scott).
—v.i. to lunch.
[earlier, a lump; origin uncertain, probably influenced by dialectal *nuncheon* lunch]

lunch·eon·ette (lun′chə net′), *n.* **1.** a restaurant that serves lunches or light meals. **2.** a light lunch.

lunch·less (lunch′ləs), *adj.* without lunch; having had no lunch.

lunch·room (lunch′rüm′, -rům′), *n.* **1.** a restaurant in which light meals already prepared or quickly made ready are served. **2.** a room in which to eat lunch, as in a school.

lunch·time (lunch′tīm′), *n.* the time at which lunch is eaten or served.

Lun·da (lün′də, lůn-), *n., pl.* **-da** or **-das. 1.** a member of a Negroid people of the Bantu linguistic family living in the northeastern district of Angola. **2.** the language of this people.

lune[1] (lün), *n.* **1.** anything shaped like a crescent or a half moon. **2.** a crescent-shaped plane figure bounded by two arcs of circles; a figure formed on a sphere by two arcs of circles that enclose a space. [< French *lune* < Latin *lūna* moon]

Lune[1] (def. 2) (shaded area)

lune[2] (lün), *n.* a leash for a hawk. [variant of Middle English *loigne* < Old French < Medieval Latin *longia* halter for a horse < Latin *longus* long]

lunes (lünz), *n.pl. Archaic.* fits of lunacy; tantrums: *Why, woman, your husband is in his old lunes again* (Shakespeare). [< Medieval Latin *luna* (literally) moon; fit of lunacy < Latin *lūna* moon]

lu·net (lü′nit), *n. Obsolete.* lunette.

lu·nette (lü net′), *n.* **1. a.** a crescent-shaped opening or space in a vaulted ceiling, dome, wall, etc. **b.** a painting or other decoration filling this space. **2.** an arched or rounded opening, window, etc., as in a vault: *The top story has no regular windows but, instead, circular lunettes* (New Yorker). **3.** a projecting part of a rampart, shaped like this ∧. **4.** a ring in the back of a towed vehicle, especially the trail of a field gun, to which the towing apparatus is attached. [< Old French *lunette* (diminutive) < *lune* moon, crescent < Latin *lūna*]

Lunettes (def. 1)

lung (lung), *n.* **1.** either one of the pair of breathing organs in vertebrates by means of which the blood receives oxygen and is relieved of carbon dioxide. It is composed of masses of spongy tissue containing many millions of tiny air sacs or alveoli, each with its own network of capillaries. *The two lungs fill almost the whole chest cavity except the part filled by the heart and windpipe* (Beauchamp, Mayfield, and West). **2.** a similar organ in certain invertebrates, such as snails and spiders.

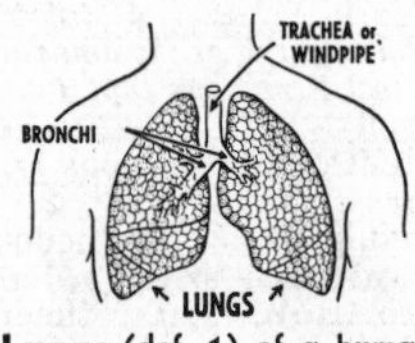

Lungs (def. 1) of a human being

at the top of one's lungs, in the loudest voice possible: *I doggedly plowed through pronoun declensions and conjugated verbs at the top of my lungs* (New Yorker).
[Old English *lungen*]

lun·gan (lung′gən), *n.* longan.

lunge[1] (lunj), *n., v.,* **lunged, lung·ing.** *—n.* **1.** any sudden forward movement; plunge; lurch: *At no time shall I be surprised to see a sudden lunge forward on that front* (H.G. Wells). **2.** a thrust, as with a sword or other weapon.
—v.i., v.t. **1.** to move suddenly forward. **2.** to thrust.
[short for earlier *allonge* < Old French *allonger* to lunge; (originally) to lengthen < *a-* a-[3] + *long* long < Latin *longus*]

lunge[2] (lunj), *n., v.,* **lunged, lung·ing.** *—n.* **1.** a long rope used in training or exercising a horse. **2.** the use of this rope in training a horse. **3.** a ring or circular track for training a horse.
—v.t. to train or exercise (a horse) by the use of a rope or in a ring. *—v.i.* (of a horse) to move in a circle within a ring or at the end of a rope. Also, **longe.**
[< French *longe* a cord, halter < Old French *loigne;* see LUNE[2]]

lunge[3] or **'lunge** (lunj), *n. Informal.* muskellunge.

-lunged, *combining form.* having ____ lungs: *Weak-lunged = having weak lungs.*

lun·gee (lůng′gē), *n.* lungi.

lun·geous (lun′jəs), *adj. Dialect.* **1.** rough or violent (in play). **2.** tending to do harm; spiteful; mischievous. [< *lunge*[1] + *-ous*]

lung·er[1] (lung′ər), *n. Slang.* a person who has tuberculosis of the lungs. [< *lung* + *-er*[2]]

lung·er[2] (lun′jər), *n.* a person who lunges.

lung·fish (lung′fish′), *n., pl.* **-fish·es** or (*collectively*) **-fish.** any of a group of fresh-water fish that can obtain oxygen by gulping air through the mouth as well as by passing water through its gills; dipnoan. Lungfishes have both lunglike air bladders and gills and are found in Australia, Africa, and South America. *The lungfishes were formerly abundant, and there are many fossil forms dating as far back as the Devonian* (John D. Black).

lung·ful (lung′fůl), *n., pl.* **-fuls.** as much as the lungs will hold: *to breathe a lungful of air.*

lun·gi (lůng′gē), *n.* **1.** a long strip of cloth worn as a loincloth in India. **2.** a headdress worn in many styles in the northwest districts of India. Also, **lungee, lungyi.** [< Hindi *lungī*]

lung·worm (lung′wėrm′), *n.* any of several nematode worms parasitic in the lungs of various vertebrates. One kind infests the lungs of sheep.

lung·wort (lung′wėrt′), *n.* **1.** a European plant of the borage family, with small purple flowers and leaves spotted with white. **2.** an American plant of the same family, having blue flowers; Virginia cowslip.

lung·y (lung′ē), *adj. Informal.* having tuberculosis.

lun·gyi (lůng′gē), *n.* lungi.

lu·ni·form (lü′nə fôrm), *adj.* lunate crescent-shaped.

Lu·nik (lü′nik), *n.* a lunar probe: *Lunik I became the first man-made planetoid.* [< Russian *lunnik*]

l'u·nion fait la force (lY nyôN′ fe lȧ fôrs′), *French.* union makes strength (the motto of Belgium).

lu·ni·so·lar (lü′nə sō′lər), *adj. Astronomy.* having to do with the mutual relations or joint action of the moon and sun: *lunisolar attraction.* [< Latin *lūna* moon + English *solar*]

lu·ni·tid·al (lü′nə tī′dəl), *adj.* having to do with the movements of the tide dependent on the moon. [< Latin *lūna* moon + English *tidal*]

lunitidal interval, the time between the transit of the moon and the next lunar high tide.

lunk (lungk), *n. U.S. Informal.* a lunkhead.

lun·ker (lung′kər), *n. Informal.* something uncommonly large of its kind, especially a game fish: *The lunkers [are] . . . much too sophisticated to be caught by the first stray dude from Peoria or Westmount* (Maclean's). [origin uncertain]

lunk·head (lungk′hed′), *n. U.S. Informal.* a blockhead. [American English; origin uncertain]

lunt (lunt, lůnt), *Scottish. —n.* **1.** a slow match. **2.** a torch. **3.** smoke; smoke with flame. **4.** pipe smoke.
set lunt to, to set fire to: *The gardener set lunt to the dead leaves.*
—v.i. **1.** to flame. **2.** to emit smoke. **3.** to smoke a pipe. *—v.t.* **1.** to kindle; light. **2.** to smoke (a pipe).
[< Dutch *lont* a match[1]]

lu·nu·la (lü′nyə lə), *n., pl.* **-lae** (-lē). **1.** a crescent-shaped mark, spot, etc., especially such a white mark at the base of the human fingernail. **2.** a lune. [< Latin *lūnula* (diminutive) < *lūna* moon]

lu·nu·lar (lü′nyə lər), *adj.* having to do with a lune or lunula; crescent-shaped.

lu·nu·late (lü′nyə lāt, -lit), *adj.* **1.** marked with crescent-shaped spots. **2.** crescent-shaped.

lu·nule (lü′nyül), *n.* lunula.

lu·nu·let (lü′nyə lit), *n. Zoology.* a small crescent-shaped mark; lunula.

lun·y (lü′nē), *adj.,* **lun·i·er, lun·i·est,** *n., pl.* **lun·ies.** loony.

Lu·o (lü ō′), *n., pl.* **Lu·o. 1.** a member of one of the principal Negro tribes in Kenya. **2.** this tribe. **3.** their Sudanic language.

Lu·per·cal (lü′pər kal), *n.* singular of **Lupercalia.**

Lu·per·ca·li·a (lü′pər kā′lē ə), *n.pl.* an ancient Roman fertility festival celebrated on February 15 in honor of Lupercus. Women were struck with thongs to insure easy childbirth.

Lu·per·ca·li·an (lü′pər kā′lē ən), *adj.* of or having to do with the Lupercalia.

Lu·per·ci (lü pėr′sī), *n.pl.* the priests of Lupercus or Faunus.

Lu·per·cus (lü pėr′kəs), *n.* a Roman rural god, the protector of the flocks, identified with Faunus and Pan.

Lu·pi (lü′pī), *n.* genitive of **Lupus.**

lu·pine[1] or **lu·pin** (lü′pən), *n.* **1.** any of a large group of plants of the pea family, that have long spikes of flowers, radiating clusters of grayish, hairy leaflets, and flat pods with bean-shaped seeds. It is grown for its showy flowers and as a food and cover crop. **2.** the seeds, often used for food. [< Latin *lupīnus,* or *lupīnum* lupine[2]]

lu·pine[2] (lü′pīn), *adj.* **1.** wolflike; fierce. **2.** related to the wolf. [< Latin *lupīnus* < *lupus* wolf] —**Syn. 1.** wolfish, savage.

lu·pu·lin (lü′pyə lin), *n.* **1.** a fine, yellow powder consisting of the small, round glands found on the stipules and fruit of hops, formerly used as an aromatic bitter and a sedative. **2.** a crystalline substance regarded as the bitter principle of the hop. [American English < Medieval Latin *lupulus* the hop (diminutive) < Latin *lupus* + English *-in*]

lu·pus (lü′pəs), *n.* a skin disease caused by the tubercle bacillus, that often scars the face. [< Medieval Latin *lupus* < Latin, wolf (apparently from its rapid eating away of the affected part)]

Lu·pus (lü′pəs), *n., genitive* **Lu·pi.** a southern constellation near Centaurus. [< Latin *Lupus* (originally) wolf]

lupus er·y·them·a·to·sus (er′ə them′ə-tō′sis), a disease that attacks the skin and connective tissues, resulting in a condition similar to rheumatoid arthritis and often in its acute form leading to disability and death.

lupus vul·ga·ris (vul gãr′is), lupus.

lur (lůr), *n.* a large, curved, bronze trumpet of Scandinavia, used in prehistoric times: *From the Bronze Age are a pair of spiraling, S-shaped lurs that represent two of the world's earliest wind instruments* (Science News Letter). [< Scandinavian (compare Old Icelandic *lūthr* trumpet)]

lurch[1] (lėrch), *n.* a sudden leaning or roll to one side, like that of a ship, a car, or a staggering person: *The car gave a lurch and upset.* —*v.i.* to lean or roll suddenly to one side; make a lurch: *The wounded man lurched forward.* —**Syn.** *v.i.* pitch, stagger, sway, lunge.

lurch[2] (lėrch), *n.* **1.** a condition in which one player in certain games, as cribbage, scores nothing or is badly beaten. **2.** a game ending in this way.

leave in the lurch, to leave in a helpless condition or difficult situation: *Dutton . . . a debauched fellow . . . leaving Win in the lurch, ran away with another man's bride* (Tobias Smollett).

[< French *lourche,* name of a game]

lurch[3] (lėrch), *v.t.* **1.** to catch (game) using a lurcher. **2.** *Archaic.* **a.** to prevent (a person) from obtaining a fair share of food, profit, etc., by getting a start before him. **b.** to cheat; rob. **3.** *Obsolete.* to pilfer; steal. —*v.i. British Dialect.* to lurk; prowl; sneak. [variant of *lurk*]

lurch·er (lėr′chər), *n.* **1.** a prowler; petty thief; poacher. **2.** a kind of crossbred hunting dog much used by poachers.

lurch·ing·ly (lėr′ching lē), *adv.* in a lurching or staggering manner.

lur·dan or **lur·dane** (lėr′dən), *Archaic.* —*n.* a lazy, stupid person; worthless loafer: *A fine thing it would be for me . . . to be afraid of a fat lurdane* (Scott). —*adj.* lazy; worthless: *lurdane knights* (Tennyson). [< Old French *lourdin* < *lourd* heavy]

lure (lůr), *n., v.,* **lured, lur·ing.** —*n.* **1.** attraction: *the lure of the sea. Monarchs, whom the lure of honour draws* (William Cowper); *that grand lure in the eyes of the savage, a pocket mirror* (Washington Irving). **2.** a decoy or bait, especially an artificial bait used in fishing: *Mr. Eisenhower asked the sailor if he had ever tried deep-sea fishing with an artificial lure instead of bait* (Newsweek). **3.** a bunch of feathers, often with meat attached, tossed or swung at the end of a long cord or thong, used as a decoy in falconry to recall a hawk to its perch. **4.** a bulb or tassellike process dangling over the head from the first dorsal ray of an angler or related fish.

—*v.t.* **1.** to lead away or into something by arousing desire; attract; tempt: *Bees are lured by the scent of flowers. Pixies; don't go near 'em, child; they'll lure you on, Lord knows where* (Henry Kingsley). **2.** to attract with a bait: *We lured the fox into a trap.* **3.** to recall (a hawk) with a lure.

[< Old French *leurre* < Germanic (compare Middle High German *luoder* bait)] —**lur′er,** *n.*

—**Syn.** *v.t.* **1. Lure, allure, entice** mean to attract or tempt. **Lure,** commonly in a bad sense, means to tempt by rousing desire and usually to lead into something bad or not to one's advantage: *The hope of high profits lured him into questionable dealings.* **Allure,** seldom in a bad sense, means to tempt by appealing to the senses and feelings and by offering pleasure or advantage: *Hawaii allures many tourists.* **Entice,** in a good or bad sense, means to tempt by appealing to hopes and desires and by using persuasion: *We enticed the kitten from the tree.*

lure·ment (lůr′mənt), *n.* allurement.

Lu·rex (lůr′eks), *n. Trademark.* a metallic fiber used in clothing, upholstery, etc.

lu·rid (lůr′id), *adj.* **1. a.** lighted up with a red or fiery glare: *lurid flashes of lightning. The sky was lurid with the flames and smoke of the burning city.* **b.** glaring in brightness or color: *a lurid red; a cheap lurid print* (Thomas B. Aldrich). **2.** terrible; sensational; startling; ghastly: *lurid crimes.* **3.** pale and dismal in color; wan and sallow. **4.** *Biology.* dirty brown. [< Latin *lūridus* pale yellow, ghastly] —**lu′rid·ly,** *adv.* —**lu′rid·ness,** *n.*

lur·ing·ly (lůr′ing lē), *adv.* in a luring or enticing manner.

lurk (lėrk), *v.i.* **1.** to stay about without arousing attention; wait out of sight: *The spy lurked in the shadows.* **2.** to be hidden; be unsuspected or latent: *A cunning politician often lurks under the clerical robe* (Washington Irving). *A fever lurked in my veins* (Charles Brockden Brown). **3.** to move about in a secret and sly manner: *the main thoroughfare . . . by which cook lurks down before daylight to scour her pots and pans* (Thackeray). [Middle English *lurken,* apparently < *louren* lower[2]] —**lurk′er,** *n.* —**lurk′ing·ly,** *adv.*

—**Syn. 1, 3. Lurk, skulk** mean to keep out of sight or move in a secret or furtive way. **Lurk** often but not always suggests an evil purpose: *A tiger was lurking in the jungle.* **Skulk,** implying sneakiness, cowardice, or shame, always suggests an evil purpose: *The cattle thieves skulked in the woods until the posse had passed.*

Lur·lei (lůr′lī), *n.* Lorelei.

Lu·sa·ti·an (lü sā′shē ən, -shən), *adj.* of or having to do with Lusatia, a region in northern Europe, or its people. —*n.* a native or inhabitant of Lusatia.

lus·cious (lush′əs), *adj.* **1.** richly sweet; delicious: *a luscious peach.* **2.** very pleasing to taste, smell, hear, see, or feel: *the luscious tones of a cello, a luscious view of a garden, a luscious description.* **3.** too sweet; cloying; sickly. [perhaps variant of *licious,* a back formation < *delicious*] —**lus′cious·ly,** *adv.* —**lus′cious·ness,** *n.* —**Syn. 1.** See **delicious. 2.** savory.

lush[1] (lush), *adj.* **1.** tender and juicy; growing thick and green: *Lush grass grows along the river bank.* **2.** characterized by abundant growth: *As the year Grows lush in juicy stalks* (Keats). **3.** abundant. **4.** very rich; too ornamented; extravagant: *lush description.* [Middle English *lache,* perhaps imitative variant of Old French *lasche* lax, soft, succulent (as young shoots) < *lascher* be careless < Vulgar Latin *lascāre* weaken < Latin *laxāre* < *laxus* lax] —**lush′ly,** *adv.* —**lush′ness,** *n.* —**Syn. 1.** succulent.

lush[2] (lush), *Slang.* —*n.* **1.** liquor; drink. **2.** a person who drinks too much: *Daddy figured him for forty-forty-five and something of a lush maybe* (Maclean's).

—*v.t.* **1.** to supply with drink. **2.** to drink: *some of the richest sort you ever lushed* (Dickens). —*v.i.* to drink liquor; drink.

[perhaps humorous use of *lush*[1] in sense of "watery"]

lush·y (lush′ē), *adj.,* **lush·i·er, lush·i·est.** tender; soft; lush.

Lu·si·ta·ni·a (lü′sə tā′nē ə), *n.* a British steamship sunk by a German submarine in 1915 with a loss of nearly 1,200 lives.

Lu·si·ta·ni·an (lü′sə tā′nē ən), *adj.* **1.** of or having to do with Lusitania, an ancient country comprising parts of Portugal and western Spain. **2.** Portuguese.

—*n.* **1.** a native of Lusitania. **2.** a Portuguese.

lust (lust), *n.* **1.** strong desire: *lust for power, lust for gold. That mere lust of fighting, common to man and animals* (Charles Kingsley). **2.** bad desire or appetite. **3.** desire for indulgence of sex. **4.** *Obsolete.* desire; inclination: *gazing upon the Greeks with little lust* (Shakespeare). **5.** *Obsolete.* pleasure; delight: *If you would consider your estate, you would have little lust to sing* (Beaumont and Fletcher). **6.** *Obsolete.* vigor; fertility: *a plant that cometh of the lust of the earth* (Francis Bacon).

—*v.i.* to have a strong desire: *A miser lusts after gold. The fruits that thy soul lusted after are departed from thee* (Revelation 18:14).

[Old English *lust* desire, pleasure]

lus·ter[1] (lus′tər), *n.* **1.** a bright shine on the surface: *the luster of pearls. Beetles, glittering with metallic luster* (Francis Parkman). **2.** brightness; radiance: *Her eyes lost their luster. The sun's mild luster warms the vital air* (Alexander Pope). *His countenance, radiant with health and the luster of innocence* (Benjamin Disraeli). **3.** fame; glory; brilliance: *The deeds of heroes add luster to a nation's history. The virtues of Claudius . . . place him in that short list of emperors who added luster to the Roman purple* (Edward Gibbon). **4. a.** a shiny, metallic, often iridescent surface on pottery or china. **b.** luster ware: *pink luster teacups.* **5.** a thin, light fabric of cotton and wool that has a lustrous surface, used for dresses and lining. **6. a.** a chandelier with glass pendants: *The luster, which had been lighted for dinner, filled the room with a festal breadth of light* (Charlotte Brontë). **b.** one of the glass pendants of such a chandelier. **7.** *Mineralogy.* the appearance of the surface of a mineral due to the reflection of light: *Cut a piece of lead or zinc, and observe the luster of its fresh surface* (Thomas Huxley). **8.** something used to give a shine or gloss to manufactured articles, furs, etc. **9.** a bright light; shining body or form.

—*v.t.* to finish with a luster or gloss. —*v.i.* to shine with luster.

[< Middle French *lustre* < Italian *lustro* < *lustrare* < Latin *lūstrāre* illuminate; (originally) purify by sacrifice < *lūstrum* a sacrifice] —**Syn.** *n.* **1.** sheen, gloss. See **polish.**

lus·ter[2] (lus′tər), *n.* a period of five years; lustrum: *So it will be the turn of you young folks, come eight more lusters, and your heads will be bald like mine* (Thackeray). [< Latin *lūstrum* lustrum]

lus·ter·less (lus′tər lis), *adj.* without luster; dull; colorless: *What Dr. Ostwald calls a "flat" voice is a smudged, lusterless, hesitant way of speaking* (Science News Letter).

luster ware, a kind of china or pottery that has a lustrous, metallic, often iridescent surface.

lust·ful (lust′fəl), *adj.* **1.** full of lust or desire; desiring indulgence of sex; sensual; lewd. **2.** *Archaic.* vigorous; lusty. —**lust′ful·ly,** *adv.* —**lust′ful·ness,** *n.* —**Syn. 1.** lecherous, lascivious.

lust·i·head (lus′tē hed), *n. Archaic.* lustiness.

lust·i·hood (lus′tē hůd), *n. Archaic.* lustiness.

lust·i·ly (lus′tə lē), *adv.* in a lusty manner; vigorously; heartily.

lust·i·ness (lus′tē nis), *n.* a being lusty; vigor; robustness.

lus·tra (lus′trə), *n.* lustrums; a plural of **lustrum.**

lus·tral (lus′trəl), *adj.* **1.** of or used in ceremonial purification: *The assistants were sprinkled with lustral water* (Edward Gibbon). *At one entrance to this building was a sunken "lustral area," where visitors made formal ablutions* (Scientific American). **2.** occurring every five years. [< Latin *lūstrālis* < *lūstrum* lustrum]

lus·trate (lus′trāt), *v.t.,* **-trat·ed, -trat·ing.** to purify by a propitiatory offering; purify by any ceremonial method. [< Latin *lūstrāre* (with English *-ate*[1]) brighten; purify by sacrifice < *lūstrum* lustrum]

lus·tra·tion (lus trā′shən), *n.* **1.** a ceremonial washing or purification: *The offender having ceased to exist, the lustration which the laws of knight-errantry prescribe was rendered impossible* (William Godwin). **2.** *Humorous.* a washing.

lus·tre[1] (lus′tər), *n. Especially British.* luster.

lus·tre[2] (lus′tər), *n. Especially British.* lustrum.

lus·tring (lus′tring), *n.* a glossy silk fabric; lutestring. [alteration of French *lustrine* < Middle French *lustre* luster[1]]

lus·trous (lus′trəs), *adj.* **1.** having luster; shining; glossy: *lustrous satin.* **2.** bright; brilliant; splendid: *He has a lustrous record.* —**lus′trous·ly,** *adv.* —**lus′trous·ness,** *n.*

lus·trum (lus′trəm), *n., pl.* **-trums** or **-tra. 1.** a ceremonial purification of the ancient Romans, performed every five years, after the taking of the census. **2.** a period of five years. [< Latin *lūstrum*]

lust·y (lus′tē), *adj.,* **lust·i·er, lust·i·est. 1.** strong and healthy; full of vigor: *a lusty boy. The churches ringing out the lustiest peals he had ever heard* (Dickens). *The savage . . . a stout, lusty fellow . . . had thrown him down* (Daniel Defoe). **2.** *Archaic.* merry; cheerful: *a lusty heart* (Chaucer); *lusty banqueting* (Scott). **3.** *Obsolete.* pleasing; agreeable: *some lusty grove* (Christopher Marlowe). **4.** *Obsolete.* beautiful; handsome. —**Syn. 1.** robust, sturdy, vigorous, hearty.

lu·sus (lü′səs), *n.* lusus naturae.

lusus na·tu·rae (nə tůr′ē, -tyůr′-), a plant, animal, etc., that deviates greatly from the normal; freak of nature. [< Latin *lūsus nātūrae* a jest of nature; *lūsus, -ūs* a playing < *lūdere* to play]

lu·ta·nist (lü′tə nist), *n.* a player on the lute: *I have heard Gog-Owza, the lutanist, playing his lute* (Lord Dunsany). Also, **lutenist.** [< Medieval Latin *lutanista* < *lutana* lute]

lute[1] (lüt), *n., v.,* **lut·ed, lut·ing.** —*n.* a stringed musical instrument, formerly much used, having a long neck and a hollow, resonant body, played with the fingers of one hand or with a plectrum. —*v.i.* **1.** to play on a lute. **2.** *Poetic.* to sound like a lute: *Her new voice luting soft, Cried, "Lycius!"* (Keats). —*v.t. Poetic.* to express with or as if with the music of a lute: *Knaves are men, that lute and flute fantastic tenderness* (Tennyson). [< Old French *lut,* or *leüt* < Old Provençal *laüt* < Arabic *al-'ūd* the lute]

Medieval Lute[1]

lute[2] (lüt), *n., v.,* **lut·ed, lut·ing.** —*n.* **1.** a sealing compound of clay used around joints in pipes, on walls, etc., to prevent leakage or seepage by gas or water. **2.** *U.S.* a tool used to scrape excess clay from a brick mold. —*v.t.* to seal (a pipe, wall, etc.) with lute. [< Old French *lut,* or Medieval Latin *lutum* < Latin, mud]

lu·te·al (lü′tē əl), *adj.* of or having to do with the corpus luteum.

lu·te·ci·um (lü tē′shē əm), *n.* lutetium.

lu·te·in (lü′tē in), *n.* **1.** a yellow pigment obtained from the corpus luteum. **2.** xanthophyll.

lu·te·in·ize (lü′tē ə nīz), *v.i.,* **-ized, -iz·ing.** (of a hormone) to stimulate the production of lutein or a corpus luteum.

lu·te·nist (lü′tə nist), *n.* lutanist.

lu·te·o·lin (lü′tē ə lin), *n.* a yellow, crystalline coloring matter present in a great many plants and used in dyeing. *Formula:* $C_{15}H_{10}O_6$ [< French *lutéoline* < New Latin *luteola* weld[2] < Latin *lūteolus* (diminutive) < *lūteus*; see LUTEOUS]

lu·te·o·troph·ic (lü′tē ə trof′ik), *adj.* that stimulates the corpus luteum. [< (corpus) *luteum* + *trophic*]

lu·te·o·troph·in (lü′tē ə trof′in), *n.* prolactin.

lu·te·ous (lü′tē əs), *adj.* golden-yellow; orange-yellow. [< Latin *lūteus* (with English *-ous*) deep yellow < *lūtum* weld[2], a plant from which the yellow used by dyers was obtained]

lu·tes·cent (lü tes′ənt), *adj.* tending to yellow; yellowish. [< Latin *lūteus* yellow + English *-escent*]

lute·string (lüt′string′), *n.* **1.** lustring. **2.** a ribbon for attaching eyeglasses, etc.

Lu·te·tian (lü tē′shən), *adj.* of or having to do with ancient Lutetia or Paris; Parisian.

lu·te·ti·um (lü tē′shē əm), *n.* a rare-earth metallic chemical element occurring with ytterbium. *Symbol:* Lu; *at. wt.:* (C^{12}) 174.97 or (O^{16}) 174.99; *at. no.:* 71; *valence:* 3. Also, **lutecium.** [< New Latin *lutecium* < Latin *Lutetia,* or *-cia* Paris]

lut·fisk (lüt′fisk′), *n.* fish soaked in a lye solution and boiled, forming one of the main dishes at a Swedish Christmas dinner. [< Swedish *lutfisk* < *luta* to wash in lye + *fisk* fish]

Luth., Lutheran.

Lu·ther·an (lü′thər ən, lüth′rən), *adj.* having to do with Martin Luther, or the church and doctrines that were named for him. —*n.* a member of the Lutheran Church.

Lu·ther·an·ism (lü′thər ə niz′əm, lüth′rə niz-), *n.* the doctrine, organization, and manner of worship of the Lutheran Church.

lu·thern (lü′thərn), *n.* a dormer window. [perhaps alteration of *lucarne*]

Lu·tine bell (lü′tēn), a bell recovered from the British frigate *Lutine,* which sank in 1799, now hanging in the offices of Lloyd's of London, where it is rung when important announcements are to be made.

lut·ing (lü′ting), *n.* **1.** a seal of lute. **2.** the act or process of sealing with lute. **3.** the material used; lute.

lut·ist (lü′tist), *n.* **1.** a lute player. **2.** a maker of lutes.

lu·trine (lü′trin), *adj.* of or like the otter; otterlike. [< New Latin *lutrinus* < Latin *lutra* otter]

lutz (lůtz), *n.* a jump in figure skating in which the skater leaps from the outside back edge of one skate, rotates in the air, and lands on the outside back edge of the other skate: *Miss Brugnera presented a dramatic programme of great athletic merit in which the only mistake was a faulty double lutz* (London Times). [origin uncertain]

lux (luks), *n., pl.* **lux·es** or **lu·ces.** the international unit of illumination, equivalent to the amount of light falling on a surface which is situated, at all points, one meter from a point source of one international candle. A lux equals one lumen per square meter. [< Latin *lūx, lūcis* light[1]]

Lux., Luxembourg.

lux·ate (luk′sāt), *v.t.,* **-at·ed, -at·ing.** to put out of joint; dislocate. [< Latin *luxāre* (with English *-ate*[1]) dislocate < *luxus* out of place]

lux·a·tion (luk sā′shən), *n.* dislocation, as of bones at a joint.

luxe (lůks, luks; *French* lYks), *n.* very fine quality; luxury; elegance. See also **de luxe.** [< French *luxe* < Latin *luxus, -ūs,* abundance, excess]

Lux·em·burg·er or **Lux·em·bourg·er** (luk′səm bėr′gər), *n.* a native or inhabitant of the grand duchy or city of Luxemburg.

Lux·em·burg·i·an or **Lux·em·bourg·i·an** (luk′səm bėr′gē ən), *adj.* of or having to do with Luxemburg, its people, or their language. —*n.* the Germanic language of Luxemburg.

lux·u·ri·ance (lug zhůr′ē əns, luk shůr′-), *n.* luxuriant growth or productiveness; rich abundance: *the faults which grow out of the luxuriance of freedom* (Edmund Burke). —**Syn.** richness, profusion.

lux·u·ri·an·cy (lug zhůr′ē ən sē, luk shůr′-), *n.* luxuriance.

lux·u·ri·ant (lug zhůr′ē ənt, luk shůr′-), *adj.* **1.** growing thick and green: *luxuriant jungle growth.* **2.** producing abundantly: *rich, luxuriant soil.* **3.** rich in ornament. [< Latin *luxuriāns, -antis,* present participle of *luxuriāre* luxuriate] —**lux·u′ri·ant·ly,** *adv.* —**Syn. 1.** lush. **2.** fertile. **3.** florid.

lux·u·ri·ate (lug zhůr′ē āt, luk shůr′-), *v.i.,* **-at·ed, -at·ing. 1.** to indulge in luxury; enjoy oneself: *The explorer planned to luxuriate in hot baths and clean clothes when he came home.* **2.** to take great delight; revel: *You luxuriate in the contemplation of nature . . . I in my snuff-box* (Frederick Marryat). **3.** to grow very abundantly. [< Latin *luxuriāre* (with English *-ate*[1]) < *luxuria* luxury] —**Syn. 2.** bask.

lux·u·ri·a·tion (lug zhůr′ē ā′shən, luk-shůr′-), *n.* the act or process of luxuriating.

lux·u·ri·ous (lug zhůr′ē əs, luk shůr′-), *adj.* **1.** fond of luxury; tending toward luxury; self-indulgent: *luxurious tastes, a luxurious city. She is too proud, too luxurious, to marry a beggar* (Charles Kingsley). **2.** giving luxury; very comfortable and beautiful: *a deep, luxurious arm-chair* (Hawthorne). *Some theaters are luxurious.* —**lux·u′ri·ous·ly,** *adv.* —**lux·u′ri·ous·ness,** *n.*

lux·u·ry (luk′shər ē, lug′zhər-), *n., pl.* **-ries. 1.** the comforts and beauties of life beyond what is really necessary: *Most Americans today live in what would have been considered luxury 100 years ago. The world declined to support the lady in luxury for nothing* (George Meredith). **2.** the use of the best and most costly food, clothes, houses, furniture, and amusements: *The movie star soon became accustomed to luxury.* **3.** a thing that a person enjoys, usually something choice and costly: *He saves some money for such luxuries as fine paintings.* **4.** a thing that is pleasant but not necessary: *Candy is a luxury. Nancy had treated herself to an expensive luxury in the shape of a husband* (Harriet Beecher Stowe). **5.** any form or means of enjoyment or self-gratification: *Learn the luxury of doing good* (Oliver Goldsmith). *I had learned . . . not to indulge in the luxury of discontent* (William Godwin). —*adj.* providing lavish comfort and enjoyment; luxurious: *a luxury hotel. The luxury liners Constitution and Independence are your floating hotels, replete with shops, pools, theaters, restaurants* (Harper's). [< Latin *luxuria* < *luxus, -ūs* excess, abundance] —**Syn.** *n.* **1.** luxuriousness. **2.** extravagance.

luxury tax, a tax put on the sale, manufacture, purchase, or use of luxury goods and services.

lv., 1. leave or leaves. **2.** livre or livres.

lve., leave or leaves.

lvs., *Botany.* leaves.

Lw, lawrencium (chemical element).

L wave, *Physics.* a long wave.

L.W.F. or **LWF** (no periods), Lutheran World Federation.

l.w.l., load waterline.

l.w.m., low-water mark.

LXX (no periods), Septuagint (Greek translation of the Old Testament).

-ly[1], *suffix forming adverbs.* **1.** in a _____ manner: *Cheerfully = in a cheerful manner.* **2.** in _____ ways or respects: *Financially = in financial respects.* **3.** to a _____ degree or extent: *Greatly = to a great degree.* **4.** in, to, or from a _____ direction: *Northwardly = to or from the north.* **5.** in the _____ place: *Thirdly = in the third place.* **6.** at a _____ time: *Recently = at a recent time.* [Middle English *-ly,* and *-li,* short for *-liche,* and *-like,* Old English *-licē* < *līc* -ly[2] + *-e,* adverb suffix]

➔ **-ly.** A few adjectives end in **-ly** (*comely, kindly, lovely*), but *-ly* is more distinctly an ending for adverbs. The suffix *-ly* is a living suffix and is freely added to adjectives to form adverbs.

-ly[2], *suffix forming adjectives.* **1.** like a _____: *Ghostly = like a ghost.* **2.** like that of a _____; characteristic of a _____: *Brotherly = like that of a brother.* **3.** suited to a _____; fit or proper for a _____: *Womanly = suited to a woman.* **4.** of each or every _____; occurring once per _____: *Daily = of every day.* **5.** being a _____; that is a _____: *Heavenly = that is a heaven.* [Middle English *-ly,* and *-li,* reduction of *-lich,* and *-lik,* Old English *-līc* < *līc* body]

ly·am-hound (lī′əm hound′), *n.* a bloodhound. Also, **lyme-hound.** [< Old French *liem* a leash, (ultimately < Latin *ligare* to bind) + English *hound*]

ly·ard (lī′ərd), *adj. Scottish.* **1.** having white or silver-gray spots: *a lyard horse.* **2.** gray; silvery gray: *lyard hair.* [< Old French *liart,* perhaps < *lie* lee[2]]

ly·art (lī′ərt), *adj.* lyard.

ly·can·thrope (lī′kən thrōp, lī kan′-), *n.* **1.** a person affected with lycanthropy. **2.** a werewolf.

ly·can·throp·ic (lī′kən throp′ik), *adj.* of, having to do with, or characteristic of lycanthropy.

ly·can·thro·py (lī kan′thrə pē), *n.* **1.** a mental disturbance, associated with schizophrenia, in which a person thinks he is a wolf or other wild animal. **2.** the supposed ability of a human being to turn into a wolf by witchcraft. [< Late Latin *lycanthrōpia* < Greek *lykanthrōpíā* < *lykánthrōpos* one who imagines himself a wolf < *lýkos* wolf + *ánthrōpos* man]

Ly·ca·on (lī kā′on), *n. Greek Legend.* a king of Arcadia who tested the divinity of Zeus by offering him human flesh to eat, and was changed into a wolf as punishment.

ly·cée (lē sā′), *n.* a French secondary school maintained by the government: *. . . far more eligible candidates than the nation's lycées could possibly handle* (Time). [< French *lycée,* learned borrowing from Latin *Lycēum.* Doublet of LYCEUM.]

ly·cé·en (lē sā′ən), *n.* a student of a lycée: *We shall expect him to appreciate the French masters as sensitively as any Parisian lycéen* (London Times). [< French *lycéen*]

Ly·ce·um (lī sē′əm, lī′sē-), *n.* **1.** an ancient outdoor grove and gymnasium near Athens, where Aristotle taught. **2.** the Aristotelian school of philosophy. [< Latin *Lycēum* < Greek *Lýkeion* (from the nearby temple of *Apollo lýkeios*). Doublet of LYCÉE.]

ly·ce·um (lī sē′əm, lī′sē-), *n.* **1.** a place where popular lectures are given; lecture hall. **2.** *U.S.* an association for instruction and entertainment through lectures, debates, and concerts, popular during the middle part of the 1800's: *Their appearances were scheduled by one or another of several lyceum bureaus* (Emory S. Bogardus). **3.** a lycée. [< *Lyceum*]

lych (lich), *n.* lich.

ly·chee (lē′chē), *n.* litchi.

lych gate, lich gate.

lych·nis (lik′nis), *n.* any of a group of plants of the pink family having showy red or white flowers, as the rose campion and the ragged robin. [< Latin *lychnis* < Greek *lychnís* some kind of brilliant red flower < *lýchnos* lamp]

Ly·ci·an (lish′ē ən), *adj.* of or having to do with Lycia, an ancient district in Asia Minor. —*n.* **1.** a native or inhabitant of Lycia. **2.** the Anatolian language of ancient Lycia.

ly·co·pod (lī′kə pod), *n.* lycopodium (def. 1).

ly·co·po·di·a·ceous (lī′kə pō′dē ā′shəs), *adj.* of or belonging to the family of plants typified by the lycopodium or club moss.

ly·co·po·di·um (lī′kə pō′dē əm), *n.* **1.** any of a group of plants that are either erect or creeping, usually mosslike, and have evergreen leaves; club moss. **2.** a fine, yellow, inflammable powder made from the spores of certain lycopodiums. [< New Latin *Lycopodium* the typical genus < Greek *lýkos* wolf + *poús, podós* foot]

Ly·cra (lī′krə), *n. Trademark.* a spandex fiber having the elastic characteristics of rubber, used in swimming suits, foundation garments, etc.

lydd·ite (lid′īt), *n.* a high explosive, consisting chiefly of picric acid. [< *Lydd,* a town in Kent, England, where it was first manufactured and tested + *-ite*[1]]

Lyd·i·an (lid′ē ən), *adj.* **1.** of Lydia (an ancient country in western Asia Minor famous for its wealth and luxury), its people, or their language: *American scientists found an inscription in the little known Lydian tongue* (Science News Letter). **2.** soft; gentle; effeminate: *Soft Lydian airs, Married to immortal verse* (Milton). *Softly sweet, in Lydian measures, Soon he sooth'd his soul to pleasures* (John Dryden).
—*n.* **1.** a native or inhabitant of Lydia. **2.** the language of Lydia.

lye (lī), *n., v.,* **lyed, ly·ing.** —*n.* **1.** any strong alkaline solution: *Lye is used in making soap and in cleaning. Sodium hydroxide and potassium hydroxide are kinds of lye.* **2.** (formerly) an alkaline solution made by leaching wood or other vegetable ashes: *soap lye, soda lye.* **3.** a crude or impure caustic soda, used for scouring, etc.
—*v.t.* to treat with lye.
[Old English *lēag.* Related to LAVE, LATHER.]

ly·go·di·um (lī gō′dē əm), *n.* a delicate climbing fern with palmately lobed fronds, native to the eastern United States. [< New Latin *Lygodium* the genus name < Greek *lygṓdēs* like a willow < *lýgos* withy + *eîdos* form]

Lygodium

ly·gus bug (lī′gəs), a common hemipterous insect that feeds on the flowers, buds, and seeds of various plants, and is especially destructive of alfalfa. [< New Latin *Lygus* the genus name]

ly·ing[1] (lī′ing), *n.* a telling a lie; the habit of telling lies. —*adj.* false; untruthful. —*v.* present participle of **lie**[1]: *I was not lying; I told the truth.* —**Syn.** *n.* mendacity, prevarication.

ly·ing[2] (lī′ing), *v.* present participle of **lie**[2]: *He was lying on the ground.*

ly·ing-in (lī′ing in′), *n.* confinement in childbirth. —*adj.* of or having to do with childbirth: *a lying-in hospital.*

ly·ing·ly (lī′ing lē), *adv.* in a lying or untruthful manner.

lyke·wake (līk′wāk′), *n.* likewake.

Lyman alpha, or **Ly·man-al·pha** (lī′mən al′fə), *adj.* of or having to do with the Lyman-alpha line: *The sun itself has been photographed in the extreme ultra-violet (the Lyman-alpha) region of the spectrum* (London Times). [< Ernest M. *Lyman,* born 1910, an American physicist]

Lyman-alpha line or **Lyman alpha line,** a line of hydrogen in the extreme ultraviolet range of the emission spectrum of the sun, representing a large part of the sun's ultraviolet radiation.

lyme-hound (līm′hound′), *n.* lyam-hound.

lymph (limf), *n.* **1.** a nearly colorless liquid in the tissues of the body, somewhat like blood without the red corpuscles. Lymph is conveyed to the blood stream by the lymphatic vessels and has a slightly alkaline quality. *The lymph carries with it most of the blood substances which can be dissolved in water* (A. F. Shull). **2.** *Medicine.* any diseased matter taken from a person or animal for use in inoculation, especially against smallpox. **3.** *Poetic.* pure, clean water or a stream of it: *I drink the virgin lymph, pure and crystalline as it gushes from the rock* (Tobias Smollett). [< New Latin *lympha* < Latin, clear water; water nymph < Greek *nýmphē* nymph]

lym·phad (lim′fad), *n.* a former type of galley with a single mast. [alteration of Gaelic *longfhada*]

lym·phad·e·nec·to·my (lim fad′ə nek′tə mē), *n.,pl.* **-mies.** the surgical removal of a lymph node.

lym·phad·e·ni·tis (lim fad′ə nī′tis, lim′fə də-), *n.* inflammation of a lymph node or gland. [< New Latin *lympha* (see LYMPH) + Greek *adēn* gland, kernel + English *-itis*]

lym·phan·gi·al (lim fan′jē əl), *adj.* of or having to do with the lymphatic vessels. [< New Latin *lympha* lymph + Greek *angeîon* vessel + English *-al*[1]]

lym·phan·gi·i·tis (lim fan′jē ī′tis), *n.* inflammation of the lymphatic vessels. [< New Latin *lympha* lymph + Greek *angeîon* vessel + English *-itis*]

lym·phan·gi·tis (lim′fan jī′tis), *n.* lymphangiitis.

lym·phat·ic (lim fat′ik), *adj.* **1.** of, carrying, or secreting lymph: *the lymphatic system, a lymphatic disease.* **2.** sluggish; lacking energy; pale (thought formerly to be due to having too much lymph in the body).
—*n.* a vessel that contains or carries lymph.
[< Latin *lymphāticus* frenzied; the meaning is < New Latin *lympha* lymph]

lymphatic gland, lymph gland.

lymphatic vessel, a tube or canal through which lymph circulates to different parts of the body.

lymph cell, a lymphocyte.

lymph corpuscle, lymphocyte.

lymph·e·de·ma (lim′fi dē′mə), *n.* edema caused by the abnormal accumulation of lymph fluid: *In lymphedema there is insufficient drainage of fluid and proteins* (Scientific American). [< New Latin *lympha* lymph + *edema*]

lymph gland, any of the bean-shaped, glandlike bodies occurring in the course of the lymphatic vessels, composed of a network of connective tissue and active as a source of lymphocytes: *Tonsils . . . have at last been pin-pointed as the primary site of polio infection, along with similar lymph glands in the small intestine* (Science News Letter).

lymph node, lymph gland.

lympho-, *combining form.* lymph: *Lymphocyte = a lymph cell.* [< New Latin *lympha;* see LYMPH]

lym·pho·blast (lim′fə blast), *n.* a lymphocyte in an early stage of development. [< *lympho-* + Greek *blastós* germ sprout]

lym·pho·blas·tic (lim′fə blas′tik), *adj.* of a lymphoblast.

lym·pho·cyte (lim′fə sīt), *n.* one of the nearly colorless cells of the blood and lymphatic system, resembling a leucocyte; lymph cell. Lymphocytes have a nucleus and are believed to serve a regenerative function, forming new leucocytes, red blood cells, etc. *The lymphocytes in leukemia, unlike normal lymphocytes, can break down the adrenal hormone, cortisone, into five compounds* (Science News Letter). [< *lympho-* + *-cyte*]

lym·pho·cyt·ic (lim′fə sit′ik), *adj.* of or having to do with a lymphocyte or lymphocytes.

lym·pho·cy·to·sis (lim′fō sī tō′sis), *n., pl.* **-ses** (-sēz). an excessive number of lymphocytes in the blood.

lym·pho·cy·tot·ic (lim′fō sī tot′ik), *adj.* of a lymphocyte.

lym·pho·gran·u·lo·ma (lim′fō gran′yə lō′mə), *n.* a venereal disease caused by a filterable virus, characterized by swelling in the groin, usually followed by ulceration leading to disturbance of the lymph nodes. [< *lympho-* + Late Latin *grānulum* small grain + Greek *-ōma* tumor, growth]

lym·pho·gran·u·lo·ma·to·sis (lim′fō gran′yə lō′mə tō′sis), *n.* Hodgkin's disease.

lymph·oid (lim′foid), *adj.* **1.** of, having to do with, or like lymph or lymphocytes. **2.** of, having to do with, or like lymphoid tissue. [< *lymph*(o)- + *-oid*]

lymphoid tissue, the tissue that forms most of the lymph glands, thymus gland, etc., consisting of connective tissue containing lymphocytes.

lym·pho·ma (lim fō′mə), *n., pl.* **-mas, -ma·ta** (-mə tə). any of various malignant tumors of the lymphatic tissue, such as Hodgkin's disease and lymphosarcoma: *The spread of the lesions and the size of the lymphomas were much larger at sea level than at high altitude* (Science News Letter).

lym·pho·ma·to·sis (lim′fō mə tō′sis), *n., pl.* **-ses** (-sēz). any of several forms of the avian leucosis complex, characterized by enlargement of the liver, paralysis, blindness, or enlargement of the bones.

lym·pho·sar·co·ma (lim′fō sär kō′mə), *n.* a sarcoma of the lymphatic tissue, characterized by enlargement of the lymph nodes: *Two of the four had lymphosarcoma, which attacks the blood-forming organs* (New York Times). [< *lympho-* + *sarcoma*]

lyn·ce·an (lin sē′ən), *adj.* like a lynx; keen; sharp-sighted. [< Latin *lyncēus* (< Greek *lýnkeios* < *lýnx* lynx) + English *-an*]

lynch (linch), *v.t.* to put (an accused person) to death without a lawful trial. [American English < *lynch* (law)] —**lynch′er,** *n.*

lyn·chet (lin′chet), *n. British.* **1.** a strip of green land between two pieces of plowed land: *The small rectangular fields are divided from one another by lynchets* (London Times). **2.** a slope or terrace along the face of a chalk down: *There was a series of clearly defined lynchets, suggesting that intensive cultivation was practised on these downs* (Manchester Guardian Weekly). [< earlier *linch* ridge, ledge (variant of *link*[1]) + *-et*]

lynch law, a putting an accused person to death without a lawful trial. [American English; (originally) *Lynch's law,* apparently from Charles *Lynch,* a planter of Virginia, who drew up a vigilante compact with his neighbors in the 1700's]

lynch·pin (linch′pin′), *n.* linchpin.

Lyn·cis (lin′sis), *n.* genitive of **Lynx.**

lynx (lingks), *n., pl.* **lynx·es** or (*collectively*) **lynx.** any of certain wildcats of the Northern Hemisphere having a short tail and rather long legs, including the Canada lynx and bobcat of North America, and several Old World varieties. [< Latin *lynx* < Greek *lýnx*] —**lynx′like′,** *adj.*

Canada Lynx
(including tail, about 3 ft. long)

Lynx (lingks), *n., genitive* **Lyn·cis.** a northern constellation near Ursa Major.

lynx eye, a sharp eye, such as the lynx is supposed to have: *His lynx eye immediately perceives the paper* (Edgar Allan Poe).

lynx-eyed (lingks′īd′), *adj.* having sharp eyes; sharp-sighted.

ly·on·naise (lī′ə nāz′), *adj.* fried with pieces of onion: *lyonnaise potatoes.* [< French *lyonnaise,* feminine of *lyonnais* of *Lyon,* a city in France]

Ly·on·nesse (lī′ə nes′), *n.* a legendary region off southwestern England, near

Cornwall, associated with Arthurian legend and supposed to have sunk beneath the sea.

ly·o·phil·ic (lī′ə fil′ik), *adj. Chemistry.* (of a colloidal system) characterized by strong attraction between the colloid and the dispersion medium: *Lyophilic colloidal systems are affected very little by electrolytes* (W.N. Jones). [< Greek *lyyén* to loosen + English *-phil* + *-ic*]

ly·oph·i·li·za·tion (lī of′ə lə zā′shən), *n.* the process of lyophilizing substances for preservation: *Refrigeration, freezing and lyophilization, the methods used almost exclusively for preserving plasma, are also the best methods for preserving viruses* (Science News Letter).

ly·oph·i·lize (lī of′ə līz), *v.t.*, **-lized, -liz·ing.** to dehydrate (a frozen material) for storage by converting its water content to a gaseous state in a vacuum, leaving it as a porous solid.

ly·o·pho·bic (lī′ə fō′bik, -fob′ik), *adj. Chemistry.* (of a colloidal system) characterized by a lack of attraction between the colloid and the dispersion medium. [< Greek *lyyén* to loosen + English *-phobe* + *-ic*]

Ly·ra (lī′rə), *n., genitive* **Ly·rae.** a small northern constellation that was once thought of as arranged in the shape of a lyre. It contains the fifth brightest star, Vega. *The brightest star of the early summer evenings, however, is Vega, which is high in the east, part of Lyra, the lyre* (Science News Letter). Also, **Lyre.** [< Latin *Lyra* < Greek *Lýrā* (literally) the lyre]

Ly·rae (lī′rē), *n.* genitive of **Lyra.**

ly·rate (lī′rāt), *adj.* shaped like a lyre, as the tail of certain birds or a leaf. [< New Latin *lyratus* < Latin *lyra* lyre]

ly·rat·ed (lī′rā tid), *adj.* lyrate.

lyre (līr), *n.* **1.** an ancient stringed musical instrument somewhat like a small harp. It was used by the ancient Greeks as accompaniment for singing and reciting. **2.** the medium of a poet's expression: *Milton's golden lyre* (Mark Akenside). *Here Poesy might wake her heav'n-taught lyre* (Robert Burns). [< Old French *lire,* and *lyre,* learned borrowing from Latin *lyra* < Greek *lýrā*]

Lyre (def. 1)

Lyre (līr), *n.* the northern constellation Lyra.

lyre·bird (līr′bėrd′), *n.* either of two Australian birds about the size of a rooster, the male of which has a long tail that resembles the shape of a lyre when spread. The lyrebird is a perching bird and exhibits elaborate courtship behavior.

lyr·ic (lir′ik), *n.* **1.** a short poem expressing personal emotions: *A love poem, a patriotic song, a lament, and a hymn might all be lyrics.* **2.** a lyric poet.

lyrics, the words for a song: *He wanted to use some Italian lyrics written for a Johann Strauss melody* (New Yorker).

—*adj.* **1.** having to do with lyric poems: *a lyric poet.* **2.** characterized by a spontaneous expression of feeling: *Elegies, sonnets, and odes are kinds of lyric poetry.* **3.** of or suitable for singing. **4. a.** tender, light in volume, and often used in the higher register: *Sopranos and tenors have lyric singing voices.* **b.** (of a singer) having such a voice. **5.** of, having to do with, or for the lyre.

[< Latin *lyricus* < Greek *lyrikós* of a lyre < *lýrā* lyre] —**Syn.** *adj.* **3.** melodious.

lyr·i·cal (lir′ə kəl), *adj.* **1.** emotional; poetic: *a lyrical landscape and still-life painter. She became almost lyrical when she described the scenery.* **2.** lyric. —**lyr′i·cal·ly,** *adv.* —**lyr′i·cal·ness,** *n.*

lyr·i·cism (lir′ə siz əm), *n.* **1.** lyric character or style: *the lyricism of Donne's songs and sonnets.* **2.** a lyric form or expression. **3.** lyric outpouring of feeling; emotionally expressed enthusiasm.

lyr·i·cist (lir′ə sist), *n.* **1.** a person who writes lyrics, especially for songs in a musical comedy: *The cards also list the song titles, the composer and lyricist . . .* (New Yorker). **2.** a lyric poet.

lyr·i·cize (lir′ə sīz), *v.*, **-cized, -ciz·ing.** —*v.i.* **1.** to sing lyrics. **2.** to compose lyrics. —*v.t.* **1.** to treat in a lyric style. **2.** to express in an emotional way.

lyr·i·co-dra·mat·ic (lir′ə kō drə mat′ik), *adj.* combining the characteristics of lyric and dramatic poetry.

lyr·i·co-ep·ic (lir′ə kō ep′ik), *adj.* having the characteristics of lyric and epic poetry.

lyr·ics (lir′iks), *n.pl.* See under **lyric,** *n.*

lyric tenor, 1. a light, high tenor voice. **2.** a man with such a voice.

lyric theater, any form of theatrical production in which dance, music, and spoken words are combined.

lyr·i·form (līr′ə fôrm), *adj.* shaped like a lyre.

lyr·ism (lir′iz əm *for 1;* līr′iz əm, lir′- *for 2*), *n.* **1.** lyricism; lyrical enthusiasm. **2.** performance on a lyre; musical performance; singing: *The lyrism . . . had gradually assumed a rather deafening and complex character* (George Eliot).

lyr·ist (lir′ist *for 1;* līr′ist, lir′- *for 2*), *n.* **1.** a lyric poet: *They . . . are both tolerably well acquainted with the minor Elizabethan lyrists* (Listener). **2.** a person who plays on the lyre; person who plays and sings to an accompaniment on the lyre.

ly·sate (lī′sāt), *n.* the product resulting from the destruction of a cell by a lysin or lysins: *A lysate . . . may contain over a hundred thousand million bacteriophage particles* (Science News Letter).

lyse (līs), *v.*, **lysed, lys·ing.** —*v.t.* to bring about the dissolution of red blood cells by lysins; subject to lysis: *These viruses prevent bacterial growth and division, eventually lysing the cells* (Science). —*v.i.* to undergo lysis. [< *lysis*]

Ly·sen·ko·ism (lə seng′kō iz əm), *n.* the theory of heredity maintained by Trofim Lysenko that acquired characteristics are inheritable, not accepted by most geneticists: *Biology has of course been made—and is still being made—nonsensical by Lysenkoism* (Alastair Mackenzie). [< Trofim D. *Lysenko,* born 1898, a Russian geneticist]

Ly·sen·ko·ist (lə seng′kō ist), *n.* a follower of Lysenko or Lysenkoism: *He was arraigned by the Lysenkoists because he had refused to compromise with their phoney science* (New Scientist). —*adj.* of, having to do with, or characteristic of Lysenkoism.

ly·ser·gic acid (lī sėr′jik), a chemical produced synthetically or extracted from ergot, with properties similar to lysergic acid diethylamide. *Formula:* $C_{16}H_{16}N_2O_2$

lysergic acid di·eth·yl·am·ide (dī-eth′ə lam′īd), a hallucinogenic compound of lysergic acid that produces temporary symptoms of schizophrenia. *Formula:* $C_{20}H_{25}N_3O$ *Abbr.:* LSD (no periods).

ly·sim·e·ter (lī sim′ə tər), *n.* an instrument for measuring the quantity of matter dissolved in a liquid: *Basically a lysimeter consists of a mass of soil so arranged that the water draining from it can be collected* (J.D. Ovington). [< Greek *lýsis* loosening + English *-meter*]

ly·sin[1] (lī′sin), *n.* any of a class of antibodies which are capable of causing the dissolution or destruction of bacteria, blood corpuscles, and other cellular elements. [special use of *lysin*[2]]

ly·sin[2] (lī′sin), *n.* lysine.

ly·sine (lī′sēn, -sin), *n.* a basic amino acid essential for growth, formed by the hydrolysis of various proteins. *Formula:* $C_6H_{14}N_2O_2$ [< Greek *lýsis* + English *-ine*[2]]

ly·sis (lī′sis), *n., pl.* **ly·ses** (lī′sēz). **1.** the destruction of a cell by dissolution of the cell membrane, as by a lysin or a virus: *For some considerable distance around the mold growth, the staphylococcal colonies were undergoing lysis (being dissolved)* (Marguerite Clark). **2.** the gradual ending of a disease (contrasted with *crisis*). [< Latin *lysis* < Greek *lýsis* a loosening < *lyyén* to loosen]

ly·so·gen·ic (lī′sə jen′ik), *adj.* **1.** causing the destruction of cells by dissolution of the cell membrane. **2.** (of bacteria) carrying a prophage within the cell. [< *lysin*[1] + *-gen* + *-ic*]

ly·sog·e·ny (lī soj′ə nē), *n.* **1.** the production of a lysin or lysins. **2.** the initiation of the process of lysis.

Ly·sol (lī′sōl, -sol), *n. Trademark.* a brown, oily liquid containing cresols and soap, used as a disinfectant and antiseptic. [< Greek *lýsis* (see LYSIS) + English *-ol*[2]]

ly·so·some (lī′sə sōm), *n.* a particle in the cytoplasm of most cells that contains destructive, hydrolytic enzymes: *The lysosomes function in many ways as the digestive system of the cell* (Scientific American). [< Greek *lýsis* (see LYSIS) + *sôma* body]

ly·so·zyme (lī′sə zīm, -zim), *n.* an enzymelike substance that hydrolyzes polysaccharidic acids present in egg white, body secretions, tears, etc.: *As early as 1922, researchers have known that the enzyme lysozyme, found in nasal secretions, has important bacteria-destroying powers* (Science News Letter). [< Greek *lýsis* (see LYSIS) + English (en)*zyme*]

lys·sa (lis′ə), *n.* rabies. [< Greek *lýssa*]

lys·sic (lis′ik), *adj.* having to do with lyssa or rabies.

lys·so·pho·bi·a (lis′ə fō′bē ə), *n.* an abnormal fear of rabies, which sometimes simulates its symptoms. [< Greek *lýssa* rage, rabies + English *-phobia*]

lyth·ra·ceous (lith rā′shəs, lī thrā′-), *adj.* of or belonging to the loosestrife family of plants. [< New Latin *Lythraceae* the family name (< *Lythrum* the typical genus < Greek *lýthron* gore) + English *-ous*]

lyt·ic (lit′ik), *adj.* having to do with or producing lysis.

lyt·ta (lit′ə), *n., pl.* **lyt·tae** (lit′ē). a long, worm-shaped cartilage in the tongue of dogs and other carnivorous animals. [< New Latin *lytta* < Greek *lýtta,* variant of *lýssa* rabies, rage]

LZ (no periods) or **L.Z.,** landing zone.

M Roman 100's A.D.

Greek 600's B.C. Phoenician 1000's B.C. Semitic 1500's B.C. Egyptian 3000's B.C.

Mm Mm *Mm Mm*

M or **m** (em), *n., pl.* **M's** or **Ms, m's** or **ms. 1.** the 13th letter of the English alphabet. **2.** any sound represented by this letter. **3.** (used as a symbol for) the 13th (of an actual or possible series): *row M in a theater*. **4.** the Roman numeral for 1,000. **5.** *Printing.* an em, the square of any size of type.

M', *prefix.* Mac or Mc, as in *M'Donald*.

m-, *prefix.* variant of **meta-** in chemical terms.

m., an abbreviation for the following:
1. male.
2. manual.
3. mark (in German money).
4. married.
5. masculine.
6. *Physics.* mass.
7. medicine.
8. medium.
9. meridian.
10. meridional.
11. meter or meters.
12. midnight.
13. mile or miles.
14. mill or mills.
15. million.
16. minim.
17. minute or minutes.
18. mist.
19. *Mathematics.* modulus.
20. *Dentistry.* molar.
21. month.
22. moon.
23. morning.
24. mountain.
25. noon (Latin, *meridies*).

M (no period), an abbreviation for the following:
1. Mach.
2. *Physics.* mass.
3. Mature (a symbol for motion pictures recommended to adult audiences).
4. medium.
5. *Linguistics.* Middle.
6. missile.

M., an abbreviation for the following:
1. majesty.
2. Manitoba.
3. *Music.* manual.
4. mark (unit of German money).
5. marquis.
6. mass.
7. medical.
8. medicine.
9. medium.
10. member.
11. midnight.
12. militia.
13. Monday.
14 Monsieur.
15. mountain.
16. noon (Latin, *meridies*).

ma (mä, mô), *n. Informal.* mamma; mother.

ma., milliampere.

mA., milliangstrom.

Ma (no period), masurium (chemical element).

MA (no periods), **1.** machine accountant. **2.** Maritime Administration. **3.** mental age.

M.A., **1.** Master of Arts (Latin, *Magister Artium*). Also, **A.M. 2.** Military Academy.

maa·ba·ra (mä bä′rä), *n., pl.* **maa·ba·rot** (mä bä rôt′). *Hebrew.* a temporary settlement for immigrants in Israel.

MAAG (no periods), Military Assistance Advisory Group.

ma'am (mam, mäm), *n. Informal.* madam.

maar (mär), *n. Geology.* the crater of a volcano formed by an explosion but with no flow of lava.

maas·bank·er (mäs′bang′kər), *n.* a small South African fish similar to the mackerel: *On that day a ravenous shoal of yellowfish drove a terrified mass of maasbankers up against the pier* (Cape Argus). [< Afrikaans *maasbanker* < *maas* mesh + *banker* of the riverbank]

Mab (mab), *n.* See **Queen Mab.**

mac (mak), *n. British Informal.* a mackintosh: *The raincoat, or mac, is as essential to an Englishman as his teeth* (H. Allen Smith)

Mac (mak), *n.* **1.** son of (used in Scottish and Irish family names): *Her Macs let Scotland boast* (Henry Fielding). **2.** *U.S. Slang.* fellow (used as a form of direct address): *"If you don't like the way the subway's being run, Mac, why don't you buy it?"* (New Yorker). [< *Mac-*]

Mac-, *prefix.* son of (used in Scottish and Irish family names). Also, **Mc-, M'.** [< Scottish Gaelic, and Irish *mac* son]

Mac., Maccabees (books of the Apocrypha).

MAC (no periods), **1.** Military Airlift Command. **2.** multiple-access computer.

mac·a·baw (mak′ə bô), *n.* maccaboy.

ma·ca·ber (mə kä′bər), *adj.* macabre.

ma·ca·bre (mə kä′brə, -bər), *adj.* **1.** gruesome; horrible; ghastly. **2.** having to do with or suggestive of the danse macabre (dance of death): *Jörgenson ... without being exactly macabre, behaved more like an indifferent but restless corpse* (Joseph Conrad). [< French *macabre* < Middle French (*danse*) *macabré* (dance of) death; origin uncertain] —**ma·ca′bre·ly,** *adv.* —**Syn. 1.** grim.

ma·ca·co[1] (mə kā′kō), *n., pl.* **-cos.** macaque. [< Portuguese *macaco* < an African (Congo) word; see MACAQUE]

ma·ca·co[2] (mə kā′kō), *n., pl.* **-cos.** a black, short-tailed lemur of Madagascar. [< French *mococo;* origin uncertain]

mac·ad·am (mə kad′əm), *n.* **1.** small, broken stones. Layers of macadam are rolled until solid and smooth to surface roads. **2.** a road or pavement made of this. [< John L. *McAdam,* 1756-1836, a Scottish engineer, who invented it]

mac·a·da·mi·a (mak′ə dā′mē ə), *n.* **1.** any of a small group of trees or tall shrubs native to eastern Australia and cultivated in Hawaii. **2.** the nutlike fruit of the macadamia. [< New Latin *Macadamia* the genus name < John *Macadam,* 1827-1865, an Australian scientist]

mac·ad·am·ise (mə kad′ə mīz), *v.t.,* **-ised, -is·ing.** *Especially British.* macadamize.

mac·ad·am·i·za·tion (mə kad′ə mə zā′shən), *n.* the act or process of macadamizing.

mac·ad·am·ize (mə kad′ə mīz), *v.t.,* **-ized, -iz·ing.** to make or cover (a road) with macadam. —**Syn.** pave.

ma·caque (mə käk′), *n.* any of a group of hardy monkeys of Asia, the East Indies, and Africa. [< French *macaque* < Portuguese *macaco;* see MACACO[1]]

Macaque or bonnet monkey (from neck to rump, 1 to 1½ ft. long)

mac·a·rize (mak′ə rīz), *v.t.,* **-rized, -riz·ing.** to call happy; consider blessed. [< Greek *makarízein* < *mákar* happy]

mac·a·ro·ni (mak′ə rō′nē), *n., pl.* **-nis** or **-nies. 1.** wheat flour paste dried, usually in the form of hollow tubes, to be cooked for food. **2.** a fashionable English dandy of the 1700's who affectedly followed French or Italian fashions in dress, food, etc. **3.** a fop; dandy: *the pigmy macaronies of these degenerate days* (Washington Irving). Also, **maccaroni.** [< earlier Italian *maccaroni,* plural of *maccarone,* perhaps ultimately < Late Greek *makariā* barley broth]

mac·a·ron·ic (mak′ə ron′ik), *adj.* **1.** characterized by a mixture of Latin words with words from another language, or with non-Latin words that are given Latin endings: *macaronic verse.* **2.** involving a mixture of languages. **3.** mixed; jumbled. —*n.* a macaronic composition; a confused heap or mixture of several things. **macaronics,** macaronic verses. [< New Latin *macaronicus* mixed (verse) < Italian *maccheronico,* < *maccarone;* see MACARONI] —**mac′a·ron′i·cal·ly,** *adv.*

mac·a·ron·i·cal (mak′ə ron′ə kəl), *adj.* macaronic.

mac·a·roon (mak′ə rün′), *n.* **1.** (originally) a small, very sweet drop cooky made of almond paste, egg whites, and sugar. **2.** (in modern use) a small, chewy cooky of similar texture, usually made of coconut, egg whites, and sugar, but sometimes with rolled oats, corn flakes, or other cereals. **3.** a mixture of eggs, sugar, and lemon juice, used as a topping for cakes. [< French *macaron* < Italian *maccarone;* see MACARONI]

Ma·cas·sar oil (mə kas′ər), an oily substance much used during the 1800's to dress the hair. [< *Macassar,* a seaport in Celebes, Indonesia, the alleged place of origin]

ma·caw (mə kô′), *n.* any of several large parrots of South America and northwestern Mexico, characterized by long tails, brilliant feathers, and harsh voices. [< Portuguese *macao,* perhaps < a Brazilian name (compare Tupi *macavuana*)]

Macaw (about 3 ft. long)

Mac·beth (mək beth′, mak-), *n.* **1.** a tragedy by Shakespeare. **2.** its principal character, who murders his king and becomes king himself.

Macc., Maccabees (books of the Apocrypha).

Mac·ca·be·an (mak′ə bē′ən), *adj.* of or having to do with Judas Maccabaeus or the Maccabees: *His party reaped the benefit of his Maccabean courage* (Quarterly Review).

Mac·ca·bees (mak′ə bēz), *n.pl.* **1.** the supporters or successors of Judas Maccabeus, the leader of a revolt of Jewish patriots against Syria in the 100's B.C.: *The patriotism of the Jew, especially in the age of the Maccabees, was an ardent passion that enabled him to overcome enemies four times his number* (H.F. Henderson). **2.** two historical books of the Old Testament Apocrypha that tell about the revolt. *Abbr.:* Macc.

mac·ca·boy (mak′ə boi), *n.* a kind of snuff. [< *Macouba,* a district in Martinique]

mac·ca·ro·ni (mak′ə rō′nē), *n., pl.* **-nis** or **-nies.** macaroni.

mac·ca·ron·ic (mak′ə ron′ik), *adj., n.* macaronic.

mac·co·boy (mak′ə boi), *n.* maccaboy.

mace[1] (mās), *n.* **1.** a war club with a heavy metal head, often spiked or flanged, used in the Middle Ages to smash armor: *Hark! how the loud and ponderous mace of Time Knocks at the golden portals of the day* (Longfellow). **2.** a staff used as a symbol of authority, carried before or by certain officials. **3.** a macebearer. **4.** a light stick with a flat head, formerly used in billiards instead of a cue. [< Old French *mace,* also *masse* < Vulgar Latin *mattea* < Latin *matteola,* variant of *mateola* a digging tool] —**Syn. 2.** truncheon.

Great Mace[1] (def. 2) of Galway, Ireland

mace[2] (mās), *n.* a spice made from the dried outer covering of nutmegs. [Middle English *mace,* taken as singular of *macis* < Old French *macis* < Latin *macir* a fragrant resin < Greek *mákir*]

mace[3] (mās), *n., v.,* **maced, mac·ing.** *Slang.* —*n.* **1.** swindling. **2.** a swindler. —*v.t.* **1.** to swindle. **2.** to dun; make demands upon; extort from: *... indicted on graft and corruption charges for passing out illegal contracts and macing state employees for political contributions* (Time). [origin unknown]

Mace (mās), *n. Trademark.* an incapacitating tear gas, used especially against rioters.

mace-bear·er (mās′bãr′ər), *n.* a person who carries a mace as a symbol of authority before some high official.

Maced., Macedonia.

mac·é·doine (mas′ā dwän′), *n.* a mixture of vegetables or fruits, sometimes in jelly, served as a salad, garnish, dessert, etc. [< French *macédoine* (literally) Macedonian, apparently a reference to Macedonia as a land of many peoples, therefore a mixture]

Mac·e·do·ni·an (mas′ə dō′nē ən), *adj.* of or having to do with Macedonia, its people, or their language.
—*n.* **1.** a native or inhabitant of Macedonia. **2.** the Slavic language of modern Macedonia. **3.** the Indo-European language of ancient Macedonia.

mac·er (mā′sər), *n.* **1.** a mace-bearer. **2.** (in Scotland) an officer who keeps order, calls the rolls, etc., in a law court. [< Old French *maissier* < *masse* mace[1]]

mac·er·ate (mas′ə rāt), *v.*, **-at·ed, -at·ing.** —*v.t.* **1.** to soften by soaking for some time: *Flowers are macerated to extract their perfume.* **2.** to break up or soften (food) by the digestive process. **3.** to cause to grow thin. **4.** *Archaic.* to oppress; vex; worry. —*v.i.* **1.** to be softened, as by soaking. **2.** to become thin; waste away. [< Latin *mācerāre* (with English *-ate*[1]) soften] —**Syn.** *v.t.* **1.** ret. **3.** emaciate.

mac·er·at·er or **mac·er·a·tor** (mas′ə-rā′tər), *n.* a person or thing that macerates.

mac·er·a·tion (mas′ə rā′shən), *n.* **1.** the act or process of macerating. **2.** the state of being macerated.

Mach (mäk, mak), *n. Aeronautics.* Mach number.

mach., **1.** machine. **2.** machinery. **3.** machinist.

ma·chaan (mə chän′), *n.* machan.

Mach·a·bees (mak′ə bēz), *n.pl.* (in the Douay Bible) Maccabees.

mach·air (maʜ′ər), *n. Gaelic.* a plain or field of low elevation.

ma·chan (mə chän′), *n. Anglo-Indian.* a platform built into a tree, used by hunters to await a tiger driven toward them by beaters. [< Hindustani *machān*]

ma chère (mȧ sher′), *French.* my dear (used in addressing a woman or girl).

ma·chet·e (mə shet′ē, -shet′; *Spanish* mä-chā′tā), *n.* a large, heavy knife, used as a tool for cutting brush, sugar cane, etc., and as a weapon in South America, Central America, and the West Indies. [American English < Spanish *machete* (diminutive) < *macho* sledge hammer, mallet, ax, probably dialectal variant of *maza* < Vulgar Latin *mattea;* see MACE[1]]

Mach·i·a·vel (mak′ē ə vel), *n.* a Machiavellian person: *The play is overwhelmingly concerned with the impact of a new type of man—the Machiavel—on the political scene* (London Times).

Mach·i·a·vel·li·an or **Mach·i·a·vel·i·an** (mak′ē ə vel′ē ən), *adj.* **1.** of or having to do with Machiavelli or his political theories: *Educated in the Machiavellian . . . school of politics, she was versed in that "dissimulation" to which liberal Anglo-Saxons give a shorter name* (John L. Motley). **2.** characterized by subtle or unscrupulous cunning; crafty; wily; astute. —*n.* a follower of the crafty political methods of Machiavelli.

Mach·i·a·vel·li·an·ism (mak′ē ə vel′ē ə-niz′əm), *n.* the principles and practices of Machiavelli or his followers; unscrupulous political cunning.

Mach·i·a·vel·lic (mak′ē ə vel′ik), *adj.* Machiavellian.

Mach·i·a·vel·lism (mak′ē ə vel′iz əm), *n.* Machiavellianism.

ma·chic·o·late (mə chik′ə lāt), *v.t.*, **-lat·ed, -lat·ing.** to build or decorate with machicolations. [< Medieval Latin *machicolare* (with English *-ate*[1]), Latinization of Old French *machicoler* < Old Provençal *machacol* projection, balcony < *macar* to crush (< a Germanic word) + *col* neck < Latin *collum*]

ma·chic·o·lat·ed (mə chik′ə lā′tid), *adj.* having machicolations.

ma·chic·o·la·tion (mə chik′ə lā′shən), *n. Architecture.* **1.** an opening in the floor of a projecting gallery or parapet, or in the roof of an entrance, through which missiles, hot liquids, stones, etc., might be cast upon attackers. Machicolations were much used in medieval fortified structures. **2.** a projecting gallery or parapet with such openings; a projection supported on corbels.

Machicolations

ma·chin·a·bil·i·ty (mə shē′nə bil′ə tē), *n.* the ability to be worked by a machine; ease of operation by machine.

ma·chin·a·ble (mə shē′nə bəl), *adj.* that can be worked or tooled.

mach·i·nate (mak′ə nāt), *v.i., v.t.*, **-nat·ed, -nat·ing.** to contrive or devise artfully or with evil purpose; plot; intrigue. [< Latin *māchinārī* (with English *-ate*[1]) < *māchina;* see MACHINE]

mach·i·na·tion (mak′ə nā′shən), *n.* evil or artful plotting; scheming against authority; intrigue.
machinations, an evil plot; secret or cunning scheme: *Was, then, the death of my father . . . the consequence of human machinations?* (Charles Brockden Brown).
—**Syn.** conspiracy, cabal.

mach·i·na·tor (mak′ə nā′tər), *n.* a person who machinates; schemer; plotter.

ma·chine (mə shēn′), *n., adj., v.*, **-chined, -chin·ing.** —*n.* **1.** an arrangement of fixed and moving parts for doing work, each part having some special thing to do: *Sewing machines and washing machines make housework easier.* **2.** any device for applying power or changing its direction: *Levers and pulleys are simple machines.* **3.** an automobile. **4.** an airplane. **5.** a person or group that acts without thinking: *Public hacknies in the schooling trade . . . Machines themselves, and governed by a clock* (William Cowper). **6.** a group of people controlling a political organization: *the Democratic machine.* **7. a.** a contrivance in the ancient theater for producing stage effects. **b.** a contrivance, such as a supernatural power or person, introduced into a literary work for effect. **8.** *Archaic.* the human or animal body. **9.** any structure or contrivance: *There was not a bed . . . except one oldfashioned machine, with a high-gilt tester* (Tobias Smollett). **10.** *Obsolete.* any vehicle, as a stagecoach.
—*adj.* **1.** of or having to do with a machine or machines: *machine action, a machine politician, the machine age.* **2.** by or with a machine, especially as distinguished from what is done by hand: *machine printing.* **3.** like that of a machine; mechanical or stereotyped.
—*v.t.* to make, prepare, or finish with a machine: *Bessemer steel normally contains more sulfur and phosphorus, and therefore is easier to machine, or cut* (World Book Encyclopedia).
[< Middle French *machine,* learned borrowing from Latin *māchina* < Greek *mēchanē* a device < *mēchos* means, expedient]
—**Syn.** *n.* **2.** mechanism. **3** motorcar. **4.** aircraft. **5.** automaton.

machine bolt, a bolt with a thread and a square or hexagonal head.

ma·chined (mə shēnd′), *adj.* made by or as if by a machine or machinery.

machine gun, a gun that fires small-arms ammunition automatically and can keep up a rapid fire of bullets.

ma·chine-gun (mə shēn′gun′), *v.*, **-gunned, -gun·ning,** *adj.* —*v.t.* to fire at with a machine gun; kill or wound with a machine gun: *The undefended Basque city of Guernica was systematically bombed and machine-gunned by German planes* (Time). —*adj.* **1.** of or having to do with a machine gun: *machine-gun fire.* **2.** rapid and staccato, like the action of a machine gun: *Speaking in either language at a machine-gun pace . . .* (New York Times).

machine gunner, **1.** one skilled in operating a machine gun, as a soldier or airman. **2.** a hired assassin or partisan fighter: *Terrorists struck for the first time in the heart of Algiers when four masked machine gunners set fire to a downtown apartment-house garage* (Newsweek).

machine language, information or instructions in the form of numbers, characters, punched tape, etc., that can be processed by an electronic computer or a data-processing machine.

ma·chine·like (mə shēn′līk′), *adj.* resembling a machine in structure or operation; steady, automatic, and unvarying: *machinelike repetition.*

ma·chine-load (mə shēn′lōd′), *n.* as much as a machine can carry or handle in its normal operation: *a machine-load of laundry.*

ma·chine-made (mə shēn′mād′), *adj.* made by machinery, not by hand.

machine minder, a machiner.

ma·chin·er (mə shē′nər), *n.* a person who works or tends a machine.

ma·chin·er·y (mə shē′nər ē, -shēn′rē), *n., pl.* **-er·ies. 1.** machines: *A factory contains much machinery.* **2.** the parts or works of a machine: *Machinery is oiled to keep it running smoothly.* **3.** any combination of persons or things by which something is kept going or something is done; system: *Policemen, judges, courts, and prisons are the machinery of the law.* **4.** persons, incidents, etc., used in the plot of a literary work.

machine screw, a threaded metal rod (1/4 inch or less in diameter), usually with a slotted head, used in holes tapped in metal parts.

Machine Screws

machine shop, a workshop for making or repairing machines or parts of machines.

machine tool, a tool or machine worked by power, with little or no direction, such as an electric drill or lathe: *Machine tools perform the heavy grinding and milling chores in metal working shops* (Wall Street Journal).

ma·chine-tool (mə shēn′tül′), *v.t.* to produce, especially to mass-produce, by or as if by a machine tool; produce automatically or with regular precision.

machine translation, **1.** translation from one language to another by an electronic computer. **2.** the result of this process.

ma·chin·ist (mə shē′nist), *n.* **1.** a skilled worker with machine tools. **2.** a person who runs a machine. **3.** a person who makes or repairs machinery. **4.** a warrant officer who acts as assistant to an engineer officer in the United States Navy.

machinist's hammer, a hammer having a straight or rounded peen.

ma·chin·i·za·tion (mə shē′nə zā′shən), *n.* **1.** the act or process of machinizing. **2.** a thing that is machinized.

ma·chin·ize (mə shē′nīz), *v.t.*, **-ized, -iz·ing.** to make into or make like a machine.

ma·chis·mo (mä chēs′mō), *n. Spanish.* **1.** manliness. **2.** (literally) maleness.

Mach·me·ter (mäk′mē′tər, mak′-), *n.* a device that indicates the speed of an aircraft relative to the speed of sound. [< *Mach (number)* + *-meter*]

Machmeter dial shows Mach number (.73 here) indicating ratio of aircraft's speed to the speed of sound.

Mach number (mäk, mak), a number expressing in decimals the ratio of the speed of an object to the speed of sound in the same medium, the speed of sound being Mach One. Thus, an aircraft traveling at half the speed of sound has a Mach number of 0.5, or subsonic; at twice the speed of sound its Mach number is 2, or supersonic: *The use of swept-back wings raises the critical Mach number for the aircraft* (Science News). [< Ernst *Mach,* 1838-1916, an Austrian physicist]

ma·cho (mä′chō), *n., pl.* **-chos,** *adj. Spanish.* —*n.* a male, especially a robust, virile male. —*adj.* masculine; manly.

Mach One, *Aeronautics.* the speed of sound (about 1,087 feet per second in dry air at 32 degrees Fahrenheit).

ma·chree (mə krē′), *n.* my heart, my love, my dearest, etc., a term of endearment in Ireland. [< Irish *mo* my + *croidhe* heart]

Macht·po·li·tik (mäʜt′pō′lē tēk′), *n. German.* power politics: *The fertilization of "ideas and cultures" which the West usually bestows on developing nations are those of Machtpolitik and the latest military technology* (Scientific American).

mac·i·lent (mas′ə lənt), *adj.* lean; thin. [< Latin *macilentus* < *macēre* to be lean]

mac·in·tosh (mak′ən tosh), *n.* mackintosh.

mack (mak), *n. British Informal.* a mackintosh (raincoat).

mack·er·el (mak′ər əl, mak′rəl), *n., pl.* **-el** or (*occasionally, especially with reference to different species*) **-els. 1.** a salt-water fish of the North Atlantic, much used for food. It is blue-green with dark bands on the back and silver below, and grows to about 18 inches long. **2.** any of various related fishes, such as the Spanish mackerel of the Atlantic coasts of North and South America. [< Old French *maquerel*]

mackerel gull, the common tern.

mackerel sky, a sky spotted with small, fleecy, white clouds.

 PRONUNCIATION KEY: hat, āge, cãre, fär; let, ēqual, tėrm; it, īce; hot, ōpen, ôrder; oil, out; cup, pu̇t, rüle;

mack·i·naw (mak′ə nô), *n.* **1.** Also, **Mackinaw coat.** a kind of short coat made of heavy woolen cloth, often in a plaid pattern. **2.** Also, **Mackinaw blanket.** a thick woolen blanket, often with bars of color. **3.** a Mackinaw boat. [American English < earlier *Mackinac,* a place name, now Mackinaw City, Michigan < Canadian French *michili-mackinac* < Algonkian (Ojibwa) *mitchi makinâk* large turtle]

Mackinaw boat, a flat-bottomed boat with a sharp prow and square stern, used on the Great Lakes.

Mackinaw trout, the namaycush; lake trout: *Mackinaw trout . . . is generally caught by the hook, and sometimes weigh ten and twelve pounds* (Southern Literary Messenger). See the picture under **namaycush.**

mack·in·tosh (mak′ən tosh), *n.* **1.** a raincoat made of a closely woven, waterproof cloth: *He put on his mackintosh and went out again in the rain* (Graham Greene). **2.** the cloth itself. Also, **macintosh.** [< Charles *Macintosh,* 1766-1843, the inventor of the waterproofing process]

mack·in·toshed (mak′ən toshd), *adj.* wearing a mackintosh.

mack·le (mak′əl), *n., v.,* **-led, -ling.** *Printing.* —*n.* a blur, as from a double impression. —*v.t., v.i.* to blur or become blurred, as from a double impression. Also, **macule.** [< Middle French *macule;* see MACULE]

ma·cle (mak′əl), *n.* **1.** a twinned crystal: *Crystals of ice, like macles of snow, were observed to form near the bottom* (Matthew F. Maury). **2.** a dark spot in a mineral. **3.** chiastolite. [< French *macle,* Old French *mascle,* perhaps < Medieval Latin *mascula* mesh of a net < Latin *macula* a spot, stain]

mac·ra·mé (mak′rə mā), *n.,* or **macramé lace,** a coarse lace or fringe, made by knotting thread or cord in patterns. [apparently < Turkish *makrama* napkin < Arabic *maḥrama* handkerchief]

mac·ro (mak′rō), *adj.* of great or comprehensive scope; large-scale: *The macro approach to human problems tends to the notion of the individual not as a unit, but as a fraction, a percentage of some whole* (Sunday Times).

macro-, *combining form.* **1.** large: *Macroclimate = the climate of a large region.* **2.** abnormally large: *Macrography = abnormally large writing.* [< Greek *makro-* < *makrós* long, large]

mac·ro·bi·ot·ic (mak′rō bī ot′ik), *adj.* **1.** long-lived. **2.** tending to prolong life. [< Greek *makrobíotos* (< *makrós* long + *bíotos* life) + English *-ic*]

mac·ro·ce·phal·ic (mak′rō sə fal′ik), *adj.* having an abnormally large head or skull. [< Greek *makroképhalos* (< *makrós* long + *kephalḗ* head) + English *-ic*]

mac·ro·ceph·a·lous (mak′rə sef′ə ləs), *adj.* macrocephalic.

mac·ro·ceph·a·ly (mak′rə sef′ə lē), *n.* a condition in which the head or skull is abnormally large.

mac·ro·chem·i·cal (mak′rō kem′ə kəl), *adj.* of or having to do with macrochemistry.

mac·ro·chem·is·try (mak′rō kem′ə strē), *n.* the branch of chemistry that deals with substances or reactions observed by the unassisted eye or without a microscope.

mac·ro·cli·mate (mak′rō klī′mit), *n.* the climate of a large region.

mac·ro·cosm (mak′rə koz əm), *n.* the universe: *The microcosm repeats the macrocosm* (Thomas Huxley). [< Old French *macrocosme,* learned borrowing from Medieval Latin *macrocosmus* < Greek *makrós* great + *kósmos* world order, universe; (originally) order; ornament] —**Syn.** cosmos.

mac·ro·cos·mic (mak′rə koz′mik), *adj.* of or having to do with the macrocosm; immense; comprehensive: *the macrocosmic ominousness of government.*

mac·ro·cyst (mak′rə sist), *n.* a large cyst or spore, as certain resting forms of slime molds.

mac·ro·cys·tis (mak′rə sis′tis), *n.* a brown seaweed of the southern seas and the northern Pacific coasts. It has the longest stems known in the vegetable kingdom, sometimes reaching a length of 700 feet. [< New Latin *Macrocystis* the genus name < Greek *makrós* long + *kýstis* bladder]

mac·ro·cyte (mak′rə sīt), *n.* an abnormally large red corpuscle found in the blood, especially in pernicious anemia. [< *macro-* + *-cyte*]

mac·ro·cyt·ic (mak′rə sit′ik), *adj.* marked by the presence of macrocytes: *Macrocytic anemia occurs not only as pernicious anemia but also with liver disease, pregnancy, sprue, and pellagra* (Science News Letter).

mac·ro·dome (mak′rə dōm), *n. Crystallography.* a dome whose planes are parallel to the longer lateral axis.

mac·ro·e·co·nom·ic (mak′rō ē′kə nom′ik, -ek′ə-), *adj.* of or having to do with macroeconomics: *macroeconomic planning, macroeconomic analysis.*

mac·ro·e·co·nom·ics (mak′rō ē′kə nom′iks, -ek′ə-), *n.* economics dealing with those national statistics that can be taken as a controlling factor in the economy as a whole.

mac·ro·ev·o·lu·tion (mak′rō ev′ə lü′shən), *n.* the evolution of animals and plants on a large scale, resulting in the classification groupings above the species level, such as families and phyla.

mac·ro·fau·na (mak′rō fô′nə), *n.* the macroscopic animals of a given habitat: . . . *and the macrofauna, represented by larger arthropods as, for example, millipedes, centipedes . . . many insects, slugs, and snails* (New Scientist). [< *macro-* + *fauna*]

mac·ro·flo·ra (mak′rō flôr′ə, -flōr′-), *n.* the macroscopic plants of a given habitat. [< *macro-* + *flora*]

mac·ro·ga·mete (mak′rō gə mēt′, -gam′ēt), *n.* the larger, usually the female, of two conjugating gametes of an organism which reproduces by the union of unlike gametes; megagamete.

mac·ro·glob·u·lin (mak′rō glob′yə lin), *n.* a globulin with an abnormally high molecular weight, found in the blood plasma of persons suffering from rheumatoid arthritis.

mac·ro·graph (mak′rə graf, -gräf), *n.* a photograph, drawing, etc., of an object that is magnified very little or not at all.

ma·crog·ra·phy (mə krog′rə fē), *n.* **1.** abnormally large writing, especially as a symptom of nervous disorder. **2.** examination and preparation of work, particularly in engineering and metallurgy, at low magnification or without use of a microscope.

ma·crom·e·ter (mə krom′ə tər), *n.* an instrument for measuring the size and distance of objects that are very far away or hard to reach. [< *macro-* + *-meter*]

mac·ro·mo·lec·u·lar (mak′rō mə lek′yə lər), *adj.* of, having to do with, or characteristic of macromolecules: *macromolecular chemistry.*

mac·ro·mol·e·cule (mak′rō mol′ə kyül), *n.* a large and complex molecule made up of many smaller molecules linked together, as in a resin or polymer.

ma·cron (mā′kron, mak′ron; mā′krən, mak′rən), *n.* a straight, horizontal line (-) placed over a vowel to show that it is long or is pronounced in a certain way. Examples: *āge, ēqual, īce, ōpen, ūse.* [< Greek *makrón,* neuter, long]

mac·ro·nu·cle·us (mak′rō nü′klē əs, -nyü′-), *n., pl.* **-cle·i** (-klē ī), **-cle·us·es.** the larger of two types of nuclei present in various ciliates, which is considered to control vegetative processes as against those of reproduction.

mac·ro·nu·tri·ent (mak′rō nü′trē ənt, -nyü′-), *n.* a major nutrient element necessary for plant or animal growth: *In contrast to the macronutrients, such as calcium, phosphorus, sulfur, sodium and potassium that are needed in relatively large amounts, the trace elements are required only in very small amounts* (Science News Letter).

mac·ro·phage (mak′rə fāj), *n.* one of several types of white blood cells which combat infection; phagocyte.

mac·ro·pho·to·graph (mak′rō fō′tə graf, -gräf), *n.* a photograph of an object that is magnified very little or not at all; a macrograph made by photography.

mac·ro·pho·tog·ra·phy (mak′rō fə tog′rə fē), *n.* the photographing of objects upon an actual or slightly magnified scale.

mac·ro·phys·ics (mak′rō fiz′iks), *n.* the branch of physics that deals with bodies that are large enough to be observed and measured.

mac·ro·phyte (mak′rə fīt), *n.* a macroscopic plant. [< *macro-* + Greek *phytón* plant]

mac·ro·phyt·ic (mak′rə fit′ik), *adj.* of or having to do with macrophytes.

mac·ro·scop·ic (mak′rə skop′ik), *adj.* visible to the naked eye. —**ma′cro·scop′i·cal·ly,** *adv.*

mac·ros·mat·ic (mak′roz mat′ik), *adj.* having the organs of smell well-developed: *Today, mammals are divided into macrosmatic (dog, cat) and microsmatic (man) classifications, according to whether they possess a high or low odour sensitivity* (New Scientist). [< *macro-* + *osmatic*]

mac·ro·spo·ran·gi·um (mak′rə spə ran′jē əm), *n.* megasporangium.

mac·ro·spore (mak′rə spôr, -spōr), *n. Botany.* a megaspore.

mac·ro·struc·tur·al (mak′rō struk′chər əl), *adj.* of or having to do with macrostructure.

mac·ro·struc·ture (mak′rō struk′chər), *n.* the macroscopic structure of bodies, objects, etc.: *Microstructure and macrostructure, too, were sufficiently heterogeneous, the grain size being particularly coarse* (New Scientist).

mac·ro·tax·o·nom·ic (mak′rō tak sə nom′ik), *adj.* of or having to do with macrotaxonomy.

mac·ro·tax·on·o·my (mak′rō tak son′ə mē), *n.* the taxonomy of the larger groupings of organisms, such as family, order, etc.

ma·cru·ral (mə krůr′əl), *adj.* macrurous.

ma·cru·ran (mə krůr′ən), *n.* a macrurous crustacean. —*adj.* macrurous.

ma·cru·roid (mə krůr′oid), *adj.* macrurous.

ma·cru·rous (mə krůr′əs), *adj.* of or belonging to a group of crustaceans that have ten legs and well-developed abdomens, including the lobsters, prawns, shrimps, etc. [< New Latin *Macrura* the suborder name (< Greek *makrós* long + *ourá* tail) + *-ous*]

mac·ta·tion (mak tā′shən), *n.* the killing of a sacrificial victim. [< Latin *mactātiō, -ōnis* < *mactāre* slay]

mac·u·la (mak′yə lə), *n., pl.* **-lae** (-lē). **1.** a spot, stain, or blotch, as on the sun, in a mineral, or in the skin. **2.** the macula lutea. [< Latin *macula* spot, stain]

macula lu·te·a (lü′tē ə), *pl.* **maculae lu·te·ae** (lü′tē ē). a yellowish spot surrounding the fovea centralis in the retina of certain vertebrates. [< New Latin *macula lutea*]

mac·u·lar (mak′yə lər), *adj.* **1.** of or having to do with the macula lutea. **2.** of, having to do with, or characteristic of a macula or maculae. **3.** having maculae; spotted.

mac·u·late (*v.* mak′yə lāt; *adj.* mak′yə lit), *v.,* **-lat·ed, -lat·ing,** *adj.* —*v.t.* to spot; stain; soil; defile. —*adj.* spotted; stained; soiled. [< Latin *maculāre* (with English *-ate*[1]) < *macula* a spot]

mac·u·la·tion (mak′yə lā′shən), *n.* **1.** a spotting or soiling. **2.** a being spotted or defiled. **3.** the pattern of spots on an animal or plant.

mac·ule (mak′yül), *n., v.,* **-uled, -ul·ing.** —*n.* **1.** macula. **2.** *Printing.* mackle. —*v.t., v.i. Printing.* to mackle; make or become blurred. [< Middle French *macule,* learned borrowing from Latin *macula* spot, stain]

ma·cush·la (mə küsh′lə), *n. Irish.* dear; darling. [< Irish Gaelic *mo cuishle* (literally) my blood]

M.A.C.V. or **MACV** (no periods), Military Assistance Command, Vietnam.

mad (mad), *adj.,* **mad·der, mad·dest,** *v.,* **mad·ded, mad·ding,** *n.* —*adj.* **1.** out of one's head; crazy; insane: *A man must be mad to cut himself on purpose.* **2.** much excited; wild: *The dog made mad efforts to catch up with the automobile.* **3.** foolish; unwise: *the same trash mad mortals wish for here* (Alexander Pope). *The maddest voyage, and the most unlikely to be performed, that ever was undertaken* (Daniel Defoe). **4. a.** blindly and unreasonably fond: *Some girls are mad about going to dances.* **b.** wildly gay or merry: *Tomorrow 'ill be of all the year the maddest merriest day* (Tennyson). **5.** *Informal.* very angry: *The insult made him mad. Mother was mad at me for coming home late for dinner.* **6.** having rabies or hydrophobia: *A mad dog foams at the mouth and may bite people.*

like mad, furiously; very hard, fast, etc.: *I ran like mad to catch the train.*

mad as a hatter. See under **hatter.**

mad as a March hare. See under **hare.**

—*v.t., v.i. Archaic.* to be or become mad; madden: *At the same time it madded some of the Republicans* (Marietta Holley).

—*n. Slang.* a fit of anger; fury: *to have a mad on.*

[Old English *gemǣded* rendered insane] —**Syn.** *adj.* **1.** See **crazy. 2.** frenzied, frantic. **3.** rash. **4. a.** infatuated. **5.** furious.

➔ **mad, angry.** Although *mad* is often substituted for *angry* in informal English, this usage is not always regarded as standard.

Mad., madam.

MAD (no periods) or **M.A.D.,** or **mad** (no periods), Magnetic Airborne Detection (a system for detecting submarines with airplanes by locating the magnetic field of the steel hull of the submarine. It is now also used in locating geological features beneath polar ice).

Madag., Madagascar, a large island in the Indian Ocean opposite southeastern Africa.

Mad·a·gas·can (mad′ə gas′kən), *adj.* of or having to do with Madagascar or its people. *—n.* a native or inhabitant of Madagascar.

Mad·a·gas·car jasmine (mad′ə gas′kər), a tropical twining shrub of Madagascar and neighboring areas, with thick, dark-green leaves and fragrant, waxy flowers, often cultivated in hothouses; stephanotis.

mad·am (mad′əm), *n., pl.* **mad·ams** or **mes·dames,** *v., —n.* **1.** a polite title used in speaking to or of a lady: *Madam, will you take my seat?* **2.** a woman who runs a brothel. *—v.t.* to address as "madam": *... the sparring scene between her and Mrs. Chatterley, wherein they "Madam" each other with genteel petulance* (Examiner). [< Old French *ma dame* my lady < Latin *mea* my, and *domina* mistress, lady]

➔ As a form of address, Madam or Dear Madam is appropriate for either a married or an unmarried woman.

mad·ame (mad′əm; *French* mȧ dȧm′), *n., pl.* **mes·dames. 1.** a French title for a married woman. **2.** a title often used by women singers, artists, etc. *Abbr.:* Mme. **3.** madam (def. 2). [< Old French *ma dame;* see MADAM]

mad·a·pol·lam (mad′ə pol′əm), *n.* a soft cotton cloth intermediate in quality between calico and muslin: *In the first decades of this century, expectant mothers could buy madapollam at sixpence a yard for baby gowns* (London Times). [< *Madapollam,* a town in India where it was first manufactured]

ma·dar (mə där′), *n.* **1.** either of two tropical Asian or African shrubs of the milkweed family whose juice and root bark yield a drug. **2.** a latex obtained from this shrub, used as a substitute for gutta-percha. **3.** a fine silky fiber obtained from the madar. Also, **mudar.** [< Hindi *madār*]

mad-brained (mad′brānd′), *adj.* hot-headed; uncontrolled; rash.

mad·cap (mad′kap′), *n.* a very impulsive person. *—adj.* impulsive; hasty; wild: *Their going along was nothing more than a madcap frolic* (Herman Melville). **—Syn.** *n.* rattlebrain. *-adj.* reckless, precipitate.

mad·cap·per·y (mad′kap′ər ē), *n.* the behavior of a madcap; reckless conduct; wildness: *Seeing the two plays ... in such quick succession ... does provide an opportunity to follow in one long sweep the two stages of Prince Hal's progress from madcappery to maturity* (Punch).

mad·den (mad′ən), *v.t.* **1.** to make crazy: *The shipwrecked sailors were nearly maddened by cold and hunger when the rescuers found them.* **2.** to make very angry or excited; irritate greatly: *The crowd was maddened by the umpire's decision.* *—v.i.* to become crazy; act crazy: *All Bedlam, or Parnassus, is let out ... They rave, recite, and madden round the land* (Alexander Pope). **—Syn.** *v.t.* **1.** derange. **2.** enrage, infuriate.

mad·den·ing (mad′ə ning), *adj.* **1.** that maddens; raging; furious: *All the people rushed along with maddening eagerness to the anticipated solace* (Thomas De Quincey). **2.** very annoying; irritating: *maddening delays.* **—mad′den·ing·ly,** *adv.*

mad·der (mad′ər), *n.* **1.** a European and Asian vine with prickly leaves and small greenish-yellow flowers. **2.** its red root. **3.** a red dye made from these roots. **4.** red; crimson. *—v.t.* to treat or dye with madder. [Old English *mædere* some plant used in dyeing]

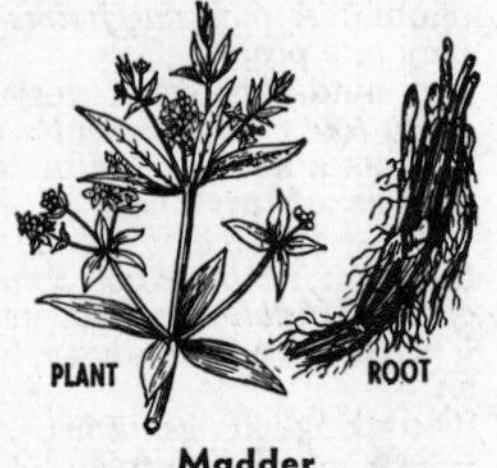

Madder

madder family, a group of dicotyledonous, chiefly tropical trees, shrubs, or herbs closely related to the honeysuckle family. The family includes the madder, cinchona, coffee, gardenia, bedstraw, and partridgeberry.

mad·ding (mad′ing), *adj.* **1.** mad; acting as if mad: *Far from the madding crowd's ignoble strife* (Thomas Gray). **2.** making mad; maddening: *the distraction of this madding fever* (Shakespeare).

mad·dish (mad′ish), *adj.* somewhat mad.

made (mād), *v.* past tense and past participle of **make:** *The baker made the cake. It was made of flour, milk, butter, eggs, and sugar.* *—adj.* **1.** built; formed: *strongly made.* **2.** specially prepared: *made gravy, a made dish.* **3.** artificially produced: *made land.* **4.** invented; made-up: *a made word.* **5.** certain of success; successful: *You are a made man, Tom, if you get on the right side of that Rajah of yours* (Joseph Conrad).

have (got) it made, *U.S. Informal.* to be assured of success: *"The Odd Couple" [a play] has it made* (New York Times). *Most Western Republicans think that ... their boy Barry's got it made* (Wall Street Journal).

Ma·dei·ra or **ma·dei·ra** (mə dir′ə), *n.* any of several fortified wines made on the island of Madeira, ranging from quite pale and dry to brownish and sweet.

Madeira vine, a basellaceous climbing plant of tropical America, with bright-green leaves and long clusters of small, fragrant, white flowers.

made·leine (mȧd len′), *n.* a small, sweet cake resembling a pound cake and usually spread with jam, icing, nuts, or fruits. [< French *madeleine* < *Sainte Madeleine* Saint Madeleine (because fruits used in the cake ripen around July 22, Saint Madeleine's Day)]

mad·e·line (mad′ə lin), *n.* madeleine.

mad·e·moi·selle (mad′ə mə zel′; *French* mȧd mwȧ zel′), *n., pl.* **mes·de·moi·selles. 1.** the French title for an unmarried woman; Miss. **2.** a French governess: *The parties of children that used to be seen hurrying along the avenue ... in the care of Nannies or Mademoiselles or Fräuleins* ... (New Yorker). *Abbr.:* Mlle. [< French *mademoiselle* < Old French *ma demoiselle* my demoiselle, young lady]

made-to-meas·ure (mād′tü mezh′ər), *adj.* made according to the buyer's measurements: *a made-to-measure suit.*

made-to-or·der (mād′tü ôr′dər), *adj.* made according to the buyer's wishes: *made-to-order clothing.*

made-up (mād′up′), *adj.* **1.** put together. **2.** invented; untrue: *a made-up story.* **3.** painted, powdered, etc., with cosmetics: *made-up lips.* **4.** resolved; decided: *a made-up mind.* **—Syn. 1.** constructed. **2.** fabricated.

made-work (mād′wėrk′), *adj.* devised to make jobs, sometimes unimportant or unnecessary, especially in public works originated during periods of economic distress: *a made-work project.*

mad-head·ed (mad′hed′id), *adj.* mad-brained: *... the inflammatory harangues of some mad-headed enthusiast* (Samuel Taylor Coleridge).

mad·house (mad′hous′), *n.* **1.** an asylum for insane people. **2.** a place of uproar and confusion.

mad·id (mad′id), *adj.* wet; moist; humid: *his large deep blue eye, madid and yet piercing* (Benjamin Disraeli). [< Latin *madidus* < *madēre* to be wet]

Mad·i·son Avenue (mad′ə sən), a street in New York City which is the locale of the major advertising agencies of America and is synonymous with the effort to mold the American taste.

Mad·i·so·ni·an (mad′ə sō′nē ən), *adj.* of or having to do with James Madison, fourth president of the United States: *... our attempt to combine the Madisonian system of checks and balances with the Jeffersonian concept of majority rule under parties* (Harper's).

mad itch, pseudorabies.

mad·ly (mad′lē), *adv.* **1.** insanely. **2.** furiously. **3.** foolishly.

mad·man (mad′man′, -mən), *n., pl.* **-men. 1.** an insane man; crazy person: *The explosion, the archbishop said, was probably "the gesture of a madman"* (Newsweek). **2.** a person who behaves madly; wildly foolish person: *I have been a madman and a fool* (David Bethune).

mad money, *U.S. Slang.* **1.** money carried by a girl or woman to use for small expenses. **2.** money carried by a girl or woman so that she is not dependent on an escort for transportation home, in the event of a quarrel or other cause for leaving him.

mad·ness (mad′nis), *n.* **1.** a being crazy; loss of one's mind: *Great wits are sure to madness near allied* (John Dryden). **2.** great rage; fury: *The madness of the people soon subsided* (Edward Gibbon). **3.** great folly: *It would be madness to try to sail a boat in this storm.* **4.** extravagant enthusiasm. **5.** rabies. **—Syn. 1.** insanity. **2.** wrath. **3.** idiocy.

ma·don·na (mə don′ə), *n.* a former Italian title for a married woman equivalent to *madame* (*signora* is now used). [< Italian *madonna* < *ma,* short for *mia* my (< Latin *mea*) + *donna* lady < Latin *domina*]

Ma·don·na (mə don′ə), *n.* **1.** Mary, the mother of Jesus. **2.** a picture or statue of her.

Madonna lily, a common, early-blooming lily whose white blossom is a symbol of purity: *An exquisite motion which an artist ... would not have wasted ... on anything less than a Madonna lily* (Elizabeth S. Phelps).

mad·ras (mad′rəs; mə dras′, -dräs′), *n.* **1.** a closely woven cotton cloth with a design on plain ground, used for shirts, dresses, etc. **2.** a thin cloth, often with a design or pattern, used for curtains, draperies, etc. **3.** a brightly colored kerchief of silk and cotton. [< *Madras,* a city and state in India]

ma·dras·ah (mə dras′ə), *n.* a Moslem school or college. Also, **medresseh.** [< Arabic *madrasa*]

Ma·dras·i (mə dras′ē, -drä′sē), *n., pl.* **-dras·i** or **-dras·is,** *adj. —n.* a native or inhabitant of Madras, a city and state in India. *—adj.* of or having to do with Madras or Madrasi.

ma·dre (*Spanish* mä′ᴛʜrā; *Italian* mä′drā), *n. Spanish and Italian.* mother.

mad·re·po·rar·i·an (mad′rə pô rãr′ē ən, -pō-), *adj.* of or belonging to a group of anthozoans with a continuous calcareous skeleton, including most of the stony corals. *—n.* a madreporarian anthozoan.

mad·re·pore (mad′rə pôr, -pōr), *n.* any of various stony corals that often form reefs in tropical seas. [< French *madrépore* < Italian *madrepora* < *madre* mother (< Latin *māter*) + *poro,* ultimately < Greek *pôros* kind of stone]

mad·re·por·ic (mad′rə pôr′ik, -por′-), *adj.* **1.** of, having to do with, or consisting of madrepores. **2.** of or having to do with a madreporite.

mad·re·por·ite (mad′rə pə rīt; mad′rə-pôr′īt, -pōr′-), *n.* the external opening of the stone canal in an echinoderm. [< *madrepor*(e) + *-ite*¹]

mad·ri·gal (mad′rə gəl), *n.* **1.** a short poem, often about love, that can be set to music: *... the spoken poetry adding greatly to the sense of the sung madrigals which follow* (Harper's). **2.** a song with parts for several voices, sung without instrumental accompaniment: *No Bach motet, no big madrigal ... relieved a succession of prettily sung choral songs* (London Times). **3.** any song. [< Italian *madrigale,* ultimately < Latin *mātrīcālis* original, invented < *mātrīx* womb; see MATRIX]

mad·ri·gal·ist (mad′rə gə list), *n.* a composer or singer of madrigals.

mad·ri·lene or **mad·ri·lène** (mad′rə len, mad′rə len′), *n.* a consommé flavored with tomato, usually served chilled or jellied. [< French *madrilène* of Madrid, Spain < Spanish *madrileño*]

Ma·dri·le·ño (mä′drə lān′yō), *n., pl.* **-ños.** a native or inhabitant of Madrid, Spain. [< Spanish *madrileño*]

ma·dro·ña (mə drō′nyə), *n.* an evergreen tree or shrub of the heath family, growing in western North America. It has a very hard wood and a smooth, reddish bark, and bears yellow, edible berries. [< American English < Spanish *madroño* arbutus; origin uncertain]

madroña apple, the berry of the madroña.

ma·dro·ño (mə drō′nyō), *n., pl.* **-ños.** madroña.

mad·stone (mad′stōn′), *n. U.S.* a concretion of mineral salts found in the stomach and intestines of deer, formerly thought to relieve or cure the effects of a poisonous bite when placed on the wound.

mad·tom (mad′tom′), *n.* any of a large group of small catfish with a poison gland at the base of the pectoral spine, found in lakes and streams.

Ma·du·ra foot (mə dür′ə), mycetoma of the foot, a fungous disease. [< *Madura,* a district in Madras State, India]

ma·du·ro (mə dür′ō), *adj., n., pl.* **-ros.** —*adj.* made with dark and strong tobacco. —*n.* a maduro cigar. [< Spanish *maduro* mature < Latin *mātūrus*]

mad·wom·an (mad′wům′ən), *n., pl.* **-wom·en. 1.** a woman who is insane. **2.** a wildly foolish woman.

mad·wort (mad′wėrt′), *n.* **1.** any of a group of low, branching herbs of the mustard family, such as the gold-of-pleasure; alyssum. **2.** a low, weedy herb of the borage family native to Europe.

mae (mā), *adj., n., adv. Scottish.* more.

Mae·ce·nas (mi sē′nəs), *n.* a generous patron of literature or art: *Are you not called . . . a mock Maecenas to second-hand authors?* (Richard Brinsley Sheridan). [< *Maecenas,* a Roman statesman, about 74-8 B.C., patron of literature and friend of Horace and Virgil]

mael·strom (māl′strəm), *n.* **1.** a great or turbulent whirlpool. **2.** a violent confusion of feelings, ideas, or conditions: *The poor man lived always in the whirl of a perfect Maelstrom of promises and engagements* (Harriet Beecher Stowe). [< earlier Dutch *maelstrom* < *malen* to grind + *stroom* stream]

mae·nad (mē′nad), *n.* **1.** *Greek and Roman Mythology.* a woman attendant or worshiper of Dionysus or Bacchus; bacchante. **2.** a woman extremely excited or in a frenzy. Also, **menad.** [< Latin *Maenas, -adis* < Greek *mainás, -ádos* a mad woman, especially a bacchante < *maínesthai* to rage, be mad]

mae·nad·ic (mi nad′ik), *adj.* of or like the maenads; frenzied; raving; frantic. Also, **menadic.**

ma·es·to·so (mä′es tō′sō), *adj., adv. Music.* stately; with dignity. [< Italian *maestoso* majestic < *maesta,* or *maestate* majesty, learned borrowing from Latin *mājestās*]

maes·tro (mīs′trō; *Italian* mä es′trō), *n., pl.* **-tros,** *Italian* **ma·es·tri** (mä es′trē). **1.** a great composer, teacher, or conductor of music: *His appearance in the dual role of pianist and maestro, was nevertheless an impressive demonstration of a remarkable musical talent* (New Yorker). **2.** a master of any art: . . . *a maestro in the field of travel and gastronomy* (Atlantic). [< Italian *maestro* < Latin *magister* a master]

Mae West (mā′ west′), an inflatable vest worn as a life preserver by an aviator in flying over water. [< *Mae West,* born 1892, an American entertainer (from a whimsical comparison of inflated vest to her celebrated bust size)]

maf·fick (maf′ik), *British.* —*v.i.* to celebrate a national victory with great demonstrations of joy. —*n.* an act of mafficking. [back formation < earlier *mafficking,* used as if a present participle, alteration of *Mafeking,* South Africa (from the kind of celebrations following the end of the siege there, on May 17, 1900)] —**maf′fick·er,** *n.*

ma·fi·a or **maf·fi·a** (mä′fē ä), *n.* the spirit of popular hostility to the law, manifesting itself frequently in criminal acts. [< Italian *mafia*]

Ma·fi·a or **Maf·fi·a** (mä′fē ä), *n.* a secret society of criminals: *The Mafia would show us how to run our backwoods criminal organizations with a new efficiency* (Maclean's). [see *mafia*]

maf·ic (maf′ik), *adj. Geology.* of, having to do with, or composed primarily of magnesium and iron: *mafic rocks.* [< *ma*(gnesium) + Latin *f*(errum) iron + English *-ic*]

Ma·fi·o·so or **ma·fi·o·so** (ma′fē ō′sō), *n., pl.* **-si** (-sē). a member of the Mafia: *A jailed mafioso traded his influence over the waterfront gangs for a remission of sentence* (Manchester Guardian Weekly). [< Italian *mafioso* < *mafia* mafia]

ma foi (mȧ fwȧ′), *French.* **1.** upon my word! indeed! **2.** (literally) my faith.

mag[1] (mag), *n. British Slang.* a halfpenny. [origin uncertain]

mag[2] (mag), *n., v.,* **magged, mag·ging.** *British Dialect.* —*n.* chatter; talk: *You go away for a while, my dear, and let me have a little mag with Emma* (E.C. Sharland). —*v.i.* to chatter: *I'll snap your backbone across my knee if you mag half a second more* (James Runciman). [shortened form of *magpie*]

mag., 1. magazine. **2.** magnetism. **3.** magnitude.

mag·a·zine (mag′ə zēn′, mag′ə zēn), *n., v.,* **-zined, -zin·ing.** —*n.* **1.** a publication appearing regularly and containing stories, articles, etc., by various writers: *Seltzer noted a switch in the roles of the newspapers, . . . and the magazines, which once dealt mainly in fiction and features . . .* (Time). *Most magazines are published either weekly or monthly.* **2.** a room in a fort or warship for storing gunpowder and other explosives: *The enemy . . . have evacuated the south side, after exploding their magazines* (London Times). **3.** a building for storing gunpowder, guns, food, or other military supplies: *A company of men . . . were stationed there until the Civil War, when the fortifications were reduced to a naval magazine with a complement of five* (New Yorker). **4.** a place for cartridges in a repeating or automatic gun: *Carruthers . . . took a box of cartridges from a niche in the wall, and proceeded to recharge his magazine* (Boyd Cable). **5.** a place for film in a camera, fuel in a stove, etc.: *A new 35-mm camera . . . featured interchangeable film magazines* (World Book Annual). **6.** a place or region rich in natural or commercial products: *This district is a magazine of mineral wealth.* **7.** a storehouse; warehouse: *a magazine of flesh, milk, butter and cheese* (Daniel Defoe). *The mind of man in a long life will become a magazine of wisdom or folly* (Sir Richard Steele).
—*v.t.* to store in or as if in a magazine.
[< Old French *magazin* < Italian *magazzino,* ultimately < Arabic *makhāzin,* plural of *makhzan* storehouse]
—**Syn.** *n.* **1.** periodical.

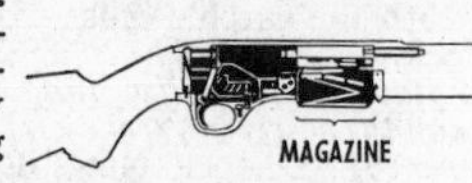

Magazine (def. 4) of Winchester Model 100

mag·a·zin·ish (mag′ə zē′nish), *adj.* having the characteristics of what is usually found in magazines; superficial; slick: *The mediocrity of the eight first lines is most miserably magazinish* (Samuel Taylor Coleridge).

mag·a·zin·ism (mag′ə zē′niz əm), *n.* writing for, editing, or producing magazines.

mag·a·zin·ist (mag′ə zē′nist), *n.* a person who writes for, edits, or produces a magazine or magazines.

mag·a·zin·y (mag′ə zē′nē), *adj.* magazinish: . . . *achieving a slightly too magaziny happy ending* (Punch).

Mag·da·len (mag′də lən), *n.* Magdalene.

Mag·da·lene (mag′də lēn), *n.* See **Mary Magdalene.**

mag·da·lene (mag′də lēn), *n.* **1.** a woman who has reformed from a sinful life; repentant prostitute. **2.** a home or reformatory for prostitutes. [< *Magdalene*]

Mag·da·le·ni·an (mag′də lē′nē ən), *adj.* belonging to or denoting a late paleolithic period represented by remains found at La Madeleine, Dordogne, France: *Magdalenian art involves portable objects and mural decorations on the walls of caves* (Beals and Hoijer). [< French *magdalénian,* Latinization of French *La Madeleine,* in Dordogne, France, a site containing remains of the period]

Mag·de·burg hemispheres (mag′də bėrg′), an early experimental apparatus for illustrating air pressure, consisting of two closely fitting hemispherical cups from which the air could be evacuated. [< *Magdeburg,* Germany, where its inventor (Otto von Guericke) was born]

mage (māj), *n. Archaic.* **1.** a magician: *And there I saw mage Merlin* (Tennyson). **2.** a wise person. [< Latin *magus;* see *Magi*]

Mag·el·lan·ic (maj′ə lan′ik), *adj.* having to do with or named after Ferdinand Magellan.

Magellanic Cloud, either of two faintly luminous patches in the heavens south of the equator. They are the two galaxies nearest to our own and consist of multitudes of stars: *In the southern sky there are two nebulae called the Magellanic Clouds which are easily resolved into individual stars by telescopes of moderate power* (Science News).

ma·gen Da·vid (mô′gən dô′vid, mä gän′ dä vēd′), a Jewish emblem, consisting of a six-pointed star formed of two interlaced triangles; Star of David. [< Hebrew *māgēn dāvīd* shield of David]

ma·gen·ta (mə jen′tə), *n.* **1.** a purplish-red aniline dye; fuchsin. **2.** a purplish red. —*adj.* purplish-red. [< the Battle of *Magenta,* Italy, 1859 (because it was discovered in that year)]

mag·got (mag′ət), *n.* **1.** the legless larva of any of various kinds of flies, often living in decaying matter. **2.** a queer notion; whim: *I thought she'd got some maggot in her head* (George Eliot). [Middle English *magot;* origin uncertain, perhaps related to Middle English *maddock,* ultimately < Old Icelandic] —**Syn. 2.** fancy.

mag·got·ry (mag′ə trē), *n., pl.* **-ries.** absurdity; stupidity.

mag·got·y (mag′ə tē), *adj.* **1.** full of maggots: *Ship's pursers . . . short-weighted everything from the rancid salt pork to the maggoty biscuits* (Maclean's). **2.** full of queer notions; whimsical.

ma·gi (mā′jī, maj′ī), *n.* plural of **magus.**

Ma·gi (mā′jī, maj′ī), *n., pl. of* **Magus. 1.** (in the Bible) the Three Wise Men who followed the star to Bethlehem and brought gifts to the infant Jesus. Matthew 2:1 and 2:7-13. **2.** the priests of an ancient Persian religion, famous as astrologers, and supposed to have supernatural powers. [< Latin *magī,* plural of *magus* < Greek *mágos* Persian priest or astrologer < Old Persian *magu* member of a priestly clan of Media]

ma·gi·an (mā′jē ən), *adj. Poetic.* magic: *Will he . . . keep me as a chosen food to draw His magian fish through hated fire and flame?* (Keats).

Ma·gi·an (mā′jē ən), *adj.* of or having to do with the Magi or priests of ancient Persia. —*n.* one of the Magi.

mag·ic (maj′ik), *n., adj., v.,* **-icked, -ick·ing.** —*n.* **1.** the pretended or supposed art of making things happen by secret charms and sayings: *The fairy's magic changed the brothers into swans.* **2.** something that produces results as if by magic; mysterious influence; unexplained power: *the magic of music. The magic of her voice charmed the audience.* **3.** the use of magic or the effects produced, as sleight of hand or optical illusion: *All these appearances could be nothing else but necromancy and magic* (Jonathan Swift). *Science is not a form of black magic* (Polykarp Kusch).
like magic, at once; with incredible swiftness: *Broiled chicken and oysters . . . disappeared from before us like magic* (Knickerbocker Magazine).
—*adj.* **1.** done by magic or as if by magic: *A magic palace stood in place of their hut.* **2.** magical: *Some of mankind's most terrible misdeeds have been committed under the spell of certain magic words or phrases* (James B. Conant).
—*v.t.* to obtain, get rid of, etc., by or as if by magic: . . . *the voluptuous wealth that could be magicked out of water colours* (Manchester Guardian Weekly).
[< Latin *magicē* < Greek *magikḗ,* feminine of *magikós* < *mágos;* see *Magi*]
—**Syn.** *n.* **1.** sorcery, necromancy, witchcraft.

mag·i·cal (maj′ə kəl), *adj.* **1.** of magic; used in magic; done by magic: *a magical spell.* **2.** like magic; mysterious; unexplained: *a magical feeling.* —**mag′i·cal·ly,** *adv.* —**Syn. 1.** occult. **2.** enchanting.

magic carpet, 1. a magically propelled carpet used for riding through the air by characters in the *Arabian Nights.* **2.** any means of transporting a person to strange and exotic places through the imagination: *Television's magic carpet takes one in a jiffy to the day of the pistol and horse.*

magic eye, one of a variety of mechanical or electronic devices designed to check consistency in manufacturing, detect trouble or danger, activate traffic signals, etc. See **electric eye.**

ma·gi·cian (mə jish′ən), *n.* **1.** a person skilled in the use of magic: *The wicked magician cast a spell over the princess.* **2.** a person skilled in sleight of hand: *The magician pulled—not one, but three rabbits out of his top hat!* [< Old French *magicien* < *magique* magic] —**Syn. 1.** sorcerer, necromancer. **2.** conjuror.

magic lantern, a device with a lamp and lenses for throwing a picture upon a screen in magnified form from a glass slide.

mag·i·co-re·li·gious (maj′ə kō ri lij′əs), *adj.* of or having to do with magic and religion, especially in the use of magic to seek the intervention of a deity or deities in the events of the natural world: *Furthermore, the inference that connected gods to dance and rain was an intellectual event,* *meditated by perception, thought, and memory and by the magico-religious world view* (Scientific American).

magic square, a square figure formed by a series of numbers so arranged in parallel and equal ranks that the sum of each row or line taken perpendicularly, horizontally, or diagonally, is constant.

2	7	6
9	5	1
4	3	8

An odd-numbered **Magic Square** whose constant sum is 15

ma·gilp (mə gilp′), *n.* megilp.

ma·gilph (mə gilf′), *n.* megilp.

Ma·gi·not Line (mazh′ə nō), an elaborate system of defense built by France against Germany after the first World War. The German Army swept around through Belgium in 1940 and completely outflanked it. [< French *la ligne Maginot* < André *Maginot,* 1877-1932, a former French minister of war]

mag·is·te·ri·al (maj′ə stir′ē əl), *adj.* **1. a.** of a magistrate; suited to a magistrate: *A judge has magisterial rank.* **b.** (of persons) holding the office of a magistrate. **2.** having or showing authority: *The captain spoke with a magisterial voice.* **3.** imperious; domineering; overbearing: *He paced up and down the room with a magisterial stride, and flashed an angry glance on every side* (William Godwin). [< Medieval Latin *magisterialis* < Late Latin *magisterius* < Latin *magister* a master] —**mag′is·te′ri·al·ly,** *adv.* —**mag′is·te′ri·al·ness,** *n.* —**Syn. 2.** authoritative. **3.** dictatorial, haughty, arrogant.

mag·is·te·ri·um (maj′ə stir′ē əm), *n. Roman Catholic Church.* the teaching function or authority of the Church: *The most important amendments concerned a passage saying that Roman Catholic couples "must not use methods which are reproved by the magisterium of the Church"* (London Times). [< Middle Latin *magisterium;* see MAGISTERY]

mag·is·ter·y (maj′ə ster′ē), *n., pl.* **-ter·ies.** (in alchemy and medieval medicine) a substance, remedy, etc., believed to be effective in curing or transmuting. [< Medieval Latin *magisterium* < Latin, office of a *magister* master]

mag·is·tra·cy (maj′ə strə sē), *n., pl.* **-cies. 1.** the position, rank, or duties of a magistrate: *A political executive magistracy . . . is a great trust* (Edmund Burke). **2.** magistrates as a group: *He went from city to city, advising with the magistracies* (John L. Motley). **3.** the district under a magistrate.

mag·is·tral (maj′ə strəl, mə jis′trəl), *adj.* **1.** *Pharmacy.* prescribed or prepared for a particular occasion: *a magistral prescription.* **2.** of or like a magistral line; principal: *The principal or magistral gallery runs all round the work* (J.M. Spearman). **3.** *Rare.* magisterial; authoritative; dogmatic: *Magistral powers . . . of the forceful and free over the weak and servile elements of life* (John Ruskin).
—*n.* a magistral line.
[< Latin *magistrālis* < *magister* a master. Doublet of MISTRAL.]

magistral line, the principal line of a military defense, from which the position of all other lines is determined.

mag·is·trate (maj′ə strāt, -strit), *n.* **1.** an officer of a government who has power to apply the law and put it into force: *The President is the chief magistrate of the United States.* **2.** a judge: *A justice of the peace is a magistrate.* [< Latin *magistrātus, -ūs* < *magistrāre* serve as a magistrate < *magister* a master]

mag·is·trate·ship (maj′ə strāt ship, -strit-), *n.* the position, duties, or term of office of a magistrate.

Mag·le·mo·sian or **Mag·le·mo·sean** (mag′lə mō′zhən), *adj.* belonging to or denoting a Mesolithic period represented by artifacts found in Denmark: *The best known culture of Boreal times in northern Europe is the Maglemosian, which extended from Denmark across the North Sea to Britain* (New Scientist). [< *Maglemose,* the name of the typical site on the island of Zeeland, Denmark + English *-ian*]

mag·ma (mag′mə), *n., pl.* **-ma·ta** (-mə tə), **-mas. 1.** any crude mixture of mineral or organic substances in the form of a thin paste. **2.** *Geology.* the molten material beneath the earth's crust from which igneous rock is formed: *The liquefied material forms a fluid mass, called magma, that is lighter than the overlying rocks and tends to rise at an opening* (Science News Letter). **3.** *Pharmacy.* a suspension of insoluble or nearly insoluble material in water: *Magnesia magma is the technical term for milk of magnesia.* [< Latin *magma* dregs of an unguent < Greek *mágma* an unguent, ultimately < *mássein* to knead, mold]

mag·mat·ic (mag mat′ik), *adj.* of or having to do with a magma: *Often the blocks represent the effect of shattering, due to the . . . unequal heating of the solid rock of magmatic contacts* (American Journal of Science).

Mag·na Char·ta or **Mag·na Car·ta** (mag′nə kär′tə), **1.** the great charter guaranteeing the personal and political liberties of the people of England, forcibly secured from King John by the English barons at Runnymede on June 15, 1215. **2.** any fundamental constitution guaranteeing civil and political rights. [< Medieval Latin *magna carta* (literally) great charter < feminine singular of Latin *magnus* great, and *charta* chart]

mag·na cum lau·de (mag′nə kum lou′də, kum lô′dē), with high honors (the second highest degree of merit on the diplomas of superior students). [< Latin *magnā cum laude* with great praise]

mag·nal·i·um (mag nā′lē əm), *n.* an alloy of aluminum and magnesium having increased hardness and good machinability, used for airplane parts and scientific instruments.

Mag·na·my·cin (mag′nə mī′sin), *n. Trademark.* an antibiotic derived from a microorganism mold, used especially against organisms which are resistant to penicillin and other antibiotics. *Formula:* $C_{42}H_{67}NO_{16}$ [< Latin *magna* great + English (strepto)*mycin*]

mag·na·nim·i·ty (mag′nə nim′ə tē), *n., pl.* **-ties. 1.** magnanimous nature or quality; nobility of soul or mind: *The soldiers showed magnanimity by treating their prisoners well. Magnanimity in politics is not seldom the truest wisdom* (Edmund Burke). **2.** a magnanimous act. —**Syn. 1.** generosity.

mag·nan·i·mous (mag nan′ə məs), *adj.* **1.** noble in soul or mind; generous in forgiving; free from mean or petty feelings or acts: *a magnanimous adversary.* **2.** showing or arising from a generous spirit: *a magnanimous attitude toward a conquered enemy. He spoke . . . with the magnanimous frankness of a man who had done great things, and could well afford to acknowledge some deficiencies* (Macaulay). [< Latin *magnanimus* (with English *-ous*) < *magnus* great + *animus* spirit, soul] —**mag·nan′i·mous·ly,** *adv.* —**mag·nan′i·mous·ness,** *n.* —**Syn. 1.** high-minded, unselfish. —**Ant. 1.** ignoble, selfish, uncharitable.

mag·nate (mag′nāt), *n.* **1.** a great man; important person: *My grandfather, a well-to-do farmer, was one of the chief magnates of the village* (Harriet Beecher Stowe). **2.** a prominent or distinguished person in any field: *a railroad magnate, a baseball magnate.* **3.** a member of the upper house of the former Hungarian or Polish parliaments. [< Late Latin *magnās, -ātis* < Latin *magnus* great]

mag·ne·form (mag′nə fôrm), *n.* a device for shaping metal, consisting of interchangeable magnetic coils of wire whose powerful magnetic fields cause metal to compress or expand to a desired shape. [< *magne*(tic) + *form*]

mag·ne·sia (mag nē′shə, -zhə), *n.* **1.** a white, tasteless, slightly alkaline powder, used in medicine as an antacid and a laxative, and in industry as an insulator, in making firebricks, etc.; magnesium oxide. *Formula:* MgO **2.** magnesium. [< Medieval Latin *magnesia* < Greek *hē Magnēsiā líthos* loadstone; also, probably talc; (literally) the Magnesian stone (from *Magnesia,* a region in Thessaly)]

mag·ne·sian (mag nē′shən, -zhən), *adj.* of, like, or containing magnesia.

magnesian limestone, dolomite.

mag·ne·sic (mag nē′sik), *adj.* of or containing magnesium.

mag·ne·site (mag′nə sīt), *n.* a mineral, carbonate of magnesium, occurring either in compact, white masses or crystalline, used for lining furnaces, in making steel, etc. *Formula:* $MgCO_3$ [< *magnes*(ium) + *-ite*[1]]

mag·ne·si·um (mag nē′shē əm, -zhē-), *n.* a very light, silver-white metallic chemical element, noted for its ductility and malleability. It is stable in dry air but tarnishes when exposed to moisture, and burns with a dazzling white light. Magnesium is used in photography, fireworks, metal alloys, etc. *Symbol:* Mg; *at. wt.:* (C^{12}) 24.312 or (O^{16}) 24.32; *at. no.:* 12; *valence:* 2. [< New Latin *magnesium* < Medieval Latin *magnesia;* see MAGNESIA]

magnesium hydroxide, 1. brucite. **2.** milk of magnesia.

magnesium light, the brilliant white light produced by the burning of magnesium, used in flares, photography, etc.

magnesium oxide, magnesia.

mag·net (mag′nit), *n.* **1.** a piece of iron, steel, etc., that has the property, either natural or induced, of attracting iron or steel; loadstone. **2.** anything that attracts: *The rabbits in our back yard were a magnet that attracted all the children in the neighborhood. The actor was the magnet that drew great audiences.* [< Old French *magnete* < Latin *magnēs, -ētis* < Greek *Mágnēs* (*líthos*) Magnesian (stone). Compare MAGNESIA.]

Magnet Shapes (def. 1) Left, horseshoe; center, bar; right, U-shape

mag·net·ic (mag net′ik), *adj.* **1.** having the properties of a magnet: *the magnetic needle of a compass.* **2. a.** of or having to do with a magnet or magnetism: *a magnetic axis.* **b.** producing, caused by, or operating by means of magnetism: *a magnetic circuit.* **3.** of or having to do with the earth's magnetism: *the magnetic north, a magnetic compass.* **4.** capable of being magnetized or of being attracted by a magnet: *magnetic nickel.* **5.** attractive: *Sympathy, the magnetic virtue . . . was extinct* (William Godwin). **6.** of or caused by hypnotism; mesmeric. —**mag·net′i·cal·ly,** *adv.* —**Syn. 5.** winning, charming.

mag·net·i·cal (mag net′ə kəl), *adj.* magnetic.

magnetic axis, *Physics.* the straight line joining the poles of a magnet.

magnetic bottle, *Nuclear Physics.* any arrangement of magnetic fields for confining or constricting charged particles in a controlled thermonuclear reaction. Magnetic bottles are formed in the pinch effect, in mirror machines, and in stellarators.

magnetic cartridge, a device consisting of a very small magnet and coils, to which a phonograph needle is attached.

magnetic circuit, the closed path taken by the magnetic flux.

magnetic compass, a device for indicating directions along the lines of the earth's magnetic field, consisting of a freely suspended magnetized pointer on a pivot. See picture under **compass.**

magnetic core, a tiny metal ring which can be magnetized in either of two directions to represent symbols used by a computer.

mag·net·ic-core memory (mag net′ik-kôr′, -kōr′), an array of magnetic cores used for storing information for a computer.

magnetic course, the course (of a ship, airplane, etc.) with reference to the north Magnetic Pole instead of the north geographic pole.

magnetic drum, (in computers) a rapidly rotating cylinder which is coated with a magnetic material on which information may be stored as small polarized spots.

magnetic equator, the line around the earth at which a magnetic needle balances horizontally without dipping.

magnetic field, 1. the space around a magnet, magnetic body (as the earth), or an electric current in which the magnetic force of the magnet or current is felt. **2.** the magnetic forces present in such a space.

magnetic flux, 1. the total magnetic induction across or through a specified area, generally expressed in maxwells or webers. **2.** the result of dividing the magnetomotive force by the reluctance.

magnetic head, a device in a recording apparatus for converting electrical impulses into magnetic impulses, for changing stored magnetic impulses back to electrical impulses, or for erasing such impulses already converted or stored, as in a tape or wire recorder.

magnetic induction, 1. the production of magnetic properties in iron or other magnetizable substances when placed in a magnetic field. 2. a measure of this phenomenon at a specified point.

magnetic ink, a specially prepared ink whose metallic properties activate electronic machines. It is useful in check processing, account coding, and other banking procedures.

magnetic iron ore, magnetite.

magnetic lines of force, a series of invisible lines passing from one pole to another of a magnet, which taken together form the magnetic field.

magnetic meridian, a line passing through both Magnetic Poles that represents the force exerted by the earth's magnetic field.

magnetic mine, an underwater mine which is exploded by the action of the metal parts of an approaching ship upon a magnetic needle.

magnetic mirror, one of the strong magnetic fields at each end of a tube having a weaker magnetic field in the middle. As a charged particle approaches one of the stronger fields, it is reflected back toward the middle. This method of trapping particles has been proposed for use in thermonuclear reactors.

magnetic moment, 1. the product of the pole strength of a magnet and the distance between the poles. 2. a magnetic force between two opposite charges in an electron or other elementary particle, associated with the spin and orbital motion of the particle.

magnetic needle, a slender bar of magnetized metal. When mounted so that it turns easily, it points approximately north and south toward the earth's Magnetic Poles.

magnetic north, the direction shown by the magnetic needle of a compass, differing in most places from the true north.

magnetic particle test or **inspection,** one of several nondestructive means of testing magnetized metals to detect cracks or other flaws.

magnetic pickup, a magnetic cartridge with a needle or needles attached.

magnetic pole, one of the two poles of a magnet.

Magnetic Pole, either of two points on the earth's surface toward which a magnetic needle points. The North Magnetic Pole is approximately in 71 degrees North latitude and 95 degrees West longitude. The South Magnetic Pole is approximately in 72 degrees South latitude and 154 degrees East longitude.

magnetic pumping, a method of heating a gas to a temperature of millions of degrees by applying an extremely high-frequency alternating current.

magnetic pyrites, pyrrhotite.

mag·net·ics (mag net′iks), *n.* the science of magnetism.

magnetic storm, a marked disturbance or variation of the earth's magnetic field, associated with solar flares.

magnetic tape, 1. a thin metal, plastic, or paper strip, usually coated or impregnated with iron oxide, on which (in a tape recorder, electronic computer, etc.) a magnetic effect is produced so that sounds can be recorded on it in the form of fluctuations in the magnetism of the tape. 2. a tape used in television to record both sound and image.

magnetic variation, declination, the deviation of the needle of a compass.

mag·net·ise (mag′nə tīz), *v.*, **-ised, -is·ing.** *Especially British.* magnetize. —**mag′net·is′er,** *n.*

mag·net·ism (mag′nə tiz əm), *n.* 1. the properties of a magnet; manifestation of magnetic properties: *the magnetism of iron and steel.* 2. the branch of physics dealing with magnets and magnetic properties. 3. the power to attract or charm: *Dick's magnetism makes him a leader among his schoolmates. Suddenly the face softened and shone with all its old magnetism* (Mrs. Humphry Ward). 4. hypnotic power; mesmerism.

mag·net·ite (mag′nə tīt), *n.* an important iron ore that is strongly attracted by a magnet; black iron oxide. Magnetite that possesses polarity is called loadstone. *Formula:* Fe_3O_4 [< German *Magnetit*]

mag·net·iz·a·bil·i·ty (mag′nə tī′zə bil′ə-tē), *n.* the power or capacity of being magnetized.

mag·net·iz·a·ble (mag′nə tī′zə bəl), *adj.* that can be magnetized.

mag·net·i·za·tion (mag′nə tə zā′shən), *n.* 1. the act of magnetizing. 2. the state of being magnetized.

mag·net·ize (mag′nə tīz), *v.*, **-ized, -iz·ing.** —*v.t.* 1. to give the properties of a magnet to: *An electric current in a coil around a bar of iron will magnetize the bar. You can magnetize a needle by rubbing it with a magnet.* 2. to attract or influence (a person); win by personal charm: *Her beautiful voice magnetized the audience. His wife was a woman ... who, coming under the dominion of a stronger nature, was perfectly magnetized by it* (Harriet Beecher Stowe). 3. to mesmerize; hypnotize: *The little white building magnetized him, as though concealed there was his only companionship* ... (Graham Greene). —*v.i.* to become magnetic. —**mag′net·iz′er,** *n.*

mag·ne·to (mag nē′tō), *n., pl.* **-tos.** a small machine, such as a dynamo or electric generator, for producing electricity; magnetoelectric machine. In some gasoline engines, such as those of the Model T Ford and of airplanes, a magneto supplies an electric spark to explode the gasoline vapor. [short for *magnetoelectric* (machine)]

magneto-, *combining form.* magnetism; magnetic forces; magnets: *Magnetometer = an instrument for measuring magnetic forces. Magnetodynamo = a dynamo having permanent magnets.* [< Greek *mágnēs, -ētis* magnet]

mag·ne·to·chem·i·cal (mag nē′tō kem′ə-kəl), *adj.* of or having to do with magnetochemistry.

mag·ne·to·chem·is·try (mag nē′tō kem′-ə strē), *n.* the science dealing with the relations between magnetism and chemistry.

mag·ne·to·dy·na·mo (mag nē′tō dī′nə-mō), *n., pl.* **-mos.** a dynamo having permanent magnets.

mag·ne·to·e·lec·tric (mag nē′tō i lek′-trik), *adj.* of or characterized by electricity produced by magnets.

mag·ne·to·e·lec·tri·cal (mag nē′tō i lek′-trə kəl), *adj.* magnetoelectric.

mag·ne·to·e·lec·tric·i·ty (mag nē′tō i-lek′tris′ə tē), *n.* 1. electricity produced by the action of magnets. 2. the science dealing with electricity and magnetism.

mag·ne·to·gen·er·a·tor (mag nē′tō jen′ə-rā′tər), *n.* a magnetoelectric generator; magneto.

mag·ne·to·gram (mag nē′tə gram), *n.* the record made by a magnetograph.

mag·ne·to·graph (mag nē′tə graf, -gräf), *n.* a device consisting of three variometers and a recording mechanism, used for detecting variations in the direction and intensity of magnetic fields.

mag·ne·to·hy·dro·dy·nam·ic (mag nē′-tō hī′drō dī nam′ik), *adj.* of or having to do with magnetohydrodynamics: *magnetohydrodynamic insulation.*

mag·ne·to·hy·dro·dy·nam·ics (mag nē′-tō hī′drō dī nam′iks), *n.* the study of the interaction of magnetic fields and electrically conducting liquids and gases, such as the highly ionized airflow about a spacecraft on reentry into the atmosphere.

mag·ne·tom·e·ter (mag′nə tom′ə tər), *n.* an instrument for measuring magnetic forces.

mag·ne·tom·e·try (mag′nə tom′ə trē), *n.* the measurement of magnetic forces with a magnetometer.

mag·ne·to·mo·tive (mag nē′tə mō′tiv), *adj.* producing magnetic effects; having to do with the production of such effects.

magnetomotive force, 1. magnetizing force or influence which produces a magnetic flux through a magnetic circuit, analogous to the electromotive force which produces an electric current or flux in an electric circuit; the quantity which, divided by the magnetic reluctance, or resistance, gives the intensity of magnetization. 2. the force required to produce magnetic flux in a magnetic circuit, measured in gilberts.

mag·ne·ton (mag′nə ton), *n. Physics.* 1. the unit of magnetic moment. 2. a theoretical ultimate magnetic particle. 3. *Obsolete.* an electron moving in a circle with the velocity of light. [< French *magnéton* < *magnétique* magnetic; influenced by English *electron*]

mag·ne·to·op·tic (mag nē′tō op′tik), *adj.* of or having to do with magnetooptics.

mag·ne·to·op·ti·cal (mag nē′tō op′tə kəl), *adj.* magnetooptic.

mag·ne·to·op·tics (mag nē′tō op′tiks), *n.* that branch of physics which deals with the influence of a magnet upon light.

mag·net·o·pause (mag nē′tə pôz, -net′ə-), *n.* the upper limits of the magnetosphere.

mag·ne·to·scope (mag nē′tə skōp, -net′ə-), *n.* a device for indicating the presence of magnetic force.

mag·ne·to·sphere (mag nē′tə sfir, -net′ə-), *n.* a zone of radiation that surrounds the earth and extends outward about 40,000 miles. The Van Allen belts are part of the magnetosphere.

mag·ne·to·spher·ic (mag nē′tə sfer′ik, -net′ə-), *adj.* of, having to do with, or characteristic of the magnetosphere: *Data from Explorer 18 ... were under intensive analysis during the year and yielded good mapping of the magnetospheric boundaries* (Hugh Odishaw).

mag·ne·to·stric·tion (mag nē′tə strik′-shən), *n.* 1. a change in the dimensions of a ferromagnetic substance when subjected to an intense magnetic field (especially characteristic of nickel). 2. a change in the magnetic properties of a body subjected to mechanical stress.

mag·ne·to·stric·tive (mag nē′tə strik′-tiv), *adj.* of, having to do with, or utilizing magnetostriction.

mag·ne·to·stric·tor (mag nē′tə strik′tər), *n.* a substance, such as nickel, which changes its dimensions when subjected to a magnetic field.

mag·ne·tron (mag′nə tron), *n.* a vacuum tube in which the flow of electrons from the heated cathode to the anode is regulated by an external magnetic field. It is used to produce microwaves.

mag·ni·cide (mag′nə sīd), *n.* the killing of an important person, especially a ruler or leader. [< Latin *magnus* great + English *-cide*[2]]

mag·nif·ic (mag nif′ik), *adj. Archaic.* 1. magnificent; splendid; imposing: *Power ... God's gift magnific* (Robert Browning). 2. pompous; grandiloquent. 3. eulogistic. [< Old French *magnifique*, learned borrowing from Latin *magnificus* < *magnus* great + *facere* to make]

mag·nif·i·cal (mag nif′ə kəl), *adj. Archaic.* magnific.

Mag·nif·i·cat (mag nif′ə kat), *n.* 1. the hymn of the Virgin Mary, beginning *Magnificat anima mea Dominum* ("My soul doth magnify the Lord"), used as a canticle at evensong or vespers. Luke 1:46-55. 2. music for this hymn. [< Latin *magnificat* it magnifies, 3rd singular present indicative of *magnificāre* glorify, extol, magnify]

mag·ni·fi·ca·tion (mag′nə fə kā′shən), *n.* 1. the act of magnifying. 2. magnified condition. 3. the power to magnify. 4. a magnified copy, model, or picture.

mag·nif·i·cence (mag nif′ə səns), *n.* richness of material, color, and ornament; grandeur; beauty; splendor: *the magnificence of mountain scenery.* [< Old French *magnificence*, learned borrowing from Latin *magnificentia* < *magnificus* noble; see MAGNIFIC] —**Syn.** majesty.

mag·nif·i·cent (mag nif′ə sənt), *adj.* 1. richly colored or decorated; making a splendid appearance; grand; stately: *the magnificent palace of a king, a magnificent spectacle.* 2. impressive; noble; exalted: *magnificent words, magnificent ideas.* 3. extraordinarily fine; superb: *a magnificent view of the mountains.*

the Magnificent, a title of certain historic persons: *Lorenzo the Magnificent was the greatest of the Medicis.*

[< Old French *magnificent* < *magnificence;* see MAGNIFICENCE] —**mag·nif′i·cent·ly,** *adv.*

—**Syn. 1, 2, 3. Magnificent, splendid, superb** mean impressive in dignity and beauty, brilliance, or excellence. **Magnificent** emphasizes impressive beauty and costly richness or stateliness of things like surroundings, jewels, or buildings, and noble greatness of ideas: *Westminster Abbey is magnificent.* **Splendid** emphasizes impressive brilliance or shining brightness in appearance or character of things, people, or deeds: *He made a splendid record in the army.* **Superb** means of the highest possible excellence, magnificence, splendor, richness, etc.: *We had a superb view of the ocean.* —**Ant. 1.** humble, simple, modest.

mag·nif·i·co (mag nif′ə kō), *n., pl.* **-coes. 1.** a Venetian nobleman: *The duke himself, and the magnificoes of greatest port* (Shakespeare). **2.** an important person: *Rockingham, a virtuous magnifico, . . . resolved to revive something of the pristine purity . . . of the old Whig connection* (Benjamin Disraeli). [< Italian *magnifico* < Latin *magnificus* magnific]

mag·ni·fi·er (mag′nə fī′ər), *n.* **1.** one that magnifies. **2.** a lens that magnifies things; magnifying glass. **3.** a small eyepiece attached to a camera to permit examination of the sharpness of focus of the image seen in the viewfinder.

ma·gni·fique (må nyē fēk′), *interj. French.* magnificent.

mag·ni·fy (mag′nə fī), *v.,* **-fied, -fy·ing.** —*v.t.* **1.** to cause to look larger than the real size: *A microscope magnifies bacteria so that they can be seen and studied.* **2.** to make too much of; go beyond the truth in telling: *She not only tells tales on her brother, but she magnifies them. My wife . . . used every art to magnify the merit of her daughter* (Oliver Goldsmith). **3.** to praise highly; glorify; extol: *My soul doth magnify the Lord* (Luke 1:46). *When the high heart we magnify . . . Ourselves are great* (John Drinkwater). —*v.i.* to increase the apparent size of an object. [< Latin *magnificāre* esteem greatly < *magnificus* magnific] —**Syn.** *v.t.* **1.** enlarge, amplify. **2.** exaggerate, overstate.

mag·ni·fy·ing glass (mag′nə fī′ing), a lens or combination of lenses that causes things to look larger than they really are.

magnifying power, 1. the ratio of the size of an image when viewed through an optical instrument to the size of the object when seen with the unaided eye. **2.** (in a telescope) the ratio of the focal length of the objective to that of the eyepiece.

mag·nil·o·quence (mag nil′ə kwəns), *n.* **1.** a high-flown, lofty style of speaking or writing; use of big and unusual words, elaborate phrases, etc.: *Cibber . . . foisted his own bombast into the company of Shakespeare's magniloquence* (Cowden Clarke). **2.** boastfulness. [< Latin *magniloquentia* < *magnus* great + *loquēns, -entis,* present participle of *loquī* speak] —**Syn. 1.** bombast.

mag·nil·o·quent (mag nil′ə kwənt), *adj.* **1.** using big and unusual words; in high-flown language. **2.** boastful: *She was a trifle more magniloquent than usual, and entertained us with stories of colonial governors and their ladies* (Thackeray). —**mag·nil′o·quent·ly,** *adv.* —**Syn. 1.** grandiloquent.

mag·ni·tude (mag′nə tüd, -tyüd), *n.* **1.** size: *the height, and strength, and magnitude of their building* (Daniel Defoe). **2.** great importance, effect, or consequence: *War brings new problems of very great magnitude to many nations.* **3.** *Astronomy.* the measure of the brightness of a star: *The brightest stars are of zero magnitude; very bright stars, of first magnitude; and so on. The scale of apparent magnitude . . . goes on up to the sixth magnitude which is the faintest that the eye alone can see* (George W. Gray). **4.** *Geometry.* the measure or extent of a particular line, area, volume, or angle. **5.** *Mathematics.* a number given to a quantity so that it may be compared with similar quantities. **6.** the measurement of the force of an earthquake, expressed on a scale of 0 to 10. *Abbr.:* mag. **7.** *Obsolete.* greatness ot character, rank, or position.

of the first magnitude, very great in some respect; excellent; overwhelming; very serious: *Thou liar of the first magnitude* (William Congreve).

[< Latin *magnitūdō* < *magnus* large] —**Syn. 1.** amplitude. **2.** moment.

mag·no·lia (mag nōl′yə), *n.* **1.** any of a group of trees or shrubs with large, generally fragrant, white, pink, or purplish flowers. The blossom of one variety is the state flower of Louisiana and Mississippi. **2.** the flower. [< New Latin *Magnolia* the genus name < Pierre *Magnol,* 1638-1715, a French botanist]

mag·no·li·a·ceous (mag nō′lē ā′shəs), *adj.* belonging to the magnolia family.

magnolia family, a group of dicotyledonous trees and shrubs, found in tropical and temperate regions of North America and Asia, and including the magnolia, tulip tree, and umbrella tree.

Magnolia State, a nickname for the State of Mississippi.

magnolia warbler, an American warbler having black back, wings, and tail banded with white, and yellow breast striped with black.

mag·num (mag′nəm), *n., pl.* **-nums** *for 1, 2;* **-na** (-nə) *for 3.* **1.** a bottle that holds about two quarts of wine or alcoholic liquor. **2.** the amount that it holds: *He . . . declared that we must have wine, and sent for a magnum of the best* (Robert Louis Stevenson). **3.** *Anatomy.* the capitate bone. [< Latin *magnum,* neuter, great]

magnum bo·num (bō′nəm), *British.* **1.** Also, **magnum bonum plum.** a large yellow plum, used for cooking. **2.** a large kind of potato. [< Latin *magnum* (see MAGNUM), and *bonum,* neuter of *bonus* good]

magnum o·pus (ō′pəs), **1.** a large or important work of literature or art: *He himself said that what he had in him was short essays rather than a magnum opus* (London Times). **2.** a person's greatest work: *Darwin turned to his friends Lyell and Hooker, who knew the many years he had been laboring upon his magnum opus* (Scientific American). [< Latin *magnum* great, and *opus* work] —**Syn. 2.** masterpiece.

mag·nus hitch (mag′nəs), a hitch or knot with one more turn than a clove hitch.

mag·ot (mag′ət, må gō′), *n.* **1.** the Barbary ape. **2.** a small, grotesque figure of porcelain, ivory, etc., common in Chinese and Japanese art: *Her rooms were crowded with hideous China magots* (Thackeray). [< French *magot*]

mag·pie (mag′pī), *n.* **1.** any of various noisy birds related to the crows and jays, with black and white plumage, a long tail, and short wings. **2.** a person who chatters. —*adj.* of or like a magpie; characterized by the habit of hoarding ascribed to magpies: *magpie gleanings; . . . Yeats's magpie fascination with collecting . . . all sorts of symbols and myths* (Canadian Forum). [< *Mag,* nickname for *Margaret* + *pie*[2]] —**Syn.** *n.* **2.** chatterbox, chatterer, babbler.

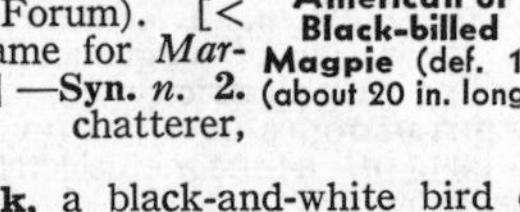

American or Black-billed Magpie (def. 1) (about 20 in. long)

magpie lark, a black-and-white bird of Australia, similar to but smaller than a magpie, peewee.

M.Agr., *U.S.* Master of Agriculture.

mags·man (magz′mən), *n., pl.* **-men.** *British Slang.* a swindler; confidence man: *[He] began his career as a pawnbroker's assistant and, by way of their duds and baubles, came into contact with the world of magsmen* (Anthony Burgess). [< *mag*[2] + *man*]

mag·tho·ri·um (mag′thôr′ē əm, -thōr′-), *n.* an alloy of magnesium and thorium, used especially in missile engines. [< *mag*(nesium) + *thorium*]

mag·uey (mag′wā; *Spanish* mä gā′), *n.* **1.** any of various agaves with pointed, fleshy leaves, found especially in Mexico, and used in making a fiber and the intoxicating drinks mescal and pulque: *The century plant is a maguey.* **2.** the fiber. [< Spanish *maguey* < Arawak (West Indies)]

ma·gus (mā′gəs), *n., pl.* **ma·gi.** an astrologer or magician: *Simon Magus* (Acts 8:9-24).

Ma·gus (mā′gəs), *n., pl.* **Ma·gi. 1.** one of the Magi or Three Wise Men. **2.** an ancient Persian priest. [< Latin *magus;* see *Magi*]

Mag·yar (mag′yär; *Hungarian* mu′dyur), *n.* **1.** a member of the chief group of people living in Hungary: *Otto von Hapsburg was in exile, and the fiercely nationalistic Magyars would never accept him as King of Hungary* (New Yorker). **2.** their Finno-Ugric language; Hungarian. —*adj.* of the Magyars or their language; Hungarian. [< Hungarian *Magyar*]

Mag·yar·i·za·tion (mag′yä rə zā′shən), *n.* the act or process of Magyarizing.

Mag·yar·ize (mag′yä rīz), *v.t.* **-ized, -iz·ing.** to make Hungarian in habits, language, customs, or character: *The "Magyarized" Jews of "Trianon Hungary" . . . and those in recently annexed territories were regarded almost as different peoples* (Hannah Arendt).

Ma·ha·bha·ra·ta (mə hä′bä′rə tə), *n.* the earlier of the two great ancient epics of Hinduism (the *Ramayana* is the other), written in Sanskrit between about 200 B.C. and 200 A.D. and combining a fabulous account of a dynastic struggle of 1200 B.C. with moral lessons in politics, law and religion, and other topics. [< Sanskrit *Mahābhārata* < *mahā* great + *Bharata,* a tribal designation]

Ma·ha·bha·ra·tam (mə hä′bä′rə təm), *n.* the Mahabharata.

ma·ha·lo (mä hä′lō), *n. Hawaiian.* thanks.

ma·hant (mə hunt′), *n.* (in India) a religious superior: *The parents of the couple to be married next morning approached the mahant to tell him the relevant details* (London Times). [< Hindi *mahant*]

ma·ha·ra·ja or **ma·ha·ra·jah** (mä′hə rä′jə), *n.* **1.** the title of certain great ruling princes in India. **2.** a person holding this title. [< Sanskrit *mahārāja* < *mahā* great + *rājan* rajah]

ma·ha·ra·nee or **ma·ha·ra·ni** (mä′hə rä′nē), *n.* **1.** the wife of a maharaja. **2.** a woman holding in her own right a rank equal to that of a maharaja. [< Hindustani *mahārānī* < *mahā* great (< Sanskrit) + *rānī* queen < Sanskrit *rājñī*]

ma·hat·ma (mə hät′mə, -hat′-), *n.* **1.** (in India) a wise and holy person who has extraordinary powers. **2.** any person thought of as resembling a mahatma in wisdom, manner, etc.

the Mahatma, Mohandas K. Gandhi, 1869-1948, Hindu political, social, and religious leader: *followers of the Mahatma.*

[< Sanskrit *mahātman* < *mahā* great + *ātman* soul]

ma·hat·ma·ism (mə hät′mə iz əm, -hat′-), *n.* the principles and practice of mahatmas.

Ma·ha·ya·na (mä′hə yä′nə, mə hä′yä′nə), *n.* a form of Buddhism, now predominant in Japan, China, Korea, Tibet, and Mongolia, which worships Buddha as a divine being. [< Sanskrit *mahāyāna* < *mahā* great + *yāna* vehicle, way]

Ma·ha·ya·nist (mä′hə yä′nist), *adj.* of or having to do with Mahayana: *The state religion was a confused amalgam of indigenous animism with imported Taoism, Confucianism, and Mahayanist Buddhism* (London Times). —*n.* a believer in Mahayana.

Mah·di (mä′dē), *n., pl.* **-dis. 1.** the leader expected by Moslems to come and establish a reign of righteousness. **2.** a person claiming to be this leader. [< Arabic *mahdīy* one who is guided aright < *hadā* he led aright]

Mah·dism (mä′diz əm), *n.* **1.** the doctrine of the coming of the Mahdi. **2.** adherence to or support of a person who claims this title: *Gordon, and Sir Samuel Baker . . . were even more responsible for the rise of Soudanese Mahdism than the Mahdi himself* (London Daily News).

Mah·dist (mä′dist), *n.* an adherent of a person claiming to be the Mahdi.

Ma·hi·can (mə hē′kən), *n.* **1.** a confederacy or tribe of Algonkian Indians who once lived in or near the upper valley of the Hudson. **2.** a member of this confederacy; Mohican. [American English < Algonkian *maingan* wolf]

ma·hi·ma·hi (mä′hē mä′hē), *n. Hawaiian.* dolphin (def. 2).

mah-jongg or **mah-jong** (mä′jông′, -jong′), *n.* a game of Chinese origin played with 144 dominolike pieces in the Orient and a varying number of pieces elsewhere. Each player tries to form winning combinations by drawing or discarding. Also, **ma-jung.** [< Shanghai dialectal Chinese *ma chiang* (literally) hemp birds, sparrows (from a design on the pieces)]

Mah·ler·i·an (mä lir′ē ən), *adj.* of or having to do with the Austrian composer Gustav Mahler or his music. —*n.* a follower, interpreter, or admirer of Mahler's music.

mahl·stick (mäl′stik′, môl′-), *n.* a light stick used by painters as a support for the painting hand and held in the other. Also, **maulstick.** [< Dutch *maalstok* < *malen* to paint + *stok* stick]

MAHLSTICK

Mahlstick

ma·hoe (mə-hō′), *n.* a tropical shrub or tree of the mallow family, important as a source of fiber for cord, sails, etc. [apparently < Carib *mahou*]

ma·hog·a·nize (mə hog′ə nīz, -hôg′-), *v.t.*, **-nized, -niz·ing.** to stain or finish (wood) to resemble mahogany.

ma·hog·a·ny (mə hog′ə nē, -hôg′-), *n., pl.* **-nies,** *adj.* —*n.* **1.** a hard, fine-grained, reddish-brown wood of a large evergreen tree growing in tropical America. It is used for fine furniture, etc. **2.** the tree itself. **3.** any of various related or similar trees or woods. **4.** a dark reddish brown. **5.** a table, especially a dinner table: *I had hoped . . . to have seen you three gentlemen . . . with your legs under the mahogany in my humble parlour* (Dickens). —*adj.* **1.** made of mahogany: *mahogany salad bowls.* **2.** dark reddish-brown. [< obsolete Spanish *mahogani,* perhaps < the Maya (Honduras) name]

mahogany family, a group of dicotyledonous tropical trees and shrubs with hard wood, frequently scented, including the mahogany and chinaberry.

Ma·hom·et·an (mə hom′ə tən), *adj., n.* Mohammedan.

Ma·hom·et·an·ism (mə hom′ə tə niz′əm), *n.* Mohammedanism.

ma·ho·nia (mə hō′nyə), *n.* any of a group of shrubs of the barberry family, having evergreen, pinnate leaves and dense racemes of yellow flowers, as the Oregon grape. [< New Latin *Mahonia* the typical genus < Bernard Mc*Mahon,* 1775-1816, an American horticulturist]

Ma·hound (mə hound′), *n.* **1.** *Archaic.* Mohammed, especially when thought of as a false prophet. **2.** *Scottish.* the Devil; Satan. [Middle English *Mahun* < Old French < *Mahomet* Mahomet]

ma·hout (mə hout′), *n.* (in India and the East Indies) the keeper and driver of an elephant. [< Hindustani *mahāut*]

Mah·rat·ta (mə rat′ə), *n.* a member of a Hindu people who live in the central and southwestern parts of India. Also, **Maratha.** [earlier *Moratta* < Hindi *Marhaṭṭa* < Sanskrit *Mahārāṣṭra*]

Mah·rat·ti (mə rat′ē), *n.* the Indic language of the Mahrattas. Also, **Marathi.**

mah·seer or **mah·sir** (mä′sər), *n.* a large fresh-water cyprinoid fish of India, resembling the barbel. [< Hindi *mahāsir*]

ma·hua (mä′wä), *n.* a south Asian tree of the sapodilla family. Its seeds yield an oil used in cooking, in making soap, etc., and its flowers are used for food and in making an intoxicating drink. [< Hindi *mahwa* < Sanskrit *madhūka* < *madhu* sweet]

mah·zor (mäH zōr′, mäH′zər), *n., pl.* **mah·zo·rim** (mäH′zō rēm′), **mah·zors.** *Judaism.* a prayer book with the prayers and devotional poetry used in the synagogue on holidays [< Hebrew *mahazōr* cycle]

Ma·ia (mā′ə, mī′-), *n.* **1.** *Greek Mythology.* the eldest of the Pleiades, who was loved by Zeus and became the mother of Hermes by him. **2.** *Roman Mythology.* an obscure goddess of spring and of fertility for whom the month of May was named; Majesta. She was a consort of Vulcan, and in later days much confused with the Greek goddess.

mai·a·moth (mā′ə môth′, -moth′), *n.* an American moth with black wings marked with white and a thick, hairy body, whose larva feeds on oak leaves. [< New Latin *maia* the species name < Latin *maia* crab < Greek *maîa*]

maid (mād), *n.* **1.** a young unmarried woman; girl: *Many a youth, and many a maid, Dancing in the chequer'd shade* (Milton). **2.** an unmarried woman; spinster: *Good old English reading . . . makes (if the worst come to the worst) most incomparable old maids* (Charles Lamb). **3.** a woman servant. **4.** *Archaic.* a virgin.

the Maid, Joan of Arc, 1412-1431, French heroine who led armies against invading England: *Rumours of the . . . miracles of the Maid were repeated even in the English camp* (J. Gairdner). [Middle English *meide,* short for *meiden,* Old English *mægden* maiden]

mai·dan (mī dän′), *n.* a level, open space in or near a town in India, etc.; esplanade. [< Persian *maidān*]

maid·en (mā′dən), *n.* **1.** a young unmarried woman; girl: *Here's to the maiden of bashful fifteen* (Richard B. Sheridan). **2. a.** a horse that has never won a race. **b.** a race or prize for such horses. **3.** *Cricket.* a maiden over. **4.** *Archaic.* **a.** a virgin. **b.** a spinster. —*adj.* **1.** of or befitting a maiden: *maiden grace.* **2.** unmarried; virgin: *a maiden aunt.* **3. a.** new; fresh; untried; unused: *maiden ground. Full bravely hast thou fleshed Thy maiden sword* (Shakespeare). **b.** made, used, etc., for the first time; first: *a ship's maiden voyage.* **4. a.** (of a horse or apprentice jockey) being a maiden. **b.** (of a race or prize, etc.) for maiden horses: . . . *the winner of a mile maiden race at Epsom* (London Times). [Old English *mægden*] —**Syn.** *n.* **1.** maid. *-adj.* **2.** single. **3. a.** virgin. **3. b.** initial.

Maid·en (mā′dən), *n.* an instrument similar to a guillotine, formerly used in Scotland for beheading criminals.

maiden assize, in British law: **1.** an assize of a criminal court at which the judge is usually presented with a pair of white gloves because there are no criminal cases to be tried. **2.** (formerly) any assize at which no person is condemned to die.

maid·en·hair (mā′dən hãr′), *n.,* or **maidenhair fern,** any of a group of ferns with very slender, dark, shining stems and delicate, finely divided fronds. See picture under **frond.**

maidenhair tree, the ginkgo.

maid·en·head (mā′dən hed), *n.* **1.** the hymen. **2.** *Archaic.* virginity; maidenhood.

maid·en·hood (mā′dən hu̇d), *n.* **1.** the condition of being a maiden. **2.** the time when one is a maiden. **3.** freshness. —**Syn. 1.** virginity.

maid·en·li·ness (mā′dən lē nis), *n.* maidenly quality or behavior.

maid·en·ly (mā′dən lē), *adj.* **1.** of or having to do with a maiden or maidenhood. **2.** like a maiden; gentle; modest. **3.** suited to a maiden: *maidenly reserve.* —*adv.* after the fashion of a maiden; modestly: *Her looks turned maidenly to ground* (Elizabeth Barrett Browning).

maiden name, a woman's surname before her marriage.

maiden over, *Cricket.* an over in which no runs are scored.

maiden speech, the first speech delivered by a member of a legislative assembly, especially one delivered in the House of Commons by a member of Parliament.

maid·hood (mād′hu̇d), *n.* maidenhood.

maid in waiting, *pl.* **maids in waiting.** an unmarried noble lady who attends a queen or princess.

Maid Marian, 1. a character in old English May Day games and morris dances. **2.** Robin Hood's companion and sweetheart.

maid of all work, a woman servant who does all kinds of housework.

maid of honor, 1. an unmarried woman who is the chief attendant of the bride at a wedding. **2.** an unmarried noble lady who attends a queen or princess.

Maid of Orleans, Joan of Arc, 1412-1431, French heroine who led armies against invading England.

maid·serv·ant (mād′sėr′vənt), *n.* a woman servant: *The maidservant met me at the front door* (Jane Welsh Carlyle). —**Syn.** maid, bonne.

ma·ieu·tic (mā yü′tik), *adj.* **1.** of or having to do with the Socratic method of helping a person to bring out ideas latent in the mind. **2.** having to do with midwifery. [< Greek *maieutikós* (literally) obstetric < *maîa* midwife]

ma·ieu·ti·cal (mā yü′tə kəl), *adj.* maieutic.

ma·ieu·tics (mā yü′tiks), *n.* the maieutic art, especially as practiced by Socrates.

mai·gre (mā′gər), *adj.* **1.** having neither flesh nor its juices and therefore permissible on days of religious abstinence: *a maigre soup.* **2.** characterized by such abstinence in diet. —*n.* a large food fish, common in the Mediterranean. —*adv.* using no meat in preparation of a food: *At last he [the doctor] consented on condition that I should . . . live maigre and drink no wine* (Hannah More). [< French *maigre* lean. Doublet of MEAGER.]

mai·hem (mā′hem), *n.* mayhem.

mai·ko (mī′kō), *n., pl.* **-ko. 1.** a young girl in training to be a geisha. **2.** a girl during her first season as a geisha: *For one year, rarely longer, she is known as a maiko* (Harper's). [< Japanese *maiko* < *mai* a dance, dancing + *ko* girl]

mail[1] (māl), *n.* **1.** *U.S. and Canada.* letters, postcards, papers, parcels, etc., sent or received by post. **2.** *Especially U.S.* the system by which such things are sent, managed by the Post Office Department: *You can pay most bills by mail.* **3.** all that comes by one post or delivery: *My mail is full of advertisements.* **4.** a train, boat, person, etc., that carries mail: *Most of us disdained all coaches except his majesty's mail* (Thomas De Quincey). **5.** *U.S.* the collection, dispatch, or delivery of postal matter at a particular time: *the 10 o'clock mail.* **6.** *Scottish.* a bag; traveling bag. —*v.t.* to send by mail; put in a mailbox; post. —*adj.* **1.** of or for mail. **2.** employed to carry the mail. [< Old French *male* wallet, bag < Germanic (compare Old High German *malha*)]

➔ In American use, **mail** is more common than **post.** In British use, **post** is the ordinary term, except for def. 4. Thus, in Britain, the **mail** or **mails** usually refers to overseas postal matter and service or the means of bringing them.

mail[2] (māl), *n.* **1.** armor made of metal rings or small loops of chain linked together, or of overlapping plates. **2.** any armor. **3.** the protective shell or scales of certain animals, as the tortoise or the lobster. —*v.t.* to cover or protect with or as if with mail. [< Old French *maille* < Latin *macula* a mesh in a net; (originally) spot, mark] —**mail′less,** *adj.*

Mail[2] (def. 1)

mail[3] (māl), *n. Obsolete or Scottish.* payment; tax; rent. [Old English *māl*]

mail·a·bil·i·ty (mā′lə bil′ə tē), *n. U.S. and Canada.* the condition of being legally acceptable for mailing: *Postal officials ordered the postmaster . . . to send in copies of the magazine's latest issue for "examination . . . as to their mailability"* (Newsweek).

mail·a·ble (mā′lə bəl), *adj. U.S. and Canada.* that can be mailed.

mail·bag (māl′bag′), *n.* a large bag for carrying mail.

mail·boat (māl′bōt′), *n.* a boat or ship that carries mail.

mail·box (māl′boks′), *n.* **1.** *U.S.* a public box from which mail is collected. **2.** a private box to which mail is delivered. [American English < *mail*[1] + *box*[1]]

mail call, the distribution of mail in the armed forces, especially on board ship: *Mail call is the height of everyone's day and the man without a letter is like a puppy without a bone* (New York Times).

mail car, a railroad car in which mail is sorted and transported.

mail carrier, a mailman.

mail·chute (māl′shüt′), *n.* a chute for depositing mail, situated in a corridor on each floor in office buildings: *The mailchutes choked up with letters, had to be taped closed* (Time).

mail clerk, an office worker who takes care of the receiving, sorting, and distributing, and frequently the sending, of mail.

mail coach, a stagecoach that carried mail: *Enough has been said to demonstrate that "town" and "city" will be . . . terms as obsolete as "mail coach"* (Harper's).

mail drop, an address used only for purposes of receiving mail: . . . *Shakespeare and Company served as their club, mail drop, meeting-house, and forum* (New Yorker).

mailed (māld), *adj.* **1.** covered or protected with mail. **2.** (of animals) having a protective covering resembling armor or mail.

mailed fist, force of arms; military power: *The massive helms are symbolic of the knight's dauntless courage, as the mailed fist is of his might* (Time). —**mailed′-fist′,** *adj.*

mail·er (mā′lər), *n.* **1.** a person who mails. **2.** a mailing machine. **3.** a vessel that carries mail. **4.** a container, usually cylindrical, in which to mail photographs, maps, etc.

mail fraud, the act of using the mails to defraud.

mail·ing (mā′ling), *n.* **1.** the sending of mail. **2.** *Scottish.* **a.** a rented farm. **b.** the rent paid for a farm: *Let the creatures stay at a moderate mailing* (Scott).

mailing list, a list of names, as of people or businesses, to whom circulars, advertisements, etc., are distributed by mail: . . . *an exceptionally fine mailing list of persons in the upper income brackets* (Harper's).

mailing machine, a machine for addressing and stamping mail.

mailing piece, a catalogue, circular, or other advertising matter to be distributed by mail.

mailing tube, a cardboard tube into which papers, maps, photographs, etc., are rolled for mailing, to prevent creasing or other damage.

maill or **maille** (māl), *n. Obsolete.* mail (tax).

mail·lot (mä yō′), *n. French.* **1.** a one-piece, close-fitting garment resembling a bathing suit, worn by dancers, acrobats, etc. **2.** a one-piece bathing suit: *There are swimming trunks and maillots of the same plaid* (New Yorker).

mail·man (māl′man′), *n., pl.* **-men.** *U.S.* a man who carries or delivers mail; postman.

mail order, an order sent by mail for goods that are to be shipped by mail or other means.

mail-or·der (māl′ôr′dər), *adj.* of or having to do with mail orders or a mail-order house. —*v.t., v.i.* to send (merchandise) upon receiving orders by mail: *More than $40,000 worth of tickets were mail-ordered before the box office opened* (Time).

mail-order catalogue, a catalogue for the advertisement of goods sold by mail order.

mail-order house, a business that receives orders and sends goods by mail: *Last month . . . sales of the nation's chain and mail-order houses were higher than a year before* (New York Times).

mail·plane (māl′plān′), *n.* an airplane for carrying mail.

mail·room (māl′rüm′, -rům′), *n.* a room used for receiving and distributing mail, as in an office.

mail·sack (māl′sak′), *n.* a mailbag.

maim (mām), *v.t.* **1.** to cut off or make useless an arm, leg, ear, etc., of; cripple; disable: *He lost two toes by the accident, but we were glad that he was not more seriously maimed.* **2.** to make defective or powerless: *You maim'd the jurisdiction of all bishops* (Shakespeare).
—*n.* **1.** a crippling or wounding of the body; injury. **2.** a serious defect, blemish, or hurt.
—*adj.* maimed.
[Middle English *maimen,* or *maheimen* < Old French *mahaignier,* perhaps < a Frankish word] —**maim′er,** *n.*
—**Syn.** *v.t.* **1.** mutilate, mangle.

maim·ed·ness (mā′mid nis, māmd′-), *n.* maimed condition.

main[1] (mān), *adj.* **1.** most important; largest: *the main street of a town, the main dish at dinner, the main line of a railway, the main branches of a river. . . . No more than an interlude in the main business of his life* (Hawthorne). **2.** designating a considerable stretch of water, land, etc.: *Over all the face of earth main ocean flowed* (Milton). **3.** *Nautical.* of or having to do with the mainmast or mainsail. **4.** *British and Scottish Dialect.* remarkable: *a main crop of apples. It were a main place for pirates once* (Robert Louis Stevenson). **5.** *Archaic.* mighty: *Soaring on main wing* (Milton).
—*n.* **1. a.** a large, central pipe or conductor for water, gas, electricity, etc.: *When the water main broke, our cellar was flooded.* **b.** *British.* an electrical outlet. **2.** *Poetic.* the open sea; ocean: *Forced from their homes . . . To traverse climes beyond the western main* (Oliver Goldsmith). **3.** *Nautical.* a mainmast or mainsail. See picture under **sail. 4.** a main line of a railroad. **5.** *Archaic.* mainland: *. . . the land they saw from our island was not the main, but an island* (Robert Louis Stevenson). **6.** *Archaic.* physical strength, force, etc. **7.** *Obsolete.* a broad expanse.
in the main, for the most part; chiefly; mostly: *Milly . . . is an excellent girl in the main* (James Fenimore Cooper).
—*adv. British and Scottish Dialect.* exceedingly; very: *I am main sorry to displease your worship* (William Godwin).
[Old English *mægen-* < *mægen* power]
—**Syn.** *adj.* **1.** principal, leading, chief.

main[2] (mān), *n.* **1.** a match between gamecocks. **2.** a number called by the caster before throwing the dice in the game of hazard: *He likes to throw a main of an evening* (Thackeray). **3.** (in dice playing) a throw, match, or stake at dice. [origin uncertain]

main·brace (mān′brās′), *n. Nautical.* the brace attached to the lower yard of the mainmast.
splice the mainbrace, *British Informal.* to serve alcoholic beverages; drink freely: *Mr. Falcon, splice the mainbrace, and call the watch* (Frederick Marryat).

main chance, the chance or probability of greatest importance or advantage to oneself: *He knew that the ladies of the stage have an ear for flattery, and an eye to the main chance* (Charles Reade).

main clause, *Grammar.* a clause in a complex sentence that can act by itself as a sentence; independent clause: [Main clause] *There are differences of opinion on the matter* [subordinate clause] *which cause a great deal of disharmony.*

main course, *Nautical.* the square sail attached to the lowest yard of the mainmast of a square-rigged vessel: *Having no sails to work the ship with, but a main course . . .* (Daniel Defoe).

main-de-fer (maN′də fer′), *n.* a defensive covering of iron for the hand, used in medieval tournaments, etc. [< Old French *main de fer* hand of iron]

Maine (mān), *n.* a United States battleship blown up in the harbor of Havana, Cuba, on February 15, 1898.

Main·er (mā′nər), *n.* a native or inhabitant of the state of Maine.

main·land (mān′land′, -lənd), *n.* the larger part of a continent or country; land that is not a small island or peninsula: *The ancient Aeolian cities on the mainland . . . amounted to eleven* (Connop Thirlwall).

main·land·er (mān′lən dər, -lan′-), *n.* a person who lives on the mainland: *We find a self-governing community, waging war with the Illyrian mainlanders* (A.J. Evans).

main·line (mān′līn′), *adj., v.,* **-lined, -lining.** —*adj.* traveling on or situated along a main line: *mainline towns.*
—*v.i., v.t. U.S. Slang.* to inject a narcotic directly into a vein.

main line, 1. a principal route of a railroad, airline, etc., as distinguished from a branch line. **2.** (of railroads) a through track, as distinguished from local or yard tracks.

main·lin·er (mān′lī′nər), *n.* **1.** a railroad, train, airplane, or boat that travels the mainline route. **2.** *U.S. Slang.* a drug addict who mainlines.

main·ly (mān′lē), *adv.* **1.** for the most part; chiefly; mostly; principally: *He is interested mainly in sports and neglects his school work.* **2.** *Obsolete.* mightily; greatly: *I think we should suit one another mainly* (Charles Lamb).

main·mast (mān′mast′, -mäst′; *Nautical* mān′məst), *n.* **1.** the principal mast of a ship. **2.** the second mast from the bow on a brig, schooner, etc. **3.** the mast nearer the bow in a yawl or ketch.

Mainmast (def. 3) carries the mainsail, and two jibs (foreward); the mizzenmast (aft) carries the mizzen sail.

mains (mānz), *n.pl. Scottish.* the farm attached to the main house of an estate; a home farm. [short for *domains*]

main·sail (mān′sāl′; *Nautical* mān′səl), *n.* **1.** the largest sail of a square-rigged vessel, attached to the lowest yard of the mainmast. See picture under **sail. 2.** the large sail set aft of the mainmast of a fore-and-aft rigged ship.

main sequence, the group of stars which, when plotted according to luminosity and spectral class on the Russel diagram, fall in a narrow diagonal band from the upper left to the lower right. Most stars fall in this sequence, showing that there is a correlation between luminosity and spectral type, and, by extension, luminosity and size.

main-se·quence star (mān′sē′kwens), any star in the main sequence, such as the sun.

main·sheet (mān′shēt′), *n.* the rope or tackle that secures the lee corner of the mainsail, or the main boom of a fore-and-aft-rigged vessel.

mains nues (manz′ nüz′; *French* maN ny′), a Basque form of handball. [< French *mains nues* (literally) bare hands]

main·spring (mān′spring′), *n.* **1.** the principal spring of a clock, watch, etc. **2.** the main cause, motive, or incentive: *The Opposition is still searching for a mainspring* (New York Times).

main stage, 1. the stage at which the greatest amount of thrust is attained in a multistage rocket. **2.** the period when the greatest amount of thrust is attained in a single-stage rocket.

main·stay (mān′stā′), *n.* **1.** a wire or rope extending forward and down from the mainmast, supporting it. **2.** main support: *Loyal friends are a person's mainstay in time of trouble.* —**Syn. 2.** prop, backbone.

main stem, *U.S. Slang.* the busiest street of a city or town; a main artery.

main·stream (mān′strēm′), *n.* a main course or direction in the historical development of an institution, art form, idea, etc.: *Kabuki continues to form the mainstream of the Japanese theater* (Atlantic). —*adj.* belonging in the main stream or course of development; not tributary or marginal: *mainstream jazz, mainstream literature.*

Main Street, 1. the chief street, usually the business section, in a small town. **2.** the ordinary behavior, point of view, and opinions of the average American community; a limited experience and outlook; a provincial attitude: *Arriving in Paris, he felt that he had finally parted with Main Street.*

main·tain (mān tān′), *v.t.* **1.** to keep; keep up; carry on: *to maintain a business, to maintain one's health. Policemen maintain order. Maintain your hold.* **2.** to bear the expenses of; provide for: *to maintain a family.* **3.** to support; uphold: *to maintain an opinion. He had a reputation to maintain.* **4.** to declare to be true: *He maintained that he was innocent. Ruth maintained that war did not pay.* **5.** to assert against opposition; affirm: *He maintains his innocence.* **6.** to keep supplied, equipped, or in repair: *This apartment house is maintained very well.* **7.** to keep or hold against attack: *to maintain one's ground.*
[< Old French *maintenir* < Latin *manū tenēre* hold by the hand; *manū,* ablative of *manus, -ūs* hand] —**main·tain′er,** *n.*
—**Syn. 1.** continue, preserve. **3.** defend. See **support. 5.** contend.

main·tain·a·bil·i·ty (mān tā′nə bil′ə tē), *n.* a being maintainable.

main·tain·a·ble (mān tā′nə bəl), *adj.* that can be maintained: *I think this action is maintainable against the husband and wife jointly* (N.C. Tindal).

main·tained school (mān tānd′), *British.* a school maintained by public funds, such as a council school: *Boys from maintained schools do not fit easily into public schools* (London Times).

main·te·nance (mān′tə nəns), *n.* **1.** a maintaining: *Maintenance of quiet is necessary in a hospital.* **2.** a being maintained; support: *A government collects taxes to pay for its maintenance.* **3.** enough to support life; means of living: *His small farm provides a maintenance, but not much more.* **4.** keeping up or in repair; upkeep: *the maintenance of an automobile.* **5.** *Law.* meddling in a lawsuit by helping either party with money or other means to prosecute or defend it: *Champerty is but a particular modification of this sin of maintenance* (Jeremy Bentham).
—**Syn. 3.** subsistence, livelihood.

maintenance man, 1. a man hired to clean a building, store, offices, etc.; janitor. **2.** a man whose work is repairing, cleaning, or renovating machines, etc.; repairman.

maintenance of membership, a clause in a union contract requiring all employees to remain paid-up members for the life of the contract or be dismissed by the employer: *The union's 650,000 basic steel workers are demanding . . . a union shop to replace an existing maintenance of membership clause* (Tuscaloosa News).

main·top (mān′top′), *n.* a platform at the head of the lower mainmast: *The war vessels . . . each flying the British ensign at the maintop* (London Standard).

main·top·gal·lant (mān′top gal′ənt; *Nautical* mān′tə gal′ənt), *n.* the mast, sail, or yard above the maintopmast. See picture under **sail.**

main·top·gal·lant·mast (mān′top gal′ənt mast′, -mäst′; *Nautical* mān′tə gal′ənt-məst), *n.* the mast next above the maintopmast.

main·top·gal·lant·sail (mān′top gal′ənt-sāl′; *Nautical* mān′tə gal′ənt səl), *n.* the sail belonging to the maintopgallantmast. See picture under **sail.**

main·top·gal·lant·yard (mān′top gal′-ənt yärd′; *Nautical* mān′tə gal′ənt yärd′), *n.* the beam or pole that supports the maintop-gallantsail.

main·top·mast (mān′top′mast′, -mäst′; *Nautical* mān′top′məst), *n.* the second section of the mainmast above the deck.

main·top·sail (mān′top′sāl′; *Nautical* mān′top′səl), *n.* the sail above the mainsail. See picture under **sail.**

main yard, the beam or pole fastened across the mainmast to support the mainsail: *We got a whip on the main yard* (Richard Henry Dana).

mai·oid (mā′oid), *adj.* of, belonging to, or like a large group of ten-footed crustaceans, typified by the spider crab. —*n.* any crab of this group, especially a spider crab. [< New Latin *Maia* the genus name (< Latin *maia* a kind of crab < Greek *maîa*) + English *-oid*]

ma·iol·i·ca (mə yol′ə kə), *n.* majolica.

mair or **maire** (mãr), *adj., n., adv. Scottish.* more.

maire (mer), *n. French.* the mayor of a French commune.

mai·rie (me rē′), *n. French.* a municipal town hall.

mai·son de san·té (me zôN′ də säN tā′), *French.* a private hospital or sanitarium.

mai·son·ette or **mai·son·nette** (mā′zə-net′), *n. British.* **1.** a house divided into apartments: *An historic house modernised and divided into flat and maisonette ...* (Observer). **2.** an apartment: *New modern Maisonettes for sale* (New York Times). [< French *maisonette* (diminutive) < Old French *maison* house; see MANSION]

maist (māst), *adj., n., adv. Scottish.* most.

mai·thu·na (mī′tü nə), *n.* sexual intercourse, one of the five elements of Shakta worship.

maî·tre (me′trə), *n. French.* the master or leader of something; a teacher; mentor.

maî·tre d′ (mā′trə dē′, mā′tər dē′), *Informal.* maître d'hôtel.

maî·tre de bal·let (me′trə də bá lā′), *French.* a ballet teacher.

maî·tre d'hô·tel (me′trə dō tel′), **1.** a butler; steward. **2.** a hotel manager: *The attentive maître d'hôtel flew past us and threw open the door of a splendid apartment* (R.H. Savage). **3.** a headwaiter. **4.** with a sauce of creamed butter, chopped parsley, and lemon juice or vinegar. [< Middle French *maître d'hôtel* (literally) master of the house; *maître* < Old French *maistre* master]

maize (māz), *n.* **1.** a kind of grain that grows on large ears; corn; Indian corn. **2.** the plant that it grows on. **3.** the color of ripe corn; yellow. [< Spanish *maíz,* earlier *mahiz, mahis,* or *mayz* < Arawak (Haiti) *mahiz*]

Maj., major.

ma·ja (mä′hä), *n.* a Spanish woman of the lower classes who dresses gaily and is a belle in her circle. [< Spanish *maja,* feminine of *majo*]

Ma·jes·ta (mə jes′tə), *n. Roman Mythology.* Maia.

ma·jes·tic (mə jes′tik), *adj.* grand; noble; dignified; stately: *His face ... Majestic though in ruin* (Milton). *In more lengthen'd notes and slow, The deep, majestic, solemn organs blow* (Alexander Pope). —**Syn.** regal, august, imposing.

ma·jes·ti·cal (mə jes′tə kəl), *adj.* majestic: *If I were ever to fall in love again ... it would be, I think, with prettiness, rather than with majestical beauty* (Abraham Cowley).

ma·jes·ti·cal·ly (mə jes′tə klē), *adv.* in a majestic manner; grandly: *Inglis ... stalked majestically out of Court, looking neither to the right hand nor to the left* (Law Times).

maj·es·ty (maj′ə stē), *n., pl.* **-ties. 1.** stately appearance; royal dignity; nobility; grandeur: *The majesty of the starry heavens is displayed above the most wretched shanty.* **2.** supreme power or authority: *Policemen and judges uphold the majesty of the law.* [< Old French *majeste* < Latin *mājestās* < *mājor,* earlier *mājus,* comparative of *magnus* great] —**Syn. 1.** sublimity. **2.** sovereignty.

Maj·es·ty (maj′ə stē), *n., pl.* **-ties.** a title used in speaking to or of a king, queen, emperor, empress, etc.: *Your Majesty, His Majesty, Her Majesty.*

Maj. Gen., major general.

Maj·lis or **maj·lis** (maj lēs′), *n.* the National Assembly of Iran, one of two houses of the legislative branch of the government: *The draft agreement ... has been submitted to the Persian Majlis for its approval* (Economist). Also, **Mejlis.** [< Persian *majlis*]

ma·jo (mä′hō), *n., pl.* **-jos.** a gaily dressed Spanish dandy of the lower classes: *The Majo glitters in velvets and filigree buttons, tags, and tassels* (Richard Ford). [< Spanish *majo* (literally) gay, fine]

ma·jol·i·ca (mə jol′ə kə, -yol′-), *n.* **1.** a kind of enameled Italian pottery richly decorated in colors: *The finest majolica was painted during the greatest days of European painting* (George Savage). **2.** any similar pottery made elsewhere: *Majolica was made in [the] U.S. in Pennsylvania and Maryland* (Carl W. Drepperd). Also, **maiolica.** [< Italian *maiolica* < Majorca, where the earliest specimens reputedly came from]

ma·jor (mā′jər), *adj.* **1.** larger; greater; more important: *Take the major share of the profits. A major part of an infant's life is spent in sleeping.* **2.** of the first rank or order: *Robert Frost and T. S. Eliot are major poets. New York is a major American port.* **3.** of legal age. **4.** *U.S.* of, having to do with, or designating a student's principal subject or course of study. **5.** *Music.* **a.** (of an interval) greater by a half step than the minor; having the difference of pitch which is found between the tonic and the second, third, sixth, or seventh tone (or step) of a major scale: *a major second, third, sixth, seventh.* **b.** (of a scale, key, or mode) in which the interval between the tonic and the third step is a major third (two whole steps): *C major scale or key.* **c.** (of a chord, especially a triad) containing a major third (two whole steps) between the root and the second tone or note. **6.** *Logic.* broader or more extensive. **7.** elder or senior: *Cato Major.*
—*n.* **1.** an officer of the army, air force, or marines, ranking next below a lieutenant colonel and next above a captain. *Abbr.:* Maj. **2.** a person of the legal age of responsibility. **3.** *U.S.* **a.** a subject or course of study to which a student gives most of his time and attention. **b.** a student engaged in such a course of study: *She is a classics major.* **4.** *Music.* one of two sets of intervals, chords, scales, or keys: *The scale of C major has neither sharps nor flats.* **5.** *Logic.* a major premise or term. **6.** a person of superior rank in a certain class: *Babe Ruth was a major among baseball players.* **7.** *U.S. Sports.* a major league.
—*v.i. U.S. and Canada.* **major in,** (of a student) to give much time and attention to a subject or course of study: *to major in mathematics. Bulbous-headed adolescents who have majored in English descend in shoals* (Publishers' Weekly).
[< Latin *mājor,* comparative of *magnus* great. Doublet of MAYOR.]

major arc, *Mathematics.* an arc that is greater than half a circle.

major axis, *Mathematics.* the diameter of an ellipse which passes through its foci.

Ma·jor·can (mə jôr′kən), *adj.* of or having to do with Majorca (the largest of the Balearic Islands): *Majorcan carpets and matting cover the floors* (C.T. Bidwell). —*n.* **1.** a native or inhabitant of Majorca. **2.** the language of the Majorcans, related to Provençal.

ma·jor-do·mo (mā′jər dō′mō), *n., pl.* **-mos. 1.** a man in charge of a royal, noble, or wealthy household: *Sir John ... seemed to be mingling the roles of major-domo and Prime Minister* (Lytton Strachey). **2.** a butler or steward: *Whose designs are so humble, as not to aspire above a major-domo, or some such domestic preferment* (Government Tongue). [< Spanish *mayordomo,* or Italian *maggiordomo* < Medieval Latin *major domus* chief of the household < Latin *mājor* (see MAJOR), *domūs,* genitive of *domus* house(hold)]

ma·jor·ette (mā′jə ret′), *n. U.S.* a girl drum major: *Co-captains, bands and majorettes all are part of big-time college football* (Wall Street Journal).

major general, an officer of the army, air forces, or marines ranking next below a lieutenant general and next above a brigadier general. *Abbr.:* Maj. Gen.

ma·jor-gen·er·al·cy (mā′jər jen′ər əl sē), *n., pl.* **-cies.** the rank or position of a major general: *I ... strongly recommended him for a major-generalcy* (Ulysses S. Grant).

ma·jor-gen·er·al·ship (mā′jər jen′ər əl-ship), *n.* major-generalcy: *His bravery on the field of Omdurman has won him his major-generalship* (London Daily News).

ma·jor·i·ty (mə jôr′ə tē, -jor′-), *n., pl.* **-ties,** *adj.* —*n.* **1.** the larger number; greater part; more than half: *A majority of the children chose red covers for their books. The will of the majority should prevail* (Thomas Jefferson). **2.** a larger number of votes than all the rest: *If Smith received 12,000 votes, Adams 7,000, and White 3,000, Smith had a majority of 2,000 and a plurality of 5,000.* **3.** the legal age of responsibility: *A person who is 21 years old or over has reached his majority and may manage his own affairs.* **4.** the rank or position of an army major. **5.** a party or group having the larger number of votes in an assembly, electoral body, etc. **6.** *Obsolete.* superiority; preponderance.

go or **pass over to,** or **join the majority,** to die: *Mirabeau's work then is done ... He has gone over to the majority* (Thomas Carlyle).
—*adj.* **1.** of a majority: *a majority vote.* **2.** representing or belonging to a majority: *the majority leader of the Senate. The court's majority opinion was delivered by Chief Justice Taft* (Manchester Guardian).

major key or **mode,** a musical key or mode based on the major scale.

major league, *U.S.* either of the two chief leagues in American professional baseball, the National League or the American League.

ma·jor-league (mā′jər lēg′), *adj.* **1.** of, having to do with, or in the major leagues: *a major-league ballplayer, major-league clubs. Babe Ruth set a major-league record by hitting sixty home runs in one season. ... The NBA offers the nearest thing yet to major-league basketball* (Newsweek). **2.** top-ranking; first-class: *Handy Associates is strictly major-league* (New Yorker).

ma·jor-lea·guer (mā′jər lē′gər), *n.* a major-league ballplayer.

major orders, holy orders.

major piece, *Chess.* a queen or a rook.

major premise, *Logic.* the premise of a syllogism that contains the major term.

Major Prophets, 1. the more important of the prophetic books of the Old Testament, including Isaiah, Jeremiah, and Ezekiel. **2.** the prophets who are believed to have written these books.

major scale, a musical scale having eight notes, with half steps instead of whole steps after the third and seventh notes.

major suit, spades or hearts, the suits having greater scoring value at auction and contract bridge.

major term, *Logic.* the term that is the predicate at the conclusion of a syllogism.

ma·jung (mä′jung′), *n.* mah-jongg.

ma·jus·cu·lar (mə jus′kyə lər), *adj.* of or like a majuscule; large: *In the beverage bold Let's renew us and grow muscular; And for those who're getting old, Glasses get of size majuscular* (Leigh Hunt).

ma·jus·cule (mə jus′kyül), *n.* a large letter in medieval writing, whether capital or uncial. —*adj.* **1.** (of a letter) large. **2.** written in majuscules. [< French *majuscule,* learned borrowing from Latin *mājusculus* somewhat larger (diminutive) < *mājor;* see MAJOR]

AB

abcde

Majuscules (above) and minuscules (below) from 12th-century manuscript

mak·a·ble (mā′kə-bəl), *adj.* that can be made.

ma·kai (mä kī′), *adv., adj. Hawaiian.* toward the ocean; seaward.

mak·ar (mak′ər), *n. Scottish.* a poet. [Middle English *makar* maker, poet]

make[1] (māk), *v.,* **made, mak·ing,** *n.* —*v.t.* **1.** to bring into being; put together; build; form; shape; create: *to make a new dress, to make a boat, to make jelly, to make a poem, to make a will. God made the country, and man made the town* (William Cowper). **2.** to have the qualities needed for: *Wood makes a good fire.* **3.** to cause; bring about: *to make trouble, to make peace, to make a noise, to make a bargain. Haste makes waste.* **4.** to cause to; force to: *He made me go. You can lead a horse to water but you cannot make him drink.* **5. a.** to cause to be or become; cause oneself to be: *to make a room warm, to make a fool of oneself. A*

sight to make an old man young (Tennyson). **b.** to appoint; constitute; render: *Who made thee a ruler and a judge over us?* (Acts 7:27). **6.** to turn out to be; become: *She will make a good teacher.* **7.** to get ready for use; arrange: *to make a bed.* **8.** to get; obtain; acquire; earn: *to make a fortune, to make one's living, to make good grades at school, to make friends.* **9. a.** to do; perform: *to make an attempt, to make a mistake. Don't make a move.* **b.** to put forth; deliver: *to make a speech.* **10.** to amount to; add up to; count as: *Two and two make four. That makes 40 cents you owe me. One good verse doesn't make a poet.* **11.** to think of as; figure to be: *I make the distance across the room 15 feet. What do you make of him?* **12.** to reach; arrive at: *The ship made port. The opposing parties made a settlement.* **13.** to go; travel: *Some airplanes can make more than 1,500 miles an hour.* **14.** to cause the success of: *One big deal made the young businessman.* **15.** *Informal.* to get on; get a place on: *He made the football team.* **16.** in card games: **a.** to win (a trick). **b.** to state (the trump or bid). **c.** to win a trick with (a card). **d.** to shuffle (the cards). **17.** *Electricity.* **a.** to complete (a circuit) and so allow the current to flow. **b.** to cause (a current) to flow by doing this. **18.** (in sports and games) to score; have a score of. **19.** *U.S. Slang.* to win the favor of (a person of the opposite sex).
—*v.i.* **1.** to attempt; start: *He made to stop me.* **2.** to move in a certain direction; proceed: *to make straight toward the barn, a boat making up stream.* **3.** to cause something to be in a certain condition: *to make sure, to make ready.* **4.** to behave or act in a certain way: *to make merry, to make bold. He beckons, and makes as he would speak* (Longfellow). **5.** to be effective: *All these facts make in his favor.* **6.** (of the tide) to flow toward the land; rise: *About nine o'clock at night, the tide making, we weighed anchor* (Charles Carrol). **7.** to construct or form something: *He can neither make nor mar. God makes; man mars.*
make after, to follow; chase; pursue: *At the signal, the hounds made after the fox.*
make as if or **as though,** to pretend that; act as if: *to make as if one is afraid.*
make away with, a. to get rid of: *I will make away with my castle and dowry to support the cause* (David Williams). **b.** to kill: *The trap made away with the rat.* **c.** to steal: *The treasurer made away with the club's funds.*
make believe. See under **believe.**
make do, to get along; manage; be contented (with): *I shall make do quite happily on biscuits and cheese* (Punch).
make fast, to attach firmly: *Make fast the boat.*
make for, a. to go toward: *Make for the hills!* **b.** to rush at; attack: *The watchdog made for the robber.* **c.** to help bring about; favor: *The new medicine made for the patient's recovery.*
make like, *U.S. Informal.* **a.** to imitate; act the part of: *The clown made like a monkey to amuse the children.* **b.** to perform the services of: *to make like a cook.*
make off, to run away; leave suddenly: *Just before the storm everybody made off for home.*
make off with, to steal: *He made off with his neighbor's car.*
make one's own, to consider (something or someone) as one's own: *He never succeeded in his own life but he made his son's success his own.*
make or break, to cause to succeed or fail: *. . . a critique written by one of the men in New York who make or break plays . . .* (George E. Sokolsky).
make out, a. to write out: *She made out a marketing list.* **b.** to show to be; prove: *It would be easy to make out a strong case for the contention* (Saturday Review). **c.** to try to prove; declare to be: *That makes me out most selfish* (A.E.W. Mason). **d.** to understand: *The boy had a hard time making out the problem.* **e.** to see with difficulty: *I can barely make out what these letters are.* **f.** to complete; fill out: *We need two more eggs to make out a dozen.* **g.** *Informal.* to get along; manage; succeed: *We must try to make out with what we have. How did you make out with your interview? You made out well with that dinner* (Harriet Beecher Stowe).
make over, a. to alter; make different: *to make over a dress.* **b.** to hand over; transfer ownership of: *He made over his business to his son.*
make up, a. to put together; compose; compound: *to make up cloth into a dress, to make up a prescription.* **b.** to invent: *to make up a story.* **c.** to settle (a dispute, etc.); reconcile: *to make up one's differences. The two gentlemen should . . . try to make matters up* (Macaulay). **d.** to pay for; compensate: *The school said it would make up all expenses the team had going to the county track meet.* **e.** to become friends again after a quarrel: *There we were, quarrelling and making up . . . by turns* (Thackeray). **f.** to put paint, powder, etc., on the face: *They have skins that would make a lemon look white; . . . but the maid makes them up; and people say how handsome they are* (New Review). **g.** to arrange (type, pictures, etc.) in the pages of a book, paper, or magazine: *to make up a page of type.* **h.** to prepare for a part on the stage by putting on suitable clothing, cosmetics, etc.: *to make up as a beggar.* **i.** to go to form or produce; constitute: *Girls make up most of that class.* **j.** to take (a test or course failed) for the second time; take (an examination missed) at a later time: *He dropped out of school for a term, which he will have to make up if he wants to graduate.* **k.** to add up and balance; adjust: *to make up a statement of accounts.*
make up for, to give or do in place of: *to make up for lost time.*
make up to, to try to get the friendship of; flatter: *If Lady Elinor was a widow, I should certainly make up to her* (Edward G. Bulwer-Lytton).
make with (the), *U.S. Slang.* **a.** to use in the usual way: *Make with the piano!* **b.** to produce; offer: *Finally, he made with the coffee.*
—*n.* **1.** the way in which a thing is made; style; fashion: *Do you like the make of that coat?* **2.** kind; brand: *What make of car is this?* **3.** nature; character: *To my natural make and my temper Painful the task is I do* (Longfellow). **4.** the act or process of making. **5.** the amount made; yield; output. **6.** the closing of an electric circuit; completion of a circuit: *Since this rate is larger on the "break" of the circuit than on the "make," the secondary voltage is much larger in one direction* (Sears and Zemansky). **7.** in card games: **a.** the naming of the trump suit. **b.** the trump suit named.
on the make, *Slang.* trying for success, profit, etc.: *. . . "What Makes Sammy Run?", Budd Schulberg's vitriolic story of a young heel on the make* (Time).
[Old English *macian*]
—**Syn.** *v.t.* **1. Make, construct, fashion** mean to put together or give form to something. **Make** is the general word meaning to bring something into existence by forming or shaping it or putting it together: *She made a cake.* **Construct** means to put parts together in proper order, and suggests a plan or design: *They constructed a bridge.* **Fashion** means to give a definite form, shape, or figure to something and usually suggests that the maker is inventive or resourceful: *He fashions beautiful bowls out of myrtle wood.*

make[2] (māk), *n. Obsolete.* **1.** a mate; companion; friend: *like a widow having lost her make* (Sir Philip Sidney). **2.** a match; equal. [Old English *gemaca*]

make and break, an apparatus for alternately making and breaking an electric circuit.

make·bate or **make·bait** (māk′bāt′), *n. Archaic.* a person or thing that causes great trouble, leads to fighting, etc.: *It was ten to one if the gold, which was the makebait of the world, did not . . . set us together by the ears* (Daniel Defoe). [< *make*[1] + (de)*bate*, confused with *bait*, verb]

make-be·lieve (māk′bi lēv′), *n.* **1.** pretense: *Goblins live in the land of make-believe. His knowledge is all make-believe.* **2.** a person who pretends; pretender. —*adj.* pretended: *Children often have make-believe playmates.*

make-do (māk′dü′), *n.* a temporary substitute, usually of an inferior kind. —*adj.* used as a make-do; characterized by makeshift methods: *When . . . prices steadily mounted to their peak, thousands of careful housewives adopted . . . a make-do policy* (London Daily Mail).

make·fast (māk′fast′, -fäst′), *n.* a buoy, piling, etc., to which a ship can be tied.

make-or-break (māk′ər brāk′), *adj.* that can be either a complete success or a complete failure: *Mr. Wilson says that 1966 is a make-or-break year for the British economy* (Manchester Guardian Weekly).

make-peace (māk′pēs′), *n.* a peacemaker.

mak·er (mā′kər), *n.* **1.** a person who makes; manufacturer: *Who was the maker of this stove?* **2.** *Law.* a person who signs a promissory note, etc.: *The maker should have a lawyer examine any document that he does not completely understand* (World Book Encyclopedia). **3.** (in card games) the player who first names the trump; declarer. **4.** *Archaic.* a poet.

Mak·er (mā′kər), *n.* God: *And three firm friends, more sure than day and night,— Himself, his Maker, and the angel Death* (Samuel Taylor Coleridge).
gone to (meet, join, etc.) one's Maker, dead: *The old man has gone to his Maker.*

make-read·y (māk′red′ē), *n.* **1.** the preparation of a form for printing by leveling the type, cuts, etc., with underlays or overlays to insure an even impression. **2.** the underlays or overlays used.

mak·er-up (mā kər up′), *n., pl.* **mak·ers-up.** **1.** *British.* a maker or manufacturer of garments. **2.** a person who makes up type, pictures, etc.

make·shift (māk′shift′), *n.* something used for a time instead of the right thing; temporary substitute: *When the electric lights went out, we used candles as a makeshift. Spools and buttons were the child's makeshifts for toys.*
—*adj.* **1.** used for a time instead of the right thing: *drowsing in the scant shade of makeshift awnings* (Mark Twain). **2.** characterized by makeshifts: *makeshift endeavors.*

make·shift·y (māk′shif′tē), *adj.* makeshift: *The hospitals at Allahabad are rather makeshifty* (Lady Canning).

mak·est (mā′kist), *v.* archaic form of the second person singular **make.**

mak·eth (mā′kith), *v. Archaic.* makes.

make·up or **make-up** (māk′up′), *n.* **1.** the way in which something is put together; composition; constitution: *The novelty of the orchestra's size and makeup . . .* (Maclean's). **2.** nature; disposition: *People of a nervous makeup are excitable.* **3. a.** the way in which an actor is dressed to look his part. **b.** the clothes, cosmetics, wigs, etc., used by an actor to look his part. **4.** rouge, lipstick, powder, etc., put on the face: *When you have plenty of makeup on, you always get served faster* (New Yorker). **5.** *Printing.* **a.** the arrangement of type, pictures, etc., in a book, paper, or magazine. **b.** the result of this: *That book has good makeup.* **6.** *Informal.* an examination, course, etc., taken to make up for having missed or failed a previous one: *Make-up injections will be given to another 300 children at the health center* (New York Times).

makeup or **make-up man,** a man whose business is making up actors and actresses or other people appearing before an audience: *Our young conductors might be expected to sew the costumes together, . . . act as make-up men, . . .* (Atlantic).

make·weight (māk′wāt′), *n.* **1.** anything added to make up for some lack: *Even a "good" Budget next month may prove no more than a temporary makeweight* (Sunday Times). **2.** something put on a scale to complete a required weight; counterpoise. —**Syn. 1.** offset.

make-work (māk′wėrk′), *n. U.S.* **1.** the contriving of unnecessary activity; featherbedding. **2.** the providing of work for unemployed people.
—*adj.* **1.** of or used for unnecessary work. **2.** devised to make jobs: *. . . top Administration planners view a huge make-work program as the last ditch move to perk up the economy* (Wall Street Journal).

ma·ki·mo·no (mä′kə mō′nō), *n., pl.* **-nos.** a Japanese picture or writing on silk, paper, or other material that is kept rolled up, and not suspended as a kakemono. [< Japanese *makimono* < *maki* scroll + *mono* thing]

mak·ing (mā′king), *n.* **1.** the cause of a person's success; means of advancement: *Early hardships were the making of him.* **2.** the material needed. **3.** the qualities needed: *I see in him the making of a hero.* **4.** something made. **5.** the amount made at one time.

in the making, in the process of being made; not fully developed: *The dress is in the making.*

makings, *U.S. Slang.* paper and tobacco for rolling cigarettes: *He had the makings for a whole pack.*

ma·ko (mä′kō), *n., pl.* **-kos.** a mako shark. [< Maori *mako*]

mako shark, a shark of warm waters that reaches a length of over 12 feet and is highly regarded as a game fish.

mal-, *combining form.* bad or badly; poor or poorly; unlawful; not ____: *Malodorous = smelling bad. Maladjusted = badly adjusted. Malnutrition = poor nutrition.* Also, **male-.** [< French *mal-* < *mal,* adverb (< Latin *male* badly), or adjective < Latin *malus* bad]

Mal., 1. Malachi (book of the Old Testament). **2.** Malayan.

mal·ab·sorp·tion (mal′ab sôrp′shən, -zôrp′-), *n. Medicine.* poor or abnormal absorption of food by the body: *malabsorption of carbohydrates. Malabsorption is almost always associated with some degree of weight loss* (Science News Letter).

Ma·lac·ca cane (mə lak′ə), a light walking stick made of rattan. [< *Malacca,* a state in the Malay Peninsula]

ma·la·ceous (mə lā′shəs), *adj.* of or belonging to a group of plants now generally classified with the rose family, as the apple and pear. [< New Latin *Malaceae* the family name (< Latin *mālum* apple) + English *-ous*]

Mal·a·chi (mal′ə kī), *n.* **1.** a Hebrew prophet who lived about 450 B.C. He was the last of the minor prophets. **2.** the last book of the Old Testament, attributed to him. *Abbr.:* Mal.

Mal·a·chi·as (mal′ə kī′əs), *n.* (in the Douay Bible) Malachi.

mal·a·chite (mal′ə kīt), *n.* a green mineral, a basic carbonate of copper, used for ornamental articles. *Formula:* $CuCO_3.Cu(OH)_2$ [< French *malachite* < Greek *maláchē* mallow (because of the similar color)]

mal·a·co·log·i·cal (mal′ə kə loj′ə kəl), *adj.* of or having to do with malacology.

mal·a·col·o·gist (mal′ə kol′ə jist), *n.* an expert in malacology.

mal·a·col·o·gy (mal′ə kol′ə jē), *n.* the branch of zoology that deals with mollusks. [< French *malacologie,* short for *malacozoologie* < *malaco-* (< Greek *malakós* soft) + *zoologie* zoology]

mal·a·cop·ter·yg·i·an (mal′ə kop′tə rij′ē ən), *adj.* of or having to do with a group of soft-finned, teleost fishes, in older classifications. [< New Latin *Malacopterygii* the division name (< Greek *malakós* soft + *ptéryx, -ygos* wing, fin < *pterón* wing) + English *-an*]

mal·a·cos·tra·can (mal′ə kos′trə kən), *adj.* of or having to do with a group of crustaceans including the lobsters, crabs, shrimps, etc. —*n.* a malacostracan crustacean. [< New Latin *Malacostraca* the order name, ultimately < Greek *malakós* soft + *óstrakon* shell + English *-an*]

mal·a·cos·tra·cous (mal′ə kos′trə kəs), *adj.* malacostracan.

mal·a·dap·ta·tion (mal′ə dap tā′shən), *n.* poor adaptation; lack of adaptation: *But there is a direct maladaptation between our inherited nature and culture that brings social disorganization* (Ogburn and Nimkoff).

mal·a·dapt·ed (mal′ə dap′tid), *adj.* **1.** maladjusted: . . . *the "maladapted" delinquent* (Listener). **2.** poorly adapted; ill-suited: *work maladapted to the assembly line.*

mal·a·dap·tive (mal′ə dap′tiv), *adj.* poorly adapting; exhibiting maladaptation: *a maladaptive response to stress. A society which denies mourning and gives no ritual support to mourners thereby produces maladaptive and neurotic responses in a large number of its citizens* (Listener).

mal·ad·dress (mal′ə dres′), *n.* clumsiness; awkwardness. [< French *maladresse,* noun to *maladroit* maladroit]

mal·a·dive (mal′ə div), *adj.* of, having to do with, or affected with sickness; sickly: *The magnificent Prescott [a singer] is nearly overgrown by a chorus of maladive voices, like a tree engulfed by poison ivy* (New Yorker). [< Old French *maladif* < *malade* ill; see MALADY]

mal·ad·just·ed (mal′ə jus′tid), *adj.* badly adjusted; not in a healthy or harmonious relation with one's environment.

mal·ad·just·ment (mal′ə just′mənt), *n.* poor or unsatisfactory adjustment; lack of adaptation: . . . *a first line of defense against delinquency, as well as against personal maladjustment and unhappiness* (New York Times).

mal·ad·min·is·ter (mal′əd min′ə stər), *v.t.* to administer badly; manage inefficiently or dishonestly: *We will never allow the cry of party to be used . . . in the defense of a man who maladministers the law* (Atlantic).

mal·ad·min·is·tra·tion (mal′əd min′ə strā′shən), *n.* bad administration; inefficient or dishonest management: *The Whigs had repeatedly assailed the maladministration of the Prince* (William E. H. Lecky). —**Syn.** misrule, misgovernment.

mal·ad·min·is·tra·tor (mal′əd min′ə strā′tər), *n.* a person guilty of maladministration.

mal·a·droit (mal′ə droit′), *adj.* unskillful; awkward; clumsy. [< French *maladroit* < *mal-* mal- + *adroit* adroit] —**mal′a·droit′ly,** *adv.* —**mal′a·droit′ness,** *n.* —**Syn.** blundering, bungling.

mal·a·dy (mal′ə dē), *n., pl.* **-dies.** a sickness; illness; disease: *Lying and cheating are social maladies.* [< Old French *maladie* < *malade* ill < Latin *male habitus* feeling unwell < *male* bad, and *habitus,* past participle of *habēre* have]

ma·la fi·de (mā′lə fī′dē), *Latin.* in bad faith; with or by fraud.

ma·la fi·des (mā′lə fī′dēz), *Latin.* bad faith.

Mal·a·ga (mal′ə gə), *n.* **1.** a large, oval, firm, sweet, white grape, grown in Spain and in California. **2.** a white dessert wine originally made in Málaga, Spain. [< *Málaga,* a province in Spain]

Mal·a·gas·y (mal′ə gas′ē), *n., pl.* **-gas·y** or **-gas·ies,** *adj.* —*n.* **1.** a native of Madagascar. **2.** the Indonesian language of Madagascar. —*adj.* of or having to do with Madagascar, its people, or their language.

ma·la·gue·ña (mä′lä gā′nyä), *n. Spanish.* a kind of fandango originating from Málaga, Spain.

ma·laise (ma lāz′), *n.* **1.** vague bodily discomfort; uneasiness, often before sickness: *It was afflicting him with a general malaise, it was affecting his energy, his temper* (H.G. Wells). **2.** uneasy, disturbed, or disordered condition: *The loss of highly trained scientists is more a symptom of an underlying malaise than the cause* (Manchester Guardian Weekly). [< French *malaise* < *mal-* imperfect (see MAL-) + *aise* ease]

ma·la·mute (mä′lə myüt), *n.* the Alaskan malamute.

mal·an·ders (mal′ən dərz), *n.* a dry, scabby rash behind the knee in horses. [< Old French *malandre* a sore on a horse's knee, learned borrowing from Latin *malandria* sores on a horse's neck]

mal·a·pert (mal′ə pėrt), *Archaic.* —*adj.* too bold; pert; saucy: *His malapert boldness might peradventure be punished* (Sir Thomas More). —*n.* a person who is too bold, pert, or saucy: *The malapert knew well enough I laughed at her* (Sir Richard Steele). [< Middle French *malapert* < *mal-* badly, mal- + *apert* adroit, expert < Latin *apertus* open] —**mal′a·pert′ly,** *adv.* —**mal′a·pert′ness,** *n.*

mal·ap·por·tioned (mal′ə pôr′shənd, -pōr′-), *adj. U.S.* wrongly or unfairly apportioned: *At stake was the necessity of readjusting Georgia's outrageously malapportioned U.S. congressional districts* (Time).

mal·ap·por·tion·ment (mal′ə pôr′shən mənt, -pōr′-), *n. U.S.* wrong or unfair assignment of representation in a legislature: *In a landmark case, Baker vs. Carr, the Court held, 7-2, that federal courts may hear claims that malapportionment of state legislatures violates the equal-protection clause of the Fourteenth Amendment* (Milton Greenberg).

mal·ap·pro·pri·ate (*v.* mal′ə prō′prē āt; *adj.* mal′ə prō′prē it), *v.,* **-at·ed, -at·ing,** *adj.* —*v.t.* to appropriate wrongly; misappropriate. —*adj.* inappropriate.

mal·ap·pro·pri·a·tion (mal′ə prō′prē ā′shən), *n.* misappropriation.

Mal·a·prop (mal′ə prop), *n.* **Mrs.,** a character in Richard Brinsley Sheridan's play *The Rivals,* noted for her ridiculous misuse of words. [< *malapropos*]

mal·a·prop·i·an (mal′ə prop′ē ən), *adj.* given to malapropisms; like a malapropism.

mal·a·prop·ism (mal′ə prop iz′əm), *n.* **1.** a ridiculous misuse of words. **2.** a misused word: *Lemaitre has reproached Shakespeare for his love of malapropisms* (Harper's). [earlier *malaprop* < Mrs. *Malaprop*]

➔ A **malapropism** is a confusion of two words somewhat similar in sound but different in meaning, as *arduous* love for *ardent* love. Malapropisms are often unconscious, but are sometimes intentionally used for humorous effect.

mal·ap·ro·pos (mal′ap rə pō′), *adv., adj.* at the wrong time or place: *Charles Lamb was frequently embarrassed by his malapropos sense of humor.* [< French *mal à propos* badly for the purpose < *mal* (see MAL-) + *à propos* apropos]

ma·lar (mā′lər), *adj.* of or having to do with the cheekbone or cheek. —*n.* the cheekbone. [< New Latin *malaris* < Latin *māla* jaw, cheek, cheekbone]

ma·lar·i·a (mə lãr′ē ə), *n.* **1.** a disease characterized by periodic chills and uncontrollable shaking, followed by fever and sweating. Malaria is caused by parasitic protozoans in the red blood corpuscles, and is transmitted by the bite of anopheles mosquitoes which have bitten infected persons. **2.** unwholesome or poisonous air, especially from marshes; miasma. [< Italian *malaria,* for *mala aria* (literally) bad air; *aria* < Latin *āēr, āeris* < Greek *āēr, āéros*]

ma·lar·i·al (mə lãr′ē əl), *adj.* **1.** having malaria: *In this circulation of the contagion the presence of malarial man is indispensable* (British Medical Journal). **2.** of or like malaria. **3.** likely to cause, or associated with, malaria: *They came to a land of encroaching sand dunes, . . . of malarial swamps and naked limestone hills* (Scientific American).

ma·lar·i·an (mə lãr′ē ən), *adj.* malarial: *A flat malarian world of reed and rush!* (Tennyson).

ma·lar·i·at·ed (mə lãr′ē ā′tid), *adj.* infected with malaria.

ma·lar·i·ol·o·gist (mə lãr′ē ol′ə jist), *n.* a person skilled in malariology.

ma·lar·i·ol·o·gy (mə lãr′ē ol′ə jē), *n.* the study of malaria, especially the relationship between malarial parasites and their hosts.

ma·lar·i·ous (mə lãr′ē əs), *adj.* malarial.

ma·lar·key (mə lär′kē), *n. U.S. Slang.* nonsense; baloney: *But this yogi business— . . . sheer nonsense. Pure malarkey* (New Yorker).

mal·as·sim·i·la·tion (mal′ə sim ə lā′shən), *n.* imperfect assimilation, especially of food by the body.

mal·ate (mal′āt, mā′lāt), *n.* a salt or ester of malic acid. [< *mal*(ic acid) + *-ate*[2]]

mal·a·thi·on (mal′ə thī′on), *n.* a residual organic phosphate widely used against many types of insect pests: *DDT, malathion, and methoxyclor are the commonest fly eradicators* (Sunset). *Formula:* $C_{10}H_{19}O_6PS_2$

Ma·la·wi·an (mä lä′wē ən), *adj.* of or having to do with the republic of Malawi (the former Nyasaland) or its people: *Tanzanian and Malawian ministers concluded their talks today at Mwanza* (London Times). —*n.* a native or inhabitant of Malawi.

mal·ax·ate (mal′ək sāt), *v.t.,* **-at·ed, -at·ing.** to soften by kneading, rubbing, mixing, making into a paste, or the like. [< Latin *malaxāre* (with English *-ate*[1]) < Greek *malássein*]

mal·ax·a·tion (mal′ək sā′shən), *n.* the act or process of malaxating.

mal·ax·a·tor (mal′ək sā′tər), *n.* a malaxating or mixing machine.

Ma·lay (mā′lā, mə lā′), *n.* **1.** a member of a brown-skinned race living in the Malay Peninsula and nearby islands. **2.** their Indonesian language. **3.** any of a breed of poultry originating in India, having a long, muscular body and red and black plumage. —*adj.* of the Malays, their country, or their language.

Mal·a·ya·lam (mal′ə yä′ləm), *n.* the Dravidian language spoken on the southwestern coast of India.

Ma·lay·an (mə lā′ən), *n., adj.* Malay.

Ma·lay·o-Pol·y·ne·sian (mə lā′ō pol′ə nē′zhən, -shən), *adj.* of or having to do with the Malays and Polynesians and the languages they speak; Austronesian.

Ma·lay·sian (mə lā′zhən, -shən), *adj.* of or having to do with Malaysia, its people, or their languages. —*n.* a native or inhabitant of Malaysia.

mal·con·duct (mal kon′dukt), *n.* bad or improper conduct, especially in office.

mal·con·for·ma·tion (mal′kon fôr mā′shən, -fər-), *n.* imperfect or faulty conformation, as of parts.

mal·con·tent (mal′kən tent′), *adj.* discontented; dissatisfied; rebellious: *The neglect of the male sex rendered her malcontent and peevish* (Tobias Smollett). *A project was even formed by the malcontent troops to deliver Harlem into the hands of Orange* (John Lothrop Motley). —*n.* a discontented or rebellious person: *It was pointed out that the Exhibition would serve as a rallying point . . . for all the malcontents in Europe . . .* (Lytton Strachey). [< Old French *malcontent* < *mal-* mal- + *content* content²]

mal de mer (mål′ də mer′), *French.* seasickness.

mal de ra·quette (mål′ də rå ket′), *Canadian French.* snowshoe sickness.

mal·de·vel·op·ment (mal′di vel′əp mənt), *n.* the improper growth or maturity of an organ, nerve, etc.: *Babies are occasionally exposed to critical stresses which initiate many of the maldevelopments not seen until birth* (Scientific American).

mal·dis·tri·bu·tion (mal′dis trə byü′shən), *n.* improper or ineffective arrangement or apportionment: *Overproduction plus maldistribution equals bootlegging* (Wall Street Journal).

Mal·div·i·an (mal div′ē ən), *adj.* of or having to do with the Maldive Islands. —*n.* **1.** a native or inhabitant of the Maldive Islands. **2.** the language of the Maldive Islands.

mal du pays (mål′ dY pā ē′), *French.* homesickness.

male (māl), *n.* **1.** a male human being; man or boy. **2.** any animal of corresponding sex. **3.** a staminate plant.
—*adj.* **1.** of or belonging to the sex that includes men, boys, and he-animals: *a male dog. A bull, a rooster, and a he-goat are all male animals.* **2. a.** of or having to do with men, boys, or he-animals: *the male love of fighting.* **b.** composed or consisting of men: *a male chorus.* **3.** *Botany.* **a.** able to fertilize the female. The same plant may have both male and female flowers. **b.** (of seed plants) having flowers which contain stamens but not pistils; staminate. **4.** fitting into a corresponding part: *a male screw.* **5.** of superior strength or vigor: *He is the most male of all these performers because he never weeps* (Edmund Wilson).
[< Old French *male, masle,* and *mascle* < Latin *masculus* masculine (diminutive) < *mās, maris* male] —**male′ness,** *n.*
—**Syn.** *adj.* **1, 3. Male, masculine, manly** mean having to do with men or the sex to which they belong. **Male** applies to plants, animals, or persons, and suggests only sex: *We have a male avocado tree.* **Masculine** applies to persons, things, or qualities, and suggests the characteristics (especially strength, vigor, etc.) of man as distinguished from woman: *He is a big, masculine man.* **Manly** suggests the finer characteristics of man, such as courage and honor: *He is a fine, clean, manly boy.*

male-, *combining form.* a variant of **mal-,** especially in borrowings from Latin, as in *maledict.*

ma·le·ate (mə lē′ət), *n.* a salt or ester of maleic acid.

Mal·e·cite (mal′ə sīt), *n., pl.* **-cite** or **-cites.** an Indian of the Abenaki group of the Algonkian linguistic stock, living in New Brunswick, Canada.

mal·e·dict (mal′ə dikt), *adj. Archaic.* accursed: *As the wings of starlings bear them on In the cold season in large band and full, So doth that blast the spirits maledict* (Longfellow). [< Latin *maledictus,* past participle of *maledīcere* < *male* ill, wrongly + *dicere* speak]

mal·e·dic·tion (mal′ə dik′shən), *n.* a speaking evil of or to a person; curse; slander: *menaces and maledictions against king and nobles* (Shakespeare). [< Latin *maledictiō, -ōnis* < *maledīcere;* see MALEDICT. Doublet of MALISON.] —**Syn.** execration, imprecation.

mal·e·dic·to·ry (mal′ə dik′tər ē), *adj.* characterized by or like malediction.

mal·e·fac·tion (mal′ə fak′shən), *n.* a crime; evil deed: *Guilty creatures . . . have proclaimed their malefactions* (Shakespeare). [< Latin *malefactiō, -ōnis* < *malefacere* to do wrong < *male* wrongly + *facere* do]

mal·e·fac·tor (mal′ə fak′tər), *n.* a criminal; evildoer: *Rank and fortune were offered to any malefactor who would compass the murder* (John L. Motley). [< Latin *malefactor* < *malefacere* < *male* badly + *facere* do]

mal·e·fac·tress (mal′ə fak′tris), *n.* a woman malefactor: *We women . . . should have the handling of such malefactresses as this Hester Prynne* (Hawthorne).

male fern, a fern whose rhizomes and stipes yield an oleoresin used medically to eradicate the tapeworm.

ma·lef·ic (mə lef′ik), *adj.* producing evil or harm; baleful. [< Latin *maleficus,* related to *malefacere;* see MALEFACTOR]

ma·lef·i·cence (mə lef′ə səns), *n.* **1.** harm; evil: *Who the perpetrator of this Parisian maleficence was, remained dark* (Thomas Carlyle). **2.** evil character; harmfulness. [< Latin *maleficentia* < *maleficus* wicked < *male* badly + *facere* do]

ma·lef·i·cent (mə lef′ə sənt), *adj.* harmful; evil. [< *maleficence,* perhaps based on *beneficent*]

male hormone, a hormone produced by the testes, as androsterone or testosterone, responsible for the secondary characteristics of males.

ma·le·ic acid (mə lē′ik), a colorless, crystalline acid, isomeric with fumaric acid, produced by the distillation of malic acid. It is used in dyeing, in organic synthesis, etc. *Formula:* $C_4H_4O_4$ [ultimately < *malic acid*]

maleic an·hy·dride (an hī′drīd), a chemical used in making paints, synthetic resins, dyes, etc. *Formula:* $C_4H_2O_3$

maleic hy·dra·zide (hī′drə zīd), a hydrazine compound that regulates the growth of plants. It is used to prevent the sprouting of potatoes and onions, retard leaf or flower development, kill weeds, etc. *Formula:* $C_4H_4N_2O_2$

ma·le·mute or **ma·le·miut** (mä′lə myüt), *n.* Alaskan malamute.

mal·en·ten·du (mål äN täN dY′), *French.* —*n.* a misunderstanding; misinterpretation. —*adj.* mistaken; misapprehended.

ma·lev·o·lence (mə lev′ə ləns), *n.* the wish that evil may happen to others; ill will; spite.

ma·lev·o·lent (mə lev′ə lənt), *adj.* wishing evil to happen to others; showing ill will; spiteful: *at the mercy of one whose purposes could not be other than malevolent* (Hawthorne). [< Old French *malivolent,* learned borrowing from Latin *malevolēns, -entis* < *male* ill + *volēns, -entis,* present participle of *velle* to wish] —**ma·lev′o·lent·ly,** *adv.*

mal·fea·sance (mal fē′zəns), *n.* official misconduct; violation of a public trust or duty: *A judge is guilty of malfeasance if he accepts a bribe.* [< French *malfaisance* < *mal-* badly, mal- + *faisant,* present participle of *faire* to do < Latin *facere*]
➤ See **feasance** for usage note.

mal·fea·sant (mal fē′zənt), *adj.* doing evil. —*n.* an evildoer; malefactor.

mal·for·ma·tion (mal′fôr mā′shən), *n.* distorted or abnormal shape; faulty structure: *A hunchback has a malformation of the spine.*

mal·formed (mal fôrmd′), *adj.* badly shaped; having a faulty structure.

mal·func·tion (mal′fungk′shən), *n.* **1.** an improper functioning; a failure to work: *"Malfunction" is the most feared word a rocket scientist can hear* (Scientific American). **2.** a disorder (of the body); sickness: *a gastrointestinal malfunction.* —*v.i.* to function badly; perform improperly: *They are full of delicate pumps and valves that often malfunction* (Time).

mal·gov·ern·ment (mal guv′ərn mənt, -ər mənt), *n.* bad government.

mal·gré (mål grā′), *prep. French.* in spite of.

mal·gré lui (mål grā lwē′), *French.* in spite of himself: *He sat the war out, a "slacker malgré lui"* (Time).

mal·gré soi (mål grā swå′), *French.* in spite of oneself or itself: *Let nothing scare me he had said, but did he know what it was to be a tramp malgré soi?* (Manchester Guardian).

Ma·li·an (mä′lē ən), *adj.* of or having to do with the republic of Mali (the former French Sudan) or its people. —*n.* a native or inhabitant of Mali.

mal·ic acid (mal′ik, mā′lik), a colorless, crystalline acid found in apples and numerous other fruits, used in making certain salts and for aging wine. *Formula:* $C_4H_6O_5$ [< French *malique acide; malique* < Latin *mālum* apple < Doric Greek *mâlon*]

mal·ice (mal′is), *n.* **1.** active ill will; wish to hurt others; spite: *I never bore malice to a brave enemy for having done me an injury* (Scott). *With malice toward none; with charity for all . . .* (Abraham Lincoln). **2.** *Law.* intent to commit an act which will result in harm to another person without justification.
[< Old French *malice,* learned borrowing from Latin *malitia* < *malus* evil]
—**Syn. 1.** spitefulness, grudge, rancor. See **spite.**

malice aforethought, *Law.* malice (def. 2).

ma·li·cious (mə lish′əs), *adj.* showing active ill will; wishing to hurt others; spiteful: *I think that story is nothing more than malicious gossip. He cursed that blind and malicious power which delighted to cross his most deep-laid schemes* (William Godwin). [< Old French *malicius* (with English *-ous*) < Latin *malitiōsus* < *malitia;* see MALICE] —**ma·li′cious·ly,** *adv.* —**ma·li′cious·ness,** *n.*

ma·lif·er·ous (mə lif′ər əs), *adj.* bringing evil; producing bad effects; unwholesome; unhealthful. [< Latin *malus* bad + English *-ferous*]

ma·lign (mə līn′), *v.t.* to speak evil of; slander: *You malign a generous person when you call him stingy. Have I not taken your part when you were maligned?* (Thackeray). [< Old French *malignier* < Late Latin *malignāre* < Latin *malignus;* see the adjective]
—*adj.* **1.** evil; injurious: *Gambling often has a malign influence.* **2.** hateful; malicious: *The devil . . . with jealous leer malign Eyed them askance* (Milton). **3.** very harmful; threatening to be fatal; cancerous: *a malign tumor.*
[< Old French *maligne,* learned borrowing from Latin *malignus,* for *male genus* < *malus* evil, and *genus* < root of *gignere* beget] —**ma·lign′er,** *n.* —**ma·lign′ly,** *adv.*
—**Ant.** *adj.* benign.

ma·lig·nance (mə lig′nəns), *n.* malignancy.

ma·lig·nan·cy (mə lig′nən sē), *n., pl.* **-cies.** **1.** malignant quality or tendency: *The malignancy of my fate might perhaps distemper yours* (Shakespeare). **2.** *Medicine.* something malignant or diseased, as a tumor.

ma·lig·nant (mə lig′nənt), *adj.* **1.** very evil; very hateful; very malicious: *Events were fatally to prove . . . that there are natures too malignant to be trusted or to be tamed* (John L. Motley). **2.** very harmful: *Unless the next word . . . Have some malignant power upon my life* (Shakespeare). **3.** very infectious; very dangerous; causing death: *Cancer is a malignant growth.* **4.** *Archaic.* disaffected; malcontent.
—*n.* a malcontent: *The supporters of the Stuarts during the English Civil War were called malignants by their opponents.*
[< Late Latin *malignāns, -antis* acting from malice, present participle of *malignāre* to injure < Latin *malignus;* see MALIGN, adjective] —**ma·lig′nant·ly,** *adv.*

malignant edema, an acute, febrile, fatal bacterial disease of domestic animals and also of man, producing hot, painful body swellings, with destruction of tissues and formation of gas in them.

malignant pustule, anthrax in man.

ma·lig·ni·ty (mə lig′nə tē), *n., pl.* **-ties. 1.** great malice; extreme hate: *Iago's soliloquy, the motive-hunting of a motiveless malignity—how awful it is!* (Samuel Taylor Coleridge). **2.** great harmfulness; dangerous quality; deadliness: *the malignity of cancer.* **3.** a malignant feeling or act. [< Old French *malignite,* learned borrowing from Latin *malignitās* < *malignus;* see MALIGN, adjective] —**Syn. 1.** enmity.

mal·ig·nol·i·pin (mal′ig nol′ə pin), *n.* a phosphatide found only in malignant tissue. [< *malignant* + *lip*(id) + *-in*]

ma·lik (mä′lik), *n.* (in Pakistan) a tribal chief. [ultimately < Arabic *mālik*]

ma·lines or **ma·line** (mə lēn′; *French* må lēn′), *n.* **1.** Mechlin lace: *Another pattern is . . . embroidered and trimmed with malines* (Harper's Magazine). **2.** a thin, stiff, silk net used in dressmaking, making women's hats, etc. [< French *malines* < *Malines,* or *Mechlin,* a town in Belgium]

ma·lin·ger (mə ling′gər), *v.i.* to pretend to be sick in order to escape work or duty; shirk: *Hastie examined him; and . . . knew not . . . whether the man was sick or malingering* (Robert Louis Stevenson). [< French *malingre* sickly < Old French, a proper

name, perhaps < *mal-* mal- + *heingre* or *haingre* sick, haggard] —**ma·lin′ger·er,** *n.*
Ma·lin·ke or **Ma·lin·ké** (mə ling′kē, -kā), *n., pl.* **-ke** or **-ké, -kes** or **-kés. 1.** a member of a Negro tribe in western Africa. **2.** this tribe. **3.** their Mandingo language.
ma·lism (mā′liz əm), *n.* the doctrine that the world is evil, or that evil generally prevails over good. [< *mal-* + *-ism*]
mal·i·son (mal′ə zən, -sən), *n. Archaic.* a curse; malediction: *Farewell, and my malison abide with thee!* (Charles Kingsley). [< Old French *maleïson,* or *maleïçon* < Latin *maledictiō, -ōnis.* Doublet of MALEDICTION.]
mal·kin (mô′kin), *n. British Dialect.* **1.** an untidy woman; a slut; slattern. **2.** a scarecrow. **3.** a cat. **4.** a mop. **5.** *Scottish.* a hare. Also, **maukin, mawkin.** [diminutive form of *Maud,* a proper name]
Mal·kin (mô′kin), *n. British Dialect.* a female demon, often in the form of a cat.
mall[1] (môl, mal), *n.* **1.** a shaded walk; public walk or promenade. **2. a.** the mallet used to strike the ball in the game of pall-mall. **b.** the game pall-mall. **c.** the alley on which the game is played. [< Old French *mail,* and *maul* mallet < Latin *malleus* hammer. Compare MAUL.]
mall[2] (môl), *n., v.t.* maul.
mal·lard (mal′ərd), *n., pl.* **-lards** or (*collectively*) **-lard.** a wild duck found in Europe, northern Asia and throughout North America. The male has a greenish-black head and a white band around the neck. Many domestic ducks are descended from mallards. [< Old French *mallart,* apparently < *male;* see MALE]

Mallard (1¾ to 2 ft. long)

mal·le·a·bil·i·ty (mal′ē ə bil′ə tē), *n.* malleable quality or condition: *The Japanese, individually and socially, has a malleability which makes it possible for him to incorporate . . . varied elements* (Atlantic).
mal·le·a·ble (mal′ē ə bəl), *adj.* **1.** that can be hammered, pressed, or extended in various shapes without being broken: *Gold, silver, copper, and tin are malleable; they can be beaten into thin sheets.* **2.** adaptable; yielding: *Human nature is often malleable . . . where religious interests are concerned* (John Lothrop Motley). [< Old French *malleable* < Latin *malleus* hammer + Old French *-able* -able] —**mal′le·a·ble·ness,** *n.*
malleable cast iron, white cast iron made tough and malleable by long heating at a high temperature followed by slow cooling.
malleable iron, 1. malleable cast iron. **2.** wrought iron.
mal·lee (mal′ē), *n.* **1.** any of several dwarf Australian kinds of eucalyptus that sometimes form large areas of brushwood. **2.** such brushwood. [< the Australian name]
mal·le·muck (mal′ə muk), *n.* any of various large sea birds, such as the fulmar or the albatross. [< Dutch *mallemok,* perhaps < *mal* foolish < *mok* gull; or perhaps alteration of a Greenland Eskimo word]
mal·le·o·lar (mə lē′ə lər), *adj.* of or having to do with the malleolus.
mal·le·o·lus (mə lē′ə ləs), *n., pl.* **-li** (-lī). the bony part that sticks out on either side of the ankle. [< Latin *malleolus* (diminutive) < *malleus* hammer]
mal·let (mal′it), *n.* a kind of hammer with a head of wood, hard rubber, etc., used to drive a chisel or other tool. Specially shaped mallets are used to play croquet and polo. [< Old French *maillet* (diminutive) < *mail* < Latin *malleus* hammer. Compare MALL[1], MAUL.]
mal·le·us (mal′ē əs), *n., pl.* **mal·le·i** (mal′ē ī). the outermost of the three small bones in the middle ear of mammals, shaped like a hammer; hammer. [< Latin *malleus* hammer]
mal·low (mal′ō), *n.* **1.** any of a group of ornamental plants with purple, pink, or white flowers, and hairy leaves and stems. See picture under **fascicle. 2.** any of various other plants of the mallow family, as the marsh mallow. [Old English *mealwe* < Latin *malva.* Doublet of MAUVE.]
mallow family, a group of dicotyledonous herbs, shrubs, and trees, most of which have sticky, gummy juice, and flowers shaped like those of the hollyhock. The family includes the mallow, hollyhock, cotton, okra, hibiscus, and althea.
mallow rose, any of certain plants of the mallow family having rose-colored flowers; rose mallow.
malm (mäm), *n. British.* **1.** a soft, friable, grayish limestone. **2.** *Dialect.* a light, loamy soil containing chalk: *To the . . . east of the village is a range of fair enclosures, consisting of what is called a white malm* (Gilbert White). [Old English *mealm-,* in *mealmstān* malm stone. Related to MEAL[2].]
malm·sey (mäm′zē), *n.* a strong, sweet wine, originally made in Cyprus: *Old Simon, the cellarer, has a rare store of malmsey and malvoisie* (G. W. Bellamy). [< Medieval Latin *malmasia,* alteration of Greek *Monembasia,* a Greek seaport. Doublet of MALVASIA, MALVOISIE.]
mal·nour·ished (mal nėr′isht), *adj.* improperly supplied with nutriments: *The malnourished American eats virtually no breakfast, has a light lunch and gorges on his evening meal* (Science News Letter).
mal·nu·tri·tion (mal′nü trish′ən, -nyü-), *n.* poor nourishment; lack of nourishment: *Improper food can cause malnutrition.*
mal·oc·clu·sion (mal′ə klü′zhən), *n.* failure of teeth opposite each other in the upper and lower jaws to close or meet properly against each other. [< *mal-* + *occlusion*]
mal·o·dor (mal ō′dər), *n.* a bad smell; stench. [< *mal-* + *odor*]
mal·o·dor·ous (mal ō′dər əs), *adj.* smelling bad: *A pestilent, malodorous home of dirt and disease* (The Century). —**mal·o′dor·ous·ly,** *adv.* —**mal·o′dor·ous·ness,** *n.* —**Syn.** unsavory, fetid.
mal·o·dour (mal ō′dər), *n. Especially British.* malodor.
ma·lo·nic acid (mə lō′nik, -lon′ik), a white, crystalline dicarboxylic acid readily decomposed by heat, derived from malic acid by oxidation. *Formula:* $C_3H_4O_4$ [< French *malonique,* alteration of *malique* (*acide*) malic (acid)]
malonic ester, a colorless liquid used as a chemical intermediate. *Formula:* $C_7H_{12}O_4$
mal·or·gan·i·za·tion (mal′ôr gə nə zā′shən), *n.* bad or faulty organization.
mal·or·gan·ized (mal ôr′gə nīzd), *adj.* badly organized.
mal·pais (mal′pīs), *n.* a volcanic rock formation characterized by a rough and jagged surface; aa: *The trail . . . to cross the rugged malpais of the Mogollones* (J.W. Fewkes). [American English < Spanish *mal país* bad country, ultimately < Latin *malus* bad, and *pāgus* district]
Mal·peque (môl′pek), *n.* a choice variety of oyster produced at Malpeque, Prince Edward Island, Canada.
mal·pigh·i·a·ceous (mal pig′ē ā′shəs), *adj.* belonging to a family of dicotyledonous tropical trees and shrubs with yellow or red flowers, some of which are grown for ornament. [< New Latin *Malpighiaceae* the order name (< *Malpighia* the typical genus < Marcello *Malpighi,* 1628-1694, an Italian anatomist) + English *-ous*]
Mal·pigh·i·an (mal pig′ē ən), *adj.* of, having to do with, or discovered by Marcello Malpighi, 1628-1694, an Italian anatomist.
Malpighian body or **corpuscle,** a renal corpuscle.
Malpighian layer, the deeper part of the epidermis, consisting of living cells which have not become hardened.
Malpighian tubules or **vessels,** slender tubules connected to the alimentary canal of insects, serving as excretory organs.
Malpighian tuft, a tuft of capillaries in the kidney.
mal·posed (mal pōzd′), *adj.* badly placed: *Mr. George J. Goldie demonstrated the usefulness of the X rays in . . . the regulation of teeth malposed in the jaw* (Lancet).
mal·po·si·tion (mal′pə zish′ən), *n.* a faulty or wrong position, especially of a part or organ of the body or of a fetus in the uterus.
mal·prac·tice (mal prak′tis), *n.* **1.** criminal neglect or unprofessional treatment of a patient by a physician or surgeon: *A professional brother, prosecuted for malpractice, is always sure you will do what you can to clear him* (Josiah G. Holland). **2.** wrong practice or conduct in any official or professional position; misconduct: *We took pains . . . to correct the malpractice of the men* (John Colborne).
mal·prac·ti·tion·er (mal′prak tish′ə nər), *n.* a person guilty of malpractice.
malt (môlt), *n.* **1.** barley or other grain soaked in water and spread until it sprouts, then dried and aged. It has a sweet taste and is used in brewing and distilling alcoholic liquors. **2.** *Informal.* beer or ale.
—*v.t.* **1.** to change (grain) into malt. **2.** to prepare or treat with malt or an extract of malt. —*v.i.* **1.** to be changed into malt. **2.** to change grain into malt.
—*adj.* of or containing malt.
[Old English *mealt.* Related to MELT, SMELT.]
Mal·ta fever (môl′tə), undulant fever; Maltese fever. [< *Malta,* an island in the Mediterranean, where it is prevalent]
malt·ase (môl′tās), *n.* an enzyme, present in saliva and other body juices and in yeast, that changes maltose to dextrose.
malt·ed milk (môl′tid), **1.** a soluble powder made of dried milk, malted barley, and wheat flour. **2.** a drink prepared by mixing this powder with milk and flavoring, and often ice cream.
Mal·tese (mol tēz′, -tēs′), *n., pl.* **-tese,** *adj.* —*n.* **1.** a native or inhabitant of Malta, a British island in the Mediterranean, south of Sicily. **2.** the native language of Malta. It is a form of Arabic with many Italian words. **3.** any of a breed of small dogs with long, silky, white hair and weighing between 2 and 7 pounds. It was popular as a lap dog among well-to-do Greeks and Romans.

Maltese (def. 3) (about 5 in. high at the shoulder)

—*adj.* **1.** of Malta, its people, or their language. **2.** of or having to do with the religious and military order of the Knights of Malta.
Maltese cat, a kind of short-haired, bluish-gray cat: *Maltese cats . . . used to be extremely popular in America* (Dick Whittington).
Maltese cross, 1. a type of cross with four equal arms resembling arrowheads pointed toward the center. See the diagram of **cross. 2.** the scarlet lychnis.
Maltese fever, Malta fever.
Maltese lace, 1. a pillow lace of silk or linen of the guipure kind. **2.** a machine-made lace of coarse cotton thread.
malt extract, a sugary substance obtained by soaking malt in water.
mal·tha (mal′thə), *n.* **1.** any of various cements or mortars, especially one containing bitumen. **2.** any of various natural mixtures of hydrocarbons, such as ozocerite. **3.** a black, tarlike substance formed from the drying of petroleum. [< Latin *maltha* < Greek *máltha,* or *málthē*]
malt·horse (môlt′hôrs′), *n. Obsolete.* a heavy horse used by maltsters.
Mal·thu·sian (mal thü′zhən, -zē ən), *adj.* of or having to do with Malthus or his theory that the world's population tends to increase faster than the food supply, and that poverty and misery are inevitable unless this trend is checked by war, famine, birth control, etc.: *There was some crisis of shortage going on at the time and my father was fond of coming out with these curt, Malthusian directives* (Punch). —*n.* a believer in his theory. [< Thomas R. *Malthus,* 1766-1834, an English social economist + *-ian*]
Mal·thu·sian·ism (mal thü′zhə niz əm, zē ə-), *n.* the theories of Malthus and his followers.
malt liquor, beer, ale, or other alcoholic liquor made with malt.
malt·ose (môl′tōs), *n.* a white, crystalline, dextrorotatory sugar made in the body by ptyalin acting on starch, and commercially by the action of diastase on starch; malt sugar. *Formula:* $C_{12}H_{22}O_{11}.H_2O$ [< French *maltose* < *malt* (< English *malt*) + *-ose* -ose[2]]
mal·treat (mal trēt′), *v.t.* to treat roughly or cruelly; abuse: *Only vicious persons maltreat animals. Many monasteries were robbed, many clerical persons maimed and maltreated* (John L. Motley). [< French *maltraiter* < *mal-* mal- + Old French *traiter* to treat]

mal·treat·ment (mal trēt′mənt), *n.* rough or cruel treatment; abuse.

malt·ster (môlt′stər), *n.* a person who makes or sells malt: *The maltsters and brewers who prefer sun ripened barley certainly have it from the home crops this year* (London Times).

malt sugar, maltose.

malt·y (môl′tē), *adj.,* **malt·i·er, malt·i·est. 1.** of, like, or containing malt: *The bread would be soft, clammy, greyish and malty* (Michael Donovan). **2.** addicted to the use of malt liquor: *'Tis degrading to see ... our malty ladies of quality* (Metropolis). **3.** *Slang.* drunk.

mal·va·ceous (mal vā′shəs), *adj.* of or belonging to the mallow family. [< Latin *malvāceus* < *malva* a mallow]

mal·va·si·a (mal′və sē′ə), *n.* **1.** a variety of sweet grape used to make malmsey. **2.** malmsey: *We entered the shanty and drank malvasia* (Chambers's Journal). [< Italian < *malvasia,* alteration of Greek *Monembasia* a Greek seaport. Doublet of MALMSEY, MALVOISIE.]

mal·ver·sa·tion (mal′vər sā′shən), *n.* corrupt conduct in a position of trust, as extortion or fraud: *Cardonnel was turned out of the House of Commons for malversation of public money* (Thackeray). [< Middle French *malversation* < *malverser* behave wrongly (in office) < *mal-* mal- + *verser* < Latin *versārī* conduct oneself, be active in]

mal·voi·sie (mal′voi zē, -və-), *n.* **1.** malmsey: *Magnificent is the word for malmsey, malvasia, or malvoisie—call it what you will* (Punch). **2.** malvasia (the grape). [alteration of Middle English *malevesie* < Old French < alteration of Greek *Monembasia.* Doublet of MALVASIA, MALMSEY.]

ma·ma (mä′mə; *especially British* mə mä′), *n.* mother: *Mama, it was all your own fault* (Oliver Goldsmith). [compare MAMMA[1]]

mama's boy, *U.S. Informal.* a boy or man lacking normal masculine interests or unwilling to accept the responsibilities of manhood; sissy. Also, **mamma's boy.**

mam·ba (mam′bə), *n.* any of several long, slender elapid snakes of Central and South Africa, whose bite is poisonous: *The swaying head and glittering eyes of a black mamba—swiftest, most vicious, most deadly of snakes* (Sir Percy Fitzpatrick). [< Kaffir *imamba*]

mam·bo (mäm′bō), *n., pl.* **-bos,** *v.,* **-boed, -bo·ing.** —*n.* **1.** a kind of rumba of Cuban origin with a syncopated four-beat rhythm, the accent on the third beat: *The fast dancing is done to a jump tune or mambo* (Harper's). **2.** the music for this dance, with a heavy beat. —*v.i.* to dance the mambo: *I mamboed into the kitchen* (Atlantic). [< Cuban Spanish *mambo*]

mam·e·luke (mam′ə lük), *n.* (in Moslem countries) a slave.

Mam·e·luke (mam′ə lük), *n.* a member of a military group that ruled Egypt from about 1250 to 1517 and had great power until 1811. The Mamelukes were originally slaves. [< Arabic *mamlūk* slave]

ma·mey (ma mā′, -mē′), *n.* mammee.

mam·ma[1] (mä′mə; *especially British* mə-mä′), *n.* mother: *I can't but say that his mamma was right* (Byron). [reduplication of infantile sound. Compare Latin *mamma,* Greek *mámmē.*]

mam·ma[2] (mam′ə), *n., pl.* **mam·mae** (mam′ē). mammary gland. [< Latin *mamma* breast]

mam·mal (mam′əl), *n.* any of a class of vertebrate animals, the females of which give milk to their young: *Human beings, horses, cattle, dogs, lions, rats, cats, and whales are mammals.* [(originally) mammals, Anglicization of *Mammalia,* plural, ultimately < Latin *mamma* breast]

mam·ma·li·an (ma mā′lē ən, -māl′yən), *adj.* of or belonging to the mammals. —*n.* one of the mammals.

mam·mal·o·gist (ma mal′ə jist), *n.* an expert in mammalogy: *The consensus among mammalogists today is: The rabbit is not a rodent!* (Science News Letter).

mam·mal·o·gy (ma mal′ə jē), *n.* the branch of zoology that deals with mammals.

mam·ma·ry (mam′ər ē), *adj.* of or having to do with the mammae or breasts.

mammary gland, the milk-secreting gland in female mammals; mamma.

mamma's boy, mama's boy.

mam·ma·to-cu·mu·lus (ma mā′tō kyü′-myə ləs), *n., pl.* **-li** (-lī). a cumulus cloud with rounded protuberances or festoons on the lower surface. It is usually a sign of rain. [< Latin *mammātus* (literally) having mammae + English *cumulus*]

mam·mee (ma mē′, -mā′), *n.* **1.** a tall, tropical American tree with fragrant white flowers and a large, edible fruit. **2.** the large, edible fruit of this tree. **3.** the sapodilla. **4.** the marmalade tree or its fruit. Also, **mamey.** [< Spanish *mamey* < Arawak (Haiti)]

mammee apple, the fruit of the mammee.

mammee colorado, the marmalade tree or its fruit.

mammee sapota, the marmalade tree or its fruit.

mam·mer (mam′ər), *British Dialect.* —*v.i.* to mutter; stammer; hesitate in speech or in thought: *I wonder ... What you would ask me, that I should deny, Or stand so mammering on* (Shakespeare). —*v.t.* to confuse; perplex. [imitative]

mam·met (mam′it), *n.* maumet.

mam·mi·fer (mam′ə fər), *n.* an animal having mammae; mammal. [< French *mammifère* < Latin *mamma* breast + *ferre* to bear, carry]

mam·mif·er·ous (ma mif′ər əs), *adj.* having mammae or breasts; mammalian. [< Latin *mamma* breast + English *-ferous*]

mam·mil·la (ma mil′ə), *n., pl.* **-mil·lae** (-mil′ē). **1.** the nipple of the female breast; teat. **2.** any nipple-shaped organ or protuberance. [< Latin *mamilla* (diminutive) < *mamma* mamma[2]]

mam·mil·lar (mam′ə lər), *adj.* mammillary.

mam·mil·lar·y (mam′ə ler′ē), *adj.* **1.** of, having to do with, or like a mammilla. **2.** having rounded protuberances, as a mineral.

mam·mil·late (mam′ə lāt), *adj.* having mammillae or nipples, or nipple-shaped protuberances.

mam·mil·lat·ed (mam′ə lā′tid), *adj.* mammillate.

mam·mock (mam′ək), *n. Archaic or British Dialect.* a scrap; fragment; shred. —*v.t.* to break, cut, or tear into mammocks: *The soft parts are cut ... and mammocked in every conceivable way* (Fraser's Magazine). [origin uncertain]

mam·mog·ra·phy (ma mog′rə fē), *n.* X-ray examination of the breast.

mam·mon (mam′ən), *n.* **1.** riches or material wealth thought of as an evil: *the worship of mammon.* **2.** greed for wealth. [< Latin *mammōna* < Greek *mamōnâs* < Aramaic *māmonā* riches]

Mam·mon (mam′ən), *n.* a personification of riches as an evil spirit or god, or a soulless wordly force: *Mammon, the least erected spirit that fell from heaven* (Milton). *Mammon wins his way where Seraphs might despair* (Byron).

mam·mon·ish (mam′ə nish), *adj.* influenced by or devoted to mammon or Mammon.

mam·mon·ism (mam′ə niz əm), *n.* devotion to the pursuit of riches; greed for wealth.

Mam·mon·ism (mam′ə niz əm), *n.* the worship of Mammon: *It was necessary to protect the Lord's Day against Mammonism* (London Daily News).

mam·mon·ist (mam′ə nist), *n.* a person devoted to the pursuit of riches.

Mam·mon·ist (mam′ə nist), *n.* a worshiper of Mammon.

mam·mon·ite (mam′ə nīt), *n.* mammonist.

mam·moth (mam′əth), *n.* a very large, extinct kind of elephant with a hairy skin and long, curved tusks. —*adj.* huge; gigantic: *Digging the Panama Canal was a mammoth undertaking.* [< earlier Russian *mamot*] —**Syn.** *adj.* colossal, immense.

Northern Mammoth (14 ft. high at the shoulder)

mam·my (mam′ē), *n., pl.* **-mies.** *Southern U.S.* **1.** mamma; mother (used especially in the Appalachians): *These too were greeted ... "daddy and mammy"* (Southern Literary Messenger). **2.** a Negro woman who takes care of white children, or is a servant in a white household: *Like most Southern children, I was brought up and cared for by a "black mammy"* (R.D. Evans).

mammy wagon, a light truck used as a bus in the rural areas of western Africa: *We were told ... that living might be rugged, that we would have no cars and would have to ride the local "mammy wagons"* (New York Times).

mam·pa·lon (mam′pə lon), *n.* a small, otterlike, viverrine animal of Borneo, having webbed feet and living in and out of water. [probably < a native name]

man (man), *n., pl.* **men,** *v.,* **manned, manning,** *adj., interj.* —*n.* **1.** an adult male person. A man is a boy grown up. *When I became a man, I put away childish things* (I Corinthians 13:11). **2.** a human being; person: *All men are created equal* (Declaration of Independence). **3.** the human race: *Man likes company. Man has existed for thousands of years. Man shall not live by bread alone ...* (Matthew 4:4). **4.** a male follower, servant, or employee: *Robin Hood and his merry men; the men at the factory.* **5. a.** a husband: *man and wife.* **b.** a male lover; suitor. **6.** one of the pieces used in games such as chess, checkers, or backgammon. **7.** a person characterized by manly qualities: *He was every inch a man. His life was gentle, and the elements So mix'd in him that Nature might stand up and say to all the world, "This was a man!"* (Shakespeare). **8.** manly character or courage. **9.** a form of address, implying contempt, impatience, etc.: *Here, read it, read it, man* (Benjamin Disraeli). **10.** *Archaic.* a vassal; liegeman.

act the man, to be courageous: *The young sailor acted the man in every way.*

as a man, from a human point of view: *He spoke as a man, not merely as a soldier.*

as one man, with complete agreement; unanimously: *The crowd voted as one man.*

be one's own man, a. to be free to do as one pleases: *So Constance Nevill may marry whom she pleases, and Tony Lumpkin is his own man again* (Oliver Goldsmith). **b.** to have complete control of oneself: *The Royal progress on Saturday will be as a sign ... that the King is indeed his own man again* (London Daily Graphic).

man alive! *U.S. Informal.* an exclamation or mild oath: *Man alive! What an exciting ball game!*

man and boy, from boyhood on; as a youth and as an adult: *... had been a peace officer, man and boy, for half a century* (Dickens).

men, the common soldiers or sailors, as distinguished from the officers: *The English had lost more than 2,400 officers and men* (James T. Wheeler).

my good man, a condescending form of address, as to an inferior: *Come here, my good man.*

the man, a. the essential human being: *Style is less important than the man.* **b.** *U.S. Slang.* the police: *Look out, here comes the man!* **c.** *U.S. Slang.* the white man: *The demonstrations, I think, suggested to "the man" that tokenism won't make it and that he has to come to grips with the problem right now* (New York Times).

to a man, without exception; all: *They obeyed him, to a man.*

wise man of Gotham. See under **Gotham.**

—*v.t.* **1.** to supply with men: *Sailors man a ship.* **2.** to serve or operate; get ready to operate: *Man the guns.* **3.** to make courageous or strong; brace: *The captive manned himself to endure the loss of his freedom.* **4.** (in falconry) to accustom (a hawk) to the presence of men; tame.

—*adj.* male: *a man dancer.*

—*interj. Informal.* an exclamation of surprise, joy, excitement, etc., or for effect: *Man, what a player! Man, that's some car!*

[Old English *mann* human being]

—**Syn.** *n.* **2.** individual, being, mortal. **3.** humanity, mankind. **4.** valet, attendant.

➔ **man, gentleman.** *Man* is now generally preferred to the more pretentious *gentleman,* unless a note of special courtesy or respect is desired.

man., manual.

Man., **1.** Manila (paper). **2.** Manitoba.

ma·na (mä′nä), *n.* supernatural or magical power or influence, especially among certain primitive peoples: *Notions of the type of mana ... are of "a nascently philosophic order"* (Times Literary Supplement). [< Maori *mana*]

man-a·bout-town (man′ə bout toun′), *n., pl.* **men-a·bout-town.** a man who spends much of his time in clubs, theaters, fashionable restaurants, etc.

man·a·cle (man′ə kəl), *n., v.,* **-cled, -cling.** —*n.* **1.** Often, **manacles.** a handcuff; fetter

for the hands: *We'll put you . . . in manacles, Then reason safely with you* (Shakespeare). **2.** a restraint: *The manacles of the all-building law* (Shakespeare).
—*v.t.* **1.** to put manacles on; handcuff: *The pirates manacled their prisoners.* **2.** to restrain; fetter.
[< Old French *manicle* < Latin *manicula* (diminutive) < *manicae* sleeves, manacles < *manus, -ūs* hand]

ma·na·da (mə nä′də), *n. Southwestern U.S.* **1.** a drove of horses, especially breeding mares. **2.** a herd of cattle. [< Spanish *manada*]

man·age (man′ij), *v.,* **-aged, -ag·ing,** *n.* —*v.t.* **1.** to control; conduct; handle; direct: *They hired a man to manage the business. He manages his horse well. Only his mother could manage him.* **2.** to succeed in accomplishing; contrive; arrange: *I shall manage to keep warm with this blanket. How did you manage to tear your new pants? The clumsy waiter managed to spill the soup. He had managed to remain poor all his life* (Edmund Wilson). **3.** to make use of: *He manages tools well.* **4.** to get one's way with (a person) by craft or by flattering: *He thoroughly understood the art of managing men, particularly his superiors* (John L. Motley). **5.** to use or change for one's own purpose; manipulate: *There has never been an administration . . . so studiously engaged in trying to manage news* (Columbia University Forum). **6.** to train or handle (a horse) in the manège. **7.** *Archaic.* to treat carefully; use sparingly; husband: *to manage one's health, resources, etc.* —*v.i.* **1.** to conduct affairs. **2.** to get along: *to manage on one's income. He managed a whole year upon the proceeds* (William Dean Howells).
—*n.* **1.** manège: *the manage of horses. The grounds extended to two acres, with a manage* (Sunday Times). **2.** *Archaic.* management.
[earlier *manege* < Italian *maneggiare* handle or train (horses) < *mano* hand < Latin *manus*]
—**Syn.** *v.t.* **1. Manage, conduct, direct** mean to guide or handle with authority. **Manage** emphasizes the idea of skillful handling of people and details so as to get results: *He manages a large department store.* **Conduct** emphasizes the idea of supervising the action of a group working together for something: *The Scoutmaster conducted his troop on a tour of the park.* **Direct** emphasizes the idea of guiding the affairs or actions of a group by giving advice and instructions to be followed: *A government man directed our bird conservation program.*

man·age·a·bil·i·ty (man′i jə bil′ə tē), *n.* the condition or quality of being manageable.

man·age·a·ble (man′i jə bəl), *adj.* that can be managed; controllable: *a package of manageable size. A meek and manageable child* (Elizabeth Barrett Browning). —**man′age·a·ble·ness,** *n.* —**Syn.** tractable, wieldy.

man·age·a·bly (man′i jə blē), *adv.* in a manageable manner.

man·aged currency (man′ijd), currency whose purchasing power is regulated by government.

man·age·ment (man′ij mənt), *n.* **1.** control; handling; direction: *Bad management caused the bank's failure.* **2.** the persons who manage a business or an institution: *a dispute between labor and management. The management of the store decided to use red wrapping paper at Christmas time.* **3.** administrative skill; skillful dealing or use: *Mark with what management their tribes divide* (John Dryden). *In the management of the heroic couplet Dryden has never been equalled* (Macaulay). —**Syn. 1.** guidance, regulation. **2.** administration.

management consultant, a person hired by a business firm to study its system of management and recommend necessary changes in it.

management engineer, an industrial engineer: *We, as management engineers, are interested in the economic utilization of human resources* (New York Times).

man·ag·er (man′i jər), *n.* **1.** a person who manages. **2.** a person in charge of the management of a business or an institution. *Abbr.:* Mgr. **3.** a person skilled in managing affairs, money, etc., as of a household: *She was neat, industrious, honest, and a good manager* (James Fenimore Cooper). **4.** *British.* a theatrical producer. —**Syn. 2.** director, executive, administrator.

man·ag·er·ess (man′i jər is), *n.* a woman manager.

man·a·ge·ri·al (man′ə jir′ē əl), *adj.* of a manager; having to do with management: *Executives . . . will be given intensive training in advanced managerial techniques* (Wall Street Journal). —**man′a·ge′ri·al·ly,** *adv.*

man·ag·er·ship (man′i jər ship), *n.* the position or control of a manager.

man·ag·ing editor (man′i jing), the executive in charge of the practical management of a publishing company or publication, as of a newspaper, magazine, or encyclopedia. The editors of the different production departments are usually responsible to the managing editor.

man·a·kin (man′ə kin), *n.* **1.** any of various small, bright-colored, songless birds of tropical America. **2.** manikin. [variant of *manikin*]

ma·ña·na (mä nyä′nä), *n., adv. Southwestern U.S.* tomorrow; some time: *Business will await, meetings, friends, jobs will be for mañana* (New Yorker). [American English < Spanish *mañana* < Latin *māne* morning]

man-ape (man′āp′), *n.* a primitive fossil man of the early Pleistocene, having both human and subhuman characteristics.

Ma·nas·seh (mə nas′ə), *n.* in the Bible: **1.** Joseph's elder son. Genesis 41:50-51. **2.** an Israelite tribe that descended from him. Joshua 17:1-6. **3.** a king of ancient Judah who ruled from about 692 to 638 B.C. II Kings 21:1-18.

man-at-arms (man′ət ärmz′), *n., pl.* **men-at-arms. 1.** a soldier. **2.** a heavily armed soldier on horseback.

man·a·tee (man′ə tē′), *n.* a large sea mammal with two flippers and a flat, oval tail, living in the warm, shallow waters of the Atlantic near the coast of tropical America and Africa; sea cow: *The manatee . . . by its quiet breathing and gentle breasts probably originated the haunting mermaid legends* (Punch). [< Spanish *manatí* < Carib (perhaps West Indies) *manati* (female) breast]

Manatee
(8 to 13 ft. long)

man·a·toid (man′ə toid), *adj.* having to do with or like a manatee.

ma·nav·el·ins or **ma·nav·il·ins** (mə nav′ə linz), *n.pl. Nautical Slang.* miscellaneous gear, equipment, etc. [origin uncertain]

Man·ches·ter terrier (man′ches′tər, -chə stər), any of a breed of slender, lively dogs, originally developed in England to catch rats, having a short, shiny-black coat marked with tan. There is a toy variety, weighing under 12 pounds, and a standard variety, from 12 to 22 pounds. [< *Manchester,* a city in England]

Manchester Terrier
(16 in. high at the shoulder)

man·chet (man′chit), *n. Archaic.* **1.** bread made of the finest white flour. **2.** a small loaf or roll of such bread. [origin uncertain]

man-child (man′chīld′), *n., pl.* **men-chil·dren.** a male child: *Bring forth men-children only* (Shakespeare).

man·chi·neel (man′chə nēl′), *n.* a tropical American tree of the spurge family, having a milky, poisonous sap, and a bitter, poisonous fruit somewhat like an apple. [< French *mancenille* < Spanish *manzanilla* (diminutive) < *manzana* apple, alteration of Old Spanish *mazana* < Latin *matiāna* (*māla*), plural, Matian fruit, probably < C. *Matius* Calvena, author of a work on cookery]

Man·chu (man′chü), *n.* **1.** a member of a Mongolian people living in Manchuria, who conquered China in 1644 and ruled it until 1912. **2.** their Ural-Altaic language. —*adj.* of the Manchus, their country, or their language.

Man·chu·ri·an (man chůr′ē ən), *adj.* of or having to do with Manchuria, a region in eastern Asia, including several provinces of China, or its people. —*n.* a native or inhabitant of Manchuria.

man·ci·pa·tion (man′sə pā′shən), *n.* **1.** a legal formality used among the ancient Romans for certain transfers of property, emancipation of slaves and children, etc. **2.** an enslaving or a being enslaved. [< Latin *mancipātiō, -ōnis* < *mancipāre* to deliver to < *manū capere* to take in hand]

man·ci·pa·to·ry (man′sə pə tôr′ē, -tōr′-), *adj.* having to do with mancipation.

man·ci·ple (man′sə pəl), *n.* a person who buys provisions for a college or other institution; steward. [< Old French *manciple, mancipe,* learned borrowing from Latin *mancipium* acquisition; a purchase, slave < *manceps, -cipis* purchaser < *manū capere* to take in hand]

Man·cu·ni·an (mang kyü′nē ən), *adj.* of or belonging to Manchester, a city in western England. —*n.* a native or inhabitant of Manchester, England: *Mancunians get incredulous responses if they say that the highest office building in the kingdom is in their city* (Manchester Guardian Weekly). [< Latin *Mancunium* Manchester + English *-an*]

Man·dae·an (man dē′ən), *n.* **1.** an adherent of an ancient religious sect, holding Gnostic beliefs with many Jewish and Zoroastrian elements, still surviving in Iraq. **2.** an Aramaic dialect used in the writings of this sect. —*adj.* of the Mandaeans or Mandaean. Also, **Mandean.** [< Aramaic *mandayyā* (translation of Greek *Gnōstikoí* the knowing ones, Gnostics) < *mandā* knowledge]

man·da·la (man′də lə), *n.* the symbol of contemplation or meditation in Buddhism and Hinduism. It is represented by a square within a circle. *The mandala is an archetypal image whose occurrence is attested throughout the ages* (Atlantic).

man·da·mus (man dā′məs), *n., v.,* **-mused, -mus·ing.** —*n. Law.* **1.** a written order from a higher court to a lower court, an official, a city, a corporation, etc., directing that a certain thing be done: *He sought . . . an order of mandamus to restore his name to the register* (London Times). **2.** any of various writs or mandates formerly issued by an English sovereign, directing that certain acts be performed. —*v.t. Informal.* to serve or threaten with a mandamus. [< Latin *mandāmus* we order, 1st plural present indicative active of *mandāre*]

Man·dan (man′dan), *n., pl.* **-dan** or **dans. 1.** a. a western plains tribe of North American Indians, famous as traders. b. a member of this tribe. **2.** the Siouan language of this tribe.

man·da·rin (man′dər in), *n.* **1.** (under the Chinese empire) an official of any of nine ranks, each distinguished by a certain button worn on the cap. **2.** a person important in political or intellectual circles, who is usually elderly or conservative. **3.** a small, sweet orange with a very loose peel; tangerine. **4.** the small tree or shrub it grows on. **5.** a bright, reddish-orange dye. —*adj.* of, or characteristic of, mandarins; intellectual, conservative, etc.: *a mandarin style, mandarin coteries. The future of Vietnam does not belong to a mandarin type of leadership* (London Times).
[< Portuguese *mandarim* < Malay *mantri* < Hindustani < Sanskrit *mantrin* advisor < a root *man-* to think]

Man·da·rin (man′dər in), *n.* the main dialect of the Chinese language, spoken by officials and educated people.

man·da·rin·ate (man′dər ə nāt), *n.* **1.** the office or authority of a mandarin. **2.** mandarins as a group. **3.** government by mandarins.

mandarin coat, a woman's long, brocaded coat for evening wear, usually of silk, having slits on the sides, elbow-length sleeves, a mandarin collar, and fastened with frogs or buttons. It is patterned after the coats worn formerly by mandarins.

mandarin collar, a narrow, turned-up collar of uniform width, with a slightly tapered split at the front.

mandarin duck, a crested duck with variegated plumage of purple, green, chestnut, and white, native to China, where it is a symbol of conjugal affection.

man·da·tar·y (man′də ter′ē), *n., pl.* **-tar·ies. 1.** a nation to which a mandate over another country has been given. **2.** *Law.* a person to whom a mandate is given. [< Late Latin *mandātārius* < Latin *mandātum* a mandate]

man·date (*n.* man′dāt, -dit; *v.* man′dāt), *n., v.,* **-dat·ed, -dat·ing.** —*n.* **1.** a command; order: *The mandate of God to His creature man is: Work!* (Thomas Carlyle). **2.** *Law.* an order from a higher court or official to a lower one: *Towards the close of Adams's term, Georgia had bid defiance to the mandates of the Supreme Court* (Theodore Roosevelt). **3.** the will of voters expressed to their representative or to a lawmaking body. **4.** a commission given to one nation by a group of nations to administer the government and affairs of a territory, colony, etc. The system of mandates established after World War I was administered by the League of Nations. *The character of the Mandate must differ according to the stage of the development of the people* (League of Nations Covenant). **5.** a mandated territory, etc. **6.** an order issued by the Pope stating that a certain person should be given a benefice. **7.** (in Roman and civil law) a contract by which one person requests another to act for him gratuitously, agreeing to indemnify him against losses. **8.** any contract of agency. **9.** (in ancient Rome) a command from the emperor, especially to the governor of a province.
—*v.t.* to put (a territory, etc.) under the administration of another nation: *The result of the late war has been to eliminate Germany from the map, her territories being mandated to the British and other nations* (Times Literary Supplement).
[< Latin *mandātum,* noun use of neuter past participle of *mandāre* to order]
—**Syn.** *n.* **1.** edict, behest, injunction.

man·da·tor (man dā′tər), *n.* the giver of a mandate.

man·da·to·ri·al (man′də tôr′ē əl, -tōr′-), *adj.* mandatory.

man·da·to·ri·ly (man′də tôr′ə lē, -tōr′-), *adv.* in a mandatory manner; by mandate.

man·da·to·ry (man′də tôr′ē, -tōr′-), *adj., n., pl.* **-ries.** —*adj.* **1.** of or like a mandate; giving a command or order: *a mandatory statement.* **2.** required by a command or order: *a mandatory sentence for manslaughter.* **3.** of, having to do with, or having received a mandate, as a nation commissioned to take care of a dependent territory.
—*n.* a mandatary.

man-day (man′dā′), *n.* one day of one man's work, used as a unit in figuring cost, time, etc., of production.

Man·de·an (man dē′ən),*n., adj.* Mandaean.

man·di·ble (man′də bəl), *n.* **1.** the jaw, especially the lower jaw. **2.** either part of a bird's beak. **3.** an organ in insects for seizing and biting: *The ant seized the dead fly with its mandibles.* [< Late Latin *mandibula* < Latin *mandere* to chew]

MANDIBLES / MAXILLAE \ UNDERSIDE

Mandibles(def. 3) of an ant

man·dib·u·lar (man dib′yə lər), *adj.* of, having to do with, or like a mandible. —*n.* a mandible (def. 1).

man·dib·u·late (man dib′yə lit, -lāt), *adj.* **1.** having a mandible or mandibles; having jaws, as most animals. **2.** adapted for chewing. —*n.* a mandibulate insect.

Man·din·gan (man ding′gən), *adj.* of or having to do with the Mandingos or their language. —*n.* **1.** a Mandingo. **2.** the language of the Mandingos.

Man·din·go (man ding′gō), *n., pl.* **-gos** or **-goes,** *adj.* —*n.* **1.** one of a number of Negro peoples forming a linguistic group in western Africa. **2.** any of the languages spoken by these peoples. —*adj.* of or having to do with the Mandingos or their languages. [< the native name]

man·di·o·ca (man′dē ō′kə), *n.* **1.** the edible root of the manioc, a staple starch foodstuff of tropical South America: *A dish of fried mandioca, the root of the manioc plant, from which the poorer natives of Brazil make flour* . . . (New Yorker). **2.** the manioc or cassava plant. [< Portuguese *mandioca* < Tupi (Brazil) *manioca.* Compare MANIOC.]

man·do·la (man dō′lə), *n.* a small lute of the 1600's and 1700's with a slightly curved handle where the tuning pegs were placed. [< Italian *mandola;* see MANDOLIN]

man·do·lin (man′də lin, man′də lin′), *n.* a musical instrument with a pear-shaped body, like that of the lute, having metal strings, usually in pairs, and played with a plectrum. [< French *mandoline* < Italian *mandolino* (diminutive) < *mandola,* variant of *mandora* < Latin *pandūra* < Greek *pandoûrā* three-stringed instrument]

man·do·lin·ist (man′də lə nist, man′də-lin′ist), *n.* a player on the mandolin.

man·dor·la (man dôr′lə; *Italian* män′-dôr lä), *n., pl.* **-las,** *Italian* **-le** (-lā). **1.** an almond-shaped or pointed oval panel, space, or piece, used as decoration. **2.** vesica piscis. [< Italian *mandorla* (literally) almond]

man·drag·o·ra (man drag′ər ə), *n.* mandrake.

man·drake (man′drāk), *n.* **1.** any of a group of poisonous herbs of the nightshade family, native to southern Europe and Asia, having very short stems and thick, often forked roots thought to resemble the human form. The mandrake has emetic and narcotic properties, and was formerly used in medicine. **2.** the root, supposed in legend to cry out when pulled up from the ground. Eating the root was believed to aid in conceiving a child. *And shrieks like mandrakes torn out of the earth* (Shakespeare). **3.** *U.S.* the May apple. [alteration (perhaps by folk etymology, with *man* and *drake*[2]) of Middle English *mandragge,* short for *mandragora* < Latin *mandragoras* < Greek *mandragóras*]

man·drel or **man·dril** (man′drəl), *n.* **1.** a spindle or bar of a lathe that supports the material being turned. **2.** a rod or core around which metal or other material is shaped. [< alteration of French *mandrin*]

man·drill (man′drəl), *n.* a large, fierce baboon of western Africa. The face of the male mandrill is marked with blue and scarlet. [perhaps < *man* + *drill*[4] baboon]

Mandrill (about 3 ft. long)

man·du·cate (man′jù kāt), *v.t.,* **-cat·ed, -cat·ing.** to chew; eat; masticate. [< Latin *mandūcāre* (with English *-ate*[1]) to chew < *mandere*]

mane (mān), *n.* **1.** the long, heavy hair on the back of the neck of a horse, lion, etc. **2.** a person's hair when long and thick. [Old English *manu*]

man-eat·er (man′ē′tər), *n.* **1.** a cannibal. **2.** a lion, tiger, or shark that attacks human beings for food.

man-eat·ing (man′ē′ting), *adj.* eating or devouring human beings.

maned (mānd), *adj.* having a mane: *a maned animal.*

maned wolf, a long-legged, red wolf of the plains of Argentina, Paraguay, and Brazil.

ma·nège or **ma·nege** (mə nezh′, -nāzh′), *n.* **1.** the art of training and riding horses; horsemanship. **2.** the movements of a trained horse. **3.** a school for training horses and teaching horsemanship. [< French *manège* < Italian *maneggio* < *maneggiare* to manage, handle]

ma·neh (mä′nā), *n.* a Hebrew unit of weight and value, equal to 1/60 of a talent. [< Hebrew *māne*]

ma·nes or **Ma·nes** (mā′nēz), *n.pl.* **1.** (among the ancient Romans) the deified souls of dead ancestors, together with the gods of the lower world. **2.** the spirit or shade of a particular dead person. [< Latin *mānēs,* plural, related to *mānus* good]

ma·neu·ver (mə nü′vər), *n., v.,* **-vered, -ver·ing.** —*n.* **1.** a planned movement of troops, ships, etc.: *Every year the army and navy hold maneuvers for practice.* **2.** a skillful plan; clever trick; adroit move: *He forced us to support him by a series of maneuvers.* **3.** the management of affairs by scheming: *when corruption shall be added to intrigue and maneuver in elections* (John Adams).
—*v.i.* **1.** to perform maneuvers. **2.** to plan skillfully; use clever tricks; scheme: *A scheming person is always maneuvering for some advantage.* —*v.t.* **1.** to cause to perform maneuvers. **2.** to force by skillful plans; get by clever tricks: *She maneuvered her lazy brother out of bed.* **3.** to move or manipulate skillfully: *to maneuver scenery on a stage, to maneuver one's defense to fool the opposition.* Also, *especially British,* **manoeuvre.**
[< French *manœuvre* manipulation, Old French *maneuvre* < Vulgar Latin *manuopera* < *manuoperāre* < Latin *manū operārī* to work by hand. Doublet of MANURE.] —**ma·neu′ver·er,** *n.*

ma·neu·ver·a·bil·i·ty (mə nü′vər ə bil′ə-tē), *n.* the quality or power of being maneuverable: *The paraboloid type of antenna has many advantages, especially maneuverability in scanning the sky* (Scientific American).

ma·neu·ver·a·ble (mə nü′vər ə bəl), *adj.* **1.** that can be maneuvered: *maneuverable scenery, a maneuverable fleet.* **2.** that can be handled with ease: *a maneuverable gearshift, a maneuverable telescope.*

ma·neu·vra·bil·i·ty (mə nü′vrə bil′ə tē), *n.* maneuverability.

ma·neu·vra·ble (mə nü′vrə bəl), *adj.* maneuverable.

man Friday, 1. a faithful servant; servile follower. **2.** Robinson Crusoe's servant, whom he called "*my man Friday.*"

man·ful (man′fəl), *adj.* manly; brave; resolute. —**man′ful·ly,** *adv.* —**man′ful·ness,** *n.*

'mang (mang), *prep. Scottish.* 'mong or among.

mang·a·bey (mang′gə bā), *n.* a tropical African monkey having a very long tail, and noted for the ease with which it is domesticated. [< *Mangabey,* a region in Madagascar]

man·ga·nate (mang′gə nāt), *n.* a salt of manganic acid. [< *mangan*(ic acid) + *-ate*[2]]

man·ga·nese (mang′gə nēs, -nēz), *n.* a hard, brittle, silver-gray, metallic chemical element with a pinkish tinge. Manganese resembles iron but is not magnetic and is softer. Substances containing manganese are used in making glass, paints, and medicines. *Symbol:* Mn; *at.wt.:* (C^{12}) 54.9380 or (O^{16}) 54.93; *at.no.:* 25; *valence:* 2,3,4,6,7. [< French *manganèse* < Italian *manganese,* alteration of Medieval Latin *magnesia;* see MAGNESIA]

manganese dioxide, a black crystal, or brownish-black powder, used in making dyes, paints, dry-cell batteries, as an oxidizing agent, etc. *Formula:* MnO_2

manganese spar, rhodonite.

manganese steel, a tough, durable cast steel containing up to 14 per cent of manganese.

man·gan·ic (man gan′ik, mang gan′-), *adj.* **1.** of or like manganese. **2.** containing manganese, especially with a valence of six.

manganic acid, an acid known only in the form of its salts. *Formula:* H_2MnO_4

man·ga·nif·er·ous (mang′gə nif′ər əs), *adj.* containing manganese.

Man·ga·nin (mang′gə nin), *n. Trademark.* an alloy of copper, manganese, and nickel, widely used in making various types of resistors: "*Standard resistors*" . . . *are constructed of wire, usually Manganin because of its low temperature coefficient of resistivity* (Sears and Zemansky). [< *mangan*(ese) + *-in*]

man·ga·nite (mang′gə nīt), *n.* **1.** a mineral, a hydrated oxide of manganese, occurring in steel-gray or iron-black masses or crystals. *Formula:* $Mn_2O_3.H_2O$ **2.** any of a group of salts containing manganese with a valence of four, formed from several manganese hydroxides, and considered to be an acid.

man·ga·nous (mang′gə nəs, man gan′əs), *adj.* containing manganese, especially with a valence of two.

mange (mānj), *n.* a skin disease of dogs, horses, sheep and cattle, caused by parasitic mites. It is much like itch in man. Tiny skin sores form, and the hair or wool falls out in patches. [< Old French *manjüe,* or *mangeue* the itch < *mangier* to eat < Latin *mandūcāre* to chew < *mandere*]

man·gel (mang′gəl), *n.* a mangel-wurzel.

man·gel-wur·zel (mang′gəl wėr′zəl), *n.* a large, coarse variety of beet, used as food for cattle. [< German *Mangelwurzel,* variant of *Mangoldwurzel* beet root]

man·ger (mān′jər), *n.* **1.** a box or trough in which hay or other food is placed for horses or cattle to eat: *She . . . wrapped him in swaddling clothes, and laid him in a manger; because there was no room for them in the inn* (Luke 2:7). *His hay storage . . . equipped with a movable manger, reduces labor* (Newsweek). **2.** *Nautical.* a small space at the forward end of a deck, divided off by a bulkhead or board to shut off any water entering by the hawseholes. [< Old French *mangeoire,* or *maingeure* < Vulgar Latin *man-*

dūcātoria feeding trough < Latin *mandūcāre* to chew < *mandere*]

man·gi·ly (mān′jə lē), *adv.* in a mangy manner.

man·gi·ness (mān′jē nis), *n.* mangy quality or condition.

man·gle[1] (mang′gəl), *v.t.*, **-gled, -gling. 1.** to cut or tear (the flesh) roughly: *The two cats bit and clawed until both were mangled.* **2.** to spoil; ruin: *to mangle words by bad pronunciation, to mangle a text in editing. The young player mangled the music badly. My mangled youth lies dead beneath the heap* (Francis Thompson). [< Anglo-French *mangler*, perhaps < *mahangler* (frequentative) < Old French *mahaigner* to maim < *mahaigne* injury] —**man′gler,** *n.* —**Syn. 1.** lacerate, mutilate.

man·gle[2] (mang′gəl), *n., v.*, **-gled, -gling.** —*n.* a machine with rollers for pressing and smoothing sheets and other flat things after washing: *Fiction turns the Muses' mangle—Of making books there is no end* (Justin H. McCarthy). —*v.t.* to press or make smooth in a mangle. [< Dutch *mangel* < Middle Dutch *mange* < Late Latin *manganum* < Greek *mánganon* contrivance] —**man′gler,** *n.*

man·go (mang′gō), *n., pl.* **-goes** or **-gos. 1.** a slightly sour, juicy fruit with a thick, yellowish-red rind. Mangoes are eaten ripe or pickled when green. **2.** the tropical evergreen tree of the cashew family that it grows on. [< Portuguese *manga* < Malay *mangga* < Tamil *mānkāy*]

man-god (man′god′), *n., pl.* **men-gods. 1.** one who is both a man and a god: *Prometheus, in the eyes of the Greek, was a man-god* (North American Review). **2.** a deified man: *The Christian world was sunk in the worship . . . of men-gods* (Thomas P. Thompson). **3.** a god having the form of a man: *The old idolaters cut down a tree and made a man-god . . . out of it* (North American Review).

man·go·nel (mang′gə nel), *n.* a machine formerly used in war for throwing large stones, etc. [< Old French *mangonel* < Vulgar Latin *manganellum* (diminutive) < Late Latin *manganum;* see MANGLE[2]]

man·go-pink (mang′gō pingk′), *adj.* of a yellowish- or reddish-pink color.

man·go·steen (mang′gə stēn), *n.* **1.** a juicy, edible fruit with a thick, reddish-brown rind. **2.** the tree of southeast Asia that it grows on. [< Malay *manggustan*]

man·grove (mang′grōv), *n.* **1.** any of a group of tropical trees and shrubs that send down many branches that take root and form new trunks. Mangroves grow in coastal swamps and along the banks of brackish rivers. **2.** any of several similar plants or trees of tropical America and the southern coast of the United States, whose flowers are rich in honey. [< Spanish *mangle*, earlier *mangue;* origin uncertain; spelling influenced by English *grove*]

man·gy (mān′jē), *adj.*, **-gi·er, -gi·est. 1.** having, caused by, or like the mange; with the hair falling out. **2.** shabby and dirty. **3.** *Informal.* mean; contemptible.

man·han·dle (man′han′dəl), *v.t.*, **-dled, -dling. 1.** to treat or handle roughly; pull or push about: *If you worry me . . . I'll catch you and manhandle you, and you'll die* (Rudyard Kipling). **2.** to move by human strength, without mechanical appliances: *The larger weapons will be marked by electricity, but are also capable of being manhandled* (London Times).

man-hat·er (man′hā′tər), *n.* **1.** a person who hates mankind; misanthrope. **2.** a person who hates men.

Man·hat·tan (man hat′ən), *n.* a cocktail consisting of rye whiskey, Italian vermouth, and usually bitters, and served with a cherry. [< *Manhattan*, a borough of New York City]

Manhattan District, an organization established in 1942 under the United States Army to administer the various scientific and industrial groups responsible for atomic research, especially in connection with the atomic bomb. It was dissolved in 1947.

Man·hat·tan·ese (man hat′ə nēz′, -nēs′), *adj., n., pl.* **-ese.** —*adj.* of the borough of Manhattan; having to do with Manhattan, New York, or its inhabitants: *I was Manhattanese, friendly, and proud* (Walt Whitman). —*n.* a Manhattanite.

Man·hat·tan·ite (man hat′ə nīt), *n.* a native or inhabitant of the borough of Manhattan: *Even a Manhattanite can find his subway way to the Coney Island Aquarium* (New York Times).

Manhattan Project, the code name for the secret project of the Manhattan District: *The Manhattan Project was initiated because the physicists had come up with a revolutionary new concept (namely the nuclear chain reaction)* (Wall Street Journal).

man·hole (man′hōl′), *n.* a hole through which a workman can enter a sewer, steam boiler, etc., to inspect or repair it.

man·hood (man′hu̇d), *n.* **1.** the condition or time of being a man: *The disappointment of manhood succeeds to the delusion of youth* (Benjamin Disraeli). **2.** courage; manliness: *Some civic manhood firm against the crowd* (Tennyson). *Peace hath higher tests of manhood than battle ever knew* (John Greenleaf Whittier). **3.** men as a group: *the manhood of the United States.* **4.** the state or condition of being human; human nature: *Yea, Manhood hath a wider span And larger privilege of life than man* (Lowell). —**Syn. 2.** virility, bravery.

man-hour (man′our′), *n.* an hour of one man's work, used as a time unit in industry: *If progress continues, the materials used in clothing will not involve the man-hours of labor traditional in the industry* (Atlantic).

man·hunt (man′hunt′), *n.*, **1.** a widespread search for a criminal, escaped prisoner, etc.: *It ended a manhunt conducted by hundreds of persons, including about 175 state patrolmen, FBI agents, sheriffs' deputies . . .* (Chicago Tribune). **2.** a dramatic entertainment based upon such a search.

ma·ni·a (mā′nē ə), *n.* **1.** a form or phase of mental disorder, characterized by extremes of joy or rage, uncontrolled and often violent activity, extravagant and irregular speech, etc., often followed by depression, as in manic-depressive psychosis. **2.** an unusual fondness; craze: *a mania for gardening, a mania for dancing, a mania for collecting old bottles.* [< Latin *mania* < Greek *maníā* madness < *maínesthai* rage, be mad]

ma·ni·ac (mā′nē ak), *n.* an insane person; raving lunatic; madman: *His eyes rolled like that of a maniac in his fever fit* (Scott). —*adj.* insane; raving: *a maniac world.* [< Late Latin *maniacus* < Latin *mania;* see MANIA]

MA·NI·AC or **Ma·ni·ac** (mā′nē ak), *n.* a complex electronic computer used in the development of the hydrogen bomb and in other projects. [< *M*(athematical) *A*(nalyzer) *N*(umerical) *I*(ntegrator) *A*(nd) *C*(omputer)]

ma·ni·a·cal (mə nī′ə kəl), *adj.* **1.** insane; raving. **2.** of or characteristic of mania or a maniac: *His industry grew almost maniacal* (Lytton Strachey). —**ma·ni′a·cal·ly,** *adv.*

ma·nic (mā′nik, man′ik), *adj.* **1.** of or like mania: *to be a manic phase.* **2.** suffering from mania. [< Greek *manikos* mad < *maníā* madness, mania]

man·ic-de·pres·sive (man′ik di pres′iv), *adj.* having or characterized by alternating attacks of mania and depression: *manic-depressive psychosis.* —*n.* a person who has this condition: *The man is a manic-depressive who brawls in his manic phases* (New Yorker).

Man·i·che·an or **Man·i·chae·an** (man′ə-kē′ən), *n.* a member of a Gnostic sect, arising in Persia in the 200's A.D., compounded of Christian, Buddhistic, Zoroastrian, and other beliefs, and maintaining a theological dualism in which the body and matter were identified with darkness and evil, and the soul, striving to liberate itself, was identified with light and goodness. —*adj.* of or having to do with the Manicheans or their doctrines. [< Late Latin *Manichaeus* (< Late Greek *Manichaîos* < *Manichaîos* of Mani, founder of the sect) + English *-an*]

Man·i·che·an·ism or **Man·i·chae·an·ism** (man′ə kē′ə niz əm), *n.* Manicheism.

Man·i·chee (man′ə kē), *n.* a Manichean.

Man·i·che·ism or **Man·i·chae·ism** (man′ə kē′iz əm), *n.* the doctrines of the Manicheans: *Manicheism, the gospel of Mani, crucified in the third century, who saw the world as a struggle between the equally balanced forces of Good and Evil, would tempt the powerful imagination of St. Augustine in Tunisia* (Hugh Trevor-Roper).

man·i·cot·ti (man′ə kot′ē), *n.* macaroni stuffed with cheese and baked in tomato sauce. [< Italian *manicotti*]

man·i·cure (man′ə kyu̇r), *v.*, **-cured, -curing,** *n.* —*v.t., v.i.* **1.** to care for (the fingernails and hands); trim, clean, and polish (the fingernails). **2.** to trim (a hedge, grounds, etc.): *. . . showed him lounging in his weeds and his neighbors slavishly manicuring their lawns* (Maclean's).
—*n.* **1.** the care of the hands; trimming, cleaning, and polishing the fingernails. **2.** a single such treatment: *She went to the beauty parlor for a manicure.* **3.** a manicurist. [< French *manicure* < Latin *manus, -ūs* hand + *cūra* care]

man·i·cur·ist (man′ə kyu̇r′ist), *n.* a person whose work is caring for the hands and the fingernails.

man·i·fest (man′ə fest), *adj.* apparent to the eye or to the mind; plain; clear: *a manifest error. Nothing is secret which shall not be made manifest* (Luke 8:17).
—*v.t.* **1.** to show plainly; reveal; display: *to manifest interest. There is nothing hid, which shall not be manifested* (Mark 4:22). **2.** to put beyond doubt; prove: *His dress . . . manifested the economy of its owner by the number and nature of its repairs* (James Fenimore Cooper). **3. a.** to record (an item) in a ship's manifest. **b.** to present the manifest of (a ship's cargo).
—*n.* **1.** a detailed list of a ship's cargo, required for presentation at a custom house: *The line's manifests made interesting reading* (New York Times). **2.** a bill of lading. **3.** a manifesto: *Jan Kadar and Elmar Klos . . . have constructed a human drama that is a moving manifest of the dark dilemma that confronted all people who were caught as witnesses to Hitler's terrible crime* (Bosley Crowther).
[< Latin *manifestus* palpable < *manus, -ūs* hand + *-festus* (able to be) seized] —**man′i·fest′ly,** *adv.* —**man′i·fest′ness,** *n.*
—**Syn.** *adj.* obvious, evident, unmistakable. *-v.t.* **1.** exhibit, disclose, evidence.

man·i·fes·tant (man′ə fes′tənt), *n.* a person who takes part in a public demonstration.

man·i·fes·ta·tion (man′ə fes tā′shən), *n.* **1.** a manifesting. **2.** a being manifested. **3.** a thing that manifests: *Entering the burning building was a manifestation of his courage.* **4.** a public demonstration by a government, political party, etc., for effect: *The manifestation planned by the party in power got off to a bad start. The principal manifestation of the British power was directed against Rangoon* (H. H. Wilson). **5.** (in spiritualism) an occurrence or occasion in which a spiritual materialization is supposed to be demonstrated: *No manifestation occurred at the first séance.*

manifest destiny, *U.S. Historical.* the belief in the 1840's in the inevitable territorial expansion of the United States, especially as advocated by southern slaveholders who wished to extend slavery into new territories.

man·i·fes·to (man′ə fes′tō), *n., pl.* **-toes,** *v.*, **-toed, to·ing.** —*n.* a public declaration of intents, purposes, or motives by an important person or group; proclamation: *The emperor issued a manifesto. A Labour Government . . . would (as stated in the party's election manifesto) set up a new Ministry of Social Welfare* (London Times). —*v.i.* to put forth a manifesto.
[< Italian *manifesto* < Latin *manifestus* manifest]

man·i·fold (man′ə fōld), *adj.* **1.** of many kinds; many and various: *manifold duties. Attractions manifold* (Wordsworth). **2.** having many parts, features, or forms: *the manifold wisdom of God* (Ephesians 3:10); *a music strange and manifold* (Tennyson). *This changeful life, So manifold in cares* (William Cowper). **3.** doing many things at the same time. **4.** *Archaic.* being such in many ways: *a manifold fool.*
—*n.* **1.** a pipe with several openings for connection with other pipes. **2.** a pipe in an internal-combustion engine, connecting the cylinders with a main inlet or outlet. **3.** one of many copies; copy made by a manifolder.
—*v.t.* **1.** to make many copies of, as

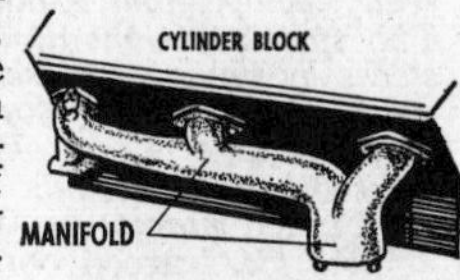

Manifold (def. 2) of an automobile engine

with a manifolder. **2.** to make manifold; multiply.
[Old English *manigfeald* < *manig* many + *feald* -fold] **—man′i·fold′ly,** *adv.* **—man′i·fold′ness,** *n.*
—Syn. *adj.* **1.** varied.
➔ See **manyfold** for usage note.
man·i·fold·er (man′ə fōl′dər), *n.* **1.** a device for making copies of a letter, document, etc., as with carbon paper. **2.** a person who makes such copies.
man·i·hot (man′ə hot), *n.* any of a group of tropical American plants of the spurge family, including the cassava and several varieties which yield a rubber. [< New Latin *manihot* the species name < French; see MANIOC]
man·i·kin (man′ə kin), *n.* **1.** a little man; dwarf; pygmy. **2.** mannequin. **3.** a model of the human body, used for teaching anatomy, surgery, etc. Also, **manakin, mannikin.** [< Dutch *manneken* (diminutive) < *man* man]
ma·nil·a (mə nil′ə), *n.* **1.** Manila hemp. **2.** Manila paper. [< *Manila,* capital of the Philippines]
Manila hemp, a strong fiber made from the leaves of a Philippine banana plant, used for making ropes, fabrics, etc.; abacá.
Manila paper, a strong, brown or brownish-yellow paper, originally made from Manila hemp, used for wrapping, sketching, etc.
Manila rope, a strong rope made from Manila hemp.
ma·nil·la[1] (mə nil′ə), *n.* manila.
ma·nil·la[2] (mə nil′ə), *n.* the next to highest trump in some card games. [alteration of Spanish *malilla* (diminutive) < *mala,* feminine, (originally) bad]
ma·nille (mə nil′), *n.* manilla[2].
man in the middle, the arbiter in a dispute.
man in the moon, a figure in the disk of the full moon popularly believed to resemble a man's face: *I was the Man in th' Moon, when time was* (Shakespeare).
not know one from the man in the moon, not to know one at all: *I don't know him from the man in the moon.*
man in the street, *U.S.* the average person, especially as typifying public opinion: *It was not read solely by naturalists and other scientists. The man in the street read it* (Science News Letter).
man in white, a doctor, especially one in a hospital.
man·i·oc (man′ē ok, mā′nē-), *n.* cassava. [< French *manioc,* and *manihot* < Tupi (Brazil) *manioca*]
man·i·ple (man′ə pəl), *n.* **1.** a subdivision of the ancient Roman legion, containing 120 or 60 men. **2.** a eucharistic vestment, consisting of an ornamental band or strip of cloth worn on the left arm near the wrist: *According to the old offices, the deacons to be ordained were presented in amice, alb, girdle and maniple* (R. W. Dixon). [< Latin *manipulus* (literally) a handful < *manus, -ūs* hand + root of *plēre* to fill]

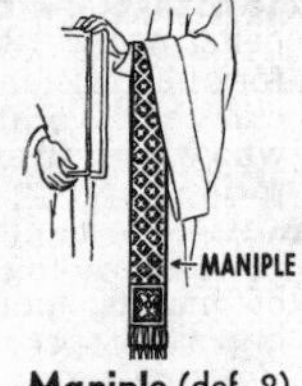

Maniple (def. 2)

ma·nip·u·lar (mə nip′yə lər), *adj.* **1.** of or having to do with an ancient Roman maniple. **2.** of or having to do with manipulation. —*n.* a Roman soldier belonging to a maniple.
ma·nip·u·late (mə nip′yə lāt), *v.t.,* **-lat·ed, -lat·ing. 1.** to handle or treat skillfully; handle: *The driver of an automobile manipulates the levers and pedals. A sailboat is steered by manipulating the sails. A clever writer manipulates his characters and plot to create interest.* **2.** to manage by clever use of personal influence, especially unfair influence: *He so manipulated the ball team that he was elected captain although they really thought John would be a better leader. The speculators manipulated the prices of stocks by buying and selling large amounts quickly.* **3.** to change for one's own purpose or advantage: *The bookkeeper manipulated the company's accounts to conceal his theft.* [< French *manipuler* (with English *-ate*[1]) < *maniple,* learned borrowing from Latin *manipulus* handful; see MANIPLE]
ma·nip·u·la·tion (mə nip′yə lā′shən), *n.* **1.** skillful handling or treatment: *Sometimes the individual must be anesthetized to straighten a fixed joint thru manipulation* (Chicago Tribune). **2.** clever use of personal influence, especially unfair influence. **3.** a change made for one's own purpose or advantage.
ma·nip·u·la·tive (mə nip′yə lā′tiv), *adj.* **1.** of or having to do with manipulation. **2.** done by manipulation.
ma·nip·u·la·tor (mə nip′yə lā′tər), *n.* a person or thing that manipulates: *I don't think they are reliable people .... They are sophisticated, clever manipulators* (Wall Street Journal).
ma·nip·u·la·to·ry (mə nip′yə lə tôr′ē, -tōr′-), *adj.* manipulative.
man·i·to (man′ə tō), *n., pl.* **-tos.** a spirit worshiped by Algonkian Indians as a force of nature; Great Spirit. [< Algonkian (probably Narragansett) *manito* supernatural power]
Man·i·to·ban (man′ə tō′bən), *adj.* of or having to do with Manitoba, a province in Canada. —*n.* a native or inhabitant of Manitoba.
man·i·tou or **man·i·tu** (man′ə tü), *n.* manito.
man jack, *Slang.* a man: *While I realize there isn't a man jack alive who doesn't know the plot ...* (New Yorker).
every man jack, every one; every single one (referring to a man): *Send them all to bed—every man jack of them* (Charles Lamb).
man·jak or **man·jack** (man′jak), *n.* a form of bitumen found in Barbados and elsewhere, used in making varnish, for insulating electric cables, etc. [< a native word]
man-kill·er (man′kil′ər), *n.* **1.** something that kills people: *What is striking about lung cancer as a man-killer is its sudden rise* (Canada Month). **2.** *Slang.* a femme fatale.
man-kill·ing (man′kil′ing), *adj.* **1.** capable of killing a man: *a man-killing tiger.* **2.** exhausting; tiring: *a man-killing job.*
man·kind (man′kīnd′ *for 1;* man′kīnd′ *for 2*), *n.* **1.** the human race; all human beings: *Let observation with extensive view Survey mankind from China to Peru* (Samuel Johnson). *To live in mankind is far more than to live in a name* (Vachel Lindsay). *The history of language is the history of mankind* (Greenough and Kittredge). **2.** men; the male sex: *Mankind and womankind both like praise. Should all despair That have revolted wives, the tenth of mankind Would hang themselves* (Shakespeare).
man·less (man′lis), *adj.* **1.** having no man. **2.** without men.
man·like (man′līk′), *adj.* **1.** like a man: *Under his forming hands a creature grew, Manlike, but different sex* (Milton). **2.** suitable for or befitting a man: *Manlike let him turn and face it* (Emerson).
man·li·ly (man′lə lē), *adv.* in a manly manner.
man·li·ness (man′lē nis), *n.* the quality or state of being manly.
man lock, an airlock or decompression chamber.
man·ly (man′lē), *adj.,* **-li·er, -li·est,** *adv.* —*adj.* **1.** like a man; as a man should be; strong, frank, brave, noble, independent, and honorable: *Now clear the ring, for, hand to hand, The manly wrestlers take their stand* (Scott). *My aunt was a lady of large frame, strong mind, and great resolution ... a very manly woman* (Washington Irving). **2.** suitable for a man; masculine: *Boxing is a manly sport. On his father's death, the boy set to work in a manly way.* —*adv. Archaic.* in a manly manner. **—Syn.** *adj.* **1.** See **male.**
man-made (man′mād′), *adj.* made or produced by human effort rather than by natural forces or by animals; artificially or synthetically created: *man-made laws, man-made radioactivity, a man-made satellite, man-made fibers and diamonds.*
man·na (man′ə), *n.* **1.** (in the Bible) the food miraculously supplied to the Israelites in the wilderness. Exodus 16:14-36. **2.** food for the soul or mind: *To some coffee-house I stray For news, the manna of a day* (Matthew Green). **3.** a much needed thing that is unexpectedly supplied: *Her inheritance came as manna from heaven.* **4.** a sweet, pale-yellow, or whitish substance obtained from the bark of certain European ash trees, formerly used as a laxative. [Old English *manna* < Late Latin < Greek *mánna* < Hebrew *mān*]
manna grass, any of a group of mostly aquatic grasses, grown as forage for cattle; meadow grass.
manna gum, an Australian eucalyptus tree that yields a crumblike, sugary manna.
manned (mand), *adj. Aeronautics.* **1.** occupied by one or more persons assigned to control flight: *a manned aircraft, a manned bomber.* **2.** occupied by one or more persons, but not under their control or guidance: *a manned satellite, a manned space vehicle.*
man·ne·quin (man′ə kin), *n.* **1.** a woman whose work is wearing new clothes to show them to potential customers. **2.** a figure of a person used by tailors, artists, stores, etc.; dummy. Also, **manikin.** [< French *mannequin* < Dutch *manneken;* see MANIKIN]
man·ner (man′ər), *n.* **1.** a way of doing, being done, or happening: *The trouble arose in this manner.* **2.** a way of acting or behaving: *He speaks in a strange manner. Urbanity of manner* (G. K. Chesterton). *Her manner made me sensible that we stood upon no real terms of confidence* (Hawthorne). **3.** kind or kinds: *We saw all manner of birds in the forest. What manner of man art thou?* (Samuel Taylor Coleridge). **4.** characteristic or customary way; mode; fashion: *a house decorated in the Italian manner.* **5.** a distinguished or fashionable air: *We country persons can have no manner at all* (Oliver Goldsmith). **6. a.** personal style in art, music, etc.: *Her manner of singing requires great effort.* **b.** a style characteristic of a particular artist, school, period, etc.: *a painting in the manner of Picasso.* **c.** affectation in style; mannerism.
by all manner of means, most certainly: *Yes, in God's name, and by all manner of means* (John Ruskin).
by no manner of means, not at all; under no circumstances: *"Basil" is by no manner of means an impeccable work of imperishable art* (Algernon Charles Swinburne).
in a manner, after a fashion; in one way; in one sense: *The bread is in a manner common* (I Samuel 21:5).
in a manner of speaking, as one might say; so to speak: *The cattle ... has been, in a manner of speaking, neglected* (Rolfe Boldrewood).
make one's manners, *U.S. Dialect.* to show one's good manners by a bow, curtsy, etc.: *good children ... who made their manners when they came into her house* (Harriet Beecher Stowe).
manners, a. ways of behaving: *good manners, bad manners.* **b.** polite ways of behaving: *Oh! ... return to us again; And give us manners, virtue, freedom, power* (Wordsworth). **c.** customs; ways of living: *a comedy of manners.*
to the manner born, a. accustomed since birth to some way or condition: *Though I am native here And to the manner born* (Shakespeare). **b.** seeming to be naturally fitted for something: *a chef to the manner born.*
[< Anglo-French *manere,* Old French *maniere* way or mode of handling, ultimately < Latin *manuārius* belonging to the hand < *manus, -ūs* hand]
—Syn. 1. See **way. 2.** bearing, demeanor, deportment.
Män·ner·chor (men′ər kōr′), *n., pl.* **-chö·re** (-kėr′ə). *German.* a German male chorus or singing society.
man·nered (man′ərd), *adj.* having many mannerisms; affected; artificial: *a mannered style of writing.*
-mannered, combining form. having ____ manners: *Well-mannered = having good manners. Mild-mannered = having mild manners.*
man·ner·ism (man′ə riz əm), *n.* **1.** too much use of some manner in speaking, writing, or behaving: *In his official contacts Mr. Galbraith has been handicapped by the mannerism of the lecture hall* (New York Times). **2.** an odd little trick; queer habit; peculiar way of acting: *the same little dainty mannerisms, the same quick turns and movements* (Charlotte Brontë). **—Syn. 1.** affectation. **2.** peculiarity.
Man·ner·ism (man′ə riz əm), *n.* a style of painting and architecture of the 1500's, chiefly Italian, which attempted to break away from the classical forms of the Renaissance by distorting scale, perspective, lighting effect, etc., within a formal framework. Its rediscovery in the early part of the 1900's was due to its affinity with some movements in modern art.
man·ner·ist (man′ər ist), *n.* a person given to mannerism, especially an artist, musician, etc.
Man·ner·ist (man′ər ist), *n.* a painter or architect whose work is characterized by

Mannerism: *Tintoretto and El Greco are sometimes referred to as essentially Mannerists.* —*adj.* of or representing Mannerism: *a Mannerist painting, a Mannerist architect.*

man·ner·is·tic (man′ər is′tik), *adj.* characterized by mannerisms. —**man′ner·is′ti·cal·ly,** *adv.*

man·ner·less (man′ər lis), *adj.* without good manners.

man·ner·li·ness (man′ər lē nis), *n.* the quality of being mannerly.

man·ner·ly (man′ər lē), *adj.* having or showing good manners; polite: *It is not mannerly to contradict one's parents. Here is mannerly forbearance* (Shakespeare). —*adv.* politely; courteously: *When we have supp'd, We'll mannerly demand thee of thy story* (Shakespeare). —**Syn.** *adj.* courteous, civil, well-behaved.

man·ners (man′ərz), *n.pl.* See under **manner.**

man·nie (man′ē), *n. Scottish.* **1.** a little man. **2.** a small boy. [< *man* + *-ie*]

man·ni·kin (man′ə kin), *n.* manikin.

man·nish (man′ish), *adj.* **1.** characteristic of a man: *a mannish way of holding a baby, a mannish argument.* **2.** imitating a man; manlike; masculine: *a mannish style of dress, a woman with a mannish walk.* —**man′nish·ly,** *adv.* —**man′nish·ness,** *n.*

man·nite (man′īt), *n.* mannitol.

man·nit·ic (mə nit′ik), *adj.* of, containing, or derived from mannite, or mannitol.

man·ni·tol (man′ə tōl, -tol), *n.* a white, odorless, crystalline alcohol obtained from glucose, seaweed, or a variety of ash tree, occurring in three optically different forms. *Formula:* $C_6H_{14}O_6$ [< *mannit*(e) + *-ol*[1]]

ma·no (mä′nō), *n. Southwestern U.S.* a hand grinding stone used by Mexicans and Indians. [American English < Spanish *mano* < Latin *manus* hand]

ma·no a ma·no (mä′nō ä mä′nō), *Spanish.* a contest in bullfighting between two matadors; hand-to-hand combat.

ma·noeu·vre (mə nü′vər), *n., v.i., v.t.,* **-vred, -vring.** *Especially British.* maneuver.

man of affairs, a man with wide experience in business, industry, public or political matters, etc.

Man of Destiny, a name given by Napoleon Bonaparte to himself.

Man of Galilee, Jesus Christ.

man of God, 1. a holy man; saint; prophet. **2.** a clergyman.

man of letters, 1. a writer. **2.** a person who has a wide knowledge of literature.

man of science, a scientist, especially one wholly dedicated to the scientific method or to scientific pursuits.

Man of Sorrows, (in the Bible) Jesus Christ (by traditional inference). Isaiah 53:3.

man of straw, an imaginary person whose arguments can easily be proved wrong.

man of the cloth, a clergyman.

man-of-the-earth (man′əv ᴛʜē ėrth′), *n., pl.* **men-** a trailing plant of the morning-glory family of the eastern United States having a very large root. [< the shape of the root]

man of the world, a man who knows people and customs, and is tolerant of both: *Temple was a man of the world among men of letters* (Macaulay).

man-of-war (man′əv wôr′), *n., pl.* **men-of-war. 1.** a warship: *All the men-of-war were burnt during the night* (London Times). **2.** Portuguese man-of-war.

man-of-war bird or **hawk,** a frigate bird.

man-of-war's-man (man′əv wôrz′mən), *n., pl.* **-men.** a sailor on a man-of-war.

ma·nom·e·ter (mə nom′ə tər), *n.* **1.** an instrument for measuring the pressure of gases or vapors. **2.** an instrument for determining blood pressure. [< French *manomètre* < Greek *mānós* thin + French *-mètre* -meter]

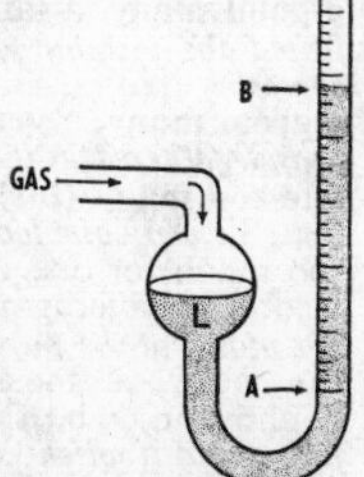

Open-air Manometer (def. 1). Pressure of gas, which enters tube at left, on liquid L is measured by height of column AB.

man·o·met·ric (man′ə met′rik), *adj.* **1.** having to do with or obtained with a manometer. **2.** having to do with the measurement of gaseous pressure. —**man′o·met′ri·cal·ly,** *adv.*

man·o·met·ri·cal (man′ə met′rə kəl), *adj.* manometric.

manometric flame, a gas flame which fluctuates in response to the movements of a diaphragm placed in an opening in the wall of an organ pipe or other resonator. The varying amounts of fluctuation are used to measure the sound vibrations in the pipe.

ma·nom·e·try (mə nom′ə trē), *n.* the measurement of the pressure of gases or vapors by means of a manometer.

man on horseback, a military leader whose influence over the people threatens the government.

man·or (man′ər), *n.* **1.** a feudal estate, part of which was set aside for the lord and the rest divided among his peasants, who paid the owner rent in goods, services, or money. In the Middle Ages, if the lord sold his manor, the peasants or serfs were sold with it. **2.** a tract of land in colonial America within which the owner had a similar arrangement. **3. a.** the main house of a nobleman's estate. **b.** the main house or mansion of any estate. [< Old French *manoir,* earlier *maneir,* noun use of infinitive < Latin *manēre* to stay, abide]

manor house, the house of the owner of a manor: *It was three stories high, of proportions not vast, though considerable; a gentleman's manor house, not a nobleman's seat* (Charlotte Brontë).

ma·no·ri·al (mə nôr′ē əl, -nōr′-), *adj.* **1.** of or having to do with a manor: *manorial rights.* **2.** forming a manor: *a manorial estate.*

manor place, a manor house.

man·pow·er (man′pou′ər), *n.* **1.** power supplied by the physical work of men. **2.** strength thought of in terms of the number of men needed or available: *China has great potential military manpower.* **3. a.** a unit equivalent to the rate at which a man can do work, equal to 1/10 horsepower. **b.** work done, expressed in terms of this unit. —*adj.* of or having to do with manpower: *the manpower problem, a manpower shortage.*

man·qué (män kā′), *adj. French.* unfulfilled; abortive; unrealized; frustrated: *a poet manqué. At heart every masseur is a doctor manqué* (New Yorker).

man·quée (män kā′), *adj. French.* the feminine form of **manqué.**

man·rope (man′rōp′), *n.* a rope used as a handrail at the side of a ladder, gangway, platform, etc.

man·sard (man′särd), *n.* **1.** Also, **mansard roof.** a four-sided roof with two slopes on each side. The lower slopes are nearly vertical and the upper slopes nearly flat, allowing greater headway throughout the top story. *The splendid mansard roof, with its double tier of dormers and fancy iron crestings* (New Yorker). **2.** the story under such a roof. [< French *mansarde,* adjective < François *Mansard,* 1598-1666, a French architect]

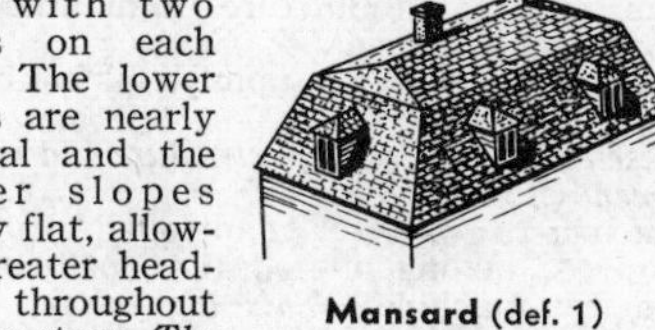

Mansard (def. 1)

manse (mans), *n.* **1.** a minister's house; parsonage, especially of a Presbyterian minister in Scotland: *The pastor may remain on salary and continue to reside in the manse* (Chicago Tribune). **2.** *Obsolete.* land sufficient to support a family. **3.** *Obsolete.* a mansion. [< Medieval Latin *mansa* a dwelling < Latin *manēre* to stay, abide]

man·serv·ant (man′sėr′vənt), *n., pl.* **men-serv·ants.** a male servant.

man-shift (man′shift′), *n.* the shift a man works each day, used as a unit in figuring cost, output, etc., of production: *The increase in productivity, as measured by output per man-shift . . . has averaged two per cent per annum cumulatively* (London Times).

-manship, *combining form.* the art or skill of being, doing, or using (something) to one's own advantage: *Companies find that premium-manship is more convincing than quality control* (Saturday Review).

man·sion (man′shən), *n.* **1.** a large house; stately residence. **2.** a manor house. **3.** *Archaic.* a place to live in; abiding place: *the village preacher's modest mansion* (Oliver Goldsmith). **4. a.** the sign of the zodiac in which the sun or a planet has its special residence: *Phebus the sun . . . was . . . in his mansion In Aries* (Chaucer). **b.** one of the twenty-eight divisions of the moon's monthly path, according to Oriental and medieval astronomy. **5.** *Obsolete.* a staying in a place; sojourn.

mansions, *British.* an apartment house or apartment: *The inhabitants of Cornwall Mansions . . . have petitioned the Kensington Council to change the name to Cornwall-place* (London Daily Chronicle). [< Old French *mansion,* learned borrowing from Latin *mānsiō, -ōnis* < *manēre* to stay, abide. Compare MANSE, MANOR.]

man·sion·ry (man′shən rē), *n.* mansions.

man-size (man′sīz′), *adj.* man-sized.

man-sized (man′sīzd′), *adj.* **1.** suitable for a full-grown man; large: *man-sized tools, man-sized portions.* **2.** *Informal.* requiring a grown man's strength or maturity of judgment: *man-sized responsibilities.*

man·slaugh·ter (man′slô′tər), *n.* **1.** the killing of a human being. **2.** *Law.* the killing of a human being unlawfully but without deliberate intent or under strong provocation: *He was indicted for involuntary manslaughter and reckless driving* (Time).

man·slay·er (man′slā′ər), *n.* **1.** a person who kills a man. **2.** a person who commits manslaughter.

man·slay·ing (man′slā′ing), *n.* the act of killing a human being; homicide. —*adj.* that kills a human being; homicidal.

man·stop·per (man′stop′ər), *n.* a man-stopping bullet.

man·stop·ping (man′stop′ing), *adj.* having great force; designed to inflict a wound that will stop an advancing soldier: *a man-stopping bullet.*

man·suete (man swēt′), *adj. Archaic.* gentle; meek; mild: *She . . . stood forth mute, mild and mansuete* (Chaucer). [< Latin *mansuētus,* past participle of *mansuēscere* become tame < *manus* hand + *suēscere* to accustom]

man·sue·tude (man′swə tüd, -tyüd), *n. Archaic.* gentleness; meekness; mildness: *our Lord Himself, made all of mansuetude* (Robert Browning). [< Latin *mansuētūdo* < *mansuēscere*; see MANSUETE]

man·swear (man′swãr′), *v.t., v.i.,* **-sworn, -swear·ing.** *Archaic.* to perjure (oneself).

man·ta (man′tə), *n.* **1.** a cloak or wrap worn by women in Spain and Latin America. **2.** a kind of horse blanket. **3.** *Military.* a movable shelter formerly used by attacking soldiers for protection; mantelet: *Seizing their mantas . . . they made a gallant assault* (Washington Irving). **4.** Also, **manta ray.** a devilfish. [< Spanish *manta* < Vulgar Latin < Late Latin *mantum,* back formation < Latin *mantellum* cloak, mantle]

man-tai·lored (man′tā′lərd), *adj.* (of women's coats, suits, etc.) tailored in the manner or style of men's clothing.

man·teau (man′tō; *French* män tō′), *n., pl.* **-teaus, -teaux** (-tōz; *French* -tō′). **1.** a mantle or cloak. **2. a.** a gown open in front to show the petticoat, formerly worn by women. **b.** a loose upper garment: *Tell my gentlewoman to bring my black scarf and manteau* (Scott). **c.** a mantua. [< French *manteau* < Old French *mantel* mantle]

man·tel (man′təl), *n.* **1.** a shelf above a fireplace with its supports. **2.** the shelf itself; mantelpiece. **3.** the decorative framework around a fireplace: *a mantel of tile.* [spelling variant of *mantle*[2]]

man·tel·et (man′tə let, mant′lit), *n.* **1.** a short mantle or cape: *a lady in a little lace mantelet* (Thackeray). **2.** manta, a military shield. **3.** a manta or devilfish. [< Old French *mantelet* (diminutive) < *mantel* mantle]

man·tel·let·ta (man′tə let′ə), *n.* a sleeveless, knee-length vestment of silk or wool, worn by cardinals, bishops, abbots, and other dignitaries of the Roman Catholic Church. [< Italian *mantelletta* (diminutive) < *mantello* < Latin *mantellum* mantle]

man·tel·piece (man′təl pēs′), *n.* a mantel (def. 2).

man·tel·shelf (man′təl shelf′), *n.* a mantel (def. 2), mantelpiece: *Though there was a clock on the mantelshelf, she preferred to consult her watch* (New Yorker).

man·tel·tree (man′təl trē′), *n.* **1.** a mantel (def. 1). **2.** a mantelpiece: *Above the fireplace . . . there was a row of old photographs on the manteltree* (Atlantic).

man·tic (man′tik), *adj.* **1.** of or having to do with divination. **2.** having the power of divination; prophetic. [< Greek *mantikós* < *mántis* prophet; see MANTIS]

man·tid (man′tid), *n.* mantis.

man·til·la (man til′ə), *n.* **1.** a veil or scarf, often of lace, covering the hair and falling down over the shoulders: *Spanish and Latin-American women often wear mantillas. Her rosepoint lace veil was arranged mantilla fashion* (New York Times). **2.** a short mantle or cape. [< Spanish *mantilla* (diminutive) < *manta* woolen blanket < *manto* cloak, mantle < Late Latin *mantus, -ūs*]

man·tis (man′tis), *n., pl.* **-tis·es, -tes** (-tēz). any of a group of large insects that hold their forelegs doubled up as if praying, and eat other insects; praying mantis. [< New Latin *Mantis* the genus name < Greek *mántis* prophet < *maínesthai* be inspired]

Mantis (from 2 to 5 in. long)

mantis crab or **shrimp,** a squilla.

man·tis·sa (man tis′ə), *n.* the decimal part of a logarithm: *In the logarithm 2.95424, the characteristic is 2 and the mantissa is .95424.* [< Latin *mantissa,* variant of *mantīsa* addition < Etruscan, apparently < Celtic]

man·tle[1] (man′təl), *n., v.,* **-tled, -tling.** —*n.* **1.** a loose cloak without sleeves. **2.** anything that covers, envelops, or conceals like a mantle: *The ground had a mantle of snow.* **3.** a lacelike tube around a gas flame that gets so hot it glows and gives light. **4.** *Zoology.* **a.** a skinlike organ of a mollusk that is responsible for the secretion of the shell and often serves largely for respiration; pallium. **b.** a pair of similar folds that secrete the shell of a brachiopod. **c.** the soft tissue that lines the shell of a tunicate or barnacle. **5.** the folded wings and back feathers of a bird that enclose the body like a cloak. **6.** a steel structure which supports the stack of a blast furnace. **7.** *Geology.* the second of the four layers of the earth, lying between the earth's crust and its outer core: *Conditions within the earth's thin crust are controlled from the mantle* (New York Times).

—*v.t.* **1.** to cover with or as if with a mantle: *a small stagnant stream, mantled over with bright green mosses* (Scott). **2.** to cover or conceal; obscure; cloak: *Clouds mantled the moon.* —*v.i.* **1.** to blush; flush; redden: *Her face mantled with shame.* **2.** to spread out like a mantle: *The rosy blush of dawn began to mantle in the east* (Washington Irving). **3.** to be or become covered with a coating or scum: *The pond has mantled.* **4.** (in falconry) to spread first one wing and then the other over the corresponding outstretched leg for exercise, as a perched hawk does.

[fusion of Old English *maentel* < Latin *mantellum,* and of Middle English *mantel* < Old French < Latin *mantellum*]

man·tle[2] (man′təl), *n.* mantel.

mantle rock, the layer of soil and loose rock fragments overlying solid rock; regolith.

mant·let (mant′lit), *n.* mantelet.

man·tling (mant′ling), *n. Heraldry.* the ornamental accessory of drapery or scrollwork frequently depicted behind and around an escutcheon.

man-to-man (man′tə man′), *adj.* **1.** frank; straightforward; direct. **2.** (in basketball, football, etc.) denoting a pattern of defense in which one player guards only his opponent, and not a certain zone. —*adv.* frankly; in a straightforward manner.

Man·toux test (man′tü), a test for tuberculosis in which old tuberculin in a diluted mixture is injected intracutaneously. [< Charles *Mantoux,* born 1877, a French physician, who developed it]

man·tra (man′trə), *n.* (in Hinduism) a prayer or invocation, sometimes held to have magical power. [< Sanskrit *mantra* (literally) instrument of thought < a root *man-* think]

man-trap (man′trap′), *n.* **1.** a trap for catching trespassers in private grounds. **2.** anything that is likely to cause injury or trouble to the unwary; trap.

man trip, a string of empty cars used to transport miners into the mine. The same cars are then used to carry out coal.

man·tu·a (man′chü ə), *n.* **1.** a loose gown or cloak formerly worn by women. **2.** a mantle. [altered < French *manteau,* by confusion with *Mantua,* a city in Italy]

Man·tu·an (man′chü ən), *adj.* of or having to do with Mantua, a city in northern Italy. —*n.* a native or inhabitant of Mantua: *Virgil was known as "the Mantuan."*

Ma·nu (ma′nü), *n. Hindu Mythology.* **1.** a legendary being, a son of the sun god, and father of the human race. He is ascribed to be the author of the system of laws known as the Code of Manu. **2.** one of a group of supernatural beings, each of whom presides over a cycle of time.

man·u·al (man′yu̇ əl), *adj.* **1.** of or having to do with the hand or hands; done with the hands: *manual labor.* **2.** like a manual or handbook: *to follow the manual procedure.*

—*n.* **1.** a book that helps its readers to understand or use something; handbook: *a laboratory manual for chemistry.* **2.** a drill in handling a rifle or other weapons. **3.** an organ keyboard played with the hands: *Most church organs have two to four manuals* (Wall Street Journal). See picture under **organ.**

[< Old French *manuel,* learned borrowing from Latin *manuālis* < *manus, -ūs* hand]

manual alphabet, finger alphabet: *Deaf and blind . . . adults can be rehabilitated. Through communication techniques such as braille and the manual alphabet, they can be a part of the world, not locked out* (New York Times).

man·u·al·ly (man′yu̇ ə lē), *adv.* **1.** by hand; with the hands. **2.** with respect to hand work.

manual training, training in work done with the hands; practice in various arts and crafts, such as woodworking, carpentry, and sheet-metal work.

ma·nu·bri·um (mə nü′brē əm, -nyü′-), *n., pl.* **-bri·a** (-brē ə). **1.** a process or part of a bone, etc., that is shaped like a handle. **2. a.** the broad upper division of the sternum of mammals, with which the two first ribs articulate; episternum. **b.** a small, tapering, curved or twisted process of the malleus of the ear. [< Latin *manūbrium* a handle, haft < *manus, -ūs* hand]

man·u·duc·tion (man′yə duk′shən), *n.* a leading by or as if by the hand; guidance. [< Medieval Latin *manuductio, -onis* < Latin *manū dūcere* to lead by hand]

man·u·duc·to·ry (man′yə duk′tər ē), *adj.* leading by or as if by the hand; guiding.

manuf., **1.** manufacture. **2.** manufacturer. **3.** manufacturing.

man·u·fac·to·ry (man′yə fak′tər ē), *n., pl.* **-ries.** a factory: *The toy manufactory itself was a curiosity in structure and management* (London Times).

man·u·fac·ture (man′yə fak′chər), *v.,* **-tured, -tur·ing,** *n.* —*v.t.* **1.** to make by hand or by machine: *This big factory manufactures goods in large quantities by using machines and dividing the work up among many people.* **2.** to make into something useful: *to manufacture aluminum into kitchenware.* **3.** to make up; invent: *The lazy boy manufactured excuses.* **4.** to produce (literary work, etc.) mechanically: *If the music is useful and effective, it also sounds manufactured* (Manchester Guardian Weekly). [< noun]

—*n.* **1.** the act or process of manufacturing. *Abbr.:* mfr. **2.** a thing manufactured. **3.** something produced mechanically, as a story.

[< Middle French *manufacture,* learned borrowing from Medieval Latin *manufactura* < Latin *manū facere* make by hand]

man·u·fac·tur·er (man′yə fak′chər ər), *n.* a person whose business is manufacturing; an owner of a factory.

ma·nu·ka (mə nü′kə; *Maori* mä′nu̇ kä), *n.* any of several Australasian trees and shrubs of the myrtle family, yielding a very hard, dark, close-grained wood, and an aromatic leaf sometimes used as a substitute for tea. [< Maori *mánuka*]

man·u·mis·sion (man′yə mish′ən), *n.* **1.** a freeing from slavery. **2.** a being freed from slavery: *Perhaps he remembers his ancestor from the Congo, who would not leave the state even for his manumission* (Time). [< Latin *manūmissiō, -ōnis* < *manūmittere;* see MANUMIT]

man·u·mit (man′yə mit′), *v.t.,* **-mit·ted, -mit·ting.** to set free from slavery: *The Christian masters were not bound to manumit their slaves, and yet were commended if they did so* (Jeremy Taylor). [< Latin *manūmittere* < *manū mittere* release from control < *manū,* ablative of *manus* hand + *ēmittere* send out, release < *ex-* from + *mittere* to send]

ma·nure (mə nu̇r′, -nyu̇r′), *n., v.,* **-nured, -nur·ing.** —*n.* a substance put in or on the soil as fertilizer, as dung or refuse from stables: *The histories of the most primitive agricultural peoples show that they knew the value of various kinds of manures* (Fred W. Emerson). [< verb] —*v.t.* to put manure in or on. [< Anglo-French *maynoverer,* Old French *manouvrer* work with the hands < *maneuvre* hand work. Doublet of MANEUVER.] —**ma·nur′er,** *n.*

manure worm, a brandling.

ma·nu·ri·al (mə nu̇r′ē əl, -nyu̇r′-), *adj.* having to do with or of the nature of manure: *The availability of ample irrigation water coupled with effective pest control and manurial treatments enabled a second cycle of growth to be initiated and sustained to maturity* (New Scientist).

ma·nus (mā′nəs), *n., pl.* **-nus.** **1.** the distal part of the forelimb of a vertebrate, including the carpus or wrist, and the forefoot or hand. **2.** (in Roman law) power or authority of a husband over his wife. [< Latin *manus, -ūs* hand]

man·u·script (man′yə skript), *n.* **1.** a book, article, etc., written by hand or with a typewriter, especially as prepared by a writer for a publisher or typesetter. *Abbr.:* MS. **2.** handwritten or typewritten condition: *His last book was three years in manuscript.* **3.** a book, document, etc., written by hand before the introduction of printing.

—*adj.* written by hand or with a typewriter.

[< Latin *manū scriptus* written by hand < *manū,* ablative of *manus* hand + *scriptus,* past participle of *scrībere* to write]

man·u·script·al (man′yə skrip′təl), *adj.* **1.** of, having to do with, or like a manuscript or manuscripts. **2.** found in a manuscript or manuscripts.

man·ward (man′wərd), *adv.* toward man; in relation to man. —*adj.* directed toward man.

man·wards (man′wərdz), *adv.* manward.

man·wise (man′wīz′), *adv.* in the manner of a man.

Manx (mangks), *adj.* of the Isle of Man, a small island west of northern England in the Irish Sea, its people, or their language. —*n.* **1.** the people of the Isle of Man. **2.** the Celtic language spoken on the Isle of Man. [earlier, *maniske,* perhaps < a Scandinavian word < the Celtic name of the island (compare Old Irish *Manu*)]

➔ **Manx,** meaning the people of the Isle of Man, is plural in use: *The Manx are hardworking people. Manx,* meaning the language of these people, is singular in use: *Manx is nearly extinct.*

Manx or **manx cat,** a breed of domestic cat that has no tail.

Manx·man (mangks′mən), *n., pl.* **-men.** a native of the Isle of Man.

Manx shearwater, a small shearwater which nests on islands of the North Atlantic and Mediterranean.

man·y (men′ē), *adj.,* **more, most,** *n.* —*adj.* consisting of a great number; numerous: *many people, many years ago.*

how many, what number of: *How many days until Christmas?*

—*n.* **1.** a great number: *many of us.* **2.** many people or things: *There were many at the dance. Many be called, but few chosen* (Matthew 20:16). *Never . . . was so much owed by so many to so few* (Sir Winston Churchill).

a good many, a fairly large number: *A few failed the test but a good many got perfect scores.*

a great many, a very large number: *A great many gathered at the scene.*

one too many (for), a. more than a match for: *We were one too many for the enemy.* **b.** too much for one's own good, especially of alcoholic beverage: *Our friend has had one too many at the party.*

the many, a. most people: *The many fail* (Tennyson). **b.** the common people: *The folly and foolish self-opinion of the half-instructed many* (Samuel Taylor Coleridge).

[Middle English *moni,* or *mani,* Old English *manig*]

—**Syn.** *adj.* **Many, innumerable** mean consisting of a large number. **Many** is the general word: *Were many people there?* **In-**

numerable means more than can be counted, or so many that counting would be very hard: *He has given innumerable excuses for being late.*

man-year (man′yir′), *n.* one year of one man's work, used as a unit in figuring cost, time, output, etc., of production: *Deaths in World War II produced a loss of 3 million man-years.*

man·y-fac·et·ed (men′ē fas′ə tid), *adj.* having many facets; many-sided.

man·y·fold (men′ē fōld′), *adv.* many times; to a great extent (usually in the expression *increase manyfold): During the past five years the number of weapons has increased manyfold* (Lewis L. Strauss).

➔ **Manyfold** is a compound recently formed on the analogy of such compounds as *twofold* and *threefold,* which denote the number of times an action recurs. **Manifold** appeared in Old English about the same time as *twofold* and *threefold* but, unlike them, it does not function as an adverb and is limited to expressing kind and variety, never time and duration.

man·y·plies (men′ē plīz′), *n.* the third stomach of a cow or other ruminant animal; omasum; psalterium. [< *many* + *plies,* plural of *ply,* noun]

man·y-sid·ed (men′ē sī′did), *adj.* **1.** having many sides. **2.** having many interests or abilities; versatile: *a many-sided person.* **3.** having many aspects, possibilities, etc.: *a many-sided problem.* —**man′y-sid′ed·ness,** *n.*

man·za·nil·la (man′zə nil′ə), *n.* a dry, light Spanish sherry with a somewhat bitter flavor: *Manzanilla is the driest sherry type of all, and may be the driest wine in the world* (New Yorker). [< Spanish *manzanilla* (originally) camomile (diminutive) < *manzana* apple; see MANCHINEEL]

man·za·ni·ta (man′zə nē′tə), *n.* **1.** any of various evergreen shrubs or trees of the heath family that grow in western North America, such as the bearberry. **2.** the fruit of any of these plants. [American English < American Spanish *manzanita* (diminutive) < *manzana* apple; see MANCHINEEL]

Mao·ism (mou′iz əm), *n.* the Communist ideology of Mao Tse-tung, Chinese Communist leader, characterized by rigid adherence to Marxian doctrine: *They seek to make of Maoism a powerful faith that would unite, guide, and inspire future generations* (London Times).

Mao·ist (mou′ist), *adj.* of or having to do with Maoism: *. . . has said that the way to win in American politics is to apply Maoist principles on "the tactics of infiltration"* (New Yorker). —*n.* a supporter of Maoism.

Ma·o·ri (mä′ō rē, mou′rē), *n., pl.* **-ris,** *adj.* —*n.* **1.** a member of the native Polynesian people of New Zealand. **2.** their Polynesian language. —*adj.* of the Maoris or their language.

Ma·o·ri·land·er (mä′ō rē lan′dər, mou′rē-), *n.* New Zealander. [< *Maoriland* a name for New Zealand + *-er*[1]]

Ma·o·ri·tan·ga (mä′ō rē tang′gə, mou′rē-), *n.* the art, customs, traditions, etc., of the Maoris. [< Maori]

map (map), *n., v.,* **mapped, map·ping.** —*n.* **1.** a drawing representing selected features of the earth's surface or part of it, usually showing countries, cities, rivers, seas, lakes, and mountains. **2.** a drawing representing the sky or part of it, showing the position of the stars. **3.** a maplike drawing of anything: *a highway map, a weather map.* —*v.t.* **1.** to make a map of; show on a map. **2.** to collect information for a map by exploring or surveying (a region, etc.). **3.** to arrange in detail; plan: *to map out the week's work. I set to work to map out a new career* (Mark Twain). **4.** *Mathematics.* to cause an element in (one set) to correspond to an element in the same or another set.

put on the map, to give importance or prominence to; make famous: *He [Gene Krupa] is credited with putting jazz drumming on the map* (New Yorker).

[< Medieval Latin *mappa* map (for earlier *mappa mundi* map of the world) < Latin *mappa* napkin, cloth (on which maps were once drawn)] —**map′like′,** *adj.* —**map′per,** *n.*

—**Syn.** *n.* **1. Map, chart** mean a drawing representing a surface or area. **Map** applies particularly to a representation of some part of the earth's surface or an area of land, showing relative geographical positions, shape, size, etc., of certain places or features: *A map of a city shows streets and parks.* **Chart** applies particularly to a map used especially in sea or air navigation, showing deep and shallow places, islands, channels, etc., in a body of water, or air currents, airlanes, etc.: *The reef that the ship struck is on the chart.*

Ma·phil·in·do (mä fi lin′dō), *n.* **1.** the plan or policy of uniting Malaysia, the Philippines, and Indonesia into a confederation. **2.** Malaysia, the Philippines, and Indonesia regarded as a geographical or political unit.

ma·ple (mā′pəl), *n.* **1.** a tree grown for its shade, its wood, or its sap. There are many kinds of maples, but all have dry fruits with two wings, and opposite leaves without stipules. **2.** its hard, light-colored wood, used for furniture, flooring, etc. **3.** the flavor of maple sugar or maple syrup. [Old English *mapeltrēow* maple tree] —**ma′ple·like′,** *adj.*

maple family, a group of dicotyledonous trees and shrubs with dry, two-winged fruit, found in mountainous, northern countries, and cultivated widely for shade and ornament.

maple leaf, 1. a leaf of the maple tree. **2.** this leaf as the official Canadian emblem.

maple sugar, sugar made by boiling the sap of the maple, usually the sugar maple, until most of the water has evaporated.

maple syrup, syrup made by boiling the sap of the maple, usually the sugar maple.

map·mak·er (map′mā′kər), *n.* cartographer: *Until recently mapmakers assumed that the mean level of the sea, observed at a chosen spot, provided a foolproof basis for measuring land heights* (New Scientist).

map·per·y (map′ər ē), *n.* the making of maps.

map·pist (map′ist), *n.* a mapmaker.

ma·quette (mȧ ket′), *n. French.* a preliminary sketch or model in clay or wax of a painting, monument, building, etc.: *The eleven maquettes on display were selected from 199 entries by a jury* (New York Times).

ma·quil·lage (mȧ kē yȧzh′), *n. French.* cosmetics applied to the face; makeup.

ma·quil·leur (mȧ kē yœr′), *n. French.* a makeup man.

Ma·quis (mȧ kē′), *n., pl.* **-quis,** *adj.* —*n.* **1.** the French underground in World War II which waged guerrilla warfare against the Germans. **2.** a member of this: *At a tank stop the train was boarded by a gang of armed Maquis* (Time). **3.** an underground resistance movement in Algeria.

—*adj.* of, resembling in tactics, or having to do with the Maquis.

[< French *maquis* (originally) scrub forest, thicket < Italian *macchia* < Latin *macula* spot, cluster. Compare MACULA, MACULE, MAIL[2].]

Ma·qui·sard (mȧ kē zärd′), *n. French.* a member of the Maquis: *Even his enemies are loath to discuss him except in privacy, among themselves, like Maquisards hiding out in cellars* (Maclean's).

mar (mär), *v.,* **marred, mar·ring,** *n.* —*v.t.* **1.** to spoil the beauty of; damage; injure: *hideously marred about the face* (Herman Melville). *Weeds mar a garden. The nails in the workmen's shoes have marred our newly finished floors.* **2.** to spoil or ruin: *Grant us felicity . . . nor let our sweet delight be marred by aught* (William Morris). —*n.* something that mars; blemish; drawback. [Old English *merran* to waste, spoil] —**Syn.** *v.t.* **1.** disfigure. **2.** impair.

mar., **1.** marine. **2.** maritime. **3.** married.

Mar., March.

mar·a·bou or **mar·a·bout**[1] (mar′ə bü), *n.* **1.** any of several varieties of large, white-bodied storks of Africa and Asia; adjutant. **2.** a furlike trimming made from its soft, white, downy feathers, used on women's hats, dresses, etc.: *a marabou feather which she wears in her turban* (Thackeray). **3. a.** a silk that is nearly pure-white in the raw state. **b.** a delicate cloth made from it. [< *marabout*[2] (because the bird appears reflective)]

mar·a·bout[2] (mar′ə büt), *n.* **1.** a Moslem holy man or ascetic of northern Africa: *a little old Turk, poorly dressed like a marabout . . . of the desert* (Scott). **2.** the tomb of such a holy man, serving as a shrine. [< French *marabout* < Arabic *murābiṭ* hermit]

ma·ra·ca (mə rä′kə, -rak′ə), *n.* a percussion instrument, consisting of seeds, lead shot, etc., enclosed in a dry gourd or gourd-shaped body and played like a rattle, usually in pairs. [American English < Portuguese *maracá* < the Brazilian name for a gourd]

ma·rae (mə rī′), *n., pl.* **-rae** or **-raes. 1.** a temple, altar, or sacred enclosure at which Polynesians worship. **2.** an enclosed space or yard in front of a Maori house. [< Polynesian]

mar·ag·ing steel (mär′ā′jing), a very strong, corrosion-resistant, low-carbon alloy of iron, chromium, nickel, titanium, silicon, and manganese, often used in spacecraft parts. [< *mar*(tensite) *aging*]

Ma·rah (mā′rə, mãr′ə), *n.* in the Bible: **1.** the place where the Israelites in their wanderings found only bitter water. Exodus 15:23. **2.** a well or stream of bitter water. [< Hebrew *mārā* bitter]

ma·rah (mā′rə, mãr′ə), *n.* bitter water; bitterness: *The wasting famine of the heart they fed, And slaked its thirst with marah of their tears* (Longfellow). [< *Marah*]

mar·a·nath·a (mar′ə nath′ə), *n.* anathema. [< Greek *maranathá.* Compare ANATHEMA.]

ma·ran·ta (mə ran′tə), *n.* any of various tropical herbs commonly grown under glass for their showy foliage; arrowroot. [< New Latin *Maranta* the genus name < Bartolomeo *Maranta,* an Italian physician and botanist of the 1500's]

mar·an·ta·ceous (mar′an tā′shəs), *adj.* belonging to the family of plants typified by the arrowroot.

ma·ran·tic (mə ran′tik), *adj.* marasmic.

ma·ras·ca (mə ras′kə), *n.* a small black cherry whose sour fruit is the source of maraschino. [< Italian *marasca,* short for *amarasca* < *amaro* bitter, sour < Latin *amārus*]

mar·a·schi·no (mar′ə skē′nō, -shē′-), *n.* a strong liqueur made from the fermented juice of marascas. [< Italian *maraschino* < *marasca;* see MARASCA]

maraschino cherries, cherries preserved in a syrup flavored with maraschino.

ma·ras·mic (mə raz′mik), *adj.* of or having to do with marasmus.

ma·ras·mus (mə raz′məs), *n.* a wasting away of the body due to malnutrition, old age, etc., rather than disease. [< New Latin *marasmus* < Greek *marasmós,* alteration of *máransis* < *maraínein* put out (a fire), die away slowly]

Ma·ra·tha (mə rä′tə), *n.* Mahratta.

Ma·ra·thi (mə rä′tē, -rat′ē), *n.* Mahratti.

Mar·a·thon (mar′ə thon), *n.* a plain in Greece about 20 miles northeast of Athens. After the Athenians defeated the Persians there in 490 B.C., a runner ran all the way to Athens with the news of the victory.

mar·a·thon (mar′ə thon), *n.* **1.** a foot race of 26 miles, 385 yards, introduced in 1896 with the revival of the Olympic Games, in memory of the runner who carried the news to Athens that the Athenians had defeated the Persians in the battle of Marathon (490 B.C.). **2.** any long race or contest: *The litigation . . . turned out to be a marathon affair* (New Yorker).

mar·a·thon·er (mar′ə thon′ər), *n.* a participant in a marathon.

Mar·a·tho·ni·an (mar′ə thō′nē ən), *adj.* of or having to do with Marathon or the battle of Marathon. —*n.* a native of Marathon.

ma·raud (mə rôd′), *v.i.* to go about in search of plunder: *The Saxon stern, the pagan Dane, Maraud on Britain's shores again* (Scott). —*v.t.* to make raids on for booty; plunder: *The tract of country they intended to maraud was far in the Moorish territories* (Washington Irving). —*n.* a marauding expedition; raid: *They were still liable to the marauds of the Blackfeet* (Washington Irving). [< French *marauder* < Middle French *maraud* rascal (perhaps as a prowler); (originally) tomcat; apparently imitative < *marau* meow]

ma·raud·er (mə rô′dər), *n.* a person or animal that goes about in search of plunder: *Tigers and leopards are night marauders of the jungle.*

ma·raud·ing (mə rô′ding), *adj.* going about in search of plunder; making raids for booty.

mar·a·ve·di (mar′ə vā′dē), *n., pl.* **-dis. 1.** a gold coin used by the Moors in Spain during the 1000's and 1100's. **2.** a former Spanish copper coin. [< Spanish *maravedí*

< Arabic *Murābiṭīn,* plural, a Moorish dynasty at Cordoba, 1087-1147. Compare MARABOU.]

mar·ble (mär′bəl), *n., adj., v.,* **-bled, -bling.** —*n.* **1.** a hard, metamorphic limestone, white or colored, capable of taking a high beautiful polish: *Marble . . . lasts quite as long as granite, and is much softer to work* (John Ruskin). **2.** a little ball of clay, glass, stone, etc., used in games. **3.** a pattern or color that looks like marble. **4.** something as cold and hard as marble: *a heart of marble.*

marbles, a. a game played with marbles: *There was the floor on which . . . I had played at marbles* (R. Chambers). **b.** a collection of sculptures: *the Elgin Marbles.* **c.** *Slang.* common sense; reason: *I think he's lost his marbles.*

—*adj.* **1.** made of marble. **2.** like marble; white, hard, cold, or unfeeling: *that seeming marble heart* (Byron). **3.** having a pattern like marble; mottled.

—*v.t.* to color in imitation of the patterns in marble: *Binders marble the edges of some books. The horizon bounded by a propitious sky, azure, marbled with pearly white* (Charlotte Brontë).

[< Old French *marble,* and *marbre* < Latin *marmor, -oris* < Greek *mármoros* marble, gleaming stone] —**mar′ble·like′,** *adj.*

➤ **Marbles,** the game, is plural in form and singular in use: *Marbles is played by many boys.*

marble cake, a cake with streaks of dark and light, made by filling the pan with alternate spoonfuls of dark and light batter.

mar·bled godwit (mär′bəld), a large brownish shore bird with an upturned bill that nests in central North America.

mar·ble·ize (mar′bə līz), *v.t.,* **-ized, -iz·ing.** to make like marble in pattern, grain, etc.

mar·bling (mär′bling), *n.* **1.** a coloring, graining, marking, etc., that suggests marble: *beefsteak with a marbling of fat.* **2.** a pattern of coloring, graining, etc., on book edges, bindings, etc., in imitation of the patterns of marble. **3.** the staining of paper, etc., with colors in imitation of marble.

mar·bly (mär′blē), *adj.,* **-bli·er, -bli·est.** like marble.

marc (märk; *French* mår), *n.* **1.** the refuse that remains after pressing grapes or other fruits: *Wine made by pressing the marc or refuse that remains after all the sound grape juice has been squeezed from the grapes* (London Times). **2.** brandy derived from this: *France's alcoholism consists mostly of excess wine drinking . . . with some help from spirits like marc, Calvados, cognac* (New Yorker). **3.** the residue that remains after extracting oil, etc., from plants, seeds, nuts, etc., by means of a solvent. [< Middle French *marc,* verbal noun of *marcher* trample under foot; see MARCH[1]]

mar·ca·site (mär′kə sīt), *n.* **1.** a native iron disulfide, white iron pyrites, similar to and of the same composition as ordinary pyrites. *Formula:* FeS_2 **2.** any crystallized iron pyrites used in the 1700's for ornaments. **3.** a crystallized piece cut and polished as an ornament: *Marcasites are among the staple stones of costume jewelry* (London Times). [< Medieval Latin *marcasita* < Arabic *marqashīṭā* < Aramaic]

mar·ca·to (mär kä′tō), *Music.* —*adj.* with strong emphasis; accentuated; marked: *The beautiful, languid tune . . . was played in quite strict time and in almost marcato rhythm* (London Times). —*adv.* in a marcato manner: . . . *horns were played staccato, flutes marcato, etc.* (Saturday Review). [< Italian *marcato* (literally) marked, past participle of *marcare* to mark]

mar·cel (mär sel′), *n., v.,* **-celled, -cel·ling.** —*n.* Also, **marcel wave.** a series of regular waves put in the hair. —*v.t.* to put a series of regular waves in (the hair). [< *Marcel,* a French hairdresser of the 1800's, who originated it] —**mar·cel′ler,** *n.*

mar·ces·cence (mär ses′əns), *n.* marcescent condition.

mar·ces·cent (mär ses′ənt), *adj.* withering but not falling off, as a part of a plant. [< Latin *marcēscēns, -entis,* present participle of *marcēscere* to wither away < *marcēre* be faint, languid]

march[1] (märch), *v.i.* **1.** to walk as soldiers do, in time and with steps of the same length: *Clinton's troops . . . marched to the cadence of their drums* (New Yorker). **2.** to walk in a very dignified or deliberate manner: *The minister marched to the altar. Miss Ophelia marched straight to her own chamber* (Harriet Beecher Stowe). **3.** to proceed steadily; advance: *History marches on.* —*v.t.* **1.** to cause to march or go: *The policeman marched the thief off to jail. March the regiment to the barracks.* **2.** to pass over, across, or through in marching.

—*n.* **1.** the act or fact of marching: *The news of the enemy's march made whole villages flee.* **2.** a manner of marching: *a slow march.* **3.** a piece of music with a rhythm suited to accompany marching. **4.** the distance covered in a single course of marching: *The camp is a day's march away.* **5.** a forward movement; advance; progress: *History records the march of events. We may resume the march of our existence* (Byron). **6.** a long, hard walk.

steal a march, to gain an advantage without being noticed: *to steal a march on one's competitors. We must be off early . . . and steal a long march upon them* (Frederick Marryat).

[< Middle French *marcher,* earlier, to trample, ultimately < Late Latin *marcus* hammer < Latin *marculus* small hammer]

march[2] (märch), *n.* the land along the border of a country; frontier: *Those low and barren tracts were the outlying marches of the empire* (John L. Motley).

the Marches, the districts along the border between England and Scotland, or between England and Wales: . . . *then occupying those parts which we now call the middle Marches, between the English and Scots* (William Warner).

—*v.i.* to border (on).

[< Old French *marche* < Germanic (compare Old High German *marcha,* English *mark*[1]). Compare MARQUIS.]

—**Syn.** *n.* boundary.

March (märch), *n.* the third month of the year. It has 31 days. *Abbr.:* Mar. [< Old French *marche* < Latin *Martius* (*mēnsis*) (month) of Mars]

March., marchioness.

M. Arch., Master of Architecture.

Mär·chen (mer′Hən), *n., pl.* **Mär·chen.** *German.* **1.** a fairy tale or folk tale. **2.** any story or tale.

march·er[1] (mär′chər), *n.* a person who marches or walks.

march·er[2] (mär′chər), *n.* **1.** an inhabitant of a march. **2.** an officer or lord having jurisdiction over border territory.

mar·che·sa (mär kā′zä), *n., pl.* **-che·se** (-kā′zā). *Italian.* the wife or widow of a marchese; marchioness: *I decided at first that she looked Italian—that she might be a faded and famous marchesa* (New Yorker).

mar·che·se (mär kā′zā), *n., pl.* **-che·si** (-kā′zē). *Italian.* a nobleman ranking next above a count and next below a prince.

March fly, any of a group of dark-colored flies, sometimes marked with red or yellow, which appear in the spring and feed on the roots of plants and decaying vegetable matter.

march·ing orders (mär′ching), **1.** *Military.* orders to proceed or to begin a march. **2.** *Informal.* notice to an employee that he has been discharged: *He referred to a recent case where the directors of a company gave the guilty executives their "marching orders"* (London Times).

mar·chion·ess (mär′shə nis), *n.* **1.** the wife or widow of a marquis. **2.** a lady equal in rank to a marquis. [< Medieval Latin *marchionissa* < *marchio, -onis* marquis < *marche* march[2]. Compare MARCH[2].]

march·land (märch′land′, -lənd), *n.* a border territory; frontier district.

march·man (märch′mən), *n., pl.* **-men.** an inhabitant of marches; marcher.

March of Dimes, *U.S.* an annual appeal for and collection of money, originally for research on poliomyelitis and rehabilitation of victims of it, and now for combating other diseases as well.

march·pane (märch′pān′), *n.* marzipan. [< Italian *marzapane;* see MARZIPAN]

march-past (märch′past′, -päst′), *n.* a parade past a reviewing stand.

Mar·co·ni (mär kō′nē), *adj.* of or designating the system of wireless telegraphy devised by Guglielmo Marconi, 1847-1937, an Italian engineer who helped to perfect wireless telegraphy.

mar·co·ni (mär kō′nē), *v.t., v.i.,* **-nied, -ni·ing.** to telegraph by the wireless system perfected by Marconi.

mar·co·ni·gram (mär kō′nē gram), *n.* a wireless telegram; radiogram.

mar·co·ni·graph (mär kō′nē graf, -gräf), *n.* the apparatus used for transmitting radiograms. —*v.t., v.i.* to transmit by wireless.

Marconi rig, a rig for a yacht, having one or more jibs and a large fore-and-aft sail hoisted on a tall mast with the foot set on a boom.

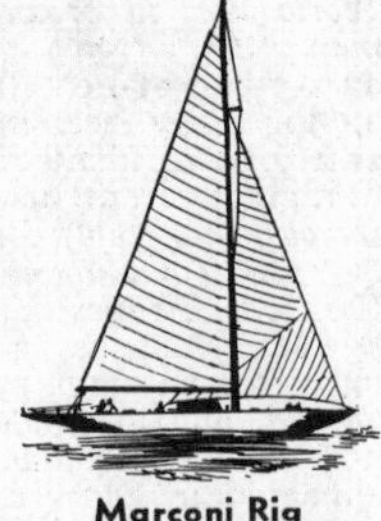

Marconi Rig

Marco Polo sheep, a large wild sheep, a variety of argali, native to the plateaus of central Asia; Pamir sheep; Tian-shan sheep: *Marco Polo sheep are notable for the great size of their curling horns.*

Mar·di gras (mär′dē grä′), the last day before Lent; Shrove Tuesday. It is celebrated in New Orleans and other cities with parades and festivities. [< French *mardi gras* fat (that is, meat-eating) Tuesday; *mardis* < Latin *Martis* (*dies*) (day) of Mars, Tuesday; *gras* < Latin *crassus*]

Mar·duk (mär′dụ̇k), *n.* the chief god of the Babylonians, originally a god of the city of Babylon only.

mare[1] (mãr), *n.* a female horse, donkey, etc.: *In two and a half hours, sixteen yearlings and 23 brood mares were auctioned off* (Newsweek). [Middle English *mare,* Old English *mearh* horse]

mare[2] (mãr), *n. Obsolete.* **1.** a goblin once believed to cause nightmares by sitting on the chest of the sleeper. **2.** the nightmare itself. [Old English *mare*]

ma·re[3] (mãr′ē), *n., pl.* **ma·ri·a. 1.** *Latin.* a sea. **2.** *Astronomy.* a broad, flat area on the moon: . . . *these dark areas appear as smooth gray plains, so uniform that Galileo and his contemporaries thought they might be seas and accordingly called them maria* . . . (John Charles Duncan).

Mare[3] (def. 2)
Flat areas (shaded) are called seas or maria.

ma·re clau·sum (mãr′ē klô′səm), *Latin.* a closed sea; waters within the sphere of control of one nation.

Ma·re Im·bri·um (mãr′ē im′brē əm), *Latin.* Sea of Rains, a great plain upon the visible face of the moon, surrounded by mountain ranges and studded with many craters.

ma·re li·be·rum (mãr′ē lib′ər əm), *Latin.* open sea; the high seas.

ma·rem·ma (mə rem′ə), *n., pl.* **-rem·me** (-rem′ē). **1.** a low, marshy, unhealthful region by the seashore. **2.** the miasma of such a region. [< Italian *maremma* < Latin *maritima,* feminine of *maritimus* maritime]

ma·re nos·trum (mãr′ē nos′trəm), *Latin.* our sea: *The Mediterranean . . . Rome's mare nostrum* . . . (Time).

mar·e·schal (mar′ə shəl), *n. Obsolete or Archaic.* marshal.

mare's-nest (mãrz′nest′), *n.* something supposed to be a great discovery that turns out to be a mistake or hoax: *In Mr. Sutliff's opinion, Mr. Kraushauer had run off after a mare's-nest* (John Stephen Strange).

mare's-tail (mãrz′tāl′), *n.* **1.** a water plant, with many circles of narrow, hairlike leaves around the stems. **2.** horsetail (the plant). **3.** a high, white, filmy cloud, shaped somewhat like a horse's tail.

Ma·re·zine (mãr′ə zēn, -zin), *n. Trademark.* an antihistaminic drug: *Marezine, one of the new drugs to control motion sickness, can be obtained at drugstores without a prescription* (New York Times). *Formula:* $C_{18}H_{22}N_2$

Mar·fan's syndrome (mär′fänz), a congenital and hereditary condition characterized by abnormal length and slenderness of the arms, legs, fingers, and toes. [< Bernard-Jean *Marfan,* 1858-1942, a French pediatrician, who first recognized the syndrome]

marg., 1. margin. **2.** marginal.

mar·gar·ic acid (mär gar′ik, -gär′-; mär′gər-), a white, crystalline, fatty acid found in lichens and produced artificially, resembling palmitic and stearic acids. *Formula:* $C_{17}H_{34}O_2$ [< French *acide margarique* < Greek *márgaron* pearl (from the appearance of its crystals)]

mar·ga·rin (mär′jər in), *n.* margarine.

mar·ga·rine (mär′jə rin, -jə rēn; -gər in, -gə rēn), *n.* a substitute for butter consisting mainly of vegetable fat derived from cottonseed and soybean oils and to a lesser extent from corn and peanut oils; oleomargarine: *Modern margarine is made from refined vegetable oils . . . grown on American farms, plus cultured skim milk* (Time). [< French *margarine* < *margarique;* see MARGARIC ACID]

mar·ga·ri·ta (mär′gə rē′tə), *n.* a Mexican cocktail of tequila and lime juice. [< Spanish *Margarita* Margaret]

mar·ga·rite (mär′gə rit), *n.* **1.** a hydrated calcium aluminum silicate, occurring as scales with a pearly luster. *Formula:* $H_2CaAl_4Si_2O_{12}$ **2.** *Archaic.* a pearl. [< Latin *margarīta* < Greek *margarī́tēs* (pearl) stone < *márgaron* pearl]

mar·ga·ri·tif·er·ous (mär′gə rə tif′ər əs), *adj.* producing or yielding pearls.

Mar·gaux (mär gō′), *n.* a claret produced in the commune of Margaux, in the region near Bordeaux: *Princess Anne relaxed . . . over a glass of red Margaux* (*vintage: '53*) (Time).

mar·gay (mär′gā), *n.* a small, long-tailed, spotted wildcat similar to the ocelot, found from Texas south to Argentina: *The elusive Texas margay . . . has only been taken one time, back in the last century* (Science News Letter).
[< French *margay*, alteration of *margaia* < Tupi (Brazil) *mbaracaïa*]

marge[1] (märj), *n. Poetic.* an edge; border: *the illuminated marge of some old book* (Lowell). *The plashy brink Of weedy lake, or marge of river wide* (William Cullen Bryant). [< Middle French *marge*, learned borrowing from Latin *margō, -inis* margin]

marge[2] (märj), *n. Especially British Informal.* margarine.

mar·gent (mär′jənt), *n. Archaic.* margin: *Across the margent of the world I fled* (Francis Thompson). [alteration of *margin*]

mar·gin (mär′jən), *n.* **1.** an edge; border: *the margin of a lake. A step or two farther brought him to one margin of a little clearing* (Robert Louis Stevenson). *Over the margin, After it, follow it, Follow the Gleam* (Tennyson). **2.** the blank space around the writing or printing on a page: *I love a broad margin to my life* (Thoreau). **3.** an extra amount; amount beyond what is necessary; difference: *a margin for error. We allow a margin of 15 minutes in catching a train.* **4.** the difference between the cost and selling price of stocks, etc. **5.** *Finance.* **a.** the money or securities deposited with a broker to protect him from loss on transactions undertaken for the real buyer or seller. **b.** the amount of such a deposit: *The reserve board raised margins from 50 to 60 per cent* (New York Times). **c.** the transaction itself, financed by both the broker and his customer: *When you buy on margin you put up only part of the total cost and the broker lends you the remainder.* **d.** the customer's profit or loss in such a transaction. **6.** the point at which an economic activity yields just enough return to cover its costs and below which the activity will result in a loss. **7.** a condition beyond which something ceases to exist or be possible; limit: *the margin of subsistence, the margin of consciousness. Abbr.:* marg.
—*v.t.* **1.** to provide with a margin; border: *The shore . . . was margined with foam* (Herman Melville). **2.** to enter (notes, comments, etc.) in the margin. **3.** to provide (a book, article, etc.) with marginal notes. **4.** *Finance.* **a.** to deposit a margin upon (stock, etc.). **b.** to secure by a margin: *Probably 45 per cent of all purchases on the Stock Exchange are margined* (New York Times).
[< Latin *margō, marginis* edge]
—**Syn.** *n.* **1.** brim, brink, rim, verge.

mar·gin·al (mär′jə nəl), *adj.* **1.** written or printed in a margin: *a marginal comment.* **2.** of or in a margin: *marginal space.* **3.** on or near the margin: *Marginal land is barely fit for farming.* **4.** existing or occurring on the fringes of anything established; only partly taken in: *a marginal culture.* **5. a.** barely producing or capable of producing goods, crops, etc., at a rate necessary to cover the costs of production: *The small, inefficient or marginal farmer* (New Yorker). **b.** of, having to do with, or obtained from goods that are so produced and marketed: *marginal income. Britain's current economic problem is marginal* (Newsweek). **6.** *Sociology.* only partially assimilated in a social group: *The marginal man is the person who belongs to two or more cultures but is not fully accepted in any* (Emory S. Bogardus).
—*n. Especially British.* a constituency where the results of an election might favor either party: *Of five by-elections pending, two are in marginals* (Sunday Times).
[< New Latin *marginalis* < Latin *margō;* see MARGIN]

mar·gi·na·li·a (mär′jə nā′lē ə), *n.pl.* marginal notes. [< New Latin *marginalia*, neuter plural of *marginalis* marginal]

mar·gin·al·i·ty (mär′jə nal′ə tē), *n.* the quality or condition of being marginal: *They are trying to solve in an explicitly political way the problems of marginality . . . that dominated the Jewish experience for so long* (New Yorker).

mar·gin·al·ly (mär′jə nə lē), *adv.* in the margin; in a marginal manner.

marginal utility, the utility derived, or expected, from a unit of a commodity which a buyer is just barely willing to purchase at the prevailing price.

mar·gin·ate (mär′jə nāt), *v.*, **-at·ed, -at·ing,** *adj.* —*v.t.* to provide with a margin; border. —*adj.* having a margin. [< Latin *margināre* (with English *-ate*[1]) furnish with a margin < *margō, marginis* margin]

mar·gin·at·ed (mär′jə nā′tid), *adj.* marginate.

mar·gin·a·tion (mär′jə nā′shən), *n.* marginate condition or appearance.

mar·go·sa (mär gō′sə), *n.* an East Indian tree of the mahogany family whose oil and bitter bark are used in medicine. [< Portuguese *amargosa*, feminine of *amargoso* bitter]

mar·gra·vate (mär′grə vāt), *n.* margraviate.

mar·grave (mär′grāv), *n.* **1.** a title of certain princes of Germany or the Holy Roman Empire. **2.** the military governor of a former German border province. [earlier *marcgrave* < Middle Dutch *markgrave* count of the marches[2]]

mar·gra·vi·ate (mär grā′vē āt, -it), *n.* the territory ruled by a margrave.

mar·gra·vine (mär′grə vēn), *n.* the wife or widow of a margrave.

mar·gue·rite (mär′gə rēt′), *n.* **1.** a kind of daisy with white petals and a yellow center, such as the oxeye daisy or the English daisy. **2.** any of several kinds of chrysanthemums that have daisylike flowers. [< French *marguerite* pearl < Old French *margarite;* see MARGARITE]

Marguerite (def. 1)
(2 to 3 ft. high)

ma·ri·a (mãr′ē ə), *n.* the plural of **mare**[3].

ma·ri·a·chi (mär′ē ăch′ē), *n.*, *pl.* **-chis.** **1.** a member of a Mexican band of strolling singers and musicians: *Professional mariachis in old times were wandering minstrels* (Saturday Review). **2.** a band of mariachis. [< Mexican Spanish *mariachi*, probably < French *mariage* marriage (because they originally played at weddings)]

ma·ri·age de con·ve·nance (mȧ ryȧzh′ də kôɴ vnäɴs′), *French.* a marriage of convenience or expediency, especially to gain prestige, wealth, etc.

Mar·i·an (mãr′ē ən), *adj.* **1.** of or having to do with the Virgin Mary. **2.** of or having to do with some other Mary, such as Mary, Queen of Scots.
—*n.* **1.** a worshiper of the Virgin Mary. **2.** a supporter of Mary, Queen of Scots.

Mar·i·an·a (mãr′ē an′ə) or **Marianas Trench,** a trench in the southern Pacific Ocean, off Guam, that is the site of the greatest ocean depth yet located, over 6½ miles.

Mar·i·an·ism (mãr′ē ə niz′əm), *n.* **1.** the worship of the Virgin Mary. **2.** the theory or belief concerning this worship: *The differences between Protestants and Roman Catholics are normally defined in terms of doctrine—papal infallibility, Marianism, the nature of the church* (Time).

Mar·i·anne (mãr′ē an′), *n.* the republic of France personified as a woman in flowing robes and wearing a liberty cap.

Marian Year, (in the Roman Catholic Church) December 8, 1954–December 8, 1955, the centenary of the promulgation of the dogma of the Immaculate Conception.

Ma·ri·a The·re·sa dollar or **thaler** (mə rē′ə tə rē′sə), the Levant dollar. [< *Maria Theresa*, 1717–1780, queen of Bohemia and Hungary from 1740 to 1780]

mar·i·cul·ture (mar′ə kul′chər), *n.* the development of the resources of the sea, especially in regard to its food potential. [< Latin *maris* sea + *cultūra* culture]

mar·i·gold (mar′ə gōld), *n.* **1.** a plant of the composite family with yellow, orange, brownish, or red flowers. See picture under **bract.** **2.** the flower. [Middle English *mary-goulden* < (the Virgin) *Mary* + *gold*]

mar·i·jua·na or **mar·i·hua·na** (mar′ə wä′nə), *n.* **1.** the hemp plant; Indian hemp. **2.** a poisonous drug made from its dried leaves and flowers, smoked in cigarettes as a narcotic; hashish. [American English < Mexican Spanish *mariguana, marihuana*]

ma·rim·ba (mə rim′bə), *n.* a musical instrument somewhat like a xylophone, consisting of small bars of hard wood that produce different sounds when they are struck with drumsticks. [ultimately < a Bantu word]

Marimba

ma·rim·e·ter (mə rim′ə tər), *n. Nautical.* a device for taking soundings. [< Latin *mare, maris* sea + English *-meter*]

ma·ri·na (mə rē′nə), *n.* a small-boat basin where supplies and moorings are available, having a service station and frequently other facilities such as sleeping accommodations, restaurant, stores, and amusements. [< Spanish, or Italian *marina* shore, coast < Latin *marīna;* see MARINE]

mar·i·nade (*n.* mar′ə nād′; *v.* mar′ə nād), *n.*, *v.*, **-nad·ed, -nad·ing.** —*n.* **1.** a spiced vinegar, wine, or oil used to pickle meat or fish. **2.** meat or fish pickled in this. —*v.t.* marinate. [< French *marinade* < *mariner* to marinate]

ma·ri·na·ra (mar′ə nar′ə), *n.* a sauce flavored with tomatoes and garlic, used in Italian cuisine: *The spaghetti, a great specialty, is presented with the usual sauces—mushroom, meat, marinara, tomato* (New York Times). [< Italian *marinare* to marinate < French *mariner;* see MARINATE]

mar·i·nate (mar′ə nāt), *v.t.*, **-nat·ed, -nat·ing.** **1.** to soak (food) in brine or marinade. **2.** to soak in oil and vinegar. [< French *mariner* (with English *-ate*[1]) to pickle in (sea)brine < Old French *marin*, adjective, marine]

mar·i·na·tion (mar′ə nā′shən), *n.* the act or process of marinating.

ma·rine (mə rēn′), *adj.* **1.** of the sea; found in the sea; produced by the sea: *Seals and whales are marine animals.* **2.** of or having to do with shipping; maritime: *marine law.* **3.** of or having to do with a navy; naval: *marine power.* **4.** for use at sea, on a ship, etc.: *marine supplies, a marine engine.* **5. a.** of or having to do with ships, sailors, etc.: *marine lore.* **b.** of or having to do with navigation at sea: *a marine compass.* **6. a.** serving or trained to serve as a marine. **b.** of or having to do with a marine or marines. **7.** underwater.
—*n.* **1.** shipping; fleet: *our merchant marine.* **2. a.** a soldier formerly serving only at sea, now also participating in land and air action. **b.** Also, **Marine.** a member of the Marine Corps. **3.** a picture of the sea, ships at sea, etc.; seascape: *His first solo show in five years comprises portraits, landscapes, and marines* (New Yorker). **4.** the government department of naval affairs in France and some other European countries.

tell that to the marines, *Informal.* an expression of contemptuous disbelief, originally implying an amount of credulity on the part of marines that would not be found in sailors: *Tell that to the marines—the sailors won't believe it* (Scott).
[< Old French *marin* < Latin *marīnus* of the sea < *mare, maris* sea]
—**Syn.** *adj.* **1.** pelagic, oceanic.

marine blue, a navy blue that is somewhat purple or green in hue.

Marine Corps, a separate branch of the Armed Forces of the United States, independently responsible to the Secretary of the Navy.

marine insurance, insurance against damage to goods in transit and their means of transportation, especially in regard to shipwrecks or disasters at sea.

marine league, a measure of nautical distance equal to 3.45 miles.

mar·i·ner (mar′ə nər), *n.* **1.** a person who navigates a ship; sailor; seaman: . . . *as reassuring a beacon as a lighthouse to a lost mariner* (New Yorker). **2.** *Law.* any person employed on a ship. [< Anglo-French *mariner,* Old French *marinier* < *marin* marine]

Mar·i·ner (mar′ə nər), *n.* a senior rank in the Girl Scouts.

mariner's compass, a sensitive, accurate compass on a ship or boat, supported in a box or bowl on gimbals, placed for the helmsman to steer by.

Mar·i·ol·a·ter (mãr′ē ol′ə tər), *n.* a worshiper of the Virgin Mary.

Ma·ri·ol·a·trous (mãr′ē ol′ə trəs), *adj.* characterized by Mariolatry.

Mar·i·ol·a·try (mãr′ē ol′ə trē), *n.* worship of the Virgin Mary. [< Greek *Mariā* + *latreiā* worship]

Mar·i·o·log·i·cal (mãr′ē ə loj′ə kəl), *adj.* of or having to do with Mariology.

Mar·i·ol·o·gy (mãr′ē ol′ə jē), *n.* the body of theory or doctrine concerning the Virgin Mary.

mar·i·o·nette (mar′ē ə net′), *n.* a small doll made to imitate a person or thing and moved by strings or the hands. A marionette show is often given on a miniature stage. *At the end of the living room, a couple who worked a marionette show were dismantling their stage* (New Yorker). [< French *marionnette* < *Marion* (diminutive) < *Marie* Mary]

Marionette

Mar·i·po·sa lily or **tulip** (mar′ə pō′sə, -zə), **1.** any of a group of plants of the lily family with tuliplike flowers, growing in the western United States and in Mexico. **2.** the flower. [American English < Spanish *mariposa* butterfly]

mar·i·schal (mar′ə shəl), *n. Obsolete or Scottish.* marshal.

mar·ish (mar′ish), *Archaic.* —*n.* a marsh: *As long as sheep shall look from the side Of Oldtown Hills on marishes wide* (John Greenleaf Whittier). —*adj.* **1.** marshy: *I . . . found, not the looked-for village, but another marish bottom* (Robert Louis Stevenson). **2.** such as is found in marshes: *a matted, marish vegetation* (Robert Louis Stevenson). [Middle English *mareis* < Old French *marais;* origin uncertain]

Mar·ist (mãr′ist), *n.* a member of a Roman Catholic missionary and teaching order, founded in 1816, devoted to the Virgin Mary. —*adj.* of or belonging to the Marists. [< French *Mariste* < *Marie* the Virgin Mary]

mar·i·tal (mar′ə təl), *adj.* **1.** of or having to do with marriage: *A man and woman take marital vows when they marry.* **2.** of or having to do with a husband: *Providing for one's wife is a marital obligation.* [< Latin *marītālis* < *marītus* married man] —**mar′i·tal·ly,** *adv.* —**Syn. 1.** matrimonial, connubial. **2.** husbandly.

marital deduction, a tax deduction in the United States of up to one-half the net value of an estate which a deceased leaves entirely to his spouse.

mar·i·time (mar′ə tīm), *adj.* **1.** on or near the sea: *Boston is a maritime city.* **2.** living near the sea: *Many maritime peoples are fishermen.* **3.** of the sea; having to do with shipping and sailing: *Ships and sailors are governed by maritime law.* **4.** characteristic of a seaman; nautical: *Solomon Gills . . . was far from having a maritime appearance* (Dickens). [< Latin *maritimus* < *mare, maris* sea]

Mar·i·time (mar′ə tīm), *adj.* of, having to do with, or characteristic of the Maritime Provinces along the Atlantic Coast of Canada: *No wonder so many Maritime boys . . . sigh for home as the grown Adam sighed for the Garden* (Maclean's). —*n.* a Maritime Province.

maritime pine, pinaster.

Mar·i·tim·er (mar′ə tī′mər), *n.* a native or inhabitant of the Maritime Provinces.

ma·ri·vau·dage (mȧ rē vō dȧzh′), *n. French.* **1.** affectedly elegant, light, and amusing conversation: *Marivaudage, that coined word which is companion to persiflage and badinage, has come to denote the very essence of light and amusing lovers' talk* (Wall Street Journal). **2.** a style of writing employing euphuisms, figures of speech, epigrams, etc.

mar·jo·ram (mär′jə rəm), *n.* **1.** any of a group of fragrant herbs of the mint family related to the oregano: *Sweet marjoram is used in cooking.* **2.** oregano. [< unrecorded Old French *marjorane,* alteration of *maiorane,* learned borrowing from Medieval Latin *majorana,* also *majoraca,* perhaps < Latin *amāracus* bitter < Greek *amárakos*]

mark[1] (märk), *n.* **1.** a trace or impression made by some object on the surface of another, as a line, dot, spot, stain, dent, or scar: *the mark of an old wound.* **2. a.** a line, dot, etc., to show position: *the high-water mark. This mark shows how far you jumped.* **b.** the line that indicates where a race starts: *On the mark; get set; go! The race will start from the mark.* **3.** something that shows what or whose a thing is; sign; indication: *a laundry mark. Remove the price mark from your new suit. Courtesy is a mark of good breeding.* **4.** a written or printed stroke or sign: *a question mark. She took up her pen and made a few marks on the paper.* **5.** a grade or rating: *a mark of A in history.* **6.** a cross or other sign made by a person who cannot write his name: *Make your mark here. Dost thou sign thy name or make thy mark?* (Herman Melville). **7.** something to be aimed at; target; goal: *Both balls had passed through the lungs—the true mark in shooting buffalo* (Francis Parkman). *So I was a mark for plunder at once, And lost my cash . . .* (Rudyard Kipling). **8.** what is usual, proper, or expected; standard: *A tired person does not feel up to the mark.* **9.** influence; impression: *A great man leaves his mark on whatever he does.* **10.** eminence; importance; distinction: *A learned clerk, a man of mark, was this Thangbrand* (Longfellow). *There was nothing of high mark in this* (Dickens). **11.** *Nautical.* **a.** a piece of bunting, bit of leather, knot, etc., used to mark depths on a lead line. **b.** a Plimsoll mark. **12.** the jack or its position in the game of bowls. **13.** *British.* a model or class: *a heavy machine gun (Mark IV).* **14.** *Boxing.* the solar plexus. **15.** *British.* a registration of the sale of stocks. **16.** *Slang.* a person marked as good pickings; sucker: *I teased my way into the pockets of a thousand marks or two* (Newsweek). **17.** *Archaic.* a border or frontier. **18.** *Obsolete.* a landmark. **19.** *Obsolete.* a memorial stone.

beside the mark, a. not hitting the thing aimed at: *The bullet went beside the mark.* **b.** not to the point; off the subject; not relevant: *To reason with such a writer is like talking to a deaf man, who catches at a stray word, makes answer beside the mark, and is led further and further into error by every attempt to explain* (Macaulay).

hit the mark, a. to succeed in doing what one tried to do: *He hit the mark when he became president of the class.* **b.** to be exactly right: *Venerable was found . . . luckily hitting the mark, as a title neither too high nor too low* (Thomas Fuller).

make one's mark, to succeed; become famous: *That fellow's a gentleman's son . . . and he'll make his mark* (Ella L. Dorsey).

miss the mark, a. to fail to do what one tried to do: *Many a preacher misses the mark because, though he knows books, he does not know men* (John Stalker). **b.** to be not exactly right: *His answer to the arithmetic problem missed the mark.*

off the mark, a. missing the desired object or end: *The projections of the Government on these outlays, . . . turned out to be pretty far off the mark* (Wall Street Journal). **b.** off the subject; inaccurate: *I leave it to them equally to decide whether my very brief and necessarily incomplete summary of Bruner's ideas is as far off the mark as he claims* (New Yorker).

of mark, important; famous: *a man of mark. And left me in reputeless banishment, A fellow of no mark nor likelihood* (Shakespeare).

save or **bless the mark,** an exclamation of deprecation, apology, impatience, or contempt: *The best of my talents (bless the mark) shut up even from my own poor view* (Carlyle).

toe the mark, a. to stand with the tips of the toes touching a certain line, mark, etc., as before a race, contest, etc.: *The child toed the mark, ready to jump.* **b.** to conform to a certain standard, as of duty, conduct, etc.: *He began to think it was high time to toe the mark* (James K. Paulding).

wide of the mark, a. missing the thing aimed at by a considerable margin: *The shot fell wide of the mark.* **b.** irrelevant: *It may, however, be . . . very wide of the mark when applied to the case of out-of-door labourers* (John R. McCulloch).

—*v.t.* **1.** to give grades to; rate: *to mark examination papers.* **2.** to put a mark or marks on: *Be careful not to mark the table.* **3.** to trace or form by marks or as if by marks. **4.** to show by a mark or as if by marks: *They never marked a man for death* (Rudyard Kipling). *Melancholy mark'd him for her own* (Thomas Gray). **5.** to show clearly; indicate; manifest: *A frown marked her disapproval. A tall pine marks the beginning of the trail.* **6.** to distinguish; set off; characterize: *Many important discoveries mark the last 150 years. His character was marked by profligacy, insolence, and ingratitude* (James Boswell). **7.** to pay attention to; notice; observe: *Mark well my words; his plan will fail. Full well I mark'd the features of his face* (Alexander Pope). *Mark my bidding, and be safe* (Charles Brockden Brown). *The cruellest error of the revolutionary bodies has been their failure to mark the limits of property rights* (Edmund Wilson). **8.** to keep (the score); record. **9.** to put a price mark on; tag: *All goods are plainly marked for sale.* **10.** to register: *The thermometer marked 90° F.* **11.** *British.* to register (a sale of stocks) so as to put it on the official price list: *On Tuesday 823 bargains were marked* (Economist). —*v.i.* **1.** to make a mark or marks. **2.** to pay attention; take notice; consider: *Mark, I pray you, and see how this man seeketh mischief* (I Kings 20:7). **3.** to keep the score in a game.

mark down, a. to write down; note down: *to mark down an appointment in a datebook.* **b.** to mark for sale at a lower price: *We have selected over $30,000 of our elegant stock and marked them down 50 per cent* (Chicago Tribune). **c.** to note where (game) has gone to cover: *It is no good to talk of having marked birds down, unless you have distinctly seen a certain toss up of the wings as they pitch* (Cornhill Magazine).

mark off or **out, a.** to make lines, etc., to show the position of or to separate: *We marked out the tennis court. The hedge marks off one yard from another.* **b.** to differentiate; distinguish: *Thus, in the last resort, what marks human history off from natural history is the fact that it is—quite deliberately—man-centered* (New Yorker).

mark out for, to set aside for; select for: *The ringleaders were marked out for punishment.*

mark up, a. to add; put: *to mark up the score.* **b.** to mark for sale at a higher price: *The prices of venison and other game was so far "marked up" that gold . . . was charged for salmon* (American Naturalist).

[Old English *mearc* boundary, mark, limit of space or time. Compare MARCH[2].]

—**Syn.** *n.* **3. Mark, sign, token,** mean an indication of something not visible or readily apparent. **Mark** particularly suggests an indication of the character of the thing: *Generosity is a mark of greatness.* **Sign** is the general word, applying to any indication, mark, or token, such as of quality, idea, or mental or physical state: *We could see no signs of life.* **Token** applies especially to something that stands as a reminder or promise of something else, as of a feeling or an event: *This gift is a token of my love.* –*v.t.* **7.** note, heed, regard, consider.

mark[2] (märk), *n.* **1.** a unit of money of Germany, now called the Deutsche mark. **2.** a coin or paper note equal to the mark. *Abbr.:* M. **3.** an old weight for gold and silver, equal to 8 ounces. **4.** a markka. **5.** a former Scottish silver coin, worth slightly more than 13 shillings. [Old English *mearc*, perhaps < Germanic (compare Middle High German *marke*)]

Mark (märk), *n.* **1.** one of the four Evangelists, a fellow worker with the Apostle Paul and the Apostle Peter; Saint Mark: *Chronologically the oldest gospel, that of Mark, does not mention the idea* [*virgin birth*] (Time). **2.** the second book of the New Testament, attributed to the Apostle Mark. It tells the story of the life of Christ. **3. King,** *Arthurian Legend.* a king of Cornwall, the uncle of Tristan and husband of Iseult. [< Latin *Mārcus*, a Roman praenomen]

mark·a·bil·i·ty (mär′kə bil′ə tē), *n.* markable quality or condition.

mark·a·ble (mär′kə bəl), *adj.* worthy or capable of being marked or noted: *The markable transparent plastic contour sheets demonstrate elevations in 3-D* (Science News Letter).

mark·down (märk′doun′), *n.* **1.** a decrease in the price of an article: *Spurts of selling—mostly in small blocks—touched off almost hourly markdowns* (Wall Street Journal). **2.** the amount of this decrease. *—adj.* of, having to do with, or characteristic of a markdown: *markdown prices.*

marked (märkt), *adj.* **1.** having a mark or marks on it: *a marked table, marked money.* **2.** very noticeable; very clear; easily recognized: *There is a marked difference between grapes and oranges.* **3.** distinguished or singled out as if by a mark: *Even as a youth he was marked for success.*
—**Syn. 2.** prominent, conspicuous, outstanding.

mark·ed·ly (mär′kid lē), *adv.* in a marked manner or degree; conspicuously; noticeably; plainly: *After this, the air temperature is known to rise markedly* (New Scientist).

marked man, a person watched or made note of as an object of suspicion, hatred, or vengeance: *When the gang discovered his hiding place, he knew he was a marked man.*

mark·ed·ness (mär′kid nis), *n.* marked condition.

mark·er (mär′kər), *n.* **1.** a person or thing that marks. **2.** a person or device that keeps the score in a game. **3.** *Sports.* **a.** a line or mark indicating position on a playing field: *. . . went over standing up from the 7-yard marker . . .* (New York Times). **b.** a score: *. . . accounted for the first West Point marker on a 2-yard plunge . . .* (New York Times). **4.** a counter, etc., used in card games. **5.** a bookmark: *Put a marker in that book . . . page seventy-four* (Samuel Lover). **6.** *U.S. Slang.* a pledge of payment, especially of a gambling debt; an I.O.U.

mar·ket (mär′kit), *n.* **1.** a meeting of people for buying and selling: *To market, to market, To buy a fat pig* (Nursery Rhyme). **2.** the people so gathered: *Excitement stirred the market.* **3.** a space or building in which provisions, cattle, etc., are shown for sale: *. . . the busy market square, where piles of vari-colored fruits and vegetables gleam* (Atlantic). **4.** a store for the sale of provisions: *a meat market.* **5.** trade, especially as regards a particular article: *the cotton market, the best shoes in the market, market research.* **6.** brokers or other persons trading extensively in a particular commodity: *the grain market.* **7.** an opportunity to sell or buy: *to lose one's market. There is always a market for wheat. Do you know, Considering the market, there are more Poems produced than any other thing?* (Robert Frost). **8.** a demand (for something); price offered: *a good market.* **9.** a region where goods can be sold: *Africa and Asia are new markets for many products.*

at the market, at the price current when a broker sells or buys (stock, etc.) for a customer: *Jackson found that brokers had put in orders to buy 77,000 shares at the market* (New Yorker).

be in the market for, to be a possible buyer of: *If you are in the market for a used car, that dealer has some fine bargains.*

glut the market, to offer on a market a quantity of a commodity, stock, etc., so greatly in excess of demand as to make the item unsalable except at a very low price: *The price for wheat dropped when the market was glutted with it.*

play the market, to speculate on the stock exchange: *He has been playing the market on tips.*

price out of the market, to lose business by setting a price above that of competitors or above what buyers will pay: *Many U.S. firms are pricing themselves out of the Far Eastern Market because of high prices and their reluctance to accept deferred payments.* (Wall Street Journal).
—v.i. to buy or sell in a market. *—v.t.* **1.** to sell: *The farmer cannot market all of his cotton.* **2.** to carry or send to market: *The peasants marketed all their surplus produce.*
—adj. of, having to do with, or characteristic of a market: *Canned food bargains, dumped into the housewife's market basket . . .* (Wall Street Journal).
[< Old North French *market*, Old French *marchiet* < Latin *mercātus, -ūs* trade, market < *mercārī* to trade, deal in < *merx, mercis* merchandise]

mar·ket·a·bil·i·ty (mär′kə tə bil′ə tē), *n.* the quality of being marketable: *Voting rights would substantially increase the marketability of the shares* (Wall Street Journal).

mar·ket·a·ble (mär′kə tə bəl), *adj.* **1.** that can be sold; salable: *Farmers therefore use less time and less food to bring stock to marketable weight* (Science News). **2.** of or having to do with buying or selling.

mar·ket·a·bly (mär′kə tə blē), *adv.* in a marketable manner: *To make their oranges marketably orange, packers can do two things . . .* (New Yorker).

market analysis, the study of the extent, characteristics, and potential of a given market.

market analyst, a person who is skilled in or practices market analysis.

mar·ke·teer (mär′kə tir′), *n.* a person who sells in a market.

mar·ket·er (mär′kə tər), *n.* **1.** a person who goes to market: *. . . They could not walk side by side in that throng of marketers—women with shopping baskets, women pushing . . .* (New Yorker). **2.** a person who buys or sells in a market: *Happily for the marketers, Americans by nature seem to relish learning to want new things* (Atlantic).

market garden, a truck farm: *The market gardens of the kolkhoz, which provide all Ashkhabad with vegetables, are right outside the city* (Atlantic).

market gardener, a truck farmer.

market house, a building in which a market is held.

mar·ket·ing (mär′kə ting), *n.* **1.** a trading in a market; buying or selling: *Marketings for the first two days of the week dwindled to the lowest point for a like period in more than three years* (Wall Street Journal). **2.** something bought or sold in a market. **3.** the bringing of merchandise, livestock, etc., to market: *The heaviest mid-week marketings in nearly four years depressed live hog prices . . .* (Wall Street Journal). **4.** a shopping for groceries, small items, etc.: *Sometimes we took her cakes for tea, or a pot of soup, or did her marketing* (New Yorker).
—adj. of, having to do with, or characteristic of marketing: *the advertising world's cadres of marketing men.*

marketing quota, *U.S.* a measure designed to cope with farm surpluses by restricting price support to only that portion of a farmer's product which was grown on his allotted acreage: *Marketing quotas theoretically limit the farmer's marketing to the amount of the crop raised on his allotted acres, and carry a much stiffer penalty for violation than the acreage allotments* (Wall Street Journal).

market letter, *U.S.* a newsletter containing information and advice on the stock market, issued by a stockbroker or investment advisory firm to its customers.

mar·ket·man (mär′kit man′), *n., pl.* **-men.** **1.** a man who sells provisions, etc., in a market. **2.** a person who buys in a market.

market order, an order to buy or sell a commodity, stock, etc., at whatever price may be current when the transaction is completed.

market place, 1. the place where a market is held, usually an open space or a square: *In open market place produced they me, To be a public spectacle to all* (Shakespeare). **2.** the world of commerce: *"The inexorable law of the market place," he argued, "is that a business which cannot compete, cannot survive"* (Wall Street Journal).

market price, the price that an article brings when sold; current price.

market research, the study of what makes people buy or not buy a product, when they do it, how long they may continue, and other similar buying habits.

mar·ket·stead (mär′kit sted), *n. Archaic.* a market place.

market town, a town in which markets are held at stated times, by privilege, as in England: *The small central-place market town usually has only one distinct primary urban function . . . which serves more than just the local settlement* (Finch and Trewartha).

market value, the worth of a given commodity, stock, etc., established as an average of the market prices over a certain period of time: *The discovery that the painting of St. Jerome is the work of the Flemish master has "vastly increased the market value" of the work, according to Edgar P. Richardson, director of the institute* (New York Times).

mar·ket·wise (mär′kit wīz′), *adv.* **1.** with regard to the stock market: *. . . the steel news yesterday had virtually no effect marketwise* (Baltimore Sun). **2.** in the market; commercially: *Mr. Morgan . . . hopes that chemical products (other than cellulose) derived from wood may become valuable marketwise* (Wall Street Journal).

mar·khor (mär′kôr), *n.* a large, wild goat of the Himalaya regions, with long, spirally twisted horns. [< Persian *mārkhōr*]

Markhor
(about 3½ ft. high at the shoulder)

mark·ing (mär′king), *n.* **1.** a mark or marks. **2.** an arrangement of marks. **3.** the act of a person or thing that marks.

mark·ka (märk′kä), *n., pl.* **-kaa** (kä). the basic Finnish monetary unit, worth about 31½ cents. [< Finnish *markka* < Swedish *mark*, probably < Old Icelandic *mork*]

Mar·kov chain (mär′kôf), *Statistics.* a succession of random events each of which is determined by the event immediately preceding it. [< Andrei *Markov*, 1856-1922, a Russian mathematician]

marks·man (märks′mən), *n., pl.* **-men. 1. a.** a person who shoots: *Some marksmen shoot badly.* **b.** a person who shoots well: *He is noted as a marksman.* **2.** a soldier in the United States Army having the lowest range of qualifying scores in firing a weapon.

marks·man·ship (märks′mən ship), *n.* the art or skill of a marksman; skill in shooting: *Ray had won a marksmanship medal at summer camp* (Time).

mark·up (märk′up′), *n.* **1.** an increase in the price of an article: *The concern is getting a slightly higher gross markup on shoes this year* (Wall Street Journal). **2.** the amount of this increase. **3.** the percentage or amount added to the cost to take care of profit and overhead when establishing the selling price of a commodity: *Many large firms are able to work on narrow markups because of enormous turnover.*

mark·wor·thy (märk′wėr′ᴛʜē), *adj.* worthy to be marked or noticed; noteworthy.

marl[1] (märl), *n.* **1.** a rock soil consisting usually of clay, sand, and calcium carbonate, used in making cement and as a fertilizer. **2.** *Poetic.* earth: *to seize upon his foe flat lying on the marl* (Edmund Spenser). *—v.t.* to fertilize with marl. [< Old French *marle* < Medieval Latin *margila* < Latin *marga*, probably < a Celtic word]

marl[2] (märl), *v.t.* to wind, cover, or fasten with marline. [< Dutch *marlen* (apparently frequentative) < Middle Dutch *merren* to tie]

mar·la·ceous (mär lā′shəs), *adj.* of or resembling marl.

marled (märld), *adj. Scottish.* marbled; mottled.

mar·lin (mär′lən), *n., pl.* **-lins** or (*collectively*) **-lin. 1.** any of various large sea fishes related to the swordfishes and sailfishes: *The Wanderer . . . was damaged by the sword of a blue marlin as they lay becalmed off the Azores* (London Times). **2.** a spearfish. [short for *marlinespike* (because of its long snout)]

mar·line (mär′lən), *n.* a small cord of two strands wound around the ends of a rope to keep it from fraying. [< Dutch *marlijn* < *marren* to tie + *lijn* line]

mar·line·spike or **mar·lin·spike** (mär′lən spīk′), *n.* a pointed iron tool used by sailors to separate the strands of a rope in splicing, etc.

Marlinespike

mar·ling (mär′ling), *n.* marline.
mar·ling·spike (mär′ling spīk′), *n.* marlinespike.
marl·ite (mär′līt), *n.* a variety of marl that resists the action of the air.
marl·it·ic (mär lit′ik), *adj.* of or like marlite.
Mar·lo·vi·an (mär lō′vē ən), *adj.* of, having to do with, or characteristic of the English dramatist and poet Christopher Marlowe or his work: *He is too eager in straining for Marlovian echoes in Shakespeare* (Manchester Guardian Weekly).
marl·stone (märl′stōn′), *n.* a rock consisting of a hardened mixture of clay, calcium carbonate, and other minerals: *. . . the marlstone formations of the Colorado region* (Gerald L. Farrar).
marl·y[1] (mär′lē), *adj.,* **marl·i·er, marl·i·est.** of, like, or full of marl.
marl·y[2] (mär′lē), *adj.,* **marl·i·er, marl·i·est.** *Scottish.* marbled; mottled.
mar·ma·lade (mär′mə lād), *n.* a preserve like jam, made of oranges or of other fruit. The peel is usually sliced up and boiled with the fruit. [< Middle French *marmelade* < Portuguese *marmelada* < *marmelo* quince < Latin *melimēlum* < Greek *melímēlon* < *méli* honey + *mêlon* apple]
marmalade cat, a tabby cat with stripes of an orange color like that of marmalade: *. . . a marmalade cat as big as a tiger* (Atlantic).
marmalade tree, an evergreen Central American tree of the sapodilla family that yields a fruit whose pulp resembles marmalade; mammee sapota. The fruit is used in preserves.
mar·mite (mär′mīt, mär mēt′), *n.* **1.** an earthenware pot in which soups are made and served: *A fireplace wide and deep and equipped with a . . . metal rod from which an earthenware marmite hangs* (New York Times). **2.** a yeast extract that has a rich vitamin content and acts as an antineuritic agent. [< French *marmite*]
mar·mo·re·al (mär môr′ē əl, -mōr′-), *adj.* **1.** of marble. **2.** like marble; cold; smooth; white: *The thronging constellations rush in crowds, Paving with fire the sky and the marmoreal floods* (Shelley). [< Latin *marmoreus* (< *marmor, -oris* marble) + English *-al*[1]]
mar·mo·re·an (mär môr′ē ən, -mōr′-), *adj.* marmoreal: *"Vast, marmorean, plate-glassy" —so Henry James . . . recalled this first architectural blockbuster of Stewart's* (New Yorker).
mar·mo·ri·za·tion (mär′mə rə zā′shən), *n.* **1.** the process of marmorizing. **2.** a being marmorized.
mar·mo·rize (mär′mə rīz), *v.t.,* **-rized, -riz·ing.** *Geology.* to convert (sedimentary limestone) into marble. [< Latin *marmor* marble + English *-ize*]
mar·mose (mär′mōs), *n.* any of several small, pouchless, South American opossums that carry the young on the back. [< French *marmose*]
mar·mo·set (mär′mə zet), *n.* any of a group of very small, Central or South American monkeys, including the tamarins, having soft, thick fur and a long, bushy tail. [< Old French *marmouset* grotesque figurine < *merme* under age < Latin *minimus* very small; influenced by Greek *mormōtós* fearful]

Marmoset (including tail, 16 in. long)

mar·mot (mär′mət), *n.* any of a group of burrowing rodents with thick bodies and short tails, including the woodchuck of North America and several European and Asiatic species. [< French *marmotte* < unrecorded Old French *murmont* < Vulgar Latin *mūrem montis* mouse of the mountain < Latin *mūs, mūris* mouse, and *mōns, montis* mountain]

Marmot (including tail, 2½ ft. long)

mar·o·cain (mar′ə kān), *n.* a dress fabric of silk and wool or cotton, having a texture like crepe. [< French *maroquin* (originally) having to do with Morocco < *Maroc* Morocco]
Mar·o·nite (mar′ə nīt), *n.* one of a group of Syrian Christians in communion with the Roman Catholic Church: *The Maronite congregation conducts its services in Syriac* (London Times). [< Late Latin *Marōnīta* < *Marōn,* who founded the sect during the 300's]
ma·roon[1] (mə rün′), *n., adj.* very dark brownish-red. [< Middle French *marron* < Italian *marrone* chestnut]
ma·roon[2] (mə rün′), *v.t.* **1.** to put (a person) ashore in a lonely place and leave him there: *Pirates used to maroon people on desert islands.* **2.** to leave in a lonely, helpless position: *The torrent rushed . . . through the* [*station*] *yard, . . . marooning several hundred passengers* (New York Post). —*v.i. Southern U.S.* to camp out for several days. [American English, (originally) to camp out < noun]
—*n.* **1.** a descendant of escaped Negro slaves living in the West Indies and Dutch Guiana. **2.** an escaped Negro slave, an ancestor of these people. **3.** a person who is marooned.
[< French *marron,* perhaps < American Spanish *cimarrón* wild; seeking refuge in the bushes on the mountains < Old Spanish *cimarra* bushes < *cima* summit < Latin *cȳma* swelling, cyma]
ma·roon·er (mə rü′nər), *n.* **1.** a person who maroons. **2.** a person who is marooned; maroon.
mar·plot (mär′plot′), *n.* a person who spoils some plan by meddling or blundering. [< *mar* + *plot*]
Marq., **1.** marquess. **2.** marquis.
marque[1] (märk), *n.* **1.** official permission from a government to capture enemy merchant ships. **2.** *Obsolete.* reprisal. [< dialectal Middle French *marque* < Old Provençal *marca* reprisal < *marcar* seize as a pledge, ultimately < a Germanic word]
marque[2] (märk), *n. British.* a mark; make; brand: *Pride of ownership has for decades made this dignified marque the choice of the discriminating motorist . . .* (Sunday Times). [< French *marque*]
mar·quee (mär kē′), *n.* **1.** *Especially British.* a large tent with sides that can be rolled up, often put up for some outdoor entertainment or exhibition. **2.** a rooflike shelter over an entrance, especially of a theater, hotel, etc.: *At eight o'clock I'd been waiting fifteen minutes under the marquee of the Bellevue theatre* (Maclean's). [new singular < French *marquise* < Old French (*tente*) *marquise* large tent for officers, (literally) for a marquis]

Theater Marquee (def. 2)

mar·que·sa (mär kā′sä), *n. Spanish.* a marchioness.
Mar·que·san (mär kā′zən, -sən), *adj.* of or having to do with the Marquesas Islands, in the South Pacific. —*n.* a native or inhabitant of the Marquesas Islands.
mar·quess (mär′kwis), *n. Especially British.* marquis.
mar·quess·ate (mär′kwə sāt), *n. Especially British.* marquisate.
mar·que·te·rie (mär′kə trē), *n.* marquetry.
mar·que·try (mär′kə trē), *n., pl.* **-tries.** decoration made with thin pieces of wood, ivory, metal, etc., fitted together to form a design on furniture: *a marquetry writing desk* (New Yorker). [< Middle French *marqueterie* < *marqueter* to inlay < *marque* mark[1]]
mar·quis (mär′kwis; *French* mȧr kē′), *n.* a nobleman ranking below a duke and above an earl or count. [< Old French *marquis,* alteration of earlier *marchis* < Medieval Latin *marchensis* (count) of the marches < *marcha* march[2]]
mar·quis·ate (mär′kwə zit), *n.* **1.** the position or rank of marquis. **2.** the territory governed by a marquis.
mar·quise (mär kēz′), *n.* **1.** the wife or widow of a marquis. **2.** a woman equal in rank to a marquis. **3. a.** a pointed oval shape into which diamonds or other gems are frequently cut. **b.** a ring setting of this shape. **4.** a marquee. **5.** an upholstered love seat. [< French *marquise,* Old French *marchise,* feminine of *marquis* marquis]
marquise ring, a finger ring set with a cluster of gems forming a pointed oval.
mar·qui·sette (mär′kə zet′, -kwə-), *n.* a very thin fabric with square meshes, made of cotton, silk, rayon, nylon, etc., and often used for window draperies, dresses, etc. [< French *marquisette* (diminutive) < *marquise* marquise]
Marquis of Queens·ber·ry rules (kwēnz′ber′ē, -bər-), **1.** the standard rules and provisions of modern boxing, formulated by the Marquis of Queensberry in 1867. **2.** any similar set of rules governing a game, contest, etc.: *We are forced to fight by Marquis of Queensberry rules while the criminals are permitted to gouge and bite* (Time).
mar·ram grass (mar′əm), a tall, coarse, perennial beach grass native to Europe, sometimes sown to prevent the drifting of sand masses. [< Scandinavian (compare Old Icelandic *maralmr* < *marr* sea + *halmr* haulm)]
mar·ra·no (mə rä′nō), *n., pl.* **-nos.** a Christianized Jew of medieval Spain, especially one who only professed conversion to escape persecution by the Inquisition. [< Spanish *marrano* pig]
mar·rer (mär′ər), *n.* a person who mars.
mar·riage (mar′ij), *n.* **1.** a living together as husband and wife; relation between husband and wife; married life: [*Their*] *marriage certainly did not seem made in heaven* (Time). **2.** the ceremony of being married; a marrying; a wedding. **3.** a close union: *the marriage of music and drama in opera.* **4.** the king and queen of the same suit in pinochle, bezique, etc. **5.** the merger of two business firms, or the acquisition of one by the other: *This major bank marriage is the fourth in less than six months* (Wall Street Journal). [< Old French *mariage* < *marier;* see MARRY[1]]
—**Syn. 1, 2. Marriage, matrimony, wedding** mean the state of being married or the act of marrying. **Marriage** is the general and common word applying to the institution, the legal and spiritual relation, the state of being married, or, less often, the ceremony. **Matrimony** is the formal and religious word, and applies especially to the spiritual relation or the religious ceremony (sacrament). **Wedding** is the common word for the ceremony or celebration.
mar·riage·a·bil·i·ty (mar′i jə bil′ə tē), *n.* a being marriageable.
mar·riage·a·ble (mar′i jə bəl), *adj.* fit for marriage; old enough to marry: *a marriageable girl.* —**mar′riage·a·ble·ness,** *n.* —**Syn.** nubile.
marriage broker, a person whose business is to arrange marriages.
marriage brokerage or **brokage,** the business of a marriage broker.
marriage bureau, marriage brokerage: *Many marriage bureaus were in essence offering clients, in consideration of a fee, introductions to prospective partners* (London Times).
marriage of convenience, mariage de convenance.
marriage portion, a dowry.
mar·ried (mar′ēd), *adj.* **1.** living together as husband and wife: *a married couple.* **2.** having a husband or wife: *a married man. Abbr.:* m. **3.** of or having to do with marriage; of husbands and wives: *Married life has many rewards.* **4.** closely united.
—*n.* **marrieds,** a married couple: *Helene and Robert Alexander are attractive young marrieds living in Palm Springs, Calif.* (New Yorker).
—**Syn.** *adj.* **3.** connubial, matrimonial.
mar·ri·er (mar′ē ər), *n.* a person who marries.
mar·ring·ly (mär′ing lē), *adv.* so as to mar or spoil.

mar·ron (mar′ən; *French* mȧ rôN′), *n.* a large, sweet European chestnut, often used in cooking, or candied or preserved in syrup. [< French *marron* < Italian *marrone.* Compare MAROON[1].]

mar·rons gla·cés (mȧ rôN′ glȧ sā′), *French.* marrons glazed with sugar or preserved in a sugar syrup: *Her admirers sent her boxes of marrons glacés* (Punch).

mar·row[1] (mar′ō), *n.* **1.** the soft, vascular, fatty tissue that fills the cavities of most bones; the medulla. **2.** this tissue obtained from animal bones and used as food. **3.** the inmost or essential part: *The icy wind chilled me to the marrow.* **4.** vitality; strength: *It takes the marrow out of a man* (Benjamin Disraeli). **5. a.** *British.* vegetable marrow. **b.** *U.S.* marrow squash. [Old English *mearg*]

mar·row[2] (mar′ō), *n. Scottish and British Dialect.* **1.** a mate; companion; associate. **2.** an equal; match. [origin uncertain. Compare Old Icelandic *margr* friendly, communicative.]

mar·row·bone (mar′ō bōn′), *n.* a bone containing edible marrow.

marrowbones, a. knees: *I jest flopped down on my marrowbones* (John Hay). **b.** crossbones: *I . . . sailed under the black flag and marrowbones* (Scott).

mar·row·fat (mar′ō fat′), *n.*, or **marrowfat pea, 1.** a tall, late variety of pea having a large, rich seed. **2.** its seed, used for food.

marrow pea, the marrowfat.

marrow squash, *U.S.* any of a group of fine-grained squashes having an oblong shape.

mar·row·y (mar′ō ē), *adj.* of, like, or full of marrow.

mar·ry[1] (mar′ē), *v.*, **-ried, -ry·ing.** *—v.t.* **1.** to join as husband and wife: *The minister married them.* **2.** to take as husband or wife: *John married Grace.* **3.** to give in marriage: *She has married all her daughters.* **4.** to unite closely. **5.** *Nautical.* to sew together or join (two ropes) without increasing the diameter. *—v.i.* **1.** to take a husband or wife; become married: *She married late in life.* **2.** to become closely united: *By that old bridge where the waters marry* (Tennyson). [< Old French *marier* < Latin *marītāre* < *marītus* husband]

mar·ry[2] (mar′ē), *interj. Archaic.* an exclamation showing surprise, indignation, etc.: *Marry, hang the idiot . . . to bring me such stuff* (Oliver Goldsmith). [< (the Virgin) *Mary*]

Mars (märz), *n.* **1.** the Roman god of war, son of Jupiter and Juno and husband or lover of Venus, identified with the Greek god Ares. **2.** war. **3.** the planet next in order beyond the earth and the fourth in distance from the sun. Its orbit about the sun lies between those of the earth and Jupiter and takes 687 days to complete, at an average distance from the sun of about 141,640,000 miles. Its mean diameter is 4,220 miles. *Mars is notable among the planets and stars for its red color* (World Book Encyclopedia). *Symbol:* ♂

Mar·sa·la (mär sä′lä), *n.* a light wine resembling sherry, originating in Marsala, Sicily.

Mar·seil·laise (mär′sə lāz′; *French* mȧr seyez′), *n.* the French national anthem, written in 1792 during the French Revolution by Claude Joseph Rouget de Lisle. [< French (*chanson*) *marseillaise* < the city of *Marseilles* (because first sung by a group from there)]

mar·seilles (mär sālz′), *n.* a thick cotton cloth woven in figures or stripes, used for bedspreads, etc.: *It is only in Switzerland that you can find the superb weaving that gave the original marseilles such a vogue* (New Yorker). [< *Marseilles,* a city in France]

marsh (märsh), *n.* low land covered at times by water; soft, wet land; swamp. *—adj.* **1.** marshy. **2.** living in marshes: *a marsh plant.* [Old English *mersc,* related to *mere* lake, mere[2]] —**Syn.** *n.* bog.

mar·shal (mär′shəl), *n.*, *v.*, **-shaled, shal·ing** or (*especially British*) **-shalled, -shal·ling.** *—n.* **1. a.** an officer of various kinds, especially a police officer: *A United States marshal is an officer of a Federal court whose duties are like those of a sheriff.* **b.** (in some states) a police officer in a city or town with duties similar to those of a sheriff or constable, including serving processes, etc. **c.** (in some cities) the chief of police or head of the fire department. **2.** an officer in an army: *A Marshal of France is a general of the highest rank in the French Army.* **3.** a person who arranges the order of march in a parade. **4.** a person in charge of events or ceremonies, as at a banquet, etc. **5.** one of the highest officials of a royal household or court, responsible in the Middle Ages for military affairs.

—v.t. **1.** to arrange in order: *The speaker won the argument because he marshaled his facts well. So to the office in the evening to marshal my papers* (Samuel Pepys). **2.** to arrange in military order; prepare for war. **3.** to conduct with ceremony; lead formally; usher: *We were marshaled before the king. The abbot marshalled him to the door of Augustine's chamber* (Scott). **4.** *Heraldry.* **a.** to combine (two or more coats of arms) upon one shield so as to form a single composition. **b.** to associate (accessories) with a shield of arms so as to form a complete composition.

—v.i. to take up positions in proper order: *no marshaling troop, no bivouac song* (Joaquin Miller).

[< Old French *mareschal* < Late Latin *mariscalcus* groom < Germanic (compare Old High German *marahscalc* < *marah* horse + *scalc* servant)] —**mar′shal·er,** *especially British,* **mar′shal·ler,** *n.*

mar·shal·cy (mär′shəl sē), *n.*, *pl.* **-cies.** the office, rank, or position of a marshal.

marshaling yard, classification yard.

Mar·shal·lese (mär′shə lēz′, -lēs′), *adj.* of or having to do with the Marshall Islands, a group of islands in the north Pacific, under U.S. trusteeship: *the Marshallese people, the Marshallese Congress.*

Mar·shall Plan (mär′shəl), a program for economic recovery of Europe after World War II. It ended in 1951. [< George C. *Marshall,* 1880-1959, Secretary of State 1947-1949, who advanced the plan]

Mar·shal·sea (mär′shəl sē), *n.* **1.** a former debtor's prison in London, abolished in 1842. **2.** a court held by the steward and marshal of the British royal household, originally for the king's servants, abolished in 1849. [alteration of Middle English *mareschalcie* < Anglo-French, Old French *mareschaucie* < Late Latin *mariscalcus;* see MARSHAL]

mar·shal·ship (mär′shəl ship), *n.* marshalcy.

marsh·buck (märsh′buk′), *n.*, *pl.* **-bucks** or (*collectively*) **-buck.** sitatunga.

marsh buggy, an amphibious vehicle much like an automobile, with mammoth tires, which can travel on land or through water, mud, swamps, etc.

marsh cress, a North American plant of the mustard family that grows in moist places.

marsh elder, any of a group of herbs or shrubs of the composite family with heads of greenish-white flowers, growing in coastal marshes and sands.

marsh·fire (märsh′fīr′), *n.* ignis fatuus; will-o'-the-wisp.

marsh gas, a gas formed by the decomposition of organic substances in marshes; methane.

marsh hare, *U.S.* a muskrat.

marsh harrier, 1. a large reddish-brown harrier of the Old World that lives in marshes and feeds on small animals. **2.** the marsh hawk.

marsh hawk, the only harrier in North America, gray or brownish with a white patch on the rump. It lives in open and marshy regions and feeds on mice, frogs, snakes, etc.

Marsh Hawk or marsh harrier (including tail, 19 in. long; wingspread, 42 in.)

marsh hen, any of certain birds that live in marshes, such as the coot and bittern.

marsh·i·ness (mär′shē nis), *n.* marshy state.

marsh·land (märsh′land′, -lənd), *n.* marshy land: *The whole place was marshland, and everything is built on concrete piles* (Observer).

marsh·land·er (märsh′lan′dər, -lən-), *n.* an inhabitant of a marshland.

marsh mallow, a shrubby herb of the mallow family that grows in marshy places. It has pink flowers and a root that is used in medicine to soothe or protect irritated mucous tissues.

marsh·mal·low (märsh′mal′ō, -mel′-), *n.* **1.** a soft, white, spongy candy, covered with powdered sugar, made from corn syrup, sugar, starch, and gelatin. **2.** a confection made from the root of the marsh mallow. **3.** the marsh mallow plant. [Old English *merscmealwe* the marsh mallow plant]

marsh·mal·low·y (märsh′mal′ō ē, -mel′-), *adj.* resembling or suggesting marshmallow in consistency, sweetness, etc.: . . . *marshmallowy reeds, booming basses* (London Times); . . . *wave to them cheerily from the marshmallowy cliffs* (Mary McCarthy).

marsh·man (märsh′mən), *n.*, *pl.* **-men.** a person who lives in a marsh or marshy region.

marsh marigold, a plant of the crowfoot family that has golden flowers and grows in moist meadows and swamps; cowslip.

marsh rabbit, 1. *U.S.* a muskrat: *For some time it* [*muskrat*] *has been sold in open market in Maryland . . . where it is offered as marsh rabbit* (Baltimore Sun). **2.** a coarse-furred rabbit, a species of cottontail, that lives in wet areas of the southeastern United States.

marsh wren, any of certain American wrens that breed in marshes, as the long-billed marsh wren.

marsh·y (mär′shē), *adj.*, **marsh·i·er, marsh·i·est. 1.** soft and wet like a marsh: *a marshy field.* **2.** having many marshes; swampy: *a marshy region.* **3.** of marshes: *a marshy odor.*

Mar·sil·id (mär sil′id), *n. Trademark.* iproniazid.

mar·si·po·branch (mär′si pə brangk), *adj.*, *n.* cyclostome. [< New Latin *Marsipobranchii* the class name < Greek *mársipos* pouch + *bránchia* gills]

mar·su·pi·al (mär sü′pē əl), *n.* a mammal that carries its young in a pouch: *Kangaroos, opossums, and wombats are marsupials. Today, pouched animals, or marsupials, are found only in North and South America, Australia and Tasmania* (Science News Letter).

—adj. **1.** of or belonging to the marsupials. **2.** having a pouch for carrying the young. **3.** having to do with or like a pouch. [< New Latin *marsupialis* < Latin *marsūpium;* see MARSUPIUM]

marsupial mouse, any of several Australian desert animals, related to the dasyure, that somewhat resemble a mouse or rat. Marsupial mice live mainly on insects.

mar·su·pi·ate (mär sü′ pē it, -āt), *n.*, *adj.* marsupial.

mar·su·pi·um (mär sü′pē əm), *n.*, *pl.* **-pi·a** (-pē ə). **1.** a pouch or fold of skin on the abdomen of a female marsupial for carrying its young. **2.** a similar pouch in certain fishes and crustaceans. [< Latin *marsūpium* < variant of Greek *marsípion* (diminutive) < *mársipos* pouch]

Mar·sy·as (mär′sē əs), *n. Greek Mythology.* a Phrygian flute player who challenged Apollo to a contest, and, when defeated, was flayed by the god for his presumption.

mart[1] (märt), *n.* **1.** a center of trade; market: *New York and London are the great marts of the world. Lisbon outshone Venice as a mart for oriental spices* (H.G.Wells). **2.** *Archaic.* a fair. [< *mart,* dialectal form of Dutch *markt* market] —**Syn. 1.** emporium.

mart[2] (märt), *n. Scottish.* an ox or cow fattened for slaughter, especially at Martinmas. [< Gaelic *mart*]

mar·ta·gon (mär′tə gən), *n.* the Turk's-cap lily. [< Middle French *martagon* < Turkish *martagan* a kind of turban]

mar·tel (mär′tel), *n. Archaic.* a hammer, especially one used as a weapon in war. [< Old French *martel*]

mar·tel·la·to (mär′tə lä′tō), *Music.* *—adj.* strongly accented (used as a direction for bowed stringed instruments and piano music). *—adv.* in a martellato manner. [< Italian *martellato* (literally) hammered, past participle of *martellare* to hammer]

Mar·tel·lo tower, or **mar·tel·lo** (mär tel′ō), *n.* a circular tower, formerly used mostly for coastal defense. [alteration (influenced by Italian *martello* hammer) of Cape *Mortella,* where one of these towers was located]

mar·ten (mär′tən), *n.*, *pl.* **-tens** or (*collectively*) **-ten. 1.** a slender carnivorous mammal like the weasels, but larger, found in northern and western North America. **2.** its valuable fur. [< Old French *martrine,* feminine of *martrin* of marten <

Pine marten (def. 1) (including tail, 2½ ft. long)

martre a marten < Germanic (compare Old High German *mardar*)]

mar·tens·ite (mär′tən zīt), *n.* a hard, brittle, solid solution of up to 2 per cent of carbon in alpha iron, a constituent of steel which is quenched rapidly: *If the steel is cooled rapidly from a higher temperature the reverse change is suppressed until the hybrid phase known as martensite forms at about 300° C* (New Scientist). [< Adolf *Martens,* 1850-1914, a German metallurgist + *-ite*[1]]

mar·tens·it·ic (mär′tən zit′ik), *adj.* having to do with or consisting of martensite: *martensitic steel.*

Mar·tha (mär′thə), *n.* (in the Bible) the sister of Lazarus and Mary; Jesus was her guest. She is often taken to represent the vigorous housekeeper. Luke 10:38-42.

mar·tial (mär′shəl), *adj.* **1.** of, having to do with, or suitable for war: *martial music.* **2.** fond of fighting; warlike; brave: *a boy of martial spirit, a martial nation.* **3.** of or having to do with the army and navy. **4.** *Obsolete.* of or containing iron. [< Latin *Mārtiālis* of Mars < *Mārs, Mārtis* Mars, Roman god of battle] —**mar′tial·ly,** *adv.* —**mar′tial·ness,** *n.* —**Syn. 1, 2.** See **military.**

Mar·tial (mär′shəl), *n.* **1.** *Astronomy.* Martian. **2.** *Astrology.* subject to the influence of Mars, as a poisonous plant or animal.

mar·tial·ism (mär′shə liz əm), *n.* martial or warlike character or spirit.

mar·tial·ist (mär′shə list), *n.* a warrior.

martial law, rule by the army, national guard, or militia with special military courts instead of by the usual civil authorities: *Martial law is declared during a time of trouble or war.*

Mar·tian (mär′shən), *adj.* **1.** of or having to do with the planet Mars: *The Martian year lasts six hundred and eighty-seven days* (New Yorker). **2.** of or having to do with Mars, the god of war. —*n.* a supposed inhabitant of the planet Mars. [< Latin *Mārtius* of Mars + English *-an*]

mar·tin (mär′tən), *n.* any of several swallows with a short beak and a forked or square tail, especially the purple martin. [apparently < French *martin* < *Martin,* a proper name]

Purple Martin (about 8 in. long)

mar·ti·net (mär′tə net′, mär′tə net), *n.* **1.** a military or naval officer who imposes very strict discipline: *The commander-in-chief was a little of a martinet* (James Fenimore Cooper). **2.** a person who enforces very strict discipline: *They soon discovered that the new teacher was a martinet.* [< Colonel *Martinet,* a French general and drillmaster of the 1600's] —**Syn. 2.** disciplinarian.

mar·ti·net·ish (mär′tə net′ish), *adj.* of, belonging to, or characteristic of a martinet: *The smug and martinetish figure of Mr. Squires loomed before them all* (Theodore Dreiser).

mar·ti·net·ism (mär′tə net′iz əm), *n.* the spirit or methods of a martinet.

mar·tin·gal (mär′tən gal), *n.* martingale.

mar·tin·gale (mär′tən gāl), *n.* **1.** a strap of a horse's harness that prevents the horse from rising on its hind legs or throwing back its head. **2. a.** a rope or stay that holds down the jib boom on a ship. **b.** a short spar to which the stay or rope is attached; dolphin striker. **3.** a system of betting in which the wager is doubled after each loss. [< Middle French *martingale* < Provençal *martengalo,* feminine of *martengo* inhabitant of *Martigues,* a small town near Marseilles, France]

Martingale (def. 2b)

mar·ti·ni (mär tē′nē), *n., pl.* **-nis.** a cocktail consisting of gin and dry vermouth, usually served with a green olive or a twisted strip of lemon peel. [< *Martini* and Rossi, an Italian company that manufactures vermouth]

Mar·ti·ni·can (mär′tə nē′kən), *n.* a native or inhabitant of Martinique. —*adj.* of or having to do with Martinique or Martinicans.

Mar·ti·ni·quan (mär′tə nē′kən), *n., adj.* Martinican.

Mar·tin·mas (mär′tən məs), *n.* November 11, a Roman Catholic church festival in honor of Saint Martin.

Mar·tle·mas (mär′təl məs), *n.* Martinmas.

mart·let (märt′lit), *n.* **1.** the European house martin. **2.** *Heraldry.* a bearing depicting a bird without feet. [< Middle French *martelet,* probably alteration of *martinet* (diminutive) < *martin;* see MARTIN]

mar·tyr (mär′tər), *n.* **1.** a person who chooses to die or suffer rather than renounce his faith or principles; person who is put to death or made to suffer greatly for his religion or other beliefs: *Many of the early Christians were martyrs.* **2.** a person who suffers great pain or anguish: *She is a martyr to dyspepsia and bad cooking* (Francis A. Kemble).
—*v.t.* **1.** to put (a person) to death or torture because of his religion or other beliefs. **2.** to cause to suffer greatly; torture; persecute: *She was ever at my side . . . martyring me by the insufferable annoyance of her vulgar loquacity* (Charles Lever).
[Old English *martyr* < Latin < Greek *mártyr* witness] —**mar′tyr·like′,** *adj.*
—**Syn.** *v.t.* **2.** torment.

mar·tyr·dom (mär′tər dəm), *n.* **1.** the death or suffering of a martyr: *Like all rebellions, this one had its . . . moments of bravery, martyrdom, and sacrifice* (Newsweek). **2.** the state of being a martyr. **3.** great suffering; torment.

mar·tyr·ess (mär′tər is), *n.* a woman martyr.

mar·tyr·i·za·tion (mär′tər ə zā′shən), *n.* **1.** a martyrizing. **2.** a being martyrized.

mar·tyr·ize (mär′tə rīz), *v.,* **-ized, -iz·ing.** —*v.t.* **1.** to make a martyr of. **2.** to torment. —*v.i.* to be or become a martyr.

mar·tyr·ol·a·try (mär′tə rol′ə trē), *n.* worship of martyrs.

mar·tyr·o·log·i·cal (mär′tər ə loj′ə kəl), *adj.* of or having to do with martyrology.

mar·tyr·ol·o·gist (mär′tə rol′ə jist), *n.* a writer of martyrology.

mar·tyr·ol·o·gy (mär′tə rol′ə jē), *n., pl.* **-gies. 1.** a list or register of martyrs, usually with an account of their lives. **2.** such accounts as a group. **3.** the part of church history or literature dealing with martyrs.

mar·tyr·y (mär′tər ē), *n., pl.* **-tyr·ies.** a shrine, chapel, etc., erected in honor of a martyr. [< Late Latin *martyrium* suffering, < Greek *martýrion* < *mártyr* witness]

mar·vel (mär′vəl), *n., v.,* **-veled, -vel·ing** or (*especially British*) **-velled, -vel·ling.** —*n.* **1.** a wonderful or astonishing thing; a wonder: *The airplane and the radio are among the marvels of science. The book is a marvel of accuracy.* **2.** *Archaic.* astonishment; wonder: *The vast acquirements of the new governor were the theme of marvel among the simple burghers* (Washington Irving).
—*v.i.* **1.** to be filled with wonder; be astonished: *I marvel at your boldness. Lancelot marvell'd at the wordless man* (Tennyson). **2.** to feel astonished curiosity: *I marvel how men toil and fare* (Andrew Lang). —*v.t.* **1.** to wonder or be curious about: *I marvel what kin thou and thy daughters are* (Shakespeare). **2.** to wonder at: *The people . . . marvelled that he tarried so long in the temple* (Luke 1:21). [< Old French *merveille* < Vulgar Latin *miribilia,* for Latin *mīrābilia* wonders, neuter plural of *mīrābilis* strange, wonderful < *mīrārī* to wonder at < *mīrus* wonderful]

mar·vel·lous (mär′və ləs), *adj. Especially British.* marvelous. —**mar′vel·lous·ly,** *adv.* —**mar′vel·lous·ness,** *n.*

mar·vel-of-Pe·ru (mär′vəl əv pə rü′), *n.* the four-o'clock (plant).

mar·vel·ous (mär′və ləs), *adj.* **1.** wonderful; extraordinary: *I thought of Chatterton, the marvelous boy* (William Wordsworth). **2.** improbable; incredible: *Children like tales of marvelous things, like that of Aladdin and his lamp.* **3.** *Informal.* excellent; splendid; fine: *a marvelous time.* —**mar′vel·ous·ly,** *adv.* —**mar′vel·ous·ness,** *n.* —**Syn. 1.** astonishing, surprising. See **wonderful.**

mar·ver (mär′vər), *n.* (in glassmaking) a slab or tablet, originally of marble, but now generally of metal, on which a gather of glass is rolled, shaped, and cooled. —*v.t.* to shape on a marver: *He marvers the glass, as it cools through red and amber, rolling it back and forth along a shining anvil* (Punch). [< French *marbre* marble; see MARBLE]

Marx·i·an (märk′sē ən), *adj.* of or having to do with Karl Marx, 1818-1883, or his theories: *They have dug up a classic Marxian dogma for the occasion* (New York Times). —*n.* a follower of Marx; believer in his theories.

Marx·i·an·ism (märk′sē ə niz′əm), *n.* Marxism: *Hence in the seven years before his* [*Lenin's*] *death in 1924 he did not make great progress in putting Marxianism into practice* (Emory S. Bogardus).

Marx·ism (märk′siz əm), *n.* the political and economic theories of Karl Marx and Friedrich Engels, who interpreted history as a continuing economic class struggle and believed that the eventual result would be the establishment of a classless society and communal ownership of all natural and industrial resources: *Mounting unemployment with attendant sliding toward Marxism is another result of too many people in too circumscribed areas* (Bulletin of Atomic Scientists).

Marx·ism-Len·in·ism (märk′siz əm len′i-niz əm), *n.* the political and economic theories of Marxism as expanded and augmented by those of Nikolai Lenin: *This fatuous optimism overlooks the peculiar character of Marxism-Leninism as a secular religion* (New York Times).

Marx·ist (märk′sist), *n.* a follower or disciple of Karl Marx; believer in Marxism: *China's leaders are devoted Marxists* (Atlantic). —*adj.* Marxian.

Marx·ist-Len·in·ist (märk′sist len′i nist), *adj.* of, having to do with, or characteristic of the theories of Marxism-Leninism.

Mar·y (mãr′ē), *n.* in the Bible: **1.** the mother of Jesus. Matthew 1:18-25. **2.** the sister of Lazarus and Martha. Luke 10:38-42. **3.** Mary Magdalene. [Old English *Maria* < Late Latin < Greek *Mariā,* variant of *Mariám* < Hebrew *Miryâm*]

mar·y·jane (mãr′ē jān′), *n. Slang.* marijuana.

Mary Jane, *Trademark.* a patent leather shoe for young girls with a low heel and a strap across the instep.

Mar·y·knoll·er (mãr′ē nōl′ər), *n.* a member of the Maryknoll Fathers, a society of Roman Catholic priests.

Mar·y·land·er (mer′ə lən dər), *n.* a native or inhabitant of Maryland.

Mar·y·land yellowthroat (mer′ə lənd), a North American warbler with olive-brown upper parts, yellow throat, and, in the male, a black mask across the face.

Mary Magdalene, (in the Bible) a woman from whom Jesus cast out seven devils. Luke 8:2. She is commonly supposed to be the repentant sinner forgiven by Jesus. Luke 7:37-50.

mar·zi·pan (mär′zə pan), *n.* a confection made of ground almonds and sugar, molded into various forms: *a thick layer of marzipan baked in the center* (London Times). Also, **marchpane.** [< German *Marzipan* < Italian *marzapane,* perhaps < Medieval Latin *matapanus* Venetian coin bearing image of a seated Christ < Arabic *mauṭabān* a seated king; porcelain container]

ma·sa (mä′sä), *n. Spanish.* the corn flour or dough with which tortillas and tamales are made: *Most of the supermarkets here carry a broad array of the basics of Spanish-American cooking including . . . masa for tamales* (New York Times).

Ma·sai (mä sī′), *n.* **1.** a tribe of tall, warlike, cattle-raising natives of East Africa: *Masai meat-and-fat-eating herdsmen and hunters in Africa are slim, healthy and get along with people* (Maclean's). **2.** a member of this tribe.

masc., masculine.

mas·car·a (mas kar′ə), *n.* a preparation used for coloring the eyelashes, made in various dark colors. [< Spanish *máscara* disguise, mask < Arabic *maskharah* buffoon]

mas·car·aed (mas kar′əd), *adj.* colored with mascara: *She smiled at us out of her beautiful green eyes . . . in their framework of mascaraed lashes* (New Yorker).

mas·ca·ron (mas′kər ən), *n.* a decorative ornament in the form of a grotesque face or head. [< French *mascaron* < Italian *mascherone* < *maschera;* see MASK]

mas·cle (mas′kəl), *n.* **1.** *Heraldry.* a bearing shaped like a voided lozenge. **2.** a small, perforated, lozenge-shaped metal plate used in making medieval armor. [< Anglo-French *mascle* (in French, *macle* mackle), probably < Germanic (compare Middle Dutch *masche*)]

mas·cot (mas′kot), *n.* an animal, person, or thing supposed to bring good luck: *The mascot of the West Point cadets is a mule.* [< French *mascotte* < Provençal *mascoto* sorcery, a fetish < *masco* witch < Old Provençal *masca*]

mas·cotte (mas′kot), *n.* mascot: *That rat's a sort of 'mascotte' to me. A mascotte's a thing that brings luck* (E. Phillpotts).

mas·cu·line (mas′kyə lin), *adj.* **1.** of or having to do with men; male. **2.** like a man; manly; strong; vigorous: *masculine courage, masculine strength.* **3.** having qualities, tastes, etc., suited to a man; mannish: *a masculine woman.* **4.** *Grammar.* of or denoting the gender to which English nouns designating males belong. *Actor, king, ram,* and *bull* are masculine nouns.
—*n.* **1.** *Grammar.* **a.** the masculine gender. **b.** a word or form of the masculine gender. *Abbr.:* masc. **2.** something that is male; male: *She flounced out of the room and left the masculines to themselves* (F. W. Robinson).
[< Latin *masculīnus* < *masculus* < *mās, maris* male. Doublet of MALE.] —**mas′cu·line·ly,** *adv.* —**mas′cu·line·ness,** *n.*
—**Syn.** *adj.* **1, 2.** See **male.**

masculine cadence, *Music.* a cadence in which the final chord falls on the strong beat.

masculine rhyme, a rhyme in which the final syllables are stressed, as in *disdain* and *complain, recline* and *divine.*

mas·cu·lin·ise (mas′kyə lə nīz), *v.t.,* **-ised, -is·ing.** *British.* masculinize.

mas·cu·lin·i·ty (mas′kyə lin′ə tē), *n.* masculine quality or condition: *Greg has colossal dignity and great masculinity* (Newsweek).

mas·cu·lin·i·za·tion (mas′kyə lə nə zā′shən), *n.* the acquiring of masculine characteristics.

mas·cu·lin·ize (mas′kyə lə nīz), *v.t.,* **-ized, -iz·ing.** to produce masculine characteristics in (a female).

ma·ser (mā′zər), *n. Electronics.* a device which amplifies or generates electromagnetic waves, especially microwaves, operating at near absolute zero temperature with great stability and accuracy, and with a very low noise level. Its primary uses are in radar and radio astronomy reception. *Low-noise amplifiers using solid-state masers may well become important in space research* (New Science). [< *m*(icrowave) *a*(mplification by) *s*(timulated) *e*(mission of) *r*(adiation)]

mash[1] (mash), *n.* **1.** a soft mixture; pulpy mass: *He beat the potato into a mash before eating it. A mash of snow covered the walk.* **2. a.** a warm mixture of bran or meal and water for horses and cattle. **b.** any of various mixtures of ground grain, often supplemented with proteins, antibiotics, etc., used as feed for poultry, livestock, etc. **3. a.** crushed malt or meal soaked in hot water to form wort, used in making beer, ale, etc. **b.** a similar preparation of rye, corn, barley, etc., used to make whiskey. **4.** a confused mixture; muddle.
—*v.t.* **1.** to beat into a soft mass; crush to a uniform mass; pound to a pulp: *I'll mash the potatoes.* **2.** to mix (crushed malt, grain, etc.) with hot water in brewing.
[Old English *māsc-, māx-,* in *māx-wyrt* mash-wort]

mash[2] (mash), *Slang.* —*v.t., v.i.* to look (at) with amorous desire; flirt (with); ogle: *Shan't I just mash the men!* (Arnold Bennett). —*n.* a person, especially a woman, who is looked at in this way. [origin uncertain]

MASH (no periods) or **M.A.S.H.,** mobile army surgical hospital.

mash·er[1] (mash′ər), *n.* a person or thing that mashes: *a potato masher.*

mash·er[2] (mash′ər), *n. Slang.* a man who tries to make advances to women: . . . *policewomen assigned to ride the subways and arrest such shady characters as mashers* (New Yorker). [< *mash*[2] + *-er*[1]]

mash·gi·ach (mäsh gē′äн), *n., pl.* **-gi·chim** (-gē нēm′). an inspector appointed to supervise the observance of Jewish law in the preparation of kosher food: *It would be operated as a strictly kosher establishment with a resident mashgiach* (New York Times). [< Hebrew *mashgiāḥ* (literally) overseer]

mash·ie or **mash·y** (mash′ē), *n., pl.* **mashies.** a golf club with a short, sloping, steel face, used especially for long approach shots. It is usually called a "number 5 iron." [perhaps < alteration of Old French *massue* club < Vulgar Latin *matteuca* < *mattea;* see MACE[1]]

mashie niblick, a golf club with a steel face that slopes more than that of a mashie, but less than that of a niblick, used especially for short approach shots. It is usually called a "number 7 iron."

Ma·sho·na (mə shō′nə), *n., pl.* **-na, -nas. 1.** a member of a Bantu tribe now inhabiting the northeastern part of Southern Rhodesia. **2.** the Bantu language of the tribe.

mas·jid (mus′jid), *n.* a mosque: *A ground plan of a house marked in white stones and evidently intended for a masjid* (Sir John Floyer). [< Arabic *masjid;* see MOSQUE]

Ma·sju·mi (mä shü′mē), *n.* a political party in Indonesia representing views of the progressive Moslems.

mask (mask, mäsk), *n.* **1.** a covering to hide or protect the face: *The burglar wore a mask. Fencers and baseball catchers wear masks.* **2.** a false face worn for amusement, as at Halloween, a masquerade, carnival, etc. **3.** a person wearing a mask: *A mask, in the character of an old woman, joined them* (Henry Fielding). **4.** something that hides or disguises: *The fox hid his plans under a mask of friendship.* **5.** a likeness of a person's face in clay, wax, or plaster: *a death mask.* **6.** the hollow figure of a human head worn by Greek and Roman actors to identify the character represented and increase the volume of the voice. **7.** masque. **8.** a carved or molded face or head, usually grotesque, used as an architectural ornament. **9.** a piece of fine gauze worn over the mouth and nose of surgeons, nurses, etc., during operations. **10.** *Military.* a screen of earth, brush, etc., used to hide or protect a battery or any military operation.

Mask (def. 8)

—*v.t.* **1.** to cover (the face) with a mask. **2.** to hide; disguise: *A smile masked his disappointment.* **3.** *Military.* to hide (a battery, etc.) from the sight of the enemy.
—*v.i.* to cover or conceal anything with a mask; put on a mask.
[< Middle French *masque* < Italian *maschera* < Arabic *maskhara* laughingstock < *sakhira* to ridicule]
—**Syn.** *n.* **4.** pretense.

mas·ka·longe (mas′kə lonj), *n.* muskellunge.

mas·ka·nonge (mas′kə nonj), *n.* muskellunge.

mask crab, a crab that has markings on its carapace suggestive of a mask.

masked (maskt, mäskt), *adj.* **1.** wearing or provided with a mask or masks. **2.** disguised; concealed. **3.** *Zoology.* **a.** marked on the face or head as if wearing a mask. **b.** having the wings, legs, etc., of the future image indicated in outline beneath the integument, as certain insect pupae. **4.** *Botany.* personate.

masked ball, a dance at which masks are worn.

mask·er (mas′kər, mäs′-), *n.* a person who wears a mask, especially at a masked ball, masquerade, or masque. Also, **masquer.**

mas·kil (mäs′kēl), *n., pl.* **mas·ki·lim** (mäs kē lēm′). a modern Jewish intellectual, especially one devoted to the Hebrew language, literature, and culture: *Theologian Cohen, 34, writes of Judaism from the standpoint of the maskil* (Time). [< Hebrew *maskīl* (literally) enlightened]

mask·ing (mas′king, mäs′-), *n.* a thing that masks or conceals something from view: *Mr. Habenicht contended he had tripped on a piece of masking covering a worn rug* (New York Times).

masking tape, a tape used to mask or protect surfaces not to be treated, painted, sprayed, etc., while work is being done on adjacent areas: *Ordinary rubber cement or two-sided masking tape probably would work* (Scientific American).

mas·lin[1] (maz′lən), *n. Especially Dialect.* **1.** a kind of brass. **2.** a vessel made of it. [Old English *mæslen*]

mas·lin[2] (maz′lən), *n. Dialect.* **1.** a mixture of grains, especially rye and wheat. **2.** bread made of it. **3.** a mixture or medley. [< Old French *mesteillon,* ultimately < Latin *miscēre* mix]

mas·och·ism (mas′ə kiz əm, maz′-), *n.* **1.** abnormal sexual pleasure derived from being dominated or physically abused. **2.** any enjoyment derived from being dominated or made to suffer. [< Leopold Von Sacher-*Masoch,* 1836-1895, an Austrian novelist, who described it in his stories + *-ism*]

mas·och·ist (mas′ə kist, maz′-), *n.* a person who derives pleasure from being dominated or physically abused; person who enjoys suffering: *Then . . . come the masochists whose only longing is to suffer, in real or in symbolic form, humiliations and tortures at the hands of the loved object* (Sigmund Freud).

mas·och·is·tic (mas′ə kis′tic, maz′-), *adj.* of or having to do with masochists or masochism: *as masochistic as the wintertime spectacle of Polar Club dunkers* (Newsweek). —**mas′och·is′ti·cal·ly,** *adv.*

ma·son (mā′sən), *n.* a man whose work is building with stone or brick; stonemason or bricklayer. —*v.t.* to build of brick, stone, etc.; strengthen with masonry: *the masoned house* (Robert Louis Stevenson). [< Old French *masson,* earlier *maçon* < Late Latin *machiō, machiōnis,* also *maciō* < Germanic (compare Old High German *steinmezzo* stonemason)]

Ma·son (mā′sən), *n.* a member of the worldwide secret society of Freemasons.

Mason and Dix·on's Line (dik′sənz), the boundary between Pennsylvania and Maryland, formerly thought of as separating the free states of the North from the slave states of the South. It was surveyed between 1763 and 1767 by Charles Mason and Jeremiah Dixon.

mason bee, a solitary bee that builds its nest of mud.

Ma·son-Dix·on line (mā′sən dik′sən), Mason and Dixon's Line.

ma·son·ic or **Ma·son·ic** (mə son′ik), *adj.* **1.** of Masons or Masonry; having to do with the Freemasons or Freemasonry: *In those expert hands the trowel seemed to assume the qualities of some lofty masonic symbol* (Lytton Strachey). **2.** in the spirit of Freemasonry; giving sympathetic understanding: *In some voiceless, masonic way, most people in that saloon had become aware that something was in process of happening* (Owen Wister).

Ma·son·ite (mā′sə nīt), *n. Trademark.* a type of fiberboard used for partitions, panels, etc.

Mason jar, a glass jar with a metal cover that can be screwed on tightly, used in home canning: *The Mason jar is the most commonly used canning jar today* (World Book Encyclopedia). [< John *Mason,* an American inventor, who patented it in 1858]

ma·son·ry (mā′sən rē), *n., pl.* **-ries. 1.** work built by a mason; stonework; brickwork. **2.** the trade or skill of a mason. **3.** Often, **Masonry. a.** the principles or doctrines of Freemasons; Freemasonry. **b.** the members of this society.

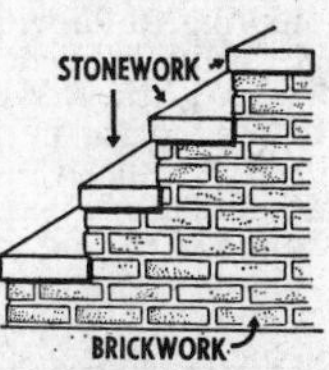

Masonry (def. 1)

ma·son·work (mā′sən wėrk′), *n.* masonry or stonework.

Ma·so·ra or **Ma·so·rah** (mə sôr′ə, -sōr′-), *n.* **1.** the tradition, compiled by Jewish critics and scholars in the 900's and earlier, regarding the correct text of the Hebrew Bible. **2. a.** the marginal notes to the Biblical text preserving this information. **b.** a book containing these. Also, **Massora, Massorah.** [earlier *Masoreth* < Hebrew *māsōrāh,* alteration of earlier *massōreth* tradition]

Mas·o·rete (mas′ə rēt), *n.* **1.** a Hebrew scholar who is skilled in the study of the Masora. **2.** one of the Jewish scholars who wrote the Masora. Also, **Masorite, Massorete, Massorite.**

Mas·o·ret·ic (mas′ə ret′ik), *adj.* of or having to do with the Masora or the Masoretes.

Mas·o·ret·i·cal (mas′ə ret′ə kəl), *adj.* Masoretic.

Mas·o·rite (mas′ə rīt), *n.* Masorete.

masque (mask, mäsk), *n.* **1.** an amateur dramatic entertainment in which fine costumes, scenery, music, and dancing are more important than the story. Masques were so named because the performers wore masks. They were much given in England in the 1500's and 1600's, at court and at the homes of nobles, often outdoors. *Masque is not opera: nor for that matter is it drama or ballet. It is something of them all* (London Times). **2.** a play written for such an entertainment: *Milton's "Comus" is a masque.* **3.** a masked ball; masquerade. Also, **mask.** [< Middle French *masque;* see MASK]

mas·quer (mas′kər, mäs′-), *n.* masker.

mas·quer·ade (mas′kə rād′), *n., v.,* **-ad·ed, -ad·ing.**—*n.* **1.** a party or dance at which masks and fancy costumes are worn: *Gaily dressed revelers . . . drumming carnival bands . . . magnificent masquerade parties* (Time). **2.** the costume and mask worn at such a party or dance. **3.** false pretense; disguise: *And, after all, what is a lie? It is but the truth in masquerade* (Byron). **4.** a going about or acting under false pretenses.
—*v.i.* **1.** to take part in a masquerade. **2.** to disguise oneself; go about under false pretenses: *In "The Prince and the Pauper," the poor boy masqueraded as the prince, and the prince masqueraded as the boy.*
[< French *mascarade* < Italian *mascarata,* variant of *mascherata* < *maschera;* see MASK] —**mas′quer·ad′er,** *n.*

mass[1] (mas), *n.* **1.** a lump: *a mass of dough.* **2.** a large quantity together; great amount or number: *a mass of treasure, a mass of books.* **3.** the greater part; main body; majority: *The great mass of men consider themselves healthy. The mass of men lead lives of quiet desperation* (Thoreau). **4.** bulk; size: *the sheer mass of an iceberg.* **5.** *Physics.* a measure of the quantity of matter a body contains; the property of a physical body which gives the body inertia. The mass of a physical body is obtained by dividing the weight of the body by the acceleration of gravity. *The mass of a piece of lead is not changed by melting it. Isotopes are atoms of the same element that differ in atomic weight, or mass* (World Book Encyclopedia). **6.** mass number; the integer closest to the atomic weight of an isotope. **7.** an expanse of color, light, shade, etc., in a painting. **8.** *Pharmacy.* a thick, pasty preparation from which pills are made.
in the mass, as a whole; without distinguishing parts or individuals: *It is difficult to speak accurately of mankind in the mass.*
the masses, the common people; the working classes; the lower classes: *The masses rebelled against the monarchy during the French Revolution.*
—*v.t., v.i.* to form or collect into a mass; assemble: *It would look better to mass the peonies behind the roses than to mix them. The great bands of caribou . . . mass up on the edge of the woods* (W. Pike).
—*adj.* **1.** on a large scale: *mass buying.* **2.** of or by many people: *a mass protest.* **3.** of or having to do with the masses: *mass culture.*
[< Middle French *masse,* learned borrowing from Latin *massa* kneaded dough, lump < Greek *mâza* barley bread, related to *mássein* to knead] —**Syn.** *n.* **2.** aggregate, accumulation. —*v.t., v.i.* gather.

Mass or **mass**[2] (mas), *n.* **1.** the central service of worship of the Roman Catholic Church and some other churches; Holy Eucharist as a sacrament. The ritual of the Mass consists of various prayers and ceremonies. *His cathedral is one of the world's most famous, but he has celebrated Mass in a Milanese printing shop* (Newsweek). **2.** music written for certain parts of it: *Bach's Mass in B Minor.* [Old English *mæsse* < Late Latin *missa* < Latin *mittere* to send away]

Mass., Massachusetts.

mas·sa (mas′ə), *n.* an old southern Negro form of **master.**

Mas·sa·chu·set (mas′ə chü′sit, -zit), *n., pl.* **-set, -sets. 1.** a member of a group of Algonkian Indians who lived near Massachusetts Bay. **2.** the Algonkian language of this group.

Mas·sa·chu·setts (mas′ə chü′sits, -zits), *n., pl.* **-setts.** Massachuset.

mas·sa·cre (mas′ə kər), *n., v.,* **-cred, -cring.** —*n.* the wholesale, pitiless slaughter of people or animals. —*v.t.* to kill (many people or animals) needlessly or cruelly; slaughter in large numbers: *The savages had massacred many of the garrison after capitulation* (Benjamin Franklin). [< French *massacre* < Old French *macecle,* and *mache-col* a shambles, butchery, perhaps ultimately < Vulgar Latin *maccāre* beat (< a Germanic word) + Latin *collum* neck] —**Syn.** *n.* butchery, carnage. -*v.t.* butcher.

mas·sa·crer (mas′ə krər), *n.* a person who massacres.

mas·sage (mə säzh′), *n., v.,* **-saged, -sag·ing.** —*n.* a rubbing and kneading of the muscles and joints to make them work better and to increase the circulation of blood, soothe the nerves, and improve functions of the organs: *A thorough massage felt good to the tired football players.* —*v.t.* to give a massage to: *Let me massage your back for you.* [< French *massage* friction, kneading < Middle French *masse* dough, mass[1]] —**mas·sag′er,** *n.*

mas·sa·geuse (mȧ sȧ zhœz′), *n. French.* a masseuse.

mas·sag·ist (mə sä′jist), *n.* a masseur or masseuse.

mas·sa·sau·ga (mas′ə sô′gə), *n.* a very small rattlesnake of the southern United States. [American English < the *Missisauga* river < Algonkian (Ojibwa) (literally) < *misi* great + *sâg,* or *sauk* river mouth]

mass communication, communication through the mass media.

mass·cult (mas′kult′), *n.* the culture created by the influence of radio, television, and other mass media: *Their [literary magazines] golden age lasted from World War I to the communications, or "masscult," revolution of the mid-1950's* (New York Times).

mass defect, the difference between the atomic weight of an atom when determined by totaling the atomic weights of the neutrons and protons comprising the atom, and the atomic weight of the atom as a whole; packing effect. The mass defect is considered as a measure of the binding energy of the atom. *The "mass defect" . . . refers to the fact that the mass of the nucleus is slightly smaller than the sum of the masses of the particles combined in it* (Scientific American).

mas·sé (ma sā′), *n.,* or **massé shot,** a stroke in billiards in which the cue ball is hit with the cue held almost vertically and with a sharp downward motion. [< French *massé,* past participle of *masser* to make such a stroke < *masse* a cue, club < Old French *mace* mace]

masse·cuite (mȧs kwēt′), *n. French.* (in sugar making) the juice of the sugar cane, a mixture of molasses and sugar crystals, after concentration by boiling.

mass-en·er·gy equation (mas′en′ər jē), an equation expressing the relation of mass and energy, formulated by Albert Einstein in 1905: $E=mc^2$; Einstein equation. E = the energy in ergs; m = the mass in grams; c = the velocity of light in centimeters per second. *What happens in the Bevatron confirms Einstein's famous mass-energy equation which says that energy can be converted into mass and mass into energy* (New York Times).

mass-energy equivalence, the theory, expressed by the mass-energy equation, that, in special relativity, mass and energy are related and mutually interchangeable.

mas·se·ter (ma sē′tər), *n.* a muscle that raises the lower jaw in chewing. [< New Latin *masseter* < Greek *masētḗr* (*mŷs*) chewer (muscle) < *masâsthai* to chew]

mas·se·ter·ic (mas′ə ter′ik), *adj.* of or having to do with the masseter.

mas·seur (ma sœr′), *n.* a man whose work is massaging people. [< French *masseur* < *masser* to massage]

mas·seuse (ma sœz′), *n.* a woman whose work is massaging people. [< French *masseuse,* feminine of *masseur* masseur]

mas·si·cot (mas′ə kot), *n.* a yellow powder, an unfused monoxide of lead, used as a pigment and drier. *Formula:* PbO [< Old French *massicot* < Italian *marzacotta* a potter's glaze < Spanish *mazacote* mortar; earlier, soda < Arabic *mashaqunyā*]

mas·sif (mas′if; *French* mȧ sēf′), *n.* **1.** a compact part of a mountain range surrounded by depressions: *The Rocky massif was already splotched with golden aspens* (Time). **2.** a large block of the earth's crust shifted upward or downward as a unit and bounded by faults. [< Middle French *massif* massive]

mass·i·ness (mas′ē nis), *n.* the quality or state of being massy; massiveness.

mas·sive (mas′iv), *adj.* **1.** forming a large mass; bulky and heavy: *a massive rock, a massive building. My master's . . . square, massive brow* (Charlotte Brontë). **2.** imposing; impressive: *Beethoven's Ninth Symphony is a massive work.* **3.** in or by great numbers; broad in scope; extensive: *a massive assault, massive retaliation.* **4.** (of gold, silver, plate, etc.) solid rather than hollow: *a chain of massive gold* (Scott). **5. a.** affecting a large area of bodily tissue: *a massive tumor.* **b.** much larger or more than usual: *a massive dose.* **6.** *Mineralogy.* not definitely crystalline. **7.** *Geology.* without definite structural divisions. [< Middle French *massive,* feminine of *massif* < *masse* mass[1]] —**mas′sive·ly,** *adv.* —**mas′sive·ness,** *n.* —**Syn. 1.** weighty, ponderous, huge.

mas·siv·i·ty (ma siv′ə tē), *n.* the fact or condition of being massive.

mass·less (mas′lis), *adj.* that has no mass: *. . . massless units of energy* (Scientific American).

mass-lu·mi·nos·i·ty (mas′lü′mə nos′ə tē), *adj.* of, having to do with, or comparing the mass and luminosity of a star.

mass man, man conceived not as an individual but as representing the anonymous multitudes of people in a mass society: *The mass man loses his independence, and more importantly, he loses the desire to be independent* (Bulletin of Atomic Scientists).

mass medium, *pl.* **mass media,** any of the modern forms of communication, such as the press, television, radio, and motion pictures, which reaches a large segment of the population: *A good deal of adult education has been accomplished by the mass media* (Bulletin of Atomic Scientists).

mass meeting, a large public gathering of people to hear or discuss some matter of common interest: *The school held a mass meeting to plan for a field day.*

mass number, the whole number that most closely indicates the atomic weight of an isotope. It is equal to the sum of the protons and neutrons in the nucleus. *For some elements that do not occur in nature, especially the radioactive elements, the term mass number is used instead of atomic weight* (World Book Encyclopedia). *Symbol:* A (no period).

mass observation, *British.* a method of studying and recording the attitudes, opinions, and habits of a large segment of the population by means of a system of surveys, interviews, and documentary analyses.

Mas·so·ra or **Mas·so·rah** (mə sôr′ə, -sōr′-), *n.* Masora.

Mas·so·rete (mas′ə rēt), *n.* Masorete.

Mas·so·rite (mas′ə rīt), *n.* Masorete.

mas·so·ther·a·py (mas′ō ther′ə pē), *n.* the treatment of a disease by massage. [< French *masser* massage + English *therapy*]

mass-pro·duce (mas′prə düs′, -dyüs′), *v.t.,* **-duced, -duc·ing.** to manufacture (anything) by or as if by mass production: *the lathe factory in Moscow which already mass-produces the cheapest lathes in the world* (New Scientist). —**mass′-pro·duc′er,** *n.*

mass-pro·duced (mas′prə düst′, -dyüst′), *adj.* made by mass-production; produced in large quantities.

mass production, 1. the manufacturing of goods, etc., in large quantities by machinery and with division of labor: *the mass production of automobiles.* **2.** any operation resembling this: *the mass production of entertainment.*

mass ratio, the ratio of the weight of a fully loaded space vehicle to its weight after its fuel is consumed and after sections no longer required have been separated: *Another important parameter is "mass ratio," the ratio of the rocket weight at take-off to the weight of remaining mechanism plus payload at burn-out* (Bulletin of Atomic Scientists).

mass society, a large, highly organized, and impersonal society consisting of masses of anonymous individuals; the society of the mass man.

mass spectrograph, an apparatus for determining the mass numbers of isotopes by passing streams of ions through an electric and magnetic field which separates those of different masses. The results are recorded on a photographic plate. *The mass spectrograph has been used to compare the ratios of mass to charge in the electron and positron* (Science News).

mass spectrometer, an apparatus similar to the mass spectrograph except that its results are recorded electrically: *Ions of the lighter isotope, 107, are deflected more quickly by the magnetic field of the mass spectrometer than those of the heavier isotope, 109* (Science News Letter).

mass spectrometry, study with or use of the mass spectrometer.

mass spectroscope, any of various devices utilizing magnetic fields, electric fields, or both, and used for separating, weighing indirectly, and studying isotopes, atomic particles, etc.: *In the simplest mass spectroscope, electrons bombard a gas at low pressure* (World Book Encyclopedia).

mass·y (mas′ē), *adj.*, **mass·i·er, mass·i·est. 1.** bulky and heavy; massive: *We closed all the massy shutters of our old building* (Edgar Allan Poe). **2.** great; impressive. **3.** solid, rather than hollow or plated, as metal.

mast[1] (mast, mäst), *n.* **1.** a long pole of wood or metal set upright on a ship to support the sails and rigging. **2.** any upright pole: *the mast of a derrick.* **abaft the mast,** *British.* in a position of authority: *He was not satisfied unless he was abaft the mast.* **before the mast, a.** as a common sailor. Sailors always slept in former times in the forward part of a ship: *He sailed for two years before the mast.* **b.** in front of the foremast; in the forecastle: *Common sailors used to be berthed before the mast.*

Mast[1] (def. 1)

—*v.t.* to equip or rig with a mast or masts. [Old English *mæst*] —**mast′like′,** *adj.*
—**Syn.** *n.* **1.** spar.

mast[2] (mast, mäst), *n.* acorns, chestnuts, beechnuts, etc., on the ground: *Pigs eat mast.* [Old English *mæst*]

mas·ta·ba or **mas·ta·bah** (mas′tə bə), *n.* an ancient Egyptian tomb set over a mummy chamber burrowed in rock. It was rectangular with a flat top and sides sloping outward to the base. [< Arabic *maṣṭaba* (literally) bench]

mast cell, a large cell in connective tissue that has a very granular cytoplasm. Under certain conditions it releases histamine and an anticoagulant, heparin. *Mast cells liberate the anti-clotting compound heparin which in turn stimulates the production of an enzyme* (Science News Letter). [*mast* < German *masten* fatten]

mas·tec·to·my (mas tek′tə mē), *n., pl.* **-mies.** the surgical removal of a woman's breast, as when cancerous. [< Greek *mastós* breast + *ektomē* a cutting out]

-masted, *combining form.* having a —— mast or masts: *A three-masted ship = a ship having three masts.*

mas·ter (mas′tər, mäs′-), *n.* **1.** a person who has power, authority or control: **a.** the man at the head of a household: *The master of the house.* **b.** the captain or officer in charge of a merchant ship. **c.** the head or presiding officer of a society or institution. **d.** an employer of workmen or servants. **e.** an owner of a slave or a horse or dog, etc. **f.** (in general) an owner; possessor: . . . *those qualities of the mind he was master of* (Jonathan Swift). **2.** a person who has the power to control, use, or dispose of something at will: *to be master of a situation. He . . . was a perfect master of both languages* (Jonathan Swift). **3.** *Especially British.* a male teacher: *The village master taught his little school* (Oliver Goldsmith). **4.** an artist, musician, or author of the highest rank. **5.** a picture, painting, or sculpture by a great artist: *an old master.* **6.** a person who knows all there is to know about his work; expert: *a master of the violin.* **7.** a skilled worker; craftsman in business for himself. **8. a.** a title of respect for a boy: *First prize goes to Master Henry Adams.* **b.** a young gentleman; boy. **9.** Also, **Master. a.** a person who has taken a certain advanced degree above bachelor and below doctor, at a college or university. **b.** Master of Arts. **c.** Master of Science. **10.** a person who overcomes another; victor: *They have marched from far away . . . And the morning saw them masters of Cremona* (Sir Arthur Conan Doyle). **11.** a court officer appointed to assist the judge. **12.** (in Scotland) the title of the heir apparent to a rank of the peerage lower than earl. **13.** a rank of excellence in contract bridge tournament play: . . . *contests for individuals, pairs and teams, in both masters' and nonmasters' classifications* (New York Times). **14.** a high-quality initial recording which is used as the source for commercial duplications.
(the) Master, Jesus Christ: *Closer drew the twelve disciples to their Master's side* (Nathaniel P. Willis).
the Masters, a golf tournament held annually at Augusta, Georgia, for the top professional players: *Ben Hogan won the Masters in 1951 and in 1953.*
—*adj.* **1.** being master; of a master: *O let me be the tune-swept fiddlestring That feels the Master Melody* (John G. Neihardt). **2.** main: *a master bedroom.* **3.** qualified to teach apprentices and carry on his trade independently; highly skilled: *a master printer.* **4.** that controls or standardizes the operation of other mechanisms or parts: *a master switch.*
—*v.t.* **1.** to become master of; conquer; control: *She learned to master her anger.* **2.** to become expert in; become skillful at: *He has mastered long division. He mastered whatever was not worth the knowing* (Lowell). **3.** to rule or direct as a master.
[fusion of Old English *mægester* (< Latin *magister*), and Middle English *meistre* < Old French *maistre* < Latin *magister*]
—**Syn.** *n.* **1.** chief, ruler, commander. *-v.t.* **1.** overcome, subjugate, subdue.
—**Ant.** *n.* **1.** servant, vassal, slave.

mas·ter-at-arms (mas′tər ət ärmz′, mäs′-), *n., pl.* **mas·ters-at-arms.** a police officer in the navy who keeps order on a ship and takes charge of prisoners, etc. The rating survives in the Royal Navy, but no longer exists in the United States Navy.

master builder, 1. a person skilled in planning buildings; architect. **2.** a person who directs the construction of buildings; contractor.

mas·ter·dom (mas′tər dəm, mäs′-), *n.* mastery; control.

mas·ter·er (mas′tər ər, mäs′-), *n.* a person or thing that masters.

mas·ter·ful (mas′tər fəl, mäs′-), *adj.* **1.** fond of power or authority; domineering: *She was attracted by his masterful ways.* **2.** expert; skillful: *a masterful performance.* —**mas′ter·ful·ly,** *adv.* —**mas′ter·ful·ness,** *n.* —**Syn. 1.** imperious, lordly, overbearing.

master gland, the pituitary.

mas·ter-hand (mas′tər hand′, mäs′-), *n.* **1.** a highly skilled craftsman; expert: *Chaucer was a master-hand at getting comic or satiric or emotional effects* (Atlantic). **2.** a high degree of skill or excellence; expertise.

mas·ter·hood (mas′tər hu̇d, mäs′-), *n.* the condition or character of being a master: *The eldest son of the head of the whole family inherited the masterhood from his father* (Bulletin of Atomic Scientists).

master key, 1. a key that opens all the different locks of a set. **2.** a key that will open many different locks of a similar type.

mas·ter·less (mas′tər lis, mäs′-), *adj.* having no master; uncontrolled or unprotected by a master: *Many a town must now be masterless, And women's voices rule* (William Morris).

mas·ter·li·ness (mas′tər lē nis, mäs′-), *n.* the quality or condition of being masterly.

mas·ter·ly (mas′tər lē, mäs′-), *adj.* expert; skillful: *In his masterly ability to render form in motion, few artists have surpassed Degas* (Time). —*adv.* expertly; skillfully. —**Syn.** *adj.* proficient, finished, excellent.

mas·ter·man (mas′tər mən, mäs′-), *n., pl.* **-men.** *British Dialect.* the head of a family; a husband.

master mason, 1. a skilled mason who can direct the work of others. **2.** Often, **Master Mason.** a fully qualified Freemason, who has passed the 3rd degree.

master mechanic, a skilled mechanic who can direct the work of others.

mas·ter·mind (mas′tər mīnd′, mäs′-), *n.* a person who plans and supervises a scheme of action, usually from behind the scenes or in the background: *Soustelle, the political mastermind of the Algiers uprising that swept DeGaulle back to power . . .* (Wall Street Journal).
—*v.t.* to devise and conduct (a plan of action) from the background: *The statement gave Burgess the credit for masterminding their escape to Russia* (Time).

Master of Arts, 1. a degree given by a college or university to a person who has completed an advanced course of study, or as an honor. *Abbr.:* M.A. or A.M. **2.** a person who has had the degree of Master of Arts conferred upon him.

master of ceremonies, a person in charge of a ceremony or an entertainment, who makes sure that all parts of it take place in the proper order.

Master of Science, 1. a degree given by a college or university to a person who has completed an advanced course of study in science, or as an honor. *Abbr.:* M.S. or M.Sc. **2.** a person who has had the degree of Master of Science conferred upon him.

Master of the Rolls, a high judicial official of Great Britain who has charge of the rolls, patents, and grants that pass the great seal.

mas·ter·piece (mas′tər pēs′, mäs′-), *n.* **1.** anything done or made with wonderful skill; perfect piece of art or workmanship: *This plan of setting our enemies to destroy one another seemed to us a masterpiece of policy* (Francis Parkman). **2.** a person's greatest work: *The Ninth Symphony was Beethoven's masterpiece.*

master plan, any general plan or design, especially one used as a blueprint for a large building project: *He helped to develop the council's master plan for hospitals in the city* (New York Times).

master point, *U.S.* a point awarded to a player of contract bridge who wins or ranks high in a national tournament: *A player with a total of three hundred master points, he went on, becomes a Life Master* (New Yorker).

master race, 1. a race that considers itself superior and therefore fit to become the dominant race. **2.** (as used by the Nazis) the German Aryans: *Most Nazis . . . intended . . . to bring the world under the hegemony of their master race* (Harper's).

master's degree, 1. the degree of master given by a college or university. **2.** a Master of Arts or Master of Science degree.

master sergeant, (in the U.S. Army, Air Force, and Marine Corps) the top grade of noncommissioned officer, above a sergeant first class in rank. He is outranked only by special designations, such as, in the Army and Marine Corps, first sergeant and sergeant major, and, in the Air Force, senior master sergeant and chief master sergeant. *Abbr.:* M. Sgt.

mas·ter·ship (mas′tər ship, mäs′-), *n.* **1.** the position of a master. **2.** the degree of master from a college or university: *Edinburgh College, where I had just received my mastership of arts* (Robert Louis Stevenson). **3.** power; rule; control. **4.** great skill; expert knowledge.
—**Syn. 3.** masterdom.

mas·ter·sing·er (mas′tər sing′ər, mäs′-), *n.* Meistersinger. [translation of German *Meistersinger*]

mas·ter-slave (mas′tər slāv′, mäs′-), *adj.* of or having to do with a system in which a master machine controls the actions of one or more duplicates of the original: . . . *he operates a master-slave manipulator to extract radioactive material from a capsule with tweezers* (Science News Letter).

master stroke, a very skillful act or achievement.

mas·ter·work (mas′tər wėrk′, mäs′-), *n.* a masterpiece: *The flowers . . . appear as the masterwork of Nature in the vegetable kingdom* (Joseph A. Smith).

master workman, 1. a person very skilled in a trade or craft. **2.** a foreman.

mas·ter·y (mas′tər ē, -trē; mäs′-), *n., pl.* **-ter·ies. 1.** the power or authority of a master; rule; control: *So far humanity has shown itself most unfit for a rational mastery of its own future* (Science News). **2.** the upper hand; victory: *Four champions fierce, Strive here for mastery* (Milton). **3.** great skill; expert knowledge; command or grasp, as over a subject: *This consummate military leader . . . was distinguished by . . . a mastery of method rarely surpassed* (Benjamin Disraeli). *Those who painfully . . . have scaled the crags of mastery over musical instruments* (Kenneth Grahame). —**Syn. 1.** command, sway. **2.** triumph.

mast-fed (mast′fed′, mäst′-), *adj.* fed on mast: *mast-fed pigs.*

mast·head (mast′hed′, mäst′-), *n.* **1.** the top of a ship's mast or the part of a lower mast where it is joined by the next higher mast: *A crow's-nest near the masthead of the lower mast is used as a lookout.* **2.** that part of a newspaper or magazine that gives the title, owner, address, rates, etc.: *The biggest category on Time's masthead . . . is that of its sixty-two girl editorial researchers* (New Yorker).

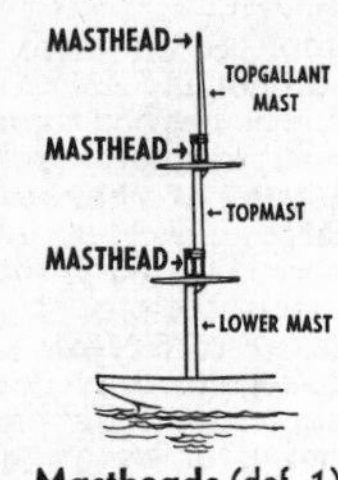

Mastheads (def. 1)

—*v.t.* **1.** to raise (a flag, yard, etc.) to the masthead. **2.** to send to the masthead as a punishment: *One of the midshipmen was mastheaded . . . for not waiting on deck until he was relieved* (Frederick Marryat).

mas·tic (mas′tik), *n.* **1.** a yellowish resin obtained from the bark of a small Mediterranean evergreen tree of the cashew family, used in making varnish, chewing gum, and incense, and as an astringent. **2.** the tree. **3.** a distilled liquor flavored with this resin. **4.** any of various cements or mortars having a pasty texture. [< Old French *mastic* < Late Latin *mastichum* < *masticha* < Greek *mastíchē* < *masâsthai* chew]

mas·ti·ca·ble (mas′tə kə bəl), *adj.* that can be masticated.

mas·ti·cate (mas′tə kāt), *v.t., v.i.,* **-cat·ed, -cat·ing.** **1.** to grind (food) to a pulp with the teeth; chew: *Americans now masticate 86 million pounds of meat every day* (Wall Street Journal). **2.** to crush or knead (rubber, etc.) to a pulp. [< Late Latin *masticāre* (with English *-ate*) < Greek *mastichân* gnash the teeth < *mástax, -akos* mouth, jaws < *masâsthai* chew]

mas·ti·ca·tion (mas′tə kā′shən), *n.* the act or process of masticating.

mas·ti·ca·tor (mas′tə kā′tər), *n.* **1.** a person, animal, or organ that chews. **2.** a machine for cutting or grinding things into small pieces.

mas·ti·ca·to·ry (mas′tə kə tôr′ē, -tōr′-), *adj., n., pl.* **-ries.** —*adj.* of, having to do with, or used in chewing: *the masticatory muscles.* —*n.* a substance chewed to increase the flow of saliva.

mas·tic·ic (mas tis′ik), *adj.* of or having to do with mastic.

mas·tiff (mas′tif, mäs′-), *n.* any of a breed of large, powerful dogs having a short, thick coat, large head, drooping ears, and hanging lips. [< Old French *mastin,* ultimately < Latin *mānsuētus* tame, gentle < *manus, -ūs* hand + *suēscere* be(come) accustomed; influenced by Old French *mestif* mongrel, ultimately < Latin *mixtus,* past participle of *miscēre* mingle]

Mastiff (27 to 33 in. high at the shoulder)

mas·ti·tis (mas tī′tis), *n.* **1.** inflammation of the breast. **2.** inflammation of the mammary glands or the udder of a cow, sow, etc., caused by bacteria or fungi; garget: *Mastitis, the most costly disease of dairy cattle in the United States* (Science News Letter). [< Greek *mastós* breast + English *-itis*]

mast·less[1] (mast′lis, mäst′-), *adj.* having no mast: *a mastless ship.*

mast·less[2] (mast′lis, mäst′-), *adj.* bearing or producing no mast: *a mastless beech.*

mas·to·don (mas′tə don), *n.* a very large, extinct mammal, much like an elephant: *Prehistoric relatives of the elephant were the mammoths and mastodons that lived in temperate and frigid climates . . .* (A.M. Winchester). [< French *mastodonte* < New Latin *Mastodon* the genus name < Greek *mastós* breast + *odoús, odóntos* tooth (from the nipplelike projections on its teeth)]

mas·to·don·ic (mas′tə don′ik), *adj.* gigantic; immense.

mas·to·don·tic (mas′tə don′tik), *adj.* of or like a mastodon; gigantic.

mas·toid (mas′toid), *n.* **1.** a projection of the temporal bone behind the ear. **2.** *Informal.* mastoiditis.
—*adj.* **1.** of, having to do with, or near the mastoid. **2.** of or designating certain air cells near the mastoid. **3.** shaped like a breast or nipple. [< Greek *mastoeidḗs* < *mastós* breast + *eîdos* form]

mas·toi·de·al (mas toi′dē əl), *adj.* mastoid.

mas·toi·de·an (mas toi′dē ən), *adj.* mastoid.

mas·toid·ec·to·my (mas′toi dek′tə mē), *n., pl.* **-mies.** removal of the mastoid.

mas·toid·i·tis (mas′toi dī′tis), *n.* infection of the mastoid.

mas·tur·bate (mas′tər bāt), *v.,* **-bat·ed, -bat·ing.** —*v.i.* to engage in masturbation. —*v.t.* to subject to masturbation. [< Latin *māsturbārī* (with English *-ate*[1]), perhaps < *manus, -ūs* hand + *stuprāre* defile < *stuprum* defilement]

mas·tur·ba·tion (mas′tər bā′shən), *n.* the producing of an orgasm or sexual excitement by manipulation of one's own genitals; self-abuse; onanism; autoerotism.

mas·tur·ba·tion·al (mas′tər bā′shə nəl), *adj.* masturbatory.

mas·tur·ba·tor (mas′tər bā′tər), *n.* a person who practices masturbation.

mas·tur·ba·to·ry (mas′tər bə tôr′ē, -tōr′-), *adj.* of or having to do with masturbation.

ma·su·ri·um (mə zůr′ē əm), *n.* the former name of the chemical element technetium. [< New Latin *masurium* < *Masuria,* formerly district in East Prussia]

mat[1] (mat), *n., v.,* **mat·ted, mat·ting.** —*n.* **1.** a piece of coarse fabric like a small rug, made of woven grass, straw, rope, etc., used as a floor covering, for wiping shoes on, etc.: *I didn't fancy that the red carpet would be out; some form of mat, perhaps* (Sunday Times). **2.** a smaller piece of material, often ornamental, set upon a table or the like, as under a dish, vase, lamp, or the like. **3.** a large, thick pad covering a ring or part of a floor, used to protect wrestlers or gymnasts. **4.** anything packed or tangled thickly together: *a mat of weeds.* **5.** *Printing.* a matrix. **6.** a bag made of matting, used to hold coffee, sugar, spices, etc.
go to the mat with, a. to meet (a person) in a contest of wrestling: *The champion went to the mat with the challenger.* **b.** to contend with over a matter at issue: *The union may go to the mat with the management over wages.*
—*v.t.* **1.** to cover with or as if with mats or matting: *This vine . . . has clothed and matted with its many branches the four walls* (Cardinal Newman). **2.** to pack or tangle thickly (together): *The swimmer's wet hair was matted together. Willow and cottonwood trees, so closely interlocked and matted together, as to be nearly impassable* (Washington Irving).
—*v.i.* to pack or tangle thickly together: *The fur collar mats when it gets wet.*
[Old English *matt, meatt* < Late Latin *matta,* probably < Semitic (compare Hebrew *mittāh* floor)]

mat[2] (mat), *n., v.,* **mat·ted, mat·ting.** —*n.* a border or background for a picture between it and the frame. —*v.t.* to put a mat around or under: *to mat a picture.* [< Old French *mat* (originally) dull, dead, perhaps < Latin *mattus* maudlin or sodden]

mat[3] (mat), *adj., n., v.,* **mat·ted, mat·ting.** —*adj.* **1.** dull; not shiny: *a mat finish.* **2.** made dull by roughening, as with a tool.
—*n.* **1.** a dull surface or finish. **2.** a tool for producing a dull surface or finish.
—*v.t.* to give a dull surface or finish to. [< French *mat;* see MAT[2]]

mat., matins.

Mat·a·be·le (mat′ə bē′lē), *n., pl.* **-le** or **-les.** a member of a powerful Bantu tribe now occupying the western part of Southern Rhodesia: *The Matabele . . . still lived for the most part in Zulu fashion, grouped in kraals, within sixty miles of Buluwayo* (Eric Walker).

mat·a·dor (mat′ə dôr), *n.* **1.** the chief performer in a bullfight, whose duty is to kill the bull: *When an apprentice bullfighter . . . is considered ready to compete with the full matadors, his manager arranges a ceremonial fight* (New Yorker). **2.** a high-ranking card in certain games such as quadrille and ombre. [< Spanish *matador* killer < Latin *mactātor* one who sacrifices < *mactāre* sacrifice (originally) honor (a god) by offerings]

Matador (def. 1)

Ma·ta Ha·ri (mä′tə hä′rē, mat′ə har′ē), a woman spy, especially one who seduces men to obtain military secrets: *. . . a Mata Hari from Minnesota who worked for British Intelligence* (Time). [< *Mata Hari* (Gertrude Margarete Zelle), 1876-1917, a Dutch dancer who lived in France and spied for the Germans during World War I]

ma·ta·ma·ta (mä′tə mä′tə), *n.* a fresh-water turtle of Guiana and Brazil, having a brown carapace covered with pyramid-shaped growths. [< a native word]

mat·a·ra (mat′ər ə), *n.* a high-quality brown seal fur much prized for women's fashions: *a coat of matara seal* (New Yorker). [perhaps < an Eskimo word]

match[1] (mach), *n.* **1.** a short, slender piece of wood, pasteboard, etc., tipped with a mixture that takes fire when rubbed on a rough or specially prepared surface: *The heads of matches have, at the very tip, a chemical called phosphorus sulfide.* **2.** a cord or fuse prepared to burn at a uniform rate, formerly used for firing guns and cannon. **3.** *Obsolete.* a piece of cord, cloth, paper, wood, etc., dipped in melted sulfur, ignited by the use of a tinderbox. [< Old French *meiche,* probably < Latin *myxa* < Greek *mýxa* lamp wick; (originally) mucus, slime; influenced by Vulgar Latin *muccāre* to snuff (a candle) < Latin *muccus* mucus]

match[2] (mach), *n.* **1.** a person able to contend or compete with another as an equal: *to meet one's match. A boy is not a match for a man.* **2.** a person or thing that equals another in some respect: *A period which . . . has not had its match in the history of the world* (John Galt). **3.** a person or thing that is like or forms an exact pair with another: *The all-seeing sun Ne'er saw her match* (Shakespeare). **4.** two persons or things that are alike or go well together: *Those two horses make a good match.* **5. a.** a game; contest: *a tennis match.* **b.** an engagement for a game or contest. **6.** a marriage: *We had projected a match between him and a gentleman's daughter in the next county* (Tobias Smollett). **7.** a person considered as a possible husband or wife: *That young man is a good match.* **8.** *Obsolete.* an agreement; compact; bargain: *A match! 'tis done* (Shakespeare).
—*v.t.* **1.** to be equal to; be a match for: *No one could match the unknown archer. The event cannot . . . match the expectation* (Charlotte Brontë). **2.** to be the same as: *The color of the skirt does not match that of the coat.* **3.** to make like; fit together: *To match our spirits to our day And make a joy of duty* (John Greenleaf Whittier). **4.** to find or produce an equal to: *To match this scenery you must go a long distance. Modern craftsmen have been unable so far to match objects produced by some of the ancient lost arts.* **5.** to arrange a match for; marry: *The duke matched his daughter with the king's son.* **6.** to put in opposition; oppose: *Tom matched his strength against Dick's.* **7.** to pair as opponents or competitors; provide with an opponent or competitor of equal power: *The champions of each league were matched for a game. A heavyweight and a lightweight cannot be matched.* —*v.i.* **1.** to be alike; go well together: *The rugs and the wallpaper match.* **2.** to marry.
[Old English *mæcca* < *gemæcca* companion. Related to MAKE[2].] —**match′er,** *n.*
—**Syn.** *n.* **5. a.** competition, tournament, tourney.

match·a·ble (mach′ə bəl), *adj.* that can be matched.

match·board (mach′bôrd′, -bōrd′), *n.* a board with a tongue cut along one edge and a groove along the opposite edge, so as to fit together with similar boards, used in floors, siding, etc.

match·book (mach′bůk′), *n.* a number of safety matches gathered together within a cardboard cover for ease of carrying, the cover bearing the striking surface: *Slowly she detached a match from the paper matchbook she held in her hand* (New Yorker).

match·box (mach′boks′), *n.* a cardboard box for holding or carrying matches, usually with a striking surface on one side.

matched order (macht), an instruction to a broker to buy and sell an equal amount of a certain commodity, stock, etc., at the same price.

match·less (mach′lis), *adj.* so great or wonderful that it cannot be equaled; peerless: *matchless courage.* —**match′less·ly,** *adv.* —**match′less·ness,** *n.* —**Syn.** unequaled, unparalleled, unrivaled.

match·lock (mach′lok′), *n.* **1.** an old form of gun fired by lighting the powder with a wick or cord. **2.** a gunlock on such gun.

match·make (mach′māk′), *v.,* **-made, -mak·ing.** —*v.i.* to arrange or try to arrange a marriage: *Nor did I matchmake for Rose, who was quite able to find her own young men* (Harper's). —*v.t.* to arrange a marriage for: *Capitol busybodies have tried to matchmake widow Smith with Georgia's Senator Richard B. Russell* (Time).

match·mak·er[1] (mach′mā′kər), *n.* **1.** a person who arranges, or tries to arrange, marriages for others. **2.** a person who arranges contests, prize fights, races, etc.: *Sam Silverman, matchmaker for the independent Andy Callahan ... booked the fifteen-round match for Boston Garden* (New York Times).

match·mak·er[2] (mach′mā′kər), *n.* a person who makes matches for burning.

match·mak·ing[1] (mach′mā′king), *n.* **1.** the business of arranging or making matches for prize fighters, etc. **2.** the practice of trying to arrange marriages. —*adj.* having to do with matchmakers or matchmaking.

match·mak·ing[2] (mach′mā′king), *n.* the business of making matches for burning. —*adj.* having to do with matchmakers or matchmaking.

match play, 1. a way of playing golf in which the player or side that wins the greatest number of holes is the winner, regardless of total strokes. **2.** a play in any match, as in handball or tennis.

match point, 1. the concluding point that is needed to win a match, as in tennis. **2.** *Especially British.* a point scored in a sports match: *The British team continued to disappoint, and although they beat Finland to-day by 53 match points ...* (London Times).

match·safe (mach′sāf′), *n.* a box for holding matches; matchbox.

match·stick (mach′stik′), *n.* a stick or slender piece of wood, of which a match is made: *The convict took the bird to his cell, fashioned a splint from a matchstick and nursed the injured fledgling back to health* (Newsweek).

match·wood (mach′wu̇d′), *n.* **1.** wood for making matches. **2.** splinters; tiny pieces.

mate[1] (māt), *n., v.,* **mat·ed, mat·ing.** —*n.* **1.** one of a pair: *Where is the mate to this glove?* **2.** a husband or wife; spouse. **3. a.** a deck officer of a merchant ship, next below the captain; first mate. **b.** any of various other deck officers in the line of command: *a second mate.* **4.** an assistant to a specialist on a ship: *a carpenter's mate, a cook's mate.* **5.** a petty officer in the United States Navy acting as assistant to a warrant officer and in charge of a certain mission, duty, or function: *a gunner's mate.* **6.** a companion; fellow worker: *Hand me a hammer, mate.* **7.** one of a pair of animals that are mated: *The eagle mourned his dead mate.* **8.** *Archaic.* an equal; match: *I know you proud to bear your name, Your pride is yet no mate for mine* (Tennyson).
—*v.t., v.i.* **1.** to join in a pair; couple; pair. **2.** to join as husband and wife; marry: *She's above mating with such as I* (Thomas Hardy). **3.** (of animals) to pair; breed: *Birds mate in the spring.* **4.** *Obsolete.* to match.
[apparently < Middle Low German *mate* messmate. Compare MEAT.]
—**Syn.** *n.* **6.** comrade, crony.

mate[2] (māt), *n., v.,* **mat·ed, mat·ing,** *interj.* —*n.* a checkmate; defeat in the game of chess. —*v.t.* to checkmate. —*interj.* checkmate. [< Old French *mater* to checkmate < *mat* checkmated, defeated < Arabic *māta* he died]

ma·té or **ma·te**[3] (mä′tā, mat′ā), *n.* **1.** a kind of tea made from the dried leaves and shoots of a South American holly. **2.** the plant itself. **3.** its leaves. Also, **Paraguay tea.** [< Spanish *mate.* (originally) the cup holding the drink < Quechua (Peru) *mati* calabash dish; *maté,* probably < French *maté* < Spanish *mate*]

Mat·e·be·le (mat′ə bē′lē), *n., pl.* **-le** or **-les.** Matabele.

mat·e·lasse (mat′ə las), *n.* matelassé.

mate·las·sé (mȧt lȧ sā′), *adj.* (of fabrics) woven with a raised pattern, as if quilted. —*n.* a matelassé fabric, as of silk, or of silk and wool: *Brocades and matelassés are at their best for these loose and voluminous evening wraps* (London Times). [< French *matelassé*]

mate·less (māt′lis), *adj.* without a mate or companion.

mate·lot (mȧt lō′), *n.* **1.** *French.* a sailor: *The drunken, moronic, embittered, panicky matelots are quite unable to steer the ship* (Observer). **2.** a sailor-type blouse [< French *matelot*]

mat·e·lote (mat′ə lōt), *n.* a fish stew cooked in red or white wine instead of water, with onions and herbs as flavoring: *... wine and eels and bacon and onion and herbs and judgment go into a matelote, and the eels should be fresh* (New Yorker). [< French *matelote* < *matelot* sailor]

mat·e·lotte (mat′ə lot), *n.* matelote.

ma·ter (mā′tər), *n. British Informal.* mother: *You're the kid whose mater kissed him goodbye, aren't you?* (New Yorker). [< Latin *māter, mātris*]

Ma·ter Do·lo·ro·sa (mā′tər dō′lə rō′sə), *Latin.* **1.** the Virgin Mary. **2.** a picture or statue of Mary grieving over the crucified Christ.

ma·ter·fa·mil·i·as (mā′tər fə mil′ē əs), *n. Latin.* the mother of a household; woman head of a house.

ma·te·ri·al (mə tir′ē əl), *n.* **1.** what a thing is made from; substance of anything manufactured or built: *building materials.* **2.** cloth: *dress material.* **3.** anything serving as crude or raw matter for working upon or developing: *His files contain enough notes, facts, ideas, and other material for a score of books.*
materials, articles necessary for making or doing something: *writing materials, teaching materials.*
—*adj.* **1.** having to do with whatever occupies space; of matter; physical: *the material world.* **2.** of or having to do with the body: *Food and shelter are material comforts.* **3.** caring too much for the things of this world and neglecting spiritual needs; worldly: *a material point of view.* **4.** that matters greatly; important: *Hard work is a material factor in success.* **5.** *Law.* providing or likely to provide information that might determine the decision of a case: *material evidence, a material witness.* **6.** *Philosophy.* of or having to do with matter as distinguished from form.
[< Latin *māteriālis* < *māteria* substance, matter < *māter* source, origin; mother. Compare MATTER. Doublet of MATÉRIEL.]
—**Syn.** *n.* **1.** See **substance.** *-adj.* **2.** bodily. **4.** essential, pertinent.

ma·te·ri·al·ise (mə tir′ē ə līz), *v.i., v.t.,* **-ised, -is·ing.** *Especially British.* materialize: *The expected increase in the volume of business duly materialised last year* (Economist).

ma·te·ri·al·ism (mə tir′ē ə liz′əm), *n.* **1.** the belief that all action, thought, and feeling can be explained by the movements and changes of matter: *In the latter half of the 1800's, materialism severely challenged the traditional spiritual view of man* (Science). **2.** the tendency to care too much for the things of this world and neglect spiritual needs: *Our materialism has produced too much dependence upon industry* (Atlantic). **3.** the ethical doctrine that material self-interest should and does determine conduct.

ma·te·ri·al·ist (mə tir′ē ə list), *n.* **1.** a believer in materialism in philosophy or ethics: *... the current split betweeen the materialists and the idealists* (London Times). **2.** a person who cares too much for the things of this world and neglects spiritual needs. —*adj.* of or having to do with materialism; materialistic.

ma·te·ri·al·is·tic (mə tir′ē ə lis′tik), *adj.* of materialists or materialism; characterized by materialism.—**ma·te′ri·al·is′ti·cal·ly,** *adv.*

ma·te·ri·al·i·ty (mə tir′ē al′ə tē), *n., pl.* **-ties. 1.** the quality of being material. **2.** material nature or character. **3.** something that is material.

ma·te·ri·al·i·za·tion (mə tir′ē ə lə zā′shən), *n.* **1.** a materializing. **2.** a being materialized.

ma·te·ri·al·ize (mə tir′ē ə līz), *v.,* **-ized, -iz·ing.** —*v.i.* **1.** to become an actual fact; be realized: *Our plans for the party did not materialize.* **2.** to appear in bodily form: *A spirit materialized from the smoke of the magician's fire. Wang vanished from the scene, to materialize presently in front of the house* (Joseph Conrad). —*v.t.* **1.** to give material form to: *An inventor materializes his ideas by building a model.* **2.** to cause to appear in bodily form: *If you materialize angels in that way, where are you going to stop?* (James M. Barrie). **3.** to make materialistic: *The system ... tends to materialize our upper class, vulgarize our middle class, brutalize our lower class* (Matthew Arnold). —**ma·te′ri·al·iz′er,** *n.*

ma·te·ri·al·ly (mə tir′ē ə lē), *adv.* **1.** with regard to material things; physically: *He improved materially and spiritually.* **2.** considerably; greatly: *The tide helped the progress of the boat materially.* **3.** in matter or substance; not in form: *What is formally correct may be materially false* (Charles S.C. Bowen). —**Syn. 2.** substantially.

ma·te·ri·al·ness (mə tir′ē əl nis), *n.* the quality of being material.

ma·te·ri·als (mə tir′ē əlz), *n.pl.* See under **material,** *n.*

ma·te·ri·a med·i·ca (mə tir′ē ə med′ə kə), **1.** the drugs or other substances used in medicine. **2.** the branch of medical science dealing with these drugs and substances. [< New Latin *materia medica* healing matter]

ma·té·ri·el (mə tir′ē el′), *n.* everything used by an army, organization, undertaking, etc.; equipment: *The general said the Iron Curtain countries had vast resources in manpower and matériel* (New York Times). [< French *matériel* material, learned borrowing of Latin *māteriālis.* Doublet of MATERIAL.]

ma·ter·nal (mə tėr′nəl), *adj.* **1.** of, having to do with, or like a mother; motherly: *maternal kindness.* **2.** related on the mother's side of the family: *Everyone has two maternal grandparents and two paternal grandparents.* **3.** received or inherited from a mother. [< Middle French *maternel,* learned borrowing from Vulgar Latin *māternālis* < Latin *māternus* maternal < *māter, mātris* mother] —**ma·ter′nal·ly,** *adv.*

ma·ter·nal·ism (mə tėr′nə liz əm), *n.* maternal quality or condition; motherliness.

ma·ter·nal·ize (mə tėr′nə līz), *v.t.,* **-ized, -iz·ing.** to make maternal.

ma·ter·ni·ty (mə tėr′nə tē), *n.* **1.** being a mother; motherhood. **2.** the qualities of a mother; motherliness.
—*adj.* **1.** for a pregnant woman: *maternity clothes.* **2.** for women in or after childbirth: *maternity care, a maternity ward.*

maternity hospital, a hospital for the care of women giving birth to children.

mate·ship (māt′ship), *n.* **1.** comradeship; fellowship. **2.** (in Australia) fellowship based on equal opportunity for all.

mat·ey (mā′tē), *adj., n., pl.* **mat·eys.** *British Informal.* —*adj.* friendly; sociable; companionable. —*n.* mate; fellow worker. —**mat′ey·ness,** *n.*

math[1] (math), *n. Obsolete.* the amount of a crop mowed; a mowing. [Old English *mǣth*]

math[2] (math), *n. U.S. Informal.* mathematics: *A guidance counselor who has not taken any math courses himself ... is likely to advise his students not to take any* (New York Times).

math., **1.** mathematical. **2.** mathematician. **3.** mathematics.

math·e·mat·ic (math′ə mat′ik, math-mat′-), *adj.* mathematical. —*n.* mathematics. [Middle English *mathematique* < Old French < Latin *mathēmatica* (*ars*) mathematical science < Greek *mathēmatikḗ* (*téchnē*), feminine singular of *mathēmatikós* relating to knowledge < *máthēma, -atos* science < *math-,* stem of *manthánein* to learn]

math·e·mat·i·cal (math′ə mat′ə kəl, math-mat′-), *adj.* **1.** of, having to do with, used in, or like mathematics: *mathematical problems.* **2.** exact; accurate: *mathematical measurements.* —**Syn. 2.** precise.

mathematical logic, symbolic logic.

math·e·mat·i·cal·ly (math′ə mat′ə klē, math mat′-), *adv.* **1.** according to mathematics. **2.** in a mathematical manner; exactly; accurately; precisely.

math·e·ma·ti·cian (math′ə mə tish′ən, math′mə-), *n.* a person skilled in mathematics: *The mathematician's work is on a higher level of abstraction and more remote from psychology as such* (Science News).

math·e·mat·ics (math′ə mat′iks, math-mat′-), *n.* the science dealing with the measurement, properties, and relationships of quantities, as expressed in numbers or symbols. Mathematics includes arithmetic, algebra, geometry, calculus, and the like. *Abbr.:* math. [see MATHEMATIC]

math·e·ma·ti·za·tion (math′ə mə tə zā′-shən, math′mə-), *n.* the formulation of something into mathematical form or terms.

math·e·mat·ize (math′ə mə tīz, math′mə-) *v.t., v.i.*, **-ized, -iz·ing.** to formulate something into mathematical terms.

ma·thet·ic (mə thet′ik), *adj.* of or having to do with learning: . . . *mathetic programming* (Harper's). [< Greek *mathētikós* < *manthánein* to learn]

maths (maths), *n. British Informal.* mathematics.

mat·ie (mā′tē), *n.* a herring having the roe or milt perfectly but not largely developed. [< Dutch *maatjes* (*haring*), literally, maiden (herring)]

mat·i·ly (mā′tə lē), *adv. British Informal.* in a matey manner; sociably: *She runs up and down, waving matily to the gallery, like Gracie Fields greeting an old Rochdale friend* (Sunday Times).

mat·in (mat′ən), *n.* **1.** *Poetic.* a morning call or song, as of birds: *The sprightly lark's shrill matin wakes the morn* (Edward Young). **2.** matins. **3.** *Obsolete.* the morning: *The glow-worm shows the matin to be near, And 'gins to pale his uneffectual fire* (Shakespeare).
—*adj.* having to do with or occurring in the early morning.
[< Old French *matin;* see MATINS]

mat·in·al (mat′ə nəl), *adj.* **1.** early; morning. **2.** early-rising.

mat·i·née or **mat·i·nee** (mat′ə nā′; *especially British* mat′ə nā), *n.* a dramatic or musical performance held in the afternoon. —*adj.* of a matinée: *a matinée audience.* [< French *matinée* < Old French *matin* morning (that is, daytime); see MATINS]

matinée or **matinee idol,** a handsome actor attractive especially to women who attend matinées: *"The Four Horsemen of the Apocalypse" brought fame to Rudolph Valentino, the matinee idol of the day* (World Book Encyclopedia).

mat·i·ness (mā′tē nis), *n. British Informal.* the quality or condition of being matey. Also, **mateyness.**

mat·ing (mā′ting), *n.* **1.** a matching. **2.** a marrying. **3.** a pairing, as of birds.

mating call, the special call or noise made by an animal, insect, etc., in trying to attract a mate.

mat·ins (mat′ənz), *n.pl.* **1.** the first of the seven canonical hours in the breviary of the Roman Catholic Church. **2.** the service for this hour, properly starting at midnight but often said as a dawn service and joined to lauds. **3.** the order for public morning prayer in the Anglican Church; mattins. **4.** *Poetic.* a morning song; matin. [< Old French *matines* < *matin* < Latin *mātūtīnus* of, or in, the morning < *Mātūta* a dawn goddess]

mat·rass (mat′rəs), *n.* **1.** a small glass tube with one end closed, used by chemists in blowpipe analysis. **2.** a round or oval glass vessel with a long neck, formerly used for distilling, evaporating, etc.; bolthead. Also, **mattrass.** [< Middle French *matheras,* perhaps < Arabic *maṭara* vase, bottle]

ma·tri·arch (mā′trē ärk), *n.* **1.** a mother who is the ruler of a family or tribe: *a crowded company of more than fifty persons, with the imperial matriarch in their midst* (Lytton Strachey). **2.** a venerable old woman. [< Latin *māter, mātris* mother + English (patri)*arch*]

ma·tri·ar·chal (mā′trē är′kəl), *adj.* **1.** of a matriarch or matriarchy. **2.** suitable for a matriarch.

ma·tri·ar·chal·ism (mā′trē är′kə liz əm), *n.* **1.** a being matriarchal. **2.** matriarchal customs or practices.

ma·tri·ar·chate (mā′trē är′kit, -kāt), *n.* **1.** a family or community governed by a matriarch. **2.** a matriarchal system.

ma·tri·ar·chic (mā′trē är′kik), *adj.* of or having to do with a matriarchy or a matriarch; matriarchal.

ma·tri·ar·chy (mā′trē är′kē), *n., pl.* **-chies.** **1.** a form of social organization in which the mother is the ruler of a family or tribe, descent being traced through the mother: *Matriarchy (absolute rule by women) and patriarchy (absolute rule by men) are exceedingly rare extremes* (Beals and Hoijer). **2.** government by women; matriarchate.

ma·tric (mə trik′), *n. British Informal.* matriculation; a matriculation examination: *Those who did not pass matric were still able to go to sea* (Cape Times).

ma·tri·cal (mat′rə kəl), *adj.* having to do with a matrix.

mat·ri·car·i·a (mat′rə kãr′ē ə), *n.* **1.** the feverfew plant. **2. a.** any of a group of daisylike plants of the composite family found chiefly in the Old World, as the camomile. **b.** the dried flower heads of the camomile used in medicine. [< Medieval Latin *matricaria* < Latin *mātrīx, -īcis* womb (for its supposed medicinal qualities)]

mat·ri·cen·tric (mat′rə sen′trik), *adj.* having or recognizing the mother as the center of the family: *Many lower-class Negro families are matricentric families: a woman and her children, with only vague or temporary associations with adult males* (Scientific American).

ma·tri·ces (mā′trə sēz, mat′rə-), *n.* a plural of **matrix.**

ma·tri·cid·al[1] (mā′trə sī′dəl, mat′rə-), *adj.* killing or tending to kill one's mother. [< *matricid*(e)[1] + *-al*[1]]

ma·tri·cid·al[2] (mā′trə sī′dəl, mat′rə-), *adj.* of or having to do with a person who is a matricide. [< *matricid*(e)[2] + *-al*[1]]

ma·tri·cide[1] (mā′trə sīd, mat′rə-), *n.* the act of killing one's mother. [< Latin *mātricīdium* < *māter* mother + *-cīdium* act of killing, -cide[2]]

ma·tri·cide[2] (mā′trə sīd, mat′rə-), *n.* a person who kills his mother. [< Latin *mātricīda* < *māter* mother + *-cīda* killer, -cide[1]]

ma·tric·u·lant (mə trik′yə lənt), *n.* a person who matriculates; candidate for matriculation.

ma·tric·u·late (*v.* mə trik′yə lāt; *n.* mə-trik′yə lit), *v.*, **-lat·ed, -lat·ing,** *n.* —*v.t., v.i.* **1.** to enroll as a student in a college or university. **2.** to enroll as a candidate for a degree: *Three years later he matriculated for advance study* (Harper's). —*n.* a person who has been matriculated. [< Latin *mātrīcula* a public register (diminutive) < *mātrīx, -īcis* register, loan-translation of Greek *mḗtrā* register of property; + English *-ate*[1]]

ma·tric·u·la·tion (mə trik′yə lā′shən), *n.* a matriculating; enrollment or admission as a student in a college or university.

ma·tric·u·la·tor (mə trik′yə lā′tər), *n.* a person who matriculates.

mat·ri·lat·er·al (mat′rə lat′ər əl), *adj.* related on the mother's side of the family; maternal.

mat·ri·lin·e·age (mat′rə lin′ē ij), *n.* the line of descent from a female ancestor or the maternal side of a family, clan, etc.

mat·ri·lin·e·al (mat′rə lin′ē əl), *adj.* having or maintaining relationship through the female line of a family, clan, tribe, etc.: *In most of Nyasaland the tribes are . . . matrilineal and uxorilocal; rights in land descend in the female line, and when a man marries he goes to live in his wife's village* (Manchester Guardian). [< Latin *māter, mātris* mother + English *lineal*] —**mat′ri·lin′e·al·ly,** *adv.*

mat·ri·lin·e·ar (mat′rə lin′ē ər), *adj.* matrilineal.

mat·ri·li·ny (mat′rə lī′nē), *n.* the taking of relationship and descent through the female line.

mat·ri·lo·cal (mat′rə lō′kəl), *adj.* having its focus in the home of the wife's family: *The Zuni have matrilocal residence which means that newlyweds make their home with the parents of the bride* (Ogburn and Nimkoff). [< Latin *māter, mātris* mother + *locus* place + English *-al*[1]]

mat·ri·lo·cal·i·ty (mat′rə lō kal′ə tē), *n.* residence in or near the home of the wife's family: *When a girl wants to live near her mother rather than her mother-in-law it is called matrilocality* (Manchester Guardian Weekly).

mat·ri·mo·ni·al (mat′rə mō′nē əl), *adj.* of or having to do with matrimony or marriage: *matrimonial vows, matrimonial agencies.* —**Syn.** nuptial, connubial.

mat·ri·mo·ni·al·ly (mat′rə mō′nē ə lē), *adv.* **1.** according to the custom or laws of matrimony. **2.** with regard to matrimony. **3.** by matrimony.

mat·ri·mo·ny (mat′rə mō′nē), *n., pl.* **-nies.** **1.** married life: *In religion and matrimony I never give advice; because I will not have anybody's torments in this world or the next laid to my charge* (Philip D. Stanhope) **2.** the rite or ceremony of marriage; act of marrying. **3.** the relation between married persons; wedlock: *to unite in holy matrimony.* **4. a.** a card game in which players score for holding certain combinations of cards. **b.** a king and queen of the same suit; marriage. [< Old French *matrimoine,* learned borrowing from Latin *mātrimōnium* < *māter, mātris* mother] —**Syn. 2, 3.** See **marriage.**

matrimony vine, the boxthorn.

ma·trix (mā′triks, mat′riks), *n., pl.* **-tri·ces** or **-trix·es. 1.** something that gives origin or form to something enclosed within it: **a.** a mold for a casting. **b.** the rock in which crystallized minerals or gems are embedded: *By etching away the limestone matrix in dilute acid, the silicified fossils, which are not affected by the acid, are freed from the rock* (World Book Encyclopedia). **2.** *Printing.* a mold for casting type faces. **3.** the womb. **4. a.** *Anatomy.* the formative part of an organ, such as the skin beneath a fingernail, toenail, etc. **b.** *Biology.* the intercellular substance of a tissue. **5.** *Mathematics.* a set of quantities in a rectangular array, subject to operations such as multiplication or inversion according to specified rules. [< Latin *mātrīx, -īcis* womb, breeding animal < *māter, mātris* mother]

matrix algebra, algebra in which the symbols are placed in a rectangular set of compartments in which an unoccupied space represents a zero.

ma·tron (mā′trən), *n.* **1.** a married woman, especially a mother, who is mature in age, character, or bearing: *a department store that caters to young matrons.* **2.** a woman who manages the household affairs or supervises the inmates of a school, hospital, or other institution: *A police matron has charge of the women in a jail.* [< Old French *matrone,* learned borrowing from Latin *mātrōna* < *māter, mātris* mother]

ma·tron·age (mā′trə nij, mat′rə-), *n.* **1.** matrons as a group. **2.** guardianship by a matron. **3.** the state of being a matron.

ma·tron·al (mā′trə nəl), *adj.* **1.** of or having to do with a matron. **2.** suitable to a matron. **3.** matronly.

ma·tron·hood (mā′trən hůd), *n.* the condition of being a matron.

ma·tron·ize (mā′trə nīz, mat′rə-), *v.t.*, **-ized, -iz·ing. 1.** to make matronly. **2.** to chaperon.

ma·tron·like (mā′trən līk′), *adj.* resembling or befitting a matron; matronly.

ma·tron·li·ness (mā′trən lē nis), *n.* matronly quality.

ma·tron·ly (mā′trən lē), *adj.* like a matron; suitable for a matron; dignified: *a plain, matronly woman, neat matronly attire.* —*adv.* in the manner of a matron.

matron of honor, a married woman who is the chief attendant of the bride at a wedding.

ma·tron·ship (mā′trən ship), *n.* the condition or position of a matron.

mat·ro·nym·ic (mat′rə nim′ik), *adj., n.* metronymic.

ma·tross (mə tros′), *n.* formerly, a soldier next in rank below a gunner in a train of artillery, who acted as an assistant or mate. [< Dutch *matroos* sailor]

Mats., matinées.

MATS (no periods) or **M.A.T.S.,** *U.S.* Military Air Transport Service.

mat·su (mat′sü), *n.* the most common tree of Japan, a pine that grows for a very long time and becomes very large. Its wood is valuable for household carpentry and furniture. [< Japanese *matsu*]

matt (mat), *adj., n., v.t.* mat[3].

Matt., Matthew (book of the New Testament).

matte (mat), *n., adj., v.*, **mat·ted, mat·ting.** —*n.* **1.** an impure and unfinished product, a mixture of sulfides, of the smelting of various sulfide ores, especially those of copper. **2.** a dull surface or finish; mat.
—*adj.* not shiny; dull; mat.
—*v.t.* to give a dull surface or finish to; mat. [< French *matte;* see MAT[2]]

mat·ted[1] (mat′id), *adj.* formed into a mat; entangled in a thick mass: *a matted growth of shrubs.*

mat·ted[2] (mat′id), *adj.* having a dull finish.

mat·ter (mat′ər), *n.* **1.** what things are made of; material; substance: *All matter is mostly vacuum, thinly populated with minute particles such as electrons and protons* (John R. Pierce). **2. a.** the substance of the ma-

terial world; the opposite of mind or spirit: *Matter occupies space.* **b.** a specific substance or body: *foreign matter, coloring matter, printed matter.* **3.** an affair: *business matters, a matter of life and death. They order, said I, this matter better in France* (Laurence Sterne). **4.** what is said or written, thought of apart from the way in which it is said or written: *the matter of his speech.* **5.** grounds; occasion; cause: *You have no matter for complaint in that. Neither can he that mindeth but his own business find much matter for envy* (Francis Bacon). **6.** a thing or things: *a matter of record, a matter of accident.* **7.** an amount; quantity: *a matter of two days, a matter of 20 miles. The matter of a fortnight* (Thomas Carlyle). **8.** importance; significance: *Let it go since it is of no matter.* **9.** mail: *Second-class matter requires less postage than first-class matter.* **10.** a substance secreted by a living body, especially pus. **11.** things written or printed: *reading matter.* **12.** *Printing.* **a.** something to be printed; copy. **b.** type that has been composed. **13.** *Law.* something to be tried or proved; statements or allegations coming before the court; something in a document.
for that matter, so far as that is concerned: *For that matter, we had intelligence* (John Dryden).
no laughing matter, a matter that is serious: *The accident was no laughing matter.*
no matter, a. never mind; it is not important: "*He has lost his key to the trunk ....*" "*No matter; we can break it open*" (Maria Edgeworth). **b.** regardless of: *No matter what excuse he gives, I will not forgive him for standing me up.*
not mince matters, to speak plainly and frankly: *A candid ferocity, if the case calls for it, is in him; he does not mince matters!* (Thomas Carlyle).
what is the matter? what is the trouble? *What is the matter with the child?*
—*v.i.* **1.** to be of importance: *Nothing seems to matter when you are sick. What they said matters little* (Bret Harte). **2.** to form pus; discharge pus; suppurate.
[< Old French *matiere* < Latin *māteria* substance, matter, growing layer in trees < *māter, mātris* mother. Compare MATERIAL.]
—**Syn.** *n.* **1.** stuff. See **substance. 4.** topic, subject. **8.** moment, concern.

mat·ter·ful (mat′ər fəl), *adj.* full of matter or substance: *a matterful book, a matterful lecture.*

mat·ter·less (mat′ər lis), *adj.* void of matter; of no consequence; immaterial.

matter of course, something to be expected: *She accepted the recurrence of his migraine at regular intervals as a matter of course.*

mat·ter-of-course (mat′ər əv kôrs′, -kōrs′), *adj.* **1.** to be expected; normal. **2.** accepting things as a matter of course: *the cool matter-of-course manner of this reply.*

matter of fact, something that is so; fact as contrasted with opinion, probability, or inference: *I was going to say when Truth broke in With all her matter of fact ...* (Robert Frost).
as a matter of fact, actually; in reality: *As a matter of fact, you are quite right* (J.K. Jerome).

mat·ter-of-fact (mat′ər əv fakt′), *adj.* dealing with facts; not fanciful; unimaginative; prosaic: *Iranian acceptance of these long-overdue exchanges has been calm and matter-of-fact* (Atlantic). —**mat′ter-of-fact′ly,** *adv.* —**mat′ter-of-fact′ness,** *n.*

matter of opinion, a debatable assertion or belief.

mat·ter·y (mat′ər ē), *adj.* full of pus; purulent.

Mat·the·an (mə thē′ən), *adj.* of, having to do with, or characteristic of the Evangelist Matthew or his gospel: *The basis upon which this constitutional position of the Pope rested was the interpretation of the crucial Matthean verses* (Listener).

Mat·thew (math′yü), *n.* **1.** one of the four Evangelists, a tax collector who was a follower of Christ. He was one of the twelve disciples chosen by Jesus as His Apostles. **2.** the first book of the New Testament, attributed to him. It tells the story of the life of Christ. *Abbr.:* Matt. [< French *Mathieu* < Late Latin *Matthaeus* < Greek *Matthaîos* < Hebrew *Mattīthyāh*]

Mat·thi·as (mə thī′əs), *n.* (in the Bible) a disciple chosen by lot to replace Judas Iscariot as one of the twelve Apostles. Acts 1:26.

mat·ting[1] (mat′ing), *n.* **1.** a fabric of grass, straw, hemp, or other fiber, for covering floors, for mats, for wrapping material, etc. **2.** mats. **3.** the making of mats.

mat·ting[2] (mat′ing), *n.* the producing of a mat surface, or such a surface itself, on metal articles, etc.

mat·tins (mat′ənz), *n.pl.* matins (the form preferred in the Anglican Church).

mat·tock (mat′ək), *n.* a tool like a pickax, but having a flat blade on one side or flat blades on both sides, used for loosening soil and cutting roots. [Old English *mattuc*]

Mattock

mat·toid (mat′oid), *n.* a person who has an abnormal mental condition bordering on insanity. [< Italian *mattoide* eccentric, half-insane < *matto* insane < Latin *mattus* tipsy, overcome by drink; see MAT[2]]

mat·trass (mat′rəs), *n.* matrass.

mat·tress (mat′ris), *n.* **1.** a covering of strong cloth stuffed with hair, cotton, straw, foam rubber, etc., used on a bed or as a bed. A spring mattress contains wire springs. **2.** a strong mat consisting of brush, rods, poles, etc., bound or twisted together, used to protect dikes, embankments, dams, etc., from erosion. [< Old French *materas* < Italian *materasso* < Arabic *al-maṭrah* the cushion; (literally) thing thrown down]

Ma·tu·ra diamond (mä′tə rə, mat′-), a colorless, brilliant variety of zircon, found in Ceylon; jargon. [< *Matura,* a town in Ceylon where it occurs]

mat·u·rate (mach′ů rāt), *v.i.,* **-rat·ed, -rat·ing. 1.** to discharge pus; suppurate. **2.** to ripen; mature. [< Latin *mātūrāre* (with English *-ate*[1]) < *mātūrus* ripe]

mat·u·ra·tion (mach′ů rā′shən), *n.* **1.** a formation of pus; suppuration. **2.** a growing and developing; a ripening; a maturing: *the germination and maturation of some truth* (Cardinal Newman). **3.** *Biology.* **a.** the final stages in the preparation of germ cells for fertilization, including meiosis and various changes in the cytoplasm: *At the close of the growth period, the reproductive cells undergo two special maturation divisions* (Beals and Hoijer). **b.** the development of a germ cell prior to meiosis. **c.** the last stage of differentiation in cellular growth.

mat·u·ra·tion·al (mach′ů rā′shə nəl), *adj.* of or having to do with maturation.

ma·tur·a·tive (mə chůr′ə tiv, mach′ə rā′-), *adj.* **1.** producing maturity; conducive to ripening. **2.** causing suppuration.

ma·ture (mə chůr′, -tůr′, -tyůr′), *adj., v.,* **-tured, -tur·ing.** —*adj.* **1. a.** full-grown; ripe: *a mature plant, a mature fruit. Fifty is a mature age.* **b.** fully developed in body and mind: *a mature person.* **c.** brought by time, treatment, etc., to the condition of full excellence: *mature wine, mature cheese.* **d.** characteristic of full development: *a mature appearance, mature wisdom.* **e.** fully worked out; carefully thought out; fully developed: *mature plans.* **2.** due; payable: *a mature note, a mature savings bond.* **3.** *Geology.* **a.** (of land) so long subjected to erosion as to show a relief of mainly smooth slopes. **b.** (of streams) fully adjusted to rock formations. **4.** in a state of suppuration.
—*v.i.* **1.** to come to full growth; ripen: *These apples are maturing fast.* **2.** to fall due: *This note to the bank matured yesterday.*
—*v.t.* **1.** to bring to full growth or development: *Her responsibilities matured her at an early age. His prudence was matured by experience* (Edward Gibbon). **2.** to work out carefully: *He matured his plans for a long trip.*
[< Latin *mātūrus* ripe] —**ma·ture′ly,** *adv.* —**ma·ture′ness,** *n.* —**ma·tur′er,** *n.*

ma·tu·ri·ty (mə chůr′ə tē, -tůr′-, -tyůr′-), *n., pl.* **-ties. 1.** a being mature; full development; ripeness: *He reached maturity at twenty years.* **2.** a being completed or ready: *We must not act until our plans and preparations reach maturity.* **3.** Also, **maturities. a.** a falling due: *U.S. Government obligations lost ground, particularly in the longer maturities, though trading volume continued quiet* (Wall Street Journal). **b.** the time a debt is payable. **4.** *Geology.* a stage in the evolutionary erosion of land areas where the flat uplands have been widely dissected by deep river valleys. —**Syn. 1.** adultness. **2.** readiness.

ma·tu·ti·nal (mə tü′tə nəl, -tyü′-), *adj.* **1.** occurring in the morning; early in the day; having to do with the morning: *A thundering sound of cowhide boots on the stairs announced that Sol's matutinal toilet was complete* (Harriet Beecher Stowe). **2.** early-rising. [< Late Latin *mātūtīnālis* < Latin *mātūtīnus* of, or in, the morning; see MATINS] —**ma·tu′ti·nal·ly,** *adv.*

mat·zah (mät′sə), *n., pl.* **-zahs.** matzo.

mat·zo (mät′sō), *n., pl.* **mat·zoth** (mät′sōth), or **mat·zos** (mät′sōs, -səz). a thin piece of unleavened bread, eaten by Jews especially during Passover. [< Yiddish *matse* < Hebrew *maṣṣāh* cake of unleavened bread]

maud (môd), *n.* **1.** a gray woolen plaid worn in southern Scotland: *The huntsmen, though hardy ... twitched their mauds, or Lowland plaids, close to their throats* (Scott). **2.** a small blanket or shawl of similar material. [origin uncertain]

maud·lin (môd′lən), *adj.* **1.** sentimental in a weak, silly way: *Sympathy for criminals is often maudlin. Is this a time ... for a maudlin universal sympathy?* (Mrs. Humphry Ward). **2.** sentimental and tearful because of drunkenness or excitement: *It is but yonder empty glass That makes me maudlin-moral* (Tennyson). [Middle English *Maudlin, Maudelen* < pronunciation of (Mary) *Magdalene,* often painted as weeping] —**maud′lin·ly,** *adv.* —**maud′lin·ness,** *n.* —**Syn. 1.** mawkish.

mau·gre or **mau·ger** (mô′gər), *prep. Archaic.* in spite of; notwithstanding: *But, maugre all these hardships, they pursued their journey cheerily* (Washington Irving). [< Old French *maugre,* earlier *malgré* (originally) ill will, spite < Latin *malō grātō* in spite of displeasure; (literally) with no thanks]

mau·ka (mou′kə), *adv., adj. Hawaiian.* toward the mountains.

mau·kin (mô′kin), *n. Dialect.* malkin.

maul (môl), *n.* **1.** a very heavy mallet or hammer for driving stakes, piles, or wedges, used in shipbuilding, mining, etc. **2.** *Archaic.* a heavy club or mace.
—*v.t.* **1.** to beat and pull about; handle roughly or carelessly; bruise: *Don't maul the cat. The lion mauled its keeper badly. He seized the gunwale, but the knives of our rowers so mauled his wrists that he was forced to quit his hold* (Herman Melville). **2.** *U.S.* to split (rails) with a maul and wedge.
[variant of Middle English *malle;* see MALL[1]] —**maul′er,** *n.*

Maul (def. 1)

maul·stick (môl′stik′), *n.* mahlstick.

Mau Mau (mou′ mou′), a secret society consisting chiefly of Kikuyu tribesmen sworn to expel Europeans from Kenya by violent means.

mau·met (mô′mit), *n.* **1.** *British Dialect.* a dressed-up figure such as a doll or puppet. **2.** *Obsolete.* a false god; idol. Also, **mammet.** [< Old French *mahumet* idol < *Mahumet* Mahomet (from the old belief that he was considered divine)]

mau·met·ry (mô′mə trē), *n. Archaic.* idolatry.

maun (mon, môn), *v.i. Scottish.* must: *Folk maun do something for their bread* (Robert Burns). [Middle English *man* < Scandinavian (compare Old Icelandic *man,* present tense of *munu* shall, will)]

maund[1] (mônd), *n. British Dialect and Scottish.* a basket; a hamper: *A thousand favours from a maund she drew* (Shakespeare). [Old English *mand*]

maund[2] (mônd), *n.* a unit of weight used in India and parts of the Middle East, usually equal to 82.28 pounds, but in some localities varying from 23 to 28 pounds: *The duty on raw jute is increased by one rupee a maund* (London Times).
[earlier, *mana* < Hindi *mān* < Sanskrit *mā* measure]

maun·der (môn′dər), *v.i.* **1.** to talk in a rambling, foolish way: *She maunders on by the hour and never says anything worth while.* **2.** to move or act in an aimless or confused manner: *The injured man maundered about in a dazed condition. The drunken man* *maundered along the street.* **3.** *Obsolete.* to grumble; mutter. [origin uncertain. Compare MEANDER.] —**maun′der·er,** *n.* —**maun′der·ing·ly,** *adv.* —**Syn. 1.** drivel.

maun·dy (môn′dē), *n., pl.* **-dies. 1.** an old ceremony of washing the feet of a number of poor people to commemorate the Last Supper and Christ's washing the feet of his disciples, performed as a religious rite, as by a sovereign or an ecclesiastic, on the Thursday before Good Friday. **2.** alms distributed at the ceremony or on this day: *In addition to the specially minted maundy coins there was a surprise for each recipient* (London Times). [< Old French *mande* < Latin *mandātum* a command, < *mandāre;* (*mandātum* is the first word of the service for that day. See John 13:5, 14, 34)]

Maun·dy (môn′dē), *n., pl.* **-dies.** the celebration of Maundy Thursday, in which the feet of the poor are washed and Maundy money given out.

Maundy money, coins given to the poor on Maundy Thursday. In England, special coins are frequently minted for the occasion in denominations of 1 to 4 pence and presented by the sovereign. *After 1661, the giving of Maundy money in Westminster Abbey in London replaced the earlier English ceremony* (World Book Encyclopedia).

Maundy Thursday, the Thursday before Easter.

Mau·resque (mə resk′), *adj., n.* Moresque.

Mau·ri·ta·ni·an (môr′ə tā′nē ən, -tān′yən), *adj.* of, having to do with, or characteristic of Mauritania, a republic in West Africa. —*n.* a native or inhabitant of Mauritania.

Mau·ri·tian (mô rish′ən), *adj.* of, having to do with, or characteristic of Mauritius, an island in the Indian Ocean. —*n.* a native or inhabitant of Mauritius.

Mau·ry·a (mou′rē ə), *n.* a member of the ancient Indian people who established an empire in northern India from 321 B.C. to 184 B.C.

Mau·ry·an (mou′rē ən), *adj.* of or having to do with the Mauryas or their civilization: *a Mauryan dynasty, the Mauryan empire.*

Mau·ser (mou′zər), *n. Trademark.* a powerful repeating rifle or pistol. [< Paul *Mauser,* 1838-1914, German inventor]

mau·so·le·an (mô′sə lē′ən), *adj.* of or having to do with a mausoleum; monumental.

Mau·so·le·um (mô′sə lē′əm), *n.* a magnificent tomb in southwest Asia Minor, at Halicarnassus, built in the 300's B.C. It was one of the seven wonders of the ancient world. [< Latin *Mausōlēum* < Greek *Mausōleîon* (tomb) of *Maúsōlos,* a king of Caria]

mau·so·le·um (mô′sə lē′əm), *n., pl.* **-le·ums, -le·a** (-lē′ə). **1.** a large, magnificent tomb: *a ponderous mausoleum with a front wall of reinforced concrete* (Newsweek). **2.** *Informal.* any large structure, building, or room similar to the Mausoleum. [< *Mausoleum*]

Mausoleum (def. 1)

mau·vaise honte (mō vez′ ôNt′), *French.* excessive modesty or shame; bashfulness.

mauve (mōv), *n.* **1.** a delicate, pale purple. **2.** a purple dye obtained from coal tar or aniline: *The beautiful purple dye mauve, synthesized by Perkin in 1856, was not found in animal and plant material* (Atlantic). —*adj.* delicate, pale-purple. [< French *mauve* < Old French, *mallow* < Latin *malva.* Doublet of MALLOW.] —**Syn.** *adj.* violet, lilac, lavender.

mauve·ine (mō′vin, -vēn), *n.* the dye mauve or its color: *mauveine, the first synthetic organic dye* (Scientific American). [< *mauve* + *-ine*²]

mav·er·ick (mav′ər ik), *n. U.S.* **1.** a calf or other animal not marked with an owner's brand. A maverick on the open range formerly became the property of anyone who branded him. **2.** *Informal.* a person who refuses to affiliate or who breaks with a regular political party: *A maverick tried unsuccessfully to unseat Mayor Edward Kelly* (Wall Street Journal). **3.** *Informal.* any person or organization which is unconventional in its actions or behavior: *All around town, there are entrancing mavericks that may have no great significance and follow no trend . . .* (New Yorker).
—*adj.* unconventional; refusing to be bound by normal procedures: *For years these maverick merchants have flourished by following a simple formula* (Wall Street Journal).
[American English < Samuel *Maverick,* 1803-1870, a Texas cattle owner who did not brand the calves of one of his herds]

ma·vis (mā′vis), *n.* the song thrush of Europe. [< Old French *mauvis,* perhaps < a Celtic word]

ma·vour·neen or **ma·vour·nin** (mə vůr′nēn, -vôr′-, -vōr′-), *n. Irish.* my darling. [< Irish *mo mhuirnīn* my treasure]

mav·ro·daph·ne (mav′rə daf′nē), *n.* a sweet red wine made in Greece, usually served after meals or with dessert. [< Greek *mauros* dark + *dáphnē* laurel]

maw (mô), *n.* **1.** the mouth, throat, or gullet of a voracious animal, as concerned in devouring: *a lion's maw.* **2.** anything thought of as resembling this in appetite: *Nations continue to pour wealth into the maw of war.* **3.** the stomach. [Old English *maga*] —**Syn. 3.** craw, crop.

maw·kin (mô′kin), *n.* malkin.

mawk·ish (mô′kish), *adj.* **1.** sickening; nauseating: *If I would drink water, I must quaff the mawkish contents of an open aqueduct* (Tobias Smollett). **2.** sickly sentimental; weakly emotional: *The portrait of Lady Mendl is sharp without being unkind and sentimental without being mawkish* (Harper's). [< Middle English *mawke* maggot < Scandinavian (compare Old Icelandic *mathkr*) + *-ish*] —**mawk′ish·ly,** *adv.* —**mawk′ish·ness,** *n.*

max., 1. maxim. **2.** maximum.

max·i (mak′sē), *adj., n., pl.* **max·is.** —*adj.* reaching to the ankle (usually in compounds such as *maxicoat, maxi-length*). —*n.* a dress, coat, etc., reaching to the ankle. [< *maxi*(mum)]

max·il·la (mak sil′ə), *n., pl.* **max·il·lae** (mak sil′ē). **1.** the upper jaw or its bones, containing the upper teeth, nasal cavity, and bottom part of the eye socket. **2.** either of the pair of appendages just behind the mandibles of insects, crabs, etc. See picture under **mandible.** [< Latin *maxilla* (upper) jaw < *māla* cheekbone, jaw]

max·il·lar·y (mak′sə ler′ē), *adj., n., pl.* **-lar·ies.** —*adj.* of or having to do with the jaw or jawbone. —*n.* a maxilla.

max·il·lo·fa·cial (mak sil′ə fā′shel), *adj.* of or having to do with the lower half of the face: *maxillofacial prosthetics.* [< *maxilla* + *facial*]

max·im (mak′səm), *n.* a short rule of conduct; statement of a general truth; proverb: "*A stitch in time saves nine*" and "*Look before you leap*" *are maxims. The trite maxim that every Englishman's house is his castle* (William E. H. Lecky). *That maxim of the heathen, "Enjoy the present, trust nothing to the future"* (Cardinal Newman). *My maxim is to obey orders* (James Fenimore Cooper). [< Middle French *maxime,* learned borrowing from Late Latin *maxima* (*prōpositiō*) axiom; (literally) greatest premise; see MAXIMUM] —**Syn.** adage, aphorism, apothegm.

max·i·ma (mak′sə mə), *n.* maximums; a plural of **maximum.**

max·i·mal (mak′sə məl), *adj.* of or being a maximum; greatest possible; highest: *an insistence on maximal loyalty.* —**max′i·mal·ly,** *adv.*

Max·i·mal·ism or **max·i·mal·ism** (mak′sə mə liz′əm), *n.* the doctrines, methods, or procedure of Maximalists.

Max·i·mal·ist (mak′sə mə list), *n.* **1.** a member of the radical section of the Social Revolutionary Party in Russia about 1903. **2.** a radical section or a radical in any party.

max·i·mate (mak′sə māt), *v.t.,* **-mat·ed, -mat·ing.** to maximize: *. . . local politicians who maximate their own importance by riding for a few hours on the train of the Presidential nominee* (Harper's).

Max·im gun (mak′səm), a type of water-cooled machine gun, in which the bolt is operated by the recoil. [< Sir Hiram S. *Maxim,* 1840-1916, a British inventor, born in the United States]

max·i·mise (mak′sə mīz), *v.t., v.i.,* **-mised, -mis·ing.** *Especially British.* maximize.

max·im·ist (mak′sə mist), *n.* a maker or user of maxims.

max·im·ite (mak′sə mīt), *n.* a powerful explosive consisting chiefly of picric acid, formerly used in shells for piercing armor. [< Hudson *Maxim,* 1853-1927, an American engineer and inventor + *-ite*¹]

max·i·mi·za·tion (mak′sə mə zā′shən), *n.* the act or process of maximizing.

max·i·mize (mak′sə mīz), *v.,* **-mized, -miz·ing.** —*v.t.* to increase or magnify to the highest possible degree: *Instead of maximizing facilities for motorcars, we should maximize the advantages of urban life* (New Yorker). —*v.i.* to maintain the most rigorous or comprehensive interpretation possible of a theological doctrine or an obligation. [< *maxim*(um) + *-ize*] —**max′i·miz′er,** *n.*

max·i·mum (mak′sə məm), *n., pl.* **-mums, -ma** (-mə), *adj.* —*n.* **1.** the largest or highest amount; greatest possible amount; highest point or degree: *Drivers must not exceed a maximum of 50 miles an hour.* **2.** relative maximum.
—*adj.* **1.** greatest possible; largest; highest: *The maximum score on the test is 100.* **2.** having to do with a maximum or maximums: *a maximum period.*
[< Latin *maximum,* neuter of *maximus* greatest, superlative of *magnus* great]
—**Syn.** *n.* **1.** limit.

max·i·mum-se·cu·ri·ty (mak′sə məm si kyůr′ ə tē), *adj.* **1.** (of a prison or penal institution) providing elaborate precautions, such as isolated cells, barred windows and doors, and a large number of armed guards, to prevent prisoners from escaping. **2.** of, belonging to, or having to do with such a prison or penal institution: *maximum-security guards, inmates, etc.*

ma·xi·xe (mə shē′shə, mak sēks′), *n.* a lively dance, originally Brazilian, formerly popular in Europe and the United States: *Brazilian dances began to spread beyond our borders and the maxixe became the rage in Paris, London, and New York* (Atlantic). [< Portuguese *maxixe*]

max·well (maks′wel, -wəl), *n.* the unit of magnetic flux in the centimeter-gram-second system; the flux through one square centimeter normal to a magnetic field, the intensity of which is one gauss. [< James Clerk *Maxwell,* 1831-1879, a British physicist]

Max·well-Boltz·mann distribution (maks′wəl bōlts′män, -wel-; -mən), *Physics.* a theory dealing with the distribution of velocities among gas particles in equilibrium and the statistical probabilities associated with these. [< James Clerk *Maxwell,* 1831-1879, and Ludwig *Boltzmann,* 1844-1906, the two physicists who formulated the theory]

may¹ (mā), *v., pres. indic. sing.* **may,** (*Archaic*) **may·est** or **mayst, may,** *pl.* **may;** *past tense* **might.** —*auxiliary. v. May* is used to express: **1.** possibility, opportunity, or permission: *We may arrive late for lunch. You may if you can. You may go now.* **2.** wish or prayer: *May you be very happy.* **3.** contingency, especially in clauses expressing condition, concession, purpose, result, etc.: *I write that you may know my plans.* **4.** ability or power (more commonly *can*). **5.** *Law.* must; shall (as interpreted by courts in documents, laws, etc.). —*v.i. Obsolete.* to be able; have power. [Old English *mæg*]
➔ See **can** for usage note.

may² (mā), *n.* **1.** the hawthorn, especially the English hawthorne. It blooms in May. **2.** any spiraea that blooms in May. [< *May*]

may³ (mā), *n. Archaic.* a maiden; virgin: *For ill beseems in a reverend friar, The love of a mortal may* (Thomas L. Peacock). [perhaps Old English *mǣg* kinswoman]

may⁴ (mā), *v.i.* to gather flowers, especially in May.

May (mā), *n.* **1.** the fifth month of the year. It has 31 days. **2.** *Poetic.* the springtime; prime of life; prime: *the May of my years* (Philip Sidney). **3.** the festivities of May Day: *I'm to be Queen o' the May, mother* (Tennyson). [Old English *maius* (< Latin), and Middle English *mai* < Old French < Latin *Māius* (*mēnsis*) (month) of May, probably related to *Māia,* an earth goddess]

ma·ya (mä′yä), *n. Hinduism.* illusion or deceptive appearance: *Reality, says the classic Vedanta doctrine is one—hence all plurality is illusion* (*maya*) (Time). [< Sanskrit *māyā*]

Ma·ya (mä′yə), *n.* **1.** a member of an ancient race of Indians living in Yucatan and Central America. The Mayas had a high degree of civilization when America was discovered. **2.** their language; Mayan.

Ma·yan (mä′yən), *adj.* of or having to do with the Mayas, their language, or the language family to which it belongs. See picture under **idol.**
—*n.* **1.** one of the Mayas. **2.** the language of the Mayas or the language family to which it belongs.

May apple, 1. a North American perennial plant of the barberry family with a large, white flower, which blooms in May; mandrake. **2.** its yellowish, slightly acid, egg-shaped fruit, which is sometimes eaten.

May basket, a basket of flowers, candy, or the like, hung on the outer knob of a house door, or otherwise surreptitiously left for the recipient, as a May Day compliment or remembrance.

may·be (mā′bē), *adv.* possibly; perhaps. —*n.* a possibility or probability; uncertainty: *There are lots of maybes in this glittering promise* (New York Times).
➔ **maybe, may be.** *Maybe* is an adverb or noun; *may be* is a verb form: *Maybe you'll have better luck next time. He may be the next mayor.*

May beetle, 1. a cockchafer. **2.** a June bug: *Most widely distributed are the ones known sometimes as May beetles, sometimes as June bugs, depending on the month in which they become most numerous* (Science News Letter).

May blob, marsh marigold.

May bug, the May beetle.

May bush, the hawthorn.

May Day, May 1. It is often celebrated by crowning the May queen and dancing around the Maypole. In some parts of the world, labor parades and meetings are held on May Day.

May·day (mā′dā′), *n.*, or **May Day,** the international radiotelephone call for help, used by a ship or aircraft when in distress: *A voice radio blared a "May Day" . . . call, then a shout from one of the B-29's eight crewmen* (Newsweek). [< French *m'aidez* help me!]

May dew, the dew of May, or of May Day, popularly reputed to have extraordinary virtue for beautifying the complexion and for medicinal and bleaching purposes.

may·est (mā′əst), *v. Archaic.* may.

May·fair (mā′fãr′), *n.* **1.** a fashionable section of London. **2.** fashionable London society.

may·flow·er (mā′flou′ər), *n.* a plant whose flowers blossom in May; the trailing arbutus and certain hepaticas and anemones (in the United States); the hawthorn, cowslip, and marsh marigold (in England).

May·flow·er (mā′flou′ər), *n.* the ship on which the Pilgrims came to America in 1620.

Mayflower Compact, a written agreement in which the Pilgrims decided on the form of self-government under majority rule to be set up in the New World, signed in the cabin of the Mayflower.

May fly, 1. a slender insect with lacy wings, and forewings much larger than the hind wings, that dies soon after reaching the adult stage; ephemerid; drake; dun; shadfly. **2.** an artificial fishing fly tied to resemble this insect.

May Fly (def. 1)

may·hap (mā′hap′, mā′hap), *adv. Archaic.* perhaps; perchance: *I'm going to the Hall Farm, but mayhap I may go to the school after* (George Eliot). [< earlier *it may hap*]

may·hap·pen (mā′hap′ən), *adv.* mayhap.

may·haps (mā′haps′), *adv.* mayhap.

may·hem (mā′hem, -əm), *n.* **1.** the crime of intentionally maiming a person or injuring him so that he is less able to defend himself. **2.** any violence inflicted upon another person: *Professional wrestling . . . has become so popular in Japan that scores of youngsters who have attempted to imitate their favorites' make-believe mayhem have wound up in hospitals* (Newsweek). Also, **maihem.** [< Anglo-French *mahem, mahaigne,* or *meshaigne,* related to *mahaignier* to maim]

May·ing (mā′ing), *n.* the celebration of May Day; taking part in May festivities.

may·n't (mā′ənt, mānt), may not.
➔ See **can't** for usage note.

may·on·naise (mā′ə nāz′, mā′ə nāz), *n.* a dressing made of egg yolks, oil, vinegar or lemon juice, and seasoning, beaten together until thick, used on salads, fish, vegetables, etc. [< French *mayonnaise,* ultimately < *Mahon,* a seaport in Minorca, captured by the Duc de Richelieu, whose chef introduced the *Mahonnaise* after his master's victory]

may·or (mā′ər, mãr), *n.* the chief official of a city or town. [< Old French *maire,* and *maor* < Latin *mājor.* Doublet of MAJOR.]

may·or·al (mā′ər əl, mãr′-), *adj.* of, having to do with, or characteristic of a mayor: *mayoral robes, mayoral duties.*

may·or·al·ty (mā′ər əl tē, mãr′-), *n., pl.* **-ties. 1.** the position of mayor. **2.** the term of office of a mayor.

may·or-coun·cil (mā′ər koun′səl, mãr′-), *adj.* of or having to do with a system of municipal government in which a popularly elected mayor and council are in charge of the city administration: *Nelson was incorporated in 1897. It has a mayor-council government* (Roderick Haig-Brown).

may·or·ess (mā′ər is, mãr′-), *n.* **1.** a woman mayor. **2.** *British.* the wife of a mayor.

may·or·ship (mā′ər ship, mãr′-), *n.* the office or dignity of mayor.

May·pole or **may·pole** (mā′pōl′), *n.* **1.** a high pole, usually decorated with flowers or ribbons, around which merrymakers dance on May Day. **2.** a tall, slender person: *the daughter, . . . a trapesing, trolloping, talkative maypole* (Oliver Goldsmith).

may·pop (mā′pop′), *n.* **1.** the small, edible, yellow fruit of a passionflower growing in the southern United States. **2.** the plant itself. [American English, earlier *maycock,* alteration of *maracock* < Algonkian (perhaps Powhatan) *mäkäk, mäkaku* a hollow receptacle; a variety of cucurbita]

May queen, a girl crowned with flowers and honored as queen on May Day.

mayst (māst), *v. Archaic.* may. "Thou mayst" means "you may."

may·thorn (mā′thôrn′), *n.* the hawthorn.

May·tide (mā′tīd′), *n.* Maytime.

May·time (mā′tīm′), *n.* the month of May.

may tree, *British.* the hawthorn.

may·weed (mā′wēd′), *n.* a weed of the composite family found in Europe, Asia, and America, having flower heads with a yellow disk and white rays and ill-smelling foliage; dog fennel. [< unrecorded *maythe-weed* < obsolete *maythe,* the same plant, Old English *mægtha, magethe*]

May wine, a punch made from a mixture of white wine, sugar, and woodruff herbs.

maz·ard (maz′ərd), *n.* **1.** *Archaic.* the head or face: *knocked about the mazard with a sexton's spade* (Shakespeare). **2.** *Obsolete.* mazer: *They . . . drank good ale in a brown mazard* (John Aubrey). Also, **mazzard.** [alteration of *mazer*]

Maz·a·rin Bible (maz′ər in), the Gutenberg Bible. [< Jules *Mazarin,* 1602-1661, a French cardinal and statesman]

maz·a·rine (maz′ə rēn′), *n.*, or **mazarine blue,** a deep, rich blue. —*adj.* of this color; deep-blue: *There are stars in the mazarine sky* (New Yorker). [perhaps < French *Mazarin,* a proper name]

Maz·da (maz′də), *n. Trademark.* a type of electric light bulb. [< Avestan *mazda* the principle of good (referring to light, a good quality). Compare ORMAZD.]

Maz·da·ism or **Maz·de·ism** (maz′də iz-əm), *n.* the religion of ancient Persia; Zoroastrianism. [< Avestan *mazda* the principle of good. Compare ORMAZD.]

Maz·da·ist or **Maz·de·ist** (maz′də ist), *n.* a believer in Mazdaism.

maze (māz), *n., v.,* **mazed, maz·ing.** —*n.* **1. a.** a network of paths through which it is difficult to find one's way: *He turned short into one of the mazes of the wood* (Scott). *A guide led us through the maze of caves.* See picture under **labyrinth. b.** any complicated arrangement, as of streets, buildings, etc.: *Bath was then a maze of only four or five hundred houses* (Macaulay). **c.** intricate windings; intricacy: *a maze of errors. Here would the good Peter . . . watch the mazes of the dance* (Washington Irving). **2.** a state of confusion; muddled condition: *He was in such a maze that he couldn't speak.*
—*v.t. Archaic.* **1.** to stupefy; daze: *Finding This tumult 'bout my door . . . It somewhat maz'd me* (Ben Jonson). **2.** to bewilder; perplex.
[variant of *amaze*] —**maze′like′,** *adj.*
—**Syn.** *n.* **1. a.** labyrinth. **2.** perplexity, bewilderment.

mazel tov, or **ma·zel·tov** (mä′zəl tōv′), *interj. Hebrew.* congratulations; good luck.

maze·ment (māz′mənt), *n. Archaic.* a stupor; trance.

ma·zer (mā′zər), *n. Obsolete.* a large goblet without a foot, originally made of a hard wood, often richly carved or ornamented. Also, **mazard.** [< Old French *masere* < Germanic (compare Old High German *maser* gall on a tree; drinking cup)]

maz·i·ly (mā′zə lē), *adv.* in a mazy manner; with intricate windings.

maz·i·ness (mā′zē nis), *n.* perplexity.

ma·zu·ma (mə zü′mə), *n. Slang.* money: *A fellow would be able to do some fancy writing at a desk which cost all that mazuma* (Cape Times). [< Yiddish *mazuma* < Hebrew *məzumon*]

ma·zur·ka or **ma·zour·ka** (mə zėr′kə, -zůr′-), *n.* **1.** a lively Polish folk dance. **2.** music for or in the rhythm of this dance, usually in 3/4 or 6/8 time. [< alteration of Polish *mazurek* (literally) dance of *Mazovia,* a region in Poland]

maz·y (mā′zē), *adj.,* **maz·i·er, maz·i·est. 1.** like a maze; full of intricate windings; intricate: *Five miles meandering with a mazy motion Through wood and dale the sacred river ran* (Samuel Taylor Coleridge). **2.** *Dialect.* dizzy; confused. —**Syn. 1.** devious.

maz·zard (maz′ərd), *n.* **1.** a wild sweet cherry used as a stock for breeding varieties of sweet and of sour cherries. **2.** mazard. [origin uncertain; perhaps Middle English *mazer,* later *mazard* a wood used for cups; a cup < Old French *masere;* see MAZER]

mb., *Meteorology.* millibar.

M.B., an abbreviation for the following:
1. *British.* Bachelor of Medicine (Latin, *Medicinae Baccalaureus*).
2. Bachelor of Music (Latin, *Musicae Baccalaureus*).

M.B.A. or **MBA** (no periods), *U.S.* Master of Business Administration.

M.B.E., Member of the Order of the British Empire.

M. b. m., thousand feet board measure.

MBS (no periods), Mutual Broadcasting System.

M·bu·ti (em bü′tē), *n., pl.* **-ti** or **-tis.** a member of certain Negroid pygmy people native to equatorial Africa and the Congo forests: *The Mbuti form the largest single group of pygmy hunters and gatherers in Africa* (New Scientist).

m.c. (em′sē′), *v.t., v.i.,* **m.c.'d, m.c.'ing.** *Informal.* to act as master of ceremonies (for): *Weaver wrote it, produced it, m.c.'d it, and, he now says, loved every minute of it* (New Yorker).

Mc- *prefix.* a variant of **Mac** ("son of"), as in *McDonald.*

mc (no period), **1.** megacycle or megacycles. **2.** millicurie or millicuries.

mc., megacycle or megacycles.

m.c. or **MC** (no periods), master of ceremonies.

M.C., an abbreviation for the following:
1. Master Commandant.
2. master of ceremonies.
3. Medical Corps.
4. Member of Congress.
5. *British.* Military Cross.

Mc·Car·thy·ism (mə kär′thē iz əm), *n.* **1.** the act or practice of publicly accusing individuals or groups of political disloyalty and subversion, usually without sufficient evidence: *McCarthyism breeds fear, suspicion and unrest. It turns neighbor against neighbor . . .* (New York Times). *So McCarthyism—a synonym for reckless accusation—was born* (Life). **2.** the public investigation of Communist activities in the United States in the early 1950's, conducted in sensational public hearings: *While this was going on, McCarthyism and attendant mental ills were preventing researchers here from even acknowledging that Russia possessed competent scientists* (New Scientist). [< Senator Joseph R. *McCarthy,* 1909-1957, chairman of the Senate Permanent Investigations Committee + *-ism*]

Mc·Car·thy·ist (mə kär′thē ist), *n., adj.* McCarthyite.

Mc·Car·thy·ite (mə kär′thē īt), *n.* a follower of Senator Joseph McCarthy or a believer in McCarthyism: *The Administration will not allow itself to be hamstrung by the McCarthyites and isolationists* (Newsweek). —*adj.* representative of or characteristic of McCarthyism.

Mc·Coy (mə koi′), *n. U.S. Informal.* Usually, **the real McCoy.** the genuine article; the real thing: *You can't fake this cigar; it's the real McCoy.* [American English < the Scottish phrase *the real Mackay,* probably < *Mackay,* a Scotch whisky exported to the U.S. and Canada by A. and M. Mackay of Glasgow; influenced by Kid *McCoy,* a celebrated boxer of the late 1880's, who was sometimes confused with another, less popular boxer called McCoy]

M.C.E., Master of Civil Engineering.

Mcfd (no periods) or **M.C.F.D.,** thousands of cubic feet per day.

Mc·Gill Fence (mə gil′), a chain of robot radar stations built by Canada roughly across its 55th parallel to serve as a warning system against missile or aircraft attack; Mid-Canada Line: *Popularly called the McGill fence, because of the part played in its development by . . . McGill University* (Newsweek).

M.Ch., Master of Surgery (Latin, *Magister Chirugiae*).

mcht., merchant.

Mc·In·tosh (mak′ən tosh), *n.,* or **McIntosh Red,** a bright-red, early fall variety of eating apple. [< John *McIntosh,* of Ontario, Canada, who cultivated it in the 1700's]

Mc·Lu·han·ism (mə klü′ə niz əm), *n.* the theories of Marshall McLuhan (born 1911), a Canadian educator, concerning the influence of electronic mass media on the information they communicate, on the people who receive it, and on the culture it creates.

Mc·Lu·han·ist (mə klü′ə nist), *n.* a student or follower of Marshall McLuhan or his theories: *The McLuhanist can observe . . . the galloping tribalism of a teenage dance party on TV; he knows that he's watching the first truly electronic generation* (Maclean's).

Mc·Naugh·ten Rule (mək nô′tən), M'Naghten Rule.

mc/s or **Mc/s,** megacycles per second.

M.C.S., Master of Commercial Science.

mcy sec, megacycles per second.

m/d or **m.d.,** *Commerce.* month's date; months after date.

Md (no period), mendelevium (chemical element).

Md., Maryland.

MD (no periods), **1.** muscular dystrophy. **2.** Doctor of Medicine (Latin, *Medicinae Doctor*).

M/D, *Banking.* memorandum of deposit.

M.D., an abbreviation for the following:
1. Medical Department.
2. *Banking.* memorandum of deposit.
3. Doctor of Medicine (Latin, *Medicinae Doctor*).

MDAP (no periods), Mutual Defense Assistance Program.

M-day (em′dā′), *n.* mobilization day; the day on which the armed forces are officially mobilized for war: *Defense mobilizers prepare to revamp M-day plans* (Wall Street Journal).

Mdlle., Mademoiselle.

mdm., madam.

Mdme., Madame.

M.D.S., Master of Dental Surgery.

mdse., *U.S.* merchandise.

me (mē; *unstressed* mi), *pron.* the objective case of **I:** *Mary said "Give the dog to me. I like it and it likes me."* [Old English *mē*]

take it from me. See under **take,** *v.*

➤ **it's I, it's me.** The first of these is formal English, the second now established in good use on the informal conversational level. The objective case of the other personal pronouns after the forms of *to be* has less status, and many speakers avoid locutions like *it's her, it was us.* Since the nominative sounds somewhat stilted, however, other constructions are often substituted, for example *we were the ones* in place of *it was we.*

m.e., marbled edges (in book manufacturing).

Me (no period), *Chemistry.* methyl.

Me., Maine.

ME (no periods), or **ME.,** Middle English.

M.E., an abbreviation for the following:
1. marine engineer.
2. Master of Engineering.
3. mechanical engineer.
4. Methodist Episcopal.
5. Middle English.
6. mining engineer.

mea·cock (mē′kok), *n. Obsolete.* an effeminate person; weakling; coward. [origin uncertain]

me·a cul·pa (mē′ə kul′pə), *Latin.* **1.** (by) my fault: *. . . I plead guilty. Mea culpa* (New Yorker). **2.** a plea or confession of guilt: *. . . polemics, Party speeches and resolutions, mea culpas of penitents confessing to scientific error . . .* (Bulletin of the Atomic Scientists). **3.** an apology: *a cringing mea culpa.* **4.** a recantation, especially of a political ideology: *Since his mea culpa, Burrows has been outspoken against Communism . . .* (New Yorker).

mead[1] (mēd), *n. Poetic.* a meadow: *Downward sloped The path through yellow meads* (Lowell). [Old English *mǣd*]

mead[2] (mēd), *n.* **1.** an alcoholic drink made from fermented honey and water, especially in Anglo-Saxon days. **2.** *U.S. Obsolete.* a soft drink of carbonated water and flavoring. [Old English *medu*]

mead·ow (med′ō), *n.* **1.** a piece of grassy land; field where hay is grown. **2.** low, grassy land near a stream or river. [Old English *mǣdwe,* oblique case of *mǣd* mead[1]]

meadow beauty, any of a group of low perennial North American herbs with showy, crimson or rose flowers: *I found growing there clumps of meadow beauty . . . their bright magenta immediately engaged my attention* (New York Times).

meadow brown, any of a family of brown or grayish butterflies that have eyespots on the wings; satyr.

meadow fescue, a tall grass grown in Europe and America for pasture and for hay.

meadow grass, 1. any of a group of grasses, such as the Kentucky bluegrass of the United States. **2.** *U.S.* manna grass.

mead·ow·land (med′ō land′, -lənd), *n.* land used as a meadow: *Expanses of meadowland, because of their proximity to New York, are becoming more attractive* (New York Times).

meadow lark, an American songbird related to the orioles, about the size of a robin, with a thick body, short tail, and a black crescent on a yellow breast; field lark.

Eastern Meadow Lark (about 10¾ in. long)

meadow lily, the Canada lily.

meadow mouse, any of various short-tailed voles living in fields and meadows; field mouse.

meadow mushroom, the common edible mushroom.

meadow rue, any of a group of plants of the crowfoot family with leaves like those of the rue.

meadow snipe, 1. the American snipe. **2.** the pectoral sandpiper.

mead·ow·sweet (med′ō swēt′), *n.* a shrub of the rose family with dense clusters of small, fragrant, pink or white flowers; spiraea.

mead·ow·y (med′ō ē), *adj.* **1.** like a meadow. **2.** of meadows: *the meadowy land* (William Morris).

mea·ger or **mea·gre** (mē′gər), *adj.* **1.** poor; scanty: *a meager meal.* **2.** lean; thin: *a meager face. A small, meagre man* (John L. Motley). *Shaggy, meager little ponies* (Francis Parkman). **3.** without fullness or richness; deficient in quality or quantity: *The report that first reached us through the newspapers was meagre and contradictory* (Thomas B. Aldrich). [< French, Old French *maigre* < Latin *macer* thin. Doublet of MAIGRE.] —**mea′ger·ly, mea′gre·ly,** *adv.* —**mea′ger·ness, mea′gre·ness,** *n.* —**Syn. 1.** sparse. See **scanty.**

meal[1] (mēl), *n.* **1.** one of the regular, daily occasions of eating, such as a breakfast, lunch, dinner, supper, or tea. **2.** the food served or eaten at one time: *Each meal is an adventure in world-famed French cuisine* (Time). [Old English *mǣl* appointed time; meal] —**Syn. 1, 2.** repast.

meal[2] (mēl), *n.* **1.** grain that is coarsely ground and not sifted. **2.** *U.S.* corn meal. **3.** anything ground to a powder: *linseed meal.* [Old English *melu.* Related to MILL.]

meal·ie (mē′lē), *n.* (in South Africa) an ear of corn: *In her hand she held the paper carrier containing the bag of mealie and the sugar and coffee that the Welfare people doled out* (New Yorker).

mealies, corn: *a sack of mealies.*

[< Afrikaans *milje* < Portuguese *milho* (*da India*) (Indian) corn < Latin *milium;* origin uncertain]

meal·i·ness (mē′lē nis), *n.* **1.** softness or smoothness, with friableness and dryness to the touch or taste. **2.** the quality of being mealy-mouthed.

meal moth, a pyralid.

meal ticket, 1. a ticket authorizing a person to obtain a meal: *We . . . were permitted to buy our meal tickets for seven shillings and sixpence* (Harper's). **2.** *Informal.* a person or thing that is a source of money: *Thomas Harrow is loved more as a meal ticket than as the man and creative genius he is* (Wall Street Journal).

meal·time (mēl′tīm′), *n.* the usual time for eating a meal: *I look forward to mealtime with real anticipation* (Time).

meal worm, the larva of a beetle that feeds on flour and meal. Meal worms are raised as food for cage birds.

ADULT LARVA

Meal Worm (Lines show actual lengths.)

meal·y[1] (mē′lē), *adj.,* **meal·i·er, meal·i·est. 1.** like meal; dry and powdery: *mealy potatoes.* **2.** of or containing meal: *the mealy treasures of the harvest bin* (James W. Riley). **3.** covered with meal: *the miller's mealy hands.* **4.** as if dusted with flour; pale: *I only know two sorts of boys. Mealy boys, and beef-faced boys* (Dickens). **5.** mealy-mouthed: *I didn't mince the matter with him. I'm never mealy with 'em* (Dickens). **6.** flecked as if with meal; spotty. [< *meal*[2] + *-y*[1]] —**Syn. 2.** farinaceous.

meal·y[2] (mē′lē), *n., pl.* **meal·ies.** mealie. [< *meal*[2] + *-y*[2]]

mealy bug, a small, soft-bodied scale insect which covers itself with a whitish secretion. It causes considerable damage by sucking the juices of plants. *I do own . . . a cactus a friend gave me . . . and a miserable old thing it is, full of mealy bugs* (New Yorker).

meal·y-mouthed (mē′lē mouᴛʜd′, -moutht′), *adj.* unwilling to tell the straight truth in plain words; using soft words insincerely: *a mealy-mouthed politician.* —**Syn.** hollow, insincere.

meal·y-mouth·ed·ness (mē′lē mou′ᴛʜid-nis, -thid-; -mouᴛʜd′-, -mouth′-), *n.* mealy-mouthed quality or character.

mean[1] (mēn), *v.,* **meant, mean·ing.** —*v.t.* **1.** to have as its thought; signify; import; denote: *What does this word mean? A poem should not mean but be* (Archibald MacLeish). **2.** to intend to express or indicate: *Keep out; that means you. Say what you mean.* **3.** to have as a purpose; have in mind; intend: *I do not mean to go. Do you think they mean to fight us? It's no use waiting any longer, if you mean to go at all, today* (William D. Howells). **4.** to design for a definite purpose; destine: *Fate meant us for each other. He was meant for a soldier.* —*v.i.* to have intentions of some kind; be minded or disposed: *She means well.*

mean well by, to have kindly feelings toward: *The manager means well by his workers.*

[Old English *mǣnan* mean, tell, say]

—**Syn.** *v.t.* **3.** design, purpose. See **intend.**

mean[2] (mēn), *adj.* **1.** low in quality or grade; poor: *the meanest of gifts.* **2.** low in social position or rank; humble. *A king is of noble birth; a groom of mean rank* (Scott). **3.** of little importance or value: *the meanest flower of the vale* (Thomas Gray). *Rightly viewed no meanest object is insignificant* (Thomas Carlyle). **4.** of poor appearance; shabby: *The poor widow lived in a mean hut.* **5.** lacking moral dignity; small-minded; ignoble: *mean thoughts. It is mean to spread gossip about your friends.* **6.** stingy; close-fisted: *A miser is mean about money.* **7.** *U.S. Informal.* humiliated; ashamed: *to feel mean.* **8.** *U.S. Informal.* **a.** hard to manage; troublesome; bad-tempered: *a mean horse.* **b.** selfish and ill-tempered; vicious; cruel:

Tell me where you hid my hat; don't be so mean! **9. a.** *Informal.* in poor physical condition; unwell: *I feel mean today.* **b.** stubborn and annoying: *a mean cold.*

no mean, very good: *He is no mean scholar.* [Middle English *mene,* Old English *gemǣne* common]

—**Syn. 2.** common, plebeian. **3.** insignificant, paltry, petty. **5.** base, contemptible, despicable. **6.** miserly.

mean[3] (mēn), *adj.* **1.** halfway between two extremes: *the mean annual air temperature. Six is the mean number between three and nine.* **2.** intermediate in kind, quality, or degree. **3.** *Mathematics.* having a value intermediate between the values of other quantities: *a mean diameter.*

—*n.* **1.** a condition, quality, or course of action halfway between two extremes: *Eight hours is a happy mean between too much sleep and too little.* **2.** *Mathematics.* **a.** a quantity having a value intermediate between the values of other quantities, especially the average obtained by dividing the sum of several quantities by their number. **b.** either the second or third term of a proportion of four terms. **3.** *Logic.* the middle term of a syllogism.

[< Old French *meien* < Latin *mediānus* (of the) middle < *medius* middle (of). Doublet of MEDIAN.]

—**Syn.** *adj.* **2.** medium, average.

mean[4] (mēn), *v.t., v.i. Especially Scottish.* to moan or lament. [apparently unrecorded Old English *mǣn,* related to *mǣnan* mean[1]]

me·an·der (mē an′dər), *v.i.* **1.** to follow a winding course: *A brook meanders through the meadow.* **2.** to wander aimlessly: *We meandered through the park. Paris is built for meandering, and for getting lost* (John O'Hara). —*v.t.* to make (one's way, etc.) by meandering. [< noun]

—*n.* **1.** a winding course or path: *the meanders of the law* (John Arbuthnot). **2.** aimless wandering. **3.** an intricate variety of fret or fretwork. **4.** a looplike, winding turn in a river or stream.

[< Latin *Maeander* < Greek *Maíandros,* a winding river in Asia Minor (now the *Menderes* River in western Turkey)] —**me·an′der·ing·ly,** *adv.*

—**Syn.** *v.i.* **2.** ramble, saunter.

mean distance, the average of the distances of the aphelion and perihelion of a planet from the sun, one of the data necessary to determine the orbit of a planet: *The earth's mean distance from the sun is about 92,900,000 miles* (Robert H. Baker).

me·an·drous (mē an′drəs), *adj.* meandering; winding: *an introspective, meandrous excursion through his own mind* (New Yorker).

mean free path, the average distance a molecule of a gas or other substance can travel before it collides with another molecule. The distance will vary according to altitude in the case of a gas. *The air density is only one trillionth of that at sea level, and the mean free path of the molecules is more than seven feet* (Scientific American).

mean·ing (mē′ning), *n.* **1.** what is meant or intended; significance: *the meaning of a story, the meaning of a sermon.* **2.** *Archaic.* intention or purpose: *I am no honest man if there be any good meaning towards you* (Shakespeare).

—*adj.* **1.** that means something; expressive: *a meaning look* (Dickens). **2.** having purpose; intending: *well meaning.* —**mean′ing·ly,** *adv.* —**mean′ing·ness,** *n.*

—**Syn.** *n.* **1. Meaning, sense, purport** mean what is expressed or meant to be. **Meaning** is the general word applying to the idea expressed or intended by a word, statement, gesture, action, painting, etc.: *The meaning of the sentence is clear.* **Sense** applies especially to a particular meaning of a word: *In other senses this word is not a synonym of "meaning."* **Purport** applies to the main idea or general drift of a longer statement: *That was the purport of the president's address.*

mean·ing·ful (mē′ning fəl), *adj.* full of meaning; having much meaning; significant: *History must be made more meaningful to the individual* (New York Times). —**mean′ing·ful·ly,** *adv.* —**mean′ing·ful·ness,** *n.*

mean·ing·less (mē′ning lis), *adj.* not making sense; without meaning; not significant: *Words such as "purpose" are . . . scientifically meaningless* (Science News). —**mean′ing·less·ly,** *adv.* —**mean′ing·less·ness,** *n.* —**Syn.** senseless, insignificant.

mean·ly (mēn′lē), *adv.* in a mean manner; poorly; basely; stingily.

mean·ness (mēn′nis), *n.* **1.** a being mean in grade or quality; poorness. **2.** a being selfish in small things; stinginess. **3.** a mean act.

mean noon, the time when the mean sun is on the meridian of the observer.

means (mēnz), *n.pl.* **1.** what a thing is done by; agency; method: *We won the game by fair means. Jean's quick thinking was the means of saving her life. There are no means that I will not resort to, to discover this infamous plot* (Frederick Marryat). **2.** wealth; resources: *a man of means.*

by all means, certainly; without fail: *I must by all means keep this feast* (Acts 18:21).

by any means, at all; in any possible way; at any cost: *None of them can by any means redeem his brother* (Psalms 49:7).

by means of, by the use of; through; with: *I found my lost dog by means of a notice in the paper.*

by no means, certainly not; not at all; under no circumstances: *But her other uncle by no means shared her sentiments* (Lytton Strachey).

means to an end, a way of getting or doing something: *This job is only a means to an end for him; he needs the experience to start his own business.*

—**Syn. 1.** device, instrumentality, expedient, shift, way. **2.** funds, income, property.

➤ **Means,** meaning what a thing is done by, is plural in form and singular or plural in use: *A means of communication is lacking. The means of helping others are never lacking. Means,* meaning wealth, is plural in form and in use: *His means permit him to live comfortably.*

mean solar day, a day of twenty-four hours, measured from midnight to midnight; civil day.

mean solar time, mean time.

mean-spir·it·ed (mēn′spir′ə tid), *adj.* having a mean spirit; small-minded: *Only a very mean-spirited reader would grudge the price of these victories* (Listener).

means test, *British.* an examination of an unemployed person's financial status when his unemployment insurance payments stop, to determine whether he should receive further financial aid: *She moved an amendment, . . . urging the Ministry to abolish the means test* (London Times).

mean sun, a hypothetical sun in various astronomical calculations that moves uniformly along the celestial equator at the mean speed with which the real sun apparently moves along the ecliptic.

meant (ment), *v.* past tense and past participle of **mean**[1]: *He explained what he meant. The sign was meant as a warning.*

mean·time (mēn′tīm′), *n.* the time between. —*adv.* **1.** in the time between. **2.** at the same time. —**Syn.** *n.* interim, interval.

mean time, time according to the hour angle of the mean sun, constituting the "ordinary time" or "clock time" of daily life.

mean·while (mēn′hwīl′), *n., adv.* meantime: *Meanwhile, the forces of the Republic of Korea and the United Nations have lived up to the commitment* (Newsweek).

meas., **1.** measurable. **2.** measure.

mea·sle (mē′zəl), *n.* one of the tapeworm larvae that produce measles in pigs and other animals. [singular of *measles*]

mea·sled (mē′zeld), *adj.* infected with measles; measly.

mea·sles (mē′zelz), *n.* **1.** an infectious virus disease, usually attacking children, characterized by fever, inflammation of the eyes and respiratory tract, and a breaking out of small red spots on the skin: *What seems to be a cold . . . often turns out to be the beginning of measles* (Newsweek). **2.** a similar but less severe disease, called German measles. **3. a.** a disease of hogs and cattle caused by the larvae of tapeworms. **b.** the larvae that cause this disease. [Middle English *maseles* blood blisters; probably influenced by *mezel* leprous < Old French < Latin *misellus* wretch < *miser* wretched]

➤ **Measles** is plural in form but usually singular in use: *Measles is a children's disease.*

mea·sly (mē′zlē), *adj.,* **-sli·er, -sli·est. 1.** of or like measles. **2.** infected with measles: *measly pork.* **3.** *Informal.* very poor; scanty; meager: *a measly portion, a measly bit of work.*

meas·ur·a·bil·i·ty (mezh′ər ə bil′ə tē, mā′zhər-), *n.* the quality or condition of being measurable.

meas·ur·a·ble (mezh′ər ə bəl, mā′zhər-), *adj.* that can be measured. —**meas′ur·a·ble·ness,** *n.*

meas·ur·a·bly (mezh′ər ə blē, mā′zhər-), *adv.* to an amount or degree that can be measured; perceptibly: *The sick man has improved measurably since yesterday.* —**Syn.** appreciably, discernibly.

meas·ure (mezh′ər, mā′zhər), *v.,* **-ured, -ur·ing,** *n.* —*v.t.* **1. a.** to find out the extent, size, quantity, capacity, etc., of (something): *We measured the room and found it was 20 feet long and 15 feet wide. We measured the pail by finding out how many quarts of water it would hold.* **b.** to estimate by some standard: *I would measure this room at about 12 by 16 feet.* **2.** to have a measurement of: *The tree measures 40 feet in height.* **3.** to get, take, or set apart by measuring: *to measure out a bushel of potatoes, to measure off 2 yards of cloth.* **4.** to serve as a measure of: *A clock measures time.* **5.** to compare; judge; estimate: *The soldier measured his strength with that of his enemy in a hand-to-hand fight.* **6.** to adjust; suit: *to measure one's behavior by the company one is in. Measure your needs to your income. Bertram carefully measured his own conduct by that of his host* (Scott). **7.** *Poetic.* to travel over; traverse: *She turned back into the room and measured its length with a restless step* (Henry James). **8.** *Poetic.* to delimit: *A cloud to measure out the marsh by day* (William Cowper). —*v.i.* **1.** to be of specified measure: *Buy some paper that measures 8 by 10 inches.* **2.** to take measurements; find out sizes or amounts: *Can he measure accurately?* **3.** to admit of measurement.

measure out, a. to divide; apportion; distribute: *I . . . Have known the evenings, mornings, afternoons, I have measured out my life with coffee spoons* (T.S. Eliot). **b.** to mete or deal out: *Sermons were measured out with no grudging hand* (Leslie Stephen).

measure up, to have the necessary qualifications: *He did not get the job because he just did not measure up.*

measure up to, to match: *The party did not measure up to her expectations.*

[< Old French *mesurer* < Late Latin *mēnsūrāre* < Latin *mēnsūra;* see the noun]

—*n.* **1.** the act or process of finding the extent, size, quantity, capacity, etc., of something, especially by comparison with a standard. **2.** the size, dimensions, quantity, etc., thus ascertained: *His waist measure is 32 inches.* **3.** an instrument for measuring. A foot rule, a yardstick, a pint measure, a quart dipper, and a bushel basket are common measures. **4.** a system of measuring: *liquid measure, dry measure, square measure.* **5.** a unit or standard of measuring. Inch, acre, mile, quart, pound, gallon, peck, and hour are common measures. **6.** any standard of comparison, estimation, or judgment, etc.; criterion: *Man is the measure of all things. Some . . . make themselves the measure of mankind* (Alexander Pope). **7.** a quantity or degree that should not be exceeded; reasonable limit: *angry beyond measure.* **8.** quantity; degree; proportion: *a measure of relief. Sickness is in great measure preventable.* **9.** rhythm, as in poetry or music; time: *the measure in which a poem or song is written.* **10.** a metrical unit; foot of verse: *the stately measures of blank verse.* **11.** a bar of music. **12.** a dance or dance movement: *"Now tread we a measure!" said young Lochinvar* (Scott). **13.** a course of action; procedure: *To adopt measures to relieve suffering. What measures shall we devise to find out the thief?* **14.** a legislative bill; law: *This measure has passed the Senate.* **15.** *Mathematics.* a number or quantity contained in another some number of times without remainder; factor. **16.** a definite quantity measured out: *to drink a measure.* **17.** *Poetic.* an air; tune; melody.

MEASURE MEASURE

Measures (def. 11)

beyond measure, greatly; exceedingly: *The bad news distressed him beyond measure.*

for good measure, as something extra; as something not necessarily expected: . . .

while for good measure there are five plays instead of the usual three (London Times).
full measure, a. ample quantity in what is sold or given by measure: *a full measure of flour.* **b.** a sufficient or just portion: *A full measure of justice was meted out to the thief.*
in a measure, to some degree; partly: *The story was funny in a measure, but it had its serious side, too.*
measures, strata or beds of a mineral: *The coal measures were found deep in the mine.*
short measure, a. deficient or defective quantity in what is sold or given by measure: *The merchant was caught selling his wares in short measure.* **b.** an insufficient or unjust portion: *a short measure of patience.*
take measures, to do something; act: *The Security Council has taken measures to avert a major crisis.*
take one's measure, to judge one's character: *I have encountered a good many of these gentlemen in actual service, and have taken their measure* (Benjamin Jowett).
tread a measure, to dance: *Let us gaily tread a measure* (Sir William S. Gilbert).
[< Old French *mesure* < Latin *mēnsūra,* noun < *mēnsus,* past participle of *mētīrī* to measure] **—meas'ur·er,** *n.*

meas·ured (mezh'ərd, mā'zhərd), *adj.* **1.** regular; uniform: *measured portions of food, the measured march of soldiers. She hears the measured beating of our horses' hoofs* (Thomas DeQuincey). **2.** rhythmical: *measured beats* **3.** written in poetry, not in prose; metrical: *For the unquiet heart and brain, A use in measured language lies* (Tennyson). **4.** deliberate and restrained; not hasty or careless: *The angry old man spoke to the boys with measured speech.* **—meas'ured·ly,** *adv.* **—Syn. 1.** regulated. **4.** moderate, temperate.

measured mile, a course exactly a mile long, either on land or water, used to check the calibration of an automobile speedometer and mileage indicator, a ship's log, etc.

meas·ure·graph (mezh'ər graf, -gräf; mā'zhər-), *n.* any of slightly differing types of devices used to measure cloth automatically while it may also be examined for flaws.

meas·ure·less (mezh'ər lis, mā'zhər-), *adj.* too great to be measured; unlimited; vast: *the measureless ocean, the measureless prairie* (Longfellow). **—meas'ure·less·ly,** *adv.* **—meas'ure·less·ness,** *n.* **—Syn.** infinite, immeasurable.

meas·ure·ment (mezh'ər mənt, mā'zhər-), *n.* **1.** a way of measuring; way of finding the size, quantity, or amount: *Clocks give us a measurement of time.* **2.** the act or fact of measuring: *The measurement of length by a yardstick is easy.* **3.** a size, quantity, or amount found by measuring; dimension: *The measurements of this room are 10 by 15 feet.* **4.** a system of measuring or of measures: *Metric measurement is used in most European countries.* **—Syn. 1.** gauge. **2.** computation, reckoning. **3.** extent, capacity.

meas·ur·ing rod (mezh'ər ing, mā'zhər-), yardstick: *By this measuring rod the United States has been moving steadily backward* (Harper's).

measuring worm, the larva of any geometrid moth; inchworm. It moves by bringing the rear end of its body forward, forming a loop, and then advancing the front end. See picture under **inchworm.**

meat (mēt), *n.* **1.** animal flesh used as food. Fish and poultry are not usually called meat. **2.** food of any kind: *meat and drink.* **3.** the part that can be eaten: *the meat of a nut. Thy head is as full of quarrels as an egg is full of meat* (Shakespeare). **4.** a meal: *Say grace before meat.* **5.** substance; food for thought: *But the real meat of the book is in the depiction of the moral conflicts keenly felt by these men* (Bulletin of Atomic Scientists). **6.** *Slang.* something a person finds easy and pleasant to do: *... peninsular warfare is traditionally the Navy's meat* (Time). [Old English *mete* food; any item of food; a meal] **—Syn. 4.** repast. **5.** gist.

meat-and-po·ta·toes (mēt'ən pə tā'tōz), *U.S. Informal.* —*n.* the principal part; foundation; basis: *Company officials still refer to [it] ... as "the meat-and-potatoes" of our business* (New Yorker). —*adj.* basic; fundamental: *One would like to urge Mr. Montecino to leave the meat-and-potatoes repertory for which his style of playing is not best suited for more contemporary cuisine* (New York Times).

meat ax or **axe, 1.** a butcher's cleaver used to chop roughly through meat and bone. **2.** a ruthless and sometimes indiscriminate hacking away: *... the House assaulted the Administration's defense request with meat axes, lopped off some $2.5 billion* (Time).

meat ball, 1. a ball of chopped or ground meat, cooked and usually served in gravy or sauce, especially with spaghetti: *a spicy Italian meat ball.* **2.** *Slang.* an uninteresting and uninspired person: *"What have these meat balls been handing you?" he inquired* (New Yorker). **3.** *Naval.* **a.** the target aimed at by an airplane landing on an aircraft carrier in a mirror landing system. It is a ball of light focused upon a mirror from four different sources. **b.** *Slang.* a battle efficiency pennant.

meat bird, the Canada jay.

meat-eat·er (mēt'ē'tər), *n.* **1.** a carnivore. **2.** a person who includes meat in his diet.

meat·head (mēt'hed'), *n. Slang.* a stupid person.

meat·i·ly (mē'tə lē), *adv.* in a meaty manner.

meat·less (mēt'lis), *adj.* **1.** without meat; foodless. **2.** on which no meat is sold or eaten: *meatless Tuesday.*

meat·man (mēt'man'), *n., pl.* **-men.** a man who sells meat; butcher.

meat packing, the business of slaughtering animals and preparing their meat for transportation and sale: *Poor returns on pork have cut earnings of the meat packing industry* (Wall Street Journal).

meat-safe (mēt'sāf'), *n.* a cupboard with walls of wire gauze, perforated zinc, or the like, for storing food.

meat tea, *British.* a tea at which meat is served; high tea.

meat tenderizer, an enzymatic preparation, either powder or liquid, used commercially and in the home to make meat more tender, usually a form of papain: *Meat tenderizers could also be better evaluated by checking tenderness before and after use* (Science News Letter).

me·a·tus (mē ā'təs), *n., pl.* **-tus·es, -tus.** a passage, duct, or opening in the body, as in the ear. [< Latin *meātus* path < *meāre* to pass]

meat wagon, *Slang.* an ambulance.

meat·work·er (mēt'wėr'kər), *n.* (in Australia) a slaughterhouse or packing-house worker.

meat·works (mēt'wėrks'), *n.* (in Australia) a slaughterhouse or packing house.

meat·y (mē'tē), *adj.,* **meat·i·er, meat·i·est. 1.** of meat; having the flavor of meat: *some choice meaty bits.* **2.** like meat: *a meaty texture.* **3.** full of meat; fleshy: *a meaty roast with little bone.* **4.** full of substance; giving food for thought; pithy: *The speech was very meaty; it contained many valuable ideas.*

me·ca·myl·a·mine (mek'ə mil'ə mēn), *n.* a nerve-blocking drug used in controlling high blood pressure: *The new drug, called "mecamylamine," appears to be more dependable than older compounds* (New York Herald Tribune). *Formula:* $C_{11}H_{21}N$

Mec·ca or **mec·ca** (mek'ə), *n.* **1.** a place that many people visit: *[The] Duquesne Club, lunchtime Mecca for some of the nation's top businessmen ...* (Wall Street Journal). **2.** a place that a person longs to visit. **3.** the goal of one's desires or ambitions. Also, **Mekka.** [< *Mecca,* the sacred city of Islam, in Saudi Arabia, where Moslems go on pilgrimages]

Mec·can (mek'ən), *adj.* of or having to do with Mecca. —*n.* a native or inhabitant of Mecca.

mech., 1. mechanical. **2.** mechanics. **3.** mechanism.

me·chan·ic (mə kan'ik), *n.* **1.** a worker skilled with tools. **2.** a worker who repairs machinery: *a typewriter mechanic, an automobile mechanic.* **3.** *Archaic.* a person who works with his hands; artisan.
—*adj.* mechanical.
[< Latin *mēchanicus* < Greek *mēchanikós* < *mēchanē* machine < *mēchos* a means, expedient]

me·chan·i·cal (mə kan'ə kəl), *adj.* **1.** of or having to do with a machine, mechanism, or machinery: *Mechanical problems are usually more interesting to boys than to girls.* **2.** made or worked by machinery. **3.** like a machine; like that of a machine; automatic; without feeling or expression: *Her reading is very mechanical.* **4.** of, having to do with, or in accordance with the science of mechanics: *a mechanical law.* **5.** *Archaic.* of or having to do with artisans. **—me·chan'i·cal·ness,** *n.* **—Syn. 3.** stereotyped.

mechanical advantage, the ratio of resistance or load to the force or effort that is applied in a machine: *We call the amount of help we get from a machine its mechanical advantage.*

mechanical brain, a complex computer; electronic brain: *... mechanical "brains" that will translate languages, create their own instructions, and prove propositions in logic* (Science News Letter).

mechanical drawing, drawing done with the help of rulers, squares, compasses, etc.

mechanical efficiency, the ratio of the horsepower of an engine actually produced to the horsepower it could theoretically produce.

mechanical energy, the kinetic plus potential energy of a body: *The largest single loss ... occurs when heat energy is converted into mechanical energy* (New Scientist).

mechanical engineer, a person skilled in mechanical engineering.

mechanical engineering, the branch of engineering that deals with the production and use of mechanical power and machinery.

me·chan·i·cal·ize (mə kan'ə kə līz), *v.t.,* **-ized, -iz·ing.** to make mechanical.

me·chan·i·cal·ly (mə kan'ə klē), *adv.* **1.** in a mechanical manner: *He greeted us mechanically.* **2.** in mechanical respects: *That new engine is mechanically perfect.* **3.** toward mechanics: *Boys are usually more mechanically inclined than girls.*

mechanical mixture, a mixture in which the several ingredients have not entered into chemical combination, but still retain their identity and can be separated by mechanical means.

mech·a·ni·cian (mek'ə nish'ən), *n.* a worker skilled in making and repairing machines; mechanic.

me·chan·ics (mə kan'iks), *n.* **1.** the branch of physics dealing with the action of forces on bodies or fluids and with motion. Mechanics includes kinetics, statics, and kinematics. **2.** knowledge dealing with machinery. **3.** the mechanical part; technique: *the mechanics of playing the piano.*

mech·a·nise (mek'ə nīz), *v.t.,* **-nised, -nis·ing.** *Especially British.* to mechanize.

mech·a·nism (mek'ə niz əm), *n.* **1.** the means or way by which something is done; machinery. **2.** a system of parts working together as the parts of a machine do: *The bones and muscles are parts of the mechanism of the body.* **3.** a machine or its working parts: *the mechanism of a watch. Something is wrong with the mechanism of our refrigerator. An automobile engine is a complex mechanism.* **4.** the mechanical part; technique, as in painting or music. **5.** *Psychology.* **a.** the arrangements in the mind or brain that determine thought, feeling, or action in regular and predictable ways. **b.** a response unconsciously selected to protect oneself or find satisfaction for an unfulfilled desire: *a defense mechanism.* **6.** the theory that everything in the universe is produced and can be explained by mechanical or material forces: *the influence of mechanism and materialism in science* (Science News).

mech·a·nist (mek'ə nist), *n.* **1.** a person who believes that all the changes in the universe are the effects of physical and chemical forces. **2.** a mechanician.

mech·a·nis·tic (mek'ə nis'tik), *adj.* of or having to do with mechanists, mechanism, mechanics, or mechanical theories: *We may regard Newton's laws of motion as the supreme model of mechanistic determinism* (Scientific American). **—mech'a·nis'ti·cal·ly,** *adv.*

mech·a·ni·za·tion (mek'ə nə zā'shən), *n.* **1.** a mechanizing. **2.** a being mechanized: *Widespread mechanization has permitted mass production and consequent lowering of consumer prices* (Bulletin of Atomic Scientists).

mech·a·nize (mek'ə nīz), *v.t.,* **-nized, -niz·ing. 1.** to make mechanical. **2.** to do by machinery, rather than by hand: *Much housework can be mechanized.* **3.** to replace men or animals by machinery in (a business, etc.): *to mechanize a factory.* **4.** to equip (a military unit) with armored vehicles, tanks, and other machines.

mech·a·no·mor·phic (mek′ə nō môr′fik), *adj.* of or having to do with mechanomorphism: *mechanomorphic psychology.*

mech·a·no·mor·phism (mek′ə nō môr′fiz əm), *n.* any doctrine or theory that conceives of or explains something only in mechanistic terms.

mech·a·no·re·cep·tor (mek′ə nō ri sep′tər), *n.* a sense organ that responds to mechanical stimuli: *The mechanoreceptors in muscle respond to . . . stimuli such as stretching and pressure* (Scientific American).

mech·a·no·ther·a·peu·tic (mek′ə nō ther′ə pyü′tik), *adj.* of or having to do with mechanotherapeutics or mechanotherapy.

mech·a·no·ther·a·peu·tics (mek′ə nō ther′ə pyü′tiks), *n.* that branch of therapeutics that deals with treatment by mechanical means. [< Greek *mēchanē* machine + English *therapeutics*]

mech·a·no·ther·a·pist (mek′ə nō ther′ə pist), *n.* a person who is skilled in or performs mechanotherapy: *The mechanotherapist aids nature with mechanical methods such as movement or exercise* (World Book Encyclopedia).

mech·a·no·ther·a·py (mek′ə nō ther′ə pē), *n.* therapy by mechanical means, as for relieving muscle stiffness. [< Greek *mēchanē* machine + English *therapy*]

mé·chant (mā shäN′), *adj. French.* malicious; mischievous; naughty; bad: *Mr. Pendennis was wicked, méchant, perfectly abominable* (Thackeray).

mé·chante (mā shäNt′), *adj. French.* the feminine form of **méchant.**

Mech·lin (mek′lən), *n.,* or **Mechlin lace,** a fine lace with the pattern clearly outlined by a distinct thread; malines. [< *Mechlin,* a city in Belgium, where it is made]

Mech·ta (mech tä′), *n. Russian.* Lunik.

mec·li·zine (mek′li zēn), *n.* Bonine.

me·con·ic (mi kon′ik), *adj.* of or derived from the poppy. [< Greek *mēkōn* poppy]

meconic acid, a white crystalline acid derived from opium. It is used in medicine. *Formula:* $C_7H_4O_7$

mec·o·nop·sis (mek′ə nop′sis), *n., pl.* **-ses** (-sēz). any of a group of plants of the poppy family with a style bearing from four to six radiating stigmas. [< Greek *mēkōn* poppy + *ópsis* appearance]

med., 1. median. **2. a.** medical. **b.** medicine. **3.** medieval. **4.** medium.

Med., 1. medieval. **2.** Mediterranean.

M.Ed., Master of Education.

Mé·daille Mi·li·taire (mā dà′yə mē lē ter′), *French.* Military Medal, the highest French decoration for bravery in war.

med·al (med′əl), *n., v.,* **-aled, -al·ing** or (*especially British*) **-alled, -al·ling.** —*n.* a flat, usually round, piece of metal with a design or words stamped on it. Medals are intended to be worn or exhibited, and are often given as awards for achievement. Other medals are sometimes worn to invoke the favor of a saint, etc. Some medals also are struck off to celebrate an important event. *The medal is in silver and bears on the obverse an effigy of the Queen* (London Times). —*v.t.* to decorate or honor with a medal: *Irving went home, medalled by the king* (Thackeray). [< Middle French *médaille* < Italian *medaglia* < Vulgar Latin *metallea* < Latin *metallum* metal, medal < Greek *métallon* mine, quarry, metal]

med·al·cup (med′əl kup′), *n.* a drinking vessel, usually of silver, in which medals or coins are set as part of the decoration.

Medal for Merit, a decoration given by the United States to a civilian for exceptional or outstanding service to the country.

med·al·ist (med′ə list), *n.* **1.** an engraver, designer, or maker of medals. **2.** a person who has won a medal.

me·dal·lic (mə dal′ik), *adj.* having to do with or like a medal.

me·dal·lion (mə dal′yən), *n.* **1.** a large medal. **2.** a design, ornament, etc., shaped like a medal: *A design on a book or a pattern in lace may be called a medallion.* [< French *médaillon* < Italian *medaglione* large medal < *medaglia* medal]

me·dal·lioned (mə dal′yənd), *adj.* ornamented with a medallion or medallions; formed into a medallion.

me·dal·lion·ist (mə dal′yə nist), *n.* a maker of medallions.

med·al·list (med′ə list), *n. Especially British.* medalist.

Medal of Freedom, Presidential Medal of Freedom.

Medal of Honor, the highest military decoration of the United States, given by Congress to members of the armed forces for bravery in combat at the risk of their lives and beyond the call of duty.

medal play, a form of golf in which the player or side that scores the lowest number of strokes is the winner.

med·dle (med′əl), *v.i.,* **-dled, -dling. 1.** to busy oneself with other people's things or affairs without being asked or needed: *Don't meddle with my books or my toys.* **2.** *Obsolete.* to fight; contend. **3.** *Obsolete.* to associate; mingle. [< Old French *medler,* ultimately < Latin *miscēre* to mix]

—**Syn. 1. Meddle, tamper, interfere** mean to concern oneself unnecessarily or unduly with someone or something. **Meddle** implies busying oneself, without right or permission, with something not one's own affair: *That old busybody is always meddling in someone's business.* **Tamper** suggests meddling in order to experiment with a thing or improperly influence a person: *Don't tamper with electrical appliances.* **Interfere** suggests meddling in a way that disturbs or hinders: *She interferes when we scold the children.*

med·dler (med′lər), *n.* a person who interferes or meddles.

med·dle·some (med′əl səm), *adj.* fond of meddling or likely to meddle in other people's affairs; meddling; interfering: *He was curious, meddlesome, gossipy* (Atlantic). —**med′dle·some·ly,** *adv.* —**med′dle·some·ness,** *n.* —**Syn.** officious.

Mede (mēd), *n.* a native or inhabitant of Media, an ancient country in southwestern Asia.

Me·de·a (mi dē′ə), *n.* **1.** *Greek Legend.* an enchantress who helped Jason get the Golden Fleece. She eloped with Jason and was later deserted by him. **2. a.** a play by Euripides. **b.** the heroine of this play.

med·e·vac (med′i vak′), *n.* a helicopter for evacuating the wounded from a combat zone. [< *med*(ical) *evac*(uation)]

Med·fly (med′flī′), *n., pl.* **-flies.** the Mediterranean fruit fly.

me·di·a[1] (mē′dē ə), *n.* a plural of **medium:** *Newspapers, magazines, and billboards are important advertising media.*
➤ See **medium** for usage note.

me·di·a[2] (mē′dē ə), *n., pl.* **-di·ae** (-dē ē). **1.** the middle layer of the wall of a blood or lymphatic vessel. **2.** *Phonetics.* a voiced stop, such as *b, d,* or *g.* [< Latin *media,* feminine of *medius* middle]

me·di·a·cy (mē′dē ə sē), *n.* **1.** a being mediate. **2.** *Obsolete.* mediation.

me·di·ae·val (mē′dē ē′vəl, med′ē-), *adj.* medieval. —**me′di·ae′val·ly,** *adv.*

me·di·ae·val·ism (mē′dē ē′və liz əm, med′ē-), *n.* medievalism.

me·di·ae·val·ist (mē′dē ē′və list, med′ē-), *n.* medievalist.

me·di·ae·val·ize (mē′dē ē′və līz), *v.t.,* **-ized, -iz·ing.** medievalize.

me·di·al (mē′dē əl), *adj.* **1.** in the middle; middle. **2.** having to do with a mathematical mean or average. **3.** average; ordinary. **4.** *Phonetics.* occurring in the middle of or within a word: *In "fairy" the "i" is in medial position.*
—*n.* **1.** a medial letter. **2.** a form of a letter used in the middle of a word.
[< Late Latin *mediālis* (of the) middle < Latin *medius* middle]
—**Syn.** *adj.* **1.** intermediate, median.

me·di·al·ly (mē′dē ə lē), *adv.* in the middle; in a medial position.

medial moraine, the moraine that occurs when the lateral moraines of two glaciers meet and merge.

me·di·a·man (mē′dē ə mən), *n., pl.* **-men.** an employee of an advertising agency who evaluates and selects media for carrying the advertisements of clients: *Newspapers, dependent on advertising . . . have to convince the mediamen and themselves that they are read by "top people" or "lively minds"* (Manchester Guardian Weekly).

me·di·an (mē′dē ən), *adj.* **1.** of, having to do with, or in the middle; middle: *the median vein of a leaf.* **2.** having to do with or designating the plane that divides something into two equal parts, especially one dividing a symmetrical animal into right and left halves. **3.** of a median; having as many above as below a certain number: *The median age of the population was found to be 21 (that is, there were as many persons above 21 as below it), while the average age was found to be 25.*
—*n.* **1.** the middle number of a series: *The median of 1, 3, 4, 8, 9 is 4.* **2.** a measurement so chosen that half the numbers in the series are above it and half are below it: *The median of 1, 3, 4, 8, 9, 10,* is *6.* **3. a.** (of a triangle) a line from a vertex to the midpoint of the opposite side. **b.** (of a trapezoid) the line joining the midpoints of the nonparallel sides. *Abbr.:* med.
[< Latin *mediānus* of the middle < *medius* middle. Doublet of MEAN[3].] —**me′di·an·ly,** *adv.*

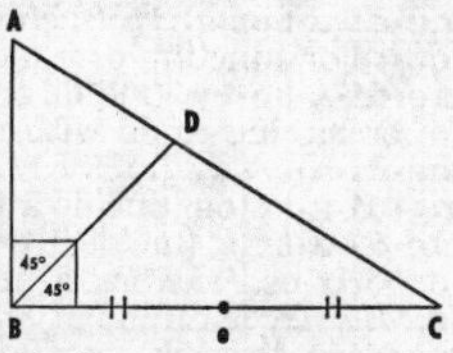

Medians (def. 3. a.) are point e and line BD. BD bisects angle ABC. Point e divides BC into 2 equal parts, Be and eC.

Me·di·an (mē′dē ən), *adj.* of Media or the Medes. —*n.* a Mede.

median strip, the strip of land, usually grass-covered or landscaped, between the lanes for traffic in either direction on some modern highways.

me·di·ant (mē′dē ənt), *n.* the third note or tone of a musical scale, halfway from the tonic or keynote to the dominant. [< Italian *mediante* < Late Latin *mediāns, -antis,* present participle of *mediārī;* see MEDIATE]

me·di·as·ti·nal (mē′dē as tī′nəl), *adj.* of or having to do with the mediastinum.

me·di·as·ti·num (mē′dē as tī′nəm), *n., pl.* **-na** (-nə). **1.** a middle partition between two body cavities or parts. **2.** a partition formed by the two pleurae between the lungs, including the enclosed space in which are all the viscera of the thorax except the lungs. [< New Latin *mediastinum* < Medieval Latin *mediastinus* intermediate; the meaning is < Latin *medius* middle; the form is < Latin *mediastīnus* inferior servant < *mediānus;* see MEDIAN]

me·di·ate (*v.* mē′dē āt; *adj.* mē′dē it), *v.,* **-at·ed, -at·ing,** *adj.* —*v.i.* **1.** to be a go-between; act in order to bring about an agreement between persons or sides: *The mayor tried to mediate between the bus company and its employees.* **2.** to occupy an intermediate place or position. —*v.t.* **1.** to effect by intervening; settle by intervening: *to mediate an agreement, to mediate a strike.* **2.** to be a connecting link between. **3.** to be the medium for effecting (a result), for conveying (a gift), or for communicating (knowledge).
—*adj.* **1.** connected, but not directly; connected through some other person or thing: *A vassal's relation with his king was mediate through the lord on whose estate he lived.* **2.** intermediate: *after many mediate preferments . . . at last he became Archbishop of Canterbury* (Thomas Fuller).
[< Late Latin *mediārī* (with English *-ate*[1]) to be in the middle, intervene < Latin *medius* middle] —**me′di·ate·ly,** *adv.* —**me′di·ate·ness,** *n.*

me·di·a·tion (mē′dē ā′shən), *n.* a mediating; effecting an agreement; friendly interference, especially to effect an agreement or reconciliation: *the mediation of friendly nations.*

Mediation Board, a United States federal agency set up in 1926 to mediate in major labor-management disputes involving railroads: *In Washington, the Mediation Board is still considering whether to offer arbitration to the Brotherhood of Locomotive Firemen and Enginemen* (Wall Street Journal).

me·di·a·tive (mē′dē ā′tiv), *adj.* mediatory.

me·di·a·ti·za·tion (mē′dē ə tə zā′shən), *n.* **1.** a mediatizing. **2.** a being mediatized.

me·di·a·tize (mē′dē ə tīz), *v.t.,* **-tized, -tiz·ing. 1.** (in the Holy Roman Empire) to reduce (a prince, principality, etc.) from a position of direct or immediate vassalage to the empire to one of indirect or mediate vassalage. **2.** to annex (a principality) to another state while leaving some rights of government to its former sovereign. **3.** to make mediate in position.

me·di·a·tor (mē′dē ā′tər), *n.* a person or group that mediates: *Mother acts as a* *mediator when John and Jim quarrel. The unions . . . had refused to accept the intervention of an official mediator* (London Times).

me·di·a·to·ri·al (mē′dē ə tôr′ē əl, -tōr′-), *adj.* mediatory.

me·di·a·tor·ship (mē′dē ā′tər ship), *n.* the office or function of a mediator.

me·di·a·to·ry (mē′dē ə tôr′ē, -tōr′-), *adj.* of or having to do with mediation.

me·di·a·tress (mē′dē ā′tris), *n.* mediatrix.

me·di·a·trice (mē′dē ā′tris), *n.* mediatrix.

me·di·a·trix (mē′dē ā′triks), *n., pl.* **-tri·ces** or **-trix·es.** a woman mediator. [< Latin *mediātrix*, feminine of *mediātor* mediator]

med·ic[1] (med′ik), *n. Informal.* **1.** a physician. **2.** a medical student. **3.** a member of the medical department of a branch of the armed services: *Army medics knocked out their [Korean POWs'] malaria* (Newsweek). [< Latin *medicus* physician; adjective, healing < *medērī* to heal]

med·ic[2] (med′ik), *n.* any of certain plants of the pea family, with purple or yellow flowers, such as alfalfa. [< Latin *Medica* < Greek (*póa*) *Medikḗ* Median (herb), lucerne]

med·i·ca·ble (med′ə kə bəl), *adj.* that can be cured or relieved by medical treatment. [< Latin *medicābilis* < *medicārī* to heal < *medicus;* see MEDIC[1]]

Med·i·caid or **med·i·caid** (med′ə kād), *n. U.S.* a program providing medical benefits for needy or disabled persons not covered by social security: *While Medicare covers persons over 65 . . . Medicaid is a federal-state-local venture to help the "medically indigent" regardless of age* (Time). [< *medic*(al) *aid*]

med·i·cal (med′ə kəl), *adj.* **1.** of or having to do with the practice or science of medicine: *medical advice, a medical school, medical treatment. Abbr.:* med. **2.** curative; medicinal.

—*n.* **1.** *Informal.* a medical student; a doctor: *I remain as skeptical as most medicals about male pattern baldness* (Maclean's). **2.** *Informal.* a medical examination: *. . . the door was flung open and a warden shouted "Get ready for your medicals"* (Punch).

[< French *médical*, learned borrowing from Late Latin *medicālis* < Latin *medicus* doctor; see MEDIC[1]]

medical examiner, 1. an official, especially a doctor or coroner, whose duties are to examine the bodies of persons who died violently or by suicide, murder, etc., perform autopsies, and attempt to determine the circumstances of death. **2.** a doctor who is in charge of examining persons applying for accident insurance, workmen's compensation, and the like: *Medical examiners can and should . . . consider the kind and location of the applicant's cancer* (Science News Letter).

medical geography, the study of the influence of geography and natural environment on health, vital functions, and diseases.

medical jurisprudence, the science that deals with the application of medical knowledge to problems in civil and criminal law; forensic medicine.

med·i·cal·ly (med′ə klē), *adv.* in medical ways or respects; for medical purposes.

medical reactor, a reactor which supplies radioactive isotopes to a local area for medical use where the radioactive life of the isotope is too short to allow for shipping from a distance: *Brookhaven's new medical reactor . . . will considerably simplify the research task* (Newsweek).

me·dic·a·ment (mə dik′ə mənt, med′ə-kə-), *n.* a substance used to cure or heal; a medicine. —*v.t.* to medicate: *He . . . had been treated and medicamented as the doctor ordained* (Thackeray). [< Latin *medicāmentum* < *medicārī* to heal < *medicus* healing; a doctor; see MEDIC[1]]

med·i·ca·men·tal (med′ə kə men′təl), *adj.* of or like a medicament; medicinal.

med·i·ca·men·ta·ry (med′ə kə men′tər ē), *adj.* medicamental.

Med·i·care or **med·i·care** (med′ə kãr′), *n.* **1.** *U.S.* a program providing medical care under social security for persons over sixty-five years old. **2.** *Canada.* a government-sponsored program of health insurance. [< *medi*(cal) *care*]

med·i·cas·ter (med′ə kas′tər), *n.* a pretender to medical skill; quack: *Impostors and visionaries and swindlers and medicasters . . . hastened to Rome* (Hendrik Van Loon). [< Latin *medicus* physician + *-aster*, a diminutive suffix]

med·i·cate (med′ə kāt), *v.t.,* **-cat·ed, -cat·ing. 1.** to treat with medicine. **2.** to put medicine on or in. [< Latin *medicārī* (with English *-ate*[1]) < *medicus* healing; a doctor; see MEDIC[1]]

med·i·cat·ed (med′ə kā′tid), *adj.* containing medicine: *medicated gauze. Cough drops are medicated.*

med·i·ca·tion (med′ə kā′shən), *n.* **1.** treatment with medicine. **2.** a putting medicine on or in. **3.** a medicament.

med·i·ca·tive (med′ə kā′tiv), *adj.* curative or healing; medicinal.

Med·i·ce·an (med′ə sē′ən, -chē′-), *adj.* of, having to do with, or like the Medici, a wealthy and powerful Florentine family of the Renaissance, the 1300's to the 1500's, famous as rulers of Tuscany and as patrons of many artists, sculptors, and writers: *He lived a life of . . . Medicean splendor* (Harper's).

me·dic·i·na·ble (mə dis′ə nə bəl), *adj. Archaic.* curative; medicinal: *Some griefs are med'cinable; that is one of them, For it doth physic love* (Shakespeare).

me·dic·i·nal (mə dis′ə nəl), *adj.* having value as medicine; healing; helping; relieving: *brandy for medicinal purposes.* —*n.* something which is or can be used as a medicine.

medicinal leech, a European leech, about four inches long, formerly used for taking blood from sick people.

me·dic·i·nal·ly (mə dis′ə nə lē), *adv.* as medicine.

med·i·cine (med′ə sən), *n., v.,* **-cined, -cin·ing.** —*n.* **1.** any substance, drug, or means used to cure disease or improve health: *The miserable have no other medicine but only hope* (Shakespeare). **2.** the science of curing disease or improving health; skill in healing; doctor's art; treatment of diseases. **3. a.** the magic power that primitive peoples believe certain men have over disease, evil spirits, and other things. **b.** any object or ceremony, such as a spell, charm, or fetish, supposed by the North American Indians or other primitive peoples to have magical power or influence. **4.** any influence that effects an improvement: *Another tax cut could well be regarded as just the right medicine* (New York Times). **5.** a medicine man: *When they come to learn you are a great medicine, they will adopt you into the tribe* (James Fenimore Cooper). **6.** *Obsolete.* a drug; love potion; poison: *If the rascal have not given me medicines to make me love him, I'll be hanged* (Shakespeare).

take one's medicine, to do what one must; do something one dislikes to do: *Canada can do nothing—she must take her medicine and make the best of it* (New York Times).

—*v.t.* to give medicine to; affect by or as if by medicine.

[< Old French *medicine, medecine*, learned borrowings from Latin *medicīna* (originally) of a doctor < *medicus* physician; see MEDIC[1]]

medicine ball, a large, heavy, leather ball tossed from one person to another for exercise.

medicine dance, a ceremonial dance of primitive peoples to cure disease or produce magic.

medicine lodge, a lodge used by North American Indians for medicine dances and other rites.

medicine man, a man believed by North American Indians and other primitive peoples to have magic power over diseases, evil spirits, and other things; shaman.

med·i·cin·er (med′ə sə nər), *n. Archaic.* a physician: *It is unbecoming a mediciner of thine eminence to interfere with the practice of another* (Scott).

medicine show, *U.S.* a cheap act or sales spiel formerly put on in towns and villages, at which medicine, sometimes represented as having originated among the Indians, was advertised and sold: *The days of the medicine show are over* (Maclean's).

med·i·co (med′ə kō), *n., pl.* **-cos.** *Informal.* **1.** a doctor; physician: *The medico held my chin in the usual way, and examined my throat* (Alexander W. Kinglake). *The delight of her husband, her aunts . . . And of medicos marveling sweetly on her ills* (John Crowe Ransom). **2.** a medical student. [< Italian *medico*, or Spanish *médico* physician, learned borrowings from Latin *medicus;* see MEDIC[1]]

med·i·co·chi·rur·gi·cal (med′ə kō kī rėr′-jə kəl), *adj.* having to do with both medicine and surgery. [< *medical* + *chirurgical*]

med·i·co·le·gal (med′ə kō lē′gəl), *adj.* of or having to do with forensic medicine; medical and legal: *. . . medicolegal problems such as the determination of disputed paternity, based on the inheritance of the various blood groups and types* (Lawrence H. Snyder). [< *medical* + *legal*]

me·di·e·val (mē′dē ē′vəl, med′ē-), *adj.* **1.** belonging to or having to do with the Middle Ages (the years from about 500 to about 1450 A.D.): *The Cathedral Church of Saint Peter . . . is the largest medieval cathedral in England* (Newsweek). *Abbr.:* med. **2.** like that of the Middle Ages. Also, **mediaeval.** [< Latin *medium*, neuter, middle + *aevum* age + English *-al*[1]] —**me′di·e′val·ly,** *adv.*

Medieval Greek, the Greek language during the Middle Ages, from about 700 A.D. to about 1500 A.D.; Middle Greek.

me·di·e·val·ism (mē′dē ē′və liz əm, med′-ē-), *n.* **1.** the spirit, ideals, and customs of the Middle Ages; medieval thought, religion, and art. **2.** devotion to medieval ideals; adoption of medieval customs. **3.** a medieval belief, custom, idea, etc. Also, **mediaevalism.**

me·di·e·val·ist (mē′dē ē′və list, med′ē-), *n.* **1.** a person who knows much about the Middle Ages: *a Cambridge University medievalist* (New Yorker). **2.** a person who is in sympathy with medieval ideals, customs, etc. Also, **mediaevalist.**

me·di·e·val·ize (mē′dē ē′və līz), *v.t.,* **-ized, -iz·ing.** to make medieval; conform to medieval types, ideas, etc. Also, **mediaevalize.**

Medieval Latin, the Latin language during the Middle Ages, from about 700 A.D. to about 1500 A.D.; Middle Latin.

me·di·na (mə dē′nə), *n.* (in Morocco) the native Arab quarter of a city: *the medina of Marrakech, the Casablanca medina.* [< Arabic *madīna* town]

me·di·o·cre (mē′dē ō′kər, mē′dē ō′-), *adj.* neither bad nor good; average; ordinary: *a mediocre student, a mediocre performance, a person of mediocre abilities.* [< Old French *mediocre*, learned borrowing from Latin *mediocris* (originally) halfway up < *medius* middle (of) + *ocris* jagged mountain] —**Syn.** medium, commonplace, indifferent.

me·di·oc·ri·ty (mē′dē ok′rə tē), *n., pl.* **-ties. 1.** mediocre quality: *Mediocrity knows nothing higher than itself, but talent instantly recognizes genius* (Sir Arthur Conan Doyle). **2.** a mediocre ability or accomplishment. **3.** a mediocre person.

Medit., Mediterranean.

med·i·tate (med′ə tāt), *v.,* **-tat·ed, -tat·ing.** —*v.i.* to think; reflect: *Monks and nuns meditate on holy things for hours at a time. He quitted her presence to meditate upon revenge* (Frederick Marryat). —*v.t.* **1.** to think about; consider; plan; intend: *They are meditating a reimposition of the tax on corn* (Manchester Examiner). *All men that meditate peace, be allowed safe conduct* (Thomas Hobbes). *Alberti had deeply meditated the remains of Roman antiquity* (Henry Hallam). **2.** to observe intently: *The ready spaniel . . . meditates the prey* (Alexander Pope). [< Latin *meditārī* (with English *-ate*[1])] —**Syn.** *v.i.* ponder, muse, cogitate. See **think.**

med·i·ta·tion (med′ə tā′shən), *n.* **1.** continued thought; reflection. **2.** contemplation on sacred or solemn subjects, especially as a devotional exercise. **3.** a contemplative or devotional writing or talk.

med·i·ta·tive (med′ə tā′tiv), *adj.* **1.** fond of meditating; inclined to meditate: *I'm just not the meditative type* (New Yorker). **2.** expressing meditation: *a meditative manner, a meditative essay.* —**med′i·ta′tive·ly,** *adv.* —**med′i·ta′tive·ness,** *n.*

med·i·ta·tor (med′ə tā′tər), *n.* a person who meditates.

med·i·ter·ra·ne·an (med′ə tə rā′nē ən, -rān′yən), *adj.* nearly or entirely enclosed by land; landlocked. [< Latin *mediterrāneus* (< *medius* middle (of) + *terra* land, earth) + English *-an*]

Med·i·ter·ra·ne·an (med′ə tə rā′nē ən, -rān′yən), *adj.* of or having to do with the Mediterranean Sea or the lands around it. —*n.* **1.** one of the generally recognized principal subgroups of the Caucasoid or Caucasian racial group, chiefly found on the shores of the Mediterranean Sea, and characterized by dark eyes, hair, and skin, narrow nose and head, and relatively short stature. **2.** a member of this group. [< Late Latin *(mare) Mediterrāneum* Mediterranean (Sea)]

Mediterranean anemia, thalassemia.

Mediterra′nean fever, undulant fever.

Mediterranean fruit fly, a very destructive fly, about the size of the common house fly, whose larvae attack fruits and vegetables. It is found in warm regions of the world. Also, **Medfly.**

me·di·um (mē′dē əm), *adj., n., pl.* **-di·ums** or **-di·a.** —*adj.* having a middle position, quality, or condition; moderate: *Eggs can be cooked hard, soft, or medium. Five feet eight inches is a medium height for a man.* —*n.* **1.** something that is in the middle; neither one extreme nor the other; middle condition: *a happy medium between city and country life.* **2.** a substance or agent through which anything acts or an effect is produced; a means: *Copper wire is a medium of electric transmission. The telephone is a medium of communication. A newspaper is an advertising medium. A negotiation was opened through the medium of the ambassador, Sam* (Charlotte Brontë). **3.** a substance in which something can live; environment: *Water is the natural medium of fish.* **4. a.** a nutritive substance, either liquid or solid, such as agar-agar or gelatin, in or upon which bacteria, fungi, and other microorganisms are grown for study; culture medium. **b.** a substance used for displaying, preserving, etc., organic specimens. **5. a.** a liquid with which pigments are mixed for painting. **b.** a type of painting: *His best medium is oil painting.* **6.** a person through whom supposed messages from the world of spirits are received and sent.
[< Latin *medium,* neuter, middle]
➔ The plural is always **mediums** in the sense of def. 6, and also in that of def. 1, although in this sense the plural rarely occurs. In other senses both *mediums* and **media** are used, but *media* is more common in technical and scientific work.

medium bomber, a bomber having a gross weight of 100,000 to 250,000 pounds.

me·di·um·is·tic (mē′dē ə mis′tik), *adj.* of or having to do with a spiritualistic medium.

medium of exchange, money or anything used as money.

me·di·um-priced (mē′dē əm prīst′), *adj.* (of a line of products) having a price ranging approximately between the cheapest and the most expensive of its kind.

me·di·um-range (mē′dē əm rānj′), *adj.* effective or operable over a moderate range.

me·di·um·ship (mē′dē əm ship′), *n.* the quality, skill, or status of a spiritualistic medium.

me·di·um-sized (mē′dē əm sīzd′), *adj.* neither large nor small of its kind.

medium steel, steel with a small percentage of carbon.

me·di·um-term (mē′dē əm tėrm′), *adj.* of or for a period of time intermediate between long-term and short-term: *This medium-term coverage expands the short-term export insurance offered since February* (Wall Street Journal).

med·lar (med′lər), *n.* **1.** a fruit that looks like a small brown apple. It is picked after frost and ripened, and usually preserved. *You'll be rotten before you are half ripe, and that's the right virtue of a medlar* (Shakespeare). **2.** the small, bushy tree of the rose family that it grows on. **3.** any of various related trees or their fruit. [< Old French *medler,* earlier *meslier* the medlar (tree) < *mesle* medlar (fruit), also *mesple* < Latin *mespila* < Greek *méspīlon*]

Branch of Medlar

med·ley (med′lē), *n., pl.* **-leys,** *adj., v.,* **-leyed** or **-lied, -ley·ing.** —*n.* **1.** a mixture of things that ordinarily do not belong together. **2.** a piece of music made up of parts from other pieces. **3.** *Archaic.* hand-to-hand fighting; melee.
—*adj.* made up of parts that are not alike; mixed: *a medley air of cunning and of impudence* (Wordsworth).
—*v.t.* to mix as in a medley.
[< Old French *medlee,* earlier *meslee,* feminine past participle of *medler,* or *mesler* to mix, ultimately < Latin *miscēre* to mix. Doublet of MELEE.]
—**Syn.** *n.* **1.** hodgepodge, jumble. *-adj.* mingled, motley.

medley relay, 1. a relay race in swimming between several teams, each of which consists of three swimmers who take turns in covering the total distance and kind of styles required. **2.** a relay race between several teams of runners, each of whom runs a certain distance out of the total required.

MEDO (no periods), Middle East Defense Organization.

Mé·doc or **Me·doc** (mā dôk′), *n.* a red wine, a kind of Bordeaux or claret. [< *Médoc,* a district in France, where it is made]

me·dres·seh (mə dras′e), *n.* madrasah.

Med·rol (med′rōl), *n. Trademark.* a synthetic hormone similar in action to cortisone but with fewer side effects in some patients, used in the treatment of arthritis and other inflammatory diseases. *Formula:* $C_{22}H_{30}O_5$

me·dul·la (mi dul′ə), *n., pl.* **-dul·lae** (-dul′ē). **1.** medulla oblongata: *the hind brain, consisting of the cerebellum and the medulla* (A.M. Winchester). **2.** the marrow of bones. **3.** the inner substance of an organ or part, as of the kidney. **4.** the pith of plants. [< Latin *medulla* marrow; origin uncertain]

medulla ob·lon·ga·ta (ob′long gā′tə, -gä′-), the lowest part of the brain, at the top end of the spinal cord. See picture under **brain.** [< New Latin *medulla oblongata* prolonged medulla]

med·ul·lar·y (med′ə ler′ē, mi dul′ər-), *adj.* of, having to do with, or like medulla or the medulla oblongata.

medullary ray, one of the radiating vertical bands or plates of parenchymatous tissue which divide the vascular bundles and connect the pith with the bark in the stems of exogenous plants.

medullary sheath, 1. a narrow ring comprising the innermost layer of woody tissue that surrounds the pith in certain plants. **2.** myelin.

med·ul·lat·ed (med′ə lā′tid, mi dul′ā-), *adj.* having a medullary sheath: *a medullated nerve fiber.*

Me·du·sa (mə dü′sə, -dyü′-; -zə), *n., pl.* **-sas.** *Greek Legend.* a horrible monster, one of the three Gorgons. She had snakes for hair, and anyone who looked upon her was turned into stone. She was slain by Perseus, and her head fixed on the shield of Athena. *Cast not thine eye upon Medusa ...* (John Gower). See picture under **Gorgoneion.**
—**Me·du′sa·like′,** *adj.*

me·du·sa (mə dü′sə, -dyü′-; -zə), *n., pl.* **-sas, -sae** (-sē, -zē). a jellyfish shaped like a bell. See picture under **jellyfish.** [< New Latin *Medusa* the genus name < Latin *Medūsa* Medusa (because one species has feelers that look like the snake hair of Medusa)]

me·du·san (mə dü′sən, -dyü′-; -zən), *adj.* of or having to do with a medusa or jellyfish. —*n.* a medusa or jellyfish.

me·du·soid (mə dü′soid, -dyü′-), *adj.* of or like a medusa or jellyfish: *The bracts, swimming bells, and gonophores are constructed on a medusoid plan* (A. Franklin Shull).

meech (mēch), *v.i., v.t.* miche. —**meech′er,** *n.*

meed (mēd), *n.* **1.** *Poetic.* what one deserves or has earned; reward: *a meed of praise, the meed of victory.* **2.** *Obsolete.* a gift. **3.** *Obsolete.* corrupt gain; bribery. **4.** *Obsolete.* merit; worth: *My meed hath got me fame* (Shakespeare). [Old English *mēd*]

meek (mēk), *adj.* **1.** not easily angered; having a mild and patient disposition: *Even the man Moses, the meekest of men, was wrathful sometimes* (George Eliot). **2.** submitting tamely when ordered about or injured by others: *The boy was meek as a lamb when he was reproved.* **3.** *Obsolete.* **a.** gentle; courteous; kind. **b.** (of a superior) merciful; compassionate.
—*adv. Obsolete.* in a meek manner; meekly.
[< Scandinavian (compare Old Icelandic *mjūkr* (originally) soft)] —**meek′ly,** *adv.* —**meek′ness,** *n.*
—**Syn.** *adj.* **1.** mild, forbearing. See **gentle. 2.** yielding, docile, submissive. See **humble.**
—**Ant.** *adj.* **1.** arrogant.

meek·en (mē′kən), *v.t., v.i.* to make or become meek. [< *meek* + *-en*[1]]

meer·kat (mir′kat), *n.* a small South African carnivorous animal allied to the mongoose; suricate: *Tortoise eggs are much sought after by jackals, meerkats and muishonds* (Cape Times). [< Afrikaans *meerkat* < Dutch *meer* sea + *kat* cat]

meer·schaum (mir′shəm, -shôm), *n.* **1.** a very soft, light mineral, a hydrous silicate of magnesium, used especially to make tobacco pipes; sepiolite: *He dried the meerschaum mug and put it back in the cabinet* (New Yorker). *Formula:* $H_4Mg_2Si_3O_{10}$ **2.** a tobacco pipe with a bowl made of this substance. Meerschaums are valued for the rich brown color they gain after continued use. [< German *Meerschaum* (literally) sea foam (compare MERE[2]), translation of Persian *kef-i-daryā* foam of (the) sea]

meet[1] (mēt), *v.,* **met, meet·ing,** *n.* —*v.t.* **1. a.** to come face to face with: *Our car met another car on a narrow road.* **b.** to go to a place at which (a person) arrives: *I must go to the station to meet my mother.* **c.** to be present at the arrival of: *to meet a plane or boat.* **2. a.** to come together; come into contact or connection with: *Sword met sword in battle.* **b.** to join; intersect: *The accident occurred where Oak Street meets Main Street.* **3.** to come into company with; be together: *The hosts met their guests at the restaurant.* **4.** to keep an appointment with: *Meet me at 1:00.* **5.** to become acquainted with; be introduced to: *Have you met my sister?* **6.** to be visible or audible to: *Of Forests, and enchantments drear, Where more is meant than meets the ear* (Milton). **7.** to satisfy: *to meet obligations, to meet objections.* **8.** to pay: *to meet bills or debts.* **9.** to fight with; deal with; oppose: *to meet threats with defiance. I only with an Oaken staff will meet thee* (Milton). **10.** to face directly: *He met her glance with a smile.* **11.** to experience: *He met open scorn before he won fame.* **12.** to conform to (a person's wishes, opinions, etc.).
—*v.i.* **1.** to come face to face: *Their cars met on the narrow road.* **2.** to assemble: *Congress will meet next month. When shall we three meet again?* (Shakespeare). **3.** to come into contact; come together; join: *The two roads met near the church.* **4.** to be united; join in harmony: *His is a nature in which courage and caution meet.*
meet up with, to meet with: *He meets up with a Bohemian sort of girl* (Atlantic).
meet with, a. to come across; light upon: *We met with bad weather.* **b.** to have; get: *The plan met with approval.*
—*n.* **1.** a meeting; gathering: *an athletic meet.* **2.** the people at a meeting. **3.** the place of meeting.
[Old English *mētan* < *mōt* meeting, moot]
—**meet′er,** *n.*
—**Syn.** *v.t.* **1. a.** confront, encounter. **7.** settle, fulfill.

meet[2] (mēt), *adj. Archaic.* **1.** fitting; becoming: *It is meet and right so to do* (Book of Common Prayer). **2.** suitable; proper: *It is meet that you should help your friends.*
—*adv. Obsolete.* in a meet or proper manner; fitly. [Old English *gemǣte*] —**meet′ness,** *n.*

meet·ing (mē′ting), *n.* **1.** a coming together: *a meeting of minds, a chance meeting with an old friend.* **2.** a gathering or assembly of people for any of various purposes, now especially discussion or legislation: *an open meeting of a Congressional committee. He [Mr. Gladstone] speaks to me as if I was a public meeting* (Queen Victoria). **3.** an assembly of people for religious worship, especially an assembly of Quakers, or, in England, of dissenters: *a Quaker meeting, a prayer meeting.* **4.** a place where things meet; junction: *a meeting of roads, the meeting of the Ohio and the Mississippi.* **5.** a hostile encounter; duel: *The meeting, was set for the next morning; the weapons: pistols at thirty paces.* **6.** a schedule of or gathering for horse races lasting several days or weeks.
—**Syn. 2. Meeting, assembly, gathering** mean a coming together of a group of people. **Meeting** applies especially when the purpose is to consider scheduled business: *The club held a meeting.* **Assembly** applies when the purpose is less explicit but suggests that the occasion is rather formal: *The principal called an assembly.* **Gathering** suggests that the occasion is informal and that it may be without any real purpose: *There was a large gathering at her house.*

meeting ground, a place where different elements meet or come together: *New York City is a meeting ground of people from almost every part of the world.*

meeting house, **1. a.** a building used for worship in the Quaker fashion. **b.** *British.* any nonconformist house of worship; conventicle. **2.** *U.S.* any place of worship; church.

meet·ly (mēt′lē), *adv.* in a meet manner; suitably; properly: . . . *where change should meetly fall* (Robert Browning).

meg-, *combining form.* the form of **mega-** before vowels, as in *megohm.*

mega-, *combining form.* **1.** large: *Megacephalic = large-headed.* **2.** one million: *Megacycle = one million cycles. Megaton = one million tons.* Also, **meg-** before vowels.
[< Greek *mégas, megálou* great]

meg·a·buck (meg′ə buk′), *n. U.S. Slang.* a million dollars: *A fifty megabuck ($50,000,000) laboratory is today a commonplace* (New York Times Magazine). [< *mega-* + *buck*[5]]

meg·a·ce·phal·ic (meg′ə sə fal′ik), *adj.* **1.** large-headed. **2.** *Anthropology.* having a skull with a cranial capacity exceeding the average for modern man (about 1,600 cubic centimeters). [< *mega-* + Greek *kephalē* head + English *-ic*]

meg·a·ceph·a·lous (meg′ə sef′ə ləs), *adj.* megacephalic.

meg·a·cit·y (meg′ə sit′ē), *n., pl.* **-cit·ies.** a city with a population of more than a million: *The United States has evolved a way to concentrate in its "megacities" vast numbers of people to optimize economic proficiency* (New Scientist).

meg·a·corpse (meg′ə kôrps′), *n.* a million dead persons, considered collectively, such as could result from nuclear warfare.

meg·a·cu·rie (meg′ə kyůr′ē), *n.* a million curies: *Since each megacurie is roughly as potent as 2,200 lbs. of pure radium, this is a large amount of radioactivity* (Time).

meg·a·cy·cle (meg′ə sī′kəl), *n. Physics.* a million cycles: *The oscillation frequency used is 200 megacycles per second* (Science News). *Abbr.:* mc.

meg·a·death (meg′ə deth′), *n.* the death of one million persons, such as could result from nuclear warfare: *The Kremlin can now destroy nearly 40 per cent of our industry and take a toll of 13 megadeaths* (Birmingham News).

Me·gae·ra (mə jē′rə), *n. Greek and Roman Mythology.* one of the three Furies (Erinyes), Alecto and Tisiphone being the other two.

meg·a·gam·ete (meg′ə gam′ēt, -gə mēt′), *n. Biology.* a macrogamete.

meg·a·hertz (meg′ə hėrts′), *n.* one million hertz.

meg·a·joule (meg′ə joul′, -jül′), *n.* a unit of work or energy, equivalent to a million joules.

meg·a·kar·y·o·cyte (meg′ə kar′ē ə sīt), *n. Biology.* a large cell of bone marrow with a lobulated nucleus that gives rise to blood platelets. [< *mega-* + *karyo-* + *-cyte*]

meg·a·lith (meg′ə lith), *n.* a stone of great size, especially in ancient construction or in monuments left by primitive people. [< *mega-* + Greek *líthos* stone]

meg·a·lith·ic (meg′ə lith′ik), *adj.* **1.** having to do with megaliths. **2.** of or having to do with a culture in western Europe in the late neolithic period, characterized by rough stone monuments and tombs of large stones.

meg·a·lo·blast (meg′ə lō blast′, -bläst′), *n.* a nucleated red blood cell, of abnormally large size, found in the blood of anemic persons. [< Greek *mégas, megálou* great + *blastós* sprout, germ]

meg·a·lo·blas·tic (meg′ə lō blas′tik, -bläs′-), *adj.* of or having megaloblasts; characterized by the presence of megaloblasts in the blood: *megaloblastic anemia.*

meg·a·lo·ce·pha·li·a (meg′ə lō sə fā′lē ə), *n.* megalocephaly.

meg·a·lo·ce·phal·ic (meg′ə lō sə fal′ik), *adj.* megacephalic.

meg·a·lo·ceph·a·lous (meg′ə lō sef′ə ləs), *adj.* megacephalic.

meg·a·lo·ceph·a·ly (meg′ə lō sef′ə lē), *n.* **1.** condition of having a large head; being megacephalic. **2.** a disease characterized by enlargement of the head. [< Greek *mégas, megálou* great + *kephalē* head]

meg·a·lo·ma·ni·a (meg′ə lō mā′nē ə), *n.* insanity marked by delusions of great personal power, importance, or wealth, associated with schizophrenia and other disorders. [< Greek *mégas, megálou* great + English *mania*]

meg·a·lo·ma·ni·ac (meg′ə lō mā′nē ak), *n.* a person who has megalomania. —*adj.* megalomaniacal: *In China, as in Russia, there is a megalomaniac desire to press forward industrialization* (Wall Street Journal).

meg·a·lo·ma·ni·a·cal (meg′ə lō mə nī′ə-kəl), *adj.* of, having to do with, or afflicted with megalomania.

meg·a·lo·mar·tyr (meg′ə lō mär′tər), *n.* a great or famous martyr. [< Greek *mégas, megálou* great + English *martyr*]

meg·a·lop·o·lis (meg′ə lop′ə lis), *n.* **1.** a city of enormous size, especially when thought of as the center of power, wealth, etc., in a country or the world: *This grim vignette symbolizes the crushing weight of the modern industrial megalopolis* (Atlantic). **2.** an area of more or less continuous urban and suburban development, with little or no intervening countryside. [< Greek *mégas, megálou* great + *pólis* city]

meg·a·lo·pol·i·tan (meg′ə lə pol′ə tən), *adj.* of or having to do with a megalopolis: *megalopolitan jungles such as New York and Chicago* (Harper's). —*n.* a person living in a megalopolis.

meg·a·lops (meg′ə lops), *n.* the final larval stage of a crab, a small organism with large, stalked eyes that swims to the shore and digs a hole in the sand where it molts into a tiny crab: *The megalops . . . must obey whatever instinct drives it shoreward* (New Yorker). [< New Latin *megalops* < Greek *megalōpós* large-eyed < *mégas, megálou* great + *ōps, ōpós* eye]

meg·a·lo·saur (meg′ə lə sôr), *n.* any of an extinct group of gigantic terrestrial, carnivorous lizards. [< New Latin *Megalosaurus* the genus name < Greek *mégas, megálou* great + *saûros* lizard]

Megalosaur
(30 to 50 ft. long)

meg·a·lo·sau·ri·an (meg′ə lə-sôr′ē ən), *adj.* having the characteristics of a megalosaur. —*n.* a megalosaur.

meg·a·lo·sau·rus (meg′ə lō sôr′əs), *n.* megalosaur.

meg·a·par·sec (meg′ə pär′sek), *n.* a unit of distance, equivalent to one million parsecs.

meg·a·phone (meg′ə fōn), *n., v.,* **-phoned, -phon·ing.** —*n.* a device, usually a large, funnel-shaped horn, used to increase the loudness of sound, as of the voice, or the distance at which it can be heard: *The cheerleader at the football game yelled through a megaphone. The megaphone has gone electronic* (Science News Letter). —*v.t., v.i.* **1.** to magnify or direct (sound) by means of a megaphone: *In desperation, Kendall megaphoned to the Storstad, "Go full speed astern!"* (Maclean's). **2.** to speak very loudly. [American English < *mega-* + *phone*]

meg·a·phon·ic (meg′ə fon′ik), *adj.* increasing the loudness of sound or the distance at which it can be heard: *She had escaped even the microscopic research and the megaphonic talk of a small country place like Highwood* (Mrs. Lynn Linton).

meg·a·pod (meg′ə pod), *adj.* having a large foot or feet. —*n.* a megapode.

meg·a·pode (meg′ə pōd), *n.* any of a family of large-footed, fowllike birds of Australia and Indonesia, that scratch up mounds of decaying vegetation, etc., bury their eggs in them, and leave them to hatch. [< New Latin *Megapodius* < Greek *mégas* great + *poús, podós* foot]

meg·a·rad (meg′ə rad′), *n.* a unit for measuring absorbed doses of radiation, equivalent to one million rads.

meg·a·ron (meg′ə ron), *n.* the central room of an ancient Greek house, having a hearth and used as a kitchen and living room. [< Greek *mégaron*]

meg·a·scope (meg′ə skōp), *n.* a kind of projector by which enlarged images of opaque objects are thrown upon a screen.

meg·a·scop·ic (meg′ə skop′ik), *adj.* **1.** having to do with the megascope. **2.** enlarged or magnified. **3.** macroscopic. —**meg′a·scop′i·cal·ly,** *adv.*

meg·a·scop·i·cal (meg′ə skop′ə kəl), *adj.* megascopic.

meg·a·seism (meg′ə sī zəm, -səm), *n.* a great or severe earthquake. [< *mega-* + Greek *seismós* earthquake]

meg·a·seis·mic (meg′ə sīz′mik, -sīs′-), *adj.* **1.** of or having to do with a severe earthquake. **2.** caused by a severe earthquake.

meg·a·spo·ran·gi·um (meg′ə spə ran′jē-əm), *n., pl.* **-gi·a** (-jē ə). a sporangium containing megaspores: *The megasporangium usually produces only four megaspores* (Fred W. Emerson). Also, **macrosporangium.** [< *mega*(spore) + *sporangium*]

meg·a·spore (meg′ə spôr, -spōr), *n.* **1.** an asexually produced spore of comparatively large size that gives rise to the female gametophyte in certain ferns. **2.** (in seed plants) the embryo sac: *Within the nucleus is found the embryo sac or megaspore* (Heber W. Youngken). Also, **macrospore.**

meg·a·spo·ro·phyll (meg′ə spôr′ə fil, -spōr′-), *n. Botany.* **1.** a sporophyll bearing only megasporangia. **2.** a carpel: *Each carpel or megasporophyll is a female organ of reproduction* (Heber W. Youngken).

me·gass or **me·gasse** (mə gas′), *n.* bagasse.

meg·a·there (meg′ə thir), *n.* any of an extinct group of huge, plant-eating mammals of the Pleistocene period, resembling the sloths, the fossil remains of which have been found in South America. [< New Latin (Cuvier) *Megatherium* < Greek *mégas* large + *thēríon* wild animal]

Megathere
(to 20 ft. long)

meg·a·the·ri·um (meg′ə thir′ē əm), *n.* megathere.

meg·a·ton (meg′ə tun′), *n.* a measure of atomic power equivalent to the energy released by one million tons of high explosive, specifically TNT: *Most estimates suggest that each megaton of dirty bomb would cause a few thousand deaths from leukaemia* (Manchester Guardian). *Abbr.:* mt.

me·ga·ton·nage (meg′ə tun′ij), *n.* the total amount of atomic power in megatons.

meg·a·volt (meg′ə vōlt′), *n.* a unit of electromotive force equivalent to one million volts.

meg·a·watt (meg′ə wot′), *n.* a million watts; a thousand kilowatts.

me·gil·lah (mə gil′ə), *n. Slang.* a long story or account: *I talked the whole megillah over with Cassius and he reckons you'd be a better draw* (Punch). [< Hebrew *megillah* scroll (especially the scroll of the Book of Esther, which is unrolled and read in the Synagogue during the festival of Purim)]

me·gilp (mə gilp′), *n.* a jellylike preparation (consisting usually of a mixture of linseed oil with turpentine or mastic varnish) used by artists as a vehicle for oil colors. Also, **magilp, magilph, megilph, meguilp.** [origin unknown]

me·gilph (mə gilf′), *n.* megilp.

Meg·i·mide (meg′ə mīd), *n. Trademark.* a compound that counteracts the influence of barbiturates, used in treating persons who have taken an overdose of sleeping pills: *Megimide . . . brings sleeping-pill victims out of dangerous comas in a few minutes* (Newsweek). *Formula:* $C_8H_{13}NO_2$ [< *me*(thylethyl)*g*(lutar)*imide*]

meg·ohm (meg′ōm′), *n.* a unit of electrical resistance, equivalent to a million ohms. [< *meg-* one million + *ohm*]

meg·ohm·me·ter (meg′ōm mē′tər), *n.* an instrument for measuring the electrical resistance of a conductor in megohms. [< *megohm* + *-meter*]

me·grim (mē′grim), *n.* **1.** migraine: *Pain at her side and Megrim at her head* (Alexander Pope). **2.** a whim; passing fancy; caprice: *It was a pity she should take such megrims into her head* (George Eliot). *The hamlet . . . has no patience with urban megrims* (J.W. R. Scott).

megrims, a. morbid low spirits; attack of the blues: *suffering from a mountainous attack of the mental megrims* (John Moyes). *She was neurotic and addicted to the megrims.* **b.** (in animals) the staggers: *The poor mare was suddenly seized with megrims* (Peter Hawker).
[earlier variant of *mygreyn* migraine. Compare HEMICRANIA.]

me·guilp (mə gilp′), *n.* megilp.

 PRONUNCIATION KEY: hat, āge, cãre, fär; let, ēqual, tėrm; it, īce; hot, ōpen, ôrder; oil, out; cup, půt, rüle;

Mei·ji (mā′jē), *n.* the reign (1868-1912) of Emperor Mutsuhito of Japan: *There was some attempt at systematic development in the Meiji era* (London Times). [< Japanese *Meiji* (literally) enlightened rule, name of the period 1868-1912]

mein·ie or **mein·y** (mā′nē), *n., pl.* **mein·ies.** 1. *Scottish.* a great number; multitude. 2. *Obsolete.* a body of feudal dependents, retainers, etc.; retinue; train: *They summon'd up their meiny, straight took horse* (Shakespeare). [< Old French *meyne*, earlier *mesnede* < Vulgar Latin *mansiōnāta* < Latin *mansiō, -ōnis* mansion]

Mein Kampf (mīn kämpf′), an autobiographical work by Adolf Hitler, written during his imprisonment in 1924 and published in 1925-26, outlining his political doctrines. [< German *Mein Kampf* (literally) my struggle]

mei·o·sis (mī ō′sis), *n., pl.* **-ses** (-sēz). **1.** *Biology.* the process whereby the number of chromosomes in germ cells is reduced to half that in somatic cells, so that after fertilization the zygote again has the diploid number characteristic of the species. It consists essentially of two cell divisions. In the first, the homologous chromosomes separate equally into the two new cells so that each contains the haploid number, or half the diploid number. In the second cell division, the pairs of chromosomes split, one of each kind of chromosome going to the four new cells. Thus each new cell again contains the haploid number of chromosomes. **2.** litotes.
[< New Latin *meiosis* < Greek *meiōsis* a lessening < *meioûn* lessen < *meiōn* less]

mei·ot·ic (mī ot′ik), *adj.* of or having to do with meiosis.

meis·je or **meis·ie** (mās′yə, mā′sē), *n.* (in South Africa) a girl: *There is enough to be done before nightfall for an idle meisje to bestir herself* (Cape Times). [< Dutch *meisje*]

Meis·sen (mī′sən), *n.* a kind of porcelain: *The sale also features old Meissen ware in the form of a pair of statuettes of bitterns* (New York Times). [< *Meissen*, a city in East Germany, where it is made]

Meis·ter·sing·er or **meis·ter·sing·er** (mīs′tər sing′ər; *German* mīs′tər zing′ər), *n.* a member of one of the guilds, chiefly of workingmen, established in the principal German cities during the 1300's, 1400's, and 1500's for the cultivation of poetry and music: *Walter studies to become a meistersinger, so that he can enter the contest* (World Book Encyclopedia). Also, **mastersinger.** [< German *Meistersinger* < *Meister* master (of a guild) + *Singer* singer]

Mej·lis (mej lēs′), *n.* Majlis.

me·ke (mā′kē), *n.* a Fijian war dance: *They stripped down to palm skirts and battle paint to demonstrate . . . mekes* (Time). [< Fijian]

Mek·ka (mek′ə), *n.* Mecca.

mel (mel), *n. Pharmacology.* honey. [< Latin *mel*]

mel·a·min (mel′ə min), *n.* melamine.

mel·a·mine (mel′ə mēn, -min; mel′ə mēn′), *n.* a colorless, crystalline substance derived from dicyandiamide. With formaldehyde it forms a group of resins which are used for coatings, insulators, etc. *During 1959, Owens-Illinois started production of melamine dinnerware* (Wall Street Journal). *Formula:* $C_3H_6N_6$ [< *mel*(am), a chemical compound + *amine*]

mel·an·cho·li·a (mel′ən kō′lē ə), *n.* a functional mental disorder characterized by great depression of spirits and activity, and gloomy thoughts and fears often accompanied by vivid delusions. [< Late Latin *melancholia* < Greek *melancholiā* < *mélās, -anos* black + *cholḗ* bile]

mel·an·cho·li·ac (mel′ən kō′lē ak), *adj.* affected with melancholia. —*n.* a person affected with melancholia.

mel·an·chol·ic (mel′ən kol′ik), *adj.* **1.** melancholy; gloomy. **2.** having to do with, like, or suffering from melancholia. —**mel′an·chol′i·cal·ly,** *adv.*

mel·an·chol·i·ly (mel′ən kol′ə lē), *adv.* in a melancholy manner.

mel·an·chol·i·ness (mel′ən kol′ē nis), *n.* the condition of being melancholy.

mel·an·cho·li·ous (mel′ən kō′lē əs), *adj. Archaic.* melancholy; gloomy.

mel·an·chol·y (mel′ən kol′ē), *n., pl.* **-chol·ies,** *adj.* —*n.* **1.** low spirits; sadness; tendency to be sad: *The chronic melancholy which is taking hold of the civilized races . . .* (Thomas Hardy). **2.** sober thoughtfulness; pensiveness: *I . . . began, Wrapp'd in a pleasing fit of melancholy, To meditate my rural minstrelsy* (Milton). **3.** one of the four humors, thought in ancient and medieval physiology to be secreted by the kidney or spleen and to be the cause of depression, gloominess, etc.; black bile: *to purge melancholy* (Shakespeare). —*adj.* **1.** sad; gloomy: *A melancholy man is not good company.* **2.** causing sadness; depressing; dismal: *a melancholy scene.* **3.** expressive of sadness: *a melancholy smile.* **4.** lamentable; deplorable: *a melancholy fact.* **5.** soberly thoughtful or pensive: *to refresh his mind with a melancholy walk* (Anthony Wood). **6.** *Obsolete.* having to do with or affected with melancholia.
[< Old French *melancolie*, and *malencollie*, learned borrowings from Late Latin *melancholia;* see MELANCHOLIA]
—**Syn.** *n.* **1.** depression, dejection, gloominess. *-adj.* **1.** depressed, despondent, downcast. —**Ant.** *n.* **1.** cheerfulness.

Mel·a·ne·sian (mel′ə nē′zhən, -shən), *n.* **1.** a member of any of the dark-skinned peoples living in Melanesia, one of the three main groups of islands in the Pacific, northeast of Australia, including New Caledonia and Fiji: *Authorities include the Melanesians . . . with the Negro group* (Ogburn and Nimkoff). **2.** any of the related languages of Melanesia, or the group that they constitute. —*adj.* of Melanesia, its people, or their languages.

mé·lange (mā länzh′), *n.* a mixture; medley: *Every nationality of the Soviet Union seemed to be represented in the mélange of peoples that paraded today before the leaders of the local Communist party and government . . .* (New York Times). [< Middle French *mélange* < *mêler* to mix < Old French *mesler* < Late Latin *misculāre* < Latin *miscēre*] —**Syn.** jumble, hodgepodge, miscellany.

me·lan·ic (mə lan′ik), *adj.* **1.** having to do with or showing melanism. **2.** affected by melanosis; melanotic.

mel·a·nin (mel′ə nin), *n.* any of several dark pigments, especially the black pigment in the choroid, retina, hair, epidermis, etc., of dark-skinned people, or one developed in certain diseases. [< Greek *mélās, -anos* black + English *-in*]

mel·a·nism (mel′ə niz əm), *n.* **1.** darkness of color resulting from an abnormal development of black pigment (melanin) in the skin, hair, and eyes of a human being, or in the skin, coat, plumage, etc., of an animal. **2.** darkness, especially near blackness, of skin, hair, etc., as a characteristic of certain peoples. [< Greek *mélās, -anos* black + English *-ism*]

mel·a·nis·tic (mel′ə nis′tik), *adj.* characterized by melanism.

mel·a·nite (mel′ə nīt), *n.* a velvet-black variety of garnet. [< Greek *mélās, -anos* black + English *-ite*[1]]

mel·a·ni·za·tion (mel′ə nə zā′shən), *n.* **1.** a melanizing. **2.** a being melanized.

mel·a·nize (mel′ə nīz), *v.t.,* **-nized, -niz·ing.** to produce melanism in.

mel·a·no (mel′ə nō), *n.* a person or animal characterized by melanism. [< Greek *mélās, -anos* black]

mel·a·no·blast (mel′ə nə blast), *n.* a cell which is capable of developing into a melanophore: *The melanomas so produced contain almost a pure culture of melanoblasts, the cells characteristic of both mouse and human black cancers* (Science News Letter). [< Greek *mélās, -anos* black + *blastós* germ, sprout]

mel·a·no·blas·to·ma (mel′ə nō blas tō′mə), *n., pl.* **-mas, -ma·ta** (-mə tə). a malignant tumor formed from melanophores, characterized by dark coloring and rapid growth; black cancer.

mel·a·no·car·ci·no·ma (mel′ə nō kär′sənō′mə), *n.* melanoblastoma.

mel·a·no·ce·tus (mel′ə nō sē′təs), *n.* a black deep-sea fish with a mouth suggesting that of a whale, and an enormously distensible belly. [< Greek *mélās, -anos* black + *kētos* any large sea animal]

Mel·a·noch·ro·i (mel′ə nok′rō ī), *n.pl.* a subdivision of the Caucasian peoples having dark hair and pale complexions. [< New Latin *Melanochroi* (coined by Thomas H. Huxley) < Greek *mélās, -anos* black + *ōchrós* pale (yellow)]

Mel·a·no·chro·ic (mel′ə nō krō′ik), *adj.* Melanochroid.

Mel·a·noch·roid (mel′ə nok′roid), *adj.* having to do with or like the Melanochroi.

mel·a·no·cyte (mel′ə nə sīt), *n.* **1.** a lymphocyte which contains black pigment. **2.** a cell which synthesizes melanin, found in the skin, the choroid of the eye, etc. [< Greek *mélās, -anos* black + English *-cyte*]

mel·a·no·gen·e·sis (mel′ə nō jen′ə sis), *n.* the formation and development of melanin. [< Greek *mélās, -anos* black + Latin *genesis*]

mel·a·noid (mel′ə noid), *adj.* **1.** of, affected by, or like melanosis. **2.** like the color of melanin; darkly pigmented; blackish.

mel·a·no·ma (mel′ə nō′mə), *n., pl.* **-mas, -ma·ta** (-mə tə). **1.** a melanoblastoma; a dark-colored or blackish tumor arising in the skin or in the pigmented layers of the eye: *Flies with no growing-up hormone develop large abdominal pigmented masses resembling the black cancers called melanoma in man* (Science News Letter). **2.** a benign tumor developed from a birthmark. [< New Latin *melanoma* < Greek *mélās, -anos* black + *-oma* -oma]

mel·a·no·phore (mel′ə nə fôr, -fōr), *n.* a chromatophore which contains a black or brown pigment, melanin.

mel·a·nose (mel′ə nōs), *n.* a common fungal disease of grapefruit that destroys the leaves and spoils the appearance of the fruit. [perhaps back formation < *melanosis*]

mel·a·no·sis (mel′ə nō′sis), *n., pl.* **-ses** (-sēz). **1.** an abnormal deposit or development of a black pigment (melanin) in various parts of the body, sometimes leading to the production of malignant pigmented tumors. **2.** a discoloration caused by this. [< New Latin *melanosis* < Late Greek *melánōsis* blackening < *melanoûsthai* become black < *mélās, -anos* black]

mel·a·not·ic (mel′ə not′ik), *adj.* **1.** characterized by or having to do with melanosis. **2.** melanistic.

mel·a·nous (mel′ə nəs), *adj.* **1.** melanic. **2.** melanoid.

mel·an·tha·ceous (mel′ən thā′shəs), *adj.* belonging to a group of bulbless plants now generally classified in the lily family, including the bellwort and white hellebore. [< New Latin *Melanthaceae* the family name (< Greek *mélās, -anos* black + *ánthos* flower) + English *-ous*]

mel·a·phyre (mel′ə fīr), *n.* any of various dark-colored igneous rocks of porphyritic texture. [< French *mélaphyre* < Greek *mélas* black + French *porphyre* porphyry]

mel·a·to·nin (mel′ə tō′nin), *n.* a hormone, the first to be isolated from the pineal gland. [< Greek *mélas* black + English *tone*, verb + *-in* (from its effect on melanocytes)]

Mel·ba toast (mel′bə), a kind of very crisp, evenly browned toast made from extremely thin slices of slightly stale white bread. [perhaps < Dame Nellie *Melba*, 1861-1931, an Australian soprano]

Mel·bur·ni·an or **Mel·bour·ni·an** (mel bėr′nē ən), *n.* a native or inhabitant of Melbourne, Australia. —*adj.* of or having to do with Melbourne or its people.

Mel·chi·or (mel′kē ôr), *n.* one of the Three Wise Men, according to medieval legend.

Mel·chite (mel′kīt), *n.* **1.** (formerly, in Syria, Palestine, and Egypt) an orthodox Eastern Christian, originally as distinguished from a Monophysite or a Nestorian. **2.** one of the Uniat Christians of these countries. —*adj.* of or having to do with the Melchites. Also, **Melkite.** [< New Greek *Melchîtai* (literally) royalists < a Syriac word]

Mel·chiz·e·dek (mel kiz′ə dek), *n.* **1.** (in the Bible) a priest and king of ancient Salem, who blessed Abraham. Genesis 14:18. **2.** (in the Mormon Church) the order of priests that has the primary responsibility of carrying out the church ordinances.

meld[1] (meld), *v.t., v.i.* to announce and show (cards for a score) in rummy, canasta, pinochle, etc.: *The veteran newspaperman melded the eight kings for a score of 800* (Charlottesville [Va.] Daily Progress). —*n.* **1.** the act of melding. **2.** any grouping of cards that can be melded. [American English < German *melden* announce]

meld[2] (meld), *v.t., v.i.* to unite; merge: *Then comes a melding of fur and flower* (New Yorker). [perhaps a blend of *melt* and *weld*]

mel·der (mel′dər), *n. Scottish.* a quantity of meal ground at one time. [< Scandinavian (compare Old Icelandic *meldr*)]

mel·e (mel′e), *n.* a native Hawaiian song or melody. [< Hawaiian *mele*]

Mel·e·a·ger (mel′ē ā′jər), *n Greek Legend.* the hero who killed the Calydonian boar. He was one of the Argonauts.

me·lee or **mê·lée** (mā′lā, mā lā′, mel′ā), *n.* **1.** a confused fight; hand-to-hand fight among a number of fighters: *Placing himself at the head of his handful of cavalry, he dashed into the mêlée* (John L. Motley). **2.** any fracas: *. . . the unions felt they must join in the general mêlée* (London Times). [< French *mêlée* < Old French *meslee.* Doublet of MEDLEY.]

me·li·a·ceous (mē′lē ā′shəs), *adj.* belonging to the mahogany family of trees and shrubs. [< New Latin *Meliaceae* the family name < *Melia* the typical genus < Greek *meliā* ash tree + English *-ous*]

Me·li·an (mē′lē ən, mēl′yən), *adj.* of or having to do with the Greek island of Melos, in the southern Aegean. —*n.* a native or inhabitant of Melos.

mel·ic (mel′ik), *adj.* **1.** intended to be sung. **2.** of or having to do with an elaborate type of Greek lyric poetry, composed in strophes, as distinguished from iambic and elegiac poetry (originally by Terpander in the 600's B.C.). [< Greek *melikós* < *mélos* song]

melic grass, any of a group of grasses widely distributed in temperate regions but of no great agricultural value. [< New Latin *Melica* the genus name < Italian *melica* sorghum < Latin *mel* honey]

mel·i·lot (mel′ə lot), *n.* any of a group of cloverlike herbs of the pea family, with racemes of small, white or yellow flowers, as the sweet clover. [< Middle French *melilot* < Latin *melilōtos* < Greek *melílōtos* a sweet clover < *méli* honey + *lōtós* clover, lotus]

me·line (mē′lin, -līn), *adj.* having to do with the badger; badgerlike. [< Latin *mēlīnus* < *mēlēs* badger, marten]

mel·i·nite (mel′ə nīt), *n.* a powerful explosive very similar to lyddite, consisting essentially of picric acid and guncotton. [< French *mélinite* < Greek *mēlinos* quince-yellow (< *mēlon* quince; any kind of tree fruit) + French *-ite* -ite[1]]

mel·io·ra·ble (mēl′yər ə bəl, mē′lē ər-), *adj.* that can be improved.

mel·io·rate (mēl′yə rāt, mē′lē ə-), *v.t., v.i.,* **-rat·ed, -rat·ing.** to make or become better or more bearable; improve; ameliorate. [< Late Latin *meliōrāre* (with English *-ate*[1]) < Latin *melior* better, comparative of *bonus* good]

mel·io·ra·tion (mēl′yə rā′shən, mē′lē ə-), *n.* **1.** a making or becoming better; improvement. **2.** an instance or form of improvement.

mel·io·ra·tive (mēl′yə rā′tiv, mē′lē ə-), *adj.* tending to improve.

mel·io·ra·tor (mēl′yə rā′tər, mē′lē ə-), *n.* a person or thing that meliorates or makes better.

mel·io·rism (mēl′yə riz əm, mē′lē ə-), *n.* the doctrine or belief, fundamental to some systems of ethics, that the world tends naturally to become better or is capable of being made better by human effort, a mean between pessimism and optimism: *Meliorism is . . . to proceed according to sociological principles and to educate the young to a higher level of intelligence and morality* (Hinkle and Hinkle). [< Latin *melior* better + English *-ism*]

mel·io·rist (mēl′yər ist, mē′lē ər-), *n.* a person who holds the doctrine of meliorism. —*adj.* melioristic.

mel·io·ris·tic (mēl′yə ris′tik, mē′lē ə-), *adj.* of or having to do with meliorism.

mel·ior·i·ty (mēl yôr′ə tē, -yor′-; mē′lē ôr′-, -or′-), *n.* the quality or condition of being better; superiority.

me·lis·ma (mə liz′mə), *n., pl.* **-mas, -ma·ta** (-mə tə). *Music.* **1.** a song, melody, or air, as contrasted with a recitative or declamatory passage. **2. a.** a long, florid melodic passage sung on one syllable, especially in Gregorian chant. **b.** any melodic decoration, grace, fioritura, or roulade. **3.** a cadenza [< Greek *mélisma*]

mel·is·mat·ic (mel′iz mat′ik), *adj.* ornate or florid in melody: *Davy's "In honore summae matris" was extremely melismatic, so that it was easy to realize the force of clerical objection to such ways of setting sacred texts* (London Times). —**mel′is·mat′i·cal·ly,** *adv.*

mel·is·mat·ics (mel′iz mat′iks), *n.* the art of florid or ornate vocalization.

Mel·kite (mel′kīt), *n., adj.* Melchite.

mell (mel), *Archaic.* —*v.t.* to mix; mingle; combine; blend. —*v.i.* **1.** to interfere; meddle. **2.** to join or engage in combat: *They are too many to mell with in the open field* (Scott). [< Old French *meller,* variant of *mesler;* see MEDDLE]

mel·lay (mel′ā), *n. Archaic.* melee: *My hat had been struck from my head in the mellay* (Robert Louis Stevenson). [< Old French *mellee, meslee;* see MELEE]

mel·ler (mel′ər), *n. Slang.* melodrama (def. 1): *The better prose doesn't conceal the fact that the story is a lurid meller* (New York Times). [shortening and alteration of *melodrama*]

mel·lif·er·ous (mə lif′ər əs), *adj.* yielding or producing honey. [< Latin *mellifer* (< *mel, mellis* honey + *ferre* to bear, produce) + English *-ous*]

mel·lif·lu·ence (mə lif′lu̇ əns), *n.* sweet sound; smooth flow (of words, etc.).

mel·lif·lu·ent (mə lif′lu̇ ənt), *adj.* mellifluous: *He is a mellifluent preacher* (Newsweek). [< Late Latin *mellifluēns, -entis* < *mel, mellis* honey + *fluēns, -entis,* present participle of *fluere* flow] —**mel·lif′lu·ent·ly,** *adv.*

mel·lif·lu·ous (mə lif′lu̇ əs), *adj.* **1.** sweetly or smoothly flowing: *mellifluous tones. We enjoyed the mellifluous speech of the orator.* **2.** flowing with honey; made sweet with or as if with honey. [< Late Latin *mellifluus* (with English *-ous*) < Latin *mel, mellis* honey + *fluere* to flow] —**mel·lif′lu·ous·ly,** *adv.* —**mel·lif′lu·ous·ness,** *n.*

mel·liv·o·rous (mə liv′ər əs), *adj.* feeding on honey. [< Latin *mel, mellis* honey + *vorāre* devour + English *-ous*]

mel·lo·phone (mel′ə fōn), *n.* a type of althorn similar to a French horn. [< *mello*(w) + *-phone*]

mel·low (mel′ō), *adj.* **1.** soft and full-flavored from ripeness; sweet and juicy: *a mellow apple.* **2.** (of wines) at or near the point of maturity: *a mellow wine.* **3.** soft and rich: *a violin with a mellow tone, a mellow light in a picture, a mellow color.* **4.** soft, rich, and loamy: *mellow soil.* **5.** softened and made wise by age or experience; having the gentleness or dignity resulting from maturity: *The baronet was . . . as merry and mellow an old bachelor as ever followed a hound* (Washington Irving). **6.** affected by liquor or drinking; slightly tipsy: *The party got gloriously mellow* (Herman Melville). —*v.t., v.i.* to make or become mellow: *Time had mellowed his youthful temper. The apples mellowed after we picked them.* [Middle English *melwe.* Related to MILD, MALT.] —**mel′low·ly,** *adv.* —**mel′low·ness,** *n.*

me·lo·de·on (mə lō′dē ən), *n.* **1.** a small reed organ in which air is sucked inward by a bellows, an American predecessor of the harmonium. **2.** a kind of accordion. [American English, variant of earlier *melodium* < *melody*]

me·lo·di·a (mə lō′dē ə), *n.* an 8-foot organ stop with wooden flue pipes, having a flute-like tone. [< Late Latin *melōdia* melody]

me·lod·ic (mə lod′ik), *adj.* **1.** having to do with melody, especially as distinguished from harmony and rhythm. **2.** melodious: *Every single instrument is largely vocal in essence—melodic, or lyric, as we call it* (Harper's). —**me·lod′i·cal·ly,** *adv.*

melodic interval, *Music.* the relation of two successive tones, in respect to pitch.

melodic minor, a version of the minor scale having the sixth and seventh steps raised in its ascending form.

me·lod·ics (mə lod′iks), *n.* the branch of musical science that is concerned with melody; melodic theory.

me·lo·di·ous (mə lō′dē əs), *adj.* **1.** sweet-sounding; pleasing to the ear; musical: *melodious verse. Man . . . forges the subtile . . . air into wise and melodious words* (Emerson). **2.** producing melody; singing sweetly: *melodious birds.* **3.** having a melody; having to do with or of the nature of melody. —**me·lo′di·ous·ly,** *adv.* —**me·lo′di·ous·ness,** *n.* —**Syn. 1.** melodic, tuneful, harmonious.

mel·o·dist (mel′ə dist), *n.* a composer or singer of melodies: *Bellini was certainly one of the greatest melodists who have ever lived* (New Yorker).

mel·o·dize (mel′ə dīz), *v.,* **-dized, -diz·ing.** —*v.t.* **1.** to make melodious. **2.** to compose a melody for (a song). —*v.i.* **1.** to blend melodiously: *Such a strain . . . Might melodize with each tumultuous sound* (Scott). **2.** to make melody or compose melodies. —**mel′o·diz′er,** *n.*

mel·o·dra·ma (mel′ə drä′mə, -dram′ə), *n.* **1.** a sensational drama with exaggerated appeal to the emotions and, usually, a happy ending: *Shakespeare's play "The Merchant of Venice" is really a fine melodrama. It is the custom on the stage, in all good murderous melodramas to present the tragic and the comic scenes, in . . . regular alternation* (Dickens). **2.** any sensational writing, speech, or action with exaggerated appeal to the emotions: *If you can identify the murderer in Agatha Christie's melodrama, you probably belong on the police force yourself* (New Yorker). **3.** (in the late 1700's and early 1800's) a romantic stage play with music interspersed. [< French *mélodrame* < Greek *mélos* music + *drâma* drama]

mel·o·dra·mat·ic (mel′ə drə mat′ik), *adj.* of, like, or suitable for melodrama; sensational and exaggerated: *His soldiers, who, save for a few rare melodramatic encounters, saw nothing of him, idolized their "Little Corporal"* (H.G. Wells). —*n.* **melodramatics,** melodramatic actions. —**mel′o·dra·mat′i·cal·ly,** *adv.* —**Syn.** *adj.* See **dramatic.**

mel·o·dram·a·tist (mel′ə dram′ə tist, -drä′mə-), *n.* a writer of melodrama.

mel·o·dram·a·tize (mel′ə dram′ə tīz, -drä′mə-), *v.t.,* **-tized, -tiz·ing. 1.** to make into a melodrama. **2.** to make melodramatic.

mel·o·dy (mel′ə dē), *n., pl.* **-dies. 1.** sweet music; any sweet sound: *The birds chant melody on every bush* (Shakespeare). **2.** musical quality: *the melody of a voice, the melody of verse.* **3.** the succession of single tones in musical composition, as distinguished from harmony and rhythm: *She sang some sweet old melodies.* **4.** the main tune in harmonized music; air. **5.** a poem suitable for singing: *Thomas Moore's "Irish Melodies."* [< Old French *melodie,* learned borrowing from Late Latin *melōdia* < Greek *melōidiā* < *mélos* song + *ōidē* song < *aeídein* sing] —**Syn. 4.** theme.

mel·oid (mel′oid), *n.* any of a family of beetles, including the blister beetles. —*adj.* of or like these beetles. [< New Latin *Meloïdae* the family name < *Meloē* the typical genus; origin uncertain]

IMAGO LARVA

Meloid or oil beetle (Line shows actual length.)

mel·o·lon·thine (mel′ə lon′thīn, -thin), *adj.* of or having to do with a subfamily of beetles, including the June bugs, chafers, etc. —*n.* a melolonthine beetle. [< New Latin *Melolontha* the typical genus (< Greek *mēlolónthē* cockchafer) + English *-ine*[1]]

mel·o·mane (mel′ə mān), *n.* melomaniac. [< French *mélomane*]

mel·o·ma·ni·a (mel′ə mā′nē ə), *n.* a mania for music. [< French *mélomanie* < Greek *mélos* song + *maniā* madness]

mel·o·ma·ni·ac (mel′ə mā′nē ak), *n.* a person who has a mania for music.

mel·o·ma·ni·a·cal (mel′ə mə nī′ə kəl), *adj.* of or characteristic of melomania or a melomaniac.

mel·on (mel′ən), *n.* **1.** the large, juicy fruit of any of several plants of the gourd family that grow on vines. Watermelons, cantaloupes or muskmelons, and honeydew melons are different kinds. **2.** a deep-pink color. **3.** *U.S. Slang.* a sum of money representing an excess of profits, or political or criminal loot, etc., for sharing by the owners of or the participants in an enterprise.

cut or **split a melon,** *U.S. Slang.* to divide extra profits among those considered to have a claim on them: *The corporation cut a melon for its stockholders at the end of the year.*

[< Old French *melon* < Late Latin *mēlō, -ōnis,* short for Latin *mēlopepō* < Greek *mēlopépōn* < *mēlon* apple + *pépōn* gourd] —**mel′on·like′,** *adj.*

melon fly, a fly whose larvae bore into melons, cucumbers, and tomatoes. It is related to the fruit fly.

mel·on-shell (mel′ən shel′), *n.* the shell of a marine gastropod, so called from the shape and markings.

mel·o·plas·ty (mel′ə plas′tē), *n., pl.* **-ties.** face lifting. [< Greek *mēlon* apple; later, cheek + *plastós* something molded + English *-y*[3]]

mel·os (mel′os, mē′los), *n.* the succession of single tones in musical composition, as distinguished from harmony and rhythm; melody: *The singer repeated endlessly a short phrase of melos* (London Times). [< Greek *mélos* song]

Me·lox·ine (me lok′sin), *n. Trademark.* a drug which increases the resistance of the skin to sunburn, taken orally in pill form. *Formula:* $C_{12}H_8O_4$

Mel·pom·e·ne (mel pom′ə nē), *n. Greek Mythology.* the Muse of tragedy.

melt (melt), *v.,* **melt·ed, melt·ed** or **mol·ten, melt·ing,** *n.* —*v.t.* **1.** to change from solid to liquid by the application of heat: *to melt ice or butter. Great heat melts iron.* **2.** to dissolve: *to melt sugar in water.* **3.** to cause to disappear gradually; disperse: *The noon sun will melt away the fog. These our actors . . . were all spirits, and Are melted into air* (Shakespeare). **4.** to blend; merge: *Dusk melted the colors of the hill into a soft gray.* **5.** to make tender or gentle; soften: *Pity melted her heart.* —*v.i.* **1.** to be changed from solid to liquid by the application of heat: *The ice on the sidewalks had melted in the sunshine.* **2.** to dissolve; appear to disintegrate: *Sugar melts in water.* **3.** to disappear gradually; vanish; disappear: *The clouds melted away, and the sun came out. The crowd melted away. Money melts away.* **4.** to waste away; dwindle: *His wealth melted away.* **5.** to change very gradually; blend; merge: *In the rainbow, the green melts into blue, the blue into violet.* **6.** to become softened; be made gentle; soften: *I had a good deal melted towards our enemy* (Robert Louis Stevenson). **7.** to suffer from the heat: *You will melt if you sit so close to the fire.* **8.** *Obsolete.* to be overwhelmed with grief.
—*n.* **1.** the act or process of melting. **2.** the state of being melted. **3.** a melted metal. **4.** a quantity of metal melted at one operation or over a specified period, especially a single charge in smelting: *A number of melters using both pig iron and scrap have begun to use more pig iron in their melt* (Baltimore Sun).
[fusion of Old English *meltan* to melt, and *mieltan* make liquid] —**melt′er,** *n.* —**melt′ing·ly,** *adv.*
—**Syn.** *v.t.* **1, 2. Melt, dissolve, thaw** mean to change from a solid state. **Melt** suggests a gradual change caused by heat, by which a solid softens, loses shape, and finally becomes liquid: *The warm air melted the butter.* **Dissolve** emphasizes a breaking up of a solid into its smallest parts, caused by putting it in a liquid that reduces it and of which it becomes a part: *Dissolve some salt in a glass of water.* **Thaw,** used only of frozen things, means to change to the unfrozen state, either liquid or less hard and stiff: *She thawed the frozen fruit.* **5.** mollify. —**Ant.** *v.t.* **1.** harden, solidify.

melt·a·bil·i·ty (mel′tə bil′ə tē), *n.* the capacity of being melted.

melt·a·ble (mel′tə bəl), *adj.* that can be melted.

melt·ing point (mel′ting), the point or degree of temperature at which a solid substance melts, especially under a pressure of one atmosphere: *At the melting point the lattice structure breaks up and the material becomes a liquid* (Science News). *Abbr.:* m.p.

melting pot, 1. a country or city thought of as a place in which various races or sorts of people are assimilated: *America is the New World, where there are no races and nations any more; She is the melting pot, from which we will cast the better state* (H.G. Wells). **2.** a pot in which metals, etc., are melted; crucible.

mel·ton (mel′tən), *n.* a smooth, heavy woolen cloth: *Overcoats are often made of melton. Melton is generally made dark and plain in color* (Bernice G. Chambers). [< *Melton* Mowbray, in Leicestershire, England, a hunting center]

melt·wa·ter (melt′wôt′ər, -wot′-), *n.* water formed from melting ice or snow, especially from a glacier: *A valley glacier . . . is far wider and thicker than the corresponding stream of meltwater* (Science News).

mem[1] (mem), *n.* the thirteenth letter of the Hebrew alphabet. [< Hebrew *mem*]

mem[2] (mem), *n. British Informal.* madam. *British mems still drove off to play bridge every morning about nine* (Punch). [alteration of *ma'am*]

mem., 1. member. **2.** memoir. **3.** memorandum. **4.** memorial.

mem·ber (mem′bər), *n.* **1.** an individual belonging to a community, club, or other group: *Every member of the family came home for Christmas. Our church has over five hundred members.* **2.** a constituent part of a whole: **a.** a part or organ of a plant, animal, or human body, especially a limb, as a leg, arm, or wing. **b.** any or either part of a logical proposition, syllogism, etc. **c.** either of the sides of an equation: *a member of an algebraic equation.* **d.** a rafter, column, or other structural unit of a building. **3.** a person elected to participate in the proceedings of a legislative body (used especially as a form of direct address by a colleague): **a.** *U.S.* a member of the Congress of the United States, especially of the House of Representatives. **b.** *British.* a member of the House of Commons. [< Old French *membre* < Latin *membrum* limb, part] —**Syn. 2.** component.

-membered, *combining form.* having —— members: *Many-membered = having many members.*

mem·ber·less (mem′bər lis), *adj.* without a member or members.

mem·ber·ship (mem′bər ship), *n.* **1.** the fact or state of being a member: *Do you enjoy your membership in the Boy Scouts?* **2.** members as a group: *Put that to a vote by the membership.* **3.** the number of members in a particular body.

mem·bral (mem′brəl), *adj.* of or having to do with a member, especially a member of the body.

mem·bra·na·ceous (mem′brə nā′shəs), *adj.* membranous.

mem·brane (mem′brān), *n.* **1.** a thin, soft sheet or layer of animal tissue lining or covering some part of the body: *Living cells are enclosed in membranes through which they obtain their food* (K.S. Spiegler). See picture under **cell. 2.** a similar layer of vegetable tissue. **3.** a skin of parchment forming part of a roll. [< Latin *membrāna* a (covering) membrane of skin < *membrum* member]

membrane bone, a bone that originates in membranous connective tissue, instead of being developed or preformed in cartilage.

mem·bra·no·phone (mem brā′nə fōn′), *n.* any musical instrument that produces its sound when a membrane stretched tightly over its frame is struck or rubbed. A drum is a kind of membranophone. [< Latin *membrāna* membrane + English *-phone*]

mem·bra·nous (mem′brə nəs, mem brā′-), *adj.* **1.** of or like membrane: *The hind pair [of wings] are membranous and are used in flying* (A.M. Winchester). **2.** characterized by the formation of a membrane: *Diphtheria is a membranous disease.*

membranous croup, a form of croup in which a membrane forms in the throat and hinders breathing.

Me·men·to (mə men′tō), *n.* (in the Roman Catholic Church) either of two prayers beginning "Memento" ("Remember") in the canon of the Mass, in which the living and the dead respectively are commemorated. [< Latin *mementō* remember, imperative of *meminisse* to remember]

me·men·to (mə men′tō), *n., pl.* **-tos** or **-toes. 1.** a souvenir, as of an event or occasion: *These postcards are mementos of our trip abroad.* **2.** something serving as a reminder of what is past or gone: *This ring is a memento of an old friend.* **3.** *Archaic.* a reminder, warning, or hint as to conduct or with regard to future events. [< *Memento*]

me·men·to mo·ri (mə men′tō môr′ī, mōr′ī), **1.** *Latin.* remember that you must die. **2.** an object or emblem used as a reminder that all men are mortal.

Mem·non (mem′non), *n.* **1.** *Greek Legend.* an Ethiopian king killed during the Trojan War by Achilles and made immortal by Zeus. **2.** a huge statue of an Egyptian king at Thebes, Egypt.

Mem·no·ni·an (mem nō′nē ən), *adj.* of, having to do with, or resembling Memnon.

mem·o (mem′ō), *n., pl.* **mem·os.** *Informal.* a memorandum: *The memo contains all the ideas being discussed at that time* (Bulletin of Atomic Scientists).

mem·oir (mem′wär, -wôr), *n.* **1.** a biography, now especially a relatively short or limited one; biographical note. **2.** a report of a scientific or scholarly study.
memoirs, a. a record of facts and events written from personal knowledge or special information: *memoirs of the Scottish clans.* **b.** a record of a person's own experiences; autobiography: *General Marshall rejected offers up to $1 million for his memoirs* (Newsweek).
[< Middle French *mémoire,* masculine < Old French *memoire,* feminine, memory. Doublet of MEMORY.]

mem·oir·ist (mem′wär ist, -wôr-), *n.* a person who writes or has written a memoir or memoirs: *Sargent has been characterized by some memoirists as a dull man* (New Yorker).

mem·o·ra·bil·i·a (mem′ər ə bil′ē ə), *n.pl.* **1.** things or events worth remembering; noteworthy things: *a full disclosure of the memorabilia of my life* (Charles J. Lever). **2.** an account of such things: *A man of gelid reserve who . . . left no paper trail of written memorabilia* (New Yorker). [< Latin *memorābilia,* neuter plural of *memorābilis;* see MEMORABLE]

mem·o·ra·bil·i·ty (mem′ər ə bil′ə tē), *n., pl.* **-ties. 1.** the quality of being memorable; memorableness. **2.** a person or thing worth remembering.

mem·o·ra·ble (mem′ər ə bəl), *adj.* worth remembering; not to be forgotten; notable: *He nothing common did or mean Upon that memorable scene* (Andrew Marvell). —*n.* Often, **memorables.** a memorable or notable thing: *When I take up my pen to record the memorables of this Ann. Dom.* (John Galt). [< Latin *memorābilis* < *memorāre* to remind < *memor, -oris* mindful] —**mem′o·ra·ble·ness,** *n.* —**Syn.** *adj.* remarkable, extraordinary.

mem·o·ra·bly (mem′ər ə blē), *adv.* in a memorable manner; so as to be remembered.

mem·o·ran·da (mem′ə ran′də), *n.* memorandums; a plural of **memorandum.**

mem·o·ran·dum (mem′ə ran′dəm), *n., pl.* **-dums** or **-da. 1.** a short written statement for future use; note to aid one's memory: *A memorandum on his desk reminded him that it was his wife's birthday. "The horror of that moment," the King went on, "I shall never, never forget!" "You will, though," the Queen said, "if you don't make a memorandum of it"* (Lewis Carroll). **2.** an informal letter, note, or report: *I contented myself . . . to write down only the most remarkable events of my life, without continuing a memorandum of other things* (Daniel Defoe). **3.** (in diplomacy) a summary of facts and arguments on some issue or arrangement that concerns two or more governments. **4.** *Commerce.* a written statement of the terms under which a shipment of goods is made, authorizing their return if they are not sold within a specified time: *Sollazzo then took to peddling jewelry . . . obtaining his wares on memorandum* (New Yorker). **5.** *Law.* a writing containing the terms of a transaction. [< Latin *memorandum* (thing) to be remembered, neuter singular of *memorandus,* gerundive of *memorāre;* see MEMORABLE]

me·mo·ri·al (mə môr′ē əl, -mōr′-), *n.* **1.** something that is a reminder of some event or person, such as a statue, an arch or column, a book, a holiday, or a park: *These stones shall be for a memorial unto the children of Israel forever* (Joshua 4:7). **2.** a statement sent to a government or person in authority, usually giving facts and asking that some wrong be corrected. **3.** (in diplomacy) any of various informal state papers. —*adj.* **1.** helping people to remember some person, thing, or event; commemorative: *a memorial window in a church.* **2.** of or having to do with memory.
[< Latin *memoriālis* < *memoria;* see MEMORY] —**me·mo′ri·al·ly,** *adv.*

Memorial Day, *U.S.* a legal holiday for honoring dead servicemen, observed by decorating graves and memorials; Decoration Day. In most states it falls on May 30; in other states, on April 26, May 10, or June 3.

me·mo·ri·al·ist (mə môr′ē ə list, -mōr′-), *n.* **1.** a writer of biographical or historical memorials: *the Duc de Saint-Simon, France's amplest secret memorialist and most illuminating historical gossip . . .* (New Yorker). **2.** a person who presents a memorial.

me·mo·ri·al·i·za·tion (mə môr′ē ə lə zā′shən, -mōr′-), *n.* **1.** the act of memorializing. **2.** the state of being memorialized.

me·mo·ri·al·ize (mə môr′ē ə līz, -mōr′-), *v.t.,* **-ized, -iz·ing. 1.** to preserve the memory of; be a memorial of; commemorate. **2.**

to submit a memorial to; petition. —**me·mo′ri·al·iz′er,** *n.*

memorial park, *U.S.* a cemetery.

me·mo·ri·a tech·ni·ca (mə môr′ē ə tek′nə kə, -mōr′-), a method of aiding the memory by a form of words or other device; system of mnemonics. [< New Latin *memoria technica* technical (artificial) memory]

mem·o·ried (mem′ər ēd), *adj.* filled or associated with memories: *a memoried castle.*

-memoried, *combining form.* having a ___ memory: *Long-memoried = having a long memory.*

mem·o·rise (mem′ə rīz), *v.t.,* **-rised, -ris·ing.** *Especially British.* memorize.

me·mo·ri·ter (mə mor′ə tər), *adv. Latin.* from memory; by heart.

mem·o·riz·a·ble (mem′ə rī′zə bəl), *adj.* that can be memorized.

mem·o·ri·za·tion (mem′ər ə zā′shən), *n.* the act of memorizing: . . . *mere memorization of fact or a formula* (Science News).

mem·o·rize (mem′ə rīz), *v.t.,* **-rized, -riz·ing.** to commit (words, numbers, etc.) to memory; learn by heart: *to memorize the alphabet. He memorized his lines for the play.* —**mem′o·riz′er,** *n.*

mem·o·ry (mem′ər ē, mem′rē), *n., pl.* **-ries. 1.** the ability to remember; capacity to retain or recall that which is learned, experienced, etc.: *Jean has a better memory than I have.* **2.** the act or process of remembering; remembrance; recollection: *the memory of things past.* **3.** all that a person remembers; what can be recalled to mind: *to examine one's memory carefully.* **4.** a person, thing, or event that is remembered: *His mother died when he was small; she is only a memory to him now.* **5.** the length of time during which the past is remembered: *This has been the hottest summer within my memory.* **6.** reputation after death: *ancient heroes of noble memory.* **7.** a system of storing information in an electronic computer on magnetic cores, magnetic drums, magnetic tape, etc.

commit to memory, to learn by heart; memorize: . . . *no longer compelled to commit to memory many thousand verses* (Benjamin Jowett).

in memory of, to help in remembering; as a reminder of: *I send you this card in memory of our happy summer together.*

[< Old French *memorie,* learned borrowing from Latin *memoria* < *memor, -oris* mindful. Doublet of MEMOIR.]

—**Syn. 2. Memory, recollection** mean the act or fact of remembering. **Memory** emphasizes keeping in mind something once learned or experienced: *That vacation lives in her memory.* **Recollection** emphasizes calling back to mind, often with effort, something not thought of for a long time: *I have little recollection of my childhood.*

memory drum, a magnetic drum.

Mem·phi·an (mem′fē ən), *adj.* **1.** having to do with Memphis in ancient Egypt. **2.** of Egypt; Egyptian.

Mem·phite (mem′fīt), *n.* **1.** a native or inhabitant of Memphis in ancient Egypt. **2.** the Coptic dialect spoken in the neighborhood of ancient Memphis, or, formerly, the dialect spoken in the neighborhood of Alexandria.

Mem·phit·ic (mem fit′ik), *adj.* Memphian.

mem·sa·hib (mem′sä′ib), *n.* (in India) a term of respect for a European woman, used by native servants: *Throughout most of the tropics it was below the dignity of the sahib, and especially the memsahib, to do physical labor* (Harper's). [Anglo-Indian *mem-sāhib* < *mem* (< English *ma'am*) + *sāhib* master < Arabic *ṣaḥib*]

men (men), *n., pl. of* **man.** human beings; people in general: *The best laid schemes o' mice and men Gang aft a-gley* (Robert Burns). *It is impossible to find any exact physical basis for the division of apes from men* (Observer).

men·ace (men′is), *n., v.,* **-aced, -ac·ing.** —*n.* a threat: *In dry weather, forest fires are a menace. A whispering menace that chilled brain and blood* (Walter de la Mare). —*v.t.* to offer a menace to; threaten: *Floods menaced the valley with destruction.* —*v.i.* to be threatening: *Earth below shook; heaven above menaced* (Edmund Burke).

[< Old French *menace* < Vulgar Latin *minācia,* singular of Latin *mināciae,* ultimately < *minae* threats, projecting points] —**men′ac·er,** *n.* —**men′ac·ing·ly,** *adv.*

—**Syn.** *v.t.* See **threaten.**

me·nad (mē′nad), *n.* maenad.

me·nad·ic (mi nad′ik), *adj.* maenadic.

mé·nage or **me·nage** (mā näzh′), *n.* **1.** a domestic establishment; household. **2.** the management of a household: *Nothing tended to make ladies so . . . inefficient in the menage as the study of dead languages* (Hannah More). [< Old French *menage* < Vulgar Latin *mansiōnāticus* household < Latin *mānsiō, -ōnis;* see MANSION]

mé·nage à trois (mā näzh′ à trwä′), *French.* **1.** a household comprising a married couple and the lover of one of them. **2.** (literally) household of three.

me·nag·er·ie (mə naj′ər ē, -nazh′-), *n.* **1.** a collection of wild animals kept in cages or enclosures, especially for exhibition, as in a zoo or a circus. **2.** the place or building in which such animals are kept. **3.** a curious assortment or collection of people: *An old quack doctor named Levett . . . completed this strange menagerie* (Macaulay). [< French *ménagerie* (literally) management of a household < *ménage;* see MÉNAGE]

me·nar·che (mə när′kē, me-), *n.* the beginning of menstruation; first menstrual period. [< Greek *mēn* month + *archē* a beginning]

men-chil·dren (men′chil′drən), *n.* the plural of **man-child.**

Menck·e·ni·an (meng kē′nē ən), *adj.* of, having to do with, or characteristic of H.L. Mencken, American author, journalist, and critic, 1880-1956, or his writings; sharply critical of existing institutions; iconoclastic: *Menckenian satire.* —*n.* an admirer or follower of H.L. Mencken or his works.

mend (mend), *v.t.* **1.** to put in good condition again; make whole or serviceable (something broken, worn, or otherwise damaged); repair: *to mend a road, to mend a broken doll, to mend clothes.* **2.** to remove or correct faults in (a person, the heart, life, etc.): *He should mend his manners.* **3.** to remove (a fault); correct (a defect): *to mend an error.* **4.** to restore to proper condition by any action: *to mend a fire by adding fuel.* **5.** to set right: *Try to mend matters with her.* **6.** to make better; improve; advance: *He . . . mended his worldly prospects by a matrimonial union with a widow lady of large property* (Harriet Beecher Stowe). **7.** *Informal.* to improve on; surpass. —*v.i.* **1.** to become better; improve: *There is no prospect of matters mending.* **2.** to get back one's health; improve. **3.** to make amends: *Least said, soonest mended.*

—*n.* **1.** a place that has been mended: *The mend in your dress scarcely shows.* **2.** a mending; improvement.

on the mend, a. improving: *Home trade in finished linens is perhaps on the mend* (London Daily News). **b.** getting well: *[My] health has been on the mend ever since Poole left town* (Samuel Taylor Coleridge).

[Middle English *menden,* probably variant of *amenden* amend] —**mend′er,** *n.*

—**Syn.** *v.t.* **1. Mend, repair, patch** mean to put in good or usable condition again. **Mend** means to make whole again something that has been broken, torn, or worn, but is now seldom used of large things: *She mended the broken cup with cement.* **Repair** means to make right again something damaged, run down, decayed, weakened, etc.: *He repaired the old barn.* **Patch** means to mend by putting a piece (or amount) of material on or in a hole, tear, or worn place: *His mother patched his torn trousers.* **2.** better. **3.** rectify.

mend·a·ble (men′də bəl), *adj.* that can be mended.

men·da·cious (men dā′shəs), *adj.* **1.** lying; untruthful: *The mendacious beggar told a different tale of woe at every house.* **2.** false; untrue: *a mendacious report, mendacious rumors.* [< Latin *mendāx, -ācis* lying + English *-ous*] —**men·da′cious·ly,** *adv.* —**men·da′cious·ness,** *n.* —**Syn. 1.** dishonest. **2.** spurious.

men·dac·i·ty (men das′ə tē), *n., pl.* **-ties. 1.** the habit of telling lies; untruthfulness: *The natural mendacity of fishermen is epitomized in "the bigger one that got away."* **2.** a lie.

Men·de (men′dē), *n., pl.* **-de** or **-des. 1.** a member of a tribe of west African people living in the central and southeastern part of Sierra Leone. **2.** the Mandingo language of this people.

Men·de·le·ev's or **Men·de·lye·ev's law** (men′də lā′əfs), *Chemistry.* the periodic law. [< Dmitri *Mendeleev,* 1834-1907, a Russian chemist, who formulated it]

men·de·le·vi·um (men′də lā′vē əm), *n.* a rare, highly radioactive, synthetic chemical element, produced as a by-product of nuclear fission: *Element 101, mendelevium, was first made in 1955, by Dr. Glenn Seaborg* (Science News Letter). *Symbol:* Md; *at.wt.:* (C^{12}) 256 or (O^{16}) 256; *at. no.:* 101; *half life:* about 30 minutes.

Men·de·li·an (men dē′lē ən), *adj.* **1.** of or having to do with Gregor Johann Mendel: *Any heredity is now considered Mendelian if it is dependent on chromosomes* (A. Franklin Shull). **2.** inherited in accordance with Mendel's laws. —*n.* an advocate of Mendel's laws.

Men·de·li·an·ism (men dē′lē ə niz′əm), *n.* Mendelism.

Men·del·ism (men′də liz əm), *n.* the doctrines of Gregor Johann Mendel.

Men·del's laws (men′dəlz), the laws or principles describing the inheritance of many characteristics in plants and animals, according to which there occurs, in the second and later generations of hybrids, every possible combination of the characteristics of the original parent animals or plants, each combination in a definite proportion of individuals. Mendel's laws were first discovered and formulated by Gregor Johann Mendel, 1822-1884, an Austrian monk and biologist, in experiments with peas. *Ideas of dominance and of independent units, together with a third, usually referred to as segregation, have come to be called Mendel's Laws* (Fred W. Emerson).

men·di·can·cy (men′də kən sē), *n.* **1.** the act of begging: *Mendicancy in the East is regarded as no disgrace.* **2.** the state of being a beggar: *After a riotous youth, ill health and bad habits reduced him to mendicancy.*

men·di·cant (men′də kənt), *adj.* begging: *Mendicant friars ask alms for charity. And with that dejected air and mendicant voice* (Samuel Richardson). —*n.* **1.** a beggar: *We were surrounded by mendicants asking for money.* **2.** a mendicant friar. [< Latin *mendīcāns, -antis,* present participle of *mendīcāre* beg < *mendīcus* beggar]

men·dic·i·ty (men dis′ə tē), *n.* beggary; mendicancy: *We find it hard to realize the problems of mendicity in Europe after great wars.* [< Middle French *mendicité,* learned borrowing from Latin *mendīcitās, -ātis* < *mendicus* beggar]

me·ne·hu·ne (men′ə hü′nə), *n., pl.* **-ne, -nes.** a legendary Polynesian dwarf or elf who worked only at night, building ponds, roads, etc. [< Hawaiian *menehune*]

Men·e·la·us (men′ə lā′əs), *n. Greek Legend.* a king of Sparta, son of Atreus, brother of Agamemnon, and husband of Helen of Troy.

men·folk (men′fōk′), *n.pl.* men: . . . *a nation of 2.5 million whose menfolk often work abroad* (Economist).

men·folks (men′fōks′), *n. pl. U.S. Dialect.* men: *She was takin' money to let menfolks come look at her dance* (New Yorker).

men-gods (men′godz′), *n.* the plural of **man-god.**

men·ha·den (men hā′dən), *n., pl.* **-den.** a marine fish of the same group as the herring, having the appearance of a shad but with a more compressed body, common along the eastern coast of the United States; mossbunker. It is rarely used for food, but it is used as a source of oil, meal, and fertilizer. [American English < Algonkian (probably Narragansett) *munnawhateaûg* a fish like a herring; (literally) they fertilize]

men·hir (men′hir), *n. Archaeology.* an upright monumental stone (megalith) standing either alone or with others, typical of the monuments of the megalithic culture of western Europe. [< French *menhir* < Breton *men hir* < *men* stone + *hir* long]

me·ni·al (mē′nē əl, mēn′yəl), *adj.* belonging to or suited to a servant; low; mean: *Cinderella had to do menial tasks. Her ladyship was of humble, I have even heard menial, station originally* (Thackeray). —*n.* **1.** a servant who does the humblest and most unpleasant tasks: *I worked for a menial's hire, Only to learn, dismayed, That any wage I had asked of Life, Life would have paid* (Jessie B. Rittenhouse). **2.** a low, mean, or servile person; flunky. [< Anglo-French *menial* < *meiniée,* variant of Old French *meisniee* household < Vulgar Latin *mansiōnāta* < Latin *mānsiō, -ōnis* habitation; see MANSION] —**me′ni·al·ly,** *adv.* —**Syn.** *adj.* servile, slavish.

Mé·nière's or **Me·nier's disease** (mā nyãrz′), a disease of the inner ear which causes dizziness and may lead to deafness. [< Prosper *Ménière,* 1799-1862, a French physician who first described it]

me·nin·ge·al (mə nin′jē əl), *adj.* of or having to do with the meninges.

me·nin·ges (mə nin′jēz), *n., pl. of* **meninx.** the three membranes that surround the brain and spinal cord. They are the pia mater, arachnoid membrane, and dura mater. [< New Latin *meninges* < Greek *mêninx, -ingos* (body) membrane]

me·nin·gi·o·ma (mə nin′jē ō′mə), *n., pl.* **-mas, -ma·ta** (-mə tə). a tumor situated in the meninges that grows by expansion, causing damage to the brain: *Meningioma . . . can often be cured by surgery* (Sunday Times). [< *mening*(es) + *-oma*]

men·in·git·ic (men′in jit′ik), *adj.* relating to, having to do with, or affected by meningitis.

men·in·gi·tis (men′in jī′tis), *n.* any of several very serious infectious diseases in which the membranes (meninges) surrounding the brain or spinal cord are inflamed: *In meningitis, several or all of the following symptoms may appear: headache, vomiting, dizziness, stiff neck, sore throat* (Sidonie M. Gruenberg). [< *mening*(es) + *-itis*]

me·nin·go·coc·cal (mə ning′gə kok′əl), *adj.* of, having to do with, or caused by meningococci.

me·nin·go·coc·cic (mə ning′gə kok′sik), *adj.* meningococcal.

me·nin·go·coc·cus (mə ning′gə kok′əs), *n., pl.* **-ci** (-sī). a bacterium or coccus that causes cerebrospinal meningitis. [< *meninge*(es) + *coccus*]

me·ninx (mē′ningks), *n.* singular o **meninges.**

me·nis·coid (mə nis′koid), *adj.* like a meniscus; crescent-shaped; concavo-convex.

me·nis·cus (mə nis′kəs), *n., pl.* **-nis·cus·es, -nis·ci** (-nis′ī). **1.** *Physics.* the curved upper surface of a column of liquid, caused by capillarity. It is concave when the walls of the container are moistened, convex when they are dry: *Most liquids wet glass, and therefore have a concave meniscus* (W.N. Jones). **2.** a lens, convex on one side and concave on the other. A miniscus is thicker in the center so that it has a crescent-shaped section. **3.** a crescent or crescent-shaped body. [< New Latin *meniscus* < Greek *mēnískos* (diminutive) of *mēnē* moon]

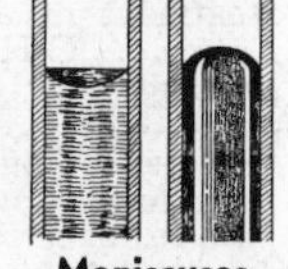
Meniscuses (def. 1) Left, concave; right, convex

men·i·sper·ma·ceous (men′ə spėr mā′shəs), *adj.* belonging to a family of dicotyledonous, chiefly tropical, woody, climbing plants, having small, usually three-parted flowers, and possessing narcotic properties, typified by the moonseed. [< New Latin *Menispermaceae* the family name (< *Menispermum* the typical genus < Greek *mēnē* moon + *spérma* seed) + English *-ous* (because of their crescent-shaped seeds)]

Men·non·ist (men′ə nist), *n.* Mennonite.

Men·non·ite (men′ə nīt), *n.* a member of one of a group of Christian denominations descended from a church that originated in 1525 in Switzerland, opposed to taking oaths, holding public office, and military service. The Mennonites wear very plain clothes and live simply. [< *Menno* Simons, 1492-1559, of Witmarsum, Holland, a leader of the group + *-ite*[1]]

me·no (mā′nō), *adv. Music.* less (used as a direction, always with another word). [< Italian *meno* (literally) less < Latin *minus* less]

men·o·branch (men′ə brangk), *n.* any of a group of salamanders characterized by persistent gills forming external tufts, and by four limbs, each having four well-developed digits. [< New Latin *Menobranchus* the typical genus < Greek *ménein* remain + *bránchia* gills]

me·nol·o·gy (mi nol′ə jē), *n., pl.* **-gies. 1.** an annotated calendar of the months. **2.** the calendar of the Greek Church with lives of the saints in the order of their festivals. **3.** a series of saints' biographies arranged according to the calendar. [< New Latin *menologium* < Late Greek *mēnológion* < *mēn* month + *lógos* an account, treatment < *légein* to tell]

Me·nom·i·nee (mə nom′ə nē), *n.* **1.** a tribe of Indians living in Wisconsin and northern Illinois, of Algonkian stock. **2.** a member of this tribe. **3.** their language.

me·no mos·so (mā′nō môs′sō), *Music.* not so fast; slower (used as a direction). [< Italian *meno mosso*]

men·o·paus·al (men′ə pô′zəl), *adj.* menopausic.

men·o·pause (men′ə pôz), *n.* the final cessation of the menses, occurring normally between the ages of 45 and 50; change of life; climacteric: *Menstrual periods . . . continue from the onset of puberty until the menopause . . .* (Harbaugh and Goodrich.) [< Greek *mēn* month + *paûsis* cessation]

men·o·paus·ic (men′ə pô′zik), *adj.* having symptoms of the menopause.

men·o·pome (men′ə pōm), *n.* any of the amphibians, such as the hellbender, with persistent branchial apertures. [< New Latin *Menopoma* the typical genus < Greek *ménein* remain + *pôma* lid]

Me·nor·ah (mə nôr′ə, -nōr′-), *n.* **1.** a candlestick having seven branches, in the ancient Temple at Jerusalem, whose flame was fed by consecrated oil. According to the Apocrypha, when the Temple was rededicated after Judas Maccabaeus and his brothers overthrew the Syrians (about 165 B.C.) the Menorah burned for eight days with only a single day's supply of oil. **2.** Also, **menorah.** a candelabrum with eight branches, used by Jews at Hanukkah to commemorate this event. Each night an additional candle is lit until finally all are lit on the last night. [< Hebrew *manorah*]

Menorah (def. 2)

men·or·rha·gi·a (men′ə rā′jē ə), *n.* excessive menstrual discharge. [< New Latin *menorrhagia* < Greek *mênes* the menses + *rhēgnýnai* burst forth, flood]

Men·sa[1] (men′sə), *n., genitive* **Men·sae.** a southern constellation

Men·sa[2] (men′sə), *n.* an international club for people of superior intelligence who must take a series of intelligence tests before being accepted as members. [< Latin *mēnsa* table]

Men·sae (men′sē), *n.* genitive of **Mensa**[1].

men·sal[1] (men′səl), *adj.* monthly. [< Latin *mēnsis* month + English *-al*[1]]

men·sal[2] (men′səl), *adj.* of, having to do with, or used at the table. [< Latin *mēnsālis* < *mēnsa* table]

mense (mens), *n. Scottish.* **1.** propriety; decorum. **2.** neatness; tidiness. [< Scandinavian (compare Old Icelandic *mennska* humanity; kindness)]

mense·ful (mens′fəl), *adj. Scottish.* **1.** proper; decorous. **2.** neat; tidy.

mense·less (mens′lis), *adj. Scottish.* lacking propriety or decorum.

men·serv·ants (men′sėr′vənts), *n.* the plural of **manservant.**

men·ses (men′sēz), *n.pl.* the discharge of bloody fluid from the uterus that normally occurs approximately every four weeks between puberty and the menopause. [< Latin *mēnses,* plural of *mēnsis* month]

Men·she·vik (men′shə vik), *n., pl.* **Men·she·viks, Men·she·vi·ki** (men′shə vē′kē). a Russian liberal political party opposed to the more radical Bolsheviks from 1903 to 1917. [< Russian *men′shevik* < *men′shij* lesser (because originally so named by Nikolai Lenin at a party congress in 1903)]

Men·she·vism or **men·she·vism** (men′shə viz əm), *n.* the doctrines or principles of the Mensheviks.

Men·she·vist or **men·she·vist** (men′shə vist), *n.* a Menshevik. —*adj.* having to do with or characteristic of the Mensheviks or Menshevism.

mens re·a (menz rē′ə), *Law.* criminal intent: *One is not anxious to multiply criminal offences in which there is no mens rea* (London Times). [< Latin *mēns rea* a guilty mind]

men's room, *U.S.* a public lavatory for men.

mens sa·na in cor·po·re sa·no (menz sā′nə in kôr′pə rē sā′nō), *Latin.* a sound mind in a sound body.

men·stru·al (men′strů əl), *adj.* **1.** of or having to do with the menses: *the menstrual discharge.* **2.** happening once in a month.

men·stru·ate (men′strů āt), *v.i.,* **-at·ed, -at·ing.** to have a discharge of bloody fluid (menses) from the uterus, normally at intervals of approximately four weeks. [< Late Latin *mēnstruāre* (with English *-ate*[1]) < Latin *mēnstrua* the menses < *mēnsis* month; see MENSES]

men·stru·a·tion (men′strů ā′shən), *n.* the act or period of menstruating: *The interval from ovulation to menstruation is about two weeks* (Sidonie Gruenberg).

men·stru·ous (men′strů əs), *adj.* **1.** menstruating. **2.** menstrual. [< Late Latin *mēnstruōsus,* or < Latin *mēnstruus* (with English *-ous*) < *mēnsis* month]

men·stru·um (men′strů əm), *n., pl.* **-stru·ums, -stru·a** (-strů ə). *Archaic.* any liquid substance that dissolves a solid; solvent. [< Medieval Latin *menstruum,* neuter of Latin *mēnstruus* menstrual, monthly; see MENSTRUOUS (from the Medieval alchemists' reputed belief in the dissolving capacity of the menses)]

men·su·al (men′shů əl, -syů-), *adj.* monthly. [< Late Latin *mēnsuālis* < Latin *mēnsis* month]

men·su·ra·bil·i·ty (men′shər ə bil′ə tē), *n.* the property of being mensurable.

men·su·ra·ble (men′shər ə bəl), *adj.* **1.** measurable. **2.** having assigned limits. [< Late Latin *mēnsūrābilis* < Latin *mēnsūrāre* to measure]

men·su·ral (men′shər əl), *adj.* having to do with measure.

men·su·rate (men′shə rāt), *v.t.,* **-rat·ed, -rat·ing.** to measure.

men·su·ra·tion (men′shə rā′shən), *n.* **1.** the action, art, or process of measuring. **2.** the branch of mathematics that deals with finding lengths, areas, and volumes. [< Late Latin *mensūrātiō, -ōnis* < *mēnsūrāre* to measure < Latin *mēnsūra* a measure]

men·su·ra·tive (men′shə rā′tiv), *adj.* adapted for or concerned with measuring.

mens·wear (menz′wãr′), *n.* **1.** clothing for men. **2.** cloth characteristically used in making suits for men. —*adj.* of or made from this cloth: *menswear flannel.*

-ment, *suffix.* **1.** the act or state or fact o ——ing: *Enjoyment = the state of enjoying.*
2. the state or condition or fact of being ——ed: *Amazement = the state of being amazed.*
3. the product or result of ——ing: *Pavement = the product of paving.*
4. the means or instrument for ——ing: *Inducement = the means of inducing.*
5. two or more of these meanings, as in *improvement, measurement, settlement.*
6. other meanings, as in *ailment, basement.*
[< Old French *-ment* < Latin *-mentum* result of]

men·tal[1] (men′təl), *adj.* **1.** of the mind: *a mental test, a mental disease.* **2.** for the mind: *a mental reminder.* **3.** done by or existing in the mind; without the use of written figures, etc.: *mental arithmetic.* **4. a.** having a mental disease or weakness: *a mental patient.* **b.** for people with a mental illness or mental deficiency: *a mental institution.* **5.** concerned with the mind and its phenomena: *a mental specialist.* [< Middle French *mental,* learned borrowing from Late Latin *mentālis* < Latin *mēns, mentis* mind]

men·tal[2] (men′təl), *adj.* of, having to do with, or in the region of the chin. [< Latin *mentum* chin + English *-al*[1]]

mental age, *Psychology.* a measure of the mental development or general intelligence of an individual in terms of the average performance of normal individuals of various ages. It is determined by a series of tests that are prepared to show natural intelligence rather than the result of education.

mental deficiency, a lack of ordinary intelligence such as to place the individual at a disadvantage in school and adult life, including idiocy, the most extreme degree: imbecility, the intermediate degree; and moronity, the least degree; feeblemindedness: *Mental deficiency, or feeblemindedness, is an arrested development of the brain* (Marguerite Clark).

mental healer, a person who heals diseases by suggestion or faith.

mental healing, the healing of diseases by suggestion or faith.

mental health, the state of being well mentally, characterized by soundness of thought and outlook, adaptability to one's environment, and balanced behavior: *On all sides we see the signs of an anxious, awakened interest in this grave problem of mental health* (New York Times).

mental hygiene, the science that deals with the preservation of mental health.

mental illness, a serious disorder of the mind, characterized by a distorted mental outlook and strange or irrational behavior: *Mental illness has become the major problem of veterans' hospitals.*

men·tal·ism (men′tə liz əm), *n.* the doctrine that mental processes are valid subjects of scientific study and experimentation: *When the behaviorists threw out mentalism, they made stimuli and responses the critical elements* (New Scientist).

men·tal·ist (men′tə list), *n.* **1.** a person who believes in mentalism. **2.** a mind reader or telepathist: *Dunninger, who says he is a mentalist, put his eyes up against the camera and, he said, transmitted a thought to those tuned in* (New York Times).

men·tal·is·tic (men′tə lis′tik), *adj.* arising from or having to do with the mind or its processes as opposed to purely physical reality or biological processes: *Bloomfield strove vigorously to avoid mentalistic terms ... in the statement of his linguistic materials and believed that every truly "scientific statement is made in physical terms"* (Charles C. Fries).

men·tal·i·ty (men tal′ə tē), *n., pl.* **-ties.** mental capacity; power of the mind to remember, learn, reason, etc.; mind: *An idiot has a very low mentality.*

men·tal·ly (men′tə lē), *adv.* **1.** in or with the mind; by a mental operation. **2.** with regard to the mind: *Police said the bomb thrower was mentally unbalanced.*

mental reservation, an unexpressed qualification of a statement.

mental telepathy, extrasensory perception.

men·ta·tion (men tā′shən), *n.* mental action.

men·tha·ceous (men thā′shəs), *adj.* belonging to the mint family of plants. [< New Latin *Menthaceae* the family name (< *Mentha* the typical genus < Latin *mentha,* variant of *menta* mint[1]) + English *-ous*]

men·thene (men′thēn), *n.* a colorless, liquid hydrocarbon, produced by the dehydration of menthol. *Formula:* $C_{10}H_{18}$ [< German *Menthen* < Latin *menta* mint[1]]

men·thol (men′thol, -thôl), *n.* a colorless, crystalline alcohol, obtained by cooling oil of peppermint and also made synthetically. It is used in relieving neuralgia and nasal inflammations, in making perfumes, and in confectionery. *Formula:* $C_{10}H_{19}OH$ [< German *Menthol* < Latin *menta* mint[1] + *oleum* oil]

men·tho·lat·ed (men′thə lā′tid), *adj.* **1.** containing menthol. **2.** treated with menthol.

men·ti·cide (men′tə sīd), *n.* brainwashing: *It was proposed that menticide, or political intervention in the individual human mind to force confessions or impose an ideology, should be declared an international crime* (Science News Letter). [< Latin *mēns, mentis* mind + English *-cide*[2]]

men·ti·cul·tur·al (men′tə kul′chər əl), *adj.* cultivating or improving the mind.

men·ti·cul·ture (men′tə kul′chər), *n.* the cultivation of the mind. [< Latin *mēns, mentis* mind + *cultūra* culture]

men·tion (men′shən), *v.t.* to speak about; refer to: *Do not mention the accident before the children.*

not to mention, not even considering; besides: *The hotel's sports activities included boating and fishing, not to mention swimming, tennis, etc.*

[< noun]

—*n.* a short statement (about); reference (to): *There was mention of the school party in the newspaper. He grows peevish at any mention of business* (Samuel Johnson).

make mention of, to speak of; refer to: *He made mention of a tiger he had shot.*

[< Old French *mention,* learned borrowing from Latin *mentiō, -ōnis* < *mēns, mentis* mind] —**men′tion·er,** *n.*

men·tion·a·ble (men′shə nə bəl), *adj.* that can be mentioned; worthy of mention.

men·ton·nière (men′tə nyãr′; *French* mäɴ-tô nyer′), *n.* a piece of armor for protecting the chin or lower part of the face and neck, used only on occasions of special danger. [< French *mentonnière* < *menton* chin < Latin *mentum*]

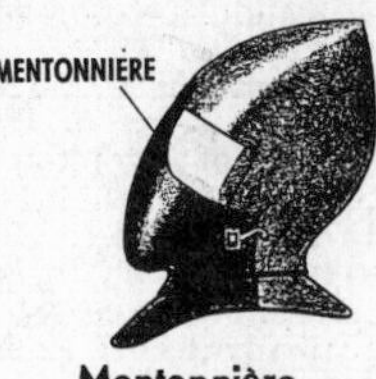

Mentonnière

Men·tor (men′tər), *n. Greek Legend.* a faithful friend of Ulysses. He was the teacher and adviser of Ulysses' son Telemachus until Ulysses finally returned from the Trojan War.

men·tor (men′tər), *n.* a wise and trusted adviser. [< *Mentor*]

men·tor·ship (men′tər ship), *n.* the office of mentor.

men·u (men′yü, mā′nyü), *n.* **1.** a list of the food served at a meal; bill of fare. **2.** the food served: *Everyone enjoyed the fine menu.* [< French *menu* < Middle French, small, detailed < Latin *minūtus* made small. Doublet of MINUTE[2].]

me·nu·et (mə nʏ e′), *n. French.* minuet (used in musical scores).

me·ow (mē ou′), *n., interj.* a sound made by a cat. —*v.i.* to make this sound. —*v.t.* to sing, utter, etc., with a voice like that of a cat. Also, **mew, miaow, miaou, miaul.** [imitative]

m.e.p., mean effective pressure.

me·per·i·dine hydrochloride (mə per′ə-dēn), a synthetic drug used as a sedative and pain reliever. It is not as powerful as morphine but can also cause addiction. *Formula:* $C_{15}H_{21}NO_2 \cdot HCl$ [< *me*(thyl) (carbethoxypi)*peridine*]

me·phen·e·sin (mə fen′ə sin), *n.* a drug that relaxes the muscles and helps to relieve nervous tension: *Thanks to the drug mephenesin, most cerebral palsy patients may now have safer and more comfortable dental care* (Science News Letter). *Formula:* $C_{10}H_{14}O_3$ [< *me*(thyl), *phen*(oxy), (cr)*es*(yl), parts of its chemical name + *-in*]

Me·phis·to (mi fis′tō), *n.* Mephistopheles.

Meph·i·stoph·e·les (mef′ə stof′ə lēz), *n.* **1.** the devil of the Faust legend. **2.** a powerful evil spirit; crafty devil. [< German *Mephistopheles;* origin uncertain]

Meph·is·to·phe·li·an or **Meph·is·to·phe·le·an** (mef′ə stə fē′lē ən), *adj.* **1.** like Mephistopheles; wicked and crafty; sardonic; scoffing. **2.** of or having to do with Mephistopheles.

me·phit·ic (mi fit′ik), *adj.* **1.** having a nasty smell. **2.** noxious; poisonous; pestilential. [< Late Latin *mephīticus* < Latin *mephītis* stench] —**me·phit′i·cal·ly,** *adv.* —**Syn. 1.** fetid. **2.** pestiferous.

me·phi·tis (mi fī′tis), *n.* **1.** a foul or nasty smell. **2.** a noxious or pestilential vapor, especially from the earth. [< Latin *mephītis*] —**Syn. 1.** stench. **2.** miasma.

me·pro·ba·mate (mə prō′bə māt), *n.* a synthetic drug widely used as a tranquilizer; Miltown; Equanil: *The Yeshiva University associate professor refers to seven reports of overdoses of meprobamate and their poisoning effects* (Science News Letter). *Formula:* $C_9H_{18}N_2O_4$ [< *me*(thyl), *pro*(pyl), (dicar)*bamate,* parts of its chemical name]

meq., milliequivalent.

mer., 1. mercury. **2. a.** meridian. **b.** meridional.

Me·rak (mē′rak), *n.* one of two stars in the Big Dipper pointing toward the North Star. Merak is the farther of the two from the North Star.

Mer·a·tran (mer′ə tran), *n. Trademark.* a tranquilizing drug that combats emotional depression, mental illness, etc.; pipradol. *Formula:* $C_{18}H_{21}NO$

Mer·cal·li scale (mer kä′lē), a scale for measuring the intensity of an earthquake, ranging from 1 to 12. [< Giuseppe *Mercalli,* an Italian scientist]

mer·can·tile (mėr′kən til, -tīl), *adj.* **1.** of or having to do with merchants or trade; commercial: *a successful mercantile venture.* **2.** engaged in trade or commerce: *a mercantile firm.* **3.** of or having to do with mercantilism (def. 1). [< French *mercantile* < Italian, < *mercante* merchant < Latin *mercāns, -antis* (literally) trading < *mercārī* to trade < *merx, mercis* wares]

mercantile agency, an organization that furnishes information about the financial standing, credit rating, etc., of individuals, commercial firms, etc.

mercantile law, law merchant;the body of principles and rules, drawn chiefly from the customs of merchants, by which the rights and obligations arising in commercial transactions are determined.

mercantile marine, merchant marine.

mercantile paper, transferable paper, such as promissory notes given by merchants for merchandise purchased or drafts drawn against purchasers of merchandise.

mercantile system, mercantilism (def. 1).

mer·can·til·ism (mėr′kən ti liz′əm, -tī-), *n.* **1.** the economic system prevailing in Europe in the 1500's and 1600's, that favored a balance of exports over imports, preferably in a nation's own ships, and through or to its own trading stations or colonies, receiving in return, whenever possible, precious metals, national wealth being measured by the amount of gold and silver possessed. A nation's agriculture, industry, and trade were regulated with that end in view. Mercantilism became dominant as feudalism waned, and the focus of national power shifted from those who owned land to those who controlled money and trade. **2.** the principles or practice characteristic of trade or commerce; commercialism.

mer·can·til·ist (mėr′kən ti list, -tī-), *n.* **1.** a believer in the supreme importance of trade and commerce. **2.** an advocate of mercantilism (def. 1) or of some similar theory. —*adj.* mercantilistic.

mer·can·ti·lis·tic (mėr′kən ti lis′tik, -tī-), *adj.* of, having to do with, or characteristic of mercantilism or mercantilists: *the mercantilistic policies of Louis XIV.*

mer·cap·tan (mər kap′tan), *n.* any of a series of organic compounds having the general formula RSH, resembling the alcohols and phenols, but containing sulfur in place of oxygen, especially ethyl mercaptan, a colorless liquid having an unpleasant odor. [< German *Mercaptan* < New Latin *(corpus) mer(curium) captan(s)* (substance) which catches mercury]

mer·cap·to·pu·rine (mər kap′tō pyu̇r′ēn, -in), *n.* a compound that inhibits the metabolism of nucleic acid, used in the treatment of acute leukemia; Purinethol. *Formula:* $C_5H_4N_4S$ [< *mercapt*(an) + *purine*]

Mer·ca·tor's chart (mėr kā′tərz), a chart made according to Mercator's projection. *A Mercator's chart represents the meridians and parallels of latitude as straight lines.*

Mercator's projection, a method of drawing maps with straight instead of curved lines for latitude and longitude. Mercator's projection is useful in navigation, but the areas near the poles appear disproportionately large. *On an American Mercator's projection of the globe, the Middle East is close to the two ends of the earth* (New Yorker). [< Gerhardus *Mercator,* 1512-1594, a Flemish cartographer]

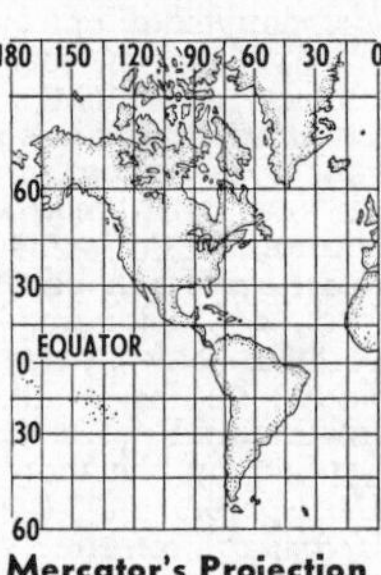

Mercator's Projection

mer·ce·nar·i·ly (mėr′sə ner′ə lē), *adv.* in a mercenary manner.

mer·ce·nar·i·ness (mėr′sə ner′ē nis), *n.* the character of being mercenary.

mer·ce·nar·y (mėr′sə ner′ē), *adj., n., pl.* **-nar·ies.** —*adj.* **1.** working for money only; acting with money as the motive: *Such wretches are kept in pay by some mercenary bookseller* (Oliver Goldsmith). **2.** done for money or gain: *a mercenary marriage.* **3.** hired to fight for a foreign ruler, army, or cause: *These ... Followed their mercenary calling And took their wages and are dead* (A.E. Housman).

—*n.* a soldier serving for pay in a foreign army.

[< Latin *mercēnārius* < *mercēs, -edis* wages < *merx, mercis* wares, merchandise]

—**Syn.** *adj.* **1.** hireling, grasping. **2.** venal.

mer·cer (mėr′sər), *n. British.* a dealer in cloth, originally in silks, velvets, etc., but now commonly in cloth of any kind. [< Old French *mercier* < *merz* wares < Latin *merx, mercis*] —**Syn.** draper.

mer·cer·ise (mėr′sə rīz), *v.t.,* **-ised, -is·ing.** *Especially British.* mercerize.

mer·cer·i·za·tion (mėr′sər ə zā′shən), *n.* the process of mercerizing: *Mercerization in-*

creases luster and strength, and enables dye to penetrate the cloth more easily (World Book Encyclopedia).

mer·cer·ize (mėr′sə rīz), *v.t.*, **-ized, -iz·ing.** to treat (cotton thread or cloth) with a solution of sodium hydroxide that strengthens the cotton, makes it hold dyes better, and gives it a silky luster. [< John *Mercer*, 1791-1866, an English inventor, who patented the process + *-ize*]

mer·cer·y (mėr′sər ē), *n.*, *pl.* **-cer·ies.** *British.* **1.** the place of business of a mercer. **2.** the ware sold by a mercer: *He left outlandish merceries stored up With many a brazen bowl and silver cup* (William Morris). [< Old French *mercerie* merchandise in general < *mercier* mercer]

mer·chan·dis·a·ble (mėr′chən dī′zə bəl), *adj.* that can be merchandised; merchantable.

mer·chan·dise (*n.* mėr′chən dīz, -dīs; *v.* mėr′chən dīz), *n.*, *v.*, **-dised, -dis·ing.** —*n.* **1.** goods for sale; articles that are or may be bought and sold; wares. *Abbr.:* mdse. **2.** *Archaic.* commercial business; trade.
—*v.t.*, *v.i.* **1.** to buy and sell; trade. **2.** to strive for increased sales or greater acceptance of goods, services, etc., by attractive display, advertising, etc.
[< Old French *marchandise* < *marchand*, earlier *marchëant* merchant] —**mer′chan·dis′er,** *n.*
—**Syn.** *n.* **1.** stock.

mer·chan·dis·ing (mėr′chən dī′zing), *n.* the planning of sales programs, including research, packaging, advertising, etc., directed toward creating a market demand for a product.

mer·chan·dize (mėr′chən dīz), *n.*, *v.t.*, *v.i.*, **-dized, -diz·ing.** merchandise.

mer·chant (mėr′chənt), *n.* **1.** a person who buys and sells commodities for profit, now especially on a relatively large scale and often with foreign countries. **2.** a storekeeper; retail shopkeeper.
—*adj.* **1.** of or having to do with the merchant marine: *a merchant seaman.* **2.** having to do with trade; trading; commercial; mercantile: *a merchant town.*
—*v.i.* to buy and sell commodities for profit. —*v.t.* to trade or sell as a commodity: *They never quite believe in the great causes that they merchant to the plain people* (Time).
[< Old French *marchëant*, later *marchand* < Vulgar Latin *mercātans, -antis*, present participle of *mercātāre* (frequentative) < Latin *mercārī* to trade < *merx, mercis* wares] —**Syn.** *n.* **1.** trader, dealer.

mer·chant·a·ble (mėr′chən tə bəl), *adj.* marketable; salable. —**Syn.** vendible.

merchant adventurer, a person, especially a member of a commercial company, engaged in the sending out of trading expeditions to foreign parts and the establishment there of factories and trading stations.

merchant bank, (in Great Britain) a banking firm that engages in accepting bills of exchange and issuing stocks and shares for British industry.

merchant banker, a person who manages or represents a merchant bank.

mer·chant·man (mėr′chənt mən), *n.*, *pl.* **-men. 1.** a ship used in commerce; trading vessel: *a stout merchantman of 350 tons. He dresses up as an ordinary seaman and sails on a merchantman* (Graham Greene). **2.** *Archaic.* a merchant (*n.* def. 1).

merchant marine, 1. the trading vessels of a nation or nations, collectively; ships used in commerce. **2.** the officers and men who serve aboard these vessels: *John's brother is in the merchant marine.*

merchant navy, *British.* merchant marine.

mer·chant·ry (mėr′chən trē), *n.* **1.** the business of a merchant; trade. **2.** merchants as a group.

merchant seaman, a seaman who works on a ship used in commerce or trade.

merchant tailor, a tailor who furnishes the cloth for the garments that he fits and makes to order.

merchant vessel, a ship used in commerce; merchantman.

mer·ci (mer sē′), *interj. French.* thank you; thanks.

Mer·cian (mėr′shən, -shē ən), *adj.* of Mercia, an ancient Anglo-Saxon kingdom in central England, its people, or their dialect: *a Mercian king, a Mercian legend.* —*n.* **1.** a native or inhabitant of Mercia: *The warlike Mercians . . .* (Spenser). **2.** the Old English dialect spoken in Mercia.

mer·ci beau·coup (mer sē′ bō kü′), *French.* thank you very much; many thanks.

mer·ci·ful (mėr′si fəl), *adj.* showing or feeling mercy; having mercy; full of mercy: *God be merciful to me a sinner* (Luke 28:13). —**mer′ci·ful·ly,** *adv.* —**mer′ci·ful·ness,** *n.* —**Syn.** compassionate, clement, kind, lenient. —**Ant.** relentless, implacable, pitiless, ruthless.

mer·ci·less (mėr′si lis), *adj.* without mercy; having or showing no mercy: *a stern prince, merciless in his exactions* (William H. Prescott). —**mer′ci·less·ly,** *adv.* —**mer·ci·less·ness,** *n.* —**Syn.** relentless, implacable, pitiless, ruthless.

mer·cu·rate (mėr′kyə rāt), *v.t.*, **-rat·ed, -rat·ing. 1.** to combine or treat with mercury or a salt of mercury. **2.** to subject to the action of mercury. [< *mercur*(y) + *-ate*[1]]

mer·cu·ri·al (mər kyůr′ē əl), *adj.* **1. a.** sprightly; quick: *I was ardent in my temperament; quick, mercurial, impetuous* (Washington Irving). **b.** changeable; fickle: *mercurial breezes. Mercurial currency exchange rates are proving to be of dollars-and-cents significance* (Wall Street Journal). **2.** caused by the use of mercury: *mercurial poisoning.* **3.** containing mercury: *a mercurial ointment.*
—*n.* a drug containing mercury.
[< Latin *mercuriālis* < *Mercurius* Mercury (originally) the god; the planet] —**mer·cu′ri·al·ly,** *adv.* —**mer·cu′ri·al·ness,** *n.*
—**Syn.** *adj.* **1. a.** agile. **1. b.** variable, volatile.

mer·cu·ri·al·ism (mər kyůr′ē ə liz′əm), *n.* poisoning caused by the absorption of mercury: *Chronic mercury poisoning, or mercurialism, was well known . . . since the first Christian century* (New Yorker).

mer·cu·ri·al·i·za·tion (mər kyůr′ē ə lə zā′shən), *n.* **1.** the act of mercurializing. **2.** the state of being mercurialized.

mer·cu·ri·al·ize (mər kyůr′ē ə līz), *v.t.*, **-ized, -iz·ing. 1.** to make mercurial in quality. **2.** to treat or impregnate with mercury or one of its compounds. **3.** *Medicine.* to affect with or subject to the action of mercury.

Mer·cu·ri·an (mėr kyůr′ē ən), *adj.* of or having to do with the planet Mercury: *Mercurian climate.* —*n.* a hypothetical native or inhabitant of Mercury.

mer·cu·ric (mər kyůr′ik), *adj.* **1.** of mercury. **2.** (of compounds) containing mercury, especially with a valence of two.

mercuric or **mercury chloride,** corrosive sublimate: *Mercuric chloride, bichloride of mercury, or corrosive sublimate is used to disinfect hands* (W.W. Bauer).

Mer·cu·ro·chrome (mər kyůr′ə krōm), *n. Trademark.* a red compound containing mercury, formed by the solution of a greenish mercury derivative in water, used externally as an antiseptic. *Formula:* $C_{20}H_8Br_2HgNa_2O_6$ [< *mercur*(y) + *chrome* color, dye]

mer·cu·rous (mər kyůr′əs, mėr′kyər-), *adj.* **1.** of mercury. **2.** (of compounds) containing mercury, especially with a valence of one.

mercurous chloride, calomel.

Mer·cu·ry (mėr′kyər ē), *n.* **1.** *Roman Mythology.* the messenger of the gods, the god of commerce, of skill of hands, quickness of wit, eloquence, and thievery, identified with the Greek Hermes. **2.** the smallest planet in the solar system, and the nearest to the sun. Its orbit about the sun takes 88 days to complete, at a mean distance of almost 36,000,000 miles. Its mean diameter is 2,900 miles. Mercury goes around the sun about four times while the earth is going around once. *Symbol:* ☿ **3.** a messenger or bearer of news: *But what says she to me? Be brief, my good She-Mercury* (Shakespeare). [< Latin *Mercurius*]

mer·cu·ry (mėr′kyər ē), *n.*, *pl.* **-ries. 1.** a heavy, silver-white, metallic chemical element, that is liquid at ordinary temperatures; quicksilver. It has the property of dissolving other metals, forming amalgams. Mercury is found native, but is more commonly obtained by sublimation from cinnabar, its most important ore. *Symbol:* Hg (hydrargyrum); *at.wt.:* (C^{12}) 200.59 or (O^{16}) 200.61; *at.no.:* 80; *valence:* 1,2. **2.** the column of mercury in a thermometer or barometer, especially with reference to the temperature or the state of the atmosphere shown by it: *The mercury dropped below freezing last night.* **3.** a go-between, especially in amorous affairs. **4.** a guide. **5.** any of a group of herbs of the spurge family, especially dog's mercury, a poisonous European weed. [< Medieval Latin *mercurius* the metal < Latin *Mercurius* Mercury]

mercury fulminate, a grayish powder, the mercury salt of fulminic acid, exploding readily when dry, used in making detonators. *Formula:* $Hg(CNO)_2$

mercury lamp, mercury vapor lamp.

mercury vapor lamp, an apparatus consisting essentially of a glass or quartz vacuum tube containing mercury vapor, that produces a bright greenish-yellow illumination when an electric current is passed through it.

Mer·cu·ti·o (mėr kyü′shē ō), *n.* the dashing friend of Romeo in Shakespeare's play *Romeo and Juliet.*

mer·cy (mėr′sē), *n.*, *pl.* **-cies. 1.** more kindness than justice requires; kindness beyond what can be claimed or expected. **2.** kindly treatment; pity: *a work of mercy.* **3.** something to be thankful for; blessing: *We thank the Lord for all His mercies. I say that we are wound with mercy round and round As if with air* (Gerard Manley Hopkins).
at the mercy of, in the power of: *at the mercy of the elements. The poor lunatic . . . was at the mercy of his servants, who robbed, laughed at, and neglected him* (Frederick Marryat).
[< Old French *merci* < *mercit* < Latin *mercēs, -ēdis* reward, wages < *merx, mercis* wares, merchandise]
—**Syn. 1. Mercy, clemency** mean kindness or mildness shown to an enemy, an offender, etc. **Mercy** applies when it is shown by anyone in any way: *The guard showed mercy to the prisoner and gave him a cigarette.* **Clemency** applies when it is shown by someone with the right or duty to be severe: *The judge showed clemency to the defendant by giving him a suspended sentence.*

mercy killing, euthanasia: *A doctor has no right to speed a patient's end by euthanasia, or "mercy killing," no matter how hopeless his condition* (Time).

mercy seat, 1. (in the Bible) the gold plate covering the Ark of the Covenant in the ancient Hebrew temple, with cherubim at either end, regarded as the place of God's presence and on which the high priest sprinkled the blood of the sin offering. Exodus 25; Leviticus 16. **2.** the throne of God in heaven.

mere[1] (mir), *adj.*, *superl.* **mer·est. 1.** nothing else than; simple; only: *The cut was the merest scratch. Even when a mere child I began my travels* (Washington Irving). **2.** *Law.* done, performed, or exercised by a person or the persons specified, without any influence or help. **3.** *Obsolete.* pure; unmixed: *mere wine.* [< Anglo-French *meer* unaided (in law) < Latin *merus* pure, unmixed] —**Syn. 1.** bare, sheer.

mere[2] (mir), *n. Poetic.* a lake; pond: *lonely mountain-meres* (Tennyson). [Old English *mere* a body of water]

mere[3] (mir), *n. Archaic.* a boundary. [Old English *gemǣre*]

mère (mer), *n. French.* mother.

mere·ly (mir′lē), *adv.* **1.** and nothing more; and that is all; simply; only: *merely as a matter of form. The multitudes Who read merely for the sake of talking* (Joseph Butler). **2.** *Obsolete.* without admixture; purely. **3.** *Obsolete.* absolutely. —**Syn. 1.** solely.

me·ren·gue (me reng′gā), *n.* a fast, gay dance of the West Indies, especially the Dominican Republic and Haiti, where it originated. Its main characteristic is a limping side step: *A new dance, the merengue, swept the United States in 1955. The merengue first became popular with the mambo fans* (World Book Annual). [< Spanish (West Indies) *merengue*]

mere·stone (mir′stōn′), *n. Archaic.* a stone marking a boundary; a stone landmark. [< *mere*[3] + *stone*]

mer·e·tri·cious (mer′ə trish′əs), *adj.* **1.** attractive in a showy way; alluring by false charms: *There is nothing showy or meretricious about the man* (William Dean Howells). *. . . the actual broadcasts have also combined the sublime and the ridiculous, the serious and the meretricious, in the kind of melange . . . found to be commercially profitable* (New Yorker). **2.** having to do with or characteristic of a prostitute. [< Latin *meretrīcius* (with English *-ous*) < *meretrīx, -icis* prostitute < *merērī* to earn (money)] —**mer′e·tri′cious·ly,** *adv.* —**mer′e·tri′cious·ness,** *n.*

mer·gan·ser (mər gan′sər), *n., pl.* **-sers** or (*collectively*) **-ser.** any of several kinds of large, fish-eating ducks having long, slender, serrated bills hooked at the tip, and great diving powers, inhabiting North America from Mexico to Alaska and Greenland. Mergansers have crested heads. [< New Latin *merganser* < Latin *mergus* waterfowl, diver (< *mergere* to dip, immerse) + *ānser* goose]

merge (mėrj), *v.,* **merged, merg·ing.** —*v.t.* **1.** to swallow up; absorb; combine and absorb; combine: *The steel trust merged various small businesses.* **2.** *Obsolete.* to immerse; sink (in): *the same forces which merged the Dane in the Englishman* (John R. Green).
—*v.i.* to become swallowed up or absorbed in something else: *The twilight merges into darkness.*
[< Latin *mergere* dip] —**Syn.** *v.t.* **1.** consolidate, fuse.

mer·gence (mėr′jəns), *n.* a merging or being merged.

merg·er (mėr′jər), *n.* **1.** a merging or being merged; absorption; combination: *One big company was formed by the merger of four small ones.* **2.** a person or thing that merges. —**Syn. 1.** coalition, amalgamation.

mer·i·carp (mer′ə kärp), *n.* one of the two single-seeded halves of the schizocarp, the fruit of most plants of the parsley family or of the maple. [< French *méricarpe* < Greek *méros* part + *karpós* fruit]

me·rid·i·an (mə rid′ē ən), *n.* **1.** a great circle passing through any place on the earth's surface and through the North and South Poles. **2.** the half of such a circle from pole to pole. All the places on the same meridian have the same longitude. *All places within one half-hour's time east and west of the 75th longitude line, or meridian, have Eastern Standard Time.*

Meridians (def. 2) of longitude

3. the highest point that the sun or a star reaches in the sky. **4.** the highest point or period of highest development or perfection; culmination: *I imagined my fortune had passed its meridian, and must now decline* (Charlotte Brontë). **5.** the middle period of a man's life, when his powers are at the full: *The meridian of life is the prime of life.*
—*adj.* **1.** highest; greatest: *Athens reached its meridian glory in the age of Pericles.* **2.** of or having to do with a meridian. **3.** (of a heavenly body) at or from the zenith: *the sun's meridian beams. The meridian moon shone full into the hovel* (Jane Porter). **4.** of or having to do with noon: *the meridian hour.*
[Middle English *meridien* midday < Latin *merīdiānus* of noon, ultimately < *medius* middle + *diēs* day]

meridian of Greenwich, the prime meridian.

me·rid·i·o·nal (mə rid′ē ə nəl), *adj.* **1.** having to do with or characteristic of the south or people living there, especially of southern France; southern; southerly: *foremost among the Spanish grandees ... stood ... a man of meridional aspect with coal-black hair and beard* (John L. Motley). **2.** of, having to do with, or resembling a meridian. **3.** along a meridian; in a north-south direction: *a meridional flow of air, a meridional chain of weather stations.*
—*n.* an inhabitant of the south, especially the south of France.
[< Late Latin *merīdiōnālis* < Latin *merīdiēs* noon, south (< *medius* middle + *diēs* day), on the pattern of *septentriōnālis* northern] —**me·rid′i·o·nal·ly,** *adv.*

me·ringue[1] (mə rang′), *n.* **1.** a mixture made of egg whites beaten stiff and sweetened with sugar, often flavored. Meringue is often made into shells for ice cream, etc., or spread on pies, puddings, etc., and lightly browned in the oven. **2.** a small shell, cooky, cake, etc., made of this mixture. [< French *meringue*]

mé·ringue or **me·ringue**[2] (mā rang′), *n.* a variant of the merengue, danced in Haiti. [< Creole *méringue* < Spanish (West Indies) *merengue*]

Me·ri·no or **me·ri·no** (mə rē′nō), *n., pl.* **-nos,** *adj.* —*n.* **1.** any of a breed of sheep of Spanish origin, having long, fine wool and (on the full-grown male) large, spiral horns. **2.** the wool of this sheep. **3.** a soft woolen yarn made from it, used for hosiery, etc. **4. a.** a thin, soft, woolen cloth made from this yarn. **b.** a similar cloth of a fine wool mixed with cotton.

Merino Ram (def. 1) (about 2 ft. high at the shoulder)

—*adj.* made of this wool, yarn, or fabric.
[< Spanish *merino,* apparently < the name of a Moorish tribe, whose sheep were imported in order to improve the local breed]

mer·i·spore (mer′ə spôr, -spōr), *n. Biology.* one of the individual cells or secondary spores of a multicellular or compound spore. [< Greek *méros* part + English *spore*]

mer·i·stem (mer′ə stem), *n. Botany.* the undifferentiated, growing cellular tissue of the younger parts of plants; actively dividing cell tissue. [< Greek *meristós* divisible, divided (< *merízein* divide < *méros* part) + *-ēma,* a noun suffix]

mer·i·ste·mat·ic (mer′ə stə mat′ik), *adj.* of or having to do with the meristem.

me·ris·tic (mə ris′tik), *adj. Biology.* of or having to do with the number or arrangement of body parts or segments: *meristic variation.* [< Greek *meristós* divisible + English *-ic*] —**me·ris′ti·cal·ly,** *adv.*

mer·it (mer′it), *n.* **1.** goodness; worth; value: *Each child will get a mark according to the merit of his work. Reputation is ... oft got without merit, and Lost without deserving* (Shakespeare). **2.** something that deserves praise or reward. **3.** a real fact or quality, whether good or bad: *The judge will consider the case on its merits.*
make a merit of, to represent (some action, circumstance, or quality) as deserving of reward or praise: *the party felon whose unblushing face ... coolly makes a merit of disgrace* (John Greenleaf Whittier).
—*v.t.* **1.** to be worthy of; deserve: *Those best can bear reproof who merit praise* (Alexander Pope). **2.** to earn by commendable action.
—*v.i.* to deserve: *a simple, religious fanatic, who felt sure that ... he was meriting well of God and his king* (John L. Motley).
[< Old French *merite,* learned borrowing from Latin *meritum* earned < *merēre* to earn, deserve]
—**Syn.** *n.* **1. Merit, worth** mean the goodness or value of someone or something. **Merit** implies achieved rather than inherent excellence, and often suggests practical value: *The merits of your plan outweigh the defects.* **Worth** implies excellence or value belonging to the person or thing by its very nature, apart from any connections or conditions affecting its usefulness, value, or importance: *The worth of the new drugs is certain, although all their uses are not yet known.*

mer·it·a·ble (mer′ə tə bəl), *adj.* merited; meritorious: *Darmon went on to score a second meritable victory* (Observer).

mer·it·ed (mer′ə tid), *adj.* deserved; well-earned. —**mer′it·ed·ly,** *adv.*

mer·it·less (mer′it lis), *adj.* without merit; without excellence or commendable qualities; undeserving.

mer·i·toc·ra·cy (mer′ə tok′rə sē), *n.* a class of people distinguished for their high intellect or talent: *If one had to choose between a class system of aristocracy and one of meritocracy, the latter would be preferable* (Manchester Guardian). [< *merit* + *-ocracy,* as in *aristocracy*]

mer·i·to·crat (mer′ə tə krat), *n.* a person who belongs to a meritocracy.

mer·i·to·crat·ic (mer′ə tə krat′ik), *adj.* **1.** having to do with a meritocracy: *a meritocratic society.* **2.** based solely upon intellectual achievement: *Higher education in Britain is in danger of becoming a "meritocratic treadmill"* (London Times).

mer·i·to·ri·ous (mer′ə tôr′ē əs, -tōr′-), *adj.* deserving reward or praise; having merit; worthy: *John's work was meritorious but not brilliant.* [< Latin *meritōrius* (with English *-ous*) of use in, or connected with, the earning of money < *merēre* to earn, deserve] —**mer′i·to′ri·ous·ly,** *adv.* —**mer′i·to′ri·ous·ness,** *n.* —**Syn.** commendable, praiseworthy.

merit system, the system in which appointments and promotions in the civil service are made on the basis of the merit of the employees.

merle or **merl** (mėrl), *n. Archaic.* the common European blackbird. [< Old French *merle* < Latin *merula*]

mer·lin (mėr′lən), *n.* **1.** a kind of small falcon, one of the smallest European birds of prey, and one of the boldest, that does not hesitate to attack birds of twice its own size. **2.** any of certain closely allied birds, as the North American pigeon hawk. [Middle English *merlyon* < Anglo-French *merilun,* Old French *esmerillon* (diminutive) < *esmeril,* probably < Germanic (compare Old High German *smirl*)]

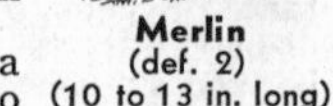
Merlin (def. 2) (10 to 13 in. long)

Mer·lin (mėr′lən), *n.* a seer and magician who helped King Arthur.

mer·lon (mėr′lən), *n.* the solid part between two openings in a battlement. [< French *merlon* < Italian *merlone* < *merlo* battlement, perhaps < Latin *mergae,* plural, (two-pronged) pitchfork]

mer·maid (mėr′mād′), *n.* **1.** a sea maiden in fairy tales, having the head and upper body of a woman, and the form of a fish from the waist down: *a mermaid fair, Singing alone, Combing her hair Under the sea* (Tennyson). **2.** an expert woman swimmer. [< *mere*[2] in the sense of "sea" + *maid*]

mer·maid·en (mėr′mā′dən), *n.* a mermaid: *... the cold strange eyes of a little Mermaiden And the gleam of her golden hair* (Matthew Arnold).

mermaid's purse, skatebarrow.

mer·man (mėr′man′), *n., pl.* **-men. 1.** a man of the sea in fairy tales, having the head and upper body of a man, and the form of a fish from the waist down. **2.** an expert male swimmer. [< *mere*[2] (see MERMAID) + *man*]

mer·o·blast (mer′ə blast), *n. Embryology.* an ovum whose contents consist of considerable nutritive as well as formative or germinal matter. [< Greek *méros* part + *blastós* germ, sprout]

mer·o·blas·tic (mer′ə blas′tik), *adj. Embryology.* (of an ovum) containing nutritive as well as germinal matter and therefore undergoing only partial segmentation, as in birds, reptiles, and most fishes: *meroblastic cleavage.*

mer·o·crys·tal·line (mer′ə kris′tə lin), *adj.* partially crystalline. [< Greek *méros* part + English *crystalline*]

me·rog·o·ny (mə rog′ə nē), *n.* the development of an embryo from a portion of an egg. [< Greek *méros* part + *-goniā* a begetting]

Mer·o·pe (mer′ō pē), *n. Greek Mythology.* one of the Pleiades. In some accounts of the story, Merope became the seventh or faint star because she married a mortal.

mer·o·sym·met·ri·cal (mer′ə si met′rə kəl), *adj.* being partially symmetrical.

mer·o·sym·me·try (mer′ə sim′ə trē), *n.* (in crystallography) partial symmetry. [< Greek *méros* part + English *symmetry*]

Mer·o·vin·gi·an (mer′ə vin′jē ən), *adj.* designating or having to do with the first Frankish line of kings that reigned in Gaul or France from about 486 A.D. to 750 A.D. —*n.* one of these kings.

mer·ri·ly (mer′ə lē), *adv.* in a merry manner.

mer·ri·ment (mer′ē mənt), *n.* laughter and gaiety; merry enjoyment; fun; mirth: *Albert was of course delighted, and his merriment at the family gathering was more pronounced than ever ...* (Lytton Strachey). —**Syn.** jollity, hilarity.

mer·ri·ness (mer′ē nis), *n.* the quality or state of being merry.

mer·ry (mer′ē), *adj.,* **-ri·er, -ri·est. 1.** laughing and gay; full of fun: *merry talk, merry laughter.* **2.** gay; joyful: *a merry Christmas. I am never merry when I hear sweet music* (Shakespeare). **3.** *Archaic.* **a.** (of things) pleasant; agreeable: *the merry* *month of May.* **b.** (of music) delightful; sweet. **c.** (of a wind) favorable. **4.** *Archaic.* **a.** amusing: *a merry jest.* **b.** facetious: *His lordship is but merry with me* (Shakespeare). **make merry,** to laugh and be gay; have fun. [Middle English *meri,* Old English *merge, myrge* pleasing, agreeable] —**Syn. 1.** jolly, jovial. See **gay.**

mer·ry-an·drew or **Mer·ry-An·drew** (mer′ē an′drü), *n.* a clown; buffoon. —**Syn.** harlequin, punchinello.

mer·ry-go-round (mer′ē gō round′), *n.* **1.** a set of animals and seats on a platform that goes round and round by machinery; carrousel: *The opera itself was tuneful as a merry-go-round* (Time). **2.** any whirl or rapid round: *The holidays were a merry-go-round of parties.*

mer·ry·make (mer′ē māk′), *v.i.,* **-made, -mak·ing.** to make merry; hold festivities.

mer·ry·mak·er (mer′ē mā′kər), *n.* a person who is being merry.

mer·ry·mak·ing (mer′ē mā′king), *n.* **1.** laughter and gaiety; fun. **2.** a gay festival; merry entertainment. —*adj.* gay and full of fun; engaged in merrymaking. —**Syn.** *n.* **1.** conviviality.

mer·ry·thought (mer′ē thôt′), *n.* a wishbone.

Mer·thi·o·late (mər thī′ə lāt), *n. Trademark.* a liquid preparation containing mercury, used as a germicide, fungicide, and antiseptic. *Formula:* $C_9H_9HgNaO_2S$

mer·y·chip·pus (mer′i kip′əs), *n.* an extinct quadruped animal believed to be an ancestor of the horse. [< New Latin *Merychippus* the genus name < Greek *mērykázein* to chew the cud + *híppos* horse]

me·sa (mā′sə), *n. U.S.* a small, isolated, high plateau with a flat top and steep, rocky sides, common in arid regions of the western and southwestern United States: *Some of the most prominent cliffs and mesas of the Colorado Plateau country are made by these Jurassic sandstones* (World Book Encyclopedia). [American English < Spanish *mesa* < Latin *mēnsa* table < *metīrī* to measure]

mé·sal·li·ance (mā zal′ē əns; *French* mā zȧ lyäNs′), *n.* marriage with a person of lower social position; misalliance. [< French *mésalliance* < *mes-* mis- + Old French *alliance* alliance]

Me·san·to·in (mə san′tō in), *n. Trademark.* a drug which depresses the nervous system, used especially to decrease the number and intensity of epileptic fits. *Formula:* $C_{12}H_{14}N_2O_2$

mes·cal (mes kal′), *n.* **1.** an alcoholic drink of Mexico made from the fermented juice of certain agaves (maguey). **2.** any of the plants yielding this. **3.** a small cactus of northern Mexico and the southwestern United States, whose buttonlike tops are dried and chewed as a stimulant by the Indians; peyote. [American English < Mexican Spanish *mescal* < Nahuatl *mexcalli* a fermented drink of maguey]

mes·cal·in (mes′kə lin), *n.* mescaline.

mes·cal·ine (mes′kə lēn, -lin), *n.* a drug obtained from mescal buttons, used to induce psychoses and hallucinations; peyote. *Formula:* $C_{11}H_{17}NO_3$ [< *mescal* + *-ine*[2]]

mes·dames (mā däm′; *French* mā dȧm′), *n.* plural of **madam** or **madame.** *Abbr.:* Mmes. ➔ **Mesdames** is used to supply a plural for *Mrs.,* particularly in reports of social affairs: *The bazaar is being organized by Mesdames Howard, Clarkson, and Reed.* In most kinds of writing, however, *Mesdames* is avoided by the repetition of Mrs. before each name.

mes·de·moi·selles (mād mwȧ zel′), *n.* the plural of **mademoiselle.**

me·seems (mi sēmz′), *v., past tense* **me·seemed.** *Archaic.* it seems to me.

mes·en·ce·phal·ic (mes′en sə fal′ik), *adj.* **1.** situated in the midst of the encephalon, as the midbrain. **2.** of or having to do with the mesencephalon: *the mesencephalic segment of the brain.*

mes·en·ceph·a·lon (mes′en sef′ə lon), *n.* the middle section of the brain, lying between the cerebellum and pons, and the forebrain; midbrain. [< Greek *mésos* middle + *enképhalon* encephalon]

mes·en·chy·ma (mes eng′kə mə), *n.* mesenchyme.

mes·en·chy·mal (mes eng′kə məl), *adj.* having to do with, consisting of, or derived from mesenchyme: *mesenchymal cells.*

mes·en·chym·a·tous (mes′eng kim′ə təs), *adj.* mesenchymal.

mes·en·chyme (mes′eng kim), *n.* that portion of the mesoderm, consisting of cells set in a gelatinous matrix, from which the connective tissues, bone, cartilage, vascular system, etc., develop. [< New Latin *mesenchyma* < Greek *mésos* middle + *enchýma* infusion < *en* in + *cheîn* pour. Compare CHYME.]

mes·en·ter·ic (mes′ən ter′ik), *adj.* of or having to do with a mesentery.

mes·en·ter·i·tis (mes en′tə rī′tis), *n.* inflammation of the mesentery.

mes·en·ter·on (mes en′tə ron), *n., pl.* **-ter·a** (-tər ə). *Embryology.* the interior of the primitive intestine (archenteron), bounded by endoderm. [< New Latin *mesenteron* < Greek *mésos* middle + *énteron* enteron]

mes·en·ter·on·ic (mes en′tə ron′ik), *adj.* of or having to do with the mesenteron.

mes·en·ter·y (mes′ən ter′ē), *n., pl.* **-ter·ies.** a membrane that enfolds and supports an internal organ, attaching it to the body wall or to another organ. [< Medieval Latin *mesenterium* < Greek *mesentérion* < *mésos* middle + *énteron* intestine, enteron]

mesh (mesh), *n.* **1.** the open space of a net or sieve: *This net has half-inch meshes. An 80-mesh screen has 80 meshes to the inch.* **2.** the cord, wire, etc., used in a net, screen, etc. **3.** a means of catching or holding fast; network; net: *Here in her hairs the painter plays the spider and hath woven a golden mesh to entrap the hearts of men* (Shakespeare). **4.** the engagement of gear teeth. See picture under **gear.**

in mesh, in gear; fitted together: *The machinery is in mesh.*

meshes, a. a network: *A fish was entangled in the meshes.* **b.** snares: *Greece has extricated it from the meshes of diplomacy* (William E. Gladstone).

—*v.t., v.i.* **1.** to catch or be caught in a net. **2.** (of gear teeth, etc.) to engage or become engaged: *The teeth of the small gear mesh with the teeth of a larger one.* **3.** to bring closely together; fit together; blend; integrate: *The [organization] never had a chance to . . . mesh all its supporters into a strong party* (Canada Month). *Both . . . plans need study to find how they might best be meshed* (Wall Street Journal).

[compare Old English *mǣscre* net]

Me·shach (mē′shak), *n.* (in the Bible) one of the three Hebrews cast into the fiery furnace by Nebuchadnezzar. Daniel 3:12-30.

meshed (mesht), *adj.* having meshes; reticulated: *meshed carpet.*

me·shu·ga or **me·shug·ga** (mə shu̇g′ə), *adj. Slang.* crazy: *This man is meshugga . . . [he] read science-fiction while awaiting trial* (Time). [< Yiddish *meshuge* < Hebrew *mĕshuggāʿ*]

mesh·work (mesh′wėrk′), *n.* a structure consisting of meshes; network.

mesh·y (mesh′ē), *adj.* formed with meshes; meshed; reticulated.

me·si·al (mē′zē əl, mes′ē-), *adj.* having to do with, situated in, or directed toward the middle line of a body; median. [< Greek *mésos* middle + English *-ial*] —**me′si·al·ly,** *adv.*

mes·ic atom (mez′ik, mē′sik), an atom in which an electron has been replaced by a negatively charged meson.

me·sit·y·lene (mə sit′ə lēn, mes′ə tə-), *n.* an oily, colorless, aromatic, liquid hydrocarbon obtained by the action of sulfuric acid on acetone. *Formula:* C_9H_{12} [< obsolete *mesite* acetic ether (< Greek *mesítēs* go-between < *mésos* middle) + *-yl* + *-ene*]

mes·mer·ic (mes mer′ik, mez-), *adj.* hypnotic: *the mesmeric driving force provided by the Marxist conception of history* (Edmund Wilson). —**mes·mer′i·cal·ly,** *adv.*

mes·mer·ism (mes′mə riz əm, mez′-), *n.* hypnotism. [< Franz *Mesmer,* 1734-1815, an Austrian physician who popularized the doctrine of animal magnetism + *-ism*]

mes·mer·ist (mes′mər ist, mez′-), *n.* a hypnotist.

mes·mer·i·za·tion (mes′mər ə zā′shən, mez′-), *n.* **1.** the act of hypnotizing. **2.** the state of being hypnotized.

mes·mer·ize (mes′mə rīz, mez′-), *v.t., v.i.,* **-ized, -iz·ing.** to hypnotize. —**mes′mer·iz′er,** *n.*

mesn·al·ty (mē′nəl tē), *n., pl.* **-ties. 1.** the estate of a mesne lord. **2.** the condition of being a mesne lord. [< law French *mesnalte* < Old French *mene, meien;* see MESNE]

mesne (mēn), *adj. Law.* middle; intermediate; intervening: *A feudal lord with vassals, but himself a vassal of a superior, was a mesne lord.* [< law French *mesne,* alteration of Anglo-French *meen,* Old French *mein, meien* mean[3]]

Mes·o·a·mer·i·can (mes′ō ə mer′ə kən, mē′sō-), *adj.* of or having to do with Mesoamerica, the central part of the American continent extending from northern Mexico through Central America to the Isthmus of Panama. —*n.* a native or inhabitant of Mesoamerica, especially in prehistoric times: *. . . the complex histories of Mesoamericans, especially the Aztec and Maya* (New Scientist).

mes·o·blast (mes′ə blast, mē′sə-), *n.* mesoderm in an embryo. [< Greek *mésos* middle + *blastós* germ, sprout]

mes·o·blas·tic (mes′ə blas′tik, mē′sə-), *adj.* of or having to do with the mesoblast: *a mesoblastic cell, the mesoblastic layer.*

mes·o·carp (mes′ə kärp, mē′sə-), *n.* the middle layer of the wall (pericarp) of a fruit or ripened ovary, such as the fleshy part of a peach or plum. See picture under **pericarp.** [< Greek *mésos* middle + *karpós* fruit]

mes·o·ce·phal·ic (mes′ō sə fal′ik, mē′sō-), *adj.* **1.** *Anthropology.* **a.** having a skull with a cranial capacity of from 1,350 to 1,450 cubic centimeters, intermediate between dolichocephalic and brachycephalic. **b.** having a skull of medium proportion. **2.** *Anatomy.* of or having to do with the mesencephalon. [< Greek *mésos* middle + *kephalē̂* head + English *-ic*]

mes·o·crat·ic (mes′ə krat′ik, mē′sə-), *adj.* (of rock) composed of light and dark minerals in about equal proportions. [< Greek *mésos* middle + *krateîn* to rule + English *-ic*]

mes·o·derm (mes′ə dėrm, mē′sə-), *n.* **1.** the middle layer of cells in an embryo: *There is a third body layer, the mesoderm, that must be produced in order to lay the foundation for the body parts that are to develop later* (A. M. Winchester). **2.** the tissues derived from this layer of cells, as the muscles, bones, and connective tissue. [< Greek *mésos* middle + *dérma* skin]

mes·o·der·mal (mes′ə dėr′məl, mē′sə-), *adj.* of or having to do with the mesoderm in plants or animals.

mes·o·der·mic (mes′ə dėr′mik, mē′sə-), *adj.* mesodermal.

mes·o·fau·na (mes′ə fô′nə, mē′sə-), *n.* the animals of a given habitat that are of intermediate size. [< Greek *mésos* middle + English *fauna*]

mes·o·gas·tric (mes′ə gas′trik, mē′sə-), *adj.* of or having to do with the mesogastrium; umbilical.

mes·o·gas·tri·um (mes′ə gas′trē əm, mē′sə-), *n.* **1.** the umbilical region of the abdomen. **2.** (in an embryo) one of the two mesenteries of the stomach. [< New Latin *mesogastrium* < Greek *mésos* middle + *gastḗr, gastrós* stomach]

mes·o·gloe·a or **mes·o·gle·a** (mes′ə glē′ə, mē′sə-), *n.* a gelatinous or fibrous layer that connects the outer and inner cell layers of a coelenterate. [< Greek *mésos* middle + *gloiā́* glue]

mes·o·gloe·al or **mes·o·gle·al** (mes′ə-glē′əl, mē′sə-), *adj.* consisting of, having to do with, or resembling mesogloea.

me·sog·na·thism (mi sog′nə thiz əm), *n.* mesognathy.

me·sog·na·thous (mi sog′nə thəs), *adj.* **1.** having jaws that are of moderate size and project only slightly. **2.** having a moderate facial angle (80 to 85 degrees); having a gnathic index that ranges between 98 and 103. [< Greek *mésos* middle + *gnáthos* jaw + English *-ous*]

me·sog·na·thy (mi sog′nə thē), *n.* the character or state of being mesognathous.

mes·o·lith·ic or **Mes·o·lith·ic** (mes′ə-lith′ik, mē′sə-), *adj.* of or having to do with the middle period of the Stone Age, transitional between the neolithic and paleolithic periods: *We know from the middens of mesolithic Man that shellfish for long remained a favourite food* (New Scientist). —*n.* this age. [< Greek *mésos* middle + *líthos* stone + English *-ic*]

mes·o·me·te·or·o·log·i·cal (mes′ə mē′tē-ər ə loj′ə kəl, mē′sə-), *adj.* of or having to do with mesometeorology.

mes·o·me·te·or·ol·o·gy (mes′ə mē′tē ə rol′ə jē, mē′sə-), *n.* the branch of meteorology that deals with atmospheric phenomena of an intermediate range, such as storms affecting an area of several tens of miles.

mes·o·morph (mes′ə môrf, mē′sə-), *n.* **1.** a mesomorphic body structure. **2.** a mesomorphic person.

mes·o·mor·phic (mes′ə môr′fik, mē′sə-), *adj.* of or designating the athletic physical type, characterized by predominance of bone, muscle, and other structures developed from the mesodermal layer of the embryo. [< Greek *mésos* middle + *morphḗ* form + English *-ic*]

mes·o·mor·phy (mes′ə môr′fē, mē′sə-), *n.* the character or state of being mesomorphic.

mes·on (mes′on, mē′son), *n.* a highly unstable particle found in the nucleus of an atom, having either a positive or negative charge and a very short lifetime (about a millionth of a second or less): *Mesons are particles believed to act as the glue that binds atomic nuclei* (Science News Letter). [< Greek *mésos* middle + English *-on*, as in *electron*]

mes·o·neph·ric (mes′ə nef′rik, mē′sə-), *adj.* of or having to do with the mesonephros.

mes·o·neph·ros (mes′ə nef′ros, mē′sə-), *n.* the middle division of the primitive kidney of vertebrate embryos, the pronephros and the metanephros being the anterior and posterior divisions, respectively. The mesonephros becomes part of the permanent kidney in fishes and amphibians. [< Greek *mésos* middle + *nephrós* kidney (because it develops between the pronephros and metanephros)]

mes·o·pause (mes′ə pôz′, mē′sə-), *n.* the area of atmospheric demarcation between the mesosphere and the exosphere: *Near the mesopause there is a change in the nature of the air motion and tidal effects begin to dominate* (New Scientist). [< Greek *mésos* middle + English *pause*, noun]

mes·o·phile (mes′ə fil′, -fil′; mē′sə-), *adj.* mesophilic.

mes·o·phil·ic (mes′ə fil′ik, mē′sə-), *adj.* (of certain bacteria) requiring moderate temperatures for development: *They studied . . . flagella from mesophilic bacteria that live under more temperate conditions* (Science News Letter). [< Greek *mésos* middle + English *-phil* + *-ic*]

mes·o·phyll or **mes·o·phyl** (mes′ə fil, mē′sə-), *n.* the inner green tissue of a leaf, lying between the upper and lower layers of epidermis; parenchyma of a leaf. [< Greek *mésos* middle + *phýllon* leaf]

mes·o·phyte (mes′ə fīt, mē′sə-), *n.* a plant that grows under conditions of average moisture and dryness. Mesophytes are intermediate between hydrophytes and xerophytes. [< Greek *mésos* middle + *phytón* plant]

mes·o·phyt·ic (mes′ə fit′ik, mē′sə-), *adj.* of, having to do with, or characteristic of a mesophyte.

mes·o·plast (mes′ə plast, mē′sə-), *n. Biology.* the nucleus of a cell; nuclear protoplasm. [< Greek *mésos* + *plastós* something formed]

mes·o·plas·tic (mes′ə plas′tik, mē′sə-), *adj.* of or having to do with mesoplast.

Mes·o·po·ta·mi·an (mes′ə pə tā′mē ən, -tām′yən), *adj.* of or having to do with Mesopotamia, a region and ancient country that is now a large part of Iraq. —*n.* a native or inhabitant of Mesopotamia.

mes·o·scaph or **mes·o·scaphe** (mes′ə-skaf, -skāf; mē′sə-), *n.* an apparatus similar to the bathyscaph, used to explore the middle depths of the ocean: *The smooth-lined mesoscaph . . . may soon be scanning the Gulf Stream* (Science News Letter). [< Greek *mésos* middle + *skáphē* a bowl, tub]

mes·o·seis·mal (mes′ō sīz′məl, -sīs′-; mē′-sō-), *adj.* having to do with the center of intensity of an earthquake. [< Greek *mésos* middle + English *seismal*]

mes·o·sphere (mes′ə sfir), *n.* **1.** the region of the earth's atmosphere between the stratosphere and the ionosphere. **2.** the region of the earth's atmosphere between the ionosphere and the exosphere.

mes·o·the·li·al (mes′ə thē′lē əl, mē′sə-), *adj.* of or having to do with mesothelium.

mes·o·the·li·um (mes′ə thē′lē əm, mē′sə-), *n., pl.* **-li·ums, -li·a** (-lē ə). that part of the mesoderm that lines the primitive body cavity of a vertebrate embryo. [< New Latin *mesothelium* < *meso(derma)* mesoderm + *(epi)thelium* epithelium]

mes·o·ther·mal (mes′ə thėr′məl, mē′sə-), *adj.* of or having to do with a moderate or intermediate temperature range. [< Greek *mésos* middle + English *thermal*]

mes·o·tho·rac·ic (mes′ə thô ras′ik, -thō-; mē′sə-), *adj.* of or having to do with the mesothorax of an insect.

mes·o·tho·rax (mes′ə thôr′aks, -thōr′-; mē′sə-), *n., pl.* **-rax·es, -ra·ces** (-rə sēz). the middle of the three divisions of the thorax of an insect, typically bearing the first pair of wings and the middle pair of legs. [< Greek *mésos* middle + English *thorax*]

mes·o·tho·ri·um (mes′ə thôr′ē əm, -thōr′-; mez′-), *n.* either of two radioactive isotopes, mesothorium I (*at.no.:* 88; *half-life:* 6.7 years), an isotope of radium, formed from thorium and yielding mesothorium II (*at. no.:* 89; *half-life:* 6.13 hours), an isotope of actinium. Both isotopes have an atomic weight of 228, and are intermediate between thorium and radiothorium. [< Greek *mésos* middle + English *thorium*]

mes·o·ton (mes′ə ton, mē′sə-), *n.* a meson.

mes·o·tron (mes′ə tron, mē′sə-),*n.* a meson.

mes·o·var·i·um (mes′ō vãr′ē əm, mē′sō-), *n.* the fold of peritoneum that suspends the ovary. [< Greek *mésos* middle + Latin *ōvārium* ovary]

Me·so·zo·ic (mes′ə zō′ik, mē′sə-), *n.* **1.** the geological era before the present era. It was characterized by the development of mammals, flying reptiles, birds, and flowering plants, the appearance and death of dinosaurs, and the age of reptiles. It comprises the Triassic, Jurassic, and Cretaceous periods. *The Mesozoic began about 205 million years ago* (Beals and Hoijer). **2.** the rocks formed in this era. —*adj.* of this era or these rocks. [< Greek *mésos* middle + *zōḗ* life + English *-ic*]

mes·quite or **mes·quit** (mes kēt′, mes′-kēt), *n.* **1.** a deep-rooted, shrublike tree of the pea family, that often grows in dense clumps or thickets in the southwestern United States, Mexico, the West Indies, and western South America; algaroba. Its bean-like pods contain much sugar, and furnish a valuable fodder for cattle. Its wood is used as fuel and lumber. *Here and there are patches of a lush green shrub—the mesquite* (Scientific American). **2.** any closely related plant, especially the screw bean. [American English < Mexican Spanish *mezquite* < Nahuatl *mizquitl*]

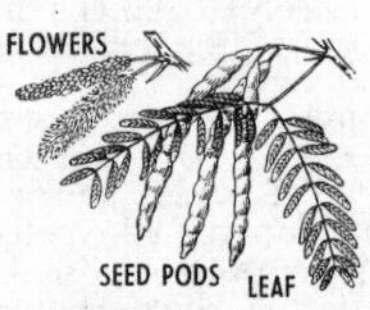

Mesquite (def. 1)

mess (mes), *n.* **1.** a dirty or untidy mass or group of things; dirty or untidy condition: *Look what a mess you have made of your dress playing in that dirt. She keeps her house in a mess.* **2.** confusion; difficulty: *His affairs are in a mess.* **3.** an unpleasant or unsuccessful affair or state of affairs: *Then maybe he would a locked her up, and this awful mess wouldn't ever happened* (Mark Twain). **4.** a group of people who take meals together regularly, especially such a group in the army or navy: *The sailor found the mess a congenial lot.* **5.** a meal of such a group: *The officers are at mess now.* **6. a.** a portion of food, especially a portion of soft food: *a mess of oatmeal.* **b.** a quantity of some edible item sufficient for a meal or meals: *He caught a large mess of fish.* **7.** food that does not look or taste good: *The first edge of hunger blunted, I perceived I had got in hand a nauseous mess* (Charlotte Brontë). **8.** *Informal.* a lot, especially a disagreeable or bothersome lot: *How about cleanin' up de whole mess of 'em and sta'tin' all over ag'in wid some new kind of animal?* (Marc Connelly). —*v.t.* **1.** to make dirty or untidy. **2.** to make a failure of; confuse; spoil. **3.** to supply with meals, as soldiers or sailors. —*v.i.* to take one's meals (with): *We turned in to bunk and mess with the crew forward* (Richard H. Dana).

mess about or **around,** to be busy without really accomplishing anything; putter around: *I mess about my flowers and read snatches of French* (Lynn Linton).

mess about or **around with,** *Informal.* to tamper with: *Miss Saloniemi is determined that one piece of tradition shall not be messed about with* (Manchester Guardian).

[< Old French *mes* < Late Latin *missus, -ūs* a course at dinner, (literally) thing put (that is, on the table) < Latin *mittere* send]

mes·sage (mes′ij), *n., v.,* **-saged, -sag·ing.** —*n.* **1.** oral or written words sent from one person, group, etc., to another: *a wireless message, a message of congratulation.* **2.** an official speech or writing: *the President's message to Congress.* **3.** a lesson or moral implied in a work or works of fiction, a motion picture, play, etc.: *Films with a message sometimes run the risk of spoiling good plots.* **4.** inspired words: *the message of a prophet.* **5.** the business entrusted to a messenger; mission; errand: *His message completed, he went on his way.*

get the message, *Informal.* to grasp the significance, implication, etc., of something: *Disgusted Detroit fans littered the ice with rubber balls and garbage, and the Red Wings got the message* (Time).

—*v.t.* to inform or communicate through a message: *We messaged him that everything was going well.* —*v.i.* to send a message: *The Philippine Coast Guard cutter Anemone messaged briefly that all towns on the tiny southern island were deserted . . .* (Charlottesville Daily Progress).

[< Old French *message* < Medieval Latin *missaticum* < Latin *missus,* past participle of *mittere* to send]

—**Syn.** *n.* **1.** communication, letter, note.

mes·sage-shell (mes′ij shel′), *n. Military.* a projectile in the interior of which messages may be placed to be propelled to a distance.

mes·sa·line (mes′ə lēn′, mes′ə lēn), *n.* a thin, soft silk cloth with a surface like satin. [< French *messaline*]

mes·san or **mes·sin** (mes′ən), *n. Scottish.* **1.** a lap dog. **2.** a miserable cur (applied to a person as a term of abuse). [perhaps < Gaelic *measan*]

mess boy, a messman.

mes·sei·gneurs (mes′ā nyėrz′; *French* mā-se nyœr′), *n.* the plural of **monseigneur.**

mes·sen·ger (mes′ən jər), *n.* **1. a.** a person who carries a message or goes on an errand: *The dying man asked his nurse to be the messenger to his family.* **b.** a person whose job it is to carry messages, run errands, etc.: *a telegraph messenger.* **2.** anything regarded as sent on an errand: *Each bullet was a messenger of death.* **3.** a sign that something is coming; forerunner: *Dawn is the messenger of day.* **4.** a government official employed to carry dispatches; courier: *. . . messenger at the British embassy in Washington* (Time). **5.** *Obsolete.* a servant sent forward to prepare the way: *. . . yon gray lines That fret the clouds are messengers of day* (Shakespeare). [Middle English *messanger,* earlier *messager* < Old French *messagier* < *message* message]

messenger RNA, a form of ribonucleic acid: *Messenger RNA carries information from DNA to the cellular particles called ribosomes, instructing them how to synthesize proteins* (Scientific American).

mes·sen·ger·ship (mes′ən jər ship), *n.* the office of a messenger.

Mes·ser·schmitt (mes′ər shmit′), *n.* a German fighter plane. [< Willy *Messerschmitt,* born 1898, a German industrialist, who built it]

mess hall, a place where a group of people eat together regularly.

Mes·si·ah (mə sī′ə), *n.* **1.** the leader and liberator of the Jews, promised by the prophets and looked for as the restorer of the theocracy. **2.** Often, **messiah.** any person hailed as or thought of as a savior, liberator, or deliverer.

the Messiah, (in Christian use) Jesus, as fulfilling the prophecy of the Lord's Anointed: *At thy nativity, a glorious quire Of angels, in the fields of Bethlehem, sung To shepherds, . . . And told them the Messiah now was born* (Milton).

[variant of Middle English *messias* < Greek *Messīās* < Hebrew *māshiaḥ*]

Mes·si·ah·ship or **mes·si·ah·ship** (mə-sī′ə ship), *n.* the character or office of a Messiah.

Mes·si·an·ic (mes′ē an′ik), *adj.* **1.** of the Messiah: *the Messianic kingdom.* **2.** Also, **messianic.** of a savior; characteristic of a Messiah or believers in a Messiah: *He is possessed by a Messianic zeal to reform mankind.*

Mes·si·an·ism (mə sī′ə niz əm), *n.* **1.** the belief in a Messiah and his coming. **2.** the belief in the betterment of mankind in preparation for or anticipation of the

Messianic age. **3.** Also, **messianism.** a visionary outlook; utopianism: *In 1925 . . . the Bolshevik Revolution turned its face away from the West, abandoned Marxist messianism, and became Russianised* (Manchester Guardian).

Mes·si·an·ist (mə sī′ə nist), *n.* **1.** a person who advocates or supports Messianism. **2.** Also, **messianist.** a person who advocates a utopian or visionary outlook.

Mes·si·as (mə sī′əs), *n.* Messiah.

Mes·si·dor (me sē dôr′), *n.* the tenth month of the French Revolutionary calendar, extending from June 19 to July 18. [< French *Messidor* < Latin *messis* harvest (< *metere* to reap) + Greek *dôron* gift]

mes·sieurs (mes′ərz; *French* mā syœ′), *n.* the plural of **monsieur.** *Abbr.:* MM.
➔ See **Messrs.** for usage note.

mess·i·ly (mes′ə lē), *adv.* in a messy manner.

mess·i·ness (mes′ē nis), *n.* the state or condition of being messy.

mes·sire (me sir′), *n.* a French title of honor and form of address formerly applied to high nobles and also to men of quality and members of the learned professions. [< French *mes sire* my lord < Latin *meus* my, and *senior* senior]

mess jacket, a short, usually white jacket, open in front and reaching to the waist, worn especially by military and naval officers as part of a semiformal dress uniform.

mess kit, 1. a shallow metal container like a skillet that folds in on itself, containing a fork, spoon, and (usually) a knife, and also a large metal cup, used by a soldier in the field, a camper, etc., as eating equipment. **2.** the stove, pots and pans, serving equipment, etc., of a field kitchen, military mess, etc.

mess·man (mes′mən), *n., pl.* **-men.** a person who serves food on a ship.

mess·mate (mes′māt′), *n.* **1.** one of a group of people who eat together regularly: *He would be more comfortable aboard a ship in which he had many old messmates and friends* (Frederick Marryat). **2.** (in Australia) any of several species of eucalyptus trees.

mess·room (mes′rüm′, -rům′), *n.* the mess hall of a ship or naval base.

Messrs., Messieurs.
➔ **Messrs.** is used as the plural of *Mr.* (*Messrs. Kennedy and Nixon*) and sometimes, though rare now in American usage, in addressing firms (*Messrs. Brown, Hubbell, and Company*).

mes·suage (mes′wij), *n. Law.* a dwelling house with its adjacent buildings and the land assigned to the use of those who live in it: *They wedded her to sixty thousand pounds, To lands in Kent and messuages in York* (Tennyson). [< Anglo-French *messuage,* ultimately < Latin *manēre* remain, dwell]

mess·y (mes′ē), *adj.,* **mess·i·er, mess·i·est. 1.** in a mess; in disorder; untidy: *a messy desk.* **2.** covered with dirt; dirty: *messy hands.*

mes·tee (mes tē′), *n.* mustee. [< variant pronunciation of Spanish *mestizo* mestizo]

mes·ti·za (mes tē′zə), *n.* a female mestizo. [< Spanish *mestiza*]

mes·ti·zo (mes tē′zō), *n., pl.* **-zos** or **-zoes.** (in Spanish or Portuguese colonies) a person of mixed blood: **a.** (in Spanish America) a person of Spanish and American Indian descent: *He was a big, simple mestizo, and his Spanish and Indian blood was evident in his dark-skinned face* (New Yorker). **b.** (in the Philippines) a person of Chinese and native descent. **c.** (in Asia and Africa) a person of European and East Indian, Negro, or Malay descent. [< Spanish *mestizo* < Late Latin *mixtīcius* < Latin *mixtus* mixed, past participle of *miscēre* mix]

met (met), *v.* the past tense and past participle of **meet**[1]: *My father met us this morning at ten. We were met at the gate by the dog.*

met-, *combining form.* the form of **meta-** before vowels, as in *metempirics, metempsychosis.*

met., 1. metaphor. **2.** metaphysics. **3.** metronome. **4.** metropolitan.

meta-, *prefix.* **1.** between; among, as in *metacarpus.*
2. reciprocal, as in *metacenter.*
3. change of place or state, as in *metabolism.*
4. behind; after, as in *metathorax, metazoic.*
5. similar in chemical composition to, as in *metaphosphate.* Also, **met-** before vowels.
[< Greek *metá* with, after]

me·tab·a·sis (mə tab′ə sis), *n., pl.* **-ses** (-sēz). transition, as from one subject to another. [< Greek *metábasis,* related to *metabaínein* change one's place < *meta-* meta- + *baínein* go]

met·a·bi·o·log·i·cal (met′ə bī ə loj′ə kəl), *adj.* of or having to do with metabiology.

met·a·bi·ol·o·gy (met′ə bī ol′ə jē), *n.* a theory or philosophy of knowledge based on established biological principles.

met·a·bol·ic (met′ə bol′ik), *adj.* of, having to do with, or produced by metabolism: *The hormone was used to treat both hypothyroidism and metabolic insufficiency* (Science News Letter). —**met′a·bol′i·cal·ly,** *adv.*

me·tab·o·lim·e·ter (mə tab′ə lim′ə tər), *n.* a device used to measure a person's basal metabolism.

me·tab·o·lism (mə tab′ə liz əm), *n.* **1.** the processes of building up food into living matter and using living matter until it is broken down into simpler substances or waste matter, giving off energy: *Only living matter is able to carry on metabolism* (A.M. Winchester). **2.** metamorphosis of an insect. [< Greek *metabolḗ* change + English *-ism*]

me·tab·o·lite (mə tab′ə līt), *n.* a substance produced by metabolism.

me·tab·o·liz·a·ble (mə tab′ə lī′zə bəl), *adj.* that can be metabolized: *Each of these is supposed to consume at least 2,200 metabolizable kilocalories per day* (Scientific American).

me·tab·o·lize (mə tab′ə līz), *v.,* **-lized, -liz·ing.** —*v.t.* to alter by or subject to metabolism. —*v.i.* to function in or undergo metabolism: *Before the seed can metabolize, all the enzymes . . . must become active* (Science News).

met·a·car·pal (met′ə kär′pəl), *adj.* of or having to do with the metacarpus. —*n.* a bone of the metacarpus: *Five metacarpals support the palm of the hand* (Harbough and Goodrich).

met·a·car·pus (met′ə kär′pəs), *n., pl.* **-pi** (-pī). **1.** the part, especially the bones, of the hand between the wrist and the fingers, comprising five bones in man. **2.** the corresponding part of the forefoot of a quadruped. [< New Latin *metacarpus* < Greek *metakárpion* < *metá* after + *karpós* wrist]

met·a·cen·ter (met′ə sen′tər), *n.* the intersecting point of the vertical line passing through the center of buoyancy of a floating body, as a ship, when in perfect equilibrium, and the vertical line passing through the center of buoyancy when the floating body is out of equilibrium. The floating body is stable if this point is above the center of gravity, and lacks stability if it is below. [< French *métacentre* < *méta-* meta- + *centre* center]

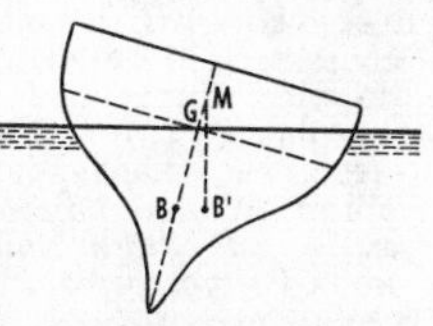

Metacenter, (M); G, center of gravity; B, center of buoyancy; B[1], center of buoyancy when ship is out of equilibrium

met·a·cen·tre (met′ə sen′tər), *n. Especially British.* metacenter.

met·a·cen·tric (met′ə sen′trik), *adj.* of or having to do with the metacenter.

met·a·chro·mat·ic (met′ə krō mat′ik), *adj.* **1.** of or having to do with metachromatism. **2.** *Anatomy.* assuming a different color from that of other tissues, when stained with a dye.

met·a·chro·ma·tism (met′ə krō′mə tiz-əm), *n.* change or variation of color, especially as a result of change of temperature or other physical condition.

met·a·chrome (met′ə krōm), *n.* a body or substance that changes color. [< *meta-* + Greek *chrôma* color]

met·a·cor·tan·dra·cin (met′ə kôr tan′drə sin), *n.* prednisone: *The drug is metacortandracin, . . . a relative of cortisone having fewer of its undesirable side effects* (Science News Letter).

met·a·cor·tan·dra·lone (met′ə kôr tan′drə lōn), *n.* prednisolone.

met·a·cy·mene (met′ə sī′mēn), *n.* one of three isomeric forms of cymene. [< *meta-* + *cymene*]

met·a·ga·lac·tic (met′ə gə lak′tik), *adj.* of or having to do with the metagalaxy.

met·a·gal·ax·y (met′ə gal′ək sē), *n., pl.* **-ax·ies.** the universe outside the Milky Way, including the whole system of external galaxies: *The metagalaxy . . . is essentially the measurable material universe* (New Scientist).

met·age (mē′tij), *n.* **1.** the official measurement of contents or weight. **2.** the charge for it. [< *met*(e)[1] + *-age*]

met·a·gen·e·sis (met′ə jen′ə sis), *n. Biology.* alternation of sexual and asexual generations supposed to occur in coelenterates.

met·a·ge·net·ic (met′ə jə net′ik), *adj.* having to do with, characterized by, or resulting from metagenesis.

me·tag·na·thism (mə tag′nə thiz əm), *n.* the condition of being metagnathous.

me·tag·na·thous (mə tag′nə thəs), *adj.* (of a bird) having the upper and lower tips of the mandibles crossed, as the crossbills. [< *meta-* + Greek *gnáthos* jaw + English *-ous*]

mé·tai·rie (mā te rē′), *n. French.* a farm or piece of land cultivated by a métayer.

met·al (met′əl), *n., adj., v.,* **-aled, -al·ing** or (*especially British*) **-alled, -al·ling.** —*n.* **1. a.** any of certain chemical elements, as iron, gold, silver, copper, lead, tin, and aluminum, typically characterized by high specific gravity, fusibility, malleability, conductivity for heat and electricity, opacity, and a characteristic, more or less identifying luster (known specifically as metallic): *Very few metals . . . exist in the earth's crust in metallic form* (Science News). **b.** any alloy or fused mixture of these, as bronze, brass, or pewter. **c.** the constituent matter of a metal or of metals collectively; metallic substance: *a mirror of polished metal.* **2.** *Chemistry.* any chemical element, or mixture of elements, that can form a salt by replacing the hydrogen of an acid. In the salt the metal takes on a positive charge. *The positive valency of metals, and the fact that they form positive ions in solution, indicate that the atoms of a metal will part readily with one or more of their outer electrons* (Sears and Zemansky). **3.** an object made of metal, as one of the rails of a railroad: *He had fallen from an engine, And been dragged along the metals* (William E. Henley). **4.** *Especially British.* broken stone, cinders, etc., used for roads or as ballast for roadbeds or railroad tracks; road metal. **5.** the melted material that becomes glass or pottery, or the glaze on pottery. **6. a.** basic stuff; material; substance: *the native metal of a man* (Lowell). *Cowards are not made of the same metal as heroes.* **b.** mettle. **7.** *Printing.* **a.** type metal. **b.** the state of being set or composed in type. **8.** the aggregate number, mass, or power of the guns of a warship. **9.** *Heraldry.* one of the three kinds of tincture (the other two being color and fur). The two heraldic metals are or (gold) and argent (silver).
—*adj.* made of metal: *Quonset huts are usually covered with metal sheeting.*
—*v.t.* to furnish, cover, or fit with metal.
[< Old French *metal,* learned borrowing from Latin *metallum* metal, mine < Greek *métallon* (originally) mine]

metal., metallurgy.

Metal Age, the prehistoric period when copper, bronze, and iron were used for making weapons and tools.

met·a·lan·guage (met′ə lang′gwij), *n.* any language used to analyze or make assertions about another language: *The language of metaphysics is the metalanguage of science* (New Scientist).

met·a·law (met′ə lô′), *n.* any system of law beyond the present human frame of reference: *Metalaw is the system for dealing with the beings we will encounter in our exploration of the vast beyond* (Science News Letter).

met·al·clad (met′əl klad′), *adj.* coated or plated with metal: *metalclad switchgear.*

metal fatigue, the cracking, disintegration, or other failure of a metal due to small but repeated stress, such as continuous vibration or tapping: *The explosions were attributed . . . to metal fatigue* (New York Times).

met·a·lin·guis·tic (met′ə ling gwis′tik), *adj.* of or having to do with metalinguistics; exolinguistic.

met·a·lin·guis·tics (met′ə ling gwis′tiks), *n.* a branch of linguistics that studies social, educational, and other cultural factors related to or involving language; exolinguistics.

met·al·ist (met′ə list), *n.* **1.** a worker in metals. **2.** a person skilled in the knowledge of metals.
met·al·i·za·tion (met′ə lə zā′shən), *n.* **1.** the act of metalizing. **2.** the state of being metalized.
met·al·ize (met′ə līz), *v.t.*, **-ized, -iz·ing.** **1.** to make metallic; give the appearance or other characteristics of metal to. **2.** to cover or treat with a metal or a compound containing a metal.
metall., metallurgy.
me·tal·lic (mə tal′ik), *adj.* **1.** of metal; containing metal; consisting of a metal or metals: *metallic reactions, metallic vaults.* **2.** like metal; characteristic of metal: *a beetle with a metallic luster.* **3.** resembling the sound produced when metal is struck: *The bird . . . broke into a gush of melody . . . rich, full, and metallic* (Henry Kingsley). **4.** *Chemistry.* having the form or outward characteristics of a metal (usually said of a metal when occurring uncombined with other substances): *metallic iron.* **—me·tal′li·cal·ly,** *adv.*
met·al·lif·er·ous (met′ə lif′ər əs), *adj.* containing or yielding metal: *metalliferous rocks, metalliferous mines.* [< Latin *metallifer* < *metallum* metal + *ferre* to bear + English *-ous*]
met·al·like (met′əl līk′), *adj.* like metal; suggesting metal; metallic.
met·al·line (met′ə lin, -līn), *adj.* **1.** metallic. **2.** containing one or more metals or metallic salts.
met·al·lise (met′ə līz), *v.t.*, **-lised, -lis·ing.** *Especially British.* metalize.
met·al·list (met′ə list), *n.* metalist.
met·al·lize (met′ə līz), *v.t.*, **-lized, -liz·ing.** metalize.
me·tal·lo·ge·net·ic (mə tal′ə jə net′ik), *adj.* producing metals: *The world's chief tin fields can be resolved into a few groups, which can be conveniently termed "metallogenetic tin provinces"* . . . (W.R. Jones).
me·tal·lo·graph (mə tal′ə graf′, -gräf′), *n.* a microscope for investigating the structure of metals and alloys: *The intricate composition of an alloy is studied by an Esso research technician who is peering into the viewer of a metallograph* (Science News Letter).
met·al·log·ra·pher (met′ə log′rə fər), *n.* a person skilled in metallography: *Metallographers use microscopes and X rays to explore the effects of heat on metal.*
me·tal·lo·graph·ic (mə tal′ə graf′ik), *adj.* of or having to do with metallography.
me·tal·lo·graph·i·cal (mə tal′ə graf′ə kəl), *adj.* metallographic.
met·al·log·ra·phy (met′ə log′rə fē), *n.* **1.** the study of metals and alloys with the aid of a microscope. **2.** *Rare.* an art or process allied to lithography, in which metal plates are used instead of stones. [< Greek *métallon* metal + *gráphein* draw, write]
met·al·loid (met′ə loid), *n. Chemistry.* **1.** an element having properties of both a metal and a nonmetal, as arsenic, antimony, or silicon. **2.** a nonmetal.
—*adj.* **1.** of or having to do with metalloids. **2.** of the nature of or like a metalloid. **3.** having the form or appearance of a metal.
me·tal·lo·phone (mə tal′ə fōn), *n.* **1.** a musical instrument similar to the xylophone but having metal bars in place of wooden ones: *a troupe of Balinese dancers, accompanied by their orchestra of gongs, gongchimes, metallophones and drums* (New York Times). **2.** a musical instrument similar to the piano but having metal bars rather than strings. [< Greek *métallon* metal + English *-phone*]
me·tal·lo·ther·a·py (mə tal′ō ther′ə pē), *n.* the use of metals, especially certain metallic salts, in the treatment of disease. [< Greek *métallon* metal + English *therapy*]
met·al·lur·gic (met′ə lėr′jik), *adj.* metallurgical.
met·al·lur·gi·cal (met′ə lėr′jə kəl), *adj.* of or having to do with metallurgy: *metallurgical coal, a metallurgical engineer.* **—met′al·lur′gi·cal·ly,** *adv.*
met·al·lur·gist (met′ə lėr′jist), *n.* a person who is trained in metallurgy.
met·al·lur·gy (met′ə lėr′jē), *n.* the science or art of working with metals. It includes the separation and refining of metals from their ores, the production of alloys, and the shaping and treatment of metals by heat, rolling, etc. *Metallurgy is very important in rocket building* (Science News). [< New Latin *metallurgia*, ultimately < Greek *métallon* metal + *érgon* work]
met·al·smith (met′əl smith′), *n.* a person skilled in metalworking.
met·al·ware (met′əl wãr′), *n.* articles or utensils made of metal.
met·al·work (met′əl wėrk′), *n.* **1.** things, especially artistic things, made out of metal. **2.** a making things out of metal.
met·al·work·er (met′əl wėr′kər), *n.* a person who makes things out of metal.
met·al·work·ing (met′əl wėr′king), *n.* the act or process of making things out of metal: *Unitron also has companion instruments for the metalworking industries* (Science).
met·a·math·e·mat·i·cal (met′ə math′ə mat′ə kəl), *adj.* of or having to do with metamathematics.
met·a·math·e·mat·ics (met′ə math′ə mat′iks), *n.* the branch of mathematics that deals with the logic and consistency of mathematical proof, formulas, equations, etc. [< German *Metamathematik*]
met·a·mer (met′ə mər), *n. Chemistry.* a compound that is metameric with another.
me·tam·er·al (mə tam′ər əl), *adj.* metameric.
met·a·mere (met′ə mir), *n.* any of a longitudinal series of more or less similar parts or segments composing the body of various animals, as the earthworm; somite. [< *meta-* + Greek *méros* part]
met·a·mer·ic (met′ə mer′ik), *adj.* **1.** *Chemistry.* (of compounds) having the same molecular weight and the same elements combined in the same proportion but with their radicals in different positions, and hence differing in structure and chemical properties. *Example:* $CH_3.CH_2.CH_2.CHO$, an aldehyde, and $CH_3.CH_2.CO.CH_3$, a ketone. **2.** *Zoology.* of or having to do with a metamere or metameres; segmental: *metameric segmentation.* **—met′a·mer′i·cal·ly,** *adv.*
me·tam·er·ism (mə tam′ə riz əm), *n.* **1.** *Zoology.* the condition of consisting of metameres: *Animals exhibiting metamerism are composed of a linear series of body segments* (A. Franklin Shull). **2.** segmentation into metameres, typically with some repetition of organs. **3.** *Chemistry.* the state of being metameric; isomerism.
met·a·mor·phic (met′ə môr′fik), *adj.* **1.** characterized by change of form; having to do with change of form; exhibiting metamorphosis. **2.** (of rocks) having undergone structural change; formed by metamorphism: *Metamorphic rocks . . . are classified on the basis of texture and composition* (World Book Encyclopedia).
met·a·mor·phism (met′ə môr′fiz əm), *n.* **1.** change of form; metamorphosis. **2.** change in the structure of a rock caused by pressure, heat, etc. **—Syn. 1.** transmutation.
met·a·mor·phose (met′ə môr′fōz, -fōs), *v.*, **-phosed, -phos·ing.** —*v.t.* **1.** to change in form; transform: *The witch metamorphosed people into animals.* **2.** to change the form or structure of by metamorphosis or metamorphism. —*v.i.* to undergo metamorphosis or metamorphism. **—Syn.** *v.t.* **1.** transmute.
met·a·mor·pho·sis (met′ə môr′fə sis), *n.*, *pl.* **-ses** (-sēz). **1.** a change of form, structure, or substance. **2.** any complete change in appearance, character, circumstances, etc.: *His visage . . . changed as from a mask to a face . . . I know not that I have ever seen in any other human face an equal metamorphosis* (Charlotte Brontë). **3.** a change in form, shape, or substance by or as if by witchcraft; transformation: *Metamorphosis is a favorite game in fairy tales: princes into swans, ogres into dragons, etc.* **4.** the changed form resulting from any such change. **5.** a marked change in the form, and usually the habits, of an animal in its development after the embryonic stage: *Tadpoles become frogs by metamorphosis; they lose their tails and grow legs. It is the process of losing the larval organs and gaining the missing adult organs which is called metamorphosis* (A. Franklin Shull). **6.** the structural or functional modification of a plant organ or structure during the course of its development. **7.** *Physiology.* metabolism. [< Latin *metamorphōsis* < Greek *metamórphōsis*, ultimately < *metá* (change) over + *morphḗ* form]

1 2 3 4

Metamorphosis (def. 5) of European swallowtail
1) Caterpillar prepares to change to chrysalis.
2) It sheds skin, exposing chrysalis.
3) Chrysalis is entirely exposed.
4) Adult emerges from chrysalis.

met·a·mor·phous (met′ə môr′fəs), *adj.* metamorphic.
met·a·neph·ric (met′ə nef′rik), *adj.* of or having to do with the metanephros.
met·a·neph·ros (met′ə nef′ros), *n.* the posterior division of the primitive renal organ or kidney of vertebrate embryos, the mesonephros and pronephros being the middle and anterior divisions, respectively. The adult kidney develops from the metanephros. [< Greek *metá* after, behind + *nephrós* kidney (because it develops after the pronephros and mesonephros)]
metaph., **1.** metaphor. **2.** metaphysics.
met·a·phase (met′ə fāz), *n.* the second stage in mitosis, characterized by the arrangement of the chromosomes along the central plane of the spindle: *In the metaphase . . . double chromosomes group together near the equator of the cell* (Fred W. Emerson). See picture under **mitosis.**
Met·a·phen (met′ə fen), *n. Trademark.* a preparation containing mercury and used in ointment form as an antiseptic for the eyes, skin, or mucous membranes and in solution or tincture as a disinfectant. *Formula:* $C_7H_5HgNO_3$
met·a·phlo·em (met′ə flō′em), *n. Botany.* the primary phloem which is formed from the procambium after the protophloem; the last primary phloem to be developed. [< *meta-* + *phloem*]
met·a·phor (met′ə fər, -fôr), *n.* an implied comparison between two different things; figure of speech in which a word or phrase that ordinarily means one thing is used of another thing in order to suggest a likeness between the two. *Examples:* "a copper sky," "a heart of stone."
mix metaphors, to confuse two or more metaphors in the same expression. *Example:* "He embarked early on the sea of public life, where he climbed at last to the very summit of success."
[< Old French *metaphore*, learned borrowing from Latin *metaphora* < Greek *metaphorá* a transfer, ultimately < *meta-* over, across + *phérein* to carry]
➔ **Metaphors** and **similes** both make comparisons, but in a *metaphor* the comparison is implied and in a *simile* it is indicated by *like* or *as.* "The sea of life" is a metaphor. "Life is like a sea" is a simile.
met·a·phor·ic (met′ə fôr′ik, -for′-), *adj.* metaphorical: *Metaphoric meat and drink Is to understand and think* (Jonathan Swift).
met·a·phor·i·cal (met′ə fôr′ə kəl, -for′-), *adj.* using metaphors; figurative. **—met′a·phor′i·cal·ly,** *adv.*
met·a·phor·ist (met′ə fər ist, -fôr′-), *n.* a person who coins or uses metaphors: *The metaphorists of high fashion made the whole thing sound startling* (Time).
met·a·phor·ize (met′ə fə rīz, -fôr′īz), *v.*, **-ized, -iz·ing.** —*v.i.* to use metaphor or metaphors; speak in or reason from metaphor. —*v.t.* **1.** to change metaphorically (into): . . . *dewdrops, metaphorized into pearls* (T. Twining). **2.** to ply with metaphors.
met·a·phos·phate (met′ə fos′fāt), *n.* a salt of metaphosphoric acid.
met·a·phos·phor·ic acid (met′ə fos fôr′ik, -for′-), an acid obtained by treating a phosphorous oxide with water and by other methods. It contains one molecule of water less than orthophosphoric acid. *Formula:* HPO_3
met·a·phrase (met′ə frāz), *n.*, *v.*, **-phrased, -phras·ing.** —*n.* a translation, especially a word-for-word translation as distinguished from a paraphrase. —*v.t.* **1.** to translate, especially word for word. **2.** to change the phrasing or literary form of. [< Greek *metáphrasis* < *meta-* + *phrázein* translate, explain; declare]
met·a·phrast (met′ə frast), *n.* a person who changes a composition into a different literary form, as prose into verse. [<

Greek *metaphrástēs* < *metaphrázein* translate]

met·a·phras·tic (met′ə fras′tik), *adj.* close or literal in translation.

met·a·phys·ic (met′ə fiz′ik), *n.* metaphysics. —*adj.* metaphysical: *He knew what's what, and that's as high As metaphysic wit can fly* (Samuel Butler).

met·a·phys·i·cal (met′ə fiz′ə kəl), *adj.* **1.** of metaphysics. **2.** highly abstract; hard to understand: *When the engineer struggles with Einstein's idea of time and space, technology becomes almost metaphysical* (Edward Weeks). **3.** philosophical; theoretical: *wars ... waged for points of metaphysical right* (Scott). **4.** concerned with abstract thought or subjects: *a metaphysical mind.* **5.** of or having to do with a group of English poets of the 1600's whose verse is characterized by abstruse conceits and the use of unexpected or elaborate imagery. The metaphysical poets included John Donne, Abraham Cowley, George Herbert, and Richard Crashaw. **6.** *Archaic.* supernatural: *metaphysical aid* (Shakespeare). **7.** *Archaic.* fanciful; imaginary. —**met′a·phys′i·cal·ly,** *adv.* —**Syn. 2.** abstruse.

met·a·phy·si·cian (met′ə fə zish′ən), *n.* a person skilled in or familiar with metaphysics: *It is a type of argument that was beloved by metaphysicians of an older generation* (Science News).

met·a·phys·i·cist (met′ə fiz′ə sist), *n.* a metaphysician.

met·a·phys·ics (met′ə fiz′iks), *n.* **1.** the branch of philosophy that tries to discover and explain reality and knowledge; the philosophical study of the real nature of the universe. Metaphysics includes epistemology (the theory of knowledge), ontology (the study of the nature of reality), and cosmology (the theory of the origin of the universe and its laws): *Youth is the time ... to circumnavigate the metaphysics* (Robert Louis Stevenson). **2.** the more abstruse or speculative divisions of philosophy, thought of as a unit. **3.** any process of reasoning thought of as abstruse or extremely subtle. [plural of earlier *metaphysic,* translation of Medieval Latin *metaphysica* < Medieval Greek (*tà*) *metaphysiká* for Greek *tà metà tà physiká* the (works) after the Physics (referring to the order of the works of Aristotle)]

met·a·pla·sia (met′ə plā′zhə), *n.* the direct formation of one type of adult tissue from another, as of bone from cartilage. [< New Latin *metaplasia* < Greek *metaplássein* transform; see METAPLASM]

met·a·plasm (met′ə plaz əm), *n.* **1.** carbohydrates, pigment, or other lifeless matter in the protoplasm of a cell. **2.** *Grammar.* the alteration of a word by addition, removal, or transposition of sounds or letters. [< Latin *metaplasmus* (rhetorical) transposition < Greek *metaplasmós* (grammatical) formation from a different stem < *metaplássein* transform < *meta-* over, changed + *plássein* mold]

met·a·plas·mic (met′ə plaz′mik), *adj.* **1.** of or having to do with the metaplasm of a cell. **2.** of or having to do with metaplasm of words.

met·a·po·di·us (met′ə pō′dē əs), *n., pl.* **-di·i** (-dē ī). a large carnivorous bug abundant in the southern United States and an important enemy of the cotton worm and the army worm. [< New Latin *Metapodius* the genus name < Greek *metá* after + *poús, podós* foot]

met·a·po·lit·i·cal (met′ə pə lit′ə kəl), *adj.* of or having to do with metapolitics.

met·a·pol·i·tics (met′ə pol′ə tiks), *n.* the study of political science on a philosophical level.

met·a·pro·tein (met′ə prō′tēn, -tē in), *n.* any of a group of products of the hydrolytic decomposition (resulting from the action of acids or alkalis) of proteins. Metaproteins are insoluble in water but soluble in acids or alkalis. [< *meta-* + *protein*]

met·a·psy·chics (met′ə sī′kiks), *n.* parapsychology.

met·a·psy·cho·log·i·cal (met′ə sī′kə loj′ə-kəl), *adj.* of or having to do with metapsychology.

met·a·psy·chol·o·gy (met′ə sī kol′ə jē), *n.* a systematic or philosophic speculation on the origin, structure, function, etc., of the mind, and on the connection between mental and physical responses or actions.

me·ta·psy·cho·sis (met′ə sī kō′sis), *n.* communication between minds without any known physical intermediary.

met·a·schiz·o·the·ri·um (met′ə skiz′ō-thir′ē əm), *n.* a large extinct mammal related to the rhinoceros, having five toes on each foot and teeth like those of hooved mammals. [< New Latin *Metaschizotherium* the genus name < Greek *meta-* + *schízein* to split + *thērion* wild animal (because of the form of the feet)]

met·a·so·mat·ic (met′ə sō mat′ik), *adj.* having to do with or resulting from metasomatism.

met·a·so·ma·tism (met′ə sō′mə tiz əm), *n.* the process by which the chemical constitution of a rock is changed, as of limestone into granite. [< *meta-* + Greek *sôma, sómatos* body + English *-ism*]

met·a·so·ma·to·sis (met′ə sō′mə tō′sis), *n.* metasomatism.

met·a·sta·bil·i·ty (met′ə stə bil′ə tē), *n.* the quality or condition of being metastable: *The scientists sought stability then, not mere metastability, not the top-heavy balancing rock on which we all breathlessly sit* (Scientific American).

met·a·sta·ble (met′ə stā′bəl), *adj.* of or having to do with a state intermediate between stability and instability, as when an excited atom requires further stimulation or an interval of time before emitting its radiation and returning to its normal state: *a world-wide metastable equilibrium of uncertain permanency* (Bulletin of Atomic Scientists). [< *meta-* + *stable*[2]]

me·tas·ta·sis (mə tas′tə sis), *n., pl.* **-ses** (-sēz). **1.** the rapid transference, as through the blood vessels or the lymphatics, or by contact, of a function, pain, or disease from one organ or part to another, especially of diseased cells, as in cancer. **2.** transformation, as in radioactive disintegration when an alpha particle is emitted. See picture under **disintegration. 3.** metabolism. **4.** *Rhetoric.* a rapid transition, as from one subject to another. [< Late Latin *metastasis* < Greek *metástasis* removal < *methistánai* to remove, change < *meta-* changed, over + *histánai* place]

me·tas·ta·sise (mə tas′tə sīz), *v.i.,* **-sised, -sis·ing.** *Especially British.* metastasize.

me·tas·ta·size (mə tas′tə sīz), *v.i.,* **-sized, -siz·ing.** (of a function, pain, or disease) to pass from one part or organ to another; undergo metastasis: *Cancer cells metastasize, or spread, through the body* (World Book Encyclopedia).

met·a·stat·ic (met′ə stat′ik), *adj.* of, having to do with, or characterized by metastasis.

met·a·tar·sal (met′ə tär′səl), *adj.* of or having to do with the metatarsus: *metatarsal bones.* —*n.* a bone of the metatarsus.

met·a·tar·sus (met′ə tär′səs), *n., pl.* **-si** (-sī). **1.** the part, especially the bones, of the foot between the ankle and the toes, comprising five bones in man. **2.** the corresponding part of the hind foot of a quadruped. **3.** a leg bone of a bird, consisting of both tarsal and metatarsal elements, extending from the tibia to the phalanges. **4.** the most basal segment of an insect's tarsus when strongly differentiated from the following segments. [< New Latin *metatarsus* < Greek *meta-* after + *tarsós* tarsal (bones), flat (of the foot)]

me·ta·te (mā tä′tā), *n.* a stone with a flat or concave upper surface, and sometimes with legs beneath, on which corn or the like is ground by hand by means of a smaller stone, used in Mexico and the southwestern United States: *A basalt metate was found in the hearth* (Science). [< Mexican Spanish *metate* < Nahuatl *metatl*]

me·tath·e·sis (mə tath′ə sis), *n., pl.* **-ses** (-sēz). **1.** the transposition of sounds, syllables, or letters in a word, as in English *bird,* Old English *bridd: By inversion of sounds, called "metathesis", many speakers change apron to apern* (Scientific American). **2.** the interchange of atoms between two molecules; double decomposition. Metathesis occurs when two compounds react with each other to form two other compounds. **3.** a change or reversal of condition. [earlier, (grammatical) interchange < Late Latin *metathesis* < Greek *metáthesis* transposition < *metatithénai* to transpose < *meta-* changed, over + *tithénai* to set] —**Syn. 3.** transposition.

met·a·thet·ic (met′ə thet′ik), *adj.* of the nature of or containing metathesis.

met·a·thet·i·cal (met′ə thet′ə kəl), *adj.* metathetic.

met·a·tho·rac·ic (met′ə thô ras′ik, -thō-), *adj.* of or having to do with the metathorax of an insect: *The flies ... each have a pair of clubbed threads ... in place of the metathoracic wings* (Hegner and Stiles).

met·a·tho·rax (met′ə thôr′aks, -thōr′-), *n., pl.* **-rax·es, -ra·ces** (-rə sēz). the posterior of the three segments of the thorax of an insect, bearing the third pair of legs and the second pair of wings.

met·a·tor·ber·nite (met′ə tôr′bər nīt), *n.* an altered form of torbernite that serves as an uranium ore.

met·a·xy·lem (met′ə zī′ləm), *n. Botany.* the primary xylem that is formed from the procambium after the protoxylem; last primary xylem to be developed: *When elongation has ceased, metaxylem ... is formed* (Fred W. Emerson).

met·a·xy·lene (met′ə zī′lēn), *n.* one of three isomeric forms of xylene.

mé·tay·age (me tā′yäzh, *French* mā te-yȧzh′), *n.* the métayer system of agriculture. [< French *métayage*]

mé·tay·er (me tā′ər; *French* mā te yā′), *n.* a farmer who cultivates land for a share of the produce, usually a half, the owner furnishing the stock, seed, tools, etc. [< French *métayer* < Medieval Latin *medietasius* < Latin *medietās* half]

met·a·zo·a (met′ə zō′ə), *n., pl. of* **metazoon.**

met·a·zo·al (met′ə zō′əl), *adj.* metazoan.

met·a·zo·an (met′ə zō′ən), *n.* any of a large division of animals, comprising all animals except the protozoans (or animal-like protistans), having the body made up of many cells arranged in tissues, developing from a single cell. —*adj.* belonging or having to do with the metazoans. [< New Latin *Metazoa* (ultimately < Greek *meta-* after + *zôia,* neuter plural of *zôion* animal) + English *-an*]

met·a·zo·ic (met′ə zō′ik), *adj.* metazoan.

met·a·zo·on (met′ə zō′on, -ən), *n., pl.* **-zo·a** (-zō′ə). metazoan.

mete[1] (mēt), *v.t.,* **met·ed met·ing. 1.** to give to each a share of; distribute; allot: *The judge will mete out praise and blame. Chance has meted you a measure of happiness* (Charlotte Brontë). **2.** *Poetic.* to measure. [Old English *metan*] —**Syn. 1.** apportion.

mete[2] (mēt), *n.* **1.** a boundary. **2.** a boundary stone. [< Old French *mete* < Latin *meta* boundary (mark) or limit] —**Syn. 1.** limit.

met·em·pir·ic (met′em pir′ik), *n.* **1.** metempirics. **2.** a supporter of the metempirical philosophy. —*adj.* metempirical.

met·em·pir·i·cal (met′em pir′ə kəl), *adj.* **1.** beyond, or outside of, the field of experience: *If then the Empirical designates the province we include within the range of Science, the province we exclude may fitly be styled the metempirical* (George H. Lewes). **2.** of or having to do with metempirics.

met·em·pir·i·cism (met′em pir′ə siz əm), *n.* metempirical philosophy.

met·em·pir·ics (met′em pir′iks), *n.* a branch of philosophy closely related to the transcendentalism of Immanuel Kant, Johann Fichte, and Georg Hegel, concerned with things outside the field of experience, but not beyond human knowledge. [< *met-* + *empir*(ic) + *-ics*]

met·em·psy·chic (met′əm sī′kik), *adj.* of or having to do with metempsychosis.

met·em·psy·cho·sis (met′əm sī kō′sis, mə-temp′sə-), *n., pl.* **-ses** (-sēz). the passing of the soul at death from one body into another body; transmigration of the soul. Some Oriental philosophies teach that by metempsychosis a person's soul lives again in an animal's body. The belief in metempsychosis is a characterizing feature of most animistic religions, and has reached a high degree of sophistication in Buddhism and Hinduism. [< Latin *metempsȳchōsis* < Greek *metempsȳchōsis* < *meta-* over, changed + *en-* in + *psȳchōsis* a livening < *psȳchē* soul]

met·en·ce·phal·ic (met′en sə fal′ik), *adj.* of or having to do with the metencephalon.

met·en·ceph·a·lon (met′en sef′ə lon), *n., pl.* **-la** (-lə). a section of the brain of the vertebrate embryo, the anterior part of the rhombencephalon, from which the cerebellum develops. [< *met-* + *encephalon*]

me·te·or (mē′tē ər), *n.* **1.** a mass of stone or metal that enters the earth's atmosphere from outer space with enormous speed; shooting star. Meteors become so hot from rushing through the air that they glow and often vaporize completely. A trail of hot gas forms in the meteor's wake. **2.** *Obsolete.* any atmospheric phenomenon, as winds, rain, a rainbow, or lightning: *In starry flake, and pellicle, All day the hoary meteor [snow] fell* (John Greenleaf Whittier). [< Late Latin *meteōrum* < Greek *meteōron* (thing) in the air < *meta-* up + *aeírein* lift]

meteor., meteorology.

me·te·or·ic (mē′tē ôr′ik, -or′-), *adj.* **1.** of, having to do with, or consisting of a meteor or meteors: *a meteoric shower.* **2.** flashing like a meteor; brilliant and soon ended; swift: *a man's meteoric rise to fame.* **3.** of the atmosphere; meteorological: *Wind and rain are meteoric phenomena.* —**me′te·or′i·cal·ly,** *adv.* —**Syn. 2.** dazzling.

meteoric shower, a meteor shower: *When the earth encounters a swarm of meteors, a meteoric shower ensues* (Robert H. Baker).

me·te·or·ite (mē′tē ə rīt), *n.* **1.** a mass of stone or metal that has reached the earth from outer space without being vaporized; fallen meteor: *Meteorites are deceptive because some are predominantly iron while others are largely stone* (Hubert J. Bernhard). **2.** a meteor or meteoroid.

Meteorite (def. 1)

me·te·or·it·ic (mē′tē ə rit′ik), *adj.* of or having to do with a meteorite or meteorites.

me·te·or·it·i·cist (mē′tē ə rit′ə sist), *n.* a person who studies meteorites, their structure, frequency, etc.

me·te·or·o·graph (mē′tē ər ə graf, -gräf; mē′tē ôr′-, -or′-), *n.* an instrument for automatically recording various meteorological conditions, as barometric pressure, temperature, and humidity, at the same time, especially one carried aloft by a balloon or airplane; aerograph.

me·te·or·oid (mē′tē ə roid), *n.* any of the many small bodies, believed often to be the remains of disintegrated comets, that travel through space and become meteors or shooting stars when they encounter the earth's atmosphere.

meteorol., meteorology.

me·te·or·o·lite (mē′tē ər ə līt), *n.* a meteorite.

me·te·or·o·log·ic (mē′tē ər ə loj′ik), *adj.* meteorological.

me·te·or·o·log·i·cal (mē′tē ər ə loj′ə kəl), *adj.* **1.** of or having to do with the atmosphere, atmospheric phenomena, or weather. **2.** of or having to do with meteorology.

COLD FRONT
WARM FRONT
STATIONARY FRONT
OCCLUDED FRONT
CLEAR
PARTLY CLOUDY
CLOUDY
HAZE
WIND N 22 MPH
SW 10 MPH
NE 28 MPH
S 5 MPH
RAIN
HEAVY RAIN
SNOW
THUNDERSTORM WITH LIGHTNING

Examples of Meteorological Symbols

me·te·or·o·log·i·cal·ly (mē′tē ər ə loj′ə klē), *adv.* in meteorological respects; by meteorology; according to meteorology.

me·te·or·ol·o·gist (mē′tē ə rol′ə jist), *n.* a person trained in meteorology.

me·te·or·ol·o·gy (mē′tē ə rol′ə jē), *n.* **1.** the science (a branch of geophysics) that treats of the atmosphere and atmospheric conditions or phenomena, especially as they relate to weather. **2.** meteorological condition; atmosphere, atmospheric phenomena, or weather: *Little can be said about the meteorology of deserts* (Science News). [< Greek *meteōrologiā* < *meteōron* (thing) in the air + *-logos* treating of]

me·te·or·ous (mē′tē ər əs), *adj.* meteoric: *a meteorous refulgence.*

meteor shower, a large number of meteors entering and burning up in the earth's atmosphere, occurring when the earth encounters a meteor swarm or a comet: *Meteor showers begin in earnest in mid-July* (New York Times).

meteor swarm, a large group of meteors that orbit together about the sun, considered to be the remains of a disintegrated comet.

me·ter[1] (mē′tər), *n.* **1.** the basic unit of length in the metric system, equal to 39.37 inches. It was intended to be, and very nearly is, equal to one ten-millionth of the distance from the equator to either pole measured on a meridian, but actually is equal to 1,650,763.73 wave-lengths of the orange-red light from the isotope Krypton-86. This standard was adopted in 1960. *Abbr.:* m. **2. a.** any kind of poetic rhythm; the arrangement of beats or accents in a line of poetry: *The meter of "Jack and Jill went up the hill" is not the meter of "One, two, buckle my shoe."* **b.** a specific kind of rhythm in verse, depending on the kind and number of feet of which the verse consists: *iambic meter, dactylic meter.* **c.** (in English hymns) the rhythmical pattern of a stanza or strophe, determined by the kind and number of lines: *short meter, long meter, common meter.* **3.** *Music.* **a.** the arrangement of beats in music; musical rhythm; rhythmic impulses as divided into parts or measures of a uniform length of time, based upon the pattern of strong and weak beats. **b.** any such division measured in number of beats: *Three-fourths meter is waltz time.* Also, *especially British,* **metre.** [(definition 1) < French *mètre,* learned borrowing from Latin *metrum* measure < Greek *métron* measure; (definitions 2,3) < Old French *metre,* learned borrowing from Latin *metrum* measure]

me·ter[2] (mē′tər), *n.* **1.** a device for measuring. **2.** a device for measuring and recording the amount of gas, water, electricity, etc., used. **3.** a person who measures, especially one whose duty or office is to see that commodities are of the proper measure. —*v.t., v.i.* to measure or record with a meter. [< *met*(e)[1] + *-er*[1]; probably influenced by *-meter*]

Electric Meter[2] (def. 2)

➔ **meter, metre.** *Meter* is the preferred spelling of this word in both U.S. and British use.

-meter, *combining form.* **1.** a device for measuring ——: *Speedometer = a device for measuring speed.*
2. meter (39.37 inches): *Kilometer = one thousand meters. Millimeter = one thousandth of a meter.*
3. having —— metrical feet: *Tetrameter = having four metrical feet.*
[< New Latin *-metrum* < Greek *métron* a measure]

me·ter·age (mē′tər ij), *n.* **1.** the act of measuring. **2.** the measurement itself. **3.** the price paid for measurement.

me·tered mail (mē′tərd), mail that has the amount to be paid for postage stamped on it by a machine. The post office controls the machines and collects the amounts from the senders. *Metered mail, already postmarked, requires less handling in the postoffice* (New Yorker).

me·ter-kil·o·gram-sec·ond (mē′tər kil′ə-gram sek′ənd), *adj.* having to do with a system of measurement in which the meter is the unit of length, the kilogram is the unit of mass, and the second is the unit of time.

meter maid, *U.S.* a woman assigned to enforce parking meter regulations.

mete·wand (mēt′wänd′), *n. Archaic.* a measuring stick or yardstick.

mete·yard (mēt′yärd′), *n.* a metewand.

meth (meth), *n. Informal.* methamphetamine.

Meth., Methodist.

meth·ac·ry·late (me thak′rə lāt), *n.* a salt or ester of methacrylic acid.

meth·a·cryl·ic acid (meth′ə kril′ik), a colorless liquid obtained artificially. Its esters are used in the manufacture of plastics. *Formula:* $C_4H_6O_2$ [< *meth*(yl) + *acrylic*]

meth·a·don (meth′ə don), *n.* methadone.

meth·a·done (meth′ə dōn), *n.* a synthetic narcotic used to relieve pain: *The Army is finding methadone a satisfactory substitute for morphine* (Newsweek). *Formula:* $C_{21}H_{27}NO.HCl$ [< (di)*meth*(yl)*a*(mino) + *d*(i-phenyl) + (heptan)*one*]

met·hae·mo·glo·bin (met hē′mə glō′bin, -hem′ə-; me thē′-), *n.* methemoglobin.

meth·am·phet·a·mine (meth′am fet′ə-mēn, -min), *n.* a drug used to combat fatigue, mental depression, etc.; Methedrine. *Formula:* $C_{10}H_{15}N.HCl$ [< *meth*(yl) + *amphetamine*]

meth·ane (meth′ān), *n.* a colorless, odorless, inflammable gas, the simplest of the hydrocarbons, and commercially important as a fuel. Methane is formed naturally by the decomposition of plant or other organic matter, as in marshes, petroleum wells, volcanoes, and coal mines, and artificially by various means. It is the principal constituent of natural gas and (in coal mines) of firedamp. *Formula:* CH_4 [< *meth*(yl) + *-ane*]

methane series, a homologous series of saturated, open-chain (aliphatic) hydrocarbons, with the group formula C_nH_{2n+2} (*n* standing for the number of carbon atoms in the molecule); alkanes. The methane series includes a larger number of known compounds than any other chain series, many of which, as methane, ethane, butane, and propane, are commercially important.

meth·a·nol (meth′ə nōl, -nol), *n.* methyl alcohol: *The nonpermanent type of antifreeze is synthetic methanol, or "wood alcohol"* (Wall Street Journal). *Formula:* CH_3OH

meth·an·the·line (mə than′thə lēn), *n.* a white, nearly odorless powder with a very bitter taste, used to inhibit cholinergic and secretory action in the treatment of various conditions; Banthine. *Formula:* $C_{21}H_{26}BrNO_3$

Meth·e·drine (meth′ə drin, -drēn), *n. Trademark.* methamphetamine.

me·theg·lin (mə theg′lin), *n.* an alcoholic drink made from fermented honey and water; a kind of mead, originally a spiced kind made in Wales. [< Welsh *meddyglyn* < *meddyg-* healing (< Latin *medicus;* see MEDIC) + *llyn* liquor]

met·he·mo·glo·bin (met hē′mə glō′bin, -hem′ə-; me thē′-), *n.* a brownish substance formed in the blood when the hematin of oxyhemoglobin is oxidized, either by spontaneous decomposition of the blood or by the action of an oxidizing agent, as potassium chlorate. [< German *Methemoglobin* < Greek *meth-,* variant of *meta-* meta- + New Latin *haemoglobin* hemoglobin]

met·he·mo·glo·bi·ne·mi·a (met hē′mə-glō′bə nē′mē ə), *n.* the presence of methemoglobin in the blood: *Dr. Singley knew that he was dealing with methemoglobinemia, in which poisoned red cells carry no oxygen, and other cells cannot deliver enough, to the tissues* (Time). [< *methemoglobin* + *-emia*]

me·the·na·min (me thē′nə min), *n.* methenamine.

me·the·na·mine (me thē′nə mēn, -min), *n.* a colorless or white, crystalline substance produced from ammonia and formaldehyde, used as a urinary antiseptic, chemical agent, in making plastics, explosives, etc. *Formula:* $C_6H_{12}N_4$ [< *methen*(e) (< *methyl* + *-ene*) + *amine*]

meth·er (meᴛʜ′ər), *n.* a square wooden drinking vessel, formerly in common use in Ireland. [< Irish *meadar*]

me·thinks (mi thingks′), *v., past tense* **me·thought.** *Archaic.* it seems to me: *The lady doth protest too much, methinks* (Shakespeare). [Old English *mē thyncth* it seems to me]

me·thi·o·nine (me thī′ə nēn, -nin), *n.* an amino acid containing sulfur, indispensable to human life, occurring in various proteins, as in casein, yeast, and egg whites: *Methionine is one of the eight essential amino acids* (Science News Letter). *Formula:* $C_5H_{11}NO_2S$ [< *met-* + Greek *theîon* sulfur + *-ine*[2]]

meth·od (meth′əd), *n.* **1.** a way of doing something, especially according to a defined plan: *a method of teaching music. Roasting is one method of cooking meat.* **2.** the habit of acting according to plan and order; system in doing things; order in thinking: *If you used more method, you wouldn't waste so much time.*
method in one's madness, system and sense in apparent folly: *There was method in Portia's madness when she disguised herself as a doctor of law in "The Merchant of Venice."*
[< Latin *methodus* < Greek *méthodos* (originally) pursuit, following after < *meta-* after + *hodós* a traveling, road, way]
—**Syn. 1.** mode, manner. See **way.**

Meth·od (meth′əd), *n.* **the,** the Stanislavsky method: *The Actors' Studio . . . is generally thought of as the home of the Method* (Lillian Ross).

me·thod·ic (mə thod′ik), *adj.* methodical.

me·thod·i·cal (mə thod′ə kəl), *adj.* **1.** according to a method; systematic; orderly: *a methodical campaign.* **2.** acting with method or order: *a methodical person.* —**me-**

thod′i·cal·ly, *adv.* —**me·thod′i·cal·ness,** *n.* —**Syn. 1.** See **orderly.**

meth·od·ism (meth′ə diz əm), *n.* adherence to a fixed method or methods.

Meth·od·ism (meth′ə diz əm), *n.* the doctrine, organization, and manner of worship of the Methodist Church.

meth·od·ist (meth′ə dist), *n.* a person who attaches great importance to method.

Meth·od·ist (meth′ə dist), *n.* a member of a church that had its origin in the teachings and work of John Wesley; adherent of Methodism; Wesleyan. —*adj.* of or having to do with the Methodists or Methodism.

Meth·od·is·tic (meth′ə dis′tik), *adj.* of, like, or suggestive of the Methodists.

Meth·od·is·ti·cal (meth′ə dis′tə kəl), *adj.* Methodistic.

meth·od·ize (meth′ə dīz), *v.t.,* **-ized, -iz·ing.** to reduce to a method; arrange with method: *I endeavored to arrange and methodize my ideas on the subject.* —**meth′od·iz′er,** *n.* —**Syn.** organize.

meth·od·less (meth′əd lis), *adj.* lacking method, order, or regularity.

meth·od·o·log·i·cal (meth′ə də loj′ə kəl), *adj.* of or having to do with methodology: *methodological tools, methodological questions.* —**meth′od·o·log′i·cal·ly,** *adv.*

meth·od·ol·o·gist (meth′ə dol′ə jist), *n.* a person who deals with or is trained in methodology.

meth·od·ol·o·gy (meth′ə dol′ə jē), *n., pl.* **-gies. 1.** the science of method. **2.** the system of methods or procedures used in any field: *the methodology of the modern historian.* **3.** a branch of logic dealing with the application of the principles of that science in the production of knowledge. **4.** the methods of teaching; the branch of education dealing with the means and ways of instruction. [< New Latin *methodologia* < Greek *méthodos* method + *-logiā* science, system, treatment < *légein* speak]

meth·o·trex·ate (meth′ə trek′sāt), *n.* amethopterin: *methotrexate, a drug widely used to treat human leukemia* (Science News Letter).

me·thought (mi thôt′), *v.* the past tense of **methinks.**

meth·ox·sal·en (me thok′sə lən), *n.* Meloxine.

meth·ox·y·chlor (me thok′sə klôr, -klōr), *n.* a chlorinated hydrocarbon insecticide less toxic than DDT. *Formula:* $C_{16}H_{15}Cl_3O_2$

Me·thu·se·lah (mə thü′zə lə), *n.* **1.** (in the Bible) a son of Enoch, said to have lived 969 years, the longest life span attributed to anyone in the Bible. Genesis 5:27. **2.** a very old man. **3.** Also, **methuselah.** a champagne bottle holding 208 ounces, equivalent to eight standard bottles.

meth·yl (meth′əl), *n.* a univalent hydrocarbon radical, occurring in methane, members of the methane series, and many other organic compounds. *Formula:* $-CH_3$ [< French *méthyle,* back formation < *méthylène* methylene]

methyl acetate, a fragrant, colorless, inflammable, volatile liquid obtained by the action of sulfuric acid on methyl alcohol and acetic acid in the presence of heat, used as a solvent, in making perfumes, and as a flavoring agent. *Formula:* $C_3H_6O_2$

meth·yl·al (meth′ə lal′, meth′ə lal), *n.* a volatile, inflammable liquid having a pleasant, ethereal odor. It is used in artificial resins, for extracting odors in making perfume, and in certain chemical tests. *Formula:* $C_3H_8O_2$ [< *methyl* + *al*(cohol)]

methyl alcohol, a colorless, volatile, inflammable, poisonous liquid made by the distillation of wood or by the combination of carbon monoxide and hydrogen in the presence of a catalyst, used in making formaldehyde, in organic synthesis, as a solvent, as a fuel, etc.; methanol; wood alcohol: *Methyl alcohol is sometimes used as a rubbing compound* (Science News Letter). *Formula:* CH_3OH

meth·yl·am·in (meth′ə lam′in), *n.* methylamine.

meth·yl·a·mine (meth′ə lə mēn′, -lam′in), *n.* a colorless, inflammable, gaseous compound with an odor like that of ammonia. It is formed by the combination of methanol and ammonia in the presence of a catalyst, and is used in organic synthesis, in tanning, dyeing, etc. *Formula:* CH_3NH_2 [< *methyl* + *amine*]

meth·yl·ate (meth′ə lāt), *n., v.,* **-at·ed, -at·ing.** —*n.* a compound derived from methyl alcohol by substituting a metal for the hydrogen of the hydroxyl group. —*v.t.* **1.** to add the radical methyl ($-CH_3$) to. **2.** to mix or saturate with methyl alcohol.

meth·yl·at·ed spirit (meth′ə lā′tid), ordinary (ethyl) alcohol mixed with methyl alcohol so as to render it unfit for drinking.

meth·yl·a·tion (meth′ə lā′shən), *n.* the substitution of the radical methyl ($-CH_3$) for an atom of hydrogen.

meth·yl·ben·zene (meth′əl ben′zēn, -ben·zēn′), *n.* toluene.

methyl bromide, a colorless liquid produced from methyl alcohol and bromine, used to extinguish fires and to fumigate grain, fruit, etc.: *Fumigants such as methyl bromide are being tested now* (Scientific American). *Formula:* CH_3Br

methyl cellulose, a white substance prepared from wood pulp or cotton, used as a thickening agent, laxative, adhesive, etc.

methyl chloride, a colorless liquefiable gas produced from hydrochloric acid and methyl alcohol, used as a refrigerant, anesthetic, solvent, etc.: *Methyl chloride is used to produce butyl rubber* (Wall Street Journal). *Formula:* CH_3Cl

meth·yl·chol·an·threne (meth′əl kə lan′thrēn), *n.* a chemical used experimentally to produce cancer in animals. *Formula:* $C_{21}H_{16}$

meth·yl·ene (meth′ə lēn), *n.* **1.** *Chemistry.* a bivalent hydrocarbon radical occurring only in combination, and regarded as derived from methane. *Formula:* $-CH_2-$ **2.** (in commercial use) methyl alcohol. [< French *méthylène* < Greek *méthy* wine + *hŷlē* wood, substance + French *-ène* -ene]

methylene blue, a dark-green, crystalline compound used as a dye, as a stain in bacteriology, in medicine as an antidote for cyanide poisoning, and in the treatment of various diseases: *The methylene blue test on a milk sample measures one type of bacterial activity* (Science News). *Formula:* $C_{16}H_{18}ClN_3S.3H_2O$

me·thyl·ic (mə thil′ik), *adj. Chemistry.* containing, relating to, or derived from the radical methyl ($-CH_3$).

methyl methacrylate, a tough, transparent plastic obtained by the polymerization of the methyl ester of methacrylic acid. It is sold under various trade names, such as Plexiglas and Lucite.

meth·yl·naph·tha·lene (meth′əl naf′thə·lēn, -nap′-), *n.* a compound obtained from coal tar, used (in the liquid alpha form) in ascertaining the cetane number of a fuel. *Formula:* $C_{11}H_{10}$

meth·y·lo·sis (meth′ə lō′sis), *n. Geology.* that variety of metamorphism which involves change of chemical substance. [< New Latin *methylosis* < Greek *meta-* change + *hŷlē* wood, substance + *osis* condition]

meth·yl·pen·ty·nol (meth′əl pen′tə nol), *n.* a drug used as a sedative and hypnotic during childbirth, dental operations, etc.: *Women in childbirth feel "pleasantly carefree" . . . when they are given a new drug, methylpentynol* (Newsweek). *Formula:* $C_6H_{10}O$

meth·yl·pred·nis·o·lone (meth′əl pred·nis′ə lōn), *n.* a drug having uses similar to those of cortisone, such as the treatment of inflammations, asthma, and allergies. *Formula:* $C_{22}H_{30}O_5$

methyl salicylate, wintergreen oil, either obtained from the leaves and bark of certain plants or prepared synthetically. It is used in perfumes, as a food flavoring, and medicinally in liniments. *A case of methyl salicylate poisoning in an eight-month-old girl* (New Yorker). *Formula:* $C_8H_8O_3$

methyl styrene, or **meth·yl·sty·rene** (meth′əl stī′rēn, -stir′ēn), *n.* a monomer used in the production of various polymers, such as heat-resistant plastics. *Formula:* C_9H_{10}

meth·yl·tes·tos·ter·one (meth′əl tes tos′·tə rōn), *n.* a synthetic male sex hormone used in the treatment of glandular deficiency, breast cancer, disorders of the uterus, etc. *Formula:* $C_{20}H_{30}O_2$

met·ic (met′ik), *n.* a resident alien in an ancient Greek city, having some of the privileges of citizenship: *A metic, or foreigner, could not be naturalized as an Athenian citizen, nor could his children become citizens* (William F. McDonald). [< Late Latin *metycus* < Greek *metoikos* < *metá* meta- + *oîkos* dwelling]

Met·i·cor·te·lone (met′ə kôr′tə lōn), *n. Trademark.* prednisolone.

Met·i·cor·ten (met′ə kôr′tən), *n. Trademark.* prednisone: *Meticorten, taken by mouth, is remarkably effective in curing stubborn ringworm of the scalp* (Newsweek).

me·tic·u·los·i·ty (mə tik′yə los′ə tē), *n. pl.* **-ties.** the quality of being meticulous.

me·tic·u·lous (mə tik′yə ləs), *adj.* extremely or excessively careful about minute details: *He had throughout been almost worryingly meticulous in his business formalities* (Arnold Bennett). [earlier, fearful < Latin *meticulōsus* < *metus, -ūs* fear] —**me·tic′u·lous·ly,** *adv.* —**Syn.** scrupulous.

me·tic·u·lous·ness (mə tik′yə ləs nis), *n.* extreme care about minute details; scrupulousness: *Only the auditor's meticulousness uncovered the embezzling teller.*

mé·tier (mā tyā′), *n.* **1.** a trade; profession. **2.** a kind of work for which a person has special ability: *a Yale boy who's finally found his métier* (New Yorker). [< French *métier* < Old French *mestier* < earlier *menestier* < Latin *ministerium.* Doublet of MINISTRY.] —**Syn. 2.** specialty.

mé·tis (mā tēs′), *n.* **1.** a person of mixed descent: *There was distinct advantage in being a métis—the offspring of a foreigner and a Vietnamese* (Time). **2.** *U.S.* an octoroon. **3.** (in Canada) a person of white (especially French) and Indian descent. [< French *métis* < Old French *mestiz* < Late Latin *mixtīcius;* see MESTIZO]

mé·tisse (mā tēs′), *n.* a female métis. [< French *métisse*]

METO (no periods), Middle East Treaty Organization.

me·toe·cious (me tē′shəs), *adj. Botany.* heteroecious. [< *met-* change + Greek *oîkos* house + English *-ous*]

me·toe·cism (me tē′siz əm), *n. Botany.* heteroecism.

Me·tol (mē′tōl, -tol), *n. Trademark.* a soluble, whitish powder, much used as the base for photographic developers. *Formula:* $C_{14}H_{20}N_2O_6S$

meton., metonymy.

Me·ton·ic (mi ton′ik), *adj.* of or having to do with Meton, an Athenian astronomer of the 400's B.C.

Metonic cycle, a cycle of 19 years or 235 lunar months, after which the phases of the moon recur on the same days of the calendar as in the previous cycle.

met·o·nym (met′ə nim), *n.* a word used in a transferred sense. [see METONYMY]

met·o·nym·ic (met′ə nim′ik), *adj.* metonymical.

met·o·nym·i·cal (met′ə nim′ə kəl), *adj.* having to do with or involving metonymy. —**met′o·nym′i·cal·ly,** *adv.*

me·ton·y·my (mə ton′ə mē), *n.* a figure of speech that consists in using the name of one thing for that of another that it naturally suggests. *Example:* The *pen* (power of literature) is mightier than the *sword* (force). [< Late Latin *metōnymia* < Greek *metōnymiā* (literally) change of name < *meta-* change, over + *ónyma* name]

me-too (mē′tü′), *adj., v.,* **-tooed, -too·ing.** *Informal.* —*adj.* (in politics) characterized by me-tooism; adopting the successful ideas of an opponent expediently: *a me-too platform, candidate, policy, etc.* —*v.t., v.i.* to say "me-too" about, in favor of, or against a political proposal, doctrine, etc.; imitate or adopt (an opponent's political platform): *A senator has little to gain politically merely by me-tooing the liberality of the House* (Newsweek). —**me′-too′er,** *n.*

me-too·ism (mē′tü′iz əm), *n. Informal.* the adoption of the political line of the opposition.

met·o·pe (met′ə pē, -ōp), *n.* one of the square spaces, decorated or plain, between the triglyphs in a Doric frieze. [< Latin *metopa* < Greek *metópē* < *meta-* between + *ópai,* plural of *ópē* holes for beams in a frieze]

Metope

me·top·ic (mi·top′ik), *adj.* of or having to do with the forehead; frontal. [< Greek *métōpon* forehead]

me·tral·gi·a (mi tral′jē ə), *n.* pain in the uterus. [< New Latin *metralgia* < Greek *mētrā* the cervix; (originally) uterus, related to *mḗtēr* mother + *-algiā* < *álgos* pain]

Met·ra·zol (met′rə zōl, -zol), *n. Trademark.* a bitter, white, crystalline substance used as a stimulant of the central nervous system, especially in narcotic depression, barbiturate poisoning, and certain mental disorders. *Formula:* $C_6H_{10}N_4$

me·tre (mē′tər), *n. Especially British.* meter[1].

Met·re·cal (met′rə kal), *n. Trademark.* a low-calorie food substitute used in weight reducing: *Clinical tests in which 100 persons took Metrecal . . . showed it was effective in reducing weight* (Science News Letter).

met·ric (met′rik), *adj.* **1.** of or having to do with the meter or system of measurement based on it. **2.** metrical. [(definition 1) < French *métrique* < *mètre* meter[1]; (definition 2) < Latin *metricus* metrical < Greek *metrikós* < *métron* measure, poetic meter]

met·ri·cal (met′rə kəl), *adj.* **1.** of meter; having a regular arrangement of accents; written in verse, not in prose: *a metrical translation of Homer.* **2.** of, having to do with, or used in measurement; metric. —**Syn. 1.** rhythmical.

met·ri·cal·ly (met′rə klē), *adv.* in meter; according to meter.

metric hundredweight, 50 kilograms.

me·tri·cian (me trish′ən), *n.* a person who studies the subject of poetic meters; metrist.

met·ri·cism (met′rə siz əm), *n.* the quality or condition of being metric.

met·ri·cize (met′rə sīz), *v.t.*, **-cized, -ciz·ing.** to put into metrical form; make or compose in meter.

metric mile, (in swimming and track competition) 1,500 meters, or 120 yards short of a statute mile.

met·rics (met′riks), *n.* the science or art of meter; art of metrical composition.

metric system, a decimal system of measurement that uses the meter (39.37 inches) as its unit of length. The gram (.0022046 pound) is the unit of mass or weight, and the liter (61.024 cubic inches or 1 cubic decimeter) is the unit of volume. A cubic centimeter of water weighs approximately one gram. The measures of length and weight are:

1 millimeter	=	1/1000 meter
1 centimeter	=	1/100 meter
1 decimeter	=	1/10 meter
1 decameter	=	10 meters
1 hectometer	=	100 meters
1 kilometer	=	1,000 meters
1 milligram	=	1/1000 gram
1 centigram	=	1/100 gram
1 decigram	=	1/10 gram
1 decagram	=	10 grams
1 hectogram	=	100 grams
1 kilogram	=	1,000 grams

metric ton, a measure of weight, 1,000 kilograms, or 2,204.62 avoirdupois pounds.

met·ri·fi·ca·tion (met′rə fə kā′shən), *n.* the making of verses.

met·ri·fi·er (met′rə fī′ər), *n.* a person skilled in poetic meter, especially one who writes verse.

met·ri·fy (met′rə fī), *v.*, **-fied, -fy·ing.** —*v.t.* to put into meter; make or compose in verse. —*v.i.* to make verse. [< Middle French *métrifier* < Medieval Latin *metrificare* < Latin *metrum* meter[1] + *facere* make]

met·rist (met′rist, mē′trist), *n.* a person skilled in the use of poetic meters.

me·tri·tis (mi trī′tis), *n.* inflammation of the uterus. [< New Latin *metritis* < Greek *mētrā* uterus, cervix + New Latin *-itis* inflammation]

Met·ro or **met·ro**[1] (met′rō), *U.S. and Canada.* —*n.* a form of municipal government whose powers extend over a metropolitan area and usually encompass a group of smaller municipalities: *Metro has amalgamated some of the services shared by all, such as police, water, conservation . . . and town planning* (Canada Month). —*adj.* **1.** of or designating such a form of government. **2.** extending over a metropolitan area: *Metro Toronto.* [< *metro*(politan) area]

Mét·ro or **met·ro**[2] (met′rō), *n., pl.* **-ros.** (in Paris and certain other European cities) the subway system; subway: *Even the buses and Métro trains are flying the tricolor* (New Yorker). [< *Métro*(politan District Railway), the unit of the London subway]

met·ro·log·i·cal (met′rə loj′ə kəl), *adj.* of or having to do with metrology.

me·trol·o·gist (mi trol′ə jist), *n.* a student of or an expert in metrology.

me·trol·o·gy (mi trol′ə jē), *n., pl.* **-gies. 1.** the science of measures and weights. **2.** a system of measures and weights. [< Greek *métron* measure + English *-logy*]

met·ro·ma·ni·a (met′rə mā′nē ə), *n.* a mania for writing verse. [< Greek *métron* measure + English *mania*]

met·ro·ma·ni·ac (met′rə mā′nē ak), *n.* a person excessively fond of writing verse.

met·ro·nome (met′rə nōm), *n.* a clocklike device with a pendulum that can be adjusted to tick at different speeds, determined by the position of an adjustable weight (the higher the weight on the pendulum, the slower the tempo). Metronomes are used especially to mark time for persons practicing on musical instruments. [< Greek *métron* measure + *nómos* regulation, law, rule]

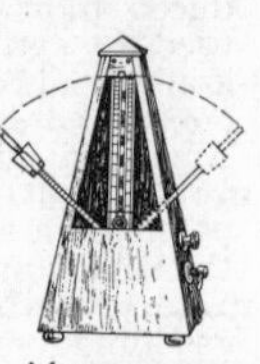

Metronome

met·ro·nom·ic (met′rə nom′ik), *adj.* **1.** of or like a metronome. **2.** having to do with tempo as indicated by a metronome: *a short, discreet, honest, and rather metronomic autobiography* (New Yorker). —**met′ro·nom′i·cal·ly,** *adv.*

me·tro·nym (mē′trə nim, met′rə-), *n.* a metronymic name.

me·tro·nym·ic (mē′trə nim′ik, met′rə-), *adj.* derived from the name of a mother or other female ancestor. —*n.* a metronymic name. Also, **matronymic.** [< Greek *mētrōnymikós* < *mḗtēr, mētrós* mother + dialectal *ónyma* name]

met·ro·pole (met′rə pōl), *n.* a metropolis, now especially an ecclesiastical metropolis.

me·trop·o·lis (mə trop′ə lis), *n.* **1.** the most important city of a country or region, usually (but not always) the one in which the government is carried on: *New York is the metropolis of the United States.* **2.** a large city; important center: *a financial metropolis. Chicago is a busy metropolis.* **3.** the chief diocese of a church province; the see of a metropolitan bishop. **4.** the mother city or parent state of a colony, especially of an ancient Greek colony. [< Latin *Metropolis,* a place name < Greek *mētrópolis* < *mḗtēr* mother + *pólis* city]

met·ro·pol·i·tan (met′rə pol′ə tən), *adj.* **1.** of a metropolis; belonging to a large city or cities: *metropolitan newspapers.* **2.** constituting a metropolis: *a metropolitan center.* **3.** of or having to do with a metropolitan of the church, or his see or province. **4.** constituting the mother city or the mainland territory of the parent state: *metropolitan France. The political connection between the people of the metropolitan country and their colonies* (James Fenimore Cooper).
—*n.* **1.** a person who lives in a large city and knows its ways. **2. a.** the chief bishop of an ecclesiastical province, having authority over the bishops (suffragans) within the territory. **b.** (in the Western Church) an archbishop presiding over a province. **c.** (in the Greek Church) a prelate ranking above an archbishop and below a patriarch. **3.** a citizen of the mother city or parent state of a colony.

metropolitan area, the area encompassing a major city and its suburbs, which may have a radius of 40 miles or more from the downtown section of the city proper and may include towns, villages, and farms: *The metropolitan area of New York goes over into New Jersey, up the Hudson River, and into Long Island* (Baltimore Sun).

met·ro·pol·i·tan·ate (met′rə pol′ə tə-nāt), *n.* the office or see of a metropolitan bishop.

met·ro·pol·i·tan·ism (met′rə pol′ə tə-niz′əm), *n.* **1.** the characteristics and manners of metropolitan living, especially as distinguished from provincialism; sophistication; urbanity: *The new metropolitanism is affecting most of our social institutions* (Science News Letter). **2.** *Sociology.* the social influence or control exerted by a central city over those who live in or on the fringes of a metropolitan area.

met·ro·pol·i·tan·ize (met′rə pol′ə tə nīz), *v.t.*, **-ized, -iz·ing.** to make metropolitan.

met·ro·po·lit·i·cal (met′rə pə lit′ə kəl), *adj.* of or having to do with a metropolitan of the church, or his see or province: *Metropolitical responsibility for the diocese of Hongkong and Macao, which the then Archbishop of Canterbury accepted in 1952, has been transferred . . .* (London Times).

me·tror·rha·gi·a (mē′trə rā′jē ə, met′rə-), *n.* a hemorrhage from the uterus not associated with menstruation. [< New Latin *metrorrhagia* < Greek *mētrā* uterus, cervix + *rhēgnýnai* to flow]

met·ro·style (met′rə stīl), *n.* a speed regulator for player pianos. [< Greek *métron* measure + English *style*]

-metry, *combining form.* process or art of measuring: *Calorimetry = the process of measuring calories.* [< Greek *-metríā* a measuring < *métron* a measure]

met·teur en scène (me tœr′ äɴ sen′), *pl.* **met·teurs en scène** (me tœr′ äɴ sen′). *French.* a stage director.

met·tle (met′əl), *n.* **1.** quality of disposition or temperament: *to try a man's mettle.* **2.** spirit; courage: *They . . . tell me flatly I am . . . a lad of mettle* (Shakespeare).
be on or **upon one's mettle,** to be ready or anxious to do one's best: *They would have to contend against cavalry, who would be upon their mettle to show their superiority over the cyclists* (London Times).
put on one's mettle, to challenge; inspire: *Her children's faith put her on her mettle to do her best by them. A whiff of . . . hostility in the atmosphere put him on his mettle* (George Meredith).
[variant of *metal*]
—**Syn. 2.** pluck, fortitude.

met·tled (met′əld), *adj.* having mettle; spirited; mettlesome.

met·tle·some (met′əl səm), *adj.* full of mettle; spirited; courageous: *a mettlesome horse.* —**Syn.** ardent, fiery.

Mett·wurst (met′vu̇rst′), *n. German.* a pork sausage with high fat content.

me·um et tu·um (mē′əm et tü′əm, tyü′-), *Latin.* mine and thine; what is my property and what is yours, thought of as expressing the universal and fundamental division of all property: *He seems to confuse meum et tuum in making out his accounts.*

Mev., Mev (no periods), **mev.,** or **MeV** (no periods) (mev), million electron volts.

mev·a·lon·ic acid (mev′ə lon′ik), a chemical compound important in the biosynthesis of steroids, carotenoids, and terpenes. *Formula:* $C_6H_{12}O_4$

mew[1] (myü), *n., interj., v.* meow: *Our kitten mews when it gets hungry.* [probably imitative]

mew[2] (myü), *n.* a gull, especially the common European gull; sea mew. [Old English *mǣw*]

mew[3] (myü), *n.* **1.** a building in which falcons are kept, especially while molting. **2.** *Dialect.* a breeding cage for any of various small, tame birds. **3.** a place of retirement or concealment; secret place; den. **4.** See **mews.**
—*v.t.* **1.** to cage (a hawk), especially at molting time. **2.** to shut up in or as if in a mew; confine; conceal: *to mew us up here until our lives' end* (Scott). **3.** *Archaic.* to change (feathers, etc.); molt. —*v.i. Archaic.* to molt.
[< Old French *müe* < *muer* to molt < Latin *mutāre* to change]

mewl (myül), *v.i., v.t.* to cry like a baby; whimper: *The infant, Mewling and puking in the nurse's arms* (Shakespeare). [imitative]

mews (myüz), *n.pl.* (*often sing. in use*). *Especially British.* **1. a.** a group of stables or garages built around a court or alley. **b.** a street or alley that was formerly part of a mews: *a mews house in Mayfair—one of those London surprises where a plain front conceals an almost Mediterranean courtyard* (Manchester Guardian). **2.** (in English history) the royal stables at London (so called because they were built on the site of the royal mews for hawks). [(originally) plural of *mew*[3]]

Mex., 1. Mexican. **2.** Mexico.

Mex·i·can (mek′sə kən), *adj.* of or having to do with Mexico or its people. —*n.* a native or inhabitant of Mexico.

Mexican bean beetle, a large, brownish-yellow ladybug of North America with eight black dots on each wing cover, that is very destructive to bean plants.

Mexican fruit fly, a fly native to Mexico and found as far south as Panama and north to southern Texas, which infests the crops of citrus and other fruits.

Mexican hairless, any of a very old breed of Mexican dogs, approximately as large as a small fox terrier, having no hair except for a tuft on the head and sometimes a little fuzz on the lower part of the tail.

Mex·i·can·i·za·tion (mek′sə kə nə zā′-shən), *n.* the act or process of making Mexican in appearance, character, etc.: . . . *a means of furthering the "Mexicanization" of Mexican industry* (Baltimore Sun).

Mex·i·can·ize (mek′sə kə nīz), *v.t., v.i.,* **-ized, -iz·ing.** to make or become Mexican in habits, customs, or character.

Mexican jumping bean, a jumping bean: *Mexican jumping beans hop about because of the movements of the larvae of leaf rollers that develop inside the beans* (World Book Encyclopedia).

Mexican onyx, onyx marble.

Mexican poppy, a prickly poppy bearing orange, yellow, or white flowers.

Mexican Spanish, the dialect of Spanish spoken in Mexico.

mez·cal (mes kal′), *n.* mescal (def. 1).

Me·zen·tian (mə zen′shən), *adj.* having to do with or suggestive of Mezentius, a legendary Etruscan king who is said to have had living men bound face to face with corpses and then left to die.

me·ze·re·on (mi zir′ē on), *n. Especially British.* mezereum.

me·ze·re·um (mi zir′ē əm), *n.* **1.** a European and Asiatic shrub, having fragrant, purplish or white flowers which appear in early spring before the leaves. **2.** the dried bark of this plant and related species, formerly used in pharmacy. [< New Latin *mezereum,* alteration of Medieval Latin *mezereon* < Arabic *māzaryūn*]

mezereum family, a family of dicotyledonous plants, mostly trees and shrubs, including the leatherwood and daphne.

me·zu·zah or **me·zu·za** (me zü′zä), *n., pl.* **-zoth** (-zōth), **-zahs, -za.** *Judaism.* a parchment scroll inserted in a small tube or box, usually of wood or metal, and attached by orthodox Jews to the right-hand doorposts of their homes, in obedience to the Biblical injunction in Deuteronomy 6:4-9 and 11:13-21, both passages being inscribed on one side of the parchment. On the other side is written "Shaddai," an ancient name of God, that is visible through a small window cut in the container. [< Hebrew *məzuzâ* doorpost]

Mezz., mezzanine (of a theater).

mez·za (met′sä, mez′ə), *adj.* the feminine form of **mezzo.**

mez·za·nine (mez′ə nēn), *n.* a low story between two higher stories or within one main story of a building; entresol. It is usually just above the ground floor. Sometimes it extends only part way over the floor below it, forming a kind of balcony. [< French *mezzanine* < Italian *mezzanino* < *mezzano* middle < Latin *mediānus;* see MEDIAN]

mez·za·vo·ce (med′zä vō′chā), *n. Italian.* a medium voice; a voice with a medium fullness of sound: *Her voice was nevertheless sufficiently ample to fill Town Hall, even when she sang—as she often did—in a safe mezza-voce* (New Yorker).

mez·zo (met′sō, mez′ō), *adj., n., pl.* **-zos.** *Music.* —*adj.* middle; medium; half, as to the dynamics or range. —*n.* mezzo-soprano: *Mezzo or not, her voice ascends to a good, strong high B* (Harper's). [< Italian *mezzo* < Latin *medius* middle]

mez·zo·for·te (met′sō fôr′tā, mez′ō-), *adj., adv. Music.* half as loud as forte; moderately loud (as a direction). *Abbr.:* mf. [< Italian *mezzo forte*]

mez·zo·re·lie·vo (met′sō ri lē′vō), *n., pl.* **-vos.** relief in which the figures project half their true proportions from the surface on which they are carved; half relief; demirelief. [< Italian *mezzo-rilievo* < *mezzo* middle + *rilievo* relievo]

mez·zo·ri·lie·vo (med′zō rē lye′vō), *n., pl.* **mez·zi·ri·lie·vi** (med′zē rē lye′vē). *Italian.* mezzo-relievo.

mez·zo·so·pran·o (met′sō sə pran′ō, -prä′-nō), *n., pl.* **-pran·os,** *adj.* —*n.* **1.** a voice or part between soprano and contralto. **2.** a singer having such a voice. —*adj.* of, for, or having to do with a mezzo-soprano. [< Italian *mezzo-soprano* < *mezzo* middle + *soprano* soprano]

mez·zo·tint (met′sō tint′, mez′ō-), *n.* **1.** an engraving on copper or steel made by polishing and scraping away parts of a roughened surface, so as to produce the effect of light and shade. **2.** a print made from such an engraving: *All that I own is a print, An etching, a mezzotint* (Robert Browning). **3.** this method of etching or engraving pictures.
—*v.t.* to engrave in mezzotint.
—*adj.* of, having to do with, or produced by mezzotint: *mezzotint engravings.*
[< Italian *mezzotinto* (literally) half-tint < *mezzo* mezzo + *tinto* < Latin *tinctus*] —**mez′zo·tint′er,** *n.*

mez·zo·tin·to (met′sō tin′tō, mez′ō-), *n., pl.* **-tos,** *v.t.,* **-toed, -to·ing.** mezzotint.

mf. or **mf** (no period), **1.** *Music.* mezzoforte. **2.** millifarad.

MF (no periods), **1.** medium frequency. **2.** Middle French.

M.F. or **MF.,** Middle French.

M.F.A., Master of Fine Arts.

mfd., **1.** manufactured. **2.** microfarad.

mfg., manufacturing.

MFH (no periods) or **M.F.H.,** master of foxhounds.

MFN (no periods) or **M.F.N.,** most favored nation.

mfr., **1.** manufacture. **2.** manufacturer.

mfrs., manufacturers.

mg., milligram or milligrams.

Mg (no period), magnesium (chemical element).

MG (no periods), **1.** machine gun. **2.** Military Government.

MGB (no periods), the Ministry of State Security of the Soviet Union. The MGB now reportedly conducts espionage and counterespionage.

m.g.d. or **mgd** (no periods), million gallons per day.

Mgr., **1.** manager. **2.** Monseigneur. **3.** Monsignor.

mh. or **mh** (no period), millihenry.

MH (no periods), Medal of Honor.

M.H., **1.** Master of Humanities. **2.** Master of Hygiene. **3.** Medal of Honor.

MHD (no periods), **1.** magnetohydrodynamic. **2.** magnetohydrodynamics.

MHG (no periods), **MHG.,** or **M.H.G.,** Middle High German.

mho (mō), *n., pl.* **mhos.** a unit of electrical conductance, equivalent to the conductance of a body whose resistance is one ohm. [reversed spelling of *ohm*]

M.Hort., Master of Horticulture.

M.H.R., Member of the House of Representatives.

m.h.w., mean high water.

mi (mē), *n. Music.* (in solmization) the third note or tone of the diatonic scale. [< Medieval Latin *mi;* see GAMUT]

mi., **1.** *U.S.* mile or miles. **2.** mill or mills.

MI (no periods) or **M.I.,** Military Intelligence.

M.I.5, the division of British Military Intelligence concerned with counterespionage and security in Great Britain.

mi·a·cis (mī′ə sis), *n.* a prehistoric carnivorous ancestor of the dog and cat, about the size of a weasel, having a long body, short legs, and a long tail. [< New Latin *Miacis* the genus name]

Mi·am·i (mī am′ē, -ə), *n., pl.* **-am·i** or **-am·is.** one of a tribe of Algonkian Indians, formerly in the Green Bay region of Wisconsin.

Mi·am·i·an (mī am′ē ən), *n.* a native or inhabitant of Miami, Florida.

mi·aow or **mi·aou** (mē ou′), *n., interj., v.* meow.

mi·asm (mī′az əm), *n.* miasma.

mi·as·ma (mī az′mə, mē-), *n., pl.* **-mas, -ma·ta** (-mə tə). **1.** poisonous vapor rising from the earth and infecting the air. The miasma of swamps was formerly supposed to cause disease: *far enough from the Dead Sea to escape its miasma* (London Times). **2.** anything considered to resemble this in its ability to spread and poison: *a miasma of fear.* [< New Latin *miasma* < Greek *míasma* pollution < *miaínein* to pollute]

mi·as·mal (mī az′məl, mē-), *adj.* containing miasma; noxious: *miasmal swamps.*

mi·as·mat·ic (mī′az mat′ik), *adj.* miasmal.

mi·as·mat·i·cal (mī′az mat′ə kəl), *adj.* miasmal.

mi·as·mic (mī az′mik, mē-), *adj.* miasmal.

mi·aul (mē oul′, -ôl′), *n., interj., v.* meow: *a miauling kitten* (Scott).

mib (mib), *n. Dialect.* a marble.
mibs, the game of marbles.
[perhaps alteration of *marbles*]

Mic., Micah (book of the Old Testament).

mi·ca (mī′kə), *n.* a mineral that divides into thin, partly transparent, and usually flexible layers, used in electric fuses, formerly in stove doors, etc., where the heat might break glass. Mica is composed essentially of silicate of aluminum, potassium, or other metals, occurring in minute, glittering plates or scales in granite and other rocks, or in crystals that separate. *An outcrop of sandstone and schist with secondary white mica* (Science News). [< Latin *mīca* grain, crumb; perhaps influenced by *micāre* to shine]

mi·ca·ceous (mī kā′shəs), *adj.* **1.** consisting of, containing, or like mica: *micaceous minerals.* **2.** of or having to do with mica.

Mi·cah (mī′kə), *n.* **1.** a Hebrew prophet of the 700's B.C. **2.** a prophetic book of the Old Testament attributed to him, placed among the minor prophets. *Abbr.:* Mic.

Mi·Ca·rême (mē kȧ rem′), *n. French.* Mid-Lent.

Mi·caw·ber (mə kô′bər), *n.* **1.** an optimistic character in Charles Dickens' novel *David Copperfield,* who is seldom able to pay his bills and is always expecting "that something will turn up." **2.** any person resembling Micawber in character or habits.

Mi·caw·ber·ish (mə kô′bər ish), *adj.* characteristic of a Micawber; improvident but habitually optimistic: *For years, the nation's biggest city has followed a Micawberish routine of using reserves and loans to meet ever-rising operating costs* (Time). —**Mi·caw′ber·ish·ly,** *adv.*

Mi·caw·ber·ism (mə kô′bər iz əm), *n.* the quality or condition of being Micawberish: *My own fear is that the present Micawberism will leave us wide open . . . to a humiliating series of defeats* (London Times).

mice (mīs), *n.* the plural of **mouse.**

mi·cel·la (mi sel′ə, mī-), *n., pl.* **-cel·lae** (-sel′ē). micelle.

mi·celle or **mi·cell** (mi sel′), *n.* a colloidal particle, especially one in a soap solution. [< New Latin *micella* (diminutive) < Latin *mīca;* see MICA]

Mich., **1.** Michaelmas. **2.** Michigan.

Mi·chael (mī′kəl), *n.* **Saint,** (in the Bible) the archangel who led the loyal angels in defeating the revolt of Lucifer. Revelation 12:7-9.

Mich·ael·mas (mik′əl məs), *n. Especially British.* **1.** an annual church festival honoring the archangel Michael and all the angels. **2.** Also, **Michaelmas Day.** September 29, the date of this festival, one of the quarter days in England.

Michaelmas daisy, **1.** a common wild aster often grown in gardens, that blooms near Michaelmas. **2.** any of several garden asters of a shrubby habit and bearing masses of small, purplish flowers.

miche (mich), *v.,* **miched, mich·ing.** *Dialect.* —*v.i.* **1.** to lurk out of sight; skulk. **2.** to play truant. **3.** to grumble; whine. —*v.t.* to pilfer. Also, **meech.** [< Old French *muchier, mucier* skulk, hide, perhaps < Celtic (compare Old Irish *mūchaim* stifle)] —**mich′er,** *n.*

Mi·che·as (mī kē′əs), *n.* (in the Douay Bible) Micah.

Mi·chel·an·gel·esque (mī′kəl an′jə lesk′, mik′əl-), *adj.* of, having to do with, or characteristic of Michelangelo or his work: *There is, in fact, something genuinely Michelangelesque about many of his paintings and drawings* (London Times). [< *Michelangelo* Buonarroti, 1475-1564, the Italian painter, sculptor, architect, and poet + *-esque*]

Mich·i·gan·der (mish′ə gan′dər), *n.* a native or inhabitant of Michigan. [American English; blend of *Michigan* and *gander,* originally the nickname of Lewis Cass, 1782-1866, an American soldier and politician who was the governor of Michigan Territory]

Mich·i·gan·ite (mish′ə gə nīt), *n.* a Michigander.

mi·chron (mī′kron), *n.* the time of vibration of a wave of one micron. [< Greek *mī(krós)* small + *chrón(os)* time]

Mick·ey or **mick·ey** (mik′ē), *n., pl.* **-eys.** a Mickey Finn.
take the mickey out of, *British Slang.* to make fun of; ridicule: *Miss Grenfell . . . helped to give us a happy satire on broadcasting itself and took the mickey out of certain familiar programmes* (London Times).

Mickey Finn or **mickey finn** (fin′), *U.S. Slang.* a drugged drink intended to make the person who unsuspectingly drinks it incapable of defending himself or of continuing whatever he may be doing.

mick·le (mik′əl), *adj., adv., n. Archaic or Dialect.* much. [Old English *micel,* also *mycel*]

Mic·mac (mik′mak), *n., pl.* **-mac** or **-macs.** an Indian of an Algonkian tribe that formerly lived in Canada and Newfoundland.

micr-, *combining form.* the form of **micro-** before vowels, as in *microhm.*

mi·cra (mī′krə), *n.* microns; a plural of **micron.**

mi·cri·fy (mī′krə fī), *v.t.,* **-fied, -fy·ing.** to make small or insignificant. [< *micr-* + *-fy,* perhaps patterned on *magnify*]

micro-, *combining form.* **1.** small; very small; microscopic: *Microorganism = a microscopic organism. Microphotograph = a very small photograph.*
2. abnormally small: *Microcephalic = having an abnormally small head.*
3. done with, or involving the use of, a microscope: *Microdissection = dissection done under a microscope.*
4. one millionth of a ——: *Microfarad = one millionth of a farad.*
5. that magnifies small ——: *Microphone = an instrument that magnifies small sounds.*
Also, **micr-** before vowels. [< Greek *mīkrós* small]

mi·cro·am·me·ter (mī′krō am′ē′ tər), *n.* an instrument which measures an electric current in microamperes.

mi·cro·am·pere (mī′krō am′pir), *n.* a unit of electrical current, equivalent to one millionth of an ampere.

mi·cro·a·nal·y·sis (mī′krō ə nal′ə sis), *n., pl.* **-ses** (-sēz). *Chemistry.* the analysis of very small quantities of matter.

mi·cro·an·a·lyst (mī′krō an′ə list), *n.* a person who is skilled in or practices microanalysis.

mi·cro·an·a·lyt·ic (mī′krō an′ə lit′ik), *adj.* microanalytical.

mi·cro·an·a·lyt·i·cal (mī′krō an′ə lit′ə-kəl), *adj.* of or having to do with microanalysis.

mi·cro·an·a·lyze (mī′krō an′ə līz), *v.t.,* **-lyzed, -lyz·ing.** to carry out microanalysis on (a substance).

mi·cro·bal·ance (mī′krō bal′əns), *n.* a very sensitive scale used to weigh minute quantities (one milligram or less) of chemicals or other substances: *microbalances that weigh lift and drag in terms of millionths of a gram* (Scientific American).

mi·cro·bar (mī′krō bär), *n.* a unit of pressure equal to one dyne per square centimeter in the centimeter-gram-second system.

mi·cro·bar·o·graph (mī′krō bar′ə graf, -gräf), *n.* an instrument for recording very small fluctuations of atmospheric pressure.

mi·crobe (mī′krōb), *n.* **1.** a microorganism. **2.** (popularly) a bacterium, especially one causing diseases or fermentation: *Pasteur, Koch, and Lister proved conclusively that germs, or microbes, were the cause of certain diseases.* [< French *microbe* < Greek *mīkrós* small + *bíos* life]

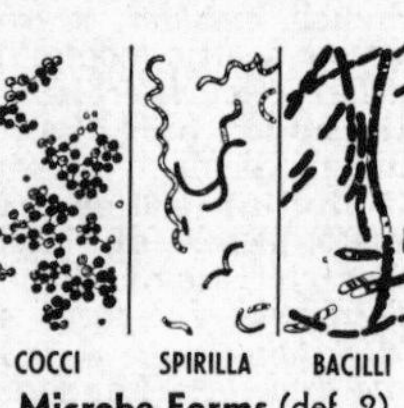

Microbe Forms (def. 2)

mi·cro·bi·al (mī krō′bē əl), *adj.* of, having to do with, or caused by microbes: *microbial disease, microbial parasites.*

mi·cro·bic (mī krō′bik), *adj.* microbial.

mi·cro·bi·cid·al (mī krō′bə sī′dəl), *adj.* having to do with the killing of microbes.

mi·cro·bi·cide (mī krō′bə sīd), *n.* something that kills microbes; germicide. [< *microbe* + *-cide*¹]

mi·cro·bi·o·log·i·cal (mī′krō bī′ə loj′ə-kəl), *adj.* **1.** of or having to do with microbiology: *microbiological research.* **2.** of, having to do with, or utilizing microorganisms: *microbiological experiments.* —**mi′cro·bi′o·log′i·cal·ly,** *adv.*

mi·cro·bi·ol·o·gist (mī′krō bī ol′ə jist), *n.* a person skilled or trained in microbiology.

mi·cro·bi·ol·o·gy (mī′krō bī ol′ə jē), *n.* the science dealing with microorganisms; study of microbes.

mi·cro·bi·on (mī krō′bē on), *n., pl.* **-bi·a** (-bē ə). a microbe. [< New Latin *microbion*]

mi·cro·card (mī′krō kärd′), *n.* a card-sized photographic print containing pages of books, newspapers, records, etc., greatly reduced in size. It is used to facilitate storage and transportation of such materials. *Sets of microcards containing weather information* (Science News Letter).

mi·cro·ce·phal·ic (mī′krō sə fal′ik), *adj.* **1.** having a cranial capacity of less than 1,350 cubic centimeters. **2.** having an abnormally small head, especially as a result of a congenital defect, as certain idiots.

mi·cro·ceph·a·lous (mī′krō sef′ə ləs), *adj.* microcephalic.

mi·cro·ceph·a·ly (mī′krō sef′ə lē), *n.* the condition of having a small or imperfectly developed head.

mi·cro·chem·i·cal (mī′krō kem′ə kəl), *adj.* of or having to do with microchemistry: *microchemical reactions.*

mi·cro·chem·is·try (mī′krō kem′ə strē), *n.* chemical analysis or investigation carried on by working with exceptionally small samples, often only a few milligrams.

mi·cro·cin·e·ma·tog·ra·phy (mī′krō-sin′ə mə tog′rə fē), *n.* the art of obtaining motion pictures of microscopic objects on a magnified scale.

mi·cro·cir·cuit (mī′krō sėr′kit), *n.* a highly miniaturized electronic circuit, usually formed of micromodules, or of extremely thin films deposited by evaporation in a high vacuum.

mi·cro·cir·cuit·ry (mī′krō sėr′kə trē), *n.* **1.** the study of microcircuits. **2.** the components of a microcircuit.

mi·cro·cli·mate (mī′krō klī′mit), *n.* the climate of a very small, specific area such as a glacier, valley bottom, corn field, or animal burrow.

mi·cro·cli·mat·ic (mī′krō klī mat′ik), *adj.* of or having to do with a microclimate or microclimatology: *Where ample water is available, redistribution . . . can cause beneficial microclimatic changes* (Bulletin of Atomic Scientists).

mi·cro·cli·ma·tol·o·gy (mī′krō klī′mə-tol′ə jē), *n.* the branch of climatology dealing with the climatic conditions of small areas.

mi·cro·cline (mī′krə klīn), *n.* a potash feldspar similar to orthoclase, white, yellow, red, or green in color. [< German *Mikroklin* < Greek *mīkrós* small + *klīnein* to incline]

mi·cro·coc·cal (mī′krə kok′əl), *adj.* relating to or caused by micrococci.

mi·cro·coc·cic (mī′krə kok′sik), *adj.* micrococcal.

mi·cro·coc·cus (mī′krə kok′əs), *n., pl.* **-coc·ci** (-kok′sī). any of a group of spherical or eggshaped, parasitic or saprophytic bacteria, aggregating in various ways. Certain micrococci cause disease; others produce fermentation. [< New Latin *Micrococcus* the typical genus < Greek *mīkrós* small + *kókkos* berry, seed, grain]

mi·cro·cop·y (mī′krə kop′ē), *n., pl.* **-cop·ies,** *v.,* **-cop·ied, -cop·y·ing.** —*n.* a copy of a book or other printed work made on microfilm. —*v.t.* to make a copy of on microfilm.

mi·cro·cosm (mī′krə koz əm), *n.* **1.** a little world; universe in miniature: *The circus comes as close to being the world in microcosm as anything I know* (New Yorker). **2.** man thought of as a miniature representation of the universe. [< Old French *microcosme* < Late Latin *microcosmus* < Late Greek *mīkròs kósmos* little world]

mi·cro·cos·mic (mī′krə koz′mik), *adj.* of, having to do with, or of the nature of a microcosm.

mi·cro·cos·mi·cal (mī′krə koz′mə kəl), *adj.* microcosmic.

microcosmic salt, a colorless, crystalline compound, a phosphate of sodium and ammonium, originally derived from human urine. It is used as a reagent in chemical analyses, especially of metallic oxides. *Formula:* $NaNH_4HPO_4 \cdot 4H_2O$

mi·cro·cos·mos (mī′krə koz′məs, -mos), *n.* microcosm: *These variations represented the microcosmos of Beethoven's genius* (London Times).

mi·cro·cou·lomb (mī′krō kü′lom), *n.* one millionth of a coulomb.

mi·cro·crys·tal (mī′krō kris′təl), *n.* a minute or microscopic crystal.

mi·cro·crys·tal·line (mī′krō kris′tə lin, -līn), *adj.* formed of microscopic crystals: *microcrystalline wax.*

mi·cro·cu·rie (mī′krō kyůr′ē), *n.* a unit of radioactivity, equivalent to one millionth of a curie.

mi·cro·cyte (mī′krə sīt), *n.* an abnormally small red blood cell. [< *micro-* + *-cyte*]

mi·cro·den·si·tom·e·ter (mī′krō den′sə-tom′ə tər), *n.* an instrument for measuring the density of very small areas of a photographic negative: *Mapping was accomplished by . . . analysis of brightness changes measured with a microdensitometer* (Donald F. Eschman). [< *micro-* + *densitometer*]

mi·cro·de·tec·tor (mī′krō di tek′tər), *n.* an instrument used to detect small quantities or changes, especially a sensitive galvanometer used to detect slight changes in electric current.

mi·cro·dis·sec·tion (mī′krō di sek′shən), *n.* dissection done under a microscope.

mi·cro·dont (mī′krə dont), *adj.* having very small teeth. —*n.* a very small tooth. [< *micr-* + Greek *odoús, odóntos* tooth]

mi·cro·don·tous (mī′krə don′təs), *adj.* microdont.

mi·cro·dot (mī′krō dot′), *n.* a microphotograph in the shape of a dot, used in espionage: *A male Russian agent . . . gave Mintkenbaugh a 35-mm. camera, along with a quick course in developing microdots and hiding microfilm* (Time).

mi·cro·dyne (mī′krə dīn), *n.* one millionth of a dyne.

mi·cro·e·co·nom·ic (mī′krō ē′kə nom′ik, -ek′ə-), *adj.* of or having to do with microeconomics: *microeconomic planning, microeconomic analysis.*

mi·cro·e·co·nom·ics (mī′krō ē′kə nom′-iks, -ek′ə-), *n.* economics that deals with individual units in the economy, such as a family or a corporation.

mi·cro·e·lec·tric (mī′krō i lek′trik), *adj.* of or having to do with very small electric quantities.

mi·cro·e·lec·trode (mī′krō i lek′trōd), *n.* a very fine electrode used to detect electrical impulses of nerve cells, muscle fibers, etc.

mi·cro·e·lec·tron·ics (mī′krō i lek′tron′-iks, -ē′lek-), *n.* the branch of electronics dealing with microminiaturization.

mi·cro·e·lec·tro·pho·re·sis (mī′krō i-lek′trō fə rē′sis), *n.* a technique for observing the electrophoresis of very small individual particles through a microscope or ultramicroscope.

mi·cro·e·lec·tro·pho·ret·ic (mī′krō i-lek′trō fə ret′ik), *adj.* having to do with or produced by microelectrophoresis: *He has developed an elegant microelectrophoretic technique that makes it possible to determine the base composition of very small amounts of RNA* (Scientific American).

mi·cro·el·e·ment (mī′krō el′ə mənt), *n.* a chemical element found only in very small amounts.

mi·cro·en·vi·ron·ment (mī′krō en vī′-rən mənt), *n.* the environment of a very small area, especially the isolated habitat of a particular species of plant or animal: *The Himalayan microenvironment shows great temperature contrasts between localities only a few inches apart* (Lawrence W. Swan).

mi·cro·ev·o·lu·tion (mī′krō ev′ə lü′shən), *n.* the evolution of animals and plants on the level of species or subspecies due to a succession of small genetic variations.

mi·cro·far·ad (mī′krō far′əd, -ad), *n.* a unit of electrical capacity, one millionth of a farad.

mi·cro·fau·na (mī′krō fô′nə), *n.* the microscopic animals of a given habitat, as in a stream. [< *micro-* + *fauna*]

mi·cro·fiche (mī′krə fēsh′), *n., pl.* **-fiches, -fiche** (-fēsh′). a single piece or strip of microfilm. [< *micro-* + French *fiche* card]

mi·cro·fi·lar·i·a (mī′krō fi lãr′ē ə), *n., pl.* **-lar·i·ae** (-lãr′ē ē). the larva of a filaria: *The tiny young larvae, called microfilariae, pour out of the mother and are transported via the lymphatic vessels to the bloodstream* (Scientific American).

mi·cro·film (mī′krə film′), *n.* **1.** a fine-grained film for making very small photographs of pages of a book, newspapers, records, etc., to preserve them in a very small space. **2.** a photograph made on such film. —*v.t., v.i.* to photograph on microfilm: *allow . . . the Treasury to microfilm tax returns* (Wall Street Journal).

mi·cro·flo·ra (mī′krō flôr′ə, -flōr′-), *n.* the microscopic plants of a given habitat, as in a cow's stomach: *the wild yeast microflora.* [< *micro-* + *flora*]

mi·cro·fos·sil (mī′krō fos′əl), *n.* a microscopic plant or animal fossil, as of foraminifera or a pollen grain, used in oil exploration and in determining early conditions on the earth.

mi·cro·ga·mete (mī′krō gə mēt′, -gam′ēt), *n. Biology.* the smaller, typically the male, of two gametes of an organism that reproduces by the union of unlike gametes.

mi·cro·gram (mī′krō gram), *n.* one millionth of a gram. *Symbol:* μg (no period).

mi·cro·gramme (mī′krō gram), *n. British.* microgram.

mi·cro·graph (mī′krə graf, -gräf), *n.* **1.** an instrument that produces very small writing or engraving. **2.** a photograph, drawing, or other representation of an object as seen through a microscope: *Other micrographs are described as showing the effects of multiple dislocations on the growth of the crystals* (Science News). **3.** a device that measures and records extremely small movements by means of the corresponding movements of a diaphragm. [< *micro-* + *-graph*]

mi·cro·graph·ic (mī′krə graf′ik), *adj.* **1.** having to do with the description of microscopic objects. **2.** of or having to do with the writing of very small characters; minutely written.

mi·crog·ra·phy (mī krog′rə fē), *n.* **1.** the description of microscopic objects. **2.** examination or study with the microscope. **3.** the art of writing in very small letters.

mi·cro·groove (mī′krə grüv′), *n.* **1.** a very narrow groove used on phonograph records, especially records designed for playing speeds of 45, 33⅓, or 16 revolutions per minute, typically requiring the use of a needle measuring 1/1000 of an inch in width at the tip: *The long-playing microgroove record . . . [is] now known familiarly to phonograph fans as "LP"* (Newsweek). **2. Microgroove,** *Trademark.* a record having such grooves: *These two symphonies have been committed to Microgroove at least twenty-two times apiece* (Atlantic).

mi·cro·hab·i·tat (mī′krō hab′ə tat), *n.* microenvironment.

mi·cro·hard·ness (mī′krō härd′nis), *n.* the degree of hardness of a metal, determined by measuring a very small indenture made on its surface.

mi·crohm (mī′krōm), *n.* one millionth of an ohm.

mi·cro·im·age (mī′krō im′ij), *n.* an image or reproduction made by microphotography: *The Bible was reproduced by what . . . the company's head of research calls photochromic microimages* (Time).

mi·cro·inch (mī′krō inch′), *n.* a unit of linear measure equal to one millionth of an inch.

mi·cro·li·ter (mī′krō lē′tər), *n.* one millionth of a liter. *Symbol:* μl (no period).

mi·cro·lith (mī′krə lith), *n.* a tiny, pointed blade or chip of stone, usually flint, that was used on arrows, tools, etc., during periods of the Stone Age. [< *micro-* + Greek *lithos* stone]

mi·cro·lith·ic (mī′krə lith′ik), *adj.* of, having to do with, or characterized by the use of microliths.

mi·cro·li·tre (mī′krō lē′tər), *n British.* microliter.

mi·cro·log·ic (mī′krə loj′ik), *adj.* micrological.

mi·cro·log·i·cal (mī′krə loj′ə kəl), *adj.* characterized by minuteness of investigation or discussion.

mi·crol·o·gy (mī krol′ə jē), *n.* the discussion or investigation of trivial things or petty affairs; hairsplitting. [< Greek *mīkrologíā* hairsplitting < *mīkrós* small + *-logíā* system, treatment < *légein* speak]

mi·cro·ma·nip·u·la·tion (mī′krō mə nip′yə lā′shən), *n.* the technique of performing delicate operations on microscopic bodies and structures such as cells, subcellular structures, crystals, and fibers.

mi·cro·ma·nip·u·la·tor (mī′krō mə nip′yə lā′tər), *n.* a device or instrument used in micromanipulation to move tiny needles, scalpels, and other tools. The operations are performed under a microscope. *With a pair of micromanipulators we were able to tease off the outer layers* (Scientific American).

mi·cro·me·te·or (mī′krō mē′tē ər), *n.* a micrometeorite: *Micrometeors, so tiny they do not burn, rain constantly upon the earth* (Science News Letter).

mi·cro·me·te·or·ic (mī′krō mē′tē ôr′ik, -or′-), *adj.* of or having to do with micrometeorites: *micrometeoric dust.*

mi·cro·me·te·or·ite (mī′krō mē′tē ə rīt), *n.* a fine particle of meteoritic dust from a few microns to about 100 microns in diameter which, because of its size, does not burn upon entering the earth's atmosphere. The impact of micrometeorites on the surface of space vehicles is the subject of much research by space scientists. *The metallized fabric balloons are susceptible to puncturing by micrometeorites* (New Scientist).

mi·cro·me·te·or·oid (mī′krō mē′tē ə roid), *n.* a micrometeorite.

mi·cro·me·te·or·ol·o·gy (mī′krō mē′tē ə-rol′ə jē), *n.* the branch of meteorology that deals with the atmospheric phenomena of very small areas.

mi·crom·e·ter (mī krom′ə tər), *n.* **1.** an instrument for measuring very small distances, angles, objects, etc., used with a microscope or telescope. **2.** a micrometer caliper. **3.** a micrometer screw. [< French *micromètre* < *micro-* micro- + *-mètre* -meter]

micrometer caliper, a caliper having a micrometer screw, used for very accurate measurement, as in working on or with machine tools or in watchmaking.

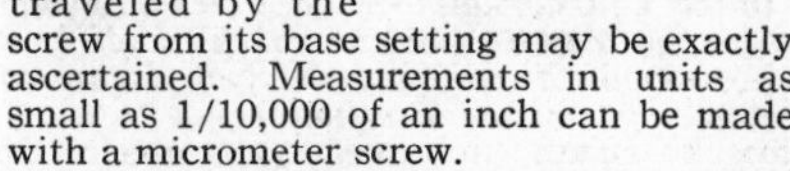

Micrometer Caliper

micrometer screw, a screw with very fine, precisely cut threads and a head graduated so that the distance traveled by the screw from its base setting may be exactly ascertained. Measurements in units as small as 1/10,000 of an inch can be made with a micrometer screw.

mi·cro·met·ric (mī′krə met′rik), *adj.* of, having to do with, or made with the micrometer: *a micrometric crispness of control.* —**mi′cro·met′ri·cal·ly,** *adv.*

mi·cro·met·ri·cal (mī′krə met′rə kəl), *adj.* micrometric.

mi·crom·e·try (mī krom′ə trē), *n.* the measurement of minute objects with a micrometer.

mi·cro·mi·cro·cu·rie (mī′krō mī′krō-kyůr′ē), *n.* one millionth of one millionth of a curie.

mi·cro·mi·cro·far·ad (mī′krō mī′krō far′-əd, -ad), *n.* one millionth of one millionth of a farad.

mi·cro·mil·li·me·ter (mī′krō mil′ə mē′-tər), *n.* **1.** one millionth of a millimeter; millicron. *Symbol:* mμ (no period). **2.** a micron.

mi·cro·mil·li·me·tre (mī′krō mil′ə mē′-tər), *n. British.* micromillimeter.

mi·cro·min·i·a·ture (mī′krō min′ē ə chər), *adj.* (of electronic or similar equipment) smaller than miniature; extremely small: *a microminiature lamp, microminiature components, microminiature transistors.*

mi·cro·min·i·a·tur·i·za·tion (mī′krō-min′ē ə chər ə zā′shən), *n.* the process of developing and producing microminiature electronic or similar devices.

mi·cro·min·i·a·tur·ize (mī′krō min′ē ə-chə rīz, -min′ə chə-), *v.t.,* **-ized, -iz·ing.** to reduce to microminiature dimensions: *The entire system is now in process of being microminiaturized* (New Scientist).

mi·cro·mod·ule (mī′krō moj′ül), *n.* a small wafer of insulation material, usually ceramic, in which an element of a microminiature electronic circuit has been deposited.

mi·cro·mo·tion (mī′krō mō′shən), *n.* an exceedingly short (in duration or length) motion or series of motions.

mi·cron (mī′kron), *n., pl.* **-crons** or **-cra. 1.** one millionth of a meter. *Symbol:* μ (no period). **2.** a colloidal particle with a diameter ranging from 1/100 to 1/5000 of a millimeter. Also, **mikron.** [< Greek *mīkrón,* neuter of *mīkrós* small]

mi·cro·nee·dle (mī′krō nē′dəl), *n.* a fine glass needle used in micromanipulation.

Mi·cro·ne·sian (mī′krə nē′zhən, -shən), *adj.* of or having to do with Micronesia (one of the three main groups of islands in the Pacific, east of the Philippines, including the Marianas and the Marshall Islands), its inhabitants, languages, etc. —*n.* **1.** one of the natives of Micronesia, of mixed Melanesian, Polynesian, and Malay stock. **2.** any of the Austronesian languages spoken by these people. [< Greek *mīkrós* small + *nēsos* island + English *-ian;* probably patterned on *Polynesian*]

mi·cro·nu·cle·us (mī′krō nü′klē əs, -nyü′-), *n., pl.* **-cle·i** (-klē ī), **-cle·us·es.** the smaller of two kinds of nuclei of ciliate protozoans, containing chromatin materials necessary for reproduction. There can be one or more micronuclei in a cell. *The nuclei are 2 in number, a large macronucleus concerned with vegetative functions, and a smaller micronucleus that is important in reproduction* (Hegner and Stiles).

mi·cro·nu·tri·ent (mī′krō nü′trē ənt, -nyü′-), *n.* a trace element.

mi·cro·or·gan·ism (mī′krō ôr′gə niz əm), *n.* an animal or vegetable organism too small to be seen except with a microscope. Bacteria are microorganisms. —**Syn.** microbe.

mi·cro·or·gan·is·mal (mī′krō ôr′gə niz′-məl), *adj.* of, having to do with, or produced by microorganisms: *Every puff of wind, every drop of water, and every handful of dust contains microorganismal life in one form or another* (Joshua Lederberg).

mi·cro·pa·lae·on·tol·o·gist (mī′krō pā′-lē on tol′ə jist, -pal′ē-), *n.* micropaleontologist.

mi·cro·pa·lae·on·tol·o·gy (mī′kro pā′lē-on tol′ə jē, -pal′ē-), *n.* micropaleontology.

mi·cro·pa·le·on·tol·o·gist (mī′krō pā′lē-on tol′ə jist, -pal′ē-), *n.* a person skilled or trained in micropaleontology.

mi·cro·pa·le·on·tol·o·gy (mī′krō pā′lē-on tol′ə jē, -pal′ē-), *n.* the branch of paleontology which studies fossils of microscopic size. It is of great importance in oil exploration.

mi·cro·par·a·site (mī′krō par′ə sīt), *n.* a parasitic microorganism.

mi·cro·par·a·sit·ic (mī′krō par′ə sit′ik), *adj.* having the character of, having to do with, or caused by microparasites: *microparasitic diseases.*

mi·cro·phone (mī′krə fōn), *n.* an instrument for magnifying small sounds or for transmitting sounds. Microphones that are used in all radio broadcasting, telephony, etc., change sound waves into variations of an electric current. [< *micro-* + *phone*]

mi·cro·phon·ic (mī′krə fon′ik), *adj.* having to do with a microphone; serving to magnify small sounds.

mi·cro·phon·ics (mī′krə fon′iks), *n.* **1.** the science of magnifying small sounds. **2.** noise caused by mechanical shocks or vibrations.

mi·cro·pho·to·graph (mī′krō fō′tə graf, -gräf), *n.* **1.** a photograph too small to be deciphered by the naked eye. **2.** a photograph made on, or printed from, microfilm. **3.** a photomicrograph.

mi·cro·pho·to·graph·ic (mī′krō fō′tə-graf′ik), *adj.* having to do with or connected with microphotography. —**mi′cro·pho′to·graph′i·cal·ly,** *adv.*

mi·cro·pho·tog·ra·phy (mī′krō fə tog′-rə fē), *n.* the photographing of objects of any size upon a microscopic or very small scale.

mi·cro·pho·tom·e·ter (mī′krō fō tom′ə-tər), *n.* a type of densitometer that measures and analyzes light passed through a photographic negative. It is particularly useful in detecting cancerous tissue and in determining the magnitude of stars: *The light the cells give off can be measured with a microphotometer* (Science News Letter).

mi·cro·phys·i·cal (mī′krō fiz′ə kəl), *adj.* of or having to do with microphysics.

mi·cro·phys·ics (mī′krō fiz′iks), *n.* the branch of physics concerned with minute masses or the ultimate particles and structure of matter: *Mr. Pierre Auger's recent book . . . studies the possible relations between microphysics and biology* (Bulletin of Atomic Scientists).

mi·cro·phyte (mī′krə fīt), *n.* a microscopic plant, especially a bacterium. [< *micro-* + Greek *phytón* plant]

mi·cro·phyt·ic (mī′krə fit′ik), *adj.* having to do with or caused by microphytes: *microphytic diseases.*

mi·cro·pi·pette (mī′krō pī pet′, -pi-), *n.* a very fine pipette used in micromanipulation.

mi·cro·po·rous (mī′krə pôr′əs, -pōr′-), *adj.* having very small pores: *These have high absorbency and a microporous structure that makes them extremely suitable for use as molecular sieves* (New Scientist).

mi·cro·print (mī′krə print′), *n.* a microphotograph of newspapers, records, etc., having such small dimensions that it must be read with a magnifying device.

mi·cro·pro·jec·tion (mī′krō prə jek′shən), *n.* the projecting of a greatly enlarged image of a minute object on a screen by means of a microprojector: *"Discovery '63" covers . . . microprojection of tiny objects and organisms* (Time).

mi·cro·pro·jec·tor (mī′krō prə jek′tər), *n.* an apparatus, consisting of a microscope lens system and an illuminator, that projects enlarged images of minute objects on a screen.

mi·crop·ter·ism (mī krop′tə riz əm), *n. Zoology.* abnormally small wing or fin development.

mi·crop·ter·ous (mī krop′tər əs), *adj. Zoology.* having small wings or fins. [< Greek *mīkrópteros* (with English *-ous*) < *mīkrós* small + *pterón* wing]

mi·cro·py·lar (mī′krə pī′lər), *adj.* having to do with or characteristic of a micropyle: *the micropylar end of the embryo sac.*

mi·cro·pyle (mī′krə pīl), *n.* **1.** any of the minute holes in the membrane covering the ovum of certain animals, through which spermatozoa enter. **2.** the minute opening in the outer layer or layers of an ovule, through which pollen enters. [< French *micropyle* < Greek *mīkrós* small + *pýlē* gate]

mi·cro·py·rom·e·ter (mī′krō pī rom′ə tər), *n.* an optical instrument used in determining the temperature of very small glowing bodies. [< *micro-* + *pyrometer*]

mi·cro·ra·di·o·graph (mī′krō rā′dē ə graf, -gräf), *n.* an enlarged radiographic image of a small specimen.

mi·cro·ra·di·o·graph·ic (mī′krō rā′dē ə-graf′ik), *adj.* of or having to do with a microradiograph or microradiography: *a microradiographic image, a microradiographic laboratory.*

mi·cro·ra·di·og·ra·phy (mī′krō rā′dē og′rə fē), *n.* the technique of producing microradiographs, used in the examination of metal structure, body tissue, paint density, etc.

mi·cro·read·er (mī′krō rē′dər), *n.* a device that projects an enlarged image of a microphotograph on a screen to make its content readable or recognizable with the naked eye.

mi·cro·roent·gen (mī′krō rent′gən), *n.* one millionth of a roentgen.

micros., microscopy.

mi·cro·scale (mī′krə skāl′), *n.* a scale or standard involving very small amounts or measurements: *These materials are . . . crude on a microscale* (New Scientist).

mi·cro·scope (mī′krə skōp), *n.* an instrument with a lens or a combination of lenses for making small things look larger. The simple microscope is merely a convex lens placed in a frame; the compound microscope consists essentially of two lenses, or systems of lenses, one of which, the objective or object glass, forms an enlarged inverted image of the object, and the other, the eyepiece or ocular, magnifies this image. *The microscope showed us the existence of small, living organisms whose existence had not been suspected* (Atlantic). [< New Latin *microscopium* < Greek *mīkrós* small + *skopeîn* look at]

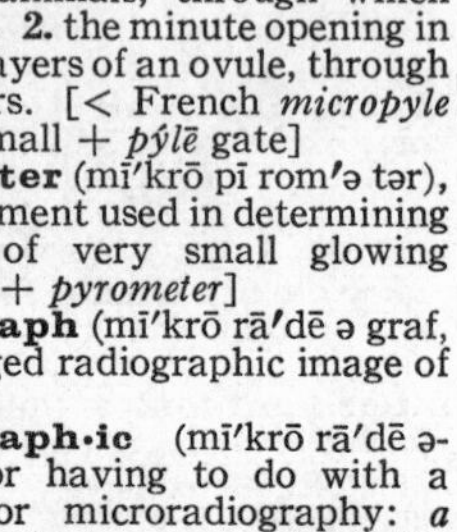

EYEPIECE
EYEPIECE ADJUSTER
FOCUS ADJUSTER
PLATFORM
MIRROR

Compound Microscope

mi·cro·scop·ic (mī′krə skop′ik), *adj.* **1.** that cannot be seen without the use of a microscope. **2.** extremely small; tiny; minute: *microscopic germs.* **3.** like that of a microscope; suggesting the use of a microscope: *a microscopic eye for mistakes, microscopic inquiry.* **4. a.** having to do with a microscope, or having its character or function: *a microscopic lens.* **b.** made or effected by a microscope: *Jean made a microscopic examination of a fly's wing.* **5.** having to do with microscopy.

mi·cro·scop·i·cal (mī′krə skop′ə kəl), *adj.* microscopic.

mi·cro·scop·i·cal·ly (mī′krə skop′ə klē), *adv.* **1.** by the use of the microscope. **2.** as if with a microscope; in great detail

Mi·cro·sco·pi·i (mī′krō skō′pē ī), *n.* genitive of **Microscopium.**

mi·cros·co·pist (mī kros′kə pist, mī′krə-skō′-), *n.* a person trained in the use of the microscope.

Mi·cro·sco·pi·um (mī′krō skō′pē əm), *n., genitive* **Mi·cro·sco·pi·i.** a southern constellation.

mi·cros·co·py (mī kros′kə pē, mī′krə-skō′-), *n.* the use of a microscope; microscopic investigation.

mi·cro·sec·ond (mī′krō sek′ənd), *n.* one millionth of a second.

mi·cro·sec·tion (mī′krō sek′shən), *n.* a very small section of animal tissue, mineral, etc., prepared for microscopic examination: *Precious Metal Depositors . . . uses a . . . microscope to examine microsections of its plating* (New Scientist).

mi·cro·seism (mī′krə sī zəm, -səm), *n.* a faint earthquake tremor, detectable only with seismographs: *Microseisms that travel about half a mile a second are the clue to changes in Great Lakes' weather detected in New York* (Science News Letter). [< *micro-* + Greek *seismós* a shaking, an earthquake < *seíein* to shake]

mi·cro·seis·mic (mī′krə sīz′mik, -sīs′-), *adj.* having to do with or of the nature of a faint earth tremor.

mi·cro·seis·mi·cal (mī′krə sīz′mə kəl, -sīs′-), *adj.* microseismic.

mi·cro·seis·mom·e·ter (mī′krə sīz mom′ə tər, -sīs-), *n.* a seismograph for detecting microseisms: *Great storms off the Greenland coast did not register on the microseismometers in the United States* (Science News Letter).

mi·cros·mat·ic (mī′krəs mat′ik), *adj.* having small or feebly developed organs of smell. [< *micro-* + *osmatic*]

mi·cro·some (mī′krə sōm), *n.* one of the submicroscopic bodies found in the cytoplasm of cells, composed of lipid and nucleoprotein, and thought to be the site of enzyme activity: *Microsomes are the tiny "protein factories" within all living cells* (Science News Letter). [< New Latin *microsoma* < Greek *mīkrós* small + *sôma* body]

mi·cro·spec·tro·pho·tom·e·ter (mī′krō-spek′trō fō tom′ə tər), *n.* a spectrophotometer used for the examination of light reflected by very small specimens: *All three made direct measurements of the light reflected by individual cone cells in the retina, using a special microspectrophotometer* (Lorus J. Milne).

mi·cro·spec·tro·pho·tom·e·try (mī′krō-spek′trō fō tom′ə trē), *n.* **1.** the science that deals with the use of the microspectrophotometer. **2.** the use of the microspectrophotometer.

mi·cro·spec·tro·scope (mī′krō spek′trə-skōp), *n.* a combination of the microscope and the spectroscope, for the examination of minute traces of substances.

mi·cro·spec·tro·scop·ic (mī′krō spek′trə skop′ik), *adj.* of or having to do with the microspectroscope.

mi·cro·spo·ran·gi·um (mī′krō spə ran′jē-əm), *n., pl.* **-gi·a** (-jē ə). *Botany.* a sporangium containing microspores, homologous with the sac containing the pollen in flowering plants: *A microsporangium contains several hundred microspores* (Fred W. Emerson). [< New Latin *microsporangium* < *micro-* micro- + *sporangium* sporangium]

mi·cro·spore (mī′krə spôr′, -spōr′), *n.* **1.** (in certain ferns) a small spore from which a male gametophyte develops. **2.** (in seed plants) a pollen grain.

mi·cro·spo·ro·phyll or **mi·cro·spo·ro·phyl** (mī′krə spôr′ə fil, -spōr′-), *n. Botany.* a leaf or other structure bearing microsporangia.

mi·cro·stom·a·tous (mī′krə stom′ə təs, -stō′mə-), *adj.* having an extremely small mouth. [< *micro-* + Greek *stóma, stómatos* mouth + English *-ous*]

mi·cros·to·mous (mī kros′tə məs), *adj.* microstomatous.

mi·cro·struc·tur·al (mī′krə struk′chər-əl), *adj.* of or having to do with microstructure.

mi·cro·struc·ture (mī′krə struk′chər), *n.* the microscopic structure of bodies, objects, etc.: *Scientists . . . have been studying the microstructure of the insect eye* (Scientific American).

mi·cro·sur·geon (mī′krō sėr′jən), *n.* a person skilled or trained in microsurgery.

mi·cro·sur·ger·y (mī′krō sėr′jər ē), *n.* micromanipulation: *The microsurgery of classical embryology is now extended by the powerful techniques of biochemistry* (Scientific American).

mi·cro·sur·gi·cal (mī′krō sėr′jə kəl), *adj.* having to do with microsurgery.

mi·cro·switch (mī′krō swich′), *n.* an electric switch used in circuits of low voltage and current: *The sleeper can turn the sound off by activating a microswitch that has been taped to his hand* (Science News Letter).

mi·cro·ther·mom·e·ter (mī′krō thər-mom′ə tər), *n.* a thermometer for measuring minute variations of temperature.

mi·cro·tome (mī′krə tōm), *n.* an instrument for cutting extremely thin sections of tissues for microscopic examination. [< *micro-* + Greek *-tomos* that cuts]

mi·cro·tom·ic (mī′krə tom′ik), *adj.* of or having to do with the microtome or microtomy.

mi·cro·tom·i·cal (mī′krə tom′ə kəl), *adj.* microtomic.

mi·crot·o·mist (mī krot′ə mist), *n.* a person expert in the use of the microtome.

mi·crot·o·my (mī krot′ə mē), *n.* the scientific use of the microtome, including the preparation of objects for microscopic examination.

mi·cro·ton·al (mī′krə tō′nəl), *adj.* having to do with or consisting of a microtone or microtones. —**mi′cro·ton′al·ly,** *adv.*

mi·cro·tone (mī′krə tōn′), *n. Music.* an interval smaller than a semitone: *The composer's restless quest for new forms of expression led him to forecast microtones and electronic music and much else long before these things descended on us* (Sunday Times).

mi·cro·volt (mī′krō vōlt′), *n.* a unit of electrical voltage, equivalent to one millionth of a volt: *The short term drift is less than 10 microvolts* (New Scientist).

mi·cro·watt (mī′krō wot′), *n.* a unit of electrical power, equivalent to one millionth of a watt.

mi·cro·wave (mī′krō wāv′), *n.* a high-frequency electromagnetic wave, having a very short wave length, usually ranging from .03937 of an inch to one foot: *Microwaves can add small amounts of energy to atoms* (World Book Annual).

mi·cro·zo·on (mī′krə zō′on), *n., pl.* **-zo·a** (-zō′ə). a microscopic animal, especially a protozoan. [< *micro-* + Greek *zôion* animal]

mi·cro·zyme (mī′krə zīm), *n.* any microorganism supposed to act like a ferment in producing disease. [< *micro-* + Greek *zýmē* leaven]

mi·crur·gi·cal (mī krėr′jə kəl), *adj.* having to do with micrurgy.

mi·crur·gy (mī′krėr jē), *n.* micromanipulation.

mic·tu·rate (mik′chə rāt), *v.i.,* **-rat·ed, -rat·ing.** to urinate. [< *mictur*(ition) + *-ate*[1]]

mic·tu·ri·tion (mik′chə rish′ən), *n.* **1.** the act of urinating; urination. **2.** (formerly) abnormally frequent passage of urine, caused by disease. **3.** *Obsolete.* the wish to urinate. [< Latin *micturīre* desire to make water (< *mingere* to urinate) + English *-tion*]

mid[1] (mid), *adj.* **1.** in the middle of; middle: *the mid days of autumn* (Keats). **2.** designating the middle or a middle: *the mid sea* (Milton). **3.** *Phonetics.* articulated with the tongue midway between high and low position, as English *e* in *bet, u* in *but.*
—*n. Obsolete.* middle: *the mid of night* (Shakespeare).
[Old English *midd,* adjective (found only in inflected forms)]

mid[2] or **'mid** (mid), *prep. Poetic.* amid: *'Mid pleasures and palaces though we may roam* (John H. Payne). [variant of *amid;* influenced by *mid*[1]]

mid-, *combining form.* mid; middle; the middle part of: *Midcontinent = the middle part of a continent.* [< *mid*[1]]

mid., 1. middle. **2.** midshipman.

mid·af·ter·noon (mid′af′tər nün′, -äf′-), *n.* the middle of the afternoon: *The judges, gourmets all, couldn't tear themselves away from a magnificent lunch until midafternoon* (Maclean's). —*adj.* occurring at, or having to do with, the middle of the afternoon: *a midafternoon snack.*

mid·air (mid′ãr′), *n.* **1.** the air; the sky (used with *in*): . . . *each of these rockets either failed to leave the pad or was destroyed in midair* (New Yorker). *This small sample is melted by electromagnetic induction while held suspended in midair by a magnetic field* (Science

(News Letter). **2.** doubt; uncertainty (used with *in*): . . . *the idea of changing the traditional Block Island race rules and the argument was left hanging in midair* (New York Times). —*adj.* **mid-air,** in mid-air: *a mid-air airplane collision.*

Mi·das (mī′dəs), *n.* **1.** *Greek Legend.* a king whose touch turned everything to gold. Having transformed even his food and his daughter, he was permitted to wash away his detested magic touch. **2.** a man of great wealth or of great moneymaking ability.
the Midas touch, the ability to profit or make money from every enterprise: *The same people who hopefully predicted that my father would lose his shirt now say that he had the Midas touch* (New Yorker).
—**Mi′das·like′,** *adj.*

mid·brain (mid′brān′), *n.* the middle part of the brain; mesencephalon.

Mid-Can·a·da Line (mid′kan′ə də), the McGill Fence.

mid·chan·nel (mid′chan′əl), *n.* the middle part of a channel.

mid·con·ti·nent (mid′kon′tə nənt), *n.* the middle part of a continent.

mid·day (mid′dā′), *n.* the middle of the day; noon. —*adj.* occurring at, or having to do with, the middle of the day; of midday: *a midday meal.* [Old English *middæg*]

mid·den (mid′ən), *n.* **1.** a kitchen midden. **2.** *Dialect.* a dunghill; refuse heap. [Middle English *myddyng*, apparently < Scandinavian (compare Danish *mødding*, alteration of *møgdynge* muck heap)]

mid·dle (mid′əl), *adj., n., v.,* **-dled, -dling.** —*adj.* **1.** halfway between; in the center; at the same distance from either end or side: *the middle house in the row.* **2.** medium: *a man of middle size.* **3.** in between; intermediate: *O, beware the middle mind That purrs and never shows a tooth* (Elinor H. Wylie). **4.** *Grammar.* intermediate between active and passive, as a voice of Greek verbs which represents the subject as acting on or for itself. **5.** *Phonetics.* medial (def. 4).
—*n.* **1.** the point or part that is the same distance from each end or side or other limit; central part: *the middle of the road.* **2.** the middle part of a person's body; waist.
—*v.t.* **1.** to set or place in the middle. **2.** to fold in the middle; double, as a rope.
[Old English *middel*]
—**Syn.** *n.* **1. Middle, center** mean a point or part halfway between certain limits. **Middle** most commonly means the part more or less the same distance from each end, side, or other limit of a thing or between the beginning and end of a period or action: *the middle of the room. He came in the middle of the day.* **Center** applies to the point in the exact middle of something having a definite outline or shape, as of a circle, sphere, or square, or to something thought of as the point from, to, or around which everything moves: *Washington is the center of our government.*

Mid·dle (mid′əl), *adj.* **1.** between ancient and modern, or old or new: *the Middle Ages, the Middle Kingdom.* **2.** of or having to do with a period in the history of a language intermediate between the periods called "Old" and "Modern" (or "New"): *Middle English.* **3.** *Geology.* of or having to do with an intermediate principal division of a period, system, or the like, between the upper and lower divisions: *Middle Cambrian.*

middle age, the time of life between youth and old age, between about 40 and 60: *He was past youth, but had not reached middle age; perhaps he might be thirty-five* (Charlotte Brontë). *Middle age has always seemed to us one of the hardest spans of life to pin down statistically* (New Yorker).

mid·dle-aged (mid′əl ājd′), *adj.* **1.** between youth and old age; being of middle age. **2.** characteristic of people in middle age.

mid·dle-ag·er (mid′əl ā′jər), *n.* a person in his or her middle age: *In "The Odd Couple," a pair of poker-playing middle-agers fled their wives to room together in bachelor bliss* (Time).

Middle Ages, the period of European history between ancient and modern times. Although different dates are assigned as the limits of this period, it is most frequently considered to extend from about 476 A.D. (the fall of Rome) to somewhere in the late 1400's.

mid·dle-ag·ing (mid′əl ā′jing), *adj.* inclined to middle age; becoming middle-aged: *Benny, middle-aging manager of a parking lot not far from Columbus Circle* . . . (New Yorker).

mid·dle-break·er (mid′əl brā′kər), *n.* a lister.

mid·dle·brow (mid′əl brou′), *Informal.* —*n.* a person who is above the average in education, taste, and knowledge, but whose attitudes and interests tend to conform to those of the average or majority of people; a person who is neither highbrow nor lowbrow: *Griffith is a discontented middlebrow* (Harper's). —*adj.* of or suitable for a middlebrow; characteristic of a middlebrow: *A professional mixture . . . it is skilfully angled at the middlebrow audience* (Punch).

middle C, the musical note on the first added line below the treble staff and the first above the bass staff.

middle class, the people between the aristocracy or the very wealthy and the working class. In Great Britain, it includes the class socially and conventionally between the aristocratic class and the laboring class, such as professional men, bankers, owners of relatively large businesses, and small gentry.

mid·dle-class (mid′əl klas′, -kläs′), *adj.* of, having to do with, or included in the middle class; bourgeois: *She was the most obnoxious variety of snob: the middle-class woman who has married into the fringe of society* (Leonard Merrick).

middle distance, 1. the part midway between the foreground and the remote region, as in a painting or the like. **2.** (in track) any race from 440 yards up to and sometimes including the mile.

middle ear, the cavity between the eardrum and the inner ear; tympanum. See picture under **ear.**

Middle Eastern, of or having to do with the Middle East, the region where Asia, Africa, and Europe meet.

Middle English, 1. the period in the development of the English language between Old English and Modern English, lasting from about 1100 to about 1500. **2.** the English language of this period: *Chaucer wrote in Middle English. Abbr.:* ME (no periods).

Middle French, the French language from about 1400 to about 1600. *Abbr.:* MF (no periods).

middle game, the middle phase of a game of chess, during which the most intricate moves are made: *As the middle game looms, Black, content to hold his own, leaves White with the choice of standing pat or overreaching himself* (New York Times).

Middle Greek, Medieval Greek.

middle ground, 1. a course between two extremes: *Between these two concepts there is no middle ground, no halfway house* (Wall Street Journal). **2.** a shallow place, such as a bank or bar: *Where a middle ground exists in a channel, each end of it will be marked by a buoy* (Sailor's Pocket Book). **3.** middle distance (def. 1).

Middle High German, the High German language spoken in central and southern Germany from about 1050 to about 1500. *Abbr.:* MHG (no periods).

Middle Irish, the Irish language from about 900 to about 1400.

middle lamella, *Botany.* the primary layer of a plant cell wall, composed chiefly of calcium pectate, on which, in older cells, secondary layers of cellulose are deposited.

Middle Low German, the Low German language spoken in northern Germany from about 1050 to about 1500.

mid·dle·man (mid′əl man′), *n., pl.* **-men.** **1.** a trader or merchant who buys goods from the producer and sells them to a retailer or directly to the consumer. **2.** a person standing in an intermediate relation to two parties concerned in some matter of business. **3.** a man in the middle of a row or line, especially the interlocutor in a minstrel troupe.

mid·dle·most (mid′əl mōst), *adj.* in the exact middle; nearest the middle; midmost.

middle name, 1. a name often following a first name and preceding a family or last name. **2.** a well-known characteristic: *Service is that company's middle name.*

mid·dle-of-the-road (mid′əl əv ᴛʜə rōd′), *adj.* moderate, especially in politics; shunning extremes: . . . *the drift of the South away from its ancient conservatism toward a more middle-of-the-road variety of politics* (Harper's).

mid·dle-of-the-road·er (mid′əl əv ᴛʜə rō′dər), *n.* a moderate, especially in politics: *Middle-of-the-roaders try to strike a balance between pleasing Washington and following their own line of thought and research* (New Yorker).

middle passage, the passage across the Atlantic Ocean formerly made by ships carrying slaves from West Africa to the West Indies or America.

mid·dle-road (mid′əl rōd′), *adj.* middle-of-the-road.

mid·dle-road·er (mid′əl rō′dər), *n.* middle-of-the-roader.

middle school, any school intermediate between elementary school and senior high school.

Middle Temple, one of the Inns of Court in London.

middle term, *Logic.* the term in the major and minor premises of a syllogism but not in the conclusion.

middle voice, *Grammar.* the form of the verb, in Greek and some other languages, which is regularly passive in form but active in meaning, and that normally expresses reflexive or reciprocal action that affects the subject or intransitive conditions.

middle way, a course between extremes.

mid·dle·weight (mid′əl wāt′), *n.* **1.** a person, especially a man, of average weight. **2.** a boxer who weighs more than 147 pounds and less than 160.

Middle Western, of or having to do with the Middle West, a part of the United States, west of the Appalachian Mountains, east of the Rocky Mountains, north of the Ohio River and the southern boundaries of Missouri and Kansas.

Middle Westerner, a native or inhabitant of the Middle West, a part of the United States, west of the Appalachian Mountains, east of the Rocky Mountains, north of the Ohio River and the southern boundaries of Missouri and Kansas.

mid·dling (mid′ling), *adj.* **1.** medium in size, quality, grade, etc.; ordinary; average: *the abundant consumption of middling literature* (Matthew Arnold). **2.** mediocre; second-rate.
—*adv. Informal or Dialect.* moderately; fairly: *I've got a middlin' tight grip, sir, On the handful o' things I know* (John Hay).
—*n.* **middlings, a.** products of medium size, quality, grade, or price: *There are often middlings in a coal-washing process* (Science News). **b.** coarse particles of ground wheat mixed with bran, used in making a very nutritious flour: *The smaller chunks go to purifiers that remove the bran by means of air currents. The purified endosperm, called middlings at this stage, is ground and sifted to produce white flour* (W.B. Dohoney). **c.** *Dialect.* pork or bacon from between the ham and shoulder: *The price of middlings has gone up this week.*
[< Scottish *middling*, probably < *mid*[1], adjective + *-ling*] —**mid′dling·ly,** *adv.*

mid·dy (mid′ē), *n., pl.* **-dies. 1.** *Informal.* a midshipman. **2.** a middy blouse.

middy blouse, a style of loosely fitting blouse having a collar with a broad flap at the back, originally worn by sailors.

Mid·east (mid′ēst′), *adj.* Middle Eastern.

mid·field (mid′fēld′), *n.* the middle of a sports field.

mid·field·er (mid′fēl′dər), *n.* (in lacrosse) a player stationed in midfield.

mid-flight (mid′flīt′), *n.* **1.** the middle of flight (used with *in*): *When bats are caught in mid-flight, their wings are often broken* (Science News Letter). **2.** the middle of any action, procedure, etc. (used with *in*): *a career in mid-flight, music in mid-flight.*

Mid·gard (mid′gärd), *n. Scandinavian Mythology.* the earth, placed between heaven and hell, and connected with heaven by a rainbow. Also, **Midgarth, Mithgarthr.**

Mid·garth (mid′gärᴛʜ), *n.* Midgard.

midge (mij), *n.* **1.** any of various very small insects; gnat: *Of course, I just call them black flies, but the guides call them midges* (New York Times). **2.** a very small person, as a child. [Old English *mycg*]

midg·et (mij′it), *n.* an extremely small person, especially an abnormally small person; dwarf: *Parson Kendall's a little midget of a man* (Harriet Beecher Stowe). —*adj.* very small; miniature; diminutive: *a midget car.* —**Syn.** *n.* See **dwarf.**

mid·gut (mid′gut′), *n.* the middle section of the alimentary canal.

mid·heav·en (mid′hev′ən), *n.* **1.** the middle of the sky. **2.** *Astronomy.* the meridian of a place.

mid·i (mid′ē), *adj., n., pl.* **mid·is.** *—adj.* reaching to the calf (usually in compounds such as *midi-skirt, midi-length*). *—n.* a dress, coat, etc., reaching to the calf. [< *mid*[1]]

Mi·di (mē dē′), *n.* the south, especially the south of France. [< French *midi* (originally) the south, midday < Old French; *mi* < Latin *medius* middle; *-di* < Latin *diēs* day. Compare MERIDIAN.]

Mid·i·an (mid′ē ən), *n.* (in the Bible) one of Abraham's sons. Genesis 25:2.

Mid·i·an·ite (mid′ē ə nīt), *n.* (in the Bible) a member of a wandering tribe of northwestern Arabia, said to be descended from Midian. They fought against the Israelites. Numbers 31:1-9.

mid·i·nette (mid′ə net′; *French* mē dē net′), *n.* a girl who works in a Paris store, dressmaking establishment, etc.: *It is the season to look at the little shopgirls and midinettes* (New Yorker). [< French *midinette,* perhaps < (*qui fait la*) *dînette* (*à*) *midi* one who takes a little dinner at midday]

mid·i·ron (mid′ī′ərn), *n.* a golf club with a steel head having a face of small slope, used for long approach shots. It is usually called a "number 2 iron."

mid·land (mid′lənd), *n.* the middle part of a country; the interior. *—adj.* **1.** in or of the midland; inland: *midland plains.* **2.** surrounded by land; mediterranean.

Mid·land (mid′lənd), *adj.* **1.** belonging to the Midlands. **2.** General American, the variety of English spoken in most of the United States.

Mid·land·er (mid′lən dər), *n.* an inhabitant of the Midland counties of England.

Midland man, an early North American human, probably predating the Folsom man.

mid·leg (mid′leg′), *n.* **1.** the middle of the leg. **2.** one of the middle or second pair of legs of an insect.

Mid-Lent (mid′lent′), *n.* the middle of Lent.

mid·line (mid′līn′), *n.* a line marking the middle of a body or object: *the midline of an organ, embryo, hoof, etc.*

mid mashie, a golf club with a steel head having a hitting surface sloped more than that of a midiron, but less than that of a mashie. It is usually called a "number 3 iron."

mid·morn·ing (mid′môr′ning), *n.* the middle of the morning: *He reached Chicago in midmorning after two nights on the train* (New Yorker). *—adj.* occurring at, or having to do with, the middle of the morning: *midmorning coffee break.*

mid·most (mid′mōst), *adj.* **1.** in the exact middle; nearest the middle; middle. **2.** most intimate.
—adv. in the midmost part; in the midst.
—prep. in the midst of.
—**Syn.** *adj.* **1.** middlemost.

mid·night (mid′nīt′), *n.* 12 o'clock at night, when the old day ends and the new one begins; the middle of the night: *We have heard the chimes at midnight* (Shakespeare). *—adj.* of or like midnight.
burn the midnight oil. See under **oil,** *n.*

mid·night·ly (mid′nīt′lē), *adj.* occurring at midnight or every midnight. *—adv.* at midnight; every midnight.

midnight sun, the sun seen at midnight in the arctic and antarctic regions during their summer: *The midnight sun is an example of a circumpolar star* (Robert H. Baker).

mid·noon (mid′nün′), *n.* the middle of the day; noon: *Gentlewomen . . . who begin their morning at midnoon* (John Lyly).

mid-o·cean (mid′ō′shən), *n.* the middle of the ocean: *stable mid-ocean research platforms* (Scientific American).

mid-off (mid′ôf′, -of′), *n.* (in cricket) the fieldsman or the area to the left of the wicket.

mid-on (mid′on′, -ôn′), *n.* (in cricket) the fieldsman or the area to the right of the wicket.

mid·point (mid′point′), *n.* the middle part of anything; midway point: *Well past midpoint in its journey, the spaceship was sailing along smoothly* (Time).

Mid·rash (mid′rash), *n.* the whole body of Jewish traditional Scriptural exegesis, partly of a legal nature, but mostly of a homiletic character. [< Hebrew *midrash* commentary]

mid·rash (mid′rash), *n., pl.* **mid·ra·shim** (mid rä′shēm) or **-shoth** (-shōth). *Judaism.* an exposition of the Scriptures or a part of them. [< *Midrash*]

mid·rash·ic (mid rash′ik), *adj.* of or having to do with a midrash or the Midrash: *His latest venture is into the vast and cloudy hinterland of Jewish midrashic lore* (Sunday Times).

mid·rib (mid′rib′), *n.* the main vein of a leaf, continuous with the petiole, extending through the central part of the blade of the leaf.

MIDRIB

Midrib

mid·riff (mid′rif), *n.* **1. a.** the diaphragm of a person. **b.** the front of the part of the body including this: *a bare midriff, a punch in the midriff.* **2.** a woman's or girl's garment, often made in two pieces, that leaves the middle portion of the body bare. *—adj.* made so as to expose the middle part of the body: *a midriff bathing suit.* [Old English *midhrif* < *midd* mid + *hrif* belly]

mid·sea·son (mid′sē′zən), *n.* the middle of a season; the busy or active part of the season in a particular business, sport, etc.: *The hotel rates were high during midseason.* *—adj.* in or for the midseason: *Counted out of the league after a disastrous midseason slump* . . . (Time).

mid·sec·tion (mid′sek′shən), *n.* **1.** the middle part of something: *The cold air pouring down into the country's midsection and Southeast is sure to shift in March* (Science News Letter). **2.** midriff: *The midsection is a bit on the heavy side and the hair is gray and thinned* (New York Times).

mid·ship (mid′ship′), *adj.* in, at, or of the middle of a ship.

mid·ship·man (mid′ship′mən), *n., pl.* **-men. 1. a.** a student at the United States Naval Academy at Annapolis or any other school for training officers for the U.S. Navy or Coast Guard. **b.** the rank held by such a student, immediately below that of a commissioned officer. **2. a.** a graduate of British naval schools until he is made sublieutenant. **b.** an officer of the same rank in training on a ship. **3.** (formerly) a boy or young man who assisted the officers of a ship.

mid·ship·mite (mid′ship′mīt), *n. Slang.* midshipman: *This linen also serves for one-piece hostess pajamas with brass ball buttons, bell-bottom trousers, and the look of a midshipmite* (New Yorker).

mid·ships (mid′ships′), *adv.* amidships.

midst[1] (midst), *n.* the middle point or part; center; middle.
in one's midst, within one's group: *a traitor in our midst.*
in the midst of, a. in the middle of; surrounded by; among: *in the midst of a forest. And Jesus called a little child unto him, and set him in the midst of them* [*His disciples*] (Matthew 18:2). **b.** in the thick of: *in the midst of a day's work.*
—adv. in the middle place: *To extol him first, him last, him midst, and without end* (Milton).
[perhaps < phrase *amidst of* (with *a-* taken as preposition)]

midst[2] or **'midst** (midst), *prep. Poetic.* in the midst of; amidst; amid: *They left me 'midst my enemies* (Shakespeare). [short for *amidst*]

mid·stream (mid′strēm′), *n.* the middle of a stream.

mid·sum·mer (mid′sum′ər), *n.* **1.** the middle of summer. **2.** the time of the summer solstice, about June 21. *—adj.* in the middle of the summer.

Midsummer Day, (in England) June 24, one of the quarter days.

midsummer madness, the height of madness: *Why, this is very midsummer madness* (Shakespeare).

mid·term (mid′tėrm′), *n.* **1.** the middle of a term of office, school, etc.: *Kennedy at midterm had changed. No longer did one think of him first as the youngest President elected by his countrymen* (John L. Steele). **2.** *U.S. Informal.* an examination held during the middle of a school term. *—adj.* occurring at, or having to do with, midterm: *The university was in midterm recess* (Time).

mid·town (mid′toun′), *n.* the middle section of a city or town: *He had reached midtown before he remembered the package.* *—adj.* of or located in midtown.

mid-Vic·to·ri·an (mid′vik tôr′ē ən, -tōr′-), *adj.* **1.** of the middle period of Queen Victoria's reign in Great Britain, or from about 1850 to 1890: *mid-Victorian architecture, a mid-Victorian novel.* **2.** like this period; strict in morals; old-fashioned.
—n. **1.** a person who lived during the middle period of Queen Victoria's reign. **2.** a person with old-fashioned ideas and tastes, and strict in morals.
—**Syn.** *adj.* **2.** prudish.

mid·way (mid′wā′), *adj.* in the middle; halfway: *a midway position.*
—n. **1.** a middle way or course: *no midway 'Twixt these extremes at all* (Shakespeare). **2.** a place for side shows and other amusements at a fair or exposition.
—adv. halfway: *Midway between the hill . . . and the city lay the ravine* (Cardinal Newman).
[Old English *midweg;* (noun, definition 2) < the *Midway Plaisance,* a boulevard area, site of the amusements at the Columbian Exposition in 1893 at St. Louis, Missouri]

mid·week (mid′wēk′), *n.* the middle of the week: *By midweek the newspapers found it necessary to give short "missiles for the layman" courses* (New York Times). *—adj.* in the middle of the week.

Mid·week (mid′wēk′), *n.* Wednesday. It is so called by the Quakers.

mid·week·ly (mid′wēk′lē), *adv., adj.* in the middle of the week.

Mid·west (mid′west′), *adj.* Middle Western.

Mid·west·ern (mid′wes′tərn), *adj.* Middle Western.

Mid·west·ern·er (mid′wes′tər nər), *n.* a person who lives in the Middle West; Middle Westerner.

mid·wife (mid′wīf′), *n., pl.* **-wives.** a woman, especially a woman trained by schooling or experience, who helps women in childbirth. [Middle English *midwyf* < Old English *mid* with + *wīf* woman]

mid·wife·ry (mid′wī′fər ē, -wīf′rē), *n.* the art or practice of helping women in childbirth; obstetrics.

mid·win·ter (mid′win′tər), *n.* **1.** the middle of winter. **2.** the time of the winter solstice, about December 21. **3.** (formerly) Christmas.
—adj. in the middle of the winter.

mid world, Midgard.

mid·year (mid′yir′), *adj. U.S.* happening in the middle of a year: *a midyear dividend, a midyear examination, etc.*
—n. **midyears,** *Informal.* **a.** midyear examinations: *The student passed all his midyears.* **b.** the period during which these examinations are held: *I'd breezed through the fall semester, been on Dean's List at midyears, . . . and now was failing* (New Yorker).

M.I.E.E., *British.* Member of the Institute of Electrical Engineers.

mien (mēn), *n.* the manner of holding the head and body; way of acting and looking: *George Washington had the mien of a soldier.* [probably short for obsolete *demean,* noun; influenced by Middle French *mine* appearance, expression of the face, perhaps < Breton *min* muzzle, beak] —**Syn.** bearing, demeanor, appearance.

miff (mif), *Informal.* *—n.* a peevish fit; petty quarrel: . . . *a little quarrel, or miff, as it is vulgarly called, rose between them* (Henry Fielding). *—v.i.* to be offended; have a petty quarrel. *—v.t.* to offend: *She was miffed at the idea that she could be mistaken.* [origin uncertain; perhaps imitative] —**Syn.** *n.* huff, tiff.

miff·y (mif′ē), *adj.,* **miff·i·er, miff·i·est.** *Informal.* easily offended; touchy.

mig or **migg** (mig), *n. Dialect.* a marble. [origin unknown]

MIG or **Mig** (mig), *n.* any of various Russian-designed jet fighter planes (the type and model being indicated by a number). [< Artem *Mi*(koyan) and Mikhail *G*(urevich) Russian airplane designers of the 1900's]

might[1] (mīt), *v.* the past tense of **may**[1]: *Mother said that we might play in the barn. He might have done it when you were not looking.* [Old English *mihte, meahte*]
➔ See **could** for usage note.

might[2] (mīt), *n.* **1.** great power; strength: *Work with all your might.* **2.** operative power (whether great or small): *To the measure of his might each fashions his desires* (Wordsworth).

with might and main, with all one's strength: *They fell to work and belabored each other with might and main* (Washington Irving). [Old English *miht*]

might-have-been (mīt′həv bin′, -əv-), *n.* **1.** something that might have happened: . . . *a junk heap of might-have-beens, the unfulfilled promises of worlds that never were* (New Yorker). **2.** a person or thing that might have been greater or more eminent: *Gustav Mahler, when he died in 1911, left behind one of the most tantalising might-have-beens in musical history: his unfinished Tenth Symphony* (Sunday Times).

might·i·ly (mī′tə lē), *adv.* **1.** in a mighty manner; powerfully; vigorously: *Samson strove mightily and pulled the pillars down.* **2.** very much; greatly: *We are mightily pleased.*

might·i·ness (mī′tē nis), *n.* **1.** power; strength. **2.** Often, **Mightiness.** with *your, his,* etc., and often preceded by *high,* a title of dignity (now used ironically).

might·less (mīt′lis), *adj.* without might; powerless; impotent.

might·y (mī′tē), *adj.,* **might·i·er, might·i·est,** *adv., n., pl.* **might·ies.** —*adj.* **1.** having or showing strength or power; powerful; strong: *a mighty ruler, mighty force.* **2.** very great: *a mighty famine, a mighty dinner.* —*adv. Informal.* very: *a mighty long time.* —*n.* a mighty or powerful person: *Eleazar . . . who was one of the three mighties* (I Chronicles 11:12).

—**Syn.** *adj.* **1. Mighty, powerful** mean strong. **Mighty** suggests great strength and size but not necessarily effective force: *The mighty battleship was so badly damaged that it had to be scuttled.* **Powerful** suggests the strength, energy, or authority to exert great force: *A battleship is a powerful weapon.* **2.** extraordinary.

mig·ma·tite (mig′mə tīt), *n. Geology.* a common type of rock formed of a complex mixture of igneous and metamorphic rocks, characterized chiefly by gneissic bands and crosscutting veins. [< Greek *mígma, -atos* compound + English *-ite*[1]]

mi·gnon (min′yon; *French* mē nyôɴ′), *adj.* delicately formed; small and pretty; dainty. [< French *mignon*]

mi·gnon·ette (min′yə net′), *n.* **1.** any of a group of herbs, especially a common garden plant having long, pointed clusters of small, fragrant, yellowish-white flowers with prominent, golden-brown anthers. **2.** a yellowish-green or grayish-green color; reseda. [< Middle French *mignonnette* < *mignon* mignon]

Mignonette (def. 1) (8 to 15 in. tall)

mi·graine (mī′grān), *n.* a severe headache, usually recurrent and on one side of the head only; megrim. [< Old French *migraigne* < Late Latin (*hē*)*micrānia* < Greek *hēmikrāniā* < *hēmi-* half + *krāníon* headache; (originally) skull. Doublet of HEMICRANIA.]

mi·grain·ous (mī grā′nəs), *adj.* having to do with or suffering from migraines: *Migrainous subjects have been found to have a disordered function in the arteries that supply the head and brain* (New Scientist).

mi·gran·cy (mī′grən sē), *n.* the state or condition of being migrant: *Until we see the connection between migrancy . . . the despairing, destitute families groping for a way to live, and the bountiful supply of fruits and vegetables on every corner fruit stand or in every supermarket, no change will come* (Atlantic).

mi·grant (mī′grənt), *n.* a person, animal, bird, or plant that migrates. —*adj.* migrating; migratory: *a migrant worker.*

mi·grate (mī′grāt), *v.i.,* **-grat·ed, -grat·ing.** **1.** to move from one place to settle in another: *Pioneers from New England migrated to all parts of the United States.* **2.** to go from one region to another with the change in the seasons: *Most birds of the Temperate Zone migrate to warmer countries in the winter.* [< Latin *migrāre* (with English *-ate*[1])]

mi·gra·tion (mī grā′shən), *n.* **1.** a migrating: *Those almighty instincts that propel the migrations of the swallow and the lemming* (Thomas De Quincey). *If migration offers little by way of a solution of the world's demographic problems, why is it so often mentioned?* (Wall Street Journal). **2.** a number of people or animals migrating together. **3. a.** a movement of one or more atoms from one place to another within the molecule. **b.** the movement of ions between the two electrodes during electrolysis.

mi·gra·tion·al (mī grā′shə nəl), *adj.* of or having to do with migration or movement to another place: *migrational ability of birds.*

mi·gra·tor (mī′grā tər), *n.* **1.** a person or thing that migrates. **2.** a migratory bird.

mi·gra·to·ry (mī′grə tôr′ē, -tōr′-), *adj.* **1.** that migrates; migrating: *migratory laborers, migratory workers.* **2.** of or having to do with migration: *the migratory pattern of elephants.* **3.** wandering: *a migratory pain.*

migratory locust, any of the grasshoppers which have short antennae and migrate in great swarms, destroying crops and other vegetation in their path. See picture under **locust.**

mih·rab (mē′rəb), *n.* a niche in a Mohammedan mosque, which points to Mecca. [< Arabic *miḥrāb*]

mi·ka·do or **Mi·ka·do** (mə kä′dō), *n., pl.* **-dos.** the title of the emperor of Japan. The Japanese seldom use this title except in poetry, and it is now decreasingly used by foreigners. [< Japanese *mikado* < *mi* honorable + *kado* gate]

mike (mīk), *n. Informal.* a microphone.

Mike (mīk), *n. U.S.* a code name for the letter *m,* used in transmitting radio messages.

mi·kron (mī′kron), *n., pl.* **-krons, -kra** (-krə). micron.

mik·vah (mik′və), *n. Judaism.* a ritual bath used in ceremonies of purification, such as the bathing of women following menstruation, and the dipping of new dishes before use: *Rabbis want to know why the mikvah attendance has fallen off* (Maclean's). [< Hebrew *mikvah*]

mil (mil), *n.* **1.** a unit of length, 0.001 of an inch, used in measuring the diameter of wires. **2.** a unit of angular measure used in adjusting the aim of a piece of artillery, equal to 1/6400 of a complete circle or about 1/18 of a degree. **3.** *Pharmacy.* a milliliter. **4.** an Israeli bronze coin, worth 1/1000 of a pound. [< Latin *mīlle* thousand; the modern senses are short for *mīllēsimum* thousandth]

mil., 1. military. **2.** militia.

mi·la·dy or **mi·la·di** (mi lā′dē), *n., pl.* **-dies. 1.** my lady: *The spittoon, once a fixture even in banks, ought to be replaced by a wall mirror so milady can look her best* (Wall Street Journal). **2.** an English lady.

➤ **Milady** originated as an appellation used by continental Europeans in speaking to or of an English noblewoman or great lady. In fashionable European hotels, shops, etc., it is often applied to any English-speaking woman whose manner, dress, or purchases are deemed to justify it: *Would milady care to pay now, or later?*

mil·age (mī′lij), *n. U.S.* mileage.

Mi·lan or **mi·lan** (mi lan′, mil′ən), *n.* a fine, closely woven straw used in the manufacture of women's hats: *a hat of red Milan* (New Yorker). [< *Milan,* a city in Italy, where it is made]

Mil·a·nese (mil′ə nēz′, -nēs′), *adj., n., pl.* **-nese.** —*adj.* of or having to do with Milan, a city in northern Italy, or its people: *a Milanese painter.* —*n.* a native or inhabitant of Milan.

milch (milch), *adj.* giving milk; kept for the milk it gives: *a milch cow.* [Old English *-milce* a milking < *mioluc* milk]

milch·er (mil′chər), *n.* a milch animal, as a cow.

mild (mīld), *adj.* **1.** gentle; kind: *a mild, inoffensive man, a mild tone of voice.* **2.** warm; temperate; moderate; not harsh or severe: *a mild climate, a mild winter.* **3.** soft or sweet to the senses; not sharp, sour, bitter, or strong in taste: *a mild cheese, a mild cigar.*

—*n. British Informal.* mild ale or beer: *Bill Flanagan, with whom I took a glass of mild at the Canonbury Working Men's Institute yesterday . . .* (Punch).

[Old English *milde* mild, generous] —**mild′ly,** *adv.* —**mild′ness,** *n.*

—**Syn.** *adj.* **1.** tender, lenient, merciful. See **gentle. 2.** clement, pleasant, bland.

—**Ant. 1.** severe, austere. **2.** harsh.

Mild (mīld), *n.* coffee grown outside of Brazil.

mild·en (mīl′dən), *v.t., v.i.* to make or become mild or milder.

mil·dew (mil′dü, -dyü), *n.* **1.** any of numerous, minute, parasitic fungi producing a whitish coating or a discoloration on plants: *Mildew spoiled the rosebuds in our garden.* **2.** the coating or discoloration, or the diseased condition, produced by such fungi. **3.** any similar discoloration due to fungi, as on cotton and linen fabrics, paper, or leather. —*v.t., v.i.* to cover or become covered with mildew: *A pile of damp clothes in his closet mildewed.*

[Old English *mildēaw, meledēaw* honeydew]

mil·dew·cide (mil′dü sīd, -dyü-), *n.* a substance for preventing or destroying mildew: *The improved "mildewcides," products which contain mercury derivatives, are now on the market* (New York Times). [< *mildew* + *-cide*[1]]

mil·dewed (mil′düd, -dyüd), *adj.* **1.** tainted with mildew: *mildewed books.* **2.** affected from lack of use; outmoded: *"Too True To Be Good," by George Bernard Shaw, is substandard . . . full of mildewed seventyish garrulities on religion, militarism, and the idle rich* (Time).

mil·dew·y (mil′dü ē, -dyü-), *adj.* of, like, or affected with mildew: *There is a mildewy odor from that old trunk.*

mild steel, soft steel.

mile (mīl), *n.* **1.** a unit of linear measure used in measuring distances on land, equal to 5,280 feet (statute mile). **2.** a unit of linear measure used especially at sea, officially fixed at 6,080.20 feet in the United States, and at 6,080 feet in Great Britain, theoretically equal to the distance traversed along one minute of a degree of a great circle of the earth (nautical or geographical mile). **3.** an international unit of linear measure for sea and air navigation, equal to 1.852 kilometers or 6,076.103 feet (international nautical mile). **4.** the ancient Roman mile, equal to 4,860 feet. **5.** the modern Swedish mile, equal to 10 kilometers. *Abbr.:* mi. [Old English *mīl* < Latin *mīlia* (*passuum*) a thousand (Roman paces), plural of *mīlle; passuum,* genitive plural of *passus, -ūs* the legionary's double pace]

mile·age (mī′lij), *n.* **1.** miles covered or traveled: *Our mileage was 350 yesterday. The mileage of this car is 50,000.* **2.** length, extent, or distance in miles: *The mileage of a railroad is its total number of miles of roadbed.* **3.** an allowance for traveling expenses at so much a mile: *Congressmen are given mileage between their homes and Washington, D.C.* **4.** a rate charged per mile, as on a toll highway or for a rented car. **5.** a mileage ticket or mileage book. **6.** *Informal.* benefit; use; gain: *The situation is not without humor but the politicians say there is no mileage in it either way* (Birmingham News). Also, **milage.**

mileage book, a book of mileage tickets or coupons.

mileage ticket, a ticket or coupon that entitles the bearer to a certain number of miles of railroad travel.

mile·post (mīl′pōst′), *n.* a post set up to show the distance in miles to a certain place: *A milepost showed that we were 38 miles from Chicago.*

mil·er (mī′lər), *n.* a person, horse, etc., competing in or trained for a mile race: *The number of sprinters and milers has increased* (Observer).

mi·les glo·ri·o·sus (mī′lēz glôr′ē ō′səs, glōr′-), *pl.* **mi·li·tes glo·ri·o·si** (mil′ə tēz glôr′ē ō′sī, glōr′-). *Latin.* a vain and boastful soldier (from the title and hero of a comedy by Plautus).

Mi·le·sian (mī lē′zhən, -shən; mə-), *adj.* Irish: *a racy Milesian brogue* (Herman Melville) —*n.* a native of Ireland. [< *Milesius,* a fabled Spanish king whose sons supposedly conquered ancient Ireland + *-ian*]

mile·stone (mīl′stōn′), *n., v.,* **-stoned, -ston·ing.** —*n.* **1.** a pillar or stone set up to show the distance in miles to a certain place. **2.** an important event: *The invention of printing was a milestone in human progress.* —*v.t.* to mark with or as with a milestone: *The road was milestoned by the parched hides . . . of horses, mules, and oxen* (J. H. M. Abbott).

mil·foil (mil′foil), *n.* yarrow, a plant. [< Old French *milfoil,* learned borrowing from Latin *millefolium* < *mille* thousand + *folium* leaf]

mil·i·ar·i·a (mil′ē ãr′ē ə), *n.* an acute, inflammatory skin disease, located about the sweat glands, characterized by an eruption of spots or blisters resembling millet seeds, accompanied by itching and considerable perspiration, and occurring especially in tropical climates; prickly heat; miliary fever. [< New Latin *miliaria*, feminine of Latin *miliārius* miliary]

mil·i·ar·y (mil′ē er′ē, mil′yər ē), *adj.* **1.** like a millet seed in size or form. **2.** (of a disease) characterized by eruptions, lesions, etc., resembling millet seeds. [< Latin *miliārius* < *milium* millet]

miliary fever, miliaria.

miliary tuberculosis, tuberculosis characterized by the appearance in various parts of the body of spherical lesions about the size of a millet seed (miliary tubercles), that are caused by tubercle bacilli carried by the blood stream.

Mi·li·bis (mī′lə bis), *n. Trademark.* an arsenical powder administered orally in the treatment of intestinal amoebiasis. *Formula:* $C_8H_9AsBiNO_6$

mi·lieu (mē lyœ′), *n., pl.* **mi·lieus** or **mi·lieux** (mē lyœz′). surroundings; environment: *He [man] takes the milieu in which he finds himself for granted* (H.G. Wells). [< French *milieu* < *mi* (< Latin *medius* middle) + *lieu* (< Latin *locus* place)]

mil·i·o·lite (mil′ē ə lit), *n.* a fossil foraminifer, the minute shells of which, occurring in immense numbers in some strata, are the chief constituent of certain limestones. [< New Latin *Miliola* the genus name (diminutive) < Latin *milium* millet + English *-ite*[1]]

milit., military.

mil·i·tan·cy (mil′ə tən sē), *n.* warlike behavior or tendency; militant spirit or policy: *The union is having trouble holding the rising militancy within bounds* (Wall Street Journal).

mil·i·tant (mil′ə tənt), *adj.* **1.** aggressive; fighting; warlike: *a militant nature.* **2.** engaged in warfare; warring. —*n.* a militant person. [< Latin *mīlitāns, -antis* serving as a soldier, present participle of *mīlitāre* serve as a soldier < *mīles, mīlitis* soldier] —**mil′i·tant·ly,** *adv.* —**Syn.** *adj.* **1.** combative.

mil·i·tar·i·ly (mil′ə ter′ə lē), *adv.* in a military manner or respect: *This nation will aid these islands militarily if they are threatened* (Wall Street Journal).

mil·i·tar·i·ness (mil′ə ter′ē nis), *n.* the state or condition of being military.

mil·i·ta·rism (mil′ə tə riz′əm), *n.* **1. a.** the policy of making military organization and power very strong. **b.** the political condition in which the military interest is predominant in government or administration. **2.** the military spirit and ideals.

mil·i·ta·rist (mil′ə tər ist), *n.* **1.** a person who believes in a very powerful military organization or the predominance of military interests. **2.** an expert in warfare and military matters. —*adj.* militaristic: *a militarist society.*

mil·i·ta·ris·tic (mil′ə tə ris′tik), *adj.* of or having to do with militarists or militarism; characterized by militarism: *militaristic empires.* —**mil′i·ta·ris′ti·cal·ly,** *adv.*

mil·i·ta·ri·za·tion (mil′ə tər ə zā′shən), *n.* **1.** the act of militarizing: *Superior air power is . . . a bulwark against the militarization of society* (Bulletin of Atomic Scientists). **2.** the state of being militarized.

mil·i·ta·rize (mil′ə tə rīz), *v.t.,* **-rized, -riz·ing.** **1.** to make the military organization of (a country) very powerful. **2.** to fill with military spirit and ideals.

mil·i·tar·y (mil′ə ter′ē), *adj.* **1.** of or for soldiers; done by soldiers: *a military victory, a military uniform, military discipline, military maneuvers.* **2.** characteristic of soldiers; soldierly. **3.** suitable for war; warlike: *military valor.* **4.** of or having to do with the army, the armed forces, affairs of war, or a state of war: *military history, military personnel.*
—*n.* **the military, a.** the army; soldiers: *Haven't you any aquaintances among the military to whom you could show your model [of a cannon]?* (William D. Howells). **b.** the military establishment of a country or countries: *Their government is now being run by the military.*
[< Latin *mīlitāris* < *mīles, mīlitis* soldier]
—**Syn.** *adj.* **4. Military, martial, warlike** mean having to do with war. **Military** emphasizes the idea of war as a serious business, and describes anything having to do with affairs of war or the armed forces (especially the army): *He has a military bearing.* **Martial** emphasizes the glory and pomp or the gallantry of fighting men: *Troops paraded in martial array.* **Warlike** suggests a fighting nature, and especially describes acts, feelings, words, etc., threatening or fit for war: *The Iroquois were a warlike people.*

military attaché, an officer in one of the armed services serving on the staff of an ambassador, minister, etc., in a foreign country.

military law, a system of rules regulating the government of armed forces and the discipline and control of persons employed in military service.
➤ **military law, martial law.** *Military law* is limited only to military personnel. *Martial law* applies to both citizens and soldiers, and operates in place of civil law when civil courts are prevented from functioning.

military police, soldiers who act as police for the army. *Abbr.:* M.P., MP (no periods).

military press, a weightlifting exercise in which the bar is lifted from the floor, brought to rest against the chest, and raised above the head.

mil·i·tate (mil′ə tāt), *v.i.,* **-tat·ed, -tat·ing.** **1.** to have or exert force; act; work; operate (against or in favor of): *Bad weather militated against the success of the picnic. Passion, in him, comprehended many of the worst emotions which militate against human happiness* (Edward G. Bulwer-Lytton). **2.** *Obsolete.* to serve in an army; be a soldier. [< Latin *mīlitāre* (with English *-ate*[1]) serve as a soldier < *mīles, mīlitis* soldier] —**Syn. 1.** contend.

mil·i·ta·tion (mil′ə tā′shən), *n.* conflict.

mi·li·tia (mə lish′ə), *n.* **1.** an authorized military force other than that of the full-time, professional military establishment, especially an army of citizens trained for war or any other emergency. Each state of the United States has an organized militia known as the National Guard, the members of which train periodically and may be called to active service in an emergency. **2.** an authorized but unorganized military force consisting of the entire body of able-bodied men in the United States or its territories who have reached the age of 18 and are not more than 45, who are or propose to become citizens, and who are not members of a National Guard or any of the regular armed services. **3.** any citizens' army; any nonprofessional armed force organized or summoned to duty in an emergency. [earlier the military art; later, administration < Latin *mīlitia* < *mīles, mīlitis* soldier]

mi·li·tia·man (mə lish′ə mən), *n., pl.* **-men.** a soldier in the militia.

mil·i·um (mil′ē əm), *n.* a hard, white or yellow tubercle in the skin resembling a millet seed, produced by the retention of a sebaceous secretion. [< New Latin *milium* < Latin, millet]

Mil·i·um (mil′ē əm), *n. Trademark.* a fabric sprayed with a metal solution, especially of aluminum, used as a lining to insulate against cold.

milk (milk), *n.* **1.** the whitish liquid secreted by the mammary glands of female mammals for the nourishment of their young, especially cow's milk, widely used by man as a food and as the source of butter, cheese, cream, etc. **2.** any liquid resembling this in appearance, taste, etc., as the juice of the coconut or the latex of certain plants.
cry over spilt milk, to waste sorrow or regret on what has happened and cannot be remedied: *The money is lost, so there's no use in crying over spilt milk.*
—*v.t.* **1. a.** to draw milk, by handling or by means of a machine, from (a cow, goat, ewe, etc.); secure the milk available in the udder of (a cow, ewe, etc.). **b.** to extract or draw (milk): *12 quarts were milked from that cow.* **2.** to extract as if by milking; drain contents, strength, information, wealth, etc., from: *to milk information from a person. The dishonest treasurer milked the club treasury.* **3.** to draw juice, poison, etc., from: *to milk a snake.* —*v.i.* to yield or produce milk.
[Old English *mioluc, milc*]

milk adder, the milk snake.

milk-and-wa·ter (milk′ən wô′tər, -wot′ər), *adj.* weak or insipid, like milk diluted with water; wishy-washy: *the milk-and-water softness of your former master* (William Godwin).

milk bar, a food counter specializing in dairy drinks and dairy products, such as ice cream or yogurt; soda fountain: *Even alcoholic Paris, thank Heaven, is being infiltrated with milk bars* (Harper's).

milk chocolate, a chocolate candy whose basic ingredients are chocolate liquor, whole milk solids, and granulated sugar.

milk·er (mil′kər), *n.* **1.** a person who milks. **2.** a machine that milks. **3.** any animal that gives milk, especially a cow.

milk fat, fat in milk containing vitamins A, D, E, and K, traces of lecithin and cholesterol, and carotene; butterfat: *Milk fat . . . provides energy and essential fatty acids that our bodies cannot make* (World Book Encyclopedia).

milk fever, 1. a slight fever sometimes occurring in women about the beginning of lactation, originally believed to be caused by a great accumulation of milk in the breasts, now thought to be caused by an infection. **2.** a disease occurring in milch cows, especially before or after calving, characterized by low sugar and calcium content of the blood and paralysis (actually not a fever).

milk·fish (milk′fish′), *n., pl.* **-fish·es** or (*collectively*) **-fish.** an edible fish of the South Pacific, related to the herrings and having a small, toothless mouth and a length of up to 4 feet.

milk float, *British.* a light wagon or cart, usually pulled by a horse, used to carry and deliver milk: *Before the average internal combustion engine utters its early morning cough, the milk floats are out in their thousands* (London Times).

milk glass, opal glass: *new Scandinavian lighting fixtures made of deliciously cool-looking milk glass* (New Yorker).

milk·i·ly (mil′kə lē), *adv.* in a milky manner; with a milky appearance.

milk·i·ness (mil′kē nis), *n.* the state of being milky or of resembling milk in appearance or quality.

milk·ing (mil′king), *n.* the amount of milk obtained at one time.

milking machine, an apparatus for milking cows mechanically.

milking shorthorn, any of a breed of dairy cattle developed from the shorthorn cattle.

milking stool, a stool for sitting on while milking a cow or other animal.

milk leg, or **milk-leg** (milk′leg′), *n.* a painful swelling of the leg caused by clots in the veins, usually due to an inflammation after childbirth.

milk·less (milk′lis), *adj.* without milk; not secreting milk.

milk-liv·ered (milk′liv′ərd), *adj.* cowardly; white-livered: *Milk-liver'd man! That bear'st a cheek for blows* (Shakespeare).

milk·maid (milk′mād′), *n.* **1.** a woman who milks cows. **2.** a woman who works in a dairy. —**Syn. 2.** dairymaid.

milk·man (milk′man′), *n., pl.* **-men.** a man who sells or delivers milk.

milk·o (mil′kō), *n. Australian Slang.* a milkman.

milk of human kindness, natural sympathy and affection.

milk of magnesia, a milky-white medicine consisting of magnesium hydroxide, suspended in water, used as a mild laxative and antacid. *Formula:* $Mg(OH)_2$

milk punch, whiskey, brandy, etc., mixed with milk, sugar, flavoring, etc.

milk room, a cool room in which milk and other food or stores of a household are kept.

milk run, *Slang.* a routine flight, especially a short reconnaissance mission in wartime.

milk shake, a beverage consisting of milk, flavoring, and often ice cream, shaken or beaten until frothy.

milk·shed (milk′shed′), *n.* **1.** the region from which a city or an area receives its milk supply: *the New York City milkshed.* **2.** a milking shed. [< *milk* + *shed,* as in *watershed*]

milk sickness, a malignant disease, formerly common in the western United States, characterized by weakness, trembling, and vomiting, and caused by the consumption of dairy products or meat from cattle that have eaten any of various poisonous plants, especially the white snakeroot; trembles.

milk snake, a harmless, gray snake of North America, with an arrow-shaped mark on the head and dark-bordered chestnut blotches on the back and sides, sometimes

confused with the copperhead and traditionally, but wrongly, supposed to milk cows.
milk·sop (milk′sop′), *n.* an effeminate, spiritless man or youth; unmanly fellow; coward: *He was no milksop; he rode, and shot, and fenced* (Lytton Strachey). [< *milk* + *sop*] —**Syn.** mollycoddle.
milk·sop·ism (milk′sop′iz əm), *n.* the character of a milksop; effeminacy.
milk sugar, lactose.
milk·toast (milk′tōst′), *n.* milquetoast.
milk toast, toast served with or in (usually hot) milk.
milk tooth, *pl.* **milk teeth.** one of the first set of teeth, of which man has twenty; temporary tooth of a young child or animal.
milk train, *U.S.* a train that carries milk to the market, usually very early in the morning.
milk vetch, 1. a European herb of the pea family, thought to increase the amount of milk secreted by goats feeding upon it. **2.** any of several allied herbs.
milk·weed (milk′wēd′), *n.* **1.** any of a group of North American and African herbs, especially a common species having a copious juice that looks like milk, and seeds tufted with long, silky hairs; silkweed. **2.** any of various other plants having a milky juice, as the butterfly weed.
milkweed butterfly, 1. the monarch butterfly. **2.** any of the related butterflies whose larvae feed on milkweed.
milkweed family, a large group of dicotyledonous herbs and shrubs, typically having a milky juice and bearing flowers in clusters. The family includes the milkweed, anglepod, and waxplant.
milk-white (milk′hwīt′), *adj.* white as milk.
milk·wort (milk′wėrt′), *n.* **1.** any of a group of showy-flowered plants, formerly thought to increase the secretion of milk in women; polygala: *I was equally glad to see and photograph the orange milkwort* (New York Times). **2.** a plant of the primrose family, common on the seacoast and in salt marshes, having small, purplish-white flowers; sea milkwort.
milk·y (mil′kē), *adj.,* **milk·i·er, milk·i·est. 1.** like milk; white as milk; whitish. **2.** of, containing, or yielding milk. **3.** mild; weak; timid: *They made . . . me (the milkiest of men) a satirist* (Byron).
milky disease, a disease that kills the larvae of Japanese beetles and other scarabaeids, caused by a type of bacteria that sporulates in the soil.
Milky Way, a broad band of faint light that stretches across the sky at night; the Galaxy. It is made up of countless stars and luminous clouds of gas, too far away to be seen separately without a telescope. *The Milky Way is an island universe composed of millions of stars grouped in the shape of a flat disc that turns like a great wheel in space* (Scientific American). [translation of Latin *Via Lactea; Via* way; *lactea,* feminine of *lacteus* < *lac, lactis* milk]
mill[1] (mil), *n.* **1.** a machine for grinding grain into flour or meal. **2.** a building specially designed and fitted with machinery for the grinding of grain into flour. **3. a.** any machine for crushing or grinding: *a coffee mill, a pepper mill.* **b.** a machine designed to extract juices by grinding or crushing: *a cider mill.* **4.** a building where manufacturing is done: *Cotton cloth is made in a cotton mill.* **5.** a roller of hardened steel having impressed upon it a pattern that is transferred by pressure to a cylinder (for printing cloth) or plate (for printing currency, bonds, etc.). **6.** a machine that performs its work by rotary motion, especially one used by lapidaries in polishing precious stones. **7.** a machine with rotary cutters or rollers for working metal. **8.** any of various other machines for performing certain operations upon material in the process of manufacture. **9.** *Slang.* a fight with the fists.
go through the mill, *Informal.* **a.** to get a thorough training or experience: *He is an excellent soldier, having gone through the mill at military school.* **b.** to learn by hard or painful experience: *He went through the mill in that business undertaking.*
put through the mill, *Informal.* **a.** to test; examine; try out: *The new car was put through the mill.* **b.** to teach by hard or painful experience: *He was put through the mill during basic training.*
—*v.t.* **1.** to grind (grain) into flour or meal. **2.** to grind into powder or pulp. **3.** to manufacture. **4.** to cut a series of fine notches or ridges in the edge of (a coin): *A dime is milled.* —*v.i.* **1.** to move (around) in confusion: *The frightened cattle began to mill around.* **2.** *Slang.* to fight with the fists; box.
[Old English *mylen* < Late Latin *molīna, molīnum,* (originally) adjectives, Latin *molīnus* having to do with a mill < *mola* millstone, mill]
mill[2] (mil), *n. U.S.* $.001, or 1/10 of a cent, used especially in expressing tax rates. Mills are used in figuring but not as coins. [American English, short for Latin *millēsimus* one thousandth < *mīlle* thousand]
mill·a·ble (mil′ə bəl), *adj.* that can be milled; suitable for milling: *It also put out last week its first guide prices for . . . millable wheat* (London Times).
mill·age (mil′ij), *n.* a rate of taxation expressed in mills per dollar.
mill·board (mil′bôrd′, -bōrd′), *n.* a stout board made of wastepaper or pulp, used for the covers of books.
mill cake, the cake or mass resulting from the incorporation of the ingredients of gunpowder, preliminary to granulation.
mill·course (mil′kôrs′, -kōrs′), *n.* millrace.
mill·dam (mil′dam′), *n.* **1.** a dam built in a stream to supply water power for a mill. **2.** a pond made by such a dam; millpond.

Milldam (def. 1)

mille (mēl), *n.* an Arabic unit of linear measure, equal to 119 miles. [< Arabic *mīl*]
milled (mild), *adj.* made or formed by milling.
mille·feuille (mēl′fœy′), *n.* a thin, crusty, sweet French pastry made with flour, butter, and eggs. [< French *mille-feuille*]
mil·le·fi·o·ri glass (mil′ə fē ôr′ē, -ōr′-), ornamental glassware made by fusing small glass tubes or rods of various colors together lengthwise and cutting the fused mass into cross sections that are then embedded in clear glass or treated in some other way. [< Italian *mille-fiori* (literally) thousand flowers]
mille·fleurs[1] (mēl′flœr′), *adj.* (of cloth, paintings, tapestry, etc.) showing a design or pattern of many flowers: *A rare Gothic Flemish tapestry of the "millefleurs" type, a weaving closely studded with bluebells, columbines, and other flowers . . .* (New Yorker). [< French *mille-fleurs* (literally) a thousand flowers]
mille·fleurs[2] (mēl′flœr′), *n.* a perfume containing extracts from a variety of flowers. [< French *(eau de) mille-fleurs* (water of) a thousand flowers]
mil·le·nar·i·an (mil′ə nãr′ē ən), *adj.* **1.** of or relating to a thousand. **2.** *Theology.* of or having to do with the prophesied millennium. —*n. Theology.* a believer in the millennium, especially one who believes it will come soon; chiliast.
mil·le·nar·i·an·ism (mil′ə nãr′ē ə niz′əm), *n.* the doctrine of or belief in the millennium.
mil·le·nar·y (mil′ə ner′ē), *adj., n., pl.* **-naries.** —*adj.* **1.** consisting of or having to do with a thousand, especially a period of a thousand years. **2.** *Theology.* of or having to do with the millennium or millenarians.
—*n.* **1. a.** an aggregate of one thousand, especially a continuous period of one thousand years: *We danced through three nights, dancing the old millenary out, dancing the new millenary in* (Cardinal Newman). **b.** a thousandth anniversary or the celebration of such an anniversary. **2.** *Theology.* **a.** a millennium; the millennium. **b.** a millenarian.
[< Late Latin *millēnārius* < *millēnī* a thousand each < *mīlle* a thousand]
mil·len·ni·al (mə len′ē əl), *adj.* **1.** of a thousand years. **2.** *Theology.* having to do with a millennium, especially the prophesied millennium. **3.** like that of the millennium; fit for the millennium: *There was to be a millennial abundance of new gates . . . and returns of ten per cent* (George Eliot).
—*n.* a thousandth anniversary or its celebration; millenary. —**mil·len′ni·al·ly,** *adv.*
Millennial Church, the Shakers.
mil·len·ni·al·ist (mə len′ē ə list), *n.* millenarian.
mil·len·ni·a·ry (mə len′ē ə rē), *adj.* millennial.
mil·len·ni·um (mə len′ē əm), *n., pl.* **-lenni·ums, -len·ni·a** (-len′ē ə). **1. a.** a period of one thousand years: *The Christian era is less than two millenniums old.* **b.** a thousandth anniversary. **2.** the period of a thousand years during which, according to the Bible, Christ is expected to reign on earth. **3.** a period of righteousness and happiness: *a catastrophic climax which would be followed by something in the nature of a millennium* (Edmund Wilson).
[< New Latin *millennium* < Latin *mīlle* thousand + *annus* year, patterned on English *biennium*]
mil·le·ped (mil′ə ped), *n.* millipede.
mil·le·pede (mil′ə pēd), *n.* millipede.
mil·le·pore (mil′ə pôr, -pōr), *n.* any of various corallike hydrozoans covered with very small openings and bearing tentacles with powerful stings. [< New Latin *millepora* < Latin *mīlle* thousand + *porus* pore]
mil·le·po·rine (mil′ə pôr′in, -pōr′-), *adj.* having to do with the millepores or having their characteristics.
mill·er (mil′ər), *n.* **1. a.** a person who owns or runs a mill, especially a flour mill. **b.** a person who operates any machine called a mill. **2.** any of certain moths whose wings are covered with a whitish powder resembling flour (from the traditional image of a miller as being dusted with flour). **3. a.** a milling machine. **b.** a tool used in a milling machine.
mill·er·ite (mil′ə rīt), *n.* a mineral, nickel sulfide, usually occurring in brassy or bronze crystals or in incrustations. *Formula:* NiS [< German *Millerit* < W.H. *Miller,* 1801-1880, a British mineralogist + *-it* -ite[1]]
Mill·er·ite (mil′ə rīt), *n.* an Adventist following the doctrine of William Miller, an American preacher, who foretold the second coming of Christ and the beginning of the millennium which would occur in the immediate future: *The Millerites . . . believed that the world would be destroyed by fire in 1843* (New Yorker).
mill·er's-thumb (mil′ərz thum′), *n.* any of various small, spiny-finned, fresh-water fishes; sculpin.
mil·les·i·mal (mə les′ə məl), *adj.* **1.** thousandth. **2.** consisting of thousandth parts. **3.** dealing with thousandths.
—*n.* a thousandth part.
[< Latin *millēsimus* a thousandth (< *mīlle* thousand) + English *-al*[1]]
mil·let (mil′it), *n.* **1.** an annual cereal grass bearing a large crop of very small, nutritious seeds on a drooping terminal panicle. It is probably native to India, but has been extensively cultivated throughout history as a food grain, in the United States mainly for fodder. **2.** any of various other grasses grown for their seeds or for forage, as durra or Indian millet, pearl millet, or Italian millet. **3.** the grain or seed of any of these plants. [< Middle French *millet* (diminutive) < *mil* millet < Latin *milium*]
mill hand, a worker in any type of mill; millman: *The Pacific Northwest's great experiment in turning plywood mill hands into capitalists* (Wall Street Journal).
milli-, *combining form.* one thousandth of a ——: *Millimeter = one thousandth of a meter.* [< Latin *milli-* < *mīlle*]
mil·li·am·me·ter (mil′ē am′mē′tər), *n.* an ammeter which measures thousandths of amperes: *A milliammeter, used to measure small electric currents, is constructed so that blind persons can feel its raised dial markings* (Science News Letter).
mil·li·amp (mil′ē amp′), *n.* a milliampere.
mil·li·am·pere (mil′ē am′pir), *n.* one thousandth of an ampere. *Abbr.:* ma.
mil·li·ang·strom (mil′ə ang′strəm), *n.* one thousandth of an angstrom.
mil·liard (mil′yərd, -yärd), *n. British.* a thousand millions; billion; 1,000,000,000. [< Middle French *milliard,* alteration of *million,* influenced by Latin *mīlliārius* containing a thousand < *mīlle* thousand]
➜ **Milliard** is the usual term for this number in Great Britain and most of Europe. The term *billion* is synonymous with *milliard* in the French system, and is applied by the British, Germans, etc., to the number 1,000,000,000,000, known as a *trillion* in the United States.
mil·li·ar·y (mil′ē er′ē), *adj., n., pl.* **-ar·ies.** —*adj.* of, having to do with, or using the

ancient Roman mile of a thousand paces. —*n.* a milestone. [< Latin *mīlliārium* a mile (stone), neuter adjective < *mīlle* (*passuum*); see MILE]

mil·li·bar (mil′ə bär), *n.* a unit of barometric pressure equal to one thousandth of a bar or 1,000 dynes per square centimeter: *Thirty-four millibars are about equal to one inch of mercury. Abbr.:* mb.

mil·li·cron (mil′ə kron), *n.* micromillimeter.

mil·li·cu·rie (mil′ə kyu̇r′ē), *n.* one thousandth of a curie: *One millicurie of radium expels thirty million alpha particles per second* (Science News). *Abbr.:* mc (no period).

mil·lieme (mēl yem′), *n.* a unit of money in Tunisia, Egypt, Libya, etc., worth one thousandth of the country's basic monetary unit. [< French *millieme* < Latin *millesimus* thousandth]

mil·li·e·quiv·a·lent (mil′ē i kwiv′ə lənt), *n.* one thousandth of the value of an equivalent weight. *Abbr.:* meq.

mil·lier (mēl yā′), *n.* a metric ton. [< French *millier* < Old French, having 1,000 < *mille* a thousand < Latin *mīlia*, plural of *mīlle*]

mil·li·far·ad (mil′ə far′əd, -ad), *n.* one thousandth of a farad. *Abbr.:* mf.

mil·li·gal (mil′ə gal), *n.* a measure of gravity, one thousandth of a gal, equal to an acceleration of one thousandth of a centimeter per second.

mil·li·gram (mil′ə gram), *n.* one thousandth of a gram, equal to 0.0154 of a grain, or about two millionths of a pound. *Abbr.:* mg.

mil·li·gramme (mil′ə gram), *n. British.* milligram.

mil·li·hen·ry (mil′ə hen′rē), *n., pl.* **-ries** or **-rys.** one thousandth of a henry. *Abbr.:* mh.

mil·li·li·ter (mil′ə lē′tər), *n.* one thousandth of a liter, equal to 1.000027 cubic centimeters, 0.061 cubic inch, or 0.0338 fluid ounce. *Abbr.:* ml.

mil·li·li·tre (mil′ə lē′tər), *n. British.* milliliter.

mil·li·me·ter (mil′ə mē′tər), *n.* one thousandth of a meter, equal to 0.03937 inch. *Abbr.:* mm (no period).

mil·li·me·tre (mil′ə mē′tər), *n. British.* millimeter.

mil·li·met·ric (mil′ə met′rik), *adj.* of or having to do with the millimeter or any system of measurement based on it.

mil·li·mi·cron (mil′ə mī′kron), *n., pl.* **-crons, -cra** (-krə). one thousandth of a micron. *Symbol:* Mμ (no period).

mil·li·mi·cro·sec·ond (mil′ə mī′krō sek′ənd), *n.* one thousandth of a microsecond: *Accuracy is said to be within a fraction of a millimicrosecond* (Science News Letter).

mil·line (mil′līn′), *n. U.S.* a unit used in buying and selling advertising space, representing one 5½-point (agate) line, one column wide, in one million copies of a newspaper, magazine, etc. [< *mil*(lion) + *line*]

mil·li·ner (mil′ə nər), *n.* **1.** a person who makes, trims, or sells women's hats. **2.** *Obsolete.* a dealer in fancy wares and articles of apparel, especially those originally of Milan manufacture. [earlier *myllener*, variant of *Milaner*, a dealer in goods from *Milan*, Italy, famous for its straw work]

mil·li·ner·y (mil′ə ner′ē, -nər-), *n., pl.* **-ner·ies. 1.** women's hats. **2.** the business of making, trimming, or selling women's hats. **3.** articles made or sold by milliners.

mill·ing (mil′ing), *n.* **1.** the business of grinding grain in a mill. **2.** manufacturing. **3.** the act or process of cutting notches or ridges on the edge of a coin. **4.** such notches or ridges. **5.** *Slang.* a thrashing.

milling machine, a machine tool with rotary cutters for working metal.

mil·lion (mil′yən), *n.* **1.** one thousand thousand; 1,000,000. *Abbr.:* m. **2.** a very large number; very many: *millions of fish. She can think of millions of reasons for not helping with the dishes.* **3.** a million coins or units of money of account of some understood value, especially a million dollars or British pounds: *He left an estate of over a million.*

the million, the multitude; the masses: *The play . . . pleased not the million* (Shakespeare).

—*adj.* **1.** one thousand thousand; 1,000,000. **2.** very large number of; very many: *a million thanks.*

[< Old French *million* < Italian *milione* < *mille* thousand < Latin *mīlle*]

mil·lion·aire or **mil·lion·naire** (mil′yə nãr′), *n.* **1.** a person whose wealth amounts to a million or more dollars, pounds, francs, etc. **2.** a very wealthy person: *Only a millionaire could afford these prices.* —**Syn. 2.** Croesus, Midas.

mil·lion·aire·dom or **mil·lion·naire·dom** (mil′yə nãr′dəm), *n.* **1.** the condition of being a millionaire. **2.** millionaires considered as a group.

mil·lion·air·ess or **mil·lion·nair·ess** (mil′yə nãr′is), *n.* a woman millionaire.

mil·lion·ar·y (mil′yə ner′ē; *especially British* mil′yə nər ē), *adj., n., pl.* **-aries.** —*adj.* possessing millions, as of money: *these millionary people* (Rudyard Kipling). —*n.* a millionaire.

mil·lioned (mil′yənd), *adj.* **1.** numbered by the million. **2.** possessed of millions, as of money.

mil·lion·fold (mil′yən fōld′), *adv., adj.* a million times as much or as many (always with the indefinite article *a*): *a millionfold increase, to increase a millionfold.*

mil·lionth (mil′yənth), *adj., n.* **1.** last in a series of one million. **2.** one, or being one, of a million equal parts.

mil·li·ped (mil′ə ped), *n.* millipede.

mil·li·pede (mil′ə pēd), *n.* any of various small, wormlike arthropods having a body consisting of many segments, most of which bear two pairs of legs: *Millipedes do not rank as a major agricultural pest* (Science News). Also, **milleped, millepede, milliped.** [< Latin *mīllepeda* < *mīlle* thousand + *pēs, pedis* foot]

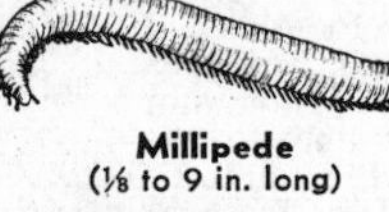
Millipede
(⅛ to 9 in. long)

Mil·li·pore (mil′ə pôr, -pōr), *n. Trademark.* a plastic, semipermeable membrane of molecular dimension, used to filter bacteria from water, air, etc., and in surgical operations to repair and protect tissues: *The apparatus consisted of a Millipore filter soaked in haemoglobin solution* (New Scientist).

mil·li·rad (mil′ə rad), *n.* one thousandth of a rad.

mil·li·rem (mil′ə rem), *n.* one thousandth of a rem.

mil·li·roent·gen (mil′ə rent′gən), *n.* one thousandth of a roentgen: *The present level of radiostrontium in the bones of young children . . . is about two milliroentgens per year* (Science News Letter).

mil·li·sec (mil′ə sek), *n.* a millisecond.

mil·li·sec·ond (mil′ə sek′ənd), *n.* one thousandth of a second: *delayed in time by several hnndred milliseconds* (Science News). *Abbr.:* ms (no period).

mil·li·stere (mil′ə stir), *n.* (in the metric system) a unit of volume equal to one thousandth of a stere, or one cubic decimeter.

mil·li·volt (mil′ə vōlt′), *n.* a unit of electrical voltage, equivalent to one thousandth of a volt.

mil·li·watt (mil′ə wot′), *n.* one thousandth of a watt.

mill·man (mil′man′, -mən), *n., pl.* **-men. 1.** a worker in any type of mill: *Miners and millmen agreed to return to work after negotiation of a new one-year contract* (Wall Street Journal). **2.** Also, **mill man.** *Informal.* a person who owns or operates a mill.

mil·lo maize (mil′ō), a variety of sorghum of the grain-sorghum group, resembling durra. [< Spanish *millo* < Latin *milium* millet]

mill·pond (mil′pond′), *n.* **1.** a pond supplying water to drive a mill wheel, especially such a pond formed by a milldam. **2.** the Atlantic, especially that part of the ocean crossed by ships passing between Great Britain and North America (used in a humorous way).

mill·race (mil′rās′), *n.* **1.** the current of water that drives a mill wheel. **2.** the channel in which the water flows to the mill. —**Syn. 2.** sluice.

Mills bomb or **grenade** (milz), a type of hand grenade long standard in the British and many other armies, about the size and shape of a goose egg and weighing about 1½ pounds: *Our retaliation was to put twelve Mills bombs into the building* (Lord Louis Mountbatten). [< Sir William *Mills*, 1856-1932, a British inventor]

mill·stone (mil′stōn′), *n.* **1.** either of a pair of round, flat stones (the upper of which rotates upon the lower), used for grinding corn, wheat, etc.: *An enormous millstone, a relic of the original mill, is imbedded in the terrace* (Wall Street Journal). **2.** a type of stone, especially a hard sandstone, suitable for the making of millstones. **3.** a heavy burden. **4.** anything that grinds or crushes: *the millstone of war.*

mill·stream (mil′strēm′), *n.* the stream in a millrace.

mill wheel, a wheel that supplies power for a mill, especially a water wheel.

MILL WHEEL

Overshot Mill Wheel

mill·work (mil′wėrk′), *n.* **1.** doors, windows, moldings, and other woodwork made separately from the main structure of a building in a planing mill. **2.** work done in a mill.

mill·wright (mil′rīt′), *n.* **1.** a person who designs, builds, or sets up mills or machinery for mills. **2.** a mechanic who sets up and takes care of machinery in a factory.

mi·lo (mī′lo, mil′ō), *n., pl.* **-los.** any of several grain-sorghums with slender, pithy stalks, introduced into the United States soon after 1880, and cultivated for grain and forage: *three cargoes of milo* (New York Times). [see MILLO, MAIZE]

Mi·lon·tin (mī lon′tin), *n. Trademark.* an anticonvulsant administered orally in the treatment of petit mal. *Formula:* $C_{11}H_{11}NO_2$

mi·lor (mi lôr′), *n.* milord.

mi·lord (mi lôrd′, -lôr′), *n.* **1.** my lord. **2.** an English gentleman. [< French *milord* < English *my lord*, a phrase of address]

➤ **Milord** originated as an appellation used by continental Europeans in speaking to or of an English lord, and subsequently came to be applied to any wealthy Englishman. A further general extension to any well-to-do, or seemingly well-to-do, English-speaking male, paralleling the development of **milady,** has not taken place.

mil·pa (mil′pä), *n.* (in Central America) a field made by clearing the jungle, farmed for only a few seasons, after which it is abandoned. [< Mexican Spanish *milpa*]

milque·toast or **Milque·toast** (milk′tōst′), *n.* an extremely timid person: *Foreign policy planners fear the U.S. gets a Milquetoast reputation abroad* (Wall Street Journal). [< the comic strip character, Caspar *Milquetoast*, probably < *milk toast*]

mil·reis (mil′rās′), *n., pl.* **-reis. 1.** a former Brazilian silver coin and monetary unit, worth 1,000 reis. **2.** an old Portuguese gold coin. [< Portuguese *milreis* (literally) a thousand reis < *mil* (< Latin *mīlle* a thousand) + *reis*, plural of *real* (literally) regal, or royal (coin) < Latin *regālis*]

milt[1] (milt), *n.* **1.** the sperm cells of male fishes with the milky fluid containing them. **2.** the reproductive gland in male fishes when containing this fluid. —*v.t.* to impregnate (fish eggs) with milt. [perhaps < Middle Dutch *milte* milt of fish, spleen; influenced by Middle English *milk* milt of fish]

milt[2] (milt), *n.* the spleen. [Old English *milte*]

milt·er (mil′tər), *n.* a male fish in breeding season.

Mil·to·ni·an (mil tō′nē ən), *adj.* Miltonic.

Mil·ton·ic (mil ton′ik), *adj.* **1.** of or having to do with John Milton. **2.** resembling Milton's literary style; solemn and majestic.

Mil·town (mil′toun), *n. Trademark.* meprobamate: *Pharmacists report big sales increases are being held by the nerve-calming tranquilizers, like Miltown* (Wall Street Journal).

mil·vine (mil′vīn, -vin), *adj.* having to do with or resembling the kites (birds). [< Latin *milvus* kite + English *-ine*[1]]

Mil·wau·kee·an (mil wô′kē ən), *n.* a native or inhabitant of Milwaukee, Wisconsin.

mim (mim), *adj. Scottish.* primly quiet; affectedly modest; prim: *Did I not say it wasna want o' spunk that made ye sae mim?* (Scott). [imitative]

mim·bar (mim′bär), *n.* the pulpit in a mosque. Also, **minbar.** [< Arabic *minbar*]

mime (mīm), *n., v.,* **mimed, mim·ing.** —*n.* **1.** a mimic; jester; clown; buffoon: *Della Scala stood among his courtiers with mimes and buffoons . . . making him heartily merry* (Thomas Carlyle). **2.** among the ancient Greeks and Romans: **a.** a coarse farce using funny actions and gestures and the ludicrous representation of familiar types: *No more*

shall wayward grief abuse The genial hour with mask and mime (Tennyson). **b.** an actor in such a farce. **c.** a dialogue written for it. **3.** an actor or dancer. **4. a.** a pantomimist. **b.** pantomime: *the art of mime. His mime is excellent . . . and he treats his dancing as a medium of art rather than a means of self-exploitation* (New York Times).
—*v.t.* **1.** to imitate; mimic: *miming Chinese laundrymen, Swedish servant girls and balloon-pants Dutch comics* (Time). **2.** to act or play (a part), usually without words: *A gang of leaping fiends . . . introduced a horrid wizard (mimed by Frederick Ashton)* (Time).
—*v.i.* to act without using words; act in a mime.
[< Latin *mīmus* < Greek *mîmos*]—**mim′er,** *n.*

mim·e·o·graph (mim′ē ə graf, -gräf), *n.* a machine for making copies of written or typewritten materials by means of stencils.
—*v.t.* to make (copies) with a mimeograph: *A resolution . . . was mimeographed on official conference stationery* (New York Times).
[< American English *Mimsograph* (originally a trademark) < Greek *mīmeîsthai* imitate + English *-graph*]

mi·me·sis (mi mē′sis, mī-), *n.* **1.** imitation; mimicry. **2.** resemblance of one animal to another or to its surroundings, which gives protection; mimicry. **3.** Also, **mimosis.** the assuming by one disease of the symptoms of another. **4.** imitation or reproduction of the supposed words of another, as in order to represent his character. **5.** the representation, by means of details from ordinary life, of reality in works of literature or art: *It implies an attempt to deny that art itself is art, a mimesis, a make-believe* (Atlantic).
[< Greek *mīmēsis* < *mīmeîsthai* imitate < *mîmos* mime]

mi·met·ic (mi met′ik, mī-), *adj.* **1.** imitative: *mimetic gestures.* **2.** mimic or make-believe: *mimetic games of children.* **3.** having to do with or exhibiting mimicry: *It is difficult for dancing to portray the beauty of physical rapture . . . since it must not be mimetic* (London Times). [< Greek *mīmētikós* < *mīmeîsthai* imitate < *mîmos* mime]

mi·met·i·cal·ly (mi met′ə klē, mī-), *adv.* in a mimetic manner; imitatively; in the manner of a mime: *Homer . . . wished to express mimetically the rolling, thundering, leaping motion of the stone* (Thomas De Quincey).

mim·e·tite (mim′ə tīt, mī′mə-), *n.* a mineral arsenate and chloride of lead, of a yellow to brown color, usually occurring in crystals. *Formula:* $Pb_5As_3O_{12}Cl$ [< German *Mimetit* < French *miméthèse* (< Greek *mīmētḗs* imitator) + German *-it* -ite[1] (because it resembles pyromorphite)]

mim·ic (mim′ik), *v.,* **-icked, -ick·ing,** *n., adj.*
—*v.t.* **1.** to make fun of by imitating or copying (a person, his speech, manner, etc.): *We like to get Tony to mimic our music teacher.* **2.** to copy closely; imitate; ape: *A parrot can mimic a person's voice.* **3.** to represent imitatively, as by drawing; simulate. **4.** (of things) to be an imitation of: *Fresh carved cedar, mimicking a glade Of palm and plantain* (Keats). **5.** *Biology.* to resemble (something else) closely in form, color, etc.: *Some insects mimic leaves.* [< noun]
—*n.* **1.** a person skillful in imitating or mimicking. **2.** one that imitates another: *Cunning is the only mimic of discretion* (Joseph Addison). **3.** *Obsolete.* a mime. [< adjective]
—*adj.* **1.** not real, but imitated or pretended for some purpose: *The soldiers staged a mimic battle for the visiting general.* **2.** imitative: *mimic gestures or expression.*
[< Latin *mīmicus* < Greek *mīmikós* < *mîmos* a mime]

mim·i·cal (mim′ə kəl), *adj.* mimic.

mim·ick·er (mim′ə kər), *n.* a person or thing that mimics.

mim·ic·ry (mim′ik rē), *n., pl.* **-ries. 1.** the act or practice of mimicking: *By the talent of mimicry . . . I could copy their pronunciation of the English language* (William Godwin). **2.** an instance, performance, or result of mimicking: *an imitation and mimicry of good nature* (Joseph Addison). **3.** *Biology.* the close outward resemblance of an animal to some different animal or to its environment, especially for protection or concealment.

Mi·mir (mē′mir), *n. Norse Mythology.* the giant who guarded the spring of wisdom beneath Yggdrasil, who knew the past and the future. His head was taken by Odin to be used as an oracle.

mi·mo·sa (mi mō′sə, -zə), *n.* **1.** any of a group of trees, shrubs, and herbs of the pea family, growing in tropical or warm regions, and usually having fernlike leaves and heads or spikes of small flowers, as the sensitive plant. **2.** the flower of any of these plants. [< New Latin *Mimosa* the genus name < Latin *mīmus* mime (< Greek *mîmos*) + *-ōsa,* feminine -ose[1] (because it mimics animal reactions)]

Mimosa (def. 1) (sensitive plant)

mim·o·sa·ceous (mim′ə sā′shəs, mī′mə-), *adj.* belonging to the mimosa family.

mimosa family, a former grouping of plants now classified as a subgroup of the pea family.

mi·mo·sis (mi mō′sis, mī-), *n.* mimesis.

mim·u·lus (mim′yə ləs), *n.* a monkey flower. [< New Latin *mimulus* (diminutive) < Latin *mīmus* mime]

min., an abbreviation for the following:
1. a. mineralogical. **b.** mineralogy.
2. minim or minims.
3. minimum.
4. mining.
5. minister.
6. minor.
7. minute or minutes.

mi·na[1] (mī′nə), *n., pl.* **-nae** (-nē), **-nas.** a unit of weight and value used by the ancient Greeks, Egyptians, and others, equal to 1/60 of a talent or about one pound. [< Latin *mina* < Greek *mnâ, mnâs* < Semitic (compare Babylonian *manū*)]

mi·na[2] (mī′nə), *n.* myna.

min·a·ble (mī′nə bəl), *adj.* that can be mined: *minable deposits, minable ores.* Also, **mineable.**

mi·na·cious (mi nā′shəs), *adj.* threatening; menacing. [< Latin *minax, minācis* (with English *-ous*) < *minārī* to threaten < *minae* projecting points, threats, menaces] —**mi·na′cious·ly,** *adv.* —**mi·na′cious·ness,** *n.* —**Syn.** minatory.

mi·nac·i·ty (mi nas′ə tē), *n.* disposition to threaten.

mi·nar (mi när′), *n.* in Moslem countries: **1.** a lighthouse. **2.** a tower. **3.** a minaret. [< Arabic *manār,* related to *nār* fire]

min·a·ret (min′ə ret′, min′ə ret), *n.* a slender, high tower of a Moslem mosque, with one or more projecting balconies from which the muezzin or crier calls the people to prayer: *Its plain red outer wall, a few dozen feet high, is topped with crenellations and minarets* (New Yorker). [< French *minaret,* or Spanish *minarete,* probably < Turkish *minare* < Arabic *manārah* < *manār;* see MANAR]

Minaret

min·a·ret·ed or **min·a·ret·ted** (min′ə ret′id, min′ə ret′-), *adj.* having a minaret or minarets: *a minareted mosque or palace.*

min·a·to·ri·al (min′ə tôr′ē əl, -tōr′-), *adj.* threatening; minatory.

min·a·to·ri·ly (min′ə tôr′ə lē, -tōr′-), *adv.* in a minatory manner; with threats.

min·a·to·ry (min′ə tôr′ē, -tōr′-), *adj.* that threatens; menacing: *A minatory inscription on one side of the gate intimated "prosecution according to law" . . . to all who should be found trespassing* (Scott). [< Late Latin *minātōrius* < Latin *minārī* threaten]

mi·nau·de·rie (mē nōd rē′), *n. French.* coquettish airs: *the minauderies of the young ladies in the ballrooms* (Thackeray).

min·bar (min′bär), *n.* mimbar.

mince (mins), *v.,* **minced, minc·ing,** *n.*
—*v.t.* **1.** to cut or chop up (meat or other food) into very small pieces; shred: *All vegetables used in this recipe are to be minced very fine.* **2.** to cut up; subdivide minutely: *The scientists extracted the gene material by mincing the cells* (Science News Letter). **3.** to speak or do in an affectedly polite or elegant manner. **4.** to make little of; disparage. **5.** to minimize in representation; soften or moderate (words, etc.), as in stating unpleasant facts: *The judge, in addressing the jury, spoke bluntly, mincing no words.*
—*v.i.* **1.** to walk with little short, affectedly dainty steps: *The daughters of Zion are haughty, and walk with stretched-forth necks . . . mincing as they go* (Isaiah 3:16). **2.** to act, behave, or speak with affected niceness or elegance: *Vanity, vanity! . . . the same sentiment that sets a lassie mincing to her glass* (Robert Louis Stevenson).
—*n.* **1.** meat cut up into very small pieces; a dish of minced meat or the like: *a mince of chicken. They dined on mince and slices of quince* (Edward Lear). **2.** mincemeat: *"We children" were employed in chopping mince for pies to a most wearisome fineness* (Harriet Beecher Stowe).
[< Old French *mincier* < Vulgar Latin *minūtiāre* < Latin *minūtus* small; see MINUTE[1]]
—**Syn.** *v.t.* **1.** hash.

minced (minst), *adj.* **1.** (of food) cut or chopped into very small pieces. **2.** (of oaths, etc.) altered to a milder or less obvious form.

mince·meat (mins′mēt′), *n.* **1.** a cooked mixture of apples, suet, raisins, currants, spices, etc., usually with chopped meat, used as a filling for pies. **2.** *British.* meat cut up into very small pieces.

make mincemeat of, to reduce as if into little pieces; cut down; defeat overwhelmingly: *The Yankees were making mincemeat of the rest of the league.*

mince pie, a pie filled with mincemeat.

minc·er (min′sər), *n.* a person or thing that minces.

minc·ing (min′sing), *adj.* **1.** too polite; too nice: *a mincing voice.* **2.** walking with little short steps: *I'll turn two mincing steps into a manly stride* (Shakespeare). —**minc′ing·ly,** *adv.* —**minc′ing·ness,** *n.*

minc·y (min′sē), *adj.,* **minc·i·er, minc·i·est.** *U.S.* using an affected delicacy or daintiness, especially in speech.

mind[1] (mīnd), *n.* **1.** that which thinks, feels, and wills, as in a human or other conscious being: *The powers or processes of the mind.* **2.** the intellect or understanding, as contrasted with the faculties of feeling and willing; intelligence: *To learn arithmetic easily, you must have a good mind. An upright heart and cultivated mind* (William Cowper). *Such statements may be repugnant to the scientific mind, which is apt to dismiss them as metaphysical or mystical nonsense* (R. Hadekel). **3.** a person who has intelligence: *A mind for ever Voyaging through strange seas of Thought, alone* (Wordsworth). **4.** the intellectual powers or capacities of a body of persons: *explanations adapted to the popular mind.* **5.** reason; sanity: *to be out of one's mind, to lose one's mind.* **6.** mental or physical activity in general, as opposed to matter. **7.** a conscious or intelligent agency or being: *the doctrine of a mind creating the universe. A pulse in the eternal mind* (Rupert Brooke). **8.** a way of thinking and feeling; opinion; view. **9.** bent or direction of thoughts, etc.: *to give one's mind to a new occupation.* **10.** tendency of thinking or feeling in social or moral respects; spirit; temper: *But the war is not ended; the hostile mind continues in full vigour* (Edmund Burke). **11.** the thinking or feeling faculty with reference to condition: *an anxious state of mind, peace of mind.* **12.** desire, purpose, intention, or will. **13.** attention; thought; mental effort: *Keep your mind on your work.* **14.** remembrance or recollection; memory: *out of sight, out of mind.* **15.** commemoration. **16.** *Psychology.* the organized total of all conscious experience of the individual. **17. Mind.** (in the belief of Christian Scientists) God.

bear in mind, to keep one's attention on; remember: *He promised to bear the subject in mind* (Macaulay).

be of one or **a mind,** to agree: *Why should we quarrel . . . when we are both of one mind?* (Frederick Marryat).

blow one's mind, *Informal.* to excite, often to the point of losing one's reason: *In one episode, some hippies offer him coffee and "blow his mind" with the new mind-expanding drug . . .* (Maclean's). *About 300 bands are inviting the faithful to "blow your mind" with the new sound* (Time).

bring or **call to mind, a.** to recall: *This brings to mind a story.* **b.** to remember: *I cannot call it to mind.*

change one's mind, a. to alter one's purpose: *Her first impulse was to change her mind and not go after all* (Francis M. Crawford). **b.** to alter one's way of thinking, opinion, etc.: *I have lived to change my mind, and*

am almost of the contrary opinion (John Duncombe).
cross one's mind, to occur to one; come into one's thoughts suddenly: *Such an idea never crossed ... our minds* (Thomas Medwin).
have a mind of one's own, to have definite or decided opinions, inclinations, or purposes: *He has a mind of his own and will not listen to reason.*
have a mind to, to intend to; think of favorably: *They thought they could deal as they had a mind to with his property* (Scott).
have half a mind to, to be somewhat inclined to; have some desire to: *I have half a mind to go.*
have in mind, a. to remember: *Others forgot her, but he still had her in mind.* **b.** to take into account; consider: *We should have in mind the benefits of the journey as well as the difficulties we might encounter.* **c.** to intend; plan: *She has in mind a trip to Europe next summer.*
in or **of two, many,** etc., **minds,** vacillating between two, many, etc., intentions: *Last week Moscow sources found the Central Committee in two minds about how to deal with the youth problem* (Time).
keep in mind, to remember: *It was hard to deal realistically with the immediate situation and yet keep in mind the ultimate goal* (Edmund Wilson).
know one's own mind, to know what one really thinks, intends, or wishes: *They are both very young and may not know their own minds* (Henry Kingsley).
make up one's mind, to decide; resolve: *We had all quietly made up our minds to treat him like one of ourselves* (Robert Louis Stevenson).
on one's mind, in one's thoughts; troubling one: *I knew my aunt sufficiently well to know that she had something of importance on her mind* (Dickens).
pass out of mind, to be forgotten: *When they are out of sight, they soon pass out of mind.*
pay no mind, *Dialect.* to pay no attention to; ignore: *Pay his insults no mind!*
put one in mind of, to remind one of: *Your joke puts me in mind of a joke my uncle told me. Rosalind Elias from the Met, New York ... put us in mind of Mr. Robert Helpmann's imitations of a certain Great Actress* (Manchester Guardian Weekly).
set one's mind on, to want very much: *He set his mind on becoming a great lawyer.*
speak one's mind, to give one's frank opinion; speak plainly or freely: *Give me leave to speak my mind* (Shakespeare).
take one's mind off, to distract one's attention from; divert from (something unpleasant): *The music took his mind off his troubles.*
to one's mind, a. in one's opinion; to one's way of thinking: *The other is but a loutish young fellow, to my mind* (Elizabeth C. Gaskell). **b.** according to one's wishes or whims: *It was ... some time before we could get a ship to our minds* (Daniel Defoe).
—*v.t.* **1.** to bear in mind; give heed to: *Mind my words!* **2.** to obey: *Mind your father and mother.* **3.** to be careful concerning: *Mind that you come on time.* **4.** to turn one's attention to; apply oneself to: *Mind your own business. Bidding him be a good child and mind his book* (Joseph Addison). **5.** to look after; take care of; tend: *Mind the baby.* **6.** to trouble oneself about; be concerned about: *I am rather faint ... but don't mind me* (Dickens). **7.** to object to; feel concern about: *Do you mind closing the door for me? I mind parting from my friends. Some people don't mind cold weather.* **8.** *Dialect.* to notice; perceive; be aware of: *Will he mind the way we are, and not tidied or washed cleanly at all?* (John M. Synge). **9.** *Dialect.* to remember: *I mind being there when I was a lad* (Robert Louis Stevenson). *The lads you leave will mind you till Ludlow tower shall fall* (A.E. Housman). **10.** *Dialect.* to remind: *They mind us of the time we made bricks in Egypt* (Tennyson). **11.** *Dialect.* to intend; contemplate.
—*v.i.* **1.** to take notice; observe: *Now mind, I don't tell you these are my idees* (James Fenimore Cooper). **2.** to be obedient: *to train a dog to mind.* **3.** to be careful: *If you don't mind, you'll get hurt.* **4.** to feel concern; care; object: *Father was furious, but Mother didn't mind.* **5.** *Dialect.* to remember.
mind one's p's and q's. See under **P.**
never mind, *Informal.* don't let it trouble you; it does not matter: *Never mind, Mother, I'll buy the dress myself.*
[Old English *gemynd* memory; thinking]
—**Syn.** *n.* **1, 2. Mind, intellect** mean the part of a human being that enables him to know, think, and act effectively. **Mind** in general usage is the inclusive word, meaning the part that knows, thinks, feels, wills, remembers, etc., thought of as distinct from the body: *To develop properly, the mind needs training and exercise.* **Intellect** applies to the knowing and thinking powers of the mind, as distinct from the powers of feeling and will: *Many motion pictures appeal to the feelings instead of the intellect.*

mind[2] (mind), *n. Archaeology.* a diadem or crescent-shaped ornament found in Ireland. [< Middle Irish *mind*]

mind-bend·er (mīnd′ben′dər), *n.* something that substantially alters the mind or one's opinions, such as a potent drug or forceful experience: *Marijuana is one of the mind-benders of antiquity. It has been used since long before Christ to ease the ills of body and soul ...* (Science News).

mind cure (mīnd), treatment of disease by the influence of a healer's mind.

mind·ed (mīn′did), *adj.* **1.** having a certain kind of mind: *high-minded, strong-minded.* **2.** inclined; disposed: *Come a little early, i you are so minded. I was minded to argue the question out with my mother* (Charles Kingsley). —**mind′ed·ness,** *n.*

Min·del (min′dəl), *n. Geology.* the second glaciation of the Pleistocene period in Europe. [< *Mindel* River, Bavaria]

mind·er (mīn′dər), *n.* **1.** a person whose business is to mind or attend to something. **2.** *British.* a child, especially an orphan or one whose parents are unable to support him, who is committed to a special school or home.

mind-ex·pand·ing (mīnd′ek span′ding), *adj.* that stimulates consciousness or enlarges mental capacity: ... *mind-expanding car-pool repartee* (New Yorker). *A Buffalo scientist reported ... evidence ... that the "mind-expanding" drug LSD might be damaging the users' chromosomes* (New York Times).

mind·ful (mīnd′fəl), *adj.* **1.** having in mind; heedful (of): *Mindful of your advice, I went slowly. What is man, that thou art mindful of him?* (Psalms 8:4). **2.** taking thought; careful (of): *We had to be mindful of every step we took on the slippery sidewalk.* —**mind′ful·ly,** *adv.* —**mind′ful·ness,** *n.* —**Syn. 1.** aware, cognizant. **2.** attentive.

mind·ing-school (mīn′ding skül′), *n. British.* a school run by a woman, mainly to keep the children out of mischief.

mind·less (mīnd′lis), *adj.* **1.** without mind or intelligence: *the shrieking of the mindless wind* (John Greenleaf Whittier). **2.** not taking thought; forgetful; careless: *Cursed Athens, mindless of thy worth, Forgetting thy great deeds* (Shakespeare). —**mind′less·ly,** *adv.* —**mind′less·ness,** *n.*

mind reader, a person who is said to be able to discern the thoughts of others.

mind reading, guessing the thoughts of others: *It is quite legitimate for a scientist to investigate whether such phenomena as ... mind reading or divination ... do exist* (Bulletin of Atomic Scientists). —**mind′-read′ing,** *adj.*

mind-set (mīnd′set′), *n.* frame of mind; mental or intellectual climate: *Whatever the explanation, the national mind-set in Sweden clearly makes major reform easier than it is in most countries* (Saturday Review).

mind's eye, mental view or vision; imagination: *In my mind's eye, Horatio* (Shakespeare). *And now crossing my mind's eye were the visions that had gone with the name* (New Yorker).

mine[1] (mīn), *pron.* a possessive form of **I. 1.** belonging to me: *This book is mine. Such as you were, I took you for mine* (Robert Browning). **2.** the one or ones belonging to me: *Please lend me your pen; I have lost mine.* **3.** those who are mine, especially my family or kindred: *me and mine.*
—*adj. Archaic.* my (used only before a vowel or *h*, or after a noun): *mine own, mine heart, sister mine.* [Old English *mīn*]

mine[2] (mīn), *n., v.,* **mined, min·ing.** —*n.* **1.** a large hole or space dug in the earth for the purpose of taking out ores, precious stones, coal, salt, etc.: *a gold mine, a coal mine.* **2.** a deposit of mineral or ore, either under the ground or at its surface. **3.** a rich or plentiful source: *The book proved to be a mine of information about radio.* **4.** an underground passage in which an explosive is placed to blow up the enemy's forts, etc. **5.** a container holding an explosive charge that is put under water and exploded by propeller vibrations (acoustic or sonic mine) or by magnetic attraction (magnetic mine), or laid on the ground or shallowly buried and exploded by contact with a vehicle, etc. (land mine). **6.** a kind of firework, consisting of a series of separate charges that scatter high in the air and explode simultaneously or in sequence.
spring a mine, to cause the gunpowder or other explosive in a mine to explode: *Be prepared to spring the mines in these bridges if the enemy should advance* (Duke of Wellington).
—*v.i.* **1.** to dig into the earth in order to extract ores, coal, etc.; make a mine. **2.** to get ores, coal, etc., from a mine. **3.** to work in a mine. **4.** to make a passage, hole, space, etc., below the surface of the earth; dig or lay explosive mines. —*v.t.* **1.** to dig into (the earth, a hill, etc.) to obtain ores, coal, etc. **2.** to extract (ores, coal, etc.) from a mine. **3.** to dig in; make (passages, etc.) by digging or burrowing. **4.** to lay explosive mines in or under: *to mine the mouth of a harbor.* **5.** to destroy secretly; ruin slowly; undermine. [< Old French *mine* < unrecorded Gaulish *meina* unrefined metal]

mine·a·ble (mī′nə bəl), *adj.* that can be mined; minable.

mine detector, an electromagnetic device used to locate explosive mines, primarily those placed underground in wartime: *Another development in mine detection is the automatic jeep-mounted mine detector* (World Book Encyclopedia).

Mine Detector

mine field, *Military.* **1.** an area throughout which explosive mines have been laid. **2.** the pattern or arrangement of mines in an area.

mine layer, a surface vessel or submarine to lay underwater mines.

Mi·nen·wer·fer (mē′nən ver′fər), *n. German.* a gun with a rifled barrel resembling a trench mortar in that it is loaded from the muzzle and fired at a high trajectory.

min·er (mī′nər), *n.* **1.** one who works in a mine: *a coal miner; the mole, the miner of the soil* (William Cowper). **2.** a soldier who digs an underground passage beneath the enemy's forts, etc., to lay mines that will blow them up; sapper. **3.** a machine used for mining. **4.** an insect that, in the larval stage, lives between the surfaces of a leaf; leaf miner.

min·er·al (min′ər əl, min′rəl), *n.* **1.** a substance obtained by mining: *Coal, quartz, feldspar, and asphalt are minerals.* **2.** *Mining.* an ore. **3.** any substance neither animal nor vegetable. **4.** *British.* mineral water.
minerals, *British.* mineral waters; soft drinks: *There will be ... supper with ale and minerals at Osborne's Hotel* (Glasgow Herald).
—*adj.* **1.** having to do with or consisting of minerals. **2.** like a mineral or minerals. **3.** containing minerals: *mineral water.* **4.** neither animal nor vegetable; inorganic.
[< Medieval Latin *minerale,* neuter adjective < *minera* a mine < Old French *minere* < *mine;* see MINE[2]]

mineral dressing, an initial process in the refining of an ore, in which the ore is crushed and ground into tiny particles which are, by flotation or some other process, then separated into mineral concentrates and waste materials.

mineral fuel, coal, petroleum, or gas.

mineral hammer, a hammer that has both square and pointed ends for pounding or prying loose crystals and other specimens embedded in solid rock.

min·er·al·i·za·tion (min′ər ə lə zā′shən, min′rə-), *n.* **1.** the act or process of mineralizing. **2.** the state of being mineralized. **3.**

a product of this process; petrifaction. **4.** *Mining.* the condition of being well supplied with ore.

min·er·al·ize (min′ər ə līz, min′rə-), *v.*, **-ized, -iz·ing.** —*v.t.* **1.** to convert into mineral substance; transform (metal) into an ore: *We had fairly unearthed an oblong chest of wood, which, from its perfect preservation and wonderful hardness, had plainly been subjected to some mineralizing process* (Edgar Allan Poe). **2.** to impregnate or supply with a mineral substance or substances. —*v.i.* to search for minerals.

min·er·al·iz·er (min′ər ə lī′zər, min′rə-), *n.* a substance that promotes the formation of minerals, especially ores around hot igneous intrusions, as water, fluorides, and borates.

mineral jelly, a kind of petrolatum that is mixed with certain explosives to make them less sensitive to shock, heat, etc., and thus easier to handle, ship, etc.

min·er·al·o·cor·ti·coid (min′ər ə lə kôr′tə koid), *n.* any of a group of steroid hormones, such as aldosterone, produced by the adrenal cortex, which play an important part in metabolism, especially in controlling the salt and water balance in the body. [< *mineral* + *corticoid*]

min·er·a·log·i·cal (min′ər ə loj′ə kəl), *adj.* of mineralogy.

min·er·a·log·i·cal·ly (min′ər ə loj′ə klē), *adv.* according to mineralogy; with reference to mineralogy.

min·er·al·o·gist (min′ə ral′ə jist, -rol′-), *n.* a person who is skilled in the study of mineralogy.

min·er·al·o·gy (min′ə ral′ə jē, -rol′-), *n.* **1.** the science of minerals. **2.** a book about this science.

➔ The second pronunciation, arising under the influence of the large group of nouns like *biology* and *geology*, is established in use. See also **genealogy.**

mineral oil, 1. any oil obtained from the earth; petroleum. **2.** any oil derived from a mineral substance, as from coal. **3.** a colorless, odorless, tasteless oil obtained from petroleum, used especially as a laxative; liquid petrolatum.

mineral pitch, asphalt.

mineral right, a right to the mineral content of a certain area of land. The holder of a mineral right is entitled to a royalty whenever a mineral is extracted from the land.

mineral rights, the land or its mineral contents: *Title litigation scared off the drillers until a recent court decision awarded the mineral rights to the government* (Time).

min·er·als (min′ər əlz, min′rəlz), *n.pl.* See under **mineral,** *n.*

mineral salt, a salt which occurs as, or is derived from, a mineral: *Over-irrigation led to the depositing of mineral salts on the soil to such an extent that crop yields were reduced sharply* (Science News Letter)

mineral tallow, hatchettin, a soft, waxy mineral substance found in Wales and Scotland.

mineral tar, a semiliquid variety of bitumen; maltha.

mineral water, water containing mineral salts or gases. People drink various mineral waters for their health.

mineral waters, *British.* soft drinks; effervescent nonalcoholic beverages, as soda water or ginger beer: *Will you have some mineral waters with your lunch?*

mineral wax, ozocerite, a waxy mixture of natural hydrocarbons.

mineral wool, a woollike material made from melted slag; rock wool. It is used in the walls, ceilings, etc., of buildings to provide insulation against heat and cold.

miner's cramp, heat cramp: *Miner's cramp quickly disappears if plain drinking water is replaced by a weak salt solution* (New Scientist).

Mi·ner·va (mə nėr′və), *n.* the Roman goddess of wisdom, the arts, and defensive war, identified with the Greek goddess Athena.

Minerva

min·e·stro·ne (min′ə strō′nē), *n.* a thick soup containing vegetables, vermicelli, etc.: *They . . . existed on a diet of minestrone while they made the rounds of the movie studios* (Newsweek). [< Italian *minestrone* < *minestra* soup < *minestrare* minister to < Latin *ministrāre* minister to < *minister;* see MINISTER]

mine·sweep·er (mīn′swē′pər), *n.* a ship used for dragging a harbor, the sea, etc., to remove mines laid by an enemy: *It was Winston Churchill . . . who conceived the idea of dispatching a fleet of old battleships and minesweepers to attack the Dardanelles* (New Yorker).

mine·sweep·ing (mīn′swē′ping), *n.* the process of dragging a harbor, the sea, etc., to remove underwater mines laid by an enemy.

mine thrower, a trench mortar.

mine·work·er (mīn′wėr′kər), *n.* a miner.

Ming (ming), *n.* **1.** the ruling Chinese dynasty from 1368 to 1644, known for the exquisitely decorated ceramics, paintings, etc., produced under it: *Brilliant best describes the color decoration and technical facility of Chinese ceramics during the Ming Dynasty* (Scientific American). **2.** a piece of fine porcelain made in China under this dynasty. [< Chinese *Ming* (literally) bright]

min·gle (ming′gəl), *v.*, **-gled, -gling.** —*v.t.* **1.** to combine in a mixture; mix; blend: *Two rivers that join mingle their waters.* **2.** to bring together or associate; unite or join in company: *Their families are mingled by marriage.* **3.** to form by mixing various ingredients: concoct: *men of strength to mingle strong drink* (Isaiah 5:22). —*v.i.* **1.** to be or become mingled; mix; blend: *The blood of all nations is mingling with our own* (Longfellow). **2.** to associate: *to mingle with important people. He is very shy and does not mingle much with the children at school.* [Middle English *mengelen* (perhaps frequentative) < Old English *mengan* to mix. Compare Middle Dutch MENGELEN.] —**min′gler,** *n.* —**Syn.** *v.t., v.i.* **1.** fuse.

min·gle·ment (ming′gəl mənt), *n.* **1.** the act of mingling. **2.** the result of mingling; a mixture.

min·gy (min′jē), *adj.*, **-gi·er, -gi·est.** *Informal.* niggardly; stingy: *We weren't mingy with our music; everybody . . . got an earful* (Punch). [perhaps < *m*(ean) + (st)*ingy*]

min·i (min′ē), *adj., n., pl.* **min·is.** —*adj.* small for its kind; miniature (usually in compounds such as *minibus, mini-home*): *A waiter serves me with three mini-sandwiches* (Punch). —*n.* **1.** a minicar: *you see him zipping by in the family mini* (London Times). **2.** a miniskirt. [< *mini*(ature)]

min·i·ate (*adj.* min′ē it; *v.* min′ē āt), *adj., v.*, **-at·ed, -at·ing.** —*adj.* of the color of minium; orange-red. —*v.t.* to color or paint with minium; rubricate or illuminate (a manuscript, etc.). [< Latin *miniāre* (with English *-ate*[1]) paint red]

min·i·a·tor (min′ē ā′tər), *n.* a person who illuminates a manuscript; rubricator.

min·i·a·ture (min′ē ə chər, min′ə chər), *n.* **1.** anything represented on a very small scale: *She is a miniature of her mother. In the museum there is a miniature of the ship "Mayflower." Tragedy is the miniature of human life* (John Dryden). **2.** a very small painting, usually a portrait on ivory or vellum: *His* [*Holbein's*] *miniatures have all the strength of oil colors joined to the most finished delicacy* (Horace Walpole). **3.** the art of painting these. **4.** a picture in an illuminated manuscript.

in miniature, on a very small scale; reduced in size: *I run over the whole history of my life in miniature, or by abridgment* (Daniel Defoe).

—*adj.* done or made on a very small scale; tiny: *The little girl had miniature furniture for her doll house.*

[< Italian *miniatura* < Medieval Latin *miniare* to rubricate, illuminate (a manuscript) in red < Latin *miniāre* paint red < *minium* red lead; later taken as related to Latin *minūtus* small] —**Syn.** *adj.* diminutive.

miniature camera, a camera using narrow film (35-millimeter or less), suitable especially for taking action photographs, informal snapshots, etc.

miniature golf, a game based on golf, played on a small course fitted out with obstacles: *Miniature golf is especially popular with teen-agers* (Time).

min·i·a·tur·ist (min′ē ə chər ist, min′ə chər-), *n.* a painter of miniatures.

min·i·a·tur·i·za·tion (min′ē ə chər ə zā′shən, min′ə chər-), *n.* **1.** the act or process of miniaturizing. **2.** the state of being miniaturized.

min·i·a·tur·ize (min′ē ə chə rīz, min′ə chə-), *v.t.*, **-ized, -iz·ing.** to reduce to miniature dimensions, especially as an improved replacement for a much larger type: *The technological skills that produced miniature radios and computers . . . should be equally successful in miniaturizing artificial organs* (Atlantic). —**min′i·a·tur·iz′er,** *n.*

min·i·bus (min′ē bus), *n., pl.* **-bus·es** or **bus·ses.** *Especially British.* **1.** any passenger van or truck seating about a dozen people. **2.** *Obsolete.* a light, four-wheeled, covered carriage.

min·i·cab (min′ē kab), *n. British.* a minicar used as a taxicab.

min·i·cam (min′ē kam), *n.* a miniature camera. [< *mini*(ature) *cam*(era)]

min·i·car (min′ē kär), *n. British.* a compact car seating two persons.

min·i·dress (min′ē dres), *n.* a very short dress, usually four to five inches above the knee: *The sleeveless minidresses had receded to the length of a pajama top* (New York Times).

Min·i·é ball or **bullet** (min′ē ā, min′ē), a conical bullet with a hollow base which expands, when fired, to fit the rifling of the gun. [< Captain Claude E. *Minié,* 1814-1879, a French inventor]

min·i·fi·ca·tion (min′ə fə kā′shən), *n.* a making smaller; lessening.

min·i·fy (min′ə fī), *v.t.*, **-fied, -fy·ing.** to make less: *The pliancy of Congress . . . during the past two sessions has greatly minified the importance of that body in the eyes of the public* (Baltimore Sun). [< Latin *minor,* neuter of *minus* less (see MINUS) + English *-fy*]

min·i·kin (min′ə kin), *n.* **1.** *Archaic.* a small or insignificant thing; a diminutive creature. **2.** *Obsolete.* a pretty girl.

—*adj.* **1.** dainty; elegant. **2.** affected; mincing. **3.** diminutive; miniature; tiny: *In the distance . . . the farmsteads* [*have become*] *minikin as if they were the fairy-finest to be packed in a box* (John Ruskin).

[alteration of earlier Dutch *minneken* small, frail thing (diminutive) < *minne* love + *-ken* -kin]

min·im (min′əm), *n.* **1.** the smallest unit of liquid measure, equal to 1/60 of a fluid dram, or about a drop. **2.** *Music.* a half note. **3.** a very small amount; the least possible portion; jot. **4.** a very small or insignificant person or thing: *Not all minims of nature; some of serpent kind, Wondrous in length and corpulence* (Milton). **5.** a single stroke made vertically downward in writing by hand, as either of the two strokes in *n.*

—*adj.* extremely small; smallest.

[< Latin *minimus* smallest, superlative of *minus* less; see MINUS]

Min·im (min′əm), *n.* a mendicant friar of the Order of Least Hermits, founded in the 1400's by Saint Francis of Paula, 1416-1507. [< *minim*]

min·i·ma (min′ə mə), *n.* minimums; a plural of **minimum.**

min·i·mal (min′ə məl), *adj.* least possible; very small; having to do with a minimum: *minimal damage, a minimal cost.* [< Latin *minimus* smallest (see MINIM) + English *-al*[1]] —**min′i·mal·ly,** *adv.*

Min·i·mal·ist (min′ə mə list), *n.* a member of a less radical section of the former Social Revolutionary Party in Russia about 1903. [adaptation of French *minimaliste* (see MINIMAL), translation of Russian *men'shevik* Menshevik]

min·i·mi (min′ə mī), *n.* plural of **minimus.**

min·i·mise (min′ə mīz), *v.t.*, **-mised, -mis·ing.** *Especially British.* minimize.

min·i·mi·za·tion (min′ə mə zā′shən), *n.* the act or process of minimizing.

min·i·mize (min′ə mīz), *v.t.*, **-mized, -miz·ing. 1.** to reduce to the least possible amount or degree: *The polar explorers took every precaution to minimize the dangers of their trip.* **2.** to state at the lowest possible estimate; make the least of: *An ungrateful person minimizes the help others have given him.* —**min′i·miz′er,** *n.* —**Syn. 2.** belittle.

min·i·mum (min′ə məm), *n., pl.* **-mums** or **-ma,** *adj.* —*n.* **1. a.** the least possible amount; lowest amount: *Each of the children had to drink some milk at breakfast; half a glass was the minimum.* **b.** the lowest amount of variation attained or recorded. **2.** *Mathematics.* a value of a variable less than or equal to any values close to it.

—*adj.* **1.** least possible: *Twenty-one is the minimum age for voting in all but two states.* **2.** lowest: *the minimum rate.*
[< Latin *minimum* smallest thing, neuter of *minimus;* see MINIM] —**Ant.** maximum.
➔ **Minimum** has two plurals: *minimums* and *minima.* The first is more common in informal English.

minimum wage, **1.** the wage agreed upon or fixed by law as the lowest payable to certain employees: *The men wanted a minimum wage of a dollar-and-a-half an hour.* **2.** a living wage.

min·i·mus (min′ə məs), *n., pl.* **-mi.** a very small or insignificant creature: *Get you gone, you dwarf, You minimus* (Shakespeare). [< Latin *minimus;* see MINIM]

min·ing (mī′ning), *n.* **1.** the working of mines for ores, coal, etc. **2.** the business of digging coal or ores from mines. **3.** the laying of explosive mines.

mining claim, **1.** the claim of a prospector to the exclusive right to work a mine that he has discovered. **2.** the mine itself. **3.** the tract of land containing the mine.

min·ion (min′yən), *n.* **1.** a servant or follower willing to do whatever he is ordered; henchman: *It is no wonder if he helps himself from the city treasury and allows his minions to do so* (James Bryce). *Let us be Diana's foresters ... minions of the moon* (Shakespeare). **2.** a favorite person or animal; darling; beloved; idol (a contemptuous use): *A son ... Who is sweet Fortune's minion and her pride* (Shakespeare). **3.** a size of printing type (7 point). This sentence is set in minion. **4.** *Obsolete.* a lady love, especially a mistress or paramour.
—*adj.* dainty; elegant.
[< Middle French *mignon* petite, dainty; favorite. Compare MIGNON.]
—**Syn.** *n.* **1.** lackey.

minion of the law, a policeman.

min·is·cule (min′ə skyūl), *adj.* minuscule. —*n.* miniature: *Our own planning of economic and military aid programs demonstrates in miniscule the way that planning can be used for democratic ... purposes* (John K. Fairbank).

min·ish (min′ish), *Archaic.* —*v.t.* to make less or fewer; diminish: *Ye shall not minish aught from your bricks of your daily task* (Exodus 5:19). —*v.i.* to become less; diminish. [alteration of Middle English *menusen,* ultimately < Old French *menuis-,* stem of *mincier* make small; see MINCE]

min·i·skirt (min′ē skėrt), *n.* **1.** a very short skirt, usually four to five inches above the knee: *DePinna's sportswear department ... has some of the miniest of the miniskirts for those who believe that legs are here to stay, no matter what the weather* (Lisa Hammel). **2.** a dress with such a skirt; minidress.

min·is·ter (min′ə stər), *n.* **1.** a clergyman serving a church; spiritual guide; pastor. **2.** a person who is given charge of a department of the government: *the Minister of War.* **3.** a person sent to a foreign country to represent his own government; a diplomat ranking below an ambassador: *the United States Minister to Switzerland.* **4.** a person or thing employed in carrying out a purpose, the will, etc., of another; agent: *The storm which killed the murderer seemed the minister of God's vengeance.* **5.** *Archaic.* a servant or attendant: *A multitude of cooks, and inferior ministers, employed in the service of the kitchens* (Edward Gibbon).
—*v.i.* **1.** to attend (to comfort or wants); act as a servant or nurse; be of service: *She ministered to the sick man's wants. For even the Son of man came not to be ministered unto, but to minister, and to give his life a ransom for many* (Mark 10:45). **2.** to be helpful; give aid; contribute: *My lord's clearness of mind ... had not ceased to minister to my amazement* (Robert Louis Stevenson).
—*v.t.* **1.** *Archaic.* to furnish; supply: *I will endeavour most faithfully not to minister any occasion of strife* (Scott). **2.** *Obsolete.* to dispense or administer (a sacrament). **3.** *Obsolete.* to apply or administer (something healing).
[< Old French *ministre,* learned borrowing from Latin *minister, -trī* servant < *minus* less; see MINUS)]
—**Syn.** *v.i.* **1.** serve. **2.** help, assist.

min·is·te·ri·al (min′ə stir′ē əl), *adj.* **1.** of a minister. **2.** of the ministry. **3.** suitable for a clergyman: *a ministerial manner.* **4.** executive; administrative: *a ministerial act.* **5.** acting as an agent; subordinate; helping. —**min′is·te′ri·al·ly,** *adv.* —**Syn. 5.** ancillary, subsidiary.

min·is·te·ri·al·ist (min′ə stir′ē ə list), *n. British.* a supporter of the ministry in political office.

minister plenipotentiary, *pl.* **ministers plenipotentiary.** a diplomatic agent given full powers by his government; plenipotentiary.

minister resident, a diplomatic agent to a minor country.

min·is·ter·ship (min′ə stər ship), *n.* the office of a minister.

minister without portfolio or **Minister without Portfolio,** a minister in a government who does not have the position and duties of a cabinet member or minister of state, but usually acts in some special capacity as the personal agent of the chief executive.

min·is·trant (min′ə strənt), *adj.* that ministers; ministering: *angels ministrant* (Milton). —*n.* a person who ministers: *I was chosen to act as ministrant and carry the cross* (New Yorker). [< Latin *ministrāns, -antis,* present participle of *ministrāre* to minister to < *minister;* see MINISTER]

min·is·tra·tion (min′ə strā′shən), *n.* **1.** service as a minister of a church. **2.** help; aid: *in sore extremity, when she most needed the ministration of her own sex* (Francis Bret Harte).

min·is·tra·tive (min′ə strā′tiv), *adj.* ministering; giving service.

min·is·try (min′ə strē), *n., pl.* **-tries. 1.** the office, duties, or time of service of a minister. **2.** the ministers of a church; clergy. **3.** the ministers of a government, especially of the British or a European government. Ministers of a government are often equivalent to cabinet members in the United States. **4.** in England and in Europe: **a.** a government department under a minister. **b.** the offices of such a department. **5.** a ministering or serving: *My idea of heaven is the perpetual ministry of one soul to another* (Tennyson). **6.** agency; instrumentality. [< Latin *ministerium* office, service < *minister;* see MINISTER. Doublet of MÉTIER.] —**Syn. 2.** ecclesiastics. **5.** ministration.

Min·i·track (min′ē trak′), *n. Trademark.* a system for following the course of satellites and rockets by means of radio signals transmitted from the satellite or rocket to receiving stations on the ground, which pool their plottings of each reading of its position. [< *mini*(mum weight) + *track*(ing)]

min·i·um (min′ē əm), *n.* **1.** vermilion (the color). **2.** red lead. [< Latin *minium* red lead]

min·i·van (min′ē van′), *n. British.* a small van or pickup truck: *Their minivan was in collision with an Army lorry* (London Times).

min·i·ver (min′ə vər), *n.* **1.** a fur or combination of furs formerly much used for lining and trimming garments. Miniver includes spotted white and gray fur, white fur symmetrically adorned with bits of dark fur, plain white fur, and ermine. **2.** *British.* any pure white fur, especially ermine. [< Old French *menu vair* small vair; *menu* < Latin *minūtus* (see MINUTE²); *vair* < Latin *varius* variegated]

mink (mingk), *n., pl.* **minks** or (*collectively*) **mink. 1.** a small, weasellike mammal of North America that lives in water part of the time. **2.** its valuable fur, most commonly a deep, lustrous brown, but occurring in other shades in certain varieties of the animal. [apparently < Swedish *mänk*] —**mink′like′,** *adj.*

Mink (def. 1) (including tail, 2 to 3 ft. long)

Minn., Minnesota.

min·ne·lied or **Min·ne·lied** (min′ə lēd, *German* -lēt), *n., pl.* **-lie·der** (-lē′dər). **1.** a minnesong. **2.** any song similar to a minnesong: *A Minnelied, "Der May," by Oswald von Wolkenstein, ... was notable for its imitations of bird cries* (London Times). **3.** any love song. [< German *Minnelied* < Middle High German *Minneliet* < *minne* love + *liet* song]

min·ne·sing·er or **Min·ne·sing·er** (min′ə sing′ər), *n.* one of a class of German lyrical poets and singers of the 1100's to the 1300's. The chief theme of their songs was love. [< German *Minnesinger,* variant of *Minnesänger* < *Minnesang* < Middle High German *minne* love + *sanc* song]

min·ne·song or **Min·ne·song** (min′ə sông, -song), *n.* **1.** one of the songs of the minnesingers; minnelied: *All the Minnesongs, even the most diversified, seem still to resemble each other* (Longfellow). **2.** such songs collectively: *English works on the subject of the German Minnesong are ... scanty in number* (F.C. Nicholson). [< German *Minnesang;* see MINNESINGER]

Min·ne·so·tan (min′ə sō′tən), *adj.* of or having to do with Minnesota. —*n.* a native or inhabitant of Minnesota.

min·nie¹ (min′ē), *n. Military Slang.* a Minenwerfer.

min·nie² (min′ē), *n. Scottish.* a familiar word for "mother": *Light loves I may get many a one, But minnie ne'er another* (Scott).

min·now (min′ō), *n., pl.* **-nows** or (*collectively*) **-now. 1.** *U.S.* any of various very small, fresh-water fish, especially those belonging to the same family as the carp, and certain of the killifishes. **2.** any very tiny fish. [Middle English *minwe.* Compare Old English *myne* (apparently) minnow.]

mi·no (mē′nō), *n., pl.* **-nos.** a kind of cloak or outer covering made of long grass, rushes, or the like, worn by laborers, etc., in Japan. [< Japanese *mino*]

Mi·no·an (mi nō′ən), *adj.* of or having to do with the civilization of Crete from about 3500 to 1400 B.C.: *Excavations by the local department of antiquities at the site of Eraclea, a city of the Minoan period, have been completed* (London Times). —*n.* a native or inhabitant of Minoan Crete: *The origin of the Minoans ... remains in darkness* (New Yorker). [< *Mino*(s) + *-an*]

mi·nor (mī′nər), *adj.* **1.** smaller; less important; lesser: *a minor fault, a minor poet, a minor gain, a minor political party. Correct the important errors in your paper before you bother with the minor ones.* **2.** under legal age. **3.** *Music.* **a.** less by a half step than the corresponding major interval: *a minor seventh, a minor chord.* **b.** denoting a scale, key, or mode whose third tone is minor in relation to the fundamental tone: *the C minor scale or key.* **4.** *U.S.* of, having to do with, or designating a minor in education: *a minor subject.* **5.** *Logic.* less broad; less extensive: *a minor premise.* **6.** (in English boys' schools) of the younger (in age or standing) of two pupils who have the same surname.
—*n.* **1.** a person under the legal age of responsibility: *You cannot vote while you are still a minor.* **2.** *U.S. Education.* a subject or course of study to which a student gives much time and attention, but less than to his major subject. **3.** *Music.* a minor key, scale, chord, interval, etc. **4.** *U.S. Sports.* a minor league.
—*v.i.* **minor in,** *U.S. Informal.* to have or take as a minor subject of study: *to minor in French.*
[< Latin *minor* lesser, comparative of *parvus* small]
—**Syn.** *adj.* **1.** subordinate, secondary, lower, inferior.

Mi·nor (mī′nər), *n.* a Minorite; Franciscan.

minor arc, *Mathematics.* an arc that is less than half a circle.

minor axis, the diameter of an ellipse perpendicular to its major axis.

Mi·nor·ca (mə nôr′kə), *n.* any of a breed of poultry of moderate size with black, buff, or white plumage and white ear lobes, notable for prolific laying. [< *Minorca,* an island in the Mediterranean < Spanish *Menorca* < Latin *minor* smaller, minor. Compare MAJORCA.]

Mi·nor·can (mə nôr′kən), *adj.* of or having to do with the island of Minorca, an island in the Mediterranean. —*n.* a native or inhabitant of Minorca.

Mi·nor·ite (mī′nə rīt), *n.* a Franciscan. [< Friars *Minor,* a name of the Franciscans + *-ite*¹]

mi·nor·i·ty (mə nôr′ə tē, -nor′-; mī-), *n., pl.* **-ties,** *adj.* —*n.* **1. a.** the smaller number or part; less than half: *The minority must often do what the majority decides to do. A minority of the children wanted a party, but the majority chose a picnic.* **b.** a group within a country, state, etc., that differs in race, religion, or national origin from the dominant group. **2.** the condition or time of being under the legal age of responsibility: *the long minority of Henry the Sixth, who was a boy nine*

months old at his father's death (John R. Green).
—*adj.* **1.** of or constituting a minority: *a minority vote, group, etc.* **2.** belonging to a minority: *a minority opinion.*
—**Syn.** *n.* **2.** nonage.

minor key, a key in the minor mode; sadly: *a song in a minor key.*

minor league, *U.S.* any professional sports league or association, especially in baseball, other than the major leagues.

mi·nor-league (mī′nər lēg′), *adj.* **1.** of or having to do with a minor league or the minor leagues: *We went to see two excellent minor-league teams play a double-header* (New Yorker). **2.** *U.S. Informal.* not first-class; inferior, cheap, or undistinguished: *a minor-league writer, a minor-league politician.*

minor leaguer, 1. a person in a minor league, especially a minor-league ballplayer. **2.** *Informal.* a person who is undistinguished, especially in a particular field of endeavor.

minor mode, the arrangement of tones found in the minor scale.

minor orders, the lesser degrees or grades of clerical office. In the Roman Catholic Church, the minor orders are acolyte, exorcist, reader, and doorkeeper.

minor piece, *Chess.* a bishop or a knight.

minor planet, an asteroid: *Ceres, the largest of the asteroids, or minor planets, was the first to be discovered* (Robert H. Baker).

minor premise, the premise which contains the minor term of a syllogism.

Minor Prophets, 1. the less important of the prophetic books of the Old Testament, including Hosea, Joel, Amos, Obadiah, Jonah, Micah, Nahum, Habakkuk, Zephaniah, Haggai, Zechariah, and Malachi. **2.** the prophets who are believed to have written these books.

minor scale, *Music.* a scale having eight notes with half steps instead of whole steps after the second and fifth tones. It is a natural scale, but in the harmonic minor the seventh step is raised to a leading tone, and in the melodic minor both the sixth and seventh steps are raised in ascending, but natural in descending.

minor suit, diamonds or clubs, the suits of lesser scoring value at auction and contract bridge.

minor term, the subject of the conclusion of a syllogism.

Mi·nos (mī′nəs, -nos), *n. Greek Legend.* **1.** a king and lawgiver of Crete, the son of Zeus and Europa, who became one of the three judges in Hades. **2.** his grandson, who built the Labyrinth at Crete and kept the Minotaur in it.

Min·o·taur (min′ə tôr), *n. Greek Legend.* a monster with a bull's head and a man's body (or, in some accounts, with a man's head and a bull's body), kept in the Labyrinth at Crete, where every year it devoured seven Athenian youths and seven maidens offered in tribute. Theseus killed the Minotaur. [< Latin *Mīnōtaurus* < Greek *Mīnṓtauros* < *Mínos* Minos + *taûros* bull]

min·ster (min′stər), *n. Especially British.* **1.** the church of a monastery. **2.** a large or important church; cathedral. [Old English *mynster* < Vulgar Latin *monistērium,* for Late Latin *monastērium.* Doublet of MONASTERY.]

min·strel (min′strəl), *n.* **1.** a singer or musician in the household of a lord in the Middle Ages: *Here to the harp did minstrels sing* (Scott). **2.** a singer or musician who went about and sang or recited poems, often of his own making: *A wandering minstrel I—a thing of shreds and patches, of ballades, songs, and snatches* (William S. Gilbert). **3.** *U.S.* a member of a group or company of theatrical performers, either Negroes or, more usually, white men whose faces and hands are blackened with burnt cork, who entertain with songs, dancing, jokes, and the like. **4.** *Poetic.* a musician, singer, or poet. [< Old French *menestrel* < Late Latin *ministeriālis* < Latin *ministerium;* see MINISTRY]

minstrel show, a performance given by minstrels: *The chiefs looked like a minstrel show cakewalk in heaven* (Bernard De Voto).

min·strel·sy (min′strəl sē), *n., pl.* **-sies. 1.** the art or practice of a minstrel: *From minstrelsy to ragtime and jazz was only a short hop, skip and jump for the banjo* (Wall Street Journal). **2.** a collection of songs and ballads. **3.** a company of minstrels: *Nodding their heads before her goes the merry minstrelsy* (Samuel Taylor Coleridge).

mint[1] (mint), *n.* **1.** any of a group of sweet-smelling herbs often used for flavoring, as the peppermint and spearmint. **2.** any other plant of the mint family. **3.** a piece of candy, usually flavored with peppermint, often eaten after dinner. [Old English *minte,* ultimately < Latin *menta*]

mint[2] (mint), *n.* **1.** a place where money is coined by public authority. **2.** a large amount: *A million dollars is a mint of money. He has a mint of reasons* (Tennyson). **3.** a place where anything is made or fabricated. **4.** *Obsolete.* a piece of money; coin.
—*v.t.* **1.** to coin (money). **2.** to make or fabricate; originate: *to mint words or phrases.*
—*adj.* **1.** (of a stamp) in the condition of issue by the Post Office. **2.** without a blemish; as good as new: *a car, house, etc., in mint condition.*
[Old English *mynet* a coin, ultimately < Latin *monēta* mint. Doublet of MONEY.]
—**mint′er,** *n.* —**Syn.** *v.t.* **2.** invent.

mint[3] (mint), *Archaic.* —*v.t.* **1.** to intend. **2.** to attempt. **3.** to aim (a blow): *I will cleave to the brisket the first man that mints another stroke* (Scott). **4.** to hint at; insinuate. —*v.i.* **1.** to aim a blow; take aim in shooting. **2.** to hint. [Old English *myntan*]

mint·age (min′tij), *n.* **1.** a minting; coinage. **2.** the product of minting; output of a mint. **3.** a charge for coining; cost of coining. **4.** the stamp impressed in minting.

mint family, a large group of dicotyledonous herbs and shrubs having square stems and opposite or whorled, aromatic leaves which usually contain a volatile, aromatic oil. The family includes many herbs used in preparing food, as the mints, sage, thyme, and basil.

mint julep, *U.S.* an alcoholic beverage of bourbon, sugar, crushed ice, and fresh mint, served in a frosted glass.

mint mark, a private mark put upon coins by mint authorities, as to indicate the place of coinage.

mint·y (min′tē), *adj.,* **mint·i·er, mint·i·est.** of or like that of mint.

min·u·end (min′yu̇ end), *n.* a number or quantity from which another is to be subtracted: *In 100 − 23 = 77, the minuend is 100.* [< Latin *minuendus* (*numerus*) (number) to be made smaller, gerundive of *minuere* diminish < *minus;* see MINUS]

min·u·et (min′yu̇ et′), *n.* **1.** a slow, stately dance in triple time. It is of French origin and was fashionable in the 1700's. *You should do everything, said Lord Chesterfield, in minuet time* (Walter Bagehot). **2.** the music for it. —*v.i.* to dance a minuet. [< French *menuet* < Old French (diminutive) < *menu* small < Latin *minūtus;* see MINUTE[2]]

mi·nus (mī′nəs), *prep.* **1.** less; decreased by: *gross earnings minus costs. 5 minus 2 leaves 3.* **2.** lacking: *a book minus its cover.*
—*adj.* **1.** less than: *A mark of B minus is not so high as B.* **2.** showing subtraction: *The minus sign is* −. **3. a.** less than zero: *If you have no money, and owe someone 10¢, you have minus 10¢.* **b.** negative in quantity. **4.** *Botany.* of or having to do with the strain of heterothallic fungi which acts as the female in reproduction.
—*n.* **1.** the sign (−) meaning that the quantity following it is to be subtracted. **2.** a negative quantity. **3.** any deficiency or shortcoming; lack. [< Latin *minus* less, neuter of *minor,* comparative of *parvus* small]
—**Syn.** *prep.* **2.** without.

mi·nus·cu·lar (mi nus′kyə lər), *adj.* **1.** like a minuscule. **2.** consisting of minuscules.

mi·nus·cule (mi nus′kyül), *adj.* **1.** extremely small: *a minuscule person.* **2.** in paleography: **a.** (of a letter) small: *Legal-size pages of written material in minuscule letters that can be blown up to reading size* (Wall Street Journal). **b.** written in minuscules.
—*n.* **1.** in paleography: **a.** a small letter, neither capital nor uncial. **b.** the small cursive script developed from the uncial during the 600's to 800's A.D. **2.** a lower-case letter.
[< French *minuscule,* learned borrowing from Latin *minuscula* (*littera*) slightly smaller (letters) < *minus* less; see MINUS]

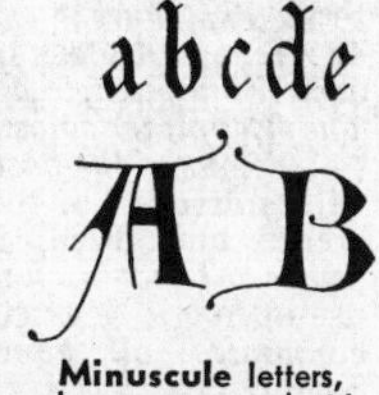

Minuscule letters, above, compared with majuscules, below

minus sign, *Mathematics.* the sign (−), indicating that the quantity following is to be subtracted, or is a negative quantity.

min·ute[1] (min′it), *n., v.,* **-ut·ed, -ut·ing.**
—*n.* **1.** sixty seconds; one sixtieth of an hour: *ten minutes to six. Abbr.:* min. **2.** a short time; instant: *I'll be there in a minute.* **3.** a point of time: *Come here this minute. The minute you see him, tell me.* **4.** one sixtieth of a degree (often indicated by the symbol ′): *10°10′ means ten degrees and ten minutes.*
at the last minute, at the latest possible time; just before the last opportunity to do something: *Labor Secretary Wirtz stepped in at the last minute to halt a strike ... which threatened opening day at the ball park* (New York Times).
minutes, a. an official record of proceedings at a meeting of a society, board, committee, etc.: *The meeting started with some disagreement as to whether executive-committee minutes should be read* (Newsweek). **b.** a rough draft or written summary; note; memorandum: *Glossin had made careful minutes of the information derived from these examinations* (Scott).
up to the minute, up to date: *She keeps her clothes up to the minute. We brought him up to the minute on the developments.*
—*v.t.* **1.** to time exactly, as movements or speed. **2.** to draft (a document, etc.); summarize in a memorandum: *I ... told them the story ... just as I have since minuted it down* (Daniel Defoe). **3.** to record in the minutes of a meeting, etc.
[< Old French *minute* < Late Latin *minūta* minute, small part < Latin *minūta,* feminine of *minūtus;* see MINUTE[2]]
—**Syn.** *n.* **2, 3. Minute, moment, instant** mean a point or extremely short period of time. **Minute** usually suggests a measurable, although very short, amount of time: *May I rest a minute?* **Moment** is less definite, suggesting a very brief period that is noticeable but not measurable: *I'll be with you in a moment.* **Instant** suggests a point of time, a period too brief to be noticed: *Come here this instant!*

mi·nute[2] (mī nüt′, -nyüt′; mə-), *adj.* **1.** very small: *minute animals, minute portions, minute variations.* **2.** going into or concerned with very small details; very precise or particular: *a minute observer. He gave me minute instructions about my work.* **3.** of very little consequence or importance; trifling; petty: *to involve the minutest details of a case.* [< Latin *minūtus* made small, past participle of *minuere* diminish < *minus* less; see MINUS. Doublet of MENU.]
—**Syn. 1.** tiny, diminutive, little. **2.** detailed.

min·ute gun (min′it), **1.** the firing of a gun, especially a cannon, once a minute as a signal of distress or formal indication of mourning. **2.** a gun used for this.

minute hand, the longer hand on a clock or watch, that indicates minutes. It moves around the whole dial once in an hour.

min·ute·ly[1] (min′it lē), *adj.* happening every minute; continually occurring; unceasing. —*adv.* every minute; minute by minute. [< *minute*[1] + *-ly*]

mi·nute·ly[2] (mī nüt′lē, -nyüt′-; mə-), *adv.* in minute manner, form, degree, or detail. [< *minute*[2] + *-ly*]

min·ute·man (min′it man′), *n., pl.* **-men.** a member of the American militia just before and during the Revolutionary War, who was ready for military service at very short notice. [American English < *minute*[1] + *man*]

Min·ute·man (min′it man′), *n., pl.* **-men.** *U.S.* a member of a secret reactionary organization formed in the 1950's to prepare militarily against a communist uprising or invasion it believes to be imminent: *The prisoners and weapons belonged to bands of Minutemen, a right-wing group* (New York Times).

mi·nute·ness (mī nüt′nis, -nyüt′-; mə-), *n.* **1.** extreme smallness. **2.** attention to very small details.

min·ute of arc (min′it), 1/60 of a degree.

min·utes (min′its), *n.pl.* See under **minute**[1], *n.*

min·ute steak (min′it), a thin, small piece of steak cut from the top round, often scored or cubed, that can be cooked very quickly: *A waiter brought in some minute steaks and beer* (New Yorker).

mi·nu·ti·a (mi nü′shē ə, -nyü′-), *n.* the singular of **minutiae.**

mi·nu·ti·ae (mi nü′shē ē, -nyü′-), *n.pl.* very small matters; trifling details: *scientific minutiae. They waited . . . for the exchange of pass-words, the delivery of keys, and all the slow minutiae attendant upon the movements of a garrison in a well-guarded fortress* (Scott). [< Latin *minūtiae* trifles, plural of *minūtia* smallness < *minūtus;* see MINUTE[2]]

mi·nu·ti·ose (mi nü′shē ōs, -nyü′-), *adj.* concerned with minutiae.

mi·nu·tious (mi nü′shəs, -nyü′-), *adj.* minutiose.

minx (mingks), *n.* **1.** a pert girl; hussy: *She liked the notion of humbling the haughty minx* (Cardinal Newman). **2.** *Obsolete.* a lewd or wanton woman. [origin uncertain. Compare Low German *minsk* person.]

min·yan (min′yən), *n., pl.* **min·ya·nim** (min′yə nēm′), **min·yans.** *Judaism.* the minimum of ten male Jews over thirteen years old required by law in order to hold a religious service or to form a congregation. [< Hebrew *minyan*]

Mi·o·cene (mī′ə sēn), *n.* **1.** a geologic epoch in which mammals achieved dominance on earth. It is the fourth epoch of the Tertiary period of the Cenozoic era, after the Oligocene and before the Pliocene. **2.** the rocks formed in this epoch. —*adj.* of this epoch or these rocks: *It is interesting to note that the Miocene fossil Proconsul . . . has an arm and hand of a very unspecialized form* (New Scientist). [< Greek *meîōn* less + *kainós* new, recent]

mi·o·sis[1] (mī ō′sis), *n., pl.* **-ses** (-sēz). excessive contraction of the pupil of the eye. Also, **myosis.** [< Greek *mȳein* to shut (the eyes) + English *-osis*]

mi·o·sis[2] (mī ō′sis), *n., pl.* **-ses** (-sēz). meiosis.

mi·ot·ic[1] (mī ot′ik), *adj.* having to do with, suffering from, or causing miosis. —*n.* a drug that causes miosis. Also, **myotic.**

mi·ot·ic[2] (mī ot′ik), *adj.* meiotic.

MIP (no periods), Monthly Investment Plan (a plan for purchasing listed securities by investing a fixed amount on a regular or monthly basis).

miq·ue·let (mik′ə lit), *n.* **1.** a Spanish guerrilla soldier who fought against the French in Spain from 1808 to 1814. **2.** a soldier belonging to any of certain regiments of Spanish militia, used especially for local escort duty. [< French *miquelet* < Spanish *miquelete,* perhaps < a proper name]

mir (mēr), *n.* a self-governing farming community that existed in Russia in the middle 1800's. [< Russian *mir*]

Mi·ra (mī′rə), *n.* the brightest and first variable star discovered, one of the largest of all stars, in the constellation Cetus. [< New Latin *Mira* < Latin *mīra,* feminine of *mīrus* wonderful]

mir·a·belle (mir′ə bel), *n.* **1.** a kind of European plum. **2.** a colorless plum brandy made from it. [< French *mirabelle*]

mi·ra·bi·le dic·tu (mi rab′ə lē dik′tü, -tyü), *Latin.* wonderful to relate; amazing as it may seem: *Mirabile dictu, the price hasn't gone up by so much as a penny* (New Yorker).

mi·ra·bi·li·a (mir′ə bil′ē ə), *n.pl. Latin.* miracles; wonderful things; wonders.

mi·ra·cid·i·um (mī′rə sid′ē əm), *n., pl.* **-i·a** (-ē ə). the minute, ciliated aquatic larva which hatches from the egg of a fluke and infects the snail, the intermediate host, in the development of the fluke. [< New Latin *miracidium* < Greek *meirakídion* little boy (diminutive) < *meirákion* boy]

mir·a·cle (mir′ə kəl), *n.* **1.** a wonderful happening that is contrary to or independent of the known laws of nature: *It would be a miracle if the sun stood still in the heavens for an hour.* **2.** something marvelous; a wonder: *It was a miracle you weren't hurt in that accident.* **3.** a remarkable example: *Mother must be a miracle of patience. What hymns are sung, what praises said For home-made miracles of bread?* (Louis Untermeyer). *They deemed the young clergyman a miracle of holiness* (Hawthorne). **4.** a miracle play. [< Old French *miracle* < Latin *mīrāculum* < *mīrārī* to marvel at < *mīrus* wonderful]

miracle drug, a drug, especially an antibiotic, considered to be a marvelous relief or cure for a disease; wonder drug.

miracle man, 1. *Informal.* a man who accomplishes something unusually difficult or previously thought impossible. **2.** a man who performs miracles; wonder-worker.

miracle play, a play based on Bible stories or on the legends of the saints, produced during the Middle Ages.

mi·rac·u·lous (mə rak′yə ləs), *adj.* **1.** contrary to or independent of the known laws of nature: *In the story, the miraculous tree grew up again in an hour after it was cut down.* **2.** wonderful; marvelous. **3.** producing a miracle; having the power to work miracles; wonder-working. [< Middle French *miraculeux* (with English *-ous*), learned borrowing from Medieval Latin *miraculosus* < Latin *mīrāculum;* see MIRACLE] —**mi·rac′u·lous·ly,** *adv.* —**mi·rac′u·lous·ness,** *n.* —**Syn. 1.** supernatural. **2.** extraordinary.

miraculous fruit, a very sweet berry of central Africa, used by natives as a sweetener when eating sour or bitter foods.

mir·a·dor (mir′ə dôr′, -dōr′), *n.* a turret, bay window, or the like, on a Spanish house, from which a fine view may be had. [< Spanish *mirador* < *mirar* to look]

mi·rage (mə räzh′), *n.* **1.** a misleading appearance or optical illusion, usually in the desert or at sea, resulting from a reflection of some distant scene in such a way as to give the impression that it is near. Often the objects reflected are inverted. *Travelers on the desert may see a mirage of palm trees and water. The sweet mirage that lured me on its track* (William W. Story). **2.** anything that does not exist; illusion. [< French *mirage* < *mirer* look at carefully < Latin *mīrāre,* variant of *mīrārī* wonder at < *mīrus* wonderful]

mi·rate (mī′rāt), *v.i.,* **-rat·ed, -rat·ing.** *U.S. Dialect.* to be full of admiration; marvel (over): *I mirated over them . . . too much, but they were the only beauteous thing she had* (Berry Morgan). [back formation < *miration*]

mi·ra·tion (mī rā′shən), *n. U.S. Dialect.* an admiring; a marveling (over). [< (ad)-*miration*]

mire (mīr), *n., v.,* **mired, mir·ing.** —*n.* **1.** soft, deep mud; slush: *I sink in deep mire, Where there is no standing* (Psalms 69:2). **2.** wet, swampy ground; bog; swamp.
—*v.t.* **1.** to get stuck in mire: *He mired his horses and had to go for help.* **2.** to soil with or as with mud or mire: *smeared thus and mired with infamy* (Shakespeare). **3.** to involve in difficulties; entangle. —*v.i.* to stick in mire; be bogged: *A path . . . that is so muddy that one mires afore he sets out* (James Fenimore Cooper).
[< Scandinavian (compare Old Icelandic *mȳrr* bog, swamp)]
—**Syn.** *v.t.* **2.** defile. **3.** embroil.

mire·poix (mir pwä′), *n., pl.* **-poix.** a mixture of chopped vegetables, herbs, seasonings, and bits of fat meat either cooked together with meat or fish or placed under meat for braising. [< French *mirepoix,* probably < the duke of *Mirepoix,* a French diplomat of the 1700's]

Mi·ri·am (mir′ē əm), *n.* (in the Bible) a Hebrew prophetess, the sister of Moses. Exodus 15:20.

mi·rif·ic (mī rif′ik), *adj.* causing wonder; wonderful; marvelous. [< Old French *mirifique,* learned borrowing from Latin *mīrificus* < *mīrus* wonderful + *facere* make]

mir·i·ness (mīr′ē nis), *n.* miry condition.

mirk (mėrk), *n., adj.* murk.

mirk·y (mėr′kē), *adj.,* **mirk·i·er, mirk·i·est.** murky.

mir·ror (mir′ər), *n.* **1.** a looking glass; surface that reflects light: *Mirrors showing stained and aging faces* (Ford Madox Ford). *The reflecting microscope . . . was made largely for the sheer fun of making a microscope with mirrors instead of lenses* (Science News). **2.** whatever reflects or gives a true description: *This book is a mirror of the life of the pioneers.* **3.** a model; example; pattern: *That knight was a mirror of chivalry.* **4.** *Archaic.* a glass or crystal used in magic art: *With a single drop of ink for a mirror, The Egyptian sorcerer undertakes to reveal . . . visions of the past* (George Eliot).
with mirrors, a. by the use of mirrors to create an optical illusion: *The magician pulled off that trick with mirrors.* **b.** by the use of magic or trickery: *It is Wizard of Oz economics—all done with mirrors* (New Scientist).
—*v.t.* **1.** to reflect as a mirror does: *The still water mirrored the trees along the bank.* **2.** to convert (glass) into a mirror by plating. [< Old French *mireor,* or *mirour* < *mirer* wonder at < Latin *mīrāre;* see MIRAGE] —**mir′ror·like′,** *adj.*

mir·rored (mir′ərd), *adj.* having a mirror or mirrors: *a mirrored hall.*

mirror image, an image in reverse; reflection: *The two ridges are roughly mirror images of each other, showing that the motion was uniform on each side* (Scientific American). *Philco is rapidly becoming a mirror image of . . . its successful parent* (Wall Street Journal).

mirror machine, *Nuclear Physics.* a tube with magnetic mirrors at each end for confining charged particles.

mirror writing, writing reversed from the usual order, as if seen reflected in a mirror. Mirror writing is sometimes a symptom of aphasia or nervous disease.

mirth (mėrth), *n.* merry fun; being joyous or gay; laughter: *a sudden outburst of mirth. I commend mirth, because a man hath no better thing under the sun, than to eat, and to drink, and to be merry* (Ecclesiastes 8:15). [Old English *myrgth* joy, pleasure, related to *myrge* merry] —**Syn.** merriment, merrymaking, jollity, gaiety, glee, hilarity.

mirth·ful (mėrth′fəl), *adj.* joyous; merry; gay; laughing. —**mirth′ful·ly,** *adv.* —**mirth′ful·ness,** *n.* —**Syn.** jolly, amused.

mirth·less (mėrth′lis), *adj.* without mirth; joyless; gloomy. —**mirth′less·ly,** *adv.* —**mirth′less·ness,** *n.* —**Syn.** cheerless.

MIRV (no periods), Multiple Independent Reëntry Vehicle (guided missile whose warhead separates into several small warheads independently directed to different targets).

mir·y (mīr′ē), *adj.,* **mir·i·er, mir·i·est. 1.** muddy; swampy: *The miry defiles . . . of the mountains* (Washington Irving). **2.** dirty; filthy.

mir·za (mir′zə, mēr′zä), *n.* in Iran: **1.** a royal prince (as a title, placed after the name). **2.** a standard title of honor, placed before the surname. [< Persian *mīrzād* < *mīr* prince, chief (< Arabic *amīr* emir) + *zādah* born]

mis-, *prefix.* **1.** bad, as in *misgovernment, misinformation.*
2. badly, as in *misform, mismade.*
3. wrong, as in *mispronunciation, misvaluation.*
4. wrongly, as in *misclassify, mislabel.*
[Old English *mis-,* or in borrowed words < Old French *mes-* < Old High German *missi-, missa-*]

mis·act (mis akt′), *v.t.* to act or perform badly.

mis·ad·dress (mis′ə dres′), *v.t.* to address improperly or incorrectly.

mis·ad·just·ment (mis′ə just′mənt), *n.* the state or condition of being badly adjusted; disagreement; lack of harmony.

mis·ad·ven·ture (mis′əd ven′chər), *n.* an unfortunate accident; bad luck; mishap. [alteration of Middle English *misaventure* < Old French *mesaventure* < *mesavenir* turn out badly; patterned on *aventure* adventure] —**Syn.** misfortune.

mis·ad·ven·tur·ous (mis′əd ven′chər əs), *adj.* unfortunate; unlucky.

mis·ad·vice (mis′əd vīs′), *n.* bad advice.

mis·ad·vise (mis′əd vīz′), *v.t.,* **-vised, -vis·ing.** to advise wrongly or incorrectly.

mis·ad·vis·ed·ly (mis′əd vī′zid lē), *adv.* under a misapprehension; imprudently.

mis·a·lign (mis′ə līn′), *v.t.* **1.** to align incorrectly: *Doors will work even if misaligned one inch* (Science News Letter). **2.** to put out of alignment: *I . . . had broken the glass of my watch and misaligned the hands* (London Times).

mis·a·lign·ment (mis′ə līn′mənt), *n.* lack of correct alignment: *. . . misalignment of upper and lower dentures* (Science News Letter).

mis·al·li·ance (mis′ə lī′əns), *n.* an unsuitable alliance or association, especially in marriage. [< *mis-* + *alliance,* probably patterned on French *mésalliance*]

mis·al·lo·cate (mis al′ə kāt), *v.t.,* **-cat·ed, -cat·ing.** to allocate improperly or incorrectly.

mis·al·lo·ca·tion (mis′al ə kā′shən), *n.* improper or incorrect allocation

mis·al·ly (mis′ə lī′), *v.t.,* **-lied, -ly·ing.** to ally inappropriately; join unsuitably.

mis·an·thrope (mis′ən thrōp, miz′-), *n.* a person who dislikes or distrusts human beings; hater of mankind: *He was also a lonely*

 PRONUNCIATION KEY: hat, āge, cãre, fär; let, ēqual, tėrm; it, īce; hot, ōpen, ôrder; oil, out; cup, pu̇t, rüle;

misanthrope who saw the world and himself with intolerable clarity (Time). [< Greek *mīsánthrōpos* < *miseîn* to hate + *ánthrōpos* man]

mis·an·throp·ic (mis′ən throp′ik), *adj.* of or like a misanthrope: *scowling on all the world from his misanthropic seclusion* (Francis Parkman). —**mis′an·throp′i·cal·ly,** *adv.*

mis·an·throp·i·cal (mis′ən throp′ə kəl), *adj.* misanthropic: *He had thrown down his pen in misanthropical despair* (Macaulay).

mis·an·thro·pist (mis an′thrə pist), *n.* a misanthrope.

mis·an·thro·pize (mis an′thrə pīz), *v.*, **-pized, -piz·ing** —*v.i.* to hate mankind. —*v.t.* to make misanthropic.

mis·an·thro·py (mis an′thrə pē), *n.* hatred, dislike, or distrust of human beings: *The outcry was so great that it . . . may well have been responsible in part for Degas's subsequent misanthropy* (New Yorker).

mis·ap·pli·ca·tion (mis′ap lə kā′shən), *n.* a wrong application; a misapplying or being misapplied.

mis·ap·plied (mis′ə plīd′), *adj.* put to a wrong use; applied wrongly.

mis·ap·ply (mis′ə plī′), *v.t.*, **-plied, -ply·ing.** to apply wrongly; make a wrong application or use of: *to misapply a fact, knowledge, wealth, etc.*

mis·ap·prais·al (mis′ə prā′zəl), *n.* incorrect appraisal: . . . *a complete misappraisal and underestimate of the military and political considerations* (New York Times).

mis·ap·pre·ci·ate (mis′ə prē′shē āt), *v.t.*, **-at·ed, -at·ing.** to estimate or value wrongly.

mis·ap·pre·ci·a·tion (mis′ə prē′shē ā′shən), *n.* wrong appreciation or estimation.

mis·ap·pre·ci·a·tive (mis′ə prē′shē ā′tiv, -shə tiv), *adj.* misappreciating.

mis·ap·pre·hend (mis′ap ri hend′), *v.t.* to misunderstand. —**Syn.** misconstrue.

mis·ap·pre·hen·sion (mis′ap ri hen′shən), *n.* a wrong idea; misunderstanding; misconception.

mis·ap·pre·hen·sive (mis′ap ri hen′siv), *adj.* misapprehending; apt to misapprehend. —**mis′ap·pre·hen′sive·ly,** *adv.*

mis·ap·pro·pri·ate (*v.* mis′ə prō′prē āt; *adj.* mis′ə prō′prē it), *v.*, **-at·ed, -at·ing,** *adj.* —*v.t.* **1.** to put to a wrong use. **2.** to use dishonestly as one's own: *The treasurer had misappropriated the club funds.* —*adj.* inappropriate. —**Syn.** *v.t.* **1.** misapply.

mis·ap·pro·pri·a·tion (mis′ə prō′prē ā′shən), *n.* **1.** dishonest use as one's own. **2.** any act of putting to a wrong use.

mis·ar·range (mis′ə rānj′), *v.t.*, **-ranged, -rang·ing.** to arrange incorrectly or poorly.

mis·ar·range·ment (mis′ə rānj′mənt), *n.* bad or incorrect arrangement.

mis·at·trib·ute (mis′ə trib′yüt), *v.t.*, **-ut·ed, -ut·ing.** to attribute incorrectly: *Acts of anonymous attack . . . may be misattributed as to source and so lead to a world holocaust* (Bulletin of Atomic Scientists).

mis·at·tri·bu·tion (mis′at rə byü′shən), *n.* incorrect attribution: *Highmore . . . has suffered from misattributions . . . of the inferior work of others to him* (London Times).

mis·be·came (mis′bi kām′), *v.* the past tense of **misbecome:** *Secundra Dass . . . wore a decent, plain black suit, which misbecame him strangely* (Robert Louis Stevenson).

mis·be·come (mis′bi kum′), *v.t.*, **-came, -come, -com·ing.** to be unbecoming to; be unfit for: *Profanity misbecomes a lady.*

mis·be·com·ing (mis′bi kum′ing), *adj.* not becoming; unbecoming; unsuitable.

mis·be·gat (mis′bi gat′), *v. Archaic.* misbegot; a past tense of **misbeget.**

mis·be·get (mis′bi get′), *v.t.*, **-got** or (*Archaic*) **-gat, -got·ten** or **-got, -get·ting.** to beget unlawfully.

mis·be·got (mis′bi got′), *adj.* misbegotten. —*v.* a past tense and a past participle of **misbeget.**

mis·be·got·ten (mis′bi got′ən), *adj.* **1.** illegitimate. **2.** *Informal.* rascally: *Three misbegotten knaves in Kendal green* (Shakespeare). —*v.* a past participle of **misbeget.**

mis·be·have (mis′bi hāv′), *v.i., v.t.*, **-haved, -hav·ing.** to behave badly; conduct oneself improperly: *She was not the woman to misbehave towards her betters* (George Eliot).

mis·be·hav·ior (mis′bi hāv′yər), *n.* bad behavior. —**Syn.** misconduct.

mis·be·hav·iour (mis′bi hāv′yər), *n. Especially British.* misbehavior.

mis·be·lief (mis′bi lēf′), *n.* **1.** an incorrect or erroneous belief. **2.** a belief in a religion that is not the regularly accepted one; heresy.

mis·be·lieve (mis′bi lēv′), *v.i.*, **-lieved, -liev·ing.** to hold an erroneous belief, especially an unorthodox or heretical religious belief.

mis·be·liev·er (mis′bi lē′vər), *n.* **1.** a person who holds an incorrect or erroneous belief. **2.** a person who believes in a religion that is not the regularly accepted one; infidel.

mis·be·stow (mis′bi stō′), *v.t.* to bestow improperly.

mis·be·stow·al (mis′bi stō′əl), *n.* wrong bestowal.

mis·brand (mis brand′), *v.t.* **1.** to brand or mark incorrectly. **2.** to label improperly or falsely, especially with the brand name or trademark of another: *The Federal Trade Commission still is studying whether his textile companies misbranded their products* (Wall Street Journal).

misc., **1.** miscellaneous. **2.** miscellany.

mis·cal·cu·late (mis kal′kyə lāt), *v.t., v.i.*, **-lat·ed, -lat·ing.** to calculate incorrectly.

mis·cal·cu·la·tion (mis′kal kyə lā′shən), *n.* incorrect calculation: [*Hitler's*] *miscalculation was not in respect of Russia; . . . his miscalculation was in respect of Britain* (Atlantic).

mis·cal·cu·la·tor (mis kal′kyə lā′tər), *n.* a person who makes miscalculations.

mis·call (mis kôl′), *v.t.* **1.** to call by an incorrect name; misname. **2.** *Archaic.* to revile; malign: *By opprobrious epithets we miscall each other* (Thomas Browne).

mis·car·riage (mis kar′ij), *n.* **1.** a failure, especially to achieve the proper result: *With infinite difficulty and repeated miscarriages I at length effected my purpose* (William Godwin). *Because the judge was unfair, that trial resulted in a miscarriage of justice.* **2.** failure to arrive: *the miscarriage of a letter.* **3.** the birth of a baby before it is able to live. —**Syn. 1.** breakdown. **3.** abortion.

mis·car·ry (mis kar′ē), *v.i.*, **-ried, -ry·ing.** **1.** to go wrong; be unsuccessful: *John's plans miscarried and he could not come. His letters to his son are a mixture of excited admiration and apprehension lest Karl's genius miscarry* (Edmund Wilson). **2.** to fail to arrive: *My letter to mother must have miscarried, for she never received it.* **3.** to have a miscarriage; be born before it can live. **4.** *Obsolete.* to go astray.

mis·cast (mis kast′, -käst′), *v.t.*, **-cast, -cast·ing.** to put in a role for which one is not suited: *The soft-spoken actor was badly miscast as Iago.*

mis·ce·ge·na·tion (mis′ə jə nā′shən), *n.* an intermarriage or interbreeding between different races, and especially, in the United States, between whites and Negroes: *Our* [*Southern white man's*] *. . . shame that even then, to justify our stand, we must becloud the issue with the bugaboo of miscegenation* (Harper's). [American English < Latin *miscēre* mix + *genus* race + English *-ation*]

mis·ce·ge·net·ic (mis′ə jə net′ik), *adj.* of or constituting miscegenation: *The rule voiding miscegenetic marriages creates another disturbing problem* (Atlantic).

mis·cel·la·ne·a (mis′ə lā′nē ə), *n.pl.* a miscellaneous collection, especially of literary compositions; miscellany. [< Latin *miscellānea* a meat hash; a (literary) medley, neuter plural of *miscellāneus* miscellaneous]

mis·cel·la·ne·i·ty (mis′ə lə nē′ə tē), *n.* the condition of being miscellaneous: . . . *lost in the general impression of fragmentation and miscellaneity* (Manchester Guardian Weekly).

mis·cel·la·ne·ous (mis′ə lā′nē əs), *adj.* **1.** not all of one kind or nature; of mixed composition or character: *The boy had a miscellaneous collection of stones, butterflies, birds' nests, and many other things. My second boy . . . received a sort of miscellaneous education* (Oliver Goldsmith). **2.** dealing with many subjects; many-sided: *a miscellaneous writer.* *Abbr.:* misc. [< Latin *miscellāneus* (with English *-ous*) < *miscellus* mixed < *miscēre* to mix] —**mis′cel·la′ne·ous·ly,** *adv.* —**mis′cel·la′ne·ous·ness,** *n.*

—**Syn. 1. Miscellaneous, indiscriminate** mean including various things or kinds, without plan or order in selection. **Miscellaneous** emphasizes the mixture that results when things are gathered together without special order, plan, or care: *A person's miscellaneous expenses include stamps and haircuts.* **Indiscriminate** emphasizes the lack of care or judgment in selection: *Indiscriminate buying is wasteful.*

mis·cel·la·nist (mis′ə lā′nist, -lə-; mi sel′ə-), *n.* a writer of miscellanies.

mis·cel·la·ny (mis′ə lā′nē, mi sel′ə-), *n., pl.* **-nies.** a miscellaneous collection; mixture: *A man who takes notes these days soon finds himself drowning in his own miscellany* (New Yorker).

miscellanies, a collection of miscellaneous articles in one book: *He has published a volume of miscellanies.*

[< Latin *miscellānea,* neuter plural of *miscellāneus;* see MISCELLANEOUS]

—**Syn.** medley, mélange.

misch (mish), *n.*, or **misch metal,** a mixture of rare-earth metals, primarily cerium and lanthanum, used to make flints for cigarette lighters and as an ingredient in alloys. [< German *mischen* to mix, ultimately < Latin *miscēre*]

mis·chance (mis chans′, -chäns′), *n.* **1.** misfortune; bad luck: *By some mischance he didn't receive my telegram.* **2.** a piece of bad luck; an unlucky accident: . . . *the vicissitudes and mischances of sublunary affairs* (Hawthorne). [alteration of Middle English *meschaunce* < Old French *mescheance* < *mes-* mis- + *cheance* chance] —**Syn. 1.** misadventure.

mis·chance·ful (mis chans′fəl, -chäns′-), *adj. Archaic.* unlucky; unfortunate.

mis·charge (mis chärj′), *n., v.*, **-charged, -charg·ing.** —*n.* an erroneous charge. —*v.t.* to charge incorrectly, as an item in an account.

mis·chief (mis′chif), *n.* **1.** injury, usually done by some person; harm: *Go away, or I'll do you mischief. The devil is seldom out of call when he is wanted for any mischief* (Daniel Defoe). *The mischief of flattery is . . . that it suppresses the influence of honest ambition* (Samuel Johnson). **2.** conduct that causes harm or trouble, often without meaning it: *A child's mischief may cause a serious fire.* **3.** a person who does harm or causes annoyance, often just in fun: *You little mischief! You have untied my apron.* **4.** merry teasing: *Her eyes were full of mischief.*

raise (the) mischief, *Informal.* to make a disturbance; create an uproar or confusion: *The head editor has been in here raising the mischief and tearing his hair* (Mark Twain).

[< Old French *meschief* < *meschever* to come (or bring) to grief < *mes-* badly, mis- + *chever* to come to an end < *chief* the head or end < Latin *caput, -itis*]

—**Syn. 1.** damage, hurt.

mis·chief-mak·er (mis′chif mā′kər), *n.* a person who makes mischief; person who stirs up trouble by gossiping, talebearing, etc.

mis·chief-mak·ing (mis′chif mā′king), *adj.* causing trouble or quarrels. —*n.* the act or practice of stirring up trouble or quarrels.

mis·chie·vous (mis′chə vəs), *adj.* **1.** harmful or injurious: *a mischievous belief.* **2.** full of mischief; causing annoyance; naughty: *mischievous children.* **3.** full of pranks and teasing fun: *a mischievous puppy.* —**mis′chie·vous·ly,** *adv.* —**mis′chie·vous·ness,** *n.*

—**Syn. 1.** hurtful. **3.** playful, teasing, roguish.

➤ In nonstandard speech **mischievous** is frequently pronounced (mis chē′vi əs).

mis·choice (mis chois′), *n.* a wrong choice.

mis·choose (mis chüz′), *v.t., v.i.*, **-chose, -cho·sen** or (*Obsolete*) **-chose, -choos·ing.** to choose wrongly.

mis·ci·bil·i·ty (mis′ə bil′ə tē), *n.* the quality or condition of being miscible; capability of being mixed.

mis·ci·ble (mis′ə bəl), *adj.* that can be mixed: *Water is not miscible with oil.* [< Latin *miscēre* mix + English *-ible*]

mis·ci·ta·tion (mis′sī tā′shən), *n.* an incorrect citation.

mis·cite (mis sīt′), *v.t.*, **-cit·ed, -cit·ing.** to cite erroneously; misquote.

mis·clas·si·fi·ca·tion (mis′klas ə fə kā′shən), *n.* incorrect or false classification: . . . *misclassification of commodities and other unlawful practices in the sale of cargo transportation* (New York Times).

mis·clas·si·fy (mis klas′ə fī), *v.t.*, **-fied, -fy·ing.** to classify incorrectly or falsely: . . . *misclassifying car buyers into higher* *risk categories and charging them stiffer premiums* (Wall Street Journal).

mis·col·or (mis kul′ər), *v.t.* to give an inaccurate color to (facts, etc.); misrepresent.

mis·col·our (mis kul′ər), *v.t. Especially British.* miscolor.

mis·com·pre·hend (mis′kom pri hend′), *v.t.* to misunderstand.

mis·com·pre·hen·sion (mis′kom pri hen′shən), *n.* a misunderstanding: . . . *in a silence of awe and great miscomprehension* (Rudyard Kipling). *A comedy of miscomprehension that explodes into sudden tragedy* (Time).

mis·con·ceive (mis′kən sēv′), *v.t., v.i.,* **-ceived, -ceiv·ing.** to have incorrect ideas about; misunderstand; misapprehend: *Things which, for want of due consideration . . . they misconceived* (Richard Hooker). **—mis′con·ceiv′er,** *n.*

mis·con·cep·tion (mis′kən sep′shən), *n.* a mistaken idea or notion; an incorrect conception: *The great errors and dangers that may result out of a misconception of the names of things* (William Harvey).

mis·con·duct (*n.* mis kon′dukt; *v.* mis′kən dukt′), *n.* **1.** bad behavior; improper conduct: *The misconduct of the city treasurer resulted in an investigation and his resignation.* **2.** bad management; mismanagement: *The misconduct of that business nearly ruined it.* **3.** *Law.* **a.** adultery. **b.** malfeasance.
—*v.i.* to behave badly. —*v.t.* to manage badly; mismanage.

mis·con·struc·tion (mis′kən struk′shən), *n.* a mistaken meaning; misunderstanding: *What you said was open to misconstruction.*

mis·con·strue (mis′kən strü′), *v.t.,* **-strued, -stru·ing.** to take in a wrong sense; misunderstand: *The little girl's shyness was sometimes misconstrued as rudeness.* **—Syn.** misinterpret.

mis·con·tent (mis′kən tent′), *adj. Archaic.* ill-content; discontented.

mis·cook (mis ku̇k′), *v.t. Especially Scottish.* **1.** to cook badly: *For unnumbered years Mrs. Butt had miscooked his meals* (Arnold Bennett). **2.** to bungle; mismanage.

mis·cop·y (mis kop′ē), *v.,* **-cop·ied, -cop·y·ing,** *n., pl.* **-cop·ies.** —*v.t.* to copy incorrectly. —*n.* **1.** an incorrect copy. **2.** an error in copying.

mis·coun·sel (mis koun′səl), *v.,* **-seled, -sel·ing** or (*especially British*) **-selled, -sel·ling,** *n.* —*v.t.* to counsel wrongly; misadvise. —*n.* wrong counsel.

mis·count (*v.* mis kount′; *n.* mis′kount′), *v.t., v.i.* to count wrongly; miscalculate; misreckon. —*n.* a wrong count or calculation.

mis·cre·ance (mis′krē əns), *n. Archaic.* false belief or faith; misbelief. [< Old French *mescreance* < *mes-* mis- + *creance,* ultimately < Latin *crēdere* believe]

mis·cre·an·cy (mis′krē ən sē), *n., pl.* **-cies.** **1.** villainy; depravity. **2.** *Archaic.* misbelief; miscreance.

mis·cre·ant (mis′krē ənt), *adj.* **1.** having very bad morals; base; depraved: *a miscreant gang of criminals.* **2.** *Archaic.* unbelieving; heretical.
—*n.* **1.** a villain: *He belongs to a . . . gang of miscreants sworn against all order and peace* (Edward G. E. L. Bulwer-Lytton). **2.** *Archaic.* an unbeliever; heretic.
[< Old French *mescreant* < *mes-* wrongly, mis- + *creant,* present participle of *creire* believe < Latin *crēdere*]
—Syn. *adj.* **1.** vile, detestable.

mis·cre·ate (mis′krē āt′), *v.,* **-at·ed, -at·ing,** *adj.* —*v.t., v.i.* to create amiss; misform. —*adj.* created or formed improperly or unnaturally; misshapen.

mis·cre·at·ed (mis′krē ā′tid), *adj.* wrongly created; misshapen; monstrous.

mis·cre·a·tion (mis′krē ā′shən), *n.* **1.** the act of miscreating. **2.** something miscreated.

mis·cue (mis kyü′), *n., v.,* **-cued, -cu·ing.** —*n.* **1.** (in billiards) a bad stroke that does not hit the ball squarely. **2.** *Informal.* an error; slip; mistake: *The miscues gave the* [*Cincinnati*] *Redlegs five unearned runs* (New York Times).
—*v.i.* **1.** (in billiards) to make a miscue. **2.** *Theater.* to miss one's cue; respond to a wrong cue.

mis·date (mis dāt′), *v.,* **-dat·ed, -dat·ing,** *n.* —*v.t.* to date incorrectly; assign or affix an incorrect date to. —*n.* an incorrect date.

mis·deal (*v.* mis dēl′; *n.* mis′dēl′), *v.,* **-dealt, -deal·ing,** *n.* —*v.t., v.i.* to deal incorrectly, especially at cards. —*n.* an incorrect deal. **—mis·deal′er,** *n.*

mis·dealt (mis delt′), *v.* the past tense and past participle of **misdeal.**

mis·deed (mis dēd′, mis′dēd′), *n.* a bad act; wicked deed. [Old English *misdǣd*] **—Syn.** misdemeanor, offense.

mis·deem (mis dēm′), *v.i.* to deem or judge wrongly. —*v.t.* to have a wrong opinion of.

mis·de·mean (mis′di mēn′), *v.t., v.i.* to behave badly; misbehave.

mis·de·mean·ant (mis′di mē′nənt), *n.* **1.** *Law.* a person convicted of a misdemeanor. **2.** a person guilty of misconduct.

mis·de·mean·or (mis′di mē′nər), *n.* **1.** a breaking of the criminal law, not so serious as a felony: *Disturbing the peace and breaking traffic laws are misdemeanors.* **2.** a wrong deed. **3.** bad behavior; misconduct. **—Syn.** **2.** misdeed. **3.** misbehavior.

mis·de·mean·our (mis′di mē′nər), *n. Especially British.* misdemeanor: . . . *an Act was passed making any attempt to hurt the Queen a misdemeanour* (Lytton Strachey).

mis·der·i·va·tion (mis′der ə vā′shən), *n.* an incorrect derivation.

mis·de·rive (mis′di rīv′), *v.t.,* **-rived, -riv·ing.** to derive incorrectly; assign an incorrect derivation to.

mis·de·scribe (mis′di skrīb′), *v.t.,* **-scribed, -scrib·ing.** to describe incorrectly or falsely.

mis·de·scrip·tion (mis′di skrip′shən), *n.* an incorrect description.

mis·di·ag·nose (mis′dī əg nōs′, -nōz′), *v.t.,* **-nosed, -nos·ing.** to diagnose incorrectly: *Did the conservatives misdiagnose their problem and/or apply the wrong treatment?* (Saturday Review).

mis·di·ag·no·sis (mis′dī əg nō′sis), *n., pl.* **-ses** (-sēz). incorrect diagnosis: *Even in recent years this same misdiagnosis has been made, and patients have been committed to mental institutions as having childhood schizophrenia when in reality they have phenylketonuria* (Atlantic).

mis·did (mis did′), *v.* the past tense of **misdo.**

mis·di·rect (mis′də rekt′, -dī-), *v.t.* to direct wrongly: *Great interests . . . which might be affected by a misdirected or careless inheritance of the colossal Walter empire* (Time). *In the hurry of a trial the ablest judge may mistake the law and misdirect the jury* (William Blackstone). **—Syn.** mislead.

mis·di·rec·tion (mis′də rek′shən, -dī-), *n.* **1.** wrong direction; improper guidance. **2.** direction to an incorrect address: *misdirection of a letter.* **3.** *Law.* an error made by a judge in his charge to a jury.

mis·di·vide (mis′də vīd′), *v.t.,* **-vid·ed, -vid·ing.** to divide incorrectly.

mis·di·vi·sion (mis′də vizh′ən), *n.* an incorrect division.

mis·do (mis dü′), *v.t., v.i.,* **-did, -done, -do·ing.** to do wrongly; perform improperly; do amiss: *I have misdone, and I endure the smart* (John Dryden). [Old English *misdōn*] **—mis·do′er,** *n.*

mis·do·ing (mis dü′ing), *n.* **1.** wrongdoing. **2.** a misdeed.

mis·done (mis dun′), *v.* the past participle of **misdo.**

mis·doubt (mis dout′), *Archaic.* —*v.t., v.i.* **1.** to have doubts about; suspect; distrust: *I do not misdoubt my wife* (Shakespeare). *We do injuriously . . . to misdoubt her* [*truth's*] *strength* (Milton). **2.** to fear.
—*n.* **1.** suspicion; distrust; doubt. **2.** fear of evil: *Change misdoubt to resolution* (Shakespeare).

mise (mēz, mīz), *n.* **1.** a settlement by agreement. **2.** *Law.* the main point or issue in a writ of right. [< Anglo-French, Old French *mise* < *mettre* set, place < Latin *mittere*]

mis·ease (mis ēz′), *n. Archaic.* **1.** uneasiness; disquiet. **2.** distress; affliction. [< Old French *mesaise* < *mes-* ill, mis- + *aise* ease] **—Syn.** **2.** discomfort, suffering.

mis·ed·u·cate (mis ej′u̇ kāt), *v.t.,* **-cat·ed, -cat·ing.** to educate improperly: *There can never be peace without freedom . . . the freedom to elect one's own representatives and government, and the right to refuse to be miseducated regarding the good or evil intentions of other nations, . . . or just other persons* (Time).

mis·ed·u·ca·tion (mis′ej u̇ kā′shən), *n.* an improper education: *Spiritual faculties, which it is as wicked to stunt . . . by miseducation as it is to maim our own limbs* (Charles Kingsley).

mise en scène (mē′ zäN sen′), *French.* **1.** surroundings; setting; milieu: *The train whistles in the background add to the mise en scène* (Harper's). **2.** the scenery, properties, etc., for a play: *The tasteful handling of the mise en scène and the subtle use of color . . . made the performance a joy to watch* (New Yorker). **3.** the placing of scenery and actors in a scene.

mis·em·ploy (mis′em ploi′), *v.t.* to use wrongly or improperly. **—Syn.** misuse.

mis·em·ploy·ment (mis′em ploi′mənt), *n.* wrong employment.

mi·ser[1] (mī′zər), *n.* **1. a.** a person who loves money for its own sake; one who lives poorly in order to save money and keep it: *A miser dislikes to spend money for anything, except to gain more money. Even to the old The hours are as a miser's coins* (Thomas B. Aldrich). **b.** any grasping person. **2.** *Obsolete.* a miserable wretch. [< Latin *miser* wretched] **—Syn.** **1. a.** skinflint, niggard.

mi·ser[2] (mī′zər), *n.* a boring tool, as for sinking wells, which forces upward the material drilled out. [origin uncertain]

mis·er·a·ble (miz′ər ə bəl, miz′rə-), *adj.* **1.** unhappy or uncomfortable. **2.** causing trouble, unhappiness, or discomfort: *miserable damp weather, a miserable cold. O, I have passed a miserable night, so full of ugly sights, of ghastly dreams* (Shakespeare). **3. a.** poor; mean; wretched: *They live in miserable surroundings. The ragged child lives in a miserable unheated house.* **b.** pitiable; deplorable; sorry: *a miserable failure, miserable sinners.*
—*n.* a person who is in misery or great want.
[< Old French *miserable,* learned borrowing from Latin *miserābilis* < *miserārī* to lament < *miser* wretched] **—mis′er·a·ble·ness,** *n.*
—Syn. *adj.* **1.** See **wretched. 3. a.** sordid.

mis·er·a·bly (miz′ər ə blē, miz′rə-), *adv.* in a miserable manner; calamitously; pitiably; deplorably; very poorly or meanly; wretchedly.

Mis·e·re·re (miz′ə rãr′ē, -rir′-), *n.* **1.** the 51st Psalm in the Revised and Authorized versions of the Bible; the 50th Psalm in the Douay Version of the Bible. **2.** the music for it. [< Latin *miserēre* have pity, singular imperative of *miserērī* (the first word of this psalm in the Vulgate)]

mis·e·re·re (miz′ə rãr′ē, -rir′-), *n.* **1.** a prayer asking mercy. **2.** a bracket on the under side of a hinged seat in a church stall, so arranged that when the seat is turned up a person standing in the stall could lean against it for support. [< *Miserere*]

mis·er·i·cord or **mis·er·i·corde** (miz′ər ə kôrd′, mi zer′ə kôrd), *n.* **1.** a specially permitted relaxation of monastic rule, as in dress or food. **2.** a room in a monastery in which certain relaxations of the rule are permitted, especially those relating to food. **3.** miserere (def. 2). **4.** (in the Middle Ages) a dagger used to give the death blow to a wounded foe. [< Latin *misericordia* < *misericors, -cordis* < *miserērī* to have pity on (< *miser* wretched) + *cor, cordis* heart]

mi·se·ri·cor·di·a (miz′ər ə kôr′dē ə), *n. Latin.* compassion; pity.

mi·ser·li·ness (mī′zər lē nis), *n.* avariciousness; niggardliness; penuriousness.

mi·ser·ly (mī′zər lē), *adj.* of, like, or suited to a miser; stingy: *miserly habits, a miserly wretch.* **—Syn.** niggardly, close, penurious.

mis·er·y (miz′ər ē, miz′rē), *n., pl.* **-er·ies.** **1.** a miserable, unhappy state of mind: *the misery of having no home or friends. It is acknowledged that rage, envy, resentment, are in themselves mere misery* (Samuel Butler). **2.** poor, mean, miserable circumstances: *the misery of poverty, companions in misery. The very poor live in misery without beauty or comfort around them.* **3.** a miserable condition or circumstance; a cause or source of wretchedness: *The explorer was exposed to unthinkable miseries and hardships. That packet of assorted miseries which we call a ship* (Rudyard Kipling). **4.** *U.S.* bodily pain: *He had the worst "misery in his back" that he had ever suffered* (George W. Cable). [< Latin *miseria* < *miser* wretched] **—Syn.** **1.** wretchedness, woe, distress.

mis·es·teem (mis′es tēm′), *v.t.* to have an incorrect estimation of; hold improperly in low esteem. —*n.* want of esteem or respect; disesteem.

mis·es·ti·mate (*v.* mis es′tə māt; *n.* mis·es′tə mit), *v.,* **-mat·ed, -mat·ing,** *n.* —*v.t.* to make an incorrect estimate of. —*n.* an incorrect estimate or valuation.

mis·es·ti·ma·tion (mis′es tə mā′shən), *n.* an incorrect estimation.

mis·faith (mis fāth′), *n.* want of faith; disbelief; mistrust: . . . *some sudden turn of anger, born of your misfaith* (Tennyson).

mis·fea·sance (mis fē′zəns), *n.* **1.** the wrongful performance of a lawful act; wrongful and injurious exercise of lawful authority. **2.** any wrong done; trespass: *General denunciation, embellished with assorted charges of misfeasance and high misdemeanors* (New York Times). [< Middle French *mesfaisance* < Old French *mesfaire* to misdo < *mes-* wrong, mis- + *faire* do < Latin *facere*] —**Syn. 1.** malfeasance. **2.** misdeed.

mis·fea·sor (mis fē′zər), *n. Law.* a person guilty of misfeasance.

mis·fea·ture (mis fē′chər), *n., v.,* **-tured, -tur·ing.** —*n.* **1.** a distorted feature. **2.** a bad feature; unfortunate trait. —*v.t.* to distort the features of.

mis·field (*v.* mis fēld′; *n.* mis′fēld′), *v.t.* to field (a ball) badly: *Hosen misfielded a short kick* (London Times). —*n.* a misfielding.

mis·file (mis fīl′), *v.t.,* **-filed, -fil·ing.** to file incorrectly: *He came across a misfiled memorandum on German relations with the Vatican* (Time).

mis·fire (mis fīr′), *v.,* **-fired, -fir·ing,** *n.* —*v.i.* **1.** to fail to be fired or exploded properly, as when the cylinders of an internal-combustion engine do not ignite the gas at the correct time, or a gun fails to shoot when the trigger is pulled: *The firings were the first of the Talos since October 15 when the missile's booster misfired shortly after takeoff* (Wall Street Journal). **2.** to go wrong; fail: *The play as a whole misfires* (New Yorker). —*n.* an instance of misfiring.

mis·fit (*n.* mis′fit′; *v.* mis fit′), *n., v.,* **-fit·ted, -fit·ting.** —*n.* **1.** a bad fit; a garment or other article which does not fit: *Do not buy shoes which are misfits.* **2.** a maladjusted individual. —*v.t., v.i.* to fit badly.

mis·form (mis fôrm′), *v.t.* to form amiss; misshape.

mis·for·ma·tion (mis′fôr mā′shən), *n.* malformation.

mis·for·tune (mis fôr′chən), *n.* **1.** bad luck. **2.** a piece of bad luck; unlucky accident: *The misfortunes hardest to bear are those which never come* (Lowell). *By misfortunes was my life prolong'd, To tell sad stories of my own mishaps* (Shakespeare).
—**Syn. 1,2. Misfortune, adversity, mishap** mean bad luck. **Misfortune** applies to a distressful condition, ordinarily not one's own fault, or to an unlucky happening: *She had the misfortune to break her arm.* **Adversity** applies chiefly to a condition of great and continued misfortune, marked by serious accidents, hardships, and distress: *Displaced persons have experienced adversity.* **Mishap** applies to a minor accident or unlucky incident: *Breaking a dish is a mishap. By some mishap the letter went astray.* —**Ant. 1.** prosperity.

mis·gauge (mis gāj′), *v.t.,* **-gauged, -gaug·ing.** to gauge incorrectly; misestimate: *No diplomatic response has fueled aggression as has appeasement—the act of misgauging the imperialist's appetite* (Wall Street Journal).

mis·gave (mis gāv′), *v.* the past tense of **misgive.**

mis·give (mis giv′), *v.,* **-gave, -giv·en, -giv·ing.** —*v.t.* to cause to feel doubt, suspicion, or anxiety: *My mind misgives me that we are lost.* —*v.i.* to have misgivings.

mis·giv·en (mis giv′ən), *v.* the past participle of **misgive.**

mis·giv·ing (mis giv′ing), *n.* a feeling of doubt, suspicion, or anxiety: *We started off through the storm with some misgivings.* —**Syn.** foreboding, apprehension.

mis·gov·ern (mis guv′ərn), *v.t.* to govern or manage badly.

mis·gov·ern·ment (mis guv′ərn mənt, -ər-), *n.* bad government or management: *Men . . . augur misgovernment at a distance and snuff the approach of tyranny in every tainted breeze* (Edmund Burke).

mis·gov·er·nor (mis guv′ər nər), *n.* a person who misgoverns.

mis·guid·ance (mis gī′dəns), *n.* bad or wrong guidance; faulty or improper direction; misdirection.

mis·guide (mis gīd′), *v.t.,* **-guid·ed, -guid·ing.** to lead into mistakes or wrongdoing; mislead. —**mis·guid′er,** *n.* —**Syn.** misdirect.

mis·guid·ed (mis gī′did), *adj.* led astray, especially into mistakes or wrongdoing; misled: *The misguided boy joined a gang of thieves.* —**mis·guid′ed·ly,** *adv.* —**mis·guid′ed·ness,** *n.*

mis·han·dle (mis han′dəl), *v.t.,* **-dled, -dling.** to handle badly or roughly; maltreat: *It is a shame to see how they have mishandled the old man among them* (Scott).

mi·shan·ter (mi shan′tər), *n. Scottish.* misadventure; mishap. [variant of earlier *misaunter,* contraction of *misaventure* misadventure]

mis·hap (mis′hap, mis hap′), *n.* **1.** an unlucky accident; misadventure: . . . *secure from worldly chances and mishaps* (Shakespeare). **2.** bad luck; misfortune. —**Syn. 1, 2.** See **misfortune.**

mis·hear (mis hir′), *v.t., v.i.,* **-heard** (-hėrd′), **-hear·ing.** to hear incorrectly or imperfectly.

mis·hit (*n.* mis′hit′; *v.* mis hit′), *n., v.,* **-hit, -hit·ting.** —*n.* a faulty or bad hit: *A club is thrown wildly away after a mishit* (Punch). —*v.t.* to hit badly: *Father Urban watched Father Feld mishit his second shot, saw it . . . roll back down ten yards—into a bad lie* (J.F. Powers).

mish·mash (mish′mash′), *n.* a confused mixture; hodgepodge; jumble: *a mishmash of unrelated facts and figures. A gastronomical mishmash of grilled and roasted and fried fishes and meats* (Atlantic). —*v.t.* to make a mishmash of. [probably imitative reduplication of *mash*[1]. Compare German *Mischmasch* < *mischen* to mix.]

Mish·na or **Mish·nah** (mish′nə), *n.* **1.** the collection of interpretations and discussions of the law of Moses by the Jewish rabbis, codified in 210 A.D.; oral law of the Hebrews. The Mishna forms the basic part of the Talmud. **2.** a paragraph of this collection. [< Hebrew *mishnâh* instruction < *shânâh* he learned; earlier, he repeated]

Mish·na·ic (mish nā′ik), *adj.* **1.** having to do with or relating to the Mishna. **2.** characteristic of the Mishna.

Mish·nic (mish′nik), *adj.* Mishnaic.

Mish·ni·cal (mish′nə kəl), *adj.* Mishnaic.

mis·im·pres·sion (mis′im presh′ən), *n.* a mistaken impression or idea: *They exaggerated the role of personal bravery . . . . Under the influence of this misimpression, they pictured warfare too much as a test of the personal qualities and spirit of a nation* (George F. Kennan).

mis·in·form (mis′in fôrm′), *v.t.* to give incorrect or misleading information to. —*v.i.* to make a false statement about someone or something. —**mis′in·form′er,** *n.*

mis·in·form·ant (mis′in fôr′mənt), *n.* a person who gives incorrect information.

mis·in·for·ma·tion (mis′in fər mā′shən), *n.* incorrect, inaccurate, or misleading information.

mis·in·ter·pret (mis′in tėr′prit), *v.t., v.i.* to interpret incorrectly; explain wrongly; misunderstand. —**mis′in·ter′pret·er,** *n.* —**Syn.** misconstrue.

mis·in·ter·pre·ta·tion (mis′in tėr′prə tā′shən), *n.* incorrect interpretation; incorrect explanation; misunderstanding.

mis·join (mis join′), *v.t.* to join incorrectly or improperly.

mis·join·der (mis join′dər), *n. Law.* a joining of parties in an action, or of causes of action in a suit, that ought not to be so joined.

mis·judge (mis juj′), *v.,* **-judged, -judg·ing.** —*v.t.* to judge wrongly or unjustly. —*v.i.* to form wrong opinions.

mis·judge·ment (mis juj′mənt), *n. Especially British.* misjudgment: *It is from . . . diplomatic misjudgements that most of the present difficulties arise* (Listener).

mis·judg·ment (mis juj′mənt), *n.* wrong or unjust judgment.

mis·kal (mis käl′), *n.* an Eastern unit of weight varying from 71 grains, as in Iran, to 74 grains, as in Turkey. [< Arabic *mithqāl*]

mis·ken (mis ken′), *v.t.,* **-kenned, -ken·ning.** *Scottish.* to fail to know, recognize, or perceive; ignore; mistake; misunderstand: *Were I you, Ranald, I would be for miskenning Sir Duncan* (Scott). [< *mis-* + *ken*]

mis·know (mis nō′), *v.t.,* **-knew** (-nü′ or -nyü′), **-known, -know·ing.** **1.** to misapprehend; misunderstand. **2.** *Scottish.* to not recognize (a person).

mis·knowl·edge (mis nol′ij), *n.* faulty knowledge; misapprehension of truth or fact.

mis·la·bel (mis lā′bəl), *v.t.,* **-beled, -bel·ing** or (*especially British*) **-belled, -bel·ling.** to label falsely or incorrectly: *Housewives in the metropolitan area may have purchased horsemeat mislabeled as beef* (New York Times).

mis·laid (mis lād′), *v.* the past tense and past participle of **mislay:** *The boy mislaid my books. I have mislaid my pen.*

mis·lay (mis lā′), *v.t.,* **-laid, -lay·ing.** **1.** to put in the wrong place. **2.** to put in a place and then forget where it is; lose temporarily: *Was ever anything so provoking —to mislay my own jewels, and force me to wear her trumpery* (Oliver Goldsmith). —**mis·lay′er,** *n.*

mis·lead (mis lēd′), *v.t.,* **-led, -lead·ing.** **1.** to lead astray; cause to go in the wrong direction: *Our guide misled us in the woods, and we got lost.* **2.** to cause to do wrong; lead into wrongdoing: *He is a good boy, but bad companions misled him.* **3.** to lead to think what is not so; deceive: *His lies misled me. Misled by fancy's meteor ray, By passion driven* (Robert Burns). —**mis·lead′er,** *n.* —**Syn. 1.** misguide, misdirect. **3.** delude, beguile, dupe.

mis·lead·ing (mis lē′ding), *adj.* causing error or wrongdoing. —**mis·lead′ing·ly,** *adv.* —**mis·lead′ing·ness,** *n.*

mis·leared (mis lird′), *adj. Scottish.* unmannerly; ill-bred. [< *mis-* + Middle English *leared,* past participle of *leren* teach, Old English *lǣran*]

mis·led (mis led′), *v.* the past tense and past participle of **mislead:** . . . *by ambition far misled* (Scott).

mis·like (mis līk′), *v.,* **-liked, -lik·ing,** *n.* —*v.t.* **1.** to disapprove of; dislike: *Mislike me not for my complexion* (Shakespeare). **2.** to displease; offend. —*n.* aversion; dislike; distaste: *Julian's mislike of the rising faith* (Richard C. Trench). —**mis·lik′er,** *n.*

mis·lik·ing (mis lī′king), *n.* **1.** a dislike (of); aversion. **2.** *Obsolete.* displeasure; indignation.

mis·made (mis mād′), *adj.* badly or wrongly made. —*v.* the past tense and past participle of **mismake.**

mis·make (mis māk′), *v.t.,* **-made, -mak·ing.** **1.** to make badly; spoil in putting together. **2.** to put (oneself) out.

mis·man·age (mis man′ij), *v.t., v.i.,* **-aged, -ag·ing.** to manage badly or improperly. —**mis·man′ag·er,** *n.*

mis·man·age·ment (mis man′ij mənt), *n.* bad management: *But by registering their disgust at ten years of mismanagement, Frenchmen had only managed to vote themselves more chaos* (Newsweek).

mis·mar·riage (mis mar′ij), *n.* an unsuitable marriage; unwise marriage; mismatch.

mis·match (mis mach′), *v.t.* to match badly or unsuitably, especially in marriage: *These seemingly mismatched mergers are not as ill-matched as they appear* (Wall Street Journal). —*n.* a bad, unwise, or unsuitable match.

mis·mate (mis māt′), *v.t., v.i.,* **-mat·ed, -mat·ing.** to mate unsuitably.

mis·move (mis müv′), *n.* **1.** *U.S.* a faulty move or step in action; misstep. **2.** any wrong move, as in a game or any course of procedure.

mis·name (mis nām′), *v.t.,* **-named, -nam·ing.** to call by a wrong name; miscall: *That lazy, careless boy is misnamed Ernest.*

mis·no·mer (mis nō′mər), *n.* **1.** a name that describes wrongly; a wrong designation: *"Lightning" is a misnomer for that slow, old horse.* **2.** an error in naming; misapplication of a term. **3.** *Law.* a mistake in naming a person in a legal instrument. [< Middle French *mesnommer* < *mes-* wrongly, mis- + *nommer* to name < Latin *nōmināre* < *nomen, -inis* name]

mi·sog·a·mist (mi sog′ə mist, mī-), *n.* a person who hates marriage.

mi·sog·a·my (mi sog′ə mē, mī-), *n.* hatred of marriage. [< Greek *mîsos* hatred + *gámos* marriage]

mis·o·gyn·ic (mis′ə jin′ik, mī′sə-), *adj.* misogynous.

mi·sog·y·nist (mi soj′ə nist, mī-), *n.* a hater of women.

mi·sog·y·nis·tic (mi soj′ə nis′tik, mī-), *n.* characteristic of misogyny or misogynists: *The misogynistic lament that "Adam ever lost a rib"* (Harper's).

mi·sog·y·nous (mi soj′ə nəs, mī-), *adj.* hating women.

mi·sog·y·ny (mi soj′ə nē, mī-), *n.* hatred of women. [< Greek *mīsogyníā* < *mīsogýnēs* woman hater < *mîsos* hatred + *gynḗ* woman]

mi·sol·o·gist (mi sol′ə jist, mī-), *n.* **1.** a hater of reason or discussion. **2.** a hater of learning.

mi·sol·o·gy (mi sol′ə jē, mī-), *n.* **1.** hatred of reason or discussion. **2.** hatred of learning. [< Greek *mīsologiā* < *mîsos* hatred + *lógos* reason, discussion]

mis·o·ne·ism (mis′ə nē′iz əm, mī′sə-), *n.* hatred or dislike of what is new; strong opposition to change. [< Italian *misoneismo* < Greek *mîsos* hatred + *néos* new + Italian *-ismo* -ism]

mis·o·ne·ist (mis′ə nē′ist, mī′sə-), *n.* a hater of what is new.

mis·o·ne·is·tic (mis′ə nē is′tik, mī′sə-), *adj.* hating what is new.

mis·per·cep·tion (mis′pər sep′shən), *n.* imperfect or erroneous perception.

mis·per·form (mis′pər fôrm′), *v.t.* to perform badly or improperly.

mis·per·form·ance (mis′pər fôr′məns), *n.* improper performance.

mis·pick·el (mis′pik′əl), *n.* arsenopyrite. [< German *Mispickel*]

mis·place (mis plās′), *v.t.,* **-placed, -placing.** **1.** to put in a wrong place: *misplaced acts of foolery* (Charles Lamb). **2.** *Informal.* to put in a place and then forget where it is; mislay. **3.** to give (one's love or trust) to the wrong person, especially to one who is unworthy: *misplaced affections.*

mis·place·ment (mis plās′mənt), *n.* **1.** the act of misplacing. **2.** the condition of being misplaced; wrong position.

mis·play (mis plā′), *n.* a wrong play, especially one not permitted by the rules of a game. *—v.t., v.i.* to play wrongly: *Anne misplayed her hand.* [American English < *mis-* + *play*]

mis·plead (mis plēd′), *v.t., v.i. Law.* to plead wrongly.

mis·plead·ing (mis plē′ding), *n. Law.* an error in pleading, as through the omission of something essential to the case.

mis·praise (mis prāz′), *v.t.,* **-praised, -praising.** **1.** to praise mistakenly or imprudently: *They, whom I have so mispraised, are the worse in the sight of God for my overpraising* (John Donne). **2.** to dispraise; blame.

mis·print (*n.* mis′print′; *v.* mis print′), *n.* a mistake in printing. *—v.t.* to print wrongly. **—Syn.** *n.* erratum.

mis·prise¹ (mis prīz′), *v.t.,* **-prised, -prising.** misprize¹.

mis·prise² (mis prīz′), *v.t.,* **-prised, -prising.** misprize².

mis·pri·sion¹ (mis prizh′ən), *n.* **1. a.** a wrongful action or omission, especially by a public official. **b.** *Law.* failure to give to the proper authority information which to a person's knowledge may lead to the apprehension of a felon: *misprision of treason.* **2.** *Archaic.* the mistaking of a thing, word, etc., for another; misunderstanding. [< Old French *mesprision* < *mesprendre* to mistake, act wrongly < *mes-* mis- + *prendre* take < Latin *prehendere*] **—Syn. 2.** misapprehension, mistake.

mis·pri·sion² (mis prizh′ən), *n. Archaic.* contempt; scorn: *those unhappy persons, who . . . have their hearts barred against conviction by prejudice and misprision* (Scott). [< *misprize*¹ + *-ion;* influenced by *misprision*¹]

mis·prize¹ (mis prīz′), *v.t.,* **-prized, -prizing.** **1.** to value too little; undervalue; slight: *Not that I have any call to misprize the event . . . since it launched me upon a commercial career* (New Yorker). **2.** to despise; scorn: *It sorrows me that you misprize my love* (Thomas Heywood). [< Old French *mesprisier* < *mes-* mis- + *prisier,* variant of *preisier* praise, prize³]

mis·prize² (mis prīz′), *v.t.,* **-prized, -prizing.** *Obsolete.* to mistake; misapprehend: *Monsieur Gaspar . . . misprize me not* (Ben Jonson). [< Old French *mespris,* past participle of *mesprendre* commit a crime]

mis·pro·nounce (mis′prə nouns′), *v.t., v.i.,* **-nounced, -nouncing.** to pronounce incorrectly.

mis·pro·nun·ci·a·tion (mis′prə nun′sē ā′shən), *n.* incorrect pronunciation.

mis·proud (mis proud′), *adj. Archaic.* wrongly or wickedly proud; arrogant: *thy misproud ambitious clan* (Scott).

mis·punc·tu·ate (mis pungk′chü āt), *v.t.,* **-at·ed, -at·ing.** to punctuate incorrectly.

mis·punc·tu·a·tion (mis′pungk chü ā′shən), *n.* incorrect punctuation.

mis·quo·ta·tion (mis′kwō tā′shən), *n.* **1.** an incorrect quotation. **2.** inaccuracy in quoting.

mis·quote (mis kwōt′), *v.t., v.i.,* **-quot·ed, -quot·ing.** to quote incorrectly: *With just enough of learning to misquote* (Byron).

mis·read¹ (mis rēd′), *v.t.,* **-read, -read·ing.** **1.** to read wrongly. **2.** to misunderstand; interpret incorrectly. [< *mis-* + *read*¹] **—Syn. 2.** misconceive.

mis·read² (mis red′), *v.* the past tense and past participle of **misread**¹.

mis·reck·on (mis rek′ən), *v.t., v.i.* to compute or count incorrectly; miscalculate; miscount.

mis·re·mem·ber (mis′ri mem′bər), *v.t., v.i.* **1.** to remember wrongly, imperfectly, or incorrectly: *I had just about given up strawberries, . . . I had lost or misremembered my own taste for them* (Atlantic). **2.** *Dialect.* to forget.

mis·ren·der (mis ren′dər), *v.t.* to render or interpret incorrectly.

mis·re·port (mis′ri pôrt′, -pōrt′), *v.t.* to report (anything) incorrectly or falsely. *—v.i. Obsolete.* to give a false report. *—n.* a false or erroneous report. **—mis′re·port′er,** *n.*

mis·rep·re·sent (mis′rep ri zent′), *v.t.* **1.** to represent falsely; give a wrong idea of: *He misrepresented this automobile when he said it was in good running order.* **2.** to fail to represent correctly or adequately as agent or official representative. *—v.i.* to make false or misleading statements. **—mis′rep·re·sent′er,** *n.*

mis·rep·re·sen·ta·tion (mis′rep ri zen tā′shən), *n.* **1.** a false representation: *He obtained the position by misrepresentation.* **2.** an incorrect story or explanation: *The report is a misrepresentation of the facts in the case.*

mis·rep·re·sent·a·tive (mis′rep ri zen′tə tiv), *adj.* misrepresenting; conveying a false impression.

mis·route (mis rüt′, -rout′), *v.t.,* **-rout·ed, -rout·ing.** to route incorrectly; send by the wrong route: *The parcels . . . were misrouted on the railways* (London Times).

mis·rule (mis rül′), *n., v.,* **-ruled, -rul·ing.** *—n.* **1.** bad or unwise rule; misgovernment. **2.** a state of disorder: *the misrule of mobs* (Lytton Strachey). *—v.t.* to rule or govern badly. **—mis·rul′er,** *n.* **—Syn.** *n.* **1.** maladministration. *-v.t.* misgovern.

miss¹ (mis), *v.t.* **1.** to fail to hit or strike: *to miss a target in shooting. John hammers away, but half the time he misses the nail.* **2. a.** to fail to find, get, meet, attend, use, catch, hear, read, do, solve, etc.: *to miss a train. I missed my music lesson today. I set out to meet my father, but in the dark I missed him.* **b.** to fail to understand or grasp: *to miss the point of a remark.* **3.** to let slip by; not seize: *I missed the chance of a ride to town.* **4.** to escape or avoid: *to miss death by a hair.* **5.** to notice the absence or loss of; feel keenly the absence of: *I miss my mother when she goes away.* *—v.i.* to fail to hit: *He fired twice, but both shots missed.*

miss fire. See under **fire.**

miss of, *Archaic.* to fail to hit, meet, obtain, or attain; miss: *Time hath a quiver full of purposes Which miss not of their aim* (Lowell).

—n. **1.** a failure to hit, attain, etc. **2.** *Obsolete.* loss; lack: *Aged people feel the miss of children* (George Eliot).

a miss is as good as a mile, a failure is a failure however near one may have been to success: *He was very near being a poet—but a miss is as good as a mile, and he always fell short of the mark* (Scott).

[Old English *missan*]

miss² (mis), *n., pl.* **miss·es.** a young unmarried woman; girl: *an arch little miss . . . to whom we strove to make ourselves particularly agreeable* (Herman Melville). [short for *mistress*]

Miss (mis), *n., pl.* **Miss·es.** a title before a girl's or unmarried woman's name: *Miss Brown.*

➔ **Miss.** Plural *Misses* is sometimes pronounced mis′ez to distinguish from mis′iz (Mrs.): *the Misses Angel and Joyce.* Of the two plural forms used in referring to unmarried women of the same family, *the Misses Thorne* is formal and somewhat old-fashioned; *the Miss Thornes* is now more usual.

Miss., Mississippi.

mis·said (mis sed′), *v.* the past tense and past participle of **missay.**

mis·sal (mis′əl), *n.* **1.** a book containing the prayers, etc., for celebrating Roman Catholic Mass throughout the year: *The religious were intent on their missals, following the recital of Mass* (Time). **2.** a devotional book: *Expert bookmen think the Pierpont Morgan Library purchase, a missal, or book of devotions, was an earlier experimental project of Johannes Gutenberg* (World Book Annual). [< Medieval Latin *missale* < Late Latin *missa* Mass]

Mis·sa So·lem·nis (mis′ə sə lem′nis), High Mass. [< Medieval Latin *missa solemnis*]

mis·saw (mis sô′), *v.* the past tense of **missee.**

mis·say (mis sā′), *v.,* **-said, -say·ing.** *—v.i.* to speak wrongly. *—v.t.* **1.** to say wrongly. **2.** *Archaic.* to speak ill of; slander: *Far liefer had I fight a score of times than hear thee so missay me and revile* (Tennyson). **—mis·say′er,** *n.*

mis·see (mis sē′), *v.t., v.i.,* **-saw, -seen, -see·ing.** to see wrongly.

mis·seem (mis sēm′), *v.t.* to be unseemly for.

mis·seen (mis sēn′), *v.* the past participle of **missee.**

mis·sel thrush (mis′əl), a large European thrush that feeds on the berries of the mistletoe. [< obsolete *mistel* mistletoe, Old English *mistel*]

mis·send (mis send′), *v.t.,* **-sent, -send·ing.** to send amiss; send to a wrong place or person.

mis·sent (mis sent′), *v.* the past tense and past participle of **missend.**

mis·set (mis set′), *v.t.,* **-set, -set·ting.** **1.** to set incorrectly; misplace: *One of these misset relays activated a circuit breaker* (New York Times). **2.** *Scottish.* to annoy; upset.

mis·shape (mis shāp′), *v.t.,* **-shaped, -shaped** or **-shap·en, -shap·ing.** to make in the wrong shape; shape badly; deform. **—Syn.** distort.

mis·shap·en (mis shā′pən), *adj.* badly shaped; deformed: *the misshapen hairy Scandinavian troll* (Emerson). *Crooked and misshapen minds* (John Florio). *—v.* misshaped; a past participle of **misshape.** **—mis·shap′en·ly,** *adv.* **—mis·shap′en·ness,** *n.*

mis·sile (mis′əl), *n.* **1.** any object that is thrown, hurled, or shot, such as a stone, an arrow, a bullet, or a lance. **2.** a self-propelled bomb or rocket: *In our diversified family of missiles, we have weapons adapted to every kind of distance, launching, and use* (Wall Street Journal). *—adj.* **1.** capable of or adapted to use as a missile: *We . . . bend the bow, or wing the missile dart* (Alexander Pope). **2.** that discharges missiles: *long-bows, slings, and other missile weapons* (Scott). [< Latin *missile,* neuter < *mittere* to send]

Missile (def. 2) U. S. Army's Nike-Hercules for ground-to-air interception

mis·sil·eer (mis′ə lir′), *n.* a missileman: *The marvelous navigational ability of birds is of particular interest to missileers* (Scientific American).

mis·sile·man (mis′əl man′), *n., pl.* **-men.** a person who works with missiles or rockets, either in construction or in use and maintenance.

missile range, a particular course or area, marked out beforehand, over which missiles are test-flown under observation: *The capsule will be . . . fired a few hundred miles down the Atlantic missile range from Cape Canaveral* (New Scientist).

mis·sile·ry (mis′əl rē), *n.* **1.** the science or art having to do with the design, manufacture, and operation of missiles and rockets: *In the fast-maturing age of missilery, a world of new wonders was in the making* (Time). **2.** missiles: *The advent of intercontinental missilery with its only multi-minute warning time . . . poses a severe dilemma for long-range civil defense planning* (Bulletin of Atomic Scientists).

mis·sil·ry (mis′əl rē), *n.* missilery.

miss·ing (mis′ing), *adj.* not found when looked for; absent; gone: *One book is missing from the set.* **—Syn.** lacking, wanting, lost.

missing link, **1.** a hypothetical creature assumed to have been the connecting link between man and the anthropoid apes. **2.**

something lacking from a series: *A small bit of evidence—an old shoe—proved to be the missing link in the murder case.*

mis·sion (mish′ən), *n.* **1.** a sending or being sent on some special work or service; errand: *An operation by one or more aircraft against the enemy is called a mission.* **2. a.** a group of persons sent on some special business, as by their government, to a foreign country to conduct negotiations: *He was one of a mission sent by our government to France.* **b.** a group of persons sent by a religious organization into other parts of the world to spread its beliefs: *A mission was sent to Africa by the Baptist Church.* **3.** the business on which a mission is sent: *Hast thou perform'd my mission which I gave?* (Tennyson). **4.** the station or headquarters of a religious mission, as the center of missionary effort in a particular area: *a mission in the slums.* **5.** a congregation or district assigned to a priest or pastor from a neighboring parish. **6.** business or purpose in life; calling: *It seemed to be her mission to care for her brother's children. When one's all right, he's prone to spite The doctor's peaceful mission* (Eugene Field).

missions, an organized effort to spread the Christian religion: *foreign missions.*

—*adj.* of or having to do with a mission or missions.

—*v.t.* **1.** to conduct a religious mission among (a people) or in (a district). **2.** to send (a person) on a mission.

[< Latin *missiō, -ōnis* < *mittere* to send]

—**Syn.** *n.* **2. a.** commission, delegation. **3.** message, charge, duty, trust.

mis·sion·al (mish′ə nəl), *adj.* of or having to do with a mission.

mis·sion·a·rize (mish′ə nə rīz), *v.i., v.t.,* **-rized, -riz·ing.** missionize: *The Unitarian Service Committee . . . does its charitable work without missionarizing* (Maclean's).

mis·sion·ar·y (mish′ə ner′ē), *n., pl.* **-ar·ies,** *adj.* —*n.* **1.** a person sent on a religious mission: *The missionary went to India to convert people to Christianity.* **2.** a person who works to advance some cause or idea. **3.** *Obsolete.* an emissary.

—*adj.* **1.** of missions or missionaries: *missionary enthusiasm.* **2.** sent on a mission; engaged in missionary work: *a missionary priest, a missionary society.*

mis·sion·er (mish′ə nər), *n.* **1.** a missionary. **2.** a person who conducts a series of inspirational religious services.

mission furniture, a kind of heavy, plain, dark furniture, resembling the furniture used in the old Spanish missions in California.

mis·sion·ize (mish′ə nīz), *v.,* **-ized, -iz·ing.** —*v.i.* to send missionaries or missions; establish a religious mission or missions: *All three religions . . . have been actively missionizing* (Alfred L. Kroeber). —*v.t.* to send missionaries or missions to; convert through evangelizing: *to missionize a pagan people.*

mis·sions (mish′ənz), *n.pl.* See under **mission,** *n.*

mis·sis (mis′iz, -is), *n. Dialect.* **1.** a wife: *And how is the missis these days?* **2.** the mistress of a household: *Missis and the young ladies and Master John are going out to tea this afternoon* (Charlotte Brontë). Also, **missus.** [variant of *mistress*]

miss·ish (mis′ish), *adj.* prim; prudish; affected: *You are not going to be missish, I hope, and pretend to be affronted at an idle report* (Jane Austen). —**miss′ish·ness,** *n.*

Mis·sis·sip·pi·an (mis′ə sip′ē ən), *n.* **1.** a native or inhabitant of Mississippi. **2.** *Geology.* the earliest period of the Carboniferous; Lower Carboniferous (the name used outside North America). **3.** the strata formed in this period.

—*adj.* **1.** of or having to do with Mississippi or the Mississippi River. **2.** *Geology.* of or having to do with the Mississippian or its rocks.

Mis·sis·sip·pi Bubble or **Scheme** (mis′ə sip′ē), a scheme for speculation in overly exaggerated business operations in French-held Louisiana and Canada during the early 1700's.

Mississippi kite, a graceful, falconlike hawk with grayish plumage and black tail, found in southeastern and central United States.

mis·sive (mis′iv), *n.* a written message; letter: *You . . . with taunts Did gibe my missive out of audience* (Shakespeare). —*adj. Obsolete.* **1.** that is or is intended to be sent. **2.** sent as a message: *a letter missive.* [< Medieval Latin *missivus* < Latin *mittere* to send]

—**Syn.** *n.* dispatch.

Mis·sou·ri (mə zůr′ē, -ə), *n.* a member of a Siouan tribe of North American Indians, formerly living in northern Missouri.

from Missouri, *Informal.* not convinced until shown clear proof; skeptical; doubtful: *The legislators, for the most part, have said that they are from Missouri* (New Yorker).

[American English < French *Missouri* < the Algonkian name of a Siouan tribe living near the mouth of the Missouri River; probably meaning people who have dugout or wooden canoes]

Mis·sou·ri·an (mə zůr′ē ən), *adj.* of Missouri or its people. —*n.* a native or inhabitant of Missouri.

Missouri Compromise, an agreement, 1820, between the proslavery and antislavery groups in the United States, providing for the exclusion of slavery from any part of the Louisiana Purchase north of the southern boundary of Missouri, except Missouri itself.

mis·speak (mis spēk′), *v.t., v.i.,* **-spoke, -spo·ken, -speak·ing.** to speak, utter, or pronounce wrongly or incorrectly.

mis·speech (mis spēch′), *n.* faulty or incorrect speech.

mis·spell (mis spel′), *v.t., v.i.,* **-spelled** or **-spelt, -spell·ing.** to spell incorrectly.

mis·spell·ing (mis spel′ing), *n.* an incorrect spelling.

mis·spelt (mis spelt′), *adj.* misspelled. —*v.* misspelled; a past tense and a past participle of **misspell.**

mis·spend (mis spend′), *v.t.,* **-spent, -spend·ing.** to spend foolishly or wrongly; waste.

mis·spent (mis spent′), *adj.* spent foolishly or wrongly; wasted: *a misspent fortune, a misspent, ruined life.* —*v.* the past tense and past participle of **misspend.**

mis·spoke (mis spōk′), *v.* the past tense of **misspeak.**

mis·spo·ken (mis spō′kən), *v.* the past participle of **misspeak.**

mis·state (mis stāt′), *v.t.,* **-stat·ed, -stat·ing.** to make wrong or misleading statements about. —**Syn.** misrepresent, distort, falsify.

mis·state·ment (mis stāt′mənt), *n.* a wrong or erroneous statement: *In justice both to Mr. Garrick and Dr. Johnson, I think it necessary to rectify this misstatement* (James Boswell). —**Syn.** misrepresentation.

mis·step (mis step′, mis′step′), *n.* **1.** a wrong step: *A misstep to the right or left was fatal.* **2.** an error or slip in conduct; faux pas.

mis·sus (mis′iz, -is), *n.* missis.

miss·y (mis′ē), *n., pl.* **miss·ies.** *Informal.* little miss; miss.

mist (mist), *n.* **1.** a suspension of very fine water droplets in the air above the ground; haze. **2.** *U.S.* a fine drizzle. **3.** a cloud of very fine drops of any liquid in the air: *A mist of perfume issued from the atomizer.* **4.** anything that dims, blurs, or obscures, as a hazy appearance before the eyes from tears: *A mist of prejudice spoiled his judgment. Things view'd . . . through the mist of fear* (Thomas Carlyle).

—*v.i.* **1.** to come down in mist; rain in very fine drops; drizzle: *It is misting.* **2.** to be covered with mist; become dim. —*v.t.* to cover with a mist; put a mist before; make dim: *Tears misted her eyes. The composer gazed absently out of the misted window* (London Times).

[Old English *mist*]

mis·tak·a·ble (mis tā′kə bəl), *adj.* that may be mistaken or misunderstood. —**Syn.** ambiguous.

mis·take (mis tāk′), *n., v.,* **-took, -tak·en, -tak·ing.** —*n.* an error; blunder; misunderstanding: *It was a mistake to leave before the snow stopped. I used your towel by mistake.*

and no mistake, without a doubt; surely: *Mary Ann was mad, and no mistake* (Harper's). [< verb]

—*v.t.* **1.** to misunderstand (what is seen or heard); take in a wrong sense. **2.** to take wrongly; take (to be some other person or thing): *to mistake a fixed star for a planet. You can't mistake him for his brother. There's no mistaking his real motive.* **3.** to estimate wrongly: *You must have mistaken the meaning of the letter.* —*v.i. Archaic.* to make a mistake; be in error.

[< Scandinavian (compare Old Icelandic *mistaka*)] —**mis·tak′er,** *n.*

—**Syn.** *n.* fault, oversight, slip. See **error.**

mis·tak·en (mis tā′kən), *adj.* **1.** wrong in opinion; having made a mistake: *A mistaken person should admit his error.* **2.** wrongly judged; wrong; misplaced: *a mistaken opinion. It was a mistaken kindness to give that boy more candy; it will make him sick.* —*v.* the past participle of **mistake:** *She was mistaken for the queen.* —**mis·tak′en·ness,** *n.*

—**Syn.** *adj.* **1.** erroneous.

mis·tak·en·ly (mis tā′kən lē), *adv.* by mistake; wrongly.

mis·taught (mis tôt′), *v.* the past tense and past participle of **misteach:** *He never recovered from having been mistaught in the lower grades.*

mis·teach (mis tēch′), *v.t.,* **-taught, -teach·ing.** to teach badly or wrongly.

mis·ter (mis′tər), *n. Informal.* sir: *"Good morning, mister," said Dominicus* (Hawthorne). —*v.t. Informal.* to address as "mister." [variant of *master*]

➤ **Mister** (spelled out in writing) is sometimes used alone as a word of address, especially by a superior officer speaking to another officer under his command, as a ship's master. Except for such traditional uses, *mister* without a name or title following is largely confined to informal English: *What's the time, mister?*

Mis·ter (mis′tər), *n.* Mr., a title put before a man's name or the name of his office: *Mr. Smith, Mr. President.*

mis·ter·i·o·so (mis tir′ē ō′sō), *Music.* —*adv.* mysteriously. —*adj.* mysterious: *The composition went into dance rhythms that turned misterioso with a ululating vibraphone* (Time). [< Italian *misterioso* mysterious]

mis·term (mis tėrm′), *v.t.* to term wrongly or incorrectly.

mist·flow·er (mist′flou′ər), *n.* a North American composite herb whose blue flowerheads resemble those of the ageratum, but are smaller.

mist·ful (mist′fəl), *adj.* abounding in mist; misty.

mis·think (mis thingk′), *v.,* **-thought, -think·ing.** —*v.i.* **1.** to think mistakenly. **2.** *Obsolete.* to think unfavorably. —*v.t. Obsolete.* to have a bad opinion of.

mis·thought (mis thôt′), *v.* the past tense and past participle of **misthink.**

mist·i·ly (mis′tə lē), *adv.* in a misty manner.

mis·time (mis tīm′), *v.t.,* **-timed, -tim·ing.** **1.** to say or do at the wrong time: *to mistime a move or a remark.* **2.** to miscalculate or misstate the time of.

mist·i·ness (mis′tē nis), *n.* misty condition.

mis·tle (mis′əl), *n.,* or **mistle thrush,** missel thrush.

mist·less (mist′lis), *adj.* free from mist.

mis·tle·toe (mis′əl tō), *n.* **1.** any of a group of plants common to Europe and America with small, waxy, white berries and yellow flowers, that grow mostly as a parasitic shrub on the branches of various trees. **2.** a sprig of mistletoe, often used as a Christmas decoration: *The mistletoe is still hung up in farm-houses and kitchens at Christmas; and the young men have the privilege of kissing the girls under it* (Washington Irving). [Old English *mistiltān* < *mistel* mistletoe + *tān* twig]

Mistletoe (def. 1)

mis·took (mis tůk′), *v.* the past tense of **mistake:** *I mistook you for your sister yesterday.*

mis·tral (mis′trəl, mis träl′), *n.* a cold, dry, northerly wind common in southern France and neighboring regions: *The mistral, a wind born some say in the valley of the Rhône, which rises with acute suddenness* (London Times). [< French *mistral* < Provençal, (originally) dominant < Latin *magistrālis* < *magister* master. Doublet of MAGISTRAL.]

mis·trans·late (mis′trans lāt′, -tranz-; mis-trans′ lāt, -tranz′-), *v.t., v.i.,* **-lat·ed, -lat·ing.** to translate incorrectly.

mis·trans·la·tion (mis′trans lā′shən, -tranz-), *n.* an incorrect translation.

mis·treat (mis trēt′), *v.t.* to treat badly or wrongly; ill-treat. —**Syn.** maltreat, abuse.

mis·treat·ment (mis trēt′mənt), *n.* bad treatment; ill-treatment. —**Syn.** maltreatment.

mis·tress (mis′tris), *n.* **1.** the woman who is at the head of a household: *Mistress Gilpin* (*careful soul!*) (William Cowper). **2.** a woman or country that is in control or can rule: *Great Britain was sometimes called mistress of the seas.* **3.** a woman owner or possessor: *The dog's mistress walks him every day. I show more mirth than I am mistress of* (Shakespeare). **4.** a woman who has a thorough knowledge or mastery: *She is a complete mistress of the art of cookery.* **5.** *British.* a woman teacher: *the dancing mistress.* **6.** a woman loved and courted by a man: *O! mistress mine, where are you roaming? O! stay and hear; your true love's coming* (Shakespeare). **7.** a woman who improperly occupies the place of a wife and is usually supported by her lover. **8.** *Archaic or Dialect.* Mrs., Madam, or Miss. [< Old French *maistresse,* feminine of *maistre;* see MASTER]

Mis·tress (mis′tris), *n.* a title of courtesy for a woman, now superseded by *Mrs.* and *Miss.*

mis·tress·hood (mis′tris hůd), *n.* the condition or status of a mistress.

mistress of ceremonies, a woman in charge of a ceremony or entertainment.

mistress of the robe, *British.* the chief attendant to the queen.

mis·tress·ship (mis′tris ship), *n.* mistresshood.

mis·tri·al (mis trī′əl), *n. Law.* **1.** a trial having no effect in law because of some error in the proceedings: *The decrepit barrister ... has defended his simple little murderer so badly that he saves his life by perpetrating a mistrial* (Listener). **2.** *Informal.* an inconclusive trial, as when the jury cannot agree on a verdict.

mis·trust (mis trust′), *v.t.* **1.** to feel no confidence in; suspect the intentions, motives, etc., of; doubt: *She mistrusted her ability to learn to swim.* **2.** to have forebodings about: *The old woman gravely mistrusted the future.* —*v.i.* to be distrustful, suspicious, or without confidence.
—*n.* lack of trust or confidence; suspicion; distrust: *Hate and mistrust are the children of blindness* (Sir William Watson). —**mis·trust′er,** *n.* —**mis·trust′ing·ly,** *adv.*
—**Syn.** *v.t.* **1.** suspect, distrust. –*n.* doubt.

mis·trust·ful (mis trust′fəl), *adj.* lacking confidence; distrustful; doubting; suspicious. —**mis·trust′ful·ly,** *adv.* —**mis·trust′ful·ness,** *n.*

mis·tryst (mis trist′), *v.t. Scottish.* **1.** to fail to keep an engagement with. **2.** to perplex, confuse, or frighten.

mist·y (mis′tē), *adj.,* **mist·i·er, mist·i·est. 1.** of mist. **2.** characterized by mist; full of or covered with mist: *misty hills, misty air.* **3.** not clearly seen or outlined: *The ghost was just a misty outline.* **4.** as if seen through a mist; vague; indistinct: *a misty notion.* [Old English *mistig*]

mist·y-eyed (mis′tē īd′), *adj.* **1.** close to tears: ... *bowed misty-eyed to the packed hall* (Time). **2.** sentimental to the point of tears: *a misty-eyed speech, misty-eyed farewells.* **3.** having dreamy eyes: *a misty-eyed youth.*

mis·un·der·stand (mis′un dər stand′), *v.t., v.i.,* **-stood, -stand·ing. 1.** to understand wrongly; not comprehend rightly; misconceive. **2.** to take in a wrong sense; give the wrong meaning to. —**mis′un·der·stand′er,** *n.* —**Syn. 1.** misapprehend. **2.** misinterpret.

mis·un·der·stand·ing (mis′un dər stan′ding), *n.* **1.** wrong understanding; failure to understand: *I shall speak in words of one syllable that there may be no misunderstanding.* **2.** a quarrel; disagreement: *Some little pique or misunderstanding between them* (George Eliot). —**Syn. 1.** misconception, misinterpretation. **2.** dissension.

mis·un·der·stood (mis′un dər stůd′), *v.* the past tense and past participle of **misunderstand:** *She misunderstood what the teacher said and did the wrong homework.*
—*adj.* **1.** not properly understood; taken in a wrong sense. **2.** not properly appreciated: *There comes a time in every woman's life when she feels herself grievously misunderstood.*

mis·us·age (mis yü′sij, -zij), *n.* **1.** a wrong or improper usage; misuse. **2.** bad treatment; maltreatment; ill-usage.

mis·use (*v.* mis yüz′; *n.* mis yüs′), *v.,* **-used, -us·ing,** *n.* —*v.t.* **1.** to use for the wrong purpose; use improperly: *He misuses his knife at the table by lifting food with it.* **2.** to abuse; ill-treat; mistreat: *He misuses his horses by giving them loads that are too heavy. Men deal with life as children with their play, Who first misuse, then cast their toys away* (William Cowper).
—*n.* **1.** a wrong or improper use; misapplication: *I notice a misuse of the word "who" in your letter.* **2.** *Obsolete.* ill-usage. **3.** *Obsolete.* evil conduct.
—**Syn.** *v.t.* **1.** misapply. **2.** maltreat.

mis·us·er (mis yü′zər), *n.* **1.** *Law.* unlawful use of a liberty, benefit, or power. **2.** a person who misuses.

mis·val·u·a·tion (mis′val yů ā′shən), *n.* false or wrong valuation; misestimation.

mis·val·ue (mis val′yü), *v.t.,* **-ued, -u·ing.** to value falsely or wrongly; misesteem.

mis·ven·ture (mis ven′chər), *n.* an unfortunate adventure; mischance.

mis·word (mis wėrd′), *v.t.* to word (a message, etc.) incorrectly.

mis·write (mis rīt′), *v.t.,* **-wrote, -writ·ten, -writ·ing.** to write improperly; make a mistake in writing (a word, etc.).

mis·writ·ten (mis rit′ən), *v.* the past participle of **miswrite.**

mis·wrote (mis rōt′), *v.* the past tense of **miswrite.**

M.I.T., Massachusetts Institute of Technology.

Mitch·ell (mich′əl), *n.* a United States long-range medium bomber. [< General William (Billy) *Mitchell,* U.S. Army, 1879–1936, who advocated the use of air power]

Mitchell grass, any of various perennial grasses of Australia, much used as fodder.

mite[1] (mīt), *n.* any of various tiny arachnids that usually live in foods, on plants, or on other animals. Mites are related to the ticks and sometimes are found as free-living scavengers in soil or water. [Old English *mīte*]

mite[2] (mīt), *n.* **1.** anything very small; little bit: *Though poor, she gave her mite to charity. I can't eat even a mite of supper. He doesn't care a mite.* **2.** a coin of slight value. **3.** a very small person; tiny child: *What a mite Dorothy is!*
—*adv. Informal.* little; a bit: *It is a mite easier to make reservations for Europe this year* (Saturday Review).
[< Middle Dutch *mite,* ultimately of same origin as *mite*[1]]
—**Syn.** *n.* **1.** particle, iota, jot, whit. **3.** tot.

mi·ter[1] (mī′tər), *n.* **1.** a tall, pointed, folded cap worn by bishops during sacred ceremonies. **2.** the office or dignity of bishop; episcopal rank. **3.** *Judaism.* the official headdress or ceremonial turban of the ancient Jewish high priest. **4.** a headband or fillet worn by women in ancient Greece.
—*v.t.* to bestow a miter on; make a bishop. Also, *especially British,* **mitre.**
[< Middle French *mitre* < Latin *mitra* < Greek *mítrā* headband]

Miter[1] (def. 1)

mi·ter[2] (mī′tər), *n.* **1.** a miter joint. **2.** the bevel on either of the pieces in a miter joint. **3.** a miter square.
—*v.t.* **1.** to join with a miter joint. **2.** to prepare (ends of wood) for joining in a miter joint. Also, *especially British,* **mitre.** [perhaps special use of *miter*[1]]

miter box, an apparatus used to cut wood for a miter joint, having cuts to guide the saw.

mi·tered[1] (mī′tərd), *adj.* having a miter joint. Also, *especially British,* **mitred.**

mi·tered[2] (mī′tərd), *adj.* **1.** wearing or privileged to wear a bishop's miter: *A mitered abbot has the privilege of using the miter and other insignia, and exercises certain of the functions of a bishop.* **2.** shaped like a bishop's miter. Also, *especially British,* **mitred.**

miter gear, a pair of beveled gear wheels of equal diameter whose axles are at right angles, and which have their teeth set at an angle of 45 degrees.

miter joint, a kind of joint or corner where two pieces of wood are fitted together at right angles with the ends cut slanting, as at the corners of a picture frame.

MITER JOINT

Miter Joint

miter shell, the fusiform shell of any of various gastropods, mostly of warm seas (so called from the shape of the spire).

miter square, 1. a carpenter's square having one arm fixed at a right angle to the other. **2.** a similar square having an arm adjustable to any angle.

miter wheels, the gear wheels of a miter gear.

mi·ter·wort (mī′tər wėrt′), *n.* **1.** any of a group of low perennial plants of the saxifrage family, having a capsule that suggests a bishop's miter; bishop's-cap. **2.** an annual plant of the southeastern United States, with small white flowers and a capsule shaped like a miter. Also, *especially British,* **mitrewort.**

Mith·gar·thr (miᴛʜ′gär′ᴛʜər), *n.* Midgard.

Mith·ra (mith′rə), *n.* Mithras.

Mith·rae·um (mith rē′əm), *n., pl.* **-rae·a** (-rē′ə). a Mithraic temple: *The holy brothers ... found ... a second-century Mithraeum, dedicated to the worship of the Persian sun god Mithras* (Harper's). [< New Latin *Mithraeum* < Latin *Mithrās* Mithras]

Mith·ra·ic (mith rā′ik), *adj.* of, having to do with, or connected with Mithras or his worship.

Mith·ra·i·cism (mith rā′ə siz əm), *n.* Mithraism.

Mith·ra·ism (mith′rā iz əm), *n.* the religion of the worshipers of Mithras: *Mithraism took on the form of a mystery religion, with elaborate rites and ceremonies* (World Book Encyclopedia).

Mith·ra·ist (mith′rā ist), *n.* a worshiper of or believer in Mithras.

Mith·ra·is·tic (mith′rā is′tik), *adj.* Mithraic.

Mith·ras (mith′ras), *n.* the Persian and Aryan god of light, truth, and justice, who opposed Ahriman, the power of evil and darkness. Mithras became the subject of an extensive cult in the late Roman Empire.

mith·ri·date (mith′rə dāt), *n. Obsolete.* a compound of many ingredients, supposed to be an antidote against all poisons. [< Medieval Latin *mithridatum,* ultimately < *Mithridates* VI, King of Pontus, who supposedly immunized himself against poison]

mith·ri·dat·ic (mith′rə dat′ik), *adj.* **1.** resembling Mithridates VI of Pontus or his alleged immunity from poisons. **2.** having to do with mithridatism. **3.** resembling mithridatism. **4.** *Obsolete.* **a.** of or having to do with mithridate. **b.** like mithridate.

mith·ri·da·tism (mith′rə dā′tiz əm), *n.* resistance to a poison produced by taking the poison in gradually increased doses.

mi·ti·cide (mī′tə sīd), *n.* a substance for killing mites. [< *mite*[1] + *-cide*[1]]

mit·i·ga·ble (mit′ə gə bəl), *adj.* that can be mitigated.

mit·i·gant (mit′ə gənt), *adj.* mitigating.

mit·i·gate (mit′ə gāt), *v.,* **-gat·ed, -gat·ing.** —*v.t.* **1.** to make (wrath, harshness, severity, etc.) less in force or degree: *The American genius for compromise could be invoked ... to mitigate possible dangers* (Bulletin of Atomic Scientists). **2.** to make less severe; make more bearable; temper; moderate: *A cool breeze mitigated the scorching heat of the day. Aspirin mitigated the pain of his headache in about half-an-hour.* **3.** to lessen the gravity of (an offense): *The principal mitigated the punishment that the teacher had given the boy in anger.* —*v.i.* to become mild; become milder or less severe. [< Latin *mītigāre* (with English *-ate*[1]) < *mītis* gentle + *agere* do, make]

mit·i·ga·tion (mit′ə gā′shən), *n.* **1.** a mitigating: *The Governor's mitigation of the death sentence to life imprisonment met with approval.* **2.** a being mitigated. **3.** something that mitigates: *The breeze was a welcome mitigation of the heat.*

mit·i·ga·tive (mit′ə gā′tiv), *adj.* tending to mitigate. —*n.* something that mitigates. —**Syn.** *n.* balm.

mit·i·ga·tor (mit′ə gā′tər), *n.* a person or thing that mitigates.

mit·i·ga·to·ry (mit′ə gə tôr′ē, -tōr′-), *adj., n., pl.* **-ries.** —*adj.* mitigative. —*n.* something which serves to mitigate.

mi·tis (mī′tis, mē′-), *n.* a mitis casting (def. 2).

mitis casting, 1. a method of producing malleable iron castings by fusing wrought iron with a minute quantity of aluminum. **2.** a casting so made. [a coined word < Latin *mītis* mild]

mitis metal, a mitis casting (def. 2).

mi·to·chon·dri·a (mī′tə kon′drē ə), *n. pl. of* **mi·to·chon·dri·on.** minute sausage-shaped structures found in the cytoplasm of cells that produce most of the energy required by the cells. Mitochondria often change their shape under certain conditions

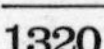

although their number in each cell remains about the same, and they contain many enzymes important for cell metabolism. [< Greek *mítos* a thread + *chóndros* lump]

mi·to·chon·dri·al (mī′tə kon′drē əl), *adj.* of or having to do with mitochondria.

mi·to·my·cin (mī′tə mī′sin), *n.* an antibiotic substance obtained from a soil microorganism, used to treat malignant tumors. [< Greek *mítos* thread + English (strepto)-*mycin*]

mi·to·sis (mi tō′sis, mī-), *n.* the usual method of cell division, which is typically divided into four stages: *prophase,* in which the chromatin of the nucleus forms into a thread that separates into segments or chromosomes, each of which in turn separates longitudinally into two parts; *metaphase,* in which the nuclear membrane disappears and the chromosomes line up near the middle of the cell; *anaphase,* in

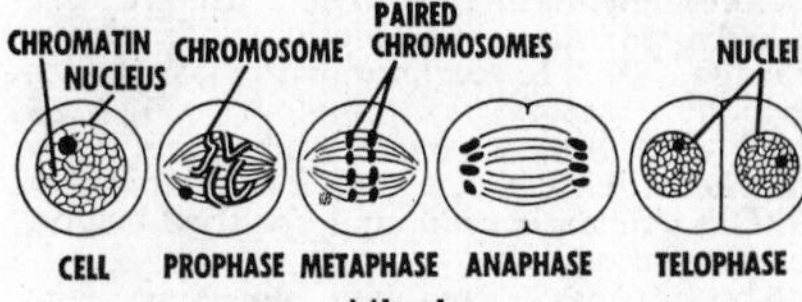

Mitosis

which one chromosome of each pair moves toward each end of the cell; and *telophase,* in which the chromosomes lose their thread-like shape and again become chromatin, two new nuclear membranes form around the chromatin, and the cytoplasm draws together in the middle, divides, and two new cells exist, each containing the same number of chromosomes as the original cell. [< New Latin *mitosis* < Greek *mítos* thread + English *-osis*]

mi·tot·ic (mi tot′ik, mī-), *adj.* of mitosis.

mi·tot·i·cal·ly (mi tot′ə klē, mī-), *adv.* by mitosis.

mi·traille (mē trä′yə), *n.* small missiles or projectiles, as pieces of iron fired in masses from a cannon, etc. [< French *mitraille* < Old French *mitaille* < *mite* a small coin]

mi·trail·leur (mē trä yœr′), *n. French.* **1.** a machine gunner. **2.** a soldier who operated a mitrailleuse. **3.** a mitrailleuse.

mi·trail·leuse (mē trä yoez′), *n. French.* **1.** an early type of machine gun consisting of a cluster of breechloading barrels around a central axis which could be fired simultaneously or in sequence, introduced into the French army in 1868. **2.** any machine gun.

mi·tral (mī′trəl), *adj.* **1.** of, having to do with, or like a miter. **2.** designating or having to do with the mitral valve.

mitral commissurotomy, surgical treatment of mitral stenosis.

mitral stenosis, the hardening or narrowing of the mitral valve, caused by rheumatic fever.

mitral valve, the valve of the heart between the left auricle and left ventricle, which prevents the blood from flowing back into the auricle; bicuspid valve.

mi·tre (mī′tər), *n., v.t.,* **-tred, -tring.** *Especially British.* miter[1] and miter[2].

mi·tred (mī′tərd), *adj. Especially British.* mitered[1] and mitered[2].

mi·tre·wort (mī′tər wėrt′), *n. Especially British.* miterwort.

mits·vah (mits′vä, -və), *n., pl.* **-voth** (-vōth), **-vahs.** mitzvah.

mitt (mit), *n.* **1.** a kind of woman's fabric glove without fingers or with very short fingers. **2.** a baseball glove with a big pad over the palm and fingers: *a catcher's mitt.* **3.** a mitten. **4.** *U.S. Slang.* a hand: *I gave him my mitt in greeting.* [short for *mitten*]

Mit·tel·schu·le (mit′əl shü′lə), *n., pl.* **-len** (-lən). *German.* (in Germany and Austria) a secondary school that emphasizes science and modern languages in preparation for the university or higher technical school.

mit·ten (mit′ən), *n.* **1.** a kind of winter glove covering the four fingers together and the thumb separately. **2.** a long glove; mitt. **3.** *Slang.* a boxing glove.

get the mitten, *Slang.* **a.** to be refused as a lover: *Young gentlemen that have got the mitten . . . always sigh* (Joseph C. Neal). **b.** to be dismissed from any office or position: *Lifeboat hands who are found shrinking get . . . the mitten* (Punch).

give the mitten to, *Slang.* **a.** to refuse as a lover: *Some said that Susan had given her young man the mitten* (Oliver Wendell Holmes). **b.** to dismiss: *Here comes Dana, . . . who'll be going to write what'll never be written till the Muse, ere he thinks of it, gives him the mitten* (James Russell Lowell).

[< Old French *mitaine* mitten, half glove < *mite* mitten. Compare Medieval Latin *mitanna.*]

mit·tened (mit′ənd), *adj.* covered with or wearing mittens.

mit·ti·mus (mit′ə məs), *n. Law.* **1.** a warrant committing someone to prison. **2.** (formerly) a writ for transferring a record from one court to another. **3.** *Humorous.* a magistrate: *Nay, 'tis but what old Mittimus commanded* (Richard Brinsley Sheridan). [< Latin *mittimus* we send]

Mit·ty (mit′ē), *n., pl.* **-ties.** a timid person who in his fantasies is a fabulous hero; a daydreaming milquetoast: *The hero of "Stern," a flabby Jewish Mitty, has . . . an imagination that flowers with persecution mania* (Manchester Guardian Weekly). [< Walter *Mitty,* the hero of the short story *The Secret Life of Walter Mitty,* by James Thurber]

Mit·ty·esque (mit′ē esk′), *adj.* characteristic of a Mitty; like an extravagant daydream: *. . . a ticket-office attendant given to Mittyesque fantasies* (London Times). *His martial derring-do sounded more Mittyesque with each telling* (Time).

mit·y (mī′tē), *adj.,* **mit·i·er, mit·i·est.** containing mites, as cheese.

mitz·vah (mits′vä, -və), *n., pl.* **-voth** (-vōth), **-vahs.** *Judaism.* **1.** a religious obligation; an act enjoined by the Bible or the rabbis. **2.** an act fulfilling a religious or ethical duty. **3.** a good deed; kind act. Also, **mitsvah.** [< Hebrew *miṣwâh* commandment]

mix (miks), *v.,* **mixed** or **mixt, mix·ing,** *n.* —*v.t.* **1.** to put together; combine and stir well together: *to mix ingredients to make a cake.* **2.** to prepare by putting different things together: *to mix a cake.* **3.** to carry on at the same time; join: *to mix business and pleasure. You mix your sadness with some fear* (Shakespeare). **4.** to cross in breeding. —*v.i.* **1.** to be mixed: *Oil and water will not mix.* **2.** to associate together; get along together: *Katy likes people and mixes well in almost any group.* **3.** to be crossed in breeding.

mix it (up), *Slang.* to fight, especially (of boxers) actively and without clinching: *If a hundred children are put to the fiddle and another hundred are made to mix it, . . . the second group will turn out some unusual bruisers* (New Yorker).

mix up, a. to confuse: *She always manages to mix up instructions.* **b.** to involve; concern: *Don't mix yourself up in other folks' affairs!*

—*n.* **1.** a mixture: *Having no experience as a bartender, he was uncertain about the mix.* **2.** *Informal.* a mixed or muddled condition; mess. **3.** the ingredients, especially dry ingredients, for a cake, pudding, etc., packaged and sold together.

[back formation < earlier *mixt* mixed < Middle French *mixte,* learned borrowing from Latin *mixtus,* past participle of *miscēre* to mix]

—**Syn.** *v.t.* **1. Mix, blend** mean to put two or more ingredients together. **Mix** applies particularly when the ingredients retain all or some of their distinct identities: *Mix gravel and cement.* **Blend** applies particularly when the ingredients lose their identity, combining to form something better, smoother, more agreeable, etc.: *Blend the flour into the melted butter. -v.i.* **2.** fraternize.

—**Ant.** *v.t.* **1.** separate.

mix·a·ble (mik′sə bəl), *adj.* that can be mixed.

mix·age (mik′sij), *n.* the editing of motion-picture film.

mixed (mikst), *adj.* **1.** put together or formed by mixing; composed of different parts or elements; of different kinds combined: *mixed candies, mixed emotions, a mixed response, blessing, etc.* **2.** of different classes, kinds, etc.; not exclusive: *a mixed society.* **3.** of or for persons of both sexes: *a mixed chorus. What Shakespeare judged could safely be absorbed by mixed company in sixteenth-century London can evidently be taken in stride by succeeding generations also* (Saturday Review). **4.** *Informal.* mentally confused, especially muddled with drink. **5.** *Botany.* (of an inflorescence) combining both determinate and indeterminate arrangements, as a thyrsus. **6.** *Law.* involving two or more kinds of legal characteristics, issues, rights, etc.: *Mixed property is property that is partly real and partly personal.* **7.** *Business, Commerce.* (of stock prices) some rising and some falling from previous levels: *Prices were mixed on the New York Stock Exchange* **8.** *Phonetics.* central; neither front nor back.

mixed bag, *Informal.* a miscellany.

mixed blood, *U.S.* **1.** descent from two or more races. **2.** a person of mixed blood.

mixed-blood (mikst′blud′), *adj.* **1.** (of a person or persons) descended from two or more races. **2.** consisting largely or entirely of such people: *a mixed-blood nation, population, etc.* **3.** interracial.

mixed-blood·ed (mikst′blud′id), *adj. U.S.* descended from two or more races.

mixed doubles, doubles played with a man and a woman on each team.

mixed economy, an economy that is partly capitalistic, partly socialistic: *[In] a mixed economy . . . cooperative private business, commercial private business, and government business compete openly and honestly in meeting the needs of the people* (Emory S. Bogardus).

mixed farming, the practice of using a farm for multiple purposes, such as cattle-raising, fruit-growing, and producing grain for sale and for livestock food.

mixed feed, a feed designed to provide a balanced diet for livestock, consisting typically of a mixture of grain, meal, and grasses with vitamins and other additives.

mixed grill, an assortment of grilled meats and vegetables served together.

mix·ed·ly (mik′sid lē, mikst′lē), *adv.* in a mixed manner; like a mixture.

mixed-manned (mikst′mand′), *adj.* (of a supranational military force or unit) supplied with men representing member nations; multinational or multilateral.

mixed marriage, a marriage in which the husband and wife are of different religions or races.

mixed media, the simultaneous use of motion pictures, tapes, phonograph records, and the like, to produce an artistic work or exhibition: *Miss Caldwell used a "mixed media" technique, with photographs and movies projected on bits of backdrop while the action was going on* (New Yorker).

mixed metaphor, an incongruous combination of metaphors. *Example:* "He set forth early on the stream of education, and climbed to a peak of wisdom."

mix·ed·ness (mik′sid nis, mikst′nis), *n.* the quality of being mixed.

mixed number, a number consisting of a whole number and a fraction, such as 16⅝.

mixed-up (mikst′up′), *adj. U.S.* confused; unstable; emotionally immature: *Some people think we're a bunch of crazy mixed-up kids because we give our client a hard time* (New York Times).

mix·en (mik′sən), *n. Archaic.* a dunghill. [Old English *mixen* < *meox* dung]

mix·er (mik′sər), *n.* **1.** a thing that mixes: *a bread mixer, an electric mixer.* **2.** a person who mixes: *A person who gets along well with others is called a good mixer.* **3.** soda, juice, etc., used with alcoholic liquors for mixing drinks. **4.** *Electronics.* **a.** a device used for sound in television and motion pictures, consisting of two or more signal inputs and a common output. It combines the outputs of individual microphones, etc., linearly and in the desired proportions, to produce the final audio output signal. **b.** a similar device which combines the outputs of two or more cameras, used in television and motion pictures.

mix·ing bowl (mik′sing), a bowl in which foods or ingredients are mixed before cooking or serving.

mix·ol·o·gist (mik sol′ə jist), *n. Slang.* a skilled mixer of drinks; bartender.

mix·o·lyd·i·an (mik′sə lid′ē ən), *n. Music.* **1.** the highest in pitch of the modes in ancient Greek music. **2.** a mode of medieval church music, beginning and ending on the note G. [< Greek *mixolýdios* half-Lydian + English *-an*]

mixt (mikst), *v.* mixed; a past tense and a past participle of **mix.**

mix·ture (miks′chər), *n.* **1.** a mixing: *The mixture took three hours.* **2.** a being mixed; mixed state or condition: *His mixture of relief and disappointment left him speechless.*

3. what has been mixed; a product of mixing: *Orange is a mixture of yellow and red. Many teas and tobaccos are mixtures. This suit is made of a mixture of dacron and wool.* 4. *Chemistry, Physics.* the product of two or more substances mixed together, but not chemically combined. 5. a fabric woven of variegated or mottled yarns: *an oxford mixture.* [< Latin *mixtūra* < *miscēre* to mix]
—**Syn.** 1. blending, fusing. 3. blend.

mix-up (miks′up′), *n. Informal.* 1. confusion; muddle; mess. 2. a confused fight: *The son took no part in the mix-up.*

Mi·zar (mī′zär), *n.* a bright star in the handle of the Big Dipper. With its companion, Alcor, it forms a visual binary.

miz·maze (miz′māz′), *n.* a confused maze: *Right at the top, a mizmaze was cut in the grass* (London Times). [varied reduplication of *maze*]

Miz·pah (miz′pə), *n.* a word used in farewell to recall these words: "The Lord watch between me and thee, when we are absent one from another." Genesis 31:49. [< Hebrew *miṣpeh* outlook point, watchtower]

miz·zen or **miz·en** (miz′ən), *n.* 1. a fore-and-aft sail on the mizzenmast; spanker. See **sail** for picture. 2. mizzenmast. —*adj.* of, having to do with, or attached to the mizzenmast. [< Middle French *misaine* foresail, foremast < Italian *mezzana* mizzen sail < Latin *mediānus* (in the) middle < *medius* middle]

miz·zen·mast (miz′ən mast′, -mäst′; *Nautical* miz′ən məst), *n.* the mast nearest the stern in a two-masted or three-masted ship, especially in certain two-masted vessels, as the yawl or ketch. See **mainmast** for picture.

miz·zen·roy·al mast, sail, yard (miz′ən roi′əl), the mast, sail, yard, etc., near the top of the mizzenmast of a square-rigged vessel next above the mizzen-topgallant mast, sail, yard. See **sail** for picture.

miz·zen·sheet (miz′ən shēt′), *n.* a rope used to control a fore-and-aft mizzen or spanker.

miz·zen·stay (miz′ən stā′), *n.* the fore-and-aft stay which helps support a mizzen lower mast.

miz·zen·stay·sail (miz′ən stā′sāl′; *Nautical* miz′ən stā′səl), *n.* a triangular sail set on the mizzenstay. See **sail** for picture.

miz·zen·top (miz′ən top′), *n.* a platform on a mizzenmast, just below the mizzen-topmast.

miz·zen·top·gal·lant mast, sail, yard (miz′ən top gal′ənt; *Nautical* miz′ən tə gal′ənt), the mast, sail, yard, etc., on the mizzen-topmast, mizzen-topsail, topsail yard. See **sail** for picture.

miz·zen·top·mast (miz′ən top′mast′, -mäst′; *Nautical* miz′ən top′məst), *n.* the mast on the mizzenmast next above the lower mast, especially on a square-rigged vessel.

miz·zen·top·sail or **yard** (miz′ən top′sāl′; *Nautical* miz′ən top′səl), the sail or yard, or either of two sails or yards, on the mizzen-top. See **sail** for picture.

miz·zen·yard (miz′ən yärd′), *n.* the yard holding the mizzen on the lower section of the mizzenmast of a square-rigged vessel; cross-jack yard.

miz·zle[1] (miz′əl), *n., v.,* **-zled, -zling.** *Dialect.* —*n.* a drizzle: *The rain, a mere mizzle when I left the restaurant . . . had got heavier* (New Yorker). —*v.i.* to drizzle: *It is mizzling.* —*v.t.* (of a cloud) to send down in a drizzle. [origin uncertain. Compare Low German *miseln.*]

miz·zle[2] (miz′əl), *v.i.,* **-zled, -zling.** *British Slang.* to disappear suddenly; decamp; vanish: *Bealby had not "mizzled" although he was conspicuously not in evidence about the camp* (H.G. Wells). [origin uncertain]

miz·zly (miz′lē), *adj. Dialect.* drizzly; misty.

M.K.S. or **MKS** (no periods), meter-kilogram-second.

MKS system, a system of units in which the meter, kilogram, and second are considered as the basic units of length, mass, and time.

mkt., market.

ml., milliliter or milliliters.

Ml., *British.* mail.

ML (no periods), **M.L.,** or **ML.,** Medieval Latin.

MLA (no periods) or **M.L.A.,** 1. Modern Language Association. 2. (in Canada) Member of the Legislative Assembly.

MLD (no periods) or **m.l.d.,** minimum lethal dose.

MLF (no periods) or **M.L.F.,** multilateral force (a proposed mixed-manned fleet of surface ships armed with nuclear weapons).

MLG (no periods) **M.L.G.,** or **MLG.,** Middle Low German.

Mlle., Mademoiselle.

Mlles., Mesdemoiselles (plural of *Mademoiselle*).

M.L.S., Master of Library Science.

mm[1] (no period), millimeter or millimeters.

mm[2] (no period) or **mm.**^{2}, square millimeter.

mm[3] (no period) or **mm.**^{3}, cubic millimeter.

mm., 1. millimeter or millimeters. 2. thousands (Latin, *millia*).

MM., 1. (Their) Majesties. 2. Messieurs. ➤ See **Messrs.** for usage note.

Mme., Madame.

Mmes., Mesdames (plural of *Madame*).

mmf (no periods) or **m.m.f.,** magnetomotive force.

mmfd (no periods) or **mmfd.,** micromicrofarad.

Mn (no period), manganese (chemical element).

M'Nagh·ten Rule (mə nä′tən, -nô′-, -na′-; mək-), *Law.* the rule that an accused person is not criminally responsible if at the time of committing the crime he was unable to distinguish between right and wrong: *The old M'Naghten Rule [is] still used in the majority of states* (Science News Letter). Also, **McNaughten Rule.** [< the name of the defendant in a trial held in England in 1843, at which the rule was formulated]

mne·mon·ic (ni mon′ik), *adj.* 1. aiding the memory. 2. intended to aid the memory: *The strongly mnemonic nature of the catchword system certainly supports the idea that the writing grew out of a memory-aid device* (Scientific American). 3. of or having to do with the memory.
—*n.* 1. a mnemonic device. 2. mnemonics. [< Greek *mnēmonikós* < *mnâsthai* remember] —**mne·mon′i·cal·ly,** *adv.*

mne·mon·i·cal (ni mon′ə kəl), *adj.* mnemonic.

mne·mon·ics (ni mon′iks), *n.* 1. (*singular in use*) the art of improving or developing the memory. 2. (*plural in use*) mnemonic aids or devices.

mne·mo·nist (nē′mə nist), *n.* an expert in mnemonics.

Mne·mos·y·ne (ni mos′ə nē), *n.* the ancient Greek goddess of memory, daughter of Uranus and Gaea, and mother of the Muses by Zeus.

mne·mo·tech·nic (nē′mə tek′nik), *adj.* mnemonic.

mne·mo·tech·nics (nē′mə tek′niks), *n.* mnemonics.

Mngr., 1. Monseigneur. 2. Monsignor.

mo (mō), *adj., n., adv. Obsolete.* more[1]. [Old English *mā*]

mo., month or months.

m.o., 1. mail order. 2. money order.

Mo (no period), molybdenum (chemical element).

Mo., 1. Missouri. 2. Monday.

MO (no periods), medical officer.

M.O., money order.

mo·a (mō′ə), *n.* any of various recently extinct, flightless birds of New Zealand, somewhat like an ostrich, but varying in size from that of a turkey to 12 feet high. [< a Maori word]

Moa or dinornis (12 ft. high)

Mo·ab·ite (mō′ə bīt), *n.* a native or inhabitant of Moab, an ancient kingdom in Syria. —*adj.* of Moab or its people.

Mo·ab·it·ess (mō′ə bī′tis), *n.* a female Moabite.

Moabite stone, a slab of black basalt bearing an inscription in Hebrew-Phoenician characters, which records the victories of Mesha, king of Moab, over the Israelites. It was discovered in 1878, and for a time was the oldest known monument, 800's B.C., of the Semitic alphabet.

Mo·ab·it·ic (mō′ə bit′ik), *adj.* Moabite.

Mo·ab·it·ish (mō′ə bī′tish), *adj.* Moabite.

moan (mōn), *n.* 1. a long, low sound of suffering: *So is mortal life, A moan, a sigh, a sob, a storm, a strife* (Sir Edwin Arnold). 2. any similar sound: *the moan of the winter wind. The moan of doves in immemorial elms* (Tennyson). 3. complaint; lamentation: *Unheard . . . Their English mother made her moan* (Lowell). 4. an instance of this: *Her moan was only that she had not been invited.*
—*v.i.* 1. to make moans. 2. to complain; lament; grieve. —*v.t.* 1. to utter with a moan: *"I'm so stiff I can't move," she moaned.* 2. to complain about; grieve for: *to moan one's fate.*
[Middle English *mone* a moan. Compare Old English *mǣnan* to complain.] —**moan′ing·ly,** *adv.*
—**Syn.** *v.i.* 1. wail. See **groan.** *-v.t.* 2. bemoan, bewail.

moat (mōt), *n.* a deep, wide ditch dug around a castle or town as a protection against enemies. Moats were usually kept filled with water. See picture under **drawbridge.** —*v.t.* to surround with or as if with a moat: *Beyond the crossroads lay a big farm with an immense, moated farmhouse* (New Yorker). [earlier *mote* mound, embankment < Old French *mote* mound, fortified height; origin uncertain]

mob (mob), *n., v.,* **mobbed, mob·bing.** —*n.* 1. a large number of people, usually crowded closely together. 2. a lawless crowd, easily moved to act without thinking: *The mob is man voluntarily descending to the nature of the beast* (Emerson). *The destruction and damage caused by the mobs were more extensive than was originally reported* (London Times). 3. *Slang.* a group of criminals who work together; gang. 4. (in Australia) a group of animals, as a flock of sheep or a herd of cattle or horses.
the mob, a. the common mass of people, thought of as lacking taste, culture, etc.; the masses: *jokes at which the mob laughs* (G.K. Chesterton); *our supreme governors, the mob* (Horace Walpole). **b.** the lawless part of the populace; the rabble. **c.** *U.S. Slang.* the dominant group in the underworld of a city, state, etc.: *The metropolis had been ruled by the mob for twenty years.*
—*v.t.* 1. to crowd around in curiosity, anger, etc.: *The eager children mobbed the candy man as soon as he appeared.* 2. to attack with violence, as a mob does: *He was mobbed as soon as he left the prison gates.* [short for earlier *mobile* < Latin *mōbile* (*vulgus*) the fickle (common people) < *mōbilis;* see MOBILE]

mob·bish (mob′ish), *adj.* moblike; vulgar; riotous: *On Cyprus, the London failure fanned mounting tension into mobbish terrorizing* (Time).

mob·bist (mob′ist), *n.* a member of a mob.

mob·cap (mob′kap′), *n.* a large, loose cap, fitting down over the ears, originally worn indoors by women in the 1700's and early 1800's: *Flowers really have their day on a mob-cap number with a white organdie crown* (New Yorker). [< obsolete *mob* an indoor cap + *cap*]

mob·dom (mob′dəm), *n.* gangsterdom.

mo·bile (mō′bəl, mō bēl′), *adj.* 1. **a.** that can move; easy to move; movable: *a mobile hospital unit. The arms and legs are mobile.* **b.** tending to be naturally fluid: *Mercury is a mobile metal.* 2. moving easily; changing easily: *a face with mobile features. A mobile mind is one that is easily moved by ideas or feeling.* 3. versatile: *mobile talents.*
—*n.* a piece of sculpture, especially abstract sculpture, composed of strips or pieces of wire, paper, etc., in balance with each other, usually suspended from a wall, ceiling, etc., so that the various parts may shift in currents of air to form different patterns: *In the middle 1900's, Alexander Calder developed a new sculptural form, the mobile, which quickly influenced other sculptors* (World Book Encyclopedia).
[< Latin *mōbilis* movable < *movēre* to move]

mobile home, a house trailer.

mobile library, a traveling branch of a library; bookmobile.

mobile unit, a specially equipped vehicle performing on-the-spot services for a larger enterprise: *Mobile units . . . offered food, clothing, and medical aid* (Time). *N.B.C.'s mobile unit [is] a 38-foot telecasting "station on wheels"* (New York Times).

mo·bi·lise (mō′bə līz), *v.t., v.i.,* **-lised, -lising.** *Especially British.* mobilize: *Ever since* *the early 1820's the French have been mobilising a succession of avant-gardes* (Sunday Observer).

mo·bi·list (mō′bə list), *n.* a maker of mobiles.

mo·bil·i·ty (mō bil′ə tē), *n., pl.* **-ties.** the ability or readiness to move or be moved; being mobile: *Reciprocity enables us to find this potential in terms of the mobilities of the ions present* (Science News).

mo·bi·liz·a·ble (mō′bə lī′zə bəl), *adj.* that can be mobilized.

mo·bi·li·za·tion (mō′bə lə zā′shən), *n.* **1.** a mobilizing; calling troops, ships, etc., into active military service: *Mobilization planning designed to guarantee a fast build-up of arms production after a future conflict starts . . . is considered largely obsolete in the missile age* (Wall Street Journal). **2.** a being mobilized.

mo·bi·lize (mō′bə līz), *v.,* **-lized, -liz·ing.** —*v.t.* **1. a.** to call (troops, warships, etc.) into active military service; organize for war. **b.** to organize or call to take part, usually during an emergency: *to mobilize Red Cross or defense units during a violent storm, to mobilize industry in time of national crisis.* **2.** to put into motion or active use: *to mobilize the wealth of a country.* **3.** to make movable: *The doctor was able to mobilize the patient's stiff elbow joint.* —*v.i.* to assemble and prepare for war: *The troops mobilized quickly.* [< French *mobiliser* (with English *-ize*) < *mobile* mobile, learned borrowing from Latin *mōbilis* mobile] —**mo′bi·liz′er,** *n.*

Mö·bi·us strip or **band** (mœ′bē əs, mō′-), *Geometry.* a strip of paper or other material which is given a half twist and then joined at the ends, thus having only one side. [< August F. *Möbius,* 1790-1868, a German mathematician]

mob·le (mob′əl), *v.t.,* **-led, -ling.** *Dialect.* to muffle, as in a hood or shawl: *But . . . who had seen the mobled Queen?* (Shakespeare). [origin uncertain]

mob·oc·ra·cy (mob ok′rə sē), *n., pl.* **-cies.** **1.** political control by a mob; mob rule: *If Congress . . . refuses to appropriate money to maintain the judiciary and executive departments, the result is mobocracy* (Baltimore Sun). **2.** the mob as a ruling class.

mob·o·crat (mob′ə krat), *n.* **1.** a supporter of mobocracy. **2.** a leader of the mob; demagogue.

mob·o·crat·ic (mob′ə krat′ik), *adj.* **1.** having to do with mobocracy. **2.** like a mobocracy. **3.** that advocates mobocracy.

mob·o·crat·i·cal (mob′ə krat′ə kəl), *adj.* mobocratic.

mob rule, rule or political control by a mob: *The President pointed out . . .* [*that*] *"mob rule cannot be allowed to override the decisions of the courts"* (Wall Street Journal).

mobs·man (mobz′mən), *n., pl.* **-men.** *British Slang.* **1.** a member of a mob or crowd. **2.** a stylishly dressed pickpocket, usually one of a gang.

mob·ster (mob′stər), *n. U.S. Slang.* a chronic lawbreaker, especially a person who specializes in crimes of violence; gangster: *I will not allow work on the piers to go to hoodlums and mobsters from New York* (New York Times).

moc·ca·sin (mok′ə sən), *n.* **1.** a soft leather shoe or sandal. Moccasins were worn by North American Indians, and are typically without heels, having the sole and the sides stitched to upper or vamp with rawhide. **2.** either of two poisonous snakes of the southeastern United States, the copperhead or especially the water moccasin. [American English < Algonkian (probably a Virginia tribe). Compare Powhatan *mäkäsĭn.*]

Moccasin (def. 1) of the Tuscarora Indian tribe

moc·ca·sined (mok′ə sənd), *adj.* wearing moccasins.

moccasin flower, a pink or white orchid shaped somewhat like a slipper; pink lady's-slipper.

mo·cha (mō′kə), *n.* **1.** a choice variety of coffee originally coming from southwestern Arabia, in what is now Yemen. **2.** a mixture of coffee and chocolate, used as a flavoring in drinks, cakes, etc.: *Strong American coffee . . . is converted into mocha by adding a tablespoon of chocolate syrup and a dab of unsweetened whipped cream* (New York Times). **3.** a kind of soft, thin leather used for gloves, usually made from Arabian goatskin. —*adj.* flavored with coffee, or chocolate and coffee: *a mocha frosting, mocha cake, etc.* [< *Mocha,* a seaport in Yemen]

Mocha stone, a kind of agate having dendritic markings due to the presence of metallic oxides; moss agate.

Mocha ware, a white pottery formerly produced in England for household use, decorated with dendritic or treelike designs on a tinted ground: *Mocha ware is so named because of its resemblance to the quartz Mocha stone* (London Times).

Mo·chi·ca (mō chē′kə), *n., pl.* **-ca** or **-cas,** *adj.* —*n.* a member of a civilization that dominated the coast of northern Peru for about a thousand years, until the 1000's A.D. The Mochica were noted for achievements in architecture and ceramics. —*adj.* of or having to do with this civilization.

mo·chi·la (mō chē′lə), *n.* a leather flap that covers a saddletree. [American English < Spanish *mochila* knapsack, caparison < Latin *mutila* shortened (thing)]

mock (mok, môk), *v.t.* **1.** to laugh at; make fun of; ridicule: *Little children . . . mocked him, and said . . . Go up, thou bald head* (II Kings 2:23). **2.** to make fun of by copying or imitating: *The thoughtless children mocked the speech of the new boy.* **3.** to imitate; copy: *Prepare To see the life as lively mock'd as ever still sleep mock'd death* (Shakespeare). **4.** to make light of; pay no attention to: *health that mocks the doctor's rules* (John Greenleaf Whittier). **5.** to deceive; disappoint: *Mind is a light which the Gods mock us with, to lead those false who trust it* (Matthew Arnold). —*v.i.* to scoff; jeer.
—*adj.* not real; copying; sham; imitation: *a mock battle, mock modesty.*
—*adv.* in a feigned or false manner; feignedly; falsely: *a mock-modest person.*
—*n.* **1.** an action or speech that mocks. **2.** a person or thing scorned or deserving scorn. **3.** an imitation; counterfeit; copy. **4.** derision; mockery.
[< Middle French, Old French *mocquer;* origin uncertain]
—**Syn.** *v.t.* **1.** deride, taunt. See **ridicule. 3.** mimic, ape. **5.** delude, fool. *-v.i.* gibe. *-adj.* feigned, pretended, counterfeit, false.

mock·a·ble (mok′ə bəl, môk′-), *adj.* that can be mocked; subject to mockery.

mock·er (mok′ər, môk′-), *n.* **1.** a person who mocks. **2.** a mockingbird: . . . *the sun was bright in the magnolia outside her window and the mockers were singing* (Margaret Mitchell).

mock·er·y (mok′ər ē, môk′-), *n., pl.* **-er·ies. 1.** a making fun; ridicule; derision: *Their mockery of my companions did not swerve me from my purpose.* **2.** a person, thing, or action to be made fun of; laughingstock: *Through his foolishness he became a mockery in the village.* **3.** a bad copy or imitation: *The children's housekeeping was a mockery of their elders'.* **4. a.** something that resembles the form but utterly disregards the spirit; a disregarding; setting at naught: *The unfair trial was a mockery of justice.* **b.** something insultingly or absurdly unfitting: *In her bitterness she felt that all rejoicing was a mockery* (George Eliot).

mock-he·ro·ic (mok′hi rō′ik, môk′-), *adj.* imitating or burlesquing what is heroic: *Alexander Pope's "Rape of the Lock" is a mock-heroic poem.* —*n.* an imitation or burlesque of what is heroic. —**mock′-he·ro′i·cal·ly,** *adv.*

mock·ing (mok′ing, môk′-), *adj.* **1.** that mocks; deriding; mimicking: *a mocking voice.* **2.** deluding: *a mocking mirage.* —**mock′-ing·ly,** *adv.* —**Syn. 1.** imitating.

mock·ing·bird (mok′ing bėrd′, môk′-), *n.* **1.** a grayish songbird, of southern North America, and Central and South America, that imitates the notes of other birds: *The mockingbird, whose song once charmed only the Southland, has been gradually spreading out toward the north* (Science News Letter). **2.** any of certain similar or related birds. [American English < *mocking* + *bird*]

Mockingbird (def. 1) (9 to 11 in. long)

mock moon, a paraselene.

mock orange, a syringa.

mock sun, a parhelion; sundog.

mock turtle soup, a soup made with calf's head in imitation of green turtle soup.

mock-up (mok′up′, môk′-), *n.* a full-sized model of an airplane, machine, etc., used for teaching purposes, for testing, or for studying details or new features of design. A mock-up is usually built to scale out of some material such as plywood, plaster, or clay. *The investigators sought to recover every possible part of the fallen plane for a mock-up on chickenwire of sections, or even all of the craft* (Wall Street Journal).

Mod or **mod** (mod), *n. British Slang.* one of a group of teen-agers affecting extreme neatness of appearance and a foppish liking for very fine or stylish clothes. [< *modern*]

mod., 1. moderate. **2.** *Music.* moderato; in moderate time. **3.** modern.

mo·dal (mō′dəl), *adj.* **1.** of or having to do with mode, manner, or form. **2.** *Grammar.* **a.** of or having to do with the mood of a verb. **b.** denoting manner or modality. **3.** *Music.* of or having to do with a mode, especially any of the medieval church modes: *One must pause before attempting to define this new music of Claude Debussy in all its tonal attributes, modal developments, and techniques* (Atlantic). **4.** *Philosophy.* of, consisting in, or relating to formal manifestation as contrasted with basic substance. **5.** *Law.* (of a legacy, contract, etc.) containing provisions defining the manner in which it is to take effect. **6.** *Logic.* displaying modality. **7.** *Physics.* of or having to do with a mode of vibration. [< Medieval Latin *modalis* < Latin *modus* a measure. Compare MODE[1].] —**mo′dal·ly,** *adv.*

modal auxiliary, one of a set of auxiliary verbs in English, including words like *may, can, must, would,* and *should,* that indicates the mood of the verb with which it is used.

mo·dal·ism (mō′də liz əm), *n. Theology.* the doctrine that the Father, Son, and Holy Spirit are merely different aspects or modes of one Divine person; Sabellianism.

mo·dal·i·ty (mō dal′ə tē), *n., pl.* **-ties. 1.** the quality or fact of being modal. **2.** a modal attribute or circumstance; mode. **3.** *Medicine.* a form, method, or apparatus of therapy, especially physiotherapy or electrotherapy. **4.** *Logic.* the character of a proposition as asserting or denying necessarily, possibly, or without such qualification.

mod. con., *pl.* **mod. cons.** *British.* modern convenience: *We live in a small flat with all mod. cons.* (Punch).

mode[1] (mōd), *n.* **1.** the manner or way in which a thing is done; method: *Riding a donkey is a slow mode of travel.* **2.** the manner or state of existence of a thing: *Heat is a mode of motion. Reflection is a mode of consciousness. The present transition of the Greenlanders' mode of life from seal-hunting to cod-fishing* (Science News). **3.** *Grammar.* **a.** the property of verbs that indicates whether the act or state is thought of as a fact, command, wish, etc.; mood: *the indicative mode, the imperative mode, the subjunctive mode.* **b.** a distinctive verb form (or set of forms) or verb phrases thus used. **4.** *Music.* **a.** any of various arrangements of the tones of an octave. **b.** either of the two classes (major and minor) of keys. **c.** any of the various scales used in ancient Greek and medieval music, having the intervals differently arranged. **d.** a rhythmical pattern, especially in medieval mensurable music. **5.** *Statistics.* the value of the variable with the highest frequency in a set of data. **6.** *Logic.* **a.** the form of a proposition with reference to the necessity, contingency, possibility, or impossibility of its content. **b.** any of the various forms of valid syllogisms, depending on the quantity and quality of their constituent propositions. **7.** the actual mineral composition of a rock, stated quantitatively in percentages by weight. **8.** *Physics.* any of various patterns in which vibration may occur. In a freely vibrating system, oscillation is restricted to certain characteristic patterns of motion at certain characteristic frequencies. **9.** *Philosophy.* a formal manifestation or particularized scheme of arrangement necessarily assumed by anything as an essential of its real existence. [< Latin *modus* measure, manner]

mode[2] (mōd), *n.* the style, fashion, or custom that prevails; the way most people are doing: *Bobbed hair became the mode* *around 1920.* [< Middle French *mode,* (originally) feminine, learned borrowing from Latin *modus* mode[1]] —**Syn.** vogue.

mod•el (mod′əl), *n., v.,* **-eled, -el•ing** or (*especially British*) **-elled, -el•ling,** *adj.* —*n.* **1.** a small copy: *a model of a ship or an engine, a model of an island.* **2.** an object or figure made in clay, wax, or the like, that is to be copied in marble, bronze, etc.: *a model for a statue.* **3.** the way in which a thing is made; design; style: *a plane of an advanced model. Our car is a late model. I want a dress like yours, for that model is becoming to me.* **4.** a thing or person to be copied or imitated; exemplar: *a model of courage. Make your father your model, and you will become a fine man.* **5.** a person who poses for artists, photographers, etc.: *Nearly every individual of their number might have been taken for a sculptor's model* (Herman Melville). **6.** a woman in a clothing store who puts on garments in order to show customers how they look.
—*v.t.* **1.** to make; shape; fashion; design; plan: *to model a horse in clay.* **2.** to follow as a model; form (something) after a particular model: *to model yourself on your father.* **3.** to wear as a model: *to model a dress.* **4.** (in drawing or painting) to give an appearance of natural relief to: *Model the trees by shading.* —*v.i.* **1.** to make models; design: *She models in plaster as a hobby.* **2.** to be a model; pose: *She models for an illustrator.* **3.** (of the portions of a drawing in progress) to assume the appearance of natural relief: *The trees model as you add shading.*
—*adj.* **1.** serving as a model: *a model house. A model home is being prepared for display by the middle of June* (New York Times). **2.** just right or perfect, especially in conduct; exemplary: *a model child.*
[< French *modèle* < Italian *modello* (diminutive) < *modo* mode[1] < Latin *modus* measure, manner]
—**Syn.** *n.* **4. Model, example, pattern** mean someone or something to be copied or followed. **Model** applies to a person or thing thought especially worth copying or imitating: *The famous surgeon is his model.* **Example** applies to a person, his conduct, or actions likely for some reason to be imitated: *He follows his father's example.* **Pattern** applies particularly to a fine example or model set up as worth imitating or following as closely as a worker follows designs in making something: *Her book gives a pattern for behavior.*

mod•el•er (mod′ə lər), *n.* a person who models, especially one who forms models or figures in clay, wax, or plaster.

mod•el•ing (mod′ə ling), *n.* **1.** the act or art of a person who models: *Miss Carter . . . said she would like to take up modeling as a profession* (Baltimore Sun). **2.** the production of designs in some plastic material, as clay or wax, especially for reproduction in a more durable material. **3.** the representation of solid form, as in sculpture. **4.** the bringing of surfaces into proper relief, as in carving. **5.** the rendering of the appearance of relief, as in painting.

mod•el•ler (mod′ə lər), *n. Especially British.* modeler.

mod•el•ling (mod′ə ling), *n. Especially British.* modeling: *Hand-made pottery is fashioned in three ways, by molding, by modelling, and by coiling* (Melville J. Herskovitz).

mo•del•lo (mō del′ō), *n., pl.* **-los.** a finished sketch or other study for a large picture or decoration: *A series of modellos by the Baroque painters brings down to a scale convenient for appreciation the compositions with which they covered vast spaces of wall and ceiling* (London Times). [< Italian *modello;* see MODEL]

Model T, 1. *Trademark.* an automobile manufactured by the Ford Motor Company from 1908 to 1927. It began the era of mass-produced automobiles in the United States. **2.** any early or outdated type or model: *The present plants being planned will soon be the Model T's of the atomic power field* (New York Times). —**Mod′el-T′,** *adj.*

mod•er•an•tism (mod′ə rən tiz′əm), *n.* a moderate political policy, especially during the French Revolution: *He exercised his influence so often in favor of sparing the accused that the bloodthirsty officials of the Terror . . . had him locked up for the crime of "moderantism"* (Edmund Wilson). [< French *modérantisme* < *modérant,* present participle of *modérer* to moderate < Latin *moderāre*]

mod•er•ate (*adj., n.* mod′ər it; *v.* mod′ə rāt), *adj., n., v.,* **-at•ed, -at•ing.** —*adj.* **1.** kept or keeping within proper bounds; not extreme: *moderate expenses, moderate styles.* **2.** not violent; calm: *moderate in speech or opinion.* **3.** fair; medium; not very large or good: *a moderate profit.* **4.** (in the U.S. Weather Bureau wind scale) denoting a breeze having a velocity of 13-18 miles per hour (on the Beaufort scale, force 4), or a gale of 32-38 miles per hour (Beaufort force 7).
—*n.* a person who holds moderate opinions, especially in politics.
—*v.t.* **1.** to make less violent: *He . . . did what he could to moderate the grief of his friend* (Anthony Trollope). **2.** to act as moderator; preside over: *The commissioner moderated the public meeting.* **3.** *Nuclear Physics.* to slow down or lower the energy of (a particle, especially a neutron). —*v.i.* **1.** to become less extreme or violent: *The wind is moderating.* **2.** to act as moderator; preside.
[< Latin *moderātus,* past participle of *moderāre* to regulate < *modus* measure, mode[1]] —**mod′er•ate•ly,** *adv.*
—**Syn.** *adj.* **1, 2. Moderate, temperate** mean not extreme in any way. **Moderate** emphasizes freedom from excess, not going beyond or above the proper, right, or reasonable limit: *He is a moderate eater.* **Temperate** emphasizes restraint, holding back within limits, especially with regard to the feelings or appetites: *He feels things deeply, but is always temperate in speech. -v.t.* **1.** *v.i.* **1.** diminish, lessen. —**Ant.** *adj.* **1.** immoderate, extreme. **2.** intemperate.

Mod•er•ate (mod′ər it), *n.* a member of a political party whose aims are considered moderate.

mod•er•ate•ness (mod′ər it nis), *n.* the state or character of being moderate; temperateness; a middle state between extremes: *the moderateness of the heat.*

mod•er•a•tion (mod′ə rā′shən), *n.* **1.** a moderating. **2.** freedom from excess; proper restraint; temperance. **3.** calmness; lack of violence: *By common understanding, by tolerance and by the virtue of moderation* (New York Times).
in moderation, within limits; not going to extremes: *The doctor advised him to eat and drink in moderation.*
Moderations, *British.* (at Oxford University) the first public examination for the degree of B.A., informally called mods: *The Tutor or Lecturer . . . will be expected to teach for Honour Moderations* (Economist).

mod•er•at•ism (mod′ər ə tiz′əm), *n.* **1.** the principles or practices of a moderate party; **2.** support of these principles or practices.

mod•er•at•ist (mod′ər ə tist), *n.* a moderate.

mod•e•ra•to (mod′ə rä′tō), *adj., adv. Music.* in moderate time (a direction). [< Italian *moderato* < Latin *moderātus* moderate]

mod•er•a•tor (mod′ə rā′tər), *n.* **1.** a presiding officer; chairman: *the moderator of a town meeting, the moderator of a church assembly.* **2.** an arbitrator; mediator. **3.** *Physics.* a material, as graphite, used in a reactor to slow down nuclear fission: *In the Florida reactor, the moderator will be heavy water, which does not absorb the atomic particles* (Wall Street Journal). —**Syn. 2.** arbiter, umpire, judge.

mod•er•a•to•ri•al (mod′ər ə tôr′ē əl, -tōr′-), *adj.* of or having to do with a moderator.

mod•er•a•tor•ship (mod′ə rā′tər ship), *n.* the office of moderator: *His service was fittingly crowned by a Double Moderatorship of the General Assembly* (London Times).

Mod•er•il (mod′ər əl), *n. Trademark.* an alkaloid derived from rauwolfia and administered orally as a tranquilizer, sedative, or agent in the control of hypertension. *Formula:* $C_{35}H_{42}N_2O_9$

mod•ern (mod′ərn), *adj.* **1.** of the present time; of times not long past: *Color television is a modern invention. All modern American literature comes from one book . . . Huckleberry Finn* (Ernest Hemingway). **2.** up-to-date; not old-fashioned: *modern views. The Justice . . . Full of wise saws and modern instances* (Shakespeare).
—*n.* **1.** a person of modern times: *Some in ancient books delight; Others prefer what moderns write* (Matthew Prior). **2.** a person who has modern ideas and tastes. **3.** *Printing.* any of various styles of type, as Bodoni, characterized by thin serifs and hairlines, heavy downstrokes, and greater symmetry and precision of cut.

This sentence is set in modern.

[earlier, extant < Late Latin *modernus* < Latin *modō* just now; (originally) in a (certain) manner, ablative of *modus* measure, mode[1]] —**mod′ern•ly,** *adv.* —**mod′ern•ness,** *n.*
—**Syn.** *adj.* **1.** See **new.** —**Ant.** *adj.* **1.** antique, ancient.

Mod•ern (mod′ərn), *adj.* designating the form of a language now in use, in contrast to an earlier form.

modern dance, the dance considered as an art form based on the principle of expression through natural bodily movements and rhythms.

mod•ern-dress (mod′ərn dres′), *adj.* **1.** (of a play) produced or performed with the actors dressed in modern fashion, or with modern scenery in the background to make it up-to-date: *a modern-dress version of Hamlet.* **2.** (of a literary work, especially fiction) up-to-date in setting, characterization, etc.; in or having a modern setting: *Faulkner's "A Fable" is a modern-dress account of the Passion of Jesus.*

mo•derne (mō därn′), *adj.* conspicuously or ostentatiously modern: *Its grandeur . . . seems moderne rather than modern* (Harper's). [< French *moderne* modern < Late Latin *modernus;* see MODERN]

Modern English, 1. a period in the development of the English language from about 1500 through the present. It is sometimes subdivided into Early Modern, 1500-1700, and Late Modern, 1700 to the present. **2.** the language of this period.

Modern French, the French language from about 1600 to the present.

Modern Greek, New Greek.

modern history, 1. history from about 1450 to the present time. **2.** history from the end of the Roman Empire to the present time.

mod•ern•ise (mod′ər nīz), *v.t., v.i.,* **-ised, -is•ing.** *Especially British.* modernize: *It is as essential to modernise administrative operations as it is production lines* (Economist). —**mod′ern•is′er,** *n.*

mod•ern•ism (mod′ər niz əm), *n.* **1.** modern attitudes or methods; sympathy with what is modern: *Modernism entered Japanese poetry with the wave of Western influence which began late in the 19th Century* (Atlantic). **2.** a tendency in religion to interpret the teachings of the Bible or the church in accordance with modern scientific theories. **3.** a modern word or phrase.

Mod•ern•ism (mod′ər niz əm), *n.* **1.** a movement among Roman Catholics to modify the teachings and tenets of the Church in the direction of the scientific, literary, and philosophic opinions of the 1800's and 1900's. It was condemned by Pope Pius X in 1907. **2.** modernism (def. 2).

mod•ern•ist (mod′ər nist), *n.* **1.** a person who holds modern views or uses modern methods: *The contemporary modernists rebel only with the established forms of Expressionism and Abstractionism* (New Yorker). **2.** a person who supports the study of modern subjects in preference to the ancient classics. **3.** a person who interprets religious teachings in a modern way: *Christianity for the modernist is a life, not a doctrine* (Newsweek).
—*adj.* of or having to do with modernists or modernism.

mod•ern•is•tic (mod′ər nis′tik), *adj.* **1.** modern: *a modernistic building, painting, etc.* **2.** having to do with modernism or modernists. —**mod′ern•is′ti•cal•ly,** *adv.*

mo•der•ni•ty (mə dėr′nə tē, mō-), *n., pl.* **-ties. 1.** a being modern: *Modernity, natural disaster, war, and hard times have . . . seriously affected many Buddhist sects* (Atlantic). **2.** something modern.

mod•ern•i•za•tion (mod′ər nə zā′shən), *n.* **1.** the act of modernizing: *The government . . . is pouring $1.4 billion worth of British pounds sterling into mechanization and modernization of mining* (Wall Street Journal). **2.** the state of being modernized.

mod•ern•ize (mod′ər nīz), *v.,* **-ized, -iz•ing.** —*v.t.* to make modern; bring up to present ways or standards: *Much expenditure has been incurred in extending, modernizing and improving the plants* (Manchester

Guardian). —*v.i.* to become modern. **—mod′ern·iz′er,** *n.*

modern jazz, a style of jazz characterized by intricate improvisation, stress on contrapuntal rhythms, and complicated harmonic development. **—mod′ern-jazz′,** *adj.*

Modern Latin, New Latin.

mod·ern-mind·ed (mod′ərn mīn′did), *adj.* given to modern ideas and methods: *a modern-minded industrialist, a modern-minded painter, a modern-minded ruler.*

modern pentathlon, (in the Olympic Games) a five-event competition consisting of horseback riding, fencing, pistol shooting, swimming, and running.

mod·est (mod′ist), *adj.* **1.** not thinking too highly of oneself; not vain; humble: *In spite of the honors he received, the scientist remained a modest man.* **2.** held back by a sense of what is fit and proper; not bold or forward: *modest pride. The Victorian definition of a modest woman is clearly outmoded.* **3.** not calling attention to or exposing too much of one's body; decent: *a modest bathing suit.* **4.** not too great; not asking too much: *a modest request.* **5.** not conspicuous; not gaudy; humble in appearance; quiet: *a modest little house, modest decorations, etc.* **6.** pure in thought and conduct; not lewd; chaste: *a modest young girl.* [< Latin *modestus* in due measure, moderate < *modus* measure] **—mod′est·ly,** *adv.*

—Syn. 1. unpretentious, unassuming. **2.** diffident. **Modest, demure** mean not bold or forward. **Modest** emphasizes a sense of what is fit and proper, a becoming lack both of conceit and of shyness: *I like a modest girl, who is neither shy nor loud.* **Demure** now suggests undue modesty or pretended shyness thought to be attractive and put on for effect: *She sipped her soda and looked demure.* **—Ant. 1.** conceited, egotistical. **2.** bold, forward.

mod·es·ty (mod′ə stē), *n., pl.* **-ties. 1.** freedom from vanity; being modest or humble: *Few "letters home" of successful men or women display the graces of modesty and self-forgetfulness* (H.G. Wells). **2.** shyness; bashfulness. **3.** a being decent or chaste: *Modesty, then, appears to be a culturally determined function of clothing, and very likely not a fundamental or original purpose* (Beals and Hoijer). **—Syn. 1.** humility. **2.** diffidence.

mod·es·ty-bit (mod′ə stē bit′), *n.* a modesty-piece.

mod·es·ty-piece (mod′ə stē pēs′), *n.* a piece or article of lace, net, embroidered muslin, or the like, worn by women over the bosom with a low-cut or open bodice.

mod·i·cum (mod′ə kəm), *n., pl.* **-cums.** a small quantity; moderate amount: *Fred is so bright that even with a modicum of effort he does excellent work.* [< Latin *modicum,* neuter of *modicus* moderate < *modus* measure, mode[1]]

mod·i·fi·a·bil·i·ty (mod′ə fī′ə bil′ə tē), *n.* the quality of being modifiable.

mod·i·fi·a·ble (mod′ə fī′ə bəl), *adj.* that can be modified. **—mod′i·fi′a·ble·ness,** *n.*

mod·i·fi·ca·tion (mod′ə fə kā′shən), *n.* **1.** a partial alteration or change: *Every modification of accepted house plans means additional cost. With some modification your composition will do for the school paper.* **2.** a modifying or being modified; a making less severe, strong, etc.; a toning down: *The modification of his anger made him able to think clearly again.* **3.** *Grammar.* **a.** qualification or limitation of meaning. **b.** an instance or result of this. **c.** a change in the form of a linguistic element when it is part of a construction. **4.** a modified form; variety. **5.** *Biology.* a change in an organism resulting from external influences, and not inheritable.

mod·i·fi·ca·tive (mod′ə fə kā′tiv), *adj.* modificatory.

mod·i·fi·ca·to·ry (mod′ə fə kā′tər ē), *adj.* modifying; tending to modify.

mod·i·fi·er (mod′ə fī′ər), *n.* **1.** a word or group of words that limits or qualifies another word or group of words. In "a very tight coat," the adjective *tight* is a modifier of *coat,* and the adverb *very* is a modifier of *tight.* **2.** a person or thing that modifies.

mod·i·fy (mod′ə fī), *v.,* **-fied, -fy·ing.** —*v.t.* **1.** to make partial changes in; change somewhat: *to modify the design of an automobile, to modify the terms of a lease.* **2.** to make less; make less severe or strong; tone down: *to modify one's demands.* **3.** to limit or qualify the meaning of: *Adverbs modify verbs and adjectives.* **4.** to change (a vowel) by umlaut. —*v.i.* to be subjected to modification; make a modification. [< Latin *modificāre* to limit, be moderate < *modus* measure, mode[1] + *facere* to make] **—Syn.** *v.t.* **1.** alter. **2.** temper.

mo·dil·lion (mō dil′yən, mə-), *n. Architecture.* **1.** one of a series of ornamental blocks or brackets placed under the corona of a cornice in the Corinthian and other orders. **2.** a block or bracket similarly used in medieval and modern styles. [earlier *modiglion* < Italian *modiglione,* ultimately < Latin *mūtulus*]

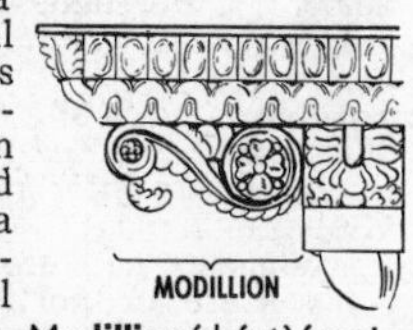

Modillion (def. 1) from interior of Pantheon, Rome

mo·di·o·lar (mō dī′ə lər, mə-), *adj.* resembling a modiolus.

mo·di·o·lus (mō dī′ə ləs, mə-), *n., pl.* **-li** (-lī). *Anatomy.* the central conical axis around which the cochlea of the ear winds. [< New Latin *modiolus* < Latin, nave of a wheel; a vessel or container < *modius* a Roman measure; also, a socket < *modus* mode[1]]

mod·ish (mō′dish), *adj.* fashionable; stylish. **—mod′ish·ly,** *adv.* **—mod′ish·ness,** *n.*

mo·diste (mō dēst′), *n.* a person who makes or sells fashionable women's dresses, hats, etc.; dressmaker. [< French *modiste* < *mode* mode[2]]

mo·di·us (mō′dē əs), *n., pl.* **-di·i** (-dē ī). **1.** an ancient Roman dry measure, equal to about a peck. **2.** a tall, cylindrical headdress worn by certain divinities as represented in ancient art. [< Latin *modius* < *modus* mode[1]]

Mo·doc (mō′dok), *n., pl.* **-doc** or **-docs.** a member of a small tribe of American Indians of southwestern Oregon and northern California, closely related to the Klamath Indians: *Basil, who was killed by the Modocs at Klamath Lake, was one of the Pathfinder's favorites* (Bernard De Voto).

Mo·dred (mō′dred), *n.* King Arthur's nephew, and one of his knights. He was a traitor and led a rebellion against Arthur. Also, **Mordred.**

Mods (modz), *n.pl. British Informal.* moderations, the first public examination for the B. A. at Oxford: *They have scarcely opened a classical text since they got their first in Mods* (London Times).

mod·u·lar (moj′ů lər), *adj.* **1.** of or having to do with a module or a modulus. **2.** made or built in units or pieces that can be interchanged to meet various needs, as furniture or building materials: *The console has three modular units that can be arranged in the room as one wishes. Basically it is an analogue computer, built up on the modular system and therefore extremely versatile* (New Scientist). **3.** of or having to do with furniture, building materials, etc., that can be interchanged: *a modular plan, a modular pattern.*

mod·u·late (moj′ů lāt), *v.,* **-lat·ed, -lat·ing.** —*v.t.* **1.** to regulate; adjust; tone down; soften. **2.** to alter (the voice) for expression; vary in pitch, tone, etc.; inflect: *He had a really noble voice which he could modulate with great skill* (Alexander Kinglake). **3.** *Music.* **a.** to attune (sounds, etc.) to a certain pitch or key. **b.** to cause to change from one key or note to another. **4.** to vary the frequency of (electromagnetic waves): *A light-beam modulated at a frequency of 8.2 megacycles per second* (Science News). **5.** to cause (a carrier wave) to vary by adding sound waves to it, the effect of one sound wave being spread over a considerable number of oscillations of the carrier wave. **6.** to intone (a prayer, response, etc.); sing softly. —*v.i.* **1.** to undergo modulation. **2.** *Music.* to change from one key to another, according to the laws of harmony. **3.** to vary electrical waves by producing oscillations. **4.** to produce modulation in a radio carrier wave. [< Latin *modulārī* (with English *-ate*[1]) < *modulus* small measure (diminutive) < *modus* measure]

mod·u·la·tion (moj′ů lā′shən), *n.* **1.** a modulating: *Modulation . . . includes the patterns of stress and intonation which frequently accompany utterances or parts of utterances* (Ralph L. Beals and Harry Hoijer). **2.** a being modulated. **3.** *Music.* a change from one key to another in the course of a piece of music, especially with a certain succession of chords: *He went to his organ and improvised with learned modulations* (Lytton Strachey). **4.** *Electronics.* a varying of high-frequency waves.

mod·u·la·tor (moj′ů lā′tər), *n.* **1.** a person or thing that modulates. **2.** a device, as a vacuum tube, for changing a radio current by adding sound waves to it.

mod·u·la·to·ry (moj′ů lə tôr′ē, -tōr′-), *adj.* serving to modulate; that modulates.

mod·ule (moj′ül), *n.* **1.** a standard unit for measuring: *Houses of the future may all be built using a four-inch cube called a module as the structural "atom"* (Science News Letter). **2.** *Architecture.* the size of some part taken as a unit of measure for other parts, especially a dimension of some part, as a column, used as a unit of measure throughout a structure, to bring all parts into correct proportion. **3.** one of several self-contained units of a projected spacecraft, each designed to serve a particular function: *At a hundred miles or so from the lunar surface retro-rockets will slow the craft into a lunar orbit; it will then be split in two, to form a mother craft and a lunar excursion module* (New Scientist). **4.** a micro-module. [earlier, a scale < Latin *modulus* (diminutive) < *modus* a measure, mode[1]]

mod·u·lus (moj′ů ləs), *n., pl.* **-li** (-lī). **1.** a quantity expressing the measure of some function, property, or the like, especially under conditions where the measure is unity. **2.** a quantity used as a multiplying factor for the conversion of units, usually consisting of pure numbers expressing a ratio of two quantities in which the dimensions cancel. [< Latin *modulus;* see MODULE]

➤modulus, coefficient. *Modulus* is used generally in describing physical relations; *coefficient* is more common for mathematical relations.

mo·dus (mō′dəs), *n., pl.* **-di** (-dī). manner or method of procedure; mode. [< Latin *modus* mode[1]]

mo·dus o·pe·ran·di (mō′dəs op′ə ran′dī), *Latin.* method or manner of working; mode of operation: *Her modus operandi in arriving at her conclusions was simplicity itself: she talked to people about politics* (Harper's).

mo·dus vi·ven·di (mō′dəs vi ven′dī), *Latin.* mode of living; way of getting along; temporary arrangement while waiting for a final settlement: *a modus vivendi between East and West.*

Moe·bi·us strip or **band** (mœ′bē əs, mō′-), Möbius strip or band.

Moe·ra (mir′ə), *n., pl.* **Moe·rae** (mir′ē). *Greek Mythology.* the goddess of fate. Also, **Moira.**

Moerae, the Fates.

Moe·so·goth (mē′sə goth), *n.* one of a Gothic tribe which settled in Moesia, an ancient Roman province corresponding nearly to modern Bulgaria and Serbia.

Moe·so·goth·ic (mē′sə goth′ik), *adj.* of or having to do with the Moesogoths or their language. —*n.* the language of the Moesogoths.

moeurs (mœrs), *n.pl. French.* mores: *She . . . transformed a historical subject . . . by endowing her characters with the moral conceptions and moeurs of her time* (Listener).

mo·fette or **mof·fette** (mō fet′), *n.* **1.** an opening or fissure in the earth from which gases, especially carbon dioxide, emanate. **2.** an emanation from such an opening. [< French *mofette* < Italian *mofetta.* Compare MEPHITIC.]

mo·fus·sil (mə fus′əl), *n.* (in India) the rural or provincial localities of a district as distinguished from the chief station; the country. [Anglo-Indian < Hindustani *mufassal* (literally) separate < Arabic *fasala* divide]

mog (mog), *v.,* **mogged, mog·ging.** *Dialect.* —*v.i.* **1.** to move on; depart; decamp. **2.** to move along slowly but steadily; jog. —*v.t.* to move (something); cause to go. [origin unknown]

mog·gie or **mog·gy** (mog′ē), *n., pl.* **-gies. 1.** *British Slang.* **a.** a cat. **b.** an untidy woman or girl. **2.** *British Dialect.* a calf or cow. [perhaps alteration of the name *Maggie*]

Mo·ghul (mō′gul, mō gul′), *n.* Mogul.

Mo·gol·lon (mō′gə yōn′), *n., pl.* **-lon** or **-lons.** a member of a tribe of North American Indians which once lived in the southwestern United States, thought to be predecessors of the Hopi and Zuñi Indians.

Mo·gul (mō′gul, mō gul′), *n.* **1.** a Mongol or Mongolian. **2. a.** one of the Mongol conquerors of India in the 1500's. **b.** one of their descendants. [< Persian and Arabic *mughal, mughul,* alteration of *Mongol,* the native name]

mo·gul (mō′gul, mō gul′), *n.* **1.** an important person: *The football captain was the mogul of the school.* **2.** a steam locomotive used especially in the late 1800's and early 1900's for hauling freight trains. [< *Mogul*]

mo·hair (mō′hãr), *n.* **1.** cloth made from the long, silky hair of the Angora goat; Angora. **2.** a similar cloth made of wool and cotton or rayon, used for upholstery and clothing. **3.** a garment of mohair. **4.** the hair of the Angora goat. [earlier *mocayare,* ultimately < Arabic *mukhayyar;* influenced by English *hair*]

Moham., Mohammedan.

Mo·ham·med·an (mō ham′ə dən), *adj.* of the Arabian prophet Mohammed, 570?-632, or the religion founded by him; Moslem. —*n.* a follower of Mohammed; a Moslem. Also, **Mahometan.**

Mohammedan calendar, the calendar used by Moslems, having cycles of 30 years, 12 months in a year, and alternate months of 30 and 29 days, with a day added to the last month every second and third year. It counts the years from 622 A.D., the date of Mohammed's flight from Mecca.

Mo·ham·med·an·ism (mō ham′ə də niz′-əm), *n.* the Mohammedan religion; Islam: *In its essence Mohammedanism . . . holds to the doctrine of the unity and omnipotence of Allah, and of the responsibility of every human being to Allah* (Emory S. Bogardus). Also, **Mahometanism.**

Mo·ham·med·an·ize (mō ham′ə də nīz), *v.t.,* **-ized, -iz·ing.** to convert to or bring into conformity with Islam; Islamize.

Mo·har·ram (mō har′əm), *n.* Muharram.

Mo·ha·ve (mō hä′vē), *n., pl.* **-ve** or **-ves.** a member of a tribe of North American Indians dwelling chiefly on the eastern side of the Colorado River. Also, **Mojave.** [American English < Yuman (Mohave) *hamakhava* (literally) the three mountains]

Mo·hawk (mō′hôk), *n., pl.* **-hawk** or **-hawks. 1.** a member of a tribe of North American Indians formerly living in central New York State, the most powerful of the Six Nations or Iroquois. **2.** the language of the Mohawks. [American English < the Algonkian (Algonkin) name *mowak* or *mowawak* (literally) they eat living things]

Mo·he·gan (mō hē′gən), *n., pl.* **-gan** or **-gans. 1.** one of a tribe of Algonkian Indians that lived in western Connecticut. **2.** Mahican. [American English, variant of *Mahican*]

Mo·hi·can (mō hē′kən), *n., pl.* **-can** or **-cans.** a member of either of two tribes of North American Indians formerly living in the upper Hudson valley and in Connecticut. Also, **Mahican.** [American English, variant of *Mahican*]

Mo·ho (mō′hō), *n.* the Mohorovicic discontinuity: *Scientists confirmed the existence of Moho . . . by sending pulses of sound down through the earth's crust* (Newsweek).

Mo·hock (mō′hok), *n.* **1.** one of a class of ruffians, often aristocrats, who roamed the streets of London at night early in the 1700's. **2.** *Obsolete.* Mohawk. [variant of *Mohawk*]

Mo·hole (mō′hōl), *n.* an experimental drilling project to bore into the earth's mantle to obtain geological specimens and to verify the Mohorovicic discontinuity. [< *Moho-*(rovicic) discontinuity + (ho)*le*]

Mo·ho·ro·vic·ic discontinuity (mō′hō-rō vē′chēch), the boundary between the earth's crust and mantle, the depth of which varies from approximately 6 to 8 miles under ocean basins, to 20 to 22 miles under the continents. [< A. *Mohorovičić,* a Yugoslav geophysicist, who discovered it in 1909 from studies of earthquake records]

Mohs scale (mōz), a scale for classifying the relative hardness of minerals, as follows: talc 1; gypsum 2; calcite 3; fluorite 4; apatite 5; feldspar 6; quartz 7; topaz 8; corundum 9; diamond 10. [< Friedrich *Mohs,* 1773-1839, a German mineralogist, who invented it]

moh·wa (mō′wä), *n.* mahua.

M.O.I., Ministry of Information (an agency of the British government during World War II, since replaced by the Central Office of Information and the British Information Service).

moi·der (moi′dər), *v.t. British.* to confuse; bother or worry; fatigue. Also, **moither.**

moi·dore (moi′dôr, -dōr), *n.* a former gold coin of Portugal and Brazil, worth about $6.50. [< Portuguese *moeda d'ouro* coin of gold < Latin *monēta* coin, money, *de* of, *aurum* gold]

moi·e·ty (moi′ə tē), *n., pl.* **-ties. 1.** half: *War, pestilence, and famine, had consumed . . . the moiety of the human species* (Edward Gibbon). **2.** part: *Only a small moiety of college students win scholarships.* **3.** a person's share or portion. **4.** *Anthropology.* each of the two strictly comparable major sections of a single society. Typically, as common among Australian aborigines, each moiety is exogamous so that all the members of any one moiety must find their spouses in the other. [earlier *moitie* < Old French *meitiet* < Late Latin *medietās* half < Latin, (coined by Cicero to translate Greek *mesótēs*) the middle < *medius* middle]

moil[1] (moil), *v.i.* **1.** to work hard; drudge. **2.** to be in a turmoil; agitate. —*v.t. Archaic.* **1.** to wet; moisten. **2.** to soil; bedaub; make dirty. —*n.* **1.** hard work; drudgery. **2.** trouble; confusion. [< Old French *moillier* to moisten (as in soup), ultimately < Latin *mollis* soft] —**moil′er,** *n.*

moil[2] (moil), *n.* the glass that adheres to the blowpipe or a piece of glassware after the piece has been blown and cracked off. [origin uncertain]

Moi·ra (moi′rə), *n., pl.* **-rai** (-rī), **-rae** (-rē). *Greek Mythology.* **1.** one of the three Fates. **2.** Also, **moira.** a person's fate, or the kind of life he has been decreed by the Fates to live: *I am going through my end, moira, my allotted part* (Atlantic).

moire (mwär; mwä rā′, mô-, mō-), *n.* **1.** (originally) a kind of watered silk. **2.** any textile fabric, especially silk, rayon, or acetate, to which a watered appearance or wavelike pattern is given by pressing it between engraved rollers: *This . . . gown is made of satin finished silk organdy, with a moire sash* (New York Times). [< French *moire,* earlier *mouaire,* apparently alteration of English *mohair*]

moi·ré (mwä rā′, mô-, mō-), *n.* **1.** moire: *. . . weaving the stuff into a fine mesh or engine-turning it into something resembling silk moiré* (New Yorker). **2.** a variegated or clouded appearance like that of watered silk, especially on metals for ornamentation. —*adj.* **1.** (of silk, paper, metal, etc.) having a wavelike pattern or clouded appearance; watered: *moiré silk.* **2.** (of a stamp) printed on the paper surface with an intricate wavy pattern to prevent forgery.
[< French *moiré* < *moirer* to give a watered look to < *moire* moire]

moire antique, silk watered in a large pattern. [< French *moire antique*]

moist (moist), *adj.* **1. a.** slightly wet; not dry; damp: *a moist cloth, a moist cellar, a moist dressing for an infection.* **b.** (of the eyes) wet with tears; tearful. **2.** rainy; wet: *The weather is moist and raw* (Dickens). **3.** associated or connected with liquid, as a disease marked by a discharge of matter, phlegm, etc. [< Old French *moiste,* perhaps < Late Latin *muscidus* moss (< Latin *muscus* moss), blended with Latin *mūcidus* slimy, musty < *mūcus* slime, mucus] —**moist′ly,** *adv.* —**moist′ness,** *n.* —**Syn. 1. a.** humid, dank. See **damp.** —**Ant. 1. a.** dry, arid, parched.

moist·en (moi′sən), *v.t.* to make moist; dampen. —*v.i.* to become moist: *Trilby's eyes moistened with tender pleasure at such a pretty compliment* (George Du Maurier). —**moist′en·er,** *n.*

mois·ture (mois′chər), *n.* slight wetness; water or other liquid spread in very small drops in the air or on a surface. [< Old French *moistour* < *moiste* moist]

mois·ture·less (mois′chər lis), *adj.* without moisture.

mois·ture·proof (mois′chər prüf′), *adj.* that will not let moisture through; impervious or resistant to moisture.

mois·tur·ize (mois′chə rīz), *v.t.,* **-ized, -iz·ing.** to supply with moisture by means of some agent: *An invisible protective film that moisturizes skin, leaving it smoother, younger-looking* (New Yorker). —**mois′-tur·iz′er,** *n.*

moist·y (mois′tē), *adj.,* **moist·i·er, moist·i·est.** moist; damp.

moi·ther (moi′ᴛʜər), *v.t.* moider.

mo·jar·ra (mō hä′rə), *n., pl.* **-ras** or (*collectively*) **-ra.** any of a group of warm-water fishes found in shallow waters on both coasts of the Americas, of small size and silvery coloration. [< American Spanish *mojarra*]

Mo·ja·ve (mō hä′vē), *n., pl.* **-ve** or **-ves.** Mohave.

moke (mōk), *n. Slang.* **1.** a donkey: *You too could ride around on this patient moke* (Sunday Times). **2.** a stupid fellow; dolt.

mol (mōl), *n. Chemistry.* the molecular weight of a substance expressed in grams; gram molecule. Also, **mole.** [apparently < *molecule*]

MOL (no periods) or **M.O.L.,** Manned Orbiting Laboratory.

mo·la (mō′lə), *n., pl.* **-las** or (*collectively*) **-la.** ocean sunfish. [< New Latin *Mola* the genus name < Latin *mola* millstone]

mo·lal (mō′ləl), *adj.* **1.** of or having to do with a mol or gram molecule. **2.** (of a solution) having one mol of solute in 1,000 grams of solvent.

mo·lar[1] (mō′lər), *n.* a tooth with a broad surface for grinding, having somewhat flattened points: *The twelve permanent back teeth in man are molars.* See also picture under **incisor.** —*adj.* **1.** adapted for grinding. **2.** of the molar teeth. [< Latin *molāris* grinding < *mola* millstone]

Molar[1]

mo·lar[2] (mō′lər), *adj.* **1.** *Physics.* of mass or a body as a whole; acting on or by means of large masses of matter. **2.** *Chemistry.* (of a solution) having one mol of solute in a liter of solution. [< Latin *mōlēs* mass + English *-ar*]

mo·lar·i·ty (mō lar′ə tē), *n. Physics.* mass.

mo·las·ses (mə las′iz), *n.* a sweet, brown syrup obtained in making sugar from sugar cane, or from raw sugar, sorghum, etc. [< Portuguese *melaço* < Late Latin *mellāceum* must[2] < Latin *mellāceus* honeylike < *mel, mellis* honey]

mold[1] (mōld), *n.* **1.** a hollow shape in which anything is formed or cast: *Melted metal is poured into a mold to harden into shape.* **2.** the shape or form which is given by a mold: *iron of an ancient mold. The molds of ice cream were turkeys and pumpkins.* **3.** a model according to which anything is shaped: *He is cast in his father's mold.* **4.** something shaped in a mold: *a mold of pudding.* **5.** nature; character: *a man of base mold.* **6.** the shape or frame on or about which something is made: *a basket mold.* **7.** an impression or cavity made in earth by the convex side of a fossil shell.
—*v.t.* **1.** to form; shape: *Children mold figures out of clay. I would mold a world of fire and dew* (William Butler Yeats). **2.** to make or form into shape: *to mold dough into loaves. Our characters are molded by our conduct.* **3.** to produce a mold of or from, so as to obtain a casting. **4.** to form into, or decorate with, moldings. **5.** to ornament by shaping or carving. Also, *especially British,* **mould.**
[< Old French *modle,* also *molle* < Latin *modulus.* Doublet of MODULE.]

mold[2] (mōld), *n.* **1.** a woolly or furry fungous growth, often greenish-blue or whitish in color, that appears on the surface of food and other animal or vegetable substances when they are left too long in a warm, moist place or when they are decaying. **2.** any fungus that forms mycelium covering the surface of its structure; mold fungus.
—*v.i.* to become covered with mold. —*v.t.* to cover with mold. Also, *especially British,* **mould.**
[probably < past participle of Middle English *moulen,* or *muwlen* grow moldy]

mold[3] (mōld), *n.* **1.** loose earth; fine, soft, rich soil: *Many wild flowers grow in the forest mold.* **2.** *Archaic.* earth as the material of the human body. **3.** *Archaic.* **a.** ground; earth, especially as used for a grave. **b.** a grave. Also, *especially British,* **mould.** [Old English *molde*] —**Syn. 1.** topsoil, humus.

mold·a·bil·i·ty (mōl′də bil′ə tē), *n.* the ability to be easily molded.

mold·a·ble (mōl′də bəl), *adj.* that can be molded or formed. Also, *especially British,* **mouldable.**

 PRONUNCIATION KEY: hat, āge, cãre, fär; let, ēqual, tėrm; it, īce; hot, ōpen, ôrder; oil, out; cup, pu̇t, rüle;

Mol·da·vi·an (mol dā′vē ən, -dāv′yən), *adj.* of or having to do with Moldavia, a Soviet republic in the southwestern Soviet Union, or its inhabitants. —*n.* a native or an inhabitant of Moldavia.

mol·da·vite (mol′də vīt), *n.* a dull-green glass similar to obsidian. [< *Moldavia,* a region of Rumania, where it is found + *-ite*[1]]

mold·board (mōld′bôrd′, -bōrd′), *n.* **1.** a curved metal plate in a plow, that turns over the earth from the furrow. **2.** one of the boards forming the sides of a concrete mold. Also, *especially British,* **mouldboard.** [alteration of Middle English *moldebred* < *mold*[3] + *bred* board, tablet]

mold·er[1] (mōl′dər), *v.i.* to turn into dust by natural decay; crumble; waste away: *John Brown's body lies a-moldering in the grave* (Charles Sprague Hall). Also, *especially British,* **moulder.** [probably < *mold*[3]. Compare dialectal Norwegian *muldra* crumble.]

mold·er[2] (mōl′dər), *n.* **1.** a person who shapes something. **2.** a maker of molds. **3.** *Printing.* an electrotype plate from which duplicate electrotypes are made. Also, *especially British,* **moulder.** [< *mold*[1] + *-er*[1]]

mold fungus, any fungus producing a woolly or furry growth that is often greenish in color and appears especially on decaying matter; mold.

mold·i·ness (mōl′dē nis), *n.* the state of being moldy.

mold·ing (mōl′ding), *n.* **1.** the act of shaping: *the molding of dishes from clay.* **2.** something molded. **3. a.** a strip, usually of wood, around the upper walls of a room, used to support pictures, to cover electric wires, etc. **b.** a decorative variety of contour or outline given to cornices, jambs, strips of woodwork, etc. Also, *especially British,* **moulding.**

molding board, a board used for kneading bread, rolling cookies, etc.

mold loft, a large room (usually a loft) in a shipyard, on the floor of which the lines of a ship are drawn in full size, in plan and elevation, from the designer's drawings.

mold·warp (mōld′wôrp′), *n. British Dialect.* the common mole of the Old World. Also, **mouldwarp.** [Middle English *moldwarp* < Old English *molde* earth, dust, mold[3] + *weorpan* throw]

mold·y (mōl′dē), *adj.,* **mold·i·er, mold·i·est.** **1.** covered with mold: *moldy bread, moldy cheese.* **2.** musty; stale: *A moldy odor of aristocracy lingered about the place* (Elizabeth Gaskell). Also, *especially British,* **mouldy.**

mole[1] (mōl), *n.* **1.** a congenital spot on the skin, usually brown: *Upon one cheek he had a mole not unbecoming* (Robert Louis Stevenson). **2.** a nevus. [Old English *māl*]

mole[2] (mōl), *n.* **1.** any of a group of small mammals that live underground most of the time eating the insects, worms, etc., that they find there. Moles have dark, velvety fur, very small eyes that cannot see well, and forelimbs adapted for digging. **2.** a person who works in obscurity, especially one who works patiently and painstakingly. [Middle English *molle,* or *molde*; origin uncertain; perhaps short for *moldwarp*]

Mole[2] (def. 1) (including tail, about 7 in. long)

mole[3] (mōl), *n.* **1.** a barrier built of stone to break the force of the waves and sometimes serving as a pier; breakwater. **2.** the harbor formed by it. [< Latin *mōlēs, -is* a mass, dam]

mole[4] (mōl), *n.* a fleshy or bloody mass occurring in the uterus. [< French *môle* < Old French *mole,* learned borrowing from Latin *mola* misconception < Greek *mýlē* tumor on the womb]

mole[5] (mōl), *n.* mol. [< German *Molekül* molecule < New Latin *molecula*]

mole·cast (mōl′kast, -käst), *n.* a molehill.

Mo·lech (mō′lek), *n.* Moloch.

mole crab, a small crustacean which buries itself in the sand under the ocean surf and gathers food with its feathery antennae: *If . . . a portion of the beach seems to rise up, move a bit, then settle down again, you are probably watching mole crabs out after their food* (Science News Letter).

mole cricket, a large insect having velvety hair and stout forelegs adapted for burrowing in the ground. It is found throughout the tropical and temperate world, feeding on insect larvae, earthworms, and root and tuber crops, including potatoes and sugar cane.

mol·ec·tron·ics (mol′ek tron′iks), *n.* molecular electronics.

mo·lec·u·lar (mə lek′yə lər), *adj.* **1.** having to do with molecules: *Some progress has been made towards interpreting the Onsager theorem in molecular terms* (Science News). **2.** consisting of molecules: *Molecular ions of deuterium are injected from an accelerating machine into a large magnetic bottle* (New Scientist). **3.** caused by molecules: *A heavy metal ball in a vessel of water . . . will be lifted to the surface by a concentration of molecular impulses* (T. Fursdon Crang). —**mo·lec′u·lar·ly,** *adv.*

molecular beam or **ray,** a stream of molecules moving in about the same direction and at approximately the same speed.

molecular biology, the branch of biology dealing with the chemical processes of life at the molecular level, especially the mechanism of the replication of cells, and the transmission of genetic information.

molecular electronics, the use of silicon crystals and other semiconductors to produce microcircuits.

molecular film, monomolecular film.

molecular gas constant, Boltzmann's constant.

mo·lec·u·lar·i·ty (mə lek′yə lar′ə tē), *n.* molecular condition or quality.

molecular sieve, a zeolite whose crystalline structure is honeycombed with regularly spaced holes of uniform size that can be used to filter out molecules: *New . . . air separation methods used molecular sieves to separate nitrogen from the oxygen in the air* (Marshall Sittig).

molecular weight, the weight of a molecule, now usually expressed on a scale on which an isotope of carbon weighs exactly 12.0000 units; the sum of the atomic weights of all the atoms in a molecule. *Abbr.:* mol. wt.

mol·e·cule (mol′ə kyül), *n.* **1.** the smallest particle into which a substance can be divided without chemical change. A molecule of an element consists of one or more atoms; a molecule of a compound consists of two or more atoms. *The rate of escape from a solid to a surrounding vapor depends on the intensity of the molecules' motion* (Scientific American). **2.** that quantity of a substance whose weight is equivalent to the molecular weight; gram molecule. **3.** a very small particle. [< New Latin *molecula* (diminutive) < Latin *mōlēs* mass, burden]

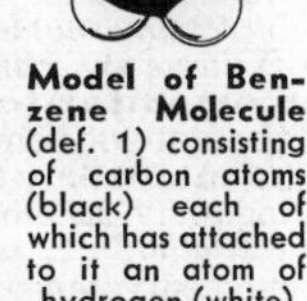

Model of Benzene Molecule (def. 1) consisting of carbon atoms (black) each of which has attached to it an atom of hydrogen (white)

mole·hill (mōl′hil′), *n.* **1.** a small mound or ridge of earth raised up by moles burrowing under the ground. **2.** something insignificant.

make a mountain (out) of a molehill. See under **mountain,** *n.*

mole·like (mōl′līk′), *adj.* resembling a mole.

mole rat, any of various Old World molelike rodents, which live underground and burrow extensively.

mole·skin (mōl′skin′), *n.* **1. a.** the skin of the mole used as fur. **b.** other skins dressed so as to resemble this. **2.** a strong, thick cotton fabric used for sportsmen's and laborers' clothing.

moleskins, garments, especially trousers, made of a strong, thick cotton fabric: *It is not unlikely that the resumption of football by his famous backfield partner . . . will accentuate a desire to don the so-called moleskins and emulate Blanchard's achievements* (Baltimore Sun).

mo·lest (mə lest′), *v.t.* to meddle with and injure; interfere with and trouble; disturb: *We did not molest the big dog, because we were afraid of him.* [< Old French *molester,* learned borrowing from Latin *molestāre* < *molestus* troublesome, related to *mōlēs, -is* burden, mass] —**mo·lest′er,** *n.* —**Syn.** harass, harry, worry, annoy.

mo·les·ta·tion (mō′les tā′shən, mol′es-), *n.* **1.** a molesting. **2.** a being molested; annoying interference: *He is not solitary by nature, but his way of life and his desire to continue it without molestation impose this penalty upon him* (Harper's). **3.** *Obsolete.* vexation; distress.

mo·line (mō′lin, mə līn′), *adj.* (of a heraldic cross) having arms which terminate in two branches resembling the rynd of a millstone. [probably < unrecorded Anglo-French *moliné* < Old French *molin* mill]

Mo·li·nism (mō′lə niz əm, mol′ə-), *n.* the religious doctrine of quietism. [< Miguel de *Molinos,* 1627-1696, a Spanish priest who propounded it + *-ism*]

Mo·li·nist (mō′lə nist, mol′ə-), *n.* a follower of Miguel de Molinos or his doctrine; quietist.

moll (mol), *n. Slang.* **1.** a female companion of a criminal or vagrant. **2.** a prostitute. [short for *Molly,* familiar variant of *Mary*]

mol·lah (mol′ə), *n.* mullah.

mol·les·cence (mə les′əns), *n.* a tendency toward softness.

mol·les·cent (mə les′ənt), *adj.* tending to become soft. [< Latin *mollēscēns, -entis,* present participle of *mollēscere* become soft < *mollīre* soften < *mollis* soft]

mol·li·fi·a·ble (mol′ə fī′ə bəl), *adj.* that can be mollified, softened, or soothed.

mol·li·fi·ca·tion (mol′ə fə kā′shən), *n.* **1.** the act of mollifying or softening: *For induration, or mollification, it is to be enquired what will make metals harder and harder, and what will make them softer and softer* (Francis Bacon). **2.** pacification; an appeasing: *No mollification of his wife's anger appeared likely.* **3.** something that will soothe: *Some mollification for your giant, sweet lady* (Shakespeare).

mol·li·fi·er (mol′ə fī′ər), *n.* a person or thing that mollifies.

mol·li·fy (mol′ə fī), *v.,* **-fied, -fy·ing.** —*v.t.* **1.** to soften, especially in temper; appease; mitigate: *He tried to mollify his father's anger by apologizing.* **2.** to make soft or supple. —*v.i. Obsolete.* **1.** to become less angry; relent. **2.** to become soft or tender. [< Late Latin *mollificāre* < *mollis* soft + *facere* make] —**mol′li·fy′ing·ly,** *adv.* —**Syn.** *v.t.* **1.** allay, pacify, calm.

mol·lusc (mol′əsk), *n. Especially British.* mollusk.

mol·lus·can (mə lus′kən), *adj.* of or having to do with mollusks. —*n.* a mollusk.

mol·lus·ci·cid·al (mə lus′kə sī′dəl), *adj.* of or by means of molluscicides.

mol·lus·ci·cide (mə lus′kə sīd), *n.* a substance for killing mollusks, especially one used to destroy the snails which are vectors of schistosomiasis. [< *mollusc* + *-cide*[1]]

mol·lus·coid (mə lus′koid), *adj.* resembling a mollusk. —*n.* an animal similar to a mollusk.

mol·lus·coi·dal (mol′ə skoi′dəl), *adj.* molluscoid.

mol·lus·cous (mə lus′kəs), *adj.* **1.** belonging to or resembling the mollusks. **2.** spineless; flabby; soft; weak.

mol·lus·cum con·ta·gi·o·sum (mə lus′kəm kən tā′jē ō′səm), an infectious skin disease of humans in which tubercles containing cheesy matter appear on the face. It is caused by a virus. [< New Latin *molluscum* a skin disease (< Latin *molluscus* soft-bodied), *contagiosum* contagious]

mol·lusk (mol′əsk), *n.* any of a large group of animals having no backbone, soft bodies not composed of segments, and usually covered with a hard shell of one or more parts. The shell of mollusks is secreted by a covering mantle and is formed on snails, clams, oysters, whelks, and mussels but not on slugs, octopuses, or squids. They make up a phylum in the animal kingdom. Also, *especially British,* **mollusc.** [< French *mollusque,* learned borrowing from New Latin *Mollusca* a Linnean order, (originally) neuter plural of Latin *molluscus* soft-bodied < *mollis* soft]

Moll·wei·de projection (môl′vī′də), a type of homolographic map projection in which the surface of the earth is represented as an ellipse, with the equator and parallels of latitude as straight lines. [< Karl *Mollweide,* 1774-1825, a German mathematician and astronomer, who devised it]

mol·ly[1] (mol′ē), *n., pl.* **-lies.** *Informal.* an effeminate man or boy; mollycoddle.

mol·ly[2] (mol′ē), *n., pl.* **-lies.** the mallemuck; fulmar. [alteration of *mallemuck*]

mol·ly·cod·dle (mol′ē kod′əl), *n., v.,* **-dled, -dling.** —*n.* a person, especially a boy or man, accustomed to being fussed over and pampered; milksop: *You have been bred up as a mollycoddle, Pen, and spoilt by the women* (Thackeray). —*v.t.* to pamper; coddle. [perhaps < *Molly* (compare MOLL) + *coddle*] —**mol′ly·cod′dler,** *n.*

Mol·ly Ma·guires (mol′ē mə gwīrz′), **1.** a lawless secret society organized in Ireland about 1843, whose members disguised themselves as women on occasion. **2.** a similar group in the mining regions of Pennsylvania, suppressed in 1877. [< *Molly Maguire,* a common Irish name]

mol·ly·mawk (môl′ē môk), *n.* mallemuck: *The fulmars—"mollymawks" to the sailors—... glide still, in twos and threes along the sea-battered cliffs* (London Times).

Mo·loch (mō′lok), *n.* **1.** a Semitic deity whose worship was marked by the sacrifice of children as burnt offerings, especially first-born males, by their parents. Moloch is mentioned in the Bible as a Canaanite god whom the Israelites worshiped secretly. **2.** anything thought of as requiring frightful sacrifice. Also, **Molech.**

mo·loch (mō′lok), *n.* a spiny Australian lizard. [< New Latin *Moloch* the genus name < English *Moloch* (because of its ugly appearance)]

Mo·lo·tov breadbasket (mô′lə tôf, mol′-ə-), *Slang.* a bomb container which rotates as it falls, scattering incendiary bombs over a considerable area. [< Vyacheslav *Molotov,* born 1890, a Russian diplomat (because it was used during the Spanish Civil War, when Molotov was involved in Russian international affairs)]

Molotov cocktail, *Slang.* a crude type of hand grenade, consisting of a bottle filled with gasoline, and having a rag as a wick. It was used in Spain by the opponents of Franco during the civil war of the late 1930's, and in World War II by various irregular or partisan troops.

molt (mōlt), *v.i.* to shed feathers, skin, hair, shell, antlers, etc., before a new growth: *Birds, snakes, insects, and crustaceans molt.* —*v.t.* to shed (feathers, skin, etc.): *We saw the snake molt its skin.* —*n.* **1.** the act or time of molting. **2.** skin, hair, antlers, etc., shed in molting. Also, *especially British,* **moult.** [alteration of Middle English *mouten,* Old English *-mūtian* (as in *bemūtian* exchange for), ultimately < Latin *mūtāre* to change] —**molt′er,** *n.*

mol·ten (mōl′tən), *adj.* **1.** made liquid by heat; melted: *molten steel.* **2.** made by melting and casting into a mold; cast: *a molten image.* —*v.* melted; a past participle of **melt.** —**mol′ten·ly,** *adv.*

molten sea, brazen sea.

mol·to (mōl′tō), *adv. Music.* much; very (used with other directions): *molto allegro.* [< Italian *molto* much; very < Latin *multum*]

molto adagio, *Music.* very slowly (used as a direction).

Mo·luc·can (mō luk′ən), *adj.* of or having to do with the Moluccas or Spice Islands, their people, or their language. —*n.* the Indonesian language of the Moluccas.

mol. wt., molecular weight.

mo·ly[1] (mō′lē), *n., pl.* **-lies. 1.** a fabulous herb with a milk-white flower and a black root, having magic properties. Hermes gave Odysseus moly to counteract the spells of Circe. **2.** a wild garlic of Europe. [< Latin *mōly* < Greek *môly*]

mol·y[2] (mol′ē), *n. Informal.* molybdenum.

mo·lyb·date (mə lib′dāt), *n.* a salt of molybdic acid.

mo·lyb·de·nite (mə lib′də nīt, mol′ib dē′-), *n.* a soft, graphitelike, native sulfide of molybdenum, a valuable ore. *Formula:* MoS_2

mo·lyb·de·nous (mə lib′də nəs, mol′ib-dē′-), *adj.* **1.** of molybdenum. **2.** containing molybdenum, especially with a valence of two; molybdous.

mo·lyb·de·num (mə lib′də nəm, mol′ib-dē′-), *n.* a heavy, hard, silver-white metallic chemical element. Molybdenum can be hammered or pressed into various shapes without being broken, but fuses with difficulty, and occurs in combination, as in molybdenite or wulfenite. It is much used in steel alloys with carbon. *Symbol:* Mo; *at. wt.:* (C^{12}) 95.94 or (O^{16}) 95.95; *at. no.:* 42; *valence:* 2,3,4,5,6 (the more common ones being 2,3,6). [earlier *molybdena* any of several ores of lead < Latin *molybdaena* < Greek *molýbdaina* < *mólybdos* lead]

mo·lyb·dic (mə lib′dik), *adj.* **1.** of molybdenum. **2.** containing molybdenum, especially with a valence of six.

molybdic acid, any of certain acids containing molybdenum.

mo·lyb·dous (mə lib′dəs), *adj.* containing molybdenum (in larger proportion than a corresponding molybdic compound).

mom (mom), *n. U.S. Informal.* mother.

mom and pop store, *U.S.* a small retail store owned and operated, often under a franchise, by a husband and wife.

mome (mōm), *n. Archaic.* a blockhead; dolt.

mo·ment (mō′mənt), *n.* **1.** a very short space of time; instant: *In a moment the house was in flames. Won't you stay for a moment? Do not delay; the golden moments fly* (Longfellow). **2. a.** a present or other particular point of time: *We both arrived at the same moment. I could not recall his name at the moment.* **b.** a definite stage, period, or turning point in a course of events. **3.** importance; weight: *The President is busy on a matter of moment.* **4.** a tendency to cause rotation around a point or axis: *Evidence is accumulating to suggest that the biosphere has its own specificity for spin and moment which may well be critical* (Atlantic). **5.** the product of a (specified) physical quantity and the length of the perpendicular from a point or axis. The moment of a force about a point is the product of the magnitude of the force and the length of the perpendicular distance from the point to the line of action of the force. **6.** *Philosophy.* a cause, motive, or stage of a logically developing process of thought or action; momentum. **7.** *Statistics.* any of several values derived from sums of powers of the variables in a set of data. [< Latin *mōmentum* movement < *movēre* to move. Doublet of MOMENTUM.] —**Syn. 1.** second. See **minute. 3.** consequence, significance.

mo·men·ta (mō men′tə), *n.* a plural of **momentum.**

mo·men·ta·ne·ous (mō′mən tā′nē əs), *adj. Obsolete.* **1.** momentary. **2.** instantaneous.

mo·men·ta·ny (mō′mən tā′nē), *adj. Obsolete.* momentary.

mo·men·tar·i·ly (mō′mən ter′ə lē, mō′-mən ter′-), *adv.* **1.** for a moment: *He hesitated momentarily.* **2.** at every moment; from moment to moment: *The danger was increasing momentarily.* **3.** at any moment: *We were expecting the postman momentarily.*

mo·men·tar·i·ness (mō′mən ter′ē nis), *n.* the state of being momentary.

mo·men·tar·y (mō′mən ter′ē), *adj.* **1.** lasting only a moment; fleeting: *momentary hesitation.* **2.** occurring or present every moment: *momentary interruptions.* **3.** occurring at any moment: *to live in fear of momentary exposure.* **4.** *Archaic.* (of living beings) ephemeral. —**Syn. 1.** transitory, temporary.

mo·ment·ly (mō′mənt lē), *adv.* **1.** from moment to moment; every moment: *The throng momently increased* (Edgar Allan Poe). **2.** at any moment; on the instant. **3.** for the moment; for a single moment: *The attack was stopped—but only momently.*

moment of truth, the point in time when a harsh truth must be faced; a moment of direct confrontation with some unpleasant fact or circumstance: *It was a shaking moment of truth for the Government and for the British public, who suddenly received a lightning, unflattering intimation of exactly how solid a risk they looked to the neighbors* (New Yorker).

mo·men·tous (mō men′təs), *adj.* very important; of great consequence; weighty: *Choosing between peace and war is a momentous decision. Momentous To himself, as I to me, Hath each man been* (Sir William Watson). —**mo·men′tous·ness,** *n.* —**Syn.** serious, critical. —**Ant.** trivial, trifling, paltry, insignificant.

mo·men·tous·ly (mō men′təs lē), *adv.* with important effect or influence.

mo·men·tum (mō men′təm), *n., pl.* **-tums** or **-ta. 1.** the quantity of the motion of a moving body, equal to its mass multiplied by its velocity: *A falling object gains momentum as it falls.* **2.** impetus resulting from movement: *Jazz rhythms create what can only be called momentum* (Harper's). **3.** *Philosophy.* a moment. [< Latin *mōmentum* moving power. Doublet of MOMENT.] —**Syn. 2.** impulse, force.

mom·ism (mom′iz əm), *n. Informal.* the emotional domination of a son by his mother. [(coined by Philip Wylie) < *mom* + *-ism*]

mom·ma (mom′ə), *n.* mamma; mother.

mom·me (mom′ē), *n., pl.* **-me.** a Japanese unit of weight, equal to 3.75 grams: *Everybody else in the world was weighing pearls in momme, the traditional Japanese unit, while Japan was determinedly using the gramme* (New Scientist). [< Japanese]

mom·my (mom′ē), *n., pl.* **-mies.** *U.S. Informal.* mother.

Mo·mus (mō′məs), *n.* **1.** *Greek Mythology.* the god of ridicule, who was banished from heaven for his censures upon the gods. **2.** a faultfinder; critic. [< Latin *Mōmus* < Greek *Mômos* god of ridicule; later, ridicule, criticism]

mon[1] (mon), *n. Scottish.* man.

mon[2] (mon), *n.* (in Japanese use) a personal or family device or insignia. [< Japanese *mon*]

mon-, *combining form.* the form of **mono-** before vowels, as in *monacid.*

mon., 1. monastery. **2.** monetary.

Mon., 1. Monaco. **2.** Monday. **3.** Monsignor.

mo·na (mō′nə), *n.* a small, long-tailed African monkey of docile disposition, often kept in captivity. [< Spanish, Portuguese *mona,* feminine of *mono* monkey]

Mon·a·can (mon′ə kən, mə nä′kən), *adj.* of or having to do with Monaco, a small country within southeastern France, on the Mediterranean Sea, or its inhabitants. —*n.* a native or inhabitant of Monaco. Also, *French,* **Monégasque.**

mon·a·chal (mon′ə kəl), *adj.* monastic. [< Late Latin *monachālis* < *monăchus* monk]

mon·a·chism (mon′ə kiz əm), *n.* monasticism.

mon·a·chi·za·tion (mon′ə kə zā′shən), *n.* the act or event of becoming a monk.

mon·a·chize (mon′ə kīz), *v.,* **-chized, -chizing.** —*v.i.* to become a monk; live a monastic life. —*v.t.* to make (a person) a monk.

mon·ac·id (mon as′id), *adj., n.* monoacid.

mon·ad (mon′ad, mō′nad), *n.* **1.** unity; a unit. **2. a.** a very simple single-celled animal or plant. **b.** a small protozoan having from one to three long, whiplike flagella. **3.** *Chemistry.* an atom, element, or radical having a valence of one. **4.** *Philosophy.* an absolutely simple entity, conceived as the ultimate unit of being.
—*adj.* of or having the nature of a monad. [< Late Latin *monas, -adis* < Greek *monás, -ádos* unit < *mónos* alone, single]

mon·a·del·phous (mon′ə del′fəs), *adj.* having stamens united by their filaments into one group, as in various legumes and mallows. [< Greek *mónos* one, single + *adelphós* brother; (literally) from the womb + English *-ous*]

mon·a·des (mon′ə dēz), *n.* plural of **monas.**

mo·nad·ic (mə nad′ik), *adj.* **1.** having to do with monads. **2.** of the nature of a monad. **3.** composed of monads. —**mo·nad′i·cal·ly,** *adv.*

mo·nad·i·cal (mə nad′ə kəl), *adj.* monadic.

mon·ad·ism (mon′ə diz əm, mō′nə-), *n.* **1.** the philosophical theory that the universe is composed of and controlled by minute, simple entities. **2.** a system based on this theory.

mon·ad·is·tic (mon′ə dis′tik), *adj.* of or having to do with monadism.

mo·nad·nock (mə nad′nok), *n.* an isolated hill or mountain of resistant rock standing in an area that is almost level from erosion. [< Mt. *Monadnock,* in New Hampshire]

mon·ad·o·log·i·cal (mon′ə də loj′ə kəl, mō′nə-), *adj.* of or having to do with monadology or the doctrine of monads.

mon·ad·ol·o·gy (mon′ə dol′ə jē, mō′nə-), *n. Philosophy.* the doctrine of monads.

mon·a·ker (mon′ə kər), *n.* moniker.

mon a·mi (môɴ ná mē′), *French.* my friend (male).

mo·nan·drous (mə nan′drəs), *adj.* **1.** having only one husband at a time; characterized by monandry: *a monandrous society.* **2.** (of a flower) having only one stamen. **3.** (of a plant) having such flowers. [< Greek *mónandros* (with English *-ous*) < *mónos* single, one + *anḗr, andrós* husband]

mo·nan·dry (mə nan′drē), *n.* **1.** the custom or condition of having only one husband at a time. **2.** the condition of having but one perfect stamen.

mo·nan·thous (mə nan′thəs), *adj.* (of a plant) single-flowered; bearing one flower on each stalk. [< Greek *mónos* single + *ánthos* flower + English *-ous*]

mon·arch (mon′ərk), *n.* **1.** a king, queen, emperor, etc.; ruler. A monarch is usually a hereditary sovereign with more or less limited powers, but more often had sole and absolute powers in earlier times. **2.** a person or thing like a monarch: *The lion is the monarch of the jungle. Mont Blanc is the monarch of mountains* (Byron). **3.** a large, widely distributed, orange-and-black butterfly whose larvae feed on milkweed. The butterfly migrates south each fall. [< Late Latin *monarcha* < Greek *mónarchos* < *mónos* alone + *árchein* to rule]

mo·nar·chal (mə när′kəl), *adj.* **1.** of or having to do with a monarch: *monarchal power, a monarchal retinue.* **2.** characteristic of a monarch: *a monarchal aloofness.* **3.** suitable for a monarch: *monarchal ceremony.* **4.** having the status of a monarch: *monarchal rank.* —**mo·nar′chal·ly,** *adv.*

mon·ar·chess (mon′ər kis), *n.* a woman monarch.

mo·nar·chi·al (mə när′kē əl), *adj.* monarchal.

mo·nar·chi·an (mə när′kē ən), *n.* an early Christian believer in monarchianism.

mo·nar·chi·an·ism (mə när′kē ə niz′əm), *n.* the theological doctrine that God is one being, not a Trinity. Monarchianism was current during the 100's and 200's A.D.

mo·nar·chi·an·ist (mə när′kē ə nist), *n.* monarchian.

mo·nar·chic (mə när′kik), *adj.* monarchical.

mo·nar·chi·cal (mə när′kə kəl), *adj.* **1.** of a monarch or monarchy. **2.** favoring a monarchy. **3.** like a monarch or monarchy. —**mo·nar′chi·cal·ly,** *adv.*

mon·ar·chism (mon′ər kiz əm), *n.* **1.** the principles of monarchy. **2.** the advocacy of monarchical principles.

mon·ar·chist (mon′ər kist), *n.* a person who supports or favors government by a monarch: *Some monarchists . . . envisage the possibility that Don Juan himself may be eventually accepted by General Franco as a candidate for the throne* (New York Times). —*adj.* monarchistic.

mon·ar·chis·tic (mon′ər kis′tik), *adj.* of or having to do with monarchism. —**mon′ar·chis′ti·cal·ly,** *adv.*

mon·ar·chize (mon′ər kīz), *v.i., v.t.,* **-chized, -chiz·ing.** to rule as or like a monarch.

mon·ar·chy (mon′ər kē), *n., pl.* **-chies. 1.** government by a monarch. In a monarchy supreme power is formally vested in a single person. *There were those who accused him of wanting to establish a monarchy with himself as king* (Newsweek). **2.** a nation governed by a monarch. **3.** *Obsolete.* absolute rule by a single person. [< Middle French *monarchie,* learned borrowing from Late Latin *monarchia* < Greek *monarchíā* < *mónos* alone, single + *árchein* to rule]

mo·nar·da (mə när′də), *n.* any of a group of North American aromatic herbs of the mint family, as the Oswego tea or the horsemint. [American English < New Latin *Monarda* the genus name < N. *Monardez,* 1493-1588, a Spanish botanist]

mon·as (mon′as, mō′nas), *n., pl.* **mon·a·des.** monad. [< Late Latin *monas* monad]

mon·as·te·ri·al (mon′ə stir′ē əl), *adj.* of or characteristic of a monastery.

mon·as·ter·y (mon′ə ster′ē), *n., pl.* **-ter·ies. 1.** a building or buildings where (usually) monks or (sometimes) nuns live a contemplative life according to fixed rules and under religious vows. **2.** the group of persons living in such a place: *a monastery of 85.* [< Late Latin *monastērium* < Greek *monastḗrion* < *monázein* to live alone. Doublet of MINSTER.] —**Syn. 1.** cloister, convent.

mo·nas·tic (mə nas′tik), *adj.* **1.** of monks or nuns: *monastic vows of poverty, chastity, and obedience.* **2.** of monasteries: *monastic architecture. He had visited . . . some monastic ruins in the county of Dumfries* (Scott). **3.** like that of monks or nuns; ascetic. —*n.* a member of a monastic order; monk: *monastics . . . who have retired to the sacred sites of Palestine* (Alexander Kinglake). [< Late Latin *monasticus* < Late Greek *monastikós* solitary, ultimately < *mónos* alone, single] —**mo·nas′ti·cal·ly,** *adv.*

mo·nas·ti·cal (mə nas′tə kəl), *adj.* monastic.

mo·nas·ti·cism (mə nas′tə siz əm), *n.* **1.** the system or condition of living according to fixed rules, in groups shut off from the world, and devoted to religion: *Here the Virgin sits serenely with hands folded across her breast in a gesture that sums up one of the great credos of monasticism: "Thy will be done"* (Time). **2.** the system of monasterial communities.

mo·nas·ti·cize (mə nas′tə sīz), *v.t.,* **-cized, -ciz·ing.** to make monastic.

mon·a·tom·ic (mon′ə tom′ik), *adj. Chemistry.* **1.** having one atom in the molecule. **2.** having one replaceable atom or group of atoms. **3.** univalent. [< *mon-* + *atom* + *-ic*]

mo·naul (mə nôl′), *n.* any of several East Indian pheasants. [< Hindustani *munāl*]

mon·au·ral (mon ôr′əl), *adj.* **1.** monophonic: *monaural recordings, monaural record players.* **2.** of, with, or for one ear: *a monaural hearing aid.* —**mon·au′ral·ly,** *adv.*

mon·ax·i·al (mon ak′sē əl), *adj.* **1.** having but one axis; uniaxial. **2.** *Botany.* having flowers growing directly from the main axis.

mon·ax·on (mon ak′son), *n.* a tiny, rod-shaped spicule found in sponges. [< *mon-* + *axon*]

mon·a·zite (mon′ə zīt), *n.* a phosphate of cerium and related rare-earth metals, found in small reddish or brownish crystals. [< German *Monazit* < Greek *monázein* be solitary (< *mónos* alone) + German *-it* -ite[1]]

mon·cher (môN sher′), *French.* my dear (masculine).

mon·dain (môN daN′), *French.* —*adj.* worldly; mundane. —*n.* a mundane person.

mon·daine (môN den′), *n. French.* a woman of the fashionable world or of society.

Mon·day (mun′dē, -dā), *n.* the second day of the week, following Sunday and coming before Tuesday. *Abbr.:* Mon. [Old English *mōnan dæg* the moon's day]

Mon·day·ish (mun′dē ish, -dā-), *adj.* affected with the indisposition typical of a Monday; exhausted or depressed: *Any Mondayish feeling the crew may have had after their weekend rest was dispelled during their outing* (London Times). —**Mon′day·ish·ness,** *n.*

Monday morning quarterback, *U.S. Slang.* **1.** a person who criticizes the errors of a football team after the game is over. **2.** a person who offers advice on how to avoid an error after the error has been committed: *President Eisenhower was talking to his Monday morning quarterback session of Senate leaders* (Birmingham News).

monde (môNd), *n. French.* **1.** the world. **2.** the world of society; the fashionable world. **3.** a particular social group or stratum: *haut monde, beau monde, etc.*

mon Dieu (môN dyœ′), *French.* my God (used as a mild interjection).

mo·ne·cious (mə nē′shəs), *adj.* monoecious.

Mo·né·gasque (mô nā gȧsk′), *n., adj. French.* Monacan.

Mo·nel metal (mō nel′), *Trademark.* a silver-colored metal made from copper (about 28 per cent), nickel (about 67 per cent), and small amounts of iron, manganese, and certain other metals. It does not rust, and is used especially in making bullets, in food handling, jewelry, etc. [< Ambrose *Monel,* president of the International Nickel Company when it introduced the metal]

mon·e·tar·i·ly (mon′ə ter′ə lē, mun′-), *adv.* as regards monetary affairs; from a monetary point of view; financially.

mon·e·tar·y (mon′ə ter′ē, mun′-), *adj.* **1.** of the money of a nation: *The American monetary system is based on the gold standard.* **2.** of money; pecuniary: *a monetary reward.* [< Late Latin *mōnetārius* < Latin *monēta;* see MONEY] —**Syn. 2.** See **financial.**

monetary unit, the unit of a currency taken as the standard of comparative value for that currency, as the dollar in the United States and Canada, and the pound in Great Britain.

mon·e·ti·za·tion (mon′ə tə zā′shən, mun′-), *n.* a monetizing.

mon·e·tize (mon′ə tīz, mun′-), *v.t.,* **-tized, -tiz·ing. 1.** to legalize as money; assign a specified value to (silver, gold, etc.). **2.** to coin into money: *to monetize gold or silver.*

mon·ey (mun′ē), *n., pl.* **mon·eys** or **mon·ies. 1.** current coin; gold, silver, or other metal made into coins; bank notes, etc., representing gold or silver; any medium of exchange, especially as issued by a government or authorized public authority: *an exhibit of money from different countries.* **2.** a particular form or denomination of money. **3.** a sum of money used for a particular purpose or belonging to a particular person: *Come back when your money's spent* (Rudyard Kipling). **4.** wealth; property of any kind having value that can be expressed in terms of money: *There is money in this contract. He agreed to pay the bill when certain moneys were realized. Wealth and money . . . are, in common language, considered in every respect synonymous* (Adam Smith). **5.** any object or material serving as a medium of exchange and a measure of value, as checks drawn on a bank, or nuggets or the dust of a precious metal: *Money in the United States consists primarily of checking accounts in the nation's banks* (World Book Annual). **6.** a money of account.

coin money, *Informal.* to become rich; have a prospering business: *The owners of horses and mules were coining money, transporting people to the fairground* (Charles Dudley Warner).

for my money, *Informal.* for my choice; in my opinion; as I see it: *Miss Day is, for our money, the most fetching star in screen musicals today* (Baltimore Sun).

in the money, *Slang.* **a.** in a winning position, especially in first, second, or third place in a horse or dog race: *That's too fast a pace for that kind of horse. She'll be lucky to finish in the money* (New York Times). **b.** having plenty of money: *Had it never occurred to him, as to most writers and artists who suddenly find themselves "in the money," to keep a reserve for tax purposes?* (Sunday Telegram).

make money, a. to get money: *The War Office ought not to make money out of, any more than they should subsidise, the rifle clubs* (Spectator). **b.** to become rich: *His ambition is to make money and retire young.*

money for jam, *British Slang.* something, especially money, that is very easily come by: *The task of the British salesman ought to be money for jam* (Homer Bigart).

out of the money, *Slang.* not in a winning position, especially in a horse or dog race: *Determine and Poona II . . . finished out of the money* (New Yorker).

[< Old French *moneie* < Latin *monēta* mint, money < *Jūnō Monēta* Juno the protectress (< *monēre* to warn), in whose temple money was coined. Doublet of MINT[2].]

➔ **money.** Exact sums of money are usually written in figures: *72¢; $4.98; $5; $168.75; $42,810.* Round sums are more likely to be written in words: *two hundred dollars, a million and a half dollars.* In factual writing with frequent references to sums of money, figures are often used throughout.

mon·ey·bag (mun′ē bag′), *n.* a bag for money.

moneybags, *Informal.* **a.** wealth; riches. **b.** a wealthy or avaricious person.

➔ **Moneybags,** meaning wealth, is plural in form and use. When *moneybags* means a wealthy person, it is plural in form and singular in use: *Old moneybags is finally giving a little money to charity.*

money belt, a belt with an inner flap or fold in which money can be secretly carried, usually under a person's clothing.

mon·ey·chang·er (mun′ē chān′jər), *n.* **1.** a person whose business it is to exchange money at a fixed or authorized rate, usually that of one country for that of another: *And Jesus went into the temple of God . . . and overthrew the tables of the money-changers* (Matthew 21:12). **2.** a banker; financier.

money cowry, the shell of a marine gastropod, used as money in parts of Asia and Africa.

money crop, *U.S.* a staple crop: *Cocoa . . . is the Gold Coast's major money crop* (New York Times).

mon·eyed (mun′ēd), *adj.* **1.** having money; wealthy: *the not too gracious bounty of moneyed relatives* (Thomas Carlyle). **2.** consisting of or representing money; derived from money: *moneyed resources.* Also, **monied.** —**Syn. 1.** rich.

mon·ey·er (mun′ē ər), *n.* **1.** a person authorized to coin money; minter. **2.** *Archaic.* a banker; financier: *F.B. moves among moneyers and City nobs* (Thackeray).

mon·ey·grub·ber (mun′ē grub′ər), *n.* a person sordidly devoted to making money or gaining wealth: *Emlen is a boor and an unscrupulous moneygrubber* (Atlantic).

mon·ey·lend·er (mun′ē len′dər), *n.* a person whose business is lending money at interest: *Understandably, the spurned student becomes a rich and ruthless moneylender* (Newsweek).

mon·ey·less (mun′ē lis), *adj.* without money; impecunious: *Her public coffers are moneyless* (R. Aastler).

mon·ey-mak·er (mun′ē mā′kər), *n.* **1.** a person who is skilled in getting money; one who is well paid: *Dr. Cary Middlecoff of Memphis, the country's No. 2 professional golf money-maker, finished second* (New York Times). **2.** a thing which yields pecuniary profit.

mon·ey-mak·ing (mun′ē mā′king), *n.* the acquisition of money. —*adj.* **1.** occupied in gaining wealth. **2.** yielding money; lucrative: *He sees the task of putting the slim, pale monthly on a money-making basis* (Time).

mon·ey·man (mun′ē man′), *n., pl.* **-men.** *Informal.* **1.** a person involved in finance; financier: *The moneymen of world finance are meeting in Washington for an accounting of the way their various governments have handled their monetary affairs* (Wall Street Journal). **2.** a financial backer; angel: *The rumpled character caught in the crush . . . had one of the most important parts in the show: he was the moneyman* (Time).

money market, 1. the market or field for the investment of money; the district or sphere within which financial operations are carried on: *Commercial paper is the money-market term for short-term borrowings of companies* (Wall Street Journal). **2.** the body of persons carrying on such operations: *Money-market observers . . . said they expected . . . only a moderate flow of funds from the U.S. to Britain* (Wall Street Journal).

mon·ey·mon·ger (mun′ē mung′gər, -mong′-), *n.* a dealer in money; moneylender.

money of account, a monetary denomination used in reckoning, especially one not issued as a coin. In the United States, the mill is a money of account but not a coin. The nickel is a coin, but not a money of account.

money order, an order for the payment of money. You can buy a money order at the post office and send it to a person in another city, who can get the money at the post office or a bank there.

money shell, a large, edible clam of the Pacific Coast of the United States; butter clam.

money spider, a small spider supposed to bring good luck in money or other matters to the person over whom it crawls.

money spinner, *British Informal.* a person, thing, or activity that brings in a lot of money: *The trees have a reputation as money spinners because of quick maturity at high prices* (London Times).

mon·ey·wort (mun′ē wėrt′), *n.* a creeping perennial plant of the primrose family, having roundish leaves and solitary, yellow, dark-spotted flowers. It is native to Europe and naturalized in the eastern United States.

Moneywort

mong (mong), *n. Australian Slang.* a dog of mixed breed; mongrel.

'mong (mung), *prep. Poetic.* among.

mon·ger (mung′gər, mong′-), *v.t.* **1.** to deal or traffic in. **2.** to spread (pernicious gossip, ill will, etc.). —*n.* a person who mongers; trafficker. [back formation < *mongering*]

-monger, *combining form.* **1.** a dealer in ——; person who sells ——: *Fishmonger = a dealer in fish.*
2. a person who exploits ——; person who spreads or busies himself with ——: *Scandalmonger = person who spreads scandal.*
[Old English *mangere,* ultimately < Latin *mangō, -ōnis* trader]

mon·ger·ing (mung′gər ing, mong′-), *n.* trading; trafficking (used especially as a second element in compounds): *All these . . . militant mongerings of moral half-truths* (Robert Louis Stevenson).

mon·ging (mung′ing), *n.* mongering.

Mon·gol (mong′gəl, -gol, -gōl), *n.* **1.** a member of the Asiatic people now inhabiting Mongolia and nearby parts of China and Siberia, but formerly extending into eastern Europe. **2.** a Mongolian. **3.** the language of the Mongols; Mongolian.
—*adj.* **1.** of this people. **2.** Mongolian.

Mon·go·li·an (mong gō′lē ən), *n.* **1.** a member of the yellow race living in Asia. Mongolians have slanting eyes, prominent cheekbones, a short, broad nose, and hair that is dark brown to brown-black. *The Chinese are Mongolians.* **2.** their language or languages. **3.** a native of Mongolia; Mongol. **4.** a person who has Mongolism.
—*adj.* **1.** of Mongolia, the Mongolians, or their languages. **2.** of or belonging to the yellow-skinned, straight-haired race of mankind. **3.** displaying characteristics of Mongolism.

Mongolian idiocy, Mongolism.

Mongolian race, Mongolians.

Mon·gol·ic (mong gol′ik), *adj.* Mongolian. —*n.* the Mongolian language.

Mon·gol·ism (mong′gə liz əm), *n.* a form of congenital idiocy characterized by a very low mentality and by abnormal body characteristics, including slanting eyes and a small, round head, flat at the back.

Mon·gol·oid (mong′gə loid), *adj.* **1.** resembling the Mongols; having characteristics of the Mongolian race. **2.** belonging to the Mongolian race.
—*n.* **1.** a person of Mongolian race. **2.** a person suffering from Mongolism: *Few Mongoloids have a mental age greater than that of a 4-year-old child* (World Book Encyclopedia).

mon·goose or **mon·goos** (mong′güs), *n., pl.* **-goos·es.** any of various slender, ferretlike carnivorous mammals of Africa and Asia (especially India), used for destroying rats, and noted for their ability to kill rats, cobras, and certain other poisonous snakes without being harmed: *The mongoose . . . is not immune to the venom of the cobra it fights* (Scientific American). Also, **mungoos, mungoose.** [< Marathi *mangūs*]

Mongoose (including tail, about 2 ft. long)

mon·grel (mung′grəl, mong′-), *n.* **1.** an animal or plant of mixed breed, especially a dog. **2.** a person not of pure race; the offspring of parents of different races or nationalities (used in an unfriendly way). **3.** anything of a haphazardly mixed nature. —*adj.* of mixed breed, race, origin, nature, etc.: *a mongrel speech that is half Spanish and half Indian. These mongrel pamphlets, part true, part false* (Thomas Fuller).
[earlier *mengrell;* perhaps influenced by obsolete *mong* mixture, Old English *gemang* mixture (compare AMONG) < *mengan* mix]

mon·grel·ism (mung′grə liz əm, mong′-), *n.* a mixture of different breeds; the condition of being of mixed breeds.

mon·grel·i·za·tion (mung′grə lə zā′shən, mong′-), *n.* the act or process of mixing different things, especially racial groups (used in an unfriendly way).

mon·grel·ize (mung′grə līz, mong′-), *v.t.,* **-ized, -iz·ing.** to mix various elements, especially the racial groups of (a country, region, etc.), usually to the injury of a dominant group of people (used in an unfriendly way).

'mongst (mungst), *prep. Poetic.* amongst.

mon·ied (mun′id), *adj.* moneyed.

mon·ies (mun′iz), *n.pl.* sums of money: *authorized by the charter to pay out monies.*

mon·i·ker or **mon·ick·er** (mon′ə kər), *n.* **1.** a person's name or signature. **2.** a nickname: *A civilizing influence has touched movie monikers* (Charlottesville Daily Progress). **3.** any mark or sign used as identification by a tramp. Also, **monaker.** [origin unknown]

mo·nil·i·al (mō nil′ē əl), *adj.* caused by one of a genus of pathogenic fungi: *monilial vaginitis.* [< Latin *monīle* necklace + English *-ial*]

mon·i·li·a·sis (mon′ə lī′ə sis, mō′nə-), *n.* **1.** an infection caused by a type of fungus, affecting different parts of the body, including the skin, mucous membrane, lungs, vagina, and gastrointestinal tract. **2.** mycosis of the digestive tract of poultry. [< Latin *monīle* necklace + English *-iasis* (because of the beaded appearance of the diseased tissue)]

mo·nil·i·form (mō nil′ə fôrm), *adj.* resembling a string of beads, as certain roots or pods, which have a series of swellings alternating regularly with contractions. [< Latin *monīle* necklace + English *-form*]

mon·ish (mon′ish), *v.t. Archaic.* to admonish.

mon·ism (mon′iz əm, mō′niz-), *n. Philosophy.* **1.** the doctrine that the universe can be explained by one substance or principle, as matter, mind, or some other single thing or force. **2.** the doctrine that reality is an indivisible, universal organism. [< New Latin *monismus* < Greek *mónos* single]

mon·ist (mon′ist, mō′nist), *n.* a person who believes in monism.

mo·nis·tic (mō nis′tik), *adj.* of or having to do with monism. —**mo·nis′ti·cal·ly,** *adv.*

mo·nis·ti·cal (mō nis′tə kəl), *adj.* monistic.

mo·ni·tion (mō nish′ən), *n.* **1.** admonition; warning: *sage monitions from his friends* (Jonathan Swift); *the monitions of Christianity* (Herman Melville). **2.** an official or legal notice: **a.** a formal court order or summons to appear and answer, as after a complaint has been filed, or to confirm title and silence adverse claims, or to commence a suit. **b.** a formal notice from a bishop to one of his subordinates to require the amendment of some ecclesiastical offense: *The bishop sent a monition to three clergymen.* [< Old French *monition,* learned borrowing from Latin *monitiō, -ōnis* < *monēre* to warn]

mon·i·tor (mon′ə tər), *n.* **1.** a pupil in school with special duties, such as helping to keep order and taking attendance. **2.** a person who gives advice or warning: *The Teamsters Union, which has been battling to rid itself of court-appointed monitors* (Wall Street Journal). **3.** something that reminds or gives warning: *Conscience . . . a most importunate monitor, paying no respect to persons and making cowards of us all* (Frederick Marryat). **4.** a low, armored warship, chiefly of the late 1800's, having one or more revolving turrets for guns. **5.** any of various large lizards of Africa, southern Asia, Australia, Indonesia, New Guinea, and the Solomon Islands. Monitors are from 4 to 10 feet long, have a forked tongue and the habit of swallowing their prey without chewing it, and exhibit other snakelike characteristics. They are the only living genus of their family, the Komodo dragon being the most familiar, and are known to have lived in America from the fossils found in Wyoming. *All of the zoo's tenants were at their best, but the . . . giant lizards or monitors virtually stole the show* (New York Times). **6.** a receiver or other device used for checking and listening to radio or television transmissions, telephone messages, etc.: *When a monitor or headphone connection is provided, it will be "live" even during recording* (Roy J. Hoopes).
—*v.t., v.i.* **1.** to check and listen to (radio or television transmissions, telephone messages, etc.) by using a receiver: *He noted that agency investigators have been monitoring broadcasts and telecasts since last fall* (Wall Street Journal). **2.** *Physics.* to test the intensity of radiations, especially of radiations produced by radioactivity. **3.** to check in order to control something: *Hearing aids now play a life-saving role in the operating room by monitoring the breathing of unconscious surgical patients* (Science News Letter).
[< Latin *monitor, -ōris* < *monēre* to admonish, warn]

mon·i·to·ri·al (mon′ə tôr′ē əl, -tōr′-), *adj.* **1.** of or having to do with a monitor: *monitorial duties.* **2.** using monitors. **3.** serving to admonish or warn. —**mon′i·to′ri·al·ly,** *adv.*

mon·i·tor·ship (mon′ə tər ship), *n.* the office, work, or period of service of a monitor: *He was compelled to raise the legal point because . . . he could not continue to serve while doubting the legality of the entire monitorship procedure* (Wall Street Journal).

mon·i·to·ry (mon′ə tôr′ē, -tōr′-), *adj., n., pl.* **-ries.** —*adj.* admonishing; warning: *He heard the monitory growl [of a dog]* (Wordsworth). *The mottoes of their families are monitory proverbs* (Emerson). —*n.* a letter containing admonition, as from the Pope or a bishop; monitory letter. [< Latin *monitōrius* < *monitor, -ōris* monitor] —**Syn.** *adj.* admonitory.

monitory letter, a monitory; letter containing admonition, sent by the Pope or a bishop.

monk (mungk), *n.* a man who gives up all worldly things and enters a monastery to live a life devoted to religion. Monks live either in solitude as hermits or as members of a religious order and are bound by the vows of poverty, celibacy, and obedience. [Old English *munuc* < Late Latin *monăchus* < Late Greek *monachós* monk < Greek, individual, solitary < *mónos* alone, single] —**Syn.** cenobite.

➤ Though the terms **monk** and **friar** are often used as synonyms, a *monk* specifically is a member of an order living a cloistered life; a *friar* is a member of a mendicant order.

monk·er·y (mung′kər ē), *n., pl.* **-er·ies. 1.** monasticism. **2.** a monastery. **3.** monks as a group.

monkeries, monastic practices or customs.

mon·key (mung′kē), *n., pl.* **-keys,** *v.,* **-keyed, -key·ing.** —*n.* **1.** any animal of the highest order of mammals, most closely allied to and resembling man and ranging from the anthropoid apes to the marmosets, but excluding man and, usually, the lemurs. **2.** any of the smaller mammals in this group, usually having a long tail, as distinguished from the chimpanzee, gorilla, or other large ape. **3.** a person, especially a child, who is full of mischief. **4.** the fur of various long-haired monkeys, often used as trimming. **5.** any of various machines or implements, especially the heavy hammer or ram of a pile driver. **6.** a small passageway in a coal mine.

Rhesus Monkey (def. 1 — including tail, about 2 ft. long)

make a monkey (out) of, *Informal.* to make (a person) look foolish; make a fool of: *He had mocked the laws and made monkeys out of the lawmen* (Time).

monkey on one's back, *U.S. Slang.* **a.** the burden of drug addiction: *The patient goes back on drugs again . . ., more convinced than ever that the monkey on his back can't be removed by any means* (Wall Street Journal). **b.** any strong addiction viewed as a burden: *Smokers may not have a full-sized monkey on their back but what they do have is just as hard to get rid of* (New Yorker). **c.** any intolerable burden: *Sometimes the pseudo-liberal can become a monkey on your back* (Floyd McKissick).

—*v.i. Informal.* to play in a mischievous way; fool; trifle: *He didn't think much of the thing, and never monkeyed with it* (Harper's).

—*v.t.* to copy, as monkeys do; mimic; ape.

[probably < Middle Low German *Moneke,* son of Martin the Ape in the *Romance of Reynard*] —**mon′key·like′,** *adj.*

monkey bars, *Informal.* jungle gym.

monkey board, a platform high in an oil derrick, on which a worker helps with the drilling operation.

monkey bread, 1. the fruit of the baobab, eaten by monkeys. **2.** the tree itself.

monkey business, *U.S. Slang.* trickery; fraud; deceit.

monkey cup, a pitcher plant of the Old World.

monkey engine, 1. a form of pile driver having a ram or monkey working in a wooden frame. **2.** the engine which lifts such a ram or monkey.

mon·key-faced owl (mung′kē fāst′), the American barn owl.

monkey flower, any of a group of plants and small shrubs of the figwort family, often grown for their brilliant flowers, which are spotted so as to suggest a grimace, as a Chilean species with deep-yellow flowers and the musk plant, native to the western United States.

mon·key·ish (mung′kē ish), *adj.* like a monkey, especially in imitativeness or mischievousness: *He drinks and smokes in a monkeyish way* (Dickens).

mon·key·ism (mung′kē iz əm), *n.* monkey-like character or behavior.

monkey jacket, a short, close-fitting jacket of heavy, coarse material, formerly worn by sailors.

monkey nut, *British.* the peanut.

mon·key·pot (mung′kē pot′), *n.* **1.** the large, woody, urn-shaped fruit, containing several edible seeds, of any of various large tropical trees. **2.** any of these trees, related to the Brazil nut tree.

monkey puzzle, an evergreen tree, a variety of araucaria native to Chile, having stiff, twisted branches and edible nuts.

mon·key·shine (mung′kē shīn′), *n. U.S. Slang.* a mischievous trick; clownish joke: *Recent weather monkeyshines hereabouts suggest that the polar air blanket may have moved south already* (Baltimore Sun).

monkey suit, *U.S. Slang.* **1.** a uniform: *. . . busboys in scarlet monkey suits* (Time). **2.** a dress suit: [*He*] *buys* [*a*] *monkey suit to serve as best man* (Saturday Review).

monkey wrench, a wrench with a movable jaw that can be adjusted to fit different sizes of nuts.

throw a monkey wrench into, *Informal.* to interfere with; subvert; destroy: *The amiable, blubber-eating Eskimos throw a monkey wrench into the dietary fat theory. In Alaska, they live for months at a time on the fat of island seal and whale, but even among their oldsters fatal atherosclerosis is rare* (Time).

monk fish, the goosefish, or angler.

Mon-Khmer (mōn′kmer′), *adj.* of a linguistic family of monosyllabic languages of southeastern Asia. It includes one great cultural language, Annamite, used by 14 million people.

monk·hood (mungk′hůd), *n.* **1.** the condition or profession of a monk. **2.** monks as a group.

monk·ish (mung′kish), *adj.* **1.** of a monk; having to do with monks or monasticism. **2.** like a monk; characteristic of a monk. **3.** like monks or their way of life (often used in an unfriendly way): *William of Occam was a monkish philosopher* (Sunday Times). —**monk′ish·ly,** *adv.* —**monk′ish·ness,** *n.*

monk's cloth, 1. a heavy worsted fabric in a basket weave, used for monks' garments. **2.** a similar fabric of cotton used for draperies, etc.

monks·hood (mungks′hůd′), *n.* a kind of aconite, so called from its hooded flowers.

mon·o[1] (mon′ō), *adj.* monophonic.

mon·o[2] (mon′ō), *n. Slang.* mononucleosis.

mono-, *combining form.* one; single: *Monorail = a single rail. Monosyllable = one syllable.* Also, sometimes **mon-** before vowels. [< Greek *mónos* single, one]

mon·o·ac·id (mon′ō as′id), *adj.* **1.** (of a base or alcohol) having one hydroxyl (-OH) group that can be replaced by an atom or radical of an acid to form a salt or ester. **2.** having one acid atom of hydrogen per molecule.

—*n.* an acid containing only one replaceable hydrogen atom. Also, **monacid.**

mon·o·a·cid·ic (mon′ō ə sid′ik), *adj.* monoacid.

mon·o·a·mine oxidase (mon′ō ə mēn′, -am′in), an enzyme present in animal and plant tissue which oxidizes and destroys amines such as norepinephrine and serotonin: *The enzyme monoamine oxidase . . . helps control blood pressure* (Science News Letter).

mon·o·ba·sic (mon′ō bā′sik), *adj.* **1. a.** (of an acid) having but one atom of hydrogen that can be replaced by an atom or radical of a base in forming salts. **b.** having one basic hydroxyl (-OH) radical per molecule. **c.** (of a salt) having one basic atom or radical which can replace a hydrogen atom of an acid. **2.** *Biology.* being the sole type of its group; monotypic.

mon·o·bath (mon′ə bath′, -bäth′), *n. Photography.* a solution in which film can be developed and fixed in one continuous procedure: *The projected monobath would allow processing in a tenth the time and a third the space now required* (Science News Letter).

mon·o·ca·ble (mon′ə kā′bəl), *n.* **1.** a single cable serving as a complete track: [*The*] *monocable . . . both supports and moves the cars* (D.L. Turner). **2.** an aerial railway having such a cable.

mon·o·carp (mon′ə kärp), *n.* a plant that bears fruit only once during its lifetime. [< *mono-* + Greek *karpós* fruit]

mon·o·car·pel·lar·y (mon′ə kär′pə ler′ē), *adj. Botany.* having or consisting of a single carpel.

mon·o·car·pic (mon′ə kär′pik), *adj.* producing fruit but once, then dying: *All annual and biennial plants are monocarpic.*

mon·o·car·pous (mon′ə kär′pəs), *adj.* **1.** (of a flower) having a gynoecium that forms only a single ovary. **2.** monocarpic.

mon·o·cel·lu·lar (mon′ə sel′yə lər), *adj.* unicellular.

Mo·noc·er·os (mə nos′ər əs), *n., genitive* **Mo·no·cer·o·tis.** a constellation near Orion. [< Latin *monoceros* (literally) unicorn (< Greek *monókerōs* < *mónos* one + *kéras* horn) + English *-ous*]

Mo·noc·er·o·tis (mə nos′ə rō′tis), *n.* genitive of **Monoceros.**

mon·o·cha·si·al (mon′ə kā′zhē əl, -zē-), *adj.* having to do with or like a monochasium.

mon·o·cha·si·um (mon′ə kā′zhē əm, -zē-), *n., pl.* **-si·a** (-zhē ə, -zē ə). *Botany.* a cyme in which the main axis produces only a single branch. [< New Latin *monochasium* < Greek *mónos* one + *chásis* chasm, separation (< *chaínein* to yawn)]

mon·o·chla·myd·e·ous (mon′ō klə mid′ē-əs), *adj.* having a single instead of a double perianth, as certain flowers. [< *mono-* + Greek *chlamýs, -ydos* mantle + English *-ous*]

mon·o·chlo·ride (mon′ə klôr′īd, -id; -klōr′-), *n.* a chloride having one chlorine atom per molecule.

mon·o·chord (mon′ə kôrd), *n.* **1.** an instrument composed of a sounding board with a single string stretched over a bridge that can be moved along a graduated scale, used for the mathematical determination of musical intervals by the division of the string into two separately vibrating parts. **2.** *Rare.* harmony; agreement: *We hear a sound of sacred and spiritual music as solemn as the central monochord of the inner main itself* (Algernon Charles Swinburne). [< Middle French *monocorde* < Late Latin *monochordos* < Greek *mónos* one + *chordḗ* string, chord[1]]

mon·o·chro·ic (mon′ə krō′ik), *adj.* of one color; monochromatic: *Arterial blood is monochroic* (James Cagney). [< Greek *monóchroos* having one color (< *mónos* one + *chróā* color) + English *-ic*]

mon·o·chro·mat·ic (mon′ə krō mat′ik), *adj.* **1.** of one color only. **2.** (of light) consisting of one wave length: *The use of monochromatic light . . . does not improve the acuity of the eye to more than a very small extent* (Science News). **3.** producing such light. —**mon′o·chro·mat′i·cal·ly,** *adv.*

mon·o·chro·ma·tic·i·ty (mon′ə krō′mə-tis′ə tē), *n.* the state, degree, or quality of being monochromatic: *Its* [*the laser's*] *monochromaticity has given new precision to measurement* (New Scientist).

mon·o·chro·ma·tor (mon′ə krō′mə tər), *n.* an instrument which can isolate and transmit a beam of monochromatic, or nearly monochromatic, light, especially useful in analyzing radiation spectra: *The filtering element in my coronagraph is a quartz monochromator* (Scientific American).

mon·o·chrome (mon′ə krōm), *n.* **1.** a painting, drawing, print, etc., in a single color or shades of a single color; monotint: *The Elgin frieze is a monochrome in a state of transition to sculpture* (John Ruskin). **2.** a stretch or mass of a single color: *A profile was visible against the dull monochrome of cloud around her* (Thomas Hardy). **3.** the art of representation in one color.

—*adj.* **1.** having or providing one color only: *a monochrome picture.* **2.** black and white: *monochrome television.*

[< Medieval Latin *monochroma* < Greek *monochrômos* < *mónos* single + *chrôma* color; complexion; skin]

mon·o·chro·mic (mon′ə krō′mik), *adj.* of a single color.

mon·o·chro·mi·cal (mon′ə krō′mə kəl), *adj.* monochromic.

mon·o·chro·mist (mon′ə krō′mist), *n.* a person who paints or draws in monochrome: *The churches . . . of one unvaried stone colour . . . have been made over periodically to the tender mercies of the monochromist* (G. Gilbert Scott).

mon·o·cle (mon′ə kəl), *n.* an eyeglass for one eye. [< French *monocle,* learned borrowing from Late Latin *monoculus* one-eyed < Greek *mónos* single + Latin *oculus* eye]

mon·o·cled (mon′ə kəld), *adj.* wearing a monocle: *The author . . . here gives us the* *further adventures of his gay, monocled hero* (Daily Telegraph).

mon·o·cli·nal (mon′ə klī′nəl), *Geology.* —*adj.* **1.** (of strata) dipping or sloping in one direction. **2.** of or having to do with strata that dip in the same direction: *Hard rocks of the folded series make hogbacks, and weak strata form monoclinal valleys* (Raymond Cecil Moore). —*n.* a monocline. [< *mono-* + Greek *klīnein* to slope, bend + English *-al*[1]] —**mon′o·cli′nal·ly,** *adv.*

mon·o·cline (mon′ə klīn), *n.* a monoclinal rock formation or fold, such as the oblique portion of a belt of strata at the place where it changes from one horizontal position to another of different level.

mon·o·clin·ic (mon′ə klin′ik), *adj.* (of crystals or crystallization) characterized by three unequal axes with one oblique intersection: *Monoclinic crystals are very transparent and are shaped like prisms* (World Book Encyclopedia).

mon·o·cli·nous (mon′ə klī′nəs, mon′ə-klī′-), *adj.* **1.** (of a plant) having both stamens and pistils in the same flower. **2.** (of a flower) having both stamens and pistils. [< French *monocline* (< Greek *mónos* one + *klīnē* bed < *klīnein* to recline, slope) + English *-ous*]

mo·no·coque (mô nô kôk′), *n. French.* a type of structure, originally used in aircraft fuselages and now also in truck trailers, which relies on a stiffened, lightweight skin or shell of metal, veneer, plastic, etc., to bear the principal stresses: *The strength of a monocoque structure . . . depends upon the way the skin is attached to the stiffeners* (Wall Street Journal).

mon·o·cot (mon′ə kot), *n.* a monocotyledon.

mon·o·cot·yl (mon′ə kot′əl), *n.* a monocotyledon.

mon·o·cot·y·le·don (mon′ə kot′ə lē′dən), *n.* a plant with only one cotyledon. The monocotyledons, which include grasses, palms, lilies, irises, etc., make up one of the two large subclasses of plants that have the seeds enclosed in an ovary. *Botanists are impressed with the fact that the Polynesians divided the plant world into monocotyledons and dicotyledons* (Scientific American). [< *mono-* + *cotyledon*]

mon·o·cot·y·le·don·ous (mon′ə kot′ə lē′-də nəs, -led′ə-), *adj.* having only one cotyledon: *The roots of monocotyledonous plants lack cambiums . . .* (Harbaugh and Goodrich).

mo·noc·ra·cy (mə nok′rə sē), *n., pl.* **-cies.** government by one person; autocracy: *A scene of wholesale bacchanalian fraud . . . which would disgust any man with a free government, and make him sigh for the monocracy of Constantinople* (Sydney Smith).

mon·o·crat (mon′ə krat), *n.* **1.** an autocrat: *Mr. Ames, the colossus of the monocrats and paper men, will either be left out or hard run* (Thomas Jefferson). **2.** a supporter of monocracy or monarchy. [American English (apparently coined by Thomas Jefferson to describe extreme Federalists) < Greek *monokratēs* ruling alone < *mónos* alone + *krateîn* rule]

mon·o·crat·ic (mon′ə krat′ik), *adj.* having to do with monocracy.

mon·o·crot·ic (mon′ə krot′ik), *adj.* **1.** denoting the single heartbeat that occurs during systole in the normal pulse. **2.** having to do with such a pulse. [< *mono-* + Greek *krótos* beat + English *-ic*]

mo·noc·ro·tism (mə nok′rə tiz əm), *n.* monocrotic condition.

mo·noc·u·lar (mə nok′yə lər), *adj.* **1.** having to do with or intended for use by one eye only: *The bird's perception of depth and distance was believed to be entirely dependent upon monocular cues* (Scientific American). **2.** having only one eye or eyepiece. —*n.* any monocular instrument. [< Late Latin *monoculus* one-eyed (< Greek *mónos* single + Latin *oculus* eye) + English *-ar*] —**mo·noc′u·lar·ly,** *adv.*

mon·o·cul·tur·al (mon′ə kul′chər əl), *adj.* of, having to do with, or characteristic of monoculture: *The livelihood of monocultural Zanzibar and Pemba . . . lies . . . in Indonesia, which takes 80 per cent of their cloves to make scented cigarettes* (Economist). —**mon′o·cul′tur·al·ly,** *adv.*

mon·o·cul·ture (mon′ə kul′chər), *n.* growing only one product: *Concentrate on grain monoculture and you are looking for trouble* (Cape Times).

mon·o·cy·cle (mon′ə sī′kəl), *n.* a unicycle: *Is he going to give us a monocycle act?* (Punch).

mon·o·cy·clic (mon′ə sī′klik, -sik′lik), *adj.* **1.** having a single circle or cycle. **2.** *Biology.* having a single whorl or series of parts, as certain crinoids with a single circlet of basal plates. **3.** *Chemistry.* having one ring (of atoms).

mon·o·cyte (mon′ə sīt), *n.* one of the major types of leucocytes in the blood, being the largest in size and comprising about 3 to 8 per cent of the total white blood cells: *They grew Brucella bacteria in tissue cultures of guinea pig monocytes without finding signs of a reduced number of organisms* (Science News Letter). [< *mono-* + *-cyte*]

mon·o·cyt·ic (mon′ə sit′ik), *adj.* of, having to do with, or characteristic of a monocyte.

mon·o·cy·to·sis (mon′ə sī tō′sis), *n.* a fatal disease of domestic fowl, characterized by cyanosis of the comb and wattles; blue comb. [< *monocyt*(e) + *-osis*]

mon·o·dac·tyl (mon′ə dak′təl), *adj.* monodactylous.

mon·o·dac·ty·lous (mon′ə dak′tə ləs), *adj.* having only one finger, toe, or claw. [< Greek *monodáktylos* (with English *-ous*) < *mónos* single + *dáktylos* finger]

mo·nod·ic (mə nod′ik), *adj.* of, having to do with, or like a monody; homophonic: *The new art of monodic writing, as opposed to the elaborate involutions of the madrigalian period . . .* (J.A.F. Maitland). [< Greek *monōdikós* < *monōidíā* monody] —**mo·nod′i·cal·ly,** *adv.*

mo·nod·i·cal (mə nod′ə kəl), *adj.* monodic.

mon·o·dist (mon′ə dist), *n.* a person who composes or sings a monody.

mon·o·dra·ma (mon′ə drä′mə, -dram′ə), *n.* a play or other dramatic piece for a single performer.

mon·o·dra·mat·ic (mon′ə drə mat′ik), *adj.* of or characteristic of a monodrama.

mon·o·dy (mon′ə dē), *n., pl.* **-dies. 1.** a mournful song; lament; dirge. **2.** a plaintive poem in which one person laments another's death: *In this Monody the Author bewails a learned Friend, unfortunately drowned* (Milton). **3. a.** a style of musical composition in which one part or melody predominates; homophony. **b.** a composition written in this style. **4.** a Greek ode sung by a single voice, as by an actor in a tragedy. [< Late Latin *monōdia* < Greek *monōidíā* < *monodós* singing alone < *mónos* single + *ōidē* ode]

mo·noe·cious (mə nē′shəs, mō-), *adj.* **1.** *Botany.* having the stamens and pistils in separate flowers on the same plant: *Corn, birches, and walnuts are monoecious plants.* **2.** *Zoology.* having both male and female organs in the same individual; hermaphroditic. Also, **monecious, monoicous.** [< New Latin *Monoecia* the class name (< Greek *mónos* single + *oikíā* dwelling place < *oîkos* property, house) + English *-ous*]

mon·o·en·er·get·ic (mon′ō en′ər jet′ik), *adj. Nuclear Physics.* (of radiation particles) having the same or nearly the same energy: *The Van de Graaf electrostatic accelerator . . . is used . . . for the production of monoenergetic fast neutron beams* (Bulletin of Atomic Scientists).

mon·o·eth·a·nol·a·mine (mon′ə eth′ə-nol′ə mēn, -nə lam′in), *n.* ethanolamine.

mon·o·fil·a·ment (mon′ə fil′ə mənt), *n.* a strand of yarn, plastic, wire, etc., composed of a single filament only, regardless of its thickness or weight: *Vyrene . . . is a silicone lubricated polyester monofilament* (New Scientist). —*adj.* made of one or more monofilaments: *a monofilament fishing line.*

mon·o·gam·ic (mon′ə gam′ik), *adj.* monogamous: *The monogamic family alone produces the highest type of affection, of altruistic love . . .* (Emory S. Bogardus).

mo·nog·a·mist (mə nog′ə mist), *n.* a person who practices, advocates, or believes in monogamy: *I valued myself upon being a strict monogamist* (Oliver Goldsmith). —*adj.* monogamous.

mo·nog·a·mis·tic (mə nog′ə mis′tik), *adj.* monogamous.

mo·nog·a·mous (mə nog′ə məs), *adj.* **1.** practicing or advocating monogamy: *We may now return to the criteria to be applied in drawing judgments concerning polygamous as against monogamous families . . .* (Melville J. Herskovits). **2.** of or having to do with monogamy: *Still, there are found among lower hunters a large number of strictly monogamous cultures, as in Pygmy tribes . . .* (Ogburn and Nimkoff). —**mo·nog′a·mous·ly,** *adv.* —**mo·nog′a·mous·ness,** *n.*

mo·nog·a·my (mə nog′ə mē), *n.* **1.** the practice or condition of being married to only one person at a time: *Monogamy . . . has been and is the leading type of marriage* (Emory S. Bogardus). **2.** (of animals) the habit of having only one mate. **3.** *Rare.* the custom or principle of marrying only once: *Moses and his spectacles, the Vicar and his monogamy . . . have caused . . . much harmless mirth* (Macaulay). [< Latin *monogamia* < Greek *monogamíā* < *mónos* single + *gámos* marriage]

mon·o·gen·e·sis (mon′ə jen′ə sis), *n.* the theory that all living things derive from a single, common origin.

mon·o·ge·net·ic (mon′ə jə net′ik), *adj.* **1.** of or having to do with monogenesis or monogenism; monogenic. **2.** having only a single host during the life cycle, as certain trematode worms. **3.** formed by one geological process: *a monogenetic mountain range.*

mon·o·gen·ic (mon′ə jen′ik), *adj.* **1.** *Biology.* monogenetic. **2.** *Zoology.* reproducing by only one method.

mo·nog·e·nism (mə noj′ə niz əm), *n.* the theory that all human beings have descended from a single pair.

mo·nog·e·nist (mə noj′ə nist), *n.* a believer in monogenism.

mo·nog·e·ny (mə noj′ə nē), *n.* monogenism.

mon·o·glot (mon′ə glot), *adj.* **1.** using or understanding only one language. **2.** written in only one language. —*n.* a person who knows only one language: *What ad. could be more helpful . . . to the monoglot abroad for the first time in Paris?* (Punch). [< Greek *monóglōttos* < *mónos* single + *glôtta* tongue]

mon·o·glyc·er·ide (mon′ə glis′ə rīd, -ər-id), *n.* any of various glycerides containing only a single hydroxyl or acid molecule, used as an emulsifier in bread and other products: *Monoglycerides give the crumb softness* (Science News Letter).

monogr., monograph.

mon·o·gram (mon′ə gram), *n.* a person's initials combined in one design. Monograms are used on note paper, table linen, clothing, jewelry, etc. [< Late Latin *monogramma* < Late Greek *monogrammon,* neuter, consisting of a single letter < Greek *mónos* single + *grámma* letter]

Monogram

mon·o·gram·mat·ic (mon′ə grə mat′ik), *adj.* having to do with or in the form of a monogram.

mon·o·grammed (mon′ə gramd), *adj.* bearing a monogram.

mon·o·graph (mon′ə graf, -gräf), *n.* a book or article, especially a scholarly one, written on a particular, narrowly limited subject: *D. O. Hebb's recent monograph on behaviour theory was an attempt to build a bridge between physiology and psychology* (F. H. George). —*v.t.* to write a monograph on; treat in a monograph: *This extraordinary object . . . has been monographed, mapped, measured, figured, and photographed* (A.M. Clerke). [< *mono-* + *-graph*] —**Syn.** *n.* treatise.

mo·nog·ra·pher (mə nog′rə fər), *n.* a writer of a monograph or monographs: *Few existing birds offer a better subject for a monographer* [*than the kakapo*] (Charles T. Newton).

mon·o·graph·ic (mon′ə graf′ik), *adj.* **1.** having to do with or like a monograph. **2.** monogrammatic. —**mon′o·graph′i·cal·ly,** *adv.*

mo·nog·y·nous (mə noj′ə nəs), *adj.* **1.** having but one wife at a time. **2.** characterized by monogyny: *a monogynous condition.* **3.** *Botany.* **a.** (of a flower) having only one pistil or style. **b.** (of a plant) having such flowers.

mo·nog·y·ny (mə noj′ə nē), *n.* the practice or the condition of having only one wife at a time. [< *mono-* + Greek *gynē* woman, female + *-y*[3]]

mon·o·hy·brid (mon′ə hī′brid), *n.* the offspring of parents who differ in a single gene or character. —*adj.* of, having to do with, or characteristic of a monohybrid.

mon·o·hy·drate (mon′ə hī′drāt), *n.* a chemical compound in which each molecule unites with one molecule of water: . . . *this maker of bicarbonate and monohydrate of soda* (Wall Street Journal).

mon·o·hy·dric (mon′ə hī′drik), *adj.* **1.**

containing a single hydroxyl (-OH) group, as an alcohol. **2.** containing one replaceable atom of hydrogen.

mo·noi·cous (mə noi′kəs), *adj.* monoecious.

mon·o·ki·ni (mon′ə kē′nē), *n.* a very scant one-piece bathing suit. [< *mono-* + (bi)*kini*]

mo·nol·a·ter (mə nol′ə tər), *n.* a person who worships but one god. [< *monolatry;* patterned on *idolater*]

mo·nol·a·trist (mə nol′ə trist), *n.* a monolater.

mo·nol·a·trous (mə nol′ə trəs), *adj.* of or having to do with monolatry.

mo·nol·a·try (mə nol′ə trē), *n.* the worship of but one god when other gods are nonetheless believed to exist. [< *mono-* + Greek *latreíā* worship]

mon·o·lay·er (mon′ə lā′ər), *n.* a monomolecular layer: *The radioactive monolayers . . . would be used instead of fuel* (New York Times). *—adj.* monomolecular.

mon·o·lin·gual (mon′ə ling′gwəl), *adj.* limited to the knowledge or use of only one language: *monolingual Americans. Bibliography of Monolingual Scientific and Technical Glossaries* (New Scientist). [< *mono-* + Latin *lingua* tongue + English *-al*[1]]

mon·o·lith (mon′ə lith), *n.* **1.** a single large block of stone, especially one forming a monument or used for building or sculpture: *Beacon Rock, an 850-foot monolith . . .* (New York Times). **2.** a monument, column, statue, etc., formed of a single large block of stone. **3.** a nation, political party, culture, etc., that is single, uniform, undifferentiated, and massive, and consequently rigid and unyielding in its attitudes and policies: *Here is a world in which Russia is a constant, a monolith, at best an enigma* (Economist).

—adj. consisting or formed of a single block of stone.

[< Latin *monolithus,* adjective < Greek *monólithos* < *mónos* single + *líthos* stone]

mon·o·lith·ic (mon′ə lith′ik), *adj.* **1.** of, having to do with, or like a monolith. **2.** consisting of monoliths: *a monolithic circle.* **3.** massively uniform, as when individuals are absolutely subservient to the state: *a monolithic society, a monolithic state.* **—mon′o·lith′i·cal·ly,** *adv.*

mon·o·lith·ism (mon′ə lith′iz əm), *n.* the state or quality of being monolithic: *It now seems clear that we are not headed for any monolithic world, Communist or American; or for a world divided into two monolithisms, the one part Communist and the other part American* (William G. Carleton).

mon·o·log (mon′ə lôg, -log), *n.* monologue.

mon·o·log·ic (mon′ə loj′ik), *adj.* of, characterized by, or like a monologue. **—mon′o·log′i·cal·ly,** *adv.*

mon·o·log·i·cal (mon′ə loj′ə kəl), *adj.* monologic.

mon·o·log·ist (mon′ə lôg′ist, -log′-), *n.* **1.** a person who talks or acts in monologue, or delivers monologues: *The comedian, a hayseed monologist . . .* (Newsweek). **2.** a person who monopolizes conversation.

mo·nol·o·gize (mə nol′ə jīz), *v.i.,* **-gized, -giz·ing.** to talk in monologue; give a monologue: *They come out of the clinches monologizing* (Time).

mon·o·logue (mon′ə lôg, -log), *n.* **1.** a long speech by one person in a group, especially a stubborn or aggressive one: *Mrs. Ellison's monologue ran on with scarcely a break from Kitty* (William Dean Howells). **2.** an entertainment by a single person. **3.** a play for a single actor. **4.** a scene or part of a play in which a single actor speaks alone. **5.** a poem or other composition in which a single person speaks alone: *Browning was master of the dramatic monologue.* [< French *monologue* < Medieval Greek *monologos* < Greek *mónos* single + *lógos* speech, discourse]

mon·o·logu·ist (mon′ə lôg′ist, -log′-), *n.* monologist: *The show is weak in comedy, despite the presence of two personable comic monologuists* (New Yorker).

mon·o·logu·ize (mon′ə lôg′īz, -log′-), *v.i.,* **-ized, -iz·ing.** monologize.

mo·nol·o·gy (mə nol′ə jē), *n., pl.* **-gies. 1.** the habit of talking to oneself. **2.** a monologue.

mo·nom·a·chist (mə nom′ə kist), *n.* a person who fights in single combat; duelist.

mo·nom·a·chy (mə nom′ə kē), *n., pl.* **-chies.** a fight or contest between single combatants. [< Latin *monomachia* < Greek *monomachíā* < *mónos* single + *máchē* duel]

mon·o·ma·ni·a (mon′ə mā′nē ə), *n.* **1.** mental disorder in which the patient's behavior is controlled by a single idea or emotion: *In "Moby Dick," Captain Ahab's pursuit of the white whale is an example of monomania.* **2.** an interest or tendency so dominant and obsessive as to seem pathologic. **3.** a dominant interest: *I call it my monomania, it is such a subject of mine* (Dickens). [< *mono-* + *mania;* patterned on French *monomanie*]

mon·o·ma·ni·ac (mon′ə mā′nē ak), *n.* a person whose behavior is characterized by monomania. *—adj.* monomaniacal.

mon·o·ma·ni·a·cal (mon′ə mə nī′ə kəl), *adj.* **1.** of or having to do with monomania. **2.** characterized by monomania: *For his monomaniacal follies, he is everywhere guffawed at* (Time). **—mon′o·ma·ni′a·cal·ly,** *adv.*

mon·o·mer (mon′ə mər), *n.* a chemical compound existing in unpolymerized form: *If the monomer contains more than one double bond, then a network is likely to form* (Michaela Leitner). [< *mono-* + Greek *méros* part]

mon·o·mer·ic (mon′ə mer′ik), *adj.* of or like a monomer: . . . *the new formulation contains a polymeric plasticizer, instead of the more usual monomeric variety* (New Scientist).

mo·nom·er·ous (mə nom′ər əs), *adj.* (of a flower) having one member in each whorl (sometimes written *1-merous*). [< New Latin *monomerus* (with English *-ous*) < Greek *monomerḗs* < *mónos* single + *méros* part]

mon·o·me·tal·lic (mon′ə mə tal′ik), *adj.* **1.** using one metal only. **2.** of, having to do with, or characterized by monometallism.

mon·o·met·al·lism (mon′ə met′ə liz əm), *n.* **1.** the use of one metal only, such as gold or silver, as the standard of money values. **2.** beliefs or policies in support of such a use.

mon·o·met·al·list (mon′ə met′ə list), *n.* an advocate of monometallism.

mon·o·met·ric (mon′ə met′rik), *adj. Crystallography.* isometric.

mo·no·mi·al (mō nō′mē əl), *adj.* **1.** *Algebra.* consisting of a single term. **2.** *Biology.* (of a name) consisting of a single word.

—n. **1.** *Algebra.* a monomial expression. In the expression $2x^2 + 3ax - \frac{3a}{b}$, $2x^2$, $3ax$, and $\frac{3a}{b}$ are monomials. **2.** *Biology.* a monomial name.

[< *mono-* + *-nomial,* patterned on *binomial*]

mon·o·mo·lec·u·lar (mon′ō mə lek′yə lər), *adj.* of or having to do with one molecule; one molecule in thickness: *a monomolecular layer.* **—mon′o·mo·lec′u·lar·ly,** *adv.*

monomolecular film, a film one molecule thick; molecular film.

mon·o·mor·phic (mon′ə môr′fik), *adj. Biology.* having only one form; having the same form throughout development. [< *mono-* + Greek *morphḗ* form + English *-ic*]

mon·o·mor·phism (mon′ə môr′fiz əm), *n.* monomorphic condition or character.

mon·o·mor·phous (mon′ə môr′fəs), *adj.* monomorphic.

mon·o·nu·cle·ar (mon′ə nü′klē ər, -nyü′-), *adj.* having only a single nucleus.

mon·o·nu·cle·o·sis (mon′ə nü′klē ō′sis, -nyü′-), *n.* **1.** a condition characterized by an abnormal increase in the number of mononuclear leucocytes in the blood: *Every couple of years he comes down with mononucleosis, a disease that is generally attributed to fatigue* (New Yorker). **2.** infectious mononucleosis; glandular fever.

mon·o·nu·cle·o·tide (mon′ə nü′klē ə tīd, -nyü′-), *n.* a principal constituent of nucleic acid; nucleotide.

mon·o·pet·al·ous (mon′ə pet′ə ləs), *adj. Botany.* **1.** having the corolla composed of united petals, as in the morning-glory; gamopetalous. **2.** (of a corolla) having only a single petal.

Monopetalous Flower (def. 1)

mon·o·phase (mon′ə fāz), *adj. Electricity.* single-phase.

mon·o·pho·bi·a (mon′ə fō′bē ə), *n.* an abnormal fear of being alone. [< *mono-* + *-phobia*]

mon·o·phon·ic (mon′ə fon′ik), *adj.* **1.** designating music sung or played in unison without accompaniment. **2.** monodic. **3.** homophonic. **4.** having to do with or characterizing the reproduction of sound by means of a single channel, without auditory perspective: *Stereo aims at a more full-bodied representation of sound than the older-type monophonic record gives* (Wall Street Journal).

—n. **1.** a monophonic sound reproduction. **2.** the system or apparatus reproducing monophonic sound.

[< *mono-* + Greek *phōnḗ* voice + English *-ic*] **—mon′o·phon′i·cal·ly,** *adv.*

mo·noph·o·ny (mə nof′ə nē), *n.* **1.** a monophonic sound reproduction; monophonic: *Stereo has a compulsive force that monophony has not; you are made to want to turn toward the source of the music* (Atlantic). **2.** homophony: *The decline of culture in musical terms—if you will excuse a bit of my own historicism—is the devolution from polyphony to monophony* (Igor Stravinsky).

mon·o·phote (mon′ə fōt), *adj.* of or having to do with an arc lamp designed to be run alone on its own electric circuit, and not to be used in series with other lamps. [< *mono-* + Greek *phôs, phōtós* light]

mon·oph·thong (mon′əf thông, -thong), *n.* a single, simple vowel sound showing little or no change in quality throughout its duration. *Example: i* in *pin.* [< Greek *monóphthongos* with one sound < *mónos* single + *phthóngos* sound, voice]

mon·oph·thon·gal (mon′əf thông′gəl, -thong′-), *adj.* having to do with or consisting of a monophthong.

mon·oph·thong·ize (mon′əf thông īz, -thong-), *v.t.,* **-ized, -iz·ing.** to make into a monophthong.

mon·o·phy·let·ic (mon′ə fī let′ik), *adj.* descended from a single, common ancestral species, usually of the same type as the extant group: *monophyletic animals.* [< *mono-* + Greek *phȳletikós* of a tribe < *phȳlḗ* tribe]

mon·o·phyl·lous (mon′ə fil′əs), *adj. Botany.* **1.** consisting of one leaf: *a monophyllous calyx.* **2.** having only one leaf. [< Greek *monóphyllos* < *mónos* single + *phýllon* leaf (with English *-ous*)]

mon·o·phy·o·dont (mon′ə fī′ə dont), *adj.* having only one set of teeth. *—n.* a monophyodont animal. [< Greek *monophyḗs* single + *odoús, odóntos* tooth]

Mo·noph·y·site (mə nof′ə sīt), *n.* a person who believes that Christ has but one nature, or a single composite nature that is both divine and human: *The Coptic Church in Egypt . . . has been an independent Monophysite Church since the fifth century* (London Times). [< Late Latin *Monophysīta* < Late Greek *Monophysī́tēs* a believer in the "one nature" < Greek *mónos* one + *phýsis* nature]

Mon·o·phy·sit·ic (mon′ə fə sit′ik), *adj.* of or having to do with the Monophysites or their doctrines.

Mo·noph·y·sit·ism (mə nof′ə sī′tiz əm), *n.* the doctrines of the Monophysites.

mon·o·plane (mon′ə plān), *n.* any airplane with a single wing, usually divided into two parts by the fuselage: *In the mid-1920's the monoplane was established as the dominant type* (Atlantic).

mon·o·plan·ist (mon′ə plā′nist), *n.* the pilot of a monoplane.

mon·o·ple·gi·a (mon′ə plē′jē ə), *n.* paralysis of only one limb or a single muscle or muscle group. [< New Latin *monoplegia* < Greek *mónos* one + *-plegíā* < *plēgḗ* stroke]

mon·o·pleg·ic (mon′ə plej′ik, -plē′jik), *adj.* of or characterized by monoplegia.

mon·o·pode (mon′ə pōd), *adj.* having only one foot.

—n. **1.** a creature having only one foot or footlike organ. **2.** a monopodium. **3.** one of a legendary race of men who had only one foot, with which, it was believed, they shaded themselves from the sun.

[< Late Latin *monopodius* with one foot < Greek *monópous* < *mónos* single + *poús, podós* foot]

mon·o·po·di·al (mon′ə pō′dē əl), *adj.* of or like a monopodium.

mon·o·po·di·um (mon′ə pō′dē əm), *n., pl.* **-di·a** (-dē ə). *Botany.* a single main axis which continues to extend at the apex in the original line of growth, producing lateral branches beneath, such as the trunk of a pine tree. [< New Latin *monopodium,* neuter (diminutive) < Late Latin *monopodius;* see MONOPODE]

mon·o·po·lar (mon′ə pō′lər), *adj.* unipolar.

mon·o·po·lar·i·ty (mon′ə pō lar′ə tē), *n.* unipolarity.

mo·nop·o·lise (mə nop′ə līz), *v.t.,* **-lised, -lis·ing.** *Especially British.* monopolize: *So long as 85 million of Indonesia's 85 million people live in crowded Java and monopolise the wealth of Indonesia, . . .* (Economist).

mo·nop·o·lism (mə nop′ə liz əm), *n.* the existence or prevalence of monopolies: *The two great national parties . . . denounce monopolism in the abstract* (James Bryce).

mo·nop·o·list (mə nop′ə list), *n.* **1.** a person who has a monopoly: *to raise the value of the possessions in the hands of the great private monopolists* (Edmund Burke). *The monopolists of political power* (John Bright). **2.** a person who favors monopoly.

mo·nop·o·lis·tic (mə nop′ə lis′tik), *adj.* **1.** that monopolizes. **2.** having to do with monopolies or monopolists: *To curb monopolistic abuses, the Interstate Commerce Act was passed in 1887* (Wall Street Journal). —**mo·nop′o·lis′ti·cal·ly,** *adv.*

mo·nop·o·li·za·tion (mə nop′ə lə zā′shən), *n.* **1.** the act or process of monopolizing: *The Justice Department appears to believe . . . [the corporation] is on the brink of illegal monopolization of the . . . industry* (Wall Street Journal). **2.** a being monopolized.

mo·nop·o·lize (mə nop′ə līz), *v.t.,* **-lized, -liz·ing. 1.** to have or get exclusive possession or control of: *This firm practically monopolizes the production of linen thread.* **2.** to occupy wholly; keep entirely to oneself: *to monopolize a person's time. The few tolerable rooms are monopolized by the friends and favourites of the house* (Tobias Smollett). —**mo·nop′o·liz′er,** *n.*

mo·nop·o·ly (mə nop′ə lē), *n., pl.* **-lies. 1.** exclusive control of a commodity or service: *In most communities, the telephone company has a monopoly. You have, in this Kingdom, an advantage in lead, that amounts to a monopoly* (Edmund Burke). **2.** such control granted by a government: *An inventor has a monopoly on his invention for a certain number of years. Raleigh held a monopoly of cards, Essex a monopoly of sweet wines* (Macaulay). **3.** control that, though not exclusive, enables the person or company to fix prices. **4.** a commercial product or service that is exclusively controlled or nearly so. **5.** a person or company having a monopoly of some commodity or service: *The pilots' association was now the compactest monopoly in the world* (Mark Twain). **6.** the exclusive possession or control of intangible assets: *No one person has a monopoly of virtue. Neither side has a monopoly of right or wrong* (Edward A. Freeman). [< Latin *monopōlium* < Greek *monopṓlion* < *mónos* single + *pōleîn* to sell]

➤ **Monopoly,** except in sense 3, is a relatively neutral word. Certain other words, such as *cartel, trust, syndicate,* and *corner* are used loosely as synonyms, but are far from neutral in current use. Some of these are precisely defined by law; all are defined in this dictionary in senses that should make clear their difference from *monopoly.*

Mo·nop·o·ly (mə nop′ə lē), *n. Trademark.* a game played upon a board, in which the players try to accumulate token real-estate parcels and put each other out of business: *"Any of you chaps play Monopoly?"* (Punch).

mon·o·pol·y·log·ist (mon′ə pol′ə lôg ist, -log-), *n.* a performer of a monopolylogue.

mon·o·pol·y·logue (mon′ə pol′ə lôg, -log), *n.* an entertainment in which a single actor plays many parts: *Miss Emma Stanley, the celebrated entertainer . . . made her third appearance in her "monopolylogue"* (Times of India). [< *mono-* + *poly-* + Greek *-logos* < *légein* speak]

mon·o·pro·pel·lant (mon′ō prə pel′ənt), *n.* a propellant for a rocket, such as hydrogen peroxide, which contains its own oxidizer and requires no additional air or oxygen for ignition.

mo·nop·so·ny (mə nop′sə nē), *n.* exclusive control of the demand for a product by a single purchaser of that product: *Where monopsony exists . . . industry must be compensated for the loss of a free market* (New Scientist). [<*mon-* + Greek *opsōniā* purchase of food]

mo·nop·ter·al (mə nop′tər əl), *adj. Architecture.* (of a temple, etc.) having a single row of columns arranged in a circle, either about a cella or, often, without a cella. [< Greek *monópteros* (< *mónos* single + *pterón* wing, row of columns) + English *-al*[1]]

mon·o·rail (mon′ə rāl′), *n.* **1.** a single rail serving as a complete track. **2.** a railway in which cars run on a single rail, either balanced on it or suspended from it: *It would be a service to every major city . . . if a definitive judgment were made on the merits of the monorail* (Harper's). —*adj.* of or having to do with a monorail: *a monorail system. He . . . is trying to interest the authorities in a form of monorail vehicle* (London Times).

mon·o·rhyme or **mon·o·rime** (mon′ə-rīm), *n.* a stanza or poem in which all the lines end in the same rhyme.

monorhymes or **monorimes,** lines having this kind of rhyming: *In this manuscript each new set of monorimes is headed by a title in Latin* (Thomas Wright).

mon·o·sac·cha·ride (mon′ə sak′ə rīd, -ər-id), *n.* any of a class of simple sugars, such as glucose, fructose, and arabinose, that occur naturally or are formed by hydrolyzing polysaccharides or glycosides. Monosaccharides cannot be decomposed by hydrolysis. [< *mono-* + *saccharide*]

mon·o·sep·al·ous (mon′ə sep′ə ləs), *adj. Botany.* **1.** having the sepals united; gamosepalous. **2.** (of a calyx) having only one sepal.

mon·o·so·di·um glutamate (mon′ə sō′dē əm), a salt of glutamic acid, derived from any of a number of vegetable proteins, as corn gluten or certain sugar-beet products, and marketed as a white, crystalline powder, which has little taste of its own but is used to enhance and point up the flavor of foods. *Formula:* $C_5H_8NNaO_4$

mon·o·some (mon′ə sōm), *n.* **1.** an impaired chromosome. **2.** a monosomic individual. **3.** a single, isolated ribosome. [< *mono-* + *-some*[3]]

mon·o·so·mic (mon′ə sō′mik), *adj.* having less than the usual number of chromosomes: *a monosomic cell, a monosomic individual.*

mon·o·sper·mal (mon′ə spėr′məl), *adj. Botany.* one-seeded; monospermous.

mon·o·sper·mous (mon′ə spėr′məs), *adj. Botany.* containing only one seed; one-seeded.

mon·o·stich (mon′ə stik), *n.* **1.** a poem or epigram consisting of a single metrical line. **2.** a single line of poetry. [< Greek *monóstichon,* neuter of *monóstichos;* see MONOSTICHOUS]

mo·nos·ti·chous (mə nos′tə kəs), *adj. Botany.* arranged in a single vertical row on one side of an axis, as flowers. [< Greek *monóstichos* (with English *-ous*) made up of one row < *mónos* single + *stíchos* row, line]

mon·o·stome (mon′ə stōm), *adj.* monostomous.

mo·nos·to·mous (mə nos′tə məs, mon′ə-stō′-), *adj. Zoology.* having a single mouth or mouthlike part: *Many jellyfish are monostomous.* [< Greek *monóstomos* < *mónos* one + *stóma* mouth]

mo·nos·tro·phe (mə nos′trə fē, mon′ə-strōf), *n.* a poem in which all the stanzas have the same metrical form. [< Greek *monóstrophos,* adjective < *mónos* single + *strophḗ* strophe]

mon·o·stroph·ic (mon′ə strof′ik), *adj.* of or like a monostrophe.

mon·o·style (mon′ə stīl), *adj. Architecture.* having or consisting of a single shaft, as a pier or pillar. [< *mono-* + Greek *stŷlos* pillar, column]

mon·o·sty·lous (mon′ə stī′ləs), *adj. Botany.* having only one style.

mon·o·sub·sti·tut·ed (mon′ə sub′stə tü′-tid, -tyü′-), *adj.* (of a chemical compound) having one substituent.

mon·o·sul·fide (mon′ə sul′fīd, -fid), *n. Chemistry.* a sulfide in which one atom of sulfur is combined with the other element or radical.

mon·o·syl·lab·ic (mon′ə sə lab′ik), *adj.* **1.** having only one syllable: *a monosyllabic word.* **2.** consisting of a word or words of one syllable: *"No, not now" is a monosyllabic reply.* **3.** using or speaking in monosyllables: *Lothair . . . was . . . somewhat monosyllabic and absent* (Benjamin Disraeli).

mon·o·syl·lab·i·cal·ly (mon′ə sə lab′ə-klē), *adv.* in monosyllables; with the use of monosyllables.

mon·o·syl·la·bism (mon′ə sil′ə biz əm), *n.* the use of monosyllables; monosyllabic character.

mon·o·syl·la·bize (mon′ə sil′ə bīz), *v.t., v.i.,* **-bized, -biz·ing.** to put or be in monosyllables.

mon·o·syl·la·ble (mon′ə sil′ə bəl), *n.* a word of one syllable: *"Yes" and "no," "man" and "child" are monosyllables.*

mon·o·sym·met·ric (mon′ə si met′rik), *adj.* **1.** monoclinic. **2.** *Botany.* bilaterally symmetrical; zygomorphic. —**mon′o·sym·met′ri·cal·ly,** *adv.*

mon·o·sym·met·ri·cal (mon′ə si met′rə-kəl), *adj.* monosymmetric.

mon·o·sym·me·try (mon′ə sim′ə trē), *n. Botany.* the condition of being monosymmetric.

mon·o·syn·ap·tic (mon′ə si nap′tik), *adj. Biology.* consisting of a single synapse: *The simplest reflex pathway in the spinal cord . . . is a monosynaptic, or two-neuron, arc consisting of a fiber from a sensory neuron forming a synapse with a motoneuron* (Scientific American).

mon·o·the·ism (mon′ə thē iz′əm), *n.* the doctrine or belief that there is only one God; worship of one God: *. . . while monotheism . . . was achieved by a few primitive peoples, a number of advanced groups like the Egyptians, Greeks, and Romans had polytheism, a hierarchy of gods* (Ogburn and Nimkoff). [< *mono-* + Greek *theós* god + English *-ism*]

mon·o·the·ist (mon′ə thē′ist), *n.* a believer in only one God. —*adj.* monotheistic.

mon·o·the·is·tic (mon′ə thē is′tik), *adj.* **1.** believing in only one God. **2.** having to do with belief in only one God. —**mon′o·the·is′ti·cal·ly,** *adv.*

mon·o·the·is·ti·cal (mon′ə thē is′tə kəl), *adj.* monotheistic.

mon·o·the·mat·ic (mon′ə thē mat′ik), *adj. Music.* **1.** having a single theme: *a monothematic symphony.* **2.** of or having to do with a single theme: *Sibelius' early symphonies foreshadowed . . . [the] same monothematic principle he revealed again in his last major work, "Tapiola"* (Howard Isham).

mon·o·thet·ic (mon′ə thet′ik), *adj.* positing or supposing a single essential element: *"Monothetic" . . . means that all the elements allocated to one class must share the character or characters under consideration. Thus the members of the class of "soluble substances" must in fact be soluble* (Scientific American).

mon·o·tint (mon′ə tint), *n.* **1.** a single color. **2.** a picture in one color.

mon·o·tone (mon′ə tōn), *n., adj., v.,* **-toned, -ton·ing.** —*n.* **1.** sameness of tone, of style of writing, of color, etc. **2.** a continuance of the same tone, as in speaking, singing, etc., without change of pitch; unvaried sound or repetition of sounds: *Don't speak in a monotone; use expression.* **3.** *Music.* **a.** a single tone without change of pitch. **b.** recitative singing, especially of liturgy, in such a tone. **4.** a person who sings or speaks in a monotone.
—*adj.* continuing on one tone; of one tone, style, or color; monotonous: *The dark figure of a watchman soldier pacing his weary round through the monotone snow, appeared the only living object* (C.P. Smyth).
—*v.t., v.i.* to recite in monotone: *He generally seized the opportunity . . . to monotone long extracts* (Eclectic Magazine).
[< Greek *monótonos;* see MONOTONOUS]
—**Syn.** *adj.* uniform.

mon·o·ton·ic (mon′ə ton′ik), *adj.* uttered in a monotone. —**mon′o·ton′i·cal·ly,** *adv.*

mo·not·o·nous (mə not′ə nəs), *adj.* **1.** continuing in the same tone: *the monotonous . . . chant of a Gaelic song* (Scott). *A voice, monotonous and hollow* (Tennyson). **2.** not varying; without change: *dull straight streets of monotonous houses* (John R. Green). **3.** wearying because of its sameness: *monotonous work.* [< Greek *monótonos* (with English *-ous*) of one tone < *mónos* single + *tónos* something stretched] —**mo·not′o·nous·ly,** *adv.* —**mo·not′o·nous·ness,** *n.* —**Syn. 1.** singsong. **2.** unvarying, uniform. **3.** tedious; humdrum.

mo·not·o·ny (mə not′ə nē), *n.* **1.** sameness of tone or pitch. **2.** lack of variety: *An occasional clump of wood . . . relieved the monotony of the waste* (Francis Parkman). **3.** wearisome sameness: *At sea, everything that breaks the monotony of the surrounding expanse, attracts attention* (Washington Irving). [< Late Greek *monotoníā* < Greek *monótonos* monotonous]

mon·o·trem·a·tous (mon′ə trem′ə təs, -trē′mə-), *adj.* of or belonging to the monotremes.

mon·o·treme (mon′ə trēm), *n.* any member of the lowest order of mammals, comprising the duckbill and the echidnas, which lay eggs and have a common opening for the genital and urinary organs and the digestive tract. [< *mono-* + Greek *trêma, -atos* hole]

mo·not·ri·cha (mə not′rə kə), *n.pl.* bacteria having a single flagellum at one end. [< New Latin *Monotricha* the genus name < Greek *mónos* single + *thríx, trichós* hair]

mon·o·trich·ic (mon′ə trik′ik), *adj.* monotrichous.

mo·not·ri·chous (mə not′rə kəs), *adj.* having a single flagellum at one end: *monotrichous bacteria.*

mon·o·tri·glyph (mon′ə trī′glif), *adj. Architecture.* having only one triglyph in the portion of the frieze over the space between two columns, as is usual in the Doric order.

mon·o·tri·glyph·ic (mon′ə trī glif′ik), *adj.* monotriglyph.

mon·o·type (mon′ə tīp), *n., v.,* **-typed, -typ·ing.** —*n.* **1.** the sole representative of its group: *A single species constituting a genus is a monotype.* **2. a.** a print from a metal plate on which a picture has been painted in color with oil or printing ink, which is transferred to paper by a rubbing process: *Degas . . . produced about 200 monotypes* (Listener). **b.** the method of producing such a print.
—*v.t.* to set (type) with a Monotype machine.

Mon·o·type (mon′ə tīp), *n. Trademark.* **1.** a set of two machines (a keyboard machine and a casting machine) for setting and casting type in separate letters. **2.** type set and cast on a Monotype.

mon·o·typ·ic (mon′ə tip′ik), *adj. Biology.* **1.** having only one type or representative. **2.** being a monotype: *a monotypic form.* **3.** (of a genus) having only one species; monobasic.

mon·o·va·lence (mon′ə vā′ləns, mə nov′ə-), *n.* monovalent character or state.

mon·o·va·len·cy (mon′ə vā′lən sē, mə-nov′ə-), *n.* monovalence.

mon·o·va·lent (mon′ə vā′lənt, mə nov′ə-), *adj.* **1.** *Chemistry.* having a valence of one; univalent: *The characteristic chemical properties of the chemist's ideal metal can be regarded as the result of its having a single valency electron which it readily loses to form a monovalent ion* (J. Crowther). **2.** *Bacteriology.* containing antibodies to only one antigen.

mon·ox·ide (mon ok′sīd, -sid; mə nok′-), *n.* a chemical compound containing one oxygen atom in each molecule.

mon·ox·yl·ic (mon′ok sil′ik), *adj.* monoxylous.

mo·nox·y·lon (mə nok′sə lon), *n., pl.* **-la** (-lə). a boat made out of a single piece of timber; dugout. [< Greek *monóxylon,* neuter of *monóxylos* made of a single piece of timber < *mónos* single + *xýlon* wood]

mo·nox·y·lous (mə nok′sə ləs), *adj.* formed of a single piece of timber.

mon·o·zy·got·ic (mon′ə zī got′ik), *adj.* produced by the splitting of a single fertilized ovum; identical: *monozygotic twins.*

Mon·roe Doctrine (mən rō′), the policy that European nations should not interfere with American nations or try to acquire more territory in the Western Hemisphere, derived from President Monroe's message to Congress on Dec. 2, 1823.

mons (monz), *n., pl.* **mon·tes.** a rounded, fatty eminence on the lower abdomen where the pubic bones meet, usually covered with hair after puberty. It is called *mons pubis* in the male and *mons veneris* in the female. [< Latin *mōns, montis* mountain]

Mons., 1. Monsieur. **2.** Monsignor.

Mon·sei·gneur or **mon·sei·gneur** (mon-sēn′yər; *French* môɴ se nyœr′), *n., pl.* **Mes·sei·gneurs** or **mes·sei·gneurs. 1.** a French title of honor given to princes, bishops, and other persons of importance. *Abbr.:* Mgr. **2.** a person having this title. [< Old French *monseigneur* my lord < *mon* my (< Latin *meum*) + *seigneur* lord, learned borrowing from Latin *senior* elder, senior. Doublet of MONSIEUR.]

mon·sieur (mə syėr′; *French* mə syœ′), *n., pl.* **mes·sieurs.** the French title of courtesy for a man; Mr.; Sir: *In the first polite step in the ladder of French merchant life, a cheery singsong "Bonjour, madame; bonjour, monsieur"* . . . (New York Times). *Abbr.:* M. [< Old French *monsieur,* earlier *mon sieur* my lord; *mon* < Latin *meum; sieur* < Latin *senior* senior. Doublet of MONSEIGNEUR.]

Mon·sieur (mə syœ′), *n.* a title given to the second son or to the next younger brother of the king of France.

Monsig., Monsignor.

Mon·si·gnor or **mon·si·gnor** (mon sēn′-yər; *Italian* mōn′sē nyōr′), *n., pl.* **-gnors, -gno·ri** (-nyō′rē). **1.** a title given to certain dignitaries in the Roman Catholic Church. *Abbr.:* Msgr. **2.** a person having this title. [< Italian *monsignore,* half-translation of Old French *monseigneur* monseigneur. Related to MONSEIGNEUR.]

Mon·si·gno·re or **mon·si·gno·re** (mōn′-sē nyō′rā), *n., pl.* **-ri** (-rē). *Italian.* Monsignor: *There were some cardinals in the apartment and several monsignori* (Benjamin Disraeli).

mon·soon (mon sün′), *n.* **1.** a seasonal wind of the Indian Ocean and southern Asia blowing from the southwest from April to October and from the northeast from October to April. **2.** a rainy season during which this wind blows from the southwest. **3.** any wind that has seasonal reversals of direction. [apparently < Portuguese *monção* < Arabic *mausim* appropriate season]

mon·soon·al (mon sü′nəl), *adj.* of, having to do with, or characteristic of a monsoon: *monsoonal rains. Communication became difficult until the advent of advanced . . . monsoonal sailing techniques, good charting, and the compass developed by the Chinese early on in the Christian era* (London Times).

mons pubis, the mons in the human male.

mon·ster (mon′stər), *n.* **1.** a huge creature or thing. **2.** a person too wicked to be human: *He is a monster of cruelty. I was a monster with whom the very earth groaned* (William Godwin). **3.** an animal or plant that is very unlike those usually found in nature: *A cow with two heads is a monster.* **4.** a grotesque legendary animal often composed of parts of different animals, as a centaur, sphinx, or griffin. **5.** something unnatural and horrible: *His imagination transformed shadows into monsters* (Charles B. Brown). **6.** *Medicine.* a congenitally malformed infant with extremely abnormal physical structure; an anomaly.
—*adj.* huge; enormous: *The purpose of the resignation is believed to be to stage a monster demonstration* (London Times).
[< Old French *monstre,* learned borrowing from Latin *mōnstrum* portent; (originally) divine warning, related to *monēre* to warn]
—**mon′ster·like′,** *adj.*
—**Syn.** *n.* **1.** giant. **3.** monstrosity. —*adj.* gigantic.

mon·ster·a (mon stir′ə), *n.* any of a group of climbing shrubs of the arum family native to tropical America, especially a greenhouse plant with aerial roots, large, perforated leaves, and a succulent, edible fruit. [< New Latin *Monstera* the genus name, apparently < Latin *mōnstrum* (because of their strange appearance); see MONSTER]

mon·strance (mon′strəns), *n.* a receptacle in which the consecrated Host is shown for adoration or is carried in procession. [< Medieval Latin *monstrantia,* showing, review (of troops) < Latin *mōnstrāre* to show < *mōnstrum* divine warning; see MONSTER]

Monstrance of Louis XVIII, Notre Dame, Paris

mon·stros·i·ty (mon-stros′ə tē), *n., pl.* **-ties. 1.** a monster. **2.** the state or character of being monstrous: . . . *the multitude . . . that numerous piece of monstrosity, which, taken asunder, seem men, and the reasonable creatures of God, but, confused together, make but one great beast and monstrosity more prodigious than Hydra* (Sir Thomas Browne). [< Late Latin *mōnstrōsitās* < Latin *mōnstrōsus* monstrous]

mon·strous (mon′strəs), *adj.* **1.** huge; enormous: *a monstrous wolf, a monstrous sum. Even while I gazed, this current acquired a monstrous velocity* (Edgar Allan Poe). **2.** having the nature or appearance of a monster of fable or legend: *With monstrous head and sickening cry And ears like errant wings* (Gilbert K. Chesterton). **3.** so wrong or absurd as to be almost unheard of. **4.** shocking; horrible; dreadful: *There was no excess too monstrous for them to commit* (Nicholas P. S. Wiseman). **5.** wrongly formed or shaped; like a monster. **6.** *Obsolete.* full of monsters: *Where thou, perhaps, under the whelming tide, Visit'st the bottom of the monstrous world* (Milton).
—*adv. Archaic.* very; extremely.
[< Old French *monstreux* (with English *-ous*), learned borrowing from Latin *mōnstrōsus* < *mōnstrum;* see MONSTER]
—**mon′strous·ly,** *adv.* —**mon′strous·ness,** *n.*
—**Syn.** *adj.* **1.** gigantic, immense, colossal, prodigious, stupendous. **4.** atrocious.

mons ve·ne·ris (ven′ər is), the mons in the human female.

mont (môɴ), *n. French.* mountain: *Mont St. Michel.*

Mont., Montana.

mon·tage (mon täzh′), *n., v.,* **-taged, -tag·ing.** —*n.* **1.** the combination of several distinct pictures to make a composite picture: *Montage is frequently used in photography.* **2.** a composite picture so made: *These dramatic photographs . . . were only montages* (Newsweek). **3.** in motion pictures and television: **a.** the use of a rapid succession of pictures, especially to suggest a train of thought. **b.** the use of a combination of images on the screen at once, often revolving or otherwise moving around or toward a focal point. **c.** a part of a motion picture using either of these devices. **4.** *Radio.* a rapid sequence of separate or blended voices, sound effects, etc., which suggest varying states of mind. **5.** any combining or blending of different elements: *His latest novel is a montage of biography, history, and fiction.*
—*v.t.* to make (pictures, scenes, etc.) into a montage: *to montage a theatrical set.*
[< French *montage* a mounting < Old French *monter* to mount[1]]

Mon·ta·gnais (mon′tə nyā′), *n., pl.* **-gnais** (-nyā′, -nyāz′), **-gnaises** (-nyāz′). **1.** a member of an Indian tribe of northern Quebec. **2.** the Cree dialect spoken by this tribe. **3.** Chipewyan. [< French *Montagnais* < *montagne* mountain]

Mon·ta·gnard or **mon·ta·gnard** (mon′-tən yärd′), *n., pl.* **-gnards** or **-gnard.** one of a large group of dark-skinned, aboriginal tribesmen living in the mountainous regions of Vietnam. [< French *montagnard* mountaineer]

mon·ta·ña (mon ta′nyä), *n.* the forested region of the upper Amazon, on the eastern slopes of the Andes. [< Spanish *montaña* mountain < Latin *montānus;* see MONTANE]

Mon·tan·an (mon tan′ən), *adj.* of or having to do with Montana. —*n.* a native or inhabitant of Montana.

mon·tane (mon′tān), *adj.* of, having to do with, or inhabiting mountains.
—*n.* the zone of plant growth on mountains below the subalpine zone. [< Latin *montānus* < *mōns, montis* mountain. Doublet of MOUNTAIN.]

mon·ta·ni sem·per li·be·ri (mon tā′nī sem′pər lib′ə rī), *Latin.* mountaineers are always free (the motto of West Virginia).

Mon·ta·nism (mon′tə niz əm), *n.* the teachings of a heretical Christian sect of the 100's A.D. whose followers believed in the prophetic inspiration of Montanus and practiced rigorous asceticism. [< *Montanus* of Phrygia, the founder of the sect + *-ism*]

Mon·ta·nist (mon′tə nist), *adj.* of or having to do with Montanism: *Of "The Third Testament," a Montanist document . . . only a few scraps have been preserved* (W.H. Auden). —*n.* a believer in Montanism.

mon·tan wax (mon′tan), a dark-brown hydrocarbon wax extracted from various lignites, peat, etc., used in making polishes, candles, etc. [apparently < German *Montan* < Latin *montānus* mountain]

mont-de-pié·té (môɴ′də pyā tā′), *n., pl.* **monts-de-pié·té** (môɴ′də pyā tā′). **1.** a former state-controlled pawnshop in certain European countries that lent money at low interest to the poor. **2.** any pawnshop. [< French *mont-de-piété,* translation of Italian *monte di pietà* (literally) hill of pity]

mon·te (mon′tē), *n.* a Spanish and Spanish-American gambling game, played with the Spanish deck of 40 cards. [American English < Spanish *monte* (originally) heap

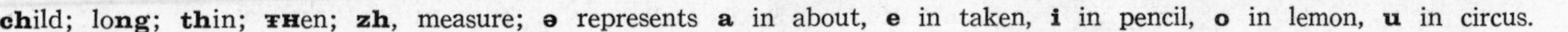

(that is, the "bank[2]"), mountain < Latin *mōns, montis*]

Mon·te Car·lo method (mon′tē kär′lō), any of various methods involving statistical techniques, such as the use of random samples, for finding solutions to mathematical and physical problems. [< *Monte Carlo,* Monaco, noted as a gambling resort (so called because of the element of chance in such methods)]

mon·teith (mon tēth′), *n.* a large bowl, usually silver, with a scalloped or notched rim from which stemmed glasses can be hung by the foot so as to cool in the water inside the bowl. It is also used as a punch bowl. [supposedly < a proper name]

Mon·te·ne·grin (mon′tə nē′grin), *adj.* of or having to do with Montenegro or its people. —*n.* a native or inhabitant of Montenegro.

mon·te·ra (môn tā′rä), *n. Spanish.* **1.** a hat; cap. **2.** a bullfighter's hat.

Mon·te·rey pine (mon′tə rā′), a pine tree of the Pacific coast, growing 40 to 60 feet in height, and widely cultivated for shelter and ornament. [< *Monterey,* city on the coast of California]

mon·te·ro (mon tãr′ō; *Spanish* môn tā′rō), *n., pl.* **-te·ros** (-tãr′ōz; *Spanish* -tā′rōs). a cap with a round crown and a flap to draw over the ears, worn by huntsmen. [< Spanish *montera* < *montero* a hunter; (literally) a mountaineer < *monte* mountain; see MONTE]

mon·tes (mon′tēz), *n.* plural of **mons.**

Mon·tes·so·ri·an (mon′tə sôr′ē ən, -sōr′-), *n.* a follower of the Montessori method: *Montessorians believe that the basic ideas of math, literature, and science are simple ones that can be taught at an early age by means of materials the child handles himself* (New York Times). —*adj.* of or having to do with the Montessori method.

Mon·tes·so·ri method or **system** (mon′tə sôr′ē, -sōr′-), a system for teaching young children that stresses training of the senses and self-education, developed by Maria Montessori, 1870-1952, Italian educator.

mont·gol·fi·er (mont gol′fē ər), *n.* a balloon raised by heated air from a fire in the lower part. [< the French brothers *Montgolfier,* who in 1783 sent up the first balloon]

month (munth), *n.* **1.** one of the 12 parts into which the year is divided; calendar month. September, April, June, and November have 30 days; February has 28 days except in leap years, when it has 29; all the other months have 31 days. *Abbr.:* mo. **2.** the time from any day of one calendar month to the corresponding day of the next month. **3.** *Astronomy.* **a.** the time it takes the moon to make one complete revolution around the earth; lunar month. **b.** the time from one new moon to the next, about 29.53 days; synodical month. **c.** one twelfth of a solar year, about 30.41 days; solar month. **d.** a sidereal month. [Old English *mōnath.* Related to MOON.]

➔ **months.** In technical and informal writing, the names of months with more than four letters are abbreviated in dates: *Jan. 21, 1963; Aug. 16, 1964.* But: *May 1, 1963; July 4, 1964.* When only the month or the month and year are given, abbreviations are rarely used: *January, 1960. Every January he tries again.* In formal writing, the names of the months are not abbreviated at all.

month·ly (munth′lē), *adj., adv., n., pl.* **-lies.** —*adj.* **1.** of a month; for a month: *a monthly report, a monthly salary.* **2.** lasting a month: *a monthly supply.* **3.** done, happening, payable, etc., once a month or every month: *a monthly meeting, a monthly examination, monthly bills.* **4.** menstrual.
—*adv.* once a month; every month; month by month: *Some magazines come monthly.*
—*n.* a magazine, review, etc., published once a month.
monthlies, the menses: *The issue is not at the usual time of the monthlies* (James G. Murphy).

monthly rose, any of several continuously blooming, hybrid varieties of rose, originally derived from the China rose.

month of Sundays, an indefinitely long time.

month's mind, 1. the commemoration of a dead person by a requiem Mass, a month after death. **2.** *British Dialect.* a mind; inclination; fancy: *Clinker has a month's mind to play the fool . . . with Mrs. Winifred Jenkins* (Tobias Smollett).

mon·ti·cle (mon′tə kəl), *n.* monticule.

mon·ti·cule (mon′tə kyül), *n.* **1.** a small hill; mound: *Seen from this monticule, everything looks tranquil and happy* (Walter Besant). **2.** a minor cone of a volcano. [< Middle French *monticule,* learned borrowing from Late Latin *monticulus* (diminutive) < Latin *mōns, montis* mountain]

mont·mo·ril·lon·ite (mont′mə ril′ə nīt), *n.* one of a group of mineral clays, a silicate of aluminum and certain other elements, used because of its absorbent structure for various industrial purposes and for safely disposing of radioactive waste materials. [< *Montmorillon,* a town in France, where it is found + *-ite*[1]]

Mont·re·al·er (mon′trē ô′lər), *n.* a native or inhabitant of Montreal, Canada: *Torontonians want to be heroes . . . but Montrealers have something to say* (Maclean's).

mon·u·ment (mon′yə mənt), *n.* **1.** an object or structure set up to keep a person or an event from being forgotten: *A monument may be a building, pillar, arch, statue, tomb, or stone.* **2.** anything that keeps alive the memory of a person, civilization, or event. **3.** an enduring or prominent instance or example: *The professor's researches were monuments of learning. The Hoover Dam is a monument of engineering.* **4.** *U.S. Law.* something set up to mark a boundary. **5.** something written or done by a person, regarded as his memorial after death: *Except some unpublished despatches . . . and a few detached sayings, he has left no monument behind him* (William E. H. Lecky). **6.** *Obsolete.* a sepulcher; tomb: *Her body sleeps in Capel's monument* (Shakespeare). **7.** *Obsolete.* an effigy. [< Latin *monumentum* < *monēre* to remind, warn] —**Syn. 2.** memorial.

mon·u·men·tal (mon′yə men′təl), *adj.* **1.** of or having to do with a monument or monuments: *monumental decorations.* **2.** serving as a monument or memorial: *He hath given her his monumental ring* (Shakespeare). **3.** having great size: *a monumental peak.* **4.** weighty and lasting; important: *The Constitution of the United States is a monumental document. A great encyclopedia is a monumental production.* **5.** very great: *monumental ignorance.* **6.** (of a statue, portrait, etc.) larger than life-size. **7.** historically prominent and significant: *the monumental achievements of the ancient Greeks.* —**mon′u·men′tal·ly,** *adv.* —**Syn. 4.** impressive. **7.** notable.

mon·u·men·tal·ism (mon′yə men′tə lizəm), *n.* monumental style or construction: *"Jacob's Ladder" marks . . . [Schoenberg's] last assault on romantic monumentalism, the pursuit of the supercolossal epic* (London Times).

mon·u·men·tal·ist (mon′yə men′tə list), *n.* an artist, writer, etc., who works on a grand or monumental scale: *There was a sudden switch of role in mid-career from a gadfly to a monumentalist* (London Times). —*adj.* of or having to do with a monumentalist or monumentalism: *monumentalist sculpture.*

mon·u·men·tal·i·ty (mon′yə men tal′ə tē), *n.* the state or quality of being monumental.

mon·u·men·tal·i·za·tion (mon′yə men′tə lə zā′shən), *n.* **1.** a making monumental: *the monumentalization of knowledge.* **2.** a being made monumental.

mon·u·men·tal·ize (mon′yə men′tə līz), *v.t.,* **-ized, -iz·ing.** to establish a lasting memorial or record of: *We consider these stepped platforms to be prototypes which were extended and monumentalized by Antiochus* (Scientific American).

mon·y (mon′ē), *adj., n. Scottish and British Dialect.* many.

mon·zo·nite (mon′zə nīt), *n.* an igneous rock composed of nearly equal amounts of plagioclase and orthoclase, plus other minerals, intermediate in composition between syenite and diorite. [< German *Monzonit* < *Monzoni,* a mountain in Tyrol + *-it* -ite[1]]

mon·zo·nit·ic (mon′zə nit′ik), *adj.* of or consisting of monzonite.

moo (mü), *n., pl.* **moos,** *v.,* **mooed, moo·ing.** —*n.* the sound made by a cow; a lowing. —*v.i.* to make the sound of a cow; low. [imitative]

mooch (müch), *Slang.* —*v.i.* **1.** to sponge or beg shamelessly. **2.** to sneak; skulk; rove about: *They sort of mooched after me, and I tells a policeman* (Lord Dunsany). —*v.t.* **1.** to get at another person's expense; beg: *He mooches a couple of cigarettes off me every day.* **2.** to pilfer; steal. Also, **mouch.** [earlier *mowche* (originally) to pretend poverty; origin uncertain. Perhaps related to MICHE.] —**mooch′er,** *n.*

mood[1] (müd), *n.* **1.** state of mind or feelings: *Are you in the mood to listen to music? I was in no mood to laugh and talk with strangers* (Mary W. Shelley). **2.** *Obsolete.* bad temper; anger.
moods, fits of depression, irritation, or bad temper: *Then turn'd Sir Torre, and being in his moods left them* (Tennyson).
[Old English *mōd* mind, heart, courage]
—**Syn. 1. Mood, humor** mean a person's state of mind or feeling at a particular time. **Mood** applies to a way of thinking and feeling determined by some emotion or desire and influencing everything a person says and does while in this frame of mind: *I am in the mood to play just now; I don't want to study.* **Humor** applies to a state of mind and spirits caused by a person's disposition or the way he feels physically, and suggests the likelihood of changing suddenly or without apparent reason: *He is in a good humor today.*

mood[2] (müd), *n.* **1.** the form of a verb or verb phrase indicating whether the act or state is thought of as a fact, a command, etc.; mode: *the indicative mood, the imperative mood, the subjunctive mood, etc.* **2.** *Logic.* mode. Also, **mode.** [alteration of *mode*[2]; influenced by *mood*[1]]

mood·i·ly (mü′də lē), *adv.* in a moody manner.

mood·i·ness (mü′dē nis), *n.* moody condition.

mood music, 1. music used to evoke or sustain a particular mood, as in connection with passages in a play or other dramatic presentation: *But in making their point the playwright and the director, with the aid of Joseph Marais's mood music . . . have covered far too much ground for theatrical comfort* (Newsweek). **2.** unobtrusive instrumental music played to provide a pleasant atmosphere for eating, drinking, or talking, as in a restaurant: *Ninety per cent of the music is played from LP records, mostly Broadway show tunes and mood music* (Harper's).

moods (müdz), *n.pl.* See under **mood**[1], *n.*

mood·y (mü′dē), *adj.,* **mood·i·er, mood·i·est. 1.** likely to have changes of mood. **2.** often having gloomy moods: *a dour, moody person. She has been moody ever since she lost her job.* **3.** sunk in sadness; gloomy; sullen: *The little girl sat in moody silence.* **4.** expressive of a mood, especially a bad mood: *a moody remark.* —**Syn. 3.** melancholy, sad.

mool (mül), *n. Scottish.* **1.** mold; earth; soil. **2.** the grave.
mools, grave clods: *Or worthy friends raked in the mools, Sad sight to see!* (Robert Burns).
[variant of *mold*[2]]

moo·la or **moo·lah** (mü′lə, -lä), *n. U.S. Slang.* money: *. . . she is going back to stuffing our moola in the mattress* (Atlantic).

moon (mün), *n.* **1.** a heavenly body that revolves around the earth once in approximately 28 days at a mean distance of 238,855 miles. The moon looks bright because it reflects the sun's light. **2.** the moon at a certain period of time. The new moon is invisible, the half moon appears as a half circle, the full moon as a circle, and the old moon as a waning crescent. **3.** a lunar month; month: *a young and tender suckling—under a moon old* (Charles Lamb). **4.** moonlight: *By the moon the reaper weary, Piling sheaves in uplands airy* (Tennyson). **5.** something shaped like the moon in any of its appearances: *a great moon of a face.* **6.** a satellite of any planet: *the moons of Jupiter.* **7.** an artificial earth satellite.

MOON'S ORBIT

MOON'S PHASES SEEN FROM EARTH

Moon
From left to right: 1, new moon (invisible); 2, waxing crescent; 3, 1st quarter; 4, gibbous; 5, full; 6, gibbous; 7, last quarter; 8, waning crescent

bark at the moon, to clamor or agitate to no effect: *Those who protested against the dictator's ruthless actions were barking at the moon, since they were few and powerless.*
once in a blue moon. See under **blue moon.**
—v.i. **1.** to wander about or gaze idly or listlessly: *to go mooning about the house and stables* (Thomas Bailey Aldrich). *If you moon at me in that stupid way ... I shall certainly end in an insane asylum* (William Dean Howells). **2.** to shine as a moon does. *—v.t.* **1.** to spend (time) idly. **2.** to expose (something) to the moon's rays. [Old English *mōna.* Related to MONTH.] **—moon′er,** *n.* **—moon′like′,** *adj.*

moon·beam (mün′bēm′), *n.* a ray of moonlight.

moon-blind (mün′blīnd′), *adj.* suffering from moon blindness: *... not to permit the men to sleep on the upper deck. We shall have many of them moon-blind* (Frederick Marryat).

moon blindness, 1. (in horses) mooneye, an intermittent inflammation of the eyes, usually resulting in blindness. **2.** (in persons) night blindness.

moon·bow (mün′bō′), *n.* a rainbow formed by moonlight; lunar rainbow: *Moonbows are due to the same cause as rainbows, but since the reflected light from the moon does not contain all the colors of sunlight the bow appears silver* (London Times).

moon·calf (mün′kaf′, -käf′), *n., pl.* **-calves. 1.** a congenital idiot: *"No," said the poor mooncalf, changing his tune at once* (Robert Louis Stevenson). **2.** a person who moons: *I have been playing, I fear, the mooncalf tonight* (Benjamin Disraeli). **3.** *Archaic.* a monstrosity: *This huge mooncalf of Sansculottism* (Thomas Carlyle).

moon·craft (mün′kraft′, -kräft′), *n.* **1.** a space vehicle designed for flight to the moon: *The first test flight of the United States Apollo "mooncraft" ended successfully with a splashdown in the Atlantic* (London Times). **2.** such vehicles collectively or as a class.

moon·creep·er (mün′krē′pər), *n.* the moonflower.

moon daisy, the oxeye daisy.

mooned (münd; *Poetic* mü′nid), *adj.* **1.** moon-shaped. **2.** ornamented with moons or crescents. **3.** having the moon as a symbol or emblem.

moon·eye (mün′ī′), *n.* **1.** an eye affected with moon blindness. **2.** moon blindness.

moon·eyed (mün′īd′), *adj.* **1.** (of horses) suffering with mooneye; moon-blind: *I have seen many a slothful and heavy horse brought to be mooneyed by the folly of his rider* (Gervase Markham). **2.** (of persons) having round, wide-open eyes, as from terror or surprise.

moon·face (mün′fās′), *n.* **1.** a round, moonlike face: *As he neared the top, he turned his happy moonface* (Time). **2.** an abnormal obesity of the face caused by various diseases.

moon·faced (mün′fāst′), *adj.* having a round face like a full moon: *the long moon-faced clock in the corner* (F. Hopkinson Smith).

moon·fish (mün′fish′), *n., pl.* **-fish·es** or (*collectively*) **-fish.** any of a number of fishes that suggest the moon by the silvery or yellowish color of their body, as various carangoids, opahs, and a Mexican top minnow.

moon·flight (mün′flīt′), *n.* space flight to the moon: *The year 1959 will be remembered as the date of the first successful moonflights, three by Soviet rockets and one by a United States rocket* (Annual Register of World Events).

moon·flow·er (mün′flou′ər), *n.* **1.** a tropical plant of the morning-glory family, having large, fragrant white flowers that open in the evening. **2.** any of various related plants. **3.** *Especially British.* the oxeye daisy.

moon·gate (mün′gāt′), *n.* (in Chinese architecture) a circular gateway through a wall: *A Chinese temple [is] ... set in intricate Chinese gardens with moongates and curiously twisted trees and rock formations* (London Times).

moon·glow (mün′glō′), *n.* moonlight: *Their only answer was to move their chairs a little closer to the great fall of moonglow outside* (Punch).

moon·i·ly (mü′nə lē), *adv.* in a moony manner.

moon·i·ness (mü′nē nis), *n.* moony quality or condition.

moon·ing (mü′ning), *n.* the act of a person who moons; listless wandering about: *Their sad moonings have transformed themselves into genuine despair* (New Yorker).

moon·ish (mü′nish), *adj.* **1.** like the moon; changeable; fickle: *at which time would I, being but a moonish youth, ... be effeminate, changeable* (Shakespeare). **2.** caused by the moon.

moon jellyfish, the most common jellyfish, disk-shaped and white or bluish, found along the Atlantic and Pacific Coasts.

moon·less (mün′lis), *adj.* **1.** having no moon: *It is by no means improbable that Mars was originally moonless* (H.C. Macpherson). **2.** not lit up by the moon: *a moonless night.*

moon·let (mün′lit), *n.* **1.** a little moon: *I pledge thee in the silver horn Of yonder moonlet bright* (William Motherwell). **2.** a small artificial earth satellite: *The man-made moonlets will circle the earth many times every day* (Science News Letter).

moon·light (mün′līt), *n.* the light of the moon: *Moonlight has a considerable influence on the activity of insects at night* (Science News).
—adj. **1.** having the light of the moon; moonlit: *a moonlight night.* **2.** while the moon is shining; at or by night: *a moonlight swim.*
—v.i. U.S. Informal. to work at a second job, usually at night, in order to supplement the wages earned at a regular job: *Workers moonlight to live on a higher plane than otherwise is possible* (Chicago Daily News).

moon·light·er (mün′lī′tər), *n. U.S. Informal.* a person who works at a second job: *Moonlighters, of course, more than make up the difference in their income with second jobs* (Wall Street Journal).

moonlight flit, *British Slang.* an absconding at night to escape creditors: *Using false names, an undischarged bankrupt started businesses in various parts of the country, then did a moonlight flit when he had incurred debts* (London Times).

moon·light·ing (mün′lī′ting), *n. U.S. Informal.* the practice of holding or working at a second job, usually at night, in addition to a regular daytime job: *One of the paradoxes and problems of the U.S. full-employment prosperity is moonlighting* (Time). [originally, performance of unlawful activities or expeditions by night < *moonlight* + *-ing*[1]]

moon·lit (mün′lit′), *adj.* lighted by the moon: *moonlit woods.*

moon·man (mün′man′, -mən), *n., pl.* **-men. 1.** a person skilled in or trained for moonflight: *Then, according to the theory, the moonmen take off, orbit, rendezvous and couple with the mother ship* (Harper's). **2.** a person engaged in research, projects, etc., concerned with moonflight.

moon probe, a lunar probe: *The other experiments carried out by the rocket will valuably supplement those of the sputniks and earlier moon probes* (Manchester Guardian).

moon·quake (mün′kwāk′), *n.* a quake or series of vibrations on the moon analogous to an earthquake: *Moonquakes cause dust storms that fill the bottoms of the moon's craters* (Science News Letter).

moon·rak·er (mün′rā′kər), *n.* **1.** a stupid or silly person. **2.** moonsail.

moon·rise (mün′rīz′), *n.* **1.** the rising of the moon: *watching a chilly autumnal moonrise over the stubbles of the cornfield* (Mrs. Humphry Ward). **2.** the time when the moon rises.

moon rocket, a rocket fired toward the moon; lunar probe: *Satellites and moon rockets promise that space travel will one day be possible* (New Scientist).

moon·sail (mün′sāl′; *Nautical* mün′səl), *n.* a light sail set above a skysail; moonraker.

moon·scape (mün′skāp′), *n.* **1.** a view of the surface of the moon: *The telescope shows the mountains themselves and other details of the moonscape as well* (Robert H. Baker). **2.** a view or landscape on earth which looks as rugged as a moonscape: *We are sometimes picking our way with him ... over the desolate moonscapes of high mountains with a young shepherd for a guide* (Manchester Guardian). [< *moon* + (land)*scape*]

moon·seed (mün′sēd′), *n.* any of a group of climbing plants having panicles of greenish-white flowers and crescent-shaped seeds, especially a variety of eastern North America grown on walls and arbors.

moon·set (mün′set′), *n.* **1.** the setting of the moon. **2.** the time of setting of the moon.

moon·shine (mün′shīn′), *n.* **1.** *U.S. Informal.* intoxicating liquor made unlawfully or smuggled: *Moonshine making may be on the rise again, revenue sleuths fear* (Wall Street Journal). **2.** empty talk; empty show; nonsense: *Making every allowance for Communist statistical moonshine ...* (Time). **3.** moonlight: *The twilight had given place to moonshine when the party halted upon the brink of a precipitous glen* (Scott).

moon·shin·er (mün′shī′nər), *n. U.S. Informal.* **1.** a person who distills intoxicating liquor contrary to law: *Vast cliffs from whose bushy brows the armed moonshiner watched the bridle-path below* (George W. Cable). **2.** a person who follows an unlawful trade at night.

moon·shin·ing (mün′shī′ning), *U.S. —n.* the unlawful distilling of whiskey: *The revenue officials ... admit that moonshining has been booming* (Newsweek). *—adj.* of or having to do with the distilling of illicit whiskey: *a moonshining ring, moonshining operations.*

moon·shin·y (mün′shī′nē), *adj.* **1.** like moonlight. **2.** lighted by the moon. **3.** unreal.

moon shoot, a moon shot: *Missilemen were busy at launching pads and hangars, preparing for two new moon shoots* (Time).

moon shot, the launching of a rocket or missile toward the moon: *In the shadow of the Russian moon shot, renewed efforts may be made to attain agreements on outer space* (New York Herald Tribune).

moon snail, a predatory, carnivorous marine snail with a globose shell: *The moon snail is a blind creature ... with an immense foot, which it uses effectively in digging and in grasping its prey, while with its radula it drills a neat round hole in the shell* (New Yorker).

moon·stone (mün′stōn′), *n.* a whitish gem with a pearly luster. Moonstone is a variety of feldspar.

moon·strick·en (mün′strik′ən), *adj.* moonstruck.

moon·struck (mün′struk′), *adj.* affected in mind, supposedly through the influence of the moon; dazed; crazed: *Deform'd in body, and Of moonstruck mind* (Robert Bridges). **—Syn.** lunatic.

Moon type, 1. a system of printing for blind people, the letters being represented by nine basic characters placed in different positions, which may be read by touch. **2.** the letters themselves: *Publication of books in Moon type also increased sharply. Elderly blind find this large alphabet easier to read than Braille* (London Times). [< William *Moon,* a British inventor of the 1900's]

moon·ward (mün′wərd), *adv.* toward the moon: *The first serious attempts to send rockets moonward were made by the Americans in 1958* (Listener). *—adj.* directed toward the moon: *... balloon-launched moonward rockets* (Time).

Moon·watch (mün′woch′, -wôch′), *n.* a program of world-wide visual observation by about 1,500 volunteers who tracked and recorded the various artificial satellites launched during the International Geophysical Year: *Moonwatch ... called its large organization of observers into action as soon as the launching was announced* (Scientific American).

moon·watch·er (mün′woch′ər, -wôch′-), *n.* a volunteer observer who took part in the Moonwatch: *The moonwatchers will report their findings to professional astronomers at key points around the world* (World Book Annual).

moon·wort (mün′wėrt′), *n.* **1.** any of a group of ferns that have fronds with crescent-shaped leaflets. **2.** the plant honesty.

moon·y (mü′nē), *adj.,* **moon·i·er, moon·i·est. 1.** of or belonging to the moon. **2.** like the moon; crescent-shaped; round: *... nor lift the moony shield* (John Dryden). **3.** mooning; dreamy; listless: *moony dreamings over inscrutable beautiful eyes* (George Meredith). **4.** illuminated by the moon; moonlit. **5.** resembling moonlight.

moor[1] (mür), *v.t.* **1.** to put or keep (a ship, boat, etc.) in place by means of ropes or chains fastened to the shore or to anchors. **2.** to fix firmly; secure. *—v.i.* **1.** to tie up a ship or boat. **2.** to be made secure by ropes, anchors, etc. [earlier *moren.* Compare Old English *mǣrels* mooring rope.]

moor² (mu̇r), *n. Especially British.* **1.** open waste land, especially when covered with coarse grasses or heather; heath. **2.** a game preserve consisting of such land. [Old English *mōr*]

Moor (mu̇r), *n.* a member of the ethnic group of mixed Berber and Arab stock living in northwestern Africa. The Moors invaded and conquered Spain in the 700's, and were finally driven out in 1492. [< Old French *More,* later *Maure* < Latin *Maurus* < Greek *Maûros*]

moor·age (mu̇r′ij), *n.* **1.** a mooring or being moored. **2.** a place for mooring. **3.** the charge for its use.

moor·ber·ry (mu̇r′ber′ē, -bər-), *n., pl.* **-ries. 1.** the bilberry. **2.** a small cranberry.

moor cock, the male red grouse.

moor·fowl (mu̇r′foul′), *n.* the red grouse.

moor hen, 1. the female red grouse; gorhen. **2.** any of various wading birds, such as the gallinule, rail, and coot.

moor·ing mast or **tower** (mu̇r′ing), a mast or tower to which an airship can be moored.

moor·ings (mu̇r′ingz), *n.pl.* **1.** the ropes, cables, anchors, etc., by which a vessel or other object is moored. **2.** the place where a vessel is moored.

moor·ish (mu̇r′ish), *adj.* **1.** of or like a moor. **2.** full of moors; covered with moors: *moorish hills.* **3.** *Archaic.* marshy: *moorish fens, low moorish ground near the sea.* [< *moor*² + *-ish*]

Moor·ish (mu̇r′ish), *adj.* **1.** of the Moors. **2.** in the style of the Moors. [< *Moor* + *-ish*]

Moorish Arch

moor·land (mu̇r′land′, -lənd), *Especially British.* —*n.* land covered with heather; moor: *. . . opportunities for studying the ecology of moorlands* (A. W. Haslett). —*adj.* **1.** of moorland. **2.** having to do with or on moorland: *Milk lorry drivers are said to be leaving crates of bottled milk at wayside points for moorland villages to collect* (London Times).

moor·land·er (mu̇r′lan′dər, -lən-), *n. Especially British.* an inhabitant of a moorland.

moor·wort (mu̇r′wėrt′), *n.* a low evergreen shrub of the heath family, growing chiefly in bogs in north temperate regions.

moor·y (mu̇r′ē), *adj.,* **moor·i·er, moor·i·est.** moorish; boggy.

moose (müs), *n., pl.* **moose. 1.** a large ruminant mammal of the deer family, living in the Northern Hemisphere throughout the world. The male has a heavy build, large head, and broad antlers. **2.** the European elk. [American English < Algonkian (compare Narragansett *moos,* apparently < *moosu* he strips off the bark of young trees as food)]

Moose (def. 1) (about 6 ft. high at the shoulder)

moose·wood (müs′wu̇d′), *n.* a small, slender maple tree having a green bark with white stripes.

moot (müt), *adj.* that can be argued; debatable; doubtful: *It is a moot point whether the family doctor "ousted from the hospital" really wants to get back* (Observer). [< noun] —*v.i.* **1.** to argue; dispute. **2.** to debate a hypothetical case of law, as was done by students in the Inns of Court. —*v.t.* **1.** to bring forward (a point, subject, case, etc.) for discussion: *The project of this conference was first mooted about two years ago* (Bulletin of Atomic Scientists). **2.** to argue (a point, case, etc.).
[Old English *mōtian* < *gemōt;* see the noun] —*n.* **1.** (in early English history) an assembly of the people of an administrative division for discussing local judicial and political affairs. **2. a.** a discussion of a hypothetical law case by students for practice. **b.** a hypothetical case that may be used for this.
[Old English *gemōt* a meeting. Related to MEET¹.] —**moot′er,** *n.*

moot court, a mock court held in a law school to give students practice.

moot hall, (in early English history) a hall in which a moot was held: *A fourteenth century moot hall at St. Albans . . . was used as a council chamber and courthouse until the early nineteenth century* (London Times).

mop¹ (mop), *n., v.,* **mopped, mop·ping.** —*n.* **1.** a bundle of coarse yarn, rags, cloth, etc., or a sponge fastened at the end of a stick, for cleaning floors, etc. **2.** a thick, tangled, or unruly mass, as of hair: *a mop of hair not a little resembling the shag of a Newfoundland dog* (Washington Irving). **3.** any of various small instruments resembling a mop, especially one used in surgery to apply medicated fluids or to remove infected matter.
—*v.t.* **1.** to wash or wipe up; clean with a mop: *to mop the floor.* **2.** to wipe sweat or tears from: *He mopped his brow with his handkerchief.* —*v.i.* to use a mop.
mop up, a. *Informal.* to finish: *Tom Sturdivant . . . will follow the fireballer, and Johnny Sain will mop up* (New York Times). **b.** *Military.* to clear out or rid (an area, town, etc.) of scattered or remaining enemy troops: *The mopping up, after an unexpected quick victory . . ., may be long and difficult* (New York Times).
[earlier *mappe,* perhaps < French (Walloon) *mappe* < Latin, or directly < Latin *mappa* napkin]

mop² (mop), *v.,* **mopped, mop·ping,** *n.* —*v.i.* to make a wry face; grimace.
mop and mow, to make faces; grimace: *At the circus, the clowns mopped and mowed.*
—*n.* a grimace.
[perhaps imitative. Compare Dutch *moppen* to pout.]

mo·pa·ne (mō pä′ne), *n.* mopani.

mo·pa·ni (mō pä′nē), *n.* a medium-sized tree of the pea family found in tropical Africa, used for lumber and as a source of copal: *The ungraceful mopani . . . with its curious bilobed butterflylike leaves* (R. H. Compton). [< a native word]

mop·board (mop′bôrd′, -bōrd′), *n. U.S.* a baseboard; board around the walls of a room next to the floor.

mope (mōp), *v.,* **moped, mop·ing,** *n.* —*v.i.* to be indifferent and silent; be gloomy: *Went moping under the long shadows at sunset* (D.G. Mitchell).
—*v.t.* to cause to mope. —*n.* a person who mopes: *She is no mope, only thoughtful and quiet* (M.C. Jackson).
the mopes, low spirits; the blues; the dumps: *Master* [*is*] *still in the mopes* (Thackeray).
[perhaps related to MOP². Compare Low German *mopen* to sulk.] —**mop′er,** *n.* —**mop′ing·ly,** *adv.* —**Syn.** *v.i.* sulk.

mo·ped (mō′ped), *n. British.* a heavily built bicycle with an auxiliary engine, used in England and other parts of Europe: *Some of the smallest internal combustion engines, such as those used on mopeds and motor-scooters, are among the most noisy* (New Scientist). [< *mo*(tor) + *ped*(al)]

mop·er·y (mō′pər ē), *n., pl.* **-er·ies.** mopish action or behavior: *. . . that apocryphal felony, mopery* (Harper's); *. . . seriously ill after a long period of mopery* (Newsweek).

mop-haired (mop′hãrd′), *adj.* having a thick or bushy head of hair: *. . . the mop-haired Aussie pulling Oxford's No. 7 sweep* (Time).

mop·head (mop′hed′), *n.* **1.** *Informal.* a mop-haired person: [*He is a*] *beefy blond mophead known better for his recordings than for his social finesse* (Maclean's). **2.** the bundle or sponge fastened at the end of a mop: *Dirty mopheads and bedside water carafes have been implicated as germ carriers* (Time).

mop·head·ed (mop′hed′id), *adj.* mop-haired: *. . . a mop-headed little old woman* (New Yorker).

mop·ish (mō′pish), *adj.* inclined to mope; listless and dejected. —**mop′ish·ly,** *adv.* —**mop′ish·ness,** *n.*

Mop·lah (mop′lə), *n.* one of a class of Moslem inhabitants of southwestern India, especially Malabar, descended from Arab settlers and native women. —*adj.* of or having to do with the Moplahs. [< Malayalam *māppila*]

mo·poke (mō pōk′), *n.* any of several Australian birds, especially a kind of goatsucker or a small owl. Also, **morepork.**

mop·per (mop′ər), *n.* a person who mops: *An army of sweepers and moppers moved in to put the Coliseum in shape for the second game* (Newsweek).

mop·per-up (mop′ər up′), *n., pl.* **mop·pers-up. 1.** *Informal.* a person who cleans up or finishes off something. **2.** *Military.* a soldier who takes part in a mop-up action.

mop·pet (mop′it), *n.* **1.** *Informal.* a little child: *Additional moppets over five travel at $1 a head extra* (Wall Street Journal). **2.** *Archaic.* darling, a term of endearment for a baby or little girl, or a rag doll. [< obsolete *mop* doll + *-et*]

mop·ping-up (mop′ing up′), *adj.* mop-up: *mopping-up operations.*

mop·py (mop′ē), *adj.,* **-pi·er, -pi·est.** like a mop: *moppy hair.*

mop-up (mop′up′), *n. Informal.* **1.** a cleaning up; a wiping out: *It was the first county in which a mop-up of gambling was ordered* (New York Times). **2.** the systematic killing or capture of defeated troops left in an area after a major battle or war: *As the mop-up continued, casualties mounted* (Time). —*adj.* of or having to do with a mop-up: *Terrorists struck at British mop-up patrols with homemade bombs and rifle fire* (Newsweek).

mop·y (mō′pē), *adj.,* **mop·i·er, mop·i·est.** mopish: *Taffy and the laird grew quite sad and mopy* (George Du Maurier).

mo·quette (mō ket′), *n.* a thick, velvety carpet or upholstery fabric made of wool and hemp or linen. [< French *moquette,* earlier *moucade;* origin uncertain]

mor (mōr), *n.* a peaty kind of humus, poor in lime and nitrogen, and unsuitable for plant growth. [< Scandinavian (compare Icelandic *mor* peat soil)]

mor., morocco (leather).

Mor., Morocco.

mo·ra¹ (môr′ə, mōr′-), *n., pl.* **mo·rae** (môr′ē, mōr′-), **mo·ras. 1.** a unit of meter, equivalent to a short syllable. *Symbol:* ◡ or ♪. **2.** *Law.* a negligent delay. [< Latin *mora* pause, delay]

mo·ra² (môr′ə), *n.* a game in which one player throws out his hand with one or more fingers extended and makes a guess at the number they will make when added to the number of fingers extended simultaneously by the other player. [< Italian *mora*]

mo·ra·ceous (mô rā′shəs, mō-), *adj.* belonging to the mulberry family: *The fig, hop, hemp, and the Osage orange are moraceous plants.* [< New Latin *Moraceae* the mulberry family (< Latin *mōrum* mulberry, or *mōrus* mulberry tree) + English *-ous*]

mo·rain·al (mə rā′nəl), *adj.* of or having to do with a moraine.

mo·raine (mə rān′), *n.* **1.** a mass of rocks, dirt, etc., deposited at the side or end of a glacier, or beneath the ice as the glacier melts. **2.** a raised border or ridge formed chiefly of stones on which plants are grown: *The one essential of the moraine is drainage of the most perfect description* (L.B. Meredith). [< French *moraine,* perhaps < Provençal *mourenne;* origin uncertain]

mo·rain·ic (mə rā′nik), *adj.* morainal: *Morainic bands bound the confluence of Malaspina and Marvine glaciers in Alaska* (Scientific American).

mor·al (môr′əl, mor′-), *adj., n., v.,* **-aled, -al·ing** or (*especially British*) **-alled, -al·ling.** —*adj.* **1.** good in character or conduct; virtuous according to civilized standards of right and wrong; right; just: *a moral act, a moral man.* **2.** capable of understanding right and wrong: *A baby has no moral ideas.* **3.** having to do with character or with the difference between right and wrong: *Whether finding should be keeping is a moral question. The Abolitionists felt a moral responsibility to free the slaves.* **4.** based on the principles of right conduct rather than on law or custom. **5.** teaching a good lesson; having a good influence. **6.** proper in sexual relations; not lewd; virtuous. **7.** depending upon considerations of what generally occurs; resting upon grounds of probability: *moral evidence, moral arguments.*

—*n.* **1.** the lesson, inner meaning, or teaching of a fable, a story, or an event: *The moral of the story was "Look before you leap."* **2.** the type of something; embodiment: *She is the very moral of old-fashioned prejudice* (Hawthorne). **3.** the image or counterpart of a person or thing: *They said I was the very moral of Lady Richmanstone, but not so pale* (Tobias Smollett). **4.** morale.
morals, a. principles, habits, or behavior with respect to right or wrong conduct: *The morals of Sedley were such as, even in that age, gave great scandal* (Macaulay). **b.** principles of conduct; ethics; moral philosophy: *In morals the action is judged by the intention* (Algernon Charles Swinburne).
—*v.i. Archaic.* to moralize: *When I did hear the motley fool thus moral on the time* (Shakespeare).
[< Latin *mōrālis* < *mōs, mōris* custom, *mōrēs* manners]
—**Syn.** *adj.* **1. Moral, ethical** mean in agreement with a standard of what is right and good in character or conduct. **Moral** refers to the customary rules and accepted standards of society: *He leads a moral life.* **Ethical** refers to the principles of right conduct expressed in a system or code, especially of the branch of philosophy that deals with moral conduct or of a profession or business: *It is not considered ethical for doctors to advertise.*
➤ **moral, morale.** A common error is writing *moral* (concerning right conduct) when *morale* (mental condition as regards courage, confidence, enthusiasm, etc.) is the word intended.

moral certainty, a probability so great that it is close to being a certainty.

mo·rale (mə ral′, -räl′), *n.* **1.** moral or mental condition as regards courage, confidence, enthusiasm, etc.: *the morale of troops.* **2.** morality; morals: *Here the . . . traveller may see more of the habits and morale of the Turkish women than he can hope to do elsewhere* (Julia S.H. Pardoe).
[< French *morale,* feminine of Old French *moral* moral, learned borrowing from Latin *mōrālis*]
➤ See **moral** for usage note.

-moraled, *combining form.* having —— morals: *High-moraled = having high morals.*

moral hazard, (in insurance) the risk taken by an insurer that the insured may not be trustworthy.

mor·al·ise (môr′ə līz, mor′-), *v.i., v.t.,* **-ised, -is·ing.** *Especially British.* moralize: *The theme has been adumbrated in English novels with sentimentality, over-earnest moralising, . . .* (Observer).

mor·al·ism (môr′ə liz əm, mor′-), *n.* **1.** a moralizing; moral counsel or advice: *. . . two notions which the Anglo-Saxon, imbued with moralism and meliorism, is apt to look upon as indulgent and defeatist* (Atlantic). **2.** a moral maxim. **3.** good morals as distinct from religion.

mor·al·ist (môr′ə list, mor′-), *n.* **1.** a person who thinks much about moral duties, sees the moral side of things, and leads a moral life. **2.** a person who teaches, studies, or writes about morals: *Writers of satires are usually moralists, because they wish to improve human conditions.*

mor·al·is·tic (môr′ə lis′tik, mor′-), *adj.* **1.** teaching the difference between right and wrong; moralizing. **2.** of or having to do with a moralist or moral teaching: *the moralistic bossiness of provincial politicians* (Santha Rama Rau). —**mor′al·is′ti·cal·ly,** *adv.*

mo·ral·i·ty (mə ral′ə tē), *n., pl.* **-ties. 1.** the relative right or wrong of an action: *They argued about the morality of dancing on Sunday.* **2.** doing right; virtue. **3.** a system of morals; set of rules or principles of conduct: *Doctor Johnson's morality was as English an article as beefsteak* (Hawthorne). **4.** a moral lesson or precept; moral instruction: *A genial optimist, who daily drew from what he saw his quaint moralities* (William Cullen Bryant). **5.** a morality play: *The book is full of such heavy symbolism, as all moralities are* (Wall Street Journal).

morality play, a type of drama popular during the 1400's and 1500's, in which vices and virtues appear as real people.

mor·al·i·za·tion (môr′ə lə zā′shən, mor′-), *n.* **1.** the act of moralizing or of becoming moral. **2.** a being moralized.

mor·al·ize (môr′ə līz, mor′-), *v.,* **-ized, -iz·ing.** —*v.i.* to think, talk, or write about questions of right and wrong: *. . . no one can moralize better after a misfortune has taken place* (Washington Irving). —*v.t.* **1.** to point out the lesson or inner meaning of: *But what said Jaques? Did he not moralize this spectacle?* (Shakespeare). **2.** to improve the morals of: *. . . a social life passed in peaceful occupation is positively moralizing* (Herbert Spencer). —**mor′al·iz′er,** *n.* —**mor′al·iz′ing·ly,** *adv.*

mor·al·ly (môr′ə lē, mor′-), *adv.* **1.** in a moral manner; virtuously: *to live morally.* **2.** in morals; as to morals: *The king was a good man morally, but too stupid for a position of importance.* **3.** from a moral point of view; ethically: *things morally considered, morally speaking.* **4.** practically; virtually: *I am morally sure that I locked the door.*

moral philosophy, ethics.

Moral Re-Armament, a religious movement of the 1900's advocating a personal form of Christianity based on ethical and moral precepts; Buchmanism.

Moral Re-Armer, a supporter of Moral Re-Armament; Buchmanite.

mor·als (môr′əlz, mor′-), *n.pl.* See under **moral,** *n.*

moral support, approval but not active help.

moral turpitude, *Law.* low or depraved conduct; conduct that offends the moral sense of a community or society: *There was a serious question as to whether the crime of draft-dodging involved moral turpitude, a deportable offense* (New York Times).

moral victory, a defeat that has the effect on the mind that a victory would have: *Labor party increased its share of the vote and therefore claimed a moral victory* (New York Times).

mo·rass (mə ras′), *n.* **1.** a piece of soft, low, wet ground; swamp; marsh: *The towing path was a morass of sticky brown mud* (Arnold Bennett). **2.** a difficult, confused, or entangled state of affairs: *The odd programme . . . generally floundered in a morass of ineptitude* (Canadian Saturday Night). [< Dutch *moeras* < Old French *marais,* perhaps < Germanic (compare Old High German *marī*)] —**Syn. 1.** bog.

mo·rass·y (mə ras′ē), *adj.* of or like a morass; marshy; swampy: *Our next operation was to build a wall of clay against the morassy sides of the well* (Erasmus Darwin).

mo·rat (môr′at, mōr′-), *n.* an old-time drink made of honey flavored with mulberries: *There was grace after meat with a fist on the board, And down went the morat, and out flew the sword* (Henry Taylor). [< Medieval Latin *moratum* < Latin *mōrus* mulberry tree]

mor·a·to·ri·um (môr′ə tôr′ē əm, -tōr′-; mor′-), *n., pl.* **-to·ri·ums, -to·ri·a** (-tôr′ē ə, -tōr′-). **1.** a legal authorization to delay payments of money due, as during an emergency. **2.** the period during which such authorization is in effect. **3.** a voluntary or negotiated temporary cessation of action on any issue: *. . . it is suggested that a moratorium on mechanical invention be declared until the lags of society have caught up* (William F. Ogburn and Meyer F. Nimkoff). [< New Latin *moratorium,* neuter of Latin *morātōrius;* see MORATORY]

mor·a·to·ry (môr′ə tôr′ē, -tōr′-; mor′-), *adj.* authorizing delay in payment: *a moratory bill or law in regard to mortgages.* [< Latin *morātōrius* tending to delay < *morārī* to delay < *mora* a delay, pause]

Mo·ra·vi·an (mō rā′vē ən, mō-), *adj.* **1.** of or having to do with Moravia, or its Slavic inhabitants. **2.** of or having to do with the Protestant church founded by John Huss: *I haven't yet found any better or quieter or forbearinger people than the Brethren and Sistern of the Moravian Church in Philadelphia* (Rudyard Kipling).
—*n.* **1.** a native or inhabitant of Moravia. **2.** a member of the Moravian Church. **3.** the Slavic language of Moravia, a dialect of Czech.

mo·ray (môr′ā, mōr′-; mō rā′, mō-), *n.* a fierce, often brilliantly colored eel of the tropical seas; muraena. One kind, found in the Mediterranean, is used as food. [< Portuguese *moreia* < Latin *murēna,* variant of *muraena* < Greek *mýraina,* feminine of *mýros*]

mor·bid (môr′bid), *adj.* **1.** unhealthy; not wholesome; sickly: *morbid fancies, a morbid look. A liking for horrors is morbid.* **2.** caused by disease; characteristic of disease; diseased. **3.** having to do with diseased parts: *morbid anatomy.* **4.** horrible; gruesome; grisly: *the morbid details of a murder.* [< Latin *morbidus* < *morbus* disease] —**mor′bid·ly,** *adv.* —**mor′bid·ness,** *n.*
—**Syn. 1.** unsound, unwholesome.

mor·bi·dez·za (môr′bē dāt′sä), *n. Italian.* the soft delicacy of living flesh as represented in painting or other forms of art.

mor·bid·i·ty (môr bid′ə tē), *n., pl.* **-ties. 1.** morbid state or quality: *He has been criticized for cynicism or coldness, as Zola was for morbidity and clinical detachment* (Observer). **2.** the proportion of sickness in a certain group or locality: *Morbidity records show the health of the men in the armed forces at an all-time high* (New York Times).

mor·bif·ic (môr bif′ik), *adj. Obsolete.* causing disease: *morbific agents.* [< Late Latin *morbificus* < Latin *morbus* disease + *facere* make, cause] —**mor·bif′i·cal·ly,** *adv.*

mor·bif·i·cal (môr bif′ə kəl), *adj.* morbific.

mor·bil·li (môr bil′ī), *n.pl.* an old term for measles. [< Medieval Latin *morbilli* measles; (originally) scarlet fever (probably diminutive) < Latin *morbus* disease]

mor·bil·li·form (môr bil′ə fôrm), *adj.* resembling measles: *morbilliform rash.*

mor·bil·lous (môr bil′əs), *adj.* of or having to do with measles.

mor·ceau (môr sō′), *n., pl.* **-ceaux** (-sō′). *French.* **1.** a short literary or musical composition: *He sat down and produced the following morceau* (Tobias Smollett). **2.** (literally) a small piece; morsel.

mor·cel·late (môr′sə lāt), *v.t.,* **-lat·ed, -lat·ing.** to divide into many pieces; break up. [< French *morceler* (with English *-ate*[1]) < *morceau* small piece < Old French *morsel;* see MORSEL]

mor·cel·la·tion (môr′sə lā′shən), *n.* division into many pieces.

mor·celle·ment (môr sel mäN′), *n. French.* **1.** division into many pieces. **2.** a dividing, as of land, into small portions.

mor·da·cious (môr dā′shəs), *adj.* **1.** given to biting; biting: *They likewise assured us the bats were very mordacious* (George Forster). **2.** caustic; mordant: *A repose freed from . . . mordacious malignity* (Isaac D'Israeli). [< Latin *mordāx, -ācis* (with English *-ous*) < *mordēre* to bite] —**mor·da′cious·ly,** *adv.*

mor·dac·i·ty (môr das′ə tē), *n.* mordancy: *We all know the vivacity, or mordacity, with which the veriest cur resents an outrage offered to his tail* (Spirit of the Public Journals).

mor·dan·cy (môr′dən sē), *n.* mordant or biting quality: *Speeches denouncing Mr. Gladstone . . . none of them equal in mordancy to the Duke of Somerset's recent jet of vitriol* (The Echo).

mor·dant (môr′dənt), *adj.* **1.** biting; cutting; sarcastic: *The mordant criticism hurt his feelings. Restraining his tongue from mordant allusions to that "prancing, red-haired fellow"* (John Galsworthy). **2.** that fixes colors in dyeing. **3.** acute; burning: *mordant pain.* **4.** corrosive.
—*n.* **1.** a substance, such as tannic acid or a salt of a metal or metallic compound, that fixes colors in dyeing. **2.** an acid that eats into metal, used in etching.
—*v.t.* to treat with a mordant: *The cloth may be . . . mordanted as usual with tin, and then dyed* (Ernest Spon).
[< Old French *mordant,* present participle of *mordre* to bite < Latin *mordēre.* Doublet of MORDENT.] —**mor′dant·ly,** *adv.*
—**Syn.** *adj.* **1.** caustic.

Mor·de·cai (môr′də kī), *n.* (in the Bible) the cousin of Esther, who helped her save the Jews from being destroyed by Haman. Esther 2-10.

mor·dent (môr′dənt), *n. Music.* **1.** a grace note or embellishment consisting of the rapid alternation of a tone with another tone usually a half step below it. There are two kinds: the single (short) with one alternation, and the double (long) with two or more. **2.** a pralltriller (inverted mordent). [< German *Mordent* < Italian *mor-*

Mordents (def. 1) Top, single; bottom, double

dente, present participle of *mordere* to bite < Latin *mordēre.* Doublet of MORDANT.]

Mor·dred (môr′dred), *n.* Modred.

more[1] (môr, mōr), *adj.* (*used as comparative of* **much** *and* **many,** *with the superlative* **most**), *n., adv.* —*adj.* **1.** greater in number, quantity, amount, degree, or importance: *more men, more help. A foot is more than an inch.* **2.** further; additional: *Take more time if you need it. This plant needs more sun.* **3.** greater: *The more fool you, to believe such a tale.*

—*n.* **1.** a greater number, quantity, amount, or degree: *The more they have, the more they want.* **2.** an additional amount: *Tell me more.* **3.** something of greater importance: *Kind hearts are more than coronets* (Tennyson).

—*adv.* **1.** in or to a greater degree or extent: *That hurts more.* **2.** in addition; further; longer; again: *Sing once more.* **3.** besides: *Drink a glass more.*

be no more, to be dead: *Cassius is no more* (Shakespeare).

more and more, a. increasingly more: *A spokesman said that more and more vehicles were taking to the highways every year* (New York Times). **b.** to an increasing degree: *The public is more and more growing to respect cleanliness and efficiency* (London Times).

more or less, a. somewhat: *Most people are more or less selfish.* **b.** nearly; approximately: *five miles more or less.*

[Old English *māra*]

➔ **More** and **most** are often used to form comparatives and superlatives, usually with adjectives or adverbs of three syllables or more, often with those of two syllables, and sometimes with those of one syllable, so that for many there are two forms: *emptier* or *more empty; emptiest* or *most empty.*

mo·re[2] (môr′ē, mōr′-), *adv. Latin.* in the manner.

mo·reen (mə rēn′), *n.* a heavy fabric of wool, or wool and cotton, usually with a watered or embossed finish, used for draperies, upholstery, etc. [compare MOIRE]

mo·re ge·o·met·ri·co (môr′ē jē′ə met′rə-kō, mōr′-), *Latin.* in the manner of geometry; with rigorous proof.

more·ish (môr′ish, mōr′-), *adj.* morish.

mo·rel[1] (mə rel′), *n.* a small edible mushroom, eaten as a table delicacy by gourmets. [< French *morille* < Germanic (compare German *Morchel* < Old High German *morhila*)]

Morel[1] **or sponge mushroom (from 2 to 6 in. high)**

mo·rel[2] or **mo·relle** (mə-rel′), *n.* any of several nightshades, especially the black nightshade. [< Old French *morele,* perhaps ultimately < Latin *mōrum* mulberry]

mo·rel·lo (mə rel′ō), *n., pl.* **-los.** a kind of sour cherry having dark-red fruit and juice. [origin uncertain; perhaps < Flemish *amarelle* < Italian *amarella* (diminutive) < *amaro* bitter < Latin *amārus;* probably influenced by Italian *morello* dark-colored]

mo·ren·do (mō ren′dō), *adj. Music.* dying away; diminuendo at the end of a cadence. [< Italian *morendo,* present participle of *morire* to die < Latin *morī*]

more·ness (môr′nis, mōr′-), *n.* **1.** the condition of being greater or more. **2.** multitude; plurality.

more·o·ver (môr ō′vər, mōr-), *adv.* also; besides; in addition to that: *I don't want to go skating; moreover, the ice is too thin. His power is absolute and, moreover, hereditary.* —**Syn.** furthermore, further.

more·pork (môr pôrk′, mōr pōrk′), *n.* mopoke.

mo·res (môr′āz, -ēz; mōr′-), *n.pl.* customs prevailing among a people or a social group that are accepted as right and obligatory; traditional rules; ways; manners: *TV . . . is having its inevitable effect on local manners and mores around the world* (Newsweek). [< Latin *mōrēs* manners, plural of *mōs, mōris* custom] —**Syn.** folkways.

Mo·resque (mə resk′), *adj.* in the Moorish style; Moorish: *Moresque architecture.* —*n.* Moorish design or decoration, as in architecture. [< French *moresque* < Italian *moresco* < *Moro* Moor < Latin *Maurus;* see MOOR]

mo·re su·o (môr′ē sü′ō, mōr′-), *Latin.* in one's own way.

Mor·gain le Fay (môr′gān lə fā′, môr′-gən), or **Morgain,** *n.* Morgan le Fay.

Mor·gan (môr′gən), *n.* any of an American breed of sturdy, relatively light horses that originated in Vermont, used as trotting horses and for work on farms: *She was a tall, clean-limbed sorrel, a Kentucky-bred Morgan* (Merwin and Webster). [< Justin *Morgan,* 1748-1798, of Vermont, who owned the first of the breed]

Mor·ga·na (môr gä′nə), *n.* Morgan le Fay.

mor·ga·nat·ic (môr′gə nat′ik), *adj.* designating or having to do with a form of marriage by which a man of high rank marries a woman of lower rank with an agreement that neither she nor her children shall have any claim to his rank or property. [< New Latin *morganaticus* < Medieval Latin (*matrimonium ad*) *morganaticam* (marriage with) morning gift (instead of a share in the husband's possessions), ultimately an adaptation of Old High German *morgangeba* < *morgan* morning + *geba* gift]

mor·ga·nat·i·cal·ly (môr′gə nat′ə klē), *adv.* by a morganatic marriage.

mor·gan·ite (môr′gə nīt), *n.* a rose-colored beryl. [< J. P. *Morgan,* 1837-1913, an American financier + *-ite*[1]]

Mor·gan le Fay (môr′gən lə fā′), the legendary half sister of King Arthur. She is usually represented as a scheming, evil fairy who seeks King Arthur's death. [< Old French *Morgain la Fée* Morgan the fairy (see FAY[1]), probably translation of Italian *Fata Morgana*]

mor·gen (môr′gən), *n., pl.* **-gen** or **-gens.** **1.** a unit of land measure used in South Africa, and formerly used in Holland and the Dutch colonies, hence in early New York, equal to about two acres: *This queer hill . . . covering at its base nearly a morgen . . . of ground* (H. Rider Haggard). **2.** a unit of land measure formerly used in Prussia, Norway, and Denmark, equal to about 2/3 of an acre. [American English < Dutch *morgen*]

morgue (môrg), *n.* **1.** a place in which the bodies of persons unidentified or killed by accident or violence are temporarily held, for identification and claim or for investigation: *The* [*police*] *headquarters contains . . . a morgue* (New York Times). **2.** *Informal.* the reference library of a newspaper, magazine, etc., in which clippings and other materials are kept. [< French *morgue* (originally) a building in Paris used as a morgue; origin uncertain]

mor·i·bund (môr′ə bund, mor′-), *adj.* at the point of death or extinction; dying: *a moribund person, a moribund political party.* —*n.* a dying person. [< Latin *moribundus* < *morī* to die] —**mor′i·bund·ly,** *adv.*

mor·i·bun·di·ty (môr′ə bun′də tē, mor′-), *n.* moribund condition.

mo·rin (môr′in, mōr′-), *n.* a substance obtained from fustic wood, used as a yellow dye, and in chemistry as a highly reliable test reagent for aluminum. *Formula:* $C_{15}H_{10}O_7$ [< French *morine* < Latin *mōrus* mulberry + French *-ine* -in]

mo·ri·on[1] (môr′ē on, mōr′-), *n.* a helmet without a visor, shaped like a hat, with a comb-shaped crest and an upturned rim forming a peak in front, worn especially by Spanish foot soldiers in the 1500's and 1600's. [< French *morion* < Spanish *morrion* < *morra* top of the head; origin uncertain]

mo·ri·on[2] (môr′ē on, mōr′-), *n.* a dark-brown or nearly black, smoky quartz. [< a misreading of Latin *mormorion,* in early editions of Pliny's *Natural History*]

Mo·ris·co (mə ris′kō), *adj., n., pl.* **-cos** or **-coes.** —*adj.* Moorish: *It was of a composite architecture, between the Morisco and the Spanish* (Frederick Marryat). —*n.* a Moor, especially one of the Moors in Spain: *These people are the undiluted descendants of Moriscos who fled the idiotic and savage persecutions under Felipe III* (Harper's). [< Spanish *morisco* < *moro* Moor < Latin *Maurus;* see MOOR]

mor·ish (môr′ish, mōr′-), *adj. Informal.* such that more is desired, as food or drink. Also, **moreish.**

mo·ri·tu·ri te sa·lu·ta·mus (môr′ə-tyu̇r′ī tē sal′yə tā′məs, mōr′-), *Latin.* we who are about to die salute thee (the salute of Roman gladiators).

Mor·mon (môr′mən), *n.* a member of the Church of Jesus Christ of Latter-day Saints, founded by Joseph Smith in 1830. The sacred book of this church is called the Book of Mormon. —*adj.* of or having to do with the Mormons or their religion. [American English < *Mormon,* the name of the alleged author of "The Book of Mormon"]

Mormon Church, the Church of Jesus Christ of Latter-day Saints.

mormon or **Mormon cricket,** a type of grasshopper (rather than a true cricket), dark-brown to black, two inches long, and highly destructive to all crops. It is native to the western United States. *Hoppers and Mormon crickets chewed up $37 million of . . . crops* (Wall Street Journal).

Mor·mon·ism (môr′mə niz əm), *n.* the religious system of the Mormons: *. . . the golden tablets that held the fundamental tenets of Mormonism* (Time).

mor·my·rid (mor mī′rid), *n.* any of a group of African fresh-water teleost fishes with a long snout bent downward and electric organs in the tail. —*adj.* of or having to do with mormyrids. [< New Latin *Mormyridae* the family name < Latin *mormyrus* a sea fish]

morn (môrn), *n.* **1.** *Poetic.* morning: *the golden light of morn* (Thomas Hood). **2.** *Scottish.* the next day; morrow. [Middle English *morwen,* Old English *morgen*]

mor·nay sauce, or **mor·nay** (môr nā′), *n.* a white sauce flavored with sharp cheese. [< Philippe de *Mornay,* 1549-1623, a French Protestant leader]

morn·ing (môr′ning), *n.* **1.** the early part of the day, ending at noon. **2.** the first or early part of anything: *the morning of life. A king lived long ago, in the morning of the world* (Robert Browning). **3.** *Poetic.* the dawn; daybreak: *Far up the solitary morning smote the streaks of virgin snow* (Tennyson). **4.** the first part of the next day or morrow: *Wait until morning. I'll come in the morning.*

—*adj.* **1.** of or in the morning: *a morning walk, the morning paper.* **2.** of the first or early part of life, etc.: *Young he appear'd, for on his cheek there shone the morning glow of health* (Robert Southey).

[Middle English *morwening* < *morwen* morn + *-ing*[1]; patterned on *evening*]

—**Syn.** *n.* **2.** dawn.

Morn·ing (môr′ning), *n.* the Roman goddess Aurora or the Greek goddess Eos.

morn·ing-af·ter (môr′ning af′tər, -äf′-), *n., pl.* **morn·ings-af·ter.** *Slang.* the morning following a night of heavy drinking of alcoholic liquor; hangover: *On various mornings-after . . . Amedeo Modigliani carved and painted in Paris a few hundred works of warmth and glamour* (Time).

morning coat, a cutaway: *My husband now appeared all dressed up in morning coat, holding top hat, white gloves, and umbrella* (Harper's).

morning gift, a gift made to a woman by her husband the morning after marriage, a former European custom.

morn·ing-glo·ry (môr′ning glôr′ē, -glōr′-), *n., pl.* **-ries.** **1.** any of various vines with heart-shaped leaves and funnel-shaped, blue, purple, red, pink, or white flowers, which bloom early in the day. **2.** the flower.

morning-glory family, a group of dicotyledonous herbs, shrubs, and small trees, having alternate leaves, bisexual, regular flowers, and often a milky juice. The family includes the morning-glory, sweet potato, dodder, and convolvulus.

morning gown, a dressing gown: *Mr. Justice was led into the parlour, in his night-cap and loose morning gown* (Tobias Smollett).

morning gun, a gun fired, usually at dawn, as a signal for reveille or the raising of the flag.

morning line, *Informal.* the probable odds against the horses running at any track, published the morning of the race: *I wish the management would do something to improve the morning line, which, after all, is supposed to give the customers some clue to a horse's chances* (New Yorker).

morning room, a room used as a sitting room during the early part of the day.

morn·ings (môr′ningz), *adv. Informal.* during the morning; in the morning: [*He*] *trains the colt and gallops him mornings* (New Yorker).

morning sickness, nausea and vomiting in the morning, a common symptom of pregnancy.

morning star, 1. a bright planet, especially Venus, when seen in the eastern sky before sunrise: *Venus, the familiar morning and evening star, is the brightest of the planets*

(Robert H. Baker). **2.** an old form of weapon consisting of a ball of metal, usually set with spikes, either mounted upon a long handle or staff or slung to one by a thong or chain.

morn·ing·tide (môr′ning tīd′), *n. Poetic.* morning: *All the gentle angels . . . glance about my dreams at morningtide* (Charles Kingsley).

morn's morning, *Scottish.* tomorrow morning; the next morning: *He would have to come for the postage the morn's morning* (John Galt).

Mo·ro (môr′ō, mōr′-), *n., pl.* **-ros,** *adj.* —*n.* **1.** a member of any of the Moslem Malay tribes in Mindanao and other southern Philippine Islands. **2.** the language of these people. —*adj.* of or having to do with these people or their language. [< Spanish *moro* a Moor < Latin *Maurus;* see MOOR]

Mo·roc·can (mə rok′ən), *adj.* of or having to do with Morocco or its people. —*n.* a native or inhabitant of Morocco.

mo·roc·co (mə rok′ō), *n., pl.* **-cos. 1.** a fine-grained leather made from goatskin tanned with vegetable extracts, used in binding books. **2.** leather made in imitation of this. [< *Morocco,* a country in Africa, where it was first made]

morocco leather, morocco.

mo·ron (môr′on, mōr′-), *n.* **1.** a person having an intelligence quotient of 50 to 70. A moron is less mentally deficient than an imbecile or idiot, and is capable of doing routine jobs. **2.** *Informal.* a stupid or annoyingly ignorant person; dullard; dunce. [American English < Greek *mōron,* neuter of *mōrós* foolish, dull]

mo·ron·ic (mə ron′ik), *adj.* of, characteristic of, or like a moron: *Miss Winters goes about her moronic chores quite convincingly* (New Yorker).

mo·ron·ism (môr′on iz əm, mōr′-), *n.* the condition of being a moron; moronity.

mo·ron·i·ty (mə ron′ə tē), *n.* moronism: *It may depend on where you draw the line between a simplicity which is endearing and outright moronity* (Wall Street Journal).

mo·rose (mə rōs′), *adj.* **1.** gloomy; sullen; ill-humored: *A morose, almost a malignant, scowl blackened his features* (Charlotte Brontë). **2.** harsh: *morose doctrines.* [< Latin *mōrōsus* (originally) set in one's ways < *mōs, mōris* habit, custom] —**mo·rose′ly,** *adv.* —**mo·rose′ness,** *n.* —**Syn. 1.** moody, surly, gruff. —**Ant. 1.** amiable, pleasant, genial.

mo·ros·i·ty (mə ros′ə tē), *n.* the state of being morose; moroseness.

morph (môrf), *n.* a minimum meaningful unit or group of speech sounds: *Any morph can be recorded as a phoneme or a pattern of phonemes* (George P. Faust). [apparently back formation < *morpheme*]

morph., morphology.

Mor·phe·an (môr′fē ən), *adj.* of or belonging to Morpheus.

mor·pheme (môr′fēm), *n. Linguistics.* a minimum meaningful element in a language, such as *un-, do, flower, -ing,* various intonation and stem patterns, etc.: *A morpheme does not necessarily* CONSIST *of phonemes, but all morphemes are statable in terms of phonemes* (H.A. Gleason, Jr.). [< French *morphème* < Greek *morphḗ* form; patterned on French *phonème* phoneme]

mor·phe·mic (môr fē′mik), *adj.* of, having to do with, or characteristic of a morpheme: *These three bound forms /iz, s, z/ may be termed allomorphs or morphemic variants* (Simeon Potter).

mor·phe·mics (môr fē′miks), *n. Linguistics.* the systematic study of the minimum meaningful elements of language and their characteristics in living speech.

Mor·phe·us (môr′fē əs, -fyüs), *n. Greek Mythology.* the god of dreams; popularly, the god of sleep.

in the arms of Morpheus, asleep; sleeping: *He was so tired that within minutes of lying down he was in the arms of Morpheus.*

[< Latin *Morpheus,* proper name meaning "fashioner" or "molder," coined by Ovid from Greek *morphḗ* form, shape (alluding to the forms seen in dreams)]

mor·phi·a (môr′fē ə), *n.* morphine: *Without the slightest hesitation, I gave him a heavy dose of morphia* (Newsweek).

mor·phic (môr′fik), *adj.* morphological.

mor·phin (môr′fin), *n.* morphine.

mor·phine (môr′fēn, -fin), *n.* a bitter, colorless or white, crystalline alkaloid obtained from opium, used in medicine to relieve pain and induce sleep: *Morphine and heroin, for example, do not give normal persons the "kick" and pleasant sensations they are supposed to give* (Science News Letter). *Formula:* $C_{17}H_{19}NO_3 \cdot H_2O$ [< French *morphine,* or German *Morphin* < Latin *Morpheus* Morpheus (because of its sleep-inducing properties)]

mor·phin·ism (môr′fə niz əm), *n.* **1.** a disordered condition caused by the habitual use of morphine. **2.** the morphine habit; addiction to the use of morphine.

mor·phin·ist (môr′fə nist), *n.* a habitual user of morphine; morphine addict; morphinomaniac.

mor·phi·no·ma·ni·a (môr′fə nə mā′nē ə), *n.* uncontrollable craving for morphine.

mor·phi·no·ma·ni·ac (môr′fə nə mā′nē-ak), *n.* a person affected with morphinomania.

mor·pho·gen·e·sis (môr′fə jen′ə sis), *n. Biology.* the origin and evolution of morphological characters.

mor·pho·ge·net·ic (môr′fə jə net′ik), *adj.* of or having to do with morphogenesis.

mor·pho·gen·ic (môr′fə jen′ik), *adj.* morphogenetic.

mor·pho·line (môr′fə lēn, -lin), *n.* a viscous liquid of basic properties, used as a solvent for dyes, waxes, and resins, as a reagent, and as an emulsifying agent: *After testing several score organic odors, we found that dilute solutions of morpholine neither attracted nor repelled salmon* (Scientific American). *Formula:* C_4H_9ON

mor·pho·log·ic (môr′fə loj′ik), *adj.* morphological: *In any discussion of phonology the only kind of contexts which can be considered are phonologic, never morphologic* (H.A. Gleason, Jr.).

mor·pho·log·i·cal (môr′fə loj′ə kəl), *adj.* of or having to do with morphology; relating to form; structural: *Every segment of every effective utterance has some degree of meaning at all levels, whether phonological, morphological, or syntactic* (Simeon Potter). —**mor′pho·log′i·cal·ly,** *adv.*

mor·phol·o·gist (môr fol′ə jist), *n.* a person skilled in morphology.

mor·phol·o·gy (môr fol′ə jē), *n., pl.* **-gies. 1.** the branch of biology dealing with the form and structure of animals and plants without regard to function. **2.** the form and structure of an organism or of one of its parts. **3. a.** the branch of grammar or linguistics dealing with forms of words as affected by inflection, derivation, etc.: *. . . the first two steps in morphology are to identify morphs and classify them* (George P. Faust). **b.** the patterns of word composition, inflection, derivation, etc., in a language: *So likewise, the syntax must be stated in terms of the morpheme sequences described in the morphology . . .* (H.A. Gleason, Jr.). **4.** the study of forms in any science, as in physical geography or geology. [< Greek *morphḗ* form + English *-logy*]

mor·pho·met·ric (môr′fə met′rik), *adj.* of or having to do with morphometry.

mor·phom·e·try (môr fom′ə trē), *n.* the measurement of the external form of any object: *. . . has worked out in detail the morphometry of the Lake of Geneva* (Nature). [< Greek *morphḗ* form + English *-metry*]

mor·phon (môr′fon), *n. Biology.* a unit or individual that is morphologically or structurally independent. [< German *Morphon* < Greek *morphḗ* form]

mor·pho·pho·ne·mic (môr′fō fə nē′mik), *adj.* **1.** of or having to do with the phonemic structure of morphemes: *. . . the plurals of substantives and the third person present singular forms of verbs show interesting morphophonemic features in English* (Simeon Potter). **2.** of or having to do with morphophonemics. —**mor′pho·pho·ne′mi·cal·ly,** *adv.*

mor·pho·pho·ne·mics (môr′fō fə nē′miks), *n.* the study of the variations in the phonemic structure of morphemes: *. . . as we proceed from morphophonemics, and morphology proper, to syntax, so we observe a rise in the scale of semantic values* (Simeon Potter).

mor·ral (mə ral′), *n. Southwestern U.S.* a feedbag. [< Spanish *morral*]

mor·rhu·ol (mor′ù ol, -ōl), *n.* a pungent, partly crystalline, oily substance extracted from cod-liver oil, that contains phosphorus, iodine, and bromine. [< New Latin *Morrhua* the cod genus (< Medieval Latin *morua* cod) + English *-ol*[2]]

mor·ris (môr′is, mor′-), *n.* morris dance.

morris or **Morris chair,** an armchair with removable cushions and an adjustable back. [< William *Morris,* 1834-1896, an English artist and poet, who invented it]

morris dance, an old English folk dance performed chiefly on May Day by people in traditional costume. The dancers frequently represented Friar Tuck, Maid Marian, and other characters of the Robin Hood legend: *Some of the warmest applause was reserved for the morris dances, named for the Moorish dances performed in early England in mummers' pageants, processionals, and May Day games* (New York Times). [earlier *moreys,* variant of *Moorish*]

mor·ris-pike (môr′is pīk′, mor′-), *n.* a kind of pike (military weapon), no longer in use. [< obsolete *morys,* a variant of *Moorish*]

Morris Plan bank, *U.S.* a private industrial bank that lends small amounts of money upon a note signed by the borrower and two acceptable endorsers, without other security than prospective wages.

mor·ro (mor′ō; *Spanish* môr′rō), *n., pl.* **mor·ros** (mor′ōz; *Spanish* môr′rōs). a round hill, hillock, or promontory. [< Spanish *morro* round object]

mor·row (môr′ō, mor′-), *n.* **1.** the following day: *Ye know not what shall be on the morrow* (James 4:14). **2.** the time immediately following a particular event: *On the morrow of a long and costly war . . .* (John Fiske). **3.** *Archaic.* morning. [Middle English *morwe,* variant of *morwen* morn]

Mors (môrz), *n.* death personified as a god by the ancient Romans, identified with the Greek Thanatos. [< Latin *Mors*]

morse[1] (môrs), *n.* the clasp or fastening of a cope, etc., often made of gold or silver and set with jewels. [< Old French *mors* < Latin *morsus* buckle clasp < *mordēre* bite]

morse[2] (môrs), *n.* the walrus. [< Lapp *morsa,* or Finnish *mursu*]

Morse (môrs), *adj.* **1.** designating or having to do with the Morse code or a telegraph system using it. **2.** having to do with a telegraphic code similar to Morse code. —*n.* **1.** the Morse code. **2.** any similar code. [< Samuel F. B. *Morse,* 1791-1872, American inventor of the telegraph]

Morse or **morse code,** a system by which letters, numbers, and spaces, etc., are expressed by dots, dashes, and spaces, used in telegraphy, signaling, etc.: *A new chapter in communications history was opened when scientists . . . transmitted the first messages in morse code and speech to America via the moon* (New Scientist).

mor·sel (môr′səl), *n., v.,* **-seled, -sel·ing** or (*especially British*) **-selled, -sel·ling.** —*n.* **1.** a small bite; mouthful: *having not eaten a morsel for some hours* (Jonathan Swift). *Take a morsel of our bread and cheese* (Hawthorne). **2.** a piece; fragment; bit; scrap: *a morsel of chalk, a morsel of earth.* **3.** a dish of food; tidbit: *a dainty morsel.* **4.** something to be enjoyed, disposed of, or endured: *to find a person a tough morsel. This decision was a bitter morsel.*

—*v.t.* to divide into small pieces; distribute (property, etc.) in small parcels.

[< Old French *morsel* (diminutive) < *mors* a bite, ultimately < Latin *mordēre* to bite]

—**Syn.** *n.* **2.** mite, particle.

Morse lamp, a blinking lamp for flashing signals that stand for the dots, dashes, and spaces used in the Morse code.

Morse telegraph, the electric telegraph in general use.

mors jan·u·a vi·tae (môrz′ jan′yů ə vī′tē), *Latin.* death is the gate of life.

mort[1] (môrt), *n.* **1.** (in hunting) a note sounded on a horn at the death of a deer. **2.** *Obsolete.* death. [< Old French *mort* death (< Latin *mors, mortis*) and *morte* dead < Latin *mortuus*]

mort[2] (môrt), *British Dialect.* —*n.* a great quantity or number: *Here's a mort o' merrymaking, hey?* (Richard Brinsley Sheridan). —*adv.* much: *You've fared better with me, ay, a mort better, than you'd have fared if the Captain had been here* (Stanley J. Weyman). [origin uncertain; perhaps < adjective use of *mortal*]

mort[3] (môrt), *n.* a salmon in its third year. [origin unknown]

mor·ta·del·la (môr′tə del′ə), *n.* a large cooked and smoked sausage made of chopped beef, pork, and pork fat and seasoned with garlic and pepper. [< Italian *mortadella* (diminutive) < Latin *murtātum* a kind of sausage]

mor·tal (môr′təl), *adj.* **1.** sure to die sometime: *all mortal creatures. Do you think your daughter is not mortal like other people?* (Charles Reade). **2.** of or having to do with man: *Mortal flesh has many pains and diseases.* **3.** of or characterized by death: *a mortal year.* **4.** causing death of the soul: *a mortal sin.* **5.** causing death; deadly; fatal: *a mortal wound, a mortal illness.* **6.** to the death; implacable; relentless: *a mortal enemy, a mortal battle, mortal hatred.* **7.** very great; deadly; dire: *mortal terror.* **8.** *Informal.* **a.** great; extreme: *I was a mortal sight younger then* (Dickens). **b.** long and tedious: *And so on for 940 mortal pages* (Edward G. Bulwer-Lytton). **c.** conceivable: *By no mortal means* (Ben Jonson).
—*n.* **1.** a being that is sure to die sometime: *All living creatures are mortals.* **2.** a human being; person: *What fools these mortals be* (Shakespeare).
—*adv. Dialect.* extremely; excessively: *Missis was mortal angry* (Thackeray).
[< Latin *mortālis* < *mors, mortis* death]
—**Syn.** *adj.* **2.** human. **5.** lethal. See **fatal.**

Mor·tal·ism (môr′tə liz əm), *n.* the belief that the soul is mortal.

Mor·tal·ist (môr′tə list), *n.* a person who believes that the soul is mortal.

mor·tal·i·ty (môr tal′ə tē), *n., pl.* **-ties. 1.** frequency of death; loss of life on a large scale: *The mortality from automobile accidents is very serious. Years of dearth ... are generally among the common people, years of sickness and mortality* (Adam Smith). **2.** the condition of being sure to die sometime; mortal nature, character, or existence: *Life's gayest scenes speak man's mortality* (Edward Young). **3.** the number of deaths per thousand cases of a disease, or per thousand persons in the population; death rate: *The mortality from typhoid fever is decreasing.* **4.** deadliness; power to kill. **5.** human nature; humanity: *Young Sir Harry is about as puny and feeble a little bit of mortality as I ever saw* (Harriet Beecher Stowe). **6.** *Obsolete.* death: *Here on my knee I beg mortality* (Shakespeare).

mortality table, a table stating the number of people of a given age that may be expected to die during a given period, survive to a certain age, etc.

mor·tal·ize (môr′tə līz), *v.t.,* **-ized, -iz·ing.** to make mortal; consider or represent as mortal: *In later times he* [*Faunus*] *was mortalized like all the other Italian gods* (Thomas Keightley).

mor·tal·ly (môr′tə lē), *adv.* **1.** so as to cause death; fatally: *mortally wounded.* **2.** bitterly; grievously: *mortally offended. Whoe'er it be That tells my faults, I hate him mortally* (Alexander Pope). **3.** *Informal.* extremely; exceedingly: *mortally ugly.* **4.** as a mortal: *Yet I was mortally brought forth, and am No other than I appear* (Shakespeare).

mortal mind, 1. (in Christian Science) the erroneous beliefs of people unguided by Christian Science. **2.** human intelligence and feelings.

mortal sin, (in Christian theology) a sin so bad that it causes the death of the soul: *Murder and blasphemy are mortal sins.*

mor·tar[1] (môr′tər), *n.* a mixture of sand, water, and lime, cement, or often both, for holding bricks or stones together. —*v.t.* to plaster with mortar; fix or hold together with or as if with mortar: *There was a real danger that the U.S.-British-French united front that Herter mortared together ... might show cracks* (Time). [< Old French *mortier* < Latin *mortārium* vessel for mixing or pounding; the material prepared in it]

mor·tar[2] (môr′tər), *n.* **1.** a bowl of very hard material, as brass, hardwood, glass, or porcelain, in which substances may be pounded to a powder. **2.** any of various mechanical devices in which limestone, shale, or other substances may be pounded or ground. **3. a.** a very short cannon with a wide, unrifled barrel and a low muzzle velocity, used to fire shells at high angles so as to drop on the target from above: *The most common type of mortar in use today is the trench mortar. A small boat nudged through the pounding Mediterranean surf to beach its ... cargo: ... cases of cartridges, mortars and shells* (Newsweek). **b.** a similar apparatus for shooting fireworks, lifelines, etc.
—*v.t.* to fire mortars at; to hit with mortar fire: *An airborne battalion ... got badly mortared* (New Yorker). —*v.i.* to fire mortars.
[(definition 1) Old English *mortere* < Latin *mortārium;* see MORTAR[1]; (definition 2) < Middle French, Old French *mortier* < Latin; (definition 3) < Old French *mortier* cannon]

PESTLE

MORTAR

Mortar[2] (def. 1) and pestle

mor·tar·board (môr′tər bôrd′, -bōrd′), *n.* **1.** a flat, square board used by masons to hold mortar while working with it. **2.** an academic cap which fits the head closely and is topped by a stiff, flat, cloth-covered square piece, worn at graduation exercises in schools and colleges, and on other academic occasions.

mort·cloth (môrt′klôth′, -kloth′), *n. Especially Scottish.* a funeral pall. [< *mort*[1] + *cloth*]

Morte d'Ar·thur (môrt′ där′thər), a collection of Arthurian legends compiled and translated from the French by Sir Thomas Malory, and published by William Caxton in 1485.

mort·gage (môr′gij), *n., v.,* **-gaged, -gag·ing.** —*n.* **1.** a claim on property, given as security to a person, bank, or firm that has loaned money, in case the money is not repaid when due. **2.** the document that gives such a claim. **3.** the rights conferred by it, or the state of the property conveyed.
—*v.t.* **1.** *Law.* to give a lender a claim to (one's property) in case a debt is not paid when due. **2.** to put under some obligation; pledge: *Faust mortgaged his soul to the Devil. He would not mortgage an inch of his independence by asking a favour from a minister* (Edward G. Bulwer-Lytton).
[< Old French *mortgage* < *mort* dead (see MORT[1]) + *gage* pledge, gage[1]]

mort·ga·gee (môr′gi jē′), *n. Law.* a person to whom property is mortgaged; the holder of a mortgage.

mort·gag·er or **mort·ga·gor** (môr′gi jər), *n.* a person who mortgages his property: *... when the mortgagor obtains a mortgage exceeding the actual cost of the project* (Atlantic).

mortgage warehousing, the practice by commercial banks of buying mortgages from other types of mortgage holders with the understanding that they will be repurchased at a later date.

mor·tice (môr′tis), *n., v.t.,* **-ticed, -tic·ing.** mortise: *Mortices break out, rectangles become obluse, shelving shrinks* (Punch).

mor·ti·cian (môr tish′ən), *n.* an undertaker: *As the jury troop out of their boxes every tread of their heels will mean another call for the mortician* (Glasgow Herald). [American English < *mort*(uary) + *-ician,* as in *logician*]

mor·tif·er·ous (môr tif′ər əs), *adj.* bringing or producing death; deadly: *Fevers are in these regions the natural expression of mortiferous influences generally* (R.F. Burton). —**mor·tif′er·ous·ly,** *adv.* —**mor·tif′er·ous·ness,** *n.*

mor·ti·fi·ca·tion (môr′tə fə kā′shən), *n.* **1.** shame; humiliation; chagrin: *mortification at having spilled food on the tablecloth.* **2.** a cause or source of shame, humiliation, or chagrin: *It is one of the vexatious mortifications of a studious man to have his thoughts disordered by a tedious wit* (Roger L'Estrange). **3.** a mortifying or being mortified: *the mortification of the body by fasting. I intend to live in continual mortification* (Jonathan Edwards). **4.** the death of tissues in one part of the body only; gangrene; necrosis: *His leg had to be amputated because mortification had set in.* —**Syn. 1.** embarrassment.

mor·ti·fi·er (môr′tə fī′ər), *n.* a person or thing that mortifies: *How sweet it is when a fallen man can thus mortify his intended mortifiers!* (Horatio Smith).

mor·ti·fy (môr′tə fī), *v.,* **-fied, -fy·ing.** —*v.t.* **1.** to make ashamed; humiliate: *A mother is mortified when her child behaves badly.* **2.** to overcome (bodily desires and feelings) by pain and self-denial: *Mortify Your flesh ... with scourges and with thorns* (Tennyson). **3.** to cause (a part of the body) to become affected with gangrene or necrosis. **4.** *Obsolete.* to reduce in strength or force; weaken.
—*v.i.* **1.** to become gangrenous; die; decay: *We had ... their fingers and toes to thaw, and take care of, lest they should mortify and fall off* (Daniel Defoe). **2.** to overcome bodily desires and feelings by pain and self-denial: *Imagine him mortifying with his barrel of oysters in dreary solitude* (Jane Austen).
[< Old French *mortifier* < Latin *mortificare* to kill, subdue < *mors, mortis* death + *facere* make] —**mor′ti·fy·ing·ly,** *adv.*
—**Syn.** *v.t.* **1.** chagrin, embarrass. See **ashamed.**

mor·tise (môr′tis), *n., v.,* **-tised, -tis·ing.** —*n.* **1.** a hole in or through one piece of wood to receive a projection on another piece (tenon) so as to form a joint (mortise and tenon joint). **2.** a groove or slot for the reception or passage of a rope, an adjustable pin, etc.
—*v.t.* **1.** to fasten or join by a mortise and tenon: *Good furniture is mortised together, not nailed.* **2.** to fasten or join securely. **3.** to cut a mortise in; provide with a mortise.
[< Old French *mortaise,* perhaps < Arabic *murtazz* be fastened]

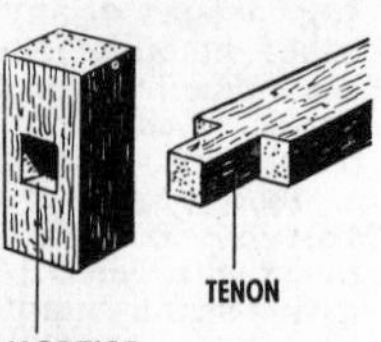

Mortise (def. 1) and tenon joint

mort·main (môrt′mān), *n. Law.* **1.** the condition of lands or tenements held without the right to sell or give them away; inalienable possession. **2.** the possession, usually perpetual, of land by a church, school, or similar corporate body. [< Middle French *morte mayn,* Old French *mortemain,* loan translation of Medieval Latin *mortus manus* dead hand (referring to corporations not being persons)]

mor·tu·ar·y (môr′chů er′ē), *n., pl.* **-ar·ies,** *adj.* —*n.* **1.** a building or room where dead bodies are kept until burial or cremation. **2.** a morgue. **3.** a gift to the priest of a parish from the estate of a dead parishioner.
—*adj.* of death, burial, or mourning.
[< Latin *mortuārius* having to do with the dead < *mortuus* dead, past participle of *morī* to die, related to *mors, mortis* death]

mor·u·la (môr′yů lə, -ů-), *n., pl.* **-lae** (-lē). the spherical mass of blastomeres forming the embryo of many animals, just after the segmentation of the ovum and before the formation of a blastula. [< New Latin *morula* (diminutive) < Latin *mōrum* mulberry]

mor·u·lar (môr′yů lər, -ů-), *adj.* of or having to do with a morula.

mor·u·la·tion (môr′yů lā′shən, -ů-), *n.* the formation of a morula.

mos., months.

MOS (no periods), *U.S.* an army military occupational specialty (designated in the service record of a soldier by a serial number or numbers).

mo·sa·ic (mō zā′ik), *n., adj., v.,* **-sa·icked, -sa·ick·ing.** —*n.* **1.** small pieces of stone, glass, wood, etc., of different colors, inlaid to form a picture or design. **2.** such a picture or design: *Mosaics are used in the floors, walls, or ceilings of buildings, for table tops, etc. This reflected the inferior role the Venetians had been forced to accept in all the arts but mosaic* (New Yorker). **3.** anything like a mosaic: *His music is a mosaic of folk melodies.* **4.** a group of aerial photographs put together to form a continuous photograph of an area. **5.** mosaic disease: *tobacco mosaic.*
—*adj.* formed by, having to do with, or resembling a mosaic.
—*v.t.* **1.** to combine, as in mosaic. **2.** to form like mosaic. **3.** to decorate with or as if with mosaics: *... brilliantly mosaicked piles of folded Persian rugs* (Atlantic).
[< Medieval Latin *mosaicus,* variant of *musaicus* having to do with music, the Muses; artistic]

Mo·sa·ic (mō zā′ik), *adj.* of or having to do with Moses or the Mosaic law. [< New Latin *Mosaicus* < Latin *Mōsēs* < Greek *Mōsēs* < Hebrew *moshe*]

Mo·sa·i·cal (mō zā′ə kəl), *adj.* Mosaic.

mosaic disease, any of various virus diseases of tobacco and other plants in which the leaves become spotted.

mosaic gold, 1. a yellow compound, stannic sulfide, used in gilding. *Formula:* SnS_2 **2.** ormolu.

mo·sa·i·cism (mō zā′ə siz əm), *n. Biology.* the presence of different or antagonistic genetic characteristics in adjacent cells of the body, chiefly due to faulty cell division.

mo·sa·i·cist (mō zā′ə sist), *n.* a maker of mosaics; dealer in mosaics.

Mosaic law, **1.** the ancient law of the Hebrews, ascribed to Moses and contained chiefly in the Pentateuch or the Torah. **2.** the part of the Bible where these laws are stated; Pentateuch.

mosaic vision, the manner of vision of compound eyes, as of insects or other arthropods, in which the visual impression is composed of the impressions of a number of the individual facets of the eye.

mo·sa·saur (mō′sə sôr, mos′ə-), *n.* a prehistoric marine lizard which reached fifty feet in length. [< New Latin *Mosasaurus* the genus name < Latin *Mosa,* the river *Meuse* (close to Maastricht, site of the fossil remains) + Greek *saûros* lizard]

mo·sa·sau·rus (mō′sə sôr′əs), *n.* mosasaur.

mos·chate (mos′kāt, -kit), *adj.* smelling like musk; musky. [< New Latin *moschatus,* variant of Late Latin *muscatus* < Latin *muscus* musk]

mos·cha·tel (mos′kə tel′, mos′kə tel), *n.* an inconspicuous perennial plant of uncertain classification but related to the honeysuckle, having greenish or yellowish flowers with a musky smell: *Moschatel and barren strawberry . . . are quickly swallowed up by springtime's rising tide of vegetation* (London Times). [< French *moscatelle* < Italian *moscatella* < *moscato* musk < Late Latin *muscus.* Related to MUSCATEL.]

Mos·co·vite (mos′kə vīt), *n. Especially British.* Muscovite.

Mo·selle or **mo·selle** (mō zel′), *n.* a light, dry white wine produced along the river Moselle: *Her preference in wines is a light and sweet one such as moselle or sauterne* (Sunday Times).

Mo·ses (mō′ziz, -zis), *n.* **1.** (in the Bible) the great leader and lawgiver of the Israelites, who led the Hebrews out of Egypt and through the desert to within sight of the Promised Land, and received the Ten Commandments from God on Mount Sinai. **2.** a person like Moses; great leader or lawgiver. [< Latin *Mōsēs;* see MOSAIC]

mo·sey (mō′zē), *v.i.,* **-seyed, -sey·ing.** *U.S. Slang.* to move along or away slowly: *I'll mosey along now* (Mark Twain). [American English; origin uncertain]

mo·shav (mō shäv′), *n., pl.* **-sha·vim** (-shä vēm′). *Hebrew.* an Israeli cooperative settlement with independent farms of equal size.

mosk (mosk), *n.* mosque.

Mos·lem (moz′ləm, mos′-), *n., pl.* **-lems** or **-lem,** *adj.* —*n.* a follower of Mohammed; a Mohammedan. —*adj.* of or having to do with the followers of Mohammed, their beliefs, customs, or culture; Mohammedan: *The Moslem world today presents a complex pattern* (Newsweek). Also, **Muslem, Muslim, Mussulman.** [< Arabic *muslim* one who submits. Related to ISLAM, SALAAM. Doublet of MUSSULMAN.] —**Syn.** *adj.* Islamic.

Mos·lem·ic (moz lem′ik, mos-), *adj.* Moslem.

Mos·lem·ism (moz′lə miz əm, mos′-), *n.* the practice of the religion of Islam, followed by Moslems; Mohammedanism.

Mos·lem·ize (moz′lə mīz, mos′-), *v.t.,* **-ized, -iz·ing.** to convert to Islam, the religion of Moslems; Mohammedanize: *The Berbers were Moslemized during the Arab invasions . . . in the 700's* (Time).

mosque (mosk), *n.* a Moslem place of public worship: *A Mohammedan mosque is as much a place of rest and refuge as of prayer . . . the houseless Arab may take shelter there by night or day* (Amelia B. Edwards). Also, **mosk, masjid, musjid.** [< Middle French *mosquée* < Italian *moschea* < Arabic *masjid*]

Mosque

mos·qui·tal (mə skē′təl), *adj.* **1.** having to do with mosquitoes. **2.** spread by mosquitoes.

mos·qui·to (mə skē′tō), *n., pl.* **-toes** or **-tos.** any of various small, slender dipterous insects. The females have mouth parts that can pierce the skin of men and animals and draw blood, causing itching. Certain mosquitoes are carriers of malaria, yellow fever, and encephalitis. *A knowledge of the biting-cycles of mosquitoes may have considerable economic and medical importance* (Science News). [< Spanish *mosquito* (diminutive) < *mosca* fly < Latin *musca*]

Common Female Mosquito (Line shows actual length.)

mosquito bar, a mosquito net: *Brett commandeered a bedroll and mosquito bar from his supply depot and turned me loose* (New Yorker).

mosquito boat, a fast motorboat carrying a gun and torpedoes, now called a PT boat.

mosquito fish, a small fresh-water fish of the southern United States, that feeds on the larvae of mosquitoes; gambusia.

mosquito fleet, a fleet of mosquito boats, used to chase and destroy submarines, do scout duty, etc.: *The Mosquito fleet sailed across the narrow Adriatic* (New York Times).

mosquito hawk, **1.** a dragonfly. **2.** *U.S.* a nighthawk.

mosquito net, a piece of mosquito netting that can be hung on a frame over a bed, chair, etc., to keep off mosquitoes.

mosquito netting, a coarse cotton fabric with small meshes, used for mosquito nets.

moss (môs, mos), *n.* **1.** any of various very small, soft, green or brown plants that grow together like a carpet on moist ground, rocks, trees, etc. **2.** a matted mass of such plants growing together. **3.** any of several superficially similar plants, such as certain lichens or lycopods. **4.** *Scottish.* a bog or swamp, especially a peat bog: *With anxious eye he wander'd o'er Mountain and meadow, moss and moor* (Scott).
—*v.t.* to cover with a growth of moss: *an oak whose boughs were moss'd with age* (Shakespeare).
[Old English *mos* bog; later, moss. Related to MIRE.] —**moss′like′,** *adj.*

moss agate, a variety of agate with dark green, brownish, or black markings that resemble a moss.

moss·back (môs′bak′, mos′-), *n.* **1.** *U.S. Slang.* a person whose ideas are out of date; extreme conservative: *He says Major Garnet means well, only he's a mossback* (George Washington Cable). **2.** *U.S.* a large and old fish, turtle, etc., with a growth of algae on its back. [American English < *moss* + *back,* noun]

moss·backed (môs′bakt′, mos′-), *adj. U.S.* behind the times; conservative; unchanging: *. . . there were some who tried to dismiss the whole matter as a mossbacked anachronism* (Time).

Möss·bau·er effect (mœs′bou ər), *Physics.* a method of producing gamma rays with a precise wave length that makes measurements by gamma radiation possible: *The experimental apparatus that employs the Mössbauer effect consists of an aluminum turntable, on the spindle of which is mounted a photon emitter, a radioactive isotope of iron* (Scientific American). [< Rudolf Ludwig *Mössbauer,* born 1929, a German physicist, who discovered it]

moss·bunk·er (môs′bung′kər, mos′-), *n. U.S. Dialect.* the menhaden (fish). [American English, probably < Dutch *marsbanker,* earlier *masbank*]

moss campion, any of several low, mosslike campions, having reddish, purplish, or white flowers and growing in arctic and mountainous regions.

moss-grown (môs′grōn′, mos′-), *adj.* **1.** overgrown with moss: *moss-grown towers* (Shakespeare). **2.** antiquated.

moss hag, *Scottish.* **1.** a hollow in a bog. **2.** a hole or pit from which peat has been dug.

moss·i·ness (môs′ē nis, mos′-), *n.* the quality or state of being mossy: *A Himalayan forest is a wealth of leafiness and mossiness* (Burrell and Cuthell).

mos·so (môs′sō), *adj. Music.* rapid (used as a direction). [< Italian *mosso* movement < *muovere* to move < Latin *movēre*]

moss pink, a low-growing phlox of the eastern United States, with pink, white, or lavender flowers; ground pink.

moss rose, a cultivated cabbage rose with mosslike growth on the calyx and stem.

moss-troop·er (môs′trü′pər, mos′-), *n.* **1.** a marauder of the Scottish border during the 1600's. **2.** a raider; brigand.

moss-troop·er·y (môs′trü′pər ē, mos′-), *n., pl.* **-er·ies.** **1.** the condition of being moss-troopers. **2.** the acts of moss-troopers.

moss-troop·ing (môs′trü′ping, mos′-), *adj.* freebooting; marauding.

moss·y (môs′ē, mos′-), *adj.,* **moss·i·er, moss·i·est.** **1.** covered or overgrown with moss: *a mossy bank. A wood of mossy distorted trees* (Francis Parkman). **2.** like moss: *mossy green.* **3.** covered as if with moss; downy; velvety: *the mossy antlers of a deer.*

moss·y-cup oak (môs′ē kup′, mos′-), the bur oak.

most (mōst), *adj.* (*used as superlative of* **much** *and* **many,** *with the comparative* **more**), *n., adv.* —*adj.* **1.** the greatest quantity, amount, measure, degree, or number of: *The winner gets the most money.* **2.** Also, **'most.** almost all: *Most children like candy.*
for the most part. See under **part,** *n.*
—*n.* **1.** the greatest quantity, amount, degree, or number: *He does most of his work at night. Most of my books are old.* **2.** the greatest number of persons; the majority: *He has a better appetite than most.*
at most or **at the most,** at the utmost extent; at furthest; at the outside: *They* [*the works of the great poets*] *have only been read as the multitude read the stars, at most astrologically, not astronomically* (Thoreau).
make the most of, to use to the best advantage: *making the most of an opportunity. Ah, make the most of what we yet may spend* (Edward FitzGerald).
the most, *Slang.* the ultimate; the absolute superlative (used predicatively): *Last week the general and even the Pentagon conceded that the bop campaign was the most, to say the least* (Time).
—*adv.* **1.** in or to the greatest extent or degree: *This tooth hurts most.* **2.** as a superlative: *most kind, most kindly, most truly, most easily, most rapid, most curious.* **3.** *Informal.* almost; nearly: *I felt so lonesome I most wished I was dead* (Mark Twain).
[Old English *māst,* and *mǣst*]
➤ **most, almost.** *Most* is the common, informal clip of *almost: A drop in prices will appeal to most everybody.* It would be used in writing conversation and in informal style, but is ordinarily out of place in written English.
➤ See **more** for another usage note.

'most (mōst), *adj.* most (def. 2).

-most, suffix forming superlatives, as in *foremost, inmost, outmost, hithermost, topmost.* [alteration (influenced by *most*) of Middle English *-mest* < Old English *-mo,* or *-ma* + *-est,* both superlative suffixes]

moste (mōst), *v.* past tense of **mote**[2].

most·est (mōs′tist), *n. Slang.* the most: *the hostess with the mostest.*

most favored nation, the nation receiving from another nation the most advantageous terms in respect to duties, tariffs, quotas of commodities, etc. Terms granted to the most favored nation are frequently taken as the standard fixing the terms to be granted by the other nation to a third, in treaties or trade agreements. —**most′-fa′vored-na′tion,** *adj.*

most·ly (mōst′lē), *adv.* for the most part; almost all; mainly; chiefly: *The work is mostly done. All afternoon we sat together, mostly in silence* (Robert Louis Stevenson). —**Syn.** principally.

mot (mō *for 1;* mot *for 2*), *n.* **1.** a clever or witty remark: *He moved easily and with a certain pleasure in political circles, loving to note down mots of Balfour and others* (London Times). **2.** *Archaic.* a note sounded on a bugle, huntsman's horn, etc.: *Three mots on this bugle will . . . bring round, at our need, a jolly band of yonder honest yeomen* (Scott). [< Old French *mot* < Vulgar Latin *mottum* < Latin *muttum* grunt, word. Doublet of MOTTO.] —**Syn. 1.** witticism.

MOT (no periods), Ministry of Transport (of Great Britain).

mote[1] (mōt), *n.* **1.** a speck of dust: *thick as motes in the sunbeam* (Chaucer). **2.** any very small thing: *And why beholdest thou the mote that is in thy brother's eye* (Matthew 7:3). [Old English *mot*]

mote[2] (mōt), *v.i., past tense* **moste** (mōst).

1. *Archaic.* may or might: *Was never knight on ground mote be with him compared* (James Thomson). 2. *Obsolete.* must: *At last their ways so fell, that they mote part* (Edmund Spenser). [Old English *mōtan*]

mot·ed (mō′tid), *adj.* full of motes: *the moted sunlight* (John Greenleaf Whittier).

mo·tel (mō tel′), *n. U.S.* a hotel or group of cottages which provide sleeping, and often eating, accommodations for motorists: *Motels in resort areas offer at least a pool. Some have washing machines, electric irons, free movies* (Saturday Review). [American English; blend of *motor* and *hotel*]

mo·tet (mō tet′), *n. Music.* a vocal composition in polyphonic style, on a Biblical or similar prose text, intended for use in a church service: *The boy and I again to the singing of Mr. Porter's motets* (Samuel Pepys). [< Old French *motet* (originally, diminutive) < *mot* word; see MOT]

moth (môth, moth), *n., pl.* **moths** (môᴛʜz, moᴛʜz, môths, moths). a broad-winged insect very much like a butterfly, but lacking knobs at the ends of the antennae, having less brightly colored wings, and flying mostly at night. Moths are destructive only in the larval stage, as the brown-tail moth larva that lives on plant tissues, and the clothes moth larva that feeds on cloth, fur, etc. Some larvae, such as the silkworm, are useful to man. See also picture under **owlet moth.** [Old English *moththe*]

Blue Underwing Moth
(wingspread, 1½ to 3 in.)

moth ball, a small ball of naphthalene or camphor, used to keep moths away from clothing, blankets, silk, fur, etc.
in or **into moth balls,** in or into storage protected against deterioration or damage: *The Navy has 3 carriers of the Midway class, . . . and 24 of the Essex class, of which 9 are in active service and 15 in moth balls* (Newsweek).

moth-ball (môth′bôl′, moth′-), *v.t. U.S.* to store (a ship, tank, etc.) protected against deterioration: *The Navy should moth-ball battleships and similar outdated ships of the line* (Time).
—*adj.* moth-balled; stored in a state protecting against deterioration: *moth-ball vessels, moth-ball wheat.*

moth-ball fleet, *U.S.* the Navy ships which have been inactivated and are being held in reserve: *One of the Navy's newest aircraft carriers . . . will be decommissioned Friday and put into the moth-ball fleet* (Baltimore Sun).

moth-eat·en (môth′ē′tən, moth′-), *adj.* 1. eaten away or destroyed by moths; having holes made by moths. 2. worn-out; out-of-date. —**Syn.** 2. passé.

moth·er[1] (muᴛʜ′ər), *n.* 1. a woman who has given birth to a child. 2. a female parent: *puppies that have lost their mother.* 3. the cause or source of anything: *Necessity, mother of invention!* (William Wycherley). *France, the mother of ideas* (Walter Besant). 4. the head of a female religious community. 5. a woman exercising control and responsibility like that of a mother. 6. a familiar name for an old woman. 7. a female ancestor. 8. the qualities characteristic of a mother; maternal affection: . . . *the mother in her soul awakes* (Alexander Pope). 9. *Archaic.* hysteria: *She is . . . much subject to fits of the mother* (Tobias Smollett).
—*v.t.* 1. to be mother of; act as mother to: *Ruth mothers her baby sister.* 2. to acknowledge oneself mother of or assume as one's own. 3. to give birth to; produce as, or as if, a mother: *The floods were mothered by another hurricane* (Time).
—*adj.* 1. that is a mother. 2. like a mother. 3. of a mother. 4. native.
[alteration of Old English *mōdor.* Compare FATHER.]

moth·er[2] (muᴛʜ′ər), *n.* a stringy, sticky substance, consisting of bacteria, formed in vinegar or on the surface of liquids that are turning to vinegar; mother of vinegar. [perhaps special use of *mother*[1], or perhaps < Middle Dutch *moeder*, or *moder*]

Mother Car·ey's chicken (kãr′iz), 1. the storm petrel. 2. any of various other petrels. [spelling for altered pronunciation of Latin *Māter cāra* dear Mother, an expression of Levantine sailors (the entire expression meant "snow," perhaps referring to the white of petrel feathers)]

mother church, a church from which or by which others have been formed.

mother country, 1. the country where a person was born. 2. a country in relation to its colonies or its natives.

moth·er·craft (muᴛʜ′ər kraft′, -kräft′), *n. British.* a mother's duties in the family; the craft or business of a mother: *Against all the rules of mothercraft, she picked herself a favourite* (London Times).

mother earth, the earth personified as the mother of its inhabitants and its products: . . . *the unbounded treasures of mother earth* (Rolf Boldrewood).

mother figure, 1. *Psychoanalysis.* a person imaginatively substituted for one's real mother and made the object of responses originally developed toward the mother. 2. a maternal figure; a kindly or warm-hearted person.

Mother Goose, the pretended author of a book of fairy tales by Charles Perrault, published in 1697.

moth·er·hood (muᴛʜ′ər hu̇d), *n.* 1. the state or fact of being a mother: *The young wife was proud of her motherhood.* 2. the qualities or spirit of a mother. 3. mothers: *All the motherhood of the town came to the exhibition of prize babies.*

mother house, 1. the monastery, convent, etc., in which the superior of a religious congregation or order lives. 2. the original monastery, convent, etc., of a congregation or order.

Mother Hub·bard (hub′ərd), 1. a full, loose garment worn by women, especially for housework. 2. the subject of a well-known Mother Goose nursery rhyme, beginning "Old Mother Hubbard went to the cupboard. . . ."

mother image, mother figure.

Moth·er·ing Sunday (muᴛʜ′ər ing), *British.* the Sunday in mid-Lent on which it is customary to visit one's parents and to give or receive presents: *Our traditional Simnel Cake is now being prepared by craftsmen in readiness for Mothering Sunday* (Sunday Times).

moth·er-in-law (muᴛʜ′ər in lô′), *n., pl.* **moth·ers-in-law.** 1. the mother of one's husband or wife. 2. *British Informal.* a stepmother.

moth·er·land (muᴛʜ′ər land′), *n.* 1. one's native country. 2. the land of one's ancestors. 3. a country as the mother or producer of anything.

moth·er·less (muᴛʜ′ər lis), *adj.* having no mother; having no living mother. —**moth′er·less·ness,** *n.*

moth·er·li·ness (muᴛʜ′ər lē nis), *n.* the quality of being motherly.

mother liquor, *Chemistry, Pharmacy.* the liquid that remains after the removal of crystallizing substances from a solution.

mother lode, a rich or main vein of ore in an area, or in a mine.

moth·er·ly (muᴛʜ′ər lē), *adj.* 1. like a mother; like a mother's; kindly: *A motherly old lady* (Dickens). 2. of a mother: *motherly affection. You from motherly lap the bright girl can sever* (Robert Ellis).

moth·er-na·ked (muᴛʜ′ər nā′kid), *adj.* naked as at birth; stark naked.

Mother of God, the Virgin Mary (a title officially defined by the Council of Ephesus in 431 A.D.).

moth·er-of-pearl (muᴛʜ′ər əv pėrl′), *n.* the hard, smooth, shining, rainbow-colored lining of certain shells, as of the pearl oyster, mussel, and abalone; nacre. It is used to make ornaments, buttons, etc. —*adj.* made of or like this substance.

mother-of-pearl cloud, nacreous cloud.

moth·er-of-thyme (muᴛʜ′ər əv tīm′), *n.* wild thyme.

mother of vinegar, mother[2].

mother's boy, mama's boy.

Mother's Day, a day set apart in the United States and Canada in honor of mothers, observed on the second Sunday in May.

mother ship, 1. an aircraft that carries aloft another aircraft, drone, or rocket, and launches it, and sometimes directs its flight: *The drone planes were flown by "pilots" in mother ships, several miles away* (Science News Letter). 2. a ship which guards, escorts, or acts as a base for, one or more torpedo boats, submarines, or the like.

moth·er-sib (muᴛʜ′ər sib′), *n. U.S., Anthropology.* a group or clan whose members trace their descent from a common ancestor through the line of the mother.

mother superior, a woman who is the head of a convent of nuns.

moth·er-to-be (muᴛʜ′ər tu̇ bē′), *n., pl.* **moth·ers-to-be.** an expectant mother: *Fashion and beauty section for mothers-to-be* (Maclean's).

mother tongue, 1. one's native language. 2. an original language to which other languages owe their origin.

mother wit, natural intelligence; common sense: *Katherine: Where did you study all this goodly speech? Petruchio: It is extempore, from my mother wit* (Shakespeare). —**Syn.** sagacity.

moth·er·wort (muᴛʜ′ər wėrt′), *n.* a bitter European plant of the mint family, whose notched leaves have whorls of purple flowers in their axils.

moth·er·y (muᴛʜ′ər ē), *adj.* containing, consisting of, or resembling mother: *mothery vinegar.* [< *mother*[2] + *-y*[1]]

moth mullein, a biennial mullein native to Europe, with smooth leaves, racemes of solitary yellow or whitish flowers, and purple, hairy filaments.

moth·proof (môth′prüf′, moth′-), *adj.* 1. repellent to moths or resistant to the attack of their larvae: *mothproof wool.* 2. impervious to moths: *a mothproof closet.* —*v.t.* to make resistant to attack by the larvae of moths.

moth·y (môth′ē, moth′-), *adj.,* **moth·i·er, moth·i·est.** infested by moths; moth-eaten.

mo·tif (mō tēf′), *n.* 1. a subject for development or treatment in art, literature, or music; a principal idea or feature; motive; theme: *This opera contains a love motif.* 2. a distinctive figure in a design. 3. *Music.* motive. [< French *motif* < Middle French, adjective < Late Latin *mōtīvus* moving. Doublet of MOTIVE.]

mo·tile (mō′təl), *adj. Biology.* able to move by itself: *motile cells, motile spores.* —*n. Psychology.* a person whose mental images are chiefly motor. [< Latin *mōtus* moved, past participle of *movēre* + *-ilis* of, like]

mo·til·i·ty (mō til′ə tē), *n.* motile quality: *A very small lesion may produce very decided impairment of motility* (A.M. Hamilton).

mo·tion (mō′shən), *n.* 1. change of position or place; movement; moving: *a sudden motion, the motion of a ship, the motion of one's hand in writing.* 2. a formal proposal made in a meeting, legislative body, etc.: *The motion to adjourn was carried.* 3. *Law.* an application made to a court or judge for an order, ruling, etc. 4. a mental or emotional impulse; inclination; volition: *He signed the agreement of his own motion.* 5. a. a mechanical apparatus that moves, causes motion, or modifies motion. b. the action of a mechanical apparatus or any of its parts. 6. *Music.* a. the melodic progression of a single part or voice from one pitch to another. b. the progression of two or more parts or voices with relation to each other. 7. *Obsolete.* a. a puppet show. b. a puppet.
in motion, moving; going: *the wheels of industry in motion.*
motions, movements; actions; activities: *Mr. Glossin was well aware that such a hint was of power sufficient to decide the motions of his . . . colleague* (Scott).
—*v.i.* to make a movement, as of the hand or head, to show one's meaning: *He motioned to show us the way.* —*v.t.* to show (a person) what to do by a motion of the hand, head, etc.: *He motioned me out.*
[< Old French *motion,* learned borrowing from Latin *mōtiō, -ōnis* < *movēre* to move]
—**Syn.** *n.* 1. **Motion, movement** imply change of place, position, or condition. **Motion** means the state of not being at rest or the process of moving, especially as thought of apart from any particular thing or when the kind of action is not stressed: *We study the laws of motion.* **Movement,** usually applying to the motion of someone or something, emphasizes a definite moving in a particular direction and regular way: *the movement of the earth.* -*v.i.* gesticulate.

mo·tion·al (mō′shə nəl), *adj.* 1. of or having to do with motion. 2. characterized by particular motions, as certain diseases.

mo·tion·less (mō′shən lis), *adj.* not moving; incapable of motion: *Some sat on horseback, motionless as equestrian statues* (Francis Parkman). —**mo′tion·less·ly,** *adv.* —**mo′tion·less·ness,** *n.* —**Syn.** inert, stationary, still, quiet.

motion picture, 1. a series of pictures photographed with a special camera on a strip of film so as to record very slight changes in position of persons or objects, and shown in succession on a screen by means of a projector at such a speed as to give the effect of continuous motion: *The motion picture began to attract attention in the United States at the close of the last century* (Emory S. Bogardus). Also called *moving picture, cinema, film,* or (in Great Britain) *pictures.* 2. a series of such pictures making up a story; photoplay.

mo·tion-pic·ture (mō′shən pik′chər), *adj.* of, having to do with, or characteristic of motion pictures: *One of the most characteristic products of the American motion-picture industry is the Western* (Saturday Review).

motion-picture projector, a machine for projecting motion pictures on a screen.

mo·tions (mō′shənz), *n.pl.* See under **motion,** *n.*

motion sickness, a condition characterized by nausea, vomiting, and dizziness, caused by the motion of a train, plane, bus, ship, etc.: *Capsules designed to prevent motion sickness ... have been added to the army's medicine chest* (Baltimore Sun).

mo·ti·vate (mō′tə vāt), *v.t.,* **-vat·ed, -vat·ing.** to provide with a motive; act upon as a motive. —**Syn.** incite.

mo·ti·va·tion (mō′tə vā′shən), *n.* the act or process of furnishing with an incentive or inducement to action: *Man's motivations emerge from his entire experience* (Atlantic).

mo·ti·va·tion·al (mō′tə vā′shə nəl), *adj.* 1. of or having to do with motivation: *motivational analysis.* 2. motivating: *... denying the very existence of those motivational drives that lead us to write to editors, to vote, to ...* (Wall Street Journal).

motivational or **motivation research,** the study of what conscious or subconscious influences actually induce people to choose or reject a course of action, especially all the factors that make potential customers buy or refrain from buying a particular commodity or brand: *Motivational research procedures already developed have proved that in many cases they can be used to boost a product's saleability* (Wall Street Journal).

motivational or **motivation researcher,** a person skilled or trained in motivational research.

mo·tive (mō′tiv), *n., adj., v.,* **-tived, -tiv·ing.** —*n.* 1. a thought or feeling that makes a person act; moving consideration or reason: *His motive in going away was a wish to travel. The poor savages ... had merely gathered together through motives of curiosity* (Washington Irving). 2. a motif in art, literature, or music: *a beautiful motive of festoons.* 3. *Music.* **a.** the briefest intelligible and rhythmically distinct fragment of a musical theme or subject. **b.** a subject. **c.** a leitmotif.
—*adj.* that makes something move.
—*v.t.* to provide with a motive; supply a motive to.
[< Late Latin *mōtīvus* moving, impelling < Latin *movēre* to move. Doublet of MOTIF.]
—**Syn.** *n.* 1. incentive. See **reason.**

mo·tive·less (mō′tiv lis), *adj.* having no motive; without object: *... a motiveless malignity* (Samuel Taylor Coleridge).

motive power, 1. power used to impart motion; source of mechanical energy: *For many years the motive power of trains was steam. Public reputation is a motive power* (Benjamin Disraeli). 2. all the locomotives and other self-propelled vehicles of a railroad.

mo·tiv·ic (mō tiv′ik), *adj. Music.* of, having to do with, or characteristic of a motif: *... in the personal works he has begun using more extended melodic themes, instead of the terse motivic ones of his earlier music ...* (Manchester Guardian).

mo·tiv·i·ty (mō tiv′ə tē), *n.* 1. the power of initiating or producing motion. 2. kinetic energy.

mot juste (mō zhYst′), *pl.* **mots justes** (mō zhYst′). *French.* a word or phrase that exactly fits the case: *Such was the general enthusiasm for her that she was credited with mots justes and insights* (New Yorker).

mot·ley (mot′lē), *n., pl.* **-leys,** *adj.* —*n.* 1. a suit of many colors worn by clowns: *Old-time fools and jesters wore motley.* 2. a mixture of things that are different. 3. a fool; jester: *I have gone here and there And made myself a motley to the view* (Shakespeare). 4. *Obsolete.* cloth of mixed colors.
—*adj.* 1. of different colors like a clown's suit: *dressed in the motley garb that jesters wear* (Longfellow). 2. wearing a motley: *a motley fool* (Shakespeare). 3. composed of unlike elements: *a motley crowd.*
[Middle English *motteley,* apparently < unrecorded Anglo-French *motelé* < Old English *mot* mote[1]] —**mot′ley·ness,** *n.*
—**Syn.** *n.* 2. medley, mélange. *-adj.* 1. variegated, harlequin. 3. heterogeneous.

mot·mot (mot′mot), *n.* any of various tropical birds, related to the kingfishers, having a serrate bill, greenish and bluish feathers, and a tail with long feathers spread like a tennis racket, found in wooded areas of Central and South America. [< New Latin *momot;* apparently imitative]

mo·to·car (mō′tō kär′), *n.* motorcar. [American English, variant of *motorcar*]

mo·to·cy·cle (mō′tō sī′kəl), *n., v.i.,* **-cled, -cling.** motorcycle.

mo·tom·e·ter (mō tom′ə tər), *n.* a device for indicating the number of revolutions made by a shaft or the like. [< Latin *mōtus* motion (< *movēre* to move) + *-meter*]

mo·to·neu·ron (mō′tə nůr′on, -nyůr′-), *n.* a motor neuron: *Nerve impulses generated by the motoneuron activate the muscle to which the stretch receptor is attached* (Scientific American).

mo·to·neu·rone (mō′tə nůr′ōn, -nyůr′-), *n.* motoneuron.

mo·tor (mō′tər), *n.* 1. an engine that makes a machine go: *an electric motor.* 2. an apparatus that converts electrical into mechanical energy by the inducing of an electrodynamic response which causes a part (the armature) of the apparatus to revolve. 3. an internal-combustion engine. 4. an apparatus that adapts the energy of some natural agent, such as water or wind, or force, such as compression, to mechanical use; prime mover, such as a water wheel or steam engine. 5. *British.* an automobile; motorcar: *The younger generation ... is habituated to motors and cinemas* (J.W.R. Scott). 6. a person or thing that imparts motion or compels action.
motors, shares of stock, bonds, etc., issued by automobile manufacturers: *The small motors were the day's most popular stocks* (Wall Street Journal).
—*adj.* 1. run by a motor: *a motor vehicle.* 2. of, by, or by means of automobiles: *a motor tour.* 3. causing or having to do with motion or action; functioning like a motor. 4. **a.** (of nerves) conveying or imparting an impulse from the central nervous system to a muscle which results or tends to result in motion. **b.** (of muscles, impulses, centers, etc.) concerned in motion. **c.** designating the effect of stimuli from the central nervous system causing motion or action. 5. *Psychology.* of, having to do with, or involving muscular or glandular activity: *a motor response.*
—*v.i.* to travel by automobile; ride in an automobile: *The two spent their time ... motoring and walking on the Downs* (John Galsworthy).
[< Latin *mōtor* mover < *movēre* to move]

mo·tor·a·ble (mō′tər ə bəl), *adj.* that can be traveled over by a motor vehicle: *There's no such thing as a railroad, and there are only 2,500 miles of motorable roads* (Wall Street Journal).

mo·tor·bi·cy·cle (mō′tər bī′sə kəl), *n.* 1. a bicycle with an auxiliary motor. 2. a light motorcycle: *In the case of motor vehicles, and in particular motorbicycles, the cost of reducing noise is more modest* (New Scientist).

mo·tor·bike (mō′tər bīk′), *n. Especially British.* a motorbicycle: *The motorbike lay on the other side of the road, its wheels in the air, like a dead bug* (Atlantic).

mo·tor·boat (mō′tər bōt′), *n.* a boat that is run by a motor.

mo·tor·boat·ing (mō′tər bō′ting), *n.* the sport of riding in a motor boat: *But motorboating did not become practical or popular until the gasoline engine was perfected in the early 1900's ...* (World Book Encyclopedia).

mo·tor·bus (mō′tər bus′), *n.* a bus run by a motor.

mo·tor·cade (mō′tər kād), *n., v.,* **-cad·ed, -cad·ing.** —*n.* a procession or long line of automobiles: *The crowd which had gathered to greet Mr. Nehru's motorcade ...* (Times of India). —*v.i. Informal.* to travel in or with a large group of automobiles: *But in Flint and Jackson, where he motorcaded through the streets ...* (Nashville Tennessean). [American English < *motor* + (caval)*cade*]

mo·tor·car (mō′tər kär′), *n. British.* an automobile: *The position commands a salary of £175 per month and a motorcar is provided by the company* (Cape Times).

motor carrier, a truck or bus line that carries passengers or freight.

mo·tor·coach (mō′tər kōch′), *n.,* or **motor coach,** a motorbus.

motor court, *U.S.* a motel: *Business composed of general store, apartments and motor court* (Wall Street Journal).

mo·tor·cy·cle (mō′tər sī′kəl), *n., v.,* **-cled, -cling.** —*n.* a two-wheeled vehicle or one with a sidecar, propelled by a gasoline engine. —*v.i.* to travel by motorcycle.

mo·tor·cy·clist (mō′tər sī′klist), *n.* a person who rides a motorcycle: *... from his early days as a motorcyclist* (Sunday Times).

mo·tor·dom (mō′tər dəm), *n.* motor vehicles, the people who use them, or those who deal in them, considered collectively: *This road had all the charms of the old English highway before the scarifying era of motordom* (Blackwood's Magazine).

motor drive, an electric motor used for operating a machine or machines.

mo·tor-driv·en (mō′tər driv′ən), *adj.* driven by a motor or motors: *The Aeronautic Show ... was somewhat of a disappointment in that none of the motor-driven heavier-than-air machines exhibited has actually flown* (Scientific American).

mo·tor·drome (mō′tər drōm′), *n.* a rounded course or track, often rising at an angle or in a curve toward its outer edge, upon which automobile and motorcycle races are run.

mo·tored (mō′tərd), *adj.* having a motor or motors.

motor generator or **motor generator set,** an apparatus consisting of a combination of one or more motors and one or more generators, used to transform electric currents, lower voltage, etc.: *The set ... is powered by a motor generator that can be carried by one of a two-man team* (Science News Letter).

motor hotel, *U.S.* a motel that provides full hotel service, especially one with garage space, in the downtown section of a city: *... a new seven-story motor hotel, to serve the tourist and convention trade* (Wall Street Journal).

mo·to·ri·al (mō tôr′ē əl, -tōr′-), *adj.* 1. of or having to do with motion. 2. of or having to do with a motor nerve.

mo·tor·ic (mō tôr′ik, -tōr′-), *adj.* having to do with or causing motion or action: *motoric rhythm, motoric music.*

mo·tor·ing (mō′tər ing), *n.* riding in a vehicle operated by a motor.

mo·tor·ise (mō′tə rīz), *v.t.,* **-ised, -is·ing.** *Especially British.* motorize.

mo·tor·ist (mō′tər ist), *n.* a person who travels by automobile, especially one who does it a great deal: *Visiting motorists could cross the frontier at Brest-Litovsk and drive to Moscow ...* (Manchester Guardian).

mo·to·ri·um (mō tôr′ē əm, -tōr′-), *n., pl.* **-to·ri·a** (-tôr′ē ə, -tōr′-). the part of an organism which is concerned with motion. [< New Latin *motorium* < Late Latin, power of motion < Latin *mōtor;* see MOTOR]

mo·tor·i·za·tion (mō′tər ə zā′shən), *n.* 1. a motorizing. 2. a being motorized.

mo·tor·ize (mō′tə rīz), *v.t.,* **-ized, -iz·ing.** 1. to furnish with a motor or motors: *The Danville voyageurs ... rode in a motorized "box car"* (Baltimore Sun). 2. to equip with motor-driven vehicles in place of horse-drawn vehicles. 3. to equip (infantry) with motor-driven transport vehicles, especially trucks, but not to alter the nature of their weapons.

mo·tor·less (mō′tər lis), *adj.* having no motor; without a motor: *motorless aircraft.*

motor lorry, *British.* a motor truck: *Even the powerful engineering exhibits, which include a monster motor lorry ...* (Listener).

mo·tor·man (mō′tər mən), *n., pl.* **-men.** 1. the operator of an electric streetcar, locomotive, etc. 2. a man who runs a motor.

motor mower, a motor-driven lawn mower; power lawn mower: *Now—the light motor mower that has everything!* (Sunday Times).

motor pool, a group of automobiles or other motor vehicles held by an organization for temporary use, as needed, by individuals, but not permanently assigned: *Several months ago the government ordered all officials ... to turn in their state-owned vehicles to a common motor pool* (Time).

mo·tors (mō′tərz), *n.pl.* See under **motor,** *n.*

motor scooter, a motor-driven vehicle for one or two passengers, generally resembling a small motorcycle except that the driver's feet rest upon a floor board and he does not sit astride: *They can out-sell us with cars, motor scooters, typewriters—not because their efficiency is high but their wage-bill is low* (Scottish Sunday Express).

Motor Scooter

mo·tor·ship (mō′tər ship′), *n.* a ship whose engine is driven by a motor, usually a Diesel engine: *A helicopter lifted the six passengers and 20 members of the crew of the disabled . . . motorship . . . during a heavy snow-storm* (Cape Times). *Abbr.:* M.S.

motor spirit, *British.* petrol: *The Government clapped a whacking increase onto the duty on oil and motor spirit* (New Yorker).

motor torpedo boat, any of a type of small, very fast, highly maneuverable naval vessels, having little or no armor, equipped with torpedo tubes and depth charges, one or more machine guns, and now also usually anti-aircraft guns and smoke-screen equipment: *When on an operation they are escorted by various types of . . . motor torpedo boat* (Combined Operations).

motor truck, a truck with an engine and chassis made for carrying heavy loads.

mo·tor·way (mō′tər wā′), *n. British.* a highway with high speed limits and no cross traffic: *New motorways will certainly not solve the problem if traffic continues to increase at the present rate* (Manchester Guardian).

mo·to·ry (mō′tər ē), *adj.* motor.

mott or **motte**[1] (mot), *n. Southwestern U.S.* a clump of trees in a prairie. [< Mexican Spanish *mata*]

motte[2] (mot), *n.* an earthen mound on which a wooden castle was built in early Norman times. [< Old French *motte* mound. Related to MOAT.]

mot·tet·to (mōt tet′tō), *n., pl.* **-ti** (-tē). *Italian.* a motet.

mot·tle (mot′əl), *v.,* **-tled, -tling,** *n.* —*v.t.* to mark with spots or streaks of different colors or shades: *the gray stone parapet, mottled with the green and gold of innumerable mosses* (Mrs. Humphry Ward). —*n.* **1.** a mottled coloring or pattern; mottling. **2.** a spot, blotch, streak, etc., on a mottled surface. [apparently < unrecorded Anglo-French *moteler* to speckle < Old English *mot* speck, mote[1]. Compare MOTLEY.]
—**Syn.** *v.t.* speckle. *-n.* **2.** variegation.

mot·tled (mot′əld), *adj.* marked with spots or streaks of different colors or shades; dappled; marbled.

mottled enamel, streaked or spotted enamel of the teeth, caused by continued use of water with excessive fluorine during the time the teeth are forming.

mot·tler (mot′lər), *n.* a person or thing that mottles.

mot·tling (mot′ling), *n.* mottled coloring.

mot·to (mot′ō), *n., pl.* **-toes** or **-tos. 1.** a brief sentence adopted as a rule of conduct: "*Think before you speak*" *is a good motto.* **2.** a word, sentence, or phrase written or engraved on some object. **3.** motto theme. [< Italian *motto* < Vulgar Latin *mottum* < Latin *muttum* grunt, word. Doublet of MOT.] —**Syn. 1.** proverb, adage, saying.

motto theme, a recurrent and sometimes transformed symbolic theme in a piece of music; leitmotif.

mo·tu pro·pri·o (mō′tü prō′prē ō, mō′tyü), *Latin.* **1.** independently; of one's own accord. **2.** (literally) by one's own motion.

mouch (müch), *v.i., v.t.* mooch.

mou·chard (mü shȧr′), *n. French.* a police spy; informer: *I think the fellow's a cursed mouchard—some Government spy* (Charles Kingsley).

mou·choir (mü shwȧr′), *n.* a handkerchief: *A mouchoir with musk his spirits to cheer* (London Magazine). [< Middle French *mouchoir* < Old French *moucher* blow, wipe the nose < Vulgar Latin *muccāre* < Latin *muccus,* variant of *mūcus* mucus]

mou·di·warp (mou′di wôrp′, mō′-, mü′-), *n. Obsolete.* moldwarp. [variant of *moldwarp*]

moue (mü), *n.* a grimace; pout: *Her pleasantly assembled features . . . can be compressed on stage into an alarming and comical moue* (New York Times). [< French *moue*]

mouf·flon (müf′lon), *n., pl.* **-flons** or (*collectively*) **-flon.** mouflon.

mouf·lon (müf′lon), *n., pl.* **-lons** or (*collectively*) **-lon. 1.** a small wild sheep of the mountainous regions of Sardinia and Corsica, the male of which has large, curving horns: *In the game-rich Gennargentu mountains there are boar, deer, and mouflon* (Atlantic). **2.** its wool, used for fur. [< French *mouflon* < Italian *muflone,* alteration of Late Latin *mufrō, -ōnis*]

mought (mout), *v. Archaic or Dialect.* might[1].
➔ **Mought** survives in nonstandard, rustic speech, chiefly in the southern United States.

mouil·lé (mü yā′), *adj. Phonetics.* **1.** palatalized by a following *y*-sound, as *l* in *million.* **2.** pronounced as palatal or palatalized, as the sounds spelled in Spanish *ll, ñ,* in Italian *gl, gn,* in French *gn,* etc. **3.** pronounced as a *y-* sound but spelled *l* or *ll,* as in certain French words. [< French *mouillé,* past participle of Old French *mouiller* to wet, moisten < Vulgar Latin *molliāre* to soften, for Latin *mollīre* < *mollis* soft]

mou·jik (mü zhik′, mü′zhik), *n.* muzhik.

mou·lage (mü läzh′), *n.* **1.** the making of molds, in plaster of Paris or the like, of objects involved in a crime, or their outlines, as a footprint or tire track, for use in identification, as evidence, etc. **2.** such a mold. **3.** a plaster, wax, or rubber imitation of an injury of the body, used in medical therapy or training. [< French *moulage* a casting < Middle French *mollage* < Old French *mouler* to mold, cast < *modle* a mold[1]]

mould (mōld), *n., v.t., v.i. Especially British.* mold[1], mold[2], and mold[3]: *Moulds often grow on the surface of the rind* (Science News).

mould·a·ble (mōl′də bəl), *adj. Especially British.* moldable.

mould·board (mōld′bôrd′, -bōrd′), *n. Especially British.* moldboard.

mould·er[1] (mōl′dər), *v.i. Especially British.* molder[1].

mould·er[2] (mōl′dər), *n. Especially British.* molder[2].

mould·ing (mōl′ding), *n. Especially British.* molding.

mould·warp (mōld′wôrp′), *n. British Dialect.* moldwarp.

mould·y (mōl′dē), *adj.,* **mould·i·er, mould·i·est.** *Especially British.* moldy.

mou·lin (mü laN′), *n.* a nearly vertical shaft or cavity worn in a glacier by surface water falling through a crack in the ice. [< French *moulin* (literally) a mill < Old French *molin;* see MOLINE]

moult (mōlt), *v.i., v.t., n. Especially British.* molt. —**moult′er,** *n.*

mound[1] (mound), *n.* **1.** a bank or heap, as of earth or stones: *a mound of hay.* **2.** a small hill; hillock: *We have Indian mounds in Ohio.* **3.** *Baseball.* the slightly elevated ground from which a pitcher pitches: *Dean, coming to the mound from center field, got the side out with only one of the runners scoring* (Tishomingo Capital-Democrat).
—*v.t.* **1.** to enclose with a mound or embankment: *A sand-built ridge of heaped hills that mound the sea* (Tennyson). **2.** to heap up: *to mound earth.* **3.** *Dialect.* to enclose with a fence. [origin uncertain]
—**Syn.** *n.* **1.** pile. **2.** knoll.

mound[2] (mound), *n.* a globe of gold or other precious material, intended to represent the earth, often surmounted by a cross and forming part of the insignia of royalty. [< Old French *monde,* learned borrowing from Latin *mundus* earth]

mound·bird (mound′bėrd′), *n.* mound builder.

mound builder, any of a number of large birds, native to Australia and the East Indies, which build large mounds mainly of decaying vegetation in which to incubate their eggs; a megapode.

Mound Builders, a largely prehistoric group of agricultural Indians who lived in central and eastern United States. They built mounds of earth as burial places or to hold temples or chiefs' houses.

mounds·man (moundz′mən), *n., pl.* **-men.** *Baseball.* a pitcher.

mount[1] (mount), *v.t.* **1.** to go or climb up; ascend: *to mount a hill, a ladder, stairs, etc. It was our design to mount the head-waters of the Hudson, to the neighbourhood of Crown Point* (Robert Louis Stevenson). **2. a.** to get up on: *to mount a platform.* **b.** to get on (a horse, bicycle, etc.) for riding. **3.** to put on a horse; furnish with a horse: *Many policemen in this city are mounted.* **4. a.** to prepare (a skeleton, organism, etc.) for examination as a specimen. **b.** to fix (an object) for microscopic examination: *to mount specimens on a slide.* **c.** to prepare (a slide). **d.** to prepare or place (a gun, etc.) in a position for use. **5.** to fix in a setting, backing, support, etc.: *to mount gems in gold, to mount a picture on cardboard.* **6.** to be equipped with or carry (guns), as a fortress or ship. **7.** to provide (a play) with scenery, costumes, etc. **8. a.** to assign (a guard) as a sentry or watch. **b.** to go on duty as (a guard or watch). **9.** to set or place upon an elevation: *a small house mounted on poles. No wonder we see more than the ancients, because we are mounted upon their shoulders* (Cardinal Newman). **10.** to put on; show oneself as wearing: *He found Dick mounting a large top-coat, and muffling up* (Samuel Lover). *It was then that I mounted the turban* (Herman Melville).
—*v.i.* **1.** to move or proceed upward: *A flush mounts to the brow. They shall mount up with wings as eagles* (Isaiah 40:31). **2.** to rise in amount; increase; rise: *The cost of living mounts steadily. The rage of each had mounted to delirium* (Frederick Marryat). **3.** to get on a horse; get up on something: *to mount and ride away. Paul Revere mounted in haste.*
—*n.* **1.** a horse or other animal, or a bicycle, provided for riding: *There was not another mount in the stable* (George Eliot). **2.** something in or on which anything is mounted; setting; backing; support: *A mount for microscopic examination is a slide.* **3.** an act or occasion of riding a horse, especially in a race. **4.** the act or manner of mounting. **5.** *Especially British.* a mat: *a picture mount.* [< Old French *monter,* or *munter* < Vulgar Latin *montāre* < Latin *mōns, montis* mountain]
—**Syn.** *v.t.* **1.** See **climb.**

mount[2] (mount), *n.* **1.** a mountain; high hill. *Mount* is often used before the names of mountains: *Mount Rainier, Mount Everest, Mount Olympus. Abbr.:* Mt. **2.** (in palmistry) a significant prominence in the palm of the hand. **3.** *Obsolete.* a mound. **4.** *Archaic.* a defensive rampart of earth. [partly Old English *munt* < Latin *mōns, montis,* and partly < Old French *mont* < Latin]

mount·a·ble (moun′tə bəl), *adj.* that can be mounted.

moun·tain (moun′tən), *n.* **1.** a very high hill; a natural elevation of the earth's surface rising high above the surrounding level in a massive and conspicuous way. **2.** something like a mountain or high hill: *a mountain of rubbish.* **3.** a huge amount: *a mountain of money.*
make a mountain (out) of a molehill, to give great importance to something which is really insignificant: *She was only five minutes late, but he made a mountain out of a molehill about it.*
mountains, a series of very high hills: *Mountains interposed make enemies of nations* (William Cowper).
the Mountain, (in French history) an extreme party, led by Danton and Robespierre, in the Legislative Assembly and the National Convention of the French Revolution: *They were deputies of the Mountain gang* (Scott).
—*adj.* **1.** of or having to do with mountains: *mountain air, mountain scenery.* **2.** living, growing, or found on mountains: *mountain plants.* **3.** resembling or suggesting a mountain.
[< Old French *montaigne* < Late Latin *montānea,* feminine of Latin *montānus* mountainous < *mōns, montis* mountain. Doublet of MONTANE.]
—**Syn.** *n.* **1.** peak.
➔ **Mountain** regularly implies a much larger and higher elevation than **hill;** but in a particular region *mountain* may designate an elevation which would be considered a *hill* elsewhere.

mountain ash, 1. any of several trees and shrubs of the rose family, having delicate pinnate leaves, white flowers, and bright-red to orange-brown berries. They grow in Europe and from Newfoundland to north-

 PRONUNCIATION KEY: hat, āge, cãre, fär; let, ēqual, tėrm; it, īce; hot, ōpen, ôrder; oil, out; cup, pu̇t, rüle;

ern Georgia. **2.** any of various Australian eucalyptus trees.

mountain avens, a low evergreen plant of the rose family with erect white flowers, growing on mountains and in arctic regions.

mountain bluebird, an American bluebird of the western United States.

mountain cat, 1. a cougar. **2.** a bobcat.

mountain chain, 1. a connected series of mountains or mountain ranges. **2.** a mountain system.

mountain chickadee, a variety of chickadee of the western United States: *The mountain chickadee has a black cap, but has a white line over each eye* (World Book Encyclopedia).

mountain climber, a mountaineer: *For four grueling days, mountain climbers struggled toward the peak* (Time).

mountain cork, a variety of asbestos.

mountain cranberry, an evergreen shrub of the heath family, growing in North America, with an edible, very tart, red berry; cowberry.

mountain damson, a West Indian tree of the quassia family, the bark of whose root is used in medicine as a tonic and astringent.

mountain dew, *Slang.* illegally distilled whiskey: *Moonshine—also known by devotees as corn squeezin's, white lightning, popskull, bumblebee stew and mountain dew* (Wall Street Journal).

moun·tained (moun′tənd), *adj. Poetic.* **1.** set on or as if on a mountain: *Like old Deucalion mountain'd o'er the flood* (Keats). **2.** covered with mountains; mountainous.

moun·tain·eer (moun′tə nir′), *n.* **1.** a person who lives in the mountains: *a Kentucky mountaineer.* **2.** a person skilled in mountain climbing; alpinist: *Fitzpatrick was a hardy and experienced mountaineer, and knew all the passes and defiles* (Washington Irving). —*v.i.* to climb mountains: *Those who mountaineer in regions where the heights are undetermined must not depend on aneroids alone* (C.T. Dent).

moun·tain·eer·ing (moun′tə nir′ing), *n.* the art or sport of mountain climbing; alpinism: *Mountaineering is all . . . patience, deliberate skill, and exaltation after long endurance* (Scientific American).

mountain goat, a white, goatlike antelope of the mountains of western North America; Rocky Mountain goat.

Mountain Goat (about 3 ft. high at the shoulder)

mountain gorilla, a gorilla of the mountain forests of the Congo region, in central Africa. It is larger and has longer and thicker hair than other gorillas.

mountain hemlock, a large hemlock of the western United States that yields a hard lumber.

mountain laurel, an evergreen shrub of the heath family with glossy leaves and pale-pink or white flowers. It is the state flower of Connecticut and Pennsylvania.

mountain lion, a large American wildcat; cougar: *Largest and probably most widely scattered of the native cats is the mountain lion* (Science News Letter).

mountain man, a person who lives in the mountains; mountaineer: *My crew was all just crude mountain men . . ., but the finest type of people* (New Yorker).

moun·tain·meal (moun′tən mēl′), *n.* bergmehl. [translation of German *Bergmehl*]

moun·tain·ous (moun′tə nəs), *adj.* **1.** covered with mountain ranges: *mountainous country.* **2.** like a mountain; large and high; huge: *mountainous waves.* —**moun′tain·ous·ly,** *adv.* —**Syn. 2.** enormous.

mountain pass, a natural passageway over or through a mountain barrier.

mountain plover, a plover of the plains of western United States, resembling the killdeer but smaller and without the black rings across the breast.

mountain quail, a grayish-brown quail with chestnut markings and a crest formed by two black feathers, found along the Pacific Coast of the United States.

mountain range, 1. a series of mountains ranged in a line and connected by more or less elevated ground. **2.** a group of mountains having any unifying arrangement.

moun·tains (moun′tənz), *n.pl.* See under **mountain,** *n.*

moun·tain·scape (moun′tən skāp′), *n.* a scene or view of mountains, pictured or in nature: *The most trivial but eye-stopping addition to the mountainscape is the seedy tangle of billboards* (Maclean's).

mountain sheep, 1. the bighorn, a wild sheep of the Rocky Mountains. **2.** any of several other wild sheep inhabiting mountains.

mountain sickness, sickness caused by the rarefied air at high altitudes. The common symptoms are difficulty in breathing, headache, and nausea.

moun·tain·side (moun′tən sīd′), *n.* the side or slope of a mountain: *A record number of Americans are sliding and careening down snow-draped mountainsides* (Wall Street Journal).

Mountain Standard Time, the standard time in the Rocky Mountain regions of the United States and Canada. Noon coincides with the apparent passage of the sun over the 105th meridian. *Abbr.:* MST

Mountain State. a nickname for West Virginia.

mountain system, a group of geographically related mountain ranges.

Mountain time, Mountain Standard Time. *Abbr.:* m.t.

mountain tobacco, a perennial herb of the composite family, used as the source of the medicine arnica.

moun·tain·top (moun′tən top′), *n.* the top or summit of a mountain.

moun·tain·ward (moun′tən wərd), *adv., adj.* toward the mountain or mountains.

moun·tain·wards (moun′tən wərdz), *adv.* mountainward.

moun·te·bank (moun′tə bangk), *n.* **1.** anybody who tries to deceive people by tricks, stories, and jokes; charlatan: *He has a reputation as one of the most corrupt and unimaginative mountebanks in Brazilian politics* (New Republic). *I am a natural-born mountebank* (George Bernard Shaw). **2.** a person who sells quack medicines in public, appealing to his audience by means of tricks, stories, jokes, etc.: *an impudent mountebank who sold pills which . . . were very good against an earthquake* (Joseph Addison).
—*v.i.* to play the mountebank.
[< Italian *montambanco* for *monta in banco* (literally) mount on bench (because such quacks usually spoke from an elevated platform)]

moun·te·bank·er·y (moun′tə bang′kər ē), *n., pl.* **-er·ies.** the practice of a mountebank; action characteristic of or suited to a mountebank: *It fills the stage with mountebankery that is broad and funny* (New York Times).

mount·ed (moun′tid), *adj.* **1.** on a horse, mule, bicycle, etc. **2.** serving on horseback: *mounted police, mounted infantry.* **3.** in a position for use: *a mounted camera, a mounted gun.* **4.** on a support; in a setting: *a mounted diamond.*

mount·er (moun′tər), *n.* a person or thing that mounts.

Mount·ie (moun′tē), *n. Informal.* a member of the Royal Canadian Mounted Police: *It's a crucial question for the RCMP as a force, because more than half the Mountie's work is done for the various provinces* (Maclean's).

mount·ing (moun′ting), *n.* **1.** a support, setting, or the like: *Her photograph is on a heavy cardboard mounting.* **2.** the act of a person or thing that mounts.

mounting block, a block, usually of stone, from which to mount on horseback, on a bus, etc.: *. . . and some kind of draught-proof mounting block for the convenience of passengers* (Punch).

mourn (môrn, mōrn), *v.i.* **1.** to feel or express deep sorrow or grief; grieve: *I left them to mourn over my folly, and now I am left to mourn under the consequence of it* (Daniel Defoe). **2.** to show the conventional signs of grief following the death of a person; go into mourning: *We mourn in black* (Shakespeare). **3.** to make a low sound indicative of pain or grief. **4.** *Poetic or Dialect.* to moan: *The dove mourned in the pine, Sad prophetess of sorrows not her own* (Shelley). —*v.t.* **1.** to feel or show sorrow for or over: *Mary mourned her lost doll. But she must die . . . and all the world shall mourn her* (Shakespeare). **2.** to utter in a very sorrowful manner: *Where the love-lorn nightingale Nightly to thee her sad song mourneth well* (Milton). [Old English *murnan* to mourn; to be anxious] —**Syn.** *v.i.* **1.** lament, sorrow. -*v.t.* **1.** lament, bewail, bemoan.

mourn·er (môr′nər, mōr′-), *n.* **1.** a person who mourns, especially at a funeral: *. . . a flock of mourners dispersing in a desolate cemetery* (Newsweek). **2.** a sinner who repents and seeks salvation at a religious revival.

mourners' bench, a front bench reserved for repenting sinners at an evangelical religious revival.

mourn·ful (môrn′fəl, mōrn′-), *adj.* **1.** full of grief; sad; sorrowful: *a mournful voice. Tell me not, in mournful numbers, Life is but an empty dream!* (Longfellow). **2.** gloomy; dreary: *a mournful occasion, the mournful howling of the wind.* **3.** expressing or used in mourning for the dead: *No mournful bell shall ring her burial* (Shakespeare). *The busy heralds hang the sable scene With mournful 'scutcheons, and dim lamps between* (William Cowper). **4.** causing or attended with sorrow or mourning: *his mournful death* (Shakespeare). —**mourn′ful·ly,** *adv.* —**mourn′ful·ness,** *n.* —**Syn. 1.** dolorous, melancholy, doleful.

mourn·ing (môr′ning, mōr′-), *n.* **1.** sorrowing; lamentation. **2. a.** the wearing of black or some other color (white in the Orient), to show sorrow for a person's death. **b.** the period during which black, etc., is worn. **3.** a draping of buildings, hanging flags at half-mast, etc., as outward signs of such sorrow. **4.** clothes, draperies, etc., used to show such sorrow: *The Houses to their Tops with Black were spread, And ev'n the Pavements were with Mourning hid* (John Dryden).
—*adj.* of mourning; used in mourning: *mourning apparel.* —**mourn′ing·ly,** *adv.*

mourning cloak, a butterfly of Europe and America, having purplish-brown wings with a yellow border; Camberwell beauty.

mourning dove, a wild dove that has a low, mournful call. It is found from southern Canada through Mexico, and, in winter, in Panama.

mourning warbler, an American warbler with a yellow breast and gray head, and in the male, a black throat.

mouse (*n.* mous; *v.* mouz), *n., pl.* **mice,** *v.,* **moused, mous·ing.** —*n.* **1.** any of various small, gnawing rodents found throughout the world, such as the deer mouse, jumping mouse, and field mouse. Some kinds, such as the house mouse, are highly destructive to stored food. The house mouse is about 3 or 4 inches long and infests human dwellings. Field mice live in the grass. **2.** a shy, timid person: *Are you a man or a mouse?* **3.** a term of affection for a woman or girl: *Let the king . . . call you his mouse* (Shakespeare). **4. a.** a knot made in a rope, or a washer or knob of cord, etc., fastened on a rope, to prevent it from slipping through an opening. **b.** a mousing. **5.** *Slang.* a black eye.
—*v.i.* **1.** to hunt for mice; catch mice for food: *Cats and owls go mousing at night.* **2.** to search as a cat does; move about as if searching; prowl. —*v.t.* **1.** *U.S.* to hunt for by patient and careful search. **2. a.** to put a mouse on (a rope, etc.). **b.** to secure (a hook) with a mousing.
[Old English *mūs*]

House Mouse (def. 1—including tail, about 6 in. long)

mouse·bird (mous′bėrd′), *n.* a colie.

mouse-col·or (mous′kul′ər), *n.* a soft, dark, dull gray.

mouse-col·ored (mous′kul′ərd), *adj.* soft, dark, dull gray: *His forehead is high and narrow, his hair mouse-colored* (New Yorker).

mouse deer, a chevrotain.

mouse-dun (mous′dun′), *n.* a dark-gray color with a brownish tinge.

mouse-ear (mous′ir′), *n.* any of several plants with small, soft, hairy leaves, such as the hawkweed and the forget-me-not: *Now I am quite content even to play croquet on a well-clipped surface of mouse-ears* (New Yorker).

mouse-ear chickweed, any of a group of plants of the pink family of temperate regions.

mouse·like (mous′līk′), *adj.* resembling a mouse in appearance, quietness, or timidity: *. . . remember her as a quiet, mouselike person off stage, with few intellectual interests . . .* (Newsweek).

mouse pox, an infectious virus disease of mice characterized by gangrene and often the loss of a limb or limbs; ectromelia. It is related to smallpox.

mouse·proof (mous′prüf′), *adj.* protected against mice.

mous·er (mou′zər), *n.* **1.** an animal that catches mice, such as a cat or an owl. **2.** a person who prowls about and pries into matters.

mouse·tail (mous′tāl′), *n.* any of a group of plants of the crowfoot family, the flowers of which have a taillike torus.

mouse·trap (mous′trap′), *n., v.,* **-trapped, -trap·ping.** —*n.* **1.** a trap for catching mice. **2.** *Football.* an attacking maneuver in which a defensive lineman is permitted to charge without initial opposition but blocked from the side while the ball carrier runs through the hole thus created: *Always they must beware the too-easy charge, the opposition that seems to fade away in front of them which warns of a mousetrap* (Time). —*v.t.* **1.** *Football.* to lure (an opposing football player) into a mousetrap. **2.** to trick; wheedle: *. . . at night I'd mousetrap the doorman at the Empire to exult in Ethel Barrymore in Déclassée . . .* (Tallulah Bankhead).

mous·ey (mou′sē), *adj.,* **mous·i·er, mous·i·est.** mousy.

mous·ie (mou′sē), *n. Scottish.* little mouse, a pet name.

mous·i·ly (mou′sə lē), *adv.* in a mousy manner.

mous·i·ness (mou′sē nis), *n.* mousy character or condition.

mous·ing (mou′zing), *n.* **1.** several turns of small rope, etc., uniting the shank and point of a hook, to keep a rope or an object from slipping off. **2.** a mouse; knot formed on rope with yarn, etc.

MOUSING

Mousing (def.1)

Mous·que·taire (müs′kə-tãr′), *n.* a member of the French royal household troops in the 1600's and 1700's, famous as dandies. [< French *mousquetaire* < *mousquet* musket]

mous·que·taire (müs′kə-tãr′), *n.* a musketeer. —*adj.* formal and colorful, in the style of the royal Mousquetaires: *Mousquetaire gloves are long closed gloves.*

mous·sa·ka (mü′sä kä′), *n.* a Greek baked dish consisting of layers of ground meat with eggplant or zucchini between them, olive oil, and a topping of cheese and dough. [< New Greek *moussaká* < Rumanian *musaca*]

mousse (müs), *n.* a fancy food made with whipped cream, either frozen or stiffened with gelatin: *chocolate mousse, tomato mousse.* [< French *mousse* < Old French, froth, scum; perhaps same as *mousse* moss, apparently < Germanic (compare Old High German *mos* moss)]

mousse·line (müs lēn′), *n.* **1.** fine muslin: *As simple as the jackets are the evening coats of . . . beige wool mousseline* (New York Times). **2.** a very thin glass used for fine wineglasses. [< French *mousseline;* see MUSLIN]

mousse·line de laine (müs lēn′ də len′), a thin woolen fabric, often having a printed pattern; delaine. [< French *mousseline de laine* mousseline of wool]

mousse·line de soie (müs lēn′ də swä′), a thin, sheer, silk fabric, slightly stiffened. [< French *mousseline de soie* mousseline of silk]

mous·tache (mus′tash, mə stash′), *n. Especially British.* mustache.

mous·ta·chio (mə stä′shō), *n., pl.* **-chios.** *Especially British.* a mustache.

Mous·te·ri·an or **Mous·tie·ri·an** (müs-tir′ē ən), *adj.* designating or having to do with a period of paleolithic culture marking the highest point of the Neanderthal race: *Prior to the Mousterian flints, there had been no evolution of flint-making* (Ogburn and Nimkoff). [< French *moustérien* < *Moustier,* a village in Dordogne, France, where cave remains were found]

mous·y (mou′sē), *adj.,* **mous·i·er, mous·i·est. 1.** resembling or suggesting a mouse in color, odor, behavior, etc.: *In one bottle . . . he found no poison, but testified he identified the mousy odor of conine* (Baltimore Sun). **2.** as quiet as a mouse: *A man ought not to remain mousy* (Sporting Magazine). **3.** infested with mice: *. . . the roomy and mousy old closet beside the fireplace* (Mary E. Braddon). Also, **mousey.**

mouth (*n.* mouth; *v.* mouᴛʜ), *n., pl.* **mouths** (mouᴛʜz), *v.* —*n.* **1.** the opening through which a person or an animal takes in food; space containing the tongue and teeth. **2. a.** an opening suggesting a mouth: *the mouth of a cave, the mouth of a well, the mouth of a bottle.* **b.** an opening out of which something shoots forth: *the mouth of a cannon, the mouth of a volcano.* **3.** a part of a river, etc., where its waters are emptied into the sea, another river, or some other body of water: *the mouth of the Ohio River.* **4.** a grimace: *The impudent boy made mouths at us.* **5.** the mouth as the structure for chewing, tasting, etc. **6.** a person or an animal requiring food and support: *He has seven mouths to feed in his family. The Lord never sends a mouth into the world without providing meat for it* (John Galt). **7. a.** the mouth as the source of spoken words: *All . . . wondered at the gracious words which proceeded out of his mouth* (Luke 4:22). *I was but the mouth of the rest, and spoke what they have dictated to me* (Samuel Pepys). **b.** utterance of words; speech: *to get news by mouth, to give mouth to one's thoughts.* **c.** a cry or bay of an animal: *My hounds are . . . match'd in mouth like bells* (Shakespeare). **8.** the fork between the open jaws of a vise, scissors, pincers, etc. **9.** *Music.* **a.** the opening of an organ flue pipe by means of which the sound is produced. **b.** an opening across which one blows, as in a flute.

down in the mouth, *Informal.* in low spirits; discouraged: *"I'm not sure," the young man said, looking a bit down in the mouth* (New Yorker).

foam at the mouth, to be vehemently angry or enraged: *He . . . foamed at the mouth, and was speechless* (Shakespeare).

from the horse's mouth. See under **horse,** *n.*

laugh on the other side or **wrong side of one's mouth,** *Informal.* to be annoyed; be made sorry: *You'll mayhap be making such a slip yourself someday; you'll laugh o' the other side of your mouth then* (George Eliot).

make one's mouth water, to arouse one's appetite or desire: *The display of exotic foods made his mouth water.*

shoot off one's mouth, or **shoot one's mouth off,** *U.S. Slang.* to talk freely and indiscreetly: *Don't you know better than to shoot your mouth off like that?* (George W. Cable).

—*v.t.* **1.** to utter (words) in an affected or pompous way: *I dislike actors who mouth their speeches. She mouthed her words in speaking; her voice was deep, its inflections very pompous* (Charlotte Brontë). **2.** to rub, press, or mumble with the mouth or lips: *Psyche . . . hugg'd . . . and in her hunger mouth'd and mumbled it* [*a baby*] (Tennyson). **3.** to put or take into the mouth; seize with the mouth or jaws. **4.** to accustom (a horse) to the bit and bridle. —*v.i.* **1.** to speak oratorically: *Stop mouthing and listen to what I have to say.* **2.** to make grimaces. [Old English *mūth*] —**mouth′like′,** *adj.*

—**Syn.** *n.* **2. a.** entrance, inlet. **3.** estuary, -*v.i.* **2.** mow.

mouth·breed·er (mouth′brē′dər), *n.* any of various small fishes that hold their eggs and their hatched young in their mouths.

mouthed (mouᴛʜd, moutht), *adj.* having a mouth or mouths: *a mouthed shell* (Keats).

-mouthed, *combining form.* having a —— mouth: *Open-mouthed = having an open mouth.*

mouth·er (mou′ᴛʜər), *n.* a long-winded talker.

mouth·ful (mouth′fu̇l), *n., pl.* **-fuls. 1.** the amount the mouth can easily hold. **2.** what is taken into the mouth at one time. **3.** a small amount.

mouth·i·ly (mou′ᴛʜə lē, -thə-), *adv.* in a mouthy manner.

mouth·i·ness (mou′ᴛʜē nis, -thē-), *n.* mouthy quality; talkativeness.

mouth·ing (mou′ᴛʜing), *n.* something which is uttered in a pompously oratorical style or with great distinctness of articulation, but often not with sincerity: *The pious mouthings of people like Mr. Sass are more exasperating than the rantings of ignorant fanatics* (Atlantic).

mouth·less (mouth′lis), *adj.* having no mouth.

mouth organ, 1. a harmonica. **2.** a Panpipe.

mouth·parts (mouth′pärts′), *n.pl. Biology.* the mouth appendages of insects, crustaceans, etc.: *The labrum, labium, mandible, and maxilla are mouthparts.*

mouth·piece (mouth′pēs′), *n.* **1.** the part of a musical instrument, such as a pipe, horn, or the like, that is placed between or against the lips. **2. a.** the part of a bit or harness of a horse that is held in the mouth. **b.** a rubber guard held in the mouth by a boxer to prevent chipped teeth or cut lips resulting from head blows: *. . . I got to feel my right crashing on his jaw, see his mouthpiece flying off with the blood and the sweat . . .* (New York Times). **3.** a piece placed at or forming the opening of something: *the mouthpiece of a telephone.* **4.** a person or medium of communication which expresses the sentiments, opinions, etc., of another or others; spokesman: *They fancied him the mouthpiece of Heaven's messages of wisdom, and rebuke, and love* (Hawthorne). *The newspaper "Democracia," considered the Government's mouthpiece . . . warned . . .* (London Times). **5.** *Slang.* a lawyer, especially a criminal lawyer.

mouth-to-mouth (mouth′tə mouth′), *adj.* of or designating a method of artificial respiration in which air is breathed directly into the victim's mouth and nose to inflate the lungs, with intervals to allow the lungs to empty: *Christopher, 2, appeared lifeless, but firemen restored his breathing by mouth-to-mouth resuscitation* (New York Times).

mouth·wash (mouth′wosh′, -wôsh′), *n.* a mildly antiseptic liquid to cleanse the mouth and teeth.

mouth-wa·ter·ing (mouth′wôt′ər ing, -wot′-), *adj.* causing the mouth to water; appetizing; tempting: *. . . items laid out in a mouth-watering display of U.S. consumer goods . . .* (Time).

mouth·y (mou′ᴛʜē, -thē), *adj.,* **mouth·i·er, mouth·i·est.** loud-mouthed; using many words to say little; ranting; bombastic: *He . . . was prone to be mouthy and magniloquent* (Washington Irving).

mou·ton[1] (mü′ton), *n.* Also, **mouton lamb.** a fur made from a sheep's pelt by shearing it to medium length, processing, and dyeing it, commonly to resemble that of beaver: *The floor of the Directeur is covered with light-blue mouton* (New Yorker). —*adj.* made of mouton: *a mouton collar, a mouton coat.* [< French *mouton* sheep < Old French; see MUTTON]

mou·ton[2] (mü′ton), *n.* gold coins bearing the figure of a lamb (Agnus Dei), used in France in the 1300's and 1400's, including coins struck by Edward III and Henry V of England for their French dominions. [< Old French *mouton* sheep]

mou·ton·née (mü′tə nā′), *adj.* (of rocks) rounded like a sheep's back by glacial erosion. [< French *moutonnée,* feminine past participle of *moutonner* to round like a sheep's back < Old French *mouton* sheep; see MUTTON]

mou·ton·néed (mü′tə nād′), *adj.* moutonnée.

mov·a·bil·i·ty (mü′və bil′ə tē), *n.* movable quality or condition. Also, **moveability.**

mov·a·ble (mü′və bəl), *adj.* **1.** that can be moved; not fixed in one place or position: *Our fingers are movable.* **2.** *Law.* of property: **a.** that can be carried from place to place. **b.** personal. **3.** changing from one date to another in different years: *Easter is a movable holy day.*

—*n.* **1.** a piece of furniture that is not a fixture but can be moved to another house or building: *The apartment . . . was destitute of all movables save a broken armchair, and an old couch or sofa* (Dickens). **2.** a thing that can be moved, removed, or set in motion. Also, **moveable.**

movables, *Law.* personal property: *Books of travel have familiarized every reader with the custom of burying a dead man's movables with him* (Herbert Spencer).

—**mov′a·ble·ness,** *n.*

—**Syn.** *adj.* **1.** mobile. **2. a.** portable, transportable.

mov·a·bly (mü′və blē), *adv.* in a movable manner; so as to be movable. Also, **moveably.**

move (müv), *v.,* **moved, mov·ing,** *n.* —*v.t.* **1.** to change the place or position of: *Do not move your hand. Move your chair to the other side of the table. She moved her lips . . .*

but could not speak (Thomas Hardy). **2.** (in games) to change the position of (a piece): *to move a pawn in chess.* **3.** to put or keep in motion; shake; stir: *The wind moves the leaves.* **4.** to cause to act: *Castor oil moves the bowels.* **5.** to prompt; impel; rouse; excite: *What moved you to do this? I have prepared such arguments as will not Fail to move them* (Byron). **6.** to affect with emotion; excite to tender feelings: *The sad story easily moved her to tears.* **7.** to bring forward formally; propose: *Mr. Chairman, I move that we adjourn.* **8.** *Commerce.* to sell; find buyers for: *That store can move these dresses.* **9.** *Archaic.* to suggest; urge: *My mother refused to move it [a proposition] to my father* (Daniel Defoe). **10.** *Obsolete.* **a.** to exhort or urge to do something: *I ... begged him ... that he would move the Captains to take some pity on me* (Jonathan Swift). **b.** to apply to for something: *The Florentine will move us For speedy aid* (Shakespeare).

—*v.i.* **1.** to change place or position; pass from one place or position to another: *The child moved in his sleep. The earth moves around the sun.* **2.** to change one's place of living: *We have moved from 96th Street to 110th Street.* **3.** to make a formal request, application, or proposal: *to move for a new trial.* **4.** in games: **a.** (of a player) to make a move: *Move quickly, don't delay the game.* **b.** (of a piece) to be moved. **5.** to act: *God moves in a mysterious way, His wonders to perform* (William Cowper). *Had the city moved sooner ... there would have been no rising, no riot* (Cardinal Newman). **6.** to be in motion; be stirred: *Then move the trees, the copses nod* (Tennyson). **7.** *Commerce.* to be sold: *These pink dresses are moving slowly.* **8.** to make progress; advance; proceed: *The train moved slowly. Then the tale Shall move on soberly* (Keats). **9.** to be active; exist: *to move in the best society.* **10.** to turn; swing; operate: *Most doors move on a hinge.* **11.** to carry oneself: *to move with dignity and grace.* **12.** *Informal.* to start off; depart: *It's time to be moving. When the ambulance had left, the crowd moved on.* **13.** (of the bowels) to be moved; act.

move in, to move oneself, one's family, one's belongings, etc., into a new place to live: *The new couple is moving in next week.*

move in on, *Informal.* **a.** to attack: *The soldiers moved in on the well-defended old house from all sides.* **b.** to take steps to dispossess (a person) of power or of control or ownership of a business, a property, etc.: *The bankers began talking of the "saturation point" in the auto market and moved in on him* (Time).

move up, to promote or be promoted: *Dr. Cabot was moved up from an associate to a full professorship.*

—*n.* **1. a.** the right or time to move in a game: *It is your move.* **b.** the moving of a piece in chess and other games: *That was a good move.* **2.** the act of moving; movement: *an impatient move of her head.* **3.** an action taken to bring about some result; step: *His next move was to earn some money. Our move to get a better place to play succeeded.* **4.** a change of a place to live.

get a move on, *Slang.* **a.** to make haste; hurry up: *A correspondent from Rhodesia says, "Get cracking, or I will come over." We would say "get a move on!"* (Holiday). **b.** to begin to move: *I remember with what excitement the Fleet received the signal: "Winston is back." Now we shall ... get a move on* (Lord Mountbatten).

on the move, moving about; traveling: *a wandering people ... continually on the move* (Washington Irving).

[< Anglo-French *mover,* Old French *moveir* < Latin *movēre*]

—**Syn.** *v.t.* **1.** shift, remove, transfer. **5. Move, actuate** mean to rouse a person to action or to act in a certain way. **Move,** the general word, does not suggest whether the thing that rouses is an outside force or influence or an inner urge or personal motive: *Praise moved him to work harder.* **Actuate,** a formal word, always implies a powerful inner force, like a strong feeling, desire, or principle: *He was actuated by desire for praise.* **6.** influence. *-v.i.* **8.** See **advance. 10.** work, revolve.

move·a·bil·i·ty (mü′və bil′ə tē), *n.* movability.

move·a·ble (mü′və bəl), *adj., n.* movable. —**move′a·ble·ness,** *n.*

move·a·bles (mü′və bəlz), *n.pl.* movables. See under **movable,** *n.*

move·a·bly (mü′və blē), *adv.* movably.

move·less (müv′lis), *adj.* without movement or motion; motionless; immovable: *His limbs were moveless in an exasperating and obstinate calm* (Arnold Bennett). —**move′less·ly,** *adv.* —**move′less·ness,** *n.*

move·ment (müv′mənt), *n.* **1.** the act or fact of moving: *We run by movements of the legs. Sometimes he binds his limbs with rope so that reflex movements will not jar his hand* (Newsweek). **2.** a change in the placing of troops, ships, etc., especially as part of a tactical maneuver. **3.** the moving parts of a machine or mechanism; special group of parts that move on each other: *The movement of a watch consists of many little wheels.* **4.** *Music.* **a.** the kind of rhythm a piece has, its speed, etc.: *The movement of a waltz is very different from the movement of a march.* **b.** one division of a long selection (a sonata, symphony, concerto, etc.): *the second movement of a symphony.* **5.** rhythmical structure or character. **6.** the suggestion of action in a painting or sculpture. **7.** action; abundance of incidents. **8.** the efforts and results of a group of people working together to bring about some one thing: *the movement for a safe and sane Fourth of July.* **9.** a notable change in the price of something. **10. a.** an emptying of the bowels. **b.** the feces discharged by it.

—**Syn. 1.** move, action, stir. See **motion.**

mov·er (mü′vər), *n.* **1.** a person or thing that moves: *We [poets] are the movers and shakers of the World* (A. W. E. O'Shaughnessy). **2.** a person whose occupation is moving furniture, etc., from one house, etc., to another: *When you plan ... a long distance move—you'll probably call several movers for quotations* (Maclean's).

mov·ie (mü′vē), *U.S. Informal.* —*n.* a motion picture: *The novel from which the movie takes its name* (Saturday Review).

the movies, a motion-picture exhibition: *We go once a week to the movies.*

—*adj.* of or having to do with motion pictures: *a movie star, a movie theater.*

[American English, short for *movi*(ng picture)]

—**Syn.** *n.* cinema.

mov·ie·dom (mü′vē dəm), *n.* filmdom: *His new movie ... [is] based on the tragic life of moviedom's ... Jean Harlow* (Wall Street Journal).

mov·ie·go·er (mü′vē gō′ər), *n.* cinemagoer; filmgoer: *They have been seen by millions of moviegoers in the nation's theaters* (Wall Street Journal).

mov·ie·go·ing (mü′vē gō′ing), *n.* the act or practice of a moviegoer; a going to the movies: *The experience of moviegoing ... gave us all a fantasy life in common* (Harper's). —*adj.* that goes to the movies: *the moviegoing public.*

movie house, a motion-picture theater: *Movie houses are crowded with friendly customers in high spirits until well after midnight* (New York Times).

mov·ie·mak·er (mü′vē mā′kər), *n.* **1.** a professional producer of motion pictures: *Moviemakers from thirty-five nations plan to show their wares at the Cannes Film Festival* (New York Times). **2.** an individual who takes his own motion pictures: *... a brand-new camera, designed as the last word for amateur moviemakers* (Time).

mov·ie·mak·ing (mü′vē mā′king), *n.* **1.** the production of a motion picture. **2.** acting in or otherwise taking part in the production of a motion picture: *Power gave up fulltime moviemaking in 1952* (Time). —*adj.* of, having to do with, or characteristic of moviemaking.

Mov·ie·o·la (mü′vē ō′lə), *n. Trademark.* a motion-picture projector used in film editing. It has a small viewing screen and allows control of the speed and direction of film movement.

mov·ing (mü′ving), *adj.* **1.** that moves: *a moving car.* **2.** causing or producing motion; having motion: *The more the moving force is distant from the center of motion, so much the more force it shall have* (John Leak). **3.** instigating or promoting action: *John was the moving spirit in planning for the party.* **4.** touching; pathetic: *a moving story. A decayed widow ... has laid her case of destitution before him in a very moving letter* (Hawthorne). —**mov′ing·ly,** *adv.* —**mov′ing·ness,** *n.*

—**Syn. 4.** affecting.

moving picture, a motion picture; series of pictures shown on a screen in which people and things seem to move.

moving-picture machine, an apparatus for presenting motion pictures, as by projection on a screen.

moving platform or **sidewalk,** a platform or sidewalk constructed on the principle of an endless belt and moving at a regular speed, for carrying along objects or persons.

moving staircase or **stairway,** a staircase constructed on the principle of an endless belt, that moves and carries people up or down; escalator.

mow[1] (mō), *v.,* **mowed, mowed** or **mown, mow·ing.** —*v.t.* **1.** to cut down with a machine or a scythe: *to mow grass.* **2.** to cut down the grass or grain from: *to mow a lawn, to mow a field.* **3.** to destroy at a sweep or in large numbers, as if by mowing: *The firing of the enemy mowed down our men like grass.* —*v.i.* to cut down grass, grain, etc.: *The men are mowing today.* [Old English *māwan*]

mow[2] (mou), *n.* **1.** a place in a barn where hay, grain, etc., is piled or stored: *Littered the stalls, and from the mows Raked down the herd's-grass for the cows* (John Greenleaf Whittier). **2.** a pile or stack of hay, grain, etc., in a barn. [Old English *mūga, mūwa*]

mow[3] or **mowe** (mō, mou), *v.,* **mowed, mow·ing,** *n.* —*v.i.* to grimace: *like apes that mow and chatter at me* (Shakespeare). —*n.* a grimace; derisive grimace: *that devil that ... made mows and mockery at his unsufferable tortures* (William Godwin). [Middle English *mouwe,* perhaps < Middle Dutch, or < Old French *moue* < Germanic (compare Middle High German *mouwe*)] —**Syn.** *v.i., n.* mop.

mow·er (mō′ər), *n.* **1.** a person who mows grass, grain, etc. **2.** a mowing machine or lawn mower.

mow·ing (mō′ing), *n.* **1.** cutting down grass, grain, etc., with a scythe or machine. **2.** *U.S.* meadowland. **3.** the amount of hay cut at one time.

mowing machine, 1. a machine with cutting blades attached to a metal arm, used to cut down tall grass, standing hay, grain, etc. **2.** a lawn mower.

mown (mōn), *v.* mowed; a past participle of **mow**[1].

mox·a (mok′sə), *n.* **1.** a soft, downy substance prepared from dried leaves of a Chinese and Japanese wormwood. It was formerly burned on the skin as a counterirritant or cauterizing agent. **2.** the plant itself. **3.** any substance similarly used. [< Japanese *mogusa*]

mox·ie (mok′sē), *n. U.S. Slang.* **1.** courage; bravery; nerve. **2.** know-how; skill; experience. [< earlier *Moxie,* a trademark for a soft drink (because the drink supposedly gave courage)]

moy·en âge (mwȧ ye nȧzh′), *French.* the medieval period; Middle Ages: *Mr. Borowsky has set his novel of King Arthur in the Middle Ages—but his moyen âge is not the time of the chivalry-loving Sir Thomas* (New York Times).

Moz·ar·ab (mō zar′əb), *n.* one of a class of Spanish Christians who submitted to the domination of the Moors and were permitted to retain their own religion. [< Spanish *Mozárabe* < Arabic *musta'rib* (literally) a "would-be" Arab]

Moz·ar·a·bic (mō zar′ə bik), *adj.* **1.** of or having to do with the Mozarabs. **2.** having to do with the ancient Christian liturgy of Spain, a modified form of which is still used in certain Spanish chapels.

Mozarabic chant, the plain song of early Christian liturgy in Spain, fragments of which continue to be used in some Spanish churches though Gregorian chant has largely superseded it.

Mo·zar·te·an or **Mo·zar·ti·an** (mō tsär′tē ən, -zär′-), *adj.* of, having to do with, or characteristic of Wolfgang Amadeus Mozart or his music: *the Mozartean touch.*

moz·za·rel·la (moz′ə rel′ə, mot′sə-), *n.* a soft Italian cheese. [< Italian *mozzarella*]

moz·zet·ta or **mo·zet·ta** (mō zet′ə), *n.* a short, hooded cape worn by the Pope, cardinals, bishops, and abbots. [< Italian *mozzetta* (diminutive) < *mozza* shortened]

mp (no period), *Music.* mezzo piano.

m.p., melting point.

M.P. or **MP** (no periods), **1.** Member of Parliament. **2.** Metropolitan Police (of London). **3.** Military Police. **4.** Mounted Police.

MPC (no periods), maximum permissible concentration (a measurement of radioactive fallout).

M.P.C., military payment certificate.

mpg (no periods) or **m.p.g.,** miles per gallon.

mph (no periods) or **m.p.h.,** miles per hour.

mpm (no periods) or **m.p.m.,** meters per minute.

M.P.P. or **MPP** (no periods), Member of the Provincial Parliament (of Canada).

mr (no period), **1.** microroentgen. **2.** milliroentgen.

Mr. or **Mr** (mis′tər), *pl.* **Messrs.** mister, a title put in front of a man's name or the name of his position: *Mr. Jackson, Mr. Chairman, Mr. President.* [(originally) abbreviation of *master*]

➔ **Mr.** is written out only when it represents informal usage and when it is used without a name: *"They're only two for five, mister."*

MR (no periods), milliroentgen.

M.R.A. or **MRA** (no periods), Moral Re-Armament.

mrad (no period), millirad.

MRBM (no periods), Medium Range Ballistic Missile; IRBM.

M.R.C.P., Member of the Royal College of Physicians (of England).

M.R.C.S., Member of the Royal College of Surgeons (of England).

mrem (no period), millirem.

mRNA (no periods), messenger RNA.

M-roof (em′rüf′, -rủf′), *n.* a roof formed by the junction of two gable roofs with a valley between, so as in transverse section to resemble somewhat the letter M.

MRP (no periods) or **M.R.P.,** Mouvement Républicain Populaire (Popular Republican Movement, a French political party in the Fourth and Fifth Republics).

Mrs. or **Mrs** (mis′iz, miz′-; miz), *pl.* **Mmes.** mistress, a title put in front of a married woman's name: *Mrs. Jackson.* [abbreviation of *mistress*]

➔ **Mrs.** is written out only in representing informal usage and is then spelled *missis* (or *missus*): *Mrs. Dorothy M. Adams, Mrs. Smith. "Where's the missis?"*

Mrs. Grundy, Grundy.

ms (no period), millisecond.

m/s, 1. meters per second. **2.** *Commerce.* months after sight.

m.s., motorship.

MS (no periods), multiple sclerosis.

MS., Ms (no period), **Ms.,** or **ms.,** manuscript.

M.S., 1. Master of Science. **2.** motorship.

MSA (no periods), Mutual Security Agency.

M.S.A., 1. Master of Science and Art. **2.** Master of Science in Agriculture.

M.Sc., Master of Science.

msec (no period), millisecond.

MSG (no periods), monosodium glutamate.

Msgr., 1. Monseigneur. **2.** Monsignor.

M/Sgt (no period) or **M.Sgt.,** master sergeant.

MSH (no periods), melanocyte-stimulating hormone; intermedin.

MSI (no periods) or **M.S.I.,** Movimento Sociale Italiano (Italian Social Movement, a political party in Italy).

m'sieur (mə syœ′), *n.* monsieur.

m.s.l., mean sea level.

MSS., MSS (no period), **Mss.,** or **mss.,** manuscripts.

M.S.S., 1. Master of Social Science. **2.** Master of Social Service.

MST (no periods), **M.S.T.,** or **m.s.t.,** Mountain Standard Time.

MsTh (no period), mesothorium.

MSTS (no periods) or **M.S.T.S.,** Military Sea Transportation Service.

M.S.W., Master of Social Work.

mt., 1. megaton. **2.** mountain.

m.t., 1. metric ton. **2.** Mountain time.

Mt., Mount: *Mt. Everest, Mt. Whitney.*

MT (no periods), machine translation.

M.T., 1. Masoretic Text (of the Old Testament). **2.** metric ton. **3.** motor transport.

MTB (no periods) or **M.T.B.,** motor torpedo boat.

mtg., 1. meeting. **2.** mortgage.

mtgd., mortgaged.

mtge., mortgage.

mtn., mountain.

MTO (no periods), Mediterranean Theater of Operations (in World War II).

Mt. Rev., Most Reverend.

mts., mountains.

mu (myü), *n.* **1.** the twelfth letter of the Greek alphabet (M, μ). **2.** micron, a unit of length. Its symbol is μ. **3.** mu-meson. [< Greek *mŷ*]

Mu (myü), *n.* a mythical lost continent, alleged to have sunk into the southwestern Pacific Ocean at about the same time Atlantis is alleged to have disappeared into the Atlantic.

much (much), *adj.*, **more, most,** *adv.*, **more, most,** *n.*, *v.*, **muched, much·ing.** —*adj.* **1.** in great quantity, amount, or degree: *much money, much time, much rain. Too much cake will make you sick. A pale yellow sun . . . showed the much dirt of the place* (Rudyard Kipling). **2.** *Obsolete.* many; numerous: *Edom came out against him with much people* (Numbers 20:20).

much of a, nearly the same: *He and his brother are much of a size. You have a son, much of his age* (Roger Ascham).

—*adv.* **1.** to a great extent or degree: *much higher. I was much pleased with the present.* **2.** nearly; about: *This is much the same as the others.*

—*n.* **1.** a great deal or amount: *Much of this is not true. I did not hear much of the talk.* **2.** a great, important, or notable thing or matter: *The rain did not amount to much. The house is not much to look at.*

make much of, to treat, represent, or consider as of great importance: *Young folks don't make so much of dinner as old ones* (Henry Kingsley).

not much of a, not very good: *$5.00 a day is not much of a wage for a grown man.*

too much for, more than a match for: *The two policemen were too much for him, and he gave himself up without a fight.*

—*v.t. Dialect.* to make much of; pet; caress: *It is the mark of a good watchdog . . . that he can't be muched by any passerby, but only by persons of rare talent* (Baltimore Sun).

[Middle English *muche*, short for *muchel*, Old English *micel*. Compare MICKLE.]

—**Syn.** *adv.* **2.** approximately.

much·ly (much′lē), *adv.* much; exceedingly: *Thanks muchly.*

much·ness (much′nis), *n.* greatness; magnitude.

much of a muchness, much alike; nearly equivalent: *much of a muchness—no better, and perhaps no worse* (Henry Kingsley).

mu·cic acid (myü′sik), a white, crystalline dibasic acid formed by oxidizing certain gums, lactose, etc., in the presence of nitric acid. *Formula:* $C_6H_{10}O_8$ [perhaps < French *mucique* < Latin *mūcus* slime, mucus]

mu·cid (myü′sid), *adj.* musty or slimy, as from decay; moldy. [< Latin *mūcidus* < *mūcus*, slime, mucus] —**mu′cid·ness,** *n.*

mu·cif·er·ous (myü sif′ər əs), *adj.* carrying or secreting mucus. [< Latin *mūcus* mucus + English *-ferous*]

mu·cig·e·nous (myü sij′ə nəs), *adj.* secreting mucus; muciparous. [< Latin *mūcus* mucus + English *-gen* + *-ous*]

mu·ci·lage (myü′sə lij), *n.* **1.** a sticky, gummy substance used to make things stick together. **2.** a substance like glue or gelatin in plants. [< Middle French *mucilage*, learned borrowing from Late Latin *mūcilāgo* musty juice < Latin *mūcus* mold[2], mucus]

mu·ci·lag·i·nous (myü′sə laj′ə nəs), *adj.* **1.** like mucilage; sticky; gummy. **2.** containing or secreting mucilage. —**Syn. 1.** glutinous, viscid.

mu·cin (myü′sin), *n.* any of various glycoproteins forming the chief constituents of mucous secretions; mucoprotein: *Lysozyme . . . interests bacteriologists because it dissolves the mucins with which the microbes are covered* (Sunday Times). [probably < French *mucine* < Latin *mūcus* mucus + French *-ine* -in]

mu·cin·ous (myü′sə nəs), *adj.* **1.** of or having to do with mucin. **2.** like mucin.

mu·cip·a·rous (myü sip′ər əs), *adj.* producing or secreting mucus: *muciparous glands.* [< Latin *mūcus* mucus + *parere* to give birth + English *-ous*]

muck (muk), *n.* **1.** dirt; filth; dirty slush. **2.** anything filthy, dirty, or disgusting. **3.** moist farmyard manure; dung. **4.** *U.S.* **a.** well-decomposed peat, used as a manure. **b.** a heavy soil containing a high percentage of this. **5.** *Informal.* an untidy condition; mess: *a muck of sweat* (Oliver Goldsmith). **6.** *Mining.* earth, rock, etc., to be removed in getting at the mineral sought.

—*v.t.* **1.** to soil or make dirty: *You can't touch pitch and not be mucked, lad* (Robert Louis Stevenson). **2.** to put muck on.

muck about or **around,** *Slang.* to waste time; putter; go about aimlessly: *The lad mucked about town all morning.*

muck in, *British Slang.* to mingle; associate (with); share quarters (with): *hurried back and forth among the confusion like a general mucking in with his troops on the eve of battle* (Manchester Guardian).

muck out, a. to clean out (a stable, mine, tunnel, etc.): *After a couple of years getting up at dawn to work horses and muck out stables . . .* (Time). **b.** *British.* to clean up (anything): *. . . spoke of the trouble she would get into if she didn't get her employer's office properly mucked out* (Punch).

muck up, *Slang.* to spoil; foul up; make a mess of: *We mucked up two hundred quids' worth . . . before getting it right, had to burn the lot . . .* (Punch).

[< Scandinavian (compare Old Icelandic *myki, mykr* cow dung). Related to MIDDEN.]

muck·er[1] (muk′ər), *n. Slang.* a very vulgar, ill-bred person: [*Mucker*] *. . . with the language and manners of the bargee and the longshoreman* (James Truslow Adams). [probably < German *Mucker* sulky person] —**Syn.** cad.

muck·er[2] (muk′ər), *n.* a person who removes muck from a mine, tunnels, etc.: *The muckers work on . . . pausing . . . to pull Their boots out of suckholes where they slosh* (Carl Sandburg). [< *muck* + *-er*[1]]

muck·le[1] (muk′əl), *adj., adv., n. Dialect.* mickle; much. [dialectal variant of *mickle*]

muck·le[2] (muk′əl), *n. U.S. Dialect.* a club used to kill fish when they are caught and landed. [perhaps specialized noun use of *muckle*[1]]

muck·luck (muk′luk), *n.* **1.** a high, soft, fur-lined, sealskin boot worn in arctic regions. **2.** a knitted wool sock, reaching the calf, to which a soft leather sole is stitched; slipper sock. Also, **mucluc, mukluk.** [American English < Eskimo *maklak* bearded seal; boot made of sealskin]

muck·rake (muk′rāk′), *n., v.,* **-raked, -raking.** —*n.* a rake for scraping and piling muck or dung: *The men with the muckrakes are often indispensable to the well-being of society* (Theodore Roosevelt). —*v.i.* to hunt for and expose corruption, especially in big business, government bureaus, etc.

muck·rak·er (muk′rā′kər), *n.* a person, especially a journalist, who muckrakes: *Lincoln Steffens was a muckraker.* [American English (coined by Theodore Roosevelt) < "man with the *muckrake*" in John Bunyan's *Pilgrim's Progress*]

muck·worm (muk′wėrm′), *n.* **1.** a worm, larva, or grub living in muck or manure. **2.** a miser.

muck·y (muk′ē), *adj.*, **muck·i·er, muck·i·est. 1.** of muck. **2.** filthy; dirty.

mu·cluc (muk′luk), *n.* muckluck.

mu·coid[1] (myü′koid), *adj.* like mucus.

mu·coid[2] (myü′koid), *n.* any of a group of glycoproteins resembling mucin. They occur in bone and connective tissue, and in the vitreous humor and cornea of the eye.

mu·co·pol·y·sac·cha·ride (myü′kō pol′ē-sak′ə rīd, -ər id), *n.* a carbohydrate compound, such as heparin, containing amino sugar and sugar acids, found mainly in the connective tissue but also present in mucous tissue, synovial fluid, etc.: *The blood group to which each of us belongs is determined by a presence . . . of a mucopolysaccharide with specific antigenic qualities* (New Scientist). [< Latin *mūcus* + English *poly-* + *saccharide*]

mu·co·pro·tein (myü′kō prō′tēn, -tē in), *n.* any of various viscous protein compounds, such as mucin, containing a mucopolysaccharide in their molecular structure, and occurring in connective tissue and other body tissues.

mu·cor (myü′kər), *n.* any of a group of molds that form small, downy, grayish-white tufts on bread, decaying fruit, decaying mushrooms, etc. [< Latin *mūcor* moldy]

mu·co·sa (myü kō′sə), *n., pl.* **-sae** (-sē). a mucous membrane. [< New Latin (*membrana*) *mucosa* mucous (membrane)]

mu·co·sal (myü kō′səl), *adj.* of, having to do with, or characteristic of a mucosa.

mucosal disease, any of several, often fatal, diseases which affect cattle, striking at their mucosae and their respiratory and digestive tracts.

mu·cos·i·ty (myü kos′ə tē), *n.* mucous quality; sliminess.

mu·cous (myü′kəs), *adj.* **1.** of mucus. **2.** like mucus. **3.** containing or secreting mucus. [< Latin *mūcōsus* slimy, like mucus < *mūcus* mucus]

mucous membrane, the tissue lining the nose, throat, anus, and other cavities of the body that are open to the air.

mu·co·vis·coi·do·sis (myü′kō vis′koi dō′-sis), *n.* cystic fibrosis. [< *muco*(us) + *viscoid* + *-osis*]

mu·cro (myü′krō), *n., pl.* **mu·cro·nes** (myü-krō′nēz). a sharp point; spinelike part: *the projecting mucro of a leaf.* [< Latin *mūcrō, -ōnis* point, sharp edge]

mu·cro·nate (myü′krə nit, -nāt), *adj.* having a sharp point: *a mucronate shell, feather, or leaf.* [< Latin *mūcrōnātus* < *mūcrō, -ōnis* point] —**mu′cro·nate·ly,** *adv.*

mu·cro·nat·ed (myü′krə nā′tid), *adj.* mucronate.

mu·cro·na·tion (myü′krə nā′-shən), *n.* **1.** mucronate condition or form. **2.** a mucronate process.

mu·cron·u·late (myü kron′yə lāt, -lit), *adj.* having a small mucro or abruptly projecting point, as a leaf. [< New Latin *mucronulatus* (diminutive) < Latin *mūcrō, -ōnis* point]

mu·cus (myü′kəs), *n.* a slimy substance that moistens the mucous membranes of the body: *A cold in the head causes a discharge of mucus.* [< Latin *mūcus* slime, mucus, mold[2], related to *ēmungere* sneeze out, blow one's nose]

Mucronate Feather

mud (mud), *n., v.,* **mud·ded, mud·ding.** —*n.* **1.** soft, sticky, wet earth: *mud on the ground after rain, mud at the bottom of a pond.* **2.** slander; libel; defamation: *They were using not criticism but mud to maintain themselves in office* (Adlai E. Stevenson). **3.** a mixture of water, clay, and certain chemicals used in well-drilling to lubricate the bit and carry debris loosened by the bit to the surface.

fling, sling, or **throw mud at,** to make disgraceful remarks about (a person, his character, etc.); slander: *A woman in my position must expect to have more mud thrown at her than a less important person* (Frederick Marryat).

—*v.t.* **1.** to muddy (a liquid): *The wolf Mudded the brook* (Tennyson). **2.** to bury in mud: *I wish Myself were mudded in that oozy bed Where my son lies* (Shakespeare). [Middle English *mudde*]

—**Syn.** *n.* **1.** mire, slime, ooze.

mu·dar (mə där′), *n.* madar; an Asian or African shrub of the milkweed family yielding a latex and a fine, silky fiber, as well as an emetic drug used in the Far East.

mud·bank (mud′bangk′), *n.* a bank or shoal of mud beside or rising from the bed of a river, lake, or sea: *Traver was shifting his position when a bullet slapped into the mudbank by his head* (Harper's).

mud bath, a bath in mud mixed with certain medicines, as a remedy for rheumatism, gout, etc.

mud·cat (mud′kat′), *n.* (in the Mississippi Valley) a large catfish.

mud dauber, any of various wasps, the females of which lay eggs in individual cells constructed of mud, and supply the larvae with insects or spiders for food.

mud·der (mud′ər), *n. Slang.* **1.** a race horse that runs well on a wet, muddy track: *Experienced horsemen can distinguish a mudder simply by watching him gallop around the track* (Cincinnati Enquirer). **2.** an athlete, such as a football player, who plays well on wet, muddy ground: *He had the most devastating weapon on the field; Navy's . . . captain, Ned Oldham, a marvelous mudder* (Time).

mud·di·ly (mud′ə lē), *adv.* in a muddy manner.

mud·di·ness (mud′ē nis), *n.* **1.** the quality or condition of being muddy: *the muddiness of a stream.* **2.** a being unclear or confused; obscurity.

mud·dle (mud′əl), *v.,* **-dled, -dling,** *n.* —*v.t.* **1.** to bring (things) into a mess; mix up: *Do you want to . . . get things all muddled up?* (Mark Twain). **2.** to make confused or stupid or slightly drunk: *The more you talk, the more you muddle me.* **3.** to make (water, etc.) muddy. **4.** to waste or squander (money, time, etc.) stupidly. —*v.i.* to think or act in a confused, blundering way: *to muddle over a problem. He meddled, or rather muddled, with literature* (Washington Irving).

muddle through, to manage somehow; succeed in one's object in spite of lack of skill and foresight: *Can it be that, faced with the serious business of self-immolation, we shall abandon the immemorial practice of muddling through, and discover logic and consistency at last?* (London Times).

—*n.* a mess; disorder; confusion: *When Mother came home, she found the house in a muddle.*

make a muddle of, to bungle: *The present Government has made an immortal muddle of the whole business* (Saturday Review).

[(originally) to mottle or obscure colors; to stir up sediment, perhaps < *mud.* Compare Middle Dutch *moddelen* to make water muddy.]

mud·dle·head (mud′əl hed′), *n.* a stupid or confused person; blockhead: . . . *unrepentant stubborn fanatics or smouldering muddleheads* (Manchester Guardian).

mud·dle·head·ed (mud′əl hed′id), *adj.* stupid; confused: *Can a country so impractical, so muddleheaded be trusted in a harsh material world?* (Harper's). —**mud′dle-head′ed·ness,** *n.*

mud·dle·ment (mud′əl mənt), *n.* muddled condition; confusion: *Many of the little muddlements that confront me in the morning are not susceptible to that kind of research* (New Yorker).

mud·dler (mud′lər), *n.* **1.** a small rod of glass, plastic, wood, or metal for stirring a drink. **2.** a person who muddles.

mud·dy (mud′ē), *adj.,* **-di·er, -di·est,** *v.,* **-died, -dy·ing.** —*adj.* **1.** of or like mud: *muddy footprints on the floor.* **2.** having much mud; covered with mud: *a muddy road, muddy shoes.* **3. a.** clouded with mud: *muddy water.* **b.** clouded with any sediment: *muddy coffee.* **4.** not clear, pure, or bright; dull: *a muddy color, a muddy yellow, a muddy sound.* **5.** not clear in mind; confused; muddled: *muddy thinking. Muddy writing is usually careless writing.* **6.** living or growing in mud.

—*v.t.* to make muddy: *Delivery difficulties and quick-changing models muddy the outlook for future sales* (Wall Street Journal). —*v.i.* to become muddy.

—**Syn.** *adj.* **3. a, b.** turbid, cloudy.

mud·fish (mud′fish′), *n., pl.* **-fish·es** or (*collectively*) **-fish.** any of certain fish that live in muddy water or burrow in mud, such as the bowfin or the killifish.

mud·flat (mud′flat′), *n.* a stretch of muddy land left uncovered at low tide: *In twisting creeks and inlets, on bird-haunted mudflats, . . . the sea anglers will soon forgather* (Sunday Times).

mud·flow (mud′flō′), *n.* **1.** an eruption of mud from a volcano: *In Java dams have been built to divert volcanic mudflows away from villages and agricultural lands* (Scientific American). **2.** a landslide of mud following spring thaws or heavy rain.

mud·guard (mud′gärd′), *n.* a guard or shield placed over or beside a wheel of a carriage, bicycle, automobile, etc., to prevent mud from splashing; fender.

mud hen, a water bird that looks like a duck and lives in marshes, such as a gallinule or coot.

mu·dir (mü dir′), *n.* (in Egypt, Turkey, etc.) a local administrator; governor. [< Arabic *mudīr*]

mud·lark (mud′lärk′), *n.* **1.** a person who dabbles, works, or lives in mud: *Illiterate mudlarks . . . used to comb the flats around the London docks looking for pilgrim's badges, towards the end of the last century* (London Times). **2.** a gamin; street urchin.

mud·pack (mud′pak′), *n.* a pack of mud applied on parts of the body for cosmetic or therapeutic purposes: *In the last decade the American man has succumbed to cologne, hairnets, mudpacks for his wrinkles, and clothes cut to accent a handsome thigh or well-turned calf* (New York Times).

mud pie, wet earth formed by children into the shape of a pie: *I stood beside my car, . . . envying her that deliberate preoccupation with mud pies and the blue innocence of the ribbon on her hair* (Atlantic).

mud puppy, 1. a large aquatic salamander of the Great Lakes, the Mississippi River, and eastern United States as far south as Georgia, having bushy, external gills; water dog. **2.** any of various other salamanders, especially the hellbender.

mu·dra (mü drä′), *n.* one of a number of symbolic finger gestures used in the dances of India: *It is not to be expected that the psychotherapist is . . . like an Indian dancer who has in the mudras, in the subtle movement of his fingers, a rich vocabulary* (Sebastian de Grazia). [< Sanskrit *mudrā* seal]

mud show, *U.S. Slang.* **1.** (formerly) a circus traveling with horses and wagons. **2.** a small circus, especially one that travels in trucks rather than trains.

mud·sill (mud′sil′), *n.* the lowest sill of a wall, dam, or other structure, usually placed in or on the ground.

mud·skip·per (mud′skip′ər), *n.* a small fish, a variety of goby, with movable pectoral fins and a muscular tail, found in shallow coastal waters from western Africa to Polynesia. It often moves about on mud flats, jumping and climbing roots after insects. *Of all living fish, the mudskippers . . . demonstrate most clearly how terrestrial vertebrates with four legs could have evolved from primitive swimmers with no legs at all* (New Scientist).

mud·sling·er (mud′sling′gər), *n.* a person given to mudslinging.

mud·sling·ing (mud′sling′ing), *n.* the use of offensive charges, misleading or slanderous accusations, etc., against an opponent in a political campaign, public meeting, or the like: *Mudslinging for however good a cause seldom pays in the end* (Sunday Times).

mud·stone (mud′stōn′), *n.* a soft, sedimentary, clayey rock nearly uniform in texture, with little or no lamination.

mud turtle, tortoise, or **terrapin,** any of various fresh-water turtles of the United States.

mud wasp, a wasp that builds its nest of mud.

mu·ez·zin (myü ez′ən), *n.* the crier who, at dawn, noon, four o'clock in the afternoon, sunset, and nightfall calls Moslems to regular hours of prayer: *There was a break in the proceedings at 5 p.m. in response to the symbolic muezzin's call* (London Times). [< Arabic *mu'adhdhin* the one who proclaims]

muff (muf), *n.* **1.** a covering of fur or other material, into which one puts both hands, one at each end, to keep them warm. **2.** a clumsy failure to catch a ball that comes into one's hands: *The catcher's muff allowed the runner to score.* **3.** awkward handling; bungling. **4. a.** a tuft or crest on the heads of certain birds. **b.** a cluster of feathers on the side of the face, characteristic of the Houdan fowl. **5.** *British Informal.* a clumsy, awkward person; bungler: *Pontifex was a young muff, a molly-coddle* (Samuel Butler).

—*v.t.* **1.** to fail to catch (a ball) when it comes into one's hands: [*He*] . . . *muffed a foul to help give the Redlegs three unearned runs* (New York Times). **2.** to handle awkwardly; bungle: *He muffs his real job without a blush* (H.G. Wells). —*v.i.* to muff a ball; bungle.

[< Dutch *mof* < French *moufle* mitten < Old French, thick glove, probably < a Germanic word]

muf·fin (muf′ən), *n.* a small, round cake made of wheat flour, corn meal, or the like, eaten with butter. [origin uncertain; perhaps < French, Old French *moufflet* soft, as in *pain moufflet* soft bread]

muf·fin·eer (muf′ə nir′), *n.* **1.** a utensil like a large saltshaker for sprinkling sugar, cinnamon, etc., over muffins: *Silver and turquoise inlaid muffineers* (London Daily News). **2.** a covered dish for keeping muffins, biscuits, etc., hot.

muffin tin, a metal dish with cup-shaped holes for baking muffins, cupcakes, etc.

muf·fle[1] (muf′əl), *v.,* **-fled, -fling,** *n.* —*v.t.* **1.** to wrap in something in order to soften or stop the sound; dull or deaden (a sound): *to muffle oars, or a drum. I heard voices, too, speaking with a hollow sound, and as if muffled by a rush of wind or water* (Charlotte Brontë). **2.** to wrap up the head of (a person) in order to keep him from speaking. **3.** to wrap or pull over so as to conceal: *to muffle one's face with a scarf. Alas, that love, whose view is muffled still Should, without eyes, see pathways to his will* (Shakespeare). **4.** to wrap or cover up in order to keep warm and dry: *She muffled her throat in a*

warm scarf. **5.** to dim (light): *through the dim length of the apartment, where crimson curtains muffled the glare of sunshine* (Hawthorne). —*v.i.* to wrap oneself in garments, etc.
—*n.* **1.** a muffled sound. **2.** a thing that muffles. **3.** *Obsolete.* a boxing glove: *Just like a black eye in a recent scuffle* (*For sometimes we must box without a muffle*) (Byron). **4.** *Scottish.* a mitten: *A muffle has only two divisions; one for the thumb and the other for the four fingers* (D. Nicholson).
[< Old French *mofler* to stuff < *moufle* thick glove, mitten. Compare MUFF.]

muf·fle[2] (muf′əl), *n.* the thick, bare part of the upper lip and nose of cows, moose, rabbits, and certain other animals. [< French *mufle;* origin unknown]

muf·fle[3] (muf′əl), *n.* **1.** an oven or arched chamber in a furnace or kiln, used for heating substances without direct contact with the fire: *Pottery and porcelain are fired in a muffle.* **2.** a furnace containing such a chamber. [< French *moufle,* probably a use of *moufle* mitten]

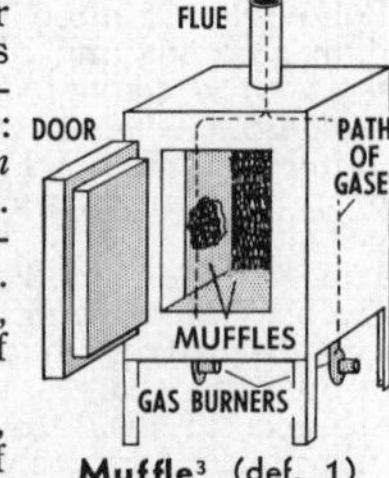

Muffle[3] (def. 1) Cutaway shows path of gases (heating element) around muffles (liners of oven, to screen object to be fired from direct heat).

muf·fler (muf′lər), *n.* **1.** a wrap or scarf worn around the neck for warmth. **2.** a thing used to deaden sound: *An automobile engine has a muffler attached to the exhaust.* **3.** any covering, such as a veil, used to conceal the face of a person. **4.** a glove or mitten. —**Syn.** **1.** tippet.

muf·ti (muf′tē), *n., pl.* **-tis.** **1.** ordinary clothes, not a uniform: *The retired general appeared in mufti.* **2.** a Moslem official who assists a judge by formal exposition of the religious law. **3.** (in Turkey) the official head of the state religion, or one of his deputies. [< Arabic *muftī* judge (apparently because of the informal costume traditional for the stage rôle of a *mufti*)]

mug[1] (mug), *n., v.,* **mugged, mug·ging.** —*n.* **1.** a heavy earthenware or metal drinking cup with a handle: *a coffee mug, a large mug of cider.* **2.** the amount a mug holds: *to drink a mug of milk.* **3.** *Slang.* **a.** the face: *an ugly mug.* **b.** the mouth: *Shut your mug!* **4.** *Slang.* a grimace. **5.** *British Slang.* a fool; dupe; simpleton. **6.** *U.S. Slang.* a ruffian; hoodlum; petty criminal: *Many a mug on the edge of the big time thinks there is a formula for dealing with newsmen: intimidate or bribe* (Time). **7.** *Slang.* **a.** a prize fighter, especially an inferior fighter: *People mostly figure once a fighter, always a mug* (New Yorker). **b.** a fighter with a disfigured face.
—*v.t. Slang.* **1.** to attack (a person) from behind by locking the forearm around the neck and choking: *Even as the raid was going on, . . . four youths mugged a 45-year-old woman* (Birmingham News). **2.** to make a photograph of (a person's face) for police purposes.
—*v.i. Slang.* to exaggerate one's facial expressions, as in acting: *None of the actors did any mugging* (New York Times).
mug up, *British Slang.* to study assiduously: *No longer do you have to mug up a set of dull figures* (Evening Standard).
[compare Norwegian *mugge,* Swedish *mugg;* definitions 3,4 < the shape of early mugs]

English Mug[1] (def. 1) (18th century)

mug[2] (mug), *n. Scottish.* a mist; drizzle; damp, gloomy state. [compare Old Icelandic *mugga*]

mug·ful (mug′fu̇l), *n., pl.* **-fuls.** enough to fill a mug: *a mugful of cocoa. Water is retailed by the bucket, and a potent brand of sherry by the mugful* (Daily Telegraph).

mug·gar (mug′ər), *n.* mugger, a man-eating crocodile of India and Ceylon.

mug·ger[1] (mug′ər), *n. Slang.* a person who mugs: *Other groups became counterfeiters, moonshiners, muggers* (Time).

mug·ger[2] (mug′ər), *n.* a man-eating crocodile of India and Ceylon, having a broad snout and growing to about 12 feet in length. [< Hindi *magar* < Sanskrit *makara* sea monster]

mug·gi·ness (mug′ē nis), *n.* muggy condition.

mug·gins (mug′inz), *n.* **1.** *Slang.* a simpleton. **2.** a certain game played with dominoes. **3.** any of various simple card games. [origin uncertain]

mug·gle (mug′əl), *n. U.S. Slang.* a marijuana cigarette.

mug·gur (mug′ər), *n.* mugger, a man-eating crocodile of India and Ceylon.

mug·gy (mug′ē), *adj.,* **-gi·er, -gi·est.** warm and humid; damp and close: *muggy weather, a muggy day.* [< *mug*[2] + *-y*[1]] —**Syn.** sultry.

Mu·ghal (mü′gul), *n. Especially British.* Mogul.

mug shot, a photograph of a person for police purposes: *Scotland Yard, the FBI and the Royal Canadian Mounted Police exchanged "mug shots" of some of their most wanted criminals* (New York Times).

mug·wort (mug′wėrt′), *n.* wormwood.

mug·wump (mug′wump′), *n. U.S.* **1.** an independent in politics: *We cannot afford to modify our principles to secure the support of a limited number of mugwumps* (Newsweek). **2.** a Republican who refused to support the party candidate, James G. Blaine, for President in 1884: *We have yet to see a Blaine organ which speaks of the Independent Republicans otherwise than as Pharisees, hypocrites, dudes, mugwumps, transcendentalists, or something of that sort* (New York Evening Post). [American English < Algonkian (Massachuset) *mugquomp* chief]

mug·wump·er·y (mug′wum′pər ē), *n., pl.* **-er·ies.** the principles or practice of mugwumps.

mug·wump·ism (mug′wum′piz əm), *n.* mugwumpery.

Mu·ham·mad (mu̇ ham′əd), *n.* Mohammed: *When, in his fortieth year, Muhammad believed he had received a fresh and divine gloss on the two testaments . . . few were those who resisted submission first to his moral and spiritual and soon to his military leadership* (Hugh Gordon Porteus).

Mu·ham·mad·an or **Mu·ham·med·an** (mu̇ ham′ə dən), *adj., n.* Mohammedan.

Mu·ham·mad·an·ism (mu̇ ham′ə də niz′-əm), *n.* Mohammedanism.

Mu·har·ram (mu̇ har′əm), *n.* **1.** the first month of the Moslem year. **2.** an annual Moslem religious celebration held during this month: *The Shia sect was taking part in a Muharram procession when some people threw bricks* (London Times). Also, **Moharram.**

muis·hond (mois′hônt′), *n. Afrikaans.* the zoril, a South African animal resembling a skunk in its markings and its ability to emit an evil-smelling liquid: *Tortoise eggs are much sought after by jackals . . . and muishonds* (Cape Times).

mu·jik (mü zhik′, mü′zhik), *n.* muzhik.

mukh·tar or **muh·tar** (mu̇k′tär, mu̇ᴴ′-), *n.* the elected headman of an Arab or Turkish town or village: *I was shown a red roof 500 yards away where the Turkish mukhtar was* (Manchester Guardian Weekly). [< Arabic *mukhtār* and Turkish *muhtar* (literally) chosen]

muk·luk (muk′luk), *n.* muckluck.

muk·tuk (muk′tuk), *n.* the thin outer skin of the beluga or white whale, or of the narwhal, used as food by the Eskimos. [< Eskimo]

mu·lat·to (mə lat′ō, myu̇-), *n., pl.* **-toes,** *adj.* —*n.* **1.** a person having one white and one Negro parent. **2.** a person having some white and some Negro blood. —*adj.* of the color of a mulatto; tawny. [< Spanish, Portuguese *mulato* < *mulo* mule < Latin *mūlus* (because of its hybrid origin)]

mul·ber·ry (mul′ber′ē, -bər-), *n., pl.* **-ries.** **1.** any of various broad, spreading trees of the mulberry family that yield a berrylike fruit, as the white mulberry, whose leaves are used for feeding silkworms. **2.** the edible, berrylike fruit of any of these trees. **3.** a dark purplish-red color: *If ever there was a wolf in a mulberry suit that 'ere Job Trotter's him* (Dickens). [Middle English *mulberie,* Old English *mōrberige* < Latin *mōrum* mulberry + Old English *berige* berry]

mul·ber·ry-col·ored (mul′ber ē kul′ərd, -bər-), *adj.* dark purplish-red.

mulberry family, a group of dicotyledonous herbs, shrubs, and trees, found chiefly in tropical regions. The family includes the fig, breadfruit, Osage orange, rubber plant, and banyan.

mulch (mulch), *n.* straw, leaves, loose earth, etc., spread on the ground around trees or plants to protect the roots from cold or heat, to prevent evaporation of moisture in the soil, to check weed growth, to decay and enrich the soil itself, or to keep the fruit clean. —*v.t.* to cover with straw, leaves, etc.; spread mulch under or around (a tree, plant, etc.): *They complain that the plants need constant spraying against aphis, caterpillars, and diseases; that they need to be pruned . . . and mulched* (London Times). [probably Middle English *molsh* soft, Old English *melsc* mellow, sweet] —**mulch′er,** *n.*

mulct (mulkt), *v.t.* **1.** to deprive of something by cunning or deceit; defraud: *He was mulcted of his money by a swindler.* **2.** to punish by a fine: *Some* [*apostates*] *. . . were again received into the Christian fold, after being severely mulcted* (Washington Irving). —*n.* a fine; penalty. [< Latin *mulctāre,* variant of *multāre* < *multa* a fine]

mule[1] (myül), *n.* **1.** the hybrid offspring of an ass and a horse, especially of a male ass and a mare, the offspring of a female ass and a stallion usually being distinguished as a *hinny.* A mule has the form and size of a horse, and the large ears, small hoofs, and tufted tail of a donkey, and is usually sterile. **2.** *Informal.* a stupid or stubborn person: *"Now don't be a young mule," said Good Mrs. Brown* (Dickens). **3.** a kind of spinning machine for drawing and twisting cotton, wool, or other fibers into yarn and winding it on spindles. **4.** any hybrid animal, especially the sterile offspring of a canary and some related bird. **5.** a tractor or small electric locomotive used to pull boats along a canal. [partly Old English *mūl* < Latin *mūlus;* partly < Old French *mule* < Latin *mūlus*]

mule[2] (myül), *n.* a loose slipper, worn by women, covering only the toes and part of the instep, and leaving the rest of the foot and the heel uncovered. [< Middle French *mule* < Dutch *muil* < Latin (*calceus*) *mulleus* red leather (shoe)]

mule·back (myül′bak′), *n.* the back of a mule: *Sometimes they came on horse- or muleback but, more often, on foot* (Harper's). —*adv.* on the back of a mule: *to ride muleback.*

mule deer, a deer of western North America having large ears and a white tail with a black tip. A mule deer of the Pacific Coast, the black-tailed deer, has a black tail with a white tip.

Mule Deer (about 3½ ft. high at the shoulder)

mule·head·ed (myül′hed′id), *adj.* stupidly obstinate or stubborn; pig-headed.

mule skinner, *U.S.* a man in charge of mules: *He knew plenty of individuals who represented the types—mule skinners, cowboys, barkeeps* (Chicago Tribune).

mu·le·ta (mü lā′tä), *n. Spanish.* (in bullfighting) a small red cloth draped over a stick, used to attract the attention of the bull: *Paeota held the folded muleta in his left hand and laid the sword across it* (Barnaby Conrad).

mu·le·teer (myü′lə tir′), *n.* a driver of mules: *muleteers hurrying forward their burdened animals* (Washington Irving). [< French *muletier* < *mulet* (diminutive) < Old French *mul* mule[1] < Latin *mūlus*]

mule train, **1.** a train of wagons drawn by mules. **2.** a train of pack mules.

mu·ley (myü′lē, mu̇l′ē), *adj., n., pl.* **-leys.** —*adj.* (of cattle) hornless. —*n.* **1.** a hornless animal. **2.** any cow. Also, **mulley.** [variant of dialectal *moiley* hornless cow < Irish *maol,* Welsh *moel* bald]

muley saw, a saw for ripping timber, having a long, stiff blade guided in a rapid reciprocating action by guide carriages at top and bottom. Also, **mully saw.**

mul·ga (mul′gə), *n.* any of various small acacias of Australia, yielding a hard, durable wood much used for carving ornaments. [< an Australian native name]

mu·li·eb·ri·ty (myü′lē eb′rə tē), *n.* **1.** womanly nature or qualities; femininity. **2.** womanhood. [< Latin *muliebritās* < *muliebris* of women < *mulier* woman]

mul·ish (myü′lish), *adj.* **1.** like a mule; obstinate; stubborn: . . . *however mulish this makes them look in the eyes of world opinion* (Economist). **2.** *Obsolete.* hybrid; sterile. —**mul′ish·ly,** *adv.* —**mul′ish·ness,** *n.* —**Syn. 1.** intractable.

mull[1] (mul), *v.t., v.i. U.S. Informal.* to think (about) without making much progress; ponder: *His subcommittee will mull the situation this fall and have a bill ready when Congress meets* (Wall Street Journal). [American English; origin uncertain] —**Syn.** ruminate.

mull[2] (mul), *v.t.* to make (wine, beer, cider, etc.) into a warm drink with sugar, spices, etc. [origin uncertain] —**mull′er,** *n.*

mull[3] (mul), *n.* a thin, soft muslin. [earlier *mulmul* < Hindustani *malmal*]

mull[4] (mul), *n. Scottish.* a snuffbox: *Hendry once offered Mr. Dishart a snuff from his mull* (James M. Barrie). [variant of *mill*[1]]

mull[5] (mul), *n.* a moist, well-aerated humus which is conducive to plant growth. [< German *Mull.* Ultimately related to MOLD[3].]

mul·lah or **mul·la** (mul′ə, mu̇l′-), *n.* (in Moslem countries) a title of respect for a person who is learned in the sacred law: *He made Kim learn whole chapters of the Koran by heart, till he could deliver them with the very roll and cadence of a mullah* (Rudyard Kipling). [< Turkish *molla,* in Persian, Hindustani *mullā* < Arabic *mawlā*]

mul·lein or **mul·len** (mul′ən), *n.* **1.** any of a group of weeds of the figwort family, with coarse, woolly leaves and spikes or racemes of yellow flowers. **2.** any of various plants similar to this group of weeds. [< Anglo-French *moleine* < Old French *mol* soft < Latin *mollis*]

mull·er (mul′ər), *n.* **1.** an implement for grinding paints, powders, etc., on a slab. **2.** a mechanical device for grinding or crushing. [Middle English *mullen* to grind to powder, or *mull* powder + *-er*[1]]

mul·let[1] (mul′it), *n., pl.* **-lets** or (*collectively*) **-let.** any of two groups of edible fish found chiefly in coastal waters, the gray mullets and the red mullets or surmullets: *Some say the mullet jump to shake off a parasite that annoys them* (New Yorker). [Middle English *molet* < Old French *mulet* < Latin *mullus* red mullet < Greek *mýllos*]

Striped Mullet[1]
(about 13 in. long)

mul·let[2] (mul′it), *n. Heraldry.* a star-shaped figure, usually with five straight or regular points. See **estoile.** [< Old French *molette* rowel]

mul·let-head·ed (mul′it hed′id), *adj.* stupid; dull. [origin uncertain]

mul·ley (mu̇l′ē, mü′lē), *adj., n., pl.* **-leys.** muley.

mul·li·gan (mul′ə gən), *n. U.S. Slang.* **1.** Also, **mulligan stew.** a stew of meat and vegetables: *Hoboes are traditionally makers of mulligan. After turkey Frost's specialties . . . are baked beans, mulligan stew, and steak-and-kidney pie* (Maclean's). **2.** *Golf.* a second drive, without penalty, off the first tee (when the first drive is bad). [American English; origin uncertain, perhaps from a proper name]

mul·li·ga·taw·ny (mul′ə gə tô′nē), *n., pl.* **-nies.** a soup made from a chicken or meat stock flavored with curry, originally made in India. [< Tamil *milagu-taṇṇi* pepper water]

mul·li·grubs (mul′i grubz), *n.pl. Slang.* **1.** low spirits; the blues. **2.** stomach ache; colic: *Where spasms were . . . afflicting him with mulligrubs and colic* (George Colman). [a coined word]

mul·lion (mul′yən), *n.* **1.** a vertical bar between the lights in a window, the panels in the wall of a room, etc.: *On the one side ran a range of windows lofty and large, divided by carved mullions of stones* (Scott). **2.** a radiating bar in a round window. —*v.t.* to divide or provide with mullions. Also, **munnion.** [alteration of Middle English *muniall* or *monial* < Old French *moienel* in the middle < *meien* < Latin *mediānus* median < *medius* middle]

mul·lioned (mul′yənd), *adj.* having mullions: *mullioned windows.*

mul·lock (mul′ək), *n.* in Australia: **1.** mining refuse. **2.** ore or earth that does not contain gold. [Middle English *mullok* rubbish < obsolete *mull* rubbish + *-ok,* a diminutive suffix]

mul·ly saw (mul′ē), *U.S.* muley saw.

mult-, *combining form.* the form of **multi-** before some vowels, as in *multangular.*

mul·ta do·cet fa·mes (mul′tə dō′set fā′mēz), *Latin.* hunger teaches many things.

mul·tan·gu·lar (mul tang′gyə lər), *n.* either of two bones of the human wrist, the greater multangular (trapezium) at the base of the thumb, or the lesser multangular (trapezoid) at the base of the forefinger in the distal row of carpal bones. —*adj.* **1.** having many angles; polygonal. **2.** of or having to do with one of the multangulars.

mul·te·i·ty (mul tē′ə tē), *n.* the quality of being many; manifoldness. [< Latin *multus* many + English *-ity*]

multi-, *combining form.* **1.** many; having many or much: *Multiform = having many forms.*
2. many times: *Multimillionaire = a millionaire many times over.*
3. much; in many ways: *Multiradial = having radii along many lines.* Also, sometimes **mult-** before vowels.
[< Latin *multi-* < *multus,* much, many]

mul·ti·ax·i·al (mul′tē ak′sē əl), *adj.* having many or several axes.

mul·ti·cel·lu·lar (mul′ti sel′yə lər), *adj.* having or consisting of many cells.

mul·ti·chan·nel (mul′ti chan′əl), *adj.* having or using several channels: *a multichannel cable, a multichannel tape recorder.*

mul·ti·coil (mul′ti koil), *adj.* having more than a single coil.

mul·ti·col·or (mul′ti kul′ər), *adj.* having or using many colors: *multicolor lacquers.*

mul·ti·col·ored (mul′ti kul′ərd), *adj.* having many colors. —**Syn.** pied.

mul·ti·cos·tate (mul′ti kos′tāt), *adj.* having many costae, ribs, or ridges.

mul·ti·cul·tur·al (mul′ti kul′chər əl), *adj.* having or blending many distinct cultures: *a multicultural nation.*

mul·ti·cul·tur·al·ism (mul′ti kul′chər ə-liz əm), *n.* the quality or state of being multicultural.

mul·ti·den·tate (mul′ti den′tāt), *adj.* having many teeth or toothlike processes.

mul·ti·di·men·sion·al (mul′ti də men′shə nəl), *adj.* having many dimensions or aspects: *Intellectual resources are multidimensional* (Science News Letter).

mul·ti·di·rec·tion·al (mul′ti də rek′shə-nəl), *adj.* having more than one direction; moving in several directions: *There is still a multidirectional market with the buying interest rotating between new issues and groups* (Wall Street Journal).

mul·ti·dis·ci·pli·nar·y (mul′ti dis′ə plə-ner′ē), *adj.* involving many branches of learning: *a multidisciplinary research program.*

mul·ti·en·gine (mul′ti en′jin), *adj.* (of an aircraft or rocket) having a number of engines: *In a multiengine missile the malfunction of any one of the engines will cause the loss of the complete missile* (U.S. Air Force Report on the Ballistic Missile).

mul·ti·fac·et·ed (mul′ti fas′ə tid), *adj.* many-faceted: *Yet Rome and the Renaissance are only two aspects of what is, when we learn to know it well, a multifaceted continuum* (Elisabeth Mann Borgese).

mul·ti·fac·to·ri·al (mul′ti fak tôr′ē əl, -tōr′-), *adj.* **1.** involving many factors. **2.** *Genetics.* of, having to do with, or caused by multiple factors.

mul·ti·fam·i·ly (mul′ti fam′ə lē, -fam′lē), *adj.* used by or intended for many families: *a multifamily residential development.*

mul·ti·far·i·ous (mul′tə fãr′ē əs), *adj.* **1.** having many different parts, elements, forms, etc.; having great variety: . . . *the machinery of high politics—the incessant and multifarious business of a great State* (Lytton Strachey). **2.** many and various. **3.** *Botany, Zoology.* arranged in many rows. [< Latin *multifārius* (with English *-ous*)] —**mul′ti·far′i·ous·ly,** *adv.* —**mul′ti·far′i·ous·ness,** *n.* —**Syn. 2.** manifold, diverse.

mul·ti·fid (mul′tə fid), *adj.* divided into many lobes or segments: *a multifid leaf.* [< Latin *multifidus* < *multus* many + *findere* to split, divide]

mul·tif·i·dous (mul tif′ə dəs), *adj.* multifid.

mul·ti·fil (mul′tə fil), *n.* multifilament.

mul·ti·fil·a·ment (mul′tə fil′ə mənt), *n.* yarn made up of many fine filaments.

mul·ti·flo·rous (mul′ti flôr′əs, -flōr′-), *adj.* bearing many flowers. [< *multi-* + Latin *flōs, flōris* flower + English *-ous*]

mul·ti·foil (mul′ti foil), *adj., n. Architecture.* polyfoil.

mul·ti·fold (mul′tə fōld), *adj.* manifold. —**Syn.** multifarious.

mul·ti·fo·li·ate (mul′tə fō′lē it, -āt), *adj. Botany.* having many leaves or leaflets. [< *multi-* + *foliate*]

mul·ti·form (mul′tə fôrm), *adj.* having many different shapes, forms, or kinds: *It includes a model, drawings, and photographs of the multiform playhouse which the Questors Theatre . . . hopes to build* (London Times). [< Middle French *multiforme,* learned borrowing from Latin *multiformis* < *multus* many + *forma* form]

mul·ti·form·i·ty (mul′tə fôr′mə tē), *n.* the character or condition of being multiform.

mul·ti·fu·el (mul′ti fyü′əl), *adj.* capable of running without adjustments on various types of fuels, such as gasoline, kerosene, diesel oil, etc.: *a multifuel engine.*

mul·ti·grade (mul′ti grād), *adj.* (of oil) combining the viscous properties of several grades.

Mul·ti·graph (mul′tə graf, -gräf), *n. Trademark.* a machine for printing circulars, letters, etc., with type similar to that of a typewriter.

mul·ti·graph (mul′tə graf, -gräf), *v.t.* to make copies of by a Multigraph: *The editors issue one new poem a day on a single, multigraphed sheet* (Saturday Review). —**mul′ti·graph·er,** *n.*

mul·ti·hued (mul′ti hyüd′), *adj.* multicolored: *a multihued sweater.*

mul·ti·jet (mul′ti jet), *adj.* (of aircraft) having a number of jet engines.

mul·ti·lam·i·nate (mul′ti lam′ə nāt, -nit), *adj.* having many laminae or layers.

mul·ti·lane (mul′ti lān′), *adj.* having more than two traffic lanes: *a multilane highway.*

mul·ti·lat·er·al (mul′ti lat′ər əl), *adj.* **1.** having many sides; many-sided. **2.** involving three or more nations: *a multilateral treaty.* —**mul′ti·lat′er·al·ly,** *adv.*

mul·ti·lat·er·al·ism (mul′ti lat′ər ə liz′-əm), *n.* **1.** a policy of reciprocity or freedom in trading with many nations (distinguished from *bilateralism*). **2.** belief in or adoption of a multilateral policy, such as the joint control of nuclear weapons by the members of an alliance (distinguished from *unilateralism*).

mul·ti·lat·er·al·ist (mul′ti lat′ər ə list), *n.* an adherent of multilateralism. —*adj.* of or having to do with multilateralism or multilateralists.

mul·ti·lay·er (mul′ti lā′ər), *adj.* **1.** consisting of several layers: *a multilayer cake, multilayer wrappers.* **2.** *Photography.* consisting of two or more layers of differently sensitized emulsions for producing differently colored images in each layer. —*n. Chemistry.* a layer consisting of several monolayers.

mul·ti·lay·ered (mul′ti lā′ərd), *adj.* multilayer.

mul·ti·lev·el (mul′ti lev′əl), *adj.* having two or more planes or levels: *a multilevel roadway.*

mul·ti·lin·e·al (mul′ti lin′ē əl), *adj.* having many lines.

mul·ti·lin·e·ar (mul′ti lin′ē ər), *adj.* having many lines; multilineal: *a multilinear map, multilinear evolution.*

mul·ti·lin·gual (mul′ti ling′gwəl), *adj.* knowing or using many languages: *Another feature is a multilingual index giving English equivalents of mathematical terms in French, German, Russian and Spanish* (Scientific American). —**mul′ti·lin′gual·ly,** *adv.*

mul·ti·lin·gual·ism (mul′ti ling′gwə liz-əm), *n.* the ability to speak more than two languages equally or almost equally well.

Mul·ti·lith (mul′ti lith), *n. Trademark.* a small offset press for printing office letters, circulars, etc.

mul·ti·lith (mul′ti lith), *v.t.* to make copies of by a Multilith.

mul·ti·lo·bate (mul′ti lō′bāt), *adj.* having many lobes: *a multilobate leaf.*

mul·ti·lobed (mul′ti lōbd′), *adj.* multilobate.

mul·ti·loc·u·lar (mul′ti lok′yə lər), *adj.* having many chambers or cells.

mul·til·o·quence (mul til′ə kwəns), *n.* the use of many words; verbosity; loquacity. [< Late Latin *multiloquentia* < Latin *multus* much + *loquentia* fluency of speech]

mul·til·o·quent (mul til′ə kwənt), *adj.* speaking much; talkative; verbose.

mul·ti·meg·a·ton (mul′ti meg′ə tun), *adj.* (of thermonuclear weapons) having a force of many megatons.

mul·ti·mil·lion·aire (mul′ti mil′yə nãr′), *n.* a millionaire many times over.

mul·ti·mil·lions (mul′ti mil′yənz), *n.pl.* millions of dollars, pounds, etc.: *When he's finally made his multimillions, he finds all he can use them for is to buy better burglar alarms* (New Scientist).

mul·ti·mo·tored (mul′ti mō′tərd), *adj.* having a number of motors.

mul·ti·na·tion·al (mul′ti nash′ə nəl, -nash′nəl), *adj.* of, representing, or having to do with many nations: *a multinational economic organization. The United States was ready to contribute to a new fund to increase multinational projects in Latin America* (Manchester Guardian Weekly).

mul·ti·no·mi·al (mul′ti nō′mē əl), *adj., n.* polynomial.

mul·ti·nom·i·nal (mul′ti nom′ə nəl), *adj.* having many names.

mul·ti·nu·cle·ar (mul′ti nü′klē ər, -nyü′-), *adj.* having more than one nucleus: *a multinuclear cell.*

mul·ti·nu·cle·ate (mul′ti nü′klē it, -nyü′-), *adj.* multinuclear.

mul·ti·nu·cle·at·ed (mul′ti nü′klē ā′tid, -nyü′-), *adj.* multinuclear.

mul·tip·a·ra (mul tip′ər ə), *n., pl.* **-a·rae** (-ə rē). a woman who has had more than one child. [< New Latin *multipara*, feminine of *multiparus* < Latin *multus* much + *parere* bring forth]

mul·ti·par·i·ty (mul′ti par′ə tē), *n.* plural birth; production of several at a birth. [< *multi-* + Latin *parere* bring forth + English *-ity*]

mul·tip·a·rous (mul tip′ər əs), *adj.* **1.** producing many, or more than one, at a birth. **2.** *Botany.* (of a cyme) having many axes.

mul·ti·par·tite (mul′ti pär′tīt), *adj.* **1.** divided into many parts; having many divisions. **2.** multilateral. [< Latin *multipartītus* < *multus* much + *partīre* to divide < *pars, partis* part]

mul·ti·par·ty (mul′ti pär′tē), *adj.* of or having to do with a number of political parties: *a multiparty system.*

mul·ti·ped (mul′tə ped), *adj.* having many feet. —*n.* an animal with many feet. [< Latin *multipēs, -pedis* < *multus* many + *pēs, pedis* foot]

mul·ti·pede (mul′tə pēd), *adj., n.* multiped.

mul·ti·phase (mul′ti fāz), *adj.* **1.** having many phases. **2.** *Electricity.* polyphase.

mul·ti·pha·sic (mul′ti fā′sik), *adj.* multiphase.

mul·ti·plane (mul′ti plān), *n.* an airplane with several main lifting surfaces.

mul·ti·ple (mul′tə pəl), *adj.* **1.** of, having, or involving many parts, elements, relations, etc.; manifold: *Benjamin Franklin was a man of multiple interests.* **2.** *Electricity.* **a.** (of a circuit) having two or more conductors in parallel. **b.** (of a group of terminals) giving access to a circuit at a number of points. **3.** *British.* of or belonging to a chain of stores or shops: *a multiple grocer.*
—*n.* **1.** a number which contains another number twice or more without remainder: *20 is a multiple of 4.* **2.** *Electricity.* a group of terminals arranged so as to give access to a circuit or group of circuits at a number of points.
in multiple, *Electricity.* in parallel: *All the motors were connected in multiple and operated individually.*
[< French *multiple* < Late Latin *multiplus* manifold]

multiple alleles, *Genetics.* a group of three or more allelomorphic genes, only two of which can be present at one time in the body cells of a diploid organism.

mul·ti·ple-choice (mul′tə pəl chois′), *adj.* containing two or more suggested answers from which the correct or best one must be chosen: *a multiple-choice test. In her two and a half years at Georgia, where even philosophy tests are usually made up of true-false and multiple-choice questions, Charlayne's grades fluctuated wildly* (New Yorker).

multiple cropping, growing two or more crops in one field in one year.

multiple factors, *Genetics.* combinations of two or more genes which act together to produce a trait, as size, yield, or skin pigmentation, or the variations in it.

multiple fruit, a fruit composed of a cluster of ripened ovaries produced by several flowers, as the mulberry; collective fruit; compound fruit. See picture under **aggregate fruit.**

multiple myeloma, a very painful cancer usually affecting a number of bones, originating in bone marrow, and causing lesions of the bone and of certain soft tissues such as the kidneys.

multiple neuritis, inflammation of several nerves at once.

multiple personality, a psychological condition in which a person exhibits the characteristics or behavior of two or more dissimilar personalities.

multiple sclerosis, a disorder of the nervous system, attacking the brain and the spinal cord, and characterized by the degeneration and scarring of patches of nerve tissue, followed by paralysis, muscle spasms, disorders of speech, tremors of the hand, etc.

multiple shop or **store,** *Especially British.* a chain store.

multiple star, a group of three or more stars comprising one gravitational system, and usually appearing to the naked eye as a single star.

mul·ti·plet (mul′tə plit), *n.* **1.** *Physics.* two or more closely associated lines in a spectrum, exhibiting characteristic differences, as of frequency. **2.** *Nuclear Physics.* two or more elementary particles exhibiting identical or similar characteristics: *The eightfold way puts nuclear particles into groups, or multiplets, and families of groups, or supermultiplets* (Science News Letter).

multiple voting, voting in more than one place at the same election. This was legally possible in Great Britain before 1918.

mul·ti·plex (mul′tə pleks), *adj.* **1.** manifold; multiple. **2.** *Telegraphy, Telephony.* of or designating a system for sending two or more messages in each direction over the same wire or circuit at the same time. **3.** *Radio, Television.* of or designating the transmission of two or more signals on one carrier wave at the same time: *Center channel output and output for multiplex adaptor assure . . . gratifying results* (Wall Street Journal).
—*v.t., v.i.* **1.** *Telegraphy, Telephony.* to send (two or more messages) over the same wire at the same time. **2.** *Radio, Television.* to send (two or more signals) on one carrier wave at the same time: *Multiplex your modulation into the intermediate frequency* (New York Times).
[< Latin *multiplex, -icis;* see MULTIPLY]
—**mul′ti·plex′er,** *n.* —**mul′ti·plex′ly,** *adv.*

mul·ti·pli·a·ble (mul′tə plī′ə bəl), *adj.* that can be or will be multiplied, especially as the consequence of some action.

mul·ti·pli·ca·ble (mul′tə plə kə bəl), *adj.* multipliable.

mul·ti·pli·cand (mul′tə plə kand′), *n.* a number or quantity to be multiplied by another: *In 5 times 497, the multiplicand is 497.* [< Latin *multiplicandus*, gerundive of *multiplicāre;* see MULTIPLY]

mul·ti·pli·cate (mul′tə plə kāt), *adj.* manifold; multifold; multiplex. [< Latin *multiplicātus*, past participle of *multiplicāre;* see MULTIPLY]

mul·ti·pli·ca·tion (mul′tə plə kā′shən), *n.* **1.** a multiplying: *I fairly cowered down . . . under this multiplication of hardships* (Herman Melville). **2.** a being multiplied: *One of the peculiarities which distinguish the present age is the multiplication of books* (Samuel Johnson). **3.** the operation of multiplying one number or quantity by another; the operation of finding a product by adding a number or quantity (the multiplicand) as many times as there are units in another (the multiplier), or of calculating this addition briefly. *Symbol:* ×.

mul·ti·pli·ca·tion·al (mul′tə plə kā′shə nəl), *adj.* of or having to do with multiplication.

multiplication table, a table that lists the products of all the simple digits, from 1 times 1 to 12 times 12.

mul·ti·pli·ca·tive (mul′tə plə kā′tiv), *adj.* tending to multiply or increase; able to multiply. —**mul′ti·pli·ca′tive·ly,** *adv.*

mul·ti·pli·cious (mul′tə plish′əs), *adj.* manifold; multiple.

mul·ti·plic·i·ty (mul′tə plis′ə tē), *n., pl.* **-ties. 1.** manifold variety; diversity: *the multiplicity of nature.* **2.** a great many; great number: *a multiplicity of gifts, a multiplicity of interests.* [< Late Latin *multiplicitās* < Latin *multiplex, -icis;* see MULTIPLY]

mul·ti·pli·er (mul′tə plī′ər), *n.* **1.** a number by which another number (the multiplicand) is to be multiplied: *In 5 times 83, the multiplier is 5.* **2.** a person or thing that multiplies. **3.** *Physics.* an instrument or device used for intensifying by repetition the intensity of a force, current, etc.

mul·ti·ply[1] (mul′tə plī), *v.,* **-plied, -plying.** —*v.t.* **1.** to increase (a number or quantity) a given number of times: *To multiply 16 by 3 means to increase 16 three times, making 48.* **2.** to increase the number, quantity, etc., of: *Fear multiplies the difficulties of life.* **3.** to increase by procreation: *that all creatures might be tempted to multiply their kind, and fill the world with inhabitants* (Joseph Addison). **4.** to produce (animals or plants) by propagation. —*v.i.* **1.** to grow in number, quantity, etc.; increase: *The difficulties of the pioneers multiplied when winter came.* **2.** to increase in number by natural generation or procreation: *Be fruitful, and multiply* (Genesis 1:22). **3.** to perform the process of multiplication: *Michael can add, subtract, and multiply, but he cannot divide.* [< Old French *multiplier* < Latin *multiplicāre* < *multiplex, -icis* < *multus* many + *-plex* -fold]

mul·ti·ply[2] (mul′tə plē), *adv.* in a multiple or manifold way; in the manner of a multiple.

mul·ti·po·lar (mul′ti pō′lər), *adj.* having many poles.

mul·tip·o·tent (mul tip′ə tənt), *adj.* having much power; very powerful: *There are still undreamed-of possibilities in the multipotent clay that is his to mold* (Atlantic). [< *multi-* + Latin *pōtens, -entis* powerful]

mul·ti·pur·pose (mul′ti pėr′pəs), *adj.* having many purposes or functions; versatile: *a multipurpose building that can be used for machinery storage, for grain storage, and for housing cattle.*

mul·ti·ra·cial (mul′ti rā′shəl), *adj.* of or having to do with a number of races: *the multiracial communities of the Caribbean.*

mul·ti·ra·cial·ism (mul′ti rā′shə liz əm), *n.* a policy or system which favors the coexistence and quality of several races in one country: *The new federation [of Malaysia] is an experiment in multiracialism* (Manchester Guardian Weekly).

mul·ti·stage (mul′ti stāj), *adj.* **1.** having a number of stages in going through a complete process: *multistage automatic washers, amplifiers, etc.; a multistage nuclear reaction.* **2.** (of a rocket or missile) having two or more propulsive sections, each operating after the preceding stage has burned out and separated: *a multistage rocket.*

mul·ti·state (mul′ti stāt), *adj.* consisting of, representing, or serving many nations or states of a nation: *a multistate conference.*

mul·ti·sto·rey (mul′ti stôr′ē, -stōr′-), *adj.* *Especially British.* multistory.

mul·ti·sto·ried (mul′ti stôr′ēd, -stōr′-), *adj.* multistory.

mul·ti·sto·ry (mul′ti stôr′ē, -stōr′-), *adj.* (of a building) having many stories.

mul·ti·syl·lab·ic (mul′ti sə lab′ik), *adj.* polysyllabic.

mul·ti·tude (mul′tə tüd, -tyüd), *n.* **1.** a great many: *a multitude of problems, a multitude of friends.* **2.** a large gathering of people; crowd: *An angry multitude collected in the street.* **3.** number: *Ye are this day as the stars of heaven for multitude* (Deuteronomy 1:10).
the multitude, the common people; the masses: *a play that appeals to the multitude.*
[< Latin *multitūdō, -inis* < *multus* much]
—**Syn. 1.** host, horde. **2.** throng.

mul·ti·tu·di·nism (mul′tə tü′də niz əm, -tyü′-), *n.* the principle according to which the interests of multitudes are placed before those of individuals.

mul·ti·tu·di·nous (mul′tə tü′də nəs, -tyü′-), *adj.* **1.** forming a multitude; existing or occurring in great numbers: *Multitudinous echoes awoke and died in the distance* (Longfellow). **2.** including many parts, elements, items, or features; very numerous: *I heard again the multitudinous murmur of the city* (George W. Curtis). **3.** crowded; thronged: *the multitudinous streets.* **4.** *Obsolete.* of or having to do with the multitude: *Pluck out The multitudinous tongue; let them not lick The sweet which is their poison* (Shakespeare). **—mul′ti·tu′di·nous·ly,** *adv.* **—mul′ti·tu′di·nous·ness,** *n.*

mul·ti·va·lence (mul′ti vā′ləns, mul tiv′ə-), *n.* multivalent quality or property.

mul·ti·va·lent (mul′ti vā′lənt, mul tiv′ə-), *adj.* **1.** having a valence of three or more. **2.** having more than one degree of valence.

mul·ti·val·ued (mul′ti val′yüd), *adj.* having many values: *a multivalued mathematical function.*

mul·ti·valve (mul′ti valv), *adj.* (of a shell) having many valves or ports. *—n.* **1.** a multivalve shell. **2.** an animal having such a shell.

mul·ti·val·vu·lar (mul′ti val′vyə lər), *adj.* multivalve.

mul·ti·var·i·ate (mul′ti vãr′ē āt), *adj.* having two or more variates.

mul·ti·verse (mul′ti vėrs), *n.* the universe regarded as lacking order or any single ruling or guiding power. [< *multi-* + (uni)*verse*]

mul·ti·ver·si·ty (mul′tə vėr′sə tē), *n., pl.* **-ties.** a large educational institution comprising several universities and their related colleges and professional schools: *The Board of Governors, whether of a small liberal arts college or a multiversity, will need . . . persuasiveness if our universities are to grow and change* (Saturday Night). [< *multi-* + (uni)*versity*]

mul·ti·vi·bra·tor (mul′ti vī′brā tər), *n.* a type of oscillator having two stages, each of which utilizes the output voltage of the other as its input. Multivibrators are used in digital computers, electronic circuits, etc.

mul·ti·vi·ta·min (mul′ti vī′tə min), *adj.* containing or combining various vitamins: *a multivitamin pill.* *—n.* a drug or similar substance containing various vitamins.

mul·tiv·o·cal (mul tiv′ə kəl), *adj.* having many meanings; equivocal; ambiguous.

mul·ti·vol·ume (mul′ti vol′yəm), *adj.* **1.** filling many volumes: . . . *the first multivolume history of Canada* (Maclean's). **2.** containing many volumes: *a multivolume set, a multivolume library.*

mul·ti·vol·umed (mul′ti vol′yəmd), *adj.* multivolume: . . . *the multivolumed shelf of books* (New York Times).

mul·ti·wall bag (mul′ti wôl), a large, heavy-duty paper bag consisting of a number of layers or sheets of kraft paper: *The cement industry has remained the top multiwall bag user* (Wall Street Journal).

mul·toc·u·lar (mul tok′yə lər), *adj.* having many eyes, or eyelike parts, as a fly or certain microscopes. [< *mult-* + *ocular*]

mul·tum in par·vo (mul′təm in pär′vō), *Latin.* much in little.

mul·ture (mul′chər), *n. Archaic.* **1.** a fee consisting of a proportion of the grain, or of the flour, paid to the miller for grinding it. **2.** the right to take this toll. [< Old French *molture,* learned borrowing from Medieval Latin *moltura,* for Late Latin *molitūra* < Latin *molere* to grind]

mum[1] (mum), *adj.* saying nothing; silent: *The company being otherwise rather mum and silent, my uncle told . . . anecdotes* (Thackeray). *—interj.* be silent! say nothing! hush!: *Mum's the word.* [perhaps imitative. Compare MUMMER, MUMMERY.] **—Syn.** *adj.* mute, speechless, dumb.

mum[2] (mum), *v.i.,* **mummed, mum·ming. 1.** to go about as a mummer, as at Christmas time. **2.** to masquerade. **3.** *Archaic.* to act in dumb show. Also, **mumm.** [perhaps back formation < *mommyng* a disguising, mummer's play; origin uncertain. Compare MUMMER.]

mum[3] (mum), *n. Informal.* a chrysanthemum. [short for *chrysanthemum*]

mum[4] (mum), *n. Informal.* mother. [short for *mummy,* (originally) dialectal variant of *mammy,* or *mommy*]

mum[5] (mum), *n.* a strong ale or beer, popular in England in the 1600's and 1700's. [< German *Mumme,* or Dutch *mom*]

mum·ble (mum′bəl), *v.,* **-bled, -bling,** *n.* *—v.i.* **1.** to speak indistinctly, as a person does when his lips are partly closed; speak in low tones; mutter: *She appeared as if she wanted to say something, and kept making signs . . . and mumbling* (Charlotte Brontë). **2.** to chew as a person does who has no teeth: *The old dog mumbled on a crust.*
—v.t. **1.** to say indistinctly, as a person does when his lips are partly closed: *He affirmed that we mumbled our speech with our lips and teeth, and ran the words together without pause or distinction* (Tobias Smollett). **2.** to chew as a person does who has no teeth: *The old dog mumbled the crust.*
—n. the act or fact of mumbling; indistinct speech: *There was a mumble of protest from the team against the umpire's decision.*
[Middle English *momelen,* perhaps (frequentative) < *mum*[2]] **—mum′bler,** *n.* **—mum′bling·ly,** *adv.* **—Syn.** *v.i., v.t.* **1.** See **murmur.**

mum·ble·ty-peg (mum′bəl ti peg′), *n.* a game in which the players in turn flip a knife from various positions, trying to make it stick in the ground; the loser has to pull a peg out of the ground with his teeth. [earlier *mumble-the-peg*]

Mum·bo Jum·bo (mum′bō jum′bō), the guardian genius of a native African village in western Sudan, represented by a masked medicine man who fends off evil and keeps the women in subjection: *Mumbo Jumbo, God of the Congo . . . will hoo-doo you* (Vachel Lindsay). [allegedly < a West African language; origin unknown]

mumbo jumbo, 1. foolish or meaningless incantation; ritualistic or ceremonial nonsense: *You are lost if you preoccupy yourself with the old mumbo jumbo . . . of an era that is done* (Harper's). **2.** an object foolishly worshiped or feared; bugaboo; bogy. **—Syn. 2.** fetish.

mum·chance (mum′chans′, -chäns′), *adj., adv. Especially British.* in silence; speechless; tongue-tied; mum: *The gunman . . . had left with £7,500 while the smirking staff stood mumchance* (Punch). [< obsolete English *mumchance,* noun, a certain game of dice < Middle Low German *mummenschanze* < *mummen* to keep silence (probably < Old French *momer* mask oneself; see MUMMER) + *schanz* game of chance < Old French *cheance;* see CHANCE]

mu-mes·on (myü′mes′on, -mē′son), *n.* a meson having a mass about 217 times that of the electron; muon. Mu-mesons are formed by the decay of pi-mesons and in turn decay to form high-energy electrons. [< Greek *mu,* arbitrary designation in a series + English *meson*]

mumm (mum), *v.i.* mum[2].

mum·mer (mum′ər), *n.* **1.** a person who wears a mask, fancy costume, or disguise for fun, as at Christmas time or at a Mardi Gras. **2.** an actor. **3.** an actor in one of the rural plays traditionally performed in England and elsewhere at Christmas: *The play was hastily rehearsed, whereupon the other mummers were delighted with the new knight* (Thomas Hardy). [< Old French *momeur* mummer < *momer* mask oneself < *momon* mask]

mum·mer·y (mum′ər ē), *n., pl.* **-mer·ies. 1.** a performance of mummers. **2.** any useless or silly show or ceremony: *Archbishop Grindal long hesitated about accepting a mitre from dislike of what he regarded as the mummery of consecration* (Macaulay). [< Middle French *mommerie* < Old French *momer* mask oneself; see MUMMER]

mum·mi·fi·ca·tion (mum′ə fə kā′shən), *n.* **1.** the act or process of mummifying: *The thighbone of a dead African king, preserved for ritual uses, represents . . . a diffusion of Egyptian mummification* (Melville J. Herskovitz). **2.** the state of being mummified.

mum·mi·fy (mum′ə fī), *v.,* **-fied, -fy·ing.** *—v.t.* to make (a dead body) into a mummy; make similar to a mummy. *—v.i.* to dry or shrivel up.

mum·my[1] (mum′ē), *n., pl.* **-mies,** *v.,* **-mied, -my·ing.** *—n.* **1.** a dead body of a human being or animal preserved from decay by the ancient Egyptian or some other method. Egyptian mummies have lasted more than 3,000 years. **2.** a dead human or animal body dried and preserved by nature. **3.** a withered or shrunken living being. **4. a.** a rich brown bituminous pigment. **b.** a rich brown color. **5.** *British Dialect.* a pulpy mass: *battering the warriors' faces into mummy by terrible yerks from their hinder hoofs* (Jonathan Swift). **6.** *Obsolete.* dead flesh; a corpse. **7.** *Obsolete.* bone or tissue matter from a mummy, formerly used as a medicine.
—v.t., v.i. to mummify.
[< Old French *mumie,* learned borrowing from Medieval Latin *mumia* < Arabic *mūmiyā* embalmed body < Persian *mūm* wax]

mum·my[2] (mum′ē), *n., pl.* **-mies.** *Informal.* mother.

mummy case, a case of wood or other material in which a mummy, wrapped in cloth, was enclosed. The case was shaped to conform to the body, and carved and painted to represent the dead person.

mump (mump), *Dialect.* *—v.i.* **1.** to mumble; mutter. **2.** to munch or chew. **3.** to mope; sulk: *It is better to enjoy a novel than to mump* (Robert Louis Stevenson). **4.** to grimace. **5.** to sponge; beg. *—v.t.* **1.** to mumble; mutter: *Old men who mump their passion* (Oliver Goldsmith). **2.** to munch or chew. **3.** to beg. **4.** to cheat. [perhaps < Icelandic *mumpa* take into the mouth]

mump·ish (mum′pish), *adj.* sullenly angry; depressed in spirits. **—mump′ish·ly,** *adv.*

mumps (mumps), *n.pl.* a contagious disease, caused by a virus, marked by inflammation and swelling of the parotid and often other salivary glands, and sometimes by inflammation of the testes or ovaries: *A person with mumps has a swollen face and neck, and finds it hard to swallow.* [plural of obsolete *mump* a grimace. Related to MUMP.]

➔ **Mumps** is usually construed as singular: *Mumps is chiefly a children's disease.*

mump·si·mus (mump′sə məs), *n.* an error obstinately clung to, regardless of right or reason: *Al is a shrewd enough showman to know that this mumpsimus is excellent publicity* (Baltimore Sun). [< misreading of Latin *sumpsimus* we took (because the reader maintained repeatedly that *mumpsimus* was correct)]

mu·mu[1] (mü′mü′), *n.* a muumuu.

mu·mu[2] (mü′mü′), *n.* filariasis: *Then he moved on to the Navy as consultant, fought a similar campaign against mumu* (Time). [perhaps < a Samoan word]

mun (mun), *auxiliary verb. Scottish.* must: *Poor folk mun get on as they can* (Charlotte Brontë). [< Scandinavian (compare Old Icelandic *mun* I shall)]

mun., municipal.

munch (munch), *v.t., v.i.* to chew vigorously and steadily; chew noisily: *The horse munched its oats. A sailor's wife had chestnuts in her lap, And munch'd, and munch'd, and munch'd* (Shakespeare). *—n.* the act or sound of munching: . . . *as crisp as the munch of a Baldwin apple* (New Yorker). [apparently imitative. Compare CRUNCH.] **—munch′er,** *n.*

Mun·chau·sen·ism (mun chô′zə niz əm), *n.* **1.** the tendency to tell exaggerated stories. **2.** an exaggerated story or statement. [< Baron *Münchausen,* 1720-1797, German cavalry officer, the supposed author of a book of incredible tales]

Mun·da (mún′dä), *n.* an Austro-Asiatic group of languages spoken on the southern slopes of the Himalayas and in central India.

mun·dane (mun′dān), *adj.* **1.** of this world; not of heaven; earthly: *mundane matters of business.* **2.** of the universe; of the world. [< Old French *mondain,* learned borrowing from Latin *mundānus* < *mundus* world] **—mun′dane·ly,** *adv.* **—mun′dane·ness,** *n.*

mun·dan·i·ty (mun dan′ə tē), *n.* mundane quality; worldliness; worldly feelings.

mun·dic (mun′dik), *n. British.* pyrites. [apparently < a Cornish word]

mun·du (mun′dü), *n.* a long sarong worn especially in southern India, usually made of thin cotton: *Small dark boys with their mundus tucked up high beckon you toward their strange primitive boats* (Santha Rama Rau).

mung bean (mung), a bean grown in areas of tropical Asia, Iran, and eastern Africa, used as food and as a forage and cover crop. [< Hindi *mūng*]

mun·go (mung′gō), *n.* cloth of inferior quality, made of used wool. It is of better quality than shoddy. [origin unknown]

mun·goos or **mun·goose** (mung′güs), *n., pl.* **-goos·es.** mongoose.

Mu·nich (myü′nik), *n.* an instance of appeasement which ultimately or immediately involves yielding to an aggressor at the expense of a principle or ally, and hence brings shame to the appeaser. [< the *Munich* Pact, a noted instance of appeasement]

Munich Pact or **Agreement,** an agreement signed September 30, 1938, by Germany, France, Great Britain, and Italy, by which the Sudetenland was given over to Germany.

mu·nic·i·pal (myü nis′ə pəl), *adj.* **1.** of or

having to do with a city, town, or other municipality: *The state police assisted the municipal police.* **2.** run by a city, town, etc.: *a municipal department store, a municipal hospital.* **3.** having local self-government: *a municipal township.* **4.** having to do with the internal affairs of a state, as distinguished from its foreign relations: *municipal or civil law.*

—*n.* **municipals,** bonds or other securities issued by a city, town, or other municipality: *The broker dealt chiefly in municipals.* [< Latin *mūnicipālis* < *mūniceps, -ipis* a citizen; an inhabitant of a *mūnicipium* or free town < *mūnia* official duties + *capere* take, assume]

mu·nic·i·pal·ise (myü nis′ə pə līz), *v.t.*, **-ised, -is·ing.** *Especially British.* municipalize: *The proposal to municipalise houses was the largest single act of nationalism* (Evening Standard).

mu·nic·i·pal·ism (myü nis′ə pə liz′əm), *n.* **1.** municipal government. **2.** the policy of increasing the power of government in cities and towns.

mu·nic·i·pal·ist (myü nis′ə pə list), *n.* **1.** a person who supports the policy of extending local self-government. **2.** *British.* a person who is skilled or experienced in municipal administration: *It was odd to hear the son of the great municipalist attacking, in his father's presence, the municipalities for their heavy borrowings* (Daily Chronicle).

mu·nic·i·pal·i·ty (myü nis′ə pal′ə tē), *n.*, *pl.* **-ties. 1.** a city, town, or other district having local self-government, especially an incorporated one: *Municipalities and cooperatives get preference over private utilities in the allocation of Federally-generated power* (Wall Street Journal). **2.** a community under municipal jurisdiction. **3.** the governing body of such a district or community. **4.** (in the Philippines, Cuba, etc.) an administrative subdivision of a province, somewhat like a county, and itself made up of still smaller communities.

mu·nic·i·pal·i·za·tion (myü nis′ə pə lə zā′shən), *n.* transference from private to municipal ownership: *Municipalization of the city's airport, as well as those of Edinburgh and Aberdeen, was first proposed in a White Paper* (London Times).

mu·nic·i·pal·ize (myü nis′ə pə līz), *v.t.*, **-ized, -iz·ing. 1.** to make into a municipality. **2.** to bring under municipal ownership or control: *to municipalize subways.* —**mu·nic′i·pal·iz′er,** *n.*

mu·nic·i·pal·ly (myü nis′ə plē), *adv.* by a city or town; with regard to a city or town or to municipal affairs: *The whole idea of the new town was municipally conceived.*

mu·nic·i·pals (myü nis′ə pəlz), *n.pl.* See under **municipal,** *n.*

mu·nif·i·cence (myü nif′ə səns), *n.* **1.** very great generosity: *My master's known munificence* (Robert Browning). *A scene which the munificence of nature had adorned with unrivalled beauties* (Charles Brockden Brown). **2.** ample measure; bountiful quality: *the munificence of a gift.* [< Latin *mūnificentia* < *mūnificus* generous, ultimately < *mūnus, -eris* gift + *facere* make]

mu·nif·i·cent (myü nif′ə sənt), *adj.* **1.** extremely generous: *My father gave me ten shillings and my mother five for pocket money and I thought them munificent* (Samuel Butler). **2.** characterized by great generosity: *a munificent reward.* —**mu·nif′i·cent·ly,** *adv.* —**Syn. 1.** bountiful, bounteous, liberal. **2.** lavish.

mu·ni·ment (myü′nə mənt), *n.* a means of defense; protection: *We cannot spare the coarsest muniment of virtue* (Emerson).

muniments, *Law.* a document, such as a title deed or charter, by which rights or privileges are defended or maintained: *The privileges of London were recognized [in 1066] by a royal writ which still remains, the most venerable of its muniments, among the city's archives* (John R. Green).

[< Middle French, Anglo-French *muniment,* learned borrowing from Medieval Latin *munimentum* document, title deed < Latin *mūnīmentum* defense, fortification < *mūnīre* to fortify; see MUNITION]

—**Syn.** stronghold.

mu·ni·tion (myü nish′ən), *n.* Often, **munitions. 1.** material used in war, such as guns, ammunition, and bombs: *to bring up reinforcements and supplies of military munition* (Scott). *Two thousand men, with seven fieldpieces, and many wagon-loads of munitions* (John L. Motley). **2.** material or equipment for carrying on any undertaking.

—*adj.* having to do with military supplies: *A munition plant is a factory for making munitions.*

—*v.t.* to provide with military supplies. [earlier, provision < Middle French *munition,* learned borrowing from Latin *mūnītiō, -ōnis* < *mūnīre* to fortify < *moenia* walls]

mu·ni·tion·eer (myü nish′ə nir′), *n.* **1.** a munitioner. **2.** a person who makes excessive profits in manufacturing or supplying munitions.

mu·ni·tion·er (myü nish′ə nər), *n.* a person who makes ammunition.

mu·ni·tion·ment (myü nish′ən mənt), *n.* a supply of munitions.

mun·nion (mun′yən), *n.*, *v.t.* mullion.

Mun·ster (mun′stər), *n.*, or **Munster cheese,** a cheese of medium softness, made from whole cow's milk. [< *Münster,* a city in West Germany]

munt·jac or **munt·jak** (munt′jak), *n.* any of certain small deer of southern and eastern Asia, Java, etc. [< Malayan (compare Sundanese *minchek*)]

mu·on (myü′on), *n.* a mu-meson.

mu·on·i·um (myü on′ē əm), *n.* a short-lived particle consisting of a positively charged mu-meson bound to a single electron. [< *muon* + *-ium,* as in *uranium*]

mu·rae·na (myů rē′nə), *n.* a moray.

mu·ral (myůr′əl), *adj.* **1.** on a wall: *A mural painting is painted for or on a wall or ceiling of a building.* **2.** of a wall; having to do with walls; like a wall: *Disburden'd heaven rejoiced, and soon repair'd her mural breach* (Milton). —*n.* a picture or decoration, usually of extensive size, painted or placed on a wall. [< Old French *muraille,* learned borrowing from Latin *mūrālis* of a wall < *mūrus* wall] —**mu′ral·ly,** *adv.*

mural crown, a golden crown formed with indentations to resemble a battlement, bestowed among the ancient Romans on the soldier who first mounted the wall of a besieged place and there lodged a standard.

mu·ral·ist (myůr′ə list), *n.* a painter or designer of murals: *Muralist Dean Cornwell captures the historic moment when Sir Walter Raleigh's men first landed on our shores* (New Yorker).

mur·der (mėr′dər), *n.* the unlawful killing of one human being by another with malice aforethought: *The murder of Abraham Lincoln was one of the world's great tragedies.*

get away with murder, *Slang.* to do something objectionable with impunity: *They [cats] refuse to make the slightest concession to human communication, and in consequence they get away with murder* (Russell Baker).

murder will out, a. murder cannot be hidden: *Murder will out, that see we day by day* (Chaucer). **b.** any great wrong will be found out: *The robbery has not been discovered yet, but murder will out eventually.*

—*v.t.* **1.** to kill (a human being) unlawfully and intentionally: *Hamilton murdered the old man in cold blood* (Macaulay). **2.** to do very badly; spoil: *to murder a song, to murder the king's English.* **3.** to spend (time) unprofitably: *Their evenings they murder in private parties* (Tobias Smollett). —*v.i.* to commit murder.

[Middle English *mordre,* variant of *murther,* Old English *morthor*]

—**Syn.** *v.t.* **1.** slay. See **kill. 2.** mangle, butcher.

mur·der·ee (mėr′də rē′), *n.* the victim of a murder: *One would never have thought that the most regretted of all Shakespeare's murderees was Polonius, with Julius Caesar, Romeo, and Juliet . . . close behind* (Punch).

mur·der·er (mėr′dər ər), *n.* a person who is guilty of murder. —**Syn.** slayer, killer.

mur·der·ess (mėr′dər is), *n.* a woman who is guilty of murder.

mur·der·ous (mėr′dər əs), *adj.* **1.** able to inflict great harm or to kill: *a murderous blow.* **2.** ready to murder; guilty or capable of murder: *a murderous villain. Enforced to fly Thence into Egypt, till the murderous king Were dead, who sought his life* (Milton). **3.** causing murder: *a murderous plot, a murderous hate.* **4.** characterized by or involving murder, death, or bloodshed; bloody: *a murderous riot. A murderous deed* (Shakespeare). —**mur′der·ous·ly,** *adv.* —**mur′der·ous·ness,** *n.*

mure (myůr), *v.*, **mured, mur·ing,** *n.* —*v.t.* *Archaic.* to shut up; imprison; immure. —*n. Obsolete.* a wall. [< Old French *murer* < Latin *mūrāre* < *mūrus* wall]

mu·rex (myůr′eks), *n.*, *pl.* **mu·ri·ces** (myůr′ə sēz), **mu·rex·es.** any of a group of marine gastropods with a rough, ridged, or spiny shell. The secretion from a gland in two species was the chief source of the famous purple dye of the ancient Phoenicians. [< Latin *mūrex*]

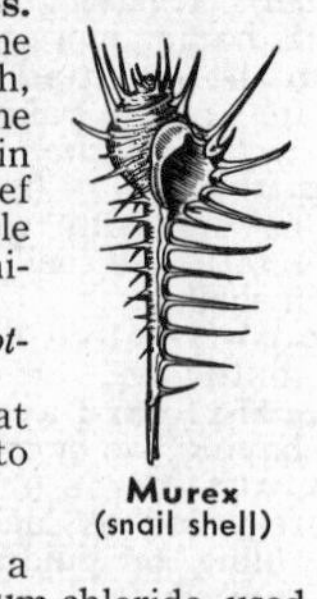

Murex (snail shell)

mur·geon (mėr′jən), *Scottish.* —*n.* a grimace.

—*v.t.* to make grimaces at (a person). —*v.i.* **1.** to grimace. **2.** to mutter. [origin unknown]

mu·ri·ate (myůr′ē āt), *n.* a chloride, especially potassium chloride, used as, or in making, fertilizer. [< French *muriate* < Latin *muria* brine]

mu·ri·at·ed (myůr′ē ā′tid), *adj.* **1.** charged with or containing a chloride or chlorides: *muriated mineral water.* **2.** salted; briny.

muriate of potash, potassium chloride: *The Treasury Department lifted restrictions on entries of muriate of potash from West Germany and France* (Wall Street Journal).

mu·ri·at·ic acid (myůr′ē at′ik), hydrochloric acid. [< Latin *muriāticus* < *muria* brine (because obtained originally from sea salt)]

mu·ri·cate (myůr′ə kāt), *adj.* covered with many sharp points; prickly. [< Latin *mūricātus* < *mūrex, -icis* murex]

mu·ri·cat·ed (myůr′ə kā′tid), *adj.* muricate.

mu·ri·form (myůr′ə fôrm), *adj. Botany.* like or suggesting a wall made of bricks arranged in courses: *muriform cellular tissue.* [< Latin *mūrus* wall + English *-form*]

mu·rine (myůr′īn, -in), *adj.* **1.** of or belonging to the family of rodents that includes many mice and rats. **2.** of or like a mouse or rat. —*n.* a rodent of this family. [< Latin *mūrīnus* having to do with mice, mouselike < *mūs, mūris* mouse]

murine typhus, a mild, endemic form of typhus spread among humans by fleas from rats, occurring in many parts of the world.

murk (mėrk), *n.* darkness; gloom: *A light flashed through the murk of the night.* —*adj. Poetic.* dark; gloomy; murky. Also, **mirk.** [perhaps < Scandinavian (compare Old Icelandic *myrkr*). Compare Old English *mirce.*]

murk·i·ly (mėr′kə lē), *adv.* in a murky manner; darkly; gloomily.

murk·i·ness (mėr′kē nis), *n.* the state of being murky; darkness; gloominess; gloom: *As if within that murkiness of mind Work'd feelings fearful, and yet undefined* (Byron).

murk·y (mėr′kē), *adj.*, **murk·i·er, murk·i·est. 1.** very dark or gloomy: *the murky blackness of the night.* **2.** very thick and dark; misty; hazy: *a murky fog. The great metropolis lay . . . buried under a homemade cloud of murky smoke* (Washington Irving). **3.** hard to understand; obscure: *a murky argument.* Also, **mirky.**

mur·mur (mėr′mər), *n.* **1.** a soft, low, indistinct sound that rises and falls a little and goes on without breaks: *the murmur of a stream, of little waves, of voices in another room. Faint murmurs from the meadows come* (Tennyson). **2.** a sound in the heart or lungs, especially an abnormal sound caused by a leaky valve in the heart. **3.** a softly spoken word or speech: *a murmur of thanks. The visitor made a grateful little murmur of acquiescence* (Hawthorne). **4.** a complaint made under the breath, not aloud: *In the City of London, lately so turbulent, scarcely a murmur was heard* (Macaulay). **5.** *Archaic.* a rumor: *There was a murmur . . . that he possesses other sciences, now lost to the world* (Scott).

—*v.i.* **1.** to make a soft, low, indistinct sound. **2.** to speak softly and indistinctly: *We saw the lights and heard The voices murmuring* (Tennyson). **3.** to complain under the breath; grumble: *Many were murmuring against the leader they had chosen, and wished to depose him* (Francis Parkman). —*v.t.* to utter in a murmur: *The angry boy murmured a threat.*

[< Old French *murmure,* learned borrowing from Latin *murmur, -uris;* probably imitative] —**mur′mur·er,** *n.*

—**Syn.** *n.* **1.** hum, babble. *-v.i.* **2.** *v.t.* **Murmur, mumble, mutter** mean to speak indistinctly. **Murmur** means to speak too softly to be clearly heard or plainly understood: *He murmured his thanks.* **Mumble** means to speak with the lips partly closed, so that the sounds are not properly formed: *Some boys mumble half the time.* **Mutter** means to mumble in a low voice, as if not wanting to be heard, and especially suggests complaining or anger: *He muttered some rude remarks.*

mur·mur·a·tion (mėr′mė rā′shən), *n.* a murmuring: *General shoe shuffling and noncommittal murmuration* (Punch).

mur·mur·ing (mėr′mər ing), *n.* a continuous murmur; low, confused noise: *As when you hear the murmuring of a throng* (Michael Drayton). —*adj.* **1.** having a low, continuous noise: *murmuring sound.* **2.** grumbling; complaining: *the . . . rock out of which Moses brought water to the murmuring Israelites* (John Evelyn).

mur·mur·ing·ly(mėr′mər ing lē), *adv.* with murmurs; with complaints.

mur·mur·ous (mėr′mər əs), *adj.* characterized by murmurs; murmuring: *There was a slight murmurous sound in the room, as of wind long pent up in many lungs suddenly exhaled* (W.H. Hudson). —**mur′mur·ous·ly,** *adv.*

mur·phy (mėr′fē), *n., pl.* **-phies.** *Slang.* **1.** a white potato. **2.** a Murphy game. [< *Murphy,* a common Irish surname]

Murphy bed, a bed that folds away on hinges into a closet.

Murphy game, a confidence game in which the confidence man exchanges an envelope with his victim's money in it for an identical one filled with paper scraps.

mur·ra (mėr′ə), *n.* a substance, perhaps fluorite, porcelain, or agate, from which the ancient Romans made vases, wine cups, etc. Also, **murrha.** [< Latin *murra*]

mur·rain (mėr′ən), *n.* **1.** any of various diseases of cattle, such as anthrax or tick fever. **2.** *Archaic.* a pestilence; plague: *A murrain on your monster!* (Shakespeare). [< Old French *morine* < Medieval Latin (England) *morina* plague < Latin *morī* die]

murre (mėr), *n.* **1.** any of a group of brown and white sea birds related to the guillemots, as a common variety of the northern Atlantic. **2.** the razor-billed auk. [origin uncertain]

murre·let (mėr′lit), *n.* any of certain small auks of the North Pacific.

Thick-billed Murre (def. 1—16 to 17 in. long)

mur·rey (mėr′ē), *n.* a dark purplish-red color. —*adj.* dark purplish-red. [< Old French *more,* adjective and *moree,* noun < Medieval Latin *moratus* and *murretus* < Latin *mōrum* mulberry]

mur·rha (mėr′ə), *n.* murra.

mur·rhine (mėr′in, -īn), *adj.* made of, having to do with, or like murra. —*n.* a murrhine vase. [< Latin *murrhinus* < *murra* murra]

murrhine glass, 1. glassware supposed to resemble the ancient Roman. **2.** glassware in which gems, metals, or colored glass are embedded.

mur·rine (mėr′in, -īn), *adj., n.* murrhine.

mur·ther (mėr′ᴛʜər), *n., v.t., v.i. Dialect.* murder. [Middle English *murther;* see MURDER]

mus., 1. museum. **2. a.** music. **b.** musical. **3.** musician.

mu·sa·ceous (myü zā′shəs), *adj.* belonging to the banana family of plants. [< New Latin *Musaceae* the family name (< *Musa* the typical genus < Arabic *mauza* the banana) + English *-ous*]

mu·sang (mü säng′, -sang′), *n.* **1.** an East Indian palm cat or palm civet. **2.** any of various related or similar animals. [< Malay *mūsang*]

Mus.B. or **Mus.Bac.,** Bachelor of Music (Latin, *Musicae Baccalaureus*).

Mus·ca (mus′kə), *n., genitive* **Mus·cae.** a southern constellation near Crux, thought of as arranged in the shape of a fly. [< Latin *musca* fly]

mus·ca·del (mus′kə del′, mus′kə del), *n.* muscatel.

mus·ca·delle (mus′kə del′), *n.* a kind of muscat grape grown especially in France. [< Old French *muscadel* muscatel]

mus·ca·din (mʏs kȧ daɴ′), *n.* **1.** a member of a party of men of fashion or of privilege that held moderate or reactionary opinions during the French Revolution. **2.** a dandy. [< French *muscadin*]

mus·ca·dine (mus′kə din, -dīn), *n.* **1.** a grape native to the southern United States, of which there are several varieties, as the scuppernong. **2.** *Obsolete.* muscatel (def. 1). [origin uncertain; perhaps < Middle French *muscade* (< Old Provençal, feminine of unrecorded *muscat*) + English *-ine*[1]]

Mus·cae (mus′sē), *n.* genitive of **Musca.**

mus·cae vo·li·tan·tes (mus′sē vol′ə tan′tēz), spots before the eyes. They may be caused by defects in the vitreous humor or in the lens. [< New Latin *muscae volitantes* (literally) flying flies]

mus·ca·rine (mus′kə rēn, -kər in), *n.* a very poisonous alkaloid present in the fly agaric and other mushrooms, and in decaying fish. [< Latin *muscārius* of the flies (< *musca* a fly) + English *-ine*[1]]

mus·cat (mus′kat, -kət), *n.* **1.** a light-colored grape with the flavor or odor of musk. **2.** muscatel (wine). [< Old French *muscat* < unrecorded Old Provençal *muscat* with the fragrance of musk < *musc* musk < Late Latin *muscus*]

mus·ca·tel (mus′kə tel′, mus′kə tel), *n.* **1.** a strong, sweet wine made from muscat grapes. **2.** the muscat (grape). [earlier *muscadell* < Old French *muscatel,* and *muscadel* < *muscat;* see MUSCAT]

mus·cid (mus′id), *adj.* of or belonging to a family of insects including the housefly and various other common flies. —*n.* a muscid insect. [< New Latin *Muscidae* the family name < Latin *musca* a fly]

mus·ci·form[1] (mus′ə fôrm), *adj.* resembling a fly. [< Latin *musca* a fly + English *-form*]

mus·ci·form[2] (mus′ə fôrm), *adj.* resembling moss. [< Latin *muscus* moss + English *-form*]

mus·cle[1] (mus′əl), *n., v.,* **-cled, -cling.** —*n.* **1.** animal tissue that contracts in response to nerve stimuli, and thus makes the body move. It is composed of bundles of fibers and is of two general types, striated muscle and smooth muscle. *Muscles are sensitive to stretch and automatically (reflexly) adjust their activity to changes in tension or stretch* (Science News). **2.** a special bundle of such tissue which moves some particular bone or part: *The biceps muscle bends the arm.* **3.** strength: *a man of more muscle than brains.*

not move a muscle, to keep perfectly still: *The injured man lay on his back, not moving a muscle.*

—*v.t. Informal.* to move or lift with effort: *Let's muscle this crate into that corner.*

—*v.i.* **muscle in,** *Slang.* to force oneself into a situation where one is not wanted: *For months he has been trying to muscle in on the Pennsylvania machine* (Baltimore Sun). [< Old French *muscle,* learned borrowing from Latin *mūsculus* (diminutive) < *mūs, mūris* mouse (from the appearance of certain muscles)]

—**Syn.** *n.* **3.** brawn, sinew.

mus·cle[2] (mus′əl), *n. Obsolete.* mussel, an edible salt-water mollusk.

mus·cle-bound (mus′əl bound′), *adj.* having some of the muscles too stiff or tight for rapid or effective movement, usually as a result of too much or too little exercise: *a muscle-bound fighter.*

-muscled, *combining form.* having —— muscles: *A well-muscled athlete = an athlete having good muscles.*

mus·cle·man (mus′əl man′), *n., pl.* **-men, 1.** *Informal.* a muscular man: . . . *another record and another reminder that U.S. musclemen will be hard to match in next fall's Olympics* (Time). **2.** *Slang.* a strong-arm man; thug: *The syndicate's musclemen forced competitors to close their businesses and leave town.*

muscle plasma, the fluid contained in muscle tissue.

muscle sense, the sensations accompanying movements of parts of the body, caused by sense receptors located in the muscles, joints, and tendons.

mus·cly (mus′lē), *adj.* muscular.

mus·coid (mus′koid), *adj.* mosslike. [< Latin *muscus* moss + English *-oid*]

mus·col·o·gist (mus kol′ə jist), *n.* a person skilled in muscology; bryologist.

mus·col·o·gy (mus kol′ə jē), *n.* the branch of botany dealing with mosses; bryology. [< Latin *muscus* moss + English *-logy*]

mus·cone (mus′kōn), *n.* a thick, liquid, closed-ring ketone derived from musk or produced synthetically, used in making perfume. *Formula:* $C_{16}H_{30}O$ [< Late Latin *muscus* musk + English *-one*]

mus·co·va·do (mus′kə vā′dō), *n.* raw sugar, a sweet, dark-brown, crystalline substance derived from the juice of the sugar cane by evaporation and draining off the molasses. —*adj.* of or having to do with raw sugar. [alteration of Spanish *mascabado* (sugar) of lowest quality < *mascabar* to depreciate, for *menoscabar* to diminish < *menos* less (< Latin *minus;* see MINUS) + *cabo* head < Latin *caput*]

mus·co·vite (mus′kə vīt), *n.* a light-colored variety of mica. [< *Muscovy* (glass) + *-ite*[1]]

Mus·co·vite (mus′kə vīt), *n.* a native or inhabitant of Muscovy; Russian. —*adj.* of or having to do with Muscovy or its inhabitants; Russian: *The Russian circus has had the most disarming effect on Paris of anything Muscovite since the October Revolution* (New Yorker). [< Middle French *Muscovie* Muscovy, the principality of Moscow, often applied to Russia generally (ultimately < Russian *Moskva* Moscow) + *-ite*[1]]

Mus·co·vit·ic (mus′kə vit′ik), *adj.* Muscovite.

mus·co·vy (mus′kə vē), *n., pl.* **-vies.** a Muscovy duck.

Muscovy duck, a large duck, originally native to tropical America, and now widely domesticated. [alteration of *musk duck;* influenced by *Muscovy*]

White Muscovy Duck (about 2½ ft. long)

mus·cu·lar (mus′kyə lər), *adj.* **1.** of the muscles; influencing the muscles: *a muscular strain.* **2.** having well-developed muscles; strong: *His figure was short, fleshy, and enormously muscular* (Charles Lever). **3.** consisting of muscle: *muscular tissue.* **4.** marked by forcefulness; powerful; virile: *The very language that Pratt used is muscular, tough and inspiring* (Canadian Saturday Night). —**mus′cu·lar·ly,** *adv.*

—**Syn. 2.** sinewy, brawny, powerful.

muscular dystrophy, a disease characterized by nerve degeneration, leading to progressive weakness and sometimes complete wasting away of the muscles.

mus·cu·lar·i·ty (mus′kyə lar′ə tē), *n.* muscular development or strength.

mus·cu·la·tion (mus′kyə lā′shən), *n.* musculature.

mus·cu·la·ture (mus′kyə lə chůr, -chər), *n.* the system or arrangement of muscles. [< French *musculature* < Latin *mūsculus* muscle]

mus·cu·lo·skel·e·tal (mus′kyə lō skel′ə təl), *adj.* of muscles and bones; both muscular and skeletal: *the musculoskeletal system.*

Mus.D., Mus.Doc., or **Mus.Dr.,** Doctor of Music (Latin, *Musicae Doctor*).

muse (myüz), *v.,* **mused, mus·ing,** *n.* —*v.i.* **1.** to think in a dreamy way; think; meditate: *The Vicar sat musing before the fire in his study* (Henry Kingsley). **2.** to look thoughtfully: *For some time Rip lay musing on this scene* (Washington Irving). **3.** *Archaic.* to wonder: *Do not muse at me, my most worthy friends* (Shakespeare). —*v.t.* **1.** to say thoughtfully. **2.** *Archaic.* to ponder over; wonder; meditate on: *I muse what this young fox may mean* (Matthew Arnold).

—*n.* **1.** *Archaic.* a fit of musing: *He would fall into a deep muse over our accounts, staring at the page or out of the window* (Robert Louis Stevenson). **2.** *Obsolete.* wonder. [< Old French *muser* ponder, loiter, apparently (originally) put one's nose in the air < *muse* muzzle. Compare MUZZLE.] —**mus′er,** *n.*

—**Syn.** *v.i.* **1.** reflect, ruminate, ponder.

Muse (myüz), *n.* **1.** one of the nine Greek goddesses of the fine arts and sciences. They were Calliope (epic poetry), Clio (history), Erato (love poetry), Euterpe (lyric poetry), Melpomene (tragedy), Polyhymnia or Polymnia (sacred song), Terpsichore (dancing), Thalia (comedy and pastoral poetry), and Urania (astronomy). **2. a.** a spirit that inspires a poet or composer; power of inspiration: *Fool, said my Muse to me, look in thy heart and write* (Philip Sidney). **b.** *Poetic.* a poet. [< Old French *Muse,* learned borrowing from Latin *Mūsa* < Greek *Moûsa*]

muse·ful (myüz′fəl), *adj.* deeply thoughtful: *museful planning.*

mu·se·o·log·i·cal (myü′zē ō loj′ə kəl), *adj.* of or having to do with museology: [*The museum's*] *whole attitude toward the museological enterprise places it under a moral and intellectual obligation* (New York Times).

mu·se·ol·o·gist (myü′zē ol′ə jist), *n.* a person skilled in museology.

mu·se·ol·o·gy (myü′zē ol′ə jē), *n.* the science of arranging, collecting for, and managing museums.

mu·sette (myü zet′), *n.* **1.** a kind of bagpipe. **2. a.** a soft pastoral melody for, or imitating the sound of, the bagpipe. **b.** a dance to such a melody. **3.** a musette bag. [< Old French *musette* < *muse* bagpipe < *muser* play the musette]

musette bag, a small canvas or leather bag carried suspended from a shoulder, used by soldiers, hikers, etc., to carry toilet articles, food, etc.

mu·se·um (myü zē′əm), *n.* a building or room where a collection of objects illustrating science, art, ancient life, or other subjects is kept and exhibited: *A museum is where you seek the work inspired by the Muses* (New Yorker). *Abbr.:* mus. [< Latin *mūsēum* < Greek *Mouseîon,* (originally) a seat or shrine of the *Muses* < *Moûsa* muse]

museum piece, 1. an article fit to receive a place in a museum; a fine example of anything, especially of manufactured articles: *... an elaborately carved Chippendale settee, a museum piece* (Horace A. Vachell). **2.** an outdated or antiquated person or thing: *The chap outside was a museum piece—cavalry mustache, single eyeglass, gray cutaway* (New Yorker).

mush[1] (mush), *n.* **1.** *U.S.* corn meal boiled in water or milk until thick. **2.** anything soft, thick, and pulpy like mush: *The rice field is stirred up into a perfect mush of mud* (E. W. Clark). **3.** *Informal.* weak or maudlin sentiment; silly talk: *The play was full of mush and impossible situations.* **4.** anything lacking force, firmness, or dignity: *I hate, where I looked for ... at least a manly resistance, to find a mush of concession* (Emerson).
—*v.t., v.i. Dialect.* to reduce to mush or a mush; mash.
[variant of *mash*[1]]

mush[2] (mush), *n.* a journey on foot through snow, driving a dog sled. —*v.i.* to travel in this way. —*interj.* a shout to a team of sled dogs to start or to speed up. [American English, perhaps for interjection *mush on,* alteration of French *marchons!* let us advance] —**mush′er,** *n.*

mush·i·ly (mush′ə lē), *adv.* in a soft or mushy manner: *"A cool hundred," said Fuzzy thoughtfully and mushily* (O. Henry).

mush·i·ness (mush′ē nis), *n.* mushy quality; weak sentimentality; sloppiness.

mush·room (mush′rüm, -rům), *n.* **1. a.** any of the larger, more conspicuous, basidiomycetous fungi that grow very fast and are shaped like an umbrella, ball, or other thickened mass. Some mushrooms are good to eat; some, such as toadstools, are poisonous. **b.** an edible basidiomycetous fungus. **2.** anything shaped or growing like a mushroom, as the mushroom-shaped cloud of radioactive matter that rises from the explosion of a nuclear bomb: *The silent trembling of seismographs and the distant mushroom in the sky* (Punch). **3.** *Archaic.* a bold and offensive newcomer; upstart: *Here is now a mushroom of opulence, who pays a cook seventy guineas a week for furnishing him with one meal a day* (Tobias Smollett).

Common (or edible) **Mushrooms** (def. 1 — 2 to 5 in. high)

—*adj.* **1.** of or like a mushroom: *The mushroom cloud of the A-bomb hung over the Nevada desert again* (Newsweek). **2.** made of or with mushrooms: *a mushroom sauce, mushroom soup.* **3.** of very rapid growth: *a mushroom town.* **4.** of very recent growth; upstart: *mushroom fame.*
—*v.i.* **1.** to grow very fast: *The little town mushroomed into a city.* **2.** to become flattened at one end: *A bullet sometimes mushrooms when it hits a very hard object.*
[alteration of Old French *mousseron,* or *moisseron,* perhaps < *mousse* moss] —**mush′room·like′,** *adj.*

mush·room·y (mush′rü mē, -rům ē), *adj.* of or like a mushroom: *Pine trees in a variety of mushroomy, distinctively Japanese shapes ...* (New Yorker).

mush·y (mush′ē), *adj.,* **mush·i·er, mush·i·est. 1.** like mush; pulpy: *Buck's feet sank into a white mushy something very like mud* (Jack London). **2.** *Informal.* weakly or foolishly sentimental: *mushy talk, a mushy scene.*

mu·sic (myü′zik), *n.* **1.** the art of putting sounds together in beautiful or pleasing arrangements. The science of music involves the study of the principles of melody, harmony, rhythm, etc. *Abbr.:* mus. **2.** beautiful or pleasing arrangements of sounds, especially as produced by the voice or instruments: *Music, when soft voices die, Vibrates in the memory* (Shelley). **3.** a pleasant sound; something delightful to hear: *the music of a thrush, of wind through the trees, or of a bubbling brook.* **4.** written or printed signs for tones; a score or scores: *Can you read music? Stacks of music lay in the corner.* **5.** appreciation of, or responsiveness to, musical sounds: *The man that hath no music in himself, Nor is moved with concord of sweet sounds, Is fit for treason, stratagems, and spoils* (Shakespeare). **6.** a group of musicians: *He says many of the music are ready to starve, they being five years behind hand for their wages* (Samuel Pepys). **7.** the cry of hounds on seeing the quarry, as in fox hunting.
face the music, *Informal.* to meet trouble boldly or bravely: *Troops of less experience and hardihood would have flinched where these faced the music* (Frank Moore).
set to music, to provide (the words of a song, etc.) with music: *... that nothing is capable of being well set to music that is not nonsense* (Joseph Addison).
[< Old French *musique,* learned borrowing from Latin *mūsica* < Greek *mousikḗ téchnē* art of the Muses < *Moûsa* Muse]

mu·si·cal (myü′zə kəl), *adj.* **1.** of or having to do with music: *musical instruments.* **2.** sounding beautiful or pleasing; like music: *a musical voice. All little sounds made musical and clear* (William Morris). **3.** set to music; accompanied by music. **4.** fond of music. **5.** skilled in music: *The English I confess, are not altogether so Musical as the French* (John Dryden).
—*n.* **1.** a musical comedy: *Musicals are the unique contribution of the United States to world theater* (Lehman Engel). **2.** *Informal.* a musicale. —**mu′si·cal·ness,** *n.*

musical box, *Especially British.* a music box.

musical chairs, 1. a game in which players march to music around chairs numbering one less than the number of players, and try to sit down when the music stops, that player failing to reach a chair being eliminated: *We played blind man's buff ... and musical chairs* (Maclean's). **2.** any switching or shifting about resembling this game: *Have you been playing musical chairs with your stocks—switching from one to another in the hope of coming out a winner?* (New Yorker).

musical comedy, a stage entertainment consisting of a story spoken in dialogue form, with songs, choruses, dances, and incidental music.

mu·si·cale (myü′zə kal′), *n.* a social gathering to enjoy music. [American English < French *musicale,* short for *soirée musicale* musical evening (party)]

musical instrument, 1. any stringed, wind, or percussion instrument, as a violin, trumpet, or drum, employed, or designed to be employed, in producing music or musical sounds. **2.** an electronic instrument used to produce, not reproduce, musical sounds.

mu·si·cal·i·ty (myü′zə kal′ə tē), *n.* **1.** musicianship: *Badura-Skoda's musicality is best conveyed ... in his three cadenzas* (Saturday Review). **2.** musical quality: *This tendency, with its emphasis on the sensuous possibilities of language, on musicality and stylistic refinement, has not ceased to attract gifted writers to whom the realistic approach seemed inadequate ...* (Atlantic).

mu·si·cal·i·za·tion (myü′zə kə lə zā′shən), *n.* the act, fact, or process of musicalizing.

mu·si·cal·ize (myü′zə kə līz), *v.t.,* **-ized, -iz·ing.** to set to music; make into a musical composition: *to musicalize a poem or play. A line like "Be sure to take your bath, Gloria" is difficult to musicalize* (Arthur Miller).

mu·si·cal·ly (myü′zə klē), *adv.* **1.** in a musical manner. **2.** in music: *She is well educated musically.*

music box, a box or case containing apparatus for producing music mechanically.

music drama, 1. an opera in which the music is the chief dramatic vehicle, typified by certain of the operas of Wagner. **2.** any opera.

music festival, a series of musical programs usually recurring at regular intervals, as annually: *the summer music festival at Tanglewood, Massachusetts.*

music hall, 1. a hall for musical entertainments. **2.** *Especially British.* a theater for vaudeville.

mu·sic-hall (myü′zik hôl′), *adj.* of or characteristic of a music hall; vaudeville.

mu·si·cian (myü zish′ən), *n.* **1.** a person skilled in music: *The Scots are all musicians. Every man you meet plays on the flute, the violin or violoncello* (Tobias Smollett). **2.** a person who sings or who plays on a musical instrument, especially as a profession or business: *An orchestra is composed of many musicians.* **3.** a composer of music.

mu·si·cian·er (myü zish′ə nər), *n. Archaic or Dialect.* a musician: *The musicianers amused the retainers ... with a tune on the clarionet, fife, or trumpet* (Samuel Lover).

mu·si·cian·ly (myü zish′ən lē), *adj.* of or suited to a musician; showing the skill and taste of a good musician: *Mr. Cole's instincts appear to be intelligent and musicianly* (New York Times).

mu·si·cian·ship (myü zish′ən ship), *n.* skill in playing, conducting, or composing music; musical ability: *She was a great artist, remarkable not for the beauty of her voice, but for musicianship, dramatic power and general intelligence* (Sunday Times).

mu·sic·less (myü′zik lis), *adj.* **1.** without music: *a musicless entertainment.* **2.** unmusical; harsh in sound; discordant. **3.** ignorant of music.

mu·si·co·dra·mat·ic (myü′zə kō drə mat′ik), *adj.* of or combining both music and the drama; musical and dramatic: *The librettist faithfully transmits the vivid bible pictures, but Milhaud fails to give them musicodramatic reality* (New York Times).

music of the spheres, beautiful harmony or music, inaudible to human beings, supposedly produced, according to Pythagoras and certain other ancient mathematicians, by the movements of the planets and other heavenly bodies: *For there is music wherever there is harmony, order, or proportion; and thus far we may maintain the music of the spheres* (Sir Thomas Browne).

mu·si·cog·ra·phy (myü′zə kog′rə fē), *n.* the art of writing down music; musical notation.

mu·si·co·log·i·cal (myü′zə kə loj′ə kəl), *adj.* of or having to do with musicology: *... to elucidate* [*all aspects of the aural experience*] *in terms of both musicological and human experience* (Abram Chasins).

mu·si·col·o·gist (myü′zə kol′ə jist), *n.* an expert in musicology: *The studies of musicologists have clearly shown that the music of all nonliterate peoples shows very definite patterns, and is not in the least random or chaotic* (Beals and Hoijer).

mu·si·col·o·gy (myü′zə kol′ə jē), *n.* the systematic study of music, especially of its literature, history, forms, methods, and principles.

mu·si·co·ma·ni·a (myü′zə kə mā′nē ə), *n.* an abnormal fondness for music; monomania for music.

mu·si·co·pho·bi·a (myü′zə kə fō′bē ə), *n.* an abnormal fear or dislike of music.

mu·si·co·ther·a·py (myü′zə kə ther′ə pē), *n.* the therapeutical use of music; listening to music as a means of promoting emotional growth and health.

music room, a room, as in a house, set apart or arranged for use in performing music: *When he was still an infant he would toddle into the music room and listen while his sisters were having their lessons* (New Yorker).

 PRONUNCIATION KEY: hat, āge, cãre, fär; let, ēqual, tėrm; it, īce; hot, ōpen, ôrder; oil, out; cup, pu̇t, rüle;

music shell, the shell of a marine gastropod, especially a volute of the Caribbean, having markings that suggest written music.

mus·ing (myü′zing), *adj.* dreamy; meditative. —*n.* meditation. —**mus′ing·ly,** *adv.* —**Syn.** *adj.* contemplative.

mu·sique con·crète (mʏ zĕk′ kôɴ kret′), *French.* **1.** a compilation of natural sounds recorded on tape and cut and spliced together to form a composition: *For 150 years the only new instruments to be invented are the saxophone, the musical saw, musique concrète and electronic devices* (Time). **2.** such compositions collectively; electronic music.

mus·jid (mus′jid), *n.* a mosque.

musk (musk), *n.* **1. a.** a substance with a strong and lasting odor, used in making perfumes. Musk is found in a special gland in the male musk deer. **b.** a strong-smelling substance found in the glands of other animals, as the mink and muskrat. **2.** an artificial imitation of this substance. **3.** the odor of musk, or a similar odor: *The woodbine spices are wafted abroad, And the musk of the rose is blown* (Tennyson). **4.** the musk deer or any animal like it, or one that has a musky smell. **5.** any plant whose leaves or flowers smell like musk, such as the musk rose. [< Old French *musc,* learned borrowing from Late Latin *muscus* < Late Greek *móschos* < Persian *mushk* < Sanskrit *muṣka* testicle (diminutive) < *mūṣ* mouse]

mus·kal·longe (mus′kə lonj), *n., pl.* **-longe.** muskellunge, a large American pike.

musk deer, a small, hornless deer of central and northeastern Asia, the male of which has a gland containing musk.

musk duck, 1. the Muscovy duck. **2.** an Australian duck, the male of which has a musky odor.

mus·keg (mus′keg), *n.* **1.** a bog or marsh filled with sphagnum moss, chiefly in the tundra or forest regions of Canada, Alaska, and northern Europe: *Much of the Arctic land is muskeg, a swampy muck which will not support even a man, much less an airstrip* (Science News Letter). **2.** any of certain mosses. [< Algonkian (Cree) *maskik,* (Ojibwa) *maskeg* swamp, wet meadow]

mus·kel·lunge (mus′kə lunj), *n., pl.* **-lunge.** a large North American pike, an important game fish that is very hard to catch. It occasionally grows to a length of about 8 feet and a weight over 75 pounds. Also, **maskalonge, maskanonge, muskallonge.** [American English < Canadian French *masquinongé* < Algonkian (Ojibwa) *mâskinonjē* (literally) big fish]

mus·ket (mus′kit), *n.* a gun introduced in the 1500's and widely used before the development of the rifle. [< Middle French *mousquet* < Italian *moschetto* (originally) a kind of hawk < *mosca* fly < Latin *musca*]

mus·ket·eer (mus′kə tir′), *n.* a soldier armed with a musket. [alteration (influenced by *musket*) of Middle French *mousquetaire* mousquetaire]

mus·ket·ry (mus′kə trē), *n., pl.* **-ries. 1.** muskets: *The storming parties were assailed with cannon, with musketry, with pistols* (John L. Motley). **2.** the art of shooting with muskets or rifles. **3.** the fire of muskets, rifles, etc.; small-arms fire: *a sudden crackle of musketry.* **4.** soldiers armed with muskets.

Mus·kho·ge·an (mus kō′gē ən), *adj.* designating or having to do with a linguistic family of North American Indians originally from the southeastern United States, including Choctaw, Chickasaw, Creek, Seminole, Yazoo, and other tribes. —*n.* this linguistic family.

mus·kie (mus′kē), *n. Informal.* a muskellunge. Also, **musky.**

mus·ki·ness (mus′kē nis), *n.* a musky quality or condition.

musk·mal·low (musk′mal′ō), *n.* the abelmosk, a bushy plant of the mallow family grown in tropical and semitropical countries for its musky seeds, which are used in perfumes.

musk·mel·on (musk′mel′ən), *n.* **1.** a round or oval melon with sweet, juicy, light-green or orange flesh and a rind with a ribbed or net-like pattern; cantaloupe. **2.** the plant it grows on.

Mus·ko·gee (mus kō′gē), *n., pl.* **-gee** or **-gees. 1.** a member of a tribe of Indians of Georgia and Alabama that formed part of the Creek confederacy of Muskhogean tribes. **2.** the language of this tribe.

musk ox, a large arctic mammal of the same family as the ox, stockily built, with a hump, covered with dense, extremely long hair, and at times giving off a musky smell: *Musk oxen . . . inhabit some of the most solitary, dreariest country on earth, where they have made a stubborn fight for survival* (Science News Letter).

Musk Ox (8 ft. long)

musk plant, a North American herb of the figwort family, having yellow flowers and musk-scented leaves.

musk·rat (musk′rat′), *n., pl.* **-rats** or (*collectively*) **-rat. 1.** a water rodent of North America, like a rat, but larger, having webbed hind feet, a glossy coat, and a musky smell. In swamps and ponds it builds small houses like those of the beaver. **2.** its valuable dark-brown fur. [American English, alteration of *musquash*]

Muskrat (def. 1) (including tail, 20 in. long)

musk rose, a rose with clusters of large, musky-smelling, white flowers, native to the Mediterranean region.

musk turtle, any of a group of small turtles of eastern United States with a narrow plastron and glands capable of producing a strong musky odor.

musk·y[1] (mus′kē), *adj.,* **musk·i·er, musk·i·est.** of or like musk; like that of musk: *a musky odor.* [< *musk* + *-y*[1]]

mus·ky[2] (mus′kē), *n., pl.* **-kies.** *Informal.* a muskellunge.

Mus·lem or **Mus·lim** (muz′ləm, mus′-), *n., adj.* Moslem.

mus·lin (muz′lən), *n.* **1.** a thin, fine cotton cloth, used for dresses, curtains, etc. **2.** a heavier cotton cloth, used for sheets, undergarments, etc. **3.** *Nautical Slang.* sails; canvas: *They staggered out of the bay . . . with a strong breeze and under all the "muslin" they could carry* (Herman Melville). **4.** *British Slang.* womankind; femininity: *That was a pretty bit of muslin hanging on your arm—who was she?* (Thackeray).
—*adj.* made of muslin.
[< French *mousseline* < Italian *mussolina* < *Mussolo* Mosul, a city in Iraq]

muslin delaine, mousseline de laine.

mus·lined (muz′lənd), *adj.* hung with or dressed in muslin.

muslin kail, *Scottish.* a broth of water, shelled barley, and greens. [< *muslin* + *kail,* variant of *kale* (perhaps because of the thinness of the broth)]

Mus.M., Master of Music.

mus·quash (mus′kwosh), *n.* a muskrat. [< Algonkian (probably Powhatan) *muscascus* (literally) it is red (because of its red color)]

muss (mus), *Informal.* —*v.t.* **1.** to make untidy; rumple: *to muss up a room. The child's dress was mussed.* **2.** to smear or soil; mess: *to muss up one's hands.*
—*n.* **1.** untidy state; disorder; mess: *Straighten up your room at once; it's in a muss!* **2.** a disturbance; row.
[variant of *mess* in sense of "disturbance, row"; probably influenced by *fuss*]
—**Syn** *n.* **1.** muddle.

mus·sel (mus′əl), *n.* **1.** any of various salt-water mollusks, some edible, that look like a small clam, with dark shells. **2.** any of various fresh-water mollusks whose shells are used in making buttons, etc. [Old English *muscle, musle* < Latin *mūsculus* mussel, muscle]

Mus·sul·man (mus′əl mən), *n., pl.* **-mans,** *adj.* Moslem: *I assembled a group of grave and worthy Mussulmans in the courtyard of the Khan* (Alexander W. Kinglake). [< Medieval Latin *Musulmani,* plural < Persian *musulmān* Mohammedan, adjective < *muslim* a Moslem < Arabic. Doublet of MOSLEM.]

muss·y (mus′ē), *adj.,* **muss·i·er, muss·i·est.** *Informal.* untidy; messy; rumpled: *a mussy room.*

must[1] (must; *unstressed* məst), *auxiliary verb, past tense* **must,** *n., adj.* —*aux. v.* **1.** to be obliged to; be forced to: *Man must eat to live. When Duty whispers low, Thou must, The youth replies, I can* (Emerson). **2.** ought to; should: *I must go home soon. I must keep my promise.* **3.** to be certain to (be, do, etc.): *I must seem very rude. The man must be crazy to talk so.* **4.** to be supposed or expected to: *You must have that book. You must know he is a great writer* (Tobias Smollett). **5.** *Must* is sometimes used with its verb omitted: *We must to horse. We must away.* —*n. Informal.* something necessary; obligation: *This rule is a must.* —*adj. Informal.* demanding attention or doing; necessary: *a must item, must legislation.*
[Old English *mōste,* past tense of *mōtan* mote[2]]

➔ **Must,** which is ordinarily an auxiliary verb, has recently become an adjective in informal English: *This is a must book for your reading.*

must[2] (must), *n.* the unfermented juice of the grape or other fruit; new wine. [Old English *must* < Latin (*vīnum*) *mustum* fresh (wine)]

must[3] (must), *n.* musty condition; mustiness; mold. —*v.t., v.i.* to make or become musty. [perhaps back formation < *musty*]

must[4] (must), *adj.* dangerously excited or irritable (used of male elephants or camels). —*n.* **1.** dangerous excitement; frenzy. **2.** a frenzied animal. Also, **musth.** [< Hindi *mast* < Persian, (literally) intoxicated]

must[5] (must), *Scottish.* —*n.* **1.** musk. **2.** a powder for the hair. —*v.t.* to put powder on (the hair). [< Old French *must,* variant of *musc* musk]

mus·tache (mus′tash, mə stash′), *n.* **1.** hair growing on a man's upper lip: *a lofty, lordly kind of man . . . with a meagre face, furnished with mustaches* (Washington Irving). **2.** hairs or bristles growing near the mouth of an animal. Also, *especially British,* **moustache.** [< French *moustache* < Italian *mostaccio,* and *mostacchio* < Medieval Latin *mustacia* < Greek *mýstax, -akos* upper lip, mustache]

mustache cup, a man's drinking cup fitted with a special piece to drink through without wetting the mustache.

mus·tached (mus′tasht, mə stasht′), *adj.* having a mustache.

mus·ta·chio (mə stä′shō), *n., pl.* **-chios.** a mustache: *His face . . . was more than half hidden by whisker and mustachio* (Edgar Allan Poe). [< Italian *mostacchio;* see MUSTACHE]

mus·ta·chioed (mə stä′shōd), *adj.* mustached.

mus·tang (mus′tang), *n.* a small, wild or half-wild horse of the American plains, descended from Spanish stock: *She [an Indian woman] was mounted on a mustang or half-wild horse* (Washington Irving). [American English < Spanish *mestengo* untamed, (literally) of the *mesta* association of graziers who divided strays or unclaimed animals < Latin *miscēre* to mix]

SEED

Mustard Plant and Seed (def.2)

mus·tard (mus′tərd), *n.* **1.** a yellow powder or paste used as a seasoning to give a pungent taste, or medicinally in a mustard plaster. **2.** the plant from whose seeds it is made. **3.** the flower of this plant. **4.** a dark yellow color: . . . *satin-finished silk that is a mass of flowers in . . . sapphire, and mustard* (New Yorker).
cut the mustard, *U.S. Slang.* to achieve a desirable end; succeed: *You can't cut the mustard at those prices* (Atlantic).
[< Old French *moustarde* < *moust* < Latin *mustum* must[2]]

mus·tard-col·ored (mus′tərd kul′ərd), *adj.* dull yellow with a tinge of green.

mustard family, a group of dicotyledonous herbs having cross-shaped, regular flowers, and bearing a two-valved capsule as the fruit. The family includes the mustard, sweet alyssum, cress, candytuft, wallflower, etc., and such vegetables as the cabbage, cauliflower, and broccoli.

mustard gas, a colorless or brown oily liquid, a poison gas that causes burns, blindness, and death: *The main war gases avail-*

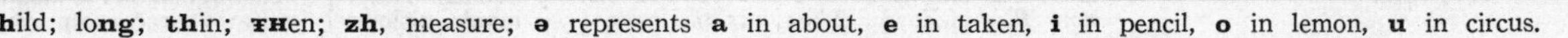

able toward the end of the last war were phosgene, . . . mustard gas, and lewisite (James Phinney Baxter). *Formula:* $C_4H_8Cl_2S$

mustard oil, oil pressed from mustard seeds.

mustard plaster, a poultice made of mustard and water, or of mustard, flour, and water, used as a counterirritant.

mustard seed, the seed of the mustard plant: *The kingdom of heaven is like to a grain of mustard seed . . . Which indeed is the least of all seeds* (Matthew 13:31-32).

mus·tee (mus tē′, mus′tē), *n.* **1.** a child of a white person and a quadroon. **2.** any half-breed. [< altered pronunciation of Spanish *mestizo* mestizo]

mus·te·line (mus′tə līn, -lin), *adj.* **1.** of or belonging to the family of mammals that includes the weasels, martens, skunks, sables, minks, badgers, and otters. **2.** like a weasel; tawny. —*n.* a musteline animal. [< Latin *mūstēlīnus* < *mūstēla* weasel, perhaps < *mūs, mūris* mouse]

mus·ter (mus′tər), *v.t.* **1.** to gather together; collect: *They could muster only a few dollars between them. Bring all the good players you can muster.* **2.** to assemble: *The starboard watch were mustered upon the quarterdeck* (Herman Melville). **3.** to summon: *Muster up your courage and fight.* **4.** to number; comprise: *The whole garrison mustered but six or eight men* (Washington Irving). **5.** (in Australia) to round up (cattle). —*v.i.* **1.** to come together; gather; assemble: *The clouds were mustering in the sky. I see them muster in a gleaming row* (Lowell). *Why does my blood thus muster to my heart?* (Shakespeare). **2.** (in Australia) to round up cattle.

muster in, to enlist; enroll: *Youths under eighteen cannot muster in.*

muster out, to discharge: *. . . mustered out of the service of the United States* (J.A. Wakefield).

—*n.* **1.** an assembly; collection. **2.** a bringing together of soldiers, sailors, etc., in formation for review, service, roll call, etc.: *a general muster of the militia.* **3.** a list of those assembled; roll: *Call the muster.* **4.** the number assembled: *Our present musters grow upon the file to five and twenty thousand men of choice* (Shakespeare). **5.** *Commerce.* a pattern; specimen; sample.

pass muster, to be inspected and approved; come up to the required standards; get by: *Double-dealers may pass muster for a while, but all parties wash their hands of them in the conclusion* (Sir Roger L'Estrange).

[< Old French *mostrer* < Latin *mōnstrāre* to show < *mōnstrum* portent; see MONSTER] —**mus′ter·er,** *n.*

—**Syn.** *v.t.* **1.** convene, marshal, array. -*v.i.* convene. —**Ant.** *v.t.* **1.** disband, dissolve, disorganize. -*v.i.* disband, dissolve.

muster roll, 1. an official roll or list, as of soldiers or sailors. **2.** roll call.

musth (must), *adj., n.* must[4].

mus·ti·ly (mus′tə lē), *adv.* **1.** in a musty manner; moldily; sourly. **2.** *Obsolete.* dully; heavily.

mus·ti·ness (mus′tē nis), *n.* musty state or quality; moldiness; damp foulness.

must·n't (mus′ənt), must not: *Father says we mustn't skate here.*

mus·ty (mus′tē), *adj.,* **-ti·er, -ti·est,** *n.* —*adj.* **1.** having a smell or taste suggesting mold, damp, poor ventilation, decay, etc.; moldy: *a musty room, musty crackers.* **2.** out-of-date; stale: *musty laws.* **3.** lacking vigor; dull: *a musty old fellow.*

—*n.* a variety of cheap, strong-smelling snuff, formerly sold in England.

[perhaps variant of *moisty*]

—**Syn.** *adj.* **1.** mildewy.

mut (mut), *n.* mutt.

mut., 1. mutilated. **2.** mutual.

mu·ta·bil·i·ty (myü′tə bil′ə tē), *n.* **1.** mutable state or quality; tendency to change: *Wherefore this lower world who can deny But to be subject still to Mutability?* (Edmund Spenser). **2.** changeableness of mind, disposition, or will; fickleness: *the mutability of opinion or purpose.*

mu·ta·ble (myü′tə bəl), *adj.* **1.** liable to change: *mutable customs.* **2.** changing; inconstant; fickle: *a mutable person. Nature is a mutable cloud . . . and never the same* (Emerson). [< Latin *mūtābilis* < *mūtāre* to change] —**mu′ta·ble·ness,** *n.* —**Syn. 1.** changeable, variable.

mu·ta·bly (myü′tə blē), *adv.* in a mutable manner; changeably.

mu·ta·gen (myü′tə jən), *n.* an agent that induces or causes mutation in an organism: *Both chemical mutagens and radiations act in an unspecific, random way on chromosomes and genes* (Laurence H. Snyder). [< Latin *mūtāre* to change + English *-gen*]

mu·ta·gen·e·sis (myü′tə jen′ə sis), *n.* the developmental process leading to mutation in an organism. [< Latin *mūtāre* to change + English *genesis*]

mu·ta·gen·ic (myü′tə jen′ik), *adj.* of, having to do with, or characteristic of a mutagen: *mutagenic radiation, a mutagenic level, mutagenic action.*

mu·tant (myü′tənt), *n.* a new variety of animal or plant resulting from mutation: *Under these conditions the mutant may be expected eventually to replace the ancestral stock in ever widening areas* (Fred W. Emerson). —*adj.* that is the result of mutation: *a mutant species.* [< Latin *mūtāns, -antis,* present participle of Latin *mūtāre* to change]

mu·ta·ro·ta·tion (myü′tə rō tā′shən), *n.* *Chemistry.* a gradual change of optical rotation taking place in freshly prepared solutions of reducing sugars. [< Latin *mūtāre* to change + English *rotation*]

mu·tate (myü′tāt), *v.t., v.i.,* **-tat·ed, -tat·ing. 1.** to change: *Sweet peas mutate from petal pink to coral* (New Yorker). **2.** to undergo or produce mutation: *Farm animals will be mutated to produce more and better meats and dairy foods* (Science News Letter). **3.** *Phonetics.* to change or be changed by umlaut. [< Latin *mūtāre* (with English *-ate*[1]) to change]

mu·ta·tion (myü tā′shən), *n.* **1.** the act or process of changing; change; alteration: *The past is exempt from mutation* (Charles Brockden Brown). **2.** a new character or feature that appears suddenly in animals or plants and can be inherited. A mutation results from a change within a gene or chromosome: *. . . many so-called gene mutations may actually be ultramicroscopic changes in chromosome structure* (The Effects of Atomic Weapons). **3.** a new genetic character or new variety of plant or animal formed in this way; mutant: *It is claimed that the first of the small African violets came as mutations* (New York Times). **4.** *Phonetics.* umlaut (def. 1): *Thus "man, men; woman, women;" . . . show mutation, . . . effected by an "i" or "j" in the succeeding syllable in Common Germanic . . .* (Simeon Potter). [< Latin *mūtātiō, -ōnis* < *mūtāre* to change]

mu·ta·tion·al (myü tā′shə nəl), *adj.* of or having to do with biological mutation: *Through a number of mutational steps, . . . it has been possible to obtain a thousand-fold increase in penicillin yield* (Bulletin of Atomic Scientists).

mu·ta·tion·ist (myü tā′shə nist), *n.* *Biology.* a person who emphasizes the importance of mutation as a factor in producing new and supposedly higher forms or species.

mutation mink, 1. a mink in captivity having fur of a color not found among wild minks, especially a shade from white to pale silver, arrived at by selective breeding. **2.** the fur of such a mink.

mu·ta·tis mu·tan·dis (myü tā′tis myü-tan′dis), *Latin.* with the necessary changes: *What would St. Francis have said to the beggar who . . . wanted to get to the Assisian equivalent of Wall Street? Mutatis mutandis, what would Robert Owen have said? Or Lenin?* (Time).

mu·ta·tive (myü′tə tiv), *adj.* of or having to do with mutation; marked by change.

mu·ta·to no·mi·ne (myü tā′tō nom′ə nē), *Latin.* with the name changed.

mutch (much), *n. Scottish.* a cap or coif, usually of linen, worn by women and young children: *an old granny in a woolen mutch* (Robert Louis Stevenson). [< Middle Dutch *mutse,* perhaps short for *almutse* or < unrecorded Latin *almutius*]

mutch·kin (much′kin), *n.* a Scottish unit of liquid measure, equal to a little less than a U.S. legal pint. [perhaps < Middle Dutch *mudseken* (diminutive) < *mudde* a Dutch measure, ultimately < Latin *modius,* or (diminutive) < Middle Dutch *mutse* a measure]

mute (myüt), *adj., n., v.,* **mut·ed, mut·ing.** —*adj.* **1.** not making any sound; silent: *The little girl stood mute with embarrassment. Mute did the minstrels stand To hear my story* (Longfellow). *Mute was the room—mute the house* (Charlotte Brontë). **2.** unable to speak; dumb. **3.** not pronounced; silent: *The "e" in "mute" is mute.* **4.** *Phonetics.* articulated as a stop; produced by the complete momentary closure of the air passage: *The "p" in "hop" and "play" is a mute consonant.* **5.** without speech or sound: *a mute refusal of an offer, mute astonishment.* **6.** *Law.* (of a prisoner) making no response when arraigned: *to stand mute.*

—*n.* **1.** a person who cannot speak, usually because of deafness, loss of or damage to the tongue, etc. **2.** a clip, pad, etc., used to soften, deaden, or muffle the sound of a musical instrument. **3.** a silent letter. **4.** *Phonetics.* a stop; mute consonant. **5.** an actor who plays pantomime. **6.** *Law.* a prisoner who fails to plead to an indictment. **7.** *Archaic.* a hired attendant at a funeral: *I saw the coffin, and the mutes, and the mourners* (John Galt).

—*v.t.* to deaden or soften the sound of (a tone, voice, a musical instrument, etc.) with or as if with a mute: *He played the violin with muted strings.*

[alteration (influenced by Latin) of Middle English *mewet* and *muet* < Old French *muet* < Latin *mūtus*] —**mute′ly,** *adv.* —**mute′ness,** *n.*

—**Syn.** *adj.* **1, 2.** See **dumb.**

mut·ed (myü′tid), *adj.* **1.** mute; silent: *They are frightened . . . and prefer their politicians to be as bland and muted as possible* (New York Times). **2.** (of musical instruments) played with a mute. —**mut′ed·ly,** *adv.*

mute swan, a common white swan of Europe and Asia that makes only hissing and snorting sounds. See **swan** for picture.

mu·ti·late (myü′tə lāt), *v.,* **-lat·ed, -lat·ing,** *adj.* —*v.t.* **1.** to cut, tear, or break off a limb or other important part of; injure seriously by cutting, tearing, or breaking off some part: *The victims of the accident were all mutilated.* **2.** to make (a book, story, song, etc.) imperfect by removing a part or parts: *Lay authorities had "mutilated" the text of the pastoral letter he issued* (New York Times).

—*adj.* **1.** *Biology.* without some organ or part, or having it only in an undeveloped or modified form. **2.** *Poetic.* mutilated.

[< Latin *mutilāre* (with English *-ate*[1]) < *mutilus* maimed]

—**Syn.** *v.t.* **1.** maim, mangle, disfigure.

mu·ti·la·tion (myü′tə lā′shən), *n.* **1.** a mutilating. **2.** a being mutilated: *Many . . . were also sentenced to mutilation . . . the hangman of Edinburgh cut off the ears of thirty-five prisoners* (Macaulay).

mu·ti·la·tive (myü′tə lā′tiv), *adj.* causing mutilation.

mu·ti·la·tor (myü′tə lā′tər), *n.* a person or thing that mutilates.

mu·tine (myü′tin), *n., v.,* **-tined, -tin·ing,** *adj. Obsolete.* —*n.* **1.** a mutinous person; mutineer: *Methought I lay Worse than the mutines in the bilboes* (Shakespeare). **2.** a mutiny.

—*v.i.* to rebel; mutiny.

—*adj.* rebellious; mutinous.

[< Old French *mutine, mutin;* see MUTINY]

mu·ti·neer (myü′tə nir′), *n.* a person who takes part in a mutiny: *Additional wireless messages received from the mutineers were accepted as indicating that they wished to bargain with the authorities* (Baltimore Sun). —*v.i.* to take part in a mutiny; mutiny. [< Middle French *mutinier* < *mutin* rebellious; see MUTINY]

mu·ti·nous (myü′tə nəs), *adj.* **1.** given to or engaged in mutiny; rebellious: *a mutinous crew. The men became mutinous and insubordinate* (Walter Besant). **2.** like or involving mutiny; characterized by mutiny: *a mutinous look.* **3.** not controllable; unruly: *mutinous passions, and conflicting fears* (Shelley). —**mu′ti·nous·ly,** *adv.* —**mu′ti·nous·ness,** *n.*

—**Syn. 1.** riotous, insubordinate, seditious.

—**Ant. 1.** obedient, submissive, tractable, compliant.

mu·ti·ny (myü′tə nē), *n., pl.* **-nies,** *v.,* **-nied, -ny·ing.** —*n.* **1.** open rebellion against lawful authority, especially by sailors or soldiers against their officers. **2.** *Obsolete.* discord; strife: *A man . . . whom right and wrong Have chose as umpire of their mutiny* (Shakespeare). —*v.i.* to take part in a mutiny; rebel: *His troops, who had received no wages for a long time, had mutinied* (John L. Motley). [< *mutine* to revolt < Old French *mutiner* < *mutin* rebellious < *meute* revolt, ultimately < Latin *movēre* to move]

—**Syn.** *n.* **1.** insurrection, revolt, uprising. *-v.i.* revolt.

mut·ism (myü′tiz əm), *n.* **1.** muteness; the state of being mute: *Paulina was awed by the savants, but not quite to mutism* (Charlotte Brontë). **2.** *Psychoanalysis.* an emotional state in which the patient seems unable, or refuses, to speak. [< obsolete French *mutisme* < Latin *mūtus* mute + French *-isme* -ism]

mu·to·graph (myü′tə graf, -gräf), *n.* an early form of motion-picture camera. [< Latin *mūtāre* to change + English *-graph*]

mu·ton (myü′ton), *n. Biology.* the smallest genetic unit capable of causing mutation: *The muton . . . may be as small as . . . a few nucleotide pairs of the chromosomal nucleic acid* (New Scientist). [< *mut*(ation) + *-on,* designating a unit]

mu·to·scope (myü′tə skōp), *n.* an early form of motion-picture projector. [< Latin *mūtāre* to change + English *-scope*]

mutt (mut), *n. Slang.* **1.** a dog, especially a mongrel: *But the alley dogs, the homeliest mutts, the dogs that nobody wants, are moved in the cages to westward* (Baltimore Sun). **2.** a stupid person. Also, **mut.** [American English; origin uncertain]

mut·ter (mut′ər), *v.i.* **1.** to speak indistinctly and in a low voice, with the lips partly closed; mumble: *He mutters of vengeance as he walks* (Lord Dunsany). **2.** to complain; grumble: *He muttered about the Army food.* **3.** to make a low rumbling sound: *We heard thunder muttering; a storm was coming on* (Francis Parkman). —*v.t.* to utter (words) low and indistinctly with lips partly closed; mumble: *The surgeon muttered his dissatisfaction* (James Fenimore Cooper).
—*n.* **1.** the act of muttering. **2.** muttered words: *We heard a mutter of discontent.*
[Middle English *muteren;* probably imitative. Compare dialectal German *muttern.*]
—**mut′ter·er,** *n.* —**mut′ter·ing·ly,** *adv.*
—**Syn.** *v.i.* **1, 2,** *v.t.* See **murmur.**

mut·ton (mut′ən), *n.* **1.** the meat of a sheep, as distinguished from that of a lamb: *We had roast mutton for dinner.* **2.** a sheep. [< Old French *mouton* < Medieval Latin *multo, -onis* a ram, perhaps < Celtic (compare Old Irish *mol*)]

mut·ton-bird (mut′ən bėrd′), *n.* a sea bird, one of the shearwaters, of the Atlantic and Pacific oceans: *The mutton-birds of the Pacific . . . spend most of the year fishing, spread out . . . from the equator to the Bering Strait* (Atlantic).

mutton chop, 1. a small piece of mutton, usually with bone from the ribs or loin, for broiling or frying. **2.** a patch of whiskers on each side of the face shaped like a mutton chop, narrow at the top and broad and rounded at the bottom, with the chin shaved both in front and beneath: *Baker wore mutton chop whiskers* (Newsweek).

mut·ton·head (mut′ən hed′), *n. Slang.* a slow, dull-witted person: *Tycho Brahe was the first to demonstrate what had already been conjectured by that strange combination of genius and muttonhead . . .* (Scientific American).

mut·ton-head·ed (mut′ən hed′id), *adj. Slang.* dull; stupid.

mut·ton·y (mut′ə nē), *adj.* like mutton; having the qualities of mutton.

mu·tu·al (myü′chü əl), *adj.* **1.** done, said, felt, etc., by each toward the other; given and received: *mutual promises. A family has mutual affection when each person likes the others and is liked by them.* **2.** each to the other: *mutual enemies.* **3.** belonging to each respectively; respective; common. **4.** *Informal.* belonging to each of several: *We are happy to have him as our mutual friend.* **5.** of or having to do with mutual insurance: *a mutual company.*
—*n.* **1.** a mutual insurance company. **2.** a mutual fund: *The mutuals seldom buy speculative stocks* (Maclean's).
[< Latin *mūtuus* reciprocal, related to *mūtāre* to change + English *-al*[1]]
—**Syn.** *adj.* **1.** reciprocal.
➔ See **common** for usage note.

mutual fund, a financial organization formed by the pooling of money by numbers of persons for the purpose of investing in a variety of securities. The fund does not have a fixed amount of capital stock but sells additional shares to investors as the demand requires: *Mutual funds . . . were switching out of lower-yielding common stocks into fixed-income securities* (Wall Street Journal).

mutual insurance or **plan,** a plan or method of insurance in which the persons who are insured jointly own and control the insurance society or company, protecting each other against loss by the payment of given amounts into a common fund, and dividing the profits as owners.

mu·tu·al·ism (myü′chü ə liz′əm), *n. Biology.* **1.** a relationship of close interdependence between two species: *Between canine and human species the predator/prey relationship appears to have developed into a mutualism, which was bound to lead eventually to the one being domesticated by the other* (New Scientist). **2.** symbiosis.

mu·tu·al·i·ty (myü′chü al′ə tē), *n.* the quality or condition of being mutual; reciprocity: *The need for a mutuality of understanding between the Joint Committee on Atomic Energy and the Atomic Energy Commission . . . is of greater importance today than ever before* (Bulletin of Atomic Scientists).

mu·tu·al·i·za·tion (myü′chü ə lə zā′shən), *n.* the act or process of mutualizing: *The meeting had been called to vote on mutualization of the firm which has operated 49 years as a stock company* (Wall Street Journal).

mu·tu·al·ize (myü′chü ə līz), *v.t., v.i.,* **-ized, -iz·ing. 1.** to make or become mutual. **2.** to sell much stock of (a corporation) to employees or customers.

mu·tu·al·ly (myü′chü ə lē), *adv.* each toward the other: *Those three girls have been mutually friendly for years.*

mutual savings bank, a savings bank with no capital, whose depositors share the profits: *Three New Jersey mutual savings banks announced plans to merge* (Wall Street Journal).

mu·tu·el (myü′chü əl), *n.* **1.** parimutuel. **2.** the money paid on a minimum winning bet, usually a two-dollar ticket, on the parimutuel: *He won the Sheepshead Bay Handicap and paid an $81.80 mutuel* (New Yorker). —*adj.* of or having to do with a mutuel: *mutuel tickets, mutuel windows.*

mu·tule (myü′tyül, myü′chül), *n. Architecture.* one of a series of projecting flat blocks under the corona of a Doric cornice. [< Latin *mūtulus* a modillion]

Mutules (M)

mu·u·mu·u (mü′mü′; *Hawaiian* mü′ü mü′ü), *n.* a long, loose-fitting cotton dress, like a Mother Hubbard, originally worn by Polynesian women, now common throughout the United States. [< Hawaiian *mu'u mu'u*]

Mu·zak (myü′zak), *n. Trademark.* music for offices, industry, and public areas, transmitted by either telephone or FM radio: *There's dinner music, too, for those who haven't been wired yet for Muzak* (New Yorker).

mu·zhik or **mu·zjik** (mü zhik′, mü′zhik), *n.* **1.** a Russian peasant: *Until the end of . . . the thirteenth century, the Russian muzhik . . . was free* (Newsweek). **2.** *U.S. Slang.* any Russian. Also, **moujik, mujik.** [< Russian *muzhik*]

muzz (muz), *Slang, Archaic.* —*v.t.* to make muzzy. —*v.i.* **1.** to study intently. **2.** to loiter aimlessly. [origin uncertain]

muz·zi·ly (muz′ə lē), *adv. Informal.* in a muzzy manner; confusedly: *He would sit at home every night reading . . . , brooding muzzily at last over his book* (Edmund Wilson).

muz·zi·ness (muz′ē nis), *n. Informal.* muzzy or befuddled character or appearance: *We lament the muzziness which seems inseparable from the process employed* (Athenæum).

muz·zle (muz′əl), *n., v.,* **-zled, -zling.** —*n.* **1.** the nose, mouth, and jaws of a four-footed animal: *the muzzle of a dog. The antler'd deer . . . thrust his muzzle in the air* (Joaquin Miller). **2. a.** a cover of straps or wires to put over an animal's head and mouth to prevent it from biting, eating, etc. **b.** any of various contrivances that resemble this, such as the respirator of a gas mask. **3.** the open front part of the barrel of a gun, pistol, etc.: *Friday . . . clapped the muzzle of his piece into his ear, and shot him dead as a stone* (Daniel Defoe).

Muzzle (def. 2a)

—*v.t.* **1.** to put a muzzle on. **2.** to compel (a person) to be silent about something: *Fear that he might betray his friends muzzled him.* **3.** to sniff at; poke a head into: *. . . a spaniel muzzling the wind* (Atlantic).
[Middle English *musell* < Old French *musel* < *muse* muzzle < Medieval Latin *musus* snout. Compare MUSE.] —**muz′zler,** *n.*

muz·zle·load·er (muz′əl lō′dər), *n.* a muzzleloading gun.

muz·zle·load·ing (muz′əl lō′ding), *adj.* (of a gun) loaded by putting gunpowder in through the open front and ramming it down.

muzzle velocity, the velocity that a gun imparts to a projectile, measured as it leaves the muzzle in feet per second: *They produced an ingenious way of measuring the muzzle velocity of guns for battleships at sea* (New Scientist).

muz·zy (muz′ē), *adj.,* **-zi·er, -zi·est.** *Informal.* **1.** befuddled; muddled; confused: *The whole company stared at me with a whimsical, muzzy look, like men whose senses were a little obfuscated by beer* (Washington Irving). **2.** dull; gloomy; spiritless. [origin uncertain]

mv (no period), millivolt.

m.v., an abbreviation for the following:
1. market value.
2. mean variation.
3. medium voltage.
4. motor vessel.
5. softly (Italian, *mezza voce*).

Mv (no period), mendelevium (chemical element).

M.V. or **M/V** (no periods), motor vessel.

MVA (no periods), Missouri Valley Authority.

MVD (no periods) or **M.V.D.,** the Ministry of Internal Affairs of the Soviet Union, an official organization of police for conventional police protection and border police activity.

M.V.O., Member of the Royal Victorian Order.

M.V.P., Most Valuable Player.

mvu·le (vü′le), *n.* an African timber tree; iroko. [< a native name]

mw (no period), milliwatt.

Mw (no period), megawatt.

MW (no periods), *British.* megawatt.

M.W., 1. Most Worshipful. **2.** Most Worthy.

M.W.A., Modern Woodmen of America.

mwa·mi (mwä′mē), *n.* the title of the ruler of Burundi, in central Africa, and formerly of the native rulers of Belgian East Africa. [< a Bantu word]

M.W.G.M., Most Worthy or Worshipful Grand Master (of a Masonic order).

my (mī), *adj.* a possessive form of **I.** of or belonging to me; that I have, hold, or possess: *my house, in my opinion. I learned my lesson.* —*interj. Informal.* an exclamation of surprise: *My! How pleasant to see you!* [Middle English *mī, mīn,* Old English *mīn*]

my-, *combining form.* the form of **myo-** before vowels, as in *myoma.*

mya., myriare.

my·al·gi·a (mī al′jē ə), *n.* muscular pain or rheumatism. [< New Latin *myalgia* < Greek *mŷs, myós* muscle + *álgos* pain]

my·al·gic (mī al′jik), *adj.* of or having to do with myalgia; affected with myalgia.

my·all (mī′ôl), *n.* (in Australia) an aborigine. [< a native name]

my·as·the·ni·a (mī′əs thē′nē ə), *n.* muscular weakness. [< New Latin *myasthenia* < Greek *mŷs, myós* muscle + *astheneiā* weakness]

myasthenia grav·is (grav′is, gräv′-; grā′vis), a disease that causes extreme weakness of the muscles, because of an interruption of nerve impulses traveling to the muscles, and related in some way to the functioning of the thymus gland.

my·as·then·ic (mī′əs then′ik), *adj.* affected with myasthenia.

my·ce·li·al (mī sē′lē əl), *adj.* of or having to do with mycelium.

my·ce·li·an (mī sē′lē ən), *adj.* mycelial.

my·ce·li·oid (mī sē′lē oid), *adj.* of or like mycelium.

my·ce·li·um (mī sē′lē əm), *n., pl.* **-li·a** (-lē ə). **1.** the vegetative part of a fungus, consisting of interwoven fibers or hyphae, often not visible on the surface: *This tubular type of mycelium, which gives to the entire plant body the form of a single complicated*

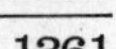

coenocytic cell (Fred W. Emerson). **2.** a similar mass of fibers formed by some higher bacteria. [< New Latin *mycelium* < Greek *mýkēs, -ētos* mushroom, fungus]

my·ce·loid (mī′sə loid), *adj.* mycelioid.

My·ce·nae·an (mī′sə nē′ən), *adj.* of or having to do with Mycenae, a very ancient city in Greece, or the civilization, culture, or art that flourished there.

my·ce·to·ma (mī′sə tō′mə), *n.* a fungous disease of the hands, feet, legs, and internal tissue, characterized by swelling, and the formation of nodules containing pus. It is most common in tropical areas and usually affects the foot, when it is called Madura foot. [< Greek *mýkēs, -ētos* fungus + English *-oma*]

my·ce·to·zo·an (mī sē′tə zō′ən), *n.* any of a group of primitive organisms, the slime molds, sometimes classified as animals and sometimes as plants; myxomycete. —*adj.* of, designating, or belonging to the mycetozoans. [< New Latin *Mycetozoa* the group name (< Greek *mýkēs, -ētos* fungus + *zôion* animal) + English *-an*]

my·co·bac·te·ri·um (mī′kō bak tir′ē əm), *n., pl.* **-te·ri·a** (-tir′ē ə). any of a group of aerobic, acid-fast, rod-shaped bacteria. One species causes leprosy; certain other species cause tuberculosis in man, cattle, and fowl. [< New Latin *Mycobacterium* the genus name < Greek *mýkēs* fungus + New Latin *bacterium* bacterium]

mycol., mycology.

my·co·log·i·cal (mī′kə loj′ə kəl), *adj.* of or having to do with mycology.

my·col·o·gist (mī kol′ə jist), *n.* a person skilled in mycology.

my·col·o·gy (mī kol′ə jē), *n.* **1.** the scientific study of fungi. **2.** the fungi of a particular region. **3.** facts about a particular fungus. [< Greek *mýkēs* fungus + English *-logy*]

my·co·plas·ma (mī′kō plaz′mə), *n., pl.* **-mas, -ma·ta** (-mə tə). any of a group of gram-negative, filterable, bacterial microorganisms, including the Eaton agent and other varieties of PPLO. [< New Latin *Mycoplasma* the genus name < Greek *mýkēs* fungus + New Latin *plasma* plasma]

my·cor·rhi·za or **my·co·rhi·za** (mī′kə-rī′zə), *n.* the symbiotic association of the mycelium of certain fungi with the roots of certain higher plants, living in close relationship with the surface cells: *It is possible with many, if not all, species of plant which normally form mycorrhizas in natural conditions to grow them in artificial surroundings without their appropriate fungi* (New Scientist). [< Greek *mýkēs* fungus + New Latin *-rrhiza* < Greek *rhíza* root]

my·cor·rhi·zal or **my·co·rhi·zal** (mī′kə-rī′zəl), *adj.* of or having to do with mycorrhiza.

my·cor·rhi·zic or **my·co·rhi·zic** (mī′kə-rī′zik), *adj.* mycorrhizal.

my·co·sis (mī kō′sis), *n., pl.* **-ses** (sēz). **1.** the presence of parasitic fungi in or on any part of the body. **2.** a disease caused by such fungi. [< Greek *mýkēs* fungus + English *-osis*]

My·co·stat·in (mī′kə stat′in), *n. Trademark.* nystatin.

my·cot·ic (mī kot′ik), *adj.* of or having to do with mycosis.

my·dri·a·sis (mi drī′ə sis, mī-), *n.* excessive dilation of the pupil of the eye, as the result of disease, drugs, or the like. [< Latin *mydriăsis* < Greek *mydríāsis*]

myd·ri·at·ic (mid′rē at′ik), *adj.* having to do with or causing mydriasis. —*n.* a drug that produces mydriasis, such as atropine: *Ephedrine and its salts are used locally to shrink mucous membranes in colds and as a mydriatic* (Heber W. Youngken).

my·e·len·ceph·a·lon (mī′ə len sef′ə lon), *n.* **1.** the brain and spinal cord taken together and considered as a whole. **2.** a posterior section of the brain of the embryo from which the medulla oblongata develops; afterbrain. [< Greek *myelós* marrow + English *encephalon*]

my·e·lin (mī′ə lin), *n.* a soft, whitish, fatty substance that forms a sheath about the core of certain nerve fibers: *The myelin sheath . . . surrounds nerve fibers much as insulating material protects electric wire* (Science News Letter). [< German *Myelin* < Greek *myelós* marrow + German *-in* -in]

my·e·lin·a·tion (mī′ə lə nā′shən), *n.* the sheathing of nerve fibers; acquisition of a myelin sheath: *Myelination . . . leads to lower levels of excitability and more mature function in the brain* (Science News Letter).

my·e·line (mī′ə lin, -lēn), *n.* myelin.

my·e·li·tis (mī′ə lī′tis), *n.* inflammation of the spinal cord or of the bone marrow. [< Greek *myelós* marrow + English *-itis*]

my·e·lo·cyte (mī′ə lə sīt), *n.* an amoeboid blood cell present in bone marrow and giving rise to leucocytes: *The marrow in early cases [of myeloid leukemia] shows an increase in . . . myelocytes* (G. E. Beaumont and E. C. Dodds). [< Greek *myelós* marrow + English *-cyte*]

my·e·lo·cyt·ic (mī′ə lə sit′ik), *adj.* of or having to do with myelocytes.

my·e·lo·cy·to·ma·to·sis (mī′ə lō sī tō′mə-tō′sis), *n.* a disease of poultry, a form of the avian leucosis complex, characterized by the formation of white tumors in the liver and along the sternum.

my·e·lo·gen·ic (mī′ə lə jen′ik), *adj.* originating or produced in the marrow. [< Greek *myelós* marrow + English *-gen* + *-ic*]

my·e·log·e·nous (mī′ə loj′ə nəs), *adj.* myelogenic.

myelogenous leukemia, a form of leukemia characterized by an excess of myelogenic leucocytes in the blood.

my·e·log·ra·phy (mī′ə log′rə fē), *n.* a method of taking X-ray pictures of the space around the spinal cord by first injecting air or certain liquids into the space. [< Greek *myelós* marrow + English *-graphy*]

my·e·loid (mī′ə loid), *adj.* **1.** of or having to do with the spinal cord. **2.** having to do with or like marrow: *Myeloid leukemia . . . involves the bone marrow and spleen primarily, the lymphoid tissue secondarily* (Science News Letter).

my·e·lo·ma (mī′ə lō′mə), *n., pl.* **-mas, -ma·ta** (-mə tə). cancer of the bone marrow. [< Greek *myelós* marrow + *-ōma* a growth]

myg., myriagram.

my·i·a·sis (mī′ə sis), *n., pl.* **-ses** (-sēz). a diseased condition of man or other animals due to the larvae of flies parasitic on or in the body. [< New Latin *myiasis* < Greek *myîa* fly + New Latin *-iasis* -iasis]

myl., myrialiter.

My·lar (mī′lär), *n. Trademark.* a tough polyester film widely used in food packaging, recording tapes, as an electrical insulator, etc.

My·le·ran (mī′lə ran), *n. Trademark.* a drug used in the treatment of myelogenic leukemia. *Formula:* $C_6H_{14}O_6S_2$

my·lo·don (mī′lə don), *n.* an extinct giant ground sloth that lived in southern South America until recent times. [< Greek *mýlos* molar + *odoús, odóntos* tooth]

my·lo·dont (mī′lə dont), *adj.* of, having to do with, or like the mylodons. —*n.* a mylodon.

my·lo·nite (mī′lə nīt, mil′ə-), *n.* a siliceous schist resulting from the crushing of quartzose rocks. [< Greek *mylṓn* mill[1] + English *-ite*[1]]

mym., myriameter.

my·na or **my·nah** (mī′nə), *n.* any of various birds related to the starlings that can mimic human speech, found in India and certain neighboring countries. Also, **mina.** [< Hindustani *mainā*]

Myn·heer (mīn hãr′), *n., pl.* **-heer·en** (-hãr′ən). *Dutch.* Sir; Mr.

myn·heer (mīn hãr′), *n.* a Dutchman.

myo-, *combining form.* muscle: *Myocardium = the muscular substance of the heart.* Also, **my-** before vowels. [< Greek *mŷs, myós* muscle; mouse; see MUSCLE]

my·o·car·di·al (mī′ə kär′dē əl), *adj.* of or having to do with the myocardium: *myocardial infarction, myocardial rupture.*

my·o·car·di·o·graph (mī′ə kär′dē ə graf, -gräf), *n.* an instrument that records heart action.

my·o·car·di·tis (mī′ō kär dī′tis), *n.* inflammation of the muscular part of the wall of the heart. [< *myocard*(ium) + *-itis*]

my·o·car·di·um (mī′ə kär′dē əm), *n.* the muscle of the heart: *The coronary arteries bring oxygen and nutriment to the most important muscle in the body, the heart muscle or myocardium* (Paul Dudley White). [< New Latin *myocardium* < Greek *mŷs, myós* muscle + *kardíā* heart]

my·o·cyte (mī′ə sīt), *n.* **1.** a muscle cell. **2.** a contractile cell around the pores of sponges. [< *myo-* + *-cyte*]

my·o·fi·bril (mī′ə fī′brəl), *n.* a striated fibril of a muscle fiber: *The striations [of the fiber] arise from a repeating variation in the density, i.e., the concentration of protein along the myofibrils* (Scientific American).

my·o·glo·bin (mī′ə glō′bin), *n.* a protein similar to hemoglobin and present in muscle cells, that takes oxygen from the blood and stores it for future use: *Muscles contain myoglobin, a compound related to haemoglobin which takes up oxygen released by haemoglobin . . . and stores it for use in time of oxygen shortage* (A.C. Allison). [< *myo-* + (hemo)*globin*]

my·o·gram (mī′ə gram), *n.* a record or tracing obtained by a myograph.

my·o·graph (mī′ə graf, -gräf), *n.* an instrument for recording muscular contractions and relaxations by means of tracings.

my·oid (mī′oid), *adj.* of or like muscle.

my·ol·o·gist (mī ol′ə jist), *n.* a person skilled in myology.

my·ol·o·gy (mī ol′ə jē), *n.* the scientific study of the structure, functions, and diseases of muscles. [< *myo-* + *-logy*]

my·o·ma (mī ō′mə), *n., pl.* **-mas, -ma·ta** (-mə tə). a tumor derived from muscular tissue. [< *my-* + *-oma*]

my·om·a·tous (mī om′ə təs, -ō′mə-), *adj.* of or characterized by myoma; affected with a myoma.

my·o·path·ic (mī′ə path′ik), *adj.* of or having to do with myopathy.

my·op·a·thy (mī op′ə thē), *n.* disease of the muscles. [< *myo-* + *-pathy*]

my·ope (mī′ōp), *n.* a person having myopia; near-sighted person: *In general, myopes become aware of their abnormality because of the difficulty of distinguishing distant objects* (Hardy and Perrin). [back formation < *myopia*]

my·o·pi·a (mī ō′pē ə), *n.* **1.** near-sightedness; an abnormal condition of the eye in which only objects close to the eye produce distinct images because parallel rays of light are brought to a focus before they reach the retina. **2.** short-sightedness: *intellectual myopia.* [< New Latin *myopia* < Greek *mýōps* < *mŷein* to shut + *ṓps* eye]

my·op·ic (mī op′ik), *adj.* near-sighted; of or affected with myopia: *Myopic children whose vision is deteriorating eat less food for every pound they increase in weight than do normally sighted children* (Science News Letter). —**my·op′i·cal·ly,** *adv.*

my·o·py (mī′ə pē), *n.* myopia.

my·o·scope (mī′ə skōp), *n.* an instrument for observing muscular contraction.

my·o·sin (mī′ə sin), *n.* a globulin found in muscle tissue, important in the elasticity and contraction of muscles.

my·o·sis (mī ō′sis), *n.* miosis; excessive contraction of the pupil of the eye.

my·o·sote (mī′ə sōt), *n.* myosotis.

my·o·so·tis (mī′ə sō′tis), *n.* any of a group of plants of the borage family, such as the forget-me-not. [earlier, hawkweed < Latin *myosōtis* < Greek *myosōtis* < *mŷs, myós* mouse + *oûs, ōtós* ear]

my·ot·ic (mī ot′ik), *adj.* producing miosis; miotic. —*n.* a drug that causes miosis; a miotic.

my·o·tis (mī ot′is), *n.* any of a widely distributed group of small bats, including varieties commonly found about buildings and caves.

myr·i·ad (mir′ē əd), *n.* **1.** a very great number: *There are myriads of stars. The grove bloomed with myriads of wild roses* (Francis Parkman). **2.** ten thousand.
—*adj.* **1.** countless; innumerable: *the City's moonlit spires and myriad lamps* (Shelley). **2.** ten thousand. **3.** having innumerable aspects or phases: *the myriad mind of Shakespeare or Da Vinci.*
[< Late Latin *mȳrias, -adis* < Greek *mȳriás, -ados* ten thousand, countless]

myr·i·ad·fold (mir′ē əd fōld), *adj.* multiplied countless times; having innumerable aspects or features. —*n.* an infinite amount.

myr·i·a·gram (mir′ē ə gram), *n.* 10 kilograms; 22.046 pounds. *Abbr.:* myg. [< Greek *mȳriás* ten thousand + English *gram*]

myr·i·a·gramme (mir′ē ə gram), *n. Especially British.* myriagram.

myr·i·a·li·ter (mir′ē ə lē′tər), *n.* 10 kiloliters; 13.08 cubic yards U.S. dry measure; 2,641.7 gallons U.S. liquid measure. *Abbr.:* myl. [< Greek *mȳriás* ten thousand + English *liter*]

myr·i·a·li·tre (mir′ē ə lē′tər), *n. Especially British.* myrialiter.

myr·i·a·me·ter (mir′ē ə mē′tər), *n.* 100 square kilometers; about 38.6 square miles. *Abbr.:* mym. [< Greek *mȳriás* ten thousand + English *-meter*]

myr·i·a·me·tre (mir′ē ə mē′tər), *n. Especially British.* myriameter.

myr·i·a·pod (mir′ē ə pod), *n.* any of a group of arthropods having a wormlike body with many segments and many legs: *Centipedes and millepedes are myriapods.* —*adj.* **1.** of or belonging to the myriapods. **2.** having many legs. [< New Latin *Myriapoda* the class name < Greek *mȳriás* ten thousand + *poús, podós* foot]

myr·i·ap·o·dal (mir′ē ap′ə dəl), *adj.* of or having to do with the myriapods.

myr·i·ap·o·dan (mir′ē ap′ə dən), *adj., n.* myriapod.

myr·i·ap·o·dous (mir′ē ap′ə dəs), *adj.* myriapod.

my·ri·are (mir′ē ãr), *n.* one square kilometer; about 247 acres. *Abbr.:* mya. [< Greek *mȳriás* ten thousand + English *are*[2]]

my·ri·ca (mi rī′kə), *n.* the dried bark of the wax myrtle or of the bayberry, formerly used in medicine. [< Latin *myrīca* < Greek *myrīkē*, perhaps ultimately < source of English *myrrh*]

myr·i·o·ra·ma (mir′ē ə rä′mə, -ram′ə), *n.* a picture made up of interchangeable parts which can be harmoniously arranged to form a great variety of picturesque scenes. [< Greek *mȳríos* countless + *hórāma* view]

my·ris·tic (mi ris′tik, mī-), *adj.* of or derived from the nutmeg. [< Medieval Latin *myristica* nutmeg tree < Greek *myrízein* to anoint]

my·ris·ti·ca·ceous (mi ris′tə kā′shəs, mī-), *adj.* belonging to the family of trees and shrubs typified by the nutmeg.

myristic acid, an organic acid such as is found in oil of nutmeg or spermaceti, used in making soap, perfumes, etc. *Formula:* $C_{14}H_{28}O_2$

myr·me·co·log·i·cal (mėr′mə kə loj′ə kəl), *adj.* of or having to do with ants.

myr·me·col·o·gist (mėr′mə kol′ə jist), *n.* an expert in myrmecology.

myr·me·col·o·gy (mėr′mə kol′ə jē), *n.* the scientific study of ants. [< Greek *mýrmēx, -ēkos* ant + English *-logy*]

myr·me·coph·a·gous (mėr′mə kof′ə gəs), *adj.* feeding on ants. [< Greek *mýrmēx, -ēkos* ant + *phageîn* to eat + English *-ous*]

myr·me·co·phile (mėr′mə kə fīl, -fil), *n.* a myrmecophilous insect.

myr·me·coph·i·lous (mėr′mə kof′ə ləs), *adj.* **1.** fond of or living with ants. Myrmecophilous insects live in ant hills. **2.** benefited by ants, as plants that are cross-fertilized by them. [< Greek *mýrmēx, -ēkos* ant + English *-phile* + *-ous*]

Myr·mi·don (mėr′mə don), *n., pl.* **Myr·mi·dons, Myr·mid·o·nes** (mėr mid′ə nēz). *Greek Mythology.* a member of a warlike people of ancient Thessaly who, according to Homer, accompanied Achilles, their king, to the Trojan War.

myr·mi·don (mėr′mə don), *n.* **1.** an obedient and unquestioning follower: *No man could now be safe, when men like him [Egmont] were in the power of Alva and his myrmidons* (John L. Motley). **2.** a policeman; bailiff; deputy sheriff: *the justice and his myrmidons* (Tobias Smollett). [< *Myrmidon*]

my·rob·a·lan (mī rob′ə lən, mi-), *n.* the dried plumlike fruit of various tropical trees, used in dyeing, tanning, and making ink. [< Old French *myrobalon* < Latin *myrobalanum* < Greek *myrobálanos* fruit of a palm that yields balsam < *mýron* any balsam + *bálanos* acorn]

myr·o·sin (mir′ə sin, mī′rə-), *n.* an enzyme found in the seeds of the mustard and of various other plants of the mustard family. [< French *myrosyne* < Greek *mýron* unguent]

myrrh (mėr), *n.* a fragrant gum resin obtained from various shrubs of Arabia and eastern Africa, used in medicine as an astringent tonic, in perfumes, and in incense. [Old English *myrre* < Latin *myrrha* < Greek *mýrrhā*, ultimately < Semitic, probably Akkadian *murrû*]

myrrh·like (mėr′līk′), *adj.* resembling myrrh.

myrrh·y (mėr′ē), *adj.* full of myrrh; fragrant with or as if with myrrh: *the myrrhy lands* (Robert Browning).

myr·ta·ceous (mėr tā′shəs), *adj.* **1.** belonging to the myrtle family: *Myrtle, clove, allspice, guava, and eucalyptus are myrtaceous plants.* **2.** of or like the myrtle. [< New Latin *Myrtaceae* the family name (< Latin *myrtāceus* < *myrtus* myrtle tree < Greek *mýrtos*) + English *-ous*]

myr·tle (mėr′təl), *n.* **1.** *U.S.* a low, creeping evergreen vine with blue flowers; periwinkle. **2.** any of a group of shrubs of the myrtle family, especially an evergreen shrub of southern Europe with shiny leaves, fragrant, white flowers, and black, aromatic berries. The myrtle was held sacred to Venus (Aphrodite) and is used as an emblem of love. **3.** a dark-green color. [earlier, fruit of the myrtle < Old French *mirtile*, probably < Medieval Latin *myrtilus* (diminutive) < Latin *myrtus* myrtle tree < Greek *mýrtos*]

Common Myrtle (def. 2)

myr·tle·ber·ry (mėr′təl ber′ē, -bər-), *n., pl.* **-ries.** the fruit of the myrtle (def. 2).

myrtle bird, myrtle warbler.

myrtle family, a group of dicotyledonous woody plants, natives of warm climates, usually having a fragrant, volatile oil. The family includes plants valued for spices, such as the clove and allspice, for edible fruit, such as the guava, and for timber or gum, such as the eucalyptus.

myrtle green, a dark green with a bluish tinge; the color of myrtle leaves.

myrtle warbler, a North American warbler with yellow patches on the crown, the rump, and each side of the breast.

myr·tle·wood (mėr′təl wu̇d′), *n.* the mountain laurel of California and the western United States.

myr·tol (mėr′tol, -tōl), *n.* an oil obtained from the leaves of the common myrtle, used as an antiseptic, stimulant, etc. [< Latin *myrt(us)* myrtle + English *-ol*[2]]

my·self (mī self′), *pron., pl.* **our·selves. 1.** the emphatic form of **me** or **I:** *I did it myself. I myself will go.* **2.** the reflexive form of **me:** *I hurt myself. I can cook for myself.* **3.** my real self; my normal self: *I am not myself today.*

➔ In informal English, **myself** is sometimes substituted for *I* or *me* in a compound subject or object: *Mrs. Johnson and myself are both very grateful. He wrote to Richards and myself.* This use is not regarded as standard.

My·so·line (mī′sə lin, -lēn), *n. Trademark.* primidone, a drug used to control or prevent convulsions in some forms of epilepsy. *Formula:* $C_{12}H_{14}N_2O_2$

my·sost (mī′sost), *n.* a hard cheese made from milk whey. [< Norwegian *mysost*]

mys·ta·gog·ic (mis′tə goj′ik), *adj.* of or having to do with a mystagogue or mystagogy.

mys·ta·gog·i·cal (mis′tə goj′ə kəl), *adj.* mystagogic.

mys·ta·gogue (mis′tə gôg, -gog), *n.* a person who initiates other persons into, or interprets, mysteries, especially religious mysteries. [< Latin *mystagōgus* < Greek *mystagōgós* < *mýstēs* one vowed to silence (< *mȳein* close the lips or eyes) + *agōgós* leading < *ágein* to lead]

mys·ta·go·gy (mis′tə gō′jē), *n.* initiation into or interpretation of mysteries, especially religious mysteries.

mys·te·ri·al (mis tir′ē əl), *adj. Rare.* mysterious.

mys·te·ri·ous (mis tir′ē əs), *adj.* **1.** full of mystery; hard to explain or understand; secret; hidden. **2.** suggesting mystery; enigmatical: *the mysterious smile of the Mona Lisa. Why are you all so mysterious, so reserved in your communications?* (Cardinal Newman). —**mys·te′ri·ous·ly,** *adv.* —**mys·te′ri·ous·ness,** *n.*

—**Syn. 1. Mysterious, inscrutable** mean hard to explain or understand. **Mysterious** describes a person, thing, or situation about which there is something secret, hidden, or unknown that arouses curiosity, conjecture, or wonder: *She had a mysterious telephone call.* **Inscrutable** describes a thing that is so mysterious or such a riddle that it is impossible to make out its meaning, or a person who keeps his feelings, thoughts, and intentions completely hidden: *His mother began to cry, but his father's face was inscrutable.* —**Ant. 1.** clear, plain, evident.

mys·ter·y[1] (mis′tər ē, -trē), *n., pl.* **-ter·ies. 1.** something that is hidden, inexplicable, or unknown; secret: *the mysteries of the universe, the mystery of love.* **2.** secrecy; obscurity: *an atmosphere of mystery, a man of mystery.* **3.** something that is not explained or understood: *It is a mystery to me how he survived the accident.* **4.** obscure, puzzling, or mysterious quality or character. **5.** a religious conception or doctrine that human reason cannot understand: *Father Deacy preached on the mystery of the Trinity* (New York Times). **6.** Often, **mysteries.** a secret religious rite to which only initiated persons are admitted. **7.** a mystery play. **8.** a novel, story, etc., in which suspense is derived from calculated development of a crime or crimes, with the solution comprising the denouement: *a writer of mysteries.* **9. a.** a sacramental rite of the Christian religion. **b.** the Eucharist; Communion; Mass. **10.** an incident in the life of Jesus or one of the saints, regarded as of special significance. [< Latin *mystērium* < Greek *mystḗrion* < *mýstēs* an initiate < *mȳein* close (the lips or eyes)] —**Syn. 1.** enigma.

mys·ter·y[2] (mis′tər ē, -trē), *n., pl.* **-ter·ies.** *Archaic.* **1.** craft; trade: *It [a town] makes pretence at some kind of cloth mystery* (Walter Besant). **2.** an association of craftsmen or merchants; guild: *Claus Hammerlein, president of the mysteries of the workers in iron* (Scott). [< Medieval Latin *misterium*, for Latin *ministerium* ministry; influenced by *mystery*[1]]

mystery play, a medieval religious play based on the Bible, often acted by the trade guilds. [< *mystery*[2]]

mys·tic (mis′tik), *adj.* **1.** mystical. **2.** having to do with the ancient religious mysteries or other occult rites: *mystic arts.* **3.** of or having to do with mystics or mysticism. **4.** of hidden meaning or nature; enigmatical; mysterious: *To him all nature is instinct with mystic influence* (Francis Parkman). —*n.* **1.** a person who believes that truth or God can be known through spiritual insight: *Lady Julian of Norwich was one of the great English mystics* (Anya Seton). **2.** a person initiated into mysteries. [< Latin *mysticus* < Greek *mystikós* < *mýstēs* an initiate; see MYSTERY[1]]

mys·ti·cal (mis′tə kəl), *adj.* **1.** having some secret meaning; beyond human understanding; mysterious. **2.** spiritually symbolic: *The lamb and the dove are mystical symbols of Christianity.* **3.** of, having to do with, or characteristic of mystics or mysticism. **4.** of or having to do with secret rites open only to the initiated. **5.** cryptic in speech or in style; enigmatic. —**mys′ti·cal·ly,** *adv.* —**mys′ti·cal·ness,** *n.*

mys·ti·cism (mis′tə siz əm), *n.* **1.** the beliefs or mode of thought of mystics: *The Gospel of St. John . . . is the charter of Christian mysticism* (William R. Inge). **2.** the doctrine that truth or God may be known through spiritual insight, independent of the mind: *Whatever it is, superstition or religion, mysticism in all its aspects is one of the most important parts of Indian life* (Santha Rama Rau). **3.** vague or fuzzy thinking; dreamy speculation: *An acute and subtile perception was often clouded by mysticism and abstraction* (William H. Prescott).

mys·tic·i·ty (mis tis′ə tē), *n.* mystic quality.

mys·ti·cize (mis′tə sīz), *v.t.,* **-cized, -cizing.** to make mystical; give a mystical character or meaning to.

mys·ti·fi·ca·tion (mis′tə fə kā′shən), *n.* **1.** a mystifying or being mystified; bewilderment; perplexity. **2.** something that mystifies or is designed to mystify; hoax.

mys·ti·fi·ca·tor (mis′tə fə kā′tər), *n.* a person who mystifies; mystifier.

mys·ti·fi·ca·to·ry (mis′tə fə kā′tər ē), *adj.* causing mystification; mystifying.

mys·ti·fi·er (mis′tə fī′ər), *n.* a person or thing that mystifies: *I am not a magician but a mystifier* (Harry Houdini).

mys·ti·fy (mis′tə fī), *v.t.,* **-fied, -fy·ing. 1.** to bewilder purposely; perplex; puzzle: *The magician's tricks mystified the audience.* **2.** to make mysterious; involve in obscurity; obscure: *the fabulous age, in which vulgar fact becomes mystified* (Washington Irving). [< French *mystifier* < *mystique* mystic + *-fier* -fy] —**mys′ti·fy′ing·ly,** *adv.* —**Syn. 1.** confuse, nonplus.

mys·tique (mis tēk′), *n.* **1.** a mystical cult: *The mystique of Mammon has seldom found* *such passionate dialectics* (Time). **2.** an aura of mystery about someone or something; mystic quality or air: *He dominated them by his reputation and his mystique, and when that was likely to fail he circumnavigated them* (Manchester Guardian). **3.** a mystic ritual: *Coloured chefs, suitably caparisoned, prepare the ducks with much devotion and mystique* (Sunday Times). [< French *mystique*]

myth (mith), *n.* **1. a.** a legend or story, usually attempting to account for something in nature: *The myth of Proserpina is the ancient Greek explanation of summer and winter.* **b.** such stories collectively; mythology: *the realm of myth.* **2.** any invented story. **3.** an imaginary person or thing: *Her wealthy uncle was a myth invented to impress the other girls.* [< New Latin *mythus* < Greek *mŷthos* word, story]

➔ See **legend** for usage note.

myth., 1. mythological. 2. mythology.

myth·ic (mith′ik), *adj.* mythical: *He sees his characters both as poor working people in Chicago and as mythic beings, descendants of the gods, larger than life* (Harper's).

myth·i·cal (mith′ə kəl), *adj.* **1.** of myths: *mythical heroes.* **2.** like a myth: *a mythical interpretation of nature.* **3.** existing only in myths: *mythical monsters.* **4.** not real; made-up; imaginary: *Their wealth is merely mythical.* —**myth′i·cal·ly,** *adv.* —**Syn. 4.** fictitious.

myth·i·cism (mith′ə siz əm), *n.* **1.** mythical treatment. **2.** interpretation of myths.

myth·i·cize (mith′ə sīz), *v.t.*, **-cized, -cizing.** to turn into a myth; treat or explain by myth.

myth·i·co-his·tor·i·cal (mith′ə kō histôr′ə kəl, -tor′-), *adj.* both mythical and historical.

myth·i·fi·ca·tion (mith′ə fə kā′shən), *n.* **1.** the act of mythifying. **2.** the state of being mythified.

myth·i·fy (mith′ə fī), *v.t.* **-fied, -fy·ing.** to make mythical; build a myth around (a person, place, etc.).

myth·mak·er (mith′mā′kər), *n.* **1.** a maker of myths; fabricator: *The Communist mythmakers labored hard to destroy the myth they had once so laboriously mouthed* ... (Time). **2.** a person who originates or preserves myths and legends: *He belonged perhaps to an older and simpler race of men, he belonged to the mythmakers* (Manchester Guardian).

myth·mak·ing (mith′mā′king), *n.* the making or construction of myths: *Frequently a respected patriarch or matriarch ... encouraged imaginative genealogy and mythmaking, so that ancestors ... became legendary heroes or beauties* (New Yorker).

my·thog·ra·pher (mi thog′rə fər), *n.* a writer or narrator of myths: *Persephone is represented by most mythographers as the daughter of Zeus* (Punch).

my·thog·ra·phy (mi thog′rə fē), *n.* **1.** descriptive mythology. **2.** the representation of myths in graphic or plastic art. [< Greek *mŷthos* word, story]

mythol., 1. mythological. 2. mythology.

myth·o·log·ic (mith′ə loj′ik), *adj.* mythological.

myth·o·log·i·cal (mith′ə loj′ə kəl), *adj.* of or having to do with mythology or myths; mythical: *The phoenix is a mythological bird.*

myth·o·log·i·cal·ly (mith′ə loj′ə klē), *adv.* according to mythology.

my·thol·o·gise (mi thol′ə jīz), *v.i.*, **-gised, -gis·ing.** *Especially British.* mythologize.

my·thol·o·gist (mi thol′ə jist), *n.* **1.** a writer of myths. **2.** a person who knows much about mythology.

my·thol·o·gize (mi thol′ə jīz), *v.i.*, **-gized, -giz·ing.** **1.** to relate or explain myths. **2.** to construct myths. —**my·thol′o·giz′er,** *n.*

my·thol·o·gy (mi thol′ə jē), *n., pl.* **-gies.** **1.** a body of myths relating to a particular country or person: *That is the miracle of Greek mythology—a humanized world, men freed from the paralyzing fear of an omnipotent Unknown* (Edith Hamilton). *The tender and delicious mythology of Arthur* (Emerson). **2.** myths collectively: *Mythology is an aspect of religion.* **3.** the study of myths. **4.** a book of myths; treatise on myths: *Cartari's book was the first popular mythology of the Renaissance* (New Yorker). [< Late Latin *mȳthologia* < Greek *mȳthologíā* < *mŷthos* word, story + *lógos* word, discourse]

myth·o·ma·ni·a (mith′ə mā′nē ə), *n.* an abnormal tendency to exaggerate and lie, especially in relating fantastic adventures as if they had really happened.

myth·o·ma·ni·ac (mith′ə mā′nē ak), *n.* a person subject to mythomania.

myth·o·pe·ic or **myth·o·poe·ic** (mith′ə-pē′ik), *adj.* making myths; having to do with making myths. [< Greek *mȳthopoiós* (< *mŷthos* myth + *poieîn* to make, compose) + English *-ic*]

myth·o·pe·ism or **myth·o·poe·ism** (mith′ə pē′iz əm), *n.* the making of myths.

myth·o·pe·ist or **myth·o·poe·ist** (mith′-ə pē′ist), *n.* a mythmaker.

myth·o·po·e·sis (mith′ə pō ē′sis), *n.* mythmaking. [< New Latin *mythopoesis* < Greek *mȳthopoiēsis* < *mȳthopoiós;* see MYTHOPEIC]

myth·o·po·et·ic (mith′ə pō et′ik), *adj.* mythopeic.

myth·o·po·et·ry (mith′ə pō′ə trē), *n.* mythological poetry.

my·thos (mī′thos), *n.* myth; mythology. [< Greek *mŷthos*]

myx·e·de·ma or **myx·oe·de·ma** (mik′sə-dē′mə), *n.* a disease characterized by thickening of the skin, blunting of the senses and intellect, and labored speech. It is associated with diminished functional activity of the thyroid gland: *Myxedema most frequently results from lack of iodine in food and drinking water* (World Book Encyclopedia). [< Greek *mýxa* mucus + *oidēma* edema]

myx·e·dem·a·tous or **myx·oe·dem·a·tous** (mik′sə dem′ə təs, -dē′mə-), *adj.* of, having to do with, or affected with myxedema.

myx·e·dem·ic or **myx·oe·dem·ic** (mik′-sə dem′ik), *adj.* myxedematous.

myx·o·ma (mik sō′mə), *n., pl.* **-mas, -ma·ta** (-mə tə). a connective-tissue tumor in which the cells are separated by mucoid. [< Greek *mýxa* mucus + English *-oma*]

myx·o·ma·to·sis (mik sō′mə tō′sis), *n.* **1.** the presence of numerous myxomas. **2.** a fatal virus disease affecting only rabbits, introduced as a means of controlling them as pests. [< Greek *mýxa* mucus + English *-oma* + *-osis*]

myx·o·my·cete (mik′sō mī sēt′), *n.* any of the slime molds that grow on damp soil and decaying vegetable matter; mycetozoan. [< New Latin *Myxomycetes* the group name < Greek *mýxa* mucus, slime + *mýkēs, -ētos* fungus, mushroom]

myx·o·my·ce·tous (mik′sō mī sē′təs), *adj.* of or belonging to the slime molds.

myx·o·phyte (mik′sə fīt), *n.* a myxomycetous organism. [< Greek *mýxa* mucus + *phytón* plant]

myx·o·vi·rus (mik′ sə vī′rəs), *n.* any of a group of viruses that agglutinate red blood cells, including the viruses which cause influenza and mumps. [< Greek *mýxa* mucus + English *virus*]

N Roman 100's A.D. — Greek 600's B.C. — Phoenician 1000's B.C. — Semitic 1500's B.C. — Egyptian 3000's B.C.

Nn Nn *Nn Nn*

N or **n** (en), *n., pl.* **N's** or **Ns, n's** or **ns.** **1.** the 14th letter of the English alphabet. **2.** any sound represented by this letter. **3.** the fourteenth, or more usually the thirteenth, of a series (either I or J being omitted). **4.** *Printing.* an en; half the width of an em.

n (no period), **1.** *Algebra.* an indefinite number, usually a general positive integer. **2.** *Physics.* neutron.

n., an abbreviation for the following:
1. born (Latin, *natus*).
2. nail or nails.
3. nephew.
4. neuter.
5. new.
6. nominative.
7. noon.
8. normal (strength of a chemical solution).
9. a. north. **b.** northern.
10. note or notes.
11. noun.
12. number.

N (no period), **1.** nitrogen (chemical element). **2. a.** North. **b.** Northern.

N., an abbreviation for the following:
1. Nationalist.
2. Navy.
3. New.
4. Noon.
5. normal (strength of a chemical solution).
6. Norse.
7. a. North. **b.** Northern.
8. November.

na (nä, nə), *Scottish.* —*adv.* **1.** no. **2.** not (in compounds with *could, should,* etc.): *He canna sit still.* —*conj. Obsolete.* nor. [Old English *nā*]

Na (no period), sodium (chemical element).

N.A., an abbreviation for the following:
1. a. National Academy. **b.** National Academician.
2. National Army.
3. Naval Auxiliary.
4. a. North Africa. **b.** North African.
5. a. North America. **b.** North American.

NAA (no periods), National Aeronautic Association.

NAACP (no periods) or **N.A.A.C.P.,** National Association for the Advancement of Colored People.

NAA·FI (na′fē), *n.* British armed forces post exchange. [< *N*(avy) + *A*(rmy) + (and) *A*(ir) + *F*(orce) + *I*(nstitutes)]

Na·a·man (nā′ə mən), *n.* (in the Bible) the Syrian captain whom Elisha cured of leprosy by bathing in the Jordan. II Kings 5:10-14.

naart·je (när′chə), *n.* a small South African tangerine. Also, **nartjie.** [< Afrikaans *nartjie* < Malayan (compare Tamil *nartei*)]

nab (nab), *v.t.,* **nabbed, nab·bing.** *Slang.* **1.** to catch or seize suddenly; grab. **2.** to snatch away; steal. **3.** to arrest. [variant of *nap*[4], probably < Scandinavian (compare Swedish *nappa,* Norwegian *nappe* catch, snatch)] —**Syn. 1.** grasp. **3.** apprehend.

NAB (no periods), National Association of Broadcasters.

Nab·a·tae·an or **Nab·a·te·an** (nab′ə tē′ən), *n.* **1.** a member of an ancient Arabian people whose kingdom extended from Syria in the west to the Persian Gulf in the east: *Little did the ancient . . . Nabataeans imagine that a people called Americans would one day wander among the ruins of their proud city* (Public Opinion). **2.** the language of the Nabataeans, an Aramaic dialect.

nabe (nāb), *n. U.S. Slang.* a neighborhood motion-picture theater: . . . *movie audiences at the large chain nabes* (New Yorker).

Na·bis (nȧ bē′), *n.pl.* a group of French artists of the late 1800's, led by Pierre Bonnard and Aristide Maillol, who broke away from impressionism. They stressed purer and less fluid colors and lines in art, sculpture, etc. [< French *nabis* (literally) prophets < Hebrew *nabi* prophet]

N.A.B.M., National Association of British Manufacturers.

na·bob (nā′bob), *n.* **1.** a native ruler in India under the Mogul empire; nawab. **2. a.** a very rich man, especially one who lives on a lavish scale: *The Colonel was one of the richest nabobs of his day* (New Yorker). **b.** any important person. **c.** (in the 1700's and 1800's) a person who came home from India with a fortune acquired there: *Major Gilchrist, a nabob from India* (John Galt). [Anglo-Indian < Hindustani *nabāb,* variant of *navvāb* < Arabic *nuwwāb,* plural of *nā'ib* deputy] —**Syn. 2. a.** tycoon. **b.** mogul.

na·bob·er·y (nā′bob ər ē, nā bob′ər-), *n., pl.* **-er·ies. 1.** a place frequented by nabobs. **2.** nabobism.

na·bob·ess (nā′bob is), *n.* **1.** a female nabob. **2.** the wife of a nabob.

na·bob·ish (nā′bob ish), *adj.* like a nabob.

na·bob·ism (nā′bob iz əm), *n.* great wealth and luxury.

Na·both (nā′both), *n.* (in the Bible) the owner of a vineyard that King Ahab coveted and seized after Naboth was slain on the orders of Jezebel. I Kings 21:1-19.

NACA (no periods) or **N.A.C.A.,** National Advisory Committee for Aeronautics, superseded in 1958 by the National Aeronautics and Space Administration.

na·celle (nə sel′), *n.* **1. a.** the pod-shaped covering of an engine on the wing of an airplane or on an engine of an airship: *The entire four-blade propeller (including the nacelle) of the starboard outboard engine ripped loose* (Newsweek). **b.** the part of the fuselage of a single-engine aircraft that contains the motor and compartment in which passengers are carried. **2. a.** the compartment in which the passengers are carried in airships and in airplanes with a twin tail boom, as the P-38 fighter plane of World War II. **b.** the basket or car of a balloon. [< Old French *nacelle* < Late Latin *nāvicella* (diminutive) < Latin *nāvicula* (diminutive) < *nāvis* ship]

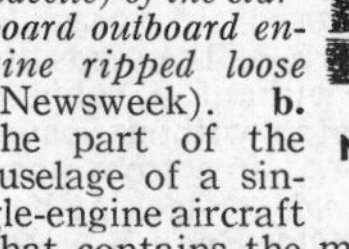

Nacelles (def. 1a) on wing of jet transport

nacht·maal (näHt′mäl′), *n. Dutch.* nagmaal.

na·cre (nā′kər), *n.* **1.** mother-of-pearl. **2.** any mollusk yielding mother-of-pearl. [< Middle French *nacre* < Italian *nacchera,* earlier *naccaro,* ultimately < Persian *nakāra* pearl oyster]

na·cré (nȧ krā′), *adj. French.* nacreous.

na·cre·ous (nā′krē əs), *adj.* **1.** of or containing nacre. **2.** like nacre; iridescent.

nacreous cloud, an iridescent cloud, resembling a cirrus, seen only in northern latitudes some 15 to 20 miles above the earth; mother-of-pearl cloud.

na·crous (nā′krəs), *adj.* nacreous.

N.A.D., National Academy of Design.

Na-Dene or **Na·dene** (nə dēn′), *n.* a group of American Indian languages, including the Athapascan family, and the languages named after the Tlingit and Haida.

NADGE (no periods), NATO Air Defense Ground Environment.

na·dir (nā′dər), *n.* **1.** the point in the heavens directly beneath the place where a person is standing; point opposite the zenith: *The two theories differed, as widely as the zenith from the nadir, in their main principles* (Hawthorne). See **zenith** for diagram. **2.** the lowest point; time of greatest misfortune or adversity: *During this second period, efforts to achieve agreement reached their nadir* (Bulletin of Atomic Scientists). [< Old French *nadir* < Arabic *naẓīr* opposite to (the zenith)]

nae (nā), *Scottish.* —*adv.* **1.** no. **2.** not. —*adj.* no.

nae·thing (nā′thing), *n., adv. Scottish.* nothing.

nae·void (nē′void), *adj.* nevoid.

nae·vus (nē′vəs), *n., pl.* **-vi** (-vī). nevus.

N. Afr., 1. North Africa. **2.** North African.

nag[1] (nag), *v.,* **nagged, nag·ging,** *n.* —*v.i.* to irritate or annoy by peevish complaints: *When Maud was sick she nagged at everybody.* —*v.t.* to find fault with (a person) all the time; scold: *A tired mother sometimes nags her children.* —*n.* **1.** the act of nagging. **2.** a person given to nagging; nagger: *She can be a terrible nag.* [compare Danish *nage* vex, Icelandic *nagga* grumble] —**nag′ger,** *n.*
—**Syn.** *v.t.* torment.

nag[2] (nag), *n.* **1.** an inferior horse: *The ancient nag, Beauty, broke into her idea of a trot* (Atlantic). **2.** *Informal.* a horse: *Bringing his nags up to the inn door in very pretty style, he gave the reins to his servant* (Charles J. Lever). **3.** a small riding horse or pony: *My Ralph, whom I left training his little Galloway nag . . . may one day attain thy years* (Scott). [Middle English *nagge* small horse, pony; origin unknown]

na·ga (nä′gə), *n.* a mythological water creature of India associated with serpents, and regarded as a spirit of peace and fertility. [< Sanskrit *nāga*]

Na·ga (nä′gə), *n.* **1.** a member of a warlike Mongoloid tribe living in Assam, a state in northeastern India: *Naga terrorists kidnaped seven pro-government villagers in broad daylight* (Time). **2.** a group of Indo-Chinese languages, chiefly spoken in eastern Assam.

na·gai·ka (nä gī′kä), *n. Russian.* a whip: *The Cossacks . . . used to run down street mobs with nagaika and saber in czarist days* (Time).

na·ga·na (nə gä′nə), *n.* a serious disease of cattle, horses, camels, and other animals, common in Africa, and caused by a trypanosome transmitted by the tsetse fly: *Nagana pursues a much slower course in cattle than in horses* (Nature). [< Zulu *nakane*]

nag·ging (nag′ing), *adj.* disturbing; bothersome; vexatious: *a vague, nagging suspicion. Canada's nagging problem of unemployment . . .* (New York Times). —**nag′ging·ly,** *adv.*

nag·gy (nag′ē), *adj.,* **-gi·er, -gi·est. 1.** inclined to nag; faultfinding. **2.** *British Dialect.* ill-natured; bad-tempered.

nag·maal (naH′mäl′), *n. Afrikaans.* the service of the Lord's Supper, administered in the Dutch Reformed Churches.

na·gor (nā′gôr), *n.* an antelope of western Africa, having the horns curved forward.

Nah., Nahum (a book of the Old Testament).

N.A.H.B. or **NAHB** (no periods), National Association of Home Builders.

Na·hua (nä′wə), *n., adj.* Nahuatl.

Na·hua·tl (nä′wä təl), *n.* any of a group of languages spoken by the Aztecs, Toltecs, and other American Indian tribes of central Mexico and parts of Central America. —*adj.* of or having to do with this group of languages.

Na·hua·tlan (nä′wä tlən), *adj., n.* Nahuatl.

Na·hum (nā′əm, -həm), *n.* **1.** a Hebrew prophet of about 600 B.C. **2.** a book of the Old Testament containing his prophecies. *Abbr.:* Nah.

N.A.I.A., National Association of Intercollegiate Athletics.

nai·ad (nā′ad, nī′-), *n., pl.* **-ads, -a·des** (-ə dēz). **1.** Also, **Naiad.** *Greek and Roman Mythology.* one of a number of beautiful young nymphs guarding a stream or spring and giving life to it: *The Naiad 'mid her reeds Press'd her cold finger closer to her lips* (Keats). **2.** a girl swimmer. **3.** any larva of water insects that changes directly to the adult stage, as the larva of the dragonfly. [< Latin *Nāias, -adis* < Greek *Naïás, -adós,* related to *nân* to flow]

na·iant (nā′ənt), *adj. Heraldry.* represented as swimming: *Beasts and monsters are passant, gardant, regardant, and statant, and fish are sometimes naiant* (New York Times). [< Old French *naiant,* present participle of *naier* to swim < Latin *natāre;* see NATANT]

na·ïf (nä ēf′), *adj.* naïve: *The naïf . . . vexation of the Irish Nationalist papers* (Saturday Review). —*n.* a naïve person; naïve: *He was no naïf piping native wood notes wild* (Harper's). [< French *naïf,* masculine of *naïve* naive]
➔ See **naïve** for usage note.

na·ik (nä′ik), *n.* in India: **1. a.** a title of nobility or authority. **b.** (formerly) a lord, prince, or governor. **2. a.** an army corporal: *A naik was cutting scrub with his kukri in order to clear a field of fire for his machine gun* (Atlantic). **b.** (formerly) a military officer of native troops under the British. [< Hindustani *nāik* < Sanskrit *nāyaka* leader]

nail (nāl), *n.* **1.** a slender piece of metal to be hammered into or through wood to hold separate pieces together or be used as a peg. Nails are usually made of steel having a point at one end and a flat or rounded head at the other end. **2.** a thin, horny plate on the upper side of the end of a finger or toe in man or a claw or talon in other vertebrates. Nails are a modified epidermis. **3.** an old measure of length for cloth, equal to 2¼ inches or 1/16 yard.

hit the nail on the head, to say or do something just right; guess or understand correctly: *Michael Harrington hit the nail on the head. There are a lot of Americans who aren't really living; they are just existing* (Clement Martin).

nail in one's coffin, something that helps to put one in his coffin or hasten his death: *Every minute he lies there is a nail in his coffin* (Scott).

on the nail, at once; immediately; without delay: *Why should a man be penalized for paying on the nail for his mistakes?* (Harper's).

—*v.t.* **1.** to fasten, close, or make secure with a nail or nails: *to nail shingles on a house, to nail a bracket to the wall, to nail a house together.* **2.** to hold or keep fixed: *Nail him down to what he promised.* **3.** *Informal.* **a.** to secure by prompt action; catch; seize: *He insisted on nailing me for dinner before he would leave me* (Thackeray). **b.** to steal: *lubbers as couldn't keep what they got, and want to nail what is another's* (Robert Louis Stevenson). **4.** *Informal.* to detect and expose (a lie, etc.): *What did Baron really think of the celebrities who made his world? Some were his friends. Some he nailed as phonies* (Scottish Sunday Express).

nail up, a. to fasten: *to nail up a picture on the wall.* **b.** to close: *to nail up a crate before shipping.*

[Old English *nægel*]

nail·a·ble (nā′lə bəl), *adj.* that can be nailed: *His use of "nailable steel" frames allowed the erection of frames for 59 buildings in 59 days* (New York Times).

nail-bit·ing (nāl′bī′ting), *n.* the habit of biting one's fingernails, especially when nervous, tense, restless, etc.: *Nail-biting may be his reaction to . . . too much scolding, punishment, or other expression of Mother's or Father's disapproval* (Sidonie M. Gruenberg). —*adj. Informal.* causing nervousness or anxiety: *It was a nail-biting finish* (London Times).

nail·er (nā′lər), *n.* **1.** a person or thing that nails. **2.** a maker of or dealer in nails.

nail·er·y (nā′lər ē), *n., pl.* **-er·ies.** a shop where nails are made.

nail file, a small, flat file used to file down, trim, and shape fingernails.

nail·head (nāl′hed′), *n.* **1.** the head or enlarged end of a nail. **2.** an ornament (usually one of a number) resembling the head of a nail driven in.

nail polish, a kind of enamel, usually tinted, used by women or girls to smooth and give gloss to the fingernails or toenails.

nail·set (nāl′set′), *n.* a tool for driving nails beneath the surface.

nain·sook (nān′sůk, nan′-), *n.* a soft, fine white cotton cloth with a shiny finish, sometimes dyed, used for underwear, dresses, and shirts. [< Hindustani *nainsukh* < *nain* eye + *sukh* pleasure]

nais·sance (nā′səns), *n.* origin; birth: *Why then this sudden renaissance, or, more properly, naissance of an art?* (New York Times). [< French *naissance* birth; see RENAISSANCE]

na·ïve or **na·ive** (nä ēv′), *adj.* simple in nature; like a child; not sophisticated; artless: *. . . this naïve simple creature, with his straightforward and friendly eyes so eager to believe appearances* (Arnold Bennett). —*n.* a naïve person: *Compared with the other partygoers, he was a complete naïve.* [< French *naïve,* feminine of *naïf* (originally) native, natural < Latin *nātīvus.* Doublet of NATIVE.] —**na·ïve′ly** or **na·ive′ly,** *adv.* —**na·ïve′ness** or **na·ive′ness,** *n.*

—**Syn.** *adj.* unaffected, natural, open, sincere.

➔ **Naïve,** although originally the feminine form of the French adjective, is used in English without reference to gender: *a naïve girl, a naïve boy.* The use of the masculine form *naïf* is now rare in English and somewhat affected.

na·ïve·té or **na·ive·te** (nä ēv′tā′), *n.* **1.** the quality of being naïve; unspoiled freshness; artlessness: *Mrs. M'Catchley was amused and pleased with his freshness and naïveté* (Edward G. Bulwer-Lytton). **2.** a naïve action, remark, etc.: *Applied with wide-eyed naivete in one instance, they may appear smartly sophisticated in another* (Saturday Review). [< Old French *naïvete* < Latin *nātīvitās* quality of being native. Doublet of NATIVITY.]

na·ive·ty or **na·ïve·ty** (nä ēv′tē), *n., pl.* **-ties.** *British.* naïveté: *They endured naivety and ignorance with almost saintly patience* (Manchester Guardian).

na·ked (nā′kid), *adj.* **1. a.** with no clothes on; bare: *naked shoulders. A barefoot boy has naked feet. They were both naked . . . and were not ashamed* (Genesis 2:25). **b.** lacking adequate or sufficient clothing: *Poor naked wretches . . . How shall . . . Your loop'd and window'd raggedness, defend you From seasons such as these?* (Shakespeare). **2.** not covered; stripped: *naked fields, a naked room.* **3. a.** not protected; exposed to attack, injury, etc.; defenseless: *. . . left me naked to mine enemies* (Shakespeare). **b.** exposed and ready for use; unsheathed: *a naked dagger.* **c.** exposed to view; plainly revealed; uncovered: *a naked nerve, a naked threat.* **4.** without addition of anything else; unadorned; plain: *the naked truth, a naked outline of facts.* **5.** *Law.* not supported or confirmed: *a naked confession.* **6.** *Botany.* **a.** (of seeds) not enclosed in a case or ovary; having no pericarp, as the seeds of a pine. **b.** (of flowers) without a calyx or corolla. **c.** (of stalks, etc.) without leaves. **d.** (of stalks, leaves, etc.) free from hairs; smooth; glabrous. **7.** *Zoology.* lacking hair, feathers, shell, etc. [Old English *nacod*] —**na′ked·ly,** *adv.* —**na′ked·ness,** *n.* —**Syn. 1. a.** nude, unclothed, undressed. See **bare. 2.** uncovered. **3. a.** unprotected. **4.** simple.

naked eye, the eye without the help of a glass, telescope, or microscope; unaided eye: *Beside those meteors visible to the naked eye, there are a great many fainter ones known as telescopic meteors* (Wasley S. Krogdahl).

na·ker (nā′kər), *n. Archaic.* a kettledrum: *the deep and hollow clang of the nakers* (Scott). [Middle English *naker* < Old French *nacre, naquere* < Arabic *nuqqārīya*]

Nal·line (nal′ēn), *n. Trademark.* nalorphine.

nal·or·phine (nal ôr′fēn, -fin), *n.* a drug resembling morphine, used to test for narcotic addiction and in the treatment of morphine poisoning. *Formula:* $C_{19}H_{21}NO_3$ [< *N-al*(lylnorm)*orphine,* the chemical name]

N. Am., 1. North America. **2.** North American.

NAM (no periods) or **N.A.M.,** National Association of Manufacturers.

Na·ma (nä′mä), *n.* Namaqua.

nam·a·ble (nā′mə bəl), *adj.* **1.** that can be named. **2.** memorable. Also, **nameable.**

Na·ma·qua (nə mä′kwə), *n.* a Hottentot people of Namaqualand, South Africa.

na·mas·te (nä mäs′te), *n.* (in India) a way of greeting by pressing together the palms of one's hands. [< Hindi *namaste* < *namas* bow]

nam·ay·cush (nam′i kush, -ā-), *n.* a large trout of the lakes of the northern United States and Canada; lake trout. [< Algonkian (perhaps Ojibwa) *namegos*]

Namaycush
(about 1½ ft. long)

na·maz (nə mäz′), *n.* the prescribed Moslem religious service or prayer, recited five times daily. [< Persian *namāz*]

nam·by-pam·by (nam′bē pam′bē), *adj., n., pl.* **-bies.** —*adj.* weakly simple or sentimental; insipid: *a namby-pamby excuse. She was a namby-pamby, milk-and-water, affected creature* (Thackeray). —*n.* **1.** namby-pamby talk or writing. **2.** a namby-pamby person. [rhyming alteration of *Ambrose* Philips, 1674-1749, a British poet satirized by Alexander Pope]

nam·by-pam·by·ism (nam′bē pam′bē izəm), *n.* **1.** weak or insipid sentimentality. **2.** an instance of this: *. . . the namby-pambyisms of the "Book of Beauty"* (Tait's Magazine).

name (nām), *n., adj., v.,* **named, nam·ing.** —*n.* **1.** the word or words by which a person, animal, place, or thing is spoken of or to: *Our son's name is Jack. What's in a name? That which we call a rose By any other name would smell as sweet* (Shakespeare). **2.** a word or words applied descriptively; appellation, title, or epithet: *Thus he bore without abuse The grand old name of gentleman* (Tennyson). **3.** a title or term as distinguished from fact: *What is friendship but a name?* (Oliver Goldsmith). *Liberty had become only a name.* **4.** persons grouped under one name; family; clan; tribe: *hostile to the name of Campbell* (Macaulay). **5. a.** reputation; fame: *to get a bad name, to make a name for oneself.* **b.** a famous or well-known person: *Sir William Osler was one of the great names in medicine.*

by name, a. the name of: *He knows all his customers by name.* **b.** by hearing about but not actually having met: *We all know George Washington by name.* **c.** by calling his or her name: *He mentioned the boy with red hair by name.*

call one names, to make fun of or ridicule, especially by giving an unfriendly name to or by swearing at or cursing: *You can call me names, but I won't change my mind one bit.*

in name only, supposed to be, but not really so: *a king in name only.*

in the name of, a. with appeal to the name of: *What, in the name of goodness, do you come hither to teach?* (Benjamin Jowett). **b.** acting for; with the authority or approval of: *I bought it in my sister's name.*

name names, to identify a person or persons by name, especially in incriminatory circumstances: *Six New York City teachers . . . were suspended because they refused to "name names" in an investigation of Communist influence* (New York Times).

take a name in vain, to use a name, properly God's name, and hence any other entitled to respect, lightly or irreverently: *Thou shalt not take the name of the Lord thy God in vain* (Exodus 20:7).

to one's name, belonging to one: *not a dollar to his name.*

—*adj.* well-known: *a name brand, a name designer. There are scarcely a dozen name musicians in the U.S. who are both able and willing to play avant-garde music* (Time).

—*v.t.* **1.** to give a name or names to: *The Hudson river is named after the English explorer Henry Hudson.* **2.** to call by name; mention by name: *Three persons were named in the report.* **3.** to give the right name for: *Can you name these flowers?* **4.** to mention; speak of; state: *to name several reasons.* **5.** to specify; fix: *to name a price.* **6.** to choose for some duty or office; nominate: *John was named for class president.* **7.** (of the Speaker of the British House of Commons) to indicate (a member) as guilty of disorderly conduct.

[Old English *nama*]

—**Syn.** *n.* **2. Name, title** mean what someone or something is called. **Name** is used of any descriptive or characterizing term applied to a person or thing: *"The Corn State" is a name for Iowa.* **Title** is used of a descriptive or characterizing term given to a book, song, play, etc., or applied to a person as a sign of honor, rank, office, or occupation: *His title is Secretary.* **5. a.** renown, note. *-v.t.* **1.** denominate, entitle, call. **2.** designate. **6.** appoint, select.

name·a·ble (nā′mə bəl), *adj.* namable.

name·board (nām′bôrd′, -bōrd′), *n.* **1. a.** a board on which the name of a ship is painted. **b.** in the absence of a board, the place on the hull where the name is painted. **2.** any signboard with the name of a station, shop, etc.: *Nameboards, carefully collected relics from closed stations, have been placed all around, telling their own sad tales* (London Times).

name-call·ing (nām′kô′ling), *n.* the act of giving a bad name to; an attacking the name of; defamation: *Name-calling—giving an idea a bad label—is used to make us reject and condemn the idea without examining the evidence* (Ogburn and Nimkoff).

name day, 1. the day sacred to the saint whose name a person bears: *The men were celebrating the Feast of St. Nicholas, the*

Czar's name day, with banquets and vodka (New Yorker). **2.** the day on which a child is named. —**name′-day′,** *adj.*

name-drop (nām′drop′), *v.i.*, **-dropped, -drop·ping.** to practice name-dropping: *This is no ordinary coffee service. Let's name-drop and you'll know why: George II period shapes for the coffee pot. . . . Elegant Chippendale design tray* (New Yorker). [back formation < *name-dropping*]

name-drop·per (nām′drop′ər), *n.* a person who practices name-dropping.

name-drop·ping (nām′drop′ing), *n.* the act of using a well-known person's name in conversation and implying acquaintance with him to make one seem important: *He mentioned associations with Russian leaders so numerous and so mighty in power as to expose himself to reproaches for name-dropping* (Harper's).

name·less (nām′lis), *adj.* **1.** having no name; unnamed: *a nameless stranger, a nameless grave.* **2.** that cannot be named or described: *a profound, nameless longing.* **3.** not fit to be mentioned: *nameless vices.* **4.** not named: *a nameless author.* **5.** unknown to fame; obscure: *Nameless in dark oblivion let them dwell* (Milton). **6.** having no legitimate name; not entitled to a father's name; illegitimate. —**name′less·ly,** *adv.* —**name′less·ness,** *n.* —**Syn. 3.** unmentionable. **4.** anonymous. **5.** inglorious.

name·ly (nām′lē), *adv.* that is to say; to wit: *This bridge connects two cities—namely, St. Paul and Minneapolis.*

name part, an important part in a play or motion picture, as that of the principal character, often having the same name as the title of the work: *He was asked to play the name part in Sherwood's "Abe Lincoln in Illinois."*

name·plate (nām′plāt′), *n.* a sign bearing the name of an occupant, contributor, manufacturer, etc., and usually mounted, as on a door or building: *They had painted the doors and put up brass nameplates.*

nam·er (nā′mər), *n.* **1.** a person who gives a name to anything. **2.** a person who calls by name.

name·sake (nām′sāk′), *n.* a person or thing having the same name as another, especially one named after another: *Theodore, namesake of President Theodore Roosevelt.* [perhaps < phrase (*the*) *name*(*'s*) *sake*]

name tape, 1. a cloth tape with a person's name woven or printed on it repeatedly, used for attaching each piece with a name on it on personal garments or other belongings for identification. **2.** a piece cut off this tape for attachment to a garment.

nan·a (nan′ə), *n.* a woman employed to care for young children; nanny. [probably alteration of *nanny*]

nance (nans), *n. Slang.* an effeminate man; a sissy. [< *Nance,* short form of *Nancy,* a feminine name]

Nan·di (nan′dē), *n., pl.* **-di** or **-dis. 1.** a member of an East African people living in western Kenya. **2.** the Sudanic language of this people.

Nandi bear, a ferocious animal believed by the natives to roam the jungles of East Africa. It is generally thought to be the spotted hyena. *It is when he gets down to cases—. . . the abominable snowman . . . and the East African Nandi bear—that Dr. Heuvelmans becomes less persuasive* (Manchester Guardian).

nan·di·na (nan dī′nə, -dē′-), *n.* an evergreen shrub of the barberry family, native to China and Japan. It reaches a height of about eight feet and is grown for its loose clusters of bright red berries and its thick foliage. [< New Latin *Nandina* the genus name < its Japanese name]

nan·dine (nan′din), *n.* a small, spotted, ring-tailed, carnivorous animal closely related to the Asiatic palm cats. [< New Latin *Nandinia* the genus name < a native name]

nan·du (nan′dü), *n.* a rhea. [< Tupi-Guarani (Brazil) *ñandú*]

ñan·du·ti (nyän′də tē′), *n.* a fine lace of intricate design made in Paraguay. [< Guarani *ñanduti* spider web]

nane (nān), *pron., adv. Scottish.* none[1].

na·nism (nā′niz əm), *n.* (in animals and plants) abnormally small size or stature; dwarfishness. [< French *nanisme* < Latin *nānus* dwarf (< Greek *nânos*) + French *-isme* -ism]

nan·keen or **nan·kin** (nan kēn′), *n.* **1. a.** a sturdy, yellow or buff cloth originally made at Nanking, China, from a yellow variety of cotton. **b.** a similar fabric made from ordinary cotton dyed that color. **2.** a pale-buff color.

nankeens, trousers made of nankeen: *You had my nankeens on . . ., and had fallen into a thicket of thistles* (Edward G. Bulwer-Lytton).

[< *Nankin,* early variant of *Nanking,* a city in China]

Nan·keen (nan kēn′), *n.* a fine Chinese porcelain, typically white with blue decorations.

nan·ny (nan′ē), *n., pl.* **-nies,** *v.t.*, **-nied, -ny·ing.** *British.* —*n.* a woman who takes care of the young children of a particular family; child's nurse: *Mistress Nellie cross-examined her on the subject of nannies* (H. Allen Smith). —*v.t. Informal.* to act like a nanny toward; treat as a child: *We don't want to nanny the firms taking part* (London Times). [probably < *Nanny,* a feminine name]

nanny goat, *Informal.* a female goat. [< *Nanny,* a feminine name + *goat*]

nan·ny·ish (nan′ē ish), *adj.* **1.** like a nanny. **2.** old-fashioned; prudish: *But people are much more robust than the nannyish fuss about undermining their faith implies* (Manchester Guardian Weekly).

nano-, *combining form.* **1.** a billionth (used by the National Bureau of Standards): *Nano-second = a billionth of a second.* **2.** very small; dwarf: *Nanoplankton = a very small plankton.* [< Greek *nânos* dwarf]

na·no·plank·ton (nā′nə plangk′tən, nan′ə-), *n.* a very small plankton.

na·no·sec·ond (nā′nə sek′ənd, nan′ə-), *n.* a billionth of a second.

Nantes (nants; *French* näNt), *n.* **Edict of,** an edict granting religious toleration to French Protestants (Huguenots), signed in 1598 by Henry IV. It was revoked in 1685.

Na·o·mi (nā ō′mē, nā′ō-), *n.* (in the Bible) Ruth's mother-in-law, a native of Judah, from whom Ruth refused to part. Ruth 1: 14-18.

na·os (nā′os), *n., pl.* **-oi** (-oi). **1.** a temple. **2.** the central chamber of an ancient Greek or Roman temple. [< Greek *nāós* temple]

nap[1] (nap), *n., v.*, **napped, nap·ping.** —*n.* a short sleep, especially one taken during the day; doze; snooze: *Baby takes a nap after his dinner.* [< verb]

—*v.i.* **1.** to take a short sleep: *Grandfather naps in his armchair.* **2.** to be off guard; be unprepared: *His question caught me napping.* [Old English *hnappian* doze]

nap[2] (nap), *n., v.*, **napped, nap·ping.** —*n.* **1.** the soft, short, woolly threads or hairs on the surface of cloth: *the nap on velvet or flannelette.* **2.** a soft, downy surface or coating, as on plants. —*v.t.* to raise a nap on (a fabric). [< Middle Dutch *noppe*]

➔ See **pile**[3] for usage note.

nap[3] (nap), *n., v.t.*, **napped, nap·ping.** —*n.* **1.** napoleon (a card game). **2.** napoleon (a coin). **3.** *British.* a tip that a particular horse is certain to win a race: *Our "Outsider's" nap of Docker for the Hainton Stakes . . .* (Starting Price).

—*v.t. British.* to recommend (a horse) as a certain winner: *Acrophel, as yet unbeaten over hurdles, . . . is napped to win Div. I of the Coronation Hurdle from Shadforth and Penvulgo, who ran well* (Daily Telegraph).

nap[4] (nap), *v.t.*, **napped, nap·ping.** *Slang.* to seize; catch; nab; steal. [see NAB]

na·palm (nā′päm, -pälm), *n.* **1.** a chemical substance used to thicken gasoline for use in certain military weapons, especially incendiary bombs. It is an aluminum soap of naphthenic, oleic, and palmitic acids. **2.** the thickened gasoline. —*v.t., v.i.* to attack with napalm. [< *na*(phthenic) and *palm*(itic) acids (the salts of these acids are used in its manufacture)]

nape (nāp, nap), *n.* the back of the neck. [Middle English *nape;* origin uncertain]

➔ **Nape, scruff.** The terms differ in that *scruff,* unlike *nape,* may be used with reference to animals: *He seized the dog by the scruff of the neck and flung him aside.* Both words are followed by the redundant, but idiomatically necessary, phrase "of the neck."

na·per·y (nā′pər ē, nāp′rē), *n.* tablecloths, napkins, and doilies: *There were flowers and cones of napery on the tables by their windows* (New Yorker). [< Old French *naperie* < *nape;* see NAPKIN]

Naph·ta·li (naf′tə lī), *n.* in the Bible: **1.** the sixth of Jacob's twelve sons. Genesis 30: 7-8. **2.** the tribe of Israel that claimed him as ancestor.

naph·tha (nap′thə, naf′-), *n.* **1.** a liquid distilled from petroleum, coal tar, or natural gas, used chiefly as fuel and to take spots from clothing; petroleum naphtha. Naphthas, which are also used as solvents and in making varnishes, are highly inflammable, consisting of various mixtures of easily vaporized hydrocarbons. **2.** *Obsolete.* petroleum. [< Latin *naphtha* < Greek *náphtha* (originally) an inflammable liquid issuing from the earth < Avestan *napta*]

naph·tha·lene or **naph·tha·line** (naf′thə lēn, nap′-), *n.* a white crystalline hydrocarbon distilled from coal tar or petroleum, used in making moth balls, dyes, explosives, lubricants, etc: *As the number of carbon atoms in the molecule reached 10, two benzene rings were fused, sharing two of the carbons between them to form naphthalene* (Scientific American). *Formula:* $C_{10}H_8$ [< *naphtha* + *al*(cohol) + *-ene, -ine*[2]]

naph·tha·lin (naf′thə lin, nap′-), *n.* naphthalene.

naph·thene (naf′thēn, nap′-), *n.* any of a group of saturated ring hydrocarbons having the general formula C_nH_{2n}, occurring in certain petroleums, as those in Baku and California: *Hydrocarbons with branched-chain molecular structure were apparently less temperature sensitive than paraffins or naphthenes* (Science News Letter). [< *naphth*(a) + *-ene*]

naph·the·nic acid (naf thē′nik, -then′ik; nap-), any of various oily liquids obtained from petroleum, used in certain soaps, paint driers, and fungicides.

naph·thol (naf′thōl, -thol; nap′-), *n.* **1.** either of two isomeric crystalline substances occurring in coal tar, and derived from naphthalene by the substitution of a hydroxyl (-OH) radical for a hydrogen atom. Both are used in making dyes and as antiseptics. *Formula:* $C_{10}H_7OH$ **2.** any of several derivatives of naphthalene that contain a hydroxyl (-OH) radical. [< *naphth*(alene) + *-ol*[2]]

naph·tol (naf′tōl, -tol; nap′-), *n.* naphthol.

Na·pier·i·an logarithms (nə pir′ē ən), **1.** natural logarithms. **2.** an early system of logarithms which formed the basis for natural and common logarithms. [< John *Napier,* 1550-1617, a Scottish mathematician, who invented the system + *-ian*]

na·pi·form (nā′pə fôrm), *adj.* shaped like a turnip; large and round above and slender below: *a napiform root.* [< Latin *nāpus* turnip (< Greek *nâpy* mustard) + English *-form*]

nap·kin (nap′kin), *n.* **1.** a piece of soft cloth or paper used at meals to wipe the lips and hands and to protect the clothes. **2.** any similar piece, such as a small towel: *cocktail napkin.* **3.** *British.* a baby's diaper. **4.** *Archaic.* a handkerchief: *. . . and the half shirt is two napkins tack'd together and thrown over the shoulders* (Shakespeare). [Middle English *napekyn* (diminutive) < Old French *nape* cloth < Latin *mappa* cloth] —**Syn. 1.** serviette.

napkin ring, a ring of silver, wood, etc., for holding a rolled-up table napkin.

nap·less (nap′lis), *adj.* **1.** having no nap on the surface. **2.** threadbare: *An old black coat, napless, not from frequent brushing, but from continual wear* (J.T. Hewlett).

na·po·le·on (nə pō′lē ən, -pōl′yən), *n.* **1.** a pastry with a cream or jam filling, usually oblong with the filling in layers. **2. a.** a card game similar to euchre. **b.** the highest bid in this game, proposing to win all five tricks of a hand. **3.** a former French gold coin, worth 20 francs. [< French *napoléon* < *Napoleon I,* Emperor of France, 1804-1815]

Na·po·le·on·a·na (nə pō′lē ə nā′nə, -nan′ə, -nā′nə), *n.pl.* writings, articles, etc., associated with Napoleon I of France; Napoleonic relics. [< *Napoleon* + *-ana*]

Na·po·le·on·ic (nə pō′lē on′ik), *adj.* of or having to do with Napoleon I, or less often, Napoleon III: *Napoleonic legend. His patience was as coldly Napoleonic as his manner* (Geoffrey Household). —**Na·po′le·on′i·cal·ly,** *adv.*

Napoleonic Code, Code Napoléon: *The Napoleonic Code . . . is the basis for law in France and seven other NATO countries* (New York Times).

napped (napt), *adj.* having a nap: *napped cloth.*

nap·per[1] (nap′ər), *n.* a person who takes naps. [< *nap*[1] + *-er*[1]]

nap·per[2] (nap′ər), *n.* a person or machine that raises a nap on cloth. [< *nap*[2] + *-er*[1]]

nap·pie (nap′ē), *n.* a nappy[2].

nap·pi·ness (nap′ē nis), *n.* the quality of having a nap, especially a thick nap, as on cloth.

nap·py[1] (nap′ē), *adj.*, **-pi·er, -pi·est,** *n. Scottish.* —*adj.* **1.** foaming. **2.** heady; strong. **3.** tipsy. —*n.* ale; liquor. [perhaps < *nappy*[3] in sense of "heady, foaming"]

nap·py[2] (nap′ē), *n., pl.* **-pies.** *U.S.* a small, round, flat-bottomed dish, often of glass, with sloping sides. Also, **nappie.** [origin uncertain. Compare obsolete *nap* bowl, Old English *hnæpp.*]

nap·py[3] (nap′ē), *adj.*, **-pi·er, -pi·est.** napped; downy; shaggy. [alteration (probably influenced by *nap*[2] + *-y*[1]) of earlier *noppy,* perhaps < Middle Dutch *noppich*]

nap·py[4] (nap′ē), *n., pl.* **-pies.** *British Informal.* diaper: *That bikini, I made it out of a baby's nappy, and it won £300 in prize money* (Evening Standard). [< *nap(kin)* + *-y*[2]]

nap·ra·path (nap′rə path), *n.* a practitioner of naprapathy.

nap·ra·path·ic (nap′rə path′ik), *adj.* of or having to do with naprapathy.

na·prap·a·thy (nə prap′ə thē), *n.* a method of treating disease by manipulating certain ligaments or connective tissues. [< Czech *napraviti* to correct + English *-pathy*]

na·pu (nä′pü), *n.* any of various kinds of chevrotain. [< Malay *napū*]

nar·ce·in (när′sē in), *n.* narceine.

nar·ce·ine (när′sē ēn, -in), *n.* a bitter, white, crystalline alkaloid obtained from opium, formerly used as a substitute for morphine. *Formula:* $C_{23}H_{27}NO_8.3H_2O$ [< French *narcéine* < Greek *nárkē* numbness + French *-ine* -ine[2]]

nar·cism (när′siz əm), *n.* narcissism.

nar·cis·sism (när sis′iz əm), *n.* **1.** excessive love of oneself. **2.** *Psychoanalysis.* gratification manifested in admiration and love of oneself, usually associated with infantile behavior and regarded as abnormally regressive in adults: *In my opinion, narcissism is the libidinal complement of egoism* (Sigmund Freud). [< German *Narzissmus* < *Narcissus*]

nar·cis·sist (när sis′ist), *n.* a person affected with narcissism: *A narcissist, ... inspired by the homage paid to great painters, may become an art student* (B. Russell).

nar·cis·sis·tic (när′si sis′tik), *adj.* **1.** of or having to do with narcissism: *I was just trying to make clear to a patient her excessive ambition, arising from narcissistic fixation* (Ernest Jones). **2.** affected with narcissism: *The child comes to admire himself, that is, becomes exhibitionistic and narcissistic* (Ogburn and Nimkoff). —**nar′cis·sis′ti·cal·ly,** *adv.*

nar·cis·sus (när sis′əs), *n., pl.* **-cis·sus·es, -cis·si** (-sis′ī). **1.** any of a group of plants of the amaryllis family, having long slender leaves, and a yellow or white flower with a crownlike tube sometimes edged with crimson or yellow in the center of the flower. It grows from a bulb and usually blooms in the spring. The daffodil and jonquil belong to this group. **2.** the flower of any of these plants. [< Latin *narcissus* < Greek *nárkissos,* associated by folk etymology (from the sedative effect of the plant) with Greek *nárkē* numbness]

Narcissus (def. 1) (jonquil)

➔ In spoken English an unchanged plural, *narcissus,* is often used, presumably to avoid the excessive sibilance of *narcissuses.*

Nar·cis·sus (när sis′əs), *n. Greek Mythology.* a beautiful youth who caused Echo to die by failing to return her love, and whom Nemesis then caused to fall in love with his own reflection in a spring. He pined away and was changed into the flower narcissus.

nar·cist (när′sist), *n.* narcissist.

nar·co·a·nal·y·sis (när′kō ə nal′ə sis), *n.* psychiatric analysis using narcosynthesis: *Narcoanalysis proved useful to physicians charged with the care of large numbers of emotional casualties in the armed forces of the U.S. during World War II and the Korean War* (Scientific American).

nar·co·lep·sy (när′kə lep′sē), *n.* **1.** abnormal sleepiness. **2.** a form of epilepsy accompanied by a brief unconsciousness; petit mal. [< Greek *nárkē* numbness + *lêpsis* a seizure]

nar·co·lep·tic (när′kə lep′tik), *adj.* affected by narcolepsy.

nar·co·ma (när kō′mə), *n., pl.* **-mas, -ma·ta** (-mə tə). stupor produced by narcotics: *Drugs such as marijuana, heroin, etc., can produce a deep and prolonged narcoma.* [< New Latin *narcoma*]

nar·co·ma·ni·a (när′kə mā′nē ə), *n.* a craving for a narcotic drug. [< *narco*(tic) + *mania*]

nar·co·ma·ni·ac (när′kə mā′nē ak), *n.* a person who craves for a narcotic drug.

nar·co·sis (när kō′sis), *n.* **1.** profound stupor; insensibility: *General anesthesia causes narcosis.* **2.** the action or effect of narcotics. [< New Latin *narcosis* < Greek *nárkōsis* < *narkoûn* to benumb < *nárkē* numbness]

nar·co·syn·the·sis (när′kō sin′thə sis), *n.* the treatment of certain psychological disorders by guiding a person toward the resolution of emotional conflicts expressed while under the influence of a hypnotic drug: *... a short psychiatric exploration of the patient's unconscious mind by narcosynthesis* (Marguerite Clark). [< *narco*(tics) + *synthesis*]

nar·cot·ic (när kot′ik), *n.* **1.** any drug that produces dullness, drowsiness, sleep, or an insensible condition, and lessens pain by dulling the nerves. Opium and drugs made from it are powerful narcotics. Narcotics are used in medicine in controlled doses, but taken in excess cause systemic poisoning, delirium, paralysis, or even death. **2.** a person who has narcotism; drug addict. **3.** anything that numbs, soothes, or dulls: *The sad, mechanic exercise Like dull narcotics, numbing pain* (Tennyson).

—*adj.* **1.** having the properties and effects of a narcotic: *He ... habitually fell asleep at that horrible council-board ... while the other murderers had found their work less narcotic* (John L. Motley). **2.** of or having to do with narcotics or their use. **3.** having to do with or intended for use in the treatment of drug addicts.

[< Greek *narkōtikós* < *narkoûn* to benumb < *nárkē* numbness]

—**Syn.** *n.* **1.** opiate, anodyne.

nar·cot·i·cal·ly (när kot′ ə klē), *adv.* by means of a narcotic.

nar·co·tine (när′kə tēn, -tin), *n.* a crystalline alkaloid of opium, formerly thought to be a narcotic. It is used to relieve coughs. *Formula:* $C_{22}H_{23}NO_7$ [< *narcot*(ic) + *-ine*[2]]

nar·co·tism (när′kə tiz əm), *n.* **1.** addiction to the use of narcotics. **2.** the effects produced by narcotics; narcosis. **3.** abnormal sleepiness; narcolepsy. **4.** anything having the influence of a narcotic.

nar·co·ti·za·tion (när′kə tə zā′shən), *n.* **1.** the act of narcotizing. **2.** the state induced by narcotic poisoning.

nar·co·tize (när′kə tīz), *v.t.*, **-tized, -tiz·ing.** **1.** to subject to the action of a narcotic; stupefy. **2.** to dull; deaden: *How much better is the restlessness of a noble ambition than the narcotized stupor of club life* (Oliver Wendell Holmes).

nard (närd), *n.* **1.** spikenard, an aromatic plant. **2.** the ointment which the ancients prepared from this plant. [< Old French *narde,* learned borrowing from Latin *nardus* < Greek *nárdos,* ultimately < Sanskrit *naladā*]

nar·doo (när dü′), *n.* an aquatic, cloverlike fern of Australia whose sporocarps are ground and eaten by the aborigines. [< the native name]

nar·es (nãr′ēz), *n. pl. of* **naris.** the nostrils; nasal passages. [< Latin *nārēs,* plural of *nāris* a nostril]

nar·ghi·le or **nar·gi·le** (när′gə lē), *n.* an oriental tobacco pipe in which the smoke is drawn through water; hookah. See picture under **hookah.** [< French *narghilé,* ultimately < Persian *nārgīleh* < *nārgīl* coconut (the original material of the tobacco holder)]

nar·gi·leh (när′gə le), *n.* narghile.

nar·i·al (nãr′ē əl), *adj.* of or having to do with the nostrils (nares). [< Latin *nāris* nostril + English *-al*]

nar·is (nãr′is), *n., pl.* **nar·es.** a nostril; a nasal passage. [< Latin *nāris*]

nark[1] (närk), *British Slang.* —*n.* a police spy; informer. —*v.i.* to turn spy or informer. [perhaps < Romany *nāk* nose < Sanskrit *nāsikā*]

nark[2] (närk), *v.t., v.i. British Slang.* to irritate or become irritated. —*n. Especially Australian Slang.* a troublesome or irritating person. [perhaps special use of *nark*[1]]

nark·y (när′kē), *adj.*, **nark·i·er, nark·i·est.** *British Slang.* narked; irritated: *By this time we got pretty narky about the advertisements* (Punch).

Nar·ra·gan·set (nar′ə gan′sit), *n., pl.* **-set.** **1.** a member of an American Indian tribe formerly living near Narragansett Bay, Rhode Island. They were of Algonkian stock, but are now extinct. **2.** this tribe. **3.** the language of this tribe. [American English < Algonkian (Narraganset) *naiagans* small point of land + *-et,* a locative suffix]

nar·rate (na rāt′, nar′āt), *v.*, **-rat·ed, -rat·ing.** —*v.t.* to tell (a story, etc.) of: *In narrating interesting facts, his comments ... often fatigue by their plenitude* (Anna Seward). —*v.i.* to tell stories, etc.: *Most men ... speak only to narrate* (Thomas Carlyle). [< Latin *nārrāre* relate (with English *-ate*[1])]

—**Syn.** *v.t.* relate, repeat, recount. See **describe.**

nar·rat·er (na rā′tər, nar′ā-), *n.* narrator.

nar·ra·tion (na rā′shən), *n.* **1.** the act of telling. **2.** the form of composition that relates an event or a story. Novels, short stories, histories, and biographies are forms of narration: *[Dante] the great master of laconic narration* (Lowell). **3.** a story; account: *a long narration.* **4.** the part of an oration in which the facts of the matter are stated. —**Syn. 3.** See **narrative.**

nar·ra·tive (nar′ə tiv), *n.* **1.** a story; account: *pages of narrative broken by occasional descriptive passages.* **2.** the practice or act of narrating; narration; storytelling: *The path of narrative with care pursue, Still making probability your clue* (William Cowper).

—*adj.* **1.** that narrates or recounts: *"Evangeline" is a narrative poem.* **2.** of or having the character of narration: *narrative conversation.* —**nar′ra·tive·ly,** *adv.*

—**Syn.** *n.* **1.** tale, anecdote. **Narrative, narration** mean something told as a story. **Narrative** applies particularly to what is told, a story or an account of real events or experiences told like a story in connected and interesting form: *His trip through the Near East made an interesting narrative.* **Narration** applies chiefly to the act of telling or to the way in which the story is put together and presented: *His narration of his trip was interesting.*

nar·ra·tor (na rā′tər, nar′ā-), *n.* a person who tells a story. Also, **narrater.**

nar·row (nar′ō), *adj.* **1.** not wide; having little width; of less than the specified, understood, or usual width: *a narrow rug. You can return the lumber if it is too narrow.* **2.** limited in extent, space, amount, range, scope, opportunity, etc.: *He had only a narrow circle of friends.* **3.** with little margin; barely possible; barely accomplished: *a narrow escape, a narrow victory.* **4.** lacking breadth of view or sympathy; not liberal; prejudiced: *a narrow point of view. As often as a study is cultivated by narrow minds, they will draw from it narrow conclusions* (John Stuart Mill). **5.** taking nothing for granted; close; careful; minute: *a narrow scrutiny.* **6.** with barely enough to live on; very poor: *to live in narrow circumstances.* **7.** *Dialect.* parsimonious; mean: *The chancellor's long robe ... was not so good as my own gown; but he is said to be a very narrow man* (John Galt). **8.** *Phonetics.* pronounced with a narrow opening of the vocal organs; tense. **9.** (of textile goods) woven less than 18 inches wide (applied to braids, ribbons, etc.). **10.** (of livestock diets, feed, etc.) containing proportionately more protein and fewer fats and carbohydrates than is usual.

—*n.* a narrow part, place, or thing.

narrows, the narrow part of a river, strait, sound, valley, pass, etc.: *Through the narrows the tide bubbles, muddy like a river* (Robert Louis Stevenson).

—*v.t., v.i.* to make or become narrower; decrease in breadth, extent, etc.; restrict or constrict; limit: *The road narrows above the bend. He deliberately narrowed his interest.*

[Old English *nearu*] —**nar′row·ly,** *adv.* —**nar′row·ness,** *n.*

—**Syn.** *adj.* **2.** confined, strait, restricted. **4.** illiberal, bigoted. **5.** detailed, scrupulous, strict, precise. **6.** scanty, meager, impoverished. —**Ant.** *adj.* **1.** wide, broad.

narrow gauge, a distance between the rails of a railroad less than the standard width of 56½ inches.

nar·row-gauge (nar′ō gāj′), *adj.* **1.** having railroad tracks less than 56½ inches apart; less than standard gauge. **2.** narrow-minded.

nar·row-mind·ed (nar′ō mīn′did), *adj.* lacking breadth of view or sympathy; prejudiced: *He is a narrow-minded man, that affects a triumph in any glorious study* (Ben Jonson). —**nar′row·mind′ed·ly,** *adv.* —**nar′row·mind′ed·ness,** *n.* —**Syn.** illiberal, intolerant, bigoted.

nar·rows (nar′ōz), *n.pl.* See under **narrow,** *n.*

narrow squeak, *Informal.* a narrow escape.

nar·thex (när′theks), *n.* **1.** a portico forming the entrance of some early Christian churches, usually at the western end. **2.** a vestibule in a church that opens onto the nave. [< Greek *nárthēx, -ēkos* vestibule, casket, small receptable; (originally) a hollow-stalked plant, the giant fennel]

nart·jie (närt′yē), *n.* naartje.

nar·wal (när′wəl), *n.* narwhal.

nar·whal (när′hwəl, -wəl), *n.* a toothed arctic whale whose body is from 15 to 20 feet long. The male narwhal has a slender, twisted tusk from 6 to 10 feet long, that extends forward from a tooth in the left upper jaw and is used for defense. Sometimes there are two such tusks. [< Danish or Swedish *narhval* < *nār* corpse + *hval* whale]

Narwhal (including tusk, 21 to 30 ft. long)

nar·whale (när′hwāl), *n.* narwhal.

nar·y (nãr′ē), *adj. Dialect.* **1.** not: *nary a one.* **2.** never a: *Three dozen steamboats and nary barge or raft* (Mark Twain). [< *ne'er a*]

NAS (no periods) or **N.A.S.,** National Academy of Science.

NASA (na′sə), *n.,* or **N.A.S.A.,** National Aeronautics and Space Administration, an agency of the United States government established to direct and aid civilian research and development in aeronautics and aerospace technology. It superseded the National Advisory Committee for Aeronautics in 1958.

na·sal[1] (nā′zəl), *adj.* **1.** of, in, or from the nose: *nasal catarrh, a nasal discharge, a nasal voice.* **2.** of or having to do with the nasal bone. **3.** *Phonetics.* requiring the nose passage to be open; spoken through the nose. *M, n,* and *ng* represent nasal sounds. —*n.* **1.** the nasal bone. **2.** *Phonetics.* a nasal sound: *We call [m] a nasal because the escape of the sound through the nose gives it the characteristic resonance of the nasal passage* (Charles Kenneth Thomas). [< Latin *nāsus* nose, related to *nāris* nostril + English *-al*[1]] —**na′sal·ly,** *adv.*

na·sal[2] (nā′zəl), *n.* a piece of armor on a helmet protecting the nose and adjacent parts of the face; nosepiece. [variant (influenced by Latin *nāsus* nose; see NASAL[1]) of Middle English *nasel* < Old French < *nes* nose < Latin *nāsus*]

nasal bone, either of two flat oblong bones forming the bridge of the nose.

nasal index, 1. the ratio of the greatest width (multiplied by 100) of the nasal opening in the skull to its height (the distance from the nasion to the lower edge of the nasal aperture), used in comparative anatomy. **2.** the ratio of the base width (multiplied by 100) of the external nose to its height, used in comparative anthropology.

na·sal·i·ty (nā zal′ə tē), *n.* nasal quality.

na·sal·i·za·tion (nā′zə lə zā′shən), *n.* the act of nasalizing or uttering with a nasal sound.

na·sal·ize (nā′zə līz), *v.t., v.i.,* **-ized, -iz·ing.** to utter or speak with a nasal sound.

NASC (no periods), National Aeronautics and Space Council; a council of nine members headed by the President of the United States, concerned with developments in aeronautics and aerospace technology.

NASCAR (no periods) or **N.A.S.C.A.R.,** National Association for Stock Car Auto Racing.

nas·cence (nas′əns, nā′səns), *n.* nascency: *Formations often disappear through the agency of fires, floods, mankind, etc., in which cases new formations may arise by nascence* (Science).

nas·cen·cy (nas′ən sē, nā′sən-), *n.* birth; beginning; origination: *In the nascency of geological ideas, a controversy flourished upon this question* (John Earle).

nas·cent (nas′ənt, nā′sənt), *adj.* **1.** in the act or process of coming into existence; just beginning to exist, grow, or develop: *a nascent sense of right and wrong. The embryos were clearly molluscan, but . . . I could not say what mollusk lay nascent within* (New Yorker). **2.** *Chemistry.* **a.** having to do with the state or condition of an element at the instant it is set free from a combination. **b.** (of an element) being in a free or uncombined state. [< Latin *nāscēns, -entis,* present participle of *nāscī* be born] —**nas′cent·ly,** *adv.* —**Syn. 1.** incipient, inchoate.

NASD (no periods), National Association of Security Dealers, an organization that supervises the over-the-counter stock market in the United States.

nase·ber·ry (nāz′ber′ē, -bər-), *n., pl.* **-ries.** the sapodilla or its fruit. [< Spanish, or Portuguese *néspera* the medlar < earlier *niéspera* < *náspila* < Latin *mespila;* influenced by *berry*]

Nash·ville warbler (nash′vil), a North American warbler with a yellow throat and breast, olive back, gray head, and white ring around the eyes.

na·si·al (nā′zē əl), *adj.* of or having to do with the nasion.

na·si·on (nā′zē on), *n.* the midpoint of the region on the skull where the nasal bones and the frontal bone meet. [< New Latin *nasion* < Latin *nāsus* nose + Greek *-ion,* a diminutive suffix]

na·so·fron·tal (nā′zō frun′təl), *adj.* of or having to do with the nasal and frontal bones: *the nasofrontal suture.* [< Latin *nāsus* nose + English *frontal*]

na·so·lac·ri·mal (nā′zō lak′rə məl), *adj.* carrying tears from the eye to the nose: *the nasolacrimal duct.* [< Latin *nāsus* nose + English *lacrimal*]

na·sol·o·gist (nā zol′ə jist), *n.* an expert in nasology: *What is your favourite perfume? asks the nasologist of his patient* (London Daily News).

na·sol·o·gy (nā zol′ə jē), *n.* the study of the nose or of noses.

na·so·pha·ryn·ge·al (nā′zō fə rin′jē əl), *adj.* of or having to do with the nasopharynx.

na·so·phar·yn·gi·tis (nā′zō far′ən jī′tis), *n.* inflammation of the nasopharynx.

na·so·phar·ynx (nā′zō far′ingks), *n.* the upper pharynx.

Nas·ser·ism (nas′ə riz əm), *n.* the policy of Arab nationalism and independence proclaimed in 1954 by President Gamal Abdel Nasser: *. . . anticipation of a struggle between Nasserism and Communism for the minds of the younger generation in the Arab world* (Sunday Times).

Nas·ser·ist (nas′ər ist), *adj., n.* Nasserite.

Nas·ser·ite (nas′ə rīt), *n.* a supporter of Nasserism. —*adj.* of or supporting the policy of Nasserism: *The Nasserite outlook and orientation and thinking becomes alarmingly clear* (Don Cook).

nas·tic (nas′tik), *adj. Botany.* of or having to do with movement or growth of cellular tissue on one surface more than on another, as in the opening of petals or young leaves: *This type contrasts with tropic responses in that the nastic response is not controlled by the direction of the stimulus* (Fred W. Emerson). [< Greek *nastós* pressed together (< *nássein* squeeze, press close) + English *-ic*]

nas·ti·ly (nas′tə lē, näs′-), *adv.* in a nasty manner.

nas·ti·ness (nas′tē nis, näs′-), *n.* **1.** the quality or state of being nasty. **2.** filth; dirt. **3.** moral filth; obscenity.

na·stur·tium (nə stėr′shəm, nas tėr′-), *n.* **1.** any of a group of plants grown in gardens for their showy yellow, orange, and red flowers. Their sharp-tasting seeds and leaves can be pickled and used as a substitute for capers. **2.** the flower of any of these plants. **3.** any of a group of plants of the mustard family, with a pungent flavor, as the water cress. **4.** reddish-orange. [< Latin *nāsturtium,* perhaps < *nāsus* nose + *torquēre* twist (from its pungent odor)]

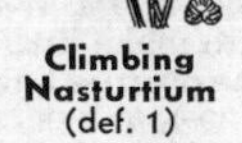
Climbing Nasturtium (def. 1)

nas·ty[1] (nas′tē, näs′-), *adj.,* **-ti·er, -ti·est. 1.** disgustingly dirty; filthy: *a nasty room, a nasty person.* **2.** morally filthy; vile: *a nasty word, a nasty mind.* **3.** offensive to smell or taste; nauseous: *a nasty medicine.* **4. a.** very unpleasant: *cold, wet, nasty weather.* **b.** obnoxious; objectionable: *He [Napoleon] was . . . no longer the embodied spirit of a world reborn; he was just a new and nastier sort of autocrat* (H. G. Wells). **5.** ill-natured; disagreeable (to another): *a nasty remark, a nasty temper.* **6.** rather serious; bad: *a nasty problem, a nasty accident.* [Middle English *nasty, nasky.* Compare Dutch *nestig* dirty, dialectal Swedish *naskug.*] —**Syn. 1.** foul, squalid. **2.** obscene, ribald, indecent. **3.** repulsive.

nas·ty[2] (nas′tē, näs′-), *n., pl.* **-ties.** *Botany.* a tendency of a plant organ, as a bud, petal, or leaf, to move in a direction determined especially by the nature and structure of the organ, rather than by external stimulus. [< Greek *nastós* pressed together (< *nássein* squeeze, press close) + English *-y*[3]]

na·sute (nā′syüt, nā syüt′), *adj.* having a large or long nose or noselike process: *the nasute termites.* [< Latin *nāsūtus* < *nāsus* nose]

na·su·tus (nā syü′təs), *n., pl.* **-ti** (-tī). any of a group of termites, or white ants, with a noselike part on the head that discharges a sticky fluid used in building nests. [< New Latin *Nasutus* < Latin *nāsūtus;* see NASUTE]

nat (nät), *n.* (in Burma and Thailand) a demon; genie: *My gardener . . . opined that it must be some nat who was either jealous of the lawn or had an unconscionable appetite for grass* (London Times). [< Thai *nat*]

nat., 1. national. **2.** native. **3.** natural. **4.** naturalist. **5.** naturalized.

na·tal (nā′təl), *adj.* **1.** of, having to do with, or dating from one's birth: *one's natal hour.* **2.** native: *The boy . . . returned from his world-wanderings to grow old and die, and mingle his dust with the natal earth* (Hawthorne). [< Latin *nātālis* < *nāscī* be born. Doublet of NOËL.]

natal day, birthday.

na·tal·i·ty (nā tal′ə tē), *n.* **1.** birth rate: *The revival of religious ideas . . . might have some effect on natality* (Popular Science Monthly). **2.** birth. [< *natal* natal + *ity.* Compare French *natalité.*]

na·tant (nā′tənt), *adj.* **1.** swimming; floating. **2.** floating on the surface of water, as a lily pad. **3.** (in heraldry) represented as swimming, or horizontally, as a fish. [< Latin *natāns, -antis,* present participle of *natāre* to float, swim]

na·ta·tion (nā tā′shən), *n.* the act or art of swimming: *There is not yet an international convention guaranteeing freedom of natation in the English Channel* (London Times). [< Latin *natātiō, -ōnis* < *natāre* to float, swim]

na·ta·tion·al (nā tā′shə nəl), *adj.* having to do with swimming.

na·ta·tor (nā tā′tər), *n.* a swimmer.

na·ta·to·ri·al (nā′tə tôr′ē əl, -tōr′-), *adj.* **1.** having to do with swimming: *the natatorial powers of a champion swimmer.* **2.** adapted for swimming: *Fins and flippers are natatorial organs.* **3.** characterized by swimming: *Fishes are natatorial animals.* [< Late Latin *natātōriālis* < *natātōria,* or *-ium* bath, natatorium]

na·ta·to·ri·um (nā′tə tôr′ē əm, -tōr′-), *n., pl.* **-to·ri·ums, -to·ri·a** (-tôr′ē ə, -tōr′-). a swimming pool, especially one in a gymnasium or other building. [< Late Latin *natātōrium* < Latin *natātor, -ōris* swimmer < *natāre* to float, swim]

na·ta·to·ry (nā′tə tôr′ē, -tōr′-), *adj.* natatorial.

natch (nach), *adv. U.S. Slang.* naturally; of course.

Natch·ez (nach′iz), *n., pl.* **-ez. 1.** an Indian of an extinct Muskhogean tribe that lived along the southern Mississippi River. **2.** the language of this tribe.

na·tes (nā′tēz), *n.pl.* **1.** the buttocks. **2.** the anterior, larger pair of the optic lobes of the brain. [< Latin *natēs,* plural of *natis* rump, buttock]

Na·than (nā′thən), *n.* (in the Bible) a prophet who rebuked King David for having Uriah killed. II Samuel 12:1-14.

Na·than·a·el (nə than′ē əl, -than′yəl), *n.* (in the Bible) one of the followers of Jesus. John 1:45-51; 21:2.

nathe·less (nāŧн′lis, nath′-), *Archaic.* —*adv.* nevertheless: *The torrid clime Smote on him sore ... Natheless he so endured* (Milton). —*prep.* notwithstanding. [Old English *nā thȳ lǣs* never the less]

nath·less (nath′lis), *adv., prep. Archaic.* natheless.

nat·i·ca (nat′ə kə), *n., pl.* **-cas, -cae** (-sē). any of a widespread group of predatory, carnivorous marine snails, having a globose shell with a flattened spire. [< New Latin *Natica* the genus name, perhaps < Medieval Latin *natica* buttock < Latin *natis*]

na·tion (nā′shən), *n.* **1. a.** the people occupying the same country, united under the same government, and mostly speaking the same language: *the English nation. The President appealed to the nation to support his policy.* **b.** a sovereign state; country: *the nations of the West.* **2.** a people, race, or tribe; those having the same language and history: *the Armenian nation, the Scottish nation.* **3.** a tribe of North American Indians, especially a member tribe of a confederation. **4.** *Archaic.* a great number; host: *What a nation of herbs he had procured* (Laurence Sterne).

the nations, a. (in the Bible) the heathen nations, or Gentiles: *All the gods of the nations are idols* (Psalms 96:5). **b.** the peoples of the earth.

[< Old French *nation,* learned borrowing from Latin *nātiō, -ōnis* stock, race < *nāscī* be born] —**Syn. 1. a.** See **people.**

na·tion·al (nash′ə nəl, nash′nəl), *adj.* **1.** of a nation; belonging to a whole nation: *national laws, a national language.* **2.** strongly upholding one's own nation; patriotic. **3.** extending throughout the nation; having chapters, branches, or members in every part of the nation: *National Academy of Sciences. Abbr.:* nat.

—*n.* **1.** a citizen of a nation: *Many nationals of Canada visit our country.* **2.** a person who owes allegiance to a nation: *Before independence, Filipinos were U.S. nationals.* **3.** a fellow countryman; compatriot.

national air, a song which by national selection or consent is usually sung or played on certain public occasions.

national anthem, the official patriotic song or hymn of a nation, sung or played on certain public occasions, as "God Save the Queen" in England, "The Star-Spangled Banner" in the United States, and the "Marseillaise" in France.

National Assembly, 1. the lower house of the French legislature. **2.** the two houses of the French parliament under the Third Republic. **3.** the first legislature during the French Revolution (from 1789 to 1792). **4.** a title for the lower house of various national governments.

National Association for the Advancement of Colored People, *U.S.* an organization founded in 1909 to promote and defend the civil rights of American Negroes. *Abbr.:* NAACP (no periods).

national bank, 1. a bank that has a charter from the national government. In the United States, the national banks are members of the Federal Reserve System and at one time were permitted to issue notes acceptable as money. **2.** a government-owned or controlled bank, usually closely associated with the financial structure of the country, as the Bank of England.

National Bureau of Standards, an agency of the United States government established in 1901 to set and regulate standards of weights and measures and to conduct research in technical fields. *Abbr.:* NBS (no periods).

National Council of Churches, a religious organization formed in 1950 by the merger of eight Protestant denominations for cooperation among their churches. *Abbr.:* NCC (no periods).

National Covenant, an agreement signed by Scottish Presbyterians in 1638, for the defense of the Presbyterian faith, especially against the efforts of Charles I to force a liturgy on Scotland.

national debt, the total amount that the government of a nation owes: *The small surplus in the budget achieved in the fiscal year just ended was used ... to make a "modest" reduction in the national debt* (New York Times).

national forest, land and forest area set aside by the President of the United States to be protected and managed by the federal government: *More than fifty million visitors are now using the National Forests alone each year* (Harper's).

National Guard, *U.S.* the reserve militia of the individual states of the United States. Units of the National Guard meet to train periodically and are subject to call in time of emergency or war by a State or the Federal government. *Abbr.:* N.G.

National Health Service, the government-financed health service of Great Britain, providing medical and dental care for every person in the country at the lowest possible rate.

National Heroes' Day, (in the Philippine Islands) November 30, a legal holiday.

national income, the total net income of a country for a year, expressed in the currency of the country and computed as the total of money received as income or taxable revenue by individuals, business organizations, and publicly-owned undertakings in the country: *The national income of a nation bears a definite relation to that country's welfare* (Emory S. Bogardus).

National Institute of Health, a division of the United States Public Health Service, of seven units for basic and clinical research in medicine, for administration of research grants and fellowships, and for the licensing of the manufacture and sale of biological products. *Abbr.:* N.I.H.

na·tion·al·ise (nash′ə nə līz, nash′nə-), *v.t.,* **-ised, -is·ing.** *Especially British.* nationalize.

na·tion·al·ism (nash′ə nə liz′əm, nash′nə liz-), *n.* **1.** patriotic feelings or efforts; devotion to the interests of one's own nation: *The spirit of nationalism is still far stronger than the spirit of world community* (Emory S. Bogardus). **2.** extreme patriotism; chauvinism: *The experience of two wars ... had shown ... what too much nationalism could mean* (New York Times). **3.** the desire and plans for national independence: *In an ... appeal to the flammable nationalism of Africa's restive millions ...* (Newsweek). **4.** a form of socialism that advocates government ownership and control of all industries. **5.** a word, phrase, trait, or custom viewed as peculiar to, and usually as an identifying sign of membership in, a given nation: *OK is probably the chief verbal nationalism of the United States.*

na·tion·al·ist or **Na·tion·al·ist** (nash′ə-nə list, nash′nə-), *n.* an upholder of nationalism; a person who believes in nationalism: *This revision would appear to be laudable only so long as the Prime Minister is able to restrict the extreme nationalists* (Atlantic). —*adj.* **1.** nationalistic. **2.** of or having to do with Nationalist China: *a Nationalist garrison on Quemoy.*

na·tion·al·is·tic (nash′ə nə lis′tik, nash′-nə-), *adj.* of nationalism or nationalists: *He has used the nationalistic instincts of the French more shrewdly than any politician of his generation* (Edmond Taylor). —**na′-tion·al·is′ti·cal·ly,** *adv.*

na·tion·al·i·ty (nash′ə nal′ə tē), *n., pl.* **-ties. 1.** a nation: *Several nationalities are represented in the ancestry of most Americans.* **2.** condition of belonging to a nation. Citizens of the same country have the same nationality: *Strictly speaking, nationality is determined by legal residence* (Beals and Hoijer). **3.** the condition of being an independent nation: *After the American Revolutionary War, the colonies attained nationality.* **4.** national quality or character: *I have little faith in that quality in literature which is commonly called nationality* (Lowell).

na·tion·al·i·za·tion (nash′ə nə lə zā′shən, nash′nə-), *n.* **1.** the act of nationalizing: *Control of industry, rather than outright nationalization, is the key to the new policy statement on public ownership by the Labor Party's national executive* (Atlantic). **2.** the state of being nationalized.

na·tion·al·ize (nash′ə nə līz, nash′nə-), *v.t.,* **-ized, -iz·ing. 1.** to bring (industries, land, railroads, etc.) under the control or ownership of a nation, usually making the government responsible for their operation: *The United States nationalized the railroads in World War I.* **2.** to make national. **3.** to make into a nation.

na·tion·al·iz·er (nash′ə nə lī′zər, nash′-nə-), *n.* a person who favors nationalization

National Labor Relations Board, an agency of the United States government, having five members, empowered to take action against unfair labor practices, supervise labor relations, etc. *Abbr.:* NLRB (no periods).

National Liberation Front, 1. the political arm of the Vietcong, formed in 1960. **2.** the EAM (a greek underground movement in World War II). *Abbr.:* NLF (no periods).

na·tion·al·ly (nash′ə nə lē, nash′nə-), *adv.* **1.** in a national manner; as a nation. **2.** throughout the nation: *The President's speech was broadcast nationally.*

national monument, an area, especially in the United States, containing some noteworthy objects of nature or historical significance, as Appomattox Court House or the Petrified Forest, usually maintained by some public agency.

national park, a relatively large area of land maintained by some governments for people to enjoy because of its natural beauty, historical or geological interest, etc.: *Mr. Kessel sets his story* ["*The Lion*"] *in Kenya, in a huge national park where every kind of wild animal roams free, protected from hunters and marauders by government law* (New Yorker).

Na·ti·o·nal·rat (nä′tsē ō näl′rät′), *n.* **1.** the lower branch of the lawmaking body of Austria, consisting of 165 members elected for four-year terms. **2.** the National Council of Switzerland consisting of 196 members elected for four-year terms.

National Service or **national service,** *British.* the military service.

National Socialism, Naziism.

National Socialist, a Nazi.

National Socialist Party, the political party led by Adolf Hitler that gained control of Germany in 1933.

National Trust, a British national organization founded in 1895 for the preservation of places of historical interest or natural beauty.

National War College, an educational institution of the United States government for training military personnel in new techniques of national defense and strategy.

na·tion·hood (nā′shən hu̇d), *n.* **1.** the state or fact of being a nation: *But the great majority of former colonial people have now gained independence and nationhood* (Harper's). **2.** nationalism: *Often it was the struggle against the foreigner that brought the first strong feeling of nationhood* (Manchester Guardian).

na·tions (nā′shənz), *n.pl.* See under **nation,** *n.*

na·tion-state (nā′shən stāt′), *n.* a country whose citizens consider themselves of a single nationality because of common descent, language, history, etc.: *In a world of nation-states ... peace in the long run will not be possible in the absence of enforceable world law* (Harrison Brown). *The Arab world is really a lot of little worlds — nation-states, kingdoms, sheikdoms ...* (Time).

na·tion·wide (nā′shən wīd′), *adj.* extending throughout the nation; national: *a nationwide election, a nationwide tour.*

na·tive (nā′tiv), *n.* **1.** a person born in a certain place or country: *The natives are the people living in a place, not visitors or foreigners.* **2.** one of the original inhabitants of a place, as contrasted with conquerors, settlers, etc., especially a member of a less civilized race. **3.** a member of a less civilized race, usually not white (now often used in an unfriendly way). **4.** an animal or plant living in the place where it originated. **5.** something grown or produced in nearby rather than remote or foreign regions. **6.** (in Great Britain) an oyster. **7.** *Astrology.* **a.** a person born under the particular planet or sign mentioned. **b.** the subject of a nativity or horoscope. [< Medieval Latin *nativus;* see the adjective]

—*adj.* **1.** born in a certain place or country: *People born in New York are native sons and daughters of New York.* **2.** belonging to a person because of his birth: *just and native rights of a human being. The United States is my native land; Argentina is yours.* **3. a.** belonging to a person because of his country or the people to which he belongs: *French is his native language.* **b.** forming the source or origin of a person or thing; original: *Is this the way I must return to native dust?* (Milton). **4.** born in a person; natural: *native ability, native courtesy.* **5. a.** of or having to do with the original inhabitants,

especially those not white: *native customs, native huts.* **b.** ruled or inhabited by such people: *the native section of a city.* **6. a.** originating, grown, or produced in a certain place: *Tobacco is native to America.* **b.** grown or produced nearby. **7.** found pure in nature: *native copper.* **8.** found in nature; not produced: *Native salt is refined for use.* **9.** in a natural state: *the native beauty of the hills.* **10.** *Astrology.* born under the particular planet or sign mentioned.
go native, to live as the less civilized natives do: *The shipwrecked seamen, befriended by the friendly islanders, decided to go native.*
[< Old French *natif, -ive,* feminine, learned borrowing from Latin *nātīvus* innate (in Medieval Latin, a native) < *nāscī* be born, related to *gignere* beget, produce. Doublet of NAÏVE.] —**na′tive·ly,** *adv.* —**na′tive·ness,** *n.*
—**Syn.** *adj.* **4. Native, natural** mean belonging to someone or something by birth or nature. **Native** emphasizes the idea of being born in a person, as contrasted with being acquired: *He has native artistic talent.* **Natural** emphasizes being part of the nature of a person, animal, or thing, belonging by birth or because of essential character: *Sugar has natural sweetness.* **5. a.** aboriginal. **6. a.** indigenous.

Native American Church, an American Indian religious sect which combines Christian beliefs with native ritual, and which uses peyote in its ceremonies.

Native American Party, an American political party founded in 1845, characterized by anti-Catholicism and extreme nativism, from which the Know-Nothing Party developed in the 1850's.

na·tive-born (nā′tiv bôrn′), *adj.* born in the place or country indicated: *a native-born New Yorker, Frenchman, etc.*

native cod, a cod in or from the coastal waters of New England.

native companion, (in Australia) brolga.

native son, *U.S.* a native of one of the States of the United States: *In New Hampshire, the Goldwater supporters tried to explain away their sharp defeat by saying that Ambassador Lodge [of Massachusetts] was almost a native son* (Atlantic).

na·tiv·ism (nā′tə viz əm), *n.* **1.** *Especially U.S.* the policy of advancing the interests of native inhabitants rather than those of immigrants: *This book attempts a general history of the anti-foreign spirit that I have defined as nativism* (New York Times). **2.** the philosophical doctrine of innate ideas.

na·tiv·ist (nā′tə vist), *n.* **1.** a person who supports or favors political nativism. **2.** a person who maintains the philosophical doctrine of innate ideas. —*adj.* nativistic: *During the Civil War many immigrant races entered the mainstream of American life and lessened nativist violence* (Canadian Saturday Night).

na·tiv·is·tic (nā′tə vis′tik), *adj.* of or having to do with nativism or nativists.

na·tiv·i·ty (nə tiv′ə tē, nā-), *n., pl.* **-ties. 1.** birth: *I have served him from the hour of my nativity to this instant* (Shakespeare). **2.** birth considered astrologically; horoscope: *He ... proceeded to calculate the nativity of the young heir of Ellangowan* (Scott).
the Nativity, a. the birth of Christ: *The cities have sobered down in their Christmas appearance. There are more models in the shop windows of the Nativity scene and fewer mink bathing suits* (Alistair Cooke). **b.** a picture of this, usually with the animals grouped about the manger: *Two famous pieces of Bassano, the one a Vulcan, the other a Nativity* (John Evelyn). **c.** Christmas; December 25: *The Nativity of our Lord Jesus Christ was now at hand* (Hamon L'Estrange).
[< Old French *nativite,* earlier *nativitet,* learned borrowing from Latin *nātīvitās* < *nātīvus;* see NATIVE. Doublet of NAÏVETÉ.]

nativity play, a play reenacting the birth of Christ.

natl., national.

NATO (nā′tō), *n.,* or **N.A.T.O.,** North Atlantic Treaty Organization, an alliance of 15 Western nations pledged under the North Atlantic Treaty to help each other in building a defense against any possible attack by Russia or the satellite nations under its control.

na·tri·um (nā′trē əm), *n.* sodium. *Abbr.:* Na (no period). [< New Latin *natrium* < *natron* natron]

nat·ro·lite (nat′rə līt, nā′trə-), *n.* a mineral, a hydrous silicate of aluminum and sodium, usually occurring in white or colorless, often needle-shaped crystals. *Formula:* $Na_2Al_2Si_3O_{10}.2H_2O$ [< German *Natrolit* < *Natron* natron + *-lit* -lite]

na·tron (nā′tron), *n.* a mineral, a native sodium carbonate. *Formula:* $Na_2CO_3.10H_2O$ [< French *natron* < Spanish *natrón* < Arabic *naṭrūn* < Greek *nítron.* Doublet of NITER.]

nat·ter (nat′ər), *v.i.* **1.** to grumble; fret: *Their voices, like the voices of tired, nattering old women, retreated up the stairs* (New Yorker). **2.** *Especially British.* to chatter; prate. —*n.* idle chatter or prating: *There is a minimum of natter in her chatter* (Time). [earlier *gnatter;* origin uncertain]

nat·ter·jack (nat′ər jak), *n.,* or **natter-jack toad,** a small European toad that runs rather than hops and has a yellow line down its back.

Natterjack

nat·ti·ly (nat′ə lē), *adv.* in a natty manner; with neatness; tidily; sprucely: *nattily dressed.*

nat·ti·ness (nat′ē nis), *n.* the quality or state of being natty or neat.

nat·ty (nat′ē), *adj.,* **-ti·er, -ti·est.** trim and tidy; neatly smart in dress or appearance; spruce: *a natty uniform, a natty young officer.* [origin uncertain] —**Syn.** dapper.

Na·tu·fi·an (nə tü′fē ən), *adj.* of or having to do with a microlithic culture of cave dwellers existing in the region of Palestine around 10,000 B.C. —*n.* a prehistoric man belonging to this culture. [< the valley of En-*Natuf,* in Palestine, where remains were found + *-ian*]

nat·u·ral (nach′ər əl, nach′rəl), *adj.* **1.** produced by nature; based on some state of things in nature: *Scenery has natural beauty.* **2. a.** not artificial: *the natural color of hair. Coal and oil are natural products. The main reason for wanting to send a rocket to the Moon is to find out more about the Earth's natural satellite* (New Scientist). **b.** (of plants) not introduced artificially. **3.** not acquired or assumed; instinctive; inborn: *natural ability.* **4.** coming in the ordinary course of events; normal: *to die a natural death.* **5.** in accordance with the nature of things or the circumstances of the case: *a natural response.* **6.** instinctively felt to be right and fair, though not prescribed by any formal law or agreement: *natural law, natural rights.* **7.** like nature; true to nature: *The picture looked natural.* **8.** free from affectation or restraint; easy: *a natural manner.* **9.** of or having to do with nature: *the natural sciences.* **10.** concerned with natural science. **11.** based on what is learned from nature by the light of human reason, rather than on supernatural revelation: *natural religion.* **12.** having a real or physical existence, as opposed to what is spiritual, intellectual, fictitious, etc.: *Which is the natural man, And which the spirit?* (Shakespeare). **13.** by birth merely, and not legally recognized; illegitimate: *a natural son.* **14.** *Music.* **a.** neither sharp nor flat; without sharps and flats. **b.** neither sharped nor flatted: *C natural.* **c.** having the pitch affected by the natural sign. **d.** produced without the aid of valves or keys, as in brass instruments. **15.** *Mathematics.* having 1 as the base of the system (applied to a function or number belonging or referred to such a system). Natural numbers are those that are positive integers, such as 1, 2, 3, etc. Natural sines, cosines, tangents, etc., are those taken in arcs whose radii are 1. They are not expressed as logarithms, but as the actual value of a ratio (of two sides of a right triangle) in which the hypotenuse of the triangle is taken as unity.
—*n.* **1.** that which is natural: *This climbing business may be a natural for monkeys, but it doesn't fit a lion's life at all* (Punch). **2.** *Music.* **a.** a natural note or tone. **b.** the sign (♮) used to cancel the effect of a preceding sharp or flat, and give a note its natural value; natural sign. **c.** a white key on a piano. **3.** a half-witted person: *She ... is not quite a natural, that is, not an absolute idiot* (Fanny Burney). **4.** *Informal.* an expert by nature: *A classmate of mine ... had proved to be a natural on the saxophone* (New Yorker). **5.** *Informal.* a sure success. [< Old French *naturel,* learned borrowing from Latin *nātūrālis* < *nātūra;* see NATURE] —**nat′u·ral·ness,** *n.*
—**Syn.** *adj.* **3.** innate, inherent. See **native. 4.** regular, usual. **8.** simple, ingenuous, artless, unaffected.

nat·u·ral-born (nach′ər əl bôrn′, nach′rəl-), *adj.* **1.** that is so by nature; born so: *a natural-born boxer, a natural-born fool.* **2.** native in a country; not alien: *a natural-born citizen or subject.*

natural cement, cement in limestone, not produced artificially.

natural childbirth, the giving birth to a child without the use of anesthetics or pain-relieving drugs.

natural draft, the draft through a room or furnace induced by a chimney or other means of natural convection.

natural frequency, *Physics.* the frequency at which a body vibrates naturally, according to set wave patterns within itself.

natural gas, a combustible gas formed naturally in the earth, consisting of methane with hydrogen and other gases: *Above the petroleum in oil wells, and in some places where no oil is found, drillers strike natural gas.*

natural gasoline, gasoline condensed from casinghead gas.

natural harmonic, one of the harmonics or overtones of an open string, produced on such stringed instruments as the viol, lute, or harp.

natural historian, a writer or authority on natural history.

natural history, 1. the study of animals, plants, minerals, and other things in nature. **2.** a book dealing with this study.

nat·u·ral·ise (nach′ər ə līz, nach′rə-), *v.t., v.i.,* **-ised, -is·ing.** *Especially British.* naturalize: *Many of you have an odd corner—perhaps a grass bank or an orchard: these are the very places for naturalising bulbs* (Listener).

nat·u·ral·ism (nach′ər ə liz′əm, nach′rə-liz-), *n.* **1.** (in art and literature) close adherence to nature and reality: *And with as little or as much as each artist needs of naturalism in his work, the essentials of the classics have always included expression and form as matters of the very first importance* (Atlantic). **2.** the principles and methods of a group of writers of the latter part of the 1800's and early 1900's whose realism of description included all the details of an environment however repulsive and whose characters were molded by their environment. This group of writers included Emile Zola, George Moore, Stephen Crane, Frank Norris, and Theodore Dreiser. **3.** action based on natural instincts. **4.** *Philosophy.* a view of the world that takes account only of natural elements and forces, excluding the supernatural or spiritual. **5.** the doctrine that all religious truth is derived from the study of nature.

nat·u·ral·ist (nach′ər ə list, nach′rə-), *n.* **1.** a person who makes a study of animals and plants, especially in their native habitats. **2.** a writer or artist who represents life exactly as it is; extreme realist. **3.** *Obsolete.* a physicist.

nat·u·ral·is·tic (nach′ər ə lis′tik, nach′rə-), *adj.* **1.** of natural history or naturalists. **2.** of naturalism, especially in art or literature: *The naturalistic painter ... deals ... with surface manifestations* (New Yorker). **3.** of or in accordance with nature. —**nat′u·ral·is′ti·cal·ly,** *adv.* —**Syn. 2.** realistic.

nat·u·ral·i·za·tion (nach′ər ə lə zā′shən, nach′rə-), *n.* **1.** the act of naturalizing: *Mr. P.G. Wodehouse ... filed a naturalization petition as a first step toward obtaining United States citizenship* (London Times). **2.** the state of being naturalized: *A suit to revoke his naturalization (which is the first step toward deportation since no U.S. citizen can be deported) was filed by the government* (Newsweek).

nat·u·ral·ize (nach′ər ə līz, nach′rə-), *v.,* **-ized, -iz·ing.** —*v.t.* **1.** to admit (a foreigner) to citizenship: *After living in the United States for a certain number of years, an immigrant can be naturalized if he passes a test.* **2.** to adopt (a foreign word or custom): *"Chauffeur" is a French word that has been naturalized in English.* **3. a.** (of animals or plants) to introduce and make at home in another country: *The English oak has been naturalized in parts of Massachusetts.* **b.** to adapt or accustom to a place or to new surroundings: *I was now in my twenty-third year of residence . . . and was . . . naturalized to the place, and to the manner of living* (Daniel Defoe). **4.** to make natural; free from conventional characteristics. **5.** to regard or explain as natural rather than supernatural: *to naturalize miracles.* —*v.i.* **1.** to become like a native. **2.** to become a citizen of another country. **3.** to be occupied with natural history. —**Syn.** *v.t.* **3. b.** acclimate, adjust.

natural law, 1. just behavior believed to result from the natural tendency of human beings to exercise right reason in dealings with others. Natural law precedes and is regarded as the basis of common law. **2.** a law or the laws of nature: *While it is apparent that natural laws are not infallible, nevertheless some of them hold within the limits of experimental accuracy* (Parks and Steinbach).

natural logarithm, a logarithm in which the base is *e*, a transcendental constant equal to 2.71828183+, used in analytical work.

nat·u·ral·ly (nach′ər ə lē, nach′rə-), *adv.* **1.** in a natural way: *to speak naturally.* **2.** by nature: *a naturally obedient child.* **3.** as might be expected; of course: *She offered me some candy; naturally, I took it.* —**Syn. 1.** unaffectedly.

natural magnet, a piece of magnetite; loadstone.

natural number, a positive integer; whole number.

natural philosopher, 1. a student of natural philosophy. **2.** a physicist.

natural philosophy, 1. physics. **2.** the study of the physical universe as a whole.

natural resources, materials supplied by nature: *Minerals, timber, land, and water power are natural resources. The effect of a diminution of natural resources is to lower the standard of living* (Ogburn and Nimkoff).

natural rights, rights instinctively felt to be right and fair, although not prescribed by any formal agreement.

natural science, 1. the science of nature. Zoology, botany, geology, chemistry, and physics are natural sciences as contrasted with such fields as pure mathematics, philosophy, or social science. **2.** these sciences or branches of knowledge collectively: *Although many concepts of the natural sciences are not applicable to the social sciences . . . training in the natural sciences could develop valuable skills in observation and an appreciation of a scientist's relationship to his data* (Science News).

natural scientist, a person who is trained or who works in the field of natural science.

natural selection, the process by which animals and plants best adapted to their environment tend to survive; tendency of the environment to permit those members of its population to survive and breed who are best adapted to it by their genetic makeup: *In the formation of races and species, in man as in other animals, natural selection rarely takes place quickly* (Atlantic).

natural sign, the sign (♮) used to cancel the effect of a preceding sharp or flat; a natural.

natural theology, the study of theology pursued only by natural reason without the aid of supernatural revelation.

natural uranium, uranium as found in nature, or refined, with little or no fissionable material added: *That reactor operation may call for an annual consumption of 8,000 metric tons of natural uranium* (New York Times).

natural year, astronomical year.

na·ture (nā′chər), *n.* **1.** the world; all things except those made by man: *the wonders of nature.* **2.** the sum total of the forces at work throughout the universe: *the laws of nature.* **3.** the instincts or inherent tendencies directing conduct: *It is against nature for a mother to hurt her child. It is . . . my nature, to believe the best of people* (George W. Curtis). **4.** reality: *true to nature.* **5.** a primitive, wild condition; condition of human beings before social organization: *The hermit lived in a state of nature.* **6.** what a thing really is; quality; character: *It is the nature of robins to fly and build nests.* **7.** a particular sort; kind: *Books of a scientific nature do not interest Helen.* **8.** a person of a particular character: *She is a gentle nature.* **9. a.** the basic functions of a living organism; physical being; vital powers: *food sufficient to sustain nature.* **b.** a natural desire or function, as that of sex or elimination: *the demands of nature.* **10.** the moral state as unaffected by grace. **11.** *Dialect.* natural feeling or affection.

by nature, because of the essential character of the person or thing: *Adeline was liberal by nature* (Byron).

of or **in the nature of,** having the nature of; being a kind of; being: *A Peace is of the nature of a Conquest* (Shakespeare).

[< Old French *nature,* learned borrowing from Latin *nātūra* birth, character < *nāscī* be born; see NATIVE] —**Syn. 1.** universe, cosmos. **3.** temperament. **7.** type.

Na·ture (nā′chər), *n.* the personification of all natural facts and forces: *Who can paint like Nature? Can imagination boast . . . hues like hers?* (James Thomson).

-natured, *combining form.* having a —— nature: *Good-natured = having a good nature.*

na·ture morte (nȧ tʏr′ môrt′), *French.* a still life: *Of his small final natures mortes, one depicts a carafe and lemon, another a wineglass and egg* (New Yorker).

nature study, the study of animals, plants, and other things and events in nature.

na·tur·ism (nā′chə riz əm), *n. Especially British.* nudism.

na·tur·ist (nā′chər ist), *n. Especially British.* a nudist.

na·tur·o·path (nā′chər ə path), *n.* a person who practices naturopathy: *After medical societies and health officers protested, Maryland state legislators turned down an appeal for legal recognition as physicians from the state's 100-odd naturopaths* (Time).

na·tur·o·path·ic (nā′chər ə path′ik), *adj.* of or having to do with naturopathy.

na·tur·op·a·thy (nā′chə rop′ə thē), *n.* a system of therapy in which natural agencies, as fresh air, exercise, etc., are preferred to drugs or surgery. [< Latin *nātūra* (see NATURE) + English *-pathy*]

naught (nôt), *n.* **1.** nothing: *to ask naught for oneself.* **2.** zero; 0.

set at naught, to slight; disregard; disdain: *I am an aristocrat and it is my whim to set good manners at naught* (Punch).

—*adv., adj.* nought: *The trial hath . . . Me naught advantaged* (Milton) (*adv.*). *Away! all will be naught else* (Shakespeare) (*adj.*). Also, **nought.**

[Old English *nāwiht* < *nā* no + *wiht* thing (wight)] —**Syn.** *n.* **1.** nil. **2.** cipher.

naugh·ti·ly (nô′tə lē), *adv.* in a naughty way.

naugh·ti·ness (nô′tē nis), *n.* the quality or state of being naughty.

naugh·ty (nô′tē), *adj.,* **-ti·er, -ti·est. 1.** not obedient; bad: *The naughty child hit his baby sister.* **2.** somewhat improper; risqué: *a naughty joke.* **3.** *Archaic.* morally bad; wicked: *naughty persons, lewdly bent* (Shakespeare). [Middle English *naughty* having nothing; later, good for nothing < *naught* nothing] —**Syn. 1.** mischievous. **2.** racy.

nau·ma·chi·a (nô mā′kē ə), *n., pl.* **-chi·ae** (-kē ē), **-chi·as. 1.** a mock sea fight staged by the ancient Romans as a spectacle. **2.** a place for staging such spectacles. [< Latin *naumachia* < Greek *naumachíā* < *naûs* ship + *máchē* a fight]

nau·ma·chy (nô′mə kē), *n., pl.* **-chies.** naumachia.

nau·pli·al (nô′plē əl), *adj.* having the character of a nauplius.

nau·pli·us (nô′plē əs), *n., pl.* **-pli·i** (-plē ī). the first stage in development of certain crustaceans, as the shrimp, after leaving the egg; a larval form with an unsegmented body, three pairs of appendages, and a single median eye. [< Latin *nauplius* a kind of shellfish < Greek *naúplios*]

Na·u·ru·an (nā′ə rü′ən), *adj.* of or having to do with Nauru, a small island in the central Pacific Ocean. —*n.* a native or inhabitant of Nauru.

nau·sea (nô′shə, -shē ə, -sē ə), *n.* **1.** the feeling that one has when about to vomit. **2.** seasickness: *Most of the ship's passengers were seized with nausea during the storm at sea.* **3.** extreme disgust; loathing: *. . . sated to nausea as we have been with the doctrines of sentimentality* (Scott). [< Latin *nausea* < Greek *nausíā* < *naûs* ship. Doublet of NOISE.] —**Syn. 3.** repugnance.

nau·se·ant (nô′shē ənt, -sē-), *adj.* inducing nausea or vomiting: *a nauseant drug.*

nau·se·ate (nô′shē āt, -sē-), *v.,* **-at·ed, -at·ing.** —*v.t.* **1.** to cause nausea in; make sick. **2.** to reject (food, etc.) with loathing or a feeling of nausea: *Many dishes are commended in one age that are nauseated in another* (Sir Thomas Browne). **3.** to cause to feel loathing. —*v.i.* to feel nausea; become sick: *the old-fashioned civility that presses food upon you until you nauseate* (Scott). [< Latin *nauseāre* (with English *-ate*[1]) be seasick < *nausea* nausea] —**nau′se·at′ing·ly,** *adv.*

nau·se·a·tion (nô′shē ā′shən, -sē-), *n.* **1.** the act of nauseating. **2.** the state of being nauseated.

nau·seous (nô′shəs, -shē əs, -sē-), *adj.* **1.** causing nausea; sickening: *a kind of slimy stuff . . . of a most nauseous, odious smell* (Daniel Defoe). **2.** disgusting; loathsome. [< Latin *nauseōsus* < *nausea* nausea] —**nau′seous·ly,** *adv.* —**nau′seous·ness,** *n.*

Nau·sic·a·ä (nô sik′ā ə, -ē ə), *n. Greek Legend.* the maiden, daughter of Alcinoüs, who, in the *Odyssey,* aided Odysseus (Ulysses) when he was shipwrecked by bringing him to her father's court.

naut., nautical.

nautch (nôch), *n.* an entertainment consisting of dancing by professional dancing girls wearing light, filmy garments, originally in India but now imitated elsewhere. [< *Hindustani nāch* < Prakrit *nacca* < Sanskrit *nṛtya* dancing < *nṛit* to dance]

nau·tic (nô′tik), *adj.* nautical.

nau·ti·cal (nô′tə kəl), *adj.* of or having to do with ships, sailors, or navigation: *nautical charts.* [< Latin *nauticus* (< Greek *nautikós* < *naûs* ship) + English *-al*[1]] —**nau′ti·cal·ly,** *adv.* —**Syn.** maritime.

nautical measure, a system of linear measure used in navigation.

nautical mile, 6,076.1033 feet, the standard unit of distance in nautical measure.

nau·ti·loid (nô′tə loid), *adj.* resembling the nautilus in form: *Nautiloid shells . . . predominate in older Paleozoic rocks* (Raymond Cecil Moore). —*n.* a nautiloid mollusk.

nau·ti·lus (nô′tə ləs), *n., pl.* **-lus·es, -li** (-lī). either of two kinds of cephalopod of warm seas. The pearly nautilus has a spiral shell with a pearly lining, divided into chambers by septa. The paper nautilus has saillike arms and a very thin shell. [< Latin *nautilus* < Greek *nautílos* (originally) sailor < *naûs* ship]

Pearly or Chambered Nautilus
(cut lengthwise)

nav., 1. naval. **2.** navigation.

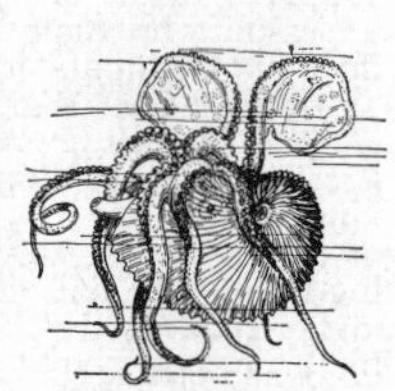

Paper Nautilus

Nav·a·ho (nav′ə hō), *n., pl.* **-hos** or **-hoes. 1.** a member of a large tribe of American Indians living in New Mexico, Arizona, and Utah. The Navahos are noted for their skill in making turquoise and silver jewelry and in weaving blankets and rugs with bright patterns, usually of black, red and white color. **2.** this tribe, of Athapascan stock. **3.** the language of this tribe. [American English < Mexican Spanish *Navajo* < Nahuatl *navajoa* place of the prickly pear cactus < *nava-* prickly pear cactus + *-joa* place of (from the abundance of this plant where the Navahos live)]

nav·aid (nav′ād′), *n.* a navigation aid: *These "navaids" range from small location-marker beacons on the ground that light a bulb on the aircraft's instrument panel as it passes overhead to huge, long-range radar systems* (Time).

Nav·a·jo (nav′ə hō), *n., pl.* **-jos** or **-joes.** Navaho.

nav·a·jo·ite (nav′ə hō′īt), *n.* a mineral of vanadium recently discovered in Arizona. [< *Navajo* + *-ite*[1] (because it was discovered on a Navajo reservation)]

na·val (nā′vəl), *adj.* **1.** of the navy; for warships or the navy: *a naval officer, naval supplies, a naval squadron.* **2.** having a navy: *the great naval powers.* **3.** accomplished by means of ships or a navy: *naval strategy.* **4.** nautical; maritime. [< Latin *nāvālis* < *nāvis* ship] —**na′val·ly,** *adv.*

naval academy, a school for training seamen. The United States Naval Academy is a school at Annapolis, Maryland, for training naval officers, founded in 1845.

naval architect, a person who designs ships.
naval dockyard, *British.* navy yard.
naval holiday, a period of cessation or reduction of naval activities, among nations not actually at war, by limitation of armaments and construction, etc., usually to promote the interests of international peace.
na·val·ism (nā′və liz əm), *n.* the principle or policy of building up or maintaining a strong navy for a country: *Armament rivalry, navalism, imperialistic conflicts, and aggressive nationalism ... had been building up for more than a generation* (New York Times).
na·val·ist (nā′və list), *n.* an advocate of navalism: *Mr. Daniels's rather flamboyant allusions to the American naval programme would be utilized by our domestic navalists* (Glasgow Herald).
naval stores, rosin, turpentine, tar, pitch, etc., as used in building and repairing wooden ships.
nave[1] (nāv), *n.* the main part of a church or cathedral between the side aisles. The nave extends from the main entrance to the transepts. [< Medieval Latin *navis* < Latin *nāvis* ship]

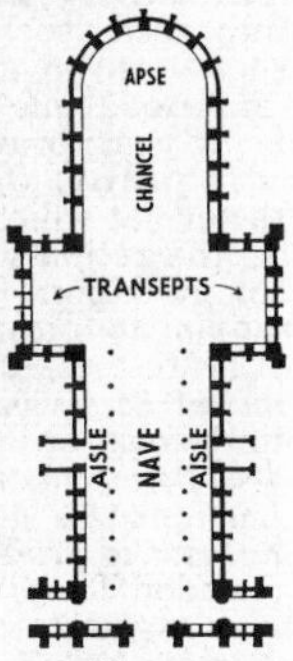

APSE
CHANCEL
TRANSEPTS
AISLE
NAVE
AISLE

Nave[1]

nave[2] (nāv), *n.* **1.** the central part of a wheel, into which the axle is fitted; hub. **2.** *Obsolete.* the navel. [Old English *nafu*]
na·vel (nā′vəl), *n.* **1.** the mark or scar, usually a puckered depression, in the middle of the surface of the abdomen where the umbilical cord was attached during prenatal development; umbilicus. **2.** the middle point of anything; center. **3.** (in heraldry) a nombril. [Old English *nafela*]
navel ill, inflammation of the navel in calves and lambs, causing redness, pain, and swelling.
navel orange, a seedless orange with a small growth at one end shaped somewhat like a navel and enclosing a small secondary fruit.
na·vel·wort (nā′vəl wėrt′), *n.* **1.** an English rock plant having fleshy and juicy tissues and greenish yellow flowers; pennywort. **2.** any of a group of herbaceous plants of the borage family, with white or blue flowers.
na·vette (nə vet′), *n.* **1.** a gem cut to a pointed oval shape: *The highest price of the morning, £14,500, was paid by an anonymous buyer for a single navette* (London Times). **2.** a ring setting of this shape; marquise. [< French *navette* (literally) small boat]
na·vew (nā′vyü), *n.* an annual weed of Europe and Asia, considered the wild form of the common turnip. [< obsolete French *naveu,* Old French *navel,* ultimately < Latin *nāpus.* Doublet of NEEP.]
nav·i·cert (nav′ə sėrt), *n.* a pass issued in time of war by a British consul or other authority in a neutral country making goods exempt from seizure or search by naval vessels of Great Britain or its allies: *These men were not criminals: they were merely breaking regulations enforced on the shipping countries by the navicert system* (Graham Greene). [< *navi*(gation) *cert*(ificate)]
na·vic·u·lar (nə vik′yə lər), *adj.* resembling a boat in shape, as certain bones; scaphoid. —*n.* **1. a.** a bone of the human foot between the talus or anklebone and the bones of the instep or metatarsals. **b.** a bone of the human wrist shaped like a comma. It is one of the eight short bones that make up this joint. **2.** a small, oval bone in the foot of a horse. [< Late Latin *nāviculāris* of a ship < Latin *nāvicula* (diminutive) < *nāvis* ship]
na·vic·u·la·re (nə vik′yə lãr′ē), *n.* navicular.
navig., navigation.
nav·i·ga·bil·i·ty (nav′ə gə bil′ə tē), *n.* the condition of being navigable.
nav·i·ga·ble (nav′ə gə bəl), *adj.* **1.** that ships can travel on or through: *The Mississippi River is deep enough to be navigable.* **2.** that can be sailed; seaworthy. **3.** that can be steered: *Without a rudder the ship was not navigable.* —**nav′i·ga·ble·ness,** *n.* —**Syn. 3.** steerable, dirigible.
nav·i·ga·bly (nav′ə gə blē), *adv.* so as to be navigable.
nav·i·gate (nav′ə gāt), *v.,* **-gat·ed, -gat·ing.** —*v.t.* **1. a.** to sail, manage, or steer (a ship, airplane, rocket, etc.) on a course or to a destination: *If the captain died, the mate was in duty bound to navigate the ship to the nearest civilized port* (Herman Melville). **b.** to direct (anything) on a course: *The President navigates the ship of state.* **2.** to sail over or on (a sea or river). **3.** to convey (goods) by water. **4.** to fly through (the air) in an airplane, rocket, etc.: *Stories of wizards and witches who navigated the upper air with the assistance of tubs and broomsticks* (C.L.M. Brown). —*v.i.* **1. a.** to travel by water; sail. **b.** (of vessels) to sail; ply. **2.** to direct or manage the course of a ship, airplane, etc.; be a navigator. [< Latin *nāvigāre* (with English *-ate*) < *nāvis* ship + *agere* to drive]
nav·i·ga·tion (nav′ə gā′shən), *n.* **1.** the act or process of navigating. **2.** the art or science of finding and planning the position and course of a ship, airplane, rocket, etc. This may be done by making various calculations based on the triangle or the arc after making certain measurements of distance in relation to the position of a craft to heavenly bodies, radio beacons, landmarks, etc.: *A completely new federal navigation system ... makes it possible for the new pilot to fly cross-country safely and efficiently* (Newsweek).
nav·i·ga·tion·al (nav′ə gā′shə nəl), *adj.* of, having to do with, or used in navigation: *The navigational system will enable the tractor to steer itself through any of the travel patterns associated with field operations* (New Scientist).
navigational satellite, an artificial earth satellite that transmits astronomical and meteorological data to earth as an aid in navigation.
navigation light, one of the lights on an aircraft to make its size, position, and course visible at night.
nav·i·ga·tor (nav′ə gā′tər), *n.* **1.** a person who has charge of the navigating of a ship or aircraft or who is skilled in navigating: *This inadequacy of knowledge results from the lack of interest in the deep seas from the point of view of the navigator, and from the difficulties of obtaining deep soundings* (Gaskell and Hill). **2.** a person who sails the seas: *The navigator set out on his long voyage.* **3.** an explorer of the seas: *Columbus, Magellan, and other great navigators.* **4.** *British.* a navvy. [< Latin *nāvigātor* < *nāvigāre;* see NAVIGATE]
nav·vy (nav′ē), *n., pl.* **-vies,** *v.,* **-vied, -vying.** *Especially British.* —*n.* an unskilled laborer employed in the excavation and construction of canals, railways, roads, etc.: *O'Casey became a navvy and bricklayer when he grew up* (New Yorker). —*v.i.* to work as a navvy: ... *Victoria Station, where he happened to be navvying at the time* (Punch). —*v.t.* to excavate. [short for *navigator*]
na·vy (nā′vē), *n., pl.* **-vies. 1.** all the ships of war of a country, with their men and the department that manages them. Most navies now have aircraft and large land areas devoted to their task of protecting a nation. **2.** the officers and men of the navy. **3.** the ships and men of the British merchant fleet. **4.** *Archaic.* a fleet of ships. **5.** navy blue. [< Old French *navie,* ultimately < Latin *nāvis* ship]
navy bean, the common white bean, dried for use as food, usually baked or in soup: *Commodore Perry coined the term "navy bean" while eating lunch one day out on Lake Erie during a British assault* (Philip Hamburger).
navy blue, a dark blue.
Navy Cross, a decoration awarded by the U.S. Navy for bravery in action.
Navy Day, October 27, a day formerly observed in honor of the U.S. Navy, now abolished in favor of Armed Forces Day.
Navy Exchange or **Navy exchange,** a general store at a naval base that sells cigarettes, candy, etc., to naval personnel.
navy yard, a government dockyard where naval vessels are built, repaired, and fitted out, and where naval stores and munitions of war are kept.
Na·wab (nə wôb′), *n.* a title given to important Moslems in India, giving princely status immediately below that of the Nizam of Hyderabad: *He routed the army of the powerful Nawab of Dir* (London Times). [< variant of Arabic *nuwwāb;* see NABOB]
na·wab (nə wôb′), *n.* **1.** a native ruler in India under the Mogul empire. Nawabs were viceroys or direct deputies of the reigning head of the government. **2. a.** a very rich man; nabob. **b.** any important or powerful person. [< *Nawab*]
nay (nā), *adv.* **1.** not only that, but also: *The daily work continued; nay, it actually increased* (Lytton Strachey). **2.** *Archaic.* no: *He woud not say her nay* (Sir Richard Steele).
—*n.* **1.** a denial or refusal; no. **2.** a negative vote or voter: *In response to a scattered voice vote, Speaker Rayburn ... facetiously remarked that the tally was three ayes and two nays, the ayes have it* (Wall Street Journal). [< Scandinavian (compare Old Icelandic *nei* < *ne* not + *ei* ever)]
na·ya pai·sa (nə yä′ pī sä′), *pl.* **na·ye pai·se** (nə yā′pī sā′), a coin of India that replaced the pice in 1957, since 1964 called paisa, worth 1/100 of a rupee. [< Hindi *nayā paisā* new pice]
nay·say (nā′sā′), *v.t., v.i.* to say nay (to); deny; oppose; vote in the negative: [*He*] *did not appear to naysay until Dirksen sent him word that his vote would make no difference* (Time). —*n. Archaic.* a denial or refusal; nay. —**nay′say′er,** *n.*
nay·word (nā′wėrd′), *n. Especially British.* **1.** a watchword. **2.** a byword.
Naz·a·rene (naz′ə rēn′, naz′ə rēn), *n.* **1.** a person born or living in Nazareth, a town in northern Palestine where Jesus lived during his boyhood. **2.** an early Christian (so called especially by Jews and Moslems): *For we have found this man* [*Paul*] ... *a ringleader of the sect of the Nazarenes* (Acts 24:5). **3.** a member of the Church of the Nazarene in the United States. **4.** one of a group of German painters of the early 1800's, who tried to recapture the primitive religious intensity of medieval Christian art.
the Nazarene, Jesus Christ: *Some versions of the New Testament use the phrase "Jesus the Nazarene" instead of "Jesus of Nazareth."* —*adj.* of or having to do with the Nazarenes or with Nazareth. [< Late Latin *Nazarēnus* < Greek *Nazarēnós* < *Nazarét* Nazareth]
Naz·a·rite (naz′ə rīt), *n.* **1.** (among the ancient Hebrews) a Jew who had taken certain strict religious vows. Numbers 6:1-27. **2.** a native of Nazareth; Nazarene. Also, **Nazirite.** [< Late Latin *Nazaraeus* (< Greek *Nāzōraîos* dedicated one < Hebrew *nāzīr*) + English *-ite*[1]]
Naz·ca (näs′kə), *n.* a member of a people who lived in Peru around the time of Christ, noted for their pottery.
Na·zi (nät′sē, nat′-), *n., pl.* **-zis,** *adj.* —*n.* **1.** a member or supporter of the National Socialist German Workers Party in Germany, organized under the leadership of Adolf Hitler. It came to power in Germany in 1933 and believed in state control of industry, denunciation of communism and Judaism, and the dominance of Germany as a world power. **2.** Often, **nazi.** a believer in similar doctrines in any country; fascist. —*adj.* of or having to do with the Nazis or their doctrines.
[< German *Nazi,* short for *Nati*(*onalsozialist*) National Socialist]
➔ **Nazi** was a political nickname for the National Socialist Party in Germany and is capitalized like *Republican* or *Democrat.* The type of party represented by the Nazis is usually referred to as *fascist* or *totalitarian.*
➔ **Nazi.** A pronunciation somewhere between (nä′zē) and (naz′ē) never gained general acceptance in the United States or Great Britain, but deserves note for its use by Sir Winston Churchill, in whose mouth during World War II it was an utterance of remarkable eloquence, conveying unmistakably Churchill's loathing and contempt for Hitler and his works.
Na·zi·dom (nät′sē dom, nat′-), *n.* the Nazi realm or power: ... *the warm story of the famed Trapp family, who sang their way out of Nazidom* (Time).
Na·zi·fi·ca·tion or **na·zi·fi·ca·tion** (nät′sə fə kā′shən, nat′-), *n.* **1.** the act of Nazifying: *Dr. Blume, who managed* (*without leaving Germany*) *not merely to abstain from these Nazifications but actually to discourage them* (Saturday Review). **2.** a being Nazified.
Na·zi·fy or **na·zi·fy** (nät′sə fī, nat′-), *v.t.,* **-fied, -fy·ing. 1.** to place under the control of the Nazis: *With Germany nazified, he settled in Paris* (Atlantic). **2.** to indoctrinate with Nazi views.

Na·zi·ism (nät′sē iz əm, nat′-), *n.* the doctrines of the Nazis, including totalitarian government and state control of industry, but opposition to communism; Nazism.

na·zir (nä′zir), *n.* **1.** the title of various officials in Moslem countries. **2.** (formerly) a native official in the Anglo-Indian courts. [< Arabic *nāzir*]

Naz·i·rite (naz′ə rīt), *n.* Nazarite.

Na·zism (nät′siz əm, nat′-), *n.* Naziism.

Nb (no period), niobium (chemical element).

n.b., note well; observe carefully (Latin, *nota bene*).

N.B., 1. New Brunswick. **2.** note well; observe carefully (Latin, *nota bene*).

➔ **N.B.** The abbreviation of the Latin *nota bene,* meaning note well, is occasionally found in formal announcements: *N.B. Members are to pay their dues not later than Monday, May 5.*

NBA (no periods) or **N.B.A.,** an abbreviation for:
1. National Bar Association.
2. National Basketball Association.
3. National Boxing Association.

NBC (no periods), National Broadcasting Company.

N-bomb (en′bom′), *n.* neutron bomb.

NBS (no periods), National Bureau of Standards.

n.c., nitrocellulose.

NC (no periods), **1.** Navy Cross. **2.** Nurse Corps.

N.C., North Carolina.

NCAA (no periods) or **N.C.A.A.,** National Collegiate Athletic Association.

NCAR (no periods), National Center for Atmospheric Research.

N.C.B. or **NCB** (no periods), National Coal Board (of Great Britain).

NCC (no periods), National Council of Churches.

NCI (no periods) or **N.C.I.,** National Cancer Institute.

NCO (no periods) or **N.C.O.,** noncommissioned officer.

Nd (no period), neodymium (chemical element).

n.d., no date; not dated.

N. Dak. or **N.D.,** North Dakota.

N.D.E.A., National Defense Education Act.

NDP (no periods), New Democratic Party (of Canada).

né (nā), *adj.* born. [< French *né,* masculine past participle of *naître* be born; see NÉE]

➔ **Né** is placed after a man's present name to show his original name: *Mark Stone* (*né Stein*) (Time).

Ne (no period), neon (chemical element).

n.e., 1. northeast. **2.** northeastern.

NE (no periods), **1.** Northeast or northeast. **2.** Northeastern or northeastern.

N.E., 1. New England. **2. a.** Northeast or northeast. **b.** Northeastern or northeastern.

NEA (no periods) or **N.E.A.,** National Education Association.

Ne·an·der·tal (nē an′dər täl; *German* nā än′dər täl), *adj.* Neanderthal.

Ne·an·der·tal·er (nē an′dər tä′lər), *n.* Neanderthaler.

Neandertal man, Neanderthal man.

Ne·an·der·thal (nē an′dər täl, -thôl; *German* nā än′dər täl), *adj.* of or like Neanderthal man, who at one time was thought to have had a brutish appearance and limited cultural development: *Here was a good example of the type of excess we could expect . . . especially on the more Neanderthal of the New York newspapers* (Atlantic).

Ne·an·der·thal·er (nē an′dər tä′lər, -thô′-), *n.* a Neanderthal man: *Unexpectedly, the latest Neanderthalers, living during the height of the last glaciation, show these simian features more strongly than those who had flourished before* (Observer).

Neanderthal man, an extinct race widespread in Europe, North Africa, and western and central Asia, in the early Stone Age, the first fossils of which were discovered in 1856 at the Neanderthal Gorge near Düsseldorf, Germany. The Neanderthal man of Europe had a large, heavy skull and low forehead, a broad, flat nose, and a heavy lower jaw with teeth intermediate in shape between those of modern man and the apes. *We now reach the immediate forerunner of modern man, homo neanderthalensis, or Neanderthal man* (Melville J. Herskovits). See picture under **humanoid.**

Ne·an·der·thal·oid (nē an′dər tä′loid), *adj.* of or like the Neanderthal man, his type of skull, or the race it is believed to represent: *Rhodesian man's limb bones show that he walked upright with his head erect, instead of in the Neanderthaloid crouch* (Scientific American).

ne·an·throp·ic (nē′an throp′ik), *adj.* of or belonging to the latest or modern period of the existence of man: *Three such stages or levels are being more and more generally recognized: Protoanthropic, Palaeoanthropic, and Neanthropic—"first," "old," and "newer" human* (Alfred L. Kroeber). [< *neo-* + *anthropic*]

neap[1] (nēp), *adj.* of or having to do with those tides that attain the least height. —*n.* a neap tide: *At London bridge the tidal range . . . at average neaps . . . is 15 feet* (New Scientist). —*v.i.* (of the tide) to become lower; tend towards the neap: . . . *in time for a tide neaping to tomorrow night's full moon* (New Yorker). [Old English *nēp*]

neap[2] (nēp), *n. U.S. Dialect.* the pole or tongue of a wagon intended to be drawn by two animals. [origin uncertain. Compare dialectal Norwegian *neip* forked pole, Old Icelandic *neip* the space between two fingers.]

neaped (nēpt), *adj.* (of a boat) grounded by neap tides and forced to wait for spring tides to get out.

Ne·a·pol·i·tan (nē′ə pol′ə tən), *adj.* of or having to do with Naples, a city in Italy. —*n.* a native or inhabitant of Naples. [< Latin *Neāpolītānus* < *Neāpolis* Naples < Greek *Neápolis* < *néā,* feminine of *néos* new + *pólis* city]

Neapolitan ice cream, ice cream or sherbet made in layers of different colors and flavors.

Neapolitan medlar, the azarole.

neap tide, a tide that occurs when the difference in height between high and low tide is least; lowest level of high tide. Neap tide comes twice a month, in the first and third quarters of the moon.

near (nir), *adv.* **1.** to or at a short distance; not far: *Christmas is drawing near. They searched near and far.* **2.** close in relation: *tribes near allied.* **3.** close to something in resemblance; almost next (to): *Fool that's near To knave* (Robert Browning). **4.** *Informal.* all but; almost; nearly: *The war lasted near a year.* **5.** thriftily: *I had lived so near and so close that in a whole year I had not spent the 15s. which I had saved* (Daniel Defoe). **6.** *Nautical.* close to the direction of the wind.

come near. See under **come.**

—*adj.* **1.** close by; not distant; less distant: *the near future. The post office is quite near.* **2.** intimate; familiar: *a near friend.* **3.** closely related: *a near relative.* **4.** approximating or resembling closely: *near silk, a near translation.* **5.** left: *The near horse and the off horse make a team.* **6.** short; direct: *Go by the nearest route.* **7.** stingy: *Mr. Barkis was something of a miser, or as Peggotty dutifully expressed it, was "a little near"* (Dickens). **8.** by a close margin; narrow: *a near escape.* **9.** closely affecting or touching one: *War is a matter of great and near concern to all of us.*

—*prep.* close to in space, time, condition, etc.: *Our house is near the river. It is near five o'clock.*

—*v.t., v.i.* to come or draw near to; approach: *The ship neared the land. The vacation was nearing its end.*

[Old English *nēar* nearer, comparative of *nēah* nigh, near]

—**Syn.** *adj.* **1.** close, nigh.

near beer, a beverage resembling beer but containing less than one half per cent alcohol.

near·by (nir′bī′), *adj., adv.* near; close by; close at hand: *a nearby house. They went nearby to visit.* —*prep. Dialect.* close to (a place, etc.).

Ne·arc·tic (nē ärk′tik, -är′tik), *adj.* having to do with the region including temperate and arctic North America and Greenland, especially with reference to the distribution of animals. [< Greek *néos* new + English *arctic*]

Near Eastern, of or having to do with the Near East, the region comprising the Balkans and the countries of southwestern Asia.

near-hand (nir′hand′), *Scottish.* —*adv.* **1.** nearby. **2.** nearly; almost: *His race is near-hand run* (Scott). —*adj.* near.

near·ly (nir′lē), *adv.* **1.** almost: *It is nearly bedtime. I nearly missed the train.* **2.** closely: *a matter that concerns you very nearly. It will cost more than we can afford as nearly as I can figure it.*

near-man or **Near-Man** (nir′man′), *n., pl.* **-men** or **-Men.** an ape man: *Some authorities conclude that the molar found in 1958 belonged to one of the Australopithecines, a primitive group of Near-Men* (Science News Letter).

near-miss (nir′mis′), *n.* **1. a.** the failure to make a direct hit on a target or other thing aimed at. **b.** a rocket, guided missile, bomb, or the like that fails to make a direct hit upon a target: *With a thermonuclear warhead the attacker can be sure of inflicting great damage even with a near-miss* (Newsweek). **2.** anything that does not fulfill but approaches very closely some standard of excellence: *The good near-misses scored by some of the first novelists* (Manchester Guardian). **3.** a narrow escape from danger or an accident: *The near-miss left me slightly shaken* (Atlantic).

near money, assets which are easily turned into cash, such as savings accounts and short-term investments.

near·ness (nir′nis), *n.* the state or fact of being near; proximity; imminence.

near point, *Optics.* the point nearest to the eye at which an image is clearly formed on the retina when there is maximum accommodation.

near·side (nir′sīd′), *n.* the side that is nearer or nearest, especially the left side: *We usually mount horses on the nearside.* —*adj.* on or to the near or left side; near; left: *blue smoke arises from the nearside mudguard* (Punch). *Lalor on his best pony, Fifty, . . . sent in Kishan to score with a good nearside shot* (London Times).

near-sight (nir′sīt′), *n.* myopia.

near-sight·ed (nir′sī′tid), *adj.* not able to see far; seeing distinctly at a short distance only; myopic: *Although Katherine Bruce was old enough to walk to the bus stop by herself, she was near-sighted and her father made the trip with her* (New Yorker). —**near′-sight′ed·ly,** *adv.* —**near′-sight′ed·ness,** *n.*

near-term (nir′tėrm′), *adj.* of or for a short period of time: *This has improved the market's near-term position* (Wall Street Journal).

neat[1] (nēt), *adj.* **1.** clean and in order: *a neat desk, a neat room, a neat dress.* **2.** able and willing to keep things in order: *a neat child.* **3.** well-formed; in proportion: *a neat design.* **4.** skillful; clever: *a neat trick, a neat turn of phrase.* **5.** without anything mixed in it; pure; straight: *He drinks his brandy neat. The gas is then enriched to the declared calorific value by the automatic addition of neat refinery gas* (London Times). **6.** *Slang.* very pleasing; fine: *a neat party.* **7.** clear; net: *a neat profit.* [< Anglo-French *neit,* Old French *net* < Latin *nitidus* gleaming < *nitēre* to shine] —**neat′ly,** *adv.* —**neat′ness,** *n.*

—**Syn. 1. Neat, tidy, trim** mean in good order. **Neat** suggests cleanness and absence of disorder or litter: *Her clothes are always neat.* **Tidy** suggests orderliness: *She keeps her room tidy.* **Trim** suggests pleasing neatness and smartness or compactness, proportion, and clean lines: *That is a trim sailboat.* **4.** deft, adroit. **5.** undiluted, clear. —**Ant. 1.** unkempt, slovenly.

neat[2] (nēt), *n. pl. or sing. Archaic.* **1.** cattle; oxen. **2.** an ox, cow, or heifer. —*adj.* of the ox kind: *neat cattle.* [Old English *nēat*]

neat·en (nē′tən), *v.t.* to put in order; clean; tidy up: *She . . . began neatening the books in a low bookshelf* (New Yorker).

neath or **'neath** (nēth, nēᴛʜ), *prep. Poetic.* beneath: *'neath the silvery moon.*

neat-hand·ed (nēt′han′did), *adj.* neat or dexterous in the use of the hands; deft: *Their savoury dinner . . . Of herbs, and other country messes, Which the neat-handed Phillis dresses* (Milton).

neat·herd (nēt′hėrd′), *n. Archaic.* cowherd.

neat's-foot oil (nēts′fu̇t′), a light-yellow oil obtained from the feet and shinbones of cattle by boiling. It is used to lubricate delicate machinery and to soften and preserve leather.

neb (neb), *n. Scottish.* **1.** the bill or beak of a bird. **2.** a person's mouth or nose: *"Woman," he said, "this is men's work. You'll keep your little turned-up neb out of it"* (Margery Allingham). **3.** an animal's snout. **4.** the tip of anything; nib. **5.** *Obsolete.* the face. [Old English *nebb*]

neb·bish (neb′ish), *n. U.S. Slang.* a drab, clumsy, inconsequential person; schlemiel. [< Yiddish *nebikh*]

Ne·bi·im (neb′ē ēm′; *Hebrew* nə vē′ēm′), *n.pl.* the books of the Prophets making up the second division of the Hebrew Old Testament canon. The first division is the Torah and the third division is the Kethubim. [< Hebrew *nəbi'im,* plural of *nābi* prophet]

Nebr. or **Neb.,** Nebraska.

Ne·bras·kan (nə bras′kən), *adj.* of or having to do with the State of Nebraska or its inhabitants. —*n.* a native or inhabitant of Nebraska.

neb·u·chad·nez·zar (neb′yə kəd nez′ər, neb′ə-), *n.* a very large bottle for alcoholic liquor that holds about 4 gallons: *nebuchadnezzars of champagne* (New Yorker). [named in honor of *Nebuchadnezzar,* died 562 B.C., a famous king of Babylon. See Daniel 1-4.]

neb·u·la (neb′yə lə), *n., pl.* **-lae** (-lē), **-las. 1.** a bright spot like a small, bright cloud, visible in the sky at night. A nebula may be either a mass of luminous gas or a cluster of stars very far away from our sun and its planets. Galactic nebulae are clouds of luminous gas within our galaxy and comparable in size with it. Extragalactic nebulae are clusters of stars outside our Milky Way. *An independent estimate was made of the distance of the Andromeda nebula by photoelectric measurements made in three colours* (A. W. Haslett). **2. a.** a cloudlike spot on the cornea of the eye. **b.** cloudiness of the urine. [< Latin *nebula* mist, cloud]

neb·u·lar (neb′yə lər), *adj.* of or concerning a nebula or nebulae.

nebular hypothesis, the theory that the solar system, and similar systems, developed from a mass of gas which drew together to form rings of matter, and in turn this matter formed planets. The theory was formulated by Pierre Simon de Laplace, 1749-1827, a French astronomer and mathematician.

ne·bu·li·um (nə byü′lē əm), *n.* a supposed chemical element to which certain green lines in the spectra of nebulae were once attributed, now known to be caused by oxygen, nitrogen, and other common gases. [< New Latin *nebulium* < Latin *nebula* mist, cloud + New Latin *-ium,* a suffix meaning "element"]

neb·u·li·za·tion (neb′yə lə zā′shən), *n.* **1.** the act of nebulizing. **2.** the state of being nebulized.

neb·u·lize (neb′yə līz), *v.t.,* **-lized, -liz·ing.** to reduce to fine mist or vapor; atomize.

neb·u·liz·er (neb′yə lī′zər), *n.* an apparatus for reducing liquid medicine to a vapor, for inhaling: *I raise these questions having just bought a nebulizer for use with an inhalant* (Atlantic).

Nebulizer

neb·u·lose (neb′yə lōs), *adj.* nebulous.

neb·u·los·i·ty (neb′yə los′ə tē), *n., pl.* **-ties. 1.** cloudlike quality; nebulous state; mistiness. **2.** cloudlike matter; nebula: *His theory is the dust and gas have been cleaned out by frequent passage through nebulosities in the Milky Way* (Science News Letter).

neb·u·lous (neb′yə ləs), *adj.* **1.** lacking form; hazy; vague; confused: *a nebulous ambition. Prestige is a nebulous word, meaning many things to many people* (Wall Street Journal). **2.** resembling a cloud or clouds; cloudlike. **3.** of or like a nebula or nebulae. [< Latin *nebulōsus* < *nebula* mist] —**neb′u·lous·ly,** *adv.* —**neb′u·lous·ness,** *n.*

n.e.c., not elsewhere classified.

nec·es·sar·i·an (nes′ə sãr′ē ən), *n., adj.* necessitarian.

nec·es·sar·i·an·ism (nes′ə sãr′ē ə niz′əm), *n.* necessitarianism.

nec·es·sar·ies (nes′ə ser′ēz), *n.pl.* See under **necessary,** *n.*

nec·es·sar·i·ly (nes′ə ser′ə lē, nes′ə-sãr′-), *adv.* **1.** because of necessity: *Leaves are not necessarily green.* **2.** as a necessary result: *War necessarily causes misery and waste.* —**Syn. 2.** inevitably.

nec·es·sar·i·ness (nes′ə ser′ē nis), *n.* the state of being necessary.

nec·es·sar·y (nes′ə ser′ē), *adj., n., pl.* **-sar·ies.** —*adj.* **1.** that must be, be had, or be done; inevitable; required; indispensable: *Death, a necessary end, will come when it will come* (Shakespeare). **2.** compelled by another or others; compulsory: *a necessary agent.* **3.** *Logic.* **a.** that cannot be denied because denial would entail contradiction of what has already been established: *a necessary truth.* **b.** that cannot be avoided or escaped because based on a premise known to be true: *a necessary inference.* **4.** *Archaic.* rendering certain essential services to a household, employer, etc.: *a necessary woman.*

—*n.* **1.** a thing impossible to do without; requisite; essential; necessity: *Water and food, clothing, and shelter are necessaries of human life.* **2.** *British Dialect.* a toilet.

necessaries, *Law.* the things, as food, shelter, clothing, etc., required to support a dependent or incompetent and suitable to his station in life: *the obligation of parents to provide their offspring with necessaries.*

the necessary, money: *"Have you the necessary for such a long trip?"*

[< Latin *necessārius* < *necesse* unavoidable, probably < *ne-* not + *cēdere* withdraw]

—**Syn.** *adj.* **1. Necessary, indispensable, essential** mean needed or required. **Necessary** applies to whatever is needed but not absolutely required: *Work is a necessary part of life.* **Indispensable** implies that, without it, the intended result or purpose cannot be achieved: *Work is an indispensable part of success.* **Essential** implies that the existence or proper functioning of something depends upon it: *Work is essential to happiness.*

necessary evil, something unpleasant that cannot be avoided: *He had profoundly disliked the Reform Bill, which he had only accepted at last as a necessary evil* (Lytton Strachey).

ne·ces·si·tar·i·an (nə ses′ə tãr′ē ən), *n.* a person who denies that the will is free, and maintains that all action is the necessary effect of prior causes. —*adj.* having to do with necessitarians or necessitarianism.

ne·ces·si·tar·i·an·ism (nə ses′ə tãr′ē ə-niz′əm), *n.* the doctrine of necessitarians, comprising a form of determination.

ne·ces·si·tate (nə ses′ə tāt), *v.t.,* **-tat·ed, -tat·ing. 1.** to make necessary: *His broken leg necessitated an operation.* **2.** to compel, oblige, or force: *I was necessitated to fight with an imaginary enemy* (Herman Melville). —**Syn. 1.** require, demand.

ne·ces·si·ta·tion (nə ses′ ə tā′shən), *n.* **1.** the act of necessitating or making necessary. **2.** the state of being made necessary; compulsion.

ne·ces·si·ta·tive (nə ses′ə tā′tiv), *adj.* tending to necessitate or make necessary.

ne·ces·si·tous (nə ses′ə təs), *adj.* very poor; needy: *He . . . grew necessitous . . . and wanted bread* (Benjamin Franklin). —**ne·ces′si·tous·ly,** *adv.* —**ne·ces′si·tous·ness,** *n.* —**Syn.** indigent, destitute.

ne·ces·si·ty (nə ses′ə tē), *n., pl.* **-ties. 1.** the fact of being necessary; extreme need: *We understand the necessity of eating.* **2.** the quality or condition of being necessary; great urgency: *He flies only in cases of necessity. His orders lack necessity.* **3.** that which cannot be done without; indispensable thing: *Water is a necessity.* **4.** that which forces one to act in a certain way: *Necessity often drives people to do disagreeable things.* **5.** that which is inevitable, especially through the operation of a law of nature: *Night follows day as a necessity.* **6.** need; poverty: *This poor family is in great necessity.* **7.** *Philosophy.* **a.** any form of compulsion, as moral, legal, physical, or logical compulsion, that causes a person to do something against his will. **b.** the inevitable connection between a cause and its effect; inevitability.

of necessity, because it must be: . . . *Marxism . . . in Russia, of necessity an outlawed movement . . . became, in its most effective form, narrow, concentrated, grim and cruel* (Edmund Wilson).

[< Old French *necessite,* learned borrowing from Latin *necessitās* (in Late Latin, poverty) < *necesse;* see NECESSARY]

—**Syn. 1.** exigency, indispensability. See **need. 3.** essential, requisite.

➔ **Necessity.** The idiom is *necessity of* or *for* doing something (not *to* do something): *Most athletes can see the necessity of* (or *for*) *keeping training. There is no necessity for an immediate decision.*

neck (nek), *n.* **1.** the part of the body that connects the head with the shoulders. The neck contains vital passages for breathing, blood supply to the head, and ingestion of food, and includes the uppermost part of the spinal column. **2.** the part of a garment that fits the neck: *the neck of a shirt.* **3.** any narrow part like a neck. **4.** a narrow strip of land: *a neck of land.* **5.** a narrow strip of water. **6.** the slender part of a bottle, flask, retort, or other container. **7.** *Architecture.* the lowest part of the capital of a column, where it joins the shaft. **8.** the long slender part of a violin or similar instrument, extending from the body to the head; finger board. **9.** the part of a tooth between the crown and the root. **10.** a slender or constricted part of a bone or organ. **11.** a long siphon occurring in certain mollusks: *the neck of a clam.* **12.** *Printing.* the part of a type between the face and shoulder; beard. **13.** (in horse racing) the length of the neck of a horse or other animal as a measure: . . . *Impasse was third, a neck behind Helianthus* (New York Times).

get (catch, take) it in the neck, to be hard hit (by something); be severely reprimanded or punished: *Unfortunately, it is the public who is getting it in the neck* (New Yorker).

neck and crop, bodily; completely; altogether: *His application was indignantly opposed, sternly put to the vote, and thrown out neck and crop* (Manchester Guardian).

neck and neck, a. abreast: *The race started with the horses nearly neck and neck.* **b.** even in a race or contest: *Neck and neck with the Poujadiste gains were those of the hard-running Communists* (Newsweek).

neck or nothing, venturing all: *Cabs are all very well in cases of expedition, when it's a matter of neck or nothing* (Dickens).

stick one's neck out, *Informal.* to put oneself in a dangerous or vulnerable position by foolish or zealous action: *He . . . has been fired for sticking his ignorant . . . neck out too far* (Sunday Times).

talk through (the back of) one's neck, *Especially British Slang.* to talk nonsense; blather: *That braggart is just talking through the back of his neck.*

up to one's neck, *Informal.* deeply taken up; thoroughly involved: *The host tends to look like a rather important civil servant up to his neck in an awkward piece of long-term diplomacy* (Manchester Guardian Weekly).

win by a neck, a. to win a horse race by the length of a head and a neck: *Capeador . . . won by a neck from Social Outcast* (New Yorker). **b.** to win by a close margin: *In his race for the city council, he won by a neck.*

—*v.i. U.S. Slang.* to embrace; hug; kiss and caress. —*v.t.* **1.** to cut or snatch off the head of (a fowl). **2.** *U.S. Slang.* to kiss and caress (a person).

[Old English *hnecca*] —**neck′er,** *n.* —**neck′less,** *adj.*

neck·band (nek′band′), *n.* **1.** a band worn around the neck. **2.** the part of a shirt to which the collar is attached.

neck-break·ing (nek′brā′king), *adj.* breakneck: *Starting from Calicut in the limousine of a rich comrade, we sped for Trichur at neck-breaking and tyre-screeching speed* (Manchester Guardian).

neck·cloth (nek′klôth′, -kloth′), *n.* a cloth worn around the neck, especially by men; cravat.

neck-deep (nek′dēp′), *adj., adv.* **1.** submerged up to the neck. **2.** very much involved: *The United States was neck-deep in political intrigue* (New York Times).

-necked, *combining form.* having a ——— neck: *Long-necked = having a long neck.*

neck·er·chief (nek′ər chif), *n.* a cloth worn around the neck. [< *neck* + *kerchief*] —**Syn.** scarf.

neck·guard (nek′gärd′), *n.* a piece of armor for the neck, usually attached to a helmet.

neck·ing (nek′ing), *n.* **1. a.** a molding or series of moldings separating the capital and shaft of a column. **b.** the space between such moldings. **2.** the part of a column between the capital and shaft; gorgerin. **3.** *U.S. Slang.* the act of caressing and kissing; amorous play.

neck·lace (nek′lis), *n.* a string or chain of jewels, gold, silver, beads, etc., worn around the neck as an ornament.

neck·let (nek′lit), *n.* an ornament to be worn about the neck; necklace.

neck·line (nek′līn′), *n.* the line around the neck where a garment ends: *Her perfect skin in the oval above her neckline was flushed* (John Updike).
neck-or-noth·ing (nek′ər nuth′ing), *adj.* headlong; reckless.
neck·piece (nek′pēs′), *n.* a fur scarf.
neck-rest (nek′rest′), *n.* a support for the neck in resting or sleeping, used in China, Japan, Africa, etc.
neck sweetbread, the thymus gland, especially of a calf, used as food.
neck·tie (nek′tī′), *n.* **1.** a narrow band or a tie worn around the neck, under the collar of a shirt, and tied in front; cravat. **2.** any bow or the like, worn in front of the neck. **3.** *Slang.* a hangman's rope.
necktie party, *U.S. Slang.* a lynching by hanging with a rope: *If Larrabee ever comes back to Tall Timber there ought to be a necktie party for him* (T.K. Holmes).
neck verse, a Latin verse printed in black-letter, usually Psalm 51:1, formerly set before an accused person claiming benefit of clergy, in order to test his ability to read; if he could read it, he was released, thus saving his neck: *Letter nor line know I never a one, Wer't my neck verse at Hairibee* (Scott).
neck·wear (nek′wãr′), *n.* collars, ties, and other articles worn around the neck.
neck-yoke (nek′yōk′), *n.* a bar, usually of wood, that is connected with the collars of a harness and from which the end of the tongue of a vehicle is suspended.
nec·ro·ba·cil·lo·sis (nek′rə bas′ə lō′sis), *n., pl.* **-ses** (-sēz). any of several diseases, especially of livestock, and occasionally of man, accompanied by necrosis and large areas of ulcerated festering tissue, caused by certain anaerobic bacilli. [< New Latin *Necrobacillus* the genus of bacteria that cause the disease (< Greek *nekrós* corpse + Late Latin *bacillus* bacillus) + English *-osis*]
nec·ro·bi·o·sis (nec′rō bī ō′sis), *n.* the natural death of one or more cells of an organism, as distinguished from necrosis, death resulting from disease. [< Greek *nekrós* corpse + *bíōsis* way of life]
nec·ro·gen·ic (nek′rə jen′ik), *adj. Pathology.* produced or caused by dead bodies or dead animal matter. [< Greek *nekrós* corpse + English *-gen* + *-ic*]
ne·crog·ra·pher (ne krog′rə fər), *n.* a writer of obituary notices.
ne·crol·a·try (ne krol′ə trē), *n.* worship of the dead. [< Greek *nekrós* dead body + *latreíā* worship]
nec·ro·log·i·cal (nek′rə loj′ə kəl), *adj.* having to do with necrology; giving an account of the dead or of deaths: *The United States . . . is about to become a forum for political discussions of a predominantly clinical and necrological nature* (New Yorker). **—nec′ro·log′i·cal·ly,** *adv.*
ne·crol·o·gist (ne krol′ə jist), *n.* a person who writes or prepares obituaries.
ne·crol·o·gy (ne krol′ə jē), *n., pl.* **-gies. 1.** a list of persons who have died. **2.** a notice of a person's death; obituary. [< Greek *nekrós* dead body + *lógos* count, reckoning]
nec·ro·mance (nek′rə mans), *n. Archaic.* necromancy.
nec·ro·man·cer (nek′rə man′sər), *n.* **1.** a person who is supposed to foretell the future by communicating with the dead. **2.** a magician; sorcerer; wizard: *He is a veritable necromancer, equipped with philters and elixirs of wondrous potency* (Harper's).
nec·ro·man·cy (nek′rə man′sē), *n.* **1.** a foretelling of the future by communicating with the dead: *By his skill in necromancy, he has a power of calling whom he pleases from the dead* (Jonathan Swift). **2.** magic; enchantment; sorcery. [alteration of Old French *nygromancie,* learned borrowing from Medieval Latin *nigromantia* < Latin *necromantīa* < Greek *nekromanteíā* < *nekrós* dead body + *manteíā* divination; confusion with Latin *niger* "black" led to translation "black art"]
nec·ro·man·tic (nek′rə man′tik), *adj.* **1.** having to do with necromancy: *old Merlin's necromantic spells* (Thomas Hood). **2.** given to the practice of necromancy. **—nec′ro·man′ti·cal·ly,** *adv.*
ne·croph·a·gous (ne krof′ə gəs), *adj.* feeding on dead bodies or carrion: *necrophagous beasts.* [< Greek *nekrós* dead body + *phageîn* eat + English *-ous*]
nec·ro·phile (nek′rə fīl, -fil), *n.* a person who is affected with necrophily.
nec·ro·phil·i·a (nek′rə fil′ē ə), *n. Psychology.* necrophily.
nec·ro·phil·i·ac (nek′rə fil′ē ak), *n.* a necrophile.
nec·ro·phil·ic (nek′rə fil′ik), *adj.* of, having to do with, or characteristic of necrophily.
ne·croph·i·ly (ne krof′ə lē), *n.* a morbid attraction to dead bodies. [< Greek *nekrós* dead body + *philíā* affection]
ne·crop·o·lis (ne krop′ə lis), *n., pl.* **-lis·es, -leis** (-līs). **1.** a cemetery. **2.** an ancient or prehistoric burying ground: *Hill and hill-slope were the necropolis of a vanished race* (John R. Green). [< Greek *nekrópolis* < *nekrós* dead body + *pólis* city] **—Syn. 1.** graveyard.
nec·rop·sy (nek′rop sē), *n., pl.* **-sies.** an autopsy.
ne·cros·co·py (ne kros′kə pē), *n., pl.* **-pies.** necropsy.
ne·crose (ne krōs′, nek′rōs), *v.t., v.i.,* **-crosed, -cros·ing.** to affect or be affected with necrosis: *The cartilages often necrose* (F.T. Roberts).
ne·cro·sis (ne krō′sis), *n., pl.* **-ses** (-sēz). **1.** the death or decay of body tissues. It may result from a degenerative disease, stoppage of the oxygen supply, infection, or destructive burning or freezing. **2.** a disease of plants characterized by small black spots of decayed tissue. [< New Latin *necrosis* < Greek *nékrōsis,* ultimately < *nekrós* dead body]
ne·crot·ic (ne krot′ik), *adj.* of, characterized by, or showing necrosis: *In one, the necrotic diseases, there is an actual destruction of host tissue* (Harbaugh and Goodrich).
necrotic enteritis, a disease of hogs that causes extensive decay of the mucous membrane of the intestines, often confused with hog cholera.
nec·ro·tize (nek′rə tīz), *v.t., v.i.,* **-tized, -tiz·ing.** to affect or be affected with necrosis.
ne·crot·o·my (ne krot′ə mē), *n., pl.* **-mies. 1.** the cutting away and removal of necrosed bone. **2.** the dissection of corpses. [< Greek *nekrós* dead body + *-tomíā* a cutting]
nec·tar (nek′tər), *n.* **1.** *Greek Mythology.* **a.** the drink of the gods: *But might I of Jove's nectar sup* (Ben Jonson). **b.** the food of the gods. **2.** any delicious drink. **3.** a sweet liquid found in many flowers, which attracts insects and birds that carry out pollination. Bees gather nectar and make it into honey. *The training of bees studied in relation to their normal feeding which is regulated by the availability of pollen and nectar . . .* (J.L. Cloudsley-Thompson). [< Latin *nectar* < Greek *néktar*]
nec·tar·e·an (nek tãr′ē ən), *adj.* nectareous.
nec·tared (nek′tərd), *adj.* filled or flavored with or as if with nectar; delicious: *a perpetual feast of nectar'd sweets* (Milton).
nec·tar·e·ous (nek tãr′ē əs), *adj.* of or like nectar; delicious; sweet: *a certain kind of beer, nectareous to the palate* (Hawthorne).
nec·tar·i·al (nek tãr′ē əl), *adj.* of or having to do with the nectary of a plant.
nec·tar·ine[1] (nek′tə rēn′, nek′tə rēn), *n.* a kind of peach with no down on its skin and a firm pulp. [< *nectarine*[2]]
nec·tar·ine[2] (nek′tər in), *adj.* like nectar; delicious. [< *nectar* + *-ine*[1]]
nec·tar·ous (nek′tər əs), *adj.* nectareous.
nec·ta·ry (nek′tər ē), *n., pl.* **-ries.** the gland of a flower or plant that secretes nectar.
NED (no periods) or **N.E.D.,** New English Dictionary (Oxford English Dictionary). See also **OED.**
NEDC (no periods), National Economic Development Council (of Great Britain).
ned·dy (ned′ē), *n., pl.* **-dies.** a donkey: *long-eared Neddies, giving themselves leonine airs* (Thackeray).
Ned·dy (ned′ē), *n., pl.* **-dies.** *British Slang.* **1.** the National Economic Development Council of Great Britain; NEDC. **2.** any similar body for developing the national economy.
née or **nee** (nā), *adj.* born. [< French *née,* feminine past participle of *naître* be born < Latin *nāscī*]
➤ **Née** is placed after the name of a married woman to show her maiden name: *Mrs. Smith, née Adams.*
need (nēd), *n.* **1.** the lack of a useful or desired thing: *For need of a nail, the shoe was lost. His writing showed need of grammar.* **2.** a useful or desired thing that is lacking: *In the jungle their need was fresh water.* **3.** necessity; requirement: *There is no real need to hurry.* **4.** a situation or time of difficulty: *a friend in need, to fail someone in his need.* **5.** extreme poverty: *The family's need was so great the children did not have shoes.*
have need to, must; should; have to: *The best of saints have need to be warned against the worst of sins* (Octavius Winslow).
if need be, if it has to be; if necessary: *They will fight to the bitter end, if need be.*
—*v.t.* to have need of; want; require: *to need money. I need a new hat. Plants need water.* —*v.i.* **1.** to be in want: *Give to those that need.* **2.** to be necessary: *The rope cuts his hands more than needs.* **3.** to have to; ought to; must; should: *He need not go. Need she go?* [Old English *nēd, nīed*] **—need′er,** *n.*
—**Syn.** *n.* **1. Need, necessity** mean lack of something required or desired. **Need** suggests pressing want, lack or absence of something required for the welfare or success of a person or thing or of something useful or satisfying: *She is in need of a rest.* **Necessity** suggests an urgent need or imperative demand, but implies a more objective attitude and has less emotional appeal than *need* sometimes does: *She realizes the necessity of getting enough sleep.* **5.** want, destitution, indigence. *-v.t.* See **lack.**
➤ **Need,** not originally a modal auxiliary, has been partly attracted into this class because of its similarity in meaning to *must* and *should.* In the present tense (especially in the negative), it often follows the pattern of the modal verbs, without *-s* in the third person singular and is followed by an infinitive without *to: He need only try* (or) *He needs only to try. He needn't go* (or) *He doesn't need to go.* It never conforms to the modal pattern in tenses other than the present or when it is not an auxiliary: *He needed to find a room. He needs money.*
need·fire (nēd′fīr′), *n. Scottish.* **1.** fire produced from dry wood by friction, formerly used to cure disease among cattle. **2.** a beacon fire or bonfire: *The ready page, with hurried hand, Awaked the needfire's slumbering brand* (Scott).
need·ful (nēd′fəl), *adj.* **1.** needed; necessary: *a needful change.* **2.** needy. —*n.* a necessary thing.
the needful, a. what is necessary or requisite: *His lawyer will do the needful in the event of the man's death.* **b.** *Informal.* the necessary funds; money; cash: *. . . to live, I must have what you call 'the needful,' which I can only get by working* (Charlotte Brontë). **—need′ful·ly,** *adv.* **—need′ful·ness,** *n.*
—**Syn.** *adj.* **1.** requisite, required, indispensable.
need·i·ness (nē′dē nis), *n.* the state of being needy; poverty; want; indigence.
nee·dle (nē′dəl), *n., v.,* **-dled, -dling.** —*n.* **1.** a very slender tool, sharp at one end and with a hole or eye to pass a thread through, used in sewing. **2.** a slender rod used in knitting. **3.** a rod with a hook at one end used in crocheting, etc. **4.** a thin steel pointer on a compass, electrical machinery, or some gauges, as a speedometer, altimeter, etc. **5.** a slender steel tube with a sharp point at the end of a hypodermic syringe used for injecting something below the skin, withdrawing blood, etc.: *The doctor jabbed the needle into my arm.* **6.** a phonograph needle. **7.** any of various small objects resembling a needle in sharpness: *needles of broken glass, ice, etc.* **8.** a slender rod that controls the opening of a valve. **9.** the thin pointed leaf of a fir tree, pine tree, etc. **10.** a pillar; obelisk: *Cleopatra's needle.* **11.** an instrument somewhat like a needle, used in engraving or etching. **12.** *Mineralogy, Chemistry.* a crystal or spicule like a needle in shape: *One such isotope, in the form of germanium oxide needles, can be inserted in the body and left there* (New York Times). **13.** *Geology.* a pinnacle of rock tapering to a point. **14.** dipole (def. 2 b): *The 400 million radio-reflecting "needles" . . . have been spotted photographically by astronomers at three observatories* (Science News Letter).

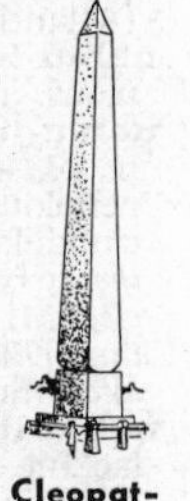

Cleopatra's Needle (def. 10)

a needle in a (or **the**) **haystack,** something extremely difficult or impossible to find or reach: *We are looking for a needle in the haystack—that one buyer in the hundreds of thousands who will see the ad* (Burnett Bear).

give one the needle, *Informal.* to urge to action or response; goad; incite; prod: *It's mostly a question of giving our personnel the needle to make them try a little harder . . .* (Wall Street Journal).
—*v.t.* **1.** *Informal.* to vex by repeated sharp prods, gibes, etc.; goad, incite, or annoy: *to needle someone into taking action. That ghoulish voice began needling me again* (S.J. Perelman). **2.** to add alcohol to (beer, ale, etc.): *The impact of the needled soft drink . . . had been such as to make him ill* (New Yorker). **3.** to sew or pierce with a needle. —*v.i.* **1.** to work with a needle. **2.** *Mineralogy, Chemistry.* to form needle-shaped crystals. [Old English *nǣdl*] —**nee′dle·like′,** *adj.*

needle bath, a bath in which the water is forced against the body in needlelike jets.

needle bug, any of the slender-bodied, long-legged hemipterous insects found in fresh-water ponds, common in the United States.

Needle Bug (about 2½ in. long)

nee·dle·fish (nē′dəl fish′), *n., pl.* **-fish·es** or (*collectively*) **-fish. 1.** any of a group of marine fishes comprising a family, similar to the fresh-water garfish although not related to them; billfish; gar. **2.** a pipefish.

nee·dle·ful (nē′dəl fu̇l), *n., pl.* **-fuls.** a suitable length of thread for using at one time with a needle.

needle gun, a breech-loading rifle in which the charge is exploded by the impact of a needle or slender steel pin, used by the Prussian army in 1866 and 1870.

needle ice, slender bits of ice formed in wet soil, the bottom of a stream, etc., during cold weather.

nee·dle-nosed (nē′dəl nōzd′), *adj.* **1.** (of airplanes and missiles) having a tapered nose to reduce air resistance at high speeds: *The cramped cockpit of a needle-nosed, stub-winged plane* (Time). **2.** having tapered ends for getting into small spaces or working with small objects: *needle-nosed pliers.*

needle point, 1. embroidery made with colored yarns on a coarse, stiff canvas cloth and used to cover chairs, footstools, etc. **2.** a lace made entirely with a needle instead of a bobbin, using a pattern of parchment or paper; point lace.

nee·dle-point (nē′dəl point′), *adj.* of or having to do with needle point.

nee·dler (nē′dlər), *n. Informal.* a person who incites or irritates others, usually by incessant nagging, heckling, reminding, or the like.

nee·dle-shaped (nē′dəl shāpt′), *adj.* shaped like a needle; long and slender, with one or both ends sharp.

need·less (nēd′lis), *adj.* not needed or wanted; unnecessary; useless: *Congress is taking a needless risk as long as it allows this important constitutional problem to remain clouded in doubt* (Newsweek). —**need′less·ly,** *adv.* —**need′less·ness,** *n.*

nee·dle·stone (nē′dəl stōn′), *n.* a mineral having needle-shaped crystals, as natrolite.

needle trade or **needle trades,** the trade or business of manufacturing clothing, including all of its members: *The inhuman working conditions of the needle trades at the beginning of the century* (New York Times).

needle valve, a valve whose very small opening is controlled by a slender, needle-shaped rod projecting into it, used especially in carburetors and other devices requiring a precise adjustment of the flow of a liquid.

nee·dle·wom·an (nē′dəl wu̇m′ən), *n., pl.* **-wom·en.** a woman who is a skillful sewer or who earns her living by sewing; seamstress.

nee·dle·work (nē′dəl wėrk′), *n.* **1.** work done with a needle; sewing; embroidery. **2.** the work or occupation of sewing with a needle.

nee·dle·work·er (nē′dəl wėr′kər), *n.* a person who does needlework: *a garment made for her by the famously skilled needleworkers of Hong Kong* (New Yorker).

nee·dly (nē′dlē), *adj.* like a needle or needles; full of needles: *a needly thorn, a needly bush.*

need·ments (nēd′mənts), *n.pl.* things needed; necessaries; requisites: *collecting from her household stores such needments as could be arranged in the smallest compass* (Harriet Beecher Stowe).

need·n't (nē′dənt), need not.

needs (nēdz), *adv.* because of necessity; necessarily: *A soldier needs must go where duty calls. You must needs be a stranger in this region . . . else you would surely have heard of Mistress Hester Prynne* (Hawthorne). [Old English *nēdes,* (originally) genitive of *nēd* need]

need·y (nē′dē), *adj.,* **need·i·er, need·i·est.** not having enough to live on; characterized by poverty or need; very poor: *a needy family, to be in needy circumstances.* —**Syn.** indigent, destitute, penniless.

neem tree (nēm), a meliaceous tree of India and Ceylon, sometimes 50 feet high, with broad, pinnate leaves; margosa. The natives chew its small twigs and use them as toothbrushes. *Most of the trees were neem trees, which look like giant versions of California's pepper trees* (Atlantic). [< Hindi *nīm*]

neep (nēp), *n. Scottish.* a turnip. [Old English *nǣp* < Latin *nāpus* turnip. Doublet of NAVEW.]

ne'er (nãr), *adv. Poetic.* never.

ne'er-do-well (nãr′dü wel′), *n.* a worthless fellow; good-for-nothing person: *The eldest son is a hard-drinking ne'er-do-well, with a bitter hostility toward his father* (Atlantic). —*adj.* worthless; good-for-nothing: *one of those ne'er-do-well lads who seem to have a . . . magnetic power for misfortunes* (Elizabeth Gaskell). —**Syn.** *n.* scapegrace.

neeze (nēz), *v.i.,* **neezed, neez·ing.** *British.* to sneeze: *And then the whole quire hold their hips and laugh, and waxen in their mirth, and neeze, and swear* (Shakespeare). [Middle English *nesen,* probably < Scandinavian (compare Old Icelandic *hnjōsa*)]

ne·fan·dous (ni fan′dəs), *adj.* unmentionable; abominable; impious: *The press restrain'd! nefandous thought! In vain our sires have nobly fought* (Matthew Green). [< Latin *nefandus* (with English *-ous*) < *ne-* not + *fandus* to be spoken, gerundive of *fārī* to speak]

ne·far·i·ous (ni fãr′ē əs), *adj.* very wicked; villainous: *a nefarious scheme.* [< Latin *nefārius* (with English *-ous*) < *nefās* < *ne-* not + *fās* right; (originally) divine decree < *fārī* speak] —**ne·far′i·ous·ly,** *adv.* —**ne·far′i·ous·ness,** *n.* —**Syn.** heinous, atrocious, infamous.

neg., **1.** negation. **2. a.** negative. **b.** negatively.

ne·gate (ni gāt′, nē′gāt), *v.t.,* **-gat·ed, -gat·ing. 1.** to destroy, nullify, or make ineffective: *If gravity can be understood scientifically and negated or neutralized in some relatively inexpensive manner . . .* (New York Herald Tribune). **2.** to declare not to exist; deny. [< Latin *negāre* (with English *-ate*[1]) say no, related to *nec* not]

ne·ga·tion (ni gā′shən), *n.* **1.** a denying; denial: *Shaking the head is a sign of negation.* **2.** the absence or opposite of some positive thing or quality: *Darkness is the negation of light. Death is nothing more than the negation of life* (Henry Fielding). **3.** a thing or object of thought, consisting in the absence of something positive [< Latin *negātiō, -ōnis* < *negāre* say no]

ne·ga·tion·ist (ni gā′shə nist), *n.* a person who denies or expresses negation, especially habitually.

neg·a·tive (neg′ə tiv), *adj., n., v.,* **-tived, -tiv·ing.** —*adj.* **1. a.** saying no; expressing or containing refusal: *His answer was negative. "I won't" is a negative expression.* **b.** prohibitory, as a command or order. **2.** not positive; consisting in the lack of the opposite: *Negative kindness means not being unkind. His negative suggestions are not helpful.* **3.** *Mathematics, Physics.* **a.** counting down from zero; minus: *Three below zero is a negative quantity.* **b.** measured or proceeding in the opposite direction to that considered as positive: *Long ago, the direction of electric current flow was defined as being from positive to negative* (John R. Pierce). **c.** lying on the side of a point, line, or plane opposite to that considered positive. **4. a.** of the kind of electricity produced on resin when it is rubbed with silk, or that present in a charged body which has an excess of electrons. **b.** characterized by the presence or production of such electricity: *Protons have positive charge, electrons negative charge* (Sears and Zemansky). **5.** *Chemistry.* having a tendency to gain electrons, and thus to become charged with negative electricity, as an element or radical. **6.** *Photography.* showing the lights and shadows reversed: *the negative image on a photographic plate.* **7.** showing an absence of the germs, symptoms, etc., of an illness; lacking the bacteria or viruses that cause a specific disease. **8.** *Biology.* moving or turning away from light, the earth, or any other stimulus: *If a plant organ reacts by turning . . . away, the response is negative* (Fred W. Emerson). **9.** *Logic.* (of a proposition) expressing denial of a predicate. **10.** *Psychology.* resisting suggestions; very uncooperative. *Abbr.:* neg.
—*n.* **1.** a word or statement that says no or denies; negative reply or answer: *The positive and the negative are set before the mind for its choice* (Jonathan Edwards). **2.** the side that says no or denies in an argument. **3.** a negative quality or characteristic. **4.** a minus quantity, sign, symbol, etc. **5.** the kind of electricity produced on resin when it is rubbed with silk. **6.** the negative element in an electric battery. **7.** a photographic image in which the lights and shadows are reversed. Positive prints are made from it. **8.** the right of veto.
in the negative, a. in favor of denying (a request, suggestion, etc.): *That should be determined in the negative* (Duke of Wellington). **b.** saying no; denying: *They unanimously answered in the negative* (Horace Walpole).
—*v.t.* **1.** to say no to; deny; vote against: *Father negatived our plan. The suggestion that it is a means of dealing with ectoparasites seems to be negatived by the following considerations* (New Scientist). **2.** to show to be false; disprove. **3.** to make useless; counteract; neutralize: *The method which both sides are using to negative the effects of atomic attack is the widest possible measure of dispersal* (London Times).
[< Latin *negātīvus* < *negāre* say no] —**neg′a·tive·ly,** *adv.* —**neg′a·tive·ness,** *n.*

negative acceleration, a decrease in velocity.

negative catalyst, a substance that retards a chemical reaction without itself being permanently affected.

negative electricity, electricity in which the electron is the elementary unit.

negative lens, diverging lens.

negative prescription, *Law.* a limitation of the time within which a claim may be made or an action brought.

negative staining, the immersing of small organisms, such as viruses and bacteria, in a stain which does not color them, so that their forms appear clearly defined against the colored background.

neg·a·tiv·ism (neg′ə tə viz′əm), *n.* **1.** a tendency to say or do the opposite of what is suggested. **2.** *Psychology.* a type of behavior marked by resistance to suggestion. Passive negativism is the kind in which the individual fails to do what is expected. Active negativism is the kind in which he does the opposite of what is expected. **3.** *Philosophy.* **a.** any doctrine of which doubt or denial is an essential characteristic, as skepticism, agnosticism, or atheism: *Even those who do not share his view of life admit that it was a product of the age and not a purely personal negativism* (Atlantic). **b.** any doctrine that rejects the validity of natural reality.

neg·a·tiv·ist (neg′ə tə vist), *n.* a negationist. —*adj.* negative.

neg·a·tiv·is·tic (neg′ə tə vis′tik), *adj.* negative.

neg·a·tiv·i·ty (neg′ə tiv′ə tē), *n.* negativeness.

ne·ga·tor (ni gā′tər), *n.* a person who denies.

neg·a·to·ry (neg′ə tôr′ē, -tōr′-), *adj.* denying; negative: *A negatory nod of his honest . . . old head* (Thackeray).

neg·a·tron (neg′ə tron), *n. Physics, Chemistry.* an electron with a negative charge, as contrasted with a positron or positively charged electron. [< *nega*(tive) + (elec)*tron*]

neg·lect (ni glekt′), *v.t.* **1.** to give too little care or attention to: *to neglect one's health, to neglect one's children.* **2.** to leave undone; not attend to: *The maid neglected her work.* **3.** to omit; fail: *Don't neglect to lock the windows or water the plants before you leave.*
—*n.* **1.** the act of neglecting; disregard: *His neglect of the truth is astonishing.* **2.** a want of attention to what should be done: *That car has been ruined by neglect.* **3.** a being neglected: *Rescue my poor remains from vile neglect* (Matthew Prior).
[< Latin *neglectus,* past participle of *negligere, neglegere,* variant of *neclegere* < *nec*

not (< *ne-* not + *que* and) + *legere* pick up] —**Syn.** *v.t.* **1.** See **slight. 2.** disregard, ignore. *-n.* **1. Neglect, negligence** mean lack of proper care or attention in the performance of a task, the carrying out of an obligation, and the like. **Neglect** applies especially to the act or fact of giving too little care or attention to one's duty or work or leaving it undone: *He has shown a persistent neglect of duty.* **Negligence** applies especially to the quality of being given to neglect, possessed by a person or group or shown in inattentiveness to work or duty or carelessness in doing it: *Many accidents in industry are caused by the negligence of the workers.*

neg·lect·a·ble (ni glek′tə bəl), *adj.* negligible: *The dangerous doctrine that Great Britain was a neglectable quantity* (London Daily News).

neg·lect·ed (ni glek′tid), *adj.* not attended to or cared for; not treated with proper attention; disregarded: *Neglected talents rust into decay* (William Cowper). —**neg·lect′ed·ly,** *adv.* —**neg·lect′ed·ness,** *n.*

neg·lect·er or **neg·lec·tor** (ni glek′tər), *n.* a person who neglects.

neg·lect·ful (ni glekt′fəl), *adj.* careless; negligent; heedless: *A man who does not vote is neglectful of his duty.* —**neg·lect′ful·ly,** *adv.* —**neg·lect′ful·ness,** *n.*

né·gli·gé (nā glē zhā′), *n. French.* negligee.

neg·li·gee (neg′lə zhā′, neg′lə zhā), *n.* **1.** a loose, usually decorative, dressing gown made of a light fabric, worn by women. **2.** any easy, informal dress or attire. [< French *négligée,* feminine past participle of *négliger* neglect, learned borrowing from Latin *negligere;* see NEGLECT]

neg·li·gence (neg′lə jəns), *n.* **1. a.** lack of proper care or attention; neglect: *Negligence was the cause of the accident.* **b.** *Law.* the failure to exercise reasonable care or the care required by the circumstances; lack of reasonable care in doing something or failing to do something. **2.** carelessness; indifference: *He dresses with easy negligence. Horace still charms with graceful negligence* (Alexander Pope). —**Syn. 1. a.** remissness, inattention. See **neglect. 2.** heedlessness.

neg·li·gent (neg′lə jənt), *adj.* **1.** neglectful; given to neglect; showing neglect: *negligent officials. O, negligent and heedless discipline* (Shakespeare). **2.** careless; indifferent. **3.** in careless disorder: *All loose her negligent attire, All loose her golden hair* (Scott). [< Latin *negligēns, -entis,* present participle of *negligere;* see NEGLECT] —**neg′li·gent·ly,** *adv.* —**Syn. 1.** remiss, derelict.

neg·li·gi·bil·i·ty (neg′lə jə bil′ə tē), *n.* a being negligible: *She had long ago been crushed into a miserable negligibility by her masterful husband* (Hugh Walpole).

neg·li·gi·ble (neg′lə jə bəl), *adj.* that can be neglected or disregarded: *In buying a suit, a difference of ten cents in price is negligible.* —**neg′li·gi·ble·ness,** *n.* —**Syn.** unimportant, insignificant.

neg·li·gi·bly (neg′lə jə blē), *adv.* in a quantity or to a degree that can be disregarded.

ne·go·tia·bil·i·ty (ni gō′shə bil′ə tē, -shē ə-), *n.* a being negotiable.

ne·go·tia·ble (ni gō′shə bəl, -shē ə-), *adj.* **1.** that can be negotiated or sold; whose ownership can be transferred, as bank drafts which are transferable by delivery, with or without endorsement: *The funds and other negotiable securities ...* (John Stuart Mill). *For accounting purposes, negotiable instruments are generally divided into two broad categories—notes receivable and notes payable* (Schmidt and Bergstrom). **2.** that can be got past or over: *a negotiable path.* —**Syn. 1.** transferable. **2.** surmountable.

ne·go·ti·ant (ni gō′shē ənt, -shənt), *n.* a person who negotiates; agent.

ne·go·ti·ate (ni gō′shē āt), *v.,* **-at·ed, -at·ing.** —*v.i.* to talk over and arrange terms: *The colonists negotiated for peace with the Indians. Negotiate, conciliate, arbitrate, try as hard as you can for agreement rather than stoppages, because strikes hurt everybody* (London Times). —*v.t.* **1.** to arrange for, agree on, bring about, or get by negotiating: *to negotiate a contract, treaty, or mortgage.* **2.** *Informal.* **a.** to get past or over: *The car negotiated the sharp curve by slowing down.* **b.** to solve (a problem) or surmount (a difficulty) so as to be able to proceed toward something. **3. a.** to sell. **b.** to circulate (a bill of exchange, etc.) by transference and assignment of claim by endorsement. **c.** to transfer or assign (a bill, etc.) to another in return for some equivalent in value. [< Latin *negōtiāre* (with English *-ate*) < *negōtium* business < *neg-* not (< *nec*) + *ōtium* ease, leisure, idleness] —**Syn.** *v.i.* parley, confer, consult.

ne·go·ti·a·tion (ni gō′shē ā′shən), *n.* **1.** a process or course of negotiating with another or others: *Negotiations for the new school are completed.* **2.** the act of negotiating; arrangement of terms with others: *the established channels of peaceable negotiation* (Duke of Wellington). *Like* [*Anthony*] *Eden, who was his tutor,* [*Selwyn*] *Lloyd is a dedicated believer in dogged negotiations* (Time).

ne·go·ti·a·tor (ni gō′shē ā′tər), *n.* a person who negotiates.

ne·go·ti·a·to·ry (ni gō′shē ə tôr′ē, -tōr′-), *adj.* of or having to do with negotiation: *For years he has been isolated from diplomatic and negotiatory give-and-take* (Christian Science Monitor).

Ne·gress (nē′gris), *n.* a Negro woman or girl (often used in an unfriendly way).

➤ See **-ess** for a usage note.

Ne·gri body (nā′grē), a stainable structure found in the nerve cells of an animal infected with rabies. It is useful in arriving at the final diagnosis for the presence of this disease. [< Adelchi *Negri,* 1876-1912, an Italian physician]

Ne·gril·lo (ni gril′ō), *n., pl.* **-los.** a Negrito, especially of Africa; Bushman or Pygmy: *Anthropologists believe ... that Negrillos, a race of small Negroes, were native to the area south of the Sahara* (George H.T. Kimble). [< Spanish *negrillo* (diminutive) < *negro* negro]

Ne·grit·ic (ni grit′ic), *adj.* of or having to do with Negroes or Negritos.

ne·gri·to (ni grē′to), *n., pl.* **-tos, -toes.** the ripened nut of the ivory palm.

Ne·gri·to (ni grē′tō), *n., pl.* **-tos** or **-toes.** a member of certain dwarfish Negroid peoples of southeastern Asia and of Africa, especially of the Philippines and East Indies: *In the shady depths of the Sumatran jungle live the Kubu and Lubu, said to be Negritos, a timid people yet unseen by anthropologists* (Atlantic). —*adj.* of or having to do with the Negritos. [< Spanish *negrito* (diminutive) < *negro* negro]

ne·gri·tude (nē′grə tüd, -tyüd), *n.* a being a Negro; Negro distinctiveness: *Black men ... have discovered the "African personality" and "negritude," and their attitude to blackness is not apologetic or resentful, but proud* (Punch). [< French *négritude* < *nègre* Negro < Latin *niger* black. Doublet of NIGRITUDE.]

Ne·gro (nē′grō), *n., pl.* **-groes,** *adj.* —*n.* **1. a.** a person belonging to any of the dark-skinned peoples of Africa: *The Negroes are the smallest in number of all races, numbering probably about 135 million, of whom 13 million live in the United States* (Ogburn and Nimkoff). **b.** a member of any other dark-skinned people. **2.** a person having some Negro ancestors (subject to precise definition by law in certain states and countries). —*adj.* of or having to do with Negroes: *Negro melodies. The first Negro slaves were brought to Jamestown in Virginia in a Dutch ship as early as 1620* (H.G. Wells).
[< Spanish, or Portuguese *negro* < Latin *niger* black]

➤ **Negro** and its derivations were formerly often written with a small *n,* but the regular practice today is to capitalize them. The pronunciations (nig′rō) and (nig′rə) occur, but are considered offensive by many, including most Negroes.

Ne·groid (nē′groid), *adj.* resembling Negroes; akin to the Negro race; of a Negro type: *On the basis of the late appearance of the Negroes in Africa, and the distribution of the Oceanic Negro, some have suggested an Asiatic origin for the Negroid stock* (Beals and Hoijer). —*n.* a person of a Negroid race: *War, conquest, and the slave trade have permitted Negroids to appear in many ... areas* (Harbaugh and Goodrich).

Ne·groi·dal (ni groi′dəl), *adj.* Negroid.

Ne·gro·phil (nē′grə fil), *n.* a person who favors the advancement of Negro interests or rights.

Ne·gro·phile (nē′grə fīl, -fil), *n.* Negrophil.

Ne·groph·i·lism (ni grof′ə liz əm), *n.* a favoring the advancement of Negro interests or rights.

Ne·groph·i·list (ni grof′ə list), *n.* a person who favors the advancement of Negro interests and rights.

Ne·gro·phobe (nē′grə fōb), *n.* a person who has hatred or very great fear of Negroes.

Ne·gro·pho·bi·a (nē′grə fō′bē ə), *n.* hatred or very great fear of Negroes.

ne·gus (nē′gəs), *n.* a drink made of port wine, hot water, sugar, lemon, and nutmeg: *He whiled away the evening with making a bottle of sherry into negus* (T.L. Peacock). [< Francis *Negus,* died 1732, a British army colonel, who concocted it]

Ne·gus (nē′gəs), *n.* the title of the sovereign of Ethiopia. [< Amharic *nəgus* king]

Neh., Nehemiah.

Ne·he·mi·ah (nē′ə mī′ə), *n.* the book of the Old Testament describing the achievements of Nehemiah, a Hebrew leader who returned from exile in Babylonia and rebuilt the walls of Jerusalem about 445 B.C. *Abbr.:* Neh.

Ne·he·mi·as (nē′ə mī′əs), *n.* (in the Douay Bible) Nehemiah.

N.E.I., Netherlands East Indies.

neigh (nā), *n.* the sound that a horse makes, long, high-pitched, and quavering. [< verb] —*v.i.* to make the sound that a horse makes. [Old English *hnǣgan*]

neigh·bor (nā′bər), *n.* **1.** a person who lives near another: *I called him my neighbour, because his plantation lay next to mine* (Daniel Defoe). **2.** a person or thing that is near another: *The big tree brought down several of its smaller neighbors as it fell.* **3.** a fellow human being: *Love thy neighbor.*
—*adj.* living or situated near to another; nearby: *two neighbor farms.*
—*v.i.* **1.** to live or be near (to): *a copse that neighbours by* (Shakespeare). *He seemed ... to suck in fresh vigour from the soil which he neighboured* (Charles Lamb). **2.** to be friendly (with). —*v.t.* **1.** to touch or border upon; adjoin. **2.** to place or bring near: *So neighbour'd to him, and yet so unseen, She stood* (Keats).
[Old English *nēahgebūr* < *nēah* nigh, nearer + *gebūr* dweller, countryman]

neigh·bor·hood (nā′bər hůd), *n.* **1.** the region near some place, thing, or person. **2.** a place; district: *Is North Street a good neighborhood?* **3.** people living near one another; people of a place: *The whole neighborhood came to the big party.* **4.** neighborly feeling or conduct; neighborliness: *I ... made them promise me to live in love and good neighbourhood with one another* (Daniel Defoe). **5.** nearness: *a large brindled cat ... kept back from its prey by our unwelcome neighbourhood* (Edward G. Bulwer-Lytton).
in the neighborhood of, a. nearby; about. **b.** *Informal.* approximately: *The literacy rate in Thailand is in the neighborhood of 60 per cent.*
—*adj.* of or having to do with a neighborhood: *a neighborhood newspaper.*
—**Syn.** *n.* **1.** vicinity, environs. **2.** locality. **5.** proximity.

neigh·bor·ing (nā′bər ing, -bring), *adj.* living or being near; bordering; adjoining; adjacent; near: *The bird calls from the neighboring wood.*

neigh·bor·less (nā′bər lis), *adj.* without neighbors: *The Londoner lives neighbourless* (J.W.R. Scott).

neigh·bor·li·ness (nā′bər lē nis), *n.* the state or quality of being neighborly: *A magazine that ... brings to more than a million homes throughout the world the ties of good neighborliness* (Newsweek).

neigh·bor·ly (nā′bər lē), *adj.* characteristic of or befitting a good neighbor; kindly; friendly; sociable: *He hath a neighbourly charity in him* (Shakespeare).

neigh·bour (nā′bər), *n., adj., v. Especially British.* neighbor: *It branded the Republicans as the cantankerous neighbour* (Manchester Guardian).

neigh·bour·hood (nā′bər hůd), *n., adj. Especially British.* neighborhood.

nei·ther (nē′ᴛʜər, nī′-), *conj.* **1.** not either: *Neither you nor I will go.* **2.** nor yet: *They toil not, neither do they spin* (Matthew 6:28).
—*adj.* not the one or the other; not either: *Neither statement is true.*
—*pron.* not either: *Neither of the statements is true.*
—*adv. Dialect.* either: *nor the old lord neither* (George Meredith).
[Middle English *neyder,* earlier *naither,* alteration (influenced by *either*) of *nauther*]

 PRONUNCIATION KEY: hat, āge, cãre, fär; let, ēqual, tėrm; it, īce; hot, ōpen, ôrder; oil, out; cup, pu̇t, rüle;

➔ The pronoun **neither** is regularly construed as a singular in formal English. In informal English, however, it is often treated as a plural, particularly if there is a dependent *of-* phrase with a plural object: *Neither of the men were at home.*

nek (nek), *n. Afrikaans.* a narrow ridge that connects two hills; saddle. [< Afrikaans *nek* < Dutch, neck]

nek·ton (nek′ton), *n.* the aggregate of all the relatively large organisms found in oceans and lakes that possess the power to swim freely, independent of water movements, as fish, in contrast to plankton that float or benthos that live on the ocean floor. [< German *Nekton* < Greek *nēktón,* neuter of *nēktós,* verbal adjective < *nḗchein* to swim, related to *neîn* swim]

nek·ton·ic (nek ton′ik), *adj.* of or having to do with nekton.

nel·ly or **nel·lie** (nel′ē), *n.*
not on your nelly (or **nellie**), *British Slang.* emphatically no; absolutely not: *"Wear bell-bottoms? Not on your nelly," said a burly, 6 ft. 3 in. corporal* (Punch). [origin unknown]

ne·lum·bi·um (ni lum′bē əm), *n.* nelumbo.

ne·lum·bo (ni lum′bō), *n., pl.* **-bos.** any of a small group of aquatic plants of the water-lily family, as the sacred lotus of India and the water chinquapin. [variant of New Latin *Nelumbium* < Singhalese *nelumbu*]

nem·a·tel·minth (nem′ə tel′minth), *n.* nemathelminth.

nem·a·thel·minth (nem′ə thel′minth), *n.* any of a former grouping of worms, including the acanthocephalans, nematodes, and various other cylindrical worms. [< Greek *nêma, -atos* thread + English *helminth*]

nem·a·to·blast (nem′ə tə blast), *n.* a cell that is able to produce a nematocyst; an embryonic nematocyst. [< Greek *nêma, -atos* thread + *blastós* sprout, germ]

nem·a·to·cide (nem′ə tə sīd), *n.* a chemical, spray, or other substance used to kill nematodes.

nem·a·to·cyst (nem′ə tə sist), *n.* one of the cells of a coelenterate that contains a coiled threadlike stinging process, discharged to capture prey and for defense. [< Greek *nêma, -atos* thread + English *cyst*]

nem·a·to·cyst·ic (nem′ə tə sis′tik), *adj.* having to do with or having the characteristics of a nematocyst.

nem·a·tode (nem′ə tōd), *adj.* **1.** belonging to the nematodes. **2.** of or having to do with the nematodes. —*n.* any of a class of slender, unsegmented, cylindrical worms, including parasitic forms such as the hookworm, pinworm, and trichina; roundworm. [< New Latin *Nematoda* the class name, ultimately < Greek *nêma, -atos* thread < *neîn* spin]

nem·a·toid (nem′ə toid), *adj.* **1.** threadlike. **2.** belonging to the order containing the typical nematodes, or sometimes all the nematodes. —*n.* a nematoid worm.

nem·a·to·log·i·cal (nem′ə tə loj′ə kəl), *adj.* of or having to do with nematology.

nem·a·tol·o·gist (nem′ə tol′ə jist), *n.* an expert in nematology.

nem·a·tol·o·gy (nem′ə tol′ə jē), *n.* the branch of parasitology that deals with nematodes. [< Greek *nêma, -atos* thread + English *-logy*]

Nem·bu·tal (nem′byə tôl, -tal), *n. Trademark.* pentobarbital sodium, used as a sedative and hypnotic. *Formula:* $C_{11}H_{17}N_2O_3Na$

nem. con., nemine contradicente.

nem. diss., nemine dissentiente.

Ne·me·an (ni mē′ən, nē′mē-), *adj.* of or having to do with Nemea, a valley in Argolis, Greece.

Nemean games, a festival held at Nemea every two years by the ancient Greeks.

Nemean lion, *Greek Mythology.* a lion killed by Hercules at Nemea as the first of his twelve tasks: *As hardy as the Nemean lion's nerve* (Shakespeare).

ne·mer·te·an or **ne·mer·ti·an** (ni mėr′tē ən), *n.* any of a group or class of chiefly marine worms, characterized by an elongated, flattened and unsegmented, contractile body, with an anal opening. Nemerteans are brightly colored, sometimes growing up to 90 feet long and have a long extensible proboscis; ribbon worm. —*adj.* **1.** belonging to the nemerteans. **2.** of or having to do with the nemerteans. [< New Latin *Nemertea* the class name (< Greek *Nēmertḗs,* a sea nymph) + English *-an, -ian*]

ne·mer·tine (ni mėr′tīn, -tin), *n., adj.* nemertean.

nem·er·tin·e·an (nem′ər tin′ē ən), *n., adj.* nemertean.

ne·me·sia (ni mē′zhə, -shē ə, -sē-), *n.* an annual or perennial plant of the figwort family, native to South Africa, often grown for decorative purposes because of its varicolored flowers. [< New Latin *Nemesia* the genus name < Greek *némesis,* a related plant]

Nem·e·sis (nem′ə sis), *n. Greek Mythology.* the goddess of vengeance. [< Greek *Némesis* < *némein* give what is due]

nem·e·sis (nem′ə sis), *n., pl.* **-ses** (-sēz). **1.** just punishment for evil deeds; retribution: *the inward suffering which is the worst form of nemesis* (George Eliot). **2.** a person who punishes another for evil deeds. [< *Nemesis*] —**Syn. 2.** avenger.

ne·mi·ne con·tra·di·cen·te (nem′ə nē kon′trə di sen′tē), *Latin.* nobody opposing; without objections.

ne·mi·ne dis·sen·ti·en·te (nem′ə nē di-sen′shē en′tē), *Latin.* nobody dissenting; without objections.

ne·mo me im·pu·ne la·ces·sit (nē′mō mē impyü′nē lə ses′it), *Latin.* nobody provokes me with impunity (the motto of Scotland).

nem·o·ral (nem′ər əl), *adj.* **1.** of or having to do with a wood or grove. **2.** inhabiting or frequenting woods, as animals. [< Latin *nemorālis* < *nemus, nemoris* grove]

ne·ne (nā′nā′), *n.* a very rare wild goose of Hawaii, grayish brown with black face and bill. It is the state bird of Hawaii. [< Hawaiian *nēnē*]

nen·u·phar (nen′yə fär), *n.* a water lily, especially the common white or yellow variety. [< Medieval Latin *nenuphar* < Arabic *nīnūfar, nīlūfar,* ultimately < Sanskrit *nīlotpala* blue lotus < *nīl* blue + *utpala* lotus]

neo-, *combining form.* **1.** new, recent: *Neoplasm = a new growth of tissue.*
2. a new, modified form of: *Neoclassicism = a new, modified form of classicism.*
3. most recent division of a geological period: *Neocene = the most recent part of the Tertiary period.*
[< Greek *néos* new]

ne·o·ars·phen·a·min (nē′ō ärs′fi nam′in), *n.* neoarsphenamine.

ne·o·ars·phen·a·mine (nē′ō ärs′fen ə-mēn′, -fi nam′in), *n.* an organic arsenic compound, a yellow powder similar to arsphenamine but more readily soluble in water, used intravenously, before the development of antibiotics, in the treatment of syphilis and other bacterial infections. *Formula:* $C_{13}H_{13}As_2N_2NaO_4S$

Ne·o·Cath·o·lic (nē′ō kath′ə lik, -kath′-lik), *adj.* **1.** of or having to do with those members of the Church of England who favor Roman Catholic principles and usages; very High-Church Anglican. **2.** of or having to do with a faction of the Roman Catholic Church in France that is opposed to papal control. —*n.* a member of either of these groups.

Ne·o·cene (nē′ə sēn), *n.* **1.** the later division of the Tertiary system of the Cenozoic era, comprising the Miocene and the Pliocene. **2.** the rocks formed during this division. —*adj.* of or having to do with this division or its rocks. [< *neo-* + Greek *kainós* new]

ne·o-Chris·ti·an·i·ty (nē′ō kris chē an′ə-tē), *n.* Christianity influenced or reshaped by a current philosophy, especially by rationalism.

ne·o·clas·sic (nē′ō klas′ik, -kläs′-), *adj.* of or having to do with the revival of ancient Greek and Roman principles or practices, especially in art and literature: *Graceful neoclassic Corinthian columns in glazed white ceramic* (New Yorker).

ne·o·clas·si·cal (nē′ō klas′ə kəl, -kläs′-), *adj.* neoclassic.

ne·o·clas·si·cism (nē′ō klas′ə siz əm, -kläs′-), *n.* **1.** neoclassic character in art or literature: *First came neoclassicism, during and shortly after the reign of Napoleon I. Its leaders . . . opposed the luxurious ornamentation of the rococo period* (Thomas Munro). **2.** a movement of the late 1600's and the 1700's, based on an interest in classical style and a desire to impose a form conceived of as embodying the formal principles of classical reason, restraint, order, and symmetry. **3.** *Music.* a movement, especially of the 1900's, based on an interest in and return to the style of the pre-Romantic composers, especially the classical style of Johann Sebastian Bach: *[Darius] Milhaud's musical idiom doggedly remains within the realm of neoclassicism* (New York Times).

ne·o·clas·si·cist (nē′ō klas′ə sist, -kläs′-), *n.* a follower of neoclassicism in art, literature, or music: *In some respects Saint-Saëns was the first of the neoclassicists* (Harold C. Schonberg).

ne·o·co·lo·ni·al·ism (nē′ō kə lō′nē ə liz′-əm), *n.* the supposed policy or practice of a large nation to dominate politically or economically smaller nations, especially former colonies; imperialism: *Indonesia and others . . . use the notion of neocolonialism to attack the former colonial Powers* (Manchester Guardian Weekly).

ne·o·co·lo·ni·al·ist (nē′ō kə lō′nē ə list), *n.* an advocate or supporter of neocolonialism. —*adj.* of or having to do with neocolonialism.

ne·o·cos·mic (nē′ō koz′mik), *adj.* belonging to the modern period of the world, especially the races of mankind in historic times.

Ne·o-Dar·win·i·an (nē′ō där win′ē ən), *adj.* having to do with Neo-Darwinism. —*n.* an advocate of Neo-Darwinism.

Ne·o-Dar·win·ism (nē′ō där′wə niz əm), *n.* the theory, based on Darwinism, that the evolution of animals and plants depends upon the operation of natural selection and upon the variability caused by mutations within a population.

Ne·o-Dar·win·ist (nē′ō där′wə nist), *n.* an advocate of Neo-Darwinism.

Ne·o-Des·tour (nē′ō des′tůr), *n.* a political party in Tunisia, a country in northern Africa. The party was founded in 1934 by Habib Bourguiba, under whose leadership the country won independence from France in 1956. [< *neo-* + Arabic *dustūr* constitution]

ne·o·dym·i·um (nē′ə dim′ē əm), *n.* a rare-earth metallic chemical element found in cerite and various other rare minerals. *Symbol:* Nd; *at.wt.:* (C^{12}) 144.27 or (O^{16}) 144.27; *at.no.:* 60; *valence:* 3.

ne·o-fas·cism (nē′ō fash′iz əm), *n.* any movement to establish or restore the former principles and beliefs of fascism.

ne·o-fas·cist or **ne·o-Fas·cist** (nē′ō fash′-ist), *n.* **1.** a member of a political party favoring neo-fascism: *The two monarchist parties and to a lesser extent the neo-fascists have lost a good deal of ground* (Economist). **2.** a person who favors or supports neo-fascism. —*adj.* of or having to do with neo-fascism or neo-fascists.

Ne·o·gae·a (nē′ə jē′ə), *n.* the Neotropical region, considered with reference to the geographical distribution of plants and animals. [< New Latin *Neogaea* < Greek *néos* new + *gaîa* earth]

Ne·o·gae·an (nē′ə jē′ən), *adj.* of or having to do with the Neogaea.

Ne·o·gae·ic (nē′ə jē′ik), *adj.* Neogaean.

Ne·o·ge·an (nē′ə jē′ən), *adj.* Neogaean.

Ne·o·ge·ic (nē′ə jē′ik), *adj.* Neogaean.

Ne·o·gene (nē′ə jēn), *n.* **1.** the later of two divisions of the Cenozoic era (comprising the Miocene, Pliocene, Pleistocene, and Recent periods). **2.** the rock strata formed during this division. **3.** Neocene. —*adj.* of or having to do with these divisions or their rocks. [< *neo-* + Greek *-genḗs* born]

ne·o-Goth·ic (nē′ō goth′ik), *adj.* of, resembling, or in the style of the Gothic Revival: *Toronto was a small town—a murmurous place of horse troughs, ice wagons, [and] neo-Gothic churches* (Maclean's).

ne·o-Greek (nē′ō grēk′), *adj.* belonging to or representing a revival of the ancient Greek style, as in architecture.

Ne·o-He·bra·ic (nē′ō hi brā′ik), *n.* Hebrew as written and spoken since the Diaspora, especially by scholars. —*adj.* of or having to do with this form of Hebrew.

ne·o-He·ge·li·an (nē′ō hā gā′lē ən, -hi-jē′-), *adj.* of or having to do with the followers and successors of Georg Hegel. —*n.* a follower of Hegel and his philosophy.

ne·o·im·pres·sion·ism (nē′ō im presh′ə-niz əm), *n.* a theory and technique of painting, developed by Georges Seurat, 1859-1891, consisting essentially in the adaptation of scientific methodology to impressionist principles through pointillism (the use of dots and squares of colors according to predetermined procedures).

ne·o·im·pres·sion·ist (nē′ō im presh′ə-nist), *n.* an artist who uses neoimpressionism.

ne·o-Kant·i·an (nē′ō kan′tē ən), *adj.* of or having to do with the followers and successors of Immanuel Kant. —*n.* a follower of Kant and his philosophy.

Ne·o-La·marck·i·an (nē′ō lə mär′kē ən), *adj.* of or having to do with Neo-Lamarckism. —*n.* Neo-Lamarckist.

Ne·o-La·marck·ism (nē′ō lə mär′kiz əm), *n.* the revival in a modified form of Lamarck's theory of organic evolution that maintains that characteristics acquired by parents during their lifetime can be inherited by their offspring.

Ne·o-La·marck·ist (nē′ō lə mär′kist), *n.* an advocate of Neo-Lamarckism.

ne·o-Lat·in (nē′ō lat′ən), *n.* Latin written and used, especially in modern scientific literature, more or less as a living language; Modern Latin. —*adj.* of or having to do with such Latin.

ne·o·lith (nē′ə lith), *n.* a neolithic stone implement.

ne·o·lith·ic or **Ne·o·lith·ic** (nē′ə lith′ik), *adj.* of the later Stone Age when polished stone weapons and tools were made and used and the appearance of agriculture and animal husbandry accompanied profound social changes: *neolithic man.* —*n.* this period. [< *neo-* + Greek *líthos* stone + English *-ic*]

ne·o·lo·gian (nē′ə lō′jən), *adj.* given to or characterized by neologism, as in views on religious subjects. —*n.* a neologist, as on religious subjects.

ne·o·log·i·cal (nē′ə loj′ə kəl), *adj.* of, having to do with, or characterized by neology or neologism. —**ne′o·log′i·cal·ly,** *adv.*

ne·ol·o·gism (nē ol′ə jiz əm), *n.* **1.** the use of new words or old words with new meanings: *His particular grievance was neologisms . . . even the newspaper, he complained, had got into the habit of using the adjective "off-colored"—properly applied only to certain diamonds—to describe the pigmentation of half-caste people* (New Yorker). **2.** a new word or expression; a new meaning for an old word: *Such neologisms are clipped words like* lube *for* lubricating oil *and* co-ed *for* co-educational; *back-formations like* to televise *(1931) from* television . . . ; *blends like* cablegram *from* cable *and* telegram . . . ; *artificial or made-up formations like* carborundum, cellophane, *and* pianola (Simeon Potter). *The paradox is, therefore, that what may appear to the individual speaker as a neologism may be in the total overview of the language a long-established form* (Harold B. Allen). **3.** the introduction of new views or doctrines, especially on religious subjects. [< French *néologisme* < Greek *néos* new + *lógos* word < *légein* speak]

ne·ol·o·gist (nē ol′ə jist), *n.* **1.** a person who introduces or uses neologisms in language. **2.** a person given to neologism in views, especially on religious subjects.

ne·ol·o·gis·tic (nē ol′ə jis′tik), *adj.* of or having to do with neologism or neologists.

ne·ol·o·gis·ti·cal (nē ol′ə jis′tə kəl), *adj.* neologistic.

ne·ol·o·gize (nē ol′ə jīz), *v.i.,* **-gized, -giz·ing. 1.** to introduce or use neologisms in language. **2.** to introduce or adopt new views, especially on religious subjects.

ne·ol·o·gy (nē ol′ə jē), *n., pl.* **-gies.** neologism.

ne·o-Mal·thu·sian (nē′ō mal thü′zhən, -zē ən), *adj.* of or having to do with the theory or view, based upon Malthusianism, which advocates selective birth control as a means of eliminating poverty and raising the standard of living. —*n.* an advocate of this theory or view: *The neo-Malthusians of the 1900's urge planned parenthood* (H.W. Spiegel).

ne·o-Mal·thu·sian·ism (nē′ō mal thü′zhə niz əm, -zē ə-), *n.* the theories of the neo-Malthusians.

Ne·o-Mel·a·ne·sian (nē′ō mel′ə nē′zhən, -shən), *n.* the pidgin English of Melanesia; bêche-de-mer.

ne·o·my·cin (nē′ə mī′sin), *n.* an antibiotic substance similar to streptomycin and obtained from a related soil actinomycete. It is used in the treatment of tuberculosis and other bacterial diseases. [< *neo-* + (strepto)*mycin*]

ne·on (nē′on), *n.* **1.** a rare chemical element that is a colorless, odorless, inert gas, forming a very small part of the air. *Symbol:* Ne; *at.wt.:* (C^{12}) 20.183 or (O^{16}) 20.183; *at.no.:* 10. **2.** a neon lamp. **3.** a sign for advertising made up of neon lamps. **4.** the light or glow of a neon lamp. —*adj.* **1.** composed of neon lamps: *a neon sign.* **2.** like a neon lamp or light: . . . *beneath the flickering neon sky* (Manchester Guardian Weekly). [< New Latin *neon* < Greek *neón,* neuter new]

ne·o·na·tal (nē′ō nā′təl), *adj.* of or having to do with newborn babies: *neonatal disease.*

ne·o·nate (nē′ə nāt), *n.* a newborn baby. [< *neo-* + Latin *nātus* born, past participle of *nāscī* be born; see NATIVE]

ne·o-Na·zi (nē′ō nät′sē), *n.* **1.** a member of a political party favoring neo-Naziism. **2.** a person who favors or supports neo-Naziism: *The neo-Nazis found some solace in . . . [the] last-act defense of Navy discipline* (Time). —*adj.* of or having to do with neo-Naziism or neo-Nazis: *The court had no doubt that both young men had been encouraged in their half-fledged anti-Semitic and neo-Nazi views by the books and papers which they had read* (Manchester Guardian).

ne·o-Na·zi·ism (nē′ō nät′sē iz əm, -nat′-siz-), *n.* any movement to restore the principles and beliefs of Naziism.

ne·o-Na·zism (nē′ō nät′siz əm, -nat′-), *n.* neo-Naziism: *A second disturbing factor is the growth of German nationalism and the accompanying widespread indifference in Germany to a revival of neo-Nazism* (New York Times).

neon lamp or **light,** a glass tube filled with neon gas and containing two electrodes instead of a filament. When voltage is applied to the electrodes, an electric discharge occurs and the tube glows fiery red.

neon tetra, a small, brightly colored fish of the upper Amazon region, commonly raised in aquariums; tetra.

ne·o·or·tho·dox (nē′ō ôr′thə doks), *adj.* of, having to do with, or characteristic of neoorthodoxy: *The older neoorthodox leaders had unwittingly "pushed God out of ordinary existence"* (New Yorker).

ne·o·or·tho·dox·y (nē′ō ôr′thə dok′sē), *n.* **1.** a movement in contemporary Protestantism reverting to traditional Christian dogmas in reaction to liberalism: *In 1943 theological liberalism looked like an outworn creed beside the fashionable stringencies of [Reinhold] Niebuhr's neoorthodoxy* (Time). **2.** any movement in other religions, such as Islam and Judaism, returning to an older form of religious beliefs and practices.

ne·o·pa·gan (nē′ō pā′gən), *adj.* of, having to do with, or characteristic of a revival of paganism: *Today, argues Driver, the world is full of neopagan sex worshippers* (Time).

ne·o·phyte (nē′ə fīt), *n.* **1.** a new convert; person recently admitted to a religious body. **2.** a person who is new at something; beginner; novice: *The employer looked upon the new office boy as a hopeful young neophyte.* **3.** in the Roman Catholic Church: **a.** a newly ordained priest. **b.** a novice of a religious order. **4.** (in the early Christian Church) a person newly baptized. **5.** *U.S.* (in fraternities) a person who has completed his pledging period, but has yet to be initiated into the fraternity. [< Latin *neophytus* < Greek *neóphytos* < *néos* new + *phýein* grow, produce] —**Syn. 2.** tyro.

ne·o·pi·li·na (nē′ō pi lī′nə), *n.* a primitive mollusk found at great depths in the Pacific Ocean. It is a living representative of an animal group which had previously been known to exist only as fossils 300 to 500 million years old. *The structure of neopilina shows it is much like the annelids, or segmented worms* (Science News Letter). [< New Latin *Neopilina* the genus name]

ne·o·pla·sia (nē′ə plā′zhə), *n.* the development of new tissue or of neoplasms.

ne·o·plasm (nē′ō plaz əm), *n.* a new, abnormal growth of tissue, as a tumor: . . . *organizations . . . devoted to improving the control of those eroding growths of many types of body cells, neoplasms collectively known as cancer* (Perspectives in Cancer Research). [< *neo-* + Greek *plásma* something formed]

ne·o·plas·tic (nē′ə plas′tik), *adj.* having to do with a neoplasm.

ne·o·plas·ti·cism (nē′ō plas′tə siz əm), *n.* a movement in modern art led by the Dutch artist Piet Mondrian, emphasizing abstract and nonrepresentational designs and forms.

ne·o·plas·ty (nē′ə plas′tē), *n., pl.* **-ties.** plastic surgery to repair or restore a part.

Ne·o·pla·ton·ic or **Ne·o-Pla·ton·ic** (nē′ō plə ton′ik), *adj.* having to do with the Neoplatonists or their doctrines: *In the proportions of some of the great cathedrals, . . . the geometry of golden sections is intimately related to . . . Neo-Platonic doctrines of light* (Economist).

Ne·o·pla·to·nism or **Ne·o-Pla·to·nism** (nē′ō plā′tə niz əm), *n.* **1.** a philosophical and religious system composed chiefly of elements of Platonism, Oriental mysticism, and, in its later phases, Christianity, represented especially in the writings of Plotinus, Porphyry, Proclus, and Philo. It originated in Alexandria in the 200's A.D. **2.** a later philosophy based upon this or upon Platonism.

Ne·o·pla·to·nist or **Ne·o-Pla·to·nist** (nē′ō plā′tə nist), *n.* a believer in the doctrines or principles of Neoplatonism.

ne·o·prene (nē′ə prēn), *n.* any of a group of synthetic rubbers made from chloroprene. It is superior to natural rubber in oil resistance, etc.: *Made of the same high tenacity nylon as is used in tire cord, the new tarpaulin is weatherproofed with neoprene* (Wall Street Journal). [< *neo-* + (chloro)*prene*]

ne·o·re·al·ism (nē′ō rē′ə liz əm), *n.* a contemporary form of realism in literature, art, and especially motion pictures, characterized by a strict adherence to physical or photographic detail, emphasis on earthy and realistic settings, and a preoccupation with social themes: *Italian neorealism . . . the . . . desire to search out life with the camera and throw it on the screen without apology or moral stricture* (Saturday Review).

ne·o·re·al·ist (nē′ō rē′ə list), *n.* a person who believes in or follows the principles of neorealism: *A story of love and squalor in equal measure, directed and written by two of Italy's most formidable neorealists* (Time). —*adj.* of or having to do with neorealism: *A new Japanese film . . . suggests that the use of the neorealist approach has been firmly adopted by the Japanese* (London Times).

ne·o·re·al·is·tic (nē′ō rē′ə lis′tik), *adj.* neorealist: *"Hiroshima" . . . can be described as a neorealistic drama* (New York Times).

ne·o-Ro·man (nē′ō rō′mən), *adj.* belonging to or representing a revival of the ancient Roman style, as in architecture.

ne·o·ro·man·tic (nē′ō rō man′tik), *adj.* of, having to do with, or characteristic of a revival of romantic style in literature, music, and art, especially in the 1900's: *His always tasteful, extremely personalized music has been called neoromantic* (Newsweek). —*n.* a person who believes in neoromanticism.

ne·o·ro·man·ti·cism (nē′ō rō man′tə siz-əm), *n.* the revival of the romantic style or spirit in literature, music, and art; neoromantic tendency.

Ne·o·sal·var·san (nē′ō sal′vər san), *n. Trademark.* a preparation of neoarsphenamine.

Ne·o-Scho·las·tic (nē′ō skə las′tik), *adj.* of or having to do with Neo-Scholasticism.

Ne·o-Scho·las·ti·cism (nē′ō skə las′tə siz-əm), *n.* a philosophical system or method consisting essentially in the application of scholasticism to modern problems, differing from medieval scholasticism especially in its acceptance of the findings and techniques of modern research.

ne·o·stig·mine (nē′ō stig′mēn, -min), *n.* a drug for treating severe muscular debility and glaucoma, usually administered as a bromide or sulfate: *Another measure . . . was giving neostigmine to prevent the dangerous heart jitters, called fibrillation* (Science News Letter). [< *neo-* + (syn)*stigmin* (bromide) the chemical name]

ne·o·style (nē′ə stīl), *n., v.,* **-styled, -styl·ing.** —*n.* a device used for making multiple copies of a document or the like; kind of cyclostyle. —*v.t.* to duplicate (printed matter) with a neostyle.

ne·o·tech·nic (nē′ō tek′nik), *adj.* of, having to do with, or characteristic of the present-day development of technology: *Soon our neotechnic society will afford us six days of rest and one of toil* (Punch).

ne·ot·e·nous (nē ot′ə nəs), *adj. Zoology.* reproducing by neoteny.

ne·ot·e·ny (nē ot′ə nē), *n. Zoology.* the phenomenon of reaching sexual maturity and of reproducing while morphologically still in a youthful or larval stage, as in certain salamanders. [< New Latin *neotenia* < Greek *néos* new + *teínein* stretch, extend]

ne·o·ter·ic (nē′ə ter′ik), *adj.* recent; new; modern. —*n.* a modern, especially a writer, thinker, or other person of modern times. [< Late Latin *neōtericus* < Greek *neōterikós* < *neṓteros*, comparative of *néos* new]

ne·ot·er·ism (nē ot′ə riz əm), *n.* a new word or expression; neologism. [< Greek *neōterismós* < *neōterízein* make innovations]

ne·ot·er·ist (nē ot′ər ist), *n.* an inventor of new words or expressions; neologist.

Ne·o·trop·ic (nē′ə trop′ik), *adj.* Neotropical.

Ne·o·trop·i·cal (nē′ə trop′ə kəl), *adj.* of or like the region that includes most of the Caribbean, tropical North America, and all of South America.

ne·o·yt·ter·bi·um (nē′ō i tėr′bē əm), *n.* ytterbium.

Ne·o·zo·ic (nē′ə zō′ik), *n.* **1.** the geologic period from the end of the Mesozoic to the present; Cenozoic. **2.** the Mesozoic and Cenozoic (as a single era). —*adj.* of or having to do with either of these geologic divisions. [< *neo-* + Greek *zōḗ* life + English *-ic*]

➔ **Neozoic** was proposed, and gained occasional use, but was never widely accepted by professional geologists.

Nep or **NEP** (nep), *n.* the New Economic Policy of the government of the Soviet Union, modifying some of the more extreme communistic policies put into effect by Lenin in 1921. Its purpose was to stimulate an economy on the verge of collapse. *Under the NEP private marketing was restored* (Newsweek). [< Russian *nèp*, abbreviation of *Novaja Ekonomičeskaja Politika* New Economic Policy]

Nep., 1. Nepal. **2.** Neptune.

Nep·a·lese (nep′ə lēz′, -lēs′), *n., pl.* **-lese,** *adj.* —*n.* a native or inhabitant of Nepal, the Himalayan kingdom between Tibet and India. —*adj.* of or having to do with Nepal or its people: *The Nepalese government said in a communique . . . that the unrest would end soon* (Cape Times).

Ne·pa·li (ne pä′lē), *n.* **1.** an Indic language used chiefly in Nepal. **2.** Nepalese: *Many of the Yeti incidents reported by the Nepalis occurred below the permanent snow line* (Harper's). —*adj.* of or having to do with Nepal; Nepalese: *Half the valley had been resettled with 3,000 Nepali families* (Sunday Times).

ne·pen·the (ni pen′thē), *n.* **1. a.** a drink or drug supposed to bring forgetfulness of sorrow or trouble. Nepenthe is supposed to be of Egyptian origin and is mentioned in Homer's Odyssey. **b.** the plant yielding this drug. **2.** anything that brings on easeful forgetfulness: *This western wind hath Lethean powers, Yon noonday cloud nepenthe showers* (John Greenleaf Whittier). [earlier *nepenthes* < Latin *nēpenthes* < Greek (*phármakon*) *nēpenthès* (drug) dispelling sorrow < *nē-* not + *pénthos* grief]

ne·pen·the·an (ni pen′thē ən), *adj.* of, having to do with, or induced by nepenthe.

ne·pen·thes (ni pen′thēz), *n.* **1.** nepenthe. **2.** any of a group of pitcher plants native chiefly to the East Indies, and cultivated also in hothouses. [< Latin *nēpenthes;* see NEPENTHE]

neph·a·lism (nef′ə liz əm), *n.* total abstinence from intoxicating drink.

neph·a·list (nef′ə list), *n.* a person who practices or advocates nephalism; teetotaler. [< Late Greek *nēphalismós* total abstinence (< *nēphálios* sober) + English *-ist*]

neph·a·nal·y·sis (nef′ə nal′ə sis), *n., pl.* **-ses** (-sēz). **1.** analysis of the cloud formations over a large area, using weather charts drawn especially from photographs taken by weather satellites. **2.** a chart of such cloud formations. [< Greek *néphos* cloud + English *analysis*]

neph·e·line (nef′ə lin), *n.* nephelite: *The Kola peninsula in the east is particularly rich in nepheline ores* (New Scientist). [< French *néphéline* < Greek *nephélē* cloud (< *néphos*) + French *-ine* -ine[2] (because it appears cloudy when fragments are put in nitric acid)]

neph·e·lin·ic (nef′ə lin′ik), *adj.* nephelitic.

neph·e·lin·ite (nef′ə lə nīt), *n.* a heavy, dark-colored, volcanic rock, essentially a basalt containing nephelite and pyroxene but no feldspar and little or no olivine. [< *nephelin*(e) + *-ite*[1]]

neph·e·lite (nef′ə līt), *n.* a mineral, a silicate of aluminum, sodium, and sometimes potassium, occurring in various volcanic rocks: *Nephelite generally forms grains and shapeless lumps or masses resembling quartz* (Fenton and Fenton). [< *nephel*(ine) + *-ite*[1]]

neph·e·lit·ic (nef′ə lit′ik), *adj.* of or like nephelite.

neph·e·lom·e·ter (nef′ə lom′ə tər), *n.* **1.** an instrument to measure the concentration of suspended matter in a liquid dispersion by measuring the amount of light transmitted or scattered by the dispersion. **2.** a similar device consisting of a group of barium chloride standards, for estimating the number of bacteria in a suspension. **3.** an instrument to measure the comparative cloudiness of the sky. [< Greek *nephélē* cloud (< *néphos*) + English *-meter*]

neph·e·lo·met·ric (nef′ə lə met′rik), *adj.* of or having to do with nephelometry: *Nephelometric standards provide four references covering the normal range of turbidities found in nephelometric studies* (Science).

neph·e·lom·e·try (nef′ə lom′ə trē), *n.* the measurement of the concentration of suspended matter in a liquid by means of a nephelometer.

neph·ew (nef′yü), *n.* **1.** a son of one's brother or sister. **2.** a son of one's brother-in-law or sister-in-law. **3.** an illegitimate son of an ecclesiastic (used as a euphemism). **4.** *Obsolete.* a grandson. **5.** *Obsolete.* a descendant, especially a remote descendant. [< Old French *neveu* < Latin *nepōs, -ōtis*]

➔ The pronunciation (nev′yü), still sometimes heard, follows the older form of the word; the pronunciation (nef′yü), now overwhelmingly the more common throughout the English-speaking world, is from the spelling.

neph·o·gram (nef′ə gram), *n.* a photograph of a cloud or clouds taken by a nephograph.

neph·o·graph (nef′ə graf, -gräf), *n.* an instrument for photographing clouds. [< Greek *néphos* cloud + English *-graph*]

neph·o·log·i·cal (nef′ə loj′ə kəl), *adj.* having to do with nephology; relating to clouds or cloudiness.

ne·phol·o·gy (ni fol′ə jē), *n.* the branch of meteorology that deals with clouds. [< Greek *néphos* cloud + English *-logy*]

neph·o·scope (nef′ə skōp), *n.* an instrument used to determine the altitude of clouds and the velocity and direction of their motion. [< Greek *néphos* cloud + English *-scope*]

neph·o·scop·ic (nef′ə skop′ik), *adj.* of, having to do with, or determined by a nephoscope.

ne·phral·gi·a (ni fral′jē ə), *n.* pain in the kidneys; renal neuralgia. [< Greek *nephrós* kidney + *-algíā* < *álgos* pain]

ne·phrec·to·my (ni frek′tə mē), *n., pl.* **-mies.** the surgical removal of a kidney. [< Greek *nephrós* kidney + *ektomḗ* a cutting out]

neph·ric (nef′rik), *adj.* renal. [< Greek *nephrós* kidney + English *-ic*]

ne·phrid·i·al (ni frid′ē əl), *adj.* of or having to do with the nephridium or nephridia.

ne·phrid·i·o·pore (ni frid′ē ə pôr, -pōr), *n.* the external opening of the excretory organ of annelids.

ne·phrid·i·um (ni frid′ē əm), *n., pl.* **-i·a** (-ē ə). a primitive excretory organ in some invertebrates and lower vertebrates, as mollusks, certain annelid worms, and brachiopods, analogous in function to the kidneys of higher animals, and in some cases serving also in reproduction. [< New Latin *nephridium* < Greek *nephrós* kidney + Latin *-idium* < Greek *-ídion*, diminutive suffix]

neph·rism (nef′riz əm), *n.* a condition of poor health caused by chronic kidney disease. [< Greek *nephrós* kidney + English *-ism*]

neph·rite (nef′rīt), *n.* a kind of jade, a silicate of calcium and either magnesium or iron, varying in color from whitish to dark green, once supposed to protect the wearer against diseases of the kidneys; greenstone. [< German *Nephrit* < Greek *nephrós* kidney + German *-it* -ite[1] (from its reputed value in curing kidney disease)]

ne·phrit·ic (ni frit′ik), *adj.* **1.** of, having to do with, or affected with kidney disease. **2.** used against kidney disease. **3.** renal. [< Late Latin *nephrīticus* < Greek *nephrītikós* < *nephrîtis* nephritis]

ne·phri·tis (ni frī′tis), *n.* any of various inflammations of the kidneys, such as Bright's disease, characterized by the presence of albumin in the urine, swelling of the tissues, etc.: *When [the kidneys] are not functioning properly, a condition develops which is known as nephritis* (Science News Letter). [< Late Latin *nephrītis* < Greek *nephrîtis* < *nephrós* kidney]

neph·ro·car·di·ac (nef′rə kär′dē ak), *adj.* of or having to do with the kidneys and the heart; both renal and cardiac. [< Greek *nephrós* kidney + English *cardiac*]

neph·ro·cele (nef′rə sēl), *n.* hernia of the kidney. [< Greek *nephrós* kidney + *kḗlē* tumor, hernia]

neph·ro·lith (nef′rə lith), *n.* a kidney stone. [< Greek *nephrós* kidney + *líthos* stone]

ne·phrol·o·gy (ni frol′ə jē), *n.* the branch of medicine dealing with the kidneys. [< Greek *nephrós* kidney + English *-logy*]

neph·ron (nef′ron), *n.* any of the more than one million functional units of the kidney serving to filter waste matter from the blood. A nephron consists of a Bowman's capsule, glomerulus, and tubule.

neph·ro·pex·i·a (nef′rə pek′sē ə), *n.* the surgical fixation of a floating kidney. [< New Latin *nephropexia* < Greek *nephrós* kidney + *pêxis* a making fast]

neph·ro·pex·y (nef′rə pek′sē), *n.,* **-pex·ies.** nephropexia.

ne·phro·sis (ni frō′sis), *n.* a degenerative disease of the kidneys, especially the renal tubules, marked by absence of inflammation: *Hospital reports also show that Meticorten has better results than cortisone in treating patients suffering from . . . nephrosis* (Newsweek). [< Greek *nephrós* kidney + English *-osis*]

neph·ro·stome (nef′rə stōm), *n. Biology.* the ciliated funnel-shaped end of the nephridium in some invertebrates and lower vertebrates. [< Greek *nephrós* kidney + *stóma* mouth]

ne·phrot·o·my (ni frot′ə mē), *n., pl.* **-mies.** surgical incision into the kidney. [< Greek *nephrós* kidney + *-tomíā* a cutting]

Neph·ta·li (nef′tə lī), *n.* (in the Douay Bible) Naphtali.

ne plus ul·tra (nē′ plus ul′trə), *Latin.* the highest or furthest point attainable; height of excellence or achievement; culmination: *The people of Leinster . . . do not vaunt Dublin as the ne plus ultra of cities* (The Nation).

nep·man (nep′mən), *n., pl.* **-men.** a person, especially a small tradesman or well-to-do peasant, allowed by the Nep to engage in private business in the Soviet Union during the early 1920's. [< Russian *nepman* < *nep* Nep + German *Mann* man]

ne·pot·ic (ni pot′ik), *adj.* nepotistical.

nep·o·tism (nep′ə tiz əm), *n.* the showing of too much favor by one in power to his relatives, especially by giving them desirable appointments: *Nepotism sometimes occurs in political appointments. Such unsavory examples of corruption and nepotism in the highest circles of government have inevitably increased that inborn skepticism with which the Italians . . . tend to treat politics and politicians* (Atlantic). [< French *népotisme* < Italian *nepotismo* < *nepote* nephew < Latin *nepōs, -ōtis* grandson, nephew + *-ismo* -ism]

nep·o·tist (nep′ə tist), *n.* a person who practices nepotism.

nep·o·tis·tic (nəp′ə tis′tik), *adj.* nepotistical.

nep·o·tis·ti·cal (nep′ə tis′tə kəl), *adj.* of or having to do with nepotism or nepotists.

Nep·tune (nep′tün, -tyün), *n.* **1.** the ancient Roman god of the sea, identified with the Greek god Poseidon. See **Poseidon** for picture. **2.** the fourth largest planet in the solar system, eighth in distance from the sun, and visible only through a telescope. Its orbit lies between those of Uranus and Pluto and takes 164.8 years to complete, at a mean distance from the sun of 2,794,100,000 miles. Symbol: ♆. [< Latin *Neptūnus*, related to *nebula* cloud, mist]

Nep·tu·ni·an (nep tü′nē ən, -tyü′-), *adj.* **1.** having to do with Neptune, the god of the sea, or the sea or ocean itself. **2.** of the planet Neptune. **3.** Also, **neptunian.** *Geology.* resulting from or produced by the action of water, particularly oceanic water.

Neptunian theory, *Geology.* an old theory that many rocks now known to be volcanic or plutonic were deposited by water.

Nep·tun·ist (nep′tü nist, -tyü-), *n. Geology.* an advocate of the Neptunian theory.

nep·tu·ni·um (nep tü′nē əm, -tyü′-), *n.* a radioactive chemical element obtained by bombardment of a uranium isotope with neutrons, used in certain types of atomic bombs. Its less stable isotope disintegrates rapidly to form an isotope of plutonium that can be used for nuclear fission. *Both neptunium and americium are artificially produced elements, heavier than uranium, not found in nature* (Science News Letter). *Symbol:* Np; *at. wt.:* (C^{12}) 237 or (O^{16}) 237; *at. no.:* 93; *valence:* 3, 4, 5, 6. [< *Neptune* + New Latin *-ium,* a suffix meaning "chemical element"]

Ne·re·id (nir′ē id), *n.* **1.** *Greek Mythology.* any of the fifty daughters of Nereus. The Nereids were sea nymphs who attended Poseidon (Neptune). **2.** the smaller of the two moons of the planet Neptune.

ne·re·id (nir′ē id), *n.* any of several polychaete worms with segmented bodies and distinct head parts, that live mostly along the seashore and reach a length of 5 feet or more. [< New Latin *Nereidae* < *Nereis* a Nereid]

Ne·re·is (nir′ē is), *n., pl.* **Ne·re·i·des** (ni-rē′ə dēz). *Greek Mythology.* a Nereid.

Ne·reus (nir′üs), *n. Greek Mythology.* a sea god, who was the father of the Nereids.

ne·ri·ne (ni rī′nē), *n.* any of a group of South African plants of the amaryllis family, with large scarlet, pink, or rose-colored flowers: *The nerine, with a head of sail, so to speak, on the top of a slender elastic stem, is forever more or less vibrating* (A. Handler Hamer). [< New Latin *Nerine* < Latin *Nērīnē,* a Nereid]

ne·rit·ic (ni rit′ik), *adj.* of or like that part of the ocean floor between the low tide mark and a depth of about 600 feet: *Life is most abundant in the shallower parts of the ocean or neritic region of the continental shelves* (Harbaugh and Goodrich). [< Latin *nērīta* a sea mussel + English *-ic* (because such life generally inhabit this depth]

ner·ka (nėr′kə), *n.* the sockeye salmon, an important salmon of the northern Pacific; blueback salmon. [apparently < a native name]

Nerka or blueback salmon (from 1 to 1½ ft. long)

Nernst lamp (nernst), an incandescent electric lamp with a filament made of a rod of magnesia and other metallic oxides, not enclosed in a vacuum. [< Walther H. *Nernst,* 1864-1941, a German chemist, physicist, and inventor]

ner·ol (nir′ōl, -ol), *n.* a colorless liquid isomeric with geraniol, occurring in neroli and other essential oils and used in perfumes. *Formula:* $C_{10}H_{18}O$ [< *neroli*]

ner·o·li (ner′ə lē, nir′-), *n.* an essential oil distilled from various flowers or prepared synthetically, used chiefly in perfumes. [< French *néroli* < Italian *neroli* < Princess *Neroli,* who reputedly discovered it]

neroli oil, neroli.

Ne·ro·ni·an (ni rō′nē ən), *adj.* of or having to do with the Roman emperor Nero, noted for his vices, cruelty, and tyranny.

Ne·ron·ic (ni ron′ik), *adj.* Neronian: *From the horrors of the . . . Neronic persecutions right up to the sufferings of the Confessing Church under Hitler, there has been a long tradition of pain and martyrdom* (Punch).

nerv·al (nėr′vəl), *adj.* of or having to do with a nerve or nerves; neural.

nerv·ate (nėr′vāt), *adj.* (of leaves) having veins; veined.

ner·va·tion (nėr vā′shən), *n.* the arrangement of the veins or ribs in a leaf or an insect's wings; venation.

nerv·a·ture (nėr′və chər), *n.* nervation.

nerve (nėrv), *n., v.,* **nerved, nerv·ing.** —*n.* **1.** a fiber or bundle of fibers connecting the brain or spinal cord with the eyes, ears, muscles, glands, etc. Nerves are elements of the peripheral nervous system that carry impulses within the body. The nerve fibers are enclosed within sheaths and are joined to each other with connective tissue. *The control of muscles is achieved via the nerves which pass from the central nervous system . . . to the various muscles of the body* (Floyd and Silver). **2.** mental strength; courage: *to continue fighting on nerve alone, icy nerve, nerves of iron. Prosperity had relaxed the nerves of discipline* (Edward Gibbon). **3.** bodily strength; vigor; energy: *He led me on to mightiest deeds, Above the nerve of mortal arm* (Milton). **4.** *Informal.* rude boldness; impudence: *He claims he is a friend of mine? The nerve of the fellow!* **5. a.** a vein of a leaf. **b.** a rib of an insect's wing; nervure. **6.** *Poetic.* sinew; tendon: *Before his tender joints with nerves are knit* (John Dryden).

get on one's nerves, to annoy or irritate one: *John Adams . . . was honest, brave, and intelligent, but he just couldn't help getting on other people's nerves* (Gerald W. Johnson).

nerves, a. nervousness: *He tried to soothe her nerves* (Graham Greene). **b.** an attack of nervousness: *to suffer from nerves.*

strain every nerve, to exert oneself to the utmost: *Both horse and jockey were straining every nerve in the race.*

—*v.t.* to arouse strength or courage in: *The soldiers nerved themselves for battle.*

[< Latin *nervus* sinew, tendon; sense influenced by Greek *neûron,* meaning both "sinew" and "nerve"]

nerve cell, 1. a neurone; cell that conducts impulses: *The other part is in a special membrane of nerve cell material wrapped around the brain capillaries* (Science News Letter). See picture under **neurone. 2.** the cell body of a neurone, excluding its fibers.

nerve center, 1. a group of nerve cells closely connected with one another and acting together in the performance of some particular function or sense: *The physiological mechanism consists of a sense organ or set of sense organs, sensory nerves leading to a nerve center* (Science News). **2. a.** any place that is the center of activity or a source of direction: *The village high street remains the nerve center of the whole community* (Manchester Guardian). **b.** the person or persons who control such a place.

nerved (nėrvd), *adj.* **1.** having nerves: *strong-nerved.* **2.** *Botany.* nervate. **3.** *Entomology.* having nervures.

-nerved, *combining form.* having —— nerves: *Strong-nerved = having strong nerves.*

nerve deafness, deafness due to disorder of the acoustic nerve: *If a violin player cannot hear his violin even when he touches his teeth to the vibrating instrument, then he knows he suffers from nerve deafness, and there is no cure* (Scientific American).

nerve fiber, any of the long threadlike fibers that constitute the chief conducting part of nerves. The long processes of certain neurons become a nerve fiber. *In all the animals he examined . . . he found a few nerve fibers that had narrow sensitivity curves with maxima in the red, green, or blue part of the spectrum* (Tansley and Weale).

nerve gas, any of various poison gases containing phosphorous that may be absorbed through the skin, as well as by breathing, and that attack the central nervous system to cause extreme weakness or death. Various types have been developed for use in warfare such as tabun and sarin. *Poisons isolated from clams and from the puffer fish have been found to be several times more toxic than the most powerful nerve gases known* (Science News Letter).

nerve·less (nėrv′lis), *adj.* **1.** without strength or vigor; feeble; weak: *Joe's pipe dropped from his nerveless fingers* (Mark Twain). **2.** without courage or firmness. **3.** without nerves. —**nerve′less·ly,** *adv.* —**nerve′less·ness,** *n.* —**Syn. 1.** flabby, flaccid.

nerve-rack·ing or **nerve-wrack·ing** (nėrv′rak′ing), *adj.* that irritates or exasperates to the limit of endurance; very trying: *a nerve-racking day at the office. He felt cool and alert, . . . and, the nerve-racking hours of waiting past, he listened for the starter's gun* (P.G. Wodehouse).

nerves (nėrvz), *n.pl.* See under **nerve,** *n.*

nerv·i·ly (nėr′və lē), *adv.* in a nervy manner: *Nervily, we pressed number 5* (New Yorker).

ner·vine (nėr′vēn, -vīn), *adj.* **1.** acting on or relieving disorders of the nerves; strengthening or soothing the nerves. **2.** of or having to do with the nerves. —*n. Obsolete.* a nerve tonic. [< New Latin *nervinus* < Late Latin *nervīnus* made of sinews < Latin *nervus;* see NERVE]

nerv·ing (nėr′ving), *n. Veterinary Medicine.* the surgical removal of part of a bundle of nerve fibers.

nerv·ous (nėr′vəs), *adj.* **1.** of the nerves: *a nervous disease. The brain is a part of the nervous system of the body.* **2.** having delicate or easily excited nerves: *a nervous driver, a nervous dog.* **3.** having or proceeding from nerves that are out of order: *a nervous patient, a nervous tapping of the fingers.* **4.** deriving from a tense or quickened condition of the nerves: *nervous energy.* **5.** restless; uneasy; timid: *Alice is nervous about staying alone at night.* **6.** having nerves. **7.** strong; vigorous; powerful; spirited: *The style is . . . nervous, masculine, and such as became a soldier* (Thomas De Quincey). *They were swept before the mettled horses and nervous arms of their antagonists like chaff before the wind* (James Fenimore Cooper). [< Latin *nervōsus* sinewy < *nervus* sinew; see NERVE] —**nerv′ous·ly,** *adv.* —**nerv′ous·ness,** *n.* —**Syn. 2.** high-strung, excitable, jumpy. **5.** apprehensive. **7.** energetic.

nervous breakdown, any disabling mental disorder requiring treatment.

nervous Nellie or **Nelly,** *pl.* **nervous Nellies.** *Slang.* a nervous or easily excited person: *He . . . denounces his critics as "nervous Nellies"* (Harper's). [< *Nellie* or *Nelly,* a feminine name]

nervous system, the system of nerve fibers, nerve cells, and other nervous tissue in a person or animal that serves to carry impulses, to bring information and activity into proper relation to one another, and, in man, to produce the phenomenon of consciousness. Man's central nervous system and that of the other vertebrates consists of the brain and spinal cord, to and from which impulses are carried by the peripheral nervous system. The peripheral nervous system consists of the cranial nerves (12 pairs in man), the spinal nerves (31 pairs in man), and the autonomic nervous system (the ganglia and nerves that regulate the involuntary muscles, viscera, glands, etc.).

ner·vure (nėr′vyůr), *n.* **1.** the principal vein of a leaf. **2.** a rib of an insect's wing. [< Middle French *nervure* < *nerf* nerve < Latin *nervus;* see NERVE]

nerv·y (nėr′vē), *adj.,* **nerv·i·er, nerv·i·est. 1.** *U.S. Slang.* rude and bold; impudent: *It is a little "nervy" . . . to walk into another man's house uninvited* (Elizabeth Robins). **2.** requiring courage or firmness: *a nervy undertaking.* **3.** strong; vigorous. **4.** *British.* suffering from nervous tension; nervous: *Jaded, nervy, overworked men, who cannot sleep after taking ordinary coffee* (Punch).

n.e.s., not elsewhere specified.

nes·cience (nesh′əns, -ē əns), *n.* **1.** lack of knowledge; ignorance: *the . . . involuntary nescience of men* (Jeremy Taylor). **2.** the philosophical doctrine, implicit in many forms of agnosticism, that knowledge cannot rest on other than the phenomena of nature, God and the supernatural being both unknowable and unprovable. [< Late Latin *nescientia* < *nesciēns;* see NESCIENT]

nes·cient (nesh′ənt, -ē ənt), *adj.* not knowing; ignorant. [< Latin *nesciēns, -entis,* present participle of *nescīre* be ignorant < *ne* not + *scīre* know]

nesh (nesh), *adj. Dialect.* **1.** soft, tender, or succulent. **2.** delicate or weakly: *the nesh hazels bending in the blast* (Robert Surtees). **3.** poor-spirited; effeminate. **4.** dainty or squeamish. [Old English *hnesce*]

ness (nes), *n.* a promontory, headland, or cape (now especially in proper names): *Loch Ness.* [Middle English *nasse,* Old English *næs, nes.* Compare Old Icelandic *nes.*]

-ness, *suffix.* **1.** quality, state, or condition of being ——: *Kindheartedness = the quality of being kindhearted. Preparedness = the state of being prepared.*

2. —— action; —— behavior: *Carefulness (in some uses) = careful action; careful behavior.*

3. a single instance of such a quality, state, or condition: *Kindness = a single instance of being kind.*

[Middle English *-nesse,* Old English *-ness, -niss*]

➔ **-ness** is a living suffix and can be freely used to form new words.

Nes·sel·rode (nes′əl rōd), *n.* Nesselrode pudding.

Nesselrode pudding, a custard made with nuts, usually chestnuts, fruits, fruit syrup, or rum, etc., frozen as ice cream or used as a pudding, to fill pies, etc. [American English, supposedly < Count Karl R. *Nesselrode,* 1780-1862, a Russian diplomat]

Nes·sus (nes′əs), *n. Greek Legend.* a centaur shot by Hercules with a poisoned arrow for attempting to carry off his wife, Deianira. Hercules was himself fatally poisoned by a robe steeped in the blood of Nessus by

Deianira, who believed it to be a love charm.

nest (nest), *n.* **1.** a place built of twigs and grass or leaves, an open hole in the ground, etc., used by birds for laying eggs and rearing young. **2.** a place used by insects, fishes, turtles, rabbits, or the like, for depositing eggs, spawn, or young: *a squirrel's nest, a wasp's nest.* **3.** a snug abode, retreat, or resting place: *The little girl snuggled down in a nest among the sofa cushions.* **4.** a place that swarms or is prevalent, usually with something bad; den: *a nest of thieves, a nest of vice.* **5.** the birds, insects, animals, etc., living in a nest. **6.** a set or series, often from large to small, such that each fits within another: *a nest of drinking cups, bowls, or tables.* **7.** *Informal.* a base for guided missiles.

Nest (def. 2) of a female potter wasp

feather one's nest, to take advantage of chances to get rich: *His spouse . . . was disposed to feather her own nest, at the expense of him and his heirs* (Tobias Smollett).

—*v.i.* **1.** to build or have a nest in a particular place: *The bluebirds are nesting here again.* **2.** to search for nests: *This is dull work for a bairn. Let's go nesting* (Robert Louis Stevenson). —*v.t.* to settle or place in, or as if in, a nest; provide with a nest or place for nesting.

[Old English *nest*]

—**Syn.** *n.* **4.** swarm.

n'est-ce pas? (nes pä'), *French.* isn't that so? don't you agree?

nest egg, 1. something laid up as the beginning of a fund or as a reserve: *She has a nice little nest egg put away for her retirement.* **2.** a natural or artificial egg left in a nest to induce a hen or other bird to lay or continue laying eggs there.

nest·er (nes'tər), *n.* **1.** *U.S.* a farmer, homesteader, or squatter seeking to settle on land used as a cattle range: *... as bitter as the Old West feud between ranchers and nesters for the one water hole in the sagebrush* (Harper's). **2.** a bird or animal that makes or lives in a nest.

nest·ing ground or **site** (nes'ting), a place used by a bird to build its nest: *A walk through a marsh in winter . . . will reveal birds' summer nesting sites by the dozens* (Science News Letter).

nes·tle (nes'əl), *v.*, **-tled, -tling.** —*v.i.* **1.** to settle oneself comfortably or cozily: *She nestled down into the big chair.* **2.** to be settled comfortably or cozily; be sheltered: *The little house nestled among the trees.* **3.** to press close in affection or for comfort: *to nestle up to one's mother.* **4.** to make or have a nest; settle in a nest. —*v.t.* **1.** to press or hold close, as in a nest; cuddle: *to nestle a kitten or a baby in one's arms.* **2.** to settle or place in or as in a nest; provide with a nest. [Old English *nestlian* build a nest < *nest* nest] —**nes'tler,** *n.*

nest·ling (nest'ling), *n.* **1.** a bird too young to leave the nest: *The author . . . describes from long and loving observation the behavior and habitat of this familiar bird, its songs and calls . . . care of the nestlings* (Scientific American). **2.** a young child.

Nes·tor (nes'tər), *n.* **1.** *Greek Legend.* the oldest and wisest of the Greeks at the siege of Troy. **2.** any wise old man: *. . . an old man, in good truth the Nestor of his tribe* (Francis Parkman). *. . . who at eighty is Nestor of the New York auction world* (Harper's).

Nes·to·ri·an (nes tôr'ē ən, -tōr'-), *n.* **1.** a follower of Nestorius; adherent of Nestorianism. **2.** one of a modern remnant of this sect in northwestern Iran and adjoining regions. —*adj.* having to do with Nestorius, his doctrine, or Nestorians.

Nes·to·ri·an·ism (nes tôr'ē ə niz'əm, -tōr'-), *n.* the doctrine of Nestorius, patriarch of Constantinople from 428 to 431. His teaching differentiated the two natures in Christ so sharply from each other as to disrupt the unity of his person and make it appear that Christ consisted of two persons, one being the Word of God and the other being a human indwelt by the other.

net[1] (net), *n., v.,* **net·ted, net·ting,** *adj.* —*n.* **1.** an open fabric made of string, cord, thread, or hair, knotted together in such a way as to leave holes regularly arranged. Nets are used to capture butterflies, birds, and fish, or to keep a woman's hair in place. Some are used to protect something, as a mosquito net or wire net used in blasting. Others are used in games like tennis over which a ball must clear after being hit: *Mrs. Fleitz . . . remained mainly at the baseline, whereas Miss Breit often came to the net to win points* (London Times). **2.** anything like net; set of things that cross each other. **3.** a lacelike cloth often used as a veil: *cotton net.* **4.** a trap or snare: *The guilty boy was caught in the net of his own lies. And I find more bitter than death the woman, whose heart is snares and nets* (Ecclesiastes 7:26). **5.** a network. **6.** a ball, bird, etc., that hits the net in tennis, badminton, and other games played with a net.

—*v.t.* **1.** to catch in a net; take with nets: *to net a fish.* **2.** to cover, confine, or protect with a net. **3.** to make into net: *to net cord.* **4.** to make with net: *to net a hammock.* **5.** to catch or capture as if with a net: *Our patrol netted three prisoners.* **6.** to hit (a ball, bird, etc.) into the net in tennis, badminton, etc., thus losing a point.

—*adj.* **1.** made of net: *a net dress.* **2.** caught in a net or nets; netted.

[Old English *nett*] —**net'ter,** *n.*

—**Syn.** *n.* **1.** mesh, network, reticulation.

net[2] (net), *adj., n., v.,* **net·ted, net·ting.** —*adj.* **1.** remaining after deductions; free from deductions. A net gain or profit is the actual gain after all working expenses have been paid. The net weight of a glass jar of candy is the weight of the candy itself. The net price of a book is the real price from which no discount can be made. **2.** sold at net prices: *a net book.*

—*n.* the net amount, as profit, price, or weight: *Final results for last year . . . show a net of $430 million* (Newsweek).

—*v.t.* to gain or yield as clear profit: *The sale netted him a thousand dollars.*

[< French *net;* see NEAT[1]]

net·ball (net'bôl'), *n.* **1.** *British.* a kind of basketball played by girls, usually on an outdoor court and with a less lively ball: *They could be taught more cookery, knitting and other housewifery arts, and less hockey, netball and lacrosse* (Cape Times). **2.** a net cord hit in tennis.

net cord, 1. the top cord holding up the net in tennis, badminton, etc. **2.** a tennis ball which glances off the top of the net but continues in play: *A miraculous flick to kill a net cord on the volley saved Rosewall* (London Times).

net·ful (net'fu̇l), *n., pl.* **-fuls. 1.** the amount that a net can hold: *As fishermen in hundreds of small boats hauled in one netful after another, the fat, red-flanked fish made the shallow water boil* (Time). **2.** the contents of a net.

Neth., Netherlands.

neth·er (neᴛʜ'ər), *adj.* **1.** lower; under: *The disappointed child's nether lip quivered.* **2.** lying or conceived as lying beneath the earth's surface: *the nether regions.* [Old English *nithera*]

Neth·er·land·er (neᴛʜ'ər lən dər), *n.* a native or inhabitant of the Netherlands, a small country in Europe, west of Germany and north of Belgium.

Neth·er·land·ish (neᴛʜ'ər lən'dish), *adj.* of, having to do with, or characteristic of the Netherlands: *London galleries specializing in the old Netherlandish masters* (London Times).

Neth·er·lands Union (neᴛʜ'ər ləndz), a federation of the kingdom of the Netherlands and its overseas territories.

nether millstone, 1. the lower of a pair of millstones in a mill for grinding grain: *His heart is as firm as a stone; yea, as hard as a piece of the nether millstone* (Job 41:24). **2.** great hardness.

neth·er·more (neᴛʜ'ər môr, -mōr), *adj.* lower.

neth·er·most (neᴛʜ'ər mōst), *adj.* lowest: *the nethermost abyss* (Milton). *From the nethermost fire . . . Thy servant deliver* (Cardinal Newman). —**Syn.** undermost.

neth·er·stock (neᴛʜ'ər stok'), *n. Archaic.* a stocking: *A dispute upon the preference due to the Spanish netherstock over the black Gascoigne hose* (Scott).

neth·er·ward (neᴛʜ'ər wərd), *adv., adj.* downward.

neth·er·wards (neᴛʜ'ər wərdz), *adv.* netherward.

nether world, 1. the lower world; world of the dead; Hades. **2.** the place of punishment after death; realm of the Devil; Hell.

net·lay·er (net'lā'ər), *n.* a ship that lays steel nets across a harbor entrance, mouth of a river, etc., to prevent enemy submarines, torpedoes, etc., from entering.

Netlayer

net national product, the part of the gross national product that remains after depreciation and the value of all capital and business products used in production for a given period have been deducted.

nets·man (nets'mən), *n., pl.* **-men.** a person who uses a net, as in fishing: *In many areas . . . the Salmon is the main, often the only, source of male employment . . . for netsmen in the commercial fisheries* (London Times).

net·su·ke (net'sü kā), *n., pl.* **-ke.** (in Japan) a small knob or button, usually ornamental, pierced with holes for tying on a purse or other article worn suspended from the sash of a kimono: *He was showing Mr. Yashamoto our authentic Japanese netsuke, a lovely little ivory carving that had been my birthday present* (New Yorker). [< Japanese *netsuke*]

nett (net), *adj., n., v.t. British.* net[2]: *It is a first-class commercial building which should show capital appreciation and a first-class nett profit yield on the capital invested* (Cape Times).

net·ting (net'ing), *n.* **1.** a netted or meshed material: *mosquito netting, wire netting for window screens.* **2.** the process of making a net, or such material. **3.** the act or privilege of fishing with a net or nets.

net·tle (net'əl), *n., v.,* **-tled, -tling.** —*n.* **1.** any of a widely distributed group of coarse herbaceous plants having sharp leaf hairs that sting the skin when touched. **2.** any of various related or similar plants.

—*v.t.* **1.** to sting the mind of; irritate; provoke; vex: *His repeating of these foolish rumors nettled me.* **2.** to beat (a person or animal) with nettles. **3.** to subject to the stinging of nettles.

Nettle (def. 1)

[Old English *netele*] —**net'tle·like',** *adj.*

—**Syn.** *v.t.* **1.** exasperate, incense, pique.

nettle rash, hives; urticaria.

net·tle·some (net'əl səm), *adj.* **1.** easily nettled; irritable. **2.** irritating: *A hot and nettlesome book and rather perplexing for a layman to handle* (Atlantic).

nettle tree, 1. a tree of Europe and Asia, belonging to the elm family, bearing a sweet, cherrylike fruit; lotus tree. **2.** some allied species, as the hackberry. **3.** an Australian tree closely related to the nettle, having stinging hairs and a bark which is used as a fiber.

net ton, a short ton; 2,000 pounds.

net tonnage, the cargo capacity of a ship, being its gross volume below decks less space allowed for fuel, engines, etc., measured in units of 100 cubic feet, called tons.

net·work (net'werk'), *n.* **1.** work or a piece of work having the texture of a net; netting. **2.** any netlike combination of filaments, lines, veins, passages, or the like: *a network of vines, a network of railroads. Their law is a network of fictions* (Emerson). **3.** anything that snares or catches, as a net does: *a police network.* **4.** a group of radio or television stations so connected that the same program can be presented by all: *Mr. Burgard mentioned two instances in which his*

corporation advised networks that it was withdrawing as a participating sponsor because of objections to scripts (New York Times).
—*v.t. Especially British.* to broadcast (a program) over a radio or television network: *Thirteen programmes on international economics . . . will be networked nationally in January* (London Times).
[< *net*[1] + *work*]

Neuf·châ·tel (nœ shä tel′), *n.*, or **Neufchâtel cheese,** a soft white cheese made from milk with or without the cream.

neuk (nyük), *n. Scottish.* nook (recess or corner).

neume or **neum** (nüm, nyüm), *n.* one of a set of signs used in the earliest plainsong notation to indicate the melody: *One of these discoveries contained the Lamentations of Jeremiah, for which Professor* [*Leo*] *Schrade put in a claim as the oldest neumes* (London Times). [< Old French *neume* < Medieval Latin *neuma, neupma* a group of sounds sung in a single respiration < Greek *pneûma* breath]

neur-, *combining form.* the form of **neuro-** before vowels, as in *neural.*

neu·ral (nůr′əl, nyůr′-), *adj.* **1.** of or having to do with a nerve, neurone, or the nervous system: *The* [*neural arch*] *encloses the neural canal which is occupied by the spinal cord* (A. Franklin Shull). **2.** having to do with or situated in the region or side of the body containing the brain and spinal cord; dorsal: *The neural processes involved in learning a given operation, such as finding the way through a maze, occur in all or most parts of the cortex* (S. A. Barnett). [< *neur-* + *-al*[1]]

neural arch, the arch on the dorsal side of a vertebra: *Each vertebra is made up of a spool-like centrum surmounted by a neural arch to house the nerve cord* (Tracy I. Storer).

neural canal, the canal formed by the vertebral foramina, enclosing and protecting the spinal cord.

neu·ral·gia (nů ral′jə, nyů-), *n.* **1.** a pain, usually sharp, along the course of a nerve. **2.** a condition characterized by such pain: *facial neuralgia, sciatic neuralgia.* [< New Latin *neuralgia* < Greek *neûron* nerve + *álgos* pain]

neu·ral·gic (nů ral′jik, nyů-), *adj.* of or having to do with neuralgia.

neural spine, a bony process on the dorsal side of a vertebra.

neu·ra·min·ic acid (nůr′ə min′ik, nyůr′-), a fatty acid found in the brain, shortage of which may be associated with schizophrenia: *Evidence that schizophrenia may be the result of a chemical immaturity of the nervous system was seen in the finding that adult schizophrenics have considerably less neuraminic acid in the spinal cord fluid* (Science News Letter). *Formula:* $C_9H_{17}NO_8$

neu·ras·the·ni·a (nůr′əs thē′nē ə, nyůr′-), *n.* **1.** nervous exhaustion or weakness, as from overwork, vitamin deficiency, disorder of the nervous system, etc. **2.** a neurosis accompanied by local digestive or circulatory upset of uncertain origin, and characterized by extreme fatigue and chronic depression: *I will tell you then that we distinguish three pure forms of actual neurosis: neurasthenia, anxiety-neurosis and hypochondria* (Sigmund Freud). [< New Latin *neurasthenia* < Greek *neûron* nerve + *asthéneia* weakness]

neu·ras·then·ic (nůr′əs then′ik, nyůr′-), *adj.* having to do with or suffering from neurasthenia. —*n.* a person suffering from neurasthenia. —**neu′ras·then′i·cal·ly,** *adv.*

neu·ra·tion (nů rā′shən, nyů-), *n.* nervation. [< *neur-* + *-ation*]

neu·rec·to·my (nů rek′tə mē, nyů-), *n., pl.* **-mies.** the surgical removal of all or part of a nerve. [< *neur-* + Greek *ektomē* a cutting out]

neu·ri·lem·ma (nůr′ə lem′ə, nyůr′-), *n.* the delicate membranous outer sheath of peripheral nerve fibers. [< Greek *neûron* nerve + *eilēma* covering; the *-lemma* spelling from confusion with Greek *lémma* husk]

neu·ril·i·ty (nů ril′ə tē, nyů-), *n.* the properties which are characteristic of nerve tissue, such as the conducting of stimuli.

neu·ris·tor (nů ris′tər, nyů-), *n.* a very small live wire having properties similar to the nerve fiber or axon in a living organism, designed for use in microminiature electronic models of the human nervous system: *A first step toward making a completely artificial nerve cell was made with the development of the neuristor* (Science News Letter). [< Greek *neur*(*ôn*) nerve + English (*trans*)*istor*]

neu·rite (nůr′īt, nyůr′-), *n. Obsolete.* an axon. [< *neur-* + *-ite*[1]]

neu·rit·ic (nů rit′ik, nyů-), *adj.* having to do with, characterized by, or affected with neuritis.

neu·ri·tis (nů rī′tis, nyů-), *n.* inflammation of a nerve or nerves, accompanied by pain, paralysis, disturbance of sensation, and loss of the reflexes. [< New Latin *neuritis* < Greek *neûron* nerve + English *-itis*]

neuro-, *combining form.* nerve; nerve tissue; nervous system: *Neuroma = a tumor growing on a nerve or nerve tissue. Neuropathy = any disease of the nervous system.* Also, **neur-** before vowels. [< Greek *neûron* nerve]

neu·ro·an·a·tom·ic·al (nůr′ō an′ə tom′ə kəl, nyůr′-), *adj.* of or having to do with neuroanatomy: *Neff . . . has emphasized the need for psycho-physiological studies to supplement the neuroanatomical and neurophysiological evidence* (Calvin P. Stone).

neu·ro·a·nat·o·mist (nůr′ō ə nat′ə mist, nyůr′-), *n.* a student or specialist in neuroanatomy: *In the physiology laboratory of Ernst Brücke, Freud worked happily and productively as a histologist and neuroanatomist* (Scientific American).

neu·ro·a·nat·o·my (nůr′ō ə nat′ə mē, nyůr′-), *n.* the branch of anatomy that deals with the structure of the nervous system: [*Man's*] *basic emotional organization has apparently evolved little in the past half million years and this is borne out by comparative neuroanatomy and physiology* (Bulletin of Atomic Scientists).

neu·ro·blast (nůr′ə blast, nyůr′-), *n.* a cell in vertebrate embryos that develops into a nerve cell. [< *neuro-* + Greek *blastós* germ, sprout]

neu·ro·blas·to·ma (nůr′ə blas tō′mə, nyůr′-), *n., pl.* **-mas, -ma·ta** (-mə tə). a malignant cancer of the sympathetic nervous system which attacks the neuroblasts of the embryo and is found usually in children. [< *neuroblast* + *-oma*]

neu·ro·chem·is·try (nůr′ō kem′ə strē, nyůr′-), *n.* the branch of biochemistry that deals with the chemical make-up and effects of the nervous system: *Since mental health is the chief medical problem today, the study of neurochemistry assumes considerable importance* (Science News Letter).

neu·ro·coele or **neu·ro·cele** (nůr′ə sēl, nyůr′-), *n. Obsolete.* the liquid-filled spaces within the central nervous system. [< *neuro-* + Greek *koiliā* a body cavity < *koîlos* hollow]

neu·ro·der·ma·ti·tis (nůr′ō dėr′mə tī′tis, nyůr′-), *n.* a chronic skin disorder of nervous origin characterized by much itching and a leathery condition of the skin. It commonly affects the neck, armpits, and pubic area: *Methedrine proved particularly useful in chronic anxiety states, neurodermatitis and acute post-traumatic anxieties* (Morris Fishbein).

neu·ro·en·do·crine (nůr′ō en′də krin, nyůr′-), *adj.* of or having to do with the nervous system and the endocrine glands: *Chromatophores are sensitive indicators of nervous, endocrine or neuro-endocrine activity* (Francis Knowles).

neu·ro·fi·bro·ma (nůr′ō fī brō′mə, nyůr′-), *n., pl.* **-mas, -ma·ta** (-mə tə). a fibrous tumor, usually benign, arising from the outer sheath of peripheral nerve fibers: *Surgery involving complete removal of a neurofibroma . . . resulted in gradual improvement of her legs* (Science News Letter). [< *neuro-* + *fibroma*]

neu·ro·gen·ic (nůr′ə jen′ik, nyůr′-), *adj.* originating in the nerves or nervous system: *Broadly speaking there are two types of heart beat in the animal kingdom: one in which the beat originates in nerve cells located in the wall of the heart* (*neurogenic*) . . . (J. Green).

neu·rog·li·a (nů rog′lē ə, nyů-), *n.* the delicate connective tissue forming a supporting network for the conducting elements of nervous tissue in the brain and the spinal cord. [< *neuro-* + Late Greek *gliā* glue]

neu·rog·li·al (nů rog′lē əl, nyů-), *adj.* neurogliar: *As well as the ten thousand million nerve cells, there are about ten times as many neuroglial cells* (New Scientist).

neu·rog·li·ar (nů rog′lē ər, nyů-), *adj.* of or having to do with neuroglia.

neu·ro·hor·mone (nůr′ō hôr′mōn, nyůr′-), *n.* a hormone that stimulates nerve cells or the nervous system: *Serotonin, a neurohormone, acts as a sedative when given in large doses* (Scientific American).

neu·ro·hu·mor (nůr′ō hyü′mər, nyůr′-), *n.* a chemical substance such as epinephrine, secreted by the endings of a nerve cell and capable of activating a muscle or another nerve cell: *An impulse, upon reaching the finely branched ends of an axone, causes the latter to produce a chemical neurohumor which sets up an impulse in the next neuron* (Tracy I. Storer).

neu·ro·hu·mor·al (nůr′ō hyü′mər əl, nyůr′-), *adj.* of or having to do with a neurohumor or the response to it: *The nerve is accustomed to this . . . because it is present on several natural neurohumoral agents such as adrenalin and histamine* (Science News Letter).

neu·ro·log·i·cal (nůr′ə loj′ə kəl, nyůr′-), *adj.* of or having to do with neurology: *Insofar as induction carries with it connotations of curious neurological mechanisms . . .* (Scientific American). —**neu′ro·log′i·cal·ly,** *adv.*

neu·rol·o·gist (nů rol′ə jist, nyů-), *n.* a person trained in neurology, especially a specialist in organic diseases of the central nervous system: *It is a condition which is all too often missed by even experienced neurologists and psychiatrists* (Sunday Times).

neu·rol·o·gy (nů rol′ə jē, nyů-), *n.* the study of the nervous system and its diseases: *Apart from the search for "hypothetic constructs" in neurology, there have been interesting developments in "molar" theory* (F. H. George). [< *neuro-* + *-logy*]

neu·ro·ma (nů rō′mə, nyů-), *n., pl.* **-ma·ta** (-mə tə), **-mas.** a tumor growing upon a nerve or in nerve tissue. [< *neur-* + *-oma*]

neu·ro·mast (nůr′ə mast, nyůr′-), *n.* a specialized sensory organ beneath the lateral line of all fishes and aquatic amphibians, consisting of a cluster of sensory cells. [< Greek *neûron* nerve + *mastós* hillock]

neu·ro·mus·cu·lar (nůr′ō mus′kyə lər, nyůr′-), *adj.* of or having to do with the relationship of nerves to the muscles: *One animal . . . was given a constant infusion of a neuromuscular blocking agent, . . . and maintained an artificial respiration* (Ruben and Sekula).

neu·ron (nůr′on, nyůr′-), *n.* one of the conducting cells of which the brain, spinal cord, and nerves are composed; nerve cell. A neuron consists of a cell body containing the nucleus, usually several dendrites or nerve processes, and commonly one axon or nerve fiber, that may be very long. *To excite or "fire" a neuron, the nerve impulse has to cross the synapse, and it is probable that two or more impulses have to summate in space and time in order to "fire" a neuron* (George M. Wyburn). Also, **neurone.** [< New Latin *neuron* < Greek *neûron* sinew, nerve]

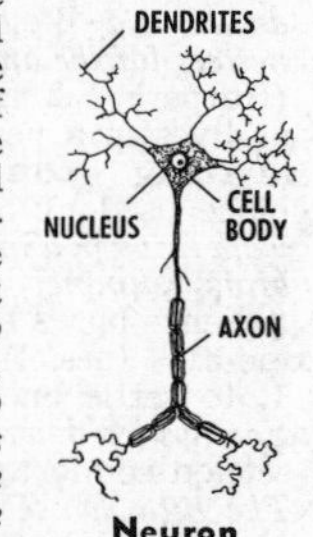

Neuron

neu·ron·al (nůr′ə nəl, nyůr′-; nů rō′-, nyů-), *adj.* of or having to do with a neuron: *Memory therefore, depends on an active neuronal mechanism which never rests* (New Scientist).

neu·rone (nůr′ōn, nyůr′-), *n.* neuron.

neu·ron·ic (nů ron′ik, nyů-), *adj.* of or having to do with a neuron.

neu·ro·path (nůr′ə path, nyůr′-), *n.* a person subject to or affected with nervous disorder, usually functional rather than organic.

neu·ro·path·ic (nůr′ə path′ik, nyůr′-), *adj.* relating to, caused by, or characterized by nervous disease. —**neu′ro·path′i·cal·ly,** *adv.*

neu·ro·path·i·cal (nůr′ə path′ə kəl, nyůr′-), *adj.* neuropathic.

neu·rop·a·thist (nů rop′ə thist, nyů-), *n.* a specialist in diseases of the nerves; neurologist.

neu·ro·path·o·log·i·cal (nůr′ō path′ə loj′ə kəl, nyůr′-), *adj.* of or having to do with neuropathology: *This together with preliminary neuropathological . . . observations, constitutes the subject of this report* (Harold Koenig).

neu·ro·pa·thol·o·gist (nůr′ō pə thol′ə jist, nyůr′-), *n.* a person skilled in neuropathology: *Adams and other neuropathologists insisted that adventitial histiocytes were also prominent* (Science).

neu·ro·pa·thol·o·gy (nu̇r′ō pə thol′ə jē, nyu̇r′-), *n.* the study of diseases of the nervous system.

neu·rop·a·thy (nu̇ rop′ə thē, nyu̇-), *n.* a disease of the nervous system.

neu·ro·phys·i·o·log·i·cal (nu̇r′ō fiz′ē ə loj′ə kəl, nyu̇r′-), *adj.* of or having to do with the physiological functions of the nervous system: *The essential first step from the neurophysiological point of view is to find out more about how images are formed by the brain* (New Scientist).

neu·ro·phys·i·ol·o·gist (nu̇r′ō fiz′ē ol′ə jist, nyu̇r′-), *n.* a person skilled in neurophysiology: *Electrical stimulation of certain areas in the brain ... evokes sensations of extreme pleasure which have recently attracted the attention of a number of neurophysiologists* (Scientific American).

neu·ro·phys·i·ol·o·gy (nu̇r′ō fiz′ē ol′ə jē, nyu̇r′-), *n.* the branch of physiology that deals with the nervous system: *[Galvani's] discovery that a muscle could be made to contract by an electrical current laid the foundation for the study of animal electricity, an important part of neurophysiology* (Caroline A. Chandler).

neu·ro·plasm (nu̇r′ə plaz′əm, nyu̇r′-), *n.* the protoplasm of the nerve cells and their fibrillae. [< Greek *neûron* nerve + *plásma* anything formed]

neu·ro·psy·chi·at·ric (nu̇r′ō sī′kē at′rik, nyu̇r′-), *adj.* of or having to do with neuropsychiatry: *The V.A. reported ... that it already had built special facilities in six neuropsychiatric hospitals* (New York Times).

neu·ro·psy·chi·a·trist (nu̇r′ō sī kī′ə trist, nyu̇r′-), *n.* a doctor of neuropsychiatry.

neu·ro·psy·chi·a·try (nu̇r′ō sī kī′ə trē, nyu̇r′-), *n.* the branch of medicine dealing with neurology and psychiatry.

neu·ro·psy·cho·sis (nu̇r′ō sī kō′sis, nyu̇r′-), *n., pl.* **-ses** (-sēz). **1.** a mental disorder associated with or caused by organic disease of the nervous system. **2.** psychoneurosis.

neu·rop·ter (nu̇ rop′tər, nyu̇-), *n.* a neuropteran insect. [< New Latin *Neuroptera* the order name < Greek *neûron* nerve, sinew + *pterón* wing]

neu·rop·ter·al (nu̇ rop′tər əl, nyu̇-), *adj., n.* neuropteran.

neu·rop·ter·an (nu̇ rop′tər ən, nyu̇-), *adj., n., pl.* **-ter·a**(-tər ə). —*adj.* of or belonging to a group of insects, having a complete metamorphosis, four large delicate wings, and mouth parts adapted for chewing, as the lace wings, ant lions, etc. —*n.* a neuropteran insect. [< New Latin *Neuroptera* the order name (< Greek *neûron* nerve, sinew + *pterón* wing) + English *-an*]

neu·rop·ter·oid (nu̇ rop′tə roid, nyu̇-), *adj.* resembling a neuropteran.

neu·rop·ter·on (nu̇ rop′tə ron, nyu̇-), *n.* a neuropteran insect.

neu·rop·ter·ous (nu̇ rop′tər əs, nyu̇-), *adj.* neuropteran.

neu·ro·se·cre·tion (nu̇r′ō si krē′shən, nyu̇r′-), *n.* **1.** the secretion of substances, such as hormones, by nerve cells whose structures have temporarily become modified and taken on the function and appearance of gland cells: *This indication of the possibility of neurosecretion in crustaceans was soon confirmed and extended by other workers* (Sir Francis Knowles). **2.** the substance secreted.

neu·ro·se·cre·to·ry (nu̇r′ō si krē′tər ē, nyu̇r′-), *adj.* of or having to do with neurosecretion: *Apparently this material "migrates" along a nervous pathway from the neurosecretory part of the brain to the adjacent corpora cardiaca* (Scientific American).

neu·ro·sis (nu̇ rō′sis, nyu̇-), *n., pl.* **-ses** (-sēz). **1.** a mild nervous disorder showing emotional disturbance with no apparent organic change. The nerve function is deranged and characterized especially by anxiety and a feeling of insecurity: *A neurosis is an emotional problem that is solved in an irrational manner* (Marguerite Clark). **2.** any action of nerve cells. [earlier, a functional disease < New Latin *neurosis* < Greek *neûron* nerve, sinew + *-ōsis* -osis]

neu·ro·spo·ra (nu̇r′ō spôr′ə, -spōr′-; nyu̇r′-), *n.* any of a group of fungi that cause red and black mold in baked goods; the bread mold: *Studies are being made ... on the tropical bread mold, neurospora, which reproduces rapidly and otherwise lends itself to genetic study* (Some Applications of Atomic Energy in Plant Science). [< *neuro-* + Greek *sporá* seed]

neu·ro·sur·geon (nu̇r′ō sėr′jən, nyu̇r′-), *n.* a doctor who specializes in neurosurgery: *The neurosurgeon decides on the precise zone of destruction by the proton beam in the brain* (Frances Burns).

neu·ro·sur·ge·ry (nu̇r′ō sėr′jər ē, nyu̇r′-), *n.* surgery of the nervous system, especially of the brain: *In the field of neurosurgery, perhaps the most important new operation is that devised by Tarnhof, of Denmark, in the treatment of trigeminal neuralgia* (Morris Fishbein).

neu·ro·sur·gi·cal (nu̇r′ō sėr′jə kəl, nyu̇r′-), *adj.* of or having to do with neurosurgery: *Drugs, conditioning, and neurosurgical procedures that modify drives, imagination, and personality have great value in treating some of the mentally ill* (Bulletin of Atomic Scientists).

neu·ro·syph·i·lis (nu̇r′ō sif′ə ləs, nyu̇r′-), *n.* syphilis which has spread to and attacked the nervous system, a characteristic of the disease in its final stage.

neu·rot·ic (nu̇ rot′ik, nyu̇-), *adj.* **1. a.** suffering from emotional instability. **b.** of or having to do with a neurosis: *Neurotic symptoms, then, just like errors and dreams, have their meaning and, like these, are related to the life of the person in whom they appear* (Sigmund Freud). **2.** *Informal.* too nervous. **3.** acting upon or stimulating the nerves.
—*n.* **1.** a person suffering from neurosis: *The problem of the neurotic, then, is suffering, but of a particular kind, suffering due to guilt* (Sebastian de Grazia). **2.** a drug or poison that acts on the nervous system. **3.** *Obsolete.* a disease of the nerves. —**neu·rot′i·cal·ly,** *adv.*

neu·rot·i·cism (nu̇ rot′ə siz əm, nyu̇-), *n.* the state or condition of being neurotic: *Bartók's music is disturbing—possessed not only of a wild beauty but also of a neuroticism* (New Yorker).

neu·rot·o·mist (nu̇ rot′ə mist, nyu̇-), *n.* a person skilled in neurotomy.

neu·rot·o·my (nu̇ rot′ə mē, nyu̇-), *n., pl.* **-mies.** the surgical incision into a nerve to relieve a painful condition, as in neuralgia. [< Greek *neûron* nerve + *-tomiā* a cutting]

neu·ro·tox·in (nu̇r′ō tok′sin, nyu̇r′-), *n.* a toxin that can damage or destroy nerve tissue. The venom of the coral snake is a neurotoxin: *All of these neurotoxins in one way or another disrupt the microchemical mechanisms that transmit nerve impulses* (Scientific American).

neu·ro·trop·ic (nu̇r′ō trop′ik, -trō′pik; nyu̇r′-), *adj.* drawn to or having an affinity for nervous tissue: *The virus of rabies is a neurotropic virus* (New Yorker). [< *neuro-* + Greek *tropē* a turning + English *-ic*]

Neus·tri·an (nüs′trē ən, nyüs′-), *adj.* of or having to do with Neustria, the western kingdom of the Franks.

neut., **1.** neuter. **2.** neutral.

neu·ter (nü′tər, nyü′tər), *adj.* **1.** *Grammar.* **a.** neither masculine nor feminine: *"It" is a neuter pronoun.* **b.** (of verbs) neither active nor passive; intransitive. *Abbr.:* neut. **2. a.** *Zoology.* having no sex organs or sex organs that are not fully developed: *Worker bees are neuter.* **b.** *Botany.* having neither stamens nor pistils; functionally asexual. **3.** being on neither side; neutral: *as to these matters I shall be impartial, though I cannot be neuter* (Richard Steele).
—*n.* **1.** *Grammar.* **a.** the neuter gender. **b.** a neuter word or form. **2.** an animal, plant, or insect that is neuter. **3.** a neutral: *which knows no neuter, owns but friends or foes* (Byron).
—*v.t.* **1.** to castrate: *They had had the animal neutered some seven years back, and it had grown gross, sulky, and resentful* (New Yorker). **2.** to counteract or make ineffective; neutralize: *A point of view that refused to neuter itself with a "nevertheless—" or a "but we must not overlook—"* (Sunday Times).
[< Latin *neuter* < *nē* not + *uter* either]

neu·tral (nü′trəl, nyü′trəl), *adj.* **1.** on neither side in a quarrel or a war: *a neutral attitude in an election. Switzerland was neutral in World War II.* **2.** of or belonging to a neutral country or neutral zone: *a neutral vessel, a neutral port.* **3.** neither one thing nor the other; indefinite. **4. a.** having little or no color; grayish: *a neutral sky.* **b.** not tinted by mixture with any other color; pure: *a neutral yellow.* **5.** neither acid nor alkaline. **6.** *Electricity.* neither positive nor negative: *Recent experiments ... have led to the discovery of ... a neutral pion, that is a pion with practically the same mass as the charged pion but with no electric charge* (H. J. Bhaba). **7.** *Biology.* not developed in sex; neuter.
—*n.* **1.** a neutral person or country; one not taking part in a quarrel or war: *We shall continue faithfully to demonstrate our complete respect for the right of self-decision by these neutrals* (Time). **2.** a position of gears when they do not transmit motion from the engine to the wheels or other working parts. **3.** a color that is neutral.
[< Latin *neutrālis* < *neuter* neuter] —**neu′tral·ly,** *adv.*

neutral corner, either of the two corners of a prize ring not occupied by the contestants between rounds.

neu·tral·ise (nü′trə līz, nyü′-), *v.t.,* **-ised, -is·ing.** *Especially British.* to neutralize: *Free acid in the mouth is very quickly neutralised by the saliva* (New Scientist).

neu·tral·ism (nü′trə liz əm, nyü′-), *n.* the practice of maintaining a position as a neutral, especially in world affairs: *Neutralism may have to become a little less neutral and may in due course even be found to be unmaintainable* (Sunday Times).

neu·tral·ist (nü′trə list, nyü′-), *n.* a person or government that practices or advocates neutrality, especially in international affairs: *It gives a new lease on life to French, British and Italian neutralists who would like to make all Western Europe neutral* (New York Times). —*adj.* practicing or advocating neutrality: *India is a neutralist country.* —**Syn.** *adj.* uncommitted, nonaligned.

neu·tral·i·ty (nü tral′ə tē, nyü-), *n.* **1. a.** a being neutral: *armed neutrality* (Woodrow Wilson). *Hemagglutination will occur ... at a pH of 7, which of course is neutrality* (Scientific American). **b.** the attitude or policy of a nation that does not take part directly or indirectly in a war between other nations: *Neutrality is not equidistant from both sides. Neutrality is not considered to exclude membership of international organizations of a non-military character, still less does it imply any ideological restraint* (London Times). **c.** a neutral character or status, especially during a time of war: *Germany violated the neutrality of Belgium in World War I.* **2.** a being neither acid nor alkaline. —**Syn. 1.** impartiality.

neu·tral·i·za·tion (nü′trə lə zā′shən, nyü′-), *n.* the act of neutralizing: *The process by which an acid and a base unite to form water and a salt is termed neutralization* (W. N. Jones).

neu·tral·ize (nü′trə līz, nyü′-), *v.t.,* **-ized, -iz·ing. 1.** to make neutral. **2.** to keep war out of; keep neutral: *Switzerland was neutralized in 1815.* **3.** to make of no effect by some opposite force; counterbalance: *Jane neutralized the bright colors in her room by using a tan rug. Alkalis neutralize acids and vice versa. Some poisons neutralize each other.* —**neu′tral·iz′er,** *n.* —**Syn. 3.** counteract, offset.

neutral spirits, unaged ethyl alcohol used with aged whisky to make blended whiskies, with flavoring to make gin, or without blending as vodka.

neutral vowel, *Phonetics.* a central vowel; schwa.

neu·tret·to (nü tret′ō, nyü-), *n., pl.* **-tos.** any of several elementary particles with a mass of or approximating zero, emitted in radioactive decay. [< *neutr*(on) + Italian *-etto,* a diminutive suffix]

neu·tri·no (nü trē′nō, nyü-), *n., pl.* **-nos.** a particle emitted, with an electron, in beta rays. It carries no electric charge and has a mass so close to zero as to be unmeasurable and, in practice, it is treated as having a mass of zero. It is believed to be stable and play an important part in the decay process of the fundamental particles which are unstable. [< *neutr*(on) + Italian *-ino,* a diminutive suffix]

neu·tron (nü′tron, nyü′-), *n.* a minute particle that is neutral electrically and has about the same mass as a proton. Neutrons form a constituent of the nucleus of all atoms except that of the ordinary isotope of hydrogen, and are used to bombard atoms in the production of fission and other nuclear reactions. *Such an [atomic] explosion is triggered by the appearance of a neutron during the particular fraction of a microsecond when the chain reaction must be started* (Arthur H. Compton). *Symbol:* n (no period). See picture under **fission.** [< *neutr*(al) + *-on,* as in *electron, proton*]

neutron bomb, a hydrogen bomb set off with little heat or shock effect. It is designed to kill personnel by the release of highly lethal, short-lived neutrons.

neutron capture, the capture of a neutron by the nucleus of an atom.

neutron flux, **1.** a flow of neutrons, as in a nuclear reactor. **2.** a measure of this flow, expressed by the number of neutrons crossing a unit area in a unit time.

neutron star, a body in interstellar space that emits intense X rays, thought to be a relatively small but extremely dense mass of neutrons remaining after the explosion of a supernova.

neu·tro·phil (nü′trə fil, nyü′-), *n.* a very abundant, phagocytic type of leucocyte that protects the body against infection, making up about 50 to 75 per cent of the total number of white blood cells.

neu·tro·phile (nü′trə fīl, -fil; nyü′-), *n.* neutrophil. [< Latin *neuter* neuter + English *-phile* (because it does not stain readily with either acid or basic dyes)]

Nev., Nevada.

Ne·vad·an (nə vad′ən, -vä′dən), *adj.* of or having to do with the state of Nevada. —*n.* a native or inhabitant of Nevada.

né·vé (nā vā′), *n.* **1.** the crystalline or granular snow on the upper part of a glacier that has not yet been compressed into ice. **2.** a field of such snow; firn. [< French *névé* < Swiss French, perhaps dialectal Savoy *névi* slope or mass of snow < Old French *neif* snow < Latin *nix, nivis* snow]

nev·er (nev′ər), *adv.* **1.** not ever; at no time: *He never has seen a more perfect copy.* **2.** in no case; not at all; to no extent or degree: *He will never be the wiser.*

never so, a. not even so: *He spoke never so much as a word.* **b.** no matter how: *Let him be weighed never so scrupulously, . . . he will not be found . . . wanting* (C.J. Fox). [Old English *nǣfre* < *ne* not + *ǣfre* ever]

nev·er·mind (nev′ər mīnd′), *n. U.S. Dialect.* **1.** attention; heed: *Grandpa Murray is still paying the girl no more nevermind than if she was a vinegar gnat* (Jesse Hill Ford). **2.** significant effect; difference: "*It don't make no real nevermind*" (Time).

nev·er·more (nev′ər môr′, -mōr′), *adv.* never again; never at any future time.

nev·er-nev·er (nev′ər nev′ər), *adj. Informal.* **1.** unreal; imaginary: *a series of pictures about never-never monsters* (New Yorker). **2.** not easily visualized or grasped and therefore seemingly unreal or imaginary; implausible: *It is a never-never world of protons, electrons, isotopic separation . . . and half-lives of the elements* (New York Times). —*n.* **1.** Also, **never never.** *British Slang.* installment plan. **2.** *Australian Slang.* the remote, thinly settled region of northwest Queensland.

never-never land, an imaginary place or unrealistic condition: *the never-never land of "total" defense* (Wall Street Journal). *A never-never land of all play and no work* (New Yorker).

nev·er-say-die (nev′ər sā′dī′), *adj.* refusing to give up; die-hard: *those never-say-die purveyors of information—the press agents* (Newsweek).

nev·er·the·less (nev′ər ᴛʜə les′), *adv.* however; none the less; for all that; in spite of it: *She was very tired; nevertheless she kept on working.* —**Syn.** but, still.

ne·void (nē′void), *adj.* like a nevus. Also, **naevoid.**

ne·vus (nē′vəs), *n., pl.* **-vi** (-vī). **1.** a discolored or pigmented spot on the skin from birth, as a mole; birthmark. **2.** a tumor of the skin, usually congenital. Also, **naevus.** [< Latin *naevus* mole, wart]

new (nü, nyü), *adj.* **1.** never having existed before; now first made, thought out, known or heard of, felt, or discovered: *a new invention.* **2.** lately grown, come, or made; not old: *a new bud, or car, new potatoes.* **3.** now first used; not worn or used up: *a new path.* **4.** beginning again: *a new attempt. The new moon is the moon when seen as a thin crescent.* **5.** different; changed; renewed: *A night's sleep will make a new man of you. The old order changeth, yielding place to new* (Tennyson). **6.** not familiar; strange: *a new country to me.* **7.** not yet accustomed: *new to the work.* **8.** later or latest; modern; recent: *new dances.* **9.** just come; having just reached the position: *a new arrival, a new president, a new author.* **10.** being the later or latest of two or more things of the same kind: *New England, the New Testament.* **11.** further; additional; more: *He sought new information on the subject.* **12.** (of a language) in use in modern times, especially since the Middle Ages, usually contrasted with *Old* and *Medieval: New Latin.*
—*adv.* **1.** recently or lately; newly; freshly: *a new-found friend.* **2.** again; anew; afresh.
—*n.* that which is new; new thing: *I prefer the old to the new.*
[Old English *nīwe*] —**new′ness,** *n.*
—**Syn.** *adj.* **1. New, novel, modern** mean having only now or recently come into existence or knowledge. **New** describes something now existing, made, seen, or known for the first time: *They own a new house.* **Novel** adds and emphasizes the idea of being unusual, strikingly different, or strange, not of the ordinary kind: *It has a novel dining room.* **Modern** describes people and things belonging to or characteristic of the present time, or recent times, and sometimes suggests being up-to-date, not old-fashioned: *The architecture is modern.* **3.** fresh, unused. **6.** unfamiliar.

Ne·war (ni wär′), *n.* a member of a Mongoloid ethnic group that ruled part of Nepal, a country between India and Tibet, before the Gurkha conquest in the late 1700's.

New Australian, a recent immigrant to Australia.

new·born (nü′bôrn′, nyü′-), *adj.* **1.** recently or only just born: *a newborn baby.* **2.** ready to start a new life; born again. —*n.* a newborn baby. —**Syn. 2.** regenerated.

new broom, a new person in charge who is very active at first.

New Canadian, 1. an immigrant who has recently arrived in Canada. **2.** a naturalized Canadian citizen.

new candle, a unit for measuring the strength or intensity of light, replacing the international candle; candela.

New·cas·tle (nü′kas′əl, -käs′-; nyü′-), *n.* **carry coals to Newcastle, a.** to do something unnecessary; waste one's time, effort, etc.: *At first sight it seems like carrying coals to Newcastle . . . when the impressive logic of senior . . . officials is applied to a process largely governed by the electronic logic of computers* (London Times). **b.** to bring something to a place where it is unneeded (as coal to Newcastle, England, where it is plentiful): *It sounds like carrying coals to Newcastle, but Lord & Taylor's cosmetics department is importing water* (New York Times).

Newcastle cloak, an inverted barrel with holes cut in it for the head and arms, and put upon a man as if it were a garment. It was a punishment formerly inflicted in England for drunkenness.

Newcastle disease, a disease of poultry, caused by a virus, forms of which attack the respiratory and nervous systems.

new chum, a new Australian.

New Church, the church of the Swedenborgians; New Jerusalem Church.

new·come (nü′kum′, nyü′-), *adj.* newly or lately come or arrived: *newcome settlers.*

new·com·er (nü′kum′ər, nyü′-), *n.* **1.** a person who has just come or who came not long ago: *As the newcomers bought land and built houses, proved friendly neighbors and good credit risks, the tensions relaxed* (Newsweek). **2.** a recent immigrant.

new-cre·ate (nü′krē āt′, nyü′-), *v.t.,* **-at·ed, -at·ing.** to create anew.

New Criticism, a form of literary criticism that originated in the United States in the 1920's, characterized by close textual analysis, complex interpretations of poems, and use of the methods or principles of linguistics and other related disciplines.

New Deal, 1. the policies and measures advocated by President Franklin D. Roosevelt as a means of improving the economic and social welfare of the United States: *The country is now assimilating the New Deal, and adjusting to the mixed economy which has been developing ever since the turn of the century* (Harper's). **2.** the administration of Franklin D. Roosevelt, 1933-1945.

New Dealer, a person who favors or advocates the policies of the New Deal.

New Deal·ish (dē′lish), characteristic of the New Deal; favoring the New Deal.

New Deal·ism (dē′liz əm), the principles and policies of the New Deal: *He was an authentic product of New Dealism* (Newsweek).

New Democrat, a member of the New Democratic Party of Canada, a political party founded in 1961.

New Economic Policy, Nep.

new·el (nü′əl, nyü′-), *n.* **1.** the post at the top or bottom of a stairway that supports the railing. **2.** the central post of a winding stairway. [< Old French *nouel,* or *noiel* newel, kernel < Late Latin *nucālis* nutlike < Latin *nux, nucis* nut; probably influenced by Old French *noel* bud, ultimately < Latin *nōdus* knot]

Newel (def. 1)

New England aster, a tall perennial aster, with purple flowers, native to northeastern North America.

New Englander, a native or inhabitant of New England, the northeastern part of the United States.

new English, *U.S. Education.* English grammar taught with the concepts and methods of structural linguistics.

Newf., Newfoundland.

new·fan·gle (nü′fang′gəl, nyü′-), *adj., n., v.,* **-gled, -gling.** *Dialect.* —*adj.* newfangled. —*n.* a new thing or fashion; novelty: *A Pedlers packe of newefangles* (John Lyly). —*v.t.* to make newfangled or fashionable; bring up to date: *. . . not hereby to control, and newfangle the Scripture* (Milton).

new·fan·gled (nü′fang′gəld, nyü′-), *adj.* **1.** lately come into fashion; of a new kind: *the newfangled doctrine of utility* (John Galt). *Thousands of tradition-minded Londoners wanted no part of such . . . newfangled devices as radio or TV* (Newsweek). **2.** fond of novelty. [Middle English *newfangle* eager for novelty < *newe* new + *fangen* to take] —**new′fan′gled·ness,** *n.* —**Syn. 1.** new-fashioned.

new·fan·gle·ment (nü′fang′gəl mənt, nyü′-), *n. Informal.* a novel or newfangled thing; novelty.

new-fash·ioned (nü′fash′ənd, nyü′-), *adj.* of a new fashion; lately come into style: *She . . . teases papa for money to buy a new-fashioned silk* (Abraham Tucker). —**Syn.** modern.

New·fie (nü′fē, nyü′-), *n. Canadian Informal.* **1.** a Newfoundlander: *The Newfies aren't really very happy about being Canadians* (Maclean's). **2.** a Newfoundland dog.

new-found (nü′found′, nyü′-), *adj.* recently found: *a new-found friend.*

New·found·land (nü found′lənd, nyü-), *n.* any of a breed of large, shaggy, intelligent dogs, usually black, developed in Newfoundland and originally used as a working animal. The Newfoundland, a powerful swimmer, has become famous for its work in rescuing people from drowning.

Newfoundland (26 to 28 in. high at the shoulder)

New·found·land·er (nü found′lən dər, nyü-), *n.* a native or inhabitant of Newfoundland.

Newfoundland Standard Time, the standard time in Newfoundland, Nova Scotia, and eastern Quebec, one hour earlier than Eastern Standard Time.

New Frontier, 1. the policies and programs advocated by President John F. Kennedy for the United States. **2.** the administration of John F. Kennedy, 1960-1963.

New Frontiersman, 1. a supporter of the policies of the New Frontier. **2.** a member of President Kennedy's administration.

New·gate (nü′gāt, nyü′-), *n.* a former prison in London, torn down in 1902.

New Greek, the Greek language as used in modern times, especially after 1500.

new·ground (nü′ground′, nyü′-), *n.* land newly cleared: *You used to open up your dinner-pails together out there in a mean piece of newground or a blistering cotton patch* (New Yorker).

New Hampshire, any of an American breed of domestic fowl having reddish-brown feathers and yellow skin, raised for eggs and meat.

new·ish (nü′ish, nyü′-), *adj.* rather new.

New Jer·sey·ite (jėr′zē īt), a native or inhabitant of the state of New Jersey.

New Jerusalem, heaven; the City of God and the blessed. Revelation 21:2.

New Jerusalem Church, the church of the Swedenborgians; New Church.

New Latin, the Latin language after 1500; Modern Latin. It contains words formed from Greek and Latin elements.

New Learning, 1. (in England, in the 1500's) the study of the Bible and Greek and Latin classical authors in the original tongues. **2.** the doctrines of the Reformation in England.

New Left, *U.S.* a diffuse political movement of the 1960's, made up chiefly of college and university students with radical or ultraliberal views on such issues as American foreign policy, civil rights, and academic freedom: *The New Left is a current expression of the drive for radical change* (New York Times).

New Lights, *Ecclesiastical.* the members of any of various parties adhering to new doctrines, or forming bodies separate from others with which they were formerly associated because of adherence to some new view of doctrine or duty.

new look, *Informal.* a striking change in appearance, policy, etc.

new·ly (nü′lē, nyü′-), *adv.* **1.** very lately; recently: *newly wedded.* **2.** once again; freshly; *newly painted walls.* **3.** in a new way. —**Syn. 2.** afresh, anew. **3.** differently.

new·ly·wed (nü′lē wed′, nyü′-), *n.* a person who has recently become married.

new-made (nü′mād′, nyü′-), *adj.* **1.** newly, recently, or freshly made: *a new-made peer, a new-made grave.* **2.** made anew; remade.

new·mar·ket (nü′mär′kit, nyü′-), *n.* **1.** Also, **Newmarket coat.** a long, close-fitting coat, worn by men and women outdoors about 1880. **2.** a card game in which cards are played in sequence, the playing of certain cards winning bets placed on them. [< *Newmarket,* a town in England]

new math or **new mathematics,** *U.S. Education.* mathematics designed to give the student an understanding of basic mathematical structures, concepts, and processes, with less emphasis on formal drills.

New Mexican, 1. of or having to do with the State of New Mexico: *Acoma is the most western of the New Mexican towns* (W.H. Emory). **2.** a native or inhabitant of the state of New Mexico.

new-mod·el (nü′mod′əl, nyü′-), *v.t.,* **-eled, -el·ing** or (*especially British*) **-elled, -el·ling.** to model anew; remodel; give a new form to: *to new-model a house, an army, or a government. To new-model opinion would be to new-model society* (Thomas L. Peacock).

new moon, 1. the moon when seen as a thin crescent with the hollow side on the left. **2.** the moon when its dark side is toward the earth, appearing almost invisible: *At times of new moon, the moon is between us and the sun* (Hubert J. Bernhard). See picture under **moon.**

New Or·le·ans jazz (ôr′lē ənz, ôr′lənz; ôr lēnz′), the jazz from which present-day jazz evolved, first played by Negro brass bands in parades and funeral processions in New Orleans during the late 1800's.

New Realism, 1. neorealism, especially in literature: *New Realism . . . has been rated a "cult of squalidity" by some proper Britons* (Time). **2.** any form of neorealistic (as opposed to abstract) art, especially pop art: *The "New Realism" . . . takes as its subject matter the most banal objects and images of commerical culture* (New Yorker).

New Realist, 1. a follower of New Realism: *Beckmann never belonged to the Bauhaus group; he was closer to . . . the New Realists* (New Yorker). **2.** having to do with or characteristic of New Realism: *New Realist works have been viewed by some critics simply as entertaining forms of social criticism* (Brie Taylor).

new-rich (nü′rich′, nyü′-), *n.* nouveau riche: *The new-rich of Texas became better dressed and better housed faster than any other new-rich in the country* (New York Times). —*adj.* **1.** recently become rich. **2.** vulgarly displaying wealth.

news (nüz, nyüz), *n.* **1.** something told as having just happened; information about something that has just happened or will soon happen. **2.** a report of a current happening or happenings in a newspaper, on television, radio, etc.: *His chief interest was in the ways in which news is gathered* (Newsweek). [Middle English *newes,* probably plural of *newe* (literally) that which is new, noun use of adjective; perhaps patterned on French *nouvelles*] —**Syn. 1.** tidings, advices, intelligence, information.

➔ **news.** Though plural in form, *news* is now invariably used as a singular: *The news from the various districts is sent to a central office.*

news agency, 1. a commercial agency that gathers and distributes news to newspapers, magazines, and radio and television stations subscribing to its service. **2.** a similar government agency.

news agent, *British.* a newsdealer.

news·beat (nüz′bēt′, nyüz′-), *n.* the securing or publication of a scoop in reporting news: *a filmed interview that would have been a newsbeat on any occasion* (Harper's).

news·boy (nüz′boi′, nyüz′-), *n.* a boy who sells or delivers newspapers: *Kid Chocolate . . . who soared in eight years from being a scrappy newsboy to $90,000 Madison Square Garden bouts* (Newsweek).

news·cast (nüz′kast′, -käst′; nyüz′-), *n.* a radio or television program devoted to current events, news bulletins, etc. —*v.t., v.i.* to broadcast (news): *I'm afraid we have to face this—why women should not replace men in general newscasting and sportscasting* (Newsweek).

news·cast·er (nüz′kas′tər, -käs′-; nyüz′-), *n.* **1.** a person who reads newscasts on radio and television: *Through open windows could be heard the cheerful voices of radio newscasters prophesying in air-conditioned studios a record [temperature] for the week end* (John Stephen Strange). **2.** a commentator on the news.

news·clip (nüz′klip′, nyüz′-), *n.* a newspaper clipping: *I have before me a Los Angeles Times newsclip* (Atlantic).

news conference, a meeting at which newspaper reporters receive information from a person or group, especially in the form of answers to questions asked by the reporters; press conference: *The President would not hold a news conference this week* (New York Times).

news·deal·er (nüz′dē′lər, nyüz′-), *n.* a person who sells newspapers and magazines.

news editor, an editor on a newspaper, magazine, or radio or television station in charge of gathering, editing, and reporting the news.

news·girl (nüz′gėrl′, nyüz′-), *n.* a girl who sells newspapers.

news·hawk (nüz′hôk′, nyüz′-), *n. Informal.* a newspaper reporter or correspondent.

news·hen (nüz′hen′, nyüz′-), *n. Informal.* a woman journalist; newspaperwoman: *I found no newspaperwomen who liked being called newshens* (Time).

news·hound (nüz′hound′, nyüz′-), *n. Informal.* a newspaper reporter.

news·let·ter (nüz′let′ər, nyüz′-), *n.* **1.** a letter or report distributed by an organization presenting an informal or confidential coverage of the news. An insurance company often issues an annual newsletter to its policyholders. *One newsletter mentions glass lamps as leading sales of metal and ceramic-based types* (Wall Street Journal). **2.** a forerunner of the modern newspaper, current in the 1600's and early 1700's, which presented news for general circulation.

news magazine, or **news·mag·a·zine** (nüz′mag′ə zēn, nyüz′-), *n.* a magazine devoted to interpretive comment on news and current events, usually published weekly.

news·man (nüz′man′, -mən; nyüz′-), *n., pl.* **-men. 1.** a man who sells or delivers newspapers and magazines. **2.** a newspaperman or newscaster.

news·mon·ger (nüz′mung′gər, -mong′-; nyüz′-), *n.* a person who gathers and spreads news, especially personal news; gossip: *a knot of anxious newsmongers, each of whom departed . . . to carry the story home to his family* (Washington Irving).

news·mon·ger·ing (nüz′mung′gər ing, -mong′-; nyüz′-), *n.* the act of gathering and spreading news; gossiping.

news·pa·per (nüz′pā′pər, nyüz′-), *n.* **1.** sheets of paper, usually printed every day of the week, telling the news, carrying advertisements, and often having stories, comics, verse, and useful information: *The newspaper, together with the telegraph, the telephone, and the radio, has created a special degree of social consciousness* (Emory S. Bogardus). **2.** the paper used; newsprint. —*v.i.* to work for a newspaper: *In Norway Willy supported himself by newspapering* (Time).

news·pa·per·dom (nüz′pā′pər dəm, nyüz′-), *n.* the world or sphere of newspapers.

news·pa·per·ing (nüz′pā′pər ing, nyüz′-), *n.* **1.** the occupation of a newspaperman. **2.** journalism: *good newspapering arises from an inner conviction of what to do* (Harper's).

news·pa·per·man (nüz′pā′pər man′, nyüz′-), *n., pl.* **-men.** a newspaper reporter, editor, etc.

news·pa·per·wom·an (nüz′pā′pər wu̇m′ən, nyüz′-), *n., pl.* **-wom·en.** a woman who works on a newspaper as journalist, reporter, editor, etc.

new·speak (nü′spēk′, nyü′-), *n.* language in which the words are made to mean the opposite of their real meanings to conform to an ideology: *"Newspeak," in which "Big Brother" has become the . . . word for "tyrant"* (Wall Street Journal). [coined by George Orwell, 1903–1950, an English novelist]

news·print (nüz′print′, nyüz′-), *n.* the soft, relatively coarse paper, made chiefly from wood pulp, on which newspapers are usually printed.

news·read·er (nüz′rē′dər, nyüz′-), *n.* a person who reads the newspapers: *A means of gratifying the curiosity of newsreaders . . .* (T. Dwight).

news·reel (nüz′rēl′, nyüz′-), *n.* a motion picture showing current events.

news·room (nüz′rüm′, -ru̇m′; nyüz′-), *n.* the part of a newspaper office or radio or television station where news is prepared for publication or broadcasting.

news service, a news agency.

news·sheet (nüz′shēt′, nyüz′-), *n.* a printed sheet issued by clubs and business organizations reporting activities and events: *notices which appeared in the club's newssheet* (Atlantic).

news stall, *British.* a newsstand.

news·stand (nüz′stand′, nyüz′-), *n. U.S.* a place where newspapers and magazines are sold: *The magazine is sold solely through subscriptions; it has no newsstand sales* (Wall Street Journal). —**Syn.** kiosk.

New·stead Abbey (nü′sted, nyü′-), an ancient building in Nottinghamshire, England, founded in 1170 by Henry II, and later for a time the home of Lord Byron.

New Stone Age, the neolithic period of the Stone Age.

New Style, the method of reckoning time according to the Gregorian calendar, adopted in England, and generally throughout the English-speaking world, in 1752. *Abbr.:* N.S.

news·ven·dor (nüz′ven′dər, nyüz′-), *n.* a seller of newspapers: *The ground floor . . . is occupied by a small newsvendor's shop* (Wilkie Collins).

news·week·ly (nüz′wēk′lē, nyüz′-), *n., pl.* **-lies.** a weekly periodical reporting current events of general interest or of specialized interest.

news·wom·an (nüz′wu̇m′ən, nyüz′-), *n., pl.* **-wom·en.** a newspaperwoman.

news·wor·thy (nüz′wėr′ᴛʜē, nyüz′-), *adj.,* **-thi·er, -thi·est.** having enough public interest to be printed in a newspaper: *Does a press photographer have the right to take a newsworthy picture even when the subject objects?* (Time).

news·y[1] (nü′zē, nyü′-), *adj.,* **news·i·er, news·i·est.** *Informal.* full of news: *a newsy letter.* [< *news* + *-y*[1]]

news·y[2] (nü′zē, nyü′-), *n., pl.* **news·ies.** *Slang.* a newsboy or newsman.

newt (nüt, nyüt), *n.* any of various small, amphibious salamanders that have lungs, lidded eyes, and are smooth-skinned as adults. [Middle English *neute,* misdivision of *an eut,* variant of *evet* eft]

Newt (3 to 6 in. long)

New Test., New Testament.

New Testament, 1. the second of the two principal divisions of the Christian Bible, which contains the life and teachings of Christ recorded by his followers, together with their own experiences and teachings. *Abbr.:* N.T. **2.** the new covenant between God and mankind established by the birth, life, teachings, and death of Jesus Christ; the new or Christian dispensation, set forth especially in the writings of Paul and other apostles.

new thing, *Jazz Slang.* a form of experimental music based on jazz rhythms, developed in the 1960's: . . . *the heretic experiments of Milford Graves, the best of the "new thing" drummers* (Whitney Balliett).

New Thought, any of several modern religious systems, not associated with Christian Science, maintaining that through good and proper ideas all bodily or mental ailments may be mastered.

new·ton (nü′tən, nyü′-), *n.* a measure of force in the MKS system, equal to 100,000 dynes. [< Sir Isaac *Newton,* 1642-1727, an English physicist]

New·to·ni·an (nü tō′nē ən, nyü-), *adj.* of or by Sir Isaac Newton, 1642-1727, the English mathematician, physicist, and philosopher: *The student of the history of ideas can render a service to science by showing the great influence exerted upon modern scientific thought by Newtonian physics* (John E. Owen). —*n.* a follower of Newton.

Newton's law of motion, any of the three fundamental statements on motion formulated by Newton: **a.** a body at rest or moving uniformly in a straight line will remain so unless acted upon by some outside force. **b.** a change in the motion of a body is proportional to and in the same direction as the force that produces it. **c.** for every action there is an equal and opposite reaction.

new town, a planned urban community where people can both live and work, designed especially to relieve the overcrowding of a nearby metropolis.

new wave, a movement in cinematography originating in France in the 1950's, characterized by extensive use of symbolism, sophisticated themes, and unconventional camerawork. [translation of French *nouvelle vague*]

new-world (nü′wėrld′, nyü′-), *adj.* of or having to do with the Western Hemisphere.

New World, the Western Hemisphere; North America and South America: *California's Imperial and Coachella Valleys form one of the wonders of the New World* (Time).

new year, the year approaching or newly begun.

New Year or **New Year's,** January 1; the first day or days of the year.

New Year's Day, January 1, the first day of the year, usually observed as a legal holiday.

New Year's Eve, the night of December 31, often observed by celebrations welcoming the New Year.

New York·er (yôr′kər), a native or inhabitant of New York City or New York State.

New York·ese (yôr kēz′, -kēs′), a type of English pronunciation heard in New York City: *Harvard accents, finishing school drawls, and plain New Yorkese mingled with the rock'n'roll racket in Greenwich Village* (New York Times).

New Zea·land·er (zē′lən dər), a native or inhabitant of New Zealand, a British dominion in the South Pacific.

New Zea·land flax or **hemp** (zē′lənd), **1.** a tall plant of New Zealand, grown also in Europe and in California, with red, honey-laden blossoms. **2.** the fiber made from the leaves of this plant, used for making ropes, fabrics, etc.

next (nekst), *adj.* following at once; nearest: *the next train, the next room. The next day after Sunday is Monday.*
—*adv.* **1.** the first time after this: *When you next come, bring it.* **2.** in the place, time, or position that is nearest: *His name comes next. I am going to do my arithmetic problems next.*
next to, a. nearest to: *Bobby is next to John in age.* **b.** almost; nearly: *It was thought next to impossible* (William H. Ireland).
—*prep.* nearest to: *the house next the church.*
[Old English *nēhst* nearest, superlative of *nēah* near] —**next′ness,** *n.*

next-door (nekst′dôr′, -dōr′), *adj.* in or at the next house, apartment, etc.: *a next-door neighbor.*

next friend, *Law.* a person who, although not the legal guardian, acts for a child or other person who cannot legally act for himself, especially in a lawsuit.

next of kin, 1. the nearest blood relative. **2.** *Law.* the blood relatives entitled to share in the estate of a person who has died intestate.

nex·us (nek′səs), *n., pl.* **-us** or **-us·es. 1.** a connection; tie; link: *The cash nexus . . . was . . . a new role for the Grocer as cosmopolitan specialist* (Harper's). *Cash Payment . . . the universal sole nexus of man to man* (Thomas Carlyle). **2.** a connected series: *A man, to [John P.] Marquand, is a nexus of institutions* (Harper's). **3.** *Grammar.* a predication or a construction akin to a predication. [< Latin *nexus,* *-ūs* < *nectere* to bind]

Nez Per·cé (nez′ pėrs′; *French* nā per sā′), *n., pl.* **Nez Per·cés** (nez′ pėr′siz; *French* nā per sā′). **1.** a member of an American Indian tribe of Shahaptian stock, that formerly lived in Idaho, Oregon, and Washington. **2.** *Obsolete.* a member of any Indian tribe that was formerly believed to pierce the nasal septum in order to wear ornaments. **3.** the language of the tribe.
[American English < French *nez percé* (literally) pierced nose (because of the alleged custom of the tribes to which it was first applied)]

n.f. or **N/F.,** *Banking.* no funds.

N.F., an abbreviation for the following:
1. National Formulary (a book containing standards for certain drugs, compiled by the American Pharmaceutical Association).
2. Newfoundland.
3. *Banking.* no funds.
4. Norman-French.

NFL (no periods) or **N.F.L.,** National Football League.

Nfld., Newfoundland.

N.F.O. or **NFO** (no periods), National Farmers Organization.

n.g., no good.

N.G., 1. National Guard. **2.** no good.

N.H., New Hampshire.

NHA (no periods), **1.** National Health Association. **2.** National Housing Agency.

N.H.I., (in Great Britain) National Health Insurance.

N.H.L., National Hockey League.

N.H.S. or **NHS** (no periods), National Health Service.

Ni (no period), nickel (chemical element).

N.I., Northern Ireland.

NIA (no periods), National Intelligence Authority.

ni·a·cin (nī′ə sin), *n.* nicotinic acid. [earlier *Niacin*(trademark) < *ni*(cotinic) *ac*(id)+-*in*]

ni·a·cin·am·ide (nī′ə sin am′īd, -id), *n.* nicotinamide.

Ni·ag·a·ra (nī ag′ər ə, -ag′rə), *n.* **1.** a cataract; torrent; deluge: *a Niagara of tears. A Niagara of water rushed in* (Maclean's). **2.** something resembling a cataract in amount and force: *a Niagara of lies and slander* (Newsweek). **3.** a variety of sweet white grape grown especially in the eastern United States. [< *Niagara* (Falls) < an Iroquoian word]

niai·se·rie (nyez rē′), *n. French.* **1.** ignorant or stupid simplicity; foolishness; silliness. **2.** an instance or example of silliness.

nib[1] (nib), *n., v.,* **nibbed, nib·bing.** —*n.* **1. a.** the point of a pen: *Ballpoint pens will be tested by the Post Office Department to replace the scratchy, ink-spilling nib pens* (Time). **b.** either of its parts. **2.** the point of anything; a peak; point; tip; prong. **3.** the beak or bill of a bird. **4.** *Dialect.* either of the two short projecting handles on the long shaft of a scythe.
—*v.t.* **1.** to mend or replace the nib of (a pen); put a nib in or on. **2.** to sharpen or trim the point of (a quill used as a pen); adapt for writing: *The lawyer nibbed his pen, spread out his paper, and prepared to write* (Washington Irving).
[Scottish variant of *neb*]

nib[2] (nib), *n.* a coffee bean.
nibs, the roasted and crushed seeds of the cacao; cocoa nibs.
[special use of *nib*[1]]

nib·ble (nib′əl), *v.,* **-bled, -bling,** *n.* —*v.t.* to eat away with quick, small bites, as a rabbit or a mouse does: *The boy was just nibbling his food.* —*v.i.* **1.** to bite gently or lightly: *The fish nibbled at the bait.* **2.** to eat little or lightly: *to nibble at one's supper.* **3.** to take apart or attack, as if by taking small bites: *critics nibbling at a new play.* —*n.* a nibbling; small bite. [origin uncertain. Compare Low German *knibbelen.*] —**nib′bler,** *n.* —**nib′bling·ly,** *adv.*

Ni·be·lung (nē′bə lůng), *n., pl.* **-lungs, lung·en** (-lůng ən). *German Legend.* **1.** any of a group of northern dwarfs, the children of the mist, who had a hoard of gold and a ring with magic powers. Siegfried and his followers captured their treasure. **2.** any of Siegfried's followers, who captured this hoard and ring. **3.** any of the Burgundian kings in the *Nibelungenlied.*

Ni·be·lung·en·lied (nē′bə lůng ən lēt′), *n.* a German epic based on the myths and legends found in the *Edda.* It was composed in its present poetic form by an unknown author in South Germany during the first half of the early 1200's. [< German *Nibelungenlied* (literally) lay of the Nibelungs]

nib·lick (nib′lik), *n.* a golf club with a heavy steel head having a deeply slanted face, used when the ball is in a sand trap, etc., or for short shots requiring sharp loft and little roll. [origin uncertain]

Ni·blung (nē′blůng), *n.* Nibelung.

nibs[1] (nibz), *n. Informal.* (with a possessive pronoun) a humorous title of respect for a person, as if in recognition of importance: *How is his nibs, or his royal nibs?* [origin uncertain]

nibs[2] (nibz), *n.pl.* See under **nib**[2].

NIC (no periods), National Incomes Commission (of Great Britain).

Ni·cae·an (nī sē′ən), *adj.* Nicene.

Nic·a·ra·guan (nik′ə rä′gwən), *adj.* of or having to do with the Central American republic of Nicaragua. —*n.* a native or inhabitant of Nicaragua.

N.I.C.B., National Industrial Conference Board.

nic·co·lite (nik′ə līt), *n.* a mineral, nickel arsenide, of a pale copper-red color and metallic luster. It usually occurs massive. *Formula:* NiAs [< New Latin *niccolum,* Latinization of *nickel* + English *-ite*[1]]

nice (nīs), *adj.,* **nic·er, nic·est,** *adv.* —*adj.* **1.** pleasing; agreeable; satisfactory: *a nice face, a nice ride, a nice day.* **2.** thoughtful and considerate; pleasant; kind: *He was nice to us.* **3.** exact; precise, discriminating; able to distinguish small differences: *a nice ear for music, weighed in the nicest scales.* **4.** minute; fine; subtle: *a nice distinction, a nice shade of meaning.* **5.** delicately skillful; requiring great care, ability, or tact: *a nice problem. It's a nice point to speak about . . . and I'm afraid o' being wrong* (George Eliot). **6.** exacting; hard to please; very particular; fastidious; dainty: *nice in his eating.* **7.** proper; suitable: *It wasn't a nice song—for a parlor, anyway* (Mark Twain). **8.** demanding a high standard of conduct; scrupulous: *too nice for a politician.* **9.** *Archaic.* affectedly modest; coyly reserved: *We'll not be nice: take hands* (Shakespeare). **10.** refined; cultured: *a nice accent.* **11.** *Obsolete.* wanton; lascivious. **12.** *Obsolete.* foolish; stupid.
—*adv. Archaic.* nicely.
[Middle English *nice* simple-minded < Old French, silly < Latin *nescius* ignorant < *ne-* not + *scīre* know] —**nice′ly,** *adv.* —**nice′ness,** *n.*
—**Syn.** *adj.* **1.** gratifying, enjoyable. **3.** accurate. **6.** delicate. **7.** fitting, seemly.

Ni·cene (nī sēn′, nī′sēn), *adj.* of or having to do with Nicaea, an ancient town in Asia Minor.

Nicene Council, either of two general ecclesiastical councils held at Nicaea, the first in 325 A.D. to deal with the Arian heresy, and the second in 787 to consider the question of images.

Nicene Creed, 1. a formal statement of the chief tenets of Christian belief, adopted by the first Nicene Council, and ultimately accepted throughout orthodox Christendom. **2.** the creed of the first Nicene Council, expanded somewhat at a later date (probably at the Council of Constantinople in 381 A.D.) and accepted by all orthodox Christians under the title of Nicene Creed.

nice Nelly or **Nellie,** *pl.* **nice Nellies.** *Slang.* a person who is overly modest or prudish: *By 1916, Dreiser was the hero of the avant-garde and the pet peeve of the nice Nellies, who denounced "The Genius" as literary sewage and got it banned by the censor* (Time). [< *Nelly* or *Nellie,* a feminine name]

nice-Nel·ly·ism (nīs′nel′ē iz əm), *n.* **1.** extreme modesty or prudishness: *Nice-Nellyism seldom wins elections in this country* (Time). **2.** circumlocution; euphemism: *Mr.*

Pyles attributes much of the nice-Nellyism that blighted polite speech and writing during the nineteenth century to Webster's Puritan prudishness (New Yorker).

Ni·ce·no-Con·stan·ti·no·pol·i·tan Creed (nī sē′nō kon stan′tə nə pol′ə tən), Nicene Creed (def. 2).

ni·ce·ty (nī′sə tē), *n., pl.* **-ties. 1.** the state or quality of being precise; exactness; accuracy; delicacy: *Television sets require nicety of adjustment.* **2.** a fine point; small distinction; detail: *I can make my car go, but I have not yet learned all the little niceties of driving.* **3.** the quality of being very particular; daintiness; refinement: *This sense of the practical is the ballast for some of Mrs. Post's more airy niceties* (Newsweek). **4.** something dainty or refined: *clean linen and other niceties of apparel* (Hawthorne). **5.** *Obsolete.* excessive refinement: *my own nicety and the nicety of my friends . . . have made me . . . an idle, helpless being* (Jane Austen). **6.** *Obsolete.* coy prudishness or squeamishness.
to a nicety, just right: *cakes browned to a nicety.*
[< Old French *nicete* < *nice;* see NICE]
—**Syn. 4.** amenity.

niche (nich), *n., v.,* **niched, nich·ing.** —*n.* **1.** a recess or hollow in a wall for a statue, vase, etc.: *Just over the grave, in a niche of the wall, is a bust of Shakespeare* (Washington Irving). **2.** a suitable place or position; place for which a person is suited: *French planemakers see the possibility of carving a modest niche in the world's air markets* (Time). **3.** *Ecology.* the function of an organism within a community.

Niche (def. 1)

—*v.t.* to place in a niche or similar recess.
[< Middle French *niche,* also *nique* < Old French *nichier* to nest, ultimately < Latin *nīdus* nest]
—**Syn.** *n.* **1.** nook, cavity.

nich·er (niʜ′ər), *v.i., v.t., n. Scottish.* nicker².

Ni·chi·ren (nē chē ren′), *n.* a militant and nationalistic Buddhist sect in Japan. [< *Nichiren,* a Japanese teacher of the 1200's, who founded it]

Nich·o·las (nik′ə ləs, nik′ləs), *n.* **Saint.** Santa Claus.

Ni·chrome (nī′krōm), *n. Trademark.* an alloy consisting of 60 per cent nickel, 16 per cent chromium, and 24 per cent iron, noted for its high heat and electrical resistance. Silicon and aluminum are sometimes added to increase its resistance to oxidation.

nicht wahr? (niʜt var′), *German.* isn't that right? isn't that so: *One doesn't shake hands with a man who is busy with both hands, nicht wahr?* (Harper's).

nick (nik), *n.* **1.** a place where a small bit has been cut or broken out; notch; groove: *to make a nick in a saucer. He cut nicks in a stick to keep count of his score.* **2.** *Printing.* a notch in the shank of a type, that serves as a guide in the identification of a font or the placing of the types. **3.** the precise moment or time of some occurrence: *In the nick of being surprised, the lovers . . . escape at a trap-door* (Sir Richard Steele). **4.** *British Slang.* a jail; prison: *five years in the nick for larceny* (Punch). **5.** *Australian.* condition; shape: *to be in good or bad nick.* **6.** *Obsolete.* the exact point aimed at; mark.
in the nick of time, just at the right moment: *He has learnt, thankfully, that atomic power is arriving in the nick of time to supplement not inexhaustible supplies of coal and oil* (London Times).
—*v.t.* **1.** to make a nick or nicks in; notch or chip: *to nick a stick or a cup.* **2.** to cut into or through: *to nick a wire.* **3.** to hit, guess, catch, etc., exactly. **4. a.** to make an incision at the root of (a horse's tail) to cause him to hold it higher. **b.** to cut (a horse) at the root of the tail. **5.** to record or score: *to nick down an address or a point won.* **6.** *Slang.* to cheat; defraud: *He nicked me out of everything I'd saved.* **7.** *Slang.* to capture, especially by surprise; nab.
[origin uncertain]
—**Syn.** *n.* **1.** dent, indentation.

Nick (nik), *n.* Usually, **Old Nick.** the Devil. [probably short for *Nicholas.* Compare German *Nickel* goblin.]

nick·el (nik′əl), *n., v.,* **-eled, -el·ing** or (*especially British*) **-elled, -el·ling.** —*n.* **1.** a hard, silvery-white, lustrous metallic chemical element that looks like silver and is somewhat like iron, much used as an alloy. It usually occurs in combination with arsenic or sulfur and is associated with cobalt. Nickel is often used in alloys and is malleable, ductile, and magnetic, but is not easily oxidized. *Symbol:* Ni; *at.wt.:* (C^{12}) 58.71 or (O^{16}) 58.71; *at.no.:* 28; *valence:* 2, 3. **2.** a coin, containing nickel, of the United States and Canada, worth 5 cents: *Hot-dog sellers, sandwich men, and jugglers peddled their offerings for nickels and dimes* (Newsweek).
—*v.t.* to cover or coat with nickel.
[< Swedish *nickel* < German *Kupfernickel* (literally) copper devil (the ore resembles copper but yields none)]

nick·el·ic (nik′ə lik, ni kel′ik), *adj.* **1.** of nickel. **2.** containing nickel, especially with a valence of three.

nick·el·if·er·ous (nik′ə lif′ər əs), *adj.* containing or yielding nickel.

nickel iron, an alloy of nickel and iron found in meteorites, small stones, etc.

nick·el·o·de·on (nik′ə lō′dē ən), *n. U.S.* **1.** (formerly) a place of amusement, such as a motion-picture theater or vaudeville, to which the price of admission was only five cents: *Loretta made her professional debut at thirteen in a Lynn, Massachusetts, nickelodeon* (Harper's). **2.** a juke box: *A nickelodeon at the end of the street emits a tinny piano tinkle* (Saturday Evening Post). [American English < *nickel* the coin + *odeon;* perhaps patterned on *Melodeon*]

nick·el·ous (nik′ə ləs), *adj.* containing nickel, especially with a valence of two.

nickel plate, a thin coating of nickel deposited on a metal object by electroplating or other means, to prevent rust, improve the appearance, etc.

nick·el-plate (nik′əl plāt′), *v.t.,* **-plat·ed, -plat·ing.** to coat with nickel by electroplating or other means.

nickel silver, German silver.

nickel steel, an alloy of steel with high nickel content to make it strong, elastic, and rust resistant: *Nickel steel is used in armor plate, automobile axles, engine forgings, and various kinds of structural work* (Harrison Ashley Schmitt).

nick·er¹ (nik′ər), *n.* **1.** a person or thing that nicks or cuts. **2.** *British Slang.* (in horse racing) **a.** one pound sterling. **b.** pounds sterling. **3.** a disorderly London youth in the 1700's, who nightly broke windows by throwing coins at them.

nick·er² (nik′ər), *v.i., v.t.* **1.** to neigh: *mounted on nags that nicker at the clash of the sword* (Scott). **2.** to laugh loudly or shrilly. —*n.* **1.** a neigh. **2.** a loud laugh. [apparently imitative. Compare NEIGH.]

nick·er³ (nik′ər), *n.,* or **nicker tree,** the bonduc. [probably < a native name]

nick·nack (nik′nak′), *n.* knickknack.

nick·name (nik′nām′), *n., v.,* **-named, -nam·ing.** —*n.* **1.** a name added to a person's real name or used instead of it: *"Ed" is a nickname for "Edward." As he [a doctor] wanted that deep magisterial voice which gives authority to a prescription . . . he . . . got the nickname of the Squeaking Doctor* (Sir Richard Steele). **2.** such a name given to a place or thing: *Hawkeye State is a nickname for Iowa.*
—*v.t.* **1.** to give a nickname to: *They nicknamed the short boy "Shorty."* **2.** to misname: *With no great care for what is nicknamed glory* (Byron).
[Middle English *neke name* < misdivision of *an eke name* < *eke* an addition, Old English *ēaca* + *name* name]
—**Syn.** *n.* **1.** sobriquet.

Nick·y (nik′ē), *n. British Slang.* the National Incomes Commission of Great Britain; NIC.

Nic·ol or **nic·ol** (nik′əl), *n.* Nicol prism.

Nicol or **nicol prism,** *Optics.* **1.** a prism made by cutting crystals of Iceland spar and cementing them together with Canada balsam, used to transform ordinary light into plane-polarized light. **2.** any prism used for that purpose. [< John P. *Nicol,* 1804-1859, a British physicist, who invented it]

ni·co·tian (ni kō′shən), *n. Obsolete.* **1.** a tobacco smoker: *It isn't for me to throw stones . . . who have been a nicotian a good deal more than half my days* (Oliver Wendell Holmes). **2.** the tobacco plant. —*adj.* having to do with tobacco or smoking.

ni·co·ti·a·na (ni kō′shē ā′nə), *n.* any of a group of plants of the nightshade family, as the tobacco plant and certain varieties grown for their showy, fragrant, night-blooming flowers. [< New Latin *Nicotiana* < (*herba*) *nicotiana;* see NICOTINE]

nic·o·tin (nik′ə tin), *n.* nicotine.

nic·o·tin·a·mide (nik′ə tin′ə mīd, -mid), *n.* the amide of nicotinic acid: *Anesthesia . . . was effective for a longer time when nicotinamide was given* (Science News Letter). *Formula:* $C_6H_6N_2O$

nic·o·tine (nik′ə tēn), *n.* a poisonous alkaloid contained in the leaves, roots, and seeds of tobacco, from which it is obtained as an oily, colorless, acrid liquid, used to kill insects, parasites, etc. *Formula:* $C_{10}H_{14}N_2$ [< French *nicotine* < *nicotiane* nicotiana < New Latin (*herba*) *nicotiana* < Jacques *Nicot,* about 1530-1600, French ambassador to Portugal who introduced tobacco into France about 1560]

nic·o·tine·less (nik′ə tēn′lis), *adj.* without nicotine: *Probably the ultimate in nicotineless smoking is represented by . . . a cigaret made from the outer leaf of romaine lettuce* (Wall Street Journal).

nic·o·tin·ic acid (nik′ə tin′ik), one of a group of vitamins that is found in all cells and especially in lean meat, milk, eggs, yeast, liver, and wheat germ; niacin. It is a vitamin of the vitamin B complex and persons who lack this vitamin often suffer from pellagra. *Formula:* $C_6H_5NO_2$

nic·o·tin·ism (nik′ə tē niz′əm, -ti-), *n.* a poisoned condition due to excessive use of nicotine or tobacco.

nic·tate (nik′tāt), *v.i.,* **-tat·ed, -tat·ing.** nictitate.

nic·tat·ing membrane (nik′tā ting), nictitating membrane.

nic·ta·tion (nik tā′shən), *n.* nictitation.

nic·ti·tate (nik′tə tāt), *v.i.,* **-tat·ed, -tat·ing.** to wink. [< unrecorded Medieval Latin *nictitare* (with English *-ate*¹) < Latin *nictāre* wink, blink]

nic·ti·tat·ing membrane (nik′tə tā′ting), a transparent inner eyelid present in birds and certain other animals that can draw over the eye to protect and moisten it.

nic·ti·ta·tion (nik′tə tā′shən), *n.* the act or habit of moving the eyelids; winking, especially with abnormal frequency.

nid·a·men·tal (nid′ə men′təl), *adj. Zoology.* **1.** having to do with an egg or eggs **2.** forming a covering or protection for an egg or eggs. [< Latin *nīdāmentum* materials for a nest (< *nīdus* nest) + English *-al*¹]

ni·da·tion (nī dā′shən), *n. Physiology.* the implantation of the fertilized egg in the lining (decidua) of the uterus: *Nidation . . . in Man takes place about a week after fertilization* (New Scientist). [< Latin *nīdus* nest + English *-ation*]

nid·der·ing (nid′ər ing), *n.* a base coward. —*adj.* base; cowardly; vile. [(used by Sir Walter Scott in *Ivanhoe*) apparently < a misreading of Old English *nīthing* < Scandinavian (compare Old Icelandic *nīthingr*)]

nide (nīd), *n.* a brood, clutch, or nest of pheasants. [< Latin *nīdus* nest]

nid·er·ing (nid′ər ing), *n., adj.* niddering.

nidge (nij), *v.t.,* **nidged, nidg·ing.** to dress (stone) with a sharp-pointed hammer instead of a chisel and mallet; nig. [origin uncertain]

nid·i·fi·cate (nid′ə fə kāt), *v.i.,* **-cat·ed, -cat·ing.** to build a nest; nidify. [< Latin *nīdificāre* (with English *-ate*¹) < *nīdus* nest + *facere* make]

nid·i·fi·ca·tion (nid′ə fə kā′shən), *n.* the process or the manner of building a nest.

nid·i·fy (nid′ə fī), *v.i.,* **-fied, -fy·ing.** to build a nest or nests. [< Latin *nīdificāre;* see NIDIFICATE]

nid·nod (nid′nod′), *v.i., v.t.,* **-nod·ded, -nod·ding.** to nod repeatedly; keep nodding: *Lady K. nidnodded her head* (Thomas Hood). [reduplicative form of *nod*]

nid·u·lant (nij′ə lənt), *adj. Botany.* **1.** lying free, or partially embedded, in a nestlike receptacle, as sporangia. **2.** lying loose in a pulp, as seeds. [< Latin *nīdulāns, -antis,* present participle of *nīdulārī* build a nest < *nīdus* nest]

ni·dus (nī′dəs), *n., pl.* **-di** (-dī), **-dus·es. 1.** a nest in which certain small animals, such as insects, snails, etc., deposit their eggs. **2.** a place or source of origin or development. [< Latin *nīdus* nest]

niece (nēs), *n.* **1.** a daughter of one's brother or sister. **2.** a daughter of one's brother-in-law or sister-in-law. **3.** an illegitimate daughter of an ecclesiastic (used as a euphemism). [< Old French *niece* < Late Latin *neptia,* alteration of Latin *neptis* granddaughter; later, niece, feminine of *nepōs;* see NEPHEW]

ni·el·list (nē el′ist), *n.* a worker in niello.

ni·el·lo (nē el′ō), *n., pl.* **-el·li** (-el′ē), **-el·los,** *v.,* **-loed, -lo·ing.** —*n.* **1.** a black alloy of silver, lead, copper, and sulfur, with which engraved designs on silver or other metals are filled in, to produce an ornamental effect. **2.** ornamental work done by the application of niello. **3.** an example of this. —*v.t.* to inlay with niello. [< Italian *niello* < Latin *nigellus* (diminutive) < *niger* black]

Nier·stein·er (nir′stī nər, -shtī-), *n.* a white Rhine wine from vineyards in Rhine Hesse, Germany. [< German *Niersteiner* < *Nierstein,* a town in Germany, where it is made]

Nie·tzsche·an (nē′chē ən), *adj.* of or having to do with the German philosopher Nietzsche or his doctrines: *The Nietzschean lady is very frank and not unjust* (New Age). —*n.* a believer in or supporter of the philosophical doctrines of Nietzsche: *The writer . . . is an enthusiastic Nietzschean* (Times Literary Supplement).

Nie·tzsche·an·ism (nē′chē ə niz′əm), *n.* Nietzscheism.

Nie·tzsche·ism (nē′chē iz əm), *n.* the doctrines of Friedrich Wilhelm Nietzsche, 1844-1900, German philosopher and writer, especially the doctrine that human beings could attain perfection only through ruthless self-assertion. From this doctrine stemmed the concept of a type of man, the superman, superior to all others, who was morally justified in using force to achieve his goals.

nieve (nēv), *n. Scottish.* a fist: *The cudgel in my nieve did shake* (Robert Burns). [Middle English *neve* < Scandinavian (compare Old Icelandic *nefi*)]

Ni·fel·heim (niv′əl hām), *n.* Niflheim.

nif·fer (nif′ər), *Scottish.* —*v.t., v.i.* to exchange. —*n.* an exchange.

Ni·fl·heim (niv′əl hām), *n. Norse Mythology.* the region of eternal cold, darkness, and fog in the extreme north. [< Old Icelandic *Niflheimr* Hades < *nifl* mist + *heimr* region]

Ni·fl·heimr (niv′əl hā′mər), *n.* Niflheim.

nif·ty (nif′tē), *adj.,* **-ti·er, -ti·est,** *n., pl.* **-ties.** *U.S. Informal.* —*adj.* attractive; stylish; fine; smart: *Hetty . . . looking so fresh and nifty and feminine* (H.L. Wilson). —*n.* something nifty, as a clever remark or act: *When the cops began throwing his complaints into their "crank" file, he came up with a real nifty* (Time). [American English; origin uncertain]

nig (nig), *v.t.,* **nigged, nig·ging.** to dress (stone) with a sharp-pointed hammer instead of a chisel and mallet; nidge.

ni·gel·la (nī jel′ə), *n.* the fennel flower.

Ni·ger-Con·go (nī′jər kong′gō), *n.* the major language group in Africa, including the Bantu languages spoken in most of West Africa.

Ni·ge·ri·an (nī jir′ē ən), *adj.* of or having to do with Nigeria, a nation in western Africa, a member of the British Commonwealth, or its people. —*n.* a native or inhabitant of Nigeria. [< *Nigeri*(a), a nation in Africa (< the river *Niger*) + English *-an*]

nig·gard (nig′ərd), *n.* a stingy person; miser: *Little niggard! . . . refusing me a pecuniary request* (Charlotte Brontë). —*adj.* stingy; miserly: *lands which a niggard nature had apparently condemned to perpetual poverty* (John L. Motley). [Middle English *negarde,* perhaps < Scandinavian (compare Old Icelandic *knöggr* stingy)] —**Syn.** *n.* skinflint.

nig·gard·ise (nig′ər dīz), *n. Obsolete.* niggardliness: *'Twere pity thou by niggardise shouldst thrive,* (Michael Drayton).

nig·gard·li·ness (nig′ərd lē nis), *n.* niggardly quality; stinginess.

nig·gard·ly (nig′ərd lē), *adj.* **1.** stingy; miserly: *Let us not be niggardly, . . . but let all our fellow prisoners have a share* (Oliver Goldsmith). **2.** meanly small or scanty: *a niggardly gift.* —*adv.* stingily; grudgingly: *[The story of his] life is niggardly doled to us in twelve short pages* (John Nettleship). —**Syn.** *adj.* **1.** illiberal, stinting. —**Ant.** *adj.* **1.** generous, liberal, munificent.

nig·ger·fish (nig′ər fish′), *n., pl.* **-fish·es** or (*collectively*) **-fish.** a red or yellowish grouper with bluish-black spots, of the Caribbean and the Florida coast.

nig·gle (nig′əl), *v.i.,* **-gled, -gling.** to do anything in a trifling way; work with too much care for petty details: *It was only to have been a sketch. And he has kept on niggling and niggling away at it* (William Black). [apparently < Scandinavian (compare dialectal Norwegian *nigla*)] —**nig′gler,** *n.*

nig·gling (nig′ling), *n.* trifling work; work with too much care for petty details: *Leadership has to be created, . . . free from niggling or pettiness* (London Times). —*adj.* trifling; mean; petty: *Neither did I like the niggling way in which they dealt with me* (Robert Southey). —**nig′gling·ly,** *adv.*

nig·gly (nig′lē), *adj.,* **-gli·er, -gli·est.** petty; niggling: *The only thing which has upset them—which shows how niggly, mean, and small they are—is that this is a person who has been on the left wing of the Labour movement* (London Times).

nigh (nī), *adv., adj.,* **nigh·er, nigh·est,** or **next,** *prep., v.* —*adv.* **1.** near: *So nigh is grandeur to our dust* (Emerson). **2.** nearly; almost: *The wood is nigh as full of thieves as leaves* (Tennyson).

nigh upon or **on** or **about,** all but; close to: *he was nigh upon twenty miles from home* (Walter S. Landor).

—*adj. Archaic.* **1.** near; close. **2.** direct. **3.** (of one of a team of horses, etc.) left; near. —*prep. Archaic or Dialect.* close to; near. —*v.t., v.i. Archaic.* to draw near (to); approach. [Old English *nēah.* Compare NEAR.]

nigh hand, *Archaic.* **1.** near at hand: *The shock made . . . woods and mountains all nigh hand resound* (Edward Fairfax). **2.** almost or nearly: *to nigh hand kill one o' my horses* (Samuel Lover).

night (nīt), *n.* **1.** the darkness between evening and morning; the time between sunset and sunrise. **2.** the darkness of night; the dark: *to go out into the night.* **3. a.** the darkness of ignorance, sin, sorrow, old age, death, etc.: *Our share of night to bear, our share of morning* (Emily Dickinson). **b.** concealment: *Robed in the long night of her deep hair* (Tennyson). **4.** evening; nightfall: *the hour of night* (Milton). **5.** a night as a particular time or during which something happens: *to travel three days and nights.*

make a night of it, to celebrate until very late at night: *Friends and neighbors also made . . . a night of it, in honor of the departed* (Scribner's Magazine).

nights, *Informal.* during the night; at night: *Some people work nights and sleep by day.*

[Old English *niht*]

night airglow, nightglow.

night ape, a small South American monkey; douricouli.

night-blind (nīt′blīnd′), *adj.* affected with night blindness: *Americans are so used to electric lights they're practically night-blind* (Newsweek).

night blindness, a condition of the eyes in which the sight is normal in the day or in a strong light, but is abnormally poor or wholly gone at night or in a dim light; nyctalopia: *The condition known as night blindness is often corrected by eating foods rich in vitamin A* (Harbaugh and Goodrich).

night-bloom·ing cereus (nīt′blü′ming), any of various American cactuses whose large, fragrant, white flowers open at night. One variety with flowers about one foot long is cultivated in the tropics as a hedge.

night·cap (nīt′kap′), *n.* **1.** a cap to be worn in bed. **2.** *Informal.* a drink, especially an alcoholic drink, taken just before going to bed. **3.** *Informal.* the last event in a sports program, especially the second baseball game of a double-header: *Gus Bell and Bob Thurman stroked two-run homers in the nightcap* (New York Times).

night·capped (nīt′kapt′), *adj.* wearing a nightcap: *The window was flung open, and Mrs. Bent's nightcapped head came out* (Mrs. Henry Wood).

night clothes, clothes to be worn in bed, as for sleeping.

night·club (nīt′klub′), *v.,* **-clubbed, -club·bing,** *n.* —*v.i.* to go to or frequent night clubs: *She has put behind her memories of the gay young girl who nightclubbed until all hours* (Newsweek). —*n.* night club. —**night′club′ber,** *n.*

night club, a place for dancing, eating, and entertainment, open only at night: *Bernardin opened a night club in the style of the wild and woolly West* (Time).

night crawler, *U.S.* any large earthworm that comes to the surface of the ground at night; nightwalker.

night·dress (nīt′dres′), *n.* **1.** a nightgown. **2.** night clothes.

night·ed (nī′tid), *adj. Archaic.* **1.** made dark as night: *nighted colour* (Shakespeare). **2.** overtaken by night; benighted: *Upon the nighted pilgrim's way* (Scott).

night·er·y (nī′tər ē), *n., pl.* **-er·ies.** *U.S. Informal.* a night club: *The blasts of jazz musicians in the Bourbon Street nighteries . . .* (Wall Street Journal). Also, **nitery.**

night·fall (nīt′fôl′), *n.* the coming of night; dusk; evening: *He walked on, and I lost him in the nightfall—I had all I could do to grope my own way home then* (Christopher Rand).

night fighter, a fighter plane designed to operate at night, especially one provided with searchlights, radar, or other special equipment for detecting enemy aircraft: *As bombardment wore on, the Nationalists used airdrop teams escorted by U.S. Marine Corps night fighters to win the supply battle* (Time).

night fire, ignis fatuus; the will-o'-the-wisp.

night glass, a telescope, usually binocular, made to concentrate as much light as possible, for use at night.

night·glow (nīt′glō′), *n.* airglow occurring at night: *Nightglow is faintest at the zenith overhead and grows in intensity down the sky until it reaches a maximum about 10 degrees above the horizon* (Scientific American).

night·gown (nīt′goun′), *n.* **1.** a loose gown worn by a woman or child in bed. **2.** a nightshirt. —**Syn. 1.** nightdress.

night·gowned (nīt′gound′), *adj.* wearing a nightgown: *At this juncture I would be leaning forward upon one nightgowned elbow, in my fourposted bed* (New Yorker).

night·hawk (nīt′hôk′), *n.* **1.** an American goatsucker, related to the whippoorwill, that flies about at dusk in search of insects, often over city roofs; bullbat; mosquito hawk. **2.** the goatsucker or nightjar of Europe. **3.** *Informal.* a person who stays up very late at night: *One evening the driver of a horse-drawn hansom cab charged him $5 for a trip. "I got to brooding over this nighthawk," Mr. Allen said* (New York Times).

Nighthawk (def. 1)
(9 to 10 in. long)

night heron, any of various medium-sized herons that are active at dusk or at night, as the black-crowned night heron.

night·ie (nī′tē), *n. Informal.* nighty.

night·in·gale (nī′tən gāl, -ting-), *n.* **1.** a small, reddish-brown bird of Europe, related to the thrush, the male of which has a sweet song heard at night as well as in the daytime: *The solemn nightingale . . . all night tuned her soft lays* (Milton). *The nightingale was anciently selected as the highest example of a perfect singer . . . credited with all the best qualities of all the other singers* (W. H. Hudson). **2.** a person who sings or speaks with a melodious voice: *As tempest in a teapot, nightingale, and cat that walks by itself, [Eartha Kitt] is just about superb* (New Yorker). [Middle English *nightingale,* for earlier *nightgale,* Old English *nihtegale* < *niht* night + unrecorded *gale* singer, related to *galan* to sing]

Nightingale (def. 1)
(6 to 7 in. long)

night·jar (nīt′jär′), *n.* any of a group of birds that fly and feed mostly at night; goatsucker. One kind sings in rapidly rising and falling sounds. *the plaintive three-syllable call of an evening bird, a nightjar common in these woods* (W. H. Hudson). [< *night* + *jar*[2] to make a harsh sound]

night lamp, a lamp for burning during the night, as in a bedroom or a sickroom.

night latch, a latch unfastened by a key from the outside or by a knob from the inside.

night·less (nīt′lis), *adj.* being without night: *the nightless period in arctic regions.* —**night′less·ness,** *n.*

night letter, a long telegram sent at night at a reduced rate and usually delivered the following morning.

night lettergram, a night letter.

night life, activity or entertainment at night, especially in night clubs, theaters, etc.: *a tourist who had heard . . . of sophisticated French-flavored night life in the Canadian metropolis* (Newsweek).

night lifer, a devotee of night life: *The City's night lifers . . . are at table until ten-thirty and then at exercise on a dance floor* (New Yorker).

night light, 1. a small light to be kept burning all night: *The night light cast the shadow of his clenched fist on the sheet and it caught the child's eye* (Graham Greene). **2.** the faint light that can be perceived during the night: *to appreciate the difference between daylight and nightlight* (A. Bruce).

night·long (nīt′lông′, -long′), *adj.* lasting all night: *Sleep . . . thou hast forged . . . A nightlong Present of the Past* (Tennyson). —*adv.* through the whole night: *Daylong and nightlong of the fourteenth and fifteenth, the undiminished flight went on* (Arthur H. Tasker).

night·ly (nīt′lē), *adj.* **1.** done, happening, or appearing every night: *nightly attacks, nightly disorder.* **2.** done, happening, or appearing at night: *nightly dew, a nightly visitor.* **3.** of or belonging to night; characteristic of night: *the nightly skies, the nightly darkness.* **4.** *Obsolete.* resembling night.
—*adv.* **1.** every night: *Performances are given nightly except on Sunday.* **2.** at night; by night.

night·mare (nīt′mãr′), *n.* **1.** a very distressing dream: *I would find myself plunged . . . in some foul and ominous nightmare, from which I would awake strangling* (Robert Louis Stevenson). **2.** a very distressing experience: *The journey was a long nightmare.* **3.** a horrible fear or dread. **4.** a sight, object, or person such as might be seen in a nightmare: *What could have made so handsome a young man lend his arm to assist such a nightmare as Sister Ursula?* (Scott). **5.** an evil spirit formerly supposed to oppress people while they are asleep: *King Arthur panted hard, Like one that feels a nightmare on his bed* (Tennyson). [Old English *niht* night + *mare* a monster oppressing men during sleep]

night·mar·ish (nīt′mãr′ish), *adj.* like a nightmare; causing fear or anxiety; wild and strange; horrible: *nightmarish visions, the more terrible for their shapelessness and vagueness* (New York Times). *They slogged 500 miles across the most nightmarish terrain on earth* (Time). —**night′mar′ish·ly,** *adv.*

night owl, 1. *Informal.* a person who habitually stays up late: *The tourist . . . can generally be classified as . . . a dedicated night owl or a dry thirster after obscure and picturesque quiet* (Newsweek). **2.** an owl active only after dark.

night rail, *Archaic.* **1.** a woman's dressing gown. **2.** a woman's nightgown.

night raven, a bird that calls in the night, such as a night heron or nightjar.

night·rid·er (nīt′rī′dər), *n. U.S.* one of a band of mounted men in the South who rode masked at night bent on mischief, intimidation, and violence.

night robe, a nightgown.

nights (nīts), *n.pl.* See under **night,** *n.*

night school, a school held in the evening for persons who work during the day: *Traditionally, night schools . . . emphasized elementary education, high-school completion, and citizenship training* (Leland P. Bradford).

night·shade (nīt′shād′), *n.* **1.** any of a large group of plants of the nightshade family, especially the black nightshade and the bittersweet or woody nightshade. **2.** the belladonna or deadly nightshade. **3.** the henbane or stinking nightshade. See picture under **belladonna.** [Old English *nihtscada* < *niht* night + unrecorded *-scada,* perhaps related to *sceatha* enemy (probably because of its narcotic or poisonous effects)]

nightshade family, a group of dicotyledonous herbs, shrubs, or small trees, many of which contain narcotic or poisonous alkaloids. The family includes the potato, tobacco, belladonna, jimson weed, mandrake, tomato, bittersweet, and petunia.

night shift, 1. a group of workers working at night: *At 11 o'clock in the forenoon the night shift . . . was relieved by the day shift* (Andrew Ure). **2.** the period of time during which they work: *Even when night shifts are not worked, many a factory will take the 24 hours' service of Muzak* (Punch).

night·shirt (nīt′shėrt′), *n.* a long, loose shirt worn by a man or boy in bed.

night soil, contents of a privy or cesspool; human excrement: *In much of China, Korea, . . . night soil is used to fertilize vegetables grown for human consumption* (R. S. J. Hawes). [because it is usually removed from privies or cesspools at night]

night spot, *U.S. Informal.* a night club: *Our jazz lives unhealthily . . . in smoky dives, back rooms, night spots* (Harper's).

night·stick (nīt′stik′), *n. U.S.* a policeman's club: *Patrolman Lemon ran in front of the approaching car and rapped loudly on the ground with his nightstick* (New York Evening Post).

night sweat, very heavy sweating occurring during the night, as in certain diseases.

night table, a small table, usually standing next to a bed, upon which certain objects necessary at night, such as a lamp, clock, etc., are often placed.

night·tide (nīt′tīd′), *n.* nighttime: *And so, all the nighttide . . .* (Edgar Allan Poe).

night·time (nīt′tīm′), *n.* the time between evening and morning; night: *In the nighttime once did Jason wake* (William Morris).

night·walk·er (nīt′wô′kər), *n.* **1.** a night crawler. **2.** a person who goes around at night, especially for a bad purpose.

night watch, 1. a watch or guard kept during the night. **2.** the person or persons keeping such a watch. **3.** a period or division of the night: *When I . . . meditate on thee in the night watches* (Psalms 63:6).

night watchman, a man who works as watchman during the night.

night·wear (nīt′wãr′), *n.* clothing to be worn in bed; night clothes.

night·y (nī′tē), *n., pl.* **night·ies.** *Informal.* a nightgown or nightshirt.

ni·gres·cence (nī gres′əns), *n.* **1.** the process of becoming black. **2.** blackness.

ni·gres·cent (nī gres′ənt), *adj.* somewhat black; blackish. [< Latin *nigrēscēns, -entis,* present participle of *nigrēscere* grow black < *niger* black]

nig·ri·fy (nig′rə fī), *v.t.,* **-fied, -fy·ing.** to blacken. [< Latin *nigrificāre* < *niger* black + *facere* make]

Ni·gri·tian (ni grish′ən), *adj.* **1.** of or having to do with Nigritia or the Sudan, or its people. **2.** of or having to do with the Negro race.
—*n.* **1.** a native or inhabitant of Nigritia; Sudanese. **2.** a Negro.

Ni·grit·ic (ni grit′ik), *adj.* of or like the Nigritians.

nig·ri·tude (nig′rə tüd, -tyüd), *n.* **1.** blackness; black color: *I like to meet a sweep . . . one of those tender novices, blooming through their first nigritude* (Charles Lamb). **2.** something black. [< Latin *nigritūdō* < *niger* black. Doublet of NEGRITUDE.]

ni·gro·sin (nī′grə sin), *n.* nigrosine.

ni·gro·sine (nī′grə sēn, -sin), *n.* any of various blue or black dyes obtained from aniline, used in dyeing textiles, leather, etc.: *The most effective repellent for sharks is a nigrosine dye that makes the water around a swimmer black and opaque* (Science News Letter). [< Latin *niger* black + English *-os*(e) + *-ine*[2]]

N.I.H. or **NIH** (no periods), National Institute of Health.

ni·hil (nī′hil), *n.* **1.** *Latin.* nothing. **2.** a thing of no worth or value.

ni·hil·ism (nī′ə liz əm), *n.* **1.** entire rejection of the usual beliefs in religion, morals, government, laws, etc. **2.** *Philosophy.* the denial of all existence; rejection of objective reality or of the possibility of an objective basis for morality: *His nihilism found a sympathetic audience among the young, and his death caused a great stir* (Atlantic). **3.** the use of violent methods against a ruler; terrorism. **4.** Nihilism. [< Latin *nihil* nothing + English *-ism*]

Ni·hil·ism (nī′ə liz əm), *n.* the beliefs of a revolutionary party in Russia that found nothing good in the old order of things and wished to clear it away to make place for a better state of society.

ni·hil·ist (nī′ə list), *n.* **1.** a person who believes in some form of nihilism. **2.** a terrorist. **3.** a Nihilist.
—*adj.* characterized by nihilism; nihilistic: *All of them were hostile to the routines of urbanization and industrialism as they found them and therefore, in terms of our society, nihilist* (Bulletin of Atomic Scientists).

Ni·hil·ist (nī′ə list), *n.* a member of the Russian revolutionary party that advocated nihilism and was prominent from the 1860's to the 1880's.

ni·hil·is·tic (nī′ə lis′tik), *adj.* of or having to do with nihilists or nihilism: *In between these two nihilistic strategies are a whole spectrum of possibilities* (Hanson Baldwin).

ni·hil·i·ty (nī hil′ə tē), *n., pl.* **-ties. 1.** nothingness; nonexistence: *Nor is there any-one who has not at some moments felt the nihility of all things* (Erasmus Darwin). **2.** a mere nothing; nullity.

ni·hil ob·stat (nī′hil ob′stat), **1.** *Latin.* nothing hinders. **2.** (in the Roman Catholic Church) a phrase on the title page of a book, preceding the name of the official censor and indicating his approval: *Milan's Roman Catholic Cardinal Montini withdrew the nihil obstat of the church* (Time). **3.** official or authoritative approval: *The Foreign Office and the Colonial Office were duly consulted, and gave their nihil obstats* (Observer).

-nik, *suffix. Slang.* a person who is greatly interested in or enthusiastic about something; devotee of a cult, concept, fad, etc.: *Jazznik = a person who is enthusiastic about jazz. Guitar-plunking protestniks . . .* (Time). *The peaceniks . . . had come to La Macaza . . . to commit nonviolent civil disobedience* (Maclean's). [< Russian *-nik* (as in *Sputnik*), a suffix meaning one that does, makes, or is connected with something; influenced by Yiddish *-nik* (as in *nudnik*) < Russian *-nik*]

Ni·ke (nī′kē, nē′kā), *n.* the Greek goddess of victory, usually represented with wings.

Nike of Samothrace
Louvre, Paris

nil (nil), *n.* nothing: *The outcome of all these elaborate tests was nil* (Harper's). [< Latin *nil,* earlier *nihil*]

nil ad·mi·ra·ri (nil ad′mi rãr′ī), *Latin.* to be astonished by nothing (an ideal of the ancient Stoics): *Sensations and excitements are now multiplying so fast in New York that . . . they will result in infusing a little of the nil admirari spirit into the population* (New Yorker).

nil de·spe·ran·dum (nil des′pə ran′dəm), *Latin.* never despair; never give up: *There is . . . a keynote running through the essays and magazine articles here reprinted, a note of nil desperandum* (London Times).

Nile blue (nīl), a pale blue with a tinge of green. [< the river *Nile;* patterned on French *bleu de Nil*]

Nile green, a pale bluish-green color.

nil·gai (nil′gī), *n., pl.* **-gais** or (*collectively*) **-gai.** a large grayish antelope of India: *The nilgai . . . male has short horns, and long hair under its chin* (Victor H. Cahalane). Also, **nylghai, nylghau.** [< Hindi *nīlgāī* < *nīl* blue + *gāī* cow]

nil·gau (nil′gô), *n., pl.* **-gaus** or (*collectively*) **-gau.** nilgai.

nill (nil), *v.t., v.i. Archaic.* to refuse; be unwilling: *Will you, nill you, I will marry you* (Shakespeare). [Old English *nyllan* < *ne* not + *willan* to will]

nil ni·si bo·num (nil nī′sī bō′nəm), *Latin.* nothing but good (abbreviated from *de mortuis nil nisi bonum,* of the dead say nothing but good).

Ni·lo-Ham·it·ic (nī′lō ha mit′ik, -hə-), *adj.* of or belonging to a group of East African tribes related by language, customs, etc., including the Masai and the Nandi: *Two-thirds of Kenya is arid, supporting at most Hamitic and Nilo-Hamitic pastoralists* (London Times). —*n.* the language division common to these tribes.

Ni·lom·e·ter (nī lom′ə tər), *n.* a graduated column used to measure the height of the

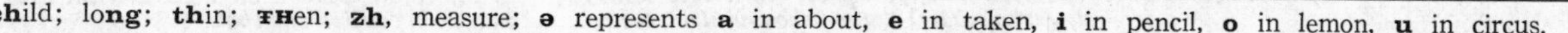

floods of the Nile, a great river in Africa. [alteration of Greek *Neilométrion* < *Neîlos* the Nile + *metríon,* neuter of *métrios* within measure]

Ni·lot·ic (nī lot′ik), *adj.* of or having to do with the Nile or the inhabitants of the Nile valley: *The tall Nilotic peoples are a modified Negro group of mixed origin who live near the headwaters of the Nile River* (George H.T. Kimble). [< Latin *Nīlus* the Nile (< Greek *Neîlos*) + Greek *-otikós* having to do with]

nil si·ne nu·mi·ne (nil sī′nē nū′mə nē), *Latin.* nothing except by the will of God (the motto of Colorado).

nim[1] (nim), *v.t.,* **nam** or **nimmed, no·men** or **nome, nim·ming.** *Archaic.* **1.** to take; seize. **2.** to steal. [< Old English *niman*]

nim[2] (nim), *n.* any of various games in which two players draw counters in turn from one or more piles, the object usually being to take the last counter, or to force the opponent to take the last counter: *Many mathematical recreations involve the binary system,* [*among them*] *the game of nim* (Scientific American). [origin unknown]

nim·ble (nim′bəl), *adj.,* **-bler, -blest. 1.** quick-moving; active and sure-footed; light and quick: *the nimble feet of a ballet dancer. Goats are nimble in climbing among the rocks.* **2.** quick to understand and to reply; clever: *a nimble mind.* [Middle English *nymel, nemel,* Old English *numol,* quick to grasp, apparently related to *niman* take] **—nim′ble·ness,** *n.* **—Syn. 1.** agile, lively, spry, brisk. **—Ant. 1.** slow, heavy.

nim·bly (nim′blē), *adv.* in a nimble manner; quickly and lightly: *We saw a stag bound nimbly by* (Goldsmith).

nim·bo·stra·tus (nim′bō strā′təs), *n., pl.* **-ti** (-tī). a low, dark-gray layer of rain or snow clouds; nimbus: *It is not necessary for precipitation to be actually falling for the cloud to be classified as nimbostratus. It is darker than stratus, has no well-defined lower surface, and its elements are not regularly arranged* (Finch and Trewartha). [< Latin *nimbus* + English *stratus*]

nim·bus (nim′bəs), *n., pl.* **-bus·es, -bi** (-bī). **1.** a light disk or other radiance about the head of a divine or sacred person in a picture; halo: *One ... knows ... a saint by his nimbus* (John Ruskin). **2.** a bright cloud surrounding a god, person, or thing; aura: *But on a deeper level ... there is a kind of nimbus about him at the end* (Time). **3.** a rain cloud; nimbostratus. [< Latin *nimbus* cloud]

Nimbuses (def. 1)
A and B, Christ;
C, Emperor Henry II

ni·mi·e·ty (ni mī′ə tē), *n., pl.* **-ties. 1.** excess; redundancy. **2.** an instance of this. [< Latin *nimietās* < *nimius* excessive < *nimis* too much]

nim·i·ny-pim·i·ny (nim′ə nē pim′ə nē), *adj.* affectedly delicate or refined; mincing: *a niminy-piminy creature, afraid of a petticoat and a bottle* (Robert Louis Stevenson). [probably imitative rhyme]

nim·i·ous (nim′ē əs), *adj.* overmuch; excessive: *Nimious state interference is ... an evil thing* (Scotsman). [< Latin *nimius* (with English *-ous*); see NIMIETY]

n'im·porte (naɴ pôrt′), *French.* it does not matter; never mind.

Nim·rod (nim′rod), *n.* **1.** (in the Bible) a son of Cush, and a great hunter, king, and builder. Genesis 10:8-9. **2.** a great hunter; hunter: *A tiger-hunting would not be the thing without some seasoned Nimrod to advise and direct us* (F. Marion Crawford).

nin·com·poop (nin′kəm pūp), *n.* a fool; simpleton. [earlier *nicompoop*]

nin·com·poop·er·y (nin′kəm pū′pər ē), *n.* lack of good judgment and sense; foolishness: *the nincompoopery of customers who persist in buying cars they cannot afford ...* (Atlantic).

nine (nīn), *n.* **1.** one more than eight; 9. **2. a.** a set of nine persons or things. **b.** a baseball team. **c.** a playing card, roll of dice, etc., with nine spots.

dressed to the nines, elaborately dressed, as for a formal occasion: *When she's dressed up to the nines for some grand party* (Thomas Hardy).

the Nine, the Muses: *For I, through grace of the Nine, Poet am also* (Charles S. C. Bowen).

—adj. being one more than eight: *"Nine little, eight little, seven little Indians."* [Old English *nigon*]

nine-band·ed armadillo (nīn′band′did), the common variety of armadillo, having nine movable bands across its carapace, found from South America through Mexico, Texas, Florida, and neighboring areas; Texas armadillo; peba. It always gives birth to identical quadruplets.

nine·bark (nīn′bärk′), *n.* any of a group of American and Asian shrubs of the rose family with alternate lobed leaves, clusters of white or pink flowers, and a bark that peels off in thin layers.

nine days' wonder, a subject of general surprise and interest for a short time.

nine-eyes (nīn′īz′), *n.* the sea lamprey: *A row of about seven small gill-openings ... behind each eye ... may have given the sea lamprey one of its common names, nine-eyes* (Science News Letter).

nine·fold (nīn′fōld′), *adj.* **1.** nine times as much or as many. **2.** having nine parts or members. *—adv.* nine times as much or as many.

nine·pence (nīn′pəns), *n.* **1.** nine British pennies, worth about 10 United States cents. **2.** a former British coin having this value.

nine·pin (nīn′pin′), *n.* one of the pins used in ninepins.

nine·pins (nīn′pinz′), *n.* a game in which nine large wooden pins are set up to be bowled down with a ball.

Ninepins

nine·teen (nīn′tēn′), *n., adj.* nine more than ten; 19. [Old English *nigontēne, nigontīene*]

nine·teenth (nīn′tēnth′), *adj.* next after the 18th; last in a series of 19. *—n.* **1.** the next after the 18th; last in a series of 19. **2.** one of 19 equal parts.

nineteenth amendment, an amendment to the Constitution of the United States granting women the right to vote, passed by Congress on August 18, 1920.

nineteenth hole, *Informal.* **1.** the time after a game when golfers relax, usually in the clubhouse. **2.** the clubhouse or other place where they relax: *Women golfers, barred from the nineteenth hole at Clacton-on-Sea, England, are not taking it quietly* (Seattle Times).

nine·ti·eth (nīn′tē ith), *adj.* next after the 89th; last in a series of 90. *—n.* **1.** the next after the 89th; last in a series of 90. **2.** one of 90 equal parts.

nine·ty (nīn′tē), *adj., n., pl.* **-ties.** *—adj.* nine times ten; 90. *—n.* nine times ten; 90. [Old English *nigontig*]

nine·ty·ish (nīn′tē ish), *adj.* of, belonging to, or characteristic of the 1890's; resembling or suggesting what was then current: *The style ... veers in its more sensitive moments to an overripe ninetyish brand of empurpled prose* (London Times).

Nine Worthies, nine famous rulers, referred to like the Seven Wonders of the World and other extraordinary things grouped together. The Nine Worthies are considered to be: Hector, Alexander, Julius Caesar, Joshua, David, Judas Maccabaeus, King Arthur, Charlemagne, and Godfrey of Bouillon and were often used as a standard of bravery.

nine·wor·thi·ness (nīn′wėr′ᴛʜē nis), *n. Obsolete.* **1.** a title of mockery and ridicule given to a person as if he were one of, or deserved to be ranked along with, the celebrated Nine Worthies: *The foe, for dread Of your nineworthiness, is fled* (Samuel Butler). **2.** valor like that of the Nine Worthies.

Nin·hy·drin (nin hī′drin), *n. Trademark.* a chemical which produces a blue color in the presence of proteins and amino acids, used in chromatographic analysis and as a test for pregnancy. *Formula:* $C_9H_6O_4$

nin·ny (nin′ē), *n., pl.* **-nies.** a fool; simpleton: *There is perhaps nothing in this calling for forfeiture of a license, but it does seem to suggest a* [*radio*] *station whose writers, editors, and managers are a sad lot of ninnies* (Atlantic). [perhaps misdivision of *an inno*(cent)]

ni·non (nē nôɴ′), *n. French.* a light-weight silk or rayon cloth with a plain weave, used for underwear, blouses, curtains, etc.

ninth (nīnth), *adj.* next after the eighth; last in a series of nine.
—n. **1.** next after the eighth; last in a series of nine. **2.** one of nine equal parts. **3.** *Music.* **a.** a tone nine diatonic degrees from a given tone. **b.** the interval between such tones. **c.** the harmonic combination of such tones.

ninth chord, *Music.* a seventh chord with a superposed third.

Ni·nus (nī′nəs), *n.* the legendary founder of Nineveh, an ancient city in Assyria, and of the Assyrian Empire, husband of Semiramis.

Ni·o·be (nī′ō bē), *n.* **1.** *Greek Mythology.* a mother whose fourteen beautiful children were slain because she boasted about them. Turned by Zeus into a stone fountain, she weeps forever for her children. **2.** a weeping or inconsolable mother: *The Niobe of nations! there she* [*Rome*] *stands, Childless and crownless in her voiceless woe* (Byron).

Ni·o·be·an (nī′ō bē′ən), *adj.* **1.** of Niobe. **2.** like Niobe.

ni·o·bic (nī ō′bik), *adj.* **1.** of niobium. **2.** containing niobium, especially with a valence of five.

ni·o·bi·um (nī ō′bē əm), *n.* a rare metallic chemical element of steel-gray color and brilliant luster, with chemical properties similar to those of tantalum. *Symbol:* Nb (no period); *at.wt.:* (C^{12}) 92.906 or (O^{16}) 92.91; *at.no.:* 41; *valence:* 3, 4, 5. Formerly called **columbium.**
[< New Latin *niobium* < Latin *Niobē* < Greek *Nióbē,* daughter of Tantalus (because it occurs with tantalum)]

ni·o·bous (nī ō′bəs), *adj.* containing niobium, especially with a valence of three.

nip[1] (nip), *v.,* **nipped, nip·ping,** *n.* *—v.t.* **1.** to squeeze tight and suddenly; pinch; bite: *The crab nipped my toe.* **2.** to take off by biting, pinching, or snipping: *to nip twigs from a bush.* **3.** to hurt at the tips; spoil; injure: *Some of our tomato plants were nipped by frost.* **4.** to have a sharp, biting effect on: *A chill wind was blowing that nipped him sharply* (Jack London). **5.** *Slang.* to steal: *Now you get hold of all the doorkeys you can find, and I'll nip all of auntie's* (Mark Twain). **6.** *Dialect.* to take suddenly or quickly; snatch: *She ... nipped up her petticoats, when she came out, as quick and sharp as ever I see* (Elizabeth C. Gaskell).
—v.i. British Informal. to move rapidly or nimbly: *I nipped in to see his mother today, and I couldn't look the old girl in the face* (Margery Allingham).
—n. **1.** a tight squeeze; pinch; sudden bite: *The little puppy gave the child a playful nip.* **2.** injury caused by frost: *So have I seen some tender slip, Sav'd with care from winter's nip* (Milton). **3.** sharp cold; chill: *There is a nip in the air on a frosty morning.* **4.** a small bit. **5.** sharp flavor: *cheese with a real nip.* **6.** a sharp or biting remark.

nip and tuck, *U.S. Informal.* even in a race or contest: *So they had it, nip and tuck, for five miles or more* (Mark Twain).
[Middle English *nyppen.* Compare Middle Dutch, Middle Low German *nippen* to pinch.]

nip[2] (nip), *n., v.,* **nipped, nip·ping.** *—n.* a small drink, especially of alcoholic liquor.
—v.i. to take nips of alcoholic liquor. *—v.t.* to drink in nips.
[origin uncertain]

ni·pa (nē′pə, nī′-), *n.* **1.** a palm of the East Indies, the Philippines, etc., with large feathery leaves that are used for thatching, mats, etc. **2.** the leaves of this palm. **3.** a thatch of them. **4.** liquor made from the juice of the nipa. [< Portuguese, or Spanish *nipa* the wine < Malay *nipah* palm tree; its wine]

nip·cheese (nip′chēz′), *n.* a person of cheeseparing habits; niggardly person; skinflint: *Small good has the tasteless agitation of these churlish nipcheeses done them* (George A. Sala).

nipped-in (nipt′in′), *adj.* pinched in at the waist; made to fit very tightly: *a nipped-in jacket and full skirt.*

nip·per (nip′ər), *n.* **1.** a person or thing that nips. **2.** one of the large claws of a lobster or crab. **3.** a cutting tooth of a horse. **4.** *Informal.* a small boy; lad: *The little nipper hit me with a snowball.*

nippers, **a.** pincers, forceps, pliers, or any tool that nips: *Its teeth are . . . so arranged that the edges cut a hook like nippers* (David Livingstone). **b.** *Slang.* (1) handcuffs: *The criminal was clapped in nippers.* (2) leg irons: *Nippers were used on the ancient galleys.*

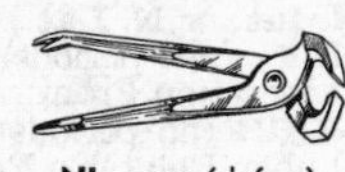
Nippers (def. a)

nip·pi·ness (nip′ē nis), *n.* nippy quality or condition: *The quicker thinking and nippiness of their halfbacks . . . were the final deciding factors* (Listener).

nip·ping (nip′ing), *adj.* that nips; sharp; cutting: *a nipping wind, a nipping remark.* —**nip′ping·ly,** *adv.*

nip·ple (nip′əl), *n.* **1.** a small projection through which a baby animal gets its mother's milk. Nipples are common to all mammals and are located on the breast or udder: *the nipple of a mother cat.* **2.** a rubber cap or mouthpiece of a baby's bottle. **3.** anything shaped or used like a nipple, such as a device on a stopcock to regulate the flow of a liquid. **4. a.** a short piece of pipe threaded at each end for use as a coupling. **b.** a threaded end of a pipe to which a faucet, hose, etc., can be attached. [earlier *nible, neble;* origin uncertain, perhaps (diminutive) < *neb.* Compare NIB.]

Nip·pon (ni pon′, nip′on), *n.* Japan. [< Japanese *Nippon,* variant of *Nihon*]

Nip·pon·ese (nip′ə nēz′, -nēs′), *adj., n., pl.* **-ese.** Japanese: *The Nipponese restraints were aimed at quieting blasts from American mills* [*about*] *. . . the volume of cloth and apparel crossing the Pacific* (Wall Street Journal). [< *Nippon* + *-ese*]

nip·py (nip′ē), *adj.,* **-pi·er, -pi·est. 1.** biting; sharp: *a nippy wind, nippy cheese.* **2.** apt to nip: *a nippy dog.* **3.** *Slang.* smart; stylish. **4.** *British Informal.* quick; keen; active. **5.** *Scottish.* stingy; grasping.

nip·up (nip′up′), *n.* **1.** (in gymnastics) a sudden leap from a reclining position on one's back to the feet. **2.** any sudden motion; jumping jerk: *My insides started to do nipups* (Tallulah Bankhead). **3.** a stunt; caper; clever performance: *Its moments of hilarity are a lot more rewarding than some of the nipups I've witnessed in farces of more recent vintage* (New Yorker). [< earlier slang *nip up* to move rapidly]

nir·va·na or **Nir·va·na** (nir vä′nə, -van′ə; nər-), *n.* **1.** the Buddhist idea of heavenly peace; perfect happiness reached by the complete absorption of oneself into the supreme universal spirit: *In the most final Heaven of the Buddhists . . . the state of Nirvana, the soul loses its separate identity and is absorbed into the Great Soul of the World* (Norbert Wiener). **2.** the Hindu idea of freedom of the soul; reunion with the world soul reached by the suppression of individual existence. **3.** any state likened to either of these: *Jazz and fast cars, in that order, are Dean's ladder to nirvana* (Phoebe Adams). [< Sanskrit *nirvāna* extinction < *nis* out + *vā* to blow]

Ni·san (nī′san; *Hebrew* ni sän′), *n.* (in the Jewish calendar) the seventh month of the civil year, and the first of the ecclesiastical year, beginning late in March or early in April. [< Hebrew *nisān*]

Ni·sei or **ni·sei** (nē′sā′), *n., pl.* **-sei,** or **-seis.** a native-born United States or Canadian citizen whose parents were Japanese immigrants. [American English < Japanese *nisei* second generation < *ni* two + *sei* generation]

ni·si (nī′sī), *conj.* unless, a term used in law after the words *decree, order,* etc., to specify or suggest some contingency. A decree nisi will take effect at a specified time, unless cause is shown against it or it is altered for some other reason. [< Latin *nisī* unless]

ni·sin (nī′sən), *n.* any of a group of antibiotics obtained from lactobacilli and streptococci, effective against mycobacteria and other gram-positive organisms, and used especially to prevent spoilage caused by clostridia in dairy products. [a coined word]

nisi pri·us (prī′əs), *Law.* **1.** unless before (applied to the trial of civil cases before a judge and jury). **2.** *U.S.* designating the court in which trial is made before a jury, as distinguished from an appellate court. [< Anglo-French *nisi prius* < Medieval Latin, (literally) unless before (that time)]

Nis·qual·ly (niz′kwä lē), *n., pl.* **-ly** or **-lys. 1.** a member of a Salishan tribe living in the region of Puget Sound, Washington. **2.** the Salishan language of this tribe.

Nis·sen hut (nis′ən), a prefabricated shelter for soldiers, made of corrugated metal with a concrete floor; Quonset hut. [< Lieutenant Colonel Peter N. *Nissen,* 1871-1930, a British mining engineer, who designed it]

ni·sus (nī′səs), *n., pl.* **-sus.** effort; endeavor; impulse. [< Latin *nīsus, -ūs* a pressing on, exertion < *nītī* press upon, strive]

nit[1] (nit), *n.* **1.** the egg of a louse or similar insect. **2.** a very young louse or similar insect. [Old English *hnitu*]

nit[2] (nit), *n. Especially British Slang.* a nitwit: *. . . a weak-willed nit* (Punch).

ni·ter (nī′tər), *n.* **1.** potassium nitrate, obtained from potash, used in making gunpowder; saltpeter. *Formula:* KNO_3 **2.** sodium nitrate, or Chile saltpeter, used as a fertilizer. *Formula:* $NaNO_3$ [< Old French *nitre,* learned borrowing from Latin *nitrum* < Greek *nítron* saltpeter; sodium carbonate < a Semitic word. Doublet of NATRON.]

nit·er·y (nī′tər ē), *n., pl.* **-er·ies.** *U.S. Informal.* a night club: *He . . . danced barefoot with Polynesian girls in the island's niteries* (Saturday Evening Post). [variant of *nightery;* influenced by *nite,* slang variant of *night*]

nit·id (nit′id), *adj.* bright; shining; glossy: *They spotted a garment less nitid than the one glittering on their own child's back* (Punch). [< Latin *nitidus* < *nitēre* shine]

ni·to (nē′tō), *n., pl.* **-tos** (-tōz). a climbing fern of the Philippines, with glossy, wiry stems that are woven into hats and other articles. [< Spanish (Philippines) *nito*]

ni·ton (nī′ton), *n.* an early name of radon. *Symbol:* Nt [< New Latin *niton* < Latin *nitēre* to shine + English *-on,* as in *argon*]

nit-pick (nit′pik′), *Informal.* —*v.t.* to pick at (something) in a petty or niggling manner, as if removing a nit or louse; examine pedantically; search for petty faults: *To make a show of debate, delegates were allowed to nit-pick a few details* (Time). —*v.i.* to pick at something nigglingly, especially with a view to finding faults; split hairs: *. . . nit-picking over who took whom to lunch . . .* (Wall Street Journal). —**nit′-pick′er,** *n.*

nitr-, *combining form.* the form of **nitro-** before vowels, as in *nitryl.*

ni·trate (nī′trāt), *n., v.,* **-trat·ed, -trat·ing.** —*n.* **1.** a salt or ester of nitric acid, containing the monovalent group $-NO_3$. **2.** potassium nitrate or sodium nitrate, used as a fertilizer.
—*v.t.* **1.** to treat with nitric acid or a nitrate. **2.** to change into a nitrate.
[< *nitr*(ic) + *-ate*[2]]

nitrate nitrogen, a chemical substance produced by nitrification through bacteria located either in the nodules of leguminous plants or in the soil and necessary to the development of plants.

ni·tra·tion (nī trā′shən), *n.* the process of nitrating; introducing the radical $-NO_2$ into a compound.

ni·tre (nī′tər), *n. Especially British.* niter.

ni·tric (nī′trik), *adj.* **1.** of or containing nitrogen, especially with a valence of five. **2.** of or derived from niter. [< French *nitrique* < Old French *nitre;* see NITER]

nitric acid, a clear, colorless liquid that eats into flesh, clothing, metal, and other substances. It has a pungent smell and is usually obtained by treating sodium nitrate with sulfuric acid. Nitric acid is used in making dyes, explosives, etc., and in etching, metallurgy, etc. *Formula:* HNO_3

nitric bacteria, bacteria that convert nitrites to nitrates by oxidation; nitrobacteria.

nitric oxide, a colorless, poisonous, gaseous compound, obtained by the oxidation of nitrogen or ammonia, or by treating copper with dilute nitric acid. *Formula:* NO

ni·trid (nī′trid), *n.* nitride.

ni·tride (nī′trīd, -trid), *n., v.,* **-trid·ed, -trid·ing.** —*n.* a compound of nitrogen with a more electropositive element or radical, such as phosphorus, boron, or a metal. —*v.t.* to transform into a nitride, as the surface of steel. [< *nitr*(ogen) + *-ide*]

ni·tri·fi·ca·tion (nī′trə fə kā′shən), *n.* the act or process of nitrifying: *Ammonia may be oxidized to nitrous acid and the latter to nitric acid by bacteria in . . . nitrification* (Harbaugh and Goodrich).

ni·tri·fi·er (nī′trə fī′ər), *n.* a thing that nitrifies: *Other organisms, called nitrifiers, convert this organic nitrogen into the mineral nitrates required by plants* (Scientific American).

ni·tri·fy (nī′trə fī), *v.t.,* **-fied, -fy·ing. 1.** to oxidize (ammonia compounds, etc.) to nitrites or nitrates, especially by bacterial action. **2.** to impregnate (soil, etc.) with nitrates. **3.** to combine or treat with nitrogen or one of its compounds. [< French *nitrifier* < Old French *nitre* (see NITER) + *-fier* -fy]

ni·tri·fy·ing bacteria (nī′trə fī′ing), nitrobacteria.

ni·tril (nī′trəl), *n.* nitrile.

ni·trile (nī′trəl, -trēl, -trīl), *n.* any of a group of organic cyanides containing the univalent radical -CN. The nitriles form acids on hydrolysis, with the elimination of ammonia. [< *nitr*(ogen) + Latin *-ilis, -īlis* having to do with]

nitrile rubber, a synthetic rubber that is resistant to the dissolving effects of gasoline, grease, oil, wax, and solvents. It contains varying proportions of butadiene and acrylonitrile and is used in gasoline hoses, paper, leather products, and many types of cloth.

ni·trite (nī′trīt), *n.* a salt or ester of nitrous acid, containing the univalent $-NO_2$ radical.

ni·tro[1] (nī′trō), *adj.* **1.** containing niter. **2.** nitric. **3.** containing the univalent radical $-NO_2$.

ni·tro[2] (nī′trō), *n. Informal.* nitroglycerin: *Pour in an explosive like nitro, give it an oxidizer, add a spark—and blooey* (Wall Street Journal).

nitro-, *combining form.* **1.** formed by the action of nitric acid, as in *nitrobenzene.*
2. indicating the presence of the $-NO_2$ radical, as in *nitrocellulose.*
3. nitrification, as in *nitrobacteria.* Also, **nitr-** before vowels.
[< Greek *nítron* saltpeter]

ni·tro·bac·te·ri·a (nī′trō bak tir′ē ə), *n.pl.* any of various bacteria living in soil that derive their energy from the oxidation of ammonium compounds. Members of one group convert ammonia to nitrites, and a second group then oxidizes the nitrite to nitrate which can be used as a source of nitrogen by higher plants.

ni·tro·ben·zene (nī′trō ben′zēn, -ben zēn′), *n.* a poisonous yellowish liquid that smells like oil of bitter almonds, obtained from benzene by the action of nitric acid, used in making aniline, in perfumery, as a reagent, etc. *Formula:* $C_6H_5NO_2$

ni·tro·ben·zol (nī′trō ben′zōl, -zol), *n.* nitrocellulose.

ni·tro·cel·lu·lose (nī′trō sel′yə lōs), *n.* cellulose nitrate.

ni·tro·chalk (nī′trə chôk′), *n.* an artificial fertilizer containing calcium carbonate and ammonium nitrate.

ni·tro·cot·ton (nī′trō kot′ən), *n.* guncotton.

ni·tro·fu·ran (nī′trə fyůr′ən), *n.* any of a group of drugs derived from corn cobs and oat husks, used against microbes and other germs.

ni·tro·fu·ran·to·in (nī′trō fyů ran′tō in), *n.* a drug used to treat bacterial infections of the prostate and the urethra. *Formula:* $C_8H_6N_4O_5$

ni·tro·fu·ra·zone (nī′trə fyůr′ə zōn), *n.* a yellow crystalline antiseptic applied on the skin, in the eyes, ears, etc., for the treatment of bacterial infections. *Formula:* $C_6H_6N_4O_4$

ni·tro·gel·a·tin (nī′trō jel′ə tən), *n.* a jellylike explosive containing nitroglycerin, guncotton, and camphor.

ni·tro·gen (nī′trə jən), *n.* a colorless, odorless, tasteless gas that forms about four-fifths of the air by volume. It is one of the most important chemical elements and is a necessary constituent of all animal and vegetable tissues. *Symbol:* N; *at.wt.:* (C^{12}) 14.0067 or (O^{16}) 14.008; *at.no.:* 7; *valence:* (chiefly) 3, 5. [< French *nitrogène* < Greek *nítron* niter + French *-gène* -gen]

nitrogen cycle, the circulation of nitrogen and its compounds by living organisms in nature. Atmospheric nitrogen passes into the soil where it is oxidized to nitrate by bacteria and used by green plants and then in turn by animals. Decaying plants and animals, and animal waste products, are in turn acted on by bacteria and the nitrogen in them is again made available for circulation.

nitrogen dioxide, an extremely poisonous, brownish gas, used in producing nitric acid, as a catalyst, and as an oxidizer for liquid rocket propellants. *Formula:* NO_2 *In the explosion of a nominal atomic bomb, something of the order of 100 tons of nitrogen dioxide are formed* (The Effects of Atomic Weapons).

nitrogen fixation, 1. the combination of free atmospheric nitrogen with other substances, as in making explosives and fertilizers. **2.** the use of atmospheric nitrogen to satisfy the requirements of certain blue-green algae and bacteria found in water and soil. Some of the algae or bacteria are free living and some live symbiotically in nodules on the roots of mostly leguminous plants. Atmospheric nitrogen is thus brought into biological circulation and can be used in combined form by other organisms. *The number of bacteria found to be capable of nitrogen fixation steadily increases* (Scientific American).

ni·tro·gen-fix·ing (nī′trə jən fik′sing), *adj.* causing atmospheric nitrogen to combine with elements in the soil: *nitrogen-fixing bacteria.*

ni·tro·gen·i·za·tion (nī′trə jə nə zā′shən), *n.* the process of nitrogenizing.

ni·tro·gen·ize (nī′trə jə nīz), *v.t.,* **-ized, -iz·ing.** to combine with nitrogen or one of its compounds.

nitrogen mustard, a substance similar to mustard gas but containing nitrogen instead of sulfur, used in medicine to treat Hodgkin's disease, leukemia, and similar malignant diseases: *There are some compounds, such as the nitrogen mustards, which imitate the action of radiation on the cell, and dislocate nuclear division* (H.O.J. Collier).

nitrogen narcosis, a stupor caused by the presence of too much nitrogen in the blood and tissues of the body, occurring in divers and others working under high atmospheric pressure: *Even at the 100-ft. depth, most divers have their thought and judgment so impaired by nitrogen narcosis that they can no longer perform simple mental or manual tasks well* (Time).

ni·trog·e·nous (nī troj′ə nəs), *adj.* of or containing nitrogen or a compound of nitrogen: *[In one] year, slightly more than two million tons of nitrogenous fertilizers were used by the nation's farmers* (Wall Street Journal).

nitrogen oxide, any of the various oxides of nitrogen, often in the form of a colorless, poisonous gas such as nitric oxide: *Nitrogen oxides . . . have been blamed for contributing to smog conditions in auto-packed Los Angeles* (Science News Letter).

nitrogen tetroxide, a poisonous compound existing in various states, used as a catalyst, oxidizing agent, etc., and considered a possible oxidizer for rocket fuels: *Nitrogen tetroxide is another bidder to replace LOX in rockets* (Science News Letter). *Formula:* N_2O_4

ni·tro·glyc·er·in (nī′trə glis′ər in), *n.* an oily, yellow or colorless, highly explosive liquid made by treating glycerol with nitric and sulfuric acids. Nitroglycerin is used in dynamite and in medicine to dilate blood vessels. *Formula:* $C_3H_5N_3O_9$

ni·tro·glyc·er·ine (nī′trə glis′ər in, -ə rēn), *n.* nitroglycerin.

nitro group, a univalent radical, $-NO_2$.

ni·tro·gua·ni·dine (nī′trə gwä′nə dēn), *n.* a chemical derived from guanidine nitrate by dissolution in sulfuric acid, used in explosives. *Formula:* $CH_4N_4O_2$

ni·trol·ic acid (nī trol′ik), any of a series of organic acids having the general formula RCN_2O_3H, obtained by treating nitroparaffin with nitrous acid.

ni·trom·e·ter (nī trom′ə tər), *n.* an apparatus for determining the amount of nitrogen, nitrates, or the like, in a substance. [< *nitro*(gen) + *-meter*]

ni·tro·meth·ane (nī′trə meth′ān), *n.* a colorless liquid used as a chemical solvent and as a fuel or fuel additive in rockets, jets, and racing cars: *The engines gleamed like platinum; for fuels some burned an explosive mixture of methyl alcohol and nitromethane* (Time). *Formula:* CH_3NO_2

ni·tro·par·af·fin (nī′trə par′ə fin), *n.* any chemical compound derived from a member of the methane series by substituting the $-NO_2$ radical for an atom of hydrogen.

ni·tros·am·in (nī′trōs am′in), *n.* nitrosamine.

ni·tros·a·mine (nī′trōs ə mēn′, -am′in), *n.* **1.** any of a series of neutral organic chemical compounds containing the bivalent group -N.NO. **2.** a compound containing the univalent group -NH.NO.

ni·tro·so (nī trō′sō), *adj.* indicating the presence of the univalent radical -NO.

nitroso group, nitrosyl.

ni·tro·syl (nī trō′səl, nī′trə sēl′, nī′trə səl), *n.* a univalent radical, -NO.

ni·tro·syl·ic (nī′trə sil′ik), *adj.* of or containing a nitrosyl.

ni·trous (nī′trəs), *adj.* **1.** of nitrogen; containing nitrogen, especially with a valence of 3. **2.** of niter. [< Latin *nitrōsus* < *nitrum* niter]

nitrous acid, an acid occurring only in solution or in the form of its salts. *Formula:* HNO_2

nitrous bacteria, nitrobacteria.

nitrous oxide, a colorless gas that causes inability to feel pain, and in some patients produces exhilaration and uncontrollable laughing; laughing gas. It is used as an anesthetic in surgery and dentistry. *Formula:* N_2O

ni·tryl (nī′trəl), *n.* a univalent radical, $-NO_2$, containing nitrogen and oxygen.

nit·ty-grit·ty (nit′ē grit′ē), *U.S. Slang.* —*n.* the essential or fundamental part: *Dr. Swanson . . . can really understand people in a gutsy way. And he's not afraid to get down to the nitty-gritty of unpleasant problems* (New York Times). —*adj.* essential, fundamental, or detailed.

nit·wit (nit′wit′), *n. Informal.* a very stupid person: *He's about the most complete nitwit I ever encountered—but useful . . . and harmless* (Saturday Evening Post). [American English < *nit* nothing (probably < dialectal German *nit* < German *nichts* nothing) + *wit*]

ni·val (nī′vəl), *adj.* **1.** of or having to do with snow. **2.** (of plants) growing in or near snow. [< Latin *nivālis* < *nix, nivis* snow]

niv·e·ous (niv′ē əs), *adj.* snowy in color; snow-white. [< Latin *niveus* (with English *-ous*) < *nix, nivis* snow]

Ni·vôse (nē vōz′), *n.* the fourth month of the French Revolutionary calendar, extending from December 21 to January 19. [< French *nivôse,* learned borrowing from Latin *nivōsus* snowy < *nix, nivis* snow]

nix[1] (niks), *Slang.* —*interj.* **1.** no! stop! **2.** watch out!
—*n.* nothing; nobody.
—*v.t.* to refuse; deny: *Russia offered Europe a 50-year "security" pact; Britain, France nixed it* (Wall Street Journal).
—*adv.* no.
[probably < German *nix,* dialectal variant of *nichts* nothing, or < dialectal Dutch *nix*]

nix[2] (niks), *n., pl.* **nix·es.** *German Legend.* a water fairy. [< colloquial Dutch or German *Nix.* Compare NIXIE[1].]

nix·ie[1] (nik′sē), *n. German Legend.* a female water fairy: *She who sits by haunted well, Is subject to the nixie's spell* (Scott). [< German *Nixe,* feminine, (originally) a legendary water creature]

nix·ie[2] or **nix·y** (nik′sē), *n., pl.* **nix·ies.** *U.S. Slang.* a letter or other mail that is not delivered because of an illegible or incorrect address: *With stamp prices up, mailers are taking a lot more care to avoid nixies* (Wall Street Journal). [< *nix*[1] + *ie, -y*[2]]

ni·zam (ni zäm′, -zam′), *n., pl.* **-zam.** a soldier in the standing army of Turkey (a term used especially in the 1800's). [< Turkish *nizam* < Urdu *niẓām;* see NIZAM]

Ni·zam (ni zäm′, -zam′), *n.* the title since 1713 of the native ruler of Hyderabad in India. [short for Hindustani *niẓām-al-mulk* governor of the empire]

ni·zam·ate (ni zäm′āt, -zam′-), *n.* the rule or domain of the Nizam.

N.J., New Jersey.

Njord (nyôrd), *n.* Njorth.

Njorth (nyôrth), *n. Scandinavian Mythology.* one of the Vanir, the father of Frey and Freya, the dispenser of riches.

NKVD (no periods) or **N.K.V.D.,** the secret police of the Soviet Union. It was renamed the MVD in 1946..

n.l., 1. it is not clear (Latin, *non liquet*). **2.** it is not permitted (Latin, *non licet*). **3.** new line (in setting type).

NL (no periods) or **N.L., 1.** *U.S.* National (Baseball) League. **2.** *British.* Navy League. **3.** New Latin.

N. lat. or **N. Lat.,** north latitude.

NLF (no periods) or **N.L.F.,** National Liberation Front.

NLRB (no periods) or **N.L.R.B.** National Labor Relations Board.

N.M. or **N. Mex.,** New Mexico.

NMB (no periods), National Mediation Board.

NMR (no periods), nuclear magnetic resonance.

N.M.U., National Maritime Union.

NNE (no periods) or **N.N.E.,** north-northeast (direction halfway between north and northeast).

NNW (no periods) or **N.N.W.,** north-northwest (direction halfway between north and northwest).

no[1] (nō), *n., pl.* **noes,** *adj., adv.* —*n.* **1.** a word used to deny, refuse, or disagree. **2.** a denial; refusal. **3.** a negative vote or voter: *The noes have it.* [< adverb]
—*adj.* **1.** not any: *He has no friends.* **2.** not a: *He is certainly no athlete. Turnbull . . . caught hold of her with no very gentle grasp* (Scott). [Middle English *no,* reduction of Old English *nān* none]
—*adv.* **1.** a word used to deny, refuse, or disagree: *Will you come? No.* **2.** not in any degree; not at all: *He is no better.* **3.** not, chiefly in phrases like *whether or no.* [Old English *nā* < *ne* not + *ā* ever]
➔ See **yes** for usage note.

no[2] or **No** (nō), *n., pl.* **no** or **nos, No** or **Nos.** a type of Japanese classical drama with formalized dancing and chanting by actors wearing symbolic masks. [< Japanese *nō*]

No[2] **Mask** representing young girl

no., *pl.* **nos.** number (Latin, *numero*).
➔ See **No.** for usage note.

No (no period), nobelium (artificial chemical element).

No., 1. north. **2.** northern. **3.** number.
➔ **No.** The abbreviation *No.* for *number* (from the Latin *numero,* "by number") is usually written with a capital. It is used chiefly in business and technical English. In the United States *No.* is not written with street numbers.

no-ac·count (nō′ə kount′), *adj. U.S. Informal.* worthless; good-for-nothing: *A lazy, no-account, good-for-nothing thief* (David Cushman). —*n.* a worthless person; good-for-nothing fellow: *dispensing wisdom to no-accounts like Billy Bigelow* (Wall Street Journal).

No·a·chi·an (nō ā′kē ən), *adj.* **1.** of or having to do with Noah or his time: *the Noachian deluge.* **2.** very ancient or old-fashioned.

No·ach·ic (nō ak′ik, -ā′kik), *adj.* Noachian.

No·ah (nō′ə), *n.* (in the Bible) a man whom God told to make an ark to save himself, his family, and a pair of each kind of animal from the Flood. Genesis 6:9-22. Also, **Noe.**

Noah's Ark, the ark built by Noah.

nob[1] (nob), *n.* **1.** *Slang.* knob; rounded part: *A man with a bottle nose—a nob of scarlet and blue on a yellow face* (Graham Greene). **2.** *Slang.* the head: *a bald, shining nob.* **3.** (in cribbage) the jack of the same suit as the card turned up, scoring one for the holder. [perhaps a variant of *knob*]

nob[2] (nob), *n. Especially British Slang.* a person of wealth or social importance: *He's not the nob I thought he was. He just took on like any other common chap* (Margery Allingham). [(originally) Scottish *knabb;* origin unknown]

no-ball (nō′bôl′), *Cricket.* —*n.* a ball illegally bowled: *The loping run, all arms and legs, and the no-ball were not forgotten* (London Times). —*v.t.* to penalize (a player) for having delivered a no-ball: *He is one of five bowlers who have been no-balled for throwing this season* (Times of India).

nob·bi·ly (nob′ə lē), *adv. Slang.* in a nobby manner; showily; smartly.

nob·ble (nob′əl), *v.t.,* **-bled, -bling.** *British Slang.* **1.** to tamper with (a horse) to prevent its winning a race, as by the use of drugs: *Tipsters whose dead certainties fail to win are often prone to complain that their favourites have been nobbled* (London Times). **2.** to bring (a person) over to one's own side by bribery or other such means. **3.** to obtain dishonestly; steal. **4.** to swindle: *I don't* *know out of how much the reverend party has nobbled his poor old sister* (Thackeray). **5.** to seize, catch, or capture. [origin uncertain] —**nob′bler,** *n.*

nob·bler (nob′lər), *n. Australian.* a glass of beer or hard liquor.

nob·by (nob′ē), *adj.,* **-bi·er, -bi·est.** *Slang.* **1.** smart; fashionable; elegant. **2.** first-rate. [< *nob*[2] + *-y*[1]]

No·bel·ist (nō bel′ist), *n.* a recipient of a Nobel prize: *Dr. Glenn T. Seaborg, chairman of the U.S. Atomic Energy Commission and 1951 Nobelist in chemistry, received the 1963 Franklin Medal* (Science News Letter).

no·be·li·um (nō bē′lē əm), *n.* a very heavy, radioactive, artificial chemical element produced by bombarding curium with carbon ions. *Symbol:* No; *at.wt.:* (C^{12}) 254 or (O^{16}) 254; *at.no.:* 102; *half life:* 10 minutes. [< New Latin *nobelium* < Alfred B. *Nobel,* who established the Nobel prizes]

No·bel prize (nō bel′), any of five money prizes, averaging $40,000 each, established by Alfred B. Nobel, 1833-1896, to be given annually to those persons or organizations who have done most in physics, chemistry, medicine, literature, and the promotion of international peace. Prizes were first awarded in 1901.

no·bil·i·ar·y (nō bil′ē er′ē), *adj.* of or having to do with the nobility: *nobiliary rank.* [earlier, list of nobles < French *nobiliaire* of the nobility, learned borrowing from Latin *nōbilis* noble]

nobiliary particle, a preposition, such as the French *de* or the German *von,* forming part of a noble title.

no·bil·i·ty (nō bil′ə tē), *n., pl.* **-ties. 1.** people of noble rank: *Earls, marquises, and counts belong to the nobility. The United States does not have a nobility.* **2.** noble birth; noble rank. **3.** noble character: *What did they have that brought them so close to nobility, when most men would have cracked?* (Time). [< Old French *nobilite,* or *noblete,* learned borrowing from Latin *nōbilitās* < *nōbilis* noble] —**Syn. 1.** peerage. **3.** greatness.

no·ble (nō′bəl), *adj.,* **-bler, -blest,** *n.* —*adj.* **1.** high and great by birth, rank, or title: *a noble family, noble blood.* **2.** high and great in character; showing greatness of mind; good: *a noble knight, a noble deed.* **3.** excellent; fine; splendid; magnificent: *a noble poem, a noble animal; a cruciform hall of noble dimensions* (Nicholas P. S. Wiseman). **4.** not easily rusted or deteriorated; precious; valuable: *Gold and silver are noble metals.* **5.** chemically inert, as helium, neon, etc.: *The nonabsorbable gas consists of nitrogen and argon, with, very likely, traces of other noble gas* (Science). **6.** (in falconry) of the long-winged hawks, as the falcons, that swoop down on the quarry: *The hawks have been classified as 'noble' or 'ignoble' according to the length and sharpness of their wings* (G. D. Campbell).
—*n.* **1.** a person high and great by birth, rank, or title: [*The Hittites*] *evolved a pioneering constitutional monarchy; their kings had to answer to a council of nobles* (Newsweek). **2.** an English gold coin of the late Middle Ages, worth 6 shillings and 8 pence. **3.** *Slang.* the leader of a group of strikebreakers. [< Old French *noble,* learned borrowing from Latin *nōbilis* noble, renowned, well known < *gnōscere* to know] —**no′ble·ness,** *n.*
—**Syn.** *adj.* **1.** aristocratic, high-born, patrician. **2.** honorable, worthy. **3.** imposing, stately. See **grand.**

Noble (def. 2) of Edward III (obverse)

noble art, *Especially British.* the art of boxing: *I was once a serious practitioner of the noble art* (Tommy Farr).

no·ble·man (nō′bəl mən), *n., pl.* **-men. 1.** a man of noble rank, title, or birth; peer. **2.** a person of some specially favored or superior class: *The warrior, from the excellence of his physical proportions, might certainly have been regarded as one of nature's noblemen* (Herman Melville).

no·blesse (nō bles′), *n.* **1.** noble birth or condition; nobility: *It roused her sense of noblesse and restored to her, brighter than before, her dream of living in style* (Jetta Carleton). **2.** persons of noble rank; the nobility: *Of the garrulous noblesse we are confronted with, the most talkative is Louis XI . . . and his vaporings make him quite a trial.* [< Old French *noblesse,* or *noblece* nobility, learned borrowing from Medieval Latin *nobilitia* < Latin *nōbilis* noble]

no·blesse o·blige (nō bles′ ō blēzh′), *French.* **1.** persons of noble rank should behave nobly: *She taught her granddaughter that noblesse oblige was the greatest virtue and that aristocracy was the only proper order of society* (New York Times). **2.** (literally) nobility obligates.

no·ble·wom·an (nō′bəl wu̇m′ən), *n., pl.* **-wom·en.** a woman of noble birth or rank; peeress.

no·bly (nō′blē), *adv.* **1.** in a noble manner; as a noble person would do; gallantly; splendidly: *a nobly fought battle.* **2.** of noble parentage: *nobly born.*

no·bod·y (nō′bod ē, -bə dē), *pron., n., pl.* **-bod·ies.** —*pron.* no one; no person.
be nobody's fool, to be hard to trick or deceive; be shrewder or cleverer than it may seem: *Miss Lesh is going to be nobody's fool on* [*the*] *courts* (London Times).
—*n.* a person of no importance: *nobodies who think they are somebodies.*
➔ **Nobody, nothing, nowhere** are written as single words. *Nobody* and *nothing* are singular, though *nobody* is informally treated as a collective: *Nothing is further from the truth. Nobody thinks that his own dog is a nuisance.* Informal: *Nobody thinks their own dog is a nuisance.*

no·car·di·a (nō kär′dē ə), *n.* any of a group of aerobic actinomycetes, certain varieties of which may cause various lesions and infections of the skin and internal organs. [< New Latin *Nocardia* < Edmund *Nocard,* 1850-1903, a French veterinarian]

no·cent (nō′sənt), *adj.* **1.** hurtful; harmful; injurious. **2.** guilty; criminal. [< Latin *nocēns, -entis,* present participle of *nocēre* to harm, related to *necāre* to kill]

no·ci·as·so·ci·a·tion (nō′sē ə sō′sē ā′shən, -sō′shē-), *n.* a loss of nervous energy as a result of traumatic injury or shock. [< Latin *nocēre* to harm + English *association.* Compare ANOCIASSOCIATION.]

nock (nok), *n.* **1.** a notch on a bow or arrow for the bowstring. **2.** *Nautical.* the forward upper corner of a sail set to a boom or of a staysail cut with a square tack. **3.** *Obsolete.* the cleft in the buttocks.
—*v.t.* **1.** to furnish (a bow or arrow) with a nock. **2.** to fit (an arrow) to the bowstring ready for shooting.
[Middle English *nocke* notch on a bow. Perhaps related to Dutch *nok* and Low German *nokk* point, tip. Compare NICK.]

no-con·fi·dence (nō′kon′fə dəns), *n.* a motion or vote by a legislative body expressing lack of confidence in the policies of a government or administration, especially in its basic policies. If such a motion is carried, the government is usually compelled to resign. —*adj.* of or having to do with a vote of no-confidence: *He squeaked through a no-confidence vote . . . intended to depose him as Premier* (Newsweek).

no-count (nō′kount′), *adj., n. U.S. Dialect.* no-account: *Ye miserable, mean-spirited, no-count critter!* (Helen Jackson).

noc·tam·bu·la·tion (nok tam′byə lā′shən), *n.* sleepwalking; somnambulism. [< Latin *nox, noctis* night + *ambulātiō, -ōnis* a walking about < *ambulāre* to walk]

noc·tam·bu·lism (nok tam′byə liz əm), *n.* noctambulation.

noc·tam·bu·list (nok tam′byə list), *n.* a sleepwalker; somnambulist.

noc·ti·flo·rous (nok′tə flôr′əs, -flōr′-), *adj. Botany.* flowering at night. [< Latin *nox, noctis* night + *flōs, flōris* + English *-ous*]

noc·ti·lu·ca (nok′tə lü′kə), *n., pl.* **-cae** (-sē). any of certain luminescent marine flagellates that gather together in great masses, often causing ocean waves to glow after nightfall. [earlier, a type of phosphorus < Latin *noctilūca* something shining at night < *nox, noctis* night + *lūcēre* to shine]

noc·ti·lu·cence (nok′tə lü′səns), *n.* noctilucent or phosphorescent quality.

noc·ti·lu·cent (nok′tə lü′sənt), *adj.* shining or luminous at night; phosphorescent: *The thin, noctilucent clouds, which can be observed only at twilight, suddenly change shape and move rapidly* (Science News Letter). [< Latin *nox, noctis* night + *lucēns, -entis,* present participle of *lūcēre* to shine]

noc·tiv·a·gant (nok tiv′ə gənt), *adj.* wandering by night. [< Latin *nox, noctis* night + *vagāns, -antis,* present participle of *vagāre* wander]

noc·to·graph (nok′tə graf, -gräf), *n.* a frame with horizontal rows of wires to help blind people write without running lines together: *He managed to surmount his physical handicap by methodical living . . . and by a simple device called a noctograph* (Samuel Eliot Morison). [< Latin *nox, noctis* night + English *-graph*]

noc·tu·id (nok′chu̇ id), *adj.* of a very large group of usually dull-colored, nocturnal moths including most of those attracted to lights at night. Many of their larvae are injurious to crops, as the cutworms, army worms, and cotton worms. —*n.* a noctuid moth. [< New Latin *Noctuidae* the family name < Latin *noctua* a night owl < *nox, noctis* night]

noc·tule (nok′chül), *n.* a large brown bat of Europe. [< French *noctule,* adaptation of Italian *nottola* bat, perhaps < Vulgar Latin *noctula* < Latin *nox, noctis* night]

noc·tur·nal (nok tėr′nəl), *adj.* **1.** of the night; in the night: *Stars are a nocturnal sight.* **2.** active in the night: *The owl is a nocturnal bird.* **3.** closed by day, open by night: *a nocturnal flower.* [< Late Latin *nocturnālis* < Latin *nocturnus* < *nox, noctis* night. Compare DIURNAL.]

nocturnal arc, *Archaic.* the part of the diurnal circle of a heavenly body below the horizon.

noc·tur·nal·i·ty (nok′tėr nal′ə tē), *n.* the quality, condition, or habit of being nocturnal.

noc·tur·nal·ly (nok tėr′nə lē), *adv.* **1.** at night. **2.** every night.

noc·turne (nok′tėrn), *n.* **1.** a dreamy or pensive musical piece: *Nocturnes in G major and G minor are among Chopin's most beautiful compositions in this most Chopinesque genre* (C. Wierzynski). **2.** a painting of a night scene. [< French, Middle French *nocturne,* learned borrowing from Latin *nocturnus* nocturnal]

noc·u·ous (nok′yu̇ əs), *adj.* noxious; hurtful; poisonous: *a nocuous gas.* [< Latin *nocuus* (with English *-ous*) < *nocēre* to harm] —**noc′u·ous·ly,** *adv.* —**noc′u·ous·ness,** *n.*

nod (nod), *v.,* **nod·ded, nod·ding,** *n.* —*v.t.* **1.** to bow (the head) slightly and raise it again quickly. **2.** to express by bowing the head: *to nod consent.* **3.** to invite, send, or bring by nodding the head: *He nodded me into the room. Cleopatra Hath nodded him to her* (Shakespeare). **4.** to cause to bend or sway: *When the whale-boats . . . nodded their slender masts at each other, and the dories pitched and tossed in the turf* (Hawthorne).
—*v.i.* **1.** to make a quick bow of the head, as in greeting, giving a command, or communicating a certain meaning: *He nods at us, as who should say, I'll be even with you* (Shakespeare). **2.** to indicate approval by nodding. **3.** to let the head fall forward and bob when sleepy or falling asleep: *The sentinel . . . began to nod at his post* (Washington Irving). **4.** to be sleepy; become careless and dull: *Reason still keeps its throne, but it nods a little, that's all* (George Farquhar). **5.** to droop, bend, or sway back and forth: *Trees nod in the wind. Or columbines, in purple dressed, Nod o'er the ground-bird's hidden nest* (William Cullen Bryant).
—*n.* **1. a.** a nodding of the head: *He gave us a nod as he passed.* **b.** a short sleep; nap. **2.** a sign of approval: *With mute obeisance, grave and slow, Repaid by nod polite* (Oliver Wendell Holmes). **3.** a bending or swaying.
get or **give the nod,** *Informal.* **a.** to receive or give approval: *The merger must get the nod from stock-holders of both banks* (Wall Street Journal). **b.** to receive or give a victory or decision to: *The judges gave the nod to the challenger.*
[Middle English *nodden;* origin uncertain]

Nod (nod), *n.* the realm of sleep; sleep; land of nod. [< *Nod,* a Biblical place name. See Genesis 4:16.]

nod·al (nō′dəl), *adj.* having to do with nodes; like a node: *Powder inside the tube will settle and collect in little piles at nodal points where the air is not vibrating* (Scientific American).

nod·der (nod′ər), *n.* person or thing that nods.

nod·ding (nod′ing), *adj.* **1.** that nods: *nodding plumes.* **2.** *Botany.* bent or drooping downward, as a flower or bud. —**nod′ding·ly,** *adv.*

nodding acquaintance, **1.** a slight acquaintance with a person or persons, extending no further than recognition by a nod: *I have met with him at dinner, and have a nodding acquaintance with him* (Edmond Yates). **2.** the person or persons with whom one has such an acquaintance. **3.** a slight or superficial acquaintance with something: *Many English people have at least a nodding acquaintance with a wider range of wines than their French equivalents* (London Times).

nodding cap, a plant of the orchid family of eastern North America, with drooping purple flowers.

nod·dle[1] (nod′əl), *n. Informal.* the head: *Slatternly girls, without an idea inside their noddles* (Anthony Trollope). *Just now I've taen the fit o' rhyme, My barmie noddle's working prime* (Robert Burns). [Middle English *nodel* or *nodul* the back of the head; origin uncertain]

nod·dle[2] (nod′əl), *v.t., v.i.,* **-dled, -dling.** to nod (the head) quickly or slightly: *The bishop . . . noddling his head and beating time with his foot* (Thomas Love Peacock). [perhaps frequentative of *nod*]

nod·dled (nod′əld), *adj. Informal.* having a noddle or head: *idle, empty-noddled boarders* (Arnold Bennett).

nod·dy (nod′ē), *n., pl.* **-dies. 1.** a fool; simpleton: *To think that I should be such a noddy!* (Dickens). **2.** a soot-colored, heavy-bodied tern with a rounded tail that breeds in the West Indies and Florida Keys. It has a habit of nodding its head to other noddies it meets, and is so fearless of man as to be easily caught. [compare NODDLE[1], NODDLE[2]]

Noddy Tern (def. 2) (15 in. long)

node (nōd), *n.* **1.** a knot; knob; swelling. **2.** any joint in a stem; the part of a stem that bears a leaf or leaves. **3.** *Physics.* a point, line, or plane in a vibrating body at which there is comparatively no vibration. **4.** a central point in any system. **5.** *Geometry.* a point at which a curve crosses itself, or a similar point on a surface. **6.** *Astronomy.* either of the two points at which the orbit of a heavenly body intersects the fundamental plane. The plane may be the ecliptic in the case of a planet or the equatorial plane of a planet in the case of a planet's satellite. The ascending node is the node at which the body moves northward, the descending node is the node at which the body moves southward. **7.** a small knotlike swelling or mass of specialized tissue on the body or an organ: *a lymph node.* **8.** a lymph gland. **9.** a knot or complication in the plot or character development of a story, play, etc.: *There are characters which are continually creating collisions and nodes for themselves in dramas which nobody is prepared to act with them* (George Eliot). [earlier, complication, tumor < Latin *nōdus* knot]

Nodes (def. 2)

nod·i·cal (nod′ə kəl, nō′də-), *adj. Astronomy.* of or having to do with nodes.

No·don valve (nō dôN′), *Electricity.* a device for transforming alternating currents into direct currents, consisting of an electrolytic cell or cells containing a solution of ammonium phosphate and electrodes of lead and aluminum.

no·dose (nō′dōs, nō dōs′), *adj.* having nodes; knotty; knobbed. [< Latin *nōdōsus* knotty < *nōdus* node, knot]

no·dos·i·ty (nō dos′ə tē), *n., pl.* **-ties. 1.** the quality or state of being nodose. **2.** a knot; knob; knotty swelling: *It is not a good imitation of Johnson; it has all his pomp without his force; it has all the nodosities of the oak without its strength* (Edmund Burke).

no·dous (nō′dəs), *adj.* full of knots; knotty.

nod·u·lar (noj′ə lər), *adj.* having nodules: *21 had nodular thyroids, 11 of which were cancerous* (Science News Letter).

nod·u·late (noj′ə lāt), *v.t.,* **-lat·ed, -lat·ing.** to form nodular growths in: *Its surface is uneven and nodulated like that of a raspberry* (Robert B. Todd).

nod·ule (noj′ül), *n.* **1.** a small knot, knob, or swelling. **2.** a small, rounded mass or lump: *nodules of pure gold.* **3.** *Botany.* an enlargement on the roots of certain plants, mostly legumes, that contains symbiotic nitrogen-fixing bacteria. < Latin *nōdulus* (diminutive) < *nōdus* knot]

nod·u·lose (noj′ə lōs, noj′ə lōs′), *adj.* having little knots or knobs.

nod·u·lous (noj′ə ləs), *adj.* nodulose.

no·dus (nō′dəs), *n., pl.* **-di** (-dī). a difficulty or complication; knotty point or situation, as in a story, play, etc.: *The whole nodus may be more of a logical cobweb, than an actual material perplexity* (Thomas Carlyle). [< Latin *nōdus* knot]

No·e (nō′ə), *n.* Noah.

No·ël (nō el′), *n.* Christmas. [< French *Noël* < Latin *nātālis* natal (day, that is, specifically, of Christ) < *gnāscī* be born. Doublet of NATAL, NOWEL.]

no·ël (nō el′), *n.* **1.** a Christmas song; carol. **2.** an expression of joy used in Christmas songs. [< *Noël*]

no·e·sis (nō ē′sis), *n.* **1.** an act of pure intellect; a comprehending by the mind alone; reason. **2.** *Psychology.* the property of yielding or being knowledge; cognition. [< Greek *nóēsis* < *noeîn* have mental perception < *nóos* mind, thought]

no·et·ic (nō et′ik), *adj.* **1.** of or having to do with the mind or intellect. **2.** originating or existing in the mind. **3.** concerned with intellectual speculation.

nog[1] (nog), *n.* eggnog or the like made with alcoholic liquor. [short for *eggnog*]

nog[2] (nog), *n. British.* a strong ale or beer.

nog[3] (nog), *n., v.,* **nogged, nog·ging.** *British.* —*n.* **1.** a wooden peg, pin, or block used in shipbuilding, mining, and for other purposes. **2.** a small block of wood set into a brick wall, for nails.
—*v.t.* **1.** to secure, support, etc., by a nog or peg. **2.** to build with or as nogging.
[origin uncertain; perhaps variant of *knag*]

No·gai (nō gī′), *n., pl.* **-gais. 1.** a member of a Tartar people of northeastern Caucasia. **2.** their Turkic language.

no·ga·ku (nō′gä′kü), *n.* a classical Japanese dramatic dance; no[2]. [< Japanese *nō-gaku*]

nogg (nog), *n.* nog[1].

nog·gin (nog′in), *n.* **1.** a small mug. **2.** a small drink, especially of an alcoholic liquor; pint: *Many a noggin of whiskey is here quaffed* (Hawthorne). **3.** *Informal.* a person's head: *This thought kept chasing through our noggin* (New York Times).

nog·ging (nog′ing), *n. British.* bricks or brickwork set between the crossed boards of a wooden frame.

no-good (nō′gůd′), *Informal.* —*n.* a worthless person; rogue: *The officer is plainly a no-good, but . . . his wife is no domestic bargain* (John McCarten). —*adj.* good-for-nothing; worthless: *Nor have we met more of a no-good scoundrel . . . who . . . suffers less for his knavery* (New York Times).

noh or **Noh** (nō), *n.* a classical Japanese dramatic dance; no[2]: *Noh, which is the oldest dramatic achievement of the Japanese originated with the Samurai class* (Atlantic). [< Japanese *nō*]

no-hit·ter (nō′hit′ər), *n. U.S.* a baseball game in which a pitcher gives up no base hits to the opposing team in nine or more innings: *The chances of a no-hitter are very slim; of some 50,000 major league games, only 86 have been no-hitters* (Time).

no-holds-barred (nō′hōldz′bärd′), *adj. Informal.* **1.** unrestrained; uninhibited; violent: *a no-holds-barred fight, a no-holds-barred jazz program.* **2.** all-out; complete: *a no-holds-barred effort or attempt.*

no-hop·er (nō′hō′pər), *n. Australian.* a worthless, lazy person.

no·how (nō′hou′), *adv. Informal or (with another negative) Dialect.* in no way; not at all: *That don't dovetail nohow* (Charles Reade).

n.o.i.b.n., not otherwise indexed by name.

noil (noil), *n.* **1.** a short fiber or knot of wool, cotton, or silk, separated from the long fiber in combing. **2.** waste material composed of such pieces. [origin unknown]

no-i·ron (nō′ī′ərn), *adj. Informal.* that does not require ironing: *a drip-dry, no-iron shirt.*

noise (noiz), *n., v.,* **noised, nois·ing.** —*n.* **1.** a sound that is not musical or pleasant: *the noise of breaking dishes, the noise of machinery, the noise of thunder.* **2.** a sound: *the little noises in the woods at night; the reapers' rustling noise* (Robert Burns). **3.** a din of voices and movements; loud shouting; outcry; clamor: *The boys made too much noise at the movie and were asked to leave. Whose noise is this that cries on murder?* (Shakespeare). **4. a.** *Physics.* a group of sound waves which are not periodic and which are produced by irregular vibrations; sound of no single fundamental frequency but many nonharmonic frequency components of varying amplitudes randomly placed. **b.** any undesired or unintended disturbance in a radio or television signal. **5.** public talk about some matter of interest or wonder: *The first [ballad] sold wonderfully, the event being recent, having made a great noise* (Benjamin Franklin). **6.** *Archaic.* music or a sound of music: *Thus all Israel brought up the ark . . . and with sound of the cornet, and with trumpets, and with cymbals, making a noise with psalteries and harps* (I Chronicles 15:28). **7.** *Archaic.* a rumor; report: *So grateful is the noise of noble deeds to noble hearts* (Tennyson). **8.** *Obsolete.* a band of musicians: *see if thou cans't find out Sneak's noise* (Shakespeare).
make a noise in the world, to arouse public talk; make a public sensation: *It was pronounced . . . the greatest poem of the age, and all anticipated the noise it would make in the great world* (Washington Irving).
—*v.t.* to spread the news of; report; tell: *It was noised about that the company was going out of business. All these sayings were noised abroad* (Luke 1:65). *It is noised he hath a mass of treasure* (Shakespeare).
—*v.i.* **1.** to make a noise or outcry: *Noising loud And threatening high* (Milton). **2.** to talk publicly or much.
[< Old French *noise* uproar, brawl < Latin *nausea,* probably in Vulgar Latin, unpleasant condition (of various kinds). Doublet of NAUSEA.]
—**Syn.** *n.* **1. Noise, din, uproar** mean disagreeably loud, confused, or harsh and clashing sound. **Noise** applies to any disagreeably unmusical or loud sound made by one or more people or things: *The noise kept me awake.* **Din** applies to a prolonged and deafening confusion or clanging or piercing noises: *The din of machines and factory whistles hurt my ears.* **Uproar** applies especially to the tumult, shouting, and loud noises of a crowd: *You should have heard the uproar when officials called back the touchdown.* **2.** See **sound**[1]. **3.** babble, uproar, hubbub, tumult.

noise·ful (noiz′fəl), *adj.* noisy.

noise·less (noiz′lis), *adj.* **1.** making no noise; silent: *a noiseless step. I stood and watched by the window The noiseless work of the sky* (Lowell). **2.** making little noise; nearly quiet: *a noiseless typewriter.* —**noise′less·ly,** *adv.* —**noise′less·ness,** *n.* —**Syn. 1.** mute.

noise·mak·er (noiz′mā′kər), *n.* **1.** a person who makes too much noise. **2.** a thing that makes noise, especially a horn, rattle, etc., used to make noise at a party: *There would be some dreadful romp on Christmas Eve with trick hats and noisemakers* (New Yorker).

noi·sette[1] (nwȧ zet′, noi-), *n.* a variety of rose, supposedly a cross between a China rose and a musk rose. [< Philippe *Noisette,* a French horticulturist, who developed it]

noi·sette[2] (nwȧ zet′), *n.* veal, lamb, mutton, etc., cooked in small, round pieces, served with vegetables. [< French *noisette* a nut (diminutive) < *noix* < Latin *nux, nucis* (because of the resemblance in shape)]

nois·i·ly (noi′zə lē), *adv.* in a noisy manner.

nois·i·ness (noi′zē nis), *n.* a being noisy; making a noise.

noi·some (noi′səm), *adj.* **1.** offensive; disgusting; smelling bad: *a noisome odor, a noisome slum; kitchens and areas with noisome sewers* (Charles Kingsley). **2.** harmful; injurious: *a noisome pestilence; the noisome beast* (Ezekiel 14:21). [Middle English *noy,* variant of *annoy* + *-some*[1]] —**noi′some·ly,** *adv.* —**noi′some·ness,** *n.* —**Syn. 1.** foul. **2.** noxious.

nois·y (noi′zē), *adj.,* **nois·i·er, nois·i·est. 1.** making much noise: *a noisy boy, a noisy crowd, a noisy engine.* **2.** full of noise: *a noisy street, a noisy house.* **3.** having much noise with it: *a noisy quarrel, a noisy party.* —**Syn. 1.** shouting, clamorous, brawling, blatant. See **loud.**

no·lens vo·lens (nō′lenz vō′lenz), *Latin.* whether willing or unwilling; willy-nilly: *Well, nolens volens, you must hold your tongue* (Scott).

no·li-me-tan·ge·re or **no·li me tan·ge·re** (nō′lī mē tan′jə rē), *Latin.* —*n.* **1.** a notice that a person or thing must not be touched or interfered with: *I see it everywhere. In your work. In the way you stand, backed up against the wall. In your books. Noli me tangere* (New Yorker). **2.** a picture portraying the appearance of Jesus to Mary Magdalene after the Resurrection. John 20:17. **3.** the touch-me-not (plant). **4.** *Medicine.* an open sore on the face or a lupus of the nose; rodent ulcer. —*adj.* (literally) touch me not: *a sort of noli me tangere manner* (Thomas De Quincey).

noll (nōl, nol), *n. Obsolete.* the head. [Old English *hnoll*]

nol·le pros·e·qui (nol′ē pros′ə kwī), *Law.* an entry made upon the records of a court by the plaintiff or prosecutor that he will proceed no further in a suit. [< Latin *nōlle prōsequī* be unwilling to pursue or prosecute]

no·lo con·ten·de·re (nō′lō kən ten′də rē), *Law.* a defendant's plea that he will accept conviction but not admit his guilt: *The agencies pleaded nolo contendere to the criminal suit, and entered into a consent decree with respect to the civil* (Time). [< Latin *nōlō contendere* I do not wish to contend]

nol·pros (nol′pros′), *v.t.,* **-prossed, -pros sing.** *Law.* to abandon (a lawsuit or indictment) by entering a nolle prosequi. [American English, short for Latin *nōlle prōsequī*]

nol. pros., nolle prosequi.

nolt (nōlt), *n. Scottish.* cattle; neat. [variant of Scottish *nowt* cattle]

nom., nominative.

no·ma (nō′mə), *n.* a gangrenous open sore of the mouth and cheeks, occurring mainly in children weakened by disease.
[< Latin *nomae,* plural, any "eating" ulcer < Greek *nomaí,* plural of *nomē* pasturage, a spreading, related to *némein* to feed, graze]

no·mad (nō′mad, nom′ad), *n.* **1.** a member of a tribe that moves from place to place to find food, have pasture for its cattle, etc.: *Moslem emirs still rule their cattle-raising nomads by the laws of the Koran* (Newsweek). **2.** a wanderer.
—*adj.* **1.** wandering from place to place to find pasture. **2.** wandering: *the nomad existence of the Gypsies.*
[< Latin *Nŏmas, -adis* a wandering tribe < Greek *nomás, -ados,* ultimately < *némein* to pasture]
—**Syn.** *n.* **2.** rover.

no·mad·ic (nō mad′ik), *adj.* **1.** of nomads or their life: *a nomadic custom. The geography of Asia and of Africa necessitated a nomadic life* (Emerson). **2.** wandering; roving: *Most of the Indians of the North American plains were nomadic.* —**no·mad′i·cal·ly,** *adv.*

no·mad·i·cal (nō mad′ə kəl), *adj.* nomadic.

no·mad·ism (nō′mad iz əm), *n.* the way that nomads live: *Nomadism cuts men off from fixed temples and intense local associations* (H.G. Wells).

no man's land, **1.** (in war) the land between opposing lines of trenches. **2.** a tract of land to which no one has a recognized or established claim. **3.** a scope of activity over which no jurisdiction or authority exists: *an ambiguous no man's land between Communism and democracy.*

nom·arch (nom′ärk), *n.* the governor of a nome or nomarchy. [earlier, a local governor < Greek *nomárchēs* < *nomós* nome + *árchein* to rule]

nom·ar·chy (nom′är kē), *n., pl.* **-ar·chies.** one of the provinces into which modern Greece is divided for administrative purposes; nomos.

nom·bles (num′bəlz), *n.pl. Archaic.* numbles.

nom·bril (nom′brəl), *n.* (in heraldry) the point in an escutcheon midway between the fess point and the middle base point; navel. [< French *nombril* navel]

Nombril
A, fess point; B, nombril; C, middle base point

nom de guerre (nôN′ də ger′), an assumed name under which to pursue a profession, undertaking, or the like; pseudonym: *Malraux . . . fought under a nom de guerre in the French Resistance* (New Yorker).
[< French *nom de guerre* (literally) war name]

nom de plume (nom′ də plüm′), a name used by a writer instead of his real name; pen name; pseudonym: *Samuel L. Clemens used "Mark Twain" as his nom de plume.*
[coined from French *nom* name, *de* of, *plume* pen]
➤ **Nom de plume** is an English usage coined from French words, as the etymology indicates, and the equivalent French phrase is *nom de guerre.*

nome[1] (nōm), *n.* **1.** a province of ancient Egypt. **2.** an administrative department of modern Greece; nomos; nomarchy. [< Greek *nomós* any of the 36 divisions of Egypt < *némein* to divide, distribute; allot for grazing]

nome[2] (nōm), *v. Archaic.* a past participle of **nim.**

no·men[1] (nō′men), *n., pl.* **nom·i·na** (nom′ə nə). (in ancient Rome) the name of one's clan or gens. *Julius* in *Gaius Julius Caesar* is his *nomen,* indicating membership in the clan of *Julii.* [< Latin *nōmen* (literally) name. Doublet of NOUN.]

no·men[2] (nō′mən), *v. Archaic.* a past participle of **nim.**

no·men·cla·tor (nō′mən klā′tər), *n.* **1.** a person who announces the names of persons or guests. **2.** a person who gives or assigns names to objects that are scientifically classified. [< Latin *nōmenclātor* < *nōmen* name + *calāre* to call (out)]

no·men·cla·to·ri·al (nō men′klə tôr′ē əl, -tōr′-), *adj.* having to do with naming or nomenclature.

no·men·cla·to·ry (nō men′klə tôr′ē, -tōr′-), *adj.* nomenclatorial.

no·men·cla·tur·al (nō′mən klā′chər əl), *adj.* of or having to do with nomenclature: *nomenclatural rules, nomenclatural oddities.* —**no′men·cla′tur·al·ly,** *adv.*

no·men·cla·ture (nō′mən klā′chər, nō-men′klə-), *n.* a set or system of names or terms as in a particular science, art, etc.: *the nomenclature of music. Another Ford venture into nomenclature, "Thunderbird," was a notable success* (New York Times). [< Latin *nōmenclātūra* < *nōmen* name + *calāre* to call (out)] —**Syn.** terminology.

no·men·cla·tur·ist (nō′mən klā′chər ist), *n.* a person who devises a nomenclature.

nom·i·nal (nom′ə nəl), *adj.* **1.** being so in name only; not real: *a position with merely nominal duties. The president is the nominal head of the club, but the secretary really runs its affairs. A state of nominal peace existed between Spain, France, and England* (John L. Motley). **2.** so small that it is not worth considering; unimportant compared with the real value: *We paid a nominal rent for the cottage—$5 a month.* **3. a.** giving the name or names: *the nominal accounts of a business, a nominal list of the students in a class.* **b.** mentioning specifically by name: *a nominal appeal.* **c.** assigned to a person by name: *a nominal share of stock.* **4.** *Grammar.* **a.** of or having to do with a noun or nouns. *Day* is the nominal root of *daily, daybreak,* and *Sunday.* **b.** (of a word or phrase) used or functioning as a noun or nouns. *Rich* and *poor* in the phrase *the rich and the poor* are nominal adjectives. **5.** of, having to do with, or consisting in a name or names.
—*n.* a word or group of words functioning as a noun.
[< Latin *nōminālis* < *nōmen, -inis* name]
—**Syn.** *adj.* **2.** trivial, negligible.

nom·i·nal·ism (nom′ə nə liz′əm), *n.* the philosophical doctrine that all abstract or general terms, such as *circle* or *man,* do not stand for real things, but exist for convenience in thought and are a necessary part of language.

nom·i·nal·ist (nom′ə nə list), *n.* a believer in nominalism. —*adj.* nominalistic.

nom·i·nal·is·tic (nom′ə nə lis′tik), *adj.* of or having to do with nominalists or nominalism.

nom·i·nal·ly (nom′ə nə lē), *adv.* **1.** in name only; as a matter of form; in a nominal way only. **2.** by name.

nominal sentence, *Grammar.* a sentence without a verb; equational sentence.

nominal value, an assigned value, as the face or par value of a share of stock.

nominal wages, wages in terms simply of money, without regard to purchasing power.

nom·i·nate (*v.* nom′ə nāt; *adj.* nom′ə nit, -nāt), *v.,* **-nat·ed, -nat·ing,** *adj.* —*v.t.* **1.** to name as candidate for an office: *Three times the Democratic Party nominated William Jennings Bryan for President, but he was never elected.* **2.** to appoint for an office or duty: *The President nominated him as Secretary of State.* **3.** to call by a certain name; mention by name. **4.** *Archaic.* to fix; specify: *Let the forfeit Be nominated for an equal pound Of your fair flesh* (Shakespeare).
—*adj.* **1.** having or mentioning a particular name. **2.** nominated, as to an office.
[< Latin *nōmināre* (with English *-ate*[1]) < *nōmen, -inis* name]
—**Syn. 1.** designate. **3.** entitle.

nom·i·na·tion (nom′ə nā′shən), *n.* **1.** a naming as a candidate for office: *In their nomination to office they will not appoint to the exercise of authority as to a pitiful job, but as to a holy function* (Edmund Burke). **2.** selection for office or duty; appointment to office or duty. **3.** a being nominated.

nom·i·na·ti·val (nom′ə nə tī′vəl, nom′-nə-), *adj.* of or having to do with the nominative case.

nom·i·na·tive (nom′ə nə tiv, -nā′-; nom′-nə-), *adj.* **1.** *Grammar.* **a.** designating the case of a noun or pronoun used as the subject of a finite verb, as the complement of a linking verb, etc., and of a noun, pronoun, or adjective in grammatical agreement with the subject, complement, etc. (as an appositive or a modifier). **b.** designating a distinctive inflectional form thus used. The Modern English pronouns *I, he, she, we, they,* and *who* are in nominative case. **2.** appointed by nomination; nominated. **3.** assigned to a person by name: *a nominative warrant, nominative shares of stock.*
—*n. Grammar.* **1.** the nominative case. **2.** a word in that case. *Abbr.:* nom.
[< Latin *nōminātīvus* < *nōmināre;* see NOMINATE]

nominative absolute, *Grammar.* a construction consisting of a substantive and its modifier (usually a participle) and not grammatically related to any other element in the sentence. *Example:* The day being warm, we took off our coats (*The day being warm* is a nominative absolute).

nominative of address, *Grammar.* a noun naming the person to whom one is speaking. *Example:* John, where is your coat? (*John* is the nominative of address).

nom·i·na·tor (nom′ə nā′tər), *n.* a person who nominates.

nom·i·nee (nom′ə nē′), *n.* a person who is nominated, especially for or to some office. —**Syn.** See **candidate.**

no·mism (nō′miz əm), *n.* the basing of religious conduct on moral law as derived from some sacred work. [< Greek *nómos* law + English *-ism*]

no·mis·tic (nō mis′tik), *adj.* of or founded on nomism.

no·moc·ra·cy (nō mok′rə sē), *n., pl.* **-cies.** government established and carried out in accordance with a code of laws. [< Greek *nomokratíā* < *nómos* law + *krátos* rule]

nom·o·gram (nom′ə gram), *n.* **1.** *Mathematics.* a chart from which one can determine by alignment of scales the value of a dependent variable for any given value of the independent variable. **2.** any device which depicts numerical relations graphically. [< Greek *nómos* law + English *-gram*]

Nomogram (def. 1) for $A^2 + B^2 = C^2$. If A = 3 and B = 4, the line drawn shows that C = 5.

nom·o·graph (nom′ə-graf, -gräf), *n.* nomogram.

no·mog·ra·phy (nō mog′rə fē), *n., pl.* **-phies.** **1. a.** the art or process of drawing up laws. **b.** a book on this subject. **2.** the science of computation by means of graphs. [< Greek *nomographíā* < *nómos* law + *gráphein* write, draw]

nom·o·log·i·cal (nom′ə loj′ə kəl), *adj.* of or having to do with nomology.

no·mol·o·gy (nō mol′ə jē), *n.* **1.** the science of law. **2.** the formulation of scientific laws. [< Greek *nómos* law + English *-logy*]

nom·o·pel·mous (nom′ə pel′məs), *adj.* (of a bird's toes) having one flexor tendon going to the first digit and the other going to the remaining three digits. [< Greek *nómos* custom, law + *pélma* sole of the foot + English *-ous*]

no·mos (nō′mos), *n., pl.* **-moi** (-moi). *Greek.* a nomarchy; a nome: *Greece is divided into 51 nomoi, or departments.*

nom·o·thet·ic (nom′ə thet′ik), *adj.* **1.** lawgiving or lawmaking; legislative. **2.** founded on law. **3.** of or having to do with a science of general or universal laws. [< Greek *nomothetikós* < *nomothétēs* a lawgiver <

nómos law + *thétēs* one who sets, gives, related to *tithénai* set, place]

nom·o·thet·i·cal (nom′ə thet′ə kəl), *adj.* nomothetic.

non (nôɴ), *n., pl.* **nons** (nôɴ). *French.* no: *The most optimistic calculations showed the treaty would get 301 nons and only 287 ouis* (Newsweek).

non-, *prefix.* not; not a; opposite of; lack of; failure of, as in *nonconformity, nonacceptance, nonpayment.* [< Latin *nōn-* < *nōn* not, not a < Old Latin *noenum* < *ne-* not + unrecorded *oinom,* accusative of *oinos* one]

➔ If an adjective formed with *non-* is not defined in this dictionary, its meaning will be clear if *not* is put in the place of the *non,* as in *nonabsorbent, noncompetitive, nongenetic, nonparental.*

If a noun formed with *non-* is not defined, its meaning will be clear if *not, not a, the opposite of,* or *the absence of* is put in place of the *non,* as in *nonadmission, noninfection, nonremission, nonsubscriber.*

Non- is a living prefix and may be used with any noun, adjective, or adverb; but if there is a commonly used word of the same meaning formed with *un-, in-,* or *dis-,* that word is usually preferable. Some of the words that have *non-* as the preferred usage, or as a respectable rival of *un-,* are defined below.

non′ab·sorb′ent
non′ab·stain′er
non′ab·stract′
non′ac·a·dem′ic
non·ac′cent
non·ac′id
non′a·cous′tic
non′ac·tin′ic
non·ac′tion
non·ac′tive
non′ad·dic′tive
non′ad·he′sive
non′ad·ja′cent
non′ad·jec·ti′val
non′ad·min′is·tra′tive
non′ad·mis′sion
non′ad·van·ta′geous
non′ad·verb′i·al
non′aes·thet′ic
non-Af′ri·can
non′ag·gres′sive
non′ag·ri·cul′tur·al
non′al·co·hol′ic
non′al·le′giance
non′al·lit′er·a′tive
non′-A·mer′i·can
non-An′gli·can
non′an·tag′o·nis′tic
non′a·pol′o·get′ic
non′ap·o·stol′ic
non′ap·peal′a·ble
non′ap·pear′ing
non′ap·pre·hen′sion
non′ap·proach′
non′a·quat′ic
non·a′que·ous
non-Ar′ab
non-Ar′a·bic
non′a·ris′to·crat′ic
non′ar·o·mat′ic
non′ar·tic′u·lat′ed
non-Ar′y·an
non′-A·si·at′ic
non′as·ser′tive
non′as·sess′a·ble
non′as·sign′a·ble
non′as·sim′i·la·ble
non′as·sim′i·la′tion
non′as·so′cia·ble
non′as·so′ci·a′tion
non′at·mos·pher′ic
non′a·tom′ic
non′at·trib′ut·a·ble
non′at·trib′u·tive
non′au·ric′u·lar
non′au·thor′i·ta′tive
non′au·to·mat′ic
non′au·to·mo′tive
non′bac·te′ri·al
non·ba′sic
non·be′ing
non′be·liev′er
non′be·liev′ing
non′bel·lig′er·ent
non′be·nev′o·lent
non-Bib′li·cal
non·bind′ing
non·bit′ing
non·bloom′ing
non-Bol′she·vist
non·break′a·ble
non·breed′ing
non-Brit′ish
non-Bud′dhist
non·bud′ding
non′bu·reau·crat′ic
non·busi′ness
non·cak′ing
non′cal·car′e·ous
non·call′a·ble
non′ca·lor′ic
non-Cal′vin·ist
non·can′cer·ous
non′ca·non′i·cal
non′cap·i·tal·is′tic
non′ca·reer′
non′car·niv′o·rous
non′cat·a·stroph′ic
non′cat·e·gor′i·cal
non-Cath′o·lic
non′-Cau·ca′sian
non·caus′a·tive
non′ce·les′tial
non·cel′lu·lar
non-Cel′tic
non·cen′tral
non·ce′re·al
non·cer′e·bral
non·cer′ti·fied
non·charge′a·ble
non·chem′i·cal
non′-Chi·nese′
non-Chris′tian
non·church′
non·cil′i·ate
non·cit′i·zen
non·civ′i·lized
non·clas′si·cal
non·clas′si·fi′a·ble
non·clas′si·fied
non·cler′i·cal
non·clin′i·cal
non·clot′ting
non′co·a·les′cing
non′co·er′cive
non·cog′ni·tive
non′co·her′ent
non′co·he′sive
non′col·lab′o·ra′tive
non′col·laps′i·ble
non′col·lect′a·ble
non·col′loid
non′co·lo′ni·al
non·com′bat
non′com·bin′ing
non′com·bus′ti·ble
non′com·mer′cial
non′com·mu′ni·ca·ble
non′com·mu′ni·cant
non′com·mu′ni·cat′ing
non′com·mu′ni·ca′tion
non·com′mu·nist
non·com′pen·sat′ing
non·com′pe·ten·cy
non′com·pet′ing
non′com·pet′i·tive
non′com·ple′tion
non′com·ply′ing
non′com·pres′si·ble
non′com·pres′sion
non′com·pul′sion
non′con·ceal′ment
non′con·cen·tra′tion
non′con·cil′i·at′ing
non′con·cord′ant
non′con·cur′rence
non′con·cur′ren·cy
non′con·den′sa·ble
non′con·du′cive
non′con·duc′ti·bil′i·ty
non′con·duc′tion
non′con·duc′tive
non′con·fer′ra·ble
non·con′fi·dence
non′con·fi·den′tial
non′con·fis′ca·ble
non′con·flict′ing
non′con·form′ing
non′con·geal′ing
non′con·gen′i·tal
non′con·ges′tion
non′-Con·gres′sion·al
non·con′gru·ent
non′con·nec′tive
non′con·niv′ance
non′con·sec′u·tive
non′con·sent′
non′con·sent′ing
non′con·ser·va′tion
non′con·serv′a·tive
non′con·sol′i·dat′ed
non′con·spir′ing
non′con·sti·tu′tion·al
non′con·struc′tive
non′con·sul′ta·tive
non′con·ta′gious
non·con′tem·pla′tive
non′con·tem′po·rar′y
non′con·ten′tious
non′con·tig′u·ous
non′con·ti·nen′tal
non′con·tin′u·ance
non′con·tin′u·ous
non·con′tra·band
non′con·trac′tile
non′con·trac′tu·al
non′con·tra·dic′to·ry
non′con·trib′u·tor
non′con·trib′u·to′ry
non′con·trolled′
non′con·tro·ver′sial
non′con·ven′tion·al
non′con·ver′gent
non′con·ver′sant
non′con·ver′ti·ble
non′con·vic′tion
non′co·or′di·na′tion
non·cor′po·rate
non′cor·rec′tive
non′cor·res·pond′ence
non′cor·re·spond′ing
non′cor·rob′o·ra′tive
non′cor·rod′ing
non′cor·ro′sive
non·cos′mic
non′cre·a′tive
non·cred′i·ble
non·cred′i·tor
non·crim′i·nal
non·crit′i·cal
non·cru′cial
non·crys′tal·line
non·cul′pa·ble
non′cul·ti·va′tion
non·cu′mu·la′tive
non·cy′clic
non·cy′cli·cal
non-Czech′
non·dam′age·a·ble
non′-Dar·win′i·an
non′de·cay′ing
non′de·cep′tive
non′de·cid′u·ous
non′de·duc′ti·ble
non′de·fam′a·to′ry
non′de·fec′tive
non′de·fense′
non′de·fen′sive
non′de·fer′a·ble
non′def·er·en′tial
non′de·file′ment
non′de·fin′ing
non′de·gen′er·a′tion
non′de·his′cent
non′de·lin′e·a′tion
non′de·lir′i·ous
non′de·liv′er·a·ble
non′de·mand′
non′dem·o·crat′ic
non′de·nom′i·na′tion·al
non′de·part·men′tal
non′de·par′ture
non′de·pend′ence
non′de·ple′tion
non′de·pos′i·tor
non′de·pre′ci·a′ting
non′de·riv′a·ble
non′de·riv′a·tive
non′de·rog′a·to′ry
non′des·pot′ic
non′de·tach′a·ble
non·det′o·nat′ing
non′de·vel′op·ment
non′de·vo′tion·al
non′di·a·bet′ic
non′di·a·lect′al
non′dic·ta·to′ri·al
non′di·dac′tic
non′dif·fer·en′ti·a′tion
non′dif·frac′tive
non′dif·fus′ing
non′dif·fu′sion
non′di·lat′a·ble
non′dip·lo·mat′ic
non′di·rec′tion·al
non·dir′i·gi·ble
non′dis·ap·pear′ing
non′dis·charg′ing
non·dis′ci·plin·ar′y
non·dis′count·a·ble
non′dis·crim′i·na′tion
non′dis·crim′i·na·to′ry
non′dis·fran′chised
non′dis·par′ag·ing
non′dis·per′sion
non′dis·pos′al
non′dis·sem′i·na′tion
non′dis·tri·bu′tion
non′dis·trib′u·tive
non′di·ver′gent
non′-di·ver′si·fied
non′di·vis′i·ble
non′doc·tri·naire′
non·doc′tri·nal
non′doc·u·men′ta·ry
non′dog·mat′ic
non′do·mes′ti·cat′ed
non′dra·mat′ic
non·dry′ing
non·du′ti·a·ble
non′dy·nas′tic
non·earn′ing
non′ec·cle′si·as′tic
non′ec·lec′tic
non′ec·o·nom′ic
non·ed′i·ble
non′ed·i·to′ri·al
non·ed′u·ca·ble
non′ed·u·ca′tion·al
non′ef·fer·ves′cent
non′ef·fi·ca′cious
non′ef·fi′cient
non′e·gal′i·tar′i·an
non′e·las′tic
non′e·lect′
non′e·lect′ed
non′e·lec′tion
non′e·lec′tive
non′e·lec′tric
non′e·lec′tri·cal
non′e·lec′tri·fied
non′e·lec′tro·lyte
non′el·e·men′ta·ry
non′e·mo′tion·al
non′em·phat′ic
non′em·pir′i·cal
non′en·cy′clo·pe′dic
non′en·dem′ic
non′en·force′a·ble
non′en·force′ment
non-Eng′lish
non′en·tailed′
non′en·vi′ron·men′tal
non′e·phem′er·al
non′e·pis′co·pal
non′-E·pis′co·pa′lian
non·e′qual
non′e·quiv′a·lent
non′e·quiv′o·cat′ing
non′e·rot′ic
non′e·ter′nal
non·eth′i·cal
non′eth·no·log′i·cal
non′Eu·clid′e·an
non′eu·gen′ic
non′-Eu·ro·pe′an
non′e·van·gel′i·cal
non′e·vic′tion
non′ev·o·lu′tion·ar′y
non′ex·change′a·ble
non′ex·clu′sive
non′ex·cus′a·ble
non′ex·e·cu′tion
non′ex·ec′u·tive
non′ex·empt′
non′ex·is′tent
non′ex·ist′ing
non′ex·ot′ic
non′ex·pan′si·ble
non′ex·pan′sive
non′ex·pe′ri·enced
non′ex·per′i·men′tal
non·ex′pert
non′ex·ploi·ta′tion
non′ex·plo′sive
non′ex·port′a·ble
non′ex·por·ta′tion
non′ex·tend′ed
non′ex·ten′sile
non′ex·ten′sion
non′ex·ter′nal
non·ex′tra·dit′a·ble
non′ex·tra′ne·ous
non·ex′tro·vert
non·fac′tu·al
non·fad′ing
non·fam′i·ly
non′fa·nat′i·cal
non·fan′ci·ful
non·farm′
non-Fas′cist
non′fas·tid′i·ous
non·fat′
non·fa′tal
non′fa·tal·is′tic
non·fed′er·al
non·fed′er·at′ed
non′fer·ment′a·ble
non·fer′tile
non·fes′tive
non·feu′dal
non·fic′tion·al
non′fi·du′ci·ar·y
non′fi·nan′cial
non·fire′proof′
non·fis′cal
non·fis′sion·a·ble
non·flow′er·ing
non·flow′ing
non·fluc′tu·at′ing
non·fo′cal
non·food′
non·for′feit·a·ble
non·for′feit·ing
non·for′fei·ture
non·for′mal
non′for·tu′i·tous
non′fos·sil·if′er·ous
non·fraud′u·lent
non·freez′ing
non-French′
non·fric′a·tive
non·func′tion·al
non·func′tion·ing
non′fun·da·men′tal
non·gas′e·ous
non′ge·lat′i·nous
non·gen′er·a′tive
non′ge·net′ic
non-Gen′tile
non-Ger′man
non′-Ger·man′ic
non-Goth′ic
non′gov·ern·men′tal
non·gran′u·lar
non-Greek′
non′gre·gar′i·ous
non·hab′it·a·ble
non′ha·bit′u·al
non′har·mo′ni·ous
non·haz′ard·ous
non·hea′then
non′he·don·is′tic
non′-Hel·len′ic
non′he·red′i·tar′y
non·her′it·a·ble
non·her′i·tor
non·hi′ber·nat′ing
non·hi′ber·na′tor
non′-Hi·ber′ni·an
non′his·tor′ic
non′his·tor′i·cal
non′ho·mo·ge′ne·ous
non·hon′o·rar′y
non·hos′tile
non·hu′man
non·hu′mor·ous
non·hy′dro·gen·at′ed
non′hy·gro·scop′ic
non′i·den′ti·cal
non′i·den′ti·ty
non·i′de·o·log′i·cal
non′id·i·o·mat′ic
non′i·dol′a·trous
non′ig·nit′i·ble
non′i·mag′i·nar′y
non·im′i·ta′tive
non′im·mune′
non′im·mu′ni·ty
non·im′mu·nized
non′im·per′a·tive
non′im·pe′ri·al
non′im·por·ta′tion
non′im·preg′nat·ed
non′im·pres′sion·ist
non′im·pres·sion·is′tic
non′in·can·des′cent
non′in·clu′sive
non′in·de·pen′dent
non-In′di·an
non′in·dict′a·ble
non′in·dict′ment
non′in·dig′e·nous
non′in·di·vid′u·al
non′in·di·vid′u·al·is′tic
non-In′do-Eu′ro·pe′an
non′in·dus′tri·al
non′in·fal′li·ble
non′in·fect′ed
non′in·fec′tion
non′in·fec′tious
non·in′fi·nite
non′in·flam′ma·to′ry
non′in·fla′tion·ary
non′in·flect′ed
non′in·flec′tion·al
non′in·form′a·tive
non′in·her′it·a·ble
non′in·ju′ri·ous
non′in·sti·tu′tion·al
non′in·struc′tion·al
non′in·stru·men′tal
non·in′te·grat·ed
non′in·tel·lec′tu·al
non′in·tel′li·gent
non′in·ter·change′a·ble
non·in′ter·course
non′in·ter·fer′ence
non′in·ter·fer′ing
non′in·ter·mit′tent
non′in·ter·na′tion·al
non′in·ter·rupt′ed
non′in·ter·sect′ing
non′in·tox′i·cant
non′in·tox′i·cat′ing
non′in·tro·spec′tive
non·in′tro·vert
non′in·tu′i·tive
non′in·vert′ed
non′in·volve′ment
non·i′o·dized
non·i′o·nized
non-I′rish
non′ir·ra′di·at′ed
non·ir′ri·ga·ble
non·ir′ri·gat′ed
non′ir·ri·ga′tion
non·ir′ri·tant
non·ir′ri·tat′ing
non′-Is·lam′ic
non-Is′ra·el·ite
non′-I·tal′ian
non·it′er·a′tive
non′-Jap·a·nese′
non-Jew′
non-Jew′ish
non′ju·di′cial
non·jur′a·ble
non′ju·rid′i·cal
non′ju·ris′tic
non·ko′sher
non-Lat′in
non·le′gal
non·le′thal
non·li′censed
non·lim′it·ing
non·liq′ue·fy′ing
non·liq′ui·dat′ing
non′liq·ui·da′tion

non·lit′er·ar′y
non′li·ti′gious
non′li·tur′gi·cal
non·lo′cal
non′lu·mi·nes′cent
non·lu′mi·nous
non·lus′trous
non-Lu′ther·an
non-Mag′yar
non·main′te·nance
non-Ma′lay
non′ma·lig′nant
non·mal′le·a·ble
non′mam·ma′li·an
non′man·u·fac′tur·ing
non′ma·rine′
non·mar′i·tal
non·mar′i·time
non·mar′riage·a·ble
non·mar′ry·ing
non·mar′tial
non′ma·te′ri·al·is′tic
non′ma·ter′nal
non′math·e·mat′i·cal
non′ma·tric′u·lat′ed
non′me·chan′i·cal
non′mech·a·nis′tic
non′me·dic′i·nal
non·med′ul·lat′ed
non′me·lo′di·ous
non·melt′ing
non·mer′can·tile
non′met·al·lif′er·ous
non′met·a·phys′i·cal
non′me·te·or′ic
non-Meth′o·dist
non·met′ri·cal
non′met·ro·pol′i·tan
non·mi′gra·to′ry
non·mil′i·tant
non·mil′i·tar′y
non′mi·met′ic
non·min′er·al
non′min·is·te′ri·al
non′mi·rac′u·lous
non·mis′chie·vous
non·mis′ci·ble
non·mo′bile
non′-Mo·ham′me-dan
non·mon′e·tar′y
non′-Mon·go′li·an
non′mo·ral′i·ty
non-Mor′mon
non·mor′tal
non-Mos′lem
non·mo′tile
non·muf′fled
non′mu·nic′i·pal
non·mus′cu·lar
non·mu′si·cal
non·mys′ti·cal
non·myth′i·cal
non′nar·cot′ic
non·na′tion·al
non′na·tion·al·is′tic
non·na′tive
non·nat′u·ral
non·nat′u·ral·is′tic
non·nau′ti·cal
non·na′val
non·nav′i·ga·ble
non′ne·ces′si·ty
non′ne·go′tia·ble
non-Ne′gro
non·neu′tral
non-Nor′man
non-Norse′
non·nu′cle·ar
non·nu′cle·at′ed
non′nu·tri′tious
non·nu′tri·tive
non′o·be′di·ence
non′ob·lig′a·to′ry
non′ob·serv′ant
non′ob·serv′er
non′ob·struc′tion·ist
non′ob·struc′tive
non′oc·cu·pa′tion·al
non′oc·cur′rence
non·o′dor·ous
non′of·fi′cial
non·op′er·at′ing
non′op·er·a′tion
non′op·er·a′tion·al
non·op′er·a′tive
non·op′ti·cal
non·op′tion·al
non′or·gan′ic
non′or·i·en′tal
non·orth′o·dox
non·ox′i·diz′a·ble
non·ox′i·diz′ing
non·ox′y·gen·at′ed
non′pa·cif′ic
non·pac′i·fist
non·pa′gan
non·pal′a·tal
non′pal·a·tal·i·za′tion
non·pa′pal
non·pa′pist
non·par′
non·par′al·lel
non′par·a·lyt′ic
non′par·a·sit′ic
non·par′ent
non′pa·ren′tal
non′pa·rish′ion·er
non′par·lia·men′ta-ry
non′pa·ro′chi·al
non′par·tic′i·pant
non′par·tic′i·pa′tion
non·par′ti·san·ship
non·par′ty
non·pas′ser·ine
non′pa·ter′nal
non′pa·ter·nal·is′tic
non′path·o·gen′ic
non·pay′ing
non′ped·es′tri·an
non·pen′sion·a·ble
non′per·cep′tu·al
non·per′for·at′ed
non′per·form′er
non′per·form′ing
non′pe·ri·od′ic
non′pe·ri·od′i·cal
non·per′ish·a·ble
non·per′ish·ing
non·per′ma·nent
non·per′me·a·ble
non′per·mis′si·ble
non′per·pen·dic′u·lar
non′per·pet′u·al
non′per·se·cu′tion
non′per·sist′ence
non′per·sist′ent
non·per′son·al
non′phil·o·soph′i·cal
non·phys′i·cal
non′phys·i·o·log′i·cal
non·plan′e·tar′y
non·plas′tic
non·plaus′i·ble
non·play′ing
non′po·et′ic
non·poi′son·ous
non·po′lar·iz′a·ble
non′po·lem′i·cal
non-Pol′ish
non′po·lit′i·cal
non·po′rous
non-Por′tu·guese′
non·prac′tic·ing
non·pred′a·to′ry
non′pre·dict′a·ble
non′pref·er·en′tial
non·preg′nant
non′pre·hen′sile
non′prej·u·di′cial
non′pre·par′a·to′ry
non′prep·o·si′tion·al
non′-Pres·by·te′ri·an
non′pre·scrip′tion
non′pre·scrip′tive
non′pres·er·va′tion
non′pres·i·den′tial
non·pres′sur·ized
non·prev′a·lent
non·priest′ly
non′pro·duc′er
non′pro·duc′ing
non′pro·duc′tion
non′pro·fes′sion·al
non′prof·es·so′ri·al
non′pro·fi′cien·cy
non′pro·fi′cient
non′prof·it·eer′ing
non·prof′it·mak′ing
non′pro·gres′sive
non′pro·hib′i·tive
non′pro·lif′ic
non′pro·mis′cu·ous
non′pro·phet′ic
non′pro·por′tion·al
non′pro·pri′e·tar′y
non′pro·scrip′tive
non′pro·tec′tive
non-Prot′es·tant
non′pro·voc′a·tive
non-Prus′sian
non′psy·chi·at′ric
non·psy′chic
non·psy′cho·an′a-lyt′ic
non·pub′lic
non·punc′tur·a·ble
non·pun′ish·a·ble
non·pu′ni·tive
non·pur′u·lent
non·ra′cial
non·ra′di·at′ing
non·rad′i·cal
non′ra·di·o·ac′tive
non·ran′dom
non·rat′a·ble
non·ra′tion·al
non′re·ac′tive
non′re·al′i·ty
non′re·ceiv′ing
non′re·cip′ro·cal
non′re·cip′ro·cat′ing
non′rec·og·ni′tion
non′re·course
non′re·cur′rent
non′re·cur′ring
non′re·deem′a·ble
non′re·fill′a·ble
non′re·flect′ing
non′re·fu′el·ing
non′re·fund′a·ble
non′re·gen′er·at′ing
non′re·gen′er·a′tive
non·reg′i·ment′ed
non·reg′is·tered
non·reg′is·tra·ble
non·reg′u·lat′ed
non·reign′ing
non′re·lat′ed
non·rel′a·tive
non′rel·a·tiv·is·tic
non′re·li′gious
non′re·mis′sion
non′re·mu′ner·a′tive
non′re·new′a·ble
non′re·pay′a·ble
non′re·pent′ance
non′re·pet′i·tive
non′rep·re·hen′si·ble
non′rep·re·sen′ta-tive
non′re·pro·duc′tive
non′res·i·den′tial
non′re·sid′u·al
non′re·sist′ing
non′re·solv′a·ble
non·res′o·nant
non′re·strict′ed
non′res·ur·rec′tion
non′re·ten′tive
non′re·tir′ing
non′re·trace′a·ble
non′re·trac′tile
non′ret·ro·ac′tive
non′re·turn′
non′re·turn′a·ble
non′re·veal′ing
non′re·ver′sal
non′re·vers′i·ble
non′re·vert′i·ble
non′re·view′a·ble
non′re·volt′ing
non′rev·o·lu′tion·ar′y
non′re·volv′ing
non′rhe·tor′i·cal
non·rhym′ing
non·rhyth′mic
non′rit·u·al·is′tic
non·ri′val
non-Ro′man
non′ro·man′tic
non·ro′tat·ing
non·roy′al
non·roy′al·ist
non·ru′mi·nant
non·ru′ral
non-Rus′sian
non′sac·er·do′tal
non′sac·ra·men′tal
non·sa′cred
non′sac·ri·fi′cial
non·sal′a·ble
non·sal′a·ried
non·sal′u·tar′y
non·sat′u·rat′ed
non′-Scan·di·na′vi-an
non′schis·mat′ic
non′schol′ar
non′scho·las′tic
non′sci·en·tif′ic
non·scor′ing
non·sea′son·al
non·se′cret
non′se·cre′tive
non′se·cre′to·ry
non·sec′tion·al
non·sec′u·lar
non·sed′en·tar′y
non′se·di′tious
non·seg′re·gat′ed
non′se·lec′tive
non-Sem′ite
non′-Se·mit′ic
non·sen′si·tive
non·sen′si·tized
non·sen′so·ry
non·sen′tient
non·ser′ous
non·ser′vile
non′-Shake·spear′e-an
non·shar′ing
non·shat′ter
non·shrink′a·ble
non·sig′na·to′ry
non′sig·nif′i·cant
non·sil′ver
non·sink′a·ble
non-Slav′ic
non·sleep′er
non·smok′er
non·smok′ing
non·so′cial
non·so′cial·ist
non′so·cial·is′tic
non·sol′id
non·sol′vent
non·sov′er·eign
non-So′vi·et
non-Span′ish
non·spar′ing
non·spa′tial
non·spe′cial·ist
non·spe′cial·ized
non′spe·cif′ic
non′spec·tac′u·lar
non·spec′tral
non·spec′u·la′tive
non·spher′i·cal
non·spir′i·tu·al
non·spir′i·tu·ous
non′spon·ta′ne·ous
non·spot′ta·ble
non·stain′able
non·stain′ing
non-Sta′lin·ist
non·stand′ard·ized
non·start′er
non·start′ing
non·stat′ic
non·sta′tion·ar′y
non′sta·tis′ti·cal
non·stat′u·to′ry
non·ster′e·o
non′stra·te′gic
non·stretch′a·ble
non·strik′er
non·strik′ing
non·struc′tur·al
non·stu′dent
non′sub·mis′sive
non′sub·scrib′er
non′sub·scrib′ing
non·sub′si·dized
non′sub·stan′tial
non′suc·cess′
non′suc·cess′ful
non′suc·ces′sive
non′sup·port′er
non′sup·port′ing
non·sup′pu·ra′tive
non·sur′gi·cal
non′sus·tain′ing
non-Swed′ish
non·swim′mer
non-Swiss′
non′sym·bol′ic
non′sym·met′ri·cal
non·sym′pa·thiz′er
non′sym·phon′ic
non′symp·to·mat′ic
non·syn′chro·nous
non′syn·tac′tic
non·syn′the·sized
non′sys·tem·at′ic
non·tar′nish·a·ble
non·tax′a·ble
non·teach′a·ble
non·teach′ing
non·tech′ni·cal
non·ter′mi·na·ble
non·ter′mi·nal
non′ter·res′tri·al
non′ter·ri·to′ri·al
non′tes·ta·men′ta·ry
non′the·at′ri·cal
non′the·is′tic
non′the·o·log′i·cal
non′ther·a·peu′tic
non·ther′mal
non·think′ing
non·tit′u·lar
non′to·tal′i·tar′i·an
non′trans·fer′a·ble
non′tran·si′tion·al
non′trans·par′ent
non·trea′son·a·ble
non·trib′u·tar′y
non·trop′i·cal
non-Turk′ish
non·typ′i·cal
non′ty·ran′ni·cal
non·ul′cer·ous
non′un·der·stand′a-ble
non·u′ni·form
non′u·ni·form′i·ty
non′-U·ni·tar′i·an
non′u·ni·ver′sal
non′u·ni·ver′si·ty
non·ur′ban
non·us′age
non·use′
non·us′er
non·u′ter·ine
non′u·til′i·tar′i·an
non·u′ti·lized
non·vas′cu·lar
non·veg′e·ta′tive
non′ve·ne′re·al
non·ven′om·ous
non·ve′nous
non·ver′bal
non′ver·nac′u·lar
non·ver′ti·cal
non′ve·sic′u·lar
non·vet′er·an
non·vi′a·ble
non·vi′bra·to′ry
non′vi·car′i·ous
non′vi·o·la′tion
non·vi′o·lent
non·vir′u·lent
non·vis′cous
non·vis′it·ing
non·vis′u·al
non·vis′u·al·ized
non·vit′re·ous
non·vo′cal
non′vo·cal′ic
non′vo·ca′tion·al
non·vol′a·tile
non′vol·can′ic
non·vol′un·tar′y
non·vot′ing
non·work′er
non·work′ing
non·yield′ing

non·ab·sorb·a·ble (non′ab sôr′bə bəl, -zôr′-), *adj.* not absorbable; that cannot be absorbed.

non·ac·cept·ance (non′ək sep′təns), *n.* failure or refusal to accept: *Fifteen articles . . . were to be proposed forthwith to the insurgents, and in case of nonacceptance to be enforced* (John L. Motley).

non·age (non′ij, nō′nij), *n.* **1.** a being under the legal age of responsibility; minority: *Mr. Graziano recovered from a twisted nonage to become a first-class citizen* (New Yorker). **2.** an early stage; period before maturity. [<Anglo-French *nonnage* < *non-* not (< Latin) + *age* age < Gallo-Romance *aetāticum* < Latin *aetās*] —**Syn. 1.** infancy. **2.** immaturity.

non·a·ge·nar·i·an (non′ə jə nãr′ē ən; nō′-nə-), *n.* a person who is 90 years old or between 90 and 100 years old: *The dinner party broke up amid jolly anecdotes about nonagenarians* (New Yorker).
—*adj.* 90 years old or between 90 and 100 years old.
[< Latin *nōnāgēnārius* containing ninety (< *nōnāgēni* ninety each, ultimately < *nōnus* ninth < *novem* nine) + English *-an*]

non·ag·gres·sion (non′ə gresh′ən), *n.* lack of aggression. —*adj.* of or having to do with the lack of aggression; specifying no aggressive action: *The idea of an East-West nonaggression pact . . . is not new—and time has not made it any more sensible* (Wall Street Journal).

non·a·gon (non′ə gon), *n.* a plane figure having nine angles and nine sides. [< Latin *nōnus* ninth + Greek *gōniā* angle]

Nonagon

non·a·ligned (non′ə līnd′), *adj.* not aligned politically; neutral: *In all its diplomatic dealings, Peking has persistently worked . . . in subtle ways to align the nonaligned nations with the Communist orbit* (Atlantic).

non·a·lign·ment (non′ə līn′mənt), *n.* the condition of being politically neutral; neutralism: *But King Mahendra refuses to swap isolation for the thralldom of any great power, steadfastly pursues a policy of nonalignment* (Time).

non·al·lel·ic (non′ə lē′lik), *adj.* not allelic.

non·ap·pear·ance (non′ə pir′əns), *n.* failure to appear, as in court. —**Syn.** absence.

non·ar·ith·met·ic (non′ar ith met′ik), *adj.* nonarithmetical.

non·ar·ith·met·i·cal (non′ar ith met′ə-kəl), *adj.* **1.** not arithmetical: *a nonarithmetical equation.* **2.** not having to do with arithmetical work.

non·art (non′ärt′), *n.* **1.** the negation of art: *He tends to look upon a good deal of Abstract Expressionism as nonart* (New Yorker). **2.** a work that rejects or parodies conventional forms and techniques of art.

non·ar·tic·u·late (non′ar tik′yə lit), *adj.* **1.** not made up of distinct parts. **2.** not jointed, hinged, or segmented.

no·na·ry (nō′nər ē), *adj.* having nine for a base: *a nonary scale.*

non·as·sent·ed (non′ə sen′tid), *adj.* of stocks or bonds whose owners have not agreed to deposit them in exchange for new stocks or bonds during the reorganization after bankruptcy.

non·at·tend·ance (non′ə ten′dəns), *n.* failure or neglect to be present: *My notice to appear arrived a good two weeks before the specified date and warned of penalties for nonattendance* (Maclean's). —**Syn.** absence.

non·bank (non bangk′), *adj.* of or having to do with an individual or institution other than a bank: *Commercial banks . . . could buy only $500 million of the issue; only nonbank buyers could apply for the rest* (Time).

non·board·ing (non bôr′ding, -bōr′-), *adj.* **1.** not living or eating in the place mentioned. **2.** not for boarding.

non·book (non′bůk′), *n.* a written work that, in its inception, form, etc., consists of gimmicks in binding, inserts, etc., and various mechanical features put together in book form merely as a salable product: *This closely printed 896-page book is more like . . . a nonbook than a disciplined treatment of a coherent theme* (Scientific American).

non·cap·i·tal murder (non kap′ə təl), (in Canadian law) murder that is not punishable by death but by life imprisonment: *The four original charges of noncapital murder . . . were reduced to charges of manslaughter* (Canada Month).

nonce (nons), *n.* the one or particular occasion or purpose: *In a nonce they are sucked into adventure* (Alfred Wright).

for the nonce, for the present time or occasion: *We must compare the Marquis of Farintosh to a lamb for the nonce* (Thackeray).

[Middle English (*for the*) *nones,* misdivision of *for than ones* for the once, that is, for the one (time or thing)]

non·cel·lu·lo·sic (non′sel yə lō′sik), *n.* a synthetic fiber made from a base other than cellulose, as nylon, Dacron, and Orlon. —*adj.* of, having to do with, or characteristic of the noncellulosics: *noncellulosic fibers.*

nonce word, a word formed and used for a single occasion: *Examples: newspaporialist* = a journalist, *planeticose* = given to wandering, *observist* = a person who makes observation his business.

non·cha·lance (non′shə ləns, non′shə läns′), *n.* a cool unconcern; indifference: *She received the prize with pretended nonchalance. The nonchalance of boys who are sure of a dinner, and would disdain as much as a lord to do or say aught to conciliate one, is the healthy attitude of human nature* (Emerson). [< French *nonchalance* < Old French < *nonchalant* nonchalant] —**Syn.** impassivity.

non·cha·lant (non′shə lənt, non′shə länt′), *adj.* without enthusiasm; coolly unconcerned; indifferent: *a nonchalant manner, a nonchalant reply.* [< French *nonchalant* < Old French < *non-* not (< Latin) + *chaloir* have concern for, care for, be warm < Latin *calēre* be warm] —**non′cha·lant·ly,** *adv.* —**Syn.** apathetic.

non·chro·mo·so·mal (non′krō mə sō′məl), *adj.* transmitting hereditary characters without chromosomes; not chromosomal or Mendelian: *The nonchromosomal system involves genes but follows rules completely different from the chromosomal one* (New York Times).

non·col·lege (non kol′ij), *adj.* **1.** not attending or not having attended a college: *The data at hand indicate that the college man outstrips the noncollege man with astonishing ease in every measure of worldly success* (Harper's). **2.** not suitable for college.

non·col·le·giate (non′kə lē′jit, -jē it), *adj.* **1.** *British.* not belonging to a college; belonging to the body of students in a university not attached to any particular college or hall. **2.** (of a university) not composed of separate colleges.

non·com (non′kom′), *Informal.* —*n.* a noncommissioned officer: *To all appearances an impeccable soldier, he is a wizard at getting the better of noncoms* (Atlantic). —*adj.* noncommissioned.

noncom., noncommissioned officer.

non·com·bat·ant (non′kəm bat′ənt, non kom′bə tənt), *n.* a person who is not a fighter in the armed forces in time of war; civilian: *Surgeons, nurses, chaplains, etc., are noncombatants even though with the army.* —*adj.* not fighting; civilian in wartime: *noncombatant personnel.*

non·com·mis·sioned (non′kə mish′ənd), *adj.* without a commission; not commissioned: *Corporals and sergeants are noncommissioned officers.*

non·com·mit·ment (non′kə mit′mənt), *n.* the state of being free of political alliance or other obligations or agreements: *Our politics are debilitated by the virus of cagey noncommitment* (Atlantic).

non·com·mit·tal (non′kə mit′əl), *adj.* not committing oneself; not saying yes or no: *"I will think it over" is a noncommittal answer.* —**non′com·mit′tal·ly,** *adv.*

non·com·pli·ance (non′kəm plī′əns), *n.* the fact of not complying; failure to comply: *They could not be punished for noncompliance with a court order* (New York Times). —*adj. U.S.* (of grain) grown in opposition to government acreage restrictions: *The Agriculture Department's announcement on price supports for noncompliance corn drew sharp protest* (Wall Street Journal).

non·com·pli·ant (non′kəm plī′ənt), *n.* a person who fails or refuses to comply.

non com·pos men·tis (non′ kom′pəs men′tis), *Latin.* mentally unable to manage one's affairs; not of sound mind: *My poor sister drank too much . . . and most of the time she was non compos mentis* (New Yorker).

non·con·duct·ing (non′kən duk′ting), *adj.* not conducting; that is a nonconductor: *Asbestos is a nonconducting material used in heat insulation.*

non·con·duc·tor (non′kən duk′tər), *n.* a substance that does not readily conduct heat, electricity, etc.: *Rubber is a nonconductor of electricity. In a nonconductor, or insulator, all the valence electrons are tied up in the chemical bonds which hold the crystal together* (Scientific American).

non·con·form·ance (non′kən fôr′məns), *n.* the fact of not conforming; failure to conform. —**Syn.** nonconformity.

non·con·form·ism or **Non·con·form·ism** (non′kən fôr′miz əm), *n.* the beliefs or practices of nonconformists or Nonconformists: *Amateur nonconformism is one of the honorable paths in American history* (Time).

non·con·form·ist (non′kən fôr′mist), *n.* **1.** a person who refuses to accept the established conventions of the social group to which he belongs: *Whoso would be a man, must be a nonconformist* (Emerson). **2.** a person who refuses to conform to an established church. —**Syn. 1.** dissenter.

Non·con·form·ist (non′kən fôr′mist), *n. British.* a Protestant who is not a member of the Church of England.

non·con·form·i·ty (non′kən fôr′mə tē), *n., pl.* **-ties. 1.** lack of conformity; failure or refusal to conform. **2.** failure or refusal to conform to an established church. **3.** *Geology.* a break between rock strata in which the earlier rock formation is deformed and eroded before being overlaid with new strata.

Non·con·form·i·ty (non′kən fôr′mə tē), *n. British.* **1.** the principles or practices of English Protestants who do not belong to the Church of England. **2.** nonconformists as a group.

non·con·tent (non′kən tent′), *n.* a negative vote or voter in the British House of Lords.

non·co·op·er·a·tion (non′kō op′ə rā′shən), *n.* **1.** failure or refusal to cooperate. **2.** refusal to cooperate with a government for political reasons or as a political weapon. Civil disobedience as originally practiced by Mahatma Gandhi and his followers in India is a form of noncooperation.

non·co·op·er·a·tion·ist (non′kō op′ə rā′shə nist), *n.* an advocate of noncooperation.

non·co·op·er·a·tive (non′kō op′ə rā′tiv, -op′rə-), *adj.* **1.** not cooperating. **2.** of or having to do with noncooperation.

non·co·op·er·a·tor (non′kō op′ə rā′tər), *n.* **1.** a person who refuses to cooperate. **2.** an advocate of noncooperation.

non·de·liv·er·y (non′di liv′ər ē, -liv′rē), *n., pl.* **-er·ies.** failure to deliver.

non·de·script (non′də skript), *adj.* not easily classified; not of any one particular kind: *eyes of nondescript shade, neither brown, blue, nor gray. A multitude of nondescript articles, indispensable on the prairies* (Francis Parkman). —*n.* a nondescript person or thing: *one of those originals and nondescripts, more frequent in German Universities than elsewhere* (Thomas Carlyle). [earlier, not yet described (said of a species) < *non-* + Latin *dēscrīptus,* past participle of *dēscrībere* describe] —**Syn.** *adj.* amorphous.

non·de·struc·tive (non′di struk′tiv), *adj.* not destructive or damaging; harmless.

non·di·rec·tive (non′də rek′tiv), *adj.* **1.** not directive. **2.** that does not attempt to guide or direct a patient, client, informant, etc., toward any particular attitude or course of action: *Nondirective therapy is one of the nonpsychoanalytic schools of psychotherapy* (John L. Herma). *Observe the . . . irrelevancy of judging an applicant by standardized interviews, nondirective techniques, forms, and tests* (Atlantic).

non·dis·junc·tion (non′dis jungk′shən), *n.* the failure of a pair of chromosomes to separate and go to different cells when the cell divides.

non·dis·tinc·tive (non′dis tingk′tiv), *adj.* **1.** that fails to be or make distinctive. **2.** *Phonetics.* that does not distinguish meanings; not phonemic: *Each phonetic symbol represents a distinctive English sound, though each may have several perceptible nondistinctive varieties* (John Kenyon).

non·dol·lar (non dol′ər), *adj.* of or having a currency unit other than the dollar: *Among the major nondollar countries, Brazil and Argentina were both undergoing continued economic difficulties* (Frances La Belle Hall).

non·dom·i·nant (non dom′ə nənt), *adj.* (of chords, especially seventh chords) standing on any step of the scale except the dominant.

non·drink·er (non dring′kər), *n.* a person who does not drink alcoholic liquor: *. . . unlimited milk for nondrinkers* (Time).

non·dur·a·ble (non důr′ə bəl), *adj.* that will not last long; that can be used up or worn out quickly; perishable: *Tomatoes are nondurable.* —*n.* something that is nondurable: *Nondurables include foodstuffs, wearing apparel, and textiles generally* (New York Times).

none[1] (nun), *pron.* **1.** not any: *We have none of that paper left. That matter is none of our business.* **2.** no one; not one: *None of these is a typical case.* **3.** no persons or things: *None have arrived. None come to the solemn feasts* (Lamentations 1:4). *I hear a voice, but none are there* (Tennyson). **4.** no part; nothing: *He had none of the appearance of a man who sailed before the mast* (Robert Louis Stevenson).

—*adv.* to no extent; in no way; not at all: *Our supply is none too great. Oh, our world is none the safer Now Great-Heart hath died!* (Rudyard Kipling).

none the less. See under **less,** *n.*

[Old English *nān* < *ne* not + *ān* one]

➔ **none, no one.** *None* is a single word, but *no one* is often used instead of *none* for emphasis. *None* may be either singular or plural: *As only ten jurors have been chosen so far, none of the witnesses were called* (or *was called*). *She tried on ten hats, but none of them were attractive. I read three books on the subject, no one of which was helpful.*

none[2] or **None** (nōn), *n.* singular of **nones**[2].

non·ef·fec·tive (non′i fek′tiv), *adj.* not fit for duty or active service, as a soldier or sailor. —*n.* such a soldier or sailor.

non·e·go (non ē′gō, -eg′ō), *n., pl.* **-gos.** *Philosophy.* **1.** all that is not part of the ego or conscious self. **2.** the object as contrasted with the subject.

non·en·ti·ty (non en′tə tē), *n., pl.* **-ties. 1.** a person or thing of little or no importance: *He was an atom, a nonentity, a very worm, and no man* (Edward G. Bulwer-Lytton). **2.** something that does not exist, or that exists only in the imagination: *Mermaids do not exist: why speak of them as if they did? How can you find interest in speaking of a nonentity?* (Charlotte Brontë). **3.** nonexistence.

nones[1] (nōnz), *n.pl.* (in the ancient Roman calendar) the ninth day before the ides, counting both days, thus being the 7th of March, May, July, and October, and the 5th of the other months. [< Latin *nōnae,* (originally) feminine plural of *nōnus* ninth]

nones[2] or **Nones** (nōnz), *n.pl.* **1.** the fifth of the seven canonical hours. **2.** the office or service for this hour, following sext, originally fixed for the ninth hour after sunrise (about 3 P.M.) but generally recited earlier: *From noon till nones The brethren* *sate; and when the quire was done Renew'd their converse till the vesper bell* (Robert Southey). [Old English *nōn*, ninth hour < Latin *nōna* (*hōra*) ninth (hour) of daylight in Roman reckoning. Doublet of NOON.]

non·es·sen·tial (non'ə sen'shəl), *adj.* not essential; not necessary: *Nonessential color is the result of an impurity in the mineral* (Frederick H. Pough). —*n.* a person or thing not essential. —**Syn.** *adj.* unnecessary.

non est (non est'), *Latin.* it is not; not there; absent.

none·such (nun'such'), *n.* **1.** a person or thing without equal or parallel; paragon: *The uncanny ability of Fiorello La Guardia to get out the vote—on his side—made him a nonesuch in New York politics* (Atlantic). **2.** *Botany.* the black medic. Also, **nonsuch.** —**Syn. 1.** nonpareil.

no·net (nō net'), *n. Music.* a composition written for nine instruments or nine voices: *The small-group sides are the best, with the nonet in particular coming through as a sparkling unit* (Saturday Review). [< Italian *nonetto* < *nono* ninth]

none·the·less (nun'ᴛʜə les'), *adv.* none the less; nevertheless: *[Henry] Everett, younger than any of these individuals, and correspondingly less of an individualist, was nonetheless a true member of the great generation* (Louis Auchincloss).

non·e·vent (non'i vent'), *n.* an event highly publicized as forthcoming but actually never taking place: *This nonevent was the great Red scare that was so confidently predicted in Europe* (Manchester Guardian).

non·ex·ist·ence (non'ig zis'təns), *n.* **1.** the condition of not existing. **2.** a thing that has no existence.

non·fea·sance (non fē'zəns), *n. Law.* the failure to perform some act which ought to have been performed.

non·fer·rous (non fer'əs), *adj.* of or denoting metal that is not or contains no iron: *nonferrous metals. Butte's troubles parallel those of many other communities whose lifeblood flows from the nonferrous mining industry* (Wall Street Journal).

non·fic·tion (non fik'shən), *n.* prose literature that is not a novel, short story, or other form of writing based on imaginary people and events: *Biographies and histories are nonfiction.*

nonfiction novel, a factual account written in the form of a novel.

non·fig·u·ra·tive (non fig'yər ə tiv), *adj.* **1.** (in art) using unrecognizable figures or symbols; not objective: *The recent emphasis on extreme abstraction—the nonobjective or nonfigurative art which has proved so controversial in the last few years* (New York Times). **2.** not figurative, as of the usage of a word.

non·fil·ter (non fil'tər), *n.* a cigarette without a filter.

non·fil·tered (non fil'tərd), *adj.* having no filter: *nonfiltered cigarettes.*

non·fis·sion·a·ble (non fish'ə nə bəl), *adj.* not capable of nuclear fission.

non·flam (non flam'), *adj.* nonflammable: *nonflam construction, nonflam plastic.*

non·flam·ma·ble (non flam'ə bəl), *adj.* that will not catch fire: *When you buy your next can of paint remover, ask for the "new nonflammable kind"* (Wall Street Journal).

non·fly·ing (non flī'ing), *adj.* that does not fly or is not capable of flying: *Before an airplane is built, a nonflying, full-scale model is made.*

non·ful·fill·ment (non'fu̇l fil'mənt), *n.* failure to fulfill; failure to be fulfilled.

non gra·ta (non grā'tə, grä'-), *Latin.* not welcome: *He was accused of conspiring ... declared non grata and thrown out of the country* (Time).

non·har·mon·ic (non'här mon'ik), *adj.* not harmonic; without harmony: *When, as in the case of a drum or a bell, [overtones] are not integral multiples of the fundamental they are called nonharmonic* (Shortley and Williams).

non·he·ro (non'hir'ō), *n., pl.* **-roes.** an antihero: *We have met ... that wistful, beset nonhero many times in recent English novels* (New Yorker).

no·nil·lion (nō nil'yən), *n.* **1.** (in the United States and France) an octillion multiplied by 1,000, equal to 1 followed by 30 zeros. **2.** (in Great Britain and Germany) a million to the ninth power, equal to 1 followed by 54 zeros. —*adj.* amounting to one nonillion in number. [< Latin *nōnus* ninth (power) + French *million* million]

no·nil·lionth (nō nil'yənth), *adj., n.* **1.** last in a series of a nonillion. **2.** one of a nonillion equal parts.

non·im·mi·grant (non im'ə grənt), *n.* **1.** a foreigner entering a country for a temporary stay only. **2.** an alien reëntering the country in which he lives after a short stay abroad.

non·in·duc·tive (non'in duk'tiv), *adj.* (of an electrical resistance) not inductive.

non·in·flam·ma·ble (non'in flam'ə bəl), *adj.* nonflammable.

non·in·stall·ment (non'in stôl'mənt), *adj.* payable all at once rather than in installments: *a noninstallment debt.*

non·in·ter·ven·tion (non'in tər ven'shən), *n.* **1.** failure or refusal to intervene. **2.** the systematic avoidance of any interference by a nation in the affairs of other nations or of its own states, etc.: *Nonintervention with "Popular Sovereignty" was the original and established Democratic doctrine with regard to Slavery in the Territories* (Horace Greeley). —**Syn. 2.** neutrality.

non·in·ter·ven·tion·ist (non'in tər ven'shə nist), *n.* a person who favors or advocates nonintervention: *The Greek ecclesiastics are noninterventionists* (Saturday Review). —*adj.* that favors or advocates nonintervention: *The government's conservative opposition ... criticized Mexico's noninterventionist stand on Cuba* (Robert J. Shafer).

non·i·on·ic (non'ī on'ik), *adj.* that does not ionize in solution: *Nonionic substances combine with water because they remove internal pressure and thereby permit formation of a crystalline compound* (Arthur N. Buswell and Worth H. Rodebush).

non·i·ron (non ī'ərn), *adj. Especially British.* no-iron.

non·join·der (non join'dər), *n. Law.* the failure of a person bringing a suit to include in it a party, person, or cause of action necessary to its determination.

non·ju·rant (non ju̇r'ənt), *adj.* that is a nonjuror; characteristic of nonjurors. —*n.* a nonjuror.

non·ju·ring (non ju̇r'ing), *adj.* refusing to take a required oath; being a nonjuror.

non·ju·ror (non ju̇r'ər), *n.* a person who refuses to take a required oath.

Non·ju·ror (non ju̇r'ər), *n.* **1.** one of the clergymen of the Church of England who in 1689 refused to swear allegiance to William and Mary and who were deprived of their benefices. **2.** a member of a separate communion founded by these clergymen. It survived until about 1800.

Non·ju·ror·ism (non ju̇r'ə riz əm), *n.* the principles or practices of the Nonjurors.

non·life (non'līf), *n.* absence or negation of life: *In the evolution from nonlife to life, atoms group themselves to form new combinations* (Science News Letter). —*adj.* of or having to do with insurance other than life insurance: *One bright feature of the companies' overseas activities—and some two-thirds of their nonlife business is conducted abroad—has been the low level of hurricane losses in the United States* (Economist).

non·lin·e·ar (non lin'ē ər), *adj.* **1.** not linear; not proportional: *The ear is a very nonlinear instrument* (New Scientist). **2.** *Electronics.* having an output not proportional to the input: *nonlinear electric circuits.*

non·lin·e·ar·i·ty (non'lin ē ar'ə tē), *n., pl.* **-ties.** the condition of being nonlinear.

non·lin·guis·tic (non'ling gwis'tik), *adj.* **1.** not consisting of or expressed in language: *Nonlinguistic communication has impact at least as profound as the spoken and printed word* (Saturday Review). **2.** not having to do with linguistics.

non·liq·uid (non lik'wid), *adj.* **1. a.** without fluids: *a nonliquid diet.* **b.** not in liquid form. **2.** lacking liquidity: *nonliquid securities.*

non·lit·er·ate (non lit'ər it), *adj.* **1. a.** not able to read or write. **b.** having no alphabet or other form of writing: *Written documents cannot, in the nature of the case, be drawn on among nonliterate peoples* (Melville J. Herskovits). **2.** having no knowledge of literature: *There is no future at all in our growingly nonliterate culture for verse drama* (Manchester Guardian).

non·liv·ing (non liv'ing), *adj.* not living: *Many of the common materials of the earth's crust may alternate between the living and the nonliving states* (Fred W. Emerson).

non·mag·net·ic (non'mag net'ik), *adj.* not having the properties of a magnet; that cannot be magnetized or attracted by a magnet.

non·mas·ter (non mas'tər, -mäs'-), *n.* a person who is not a master in contract bridge tournament play.

non·ma·te·ri·al (non'mə tir'ē əl), *adj.* having no material properties; not substantial: *The majority of people really long to experience that moment of pure, disinterested, nonmaterial satisfaction which causes them to ejaculate the word "beautiful"* (Kenneth Clark).

non·med·i·cal (non med'ə kəl), *adj.* having nothing to do with medicine, medical practice, or study.

non·mem·ber (non mem'bər), *n.* a person or thing that is not a member; one that does not belong.

non·met·al (non'met'əl), *n.* a chemical element, such as carbon or nitrogen, that lacks the physical properties of a metal. A nonmetal forms acidic oxides and is electronegative in solution: *... the halogen family —the family that begins with fluorine, the supreme example of a nonmetal* (J. Crowther).

non·me·tal·lic (non'mə tal'ik), *adj.* not like a metal. Carbon, oxygen, sulfur, and nitrogen are nonmetallic chemical elements. —*n.* a nonmetallic substance: *In addition to its leading position in diamonds and lithium minerals, Africa produced important quantities of other nonmetallics* (Berenice B. Mitchell).

non·mor·al (non môr'əl, -mor'-), *adj.* having no relation to morality; neither moral nor immoral: *Keats ... the most absolutely nonmoral of all serious writers* (Algernon Charles Swinburne).

non·ni·trog·e·nous (non'nī troj'ə nəs), *adj.* not containing nitrogen.

non·ob·jec·tive (non'əb jek'tiv), *adj.* **1.** lacking objectivity. **2. a.** not portraying or resembling natural objects, persons, etc. **b.** of or having to do with a type of abstract art created from the interplay of forms, colors, and lines, without reference to other elements of the artist's experience: *The first ascertainable nonobjective painting was done by Kandinsky in about 1909* (New York Times).

non·ob·jec·tiv·ism (non'əb jek'tə viz əm), *n.* **1.** nonobjective art: *... the wide variety of American styles, from realism to nonobjectivism* (Newsweek). **2.** nonobjectivity (def. 2).

non·ob·jec·tiv·ist (non'əb jek'tə vist), *n.* an artist whose work follows the principles of nonobjectivism.

non·ob·jec·tiv·i·ty (non'ob jek tiv'ə tē), *n.* **1.** a lack of objectivity: *His views were probably biased; he was, so to speak, objective about his nonobjectivity* (New Yorker). **2.** the principles or practices of the nonobjective school of art: *Here we have two members of the same generation, one realizing a visionary expressionism in nonobjectivity, the other a supercharged dynamism* (Atlantic).

non·ob·serv·ance (non'əb zėr'vəns), *n.* the act or fact of not observing laws or customs.

non obst., non obstante.

non ob·stan·te (non ob stan'tē), *Latin.* notwithstanding.

no-non·sense (nō'non'sens), *adj.* down-to-earth; practical; matter-of-fact: *It wasn't long before a stranger, a stout, no-nonsense type, suggested we find another vantage point* (New Yorker).

non·op·er·at·ing (non op'ə rā'ting), *adj.* of or having to do with railroad workers not directly concerned with the operation of trains, such as ticket agents or dispatchers: *a nonoperating union.*

non·own·er (non ō'nər), *n.* a person or group that is not an owner.

non·pa·reil (non'pə rel'), *adj.* having no equal; peerless: *The literary salons have had a major part in making Paris the city nonpareil, for centuries the undisputed cultural centre of the world* (Canadian Forum). —*n.* **1.** a person or thing having no equal: *Though you were crown'd The nonpareil of beauty* (Shakespeare). **2.** a beautifully colored finch of the southern United States;

Nonpareil (def. 2) (5¼ in. long)

painted bunting. **3.** a kind of apple. **4.** *Printing.* **a.** a size of type; 6-point. This sentence is set in nonpareil. **b.** a slug 6 points high used between lines. **5.** a small chocolate drop covered with tiny white pellets of sugar.
[< Middle French *nonpareil* < *non-* not (< Latin) + *pareil* equal < Vulgar Latin *pāriculus* (diminutive) < Latin *pār, paris* equal]

non·par·ous (non par′əs), *adj.* not having given birth to a child. [< *non-* + Latin *parere* to give birth + English *-ous*]

non·par·tic·i·pat·ing (non′pər tis′ə pā′-ting), *adj.* **1.** not participating: *The United States was a nonparticipating country in the League of Nations.* **2.** *Insurance.* that does not give its owner the right to share in profits or surplus: *a nonparticipating policy.*

non·par·ti·san or **non·par·ti·zan** (non-pär′tə zən), *adj.* **1.** not partisan: *a nonpartisan committee.* **2.** not supporting, or controlled by, any of the regular political parties: *a nonpartisan voter.* —*n.* a nonpartisan person: *Five of the fifteen candidates at-large would . . . be nonpartisans* (New York Times). —**Syn.** *adj.* **1.** impartial. **2.** independent.

Nonpartisan League, *U.S.* an organization of farmers that helped to create the Farmer-Labor Party, founded in North Dakota in 1915 to restore government control to the farmers and to establish state-owned institutions for their benefit.

non·pay·ment (non pā′mənt), *n.* failure to pay; condition of not being paid: *The family had been evicted for nonpayment of rent* (New York Times). —**Syn.** default.

non·per·form·ance (non′pər fôr′məns), *n.* the fact of not performing; failure to perform.

non pla·cet (non plā′set), *Latin.* **1.** a vote in the negative; veto. **2.** (literally) it does not please.

non·plus (non plus′, non′plus), *v.*, **-plused, -plus·ing** or (*especially British*) **-plussed, -plus·sing,** *n.* —*v.t.* to puzzle completely; make unable to say or do anything: *We were nonplused to see two roads leading off to the left where we had expected only one. Right or wrong, he ne'er was nonplus't* (Samuel Butler).
—*n.* a state of being nonplused: *Prophets are never at a nonplus, and never surprised by a question* (Augustus Jessopp).
[< Latin *nōn plūs* no more, no further]
—**Syn.** *v.t.* confound, confuse, mystify, embarrass. —*n.* confusion, embarrassment.

non pos·su·mus (non pos′yu̇ məs), *Latin.* **1.** a plea of being unable to consider, or act in, a matter. **2.** (literally) we cannot.

non·prin·ci·pled (non prin′sə pəld), *adj.* rejecting moral principles; nonmoral: *The antinomian, or nonprincipled, approach of the existentialists leads to anarchy and to moral decisions that are "random, unpredictable, erratic, and quite anomalous"* (Time).

non·pro·duc·tive (non′prə duk′tiv), *adj.* **1.** not productive. **2.** not directly connected with production: *nonproductive charges or expenses. Clerks and supervisors are nonproductive workers.*
—**non′pro·duc′tive·ness,** *n.*

non·prof·it (non prof′it), *adj.* not for profit; without profit: *The Salvation Army is a nonprofit organization.*

non·pro·lif·er·a·tion (non′prō lif′ə rā′-shən), *n.* the regulation of the spread of nuclear weapons among nations, especially by means of an agreement.

non·pros (non′pros′), *v.t.*, **-prossed, -pros·sing.** *Law.* to enter a judgment of non prosequitur against (a plaintiff). [earlier, noun, abbreviation of *nōn prōsequitur*]

non pros., non prosequitur.

non pro·se·qui·tur (non prō sek′wə tər), *Law.* a judgment entered against the plaintiff in a suit when he does not appear to prosecute it. [< Latin *nōn prōsequitur* he does not pursue (the suit)]

non·pro·tein (non prō′tēn, -tē in), *n.* a substance that is not a protein or does not contain protein. —*adj.* having no protein or proteins: *a nonprotein molecule, food, or diet.*

non·quo·ta immigrant (non kwō′tə), an immigrant whose national or other group is not subject to a quota set by immigration law: *Nonquota immigrants are not restricted numerically, although they must meet all other standards of health, morals, literacy, and economics established for all immigrants* (Joseph M. Strong).

non·read·er (non′rē′dər), *n.* **1.** a child who cannot read: *Many boys are poor readers or nonreaders* (Maclean's). **2.** a person who reads little: *The number of nonreaders will diminish if and when he can find more salesmen . . . to sell books from door to door* (Time).

non·re·cov·er·a·ble (non′ri kuv′ər ə bəl, -kuv′rə), *adj.* **1.** from which a person cannot recover: *A large part of the radiation injury is recovered from in time, but . . . there is also a nonrecoverable fraction* (Bulletin of Atomic Scientists). **2.** that cannot be recovered: *This will . . . involve high expenses and nonrecoverable outlays* (Wall Street Journal).

non·rep·re·sen·ta·tion·al (non′rep ri-zen tā′shə nəl), *adj.* not representing or resembling natural objects; abstract: *nonrepresentational art.*

non·res·i·dence (non rez′ə dəns), *n.* a being nonresident.

non·res·i·den·cy (non rez′ə dən sē), *n.* nonresidence.

non·res·i·dent (non rez′ə dənt), *adj.* **1.** not residing in a particular place: *a nonresident voter.* **2.** not residing where official duties require one to reside. —*n.* a nonresident person.

non·re·sist·ance (non′ri zis′təns), *n.* the fact or conditon of not resisting; lack of resistance.

non·re·sist·ant (non′ri zis′tənt), *adj.* not resisting; passively obedient. —*n.* a person who does not resist authority or force; person who maintains that violence should never be resisted by force: . . . *released on parole as a nonresistant* (Thomas W. Higginson).

non·re·straint (non′ri strānt′), *n.* **1.** absence of restraint. **2.** the controlling of psychotic persons without the use of force, strait jackets, etc., as by tranquilizing drugs or other placid means.

non·re·stric·tive (non′ri strik′tiv), *adj.* **1.** *Grammar.* adding descriptive detail. Modifiers which do not limit the meaning of a noun but add a descriptive detail are nonrestrictive modifiers: *a nonrestrictive phrase or clause. Example:* President Kennedy, *who just entered the room,* was smiling. (Contrast the same clause used in a restrictive sense: The man *who just entered the room* is President Kennedy.) **2.** that does not restrict: *nonrestrictive legislation.*

non·rig·id (non rij′id), *adj.* **1.** not rigid. **2.** (of an airship) having no supporting internal structure; given shape solely through inflation with a gas: *The initial flight of a new and larger class of nonrigid airships for airborne early warning "picket patrol" was made here* (Wall Street Journal).

non sans droit (non sanz droit′), not without right (an Old French motto on Shakespeare's coat of arms).

non·sched·uled (non skej′u̇ld), *adj.* **1.** not operating or proceeding according to a regular schedule: *a nonscheduled airline, a nonscheduled flight.* **2.** not according to a program or plan: *The train made a nonscheduled stop.*

non·sci·en·tist (non sī′ən tist), *n.* a person who is not trained in science: *Nonscientists have trouble understanding the scientific method and attitude* (Science News Letter).

non·sec·tar·i·an (non′sek tãr′ē ən), *adj.* not connected with any religious denomination: *a nonsectarian college or hospital.*

non·self-gov·ern·ing (non self′guv′ər-ning), *adj.* not having self-government; not autonomous: . . . *a United Nations ruling that all non-self-governing territories should hold a plebiscite to determine whether they wanted to continue in their present status, become independent, or seek alignment with some other nation* (Atlantic).

non·sense (non′sens), *n.* **1.** words, ideas, or acts without meaning; foolish talk or doings; a plan or suggestion that is foolish: *He says we must wait with patience, and trust to Providence, and such nonsense* (Tobias Smollett). *You are talking the greatest nonsense; and you know it* (George Bernard Shaw). **2.** worthless stuff; junk: *a kitchen drawer full of useless gadgets, and similar nonsense.*
take the nonsense out of, to make (a person) behave or think rightly: *The instructor soon took the nonsense out of the students.*
[probably < *non-* + *sense.* Compare Old French *nonsens,* Latin *nonsensus.*]
—**Syn. 1.** foolishness, absurdity, humbug.

nonsense syllable, a syllable formed by putting a vowel between any two consonants, used in various psychological and educational experiments, tests, etc.: *When Ebbinghaus began his . . . study of memory and association, he chose as his materials nonsense syllables* (Edward B. Titchener).

non·sen·si·cal (non sen′sə kəl), *adj.* foolish; ridiculous; absurd: *a nonsensical person.* —**non·sen′si·cal·ly,** *adv.* —**non·sen′si·cal·ness,** *n.* —**Syn.** senseless, silly, preposterous.

non seq., non sequitur.

non se·qui·tur (non sek′wə tər), **1.** a remark that has no bearing on what the speaker is talking about or has just said: *It is ridiculous . . . to mutilate the libretto so that the dialogue . . . becomes a running non sequitur* (Harper's). *If he decides to defend the islands, some U.S. allies (and some U.S. citizens) will immediately cry that a little war will inevitably lead to a big war, a non sequitur that is being pounded home in speeches, editorials, and sermons* (Time). **2.** an inference or conclusion that does not follow from the premise: *"How does theatre and cooking mix?" the pamphlet inquired, mixing its syntax and laying the groundwork for a solid non sequitur* (New Yorker). [< Latin *non sequitur* it does not follow]

non·sex·u·al (non sek′shu̇ əl), *adj.* **1.** having no sex; sexless; asexual. **2.** done by or characteristic of sexless animals: *the nonsexual conjugation of protozoans.*

non·sked (non′sked′), *n. U.S. Informal.* a nonscheduled airline: *The nonskeds . . . were willing to carry anything, anywhere, and at any time* (Harper's).

non·skid (non′skid′), *adj.* made so as to prevent or reduce skidding: *nonskid tires, nonskid floor wax.*

non·skid·ding (non skid′ing), *adj.* nonskid.

non·stand·ard (non stan′dərd), *adj.* **1.** not conforming to the existing regulations, accepted specifications, etc.: *In the case of nonstandard items, the Government from now on will call for disclosure of proprietary information* (Wall Street Journal). **2.** (of language) not in the generally accepted pattern; not standard: *The social status of many nonstandard [language habits] is often different in different sections* (Harold B. Allen).

non·ster·ling (non stėr′ling), *adj.* of or having to do with countries outside the sterling area: *The present basic allowances for foreign travel are the equivalent of . . . $280 for the . . . nonsterling area* (Wall Street Journal).

non·stop (non′stop′), *adj.* that travels between two places without stopping, or without scheduled stops for passengers: *a nonstop flight, a nonstop train from New York to Chicago.* —*adv.* without stopping: *That plane flies nonstop to Paris.* —*n.* a nonstop airplane or flight: *2 nonstops daily—the only all first-class service* (Wall Street Journal).

non·stri·at·ed (non strī′ā tid), *adj.* not striped; smooth: *Nonstriated or smooth muscle consists of delicate spindle-shape cells . . .* (Tracy I. Storer).

non·such (nun′such′), *n.* nonesuch.

non·sug·ar (non shu̇g′ər), *n.* a substance that is not a sugar or does not contain sugar.

non·suit (non′süt′), *n. Law.* a judgment given against a person beginning a lawsuit who neglects to prosecute, fails to show a legal case, or fails to bring sufficient evidence. —*v.t.* to stop (a plaintiff) by a nonsuit. [Middle English *noun suyt* < Anglo-French *noun sute* < *noun* non- + *sute* suit]

non·sup·port (non′sə pôrt′, -pōrt′), *n.* **1.** lack of support. **2.** *Law.* failure to provide for someone for whom one is legally responsible.

non·tel·e·vised (non tel′ə vīzd), *adj.* **1.** not shown on television: *a nontelevised boxing match.* **2.** not exposed to television broadcasts: *Children exposed to this type of entertainment were 35 per cent less healthy than nontelevised children* (Birmingham News).

non·tox·ic (non tok′sik), *adj.* not toxic or poisonous: *Most paint used on children's toys is now required to be nontoxic.*

non·tra·di·tion·al (non′trə dish′ə nəl), not traditional or customary: *Charlotte Negroes have now begun to break into "non-*

traditional" jobs as store clerks, secretaries, bank tellers (Harper's).

non trop·po (nōn trôp′pō), *Music.* not too much; moderately (as part of a direction). [< Italian *non troppo*]

no·nu (nō′nü), *n.* a tree of the madder family found in the East Indies and other Pacific islands, having a composite fruit full of seeds and a bark from which a dye is made. [< Samoan *nonu*]

non-U (non′yü′), *Especially British Slang.* —*adj.* that is not generally acceptable in British upper class society; tending to be common or informal: *Such non-U usages as "met up with," "take in a show," "go steady," and "formal" used as a noun* (New Yorker). —*n.* a person or thing that is non-U. [< *non-u*(pper class)]

non·un·ion (non yün′yən), *adj.* **1.** not belonging to a trade union: *a nonunion worker.* **2.** not following trade-union rules: *nonunion working conditions.* **3.** not recognizing or favoring trade unions: *a nonunion company.* **4.** manufactured by other than union labor.
—*n.* **1.** the condition of a broken bone in which the ends fail to unite. **2.** failure to unite.

non·un·ion·ism (non yün′yə niz əm), *n.* the theories or practices of those opposed to trade unions: *Local trades councils should organize campaigns against nonunionism in their districts* (London Times).

non·un·ion·ist (non yün′yə nist), *n.* **1.** a person who is opposed to trade unions. **2.** a person who does not belong to a trade union: *The union reports claimed that most of those at work were nonunionists* (London Times).

nonunion shop, a business or industrial establishment in which the employer does not recognize and will not bargain with a labor union in determining wages, conditions of employment, etc.

non·vi·o·lence (non vī′ə ləns), *n.* **1.** the absence of violence: *He believes that the world no longer has a choice between violence and nonviolence* (Manchester Guardian). **2.** a political or philosophical belief based on refraining from violence: *International nonviolence is no longer merely the fond hope of a few imaginative or saintly cranks* (Observer).

non·vot·er (non vō′tər), *n.* a person who does not vote or does not have the right to vote: *It's believed that the nonvoters are more in the middle class than among the extremely poor and illiterate* (Wall Street Journal).

non·white (non hwīt′), *n.* **1.** a person who is not a Caucasian. **2.** (in South Africa) a person who is not of European origin: *Until now the Forest Town church has been the only Methodist one serving Johannesburg's nonwhites* (Cape Times).
—*adj.* **1.** not Caucasian: *Moscow is representing itself as the champion of African colonial peoples . . . and of the emergence of the nonwhite peoples everywhere* (Christian Science Monitor). **2.** of or having to do with nonwhites: *a nonwhite association.*

non·wo·ven (non wō′vən), *n.* a fabric made by a method other than weaving: *Nonwovens . . . disdain the spindle and the shuttle* (Wall Street Journal). —*adj.* **1.** made by a method other than weaving: *a nonwoven fabric.* **2.** made of a nonwoven fabric: *nonwoven raincoats and aprons.*

non·ze·ro (non zē′rō), *adj.* not having to do with or being equal to zero: *nonzero calculations, nonzero integers.*

noo·dle[1] (nü′dəl), *n.* a mixture of flour and water, or flour and eggs, like macaroni, but made in flat strips: *The noodles of Rome, however, were a revelation—the very nonpareil of noodles* (New Yorker). [< German *Nudel*]

noo·dle[2] (nü′dəl), *n., v.,* **noo·dled, noo·dling.** —*n.* **1.** a very stupid or silly person; fool: *The fashionable left-wing stereotype of Lord Home as an effete upper-class noodle is ludicrously wide of the mark* (Spectator). **2.** *Slang.* the head. —*v.i. Slang.* to play music in a casual, offhand manner: *A couple of easygoing . . . dance bands noodle around in the Grill most of the evening* (New Yorker). [origin uncertain. Compare NODDY.] —**Syn.** *n.* **1.** simpleton.

nook (nůk), *n.* **1.** a cozy little corner: *a nook facing the fire.* **2.** a hidden or remote spot; sheltered place: *a shady nook* **3.** an interior angle formed by the meeting of two walls, partitions, etc.; corner: *The shades of twilight still hide themselves among the nooks of the adjacent buildings* (Hawthorne). *He wants my poor little farm because it makes a nook in his park wall* (John Arbuthnot). **4.** a corner or angular piece of land; small triangular field. **5.** a piece at a corner or broken from a corner. [Middle English *noke*] —**nook′like′,** *adj.* —**Syn. 1.** recess, niche.

nook-shot·ten (nůk′shot′ən), *adj. Archaic.* running out into corners or angles: *that nook-shotten isle of Albion* (Shakespeare). [origin uncertain; perhaps < Middle English *noke* nook + *shotten,* Old English *scotan* to shoot]

nook·y (nůk′ē), *adj.,* **nook·i·er, nook·i·est. 1.** full of nooks. **2.** nooklike.

no·ol·o·gy (nō ol′ə jē), *n.* the science of the understanding. [< Greek *nóos* mind]

noon (nün), *n., adj., v.,* **nooned, noon·ing.** —*n.* **1.** twelve o'clock in the daytime; middle of the day; midday. *Abbr.:* m. **2.** the highest, finest, or brightest point or part: *the noon of life. To behold the wandering moon Riding near the highest noon* (Milton). **3.** *Poetic.* the middle point of night; midnight: *at noon of night* (John Dryden).
—*adj.* of noon.
—*v.i. Dialect.* to halt for or take a noonday rest or meal: *We traveled six or seven miles farther, and 'nooned' near a brook* (Francis Parkman).
[Middle English *nōne* midday < Old English *nōn* the ninth hour < Latin *nōna* (*hōra*) ninth (hour of daylight by Roman reckoning), about 3 P.M.; the meaning shifted with a change in time of church service. Doublet of NONES[2].]

noon·day (nün′dā′), *n., adj.* noon.

no one, or **no-one** (nō′wun′, -wən), *pron.* no person; nobody.
➔ See **none** for usage note.

noon·ing (nü′ning), *n. Dialect.* **1.** a rest or time for rest at noon: *She had said she would look at pictures all through the nooning* [*at school*] (Mark Twain). **2.** a meal, snack, etc., taken at noon. **3.** noon.

noon·tide (nün′tīd′), *n., adj.* noon: *the noontide of your prosperity* (Charles Lamb).

noon·time (nün′tīm′), *n., adj.* noon; noontide.

noose (nüs), *n., v.,* **noosed, noos·ing.** —*n.* **1.** a loop with a slip knot that tightens as the string or rope is pulled. Nooses are used especially in lassos and snares. **2.** a similar loop used in execution by hanging. **3.** a snare or bond: *the noose of marriage.*
the noose, death by hanging: *He was sentenced to the noose for his crimes.*
—*v.t.* **1.** to make a noose with; tie a noose in. **2.** to catch with a noose: *They run out, and with the lasso, dexterously noose him* [*a bear*] *by either leg* (Washington Irving). **3.** to snare; ensnare: *as dexterous a gipsy as ever . . . noosed a hare* (George J. Whyte-Melville). **4.** to put to death by hanging. **5.** to marry.
[Middle English *nose,* probably < Old French *nous,* perhaps < Old Provençal *nous* < Latin *nōdus* knot, node]

Noose (def. 1)

no·o·sphere (nō′əs fir), *n.* human thought and feeling conceived as a region above and surrounding the biosphere: . . . *the "noosphere"* [*is*] *the psychological habitat in which we live and on whose resources we must draw* (Sir Julian Huxley). [< Greek *nóos* mind + English (bio)*sphere*]

Noot·ka (nüt′kə), *n.* a Wakashan language spoken by Indians on Vancouver Island and in northwestern Washington.

n.o.p., not otherwise provided for.

no·pal (nō′pəl), *n.* **1.** any of various cactuses, especially a variety grown to nourish the cochineal insect. **2.** the prickly pear. [< Mexican Spanish *nopal* < Nahuatl *nopalli*]

no·pal·ry (nō′pəl rē), *n., pl.* **-ries.** a plantation of nopals for raising cochineal insects.

no-par (nō′pär′), *adj.* without any face value; issued without a par: *no-par stock.*

nope (nōp), *adv. U.S. Informal.* no: *"Will you help me win an argument?"* . . . *"Nope. Slug it out."* (New Yorker).

nor[1] (nôr; *unstressed* nər), *conj.* and not; or not; neither; and not either. *Nor* is used: **1.** with a preceding *neither* or other negative: *I have not gone there, nor will I ever go. There was neither stream nor spring in that desert. He had neither food nor drink left.* **2.** *Poetic.* with a preceding *neither* or *not* left out: *Great brother, thou nor I have made the world* (Tennyson). **3.** *Poetic.* instead of *neither* as correlative to a following *nor: Nor bits nor bridles can his rage restrain* (John Dryden). *Drake nor devil nor Spaniard feared* (Henry Newboldt). [Middle English contraction of *nauther,* and *nother* neither, reduction of Old English *nāhwæther* < *ne* not + *āhwæther* either]

nor[2] (nôr), *conj. Scottish.* than: *Hev a dog, Miss!—they're better friends nor any Christian* (George Eliot). *Mighty small specimen . . . Ain't bigger nor a derringer* (Bret Harte). [origin uncertain]

nor' (nôr), *adj., adv.* north.

Nor., 1. Norman. **2.** North. **3.** Norway. **4.** Norwegian.

NORAD (no periods), North American Air Defense Command.

nor·ad·ren·a·lin (nôr′ə dren′ə lin), *n.* norepinephrine: *He has worked mainly on the sympathetic nervous system and on the factors controlling the release of noradrenalin* (New Scientist).

nor·ad·ren·a·line (nôr′ə dren′ə lin, -lēn), *n.* norepinephrine.

Nord (nôrd), *n.* a member of the Nordic race.

Nor·dic (nôr′dik), *adj.* designating, belonging to, or having to do with a race or type characterized by tall stature, blond hair, blue eyes, and long heads: *The Nordic peoples came into Italy and Greece under leader kings* (H. G. Wells). —*n.* a member of the Nordic race: *Scandinavians are Nordics.* [< French *nordique* < *nord* north < Germanic (compare Old Icelandic *northr*)]

nor'·east·er (nôr′ēs′tər), *n.* northeaster.

nor·ep·i·neph·rine (nôr′ep ə nef′rin), *n.* a hormone similar to epinephrine produced by the endings of the sympathetic nerves and found also in the adrenal medulla; noradrenalin. It stimulates the contraction of small blood vessels, and is used in the treatment of hypotension and shock. *Serotonin and norepinephrine are essential to the mosquito and . . . motivate the insect to bite* (Science News Letter). *Formula:* $C_8H_{11}NO_3$ [< *nor*(mal) + *epinephrine*]

nor·eth·an·dro·lone (nôr′eth an′drə lōn), *n.* a synthetic androgen administered orally in treating severe burns, paralytic polio, malnutrition, tuberculosis, and other conditions. *Formula:* $C_{20}H_{30}O_2$

nor·eth·in·drone (nôr eth′ən drōn), *n.* a synthetic hormone used in treating uterine bleeding, premenstrual tension, habitual abortion, and other conditions associated with the female reproductive system. *Formula:* $C_{20}H_{26}O_2$

nor·eth·y·no·drel (nôr′eth i nō′drəl), *n.* Enovid.

Nor·folk Island pine (nôr′fək), a tall pine tree native to Norfolk Island, near Australia, having tough, close-grained wood. It is a kind of araucaria, and is often raised dwarfed as a house plant.

Norfolk jacket or **coat,** a loose-fitting, single-breasted jacket with a belt and box pleats in front and back: . . . *a quartet clad in rough shooting clothes—Norfolk jackets, gaiters, and waterproofs* (New Yorker). [< *Norfolk,* a county in England]

no·ri·a (nôr′ē ə, nōr′-), *n.* a device for raising water, used in Spain, North Africa, and Asia, consisting of a water wheel carrying buckets which fill as they pass through the water and empty on reaching the high point of the turning wheel. [< Spanish *noria* < Arabic *nā'ūra*]

nor·ite (nôr′īt), *n.* a granular igneous rock containing pyroxene in orthorhombic form, often associated with ore deposits. It is a variety of gabbro. [< *Nor*(way), where it is found + *-ite*[1]]

nor·land (nôr′lənd), *n. Poetic.* the north country; northland. [variant of *northland*]

Nor·lu·tin (nôr lü′tin), *n. Trademark.* norethindrone.

norm (nôrm), *n.* a standard for a certain group; type; model; pattern: *to determine the norm for a test. In mathematics this class is above the norm for the senior year.* [< Latin *nōrma* rule, pattern]

Nor·ma (nôr′mə), *n., genitive* **Nor·mae.** a southern constellation near Ara. [< New Latin *Norma*]

Nor·mae (nôr′mē), *n.* genitive of **Norma.**

nor·mal (nôr′məl), *adj.* **1.** of the usual standard or type; regular; usual: *The normal temperature of the human body is 98.6 degrees. A normal day's work is eight hours.* **2.** *Psychology.* **a.** not mentally ill; fairly well adjusted; sane: *the note . . . of the strange and sinister embroidered on the very type of the normal and easy* (Henry James). **b.** of average intelligence, emotional stability, etc. **3.** *Biology, Medicine, etc.* well; healthy; not diseased; functioning normally. **4.** *Geometry.* **a.** being at right angles; perpendicular. **b.** of or like a normal line or plane. **5.** *Chemistry.* **a.** (of an acidic or basic solution) containing the equivalent of one gram of hydrogen ion per liter. *Abbr.:* N. **b.** of or denoting an aliphatic hydrocarbon or hydrocarbon derivative consisting of a straight unbranched chain of carbon atoms, each carbon atom of which is united with no more than two other carbon atoms. **c.** not found in association, as molecules. **6.** *Electricity.* (of a galvanic cell) having a voltage that can be reproduced.
—*n.* **1.** the usual state or level: *He is ten pounds above normal for his age.* **2.** *Geometry.* **a.** a line or plane that is at right angles to another. **b.** the intercepted part of the line (on the normal line) between the curve and the x-axis. **3.** a normal person in mental ability or adjustment. **4.** *Psychology.* average intelligence, average emotional stability, etc.
[< Latin *nōrmālis* < *nōrma* a rule, pattern]
—**nor′mal·ness,** *n.*
—**Syn.** *adj.* **1.** natural, typical. *-n.* **1.** average.

normal curve or **distribution,** *Statistics.* a bell-shaped curve which represents the theoretical frequency distribution of a series of chance happenings, occurrences of human characteristics, etc.; probability curve.

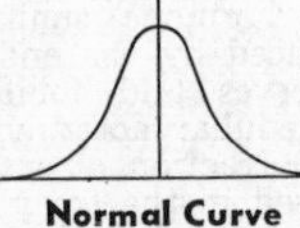

Normal Curve

nor·mal·cy (nôr′məl sē), *n.* a being normal; normal condition; normality: *back to normalcy. We must . . . strive for normalcy* (Warren G. Harding).

nor·mal·ise (nôr′mə līz), *v.t.,* **-ised, -is·ing.** *Especially British.* normalize: *He says the situation there must be "normalised under all circumstances"* (Manchester Guardian).

nor·mal·i·ty (nôr mal′ə tē), *n.* normal condition; normalcy: *A series of shattering experiences brings home to him that the normality he has pursued is a mirage* (Atlantic).

nor·mal·i·za·tion (nôr′mə lə zā′shən), *n.* the act or process of making normal: *Two Communist countries "have agreed to take further steps toward the normalization of their relations"* (Wall Street Journal).

nor·mal·ize (nôr′mə līz), *v.t.,* **-ized, -iz·ing.** to make normal: *The Yugoslavs maintain the purpose of the conference is . . . to normalize relations between Moscow and Belgrade* (New York Times). —**nor′mal·iz′er,** *n.*

nor·mal·ly (nôr′mə lē), *adv.* in the normal way; regularly; if things are normal: *to speak normally. A child normally begins to lose his first teeth when he is six or seven years old. I wouldn't normally approve of that.*
—**Syn.** generally, ordinarily.

normal pressure, one atmosphere or 76 centimeters of mercury.

normal salt, a salt formed from an acid of which all of the hydrogen has been replaced.

normal school, a school where people, usually high school graduates, are trained to become teachers, especially a separate institution for teacher education offering a two-year course and a certificate. [after French *école normale*]

normal solution, a solution containing one gram equivalent of a dissolved substance per liter.

normal temperature, zero degrees centigrade; 273 degrees absolute.

Nor·man (nôr′mən), *n.* **1.** a native or inhabitant of Normandy in France. **2.** a member of the mixed ethnic group descended from the Scandinavians who settled in Normandy and the French. **3.** one of the Scandinavian ancestors of these people; Norsemen; Northman. **4.** Norman-French.
—*adj.* **1.** of or like the Normans or Normandy. **2.** Norman-French. **3.** of or having to do with the architecture of Normandy, characterized by simplicity, massiveness, and use of the rounded arch. It is a variety of Romanesque developed there in the 900's and later introduced into England, southern Italy, and Sicily.
[< Old French *Normans,* plural of *Normant* < Germanic (compare Old High German *Northman*)]

Norman Façade of Anglo-Saxon Church

Norman Conquest, the conquest of England by the Normans in 1066, under the leadership of William the Conqueror.

Nor·man·esque (nôr′mə nesk′), *adj.* after the Norman style, as of architecture.

Nor·man-French (nôr′mən french′), *n.* **1.** a dialect of the French language spoken by the Normans who conquered England in 1066; Anglo-French. **2.** a later form of this dialect, surviving in certain English legal phrases; law French. —*adj.* of or having to do with this dialect or those who spoke it; Anglo-French; Anglo-Norman.

Nor·man·i·za·tion (nôr′mə nə zā′shən), *n.* the process of Normanizing.

Nor·man·ize (nôr′mə nīz), *v.,* **-ized, -iz·ing.** —*v.i.* to adopt the Norman dialect or manners. —*v.t.* to make Norman or like the Normans: *There is no wavering here—as there was none in the ruthless policy of William the Conqueror in subduing and Normanizing England* (Nikolaus Pevsner).

nor·ma·tive (nôr′mə tiv), *adj.* **1.** establishing or setting up a norm or standard: *The normative judgments themselves are more clearly anchored in fact than in most other books dealing with this difficult topic* (Harold P. Green). **2.** based on or prescribing standards of usage: *normative grammar.*

nor·mo·cyte (nôr′mə sīt), *n.* a red blood corpuscle of normal size, shape, and color. [< Latin *nōrma* a rule, pattern + English *-cyte*]

Norn (nôrn), *n.* any of the three Norse goddesses of fate, Urd, Verdande and Skuld, to whose decrees the gods as well as men are subject: *Skuld, the younger Norn, Who watches over birth and death* (John Greenleaf Whittier).
[< Old Icelandic *Norn*]

Nor·roy (nor′oi), *n.* the title of the third English King-of-arms, ranking after Clarencieux. [< Anglo-French *nor-* north + *roy* king]

Norse (nôrs), *adj.* **1.** of or having to do with ancient Scandinavia, its people, or their language. **2.** of or having to do with Norway or its people; Norwegian.
—*n.* **1.** the people of ancient Scandinavia; Norsemen; Northmen. **2. a.** the Norwegians. **b.** the ancient Norwegians. **3.** the language of the ancient Scandinavians, often called Old Norse. **4.** the language of Norway.
[probably < Dutch *Noorsch* Norwegian]
➔ **Norse,** meaning the people of ancient Scandinavia and Norwegians, is singular in form and plural in use: *The Norse are a hardy race.* When *Norse* means language it is singular in form and use.

Norse·man (nôrs′mən), *n., pl.* **-men.** a member of a tall, blond ethnic group that lived in ancient Scandinavia; Northman: *The Vikings were Norsemen.*

nor·te·a·mer·i·ca·no (nôr′tā ä mä′rē kä′nō), *n., pl.* **-ca·nos** (-kä′nōs). *Spanish.* a citizen of the United States: *Add here a small but nice point of courtesy: speak of yourself always as a norteamericano* (Harper's).

north (nôrth), *n.* **1.** the direction to which a compass needle points; direction to the right as one faces the setting sun. *Abbr.:* N (no period). **2.** the part of any country toward the north, especially that part of Great Britain north of the Humber. Also, **North. 3.** *Especially Poetic.* the north wind.
—*adj.* **1.** toward the north: *the north side of town.* **2.** from the north: *a north wind.* **3.** in the north; facing the north: *the north wing of the house.* **4.** in the northern part; northern.
—*adv.* **1.** toward the north; northward: *a train moving north.* **2.** in the north: *The city is north of us.* [Old English *north*]

North (def. 1) on a compass

North (nôrth), *n.* **1.** the north part of a country. **2.** the northern part of the United States; the States north of Maryland, the Ohio River, and Missouri, making up most of the states that formed the Union side in the Civil War. **3.** the player in the game of bridge sitting opposite and in partnership with South: *North responded by confirming interest in the slam and cue bidding the Ace of Diamonds* (London Times).
—*adj.* in the northern part; northern.

North American, 1. of or having to do with North America. **2.** a native or inhabitant of North America.

North American Newspaper Alliance, a world-wide independent news agency specializing in exclusive news coverage and in articles by famous persons.

North Atlantic Treaty, the treaty of alliance signed by the 15 western nations that are members of NATO; Atlantic Pact.

North Atlantic Treaty Organization, NATO.

North Briton, a Scot.

north·bound (nôrth′bound′), *adj.* bound northward; going north.

north by east, the point of the compass or the direction one point or 11 degrees 15 minutes to the east of north.

north by west, the point of the compass or the direction one point or 11 degrees 15 minutes to the west of north.

North Carolinian, 1. of or having to do with North Carolina or its people. **2.** a native or inhabitant of North Carolina.

north celestial pole, the zenith of the northern end of the earth's axis from which every direction is south. It is just over 1 degree from the North Star; North Pole. See picture under **celestial sphere.**

North Da·ko·tan (də kō′tən), **1.** of or having to do with North Dakota. **2.** a native or inhabitant of North Dakota.

north·east (nôrth′ēst′; *Nautical* nôr′ēst′), *adj.* **1.** halfway between north and east. **2.** lying toward or situated in the northeast: *a northeast district.* **3.** coming from the northeast: *a northeast wind.* **4.** directed toward the northeast.
—*n.* **1.** a direction midway between north and east. *Abbr.:* NE (no periods). **2.** a place in the northeast part or direction.
—*adv.* **1.** toward the northeast: *At this point the road turns northeast.* **2.** from the northeast. **3.** in the northeast.

northeast by east, the point of the compass or the direction one point or 11 degrees 15 minutes to the east of northeast.

northeast by north, the point of the compass or the direction one point or 11 degrees 15 minutes to the north of northeast.

north·east·er (nôrth′ēs′tər), *n.* a wind or storm from the northeast: *The northeaster blew in fresh and cool.* Also, **nor′easter.**

north·east·er·ly (nôrth′ēs′tər lē), *adj., adv.* **1.** toward the northeast. **2.** from the northeast.

north·east·ern (nôrth′ēs′tərn; *Nautical* nôr′ēs′tərn), *adj.* **1.** toward the northeast. **2.** from the northeast. **3.** of the northeast; having to do with the northeast.

North·east·ern (nôrth′ēs′tərn), *adj.* of, having to do with, or in the northeastern states of the United States.

Northeast Passage, a sea route from the North Atlantic to the Pacific along the northern coast of Europe and Asia, first traveled in 1878-1879.

north·east·ward (nôrth′ēst′wərd; *Nautical* nôr′ēst′wərd), *adv., adj.* **1.** toward the northeast. **2.** northeast. —*n.* northeast.

north·east·ward·ly (nôrth′ēst′wərd lē; *Nautical* nôr′ēst′wərd lē), *adj.* **1.** toward the northeast. **2.** (of winds) from the northeast. —*adv.* toward the northeast.

north·east·wards (nôrth′ēst′wərdz; *Nautical* nôr′ēst′wərdz), *adv.* northeastward.

north·er (nôr′ᴛʜər), *n.* **1.** a wind or storm coming from the north. **2.** *U.S.* a strong, intensely cold north wind which blows over Texas, the Gulf Coast, Florida, and the Gulf of Mexico during the autumn and winter months.

north·er·li·ness (nôr′ᴛʜər lē nis), *n.* the state of being northerly.

north·er·ly (nôr′ᴛʜər lē), *adj.* **1.** toward the north: *the northerly window of the bedroom.* **2.** from the north: *a northerly wind.* **3.** of the north.

—*adv.* **1.** toward the north; northward. **2.** from the north. —*n.* a northerly wind.
north·ern (nôr′ᴛʜərn), *adj.* **1.** toward the north: *the northern side of a building.* **2.** coming from the north: *a northern breeze.* **3.** of the north: *He has traveled in northern countries.* **4.** *Astronomy.* of or in the northern half of the celestial sphere: *the northern signs of the zodiac, a northern constellation.*
—*n.* **1.** Often, **Northern,** a Northerner. **2.** a north wind; norther. [Old English *northerne*]
North·ern (nôr′ᴛʜərn), *adj.* of or in the North of the United States: *Seattle is a Northern city.* —*n.* a Northerner.
Northern Car, *Astronomy.* Charles's Wain; the Big Dipper.
Northern Coalsack, one of the large dark spaces in the Milky Way near Deneb.
Northern Cross, a cross of six stars in the northern constellation Cygnus.
Northern Crown, Corona Borealis.
northern eider, a variety of eider duck of northeastern North America and Greenland, black and white in the male and brown in the female.
Northern English, the English language as spoken in the north of England.
north·ern·er (nôr′ᴛʜər nər), *n.* a native or inhabitant of the north.
North·ern·er (nôr′ᴛʜər nər), *n.* a native or inhabitant of the North of the United States.
northern fur seal, a fur seal found in the Bering Sea, a sea in the North Pacific.
Northern Hemisphere, the half of the earth that is north of the equator.
northern lights, the aurora borealis: *The northern lights seem to wax and wane in frequency with the rise and fall of the sunspot cycle* (Hubert J. Bernhard).
northern mammoth, a mammoth, formerly native to Europe and Northern Asia, remains of which have been found in Siberia; woolly mammoth. See picture under **mammoth.**
north·ern·most (nôr′ᴛʜərn mōst), *adj.* farthest north: *A few of the northernmost stars in this constellation* (Science News Letter).
northern phalarope, a gray and white phalarope of arctic regions that migrates in winter to the southern Atlantic.
northern pike, a slender predatory food fish of the Northern Hemisphere reaching a length of over 4 feet and having spiny fins and a narrow, pointed head.
northern sea lion, Steller's sea lion.
Northern Spy, a tart, American winter apple, marked with yellow and red stripes.
northern star, the North Star.
northern water thrush, a water thrush found in wooded swampy areas of North America.
northern whiting, a whiting of the Atlantic coast of the United States.
north geographic pole, North Pole.
North Germanic, the Scandinavian group of languages.
north·ing (nôr′thing, -ᴛʜing), *n.* **1.** the distance of latitude reckoned northward from the last point of reckoning. **2.** the distance northward covered by a ship on any northerly course. **3.** *Astronomy.* declination measured northward.
north·land (nôrth′lənd), *n.* the land in the north; the northern part of a country. [Old English *northland*]
North·land (nôrth′lənd), *n.* **1.** the northern regions of the world. **2.** the peninsula containing Norway and Sweden: *I am the God Thor ... Here in my Northland ... Reign I forever!* (Longfellow).
north·land·er (nôrth′lən dər), *n.* an inhabitant of the northland.
north magnetic pole, the point on the earth's surface toward which a magnetic needle points; the pole of the earth's magnetic field. Its location varies slightly from year to year but is about 1,100 miles from the North Pole (71 degrees north, latitude, and 95 degrees west, longitude), near Prince of Wales Island.
North·man (nôrth′mən), *n., pl.* **-men. 1.** Norseman; one of the ancient Scandinavians. **2.** a native or inhabitant of northern Europe.
north·most (nôrth′mōst), *adj.* northernmost: *the northmost part of the coast of Mozambique* (Daniel Defoe).
north-north·east (nôrth′nôrth ēst′; *Nautical* nôr′nôr ēst′), *n.* the point of the compass or the direction midway between north and northeast, two points or 22 degrees 30 minutes to the east of north. —*adj., adv.* of, from, or toward the north-northeast.
north-north·west (nôrth′nôrth west′; *Nautical* nôr′nôr west′), *n.* the point of the compass or the direction midway between north and northwest, two points or 22 degrees 30 minutes to the west of north. —*adj., adv.* of, from, or toward the north-northwest.
North Pole, 1. the northern end of the earth's axis; that point on the earth's surface from which every direction is south: *The North Pole is surrounded by water and is at sea level* (Gabriele Rabel). **2.** the north magnetic pole. **3.** the north celestial pole.
North Star, the bright star almost directly above the North Pole; Polaris: *The North Star, which has guided navigators throughout history, is not a lonely star like the sun* (Time).
North·um·bri·an (nôr thum′brē ən), *adj.* **1.** of or having to do with Northumbria, its people, or their dialect: *This uvular trill developed in the north of England, where it came to be known as the Northumbrian burr* (Charles Kenneth Thomas). **2.** of or having to do with Northumberland, its people, or their dialect.
—*n.* **1.** a native or inhabitant of Northumbria, an ancient kingdom in northern England. **2.** the dialect of Old English spoken in Northumbria. **3.** a native or inhabitant of Northumberland. **4.** the Northumberland dialect of Modern English.
north·ward (nôrth′wərd; *Nautical* nôr′ᴛʜərd), *adv.* toward the north; in a northerly direction: *Rocks lay northward of the ship's course.* —*adj.* toward the north; north: *the northward slope of a hill.* —*n.* north.
north·ward·ly (nôrth′wərd lē; *Nautical* nôr′ᴛʜərd lē), *adj.* **1.** toward the north. **2.** (of winds) from the north. —*adv.* toward the north.
north·wards (nôrth′wərdz; *Nautical* nôr′ᴛʜərdz), *adv.* northward.
north·west (nôrth′west′; *Nautical* nôr′west′), *adj.* **1.** halfway between north and west. **2.** lying toward or situated in the northwest. **3.** coming from the northwest: *a northwest wind.* **4.** directed toward the northwest: *a northwest window.*
—*n.* **1.** a northwest direction midway between north and west. *Abbr.:* NW (no periods). **2.** a place that is in the northwest part or direction.
—*adv.* **1.** toward the northwest: *The road from Chicago to Minneapolis runs northwest.* **2.** from the northwest. **3.** in the northwest.
northwest by north, the point of the compass or the direction one point or 11 degrees 15 minutes to the north of northwest.
northwest by west, the point of the compass or the direction one point or 11 degrees 15 minutes to the west of northwest.
north·west·er (nôrth′wes′tər; *Nautical* nôr′wes′tər), *n.* **1.** a wind or storm from the northwest. **2.** the strong wind which blows over Bengal, India, in March and April. Also, **nor'wester.**
north·west·er·ly (nôrth′wes′tər lē; *Nautical* nôr′wes′tər lē), *adj., adv.* **1.** toward the northwest. **2.** from the northwest.
north·west·ern (nôrth′wes′tərn; *Nautical* nôr′wes′tərn), *adj.* **1.** toward the northwest. **2.** from the northwest. **3.** of the northwest; having to do with the northwest.
North·west·ern (nôrth′wes′tərn), *adj.* of, having to do with, or in the northwestern states of the United States.
Northwest Passage, a passage for ships from the Atlantic to the Pacific along the northern coast of North America, first successfully traveled in 1906-1909: *Both Pond and Mackenzie hoped that this river, if anyone could find it, might turn out to be the Northwest Passage to the Pacific Ocean* (Maclean's).
Northwest Territory, the region north of the Ohio River, organized by Congress in 1787, now forming the states of Ohio, Indiana, Illinois, Michigan, Wisconsin, and part of Minnesota.
north·west·ward (nôrth′west′wərd; *Nautical* nôr′west′wərd), *adv., adj.* **1.** toward the northwest. **2.** northwest. —*n.* northwest.
north·west·ward·ly (nôrth′west′wərd lē; *Nautical* nôr′west′wərd lē), *adj.* **1.** toward the northwest. **2.** (of winds) from the northwest. —*adv.* toward the northwest.
north·west·wards (nôrth′west′wərdz; *Nautical* nôr′west′wərdz), *adv.* northwestward.
Norw., 1. Norway. **2.** Norwegian.
nor·ward (nôr′wərd), *adv., adj., n.* northward.
Norway pine (nôr′wā), the red pine.
Norway rat, the common brown rat found about buildings, refuse, etc.; brown rat.
Norway spruce, a tall spruce native to Europe and Asia, an important source of lumber, wood pulp, etc. Various dwarf varieties are grown for ornament.
Nor·we·gian (nôr wē′jən), *adj.* of Norway, a country in northern Europe, west and north of Sweden, its people, or their language: *a Norwegian village.* —*n.* **1.** a native or inhabitant of Norway. **2.** the Scandinavian language of Norway.
Norwegian elkhound, any of an ancient breed of Norwegian hunting dogs having a short body, gray coat, pointed ears, and a tail curled over the back, used for tracking elk and other game.

Norwegian Elkhound
(18 to 20½ in. high at the shoulder)

nor'west·er (nôr-wes′tər), *n.* **1.** a heavy, waterproof oilskin hat or coat worn by seamen. **2.** northwester.
Nor·wich terrier (nôr′ij, -ich; nor′-), any of a breed of small, short-legged terriers with a wiry, usually red coat, weighing from 10 to 15 pounds. It is used for hunting rabbits or kept as a house dog. [< *Norwich,* a city in England]
n.o.s., not otherwise specified.
Nos. or **nos.,** numbers.
nose (nōz), *n., v.,* **nosed, nos·ing.** —*n.* **1.** the part of the face or head just above the mouth, serving as an opening for breathing and as the organ of smell: *Savory odors greeted the nose.* **2.** the sense of smell: *A mouse has a good nose for cheese.* **3.** a faculty for perceiving or detecting: *A reporter must have a nose for news.* **4.** a part that stands out, especially at the front of anything: *The bow of a ship or airplane is often called the nose. We saw the little steamer's nose poking around the cliff.* **5.** odor. **6.** *British Slang.* an informer.
count noses, *Informal.* to find out how many people are present, in favor of something, etc.; make a nose count: *Some modern zealots appear to have no better knowledge of truth, nor better manner of judging it, than by counting noses* (Anthony Shaftesbury).
cut off one's nose to spite one's face, to be spiteful in such a way as to hurt oneself: *To threaten such a tragic thing as moving the Stock Exchange out of Lower Manhattan is . . . cutting off one's nose to spite one's face* (New York Times).
follow one's nose, a. to go straight ahead: *Adams asked him if he could direct him to an alehouse. The fellow . . . bade him follow his nose* (Henry Fielding). **b.** to be guided by one's instinct: *All that follow their noses are led by their eyes, but blind men* (Shakespeare). **c.** to be guided by one's sense of smell: *The hounds ran ahead, following their noses.*
have, keep, or **put one's nose to the grindstone,** to work long and hard: *People whose heads are a little up in the world, have no occasion to keep their nose to the grindstone* (Lights and Shades).
lead by the nose, to have complete control over: *Seven-eighths of the town are led by the nose by this or that periodical work* (Frederick Marryat).
look down one's nose at, to feel contempt for: *People who prefer symphony concerts or chamber music tend to look down their noses at . . . opera* (Winthrop Sargeant).
on the nose, a. exactly: *He was an instinctive showman, and he could hit it right on the nose* (New Yorker). **b.** solidly: *He won the race on the nose.*
pay through the nose, to pay excessively; be charged exorbitantly: *The Russians have been making them pay through the nose for the war supplies they've received* (Wall Street Journal).
poke one's nose into, to pry into; meddle in: *A flourishing Evangelical, who poked his nose into everything* (Mark Pattison).

put one's nose out of joint, a. to displace or supplant one: *The king is pleased enough with her: which, I fear, will put Madam Castlemaine's nose out of joint* (Samuel Pepys). **b.** to put in a bad humor; disconcert: *It always put his nose out of joint to see someone else getting attention.*
thumb one's nose at, a. to put one's thumb to one's nose in scorn of: *The boys thumbed their noses at each other.* **b.** to dismiss scornfully; disdain: *His film defiantly thumbs its nose at the fate all men fear* (Time).
turn up one's nose at, to treat with contempt or scorn: *What learning there was in those days . . . turned up its nose at the strains of the native minstrels* (Bayard Taylor).
under one's nose, in plain sight; very easy to notice: *A wagon-load of valuable merchandise had been smuggled ashore . . . directly beneath their unsuspicious noses* (Hawthorne).
win by a nose, a. to win a horse race by no more than the length of a horse's nose: *Lucky Day won the race at Churchill Downs by a nose.* **b.** to win by a small margin: *The 1960 presidential election was won by a nose.*
—*v.t.* **1.** to discover by smell; smell out; scent: *A dozen times, Perrault, nosing the way, broke through the ice bridges* (Jack London). **2.** to examine with the nose; smell. **3.** to rub with the nose; nuzzle: *The cat nosed her kittens.* **4.** to push with the nose or forward end: *The bulldozer nosed the rock off the road.* —*v.i.* **1.** to sniff. **2.** to push forward or move, especially slowly, cautiously, or hesitantly: *The little boat nosed carefully between the rocks.* **3.** to search (for); pry (into): *Don't nose into my affairs.* **4.** *British Slang.* to be an informer; serve as a police spy.
nose out, a. to find out by looking around quietly or secretly: *to nose out the truth.* **b.** to win (over someone) by a small margin; win by a nose: *Kennedy nosed out Nixon in the 1960 presidential race.*
[Old English *nosu*]

nose bag, a bag containing food, to be hung on a horse's head.

nose•band (nōz′band′), *n.* the part of a bridle that goes over the animal's nose.

nose•bleed (nōz′blēd′), *n.* bleeding from the nose; epistaxis.

nose cone, the front section of a missile or rocket made to carry a bomb to a target or to carry instruments or a man into space. The nose cone is made to withstand high temperatures from friction with air particles and usually separates from the rest of the missile or rocket after the fuel runs out. *A one-degree launch error could cause the nose cone to miss its bull's-eye by about 100 miles* (Science News Letter).

NOSE CONE

Nose Cone on Juno-I Explorer missile

nose count, *Informal.* the act of determining the number of those people present or of finding out how many people are in favor of or against something; survey; poll: *House Democratic leaders have started a nose count of their party's House members on the natural gas bill* (Wall Street Journal).

-nosed, *combining form.* having a ___ nose: *Long-nosed = having a long nose.*

nose dive, 1. a swift plunge straight downward by an airplane, etc. **2.** *Informal.* a sudden, sharp drop: *The thermometer took a nose dive after the warm spell in January.*

nose-dive (nōz′dīv′), *v.i.,* **-dived, -div•ing.** to take a nose dive: *After the war, the seed business nose-dived, just as rapidly as it had expanded* (Wall Street Journal).

nose drops, liquid medicine administered in drops put in the nose especially to make breathing through the nose easier.

no-see-um (nō sē′əm), *n.* a minute biting fly or midge; punkie.

nose flute, a musical instrument blown with the nose, used in Thailand, in the Fiji and Society Islands, etc.

nose•gay (nōz′gā′), *n.* a bunch of flowers; bouquet: *a garden where I had . . . gathered many a nosegay* (Samuel Butler). [< *nose* + obsolete *gay* something gay or pretty] —**Syn.** posy.

nose•piece (nōz′pēs′), *n.* **1.** the part of a helmet that covers and protects the nose. **2.** a noseband for an animal. **3.** the part of a microscope to which the objective is attached: *The instrument is provided with a rotating nosepiece to which are permanently attached three objectives of different magnifications* (Sears and Zemansky). **4.** a piece of wood inserted to form the nose of a stuffed animal. **5.** the nozzle of a hose or pipe.

nose ring, 1. a ring fixed in an animal's nose for leading it: *His bull had broken and dislodged its nose ring, which is, of course, the only means by which it is controlled* (Punch). **2.** a ring worn in the nose for ornament by some peoples.

nose•wheel (nōz′hwēl′), *n.* a retractable landing wheel located at the nose of an airplane.

nos•ey (nō′zē), *adj.,* **nos•i•er, nos•i•est,** *n.* nosy.

Nosey Parker, Nosy Parker.

nosh (nosh), *British Slang.* —*n.* a meal or snack: *Evening nosh depended on what was going on at special prices* (Punch). —*v.t., v.i.* to have a meal or snack: *He had called to see if my son would go out to nosh with him* (Punch). [probably < Yiddish *nosh, nash* < *nashen* to snack, nibble < German *naschen*]

no-show (nō′shō′), *n. U.S.* a person who reserves a seat or other space, especially on an airplane, and fails either to cancel it or to use it: *Domestic air carriers themselves have twice experimented with penalty rules for no-shows* (Wall Street Journal). [< *no*[1] + *show* (up to claim or use)]

no-side (nō′sīd′), *n. British.* the conclusion of a game of Rugby.

nos•i•ness (nō′zē nis), *n.* the quality or fact of being nosy: *More than indiscreet nosiness was involved* (Newsweek).

nos•ing (nō′zing), *n.* a horizontal edge that projects over a vertical surface, as the edge of a stair tread.

nos•o•co•mi•al (nos′ə kō′mē əl), *adj.* of or having to do with a hospital. [< Late Latin *nosocomīum* hospital (< Greek *nosokomeîon* < *nósos* disease + *komeîn* take care of) + English *-al*[1]]

nos•o•ge•o•graph•ic (nos′ō jē′ə graf′ik), *adj.* of or having to do with nosogeography.

nos•o•ge•o•graph•i•cal (nos′ō jē′ə graf′ə kəl), *adj.* nosogeographic.

nos•o•ge•og•ra•phy (nos′ō jē og′rə fē), *n.* the study of disease in relation to geographical factors. [< Greek *nósos* disease + English *geography*]

no•sog•ra•pher (nō sog′rə fər), *n.* an expert in nosography; a person who describes diseases.

nos•o•graph•ic (nos′ə graf′ik), *adj.* of or having to do with nosography.

no•sog•ra•phy (nō sog′rə fē), *n.* the systematic description of diseases. [< Greek *nósos* disease + English *-graphy*]

nos•o•log•i•cal (nos′ə loj′ə kəl), *adj.* having to do with nosology.

no•sol•o•gist (nō sol′ə jist), *n.* an expert in nosology; a classifier of diseases.

no•sol•o•gy (nō sol′ə jē), *n.* **1.** the classification of diseases. **2.** the branch of medicine dealing with the classification of diseases. **3.** the special symptoms or characteristics of a disease, comprising the chief basis for diagnosis. [< Greek *nósos* disease + English *-logy*]

nos•tal•gia (nos tal′jə, -jē ə), *n.* **1.** painful yearning for one's home country, city, etc.; homesickness: *One who has to spend so much of his life in the East . . . should not be hampered by ties and habits calculated . . . to foster nostalgia* (Sidney J. Owen). **2.** a painful or wistful yearning for anything far removed in space or time: *the nostalgia of the heathen past* (David H. Lawrence). [< New Latin *nostalgia* < Greek *nóstos* homecoming (< *neîsthai* come, go) + *-algiā* < *álgos* pain]

nos•tal•gic (nos tal′jik), *adj.* feeling or showing nostalgia; homesick: *Nostalgic Southerners . . . speak of Jefferson Davis with respect but not with affection* (New York Times). —**nos•tal′gi•cal•ly,** *adv.*

nos•toc (nos′tok), *n.* any of a group of bluish-green algae that live in jellylike colonies in moist places, fresh water, or on plants. [< New Latin *Nostoc* (coined by Paracelsus)]

nos•to•log•ic (nos′tə loj′ik), *adj.* **1.** characterized by extreme senility. **2.** having to do with gerontology.

nos•tol•o•gy (nos tol′ə jē), *n.* gerontology. [< Greek *nóstos* homecoming (see NOSTALGIA) + English *-logy*]

nos•to•ma•ni•a (nos′tō mā′nē ə), *n.* obsessive nostalgia.

Nos•tra•da•mus (nos′trə dā′məs), *n.* a person who professes to foretell future events; prophet; seer. [< Latinization of Michel de *Notredame,* 1503-1566, a French physician and astrologer]

nos•tril (nos′trəl), *n.* either of the two openings in the nose. Air is breathed into the lungs, and smells come into the sensitive parts of the nose, through the nostrils. [Old English *nosthyrl* < *nosu* nose + *thyrel* hole]

nos•triled or **nos•trilled** (nos′trəld), *adj.* having nostrils.

nos•trum (nos′trəm), *n., pl.* **-trums. 1.** a medicine for which great claims are made by the person who makes and sells it; quack remedy; patent medicine: *What drop or nostrum can this plague remove* (Alexander Pope). *The doctors and quack-salvers . . . experimenting on his poor little body with every conceivable nostrum* (Thackeray). **2.** a pet scheme for producing wonderful results; cure-all: *World government, his nostrum, is probably accepted by most thinking people today as a necessity at some time in the not too distant future* (Bulletin of Atomic Scientists). [< Latin *nostrum* (*remedium*) our (remedy) (because it is usually prepared by the person recommending it)] —**Syn. 2.** panacea.

nos•y (nō′zē), *adj.,* **nos•i•er, nos•i•est,** *n. Informal.* —*adj.* rudely or improperly inquisitive; prying: *He said that those of his followers who had chased nosy tax collectors out of their shops . . . were only fighting for their liberties* (New Yorker). —*n.* **1.** a person with a large or prominent nose. **2.** a busybody; meddler. Also, **nosey.**

Nosy Parker, an offensively inquisitive person; one who is insatiably curious about things that are none of his business: *The jolt would no doubt fling the book a good distance from one, but some Nosey Parker would be sure to retrieve it* (Frank Sullivan).

not (not), *adv.* a word that says no; a negative: *not in any way or fashion, not to any extent or degree. That is not true. Is it true or not? It is a fine day, is it not?* (used elliptically).
whether or not or **no,** in any case; no matter what happens: *You may say that this is to degrade the state. Possibly. But whether or no, this is the principle already . . . acted upon* (John Morley).
[unstressed variant of *nought*]

no•ta be•ne (nō′tə bē′nē), *Latin.* note well; observe what follows; take notice. *Abbr.:* N.B., n.b.

no•ta•bil•i•a (nō′tə bil′ē ə), *n.pl.* things or events worth noting; notable things: *I reached for the stout . . . book of notabilia I had been reading in bed* (J.W.R. Scott). [< Latin *notābilia,* neuter plural of *notābilis;* see NOTABLE]

no•ta•bil•i•ty (nō′tə bil′ə tē), *n., pl.* **-ties. 1.** the quality of being notable; distinction. **2.** a prominent person; notable: *All sorts of cosmopolites and notabilities stopped over, summered, wintered there* (Atlantic). —**Syn. 1.** eminence.

no•ta•ble (nō′tə bəl; *also* not′ə bəl *for adj. 3*), *adj.* **1.** worthy of notice; striking; remarkable: *a notable event, a notable book, a notable painter.* **2.** that can be noted or perceived; perceptible; appreciable: *a notable quantity.* **3.** capable; thrifty and industrious as a housewife: *His notable little wife, too, had enough to do to attend to her housekeeping* (Washington Irving). —*n.* **1.** a person who is notable: *Many notables came to the President's reception.* **2.** Often, **Notable.** (in French history) one of a number of prominent men from the three estates, before the Revolution, called together by the king as a deliberative body in times of crisis.
[< Latin *notābilis* < *notāre* to note < *nota* a mark] —**no′ta•ble•ness,** *n.*
—**Syn.** *adj.* **1.** memorable, conspicuous, famous.

no•ta•bly (nō′tə blē), *adv.* in a notable manner; to a notable degree.

no•tan•dum (nō tan′dəm), *n., pl.* **-dums, -da** (-də). **1.** a thing to be noted. **2.** a record of something to be noted; memorandum. [< Latin *notandum,* gerund of *notāre;* see NOTABLE]

no·tar·i·al (nō tãr′ē əl), *adj.* **1.** of or having to do with a notary public. **2.** made or done by a notary public. —**no·tar′i·al·ly,** *adv.*

no·ta·rize (nō′tə rīz), *v.t.,* **-rized, -riz·ing.** to certify (a contract, deed, will, etc.), as a notary public does; give legal authenticity to: *Many documents must be notarized before they become legally effective. The purpose of notarizing a document is to protect those who use it from forgeries* (World Book Encyclopedia).

no·ta·ry (nō′tər ē), *n., pl.* **-ries.** a notary public. [< Latin *notārius* clerk, ultimately < *nota* a mark, note]

notary public, *pl.* **notaries public.** a public officer authorized to certify deeds and contracts, to record the fact that a certain person swears that something is true, and to attend to other legal matters.

no·ta·tion (nō tā′shən), *n.* **1.** a set of signs or symbols used to represent numbers, quantities, or other values: *In arithmetic we use the Arabic notation (1, 2, 3, 4, etc.).* **2.** the representing of numbers, quantities, or other values by symbols or signs: *Music has a special system of notation, and so has chemistry.* **3.** a note to assist the memory; record; jotting: *He made a notation in the margin of the book.* **4.** the act of noting. [< Latin *notātiō, -ōnis* < *notāre* to note < *nota* a mark] —**Syn. 3.** memorandum.

no·ta·tion·al (nō tā′shə nəl), *adj.* of or having to do with notation.

notch (noch), *n.* **1.** a V-shaped nick or cut made in an edge or on a curving surface, as for keeping a score or record: *a pole with notches for aid in climbing. The Indians cut notches on a stick to keep count of numbers.* **2.** *U.S.* a deep narrow pass or gap between mountains. **3.** *Informal.* a grade; step; degree: *In the hot weather many people set their air conditioners several notches higher. A mark of A-minus is a slight notch below an A.*
—*v.t.* **1.** to make a notch or notches in. **2.** to record by notches; score; tally: *British industry has already notched some impressive victories* (Punch).
[apparently earlier *a noch,* by misdivision of Middle English *an och* < French *oche* < Old French *oschier* to notch]
—**Syn.** *n.* **1.** dent, indentation.

note (nōt), *n., v.,* **not·ed, not·ing.** —*n.* **1.** words written down to remind one of something: *Her notes helped her remember what the speaker said.* **2.** notice; heed; observation: *Give careful note to his words. A streaming flight of wild geese . . . gave note of the waning year* (Washington Irving). **3.** a piece of information; comment; remark: *a marginal note. See the note below. Her chemistry book has many helpful notes at the back.* **4. a.** a very short letter: *Drop me a note when you arrive.* **b.** any short written instruction, list, etc.: *a note to the milkman.* **5.** a letter from one government to another; diplomatic or official communication in writing: *Britain has informed Russia in a note delivered in Moscow . . . of her grave concern* (London Times). **6.** a single sound of definite pitch made by a musical instrument or voice: *a sudden shrill note from the clarinet. Sing this note for me.* **7.** *Music.* **a.** a written sign to show the pitch and length of

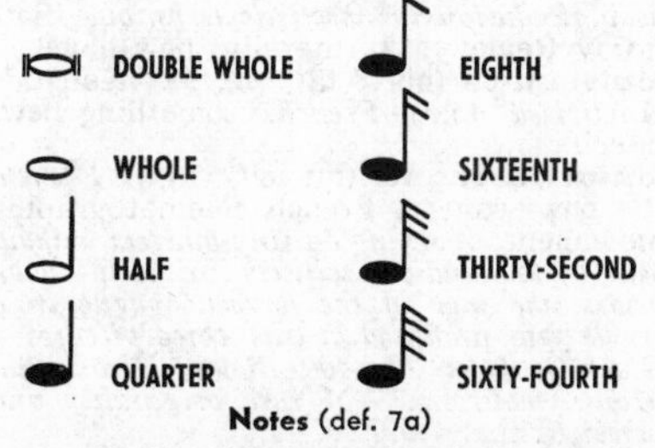

Notes (def. 7a)

a sound. **b.** a black or white key of a piano or other instrument: *to strike the wrong note.* **8.** a bird's song or call: *the robin's cheerful note.* **9.** *Poetic.* a song; melody; tune: *The pealing anthem swells the note of praise* (Thomas Gray). **10.** a significant tone, sound, or way of expression: *There was a note of anxiety in her voice.* **11.** a sign, token, or proof of genuineness; characteristic or distinguishing feature: *the wailing note of a siren. His writing displays the note of scholarship.* **12.** true importance; distinction; consequence. **13.** a written promise to pay a certain sum of money at a certain time; promissory note: *The notes will come due . . . this year* (New York Times). **14.** a certificate of a government or bank passing current as money; piece of paper money; bank note. **15.** a mark or sign, as of punctuation, used in writing or printing.

compare notes, to exchange ideas or opinions: *Everybody put questions to everybody, and all compared notes* (Charles Reade).

make a note of, to write down as something to be remembered: *When found, make a note of* (Dickens).

of note, a. that is important, great, or notable: *Washington is a person of note.* **b.** of being noticed: *The manner in which these statutes were interpreted is worthy of note* (Law Quarterly Review).

strike the right note, to say or do something suitable: *The mediator struck the right note in his dealings with the union.*

take note of, to take notice of; give attention to; observe: *What if thou withdraw in silence from the living and no friend take note of thy departure?* (William Cullen Bryant).

take notes, to write down things to be remembered: *Mr. L——l was so kind as to accede to my desire that he would take notes of all that occurred* (Edgar Allan Poe).
—*v.t.* **1.** to write down as a thing to be remembered: *Write it before them in a table, and note it in a book, that it may be for the time to come* (Isaiah 30:8). **2.** to observe carefully; give attention to; take notice of: *to note a change in the temperature. Note the sly smile on his face.* **3.** to mention especially; dwell on; emphasize. **4.** to indicate; signify; denote. **5.** to furnish with notes or annotations; annotate. **6.** to set down in or furnish with musical notes.
[Old French *note,* learned borrowing from Latin *nota* a mark, note] —**not′er,** *n.*
—**Syn.** *n.* **11.** mark, symbol, character. **12.** repute, significance. *-v.t.* **1.** record. **2.** regard, perceive.

note·book (nōt′bu̇k′), *n.* **1.** a book in which to write or keep notes, memorandums, etc.: *a loose-leaf notebook.* **2.** a book for the registering of promissory notes.

note-case (nōt′kās′), *n. Especially British.* a billfold.

not·ed (nō′tid), *adj.* especially noticed; conspicuous; well-known; celebrated; famous: *Samson was noted for his strength. Robert Frost is a noted American poet.* —**not′ed·ly,** *adv.* —**not′ed·ness,** *n.* —**Syn.** renowned, distinguished. See **famous.**

note·hold·er (nōt′hōl′dər), *n.* a holder of notes issued by a business company for temporary financing: *The fair's obligations to its noteholders might not be met in full* (Robert Alden).

note·less (nōt′lis), *adj.* **1.** without note; undistinguished; unnoticed. **2.** unmusical. **3.** voiceless.

note·let (nōt′lit), *n.* a short note.

note of hand, a promissory note; note.

note paper, paper used for writing letters.

note shaver, *U.S. Slang.* a promoter of bogus financial companies: *The wrinkled note shaver will have taken his railroad trip in vain* (Nathaniel Hawthorne).

notes payable (nōts), **1.** current liabilities in the form of promissory notes given to creditors. **2.** a record of this.

notes receivable, 1. current assets in the form of promissory notes presented by debtors. **2.** a record of this.

note ver·bale (nōt′ ver bàl′), *French.* **1.** a diplomatic message written in the third person and sent unsigned. A note verbale is more formal than an aide-mémoire but less so than a note. *The Greek government addressed a note verbale to the signatories of the Treaty of Lausanne, protesting against Turkey's violation of that treaty's provisions* (Alexander A. Pallis). **2.** (literally) verbal note.

note·wor·thi·ly (nōt′wėr′ᴛʜə lē), *adv.* in a manner worthy of being noted; noticeably.

note·wor·thi·ness (nōt′wėr′ᴛʜē nis), *n.* the state or fact of being noteworthy.

note·wor·thy (nōt′wėr′ᴛʜē), *adj.* worthy of notice; remarkable; notable: *Lindbergh's flight across the Atlantic in 1927 was a noteworthy achievement.* —**Syn.** extraordinary.

noth·ing (nuth′ing), *n.* **1. a.** not anything; no thing: *He believes in nothing. Nothing arrived by mail.* **b.** no part, share, or trace: *There is nothing of his father about him.* **2.** a thing that does not exist: *to create a world out of nothing. Dead men rotting to nothing* (William Morris). **3.** a thing of no importance or significance; a person of no importance: *People regard him as a nothing. Gratiano speaks an infinite deal of nothing* (Shakespeare). **4.** zero; naught.

make nothing of, a. to be unable to understand: *Bella could make nothing of it but that John was in the right* (Dickens). **b.** to fail to use or do: *Tom made nothing of the opportunity afforded him.* **c.** to consider as easy to do: *She makes nothing of leaping over a six-bar gate* (Joseph Addison). **d.** to treat as unimportant or worthless: *The river makes nothing of washing away . . . islands* (S. Parker).

nothing less than, just the same as: *But yet, methinks, my father's execution was nothing less than bloody tyranny* (Shakespeare).

think nothing of, a. to consider as easy to do: *Harry thought nothing of swimming a mile.* **b.** to treat as unimportant or worthless: *The executive thought nothing of his employee's advice.*
—*adv.* not at all; in no way: *He was nothing wiser than before. We were nothing loath to go.*
[Middle English *nothing* < Old English *nān* no + *thing* thing]
➔ See **nobody** for usage note.

noth·ing·ness (nuth′ing nis), *n.* **1.** a being nothing; nonexistence: *A thing of beauty is a joy for ever . . . it will never Pass into nothingness* (Keats). **2.** a being of no value; worthlessness; insignificance: *the vanity and nothingness of the things of time in comparison to those of eternity* (Scott). **3.** an unimportant or worthless thing. **4.** unconsciousness: *in the nothingness of sleep.*

noth·o·fa·gus (noth′ə fā′gəs), *n.* any of a group of trees or shrubs of southern South America, Australia, and New Zealand, closely related to the beech but having usually much smaller leaves, and the male and female flowers on separate plants. [< New Latin *Nothofagus* the genus name < Greek *nóthos* bastard + Latin *fāgus* beech]

noth·o·saur (noth′ə sôr), *n.* any of a group of extinct marine reptiles, common in the Triassic period, similar to the plesiosaurs but smaller. [< New Latin *Nothosaurus* the genus name < Greek *nóthos* bastard + *saûros* lizard]

no·tice (nō′tis), *n., v.,* **-ticed, -tic·ing.** —*n.* **1. a.** observation; heed; attention: *to escape one's notice. A sudden movement caught his notice.* **b.** a polite ear; sympathetic attention; courteous heed: *I beg your notice of my needs.* **2.** information; announcement; warning: *The whistle blew to give notice that the boat was about to leave.* **3.** a written or printed sign; a paper posted in a public place, especially to give information, a warning, etc.: *We saw a notice of today's motion picture outside the theater.* **4.** a warning that one will end an agreement with another at a certain time: *He gave a month's notice that he was leaving to take another job.* **5.** a paragraph or article about something, as a review of a book, play, etc.: *The new book got a favorable notice.*

serve notice, to give warning; inform; announce: *Before the blasting occurred, the builder served notice to the neighboring houses.*

take notice, to give attention; observe; give attention to; see: *Taking no notice that she is so nigh* (Shakespeare).
—*v.t.* **1.** to take notice of; give attention to; observe; perceive: *I noticed a big difference at once. If you notice her so much she will be vain* (Harriet Beecher Stowe). **2.** to mention; refer to: *to notice a matter in a speech or book.* **3.** to serve with a notice; give notice to: *The attorneys have noticed us that they have withdrawn the suit* (Anthony Trollope). **4.** to write a notice of (a book, play, etc.); review.
[< Middle French *notice,* learned borrowing from Latin *nōtitia* cognizance (in Late Latin, list) < *nōscere* know]
—**Syn.** *n.* **1. a, b.** regard, note. **2.** notification. **3.** bulletin, placard. *-v.t.* **1.** see, mark, note, heed. —**Ant.** *v.t.* **1.** overlook, skip, disregard, ignore.

no·tice·a·ble (nō′ti sə bəl), *adj.* **1.** easily seen or noticed: *The class has made noticeable improvement.* **2.** worth noticing; deserving notice. —**Syn. 1.** discernible, observable, conspicuous. —**no′tice·a·ble·ness,** *n.*

no·tice·a·bly (nō′ti sə blē), *adv.* to a noticeable degree: *It is noticeably cooler in the shade.*

notice board, *British.* a bulletin board.

no·ti·fi·a·ble (nō′tə fī′ə bəl), *adj. Especially British.* that must be reported to medical or other authorities: *The Government has recently declared kwashiorkor to be a notifiable disease* (Manchester Guardian Weekly).

no·ti·fi·ca·tion (nō′tə fə kā′shən), *n.* **1.** a notifying or making known. **2.** a notice, especially printed, written, or spoken.

no·ti·fi·er (nō′tə fī′ər), *n.* a person or thing that notifies.

no·ti·fy (nō′tə fī), *v.t.,* **-fied, -fy·ing. 1.** to give notice to; let know; inform; announce to: *Our teacher notified us that there would be a test on Monday.* **2.** *Especially British.* **a.** to make (something) known; proclaim. **b.** to warn of. [< Old French *notifier,* learned borrowing from Latin *nōtificāre* < *nōscere* know + *facere* make] —**Syn. 1.** apprise, acquaint. See **inform.**

no·tion (nō′shən), *n.* **1.** an idea; understanding: *He has no notion of what I mean. Her notion of a joke is not very delicate* (Samuel Johnson). *He had no thoughts, no notion of its being me* (Daniel Defoe). *I considered that my notions of an advocate were false* (James Boswell). **2.** an opinion; view; belief: *modern notions about the training of children. One common notion is that red hair means a quick temper.* **3. a.** intention: *He has no notion of risking his money.* **b.** an inclination or desire; fancy; whim: *That silly girl has too many notions.* **4.** a foolish idea or opinion: *Grow oranges in Alaska? What a notion!*
notions, *U.S.* small, useful articles; pins, needles, thread, tape, etc.: *A dime store sells notions.*
[< Latin *nōtiō, -ōnis* < *nōscere* know]
—**Syn. 1.** concept, impression. See **idea.**

no·tion·al (nō′shə nəl), *adj.* **1.** having to do with ideas or opinions; characterized by abstract concepts, speculation, etc.: *a notional work as distinguished from an experimental work* (Matthew Arnold). **2.** in a person's imagination or thought only; not real; imaginary. **3.** *U.S.* full of notions; having strange notions. **4.** *Grammar.* **a.** having to do with the meaning of a linguistic form. **b.** (of meaning) lexical rather than syntactic. **5.** *Semantics.* presentive. —**no′tion·al·ly,** *adv.* —**Syn. 3.** whimsical.

no·tion·ate (nō′shə nāt, -nit), *adj. Informal.* **1.** full of notions or fancies. **2.** having a notion; opinionated.

no·to·chord (nō′tə kôrd), *n.* **1.** a rodlike structure that is the backbone of many of the lowest chordates, as the lancelet. It is a band of cells, enclosed by a fibrous sheath running lengthwise in the back. **2.** a similar structure in the embryos of higher vertebrates, considered to be the basis upon which the spinal column is laid down during development. [< Greek *nōton* the back + English *chord*[2]]

no·to·chord·al (nō′tə kôr′dəl), *adj.* **1.** of or having to do with the notochord: *Changes occur in the notochordal region, whereby some of the tissue becomes converted into [the] cartilage of ... contemporary adult sharks* (Harbaugh and Goodrich). **2.** like a notochord.

no·to·don·tid (nō′tə don′tid), *n.* any of a family of common North American moths whose larva eats the leaves of the apple, plum, etc. —*adj.* belonging to or having to do with this family of moths. [< New Latin *Notodontidae* the family name < Greek *nōton* the back + *odoús, odóntos* tooth]

No·to·gae·a (nō′tə jē′ə), *n.* a zoogeographic region of the earth's surface that includes Australia, New Zealand, South America, and tropical North America. [< Greek *nótos* south (wind) + *gaîa* earth, land]

No·to·gae·an (nō′tə jē′ən), *adj.* of or having to do with the Notogaea.

No·to·gae·ic (nō′tə jē′ik), *adj.* Notogaean.

no·to·ri·e·ty (nō′tə rī′ə tē), *n., pl.* **-ties. 1.** a being famous for something bad; ill fame: *Scandal brings much notoriety to those involved in it.* **2.** a being widely known: *The newspapers gave the plan notoriety overnight.* **3.** a well-known person; celebrity: *They ... enjoy the vicarious pleasure of mixing with society notorieties* (New Statesman). —**Syn. 1.** notoriousness.

no·to·ri·ous (nō tôr′ē əs, -tōr′-), *adj.* **1.** well known because of something bad; having a bad reputation: *The notorious thief was sent to prison for his many crimes.* **2.** well-known; celebrated: *Sir Winston Churchill's taste for cigars is notorious.* [< Medieval Latin *notorius* (with English *-ous*) < Latin *nōtus* known, past participle of *nōscere* know] —**no·to′ri·ous·ly,** *adv.* —**no·to′ri·ous·ness,** *n.* —**Syn. 1.** infamous.
➔ **Notorious** generally means well-known for unfavorable or unsavory reasons: *a notorious cheat.* **Famous** means well-known for accomplishments or excellence: *a famous writer or aviator.*

no·tor·nis (nō tôr′nis), *n.* any of a group of almost extinct flightless rails that inhabit New Zealand. [< New Latin *Notornis* < Greek *nótos* south + *órnis* bird]

Notornis

no·tos·tra·can (nō tos′trə kən), *n.* any of a group of branchiopods with sessile eyes and a low, oval carapace.

No·tre Dame (nō′trə däm′), Our Lady, the Virgin Mary. [< French *notre dame*]

no-trump (nō′trump′), *adj.* without any trumps, especially in bridge. —*n.* **1.** a declaration in bridge to play with no suit as trumps. **2.** a hand in bridge that is, or is suitable to be, so played

no-trump·er (nō′trum′pər), *n.* a no-trump hand.

not-self (not′self′), *n.* **1.** *Philosophy.* all that is not part of the self: *Hinduism and Buddhism are religions of renunciation: the self must be denied in the name of the not-self* (Observer). **2.** *Medicine.* all that is not part of the individual physical self: *The body has a remarkably efficient mechanism for distinguishing between protein that properly belongs to it, and proteins that do not belong—to use current terminology, the body can distinguish between "self" and "not-self"* (New Scientist).

no·tun·gu·late (nō tung′gyə lāt), *adj.* of or belonging to a group of extinct herbivorous mammals abundant in South America during the Cenozoic period. —*n.* a notungulate animal. [< New Latin *Notungulata* the order name < Greek *nôton* the back + Latin *ungulātus* ungulate]

not·with·stand·ing (not′wiᴛʜ stan′ding, -with-), *prep.* in spite of: *He bought it notwithstanding the high price.*
—*conj.* in spite of the fact that: *Notwithstanding there was need for haste, he still delayed.*
—*adv.* **1.** in spite of it; nevertheless: *It is raining; but I shall go, notwithstanding.* **2.** in spite of anything; still; yet: *He is, notwithstanding, entitled to decent treatment.*
—**Syn.** *prep.* despite. *-conj.* although.

nou·gat (nü′gət, -gä), *n.* a kind of soft candy made chiefly from sugar and egg whites and containing nuts. [< French *nougat* < Provençal < Old Provençal *nogat* < Vulgar Latin *nucātus* made with nuts < Latin *nux, nucis* nut]

nought (nôt), *n.* **1.** naught; nothing: *All my work came to nought. Nought's had, all's spent Where our desire is got without content* (Shakespeare). **2.** zero; a cipher; 0: *Two noughts after a six make six hundred.* **3.** a person or thing of no worth, importance, etc.; a mere nothing.
—*adv. Archaic.* in no way; not at all: *Say not the struggle nought availeth* (Arthur H. Clough).
—*adj.* **1.** good for nothing; worthless; useless. **2.** *Obsolete.* **a.** (of things) bad in condition: *'Tis too plain the materials are nought* (Jonathan Swift). **b.** (of actions) injurious or wicked.
[Old English *nōwiht;* see NAUGHT]

noughts-and-cross·es (nôts′ən krôs′iz, -kros′-), *n.* tick-tack-toe (children's game).

nou·me·na (nü′mə nə, nou′-), *n.* the plural of **noumenon.**

nou·me·nal (nü′mə nəl, nou′-), *adj.* **1.** having to do with noumena. **2.** consisting of noumena; understood only by intuition; not phenomenal. —**nou′me·nal·ly,** *adv.*

nou·me·nal·ism (nü′mə nə liz′əm, nou′-), *n.* a philosophical system dealing with, or based on, noumena.

nou·me·nal·ist (nü′mə nə list, nou′-), *n.* a believer in noumenalism.

nou·me·non (nü′mə non, nou′-), *n., pl.* **-na** (-nə). **1.** (in Kantian philosophy) something that seems real, but cannot be truly understood, although people have some intuitive idea of it, as God or the soul. **2.** a thing in itself; something that remains of an object of thought after all the categories of understanding, such as space, time, etc., have been removed from it. [< Greek *nooúmenon,* neuter passive present participle of *noeîn* apprehend]

noun (noun), *n.* **1.** a word used as the name of a person, place, thing, quality, event, etc. Words like *John, table, school, kindness, skill,* and *party* are nouns. **2.** the part of speech or form class to which such words belong. **3.** a word, phrase, clause, etc., functioning as a noun; nominal. *Abbr.:* n.
—*adj.* like or used as a noun.
[< Anglo-French *noun,* variant of Old French *nom* < Latin *nōmen, -inis* name, noun. Doublet of NOMEN[1].]
➔ **forms of English nouns.** *Nouns* may be single words or compound words written solid or as two words or hyphenated: *ceremony, bookcase, high school, go-getter.* Most nouns change their form to make the plural, most of them adding *-s* or *-es: boys, kindnesses, manufacturers. Nouns* change their form for case only in the genitive or possessive, typically by adding *'s: boy's, Harriet's.* A few nouns may have different forms for male and female sex: *confidant-confidante, executor-executrix, actor-actress.*

noun·al (nou′nəl), *adj.* **1.** of a noun. **2.** like a noun. —**noun′al·ly,** *adv.*

nour·ish (nėr′ish), *v.t.* **1. a.** to make grow or keep alive and well, with food; feed: *Milk nourishes a baby. It's a' for the apple he'll nourish the tree* (Robert Burns). **b.** to supply; sustain; support: *a river nourished by many small streams.* **2.** to maintain; foster: *to nourish a hope. I could find nothing to nourish my suspicion* (Daniel Defoe). [< Old French *noriss-,* stem of *norrir,* or *nurrir* < Latin *nūtrīre* feed] —**nour′ish·er,** *n.* —**nour′ish·ing·ly,** *adv.* —**Syn. 1. a.** nurture. **2.** encourage, support.

nour·ish·ment (nėr′ish mənt), *n.* **1.** food; nutriment; sustenance: *Their nourishment consisted entirely of the vegetables of their garden, and the milk of one cow* (Mary W. Shelley). **2.** a nourishing. **3.** a being nourished.

nous (nüs, nous), *n.* **1.** the mind as the seat of reason; intellect: *Professor Laski would certainly not have concluded that his promising pupil had failed to develop his political nous with the years* (Observer). **2.** *Informal.* common sense or gumption. [< Greek *noûs,* contraction of *nóos* mind]

Nous (nüs, nous), *n.* God (as the Supreme Intellect).

nou·veau riche (nü vō rēsh′), *pl.* **nouveaux riches** (nü vō rēsh′), *French.* **1. a.** a person who has recently become rich: *Many energetic nouveaux riches ... lavish their funds on music, art, giving Chicago a fast start toward high cosmopolitanism* (Newsweek). **b.** a person who makes a vulgar display of his wealth: *False pewter objects [were] cooked up ... when Renaissance goblets and plates became a fad among the nouveaux riches* (New Yorker). **2.** (literally) new rich.

nou·veau ro·man (nü vō′ rô mäɴ′), *pl.* **nou·veaux ro·mans** (nü vō′ rô mäɴ′), *French.* **1.** the antinovel: *The widely discussed "nouveau roman" is generally described as a revolution in novelistic technique* (Saturday Review). **2.** (literally) new novel.

nou·veau·té (nü vō tā′), *n., pl.* **-tés** (-tā′; *Anglicized* -tāz′), *French.* something new; novelty.

nou·velle vague (nü vel′ väg′), *French.* the new wave, a French cinematographic movement: *Working on tiny budgets without benefit of studio facilities or well-known actors, the men of the nouvelle vague in a single year produced at least three pictures—Black Orpheus, The 400 Blows, Hiroshima, Mon Amour ... —of rare originality and power* (Time).

Nov., November.

nov., **1.** novel. **2.** novelist.

no·va (nō′və), *n., pl.* **-vae** (-vē), **-vas.** *Astronomy.* a star that suddenly becomes much brighter and then gradually fades, usually to its normal brightness over a period of some hundreds of days: *[Stars] occasionally boil up to a state of instability that results in their exploding as a nova* (William A. Fowler). [< Latin *nova,* feminine singular of *novus* new]

No·va·chord (nō′və kôrd), *n. Trademark.* an electronic keyboard instrument somewhat like a spinet, capable of producing a variety of tones approximating the sounds of an organ, piano, stringed instrument, or woodwind, or a combination of these. [< Latin *nova* (see NOVA) + English *chord*[1]]

no·vac·u·lite (nō vak′yə līt), *n.* a very hard, dense, siliceous rock used for hones, etc. [< Latin *novācula* razor + English *-ite*[1]]

No·va Sco·tian (nō′və skō′shən), **1.** of or having to do with Nova Scotia, a province in southeastern Canada, or its inhabitants. **2.** a native or inhabitant of Nova Scotia.

no·vate (nō′vāt, nō vāt′), *v.t.*, **-vat·ed, -vat·ing. 1.** to replace by something new. **2.** *Law.* to replace by a new obligation, debt, etc. [< Latin *novāre* (with English *-ate*[1]) < *novus* new]

No·va·tian (nō vā′shən), *n.* one of a sect founded in the 200's A.D., by Novatianus, or Novatian, a Roman schismatic bishop. He denied that the church had power to restore to communion those guilty of idolatry after Christian baptism, and his followers appear to have refused the grant of forgiveness for all grave sin committed after baptism.

No·va·tian·ism (nō vā′shə niz əm), *n.* the doctrine of the Novatians.

no·va·tion (nō vā′shən), *n.* **1.** *Law.* the substitution of a new obligation for an old one, as by replacing the old debtor or creditor with a new one or by altering the names. **2.** a change; innovation. **3.** *Obsolete.* alteration; renewal.

nov·el[1] (nov′əl), *adj.* of a new kind or nature; not known before; strange; new: *Red snow is a novel idea to us.* [< Old French *novel,* learned borrowing from Latin *novellus* (diminutive) < *novus* new] —**Syn.** unfamiliar. See **new.**

nov·el[2] (nov′əl), *n.* **1.** a story with characters and a plot, long enough to fill one or more volumes: *It is absurd to ignore Cervantes, as many literary historians do . . . , for the novel is there, complete and glorious, in "Don Quixote"* (J.B. Priestley). *Only a novel . . . only some work in which the most thorough knowledge of human nature . . . the liveliest effusions of wit and humour are conveyed in the best chosen language* (Jane Austen). **2.** a novella.

the novel, the branch of literature represented by such stories: *The novel is about experience, and experience is always changing* (Newsweek).

[partly < Middle French *nouvelle* < Italian *novella,* partly < Italian < Latin, new things, neuter plural of *novellus* (see NOVEL[1])]

—**Syn. Novel, romance** mean a long fictitious story. **Novel** applies to a long work of prose fiction dealing with characters, situations, and scenes that represent those of real life and setting forth the action in the form of a plot. **Romance,** in its modern sense, applies particularly to a story, often a novel in form, presenting characters and situations not likely to be found in real life and emphasizing exciting or amazing adventures, love, etc., usually set in distant or unfamiliar times or places: *W.H. Hudson's novel, "Green Mansions," is accurately subtitled, "A Romance of the Venezuelan Jungle."*

nov·el[3] (nov′əl), *n.* **1.** (in Roman law) a new decree or constitution supplementary to a code. **2.** (in civil law) a supplement to a law. [< Late Latin *novella* (*cōnstitūtiō*) new (constitution), feminine of *novellus* new, novel[1]]

nov·el·ette (nov′ə let′), *n.* a short novel or very long short story: *For so small a book, "Bonjour Tristesse" is creating quite a large stir. The Françoise Sagan novel (novelette really) . . .* (Publishers' Weekly).

nov·el·et·tish (nov′ə let′ish), *adj.* **1.** characteristic of a second-rate novelette. **2.** *Especially British.* sentimental; trite: *an absurdly novelettish romance which I am sure will run for ages, for its heroine is that sure-fire draw, a tart with a golden heart* (Punch).

nov·el·ist (nov′ə list), *n.* a writer of novels: *It is the duty of the novelist to make us believe in his people* (Atlantic).

nov·el·is·tic (nov′ə lis′tik), *adj.* of or like novels: *[The characters in my novel] must be vastly more bizarre than living people in order to exist upon a printed page . . . The same is true with all novelistic settings* (John P. Marquand). —**nov′el·is′ti·cal·ly,** *adv.*

nov·el·i·za·tion (nov′ə lə zā′shən), *n.* **1.** the process of novelizing; conversion into a novel. **2.** the result of this process; a novelized work: *Turning a screenplay into a novel is generally fast work. Some authors bang out novelizations in as little as three weeks* (Wall Street Journal).

nov·el·ize (nov′ə līz), *v.t.*, **-ized, -iz·ing.** to put into the form of a novel; make a novel from: *to novelize history.*

no·vel·la (nō vel′ə; *Italian* nō vel′lä), *n., pl.* **no·vel·las,** *Italian* **no·vel·le** (nō vel′lā). **1.** a short story or novelette with a simple plot: *The title novella depicts an unusual heroine who would be more at home in the medieval world of folk ballads than in the upper Mississippi valley town into which fate . . . cast her* (Saturday Review). **2.** a short prose tale, usually moral or satiric, as in Boccaccio's *Decameron.* [< Italian *novella;* see NOVEL[2]]

nov·el·ly (nov′ə lē, -əl lē), *adv.* **1.** in a novel manner; by a new method. **2.** as in a novel.

Nov·els (nov′əlz), *n.pl.* the statutes issued by Justinian, emperor of the Eastern Roman Empire from 518 to 565 A.D., and his successors after Justinian's codification of Roman Law and now incorporated in the Corpus Juris Civilis.

nov·el·ty (nov′əl tē), *n., pl.* **-ties. 1.** novel character; newness: *After the novelty of washing dishes wore off, Mary did not want to do it anymore.* **2.** a new or unusual thing or occurrence; innovation: *Staying up late was a novelty to the children, and they enjoyed it.*

novelties, small, unusual articles; toys, cheap jewelry, etc.: *Susan bought some novelties on the boardwalk.*

[< Old French *novelte,* or *novelite* < Latin *novellitās* < *novellus;* see NOVEL[1]] —**Syn. 1.** recentness, freshness.

No·vem·ber (nō vem′bər), *n.* **1.** the eleventh month of the calendar year. It has 30 days. *Abbr.:* Nov. **2.** *U.S.* a code name for the letter *n,* used in transmitting radio messages. [< Latin *November* < *novem* nine (because of its position in the early Roman calendar)]

no·ve·na (nō vē′nə), *n., pl.* **-nas, -nae** (-nē). (in the Roman Catholic Church) a religious exercise consisting of prayers or services on nine days, or sometimes nine corresponding days in consecutive months: *a novena of nine first Fridays.* [< Medieval Latin *novena,* ultimately < Latin *novem* nine]

no·ven·ni·al (nō ven′ē əl), *adj.* occurring every nine years. [< Latin *novennis* (< *novem* nine + *annus* year) + English *-ial*]

no·ver·cal (nō vėr′kəl), *adj.* **1.** characteristic of or resembling a stepmother. **2.** befitting a stepmother. [< Latin *novercālis* < *noverca* stepmother, related to *novus* new]

nov·ice (nov′is), *n.* **1.** a person who is new to what he is doing; beginner: *Novices are likely to make some mistakes.* **2.** a person who is received into a religious group on trial, before taking vows. Before becoming a monk or a nun, a person is a novice: *After six months a postulant may receive the habit and white veil of a novice together with a new name* (Time). **3.** a new member of the church. **4.** a new convert to Christianity. [< Old French *novice, novisse,* learned borrowing from Latin *novīcius* < *novus* new] —**Syn. 1.** tyro, apprentice.

nov·ice·hood (nov′is hůd), *n.* the condition of a novice.

nov·ice·ship (nov′is ship), *n.* novitiate.

no·vil·le·ro (nō′vē lyā′rō), *n., pl.* **-ros.** *Spanish.* an apprentice bullfighter: *He had semi-flopped in his presentation as a novillero in Madrid nine years ago* (Barnaby Conrad).

no·vi·ti·ate or **no·vi·ci·ate** (nō vish′ē it, -āt), *n.* **1.** the period of trial and preparation of a novice in a religious order. **2.** a novice. **3.** the house or rooms occupied by religious novices. **4.** the state or period of being a beginner in anything. [< Medieval Latin *novitiatus* or *noviciatus* < Latin *novīcius* < *novus* new]

no·vo·bi·o·cin (nō′və bī′ə sin), *n.* an antibiotic effective against gram-positive bacteria, especially in infections where bacteria are resistant to other antibiotics. *Formula:* $C_{31}H_{36}N_2O_{11}$

no·vo·caine or **no·vo·cain** (nō′və kān), *n.* **1.** an alkaloid compound, used as a local anesthetic; procaine. **2. Novocaine,** a trademark for this compound. [< Latin *novus* new + English (co)*caine*]

NOVS (no periods), National Office of Vital Statistics.

no·vus or·do se·clo·rum (nō′vəs ôr′dō se klôr′əm, -klōr′-), *Latin.* a new order of the ages (the motto on the Great Seal of the United States, from Virgil, *Eclogues,* 4,5): *Novus Ordo Seclorum. When the Founding Fathers set these words—A New Order of the Ages—in the Great Seal of the United States, they had in mind a social order that would guarantee the individual political and personal freedom under law* (Time).

now (nou), *adv.* **1.** at the present time; at this moment: *He is here now. Most people do not believe in ghosts now.* **2.** by this time: *She must have reached the city now.* **3.** at once: *Do it now!* **4.** then; next: *If passed, the bill now goes to the President.* **5.** at the time referred to: *The clock now struck three. Night was now approaching.* **6.** a little while ago: *I just now saw him.* **7.** under the present circumstances; as things are; as it is: *I would believe almost anything now.* **8.** *Now* is also used to introduce or emphasize: *Now what do you mean? Oh, come now! Now you knew that was wrong.*

now and again, from time to time; once in a while: *I see my old neighbor now and again.*

now and then, from time to time; once in a while: *These Gypsies now and then foretold very strange things* (Joseph Addison).

now . . . now, at one time . . . at another time: *like a stormy day, now wind, now rain* (Shakespeare).

—*n.* the present; this time: *by now, until now, from now on. An everlasting Now reigns in Nature* (Emerson).

—*conj.* since; inasmuch as: *Now that you are older, you should know better.*

—*interj.* be careful! please!

[Old English *nū*]

—**Syn.** *adv.* **1.** currently. **3.** immediately.

now·a·days (nou′ə dāz′), *adv.* at the present day; in these times: *Nowadays people travel distances by air more than by train.* —*n.* the present day; these times: *the sports of nowadays.*

no·way (nō′wā), *adv.* nowise.

no·ways (nō′wāz), *adv.* nowise.

now·el or **now·ell** (nō el′, nō′el), *n. Archaic.* noël. [< Old French *nouel,* variant of *noël.* Doublet of NOËL, NATAL.]

no·where (nō′hwãr), *adv.* in no place; at no place; to no place; not anywhere: *a plant found nowhere else, to go nowhere.*

nowhere near, *Informal.* not nearly; not by a long way: *Though the deed were nowhere near so great, yet is it a manner of resemblance* (William Caxton).

—*n.* a nonexistent place.

[Old English *nāhwǣr* or *nōhwǣr*]

➤ See **nobody** for usage note.

no·wheres (nō′hwãrz), *adv., n. U.S. Dialect.* nowhere.

no·whith·er (nō′hwiᴛʜ′ər), *adv.* nowhere.

no·wise (nō′wīz), *adv.* in no way; not at all: *The price decline, nowise limited to cotton farmers, is reflected in the skidding national farm income* (Wall Street Journal). [< *no*[1] + *-wise* < *wise*[2]]

nowt (nout), *n. Scottish.* **1.** cattle; oxen. **2.** an ox; bullock. **3.** a clumsy or stupid person. [< Scandinavian (compare Old Icelandic *naut* cattle)]

now·y (nou′ē, nō′-), *adj.* in heraldry: **1.** having a small semicircular projection at or near the middle, as a line or fesse. **2.** (of a cross) having a projection in each angle between the arms. [< Old French *noe,* past participle of *noer* to knot < Latin *nōdāre* < *nōdus* knot]

Nox (noks), *n.* the Roman goddess of night, identified with the Greek Nyx.

nox·al (nok′səl), *adj. Roman Law.* relating to wrongful injury: *a noxal action.* [< Latin *noxālis* < *noxa* a hurt < *nocēre* to hurt]

nox·ious (nok′shəs), *adj.* **1.** very harmful; poisonous: *Fumes from the exhaust of an automobile are noxious. Poison ivy is a noxious plant.* **2.** morally hurtful; corrupting: *an unjust and noxious tyranny* (Macaulay). **3.** *Obsolete.* criminal. [< Latin *noxius* (with English *-ous*) < *noxa* a hurt < *nocēre* to hurt] —**nox′ious·ly,** *adv.* —**nox′ious·ness,** *n.* —**Syn. 1.** unhealthful, deadly, unwholesome. —**Ant. 1.** healthful.

no·yade (nwä yäd′), *n., v.,* **-yad·ed, -yad·ing.** —*n.* death by drowning. —*v.t.* to put to death by drowning. [< French *noyade* < *noyer* to drown < Old French < Late Latin *necāre* drown < Latin, to kill]

No·yade (nwä yäd′), *n.pl.* the mass executions by drowning at Nantes, France (1793-94), during the Reign of Terror.

noy·ance (noi′əns), *n. Obsolete.* annoyance.

no·yau (nwä yō′), *n.* a cordial or liqueur flavored with the kernels of peaches, cherries, or other fruit, or with some substitute. [< French *noyau* (literally) kernel]

noz·zle (noz′əl), *n.* **1.** a tip put on a hose, etc., forming an outlet. **2.** a socket on a candlestick or sconce. **3.** *Slang.* the nose: *His whole face was overshadowed by this tremendous nozzle* (Tobias Smollett). [diminutive of *nose*]

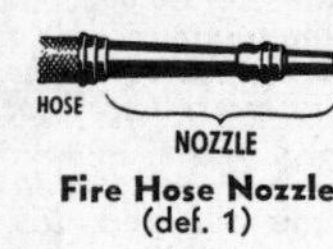

Fire Hose Nozzle (def. 1)

Np (no period), neptunium (chemical element).

NP (no periods), **1.** neuropsychiatric. **2.** neuropsychiatrist. **3.** neuropsychiatry.

N.P., **1.** Nobel Prize. **2.** Notary Public.

NPA (no periods) or **N.P.A.,** National Planning Association.

N.P.D., **1.** National Democratic Party (of West Germany): *Undoubtedly some members of the neo-Nazi . . . N.P.D. are genuine conservative nationalists* (New York Times). **2.** North Polar Distance.

NPS (no periods), National Park Service.

nr., near.

NRA (no periods) or **N.R.A.,** **1.** National Recovery Administration (a United States government agency from 1933 to 1936, established to administer codes of fair competition for industry). **2.** National Rifle Association.

NRAB (no periods), National Railroad Adjustment Board.

NRB (no periods), National Resources Board.

NRC (no periods), National Research Council.

NRDC (no periods) or **N.R.D.C.,** National Research Development Corporation (a British government-financed but independent corporation for developing scientific projects).

NRL (no periods) or **N.R.L.,** Naval Research Laboratory.

NROTC (no periods) or **N.R.O.T.C.,** Naval Reserve Officer Training Corps.

n/s, *Banking.* not sufficient (funds).

n.s., not specified.

NS (no periods), nuclear ship.

N.S., **1.** National Society. **2.** New Series. **3.** New Style. **4.** Nova Scotia. **5.** nuclear ship.

N.S.A., National Student Association.

NSC (no periods), **1.** National Safety Council. **2.** National Security Council (a board of advisers to the President of the United States on military, economic, and diplomatic affairs relating to the national security).

NSF (no periods) or **N.S.F.,** National Science Foundation.

N.S.P.C.A., National Society for the Prevention of Cruelty to Animals.

N.S.P.C.C., National Society for the Prevention of Cruelty to Children.

n.s.p.f., not specifically provided for.

NSRB (no periods), National Security Resources Board.

N.S.W., New South Wales.

Nt (no period), niton (the former name of radon, now replaced by the symbol Rn).

N.T., **1.** New Testament. **2.** Northern Territory (in Australia).

NTA (no periods) or **N.T.A.,** National Tuberculosis Association.

nth (enth), *adj.* **1.** last in the series 1,2,3,4, . . .n, n representing an ordinal number of indefinite size; of the indefinitely large or small amount denoted by *n: the nth term in a series, the nth power of a number.* **2.** *Informal.* umpteenth: *I was reading Goldsworthy Lowes Dickinson's "A Modern Symposium" for the nth time the other day* (London Times).
to the nth degree, to the utmost: *He was dressed to the nth degree for the occasion. As the finale approached, the excitement rose to the nth degree.* [< *n*(umber)]

N.T.P., normal temperature and pressure; standard temperature and pressure.

nt. wt., net weight.

n-type (en′tīp′), *adj.* of or having to do with semiconductor materials such as germanium and silicon, with electrical conducting properties that depend upon the presence of impurities such as phosphorus, antimony, and arsenic. The impurities have a density of free electrons greater than the density of holes (vacant spots not occupied by electrons).

nu (nü, nyü), *n.* the 13th letter (N, ν) of the Greek alphabet. [< Greek *ny̆*]

nu·ance (nü äns′, nyü-; nü′äns, nyü′-), *n.* **1.** a shade of expression, meaning, feeling, etc.: *I heard the Brahms Sonata in E Minor, which he interpreted with a subtle feeling for nuance* (New Yorker). **2.** a slight difference in the shade of a color or tone: *A single primary colour alone may have a surprisingly large number of nuances* (London Times). [< French *nuance* < *nuer* to shade < *nue* cloud < Vulgar Latin *nūba,* for Latin *nūbēs*]

nu·anced (nü änst′, nyü-; nü′änst, nyü′-), *adj.* marked by or exhibiting nuances.

nub (nub), *n.* **1.** a knob or knotlike lump; protuberance. **2.** a lump or small piece; nubbin. **3.** *U.S. Informal.* the point or gist of anything: *The nub of this matter is that we must not fall into the egregious sin of lack of faith in . . . our youth* (Eugene Youngert). [apparently variant of obsolete *knub* knob]

nub·bin (nub′in), *n.* **1.** a small lump or piece. **2.** *U.S.* a small or imperfect ear of corn. **3.** an undeveloped fruit. [American English, diminutive form of *nub*]

nub·ble (nub′əl), *n.* a nub or nubbin: *He was lying on a piece of dingy ticking full of lumps and nubbles* (Rudyard Kipling). [diminutive form of *nub*]

nub·bly (nub′lē), *adj.,* **-bli·er, -bli·est.** knobby; lumpy: . . . *nubbly daytime tweeds* (New Yorker).

nub·by (nub′ē), *adj.,* **-bi·er, -bi·est.** nubbly.

nu·bi·a (nü′bē ə, nyü′-), *n.* a soft, fleecy wrap for the head and neck, worn by women. [< Latin *nūbēs, -is* cloud]

Nu·bi·an (nü′bē ən, nyü′-), *adj.* of or having to do with Nubia, a region in northeastern Africa south of Egypt and bordering on the Red Sea, its inhabitants, or their language. —*n.* **1.** a member of the Negroid people inhabiting Nubia. **2.** the language spoken by this people.

nu·bile (nü′bəl, nyü′-), *adj.* (of a girl) old enough to be married; marriageable: *The moon's three phases of new, full, and old recalled the matriarch's three phases of maiden, nymph (nubile woman) and crone* (Robert Graves). [< Latin *nūbilis* < *nūbere* take a husband. Compare NUPTIAL.]

nu·bil·i·ty (nü bil′ə tē, nyü-), *n.* (of women) the state of being old enough to marry

nu·bi·lous (nü′bə ləs, nyü′-), *adj.* **1.** cloudy; foggy; misty. **2.** obscure; indefinite. [< Latin *nūbilōsus* < *nūbilus* cloudy < *nūbēs* cloud]

nu·cel·lar (nü sel′ər, nyü-), *adj.* **1.** of or having to do with a nucellus. **2.** like a nucellus.

nu·cel·lus (nü sel′əs, nyü-), *n., pl.* **-cel·li** (-sel′ī). *Botany.* the central mass of cells within the integument of the ovule containing the embryo sac; megasporangium. [< New Latin *nucellus* < Late Latin *nucella* hazelnut (diminutive) < *nucula* (diminutive) < *nux, nucis* nut]

nu·cha (nü′kə, nyü′-), *n., pl.* **-chae** (-kē). the nape of the neck. [< Medieval Latin *nucha* nape of the neck < Arabic *nukha'* spinal marrow]

nu·chal (nü′kəl, nyü′-), *adj.* **1.** of or having to do with the nape of the neck: *the nuchal muscles.* **2.** *Entomology.* situated on the thorax just behind the head, as certain markings on an insect larva.

nu·cif·er·ous (nü sif′ər əs, nyü-), *adj.* bearing nuts. [< Latin *nux, nucis* nut + English *-ferous*]

nu·ci·form (nü′sə fôrm, nyü′-), *adj.* shaped like a nut.

nu·cle·ar (nü′klē ər, nyü′-), *adj.* **1.** forming a nucleus. **2.** of or having to do with a nucleus, as of a cell or an atom or the particles contained within the nucleus: *nuclear disintegration, a nuclear charge.* **3.** having the character or position of a nucleus; like a nucleus. **4. a.** of or having to do with atomic energy: *nuclear age, nuclear processes.* **b.** used in atomic energy; using atomic energy: *nuclear materials, a nuclear submarine.* **c.** of or having to do with nuclear weapons or their use: *nuclear disarmament; . . . to see this crisis through even to a nuclear conclusion* (Observer).

nuclear chemist, an expert in nuclear chemistry.

nuclear chemistry, the branch of chemistry dealing with atoms and atomic nuclei, and their relation to chemical processes and reactions, especially reactions producing new elements.

nuclear club, the group of nations armed with nuclear weapons: *Much of the disarmament negotiation turns on whether and how the nuclear club could be closed* (Christian Science Monitor).

nuclear energy, atomic energy.

nuclear family, the group consisting of a father, a mother, and their children: *The nuclear family is universal either as the sole prevailing form or as the basic unit form from which more complex familiar forms are compounded* (Clyde Kluckhohn).

nuclear fission, the splitting that occurs when the nucleus of an atom under bombardment absorbs a neutron and divides into two nearly equal parts: *As a result of attempts to prepare isotopes of elements of atomic number greater than 92 [uranium] . . . nuclear fission was discovered* (W.N. Jones).

nuclear fuel, a fissile substance which will sustain a chain reaction: *There was freedom also in discussing the relative roles of uranium and thorium as nuclear fuels* (A.W. Haslett).

nuclear fusion, the combining of two atomic nuclei to create a nucleus of greater mass.

nu·cle·ar·ise (nü′klē ə rīz, nyü′-), *v.t.,* **-ised, -is·ing.** *Especially British.* nuclearize.

nu·cle·ar·i·za·tion (nü′klē ər ə zā′shən, nyü′-), *n.* the act or process of nuclearizing.

nu·cle·ar·ize (nü′klē ə rīz, nyü′-), *v.t.,* **-ized, -iz·ing.** to furnish with nuclear weapons or nuclear power; convert to the use of nuclear weapons or power: *to nuclearize a country. By the end of this fiscal year, $1.5 billion will have been spent to nuclearize the Navy* (Wall Street Journal).

nuclear particle, a particle within, or emitted by, an atomic nucleus. Nuclear particles include neutrons, protons, deuterons, and alpha particles. *If the energy of the incident particle is high enough it can enter the target nucleus and cause it to break up with the emission of a number of nuclear particles* (P.E. Hodgson).

nuclear physicist, an expert in nuclear physics: *Between Copenhagen and Cambridge, there was a stream of travelers, all the nuclear physicists of the world* (C.P. Snow).

nuclear physics, the branch of physics that is concerned with atoms and their nuclear structure: *In nuclear physics, the scientist is interested in the behavior within the nucleus of an atom* (World Book Annual).

nu·cle·ar-pow·ered (nü′klē ər pou′ərd, nyü′-), *adj.* operating on atomic power.

nuclear reaction, reaction (def. 8): *In the case of a rocket, the nuclear reaction would heat up the . . . liquid reaction to any desired temperature* (Science News).

nuclear reactor, a reactor: *The temperature limitation inherent in the solid-core nuclear reactor has inspired a number of alternative systems* (Scientific American).

nuclear test, the experimental firing or exploding of a nuclear weapon.

nuclear transmutation, transmutation (def. 3).

nuclear warfare, warfare using nuclear weapons: *There seems to be a growing realization by all that nuclear warfare, pursued to the ultimate, could be possibly race suicide* (Dwight D. Eisenhower).

nuclear warhead, a warhead containing fissionable or fusionable material as its explosive charge: *The world is instead putting its most concentrated imaginative efforts on the development of missiles with nuclear warheads* (Bulletin of Atomic Scientists).

NUCLEAR WARHEAD

Nuclear Warhead on a missile

nuclear weapon, a bomb, shell, rocket, guided missile, or other weapon carrying a nuclear warhead: *Fear of general annihilation may forestall indiscriminate use of nuclear weapons* (Newsweek).

nu·cle·ar·y (nü′klē er′ē, nyü′-; *especially British* nü′klē ər ē), *adj.* nuclear.

nu·cle·ase (nü′klē ās, nyü′-), *n.* any enzyme that hydrolyzes nucleic acids.

nu·cle·ate (*v.* nü′klē āt, nyü′-; *adj.* nü′klē it, nyü′-; -āt), *v.,* **-at·ed, -at·ing,** *adj.* —*v.t., v.i.* to form into a nucleus or around a nucleus. —*adj.* having a nucleus. [< Late Latin *nucleāre* (with English *-ate*[1]) become full of kernels < Latin *nucleus* kernel (diminutive) < *nux, nucis* nut]

nu·cle·a·tion (nü'klē ā'shən, nyü'-), *n.* the formation of nuclei: *Dust particles of the proper configuration . . . start the nucleation of snow crystals* (Scientific American).

nu·cle·a·tor (nü'klē ā'tər, nyü'-), *n.* a substance or agent that produces nuclei in gases or liquids.

nu·cle·i (nü'klē ī, nyü'-), *n.* a plural of **nucleus.**

nu·cle·ic (nü klē'ik, nyü-), *adj.* nucleinic.

nucleic acid, any of a group of compounds occurring, chiefly in association with proteins, in the nucleus of cells. Nucleic acids consist of a pentose combined with phosphoric acid and basic nitrogen compounds, purine, and pyrimidine. They determine genetic specificity and function in the control of cellular activities. *The [Nobel] prize in medicine and physiology was given to two U.S. biologists: Severo Ochoa . . . and Arthur Kornberg . . . for artificial production of nucleic acids found in living cells* (Bulletin of Atomic Scientists). See also **deoxyribonucleic acid** and **ribonucleic acid.**

nu·cle·in (nü'klē in, nyü'-), *n.* any of a class of substances present in the nuclei of cells, consisting chiefly of proteins, phosphoric acids, and nucleic acids.

nu·cle·in·ic (nü'klē in'ik, nyü'-), *adj.* **1.** of or having to do with a nuclein or nucleins. **2.** like a nuclein or nucleins.

nu·cle·o·lar (nü klē'ə lər, nyü-), *adj.* **1.** of the nature of a nucleolus. **2.** having to do with a nucleolus.

nu·cle·o·late (nü'klē ə lāt, nyü'-), *adj.* nucleolated.

nu·cle·o·lat·ed (nü'klē ə lā'tid, nyü'-), *adj.* having a nucleolus or nucleoli.

nu·cle·ole (nü'klē ōl, nyü'-), *n.* nucleolus.

nu·cle·o·lus (nü klē'ə ləs, nyü-), *n., pl.* **-li** (-lī). a small, usually round structure found within the nucleus in most cells containing a high concentration of ribonucleic acid. [< Late Latin *nucleolus* (diminutive) < Latin *nucleus* kernel (diminutive) < *nux, nucis* nut]

nu·cle·on (nü'klē on, nyü'-), *n.* one of the atomic particles that make up the nucleus of an atom, such as a neutron or proton: *It seems that each nucleon . . . cannot interact with all the other particles in the nucleus, but only with its neighbors* (J. Little). [< *nucle-*(us) + *-on,* as in *electron*]

nu·cle·on·ic (nü'klē on'ik, nyü'-), *adj.* **1.** of or having to do with nucleonics: *nucleonic equipment, nucleonic research.* **2.** of or having to do with an atomic nucleus: *a nucleonic charge, nucleonic radiation.*

nu·cle·on·ics (nü'klē on'iks, nyü'-), *n.* the science of the behavior and characteristics of nucleons, or of nuclear phenomena: *It was toward the end of the war that nucleonics entered as the third decisive element of the new technology* (Science News Letter).

nu·cle·o·phil·ic (nü'klē ə fil'ik, nyü'-), *adj.* strongly attracted to the nuclei of atoms: *nucleophilic ions or molecules.*

nu·cle·o·plasm (nü'klē ə plaz'əm, nyü'-), *n.* the material found in the nucleus of a cell, not including the nucleoli; karyoplasm. [< *nucleus* + *-plasm,* as in *protoplasm*]

nu·cle·o·plas·mic (nü'klē ə plaz'mik, nyü'-), *adj.* **1.** having to do with nucleoplasm. **2.** like nucleoplasm.

nu·cle·o·pro·tein (nü'klē ō prō'tēn, -tē in; nyü'-), *n.* any of a group of substances present in the nuclei of cells, consisting of proteins in combination with nucleic acids and carbohydrates.

nu·cle·o·side (nü'klē ə sīd, nyü'-; -sid), *n.* a compound of pyrimidine and various sugars, similar to nucleotide but lacking phosphoric acid.

nu·cle·o·tide (nü'klē ə tīd, nyü'-; -tid), *n.* a compound of sugar, phosphoric acid, and a nitrogen base. It is the principal constituent of nucleic acid and determines the structure of genes. *Inert molecules known as nucleotides and found in DNA were used as the starting material* (Science News Letter).

nu·cle·us (nü'klē əs, nyü'-), *n., pl.* **-cle·i** or **-cle·us·es. 1.** a beginning to which additions are to be made: *A five-dollar bill can become the nucleus of a flourishing bank account. He had the nucleus of a good plan, but it required working out.* **2.** a central part or thing around which other parts or things are collected: *A very strange old gentleman, whose eccentricity had become the nucleus for a thousand fantastic stories* (Hawthorne). *The few hundred families, which formed the original nucleus of her citizenship* (Charles Merivale). **3.** a proton, or a group of protons and neutrons, or other nuclear particles, forming the central part of an atom and carrying a positive charge. The nucleus forms the core around which the electrons revolve in orbits. It also contains most of the mass of the whole atom. *The exact ratio of protons to neutrons in a stable nucleus depends on the total number of particles it contains* (J. Little). **4.** the basic arrangement of atoms in a particular compound, to which other atoms may be joined in various ways. **5.** *Biology.* an active body lying within the protoplasm of a cell of an animal or a plant without which the cell cannot grow and divide. A nucleus is different in structure from the rest of the cell. It consists of complex arrangements of proteins, nucleic acids, and lipids surrounded by a delicate membrane, and typically containing such structures as chromosomes and nucleoli. The nucleus controls growth, cell division, and other activities, and contains DNA, a nucleic acid which passes on the genetic characteristics of the cell. *The hereditary endowment of a plant or animal is now known to be determined by a very special kind of material found primarily in the threadlike chromosomes that may be seen under the microscope in the nucleus of the cell* (Atlantic). **6.** one of a number of anatomically distinct masses of gray matter in the brain of vertebrates, consisting of the cell bodies of nerve cells, having special functions, and connected to one another by nerve fibers. **7.** the relatively dense central part of a comet's head: *The astronomers tell us that some of these comets have no visible nucleuses* (James Fenimore Cooper). **8.** *Meteorology.* a particle of dust, etc., upon which water vapor condenses, as to form a drop. **9.** the kernel of a seed.
[< Latin *nucleus* kernel (diminutive) < *nux, nucis* nut] —**Syn. 2.** center, core, heart.

nu·clide (nü'klīd, nyü'-), *n.* a particular type of atom having a characteristic nucleus and a measurable life span.

nu·cule (nü'kyül, nyü'-), *n. Botany.* a nutlet. [< Latin *nucula* (diminutive) < *nux, nucis* nut]

nude (nüd, nyüd), *adj.* **1.** naked; bare; unclothed: *the nude trees of winter.* **2.** *Law.* not supported or confirmed; made without a consideration; not actionable, as of an agreement.
—*n.* a naked human figure in painting, sculpture, or photography: *oldfashioned Rubenslike nudes* (New Yorker).
the nude, a. the naked human figure: *Modern chalk drawings, studies from the nude* (Robert Browning). **b.** a naked condition: *to swim in the nude. Stands sublimely in the nude, as chaste As Medicean Venus* (Elizabeth Barrett Browning).
[< Latin *nūdus*] —**nude'ly,** *adv.* —**nude'ness,** *n.*
—**Syn.** *adj.* **1.** undraped, stripped. See **bare.**

nudge (nuj), *v.,* **nudged, nudg·ing,** *n.* —*v.t.* **1.** to push or poke slightly; jog with the elbow to attract attention, etc.: *His next neighbors nudged him* (Dickens). **2.** to prod; stimulate: *to nudge one's memory.*
—*v.i.* to give a nudge or slight push.
—*n.* a slight push or jog, as with the elbow.
[origin uncertain. Compare dialectal Norwegian *nyggja* to jostle.]

nu·di·branch (nü'də brangk, nyü'-), *n.* any of a group of marine mollusks that usually have external adaptive gills and no shell when adult.
—*adj.* of or belonging to this group.
[< New Latin *Nudibranchiata* the suborder name < French *nudibranche* < Latin *nūdus* naked + Greek *bránchia* gills]

nu·di·bran·chi·ate (nü'də brang'kē it, -āt; nyü'-), *n., adj.* nudibranch.

nu·di·caul (nü'də kôl, nyü'-), *adj. Botany.* having leafless stems. [< Latin *nūdus* + *caulis* stem, caulis]

nu·di·cau·lous (nü'də kô'ləs, nyü'-), *adj.* nudicaul.

nu·die (nü'dē, nyü'-), *n.* a motion picture, magazine, etc., showing nude figures.

nud·ism (nü'diz əm, nyü'-), *n.* the practice of going naked for health or as a fad: *The meeting was presided over by state representative G. S. Sampsel, who had offered to sponsor legislation against nudism* (Harper's).

nud·ist (nü'dist, nyü'-), *n.* a person who goes naked for health or as a fad: *The nudists of France are pursued by the police, by the clergy, by the wit of Parisian cartoonists* (John O'London's Weekly). —*adj.* of nudism or nudists: *a nudist colony.*

nu·di·ty (nü'də tē, nyü'-), *n., pl.* **-ties. 1.** nakedness. **2.** a nude figure, especially as represented in painting or sculpture.

nud·nik or **nud·nick** (nůd'nik), *n. Slang.* a tiresome, annoying person; bore; pest; crank: *I have another nudnick here wants a round table like King Arthur's* (S.J. Perelman). [< Yiddish *nudnik* < Russian *nudnyi* tedious + *-nik,* a personal suffix]

nu·dum pac·tum (nyü'dəm pak'təm), *pl.* **nu·da pac·ta** (nyü'də pak'tə). *Latin.* **1.** a contract made without fee or compensation. **2.** an agreement which is not actionable. **3.** (literally) a nude pact.

nug (nug), *n. British Dialect.* **1.** a lump or mass of something. **2.** a knot or protuberance.

nu·gae (nyü'jē), *n.pl. Latin.* trifles; nonsense.

nu·ga·to·ry (nü'gə tôr'ē, -tōr'-; nyü'-), *adj.* **1.** of no value or importance; trifling; worthless: *. . . sentimental interpretation of small part-songs of nugatory musical merit* (London Times). **2.** of no force; invalid. **3.** ineffective; useless. [< Latin *nūgātōrius* < *nūgārī* to trifle < *nūgae* trifles] —**Syn. 3.** futile.

nug·gar (nug'ər), *n.* a large, broad boat used on the Nile River for the carrying of cargo, troops, etc. [< Arabic *nuqqār*]

nug·get (nug'it), *n.* **1.** a lump: *Pea and lima bean nuggets can be ground into soup powders that reconstitute in hot water in a few minutes* (Wall Street Journal). *Stone Age man probably knew metals only as occasional nuggets of the precious metals* (J. Growther). **2.** a lump of native gold. **3.** anything valuable: *a nugget of wisdom.* **4.** *Australian.* a short, thick-set person or beast [perhaps related to NUG]

nug·get·y (nug'ə tē), *adj.* **1.** having the form of a nugget; occurring in nuggets or lumps. **2.** *Australian.* short and sturdy.

nui·sance (nü'səns, nyü'-), *n.* **1.** a thing or person that annoys, troubles, offends, or is disagreeable; source of annoyance: *Flies are a nuisance. The quartering of soldiers upon the colonists was a great nuisance* (H. G. Wells). **2.** *Law.* anything annoying, harmful, or offensive to a community, or a member of it, especially to a property owner, and always as defined by law. [Middle English *nusance* harm < Old French *nuisance* < *nuis-,* stem of *nuire* to harm < Latin *nocēre*]
—**Syn. 1.** annoyance, plague, trouble, inconvenience.

nuisance tax, a tax that is annoying because it is collected in very small amounts from the consumer.

nuke (nük), *n. Slang.* **1.** an atomic nucleus: *Stage I involves the firing of an inner "nuke" . . . of U-235 or plutonium* (Bulletin of Atomic Scientists). **2.** a nuclear weapon: *The enemy's temptation to . . . use "nukes" against Taiwan would be discouraged* (Atlantic).

N.U.L., National Urban League.

null (nul), *adj.* **1.** not binding, especially under law; of no effect; as if not existing: *A promise obtained by force is legally null.* **2.** of no value; unimportant; useless; meaningless: *Here the principle of contribution . . . is reprobated as null, and destructive to equality* (Edmund Burke). **3.** not any; nothing; zero: *The effect was small or null.*
null and void, without force or effect, especially legally; not binding; worthless: *That all acts done by the authority of the usurper Harold were held to be null and void* (Edward A. Freeman).
[< Latin *nūllus* not any < *nē-* not + *ūllus* any (diminutive) < *ūnus* one]
—**Syn. 2.** nugatory.

nul·lah (nul'ə), *n.* (in India) a watercourse, especially one which is dry except after a heavy rain. [Anglo-Indian < Hindi *nālā*]

nul·la-nul·la (nul'ə nul'ə), *n.* a club used as a weapon by Australian aborigines.

nul·li·fi·ca·tion (nul'ə fə kā'shən), *n.* **1.** a making null: *What labor really wants is nullification of right-to-work laws now in effect in eighteen states* (Newsweek). **2.** a being nullified: *the nullification of a treaty.*

3. Often, **Nullification.** *U.S.* the unwillingness of a state to allow a Federal law or judicial decision to be enforced within its territory.

nul·li·fi·ca·tion·ist or **Nul·li·fi·ca·tion·ist** (nul′ə fə kā′shə nist), *n. U.S.* a supporter of the nullification of a Federal law.

nul·li·fid·i·an (nul′ə fid′ē ən), *n.* a person who lacks any faith or religion; skeptic; unbeliever. [< Latin *nūllus* not any + *fidēs* faith + English *-ian*]

nul·li·fi·er (nul′ə fī′ər), *n.* **1.** a person who nullifies. **2.** *U.S.* a person who maintains the right of any state to annul, within its own boundaries, laws passed by Congress.

nul·li·fy (nul′ə fī), *v.t.*, **-fied, -fy·ing. 1.** to make not binding, especially legally; render void: *to nullify a will or a law.* **2.** to make unimportant, useless, or meaningless; destroy; cancel: *The difficulties of the plan nullify its advantages.* [< Latin *nūllificāre* < *nūllus* not any (see NULL) + *facere* make] —**Syn. 1.** annul, repeal.

nul·lip·a·ra (nə lip′ər ə), *n., pl.* **-a·rae** (-ə rē). a woman who has never borne a child. [< New Latin *nullipara* < Latin *nūllus* not any + *parere* bear young]

nul·li·par·i·ty (nul′ə par′ə tē), *n.* the state of having never borne a child.

nul·lip·a·rous (nə lip′ər əs), *adj.* (of a woman) having never borne a child.

nul·li·pen·nate (nul′ə pen′āt), *adj.* having no flight feathers, as the penguin. [< Latin *nūllus* not any + *penna* feather + English *-ate*[1]]

nul·li·pore (nul′ə pôr, -pōr), *n.* any of various marine red algae having the power of secreting lime, as a coralline. [< Latin *nūllus* not any + English *pore*[2]]

nul·li·ty (nul′ə tē), *n., pl.* **-ties. 1.** futility; nothingness. **2.** the state of being legally null and void; invalidity. **3.** a mere nothing; nobody; nonentity. **4.** something that is null and especially without legal force or effect: *The Declaration was, in the eye of the law, a nullity* (Macaulay). [< Medieval Latin *nullitas* < Latin *nūllus* not any; see NULL]

num., 1. number or numbers. **2.** numeral or numerals.

Num., Numbers (book of the Old Testament).

numb (num), *adj.* having lost the power of feeling or moving: *My fingers are numb with cold.* —*v.t.* **1.** to make numb: *arms and ankles, . . . numbed and stiff with . . . binding* (Daniel Defoe). **2.** to dull the feelings of: *numbed with grief.*
[Middle English *nome* < Old English *numen*, past participle of *niman* to take, seize] —**numb′ly,** *adv.* —**numb′ness,** *n.*
—**Syn.** *adj.* deadened, insensible, benumbed.

num·bat (num′bat), *n.* the banded anteater.

num·ber (num′bər), *n.* **1.** a word or symbol used in counting; numeral: *Two, fourteen, twenty-six (or 2, 14, and 26) are cardinal numbers; second, fourteenth, twenty-sixth (or 2nd, 14th, 26th) are ordinal numbers. Abbr.:* no. **2.** the amount of units; sum; total: *The number of your fingers is ten.* **3.** a quantity: *a number of reasons. A large number cannot read.* **4.** a collection or company: *the number of saints. Two more are still required to make up the number.* **5.** the particular number that indicates the place of a person or object in a series, and is a means of identifying it: *an apartment number, a license number.* **6.** one of a numbered series; single part of a program, etc. **7.** a song or other piece of music: *She sings many old numbers.* **8. a.** a single issue of a periodical: *the latest number of the "Saturday Review."* **b.** a single part of a book published in parts. **9.** *Informal.* any thing or person viewed apart or thought of as standing apart from a collection or company: *That dress is the most fashionable number in the store. He's a shrewd number, isn't he?* **10.** *Grammar.* **a.** the property or feature of words that indicates whether they refer to one, or more than one, person or thing. *Boy, ox,* and *this* are in the singular number; *boys, oxen,* and *these* are in the plural number. **b.** the form or group of forms indicating this. **11.** regularity of beat or measure in verse or music; rhythm: *instrumental sounds in full harmonic number joined* (Milton).

a number of, several; many: *a number of books, a number of people.*

beyond number, too many to count: *There were people beyond number at the circus.*

numbers, a. arithmetic: *He is very clever at numbers.* **b.** many: *Numbers were turned away.* **c.** a being greater or more powerful in size or number: *to win a battle by force of numbers.* **d.** poetry; lines of verse: *I lisp'd in numbers, for the numbers came* (Alexander Pope). **e.** groups of musical notes or measures: *Harp of the North! that . . . down the fitful breeze thy numbers flung* (Scott). **f.** numbers game: *He hoped to make his fortune by playing the numbers.*

one's number is up, *Informal.* one is doomed: *When the bandits ambushed the stagecoach, the driver was sure that his number was up.*

without number, too many to be counted: *stars without number.*

—*v.t.* **1.** to assign a number to; mark with a number; distinguish with a number: *The pages of this book are numbered.* **2.** to be able to show; have; contain: *This city numbers a million inhabitants.* **3.** to amount to; equal: *a crew numbering 20 men.* **4.** to reckon as one of a class or collection; classify: *numbered among his followers.* **5.** to fix the number of; limit: *That very old man's years are numbered.* **6.** to live or have lived (so many years): *The brave soldier had already numbered, nearly or quite, his threescore years and ten* (Hawthorne). **7. a.** to enumerate; count: *The business of the poet . . . is to examine, not the individual, but the species . . . he does not number the streaks of the tulip* (Samuel Johnson). **b.** *Archaic.* to allot; apportion: *So teach us to number our days, that we may apply our hearts unto wisdom* (Psalm 90:12). **8.** *Obsolete.* to levy (a number of, as soldiers).

—*v.i.* **1.** to make a count: *Many of us can number automatically.* **2.** to be numbered or included with: *Tho' thou numberest with the followers of one who cried "leave all and follow me"* (Tennyson).

[< Old French *nombre* < Latin *numerus*] —**num′ber·er,** *n.*

—**Syn.** *n.* **2. Number, sum** mean total of two or more persons, things, or units taken together. **Number** applies to the total reached by counting the persons or things in a group or collection: *Only twelve came—a smaller number than usual.* **Sum** applies to the total reached by adding figures or things: *The sum of two and two is four.*

➔ **Number** is a collective noun, requiring a singular or plural verb according as the total or the individual units are meant: *A number of tickets have already been sold. The number of tickets sold is astonishing.* See **amount** for another usage note.

➔ **numbers.** In informal writing, figures are usually used for numbers over ten, words for smaller numbers. In formal writing, figures are usually used for numbers over 100 except when they can be written in two words: Informal: *four, ten, 15, 92, 114, 200.* Formal: *four, ten, fifteen, ninety-two, 114, two hundred.* But practice is not consistent.

num·ber·less (num′bər lis), *adj.* **1.** very numerous; too many to count: *the numberless fish in the sea.* **2.** without a number; not numbered. —**Syn. 1.** countless, myriad, infinite.

number one, 1. *Informal.* oneself, as the chief interest of the selfish: *He always looks out for number one.* **2.** the first or best of a group or series: *to be number one in the class.*

num·ber-one (num′bər wun′), *adj.* chief; leading; principal: *Television . . . now seems to be firmly entrenched as the number-one medium for national advertising* (C. Jackson Shuttleworth).

Number One, *British.* the officer second in command of a naval vessel; first lieutenant or first mate.

number plate, *British.* a license plate.

num·bers (num′bərz), *n.pl.* See under **number,** *n.*

Num·bers (num′bərz), *n.* the fourth book of the Old Testament. It tells about the counting of the Israelites after they left Egypt. *Abbr.:* Num.

numbers game, racket, or **pool,** *U.S.* an illegal daily lottery in which bets are made on the appearance of any three digit numbers in a published statistic, as of the total amount bet at a race track, a stock market total, etc.

number theory, the study of integers and their relationships.

numb·fish (num′fish′), *n., pl.* **-fish·es** or (*collectively*) **-fish.** an electric ray or torpedo fish that numbs its prey by electric shock.

numb·ing (num′ing), *adj.* that numbs or induces numbness: *numbing cold or grief, etc.* —**numb′ing·ly,** *adv.*

num·bles (num′bəlz), *n.pl. Archaic.* the heart, liver, or certain other internal organs of an animal, especially of a deer, used as food. Also, **nombles.** [< Old French *nombles,* or *numbles* a loin or fillet, apparently an alteration of unrecorded *lombles* < Latin *lumbulus* (diminutive) < *lumbus* loin]

numb·skull (num′skul′), *n.* numskull.

nu·men (nü′mən, nyü′-), *n., pl.* **-mi·na** (-mə nə). *Roman Mythology.* a spirit presiding over the affairs of men; deity. [< Latin *nūmen* divine power; (originally) a nod, related to *nuere* nod]

nu·mer·a·ble (nü′mər ə bəl, nyü′-), *adj.* that can be counted: *The friend does not count his friends on his fingers; they are not numerable* (Thoreau). [< Latin *numerābilis* < *numerāre* to number, numerate]

nu·mer·a·cy (nü′mər ə sē, nyü′-), *n.* competence in mathematics; the quality of being numerate: *Literacy and numeracy [together] . . . cover whatever extensions of the three Rs are now required by the recharged meaning of "educated"* (London Times). [back formation < *innumerate*]

nu·mer·al (nü′mər əl, nyü′-), *n.* **1. a.** a figure, letter, or word standing for a number. **b.** group of figures, letters, or words standing for a number: *1, 5, 10, 50, 100, and 1,000 are Arabic numerals; I, V, X, L, C, and M are Roman numerals.* **2.** one of the figures or symbols used to express a number; digit.

numerals, big cloth numbers given by a school for excellence in some sport. They state the year in which the person who wins them will graduate. *John wore his varsity numerals with pride.*

—*adj.* **1.** of numbers; standing for a number: *a numeral word or adjective.* **2.** belonging or having to do with number.

[< Late Latin *numerālis* < Latin *numerus* number] —**nu′mer·al·ly,** *adv.*

nu·mer·ar·y (nü′mə rer′ē, nyü′-), *adj.* of or having to do with a number or numbers.

nu·mer·ate[1] (nü′mə rāt, nyü′-), *v.t.*, **-at·ed, -at·ing. 1.** to number; count; enumerate. **2.** to read (an expression in numbers). [< Latin *numerāre* (with English *-ate*[1]) to number < *numerus* a number]

nu·mer·ate[2] (nü′mər it, nyü′-), *adj.* able to understand or use mathematics: *In the nineteenth century we recognized that to achieve commercial leadership we needed a literate population. We are now learning that technological leadership requires a numerate population* (New Scientist). [back formation < *innumerate*]

nu·mer·a·tion (nü′mə rā′shən, nyü′-), *n.* **1.** a numbering; a counting; a calculating: *Numeration is but still the adding of one unit more* (John Locke). **2.** the reading of numbers expressed in figures.

nu·mer·a·tor (nü′mə rā′tər, nyü′-), *n.* **1.** the number above the line in a fraction, which shows how many parts are taken: *In* $\frac{3}{8}$, *3 is the numerator and 8 the denominator.* **2.** a person or thing that makes a count, takes a census, etc. [< Late Latin *numerātor* counter < Latin *numerāre* numerate]

nu·mer·ic (nü mer′ik, nyü-), *adj.* numerical.

nu·mer·i·cal (nü mer′ə kəl, nyü-), *adj.* **1.** of a number; having to do with numbers; in numbers; by numbers: *It can sort cards in numerical or alphabetical order at the rate of 1,000 a minute* (Wall Street Journal). **2.** shown by numbers, not by letters: *10 is a numerical quantity; bx is a literal or algebraic quantity.* **3.** (of a mathematical quantity) designating the value in figures without considering the sign: *The numerical value of +4 is less than that of −7, though its algebraic value is more.*

numerical forecasting, a method of weather forecasting in which an electronic computer is fed numerical data on the current weather situation to compute the conditions likely to prevail in a short period of time. It then uses the resulting prediction as the basis for computing the weather at the end of the next period, and so on until a 24-hour forecast is obtained.

nu·mer·i·cal·ly (nü mer′ə klē, nyü-), *adv.* **1.** by numbers; in a numerical manner: *to state one's findings numerically.* **2.** in numerical respects; so far as numbers are concerned: *The other team is numerically superior.*

nu·mer·o·log·i·cal (nü′mər ə loj′ə kəl, nyü′-), *adj.* of or having to do with numerology: *numerological tables, numerological analysis.*

nu·mer·ol·o·gist (nü′mə rol′ə jist, nyü′-), *n.* a person who practices numerology: *Canada's 6,195 tax collectors claim the most difficult cases to keep track of are the obsessed numerologists who change their name when the stars tell them to* (Maclean's).

nu·mer·ol·o·gy (nü′mə rol′ə jē, nyü′-), *n.* foretelling the future of an individual through supposedly meaningful numbers or combinations of numbers based on a date of birth, the letters of a name, etc.; the occultism of numbers: *astrology, palmistry, and numerology arouse interest mainly as novelties* (World Book Encyclopedia). [< Latin *numerus* number + English *-logy*]

nu·mer·os·i·ty (nü′mə ros′ə tē, nyü′-), *n., pl.* **-ties. 1.** large number; numerousness. **2.** harmonious flow; poetical rhythm; harmony.

nu·mer·ous (nü′mər əs, nyü′-), *adj.* **1.** very many; of great number: *The child asked numerous questions.* **2.** in great numbers; consisting of many; plentiful: *He has numerous acquaintances among politicians.* [< Latin *numerōsus* (with English *-ous*) < *numerus* number] —**nu′mer·ous·ly,** *adv.* —**nu′mer·ous·ness,** *n.* —**Syn. 1.** manifold, several, innumerable.

Nu·mid·i·an (nü mid′ē ən, nyü-), *adj.* of or having to do with Numidia, an ancient country in northern Africa, its people, or their language. —*n.* **1.** a native or inhabitant of Numidia. **2.** the Hamitic language of ancient Numidia.

Numidian crane, a demoiselle.

nu·mi·na (nü′mə nə, nyü′-), *n.* plural of **numen.**

nu·mi·nous (nü′mə nəs), *adj.* **1.** spiritual; holy; divine: *a numinous light. Certain human beings are publicly regarded as numinous* (W.H. Auden). **2.** ethereal; nebulous; intangible: *everything for her was numinous —the butcher with his cleaver, the hunters in the woods* (New Yorker). [< Latin *nūmen, -inis* (see NUMEN) + English *-ous*]

numis., numismatic or numismatics.

nu·mis·mat·ic (nü′miz mat′ik, nyü′-), *adj.* **1.** of numismatics or numismatists. **2.** of coins and medals. —**nu′mis·mat′i·cal·ly,** *adv.*

nu·mis·mat·i·cal (nü′miz mat′ə kəl, nyü′-), *adj.* numismatic.

nu·mis·ma·ti·cian (nü miz′mə tish′ən, nyü-), *n.* a numismatist.

nu·mis·mat·ics (nü′miz mat′iks, nyü′-), *n.* the study or collecting of coins or paper currency, medals, tokens, etc. [< French *numismatique* < Latin *numisma, -atis* coin, currency < Greek *nómisma, -atos* < *nomízein* have in use]

nu·mis·ma·tist (nü miz′mə tist, nyü-), *n.* a person skilled in numismatics: *A numismatist asked for a spot to spread coins* (Wall Street Journal).

nu·mis·ma·tol·o·gist (nü miz′mə tol′ə jist, nyü-), *n.* numismatist.

nu·mis·ma·tol·o·gy (nü miz′mə tol′ə jē, nyü-), *n.* numismatics.

num·ma·ry (num′ər ē), *adj.* of or having to do with coins or money; occupied with coins or money. [< Latin *nummārius* < *nummus* coin]

num·mu·lar (num′yə lər), *adj. Medicine.* somewhat flat and nearly round; shaped like a coin. [< Latin *nummulus* money (diminutive) < *nummus* a coin + English *-ar*]

num·mu·lar·y (num′yə ler′ē), *adj.* nummary.

num·mu·lat·ed (num′yə lā′tid), *adj. Medicine.* nummular.

num·mu·la·tion (num′yə lā′shən), *n. Medicine.* the arrangement, like that of rolls of coins, assumed by red blood cells in freshly drawn blood. [< Latin *nummulus* money (see NUMMULAR) + English *-ation*]

num·mu·lite (num′yə līt), *n.* any of an extinct group of foraminifers of the early Tertiary period, having a flat spiral shell. Their fossils are especially abundant in limestones of the Mediterranean area. [< Latin *nummulus* (diminutive) < *nummus* coin + English *-ite*[1]]

num·mu·lit·ic (num′yə lit′ik), *adj.* **1.** containing nummulites: *nummulitic limestone.* **2.** characterized by nummulites.

num·skull (num′skul′), *n. Informal.* a stupid person; blockhead; dolt: *We considered them to be numskulls and little better than idiots* (Anthony Trollope). *You numskulls! and so while . . . you are quarrelling for places, the guests must be starved* (Oliver Goldsmith). Also, **numbskull.**

nun[1] (nun), *n.* **1.** a woman who devotes her life to religion and lives under religious vows with a group of women like her. Some nuns teach; others take care of sick people. **2.** any of various birds, as the European blue titmouse, the smew, or a variety of domestic pigeon with a veil-like crest. [Old English *nunne* < Late Latin *nonna,* feminine of *nonnus* monk (originally) a term of address] —**nun′like′,** *adj.*

Nun (def. 2) or European blue titmouse (to 6 in. long)

nun[2] (nün), *n.* the fourteenth letter of the Hebrew alphabet. [< Hebrew *nūn*]

nu·na·tak (nü′nə tak), *n.* the peak of a mountain or hill which projects above a surrounding glacier. [< an Eskimo word]

nun·bird (nun′bėrd′), *n.* any of the South American puffbirds, with dark feathers on the body, wings, and tail, and white on the head.

nun buoy, a buoy that is round in the middle and tapering toward each end. [perhaps obsolete *nun* top, a child's toy (because of the shape)]

nunc di·mit·tis (nungk′ di mit′is), *Latin.* permission to depart; departure; dismissal.

Nunc Di·mit·tis (nungk′ di mit′is), a canticle of Simeon, beginning "Lord, now lettest thou thy servant depart in peace," from the words of Simeon on recognizing the infant Jesus as the Christ. Luke 2:29-32. [< Latin *Nunc dimittis* now lettest thou depart]

nun·cheon (nun′chən), *n. British Informal or Dialect.* a light refreshment taken between meals: *I left London this morning . . . and the only ten minutes I have spent out of my chaise . . . procured me a nuncheon at Marlborough* (Jane Austen). [reduction of Middle English *nonechenche* < Old English *nōn* noon + *scenc* drink]

nun·ci·a·ture (nun′shē ə chər), *n.* the office or term of service of a nuncio. [Latinization of Italian *nunziatura* < *nunzio* nuncio]

nun·ci·o (nun′shē ō), *n., pl.* **-ci·os.** an ambassador from the Pope to a government: *With the papal nuncio threatening, the Doge felt obliged to decline the gift* (New Yorker). [< Italian *nuncio,* or *nunzio* < Latin *nūntius* messenger] —**Syn.** legate.

nun·cle (nung′kəl), *n. Dialect.* uncle. [< misdivision of *an uncle*]

nun·cu·pa·tive (nung′kyə pā′tiv, nung-kyü′pə-), *adj.* (of wills) not in writing; oral: *He left me a small legacy in a nuncupative will, as a token of his kindness for me* (Benjamin Franklin). [< Late Latin *nuncupātīvus* < *nuncupāre* to name, call by name < *nōmen* name + *capere* take]

nun·di·nal (nun′də nəl), *adj.* **1.** having to do with a fair or market. **2.** connected with the Roman nundines.

nun·dine (nun′dīn, -din), *n.* a periodical market day among the ancient Romans, being the ninth day as reckoned from the preceding market day taken as the first, or, as expressed in modern reckoning, occurring every eighth day. [< Latin *nundinae,* feminine plural of *nundinus* < *novem* nine + *diēs* day]

nun moth, a European moth, whose larva does great damage to forest trees.

nun·na·tion (nu nā′shən), *n.* the addition of a final *n* in the declension of nouns, as in Middle English and Arabic. [< New Latin *nunnatio, -onis* < Arabic *nūn* the letter "n"]

nun·ner·y (nun′ər ē), *n., pl.* **-ner·ies.** the building or buildings where nuns live; convent: *I shall take up my abode in a religious house, near Lisle—a nunnery, you would call it* (Charlotte Brontë).

nun's cotton, fine cotton embroidery thread, so called from its use by nuns.

nun's veiling, a thin, plain-woven woolen fabric, used mainly for women's dresses and sometimes for religious habits.

nu·phar (nü′fər, nyü′-), *n.* any of a group of perennial aquatic herbs of the water-lily family, with large floating or erect leaves and yellow or purplish flowers; yellow water lily; spatterdock. [< New Latin *nuphar* < Arabic, and Persian *nūfar,* reduction of *nīnūfar* nenuphar]

nup·tial (nup′shəl), *adj.* of marriage or weddings: *nuptial vows. I chose a Wife . . . And in your City held my Nuptial Feast* (Milton). —*n.* **nuptials,** a wedding; the wedding ceremony: *a feast . . . rich as for the nuptials of a king* (Tennyson). [< Middle French *nuptial,* learned borrowing from Latin *nuptiālis* < *nuptiae, -ārum* wedding < *nūbere* take a husband]

Nuptial Blessing, (in the Roman Catholic Church) a special blessing bestowed upon the bride and groom at a Nuptial Mass.

Nuptial Mass, in the Roman Catholic and some other churches: **1.** a Mass for the bride and groom incorporated into the wedding ceremony. **2.** the wedding ceremony including this.

N.U.R., National Union of Railwaymen.

nu·ra·ghe (nü rä′gā), *n., pl.* **-ghi** (-gē). a towerlike structure of ancient date, of a kind peculiar to Sardinia: *The link with Mycenaean civilization has been confirmed in recent years by the discovery of bronze ingots in several nuraghi* (Scientific American). [< a dialectal Sardinian word]

nurse (nėrs), *n., v.,* **nursed, nurs·ing.** —*n.* **1.** a person who takes care of the sick, the injured, or the old, or is trained to do this: *Hospitals employ many nurses.* **2.** a woman who cares for and brings up the young children or babies of another person: *Mrs. Jones has hired a new nurse.* **3.** a wet nurse. **4.** a person, animal, or thing that feeds, protects, or gives any sort of aid or comfort: *Gentle sleep, Nature's soft nurse* (Shakespeare). **5.** a worker in a colony of bees or ants that cares for the young. **6.** (in billiards) the act of controlling the balls for a series of shots.
—*v.i.* **1.** to be a nurse; act as a nurse; work as a nurse. **2.** to suck milk from a mother or nurse. —*v.t.* **1.** to act as a nurse for; wait on or try to cure (the sick); take care of (sick, injured, or old people). **2.** to cure or try to cure by care: *She nursed a bad cold by going to bed.* **3.** to take care of and bring up (another's baby or young child). **4.** to nourish; protect; make grow: *to nurse a plant, nurse a fire, nurse a grudge, to nurse a hope in one's heart. He nursed what property was yet left to him* (Scott). **5.** to use or treat with special care: *He nursed his sore arm by using it very little.* **6.** to hold closely; clasp fondly: *Here I found my lord seated, nursing his cane* (Robert Louis Stevenson). **7.** to give milk to (a baby). **8.** (in billiards) to hit (balls) softly so as to keep them close together for a series of shots. **9.** *Informal.* to drink very slowly in sips: *to nurse a cocktail.*
[Middle English *nurice* < Old French *nurrice* < Latin *nūtrīcia* < *nūtrīre* to feed. Compare NOURISH.] —**nurs′er,** *n.*

nurse balloon, *Aeronautics.* a small portable balloon of heavy fabric, used for storing gas, as for replenishing the supply of gas of another balloon.

nurse·ling (nėrs′ling), *n.* nursling.

nurse·maid (nėrs′mād′), *n.* a maid employed to care for children.

nurs·er·y (nėrs′ər ē, nėrs′rē), *n., pl.* **-er·ies. 1.** a room set apart for the use of small children and babies: *What I should like best . . . would be to go to the nursery, and see your dear little children* (Thackeray). **2.** a piece of ground or place where young trees and plants are raised for transplanting or sale. **3.** a place or condition that helps something to grow and develop: *Family life, the first and last nursery of the higher sympathies* (H. Drummond). **4.** the brood or chambers in which larval, social insects attain maturity. **5.** a nursery school. **6.** *Obsolete.* upbringing.

nurs·er·y·maid (nėr′sər ē mād′, nėrs′rē-), *n.* nursemaid: *A nurserymaid is not afraid of what you gentlemen call work* (William S. Gibert).

nurs·er·y·man (nėr′sər ē mən, nėrs′rē-), *n., pl.* **-men.** a man who grows or sells young trees and plants: *Nurserymen expect big . . . sales to gardeners replacing dead shrubs* (Wall Street Journal).

nursery rhyme, a little poem for children: *"Sing a Song of Sixpence" is a favorite nursery rhyme. The origins of many nursery rhymes are shrouded in the fumes of taverns and mughouses* (Time).

nursery school, a school for children not old enough to go to kindergarten, especially children between the ages of three and five: *Nursery school gives young children space to play freely and actively* (Sidonie Gruenberg).

nurse shark, any of various sharks that rest for a long time between movements, especially the gata-nosed shark.
nurs·ing bottle (nėr′sing), a bottle to which a rubber nipple is attached, for feeding infants.
nursing home, a private hospital, especially for convalescent patients.
nurs·ling (nėrs′ling), *n.* **1.** a baby that is being nursed. **2.** any person or thing that is having tender care: *I am the daughter of Earth and Water, And the nursling of the sky* (Shelley).
nur·ture (nėr′chər), *v.*, **-tured, -tur·ing,** *n.* —*v.t.* **1.** to rear; bring up; care for; foster; train: *She nurtured the child as if he had been her own.* **2.** to nourish; feed: *to nurture resentment.* [< noun]
—*n.* **1.** a rearing; bringing up; training; education: *The two sisters had received very different nurture, one at home and the other at a convent.* **2.** nourishment; food: *Where ... from the heart we took our first and sweetest nurture* (Byron).
[< Old French *nourture,* or *norreture,* adaptation < Late Latin *nūtrītūra* a nursing, suckling < Latin *nūtrīre* to nurse, nourish. Compare NUTRITIOUS.] —**nur′tur·er,** *n.*
nut (nut), *n., v.,* **nut·ted, nut·ting.** —*n.* **1.** a dry fruit or seed with a hard, woody or leathery shell and a kernel inside which is often good to eat: *... two or three cents to buy candy, and nuts and raisins* (Hawthorne). **2. a.** the kernel of a nut; nutmeat. **b.** *Botany.* a dry, one-seeded, indehiscent fruit similar to an achene, but larger and having a harder and thicker pericarp, as an acorn, hazelnut, or beechnut. **3.** a small block, usually of metal, with a threaded hole in the center, that screws on to a bolt to hold the bolt in place. **4. a.** a piece at the upper end of a violin, cello, etc., over which the strings pass. **b.** a device at the lower end of the bow, by which the horsehair may be relaxed or tightened. **5.** *Slang.* the head. **6.** *Slang.* an odd or crazy person.

Nuts (def. 3)
From left to right: square, hexagon, castellated hexagon, wing and hexagon cap

from soup to nuts. See under **soup,** *n.*
hard nut to crack, *Informal.* a difficult question, problem, or undertaking: *Miss Lawrence, the Scottish champion, found Miss Cross too hard a nut to crack and for the second time in the day missed a holeable putt on the last green for a halved match* (London Times).
nuts, *Informal.* something especially enjoyable or delightful: *Tom had his store clothes on, and an audience—and that was always nuts for Tom Sawyer* (Mark Twain).
—*v.i.* to gather nuts: *The younger people, making holiday, with bag and sack and basket, great and small, went nutting to the hazels* (Tennyson).
[Old English *hnutu*] —**nut′like′,** *adj.*
NUT (no periods) or **N.U.T.,** National Union of Teachers: *It was hoped that the NUT would be successful in its negotiations to combat famine in the primary school teaching profession* (Alan Coren).
nu·tant (nü′tənt, nyü′-), *adj.* **1.** *Botany.* drooping; nodding. **2.** *Zoology.* **a.** sloping in relation to the parts behind it or with the axis of the body: *a nutant head.* **b.** bent or curved toward the anterior extremity of the body: *a nutant horn.*
[< Latin *nutāns, -antis,* present participle of *nūtāre;* see NUTATION]
nu·ta·tion (nü tā′shən, nyü-), *n.* **1.** the act of nodding the head. **2.** an instance of nodding the head. **3.** *Botany.* a twisting or rotation of the growing tip of a plant due to consecutive differences in growth rates of different sides: *Nutation is the spiral twisting of a stem as it grows* (Scientific American). **4.** *Astronomy.* a slight oscillation of the earth's axis, which makes the motion of the precession of the equinoxes irregular. [< Latin *nūtātiō, -ōnis* < *nūtāre* to nod, sway (frequentative) < *nuere* to nod]
nu·ta·tion·al (nü tā′shə nəl, nyü-), *adj.* **1.** of or having to do with nutation. **2.** exhibiting nutation.
nut-brown (nut′broun′), *adj.* brown as a ripe nut: *spicy nut-brown ale* (Milton).
nut cake, 1. a doughnut. **2.** a cake with nuts.
nut·crack·er (nut′krak′ər), *n.* **1.** an instrument for cracking the shells of nuts. **2.** either of two birds related to the crow, that feed generally on coniferous seeds, as Clark's nutcracker living in the mountains of western North America.

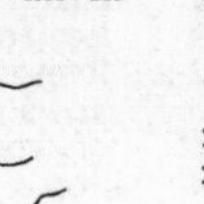
Nutcracker (def. 1)

Nutcracker Man, Zinjanthropus.
nut·gall (nut′gôl′), *n.* a lump or ball that swells up, especially on an oak tree, where the tree has been injured by an insect; any of various galls resembling a nut.

Clark's Nutcracker (def. 2—12½ in. long)

nut grass, any of a group of sedges having small tuberous roots.
nut·hatch (nut′hach′), *n.* any of a group of small, stout, climbing birds that feed on small nuts, seeds, and insects, and have strong beaks, large feet, and live mostly in trees. [Middle English *notehache* (literally) nut hacker. Compare HACK.]
nut·house (nut′hous′), *n. Slang.* an insane asylum.
nut·let (nut′lit), *n.* **1.** a small nut or nutlike fruit. **2.** the stone of a drupe, especially a small drupe.
nut·meat (nut′mēt′), *n.* kernel of a nut.
nut·meg (nut′meg), *n.* **1.** a hard, spicy seed about as big as a marble, obtained from the fruit of a tall East Indian evergreen tree. The seed is grated and used for flavoring food: *Nutmeg and mace are the only two different spices harvested from the same fruit* (Science News Letter). **2.** the tree that it grows on. **3.** the similar product of various related trees. [Middle English *notemuga,* half-translation of unrecorded Old French *nois mugue* nut smelling like musk < *nois* nut (< Latin *nux*) + *mugue* musk < Late Latin *muscus*]
nutmeg melon, a variety of small muskmelon with a netted rind.
Nutmeg State, a nickname of Connecticut.
nut·pick (nut′pik′), *n.* a pointed instrument to remove nuts from their shells.
nut pine, any of several North American pines producing large edible seeds, especially a pine of the western United States.
nu·tri·a (nü′trē ə, nyü′-), *n.* **1.** the coypu, an aquatic rodent of South America resembling the muskrat. It has become established in parts of southern and western United States. **2.** its dark, lustrous beaver-like fur. [< Spanish *nutria,* variant of *lutria* otter < Latin *lutra*]
nu·tri·ent (nü′trē ənt, nyü′-), *adj.* nourishing. —*n.* a nourishing substance, especially as an element or ingredient of a foodstuff: *a diet rich in nutrients.* [< Latin *nūtriēns, -entis,* present participle of *nūtrīre* nourish]
nutrient solution, a chemical solution of minerals required for plant growth, used in growing plants without soil or in poor soil.
nutrient X, anti-anemic constituent of milk, supposedly the same as vitamin B_{12}.
nu·tri·ment (nü′trə mənt, nyü′-), *n.* **1.** that which is required by an organism as building material and fuel; nourishment; food. **2.** something that maintains anything, or by which its development is made possible.
nu·tri·men·tal (nü′trə men′təl, nyü′-), *adj.* having the qualities of food; nutritious.
nu·tri·tion (nü trish′ən, nyü-), *n.* **1.** food; nutriment. **2.** processes by which food is changed to living tissues. **3.** the act or process of supplying or receiving nourishment.
nu·tri·tion·al (nü trish′ə nəl, nyü-), *adj.* having to do with nutrition. —**nu·tri′tion·al·ly,** *adv.*
nu·tri·tion·ist (nü trish′ə nist, nyü-), *n.* an expert in nutrition.
nu·tri·tious (nü trish′əs, nyü-), *adj.* valuable as food; nourishing: *Fruits are nutritious.* [< Latin *nūtrītius* or *nūtrīcius* < *nutrīx, -īcis* a nurse < *nūtrīre* nourish] —**nu·tri′tious·ly,** *adv.* —**nu·tri′tious·ness,** *n.*
nu·tri·tive (nü′trə tiv, nyü′-), *adj.* **1.** having to do with foods and the use of foods: **2.** giving nourishment; nutritious. —**nu′tri·tive·ly,** *adv.* —**nu′tri·tive·ness,** *n.*
nuts[1] (nuts), *adj. U.S. Slang.* crazy.
be nuts about, to be very fond of or delighted with (a person or thing): *Larry is nuts about detective stories.*
nuts[2] (nuts), *n., pl.* See under **nut,** *n.*
nuts and bolts, small but essential features, especially those that form an integral framework or make up practical details, as of a plan: *the busy executive who wants to see the underlying realities, the economic nuts and bolts, that are common to all business enterprises* (London Sunday Times).
nut·shell (nut′shel′), *n.* **1.** the shell of a nut; hard outside covering within which the kernel of a nut is enclosed. **2.** something extremely small or scanty.
in a nutshell, in very brief form; in a few words: *You have my history in a nutshell* (Robert Browning).
—*v.t.* to put in a nutshell; summarize.
Nut·tall's woodpecker (nut′ôlz), a black and white, barred woodpecker with a black crown and, in the male, red on the back of the head and neck, found in Oregon, California, and Baja California. [< Thomas *Nuttall,* 1786–1859, Anglo-American ornithologist]
nut·ter (nut′ər), *n.* a person who gathers nuts.
nut·ti·ness (nut′ē nis), *n.* **1.** the quality of being nutty. **2.** nutty flavor.
nut·ting (nut′ing), *n.* the act of looking for nuts; gathering nuts.
nut·ty (nut′ē), *adj.,* **-ti·er, -ti·est. 1.** containing many nuts: *nutty cake.* **2.** like nuts; tasting like nuts. **3.** *Slang.* odd; crazy. **4.** *Slang.* greatly interested or enthusiastic. **5.** full of zest or flavor; pleasant; rich: *the nutty Spanish ale* (John Masefield). **6.** *Slang.* witless; crazy; nuts.
nut weevil, a weevil that feeds on the insides of nuts.
nut·wood (nut′wu̇d′), *n.* **1.** a tree bearing nuts, as the hickory, walnut, etc. **2.** the wood of such a tree.

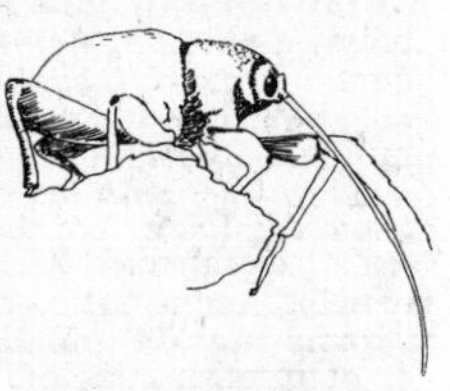
Acorn Nut Weevil (⅝ in. long)

nux vom·i·ca (nuks vom′ə kə), **1.** a bitter yellowish powder containing strychnine and made from the seed of a tree growing in southern Asia and Northern Australia. It is used as a stomachic and tonic. **2.** the poisonous seed from which nux vomica is prepared. **3.** the tree itself. See **strychnos** for picture. [< New Latin *nux vomica* (literally) vomiting nut < Latin *nux* nut, *vomere* to vomit]
nuz·zle[1] (nuz′əl), *v.,* **-zled, -zling.** —*v.t.* **1.** to poke or rub with the nose; press the nose against: *The calf nuzzles his mother.* **2.** to burrow or dig (the snout) into, as a horse with grain or a hog with swill. —*v.i.* **1.** to nestle; snuggle; cuddle. **2.** to burrow or dig with the nose. [< *nose* + *-le;* influenced by *nestle.* Compare NOZZLE.]
nuz·zle[2] (nuz′əl), *v.t.,* **-zled, -zling.** to cherish fondly; nurse. [perhaps related to NUZZLE[1] and NOSE]
n.w., 1. net weight. **2. a.** northwest. **b.** northwestern.
NW (no periods), **1.** Northwest or northwest. **2.** Northwestern or northwestern.
N.W., 1. North Wales. **2.** Northwest or northwest. **3.** Northwestern or northwestern.
N.W.T., Northwest Territories (in Canada).
N.Y., 1. New York State. **2.** New York City.
NYA (no periods), National Youth Administration.
ny·al·a (nī al′ə), *n.* a South African antelope related to the bushbuck and having vertical stripes of a bluish-gray and faint white color: *The Mkuzi Reserve is the headquarters of the rare and beautiful nyala* (Cape Times). [< Bantu *inyala*]
ny·an·za (nē an′zə, nī-), *n.* any relatively large body of water in the interior of Africa, especially

Nyala (about 3½ ft. high at the shoulder)

a lake: *Albert Nyanza.* [< a native word appearing in several African languages]

Ny·as·a (nī as′ə, nē-), *adj., n.* Nyasalander.

Ny·as·a·land·er (nī as′ə lan′dər, nē-), *adj.* of or having to do with Nyasaland (now Malawi), in southeastern Africa, or its people. —*n.* a native or inhabitant of Nyasaland.

N.Y.C., New York City.

nyck·el·har·pa (nik′əl här′pə), *n.* a stringed instrument of Sweden, similar to a hurdy-gurdy but played with a bow. [< Swedish *nyckelharpa* (literally) key harp]

nyc·ta·gi·na·ceous (nik′tə jə nā′shəs), *adj.* belonging to the four-o'clock family. [< New Latin *Nyctaginaceae* the family name (< *Nyctago, -inis* the former genus name < Greek *nýx, nýktos* night) + English *-ous*]

nyc·ta·lo·pi·a (nik′tə lō′pē ə), *n.* night blindness, a visual defect characterized by poor adaptation of the eyes to darkness, associated with vitamin-A deficiency and xerophthalmia; moon blindness. [< Late Latin *nyctalopia* < Greek *nyktálōps* (originally) night-blindness < *nýx, nýktos* night + *alaós* blind + *ōps* eye]

nyc·ta·lop·ic (nik′tə lop′ik), *adj.* **1.** having to do with nyctalopia. **2.** like nyctalopia. **3.** affected with nyctalopia.

nyc·ti·trop·ic (nik′tə trop′ik), *adj. Botany.* turning in a different direction at night, as the leaves of certain plants. [< Greek *nýx, nýktos* night + English *tropic*]

nyc·tit·ro·pism (nik tit′rə piz əm), *n. Botany.* a tendency to assume at, or just before, nightfall, certain positions unlike those maintained during the day, as the leaves of certain plants. [< Greek *nýx, nýktos* night + English *tropism*]

nyc·to·pho·bi·a (nik′tə fō′bē ə), *n.* an abnormal fear of the dark and of night. [< Greek *nýx, nýktos* night + English *-phobia*]

nyet (nyet), *n., adj., adv. Russian.* no.

nyl·ghai (nil′gī), *n.* nilgai.

nyl·ghau (nil′gô), *n.* nilgai.

ny·lon (nī′lon), *n.* any of a group of extremely strong, elastic, and durable synthetic substances resembling proteins in structure. Nylon is made by polymerization of aliphatic dicarboxylic acids, such as adipic acid, and aliphatic diamines, and is used to make clothing, stockings, bristles, etc.

nylons, stockings made of nylon.

—*adj.* made of nylon: *Many toothbrushes have nylon bristles.* [< *Nylon,* a trademark]

nymph (nimf), *n.* **1.** one of the lesser Greek and Roman goddesses of nature, who lived in seas, rivers, springs, hills, woods, or trees. **2.** *Poetic.* a beautiful or graceful young woman: *Nymph, in thy orisons Be all my sins remember'd* (Shakespeare). **3.** the stage of development in certain insects immediately after hatching, resembling the adult but lacking fully developed wings. See **mayfly** for picture. [< Old French *nymphe,* or *nimphe,* learned borrowing from Latin *nympha* < Greek *nýmphē*] —**nymph′like′,** *adj.*

nym·pha (nim′fə), *n., pl.* **-phae** (-fē). **1.** *Anatomy.* either of the labia minora. **2.** nymph. [< New Latin *nympha* < Greek *nýmphē* the clitoris, probably as "source of water," transferred meaning from river goddess, nymph]

nym·phae·a·ceous (nim′fē ā′shəs), *adj.* belonging to the water-lily family of aquatic plants.

nym·phal (nim′fəl), *adj.* of or having to do with a nymph or nymphs.

nym·pha·lid (nim′fə lid), *n.* any of a family of butterflies having the forelegs much reduced, including the admiral, mourning cloak, viceroy, etc. —*adj.* of or belonging to this family. [< New Latin *Nymphalis, -idis* the genus name < Latin *nympha* nymph]

nym·phe·an (nim fē′ən), *adj.* nymphal.

nym·phet (nim fet′, nim′fit), *n.* a young girl, especially one in her teens, who attracts older men: *The novel* ["*Lolita*"] *by Vladimir Nabokov is about a man who has a passion for . . . nymphets* (Manchester Guardian).

nym·phic (nim′fik), *adj.* nymphal.

nym·pho (nim′fō), *adj., n. Informal.* nymphomaniac.

nym·pho·lep·si·a (nim′fə lep′sē ə), *n.* nympholepsy.

nym·pho·lep·sy (nim′fə lep′sē), *n.* **1.** a state of rapture supposed to be inspired in men by nymphs. **2.** a frenzy of emotion, especially that inspired by something unattainable. [< Greek *nymphólēptos* one bewitched by a nymph < *nýmphē* nymph + *lēptos,* stem of *lambánein* to seize; perhaps patterned on English *epilepsy*]

nym·pho·lept (nim′fə lept), *n.* a person seized with nympholepsy.

nym·pho·lep·tic (nim′fə lep′tik), *adj.* **1.** of or belonging to nympholepsy. **2.** possessed by nympholepsy; ecstatic; frenzied.

nym·pho·ma·ni·a (nim′fə mā′nē ə), *n.* **1.** abnormal, uncontrollable sexual desire in a woman. **2.** uncontrollable sexual desire in animals, especially in cattle. [< Greek *nýmphē* nymph, bride + English *mania*]

nym·pho·ma·ni·ac (nim′fə mā′nē ak), *adj.* **1.** characterized by nymphomania. **2.** suffering from nymphomania. —*n.* a woman who is affected with nymphomania.

NYSE (no periods) or **N.Y.S.E.,** New York Stock Exchange.

nys·tag·mic (nis tag′mik), *adj.* of or like nystagmus.

nys·tag·mus (nis tag′məs), *n.* an involuntary movement of the eyeballs, frequently a symptom of disease. [< New Latin *nystagmus* < Greek *nystagmós* drowsiness; (literally) nodding < *nystázein* to nod, be sleepy]

nys·tat·in (nis tat′in), *n.* an antibiotic used to combat fungus diseases such as moniliasis, ringworm, and athlete's foot. *Formula:* $C_{46}H_{77}NO_{19}$

NYU (no periods) or **N.Y.U.,** New York University.

Nyx (niks), *n.* the ancient Greek goddess of night, identified with the Roman Nox.

N.Z. or **N.Zeal.,** New Zealand.

Roman
100's A.D.

O
Greek
600's B.C.

O
Phoenician
1000's B.C.

Semitic
1500's B.C.

Egyptian
3000's B.C.

Oo Oo *Oo* *Oo*

O[1] or **o** (ō), *n., pl.* **O's** or **o's, Os, os,** or **oes. 1.** the 15th letter of the English alphabet: *There are two o's in Ohio.* **2.** any sound represented by this letter. **3.** (used as a symbol) the 15th, or more usually the 14th, of a series (either I or J being omitted). **4.** something like the letter O in shape: *May we cram Within this wooden O [theater] the very casques That did affright the air at Agincourt?* (Shakespeare). **5.** zero. **6.** a mere nothing.

O[2] (ō), *interj., n., pl.* **O's.** —*interj.* oh!: *Praise the Lord, O Jerusalem* (Psalms 147:12). *O say, can you see, by the dawn's early light* (Francis Scott Key). —*n.* an exclamation of oh: *O's of admiration* (Thackeray). [Middle English *O*]

O[3] (ō), *n., pl.* **O's** (ōz). a person whose name begins with the prefix O'-: *Ireland her O's, her Macs let Scotland boast* (Henry Fielding).

o' (ə, ō), *prep.* **1.** of: *man-o'-war, o'clock, will-o'-the-wisp.* **2.** on: *Being knocked o' the head . . .* (Richard Brinsley Sheridan).

O', *prefix.* descendant, used as a prefix in Irish family names, as in *O'Connell, O'Connor, O'Neil.* [< Irish *ó* descendant]

o-, *combining form.* the form of **ob-** before *m,* as in *omit.*

o (no period), ohm (unit of electrical resistance).

o., an abbreviation for the following:
1. octavo.
2. off.
3. officer.
4. old.
5. only.
6. order.
7. (in baseball) outs or put-outs (in scoring).
8. *Pharmacy.* pint (Latin, *octarius* or *octavus*).

O (no period), **1.** Old: *OHG* (Old High German). **2.** oxygen (chemical element). **3.** one of the four major blood factors or groups widely used to determine blood compatibility in transfusions. A person with O type blood can receive blood of the O group only.

O., an abbreviation for the following:
1. Ocean.
2. Octavo.
3. Ohio.
4. Old.
5. Ontario.
6. Order: *D.S.O.* (Distinguished Service Order).

oaf (ōf), *n., pl.* **oafs** or **oaves. 1.** a very stupid child or man: *a great oaf, in wooden shoes and a blouse* (Charles Lever). **2.** a clumsy person. **3.** a deformed child. **4.** *Obsolete.* an elf's child; changeling. [earlier *auf,* or *aulf* < Scandinavian (compare Old Icelandic *ālfr* silly person, elf)]

oaf·ish (ō'fish), *adj.* very stupid; clumsy. —**oaf'ish·ly,** *adv.* —**oaf'ish·ness,** *n.* —**Syn.** lubberly.

oak (ōk), *n.* **1.** any of a group of trees or shrubs of the beech family, found in all parts of the world, with strong, hard, durable wood and nuts called acorns. **2.** the wood, used in building, for flooring, cabinetwork, etc. **3.** a tree or shrub resembling or suggesting an oak. **4.** the leaves of an oak worn in a chaplet or garland. **5.** *British Slang.* a door of oak or other wood.

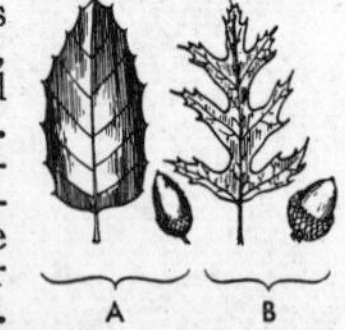

Oak Leaves and Acorns (def. 1)
A, European;
B, American

sport one's oak, *British University Slang.* to shut one's outer door to show one is out or busy: *Your oak was sported and you were not at home to anybody* (Walter Besant).

—*adj.* **1.** of an oak: *oak leaves.* **2.** made of oak; oaken: *an oak table.*
[Old English *āc*] —**oak'like',** *adj.*

oak apple, a lump or ball on an oak leaf or stem due to injury by an insect.

oak·en (ō'kən), *adj.* **1.** made of oak wood: *the old oaken bucket.* **2.** *Archaic.* of or having to do with the oak. **3.** consisting of oak trees.

oak gall, oak apple.

Oa·kie (ō'kē), *n.* Okie.

oak-leaf cluster (ōk'lēf'), a cluster of bronze or silver oak leaves and acorns given as an honor to a person in the United States armed forces who has already earned the same award for an earlier act of valor.

Oak·ley (ōk'lē), *n. Slang.* Annie Oakley.

oak-o·pen·ing (ōk'ō'pə ning, -ōp'ning), *n. U.S.* an opening, meadow, or thinly wooded tract in a forest of oak trees.

oa·kum (ō'kəm), *n.* loose fiber obtained by untwisting and picking apart old hemp ropes, used for stopping up the seams or cracks in ships. [Old English *ācumba* < *ā-* out + *cemban* to comb < *camb* a comb]

oak wilt, a serious fungus disease of oak trees that is spread by root grafts and insects. It was first reported in 1943 in Wisconsin, Iowa, and Minnesota. *Oak wilt is caused by . . . a fungus that grows in the sapwood of oaks and stops the exchange of nutrients between roots and leaves* (Atomic Energy Commission Report).

OAO (no periods), orbiting astronomical observatory.

OAP (no periods) or **O.A.P., 1.** old-age pension. **2.** old-age pensioner.

oar (ôr, ōr), *n.* **1.** a long pole with a flat end, used in rowing. Sometimes an oar is used to steer a boat. **2.** a person who rows; oarsman. **3.** a paddle or pole for stirring.

put or **stick one's oar in,** to meddle; interfere: *Already Mr. Khrushchev has been given the opportunity to stick his oar in* (London Times).

rest on one's oars, to stop working or trying and take a rest: *The managers of the usual autumn gathering of paintings . . . will rest on their oars* (Athenaeum).

ship oars, to lift oars from the rowlocks and put them in the boat: *The sailors stopped rowing and shipped their oars.*

—*v.t.* **1.** to row (a boat). **2. a.** to travel across (a body of water). **b.** to make (one's way) by or as if by rowing: *He . . . oared himself with his good arms . . . to the shore* (Shakespeare). **3.** to move or use (an arm, hand, etc.) as an oar.

—*v.i.* to row.
[Old English *ār*] —**oar'like',** *adj.*

oar·age (ôr'ij, ōr'-), *n.* **1.** the use of oars; rowing: *the Viking ship, its rowers oarage boiling up the sea.* **2.** rowing apparatus.

oared (ôrd, ōrd), *adj.* furnished with oars; moved by oars.

oar·fish (ôr'fish', ōr'-), *n., pl.* **-fish·es** or (*collectively*) **-fish.** a deep-sea fish with a slender, tapelike body from 12 to 30 feet long. It has a long flat fin along the length of its body making it look somewhat like an oar, and is sometimes mistaken for a sea serpent.

oar·less (ôr'lis, ōr'-), *adj.* **1.** without oars: *an oarless boat.* **2.** undisturbed by oars: *the . . . oarless sea* (Tennyson).

oar·lock (ôr'lok', ōr'-), *n.* a notch or U-shaped support in which the oar rests in rowing; rowlock. [Old English *ārloc* < *ār* oar + *loc* lock[1]]

oars·man (ôrz'mən, ōrz'-), *n., pl.* **-men. 1.** a man who rows: *The British Foreign Office today cleared the way to give visas to nineteen Soviet oarsmen expected here for the Henley regatta* (New York Times). **2.** a man who rows well.

oars·man·ship (ôrz'mən ship, ōrz'-), *n.* the art of rowing; skill as a rower.

oar·weed (ôr'wēd', ōr'-), *n.* a type of kelp, one of the brown algae. It has been used as a fertilizer in coastal areas of England and Scotland.

oar·y (ôr'ē, ōr'-), *adj.* **1.** *Poetic.* shaped or used like an oar. **2.** having oars; oared: *the oary trireme.*

OAS (no periods) or **O.A.S.,** Organization of American States (an organization of 21 American republics, founded in 1948 to succeed the Pan American Union).

OASDI (no periods) or **O.A.S.D.I.,** Old-Age, Survivors, and Disability Insurance.

OASI (no periods) or **O.A.S.I.,** Old-Age and Survivors Insurance.

o·a·sis (ō ā'sis, ō'ə-), *n., pl.* **-ses** (-sēz). **1.** a fertile spot in the desert where there is water and usually trees and other vegetation: *a tiny oasis where there were camels, and a well . . . and a patch of emerald-green barley* (Amelia B. Edwards). **2.** a plot or spot refreshingly different from others around it: *a cultural oasis on the western frontier.* [< Latin *oasis* < Greek *Óasis,* name of various cities in the Libyan Desert, apparently of Egyptian origin]

Oasis (def. 1)

oast (ōst), *n.* a kiln for drying hops, malt, or tobacco. [Old English *āst*]

oat (ōt), *n.* **1. a.** Often, **oats.** a tall cereal grass whose grain is used in making oatmeal and other cereals and baked goods, and as food for horses and other livestock. **b.** the wild oat. **c.** the seeds or grains of the oat plant. **2.** *Poetic.* a musical pipe made of an oat straw: *That strain I heard was of a higher mood: But now my oat proceeds* (Milton).

feel one's oats, *Informal.* **a.** to be lively or frisky: *The youngster was feeling his oats as he bounced his ball against the side of the house.* **b.** to feel pleased or important and show it: *American women are feeling their political oats* (Harper's).

sow one's oats, to sow one's wild oats; indulge in youthful dissipation before settling down in life: *Alberto Sordi plays an Italian fur merchant testing some hopelessly romantic notions about sowing one's oats in Stockholm* (Time).

[Old English *āte* grain of oats] —**oat'like',** *adj.*

oat·cake (ōt'kāk'), *n.* a thin cake made of oatmeal: *England,—that land of Calvin, oatcakes, and sulphur* (Sydney Smith).

oat·en (ō'tən), *adj.* **1.** made of oats or oatmeal: *an oaten cake.* **2.** made of oat straw: *his oaten pype* (Edmund Spenser). **3.** of or having to do with the oat: *oaten straws* (Shakespeare).

oat·er (ō'tər), *n. U.S. Slang.* a motion picture or television show about the United States West; western: *The fact that he owns 15% of Wells Fargo does not keep him from writing script for other oaters* (Time).

oat grass, 1. any of various oatlike grasses. **2.** any wild oat.

oath (ōth), *n., pl.* **oaths** (ōᴛʜz, ōths). **1. a.** a solemn promise or statement that something is true, which God or some holy person or thing is called on to witness: *to repeat an oath on the Bible. He made an oath that he would tell the whole truth and nothing but the truth.* **b.** the form of words in which such a statement or promise is made: *the President's oath of office, the Hippocratic oath.* **2.** the name of God or some holy person or thing used as an exclamation to add force or to express anger. **3.** a curse; swearword: *At last he broke out with a villainous low oath* (Robert Louis Stevenson).

take oath, to make an oath; promise or state solemnly: *He took oath to give up smoking.*

under oath, sworn to tell the truth: *He had said under oath that his birthplace was Passaic, N.J., [but] . . . two grand juries preferred to believe that he had been born in Italy* (Newsweek).

upon one's oath, sworn to tell the truth: *They cannot speak always as if they were upon their oath—but must be understood, speaking or writing, with some abatement* (Charles Lamb).

[Old English *āth*]

—**Syn. 1. a.** vow, pledge. **3.** expletive.

oat·meal (ōt'mēl'), *n.* **1.** oats made into meal; ground oats; rolled oats. **2.** porridge made from oatmeal. **3.** a yellowish-gray color. —*adj.* yellowish-gray: *an oatmeal tweed.*

oat opera, *U.S. Slang.* a horse opera: *California's High Sierra country fills the wide screen with some breathtaking acreage that no TV oat opera can duplicate* (Time).

oats (ōts), *n.pl.* See under **oat,** *n.*

O.A.U. or **OAU** (no periods), Organization of African Unity (an alliance of over 30 African countries formed in 1963).
oaves (ōvz), *n.* a plural of **oaf.**
ob-, *prefix.* **1.** against; in the way; opposing; hindering, as in *obstruct.*
2. inversely; contrary to the usual position, as in *oblate.*
3. toward; to, as in *obvert.*
4. on; over, as in *obscure.* Also: **o-** before *m;* **oc-** before *c;* **of-** before *f;* **op-** before *p;* **os-** in some cases before *c* and *t.*
[< Latin *ob-*, related to *ob* against]
ob., **1.** he, she, or it died (Latin, *obiit*). **2.** in passing; incidentally (Latin, *obiter*). **3.** oboe.
o•ba (ō′bə), *n.* a traditional tribal ruler or king in Nigeria: *In western Nigeria the obas combine grass-roots machine politics with honorific tribal positions* (London Times). [< the native name]
Obad. or **Ob** (no period), Obadiah (a book of the Old Testament).
O•ba•di•ah (ō′bə dī′ə), *n.* **1.** a Hebrew prophet. **2.** a book of the Old Testament containing his prophecies, placed among the minor prophets. *Abbr.:* Obad.
obb., obbligato.
ob•bli•ga•to (ob′lə gä′tō), *adj., n., pl.* **-tos, -ti** (-tē). *Music.* —*adj.* accompanying a solo, but having a distinct character and independent importance. —*n.* an obbligato part or accompaniment: *Bach's orchestra was unshakably architectural, with its own themes, counterpoints and obbligati* (Edward Tatnall Canby). Also, **obligato.** [< Italian *obbligato* (literally) obliged]
ob•com•pressed (ob′kəm prest′), *adj. Biology.* compressed or flattened in the opposite of the usual direction.
ob•con•ic (ob kon′ik), *adj. Botany.* conical, with the base upward or outward; inversely conical. —**ob•con′i•cal•ly,** *adv.*
ob•con•i•cal (ob kon′ə kəl), *adj.* obconic.
ob•cor•date (ob kôr′dāt), *adj.* (of a leaf) heart-shaped, with the attachment at the pointed end; inversely cordate. [< *ob-* + *cordate*]
obdt., obedient.
ob•du•ra•cy (ob′dər ə sē, -dyər ə-), *n.* a being obdurate: *The President's search for peace will again have foundered on the rock of Communist obduracy* (Newsweek).
ob•du•rate (ob′dər it, -dyər-), *adj.* **1.** stubborn; unyielding: *an obdurate refusal.* **2.** hardened in feelings or heart; unfeeling; pitiless: *an obdurate criminal. Be ... obdurate, do not hear him plead* (Shakespeare). [< Latin *obdūrātus*, past participle of *obdūrāre* < *ob-* against + *dūrāre* harden < *dūrus* hard] —**ob′du•rate•ly,** *adv.* —**ob′du•rate•ness,** *n.* —**Syn. 1.** obstinate, unbending, inexorable. **2.** impenitent, callous.
OBE (no periods), Office of Business Economics (an agency of the United States Department of Commerce).
O.B.E. or **OBE** (no periods), Officer of the Order of the British Empire.
o•be•ah (ō′bē ə), *n.* **1.** a kind of witchcraft practiced by certain Negroes in Africa, and formerly in the West Indies and the United States: *The same village recently held a trial for three women accused of practicing obeah* (New Yorker). **2.** an amulet, charm, or fetish used in this witchcraft. Also, **obi.** [American English; ultimately of West African origin]
o•be•ah•ism (ō′bē ə iz′əm), *n.* the practice of or belief in obeah.
o•be•di•ence (ō bē′dē əns), *n.* **1.** doing what one is told; submission to authority or law: *Parents desire obedience from their children. Soldiers act in obedience to the orders of their officers.* **2.** a sphere of authority, or a group of persons subject to some particular authority: *a church of the Roman Catholic obedience.* **3.** *Archaic.* a bow or curtsy; obeisance: *to make one's obedience.* —**Syn. 1.** compliance, subservience. —**Ant. 1.** disobedience, defiance.
obedience trial, a test given to dogs to determine their ability to follow commands, usually as a competitive exercise with a prize for the winner: *More than a thousand dog shows, field trials, and obedience trials were held* (New Yorker).
o•be•di•ent (ō bē′dē ənt), *adj.* doing what one is told; willing to obey; dutiful: *Servants, be obedient to them that are your masters* (Ephesians 6:5). [< Latin *oboediēns, -entis,* present participle of *oboedīre* obey] —**o•be′di•ent•ly,** *adv.*
—**Syn. Obedient, compliant, docile** mean acting as another asks or commands. **Obedient** emphasizes being willing to follow instructions and carry out orders of someone whose authority or control one acknowledges: *The obedient dog came at his master's whistle.* **Compliant** emphasizes bending easily, sometimes too easily, to another's will and being ready to do whatever he wishes or commands: *Compliant people are not good leaders.* **Docile** emphasizes having a submissive disposition and no desire to rebel against authority or control: *Janet always rides a docile horse.* —**Ant.** disobedient, refractory.
o•bei•sance (ō bā′səns, -bē′-), *n.* **1.** a movement of the body expressing deep respect or reverence; deep bow or curtsy: *After three profound obeisances ... we were permitted to sit on three stools ... near his Highness's throne* (Jonathan Swift). **2.** deference; homage: *He ... made the usual humiliating acts of obeisance* (William H. Prescott). [< Old French *obeissance* obedience < *obeir* obey] —**Syn. 2.** veneration.
o•bei•sant (ō bā′sənt, -bē′-), *adj.* obedient; deferential; subject. [< Old French *obeissant,* present participle of *obeir* obey]
ob•e•lis•cal (ob′ə lis′kəl), *adj.* of or in the form of an obelisk: *obeliscal stones.*
ob•e•lisk (ob′ə lisk), *n.* **1.** a tapering, four-sided shaft of stone with a top shaped like a pyramid: *The obelisk is of red, highly polished, and covered on all four sides with superb hieroglyphs* ... (Amelia B. Edwards). See also picture under **needle. 2.** something resembling such a shaft: *She strode like a grenadier, strong and upright like an obelisk* (Joseph Conrad). **3.** *Printing.* the dagger (†). **4.** an obelus. [< Latin *obeliscus* < Greek *obelískos* (diminutive) < *obelós* pointed pillar]

Egyptian Obelisk (def. 1)

ob•e•lize (ob′ə līz), *v.t.,* **-lized, -liz•ing.** to mark (a word or passage) with an obelus; condemn as corrupt or not genuine.
ob•e•lus (ob′ə ləs), *n., pl.* **-li** (-lī). **1.** a mark (— or ÷) used in old manuscripts to point out a word or passage that is corrupt, doubtful, or not genuine. **2.** an obelisk in printing. [< Late Latin *obelus* < Greek *obelós* (literally) a spit]
O•ber•bür•ger•meis•ter (ō′bər bʏr′gər-mīs′tər), *n. German.* lord mayor: *Willy Brandt was Oberbürgermeister of western Berlin, appointed by an elected city assembly* (Terence C. Prittie).
o•be•rek (ō′bə rek), *n.* a lively Polish folk dance: *Dances such as the mazurka and oberek resemble American square dances* (M. Kamil Dziewanowski). [< Polish *oberek*]
O•ber•on (ō′bə ron), *n.* **1.** (in medieval folklore) the king of the fairies and husband of Titania. He is a main character in Shakespeare's *Midsummer Night's Dream.* **2.** one of the five satellites of the planet Uranus.
o•bese (ō bēs′), *adj.* extremely fat; corpulent: ... *a woman of robust frame ... though stout, not obese* (Charlotte Brontë). [< Latin *obēsus,* past participle of *obedere* devour < *ob-* away + *edere* eat] —**o•bese′ly,** *adv.* —**o•bese′ness,** *n.* —**Syn.** portly.
o•bes•i•ty (ō bē′sə tē, -bes′ə-), *n.* extreme fatness; corpulence: *Obesity has become a national obsession* (Atlantic).
o•bey (ō bā′), *v.i.* to do what one is told: *The dog obeyed and went back home.* —*v.t.* **1.** to follow the orders of: *to obey a superior officer. Obey your father. Children, obey your parents in all things* (Colossians 3:20). *He commandeth even the winds and water, and they obey him* (Luke 8:25). **2.** to yield or submit to (authority or law, etc.): *to obey the requirements of simple decency. Obey that impulse* (Thomas L. Masson). **3.** to yield to the control of: *to obey one's conscience; ... thou great Anna! whom the three realms obey* (Alexander Pope). *A ship obeys the helm.* [< Old French *obeir* < Latin *oboedīre* < *ob-* to + *audīre* listen, give ear] —**o•bey′er,** *n.* —**o•bey′ing•ly,** *adv.*
ob•fus•cate (ob fus′kāt, ob′fus-), *v.t.,* **-cat•ed, -cat•ing. 1.** to confuse; bewilder; stupefy: *The whole company stared ... like men whose senses were a little obfuscated by beer* (Washington Irving). **2.** to darken; obscure. Also, **offuscate.** [< Latin *obfuscāre* (with English *-ate*[1]) to darken < *ob-* against, in the way of + *fuscus* dark] —**Syn. 1.** perplex. **2.** becloud.
ob•fus•ca•tion (ob′fus kā′shən), *n.* **1.** an obfuscating or being obfuscated: *In style they are admirably simple, direct, and uncluttered with medical obfuscation* (Harper's). **2.** something that obfuscates.
ob•fus•ca•tor (ob fus′kā tər), *n.* a thing that obfuscates.
ob•fus•ca•to•ry (ob fus′kə tôr′ē, -tōr′-), *adj.* that obfuscates; confusing: ... *hurried, well-meant but often obfuscatory explanations* (New York Times).
o•bi[1] (ō′bē), *n.* a long, broad, often brightly colored sash, worn around the waist of a kimono by Japanese women and children: ... *geishas wearing their gaudy silks and brocaded obis* (Harper's). [< Japanese *obi*]

OBI
Obi[1]

o•bi[2] (ō′bē), *n.* obeah, a kind of witchcraft.
o•bi•ism (ō′bē iz əm), *n.* obeahism.
ob•i•it (ob′ē it, ō′bē-), *Latin.* he, she, or it died. *Abbr.:* ob.
o•bis•po (ō bis′pō), *n., pl.* **-poes.** a four-horned sheep of Bolivia and Peru. [< Spanish *obispo* (literally) bishop]
o•bit (ō′bit, ob′it), *n.* **1.** an obituary. **2.** a ceremony performed in memory of a dead person on the anniversary of his death. [< Old French *obit,* learned borrowing from Latin *obitus, -ūs* a departure, going down < *obīre* perish < *ob-* away, down + *īre* to go]
ob•i•ter (ob′ə tər), *adv.* by the way; in passing; incidentally: *His Lordship thought his observations, which were obiter, went too far* (London Times). [< Latin *obiter* < *ob-* to, against + *iter* route; journey]
ob•i•ter dic•tum (ob′ə tər dik′təm, ō′bə-tər), *pl.* **ob•i•ter dic•ta** (ob′ə tər dik′tə, ō′-bə tər). **1.** an incidental statement; passing remark: *The Western world so excited about Soviet penetration and so affronted by Mr. Kruschchev's obiter dicta about the doom of capitalism* ... (Edward Crankshaw). **2.** an incidental opinion given by a judge on a rule of law not concerned with the case before him, and not binding: ... *a few well-phrased obiter dicta on civil rights* (Time). [< Latin *obiter dictum* said by the way; *dictum* (a thing) said < *dīcere* to say]
o•bit•u•ar•ist (ō bich′ů er′ist), *n.* the writer of an obituary or obituaries.
o•bit•u•ar•y (ō bich′ů er′ē), *n., pl.* **-ar•ies,** *adj.* —*n.* a notice of death, often with a brief account of the person's life. —*adj.* of a death; recording a death or deaths: *an obituary notice, the obituary column.* [< Medieval Latin *obituarius* < Latin *obitus;* see OBIT] —**Syn.** *n.* necrology.
obj., 1. object. **2.** objection. **3.** objective.
ob•ject (*n.* ob′jikt, -jekt; *v.* əb jekt′), *n.* **1.** something that can be seen or touched; thing: *What is that object by the fence? Children, from their very birth, are daily growing acquainted with the objects about them* (Joseph Butler). **2.** a person or thing toward which feeling, thought, or action is directed: *an object of charity, an object of study. He was the object of his dog's affection.* **3.** a person or thing that is absurd, funny, or foolish; sight; spectacle: *What an object you are with your hair pulled down over your face that way.* **4.** a thing aimed at; end; purpose: *My object in coming here was to get her address. Napoleon assumed that the objects of society were perpetual war and conquest, whereas its actual objects were production and consumption* (Edmund Wilson). **5.** *Grammar.* the word or group of words toward which the action of the verb is directed or to which a preposition expresses some relation. In "He threw the ball to his brother," *ball* is the object of *threw,* and *brother* is the object of *to.* **6. a.** anything that can be presented to the mind: *objects of thought.* **b.** a thing with reference to the impression it makes on the mind: ... *objects of terror, pity, and of love* (Macaulay). **7.** *Philosophy.* a thing that is or can be thought of.
no object, not taken into account; forming no obstacle: *Price is no object. The colour of the solder is no object, as the joint will be hidden* (English Mechanic).
—*v.i.* to make an objection or objections;

be opposed; feel dislike: *Many people object to loud noise. Do you object to my going now?* —*v.t.* **1.** to give a reason against; bring forward in opposition; oppose: *Mother objected that the weather was too wet to play outdoors.* **2.** *Archaic.* to bring forward; adduce. **3.** *Archaic.* to throw or place in the way: *Pallas to their eyes The mist objected* (Alexander Pope).
[< Medieval Latin *objectum* thing presented to the mind or thought < neuter of Latin *objectus,* past participle of *obicere* oppose something (to) < *ob-* against + *jacere* to throw] —**ob·ject′ing·ly,** *adv.*
—**Syn.** *n.* **1.** article. **4.** goal, aim. —**Ant.** *v.i.* acquiesce, approve. -*v.t.* **1.** agree.

object., objective.

object ball, in billiards and pool: **1.** the ball at which the player aims the cue ball. **2.** any ball other than the cue ball.

object glass, a lens or combination of lenses (in a telescope, microscope, etc.) that first receives light rays from the object and forms the image viewed through the eyepiece; objective.

ob·jec·ti·fi·ca·tion (əb jek′tə fə kā′shən), *n.* the act or process of objectifying or of making objective: *Texts which have so far failed to show predictiveness when subjected to objectification and quantification may still provide a maximum of information . . .* (Stone and Taylor).

ob·jec·ti·fy (əb jek′tə fī), *v.t.,* **-fied, -fy·ing.** to make objective; externalize: *Experiments in chemistry objectify the principles. Kind acts objectify kindness.* [< *object* + *-fy*]

ob·jec·tion (əb jek′shən), *n.* **1.** something said or written in objecting; reason or argument against something: *One of his objections to the plan was that it would cost too much. Do I hear any objections?* **2.** a feeling of disapproval or dislike: *A lazy person has an objection to working.* **3.** the act of objecting: *What is the basis for your objection?* **4.** a ground or cause of objecting: *It was his obesity that was the great objection to him* (Frederick Marryat). —**Syn. 2.** opposition.

ob·jec·tion·a·ble (əb jek′shə nə bəl), *adj.* **1.** likely to be objected to: *an objectionable movie, objectionable scenes.* **2.** unpleasant; disagreeable: *an objectionable odor or manner.* —**Syn. 2.** undesirable, offensive.

ob·jec·tion·a·bly (əb jek′shə nə blē), *adv.* in an objectionable manner; to an objectionable degree; so as to be objectionable.

ob·jec·ti·vate (əb jek′tə vāt), *v.t.,* **-vat·ed, -vat·ing.** to make objective; objectify.

ob·jec·ti·va·tion (əb jek′tə vā′shən), *n.* objectification: *This is the core of the real-world hypothesis, the root of objectivation* (James R. Newman).

ob·jec·tive (əb jek′tiv), *n.* **1.** something aimed at: *My objective this summer will be learning to drive a car.* **2.** something real and observable. **3.** *Grammar.* **a.** the objective case. **b.** a word in the objective case. *Whom* and *me* are objectives. **4.** lens or lenses nearest to the thing seen through a telescope, microscope, etc.; object glass: *The instrument is provided with a rotating nosepiece to which are permanently attached three objectives of different magnifications* (Sears and Zemansky). See picture under **refracting telescope. 5.** the goal or target of a military operation: *Paris was the real objective of the invading German army.*
—*adj.* **1.** being the object of endeavor. **2.** existing outside the mind as an actual object and not merely in the mind as an idea; real: *Actions are objective; ideas are subjective.* **3.** about outward things, not about the thoughts and feelings of the speaker, writer, painter, etc.; giving facts as they are without a bias toward either side; impersonal: *an objective report of an accident, an objective analysis of a poem or painting. An "objective test" is often true and false or multiple choice. A scientist must be objective in his experiments.* **4.** *Grammar.* **a.** showing the case of a noun or pronoun used as the direct object of a verb, the object of a preposition, etc. In "John hit me," *me* is in the objective case. **b.** having to do with or being in this case. **5.** perceptible to other persons as well as to the patient: *an objective symptom.* **6. a.** (of a work of art) representing or resembling natural objects; not abstract. **b.** (in perspective) that is, or belongs to, the object of which the delineation is required: *an objective point.*
[< Medieval Latin *objectivus* having to do with things as they are presented to the mind < *objectum;* see OBJECT] —**ob·jec′tive·ly,** *adv.* —**ob·jec′tive·ness,** *n.*
—**Syn.** *n.* **1.** goal, object, aim.

objective complement, *Grammar.* a word, such as a noun, pronoun, or adjective, used as a complement to a factitive verb. In "I consider him *smart,*" *smart* is the objective complement of *consider.*

ob·jec·tiv·ism (əb jek′tə viz əm), *n.* **1.** any doctrine or philosophy that holds that external or objective elements of perception are the only real or worthwhile things: *It is the radical utilitarianism of our age, the fruit of our scientific objectivism, that speaks here* (Bulletin of Atomic Scientists). **2.** the tendency to deal with objective things rather than thoughts or feelings, as in literature, art, etc.

ob·jec·tiv·ist (əb jek′tə vist), *n.* a believer in objectivism. —*adj.* objectivistic.

ob·jec·ti·vis·tic (əb jek′tə vis′tik), *adj.* having to do with objectivism or objectivists: *objectivistic logic.*

ob·jec·tiv·i·ty (ob′jek tiv′ə tē), *n.* the state or quality of being objective; intentness on objects external to the mind; external reality: *Values are also determined by their objectivity, or how well they are met by objects themselves* (James Collins).

object lens, objective; the lens or lenses other than the eyepiece on an optical instrument.

ob·ject·less (ob′jikt lis, -jekt-), *adj.* without an object or end in view; aimless; purposeless: *Strangers would wonder what I am doing, lingering here at the sign-post, evidently objectless and lost* (Charlotte Brontë).

object lesson, 1. instructions conveyed by means of material objects. **2.** a practical illustration of a principle: *Many automobile accidents are object lessons in the dangers of speeding.*

ob·jec·tor (əb jek′tər), *n.* a person who objects.

ob·jet d'art (ôb zhe′ där′), *pl.* **ob·jets d'art** (ôb zhe′ där′), *French.* **1.** a small picture, vase, etc., of some artistic value: *The drawing-room was crowded with objets d'art* (London Times). **2.** (literally) an object of art.

ob·jet trou·vé (ôb zhe′ trü vā′), *pl.* **ob·jets trou·vés** (ôb zhe′ trü vā′). *French.* **1.** any object found lying about, such as a piece of driftwood, shell, etc., regarded as a work of art by surrealists: *. . . some excellent pots on shelves and an odd variety of objets trouvés* (Punch). **2.** (literally) a found object.

ob·jur·gate (ob′jər gāt, əb jėr′-), *v.t.,* **-gat·ed, -gat·ing.** to reproach vehemently; upbraid violently; berate: *Command all to do their duty. Command, but not objurgate* (Jeremy Taylor). [< Latin *objūrgāre* (with English *-ate*[1]) < *ob-* against + *jūrgāre* to scold, rebuke < *jūs, jūris* law + *agere* drive, lead] —**Syn.** vituperate, denounce, rebuke.

ob·jur·ga·tion (ob′jər gā′shən), *n.* an objurgating; vehement reproach: *Except for a pair of spurious Hungarians crouched over their [drinks], hissing objurgations at Sir Alexander Korda, the place was empty of customers* (New Yorker).

ob·jur·ga·tor (ob′jər gā′tər), *n.* a person who objurgates.

ob·jur·ga·to·ry (əb jėr′gə tôr′ē, -tōr′-), *adj.* vehemently reproachful; upbraiding; berating. —**Syn.** vituperative.

obl., 1. obligation. **2.** oblique. **3.** oblong.

ob·lan·ce·o·late (ob lan′sē ə lit, -lāt), *adj.* shaped like a lance head but with the tapering end at the base: *an oblanceolate leaf.*

ob·last (ob′ləst), *n., pl.* **-lasts, -las·ti** (-ləs tē). any of the regional subdivisions of the constituent republics of the Soviet Union that are subdivided into provincial districts: *. . . pictures life in the Jewish autonomous oblast . . . of the Soviet Union as busy, productive and growing* (New York Times). [< Russian *oblast′*]

ob·late[1] (ob′lāt, ob lāt′), *adj.* flattened at the poles: *The earth is an oblate spheroid.* [< New Latin *oblatus* < Latin *ob-* inversely + (*pro*)*lātus* prolate] —**ob′late·ly,** *adv.* —**ob′late·ness,** *n.*

ob·late[2] (ob′lāt, o blāt′), *n.* **1.** a person devoted to the service of a monastery as a lay brother. **2.** a member of any of various secular societies in the Roman Catholic Church devoted to religious work. —*adj.* dedicated to religious work; consecrated. [< Medieval Latin *oblatus,* noun use of past participle of Latin *offerre* offer]

ob·la·tion (ob lā′shən), *n.* **1.** something offered, now especially to God or a deity: *Bring no more vain oblations; incense is an abomination unto me* (Isaiah 1:13). **2. a.** the offering of bread and wine in the Communion service: *a full, perfect and sufficient sacrifice, oblation and satisfaction* (Book of Common Prayer). **b.** the Communion service. **3.** any donation or gift for religious or charitable uses: *We humbly beseech thee to accept our alms and oblations* (Book of Common Prayer). [< Old French *oblation,* learned borrowing from Late Latin *oblātiō, -ōnis* < *offerre* bring, offer. Compare OFFERTORY.]

ob·la·tion·al (ob lā′shə nəl), *adj.* of, having to do with, or like an oblation.

ob·la·to·ry (ob′lə tôr′ē, -tōr′-), *adj.* oblational.

ob·li·ga·ble (ob′lə gə bəl), *adj.* capable of being bound by an obligation: *One man can come under obligations on which you can rely,—is obligable; and another is not* (Emerson).

ob·li·gate (*v.* ob′lə gāt; *adj.* ob′lə git, -gāt), *v.,* **-gat·ed, -gat·ing,** *adj.* —*v.t.* **1.** to bind morally or legally; pledge: *A witness in court is obligated to tell the truth.* **2.** to compel; oblige: *Don't feel obligated to answer.*
—*adj.* **1.** *Biology.* able to exist under or restricted to only one set of environmental conditions, as a parasite which can survive only by living in close association with its host: *Obligate parasites . . . are completely dependent upon living hosts for their food* (Harbaugh and Goodrich). **2.** obligated; bound.
[< Latin *obligāre* (with English *-ate*[1]) < *ob-* to + *ligāre* bind. Doublet of OBLIGE.]

ob·li·ga·tion (ob′lə gā′shən), *n.* **1.** duty under the law; duty due to a promise or contract; duty on account of social relationship or kindness received: *A man's first obligation is to his wife and children. Taxes are an obligation which may fall on everybody. The painter is really under obligation to paint our house first.* **2.** binding power (of a law, promise, sense of duty, etc.): *The one who did the damage is under obligation to pay for it. "The cultivation of the soil," we are told, "is an obligation imposed by nature on mankind* (Washington Irving). **3. a.** a binding legal agreement; bond; contract: *The firm was not able to meet its obligations.* **b.** a bond containing such an agreement, with a condition or penalty attached. **c.** a bond, note, bill, or certificate serving as security for payment of indebtedness, as of a government or corporation. **4.** the condition of being in debt for a favor, service, or the like: *Every opportunity implies an obligation* (John D. Rockefeller, Jr.). *It was George's obligation to return Mary's favor by asking her to his birthday party.* **5.** a service; favor; benefit: *A self-reliant person likes to repay all obligations.* **6. a.** a binding oneself by oath, promise, or contract to do or not to do something. **b.** an agreement whereby one person is bound to another, or two or more persons are mutually bound. —**Syn. 1.** responsibility. See **duty.**

ob·li·ga·tion·al (ob′lə gā′shə nəl), *adj.* obligatory: *The obligational delivery of agricultural products to the government warehouses was abolished* (Jonas Paplenas).

obligational authority, *U.S.* the authority given by Congress to an administrative agency in the Federal Government to spend a given amount of money in a given period: *The obligational authority, usually granted by Congress through appropriations, must precede all budget spending* (Wall Street Journal).

ob·li·ga·tive (ob′lə gā′tiv), *adj.* imposing or implying obligation. —**ob′li·ga′tive·ness,** *n.*

ob·li·ga·to (ob′lə gä′tō), *adj., n., pl.* **-tos, -ti** (-tē). *Music.* obbligato.

ob·li·ga·tor (ob′lə gā′tər), *n.* **1.** *Law.* a person who binds himself or gives his bond to another; obligor. **2.** a peron who obliges another.

ob·lig·a·to·ri·ly (ə blig′ə tôr′ə lē, -tōr′-; ob′lə gə-), *adv.* in an obligatory manner; by obligation.

ob·lig·a·to·ri·ness (ə blig′ə tôr′ē nis, -tōr′-; ob′lə gə-), *n.* the state or quality of being obligatory.

ob·lig·a·to·ry (ə blig′ə tôr′ē, -tōr′-; ob′lə gə-), *adj.* binding morally or legally; compulsory; required: *Attendance at primary school is obligatory.* [< Late Latin *obligātōrius* < Latin *obligāre;* see OBLIGATE] —**Syn.** coercive, mandatory.

o·blige (ə blīj′), *v.,* **o·bliged, o·blig·ing.** —*v.t.* **1.** to bind by a promise, contract, duty, etc.; compel; force; require: *The law obliges parents to send their children to school. I am obliged to leave early to catch my train.* **2.** to put under a debt of thanks for some favor or service: *We are very much obliged for your kind offer. She obliged us with a song.* —*v.i. Informal.* to do a favor: *She obliged graciously by singing another song.* [< Old French *obliger,* learned borrowing from Latin *obligāre.* Doublet of OBLIGATE.] —**o·blig′er,** *n.* —**Syn.** *v.t.* **1.** constrain. **2.** accommodate.

ob·li·gee (ob′lə jē′), *n.* **1.** *Law.* a person to whom another is bound by contract; person to whom a bond is given. **2.** a person under obligation to another.

o·blig·ing (ə blī′jing), *adj.* **1.** willing to do favors; helpful; accommodating: *an obliging neighbor.* **2.** obligatory. —**o·blig′ing·ly,** *adv.* —**o·blig′ing·ness,** *n.*

ob·li·gor (ob′lə gôr′, ob′lə gôr), *n. Law.* a person who binds himself to another by contract; person who gives a bond.

ob·lique (ə blēk′, -blīk′), *adj., v.,* **-liqued, -liqu·ing.** —*adj.* **1.** not straight up and down; not straight across; slanting: *This terrace or garden ... took an oblique view of the open sea* (Thomas L. Peacock). *Upon others we can look but in oblique; only upon ourselves in direct* (John Donne). **2.** not straightforward; indirect: *She made an oblique reference to her illness, but did not mention it directly. All censure of a man's self is oblique praise* (Samuel Johnson). **3.** not upright and moral; underhanded: *oblique dealings.* **4.** (of a solid figure) not having the axis perpendicular to the plane of the base. **5.** *Grammar.* of or in an oblique case. **6.** *Botany.* having unequal sides: *an oblique leaf.*
—*v.i., v.t.* **1.** to have or take an oblique direction; slant. **2.** (in military use) to advance obliquely by turning 45 degrees to the right or left and marching in the new direction.
[< Latin *obliquus* < *ob-* against + a root *līc-* to bend, as in *licinus* bent upward] —**ob·lique′ly,** *adv.* —**ob·lique′ness,** *n.*

oblique angle, any angle that is not a right angle.

oblique case, any case except the nominative and vocative, or sometimes except the nominative and objective.

OBLIQUE ANGLES RIGHT ANGLE

Oblique Angles: more or less than 90 degrees

oblique motion, *Music.* the motion of the parts of a composition in which one part repeats the same tone while the other rises or descends in pitch.

oblique sailing, the sailing of a ship on a course which crosses each meridian obliquely at the same angle.

Oblique Motion
Notes D through A ascend while C repeats.

ob·liq·ui·tous (ə blik′wə təs), *adj.* exhibiting intellectual or moral obliquity.

ob·liq·ui·ty (ə blik′wə tē), *n., pl.* **-ties.** **1.** indirectness or crookedness of thought, speech, or behavior; conduct that is not upright and moral: *a moral obliquity which grated very harshly against Ilbrahim's instinctive rectitude* (Hawthorne). **2.** a being oblique. **3.** *Astronomy.* the angle (about 23 degrees 27 minutes) between the planes of the ecliptic and the equator. —**Syn. 1.** deviation.

ob·lit·er·ate (ə blit′ə rāt), *v.t.,* **-at·ed, -at·ing.** to remove all traces of; blot out; destroy: *The heavy rain obliterated all footprints. By the destruction of that city, [they] obliterated the memory of their former disgrace* (Edward Gibbon). [< Latin *obliterāre* (with English *-ate*[1]) < *ob litterās scrībere* to strike out, erase; (literally) draw across the letters] —**Syn.** efface, expunge, erase.

ob·lit·er·a·tion (ə blit′ə rā′shən), *n.* an obliterating or being obliterated; effacement: *Mutual obliteration ... is "moral as well as practical nonsense"* (Bulletin of Atomic Scientists).

ob·lit·er·a·tive (ə blit′ə rā′tiv), *adj.* tending to obliterate: *Obliterative coloration [obscures] ... the outlines of the animal, save when it moves* (Tracy I. Storer).

ob·lit·er·a·tor (ə blit′ə rā′tər), *n.* a person or thing that obliterates.

ob·liv·i·on (ə bliv′ē ən), *n.* **1.** the condition of being entirely forgotten: *to consign ... to total neglect and oblivion* (Charles Lamb). *Pompeii and Herculaneum might have passed into oblivion, with a herd of their contemporaries, had they not been fortunately overwhelmed by a volcano* (Washington Irving). *The very names of many plays have gone to oblivion* (Ashley Thorndike). **2.** the fact of forgetting or having forgotten; forgetfulness: *Grandfather sat by the fire in peaceful oblivion. Oh, what would he have given for one five minutes of oblivion, of slumber, of relief from the burning thirst!* (Cardinal Newman). **3.** intentional overlooking or disregard, especially of political offenses; pardon: *He [William III] expressed his hope that a bill of general pardon and oblivion would be ... presented for his sanction* (Macaulay). [< Latin *oblīviō, -ōnis* < *oblīviscī* forget; (originally) even off, smooth out < *ob-* out + *lēvis* smooth]

ob·liv·i·ous (ə bliv′ē əs), *adj.* **1.** not mindful; forgetful: *The book was so interesting that I was oblivious of my surroundings. She could hardly have been oblivious of Yuba Bill's adoration* (Bret Harte). **2.** bringing or causing forgetfulness: *an oblivious sleep.* **3.** *Obsolete.* of or for forgotten things; forgotten. [< Latin *oblīviōsus* (with English *-ous*) < *oblīvium* forgetfulness < *oblīviscī* forget; see OBLIVION] —**ob·liv′i·ous·ly,** *adv.* —**ob·liv′i·ous·ness,** *n.* —**Syn. 1.** unmindful.

ob·li·vis·cence (ob′lə vis′əns), *n.* a forgetting; forgetfulness.

ob·long (ob′lông, -long), *adj.* **1.** longer than broad: *an oblong loaf of bread, an oblong leaf.* **2.** *Geometry.* having the opposite sides parallel and the adjacent sides at right angles but not square. —*n.* a rectangle that is not a square; something oblong in form. [< Latin *oblongus* < *ob-* + *longus* long]

ob·lo·quy (ob′lə kwē), *n., pl.* **-quies.** **1.** public reproach; abuse; blame: *Was he not himself the mark of obloquy among the Reformers, because of his leniency to Catholics?* (John L. Motley). **2.** disgrace; shame: *his long public life, so singularly chequered with good and evil, with glory and obloquy* (Macaulay). **3.** a speaking evil against a person or thing; slander. **4.** *Obsolete.* a cause of reproach. [< Late Latin *obloquium* abusive contradiction < Latin *ob-* against + *loquī* speak] —**Syn. 1.** censure. **3.** calumny.

ob·nounce (əb nouns′), *v.i.,* **-nounced, -nounc·ing.** (in ancient Rome) to announce an unfavorable omen for a proposed public action. [< Latin *obnuntiāre* < *ob-* against + *nuntiāre* announce]

ob·nox·ious (əb nok′shəs), *adj.* **1.** very disagreeable; offensive; hateful: *His disgusting table manners made him obnoxious to us. Persons obnoxious to the government were frequently imprisoned without any other authority than a royal order* (Macaulay). *It should be as easy to expel an obnoxious thought from your mind as shake a stone out of your shoe* (Edward Carpenter). **2.** *Archaic.* exposed or liable to harm, injury, or evil: *Made hereby obnoxious more To all the miseries of life* (Milton). **3.** *Obsolete.* **a.** harmful; injurious. **b.** liable to punishment or censure. [< Latin *obnoxiōsus* (with English *-ous*) ultimately < *ob-* against + *noxa* injury < *nocēre* to harm] —**ob·nox′ious·ly,** *adv.* —**ob·nox′ious·ness,** *n.* —**Syn. 1.** objectionable. See **hateful.**

o·boe (ō′bō), *n.* **1.** a slender wooden wind instrument in which a thin, poignant tone is produced by a double reed. **2.** a reed stop in an organ that produces a penetrating tone like that of the oboe. [< Italian *oboe* < French *hautbois* hautboy]

Oboe (def. 1)

o·bo·ist (ō′bō ist), *n.* a player on the oboe.

ob·ol (ob′əl, ō′bəl), *n.* obolus, an ancient Greek coin.

ob·o·lus (ob′ə ləs), *n., pl.* **-li** (-lī). **1. a.** an ancient Greek silver coin worth $\frac{1}{6}$ of a drachma. **b.** any of various former European coins of small value. **2.** *Obsolete.* a unit of apothecaries' weight, equal to 10 grains. [< Latin *obolus* < Greek *obolós,* variant of *obelós* nail (because nails were used for money)]

O-Bon or **O'Bon** (ō′bon′), *n.* a Buddhist festival celebrating the dead whose spirits are believed to return to the world of the living for the duration of the festival: *O'Bon has evolved from a strictly Buddhist to a national [Japanese] festival with all faiths participating* (New York Times). [compare Japanese *bon* Buddhist festival]

ob·o·vate (ob ō′vāt), *adj.* (of a leaf) inversely ovate.

ob·o·void (ob ō′void), *adj.* (of certain fruits) inversely ovoid.

ob·py·ram·i·dal (ob′pə ram′ə dəl), *adj. Botany.* having the form of an inverted pyramid; inversely pyramidal.

obs. or **Obs.,** **1.** observation. **2.** observatory. **3.** obsolete; used formerly but not now.

ob·scene (əb sēn′), *adj.* **1.** offending modesty or decency; impure; filthy; vile: *obscene language, books, or pictures, an obscene joke or dance.* **2.** *Archaic.* loathsome; disgusting; repulsive: *so heinous, black, obscene a deed* (Shakespeare). **3.** *Obsolete.* ill-boding; ominous: *The boding bird ... Which ... beats about the tombs with nightly wings, Where songs obscene on sepulchers she sings* (John Dryden). [< Latin *obscēnus, obscaenus*] —**ob·scene′ly,** *adv.* —**ob·scene′ness,** *n.* —**Syn.** *adj.* indecent, gross, lewd, ribald.

ob·scen·i·ty (əb sen′ə tē, -sē′nə-), *n., pl.* **-ties.** **1.** obscene quality. **2.** obscene language or behavior; an obscene word or act: *It is possible that the proposed new definition of literary obscenity ... may not entirely satisfy* (New Yorker).

ob·scur·ant (əb skyůr′ənt), *n.* **1.** an obscurantist. **2.** a person or thing that obscures.
—*adj.* **1.** that obscures or darkens. **2.** obscurantist.
[< German *Obskurant* < Latin *obscūrāns, -antis,* present participle of *obscūrāre* darken < *obscūrus* obscure]

ob·scur·ant·ism (əb skyůr′ən tiz əm), *n.* opposition to progress and the spread of knowledge, especially through great complexity of language, ritual, etc.: *the obscurantism of modern poetry.* [probably < German *Obskurantismus* < *Obskurant,* noun, obscurant + *-ismus* -ism]

ob·scur·ant·ist (əb skyůr′ən tist), *n.* a person who is opposed to progress and the spread of knowledge; obscurant: *... that ordinary, average man whose lack of spiritual life and resource Mr. Eliot and his followers among the new obscurantists have been urging us to despise* (New Yorker). —*adj.* of obscurantists or obscurantism: *It is a tribute to the obscurantist techniques of these zealots that they can even begin to smother the real issue under tons of gobbledygook* (Wall Street Journal).

ob·scu·ra·tion (ob′skyů rā′shən), *n.* **1.** the act of obscuring. **2.** the condition of being obscured: *The obscuration of the star [is caused] by a small dense cloud of dust which has drifted in front of it* (F.D. Kahn).

ob·scure (əb skyůr′), *adj.,* **-scur·er, -scur·est,** *v.,* **-scured, -scur·ing,** *n.* —*adj.* **1.** not clearly expressed; hard to understand: *an obscure passage in a book.* **2.** not expressing meaning clearly: *an obscure style of writing. This obscure saying baffled him* (Arnold Bennett). **3. a.** not well known; attracting no notice: *an obscure little village, an obscure position in the government, an obscure poet.* **b.** not prominent; humble: *a person of obscure lineage; this obscure family of ours* (Benjamin Franklin). **4.** not easily discovered; hidden: *an obscure path, an obscure meaning.* **5.** not distinct; not clear: *an obscure form, obscure sounds, an obscure view.* **6. a.** dark; dim; murky: *an obscure corner. Obscurest night involv'd the sky* (William Cowper). **b.** hidden by darkness: *Thus wrapp'd in mist of midnight vapour glide obscure* (Milton). **7.** indefinite: *an obscure brown, an obscure vowel.*
—*v.t.* **1.** to hide from view; make obscure; dim; darken: *mountains obscured by mists.*

Gloomy clouds obscure the cheerful day (Alexander Pope). **2.** to make dim or vague to the understanding: *His difficult style obscures his meaning.* **3.** *Phonetics.* to make (a vowel) central or neutral in quality. —*v.i.* to conceal from knowledge: *This language . . . serves not to elucidate, but to disguise and obscure* (John S. Mill).
—*n.* obscurity; darkness: *a . . . feeling as though a palpable obscure had dimmed the face of things* (Charles Lamb).
[< Middle French *obscur* < Old French *oscur*, learned borrowing from Latin *obscūrus*] —**ob·scure′ly,** *adv.* —**ob·scure′ness,** *n.* —**ob·scur′er,** *n.*
—**Syn.** *adj.* **1. Obscure, vague, ambiguous** mean not clearly expressed or understood. **Obscure** suggests that the meaning of something is hidden either because it is not plainly expressed or because the reader lacks the necessary knowledge to understand it: *To a layman much legal language is obscure.* **Vague** means not definite, too general in meaning or statement or not clearly and completely thought out: *No one can be sure what a vague statement means.* **Ambiguous** means so expressed that either of two meanings is possible: "*She kissed her when she left" is an ambiguous statement.* **3. a.** unknown, inconspicuous. **b.** undistinguished. **4.** secluded. **6. a.** dusky, gloomy. —*v.t.* **1.** eclipse, conceal, shroud, veil, cloak, mask.

ob·scu·ri·ty (əb skyůr′ə tē), *n., pl.* **-ties. 1.** lack of clearness; difficulty in being understood: *The obscurity of the passage makes several interpretations possible. One of the most pernicious effects of haste is obscurity* (Samuel Johnson). **2.** something obscure; thing hard to understand; point or passage not clearly expressed; doubtful or vague meaning. **3.** a being unknown: *Lincoln rose from obscurity to fame.* **4.** a little-known person or place. **5.** lack of light; dimness: *The dog hid in the obscurity of the thick bushes.* —**Syn. 1.** ambiguity, vagueness. **5.** darkness, shade.

ob·se·crate (ob′sə krāt), *v.t.,* **-crat·ed, -crat·ing. 1.** to beg (a person, etc.) solemnly; beseech. **2.** to beg for (a thing): *Andrew Fairservice employed his lungs in obsecrating a share of Dougal's protection* (Scott). [< Latin *obsecrāre* (with English *-ate*[1]) entreat (in the name of something sacred) < *ob-* for + *sacer, sacris* sacred] —**Syn. 1.** implore, supplicate.

ob·se·cra·tion (ob′sə krā′shən), *n.* **1.** the act of obsecrating; entreaty; supplication: *Let us fly to God at all times with humble obsecrations* (Francis Bacon). **2.** one of the prayers of the Litany beginning with the word *by*, especially a petition of the Litany for deliverance from evil: "By thy baptism, fasting and temptation, Good Lord, deliver us." **3.** *Rhetoric.* a figure in which the orator implores the help of God or man.

ob·se·quies (ob′sə kwēz), *n.pl.* funeral rites or ceremonies; stately funeral: *His funeral obsequies were celebrated with the utmost grandeur and solemnity* (Washington Irving). [< Medieval Latin *obsequiae*, plural, for Latin *exsequiae* funeral rites < *ex-* out + *sequī* follow]

ob·se·qui·ous (əb sē′kwē əs), *adj.* **1.** polite or obedient from hope of gain or from fear; servile; fawning: *Obsequious courtiers greeted the king.* **2.** properly obedient; dutiful. **3.** *Obsolete.* dutiful and proper in observing funeral rites or in mourning for the dead: *The survivor bound In filial obligation for some term To do obsequious sorrow* (Shakespeare). [< Latin *obsequiōsus* (with English *-ous*) < *obsequium* dutiful service < *ob-* after + *sequī* follow] —**ob·se′qui·ous·ly,** *adv.* —**ob·se′qui·ous·ness,** *n.* —**Syn. 1.** slavish.

ob·se·quy (ob′sə kwē), *n. Obsolete.* singular of **obsequies.**

ob·serv·a·ble (əb zėr′və bəl), *adj.* **1.** that can be or is noticed; noticeable; easily seen: *a star barely observable by the naked eye, an observable loss of weight.* **2.** that can be or is observed: *Lent is observable by some churches.* —*n.* something that can be observed or perceived by the senses: *No one denies that physical theories involving unobservables enable us to predict the behaviour of observables* (Bernard Mayo). —**ob·serv′a·ble·ness,** *n.*

ob·serv·a·bly (əb zėr′və blē), *adv.* so as to be observed; to an observable degree; remarkably; noticeably.

ob·serv·ance (əb zėr′vəns), *n.* **1.** the act of observing or keeping laws or customs: *the observance of traffic regulations, the observance of the Sabbath.* **2.** an act performed as a sign of worship or respect; religious ceremony: *Our Sundays, at Blithedale, were not ordinarily kept with such rigid observance as might have befitted the descendants of the Pilgrims* (Hawthorne). **3.** a rule or custom to be observed: *strict observances.* **4.** *Archaic.* respectful attention or service: *I have long loved her . . . followed her with a doting observance* (Shakespeare). *He compass'd her with sweet observances and worship* (Tennyson). **5.** observation; notice: *I passed, And pried, in every place, without observance* (Philip Massinger). **6. a.** the rules or laws of a Roman Catholic religious order or community. **b.** an order or group following such rule or discipline. —**Syn. 1.** celebration. **2.** rite.
➤ See **observation** for usage note.

ob·serv·ant (əb zėr vənt), *adj.* **1.** quick to notice; watchful; observing: *If you are observant in the fields and woods, you will find many flowers that others fail to notice. He was observant and thoughtful, and given to asking sagacious questions* (John Galt). **2.** careful in observing (a law, rule, custom, etc.); properly mindful: *A careful driver is observant of the traffic rules. No man . . . could have been more observant of religious rites* (John L. Motley). [< noun]
—*n.* **1.** a person who is strict in observing a law, rule, custom, etc. **2.** an observer: *The nonparticipant observant remains aloof, and describes the [subjects'] behavior by time intervals* (Emory S. Bogardus). **3.** *Obsolete.* a dutiful follower; obsequious attendant.
[< Latin *observāns, -antis*, present participle of *observāre* observe] —**ob·serv′ant·ly,** *adv.*
—**Syn.** *adj.* **1.** heedful, regardful, attentive. **2.** aware, cognizant.

Ob·serv·ant (əb zėr′vənt), *n.* a member of the branch of the Franciscans which followed the strict rule of Saint Francis and separated in the 1400's from the Conventuals.

Ob·ser·vant·ine (əb zėr′vən tīn, -tēn), *n.* an Observant (Franciscan friar).

Ob·ser·vant·ist (əb zėr′vən tist), *n.* an Observant.

ob·ser·va·tion (ob′zər vā′shən), *n.* **1.** the act, habit, or power of seeing and noting: *By his trained observation the doctor knew that the unconscious man was not dead.* **2.** being seen; notice: *The tramp avoided observation.* **3.** something seen and noted: *The student of bird life kept a record of his observations.* **4.** act of watching for some special purpose; study: *The observation of nature is important in science.* **5.** a remark; comment: "*Haste makes waste," was Father's observation when I spilled the ice cream.* **6.** the measuring by a sextant or similar instrument of the altitude of the sun or other heavenly body to determine the latitude and longitude of a ship, airplane, etc. **7.** *Obsolete.* observance.
—*adj.* **1.** from which to observe: *an observation balloon. There were also observation towers which I was able to climb to look out across the forest and the mountains* (Manchester Guardian). *Moscow is a priceless listening and observation post . . . within the lines of our "cold-war" enemy* (New York Times). **2.** within which persons, animals, etc., can be watched, studied, etc.: *an observation cell or ward equipped with one-way glass.*
➤ **Observation, observance** are sometimes confused because both are related to the verb **observe. Observation,** connected with the meaning watch closely, applies especially to the act or power of noticing things or watching closely, or to being watched or noticed: *An observatory is for the observation of the stars.* **Observance,** connected with the meaning keep, applies to the act of keeping and following customs or duties, or to a rule, rite, etc., kept or celebrated: *You go to church for the observance of religious duties. Observation* is sometimes used in this sense, but this usage is now rare or obsolete.

ob·ser·va·tion·al (ob′zər vā′shə nəl), *adj.* of, having to do with, or founded on observation, especially as contrasted with experiment: *This process of continuous creation of matter is completely speculative, and no observational evidence exists to support the idea* (Atlantic). —**ob′ser·va′tion·al·ly,** *adv.*

observation balloon, a captive balloon used for purposes of observation.

observation car, a railroad passenger car with a transparent dome, large windows, or an open platform at one end, so that passengers may view the scenery.

observation station, 1. a place from which to observe and report what is happening nearby: *A possible . . . immediate objective . . . would be . . . to . . . seek prompt agreement to stop all nuclear tests, with compliance assured by a network of internationally manned observation stations* (David R. Inglis). **2.** a building or camp equipped with instruments for making a scientific study over a period of time: *an observation station on a mountain for studying weather.*

Plastic Observation Balloon with transmitter for obtaining high altitude weather data

observation train, a train that runs along the water's edge parallel to the course of a boat race, so that its passengers may see the race from start to finish.

ob·serv·a·to·ri·al (əb zėr′və tôr′ē əl, -tōr′-), *adj.* **1.** of or belonging to a scientific observer. **2.** like an observatory.

ob·serv·a·to·ry (əb zėr′və tôr′ē, -tōr′-), *n., pl.* **-ries. 1.** a place or building with a telescope for observing the stars and other heavenly bodies. **2.** a place or building for observing facts or happenings of nature: *a meteorological observatory.* **3.** a high place or building giving a wide view: *I never knew of a ship sailing . . . but I went up to the State House cupola or to the observatory on some friend's house . . . and there watched the departure* (George W. Curtis).

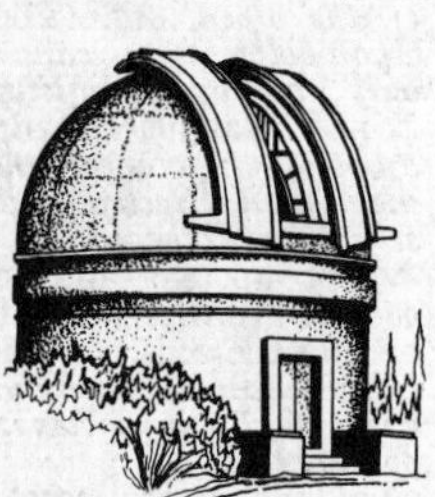

Observatory (def. 1) at Mt. Palomar

ob·serve (əb zėrv′), *v.,* **-served, -serv·ing,** *n.* —*v.t.* **1.** to see and note; notice: *I observed nothing odd in his behavior. I saw the pots . . . red-hot . . . and observed that they did not crack at all* (Daniel Defoe). *. . . the distant radio sources observed by radio-astronomers* (Fred Hoyle). **2.** to watch carefully or examine for some special purpose; watch; study: *An astronomer observes the stars. The spy observed the enemy's military installations.* **3.** to remark; comment. "*It's a rare lot of money," he observed* (Arnold Bennett). **4.** to follow in practice; keep: *We must observe silence in the classroom. Please observe the rule about not walking on the grass.* **5.** to show proper regard for; celebrate: *to observe the Sabbath, to observe birthdays and anniversaries.* **6.** *Obsolete.* to treat with respect or consideration. —*v.i.* **1.** to take notice. **2.** to make observations. **3.** to make a remark or observation; comment (on).
—*n. Scottish.* a remark; observation: *Thomas said he had not heard a mair sound observe for some time* (John Galt).
[< Latin *observāre* < *ob-* over + *servāre* to watch, keep] —**ob·serv′er,** *n.*
—**Syn.** *v.t.* **1.** perceive. See **see. 2.** survey. **3.** mention.

ob·serv·er force (əb zėrv′ər), a group of military or civilian personnel sent to observe and report the social, military, or political situation of some area, and to perform certain administrative functions: *. . . a United Nations observer force taking over from the British Army* (Manchester Guardian).

ob·serv·ing (əb zėr′ving), *adj.* observant. —**ob·serv′ing·ly,** *adv.*

ob·sess (əb ses′), *v.t.* **1.** to fill the mind of; keep the attention of; haunt: *Fear that someone might steal his money obsessed the miser.* **2.** (of an evil spirit) to beset or dominate (a person). [< Latin *obsessus*, past participle of *obsidēre* to sit at < *ob-* by, against + *sedēre* sit]

ob·ses·sion (əb sesh′ən), *n.* **1.** an obsessing or being obsessed; influence of a feeling, idea, or impulse that a person cannot escape. **2.** the feeling, idea, or impulse itself. **3.** *Psychiatry.* a compelling or fixed idea or feeling, usually irrational, over which a person has little conscious control; compulsion. **4.** domination by an evil spirit.

ob·ses·sion·al (əb sesh′ə nəl), *adj.* obsessive: *"Raven" . . . so Emperor Napoleon called Germaine de Staël, who became almost an obsessional hatred* (Time). —*n.* a person who has an obsessional neurosis: *treatment of psychotics and obsessionals* (Scientific American). —**ob·ses′sion·al·ly,** *adv.*

obsessional neurosis, a neurosis in which a person is obsessed with one idea or emotion, or compulsively repeats certain actions, as handwashing, looking in mirrors, etc.; compulsion neurosis: *The morbid ideas, impulses, and actions are not by any means combined in the same proportions in individual types and cases of the obsessional neurosis . . .* (Sigmund Freud).

ob·ses·sive (əb ses′iv), *adj.* of, having to do with, or causing obsession; obsessing. —*n.* a person having an obsession or obsessions: *There is, of course, a set of middle-class obsessives . . . who live in a nightmarish world where they are threatened by juvenile delinquents, coloured immigrants, tax inspectors, trade union leaders, motorcyclists, and libertine publishers* (New Statesman). —**ob·ses′sive·ly,** *adv.*

ob·ses·sive-com·pul·sive (ob ses′iv kəm-pul′siv), *adj.* of or having to do with an obsessional neurosis. —*n.* a person suffering from an obsessional neurosis: *Most gratifying was the success with victims of notoriously resistant types of illness — addicts and obsessive-compulsives* (Time).

ob·sid·i·an (ob sid′ē ən), *n.* a hard, dark, glassy rock that is formed when lava cools; volcanic glass. [< Latin *obsidiānus,* misreading of *obsiānus* (*lapis*) (stone) of *Obsius,* its alleged discoverer]

ob·sid·i·o·nal (ob sid′ē ə nəl), *adj.* of or having to do with a siege: *An obsidional crown was a crown or wreath conferred upon a Roman general who had delivered a besieged place. Obsidional coins were coins struck in besieged places, as a substitute for current money.* [< Latin *obsidiōnālis* < *obsidiō, -ōnis* a siege < *obsidēre* sit at; see OBSESS]

ob·sid·i·o·nar·y (ob sid′ē ə ner′ē), *adj.* obsidional.

ob·so·lesce (ob′sə les′), *v.i.,* **-lesced, -lesc·ing.** to be obsolescent; fall into disuse: *Service aircraft tend to obsolesce . . . soon after leaving the drawing board* (Punch). [< Latin *obsolēscere;* see OBSOLESCENT]

ob·so·les·cence (ob′sə les′əns), *n.* **1.** a passing out of use; getting out of date; becoming obsolete: *Office buildings face obsolescence in five years unless they're air-conditioned* (Wall Street Journal). **2.** *Entomology.* an indistinct or blurred part of a mark, stria, etc.: *a band with a central obsolescence.*

ob·so·les·cent (ob′sə les′ənt), *adj.* **1.** passing out of use; tending to become out of date: *Horse-drawn delivery trucks are obsolescent.* **2.** *Biology.* gradually disappearing; imperfectly or slightly developed: *obsolescent organs.* [< Latin *obsolēscēns, -entis,* present participle of *obsolēscere* to fall into disuse, ultimately < *ob-* away + *solēre* be usual, be customary] —**ob′so·les′cent·ly,** *adv.*

ob·so·lete (ob′sə lēt), *adj., v.,* **-let·ed, -let·ing.** —*adj.* **1.** no longer in use: *an obsolete custom, obsolete methods. "Eft" (meaning again) is an obsolete word. Wooden warships are obsolete. Abbr.:* obs. **2.** out-of-date: *We still use this machine though it is obsolete.* **3.** *Biology.* imperfectly developed and of little use; indistinct, especially in comparison with the corresponding character in other individuals or related species. —*v.t.* to make obsolete; discard or disuse as being out of date: *We are about to obsolete the wheel, just as the wheel and axle invention obsoleted the skid, some ten thousand years ago* (Atlantic).
[< Latin *obsolētus,* past participle of *obsolēscere* become out-of-date; see OBSOLESCENT] —**ob′so·lete·ly,** *adv.* —**ob′so·lete·ness,** *n.*
—**Syn.** *adj.* **1.** disused. **2.** antiquated.

ob·so·let·ism (ob′sə lēt′iz əm), *n.* **1.** an obsolete custom, expression, word, or the like. **2.** the condition of being obsolete.

ob·sta·cle (ob′stə kəl), *n.* something that stands in the way or stops progress: *. . . the grim obstacle of the mountain hidden in the storm* (Manchester Guardian). *Blindness is an obstacle in most occupations.* [< Old French *obstacle,* learned borrowing from Latin *obstāculum* < *obstāre* to block, hinder < *ob-* in the way of + *stāre* to stand]
—**Syn. Obstacle, obstruction, hindrance** mean something that gets in the way of action or progress. **Obstacle** applies to an object, condition, etc., that stands in the way and must be moved or overcome before continuing toward a goal: *A fallen tree across the road was an obstacle to our car.* **Obstruction** applies especially to something that blocks a passage: *The enemy built obstructions in the road.* **Hindrance** applies to a person or thing that holds back or makes progress difficult: *Noise is a hindrance to studying.*

obstacle race, a foot race in which various devices, such as walls, streams, fences, etc., have to be jumped or climbed over.

obstet., **1. a.** obstetric. **b.** obstetrical. **2.** obstetrics.

ob·stet·ric (ob stet′rik), *adj.* having to do with the care of women in childbirth.

ob·stet·ri·cal (ob stet′rə kəl), *adj.* of or having to do with obstetrics; obstetric. —**ob·stet′ri·cal·ly,** *adv.*

ob·ste·tri·cian (ob′stə trish′ən), *n.* a doctor who specializes in obstetrics.

ob·stet·rics (ob stet′riks), *n.* the branch of medicine and surgery concerned with caring for and treating women before, in, and after childbirth. [adaptation of Latin *obstetrīcia* midwifery (with English *-ics*) < *obstetrīx, -īcis* midwife < *ob-* by + *stāre* to stand]

ob·sti·na·cy (ob′stə nə sē), *n., pl.* **-cies. 1.** stubbornness; a being obstinate: *Obstinacy drove the boy to repeat the statement even after he knew it was wrong.* **2.** stubborn persistence; unyielding nature: *Obstinacy in a bad cause is but constancy in a good* (Thomas Browne). **3.** an obstinate act: *rebuke for their pedantries and obstinacies* (Thomas Carlyle). [< Medieval Latin *obstinatia* < Latin *obstinātus,* past participle of *obstināre;* see OBSTINATE]

ob·sti·nate (ob′stə nit), *adj.* **1.** not giving in; stubborn: *The obstinate girl would go her own way, in spite of all warnings.* **2.** hard to control or treat: *an obstinate cough; the stiff, obstinate growth of the endless wild-sage bushes* (Francis Parkman). [< Latin *obstinātus,* past participle of *obstināre* be determined, ultimately < *ob-* by + *stāre* to stand. Compare DESTINE.] —**ob′sti·nate·ly,** *adv.*—**ob′sti·nate·ness,** *n.*
—**Syn. 1. Obstinate, stubborn** mean fixed in purpose or opinion. **Obstinate** suggests persistent holding to a purpose, opinion, or way of doing something and sometimes being unreasonable or contrary: *The obstinate man refused to obey orders.* **Stubborn** suggests a quality which makes a person withstand attempts to change his mind, or makes an animal or thing hard to handle: *He is as stubborn as a mule.* **2.** persistent, intractable.

ob·sti·na·tion (ob′stə nā′shən), *n.* obstinacy.

ob·sti·pant (ob′stə pənt), *n. Medicine, Obsolete.* any substance that induces severe constipation.

ob·sti·pa·tion (ob′stə pā′shən), *n. Medicine, Obsolete.* a severe form of constipation. [< Late Latin *obstīpātiō, -ōnis* < Latin *ob-* against + *stīpāre* cram, pack together]

ob·strep·er·ous (əb strep′ər əs), *adj.* **1.** noisy; boisterous: *Most boys are naturally obstreperous.* **2.** unruly; disorderly: *It means reaching directly a pretty obstreperous sector of youth, some of them before they get into serious trouble* (New York Times). [< Latin *obstreperus* (with English *-ous*) < *ob-* against + *strepere* make a noise] —**ob·strep′er·ous·ly,** *adv.* —**ob·strep′er·ous·ness,** *n.* —**Syn. 1.** clamorous, vociferous.

ob·struct (əb strukt′), *v.t.* **1.** to make hard to pass through; block up: *Fallen trees obstruct the road.* **2. a.** to be in the way of: *Trees obstruct our view of the ocean.* **b.** to oppose the course of; hinder: *to obstruct justice.* [< Latin *obstrūctus,* past participle of *obstruere* < *ob-* in the way of + *struere* to pile] —**Syn. 1.** close, choke, clog. **2. a,b.** impede. —**Ant. 1.** open, clear.

ob·struct·er (əb struk′tər), *n.* a person or thing that obstructs.

ob·struc·tion (əb struk′shən), *n.* **1.** a thing that obstructs; something in the way: *The soldiers had to get over such obstructions as ditches and barbed wire. Ignorance is an obstruction to progress.* **2.** a blocking; a hindering, as of legislation by filibuster or other tactics: *the obstruction of progress by prejudices.* —**Syn. 1.** impediment, barrier, hindrance. See **obstacle.**

ob·struc·tion·ism (əb struk′shə niz əm), *n.* action, behavior, or speech hindering the progress of business as in a meeting, legislature, etc.: *What policies they will follow, beyond sheer obstructionism, are clear to no one in France* (Newsweek).

ob·struc·tion·ist (əb struk′shə nist), *n.* a person who hinders (progress, legislation, reform, etc.). —*adj.* of or having to do with obstructionism or obstructionists.

ob·struc·tive (əb struk′tiv), *adj.* tending or serving to obstruct: *Many Western Commentators speculated as to why . . . the Kremlin was now being so obstructive . . .* (Listener). *Academies may be said to be obstructive to energy and inventive genius* (Matthew Arnold). —*n.* a person or thing that obstructs. —**ob·struc′tive·ly,** *adv.* —**ob·struc′tive·ness,** *n.*

ob·struc·tor (əb struk′tər), *n.* obstructer.

ob·stru·ent (ob′strů ənt), *adj.* obstructing natural openings or passages in the body. —*n.* **1.** something that obstructs a natural opening or passage in the body. **2.** *Phonetics.* a stop or fricative. [< Latin *obstruēns, -entis,* present participle of *obstruere* obstruct]

ob·tain (əb tān′), *v.t.* **1.** to get or procure through diligence or effort; come to have; acquire: *to obtain a prize, to obtain possession of a house one has rented, to obtain knowledge through study.* **2.** *Archaic.* to attain; reach. **3.** *Obsolete.* to hold; possess: *His mother then is mortal, but his Sire He who obtains the monarchy of Heaven* (Milton). —*v.i.* **1.** to be in use; be customary: *the low standard of civilization that obtained at Logport in the year 1860* (Bret Harte). *Different rules obtain in different schools.* **2.** to get what is desired: *The simple heart, that freely asks In love, obtains* (John Greenleaf Whittier). **3.** *Archaic.* to prevail; succeed: *This, though it failed at present, yet afterwards obtained* (Jonathan Swift). **4.** *Obsolete.* to attain (to): *if a man cannot obtain to that judgment* (Francis Bacon). [< Middle English *obteynen* < Middle French *obtenir* < Latin *obtinēre* < *ob-* to + *tenēre* to hold] —**ob·tain′er,** *n.* —**Syn.** *v.t.* **1.** secure, gain. See **get.**

ob·tain·a·ble (əb tā′nə bəl), *adj.* that can be obtained.

ob·tain·ment (əb tān′mənt), *n.* the act of obtaining.

ob·tect (ob tekt′), *adj.* obtected.

ob·tect·ed (ob tek′tid), *adj.* having the appendages covered or protected by a hard shell or horny case, as the pupae of many insects, especially butterflies. [< Latin *obtēctus,* past participle of *obtegere* cover up, protect (< *ob-* against + *tegere* to cover) + English *-ed*[2]]

ob·ten·tion (əb ten′shən), *n.* the act of obtaining; obtainment.

ob·test (ob test′), *v.t.* **1.** to call upon (God or something sacred) as witness; invoke. **2.** to beg earnestly; beseech; entreat; implore. [< Latin *obtestārī* < *ob-* on account of + *testārī* bear witness]

ob·tes·ta·tion (ob′tes tā′shən), *n.* an obtesting; entreaty; supplication: *Our humblest petitions and obtestations at his feet* (Milton).

ob·trude (əb trüd′), *v.,* **-trud·ed, -trud·ing.** —*v.t.* **1.** to put forward unasked and unwanted; force: *Don't obtrude your opinions on others. He would obtrude his assistance, if it were declined* (John L. Motley). **2.** to push out; thrust forward: *A turtle obtrudes its head from its shell.* —*v.i.* to come unasked and unwanted; force oneself; intrude: *imagination . . . that forward, delusive faculty, ever obtruding beyond its sphere* (Joseph Butler). *The remembrance that our poor captain was lying dead in the cabin was constantly obtruding* (Frederick Marryat). [< Latin *obtrūdere* < *ob-* toward + *trūdere* to thrust] —**ob·trud′er,** *n.* —**Syn.** *v.t.* **2.** eject.

ob·trun·cate (ob trung′kāt), *v.t.,* **-cat·ed, -cat·ing.** to cut or lop off the head or top from: *the stumps of obtruncated trees* (Hawthorne). [< *ob-* + *truncate*]

ob·tru·sion (əb trü′zhən), *n.* **1.** an obtruding. **2.** something obtruded: *disturbed by the obtrusion of new ideas* (Samuel Johnson).

[< Late Latin *obtrūsiō, -ōnis* < Latin *obtrūdere* obtrude]
ob•tru•sive (əb trü′siv), *adj.* **1.** inclined to obtrude; intrusive: *What matters if you are considered obtrusive?* (Thackeray). **2.** projecting; protruding. **—ob•tru′sive•ly,** *adv.* **—ob•tru′sive•ness,** *n.* **—Syn. 1.** meddlesome, officious, pushing, forward.
ob•tund (ob tund′), *v.t.* to blunt; dull; deaden. [< Latin *obtundere* to blunt, dull; see OBTUSE]
ob•tund•ent (ob tun′dənt), *adj.* dulling sensibility, as of nerves. *—n.* an obtundent agent or anesthetic.
ob•tu•rate (ob′tyə rāt), *v.t.,* **-rat•ed, -rat•ing. 1.** to stop up; close; obstruct. **2.** to close (a hole, joint, etc., in a gun breech) to prevent the escape of gas after firing. [< Latin *obtūrāre* (with English *-ate*[1]) to stop up]
ob•tu•ra•tion (ob′tyə rā′shən), *n.* **1. a.** an obturating. **b.** a being obturated. **2.** the act of closing a hole, joint, or cavity so as to prevent the flow of gas through it: *the obturation of a vent or a powder chamber.*
ob•tu•ra•tor (ob′tyə rā′tər), *n.* a thing that closes or stops up an entrance, cavity, or the like.
ob•tuse (əb tüs′, -tyüs′), *adj.* **1.** not sharp or acute; blunt. **2.** having an angle of more than 90 degrees but less than 180 degrees: *an obtuse triangle.* **3.** slow in understanding; stupid: *He was too obtuse to take the hint.* **4. a.** not sensitive; dull: *a person . . . obtuse in sensibility and unimaginative in temperament* (Harriet Beecher Stowe). *One's hearing often becomes obtuse in old age.* **b.** indistinctly felt or perceived: *an obtuse pain, an obtuse sound.* **5.** rounded at the top: *an obtuse leaf or petal.* [< Latin *obtūsus* blunt, dulled, past participle of *obtundere* < *ob-* on + *tundere* to beat] **—ob•tuse′ly,** *adv.* **—ob•tuse′ness,** *n.*
obtuse angle, an angle larger than a right angle but smaller than 180 degrees.
ob•tuse-an•gled (əb tüs′ang′gəld, -tyüs′-), *adj.* having an obtuse angle.

OBTUSE ANGLE RIGHT ANGLE
Obtuse Angle: more than 90 degrees and less than 180 degrees

ob•tu•si•ty (əb tü′sə tē, -tyü′-), *n., pl.* **-ties. 1.** insensibility; dullness: *obtusity of the ear.* **2.** folly; stupidity: *Mr. Johnson's purpose in parading this gallery of prophets is not to entertain us with the obtusities of our forebears but to save us from our own* (New Yorker).
o•bus (ō′bəs; *French* ō bʏ′, -bʏs′), *n., pl.* **o•bus.** *Military.* a shell. [< French *obus* < German *Haubitze* howitzer]
ob•verse (*n.* ob′vėrs; *adj.* ob vėrs′, ob′vėrs), *n.* **1.** the side of a coin, medal, seal, etc., that has the principal design. See picture under **noble. 2.** the face of anything that is meant to be turned toward the observer; front. **3.** a counterpart: *Alchemy is the medieval obverse of modern science.* **4.** *Logic.* a proposition derived through obversion; the negative (or affirmative) counterpart of a given affirmative (or negative) proposition. [< adjective]
—adj. **1.** turned toward the observer. **2.** being a counterpart to something else: . . . *he was the malevolent obverse side of the rebel benefactor of man* (Edmund Wilson). **3.** having the base narrower than the top or tip: *an obverse leaf.*
[< Latin *obversus,* past participle of *obvertere* < *ob-* toward + *vertere* to turn] **—ob•verse′ly,** *adv.*
ob•ver•sion (ob vėr′zhən, -shən), *n.* **1.** the formation of an obverse or counterpart; an obverting. **2.** *Logic.* inferring the negative or opposite of a proposition. By obversion the statement "All men are mortal" means also "No men are immortal."
ob•vert (ob vėrt′), *v.t.* **1.** to turn (something) toward an object or in a contrary direction. **2.** *Logic.* to change (a proposition) to the denial of its opposite. [< Latin *obvertere* to turn toward; see OBVERSE]
ob•vi•ate (ob′vē āt), *v.t.,* **-at•ed, -at•ing.** to meet and dispose of; clear out of the way; remove: *to obviate a difficulty, to obviate danger, to obviate objections.* [< Late Latin *obviāre* (with English *-ate*[1]) < Latin *obvius* in the way; see OBVIOUS] **—Syn.** intercept, avert, preclude.
ob•vi•a•tion (ob′vē ā′shən), *n.* **1.** an obviating. **2.** a being obviated.
ob•vi•a•tor (ob′vē ā′tər), *n.* a person or thing that obviates.
ob•vi•ous (ob′vē əs), *adj.* **1.** easily seen or understood; clear to the eye or mind; not to be doubted; plain: *It is obvious that two and two make four. That a blind man ought not to drive an automobile is too obvious to need proof. The frail child was in obvious need of food and sunshine.* **2.** *Obsolete.* being or standing in the way; fronting. **3.** *Obsolete.* exposed or open (to): *The pedant is . . . obvious to ridicule* (Sir Richard Steele). [< Latin *obvius* (with English *-ous*) < *obviam* in the way < *ob* across + *via* way] **—ob′vi•ous•ly,** *adv.* **—ob′vi•ous•ness,** *n.*
—Syn. 1. Obvious, apparent, evident mean plain to see, easy to understand. **Obvious** suggests standing out so prominently that the eye or mind cannot miss it: *His exhaustion was obvious when he fell asleep standing up.* **Apparent** means plainly to be seen as soon as one looks (with eye or mind) toward it: *A dent in the fender is apparent.* **Evident** means plainly to be seen because all the apparent facts point to it: *When he did not drive the car home, it was evident that he had had an accident.*
ob•vo•lute (ob′və lüt), *adj.* **1.** overlapping. **2.** (of two leaves in a bud) folded together so that one half of each is exterior and the other interior, as in the poppy. [< Latin *obvolūtus,* past participle of *obvolvere* to wrap around < *ob-* against, over + *volvere* wind, roll]
ob•vo•lu•tion (ob′və lü′shən), *n.* **1.** the wrapping or folding of a bandage around a limb. **2.** *Obsolete.* a fold, twist, or turn.
ob•vo•lu•tive (ob′və lü′tiv), *adj.* obvolute.
oc-, *combining form.* the form of **ob-** before *c,* as in *occasion.*
o/c, overcharge.
o.c., in the work cited (Latin, *opere citato*). ➔ **op. cit.** is the abbreviation now more commonly used.
Oc. or **oc.,** ocean.
O.C., 1. Officer Candidate. **2.** *British.* Officer Commanding (*C.O.* in American use).
oc•a•ri•na (ok′ə rē′nə), *n.* a simple musical instrument shaped something like a sweet potato, with finger holes and a whistlelike mouthpiece. [< Italian *ocarina* (diminutive) < *oca* goose (because of its shape)]

Ocarina

OCAS (no periods), Organization of Central American States.
Oc•cam•ism (ok′ə miz əm), *n.* the doctrine or system of the English scholastic philosopher, William of Occam, who revived the tenets of nominalism, maintaining that abstract ideas have no objective reality but are merely products of the mind. Also, **Ockhamism.**
Oc•cam•ist (ok′ə mist), *n.* a disciple or follower of William of Occam. Also, **Ockhamist.**
Oc•cam's Razor (ok′əmz), a principle devised by the English philosopher, William of Occam, which states that entities must not be multiplied beyond what is necessary. In a scientific evaluation, Occam's Razor is the choice of the simplest theory from among the theories which fit the facts we know. In logic, Occam's Razor is the statement of an argument in its essential and simplest terms. Also, **Ockham's Razor.** [*Razor* refers to the idea in this principle of shaving an argument to its simplest terms]
occas., 1. occasional. **2.** occasionally.
oc•ca•sion (ə kā′zhən), *n.* **1.** a particular time: *upon the next occasion that we meet* (Shakespeare). *He has said this on several occasions.* **2.** a special event; important time: *a pair of gloves . . . which were to be worn on some great occasion of state* (Hawthorne). **3.** a good chance; opportunity: *The trip gave us an occasion to get better acquainted.* **4.** a cause; reason; ground: *the woman who was the occasion of the quarrel.* **5.** need; necessity: *A simple cold is no occasion for alarm.* **6.** *Scottish.* a religious function: *They should see about getting him [a minister] to help at the summer Occasion* (John Galt). **7.** *Obsolete.* excuse; pretext: *Delay . . . Whose manner was all passengers to stay And entertaine with her occasions sly* (Edmund Spenser). **8.** *Obsolete.* occurrence.
improve the occasion, to take advantage of an opportunity: *The friends improved the occasion of their meeting by celebrating it with a party.*
occasions, *Obsolete.* **a.** particular needs or requirements: *Martin . . . could not supply his occasions any other way than by taking to the road* (Tobias Smollett). **b.** affairs; business: *Such as pass on the seas upon their lawful occasions* (Book of Common Prayer).
on occasion, now and then; once in a while: *[Jenny Marx] had had herself on occasion to write begging letters to Engels . . .* (Edmund Wilson).
—v.t. to cause; bring about: *to occasion an argument. His queer behavior occasioned talk. I said nothing: I was afraid of occasioning some shock by declaring my identity* (Charlotte Brontë).
[< Latin *occāsiō, -ōnis* convenient time < *occāsus,* past participle of *occidere* to fall; see OCCIDENT]
—Syn. *n.* **4.** See **cause.**
oc•ca•sion•al (ə kā′zhə nəl, -kāzh′nəl), *adj.* **1.** happening or coming now and then, or once in a while: *an occasional thunderstorm, occasional visits.* **2.** caused by or used for some special time or event: *occasional poetry. The ruin of the ancient democracies was, that they ruled . . . by occasional decrees* (Edmund Burke). **3.** intended for use when needed: *Upon a little occasional table, was a tray with breakfast things* (H.G. Wells) **4.** acting or serving for the occasion or on certain occasions: *The occasional soldier is no match for the professional soldier* (Macaulay). **—Syn. 1.** irregular, sporadic.
oc•ca•sion•al•ism (ə kā′zhə nə liz′əm, -kāzh′nə liz-), *n. Philosophy.* the doctrine that the apparent interaction of mind and matter is to be explained by the supposition that God takes an act of the will as the occasion of producing a corresponding movement of the body, and a state of the body as the occasion of producing a corresponding mental state.
oc•ca•sion•al•ist (ə kā′zhə nə list, -kāzh′nə-), *n.* an adherent of occasionalism.
oc•ca•sion•al•ly (ə kā′zhə nə lē, -kāzh′nə-), *adv.* at times; now and then; once in a while.
Oc•ci•dent (ok′sə dənt), *n.* **1.** the countries in Europe and America; the West: *The Occident and the Orient have different ideals and customs.* **2.** the Western Hemisphere. [< Latin *occidēns, -entis,* present participle of *occidere* fall down; go down < *ob-* down, away + *cadere* to fall (in reference to the setting sun)]
oc•ci•dent (ok′sə dənt), *n. Archaic.* the west.
Oc•ci•den•tal (ok′sə den′təl), *adj.* Western; of the Occident. *—n.* a native of the West. Europeans and Americans are Occidentals. [< Latin *occidentālis* < *occidēns* Occident]
oc•ci•den•tal (ok′sə den′təl), *adj.* western.
Oc•ci•den•tal•ism (ok′sə den′tə liz əm), *n.* the customs, characteristics, institutions, etc., of the peoples and countries of the Occident.
Oc•ci•den•tal•ist (ok′sə den′tə list), *n.* a student or admirer of Occidental habits, customs, or institutions. *—adj.* of or having to do with Occidentalism or Occidentalists.
Oc•ci•den•tal•i•za•tion (ok′sə den′tə lə zā′shən), *n.* a making Occidental, especially in habits, customs, or character.
Oc•ci•den•tal•ize (ok′sə den′tə līz), *v.t.,* **-ized, -iz•ing.** to make Occidental in habits, customs, or character.
oc•ci•den•tal•ly (ok′sə den′tə lē), *adv.* in an occidental manner or situation.
Oc•ci•den•tal•ly (ok′sə den′tə lē), *adv.* **1.** in an Occidental or Western manner. **2.** in the West.
oc•cip•i•tal (ok sip′ə təl), *adj.* of or having to do with the back part of the head or skull. *—n.* the occipital bone. [< Medieval Latin *occipitalis* < Latin *occiput* occiput]
occipital bone, the compound bone forming the lower back part of the skull.
oc•ci•put (ok′sə pət), *n., pl.* **oc•ci•pi•ta** (ok sip′ə tə). the back part of the head or skull. [< Latin *occiput, -cipitis* < *ob-* behind + *caput, capitis* head]
oc•clude (ə klüd′), *v.,* **-clud•ed, -clud•ing.** *—v.t.* **1.** to stop up (a passage, pores, etc.); close. **2.** to shut in, out, or off: *The rain, in a grey occluding storm, thrashed the windows*

(Eric Linklater). **3.** *Chemistry.* to absorb and retain (gases): *Platinum occludes hydrogen.* —*v.i. Dentistry.* to meet closely: *The teeth in the upper jaw and those in the lower jaw should occlude.* [< Latin *occlūdere* < *ob-* up + *claudere* to close]

oc·clud·ed front (ə klü′did), *Meteorology.* the front formed in a system of low barometric pressure when a cold air mass overtakes a warm air mass and displaces it upward: *Occluded fronts . . . move more slowly than ordinary fronts and therefore bring persistent bad weather over the affected area* (Neuberger and Stephens).

oc·clud·ent (ə klü′dənt), *adj.* serving to shut up or close so as to prevent passage in or out. —*n.* anything that closes.

oc·clu·sion (ə klü′zhən), *n.* **1.** an occluding or being occluded. **2.** *Medicine.* the blocking of a blood vessel, as by thrombosis, embolism, or gradual narrowing: *The President had suffered a mild cerebral occlusion* (Wall Street Journal). **3.** *Dentistry.* the meeting of the teeth of the upper and lower jaws when closed. **4.** *Phonetics.* the momentary cutting off of the stream of air in the articulation of a stop, produced by pressing the lips together, the tongue against the upper teeth, etc.: *Nasal consonants are produced by the obstruction or occlusion of the buccal passage . . .* (Simeon Potter). **5.** *Meteorology.* **a.** the process in which a cold air mass overtakes and forces upward a warm air mass in a cyclone, thereby meeting a second cold air mass originally in front of the warm air mass. Occlusion increases the intensity of a cyclone. **b.** the contact between these two cold air masses. [< Latin *occlūsus,* past participle of *occlūdere* occlude + English *-ion*]

oc·clu·sive (ə klü′siv), *adj.* serving to close; closing: *an occlusive dressing for a wound.*

oc·cult (ə kult′, ok′ult), *adj.* **1.** beyond the bounds of ordinary knowledge; mysterious: *At once the metaphysical panic turned into something physical—physical but at the same time occult* (Harper's). **2. a.** outside the laws of the natural world. **b.** of or having to do with laws or forces outside of the natural world; magical: *Astrology and alchemy are occult sciences.* **3.** not disclosed; secret; revealed only to the initiated. **4.** *Archaic.* hidden from sight; concealed: *We two will stand beside that shrine, Occult, withheld, untrod* (Dante Gabriel Rossetti).
—*v.t., v.i.* to cut off, or be cut off, from view by interposing some other body, as one heavenly body hiding another by passing in front of it; eclipse: *Because the corona-graph occults the photosphere it is difficult to observe the low- and high-altitude components of a flare simultaneously* (Harold Zirin).
—*n.* **the occult,** the occult sciences: *There were many students of the occult in northern Europe in the 1100's and 1200's.*
[< Latin *occultus* hidden, past participle of *occulere,* ultimately < *ob-* up + *cēlāre* conceal] —**oc·cult′ly,** *adv.* —**oc·cult′ness,** *n.*
—**Syn.** *adj.* **1.** secret, hidden, mystic.

oc·cul·ta·tion (ok′ul tā′shən), *n.* **1.** a hiding of one heavenly body by another passing between it and the observer: *the occultation of a star by the moon.* **2.** disappearance from view or notice; concealment; hiding.

oc·cult·er (ə kul′tər), *n.* an apparatus for occulting light, such as a device in a lighthouse that periodically interrupts the beam of light.

oc·cult·ism (ə kul′tiz əm, ok′ul-), *n.* **1.** belief in occult powers. **2.** the study or use of occult sciences.

oc·cult·ist (ə kul′tist, ok′ul-), *n.* a person who believes or is skilled in occultism: *Moricand was not only an astrologer and a scholar steeped in the hermetic philosophies, but an occultist* (Time).

oc·cu·pance (ok′yə pəns), *n.* occupancy.

oc·cu·pan·cy (ok′yə pən sē), *n.* **1.** the act or fact of occupying; holding (land, houses, a pew, etc.) by being in possession: *The occupancy of the land by farmers was disputed by the cattlemen.* **2.** *Law.* the act of taking possession of a thing belonging to no one in order to become its owner. —**Syn. 1.** tenure.

oc·cu·pant (ok′yə pənt), *n.* **1.** a person who occupies: *The occupant of the shack stepped out as I approached.* **2.** a person in actual possession of a house, office, etc. **3.** *Law.* a person who becomes an owner by occupancy. [< Latin *occupāns, -antis,* present participle of *occupāre* occupy]

oc·cu·pa·tion (ok′yə pā′shən), *n.* **1.** business; employment; trade: *Caring for the sick is a nurse's occupation.* **2.** a being occupied; possession; occupying: *the occupation of a house by a family, the occupation of a town by soldiers. Stooping down in complete occupation of the footpath* (Jane Austen). **3.** something to do: *to be bored for lack of occupation.* [Middle English *occupacioun* < Anglo-French, Old French *occupation,* learned borrowing from Latin *occupātiō, -ōnis* < *occupāre* occupy]
—**Syn. 1. Occupation, business, employment** mean work a person does regularly or to earn his living. **Occupation** means work of any kind one does regularly or for which he is trained, whether or not he is working at the moment or is paid: *By occupation she is a housewife.* **Business** means work done for profit, often for oneself, especially in commerce, banking, merchandising, etc.: *My business is real estate.* **Employment** means work done for another, for which one is paid: *He has no employment at present.*

oc·cu·pa·tion·al (ok′yə pā′shə nəl, -pāsh′-nəl), *adj.* of or having to do with an occupation, especially with trades, callings, etc.: *an occupational hazard. Beginning in 1933 there had been reports from Germany, Italy and the U.S.S.R. of an occupational disease peculiar to beryllium workers* (Scientific American). —**oc′cu·pa′tion·al·ly,** *adv.*

occupational therapist, a specialist in occupational therapy.

occupational therapy, the treatment of persons having physical or mental disabilities through specific types of exercises, work, etc., to promote rehabilitation.

oc·cu·pi·er (ok′yə pī′ər), *n.* a person who occupies; occupant: *Two hotels at Lancaster Gate were bought by their present occupiers* (London Times).

oc·cu·py (ok′yə pī), *v.,* **-pied, -py·ing.** —*v.t.* **1.** to take up; fill: *The building occupies an entire block. That radio program occupies a whole hour.* **2.** to keep busy; engage; employ: *Sports often occupy a boy's attention.* **3.** to take possession of, as by invasion: *The enemy occupied our fort. The . . . commanders . . . descended upon Rhode Island, and occupied it without resistance* (William E. H. Lecky). **4.** to keep possession of; hold: *A judge occupies an important position.* **5.** to live in: *The owner and his family occupy the house.* **6.** *Obsolete.* to use: *new ropes that never were occupied* (Judges 16:11). —*v.i.* **1.** to take possession. **2.** *Obsolete.* to trade; exchange: *He called his ten servants, and then delivered them ten pounds, and said unto them, Occupy till I come* (Luke 19:13). [< Old French *occuper,* learned borrowing from Latin *occupāre* seize < *ob-* onto + *capere* to grasp, seize] —**Syn.** *v.t.* **2.** absorb. **4.** possess.

oc·cur (ə kėr′), *v.i.,* **-curred, -cur·ring. 1.** to take place; happen: *Storms often occur in winter. Delays are liable to occur.* **2.** to be found; appear; exist: *"E" occurs in print more than any other letter.* **3.** to come to mind; suggest itself: *It never seems to occur to him to say "thanks."* [< Latin *occurrere* < *ob-* in the way (of) + *currere* to run]
—**Syn. 1.** See **happen.**

oc·cur·rence (ə kėr′əns), *n.* **1.** an occurring: *The occurrence of storms delayed our trip.* **2.** an event: *an unexpected occurrence. Newspapers record the chief occurrences of the day.* —**Syn. 2.** incident, happening. See **event.**

oc·cur·rent (ə kėr′ənt), *adj.* occurring; happening. —*n. Obsolete.* an occurrence: *He has my dying voice; So tell him, with the occurrents, more and less* (Shakespeare). [< Latin *occurrēns, -entis,* present participle of *occurrere* occur]

OCD (no periods), Office of Civilian Defense.

OCDM (no periods) or **O.C.D.M.,** Office of Civil and Defense Mobilization.

o·cean (ō′shən), *n.* **1.** the great body of salt water that covers almost three fourths of the earth's surface: *Roll on, thou deep and dark blue ocean, roll* (Byron). **2.** any of its four main divisions; the Atlantic, Pacific, Indian, and Arctic oceans. **3.** a vast expanse or quantity: *oceans of trouble. I turned and looked back over the undulating ocean of grass* (Francis Parkman). [< Old French *ocean,* learned borrowing from Latin *ōceanus* < Greek *Okeanós* Oceanus] —**Syn. 1.** sea, main, deep.

o·cean·ar·i·um (ō′shə nãr′ē əm), *n., pl.* **-i·ums, -i·a** (-ē ə). a very large salt-water aquarium built near an ocean to display living fish and other animals of the ocean: *Anyone who cares to will be able to get a ringside seat at the two new oceanariums* (Cape Times). [< *ocean* + (aqu)*arium*]

o·cean·aut (ō′shə nôt), *n.* an explorer of an ocean or sea: *French oceanauts last summer (1963) lived in a prefabricated village 36 feet below surface in the Red Sea* (Science News Letter). [< *ocea*(n) + *-naut,* as in *astronaut*]

ocean bed, the bottom of the ocean.

ocean carrier, any commercial ship crossing the ocean.

o·cean·front (ō′shən frunt′), *n.* the land along the ocean; seashore: *The Nautilus cooperative apartments on the oceanfront* (New Yorker). —*adj.* having to do with or at the oceanfront: *several hundred acres of oceanfront land . . .* (New Yorker).

o·cean-go·ing (ō′shən gō′ing), *adj.* **1.** going by sea: *A case might indeed be made that the purely passenger ocean-going ship is already obsolescent* (New Scientist). **2.** fit to meet the dangers of sea travel: *Ocean-going freighters go about 25 per cent faster than lake vessels* (Wall Street Journal). **3.** having to do with sea travel or commerce: *The success of the S.S. United States promises an enormous use for aluminum throughout the ocean-going world . . .* (Newsweek).

o·cean-gray (ō′shən grā′), *n.* a light pearly- or silvery gray. —*adj.* light pearly- or silvery-gray.

O·ce·an·i·an (ō′shē an′ē ən), *adj.* of or having to do with Oceania, a division of the world which comprises Polynesia, Micronesia, and Melanesia, a group of islands in the southern Pacific, or its people. —*n.* a native or inhabitant of Oceania.

o·ce·an·ic (ō′shē an′ik), *adj.* **1.** of the ocean: *oceanic islands. In the deep sea . . . the rocks over vast areas are covered with oceanic sediments which may be thousands of feet in thickness* (Gaskell and Hill). **2.** living in or by the ocean: *oceanic fish.* **3.** like the ocean; wide; vast: *A year ago the price supporters were burdened with an oceanic one billion pounds of [vegetable oil]* (Wall Street Journal). —**o′ce·an′i·cal·ly,** *adv.*

O·ce·an·ic (ō′shē an′ik), *adj.* of or having to do with Oceania, its inhabitants, or its culture; Oceanian: *The Baltimore Museum of Art acquired a rare collection of . . . Oceanic art, [including] masks, figures, shields, jewelry* (Frederick A. Sweet).

o·ce·an·ics (ō′shē an′iks), *n.* the group of sciences dealing with the exploration and study of the ocean.

O·ce·a·nid (ō sē′ə nid), *n. Greek Mythology.* a sea nymph, daughter of Oceanus, the ocean god. [< Greek *Okeanís, -ides* < *Okeanós* Oceanus]

o·ce·an·i·ty (ō′shē an′ə tē), *n.* **1.** the condition of being oceanic. **2.** *Meteorology.* the characteristics of an oceanic climate.

ocean liner, a ship used to carry passengers and some freight across the ocean, usually on regularly scheduled trips: *A tugboat strike had been in progress for two weeks . . . forcing ocean liners into the tricky business of docking under their own power* (Newsweek).

o·cean·og·ra·pher (ō′shə nog′rə fər), *n.* a person skilled in oceanography.

o·cean·o·graph·ic (ō′shə nə graf′ik), *adj.* of or having to do with oceanography: *They will take samples of the marine life, and make gravitational, magnetic and oceanographic studies* (Science News Letter). —**o′cean·o·graph′i·cal·ly,** *adv.*

o·cean·o·graph·i·cal (ō′shə nə graf′ə kəl), *adj.* oceanographic.

o·cean·og·ra·phy (ō′shə nog′rə fē), *n.* the branch of physical geography dealing with oceans and ocean life: *The importance of his own extensive experimental work have given his previous writings a prominent and influential place in oceanography* (Science).

o·cean·ol·o·gist (ō′shə nol′ə jist), *n.* an oceanographer.

o·cean·ol·o·gy (ō′shə nol′ə jē), *n.* the study of oceans; oceanography.

ocean perch, the rosefish, an edible fish of the North Atlantic.

o·cean-span·ning (ō′shən span′ing), *adj.* that crosses or is able to cross the ocean: *The cigar-shaped Atlas [missile] is designed for ocean-spanning, H-bomb missions* (Newsweek).

ocean sunfish, a large marine fish with a compressed body, found in warm and temperate seas throughout the world; headfish; mola. See **sunfish** for picture.

O·ce·a·nus (ō sē′ə nəs), *n. Greek Mythology.* **1.** the god of the great stream that was supposed to surround all the land. **2.** this stream.

o·cean·ward (ō′shən wərd), *adv.* toward the ocean.

o·cean·wards (ō′shən wərdz), *adv.* oceanward.

o·cel·lar (ō sel′ər), *adj.* of or having to do with an ocellus or ocelli.

oc·el·late (os′ə lāt; ō sel′āt, -it), *adj.* ocellated.

oc·el·lat·ed (os′ə lā′tid, ō sel′ā-), *adj.* **1.** having ocelli or eyelike spots. **2.** eyelike: *ocellated spots or markings.* [< Latin *ocellātus* having eye-spots (< *ocellus* ocellus) + English *-ed*[2]]

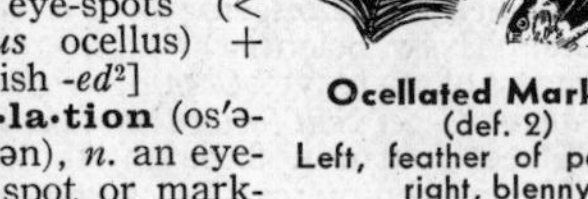
Ocellated Markings (def. 2)
Left, feather of peacock; right, blenny

oc·el·la·tion (os′ə-lā′shən), *n.* an eyelike spot or marking.

o·cel·lus (ō sel′əs), *n., pl.* **o·cel·li** (ō sel′ī). **1.** a little eye; one of the rudimentary, single-lens eyes found in certain invertebrates, especially one of the simple eyes, usually three in number, situated between the compound eyes of insects: *Ocelli . . . may function in increasing the irritability of the organism to light* (Harbaugh and Goodrich). **2.** an eyelike spot or marking. There are ocelli on peacock feathers and certain butterfly wings. [< Latin *ocellus* (diminutive) < *oculus* eye]

o·ce·lot (ō′sə lot, os′ə-), *n.* a spotted and streaked wildcat somewhat like a leopard, but smaller, found from Texas through South America: *The ocelot, . . . a nocturnal cat, lives in forests and thick vegetation [and] makes his meals off small mammals and birds* (Science News Letter). [< French *ocelot* < Nahuatl *ocelotl*]

Ocelot (including tail, about 4 ft. long)

och (OH), *interj. Irish and Scottish.* an exclamation of surprise, regret, sorrow, etc.

o·cher (ō′kər), *n.* **1.** any of various natural earths ranging in coloring from pale yellow to orange, brown, and red, used as pigments. The ochers consist of mixtures of hydrated oxides of iron with varying proportions of clay. **2.** a pale brownish yellow. **3.** *Slang.* money.
—*adj.* pale brownish-yellow.
—*v.t.* to color or mark with ocher. Also, **ochre.**
[< Old French *ocre,* learned borrowing from Latin *ōchra* < Greek *ṓchra* < *ōchrós* pale-yellow]

o·cher·ous (ō′kər əs), *adj.* **1.** of or containing ocher. **2.** like ocher; brownish-yellow.

o·cher·y (ō′kər ē), *adj.* ocherous. Also, **ochry.**

och·loc·ra·cy (ok lok′rə sē), *n., pl.* **-cies.** government by the mob; mob rule: *The commonest of the old charges against democracy was that it passed into ochlocracy* (James Bryce). [< French *ochlocratie* < Greek *ochlokratíā* < *óchlos* a crowd + *-kratíā* < *krátein* to rule]

och·lo·crat (ok′lə krat), *n.* an advocate of ochlocracy.

och·lo·crat·ic (ok′lə krat′ik), *adj.* of, having to do with, or having the form of ochlocracy. —**och′lo·crat′i·cal·ly,** *adv.*

och·lo·crat·i·cal (ok′lə krat′ə kəl), *adj.* ochlocratic.

och·loc·ra·ty (ok lok′rə tē), *n., pl.* **-ties.** ochlocracy.

och·one (OH ōn′), *interj. Scottish and Irish.* an exclamation of lamentation.

o·chre (ō′kər), *n., adj., v.t.,* **o·chred, o·chring.** ocher.

och·re·a (ok′rē ə, ō′krē-), *n., pl.* **och·re·ae** (ok′rē ē, ō′krē-). ocrea.

o·chre·ous (ō′kər əs, -krē-), *adj.* ocherous.

o·chroid (ō′kroid), *adj.* like ocher in color; brownish-yellow. [< Late Greek *ōchroeidḗs* pale-yellow colored < Greek *ṓchra* ochre + *eîdos* form]

o·chry (ō′krē), *adj.* ochery.

-ock, *suffix.* diminutive, as in *dunnock, hillock.* [Middle English *-ok,* Old English *-oc, -uc*]

Ock·ham·ism (ok′ə miz əm), *n.* Occamism.

Ock·ham·ist (ok′ə mist), *n.* Occamist.

Ock·ham's Razor (ok′əmz), Occam's Razor.

o'clock (ə klok′), of the clock; by the clock: *What o'clock is it? Eight o'clock.*

o·co·til·lo (ō′kə tēl′yō, -tē′yō), *n., pl.* **-los.** a spiny, scarlet-flowered shrub, a candlewood, growing in the southwestern United States and in Mexico. When the plants are not blooming, they look like dead sticks. [American English < Mexican Spanish *ocotillo* (diminutive) < *ocote* pine tree < Nahuatl *ocotl* a type of conifer]

oc·re·a (ok′rē ə, ō′krē-), *n., pl.* **oc·re·ae** (ok′rē ē, ō′krē-). **1.** a tubular stipule or stipules sheathing the stem above the node, as in buckwheat. **2.** a similar part or growth on an animal, as on the legs of some birds. Also, **ochrea.** [< Latin *ocrea* legging]

oc·re·ate (ok′rē it, -āt), *adj.* having an ocrea or ocreae; sheathed.

OCS (no periods), *U.S.* Officer Candidate School.

oct-, *combining form.* the form of **octo-,** or **octa-,** before vowels, as in *octane.*

oct., octavo.

Oct., October.

octa-, *combining form.* a variant of **octo-,** as in *octachord.* [< Greek *okta-* < *oktṓ* eight]

oc·ta·chord (ok′tə kôrd), *n. Music.* **1.** an instrument having eight strings. **2.** a diatonic series of eight notes or tones.

oc·ta·chord·al (ok′tə kôr′dəl), *adj.* of the octachord.

oc·tad (ok′tad), *n.* **1.** a group or series of eight. **2.** *Chemistry.* an element, atom, or radical with a valence of eight. [< Greek *oktás, -ádos* eight]

oc·tad·ic (ok tad′ik), *adj.* of or having to do with an octad.

oc·ta·gon (ok′tə gon, -gən), *n.* a plane figure having eight angles and eight sides. [< Greek *oktágōnos* < *okta-* eight + *gōníā* angle]

Octagon

oc·tag·o·nal (ok tag′ə nəl), *adj.* having eight angles and eight sides. —**oc·tag′o·nal·ly,** *adv.*

oc·ta·he·dral (ok′tə hē′drəl), *adj.* **1.** having eight plane faces: *The direction . . . at right angles to an octahedral plane is called an octahedral direction* (Science News). **2.** of or like an octahedron. —**oc′ta·he′dral·ly,** *adv.*

oc·ta·he·drite (ok′tə hē′drīt), *n.* a mineral, titanium dioxide, commonly occurring in octahedral crystals. *Formula:* TiO_2

oc·ta·he·dron (ok′tə hē′drən), *n., pl.* **-drons, -dra** (-drə). a solid figure having eight plane faces or sides. [< Greek *oktáedron,* neuter of *oktáedros* eight-sided < *okta-* eight + *hédra* seat, base]

Octahedron

oc·tal (ok′təl), *adj.* of, having to do with, or based upon the number eight, as a numbering system based upon units of eight.

oc·tam·er·ism (ok tam′ə riz əm), *n.* **1.** a being octamerous. **2.** *Humorous.* a being in eight parts.

oc·tam·er·ous (ok tam′ər əs), *adj.* **1.** (of an animal) having eight radiating parts or organs. **2.** (of a flower) having eight members in each whorl. [< Greek *oktamerḗs* (with English *-ous*) < *okta-* eight + *méros* part]

oc·tam·e·ter (ok tam′ə tər), *adj.* consisting of eight feet or measures. —*n.* a line of verse having eight feet or measures. [< Late Latin *octameter* < Greek *oktámetros* < *okta-* eight + *métron* measure]

oc·tan (ok′tən), *adj.* characterized by paroxysms which recur every eighth day, as a fever. [< French *octane* < Latin *octānus* eighth]

oc·tane (ok′tān), *n.* a colorless, liquid hydrocarbon that occurs in petroleum and belongs to the methane series. High quality gasoline contains more octane than the lower grades. *Formula:* C_8H_{18}

octane number or **rating,** a number indicating the quality of a motor fuel, based on its antiknock properties. The higher the compression ratio of an engine, the higher must be the octane number of its fuel to have satisfactory performance.

oc·tan·gle (ok′tang gəl), *n.* an octagon. —*adj.* octagonal.

oc·tan·gu·lar (ok tang′gyə lər), *adj.* having eight sides; octagonal. [< Latin *octangulus* eight-cornered < *octō* eight + *angulus* angle, corner]

Oc·tans (ok′tanz), *n., genitive* **Oc·tan·tis.** a southern constellation near the south celestial pole. [< New Latin *Octans* < Latin *octāns;* see OCTANT]

oc·tant (ok′tənt), *n.* **1.** one eighth of a circle; a 45-degree angle or arc. **2.** one of the eight parts into which a space is divided by three planes intersecting at one point. **3. a.** an instrument having an arc of 45 degrees, used in measuring angles in navigation. **b.** an aircraft sextant by which angles up to 90 degrees may be measured against an artificial horizon of the bubble type. **4.** *Astronomy.* the position of a planet, the moon, or other heavenly body when 45 degrees distant from another. [< Latin *octāns, -antis* < *octō* eight]

oc·tan·tal (ok tan′təl), *adj.* of or having to do with an octant. —**oc·tan′tal·ly,** *adv.*

Oc·tan·tis (ok tan′tis), *n.* genitive of **Octans.**

oc·tar·chy (ok′tär kē), *n., pl.* **-chies. 1.** government by eight persons. **2.** a group of eight states, each under its own ruler. [< Greek *oktṓ* eight + *-archíā* empire (< *árchein* to rule) + English *-y*[3]]

Oc·tar·chy (ok′tär kē), *n.* the eight kingdoms of Anglo-Saxon England (usually reckoned as seven and called the Heptarchy).

➔ **Octarchy** is rarely used but is preferred by those historians who count Deira and Bernicia as separate kingdoms of Anglo-Saxon England rather than as the single kingdom of Northumbria.

oc·ta·val (ok tā′vəl, ok′tə-), *adj.* of or having to do with an octave or series of eight; numbered or proceeding by eights.

oc·ta·va·lent (ok′tə vā′lənt, ok tav′ə-), *adj. Chemistry.* having a valence of eight.

oc·tave (ok′tiv, -tāv), *n.* **1.** the interval between a musical note and another note having twice or half as many vibrations. From middle C to the C above it is an octave. **2.** the eighth note above or below a given tone, having twice or half as many vibrations per second. **3.** the series of notes, or of keys of an instrument, filling the interval between a note and its octave. **4.** the combination of a note and its octave. **5.** a group of eight. **6.** a group of eight lines of poetry. **7.** the first eight lines of a sonnet. **8.** a church festival and the week after it. **9.** the last day of such a week. **10.** the eighth in a series of eight parries in fencing.
—*adj.* **1.** consisting of eight (of anything). **2.** producing notes one octave higher: *an octave flute (piccolo), the octave stop of an organ.* [< Latin *octāvus* eighth < *octō* eight]

Octaves (def. 3)

oc·ta·vo (ok tā′vō, -tä′-), *n., pl.* **-vos,** *adj.* —*n.* **1.** the page size of a book in which each leaf is one eighth of a whole sheet of paper. **2.** a book having pages of this size, usually about 6 by 9½ inches. *Abbr.:* 8vo, 8°. —*adj.* in or of this size. [< Medieval Latin *in octavo* in an eighth]

oc·ten·ni·al (ok ten′ē əl), *adj.* **1.** of or for eight years. **2.** occurring every eight years. [< Late Latin *octennius* a period of eight years] —**oc·ten′ni·al·ly,** *adv.*

oc·tet or **oc·tette** (ok tet′), *n.* **1.** a musical composition for eight instruments or voices. **2.** eight singers or players who perform together. **3.** a group of eight lines of verse; octave. **4.** the first eight lines of a sonnet. **5.** any group of eight. [< *oct-* eight + *-et,* patterned on *duet*]

oc·til·lion (ok til′yən), *n.* **1.** (in the United States and France) 1 followed by 27 zeros. **2.** (in Great Britain and Germany) 1 followed by 48 zeros. [< French *octillion* < Latin *octō* eight (in the sense "eighth power") + French *million* million]

oc·til·lionth (ok til′yənth), *n., adj.* **1.** last in a series of an octillion. **2.** one of an octillion equal parts.

octo-, *combining form.* eight: *Octosyllable = a verse of eight syllables.* Also, **oct-** before vowels, **octa-.** [< Latin *octō* and Greek *oktṓ*]

Oc·to·ber (ok tō′bər), *n.* **1.** the tenth month of the calendar year. It has 31 days. *Abbr.:* Oct. **2.** *British.* ale brewed in October: *a bumper of October* (Tobias Smollett). [< Latin *Octōber* < *octō* eight (because of its place in the early Roman calendar)]

October Revolution, the revolution in 1917 in which the Bolsheviks overthrew the provisional government led by A.F. Kerensky, and seized power in Russia.
➔ See note under **Russian Revolution.**

Oc·to·brist (ok tō′brist), *n.* a member of a liberal political party existing in Russia before the Russian Revolution. [translation of Russian *oktyabrist;* because the party adhered to the Czar's manifesto of October 17 (Old Style), 1905]

oc·to·dec·i·mo (ok′tə des′ə mō), *n., pl.* **-mos,** *adj.* —*n.* **1.** the page size of a book in which each leaf is one eighteenth of a whole sheet of paper; 18mo. **2.** a book having pages of this size, usually about 4 by 6½ inches. —*adj.* in or of this size. [< New Latin *in octodecimo; octodecimo,* ablative of Latin *octōdecimus* eighteen(th) < *octō* eight + *decimus* ten]

oc·to·ge·nar·i·an (ok′tə jə nãr′ē ən), *n.* a person who is 80 years old or between 80 and 90 years old: *The dapper, athletic little octogenarian spoke from the assembly rostrum with vigour* (Clare Hollingworth). —*adj.* **1.** 80 years old or between 80 and 90 years old. **2.** of or belonging to such a person. [< Latin *octōgēnārius* containing eighty (< *octogēnī* eighty each, ultimately < *octō* eight) + English *-an*]

oc·tog·e·nar·y (ok toj′ə ner′ē), *n., pl.* **-nar·ies,** *adj.* octogenarian.

oc·to·nal (ok′tə nəl), *adj.* based on the number eight, as a system of reckoning; octonary. [< Latin *octōnī* by eights (< *octō* eight) + English *-al*[1]]

oc·to·nar·y (ok′tə ner′ē), *adj., n., pl.* **-nar·ies.** —*adj.* **1.** having to do with the number eight; consisting of eight. **2.** proceeding by eights; having eight as its base: *an octonary system of counting.* —*n.* **1.** a group of eight; ogdoad. **2.** an octave or octet. [< Latin *octōnārius* containing eight < *octōnī* by eights < *octō* eight]

oc·to·pod (ok′tə pod), *n.* any of a group of two-gilled cephalopods having eight arms, such as the argonaut and the octopus. —*adj.* having eight feet or arms. [< New Latin *Octopoda* the order name < Greek *oktōpous, -podos* eight-footed; see OCTOPUS]

oc·top·o·dous (ok top′ə dəs), *adj.* octopod.

oc·to·pus (ok′tə pəs), *n., pl.* **-pus·es, -pi** (-pī), **oc·top·o·des** (ok top′ə dēz). **1.** a sea mollusk having a soft body and eight arms with suckers on them. **2.** anything like an octopus; powerful, grasping organization with far-reaching influence. [< New Latin *octopus* < Greek *oktōpous* eight-footed < *oktō* eight + *poús podós* foot]

Common Octopus (def. 1) (from 6 in. to 20 ft. across)

oc·to·roon (ok′tə rün′), *n.* a person who is one-eighth Negro in ancestry. [American English < *octo-* + *-roon,* as in *quadroon*]

oc·to·syl·lab·ic (ok′tə sə lab′ik) *adj.* having eight syllables: *the fatal facility of the octosyllabic verse* (Byron). —*n.* octosyllable.

oc·to·syl·la·ble (ok′tə sil′ə bəl, ok′tə sil′-), *n.* **1.** a line of verse having eight syllables. **2.** a word having eight syllables. —*adj.* octosyllabic.

oc·troi (ok′troi; *French* ôk trwä′), *n., pl.* **-trois** (-troiz; *French* -trwä′). **1.** a local tax levied on certain articles on their admission into a town. **2.** the barrier or place at which this tax is collected. **3.** the officials who collect it: *This is the criminal Saint-Rambertese Who smuggled in tobacco, half-a-pound! The octroi found it out and fined the wretch* (Robert Browning). [< French *octroi* < Middle French *octroyer* to grant, ultimately < Medieval Latin *auctorizare* to guarantee, authorize]

O.C.T.U., Officer Cadet Training Unit.

oc·tu·ple (ok′tu̇ pəl, -tyu̇-; ok tü′-, -tyü′-), *adj., n., v.,* **-pled, -pling.** —*adj.* **1.** consisting of eight parts; eightfold. **2.** eight times as great.
—*n.* a number or amount eight times as great as another.
—*v.t., v.i.* to make or become eight times as great.
[< Latin *octuplus* < *octō* eight + *-plus,* as in *duplus* double]

oc·tu·ply (ok′tu̇ plē, -tyu̇-; ok tü′-, -tyü′-), *adv.* in an octuple manner; to an octuple degree.

oc·u·lar (ok′yə lər), *adj.* **1.** of or having to do with the eye: *an ocular muscle, ocular movements.* **2.** like an eye; eyelike: *an ocular organ.* **3.** received by actual sight; seen: *ocular proof.*
—*n.* the eyepiece of a telescope, microscope, etc.: *An ocular . . . is a magnifier used for viewing an image formed by a lens or lenses preceding it in an optical system* (Sears and Zemansky).
[< Late Latin *oculāris* of the eyes < Latin *oculus* eye] —**oc′u·lar·ly,** *adv.*
—**Syn.** *adj.* **3.** visual.

oc·u·list (ok′yə list), *n.* an ophthalmologist; a doctor skilled in the examination and treatment of the eye. [< French *oculiste* < Latin *oculus* eye + French *-iste* -ist]

oc·u·lo·mo·tor (ok′yə lō mō′tər), *adj.* of or having to do with the moving of the eyeball in its socket: *an oculomotor muscle, an oculomotor nerve.* —*n.* either of a pair of cranial nerves that supply most of the muscles moving the eyeball. [< Latin *oculus* eye + *mōtor* that which moves < *movēre* move]

oc·u·lus (ok′yə ləs), *n., pl.* **-li** (-lī). **1.** *Architecture.* **a.** an opening at the summit of a dome. **b.** a circular window, usually a small one without tracery or other special subdivision; oeil-de-boeuf. **2.** *Anatomy.* an eye, especially a compound eye. [< Latin *oculus* eye]

od[1] (od, ōd), *n.* an imaginary force formerly believed to pervade all nature and to manifest itself in magnetism, mesmerism, chemical action, etc. Also, **odyl, odyle.** [< German *Od,* coined by Baron Karl von Reichenbach, 1788-1869, a German naturalist]

Od, od[2] or **'Od, 'od** (od), *interj. Archaic.* a short form of *God,* used in oaths: *Od rot 'em! Od's wounds! Od, ye are a clever birkie!* (Scott). Also, **Odd.**

o/d, *Banking.* **a.** overdraft. **b.** overdrawn.

o.d., an abbreviation for the following:
1. olive drab (uniform).
2. on duty.
3. outside diameter.
4. outside dimension.
5. on demand.

O.D., an abbreviation for the following:
1. Officer of the Day.
2. olive drab (uniform).
3. Ordinary Seaman.
4. *Banking.* **a.** overdraft; **b.** overdrawn.

o·da·lisque or **o·da·lisk** (ō′də lisk), *n.* a female slave in an Oriental harem, especially in that of a sultan of Turkey. [< French *odalisque,* also *odalique* < Turkish *odalik* < *oda* (originally) room in a harem + *-lık,* a noun suffix]

ODB (no periods), Office of Dependency Benefits.

odd (od), *adj.* **1.** left over: *Pay the bill with this money and keep the odd change.* **2.** being one of a pair or set of which the rest is missing: *an odd stocking.* **3.** extra; occasional; casual: *odd jobs, odd moments, odd volumes of a magazine.* **4.** with some extra: *six hundred odd children in school. Eighty odd years of sorrow have I seen* (Shakespeare). **5. a.** (of a whole number) leaving a remainder of 1 when divided by 2: *Seven is an odd number.* **b.** of such a number: *the odd symphonies of Beethoven.* **6.** strange; peculiar; queer: *a very odd fellow. It is odd that I cannot remember his name.* **7.** out-of-the-way; secluded: *from some odd corner of the brain* (Tennyson).
—*n.* **1.** an odd thing; oddity. **2.** in golf: **a.** a stroke more than the opponent, caused by hitting first during the playing of a hole. **b.** *British.* a stroke taken from a player's total score before playing a hole to give him an advantage.
[< Scandinavian (compare Old Icelandic *odda-* odd, and *oddi* odd number)] —**odd′ness,** *n.*
—**Syn.** *adj.* **2.** unmatched, unmated, single. **6.** freakish, uncommon. See **strange.**

Odd (od), *interj.* Od.

odd·ball (od′bôl′), *U.S. Slang.* —*n.* a person or thing that is a member of some group, type, or other classification but differs from the usual or accepted standards in its features, behavior, habits, etc.: *The platypus has been the oddball of the animal world* (New York Journal American). *The round, owl-eyed, oddball in horn-rimmed glasses* . . . (Time). *Among the motley crew . . . were some oddballs engaged in what was known as black propaganda* (Maclean's). —*adj.* unusual for its type and often somewhat amusing; odd; eccentric: . . . *a master of zany oddball humor* . . . (New Yorker).

Odd Fellow, a member of the Independent Order of Odd Fellows, a secret social and benevolent society.

odd fish, *Informal.* an odd or singular person: *He was an odd fish; ignorant of common life, fond of rudely opposing received opinions, slovenly to extreme dirtiness, enthusiastic in some points of religion, and a little knavish withal* (Benjamin Franklin).

odd·i·ty (od′ə tē), *n., pl.* **-ties. 1.** strangeness; queerness; peculiarity: *the oddity of wearing a fur coat over a bathing suit. All people have their oddities* (Benjamin Disraeli). *By a hundred whimsical oddities, my long friend became a great favorite with these people* (Herman Melville). **2.** a strange, queer, or peculiar person or thing: *Here is a strange, fantastical oddity . . . who harangues every day in the pump room* (Tobias Smollett). —**Syn. 1.** singularity. **2.** freak, curiosity.

odd-job·ber (od′job′ər), *n. British.* an odd-job man: *He finds a . . . village and ends up as apprentice to an old craftsman turned odd-jobber* (Manchester Guardian Weekly).

odd-job man (od′job′), *British.* a man who does odd jobs; handyman.

odd lot, a quantity of goods or securities smaller than the normal or standard amount used in the trading: *On the New York Stock Exchange, the usual unit of trading is 100 shares, called a "round lot." Smaller units are referred to as "odd lots"* (Wall Street Journal). —**odd′-lot′,** *adj.*

odd-lot·ter (od′lot′ər), *n.* one who buys shares in odd lots (less than 100 shares): *The characteristic odd-lotter . . . does not buy when the market soars* (Time).

odd·ly (od′lē), *adv.* in an odd manner; queerly; strangely: *Her oddly titled latest book again set in Maine, is woven in the same serene prose as its predecessors* (Newsweek).

odd-man-out (od′man′out′), *n.* **1.** a person or thing left out of a group; a person who does not fit or belong in a group: *He is an odd-man-out of his native world* (Harper's). **2. a.** the person singled out, as by tossing a coin or in some similar way, from among a number of people to perform some special act or service. **b.** this way of selection. —*adj.* left out or eliminated, especially for being different from the rest of the group.

odd·ment (od′mənt), *n.* a thing left over; extra bit.
oddments, a. *Printing.* parts of a book other than the text, such as the title page, preface, table of contents, etc.: *The oddments of this book are set in brevier and great primer.* **b.** odds and ends: *oddments of furniture, including a desk* (Arnold Bennett).

odd-num·bered (od′num′bərd), *adj.* having a whole number which, when divided by 2, leaves a remainder of one: *May 19 is an odd-numbered day. 1939 is an odd-numbered year.*

odd-pin·nate (od′pin′āt, -it), *adj.* (of a leaf) pinnate with an odd terminal leaflet; imparipinnate.

odds (odz), *n. pl. or sing.* **1.** difference in favor of one and against another; advantage. In betting, odds of 3 to 1 mean that 3 will be paid if the bet is lost for every 1 that is received if the bet is won. *How can man die better Than facing fearful odds, For the ashes of his Fathers, And the temples of his Gods?* (Macaulay). **2.** (in games) an extra allowance given to the weaker player or side. **3.** things that are odd, uneven, or unequal: *Yet death we fear, That makes these odds all even* (Shakespeare). **4.** difference or the amount of difference: *It makes no odds when he goes.*
at odds, quarreling; disagreeing: *Pity 'tis you lived at odds so long* (Shakespeare).
by all odds, by any reckoning; without doubt: *Herblock is by all odds one of the most . . . useful commentators on the American scene . . . . He can think, he can draw, and he can write* (New Yorker).
odds and ends, things left over; extra bits; scraps; remnants: *If there's ever a bit o' odds an' ends as nobody else 'ud eat, you're sure to pick it out* (George Eliot).
the odds are, the chances are; the prob-

ability is: *The odds are in our favor and we should win. The odds are, that she has a thousands faults, at least* (Maria Edgeworth). ➔ **Odds** is sometimes construed as a singular, as in *What's the odds?* The plural, however, is usual: *The odds are against him.*

odds board, a large, usually illuminated board at a race track, on which are posted the betting odds on the horses entered in a given race: *There are odds boards all over the place to keep you posted on the progress of the betting* (New Yorker).

odds-mak·er (odz′mā′kər), *n.* a person who makes a business of establishing the odds for betting, especially in a sporting event: *The professional odds-makers have established the slugging Marciano a 13–5 favorite to retain his crown* (New York Times).

odds-on (odz′on′), *adj.* having the odds in one's favor; having a good chance to win in a contest: *Macmillan seems an odds-on favorite in the October 8 election* (Wall Street Journal). —*n.* favorable odds; a good chance to win: *Silver Spoon started at odds-on . . . and the best she could do was finish third* (New Yorker).

ode (ōd), *n.* **1.** a lyric poem, usually rhymed and sometimes in irregular meter, full of noble or enthusiastic feeling and expressed with dignity, often addressed to some person or thing: *This poem which is more nearly an ode than any other of the lyrical forms, obviously was written to be read before an audience* (Lorenzo D. Turner). **2.** a poem intended to be sung. [< Middle French *ode*, learned borrowing from Latin *ōdē* < Greek *ōidḗ*, related to *aeidein* to sing]

ODECA (no periods), (ō dek′ə), *n.* Organization of Central American States (in Spanish, *Organización de Estados Centroamericanos*).

o·dels·ting or **o·dels·thing** (ō′dəls ting), *n.* the lower house of the national legislature of Norway, a country in northern Europe. [< Norwegian *odelsthing* < *odel* land + *thing* legislative meeting]

o·de·on (ō dē′on), *n.* a theater or music hall; odeum: *Six years later . . . [he] sought surcease in an odeon on the Champs Élysées* (Tallulah Bankhead). [< Greek *ōideîon*; see ODEUM]

o·de·um (ō dē′əm), *n., pl.* **o·de·a** (ō dē′ə). **1.** a theater, hall, etc., used for musical or dramatic performances. **2.** (in ancient Greece and Rome) a roofed building in which vocal and instrumental music was performed. [< Late Latin *ōdēum* < Greek *ōideîon* place for musical performances, related to *ōidḗ* song; see ODE]

Ruins of Odeum (def. 2) of Herodes Atticus, Greece

od·ic[1] (ō′dik), *adj.* of or having to do with an ode. [< *od*(e) + *-ic*]

od·ic[2] (od′ik, ō′dik), *adj.* of or having to do with the imaginary force od. [< *od*[1] + *-ic*]

o·dif·er·ous (ō dif′ər əs), *adj.* odoriferous: *We saw close-packed slum houses of crumbling cement—one- and two-room barracks fronting on streets of odiferous mud that served both as thoroughfare and plumbing* (Maclean's). [shortened form of *odoriferous*]

O·din (ō′din), *n.* the chief Norse god, the god of wisdom, culture, war, and the dead. The Germans and Anglo-Saxons identified him with Woden. Also, **Othin.** [< Old Icelandic *Ōthinn*, or Danish *Odin*. Compare WOTAN.]

o·di·ous (ō′dē əs), *adj.* very displeasing; hateful; offensive: *a kind of slimy stuff . . . of a most nauseous, odious smell* (Daniel Defoe); *consequences odious to those you govern* (Edmund Burke). *The unhappy woman . . . whose image became more odious to him every day* (George Eliot). *You told a lie, an odious damned lie* (Shakespeare). [< Latin *odiōsus* < *odium* odium] —**o′di·ous·ly,** *adv.* —**o′di·ous·ness,** *n.* —**Syn.** detestable, abominable, abhorrent, repulsive. See **hateful.**

o·di·um (ō′dē əm), *n.* **1.** hatred; dislike: *It was his lot to taste the bitterness of popular odium* (Hawthorne). **2.** reproach; blame: *to bear the odium of having betrayed one's friend. The West would surely be wise to let the Russians take on the odium of being the first to resume testing* (Manchester Guardian). [< Latin *odium*] —**Syn. 1.** detestation, aversion, opprobrium. **2.** disgrace, stigma, disfavor.

odium the·o·log·i·cum (thē′ə loj′ə kəm), rancor or acrimony characterizing or resembling theological dissensions: *The question, then, arises whether the college to which he belongs and the cause of education in Oxford are to be sacrificed to the odium theologicum of a few infatuated dignitaries* (London Times). [< New Latin *odium theologicum* (literally) theological hatred]

o·do·graph (ō′də graf, -gräf), *n.* **1.** an odometer that makes a record of what it measures. **2.** a pedometer. [< Greek *hodós* way, course + English *-graph*]

o·dom·e·ter (ō dom′ə tər), *n.* a device for measuring distance traveled by a vehicle, by recording the number of revolutions of a wheel: *Odometers are as unreliable as speedometers because they operate from the same shaft that rotates the speedometer magnet* (New York Times). [American English < Greek *hodómetron* < *hodós* way + *métron* a measure; probably patterned on French *odomètre*]

o·dom·e·try (ō dom′ə trē), *n.* the measurement by some mechanical device of distances traveled.

odont-, *combining form.* the form of **odonto-** before vowels, as in *odontalgia.*

o·don·tal·gi·a (ō′don tal′jē ə), *n.* toothache. [< New Latin *odontalgia* < Greek *odontalgíā* < *odoús, odóntos* tooth + *álgos* pain]

o·don·tal·gic (ō′don tal′jik), *adj.* of, having to do with, or suffering from toothache. —*n.* a remedy for a toothache.

o·don·ti·a·sis (ō′don tī′ə sis), *n.* the process of cutting teeth; teething.

odonto-, *combining form.* tooth; teeth: *Odontology = the scientific study of the teeth.* Also, **odont-** before vowels. [< Greek *odoús, odóntos* tooth]

o·don·to·blast (ō don′tə blast), *n.* one of a layer of cells that produce dentine as a tooth develops. [< *odonto-* + Greek *blastós* germ, sprout]

o·don·to·blas·tic (ō don′tə blas′tik), *adj.* of or having to do with odontoblasts.

o·don·to·glos·sum (ō don′tə glos′əm), *n.* any of a group of epiphytic orchids found in tropical American mountains, some of which are raised for their showy flowers. [< New Latin *Odontoglossum* the genus name < Greek *odoús, odóntos* tooth + *glôssa* tongue]

o·don·to·graph (ō don′tə graf, -gräf), *n.* **1.** a kind of template for marking the outlines of teeth on a gear. **2.** an instrument for showing the pattern of irregularity on the surface of tooth enamel.

o·don·toid (ō don′toid), *adj.* **1.** of or having to do with a toothlike projection of the second cervical vertebra, upon which the first cervical vertebra rotates: *the odontoid process or peg.* **2.** toothlike. —*n.* the odontoid process. [< Greek *odontoeidḗs* < *odoús, odóntos* tooth + *eîdos* form]

o·don·to·log·i·cal (ō don′tə loj′ə kəl), *adj.* of or having to do with odontology. —**o·don′to·log′i·cal·ly,** *adv.*

o·don·tol·o·gist (ō′don tol′ə jist), *n.* a specialist in odontology.

o·don·tol·o·gy (ō′don tol′ə jē), *n.* the branch of anatomy dealing with the structure, development, and diseases of the teeth; dentistry. [< *odonto-* + *-logy*]

o·don·toph·o·ral (ō′don tof′ər əl), *adj.* of or having to do with the odontophore of a mollusk: *the odontophoral apparatus.*

o·don·to·phore (ō don′tə fôr, -fōr), *n.* a structure in the mouth of most mollusks (other than bivalve mollusks) over which the radula is drawn backward and forward in the process of breaking up food. [< Greek *odontophóros* < *odoús, odóntos* tooth + *-phóros* < *phérein* to bear]

o·don·toph·o·rous (ō′don tof′ər əs), *adj.* having an odontophore.

o·don·tor·nith·ic (ō don′tôr nith′ik), *adj.* of or belonging to a group of extinct birds of the Mesozoic era, which had true teeth. [< New Latin *Odontornithes* the group name (< Greek *odoús, odóntos* tooth + *órnīs, -īthos* bird) + English *-ic*]

o·don·to·scope (ō don′tə skōp), *n.* a small mirror with a long slender handle, for examining the teeth. [< *odonto-* + *-scope*]

o·do·phone (ō′də fōn), *n.* a scale of odors or scents, used in grading perfumes. [< Latin *odor* odor + Greek *phōnḗ* sound (because of the analogy to the musical scale)]

o·dor (ō′dər), *n.* **1.** smell: *the odor of roses, the odor of garbage, a gas without odor.* **2.** reputation. **3.** fragrance; perfume. **4.** a taste or quality characteristic or suggestive of something: *There is no odor of impropriety about the case.* **5.** *Archaic.* a fragrant substance, flower, or plant: *Through groves of myrrh, And flowering odors, cassia nard, and balm* (Milton).

be in bad odor, to have a bad reputation or inferior standing: *Those boys were in bad odor because they were suspected of stealing. These Sydney gentry . . . are in excessively bad odor* (Herman Melville). Also, *especially British* **odour.**

[< Old French *odor*, learned borrowing from Latin *odor*]

—**Syn. 1.** scent. See **smell. 3.** aroma.

O·dor·a·ma (ō′də rä′mə, -ram′ə), *n. Trademark.* a device in a motion-picture theater that reproduces the smells of objects, places, etc., shown on the screen.

o·dor·ant (ō′dər ənt), *n.* anything that gives off or produces an odor: *Richfield Oil considers devising a synthetic skunk odorant to protect campers against rattlers; research shows the snakes flee from the smell of the natural skunk odor* (Wall Street Journal). —*adj.* that emits a smell; odorous; fragrant.

o·dored (ō′dərd), *adj.* having an odor; scented.

o·dor·if·er·ous (ō′də rif′ər əs), *adj.* **1.** giving forth an odor; fragrant: *The rose is an odoriferous flower.* **2.** giving forth an unpleasant or foul odor: *an odoriferous slum, odoriferous stagnant canal; warehouses, ships, and smell of tar, and other odoriferous circumstances of fishery and the sea* (John Galt). [< Latin *odōrifer* (< *odor, odōris* odor + *ferre* to bear) + English *-ous*] —**o′dor·if′er·ous·ly,** *adv.* —**o′dor·if′er·ous·ness,** *n.* —**Syn. 1.** aromatic. **2.** malodorous.

o·dor·less (ō′dər lis), *adj.* without an odor; having no odor: *Carbon monoxide is an odorless gas.*

odor of sanctity, 1. a sweet odor said to have been exhaled from the bodies of certain saints at death or on disinterment, and held to be evidence of their sanctity. **2.** established reputation for sanctity or holiness: *. . . the odor of its sanctity—and golly how it stank* (G.K. Chesterton).

o·dor·os·i·ty (ō′də ros′ə tē), *n.* the quality of being odorous; odorousness.

o·dor·ous (ō′dər əs), *adj.* giving forth an odor; having an odor; sweet-smelling; fragrant: *odorous spices; the odorous breath of morn* (Milton). [< Latin *odorus* (with English *-ous*)] —**o′dor·ous·ly,** *adv.* —**o′dor·ous·ness,** *n.* —**Syn.** aromatic.

o·dour (ō′dər), *n. Especially British.* odor.

ODT (no periods), Office of Defense Transportation.

od·yl or **od·yle** (od′əl, ō′dəl), *n.* od[1].

o·dyl·ic (ō dil′ik), *adj.* of or having to do with the supposed force od; odic[2].

Od·ys·se·an (od′ə sē′ən), *adj.* of or like the Odyssey or its hero.

O·dys·se·us (ō dis′ē əs, -dis′yüs), *n.* the hero of Homer's *Odyssey*, a king of Ithaca, known for his wisdom and shrewd resourcefulness; Ulysses.

Od·ys·sey (od′ə sē), *n., pl.* **-seys. 1.** a long Greek epic poem, by Homer, describing the adventures and wandering of Odysseus (Ulysses) during the ten years after the Trojan War and of his final return home to Ithaca. **2.** Also, **odyssey.** any long series of wanderings and adventures: *"The Grapes of Wrath" tells of the odyssey of migratory workers to California.* [< Latin *Odyssēa* < Greek *Odýsseia* < *Odysseús* Odysseus]

oe (oi), *n. Scottish.* oy.

o.e., omissions excepted.

OE (no periods), **O.E.,** or **OE.,** Old English (Anglo-Saxon).

O.E.C.D. or **OECD** (no periods), Organization for Economic Cooperation and Development (an organization established in 1961 to succeed the O.E.E.C.).

oec·u·men·ic (ek′yů men′ik), *adj.* ecumenic.

oec·u·men·i·cal (ek′yů men′ə kəl), *adj. British.* ecumenical.

oec·u·men·i·cal·ism (ek′yů men′ə kə liz′əm), *n.* ecumenicalism.

oec·u·me·nic·i·ty (ek′yů me nis′ə tē), *n.* ecumenicity.

O.E.D. or **OED** (no periods), Oxford English Dictionary. Also, **N.E.D.**

oe·de·ma (i dē′mə), *n. Especially British.* edema.

oe·dem·a·tous (i dem′ə təs), *adj. Especially British.* edematous.

Oed·i·pal or **oed·i·pal** (ed′ə pəl, ē′də-), *adj.* of, having to do with, or characteristic of Oedipus or the Oedipus complex: [*He*] *has succeeded in a most difficult biographical enterprise—to write of a famous father without ... indulging in Oedipal iconoclasm* (Time).

Oed·i·pus (ed′ə pəs, ē′də-), *n. Greek Legend.* a Greek king who unknowingly killed his father and married his mother. When he learned this, he blinded himself and passed the rest of his life wandering miserably.

Oedipus complex, *Psychoanalysis.* a strong childhood attachment for the parent of the opposite sex, based on early sexual desire and often accompanied by a feeling of rivalry, hostility, or fear toward the other parent. According to Freudian theory, it is a normal phase of personality development, but it is sometimes carried over into adulthood and then becomes a psychoneurotic tendency.

O.E.E.C. or **OEEC** (no periods), Organization for European Economic Cooperation (an organization established in 1948 to administer the European Recovery Program, succeeded in 1961 by the O.E.C.D.).

oeil-de-boeuf (œ′yə də bœf′), *n., pl.* **oeils-de-boeuf** (œ′yə də-bœf′) *French.* **1.** a small round or oval window, as in a frieze. **2.** (literally) bull's-eye.

Oeil-de-boeuf (def. 1)

oeil-de-per·drix (œ′yə də per drē′), *n., pl.* **oeils-de-per·drix** (œ′yə də-per drē′). *French.* **1.** tawny wine. **2.** (literally) partridge eye.

oeil·lade (œ yád′), *n. French.* an amorous or flirtatious glance; ogle.

OEM (no periods), Office for Emergency Management.

oe·no·log·i·cal (ē′nə loj′ə kəl), *adj.* of or having to do with oenology.

oe·nol·o·gist (ē nol′ə jist), *n.* a person skilled in oenology; wine connoisseur.

oe·nol·o·gy (ē nol′ə jē), *n.* the knowledge or study of wines. [< Greek *oînos* wine + English *-logy*]

oe·no·mel (ē′nə mel, en′ə-), *n.* **1.** a drink made of wine and honey, drunk by the ancient Greeks. **2.** *Poetic.* language or thought combining strength and sweetness. [< Late Latin *oenomelum,* variant of Latin *oenomeli* < Greek *oinómeli* < *oînos* wine + *méli* honey]

Oe·no·ne (ē nō′nē), *n. Greek Legend.* a nymph of Mt. Ida, who became the wife of Paris, but was deserted by him when he fell in love with Helen of Troy.

oe·no·phile (ē′nə fīl, -fil), *n.* oenophilist.

oe·noph·i·list (ē nof′ə list), *n.* a lover of wine; an expert on wines: ... *as heady a discovery as a rare wine might be to an oenophilist touring the domains of his dreams* (New Yorker).

OEO (no periods) or **O.E.O.,** Office of Economic Opportunity (an antipoverty agency of the U.S. government, established in 1964).

OEP (no periods), Office of Emergency Planning (an agency concerned with the nonmilitary aspects of national civil defense, which replaced the OCDM in 1961).

o'er (ôr, ōr), *prep., adv. Poetic.* over.

Oer·li·kon (ėr′lə kon), *n.* any of certain 20-millimeter automatic aircraft or anti-aircraft cannon which shoot greased ammunition. [< *Oerlikon,* Switzerland, where this type of cannon was developed]

oer·sted (ėr′sted), *n.* **1.** the unit of magnetic intensity in the cgs (centimeter-gram-second) system, equivalent to the intensity in a vacuum of a magnetic pole of unit strength at a distance of one centimeter. **2.** a former unit of magnetic reluctance. [< Hans Christian *Oersted,* 1777-1851, a Danish physicist]

OES (no periods), Office of Economic Stabilization.

oe·so·phag·e·al (ē′sə faj′ē əl), *adj.* esophageal.

oe·so·phag·e·an (ē′sə faj′ē ən), *adj.* esophageal.

oe·soph·a·gus (ē sof′ə gəs), *n., pl.* **-gi** (-jī). esophagus.

oes·tra·di·ol (es′trə dī′ōl, -ol), *n.* estradiol.

oes·trin (es′trin, ēs′-), *n.* estrin.

oes·tri·ol (es′trē ōl, -ol; ēs′-), *n.* estriol.

oes·tro·gen (es′trə jən, ēs′-), *n.* estrogen.

oes·tro·gen·ic (es′trə jen′ik, ēs′-), *adj.* estrogenic.

oes·trone (es′trōn), *n.* estrone.

oes·trous (es′trəs, ēs′-), *adj.* estrous.

oestrous cycle, estrous cycle.

oes·tru·al (es′trů əl), *adj.* estrual; estrous.

oes·trum (es′trəm, ēs′-), *n.* estrus.

oes·trus (es′trəs, ēs′-), *n.* estrus.

oestrus cycle, estrous cycle.

oeu·vre (œ′vrə), *n., pl.* **oeu·vres** (œ′vrə). *French.* **1.** a literary or artistic work; lifework of an artist. **2.** (literally) work.

OEW (no periods), Office of Economic Warfare.

of (ov, uv; *unstressed* əv), *prep.* **1.** belonging to: *the children of a family, a friend of his boyhood, the news of the day, the captain of a ship, the cause of the quarrel.* **2.** made from: *a house of bricks, castles of sand.* **3.** that has; containing; with: *a house of six rooms.* **4.** that has as a quality: *a look of pity, a word of encouragement, a woman of good judgment.* **5.** that is the same as; that is; named: *the city of Chicago.* **6.** away from; from: *north of Boston, wide of the mark, to take leave of a friend.* **7.** having to do with; in regard to; concerning; about: *to think well of someone, to be fond of, to be hard of heart, to be fifteen years of age, hard of hearing, short of stature.* **8.** that has as a purpose: *a house of prayer.* **9.** by: *the writings of Shakespeare, Darwin, Freud, the symphonies of Beethoven.* **10.** as a result of having or using; through: *to die of a disease, to expect much of a new medicine.* **11.** out of: *She came of a noble family. His second marriage ... took place in 1922 and there was a son of the marriage* (London Times). **12.** among: *a mind of the finest, a friend of mine. Two of us went and two of us stayed at home.* **13.** during: *of late years.* **14.** (in telling time) before: *ten minutes of six.* **15.** *Of* connects nouns and adjectives having the meaning of a verb with what would be the object of the verb; indicating the object or goal (especially of a verbal noun): *the eating of fruit, his drinking of milk, the love of truth, a man sparing of words.* [Old English (unstressed) *of;* see OFF]

➔ **of, have.** In representations of nonstandard speech the form *of* is often written instead of *have,* since in unstressed position both are pronounced (əv): *You could of been a great athlete* (New Yorker). *I'd of chased them rascals myself* (Atlantic).

➔ **of, off.** A redundant *of* (as in *off of, inside of,* etc.) is sometimes used in informal English, but the usage is not regarded as standard: *He stepped off* (not *off of*) *the sidewalk.*

of-, *prefix.* the form of **ob-** before *f,* as in *offer.*

OF (no periods), **O.F.,** or **OF.,** Old French.

o·fay (ō′fā, ō fā′), *n. U.S. Slang.* a white person (used in an unfriendly way).

off (ôf, of), *prep.* **1.** not in the usual or correct position on; not in the usual or correct condition of; not on: *A button is off his coat.* **2. a.** from; away from: *miles off the main road. He will be off duty at four o'clock.* **b.** subtracted from: *25 per cent off the marked price.* **3.** seaward from: *The ship anchored off Maine.* **4.** leading out of: *an alley off 12th Street.* **5.** *Informal.* from the possession of: *I bought it off a complete stranger.*
—*adv.* **1.** from the usual or correct position, condition, etc.: *He took off his hat.* **2.** away: *to go off on a journey.* **3.** distant in time or space: *Christmas is only five weeks off. He stopped twenty yards off.* **4.** so as to stop or lessen: *Turn the water off. The game was called off.* **5.** without work: *an afternoon off.* **6.** in full; wholly; entirely: *Clear off the table. They paid off the mortgage.* **7.** on one's way: *The train started and we were off on our trip.*

be off. See under **be.**

off and on, at some times and not at others; now and then: *He has lived in Europe off and on for ten years. It has been turning up off and on since at least 1757 in various collections of songs* (St. Louis Post Dispatch).
—*adj.* **1.** not connected; not continued; stopped: *The electricity is off. The game is off.* **2.** without work: *He pursues his hobby during off hours. It was with a team of those very horses* [*used for plowing, etc.*], *on an off day, that Miss Sharp was brought to the Hall* (Thackeray). **3.** in a specified condition in regard to money, property, etc.: *How well off are the Smiths?* **4.** not very good; not up to average: *Bad weather made last summer an off season for fruit. All drivers have their off moments, which may be due to fatigue, frustration, worry, boredom or alcohol* (New Scientist). **5.** possible but not likely: *There is an off chance of rain. I came on the off chance that I would find you.* **6.** on one's way. **7.** more distant; farther: *the off side of a wall.* **8.** on the right-hand side: *The nigh horse and the off horse make a team.* **9.** seaward: *Our men ... were at work ... on the off side* (Daniel Defoe). **10.** in error; wrong: *Your figures are way off.* **11.** *Informal.* not normal or stable; abnormal: *Their personal lives ... are rather off and strange* (James Jones). **12.** *Cricket.* in, at, of, or directed toward that side of the wicket or ground which the batsman faces as he stands at bat.
—*interj.* go away! stay away!

off with, a. take off: *Off with those wet clothes.* **b.** away with!: *Off with the old and on with the new!*
—*n.* **1.** the fact or state of being off: *The thermostat is set at "off."* **2.** the side in cricket opposite to the batsman: *Johnson the young bowler is getting wild, and bowls a ball almost wide to the off* (Thomas Hughes). [Middle English *off,* Old English *of,* in stressed position]

➔See **of** for usage note.

off., an abreviation for the following:
1. offered.
2. office.
3. officer.
4. official.
5. officinal.

off-a·gain on-a·gain, or **off-a·gain-on-a·gain** (ôf′ə gen′ on′ə gen′; of′-; -ôn′-), *adj.* wavering; inconclusive; unresolved: *The dispute over production standards ... has caused a topsy-turvy, off-again on-again work situation for many of the company's employes in the Detroit area* (Wall Street Journal). Also, **on-again off-again.**

of·fal (ôf′əl, of′-), *n.* **1.** the waste parts of an animal, fish, etc., killed for food. **2.** garbage; refuse; rubbish. **3.** the waste produced by any of various industrial processes, as chips in milling wood, scraps of leather in trimming hides, etc. **4.** dead or decaying flesh; carrion. [probably < *off* + *fall.* Compare Dutch *afval* refuse, shavings, German *Abfall* waste, garbage.]

off-and-on (ôf′ən on′, of′-; -ôn′), *adj.* occasional; interrupted; irregular; uncertain: *Orpheus and Euridice ... has had an off-and-on career with American audiences* (Wall Street Journal). Also, **on-and-off.**

off-bal·ance (ôf′bal′əns, of′-), *adj., adv.* **1.** in an unsteady position: *When Patterson, a little off-balance ... suddenly went to the floor in the second round ...* (Newsweek). **2.** by surprise: *Mr. Nixon was plainly caught off-balance at the first thrusts from his host on an occasion which ... called for informality, friendliness and courtesy* (Wall Street Journal).

off·beat (ôf′bēt′, of′-), *adj.* **1.** unusual; not orthodox; unconventional: *an offbeat display, offbeat drama.* **2.** *Music.* of or characterized by offbeats: *an offbeat rhythm, offbeat melody.*
—*n. Music.* a beat which normally has little or no accent: *Gradually, the beat began to ricochet from the audience as more and more fans began to clap hands on the offbeats* (Time).

off-board (ôf′bôrd′, of′-; -bōrd′), *adj., adv.* through a broker's office instead of a regular exchange; over-the-counter: (*adj.*) *off-board trading.* (*adv.*) *Exchange members were prohibited from going off-board* (London Times).

off break, *Cricket.* a ball that travels away from a line between the bowler and batsman but breaks back toward the batsman upon hitting the ground.

off-Broad·way (ôf′brôd′wā′, of′-), *adj.* **1.** outside the main theater district in New York City: *an off-Broadway play or theater.* **2.** close to, but not on, Broadway, in New York City: *an off-Broadway restaurant.*

off·cast (ôf′kast′, -käst′; of′-), *adj.* cast off; rejected. —*n.* a thing that is cast off; person who is rejected: *This wood ... is the offcast of the great Siberian and American rivers* (Elisha K. Kane).

off-cen·ter (ôf′sen′tər, of′-), *adj.* **1.** not in the center; away from the center: *Some* *engines are off-center so that the drive shaft bypasses the driver and permits lower seating* (Newsweek). **2.** unconventional; strange; eccentric: *... an engaging parasite whose code is in part peculiarly off-center and in part gentlemanly to the point of being quixotic* (Atlantic).

off-col·or (ôf′kul′ər, of′-), *adj.* **1.** not of the right or required color or shade; defective in color: *an off-color diamond.* **2.** somewhat improper; objectionable: *an off-color joke, an off-color song.* —**Syn. 2.** risqué.

off-col·ored (ôf′kul′ərd, of′-), *adj.* off-color.

off-course (ôf′kôrs′, of′-; -kōrs′), *adj.* **1.** off-track: *If off-course betting does come, it will do racing no good* (New Yorker). **2.** not on the right course; deviating: *The slightly off-course landing of the Molly Brown ... illustrates the sort of error that can arise from depending on men instead of computers* (Science News Letter).

off·cut (ôf′kut′, of′-), *n.* **1.** one of the pieces cut off in shaping a block of stone, a piece of lumber, etc.: *Timber has been used in the length in which it is imported, instead of having wasteful offcuts* (Manchester Guardian Weekly). **2.** *Printing.* **a.** a piece cut off from a sheet to reduce it to the proper size. **b.** a part cut off the main sheet and folded separately, as in a sheet of duodecimo.

off-du·ty (ôf′dü′tē, of′-; -dyü′-), *adj.* **1.** not engaged or occupied with one's normal work: *an off-duty policeman.* **2.** of or for a person who is not on duty: *off-duty entertainment, off-duty offense.*

of·fence (ə fens′), *n. Especially British.* offense.

of·fence·less (ə fens′lis), *adj. Especially British.* offenseless. —**of·fence′less·ly,** *adv.*

of·fend (ə fend′), *v.t.* **1.** to hurt the feelings of; make angry; displease: *He offends first one side and then the other* (Manchester Guardian). *He often offended men who might have been useful friends* (John L. Motley). **2.** to affect in an unpleasant or disagreeable way: *the rankest compound of villainous smell that ever offended nostril* (Shakespeare). *Far voices, sudden loud, offend my ear* (William E. Henley). **3.** *Obsolete.* to cause to sin: *If thy right eye offend thee, pluck it out* (Matthew 5:29). **4.** *Obsolete.* **a.** to sin against; wrong (a person). **b.** to violate; transgress (a law).
—*v.i.* **1.** to sin; do wrong: *In what way have I offended? We have offended against thy holy laws* (Book of Common Prayer). **2.** to give offense; cause displeasure. **3.** *Archaic.* to act on the offensive: *the stroke and parry of two swords, offending on the one side and keeping the defensive on the other* (Scott).
[< Old French *offendre* < Latin *offendere* < *ob-* against + *-fendere* to strike]
—**Syn.** *v.t.* **1.** affront, provoke. —*v.i.* **1.** transgress.

of·fend·ed·ly (ə fen′did lē), *adv.* in an offended manner.

of·fend·er (ə fen′dər), *n.* **1.** a person who offends. **2.** a person who does wrong or breaks a law: *No trespassing; offenders will be prosecuted.*

of·fend·ress (ə fen′dris), *n.* a woman offender.

of·fense (ə fens′), *n.* **1.** a breaking of the law; sin; crime: *a penal offense. Offenses against the law are punished by fines or imprisonment.* **2.** a cause of wrongdoing. **3.** the condition of being offended; hurt feelings; anger: *He tried not to cause offense.* **4.** the act of offending; hurting someone's feelings: *No offense was meant.* **5.** something that offends or causes displeasure. **6.** the act of attacking: *A gun is a weapon of offense. He drew his sword, and with a deliberate and prepared attitude of offence, moved slowly to the encounter* (Scott). **7.** those who are attacking: *On a professional football team, players on the offense seldom play defense.* **8.** *Obsolete.* hurt; harm; injury: *So shall he waste his means, weary his soldiers, Doing himself offence* (Shakespeare). **9.** *Obsolete.* stumbling: *He shall be ... for a stone of stumbling and for a rock of offence to both the houses of Israel* (Isaiah 8:14).
give offense, to offend: *Pleasing the most delicate reader, without giving offense to the most scrupulous* (Joseph Addison).
take offense, to be offended: *Unfortunately, offense is usually taken where offense is meant* (A.W. Ward).
Also, *especially British,* **offence.**
[fusion of Middle English *offens* (< Old French *offense* < Latin *offensus* a striking upon, annoyance), and of *offense* (< Old French *offense* < Latin *offensa* an injury, affront); both Latin nouns < *offendere* offend]
—**Syn. 1.** misdemeanor, transgression. See **crime. 3.** resentment, displeasure.
➤ See **defense** for usage note.

of·fense·less (ə fens′lis), *adj.* **1.** without offense; unable to attack. **2.** not offending; inoffensive. —**of·fense′less·ly,** *adv.*

of·fen·sive (ə fen′siv), *adj.* **1.** giving offense; irritating; annoying; insulting: "*Shut up*" *is an offensive remark.* **2.** unpleasant; disagreeable; disgusting: *Bad eggs have an offensive odor.* **3.** ready to attack; attacking: *an offensive army.* **4.** used for attack; having to do with attack: *offensive weapons, an offensive war for conquest.*
—*n.* **1.** a position or attitude of attack: *The army took the offensive.* **2.** an attack; assault: *Our planes bombed the enemy lines on the night before the offensive.* —**of·fen′sive·ly,** *adv.* —**of·fen′sive·ness,** *n.*
—**Syn.** *adj.* **2.** displeasing, distasteful. **3.** aggressive.

of·fer (ôf′ər, of′-), *v.t.* **1. a.** to hold out to be taken or refused; put forward; present: *He offered us his help. Bets were freely offered and taken regarding the result* (Bret Harte). *Mr. Arbuton has offered himself to Kitty* (William Dean Howells). **b.** to present for sale: *to offer suits at reduced prices.* **c.** to bid as a price: *He offered twenty dollars for our old stove.* **2.** to be willing if another approves: *He offered to help us. Shaw offered to accompany him* (Francis Parkman). **3.** to bring forth for consideration; propose: *She offered a few ideas to improve the plan.* **4.** to present in worship or devotion: *to offer prayers, to offer sacrifices.* **5.** to give; show: *The enemy offered strong resistance to the attack. That hath enrag'd him on, to offer strokes* (Shakespeare). **6.** to show intention; attempt; try: *When they offered to depart he entreated their stay* (Samuel Johnson). **7.** to present to sight or notice: *the scene ... offered to his view* (James Fenimore Cooper).
—*v.i.* **1.** to make an offer or proposal. **2.** to make an offer of marriage: *Miss Pole had a cousin ... who had offered to Miss Matty long ago* (Elizabeth C. Gaskell). **3.** to present itself; occur: *I will come if the opportunity offers.* **4.** to present a sacrifice or offering as an act of worship. **5.** *Archaic.* to make an attempt (at).
—*n.* **1.** the act of offering: *an offer to sing, an offer of money, an offer of marriage, an offer of $25,000 for a house.* **2.** a thing that is offered. **3.** *Law.* a proposal from one person to another which, if accepted, will become a contract. **4.** an attempt or show of intention: *He had no sooner spoke these words, but he made an offer of throwing himself into the water* (Sir Richard Steele).
[Old English *offrian* < Latin *offerre* < *ob-* to + *ferre* bring] —**of′fer·er,** *n.*
—**Syn.** *v.t.* **1. a. Offer, proffer, tender** mean to hold out something to someone to be accepted. **Offer** is the common word: *She offered him coffee.* **Proffer** is a literary word, and usually suggests offering with warmth, courtesy, or earnest sincerity: *He refused the proffered hospitality.* **Tender** is a formal word, and usually applies to an obligation or politeness rather than to an object: *He tendered his apologies.* **3.** advance, suggest. **6.** endeavor.

of·fer·ing (ôf′ər ing, of′-; ôf′ring, of′-), *n.* **1.** the giving of something as an act of worship or devotion. **2. a.** a contribution or gift, as to a church, for some special purpose. **b.** stocks, bonds, and other securities offered to the public for sale: *No big offerings came into the market last week ...* (Wall Street Journal). **3.** the act of one that offers. —**Syn. 1.** oblation. **2. a.** donation.

of·fer·to·ri·al (ôf′ər tôr′ē əl, -tōr′-; of′-), *adj.* **1.** of or having to do with an offertory: *an offertorial hymn.* **2.** used in sacrificial offerings.

of·fer·to·ry (ôf′ər tôr′ē, -tōr′-; of′-), *n., pl.* **-ries. 1.** a collection of offerings, as of money, at a religious service. **2.** verses said or the music sung or played while the offering is received. **3.** Sometimes, **Offertory. a.** (in the Roman Catholic Church) the part of the Mass at which bread and wine are offered to God. **b.** (in the Anglican Church) a similar offering of bread and wine to God. **c.** the prayers said or sung at this time. [< Late Latin *offertōrium* place to which offerings were brought < Latin *offerre* to offer]

off-fla·vor (ôf′flā′vər, of′-), *n.* an undesirable or unnatural flavor: *The off-flavor from one egg can cause off-flavor to an entire case of eggs* (Seattle Times Magazine). *Off-flavors result from such things as feeding the cow silage just before milking* (Atlantic).

off-glide (ôf′glīd′, of′-), *n. Phonetics.* a transitional sound produced by the movement of the articulators away from the position first taken: *The English tʃ and dʒ sounds are instances in which the principal acoustic feature was once a mere off-glide ...* (John Samuel Kenyon).

off-grade (ôf′grād′, of′-), *adj.* of average or less than average quality; intermediate between high-grade and low-grade: *off-grade steel, off-grade paper.*

off·hand (*adv.* ôf′hand′, of′-; *adj.* ôf′hand′, of′-), *adv.* without previous thought or preparation; at once: *That question is too important to answer offhand. The carpenter could not tell offhand how much the work would cost.* —*adj.* **1.** done or made offhand: *His offhand remarks were sometimes very wise.* **2.** free and easy; casual; informal: *He had gone about next day with his usual cool, offhand manner* (John Galsworthy). —**Syn.** *adj.* **1.** unpremeditated, unstudied, impromptu, extemporaneous. **2.** unceremonious.

off·hand·ed (ôf′han′did, of′-), *adj.* offhand. —**off′hand′ed·ly,** *adv.* —**off′hand′ed·ness,** *n.*

off-hour (ôf′our′, of′-), *n.* **1.** a period of leisure time: *Clegg collects butterflies in his off-hours* (Time). **2.** a period of lessened activity: *The tube trains are designed to handle express cargo ... during off-hours, providing ballast* (Scientific American).
—*adj.* **1.** of or for off-hours: *off-hour diversions.* **2.** having off-hours: *The government [permits] private persons—chiefly off-hour craftsmen and the unemployed—to perform repairs* (Richard A. Pierce).

offic., official.

of·fice (ôf′is, of′-), *n.* **1.** a place in which the work of a position is done; room or rooms for clerical or other work: *a doctor's office, a ticket office. The post office is on Main Street.* **2.** a position, especially in the public service: *The President holds the highest public office in the United States. Men too conversant with office are rarely minds of remarkable enlargement* (Edmund Burke). **3.** the duty of one's position; task; job; work: *A teacher's office is teaching. It has been the office of art to educate the perception of beauty* (Emerson). **4.** a person or staff of persons carrying on work in an office: *Half the office is on vacation. Will the office approve such an expense?* **5.** an administrative department of a governmental organization: *the Office of Civil and Defense Mobilization.* **6.** an act of kindness or unkindness; attention; service: *Through the good offices of a friend, he was able to get a job.* **7.** a religious ceremony or prayer: *the communion office, last offices.*
offices, the parts of a house devoted to household work, such as kitchen, pantry, laundry, etc., often also stables and buildings.
the office, *Slang.* a signal, usually a secret or special one; hint: *If the bloke you're working with is going too strong you give him what we call the office, you press his arm with finger and thumb, pincers like. That means take it a bit easy* (Manchester Guardian Weekly).
[< Old French *office,* learned borrowing from Latin *officium* service (in Medieval Latin, place for work) < *opus* work + *facere* do]
—**Syn. 2.** post, situation. **3.** function, charge.

office block, *British.* an office building: *Applications have also been received ... for an office block on the site of the Old Gaiety Theatre* (London Times).

office boy, a boy whose work is doing odd jobs in an office.

office building, *U.S.* a building with offices for one or more businesses or professions: *The solar-heated office building, claimed to be the first such building in the world, is located in Albuquerque, N.M.* (Science News Letter).

of·fice·hold·er (ôf′is hōl′dər, of′-), *n.* a person who holds a public office; government official: *Already many Moslem officeholders* *appointed by the French have resigned from municipal and regional councils* (Newsweek).

office hours, the hours during the day when an office is open for work or business.

of·fi·cer (ôf′ə sər, of′-), *n.* **1.** a person who commands others in the armed forces. An officer's authority is usually defined by his commission. **2.** the captain of a ship or any of his chief assistants, such as the first mate, chief engineer, etc. **3.** a person who holds a public, church, or government office: *a health officer, a police officer.* **4.** a person appointed or elected to an administrative position in a club, society, etc. **5.** an executive in a corporation, company, etc. **6.** a member above the lowest rank in some honorary societies. **7.** *Obsolete.* an agent; minister: *slavish officers of vengeance* (Milton).
—*v.t.* **1.** to provide with officers: *They have . . . officered the ships, and maintained the public utilities* (Newsweek). **2.** to direct; conduct; manage: *The Students' Union, the Zengakuren, is officered largely by Communists* (Atlantic). *Most of the cavalry regiments . . . were led and officered by gentlemen from the south* (James Fenimore Cooper).
[< Anglo-French *officer*, variant of Old French *officier*, learned borrowing from Medieval Latin *officiarius* < Latin *officium* service, office]

of·fi·cer·less (ôf′ə sər lis, of′-), *adj.* without officers.

officer of the day, a military officer who has charge, for the time being, of the guards, prisoners, barracks, etc. *Abbr.:* O.D.

officer of the guard, an officer, under the officer of the day, who has charge of the guard detail on a military post, ship, etc.

officer of the watch, an officer in charge of a ship during a watch at sea, usually the first, second, third, or fourth mate.

of·fi·cer·ship (ôf′ə sər ship, of′-), *n.* **1.** the position, rank, or leadership of an officer: *Regiments of troops were abandoned or lost due to almost ridiculous officership* (Wall Street Journal). **2.** a group of officers.

of·fic·es (ôf′is iz, of′-), *n.pl.* See under **office,** *n.*

office seeker, a person who tries to obtain a public office: *Don John . . . was soon surrounded by courtiers, time-servers, noble office seekers* (John L. Motley).

of·fi·cial (ə fish′əl), *n.* **1.** a person who holds a public position or who is in charge of some public work or duty: *Postmasters are government officials.* **2.** a person holding office; officer: *bank officials.*
—*adj.* **1.** of or having to do with an office: *Policemen wear an official uniform.* **2.** authorized by government or other authority; having authority; authoritative: *An official record is kept of the proceedings of Congress. Since the previous August [1792] the guillotine had been in use as the official instrument in French executions* (H.G. Wells). **3.** being an official: *Each State has its own official representatives in Congress. The unions . . . refused to accept the intervention of an official mediator* (London Times). **4.** suitable for a person in office: *the official dignity of a judge.* **5.** holding office: *an official body.* **6.** *Pharmacy.* authorized by the pharmacopoeia; officinal.
[< Old French *official*, learned borrowing from Latin *officiālis* < *officium* service]

of·fi·cial·dom (ə fish′əl dəm), *n.* **1.** the position or domain of officials. **2.** officials or the official class: *. . . the officialdom of the political and military police and full-time party whips, accustomed to ruthless doctrinal rather than practical empirical solutions* (Wall Street Journal). [< *official* + *-dom*]

of·fi·cial·ese (ə fish′ə lēz′, -lēs′), *n.* the language characteristic of officials or official documents, often formal and excessively wordy in style: *DP 32 . . . is a certificate to be signed by a "medical practitioner" (officialese for a doctor, I suppose) . . .* (Punch).

of·fi·cial·ism (ə fish′ə liz əm), *n.* **1.** official methods or system. **2.** excessive attention to official routine. **3.** officials as a group.

of·fi·cial·i·za·tion (ə fish′ə lə zā′shən), *n.* the act or process of officializing: *The officialization of Hindi has long been fought by non-Hindi regions* (Time).

of·fi·cial·ize (ə fish′ə līz), *v.t.*, **-ized, -iz·ing.** to make official in character: *They have popularized, officialized, and standardized the modern vocabulary* (Atlantic).

of·fi·cial·ly (ə fish′ə lē), *adv.* in an official manner; as an official: *How far [the Administration feels] they can go officially is something else* (Newsweek).

of·fi·ci·ant (ə fish′ē ənt), *n.* a person who officiates at a religious service or ceremony. [< Medieval Latin *officians, -antis*, present participle of *officiare* officiate]

of·fi·ci·ar·y (ə fish′ē er′ē), *adj., n., pl.* **-ar·ies.** —*adj.* **1.** (of a title) attached to or derived from an office. **2.** (of a dignitary) having a title or rank derived from office.
—*n.* **1.** officials as a group. **2.** an officer or official.

of·fi·ci·ate (ə fish′ē āt), *v.i.*, **-at·ed, -at·ing. 1.** to perform the duties of any office or position; act or serve as: *The president officiates as chairman at all club meetings. The apothecary occasionally officiated as a barber* (William Godwin). **2.** to perform the duties of a priest, minister, or rabbi: *The bishop officiated at the service in the cathedral.* **3.** to do anything as a ritual or ceremony: *to officiate in carving the Thanksgiving turkey.*
—*v.t. Obsolete.* to supply; minister: *Stars, that seem to roll Spaces incomprehensible . . . merely to officiate light Round this opacous earth* (Milton). [< Medieval Latin *officiare* (with English *-ate*[1]) < Latin *officium* service, office]

of·fi·ci·a·tion (ə fish′ē ā′shən), *n.* the act of officiating; performance of a religious, ceremonial, or public duty.

of·fi·ci·a·tor (ə fish′ē ā′tər), *n.* a person who officiates.

of·fic·i·nal (ə fis′ə nəl), *adj.* **1.** kept in stock by druggists; not made by prescription: *officinal drugs or medicines.* **2.** recognized by the pharmacopoeia; official. **3.** of or having to do with a shop.
—*n.* a drug that is kept in stock.
[< Medieval Latin *officinalis* of a monastery < Latin *officīna* shop, storeroom (in Medieval Latin, monastery) < *officium* service, office]

of·fi·cious (ə fish′əs), *adj.* **1.** too ready to offer services or advice; minding other people's business; fond of meddling: *One of those officious, noisy little men who are always ready to give you unasked information* (Benjamin Disraeli). **2.** (in diplomacy) casual and friendly; unofficial; informal: *an officious exchange of views.* **3.** *Obsolete.* eager to serve; obliging. [< Latin *officiōsus* dutiful < *officium* service, office] —**of·fi′cious·ly,** *adv.* —**of·fi′cious·ness,** *n.* —**Syn. 1.** meddlesome; intrusive.

off·ing (ôf′ing, of′-), *n.* **1.** the more distant part of the sea or other large body of water as seen from the shore. **2.** a position at a distance from the shore.
in the offing, a. just visible from the shore: *a schooner in the offing.* **b.** impending; in the making: *In sum, the Washington view is that . . . an Arab-Israeli war was in the offing* (Atlantic).

off·ish (ôf′ish, of′-), *adj. Informal.* inclined to keep aloof; distant and reserved in manner. —**off′ish·ness,** *n.*

off-key (ôf′kē′, of′-), *adj.* **1.** not in the right musical key; not in harmony; discordant: *Her voice, slightly off-key, was that of the Parisian street hawkers* (New Yorker). **2.** somewhat improper; inconsistent; rash: *An irreverent, off-key assault on an assortment of sacred cows* (Time).

off-li·cence or **off-li·cense** (ôf′lī′səns, of′-), *n. British.* **1.** a license for the sale by the bottle of alcoholic liquor for consumption off the premises: *A number of off-licenses had been granted to Pakistanis in the city, but this was the first on-licence* (London Times). **2.** an establishment with an off-licence; package store: *On the way home I called at the off-licence to collect six large tonics, a bottle of vodka, and a bottle of brandy* (Patrick Campbell).

off-lim·its (ôf′lim′its, of′-), *adj.* not to be entered; out of bounds: *. . . the entire control area would remain off-limits until official notices were published lifting restrictions* (New York Times).

off-line (ôf′līn′, of′-), *adj.* **1. a.** (of equipment associated with an electronic computer) operating outside of direct control by the central equipment. **b.** not operating in real-time. **2.** (of a railroad operation, service, etc.) being outside of the area served by the line. —*adv.* outside the direct control of central equipment: *These tapes have to be . . . analyzed by a Mercury or Atlas computer working off-line* (New Scientist).

off-load (ôf′lōd′, of′-), *v.t., v.i.* to unload or discharge a cargo: *Flight C knew they were not needed and wheeled away to off-load their bombs on the railway marshalling yards* (Terence Robertson).

off-mike (ôf′mīk′, of′-), *adj., adv.* **1.** not heard clearly through the microphone: *Jane herself was distinctly off-mike some of the time (one turned up the volume control, only to have to turn it down lest Rochester blasted one's head off)* (Listener). **2.** while not engaged in broadcasting; off the air: *. . . a B.B.C. radio actress who is famed as a kindly district nurse on the airwaves but is a sadistic, cigar-smoking old horror off-mike* (New Yorker).

off-off-Broad·way (ôf′ôf′brôd′wā′, of′-of′-), *adj.* outside the main theater district and off-Broadway theatrical centers in New York City: *The flourishing off-off-Broadway movement . . . owes much of its vigor to two Protestant churches in Greenwich Village* (New York Times).

off-peak (ôf′pēk′, of′-), *adj.* **1.** less than what is usual or possible as a maximum: *off-peak production.* **2.** characterized by reduced demand, output, etc.: *an off-peak season.*

off·print (ôf′print′, of′-), *n.* a separate reprint of an article, story, etc., originally printed as a part of a magazine, book, etc.; printed excerpt: *. . . an offprint of a piece of his published in some journal I had never heard of* (Harper's). —*v.t.* to reprint separately or as an excerpt.

off-put·ting (ôf′pu̇t′ing, of′-), *adj. Especially British Informal.* disconcerting; annoying. —**off′put′ting·ly,** *adv.*

off·sad·dle (ôf′sad′əl, of′-), *v.t., v.i.*, **-dled, -dling.** (in South Africa) to take the saddle off (a horse), as at a halt in a journey.

off·scour·ings (ôf′skour′ingz, of′-), *n.pl.* **1.** low, worthless, or depraved people. **2.** filth; refuse; rubbish.

off·screen (ôf′skrēn′, of′-), *adj., adv.* **1.** not seen on the motion picture or television screen: *an offscreen voice or commentary.* **2.** while not acting for motion pictures or television: *Japanese actors, offscreen, are less excitable than American actors* (New Yorker).

off·scum (ôf′skum′, of′-), *n.* something skimmed off; scum; refuse.

off-sea·son (ôf′sē′zən, of′-), *n.* the period when something is out of season; the slack or inactive season of a business, sport, etc.: *We work during the summer months, and in the off-season the three of us sometimes travel* (Maclean's). —*adj.* in or for the off-season: *off-season travel, off-season hotel rates.*

off·set (*v.* ôf′set′, of′-; *n., adj.* ôf′set′, of′-), *v.*, **-set, -set·ting,** *n., adj.* —*v.t.* **1.** to make up for; compensate for: *The better roads offset the greater distance.* **2.** to balance (one thing) by another as an equivalent: *We offset the greater distance by the better roads.* **3.** to set off or balance: *to offset the better roads against the greater distance.* **4. a.** to furnish (a pipe, bar, etc.) with an offset or offsets. **b.** to make offsets or setoffs in (a wall, etc.). **5.** *Printing.* to make an offset of.
—*v.i.* to form or make an offset or offsets.
—*n.* **1.** something which makes up for something else; compensation: *In football, his speed and cleverness were an offset to his small size.* **2.** a short side shoot from a main stem or root that starts a new plant, as in the houseleek or date palm. **3.** any offshoot. **4.** *Printing.* **a.** a process in which the inked impression is first made on a rubber roller and then on the paper, instead of directly on the paper. **b.** the impression thus made. **c.** the transfer or blotting of an impression onto another sheet because the ink is still wet. **5.** a short distance measured perpendicularly from a main line in surveying. **6.** *Architecture.* a ledge formed on a wall by lessening its thickness above; setoff. **7.** an abrupt bend in a pipe or bar to carry it past something in the way. **8.** a minor branch of a mountain range; spur. **9.** *Electricity.* a conductor going out from a principal conductor.
—*adj.* of, having to do with, or produced by offset: *The local printer makes offset plates directly from the film* (Time).
—**Syn.** *v.t.* **1.** counterbalance, neutralize.

off·shoot (ôf′shüt′, of′-), *n.* **1.** a shoot or branch growing out from the main stem of a plant, tree, etc. **2.** anything coming, or thought of as coming, from a main part, stock, race, etc.; branch: *The nation's annual spending for road construction . . . is obviously a direct offshoot of the swelling auto population* (Newsweek).

off·shore (*adv., adj.* ôf′shôr′, -shōr′; of′-; *adj.* -shôr′), *adv., adj.* **1.** off or away from the shore: *a wind blowing offshore, ships lying offshore.* **2.** *U.S.* outside the United States; foreign: *Offshore procurements are American purchases of airplanes, tanks, ammunition and other munitions in European countries* (Wall Street Journal).

offshore bar, barrier beach.

off·side or **off-side** (ôf′sīd′, of′-), *adj., adv.* away from one's own or the proper side; being on the wrong side. —*n.* a play in football, etc., that is offside.

off·sid·er (ôf′sī′dər, of′-), *n.* (in Australia) a person who assists another; helper: *After eight months representing the State Department abroad this distinguished scholar ... was debriefed in ... interviews which consisted mostly of chit-chat by his official offsider* (Stan Swinton).

off-spin (ôf′spin′, of′-), *n. Cricket.* a spin that results in an off break.

off-spin·ner (ôf′spin′ər, of′-), *n. Cricket.* **1.** an off break. **2.** a bowler who specializes in off breaks.

off·spring (ôf′spring′, of′-), *n.* **1.** what is born from or grows out of something; child or children; descendant: *Everyone of his offspring had red hair just like his own.* **2.** a result; effect: *He appeared to consider it* [*an assertion*] *as the offspring of delirium* (Mary W. Shelley). [Old English *ofspring*] —**Syn. 1.** progeny, issue, young.

off-stage (ôf′stāj′, of′-), *adj., adv.* **1.** away from the part of the stage that the audience can see; behind the scenes: *He is about to start taking lessons so that the set of his lips and finger movements will correspond to the melody to be played off-stage by an expert musician* (New York Times). **2.** while not acting for an audience.

off-street (ôf′strēt′, of′-), *adj.* away from the street, as for easing traffic or preventing congestion: *off-street parking.*

off stump, *Cricket.* the stump farthest from the batsman.

off·take (ôf′tāk′, of′-), *n. British.* **1.** a taking off, as when purchase of goods takes them off the market; consumption: *The United States' offtake of Brazilian cocoa is now more consistent—thanks to the devaluation of the "cocoa cruzeiro"* (London Times). **2.** that which is taken off; a deduction. **3.** a means of drawing off or away, as a pipe, tube, or course.

off-the-cuff (ôf′ᴛʜə kuf′, of′-), *U.S. Informal.* —*adj.* not prepared in advance; extemporaneous; impromptu: *Armed for his off-the-cuff speeches only with a list of candidates' names, he interweaves their names into his talk as if the speech had been built on that basis* (Wall Street Journal). —*adv.* offhand; extemporaneously: *Only ... where he spoke completely off-the-cuff did he seem to be establishing any great rapport with his audience* (Alan Otten).

off-the-face (ôf′ᴛʜə fās′, of′-), *adj.* (of a woman's hat) being without a brim or with a narrow, usually upturned brim: *... an off-the-face turban of natural raffia* (New Yorker).

off-the-peg (ôf′ᴛʜə peg′, of′-), *adj. British.* ready-made: *An off-the-peg dress may cost £20 in a Geneva shop* (London Times). *I sensed ... that personality was more important to a room than any amount of off-the-peg convention* (Punch).

off-the-rec·ord (ôf′ᴛʜə rek′ərd, of′-), *adj.* not intended for publication; not to be repeated publicly or issued as news: *an off-the-record opinion. Two unions have held several off-the-record meetings here recently to discuss pending contract negotiations* (Wall Street Journal). —*adv.* not to be recorded or quoted; so as to be off-the-record: *to speak off-the-record. Officials maintained a discreet public silence, but off-the-record they complained bitterly* (New York Times).

off-the-shelf (ôf′ᴛʜə shelf′, of′-), *adj.* suitable for use without major or extensive modification: *Off-the-shelf instruments and propulsion units ... give as economic a launcher as possible* (New Scientist). —*adv.* without major modification: *Deliveries in practically all small items of construction equipment can be made off-the-shelf* (Wall Street Journal).

off-track (ôf′trak′, of′-), *adj.* **1.** that is conducted away from the race track: *off-track horserace betting.* **2.** off the beaten track; out of the way: *... wanderings in the off-track Caribbean islands occupied by poor-white Frenchmen* (Punch). **3.** that is not a usual function of railroading: *Southern Pacific ... has never had an eye for off-track business ventures* (New York Times).

off-train (ôf′trān′, of′-), *adj.* nonoperating: *Off-train railroad unions demanded improved benefits* (Wall Street Journal).

off-white (ôf′hwīt′, of′-), *n.* a very light shade of color, verging on white: *White and gray, off-whites and beiges are leading daytime colors* (Seattle Times). —*adj.* that is nearly white: *an off-white ceiling.*

off-year (ôf′yir′, of′-), *U.S.* —*n.* **1.** a year of unfavorable conditions or lower than average yield: *This one is an off-year for domestic exports.* **2. a.** a year in which national elections are held for offices other than the presidency: *President Eisenhower hopped into the campaign more vigorously than any President ever had in an off-year* (New York Times). **b.** a year in which elections are held on a state or local level for offices other than the governorship, mayoralty, etc. —*adj.* of or taking place in an off-year: *off-year elections.*

O.F.M., Order of Friars Minor; Franciscans (Latin, *Ordo Fratrum Minorum*).

OFr (no periods), **O.Fr.,** or **OFr.,** Old French.

O.F.S. or **OFS** (no periods), Orange Free State.

oft (ôft, oft), *adv. Archaic.* often; frequently: *Oft I talked with him apart* (Tennyson). —*adj. Obsolete.* frequent. [Old English *oft*]

of·ten (ôf′ən, of′-; -tən), *adv.* in many cases; many times; frequently: *Blame is often misdirected. He comes here often.* —*adj. Archaic.* frequent: *Use a little wine for ... thine often infirmities* (I Timothy 5:23). [Middle English *often;* extension of *ofte* oft] —**Syn.** *adv.* **Often, frequently** mean many times or in many instances, and are often interchangeable. But **often** suggests only that something happens or occurs a number of times or in a considerable proportion of the total number of instances: *We often see him.* **Frequently** emphasizes happening or occurring again and again, regularly or at short intervals: *We saw him frequently last week.*

of·ten·times (ôf′ən tīmz′, of′-; -tən-), *adv.* often: *This song to myself did I oftentimes repeat* (Wordsworth).

oft·time (ôft′tīm′, oft′-), *Archaic.* —*adv.* ofttimes. —*adj.* frequent.

oft·times (ôft′tīmz′, oft′-), *adv. Poetic.* often: *The fabled Haroun-al-Rashid ofttimes used to dress up in rags and mingle with his subjects in the bazaar* (New Yorker).

O.G., an abbreviation for the following:
1. Officer of the Guard.
2. Olympic Games.
3. Also, **o.g.** *Philately.* Original Gum (a stamp in mint condition with the original mucilage).

og·am (og′əm, ōg′əm), *n.* **1.** an alphabet of 20 characters used in ancient Britain and Ireland. **2.** an inscription in such characters. **3.** one of the characters. Also, **ogham.** [< Old Irish *ogam*]

Ogam (def. 2) on Irish tablet

og·am·ic (og′ə mik, ō gam′ik), *adj.* **1.** of or having to do with the ogam. **2.** consisting of ogams. Also, **oghamic, ogmic.**

og·do·ad (og′dō ad), *n.* **1.** the number eight. **2.** a group, set, or series of eight. [< Latin *ogdoas, -adis* < Greek *ogdoás, -ádos* < stem of *oktṓ* eight]

o·gee (ō jē′, ō′jē), *n.* **1.** an S-shaped curve or line. **2.** a molding with such a curve; cyma. **3.** an ogee arch. **4.** *Obsolete.* a diagonal rib or pointed arch; ogive. [variant of *ogive*]

ogee arch, a form of pointed arch each side of which has the curve of an S-shape.

Ogee Arch

og·ham (og′əm, ō′əm), *n.* ogam.

og·ham·ic (og′ə mik, ō-gam′ik), *adj.* ogamic.

o·gi·val (ō jī′vəl), *adj. Architecture.* **1.** of or like a diagonal rib or pointed arch in a building. **2.** having pointed arches or diagonally ribbed vaulting: *Their ogival architecture was too foreign to impress the Renaissance world, except by the richness of its decoration* (New Yorker).

o·give (ō′jīv, ō jīv′), *n.* **1.** *Architecture.* **a.** a diagonal rib of a vault. **b.** a pointed arch. **2.** *Statistics.* a distribution curve in which the frequencies are cumulative. In an ogive of wage levels in which 10 people earn less than $50, 60 people $50 to $100, and 40 people $100 to $150, the abscissas of the curve would be 50, 100, and 150 and the ordinates 10, 70, 110. [< Middle French *ogive;* origin uncertain]

Equilateral Ogive (def. 1b)

o·gle (ō′gəl), *v.,* **o·gled, o·gling,** *n.* —*v.t.* **1.** to look at with desire; make eyes at: *He ogled the ladies with an air of supreme satisfaction* (Herman Melville). **2.** to look at; eye. —*v.i.* to look with desire; make eyes: *She ogled, and nodded, and kissed her hands quite affectionately to Kew* (Thackeray). —*n.* an ogling look: *Miss Brindle ... gave him two or three ogles* (Thomas L. Peacock). [< Low German *oeglen* (frequentative) < *oegen* look at < *oege* eye] —**o′gler,** *n.*

og·mic (og′mik), *adj.* ogamic.

OGO (no periods), Orbiting Geophysical Observatory: *An OGO ... is scheduled for orbit late in 1963 and will carry aloft a series of individual experiments to probe earth-space relationships* (Science News Letter).

Og·pu (og′pü), *n.* the official organization of secret police and detectives in the Soviet Union from 1922 to 1935. It was named the NKVD in 1935, and, later, the MVD. [< Russian *O(b″edinennoe) G(osudarstvennoe) P(oliticheskoe) U(pravlenie)* "Unified State Political Administration"]

o·gre (ō′gər), *n.* **1.** (in folklore and fairy tales) a hideous giant or monster that supposedly eats people. **2.** a man like such a monster in appearance or character: *If those robber-barons were somewhat grim and drunken ogres, they had a certain grandeur of the wild beast in them* (George Eliot). [< French *ogre;* origin uncertain]

o·gre·ish (ō′gər ish), *adj.* of, having to do with, or like an ogre.

o·gress[1] (ō′gris), *n.* a female ogre.

o·gress[2] (ō′gris), *n.* (in heraldry) a black, round spot on a shield, representing a cannon ball; a roundel sable. [origin unknown]

o·grish (ō′grish), *adj.* ogreish.

oh or **Oh** (ō), *interj., n., pl.* **oh's, Oh's, ohs, Ohs.** —*interj.* **1.** a word used before names in addressing persons: *Oh Mary, look!* **2.** an expression of surprise, joy, grief, pain, and other feelings: *Oh, dear me! Oh! that hurt! Oh, what a pity!* —*n.* the interjection or exclamation *Oh: You should have heard their Oh's and Ah's when they got the news.*

OHE (no periods) or **O.H.E.,** Office of the Housing Expediter.

OHG (no periods) or **O.H.G.,** Old High German.

O·hi·an (ō hī′ən), *n.* Ohioan.

O·hi·o·an (ō hī′ō ən), *adj.* of or having to do with Ohio. —*n.* a native or an inhabitant of Ohio.

ohm (ōm), *n.* the unit of electrical resistance. One ohm is the resistance of a conductor through which one volt can send a current of one ampere. [< Georg S. *Ohm,* 1787-1854, a German physicist]

ohm·age (ō′mij), *n.* the electrical resistance of a conductor, expressed in ohms.

ohm·ic (ō′mik), *adj.* **1.** of or having to do with the ohm: *It is the ohmic resistance of the gas that generates the heat on passage of the current* (Lyman Spitzer, Jr.). **2.** measured in ohms.

ohm·me·ter (ōm′mē′tər), *n.* an instrument for measuring the electrical resistance of a conductor in ohms.

O.H.M.S., On His or Her Majesty's Service.

Ohm's law (ōmz), a law expressing the strength of an electric current, in which the current in amperes is directly proportional to the electromotive force in volts and inversely proportional to the resistance in ohms.

o·ho (ō hō′), *interj.* an exclamation expressing surprise, taunting, or exultation.

o·hone (ō hōn′), *interj. Scottish and Irish.* ochone.

-oid, *suffix.* **1.** like; like that of: *Amoeboid = like an amoeba.*
2. a thing like a ——: *Spheroid = a thing like a sphere (in shape).*

[< New Latin *-oides,* reduction of Greek *-oeidēs* in the form of < *eîdos* form]

oil (oil), *n.* **1.** any of several kinds of fatty or greasy liquids that are lighter than water, that burn easily, and that dissolve in alcohol but not in water. Mineral oils, such as kerosene, are used for fuel; animal and vegetable oils, such as olive oil, peanut oil, etc., are used in cooking, medicine and in many other ways. Essential or volatile oils, such as oil of peppermint, are distilled from plants, leaves, flowers, etc., and are thin and evaporate very quickly. **2.** mineral oil; petroleum. **3.** olive oil. **4.** a substance that resembles oil in some respect: *Sulfuric acid is called oil of vitriol.* **5.** oil paint: *a landscape in oil.* **6.** an oil painting: *The exhibition has more oils than water colors.*
burn the midnight oil, to study or work late at night: *I cannot say that I burnt much midnight oil* (William Ballantine).
pour oil on troubled waters, to make things calm and peaceful: *The fight between the boys had become so fierce that the teacher had to come out to pour oil on troubled waters.*
strike oil, a. to find oil by boring a hole in the earth: *He struck oil in Oklahoma.* **b.** to find something very profitable; succeed: *He has certainly struck oil in the . . . loans* (Punch). *We are a nation which has struck oil* (James Russell Lowell).
—*v.i.* to become oil: *Butter oils when heated.*
—*v.t.* **1.** to put oil on or in: *to oil the squeaky hinges of a door, to oil a tanker.* **2.** *Informal.* to bribe.
—*adj.* **1.** of, having to do with, or for oil: *an oil filter, an oil company.* **2.** containing or carrying oil: *an oil drum, an oil car.* **3.** using oil as fuel: *an oil lamp.*
[Middle English *olie, oyle* < Old North French *olie,* Old French *oille* < Latin *oleum* olive oil < Greek *élaion* oil]
—**Syn.** *v.t.* **1.** lubricate, grease.

oil beetle, a beetle that gives off an oily liquid when alarmed. See picture under **meloid.**

oil·bird (oil′bėrd′), *n.* the guacharo.

oil·bug (oil′bug′), *n.* the synura, a tiny water animal that gives off an oily substance that makes water distasteful.

oil burner, a furnace, ship, etc., that uses oil for fuel.

oil cake, a mass of cottonseed, linseed, coconut meat, etc., from which the oil has been pressed. Oil cakes are used as a food for cattle and sheep or as a fertilizer.

oil can, 1. a can to hold oil. **2.** a can with a narrow nozzle, used in lubricating machinery, moving parts, etc.: *He lovingly wiped the wheel with a handful of grass and produced an oil can from his pocket and gave it a squirt* (V. S. Pritchett).

oil·cloth (oil′klôth′, -kloth′), *n.* **1.** a cloth made waterproof by coating it with paint or oil, used to cover tables, shelves, etc.: *The thresholds and doorsteps were covered with the neatest and brightest oilcloth* (William Dean Howells). **2.** cloth made waterproof by treating it with oil; oilskin: *a hat covered with an oilcloth* (Hawthorne).

oil color, 1. a paint made by mixing pigment with oil; oil paint. **2.** a painting done in such colors.

oil crop, a crop, such as soybeans, cottonseed, peanuts, or coconuts, that supplies oil used in cooking and in making paints and other products.

oil derrick, a tall steel structure that raises and lowers the equipment used in drilling an oil well.

oiled (oild), *adj.* **1.** saturated with oil so as to be waterproof: *oiled silk.* **2.** *U.S. Slang.* drunk.

oil·er (oi′lər), *n.* **1.** a person or thing that oils. **2.** a can with a long spout used in oiling machinery; oil can. **3.** *U.S. Informal.* an oilskin coat. **4.** an oil tanker: *Dozens of destroyers, oilers and auxiliaries were included in that part of the fleet that anchored in the Clyde* (New York Times). **5.** *U.S. Informal.* an oilman.

oil field, an area where petroleum has been found.

oil-fired (oil′fīrd′), *adj.* using oil as the fuel or source of heat.

oil·fish (oil′fish′), *n., pl.* **-fish·es** or (*collectively*) **-fish.** escolar.

oil gas, any of various hydrocarbon gases produced by heating oil vapor and steam: *The production of straight oil gas follows to some extent the process outlined for carbureted water gas* (World Book Encyclopedia).

oil·i·ly (oi′lə lē), *adv.* in an oily manner.

oil·i·ness (oi′lē nis), *n.* oily quality or state.

oil lamp, a lamp which uses kerosene or other oils as a fuel: *He slowed up and stopped outside a small baker's shop, which was opened to the street and upon the counter of which an oil lamp was burning* (Atlantic).

oil·man (oil′man′, -mən), *n., pl.* **-men.** an owner, administrator, worker, or other person engaged in the business of producing or selling oil: *U.S. oilmen are winning battles against imports, but can lose the war* (Wall Street Journal).

oil nut, 1. any of various nuts and seeds yielding oil, such as the buffalo nut, butternut, peanut, or castor bean. **2.** any of the plants producing them.

oil of cinnamon, 1. an oil used in perfumes and as a flavoring derived from the twigs and leaves of the cinnamon tree. **2.** a somewhat similar oil derived from the twigs and leaves of the cassia tree; cassia oil.

oil of thuja, an aromatic oil of an American species of thuja, used in medicine and in polishes.

oil of turpentine, a colorless, inflammable, volatile oil made from turpentine, used in mixing paints.

oil of vitriol, sulfuric acid.

oil of wintergreen, a heavy, volatile oil of the wintergreen plant, used in medicine and as a flavoring.

oil paint, paint made by mixing a pigment with oil: [*Synthetic latex paint*] *does not leave a paint odor so characteristic of most oil paints* (Wall Street Journal).

oil painting, 1. a picture painted with oil colors, usually on canvas. **2.** the art of painting with oil colors.

oil palm, an African palm whose fruit and seeds yield palm oil.

oil pan, a detachable metal housing of an engine containing the lubricating oil.

oil·pa·per (oil′pā′pər), *n.* paper oiled to make it transparent and waterproof.

oil pool, pool (def. 5).

oil press, an apparatus for expressing oil from fruits, seeds, etc.

oil·proof (oil′prüf′), *adj.* resistant to oil: *A new treatment for cotton fabric made it . . . waterproof, oilproof, and resistant to heat and rot* (Science News Letter). —*v.t.* to make oilproof.

oil sand, any sandstone or rock that yields oil: *Oil may be obtained through underground nuclear explosions from two untapped sources, oil sands and tar sands* (Science News Letter).

oil seal, a device packed with material impermeable by oil, used to prevent leakage of oil in a machine, etc.

oil·seed (oil′sēd′), *n.* any seed that yields oil, such as peanut, coconut, soybean, and cottonseed, especially the seed of an East Indian composite plant whose oil is used for lamps and as a condiment.

oil shale, shale containing kerogen, that yields oil upon distillation in the absence of air: *One of the largest potential reserves of oil in the world is that locked up in oil shale* (New Scientist).

oil·skin (oil′skin′), *n.* a cloth treated with oil to make it waterproof; oilcloth.
oilskins, a coat and trousers made of this cloth: *There were two men at the wheel in yellow oilskins* (Clark Russell).

oil·skinned (oil′skind′), *adj.* dressed in oilskins: *He saw a black-hulled fishing schooner scudding before the wind with reefed sails, saw the oilskinned men on her deck . . .* (Maclean's).

oil slick, a smooth place on the surface of water caused by the presence of oil.

oil·stone (oil′stōn′), *n.* a fine-grained stone used for sharpening tools, the rubbing surface of which is oiled.

oil stove, a stove using kerosene, naphtha, or similar oil for fuel.

oil tanker, a ship with special tanks for transporting oil: *a Maritime Administration request for a nuclear-powered oil tanker* (Wall Street Journal).

oil well, a well drilled in the earth to get oil.

oil·y (oi′lē), *adj.,* **oil·i·er, oil·i·est. 1.** of oil. **2.** containing oil. **3.** covered or soaked with oil: *oily rags. He mopped his oily pate* (Robert Browning). **4.** like oil; smooth; slippery. **5.** too smooth; suspiciously or disagreeably smooth: *an oily smile, an oily manner.* —**Syn. 5.** unctuous.

oink (oingk), *n.* **1.** the sound a hog makes. **2.** a sound resembling or imitating this; grunt. —*v.i.* to make the sound that a hog makes, or one resembling it.

oi·noch·o·e (oi nok′ō ē), *n.* (in ancient Greece) a pitcherlike vessel with a three-lobed rim, for dipping wine from the crater or bowl and pouring it into the drinking cups. [< Greek *oinochóē* < *oînos* wine + *chein* pour]

Oinochoe of Rhodes

oint·ment (oint′mənt), *n.* a substance made from oils, fats, waxes, or hydrocarbons, often containing medicine, used on the skin to heal, or to make it soft and white. Cold cream and salve are ointments. [Middle English *oignement* < Old French < *oindre* anoint < Latin *unguere;* influenced by English *anoint*] —**Syn.** unguent, salve, balm.

Oir·each·tas (er′əᴛʜ thəs), *n.* the legislature of the Irish Republic. The lower house is called the Dail Eireann, and the upper house the Seanad Eireann. [< Irish *oireachtas* assembly]

OIT (no periods), Office of International Trade.

oi·ti·ci·ca (oi′tə sē′kə), *n.* a South American tree of the rose family, whose seeds yield an oil used in paints, varnishes, etc. [< a native word]

o·jam (ō′jəm), *n.* galago.

O·jib·wa (ō jib′wā), *n., pl.* **-wa** or **-was. 1.** a member of a large tribe of American Indians of Algonkian stock formerly living near the Great Lakes; Chippewa. **2.** the language of these Indians. [American English < Algonkian (Ojibwa) *ojib* pucker up + *ub-way* roast (in reference to the puckered seam on their moccasins)]

O·jib·way (ō jib′wā), *n., pl.* **-way** or **-ways.** Ojibwa.

OK (no periods) or **O.K.** (ō′kā′), *adj., adv., v.,* **OK'd, OK'ing** or **O.K.'d, O.K.'ing;** *n., pl.* **OK's** or **O.K.'s,** *interj. Informal.*
—*adj., adv.* all right; correct; approved.
—*v.t.* to put "OK" on to show that something is correct or has been approved; approve; endorse: *to OK a request for a loan. Barney grinned, "Pink has O.K.'d the article"* (John Stephen Strange).
—*n.* approval: *The foreman put his OK on the shipment.*
—*interj.* all right: *OK, you can go if you come home before dark. The policemen called back faintly, "O.K.!"* (New Yorker).
[American English; apparently < the initial letters of "oll korrect," a phonetic respelling of *all correct*]
➤ **OK, O.K.** Business and informal English for correct, all right, approved.

o·ka (ō′kə), *n.* in Greece, Turkey, Egypt, etc.: **1.** a unit of weight, equal to about 2¾ lbs. **2.** a unit of liquid measure, equal to about 1⅓ United States quarts. [< Turkish *okka* < Arabic *ūqiya,* ultimately < Greek *ounkíā* < Latin *uncia.* Doublet of OUNCE[1], INCH.]

O·ka (ō′kə), *n.* a cheese cured with brine and similar to Port du Salut, made by Trappist monks in Oka, a village in Quebec.

o·ka·pi (ō kä′pē), *n., pl.* **-pis** or **-pi.** an African ruminant mammal related to the giraffe, but smaller, unspotted, and with a much shorter neck. [< a native word]

Okapi (about 4 ft. high at the shoulder)

o·kay or **o·keh** (ō′kā′), *adj., adv., v.t., n., interj. Informal.* OK: *I muttered, "Okay," not feeling very sure that I could survive two hours of Devon* (Guy Endore). [American English; spelling for pronunciation of *O.K.*]

oke (ōk), *n.* oka.

o·key-do·key (ō′kē dō kē), *interj. Informal.* OK. [reduplication of *okeh*]

O·kie (ō′kē), *n. U.S. Informal.* a migratory farm worker, originally one from Oklahoma, who wandered from place to place in search of work during the depression of the 1930's: *Okies—the owners hated them because the owners knew they were soft and the Okies strong, that they were fed and the Okies hungry* (John Steinbeck). Also, **Oakie.** [American English < *Ok*(lahoma) + *-ie*]

O·ki·na·wan (ō′kə nä′wən), *adj.* of or having to do with Okinawa, an island in the northern Pacific, or its people. —*n.* a native or inhabitant of Okinawa.

Okla., Oklahoma.

O·kla·ho·man (ō′klə hō′mən), *adj.* of or having to do with Oklahoma. —*n.* a native or inhabitant of Oklahoma.

o·ko·le·hao (ō′kə lā hou′), *n. Hawaiian.* an alcoholic liquor usually distilled from the root of the ti palm. Other ingredients sometimes used are rice, pineapple, and molasses. *Okolehao [is] a powerful spirit that resembles whisky in color and transparency* (New York Times).

o·kou·mé or **o·kou·me** (ō′kə mā′), *n.* **1.** any of several tropical African trees whose fine softwood is much used for veneer. **2.** the wood. [< French *okoumé* < a Gabonese word]

o·kra (ō′krə), *n.* **1.** a tall plant of the mallow family, grown in the southern United States and elsewhere for its sticky green pods, which are used in soups and as a vegetable; gumbo. **2.** the pods. **3.** a stew or soup made with okra pods; gumbo. [< a West African word]

-ol[1], *suffix.* **1.** containing, derived from, or like alcohol, as in *carbinol, phenol.*
2. the phenols and phenol derivatives, as in *thymol.*
[< (alcoh)*ol*]

-ol[2], *suffix.* a variant of **-ole,** as in *terpinol.*

OL (no periods), **O.L.,** or **OL.,** Old Latin.

old (ōld), *adj.,* **old·er** or **eld·er, old·est** or **eld·est,** *n.* —*adj.* **1.** having existed long; aged: *An old wall surrounds the castle. I love everything that's old; old friends, old times, old manners, old books, old wines* (Oliver Goldsmith). **2.** of age; in age: *The baby is one year old.* **3.** not new; made long ago; ancient: *an old excuse, an old custom, an old tomb, an old debt, an old family.* **4.** much worn by age or use: *old clothes. Neither do men put new wine into old bottles; else the bottles break* (Matthew 9:17). *Your fooling grows old, and people dislike it* (Shakespeare). **5.** looking or seeming old; mature: *That child is old for her years.* **6.** having much experience: *to be old in wrongdoing, to be an old hand at it.* **7.** former: *the old days before the war. An old student came back to visit his teacher.* **8.** earlier or earliest: *Old English, the Old Testament.* **9.** familiar; dear: *a good old fellow.* **10.** *Informal.* good; fine; splendid: *We had a high old time at the party.* **11.** (of topographical features) well advanced in the process of erosion to base level.
—*n.* the time long ago; earlier or ancient time: *the heroes of old. Of old hast thou laid the foundation of the earth* (Psalms 102:25).
the old, old people: *a home for the old.*
[Old English *ald, eald*] —**old′ness,** *n.*
—**Syn.** *adj.* **1. Old, elderly, ancient** mean having existed a long time. **Old,** describing people, animals, or things, means not young or new, but near the end of life or having been in existence, use, or a particular relation, a long or relatively long time: *We are old friends.* **Elderly,** describing people, means past middle age and getting old: *He is an elderly man, about seventy.* **Ancient** means having come into existence or use, or having existed or happened, in the distant past: *Jerusalem is an ancient city.* **4.** dilapidated, decayed, shabby, outworn. **6.** experienced, practiced.
➤ See **elder** for usage note.

old age, the years of life from about 65 on in human beings. —**old′-age′,** *adj.*

old-age pension (ōld′āj′), a pension paid to retired employees or their beneficiaries, the cost of which is either shared by the pensioner and the administrator of the pension or financed entirely by the employer.

Old Arabic, the earliest form of Arabic, used from about the 100's A.D. to the 600's.

Old Bai·ley (bā′lē), the chief court in London for trying criminal cases: *Haul the culprit to Old Bailey* (Wall Street Journal). [< *Old Bailey,* the common name for Newgate Prison, that once stood on this site < *bailey*]

old bean, *British Slang.* old fellow; old man (as a familiar form of address): *The child of two and a half years . . . addressed her learned parent as "old bean"* (Punch).

Old Believer, a dissenter from the Russian Church; Raskolnik: *Old Believers . . . split from the Russian Orthodox Church in the 17th century* (New York Times).

old Bogy, the Devil.

old boy, 1. old man. **2.** Often, **Old Boy.** *Informal.* an alumnus, especially of an English boarding school. **3.** the Devil (a humorous use).

Old Bulgarian, Old Church Slavic.

Old Catholics, an independent church organization that developed from a party formed in the Roman Catholic Church in 1870 in opposition to the dogma of papal infallibility.

old chum, (in Australia) an old and experienced settler.

Old Church Slavic or **Slavonic,** a Slavic language preserved in Russian Orthodox religious texts of the 800's and 900's, and still used in the liturgy of some Orthodox Churches; Old Bulgarian.

old-clothes-man (ōld′klōz′man, -klōᴛʜz′-), *n., pl.* **-men.** a dealer in old or second-hand clothes.

old country, the country of origin of an immigrant.

Old Dominion, a nickname for Virginia.

olde (ōld), *adj.* old.
➤ This archaic spelling is used for humorous, nostalgic, or eye-catching effect: . . . *travelogue shots of Olde England* (Time).

old·en[1] (ōl′dən), *adj. Poetic.* of old; old; ancient: *olden times; islands which the olden voyages had so glowingly described* (Herman Melville). [< *old* + *-en*[2]] —**Syn.** bygone.

old·en[2] (ōl′dən), *v.i.* to grow old; age: *In six weeks he oldened more time than he had done for fifteen years before* (Thackeray). —*v.t.* to cause to grow or appear old. [< *old* + *-en*[1]]

Ol·den·burg (ōl′dən bėrg), *n.* a variety of apple which ripens early. [American English < earlier Duchess of *Oldenburg*]

Old English, 1. the period in the history of the English language and literature before 1100 A.D. **2.** the language of this period; Anglo-Saxon. *Abbr.:* OE (no periods). **3.** *Printing.* a kind of blackletter type.

This sentence is set in Old English.

Old English sheepdog, any of a breed of English working dogs having a long, shaggy, blue or grizzly gray coat, docked tail, and standing about 22 inches high.

Old Faithful, a geyser in Yellowstone National Park which spouts to a height of up to 170 feet about every 65 minutes.

old·fan·gled (ōld′fang′gəld), *adj.* old-fashioned: *his vesture so oldfangled* (Robert Browning). *Now for a few words about recorders—not the newfangled machines but the oldfangled musical instruments* (New Yorker). [patterned on *newfangled*]

old-fash·ioned (ōld′fash′ənd), *adj.* **1.** of an old fashion; out of fashion: *an old-fashioned dress. The writing was old-fashioned and rather uncertain, like that of an elderly lady* (Charlotte Brontë). **2.** keeping to old ways, ideas, etc.: *an old-fashioned housekeeper.* **3.** (of a child) old or mature in ways, thoughts, etc.: *"Oh! the old-fashioned little soul!" cried Mrs. Blimber* (Dickens). —**old′-fash′ioned·ly,** *adv.* —**Syn. 1.** out-of-date, fusty.

old fashioned, a cocktail made of whiskey, sugar, and bitters with a slice of orange and a cherry, mixed with soda and served cold.

old·field (ōld′fēld′), *n.* a field left abandoned because of its poor yield.

old fogy or **fogey,** an old-fashioned or very conservative person.

old-fo·gy or **old-fo·gey** (ōld′fō′gē), *adj.* out-of-date; behind the times.

old-fo·gy·ish or **old-fo·gey·ish** (ōld′fō′gē ish), *adj.* old-fogy.

old-fo·gy·ism or **old-fo·gey·ism** (ōld′fō′gē iz əm), *n.* the ideas or behavior characteristic of old fogies; old-fashioned ways: *So we adopt the traditional defense, which is old-fogyism* (Harper's).

old folks, 1. old or aged people. **2.** persons of an older generation in a family, such as the parents: *The old folks encouraged me by continual invitations to supper, and by leaving us together* (Benjamin Franklin).

Old French, the French language from about 800 A.D. to about 1400. *Abbr.:* OF (no periods).

old gentleman, the Devil.

Old Glory, the flag of the United States; Stars and Stripes.

old gold, a dull-gold color; soft, rich yellow that is nearly brown.

old-gold (ōld′gōld′), *adj.* of the color old gold; dull-gold.

Old Guard, 1. *U.S.* a very conservative section of the Republican Party of the United States: *The Republican National Committee . . . remained an Old Guard stronghold even after Mr. Eisenhower's election* (Newsweek). **2.** the imperial guard of Napoleon I, created in 1804. It made the last French charge at Waterloo. **3.** the conservative members of a country, community, organization, etc. [translation of French *Vieille Garde* (of Napoleon I)]

Old Guardsman, a member of the Old Guard.

old hand, 1. a very skilled or experienced person; expert: *an old hand at selling, an old hand at swimming.* **2.** (in Australia) an ex-convict. —**old′-hand′,** *adj.*

Old Harry, the Devil.

old hat, 1. out-of-date; old-fashioned: *One of her earliest campaigns had been of the feminist persuasion; it was rather old hat now, but a whiff of it was still not offensive to her* (New Yorker). **2.** familiar; well-known.

Old High German, the form of the German language used in southern Germany from about 800 A.D. to 1100. Modern standard German is descended from Old High German. *Abbr.:* OHG (no periods).

Old Icelandic, the Icelandic language of the Middle Ages; Old Norse.

old identity, (in Australia) a well-known, long-time resident of a place.

old·ie (ōl′dē), *n. Informal.* something old and, often, well-known, as a motion picture or song: . . . *two real oldies, "Little Caesar" (1930) and "Public Enemy" (1931)* (Wall Street Journal). Also, **oldy.**

Old Ionic, the form of the Greek language spoken in the time of Homer. The *Iliad* and *Odyssey* were written in Old Ionic.

Old Irish, the Irish language before 1200 A.D.

Old Ironsides, the American frigate *Constitution,* famous for its exploits in the War of 1812; subject of Oliver Wendell Holmes' poem, "Old Ironsides."

Old Ironsides

old·ish (ōl′dish), *adj.* somewhat old; no longer young: *I'm getting an oldish man* (Arnold Bennett).

old lady, 1. a familiar term for a mother or wife. **2.** a prim, fussy person.

Old Lady, a nickname for the Bank of England: *"The Old Lady" is committed to helping maintain the integrity of the dollar* (Wall Street Journal).

old lag, *British.* a person who has been convicted more than once: . . . *a semi-security centre for old lags regarded as past the escaping age* (Sunday Times).

Old Latin, the Latin language before the 100's B.C.

Old Lights, the members of any of various church parties adhering to old doctrines.

old-line (ōld′līn′), *adj.* **1.** keeping to old ideas and ways; conservative: *an old-line banker.* **2.** having a long history; long established: *an old-line company.* **3.** of an old family or lineage. [American English, perhaps < the *Old-line* regiments, which Maryland contributed in the American Revolutionary War]

old-lin·er (ōld′lī′nər), *n.* an advocate of old or traditional ideas, policies, etc.; conservative: . . . *the straight old-liners, some of them men of fossilized ideas* (Harper's).

Old Line State, a nickname for Maryland.

Old Low German, the form of the German language used in northern Germany and the Netherlands from about 800 A.D. to 1100. Modern Low German is descended from Old Low German.

old maid, 1. a woman who has not married and seems unlikely to. **2.** a prim, fussy person. **3.** a very simple card game in which players draw cards from each other's hands to make pairs. —**Syn. 1.** spinster.

old-maid·ish (ōld′mā′dish), *adj.* like, suggesting, or befitting an old maid; prim; fussy. —**Syn.** spinsterish.

old man, **1.** a familiar term of affection. **2.** a familiar term for a father or husband: *His old man and his uncles also wore the "tools of ignorance"* (Time). **3.** a familiar term for the man in charge of anything, as a school principal, captain of a ship, commander of a military unit, etc.

Old Man of the Sea, **1.** (in *The Arabian Nights*) a horrible old man who clung to the back of Sinbad. **2.** a person or thing that is hard to get rid of.

old-man's-beard (ōld′manz′bird′), *n.*, or **old-man's beard.** **1.** the beard lichen. **2.** the fringe tree. **3.** *British.* a European clematis with fragrant, greenish-white flowers.

old master, **1.** any great painter who lived before 1700: *About suffering they were never wrong, The Old Masters: how well they understood Its human position* (W. H. Auden). **2.** a painting by such a painter.

old moon, the moon when seen as a thin crescent with the hollow side on the right.

Old Nick, the Devil: *"Old Nick" (Niccoló Machiavelli) became in English a synonym for the Devil* (Mary McCarthy).

Old Norse, **1.** the Scandinavian language to about 1300. **2.** the Icelandic language in the Middle Ages; Old Icelandic. *Abbr.:* ON (no periods).

Old North French, the dialects of northern France from the 800's A.D. to the 1500's, especially those of Normandy and Picardy.

Old North State, a nickname of North Carolina.

Old One, the Devil.

Old Order Amish, the conservative branch of the Amish sect, or its members: *For geneticists the fascinating fact about the Old Order Amish . . . is that they all are descended from about 200 immigrants of 200 years ago* (Time).

Ol·do·wan (ol′də wən, ōl′-), *adj.* of or having to do with a pebble culture of eastern Africa that preceded the Abbevillean and Acheulian cultures, represented by tools discovered in Oldoway (or Olduvai) Gorge, Tanganyika; Olduvai. Also, **Olduwan.**

Old Persian, an ancient Iranian language, recorded in cuneiform inscriptions.

Old Pretender, James Stuart, 1688-1766, the son of James II of England, who claimed the throne which William III occupied. (His son, Charles Stuart, 1720-1788, was called the *Young Pretender.*)

Old Provençal, the form of Provençal from about the 1000's A.D. to the 1500's.

Old Prussian, an extinct Baltic language preserved in records of the 1400's and 1500's.

old rose, a rose color with a purplish or grayish tinge.

old-rose (ōld′rōz′), *adj.* of the color old rose.

old salt, an old and experienced sailor: *Old salts insist that the quality of the bluefishing . . . during the summer can be forecast* (New York Times).

Old Saxon, the form of Low German used in northwestern Germany from about 800 A.D. to about 1100.

old school, a group of people who have old-fashioned or conservative ideas: *a doctor of the old school, a lady of the old school.*

old-school (ōld′skül′), *adj.* old-fashioned; conservative: *an old-school doctor, old-school attitudes.*

old school tie, **1.** loyalty among members of a group, especially among graduates of the same school or college. **2.** a necktie worn by members of a group, as a sign of their association and loyalty.

Old Scratch, the Devil.

old-shoe (ōld′shü′), *adj. U.S.* pleasantly casual; informal: *Buchwald's manner is so ingenuous and old-shoe that the subjects of his interviews are soon disarmed into chattering away like old friends* (Time).

old sledge, the card game seven-up.

Old South, *U.S.* the South or its ways of life before the Civil War: *The region south of Baltimore resembles the Old South* (Francis C. Haber).

Old Spanish, the Spanish language from the 1100's A.D. to the 1500's.

old squaw, a long-tailed sea duck of northern regions.

old stager, a person of long experience; veteran; old hand.

old·ster (ōld′stər), *n. Informal.* **1.** an old or older person: *The discreet and sober conversation of the oldsters was much disturbed by the loud laughter of the younger folks* (Henry Kingsley). **2.** (in the British Navy) a midshipman with four years in grade. [< *old* + *-ster*, as in *youngster*]

Old Stone Age, the Paleolithic period.

old story, **1.** a story long told or often repeated; something that has lost all its novelty: *Airplanes are an old story to them. You must find the trip quite an old story.* **2.** a statement, excuse, complaint, or the like, that is repeatedly heard, or a thing that is repeatedly encountered.

old stuff, *Informal.* familiar; well-known: *To the sophisticated grade-schooler now happily on the verge of leaving classroom routine behind, returning to the fold next fall will be old stuff* (New York Times).

old style, a kind of type, such as Garamond, Caslon, etc., characterized by slanting serifs and strokes of almost equal thickness. This sentence is printed in old style.

old-style (ōld′stīl′), *adj.* of or in old style.

Old Style, the method of reckoning time according to the calendar used until 1582, when the date was moved ahead 10 days. In Great Britain the Old Style or Julian calendar was used until 1752, when all dates were moved ahead 11 days. It was used in Russia until 1918. *Abbr.:* O.S.

Old Test., Old Testament.

Old Testament, **1.** the earlier and largest part of the Bible, which contains the religious and social laws of the Hebrews, a record of their history, their important literature, and writings of their prophets. *Abbr.:* O.T. **2.** the covenant between God and the Hebrew people established through Moses on Mount Sinai. Exodus 19:5.

old thing, *British Informal.* a familiar form of address used to a person: *By-bye, old thing* (Arnold Bennett).

old-time (ōld′tīm′), *adj.* of former times; like that of old times: *old-time religion.*

old-tim·er (ōld′tī′mər), *n. Informal.* **1.** a person who has long been a resident, member, worker, etc., and whose experience goes back to an earlier day: *. . . some skilled old-timers at the forge plants earning $10,000 a year* (Time). **2.** a person who favors old ideas and ways: *Old-timers rule the Republican side of Congress* (Wall Street Journal).

old-times (ōld′tīmz′), *adj.* old-time.

old-tim·ey (ōld′tī′mē), *adj. Informal.* **1.** old-time: *They had her in a Sunday-go-to-meeting dress, old-timey looking and too big for her* (New Yorker). **2.** from the old days; veteran: *Our newspaper has an old-timey correspondent in London.*

old top, *British Informal.* a familiar form of address used to a person.

Ol·du·vai (ol′də vā, -wā; ōl′-), *adj.* Oldowan.

Ol·du·wan (ol′də wən, ōl′-), *adj.* Oldowan.

Old Vic, **1.** a British acting company specializing in Shakespearean productions: *London has recently seen a fine Old Vic production of "Ghosts"* (New Yorker). **2.** the theater in which these productions take place: *It is a great shock to find the courts and battlefields of Shakespeare banished from the Old Vic's stage* (Punch).

old·wife (ōld′wīf′), *n., pl.* **-wives,** or **old wife,** **1.** any of various fishes, such as the alewife, menhaden, and certain triggerfish. **2.** the old squaw (duck). [(definition 1) probably variant of *alewife*]

old wives' tale, a foolish story; silly or superstitious belief: *This [body of anthropological fact] came from travelers, missionaries, and soldiers, and formed a collection in which careful and precise description was often combined with folklore and old wives' tales* (Beals and Hoijer).

old-wom·an·ish (ōld′wu̇m′ə nish), *adj.* suggesting or befitting an old woman; fussy.

old-world (ōld′wėrld′), *adj.* **1.** belonging to or characteristic of a former period: *old-world courtesy.* **2.** of or having to do with the ancient world: *The mammoth was an old-world elephant.* **3.** Also, **Old-World.** of or having to do with the Eastern Hemisphere; not American: *old-world folk songs.* —**old′-world′ly,** *adv.*

Old World, **1.** Europe. **2.** Asia and Africa; Eastern Hemisphere.

old·y (ōl′dē), *n., pl.* **old·ies.** oldie.

o·lé or **o·le** (ō lā′, ō′lā), *interj. Spanish.* a cheer of enthusiasm or approval.

-ole, *suffix.* **1.** containing a five-part ring, as in *pyrrole.*
2. belonging to the ethers or aldehydes, as in *anethole.* Also, **-ol.**
[short for Latin *oleum* oil]

o·le·a·ceous (ō′lē ā′shəs), *adj.* belonging to the olive family of plants, including the ash, jasmine, etc. [< New Latin *Oleaceae* the order (< Latin *olea* olive tree, alteration of *olīva* olive) + English *-ous*]

o·le·ag·i·nous (ō′lē aj′ə nəs), *adj.* **1.** oily; greasy: *. . . the oleaginous scum that pollutes the surface of a city river* (Mary E. Braddon). **2.** unctuous: *an oleaginous hypocrite.* [< Latin *oleāginus* (with English *-ous*) of the olive < *olea* olive, alteration of *olīva* olive] —**o′le·ag′i·nous·ness,** *n.*

o·le·ag·i·nous·ly (ō′lē aj′ə nəs lē), *adv.* in an oleaginous manner: *Anyone who tried to play Uriah Heep importantly would miss the essence of an oleaginously obsequious character* (Harper's).

o·le·an·der (ō′lē an′dər), *n.* a poisonous evergreen shrub of the dogbane family, with fragrant red, pink, or white flowers. [< Medieval Latin *oleander;* origin uncertain]

o·le·an·do·my·cin (ō′lē an′də mī′sin), *n.* an antibiotic used in treating infections caused by bacteria, viruses, and other microorganisms, especially those immune to other antibiotics. *Formula:* $C_{35}H_{63}NO_{12}$

o·le·as·ter (ō′lē as′tər), *n.* **1.** a shrub or small tree of southern Europe and western Asia, having fragrant yellow flowers and yellowish olivelike fruit. **2.** the wild form of the olive. [< Latin *oleaster* < *olea* olive tree + *-aster*, a diminutive suffix]

o·le·ate (ō′lē āt), *n.* a salt or ester of oleic acid. [< *ole(ic)* + *-ate*[2]]

o·lec·ra·non (ō lek′rə non, ō′lə krā′-), *n.* a part of the ulna that forms the point of the elbow. [< Greek *ōlékrānon* point of the elbow, short for *ōlenókrānon* < *ōlénē* elbow + *krāníon* head]

o·le·fi·ant (ō′lə fī′ənt), *adj.* forming oil. [< French *oléfiant* < Latin *oleum* oil + *facere* make]

o·le·fin (ō′lə fin), *n.* one of a series of hydrocarbons homologous with ethylene, having the general formula C_nH_{2n}, which form with bromine and chlorine oily bromides and chlorides. [< French *(gaz) oléfiant* oil-forming (gas), ethylene + English *-in*]

o·le·fine (ō′lə fin, -fēn), *n.* olefin.

o·le·fin·ic (ō′lə fin′ik), *adj.* of or having to do with an olefin.

o·le·ic (ō lē′ik, ō′lē-), *adj.* of or derived from oil.

oleic acid, an oily liquid obtained by hydrolyzing various animal and vegetable oils and fats, much used in making soaps. *Formula:* $C_{18}H_{34}O_2$ [< Latin *oleum* (olive) oil (< *olea* olive, alteration of *olīva*) + English *-ic*]

o·le·in (ō′lē in), *n.* **1.** the ester of oleic acid and glycerin, one of the most abundant natural fats. Lard, olive oil, and cottonseed oil are mostly olein. *Formula:* $C_{57}H_{104}O_6$ **2. a.** the liquid or lower melting portions of any fat. **b.** oleic acid. [< Latin *oleum* (olive) oil + English *-in*]

o·le·ine (ō′lē in, -ēn), *n.* **1.** the liquid part of any fat; olein. **2.** oleic acid.

o·lent (ō′lənt), *adj. Archaic.* odorous; scented. [< Latin *olēns, olentis,* present participle of *olēre* to smell]

o·le·o (ō′lē ō), *n.* **1.** oleomargarine: *[The F.T.C.] ordered two oleo manufacturers to stop using ads that might give [a misleading] impression* (New York Times). **2.** oleo oil.

o·le·o·graph (ō′lē ə graf, -gräf), *n.* a chromolithograph made to look like an oil painting: *The . . . portrait . . . is made to look in this setting even more like a cheap oleograph than it usually does* (Listener). [< Latin *oleum* oil + English *-graph*]

o·le·o·graph·ic (ō′lē ə graf′ik), *adj.* of or having to do with oleography. —**o′le·o·graph′i·cal·ly,** *adv.*

o·le·og·ra·phy (ō′lē og′rə fē), *n.* the art or process of preparing oleographs.

o·le·o·mar·ga·rin (ō′lē ō mär′jər in, -gər-), *n.* oleomargarine.

o·le·o·mar·ga·rine (ō′lē ō mär′jər in, -jə-rēn; -gər in, -gə rēn), *n.* a substitute for butter made from animal fats and vegetable oils or from pure vegetable oils; margarine. [American English < French *oléo-margarine* < *oléine* olein + *margarine* margarine (the original substance was thought to be a compound of these two)]

o·le·om·e·ter (ō′lē om′ə tər), *n.* a hydrometer for testing the purity of an oil by means of its density. [< Latin *oleum* oil + English *-meter*]

oleo oil, *U.S.* oil obtained by pressing beef fat, used for making substitutes for butter.

o·le·o·res·in (ō′lē ō rez′ən), *n.* a natural or prepared solution of resin in oil, as that obtained from a plant by means of a volatile solvent. [< Latin *oleum* oil + English *resin*]

o·le·o·res·in·ous (ō′lē ō rez′ə nəs), *adj.* of or like an oleoresin.

oleo strut, a tubular, telescoping strut in the landing gear of an aircraft, which contains a shock absorber consisting of a hollow piston that moves in an oil-filled chamber.

ol·er·a·ceous (ol′ə rā′shəs), *adj.* of or like a potherb or vegetable. [< Latin *holerāceus* (with English *-ous*) < *holus, -eris* potherb]

ol·er·i·cul·tur·al·ly (ol′ər ə kul′chər ə lē), *adv.* with reference to olericulture.

ol·er·i·cul·ture (ol′ər ə kul′chər), *n.* the raising of potherbs and vegetables. [< Latin *holus, -eris* potherb + *cultūra* culture]

o·le·um (ō′lē əm), *n.* a solution of sulfur trioxide and concentrated sulfuric acid, used in dyes and explosives, as an agent in chemical processes, etc. [< New Latin *oleum* < Latin, oil]

O level, *British.* the ordinary level, lowest of three levels of examination given to secondary school students who wish to obtain a General Certificate of Education.

ol·fac·tion (ol fak′shən), *n.* **1.** the act of smelling. **2.** the sense of smell. [< obsolete verb *olfact* (< Latin *olfactus,* past participle *olfacere* smell out, detect < *olēre* emit a smell + *facere* make) + *-ion*]

ol·fac·tive (ol fak′tiv), *adj.* olfactory.

ol·fac·tom·e·ter (ol′fak tom′ə tər), *n.* an instrument for measuring the acuteness of the sense of smell. [< *olfact*(ion) + *-meter*]

ol·fac·to·ry (ol fak′tər ē, -trē), *adj., n., pl.* **-ries.** —*adj.* of smell; having to do with smelling. The nose is an olfactory organ. *holding a book . . . close . . . to her nose, as if with the hope of gaining an olfactory acquaintance with its contents* (Hawthorne).
—*n.* **olfactories, a.** an olfactory organ. **b.** the ability to smell.
[< Latin *olfactōrius* < *olfacere;* see OLFACTION]

ol·fac·tron·ics (ol′fak tron′iks), *n.* the use of electronic instruments to detect and identify anything by its odor: *Eventually olfactronics may be used to guard bank vaults against burglars . . .* (New York Times). [< *olfac*(tory) (elec)*tronics*]

o·lib·a·num (ō lib′ə nəm), *n.* frankincense. [< Medieval Latin *olibanum,* alteration of Late Latin *libanus* frankincense < Greek *líbanos* fragrant gum, the gum-tree.

olig-, *combining form.* the form of **oligo-** before vowels, as in *oligarch.*

ol·i·garch (ol′ə gärk), *n.* one of a small number of persons holding the ruling power in a state: *The oligarchs, the political parties, the middle class . . . hated him* (Newsweek). [< Greek *oligárchēs* < *olígos* few + *árchein* to rule < *archós* leader]

ol·i·gar·chic (ol′ə gär′kik), *adj.* of an oligarchy or oligarchs; having to do with rule by few: *In autocratic or oligarchic societies . . . the moral and intellectual flabbiness of only a few men in the seats of power will lead to the disintegration of great empires* (Harper's). —**ol′i·gar′chi·cal·ly,** *adv.*

ol·i·gar·chi·cal (ol′ə gär′kə kəl), *adj.* oligarchic.

ol·i·gar·chy (ol′ə gär′kē), *n., pl.* **-chies. 1.** a form of government in which a few people have the power: *The Pilgrims at Plymouth Colony were governed by a Puritan oligarchy.* **2.** a country or state having such a government: *Ancient Sparta was really an oligarchy, though it had two kings.* **3.** the ruling few. **4.** any organization, such as a business or a church, having an administration controlled by a few people. [< Greek *oligarchiā,* ultimately < *olígos* few + *árchein* to rule < *archós* leader]

oligo-, *combining form.* small; little; few: *Oligarchy = rule by a few.* Also, **olig-** before vowels. [< Greek *olígos* few]

ol·i·go·car·pous (ol′ə gō kär′pəs), *adj. Botany.* having few fruits. [< *oligo-* + Greek *karpós* fruit + English *-ous*]

Ol·i·go·cene (ol′ə gō sēn), *n.* **1.** the third epoch of the Tertiary period of the Cenozoic era, after the Eocene and before the Miocene. **2.** the rocks formed in this epoch. —*adj.* of this epoch or these rocks. [< *oligo-* + Greek *kainós* new, recent]

ol·i·go·chaete (ol′ə gō kēt), *n.* any of a group of hermaphroditic annelid worms, such as the earthworms and various aquatic groups, having only a few setae projecting from each body segment, and lacking a distinct head. [< New Latin *Oligochaeta* < Greek *olígos* few + *chaítē* bristle]

ol·i·go·chae·tous (ol′ə gō kē′təs), *adj.* having the character of the oligochaetes.

ol·i·go·chrome (ol′ə gō krōm), *adj.* painted or done in few colors, as decorative work. —*n.* a design in a few colors.

ol·i·go·clase (ol′ə gō klās), *n.* a feldspar containing sodium and calcium, occurring in light gray, yellow, or greenish crystals. [< *oligo-* + Greek *klásis* a breaking (because it was thought to be less perfect in cleavage than albite, another feldspar)]

ol·i·go·cy·the·mi·a or **ol·i·go·cy·thae·mi·a** (ol′ə gō sī thē′mē ə), *n.* a form of anemia characterized by a deficiency of red cells in the blood. [< New Latin *oligocythaemia* < Greek *olígos* few + *kýtos* hollow + *haîma* blood]

ol·i·go·my·cin (ol′ə gə mī′sin), *n.* either of three related antibiotics obtained from an actinomycete, used in treating various fungus diseases of animals and plants. [< *oligo-* + *mycin,* as in *streptomycin*]

ol·i·go·phre·ni·a (ol′ə gō frē′nē ə, -frēn′yə), *n.* mental deficiency.

ol·i·go·phren·ic (ol′ə gō fren′ik), *adj.* of, having to do with, or displaying mental deficiency.

ol·i·gop·o·list (ol′ə gop′ə list), *n.* a person or firm that creates or maintains an oligopoly: *The principal defect of present antitrust law is its inability to cope with market power created by jointly acting oligopolists—small groups of large companies that dominate an industry* (New York Times).

ol·i·gop·o·lis·tic (ol′ə gop′ə lis′tik), *adj.* of or having to do with oligopoly.

ol·i·gop·o·ly (ol′ə gop′ə lē), *n., pl.* **-lies.** a condition in which so few producers supply a commodity or service that each of them can influence its price, with or without an agreement between them: *Ultimately, it is the oligopolies and not the State that set the economic priorities of our society* (Manchester Guardian). [< *oligo-* + *-poly,* as in *monopoly*]

ol·i·gop·so·ny (ol′ə gop′sə nē), *n.* a condition in which a few buyers have a strong influence on the demand for a commodity or service. [< *oligo-* + Greek *opsōnía* purchase of food]

ol·i·go·sac·cha·ride (ol′ə gō sak′ə rīd, -ər-id), *n.* a carbohydrate that on hydrolysis yields a relatively small number of monosaccharides as compared to a polysaccharide.

ol·i·go·troph·ic (ol′ə gō trof′ik), *adj.* not providing nutrition, as a lake with scant vegetation.

ol·i·got·ro·phy (ol′ə got′rə fē), *n.* deficiency of nutrition. [< Greek *oligotrophiā* < *olígos* few, little + *tréphein* nourish]

ol·i·gu·re·sis (ol′ə gyu̇ rē′sis), *n.* oliguria.

ol·i·gu·ri·a (ol′ə gyu̇r′ē ə), *n.* insufficient or diminished elimination of urine in relation to intake of fluids. [< New Latin *oliguria* < Greek *olígos* little + *oúrios* of urine < *oûron* urine]

ol·in·go (ol′ing gō), *n.* a mammal related to the raccoon, found from Ecuador to Nicaragua, having golden-brown fur and a bushy tail. [< a native name]

o·li·o (ō′lē ō), *n., pl.* **-os. 1. a.** olla-podrida, a stew. **b.** any dish made of many ingredients. **2.** any mixture; jumble; hodgepodge. **3. a.** a collection of artistic or literary pieces; miscellany: *Ben Jonson, in his "Sejanus and Catiline" has given us this olio of a play* (John Dryden). **b.** a musical medley; potpourri. [< Spanish *olla* pot, stew < Latin *ōlla* pot, jar. Compare OLLA.]

ol·i·to·ry (ol′ə tôr′ē, -tōr′-), *adj.* of or producing potherbs or vegetables. [< Latin *olitōrius* < *olitor* kitchen gardener]

ol·i·va·ceous (ol′ə vā′shəs), *adj.* olive; olive-green. [< Latin *olīva* olive (tree) + English *-aceous*]

ol·i·var·y (ol′ə ver′ē), *adj.* **1.** shaped like an olive. **2.** of or having to do with either of two olive-shaped bodies, one on each side of the anterior surface of the medulla oblongata. [< Latin *olīvārius* of olives < *olīva* olive]

ol·ive (ol′iv), *n.* **1.** a kind of evergreen tree with gray-green leaves, that grows in southern Europe and other warm regions. **2.** the fruit of this tree, with a hard stone and a bitter pulp: *Olives are eaten green or ripe. Olive oil is pressed from olives.* **3.** the wood of the olive tree. **4.** a wreath of olive leaves; olive branch: *I hold the olive in my hand; my words are as full of peace as matter* (Shakespeare). **5. a.** a yellowish green; olive green. **b.** a yellowish brown; olive brown. **6.** a gastropod mollusk with an elongated oval shell, found in tropical seas. —*adj.* **1. a.** yellowish-green. **b.** yellowish-brown. **2.** of the olive.
[< Old French *olive,* learned borrowing from Latin *olīva* olive]

ol·ive-backed thrush (ol′iv bakt′), an American thrush with a grayish or olive-brown back, and a conspicuous eye ring, that breeds chiefly in the coniferous forests of Canada and the northern United States.

olive branch, 1. a branch of the olive tree as an emblem of peace. **2.** anything offered as a sign of peace. **3.** a child: *The wife and olive branches of one Mr. Kenwigs* (Dickens). —Syn. **3.** scion.

Olive Branches
Left, branch of olive tree; right, two olive branches as sign of peace in UN emblem

olive brown, a yellowish-brown color.

ol·ive-brown (ol′iv broun′), *adj.* brown with a yellowish tinge.

olive drab, 1. a dark greenish-yellow color. **2.** a dark greenish-yellow woolen cloth, formerly used by the United States Army for uniforms. *Abbr.:* o.d.

ol·ive-drab (ol′iv drab′), *adj.* of, in, or like olive drab: *Olive-drab slacks of imported corduroy* (New Yorker).

olive family, a group of dicotyledonous trees and shrubs, native to warm and temperate regions. The family includes the olive, ash, jasmine, lilac, forsythia, and fringe tree.

olive green, a dull, yellowish green; olive.

ol·ive-green (ol′iv grēn′), *adj.* dull yellowish-green.

o·liv·en·ite (ō liv′ə nīt, ol′ə və-), *n.* a mineral, an arsenate of copper, usually occurring in olive-green crystals or masses. *Formula:* $Cu_3As_2O_8.Cu(OH)_2$ [< German *Olivenerz* olive ore + English *-ite*[1]]

olive oil, oil pressed from olives, used as food, especially in cooking, in salad dressings, and in medicine, soap making, etc.

Ol·i·ver (ol′ə vər), *n.* one of Charlemagne's heroic followers and a friend of Roland.

olive shell, 1. the elongated oval shell of an olive or gastropod mollusk, having a fine polish and colorful markings. **2.** a mollusk with such a shell.

olive sparrow, an olive-green finch of southern Texas and Mexico, with yellow and reddish markings; Texas sparrow; greenfinch.

ol·i·vette (ol′ə vet′), *n.* a piece of ground planted with olive trees; olive grove. [< French *olivette* < Latin *olīvētum* olive grove]

olive warbler, a grayish-and-white warbler of southwestern United States, Mexico, and Central America, the male of which has a tawny head, neck, and breast. See picture under **warbler.**

ol·ive·wood (ol′iv wu̇d′), *n.* the hard, yellow wood of the olive tree, used in cabinet making, for inlays, etc.

ol·i·vine (ol′ə vēn, ol′ə vēn′), *n.* a chrysolite, especially when greenish; silicate of iron and magnesium: *The rigid mantle of the earth is thought to consist largely of olivine, an insulator under normal conditions* (Science News Letter). [< *oliv*(e) + *-ine*[1]]

ol·la (ol′ə), *n.* **1.** an earthen water jar or cooking pot. **2.** olla-podrida, a stew. [< Spanish *olla* < Latin *ōlla* pot, jar]

ol·la-po·dri·da (ol′ə pə drē′də), *n.* **1.** a stew made from fresh and smoked meats, chicken, chickpeas, onions, garlic, a variety of green vegetables, and seasonings. It is a Spanish national dish eaten throughout the Spanish-speaking world. **2.** a hodgepodge; olio: *And instead of making up an olla-podrida of Gothic and Renaissance . . . they were headstrong and imaginative enough to invent something for themselves* (Nikolaus Pevsner). [< Spanish *olla podrida* (literally) rotten pot < *olla* olla + *podrida* < Latin *putrida* putrid, rotten. Compare POTPOURRI.]

Ol·mec (ōl′mek), *n.* a member of a highly civilized people who lived in southeastern Mexico before the Aztecs, from about 800 B.C. to 200 A.D. —*adj.* of the Olmecs or their culture.

ol·o·gist (ol′ə jist), *n. Informal.* a specialist in any science or branch of knowledge: *. . . the enthronement of the intellectual and the ologist* (Atlantic).

ol·o·gy (ol′ə jē), *n., pl.* **-gies.** *Informal.* any science or branch of knowledge: *Etymology is an unpredictable ology* (New Yorker). [abstracted < words ending in *-ology*]

O·lo·ro·so or **o·lo·ro·so** (ō′lə rō′sō), *n., pl.* **-sos.** a sweet Spanish sherry: *No choice liqueur is so delicious as this rarest of Spanish Olorosos* (Wall Street Journal). [< Spanish *oloroso* (literally) fragrant]

ol·pe (ol′pē), *n.* in ancient Greece: **1.** a leather oil flask, used especially in the palestra. **2.** a small pitcherlike vessel resembling an oinochoe but having a more slender body. [< Greek *ólpē*]

O·lym·pi·ad or **o·lym·pi·ad** (ō lim′pē ad), *n.* **1.** a period of four years reckoned from one celebration of the Olympic games to the next, by which the Greeks computed time from 776 B.C. **2.** a celebration of the modern Olympic games: *As the first man ever to sweep all three Olympic Alpine skiing races . . . Toni Sailer was beyond question the hero of* [*the*] *Olympiad* (Newsweek). [probably < Middle French, Old French *olympiade,* learned borrowing from Latin *Olympias, -adis,* < Greek *Olympiás, -ádos,* ultimately < *Ólympus* the village (where games were held), and the mountain]

O·lym·pi·an (ō lim′pē ən), *adj.* **1.** having to do with Olympia or Mount Olympus; Olympic. **2.** like a god; heavenly. **3.** rather too gracious: *Olympian manners. Kennan himself approached his delicate* [*diplomatic*] *mission with Olympian calm* (Saturday Evening Post).
—*n.* **1.** one of the major Greek gods, led by Zeus, that lived on Mount Olympus. **2.** a contender in the Olympic games.
—**Syn.** *adj.* **3.** magnificent, superior.

Olympian games, Olympic games.

O·lym·pic (ō lim′pik), *adj.* **1.** of or having to do with Olympia in ancient Greece. **2.** of or having to do with Mount Olympus. **3.** of or having to do with the Olympic games: *If he has no bad luck, he can win the Olympic slalom* (Newsweek).

Olympic games, 1. contests in athletics, poetry, and music, held every four years by the ancient Greeks in honor of Zeus. **2.** modern athletic contests in the tradition of the athletic contests of these games. They are held once every four years in a different country, and athletes from many nations compete in them.

O·lym·pics (ō lim′piks), *n.pl.* the Olympic games: *He learned that . . .* [*the*] *two young men were international stars practicing for the Olympics* (New Yorker).

O·lym·pus (ō lim′pəs), *n.* heaven. [< Mount *Olympus,* in Greece, regarded as the home of the Greek deities]

om (ôm), *n.* a Hindu sacred word that symbolizes Brahma, used as a spell, spoken before reciting mantras, or mystically contemplated in its written or spoken form. [< Sanskrit *om*]

O.M., *British.* Order of Merit.

-oma, *suffix, pl.* **-omas** or **-omata.** a growth, as a tumor or neoplasm, as in *adenoma, carcinoma.* [< Greek *-ōma, -ōmatos* a noun suffix]

om·a·dhaun (om′ə dôn, -ᴛʜôn), *n. Irish.* a fool; simpleton.

O·ma·gua (ō mä′gwä), *n., pl.* **-gua** or **-guas.** a member of a small tribe of South American Indians living on the upper Amazon River. The Omagua Indians, who are of Tupi-Guarani stock, were very powerful at the time of the Spanish Conquest.

O·ma·ha (ō′mə hô, -hä), *n., pl.* **-ha** or **-has.** a member of an American Indian tribe of Siouan stock, now living in Nebraska.

O·ma·han (ō′mə hôn, -hän), *n.* a native or inhabitant of Omaha, Nebraska.

O·ma·ni (ō mä′nē), *adj.* of or having to do with Muscat and Oman, a country in southeastern Arabia. —*n.* a native or inhabitant of Muscat and Oman.

o·ma·sum (ō mā′səm), *n., pl.* **-sa** (-sə). the third stomach of a cow or other ruminant; manyplies. It receives the food when swallowed the second time, after having been chewed as a cud. See picture under **abomasum.** [< Latin *omāsum* bullock's tripe]

O·may·yad (ō mī′ad), *n., pl.* **-yads, -ya·des** (-ə dēz). **1.** a member of the dynasty of Moslem caliphs (661-750 A.D.) that preceded the Abbassids and had its seat at Damascus. **2.** a member of a branch of this dynasty which founded the caliphate of Córdoba in Spain (756 A.D.). Also, **Ommiad, Umayyad.**
[< *Omayya,* an ancestor of the first caliph of the dynasty + Greek *-ad,* a noun suffix]

om·ber (om′bər), *n.* **1.** a card game, popular in the 1600's and 1700's, played by three persons with 40 cards, the eights, nines, and tens being left out. **2.** the player who tries to win the pool in this game. [< Spanish *hombre* man (in this game, the challenger) < Latin *homō*]

om·bre[1] (om′bər), *n. Especially British.* omber.

om·bré or **om·bre**[2] (om brā′, om′brā; *French* ôɴ brā′), *adj.* (of a fabric color) running gradually from light to darker shades to give a shaded or striped effect; shadowy; shaded. —*n.* an ombré fabric. [< French *ombré* < *ombre* shadow < Latin *umbra*]

om·bréd or **om·bred** (om brād′, om′brād), *adj.* ombré.

om·bu (om bü′), *n.* a rapidly growing, evergreen, dioecious shade tree of South America, having very dense foliage and a width of up to fifteen feet at the base. [< American Spanish *ombú*]

om·buds·man (om′budz man′, -mən; ombudz′mən), *n., pl.* **-men.** a public official appointed to protect the private rights of citizens, especially by investigating individual complaints against government departments or officials. The office of ombudsman originated in the Scandinavian countries. [< Swedish *ombudsman* (literally) grievance man]

o·meg·a (ō meg′ə; -mē′gə, -mā′-), *n.* **1.** the last of any series; end. **2.** the 24th and last letter of the Greek alphabet (Ω or ω), corresponding to English *O, o,* especially with the sound *ō.* [< Medieval Greek *o mega* large o (because of the length of the vowel)]

omega minus, *Nuclear Physics.* a negatively-charged elementary particle of extremely short life, produced in a nuclear accelerator after its existence and properties were predicted by the eightfold way.

om·e·let or **om·e·lette** (om′ə lit, om′lit), *n.* eggs beaten up with milk or water, fried or baked in very hot oil or butter in a shallow pan, and then folded over on a plate when done, often filled with minced ham, tomato sauce, cheese, etc. [< Middle French *omelette,* alteration of *alemette,* alteration of *alemelle* < Latin *lāmella* (diminutive) < *lāmina* metal plate]

o·men (ō′mən), *n.* **1.** a sign of what is to happen; object or event that is believed to mean good or bad fortune: *Spilling salt is said to be an omen of misfortune. The brave man . . . asks no omen but his country's cause* (Alexander Pope). *Scarce landed, the first omens I beheld Were four white steeds . . . "War, war is threaten'd . . ." My father cried, "where warlike steeds are found"* (John Dryden). **2.** prophetic meaning; foreboding: *birds of evil omen. Some people consider a black cat a creature of ill omen.*
—*v.t.* **1.** to be a sign of; presage; forebode. **2.** to predict as if from omens; divine: *the yet unknown verdict, of which, however, all omened the tragical contents* (Scott).
[< Latin *ōmen*] —**Syn.** *n.* **1.** augury, portent, presage. See **sign.**

o·mened (ō′mənd), *adj.* preceded by or attended with omens.

-omened, *combining form.* containing a —— omen: *Ill-omened = containing an ill omen*

o·men·tal (ō men′təl), *adj.* of or having to do with the omentum.

o·men·tum (ō men′təm), *n., pl.* **-ta** (-tə). a fold of the peritoneum connecting the stomach with certain of the other viscera. The great omentum is attached to the stomach and enfolds the transverse colon; the lesser omentum lies between the stomach and the liver. [< Latin *ōmentum*]

o·mer (ō′mər), *n.* **1.** an ancient Hebrew unit of dry measure, equal to 1/10 of an ephah, about 3½ quarts. **2.** the 49 days between Passover and Shabuoth during which weddings and other celebrations are prohibited to Orthodox Jews, except on the day of Lag Ba'Omer. [< Hebrew *'omer,* confused with *homer*[3]]

o·mer·tà or **o·mer·ta** (ō′mər tä′; *Italian* ō′-mer tä′), *n.* a Sicilian code of honor which forbids informing about crimes thought to be the private affairs of the persons involved. [< Italian (Naples) *omerta,* variant of *umilta* (literally) humility]

om·i·cron (om′ə kron, ō′mə-), *n.* the 15th letter of the Greek alphabet (O or o). [< Greek *ò micrón* small o (because of the shorter length of the vowel)]

om·i·nous (om′ə nəs), *adj.* **1.** of bad omen; unfavorable; threatening: *a dull, ominous rumble* (Bret Harte). *Those clouds look ominous for our picnic.* **2.** of or like an omen; prophetic; portentous: *I feel a thousand fears Which are not ominous of right* (Byron). [< Latin *ōminōsus* (with English *-ous*) < *ōmen, -inis* omen] —**om′i·nous·ly,** *adv.* —**om′i·nous·ness,** *n.* —**Syn. 1.** inauspicious, foreboding.

o·mis·si·ble (ō mis′ə bəl), *adj.* that can be omitted.

o·mis·sion (ō mish′ən), *n.* **1.** an omitting or being omitted: *the omission of a paragraph in copying a story.* **2.** a thing omitted. [< Late Latin *omissiō, -ōnis* < Latin *omittere* omit] —**Syn. 1.** exclusion.

o·mis·sive (ō mis′iv), *adj.* characterized by omission; omitting.

o·mit (ō mit′), *v.t.,* **o·mit·ted, o·mit·ting. 1.** to leave out: *to omit a letter in a word. I must not omit that Sir Roger is a justice of the quorum* (Sir Richard Steele). **2.** to fail to do; neglect: *to omit to say thanks. He omitted to state his reasons.* **3.** *Obsolete.* to let go; lay aside: *Tempests themselves . . . As having sense of beauty, do omit Their mortal natures, letting go safely by The divine Desdemona* (Shakespeare). [< Latin *omittere* < *ob-* by + *mittere* let go, send] —**Syn. 2.** overlook, ignore, skip.

o·mit·tance (ō mit′əns), *n. Archaic.* omission.

om·ma·te·um (om′ə tē′əm), *n., pl.* **-te·a** (-tē′ə). a compound eye of an insect, crustacean, etc. [< New Latin *ommateum* < Greek *ómma, -atos* eye]

om·ma·tid·i·al (om′ə tid′ē əl), *adj.* of or having to do with the ommatidium.

om·ma·tid·i·um (om′ə tid′ē əm), *n., pl.* **-i·a** (-ē ə). one of the radial elements or segments that make up the compound eye of insects, crustaceans, etc. [< New Latin *ommatidium* < Greek *ómma, -atos* eye + Latin *-idium,* a diminutive suffix]

om·mat·o·phore (ə mat′ə fôr, -fōr), *n.* a movable eyestalk, as in certain snails. [< New Latin *ommatophorus* < Greek *ómma, -atos* eye + *-phóros* bearing < *phérein* to bear]

om·ma·toph·o·rous (om′ə tof′ər əs), *adj.* **1.** bearing eyes, as an eyestalk. **2.** functioning as an ommatophore.

Om·mi·ad (ō mī′ad), *n., pl.* **-ads, -a·des** (-ə dēz). Omayyad.

omni-, *combining form.* all; completely: *Omnipotent = all powerful.* [< Latin *omnis* all]

om·ni·a vin·cit a·mor (om′nē ə vin′sit ā′môr), *Latin.* love conquers all.

om·ni·bus (om′nə bus), *n., pl.* **-bus·es,** *adj.* —*n.* **1.** a large vehicle with seats inside and sometimes also on the roof; bus. An omnibus is used for carrying passengers between fixed stations along a route. **2.** a volume of works by a single author, or of works by many authors, usually arranged according to literary types or themes; anthology: *an omnibus of detective stories.* —*adj.* covering many things at once: *an omnibus law.* [< French (*voiture*) *omnibus* common (conveyance) < Latin *omnibus* for all, dative plural of *omnis* all. Compare BUS, AUTOBUS.]

om·ni·com·pe·tence (om′nə kom′pə-təns), *n.* complete or unlimited competence: *America's contemporary welfare state is "exhibiting delusions of omnicompetence"* (Wall Street Journal).

om·ni·com·pe·tent (om′nə kom′pə tənt), *adj.* competent in all matters; legally qualified in all cases: *The younger so-called Communist technocrats . . . trained by an omnipotent but far from omnicompetent state . . .* (Times Literary Supplement).

om·ni·di·rec·tion·al (om′nə də rek′shə-nəl, -dī-), *adj.* directed to or extending in every direction: *an omnidirectional radio beacon, an omnidirectional microphone.*

om·ni·far·i·ous (om′nə fãr′ē əs), *adj.* of all forms, varieties, or kinds: *omnifarious reading.* [< Late Latin *omnifārius* (with English *-ous*) < Latin *omnis* all + *fās, fāris* (originally) pronouncement of divine law < *fārī* speak] —**om′ni·far′i·ous·ness,** *n.*

om·nif·ic (om nif′ik), *adj.* creating all things: *Silence, ye troubled waves, and thou deep, peace, Said then the omnific Word* (Milton). [< Latin *omnis* all + *facere* make]

om·ni·fo·cal (om′nə fō′kəl), *adj.* having continuously varying focal lengths: *Omnifocal lenses eliminate a typical sharp break between lens segments of bifocals* (Chicago Tribune).

om·ni·form (om′nə fôrm), *adj.* of all forms or shapes; taking any form or shape: *the omniform sea.* [< Latin *omniformis* < *omnis* all + *forma* form]

om·ni·form·i·ty (om′nə fôr′mə tē), *n.* omniform quality: *The sole truth of which we must again refer to the divine imagination, in virtue of its omniformity* (Samuel Taylor Coleridge).

om·nig·e·nous (om nij′ə nəs), *adj.* of all kinds: *a vast and omnigenous mass of information* (Cardinal Newman). [< Latin *omnigenus* (with English *-ous*) < *omnis* all + *genus* noun, kind]

om·nip·o·tence (om nip′ə təns), *n.* complete power; unlimited power: *the omnipotence of God, pursuing the guilty sinner* (William Godwin).

Om·nip·o·tence (om nip′ə təns), *n.* God.

om·nip·o·tent (om nip′ə tənt), *adj.* **1.** having all power; almighty: *Alleluia: for the Lord God omnipotent reigneth* (Revelation 19:6). *The Senate was . . . made omnipotent and irresponsible* (James A. Froude). **2.** capable of anything; utter: *The most omnipotent villain that ever cried "Stand" to a true man* (Shakespeare). —*n.* an omnipotent being. [< Latin *omnipotēns, -potentis* < *omnis* all + *potēns*, present participle of *posse* be able] —**om·nip′o·tent·ly,** *adv.*

Om·nip·o·tent (om nip′ə tənt), *n.* God: *Boasting I could subdue The Omnipotent* (Milton).

om·ni·pres·ence (om′nə prez′əns), *n.* presence everywhere at the same time: *God's omnipresence. His omnipresence fills Land, sea, and air* (Milton). —**Syn.** ubiquity.

om·ni·pres·ent (om′nə prez′ənt), *adj.* **1.** present everywhere at the same time; ubiquitous: *the omnipresent God* (William Godwin). **2.** found everywhere: *the omnipresent Times newspaper* (Alexander W. Kinglake). [< Medieval Latin *omnipraesēns, -praesentis* < Latin *omnis* all + *praesēns* present, adjective]

om·ni·range (om′nə rānj′), *n.* a navigational system for aircraft, in which position is determined by picking up omnidirectional radio signals from a ground station.

om·nis·cience (om nish′əns), *n.* knowledge of everything; complete or infinite knowledge: *For many patients the notion that the doctor lacks omniscience or omnipotence in his domain is extremely disturbing* (Scientific American). *Science is his forte and omniscience his foible* (Sydney Smith). [< Medieval Latin *omniscientia* < Latin *omnis* all + *scientia* knowledge < *sciēns, -entis*, present participle of *scīre* to know]

Om·nis·cience (om nish′əns), *n.* God: *the eye of Omniscience.*

om·nis·cient (om nish′ənt), *adj.* knowing everything; having complete or infinite knowledge: *By no means trust to your own judgment alone; for no man is omniscient* (Francis Bacon). —**om·nis′cient·ly,** *adv.*

Om·nis·cient (om nish′ənt), *n.* God.

om·ni·tude (om′nə tüd, -tyüd), *n.* the state or fact of being or comprising all; universality. [< Latin *omnis* all + *-tude*]

om·ni·um·gath·er·um (om′nē əm gaᴛʜ′ər əm), *n.* a miscellaneous collection; confused mixture: *I reached for the stout omnium-gatherum book of notabilia I had been reading in bed the night before* (J.W.R. Scott). [< Latin *omnium* of all, genitive plural of *omnis* + *gatherum*, a Latinization coined from English *gather*] —**Syn.** medley.

om·ni·vore (om′nə vôr, -vōr), *n.* an omnivorous animal or person.

om·niv·o·rous (om niv′ər əs), *adj.* **1.** eating every kind of food. **2.** eating both animal and vegetable food: *Man is an omnivorous animal.* **3.** taking in everything; fond of all kinds: *An omnivorous reader reads all kinds of books.* [< Latin *omnivorus* (with English *-ous*) < *omnis* all + *vorāre* eat greedily] —**om·niv′o·rous·ly,** *adv.* —**om·niv′o·rous·ness,** *n.*

omnivorous looper, a kind of measuring worm native to California, that feeds on a large variety of trees and shrubs, especially the avocado. It is yellow, green, or pink, with various colored markings on the body.

o·mo·pha·gi·a (ō′mə fā′jē ə), *n.* the eating of raw flesh or raw food. [< New Latin *omophagia*]

o·mo·phag·ic (ō′mə faj′ik), *adj.* omophagous.

o·moph·a·gist (ō mof′ə jist), *n.* an eater of raw flesh.

o·moph·a·gous (ō mof′ə gəs), *adj.* eating raw flesh or raw food. [< Greek *ōmophágos* < *ōmós* raw + *phágos* eating < *phageîn* eat]

o·mo·plate (ō′mə plāt), *n.* the shoulder blade or scapula. [< French *omoplate* < Greek *ōmoplátē* < *ômos* shoulder + *plátē* flat surface]

Om·pha·le (om′fə lē), *n. Greek Mythology.* a queen of Lydia whom Hercules had to serve for three years, dressed as a woman, to atone for a murder.

om·pha·li·tis (om′fə lī′tis), *n.* inflammation of the navel in young animals. [< Greek *omphalós* navel + English *-itis*]

om·pha·los (om′fə ləs), *n., pl.* **-li** (-lī). **1.** the navel. **2.** a central point or part; center; hub. **3.** a round or conical stone in the temple of Apollo at Delphi, believed by the ancient Greeks to mark the center of the earth. [< Greek *omphalós* navel, boss[2], hub]

Omphalos (def. 3)
Apollo seated on the Omphalos
(from Greek vase)

om·pha·lo·skep·sis (om′fə lō skep′sis), *n.* the act of gazing steadily at one's navel in the process of mystical contemplation: *Omphaloskepsis, then, is no longer the métier of only the Buddhists* (Time). [< Greek *omphalós* navel + *sképsis* a looking at]

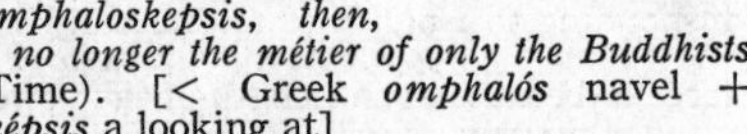

O.M.S., output per man-shift.

on (on, ôn), *prep.* **1.** above and supported by: *to stand on one foot, to ride on a train. The book is on the table.* **2.** touching so as to cover, be around, etc.: *a blister on one's heel, shoes on one's feet, a ring on one's finger.* **3.** close to; near: *a house on the shore, to border on absurdity.* **4.** in the direction of; toward: *The workers marched on the capitol.* **5.** against; upon: *the picture on the wall.* **6.** by means of; by the use of: *to talk on the telephone. This news is on good authority.* **7.** in the condition of; in the process of; in the way of: *on half pay, on fire, on purpose, on duty, on sale.* **8.** at the time of; during: *They greeted us on our arrival.* **9.** in relation to; in connection with; concerning: *a book on animals, a poem on winter.* **10.** for the purpose of: *He went on an errand.* **11.** in addition to: *Defeat on defeat discouraged them.* **12.** among: *on a committee, on a team.* **13.** indicating risk or liability: *on pain of death.*

—*adv.* **1.** on something: *The walls are up, and the roof is on. Put on a clean shirt.* **2.** to something: *Hold on, or you may fall.* **3.** toward something: *Some played; the others looked on.* **4.** farther: *March on.* **5.** in or into a condition, process, manner, action, etc.: *Turn on the gas.* **6.** from a time; forward: *later on, from that day on.*

and so on. See under **so**[1], *adv.*

on and off, now and then: *He looked out of the window on and off.*

on and on, without stopping: *The President showed signs of restlessness as the oratory went on and on throughout the afternoon* (New York Times).

—*adj.* **1.** taking place: *The race is on.* **2.** near: *the on side.* **3.** (of a brake) operating etc. **4.** *Cricket.* of or on the side of the wicket or the field on which the batsman stands.

on to, *Slang.* aware of the truth about: *Some of the kids are sweet, though I have a feeling they're on to me* (Punch).

—*n. Cricket.* the on side.

[Old English *on,* also *an* in, on, into. Compare ᴀ-[1].]

ON (no periods), **O.N.,** or **ON.,** Old Norse.

O·na (ō′nə), *n., pl.* **-na** or **-nas.** a member of a tribe of American Indians formerly living on the island of Tierra del Fuego at the southernmost tip of South America: *The Ona hunted the guanaco, a small wild relative of the llama* (Charles Wagley).

on-a·gain off-a·gain, or **on-a·gain-off-a·gain** (on′ə gen′ ôf′ə gen′; ôn′-; -of′-), *adj.* that is not steadily pursued or carried out; wavering; faltering; inconclusive; unresolved: *The fund was meant to free economic aid from the jerking, jolting, on-again-off-again procedures imposed by the annual cycle of appropriations* (Economist).

on·a·ger (on′ə jər), *n., pl.* **-gri** (-grī), **-gers.** **1.** a wild ass of the dry plains of western central Asia, light brownish with a black stripe along its back. **2.** an ancient and medieval machine of war for throwing stones. [< Latin *onager* < Greek *ónagros* < *ónos ágrios* ass of the fields]

Onager (def. 1)
(from 3½ to 4 ft. high at the shoulder)

on·a·gra·ceous (on′ə grā′shəs), *adj.* belonging to the evening-primrose family. [< New Latin *Onagraceae* the family name < *Onagra* the former typical genus < Latin *onagra*, feminine of *onager* onager]

on-and-off (on′ən ôf′, ôn′-; -of′), *adj.* off-and-on: *After on-and-off contract negotiations for several months, the union called a strike* (Wall Street Journal).

o·nan·ism (ō′nə niz əm), *n.* **1.** masturbation. **2.** sexual intercourse stopped suddenly before ejaculation. [< *Onan* (see Genesis 38:9) + *-ism*]

o·nan·ist (ō′nə nist), *n.* a person who practices onanism.

on-board (on′bôrd′, -bōrd′; ôn′-), *adj.* on or within a vehicle; installed aboard: *The Gemini 5 rendezvous experiment will be the first to use an on-board computer linked with on-board radar* (New York Times).

O.N.C., Ordinary National Certificate (the O-level diploma in Great Britain).

once (wuns), *adv.* **1.** one time: *He comes once a day. Read it once more. A man can die but once* (Shakespeare). **2.** at some one time in the past; formerly: *a once powerful nation. That big man was once a little baby.* **3.** even a single time; ever: *if the facts once become known; once seen, never forgotten.* **4.** *Archaic.* at some future time: *meditating that she must die once* (Shakespeare).

once and again, repeatedly: *That good woman would open the door once and again in the morning, and put her head through* (Mrs. Humphry Ward).

once (and) for all. See under **all,** *n.*

once in a while. See under **while,** *n.*

once or twice, a few times: *So the merchants . . . lodged without Jerusalem once or twice* (Nehemiah 13:20).

once upon a time. See under **time,** *n.*

—*n.* a single occasion: *I think he might as well have favoured me this once* (Shelley).

all at once, suddenly: *All at once the sun disappeared and rain began to fall.*

at once, a. immediately: *You must come at once.* **b.** at one and the same time: *All three boys spoke at once.*

for once, for one time at least: *For once I wasn't thinking of you. I had other things in mind* (Graham Greene).

—*conj.* if ever; whenever: *Most boys like to swim once they have learned how.*

—*adj.* former: *a once friend.*

[Middle English *ones,* or *anes,* Old English *ānes, ǣnes* < *ān* one + adverbial genitive *-es*] —**Syn.** *adj.* quondam.

once-o·ver (wuns′ō′vər), *n. Informal.* short, quick look, as for inspection, evaluation, etc.: *to give the new plans a quick once-over.*

once-o·ver-light·ly (wuns′ō′vər līt′lē), *n. Informal.* a light or superficial look, survey, etc.; a casual once-over: *The religious essays . . . are a once-over-lightly in the principles of Catholicism* (Time). —*adj.* superficial; casual: *once-over-lightly coverage of the news.*

on·cho·cer·ci·a·sis (ong′kō sėr sī′ə sis), *n.* a tropical disease that causes nodules under the skin and lesions of the eye which may result in blindness; river blindness. It is caused by a filarial worm whose carrier is a gnat. [< New Latin *Onchocera* genus of nematode that causes the disease (< Greek *ónkos* barb + *kérkos* tail) + English *-iasis*]

on·cid·i·um (on sid′ē əm), *n.* any of a group of tropical American epiphytic orchids. Some kinds have flowers resembling butterflies. [< New Latin *oncidium* < Greek *ónkos* barb of an arrow (because of the shape of the corolla) + Latin *-idium*, a diminutive suffix]

on·co·gen·ic (ong′kə jen′ik), *adj.* tending to produce tumors: *No . . . evidence is yet available to suggest that human breast cancer is actually caused by a milk-transmitted oncogenic virus* (New Scientist). [< Greek *ónkos* tumor; mass, bulk + English *-gen* + *-ic*]

on·co·log·ic (ong′kə loj′ik), *adj.* oncological.

on·co·log·i·cal (ong′kə loj′ə kəl), *adj.* of or having to do with oncology: *The U.S.S.R. has embarked on a nationwide specialist oncological service to deal with all growth disorders, benign and malignant* (London Times).

on·col·o·gy (ong kol′ə jē), *n.* the branch of medicine dealing with the study of tumors. [< Greek *ónkos* tumor; mass, bulk + English *-logy*]

on·co·lyt·ic (ong′kə lit′ik), *adj.* of or having to do with the destruction of cells comprising a tumor: *These oncolytic properties could effect permanent cure of cancer in animals and humans, he believes* (Science News Letter). [< Greek *ónkos* tumor; mass, bulk + English *lytic*]

on·com·ing (on′kum′ing, ôn′-), *adj.* approaching; advancing: *oncoming winter, the oncoming tide, oncoming traffic.* —*n.* approach; advance: *the oncoming of the storm; the oncoming of numbness* (George Eliot).

ondes Mar·te·not (ōnd′ mär tə nō′), *pl.* **ondes Mar·te·not** (ōnd′ mär tə nō′). an electrophonic keyboard instrument: *the seductive wailing whistle of two ondes Martenot* (London Times). [< French *ondes Martenot* (literally) waves of Martenot, after the inventor, Maurice *Martenot*, a French musician]

on·ding (on′ding′), *n. Scottish.* a very heavy fall of rain or snow. [< *on* + Scottish *ding* rain heavily, probably < Scandinavian (compare Icelandic *dengya* to hammer, beat)]

on dit (ôn dē′), *French.* **1.** they say; it is said. **2.** a piece of gossip; report: *I thought it was a mere on dit* (Benjamin Disraeli).

on·do·gram (on′də gram), *n.* a record made by an ondograph.

on·do·graph (on′də graf, -gräf), *n.* an instrument for recording the oscillatory variations of electric currents, especially of alternating currents. [< French *onde* wave (< Latin *unda*) + English *-graph*]

on·dom·e·ter (on dom′ə tər), *n.* a device for measuring the length of radio waves. [< French *onde* wave (< Latin *unda*) + English *-meter*]

one (wun), *n.* **1.** the first and lowest whole number; 1. **2.** a single person or thing indicated: *I gave him the one he wanted. I like the ones in that box. Is this the one I gave you? Are you the one who is going to help?*

at one, in agreement or harmony: *Where Conservative and Labour critics of the Government's policy are at one is their common belief that the Prices and Incomes Bill will not achieve the restraints which the Government desires* (Manchester Guardian Weekly).

make one, a. to form or be one of a number, assembly, or party: *I made one upon that winter's journey of which so many tales have gone abroad* (Robert Louis Stevenson). **b.** to join together; unite in marriage: *The parson pronounced the words that made the couple one.*

one and all, everyone: *Towards this great end it behooves us one and all to work* (London Daily News).

one by one, one after another: *It was a hot day, and Whitey stripped to his shorts and rubbed his charges, one by one* (New Yorker).

one up on, *Informal.* an advantage over: *Ever since the Russians put Sputnik I into orbit in 1957 the United States and Soviet Union have been trying to get one up on each other in the space race* (Observer).

—*adj.* **1.** being a single unit or individual: *one apple, one dollar. A man has one head and one neck.* **2.** some: *One day he will be sorry.* **3.** of a single kind, nature, or character; the same: *They held one opinion. Graphite and diamond are chemically one substance.* **4.** joined together; united: *They replied in one voice.* **5.** a certain; particular: *One John Smith was elected.*

all one, just the same: *'Twere all one That I should love a bright particular star, And think to wed it, he is so above me* (Shakespeare).

—*pron.* **1.** some person or thing: *Two may go, but one must stay. One of the poems was selected for the book.* **2.** any person or thing: *One must work hard to achieve success. One does not like to be left out.* **3.** the same person or thing: *Doctor Jekyll and Mr. Hyde were one and the same.*

[Old English *ān*. Compare A², AN¹.]

—**Syn.** *adj.* **1.** a, any. **3.** identical. **4.** undivided.

➔ **one.** The use of the impersonal pronoun *one,* especially when repeated, is characteristically formal: *One can't be too careful, can one?*

-one, *suffix.* ketone, as in *acetone, progesterone.* [< Greek *-ōnē*, a feminine suffix]

one-act·er (wun′ak′tər), *n. Informal.* a one-act play or opera: *Thornton Wilder has gone to Europe for peace and quiet to finish up his six one-acters called "The Seven Deadly Sins"* (Saturday Review).

one another, one the other: *They struck at one another. They were in one another's way.*

➔ **one another, each other.** As a reciprocal pronoun, *one another* is usually used with reference to more than two, *each other* with reference to two: *The members of the team support one another. The two hate each other.*

one-arm bandit (wun′ärm′), *U.S. Slang.* a gambling device having a lever at one side, operated by dropping a coin into a slot; slot machine: *Undaunted tourists kept yanking undaunted one-arm bandits* (Time).

one-armed bandit (wun′ärmd′), *U.S. Slang.* one-arm bandit.

one-celled (wun′seld′), *adj.* having only one cell: *The one-celled protozoa have no nerves and no complex cellular sense organs* (Science News Letter).

one-di·men·sion·al (wun′də men′shə nəl), *adj.* **1.** having no depth; of little scope; not profound; fanciful: *Their stereotypes, their one-dimensional world of bad men and good men, prevent growth in understanding of one's self and other people* (New York Times). **2.** having only one dimension: *Time is one-dimensional.* —**one′-di·men′sion·al·ly,** *adv.*

one-eyed (wun′īd′), *adj.* **1.** having only one eye: . . . *Cyclops, the one-eyed giant* (Theodore H. Ingalls). **2.** blind in one eye.

one·fold (wun′fōld′), *adj.* consisting of but one; single; simple.

one-for-one (wun′fər wun′), *adj.* one-to-one.

one-hand·ed (wun′han′did), *adj.* **1.** having or using only one hand: *a one-handed clock.* **2.** used, worked, or performed with one hand: . . . *spectacular one-handed catches* (New Yorker). —*adv.* with one hand: *He was caught . . . finishing his stroke one-handed* (London Times).

one-horse (wun′hôrs′), *adj.* **1.** drawn or worked by a single horse: *a little one-horse sleigh* (Harriet Beecher Stowe). **2.** using or having only a single horse: *a one-horse farmer.* **3.** *Informal.* of little scope, capacity, or importance; minor: *a one-horse town; some one-horse junction near the Dutch frontier that I can't even learn the name of* (H. G. Wells).

O·nei·da (ō nī′də), *n., pl.* **-da** or **-das. 1.** a member of an American Indian tribe of Iroquoian stock formerly living in New York State. **2.** the language of this tribe. [American English < reduction of Iroquoian (Oneida) *tiionĕñ′iote′* "standing rock" (because such a rock was a landmark near one of their villages)]

o·nei·ric (ō nī′rik), *adj.* of or having to do with dreams.

o·nei·ro·crit·ic (ō nī′rə krit′ik), *n.* an interpreter of dreams.

o·nei·ro·crit·i·cal (ō nī′rə krit′ə kəl), *adj.* having to do with or practicing the interpretation of dreams. [< Greek *oneirokritikós* (< *óneiros* dream + *kritikós* critic, student (of) < *krítēs* a judge < *krīnein* to judge) + English *-al*¹]

o·nei·ro·crit·i·cism (ō nī′rə krit′ə siz əm), *n.* the art of interpreting dreams.

o·nei·ro·crit·ics (ō nī′rə krit′iks), *n.* oneirocriticism.

o·nei·rol·o·gy (ō′nī rol′ə jē), *n.* the science or subject of dreams, or of their interpretation. [< Greek *óneiros* dream + English *-logy*]

o·nei·ro·man·cer (ō nī′rə man′sər), *n.* a person who divines by dreams.

o·nei·ro·man·cy (ō nī′rə man′sē), *n.* divination by dreams. [< Greek *óneiros* dream + *manteíā* divination < *mántis* seer]

one-leg·ged (wun′leg′id, -legd′), *adj.* **1.** having only one leg: . . . *one-legged, pedestal-based chairs, dining tables and coffee tables that have all the weightless elegance of a stemmed wine glass* (Time). **2.** one-sided: *a one-legged argument.*

one-lin·er (wun′lī′nər), *n.* a snappy or pithy remark, usually of one sentence; wisecrack: *He even scored with an old one-liner about banks: "Never trust a place where they pull the shades down at three o'clock in the afternoon"* (Time).

one-lung (wun′lung′), *adj.* **1.** having only one lung. **2.** *Slang.* having only one cylinder: *The rice comes down to Bangkok . . . in boats powered by one-lung motors* (Harper's).

one-man (wun′man′), *adj.* **1.** consisting of only one person; exercised or managed by only one man: *a one-man rule or dictatorship, a one-man job.* **2.** of or for a single person; designed to be carried, worn, used, etc., by one man: *a one-man submarine.*

one-man show, an exhibition of the work of one man; display or performance of the skill of a particular man: *One-man shows of painting opening tomorrow include those of work by Picasso* (New York Times).

one·ness (wun′nis), *n.* **1.** singleness. **2.** sameness; identity: *the solidarity and oneness of humanity* (John Greenleaf Whittier). **3.** unity; union: *the oneness of marriage.* **4.** agreement; harmony: *oneness of mind.* —**Syn. 1.** individuality.

one-night·er (wun′nī′tər), *n. U.S.* **1.** a one-night stand: *A few units like Dave Brubeck's and the Modern Jazz Quartet are spending an increasing amount of their time playing one-nighters* (Nat Hentoff). **2.** an actor or performer who plays one-night stands.

one-night stand (wun′nīt′), *U.S.* **1.** a show for one night in a town by a touring company of actors or other performers. **2.** the place where such a show is given.

one-o-cat or **one-o'-cat** (wun′ə kat′), *n.* a ball game in which there is one batter, 3 to 6 fielders, a pitcher, and one base in addition to home plate. It is a forerunner of baseball. *He spells me increasingly in romps and games of one-o-cat* (New Yorker).

one old cat, one-o-cat.

one-piece (wun′pēs′), *adj.* of or in one piece; not having separate parts: *a one-piece garment.*

one-piec·er (wun′pē′sər), *n.* a one-piece garment.

on·er (wun′ər), *n.* **1.** *Slang.* a person or thing of a unique or remarkable kind. **2.** *Slang.* a person expert at or much addicted to something: *Miss Sally's such a oner for that* (Dickens). **3.** *Informal.* something known by or in some way connected with the number one.

one-reel·er (wun′rē′lər), *n. U.S.* a short motion picture, as a newsreel or cartoon, contained in a single reel of film that runs approximately twelve minutes.

on·er·ous (on′ər əs), *adj.* **1.** burdensome; oppressive; troublesome: *Overtime work is well paid, but it is often onerous.* **2.** *Law.* of the nature of a legal burden or obligation. [< Old French *onereus* (with English *-ous*), learned borrowing from Latin *onerōsus* < *onus, -eris* burden] —**on′er·ous·ly,** *adv.* —**on′er·ous·ness,** *n.* —**Syn. 1.** heavy, weighty, arduous.

one·self (wun self′, wunz-), *pron.* one's own self: *One should not praise oneself. To be pleased with oneself is the surest way of offending everybody else* (Edward G. Bulwer-Lytton).

be oneself, a. to have full control of one's mind or body: *He was not himself after he heard the news that his son had been in a serious accident.* **b.** to act naturally: *Be yourself and stop putting on airs.*

by oneself, a. having no company; alone: *To sit down to dinner all by oneself!* (Anthony Trollope). **b.** single-handed; unaided: *It was the first time that he did his homework by himself, without any help whatever.*

one-shot (wun′shot′), *U.S. Informal.* —*adj.* **1.** intended for use on only one occasion, and sometimes as a quick, temporary measure: *The one-shot boycott was a low-pressure affair* (Wall Street Journal). **2.** undertaken, issued, or occurring one time only; formed for a single project or venture: *a one-shot magazine. Solutions will not be easy, one-shot solutions* (Saturday Review).

—*n.* **1.** a magazine or booklet, issued once, and usually devoted to a subject popular at the moment: *Sputnik's beep-beep already has signaled the start of a bunch of one-shots on space travel, satellites, moon missions* (Wall Street Journal). **2.** a single subject or theme to the exclusion or neglect of others: *The*

Western was the one-shot of last season's television. **3.** anything done or occurring only once: *His attempt to cross the English Channel was a one-shot, but he tried the Thames more than once.*

one-sid·ed (wun′sī′did), *adj.* **1.** seeing only one side of a question; partial: *The umpire seemed one-sided in his decisions.* **2.** uneven; unequal: *If one team is much better than the other, a game is one-sided.* **3.** having but one side. **4.** on only one side. **5.** having one side larger or more developed than the other. **6.** *Law.* involving but one side; unilateral: *a one-sided obligation.* —**one′-sid′ed·ly,** *adv.* —**one′-sid′ed·ness,** *n.* —**Syn. 1.** unfair, prejudiced.

one's self, oneself.

one-step (wun′step′), *n., v.,* **-stepped, -step·ping.** —*n.* **1.** a dance much like a quick walk. Its original version, popular in the 1920's, was based on the turkey trot. **2.** the music for it, in two-quarter time. —*v.i.* to dance the one-step.

one·time (wun′tīm′), *adj.* of the past; former: *a onetime millionaire; the onetime home of one of the nation's great amateur scientists* . . . (Scientific American).

one-to-one (wun′tə wun′), *adj.* of or having to do with a relationship between two groups of elements such that every element of each is paired with one and only one element of the other: *The correspondence between a list of five boys' names and the five boys whose names are listed is one-to-one.*

one-track (wun′trak′), *adj.* **1.** having only one track: *a one-track railroad line.* **2.** *Informal.* understanding or doing only one thing at a time; narrow: *a one-track mind.*

one-two (wun′tü′), *n.* **1.** (in boxing) two punches given in quick succession, usually one with the left hand followed by one with the right hand: *a lightning one-two on the jaw.* **2.** *Slang.* a quick retort: *He countered each question with a stunning one-two.*

one-up (wun′up′), *v.t.,* **-upped, -up·ping.** *Informal.* to gain one up on; outstrip: *The party's 46-year-old leader . . . one-upped the socialists by endorsing the Saskatchewan plan* (Canada Month).

one-up·man·ship (wun′up′mən ship), *n.* *Informal.* the skill of being able to gain the advantage over one's opponent: *Committees have their inhibitions—compromise, diplomacy, and careful one-upmanship* (Wall Street Journal). [< *one up* (*on*), idiom; patterned on *gamesmanship*]

one-way (wun′wā′), *adj.* **1.** moving or allowing movement in only one direction: *one-way traffic, a one-way street, a one-way ticket.* **2.** leading or developing in only one direction: *a one-way argument.* **3.** that works in only one direction: *One-way glass looks like a mirror on one side but can be seen through on the other side.*

one world or **One World,** the idea that the world is a single unit in which a way must be found to keep it going and make it safe for different opinions: *He agreed . . . that the one world concept of Mr. Willkie was largely misunderstood today* (New York Times).

one-world·er (wun′wėrl′dər), *n.* *U.S. Informal.* a person who favors internationalism: *In both parties, the one-worlders . . . have taken a licking* (New Yorker).

one-world·ism (wun′wėrl′diz əm), *n.* *Informal.* internationalism: *A new group, firm in their old belief that foreign entanglements are dangerous, . . . will combat . . . one-worldism and Communism in America* (Time).

one-world·ness (wun′wėrld′nis), *n.* the state or condition of having internationalism.

on·fall (on′fôl′, ôn′-), *n.* an onset; attack: *I was all strung up to meet and to resist an onfall* (Robert Louis Stevenson).

on·flow (on′flō′, ôn′-), *n.* an onward flow.

on-glide (on′glīd′, ôn′-), *n.* *Phonetics.* a transitional sound produced at the movement of the articulars to a position for a speech sound different from their first position.

on·go·ing (on′gō′ing, ôn′-), *adj.* continuous; uninterrupted.
—*n.* **ongoings,** goings on: *It breaks my heart to hear you upholding such ongoings* (Samuel R. Crockett).

ONI (no periods), *U.S.* Office of Naval Intelligence.

on·ion (un′yən), *n.* **1.** the bulb of a plant of the amaryllis family, having a sharp, strong smell and taste, and eaten raw or used in cooking. The bulb is formed of concentric layers of modified leaves. *Indeed, the tears live in an onion that should water this sorrow* (Shakespeare). **2.** the plant it grows on. **3.** any of various similar or related plants.
know one's onions, *Informal.* to have the knowledge and skill necessary for competence: *The author is a little pretentious . . . but on the whole he does know his onions* (T.S. Eliot).
[< Old French *oignon* < Latin *uniō, -ōnis* onion] —**on′ion·like′,** *adj.*

onion fly, a dipterous insect whose larva feeds underground on the onion.

onion maggot, the larva of an onion fly.

on·ion·skin (un′yən skin′), *n.* a very thin, translucent paper used especially for carbon copies.

on·ion·y (un′yə nē), *adj.* having the taste or smell of onions; onionlike: *Some bacterial cultures produce distinct fruity and oniony odors* (Science News Letter).

on-li·cence or **on-li·cense** (on′lī′səns, ôn′-), *n.* *British.* a license for the sale of alcoholic liquor to be consumed on the premises.

on·li·est (ōn′lē ist), *adj.,* superlative of **only.** best; finest: *I went there on the one and onliest trip I made on a tanker, when I was younger'n Davy* (New Yorker).

on-line (on′līn′, ôn′-), *adj.* **1. a.** (of equipment associated with an electronic computer) operating under the direct control of the central equipment. **b.** operating in real-time. **2.** (of a railroad operation, service, etc.) being or taking place on the regular line. —*adv.* under the direct control of central equipment: [*The*] *computer is connected "on-line" to the plant* (London Daily Telegraph).

on·look·er (on′lu̇k′ər, ôn′-), *n.* a person who watches without taking part: *It is the onlooker that sees most of the game* (Macmillan's Magazine). —**Syn.** bystander.

on·look·ing (on′lu̇k′ing, ôn′-), *adj., n.* watching; seeing; noticing.

on·ly (ōn′lē), *adj.* **1.** by itself or themselves; sole, single, or few of the kind or class: *an only son.* **2.** best; finest: *She is the only woman for me. He is the only writer for my taste. He is the only man of Italy, Always excepted my dear Claudio* (Shakespeare).
—*adv.* **1.** merely; just: *He sold only two.* **2.** and no one else; and nothing more; and that is all: *Only he remained. I did it only through friendship.*
if only, I wish: *If you would only say yes. If only wars would cease!*
only too, very: *She was only too glad to help.*
—*conj.* *Informal.* except that; but: *I would have gone only you objected.*
[Old English *ānlīc, ǣnlīc*]
—**Syn.** *adj.* **1.** solitary, unique. See **single.**
➔ **Only** and several other limiting adverbs such as *scarcely* and *just* are often placed immediately before the verb even when they modify some other element in the sentence: *I only know this* (instead of *I know only this*); *I only see them when I go to New York* (instead of *only when I go to New York*); *I scarcely had enough time to finish* (instead of *scarcely enough time*). Although this construction has often been condemned as illogical and ambiguous, it has been firmly established for centuries, both in literary English and in ordinary speech. In actual fact, this word order is rarely ambiguous: in speaking, stress and intonation make clear which element is modified by the adverb; in writing, the context ordinarily excludes all meanings but the one intended.

on·ly-be·got·ten (ōn′lē bi got′ən), *adj.* begotten as an only child.

on·o·mas·tic (on′ə mas′tik), *adj.* **1.** of or connected with a name or names, or with the naming of something: *Naming a horse is not an easy matter . . . The result was that for the seven years we had him the onomastic question remained pending* (New Yorker). **2.** *Law.* designating the signature of a legal document the body of which is in the handwriting of another person. [< Greek *onomastikós* < *onomázein* to name < *ónoma* name]

on·o·mas·ti·con (on′ə mas′tə kon), *n.* a vocabulary of names, especially of persons, arranged in alphabetical or other order.

on·o·mas·tics (on′ə mas′tiks), *n.* the study of names.

on·o·mat·o·poe·ia (on′ə mat′ə pē′ə), *n.* **1.** the formation of a name or word by imitating the sound associated with the thing designated, as in *buzz, hum, cuckoo, hiss, slap, splash.* **2.** a word or phrase so formed. **3.** the adaptation of the sound to the sense for rhetorical effect. *Examples:* The tintinnabulation that so musically wells From the bells (Edgar Allan Poe). The double double double beat of the thundering drum (John Dryden). [< Latin *onomatopoeia* < Greek *onomatopoiīā* < *ónoma* word, name + *poieîn* make, do]

on·o·mat·o·poe·ic (on′ə mat′ə pē′ik), *adj.* having to do with or like onomatopoeia; imitative in sound.

on·o·mat·o·po·e·sis (on′ə mat′ə pō ē′sis), *n.* onomatopoeia.

on·o·mat·o·po·et·ic (on′ə mat′ə pō et′ik), *adj.* onomatopoeic. —**on′o·mat′o·po·et′i·cal·ly,** *adv.*

On·on·da·ga (on′ən dô′gə, -dä′-), *n., pl.* **-ga** or **-gas. 1.** a member of a tribe of American Indians of Iroquoian stock formerly living in central New York State. **2.** the Iroquoian language of this tribe. [American English < Iroquoian (Onondaga) *Ononta'gé,* place name, (literally) on top of the hill]

on·rush (on′rush′, ôn′-), *n.* a violent forward rush: *the tremendous onrush and check of the German attack in the west that opened the great war* (H.G. Wells).

on·rush·ing (on′rush′ing, ôn′-), *adj.* that rushes on; moving forward rapidly: *the onrushing crowd at a bargain sale, onrushing vehicles; the onrushing advent of television* (Maclean's).

on·screen (on′skrēn′, ôn′-), *adj., adv.* **1.** seen on the motion-picture or television screen: *an onscreen moderator.* **2.** while acting for motion pictures or television: *onscreen showmanship.*

on·set (on′set′, ôn′-), *n.* **1.** attack: *The onset of the enemy took us by surprise.* **2.** beginning; start: *The onset of this disease is gradual.* —**Syn. 1.** assault, onslaught. **2.** commencement.

on·shore (on′shôr′, -shōr′; ôn′-), *adv., adj.* **1.** toward the land. **2.** on the land.

on·side (on′sīd′, ôn′-), *adj., adv.* in a position allowed by the rules of the game.

on-site (on′sīt′, ôn′-), *adj.* at the location of something; on the actual site where something takes place regularly: *on-site maintenance of aircraft. The working group of seismologists and physicists failed to agree on criteria for on-site inspection* (Bulletin of Atomic Scientists).

on·slaught (on′slôt′, ôn′-), *n.* a vigorous attack: *The Indians made an onslaught on the settlers' fort.* [< Germanic (compare Middle Low German *anslach* attack)] —**Syn.** onset.

on·stage (on′stāj′, ôn′-), *adj., adv.* **1.** on the part of the stage that the audience can see: *During the battle scene, a ship was sunk onstage.* **2.** while acting for an audience: *The children begin their onstage Kabuki experience from the age of five* (Atlantic).

on-stream (on′strēm′, ôn′-), *adj.* operating in a fluid manner; using a fluid method; of or by means of flow: *On-stream process control by fluorescent spectrometry has become established . . . for control of the zinc coating of sheet metal* (G.L. Clark). —*adv.* into fluid operation: *The plant . . . is expected to come on-stream early next year* (New Scientist).

on·sweep (on′swēp′, ôn′-), *n.* a sweeping onward: *the onsweep of our van* (Rudyard Kipling).

Ont., Ontario.

On·tar·i·an (on tãr′ē ən), *adj.* of or having to do with Ontario, a province in Canada, north of the Great Lakes. —*n.* a native or inhabitant of Ontario.

on-the-cuff (on ᴛʜə kuf′, ôn-), *adj., adv.* *U.S. Informal.* on credit: *And the proud symbol of the growing enthusiasm for on-the-cuff spending is the credit card* (Newsweek).

on-the-job (on ᴛʜə job′, ôn-), *adj.* *Informal.* during the actual performance of one's job or duties; not prior to or in preparation for a job: *on-the-job teaching, study, experience, etc. The boys would be put into on-the-job training situations throughout the conservation field* (Harper's).

on-the-rec·ord (on ᴛʜə rek′ərd, ôn-), *adj.* **1.** for public consumption; not off-the-record: *In both on-the-record statements and private comments, leading officials portrayed* [*him*] *as a man of uncertain political purpose* (New York Times). **2.** official: *Chiang's demand for an on-the-record commitment from Washington held up . . . the planned evacuation* (New York Times).

on-the-scene (on ᴛʜə sēn′, ôn-), *adj.* on-the-spot: . . . *television's on-the-scene presentation of events as they occurred* (Dwight Bentel). *Portable welders . . . lend themselves to rapid on-the-scene repairs* (Wall Street Journal).

on-the-spot (on ᴛʜə spot′, ôn-), *adj. Informal.* **1.** on the location of; at that very place: *on-the-spot news coverage. On-the-spot camerawork in Europe . . .* (Maclean's). **2.** that takes place immediately and usually without formality: *on-the-spot diagnoses of illnesses, an on-the-spot business deal.*

on·to (on′tü, ôn′-; *before consonants often* on′tə, ôn′-), *prep.* **1.** on to; to a position on or upon: *to throw a ball onto the roof, get onto a horse, a boat driven onto the rocks.* **2.** *Slang.* familiar with; aware of; experienced in: *to get onto a new job. It doesn't take long to get onto him and his alibis.*

➤ **onto, on to.** When *on* is clearly an adverb, the two words should of course be separated: *The rest of us drove on to the city.* When *on* is not clearly an adverb, they are usually written solid: *The team trotted onto the floor. They looked out onto the park.*

on·to·gen·e·sis (on′tə jen′ə sis), *n.* ontogeny.

on·to·ge·net·ic (on′tō jə net′ik), *adj.* of or having to do with ontogeny: *It is Gesell who has uniquely been the draftsman of the architecture of the developing mind—what he calls "the ontogenetic patterning of behavior"* (Harper's). —**on′to·ge·net′i·cal·ly,** *adv.*

on·to·gen·ic (on′tə jen′ik), *adj.* ontogenetic.

on·tog·e·nist (on toj′ə nist), *n.* a person skilled in the study of ontogeny.

on·tog·e·ny (on toj′ə nē), *n. Biology.* the development of an individual organism: *The development of any organism demonstrates the biological law that ontogeny repeats phylogeny* (New Yorker). [< Greek *ṓn, óntos* being + *-geneia* origin < *-genḗs* born, produced]

on·to·log·i·cal (on′tə loj′ə kəl), *adj.* of or having to do with ontology: *The root of every philosophy, says Tillich, is the ontological question. What is "being," what is "real," what is "ultimate reality beyond everything that seems to be real?"* (Time). —**on′to·log′i·cal·ly,** *adv.*

ontological argument or **proof,** the contention that since our idea of God is that of a perfect being and since existence is part of perfection, our idea of God is an idea of a necessarily existent being. This argument, used by Anselm and Descartes, is repeated by Thomas Aquinas and most of the theologians.

on·tol·o·gism (on tol′ə jiz əm), *n.* the doctrine that human beings have an intuitive knowledge of God and that this knowledge is the basis of all other knowledge.

on·tol·o·gist (on tol′ə jist), *n.* a person skilled in ontology.

on·tol·o·gy (on tol′ə jē), *n.* the branch of philosophy that deals with the nature of reality. [< New Latin *ontologia* < Greek *ṓn, óntos* being + *-logíā* -logy]

o·nus (ō′nəs), *n.* a burden; responsibility: *The onus of housekeeping fell upon the daughters. The onus of proving it was not right lay with those who disputed its being so* (Samuel Butler). [< Latin *onus*] —**Syn.** duty, obligation.

o·nus pro·ban·di (ō′nəs prō ban′dī), *Latin.* the burden of proof.

on·ward (on′wərd, ôn′-), *adv.* **1.** toward the front; further on; on; forward: *The crowd around the store window began to move onward.* **2.** *Archaic.* at a position in advance: *My grief lies onward and my joy behind* (Shakespeare). —*adj.* on; further on; toward the front; forward: *Resuming his onward course* (Washington Irving). [Middle English *onward*] —**Syn.** *adv.* **1.** forth. See **forward.**

on·wards (on′wərdz, ôn′-), *adv.* onward: *Birds which nest in the wildest of wild places . . . are returning to the coastal mudflats which, from August onwards through the autumn, will be their home* (London Times).

on·y·cha (on′ə kə), *n.* an ingredient of the incense used in the Mosaic ritual, supposed to be the operculum of a marine gastropod. [< Late Latin *onycha* < Greek *ónycha,* accusative of *ónyx* a kind of aromatic substance]

o·nych·i·a (ō nik′ē ə), *n.* inflammation of the matrix of the nails or claws. [< New Latin *onychia* < Greek *ónyx, ónychos* claw]

on·y·cho·my·co·sis (on′ə kō mī kō′sis), *n.* a fungous disease of the nails characterized by thickened, brittle, white nails. [< Greek *ónyx, ónychos* claw + *mýkēs, -ētos* fungus + English *-osis*]

on·yx (on′iks), *n.* a semiprecious variety of quartz with layers of different colors and shades, often used for cameos. [< Latin *onyx* < Greek *ónyx, ónychos* claw, fingernail (because of its color)]

Onyx

onyx marble, a variety of calcite resembling true onyx, used for ornamental stonework; Mexican onyx. It is formed by water deposition, and is commonly found in caves.

oö-, *combining form.* **1.** egg or eggs: *Oölogy = the science of (birds') eggs.* **2.** ovum: *Oöblast = a primitive ovum.* [< Greek *ōión* egg]

oo (ü), *interj., n., v.i.* ooh.

o·ö·blast (ō′ə blast), *n. Biology.* a primitive or formative ovum not yet developed into a true ovum. [< *oö-* + Greek *blastós* germ, sprout]

o·ö·cyst (ō′ə sist), *n.* a cyst in sporozoans that contains developing sporozoites, present within a host organism. [< *oö-* + *cyst*]

o·ö·cyte (ō′ə sīt), *n. Biology.* an egg in the stage that precedes maturation.

oo·dles (ü′dəlz), *n.pl. Informal.* large or unlimited quantities; heaps; loads: *oodles of money. As for the den, we converted that into a Polynesian-style bar—oodles of rattan and hogsheads to roost on* (S. J. Perelman).

oof (üf), *n. British Slang.* cash; money. [earlier *ooftish* < Yiddish *auf tische* on the table (as "cash down")]

oof-bird (üf′bėrd′), *n. British Slang.* **1.** the imaginary bird that produces oof. **2.** a person from whom money is obtained.

oof·y (ü′fē), *adj.,* **oof·i·er, oof·i·est.** *British Slang.* rich; wealthy.

o·ög·a·mous (ō og′ə məs), *adj. Biology.* heterogamous.

o·ög·a·my (ō og′a mē), *n. Biology.* the conjugation of two gametes of dissimilar form. [< *oö-* + *-gamy*]

o·ö·gen·e·sis (ō′ə jen′ə sis), *n. Biology.* the origin and development of the ovum: *Different stages of spermatogenesis and oögenesis differ considerably in sensitivity* (C. Auerbach). [< *oö-* + *genesis*]

o·ö·ge·net·ic (ō′ə jə net′ik), *adj.* of or having to do with oögenesis.

o·ö·go·ni·al (ō′ə gō′nē əl), *adj.* of or having to do with an oögonium.

o·ö·go·ni·um (ō′ə gō′nē əm), *n., pl.* **-ni·a** (-nē ə), **-ni·ums. 1.** *Biology.* a primitive germ cell that divides and gives rise to the oöcytes. **2.** *Botany.* the female reproductive organ in various thallophytes, usually a rounded cell or sac containing one or more oöspheres. [< New Latin *oögonium* < Greek *ōión* egg + *gónos* producing]

ooh (ü), *Informal.* —*interj., n.* an exclamation of surprise, admiration, delight, fear, etc.: *The oohs and ahs of shoppers this week will not signal a rest for the display staff* (New York Times). —*v.i.* to exclaim "ooh" in admiration, delight, etc.: *Women oohed at the black-and-white sari worn by Madame Vijaya Lakshmi Pandit of India* (Newsweek). Also, **oo.**

oo·la·kan or **oo·la·chan** (ü′lə kən), *n.* the candlefish of the northwestern coast of America; eulachon. [< a native Chinook name]

o·ö·lite (ō′ə līt), *n.* a rock, usually limestone, composed of rounded concretions resembling the roe of fish. [probably an adaptation of French *oölithe* < Greek *ōión* egg + *líthos* stone]

o·ö·lit·ic (ō′ə lit′ik), *adj.* of or like oölite.

o·ö·log·i·cal (ō′ə loj′ə kəl), *adj.* of or having to do with oölogy.

o·öl·o·gist (ō ol′ə jist), *n.* **1.** a person skilled in oölogy. **2.** a collector of birds' eggs.

o·öl·o·gy (ō ol′ə jē), *n.* the branch of ornithology that deals with birds' eggs. [< *oö-* + *-logy*]

oo·long (ü′lông, -long), *n.* a black tea consisting of leaves that were partially fermented before they were dried. [< Chinese *wu-lung* black dragon]

oom (ōm), *n.* (in Dutch use) uncle, used affectionately before the name of an elderly man. [< Dutch *oom*]

Oom (ōm, üm, ům), *n. Afrikaans.* uncle: *Then Oom Dawie came to my rescue* (Cape Times). [< Afrikaans *oom* < Dutch]

oo·mi·ak or **oo·mi·ac** (ü′mē ak), *n.* umiak.

oo·ming·mack (ü′ming mak), *n.* musk ox: *The oomingmack is no longer in danger of extermination* (Science News Letter). [< an Eskimo word]

oom·pah (üm′pä′), *n.* **1.** the low, continuous, puffing sound of a large brass instrument, as the tuba: *The ubiquitous beer halls echo to the oompah of brass bands* (Newsweek). **2.** *Slang.* a brassy, monotonous manner or style. [imitative]

oomph (ůmf), *n. U.S. Slang.* **1.** spirit; vigor; vitality; enthusiasm: *"Fellas, let's have all the oomph you can give these bass notes—just a little stronger"* (New York Times). **2.** sex appeal: *His clothes have oomph, said a buyer* (New York Times). [imitative]

o·ö·phore (ō′ə fôr, -fōr), *n. Obsolete.* oöphyte. [< *oö-* + *-phore*]

o·ö·pho·rec·to·my (ō′ə fə rek′tə mē), *n., pl.* **-mies.** the surgical removal of one or both ovaries. [< New Latin *oöphoron* ovary + Greek *ektomḗ* a cutting out]

o·ö·phor·ic (ō′ə fôr′ik, -for′-), *adj. Obsolete.* of or having to do with the oöphore.

o·ö·pho·ri·tis (ō′ə fə rī′tis), *n.* inflammation of the ovary.

o·ö·phyte (ō′ə fīt), *n.* the generation or form of a plant that bears the sexual organs in the alternation of generations, as in ferns, mosses, and liverworts.

o·ö·phyt·ic (ō′ə fit′ik), *adj.* of or having to do with the oöphyte.

oops (wups, üps, ups), *interj.* an exclamation of apology or dismay, as at a blunder: *Last week the court said oops, and . . . withdrew both opinions* (Time). [origin unknown]

oo·ra·li (ü rä′lē), *n.* curare. [< a Tupi word]

oo·ri·al (ůr′ē əl), *n.* the urial, a wild sheep of Asia.

oo·rie (ůr′ē), *adj.* ourie.

o·ö·sperm (ō′ə spėrm), *n.* **1.** *Zoology.* a fertilized ovum; zygote. **2.** *Botany. Obsolete.* an oöspore. [< *oö-* + Greek *spérma* seed]

o·ö·sphere (ō′ə sfir), *n. Botany.* a female reproductive cell contained in an oögonium which when fertilized becomes an oöspore.

o·ö·spore (ō′ə spôr, -spōr), *n. Botany.* the fertilized female cell or oösphere within an oögonium which forms the cell of a future plant. [< *oö-* + Greek *spóros* seed, spore]

o·ö·spor·ic (ō′ə spôr′ik, -spōr′-), *adj. Botany.* of or having to do with the oöspore.

o·ös·po·rous (ō os′pər əs; ō′ə spôr′-, -spōr′-), *adj.* oösporic.

o·ö·the·ca (ō′ə thē′kə), *n., pl.* **-cae** (-sē). an egg case or capsule of certain mollusks and insects, especially cockroaches and mantises. [< *oö-* + Greek *thḗkē* receptacle]

ooze[1] (üz), *v.,* **oozed, ooz·ing,** *n.* —*v.i.* **1.** to pass out slowly through small openings; leak out slowly and quietly: *Blood still oozed from the cut.* **2.** to give forth moisture little by little: *Swamp ground oozes when you step on it.* —*v.t.* to give out slowly; make by oozing; exude: *The cut oozed blood. A scarcely perceptible creek, oozing its way through a wilderness of reeds and slime* (Edgar Allan Poe).
[Middle English *wosen* < *wose;* see the noun]
—*n.* **1.** a slow flow. **2.** something that oozes. **3.** a liquid used in tanning leather, obtained as an infusion from the bark of oak, sumac, etc.
[alteration of Middle English *wose,* Old English *wōs* juice]

ooze[2] (üz), *n.* **1.** a soft mud or slime, especially at the bottom of a pond or river or on the ocean bottom: *Whereas the deep-sea bed elsewhere consisted of thick deposits of fine oozes and clays, here the bed was mainly composed . . . of sand and silt* (Bruce C. Heezen). **2.** white or gray fine-grained matter, often calcareous, and largely composed of the shells and other remains of small organisms, covering large areas of the ocean floor. **3.** a piece of soft, boggy ground; marsh: *Fishing a manuscript out of the ooze of oblivion* (Lowell). [probably earlier *wooze,* Middle English *wose,* Old English *wāse* mud, mire]

ooze leather, leather with a soft, velvety finish on the flesh side, made from calfskin, etc.

oo·zie (ü′zē), *n.* (in Burma) the keeper and driver of an elephant; mahout. [< a native word]
oo·zi·ly (ü′zə lē), *adv.* in an oozy manner.
oo·zi·ness (ü′zē nis), *n.* oozy quality or condition.
oo·zy[1] (ü′zē), *adj.* oozing. [< *ooz*(e)[1] + *-y*[1]]
oo·zy[2] (ü′zē), *adj.*, **-zi·er, -zi·est.** containing ooze; muddy and soft; slimy: *a low oozy meadow* (Francis Parkman). [Middle English *wosie* < *wose* ooze[2]]
op (op), *adj.* having to do with optical art: *op artists, an op show; . . . new op paintings and textile designs* (Scientific American). —*n.* optical art: *Opinions vary as to how influential op will be* (New York Times). [< *op* art]
op-, *prefix.* the form of **ob-** before *p*, as in *oppress.*
op., **1.** opera. **2.** operation. **3.** opposite. **4.** opus.
o.p. or **O.P.**, **1.** out of print. **2.** overprint (on a stamp). **3.** overproof.
OP (no periods) or **O.P.**, observation post.
O.P., (among Dominicans) Order of Preachers (Latin, *Ordo Praedicatorum*).
OPA (no periods), Office of Price Administration.
o·pac·i·fi·ca·tion (ō pas′ə fə kā′shən), *n.* **1.** the act of opacifying. **2.** the state of being opacified: . . . *the permanent opacification of the pupil, which produces blindness* (Frank P. Mathews).
o·pac·i·fi·er (ō pas′ə fī′ər), *n.* a substance used to opacify a material such as glass, paper, etc.
o·pac·i·fy (ō pas′ə fī), *v.t., v.i.*, **-fied, -fy·ing.** to make or become opaque.
o·pac·i·ty (ō pas′ə tē), *n., pl.* **-ties. 1.** the quality or condition of being opaque; being impervious to light; darkness: *The small triangular area . . . at the edge of the nebula is a dark cloud of very high opacity* (Scientific American). **2.** a being impervious to heat, sound, etc. **3.** obscurity of meaning. **4.** something opaque. **5.** denseness or stupidity. [< Latin *opācitās* < *opācus* dark]
o·pa·cous (ō pā′kəs), *adj. Archaic.* opaque.
o·pah (ō′pə), *n.* a large, brilliantly colored deep-sea fish, found especially in the warmer parts of the Atlantic Ocean. [< West African *ùbà*]

Opah (4 ft. long)

o·pal (ō′pəl), *n.* a mineral, an amorphous form of hydrous silica, somewhat like quartz, found in many varieties and colors, certain of which reflect light with a peculiar rainbow play of color and are valued as gems. Black opals are green and blue with brilliant reflected colors; some are so dark as to seem almost black. Milk opals are milky white with rather pale colors. Fire opals are similar with more red and yellow flashes of color. —*adj.* like an opal: *The opal murmuring sea* (Jean Ingelow). [< Latin *opalus* < Greek *opállios* < Sanskrit *upala* gem]
o·pal·esce (ō′pə les′), *v.i.*, **-esced, -esc·ing.** to exhibit a play of colors like that of the opal.
o·pal·es·cence (ō′pə les′əns), *n.* the exhibition of a play of colors like an opal's.
o·pal·es·cent (ō′pə les′ənt), *adj.* having a play of colors like that of an opal, especially the milk opal. [< *opal* + *-escent*]
o·pal·esque (ō′pə lesk′), *adj.* like an opal; opalescent.
o·pal·eye (ō′pə lī′), *n., pl.* **-eyes** or (*collectively*) **-eye.** a greenish, herbivorous fish found off the California coast, sometimes used for food; greenfish.
opal glass, a glass with a milky-white appearance caused by the addition of small colloidal particles which disperse the light passing through it; milk glass.
o·pal·ine (ō′pə lin, -līn), *adj.* of or like opal; opalescent. —*n.* opal glass.
o·pal·ize (ō′pə līz), *v.t.*, **-ized, -iz·ing. 1.** to convert into opal. **2.** to make opaline or opalescent.
o·paque (ō pāk′), *adj.* **1. a.** not letting light through; not transparent: *It was so dark that . . . he could scarcely distinguish the transparent window from the opaque walls of his chamber* (Dickens). *The water is so charged with mud and sand that it is opaque* (Francis Parkman). **b.** not conducting heat, sound, electricity, etc.: *Even on the clearest day, the atmosphere is as opaque to many kinds of radiation as if it were an ocean of ink* (Time). **2.** not shining; dark; dull. **3.** hard to understand; obscure: *The Critique of Political Economy . . . had baffled even Marx's disciples by its relentless and opaque abstraction* (Edmund Wilson). **4.** stupid; dense. —*n.* **1.** something opaque. **2.** *Photography.* a pigment used to shade parts of a negative. [< Latin *opācus* dark, shady] —**o·paque′ly,** *adv.* —**o·paque′ness,** *n.*
opaque projector, a projector having a series of mirrors and lenses to throw the image of a drawing, page of a book, map, or other opaque object on a screen.
op art (op), optical art: *'Op art' [is] a play of words on 'pop art'. . . . 'Op' means 'optical'* (New Yorker).
Op. Atty. Gen., Opinions of the Attorney General of the United States.
op. cit., in the work (previously) cited; in the book, etc., referred to (Latin, *opere citato*).
ope (ōp), *v.*, **oped, op·ing,** *adj. Archaic.* —*v.t., v.i.* to open: *Lord, ope their eyes that they may see!* (John Greenleaf Whittier). —*adj.* open: *With both eyes wide ope* (Robert Browning).
o·pen (ō′pən), *adj.* **1.** not shut; not closed: *an open drawer. The open windows let in the fresh air.* **2.** not having its door, gate, lid, etc., closed: *an open box, an open house.* **3.** not closed in: *the open sea, an open field.* **4.** unfilled; not taken: *a position still open, to have an hour open.* **5. a.** that may be entered, used, shared, or competed for, etc., by all: *an open meeting, an open market.* **b.** ready for business or admission of the public: *The exhibition is now open.* **6.** accessible or available: *the only course still open. The invitation is still open to you.* **7.** without prohibition or restriction: *an open season for hunting. It will be an open season for Congressional investigations* (Newsweek). **8.** *U.S. Informal.* allowing saloons, gambling, etc.: *an open town.* **9. a.** not finally settled or determined; undecided: *an open question.* **b.** ready to listen to new ideas and judge them fairly; not prejudiced: *an open mind.* **10.** having no cover, roof, etc.; letting in air freely: *an open car, an open boat.* **11.** not covered or protected; exposed: *an open fire, an open wound, open to temptation.* **12.** not obstructed: *an open view, an open harbor.* **13.** exposed to general view, knowledge, etc.; not hidden or secret: *open disregard of rules.* **14.** having spaces or holes: *open ranks, cloth of open texture.* **15.** *Music.* **a.** (of an organ pipe) not closed at the upper end. **b.** (of a string) not stopped by the finger. **c.** (of a note) produced by such a pipe or string, or without aid of slide, key, etc. **16.** *Phonetics.* **a.** (of a vowel) uttered with a relatively wide opening above the tongue; low. **b.** (of a syllable) ending in a vowel or diphthong, as *clo-* in *clover.* **c.** (of a consonant) fricative; spirant. **17.** unreserved, candid, or frank; sincere: *an open face. Please be open with me.* **18.** that is spread out; unfolded; expanded: *an open flower, an open newspaper.* **19.** generous; liberal: *Give with an open hand.* **20. a.** free from frost: *an open winter.* **b.** free from ice; not frozen: *open water on the lake.* **c.** *Nautical.* free of fog. **21.** (of a city, town, etc.) unfortified; without strategic importance, or containing historic buildings and works of art of such value as to outweigh its military importance; protected from enemy attack under international law: *Rome was declared an open city in World War II.* **22.** (of an electric circuit) not complete or closed. **23.** *Printing.* **a.** (of type) consisting of outlines; not solid black. **b.** (of printed matter) widely spaced or leaded. **24.** (of an account, etc.) not yet balanced or closed.
lay oneself or **one open.** See under **lay**[1], *v.*
lay open. See under **lay**[1], *v.*
open to, a. ready to take; willing to consider: *open to suggestions.* **b.** liable to; exposed to: *The service . . . left me open to all injuries* (Shakespeare). **c.** to be had or used by: *The old universities are open to all, without distinction of rank or creed* (The Speaker). **d.** available to; within the discretion of: *It was open to Mr. Smith to sign an agreement covering all the issues providing for an immediate return to constitutional rule* (Manchester Guardian Weekly).
—*n.* **1.** an open or clear space; opening. **2.** an open competition, tournament, etc.: *to play in a golf open.*
the open, a. the open country, air, sea, etc.: *to sleep out in the open.* **b.** public view or knowledge: *to act in the open. Mr. Waddington challenges them to "come out into the open and make a realistic offer for the whole of the share capital"* (London Times).
—*v.t.* **1.** to move or turn away from a shut or closed position to allow passage; give access to: *to open a door, to open a bottle.* **2.** to cause to be open or more open; make accessible: *to open a path through the woods.* **3.** to clear of obstructions; make (a passage, etc.) clear: *to open a road.* **4.** to make accessible to knowledge, sympathy, etc.; enlighten: *Then opened he their understanding, that they might understand the scriptures* (Luke 24:45). **5.** to lay bare; expose to view; uncover; disclose; reveal; divulge: *The spy opened our plans to the enemy. Herbs . . . that sudden flower'd, Opening their various colours* (Milton). **6.** to expand, extend, or spread out; make less compact: *to open a newspaper.* **7.** to establish or set going: *to open an account. He opened a new store. The President opened his campaign for a second term.* **8.** to cut into: *to open a wound.* **9.** to come to view: *keeping a yellow warehouse on our starboard hand till we opened a white church to the larboard* (Herman Melville). **10.** *Law.* to make the first statement of (a case) to the court or jury.
—*v.i.* **1.** to afford access (into, to, etc.); have an opening: *This door opens into the dining room.* **2.** to become open or more open; become accessible. **3.** to become accessible to knowledge, sympathy, etc.; become enlightened. **4.** to become disclosed or revealed: *A new field of science opened to our view.* **5.** to become more and more visible, especially as one approaches: *A large valley opened to our gaze.* **6.** to move apart; become less compact: *The ranks opened.* **7. a.** to begin; start: *Congress opens tomorrow. School opens soon.* **b.** (of a theatrical company) to begin a season or tour: *They opened in Boston.* **8.** to come apart, especially so as to allow passage or show the contents: *the wound opened. The clouds opened and the sun shone through.* **9.** (of hounds) to begin to bark when in pursuit on a scent. **10.** (in poker) to begin the betting, as in a game requiring openers.
open up, a. to make accessible: *By schemes such as this it is hoped to . . . open up the almost undeveloped southeast* (London Times). **b.** to become accessible: *Avenues of wealth opening up so readily* (David Livingstone). **c.** to bring to light: *The view of political economy which his [Ricardo's] genius was the first to open up* (John Stuart Mill). **d.** to unfold; spread out: *to open up a folder.* **e.** to begin; start: *to open up a new business.* **f.** to speak freely: *He was opening up because he knew that I was not making fun of him* (Atlantic).
[Old English. Related to UP.] —**o′pen·ly,** *adv.*
—**Syn.** *adj.* **1.** unclosed, ajar, unlocked. **4.** unoccupied, free. **9. a.** unsettled, debatable. **11.** uncovered, unprotected. **13.** public. **14.** perforated, porous. **17.** straightforward.
o·pen·a·ble (ō′pə nə bəl), *adj.* that can be opened; fitted to be opened.
open account, 1. a course of business dealings still continuing between two parties. **2.** an account not in balance.
open air, the outdoors.
o·pen-air (ō′pən ãr′), *adj.* **1.** outdoor. **2.** *Painting.* plein-air. —**Syn. 1.** alfresco.
o·pen-and-shut (ō′pən ən shut′), *adj. U.S. Informal.* simple and direct; obvious; straightforward: *an open-and-shut case.*
open·bill (ō′pən bil′), *n.* any of a group of small storks, with species in Africa and southern Asia, having a bill with mandibles separated by an interval before meeting at the tip.

Indian Openbill (about 4 ft. long)

open book, 1. something that is readily known or understood: *His life is an open book, which we cannot deny when we recall his winter outings in the West Indies, his cars, camps, summer home, all open and aboveboard, with* *never an attempt to conceal any of it* (Charles W. Morton). **2.** a person who conceals nothing; one whose thoughts or actions are readily understood: *There's no mystery about me. I'm an open book* (P.G. Wodehouse).

o·pen-cast (ō′pən kast′, -käst′), *adj.* open-pit: *All open-cast mining in South Wales should cease for the time being* (London Times).

open chain, *Chemistry.* atoms in an organic molecule represented in a structural formula by a chain with open ends rather than by a ring. —**o′pen-chain′,** *adj.*

open champion, (in sports and games) the holder of an open championship.

open championship, a title in a sport or game that may be competed for by all.

o·pen-cir·cuit (o′pən sėr′kit), *adj.* **1.** of or having to do with a television or radio program which is broadcast over the air to any viewers. **2.** having to do with a device used in skin-diving that permits exhaled air to escape in a chain of fine bubbles.

open circuit cell, an electric cell, as a dry-cell battery, having two poles connected by a flashlight switch or other device to make a closed circuit. Bubbles of hydrogen ions on the positive electrode finally stop the current, making open circuit cells useful only for short periods.

open cluster, a galactic cluster.

open couplet, a couplet in which the second line does not complete a thought but depends on the line or lines that follow.

open court, 1. a court of law which has been formally convened to carry on its proper business. **2.** a court of law which is open to the public: *The resolution added: "If the prosecution's case was made in open court that would, in our opinion, be the quickest way of clearing the air of rumour and speculation"* (London Times).

o·pen-cut (ō′pən kut′), *adj.* **1.** open-pit: *Soviet efforts to expand open-cut coal extraction, whose output is much cheaper than mined coal, have progressed slowly* (New York Times). **2.** of or having to do with a subway, railroad line, road, etc., which runs below ground level in an uncovered trench: *Brussels, Belgium, opened a 2-mile, 6-track, open-cut railway connection between its Nord and Midi Stations* (John W. Hazen).

open diapason, an organ stop that gives full, majestic tones.

open door, the free and equal chance for all countries to do business in another country.

o·pen-door (ō′pən dôr′, -dōr′), *adj.* of or having to do with the doctrine of the open door: *The scientific and technological open-door policy which prevailed in east Asia* (Bulletin of Atomic Scientists).

o·pen-doored (ō′pən dôrd′, -dōrd′), *adj.* accessible; hospitable: *A house Once rich, now poor, but ever open-door'd* (Tennyson).

o·pen-end (ō′pən end′), *adj.* **1.** of or having to do with investment trusts, as mutual funds, that have no fixed capitalization and continually issue shares on request to old or new investors: *Open-end funds stand ready to repurchase shares at net asset value at all times* (Wall Street Journal). **2.** that allows for adjusting or revising details later on: *an open-end contract, an open-end mortgage.* **3.** (in poker) of a 4-card straight that can be filled at either end, such as 7,8,9,10.

o·pen-end·ed (ō′pən en′did), *adj.* **1.** open to later consideration, revision, or adjustment: *It is good to make open-ended settlements to allow for further manifestation of injury* (Bulletin of Atomic Scientists). **2.** not closed at either end: *an open-ended stovepipe.* **3.** not committed or predisposed; admitting many views or interpretations: *His exchanges between Mr. White and Mr. Black abounded in ambiguously open-ended clues to their real identity* (Time). **4.** limitless, as in power, effect, or consequence: *The hydrogen bomb is an open-ended weapon. ... if you want to make it more powerful, you just shovel in more of the heavy-hydrogen mixture* (Saturday Evening Post).

open enrollment, *U.S.* the transfer of children from neighborhood public schools attended chiefly by one racial group into other neighborhood public schools in order to attain racial balance in the enrollments.

o·pen·er (ō′pə nər), *n.* **1.** a person or thing that opens: *In the afternoon Cardiff had welcomed its official opener, the Duke of Gloucester* (Manchester Guardian). **2.** (in poker) the first better in a jack pot. **3.** *U.S. Informal.* the first game of a scheduled series. **4.** the first part of anything; opening: *the opener of a speech.*

openers, (in poker) a pair of jacks, or better cards, in a jack pot: *I didn't hold openers, an' yet if I didn't draw some cards an' see it out, I stood to lose entirely* (R.A. Wason).

o·pen-eyed (ō′pən īd′), *adj.* **1.** having eyes wide open, as in wonder: *We saw him now, dumb with fear and astonishment, staring open-eyed at the emperor* (Sir Arthur Conan Doyle). **2.** having the eyes open; watchful or vigilant; observant. **3.** done or experienced with the eyes open; frank and honest: *an open-eyed conspiracy* (William Dean Howells). —**Syn. 2.** alert.

o·pen-face (ō′pən fās′), *adj.* (of a sandwich) made without a slice of bread or toast on top.

o·pen-faced (ō′pən fāst′), *adj.* **1.** having the face uncovered. **2. a.** having a frank and ingenuous face: *a blond, open-faced Scot* (Time). **b.** done in a frank and honest way. **3.** (of a watch) having no protective cover over the crystal. **4.** open-face.

o·pen-field (ō′pən fēld′), *adj.* **1.** of or having to do with the division of the arable land of a community into unenclosed strips, each of which is owned or used by a person or family: *... walking along a dirt road, in high, open-field country like the farm* (New Yorker). **2.** in the part of the playing field beyond the line of scrimmage, in football.

open file, *Chess.* a file on which there are neither pieces nor pawns. A player may obtain possession of an open file by playing his queen or rook on any of its squares.

open forum, a forum or assembly for the discussion of questions of public interest, open to all who wish to take part.

open fracture, a compound fracture.

o·pen-hand·ed (ō′pən han′did), *adj.* generous; liberal. —**o′pen-hand′ed·ly,** *adv.* —**o′pen-hand′ed·ness,** *n.*

o·pen-heart (o′pən härt′), *adj.* with the pericardium opened for direct access to the heart. Open-heart surgery is performed within the heart to repair a damaged valve or a defective chamber wall while a heart-lung machine performs the circulatory function of the heart. *Direct vision or open-heart operations have become a reality* (Science News Letter).

o·pen-heart·ed (ō′pən här′tid), *adj.* **1.** candid; frank; unreserved: *a good, honest, open-hearted, and positive naval officer of the old school* (Alexander W. Kinglake). **2.** kindly; generous. —**o′pen-heart′ed·ly,** *adv.* —**o′pen-heart′ed·ness,** *n.*

o·pen-hearth (ō′pən härth′), *adj.* **1. a.** of or having an open hearth: *an open hearth furnace.* **b.** using a furnace with an open-hearth. **2.** made by the open-hearth process: *open-hearth steel.*
—*n.* an open-hearth furnace: *The Republic plant is now operating six of its nine steel-making open-hearths* (Wall Street Journal).

open-hearth process, a process of making steel in a furnace in which the flame is directed onto the raw material, the impurities becoming oxidized.

open house, 1. a house that is open to all friends who wish to visit. **2.** an occasion on which an open house is maintained: *The High School open house is every other Friday evening.*

keep open house, to offer food, or food and lodging, to all visitors: *The Joneses are keeping open house this weekend at their summer ranch.*

o·pen·ing (ō′pə ning, ōp′ning), *n.* **1.** an open or clear space; gap; hole: *an opening in a wall, an opening in the forest.* **2.** the first part; beginning: *the opening of a lecture.* **3.** a formal beginning: *The opening will be at three o'clock tomorrow afternoon.* **4.** a place or position that is open or vacant: *an opening in a bank.* **5.** a favorable chance or opportunity: *In talking with your mother, I made an opening to ask her about sending you to camp. Here is an opening which, if neglected by our government ... they will one day sorely repent* (Edmund Burke). **6.** *Law.* the statement of the case made by the lawyer to the court or jury before adducing evidence. **7.** *Chess.* **a.** the beginning of a game, distinguished from the moves that follow. **b.** a standard series of moves beginning a game, especially such a series adopted by a player to establish an attack or defense. —**Syn. 1.** aperture, fissure, orifice. **2.** start, commencement, introduction. **4.** vacancy.

opening gun, *Informal.* something that forms the beginning of a major event or proceeding: *The San Diego address was the opening gun in a campaign of executive leadership* (New York Times).

opening night, the evening of the first formal performance of a new play, motion picture, broadcast series, or other type of entertainment: *There is nothing to match the experience of an opening night on Broadway* (Atlantic). —**o′pen·ing-night′,** *adj.*

open letter, a letter addressed to a person or organization but published in a newspaper, magazine, etc., to bring some error, argument, grievance, etc., to the attention of the public.

open loop, the path or flow of input in an automated system without feedback, as distinguished from a closed or feedback loop.

open market, 1. the general market; a market open to anyone, with no restrictions as to source of purchase or destination of sale; free market. **2.** the buying and selling of government securities in a free market, especially as controlled or influenced by the activities of the Federal Reserve Bank. —**o′pen-mar′ket,** *adj.*

o·pen-mind·ed (ō′pən mīn′did), *adj.* having or showing a mind open to new arguments or ideas: *The claim of scientific inquiry to be impartial and open-minded is erroneously associated with a definition of "open-mindedness" as a freedom from assumptions and presuppositions* (John E. Owen). —**o′pen-mind′ed·ly,** *adv.* —**o′pen-mind′ed·ness,** *n.* —**Syn.** unprejudiced.

o·pen-mouthed (ō′pən mouᴛʜd′, -moutht′), *adj.* **1.** having the mouth open. **2.** gaping with surprise or astonishment: *Countless men ... stared open-mouthed at the news* (H.G. Wells). **3.** greedy, ravenous, or rapacious. **4.** vociferous or clamorous: *open-mouthed hounds. Officers who are open-mouthed against the government* (Thomas Jefferson). **5.** having a wide mouth: *an open-mouthed pitcher or jug.*

o·pen-necked (ō′pən nekt′), *adj.* open at the neck: *an open-necked shirt. An open-necked balloon allows gas within the balloon to expand as it rises, and has no tendency to burst at great altitudes* (Herz and Tennent).

o·pen·ness (ō′pən nis), *n.* **1.** the state or quality of being open. **2.** lack of secrecy. **3.** frankness; candor: *I will answer him as clearly as I am able, and with great openness* (Edmund Burke). **4.** a willingness to consider new ideas or arguments. —**Syn. 4.** open-mindedness.

open order, an arrangement of military or naval units at a relatively great distance from each other, especially as a tactical device to offer a difficult target.

o·pen-pit (ō′pən pit′), *adj.* exposed on the surface; worked on or slightly below the surface; not underground: *open-pit mining or a mine.*

o·pen-plan (o′pən plan′), *adj.* (of an apartment, a house, etc.) designed with an open, spacious interior; having the living or working parts divided into general areas instead of conventional rooms: *The suburban family, with its garden, its barbecue, its lack of privacy in the open-plan house ...* (David Riesman).

open policy, an insurance policy on varying amounts of goods, thus requiring a periodic, usually monthly, computation of premium charges.

open primary, *U.S.* a primary in which any registered voter of the state, city, etc., may vote, whether or not he is an enrolled member of a political party.

open prison, a prison designed to give inmates maximum freedom from custody and restraint: *He said that every escape from an open prison was to some extent a failure in selection, and special attention was being given to the selection processes* (London Times).

open question, something undecided or uncertain: *Whether nations can settle their differences without war is an open question.*

open sea, 1. the part of the sea which is not enclosed by land. **2.** the part of the sea which is outside the sphere of control of any nation.

open season, 1. any of various periods during which the hunting, trapping, or fishing of certain game is permitted. **2.** a time when complete freedom of action or expression prevails, especially in a matter usually subject to control or restraint: *A weak season on Broadway means open season on reviewers* (Walter Kerr).

open secret, a secret that everyone knows about.

open sesame, 1. a password at which doors or barriers fly open: *Your note was an open sesame to the president's office.* 2. the magic command that made the door of the robbers' cave fly open, in the tale of Ali Baba and the Forty Thieves, in the "Arabian Nights' Entertainments."

o·pen-shelf (ō′pən shelf′), *adj.* of or having to do with a method of library organization under which patrons have access to the bookshelves: *an open-shelf library.*

open shop, a factory, shop, or other establishment that will employ both union and nonunion workers. —**o′pen-shop′,** *adj.*

open sight, a rear sight on rifles, shotguns, etc., consisting of a small metal plate with a V-shaped notch through which the front sight and target are brought into alignment.

open stock, a stock or reserve of a particular item of merchandise which is carried at all times and from which a person can purchase in any desired quantity.

o·pen·work (ō′pən wėrk′), *n.* ornamental work that shows openings. —*adj.* of openwork: *an openwork screen.*

op·er·a[1] (op′ər ə, op′rə), *n.* 1. a play that is mostly sung, with costumes, scenery, acting, and music to go with the singing: *"Faust" and "Lohengrin" are well-known operas.* 2. the branch of art represented by such plays: *the history of opera, to sing in opera. Opera is a blend of all the performing arts—song, instrumental music, dance and drama* (New York Times). 3. a performance of an opera. 4. a theater where operas are performed. 5. the libretto or the score for an opera. [< Italian *opera,* for *opera in musica* a (dramatic) work to music; *opera* < Latin *opera* effort, (originally) neuter plural of *opus, -eris* a work]

op·er·a[2] (op′ər ə), *n.* a plural of **opus.**

op·er·a·ble (op′ər ə bəl, op′rə-), *adj.* 1. fit for, or admitting of, a surgical operation. 2. that can or should be done; practicable. 3. that can be operated; in a condition to be used: *... how rapidly he can shift aircraft or salvaged equipment from an inoperable to an operable field* (Bulletin of Atomic Scientists). [< Latin *operārī* to operate + English *-able*]

o·pé·ra bouffe (op′ər ə büf′, op′rə; *French* ô pā rä büf′), 1. comic opera; light opera. 2. an absurd situation; ridiculous arrangement: *The bureaucratic opéra bouffe which is more or less inseparable from the attempt to administer a gigantic philanthropic enterprise* (Atlantic). [< French *opéra bouffe* < Italian *opera buffa;* see OPERA; *buffa* buffoon]

ò·pe·ra buf·fa (ô′pe rä büf′fä), *Italian.* opéra bouffe; comic opera: *Donizetti's òpera buffa "Don Pasquale"* (New York Times).

o·pé·ra co·mique (ô pā rä kô mēk′), *French.* comic opera: *Opéra comique is the French name for opera in which the dialogue is spoken instead of sung* (Konrad Neuger).

opera glasses or **glass,** a small binocular telescope for use at the opera and in theaters. An opera glass is like a field glass, but smaller. —**Syn.** lorgnette.

Opera Glasses

op·er·a·go·er (op′ər ə gō′ər, op′rə-), *n.* a person who regularly attends the opera: *It was one of those memorable events that operagoers are privileged to witness only now and again in a lifetime* (New Yorker).

opera hat, a tall collapsible hat worn by a man with formal clothes.

opera house, 1. a theater where operas are presented. 2. *U.S.* any theater, especially a rural one.

op·er·am·e·ter (op′ə ram′ə tər), *n.* an instrument for indicating the number of movements made by a part of a machine or the like, as the turns made by a shaft. [< Latin *opera* work + English *-meter*]

op·er·and (op′ə rand), *n. Mathematics.* the quantity or expression that is to be subjected to a mathematical operation: *The second operand is in the accumulator register as a result of a previous operation* (New Scientist). [< Latin *operandum,* neuter gerundive of *operārī;* see OPERATE]

op·er·ant (op′ər ənt), *adj.* in operation; working: *In operant conditioning, the patient does not have to pull the lever, or make a response* (Science News Letter). —*n.* 1. a person or thing that operates. 2. *Rare.* a workman; operator. [< Latin *operāns, -antis,* present participle of *operārī* work; see OPERATE]

opera pump, a low-cut, untrimmed shoe for women: *Low-heeled shoes ... have been replaced by blunt opera pumps with thick high heels* (Charlotte Curtis).

ò·pe·ra se·ri·a (ô′pe rä se′rē ä), *Italian.* serious or tragic opera.

op·er·at·a·ble (op′ə rā′tə bəl), *adj.* 1. that can be operated. 2. admitting of a surgical operation; operable.

op·er·ate (op′ə rāt), *v.,* **-at·ed, -at·ing.** —*v.i.* 1. to be at work; run: *Power plants operate night and day.* 2. to produce an effect; work; act: *Several causes operated to bring on the war.* 3. to produce a desired effect: *Some medicines operate more quickly than others.* 4. to do something to the body, usually with instruments, to improve health: *The doctor operated on the injured man.* 5. to carry on military movements, duties, or functions. 6. to buy and sell stocks and bonds: *to operate in stocks or grain futures.*
—*v.t.* 1. to keep at work; drive; run: *Who operates this elevator?* 2. to direct the working of as owner or manager; manage: *That company operates factories in seven countries.* 3. to bring about; produce some effect: *We admitted that the Book ... had even operated changes in our way of thought* (Thomas Carlyle).
[< Latin *operārī* (with English *-ate*[1]) < *opus, -eris* a work] —**Syn.** *v.i.* 1. perform, function.

op·er·at·ic (op′ə rat′ik), *adj.* of or like the opera. —**op′er·at′i·cal·ly,** *adv.*

op·er·at·ing (op′ə rā′ting), *adj.* 1. used in performing operations: *... the high operating speed of a computer* (Science News). 2. of or involving business operations: *Bethlehem Steel sees the possibility of steel price reductions if the Steelworkers accept contract changes in working practices that would cut operating costs* (Wall Street Journal). 3. that operates: *an operating surgeon.*

op·er·at·ing room (op′ə rā′ting), a room, usually in a hospital, that is specially equipped for surgical operations: *Ten years from now, no operating rooms are likely to be constructed without provision for television* (New Scientist).

operating table, the table for a patient to lie on during a surgical operation: *He lay on an operating table ... his head held in position by clamps* (Science News Letter).

operating union, a union of railroad workers who are directly involved in the operation of trains, as engineers, conductors, switchmen, etc.

op·er·a·tion (op′ə rā′shən), *n.* 1. the working: *The operation of a railroad requires many men. The operation of natural law is constant.* 2. the way a thing works; manner of working: *the operation of a machine.* 3. the performance of something; action; activity: *the operation of reading, the operation of brushing one's teeth.* 4. something done to the body, usually with instruments, to improve health: *Taking out the tonsils is a common operation.* 5. a. the movements of soldiers, ships, supplies, etc., for war purposes: *The assembling of an invasion force is a major operation.* b. a particular military movement or undertaking, usually with a code name added. *Example:* Operation Overlord (the Allied invasion of Europe across the English Channel in June, 1944). c. any plan, project, or undertaking designated by a code name: *Since 1953 the area has engaged in a strenuous "Operation Bootstrap" program of self-help* (Wall Street Journal). 6. a. something done to a number or quantity in mathematics: *Addition, subtraction, multiplication, and division are the four commonest operations in arithmetic.* b. the act of making such a change. 7. a commercial transaction, especially one that is speculative and on a large scale: *operations in stocks or wheat.* 8. the power to operate or work; efficacy; force (now used chiefly of legal documents).
in operation, a. running; working; in action: *The machine is in operation.* b. in use or effect: *The new law has been in operation since Monday.* —**Syn.** 5. a. maneuver.

op·er·a·tion·al (op′ə rā′shə nəl), *adj.* 1. of or having to do with operations of any kind: *The problems uncovered by this report, and the present criticism by operational managers ... indicate that this emphasis has not been misplaced* (London Times Literary Supplement). 2. (of equipment) in condition to operate effectively: *The Hunter, which is comparable in performance with the Sabre Jet ... flies about 650 miles an hour in operational trim* (New York Times). 3. used in a military operation; trained or equipped to carry out a particular mission: *operational troops.* —**op′er·a′tion·al·ly,** *adv.*

Operation Alert, *U.S.* an annual civil defense mobilization alert.

op·er·a·tion·al·ism (op′ə rā′shə nə liz′əm), *n. Philosophy.* the doctrine that statements or ideas do not have meaning except for what they signify in actual practice. Only operation gives meaning.

op·er·a·tion·al·ist (op′ə rā′shə nə list), *n.* a person who maintains the doctrine of operationalism. —*adj.* of or having to do with operationalists or operationalism.

operational research, *British.* operations research.

Operation Deepfreeze, any of the expeditions to Antarctica by the United States Navy.

op·er·a·tion·ism (op′ə rā′shə niz əm), *n.* operationalism.

operations analysis, systems analysis.

operations research, *U.S.* the use of scientific and mathematical methods in analyzing and solving problems dealing with the operation of any system or organization.

op·er·a·tive (op′ə rā′tiv, -ər ə tiv; op′rə-), *adj.* 1. exerting force or influence; effective: *the laws operative in a community, an operative medicine.* 2. having to do with work or productiveness: *the operative departments of a manufacturing establishment.* 3. of or concerned with surgical operations: *Treatment of the disease requires operative measures.* —*n.* 1. a worker, especially one who works with a machine; trained or experienced laborer. 2. a. a detective. b. a foreign spy. —**op′er·a′tive·ly,** *adv.* —**op′er·a′tive·ness,** *n.* —**Syn.** *n.* 1. workman, hand.

op·er·a·tize (op′ər ə tīz), *v.t.,* **-tized, -tiz·ing.** to put (a play, etc.) into the form of an opera. [< *opera*[1] + *-ize,* as in *dramatize*]

op·er·a·tor (op′ə rā′tər), *n.* 1. a person who operates. 2. a skilled worker who operates a machine, telephone switchboard, telegraph, etc.: *a telegraph or telephone operator. Operators taken off other machines say they "feel" the sensation of* [*the computer's*] *cosmic speed* (Newsweek). 3. a person who runs a factory, mine, etc. 4. *U.S. Informal.* a shrewd individual who maneuvers people and events for his own purposes: *The musical stars Robert Preston, as a fast operator who is redeemed by contact with prairie honesty* (New Yorker). 5. a person who speculates in stocks or a commodity. 6. a doctor who performs surgical operations; surgeon.

operator gene, a gene which initiates the process resulting in the synthesis of messenger RNA. See also **operon.**

o·per·cu·lar (ō pėr′kyə lər), *adj.* of, having to do with, or of the nature of an operculum. —**o·per′cu·lar·ly,** *adv.*

o·per·cu·late (ō pėr′kyə lit, -lāt), *adj.* having an operculum.

o·per·cu·lat·ed (ō pėr′kyə lā′tid), *adj.* operculate.

o·per·cu·li·form (ō pėr′kyə lə fôrm), *adj.* having the form of an operculum; lidlike.

o·per·cu·lum (ō pėr′kyə ləm), *n., pl.* **-la** (-lə), **-lums.** *Biology.* a lidlike part or organ; any flap covering an opening, as the lid of the spore case in mosses, the plate of some gastropods that closes the opening of the shell, the gill cover of a fish, or the limb of the calyx on a species of eucalyptus. [< Latin *operculum* < *operīre* to cover]

o·pe·re ci·ta·to (op′ə rē sī tā′tō), *Latin.* in the work (previously) quoted. *Abbr.:* op. cit.

op·er·et·ta (op′ə ret′ə), *n., pl.* **-tas.** a short, amusing opera, with spoken dialogue: *Whenever a production of Porgy really succeeds, you find that it's been changed into a sort of operetta* (Atlantic). [< Italian *operetta* (diminutive) < *opera* opera]

op·er·ette (op′ə ret′), *n.* operetta: *The most popular theatrical genres are still comedies, musicals, and operettes* (London Times). [< French *opérette* < Italian *operetta*]

op·er·on (op′ər on), *n.* the region of a chromosome which contains the operator gene and any structural genes involved in the production of messenger RNA for a given synthesis. [< *oper*(ator) + *-on,* as in *-ion*]

op·er·ose (op′ə rōs), *adj.* **1.** involving much labor; laborious: *What an operose method! What a train of means to secure a little conversation!* (Emerson). **2.** (of a person) industrious. [< Latin *operōsus* < *opus, -eris* work] —**op′er·ose′ly,** *adv.* —**op′er·ose′ness,** *n.*

O·phel·ia (ə fēl′yə), *n.* in Shakespeare's *Hamlet,* the daughter of Polonius who was driven to madness and suicide by Hamlet's capricious treatment of her.

oph·i·cleide (of′ə klīd), *n.* a low-pitched wind instrument consisting of a conical metal tube bent double, usually with eleven keys, replaced, since about 1850, by the bass tuba. [< French *ophicléide* < Greek *óphis, -eōs* serpent + *kleís, kleidós* key (a similar instrument is called a serpent)]

o·phid·i·an (ō fid′ē ən), *n.* a snake. —*adj.* **1.** like a snake: *the tremendous ophidian head . . . with glistening scales and symmetrical markings* (W.H. Hudson). **2.** of or having to do with snakes or serpents. [< New Latin *Ophidia* the serpent order < Greek *óphis, ópheōs* serpent]

o·phid·i·ar·i·um (ō fid′ē ãr′ē əm), *n., pl.* **-ar·i·ums, -ar·i·a** (-ãr′ē ə). a place where snakes are kept in confinement, for exhibition or for other purposes. [< New Latin *ophidiarium* < *Ophidia;* see OPHIDIAN]

oph·i·ol·a·ter (of′ē ol′ə tər, ō′fē-), *n.* a person who worships snakes.

oph·i·ol·a·trous (of′ē ol′ə trəs, ō′fē-), *adj.* **1.** worshiping snakes. **2.** having to do with ophiolatry.

oph·i·ol·a·try (of′ē ol′ə trē, ō′fē-), *n.* the worship of serpents. [< Greek *óphis, ópheōs* snake + *latreíā* worship]

oph·i·o·log·i·cal (of′ē ə loj′ə kəl, ō′fē-), *adj.* of or having to do with ophiology.

oph·i·ol·o·gist (of′ē ol′ə jist, ō′fē-), *n.* a person skilled in the study of snakes.

oph·i·ol·o·gy (of′ē ol′ə jē, ō′fē-), *n.* the branch of zoology dealing with snakes. [< Greek *óphis, ópheōs* snake + English *-logy*]

oph·i·oph·a·gous (of′ē of′ə gəs, ō′fē-), *adj.* feeding on snakes. [< Greek *óphis, ópheōs* serpent + *phageîn* to feed + English *-ous*]

O·phir (ō′fər), *n.* a place spoken of in the Bible, probably in Arabia or Africa, from which Solomon obtained gold, precious stones, and wood for the Temple. I Kings 9:28; 10:11.

oph·ite (of′īt, ō′fīt), *n.* a greenish altered diabase, produced by the change of augite into uralite. [< Latin *ophītēs* < Greek *ophī́tēs líthos* serpentine[2] (stone), or a similar marble < *óphis* serpent]

o·phit·ic (ō fit′ik), *adj.* **1.** of or like ophite. **2.** of or having to do with certain rocks in which crystals of feldspar are embedded in a matrix of augite.

Oph·i·u·chi (of′ē yü′kī, ō′fē-), *n.* genitive of **Ophiuchus.**

Oph·i·u·chus (of′ē yü′kəs, ō′fē-), *n., genitive* **Oph·i·u·chi.** a constellation on the celestial equator, south of Hercules.

oph·i·u·ran (of′ē yu̇r′ən, ō′fē-), *adj.* of or belonging to a group of echinoderms resembling the starfishes (asteroids) but having slender arms that are sharply marked off from the central disk. —*n.* an ophiuran echinoderm, such as the brittle star. [< New Latin *Ophiura* the typical genus (< Greek *óphis* serpent + *ourá* tail) + English *-an*]

oph·i·u·roid (of′ē yu̇r′oid, ō′fē-), *adj., n.* ophiuran.

oph·thal·mi·a (of thal′mē ə), *n.* an acute inflammation of the eye or the membrane around the eye, sometimes causing blindness. [< Late Latin *ophthalmia* < Greek *ophthálmia* region of the eyes < *opthalmós* eye. Compare *ṓps, ōpós* eye, and *thálamos* chamber.]

ophthalmia ne·o·na·to·rum (nē′ō nə-tôr′əm, -tōr′-), an acute inflammation of the eyes of newborn babies, often caused by gonorrheal infection.

oph·thal·mic (of thal′mik), *adj.* **1.** of or having to do with the eye. **2.** having to do with or affected with ophthalmia. —**Syn. 1.** ocular, optic.

oph·thal·mi·tis (of′thal mī′tis), *n.* ophthalmia.

oph·thal·mo·log·i·cal (of thal′mə loj′ə-kəl), *adj.* of or having to do with ophthalmology. —**oph·thal′mo·log′i·cal·ly,** *adv.*

oph·thal·mol·o·gist (of′thal mol′ə jist), *n.* a doctor who specializes in ophthalmology.

oph·thal·mol·o·gy (of′thal mol′ə jē), *n.* the branch of medicine dealing with the structure, functions, and diseases of the eye.

oph·thal·mom·e·ter (of′thal mom′ə tər), *n.* an instrument for determining the curvature of the cornea of the eye.

oph·thal·mo·ple·gi·a (of thal′mə plē′jē ə), *n.* paralysis of one or more of the muscles of the eye. [< Greek *ophthalmós* eye + *plēgḗ* a stroke, a blow]

oph·thal·mo·scope (of thal′mə skōp), *n.* an instrument for examining the interior of the eye or the retina. It has a small mirror that reflects light into the eye and a hole in the middle of the mirror through which the eye can be examined. [< Greek *ophthalmós* eye + English *-scope*]

oph·thal·mo·scop·ic (of thal′mə skop′ik), *adj.* **1.** of or having to do with the ophthalmoscope or its use. **2.** performed or obtained with an ophthalmoscope: *an ophthalmoscopic analysis.* —**oph·thal′mo·scop′i·cal·ly,** *adv.*

oph·thal·mo·scop·i·cal (of thal′mə-skop′ə kəl), *adj.* ophthalmoscopic.

oph·thal·mos·co·py (of′thal mos′kə pē), *n., pl.* **-pies.** the examination of the interior of the eye with an ophthalmoscope. [< Greek *ophthalmós* eye + English *-scopy*]

o·pi·ate (*n., adj.* ō′pē it, -āt; *v.* ō′pē āt), *n., adj., v.,* **-at·ed, -at·ing.** —*n.* **1.** a drug that contains opium and so dulls pain or brings sleep. **2.** anything that quiets: *opiates to grief.* [*She*] *found the opiate for her discontent in the exertion of her will about smaller things* (George Eliot).

—*adj.* **1.** containing opium. **2.** bringing sleep or ease.

—*v.t.* to subject to an opiate.

[< Medieval Latin *opiatus* < Latin *opium* opium]

o·pi·at·ic (ō′pē at′ik), *adj.* of, having to do with, or caused by an opiate.

o·pine (ō pīn′), *v.t., v.i.,* **o·pined, o·pin·ing.** *Informal* (*now usually humorous*). to hold or express an opinion; think: *Mr. Squeers yawned fearfully and opined that it was high time to go to bed* (Dickens). [< Middle French *opiner,* learned borrowing from Latin *opīnārī*] —**o·pin′er,** *n.*

o·pin·i·a·tive (ə pin′ē ā′tiv, -ə tiv), *adj.* opinionative. —**o·pin′i·a′tive·ly,** *adv.* —**o·pin′i·a′tive·ness,** *n.*

o·pin·ion (ə pin′yən), *n.* **1.** what one thinks; belief not so strong as knowledge; judgment: *Opinion in good men is but knowledge in the making* (Milton). **2.** an impression; estimate: *What is your opinion of him as a candidate? Everyone has a poor opinion of a liar.* **3.** a formal judgment by an expert; professional advice: *He wanted the doctor's opinion about his headaches.* **4.** *Law.* a statement by a judge or jury of the reasons for the decision of the court. **5.** *Obsolete.* self-esteem; self-conceit: *audacious without impudency, learned without opinion* (Shakespeare). **6.** *Obsolete.* reputation; credit: *Thou hast redeem'd thy lost opinion* (Shakespeare).

be of the opinion, to hold the belief or view: *American officers are of the opinion that the Cambodians are incapable of standing up to the Thais or Vietnamese in battle* (New Yorker).

have no opinion, to have an indifferent or unfavorable estimate of someone: *Old Mr. Benjamin Bunny had no opinion of cats whatever* (Beatrix Potter). *She . . . is a hypocritical woman and I have no opinion of her* (Jane Austen).

[< Latin *opīniō, -ōnis*]

—**Syn. 1. Opinion, view** mean what a person thinks about something. **Opinion** suggests a carefully thought out conclusion based on facts, but without the certainty of knowledge: *I try to learn the facts and form my own opinions.* **View** suggests an opinion affected by personal leanings or feelings: *His views are conservative.*

o·pin·ion·al (ə pin′yə nəl), *adj.* of, having to do with, or like opinion.

o·pin·ion·at·ed (ə pin′yə nā′tid), *adj.* obstinate or conceited with regard to one's opinions; dogmatic: *The general is too opinionated to listen to anyone else.* —**o·pin′ion·at′ed·ness,** *n.*

o·pin·ion·a·tive (ə pin′yə nā′tiv), *adj.* **1.** opinionated: *Young men are too opinionative and volatile to be guided by the sober dictates of their seniors* (Jonathan Swift). **2.** having to do with opinion or belief; doctrinal. —**o·pin′ion·a′tive·ly,** *adv.* —**o·pin′ion·a′tive·ness,** *n.*

o·pin·ioned (ə pin′yənd), *adj.* **1.** having an opinion: *to be otherwise opinioned.* **2.** opinionated.

o·pi·ol·o·gy (ō′pē ol′ə jē), *n.* the study of the nature and properties of opium. [< Greek *ópion* (see OPIUM) + English *-logy*]

o·pi·o·ma·ni·a (ō′pē ə mā′nē ə), *n.* an uncontrollable craving for opium.

o·pi·o·ma·ni·ac (ō′pē ə mā′nē ak), *n.* a person affected with opiomania.

o·pi·oph·a·gy (ō′pē of′ə jē), *n.* the eating of opium. [< Greek *ópion* (see OPIUM) + *phageîn* eat + English *-y*[3]]

op·is·thog·na·thism (op′is thog′nə thiz-əm), *n.* the condition of being opisthognathous.

op·is·thog·na·thous (op′is thog′nə thəs), *adj.* **1.** having receding jaws. **2.** (of a jaw) receding. [< Greek *ópisthen* behind + *gnáthos* jaw + English *-ous*]

o·pi·um (ō′pē əm), *n.* **1.** a powerful drug that causes sleep and eases pain. It is also used to stimulate and intoxicate. Opium is a narcotic made from the unripened capsule of the opium poppy and is a bitter substance, containing morphine and other alkaloids. **2.** any thing having the properties or effects of opium: *There is no antidote against the opium of Time* (Sir Thomas Browne). —*adj.* of or having to do with opium: *an opium dream, the opium traffic.* [< Latin *opium* < Greek *ópion* poppy juice, poppy (diminutive) < *opós* vegetable juice]

opium eater, a person addicted to opium eating.

opium eating, the habitual eating or swallowing of opium in some form, as a narcotic.

o·pi·um·ism (ō′pē ə miz′əm), *n.* **1.** the habitual use of opium as a narcotic. **2.** the condition caused by such habitual use.

opium poppy, a kind of poppy from which opium is derived.

opium smoker, a person addicted to opium smoking.

opium smoking, the practice or habit of smoking opium as a stimulant or intoxicant.

opium tincture, *Pharmacy.* laudanum.

OPM (no periods) or **O.P.M.,** Office of Production Management (an agency of the U.S. government during World War II).

op·o·del·doc (op′ə del′dok), *n.* a liniment containing soap and camphor or alcohol, formerly common in medical use. [< New Latin *oppodeltoch* a medical plaster (apparently coined by Paracelsus)]

o·pop·a·nax (ō pop′ə naks), *n.* **1.** a gum resin formerly used in medicine, obtained from the root of a southern European plant of the parsley family. **2.** the plant itself. **3.** a gum resin like myrrh, used in perfumery, obtained from an African tree. [< Latin *opopanax* < Greek *opopánax* < *opós* juice + *pánax* a kind of plant]

o·pos·sum (ə pos′əm), *n.* any of a family of small mammals that carries its young in a pouch or on its back, and lives mostly in trees, especially the Virginia opossum of North and South America. The opossum feeds at night, and when caught pretends to be dead. [American English < Algonkian (Powhatan) *âpäsûm* white animal]

Opossum (including tail, 33 in. long)

opossum shrew, a solenodon.

opossum shrimp, any of a family of small crustaceans resembling shrimps, the females of which carry their eggs in a pouch on the underside of the body.

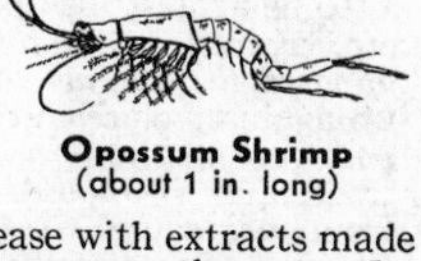

Opossum Shrimp (about 1 in. long)

op·o·ther·a·py (op′ə ther′ə pē), *n.* the treatment of disease with extracts made from animal organs; organotherapy. [< Greek *opós* juice + English *therapy*]

opp., 1. opposed. **2.** opposite. **3.** opposition.

op·pi·dan (op′ə dən), *adj.* of or having to do with a town; urban. —*n.* **1.** an inhabitant of a town; townsman. **2.** *British.* a student boarding in the town, as at Eton College. [< Latin *oppidānus* of a town; urban < *oppidum* town]

op·pi·dum (op′ə dəm), *n., pl.* **-da** (-də). an ancient Roman provincial town: *Vespasian overcame 20 oppida, fought 30 battles, and took the Isle of Wight* (London Times). [< Latin *oppidum*]

op·pi·late (op′ə lāt), *v.t.,* **-lat·ed, -lat·ing.** to fill with obstructing matter; stop up; obstruct. [< Latin *oppīlāre* (with English *-ate*[1]) < *ob-* + *pīlāre* to ram down]

op·pi·la·tion (op′ə lā′shən), *n.* **1.** the act of oppilating. **2.** the state of being oppilated.

op·po·nen·cy (ə pō′nən sē), *n.* the act of opposing or resisting; antagonism; opposition.

op·po·nent (ə pō′nənt), *n.* a person who is on the other side in a fight, game, or discussion; a person fighting, struggling, or speaking against one: *two men, one . . . a zealous supporter and the other a zealous opponent of the system pursued* (Macaulay).
—*adj.* **1.** being opposite; opposing. **2.** of or having to do with those muscles of the hand by which the fingers and thumb may be placed against each other, so as to pick up or hold something.
[< Latin *oppōnēns, -entis,* present participle of *oppōnere* set against < *ob-* against + *pōnere* place]
—**Syn.** *n.* **Opponent, antagonist, adversary** mean someone against a person or thing. **Opponent** applies to someone on the other side in an argument, game, or other contest, or against a proposed plan, law, etc., but does not suggest personal ill will: *He defeated his opponent in the election.* **Antagonist,** more formal, suggests active, personal, and unfriendly opposition, often in a fight for power or control: *Hamlet and his uncle were antagonists.* **Adversary** now usually means a hostile antagonist actively blocking or openly fighting another: *Gamblers found a formidable adversary in the new district attorney.*

op·por·tune (op′ər tün′, -tyün′), *adj.* fortunate; well-chosen; suitable; favorable: *You have come at a most opportune moment, for I need your advice.* [< Middle French *opportune,* learned borrowing from Latin *opportūnus* favorable < *ob portum* (*veniēns*) (going) toward a port[1] (said of the wind)] —**op′por·tune′ly,** *adv.* —**op′por·tune′ness,** *n.* —**Syn.** See **timely.**

op·por·tun·ism (op′ər tü′niz əm, -tyü′-), *n.* the policy or practice of adapting thought and action to particular circumstances rather than to general principles: *Nehru's principles may keep him from this path to oblivion even if opportunism does not* (New Yorker). —**Syn.** expediency.

op·por·tun·ist (op′ər tü′nist, -tyü′-), *n.* a person influenced more by particular circumstances than by general principles: *He was surrounded by adventurers, slick opportunists, intriguers* (Atlantic). —*adj.* opportunistic.

op·por·tun·is·tic (op′ər tü nis′tik, -tyü-), *adj.* of opportunism; characteristic of opportunists. —**op′por·tun·is′ti·cal·ly,** *adv.*

op·por·tu·ni·ty (op′ər tü′nə tē, -tyü′-), *n., pl.* **-ties.** a good chance; favorable time; convenient occasion: *I had an opportunity to earn some money picking blueberries. I have had no opportunity to give John your message, because I have not seen him.*

op·pos·a·bil·i·ty (ə pō′zə bil′ə tē), *n.* the state or property of being opposable: *the opposability of the jaws.*

op·pos·a·ble (ə pō′zə bəl), *adj.* **1.** that can be opposed. **2.** that can be placed opposite something else: *The human thumb is opposable to the fingers.*

op·pose (ə pōz′), *v.,* **-posed, -pos·ing.** —*v.t.* **1.** to be against; be in the way of; act, fight, etc., against; try to hinder; resist: *A swamp opposed the advance of the army.* **2.** to set up against; place in the way of: *Let us oppose good nature to anger.* **3.** to put in contrast: *Love is opposed to hate.* **4.** to put in front of; cause to face: *to oppose one's finger to one's thumb.* —*v.i.* to be or act in opposition; create resistance: *to take arms against a sea of troubles And, by opposing, end them* (Shakespeare). [< Old French *opposer* < *op-* against + *poser* put, pose[1]] —**op·pos′er,** *n.* —**op·pos′ing·ly,** *adv.*
—**Syn.** *v.t.* **1. Oppose, resist, withstand** mean to act or be against someone or something. **Oppose** implies setting oneself against a person or thing, especially an idea, plan, etc., but does not suggest the nature, purpose, form, or effectiveness of the action or stand taken: *We opposed the plan because of the cost.* **Resist** implies making a stand and actively striving against an attack or force of some kind: *The bank messenger resisted the attempt to rob him.* **Withstand** implies holding firm against attack: *The bridge withstood the flood.*

op·pose·less (ə pōz′lis), *adj.* not to be opposed; not resisting: *your great opposeless wills* (Shakespeare).

op·po·site (op′ə zit), *adj.* **1.** placed against; as different in direction as can be; face to face; back to back: *The house straight across the street is opposite to ours.* **2.** as different as can be; just contrary: *Sour is opposite to sweet.* **3.** *Botany.* **a.** situated in pairs on diametrically opposed sides of an axis: *opposite leaves.* **b.** in front of an organ, coming between it and its axis, as a stamen in front of a sepal or petal. **4.** *Obsolete.* opposed in feeling or action; adverse; inimical: *a design of strengthening a party opposite to the public interest* (Jonathan Swift).

Opposite Leaves (def.3a)

—*n.* **1.** a thing or person that is opposite: *Black is the opposite of white.* **2.** *Obsolete.* an antagonist; adversary; opponent: *By the law of arms thou wast not bound to answer An unknown opposite* (Shakespeare).
—*prep.* opposite to: *Wait for me in the building opposite the bank.*
—*adv.* in an opposite position or direction: *to sit opposite.*
[< Latin *oppositus,* past participle of *oppōnere* < *ob-* against + *pōnere* place] —**op′po·site·ly,** *adv.* —**op′po·site·ness,** *n.*
—**Syn.** *adj.* **2. Opposite, contrary** mean completely different (from each other). **Opposite** particularly applies to two things so far apart in position, nature, meaning, etc., that they can never be brought together: *"True" and "false" have opposite meanings.* **Contrary** particularly applies to two things going in opposite directions, or set against each other, often in strong disagreement or conflict: *Your statement is contrary to the facts.*

opposite number, the person who has a similar or corresponding position, duty, or the like, to another; a person's counterpart.

op·po·si·tion (op′ə zish′ən), *n.* **1. a.** action against; resistance: *The mob offered opposition to the police.* **b.** a being opposed or adverse: *Their opposition to the new law is surprising.* **2.** contrast: *high in opposition to low. Between him and Darcy there was a very steady friendship, in spite of great opposition of character* (Jane Austen). **3. a.** Also, **Opposition.** a political party opposed to the party that is in power: *On both occasions the Opposition managed to get themselves on the wrong foot* (Economist). **b.** any party or body of opponents. **4.** a placing opposite. **5.** opposite direction or position: *Before mine eyes in opposition sits Grim Death* (Milton). **6.** the position of two heavenly bodies when their longitude differs by 180 degrees, especially such a position of a heavenly body with respect to the sun. **7.** *Logic.* **a.** the relation between two propositions that have the same subject and predicate but differ in quantity or quality, or in both. **b.** the relation between two propositions that differ in quantity and quality, so that from the truth or falsity of one, the truth or falsity of the other may be determined.
—*adj.* of or having to do with an opposition: *opposition forces, an opposition leader.*
[< Old French *opposicion,* learned borrowing from Latin *oppositiō, -ōnis* < *oppōnere;* see OPPOSITE]
—**Syn.** *n.* **1. b.** antagonism, hostility. **2.** antithesis.

op·po·si·tion·al (op′ə zish′ə nəl), *adj.* of or having to do with opposition or opponents.

op·po·si·tion·ist (op′ə zish′ə nist), *n.* a member of the opposition; person who belongs to the party opposing the existing administration or the party in power: *If the Democrats want to function as stubborn oppositionists, they can take encouragement* (New Yorker).

op·pos·i·tive (ə poz′ə tiv), *adj.* characterized by or expressing opposition; adversative.

op·press (ə pres′), *v.t.* **1.** to govern harshly; keep down unjustly or by cruelty: *A good ruler will not oppress the people.* **2.** to weigh down; lie heavily on; burden: *A sense of trouble ahead oppressed my spirits.* **3.** *Obsolete.* to press down by force; trample down. **4.** *Obsolete.* to put down; suppress. [< Medieval Latin *oppressare* (frequentative) < Latin *opprimere* oppress < *ob-* against + *premere* press] —**Syn. 2.** overburden, crush.

op·pres·sion (ə presh′ən), *n.* **1.** an oppressing; burdening: *The oppression of the people by the nobles caused the war.* **2.** a being oppressed or burdened: *They fought against oppression.* **3.** cruel or unjust treatment. **4.** a heavy, weary feeling. —**Syn. 3.** tyranny, persecution, despotism. **4.** weariness, lassitude, depression.

op·pres·sive (ə pres′iv), *adj.* **1.** harsh; severe; unjust: *Oppressive measures were taken to crush the rebellion.* **2.** hard to bear; burdensome: *an oppressive modesty that found vent in endless apologies* (Elizabeth Gaskell). —**op·pres′sive·ly,** *adv.* —**op·pres′sive·ness,** *n.* —**Syn. 1.** tyrannical.

op·pres·sor (ə pres′ər), *n.* a person who is cruel or unjust to people under him. —**Syn.** despot, tyrant.

op·pro·bri·ous (ə prō′brē əs), *adj.* **1.** expressing scorn, reproach, or abuse: *"Coward," "liar," and "thief" are opprobrious names.* **2.** disgraceful; shameful; infamous: *this dark opprobrious den of shame* (Milton). [< Late Latin *opprobriōsus;* see OPPROBRIUM] —**op·pro′bri·ous·ly,** *adv.* —**op·pro′bri·ous·ness,** *n.* —**Syn. 1.** vituperative, abusive.

op·pro·bri·um (ə prō′brē əm), *n.* **1.** the disgrace or reproach caused by shameful conduct; infamy; scorn; abuse: *Because I had turned against him . . . I was loaded with general opprobrium* (Charlotte Brontë). *There might very well arise the ill-considered compromise such as made the mere words "Munich" and "Yalta" terms of opprobrium* (Wall Street Journal). **2.** a cause or object of such reproach: *The village drunkard was the opprobrium of the community.* [< Latin *opprobrium* < *opprobrāre* to reproach, taunt < *ob-* at + *probrum* infamy, a shameful act] —**Syn. 1.** odium, disrepute.

op·pugn (ə pyün′), *v.t.* **1.** to call in question (rights, merits, judgment, etc.). **2.** to dispute (a statement, belief, etc.): *When Law and Conscience . . . seem to oppugn one another* (Thomas Hobbes). **3.** *Obsolete.* to attack in fight or war. [< Latin *oppūgnāre* attack, besiege < *ob-* against + *pūgnāre* to fight < *pūgna* a fight] —**op·pugn′er,** *n.*

op·pug·nance (ə pug′nəns), *n.* oppugnancy.

op·pug·nan·cy (ə pug′nən sē), *n.* the fact or act of oppugning or opposing.

op·pug·nant (ə pug′nənt), *adj.* opposing; antagonistic; contrary. [< Latin *oppūgnāns, -antis,* present participle of *oppūgnāre;* see OPPUGN]

op·pug·na·tion (op′ug nā′shən), *n. Rare.* the act of oppugning; opposition.

Ops (ops), *n. Roman Mythology.* the wife of Saturn and goddess of plenty, identified by the Greeks with Rhea.

OPS (no periods) or **O.P.S.,** Office of Price Stabilization.

op·si·math (op′sə math), *n.* a person who begins to learn or study late in life: *He is what the Greeks called an opsimath; not ignorant, but a laggard in learning* (Saturday Review). [< Greek *opsimathḗs* late in learning < *opsé* late + *manthánein* learn]

op·sim·a·thy (op sim′ə thē), *n., pl.* **-thies.** **1.** learning or education late in life. **2.** something learned late.

op·sin (op′sin), *n.* a protein formed in the retina, one of the constituents of the visual pigments, such as rhodopsin. [< Greek *ṓps, ōpós* eye + English *-in*]

op·son·ic (op son′ik), *adj.* of, having to do with, produced by, or arising from opsonin.

opsonic index, the ratio of bacteria destroyed by the phagocytes in the blood serum of a given individual to the number destroyed in normal blood serum.

op·son·i·fi·ca·tion (op son′ə fə kā′shən), *n.* **1.** the act of opsonifying. **2.** the state of being opsonified.

op·son·i·fy (op son′ə fī), *v.t.,* **-fied, -fy·ing.** to make (bacteria) more susceptible to destruction by phagocytes by the action of opsonins.

op·so·nin (op′sə nin), *n.* a substance in blood serum that weakens bacteria, so that the white blood cells can destroy them more easily. [< Greek *ópson* a relish (as meat, fish) + English *-in*]

op·so·nize (op′sə nīz), *v.t.*, **-nized, -niz·ing.** 1. to increase the opsonins in, as by immunization. 2. to make (bacteria) more susceptible to destruction by leucocytes.

opt (opt), *v.i.* to make a choice; choose: *British legion women . . . opted to ban knitting at all conferences on the ground that it stops concentration* (Punch).

opt for, to decide to choose; favor; choose: *Those colonies which choose to stay within the French community . . . will have the chance to change their minds later and opt for independence* (Observer).

opt out, to choose to back out; withdraw; resign: *Union members pay a political levy, part of which goes to the party, unless they specifically opt out* (New York Times).

[< French *opter,* learned borrowing from Latin *optāre* choose, desire]

opt., 1. operation. 2. optative. 3. a. optical. b. optician. c. optics. 4. optional.

op·tate (op′tāt), *v.i.*, **-tat·ed, -tat·ing.** to opt.

op·ta·tive (op′tə tiv), *Grammar.* —*adj.* 1. expressing a wish: *"Oh! that I had wings to fly!" is an optative expression.* 2. a. (in Greek and certain other languages) having to do with the verbal mood that expresses desire, wish, etc. b. having to do with distinctive verb forms with such meaning or function.

—*n.* 1. the optative mood. 2. a verb in the optative mood. [< Latin *optātīvus* (*modus*) optative (mood) < *optāre* to wish, choose]

—**op′ta·tive·ly,** *adv.*

op·tic (op′tik), *adj.* of the eye; of the sense of sight. —*n. Informal.* the eye: *I concluded that, by the position of their optics, their sight was so directed downward, that they did not readily see objects that were above them* (Daniel Defoe). [< Middle French *optique,* learned borrowing from Medieval Latin *opticus* < Greek *optikós* < *op-*, stem of *ópsomai,* future of *horân* see]

op·ti·cal (op′tə kəl), *adj.* 1. of the eye; visual: *Near-sightedness is an optical defect.* 2. made to assist sight: *A telescope is an optical instrument.* 3. of vision and light in relation to each other. 4. having to do with optics. —**op′ti·cal·ly,** *adv.* —**Syn.** 1. ocular.

optical activity, *Chemistry.* the ability of a compound to turn the plane of vibration of polarized light.

optical art, a form of abstract painting in which unusual optical illusions and effects are produced by means of highly complex geometrical designs; op art: *What optical art loses through impersonality it gains in universality of appeal* (John Canaday).

optical center, a point in the axis of a lens so situated that all rays pass through the axis and the lens without being refracted.

optical maser, the laser, a device for amplifying and directing light waves.

optical scanner, scanner (def. 4).

optical square, a reflecting instrument used especially by surveyors to mark off right angles.

optic axis, the line in a doubly refracting crystal in the direction of which no double refraction occurs. Crystals having a single such line are uniaxial; crystals having two such lines are biaxial.

op·ti·cian (op tish′ən), *n.* a maker or seller of eyeglasses and other optical instruments: *An optician . . . fills prescriptions for glasses . . . but he does not have the training to treat visual defects* (World Book Encyclopedia). [< French *opticien* < Medieval Latin *optica* optics + French *-ien* -ian]

op·ti·cist (op′tə sist), *n.* a person who studies or is skilled in optics.

optic nerve, the nerve that goes from the eye to the brain. See **eye** for diagram.

op·tics (op′tiks), *n.* the branch of physics that deals with light and vision. [translation of Medieval Latin *optica* < Greek (*tà*) *optiká* (the) optics, neuter plural of *optikós* optic]

optic thalamus, *Anatomy.* thalamus.

op·ti·mal (op′tə məl), *adj.* most favorable; best; optimum. —**op′ti·mal·ly,** *adv.*

op·ti·me (op′tə mē), *n. British.* a candidate for honors in mathematics at Cambridge University. Those in the second grade of honors are called senior optimes; those in the third grade are called junior optimes. [apparently < New Latin *optime* (*disputasti*) (you have disputed) very well < Latin *optimē,* adverb < *optimus;* see OPTIMISM]

op·ti·mism (op′tə miz əm), *n.* 1. a tendency to look on the bright side of things. 2. the belief that everything will turn out for the best. 3. *Philosophy.* a. the doctrine that the existing world is the best of all possible worlds. Optimism, as propounded by Leibnitz, stated that any other doctrine would be inconsistent with the nature of God. b. any doctrine that assumes that good will finally prevail over evil in the universe. [< French *optimisme* < New Latin *optimum* the greatest good (in Leibnitz' philosophy); the best, neuter of Latin *optimus,* superlative of *bonus* good]

op·ti·mist (op′tə mist), *n.* 1. a person who looks on the bright side of things. 2. a person who believes that everything in life will turn out for the best. 3. a person who believes in or supports a doctrine of optimism.

op·ti·mis·tic (op′tə mis′tik), *adj.* 1. inclined to look on the bright side of things. 2. hoping for the best: *I am optimistic about the chance of good weather this weekend.* 3. having to do with optimism. —**op′ti·mis′ti·cal·ly,** *adv.* —**Syn.** 1. sanguine.

op·ti·mis·ti·cal (op′tə mis′tə kəl), *adj.* optimistic.

op·ti·mi·za·tion (op′tə mə zā′shən), *n.* a making the best or most of anything.

op·ti·mize (op′tə mīz), *v.*, **-mized, -miz·ing.** —*v.t.* to make the best or most of; develop to the utmost: *One of the airlines wants to optimize the assignment of its maintenance help* (New Yorker). —*v.i.* to hold or express optimistic views.

op·ti·mum (op′tə məm), *n., pl.* **-mums, -ma** (-mə), *adj.* —*n.* 1. the best or most favorable point, degree, amount, etc., for the purpose. 2. *Biology.* the degree or amount of heat, light, food, moisture, etc., most favorable for the reproduction or other vital process of an organism: *There is usually for each species a rather narrow range, the optimum, in which the organism lives most effectively* (Harbaugh and Goodrich). —*adj.* best or most favorable: *An optimum population is one of a size and quality best fitted to achieve some social goal* (Emory S. Bogardus). [< Latin *optimum,* neuter of *optimus;* see OPTIMISM]

op·tion (op′shən), *n.* 1. the right or freedom of choice: *Each State has local option about daylight-saving time.* 2. a. a choosing; choice: *Pupils in our school have the option of taking Spanish, French, or German.* b. a thing that is or can be chosen. 3. the right to buy something at a certain price within a certain time: *The man paid $500 for an option on the land.* 4. *Insurance.* the right of an insured person to decide how he shall receive the money due him on a policy.

—*v.t.* to obtain or grant an option in reference to (something): *I've written five unproduced plays. One of them . . . has been optioned so often I've made five thousand dollars out of it* (New Yorker).

[< Latin *optiō, -ōnis,* related to *optāre* to desire, choose]

—**Syn.** *n.* 2.a. See **choice.** b. preference.

op·tion·al (op′shə nəl), *adj.* left to one's choice; not required: *Attendance is optional.* —**op′tion·al·ly,** *adv.* —**Syn.** elective.

optional writ, *Law.* a writ that commands the defendant to do the thing required, or show the reason why he has not done it.

op·to·e·lec·tron·ic (op′tō i lek′tron′ik, -ē′lek-), *adj.* combining optical and electrical properties; using light and electricity to transmit signals: *an optoelectronic computer.* [< Greek *optós* seen + English *electronic*]

op·to·ki·net·ic (op′tō ki net′ik), *adj.*, of or having to do with movement of the eyes: *. . . the phenomenon of "optokinetic nystagmus," which is a to and fro movement of the eye* (New Scientist).

op·tom·e·ter (op tom′ə tər), *n.* any of various instruments for testing or measuring the vision, especially the refractive power of the eye. [< Greek *optós* seen + English *-meter*]

op·to·met·ric (op′tə met′rik), *adj.* of or having to do with optometry. —**op′to·met′ri·cal·ly,** *adv.*

op·tom·e·trist (op tom′ə trist), *n.* a person skilled in examining the eyes and prescribing the kind of glasses needed, and legally authorized to do such work, but not a doctor of medicine. [American English < *optometr*(y) + *-ist*]

op·tom·e·try (op tom′ə trē), *n.* the measurement of powers of sight; practice or art of testing eyes in order to fit them with glasses.

op·to·phone (op′tə fōn), *n.* an apparatus for converting optical effects into acoustic effects, especially a telephonic device for enabling the blind to read, the light effects peculiar to each printed letter being made to give rise to a characteristic sound. [< Greek *optós* seen + English *-phone*]

op·u·lence (op′yə ləns), *n.* 1. wealth; riches: *The most meritorious public services have always been performed by persons in a condition of life removed from opulence* (C.J. Fox). 2. abundance; plenty: *He has that opulence which furnishes, at every turn, the precise weapon he needs* (Emerson). —**Syn.** 1. affluence.

op·u·len·cy (op′yə lən sē), *n. Obsolete.* opulence.

op·u·lent (op′yə lənt), *adj.* 1. a. wealthy; rich: *an opulent merchant.* b. showing wealth; costly and luxurious: *an opulent home.* 2. abundant; plentiful: *opulent sunshine.* [< Latin *opulentus* < *ops, opis* power, resources + *-lentus* abounding in] —**op′u·lent·ly,** *adv.* —**Syn.** 1. a. affluent. 2. profuse.

o·pun·ti·a (ō pun′shē ə), *n.* 1. any of a large group of cactuses comprising fleshy herbs, shrubby plants, and sometimes trees; prickly pear. Opuntias have branches of flattened, globose, or cylindrical joints with hairy tubercles set with sharp spines, and commonly bear yellow flowers succeeded by a pear-shaped pulpy berry that is often edible. 2. the fruit of any of these plants. [< New Latin *Opuntia* the genus name < Latin *opuntia* a kind of prickly pear, apparently < *Opus, -untis,* a city of Locris, Greece, where it grew]

o·pus (ō′pəs), *n., pl.* **op·er·a** or **o·pus·es.** a work; composition: *The violinist played his own opus, No. 16.* [< Latin *opus, -eris* a work] —**Syn.** creation, production.

➔ Because the Latin plural is identical with *opera* "musical drama," it is now generally replaced, except in learned use, by *opuses.*

o·pus·cule (ō pus′kyül), *n.* a small work, especially a literary or musical work of small size or limited scope: *In this opuscule he points out that Modern Society is passing through a great crisis* (John Morley). [< Latin *opusculum* (diminutive) < *opus, -eris* a work]

o·pus·cu·lum (ō pus′kyə ləm), *n., pl.* **-la** (-lə). an opuscule: *She . . . proudly showed me her book collection, which contained one of your opuscula* (John Pearson). [< Latin *opusculum;* see OPUSCULE]

o·quas·sa (ō kwas′ə), *n.* a small, bluish trout, found especially in the lakes of central Maine. [American English, apparently < *Oquassa* Lake, Maine]

Oquassa (8 in. long)

or[1] (ôr; *unstressed* ər), *conj.* 1. a word used to express a choice, difference, etc.: *You may go or stay. Is it sweet or sour?* 2. and if not; otherwise: *Either eat this or go hungry. Hurry, or you will be late.* 3. that is; being the same as: *This is the end or last part.* [Middle English *or,* reduction of *other,* perhaps fusion of Old English *oththe* or, and *āther* either]

or[2] (ôr), *prep., conj. Archaic.* before; ere: *I'll be there long or that* (Robert Louis Stevenson). [Old English *ār* early, confused in sense with *ǣr* ere]

or[3] (ôr), *n.* (in heraldry) the gold or yellow in coats of arms. [< French *or* < Old French < Latin *aurum* gold]

-or, *suffix.* 1. person or thing that ——s: *Actor = a person that acts. Accelerator = a thing that accelerates.*

2. act, state, condition, quality, characteristic, etc., especially in words from Latin, as in *error, horror, labor, terror.*

[< Middle French *-our* < Old French < Latin *-or*]

➔ **-or, -our.** American spelling prefers *-or* in such words as *color, governor, honor.* When referring to Jesus Christ, *Saviour* is frequently spelled with the *u,* but in other senses without it. *Glamour* still survives, but the *u* is rapidly being dropped from this word. British usage is divided on this point, though of course to an American reader the words in *-our* are conspicuous.

OR (no periods) or **O.R.**, operations research.

o·ra (ôr′ə, or′-), *n. Latin.* plural of **os**².

or·ach or **or·ache** (ôr′ək, or′-), *n.* any of a group of plants of the goosefoot family, especially a tall annual whose leaves can be eaten like spinach. [Middle English *orage, arage* < Old French (Picard) *arrache,* ultimately < Latin *atriplex, -icis* < Greek *atráphaxys*]

or·a·cle (ôr′ə kəl, or′-), *n.* **1.** in ancient Greece and Rome: **a.** the answer of a god to some question. It often had a hidden meaning that was hard to understand. **b.** a place where the god gave such answers: *A famous oracle was at Delphi.* **c.** the priest, priestess, or other means by which the god's answer was given. **2.** a very wise person: *Under the instructions of these political oracles the good people . . . became exceedingly enlightened* (Washington Irving). **3.** a very wise answer. **4.** something regarded as a reliable or sure guide, as a compass or a watch. **5.** divine revelation; a message from God. **6.** a prophet. **7.** the holy of holies in the ancient Jewish Temple.

oracles, the Bible: . . . *unto them were committed the oracles of God* (Romans 3:2).

work the oracle. a. to scheme; pull strings: *Every reader will be able to form his own judgment of the methods which* [*certain publishers*] *adopt to work the oracle in their favour* (Pall Mall Gazette). **b.** *Slang.* to raise money: *With . . . big local loan mongers to work the oracle* (John Newman).

[< Old French *oracle,* learned borrowing from Latin *ōrāculum* < *ōrāre* (originally) recite solemnly]

—**Syn. 2.** sage.

o·rac·u·lar (ô rak′yə lər, ō-), *adj.* **1.** of or like an oracle: *That irrepressibly oracular figure, Dr. Samuel Johnson* (Atlantic). **2.** with a hidden meaning that is difficult to make out. **3.** very wise: *an oracular statement or manner. They referred to each other as oracular sources of wisdom and good taste* (Arnold Bennett).

[< Latin *ōrāculum* oracle + English *-ar*]

—**o·rac′u·lar·ly,** *adv.*

—**Syn. 3.** sagacious.

o·rac·u·lar·i·ty (ô rak′yə lar′ə tē, ō-), *n.* the quality or character of being oracular.

o·ral (ôr′əl, ōr′-), *adj.* **1.** using speech; spoken: *An oral agreement is not enough; we must have a written promise.* **2.** of the mouth: *oral hygiene. The oral opening in an earthworm is small.* **3.** through or by the mouth: *an oral dose of morphine.* **4.** *Phonetics.* articulated with the breath stream passing out entirely through the mouth: *Most sounds are, in fact, oral, or better perhaps, buccal* (Simeon Potter). **5.** of or having to do with instruction of the deaf and dumb by or in lip reading.

—*n.* an oral examination.

orals, a series of oral examinations taken by a candidate for a doctoral degree: *He handed in his thesis in March, and passed his orals four months later.*

[< Latin *ōs, ōris* mouth + English *-al*¹]

➤ **oral, verbal.** Strictly, *oral* means spoken, and *verbal* means in words; but the distinction is often ignored: *He gave an oral report. They had only a verbal agreement.*

o·ral·i·ty (ô ral′ə tē, ō-), *n.* **1.** the quality of being oral. **2.** *Psychology.* the derivation of sexual pleasure from stimulation of the mouth.

o·ral·ly (ôr′ə lē, ōr′-), *adv.* **1.** by spoken words. **2.** by the mouth.

o·rang (ō rang′), *n.* orang-utan.

or·ange (ôr′inj, or′-), *n.* **1.** a round, reddish-yellow, juicy, edible citrus fruit that grows in warm climates. **2.** any of the evergreen trees of the rue family bearing this fruit. The orange has fragrant white blossoms and oval or elliptical leaves. Its blossom is the floral emblem of Florida. **3.** a fruit or tree that suggests an orange, such as the Osage orange and a hardy Japanese tree grown chiefly for hedges in the United States. **4.** a reddish yellow.

Orange Branch (def. 2)

—*adj.* **1.** of or like an orange. **2.** reddish-yellow.

[< Old French *pomme d'orenge* < Spanish *naranja* < Arabic *nāranj* < Persian *nārang;* influenced in Old French by *or* gold, and the *n* was lost by misdivision of the article *un*] —**or′ange·like′,** *adj.*

or·ange·ade (ôr′inj ād′, or′-), *n.* a drink made of orange juice, sugar, and water.

orange blossom, the fragrant white flower of the orange, much worn by brides in wreaths, or carried in bridal bouquets.

or·ange-crowned warbler (ôr′inj-kround′, or′-), a North American warbler with dull greenish plumage and an inconspicuous tawny patch on the crown.

or·ange-cup lily (ôr′inj kup′, or′-), a lily of the eastern United States that bears a cup-shaped orange flower with purple spots.

orange hawkweed, a European variety of hawkweed with orange-red clusters of flowers, that has become naturalized in eastern North America.

Or·ange·ism (ôr′in jiz əm, or′-), *n.* the principles and practices of the Orangemen; the principle of Protestant political supremacy in Ireland.

Or·ange·ist (ôr′in jist, or′-), *n.* an advocate of Orangeism.

Or·ange·man (ôr′inj mən, or′-), *n., pl.* **-men.** a member of a secret society formed in the north of Ireland in 1795, to uphold the Protestant religion and Protestant control in Ireland.

orange pekoe, a black tea that comes from Ceylon or India, usually made from the smallest leaves at the tips of the branches.

or·ange·root (ôr′inj rüt′, or′-; -růt′), *n.* goldenseal; a North American plant whose rootstock is used in medicine.

or·ange·ry (ôr′inj rē, or′-), *n., pl.* **-ries.** a place, usually a greenhouse, for growing orange trees in cool climates. Orangeries were formerly common to the formal gardens of great estates. [< French *orangerie* < *orange* orange]

oranges and lemons, a children's singing game in which the players take sides according to their answer to the question, "Which will you have, oranges or lemons?": *The brother and sister, deciding which side to elect, seem to be playing oranges and lemons* (London Times).

orange squash, *Especially British.* orangeade.

orange stick, a small stick used in manicuring, originally of orangewood, and pointed at one end, with the other end broad and tapered.

or·ange·wood (ôr′inj wůd′, or′-), *n.* the hard, fine-grained wood of the orange tree, used as a cabinet wood, for small dental tools, and for manicuring the nails. —*adj.* of this wood.

or·ange·y (ôr′in jē, or′-), *adj.* like an orange in color, taste, etc.

Or·an·gism (ôr′in jiz əm, or′-), *n.* Orangeism.

Or·an·gist (ôr′in jist, or′-), *n.* **1.** Orangeist. **2.** an adherent of the House of Orange, in the Netherlands.

o·rang-ou·tang (ō rang′ů tang′), *n.* orang-utan.

o·rang-u·tan or **o·rang·u·tan** (ō rang′ů-tan′), *n.* a large ape of the forests of Borneo and Sumatra, that has long, reddish-brown hair and very long arms. The orang-utan is an anthropoid ape and lives mostly in trees, eating fruits and leaves. Also, **ourang-outang.** [ultimately < Malay *orangutan* wild man < *orang* man + *utan* of the woods]

Orang-utan
(5 ft. tall when standing)

o·rant (ôr′ənt, ōr′-), *n.* orante: . . . *a free-standing orant, probably Jonah, which Wixom calls "one of the most moving depictions of a figure in prayer in the entire history of art"* (Time). [< Latin *ōrāns, -āntis;* see ORANTE]

o·ran·te (ô ran′tē, ō-), *n.* (in early Christian art) a figure, usually female, standing with arms outspread or raised in prayer. [< Italian *orante* < Latin *ōrāns, -āntis,* present participle of *ōrāre* recite, pray]

o·ra pro no·bis (ôr′ə prō nō′bis, ōr′-), *Latin.* **1.** pray for us. **2.** (in the Roman Catholic liturgy) the refrain of a litany to the Virgin Mary.

o·rate (ô rāt′, ō-; ôr′āt, ōr′-), *v.,* **o·rat·ed, o·rat·ing.** *Informal.* —*v.i.* to make an oration; talk in a grand manner. —*v.t.* to harangue. [apparently back formation < *oration*]

o·ra·tion (ô rā′shən, ō-), *n.* **1.** a formal public speech delivered on a special occasion: *the orations of Cicero.* **2.** a speech given in an overly formal or affected style. [< Latin *ōrātiō, -ōnis* < *ōrāre* speak formally, recite. Doublet of ORISON.] —**Syn. 1.** address. See **speech.**

o·ra·ti·o o·bli·qua (ô rā′shē ō ə blē′-kwə, ō-; -shō-), *Latin.* **1.** indirect use of language: . . . *muttering in brave oratio obliqua so that no foreign queue-jumper can actually catch them criticising* (Manchester Guardian). **2.** (literally) oblique oration.

or·a·tor (ôr′ə tər, or′-), *n.* **1.** a person who makes an oration. **2.** a person who can speak very well in public and often with great eloquence: *I come not, friends, to steal away your hearts: I am no orator, as Brutus is* (Shakespeare). **3.** *Law, Obsolete.* the plaintiff in a suit in chancery. [< Latin *ōrātor* speaker < *ōrāre;* see ORATION]

or·a·to·ri·al (ôr′ə tôr′ē əl, -tōr′-; or′-), *adj.* **1.** of, having to do with, or befitting an orator. **2.** of or having to do with an oratorio. —**or′a·to′ri·al·ly,** *adv.*

Or·a·to·ri·an (ôr′ə tôr′ē ən, -tōr′-; or′-), *adj.* of or having to do with an Oratory. —*n.* a member of an Oratory.

or·a·tor·ic (ôr′ə tôr′ik, or′ə tor′-), *adj.* oratorical.

or·a·tor·i·cal (ôr′ə tôr′ə kəl, or′ə tor′-), *adj.* **1.** of oratory; having to do with orators or oratory: *an oratorical contest.* **2.** characteristic of orators or oratory: *an oratorical manner.* —**or′a·tor′i·cal·ly,** *adv.* —**Syn. 1.** declamatory. **2.** eloquent.

or·a·to·ri·o (ôr′ə tôr′ē ō, -tōr′-; or′-), *n., pl.* **-ri·os.** a musical composition, usually based on a religious theme, for solo voices, chorus, and orchestra, dramatic in character, but performed without action, costumes, or scenery. [< Italian *oratorio* (originally) place of prayer < Late Latin *ōrātōrium.* Doublet of ORATORY².]

or·a·tor·ize (ôr′ə tə rīz, or′-), *v.i.,* **-ized, -iz·ing.** to play the orator; orate: *They reached the magistrate's house . . . Mr. Pickwick oratorizing and the crowd shouting* (Dickens).

or·a·to·ry¹ (ôr′ə tôr′ē, -tōr′-; or′-), *n.* **1.** skill in public speaking; fine speaking: *Their leader's rabble-rousing oratory had parlayed the seething resentments* (Newsweek). **2.** the art of public speaking, especially according to definite rules. [< Latin (*ars*) *ōrātōria* oratorical (art), feminine adjective < *ōrāre* plead, speak formally]

—**Syn. 1.** eloquence. **2.** declamation.

or·a·to·ry² (ôr′ə tôr′ē, -tōr′-; or′-), *n., pl.* **-ries.** a small chapel; room set apart for prayer. [< Late Latin *ōrātōrium,* noun use of adjective < Latin *ōrāre* pray, recite formally. Doublet of ORATORIO.]

Or·a·to·ry (ôr′ə tôr′ē, -tōr′-; or′-), *n., pl.* **-ries. 1.** any of certain religious societies of the Roman Catholic Church, especially one composed of secular priests, not bound by vows, devoted to simple and familiar preaching. **2.** a local branch or house of an Oratory society.

or·a·tress (ôr′ə tris, or′-), *n.* a woman orator.

orb (ôrb), *n.* **1.** a sphere; globe: *What a hell of witchcraft lies In the small orb of one particular tear!* (Shakespeare). **2. a.** the sun, the moon, a planet, or a star: *the orb of day, the sun; the orb of night, the moon.* **b.** the earth; the world. **3.** *Poetic.* the eyeball or eye: *His eyelids heavily closed over their orbs* (Washington Irving). **4.** Also, **Orb.** a globe surmounted by a cross, symbolizing royal sovereignty. **5.** an organized or collective whole. **6.** *Astrology.* the space within which the influence of a planet, star, or house is supposed to act. **7.** *Obsolete.* anything of circular form.

—*v.t.* **1.** to form into a circle, disk, or sphere; make round. **2.** to encircle; enclose. —*v.i.* **1.** to form itself into an orb. **2.** to move in an orbit.

[< Old French *orbe,* learned borrowing from Latin *orbis* circle]

—**Syn.** *n.* **1.** ball.

or·bic·u·lar (ôr bik′yə lər), *adj.* **1.** like a circle or sphere; rounded. **2.** *Botany.* having the shape of a flat body with a nearly circular outline, as a leaf. [< Late Latin *orbiculāris* < Latin *orbiculus* (diminutive) < *orbis* circle] —**or·bic′u·lar·ly,** *adv.* —**or·bic′u·lar·ness,** *n.* —**Syn. 1.** circular, spherical.

Orbicular Leaf (def. 2)

or·bic·u·lar·i·ty (ôr bik′yə lar′ə tē), *n., pl.* **-ties.** an orbicular quality or form.

or·bic·u·late (ôr bik′yə lit, -lāt), *adj.* orbicular. [< Latin *orbiculātus* < *orbiculus;* see ORBICULAR] —**or·bic′u·late·ly,** *adv.*

or·bic·u·lat·ed (ôr bik′yə lā′tid), *adj.* orbicular.

or·bis sci·en·ti·a·rum (ôr′bis sī en′shē ãr′əm), *Latin.* the world of science; sum of what is known in science.

or·bit (ôr′bit), *n.* **1.** the path of the earth or any one of the planets about the sun: *the orbit of Mars.* **2.** the path of any heavenly body about another heavenly body. **3.** the path of a man-made satellite about any heavenly body: *to put a satellite into orbit about the earth.* **4.** the regular path traveled by any particle of matter. **5.** the regular course of life or experience; area of knowledge or skill: *a problem not in his orbit. They knew each other by sight, but their orbits did not touch* (Arnold Bennett). **6.** the sphere of influence of a country in politics, trade, etc.: *The U.S.S.R. makes constant efforts to woo Asian neutrals into the Communist orbit.* **7. a.** the bony cavity or socket in which the eyeball is set. **b.** the eye; eyeball.
—*v.t.* **1.** to put into an orbit: ... *whether one nation will want another nation to orbit numbers of satellites over its country* (Bulletin of Atomic Scientists). **2.** to travel in an orbit around: *Some satellites can orbit the earth in less than an hour.*
—*v.i.* **1.** to travel in an orbit: *The satellite itself will orbit around the earth for a period of days* (New York Times). **2.** (of a satellite, etc.) to arrive in its orbit; achieve orbital velocity.
[< Latin *orbita* wheel track < *orbis* circle, wheel]
—**Syn.** *n.* **5.** field.

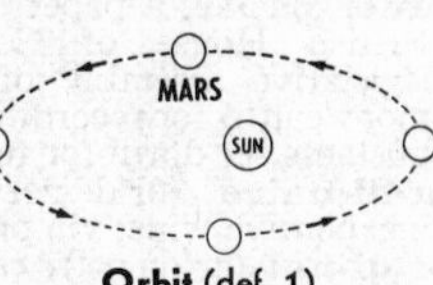

Orbit (def. 1)

or·bi·tal (ôr′bə təl), *adj.* **1.** of an orbit: *A Discoverer IX satellite rocket ... failed to reach orbital speed and burned up while falling back into the earth's atmosphere* (Wall Street Journal). **2.** of or having to do with the orbit of the eye. —*n. Physics.* the wave function of an electron moving in a molecule or atom, corresponding to the orbit or path of an electron in earlier theory.

orbital index, the ratio of length to height of the orbit of the eye.

orbital velocity, 1. the velocity at which a body, as a satellite, revolves about another body: *Orbital velocity is 18,000 miles per hour 24,200 feet per second for a circular orbit at 300 miles altitude* (United States Air Force Report on the Ballistic Missile). **2.** the velocity a body must achieve and maintain to go into or remain in orbit.

or·bit·er (ôr′bit ər), *n.* something that orbits, as an artificial satellite.

or·bi·to·sphe·noid (ôr′bə tō sfē′noid), *adj.* having to do with the orbitosphenoid bone. —*n.* the orbitosphenoid bone.

orbitosphenoid bone, a section of the sphenoid bone forming a part of the bony orbit of the eye.

orb weaver, any of a group of strong-jawed spiders that spin nearly circular webs, anchored at various points around the circumference.

orb web, the web spun by an orb weaver: ... *the orb webs of the nearly blind cave spiders* (Scientific American).

orc (ôrk), *n.* any of various marine mammals, as the grampus or killer whale: *The haunt of seals, and orcs, and sea-mews' clang* (Milton). Also, **ork.** [< Latin *orca* a kind of whale]

ORC (no periods) or **O.R.C., 1.** Officers' Reserve Corps. **2.** Organized Reserve Corps (of the U.S. Army).

Or·ca·di·an (ôr kā′dē ən), *adj.* of or having to do with the Orkney Islands, north of Scotland. —*n.* a native or inhabitant of the Orkney Islands. [< Latin *Orcadēs* the Orkney Islands + English *-ian*]

or·ce·in (ôr′sē in), *n.* a reddish or purplish nitrogenous dye obtained from orcinol by the action of ammonia and oxygen, or from the dye orchil. It is used in microscopic stains and as a reagent. *Formula:* $C_{28}H_{24}O_7N_2$ [< French *orcein,* alteration of earlier English *orcin;* see ORCINOL]

orch., orchestra.

or·chal (ôr′kəl), *n.* orchil.

or·chard (ôr′chərd), *n.* **1.** a piece of ground on which fruit trees are grown. **2.** the trees in an orchard: *The orchard is bearing well this year.* [Old English *orcgeard,* and *ortgeard,* perhaps < Latin *hortus* garden. Compare Old English *geard* yard[1].]

orchard grass, cocksfoot; a perennial grass, valuable for hay and pasture.

or·chard·ing (ôr′chər ding), *n.* the care and management of an orchard.

or·chard·ist (ôr′chər dist), *n.* a person who grows or cares for an orchard.

or·chard·man (ôr′chərd mən), *n., pl.* **-men.** orchardist.

orchard oriole, an oriole of the eastern and central United States and Mexico, similar to the Baltimore oriole but having chestnut instead of orange feathers on its body. It suspends its nest from the branches of fruit and shade trees.

or·ches·tic (ôr kes′tik), *adj.* of or having to do with dancing. [< Greek *orchēstikós* < *orcheîsthai* to dance]

or·ches·tra (ôr′kə strə), *n.* **1.** a group of musicians playing at a concert, an opera, or a play. An orchestra is usually distinguished from a band by the use of violins and other stringed instruments: *a symphony orchestra, a dance orchestra.* **2.** violins, cellos, clarinets, and other instruments played together by the musicians in an orchestra. **3.** the part of a theater, auditorium, etc., just in front of the stage, where musicians sit to play. **4.** the main floor of a theater, especially the part near the front: *Buy two seats in the orchestra.* **5.** (in the ancient Greek theater) a large semicircular space in front of the stage, where the chorus sang and danced. **6.** (in the Roman theater) a similar space reserved for the seats of senators and other persons of distinction.
—*adj.* of or having to do with an orchestra: *the orchestra pit, orchestra seats.*
[< Latin *orchēstra* < Greek *orchḗstra* the space where the chorus of dancers performed, ultimately < *orcheîsthai* to dance]

or·ches·tral (ôr kes′trəl), *adj.* of an orchestra; composed for or performed by an orchestra. —**or·ches′tral·ly,** *adv.*

or·ches·trate (ôr′kə strāt), *v.t., v.i.,* **-trat·ed, -trat·ing. 1.** to compose or arrange (music) for an orchestra. **2.** to combine or arrange harmoniously: *These flashbacks are so orchestrated that changes in location and pace ... have a cumulative effect* (Listener).

or·ches·tra·tion (ôr′kə strā′shən), *n.* **1.** the arrangement of music for an orchestra: *The orchestration is so thick that the tunes can't emerge as buoyantly as they should* (New Yorker). **2.** any harmonious arrangement: ... *a wonderful orchestration of deep and pale colours* (Manchester Guardian Weekly).

or·ches·tra·tor (ôr′kə strā′tər), *n.* a person who composes or arranges music for performance by an orchestra: *He is a superb orchestrator, after Berlioz; his work is transparent and as mobile as quicksilver* (Harper's).

or·ches·tri·na (ôr′kə strē′nə), *n.* a reed organ that can imitate instruments such as the flute, clarinet, oboe, bassoon, and French horn by varying the form of the reeds or wind channels.

or·ches·tri·on (ôr kes′trē ən), *n.* a mechanical musical instrument, resembling a barrel organ, for producing the effect of an orchestra: *The Black Forest is famous for .. orchestrions* (C.W. Wood). [< German *Orchestrion* < Greek *orchēstra;* see ORCHESTRA]

or·chid (ôr′kid), *n.* **1.** a plant with beautiful, queerly shaped flowers that are formed of three petallike sepals and three petals, one petal being very different from the other two. **2.** the flower of any of these plants. **3.** a light purple.
—*adj.* light-purple.
[< New Latin *orchid-,* erroneous stem of Latin *orchis* a kind of orchid < Greek *órchis* an orchid; (originally) testicle (because of the shape of its root)]

or·chi·da·ceous (ôr′kə dā′shəs), *adj.* belonging to the orchid family of plants.

orchid family, any of a family of terrestrial and epiphytic monocotyledonous herbs, widely distributed in temperate and tropical regions. Orchids have beautiful, queerly shaped flowers that are characterized by having their style, stigma, and stamens united into a central body (the column). The orchid family includes the lady's-slipper, arethusa, rattlesnake plantain, twayblade, showy orchis, and lady's-tresses.

or·chid·ist (ôr′kə dist), *n.* a person who cultivates orchids.

or·chid·ol·o·gist (ôr′kə dol′ə jist), *n.* a person skilled in orchidology.

or·chid·ol·o·gy (ôr′kə dol′ə jē), *n.* the branch of botany, or of horticulture, that deals with orchids.

or·chil (ôr′kəl, -chəl), *n.* **1.** a red or violet coloring matter obtained from certain lichens. **2.** any lichen that yields it. Also, **archil, orchal.** [Middle English *orchell* < Old French *orcheil*]

or·chis (ôr′kis), *n.* **1.** an orchid. **2.** any of a group of terrestrial orchids of temperate regions. The showy orchis, a common North American kind, has a spike of pink-purple flowers with a white lip. **3.** any related orchid, such as the fringed orchis. [< Latin *orchis* < Greek *órchis* (originally) testicle; see ORCHID]

or·chit·ic (ôr kit′ik), *adj.* having to do with orchitis.

or·chi·tis (ôr kī′tis), *n.* inflammation of a testicle. [< Greek *órchis* testicle + English *-itis*]

or·cin (ôr′sin), *n.* orcinol.

or·cin·ol (ôr′sə nōl, -nol), *n.* a white crystalline substance, a phenol, obtained from various lichens or prepared artificially. It is used chiefly as a reagent and also as an antiseptic. *Formula:* $C_7H_8O_2.H_2O$ [< *orcin* ultimately < New Latin *Variolaria orcina* orchil (because it was originally prepared from this lichen) + *-ol*[2]]

Or·cus (ôr′kəs), *n. Roman Mythology.* **1.** the abode of the dead; Hades. **2.** the god of the abode of the dead; Pluto.

ord., an abbreviation for the following:
1. ordained.
2. order.
3. ordinal.
4. ordinance.
5. ordinary.
6. ordnance.

or·dain (ôr dān′), *v.t.* **1.** to establish as a law; order; fix; decide; appoint: *In some places the law ordains that murderers shall be hanged. The eternal rules of order and right, which Heaven itself has ordained* (Time). **2.** to appoint or consecrate officially as a clergyman. **3.** to appoint (a person, etc.) to a charge, duty, or office. —*v.i.* to command.
[< Anglo-French *ordeigner,* Old French *ordener,* learned borrowing from Latin *ōrdināre* arrange (in Medieval Latin, consecrate; take holy orders) < *ōrdō, -inis* order] —**or·dain′er,** *n.* —**Syn.** *v.t.* **1.** decree, prescribe.

or·dain·ment (ôr dān′mənt), *n.* **1.** the act of ordaining. **2.** the state of being ordained.

or·deal (ôr dēl′, ôr′dēl), *n.* **1.** a severe test or experience: *Jack dreaded the ordeal of a visit to the dentist. She wondered how he, and how she, would comport themselves in the ordeal of adieu* (Arnold Bennett). **2.** (in early times) an effort to decide the guilt or innocence of an accused person by making him do something dangerous like holding fire or taking poison. It was supposed that an innocent person would not be harmed by such danger.
[Old English *ordāl, ordēl* judgment; influenced by *deal*]
—**Syn. 1.** trial.

ordeal bean, the poisonous Calabar bean of Africa, used by certain tribesmen in an ordeal to decide guilt.

or·der (ôr′dər), *n.* **1.** the way one thing follows another: *in order of size, in alphabetical order, the order of history.* **2. a.** the condition in which every part or piece is in its right place: *to put a room in order.* **b.** a regular, methodical, or harmonious arrangement: *the order of a fleet of ships.* **3.** condition; state: *a machine in good working order. My affairs are in good order.* **4.** the way the world works; way things happen: *the order of nature.* **5.** the state or condition of things in which the law is obeyed and there is no trouble: *The police maintained order.* **6.** the principles and rules by which a meeting is run: *to rise to a point of order.* **7.** a telling what to do; command: *The orders of the captain must be obeyed.* **8.** a direction of a court or judge, especially one made in writing and not included in a judgment. **9. a.** a paper saying that money is to be given or paid, or something handed over: *a postal money order.* **b.** the account of someone; someone's disposition of money: *He received a note for $1,000 payable to his order after one year.* **10.** a statement or list of things telling a store or tradesman what you wish sent: *a grocery order.* **11.** a kind or sort: *He had ability of a high order.* **12.** *Biology.* a group in the classifying of plants and animals that is below or smaller than a class, but larger than a family: *The rose family, the pea family, and several others belong to one order.* **13.** a social rank, grade, or class: *all orders of society. He had found, in general, the lower orders debased; the superior immersed in sordid pursuits* (Benjamin Disraeli). **14.** a rank or position in the church: *the order of bishops.* **15. a.** ordination. **b.** the rite of ordination; holy orders. **16. a.** a brotherhood of monks, friars, or knights: *the Benedictine Order.* **b.** a sisterhood of nuns. **17.** a society to which one is admitted as an honor: *the Order of the Golden Fleece, the Order of the Garter.* **18.** a modern fraternal organization: *the Order of Masons.* **19.** the badge worn by those belonging to an honorary order. **20. a.** any one of the typical

DORIC

IONIC

CORINTHIAN

Greek Orders (def. 20a)

styles of columns and architecture, having differences in proportion, decoration, etc.: *the Doric, Ionic, and Corinthian orders.* **b.** a style of building. **21.** the regular form of worship for a given occasion. **22.** a portion or serving of food served in a restaurant, etc. **23.** *Mathematics.* the degree (of complexity). **24.** the arrangement of the constituents in a linguistic expression. **25.** *Military.* the command or position of order arms. **26.** any of the nine ranks or grades of angels in medieval angelology. **27.** *Especially British.* a pass for admission, without payment or at a reduced price, to a theater, museum, etc.

by order, according to an order given by the proper person: *by order of the governor.*

call to order, a. to open (a convention, meeting, etc.) for formal proceedings: *The annual town meeting of the town of Seekonk was called to order Monday by Town Clerk Hill* (Providence Journal). **b.** to ask to be quiet and start work: *The teacher called the class to order.*

in order, a. in proper sequence or succession: *The lowest first, and without stop the rest in order to the top* (William Cowper). **b.** in proper condition; working properly: *Having set all things in order for that voyage . . .* (Miles Coverdale). **c.** in obedience to authority: *One of the chief duties of these societies is to keep the women in order* (Mary Kingsley). **d.** allowed by the rules of a meeting, etc.: *The motion is in order.* **e.** natural; logical; likely to be done: *A visit to the place seemed in order.* **f.** current; in fashion; appropriate: *A quotation from Professor James on any subject which his brilliant pen has touched is always in order* (H.H. Horne).

in orders, being a clergyman: *A master of arts, in full orders, is desirous of a curacy* (Harriet Martineau).

in order that, so that; with the purpose that: *Come early in order that you may see him.*

in order to, as a means to; to: *He ran in order to catch the train.*

in short order, without delay; quickly: *He hurried away and returned in short order.*

on order, having been ordered but not yet received: *American Airlines Inc. hopes to get two to four of the 35 Electras it has on order this year* (Wall Street Journal).

on or of the order of, somewhat like; similar to: *a house on the order of ours. The next day the photographer arrived, a nice tall thin man of the order of Mel Ferrer* (Punch).

out of order, a. not in proper sequence or succession: *He listed the States alphabetically, but California was out of order.* **b.** not in working condition: *The watch is out of order.* **c.** against the rules of a meeting, etc.: *Senator W. Kerr Scott . . . ruled the motion out of order on grounds that a quorum was not present* (New York Times). **d.** indisposed; sick: *His . . . Majesty being out of order, by reason of a cold* (London Gazette). **e.** in confusion or disorder: *The boy's room was out of order.* **f.** inappropriate; uncalled-for: *It was out of order to make such a tactless remark.*

take orders. See under **holy orders.**

to order, according to the buyer's wishes or requirements: *a coat made to order.*

—*v.t.* **1.** to put in order; arrange: *to order one's affairs. I had to order my life methodically* (Joseph Conrad). **2.** to tell what to do; give an order to; command; bid: *to order a person to leave. He ordered that the prisoners be handcuffed.* **3.** to prescribe as medicine: *to order a tonic for a patient.* **4.** to give (a store, etc.) an order for; direct (a thing) to be made or furnished: *to order dinner, to order a cab. She ordered a chicken from the butcher.* **5.** to decide; will; determine: *The authorities ordered it otherwise.* **6.** *Ecclesiastical.* to invest with clerical rank and authority. **7.** *Archaic.* to draw up in order of battle.

—*v.i.* to give orders, directions, etc.: *Please order for me.*

order about or **around,** to send here and there; tell to do this and that: *He was exasperated by the thought that he was ordered about and overruled by Russell* (Macaulay).

[earlier, class, division < Old French *ordre* < *ordene,* learned borrowing from Latin *ōrdō, -inis* row, series, regular arrangement] —**or′der·er,** *n.*

—**Syn.** *n.* **1.** sequence, succession. —*v.t.* **1.** regulate. **2.** direct, instruct. See **command.**

order arms, 1. the command to bring a weapon to a prescribed position, especially to bring a rifle to an erect position at the side with the butt on the ground while one is standing at attention. **2.** the position in the manual of arms in which a weapon is thus held.

or·dered pair (ôr′dərd), *Mathematics.* any two numbers written in a meaningful order, so that one can be considered as the first and the other as the second of the pair.

order in council, *British.* an order by the sovereign with the advice of the privy council. Such an order generally has previously been authorized by Parliament. *An order in council to proceed immediately with the work was applied for.*

or·der·less (ôr′dər lis), *adj.* without order, arrangement, method, or regularity; disorderly: *The orderless lives of society's cast-offs and stepchildren.*

or·der·li·ness (ôr′dər lē nis), *n.* **1.** orderly state or character. **2.** orderly manner or behavior: *He bears testimony to the orderliness of the crowd* (Hawthorne).

or·der·ly (ôr′dər lē), *adj., n., pl.* **-lies,** *adv.* —*adj.* **1.** in order; with regular arrangement, method, or system: *an orderly arrangement of dishes on shelves, an orderly mind.* **2.** keeping order; well-behaved or regulated: *an orderly class.* **3.** concerned with carrying out orders; being on duty.

—*n.* **1.** a noncommissioned officer or private soldier who attends a superior officer to carry orders, etc.: *The general's orderly delivered the message.* **2.** a hospital attendant who keeps things clean and in order.

—*adv.* in or with due order; methodically: *We'll do this orderly* (Time).

—**Syn.** *adj.* **1. Orderly, methodical, systematic** mean following a plan of arrangement or action. **Orderly** suggests lack of confusion and arrangement of details or things in proper relation to each other according to some rule or scheme: *The chairs are in orderly rows.* **Methodical** suggests an orderly way of doing something, following step by step a plan carefully worked out in advance or regularly followed: *The police made a methodical search for the weapon.* **Systematic** adds to *methodical* and emphasizes the idea of thoroughness and completeness: *The committee began a systematic investigation of crime.*

orderly officer, *British.* the officer of the day.

orderly room, the office of the commanding officer of an infantry company or equivalent military unit, in which (in the U.S. Army, Marine Corps, etc.) the first sergeant and company clerk are also situated: *The sergeant in the orderly room . . . was already stuffing the papers back into the box* (Ralph Ingersoll).

order of battle, an arrangement or disposition of the different parts of an army or fleet for the purpose of engaging in battle, to be reviewed, etc.

order of the day, 1. the business to be considered on a particular day, especially by a legislature. **2.** specific commands or notices issued by a commanding officer to his troops. **3.** the prevailing rule or custom: *In Wall Street, . . . giant money maneuvers are the order of the day* (New York Times).

Order of the Garter, the oldest and most important order of knighthood in Great Britain, established about 1349.

order paper, a paper or form used in the British House of Commons (or other legislative assembly of the British Commonwealth) for recording questions or other business set down for future debate.

or·di·naire (ôr dē ner′), *n. French.* an inexpensive wine; vin ordinaire.

or·di·nal (ôr′də nəl), *adj.* **1.** showing order or position in a series. **2.** having to do with an order of animals or plants.

—*n.* **1.** an ordinal number. **2.** Also, **Ordinal.** a book of special forms for certain church ceremonies, as the conferring of holy orders in the Church of England or the conducting of the daily office in the Roman Catholic Church.

[< Late Latin *ōrdinālis* < Latin *ōrdō, -inis* row, series] —**or′di·nal·ly,** *adv.*

ordinal number or **numeral,** a number that shows order or position in a series: *First, second, third, fourth, etc., are ordinal numbers; one, two, three, four, etc., are cardinal numbers.*

➤ See **cardinal number** for usage note.

or·di·nance (ôr′də nəns), *n.* **1.** a rule or law made by authority, especially one adopted and enforced by a municipal or other local authority; decree: *a traffic ordinance. Some cities have ordinances forbidding Sunday amusements.* **2.** an established religious ceremony, especially the sacrament of Holy Communion. **3.** what is ordained or decreed by God or by fate. **4.** *Archaic.* direction or management.

[Middle English *ordynaunce* < Old French *ordenance* < Latin *ōrdināre* arrange, regulate; see ORDAIN]

—**Syn. 1.** regulation, canon.

or·di·nand (ôr′də nand), *n.* a person about to be ordained or to receive holy orders: *At the mass ordination . . . one thousand relatives and friends of the ordinands were present* (New York Times). [< Latin *ōrdinandus,* gerundive of *ōrdināre* ordain]

or·di·nant (ôr′də nənt), *adj.* ordering; directing; ordaining: *Why, even in that was heaven ordinant* (Shakespeare). —*n.* a person who ordains or confers holy orders. [< Latin *ōrdināns, -antis,* present participle of *ōrdināre* ordain]

or·di·nar·i·ate (ôr′də ner′ē it), *n.* the church district under the charge of an ordinary.

or·di·nar·i·ly (ôr′də ner′ə lē, ôr′də nãr′-), *adv.* **1.** usually; regularly: *We ordinarily go to the movies on Saturday.* **2.** to the usual extent.

or·di·nar·i·ness (ôr′də ner′ē nis), *n.* ordinary quality or condition; commonness: *the ordinariness of these stories.*

or·di·nar·y (ôr′də ner′ē), *adj., n., pl.* **-nar·ies.** —*adj.* **1.** usual; regular; customary: *an ordinary day's work. In ordinary life we use a great many words with a total disregard of logical precision* (William S. Jevons). **2.** somewhat below the average: *The speaker was ordinary and tiresome.* **3. a.** having authority in his own right, by virtue of office: *a judge or bishop ordinary.* **b.** immediate or original, not delegated: *jurisdiction ordinary.*

—*n.* **1.** a meal served at a fixed price: *A board hung out of a window signifying, "An excellent Ordinary on Saturdays and Sundays"* (Henry Mackenzie). **2. a.** an inn. **b.** the dining room of an inn. **3.** a person who has authority in his own right, as a bishop or a judge, especially a judge of a probate court. **4. a.** Also, **Ordinary.** the form for saying Mass. **b.** a book containing this form. **5.** (in heraldry) a bearing of the earliest, simplest, and commonest kind, usually bounded by straight lines. **6.** an early kind of bicycle having a high wheel in front with the seat on top, and a small wheel behind. **7.** *Obsolete.* a clergyman appointed to prepare condemned criminals for death.

Ordinary (def. 6)

in ordinary, in regular service: *physician in ordinary to the king.*
out of the ordinary, not regular or customary; unusual: *Such a long delay is out of the ordinary. This ormolu clock is certainly out of the ordinary.*
[< Latin *ōrdinārius* < *ōrdō, -inis* row, rank; see ORDER]
—**Syn.** *adj.* **1.** normal, habitual, wonted. See **common. 2.** mediocre, inferior. —**Ant.** *adj.* **1.** extraordinary, uncommon, exceptional.

ordinary seaman, a sailor having some experience, but not yet an able seaman.

ordinary share or **stock,** *British.* a share of common stock: *Ordinary shares have far outpaced the average growth in industrial shares* (London Times).

or·di·nate (ôr′də nit, -nāt), *n.* the distance of a point on a graph from the origin of a system of coordinates, measured along a line extending up or down from the x-axis. The ordinate and the abscissa together are coordinates of the point. See **abscissa** for a diagram. [< Latin *ōrdinātus,* past participle of *ōrdināre* arrange; see ORDAIN]

or·di·na·tion (ôr′də nā′shən), *n.* **1.** the act or ceremony of admitting a person to the ministry of a church. **2.** a being admitted as a minister in a church. Ordination gives a person the right to baptize or marry people. **3.** arrangement; disposition. [< Latin *ōrdinātiō, -ōnis* < *ōrdināre;* see ORDAIN]

or·di·nee (ôr′də nē′), *n.* a person who receives ordination.

ordn., ordnance.

ord·nance (ôrd′nəns), *n.* **1.** cannon; artillery: *heavy ordnance.* **2.** military weapons of all kinds, as guns, vehicles, ammunition, etc. [reduction of *ordinance*] —**Syn. 2.** arms, armament.

Ordnance Survey, the government survey of Great Britain and Ireland, originally carried out under the direction of the ordnance department.

or·do (ôr′dō), *n., pl.* **or·di·nes** (ôr′də nēz). (in the Roman Catholic Church) the schedule of offices, services, and festivals for every day of the year. [< Latin *ōrdō, -inis* row, rank, series, regular order]

or·don·nance (ôr′də nəns; *French* ôr dô-näɴs′), *n.* **1.** the arrangement or disposition of parts, as of a building, a picture, or a literary composition. **2.** a decree or law, as, in France: **a.** (under the monarchy) a decree of the king or the regent, especially one of the partial codes issued by Louis XIV and his successors. **b.** an order of a criminal court. [< Middle French *ordonnance,* alteration of Old French *ordenance;* see ORDINANCE]

Or·do·vi·cian (ôr′də vish′ən), *n.* **1.** a geological period, the second in the Paleozoic era, after the Cambrian and before the Silurian. The Ordovician is characterized by the first appearance of vertebrates and the development of many trilobites, brachiopods, and other invertebrates. **2.** the rocks formed in this period. —*adj.* of the Ordovician or the rocks formed in the Ordovician. [< Latin *Ordovicēs* ancient Celtic tribe in Wales + English *-ian*]

or·dure (ôr′jər, -dyůr), *n.* **1.** filth; dung. **2.** vile language: *Those let me curse; what vengeance will they urge, Whose ordures neither plague nor fire can purge?* (John Dryden). [< Old French *ordure* < *ord* filthy < Latin *horridus* repulsive, horrid]

ore (ôr, ōr), *n.* **1.** a rock, sand, or dirt containing some metal: *Gold ore was discovered in California in 1849.* **2.** a natural substance yielding a nonmetallic material, as sulfur. [Middle English *ure, ore,* fusion of Old English *ōra* ore, unworked metal, and of *ār* brass]

ö·re (œ′rə), *n.* **1.** a unit of money, 1/100 of a Danish or Norwegian krone or of a Swedish krona. **2.** a bronze coin having this value. [< Danish, Norwegian *øre,* Swedish *öre*]

Ore., Oregon.

O·re·ad or **o·re·ad** (ôr′ē ad, ōr′-), *n. Greek Mythology.* a mountain nymph. [< Latin *Oreas, -adis* < Greek *Oreiás, -ádos* < *óros, óreos* mountain]

ore·bod·y (ôr′bod′ē, ōr′-), *n., pl.* **-bod·ies.** a bed or vein of ore: *The mine has been closed and the equipment is being transferred to a new orebody* (Wall Street Journal).

ore carrier, a ship that carries ore.

o·rec·tic (ô rek′tik, ō-), *adj.* of or having to do with appetite or desire; appetitive. [< Greek *orektikós* < *orektós* longed for; (literally) stretched out (for) < *orégein* to desire, stretch after]

ore dressing, the act or process of obtaining the valuable minerals contained in an ore by means involving physical changes only, as by crushing or washing.

Oreg., Oregon.

o·reg·a·no or **o·ré·ga·no** (ə reg′ə nō, -rig′-; ôr′ə gä′-), *n.* any of various aromatic herbs of the mint family. The leaves are used for seasoning food. [< Spanish *orégano* < Latin *orīganum;* see ORIGAN]

Or·e·gon grape (ôr′ə gon, -gən; or′-), **1.** an evergreen shrub of the barberry family, growing in the western United States and bearing clusters of yellow flowers and small blue-black berries. It is the state flower of Oregon. **2.** the berry.

Or·e·go·ni·an (ôr′ə gō′nē ən, or′-), *adj.* of or having to do with Oregon or its people. —*n.* a native or inhabitant of Oregon.

Oregon pine or **fir,** the Douglas fir.

Oregon towhee, a towhee of the Pacific Coast region of the United States and Canada.

Or·e·o·pith·e·cus (ôr′ē ō pith′ə kəs), *n.* a humanoid that lived between ten and twelve million years ago, whose remains have been found in coalbeds in Italy. Opinion varies as to whether or not it is a true ancestor of man. [< New Latin *Oreopithecus* < Greek *óros, óreos* mountain + *píthekos* ape]

o·re ro·tun·do (ôr′ē rō tun′dō, ōr′-), *Latin.* **1.** clearly and distinctly. **2.** (literally) with round mouth.

ore shoot, a concentration of mineral ore within an orebody: *In veins and dikes ore generally is concentrated into irregularly shaped bodies called ore shoots* (Fenton and Fenton).

O·res·tes (ô res′tēz, ō-), *n. Greek Legend.* the son of Agamemnon and Clytemnestra, who killed his mother because she had murdered his father. He was pursued by the Furies for this crime.

o·rex·is (ô rek′sis, ō-), *n.* appetite; desire. [< Latin *orexis* < Greek *órexis* < *orégein* to desire]

orf (ôrf), *n.* an acute, contagious viral disease of sheep and goats, characterized by blisters, pustules, and ulcers of the lips and mouth. [Old English *orf* livestock, cattle]

org., **1.** organ. **2.** organic. **3.** organist. **4.** organized.

or·gan (ôr′gən), *n.* **1. a.** a musical instrument made of pipes of different lengths, which are sounded by compressed air blown by a bellows, and played by keys. Organs are used especially in church, and the modern organ is the most comprehensive of all musical instruments. **b.** any of certain smaller instruments that are somewhat similar to the pipe organ but are sounded by an electronic device. **2.** any of various other musical instruments: **a.** a street organ or hand organ. **b.** a parlor organ or reed organ. **c.** a mouth organ or harmonica. **d.** (in the Bible) any wind instrument. **3.** any part or member of an animal or plant that is composed of various tissues organized to perform some particular function: *An eye, lung, stomach, root, stamen, or pistil is an organ. In most complex organisms, some organs become specialized to perform only a portion of a process* (Harbaugh and Goodrich). **4.** a means of action; instrument: *A court is an organ of government.* **5.** a means of giving information or expressing opinions; newspaper, magazine, or the like, that speaks for and gives the views of a political party or some other organization. [< Latin *organum* < Greek *órganon* instrument, body organ, related to *érgon* work. Compare ERG.] —**Syn. 4.** agency.

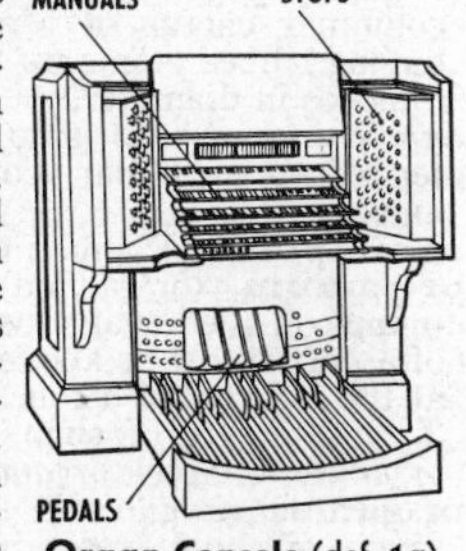

Organ Console (def. 1a)

or·ga·na (ôr′gə nə), *n.* a plural of **organum** and a plural of **organon.**

or·gan·dy or **or·gan·die** (ôr′gən dē), *n., pl.* **-dies.** a fine, thin, stiff muslin, used for dresses, curtains, trimming, etc. [< French *organdi;* origin uncertain]

or·gan·elle (ôr′gə nel′), *n. Biology.* a minute specialized part of a cell, such as a vacuole in protozoans, similar in function to an organ of higher animals.

organ grinder, a person, especially a wandering street musician, who plays a hand organ by turning a crank.

or·gan·ic (ôr gan′ik), *adj.* **1.** of the bodily organs; vital; affecting the structure of an organ: *an organic disease, an organic process.* **2.** produced by animal or plant activities; containing carbon: *Starch is an organic compound.* **3.** having organs, or an organized physical structure, as plants and animals have; not of the mineral kingdom. **4.** made up of related parts, but being a unit; coordinated: *The United States is an organic whole made up of 50 states.* **5.** that is part of the structure or constitution of a person or thing; fundamental: *The Constitution is the organic law of the United States.* [< Latin *organicus* < Greek *organikós* < *órganon* instrument; see ORGAN]
—**Syn. 4.** organized. **5.** inherent, innate, constitutional.

organic acid, any carbon compound that displays typical acidic properties, especially one containing the carboxyl radical—COOH.

or·gan·i·cal (ôr gan′ə kəl), *adj.* organic.

or·gan·i·cal·ly (ôr gan′ə klē), *adv.* **1.** in an organic manner. **2.** by or with animal or plant organs. **3.** in organization. **4.** as part of an organization.

organic chemistry, the branch of chemistry that deals with compounds of carbon; the chemistry of organic compounds, as foods and fuels.

or·gan·ic-cooled (ôr gan′ik küld′), *adj.* (of a nuclear reactor) cooled by an organic compound.

or·gan·i·cism (ôr gan′ə siz əm), *n.* **1. a.** the doctrine that everything in nature has an organic basis or explanation. **b.** the medical theory that all symptoms of disease can be traced back to an organic lesion or defect. **2.** the doctrine that organic structure is merely the result of an inherent property in matter to adapt itself to circumstances.

or·gan·i·cist (ôr gan′ə sist), *n.* **1.** a person who believes that all symptoms of disease have an organic cause: *The organicists, some of whom are psychiatrists, point out that the discovery of the thyroid hormone, the infectious agent of syphilis, and the vitamin niacin, removed from the lists of the insane asylum those afflicted not with mental disease but with myxedema, syphilis, and pellagra masquerading as mental disease* (John H. Knowles). **2.** a person who favors or advocates a doctrine of organicism.

or·gan·ic·i·ty (ôr′gə nis′ə tē), *n.* organic quality: *A generation which knew so rightly to stress (if not overstress) the organicity of a complex poetic structure could not be interested in what is actually an abstraction* (Benjamin Hrushovski).

or·gan·ic-mod·er·at·ed (ôr gan′ik mod′ə rā′tid), *adj.* organic-cooled.

or·gan·ise (ôr′gə nīz), *v.,* **-ised, -is·ing.** *Especially British.* organize: *It is very undisciplined and irregular that school-children should organise a sit-down strike* (Manchester Guardian).

or·gan·ism (ôr′gə niz əm), *n.* **1.** a living body having organs or an organized structure, constituted to carry on the processes of life; individual animal or plant: *It is almost impossible to keep any space in the habitable parts of the earth's surface free from organisms* (Fred W. Emerson). **2.** a very tiny animal or plant; microorganism. **3.** a whole made up of related parts that work together: *Human society, or any community, may be spoken of as a social organism.*

or·gan·is·mal (ôr′gə niz′məl), *adj.* of or produced by living organisms.

or·gan·is·mic (ôr′gə niz′mik), *adj.* organismal.

or·gan·ist (ôr′gə nist), *n.* a person who plays an organ: *a church organist.*

or·gan·is·tic (ôr′gə nis′tik), *adj.* **1.** of, having to do with, or characteristic of the organ or organ music: *These pieces both are rather "organistic," but so was the aim of the record, which is achieved gloriously* (John M. Conly). **2.** of or having to do with animal or plant organs: *Until quite recently, the theories proposed for anesthesia have been based on gross and organistic concepts rather than upon concepts arising out of actions at the molecular level* (Raymond C. Ingraham).

or·gan·iz·a·bil·i·ty (ôr′gə nī′zə bil′ə tē), *n.* **1.** capability for organization or for being turned into living tissue: *the organizability of fibrin.* **2.** the quality of being organizable.

or·gan·iz·a·ble (ôr′gə nī′zə bəl), *adj.* **1.** that can be organized. **2.** *Biology.* that can be converted into living tissue.

or·gan·i·za·tion (ôr′gə nə zā′shən), *n.* **1.** a group of persons united for some purpose: *Churches, clubs, and political parties are organizations.* **2.** a grouping and arranging parts to form a whole; an organizing: *The organization of a big picnic takes time and thought.* **3.** the way in which a thing's parts are arranged to work together: *The organization of the human body is very complicated.* **4.** a thing made up of related parts, each having a special duty; organism: *A tree is an organization of roots, trunks, branches, leaves, and fruit.* **5.** the people who manage an organization, as in a political party or business: *Politics is a business ... you got to have organization* (Newsweek). —**Syn. 1.** association. **2.** arrangement. **3.** constitution.

or·gan·i·za·tion·al (ôr′gə nə zā′shə nəl), *adj.* of or having to do with organization: *This results in a vote-getting free-for-all and minimizes party loyalty and organizational possibilities* (New York Times). —**or′gan·i·za′tion·al·ly,** *adv.*

or·gan·i·za·tion·ist (ôr′gə nə zā′shə nist), *n.* a person who advocates or is skilled in organization.

organization man, an employee of a large corporation, generally an executive, who has absorbed the philosophy of such companies and has merged his personality, habits, and activities to the extent that he has lost his identity as an individual. [suggested and popularized by *The Organization Man,* a book by William H. Whyte, that deals with this concept]

or·gan·ize (ôr′gə nīz), *v.,* **-ized, -iz·ing.** —*v.t.* **1.** to put into working order; get together and arrange: *The explorer organized an expedition to the North Pole.* **2.** to bring together into a labor union, as the workers of a particular industry: *to organize the truckers, to organize the steel industry.* **3.** to furnish with organs; provide with an organic structure; make organic. **4.** *Slang.* to steal; talk someone out of something: *We tracked the group down in a butcher shop, where they were busy organizing some sausage from the reluctant proprietor* (New Yorker). —*v.i.* **1.** to combine in a company, party, labor union, etc.; form an organization. **2.** to assume organic structure; become living tissue. [< Late Latin *organizāre* to play on the organ (in Medieval Latin, organize) < Latin *organum* < Greek *órganon* organ] —**Syn.** *v.t.* **1.** form, systematize.

or·gan·ized (ôr′gə nīzd), *adj.* **1.** combined in an organization, such as a company, party, labor union, etc.: *Vito Genovese, who has been called the leader of organized crime in the U.S., won court review of the narcotic conviction that sent him to prison* (Wall Street Journal). **2.** put into working order; systematically arranged: *An assembly governs each organized borough. . . . The state legislature governs all unorganized boroughs* (Lyman E. Allen). **3.** having organs or organic structure: *A rose is a highly organized plant.*

or·gan·ized ferment (ôr′gə nīzd), a living organism, such as yeast or other fungi, which is used to cause fermentation.

organized labor, 1. the workers who belong to labor unions. **2.** labor unions as a group.

or·gan·iz·er (ôr′gə nī′zər), *n.* **1.** a person who brings elements or parts together; one who brings into being, action, etc. **2.** *Biology* an inductor.

or·ga·no·chlo·rine (ôr′gə nō klôr′ēn, -in; -klōr′-), *n.* organic compound containing chlorine, as methyl chloride, chlordane, etc.

organ of Cor·ti (kôr′tē), a part of the structure of the internal ear that lies along the basilar membrane of the cochlea. It contains over 15,000 hair cells which transmit sound vibrations to the nerve fibers. [< Alfonso *Corti,* 1822-1888, an Italian anatomist]

or·ga·no·gen·e·sis (ôr′gə nō jen′ə sis), *n.* *Biology.* the origin or development of the organs of an animal or plant: *The genes engaged in flower organogenesis have widely different alternative reaction modes* (J. Heslop-Harrison).

or·ga·nog·en·y (ôr′gə noj′ə nē), *n.* organogenesis.

or·ga·nog·ra·phy (ôr′gə nog′rə fē), *n.* the description of the organs of living beings; descriptive organology.

or·ga·no·lep·tic (ôr′gə nō lep′tik), *adj.* using various sense organs to determine flavor, texture, or other quality: *Quality-control men ... make an "organoleptic" test in which they bite sample peas, taste, swallow, and hopefully, like them* (Time). [< *organ* + Greek *lēptós* fine, delicate + English *-ic*] —**or′ga·no·lep′ti·cal·ly,** *adv.*

or·ga·nol·o·gy (ôr′gə nol′ə jē), *n.* **1.** the branch of biology that deals with the structure and function of animal and plant organs. **2.** phrenology.

or·ga·no·me·tal·lic (ôr′gə nō mə tal′ik), *adj.* consisting of an atom of a metal in combination with one or more alkyl radicals. —*n.* an organometallic compound.

or·ga·non (ôr′gə non), *n., pl.* **-na** (-nə), **-nons. 1.** an instrument of thought or knowledge; means by which some process of reasoning, discovery, etc., is carried on: *Language has been called "the supreme organon of the mind's self-ordering growth." It is the means by which we not only communicate our thoughts to others but interpret our thoughts to ourselves* (Wall Street Journal). **2.** a system of rules or principles for investigation of a field of knowledge. [< Greek *órganon*]

or·ga·no·phos·pho·rus (ôr′gə nō fos′fər-əs), *n.* a chemical compound consisting of an atom of phosphorus combined with an atom of carbon and one or more alkyl radicals, used especially as an insecticide.

or·ga·no·sil·i·con (ôr′gə nō sil′ə kən), *n.* an organic compound that contains silicon, as one of the silicones.

or·gan·o·sol (ôr gan′ə sol), *n.* **1.** any organic liquid containing a colloidal suspension. **2.** plastisol.

or·ga·no·ther·a·peu·tic (ôr′gə nō ther′-ə pyü′tik), *adj.* of, having to do with, or treated by organotherapy.

or·ga·no·ther·a·peu·tics (ôr′gə nō ther′-ə pyü′tiks), *n.* organotherapy.

or·ga·no·ther·a·py (ôr′gə nō ther′ə pē), *n.* therapy in which preparations from the organs of animals are used, as the thyroid gland, the pancreas, and suprarenal bodies.

organ pipe, one of the pipes of a pipe organ.

or·gan-pipe cactus (ôr′gən pīp′), a large columnar cactus of Mexico and Arizona, having ribbed stems up to 25 feet high and 6 inches in diameter.

organ-pipe coral, a colonial coral characterized by tubular corallites united in masses.

organ point, *Music.* a pedal point.

or·ga·num (ôr′gə nəm), *n., pl.* **-na** or **-nums.** in medieval music: **1.** the addition of a part below or above a melody, usually at the interval of a fourth, fifth, or octave. **2.** the singing of such a part. [< Latin *organum* < Greek *órganon* organ]

or·gan·za (ôr gan′zə), *n.* a sheer cloth of rayon, silk, etc., resembling organdy, used especially for dresses. [origin uncertain]

or·gan·zine (ôr′gən zēn), *n.* a very fine quality of silk thread made of several single threads twisted together, used for the warp in weaving. [< French *organsin* < Italian *organzino,* perhaps < *Organzi,* medieval form of *Urganj,* a silk center in Turkestan]

or·gasm (ôr′gaz əm), *n.* **1.** the culmination of sexual excitement; climax of an act of coition. **2.** a paroxysm of excitement; rage; fury: *the periodic orgasm of war.* [< Greek *orgasmós* < *orgân* be in heat, become ripe for; (literally) to swell]

or·gas·mic (ôr gaz′mik), *adj.* of, characteristic of, or like an orgasm.

or·gas·tic (ôr gas′tik), *adj.* characterized by or exhibiting orgasm.

Org·bu·ro (ôrg′byůr′ō), *n.* the Organization Bureau of the Communist Party of the Soviet Union until 1952, when it was combined with the Politburo to form the party Presidium.

or·geat (ôr′zhat; *French* ôr zhá′), *n.* a syrup flavored with almonds (formerly, barley) and water in which orange flowers have been steeped. [< Middle French *orgeat* < Provençal *ourjat* < Old French *orge* (in Old Provençal, *ordi*) barley < Latin *hordeum*]

or·gi·ac (ôr′jē ak), *adj.* having to do with orgies; orgiastic.

or·gi·ast (ôr′jē ast), *n.* one who celebrates orgies.

or·gi·as·tic (ôr′jē as′tik), *adj.* of, having to do with, or of the nature of orgies; wild; frenzied: *an orgiastic carnival, gross in all its manifestations of joy* (Arnold Bennett). [< Greek *orgiastikós* < *orgiázein* celebrate < *orgiā* secret rites < *érgon* act, deed] —**or′gi·as′ti·cal·ly,** *adv.*

or·gic (ôr′jik), *adj.* orgiac.

or·gu·lous (ôr′gyə ləs), *adj. Archaic.* proud; haughty: *From isles of Greece The princes orgulous, their high blood chafed, Have to the port of Athens sent their ships* (Shakespeare). [< Old French *orguillus* (with English *-ous*) < *orguil* pride; origin uncertain]

or·gy (ôr′jē), *n., pl.* **-gies. 1.** a wild, drunken revel. **2. a.** a period of uncontrolled indulgence: *an orgy of eating.* **b.** a period within which controls are lacking or ineffective: *an orgy of bloodshed or crime. The worship of the beautiful always ends in an orgy* (Benjamin Disraeli).

orgies, secret rites or ceremonies in the worship of certain Greek and Roman gods, especially Dionysus, the god of wine, celebrated by drinking, wild dancing, and singing: *The orgies of Bacchus ... were famed through all the Ages of Antiquity* (John Brown).

[originally, plural < Middle French *orgies,* learned borrowing from Latin *orgia,* plural < Greek *orgiā* secret rites; see ORGIASTIC]

O·ri·an·a (ôr′ē an′ə), *n.* the daughter of a legendary king of Britain and the beloved of Amadis of Gaul, hero of a medieval romance of chivalry.

or·i·bi (ôr′ə bē, or′-), *n., pl.* **-bis** or (*collectively*) **-bi.** any of several small, brownish African antelopes with short, straight horns in the male. [< Afrikaans *oribi,* apparently < a Hottentot word]

or·i·chalc (ôr′ə kalk), *n.* a yellow metal or metallic alloy, highly prized by the ancients. It is believed to have been brass. [< Latin *orichalchum* < Greek *oreíchalkos* < *óros, óreos* mountain + *chalkós* copper]

o·ri·el (ôr′ē əl, ōr′-), *n.* a bay window projecting from the outer face of a wall. [< Old French *oriol* porch, corridor, gallery; origin uncertain]

Oriel

o·ri·ent (*n., adj.* ôr′ē ənt, ōr′-; *v.* ôr′ē ent, ōr′-), *n.* **1.** *Poetic.* the east. **2. a.** the soft, glowing luster or sheen of a pearl of excellent quality: *In every nobler mood We feel the orient of their spirit glow* (Lowell). **b.** a natural pearl having such a luster: *a very Sea of Thought ... wherein the toughest pearl-diver may dive ... and return ... with true orients* (Thomas Carlyle).
—*adj.* **1.** *Poetic.* eastern: *Now morning from her orient chamber came* (Keats). **2.** bright; shining: *Ten thousand banners ... With orient colours waving* (Milton). **3.** (of a pearl or other gem) of the best or very fine quality; brilliant or lustrous. **4.** *Poetic.* rising: *the orient moon of Islam* (Shelley).
—*v.t.* **1.** to put facing east, as a church built with the chief altar to the east. **2.** to place so that it faces in any indicated direction: *The building is oriented north and south.* **3.** to find the direction of. **4.** to place in the right position; bring into accord with facts or principles; adjust; correct: *These men will ask for nothing specific in return although they will help to orient and determine the general course of party policies* (Paul H. Douglas). **5.** *Surveying.* to place (a map) so that a north and south line on the map is pointed to the north and south direction on the earth. —*v.i.* **1.** to turn to-

ward the east. **2.** to turn toward any specified direction.
orient oneself, to get in the right relations to the things or persons about one: *Mistress Kitty accepted Mrs. Hopkins's hospitable offer, and presently began orienting herself, and getting ready to make herself agreeable* (Oliver Wendell Holmes).
[< Old French *orient,* learned borrowing from Latin *oriēns, -entis* the East; the Orient; (literally) the rising sun, properly, present participle of *orīrī* to rise] —**o'ri•ent•er,** *n.*
—**Syn.** *adj.* **1.** oriental. **2.** radiant, effulgent.

O•ri•ent (ôr'ē ənt, ōr'-), *n.* the countries in Asia; the East: *China and Japan are important nations of the Orient.* —*adj.* of the Orient; Oriental.

o•ri•en•tal (ôr'ē en'təl, ōr'-), *adj.* eastern. —**o'ri•en'tal•ly,** *adv.*

O•ri•en•tal (ôr'ē en'təl), ōr'-), *adj.* **1.** Eastern; of the Orient. **2.** Also, **oriental.** belonging to the region that includes Asia south of the Himalayas, the Philippines, and the East Indies. **3. a.** (of a gem, especially a sapphire) that resembles in color a gem of the type indicated. An Oriental topaz is actually a yellow sapphire. **b.** Also, **oriental.** (of a gem) of the best or very fine quality; orient.
—*n.* **1. a.** a native or inhabitant of the East: *Turks, Arabs, Persians, Hindus, Japanese, and Chinese are Orientals belonging to the ethnic group of Asia.* **b.** an Asian (now often used in an unfriendly way). **2.** a person who is trained in or adopts any one of the cultures of Asia.
[< Old French *oriental,* learned borrowing from Latin *orientālis* < *oriēns;* see ORIENT]

Oriental carpet, Oriental rug.

O•ri•en•ta•li•a (ôr'ē ən tā'lē ə, ōr'-; -tāl'-yə), *n.pl.* **1.** a collection of books, documents, facts, etc., about the Orient. **2.** a collection of objects of or from the Orient.

O•ri•en•tal•ism or **o•ri•en•tal•ism** (ôr'ē-en'tə liz əm, ōr'-), *n.* **1.** Oriental character or characteristics: *To Eastern ears this may seem about as exotic as Rimsky-Korsakov's orientalism is to our own* (Harper's). **2.** the knowledge or study of Oriental languages, literature, and culture.

O•ri•en•tal•ist or **o•ri•en•tal•ist** (ôr'ē en'-tə list, ōr'-), *n.* a person skilled in Oriental languages, literature, history, and culture.

O•ri•en•tal•ize (ôr'ē en'tə līz, ōr'-), *v.t., v.i.,* **-ized, -iz•ing.** to make or become Oriental.

Oriental rug, a handmade rug in one piece with a distinctive pattern, made especially in the Middle East.

Oriental sore, a type of leishmaniasis characterized by ulcerous infections of the skin, occurring chiefly in central Asia and the Mediterranean region.

o•ri•en•tate (ôr'ē en tāt, ōr'-), *v.t., v.i.,* **-tat•ed, -tat•ing.** to orient. [< *orient* + *-ate*[1]]

o•ri•en•ta•tion (ôr'ē en tā'shən, ōr'-), *n.* **1.** an orienting. **2.** a being oriented. **3.** the direction that any process, movement, or development follows: *The present orientation of Soviet policy* (Bulletin of Atomic Scientists). **4.** a finding out of the actual facts and conditions and putting oneself in the right relation to them. **5.** the ability of many birds and other animals to find their way back to their usual habitat after going to another point distant from it. **6.** a general point of view toward a topic or object. **7.** *Chemistry.* **a.** the relative position of atoms or radicals in complex molecules. **b.** the determination of the position of atoms and radicals to be substituted in a substance. —**Syn. 4.** adjustment, adaptation.

or•i•fice (ôr'ə fis, or'-), *n.* a mouth; opening; hole: *the orifice of a tube, pipe, or furnace.* [< Middle French *orifice,* learned borrowing from Latin *ōrificium* < *ōs, ōris* mouth + *facere* make] —**Syn.** aperture, vent.

or•i•fi•cial (ôr'ə fish'əl, or'-), *adj.* of or having to do with an orifice.

or•i•flamme (ôr'ə flam, or'-), *n.* **1.** the red banner of Saint Denis carried as a military ensign by the early kings of France from the time of the Crusades until the early Renaissance. A deep V was cut laterally into its central part. **2.** any banner used as an ensign or standard. **3.** anything that serves as a rallying point in a struggle: *And be your oriflamme today the helmet of Navarre* (Macaulay). **4.** anything that is bright, colorful, or showy: *the oriflamme of day* (John Greenleaf Whittier). [< Old French *orie flambe; orie,* learned borrowing from Latin *aureus* golden, and *flambe,* ultimately < Latin *flamma* flame]

orig., **1.** origin. **2. a.** original. **b.** originally. **3.** originated.

or•i•ga•mi (ôr'ə gä'mē), *n., pl.* **-mis** or **-mi.** **1.** the Japanese art of folding paper to make decorative objects, such as birds and flowers. **2.** an object thus made. [< Japanese *origami* < *ori* fold + *kami* paper]

or•i•gan (ôr'ə gən, or'-), *n.* **1.** oregano. **2.** marjoram. [< Old French *origane,* learned borrowing from Latin *orīganum* < Greek *orīganon* wild marjoram]

or•i•gin (ôr'ə jin, or'-), *n.* **1.** the thing from which anything comes; source; beginning: *the origin of a quarrel, the origin of a disease. Ancient Greece has been called the origin of Western civilization.* **2.** parentage; ancestry; birth: *a man of humble origin.* **3.** the act or fact of rising or springing from a particular source; derivation: *these and other reports of like origin.* **4.** *Anatomy.* the more fixed attachment of a muscle, which does not change position during the muscle's contraction. **5.** *Mathematics.* the intersection of the x-axis and the y-axis in a coordinate system. [< Latin *orīgō, -īginis* < *orīrī* to rise] —**Syn. 1.** root.

o•rig•i•nal (ə rij'ə nəl), *adj.* **1.** belonging to the beginning; first; earliest: *the original settlers, a hat marked down from its original price. Which is the original error?* **2.** new; fresh; novel: *to plan an original game for the party.* **3.** able to do, make, or think something new; inventive: *Edison had an original mind.* **4.** not copied, imitated, or translated from something else; firsthand: *an original poem, sketch, or design.*
—*n.* **1.** a thing from which another is copied, imitated, or translated: *The original of this picture is in Rome.* **2.** a new written work, picture, etc., that is not a copy or imitation. **3.** the language in which a book was first written: *Our minister can read the Bible in the original.* **4.** an unusual person; odd person: *Teufelsdröckh passed . . . as one of those originals and nondescripts, more frequent in German universities than elsewhere* (Thomas Carlyle). **5.** *Archaic.* origin; source. —**o•rig'i•nal•ness,** *n.*
—**Syn.** *adj.* **1.** initial. **3.** creative, ingenious.

original gum, the adhesive gum put on a stamp by postal authorities. Its presence on a stamp certifies it is in mint condition.

o•rig•i•nal•i•ty (ə rij'ə nal'ə tē), *n.* **1.** the ability to do, make, or think up something new: *Originality is the seeing nature differently from others, yet as it is in itself* (William Hazlitt). **2.** freshness; novelty. **3.** a being original. —**Syn. 1.** inventiveness, imagination.

o•rig•i•nal•ly (ə rij'ə nə lē), *adv.* **1.** by origin; indigenously: *a plant originally African.* **2. a.** at first; in the first place: *a house originally small.* **b.** from the beginning; from the first: *Originally conceived as an emergency measure, it has taken on the look of a long-range policy* (Time). **3.** in an original manner: *We want this room decorated originally.* —**Syn. 2. a.** initially.

original sin, **1.** *Theology.* a depravity, or tendency to evil, held to be innate in mankind and transmitted from Adam to the race of man in consequence of his sin. **2.** (in Roman Catholic theology) the privation of sanctifying grace in consequence of Adam's sin.

o•rig•i•nate (ə rij'ə nāt), *v.,* **-nat•ed, -nat•ing.** —*v.t.* to cause to be; invent: *to originate a new style of painting.* —*v.i.* to come into being; begin; arise: *Where did that report originate?* [< *origin* + *-ate*[1]] —**Syn.** *v.i.* commence.

o•rig•i•na•tion (ə rij'ə nā'shən), *n.* **1.** an originating. **2.** origin.

o•rig•i•na•tive (ə rij'ə nā'tiv), *adj.* **1.** having originality; inventive; creative. **2.** productive. —**o•rig'i•na'tive•ly,** *adv.*

o•rig•i•na•tor (ə rij'ə nā'tər), *n.* a person who originates: *Next to the originator of a good sentence is the first quoter of it* (Emerson).

o•ri•na•sal (ôr'i nā'zəl, ōr'-), *Phonetics.* —*adj.* articulated with the breath stream passing out through both nose and mouth, as the French nasal vowels. —*n.* an orinasal sound. [< Latin *ōs, ōris* mouth + English *nasal*]

Or•i•nase (ôr'ə nās), *n. Trademark.* tolbutamide.

O ring, a rubber ring similar to a washer or gasket, used especially in hydraulic equipment.

o•ri•ole (ôr'ē ōl, ōr'-), *n.* **1.** any of several American songbirds of a family that also includes the blackbirds, meadow larks, grackles, and bobolinks. Orioles build hanging nests and usually have orange or yellow and black feathers. **2.** any of several birds of Europe, Asia, Africa, and Australia, having rich yellow and black feathers, as the golden oriole. [< New Latin *oriolus* < Old French *oriol* < Latin *aureolus* (diminutive) < *aureus* golden < *aurum* gold]

Baltimore Oriole
(def. 1)
(7½ in. long)

O•ri•on (ô rī'ən, ō-), *n., genitive (def. 1)* **O•ri•on•is.** **1.** a constellation near the celestial equator, that contains the extremely bright stars Betelgeuse and Rigel. To the ancients they suggested a man with a belt around his waist and a sword by his side. **2.** *Greek Mythology.* a giant hunter of great strength, who was slain by Artemis. After his death Orion was supposedly placed in the heavens with his belt and sword.

O•ri•on•id (ô rī'ə nid, ō-), *n.* any of a shower of meteors occurring in October and appearing to radiate from the constellation Orion.

O•ri•on•is (ô rī'ə nis, ō-; or'ē ō'nis), *n.* genitive of **Orion** (the constellation).

or•i•son (ôr'ə zən, or'-), *n. Archaic.* a prayer: *Nymph, in thy orisons be all my sins remembered* (Shakespeare). [< Old French *oreisoun,* learned borrowing from Late Latin *ōrātiō, -ōnis* prayer < *ōrāre* pray, speak formally. Doublet of ORATION.]

O•ri•ya (ō rē'yä), *n.* an Indo-European language spoken in India, mainly in the province of Orissa and adjoining areas: *The faithful sat down in concentric circles to hear Vinoba read from the Hindu classics—in Oriya* (New Yorker).

ork (ôrk), *n.* orc.

orle (ôrl), *n.* (in heraldry) a narrow band of half the width of the bordure (an outside bearing), following the outline, but not reaching the edge, of the shield. [< Old French *ourle* border < Vulgar Latin *ōrulus* (diminutive) < Latin *ōra* edge, boundary]

Or•le•an•ist (ôr'lē ə nist), *n.* (in French politics) an adherent of the Orléans family, descendants of the brother of Louis XIV. The last French king, Louis Philippe, was a member of this family.

Or•lon (ôr'lon), *n. Trademark.* a lightweight synthetic acrylic fiber that is very resistant to sun, rain, and acids, used for clothing, sails, awnings, etc.

or•lop (ôr'lop), *n.,* or **orlop deck,** the lowest deck of a ship, especially of a warship, laid over the beams of the hold. [reduction of Scottish *ouerlop, overloppe,* probably < Middle Low German *overlōp* < *overlopen* run over]

Or•mazd (ôr'məzd), *n.* (in the Zoroastrian religion) the principle of good, light, and law in ceaseless conflict with Ahriman, the spirit of evil; Ahura Mazda. Also, **Ormuzd.** [< Persian *Ormazd* < Avestan *Ahura Mazda* wise lord]

or•mer (ôr'mər), *n.* a kind of abalone found especially in the English Channel. [< French dialectal *ormer,* variant of French *ormier,* perhaps < *oreille-de-mer* or < Latin *auris maris,* both (literally) ear of the sea]

or•mo•lu (ôr'mə lü), *n.* an alloy of copper, containing zinc or tin, used to imitate gold. Ormolu is used in decorating furniture, clocks, etc.: *an eighteenth-century Chinese . . . vase, with ormolu mounts* (London Times). [< French *or moulu* (literally) ground gold < *or* gold + *moulu* ground up, past participle of *moudre* to grind < Latin *molere* < *mola* millstone]

Or•muzd (ôr'məzd), *n.* Ormazd.

or•na•ment (*n.* ôr'nə mənt; *v.* ôr'nə ment), *n.* **1.** something pretty; something to add beauty: *ornaments for a Christmas tree. Jewelry and vases are ornaments.* **2.** the use of ornaments: *Loveliness Needs not the*

foreign aid of ornament (James Thomson). **3.** the condition of having an ornament or ornaments. **4.** a person or act that adds beauty, grace, or honor: *She is so charming she would be an ornament to any society. But let it be the hidden man of the heart, in that which is not corruptible, even the ornament of a meek and quiet spirit, which is in the sight of God of great price* (I Peter 3:4). **5.** the things used in church services, such as the organ, bells, silver plate, etc. **6.** *Music.* an additional note or notes introduced as an embellishment but not essential to the harmony or melody: *His ornaments are correct ... and his tempi are relatively strict* (Edward Tatnall Canby).
—*v.t.* to add beauty to; make more pleasing or attractive; decorate; embellish: *A man, formed to ornament, to enlighten, and to defend his country* (Scott).
[alteration of Old French *ornement,* learned borrowing from Latin *ōrnāmentum* < *ōrnāre* adorn]
—**Syn.** *n.* **1.** adornment, decoration, embellishment. *-v.t.* deck, beautify, adorn. See **decorate.**

or·na·men·tal (ôr′nə men′təl), *adj.* **1.** of or having to do with ornament: *ornamental purposes.* **2.** for ornament; used as an ornament: *ornamental plants.* **3.** decorative: *ornamental vases.*
—*n.* a plant cultivated for decorative uses: *No doubt the Russian olive came West as a workhorse tree, not as an ornamental* (Sunset). —**or′na·men′tal·ly,** *adv.* —**or′na·men′tal·ness,** *n.*

or·na·men·tal·ism (ôr′nə men′tə liz əm), *n.* **1.** the character of being ornamental. **2.** ornamental style in art, literature, etc.

or·na·men·ta·tion (ôr′nə men tā′shən), *n.* **1.** an ornamenting or being ornamented. **2.** decorations; ornaments: *She was dressed simply, with no ornamentation. The Quaker meeting house in our city has no ornamentation.*

or·nate (ôr nāt′), *adj.* **1.** much adorned; much ornamented: *a taste for ornate furniture.* **2.** characterized by the use of elaborate figures of speech, flowery language, etc.: *an ornate style of writing. In diction, Virgil is ornate and Homer simple* (William Ewart Gladstone). **3.** *Archaic.* adorned; ornamented (with). [< Latin *ōrnātus,* past participle of *ōrnāre* adorn] —**or·nate′ly,** *adv.* —**or·nate′ness,** *n.* —**Syn. 1.** elaborate, showy, sumptuous.

or·ner·i·ness (ôr′nər ē nis), *n. Especially U.S. Informal.* the fact or condition of being ornery: *They ... let loose their deviltries just for pure orneriness* (Booth Tarkington).

or·ner·y (ôr′nər ē), *adj.,* **-ner·i·er, -ner·i·est.** *Especially U.S. Informal.* **1. a.** mean in disposition: *an ornery horse.* **b.** of a mean kind: *an ornery remark.* **2.** inferior. **3.** homely. **4.** low; vile. [American English; reduction of *ordinary,* in the sense of "mean, vile"] —**Syn. 1. a.** contrary. **4.** contemptible.

or·nis (ôr′nis), *n.* the birds or bird life of a region or country; avifauna. [< German *Ornis* < Greek *órnīs* bird]

ornith., 1. ornithological. **2.** ornithology.

or·nith·ic (ôr nith′ik), *adj.* of, having to do with, or characteristic of birds. [< Greek *ornīthikós* < *órnīs, -īthos* bird]

or·ni·thine (ôr′nə thin), *n.* an amino acid formed by hydrolyzing arginine. *Formula:* $C_5H_{12}O_2N_2$ [< Greek *órnīs, -īthos* bird (because it is found in their excrement) + English *-ine*]

or·ni·this·chi·an (ôr′nə this′kē ən), *adj.* of or having to do with a group of dinosaurs that lived during the Jurassic and Cretaceous periods and had birdlike pelvic bones. —*n.* an ornithischian dinosaur. [< Greek *órnīs, -īthos* bird + *ischíon* hip + English *-ian*]

or·ni·thoid (ôr′nə thoid), *adj.* having a certain structural resemblance to a bird: *an ornithoid lizard.* [< Greek *órnīs, -īthos* bird + English *-oid*]

ornithol., 1. ornithological. **2.** ornithology.

or·nith·o·lite (ôr nith′ə līt), *n.* the fossilized remains of a bird. [< Greek *órnīs, -īthos* bird + English *-lite*]

or·ni·tho·log·i·cal (ôr′nə thə loj′ə kəl), *adj.* of or having to do with birds. —**or′ni·tho·log′i·cal·ly,** *adv.*

or·ni·thol·o·gist (ôr′nə thol′ə jist), *n.* a person who studies birds and their habits.

or·ni·thol·o·gy (ôr′nə thol′ə jē), *n.* **1.** the branch of zoology dealing with the study of birds. **2.** a book on this subject. [< New Latin *ornithologia* < Greek *órnīs, -īthos* bird + *-logiā* -logy]

or·ni·tho·man·cy (ôr′nith ə man′sē), *n., pl.* **-cies.** divination from birds. [< Greek *órnīs, -īthos* bird + *manteíā* divination]

or·ni·tho·pod (ôr′nə thə pod, ôr nī′-), *adj.* belonging to or having to do with a group of extinct saurians, containing herbivorous dinosaurs, whose hind feet resembled those of birds and left similar tracks. —*n.* a member of this group. [< New Latin *Ornithopoda* the group name < Greek *órnīs, -īthos* bird + *poús, podós* foot]

or·ni·thop·ter (ôr′nə thop′tər), *n.* a machine designed to fly by flapping its wings. Examples are cited from ancient times until the present. *Observing the flight of birds,* [*Leonardo da Vinci*] *invented the ornithopter* (Atlantic). Also, **orthopter.** [< Greek *órnīs, -īthos* bird + *pterón* wing]

Ornithopter
(Leonardo da Vinci, 1490)

or·ni·tho·rhyn·chus (ôr′nə thə ring′kəs, ôr nī′-), *n.* a duckbill; platypus. [< Greek *órnīs, -īthos* bird + *rhýnchos* bill, beak]

or·ni·thos·co·pist (ôr′nə thos′kə pist), *n.* a bird watcher: *... bird-chasing ornithoscopists, tracking down rarity records with the zeal of collectors of cigarette cards or obsolete bus tickets* (John Hillaby). [< Greek *órnīs, -īthos* bird + *skopeîn* look at + English *-ist*]

or·ni·tho·sis (ôr′nə thō′sis), *n.* a contagious virus disease of birds other than parrots, such as pigeons, chickens, and other fowl. It is communicable to man. The similar disease occurring in parrots and related birds is called psittacosis. [< Greek *órnīs, -īthos* bird + English *-osis*]

or·o·ban·cha·ceous (ôr′ō bang kā′shəs, or′-), *adj.* belonging to a family of dicotyledonous, parasitic herbs that lack green foliage, typified by the broomrape. [< New Latin *Orobanchaceae* the order name (< *Orobanche* the genus name < Greek *orobánchē* < *órobos* a kind of vetch + *ánchein* to throttle) + English *-ous*]

or·o·gen·e·sis (ôr′ə jen′ə sis, or′-), *n.* orogeny.

or·o·ge·net·ic (ôr′ə jə net′ik, or′-), *adj.* orogenic: *We do not know how much carbon dioxide may have been emitted by the volcanoes of Venus in some recent orogenetic spasm* (Science News).

or·o·gen·ic (ôr′ə jen′ik, or′-), *adj.* having to do with the formation of mountains.

o·rog·e·ny (ô roj′ə nē, ō-), *n., pl.* **-nies.** the formation of mountains, as by the folding of the earth's crust: *The deposits comprise mostly shale and sandstone which represent rock materials eroded from adjacent mountain areas formed in the Nevadan orogeny* (Raymond Cecil Moore). [< Greek *óros* mountain + English *-gen* + *-y*[3]]

or·o·graph·ic (ôr′ə graf′ik, or′-), *adj.* **1.** of or having to do with orography. **2.** *Meteorology.* produced by the forced ascent of warm air into cooler regions because of a mountain range lying in its path: *orographic rainfall.* —**or′o·graph′i·cal·ly,** *adv.*

or·o·graph·i·cal (ôr′ə graf′ə kəl, or′-), *adj.* orographic.

o·rog·ra·phy (ô rog′rə fē, ō-), *n.* the branch of physical geography that deals with the formation and features of mountains. [< Greek *óros* mountain + English *-graphy*]

or·o·ide (ôr′ō īd, -id; ōr′-), *n.* an alloy consisting chiefly of copper and tin or zinc, resembling gold in appearance, used in making inexpensive jewelry. [American English < French *or* gold + *-oïde* -oid]

or·o·log·i·cal (ôr′ə loj′ə kəl, or′-), *adj.* of or having to do with orology.

o·rol·o·gist[1] (ô rol′ə jist, ō-), *n. Obsolete.* horologist.

o·rol·o·gist[2] (ô rol′ə jist, ō-), *n.* a person skilled in orology. [< *orolog*(y) + *-ist*]

o·rol·o·gy (ô rol′ə jē, ō-), *n.* orography. [< Greek *óros* mountain + English *-logy*]

o·rom·e·ter (ô rom′ə tər, ō-), *n.* an aneroid barometer with a scale giving elevations above sea level, used for measuring the altitudes of mountains. [< Greek *óros* mountain + English *-meter*]

or·o·met·ric (ôr′ə met′rik, or′-), *adj.* of or having to do with the measurement of mountains.

o·rom·e·try (ô rom′ə trē, ō-), *n.* the measurement of mountains.

o·ro·phar·ynx (ôr′ō far′ingks, ōr′-), *n., pl.* **-pha·ryn·ges** (-fə rin′jēz), **-phar·ynx·es.** the part of the pharynx directly continuous with the cavity of the mouth. [< Latin *ōs, ōris* mouth + English *pharynx*]

o·ro·tund (ôr′ə tund, ōr′-), *adj.* **1.** strong, full, rich, and clear in voice or speech. **2.** wordy and pompous in speech or writing; bombastic: *The actors have fallen into the classical cliches—strutting figures in flowing costumes, orotund, expressionless voices* (New York Times). [alteration of Latin *ōre rotundō* in well-rounded phrases; (literally) with round mouth] —**o′ro·tund′ly,** *adv.* —**Syn. 1.** resonant.

o·ro·tun·di·ty (ôr′ə tun′də tē, ōr′-), *n., pl.* **-ties. 1.** the quality of being orotund: *Max's voice boomed into orotundity again* (New Yorker). **2.** pompousness and ornateness of style: *Despite the orotundity of Mr. Levy's lines the actors do remarkably well* (Wall Street Journal). **3.** orotund expression or writing: *Wordsworthians were there to discover the hallmark of genius on his most insignificant orotundities* (J.M. Murry).

O·roy·a fever (ō rō′yə), an infectious disease prevalent in South America, caused by a germ carried by sandflies and characterized by fever, anemia, headaches and, often, wartlike spots on the skin. [< *Oroya,* Peru, where the disease was first discovered]

o·ro y pla·ta (ō′rō ē plä′tä), *Spanish.* gold and silver (the motto of Montana).

or·phan (ôr′fən), *n.* **1.** a child whose parents are dead; child whose father or mother is dead. **2.** an infant animal whose mother is dead.
—*adj.* **1.** of or for orphans: *an orphan asylum.* **2.** without a mother or father or both.
—*v.t.* to make an orphan of: *The war orphaned her at an early age.*
[< Late Latin *orphanus* < Greek *orphanós* bereaved]

or·phan·age (ôr′fə nij), *n.* **1.** a home for orphans: *A boys' orphanage near Palermo, Sicily, which the I.L.G.W.U. has supported* (Time). **2.** a being an orphan. **3.** orphans as a group.

or·phan·hood (ôr′fən hůd), *n.* the condition of being an orphan.

Or·phe·an (ôr fē′ən), *adj.* **1.** of or having to do with Orpheus: *the Orphean lyre* (Milton). **2.** like the music of Orpheus.

Or·phe·us (ôr′fē əs, -fyüs), *n. Greek Mythology.* a Thracian musician, son of Calliope and Apollo, who played his lyre so sweetly that animals and even trees and rocks followed him.

Or·phic (ôr′fik), *adj.* **1.** of or having to do with Orpheus. **2.** having to do with religious or philosophical cults, ascribed to Orpheus as founder. **3.** Also, **orphic.** having a hidden meaning; mystic; oracular: "*No summer ever came back ...*" *said I, with a degree of Orphic wisdom that astonished myself* (Hawthorne). **4.** like the music or verses of Orpheus; melodious; entrancing.

Or·phism (ôr′fiz əm), *n.* **1.** a religion or philosophical system based on the mysteries and verses attributed to Orpheus. **2.** a style of abstract painting current in France in the early 1900's, characterized by the use of geometric forms painted in rich, glowing colors to produce prismatic effects.

Or·phist (ôr′fist), *n.* an artist who follows the style of Orphism: *... a style that is reminiscent of the early Orphists in its massings of dappled color and swirling, striated movement* (New Yorker).

or·phrey (ôr′frē), *n., pl.* **-phreys. 1.** an ornamental border or band, often embroidered, on an ecclesiastical vestment. **2.** *Archaic.* gold embroidery or any similarly rich embroidery. [Middle English *orfreis,* singular < Old French *orfreis,* probably ultimately < Latin *aurum* gold + *phrygium* of Phrygia (because the region was noted for its gold embroidery)]

or·pi·ment (ôr′pə mənt), *n.* a bright-yellow mineral, arsenic trisulfide, found in soft, foliated masses or prepared synthetically as a yellow powder, used as a pigment. *Formula:* As_2S_3 [< Old French *orpiment,* also *or pigment,* learned borrowing from Latin *auripigmentum* < *aurum* gold + *pigmentum* pigment]

or·pine or **or·pin** (ôr′pin), *n.* a succulent herb of the Old World, a variety of stonecrop, with smooth, fleshy leaves and clusters (corymbs) of purple flowers. It was formerly used as a remedy for wounds. [< Old French *orpin,* (originally) reduction of *orpiment*]

orpine family, a widely distributed group of dicotyledonous, succulent herbs or low shrubs, commonly grown in rock gardens or greenhouses. The family includes the orpine, houseleek, kalanchoe, and live-forever.

Or·ping·ton (ôr′ping tən), *n.* one of a breed of large, sturdy domestic fowl, originally from England, raised for the production of both meat and eggs. The skin is white and the eggs are brown. The plumage is buff, black, white, or bluish, depending on the variety. [< *Orpington,* a town in Kent, England]

or·ra (ôr′ə), *adj. Scottish.* not one of a pair; left over; odd; extra: *I daresay you would both take an orra thought upon the gallows* (Robert Louis Stevenson). [origin unknown]

or·rer·y (ôr′ər ē, or′-), *n., pl.* **-rer·ies. 1.** a device with balls representing various planets that are moved by clockwork to illustrate motions of the solar system. **2.** a planetarium or similar device. [< Charles Boyle, Earl of *Orrery,* 1676-1731, who first had such a device made]

or·ris (ôr′is, or′-), *n.* **1.** any of certain European species of iris with a fragrant rootstock. **2.** its rootstock; orrisroot. [apparently alteration of *iris*]

or·ris·root (ôr′is rüt′, -rút′; or′-), *n.* the fragrant rootstock of orris, a variety of iris, used in making perfume and formerly used in cosmetic powders and toothpaste.

or·thi·con (ôr′thə kon), *n.* a television camera tube, similar to the iconoscope but using a low-velocity electron beam. [< *orth*(o)- + *icon*(oscope)]

or·tho (ôr′thō), *adj.* (of a salt or acid) having the highest number of water molecules within a series. [< *ortho-*]

ortho-, *combining form.* **1.** straight: *Orthognathous = having a straight jaw.*
2. correct; proper: *Orthoëpy = correct pronunciation.*
3. ortho, as in *orthophosphoric acid.*
[< Greek *orthós* straight]

or·tho·bo·ric acid (ôr′thō bô′rik, -bō′-), boric acid.

or·tho·cen·ter (ôr′thə sen′tər), *n.* the point at which the altitudes of a triangle intersect. [< *ortho-* + *center*]

or·tho·ce·phal·ic (ôr′thə sə fal′ik), *adj.* having a skull that is of medium height for its breadth or length; intermediate between brachycephalic and dolichocephalic. [< *ortho-* + Greek *kephalḗ* head + English *-ic*]

or·tho·ceph·a·lous (ôr′thə sef′ə ləs), *adj.* orthocephalic.

or·tho·ceph·a·ly (ôr′thə sef′ə lē), *n.* orthocephalic character or structure.

or·tho·chro·mat·ic (ôr′thə krə mat′ik), *adj. Photography.* **1.** of, having to do with, or reproducing the tones of light and shade as they appear in nature. **2.** (of film) sensitive to all colors except red. [< *ortho-* + Greek *chrōmatikós* chromatic]

or·tho·chro·ma·tism (ôr′thə krō′mə tizəm), *n.* the representation of the tones of light and shade as they appear in nature.

or·tho·clase (ôr′thə klās, -klāz), *n.* common or potash feldspar, a silicate of aluminum and potassium, occurring in orthoclastic crystals or masses of various colors. *Formula:* $KAlSi_3O_8$ [< *ortho-* + Greek *klásis* cleavage (because of the way it breaks)]

or·tho·clas·tic (ôr′thə klas′tik), *adj. Mineralogy.* having cleavages at right angles to each other, as certain feldspars, especially orthoclase.

or·tho·cous·in (ôr′thə kuz′ən), *n.* a parallel cousin.

or·tho·cy·mene (ôr′thə sī′mēn), *n.* one of three isomeric forms of cymene.

or·tho·don·tia (ôr′thə don′shə, -shē ə), *n.* the branch of dentistry that deals with straightening and adjusting teeth. [< New Latin *orthodontia* < Greek *orthós* straight + *odoús, odóntos* tooth]

or·tho·don·tic (ôr′thə don′tik), *adj.* of or having to do with orthodontia: *The condition can usually be corrected by orthodontic treatments, during which the teeth are moved gently and gradually to acceptable positions* (Peter J. Brekhus).

or·tho·don·tics (ôr′thə don′tiks), *n.* the science or practice of orthodontia.

or·tho·don·tist (ôr′thə don′tist), *n.* a dentist who specializes in orthodontia.

or·tho·dox (ôr′thə doks), *adj.* **1.** generally accepted, especially in religion: *orthodox beliefs. And prove their doctrines orthodox By apostolic blows and knocks* (Samuel Butler). **2.** having generally accepted views or opinions, especially in religion: *an orthodox Methodist, a very orthodox young man.* **3.** approved by convention; usual; customary. **4. a.** conforming to the basic Christian faith as established in the early creeds. **b.** *Especially U.S.* Trinitarian.
—*n.* **1.** a person who is orthodox. **2** such persons as a group.
[< Late Latin *orthodoxus* < Greek *orthodóxos* < *orthós* correct + *dóxa* opinion] —**or′tho·dox′ly,** *adv.*
—**Syn.** *adj.* **1.** canonical. **3.** conventional, standard.

Or·tho·dox (ôr′thə doks), *adj.* **1.** of or having to do with the Greek or Russian Church or one of the national churches conforming to its doctrine. **2.** of or having to do with the branch of Judaism that adheres most closely to the traditionally prescribed ritual, customs, etc.: *The Orthodox and Conservative branches [of Judaism] emphasize the binding authority of that law* (New York Times). **3.** of or having to do with the body of Quakers that adheres most closely to the austere manner of worship and life originally associated with members of the Society of Friends.

Orthodox Church, the group of Christian churches in eastern Europe, western Asia, and Egypt, that do not recognize the Pope as the supreme head of the Catholic Church; Greek Orthodox Church.

or·tho·dox·y (ôr′thə dok′sē), *n., pl.* **-dox·ies.** the holding of correct or generally accepted beliefs; orthodox practice, especially in religion; being orthodox: *All the royal children were brought up in complete orthodoxy* (Lytton Strachey). *It is the theorist ... who is more likely to see the dangers of a scientific orthodoxy* (John E. Owen). *Orthodoxy is my doxy; heterodoxy is another man's doxy* (William Warburton).

or·tho·ëp·ic (ôr′thō ep′ik), *adj.* of or having to do with orthoëpy: *It is often impossible to suggest any explanation of orthoëpic mutations* (G.P. Marsh).

or·tho·ëp·i·cal (ôr′thō ep′ə kəl), *adj.* orthoëpic: *Final "e" in the 16th Century ... had come to be regarded mainly as an orthoëpical symbol* (A.J. Ellis).

or·tho·ë·pist (ôr thō′ə pist, ôr′thō-), *n.* a person who knows much about the pronunciation of words: *The polished language of seventeenth-century classical authors resulted from a remarkable collaboration between ... professional orthoëpists and grammarians* (Simeon Potter).

or·tho·ë·py (ôr thō′ə pē, ôr′thō-), *n.* **1.** correct, accepted, or customary pronunciation. **2.** the part of grammar that deals with pronunciation; phonology. [< Greek *orthoépeia* < *orthós* correct + *épos* utterance, word]

or·thog·a·mous (ôr thog′ə məs), *adj. Botany.* having direct or immediate methods of pollination.

or·thog·a·my (ôr thog′ə mē), *n. Botany.* orthogamous condition. [< *ortho-* + *-gamy*]

or·tho·gen·e·sis (ôr′thə jen′ə sis), *n.* **1.** *Biology.* the alleged development of one species into another in a definite line which is predetermined by the constitution which outward circumstances have given to each organism. **2.** *Anthropology.* the theory that social patterns follow an identical, predictable course in every culture, regardless of external pressures, conditions, etc.

or·tho·ge·net·ic (ôr′thə jə net′ik), *adj.* of, having to do with, or exhibiting orthogenesis.

or·tho·gen·ic (ôr′thə jen′ik), *adj.* of, having to do with, or providing care and training for children who are mentally retarded or emotionally disturbed: *an orthogenic center or institution.* [< *ortho-* + *-gen* + *-ic*]

or·thog·nath·ic (ôr′thog nath′ik), *adj.* orthognathous.

or·thog·na·thism (ôr thog′nə thiz əm), *n.* the character of being orthognathous.

or·thog·na·thous (ôr thog′nə thəs), *adj. Anthropology.* straight-jawed; not having the jaws projecting beyond the vertical line drawn from the forehead. [< *ortho-* + Greek *gnáthos* jaw + English *-ous*]

or·thog·na·thy (ôr thog′nə thē), *n.* orthognathism.

or·tho·gon (ôr′thə gon), *n.* a rectangular figure. [< Latin *orthogōnium,* neuter of Latin *orthogōnius;* see ORTHOGONAL]

or·thog·o·nal (ôr thog′ə nəl), *adj.* **1.** having to do with or involving right angles; rectangular. **2.** orthorhombic. —*n.* an orthogonal line or plane: *... reading in both directions along all orthogonals and main diagonals* (Scientific American). [< Latin *orthogōnius* right-angled (< Greek *orthogṓnios* < *orthós* right + *gōníā* angle) + English *-al*[1]] —**Syn.** *adj.* **1.** right-angled.

or·thog·o·nal·i·ty (ôr′thog ə nal′ə tē), *n.* orthogonal quality or state.

or·thog·ra·pher (ôr thog′rə fər), *n.* **1.** a person skilled in orthography. **2.** a person who spells correctly.

or·tho·graph·ic (ôr′thə graf′ik), *adj.* **1.** having to do with orthography: *an orthographic mistake.* **2.** correct in spelling: *For the sake of simplicity only the orthographic spellings are here given* (Simeon Potter). **3.** *Geometry.* orthogonal.

or·tho·graph·i·cal (ôr′thə graf′ə kəl), *adj.* orthographic.

or·tho·graph·i·cal·ly (ôr′thə graf′ə klē), *adv.* in an orthographic manner; according to the rules of proper spelling.

orthographic projection, a projection on a plane by lines perpendicular to the plane.

or·thog·ra·phist (ôr thog′rə fist), *n.* an orthographer.

or·thog·ra·phy (ôr thog′rə fē), *n., pl.* **-phies. 1. a.** correct spelling; spelling considered as right or wrong. **b.** any system of spelling: *The function of orthography is to identify the phonemes, or distinctive vowels and consonants, of a language* (Harold B. Allen). **2.** the art of spelling; study of spelling. **3.** a drawing in a kind of projection in which the object is projected on a plane by lines perpendicular to the plane. [< Latin *orthographia* < Greek *orthographíā* < *orthós* correct + *gráphein* write]

or·tho·hy·dro·gen (ôr′thō hī′drə jən), *n.* a form of hydrogen consisting of molecules whose pairs of nuclei have spins in the same direction: *Three quarters of hydrogen gas is ortho-hydrogen* (Monroe M. Offner).

or·tho·pae·dic (ôr′thə pē′dik), *adj.* orthopedic.

or·tho·pe·di·a (ôr′thə pē′dē ə), *n.* orthopedics.

or·tho·pe·dic (ôr′thə pē′dik), *adj.* of or having to do with orthopedics: *an orthopedic surgeon.* —**or′tho·pe′di·cal·ly,** *adv.*

or·tho·pe·dics (ôr′thə pē′diks), *n.* the branch of surgery that deals with the deformities and diseases of bones and joints, especially in children. [< French *orthopédique* < *orthopédie* < New Latin *orthopaedia* < Greek *orthós* straight + *paideíā* rearing of children < *paîs, paidós* child]

or·tho·pe·dist (ôr′thə pē′dist), *n.* a surgeon who specializes in orthopedics: *The big Cornell athletic clinic, headed by a crack team of orthopedists and physiotherapists, is equipped to handle everything from mild Charley horses to severe skull fractures* (Newsweek).

or·tho·pe·dy (ôr′thə pē′dē), *n.* orthopedics.

or·tho·phos·phor·ic acid (ôr′thō fos fôr′ik, -for′-), phosphoric acid.

or·tho·phyre (ôr′thə fīr), *n.* porphyry in which the embedded crystals consist chiefly of orthoclase. [< French *orthophyre* < *orthose* orthoclase + (por)*phyre* porphyry]

or·thop·ne·a (ôr thop′nē ə), *n.* a condition, associated with asthma and certain heart ailments, in which satisfactory breathing can take place only when one is in an erect position. [< Latin *orthopnoea* < Greek *orthópnoia* < *orthós* straight + *pneîn* blow, breathe]

or·tho·prax·y (ôr′thə prak′sē), *n.* **1.** correctness of practice, action, or procedure. **2.** corrective treatment of deformities; orthopedics. [< *ortho-* + Greek *prâxis* a doing, acting]

or·tho·psy·chi·at·ric (ôr′thō sī′kē at′rik), *adj.* of or having to do with orthopsychiatry. —**or′tho·psy′chi·at′ri·cal·ly,** *adv.*

or·tho·psy·chi·at·ri·cal (ôr′thō sī′kē at′rə kəl), *adj.* orthopsychiatric.

or·tho·psy·chi·a·trist (ôr′thō sī kī′ə trist), *n.* a person who practices orthopsychiatry.

or·tho·psy·chi·a·try (ôr′thō sī kī′ə trē), *n.* the branch of psychiatry dealing with the prevention or early correction of mental disorders, as personality and behavior problems, especially in young people. [< *ortho-* + *psychiatry*]

or·thop·ter (ôr thop′tər), *n.* **1.** ornithopter. **2.** an orthopterous insect. [< French *orthoptère* < Greek *orthós* straight + *pterón* wing]

or·thop·ter·an (ôr thop′tər ən), *adj.* orthopterous. —*n.* an orthopterous insect.

or·thop·ter·on (ôr thop′tə ron), *n., pl.* **-ter·a** (-tər ə). an orthopterous insect; orthopter.

or·thop·ter·ous (ôr thop′tər əs), *adj.* of or belonging to an order of insects characterized by longitudinally folded, membranous hind wings covered by hard, narrow outer wings, and having mouth parts adapted for chewing. Orthopterous insects have an incomplete metamorphosis. The order includes crickets, grasshoppers, locusts, and cockroaches.

or·thop·tic (ôr thop′tik), *adj.* of, having to do with, or producing normal binocular vision. [< *ortho-* + Greek *optikós* having to do with sight]

orthoptic exercises, a method of exercising the muscles of the eye to correct cross-eye, muscular weaknesses, etc.

or·thop·tics (ôr thop′tiks), *n.* the treatment of certain visual defects by exercising and training the eye muscles. [< *ortho-* + *optics*]

or·tho·rhom·bic (ôr′thə rom′bik), *adj.* having to do with a system of crystallization in which the three unequal axes intersect at right angles. [< *ortho-* + *rhombic*]

or·tho·scop·ic (ôr′thə skop′ik), *adj.* having to do with or producing correct or normal vision: *orthoscopic glasses, an orthoscopic eyepiece on a telescope.* [< *ortho-* + *-scop*(e) + *-ic*]

or·tho·stat·ic (ôr′thə stat′ik), *adj. Medicine.* caused by standing up, especially for long periods of time; affecting the body in a vertical position: *orthostatic hypotension, orthostatic albuminuria.* [< *ortho-* + *static*]

or·thos·ti·chous (ôr thos′tə kəs), *adj. Botany.* exhibiting orthostichy; vertically ranked.

or·thos·ti·chy (ôr thos′tə kē), *n., pl.* **-chies.** *Botany.* a vertical rank or row; an arrangement of lateral members, such as leaves, at different heights on an axis or stem so that their median planes coincide. [< *ortho-* + Greek *stíchos* row, line + English *-y*[3]]

or·tho·tone (ôr′thə tōn), *adj.* **1.** having an accent, as a word. **2.** acquiring an accent, as from position, though not ordinarily accented. —*n.* an orthotone word. The English articles, usually proclitics, are orthotones when emphasized. *Example:* "I did not say *a* man, I said *the* man." [< Greek *orthótonos* having the right accent < *orthós* right, correct + *tónos* tone]

or·tho·trop·ic (ôr′thə trop′ik), *adj. Botany.* of, having to do with, or exhibiting orthotropism; growing vertically upward or downward, as a stem or root.

or·thot·ro·pism (ôr thot′rə piz əm), *n. Botany.* a tendency to grow in a vertical direction, upward or downward.

or·thot·ro·pous (ôr thot′rə pəs), *adj. Botany.* (of an ovule) having the nucellus straight, or not inverted, so that the chalaza is at the evident base and the micropyle at the opposite end. [< New Latin *orthotropus* (with English *-ous*) < Greek *orthós* straight + *-tropos* turned]

or·thot·ro·py (ôr thot′rə pē), *n. Botany.* orthotropous condition.

or·tho·xy·lene (ôr′thə zī′lēn), *n.* one of three isomeric forms of xylene: *Orthoxylene is produced in pure form and from it is derived phthalic anhydride, a chemical raw material used in manufacturing certain plastic materials* (Wall Street Journal).

or·to·lan (ôr′tə lən), *n.* **1.** a small bunting of Europe, northern Africa, and western Asia, the meat of which is regarded as a delicacy: *Let me die eating ortolans to the sound of soft music* (Benjamin Disraeli). **2.** *U.S.* any of various small wild birds, such as the bobolink and the sora. [< French *ortolan* (literally) gardener < Provençal < Latin *hortulānus* of gardens < *hortulus* (diminutive) < *hortus* garden]

orts (ôrts), *n.pl.* leftover fragments of food, fodder, etc.; scraps; leavings: *Besides, their feasting caused a multiplication of orts, which were the heirlooms of the poor* (George Eliot). [Middle English *ort.* Compare Middle Dutch *orte,* and Low German *ort.*]

Or·well·i·an (ôr wel′ē ən), *adj.* **1.** of, having to do with, or in the style and words of George Orwell: *The Politburo and the Orgburo will be merged and the two ugly Orwellian names replaced by the stern old Latin "Presidium"* (Time). **2.** characteristic of the regimented and dehumanized society described in George Orwell's novel *1984: . . . for those Chinese whose life last year was changed into an Orwellian inferno* (Sunday Times). —*n.* a person who supports the form of society as presented in *1984: Left-wing Orwellians noted . . . how the benevolent Tory mask slipped* (Punch).

-ory, *suffix.* **1.** ——ing, as in *compensatory, contradictory.*
2. of or having to do with ——; of or having to do with ——ion, as in *advisory, auditory.*
3. characterized by ——ion, as in *adulatory.*
4. serving to ——, as in *expiatory.*
5. tending to or inclined to ——, as in *conciliatory.*
6. place for ——ing; establishment for —ing, as in *depository.*
7. other meanings, as in *conservatory.*
[< Old North French *-ory, -orie,* Old French *-oir, -oire* < Latin *-ōrius, -ōria, -ōrium* < *-or, -ōris* -or + *-ius* -y[3]]

o·ryx (ôr′iks, ōr′-), *n., pl.* **o·ryx·es** or (*collectively*) **o·ryx.** any of a group of African antelope with long, nearly straight horns in the adult of both sexes: *In Arabia Talbot found that the oryx, a handsome black-and-white antelope, is almost extinct* (Time). [< Latin *oryx* < Greek *óryx, -ygos* an antelope (in Biblical Latin and Greek, wild ox)]

Oryx
(6 ft. long; 4 ft. high at the shoulder)

os[1] (os), *n., pl.* **os·sa** (os′ə). *Latin.* a bone.

os[2] (os), *n., pl.* **o·ra** (ôr′ə, ōr′-). *Latin.* a mouth; opening.

os[3] (ōs), *n., pl.* **o·sar** (ō′sär). *Geology.* an esker. [< Swedish *ås* ridge (of a hill or roof); *åsar,* plural]

os-, *prefix.* the form of **ob-** in some cases before *c* and *t,* as in *oscine, ostensible.*

o.s. or **o/s** (no periods), out of stock.

Os (no periods), osmium (chemical element).

OS (no periods) or **O.S.,** Old Saxon.

O.S., **1.** Old Style. **2.** ordinary seaman.

O.S.A., **1.** Ontario Society of Artists. **2.** Order of Saint Augustine; Augustinians (Latin, *Ordinis Sancti Augustini*).

O·sage (ō′sāj, ō sāj′), *n.* **1.** a member of a tribe of American Indians, originally inhabiting the region of the Arkansas River. **2.** their Siouan language. [American English < Siouan (Osage) *Wazhazhe* "war people," originally applied to one of the three Osage bands]

Osage orange, **1.** an ornamental, spreading tree of the mulberry family, with glossy leaves and hard, bright-orange wood; yellowwood. It was originally native to Arkansas and surrounding regions. **2.** its inedible, greenish fruit that looks somewhat like an orange.

O·sag·yef·o (ō′säg yef′ō), *n.* title of the first president of Ghana, Kwame Nkrumah; *[The] title Osagyefo can mean anything from leader to saviour* (Maclean's).

o·sar (ō′sär), *n.* plural of **os**[3].

O.S.B., Order of Saint Benedict; Benedictines (Latin, *Ordinis Sancti Benedicti*).

Os·can (os′kən), *n.* **1.** one of the ancient inhabitants of Campania, a region in southern Italy. **2.** the ancient Italic dialect of Campania, closely related to Umbrian.

Os·car[1] or **os·car** (os′kər), *n.* **1.** a small statuette awarded annually by the Academy of Motion Picture Arts and Sciences for the best performances, production, photography, etc., during the year: *Candidates in the Academy Awards show last week sweated fearfully until each gleaming Oscar was firmly in hand* (Newsweek). **2.** a prize: *Last week's Oscar for the most dramatic bomb story went unquestionably to the Star, whose reporter described the South Bank discovery as "the bomb that made London hold its breath for ten hours"* (Punch). [American English; supposedly from the remark, "He reminds me of my Uncle Oscar," made by the secretary of the Academy when he saw one of the statuettes]

Os·car[2] (os′kər), *n. U.S.* a code name for the letter *o,* used in transmitting radio messages.

os·cil·late (os′ə lāt), *v.,* **-lat·ed, -lat·ing.** —*v.i.* **1.** to swing to and fro like a pendulum; move to and fro between two points. **2.** to vary between opinions, purposes, etc.: *Human nature oscillates between good and evil* (Benjamin Jowett). **3.** *Electricity.* to have or produce oscillations. **4.** *Physics.* to swing from one limit to another. —*v.t.* **1.** to cause to swing to and fro. **2.** *Electricity.* to cause (an electric current) to alternate at a high frequency. [< Latin *ōscillāre* (with English *-ate*[1]) to swing, rock < *ōscillum* a swing] —**Syn.** *v.i.* **2.** vacillate.

os·cil·la·tion (os′ə lā′shən), *n.* **1.** the fact or process of oscillating. **2.** a single swing of a vibrating body. **3.** *Physics.* **a.** a single forward and backward surge of a charge of electricity: *Oscillations may be sustained in a circuit if some provision is made for returning energy at the same rate as it is removed* (Sears and Zemansky). **b.** a rapid change in electromotive force. **c.** a single complete cycle of an electric wave. **d.** an electric wave.

os·cil·la·tor (os′ə lā′tər), *n.* **1.** a person or thing that oscillates. **2.** a device producing the oscillations that give rise to an alternating electric current, as the vacuum tube of a radio transmitting apparatus: *It is also proposed to use a number of electrical oscillators to provide acceleration* (A.W. Haslett).

os·cil·la·to·ry (os′ə lə tôr′ē, -tōr′-), *adj.* oscillating: *The small oscillatory movements of a fixating eye have been observed.*

oscillatory discharge, **1.** the electric discharge characteristic of a Leyden jar; a backward and forward surging of the charge, with a continual decrease in magnitude. **2.** any corresponding electric discharge.

os·cil·lo·gram (os′ə lə gram, ə sil′ə-), *n.* a record made by an oscillograph: *An oscillogram . . . pictures the slightest flaw that anxious eyes and modern microscopes can see* (New Yorker). [< Latin *ōscillāre* to swing + English *-gram*]

os·cil·lo·graph (os′ə lə graf, -gräf; ə sil′ə-), *n.* an instrument for recording electric oscillations, as of currents and voltages: *The electrical potentials can be . . . then recorded either photographically or by an ink-writing oscillograph* (Floyd and Silver). [< French *oscillographe* < Latin *ōscillāre* to swing + French *-graphe* -graph]

os·cil·lo·graph·ic (os′ə lə graf′ik), *adj.* of or produced by an oscillograph. —**os′cil·lo·graph′i·cal·ly,** *adv.*

os·cil·log·ra·phy (os′ə log′rə fē), *n.* the recording of electric oscillations with an oscillograph.

os·cil·lo·scope (ə sil′ə skōp), *n. Electricity.* an instrument for representing the oscillations of a varying voltage or current on the fluorescent screen of a cathode-ray tube. [< Latin *ōscillāre* to swing + English *-scope*]

os·cine (os′in, -īn), *n.* any of a large group of perching birds that have well-developed vocal organs and usually sing. —*adj.* of or belonging to this group of birds. [< New Latin *Oscines* the suborder name < Latin *oscinēs,* plural of *oscen, -inis* bird with a voice (usable in augury) < *ob-* to + *canere* sing]

os·ci·tance (os′ə təns), *n.* oscitancy.

os·ci·tan·cy (os′ə tən sē), *n.* **1.** a gaping or yawning; drowsiness: *In the case of oscitancy, when one person has extended or dilated his jaws, he has set the whole company into the same posture* (Entertainer). **2.** negligence; inattention; dullness.

os·ci·tant (os′ə tənt), *adj.* **1.** gaping; yawning; drowsy. **2.** inattentive; negligent; dull. [< Latin *ōscitāns, -antis,* present participle of *ōscitāre* yawn, gape, probably < *ōs* mouth + *citāre* move, agitate]

os·ci·tate (os′ə tāt), *v.i.,* **-tat·ed, -tat·ing.** to yawn or gape with sleepiness.

os·ci·ta·tion (os′ə tā′shən), *n.* the act of gaping or yawning; drowsiness; inattention.

Os·co-Um·bri·an (os′kō um′brē ən), *adj.* of or having to do with the group of Italic dialects comprising Oscan and Umbrian.

os·cu·la (os′kyə lə), *n.* plural of **osculum.**

os·cu·lant (os′kyə lənt), *adj.* **1.** *Biology.* intermediate between two or more groups (applied to genera, families, etc., that connect or link others together). **2.** *Zoology.* adhering closely; embracing. [< Latin

 PRONUNCIATION KEY: hat, āge, cãre, fär; let, ēqual, tėrm; it, īce; hot, ōpen, ôrder; oil, out; cup, pu̇t, rüle;

ōsculāns, -antis, present participle of *ōsculārī* to kiss; see OSCULATE]

os·cu·lar (os′kyə lər), *adj.* **1.** *Zoology.* of or having to do with the osculum of a sponge or the like. **2.** of or having to do with the mouth or with kissing.

os·cu·late (os′kyə lāt), *v.,* **-lat·ed, -lat·ing.** —*v.t.* **1.** to kiss. **2.** to come into close contact with. **3.** *Geometry.* to have three or more points coincident with: *A plane or a circle is said to osculate a curve when it has three coincident points in common with the curve.* —*v.i.* **1.** to kiss. **2.** *Geometry.* (of two curves, surfaces, etc.) to osculate each other. **3.** *Biology.* to share the characters of two or more groups; be intermediate. [< Latin *ōsculārī* (with English *-ate*[1]) to kiss < *ōsculum* kiss (literally) little mouth (diminutive) < *ōs, -ōris* mouth]

os·cu·la·tion (os′kyə lā′shən), *n.* **1.** the act of kissing. **2.** a kiss: *And here, I suppose, follow osculations between the sisters* (Thackeray). **3.** *Geometry.* a contact between two curves, surfaces, etc., at three or more common points.

os·cu·la·to·ry (os′kyə lə tôr′ē, -tōr′-), *adj., n., pl.* **-ries.** —*adj.* **1.** of or having to do with kissing. **2.** coming into close contact. **3.** *Geometry.* osculating.
[< Latin *ōsculātus,* past participle of *ōsculārī* (see OSCULATE) + English *-ory*]
—*n.* (in the Roman Catholic Church) a small tablet in former times kissed by priest and congregation in the Mass.
[< Medieval Latin *osculatorium* < Latin *ōsculārī* to kiss]

os·cule (os′kyül), *n.* osculum.

os·cu·lum (os′kyə ləm), *n., pl.* **-la** (-lə). *Zoology.* a mouth or mouthlike opening, as of a sponge or tapeworm. [< Latin *ōsculum;* see OSCULATE]

OSCULUM

Osculum of a sponge

O.S.D., Order of Saint Dominic; Dominicans (Latin, *Ordinis Sancti Dominici*).

-ose[1], *suffix.* **1.** full of; having much or many, as in *verbose.*
2. inclined to; fond of, as in *jocose.*
3. like, as in *schistose.*
[< Latin *-ōsus*]

-ose[2], a suffix used to form chemical terms, especially names of sugars and other carbohydrates, as in *fructose, lactose,* and of protein derivatives, as in *proteose.* [< French *-ose,* in *glucose* glucose]

O·see (ō′zē, -sē), *n.* (in the Douay Bible) Hosea.

O·se·tian (o sē′shən), *adj., n.* Ossetian.

O·set·ic (o set′ik), *n., adj.* Ossetic.

O.S.F., Order of Saint Francis; Franciscans (Latin, *Ordinis Sancti Francisci*).

o·sier (ō′zhər), *n.* **1.** *Especially British.* **a.** any of various willows with tough, flexible branches or shoots. **b.** one of these branches, used in weaving baskets or other wickerwork. **2.** any of various shrubby dogwoods of North America. —*adj.* made of osiers. [< French *osier* < Old French *osiere,* perhaps related to Medieval Latin *auseria*] —**Syn.** *n.* **1. b.** withe.

o·siered (ō′zhərd), *adj.* covered with osiers; consisting of osiers.

O·si·ri·an (ō sī′rē ən), *adj.* of, having to do with, or representing Osiris: . . . *one of the Osirian pillars in the hypostyle hall of the Great Temple* (Karl H. Martini).

O·si·ris (ō sī′ris), *n.* the chief god of ancient Egypt, brother and husband of Isis, ruler of the lower world, and judge of the dead. He represented good and productivity and was identified with the Nile.

-osis, *pl.* **-oses.** *suffix.* **1.** act or process of ——, or state or condition of ——, as in *osmosis, cyanosis.*
2. a morbid or abnormal condition, as in *mononucleosis, neurosis, trichinosis, thrombosis.*
[< Latin *-osis* < Greek *-ōsis*]

Os·man·li (oz man′lē, os-), *n., pl.* **-lis,** *adj.* —*n.* **1.** Ottoman. **2.** the language of the Ottoman Turks. —*adj.* Ottoman. [< Turkish *Osmanlı* belonging to *Osman,* 1259-1326, founder of the Ottoman Empire. Compare OTTOMAN.]

os·mat·ic (oz mat′ik, os-), *adj.* of, having to do with, or possessing the sense of smell. [< Greek *osmḗ* smell + English *-ate*[1] + *-ic*]

os·mic (oz′mik, os′-), *adj. Chemistry.* **1.** of osmium. **2.** containing osmium, especially with a valence of four.

os·mics (oz′miks, os′-), *n.* the science that deals with the sense of smell. [< Greek *osmḗ* smell, odor + English *-ics*]

os·mi·ous (oz′mē əs, os′-), *adj. Chemistry.* **1.** of osmium. **2.** containing osmium, especially with a valence of three.

os·mi·rid·i·um (oz′mə rid′ē əm, os′-), *n.* iridosmine.

os·mi·um (oz′mē əm, os′-), *n.* a hard, heavy, grayish metallic chemical element of the platinum group, generally found associated with platinum in the alloy iridosmine. Osmium is the heaviest known material and is used for electric-light filaments, phonograph needles, etc. *Symbol:* Os; *at.wt.:* (C^{12}) 190.2 or (O^{16}) 190.2; *at no.:* 76; *valence:* 2,3,4,5,6,8. [< New Latin *osmium* < Greek *osmḗ* smell, odor (from the odor of one of the osmium oxides)]

os·mom·e·ter (oz mom′ə tər, os-), *n.* a device for measuring osmotic pressure. [< Greek *ōsmós* a thrust + English *-meter*]

os·mom·e·try (oz mom′ə trē, os-), *n.* the measurement of osmotic pressure.

os·mo·reg·u·la·tion (oz′mō reg′yə lā′shən, os′-), *n.* the process by which the osmotic activity of a living cell is increased or decreased by the organism in order to maintain the most favorable conditions for the vital processes of the cell and the organism.

os·mo·reg·u·la·to·ry mechanism (oz′mō reg′yə lə tôr′ē, -tōr′-; os′-), a biological device or chemical reaction by which an organism carries out osmoregulation: *It would seem that the organism's osmoregulatory mechanism is strained to its limit* (A.J. Brook).

os·mose (oz mōs′, os-), *v.,* **-mosed, -mosing,** *n.* —*v.t.* to subject to osmosis. —*v.i.* to pass by osmosis. —*n.* osmosis.

os·mo·sis (oz mō′sis, os-), *n.* **1.** the tendency of two fluids of different strengths that are separated by something porous to go through it and become mixed. Osmosis is the chief means by which the body absorbs food and is specifically the tendency of a fluid of lower concentration to pass through a semipermeable membrane into a solution of higher concentration. **2.** the diffusion or spreading of fluids through a membrane or partition till they are mixed. **3.** a gradual, often unconscious, absorbing or understanding of facts, theories, ideas, and the like: *A hilarious round of sport and pleasure which could only be described as the broadest education by osmosis* (Harper's). [Grecized variant (as in *endosmosis*) of *osmose* < French < Greek *ōsmós* a thrust]

os·mot·ic (oz mot′ik, os-), *adj.* of or having to do with osmosis.

os·mot·i·cal·ly (oz mot′ə klē, os-), *adv.* by osmosis; diffusively: *"Concentration" for this purpose means the total concentration of osmotically active particles—ions and molecules* (G.R. Hervey).

osmotic pressure, the force acting upon a semipermeable membrane placed between a solution and its pure solvent, caused by the flow of solute molecules through the membrane toward the pure solvent: *One cell contains a solution of high osmotic pressure, such as a solution of sugar* (Susann and Orlin Biddulph).

os·mund (oz′mund, os′-), *n.* any of a group of ferns, with large, upright, pinnate or bipinnate fronds, as the royal fern. [< Anglo-French *osmunde,* Old French *osmonde*]

Os·na·burg (oz′nə bėrg), *n.* **1.** a coarse linen fabric originally made in Osnabrück, Germany. **2.** a similar cotton fabric, used for sacking, upholstery, etc.: *The cheapest-quality coarse cotton goods used for wearing apparel is Osnaburg* (Bernice G. Chambers). [< *Osnaburg* (*Osnabrück*), a city in West Germany]

OSO (no periods), orbiting solar observatory: *OSO was launched in March 1962* (New Scientist).

os·prey (os′prē), *n., pl.* **-preys.** **1.** a large fish-eating hawk with white underparts and dark-brown back and wings; fish hawk; sea eagle. **2.** an ornamental feather, used for trimming hats, etc. [Middle English *ospray,* apparently < Latin *ossifraga;* see OSSIFRAGE]

Osprey (def. 1) (23 in. long; wingspread, 68 in.)

OSS (no periods) or **O.S.S.,** Office of Strategic Services (an agency of the United States government during World War II).

os·sa (os′ə), *n. Latin.* plural of **os**[1].

os·se·in (os′ē in), *n.* the organic basis of bone tissue, remaining after the mineral matter has been removed; ostein. [< Latin *osseus* bony, osseous + English *-in*]

os·se·let (os′ə lit), *n.* **1.** a hard substance growing on the inside of a horse's leg above the knee: *The horse was found to be afflicted with popped osselets* (New York Times). **2.** a small, bonelike part; ossicle. [< Old French *osselet* a little bone < Latin *os, ossis* bone]

os·se·ous (os′ē əs), *adj.* **1.** bony: *True bone or osseous tissue occurs only in the skeletons of bony fishes and land vertebrates* (Tracy I. Storer). **2.** containing bones. [< Latin *osseus* (with English *-ous*) < *os, ossis* bone] —**os′se·ous·ly,** *adv.*

Os·set (os′et), *n.* a native or inhabitant of Ossetia, in the southern Soviet Union.

Os·se·tian (o sē′shən), *adj.* Ossetic. —*n.* Osset. Also, **Osetian.**

Os·set·ic (o set′ik), *n.* the Iranian language spoken by the Ossets. —*adj.* of or having to do with the Ossets or their language. Also, **Osetic.**

Os·si·an·ic (osh′ē an′ik, os′-), *adj.* **1.** of or having to do with the style of poetry or rhythmic prose used by James Macpherson in *Poems of Ossian* (1762) and *Temora* (1763), purporting to be translations of works by Ossian, but which Samuel Johnson and Thomas Gray, among others, declared to be forgeries, contrived by Macpherson himself. **2.** grandiloquent; bombastic. **3.** of or having to do with Ossian, a legendary Gaelic poet and hero of the 200's A.D.

os·si·cle (os′ə kəl), *n.* **1.** a small bone, especially of the ear: *As vibrations strike against this drum they set in motion the chain of bones or ossicles of the middle ear* (Simeon Potter). **2.** a small bony or bonelike part: *The individual portions of the skeleton of a starfish, sea urchin, or sea cucumber are termed ossicles* (Harbaugh and Goodrich). [< Latin *ossiculum* little bone (diminutive) < *os, ossis* bone]

os·si·cu·lar (o sik′yə lər), *adj.* of or having to do with an ossicle or ossicles.

ossicular chain, a series of three small bones, the malleus, incus, and stapes, located in the middle ear of mammals and connecting the tympanic membrane with the vestibule.

os·sif·er·ous (o sif′ər əs), *adj.* containing or yielding bones, as a cave or a geological deposit. [< Latin *os, ossis* bone + English *-ferous*]

os·sif·ic (o sif′ik), *adj.* making or forming bone; ossifying.

os·si·fi·ca·tion (os′ə fə kā′shən), *n.* **1.** the process of changing into bone. **2.** a being changed into bone. **3.** a part that is ossified; bony formation. **4.** a becoming fixed, hardened, or very conservative; an ossifying: . . . *to prevent the ossification that can easily overtake state theatrical enterprises* (London Times).

os·si·frage (os′ə frij), *n.* **1.** the lammergeier, a vulture: *Such kin they seemed to their conquerors as the dog to the wolf, the ossifrage to the eagle* (J.G. Whyte-Melville). **2.** *Obsolete.* the osprey: *Crook'd claw o' the creature, cormorant, Or ossifrage, that . . . hangs Afloat i' the foam* (Robert Browning). [< Latin *ossifragus,* or *ossifraga* sea eagle, osprey < *os, ossis* bone + *-fragus* breaker < *frangere* to break]

os·si·fy (os′ə fī), *v.t., v.i.,* **-fied, -fy·ing.** **1.** to change into bone; become bone: *The soft parts of a baby's skull ossify as he grows older.* **2.** to make or become fixed, hard-hearted, or very conservative; harden like bone: *Long-continued doubt . . . must in the end ossify the higher parts of the mind* (R.H. Hutton). [< Latin *os, ossis* bone + English *-fy*]

os·su·ar·i·um (os′yü ãr′ē əm, osh′-), *n., pl.* **-i·a** (-ē ə). an ossuary: *I visited an ossuarium which originally housed the bones of both French and Prussian soldiers* (Sunday Times). [< Late Latin *ossuārium;* see OSSUARY]

os·su·ar·y (os′yü er′ē, osh′-), *n., pl.* **-ar·ies.** a vault, urn, or the like for the bones of the dead: *In addition to the crematory jar, there was an ossuary under the daislike steps before* *the altar* (Science News Letter). [< Late Latin *ossuārium,* neuter of *ossuārius* of bones < Latin *os, ossis* bone]

os·te·al (os′tē əl), *adj.* bony; osseous. [< Greek *ostéon* bone + English *-al*[1]]

os·te·in (os′tē ən), *n.* ossein.

os·te·it·ic (os′tē it′ik), *adj.* having to do with or affected with osteitis. Also, **ostitic.**

os·te·i·tis (os′tē ī′tis), *n.* inflammation of the substance of bone. [< Greek *ostéon* bone + English *-itis*]

os·ten·si·ble (os ten′sə bəl), *adj.* apparent; pretended; professed: *Her ostensible purpose was to borrow sugar, but she really wanted to see the new furniture.* [< French *ostensible* < Latin *ostēnsus,* past participle of *ostendere* to show < *ob-* toward + *tendere* stretch] —**Syn.** seeming.

os·ten·si·bly (os ten′sə blē), *adv.* on the face of it; as openly stated or shown; apparently: *Though ostensibly studying his history, Tom was really drawing pictures behind the big book.*

os·ten·sive (os ten′siv), *adj.* **1. a.** manifestly or directly demonstrative: *It has been manifested . . . by ostensive proof from Scriptures* (Thomas Jackson). **b.** (of a definition) giving meaning to a word by referring to examples coming after it. **2.** ostensible: *I have always observed, that where one scheme answers two purposes, the ostensive is never the purpose most at heart* (Frances Burney). —**os·ten′sive·ly,** *adv.*

os·ten·so·ri·um (os′ten sôr′ē əm, -sōr′-), *n., pl.* **-so·ri·a** (-sôr′ē ə, -sōr′-). (in the Roman Catholic Church) a monstrance: *The priest . . . walked under the canopy, and held the ostensorium up in an imposing manner as high as his head* (Harper's Magazine). See picture under **monstrance.** [< Medieval Latin *ostensorium* < Latin *ostendere;* see OSTENSIBLE]

os·ten·so·ry (os ten′sər ē), *n., pl.* **-ries.** ostensorium.

os·tent (os tent′), *n. Archaic.* **1. a.** the act of showing; a show or display: *fair ostents of love* (Shakespeare). **b.** ostentatious display. **2.** a sign, portent, or prodigy: *Latinus, frighted with this dire ostent, For counsel to his father Faunus went* (John Dryden). [< Latin *ostentum,* noun use of neuter past participle of *ostendere;* see OSTENSIBLE]

os·ten·ta·tion (os′ten tā′shən), *n.* **1.** a showing off; display intended to impress others: *the ostentation of a rich, vain man.* **2.** *Archaic.* a show, exhibition, or display of something: *to hide the distress and danger . . . under an ostentation of festivity* (Hawthorne). [< Latin *ostentātiō, -ōnis* < *ostentāre* to display (frequentative) < *ostendere* to show; see OSTENSIBLE] —**Syn. 1.** parade, pomp. —**Ant. 1.** modesty, reserve, simplicity.

os·ten·ta·tious (os′ten tā′shəs), *adj.* **1.** done for display; intended to attract notice: *Tom rode his new bicycle up and down in front of Dick's house in an ostentatious way. His religion was sincere, not ostentatious* (Joseph Addison). **2.** showing off; liking to attract notice: *Were I to detail the books which I have consulted . . . I should probably be thought ridiculously ostentatious* (James Boswell). —**os′ten·ta′tious·ly,** *adv.* —**os′ten·ta′tious·ness,** *n.* —**Syn. 1.** showy, spectacular, pretentious, gaudy.

osteo-, *combining form.* bone: *Osteogenesis = the development or formation of bone.* [< Greek *ostéon*]

os·te·o·ar·thri·tis (os′tē ō är thrī′tis), *n.* arthritis caused by degeneration of the cartilage of the joints, especially in older people: *Most people over 50 years old have osteoarthritis in some degree* (Joseph Lee Hollander).

os·te·o·blast (os′tē ə blast), *n.* a bone-forming cell. [< German *Osteoblast* < Greek *ostéon* bone + *blastós* germ, sprout]

os·te·oc·la·sis (os′tē ok′lə sis), *n.* **1.** the breaking down or absorption of bone tissue. **2.** the surgical breaking of a bone to correct deformity. [< *osteo-* + Greek *klásis* fracture < *klân* to break]

os·te·o·clast (os′tē ə klast), *n.* **1.** one of the large multinuclear cells found in growing bone which absorb bony tissue as canals, cavities, etc., are formed. **2.** a surgical instrument for performing an osteoclasis. [< German *Osteoklast* < Greek *ostéon* bone + *klastós* broken]

os·te·o·cyte (os′tē ə sīt), *n.* a bone cell: *Many of the bone-tending osteocytes are situated at relatively large distances from blood vessels* (Andrew L. Bassett). [< *osteo-* + *-cyte*]

os·te·o·gen·e·sis (os′tē ə jen′ə sis), *n.* the formation or growth of bone.

os·te·o·ge·net·ic (os′tē ō jə net′ik), *adj.* of or having to do with osteogenesis; ossific: *an osteogenetic process, an osteogenetic theory.*

osteogenetic cell, an osteoblast.

os·te·o·gen·ic (os′tē ə jen′ik), *adj.* osteogenetic.

os·te·oid (os′tē oid), *adj.* bonelike; bony. [< *oste*(o)- + *-oid*]

os·te·o·log·i·cal (os′tē ə loj′ə kəl), *adj.* of or having to do with osteology.

os·te·ol·o·gist (os′tē ol′ə jist), *n.* a person skilled in osteology.

os·te·ol·o·gy (os′tē ol′ə jē), *n., pl.* **-gies. 1.** the branch of anatomy that deals with bones. **2.** the bony structure or system of bones of an animal or major part of an animal, as the head, trunk, etc. [< New Latin *osteologia* < Greek *ostéon* bone + *-logiā* -logy]

os·te·o·ma (os′tē ō′mə), *n., pl.* **-mas, -ma·ta** (-mə tə). a tumor composed of bony tissue, usually benign. [< New Latin *osteoma* < Greek *ostéon* bone + *-ōma* -oma]

os·te·o·ma·la·cia (os′tē ō mə lā′shə), *n.* a softening of the bones, usually in adults, caused by the gradual disappearance of calcium salts. [< *osteo-* + Greek *malakía* softness < *malakós* soft]

os·te·o·ma·lac·ic (os′tē ō mə las′ik), *adj.* of or affected with osteomalacia: *Rickety children born of these osteomalacic mothers showed a similar comparative immunity to caries* (New Biology).

os·te·o·my·e·li·tis (os′tē ō mī′ə lī′tis), *n.* an infection of the bone, usually caused by pus-forming microorganisms, as certain strains of streptococcus. [< *osteo-* + Greek *myelós* marrow + English *-itis*]

os·te·o·path (os′tē ə path), *n.* a person who treats disease by osteopathy. [American English < *osteopathy*]

os·te·o·path·ic (os′tē ə path′ik), *adj.* of osteopathy or osteopaths.

os·te·op·a·thist (os′tē op′ə thist), *n.* an osteopath.

os·te·op·a·thy (os′tē op′ə thē), *n.* a theory and treatment of disease based on the concept that both the structure and functions of a body and its organs are interdependent and any structural deformity may lead to functional breakdown. Osteopathy emphasizes treatment by manipulation of the bones and muscles but includes all types of medical and physical therapy. [American English < *osteo-* + *-pathy*]

os·te·o·phyte (os′tē ə fīt), *n.* a bony outgrowth. [< *osteo-* + Greek *phytón* plant]

os·te·o·phyt·ic (os′tē ə fit′ik), *adj.* of or like an osteophyte.

os·te·o·plas·tic (os′tē ə plas′tik), *adj.* **1.** of or having to do with osteoplasty. **2.** of or having to do with the formation of bone.

os·te·o·plas·ty (os′tē ə plas′tē), *n., pl.* **-ties.** the surgical transplanting or inserting of bone to supply a defect or loss. [< *osteo-* + Greek *plastós* something formed]

os·te·o·po·ro·sis (os′tē ō pə rō′sis), *n.* a disease in which the bone spaces or Haversian Canals become enlarged and the bones become weak and brittle. It occurs especially among old people, causing the bones to break easily and heal slowly. *Horses stabled indoors may go lame because they get so little sunlight that they get a mild form of the porous bone disease, osteoporosis* (Science News Letter).

os·te·o·scle·ro·sis (os′tē ō skli rō′sis), *n.* an abnormal hardening of a bone, especially at the ends or outer surface.

os·te·o·tome (os′tē ə tōm), *n.* a surgical instrument for cutting or dividing bone. [< *osteo-* + Greek *-tomiā* a cutting]

os·te·ot·o·mist (os′tē ot′ə mist), *n.* a surgeon who performs osteotomies.

os·te·ot·o·my (os′tē ot′ə mē), *n., pl.* **-mies.** the surgical operation of dividing or cutting away bone. [< *osteo-* + Greek *-tomos* that cuts]

os·te·ri·a (os′tə rē′ə), *n.* a hostelry; inn; tavern; restaurant: *Austrians or Germans as well as British and Scandinavians throng the wine shops and osterias below the Brenner to sample wines inferior to their own* (Cyril Connolly). [< Italian *osteria* < Medieval Latin *hospitale* inn; see HOSPITAL]

os·ti·ar·y (os′tē er′ē), *n., pl.* **-ar·ies. 1.** a doorkeeper, especially of a church. **2.** in the Roman Catholic Church: **a.** the lowest of the four minor orders. **b.** a person ordained in this order. [< Latin *ōstiārius* < *ōstium* door, opening, related to *ōs* mouth]

os·ti·na·to (os′tə nä′tō), *n., pl.* **-tos.** *Music.* a constantly repeated melody, usually in the bass, but occasionally in other voices: *It is impossible not to admire the deftness and complexity of his orchestral scoring, which is full of ostinatos* (New Yorker). [< Italian *ostinato* (literally) obstinate < Latin *obstinātus*]

os·ti·o·lar (os′tē ə lər, os tī′-), *adj.* of or having to do with any ostiole: *the ostiolar filaments of certain lichens.*

os·ti·ole (os′tē ōl), *n.* a very small orifice or opening, as those in certain algae and fungi through which the spores are discharged. [< Latin *ōstiolum* (diminutive) < *ōstium* door, opening]

os·tit·ic (os tit′ik), *adj.* osteitic.

os·ti·um (os′tē əm), *n., pl.* **-ti·a** (-tē ə). an opening or mouthlike hole, as in the heart of an arthropod: *Blood is taken into the heart from the surrounding pericardial sinus through . . . the ostia* (A. M. Winchester). [< Latin *ōstium*]

ost·ler (os′lər), *n.* hostler.

➤ **Ostler, hostler.** In British use, *ostler* was generally preferred in Shakespeare's day, yielding to *hostler* in the 1700's, and regaining favor in the 1800's (although agreement was and remains far from unanimous; one finds *ostler* in George Eliot, *hostler* in Dickens). American usage has always favored *hostler.*

ost·mark (ôst′märk′), *n.* a unit of money in East Germany, worth about 24 cents. [< German *Ostmark* < *Ost* east + *Mark* mark[2]]

os·to·sis (os tō′sis), *n.* the formation of bone. [< Greek *osto-* < *ostéon* bone + English *-osis*]

os·to·the·ca (os′tə thē′kə), *n., pl.* **-cae** (-sē). (in ancient Greece) a receptacle for the bones of the dead. [< New Latin *ostotheca* < Greek *ostothḗkē* < *ostéon* bone + *thḗkē* case, box]

os·tra·cise (os′trə sīz), *v.t.,* **-cised, -cis·ing.** *Especially British.* ostracize: *An American who speaks perfect French and had many French friends . . . has been ostracised by the people he knew because he was seen talking with "etrangers"* (Observer).

os·tra·cism (os′trə siz əm), *n.* **1.** banishment from one's native country. **2.** a being shut out from society, from favor, from privileges, or from association with one's fellows: *His continued rudeness led finally to ostracism.*

os·tra·ci·za·tion (os′trə sə zā′shən), *n.* ostracism: *Social ostracization, particularly in small communities, can just as effectively silence the religious dissenter as can a powerful government* (Clayton and Heinz).

os·tra·cize (os′trə sīz), *v.t.,* **-cized, -ciz·ing. 1.** to banish: *The ancient Greeks ostracized a dangerous or unpopular citizen by public vote on ballots consisting of potsherds or tiles.* **2.** to shut out from society, from favor, from privileges, etc.: *A boy who boasts too much or tries to show off in a new school is sometimes ostracized until he learns how to get on with his new schoolmates.* [< Greek *ostrakízein* < *óstrakon* tile, potsherd, related to *ostéon* bone] —**os′tra·ciz′er,** *n.*

os·tra·cod (os′trə kod), *n.* any of a group of very small, free-swimming, bivalved crustaceans living in fresh or salt water, and found in fossil form in all geologic strata since the early Paleozoic. [< New Latin *Ostracoda* < Greek *ostrakṓdēs* like a shell < *óstrakon;* see OSTRACIZE]

os·tra·code (os′trə kōd), *n.* ostracod.

os·tra·co·derm (os′trə kō dėrm), *n.* any of a large group of jawless, bony-plated vertebrates of the Ordovician, Silurian, and Devonian periods: *The earliest vertebrates of which there is any definite knowledge were a varied group of fishlike animals, the ostracoderms* (L. Beverly Tarlo). [< New Latin *ostracodermi* name of the group < Greek *ostrakódermos* having a shell < *óstrakon* shell, tile + *dérma* skin]

os·tra·con (os′trə kon), *n., pl.* **-ca** (-kə), **-cons.** ostrakon.

os·tra·kon (os′trə kon), *n., pl.* **-ka** (-kə), **-kons. 1.** a potsherd or tile used in ancient Greece as a ballot on which the name of a citizen to be ostracized was inscribed. **2.** *Archaeology.* a fragment of pottery or limestone on which an inscription is written: *Nearly 200 ostrakons (ink descrip-*

tions on pottery) have been found (Scotsman). [< Greek *óstrakon;* see OSTRACIZE]

os·tre·i·cul·tur·al (os′trē ə kul′chər əl), *adj.* of or having to do with ostreiculture.

os·tre·i·cul·ture (os′trē ə kul′chər), *n.* the artificial breeding and cultivation of oysters. [< Latin *ostrea* oyster + *cultūra* culture]

os·tre·i·cul·tur·ist (os′trē ə kul′chər ist), *n.* a person who cultivates oysters artificially.

os·trich (ôs′trich, os′-), *n.* **1.** a large African and Arabian bird that can run swiftly but cannot fly. Ostriches have two toes and are the largest of existing birds. They have large feathers or plumes which were much used for decorating hats, fans, etc. **2.** a rhea. **3.** a person who refuses to face reality or an approaching danger, like the ostrich, which is supposed to bury its head in the sand to avoid oncoming dangers: *Over the last decade Ministers had acted like economic ostriches* (London Times). —*adj.* ostrichlike: *These ostrich attitudes are like the frivolity of those who deny the reality of* [*evil*] *by refusing to think about it* (Time). [< Old French *ostrusce* < Vulgar Latin *avis strūthiō* < Latin *avis* bird + Late Latin *strūthiō, -ōnis* ostrich < Late Greek *strouthíōn* < Greek *strouthós* (*mégas*) (great) sparrow]

African Ostrich (def. 1) (to 8 ft. tall)

os·trich·ism (ôs′tri chiz əm, os′-), *n.* refusal to face reality or an approaching danger: *It is stupid ostrichism . . . to pretend that history will never, under any circumstances, be invited to repeat itself* (Bernard Hollowood).

os·trich·like (ôs′trich līk′, os′-), *adj.* like an ostrich: *He was "unwilling to accept the ostrichlike materialistic viewpoint that such a problem does not exist"* (Science News Letter).

Os·tro·goth (os′trə goth), *n.* a member of the eastern division of Goths that overran the Roman Empire and controlled Italy from 493 to 555 A.D. [< Late Latin *Ostrogothi,* earlier *Austrogothi* < Germanic; perhaps earlier taken as "the splendid Goths," but later taken as "the eastern Goths"]

Os·tro·goth·ic (os′trə goth′ik), *adj.* of or having to do with the Ostrogoths.

Os·ty·ak (os′tē ak), *n.* an Ugric language spoken in western Siberia, in the northern Soviet Union.

Os·we·go tea (os wē′gō), a North American plant of the mint family, with showy, bright-red flowers; bee balm. An excellent tea can be brewed from its leaves, and its flowers attract hummingbirds. [< the *Oswego* River, in New York State]

O.T., Old Testament.

o·tal·gi·a (ō tal′jē ə), *n.* earache. [< New Latin *otalgia* < Greek *ōtalgíā* < *oûs, ōtós* ear + *álgos* pain]

o·tal·gic (ō tal′jik), *adj.* having to do with earache. —*n.* a remedy for earache.

o·ta·rine (ō′tə rīn, -tər in), *adj.* having to do with otaries or eared seals

o·ta·ry (ō′tər ē), *n., pl.* **-ries.** any of the eared seals, as the sea lions and fur seals. [< New Latin *Otaria* the typical genus < Greek *oûs, ōtós* ear]

OTC (no periods) or **O.T.C.,** an abbreviation for the following:
1. Officers' Training Camp.
2. *British.* Officer Training Corps (correlative with the American OCS).
3. Organization for Trade Cooperation.
4. over-the-counter: *The O.T.C. market deals in thousands of tightly held and rarely traded stocks such as Upjohn Co.* (Wall Street Journal).

O tem·po·ra! O mo·res! (ō tem′pər ə ō môr′ēz, mōr′-), *Latin.* Oh the times! Oh the manners! (from the first of Cicero's orations against Catiline).

oth·er (uᴛʜ′ər), *adj.* **1.** remaining: *John is here, but the other boys are at school.* **2.** additional or further: *I have no other place to go.* **3.** not the same as one or more already mentioned: *Come some other day.* **4.** different: *I would not have him other than he is.*
every other. See under **every.**
the other day (night, etc.), recently: *What did you do the other night? I bought this dress the other day.*
—*pron.* **1.** the other one; not the same ones: *Each praises the other.* **2.** another person or thing: *There are others to be considered.*
of all others, more than all others: *Of tame beasts . . . the most gross and indocile of all others, namely an ass* (Philemon Holland).
—*adv.* otherwise; differently: *I can't do other than to go.*
[Old English *ōther* the second; other]

oth·er-di·rect·ed (uᴛʜ′ər də rek′tid, -dī-), *adj.* conforming to the practices, ideas, expectations, etc., of one's personal group or society rather than following personal convictions; practicing conformity: *Your intransigence in this other-directed world we live in is a delightful curiosity* (New Yorker). —*n.* a person who is other-directed: *David Riesman consoles the radar-flaunting other-directeds* (Atlantic). —**oth′er-di·rect′ed·ness,** *n.*

oth·er-di·rec·tion (uᴛʜ′ər də rek′shən, -dī-), *n.* the tendency to be other-directed; other-directedness; conformity: *In the United States inner-direction has largely been supplanted by other-direction, at least among the middle classes* (David Riesman).

oth·er·gates (uᴛʜ′ər gāts′), *British Dialect.* —*adv.* in another manner; differently; otherwise. —*adj.* of another, different kind. [< *other* + *gate*[3] + adverbial genitive *-s*]

oth·er·guess (uᴛʜ′ər ges′), *Archaic.* —*adj.* of another kind or sort: *It was otherguess work with Bellamy* (Pall Mall Gazette). —*adv.* otherwise. [variant of *othergates*]

oth·er·ness (uᴛʜ′ər nis), *n.* **1.** the quality of being other; difference; diversity. **2.** the fact of being other.

oth·er·where (uᴛʜ′ər hwãr′), *adv. Archaic.* in another place; somewhere else; elsewhere: *His chair desires him here in vain, However they may crown him otherwhere* (Tennyson).

oth·er·wheres (uᴛʜ′ər hwãrz′), *adv. Archaic.* otherwhere.

oth·er·while (uᴛʜ′ər hwīl′), *adv. Archaic.* **1.** at another time or times. **2.** sometimes.

oth·er·whiles (uᴛʜ′ər hwīlz′), *adv. Archaic.* otherwhile. [< *otherwhile* + adverbial genitive *-s*]

oth·er·wise (uᴛʜ′ər wīz′), *adv.* **1.** in a different way; differently: *I could not do otherwise.* **2.** in other ways: *He is noisy, but otherwise a very nice boy.* **3.** under other circumstances; in a different condition: *He reminded me of what I should otherwise have forgotten.*
—*adj.* different: *It might have been otherwise.*
—*conj.* or else; if not: *Come at once; otherwise you will be too late.*
[< Old English *on ōthre wīsan* in another way]

oth·er·world (uᴛʜ′ər wėrld′), *n.* the world to come; life after death.

oth·er·world·li·ness (uᴛʜ′ər wėrld′lē nis), *n.* the quality of being otherworldly.

oth·er·world·ly (uᴛʜ′ər wėrld′lē), *adj.* **1.** of or devoted to another world, such as the world of mind or imagination, or the world to come: *The strange world of the Byzantine Empire had an art type all its own—intellectualized, otherworldly* (Newsweek). **2.** supernatural; weird: *The sound above is rather otherworldly* (New Yorker).

O·thin (ō′ᴛʜin), *n.* Odin.

o·tic (ō′tik, ot′ik), *adj.* of, having to do with, or in the region of the ear. [< Greek *ōtikós* < *oûs, ōtós* ear + *-ikós* -ic]

o·ti·ose (ō′shē ōs, -tē-), *adj.* **1.** lazy; idle; inactive: *Our policy in Turkey has now dwindled into an otiose support of the Government* (Saturday Review). **2.** of no value; trifling; nugatory: *Such stories . . . require . . . nothing more than an otiose assent* (William Paley). **3.** having no practical function; superfluous; useless: *An alphabet which . . . possesses otiose and needless letters* (Nature). [< Latin *ōtiōsus* unemployed < *ōtium* leisure] —**o′ti·ose′ly,** *adv.*

o·ti·os·i·ty (ō′shē os′ə tē, -tē-), *n.* **1.** laziness; idleness: *Joseph Sedley then led a life of dignified otiosity, such as became a person of his eminence* (Thackeray). **2.** worthlessness. **3.** uselessness.

o·ti·tis (ō tī′tis), *n.* inflammation of the ear. [< New Latin *otitis* < Greek *oûs, ōtós* ear + *-ītis* -itis]

otitis ex·ter·na (ek stėr′nə), inflammation of the external ear. [< New Latin *otitis* otitis, Latin *externa,* feminine of *externus* external]

otitis me·di·a (mē′dē ə), inflammation of the middle ear. [< New Latin *otitis* otitis, Latin *media,* feminine of *medius* middle]

o·ti·um cum dig·ni·ta·te (ō′shē əm kum dig′nə tā′tē), *Latin.* leisure with dignity; dignified ease: *Intending there to lead my future life in the otium cum dignitate of half-pay and annuity* (Scott).

o·to·cyst (ō′tə sist), *n.* an organ in many invertebrates, probably of sense of direction and balance, containing fluid and otoliths, once supposed to be an organ of hearing. [< Greek *oûs, ōtós* ear + English *cyst*]

o·to·la·ryn·go·log·ic (ō′tə lə ring′gə loj′ik), *adj.* **1.** of or having to do with otolaryngology. **2.** of or having to do with the nose, throat, and ear: *serious otolaryngologic diseases.*

o·to·la·ryn·go·log·i·cal (ō′tə lə ring′gə loj′ə kəl), *adj.* otolaryngologic.

o·to·lar·yn·gol·o·gist (ō′tə lar′ing gol′ə jist), *n.* a doctor who specializes in otolaryngology.

o·to·lar·yn·gol·o·gy (ō′tə lar′ing gol′ə jē), *n.* the branch of medicine that deals with diseases of the ear, nose, and throat and their treatment. [< Greek *oûs, ōtós* ear + English *laryngology*]

o·to·lith (ō′tə lith), *n.* one of the calcareous bodies formed in the internal ear of vertebrates and some invertebrates, often very large in fishes. It helps maintain equilibrium. [< French *otolithe* < Greek *oûs, ōtós* ear + *líthos* stone]

o·to·log·ic (ō′tə loj′ik), *adj.* otological.

o·to·log·i·cal (ō′tə loj′ə kəl), *adj.* of or having to do with otology.

o·tol·o·gist (ō tol′ə jist), *n.* a doctor who specializes in otology: *The otologists are trying to find why the nerve type of aging deafness can occur in the 50's* (Newsweek).

o·tol·o·gy (ō tol′ə jē), *n.* the branch of medicine that deals with the ear and the diagnosis and treatment of its diseases. [< American English < Greek *oûs, ōtós* ear + *-logíā* -logy]

o·to·rhi·no·lar·yn·gol·o·gy (ō′tə rī′nō-lar′ing gol′ə jē), *n.* otolaryngology.

o·to·scle·ro·sis (ō′tə skli rō′sis), *n.* a disorder of the ear, in which the base of the stapes becomes immobile because of bony growths in the inner ear. It results in deafness. *The two principal types of deafness are those caused by destruction of the auditory nerves and by otosclerosis* (Scientific American). [< Greek *oûs, ōtós* ear + English *sclerosis*]

o·to·scle·rot·ic (ō′tə skli rot′ik), *adj.* of or having to do with otosclerosis.

o·to·scope (ō′tə skōp), *n.* **1.** an instrument for examining the ear, especially the eardrum. **2.** a modification of the stethoscope for listening in the ear. [< Greek *oûs, ōtós* ear + English *-scope*]

ot·tar (ot′ər), *n.* attar.

ot·ta·va (ōt tä′vä), *n., pl.* **-ve** (-vā). *Music.* an octave.

ot·ta·va ri·ma (ə tä′və rē′mə; *Italian* ōt-tä′vä rē′mä), a stanza of eight lines with the lines according to the rhyme scheme *a b a b a b c c.* In Italian each line normally has eleven syllables; in English ten. *It is true that since* [*Byron*] *could read Italian well, he might have discovered the latent possibilities of the mock-heroic ottava rima for himself* (W.H. Auden). [< Italian *ottava rima* (literally) octave rhyme]

Ot·ta·wa (ot′ə wə, -wä), *n., pl.* **-wa** or **-was.** **1.** a member of a tribe of Algonkian Indians who lived near Lake Superior. **2.** this tribe. [American English < Canadian French *Otaua* < Algonkian (probably Cree) *atāwāyoo* trader]

Ot·ta·wan (ot′ə wən), *n.* a native or inhabitant of Ottawa, the capital of Canada.

ot·ter (ot′ər), *n., pl.* **-ters** or (*collectively*) **-ter.** **1.** any of several aquatic, fur-bearing, carnivorous mammals, related to the minks and weasels, that are good swimmers and have short legs with webbed toes and claws and a thick, tapered tail. **2.** the fur of an otter. Otter is short, thick, and glossy, somewhat like seal or beaver. **3. a.** a kind of tackle

Otter (def. 1) (to 4 ft. long)

with float, line, and hooks, used in fresh-water fishing. **b.** a kind of gear used in deep-sea trawling. **4.** a device towed by a ship for cutting the mooring cables of mines; paravane. **5.** the larva of a moth that is very destructive to hop vines. [Old English *oter*]

otter gear, **1.** a kind of tackle used in trawling; otter. **2.** a paravane.

otter hound, any of a breed of sturdy dogs developed in Great Britain for the hunting of otter. It has a thick, oily coat and slightly webbed feet and is an excellent swimmer.

ot·to (ot′ō), *n.* attar.

Ot·to cycle (ot′ō), the cycle in common internal-combustion engines in which one piston stroke out of every four is a working stroke. [< Nikolaus *Otto*, 1832-1891, a German scientist, who invented it]

ot·to·man (ot′ə mən), *n.* **1. a.** a low, cushioned seat without back or arms. **b.** a cushioned footstool. **2.** a cushioned, armless sofa, with or without a back. **3.** a heavy, corded fabric of silk or rayon, often with a cotton woof, used for coats and trimming: [*a coat of*] *heavily ribbed black ottoman with a high, round neck* (New Yorker). [< French *ottomane* (literally) Ottoman (to suggest the Oriental style of the seat)]

Ot·to·man (ot′ə mən), *n., pl.* **-mans,** *adj.* —*n.* **1.** a Turk. **2.** a Turk descended from or belonging to the tribe of Osman, the founder of the Ottoman Empire.
—*adj.* **1.** Turkish; Osmanli. **2.** of or having to do with the Turkish dynasty founded by Osman I about 1300 or the Ottoman Empire. [< Middle French *Ottoman* < Italian *Ottomano* < Arabic *'uthmānī* belonging to *'uthmān* < Turkish *Osman;* see OSMANLI]

Ot·to·ni·an (ə tō′nē ən), *adj.* of or having to do with the period of the German dynasty beginning with Otto the Great and including Otto II and III, which ruled the Holy Roman Empire from 962 to 1002: . . . *a late eleventh century Ottonian ivory plaque* (London Times). [< German *Ottonen* Ottos]

oua·ba·in (wä bä′in), *n.* a poisonous glucoside obtained from the seeds of various African plants of the dogbane family, used as an arrow poison and as a substitute for digitalis. *Formula:* $C_{29}H_{44}O_{12}.8H_2O$ [< earlier *ouabaio* the plant name; its juice (< French < Somali *wabāyo*) + *-in*]

oua·ka·ri (wä kä′rē), *n., pl.* **-ris.** a South American monkey having a short tail, and long, light-colored hair, part of which it loses upon reaching adulthood. Also, **uakari.** [< Tupi *uakari*]

oua·na·niche (wä′nä nēsh′), *n., pl.* **-niche.** a fresh-water salmon of eastern Canada. [< Canadian French *Ouananiche* < Algonkian (Cree), diminutive form of *wanans* salmon]

ou·bli·ette (ü′blē et′), *n.* **1.** a secret dungeon with an opening only at the top. **2.** a deep pit in the floor of a dungeon: *The . . . oubliette, Down thirty feet below the smiling day* (Tennyson). [< French, Middle French *oubliette* < Old French *oublier* forget < Vulgar Latin *oblītāre* (frequentative) < Latin *oblīvīscī* forget]

ouch[1] (ouch), *interj.* an exclamation expressing sudden pain. [probably < Pennsylvania German *autsch*]

ouch[2] (ouch), *Obsolete.* —*n.* **1.** a brooch or buckle worn as an ornament. **2.** the setting of a precious stone, usually part of a brooch or buckle: *onyx stones inclosed in ouches of gold* (Exodus 39:6). **3.** a glittering jewel; precious ornament; gem.
—*v.t.* to adorn with or as if with gems: *A lamplit bridge ouching the troubled sky* (William E. Henley).
[Middle English *ouche*, by misdivision < *a nouche* < Anglo-French, Old French *nouche* < Late Latin *nusca* < Germanic (compare Old High German *nusche*)]

oud (üd), *n.* an Arabian lute, usually having seven pairs of strings. It was the prototype of the medieval European lute. *The oud, a large Egyptian stringed instrument . . . resembles a gourd sliced in half and . . . emits an urgent nasal, tingling sound* (New Yorker). [< Arabic *'ud* (literally) wood]

oud·stry·der (oud′strī′dər), *n. Afrikaans.* a South African who fought (on either side) in the Boer War of 1899 to 1902: *He was bitterly disappointed that the outstryders had been lumped with other pensioners and not treated as a separate group* (Cape Argus).

oued (wed), *n.* wadi: *The Romans had worked out means of harnessing the oueds—seasonal watercourses which are to be found all over the area* (London Times).

ough (üH, úH), *interj.* an exclamation expressing disgust.

ought[1] (ôt), *auxiliary verb.* **1.** to have a duty; be obliged: *You ought to obey your parents.* **2.** to be right or suitable: *It ought to be allowed.* **3.** to be wise: *I ought to go before it rains.* **4.** to be expected: *At your age you ought to know better.* **5.** to be very likely: *The defending champion ought to win the race.* [Old English *āhte*, past tense of *āgan* owe; own] —**Syn. 1.** must, should.

➤ **ought.** Originally a past tense, *ought* now has present or future meaning. The past sense is expressed by a dependent perfect infinitive: *He ought to have answered* (not *had ought to answer*, which is substandard).

ought[2] (ôt), *n., adv.* aught; anything. [variant of *aught*]

ought[3] (ôt), *n. Informal.* nought; zero; 0. [earlier *an ought*, apparently misdivision of *a nought;* perhaps influenced by *aught*]

oui (wē), *adv., n., pl.* **ouis** (wē). *French.* yes.

Oui·ja (wē′jə), *n. Trademark.* a device that consists of a small board on legs that rests on a larger board marked with words, letters of the alphabet, or other characters. The person wishing an answer to questions rests his fingers lightly on the small board which may then move and touch letters or words. Ouijas are sometimes used at spiritualistic meetings and as games. [American English, supposedly < French *oui* yes + German *ja* yes]

ounce[1] (ouns), *n.* **1.** a unit of weight, 1/16 of a pound in avoirdupois, and 1/12 of a pound in troy weight. **2.** a measure for liquids; fluid ounce. 16 ounces = 1 pint in the United States. *Abbr.:* oz. **3.** a little bit; very small amount: *An ounce of prevention is worth a pound of cure.* [< Old French *unce* < Latin *uncia* twelfth part (of various measures). Doublet of INCH, OKA.]

ounce[2] (ouns), *n.* **1.** a large, whitish, carnivorous catlike mammal, with brown spots somewhat like a leopard, found in the mountains of central Asia; snow leopard. **2.** *Obsolete.* a lynx. [< Old French *once*, for *lonce* < Vulgar Latin *lyncea* < Latin *lynx* lynx < Greek *lýnx, lynkós*]

Ounce[2] **(def. 1)**
(6 to 8 ft. long)

ouph or **ouphe** (ouf, üf), *n. Archaic.* an elf, sprite, or goblin: *We'll dress like urchins, ouphes, and fairies, green and white* (Shakespeare). [variant of *oaf*, earlier *oaph*]

our (our, är), *adj.* a possessive form of **we. 1.** of us; belonging to us: *We need our coats now.* **2.** of me (an imperial or royal use, instead of *my*). [Old English *ūre* of us, genitive plural of *ic* I]

ou·rang-ou·tang (ü rang′ü tang′), *n.* orang-utan.

ou·ra·nog·ra·phy (úr′ə nog′rə fē), *n.* uranography.

ou·ra·ri (ü rä′rē), *n.* curare.

ou·rie (úr′ē), *adj. Scottish.* poor in appearance; shabby; dingy; dreary. [origin uncertain. Compare Old Icelandic *ūrig* wet.]

Our Lady, the Virgin Mary.

Our Lady's bedstraw, a variety of bedstraw having yellow flowers, believed to have been in the manger where the infant Jesus was placed.

ourn (ourn), *pron. Dialect.* ours.

ou·rol·o·gy (ü rol′ə jē), *n.* urology.

ou·ros·co·py (ü ros′kə pē), *n.* uroscopy.

ours (ourz, ärz), *pron.* a possessive form of **we. 1.** of us; belonging to us: *This garden is ours.* **2.** the one or ones belonging to us: *Ours is a large house.*

our·self (our self′, är-), *pron.* myself: *Ourself behind ourself* (Emily Dickinson).

➤ **Ourself** is used by an author, king, judge, etc.: *"We will ourself reward the victor," said the queen.*

our·selves (our selvz′, är-), *pron.pl.* **1.** the intensifying form of **we** or **us:** *We did it ourselves.* **2.** the reflexive form of **us:** *We hurt ourselves. We cannot see ourselves as others see us.*

-ous, *suffix.* **1.** having; having much; full of: *Joyous = full of joy.*
2. characterized by ——: *Zealous = characterized by zeal. Blasphemous = characterized by blasphemy.*
3. having the nature of: *Idolatrous = having the nature of an idolater.*
4. of or having to do with: *Monogamous = having to do with monogamy.*
5. like: *Thunderous = like thunder.*
6. committing or practicing: *Bigamous = practicing bigamy.*
7. inclined to: *Blusterous = inclined to bluster.*
8. in chemical terms, implying a larger proportion of the element indicated by the word than *-ic* implies. *Stannous* means containing tin in larger proportions than a corresponding *stannic* compound.
[< Old French *-os, -us* < Latin *-ōsus. -ous* is often used to represent the Latin adjective ending, *-us*, as in Latin *omnivorus* omnivorous, or the Greek adjective ending, *-os*, as in Greek *anṓnymos* anonymous]

ou·sel (ü′zəl), *n.* ouzel.

ou·si·a (ü sē′ä), *n. Greek.* essence.

oust (oust), *v.t.* **1.** to force out; drive out: *The sparrows have ousted the bluebirds from the birdhouse. The war problem . . . ousted for a time all other intellectual interests* (H. G. Wells). **2.** *Law.* to deprive of the possession of; dispossess. [< Anglo-French *ouster*, Old French *oster*, perhaps < Latin *obstāre* to block, hinder < *ob-* in the way of + *stāre* stand. Compare OBSTACLE.] —**Syn. 1.** eject, expel. **2.** evict.

oust·er (ous′tər), *n.* **1.** an ousting, especially an illegal forcing of a person from or out of his property. **2.** a person who ousts.

out (out), *adv.* **1.** away; forth: *to rush out. Spread the rug out.* **2.** not in or at a place, position, state, etc.: *That style went out of fashion. The miners are going out on strike.* **3.** into the open air: *He went out at noon.* **4.** to or at an end: *to play a game out, to fight it out.* **5.** from the usual place, condition, position, etc.: *Put the light out. The boy turned his pockets out.* **6.** completely; effectively: *to fit out for an expedition.* **7.** so as to project or extend: *to stand out, to stick out one's hand.* **8.** into or in existence, activity, or outward manifestation: *Fever broke out. Flowers came out.* **9.** aloud; loudly: *Speak out.* **10.** to others: *Give out the books.* **11.** from a number, stock, store, source, cause, material, etc.: *She picked out a new coat.* **12.** in the wrong: *to be out in one's calculations.* **13.** from a state of composure, satisfaction, or harmony: *to feel put out, to fall out with a friend.* **14.** at a money loss: *to be out ten dollars.* **15.** not in play; no longer at bat or on base in baseball, etc. **16.** into society: *She came out last year.*

out and away, beyond all others; by far: *He is out and away the best player.*

out of, a. from within: *She took a piece of candy out of the box. I sipped some soup out of the bowl.* **b.** so as to have left; no longer in: *He is out of the house. In another year he will be out of the army.* **c.** not within; away from; outside of; beyond: *The jet plane was soon out of sight. He moved out of hearing.* **d.** not having; without: *We are out of coffee.* **e.** so as to take away: *She was cheated out of her money.* **f.** from: *a house made out of brick. My dress is made out of silk.* **g.** from among; from the group of: *We picked our puppy out of that litter.* **h.** because of; by reason of: *I only went out of curiosity.* **i.** from the proceeds of; by the pursuit of: *Few of them managed to make a good living out of their art alone, without running a sideline such as a brewery or an insurance office* (Ellis Waterhouse). **j.** born of: *a colt out of a good dam.*

out of it, *Informal.* left out of what is going on; lacking a sense of being part of the proceedings: *The Bishop had never felt so out of it as he did late in July, at the dedication of the new cathedral* (New Yorker).
—*adj.* **1.** not in possession or control: *The Republicans are out, the Democrats in.* **2.** not in use, action, fashion, etc.: *The fire is out. Full skirts are out this season.* **3.** (in baseball) not having its inning: *the out side.* **4.** external; exterior; outer; outlying: *an out island or town.* **5.** not usual or normal: *an out size.* **6.** *Slang.* not up-to-date or fashionable; not in: *Fantasy, we keep being told, is "out"; but those of us who are not "in" can keep right on enjoying fantasy* (Punch).

out for, looking for; trying to get: *to be out for a good time at any cost.*

 PRONUNCIATION KEY: hat, āge, cãre, fär; let, ēqual, tėrm; it, īce; hot, ōpen, ôrder; oil, out; cup, pu̇t, rüle;

out to, eagerly or determinedly trying to: *to be out to show him up.*
—*n.* **1.** a person who is out: *An internal struggle is now taking place that is more than an effort by the outs to get in* (Time). **2.** something wrong. **3.** that which is omitted. **4.** a being out or putting out in baseball. **5.** a defense or excuse: *to have an out for stealing.* **6.** an answer or solution: *The other possible "out" for bondholders is a proposed bill pending before Congress* (Wall Street Journal). **7.** (in tennis) a serve or return that lands outside the lines. **8.** *Dialect.* an excursion; outing: *Us London lawyers don't often get an out* (Dickens).
at outs or **on the outs,** quarreling; disagreeing: *to be on the outs with a friend.*
—*prep.* **1.** from out; forth from: *He went out the door.* **2.** out along: *Drive out Main Street.*
—*interj.* *Archaic.* an exclamation of indignation, reproach, etc.: *Out upon you!*
—*v.i.* to go or come out; be disclosed: *The truth will out.* —*v.t.* to put out: *Please out the fire.* [Old English *ūt*]

out-, *prefix.* **1.** movement outward; forth; away, as in *outcry, outgoing, outlet, outburst, outstanding.* Other examples are:

out·beam′
out′bent
out′blow′ing
out′bowed
out′branch′ing
out·breathe′
out·bulge′
out′drawn
out′flight
out′flood
out·flung′
out·fly′
out′gleam
out·is′sue
out′jet
out′jut
out·launch′
out·leaf′
out·length′en
out′lipped
out·pass′
out′path
out·ring′
out·shape′
out·slide′
out·spew′
out·spill′
out′spring
out′spurt
out·strain′
out·stream′
out′throw
out′thrust
out′voy′age
out·weep′
out·wrench′

2. outside, in literal or figurative positions; at a distance; living or acting outside boundaries (opposed to those within), as in *outbuilding, outfield, outlying, outpatient, outdoor.* Other examples are:

out′cit′y
out′clerk′
out′coun′try
out′dis′trict
out′dwell′er
out′dwell′ing
out′gate′
out′kit′chen
out′lodg′ing
out′lot
out′mer′chant
out′of′fice
out′pick′et
out′port′
out′pu′pil
out′quar′ters
out′serv′ant
out′set′tle·ment
out′set′tler
out′vil′lage
out′world′

3. more than; longer than, as in *outbid, outlive, outnumber.* Other examples are:

out′ar·tic′u·late
out·bar′gain
out·bawl′
out·bel′low
out·bluff′
out·blus′ter
out·brag′
out·bra′zen
out·bribe′
out·chat′ter
out·chide′
out·dance′
out·drink′
out·eat′
out·glare′
out·gross′
out·howl′
out·laugh′
out·lin′ger
out·reign′
out·ring′
out·scold′
out·scream′
out·serve′
out·shout′
out·shriek′
out·snore′
out·speed′
out·strain′
out·stride′
out·strike′
out·sulk′
out·swag′ger
out·thun′der
out·wait′
out·waltz′
out·weep′

4. better than, as in *outdo, outrun, outsail.* Other examples are:

out·bowl′
out·box′
out·curse′
out·daz′zle
out·dress′
out·fly′
out·gain′
out·gal′lop
out·gam′ble
out·glit′ter
out·jest′
out·jump′
out·kill′
out·la′bor
out·love′
out·meas′ure
out·pass′
out·plan′
out·plot′
out·preach′
out·pro·duce′
out·prom′ise
out·race′
out·rate′
out·rea′son
out·score′
out·sprint′
out·spy′
out·strive′
out·swim′
out·swin′dle
out·think′
out·trade′
out·trick′
out·trot′
out·wres′tle

out·act (out akt′), *v.t.* to surpass in acting.
out·age (ou′tij), *n.* **1.** a period of interrupted service; time during which the providing of something, as electric power, gas, or water, is halted. **2.** the condition of being interrupted.
out-and-out (out′ən out′), *adj.* thorough; complete; unqualified: *an out-and-out defeat. Ladies and gentlemen claiming to be out-and-out Christians* (Dickens).
out-and-out·er (out′ən ou′tər), *n.* a thoroughgoing person or thing; perfect example of the kind.
out·ar·gue (out är′gyü), *v.t.,* **-gued, -gu·ing.** to outdo or defeat in arguing.
out·back (out′bak′), *n.* **1.** the Australian hinterland or back country. **2.** the hinterland of any country: *the Canadian outback.* —*adj.* of, belonging to, or located in the outback: *In the outback country he found a shifting population of aborigines* (Time).
out·back·er (out′bak′ər), *n.* a person who lives or settles in the back country of Australia.
out·bal·ance (out bal′əns), *v.t.,* **-anced, -anc·ing. 1.** to weigh more than. **2.** to exceed in value, importance, influence, etc.
out·bas·ket (out′bas′kit, -bäs′-), *n.* a shallow container with a low rim, used to hold completed or outgoing work, mail, memoranda, etc.; out-tray.
out·bid (out bid′), *v.t.,* **-bid, -bid** or **-bid·den, -bid·ding. 1.** to bid higher than (someone else), as in a card game. **2.** to underbid: *Three firms from the United States . . . outbid British and Belgian companies for Government contracts* (London Times).
out·bloom (out blüm′), *v.t.* to surpass in bloom.
out·board (out′bôrd′, -bōrd′), *adj., adv.* **1.** outside of the hull of a ship or boat. **2.** away from the middle of a ship or boat. **3.** (in machinery) outside; outer.
—*n.* **1.** a small boat with an outboard motor: *. . . palm-lined lagoons plied by luxury yachts and busy little outboards* (Time). **2.** an outboard motor.
outboard bearing, the bearing farthest from the crank or other driving part.
out·board·ing (out′bôr′ding, -bōr′-), *n.* riding in a boat that has an outboard motor: *One of Long Island's busy regatta officials . . . feels that boating, especially outboarding, has caught on with youngsters* (New York Times).
outboard motor, a portable gasoline or electric motor attached to the stern of a boat or canoe and usually having a vertical driveshaft connected to a propeller.
out·bound (out′bound′), *adj.* outward bound: *an outbound vessel.*
out·brave (out brāv′), *v.t.,* **-braved, -brav·ing. 1.** to face bravely, especially with a show of defiance. **2.** to be braver than; surpass in daring or courage: *I would . . . Outbrave the heart most daring on earth . . . To win thee, lady* (Shakespeare). **3.** to outdo or excel in beauty, splendor, finery, etc.
out·break (*n.* out′brāk′; *v.* out brāk′), *n., v.,* **-broke, -bro·ken, -break·ing.** —*n.* **1.** a breaking out: *outbreaks of anger.* **2.** a public disturbance; riot: *The outbreak was mastered in two hours and no one was injured* (London Times). —*v.i. Poetic.* to break out; burst forth: *The blare of horns outbroke* (William Morris). —**Syn.** *n.* **1.** outburst.
out·breed (out brēd′), *v.t.,* **-bred, -breed·ing.** to breed from individuals or stocks that are not closely related.
out·breed·ing (out′brē′ding), *n.* a breeding from individuals or stocks that are not closely related.
out·build (out bild′), *v.t.,* **-built, -build·ing.** to build more or better than: *We propose to outbuild, outperform . . . our competitors at home and abroad* (Harper's).
out·build·ing (out′bil′ding), *n.* a shed or building built near a main building: *Barns are outbuildings on a farm.*
out·burn (out bėrn′), *v.,* **-burned** or **-burnt, -burn·ing.** —*v.i.* to burn out, or until consumed: *She burn'd out love, as soon as straw outburneth* (Shakespeare). —*v.t.* to surpass in burning; burn brighter than: *We lit Lamps which outburn'd Canopus* (Tennyson).
out·burst (out′bėrst′), *n.* **1.** a bursting forth: *an outburst of laughter, anger, or smoke.* **2.** a sunspot or stellar explosion: *Outbursts therefore now join that extremely restricted list of phenomena for which we can associate something observed on the earth with something seen on the sun* (A. J. Higgs). **3.** an outbreak; violent disorder; riot: *racial outbursts.*
out·bye (out′bī′), *adv. Scottish.* out a little way; outside: *Step outbye to the door a minute* (Robert Louis Stevenson).
out·cast[1] (*n., adj.* out′kast′, -käst′; *v.* out kast′, -käst′), *n., adj., v.,* **-cast, -cast·ing.** —*n.* **1.** a person or animal cast out from home and friends: *Criminals are outcasts of society. Pearl was a born outcast of the infantile world* (Hawthorne). **2. a.** refuse; offal. **b.** a plant thrown out from a garden.
—*adj.* **1.** being an outcast; homeless; friendless. **2.** (of things) rejected; discarded.
—*v.t.* to cast out; reject; banish: *The patient was outcast by society, left on a barren island* (Philip Hope-Wallace).
[< *out* + *cast,* verb]
out·cast[2] (out′kast′, -käst′), *n. Scottish.* a falling out; quarrel. [< *out-* to the end + dialectal *cast* disagree]
out·caste (out′kast′, -käst′), *n.* in India: **1.** a Hindu who has lost or is put out of his caste. **2.** a person not of one of the four principal castes, as a Pariah; a person without caste or of so low a caste as to be for all practical purposes without caste; an untouchable. Such persons were formerly denied virtually all ordinary social privileges. This is now forbidden by law under the constitution of the Republic of India.
out·class (out klas′, -kläs′), *v.t.* to be of higher class than; be much better than: . . . *and found themselves outclassed financially and socially by the flashy ringside crew* (Harper's).
out·climb (out klīm′), *v.t.,* **-climbed** or (*Archaic*) **-clomb, -climb·ing.** to surpass in climbing: *This '63 truck can outspeed, outclimb, outdo any other VW Truck on the road today* (New York Times).
out·come (out′kum′), *n.* a result; consequence. —**Syn.** upshot, issue.
out·crop (*n.* out′krop′; *v.* out krop′), *n., v.,* **-cropped, -crop·ping.**
—*n.* **1.** a coming (of a rock, stratum, etc.) to the surface of the earth: *the outcrop of a vein of coal.* **2.** such rock exposed at the surface or covered only by soil: *The outcrop that we found proved to be very rich in gold.* —*v.i.* to come to the surface; appear.

Outcrop (def. 1)

out·crop·ping (out′krop′ing), *n.* **1.** the act or fact of cropping out. **2.** a part that crops out: *Its white houses look like the outcroppings of quartz on the mountain-side* (Bret Harte).
out·cross (*v.* out krôs′, -kros′; *n.* out′krôs′, -kros′), *v.t.* **1.** to subject to outcrossing. **2.** to cross with an unrelated breed or race; outbreed. —*n.* the offspring resulting from outcrossing.
out·cross·ing (out′krôs′ing, -kros′-), *n.* the mating of livestock of different strains but the same breed.
out·cry (out′krī′), *n., pl.* **-cries,** *v.,* **-cried, -cry·ing.** —*n.* **1.** a crying out; sudden cry or scream. **2.** a great noise or clamor: *an outcry of public indignation.* **3.** *Archaic.* an auction: *I . . . sold my furniture by public outcry* (Daniel Defoe).
—*v.t.* to outdo in clamor; shout down.
—**Syn.** *n.* **1.** shout. **2.** uproar.
out·curve (out′kėrv′), *n.* a baseball pitch that curves away from the batter.
out·dare (out dãr′), *v.t.,* **-dared** or **-durst, -dared, -dar·ing. 1.** to dare or meet defiantly; outbrave: *And boldly did outdare The dangers of the time* (Shakespeare). **2.** to surpass in daring.
out·date (out dāt′), *v.t.,* **-dat·ed, -dat·ing.** to make out of date or obsolete: *Constantly improving communications are steadily outdating many of the old reasons for divided authority* (Roderick Haig-Brown).

out·dat·ed (out dā′tid), *adj.* out-of-date; old-fashioned: *Middle-of-the-roaders . . . feel Attlee and those around him are simply outdated and too old to lead* (Newsweek).

out·did (out did′), *v.* the past tense of **outdo:** *The girls outdid the boys in neatness.*

out·dis·tance (out dis′təns), *v.t.*, **-tanced, -tanc·ing.** to leave behind; outstrip: *The Bolsheviks brought out a paper called Pravda (Truth) in April, and its circulation outdistanced the Menshevik paper* (Edmund Wilson).

out·do (out dü′), *v.t.*, **-did, -done, -do·ing.** to do more or better than; surpass: *Men will outdo boys in most things.* —**out·do′er,** *n.* —**Syn.** exceed, beat. See **excel.**

out·done (out dun′), *v.* the past participle of **outdo:** *The girls were outdone by the boys in baseball.*

out·door (out′dôr′, -dōr′), *adj.* **1.** done, used, or living outdoors: *outdoor games, an outdoor meal.* **2.** outside of a hospital, poorhouse, etc., as a person supported by public or private charity, but not living in an institution: *outdoor relief.*

out·doors (out′dorz′, -dōrz′), *adv.* out in the open air; not indoors or in the house: *to sleep outdoors.* —*n.* the world outside of houses; the open air: *to love the outdoors.*

out·doors·man (out′dôrz′mən, -dōrz′-; -man′), *n., pl.* **-men.** a man, such as a hunter, fisherman, or camper, who spends much time outdoors for pleasure: *Still incredulous, a few intrepid outdoorsmen offered to enter a bear's den* (Science News Letter).

out·door·sy (out′dôr′zē, -dōr′-), *adj.* characteristic of or suitable for the outdoors or for outdoorsmen: *an outdoorsy spirit, outdoorsy clothing.*

out·draw (out drô′), *v.t., v.i.*, **-drew, -drawn, -draw·ing. 1.** to attract more people or attention than (something else): *The football games outdrew all the other college sports combined.* **2.** to pull out a pistol, sword, or other weapon faster than (an opponent).

out·drive (out drīv′), *v.t.*, **-drove, -driv·en, -driv·ing. 1.** to drive a vehicle faster or more skillfully than (someone else). **2.** to drive a golf ball farther than (someone else).

out·en (ou′tən), *prep. Dialect.* out; out of; out from. [Middle English *outen, uten,* Old English *ūtan* from without]

out·er (ou′tər), *adj.* farther out; outside: *an outer garment.* [< *out* + *-er*[3]] —**Syn.** outward, exterior, external.

out·er·coat (ou′tər kōt′), *n.* a coat worn over the regular clothing, such as a topcoat or overcoat, but usually not a raincoat: *These fine suits, sport coats and outercoats are coordinated in patterns . . . and models* (New Yorker).

outer core, the third of the four layers of the earth, lying between the mantle and the inner core.

out·er-di·rec·ted (out′ər də rek′tid, -dī-), *adj.* extroverted: . . . *almost 28 per cent feel that a minister should be an "outer-directed person" or "radiant personality"* (Time).

out·er·most (ou′tər mōst), *adj.* farthest out; most outward: *an atom which has only one electron in its outermost electron shell* (W. H. Haslett). —*adv.* in the most outward position.

Outer Seven, the seven original members of the European Free Trade Association (EFTA); Great Britain, Sweden, Norway, Denmark, Switzerland, Portugal, and Austria.

outer shell, the first of the four layers of the earth, lying above the mantle; crust.

outer space, 1. space beyond the earth's atmosphere: *Far up in outer space, U.S. satellites derive their radio voices from the transistor* (New Yorker). **2.** space beyond the solar system: *Micro-meteorites from outer space smash into missile shells and satellite skins* (Science News Letter). —**out′er-space′,** *adj.*

out·er·wear (ou′tər wãr′), *n.* clothing worn over underwear or other clothing: *shirts, slacks, jackets and other outerwear* (Wall Street Journal).

out·face (out fās′), *v.t.*, **-faced, -fac·ing. 1.** to face boldly; defy: *The world's hostility, steadily increasing, was confronted and outfaced by . . . Victoria* (Lytton Strachey). **2. a.** to stare at (a person) until he stops staring back. **b.** to bully; frighten into doing something by overbearing looks or words. —**Syn. 1.** brave. **2. a, b.** abash.

out·fall (out′fôl′), *n.* the outlet or mouth of a river, drain, sewer, etc.

out·field (out′fēld′), *n.* **1.** in baseball: **a.** the part of the field beyond the diamond or infield. **b.** the three players in the outfield. **2.** (in cricket) the part of the field farthest from the batsman. **3.** *Scottish.* the outlying land of a farm, that is not enclosed and seldom, tilled.

out·field·er (out′fēl′dər), *n.* (in baseball) a player stationed in the outfield.

out·fight (out fīt′), *v.t.*, **-fought, -fight·ing.** to fight better than; surpass in a fight: *Our first hero of the frontier was a superman, Davy Crockett, who could outshoot, outfight and outwoo anyone* (Atlantic).

out·fit (out′fit), *n., v.*, **-fit·ted, -fit·ting.** —*n.* **1.** all the articles necessary for any undertaking or purpose: *a sailor's outfit, an outfit for a camping trip, a bride's outfit.* **2.** *U.S.* **a.** a group working together, as a group of cowboys from a particular ranch, or a military group: *This Regular Army outfit will play a major role throughout . . . training this summer* (New York Times). **b.** *Informal.* an industrial company or business organization: *A television outfit went there to shoot the story* (New Yorker). **3. a.** a fitting out, as for an expedition. **b.** the expense of fitting out.

—*v.t.* to furnish with everything necessary for any purpose; equip: *John outfitted himself for camp.* —*v.i.* to secure an outfit or equipment: *We will outfit two days before sailing.*

—**Syn.** *n.* **1.** equipment, gear.

out·fit·ter (out′fit′ər), *n.* **1.** a person who sells clothing at retail, especially men's clothing. **2.** a person who outfits, especially a dealer in outfits for traveling, athletic sports, etc.

out·flank (out flangk′), *v.t.* **1.** to go around or extend beyond the flank of (an opposing army, etc.); turn the flank of: *The city was perilously outflanked, and [George] Washington had to pull back* (New Yorker). **2.** to get the better of; circumvent.

out·flow (out′flō′), *n.* **1.** a flowing out: *the outflow from a waterpipe, an outflow of sympathy.* **2.** that which flows out.

out·foot (out fu̇t′), *v.t.* **1.** (of a boat, especially a sailboat) to go faster than (another). **2.** to surpass in walking, running, etc.

out·fox (out foks′), *v.t.* to outsmart: *Since I couldn't outrun him I had to outfox him* (New York Times).

out·frown (out froun′), *v.t.* to outdo in frowning; frown down.

out·game (out gām′), *v.t.*, **-gamed, -gam·ing.** to surpass in gaminess or mettle: *The infantry, man for man, outgamed the Red Chinese* (Time).

out·gas (out gas′), *v.t.*, **-gassed, -gas·sing.** to drive out or free gases from: *to outgas a metal, a vessel, etc.*

out·gate (out′gāt′), *n.* **1.** a way to go out; exit. **2.** a passage or way out; outlet.

out·gen·er·al (out jen′ər əl, -jen′rəl), *v.t.*, **-aled, -al·ing** or (*especially British*) **-alled, -al·ling.** to be a better general than; get the better of, as by superior strategy: *Coligny had to retire from the field—his rival had outgeneralled him* (Walter Besant).

out·giv·ing (out′giv′ing), *n.* **1.** the act of giving out something. **2.** that which is given out. **3.** an utterance or statement.

outgivings, money spent; outgoings: . . . *the outgivings and disbursements to traders* (Robert Blair).

—*adj.* very friendly; outgoing: *They are outgiving, they apparently like to have fun, they appreciate a joke* (Wall Street Journal).

out·go (out′gō′), *n., pl.* **-goes,** *v.*, **-went, -gone, -go·ing.** —*n.* **1.** what goes out, especially what is paid out; amount that is spent: *Damage to their economy through these restrictions is costing the Mexican Government more than it loses in dollar outgo* (New York Times). **2.** the fact of going out. **3.** a going out; outflow; efflux.

—*v.t.* **1.** to exceed or surpass; excel; outstrip; outdo: *In worth and excellence he shall outgo them* (Milton). **2.** *Archaic.* to pass; outdistance.

out·go·ing (out′gō′ing), *n.* **1.** a going out. **2.** that which goes out.

outgoings, an amount of money spent: . . . *causing the Chairman's eyebrows to lift when he looks at the outgoings for stationery on the Balance Sheet* (Observer).

—*adj.* **1. a.** outward bound; departing: *an outgoing ship, the outgoing tide.* **b.** retiring or defeated: *an outgoing legislator.* **2.** inclined to offer one's time, ideas, energy, or the like, without much urging; very friendly and helpful to others; sociable; outgiving: *a very outgoing person.*

out·go·ing·ness (out′gō′ing nis), *n.* the quality of being outgoing; sociability; friendliness: *so extreme in his expansiveness and outgoingness* (Harper's).

out-group (out′grüp′), *n. Sociology.* everyone outside the group of which one is a member: *One of the surest ways of jeopardizing a reform program . . . is for members of the out-group to propose it* (Ogburn and Nimkoff).

out·grow (out grō′), *v.*, **-grew, -grown, -grow·ing.** —*v.t.* **1.** to grow too large for: *to outgrow one's clothes.* **2.** to grow beyond or away from; get rid of by growing older: *to outgrow boyhood friends, to outgrow a babyish habit.* **3.** to grow faster, or taller, or bigger than: *By the time he was ten Tom had outgrown his elder brother.* —*v.i.* to grow out; project; protrude.

out·growth (out′grōth′), *n.* **1.** a natural development, product, or result: *This big store is the outgrowth of the little shop started ten years ago. Many American cities are the outgrowths of small frontier settlements.* **2.** something that has grown out; offshoot: *A corn is an outgrowth on a toe.* **3.** a growing out or forth: *the outgrowth of new leaves in the spring.*

out·guard (out′gärd′), *n.* a guard at a distance from the main body of an army; advance guard; outpost.

out·guess (out ges′), *v.t.* to be too clever for; get the better of.

out·gun (out gun′), *v.t.*, **-gunned, -gun·ning. 1.** to have more weapons than (the opposition): *Admittedly the Reds . . . outnumbered U.N. troops by 2 1/2 to 1 and outgunned U.N. artillery by 2 to 1* (Newsweek). **2.** to outshoot: *Viewers will not be surprised that Cooper outfoxes and outguns every one of that old gang of his* (Time). **3.** to defeat: *Columbia outgunned Yale in the second half today* (New York Times).

out·gush (*v.* out gush′; *n.* out′gush), *v.i.* to gush out or forth. —*n.* a gushing out; sudden outflow: *A lovely, peaceful old lady . . . came to us with a perfect outgush of motherly kindness* (Harriet Beecher Stowe).

out·haul (out′hôl′), *n. Nautical.* a rope by which a sail is hauled out to the end of a boom, yard, etc.

out-Her·od (out her′əd), *v.t.* to surpass (anyone) in something not worth doing, ridiculous, etc.

out-Herod Herod, a. to outdo Herod (represented in the old mystery plays as a blustering tyrant) in violence: *I could have such a fellow whipt for overdoing Termagant: it out-Herods Herod* (Shakespeare). **b.** to outdo in any excess of evil or extravagance: *The figure in question had out-Heroded Herod, and gone beyond the bounds of even the prince's indefinite decorum* (Edgar Allan Poe).

out·hit (out hit′), *v.t.*, **-hit, -hit·ting.** to surpass in hitting skill or number of hits: *Williams, 39, but still pulling the ball sharply, outhit Mickey Mantle, 25, by some 21 points* (Newsweek).

out·house (out′hous′), *n.* **1.** an enclosed outdoor toilet; privy. **2.** a separate building used in connection with a main building; outbuilding.

out·ing (ou′ting), *n.* **1. a.** a short pleasure trip or excursion; walk or airing: *He liked . . . outings into the country on a Sunday* (Samuel Butler). **b.** a holiday spent outdoors away from home: *a weekend outing on the sea.* **2.** the part of the sea out from the shore; offing.

—*adj.* of or for an outing: *an outing dress.*

outing flannel or **cloth,** a soft cotton cloth with a short nap, woven to look like flannel.

out-is·land (out′ī′lənd), *n.* an outlying island: *I would rather make for an out-island like Eleuthera, which is well-spoken of, or remote Inagua with its flamingoes and spoonbills* (Cyril Connolly).

out-is·land·er (out′ī′lən dər), *n.* a native or inhabitant of an out-island.

out·jock·ey (out jok′ē), *v.t.*, **-eyed, -ey·ing.** to get the better of by adroitness or trickery; outwit; overreach.

out·laid (out lād′), *v.* the past tense and past participle of **outlay.**

out·lain (out lān′), *v.* the past participle of **outlie**[1].

out·land (out′land′), *adj.* **1.** outlying: *outland districts.* **2.** *Archaic.* foreign; alien: *outland merchants* (William Morris).

—*n.* **1.** outlying land: *the outland of an estate.* **2.** *Archaic.* a foreign land.
[Old English *ūtland* < *ūt* out + *land* land]
out·land·er (out′lan′dər), *n.* **1.** *Informal.* an outsider; stranger: *Shaw's remark that the Englishman thinks he is being virtuous when he is only being uncomfortable was an outlander's satirical rapier-thrust* (Carlos Baker). **2.** a foreigner; alien.
out·land·ish (out lan′dish), *adj.* **1.** not familiar; strange or ridiculous; queer: *an outlandish hat. What outlandish manners!* **2.** looking or sounding as if it belonged to a foreign country: *an outlandish custom or dialect.* **3.** far removed from civilization; out-of-the-way; remote: *Alaska was once regarded as an outlandish place.* **4.** *Archaic.* foreign: *outlandish women* (Nehemiah 13:26). —**out·land′ish·ly,** *adv.* —**out·land′ish·ness,** *n.* —**Syn. 1.** odd, bizarre.
out·last (out last′, -läst′), *v.t.* to last longer than; survive; outlive: *a work to outlast immortal Rome* (Alexander Pope).
out·law (out′lô′), *n.* **1.** a lawless person; criminal. **2.** a person outside the protection of the law; exile; outcast. **3.** an untamed or untamable horse or other animal.
—*v.t.* **1.** to make or declare illegal: *A group of nations agreed to outlaw war.* **2.** to make or declare (a person) an outlaw. **3.** *U.S.* to deprive of legal force: *An outlawed debt is one that cannot be collected because it has been due too long.*
[Old English *ūtlaga*, noun, *ūtlah*, adjective < Scandinavian (compare Old Icelandic *ūtlagi*, noun, *ūtlaga*, adjective)]
—**Syn.** *n.* **1.** bandit, highwayman, desperado. *-v.t.* **1.** proscribe.
out·law·ry (out′lô′rē), *n., pl.* **-ries. 1.** the act of making or declaring illegal; an outlawing: *the outlawry of war.* **2.** the condition of being an outlaw. **3.** the condition of being condemned as an outlaw. In England before the 1200's outlawry was used as a punishment and meant forfeiture of all possessions to the Crown, and liability to be killed with impunity.
out·lay (*n.* out′lā′; *v.* out lā′), *n., v.,* **-laid, -lay·ing.** —*n.* **1.** a spending or laying out money; expense: *a large outlay for clothing.* **2.** the amount spent; expenditure. —*v.t.* to lay out; spend: *to outlay money in improvements.*
out·leap (out lēp′), *v.,* **-leaped** or **-leapt, -leap·ing.** —*v.i.* to leap out or forth. —*v.t.* **1.** to leap over or beyond. **2.** to surpass in leaping.
out·let (out′let), *n.* **1. a.** a means or place of letting out or getting out; way out: *an outlet of a spring or an express highway, an outlet for one's energies.* **b.** a stream that drains or flows out of a lake or other body of water. **2. a.** a market for a product: *Discount houses are a growing and virtually indispensable outlet for goods* (Newsweek). **b.** a store selling the products of a particular manufacturer: *The shoe manufacturer had several outlets.* **3. a.** the place in a wall, etc., for inserting an electric plug. **b.** an outlet box. —**Syn. 1. a.** vent, opening, exit.
outlet box, a metal box containing the wires to connect lamps, fixtures, and other devices to a system of electric wiring.
out·lie[1] (out lī′), *v.,* **-lay, -lain, -ly·ing.** —*v.i.* **1.** to lie outside. **2.** to camp out. —*v.t.* to lie outside of or beyond.
out·lie[2] (out lī′), *v.t.,* **-lied, -ly·ing.** to outdo in telling lies.
out·li·er (out′lī′ər), *n.* **1.** an outlying part of anything, detached from the main mass, body, or system to which it belongs. **2.** a part of a geological formation left detached through the removal of surrounding parts by denudation: *An outlier is surrounded by rocks older than itself.* **3.** a person who lives away from the place with which he is connected by business or otherwise.
out·line (out′līn′), *n., v.,* **-lined, -lin·ing.** —*n.* **1.** a line that shows the shape of an object; line that bounds a figure: *We saw the outlines of the mountains against the evening sky.* **2.** a drawing or style of drawing that gives only outer lines without shading. **3.** a general plan; rough draft: *Make an outline before trying to write a composition. The teacher gave a brief outline of the work planned for the term.*

Outline (def. 2) of North America

in outline, a. with only the outline shown: *Carrick shore, dim seen in outline faintly blue* (Scott). **b.** with only the main features: *He presented his idea in outline before preparing a detailed plan.*
outlines, the main features or leading characteristics of any subject; general principles: *the outlines of science.*
—*v.t.* **1.** to draw or trace the outer line of; draw in outline: *Outline a map of North America.* **2.** to indicate or define the outline of: *hills outlined against the sky. Each rib and every bone in his [a dog's] frame were outlined cleanly through the loose hide* (Jack London). **3.** to give a plan of; describe in general terms; sketch out: *She outlined her plans for a trip abroad.* —**out′lin′er,** *n.*
—**Syn.** *n.* **1. Outline, contour, profile** mean the line or lines showing the shape of something. **Outline** applies to the line marking the outer limits or edge of an object, figure, or shape: *We could see the outline of a man.* **Contour** emphasizes the shape shown by the outline: *The contours of his face are rugged.* **Profile** applies to the side view of something in outline, especially the face in a side view, seen against a background: *a sketch of the model's head in profile. You would stand up straight if you could see your profile when you slouch.*
out·live (out liv′), *v.t.,* **-lived, -liv·ing.** to live or last longer than: *The idea was good once, but it has outlived its usefulness.* —**Syn.** survive, outlast.
out·look (*n.* out′lu̇k′; *v.* out lu̇k′), *n.* **1.** what one sees on looking out; view: *The room has a pleasant outlook.* **2.** what seems likely to happen; prospect: *the outlook for better times, the weather outlook.* **3.** a way of thinking about things; attitude of mind; point of view: *a gloomy outlook on life.* **4.** a tower or other place to watch from; lookout. **5.** a vigilant watching.
—*v.t.* **1.** to outdo in looks or appearance: *He tells the King he's going to outlook him* (Calvin Trillin). **2.** to disconcert by looking; stare down. —*v.i.* to look out or forth: *I saw those three wan shapes outlooking from the greenness of the woods* (R. Buchanan).
—**Syn.** *n.* **1.** scene.
out·ly·ing (out′lī′ing), *adj.* **1.** lying outside the boundary; far from the center; remote: *outlying suburbs.* **2.** lying or situated outside certain limits: *a few outlying shoals, well beyond the marked channel.* —**Syn. 1.** distant, isolated, out-of-the-way.
out·man[1] (out man′), *v.t.,* **-manned, -man·ning. 1.** to surpass in man power, or number of men: *Outmanned and outgunned, they still fought on bravely.* **2.** to surpass in manly qualities or achievements.
out·man[2] (out′mən), *n., pl.* **-men.** an outsider: *Howard seems to be a bit of an outman in the local community* (Cyril Dunn).
out·ma·neu·ver (out′mə nü′vər), *v.t.,* **-vered, -ver·ing.** to outdo in maneuvering; get the better of by maneuvering: *Southerners were grateful for the help—and sore at the Republicans for outmaneuvering them* (Time).
out·ma·noeu·vre (out′mə nü′vər), *v.t.,* **-vred, -vring.** *Especially British.* outmaneuver: *It is very difficult to outmanoeuvre a Frenchman, as you know* (Joseph Conrad).
out·march (out märch′), *v.t.* to outstrip or outdo in marching.
out·match (out mach′), *v.t.* to overmatch; surpass; outdo: *The addition of sixty to seventy . . . divisions to the Soviet strength would outmatch in numbers the new-found Allied strength* (New York Times).
out·mode (out mōd′), *v.t.,* **-mod·ed, -mod·ing.** to make out of fashion or out-of-date: *The arrival of the . . . shorter skirts, outmoding the extreme chemise* (New York Times).
out·mod·ed (out mō′did), *adj.* no longer in fashion; out-of-date: *an outmoded dress, an outmoded airplane, ship, or typewriter.*
out·most (out′mōst), *adj.* farthest out from the inside or center; outermost.
out·ness (out′nis), *n.* the state of being out or external; externality.
out·num·ber (out num′bər), *v.t.* to be more than; exceed in number: *They outnumbered us three to one.*
out-of-bounds (out′əv boundz′), *adj., adv.* **1.** outside the established limits or boundaries; not to be crossed, entered, or used: *We consider bad manners out-of-bounds here. Some of its offices and workshops are completely out-of-bounds to everyone except an authorized handful of research men* (Johns Hopkins Magazine). **2.** beyond the expected limits; surpassing expectations: *Our cars are having a formidable out-of-bounds sale this year.* **3.** *Sports.* outside the boundary line; out of play: *an out-of-bounds ball. He kicked the ball out-of-bounds.*
out-of-court settlement (out′əv kôrt′, -kōrt′), the settlement of a litigation between parties without the aid or sponsorship of the court. Such a settlement is not binding upon the court, but the court usually permits withdrawal of the suit. *The out-of-court settlement terminates a legal battle among shareholders* (Wall Street Journal).
out-of-date (out′əv dāt′), *adj.* not in present use; old-fashioned: *a horse and buggy is an out-of-date method of transportation.* —**out′-of-date′ness,** *n.*
➤ **Out-of-date, out-of-doors** are usually, but not invariably, hyphenated when they stand before a noun: *He has an out-of-date model.*
out-of-door (out′əv dôr′, -dōr′), *adj.* outdoor.
out-of-doors (out′əv dôrz′, -dōrz′), *adj.* outdoor. —*n., adv.* outdoors.
➤ See **out-of-date** for usage note.
out-of-phase (out′əv fāz′), *adj.* (of electric currents) of different phases: *The resulting interference of the out-of-phase waves reduces the strength of the signal* (Scientific American).
out-of-pock·et (out′əv pok′it), *adj.* (of expenses, deficits, etc.) requiring or incurred through direct cash payment: *The government's actual out-of-pocket expenditures will not exceed the total revenue taken in* (Wall Street Journal).
out-of-print (out′əv print′), *adj.* no longer sold by the publisher: *He loaned us out-of-print books* (Kathryn Hulme). —*n.* an out-of-print book.
out-of-the-way (out′əv ᴛʜə wā′), *adj.* **1.** remote; unfrequented; secluded: *an out-of-the-way cottage.* **2.** seldom met with; unusual: *out-of-the-way bits of information.*
out-of-town (out′əv toun′), *adj.* living or situated in, coming from, or having to do with territory outside the limits of a town or city specified or understood: *We're treating all rehearsals . . . as if they were out-of-town tryouts* (Saturday Review).
out-of-town·er (out′əv tou′nər), *n. Informal.* a person who lives outside the limits of a town or city.
out-of-work (out′əv wėrk′), *n.* a person who is unemployed: *Lord Rowton started the first hostels in 1892 to meet the urgent need for clean, cheap accommodation for . . . the out-of-work* (Manchester Guardian Weekly). —*adj.* unemployed: *The Office had sent us a couple of students, an out-of-work actor . . .* (Manchester Guardian Weekly).
out·pace (out pās′), *v.t.,* **-paced, -pac·ing. 1.** to outstrip; outdo; surpass: *As state spending has continued to outpace revenues, the states have been running more deeply into debt* (Wall Street Journal). **2.** to run faster than: *. . . outpacing two other defenders, he cut in* (London Times).
out·par·ish (out′par′ish), *n. British.* an outlying or rural parish; a parish lying outside the boundaries of a city or town, with which it is in some way connected.
out·pa·tient (out′pā′shənt), *n.* a patient receiving treatment at a hospital but not staying there: *A psychiatrist concluded that [she] needed more treatment than he could give her as an outpatient, but not enough to require admission to the full-time inpatient hospital* (Time).
out·pay·ment (out′pā′mənt), *n.* **1.** a paying out. **2.** an amount paid out: *One way to help the balance of payments problem would be to cut down on the Government's own huge outpayments of dollars* (Wall Street Journal).
out·pen·sion (out′pen′shən), *n.* a pension granted to one not required to reside in a particular charitable institution. —*v.t.* to grant an outpension to.
out·pen·sion·er (out′pen′shə nər), *n.* a person who receives an outpension; nonresident pensioner.
out·per·form (out′pər fôrm′), *v.t.* to outdo; surpass.
out·play (out′plā′), *v.t.,* **-played, -play·ing.** to play better than; beat or surpass in playing.
out·pock·et·ing (out′pok′ə ting), *n.* an evagination: *The lateral appendages or*

parapodia are formed by outpocketings of the lateral body walls (Hegner and Stiles).
out·point (out point′), *v.t.* **1.** to score more points than, as in a game or contest: *[Marciano] outpointed Ezzard Charles last June, as well as knocking him out in September* (New York Times). **2.** to sail closer to the wind than; move on a tack nearer the direction of the wind than (another sailing vessel).
out·poll (out pōl′), *v.t.* to receive more votes than: *To win her award as TV's best actress, Polly Bergen outpolled such veteran rivals as the theater's Helen Hayes and the movies' Teresa Wright* (Time).
out·port (out′pôrt′, -pōrt′), *n.* **1.** an outlying port: *The union itself is expected to put pressure on the outports* (New York Times). **2.** (in Canada) an isolated fishing village, especially in Newfoundland.
out·port·er (out′pôr′tər, -pōr′-), *n.* a native or inhabitant of an outport: *Smallwood interspersed the yarns with friendly greetings and messages to outporters* (Ian Sclanders).
out·post (out′pōst′), *n.* **1. a.** a guard or small number of soldiers placed at some distance from an army or camp to prevent a surprise attack. **b.** the place where they are stationed. **2.** anything thought of as an outpost or advance guard: *Missionaries and traders have been outposts of civilization.*
out·pour (*n.* out′pôr′, -pōr′; *v.* out pôr′, -pōr′), *n.* **1.** a pouring out. **2.** that which is poured out; overflow. —*v.t., v.i.* to pour out.
out·pour·ing (out′pôr′ing, -pōr′-), *n.* **1.** anything that is poured out; outflow: *The outpouring from the factory has mounted in startling style* (Wall Street Journal). **2.** an uncontrolled expression of thoughts or feelings: *an outpouring of grief.*
out·pull (out pu̇l′), *v.t.* to outdo; outdraw.
out·put (*n.* out′pu̇t′; *v.* out′pu̇t′, out pu̇t′), *n., v.,* **-put, -put·ting.** —*n.* **1.** the amount produced; product or yield: *the daily output of automobiles.* **2.** a putting forth; production: *With a sudden output of effort John moved the rock.* **3.** the power or energy produced by a machine, etc.: *The power output of a transformer is necessarily less than the power input because of the unavoidable loss in the form of heat* (Sears and Zemansky). **4.** information put out by or delivered from the storage unit of a computer.
—*v.t.* (of a computer) to put out or deliver from the storage unit: *The computer, though it may hoard a large quantity of information, will output only a very small quantity: the replies to specific questions that are put to it* (Tom Margerison).
out·rage (out′rāj), *n., v.,* **-raged, -rag·ing.** —*n.* **1. a.** an act showing no regard for the rights or feelings of others; offense; insult: *His request is an outrage.* **b.** an overturning of the rights of others by force or the threat of force; act of violence: *the outrages of the Nazis against the Jews.* **2.** *Archaic.* violent behavior, or violence of language; fury: *I fear some outrage, and I'll follow her* (Shakespeare).
—*v.t.* **1.** to offend greatly; do violence to; insult: *Gentleman and peasant . . . priest and layman, all were plundered, maltreated, outraged* (John L. Motley). **2.** to break (the law, a rule of morality, etc.) openly; treat as nothing at all: *to outrage good taste.* **3.** to rape.
[< Old French *outrage* < *outre* < Latin *ultrā* beyond]
—**Syn.** *n.* **1. a.** affront, indignity.
out·ra·geous (out rā′jəs), *adj.* **1.** very offensive or insulting; shocking: *outrageous behavior in public, outrageous language.* **2.** of or involving gross injury or wrong: *outrageous injustice.* **3. a.** unrestrained in action; violent; furious: *At these words the squire grew still more outrageous than before* (Henry Fielding). **b.** *Obsolete.* excessively bold or fierce. —**out·ra′geous·ly,** *adv.* —**out·ra′geous·ness,** *n.* —**Syn. 1.** atrocious, flagrant. **2.** villainous, heinous.
out·ran (out ran′), *v.* the past tense of **outrun:** *He outran me easily.*
ou·trance (ü träns′), *n. French.* the last extremity; the end: *To fight the owner to extremity or outrance* (Tobias Smollett).
out·range (out rānj′), *v.t.,* **-ranged, -rang·ing. 1.** to have a greater range or firing power than, as a military weapon, craft, etc. **2.** to be able to fly, cruise, etc., farther than.
out·rank (out rangk′), *v.t.* to rank higher than: *A captain outranks a lieutenant.*
ou·tré (ü trā′), *adj.* passing the bounds of what is usual and considered proper; eccentric; bizarre: *Ernest was always so outré and strange; there was never any knowing what he would do next* (Samuel Butler). [< French *outré,* past participle of *outrer* exaggerate, push to excess < Old French *outre* beyond < Latin *ultrā*]
out·reach (*v.* out rēch′; *n.* out′rēch′), *v.t.* **1.** to reach beyond: *He outreached his own ambitions by his spectacular success.* **2.** to reach out; stretch out. —*v.i.* **1.** to reach too far. **2.** to stretch; exceed; surpass.
—*n.* the act of reaching out.
ou·tre·cui·dance (ü′tėr kwē′dəns; *French* ü trə kwē däns′), *n.* excessive self-confidence; overweening conceit. [< Old French *outrecuidance* < *outre* (< Latin *ultrā* beyond) + *cuider* < Latin *cogitāre* think]
ou·tre·mer (ü trə mer′), *French.* —*n.* **1.** the lands beyond the sea; foreign countries. **2.** ultramarine. —*adv.* beyond the sea.
out·ride (*v.* out rīd′; *n.* out′rīd′), *v.,* **-rode, -rid·den, -rid·ing,** *n.* —*v.t.* **1.** to ride faster, better, or farther than: *like a tempest that outrides the wind* (John Dryden). **2.** (of ships) to last through (a storm); ride out (a gale, hurricane, etc.).
—*n.* **1. a.** a riding out; excursion. **b.** a place for riding. **2.** *Prosody.* one to three unaccented syllables added to a foot, especially in sprung rhythm.
out·rid·er (out′rī′dər), *n.* **1.** a servant or attendant riding on a horse before or beside a carriage. **2.** a person who rides out or forth.
out·rigged (out′rigd′), *adj.* fitted with outriggers.
out·rig·ger (out′rig′ər), *n.* **1.** a framework ending in a float, extending outward from the side of a light boat or canoe, to prevent upsetting: *With the outrigger not only was danger of capsizing reduced . . . but the craft could tack, that is, sail into the wind at an angle* (Beals and Hoijer). **2. a.** a bracket extending outward from either side of a boat to hold a rowlock. **b.** a boat equipped with such brackets. **3.** a spar projecting outward from the rail of a ship on which a sail may be set. **4.** a projecting spar, framework, or part: *Tubular outriggers give the launcher good stability with maximum weight conservation* (Scientific American).

Outrigger (def. 1)

out·rig·gered (out′rig′ərd), *adj.* fitted with an outrigger.
out·right (out′rīt′), *adv.* **1.** not gradually; altogether; entirely: *to sell a thing outright. We paid for our car outright.* **2.** without restraint, reserve, or concealment; openly: *I laughed outright.* **3.** at once; on the spot: *to kill a person outright.* **4.** directly onward; straight ahead: *I never travelled in this journey above two miles outright in a day* (Daniel Defoe).
—*adj.* **1.** complete; thorough: *an outright loss. The gift outright* (Robert Frost). **2.** downright; straightforward; direct: *an outright refusal.* **3.** entire; total. **4.** directed or going straight on: *The river . . . glided seaward with an even, outright, but imperceptible speed* (Robert Louis Stevenson). —**out′right′ly,** *adv.* —**out′right′ness,** *n.*
out·ri·val (out rī′vəl), *v.t.,* **-valed, -val·ing;** (*especially British*) **-valled, -val·ling.** to outdo as a rival; surpass in competition: *Having tried to outrival one another upon that subject* (Joseph Addison).
out·road (out′rōd′), *n. Archaic.* a hostile or predatory excursion; raid.
out·roar (out rôr′, -rōr′), *v.t.* to outdo in roaring; roar louder than: *This animal—miscalled "howler" . . . would outroar the mightiest lion that ever woke the echoes of an African wilderness* (W.H. Hudson).
out·rode (out rōd′), *v.* the past tense of **outride.**
out·root (out rüt′, -ru̇t′), *v.t.* to root out; eradicate; exterminate.
out·row (out rō′), *v.t.* to outdo in rowing.
out·run (out run′), *v.t.,* **-ran, -run, -running. 1.** to run faster than. **2.** to leave behind; run beyond; pass the limits of: *I am afraid your story outruns the facts.*
out·run·ner (out′run′ər), *n.* **1.** an attendant who runs in advance of or beside a carriage. **2.** the lead dog of a team pulling a sledge. **3.** a forerunner.
out·rush (out′rush′), *n.* rushing out; violent overflow: *Ow! he shouted, with a tremendous outrush of scandalised breath* (Manchester Guardian). —*v.i.* to rush out or forth.
out·sail (out sāl′), *v.t.* to outdo in sailing: *We were several times chased in our passage, but outsailed everything* (Benjamin Franklin).
out·scorn (out skôrn′), *v.t.* to overcome or defeat by scorn.
out·sell (out sel′), *v.t.,* **-sold, -sell·ing. 1.** to outdo in selling; sell more than: *Financially, it outsold by far previous French loans for the same period of subscription* (Wall Street Journal). **2.** to sell for more than.
out·sen·try (out′sen′trē), *n., pl.* **-tries.** a sentry placed considerably in advance; picket.
out·sert (out′sėrt′), *n.* a section printed and arranged so that it can be folded around another section in a magazine, book, etc. [< *out-,* patterned on *insert*]
out·set (out′set′), *n.* a setting out; start; a beginning: *At the outset, it looked like a nice day.*
out·shine (out shīn′), *v.,* **-shone, -shin·ing.** —*v.t.* **1.** to shine more brightly than. **2.** to be more brilliant or excellent than; surpass: *Russia far outshone any of her satellites by building at a rate . . . a little better than the European-wide average* (Time). —*v.i.* to shine forth or out: *From the east faint yellow light outshone* (William Morris).
—**Syn.** *v.t.* **2.** excel.
out·shoot (*v.* out shüt′; *n.* out′shüt′), *v.,* **-shot, -shoot·ing,** *n.* —*v.t., v.i.* **1.** to shoot better or farther than: *they outshot Robin Hood* (Philip Sidney). **2.** to shoot or send forth.
—*n.* **1.** a projection. **2.** an offshoot. **3.** the act or fact of shooting or thrusting out. **4.** (in baseball) an outcurve.
out·side (out′sīd′; *prep. also* out′side′), *n.* **1.** the side or surface that is out; outer part. **2.** external appearance: *O, what a goodly outside falsehood hath!* (Shakespeare). **3.** the space or position without: *to wait on the outside.*
at the outside, *Informal.* at the utmost limit: *I can do it in a week, at the outside.*
outside in, so that what would ordinarily be outside is inside; with the outside not showing: *He did not know that a keeper is only a poacher turned outside in, and a poacher a keeper turned inside out* (Charles Kingsley).
—*adj.* **1.** on the outside; of or nearer the outside: *the outside leaves.* **2.** not belonging to or included in a certain group, set, district, etc.: *Outside people tried to get control of the business.* **3.** being, acting, done, or originating without or beyond a wall, boundary, etc.: *the outside world. Outside noises disturbed the class.* **4.** *Informal.* reaching the utmost limit; highest; largest: *an outside estimate of the cost.* **5.** *Informal.* barely possible; very slight: *The team has an outside chance to win.* **6.** covering the greater distance in making a turn or following a circular course: *The righthand wheels are the outside wheels in a turn to the left.* **7.** *Obsolete.* superficial.
—*adv.* **1.** on or to the outside: *Both had lost faith . . . in the liberal politics of the period and both stood outside its conventional culture* (Edmund Wilson). **2.** out in the open air; outdoors: *Run outside and play.*
—*prep.* **1.** *U.S. Informal.* with the exception (of): *Outside of John, none of us liked the play.* **2.** out of; beyond the limits of: *Stay outside the house.*
—**Syn.** *n.* **1.** exterior.
out·side·ness (out′sīd′nis), *n.* the state or quality of being outside; externality.
out·sid·er (out′sī′dər), *n.* **1.** a person who is outside. **2.** a person not belonging to a particular group, set, company, party, district, etc.: *What good did an outsider ever get by meddling in a love affair?* (Mrs. Humphry Ward). **3.** a person unconnected or unacquainted with the matter in question. **4.** a horse, contestant, etc., not favored to win.

out·sing (out sing′), *v.*, **-sang** or **-sung, -sung, -sing·ing.** —*v.t.* **1.** to surpass or excel in singing; sing better than: *Each appeared to be trying to outsing the other* (The Athenaeum). **2.** to sing louder than: *She would sing over the washing tub . . . outsinging Martha's scolding* (Mary Russell Mitford). —*v.i.* to sing out: *When once more . . . The meadow-lark outsang* (John Greenleaf Whittier).

out sister, a nun, especially of a secluded order, working outside a convent.

out·sit (out sit′), *v.t.*, **-sat, -sit·ting. 1.** to sit beyond the time of: *to outsit the twilight.* **2.** to sit longer than.

out·size (out′sīz′), *adj.* larger than the usual size: *An outsize nylon umbrella, as big as a doorman's* (New Yorker). —*n.* an article of clothing, etc., larger than the usual size.

out·sized (out′sīzd′), *adj.* outsize: *a study where John kept bound outsized volumes* (Saturday Review).

out·skirts (out′skėrts′), *n.pl.* the outer parts or edges of a town, district, etc.; outlying parts: *to continue their walk to the outskirts of the village* (Frederick Marryat).

out·sleep (out slēp′), *v.t.*, **-slept, -sleep·ing. 1.** to sleep beyond; oversleep. **2.** to sleep longer than (another). **3.** to sleep to the end of: *he has outslept the winter* (William Cowper).

out·slick (out slik′), *v.t. Slang.* outslicker.

out·slick·er (out slik′ər) *v.t. Slang.* to outdo in slickering; outwit; outsmart: *Casey Stengel . . . frankly admitted he had been grossly outslickered* (New York Times).

out·smart (out smärt′), *v.t. U.S. Informal.* to outdo in cleverness; outwit: *This was demagogy outsmarting itself* (Newsweek).

out·soar (out sôr′, -sōr′), *v.t.* to soar above or beyond; exceed in height of flight: *He has outsoared the shadow of our night* (Shelley).

out·sold (out sōld′), *v.* the past tense and past participle of **outsell.**

out·sole (out′sōl′), *n.* the outer sole of a shoe or boot: *The postmen's walking experiments showed that after original outsoles and two resoles were worn through . . .* (Science News Letter).

out·span (out span′), *v.*, **-spanned, -spanning,** *n.* in South Africa: —*v.t., v.i.* **1.** to unyoke or unharness (horses, etc.) from a wagon: *They very frequently unyoke, or outspan . . . at Salt River* (W.J. Burchell). **2.** to encamp: *They outspan and picnic just outside the town* (Beatrice M. Hicks).
—*n.* **1.** the act of outspanning. **2.** the time or place of outspanning; encampment.
[< Afrikaans *uitspannen* unharness < Dutch < *uit* out + *spannen* to hitch, harness, span². Compare INSPAN.]

out·spar·kle (out spär′kəl), *v.t.*, **-kled, -kling.** to surpass in sparkling.

out·speak (out spēk′), *v.*, **-spoke, -spo·ken, -speak·ing.** —*v.t.* **1.** to outdo or excel in speaking. **2.** to speak (something) out; utter frankly or boldly. —*v.i.* to speak out.

out·spend (out spend′), *v.t.*, **-spent, -spending.** to exceed or surpass in spending.

out·spent (out spent′), *adj.* completely spent; exhausted. —*v.* the past tense and past participle of **outspend.**

out·spo·ken (out′spō′kən), *adj.* frank; not reserved. —**out′spo′ken·ly,** *adv.* —**out′spo′ken·ness,** *n.* —Syn. blunt. See **frank.**

out·spread (*adj., n.* out′spred′; *v.* out spred′), *adj., v.*, **-spread, -spread·ing,** *n.* —*adj.* spread out; extended: *an eagle with outspread wings, the outspread stars above.*
—*v.t.* **1.** to spread out; stretch out; expand; extend. **2.** *Obsolete.* to exceed in expanse.
—*n.* **1.** a spreading out. **2.** an expanse or expansion.

out·stand (out stand′), *v.*, **-stood, -standing.** —*v.i.* **1.** to stand out distinctly or prominently. **2.** (of a ship) to sail away from land; move from the shore: *Many a keel shall seaward turn, And many a sail outstand* (John Greenleaf Whittier). —*v.t. Dialect.* to stand or hold out against.

out·stand·ing (out stan′ding), *adj.* **1.** standing out from others; well-known; important: *an outstanding work of fiction, an outstanding statesman.* **2.** unsettled; unpaid: *outstanding bills.* **3.** projecting: *outstanding ears.* —**out·stand′ing·ly,** *adv.*

out·stare (out stãr′), *v.t.*, **-stared, -staring.** to outdo in staring.

out·state (out′stāt′), *U.S.* —*n.* the area away from metropolitan or industrial centers in any of certain States, especially Michigan and Wisconsin. —*adj.* **1.** in, of, or toward outstate. **2.** coming from or living in another State: *an outstate visitor.*

out·sta·tion (out′stā′shən), *Especially British.* —*n.* an outlying military post, trading post, etc., in a sparsely settled region, as in parts of Australia or a place in which Europeans are relatively few, as in parts of Africa. —*adj.* of or having to do with such a place: *outstation life.*

out·stay (out stā′), *v.t.*, **1.** to stay longer than. **2.** to stay beyond the limit of; overstay.

out·stood (out stu̇d′), *v.* the past tense and past participle of **outstand.**

out·stretch (out strech′), *v.t.* **1.** to stretch out or forth. **2.** to extend in area or content; expand.

out·stretched (out′strecht′), *adj.* stretched out; extended.

out·strip (out strip′), *v.t.*, **-stripped, -stripping. 1.** to go faster than; leave behind in a race: *A horse can outstrip a man.* **2.** to do better than; excel: *Tom can outstrip most boys both in sports and studies.* **3.** *Obsolete.* to pass beyond (a place).

out·stroke (out′strōk′), *n.* a stroke directed outward, especially the stroke of a piston in an engine during which the piston moves toward the crankshaft.

out·swear (out swãr′), *v.t.*, **-swore, -sworn, -swear·ing. 1.** to outdo in swearing. **2.** to overcome by swearing.

out·swing·er (out′swing′ər), *n.* (in cricket) a bowl which curves to the outside of the wicket.

out·talk (out tôk′), *v.t.* to talk better, faster, longer, or louder than; get the better of by talking.

out·tell (out tel′), *v.t.*, **-told, -tell·ing. 1.** to declare. **2.** to tell to the end; tell completely. **3.** to tell better than; outtalk.

out·tongue (out tung′), *v.t.*, **-tongued, -tongu·ing. 1.** to excel in speaking. **2.** to speak louder than; drown the sound of.

out·top (out top′), *v.t.*, **-topped, -top·ping.** to rise above; surpass.

out·tray (out′trā′), *n. Especially British.* out-basket.

out·trump (out trump′), *v.t.* **1.** to lay down a higher trump at cards than. **2.** to get the better of.

out·turn (out′tėrn′), *n.* the quantity turned out or yielded; produce; output.

out·val·ue (out val′yü), *v.t.*, **-ued, -u·ing.** to exceed in value.

out·vie (out vī′), *v.t.*, **-vied, -vy·ing.** to outdo in competition or rivalry: *. . . he outvied them all by the reach and freshness of his imagination and the variety and inventiveness of his resource* (London Times).

out·vote (out vōt′), *v.t.*, **-vot·ed, -vot·ing.** to defeat in voting; cast more votes than.

out·walk (out wôk′), *v.t.* to walk faster or farther than.

out·wall (out′wôl′), *n.* **1.** the outer wall. **2.** the exterior.

out·ward (out′wərd), *adj.* **1.** going toward the outside; turned toward the outside: *an outward motion, an outward glance.* **2.** outer: *to all outward appearances.* **3.** that can be seen; plain to see: *He [John Bunyan] must have still been a very young man when that outward reformation took place* (Robert Southey). **4.** on the surface; seeming: *the outward man, an outward and misleading air of kindness.* **5.** *Obsolete.* lying outside some sphere of work, duty, or interest; external. **6.** *Obsolete.* done or situated outside; outdoor.
—*adv.* **1.** toward the outside; away: *Porches extended outward from the house.* **2.** away from the dock, station, etc.: *That ship is outward bound.* **3.** on the outside; without. **4.** *Obsolete.* in outward appearance as opposed to inner reality; outwardly; externally.
—*n.* **1.** outward appearance; the outside; exterior. **2.** that which is outside the mind; external or material world. **3.** *Obsolete.* an outer part of anything.
outwards, outward things; externals: *Nature . . . makes us all equal; we are differenc'd but by accident and outwards* (Owen Feltham).
[Old English *ūtweard* < *ūt* out (ward) + *-weard* -ward]
—**Syn.** *adj.* **2.** external, exterior, superficial.

out·ward·ly (out′wərd lē), *adv.* **1.** on the outside or outer surface; externally. **2.** toward the outside. **3.** as regards appearance or outward manifestation: *Though frightened, the boy remained outwardly calm.*

out·ward·ness (out′wərd nis), *n.* **1.** the state of being outward; outward existence; externality. **2.** occupation with outward things.

out·wards (out′wərdz), *adv.* outward.

out·wash (out′wôsh′, -wosh′), *n. Geology.* glacial debris, such as rock fragments, deposited beyond a glacier by streams of water from the melting ice: *There was, however, a sufficient supply of debris, lake deposits . . . sandy and gravelly outwash to fill the basin completely so that in the end the lake consisted only of a thin skin of water* (G.H. Drury)

out·watch (out woch′, -wôch′), *v.t.* **1.** to watch longer or more carefully than. **2.** to watch until the disappearance or end of.

out·wear (out wãr′), *v.t.*, **-wore, -worn, -wear·ing. 1.** to wear longer than; be useful, serviceable, etc., for a greater time than: *Some plastics can outwear leather. I have made a Calender for every yeare, That steele in strength, and time in durance, shall outweare* (Edmund Spenser). **2. a.** to wear out or to an end: *to outwear someone's patience.* **b.** to exhaust in strength or endurance. **3.** to outlive; outgrow: *to outwear sorrow.*

out·wear·y (out wir′ē), *v.t.*, **-wear·ied, -wear·y·ing.** to weary to exhaustion; tire out.

out·weigh (out wā′), *v.t.* **1.** to weigh more than: *Sam Langford . . . once held heavyweight Jack Johnson—who outweighed him by 53 pounds—to a fifteen-round decision* (Newsweek). **2.** to exceed in value, importance, influence, etc.

out·well (out wel′), *v.i.* to well or gush out.

out·went (out′went′), *v.* the past tense of **outgo.**

out·wind (out wind′), *v.t.*, **-wind·ed, -winding.** to put out of wind or breath.

out·wit (out wit′), *v.t.*, **-wit·ted, -wit·ting. 1.** to get the better of by being more intelligent; be too clever for: *The prisoner outwitted his guards and escaped.* **2.** *Archaic.* to surpass in wisdom or knowledge.

out·woo (out wü′), *v.t.* to woo or court better than.

out·work (*n.* out′wėrk′; *v.* out wėrk′), *n., v.*, **-worked** or **-wrought, -work·ing.** —*n.* **1.** the part of the fortifications of a place lying outside the main ones; a less important defense: *the outworks of a castle.* **2.** work upon the outside or exterior of anything.
—*v.t.* **1.** to surpass in working; work harder, longer, or faster than. **2.** *Poetic.* to work out to a conclusion; complete.

out·work·er (out′wėr′kər), *n.* a person who works outside, as outdoors or outside a factory.

out·worn (*adj.* out′wôrn′, -wōrn′; *v.* out wôrn′, -wōrn′), *adj.* **1.** worn out: *outworn clothes.* **2.** out-of-date: *outworn opinions.* **3.** outgrown: *outworn habits.*
—*v.* the past participle of **outwear.**

out·write (out rīt′), *v.t.*, **-wrote, -writ·ten, -writ·ing.** to surpass or excel in writing; write better than.

out·wrought (out rôt′), *v.* outworked; a past tense and a past participle of **outwork.**

out·yield (out yēld′), *v.t.* to yield more than: *. . . late sown spring wheats have outyielded winter varieties locally* (London Times).

ou·zel (ü′zəl), *n.* **1.** any of certain European birds of the thrush family, as the blackbird and the ring ouzel, black with a white ring or bar on the breast. **2.** the water ouzel or dipper that often wades into deep water: *The ouzel alone of all birds dares to enter a white torrent* (John Muir). Also, **ousel.** [Old English *ōsle* blackbird, merle]

Ouzel (def. 2) (about 6 in. long)

ou·zo (ü′zō), *n.* a licorice-flavored apéritif derived from resinated Greek wine. [< New Greek *ouzōn*]

o·va (ō′və), *n.* the plural of **ovum.**

o·val (ō′vəl), *adj.* **1.** egg-shaped. **2.** shaped like an ellipse; ellipsoidal.
—*n.* **1.** something having an oval shape, such as some athletic fields, a track, or a plane figure. **2.** *U.S. Informal.* a football.
[< New Latin *ovalis* < Latin *ōvum* egg]
—**o′val·ness,** *n.*

Ovals

o·val·bu·min (ōv′al byü′mən), *n.* the albumin of egg white.

o·val·ly (ō′vəl lē), *adv.* in an oval form.

o·val·oid (ō′və loid), *adj.* resembling an oval; ovoid.

oval window, a membrane in the ears of mammals and other vertebrates connecting the middle ear with the inner ear.

O·vam·bo (ō väm′bō), *n., pl.* **-bo, -bos.** a member of a people of southwest Africa whose language is Bantu.

o·var·i·an (ō vãr′ē ən), *adj.* of or having to do with an ovary.

o·var·i·ec·to·mize (ō vãr′ē ek′tə mīz), *v.t.,* **-mized, -miz·ing.** to remove (an ovary) by surgery.

o·var·i·ec·to·my (ō vãr′ē ek′tə mē), *n., pl.* **-mies.** ovariotomy.

o·var·i·ot·o·my (ō vãr′ē ot′ə mē), *n., pl.* **-mies.** surgical incision into or removal of an ovary. [< New Latin *ovarium* ovary + Greek *-tomĭā* a cutting]

o·va·ri·tis (ō′və rī′tis), *n.* inflammation of an ovary.

o·var·i·um (ō vãr′ē əm), *n., pl.* **-i·a** (-ē ə). ovary.

o·va·ry (ō′vər ē), *n., pl.* **-ries.** **1.** the organ of a female in which eggs and sex hormones are produced. **2.** the enlarged lower part of the pistil of a flowering plant, enclosing the young seeds. **3.** the core or pit of a fleshy fruit. [< New Latin *ovarium* < Latin *ōvum* egg + *-ārium* -ary]

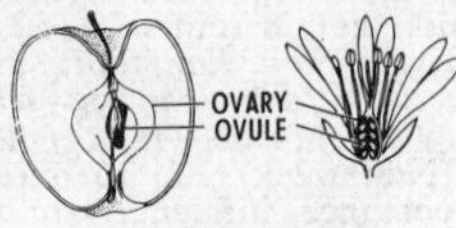

Ovaries
Left, apple (def. 3); right, chickweed (def. 2)

o·vate[1] (ō′vāt), *adj.* egg-shaped: *an ovate leaf.* [< Latin *ōvātus* < *ōvum* egg] **—o′vate·ly,** *adv.*

o·vate[2] (ō′vāt), *n.* a person awarded the third degree of achievement in poetry and music at an eisteddfod: . . . *the green robes of the ovates and the bards' blue ones* (Punch). [< Greek *ouateis,* probably < Gaulish]

Ovate Leaf

o·va·tion (ō vā′shən), *n.* **1.** an enthusiastic public welcome; burst of loud clapping or cheering: *The President received a great ovation.* **2.** (in ancient Rome) a lesser celebration than a triumph, given to a victorious commander. [< Latin *ovātiō, -ōnis* < *ovāre* rejoice]

ov·en (uv′ən), *n.* **1.** an enclosed space usually in a stove or near a fireplace, for baking food. **2.** a small furnace for heating or drying; kiln. [Old English *ofen*]

ov·en·bird (uv′ən bėrd′), *n.* any of various birds that build nests with dome-shaped roofs shaped something like a primitive oven. The ovenbird of North America is a wood warbler that has an olive-brown back, black-streaked white breast, and orange crown.

Ovenbird (6 in. long)

ov·en·proof (uv′ən prüf′), *adj.* made of material that can withstand the heat of an oven without cracking.

ov·en·ware (uv′ən wãr′), *n.* a dish or dishes for baking that can withstand the heat of an oven.

o·ver (ō′vər), *prep.* **1.** above in place or position: *the roof over one's head.* **2.** above in authority, power, etc.: *We have a captain over us.* **3.** on; upon: *a coat over one's shoulders, a blanket lying over a bed.* **4.** at all or various places on: *A blush came over her face. Farms were scattered over the valley.* **5.** above and to the other side of; from side to side of; across: *to jump over a fence, to fly over the ocean, to cross over the road, to walk over a bridge.* **6.** on the other side of: *lands over the sea.* **7.** out and down from: *He fell over the edge of the cliff.* **8.** more than; beyond: *over sixty miles. It costs over ten dollars. He likes golf over all other sports.* **9.** here and there on or in; roundabout; all through: *We shall travel over Europe. The student went over his notes before the test. He went over everything in his pockets looking for the letter.* **10.** from end to end of; along: *We drove over the new thruway. A report has come over the wire.* **11.** during: *payments lasting over a period of years.* **12.** in reference to; concerning; about: *He is worried over his health.* **13.** while engaged in or concerned with: *to talk over dinner.* **14.** until the end of: *to stay over the weekend.*
—*adv.* **1.** above: *to hang over.* **2.** so as to cover the surface, or affect the whole surface: *to paint a wall over. Spread the canvas over the new cement.* **3.** from side to side; across any intervening space; to the other side. **4.** from one to another: *Hand the money over. He willed the house over to his son. Climb over into the garden.* **5.** on the other side; at some distance: *over in Europe, over by the hill.* **6.** down; out and down: *to boil over. She went too near the edge and fell over.* **7.** so as to bring the upper side or end down or under: *to turn over a page.* **8.** again; once more; in repetition: *to do a thing over.* **9.** excessively; too (used chiefly in compounds): *overnice. He is not over well.* **10.** through a region, area, etc.: *to travel all over.* **11.** from beginning to end: *to talk a matter over, to read a newspaper over.* **12.** throughout or beyond a period of time: *Please stay over until Monday.* **13.** in excess or addition: *to receive the full sum and something over.*

over again, once more: *to try over again.*

over against, a. opposite to; in front of: *a house over against the park.* **b.** so as to bring out a difference: *to consider one book over against another.*

over and above, in addition to; besides: *over and above what it had cost him.*

over and over, again and again; repeatedly: *I have told them over and over; they lack no direction* (Shakespeare).

over there, *U.S. Informal.* in Europe at the scene of World War I: *The Yanks are coming . . . and we won't be back till it's over over there* (George M. Cohan).

over with, *Informal.* done; finished: *Let's hurry and get the job over with.*

—*adj.* **1.** at an end; done; past: *The day is over.* **2.** higher in authority, station, etc. (used chiefly in compounds): *an overlord.* **3.** extra; surplus (used chiefly in compounds): *pay for overtime.* **4.** too much; too great; excessive (used chiefly in compounds): *an overuse of drugs.* **5.** upper; higher up: *an over drapery.*
—*n.* **1.** an amount in excess; an extra. **2.** in cricket: **a.** the number of balls (usually six) delivered between successive changes of bowlers. **b.** the part of the game between such changes. **3.** *Military.* a shot which strikes beyond the target, especially while firing to adjust the range.
—*v.t. Archaic.* to leap or jump over; clear.
—*v.i. Archaic.* to go over; pass over.
[Old English *ofer*]
—**Syn.** *prep.* **1, 2. Over, above** express a relation in which one thing is thought of as being higher than another. **Over,** the opposite of *under,* suggests being directly higher or in the position or space immediately higher up: *Carry the umbrella over your head. A sergeant is over a corporal.* **Above,** opposed to *below* and *beneath,* suggests being on or at or rising to a higher level, but seldom suggests being straight up or in a direct connection: *The plane flew above the clouds. An admiral is above a sergeant.*
—**Ant.** *prep.* **1.** under, below.

➔ **Over with** is used in informal speech and writing to mean over or finished. Spoken: *I'd like to get this over with today.* More formal: *I'd like to get this finished today.*

over-, *prefix.* **1.** too; too much; too long, etc., as in *overcrowded, overfull, overburden, overpay, oversleep.* **2.** extra, as in *oversize, overtime.* **3.** over, as in *overflow, overlord, overseas, overthrow.*

If an adjective beginning with *over-* is not specially defined in this dictionary, its meaning may be learned by putting *too* in place of *over.* Some such words are:—

o′ver·ab·ste′mi·ous
o′ver·a·cute′
o′ver·ag·gres′sive
o′ver·am·bi′tious
o′ver·ap′pre·hen′sive
o′ver·apt′
o′ver·at·ten′tive
o′ver·bash′ful
o′ver·big′
o′ver·bit′ter
o′ver·boun′te·ous
o′ver·bred′
o′ver·bright′
o′ver·ca′pa·ble
o′ver·cap′tious
o′ver·care′less
o′ver·cas′u·al
o′ver·char′i·ta·ble
o′ver·child′ish
o′ver·cir′cum·spect
o′ver·civ′il
o′ver·civ′il·ized
o′ver·clean′
o′ver·cold′
o′ver·com′mon
o′ver·com·pet′i·tive
o′ver·con′sci·en′tious
o′ver·con′scious
o′ver·con·serv′a·tive
o′ver·con·sid′er·ate
o′ver·cor·rect′
o′ver·cor·rupt′
o′ver·cost′ly
o′ver·cour′te·ous
o′ver·cov′e·tous
o′ver·cred′u·lous
o′ver·cun′ning
o′ver·dain′ty
o′ver·dear′
o′ver·de·lib′er·ate
o′ver·del′i·cate
o′ver·de·sir′ous
o′ver·de·tailed′
o′ver·dig′ni·fied
o′ver·dis′ci·plined
o′ver·dra·mat′ic
o′ver·ear′ly
o′ver·ear′nest
o′ver·eas′y
o′ver·e·lab′o·rate
o′ver·e·mo′tion·al
o′ver·em·phat′ic
o′ver·en·thu′si·as′tic
o′ver·ex·act′
o′ver·ex·cit′a·ble
o′ver·ex·plic′it
o′ver·ex·u′ber·ant
o′ver·fa·mil′iar
o′ver·far′
o′ver·fast′
o′ver·fas·tid′i·ous
o′ver·fat′
o′ver·fear′ful
o′ver·flu′ent
o′ver·fool′ish
o′ver·for′mal
o′ver·for′ward
o′ver·frail′
o′ver·fre′quent
o′ver·fruit′ful
o′ver·gen′er·ous
o′ver·gen′ial
o′ver·gen′tle
o′ver·glad′
o′ver·grate′ful
o′ver·greas′y
o′ver·greed′y
o′ver·hap′py
o′ver·har′dy
o′ver·harsh′
o′ver·haugh′ty
o′ver·ir′ri·ta·ble
o′ver·jeal′ous
o′ver·joy′ful
o′ver·joy′ous
o′ver·ju·di′cious
o′ver·keen′
o′ver·kind′
o′ver·late′
o′ver·lav′ish
o′ver·lean′
o′ver·lib′er·al
o′ver·lit′tle
o′ver·live′ly
o′ver·log′i·cal
o′ver·lov′ing
o′ver·lus′cious
o′ver·lust′y
o′ver·lux·u′ri·ant
o′ver·man′y
o′ver·mas′ter·ful
o′ver·ma·ture′
o′ver·meek′
o′ver·mel′low
o′ver·mer′ci·ful
o′ver·mer′ry
o′ver·mild′
o′ver·mod′est
o′ver·moist′
o′ver·mourn′ful
o′ver·neat′
o′ver·neg′li·gent
o′ver·nerv′ous
o′ver·nu′mer·ous
o′ver·o·be′di·ent
o′ver·ob·se′qui·ous
o′ver·of·fi′cious
o′ver·of′ten
o′ver·op′ti·mis′tic
o′ver·par′tial
o′ver·par·tic′u·lar
o′ver·pas′sion·ate
o′ver·per·emp′to·ry
o′ver·plau′si·ble
o′ver·plen′ti·ful
o′ver·plump′
o′ver·pop′u·lar
o′ver·pop′u·lous
o′ver·pos′i·tive
o′ver·pow′er·ful
o′ver·pre·cise′
o′ver·pre·sump′tu·ous
o′ver·priv′i·leged
o′ver·prompt′
o′ver·pub′li·cized
o′ver·quick′
o′ver·rash′
o′ver·read′y
o′ver·re·fined′
o′ver·re·li′gious
o′ver·rep′re·sent′ed
o′ver·res′o·lute
o′ver·rich′
o′ver·rife′
o′ver·right′eous
o′ver·rig′id
o′ver·rig′or·ous
o′ver·rude′
o′ver·sad′
o′ver·san′guine
o′ver·sau′cy
o′ver·scent′ed
o′ver·scru′pu·lous
o′ver·sea′soned
o′ver·sen′si·ble
o′ver·sen′si·tive
o′ver·sen′ti·men′tal
o′ver·se′ri·ous
o′ver·ser′vile
o′ver·se·vere′
o′ver·sharp′
o′ver·short′
o′ver·si′lent
o′ver·sim′ple
o′ver·skep′ti·cal
o′ver·slow′
o′ver·small′
o′ver·soft′
o′ver·sol′emn
o′ver·so·lic′i·tous
o′ver·soon′
o′ver·squeam′ish
o′ver·stiff′
o′ver·strong′
o′ver·stu′di·ous
o′ver·suf·fi′cient
o′ver·su′per·sti′tious
o′ver·sure′
o′ver·sus·cep′ti·ble
o′ver·sus·pi′cious
o′ver·sweet′
o′ver·swift′
o′ver·talk′a·tive
o′ver·tame′
o′ver·tech′ni·cal
o′ver·te′di·ous
o′ver·ten′der
o′ver·thick′
o′ver·thought′ful
o′ver·thrif′ty
o′ver·tight′
o′ver·tim′or·ous
o′ver·trim′
o′ver·truth′ful
o′ver·ve′he·ment
o′ver·ven′ture·some
o′ver·vig′or·ous
o′ver·vit′ri·fied
o′ver·weak′
o′ver·well′
o′ver·wet′
o′ver·word′y
o′ver·zeal′ous

If a noun beginning with *over* is not specially defined in this dictionary, its meaning may be learned by putting *too much* or *excessive* in place of *over.* Some such words are:—

o′ver·a·nal′y·sis
o′ver·at·ten′tion
o′ver·cau′tious·ness
o′ver·cen′tral·i·za′tion
o′ver·civ′i·li·za′tion
o′ver·clas′si·fi·ca′tion
o′ver·con′cen·tra′tion
o′ver·con·cern′
o′ver·con·ges′tion

o′ver·con·sump′tion
o′ver·cre·du′li·ty
o′ver·cul′ti·va′tion
o′ver·cut′
o′ver·de·mand′
o′ver·de·pend′ence
o′ver·de·sign′
o′ver·dil′i·gence
o′ver·dos′age
o′ver·e·lab′o·ra′tion
o′ver·em·ploy′ment
o′ver·en·thu′si·asm
o′ver·ex·pan′sion
o′ver·ex′ploi·ta′tion
o′ver·fre′quen·cy
o′ver·gen′er·al·i·za′-tion
o′ver·in·fla′tion
o′ver·in·sist′ence
o′ver·in·ten′si·ty
o′ver·in·ter′pre·ta′-tion
o′ver·loud′ness
o′ver·neg′li·gence
o′ver·op′ti·mism
o′ver·or′gan·i·za′tion
o′ver·pro·vi′sion
o′ver·reg′u·la′tion
o′ver·re·li′ance
o′ver·rep′re·sen-ta′tion
o′ver·se·ver′i·ty
o′ver·sim·plic′i·ty
o′ver·spec′u·la′tion
o′ver·stim′u·la′tion
o′ver·stud′y
o′ver·wor′ry
o′ver·zeal′ous·ness

If a verb beginning with *over* is not specially defined in this dictionary, its meaning may be learned by putting —— *too much* in place of *over* ——. Some such words are:—

o′ver·as·sess′
o′ver·bake′
o′ver·boil′
o′ver·book′
o′ver·bor′row
o′ver·breed′
o′ver·broil′
o′ver·com′pli·cate
o′ver·con·trol′
o′ver·cook′
o′ver·cor·rect′
o′ver·cor·rupt′
o′ver·cul′ti·vate
o′ver·cut′
o′ver·dec′o·rate
o′ver·de·mand′
o′ver·de·sign′
o′ver·ed′it
o′ver·ed′u·cate
o′ver·e·lab′o·rate
o′ver·es·teem′
o′ver·ex′er·cise
o′ver·ex·pand′
o′ver·glo′ri·fy
o′ver·gov′ern
o′ver·grat′i·fy
o′ver·hard′en
o′ver·im·press′
o′ver·in·crease′
o′ver·in·flate′
o′ver·in′tel·lec′tu-al·ize
o′ver·in·ter′pret
o′ver·lean′
o′ver·learn′
o′ver·light′
o′ver·lin′ger
o′ver·meas′ure
o′ver·mech′a·nize
o′ver·mix′
o′ver·mort′gage
o′ver·mourn′
o′ver·mul′ti·ply
o′ver·nour′ish
o′ver·pam′per
o′ver·plant′
o′ver·press′
o′ver·pro·mote′
o′ver·pro·tect′
o′ver·prove′
o′ver·pro·vide′
o′ver·pro·voke′
o′ver·pun′ish
o′ver·pur′chase
o′ver·rank′
o′ver·reg′u·late
o′ver·rip′en
o′ver·salt′
o′ver·sen′ti·men′-tal·ize
o′ver·short′en
o′ver·sim′pli·fy
o′ver·spe′cial·ize
o′ver·spec′u·late
o′ver·staff′
o′ver·steer′
o′ver·stim′u·late
o′ver·study
o′ver·tar′ry
o′ver·trim′
o′ver·trust′
o′ver·wor′ry

o·ver·a·bound (ō′vər ə bound′), *v.i.* to abound to excess.

o·ver·a·bun·dance (ō′vər ə bun′dəns), *n.* excessive abundance; too abundant a supply.

o·ver·a·bun·dant (ō′vər ə bun′dənt), *adj.* too abundant; superabundant. **—o′ver·a·bun′dant·ly,** *adv.*

o·ver·a·chieve·ment (ō′vər ə chēv′ment), *n* achievement above expectations, especially in schoolwork.

o·ver·a·chiev·er (ō′vər ə chēv′ər), *n.* a pupil whose work is better than it might be expected from his intelligence tests.

o·ver·a·cid·i·ty (ō′vər ə sid′ə tē), *n.* excessive acidity; hyperacidity.

o·ver·act (ō′vər akt′), *v.t., v.i.* to act to excess; overdo in acting; act (a part) in an exaggerated manner.

o·ver·ac·tion (ō′vər ak′shən), *n.* action carried to excess.

o·ver·ac·tive (ō′vər ak′tiv), *adj.* too active; active to excess: *Most of the 108 children in the study were overactive, overirritable . . . and doing poorly scholastically* (Science News Letter). **—o′ver·ac′tive·ly,** *adv.*

o·ver·ac·tiv·i·ty (ō′vər ak tiv′ə tē), *n.* excessive activity.

o·ver·age[1] (ō′vər āj′), *adj.* past a certain age; past the age of greatest use, eligibility, etc.

o·ver·age[2] (ō′vər ij), *n.* **1.** a surplus of any commodity. **2. a.** the value of surplus goods not included in records of stock. **b.** surplus money not accounted for in records of sales.

o·ver·all (ō′vər ôl′), *adj.* **1.** from one end to the other: *an overall length of 10 feet.* **2.** including everything: *the overall cost of a year at college.* —*n. British.* an outer garment, such as a smock, worn over clothing to protect against wet, dirt, etc.

o·ver·alled (ō′vər ôld′), *adj.* wearing overalls: *Booted and overalled farmers gather on benches . . .* (Newsweek).

o·ver·alls (ō′vər ôlz′), *n.pl.* **1.** loose trousers, usually of denim and with a piece covering the chest, worn either with a shirt or over clothes to keep them clean. **2.** *British.* long leather or waterproof leggings reaching to the thigh.

o·ver-and-un·der (ō′vər ən un′dər), *n.* a double-barreled shotgun in which the barrels are placed one above the other rather than side by side.

o·ver·anx·i·e·ty (ō′vər ang zī′ə tē), *n.* excessive anxiety.

o·ver·anx·ious (ō′vər angk′shəs, -ang′-), *adj.* unnecessarily anxious; too anxious. **—o′ver·anx′ious·ly,** *adv.*

o·ver·arch (ō′vər ärch′), *v.t.* **1.** to arch over; span with or like an arch: *The street was overarched by elm trees.* **2.** to curve like an arch.
—*v.i.* to form an arch over something.

o·ver·arm (ō′vər ärm′), *adj.* with the arm raised above the shoulder; overhand: *an overarm pitch.*

o·ver·as·sess·ment (ō′vər ə ses′mənt), *n.* an assessment that is too high or higher than usual: *The Mayor . . . caused property owners to lose $100 million in overassessments* (New York Times).

o·ver·ate (o′vər āt′), *v.* past tense of **overeat:** *He and I overate, overdrank, overslept, just generally overdid things* (New Yorker).

o·ver·awe (ō′vər ô′), *v.t.,* **-awed, -aw·ing.** to overcome or restrain with awe: *Seeing an airplane overawed the savages.* **—Syn.** intimidate, cow.

o·ver·bal·ance (ō′vər bal′əns), *v.,* **-anced, -anc·ing,** *n.* —*v.t.* **1.** to be greater than in weight, importance, value, etc.; outweigh: *The gains overbalanced the losses.* **2.** to cause to lose balance: *Tom's weight as he leaned over the side overbalanced the canoe and it upset.*
—*n.* an excess of weight, value, or amount: *There is an overbalance of chemistry courses in your program.* **—Syn.** *v.t.* **2.** upset.

o·ver·bear (ō′vər bãr′), *v.,* **-bore, -borne** or **-born, -bear·ing.** —*v.t.* **1.** to overcome by weight or force; oppress; master: *He overbore all my objections.* **2.** to bear down by weight or force; overthrow; upset: *As a wild wave . . . overbears the bark . . . so they overbore Sir Lancelot and his charger* (Tennyson). **3.** to overbalance; outweigh. —*v.i.* to bear or produce too much or too many. **—Syn.** *v.t.* **1.** overpower, subdue.

o·ver·bear·ing (ō′vər bãr′ing), *adj.* inclined to dictate; forcing others to one's own will; masterful; domineering: *That old man is a very overbearing person. We found it hard to like the new boy because of his overbearing manners.* **—o′ver·bear′ing·ly,** *adv.* **—o′ver·bear′ing·ness,** *n.*
—Syn. dictatorial, imperious, arrogant. See **proud.**
—Ant. meek, humble.

o·ver·be·lief (ō′vər bi lēf′), *n.* belief in more than is warranted by the evidence or in that which cannot be verified: *Faith in the literal construction of the word was pushed to an excess . . . resembling a true superstition or overbelief* (John Morley).

o·ver·bid (ō′vər bid′), *v.,* **-bid, -bid** or **-bid·den, -bid·ding,** *n.* —*v.t.* **1.** to bid more than the value of (a thing). **2.** to bid higher than (a person); outbid. —*v.i.* to bid too high. —*n.* an overbidding.

o·ver·bite (ō′vər bīt′), *n.* the overlapping by the upper incisors of the lower incisors when the mouth is closed.

o·ver·blouse (ō′vər blous′), *n.* a blouse that is worn outside a skirt, shorts, or slacks, rather than being tucked in: *Overblouses of red cotton poplin have broad self bands at the bottom* (New Yorker).

o·ver·blow (ō′vər blō′), *v.,* **-blew, -blown, -blow·ing.** —*v.t.* **1.** to blow over or away. **2.** to blow down; overthrow by blowing. **3.** to cover by blowing over, as wind, sand, or snow. —*v.i.* to blow hard or with too much violence: *Finding it was likely to overblow, we took in our spritsail* (Jonathan Swift).

o·ver·blown (ō′vər blōn′), *adj.* **1.** more than fullblown; between ripeness and decay: *an overblown flower.* **2.** blown over, down, or away: *The tempest is o'erblown, the skies are clear* (John Dryden). **3.** carried too far; exaggerated; extreme; overdone: *one of those overblown interpretations of Biblical stories that Hollywood indulges in* (New Yorker).

o·ver·board (ō′vər bôrd′, -bōrd′), *adv.* from a ship into the water: *to fall overboard.*
go overboard, to go too far in an effort, especially because of extreme enthusiasm: *She went overboard and bought three new hats at once.*
throw overboard, a. to throw into the water: *The Pearl . . . had thrown about 14 tons of water overboard* (Pascoe Thomas). **b.** *Informal.* to get rid of; give up; abandon; discard: *The turncoats threw overboard all their former beliefs and abjectly joined the enemy's cause.* [< Old English *ofer bord*]

o·ver·bod·ice (ō′vər bod′is), *n.* an outer bodice.

o·ver·bold (ō′vər bōld′), *adj.* too bold; impudent: *The bee goes singing . . . Drunken and overbold* (Robert Browning). **—o′ver·bold′ly,** *adv.* **—o′ver·bold′ness,** *n.*

o·ver·bore (ō′vər bôr′, -bōr′), *v.* the past tense of **overbear.**

o·ver·born (ō′vər bôrn′), *v.* a past participle of **overbear.**

o·ver·borne (ō′vər bôrn′, -bōrn′), *v.* a past participle of **overbear.**

o·ver·bought (ō′vər bôt′), *v.* the past tense and past participle of **overbuy.**

o·ver·bowed (ō′vər bōd′), *adj.* (in archery) equipped with too strong a bow.

o·ver·bridge (ō′vər brij′), *n.* overpass.

o·ver·bril·liant (ō′vər bril′yənt), *adj.* too brilliant; overly splendid or ornate.

o·ver·brim (ō′vər brim′), *v.,* **-brimmed, -brim·ming.** —*v.i.* to brim over; overflow at the brim: *If the pitcher shall overbrim with water* (Scott). —*v.t.* to flow over the brim of: *The liquor that o'erbrims the cup* (Robert Browning).

o·ver·build (ō′vər bild′), *v.t.,* **-built, -build·ing. 1.** to build over or upon: *aquiline his nose, and overbuilt with most impending brows* (William Cowper). **2.** to build too much or too elaborately: *The administrative structure was overbuilt.* **3.** to build too much upon: *A city which has been overbuilt, which has 'superfluous' houses and flats by the block and mile* (Chicago Advance).

o·ver·bur·den (*v.* ō′vər bėr′dən; *n.* ō′vər-bėr′dən), *v.t.* to load with too great a burden: *A catalogue of the absurdities in which we have indulged under the influence of fear would overburden this document* (Bulletin of Atomic Scientists).
—*n.* **1.** too great a burden. **2.** *Mining.* clay, rock, etc., which has to be removed to get at a deposit of ore.

o·ver·bur·den·some (ō′vər bėr′dən səm), *adj.* excessively burdensome.

o·ver·burn (ō′vər bėrn′), *v.,* **-burned, -burnt, -burn·ing.** —*v.i.* **1.** to burn too much. **2.** to be overzealous: *overburning with ambition.* **3.** to be excessive. —*v.t.* to burn too much.

o·ver·bur·then (ō′vər bėr′ᴛʜən), *v.t. Archaic.* overburden.

o·ver·bus·y (ō′vər biz′ē), *adj.* **1.** too busy. **2.** obtrusively officious.

o·ver·buy (ō′vər bī′), *v.,* **-bought, -buy·ing.** —*v.t.* to buy on margin more (stock, etc.) than one can support if prices drop. —*v.i.* to buy too much or beyond one's means.

o·ver·by (ō′vər bī′), *adv.* a little way over or across.

o·ver·call (*v.* ō′vər kôl′; *n.* ō′vər kôl′), *v.t.* to outbid at cards. —*v.i.* **1.** to bid higher than a previous bid. **2.** to make an overcall in cards: *Opponents will hardly suspect you of being strong in their suit if you choose to overcall instead of remaining silent* (Manchester Guardian Weekly).
—*n.* a higher bid at cards, especially one made with minimal values over an opponent's bid when one's partner has passed or not bid: *. . . to make shutout calls when partner has opened the bidding and an opponent has made a simple overcall* (Observer).

o·ver·came (ō′vər kām′), *v.* the past tense of **overcome:** *She overcame her shyness.*

o·ver·can·o·py (ō′vər kan′ə pē), *v.t.,* **-pied, -py·ing.** to cover over with or as if with a canopy: *I know a bank where the wild thyme blows . . . Quite overcanopied with luscious woodbine* (Shakespeare).

o·ver·ca·pac·i·ty (ō′vər kə pas′ə tē), *n., pl.* **-ties.** productive capacity above what is required or profitable.

o·ver·cap·i·tal·i·za·tion (ō′vər kap′ə tə-lə zā′shən), *n.* **1.** an overcapitalizing. **2.** a being overcapitalized.

o·ver·cap·i·tal·ize (ō′vər kap′ə tə līz), *v.t.,* **-ized, -iz·ing.** to fix or estimate the capital of (a company, enterprise, etc.) at too high an amount.

o·ver·care (ō′vər kãr′), *n.* excessive care or anxiety: *The very overcare And nauseous pomp would hinder half the prayer* (John Dryden).

o·ver·care·ful (ō′vər kãr′fəl), *adj.* too careful. —**o′ver·care′ful·ly,** *adv.* —**o′ver·care′ful·ness,** *n.*

o·ver·cast (ō′vər kast′, -käst′), *adj., v.,* **-cast, -cast·ing,** *n.* —*adj.* **1.** cloudy; dark; gloomy: *It was a dull, close, overcast summer evening.* **2.** sewn with overcast stitches.
—*v.t.* **1.** to cover with clouds or darkness; make gloomy: *The distress spreads as wintry gray overcasts a sky* (George W. Cable). **2.** to sew over and through (the edges of a seam) with long stitches to prevent raveling. —*v.i.* to become dark or cloudy; become gloomy.
—*n.* **1.** a sky covered with clouds: *... straight up into the grey overcast* (Time). **2.** the clouds covering the sky: *The sun was obscured by a cloudy overcast.*
—**Syn.** *v.t.* **1.** obscure, becloud.

o·ver·cast·ing (ō′vər kas′ting, -käs′-), *n.* **1.** the act or process of coating a brick or stone surface with a layer of plaster or other material. **2.** the use of overcast stitching to edge a fabric.

o·ver·cau·tion (ō′vər kô′shən), *n.* excessive caution.

o·ver·cau·tious (ō′vər kô′shəs), *adj.* too cautious: *Many thought this was an overcautious estimate* (Charles Darwin).

o·ver·cen·tral·ize (ō′vər sen′trə līz), *v.t.,* **-ized, -iz·ing.** to centralize in excess of what is necessary, profitable, or desirable: *We are one of the largest countries in the world (in numbers, I mean, not geographical size) ruled by a unitary centralized system, and in my opinion, at least, we are ... overcentralized* (London Times).

o·ver·cer·ti·fi·ca·tion (ō′vər sėr′tə fə kā′shən), *n.* **1.** an overcertifying. **2.** a being overcertified.

o·ver·cer·ti·fy (ō′vər sėr′tə fī), *v.t.,* **-fied, -fy·ing.** to certify (a check) drawn for an amount greater than the balance in the drawer's account.

o·ver·charge (*v.* ō′vər chärj′; *n.* ō′vər-chärj′), *v.,* **-charged, -charg·ing,** *n.* —*v.t.* **1.** to charge too high a price: *The grocer overcharged you for the eggs.* **2.** to load too heavily; fill too full: *The overcharged old musket burst.* **3.** to exaggerate. —*v.i.* to charge too much.
—*n.* **1.** a charge that is too great. **2.** too heavy or too full a load.

o·ver·check[1] (ō′vər chek′), *n.* an overcheck rein or bridle.

o·ver·check[2] (ō′vər chek′), *n.* a checked pattern in one color or design superimposed on a different pattern of checks on a fabric: *A huge-patterned gray-and-black plaid covers the cotton, and the red overcheck on it matches the jersey sash* (New Yorker).

overcheck bridle, a bridle fitted with an overcheck rein.

overcheck rein, a kind of checkrein passing over a horse's head between the ears.

o·ver·climb (ō′vər klīm′), *v.t.,* **-climbed** or (*Archaic*) **-clomb, -climb·ing.** to climb over.

o·ver·close (ō′vər klōs′), *adj., adv.* too close: *Best unbar the doors Which Peter's heirs keep locked so overclose* (Elizabeth Barrett Browning).

o·ver·clothes (ō′vər klōz′, -klōᴛʜz′), *n.pl.* outer garments.

o·ver·cloud (ō′vər kloud′), *v.t., v.i.* **1.** to cloud over; become clouded over; darken. **2.** to make or become gloomy.

o·ver·coat (ō′vər kōt′), *n.* **1.** a heavy coat worn over the regular clothing: *the only argument available with an east wind is to put on your overcoat* (Lowell). **2.** an outer coat or covering: *Photomicrographs show the emptied protein overcoat that encloses a virus* (Scientific American).

o·ver·coat·ing (ō′vər kō′ting), *n.* the stuff or material from which overcoats are made.

o·ver·col·lar (ō′vər kol′ər), *n.* a collar on a coat that is made of a different fabric or color than the coat itself: *An overcollar of black Russian sable or chinchilla can be snapped in* (New Yorker).

o·ver·col·or (ō′vər kul′ər), *v.t.* **1.** to color too highly. **2.** to exaggerate.

o·ver·col·ored (ō′vər kul′ərd), *adj.* brightly colored, so as to be in bad taste: *The overlarge and overcolored automobile* (Alfred Kazin).

o·ver·com·a·ble (ō′vər kum′ə bəl), *adj.* that can be overcome.

o·ver·come (ō′vər kum′), *v.,* **-came, -come, -com·ing.** —*v.t.* **1.** to get the better of; win the victory over; conquer; defeat: *to overcome an enemy, one's faults, all difficulties. Rage overcame her and she burst into angry tears.* **2.** to make weak or helpless; overwhelm: *to be overcome by weariness.* **3.** *Archaic.* to spread over; overrun: *Trees ... o'ercome with moss and baleful mistletoe* (Shakespeare). —*v.i.* to gain the victory; conquer: *To him that overcometh will I grant to sit with me in my throne* (Revelation 3:21). [Old English *ofercuman*] —**Syn.** *v.t.* **1.** overpower, vanquish, master. See **defeat.**

o·ver·com·er (ō′vər kum′ər), *n.* a person who overcomes, vanquishes, or surmounts.

o·ver·com·mer·cial·ism (ō′vər kə mėr′shə liz əm), *n.* excessive or undue commercialism: *We can go along with his sniping at such dangers as ... overcommercialism of research to the sacrifice of teaching craft* (Harper's).

o·ver·com·mer·cial·i·za·tion (ō′vər kə-mėr′shə lə zā′shən), *n.* excessive or undue commercialization: *Advertisers howl at any suggestion of a tax on commercials, yet a tax may be the only way to curb the overcommercialization of television and radio* (Vance Packard).

o·ver·com·mit (ō′vər kə mit′), *v.t.,* **-mitted, -mit·ting.** to commit, involve, or pledge beyond what is required or expected: *U.A.R. President Nasser ... will not overcommit himself to the Soviets* (Wall Street Journal).

o·ver·com·mit·ment (ō′vər kə mit′ mənt), *n.* a commitment beyond what is required or expected: *Perhaps it is time ... to investigate the drives and compulsions that have led to our overcommitment to technology* (Lewis Mumford).

o·ver·com·pen·sa·tion (ō′vər kom′pən-sā′shən), *n. Psychology.* an excessive effort or exaggerated attempt to make up for a shortcoming in one's personality, as by overemphasizing a particular ability or concealing one's inadequacy with a display of overconfidence: *The little man who talks too loudly and too much, who is always itching to fight a bigger fellow ... illustrates overcompensation to a feeling of inferiority* (Floyd L. Ruch).

o·ver·con·fi·dence (o′vər kon′fə dəns), *n.* a being overconfident; too much confidence.

o·ver·con·fi·dent (ō′vər kon′fə dənt), *adj.* too confident. —**o′ver·con′fi·dent·ly,** *adv.*

o·ver·cooked (ō′vər ku̇kt′), *adj.* cooked too much or too long.

o·ver·cool (ō′vər kül′), *v.t.* to cool below the temperature of fusion without bringing about solidification. It is possible, under certain conditions, to cool water to a temperature several degrees below its freezing-point, without converting it into ice.

o·ver·cor·rec·tion (ō′vər kə rek′shən), *n.* **1.** correction beyond the normal or necessary degree: *Tax increases contain certain risks —above all, of the sort of overcorrection which initiates a recession instead of checking an inflation* (Atlantic). **2.** the conversion of one defect of vision into its opposite by means of a too powerful lens. **3.** the surgical correction of a deformity beyond the usual degree to allow for later modification of the correction.

o·ver·count (ō′vər kount′), *v.t.* **1.** to overestimate. **2.** to outnumber.

o·ver·cov·er (ō′vər kuv′ər), *v.t.* to cover over; cover completely.

o·ver·crit·i·cal (ō′vər krit′ə kəl), *adj.* too critical; hypercritical.

o·ver·crop (ō′vər krop′), *v.t.,* **-cropped, -crop·ping.** to exhaust the fertility of (soil) by uninterrupted planting and harvesting.

o·ver·crow (ō′vər krō′), *v.t.* **1.** to crow or exult over. **2.** to triumph over; overcome.

o·ver·crowd (ō′vər kroud′), *v.t., v.i.* to crowd too much: *These people overcrowd into the already overcrowded smaller properties that lie around* (London Daily News).

o·ver·cu·ri·ous (ō′vər kyu̇r′ē əs), *adj.* curious or nice to excess.

o·ver·cur·tain (ō′vər kėr′tən), *v.t.* to cover; shadow; obscure.

o·ver·dare (ō′vər dãr′), *v.,* **-dared, -dar·ing.** —*v.i.* to exceed in daring; dare too much or rashly; be too daring. —*v.t.* to dishearten; discourage; daunt.

o·ver·dar·ing (ō′vər dãr′ing), *adj.* unduly or imprudently bold; foolhardy.

o·ver·date (ō′vər dāt′), *v.t.,* **-dat·ed, -dat·ing.** **1.** to date beyond the proper period. **2.** to cause to continue beyond the proper date

o·ver·de·stroy (ō′vər di stroi′), *v.i.* (of bombs) to develop more energy at the explosion center than is necessary for total destruction, thereby wasting considerable energy. —*v.t.* to destroy in this way: *The high-pressure region of a bomb burst on or close to the ground would overdestroy the target in the near vicinity of the bomb* (The Effects of Atomic Weapons).

o·ver·de·struc·tion (ō′vər di struk′shən), *n.* **1.** the process of overdestroying. **2.** an instance of this.

o·ver·de·vel·op (ō′vər di vel′əp), *v.t.* to develop too much or too long: *overdeveloped curiosity, overdeveloped muscles. Overdeveloping fast film will step up the camera's rate to about five frames a second* (Science News Letter).

o·ver·de·vel·op·ment (ō′vər di vel′əp-mənt), *n.* development carried too far or continued too long: *Weightlifters show overdevelopment.*

o·ver·dil·i·gent (ō′vər dil′ə jənt), *adj.* diligent to excess.

o·ver·dis·charge (ō′vər dis chärj′), *n. Electricity.* the discharge of an accumulator or storage battery beyond the usual limit.

o·ver·do (ō′vər dü′), *v.,* **-did, -done, -do·ing.** —*v.t.* **1.** to do too much; carry to excess: *She overdoes exercise.* **2.** to make too much of; exaggerate: *The funny scenes in the play were overdone.* **3.** to cook too much: *to overdo a roast.* **4.** to overtax the strength of; exhaust; tire: *It might be that she was a little overdone with work and anxiety* (George Eliot). —*v.i.* to do or attempt to do too much: *She overdid and became tired.* [Old English *oferdōn*] —**Syn.** *v.t.* **1.** overwork. **4.** fatigue. —*v.i.* overwork.

o·ver·do·er (ō′vər dü′ər), *n.* a person who does more than is necessary or expedient.

o·ver·done (ō′vər dun′), *adj.* **1.** carried to excess: *The wonderfully overdone upper-class interiors ... are photographed ... [so] that moviegoers ... will recognize [them]* (Time). **2.** overcooked: *overdone vegetables.* —*v.* past participle of **overdo:** *Yet the harshness can be and has been overdone* (Observer).

o·ver·door (ō′vər dôr′, -dōr′), *adj.* placed, or to be placed, over a door, as a decorative piece. —*n.* a piece of decorative work over a door.

o·ver·dose (*n.* ō′vər dōs′; *v.* ō′vər dōs′), *n., v.,* **-dosed, -dos·ing.** —*n.* too big a dose; more than is needed or wanted: *an overdose of sleeping pills, an overdose of criticism.* —*v.t.* to give too large a dose to.

o·ver·draft (ō′vər draft′, -dräft′), *n.* **1. a.** an overdrawing of an account, especially a bank account: *Mr. Orrin also told the witness that he (the witness) was improvident and had an overdraft* (London Times). **b.** the amount of the excess. **2.** a draft passing over a fire, as in a furnace, or downward through a kiln. Also, **overdraught.**

o·ver·dram·a·tise (ō′vər dram′ə tīz, -drä′mə-), *v.t.,* **-tised, -tis·ing.** *Especially British.* overdramatize.

o·ver·dram·a·tize (ō′vər dram′ə tīz, -drä′mə-), *v.t.,* **-tized, -tiz·ing.** to present in a melodramatic way; overstate so as to impress: *A political aspirant who constantly overstates or overdramatizes his case to create shock effect* (Saturday Review).

o·ver·draught (ō′vər draft′, dräft′), *n.* overdraft.

o·ver·draw (ō′vər drô′), *v.,* **-drew, -drawn, -draw·ing.** —*v t.* **1.** to draw more money from (a bank account, allowance, etc.) than one has a right to: *The careless man overdrew his bank account.* **2.** to exaggerate: *The characters in the book were greatly overdrawn.* **3.** to draw or strain too much. —*v.i.* **1.** to make an overdraft. **2.** to exaggerate.

o·ver·dress (*v.* ō′vər dres′; *n.* ō′vər dres′), *v.t., v.i.* to dress too richly. —*n.* a dress worn over the main dress: *These are covered by chiffon overdresses that have a bloused top* (New Yorker).

o·ver·drink (ō′vər dringk′), *v.i.,* **-drank, -drunk·en, -drink·ing.** to drink to excess: *They overeat and overdrink, and they try to forget what they really want* (J.O. Hobbes).

o·ver·drive[1] (ō′vər drīv′), *n.* an arrangement of gears in an automobile, machine, etc., whereby even more speed and less power are produced than in high gear: *Overdrive permits the drive shaft to turn four* *times for every three revolutions of the engine crankshaft* (Franklin M. Reck).

o·ver·drive[2] (ō′vər drīv′), *v.t.*, **-drove, -driv·en, -driv·ing.** **1.** to drive too hard: *If men should overdrive them one day, all the flock will die* (Genesis 33:13). **2.** to push or carry to excess; overwork: *You must not fancy I am sick, only overdriven and under the weather* (Robert Louis Stevenson). **3.** to hit a golf ball beyond.

o·ver·drop (ō′vər drop′), *v.t.*, **-dropped, -drop·ping.** to drop over; overhang; overshadow.

o·ver·dry (ō′vər drī′), *v.t.*, **-dried, -dry·ing.** to make too dry.

o·ver·due (ō′vər dü′, -dyü′), *adj.* more than due; due some time ago but not yet arrived, paid, etc.: *The train is overdue. This bill is overdue.* —**Syn.** belated, tardy.

o·ver·dye (ō′vər dī′), *v.t.*, **-dyed, -dye·ing.** **1.** to dye (cloth, etc.) with a second color over the first. **2.** to dye (cloth, etc.) too long or with too dark a color.

o·ver·ea·ger (ō′vər ē′gər), *adj.* too eager; overanxious. —**o′ver·ea′ger·ly,** *adv.* —**o′ver·ea′ger·ness,** *n.*

o·ver·eat (ō′vər ēt′), *v.*, **-ate, -eat·en, -eat·ing.** —*v.i.* to eat too much. —*v.t.* to eat more than is good for (oneself): *Without doubt, the most of mankind grossly overeat themselves* (Robert Louis Stevenson).

o·ver·e·lec·tri·fi·ca·tion (ō′vər i lek′trə fə kā′shən), *n.* **1.** an overelectrifying. **2.** a being overelectrified.

o·ver·e·lec·tri·fy (ō′vər i lek′trə fī), *v.t.*, **-fied, -fy·ing.** to electrify too much or beyond necessary or desirable limits: *Government regulation of competing power companies is necessary to prevent the overelectrifying of an area.*

o·ver·em·pha·sis (ō′vər em′fə sis), *n.* **1.** too much force; undue stress; unjustified importance, often resulting in an undesirable outcome: ... *the slightest overemphasis can transmute its simplicity into banality* (New Yorker). **2.** too much force given to a particular syllable, word, or phrase.

o·ver·em·pha·size (ō′vər em′fə sīz), *v.t.*, **-sized, -siz·ing.** **1.** to give too much force to; stress unduly; overestimate the importance of: *He overemphasized the details and ruined the story.* **2.** to call too much attention to: *By overemphasizing the scenery with loud colors nobody paid any attention to the actors.*

o·ver·en·dowed (ō′vər en doud′), *adj.* having an abundance of; being well supplied with: *The villages ... are overendowed with supermarkets* (Maclean's).

o·ver·en·treat (ō′vər en trēt′), *v.t.* to persuade or gain over by entreaty.

o·ver·es·ti·mate (*v.* ō′vər es′tə māt; *n.* ō′vər es′tə mit), *v.*, **-mat·ed, -mat·ing,** *n.* —*v.t., v.i.* to estimate at too high a value, amount, rate, etc.: *Men often overestimate their capacity for evil* (Hawthorne). —*n.* an estimate that is too high. —**Syn.** *v.t.* overrate. -*n.* overvaluation.

o·ver·es·ti·ma·tion (ō′vər es′tə mā′shən), *n.* **1.** an overestimating. **2.** a being overestimated.

o·ver·ex·cite (ō′vər ik sīt′), *v.t.*, **-cit·ed, -cit·ing.** to excite too much.

o·ver·ex·cite·ment (ō′vər ik sīt′mənt), *n.* **1.** a being overexcited. **2.** too much excitement.

o·ver·ex·ert (ō′vər ig zėrt′), *v.t.* to exert too much.

o·ver·ex·er·tion (ō′vər ig zėr′shən), *n.* too much exertion.

o·ver·ex·pose (ō′vər ik spōz′), *v.t.*, **-posed, -pos·ing.** **1.** to expose too much. **2.** *Photography.* to expose (a film or negative) too long to light.

o·ver·ex·po·sure (ō′vər ik spō′zhər), *n.* too much or too long an exposure: *Underexposing the negative results in loss of detail in the shadows, whereas overexposure results in loss of detail in the high lights* (Hardy and Perrin).

o·ver·ex·qui·site (ō′vər ek′skwi zit, -ik skwiz′it), *adj.* excessively or unduly exquisite or exact; too nice; too careful or anxious.

o·ver·ex·tend (ō′vər ik stend′), *v.t.* **1.** to spread (something) out too far; to expand over too large an area: *Dulles ... said Russia had overextended herself in her drive for world domination* (New York Times). **2.** to overdo or belabor (something) to the point of fatigue or unwarranted excess: *to overextend one's visit. However much Miss West overextends her material, her turn of phrase is a delight* (Charles J. Rolo). **3.** *Finance.* to take on financial obligations to the point where there are too few assets to cover them and bankruptcy is imminent: *Typically, the small businessman stretches his limited capital too far, overextends his credit in order to get customers* (George S. Odiorne).

o·ver·ex·tend·ed (ō′vər ik sten′did), *adj.* having greater liabilities than assets: *The American family, buying hard goods on the newly discovered installment plan, was equally exposed to the hazard of overextended credit* (Bulletin of Atomic Scientists).

o·ver·ex·ten·sion (ō′vər ik sten′shən), *n.* **1.** an overextending. **2.** something overextended: *The play had been little more than "an overextension of a quite small idea"* (Time).

o·ver·eye (ō′vər ī′), *v.t.*, **eyed, ey·ing** or **eye·ing.** *Obsolete.* to survey; oversee.

o·ver·fall (ō′vər fôl′), *n.* **1. a.** a turbulent stretch of water caused by the meeting of currents or by a strong current running over a submerged ridge or shoal. **b.** such a ridge or shoal. **2.** a sudden drop in the sea bottom. **3.** a place for the overflow of water, as from a canal.

o·ver·fa·mil·iar·i·ty (ō′vər fə mil′yar′ə tē), *n.* too much familiarity.

o·ver·fa·tigue (ō′vər fə tēg′), *n.* fatigue beyond the normal limits of recovery.

o·ver·feed (ō′vər fēd′), *v.t., v.i.*, **-fed, -feed·ing.** to feed too much; feed to excess.

o·ver·fill (ō′vər fil′), *v.t., v.i.* to fill too full; fill so as to cause overflowing.

o·ver·fine (ō′vər fīn′), *adj.* too fine. —**o′ver·fine′ness,** *n.*

o·ver·fired (ō′vər fīrd′), *adj.* (in ceramics) exposed to too great a heat in firing, resulting in the running together of the colors, or the melting of the enamel or the work itself.

o·ver·fish (ō′vər fish′), *v.i.* to catch fish faster than they can reproduce, thereby gradually depleting the fisheries. —*v.t.* to deplete (a fishery or a kind of fish) by excessive fishing: *Many of the area's salmon fisheries [are] overfished* (Science News Letter).

o·ver·flight (ō′vər flīt′), *n.* the act of flying over the territory of a country: *Israel was about to ban the overflights of U.S. and British planes across Israeli territory* (Time).

o·ver·flood (ō′vər flud′), *v.t.* to pour over in or as if in a flood.

o·ver·flow (*v.* ō′vər flō′; *n., adj.* ō′vər flō′), *v.*, **-flowed, -flown, -flow·ing,** *n., adj.* —*v.i.* **1.** to flow over the bounds: *Rivers often overflow in the spring.* **2.** to have the contents flowing over: *My cup is overflowing.* **3.** to pass from one part to another because of lack of room: *The crowd overflowed from the auditorium into the hall.* **4.** to be very abundant: *an overflowing harvest, overflowing kindness; to make the coming hour o'erflow with joy* (Shakespeare).
—*v.t.* **1.** to cover; flood: *The river overflowed my garden. Waters rise up ... and shall overflow the land, and all that is therein* (Jeremiah 47:2). **2. a.** to flow over the top of: *The dough overflowed the pan.* **b.** to fill to the point of overflowing: *So they overflowed his house, smoked his cigars and drank his health* (Rudyard Kipling). **3.** to extend out beyond; be too many for: *The crowd overflowed the auditorium and filled the hall.*
—*n.* **1.** an overflowing; excess: *the annual overflow of the Nile.* **2.** something that flows or runs over: *an overflow of people from the cities, to carry off the overflow from a fountain.* **3.** an outlet or container for overflowing liquid.
—*adj.* superabundant; overflowing: *In theaters and student hostels from White Russia to Central Asia, overflow crowds listen to poets with almost religious fervor* (Time).
[Old English *oferflōwan*] —**o′ver·flow′ing·ly,** *adv.*
—**Syn.** *v.t.* **1.** inundate, overrun.

o·ver·fly (ō′vər flī′), *v.t.*, **-flew, -flown, -fly·ing.** **1.** to make an overflight above: *The U-2 has been overflying Russia* (Time). **2.** to fly over or past, as in an unscheduled flight; fly without landing for a scheduled stop: *If no passengers are to be dropped or picked up ... stops are overflown* (Newsweek). **3.** to fly faster, farther, or higher than.

o·ver·fond (ō′vər fond′), *adj.* too fond. —**o′ver·fond′ly,** *adv.* —**o′ver·fond′ness,** *n.*

o·ver·fraught (ō′vər frôt′), *adj.* fraught or laden too heavily; overladen.

o·ver·free (ō′vər frē′), *adj.* too free. —**o′ver·free′ly,** *adv.*

o·ver·ful·fill or **o·ver·ful·fil** (ō′vər fu̇l fil′), *v.t.*, **-filled, -fill·ing.** to go beyond a required duty, quota, or norm; do more than is expected: *He receives a pat-on-the-back from his ... boss ... when he overfulfills quotas* (Saturday Review).

o·ver·ful·fill·ment or **o·ver·ful·fil·ment** (ō′vər fu̇l fil′mənt), *n.* a state of being overfulfilled: *The director ... promised him an extra bonus besides the one due for overfulfillment of quota* (Sergei Antonov).

o·ver·full (ō′vər fu̇l′), *adj.* too full: *There has been excess demand and overfull employment* (Economist). —**o′ver·full′ness,** *n.*

o·ver·gar·ment (ō′vər gär′mənt), *n.* an outer garment: *The cloth used for overgarments ... was completely windproof* (Scientific American).

o·ver·gild (ō′vər gild′), *v.t.*, **-gild·ed** or **-gilt, -gild·ing.** **1.** to cover with gilding. **2.** to tinge with a golden color.

o·ver·glaze (*n.* ō′vər glāz′; *v.* ō′vər glāz′), *n., v.*, **-glazed, -glaz·ing.** —*n.* a glaze applied over another glaze on pottery. —*v.t.* to apply an overglaze to.

o·ver·go (ō′vər gō′), *v.*, **-went, -gone, -go·ing.** *Archaic.* —*v.t.* **1.** to pass over or through. **2.** to go beyond; exceed; surpass. **3.** to overcome. **4.** to overwhelm; weigh down. —*v.i.* **1.** to go by; pass away; disappear. **2.** to go to excess.

o·ver·gorge (ō′vər gôrj′), *v.t., v.i.*, **-gorged, -gorg·ing.** to gorge too much.

o·ver·graze (ō′vər grāz′), *v.*, **-grazed, -graz·ing.** —*v.i.* to graze so long and uninterruptedly as to reduce seriously or destroy the grass cover of a pasture. —*v.t.* to destroy (pasture land) in that way: *Most of the range in the West has been or is being overgrazed* (Bernard De Voto).

o·ver·great (ō′vər grāt′), *adj.* too great.

o·ver·ground (ō′vər ground′), *adj.* above the ground.

o·ver·grow (ō′vər grō′), *v.*, **-grew, -grown, -grow·ing.** —*v.t.* **1.** to grow over: *The wall is overgrown with vines.* **2.** to grow out of or beyond; outgrow: *The rosebush has overgrown its support.* **3.** to outdo in growing; choke or replace by a more profuse growth: *seeds of a new and rampant quality, which were destined to overgrow them all* (Harriet Beecher Stowe). —*v.i.* to grow too fast; become too big.

o·ver·grown (ō′vər grōn′), *adj.* **1.** grown too big: *an overgrown boy.* **2.** grown over with vegetation, weeds, etc. —*v.* the past participle of **overgrow.**

o·ver·growth (ō′vər grōth′), *n.* **1.** too great or too rapid growth. **2.** a growth overspreading or covering something: ... *the selective overgrowth of the culture by a few individuals that are able to multiply in its presence* (Evelyn M. Witkin).

o·ver·hand (ō′vər hand′), *adj., adv.* **1.** with the hand raised above the shoulder; overarm: *an overhand throw, to pitch overhand.* **2.** with the knuckles upward. **3.** over and over; with stitches passing successively over an edge: *an overhand stitch.*
—*n.* performance, or style of performance, in making overhand plays, as in tennis: *He has a strong overhand.*
—*v.t.* to sew with overhand stitches.

o·ver·hand·ed (ō′vər han′did), *adj.* **1.** overhand. **2.** supplied with too many workers.

overhand knot, a simple knot, used in beginning other knots. See picture under **knot**[1].

o·ver·hang (*v.* ō′vər hang′; *n.* ō′vər hang′), *v.*, **-hung, -hang·ing,** *n.* —*v.t.* **1.** to hang over; project over: *Trees overhang the street to form an arch of branches.* **2.** to hang over so as to darken, sadden, or threaten: *The threat of war overhangs mankind.* **3.** to drape or decorate with hangings. —*v.i.* to hang over; jut out over something below: *The granite walls, overhanging, bend forward above to meet one another, almost forming an arch* (Henry Kingsley).
—*n.* **1.** something that projects: *The overhang of the roof shaded the flower bed beneath. The overhang of the stern or bow of a ship is between the water line and the deck.* **2.** amount of projecting: *Frames generally will be stretched to reduce front and rear overhang* (Wall Street Journal). **3.** the distance the tip of the upper wing of a biplane extends beyond the tip of the lower wing.

o·ver·hard (ō′vər härd′), *adj.* too hard.

o·ver·hast·i·ly (ō′vər hās′tə lē), *adv.* in an overhasty manner; with too much haste.

o·ver·hast·i·ness (ō′vər hās′tē nis), *n.* a being overhasty; too much haste: *failure because of dilatoriness or overhastiness.*

o·ver·hast·y (ō′vər hās′tē), *adj.* too hasty: *It would be overhasty to start drawing unfavorable conclusions now about Sword Dancer* (New Yorker).

o·ver·haul (*v.* ō′vər hôl′; *n.* ō′vər hôl′), *v.t.* **1.** to examine thoroughly so as to make any repairs or changes that are needed: *to overhaul an automobile, to overhaul a government department.* **2.** to gain upon; overtake: . . . *victory going to Golden Thread, who overhauled Brilliant Star to win by a head* (London Times). **3.** *Nautical.* **a.** to slacken (a rope) by hauling in the opposite direction to that in which it was drawn taut. **b.** to release the blocks of (a tackle).
—*n.* an overhauling: *The repair bill . . . was $411.92 for two transmission overhauls* (Time).

o·ver·haul·ing (ō′vər hô′ling), *n.* a thorough examination to find and make any needed repairs or changes: *The proposed change . . . was included in a bill to provide extensive overhauling of the Federal excise laws* (Wall Street Journal).

o·ver·head[1] (*adv.* ō′vər hed′; *adj., n.* ō′vər-hed′), *adv.* **1.** in the sky; on high; far above: *birds flying overhead. Overhead was a gray expanse of cloud* (Hawthorne). **2.** on the floor above; just above: *people dancing overhead.*
—*adj.* being, working, or passing overhead: *overhead wires.*
—*n.* a tennis stroke made with an overhand motion downward from above the head: *She never went to the net voluntarily, though she won with her overhead when drawn in* (New York Times).
—**Syn.** *adv.* **1.** aloft.

o·ver·head[2] (ō′vər hed′), *n.* general expenses or charges of a business which cannot be charged against a particular operation, including rent, lighting, heating, taxes, and repairs. —*adj.* of or having to do with overhead in business: *overhead charges or expenses.*

o·ver·head[3] (ō′vər hed′), *adj. Especially British.* applying to one and all; general: *an overhead tax.* [Middle English *overheved,* Old English *ofer hēafod,* in the earlier sense of "taking everything together"]

overhead railway, *British.* an elevated railroad.

overhead valve, a valve in the cylinder head, above the piston in certain automobile engines.

o·ver·hear (ō′vər hir′), *v.t.,* **-heard, -hear·ing.** to hear when one is not meant to hear: *They spoke so loud that I could not help overhearing what they said.* [Old English *oferhēran*]

o·ver·hear·er (ō′vər hir′ər), *n.* a person who overhears.

o·ver·heat (*v.* ō′vər hēt′; *n.* ō′vər hēt′), *v.t., v.i.* to heat too much: *It may be found that the rocket overheats in spite of this cooling* (D. Hurden). —*n.* too much heat.

o·ver·high (ō′vər hī′), *adj., adv.* too high.

o·ver·hours (ō′vər ourz′), *n.pl.* **1.** extra hours of work; overtime. **2.** spare or odd hours: *I only worked at it in overhours—often late at night* (George Eliot).

o·ver·hung (*adj.* ō′vər hung′; *v.* ō′vər-hung′), *adj.* **1.** hung from above: *an overhung door.* **2.** (of the upper jaw) projecting beyond the lower jaw. —*v.* the past tense and past participle of **overhang:** *A big awning overhung the sidewalk.*

o·ver·in·dulge (ō′vər in dulj′), *v.t., v.i.,* **-dulged, -dulg·ing.** to indulge too much.

o·ver·in·dul·gence (ō′vər in dul′jəns), *n.* excessive or too much indulgence: *Overindulgence is as bad for children as overstrictness* (Sidonie M. Gruenberg).

o·ver·in·dul·gent (ō′vər in dul′jənt), *adj.* too indulgent.

o·ver·in·sure (ō′vər in shůr′), *v.t.,* **-sured, -sur·ing.** to insure for more than the real value: *Ship and cargo are overinsured about ten times, I suppose?* (Blackwood's Magazine).

o·ver·is·sue (ō′vər ish′ü; *especially British,* ō′vər is′yü), *n., v.,* **-sued, -su·ing.** —*n.* an issue of stocks, bonds, etc., in excess of what is authorized or needed. —*v.t.* to issue (notes, securities, etc.) in excess of a proper or authorized amount.

o·ver·joy (ō′vər joi′), *v.t.* to make extremely joyful: *My sister . . . was overjoyed at the intelligence of my safe return* (Frederick Marryat). —**Syn.** delight.

o·ver·joyed (ō′vər joid′), *adj.* very joyful; filled with joy; delighted.

o·ver·jump (ō′vər jump′), *v.t., v.i.* **1.** to jump over. **2.** to jump too far over. **3.** to transcend; pass over.

o·ver·kill (*v.* ō′vər kil′; *n.* ō′vər kil′), *v.t.* to overdestroy: *We can both overkill the other, to use the new charming nomenclature* (Bulletin of Atomic Scientists). —*n.* overdestruction: *SAC alone will provide an abundance of what the Pentagon calls "overkill"* (Time).

o·ver·la·bor (ō′vər lā′bər), *v.t.* **1.** to overwork. **2.** to labor too much over; elaborate too much.

o·ver·lad·en (ō′vər lā′dən), *adj.* overloaded.

o·ver·laid (ō′vər lād′), *v.* the past tense and past participle of **overlay**[1]**:** *The workmen overlaid the dome with gold. The iron had become overlaid with rust.*

o·ver·lain (ō′vər lān′), *v.* the past participle of **overlie:** *In most oceanic areas, however, the crust seems to be overlain with half a mile of sediment* (Willard Bascom).

o·ver·land (ō′vər land′, -lənd), *adv., adj., v.* —*adv., adj.* on land; by land; across land: *to travel overland.* —*v.t.* (in Australia) to drive (livestock) overland, especially for long distances. —*v.i.* (in Australia) to travel overland driving livestock. —**o′ver·land′er,** *n.*

overland stage, *U.S.* a sturdy stagecoach that carried passengers and mail in the West before the railroads, in the mid-1800's.

Overland Stage

o·ver·lap (*v.* ō′vər lap′; *n.* ō′vər lap′), *v.,* **-lapped, -lap·ping,** *n.* —*v.t.* **1.** to lap over; cover and extend beyond: *Shingles are laid so that they overlap each other.* **2.** to coincide partly with. —*v.i.* to overlap another thing or each other: *The shingles overlap. Our arguments seem to overlap.*
—*n.* **1.** a lapping over: *Overlaps do not matter and thin spots can be touched up at any time* (New York Times). **2.** the amount by which one thing laps over another. **3.** a part that overlaps.

o·ver·large (ō′vər lärj′), *adj.* too large; oversized.

o·ver·lay[1] (*v.* ō′vər lā′; *n.* ō′vər lā′), *v.,* **-laid, -lay·ing,** *n.* —*v.t.* **1.** to lay or place (one thing) over or upon another. **2. a.** to cover, overspread, or surmount with something. **b.** to finish with a layer or applied decoration of something: *wood overlaid with gold; bright ivory overlaid with sapphires* (Canticles 5:14). **3.** to weigh down: *to be overlaid with responsibilities.* **4.** *Printing.* to place an overlay on. **5.** to conceal or obscure as if by covering. **6.** to overlie.
—*n.* **1. a.** something laid over something else; covering. **b.** a layer or decoration of something applied: *an overlay of fine wood, an overlay of gold.* **2.** a sheet of some transparent substance by means of which special geographical or other information, as the location of military units, may be obtained when it is placed over the map to which it is keyed, and by which the marks on the overlay are made meaningful. **3.** *Printing.* a piece of paper, or a sheet with pieces pasted on it, laid on the press cylinder as part of make-ready to compensate for low spots in the form. **4.** *Scottish.* a necktie.
—**Syn.** *v.t.* **1.** superimpose. **3.** encumber, overburden.

o·ver·lay[2] (ō′vər lā′), *v.* the past tense of **overlie.**

o·ver·leaf (ō′vər lēf′), *adv., adj.* on the reverse side of a piece of paper.

o·ver·leap (ō′vər lēp′), *v.t.* **1.** to leap over or across; pass beyond: *Her joy overleaped all bounds.* **2.** to overreach (oneself) by leaping too far: *Vaulting ambition, which o'erleaps itself* (Shakespeare). **3.** to pass over; omit; skip. **4.** to leap farther than; outleap.

o·ver·lie (ō′vər lī′), *v.t.,* **-lay, -lain, -ly·ing.** **1.** to lie over; lie upon. **2.** to smother by lying on; overlay: *The old idiot wretch Screamed feebly, like a baby overlain* (Elizabeth Barrett Browning).

o·ver·ling (ō′vər ling), *n.* a person who is over others in position or authority (used in an unfriendly way).

o·ver·live (ō′vər liv′), *v.,* **-lived, -liv·ing.** —*v.t.* to live longer than or beyond; outlast; outlive: *The mighty Pyramids . . . have overlived the feeble generations of mankind* (Robert Southey). —*v.i.* to continue to live; survive: *Why do I overlive? Why am I mocked with death, and lengthen'd out To deathless pain?* (Milton).

o·ver·load (*v.* ō′vər lōd′; *n.* ō′vər lōd′), *v.t.* **1.** to load too heavily; overburden: *to overload a boat, to overload an electric circuit.* **2.** to overcharge (a gun). —*n.* too great a load or charge: *One of the most familiar dissatisfactions in the Doing Period of thirty-five to fifty is work overload, especially for teachers* (Harper's).

o·ver·long (ō′vər long′), *adj., adv.* too long.

o·ver·look (*v.* ō′vər lůk′; *n.* ō′vər lůk′), *v.t.* **1.** to fail to see; neglect: *Here are the letters you overlooked.* **2.** to pay no attention to; excuse: *I will overlook your bad behavior this time.* **3.** to have a view of from above; be higher than: *This high window overlooks half the city.* **4.** to look after and direct; manage. **5.** to look over; watch: *Utterly absorbed in her task, she had no suspicion that she was being overlooked* (Arnold Bennett). **6.** to look over the top of; rise above; overtop. **7.** to look upon with the evil eye; bewitch: *I tell you she has overlooked me; and all this doctor's stuff is no use, unless you can say a charm as will undo her devil's work* (Henry Kingsley).
—*n.* a lookout: *The overlook is a short hike from the road's end. The view down has a smashing impact* (New York Times).
—**o′ver·look′er,** *n.* —**Syn.** *v.t.* **1.** disregard, ignore. See **slight. 2.** forgive, condone. **4.** oversee, superintend. **5.** survey, scrutinize.

o·ver·lord (ō′vər lôrd′), *n.* **1.** a person who is lord over another lord or other lords: *The duke was the overlord of barons and knights who held land from him.* **2.** any person, group, or government having comparable status or authority.

o·ver·lord·ship (ō′vər lôrd′ship), *n.* the position, rank, or authority of an overlord: . . . *the last Jewish revolt against Roman overlordship* (New York Times).

o·ver·ly (ō′vər lē), *adv.* overmuch; excessively; too: *a voyage . . . not overly dangerous* (John Galt).

o·ver·ly·ing (ō′vər lī′ing), *v.* the present participle of **overlie.**

o·ver·man (*n. 1 and 2* ō′vər mən; *3* ō′vər-man′; *v.*ō′vər man′), *n.,pl.* **-men,** *v.,* **-manned, -man·ning.** —*n.* **1.** *Especially British.* a foreman or overseer, especially in a coal mine: *This sparking had been observed by workmen, deputies, and the overman* (London Times). **2.** *Especially British.* an arbiter; arbitrator; umpire. **3.** a superman.
—*v.t.* to supply with too many workers: *The union-owned Vulcan Foundries, Ltd., decided it was overmanned and dismissed some union members* (Wall Street Journal).

o·ver·man·tel (ō′vər man′təl), *n.* a piece of decorative work placed above a mantelpiece, often a piece of ornamental cabinet-work with or without a mirror.

o·ver·mas·ter (ō′vər mas′tər, -mäs′-), *v.t.* to overcome; overpower. —**o′ver·mas′ter·ing·ly,** *adv.* —**Syn.** defeat, surmount.

o·ver·match (ō′vər mach′), *v.t.* to be more than a match for; surpass; outdo. —*n.* a person or thing that is more than a match.

o·ver·much (ō′vər much′), *adj., adv., n.* too much.

o·ver·nice (ō′vər nīs′), *adj.* too fastidious. —**Syn.** finical.

o·ver·night (*adv., v.i.* ō′vər nīt′; *adj., n.* ō′vər nīt′), *adv.* **1.** during the night; through the night: *to stay overnight with a friend.* **2.** at once; immediately; in a very short time: *Everyday life will not be changed radically and overnight* (Science News Letter). **3.** on the night before: *Preparations were made overnight for an early start.*
—*adj.* **1.** done, occurring, lasting, etc., during the night: *an overnight stop, overnight hospitality.* **2.** for the night: *overnight guests. An overnight bag contains articles needed for one night's stay.* **3.** of or having to do with the night before.
—*n.* the previous evening.
—*v.i.* to stay overnight: *to overnight at a hotel.*

o·ver·num·ber (ō′vər num′bər), *v.t.* to outnumber.

o·ver·or·gan·ize (ō′vər ôr′gə nīz), *v.t., v.i.,* **-ized, -iz·ing.** to subject to excessive organization; organize too much.

o·ver·paid (ō′vər pād′), *v.* the past tense and past participle of **overpay.**

o·ver·paint (ō′vər pānt′), *v.t.* **1.** to paint (one picture, layer, etc.) over or upon another: *Icons were heavily overpainted and smudged by centuries of candle smoke* (Time). **2.** to overemphasize; exaggerate.

o·ver·part·ed (ō′vər pär′tid), *adj.* having too difficult a part, or too many parts, to play: *to be overparted in a play.*

o·ver·pass (*v.* ō′vər pas′, -päs′; *n.* ō′vər-pas′, -päs′), *v.*, **-passed** or **-past, -pass·ing,** *n.* —*v.t.* **1.** to pass over (a region, bounds, etc.): *The next few miles would be no light thing for the whale-boats to overpass* (Rudyard Kipling). **2.** to go beyond; exceed; surpass: *Men Who overpass their kind* (Robert Browning). **3.** to overlook; disregard: *All the beauties of the East He slightly view'd, and slightly overpass'd* (Milton). —*v.i.* **1.** to pass over or across something. **2.** to pass by or away: *I view her ... As a sweet sunset almost overpast* (William E. Henley). **3.** to remain unnoticed.
—*n.* a bridge over a road, railroad, canal, etc.: *Drive several miles down the turnpike, around a cloverleaf, under an overpass* (Atlantic).

o·ver·pay (ō′vər pā′), *v.t.*, **-paid, -pay·ing. 1.** to pay too much: *This high official ... Is grossly overpaid* (A.P. Herbert). **2.** to pay more than (an amount due).

o·ver·pay·ment (ō′vər pā′mənt), *n.* too great a payment.

o·ver·peer[1] (ō′vər pir′), *v.t.* **1.** to rise or tower above; overtop: *The cedar ... Whose top-branch overpeer'd Jove's spreading tree* (Shakespeare). **2.** to excel.

o·ver·peer[2] (ō′vər pir′), *v.t.* to peer over; look down over.

o·ver·peo·ple (ō′vər pē′pəl), *v.t.*, **-pled, -pling.** to fill with too many people; overpopulate.

o·ver·per·suade (ō′vər pər swād′), *v.t.*, **-suad·ed, -suad·ing.** to bring over by persuasion, especially against one's inclination or intention: *I should have left you before now, if Mrs. Jakeman had not overpersuaded me* (William Godwin).

o·ver·per·sua·sion (ō′vər pər swā′zhən), *n.* **1.** an overpersuading. **2.** a being overpersuaded.

o·ver·plaid (ō′vər plad′), *n.* **1.** a plaid pattern appearing over another pattern on woven fabrics. **2.** cloth with such a combination of patterns.

o·ver·plant (ō′vər plant′, -plänt′), *v.t., v.i.* to plant in excess or beyond what is required: *A drought in one area of the country encourages farmers in another area to overplant their crops in the hope of making a better profit.*

o·ver·play (ō′vər plā′), *v.t.* **1.** to play (a part, etc.) in an exaggerated manner; overact. **2.** to seek to obtain too much or too great an advantage from; exploit too vigorously: *The Southern leaders had overplayed their hand* (New Republic). **3.** to play better than; surpass; defeat. **4.** (in golf) to hit (the ball) past the green.

o·ver·please (ō′vər plēz′), *v.t.*, **-pleased, -pleas·ing.** to please too much: *He was not overpleased with your reply.*

o·ver·plus (ō′vər plus′), *n.* **1.** an amount left over; surplus. **2.** too great an amount; excess: *He was ruined, morally, by an overplus of the very same ingredient [purpose]* (Hawthorne).

o·ver·pop·u·late (ō′vər pop′yə lāt), *v.t.*, **-lat·ed, -lat·ing.** to overpeople.

o·ver·pop·u·la·tion (ō′vər pop′yə lā′shən), *n.* too great a population: *Overpopulation ... affects a great many other needs of mankind besides bread* (Julian Huxley).

o·ver·pow·er (ō′vər pou′ər), *v.t.* **1.** to overcome; master; overwhelm: *to overpower one's enemies. He overpowered his assailant. The thought of one man owning all those books overpowered him* (Winston Churchill). **2.** to be so much greater than, that nothing else is felt: *Sudden anger overpowered every other feeling.* **3.** to provide with an excess of power: *to overpower an automobile.* —**o′ver·pow′er·ing·ly,** *adv.* —**Syn. 1.** conquer, vanquish, defeat, overthrow.

o·ver·praise (*v.* ō′vər prāz′; *n.* ō′vər-), *v.*, **-praised, -prais·ing,** *n.* —*v.t.* to praise too much or too highly. —*n.* too much or too high praise.

o·ver·pre·scribe (ō′vər pri skrīb′), *v.i.*, **-scribed, -scrib·ing.** to prescribe drugs, especially narcotics, in excess of the patient's actual need.

o·ver·pres·sure (ō′vər presh′ər), *n.* **1.** excessive pressure; a pressing or being pressed too hard, especially with study or intellectual work: *The intellectual overpressure of children in the schools* (Popular Science Monthly). **2.** pressure over and above the normal atmospheric pressure, such as that generated by explosions: *Any target within this radius and vulnerable to the specified overpressure will be destroyed* (United States Air Force Report on the Ballistic Missile).

o·ver·price (ō′vər prīs′), *v.t.*, **-priced, -pric·ing.** to put or set at too high a price; price higher than the real value: *The phrase "do it yourself" is just an excuse to go out and buy an overpriced gadget to do it for you* (Maclean's).

o·ver·print (*v.* ō′vər print′; *n.* ō′vər print′), *v.t.* **1.** to print or stamp over with additional marks or matter, as in making revisions, in color work, etc. **2.** *Photography.* to print (a positive) darker than intended.
—*n.* **1.** any mark, design, or writing printed across a stamp to change its use, value, etc. **2.** a postage stamp printed with such a mark.

o·ver·prize (ō′vər prīz′), *v.t.*, **-prized, -priz·ing.** to prize or value too highly; overrate.

o·ver·pro·duce (ō′vər prə düs′, -dyüs′), *v.t., v.i.*, **-duced, -duc·ing. 1.** to produce more than is needed. **2.** to produce more than can be sold, or more than can be sold at a profit: *Pig iron has been overproduced ... in recent years* (London Daily News).

o·ver·pro·duc·tion (ō′vər prə duk′shən), *n.* **1.** the production of more than is needed: *Today the real farm problem is overstorage not overproduction* (Time). **2.** the production of more than can be sold at a profit.

o·ver·proof (ō′vər prüf′), *adj.* containing a greater proportion of alcohol than proof spirit contains; higher than 100 proof. In the United States, overproof liquor contains more than 50 per cent alcohol by volume.

o·ver·pro·por·tion (ō′vər prə pôr′shən, -pōr′-), *n.* excess of one thing in proportion to another. —*v.t.* to make or estimate in excess of the true or proper proportion.

o·ver·pro·por·tion·ate (ō′vər prə pôr′shə nit, -pōr′-), *adj.* in excess of the true or proper proportion; disproportionate.

o·ver·pro·por·tioned (ō′vər prə pôr′shənd, -pōr′-), *adj.* overproportionate.

o·ver·pro·tec·tive (ō′vər prə tek′tiv), *adj.* excessively protective. —**o′ver·pro·tec′tive·ness,** *n.*

o·ver·proud (ō′vər proud′), *adj.* too proud.

o·ver·ran (o′vər ran′), *v.* the past tense of **overrun.**

o·ver·rate (ō′vər rāt′), *v.t.*, **-rat·ed, -rat·ing. 1.** to rate or estimate too highly: *His fortune has been greatly overrated.* **2.** *British.* to assess too highly for purposes of taxing.
—**Syn. 1.** overvalue, overestimate.

o·ver·reach (ō′vər rēch′), *v.t.* **1.** to reach over or beyond. **2.** to get the better of by cunning: *to overreach a man in a bargain.* **3.** to get the better of by trickery or fraud; cheat. **4.** *Archaic.* **a.** to overtake. **b.** to overcome. —*v.i.* **1.** to reach too far. **2.** to cheat. **3.** (of a horse) to bring a hind foot against a forefoot and injure it in walking or running.

overreach oneself, a. to fail or miss by trying for too much: *A common error when working to windward in a race ... is for a boat to overreach herself* (Edward F. Qualtrough). **b.** to be too anxious; try for too much: *Rudeness is another matter, and any interviewer who overreaches himself should be nailed in his place* (Punch). —**o′ver·reach′er,** *n.*
—**Syn.** *v.t.* **2.** outwit. **3.** defraud, swindle, dupe.

o·ver·re·act (ō′vər ri akt′), *v.i.* to react with greater force, intensity or emotion than is necessary or expected.

o·ver·re·ac·tion (ō′vər ri ak′shən), *n.* a reaction of greater force, intensity, or emotion than is necessary or expected: *Americans so long ignored their Latin neighbors to the South that an overreaction probably was inevitable once they woke up to the trouble south of the border* (Atlantic).

o·ver·re·fine (ō′vər ri fīn′), *v.t., v.i.*, **-fined, -fin·ing.** to refine too much.

o·ver·re·fine·ment (ō′vər ri fīn′mənt), *n.* too much refinement: *If Twain suffered from a certain crudity of sensibility, James's defect was overrefinement* (Time).

o·ver·rep·re·sent (ō′vər rep′ri zent′), *v.t* to represent by more than a proper proportion: *... whether the state actually intended to overrepresent certain groups or merely let this happen by failure to reapportion while cities grew* (Wall Street Journal).

o·ver·ride (ō′vər rīd′), *v.t.*, **-rode, -rid·den, -rid·ing.** *n.* —*v.t.* **1.** to act in spite of: *to override advice or objections.* **2.** to prevail over; set aside: *The chairman's veto was overridden by the committee.* **3.** to ride over; trample on: *overriding another's happiness in pursuit of your own* (George W. Cable). **4.** to ride over or across (a region, place, etc.). **5.** to tire out (a horse) by riding; ride too much. **6.** to pass or extend over; overlap, as the pieces of a fractured bone, ice floes forced against each other, etc.
—*n.* a commission paid to a sales manager, in addition to his basic wage, based on the total sales in his territory.
[Old English *oferrīdan*] —**o′ver·ri′ding·ly,** *adv.*

o·ver·rid·er (ō′vər rī′dər), *n. British.* a protective metal guard on an automobile bumper: *The car has rubber cushioned overriders* (London Times).

o·ver·ripe (ō′vər rīp′), *adj.* too ripe; more than ripe: *The time is overripe for a new translation of the American theme—freedom through order* (Time). —**o′ver·ripe′ness,** *n.*

o·ver·roast (ō′vər rōst′), *v.t.* to roast too much.

o·ver·roof (ō′vər rüf′, -rúf′), *v.t.* to cover over with or as if with a roof.

o·ver·ruff (*v.* ō′vər ruf′; *n.* ō′vər ruf′), *v.t., v.i.* to trump with a card higher than that with which a previous player has already trumped: *If the diamonds do not break favourably there is a chance that West will overruff* (Manchester Guardian Weekly).
—*n.* an act or instance of overruffing: *It was East's overruff that set the contract.*

o·ver·rule (ō′vər rül′), *v.t.*, **-ruled, -rul·ing. 1.** to rule or decide against (a plea, argument, objection, etc.); set aside: *The president overruled my plan.* **2.** to prevail over; be stronger than: *I was overruled by the majority.* —**o′ver·rul′ing·ly,** *adv.* —**Syn. 1.** override, reject, annul, disallow.

o·ver·run (*v.* ō′vər run′; *n.* ō′vər run′), *v.*, **-ran, -run, -run·ning,** *n.* —*v.t.* **1.** to spread over and spoil or harm in some way: *Weeds had overrun the old garden. The conquering army overran the village.* **2.** to spread over: *Ivy overran the wall.* **3.** to run or go beyond; exceed: *The speaker overran the time set for him.* **4.** *Printing.* **a.** to carry over (words or lines of type) into another line or page to provide for addition or removal of other matter. **b.** to remake (columns, pages, etc.) by carrying over words, lines, etc. **5.** to run over; crush: *Like a gallant horse fall'n ... O'errun and trampled on* (Shakespeare). **6.** *Archaic.* to outrun; surpass: *Atalanta ... overran A white high-crested bull* (William Morris). —*v.i.* to run over; overflow; extend beyond the proper or desired limit.
—*n.* **1.** an overrunning. **2.** amount overrunning or carried over, as a balance or surplus; an excess: *The principal problem ... has been the overrun in the capital expenditure of the uranium mines* (Economist). —**o′ver·run′ner,** *n.*
—**Syn.** *v.t.* **1.** invade, ravage, infest.

o·ver·saw (ō′vər sô′), *v.* the past tense of **oversee.**

o·ver·score (*n.* ō′vər skôr′, -skōr′; *v.* ō′vər-skôr′, -skōr′), *n., v.*, **-scored, -scor·ing.** —*n.* one or more tricks over the contract in the game of contract bridge. —*v.i.* to make more tricks than bid for in contract bridge. —*v.t.* to make strokes or lines over: *to overscore a word or sentence.*

o·ver·sea (*adv.* ō′vər sē′; *adj.* ō′vər sē′), *adv., adj.* overseas: *Elections ... will be held on Sunday in 36 French departments, two departments oversea ...* (London Times).

o·ver·seam (*n.* ō′vər sēm′; *v.* ō′vər sēm′), *n.* a seam made by oversewing edges: *The overseam is finished with a thread holding the seam together, with the threads going over the edge of the seam* (Bernice G. Chambers). —*v.t., v.i.* to sew with an overseam.

o·ver·seas (*adv.* ō′vər sēz′; *adj.* ō′vər sēz′), *adv.* across the sea; beyond the sea; abroad: *While the presses are still rolling in the U.S., negatives of each page are on their way overseas* (Newsweek). —*adj.* **1.** done, used, or serving overseas: *overseas service, overseas equipment.* **2.** of or in countries across the sea; foreign: *overseas investments.*

overseas cap, *U.S. Military.* garrison cap; a small, soft hat without a visor.

o·ver·see (ō′vər sē′), *v.t.*, **-saw, -seen, -see·ing.** **1.** to look after and direct; superintend; manage: *to oversee a factory. None but a grandmother should ever oversee a child. Mothers are only fit for bearing* (Rudyard Kipling). **2.** to overlook, as from a higher position; survey. **3.** *Archaic.* to examine. [Old English *ofersēon*] —**Syn. 1.** supervise.

o·ver·se·er (ō′vər sē′ər), *n.* a person who oversees, the work of others.

overseer of the poor, an officer of parish administration in England.

o·ver·se·er·ship (ō′vər sē′ər ship), *n.* the position, rank, or authority of an overseer.

o·ver·sell (ō′vər sel′), *v.t.*, **-sold, -sell·ing.** **1.** to sell to excess: *At LaGuardia it turned out that the flight she was booked on was oversold* (New Yorker). **2. a.** to sell more of (a commodity, stock, etc.) than can be delivered: *We are badly oversold beyond our production capacity* (Wall Street Journal). **b.** to sell more of (a stock, etc.) than one can support if prices rise. **3.** *U.S. Informal.* to urge (a person) to buy something too aggressively or too long, often at the risk of losing a sale.

o·ver·set (*v.* ō′vər set′; *n.* ō′vər set′), *v.*, **-set, -set·ting,** *n.* —*v.t.* **1.** to upset; overturn: *The boat was overset by a sudden flurry from the north* (Jonathan Swift). **2.** to disturb mentally or physically: *So overset was she by the dramatic surprise of his challenging remark . . . that her manner changed in an instant* (Arnold Bennett). **3.** *Printing.* to set too much type for: *to overset a page by three lines.* —*v.i.* **1.** to become upset or overturned: *This raft . . . overset, and threw me . . . into the water* (Daniel Defoe). **2.** *Printing.* to set too much type.
—*n.* **1.** an overturn; upset. **2.** *Printing.* matter set in type in excess of available space.

o·ver·sew (ō′vər sō′, ō′vər sō′), *v.t.*, **-sewed, -sewed** or **-sewn, -sew·ing.** to sew over (an edge or edges of material) with many close stitches.

o·ver·sexed (ō′vər sekst′), *adj.* having an excessive interest in or capacity for sexual activity.

o·ver·shade (ō′vər shād′), *v.t.*, **-shad·ed, -shad·ing.** to overshadow.

o·ver·shad·ow (ō′vər shad′ō), *v.t.* **1.** to be more important than: *Mr. Gamaliel Ives . . . would have been the first citizen if that other first citizen had not . . . so completely overshadowed him* (Winston Churchill). **2.** to cast a shadow over; make dark or gloomy: *Those misfortunes which were soon to overshadow her* (James A. Froude). **3.** *Archaic.* to shelter; protect: *The power of the Highest shall overshadow thee* (Luke 1:35). —**Syn.** *v.t.* **1.** outrival, surpass. **2.** darken.

o·ver·shine (ō′vər shīn′), *v.t.*, **-shone, -shin·ing. 1.** to shine over or upon; illumine. **2.** to surpass; outshine.

o·ver·shoe (ō′vər shü′), *n.* a rubber shoe or a fabric shoe with a rubber sole worn over another shoe to keep the foot dry and warm; a galosh. [American English; Compare Dutch *overschoe,* German *Überschuh.*]

o·ver·shoot (ō′vər shüt′), *v.*, **-shot, -shoot·ing.** —*v.t.* **1.** to shoot over, higher than, or beyond: *to overshoot a target.* **2.** to go over, higher than, or beyond. **3.** to force or drive beyond the proper limit. —*v.i.* to go, run, or shoot too far.

overshoot oneself, to go too far in any course or matter; overreach oneself: *He was the first, in a manner, that put his hand to write Commentaries . . . and therefore no marvel, if he overshot himself many times* (Translators' Preface to the King James Version).
—*n.* the act of overshooting

o·ver·shot (*adj.* ō′vər shot′; *v.* ō′vər shot′), *adj.* **1.** having the upper jaw projecting beyond the lower: *The mouths of some collies are slightly overshot.* **2.** driven by water flowing over from above: *an overshot water wheel.* —*v.* the past tense and the past participle of **overshoot.**

Overshot Water Wheel (def. 2)

o·ver·side (*adv.* ō′vər sīd′; *adj., n.* ō′vər sīd′), *adv.* over the side, as of a ship. —*adj.* **1.** done over the side of a ship: *an overside delivery of coal.* **2.** unloading or unloaded over the side.
—*n.* the second or reverse side: *The folksongs, on the overside of the record, are authoritative* (Atlantic).

o·ver·sight (ō′vər sīt′), *n.* **1.** failure to notice or think of something: *By an oversight that cut me to the quick, my place had been forgotten* (Robert Louis Stevenson). **2.** watchful care: *While children are at school, they are under their teacher's oversight and direction.* —**Syn. 1.** overlooking, inadvertence, omission, slip. **2.** supervision, superintendence, charge.

o·ver·sim·pli·fi·ca·tion (ō′vər sim′plə fə kā′shən), *n.* excessive or undue simplification of something complicated, leading to distortion or misrepresentation.

o·ver·size (ō′vər sīz′), *adj.* too big. —*n.* **1.** a size larger than the proper or usual size. **2.** something larger than is necessary.

o·ver·sized (ō′vər sīzd′), *adj.* over the usual size; very large.

o·ver·skirt (ō′vər skėrt′), *n.* **1.** an outer skirt. **2.** a separate skirt over the upper part of the main skirt or slacks.

o·ver·slaugh (ō′vər slô′), *v.t.* **1.** *U.S.* to pass over in favor of another, as in a promotion or appointment to an office. **2.** *British.* **a.** to excuse from (military duty). **b.** to excuse (a soldier, etc.) from one duty in order to perform some other duty. **3.** to ignore. **4.** to hinder; obstruct.
—*n.* **1.** *British.* an excusing or exemption from duty. **2.** *U.S.* a sandbank or bar obstructing navigation in a river.
[< Dutch *overslaan.* Compare German *überschlagen.*]

o·ver·sleep (ō′vər slēp′), *v.*, **-slept, -sleep·ing.** —*v.i.* to sleep too long: *I overslept and missed the bus.* —*v.t.* to sleep beyond (a particular time)

o·ver·slip (ō′vər slip′), *v.t.*, **-slipped, -slip·ping. 1.** to slip past or beyond, especially in secret. **2.** to pass by; omit; miss.

o·ver·snow (ō′vər snō′), *adj.* **1.** done or taking place on or across snow-covered ground or ice: *The results of United States IGY oversnow traverses reveal the nature of a large portion of ice-covered Antarctica* (Science). **2.** of or for use in traveling over such ground or ice: *oversnow equipment.*

o·ver·sold (ō′vər sōld′), *v.* the past tense and past participle of **oversell.**

O·ver·soul or **o·ver·soul** (ō′vər sōl′), *n.* the Deity as the spiritual unity of all being in the philosophy of Emerson and other transcendentalists: *that Unity, that Oversoul, within which every man's particular being is contained and made one with all other* (Emerson).

o·ver·spe·cial·i·za·tion (ō′vər spesh′ə lə zā′shən), *n.* excessive or undue specialization: *Both must somehow steer a course between superficiality and overspecialization* (Scientific American).

o·ver·speed (*v.* ō′vər spēd′; *n.* ō′vər spēd′), *v.*, **-sped** or **-speed·ed, -speed·ing,** *n.* —*v.t.* to operate (a motor, vehicle, etc.) at excessive speeds. —*v.i.* to run at too high a speed: *Then an indicator showed that one of the six engines was overspeeding* (Time). —*n.* speed that is more than normal: *An audible speed warning system which conveys . . . the degree of overspeed* (New Scientist).

o·ver·spend (ō′vər spend′), *v.*, **-spent, -spend·ing.** —*v.i.* to spend more than one can afford. —*v.t.* **1.** to spend more than (a specified amount). **2.** to spend more than is necessary. **3.** *Archaic.* to wear out; exhaust.

o·ver·spill (*n., adj.* ō′vər spil′; *v.* ō′vər spil′), *n., v.*, **-spilled** or **spilt, -spill·ing,** *adj.* —*n.* *Especially British.* **1.** the act of spilling over: *There should be such an overspill of compressed air outwards . . .* (New Scientist). **2.** something which has spilled over; an excess: *Even to pass along the street outside is difficult because of the overspill of customers* (Punch). —*v.i.* to spill over; overflow: *Something, it seems, has overspilled, And trickled half the way to Hants* (Punch).
—*adj.* spilling over; overflowing: *overspill population.*

o·ver·spin (ō′vər spin′), *n.* **1.** a forward rolling motion given a ball in the direction of flight: *The ball . . . carried overspin which gave it the necessary impetus* (London Times). **2.** a ball with overspin: *Playing faultlessly, he got off smashes, drop shots, overspins . . . and cannonball serves* (Time).

o·ver·spray (*n.* ō′vər sprā′; *v.* ō′vər sprā′), *n.* **1.** a spray that does not adhere to a surface: *Overspray dries as it falls—turns to a harmless dust easily wiped or swept away* (Wall Street Journal). **2.** a spraying beyond the intended area. —*v.t.* to spray over, as one color or layer on another: *The design . . . is built up by overspraying the base coat with contrasting colors of the same material* (New Scientist).

o·ver·spread (ō′vər spred′), *v.*, **-spread, -spread·ing.** —*v.t.* to spread over: *A smile overspread his broad face. The hot lava overspread the mountain side.* —*v.i.* to be spread over. —**Syn.** *v.t.* cover.

o·ver·stand (ō′vər stand′), *v.t., v.i.*, **-stood, -stand·ing.** *Nautical.* to go beyond (a mark), especially in making way by tacking against the wind: *"Gretel" took one tack too many and overstood the mark by over a hundred yards* (London Times).

o·ver·state (ō′vər stāt′), *v.t.*, **-stat·ed, -stat·ing.** to state too strongly; exaggerate: *She was . . . anxious to overstate . . . her real social status* (H. G. Wells).

o·ver·state·ment (ō′vər stāt′mənt), *n.* too strong a statement; exaggeration: *There had been, said president Henry Ford II, "a certain amount of overstatement about the potential value of Ford stock"* (Newsweek).

o·ver·stay (ō′vər stā′), *v.t.* **1.** to stay beyond the time of: *to overstay one's welcome.* **2.** *Commerce, Informal.* to hold a stock, commodity, etc., beyond the most profitable time to sell.
—**Syn. 1.** outstay.

o·ver·step (ō′vər step′), *v.t., v.i.*, **-stepped, -step·ping.** to go beyond; exceed: *to overstep the limits of good manners.*

o·ver·stock (*v.* ō′vər stok′; *n.* ō′vər stok′), *v.t.* to supply with more than is needed. —*n.* too great a stock or supply.

o·ver·stor·age (ō′vər stôr′ij, -stōr′-), *n.* excessive storage; the storing of more goods, supplies, etc., than is needed.

o·ver·strain (*v.* ō′vər strān′; *n.* ō′vər-strān′), *v.t., v.i.* to strain too much. —*n.* excessive strain: *The economy is entering . . . a period of overstrain* (New York Times).

o·ver·stress (ō′vər stres′), *v.t.* to give excessive or undue stress to: *It is impossible to overstress the importance of this remarkable assemblage of soil organisms* (New Scientist).

o·ver·stretch (ō′vər strech′), *v.t.* to stretch beyond the proper length, amount, or degree: *The amount of capital which this country can provide without overstretching itself is something of a puzzle* (Manchester Guardian).

o·ver·strict (ō′vər strikt′), *adj.* too strict. —**o′ver·strict′ness,** *n.*

o·ver·stride (ō′vər strīd′), *v.t.*, **-strode, -strid·den, -strid·ing. 1.** to stride over or across. **2.** to stride or go beyond; surpass. **3.** to bestride.

o·ver·strung (ō′vər strung′), *adj.* too highly strung; too nervous or sensitive: *overstrung nerves.*

o·ver·stuff (ō′vər stuf′), *v.t.* **1.** to stuff too full. **2.** to make (upholstered furniture) soft and comfortable by thick padding: *an overstuffed chair.*

o·ver·sub·scribe (ō′vər səb skrīb′), *v.t., v.i.*, **-scribed, -scrib·ing.** to subscribe for in excess of what is available or required: *The concert series was oversubscribed and many people could not buy tickets.*

o·ver·sub·scrip·tion (ō′vər səb skrip′-shən), *n.* **1.** an oversubscribing. **2.** an amount subscribed for in excess.

o·ver·sub·tle (ō′vər sut′əl), *adj.* too subtle.

o·ver·sub·tle·ty (ō′vər sut′əl tē), *n., pl.* **-ties.** too great subtlety: *Resisting . . . the orthodox doctrine from oversubtlety, timidity, pride, restlessness, or other weakness of mind* (Cardinal Newman).

o·ver·sup·ply (*v.* ō′vər sə plī′; *n.* ō′vər sə-plī′), *v.*, **-plied, -ply·ing,** *n., pl.* **-plies.** —*v.t.* to supply in excess: *to oversupply buyers with oil, to oversupply oil.* —*n.* an excessive supply: *It is futile economically . . . to give governmental authorities the right . . . to ration the oversupply* (Newsweek).

o·ver·swarm (ō′vər swôrm′), *v.t.* **1.** to swarm over; spread over in swarms. **2.** to swarm in excess of.

o·ver·sway (ō′vər swā′), *v.t.* **1.** to sway over, or cause to incline to one side or fall over. **2.** *Obsolete.* to persuade, as to some course of action: *If he be so resolved, I can o'ersway him* (Shakespeare).

o·ver·sweep (ō′vər swēp′), *v.t.*, **-swept, -sweep·ing.** to sweep over.

o·ver·swell (ō′vər swel′), *v.*, **-swelled, -swelled** or **-swol·len, -swell·ing.** —*v.t.* to swell so as to pass over or beyond; overflow. —*v.i.* to swell beyond the bounds or limits.

o·vert (ō′vėrt, ō vėrt′), *adj.* **1.** not hidden; open; evident: *Hitting someone is an overt act. I know only his overt reasons for refusing; he may have others.* **2.** *Heraldry.* (of a bearing) having an open figure; outspread, as the wings of a bird in flight. [< Old French *overt* < Vulgar Latin *ōpertus,* alteration of Latin *apertus,* past participle of *aperīre* open] —**o′vert·ly,** *adv.* —**o′vert·ness,** *n.*
—**Syn. 1.** plain, manifest, apparent. —**Ant. 1.** covert, latent.

overt act, *Law.* an open or outward act from which criminal intent is inferred.

o·ver·take (ō′vər tāk′), *v.*, **-took, -tak·en, -tak·ing.** —*v.t.* **1.** to come up with; catch up to: *The blue car overtook ours.* **2.** to come upon suddenly or unexpectedly: *A storm overtook the children. Fearful was the fate that . . . overtook some of the members of that party* (Francis Parkman). **3.** *Scottish.* to get through when pressed for time, or within the time: *It's a job you could doubtless overtake with the other* (Robert Louis Stevenson). **4.** *Dialect.* to overcome the mind or senses of; intoxicate: *I don't appear to carry drink the way I used to . . . I get overtaken* (Robert Louis Stevenson). —*v.i. British.* to pass a motor vehicle: *At peak hour in English cities English drivers mount the pavement, overtake on the wrong side, and weave in and out like lunatic dancers in a ballet* (Listener). —**Syn.** *v.t.* **2.** surprise.

o·ver·task (ō′vər task′, -täsk′), *v.t.* to give too long or too hard tasks to: *In those days children's brains were not overtasked, as they are now* (Samuel Butler).

o·ver·tax (ō′vər taks′), *v.t.* **1.** to tax too heavily; overburden or oppress with taxes. **2.** to put too heavy a burden on; make too great demands on: *I had overtaxed my strength* (Mary W. Shelley). *Our credulity is overtaxed* (Lord Dunsany).

o·ver·tax·a·tion (ō′vər tak sā′shən), *n.* **1.** an overtaxing: *Overtaxation in the middle and higher brackets produces only 17% . . of total income tax revenues* (Wall Street Journal). **2.** a being overtaxed: . . . *attributed his death to a general prostration of the system from overtaxation of its powers* (New Yorker).

o·ver·teem (ō′vər tēm′), *v. i.* to teem, breed, or produce too much. —*v.t.* to wear out or exhaust with too much breeding or production.

o·ver-the-count·er (ō′vər ᴛʜə koun′tər), *adj.* **1.** not bought or sold through a regular exchange; not listed on a stock exchange: *over-the-counter securities.* **2.** that may be dispensed without a doctor's prescription: *over-the-counter drugs.*

o·ver-the-ho·ri·zon (ō′vər ᴛʜə hə rī′zən), *adj.* of or having to do with a system of communication using ultrahigh-frequency radio waves transmitted beyond the curvature of the earth by reflection off the troposphere.

o·ver-the-road (ō′vər ᴛʜə rōd′), *adj.* of or having to do with long-distance transportation by road or highway: *They include modest pick-up vehicles and huge over-the-road truck trailers* (Wall Street Journal).

o·ver-the-shoul·der (ō′vər ᴛʜə shōl′dər), *adj.* **1.** worn or carried over the shoulder: *an over-the-shoulder bag.* **2.** obtained by or as if by watching over someone's shoulder as he works: . . . *to learn what can be learned only by over-the-shoulder training* (United States Air Force Report on the Ballistic Missile).

over-the-shoulder bombing, loft-bombing.

o·ver·threw (ō′vər thrü′), *v.* the past tense of **overthrow.**

o·ver·throw (*v.* ō′vər thrō′; *n.* ō′vər thrō′), *v.*, **-threw, -thrown, -throw·ing,** *n.* —*v.t.* **1.** to take away the power of; defeat: *to overthrow a dictator. A fierce, bloody, and confused action succeeded, in which the patriots were completely overthrown* (John L. Motley). **2.** to put an end to; destroy; ruin: *to overthrow slavery. Much of the city was overthrown by the earthquake and a great fire. O, what a noble mind is here o'erthrown* (Shakespeare). **3.** to overturn; upset; knock down. **4.** to throw (a ball) past the intended place. —*n.* **1.** an overthrowing or being overthrown; defeat; upset: *The overthrow of the party in power left the country in a turmoil.* **2.** a ball thrown past the place for which it is intended: . . . *helped by indiscriminate throwing, which led to many overthrows* (London Times). —**o′ver·throw′er,** *n.*
—**Syn.** *v.t.* **1.** rout, conquer, vanquish, overcome. *-n.* **1.** destruction.

o·ver·thrown (ō′vər thrōn′), *v.* the past participle of **overthrow.**

o·ver·thrust (ō′vər thrust′), *n.* a geological fault in which the earth's surface has cracked and been forced upward by internal pressure, pushing rocks of an earlier formation horizontally over those of later formation. —*adj.* of or like an overthrust: *an overthrust fault.*

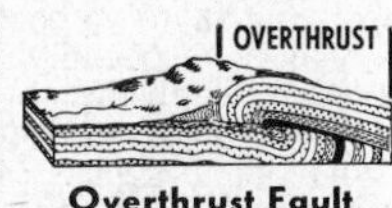

Overthrust Fault

o·ver·thwart (*adv., prep.* ō′vər thwôrt′; *adj.* ō′vər thwôrt′), *Dialect.* —*adv., prep.* across; athwart. —*adj.* **1.** lying across; situated across or opposite. **2.** contrary; perverse; cross.

o·ver·time (*n., adv., adj.* ō′vər tīm′; *v.* ō′vər tīm′), *n., adv., adj., v.*, **-timed, -tim·ing.** —*n.* **1.** time beyond the regular hours; extra time. **2.** wages for this period: *to pay overtime.* **3.** the time added to the normal length of an athletic contest to break a tie in the score: *The Gophers lagged for much of the first overtime, but tied it up . . . with 40 seconds remaining* (New York Times).
—*adv.* beyond the regular hours; during overtime: *to work overtime.*
—*adj.* **1.** of or for overtime: *overtime work, overtime pay.* **2.** beyond the allotted or permitted time: *overtime parking.*
—*v.t.* to give too much time to: *to overtime a camera exposure.*

o·ver·tire (ō′vər tīr′), *v.t.*, **-tired, -tir·ing.** to tire too much.

o·ver·tone (ō′vər tōn′), *n.* **1.** *Music.* a fainter and higher tone heard along with the main or fundamental tone; harmonic: *It is the overtones which give a musical tone its characteristic timbre or quality* (New York Times). **2.** the color of the light reflected from a painted or glazed surface or the like. **3.** a hint or suggestion of something felt, believed, etc.: *an overtone of anger.*

overtone series, *Music.* the entire range of overtones having frequencies that are integral multiples of the fundamental tone; harmonic series.

o·ver·took (ō′vər tůk′), *v.* the past tense of **overtake.**

o·ver·top (ō′vər top′), *v.t.*, **-topped, -top·ping.** **1.** to rise above; be higher than: *One . . . building, in course of construction, had already far overtopped the highest of its neighbours* (Arnold Bennett). **2.** to surpass; excel: *In them the man somehow overtops the author* (Lowell). *She overtops now her previous appearances on the screen* (London Times). —**Syn. 1.** surmount.

o·ver·trade (ō′vər trād′), *v.i.*, **-trad·ed, -trad·ing.** to purchase goods or lay in stock beyond the limit of one's capital or the requirements of the market.

o·ver·train (ō′vər trān′), *v.t., v.i.* to subject to or undergo so much athletic training that the condition is injured rather than improved; train to excess, resulting in going stale.

o·ver·trick (ō′vər trik′), *n.* (in card games) a trick more than the number bid for or needed for game: . . . *a contract made with two overtricks for a score of 1,750* (London Times).

o·ver·trump (ō′vər trump′), *v.i.* (in card games) to play a higher trump: *East did not overtrump on the third spade* (New York Times). —*v.t.* (in card games) to play a higher trump than: *to overtrump an opponent, to overtrump a trump.*

o·ver·ture (ō′vər chůr, -chər), *n., v.*, **-tured, -tur·ing.** —*n.* **1.** a proposal; offer: *The enemy is making overtures for peace.* **2.** a musical composition played by the orchestra as an introduction to an opera, oratorio, etc.: *Once the musicians were seated, Rapee . . . raised his baton and the band swung into its booming overture* (New Yorker). **3.** an introductory part, as of a poem. **4.** in Presbyterian churches: **a.** the sending of a proposal or question to the highest court or to the presbyteries. **b.** the proposal or question itself.
—*v.t.* **1.** to bring or put forward as an overture. **2.** to introduce with a musical overture.
[earlier, an opening, aperture < Old French *overture,* alteration of Latin *apertūra* opening. Compare OVERT. Doublet of APERTURE.]
—**Syn.** *n.* **1.** proposition. **2.** prelude.

o·ver·turn (*v.* ō′vər tėrn′; *n.* ō′vər tėrn′), *v.t.* **1.** to turn upside down; upset. **2.** to make fall down; overthrow; destroy the power of: *The rebels overturned the government.* —*v.i.* to fall down; turn over; upset: *The boat overturned.*
—*n.* **1.** an overturning. **2.** the turnover (of merchandise, etc.). —**o′ver·turn′er,** *n.*
—**Syn.** *v.t.* **1.** invert. -*v.i.* capsize. See **upset.**

o·ver-un·der (ō′vər un′dər), *n.* over-and-under.

o·ver·use (*v.* ō′vər yüz′; *n.* ō′vər yüs′), *v.*, **-used, -us·ing,** *n.* —*v.t.* **1.** to use too much. **2.** to use too hard or too often. —*n.* too much or too hard use: *The easy overuse of "pretty" and "little" exacerbated his uneasy mind* (James Thurber).

o·ver·val·u·a·tion (ō′vər val′yů ā′shən), *n.* too high valuation; overestimate.

o·ver·val·ue (ō′vər val′yü), *v.t.*, **-ued, -u·ing.** to value too highly; put too high a value on.

o·ver·view (ō′vər vyü′), *n.* a broad survey; inspection; examination: *An overview of the published studies of this year reveals some gaps and some significant trends* (Stone and Taylor).

o·ver·volt·age (ō′vər vōl′tij), *n.* the difference between the theoretical voltage and the actual required voltage of an electrode in an electrolytic process.

o·ver·warm (ō′vər wôrm′), *adj.* too warm or solicitous: *Her voice was as overwarm as if she were coaxing a shy child* (New Yorker).

o·ver·watch (ō′vər woch′, -wôch′), *v.t.* **1.** to watch over. **2.** to make weary by watching: *Morning was well advanced, when Tressilian, fatigued and overwatched, came down to the hall* (Scott).

o·ver·wa·ter (ō′vər wôt′ər, -wot′-), *adj.* above or across water: *overwater travel, an overwater flight.* —*v.t.* to water too much: . . . *it would be easy to overwater it, and this would rot the roots* (Sunset).

o·ver·wear (ō′vər wãr′), *v.t.*, **-wore, -worn, -wear·ing.** **1.** to wear out; exhaust. **2** to outwear; outgrow.

o·ver·wea·ry (ō′vər wir′ē), *adj., v.*, **-ried, -ry·ing.** —*adj.* very weary; tired out: *The little girl, overweary, had . . . fallen asleep* (Harriet Beecher Stowe). —*v.t.* to weary to excess.

o·ver·weath·er (ō′vər weᴛʜ′ər), *adj.* of or at altitudes high enough to avoid unfavorable weather conditions: *an overweather flight.*

o·ver·ween (ō′vər wēn′), *v.i.* to have too high an opinion of oneself; be conceited or arrogant; presume.

o·ver·ween·ing (ō′vər wē′ning), *adj.* **1.** thinking too much of oneself; self-confident; conceited; presumptuous: *overweening confidence in his own powers* (William H. Prescott). **2.** excessive; exaggerated: *an overweening opinion, an overweening desire.* —*n.* excessive esteem; overestimation. [present participle of Middle English *overween* < *over-* + *ween* expect] —**o′ver·ween′ing·ly,** *adv.* —**o′ver·ween′ing·ness,** *n.*

o·ver·weigh (ō′vər wā′), *v.t.* **1.** to be greater than weight, importance, etc.; outweigh: *My duty is imperative, and must overweigh my private feelings* (Nicholas P.S. Wiseman). **2.** to weigh down; oppress.

o·ver·weight (*adj., n.* ō′vər wāt′; *v.* ō′vər wāt′), *adj.* having too much weight: *a boy overweight for his age.*
—*n.* **1.** extra weight: *The butcher gave us overweight on this roast.* **2.** too much weight: *an overweight of people on a floor, an overweight of care on the mind.*
—*v.t.* **1.** to overburden: *a small child overweighted by heavy schoolbooks.* **2.** to weigh too heavily; give too much attention to; overstress: *Our efforts . . . may leave the impression that we are overweighting the Arab side* (Wall Street Journal).

o·ver·went (ō′vər went′), *v.* the past tense of **overgo.**

o·ver·whelm (ō′vər hwelm′), *v.t.* **1.** to overcome completely; crush: *to overwhelm with grief.* **2.** to cover completely, as a flood would: *A great wave overwhelmed the*

boat. **3.** to heap, treat, or address with an excessive amount of anything: *He ... overwhelmed her with a profusion of compliment* (Tobias Smollett). [< *over-* + *whelm* roll, submerge]
—**Syn. 2.** submerge.

o·ver·whelm·ing (ō′vər hwel′ming), *adj.* too many, too great, or too much to be resisted; overpowering: *an overwhelming majority of votes.* —**o′ver·whelm′ing·ly,** *adv.*

o·ver·wind (ō′vər wīnd′), *v.t.,* **-wound, -wind·ing.** to wind beyond the proper limit; wind too far: *to overwind a watch.*

o·ver·win·ter (ō′vər win′tər), *v.i.* to stay through the winter enduring cold and snow: *Dahlia tubers can overwinter, right in the ground ...* (Sunset).

o·ver·wise (ō′vər wīz′), *adj.* too wise. —**o′ver·wise′ly,** *adv.*

o·ver·word (ō′vər wėrd′), *n. Scottish.* a word or phrase repeated, such as the refrain of a song.

o·ver·wore (ō′vər wôr′, -wōr′), *v.* the past tense of **overwear.**

o·ver·work (*n.* ō′vər wėrk′; *v.* ō′vər wėrk′), *n., v.,* **-worked** or **-wrought, -work·ing.** —*n.* **1.** too much or too hard work. **2.** extra work.
—*v.t.* **1.** to cause to work too hard or too long: *I know how busy you are; you mustn't overwork yourself* (G. K. Chesterton). **2.** *Informal.* to use to excess: *to overwork a pose of childlike innocence.* **3.** to fill too full with work. **4.** to work too much upon (a book, speech, etc.); elaborate too much. **5.** to stir up or excite too much. **6.** to figure or decorate the surface of.
—*v.i.* to work too hard or too much.

o·ver·world (ō′vər wėrld′), *n.* **1.** the respectable section of society: *They lapse in time into what sociologists call a subculture, an underworld of mores subtly opposed to those of the overworld* (Maclean's). **2.** a section of society seeking privileges because of wealth or position: *As if the underworld weren't enough of a problem, Dist. Atty. McKesson has come up with something new to worry about, the overworld* (Tuscaloosa News). **3.** a world above or higher than this; heaven: *They [primitive men] believed there was an overworld where God resided in space, and an underworld where all departed spirits were gathered together* (Edmund Hamilton Sears).

o·ver·worn (ō′vər wôrn′, -wōrn′), *v.* the past participle of **overwear.**

o·ver·wound (ō′vər wound′), *v.* the past tense and past participle of **overwind:** *The clock broke when it was overwound.*

o·ver·wrap (ō′vər rap′), *n.* a material, usually transparent such as cellophane, often used as a second, outside wrapping for cigarettes, bread, and other items that have to be kept fresh.

o·ver·write (ō′vər rīt′), *v.t., v.i.,* **-wrote, -writ·ten, -writ·ing.** to write too much (about a subject); write ornately or pretentiously: *Why should books about the Arab world be ... grossly overwritten?* (Manchester Guardian Weekly).

o·ver·wrought (ō′vər rôt′), *adj.* **1.** wearied; exhausted: *overwrought nerves.* **2.** worked up to too high a pitch; too excited. **3.** decorated all over: *an overwrought platter. Of Gothic structure was the Northern side, O'erwrought with ornaments of barbarous pride* (Alexander Pope). **4.** too elaborate.
—*v.* a past tense and a past participle of **overwork.**
—**Syn.** *adj.* **4.** overdone.

o·vi·bos (ō′və bos), *n.* a musk ox. [< New Latin *ovibos* < Latin *ovis* sheep + *bōs* ox]

O·vid·i·an (ō vid′ē ən), *adj.* of or having to do with the Roman poet Ovid, 43 B.C.-A.D. 17? or his poetry: *... a series of Ovidian allusions* (London Times).

o·vi·duct (ō′və dukt), *n.* the tube through which the ovum or egg passes from the ovary. In human beings the oviduct connects with the uterus and is called the Fallopian tube. [< New Latin *oviductus* < Latin *ōvum* egg + *ductus,* past participle of *dūcere* to lead]

o·vif·er·ous (ō vif′ər əs), *adj.* producing or bearing eggs. [< Latin *ōvum* egg + English *-ferous*]

o·vi·form (ō′və fôrm), *adj.* egg-shaped. [< Latin *ōvum* egg + English *-form*]

o·vine (ō′vīn, -vin), *adj.* of, having to do with, or like sheep. [< Latin *ovīnus* < *ovis* sheep]

o·vip·a·ra (ō vip′ər ə), *n.pl.* egg-laying animals as a formerly recognized group. [< New Latin *Ovipara*]

o·vi·par·i·ty (ō′və par′ə tē), *n.* condition of being oviparous; the laying of eggs to be hatched outside the body.

o·vip·a·rous (ō vip′ər əs), *adj.* producing eggs that hatch after leaving the body: *Birds, and most reptiles, fishes, and insects are oviparous.* [< Latin *ōviparus* (with English *-ous*) < *ōvum* egg + *parere* bring forth]

o·vi·pos·it (ō′və poz′it), *v.i.* to deposit or lay eggs, especially by means of an ovipositor, as an insect. [< Latin *ōvum* egg + *positus,* past participle of *pōnere* to place, put]

o·vi·po·si·tion (ō′və pə zish′ən), *n.* the laying of eggs by means of an ovipositor.

o·vi·pos·i·tor (ō′və poz′ə tər), *n.* an organ or set of organs at the end of the abdomen in certain female insects, by which eggs are deposited. [< Latin *ōvum* egg + *positor* builder; (literally) one who places < *pōnere* to place]

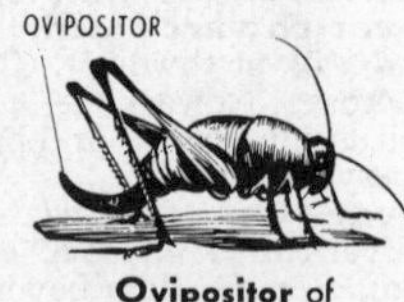

Ovipositor of a field cricket

o·vi·sac (ō′və sak), *n.* **1.** a sac, cell, or capsule containing an ovum or ova. **2.** a Graafian follicle.

o·vism (ō′viz əm), *n. Biology.* the old doctrine that the egg contains all the organs of the future animal.

o·vis po·li (ō′vis pō′lī, -lē), *n., pl.* **-lis.** Marco Polo sheep. [< New Latin *Ovis poli* the genus and species name; (literally) sheep of Polo (in reference to Marco Polo, about 1254-1324, the Venetian traveler, who described it in his book)]

o·vist (ō′vist), *n.* an adherent of the doctrine of ovism.

o·vo·gen·e·sis (ō′və jen′ə sis), *n.* oogenesis.

o·vo·ge·net·ic (ō′və jə net′ik), *adj.* oogenetic.

o·void (ō′void), *adj.* **1.** oval with one end more pointed than the other; egg-shaped. **2.** of this form with the broader end at the base, as a pear or avocado. —*n.* an egg-shaped object.

o·voi·dal (ō voi′dəl), *adj.* ovoid.

o·vo·lo (ō′və lō), *n., pl.* **-li** (-lē). *Architecture.* a convex molding whose cross section is approximately a quarter of a circle or an ellipse. [< Italian *ovolo* (diminutive) < *ovo* < Latin *ōvum* egg. Compare OVULE.]

o·vo·tes·tis (ō′və tes′tis), *n., pl.* **-tes** (-tēz). a combined male and female reproductive organ, as in the snail. [< New Latin *ovotestis* < Latin *ōvum* egg + *testis* testis]

o·vo·vi·tel·lin (ō′vō vī tel′in, -vi-), *n.* a protein contained in the yolk of eggs. [< Latin *ōvum* egg + *vitellin*]

o·vo·vi·vip·a·rous (ō′vō vī vip′ər əs), *adj.* producing eggs that are hatched within the body of the parent, so that young are born alive but without placental attachment, as certain reptiles and fishes and many invertebrate animals. [< Latin *ōvum* egg + *viviparous*] —**o′vo·vi·vip′a·rous·ly,** *adv.* —**o′vo·vi·vip′a·rous·ness,** *n.*

o·vu·lar (ō′vyə lər), *adj.* of an ovule; being an ovule.

o·vu·lar·y (ō′vyə ler ē), *adj.* ovular.

o·vu·late (ō′vyə lāt), *v.i.,* **-lat·ed, -lat·ing. 1.** to produce ova, oocytes, or ovules. **2.** to discharge ova or oocytes from the ovary. [< New Latin *ovulum* ovule + English *-ate*[1]]

o·vu·la·tion (ō′vyə lā′shən), *n.* **1.** the formation or production of ova or ovules: *In 1936 F.H.A. Marshall and E.B. Verney found that strong electrical stimulation of the nervous system of the rabbit caused ovulation* (Science News). **2.** the discharge of an ovum from the ovary.

o·vu·la·to·ry (ō′vyə lə tôr′ē, -tōr′-), *adj.* of or having to do with ovulation: *A ... gynecologist recently announced a new concept of ovulatory timing* (Wall Street Journal).

o·vule (ō′vyül), *n.* **1.** *Biology.* a little ovum, especially when immature or unfertilized; the ovum before its release from the ovarian follicle. **2.** *Botany.* **a.** the part of a plant that develops into a seed. In higher plants, the ovule contains the female germ cell or egg, which after fertilization develops into an embryo. **b.** a young seed. See picture under **ovary.** [< New Latin *ovulum* (diminutive) < Latin *ōvum* egg]

o·vu·lif·er·ous (ō′vyə lif′ər əs), *adj.* producing ovules.

o·vum (ō′vəm), *n., pl.* **o·va. 1.** *Biology.* a female gamete; egg. **2.** *Architecture.* an egg-shaped ornament. [< Latin *ōvum* egg]

owe (ō), *v.,* **owed, ow·ing.** —*v.t.* **1.** to have to pay; be in debt for: *I owe the grocer $10. He owes not any man* (Longfellow). **2.** to be obliged or indebted for: *Never in the field of human conflict was so much owed by so many to so few* (Sir Winston Churchill). *She owes her blue eyes to her mother.* **3.** to have or cherish toward another: *to owe a grudge.* **4.** *Obsolete.* to own; possess. —*v.i.* to be in debt: *He is always owing for something.* [Old English *āgan* to own, have an obligation to]

O·wen·ism (ō′ə niz əm), *n.* the theory or system of Robert Owen, 1771-1858, a British social reformer who advocated the reorganization of society into a system of communistic cooperation, which he tried to put into practice in several experimental communities: *Owenism remained the creed of a substantial body of followers, who turned back to the attempt to establish villages of cooperation* (G.D.H. Cole).

O·wen·ite (ō′ə nīt), *n.* a follower of Robert Owen; a believer in Owenism: *A community of Owenites, early Utopian socialists, set up a short-lived colony ... in 1826* (New York Times).

OWI (no periods), Office of War Information.

ow·ing (ō′ing), *adj.* **1.** that owes: *a man owing money.* **2.** due; owed: *to pay what is owing.* **3.** *Archaic.* indebted; beholden: *I am greatly owing to your Lordship for your last favour* (Samuel Pepys).
owing to, on account of; because of; due to; as a result of: *Owing to a change of administrations, he lost his job. I could not see many yards ahead owing to the bushes* (W.H. Hudson).
—**Syn. 2.** outstanding.

owl (oul), *n.* **1.** a bird with a big head, a short hooked beak, and large eyes which look forward from a rounded face, and very soft feathers that enable them to fly noiselessly. Most owls hunt at night and live on mice, small birds, and reptiles. **2.** any of various domestic pigeons that look like owls. **3.** a person who stays up late at night. **4.** a person who looks solemn and wise, as an owl is supposed to be. [Old English *ūle*] —**owl′like′,** *adj.*

Great Horned Owl (def. 1) (18 to 25 in. long)

owl·et (ou′lit), *n.* **1.** a young owl. **2.** a small owl.

owlet moth, a noctuid or phalaenid moth.

owl-eyed (oul′īd′), *adj.* **1.** having eyes like those of an owl; seeing best in the dark. **2.** looking somewhat strange or staring, and having a wide-eyed appearance: *The round, owl-eyed, oddball in horn-rimmed glasses* (Time).

Spiderwort Owlet Moth

owl·ish (ou′lish), *adj.* **1.** like an owl; like an owl's: *round owlish eyes* (Francis Parkman). **2.** trying to look wise: *an owlish air of wisdom.* —**owl′ish·ly,** *adv.* —**owl′ish·ness,** *n.*

owl·light (oul′līt′), *n.* twilight; dusk.

owl's-clo·ver (oulz′klō′vər), *n.* any of a group of herbs of the figwort family, growing especially in California.

owl train, *U.S.* a railroad train that makes its trip late at night.

owl·wise[1] (oul′wīz′), *adj.* as wise as an owl.

owl·wise[2] (oul′wīz′), *adv.* in the manner of an owl.

own (ōn), *adj.* **1.** of oneself or itself; belonging to oneself or itself: *This is my own book. She makes her own dresses.* **2.** in closest relationship: *Own brothers have the same parents.*
—*n.* the one or ones belonging to oneself or itself: *The cup ... from which our Lord Drank at the last sad supper with his own* (Tennyson).
come into one's own, a. to get what belongs to one: *His inheritance was held in trust; not until he was twenty-one would he come into his own.* **b.** to get the success or credit that one deserves: *It was when the primitive vigor of his carving united with the human sensuality of his life drawing, at the end of the*

twenties, that he [Henry Moore] came into his own as a sculptor (Donald Hall).
hold one's own, a. to maintain one's position against opposition; stand one's ground; make no concessions: *Frightful superstitions still hold their own over two-thirds of the inhabited globe* (John Ruskin). **b.** to maintain one's strength or state of health; lose no ground: *The doctor assured us that grandfather was holding his own, despite the new complications.*
of one's own, belonging to oneself: *You have a good sword and a good mother-wit of your own* (George J. Whyte-Melville).
on one's own, *Informal.* on one's own account, responsibility, resources, etc.: *knocking about the world on his own* (Joseph Conrad).
—*v.t.* **1.** to have; possess: *I own many books. Enjoy the land but own it not* (Henry David Thoreau). **2.** to acknowledge; admit; confess: *He owned his guilt. I own you are right.* **3.** to acknowledge as one's own: *His father will not own him.* —*v.i.* to confess: *She owns to many faults. I own to being afraid.*
own up, to confess fully: *The boy owned up to his part in the Hallowe'en prank.*
[Old English *āgen*]
—**Syn.** *v.t.* **1.** hold. See **have. 2.** concede, grant.

own·er (ō′nər), *n.* a person who owns: *The owner of the dog bought him a collar.* —**Syn.** proprietor.

own·er·less (ō′nər lis), *adj.* having no owner: *an ownerless dog.*

own·er-oc·cu·pi·er (ō′nər ok′yə pī′ər), *n. British.* a homeowner: *Nobody could tell whether 200,000 houses for sale each year would be the right number . . . but he was certain that at least three-fifths of the population would want to be owner-occupiers* (London Times).

own·er·ship (ō′nər ship), *n.* the state of being an owner; the possessing (of something); right of possession: *He claimed ownership of a boat he found drifting down the river.*

owse (ous), *n., pl.* **ow·sen, ows·sen** (ou′sən, -zən). *Scottish.* ox.

ox (oks), *n., pl.* **ox·en. 1.** the full-grown male of cattle, that has been castrated and is used as a draft animal or for beef. **2.** any cattlelike member of a group of mammals with horns and cloven hoofs, including domestic cattle, buffaloes, and bison; a bovine animal. [Old English *oxa,* singular of *oxan*]

ox·a·late (ok′sə lāt), *n.* a salt or ester of oxalic acid. [< *oxal*(ic) + *-ate*[2]]

ox·al·ic (ok sal′ik), *adj.* **1.** of or derived from oxalis. **2.** of oxalic acid.

oxalic acid, a colorless, crystalline, poisonous organic acid that occurs in wood sorrel, the leaves of rhubarb, and many other plants, and is produced artificially. It is used for bleaching, removing stains, making dyes, as a reagent, etc. *Formula:* $C_2H_2O_4 \cdot 2H_2O$ [< French *acide oxalique* < Latin *oxalis;* see OXALIS]

ox·al·i·da·ceous (ok sal′ə dā′shəs), *adj.* belonging to the family of plants typified by the wood sorrel. [< New Latin *Oxalidaceae* the family name (< *Oxalis* the typical genus) < Latin; see OXALIS + *-aceous*]

ox·a·lis (ok′sə lis), *n.* any of a group of plants with acid juice, usually having leaves composed of three heart-shaped leaflets, and delicate white, yellow, or pink flowers; wood sorrel. [< Latin *oxalis* sorrel[2] < Greek *oxalís* < *oxýs* sour, sharp]

ox·a·zin (ok′sə zin), *n.* oxazine.

ox·a·zine (ok′sə zēn, -zin), *n.* one of a series of isomeric chemical compounds consisting of one oxygen, one nitrogen, and four carbon atoms arranged in a ring. *Formula:* C_4H_5ON [< *ox*(ygen) + *azine*]

ox·blood (oks′blud′), *n.* a deep-red color.

ox·bow (oks′bō′), *n.* **1.** *U.S.* a U-shaped piece of wood placed under and around the neck of an ox, with the upper ends inserted in the bar of the yoke. **2.** a U-shaped bend in a river. **3.** the land contained within it.

oxbow lake, a small lake or pond formed by a river that has straightened its meandering bed, so that a former oxbow becomes separated from the river.

Ox·bridge (oks′brij′), *adj. British.* of or having to do with Oxford and Cambridge Universities, together contrasted with redbrick universities. —*n.* a student or graduate of Oxford or Cambridge.

ox·cart (oks′kärt′), *n.* a cart drawn by an ox or oxen.

ox·en (ok′sən), *n.* the plural of **ox.**

ox·er (ok′sər), *n. British Slang.* **1.** a fence to keep oxen from straying. **2.** (in foxhunting) a fence consisting of a wide ditch bordered by a strong hedge, beyond which is a railing: *The fence . . . was an oxer, about seven feet high, and impervious to a bird* (G.J. Whyte-Melville).

ox·eye (oks′ī′), *n.* **1.** the common American daisy; oxeye daisy. **2.** any of several plants like it. **3.** any of various shore birds, such as the semipalmated sandpiper and the black-bellied plover of North America.

ox-eyed (oks′īd′), *adj.* having large, full eyes like those of an ox.

oxeye daisy, the common American daisy, having flower heads with a yellow disk and white rays; oxeye.

ox·fly (oks′flī′), *n., pl.* **-flies.** a fly troublesome to cattle.

ox·ford or **Ox·ford** (oks′fərd), *n.* **1.** *U.S.* a kind of low shoe, laced over the instep, usually with three or more eyelets. **2.** a very dark gray. **3.** a cotton cloth in a basket weave, used for men's shirts or women's blouses. **4.** *British Slang.* five shillings. [< *Oxford,* a city in England]

Oxford bags, a style of trousers very wide at the ankles, worn especially in the 1920's.

Oxford corners, *Printing.* ruled borderlines around the print of a book, etc., that cross and extend beyond the corners.

Oxford Down, any of an English breed of hornless sheep.

Oxford gray or **oxford gray,** a very dark gray.

Oxford Group or **Oxford Group movement,** Buchmanism; Moral Rearmament Group.

Ox·for·di·an (oks fôr′dē ən), *n.* a supporter of the theory that the Earl of Oxford was the author of Shakespeare's plays: *What can the Oxfordians say about the fact that the Earl of Oxford died in 1604 and the author of the plays was writing until 1613?* (New Yorker).

Oxford movement, 1. a movement in the Church of England favoring High-Church principles, which originated at Oxford University about 1833. **2.** Buchmanism; Oxford Group.

Oxford shoe, a kind of low shoe; oxford.

Oxford theory, the theory that the Earl of Oxford was the author of Shakespeare's plays.

Oxford tie, a kind of low shoe; oxford.

ox·heart (oks′härt′), *n.* a large, heart-shaped cherry.

ox·hide (oks′hīd′), *n.* **1.** the hide of an ox. **2.** leather made from it: *It was an exhilarating feeling to be hauled up on a length of oxhide tied around the waist* (London Times).

ox·id (ok′sid), *n.* oxide.

ox·i·dant (ok′sə dənt), *n.* an oxidizer, such as liquid oxygen, used for burning the fuel of missiles and rockets.

ox·i·dase (ok′sə dās, -dāz), *n.* any of a group of enzymes that cause or promote oxidation.

ox·i·date (ok′sə dāt), *v.t., v.i.,* **-dat·ed, -dat·ing.** oxidize.

ox·i·da·tion (ok′sə dā′shən), *n.* **1.** an oxidizing; the combining of oxygen with another element to form one or more new substances: *Burning is one kind of oxidation.* **2.** a being oxidized. Also, **oxydation.**

oxidation enzyme, an oxidase: *Oxidation enzymes are required in all living matter to help cells burn oxygen* (Wall Street Journal).

ox·i·da·tive (ok′sə dā′tiv), *adj.* having the property of oxidizing: *The metabolic significance of porphyrins in cellular oxidative processes is well known to biochemists* (B. Nickerson).

ox·ide (ok′sīd, -sid), *n.* a compound of oxygen with another element or radical. [< earlier French *oxide* < *ox(ygène)* oxygen + *(ac)ide* acid]

ox·i·dim·e·try (ok′sə dim′ə trē), *n. Chemistry.* an analytical method using oxidizing agents for titrations.

ox·i·dise (ok′sə dīz), *v.,* **-dised, -dis·ing.** *Especially British.* oxidize.

ox·i·diz·a·ble (ok′sə dī′zə bəl), *adj.* that can be oxidized: *The iron atom is in its "reduced," or oxidizable form* (Martin D. Kamen).

ox·i·di·za·tion (ok′sə də zā′shən), *n.* oxidation.

ox·i·dize (ok′sə dīz), *v.,* **-dized, -diz·ing.** —*v.t.* **1.** to combine with oxygen; make into an oxide. When a substance burns or rusts, it is oxidized. *The normal liver of the rat utilized acetic acid to synthesize fatty acids and oxidized (burned) it to carbon dioxide and water* (New York Times). **2.** to cover (a metal) with a coating of oxide; rust. **3.** to cause to lose hydrogen by the action of oxygen; dehydrogenate. **4.** to change (the atoms of an element) to a higher positive valence, as by loss of electrons. —*v.i.* to become oxidized. Also, *especially British,* **oxidise.**

ox·i·diz·er (ok′sə dī′zər), *n.* **1.** something that oxidizes; oxidizing agent. **2.** *Aerospace.* a substance that supports the combustion of a fuel.

ox·im (ok′sim), *n.* oxime.

ox·ime (ok′sēm, -sim), *n.* any of a group of chemical compounds having the general formula RC:NOH, where R is an alkyl group or hydrogen. Oximes are formed by treating aldehydes or ketones with hydroxylamine.

ox·im·e·ter (ok sim′ə tər), *n.* a device for measuring the oxygen saturation of hemoglobin, operating on the basis of photoelectricity: *Oxygen tension in the blood flowing through the skin can be measured . . . by means of an oximeter* (New Scientist).

ox·like (oks′līk′), *adj.* like an ox; resembling that of an ox.

ox·lip (oks′lip′), *n.* **1.** a primrose that has clusters of pale-yellow flowers. **2.** a natural hybrid between the cowslip and other varieties of primrose; polyanthus. [Old English *oxanslyppe* < *oxan* ox's + *slyppe* slime. Compare COWSLIP.]

Oxon., 1. of Oxford (Latin, *Oxoniensis*). **2.** Oxford (Latin, *Oxonia*). **3.** Oxfordshire.

Ox·o·ni·an (ok sō′nē ən), *adj.* of or having to do with Oxford University or Oxford, a city in southern England. —*n.* **1.** a member or graduate of Oxford University. **2.** a native or inhabitant of Oxford. [< Medieval Latin *Oxonia* Oxford + English *-an*]

ox·o·ni·um compound (ok sō′nē əm), a chemical compound formed when an organic compound containing a basic atom of oxygen reacts with a strong acid. [< *ox*(ygen) + (amm)*onium*]

ox·peck·er (oks′pek′ər), *n.* a small African starling that feeds on external parasites that infest the hides of cattle and other animals; tickbird.

ox·tail (oks′tāl′), *n.* the skinned tail of a steer, ox, or cow, used in making soup.

ox·ter (oks′tər), *Scottish.* —*n.* the armpit: *Wi' his sleeves up tae his oxters* (Ian Maclaren). —*v.t.* to support or lift by the arm or armpit. [apparently Old English *ōxta.* Related to AXLE.]

ox·tongue (oks′tung′), *n.* **1.** the tongue of an ox. **2.** a composite plant with yellow flowers and prickly leaves, growing on clayey soil. **3.** any of various plants with rough tongue-shaped leaves, such as the bugloss.

ox·y·a·cet·y·lene (ok′sē ə set′ə lēn, -lin), *adj.* of, having to do with, or using a mixture of oxygen and acetylene.

oxyacetylene torch, a tool producing a very hot flame for welding or cutting metals. It burns a mixture of oxygen and acetylene.

ox·y·ac·id (ok′sē as′id), *n.* **1.** an acid that contains oxygen, such as sulfuric acid; oxygen acid. **2.** any organic acid containing both a carboxyl and a hydroxyl group.

ox·y·cal·ci·um (ok′sē kal′sē əm), *adj.* of, having to do with, or using oxygen and calcium.

oxycalcium light, limelight.

ox·y·chlo·ride (ok′sē klôr′īd, -klōr′-; -id), *n.* **1.** a combination of oxygen and chlorine with another element. **2.** a compound of a metallic chloride with the oxide of the same metal.

ox·y·da·tion (ok′sə dā′shən), *n.* oxidation.

ox·y·gen (ok′sə jən), *n.* a gas without color or odor that forms about one fifth of the air. Animals and plants cannot live, and fire will not burn, without oxygen. Oxygen is a chemical element present in a combined form in many substances and is used as an oxidizer for rocket fuels. *Symbol:* O; *at.wt.:* (C^{12}) 15.9994 or (O^{16}) 16; *at.no.:* 8; *valence:* 2. [< French *oxygène,* intended as "acidifying (principle)" < Greek *oxýs* sharp + *-genēs* born, ultimately < *gignesthai* be born]

oxygen acid, an oxyacid.

ox·y·gen·ate (ok′sə jə nāt), *v.t.,* **-at·ed, -at·ing. 1.** to treat or combine with oxygen. **2.** to oxidize.

ox·y·gen·a·tion (ok′sə jə nā′shən), *n.* **1.** the act or process of oxygenating: *He assists* *in work on physiochemical problems associated with the oxygenation of the blood* (Science News). **2.** oxidation.

ox·y·gen·a·tor (ok′sə jə nā′tər), *n.* a device for oxygenating blood as it passes through the heart-lung machine that maintains circulation during open-heart operations: *The all-glass dispersion oxygenator introduces the oxygen as fine bubbles freed from extra gas by a siliconed surface* (Science News Letter).

oxygen debt, depletion of oxygen stored in the tissues and red blood cells due to a burst of exercise. Oxygen is restored after the exercise is completed. *Although the other tissues can accumulate an oxygen debt, it is essential for the brain to maintain its oxygen supply* (New Scientist).

ox·y·gen·ic (ok′sə jen′ik), *adj.* having to do with, consisting of, or containing oxygen; oxygenous.

ox·y·gen·ise (ok′sə jə nīz), *v.t.*, **-ised, -is·ing.** *Especially British.* oxygenize.

ox·y·gen·iz·a·ble (ok′sə jə nī′zə bəl), *adj.* that can be oxygenized.

ox·y·gen·ize (ok′sə jə nīz), *v.t.*, **-ized, -iz·ing.** to treat with oxygen; combine with oxygen; oxygenate.

ox·y·gen·ize·ment (ok′sə jə nīz′mənt), *n.* oxidation.

ox·y·gen·iz·er (ok′sə jə nī′zər), *n.* thing that oxidates or converts into an oxide.

oxygen mask, a device worn over the nose and mouth by aviators and climbers at very high altitudes, through which supplementary oxygen is supplied from an attached container.

ox·yg·e·nous (ok sij′ə nəs), *adj.* consisting of or containing oxygen; oxygenic.

oxygen tent, a small tent or tentlike device that can be placed over a patient and filled with oxygen, used in treating pneumonia and other diseases.

ox·y·he·mo·glo·bin or **ox·y·hae·mo·glo·bin** (ok′si hē′mə glō′bin, -hem′ə-), *n.* the combination of hemoglobin and oxygen in arterial blood.

ox·y·hy·dro·gen (ok′si hī′drə jən), *adj.* of, having to do with, or using a mixture of oxygen and hydrogen: *By 1875 . . . limelight —created by directing an oxyhydrogen flame against a block of lime enclosed in a lamp with a powerful lens—had made its appearance* (New Yorker).

oxyhydrogen torch, a tool with a very hot flame for welding or cutting through metals. It uses a mixture of oxygen and hydrogen.

ox·y·mel (ok′si mel), *n.* a mixture of acetic acid or vinegar and honey, formerly used in medicines: *The patient took a draught made with oxymel of squills* (Tobias Smollett). [< Latin *oxymeli* < Greek *oxýmeli* < *oxýs* sharp, acid + *méli* honey]

ox·y·mo·ron (ok′si môr′on, -mōr′-), *n.*, *pl.* **-mo·ra** (-môr′ə, -mōr′-). a figure of speech in which words of opposite meaning or suggestion are used together. Examples: *a wise fool, cruel kindness, to make haste slowly. Perhaps it is an oxymoron . . . to say that the President was both resolute and restrained* (Richard B. Russell). [< Greek *oxýmōron*, noun use of neuter of *oxýmōros*, adjective, pointedly foolish < *oxýs* sharp + *mōrós* stupid]

ox·y·salt (ok′si sôlt′), *n.* a salt containing oxygen in place of other electronegative radicals, BiOCl.

ox·y·sul·fid or **ox·y·sul·phid** (ok′si sul′fid), *n.* oxysulfide.

ox·y·sul·fide or **ox·y·sul·phide** (ok′si-sul′fīd, -fid), *n.* a sulfide compound in which one part of the sulfur is replaced by oxygen.

ox·y·tet·ra·cy·cline (ox′si tet′rə sī′klin), *n.* an antibiotic obtained from a soil microorganism, which is effective against a wide range of disease organisms, including bacteria, viruses, and protozoa; Terramycin: *Injecting livestock . . . with . . . oxytetracycline permits the high temperature aging of meat, without spoilage* (Science News Letter). *Formula:* $C_{22}H_{24}N_2O_9.2H_2O$

ox·y·to·cia (ok′si tō′shə), *n.* rapid childbirth. [< New Latin *oxytocia* < Greek *oxytokiā* < *oxýs* sharp + *tókos* birth < *tiktein* give birth to]

ox·y·to·cic (ok′si tō′sik, -tos′ik), *adj.* hastening childbirth, especially by stimulating the contraction of the uterine muscles. —*n.* an oxytocic drug or medicine.

ox·y·to·cin (ok′si tō′sin, -tos′in), *n.* a hormone of the pituitary gland effecting contraction of the uterus in childbirth and stimulating lactation.

ox·y·tone (ok′si tōn), *adj.* having an acute accent on the last syllable. —*n.* an oxytone word. [< Greek *oxýtonos* < *oxýs* sharp + *tónos* accent, tone]

oy or **oye** (oi), *n. Scottish.* a grandchild. Also, **oe.** [< Gaelic *ogha.* Compare Irish *úa.*]

o·yer (ō′yər, oi′ər), *n. Law.* **1.** a hearing; a criminal trial (abbreviation of *oyer and terminer*). **2. a.** the hearing in court of some document demanded by one party, which the other is compelled to produce (make profert of). **b.** such a demand. [< Anglo-French *oyer*, noun, variant of Old French *oïr*, to hear < Latin *audīre*]

oyer and ter·mi·ner (tėr′mə nər), *Law.* a hearing and determining; a trial. It is used in England of a writ directing the holding of a court or commission of assize to try indictable offenses, and in the United States of various higher criminal courts. [< *oyer*, and Old French *terminer* terminate < Latin *termināre*]

o·yez or **o·yes** (ō′yes, -yez), *interj.*, *n.* "hear! attend!" a cry uttered, usually three times, by a public or court crier to command silence and attention before a proclamation, etc., is made. [< Anglo-French *oyez* hear ye, imperative of *oyer* to hear; see OYER]

oys·ter (ois′tər), *n.* **1.** a kind of mollusk much used as food, having a rough, irregular shell in two halves, and living in shallow water along seacoasts. Some kinds yield pearls. **2.** an oyster-shaped bit of dark meat found on either side of the back of a fowl. **3.** *Informal.* a very reserved or uncommunicative person: *Secret, and self-contained, and solitary as an oyster* (Dickens). **4.** something from which to take or derive advantage: *The world's mine oyster, Which I with sword will open* (Shakespeare). [< Old French *oistre* < Latin *ostrea* < Greek *óstreon*, related to *osteón* bone]

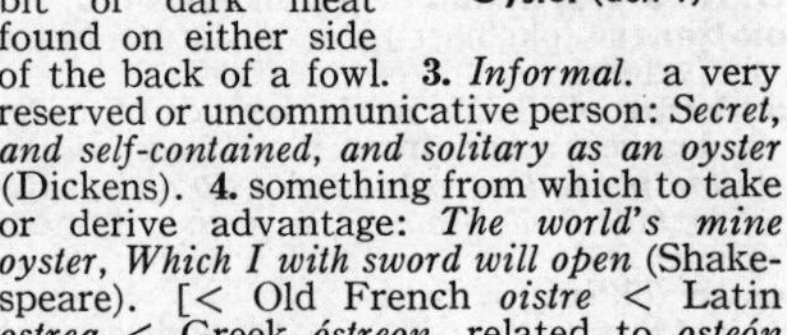

Oyster (def. 1)

oys·ter·age (ois′tər ij), *n.* an oyster bed.

oyster bed, a place where oysters breed or are cultivated.

oyster catcher, any of various wading birds of world-wide distribution that are black and white, have red, wedge-shaped bills for opening shellfish, and grow to about 20 inches long.

oyster crab, a small crab that lives harmlessly within the shell of a live oyster. Related kinds live similarly in mussels and scallops.

oyster cracker, a small, round or hexagonal, salted cracker eaten with oysters, soups, etc.

oyster farm, a place where oysters are raised for the market.

oyster gray, a slightly dark, silvery color.

oys·ter·ing (oi′stər ing), *adj.* having to do with taking or cultivating oysters: *. . . near the oystering grounds of Louisiana . . .* (Atlantic). —*n.* the act or business of taking oysters: *Oystering was his livelihood.*

oyster leaf, the sea lungwort.

oys·ter·man (ois′tər mən), *n.*, *pl.* **-men. 1.** a man who gathers, sells, or raises oysters. **2.** a boat or ship used to gather oysters.

oyster plant, 1. the salsify, a vegetable like a parsnip with a root that tastes somewhat like an oyster. **2.** the sea lungwort.

oyster rake, a rake with a long handle and long, curved teeth, used for gathering oysters from oyster beds.

oyster rock, an oyster bed, often containing masses of old shells.

oys·ter·root (ois′tər rüt′, -rụ̇t′), *n.* the salsify.

oyster tongs, an implement for dredging up oysters.

oyster white, white with a greenish-gray or yellowish-gray tinge.

oz., 1. ounce. **2.** ounces.

oz. ap., ounce (apothecaries' weight).

oz. av., ounce (avoirdupois weight).

o·zo·ce·rite (ō zō′kə rīt, -sə-; ō′zō sir′īt), *n.* a mineral, a waxlike fossil resin of brownish-yellow color and aromatic odor, consisting of a mixture of natural hydrocarbons, and sometimes occurring in sandstones; mineral wax. It is used in making candles, for insulating electrical conductors, etc. [< German *Ozokerit* < Greek *ózein* to smell (because it is aromatic) + *kērós* beeswax + German *-it* -ite[1]]

o·zo·ke·rite (ō zō′kə rīt), *n.* ozocerite.

o·zone (ō′zōn), *n.* **1.** a form of oxygen produced by electricity and present in the air, especially after a thunderstorm. Ozone has a peculiar odor like that of weak chlorine, and is a strong oxidizing agent, used for bleaching, for sterilizing water, etc. *Formula:* O_3 **2.** *Informal.* pure air that is refreshing. [< French *ozone* < Greek *ózein* to smell (because of its odor)]

ozone layer, the ozonosphere.

o·zon·er (ō′zō nər), *n. U.S. Slang.* a drive-in motion-picture theater: *In the movie trade, drive-ins or ozoners . . . are "passion pits with pix"* (New York Times).

o·zon·ic (ō zon′ik, -zō′nik), *adj.* of, having to do with, or containing ozone.

ozonic ether, a solution of hydrogen peroxide in ether.

o·zo·nid (ō′zə nid), *n.* ozonide.

o·zo·nide (ō′zə nīd), *n.* any of a group of organic compounds formed when ozone is added to an unsaturated hydrocarbon.

o·zo·nif·er·ous (ō′zə nif′ər əs), *adj.* containing ozone. [< *ozon*(e) + *-ferous*]

o·zo·nise (ō′zə nīz), *v.t.*, **-nised, -nis·ing.** *Especially British.* ozonize.

o·zo·ni·za·tion (ō′zə nə zā′shən), *n.* **1.** the act or process of ozonizing. **2.** the state or condition of being ozonized.

o·zo·nize (ō′zə nīz), *v.t.*, **-nized, -niz·ing. 1.** to charge or treat with ozone. **2.** to convert (oxygen) into ozone. [< *ozon*(e) + *-ize*]

o·zo·niz·er (ō′zə nī′zər), *n.* an apparatus for producing ozone.

o·zo·nol·y·sis (ō′zə nol′ə sis), *n.* **1.** the process of treating a hydrocarbon with ozone followed by hydrolysis. **2.** decomposition following treatment with ozone. [< *ozon*(e) + Greek *lýsis* a loosening]

o·zo·nom·e·ter (ō′zə nom′ə tər), *n.* a device for determining the amount of ozone in air, etc. [< *ozone* + *-meter*]

o·zo·nom·e·try (ō′zə nom′ə trē), *n.* the art of measuring the amount of ozone in the atmosphere.

o·zon·o·sphere (ō zon′ə sfir), *n.* a layer of concentrated ozone in the outer stratosphere, located about 20 to 40 miles above the earth's surface. It shields the earth from excessive ultraviolet radiation.

o·zo·nous (ō′zə nəs), *adj.* of, like, or containing ozone. [< *ozon*(e) + *-ous*]

o·zos·to·mi·a (ō′zos tō′mē ə), *n.* an offensive breath. [< New Latin *ozostomia* < Greek *ózein* to smell + *stóma* mouth]

ozs., ounces.

oz. t., ounce (troy weight).

P

Roman
100's A.D.

Greek
600's B.C.

Phoenician
1000's B.C.

Semitic
1500's B.C.

Egyptian
3000's B.C.

Pp Pp *Pp* *Pp*

P or **p** (pē), *n., pl.* **P's** or **Ps, p's** or **ps. 1.** the 16th letter of the English alphabet. **2.** any sound represented by this letter. **3.** the sixteenth, or more usually the fifteenth of a series (either *I* or *J* being omitted). **4.** *Genetics.* (as a symbol) parental generation (used with a subscript number, as P_1 or the parents, P_2, the grandparents, etc.).

mind one's p's and q's, to be careful or particular about what one says or does: *Even the cleverest must mind their p's and q's with such a lady* (Arnold Bennett).

p-, *prefix.* para-[1].

p (no period), *Music.* **1.** soft. **2.** softly (Italian, *piano*).

p., an abbreviation for the following:
1. after (Latin, *post*).
2. father (Latin, *pater;* French, *père*).
3. first (Latin, *primus*).
4. for (Latin, *pro*).
5. in part (Latin, *partim*).
6. page.
7. part.
8. participle.
9. *Meteorology.* passing (showers).
10. past.
11. *Chess.* pawn.
12. penny.
13. per.
14. perch (unit of measure).
15. perishable.
16. peseta.
17. peso.
18. pint.
19. pipe.
[illegible] (in baseball) pitcher.
[illegible] *Music.* poco.
22. [illegible] (unit of measure).
23. population.
24. president.
25. pressure.
26. priest.
27. *Music.* **a.** soft. **b.** softly (Italian, *piano*).

P (no period), **1.** phosphorus (chemical element). **2.** *Physics.* **a.** parity. **b.** pressure.

P., an abbreviation for the following:
1. Father (Latin, *Pater;* French, *Père*).
2. Pastor.
3. *Chess.* pawn.
4. Pope.
5. post.
6. President.
7. Priest.
8. Prince.
9. Progressive.
10. Province.

pa[1] (pä, pô), *n. Informal.* papa; father.

pa[2] (pä), *n. Maori.* a village.

p.a., 1. participial adjective. **2.** per annum. **3.** public address.

Pa (no period), protactinium (chemical element).

Pa., Pennsylvania.

P/A (no periods), power of attorney.

P.A., an abbreviation for the following:
1. Passenger Agent.
2. Post Adjutant.
3. power of attorney.
4. Press Agent.
5. Press Association.
6. public address.
7. Purchasing Agent.

paa·uw (pä'ü, pou), *n.* any of several South African species of bustards. [< Dutch *paauw* peacock]

PABA (no periods), para-aminobenzoic acid.

pa·bouche (pä büsh'), *n.* babouche.

pab·u·lum (pab'yə ləm), *n.* **1.** food; anything taken in by an animal or plant to maintain life and growth. **2.** fuel. **3.** intellectual or spiritual nourishment; food for the mind: *The idea that it is "progressive" to hold that "democracy" consists of giving the same educational pabulum to everybody . . . is weakening* (Wall Street Journal). [< Latin *pābulum* fodder, related to *pāscere* to feed] —**Syn. 1.** aliment, nutriment.

Pac., Pacific.

PAC (no periods) or **P.A.C.,** Political Action Committee (of the Congress of Industrial Organizations).

pa·ca (pä'kə, pak'ə), *n.* any of a group of large rodents of Central and South America, related to the agouti; spotted cavy. [< Spanish and Portuguese *paca* < Tupi *páca,* or perhaps < Quechua *paco* reddish]

Paca
(2 ft. long)

pa·ca·ble (pā'kə bəl), *adj.* that can be pacified; placable: *He was the most easy-going and pacable of men.* [< Latin *pācāre* pacify (< *pāx, pācis* peace) + English *-able*]

Pac·chi·o·ni·an (pak'ē ō'nē ən), *adj.* of, having to do with, or described by Antonio Pacchioni, an Italian anatomist.

Pacchionian bodies or **glands,** small villi, not glandular in character, found in clusters on the membranes enveloping the brain. Cerebrospinal fluid passes through them into the veins.

pace[1] (pās), *n., v.,* **paced, pac·ing.** —*n.* **1.** rate of movement; speed: *a fast pace in walking, the deliberate pace of a Haydn symphony.* **2.** a step: *Behind her Death following pace for pace* (Milton). **3.** the length of a step in walking, sometimes used as a rough unit of measure; about 2½ feet: *There were perhaps ten paces between me and the bear.* **4.** way of stepping; gait: *The walk, trot, and gallop are some of the paces of a horse.* **5.** a particular gait of some horses in which the feet on the same side are lifted and put down together.

keep pace (with), a. to go as fast as: [*He*] *walked so fast that they could hardly keep pace with him* (Frances Burney). **b.** to keep up (with): *A lot of things are changing, and the . . . Bank must surely try to keep pace* (Punch).

put one through his paces, to try one out; find out what one can do: *The captain ordered the Nautilus put through her paces* (Time).

set the pace, a. to fix or regulate the speed: *He set a rapid pace for solving the algebra problem.* **b.** to be an example or model for others to follow: *Right up with the pace set by this is Trigère's ensemble of heavy wool in black, chestnut, and white* (New Yorker).

—*v.t.* **1.** to set the pace for: *A motor boat will pace the boys training for the rowing match.* **2.** to walk over with regular steps: *to pace the floor. Then, pale and worn, he paced his deck* (Joaquin Miller). **3.** to measure by pacing or in paces: *We paced off the distance and found it to be 69 paces.* **4.** to train (a horse) to a certain step, especially to lift and put down the feet on the same side together. —*v.i.* **1.** to walk with regular steps: *The tiger paced back and forth in his cage.* **2.** (of a horse) to move at a pace. [< Old French *pas* < Latin *passus, -ūs* a step < *pandere* to stretch. Doublet of PASS[1], noun.]

pa·ce[2] (pā'sē), *prep., adv. Latin.* with the indulgence of; by the leave of; with regrets for differing from: *But it is not* (*pace the 618 scientists who wrote to Mr. Macmillan*) *radioactivity that really matters in stopping the tests* (Economist).

paced (pāst), *adj.* **1.** having a pace: *slow-paced.* **2.** traversed or measured by pacing. **3.** (in racing) having the speed set by a pacemaker or run at a set speed.

pace egg (pās), *British Dialect.* Easter egg. [*pace* < earlier *pase* < Middle French *pasche* < Old French *pasche, pasque;* see PASCH]

pace·mak·er (pās'mā'kər), *n.* **1.** a person, animal, or thing that sets the pace: *These enzyme proteins in turn act as catalyzers or pacemakers of the chemical reactions that take place in the cell* (Scientific American). **2.** a node of specialized tissue near the top of the wall of the right auricle of the heart where the impulse that results in the heartbeat begins: *Normally the ventricles . . . beat regularly in rhythmic response to the heart's pacemaker* (Paul Dudley White). **3.** an electrical device applied to the wall of the heart when the natural pacemaker does not function, to maintain or restore the rhythm of the heartbeat: *The solution to this condition would be to supply the heart with an artificial pacemaker* (New Scientist).

pace·mak·ing (pās'mā'king), *n.* the act of setting the pace. —*adj.* that sets the pace: *Within the span of my own memory there was considerable evidence for the view that the pacemaking impulses were generated by nerve cells in the right atrium and transmitted by nerve fibers to the heart-muscle cells* (Scientific American).

pac·er (pā'sər), *n.* **1.** a person or thing that paces. **2.** a horse that lifts and puts down the feet on the same side together, whether natural or taught: *Adios Boy and Adios Harry, regarded as the best pacers in harness racing . . . will meet in a special one-mile match* (New York Times). **3.** a pacemaker.

pace·set·ter (pās'set'ər), *n.* a person, animal, or thing that sets the pace; leader; pacemaker: *The auto industry is regarded as a pacesetter* (Wall Street Journal).

pace·set·ting (pās'set'ing), *adj.* that sets the pace; that serves as an example for others to follow; leading: *Outlook for labor peace will of course hinge largely on what happens in the two pacesetting industries, automobiles and steel* (Newsweek).

pa·cha (pə shä', pash'ə, pä'shə), *n.* pasha.

pa·cha·lic (pə shä'lik), *n.* pashalik.

pa·chan·ga (pə chang'gə), *n.* a fast, hopping dance of Cuban origin, with intricate step patterns that blend elements of the merengue and the samba. [< Cuban Spanish *pachanga*]

pa·chin·ko (pä'chin kō'), *n.* a pinball game played in Japan. [< Japanese *pachinko*]

pa·chi·si (pə chē'zē), *n.* **1.** a game somewhat resembling backgammon, originating in India, played on a cross-shaped board. **2.** parcheesi. [< Hindustani *pachīsī* (literally), adjective < *pachīs* twenty-five (the highest throw on the dice)]

pach·ou·li (pach'ù lē, pə chü'-), *n.* patchouli.

pa·chu·co (pə chü'kō), *n. U.S.* a zoot-suited young tough of Mexico or of Mexican descent. [< Mexican Spanish *pachuco*]

pach·y·derm (pak'ə dėrm), *n.* **1.** any of certain thick-skinned mammals with hoofs, as the elephant, hippopotamus, and rhinoceros: *He* [*the Elephant's Child*] *was a Tidy Pachyderm* (Rudyard Kipling). **2.** a person who is not sensitive to criticism or ridicule; thick-skinned person. [< French *pachyderme* < Greek *pachýdermos* thick-skinned < *pachýs* thick + *dérma* skin]

pach·y·der·ma·tous (pak'ə dėr'mə təs), *adj.* **1.** belonging or having to do with pachyderms. **2.** insensitive to criticism, rebuff, etc.; thick-skinned: *A distinct impression of pachydermatous personality emerges, but Mr. Shebbeare refrains from any undue anthropomorphism* (Observer).

pach·y·der·mous (pak'ə dėr'məs), *adj.* pachydermatous. —**pach'y·der'mous·ly,** *adv.*

pach·y·san·dra (pak'ə san'drə), *n.* any of a group of trailing, usually evergreen plants of the box family, commonly planted for ground cover. [< New Latin *Pachysandra* the genus name < Greek *pachýs* thick + New Latin *-andrus* man, male]

Pacif., Pacific.

pac·i·fi·a·ble (pas'ə fī'ə bəl), *adj.* that can be pacified or appeased.

pa·cif·ic (pə sif'ik), *adj.* **1.** tending to make peace; making peace: *The policy of the Prince was pacific and temporizing* (John L. Motley). **2.** loving peace; not warlike: *a pacific nature.* **3.** peaceful; calm; quiet: *pacific weather. Mr. Britling . . . marked the steady conversion of the old pacific countryside into an armed camp* (H.G. Wells). [< Middle French *pacifique,* learned borrowing from Latin *pācificus* < *pāx, pācis* peace + *facere* make] —**Syn. 1.** peaceable, conciliatory. **3.** placid, tranquil. —**Ant. 2.** quarrelsome, belligerent.

Pa·cif·ic (pə sif'ik), *adj.* **1.** of the Pacific Ocean: *Pacific fish.* **2.** on or near the Pacific Ocean: *a Pacific storm.*

pa·cif·i·cal (pə sif'ə kəl), *adj.* pacific.

pa·cif·i·cal·ly (pə sif'ə klē), *adv.* peacefully.

pa·cif·i·cate (pə sif′ə kāt), *v.t.*, **-cat·ed, -cat·ing.** to bring into a state of peace; pacify: *The remaining dominions . . . will doubtless by degrees be conquered and pacificated* (Thomas Carlyle). [< Latin *pācificāre* (with English *-ate*[1]) < *pācificus* pacific]

pac·i·fi·ca·tion (pas′ə fə kā′shən), *n.* **1.** the act of pacifying: *French forces are engaged, so the official thesis goes, in an effort at "pacification"* (Wall Street Journal). **2.** the state of being pacified: *"I . . . offer my retirement if that will be a guarantee of pacification," Peron declared* (Wall Street Journal). **3.** a compact or treaty establishing peace: *The pacification had just been signed at Ghent* (John L. Motley).

pa·cif·i·ca·tor (pə sif′ə kā′tər), *n.* a person who pacifies; peacemaker.

pa·cif·i·ca·to·ry (pə sif′ə kə tôr′ē, -tōr′-), *adj.* tending to make peace; conciliatory.

pa·cif·i·cism (pə sif′ə siz əm), *n.* pacifism.

pa·cif·i·cist (pə sif′ə sist), *n., adj.* pacifist.

pa·cif·i·co (pə sif′ə kō; *Spanish* pä sē′fē-kō), *n., pl.* **-cos** (-kōz; *Spanish* -kōs). (in Spanish America, the Philippines, etc.) a peaceable person; a non-belligerent. [< Spanish *pacífico*, learned borrowing from Latin *pācificus* pacific]

Pacific Standard Time, the standard time in the western parts of the continental United States and Canada, a belt centered on the 120th meridian. Pacific Standard Time is eight hours behind Greenwich time. *Abbr.:* P.S.T.

Pacific time, Pacific Standard Time. *Abbr.:* P.t.

pac·i·fi·er (pas′ə fī′ər), *n.* **1.** a person or thing that pacifies. **2.** a rubber nipple or ring given to a baby to suck: *But certainly a pacifier should not be offered to a child who shows no need for it* (Sidonie M. Gruenberg).

pac·i·fism (pas′ə fiz əm), *n.* the principle or policy of establishing and maintaining universal peace; settlement of all differences between nations by peaceful means; opposition to war: *Liberalism, the social gospel, pacifism, and prohibition are only a few of the causes for which it has fought at one time or another, and it has fought for each one with wit, conviction, and strong journalistic punch* (Newsweek). [< *pacif*(ic) + *-ism;* probably patterned on French *pacifisme*]

pac·i·fist (pas′ə fist), *n.* a person who is opposed to war and favors settling all disputes between nations by peaceful means: *This is to confuse pacifism with appeasement. The pacifist is definitely not a passivist* (Bulletin of Atomic Scientists). *—adj.* belonging to or like pacifists: *He has often publicly praised the pacifist provision of the new Japanese Constitution, renouncing war and the use of armed force* (Wall Street Journal).

pac·i·fis·tic (pas′ə fis′tik), *adj.* of pacifism or pacifists: *Opinion polls showed the people very pacifistic, and this attitude was reflected in the smallness of Britain's army and air force, in comparison with the much superior numbers of Germany and Italy* (Ogburn and Nimkoff). —**pac′i·fis′ti·cal·ly,** *adv.*

pac·i·fy (pas′ə fī), *v.t.*, **-fied, -fy·ing. 1.** to make calm; quiet down: *Can't you pacify that screaming baby? We tried to pacify the man we ran into.* **2.** to bring peace to: *Soldiers were sent to pacify the country.* [< Middle French *pacifier*, Old French, make peace, learned borrowing from Latin *pācificāre* < *pācificus* pacific] —**Syn. 1.** See **appease.**

Pa·cin·i·an (pə sin′ē ən), *adj.* having to do with, discovered, or described by Filippo Pacini, an Italian anatomist.

Pacinian body or **corpuscle,** one of the numerous oval, seedlike bodies attached to nerve endings, especially in the subcutaneous tissue of the hand and foot: *There is evidence that in the body the pressure-sensitive nerve endings known as Pacinian corpuscles work in much the same way* (Scientific American).

pack[1] (pak), *n.* **1.** a bundle of things wrapped up or tied together for carrying: *a pack of cigarettes, letters, etc. The soldier carried a pack on his back.* **2.** the amount packed: *This year's pack of fish is larger than last year's.* **3.** a set; lot; a number together: *a pack of thieves, a pack of nonsense. Would you rather that I should write you a pack of lies?* (Thomas Jefferson). *It's a wicked, thieving, lying, scheming lot you are — the pack of you* (John M. Synge). **4. a.** a number of animals hunting or living together: *Wolves often hunt in packs; lions usually hunt alone.* **b.** a number of dogs kept together for hunting. **5.** a complete set of playing cards, usually 52; deck. **6.** a large area of floating pieces of ice pushed together; ice pack: *A ship forced its way through the pack.* **7. a.** something put on the body or skin as a treatment. A cloth soaked in hot or cold water is often used as a pack. **b.** the cloth, sheet, blanket, etc., so used. **c.** a small, absorbent cotton pad that is applied to open wounds or body cavities in order to check the flow of blood; tampon: *Tapes were regarded by many surgeons . . . as a help towards finding packs and ensuring their removal after operation* (London Times). **8.** several groups of Cub Scouts or Brownies joined together and led by an adult: *A feature of the evening was the presentation of group flags to the 61st Boy Scout Troop and the 61st Cub Pack* (Ottawa Citizen). *The 111th Brownie pack, Leaside, voted to send them a cheque for $20* (Toronto Daily Star). **9.** *U.S.* the practice of raising the price of an automobile to offer a larger discount: *Price packs and overallowances fret auto finance men* (Wall Street Journal). **10.** *British.* **a.** the players on a Rugby team who are in the front line; all of the forwards together: *Both sides played excellent rugby, with two well-matched packs concentrating on getting the ball back* (London Times). **b.** the scrummage. **11.** *Archaic.* a worthless person: *a naughty pack.* **12.** *Obsolete.* a plot; conspiracy: *There's a knot, a ging, a pack, a conspiracy against me* (Shakespeare).

—*v.t.* **1.** to put together in a bundle, box, bale, etc.: *Pack your books in this box. We pack onions in bags.* **2.** to fill with things; put one's things into: *Pack your trunk. Pack the car for a trip.* **3.** to press or crowd closely together: *The air became stifling, for now the front of the gallery was packed* (Winston Churchill). **4.** to press together; make firm: *The heavy trucks packed the snow on the highway.* **5.** to fill (a space) with all that it will hold: *to pack a small theater with a large audience.* **6.** to put into a container to be sold or stored: *Meat, fish, and vegetables are often packed in cans.* **7.** to make tight with something that water, steam, air, etc., cannot leak through: *The plumber packed the joint in the two sections of the pipe with string and a special compound.* **8.** to load (an animal) with a pack; burden. **9.** *Informal.* to carry: *Be careful! He packs a gun.* **10.** *U.S.* to raise (the price of an automobile) to offer a larger discount: *Some dealers pack their prices from $50 to $500, depending on the strength of competition.* **11.** *U.S.* to carry in a pack: *to pack supplies up a mountain.* **12.** to form (hounds) into a pack. **13. a.** to put (cards) together in a pack. **b.** *Archaic.* to shuffle (playing cards) so as to cheat. **14.** to drive (floating ice) into a pack. **15.** to cover, surround, or protect with closely applied materials; treat with a therapeutic pack: *The dentist packed my gum after he extracted my tooth.* **16.** *Informal.* **a.** to possess as a characteristic or power: *That mule packs a knockout punch in its hind feet.* **b.** to be capable of administering.

—*v.i.* **1.** to put things together in a bag, box, bundle, bale, etc.: *Are you ready to pack?* **2.** to fit together closely; admit of storing and shipping: *These small cans will pack well.* **3.** to become or be packed; crowd together: *The whole group packed into one small room.* **4.** to become relatively compact: *The Navaho Indians found that mud will pack easily to make bricks.* **5.** to gather into a pack or packs, as animals. **6.** to be off; to take oneself off: *Seek shelter! Pack!* (Shakespeare).

pack in, *Informal.* to stop working; fail: *If your kidney happened to pack in when you were thirty but the rest of you was going to last you until you were seventy, then obviously there would be a good case for replacing your kidney* (Listener).

pack it in, *Informal.* to give up, abandon, or leave something or someplace: *Southampton, too, Infancy, would suffer similarly should Melia decide to pack it in* (Listener).

pack off or **away, a.** to send away: *to pack a child off to bed.* **b.** to go away suddenly; depart: *to pack off at dawn.*

pack out, to sell out: *We're packed out, and again chiefly* [*to*] *young people. Godot has become a box-office draw* (London Times).

pack up, *Informal.* **a.** to stop working; cease operating; fail: *One of the aircraft's engines packed up.* **b.** to die: *The old dog quietly packed up in his sleep.*

send packing. See under **send,** *v.*

[probably < Middle Dutch *pac*]

—**Syn.** *n.* **1.** parcel, bale, package, packet. *–v.t.* **3.** cram.

pack[2] (pak), *v.t.* **1.** to arrange unfairly; fill (a jury, court, legislature, convention, etc.) with those who will favor one side or who believe in a certain cause: *to pack the convention with bought delegates.* **2.** *Archaic.* to shuffle (playing cards) so as to cheat. [origin uncertain; perhaps influenced by *pack*[1]]

pack[3] (pak), *Scottish.* —*adj.* **1.** (of persons) intimate; friendly. **2.** (of animals) tame. —*adv.* intimately. [origin uncertain]

pack·a·ble (pak′ə bəl), *adj.* that can be packed easily without damage: *You must give a woman a wardrobe which is practical, packable, transformable, and uncrushable* (Sunday Times).

pack·age (pak′ij), *n., adj., v.*, **-aged, -ag·ing.** —*n.* **1.** a bundle of things packed or wrapped together; box with things packed in it; parcel: *a package of books, a package of laundry.* **2. a.** a box, can, bottle, jar, case, or other receptacle for packing goods, especially one designed for a particular commodity and printed with matter intended both to identify it and to attract buyers: *We need the best package we can get for this new breakfast food.* **b.** such a package with its contents, as offered for sale: *a package of soap, a package of frozen peas.* **3.** a group of related items or elements, as goods, services, laws, articles of agreement in a negotiation, etc., offered, provided, sold, accepted, or rejected as a unit, often as an indivisible unit: *a house, lot, major appliances, and financing as a package for $2,000 down. Our Florida package includes transportation, hotel, and meals for a week. The guaranteed wage, pension and welfare clauses of the auto package* (New York Times).

—*adj.* **1.** including a number of elements or items provided or offered as a unit: *a package summer vacation, a package wage increase.* **2.** of or having to do with a package deal: *NBC hoped to encourage non-network package producers to use the talents of its comedy unit writers* (Saturday Review).

—*v.t.* **1.** to put in a package or packages; box, can, bottle, etc., in order to sell: *to package meat.* **2.** to make a package or packages out of: *to wrap and package Christmas presents.*

—**Syn.** *n.* **1.** packet, bale. *-v.t.* **1.** pack.

pack·age·a·ble (pak′i jə bəl), *adj.* that can be packaged: *a packageable present.*

package deal, an offer or transaction involving a number of elements or items grouped as a unit, often as an indivisible unit: *The proposal was presented as a final, take-it-or-leave-it package deal.*

package power reactor, a relatively small assembly for the production of atomic power, that can be stripped down and transported by air to isolated outposts: *The Army awarded contracts for small power plants, known as "package power reactors," . . . designed to supply power, light, and heat for isolated military outposts* (London Times).

pack·ag·er (pak′i jər), *n.* **1.** a person or thing that packages. **2.** a producer who makes and sells a group of television programs, etc.: *The show is a film series produced by an independent packager and merely purchased by the agency for its client* (Harper's).

package store, *U.S.* a store selling by the bottle distilled alcoholic liquors and other intoxicating beverages, including (in some states) wine and beer.

pack·ag·ing (pak′i jing), *n.* **1.** the act of putting in a package: *the packaging of glassware.* **2.** a package: *The best packaging for this new cereal is one which will attract attention.*

pack animal, a horse, mule, donkey, or other animal used for carrying loads or packs. See picture under **burro.**

pack drill, a military punishment in which the offender must walk up and down for a certain amount of time in full uniform and gear: *Mulvaney was doing pack drill . . ., with rifle, bayonet, ammunition, knapsack, and overcoat* (Rudyard Kipling).

pack·er (pak′ər), *n.* **1.** a person or thing that packs, especially a person or company that packs meat, fruit, vegetables, etc., to be sold at wholesale or to wholesalers: *a meat packer.* **2.** *U.S., Canada, and Australia.* a person who transports goods by means of pack animals: *The peaks were heavy with wet snow and the pass so treacherous that the experienced packers flatly refused to climb it* (Maclean's).

pack·er·y (pak′ər ē), *n., pl.* **-er·ies.** a packing house.

pack·et (pak′it), *n.* **1.** a small package; parcel: *a packet of letters, a packet of cigarettes, a packet of pins.* **2.** a packet boat: *I had agreed with Captain Morris, of the packet at New York, for my passage* (Benjamin Franklin).

cost a packet, *British Slang.* to cost a large sum of money: *Well, it cost him a packet but it cured his indigestion* (Cape Times).

—*v.t.* to make into or wrap in a packet; package.

[earlier *pacquet,* perhaps < an Anglo-French diminutive form of Middle English *pakke* pack[1]]

packet boat, a boat that carries mail, passengers, and goods regularly on a fixed route, usually along a river or the coast.

pack horse, a horse used to carry loads or packs: *Bridges (3), just wide enough for pack horses, survive across the rapid streams below the Moor* (Punch).

pack·house (pak′hous′), *n.* a warehouse.

pack ice, the ice forming a pack, often squeezed or piled into fantastic formations: *Here among the desolate mountains and pack ice next to the Arctic Circle, where in the springtime the snow still drifts as high as the houses . . . a new little city is being born* (Wall Street Journal).

pack·ing (pak′ing), *n.* **1.** material used to pack or to make watertight, steamtight, etc.: *the packing around the valves of a radiator.* **2.** the business of preparing and packing meat, fish, fruit, vegetables, etc., to be sold: *This spring, packing companies will be shifting summer sausage production to the new culture* (Wall Street Journal). **3.** *Nuclear Physics.* the building up of a nucleus from protons and neutrons, resulting in a loss of mass (packing loss) and a formation of energy. —**Syn. 1.** stuffing.

packing box, a box for packing goods in: *His friends wondered how it was that he could reach into the packing box and . . . produce the desired episode, even if it had been written . . . years before* (Malcolm Cowley).

packing case, a case or framework in which articles may be packed securely for shipment to a distance: *. . . four Army trucks required to carry to the airfield the cabinets and packing cases containing the Presidential files* (Alistair Cooke).

packing effect, *Physics.* mass defect.

packing house, a place where meat, fruit, vegetables, etc., are prepared and packed to be sold: *Infinitely more important is the fact that these animals will be spared many of the horrors of the packing house* (Science News Letter).

pack load, the weight or amount that can be put or carried in a pack: *The pack load for a mule is about 300 pounds; for a burro, about 150 pounds.*

pack·man (pak′mən), *n., pl.* **-men.** a man who travels about carrying goods in a pack for sale; peddler.

pack mule, a mule used for carrying loads: *They met 60 allies leading pack mules and horses and headed into the trackless jungle* (Time).

pack rat, any of a group of large North American rats, with a hairy tail, that carries away and hides food, clothing, tools, etc., often leaving something else, as if in exchange; wood rat.

pack·sack (pak′sak′), *n.* a bag of strong material to hold equipment when traveling: *Climbers carry packsacks loaded with first-aid supplies, food, and extra clothing for sudden changes in weather* (Paul W. Wiseman).

pack·sad·dle (pak′sad′əl), *n., v.,* **-dled, -dling.** —*n.* a saddle specially adapted for supporting the load on a pack animal. —*v.t.* to convey on a packsaddle; transport by a pack animal.

packsaddle roof, a saddle roof.

pack·thread (pak′thred′), *n.* a strong thread or twine for sewing or tying up packages.

pack train, a line or group of animals carrying loads: *According to one version . . . Don Miguel's pack train of 50 mules and 100 men was attacked and massacred by a band of Apaches* (Time).

pact (pakt), *n.* an agreement; compact: *The U.S. joined the Military Committee of the Baghdad Pact* (Wall Street Journal). [< Latin *pactum,* (originally) neuter past participle of *pacīscī* to covenant, agree] —**Syn.** covenant, treaty.

pac·tion (pak′shən), *n.* **1.** agreement. **2.** an agreement, compact, or pact.

pac·tion·al (pak′shə nəl), *adj.* of the nature of a pact.

Pac·to·li·an (pak tō′lē ən), *adj.* **1.** of or having to do with the river Pactolus in ancient Lydia, Asia Minor, famed for the gold obtained from the sands. **2.** golden.

pad[1] (pad), *n., v.,* **pad·ded, pad·ding.** —*n.* **1.** a soft mass used for comfort, protection, or stuffing; cushion: *to put a pad on a bench or under a rug, to wear pads on one's knees in hockey, to put a pad under a hot plate.* **2.** a soft, stuffed saddle. **3.** one of the cushionlike parts on the bottom side of the feet of dogs, foxes, camels, and some other animals. It is a fleshy and elastic part forming the sole. **4. a.** the foot of a fox, dog, wolf, rabbit, or other animal. **b.** the footprint of such an animal. **5.** a tarsal cushion of an insect's foot; pulvillus. **6.** any cushionlike part of an animal body. **7.** *U.S.* the large floating leaf of the water lily; lily pad. **8.** a number of sheets of paper fastened tightly together along an edge or edges; tablet. **9.** a cushionlike piece of cloth or other absorbent material soaked with ink to use with a rubber stamp. **10.** a launching pad: *Gravity is what makes it so hard for rockets to hop off their pads and hit the moon* (New Yorker). **11.** the socket of a brace, in which the bit is inserted. **12.** a tool handle for various sizes or kinds of tools. **13.** *Obsolete.* a bundle of straw or the like to lie on. **14.** *U.S. Slang.* a place where a person sleeps, as a bed, a room, an apartment, etc.

—*v.t.* **1.** to fill with something soft; stuff: *to pad a chair.* **2.** to expand or lengthen (a story, composition, etc.) by including unnecessary material: *to pad a short story with anecdotes. Mr. Killmayer never padded a song beyond what it was worth* (New York Times). **3.** to increase the amount of (a bill, expense account, etc.) by false entries.

[origin uncertain]

pad[2] (pad), *v.,* **pad·ded, pad·ding,** *n.* —*v.t.* **1.** to walk along (a path, road, etc.); tramp; trudge: *to pad the same path everyday.* **2.** to beat down by treading. —*v.i.* **1.** to travel on foot; tramp or trudge along. **2.** to walk or trot steadily and softly: *a wolf padding through the forest.*

—*n.* **1.** a dull sound, as of footsteps on the ground: *'Tis the regular pad of the wolves in pursuit of the life in the sledge* (Robert Browning). **2.** a slow horse for riding on a road, as for journeying: *an abbot on an ambling pad* (Tennyson). **3.** *British.* a path or track: *It is a curious fact that wild animals do not seem to notice anything above the pad* (Observer). **4.** *Obsolete.* a highway robber; highwayman; footpad: *Four pads in ambush lay* (Byron).

[probably < earlier Dutch or Low German *pad* path. Compare Low German *padden* to tread.]

pad·ded cell (pad′id), a room in an insane asylum or prison, having the walls padded to prevent the person confined in it from injuring himself.

pad·ding[1] (pad′ing), *n.* **1.** material used to pad with, such as cotton, felt, straw, or hair. **2.** unnecessary words used just to fill space in making a speech or a written paper longer: *His letters were usually all common form and padding* (Samuel Butler). [< *pad*[1] + *-ing*[1]] —**Syn. 1.** wadding.

pad·ding[2] (pad′ing), *n.* the act of a person or thing that pads. [< *pad*[2] + *-ing*[1]]

pad·dle[1] (pad′əl), *n., v.,* **-dled, -dling.** —*n.* **1.** a short oar with a broad blade at one end or both ends, used without resting it against the boat. **2.** the act of paddling; turn at the paddle. **3. a.** one of the broad boards fixed around a water wheel or a paddle wheel to push, or be pushed by, the water. **b.** a paddle wheel. **4.** a paddle-shaped piece of wood used for stirring, for mixing, for beating clothes in washing, etc. **5.** an instrument or tool of this shape, used in various trades or industries, especially for stirring and mixing. **6.** a flipper or similar limb, as of a turtle, whale, or penguin. **7.** a small wooden implement used to hit the ball in table tennis; racket. **8.** Also, **pettle.** *British.* a small, long-handled, spadelike tool used for cleaning a plowshare, digging up thistles, etc.

Paddle[1] **(def. 1)**

—*v.t.* **1.** to move (a boat or canoe) with a paddle or paddles. **2.** to transport or convey, as in a canoe, by paddling: *She would herself paddle me off to the ship* (Herman Melville). **3.** *U.S. Informal.* to beat with a paddle; spank. —*v.i.* **1.** to use a paddle to move a canoe or boat through water: *Being fatigued with rowing, or paddling, as it is called* (Daniel Defoe). **2.** to row gently, so as barely to move through the water or simply to hold a boat steady against the current: *a rainbow shell That paddles in a halcyon sea* (Christina G. Rossetti).

pad·dle[2] (pad′əl), *v.i.,* **-dled, -dling. 1.** to move the hands or feet about in water: *the children paddling in the mud puddle.* **2.** to toy with the fingers. **3.** to walk with short, unsteady steps, like those of a young child; toddle. [apparently related to PAD[2]. Compare Low German *paddlen* tramp about < *padden* to tread, pad[2].] —**Syn. 1.** dabble.

pad·dle·ball (pad′əl bôl′), *n.* a game in which two opposing sides alternate in hitting a tennis ball with a wooden paddle against the four walls of a court.

pad·dle·boat (pad′əl bōt′), *n.* a steamboat equipped with a paddle wheel on each side or one at the stern: *We weaved in between the gaily coloured canoes and paddleboats, our gun ports open and bold, our little Morris engine throbbing softly* (Manchester Guardian).

paddle box, the guard or casing covering the upper part of a paddle wheel.

pad·dle·fish (pad′əl fish′), *n., pl.* **-fish·es** or (*collectively*) **-fish.** a large scaleless fish of the Mississippi and Great Lakes, allied to the sturgeons, having a long, flat snout that looks somewhat like a canoe paddle; spoonbill. It sometimes grows to a length of over 6 feet.

paddle foot, *Slang.* an infantry soldier.

pad·dler[1] (pad′lər), *n.* **1.** a person who paddles a canoe or boat. **2.** *Obsolete.* a paddle.

pad·dler[2] (pad′lər), *n.* a person or thing that paddles, as in water or mud.

pad·dle·steam·er (pad′əl stē′mər), *n.* paddleboat: *The vessel is a paddlesteamer, her dimensions being: length, 75 feet; breadth, 8 feet; and depth 3 feet* (Scientific American).

paddle tennis, a game of tennis played with wooden paddles on a court half the size of a tennis court and using a lower net than that of a tennis court.

paddle wheel, a wheel with paddles fixed around it for propelling a ship over the water.

pad·dle·wheel·er (pad′əl hwē′lər), *n.* a boat or ship equipped with paddle wheels or a paddle wheel: *In Montreal, paddlewheelers picked up freight for other St. Lawrence ports* (Maclean's).

pad·dock[1] (pad′ək), *n.* **1.** a small field near a stable or house, used as a pasture, especially for horses: *Ten cows were grazed in each break and moved into a new paddock every morning* (John Hancock). **2.** a pen for horses at a race track. **3.** (in Australia) any field or piece of tillable land enclosed by a fence.

—*v.t.* **1.** to put or keep in or as in a paddock: *Shakespeare himself would have been commonplace had he been paddocked in a thinly-shaven vocabulary* (Lowell). **2.** (in Australia) to fence in (land).

[variant of *parrock,* Old English *pearroc* enclosed space; fence. Compare PARK.]

pad·dock[2] (pad′ək), *n. Scottish.* **1.** a frog. **2.** a toad: *Paddock calls* (Shakespeare). [Middle English *paddoke* < *pade* toad, frog + *-ok* diminutive suffix]

pad·dy[1] (pad′ē), *n., pl.* **-dies. 1.** rice: *The country, like most parts of India near to the coast, consisted of paddy or rice fields, under water* (Frederick Marryat). **2.** rice in the husk, uncut or gathered. **3.** a field of rice: *From 4,300 acres of paddy the family's holding dropped to 10 acres* (London Times). Also, **padi.** [< Malay *padi* rice in the husk]

pad·dy[2] (pad′ē), *n., pl.* **-dies.** *British Informal.* a tantrum; paddywhack.

Pad·dy (pad′ē), *n., pl.* **-dies.** *Slang.* a nickname for an Irishman. [< nickname for Irish *Pādraig* Patrick]

pad·dy·bird (pad′ē bėrd′), *n.* any of various birds that frequent rice fields, as the Java sparrow.

pad·dy·field (pad′ē fēld′), *n.* a field in which rice is grown; paddy: *The dry season drains the swamps and paddyfields, making fighting easier* (Time).

pad·dy·mel·on (pad′ē mel′ən), *n.* pademelon.

pad·dy·wack (pad′ē wak′), *n. Informal.* paddywhack.

paddy wagon, *U.S. Slang.* a patrol wagon: *Three paddy wagons shuttled back and forth ... hauling 276 men and three women to headquarters for questioning* (Time).

pad·dy·whack (pad′ē hwak′), *n.* **1.** *U.S. Informal.* a spanking or beating. **2.** *British Informal.* a rage; passion; temper. [apparently < *Paddy*]

pad·e·mel·on (pad′ē mel′ən), *n.* a small Australian kangaroo. [< a native name]

pad foot, a flattened ornamental foot at the end of a cabriole leg: *A Queen Anne table with ... cabriole legs and pad feet has come through unscathed* (New York Times).

pad·i (pad′ē), *n., pl.* **-is.** paddy[1].

pa·di·shah or **Pa·di·shah** (pä′di shä), *n.* great king; emperor (a title applied especially to the Shah of Iran and, formerly, to the Sultan of Turkey or to the British sovereign as emperor of India). [< Persian *pādshah*]

pa·dle (pā′dəl), *n., v.,* **-dled, -dling.** *Scottish.* —*n.* a hoe. —*v.t.* to hoe. [variant of *paddle*[1]]

pad·lock (pad′lok′), *n.* a lock that can be put on and removed. It hangs by a curved bar, hinged at one end and snapped shut at the other. —*v.t.* to fasten with a padlock: *At other schools the playgrounds were left open for afterhours recreation, but at Quincy Adams the playground gates were padlocked as soon as school was out* (Atlantic). [< *pad*, perhaps variant of *pod*[3] + *lock*[1]]

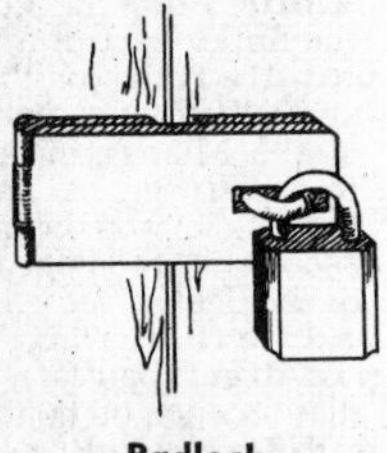

Padlock

pad·nag (pad′nag′), *n.* a horse with an easy gait; pad. [< *pad*[2] + *nag*[2]]

Pa·douk wood (pə dük′), the ornamental wood of an Indian and Malayan tree of the pea family; Amboina wood. [< the Burmese name]

pa·dre (pä′drā), *n.* **1.** father. It is used as a name for a priest, especially in regions where Spanish, Portuguese, or Italian is spoken. **2.** *Informal.* a chaplain in the armed forces: *To some villages a padre has come from the services who has faced the grimmest realities* (J.W.R. Scott). [< Italian, Spanish, and Portuguese *padre* < Latin *pater, patris* father]

pa·dro·ne (pä drō′nā *for 1;* pə drō′nē *for 2*), *n., pl.* **pa·dro·ni** (pä drō′nē), *for 1;* **pa·dro·nes** (pə drō′nēz) *for 2.* **1.** *Italian.* **a.** a master; boss: *Everything tangible is Florentine in actuality, including the padrone, Arturo Sacco, for fifteen years viceroy of the Blue Angel* (New Yorker). **b.** the master of a small coastal vessel. **c.** an innkeeper. **2.** a man who controls and supplies Italian laborers on contract with an employer, as in America. Originally he was paid by the employer, and his force of recent immigrant laborers was given a nominal wage by the padrone. [< Italian *padrone* < Latin *patrōnus.* Doublet of PATRON, PATROON.]

pa·dro·nism (pə drō′niz əm), *n.* boss control of Italian laborers.

Pad·u·an (paj′ů ən, pad′yů ən), *adj.* of or having to do with Padua, a city in northeastern Italy, or its people: *The sharp geometric definition of form in "Lamentation over the Dead Christ" by the Paduan artist Bartolommeo Bellano is "very modern"* (London Times). —*n.* a native or inhabitant of Padua.

pad·u·a·soy (paj′ů ə soi), *n.* **1.** a smooth, strong, heavy, rich fabric of corded silk, much worn by both men and women in the 1700's. **2.** a garment of this fabric: *The paduasoy ... was being made into a christening cloak for the baby* (Elizabeth Gaskell). —*adj.* made of this fabric. [< French *pou-de-soie;* origin uncertain; spelling influenced by earlier English *padou* (or *Padua*) *say* (literally) silk serge of Padua]

pae·an (pē′ən), *n.* **1.** a song of praise, joy, or triumph: *Loud paeans chanted through the valley announced the approach of the victors* (Herman Melville). *He ended with a fervent paean to the country he has served so long* (Newsweek). **2.** (in ancient Greece) a hymn or chant of triumph or thanksgiving to a deity, especially to Apollo or Artemis. Also, **pean.** [< Latin *paean* < Greek *paiân, -ânos* hymn to Apollo] —**Syn. 1.** hallelujah.

pae·di·at·ric (pē′dē at′rik, ped′ē-), *adj. Especially British.* pediatric.

pae·di·a·tri·cian (pē′dē ə trish′ən, ped′ē-), *n. Especially British.* pediatrician.

pae·di·at·rics (pē′dē at′riks, ped′ē-), *n. Especially British.* pediatrics.

pae·do·gen·e·sis (pē′dō jen′ə sis), *n.* pedogenesis.

pa·el·la (pä el′ə), *n. Spanish.* a spicy dish, originally Basque, consisting of seasoned rice, cooked in oil with saffron, and of lobster or shrimp, scraps of chicken, or of beef and pork, and fresh vegetables: *At about three o'clock we sat down to eat a paella and some veal* (New Yorker).

pae·on (pē′ən), *n.* (in Greek and Latin verse) a foot of four syllables, one long and three short. The long syllable may come anywhere in the foot. [< Latin *paeon* < Greek *peiōn, paiân* paean]

pae·o·ny (pē′ə nē), *n., pl.* **-nies.** *Especially British.* peony.

pa·gan (pā′gən), *n.* **1.** a person who is not a Christian, Jew, or Moslem; person who worships false gods; heathen. The ancient Greeks and Romans were pagans: *I'd rather be a pagan, suckled in a creed outworn* (Wordsworth). **2.** a person who has no religion.
—*adj.* **1.** having to do with pagans; not Christian, Jewish, or Moslem. **2.** not religious.
[< Latin *pāgānus* rustic (in Late Latin, heathen) (at a time when Christianity was accepted by urban populations) < *pāgus* village]
—**Syn.** *n.* **1.** See **heathen.**

pa·gan·dom (pā′gən dəm), *n.* **1.** the pagan world; region or regions inhabited by pagans. **2.** all pagans; pagans collectively.

pa·gan·ish (pā′gə nish), *adj.* having to do with or characteristic of pagans; heathenish.

pa·gan·ism (pā′gə niz əm), *n.* **1.** a pagan attitude toward religion or morality. **2.** the beliefs and practices of pagans. **3.** the condition of being pagan: *The divisions of Christianity suspended the ruin of Paganism* (Edward Gibbon). *The rising paganism of the western world will make our civilization as cold as interstellar spaces* (Time).

pa·gan·i·za·tion (pā′gə nə zā′shən), *n.* **1.** the act of paganizing. **2.** the state of being paganized.

pa·gan·ize (pā′gə nīz), *v.,* **-ized, iz·ing.** —*v.t.* to make pagan. —*v.i.* to become pagan: *In spite of the commercializing—even the paganizing—of a religious festival, people are forcibly aware of it* (Newsweek).

page[1] (pāj), *n., v.,* **paged, pag·ing.** —*n.* **1.** one side of a leaf or sheet of paper: *a page in this book. Abbr.:* p. **2. a.** the print or writing on one side of a leaf. **b.** *Printing.* the type set and made up to be printed as a page. **3. a.** a record: *the pages of history.* **b.** a happening or time considered as part of history: *The settling of the West is an exciting page in the history of the United States.*
—*v.t.* to number the pages of (a manuscript, etc.); folio (a book, etc.); paginate.
[< French *page* < Old French *pagene*, learned borrowing from Latin *pāgina*, related to *pangere* to fasten]

page[2] (pāj), *n., v.,* **paged, pag·ing.** —*n.* **1.** a boy employed by a hotel, club, legislature, theater, etc., to run errands, carry parcels, deliver messages, etc.; errand boy; bell boy. **2.** a very small boy, usually elaborately dressed, who is a nominal attendant of the bride in a wedding ceremony. **3. a.** a youth employed as the personal attendant of a person of high rank, from whom he received an education in social customs, etc. **b.** a youth who was preparing to be a knight, and who was attached to the household of a lord or knight whom he followed in the course of training for knighthood. **4.** *Obsolete.* a boy; youth; lad.
—*v.t.* **1.** *U.S.* **a.** to try to find (a person) at a hotel, club, etc., by having his name called out. **b.** (of a page or bellhop) to try at find (a person) by calling out his name: *The bellhop is paging Mr. Saunders in the lobby.* **2.** to wait on, attend, or follow like a page. —*v.i.* to act as page; be a page.
[< Old French *page*, perhaps < Medieval Latin *pagius* rustic < Latin *pāgus* country district]

pag·eant (paj′ənt), *n.* **1.** an elaborate spectacle; procession in costume; pomp; display: *The coronation of the new king was a splendid pageant.* **2. a.** a public entertainment that represents scenes from history, legends, or the like: *Our school gave a pageant of the coming of the Pilgrims to America.* **b.** a drama or series of scenes played outdoors by local actors: *a children's Christmas pageant.* **3.** an empty show, not reality: *Once in a while one meets with a single soul greater than all the living pageant which passes before it* (Oliver Wendell Holmes). *These our actors, As I foretold you, were all spirits and Are melted into air, into thin air ... And like this insubstantial pageant faded, Leave not a rack behind* (Shakespeare). **4. a.** *Archaic.* a stage or platform, usually moving on wheels, on which scenes from medieval mystery plays were presented. **b.** a similar stage bearing any kind of a spectacle. **5.** *Archaic.* any dramatic piece or play: *This wide and universal theatre Presents more woeful pageants than the scene Wherein we play in* (Shakespeare). **6.** *Archaic.* anything viewed as a drama within which one has a part, as a course of duty or the course of a life.
—*v.t.* to honor with a pageant; celebrate with pageantry: *He pageants us* (Shakespeare).
[Middle English *pagent, pagen;* origin uncertain; probably < Late Latin *pāgina* scaffold, stage; plank < Latin, page[1]]

pag·eant·ry (paj′ən trē), *n., pl.* **-ries. 1.** a splendid show; gorgeous display; pomp: *The large Stratford company of some 90-odd players manages swordplay and panoplied pageantry with great facility* (Newsweek). **2.** mere show; empty display. **3.** a pageant, or pageants collectively. —**Syn. 1.** spectacle. **2.** ostentation, pretension.

page boy, 1. a person, usually a boy, who works as a page: *After breakfast Mr. Truman met with a group of eight Senate page boys, who brought photographs of the former President to be autographed* (New York Times). **2.** a shoulder-length hair style for women in which the hair in the back is turned under at the ends in a soft roll.

page·hood (pāj′hůd), *n.* the state or condition of being a page.

page proof, *Printing.* a proof taken after type has been made up into a page.

pag·i·nal (paj′ə nəl), *adj.* **1.** of, having to do with, or consisting of a page or pages. **2.** page for page: *a paginal reprint.* [< Latin *pāginālis* < *pāgina* page[1]]

pag·i·nar·y (paj′ə ner′ē), *adj.* paginal.

pag·i·nate (paj′ə nāt), *v.t.,* **-nat·ed, -nat·ing.** to mark the number of pages of; page (a book, etc.); folio.

pag·i·na·tion (paj′ə nā′shən), *n.* **1.** the act or process of numbering the pages of books, etc. **2.** the figures with which pages are numbered; numbering of pages. **3.** the number of pages or (now rarely) leaves in a book, etc.

pag·ing (pā′jing), *n.* pagination.

pag·od (pag′əd, pə god′), *n. Archaic.* **1.** pagoda. **2.** an idol.

pa·go·da (pə gō′də), *n.* **1.** a temple or other sacred building with many stories forming a tower. Pagodas are built in China, Japan, and in parts of India and southeastern Asia. **2.** a gold or silver coin formerly current in India. [< Portuguese *pagode*, perhaps < Tamil *pagavadi* < Sanskrit *bhagavatī* goddess]

Pagoda (def. 1)

pagoda tree, 1. any of several trees so called from their resemblance to or their association with pagodas, as the banyan of India. **2.** a mythical East Indian tree fabled to let fall pagodas (the coins) when shaken.

shake the pagoda tree, to make a fortune in India: *The service of John*

Company, under whose flag, as we know, the pagoda tree was worth shaking (Mrs. Lynn Linton).

pa·go·dite (pə gō′dīt), *n.* agalmatolite.

pa·gu·ri·an (pə gyůr′ē ən), *adj.* of or belonging to a family of crustaceans comprising the hermit crabs.
—*n.* a hermit crab.
[< New Latin *Pagurus* the typical genus (< Latin *pagūrus* a kind of crab < Greek *págouros*) + English *-ian*]

pa·gu·rid (pə gyůr′id, pag′yər-), *n.* pagurian.

pah (pä), *interj.* an exclamation of disgust.

pah·la·vi (pä′lə vē), *n.* a gold coin of Iran, worth 20 rials. [< Persian *pahlavi* < Riza Khan *Pahlavi,* the Shah of Iran (Persia)]

Pah·la·vi (pä′lə vē), *n.* the principal language of Persia from the 200's to the 800's, an Iranian language using a Semitic alphabet and word forms representing the Persian equivalents. Also, **Pehlevi.** [< Persian *Pahlavi* Parthian < Old Persian *Parthava* Parthia]

pa·hoe·hoe (pä hō′ē hō′ē), *n.* lava that has hardened into a smooth, shiny surface. [< Hawaiian *pāhoehoe*]

paid (pād), *adj.* **1.** receiving money; hired: *a paid worker, a paid informer.* **2.** no longer owed; settled: *a paid mortgage. Abbr.:* pd. **3.** cashed: *a paid check.*

put paid to, *British Informal.* to dispose of; finish off; settle: *We became fast friends after we decided to put paid to our quarrel once and for all.*
—*v.* the past tense and past participle of **pay**[1]: *I have paid my bills. These bills are all paid.*

➤ **paid, payed.** *Paid* is the spelling of the past tense and past participle of pay[1] (*He paid his bills*) in all senses except let out (*They payed out the rope*), and occasionally in that sense also.

paid-in surplus (pād′in′), capital surplus obtained by selling shares of stock above their face value.

paid-up (pād′up′), *adj.* that has paid in full; not in arrears: *a paid-up member; . . . our club for paid-up party hacks* (Punch).

paik (pāk), *Scottish. n.* a hard blow, especially against the body.

one's paiks, the thrashing that is due to one or that one receives: *He got his paiks—having acted like an assassin* (Byron).
—*v.t.* to beat; pummel; thrash.
[origin unknown]

pail (pāl), *n.* **1.** a round container, used for carrying liquids, etc.; bucket. **2.** amount a pail holds; a pailful. [Old English *pægel* wine vessel; gill, and < Old French *paielle* warming pan, both < Medieval Latin *pagella* a measure (diminutive) < Latin *pāgina* (originally) something fixed]

pail·ful (pāl′fůl), *n., pl.* **-fuls.** the amount that fills a pail: *The rain was falling by pailfuls* (Macaulay).

pail·lasse (pal yas′, pal′yas), *n.* a mattress or under mattress filled with straw or some similarly simple, inexpensive material. Also, **palliasse.** [< Old French *paillasse* < *paille* straw < Latin *palea* chaff, straw]

pail·lette (pal yet′), *n.* **1.** a spangle. **2.** a piece of bright metal or thin metal foil used in enamel painting: *Stylized flowers embroidered with mother-of-pearl and gold paillettes outline its strapless top* (New Yorker). [< Middle French *paillette* (diminutive) < *paille* chaff < Latin *palea*]

pail·let·ted (pal yet′id), *adj.* spangled.

pail·lon (pä yôɴ′), *n., pl.* **-lons** (-yôɴ′). *French.* thin metal foil, used in gilding or for other decorations.

pai·lou (pī′lō′), *n.* (in China) an elaborate structure forming or resembling a gateway, erected as a memorial. [< Chinese (Peking) *p'ai lou*]

pain (pān), *n.* **1.** a feeling of being hurt; suffering: *A cut gives pain. The death of one we love causes pain.* **2.** a single or localized feeling of hurt: *a sharp pain in one's back.* **3.** *Obsolete.* labor; effort; work: *'Tis most strange Nature should be so conversant with pain* (Shakespeare). **4.** *Obsolete.* punishment; penalty: *liable to the pains and penalties of high treason* (Jonathan Swift).

feel no pain, to be intoxicated: *Having come down out of the woods to Berlin, Jack was feeling no pain* (Atlantic).

on or **under pain of,** with the punishment or penalty of, unless a certain thing is done: *A proclamation ordering the tribes to join him under pain of death . . .* (London Times).

pain in the neck, *Slang.* a very troublesome or irritating thing or person: *O'Malley is tall and gentle, and has a wife who is a pain in the neck* (Frank O'Connor).

pains, a. trouble to do something; effort; care: *Great . . . pains have been taken to inflame our minds* (Edmund Burke). *You . . . are like to have nothing but your travel for your pains* (John Bunyan). **b.** the sufferings of childbirth: *labor pains.*
—*v.t.* to cause to suffer; give pain to: *Does your tooth pain you?* —*v.i.* to cause suffering; give pain: *a natural desire to pain* (Rudyard Kipling).
[< Old French *peine* < Latin *poena* penalty < Greek *poinē*]
—**Syn.** *n.* **1, 2. Pain, ache** mean a feeling of being hurt, bodily or mentally. **Pain** particularly suggests a sharp hurt, but of any degree from a sudden jab in one spot to a very severe and sometimes long-lasting hurt of the whole body or, figuratively, a sorrow that causes severe mental suffering: *I have pains in my side.* **Ache** suggests a steady and usually dull hurt or, figuratively, a longing for something: *I have an earache.* -*v.t.* hurt, afflict, torture.

pained (pānd), *adj.* **1.** hurt, distressed, grieved, etc.: *I am greatly pained to learn of your refusal.* **2.** expressing or showing pain: *a pained look.*

pain·ful (pān′fəl), *adj.* **1.** causing pain; unpleasant; hurting: *a painful illness, a painful duty, a painful back.* **2.** difficult: *a painful ascent of a mountain by its steepest face.* **3.** *Archaic.* painstaking; careful: *The painful chronicle of honest John Stowe* (Robert Southey). —**pain′ful·ly,** *adv.* —**pain′ful·ness,** *n.* —**Syn. 2.** toilsome.

pain·kill·er (pān′kil′ər), *n.* **1.** *U.S. Informal.* **a.** any drug or remedy for abolishing or alleviating pain, such as morphine, novocaine, etc.: *A new painkiller, propoxyphene hydrochloride, is as effective as codeine* (Newsweek). **b.** anything that serves to relieve pain: *Some dental patients have found stereophonic sound to be an effective painkiller* (Science News Letter). **2.** *U.S. Slang.* an alcoholic drink, especially whiskey: *The man looked away; he wasn't sharing his painkiller with anyone* (New Yorker).

pain·kill·ing (pān′kil′ing), *adj. U.S. Informal.* relieving pain: *a painkilling drug, medicine, or sedative.*

pain·less (pān′lis), *adj.* without pain; causing no pain: *Unclarified explicitly by him until last week was the question of the morality of enabling mothers to perform so-called "natural, painless" childbirth, a procedure which dispenses with artificial helps* (Newsweek). —**pain′less·ly,** *adv.* —**pain′less·ness,** *n.*

pains·tak·ing (pānz′tā′king), *adj.* **1.** very careful: *a painstaking writer.* **2.** marked or characterized by attentive care; carefully done: *a painstaking reproduction.* —*n.* the taking of pains; careful effort in doing anything: *I afterwards, with a little painstaking, acquired as much of the Spanish as to read their books* (Benjamin Franklin). —**pains′tak′ing·ly,** *adv.* —**Syn.** *adj.* **1.** particular, scrupulous, assiduous.

paint[1] (pānt), *n.* **1. a.** a substance consisting of solid coloring matter or pigment mixed with a liquid, that can be spread on a surface to make a layer or film of white, black, or colored matter. **b.** the solid coloring matter alone; pigment: *a box of paints.* **2.** any cosmetic that colors or tints, especially one applied to the face, as rouge. **3.** the act or fact of painting or coloring. [< verb]
—*v.t.* **1.** to cover or decorate with paint: *to paint a house or a room.* **2.** to represent (an object, etc.) in colors, usually on a prepared surface: *The artist painted cherubs and angels. Paint me a cavernous waste shore* (T.S. Eliot). **3.** to show as if by painting: *A lively surprise . . . was painted on his countenance* (Mary W. Shelley). **4.** to picture vividly in words: *I shall . . . paint to you . . . something like the true form of the whale as he actually appears to the eye of the whaleman* (Herman Melville). **5. a.** to put on like paint: *The doctor painted iodine on the cut.* **b.** to treat (a wound, any part, etc.) in this way. **6.** to put color on (the face) in order to beautify it artificially. —*v.i.* **1.** to use paint in covering, decorating, or coloring. **2.** to practice the art of painting; make pictures. **3.** *Obsolete.* to apply rouge, etc.: *Nor could it sure be such a sin to paint* (Alexander Pope).
[< Old French *peint,* past participle of *peindre* to paint < Latin *pingere*]

paint[2] (pānt), *n. U.S. Informal.* a piebald or particolored horse: *I ride an old paint . . .* (American cowboy song). [< Spanish *pinto*]

paint·a·ble (pān′tə bəl), *adj.* that can be painted; suitable for being painted: *It had never before occurred to him that she was paintable* (Edith Wharton).

paint·box (pānt′boks′), *n.* a box used by artists for holding cakes or tubes of pigment: *In their earliest days they had been given paintboxes and sketching blocks* (New Yorker).

paint·brush (pānt′brush′), *n.* **1.** a brush for putting on paint. **2.** the painted cup.

paint cards, *U.S. Slang.* the picture cards (king, queen, etc.) in a deck of cards.

paint·ed (pān′tid), *adj.* **1.** depicted or executed in colors; coated or decorated with paint: *Painted Bulletins, the next most popular form of outdoor advertising, are usually larger than posters, and are often illuminated* (World Book Encyclopedia). **2.** of bright or variegated coloring, as certain animals. **3.** *Archaic.* feigned, artificial, or insincere.

painted bunting, 1. a small bright-colored finch of the southern United States, the male of which has a purple head, red breast, and green back; nonpareil. See picture under **nonpareil. 2.** a longspur of the arctic and central North America.

painted cup, any of a group of plants of the figwort family, having bright-colored bracts about the flowers, especially the Indian paintbrush.

painted lady, 1. a very common, handsome butterfly of an orange-red color spotted with black and white, found in temperate regions throughout the world: *The painted lady is abundant in Africa from where it frequently migrates in great numbers across the Mediterranean Sea into Europe reaching England and the Scandinavian countries* (Science News Letter). **2.** a gladiolus with pink splashes upon its flowers.

Painted Porch, 1. the public portico in ancient Athens where the Stoic philosopher Zeno taught; Porch. **2.** the Stoic school of philosophy.

painted redstart, a warbler of southwestern North America, black with red and white markings.

painted turtle, a common freshwater turtle of North America, having a slate-colored carapace and yellow underside, with red and yellow markings on the head, legs, and shell.

paint·er[1] (pān′tər), *n.* **1.** a person who paints pictures; artist: *Bonnard may not have been the most profound of modern painters, but he was one of the most charming* (London Times). **2.** a person who paints houses, woodwork, etc. [< Anglo-French *painter,* Old French *peinteur* < Vulgar Latin *pinctor,* for Latin *pictor* < *pingere* to paint]

paint·er[2] (pān′tər), *n.* a rope, usually fastened to the bow of a boat, for tying it to a ship, pier, etc. [probably < Old French *pentoir,* and *pentour* cordage for hanging, ultimately < Latin *pendēre* to hang]

paint·er[3] (pān′tər), *n.* the American panther or mountain lion; cougar (so called especially by early settlers in the eastern United States): *The painters (panthers) used to come round their log cabin at night* (Harriet Beecher Stowe). [American English, variant of earlier English *panter* panther]

pain·ter·ish (pān′tər ish), *adj.* painterly: *The stage pictures [are] . . . beautiful in their painterish and highly coloured way* (Manchester Guardian Weekly).

paint·er·li·ness (pān′tər lē nis), *n.* painterly quality; artistry in painting.

paint·er·ly (pān′tər lē), *adj.* having to do with, like, or characteristic of a painter; artistic: *. . . four pictures which are sensitive, workmanlike and painterly* (Manchester Guardian). —*adv.* in a way proper to a painter; artistically.

painter's colic, severe and continuing abdominal pain resulting from chronic lead poisoning: *Lead poisoning is commonly known as painter's colic, and vitamin C has been shown to be beneficial in its treatment* (W.N. Jones).

paint·ing (pān′ting), *n.* **1.** something painted; picture: *a very lifelike painting.* **2.** the act or process of a person who paints: *You must clean the walls before painting.* **3.** the art of representation, decoration, and creating beauty with paints: *She studied painting at the Academy of Design. The power and force of painting lie in the method of presenting fundamental truth, current and historical, so as to influence social conditions or countless human beings* (Emory S. Bogardus).

paint·less (pānt′lis), *adj.* without paint.

paint·pot (pānt′pot′), *n.* **1.** a container for holding paint: *We sat, with our brushes and paintpots by us* (Richard Henry Dana). **2.** *Geology.* a type of hot spring containing brightly colored boiling mud.

paint·ress (pān′tris), *n.* **1.** a woman who paints. **2.** a woman whose work is painting pottery.

paint·work (pānt′wėrk′), *n.* **1.** paint spread and dried on a surface: *A raised strip of chromium protects the paintwork.* **2.** the manner or quality of work in applying paint: *Only the most painstaking paintwork could produce such a satiny finish.*

paint·y (pān′tē), *adj.* of, having to do with, or containing too much paint: *a painty odor. The portrait is a bit too painty.*

pair (pãr), *n., pl.* **pairs** or (*sometimes after a numeral*) **pair,** *v.* —*n.* **1.** a set of two; two that go or are used together: *a pair of shoes, a pair of eyes, a pair of horses, a pair of pistols.* **2.** a single thing consisting of two parts that cannot be used separately: *a pair of scissors, a pair of trousers.* **3.** a man and woman who are married or are engaged to be married: *Among the members of the household of Claremont, near Esher, where the royal pair were established, was a young German physician, Christian Friedrich Stockmar* (Lytton Strachey). **4.** two partners in a dance. **5.** two animals that are mated: *In many cases one or a few pairs of a species are entirely inadequate for the establishment or for the preservation of an animal species* (Science News Letter). **6. a.** two members on opposite sides in a legislative body who arrange not to vote on a certain question or for a certain time, especially so that their absence may not affect the voting. **b.** the arrangement thus made. **7.** (in cards) **a.** two cards of the same value in different suits, viewed as a unit in one's hand: *a pair of sixes, jacks, etc.* **b.** (in games using a multiple deck) two identical cards. **c.** a team of two who remain partners through the several rounds of a match, as in duplicate bridge. **8.** *Mechanics.* a set of two parts (elements) so connected as to act mutually to constrain relative motion. **9.** *Dialect.* a set, not limited to two: *a pair of beads.*
—*v.t.* to arrange as a pair or in pairs: *to pair stockings. Her gloves were neatly paired in a drawer.* —*v.i.* **1.** to be arranged as a pair or in pairs; match. **2.** to join in love and marriage. **3.** to mate; couple. **4.** to agree with a member of the opposite party in a legislative body that both shall abstain from voting on a certain question or for a certain time: *At the time the vote to "censure" McCarthy was taken, Kennedy was ill. He did not vote, nor was he paired* (Newsweek).

pair off, to arrange in pairs; form into pairs: *Suppose the three hundred heroes at Thermopylae had paired off with three hundred Persians* (Emerson).
[< Old French *paire* < Latin *paria* equals, neuter plural of *pār, paris* part, share]
—**Syn.** *n.* **1. Pair, couple** mean two of the same kind. **Pair** applies to two things that belong together because they match or complement each other: *I bought a new pair of gloves.* **Couple** usually applies to any two of the same kind: *I bought a couple of shirts.*
➔ **pair.** The plural form *pair* is used only after a numeral or *many, several, few,* etc.: *I bought six pair* (or *pairs*).

pair·ing (pãr′ing), *n.* **1.** the act of arranging in pairs: *The pairing of couples at the high-school dance took place slowly.* **2.** a pair: *Coles and Player, of South Africa,* [*are*] *an exciting first round pairing in the ... tournament at Wentworth next week* (London Times).

pair-oar (pãr′ôr′, -ōr′), *n.* a shell or boat rowed by two oarsmen, one seated behind the other, each pulling one oar in unison with the other. —*adj.* of or having to do with a pair-oar.

pair-oared (pãr′ôrd′, -ōrd′), *adj.* pair-oar.

pair of compasses, a drawing compass. See **compass** for picture.

pair of stairs, a flight of stairs.

pair production, *Physics.* the simultaneous formation of an electron and a positron from a photon passing through a strong electric field.

pai·sa (pī sä′, pī′sä), *n., pl.* **pai·se** (pī sā′, pī′sā), a coin of India and Pakistan that replaced the naya paisa in 1964, worth 1/100 of a rupee. [< Hindustani *paisā* pice]

pai·sa·no (pī sä′nō), *n. Spanish.* countryman: *In the film we find Mr. Cain's questionable fellow ... working as a singing paisano in a grapegrowing area of California* (New Yorker).

pais·ley or **Pais·ley** (pāz′lē), *n., pl.* **-leys,** *adj.* —*n.* **1.** a soft woolen cloth with a very elaborate and colorful pattern. **2.** something made of paisley: *Liberty's lovely blouses are available in breath-taking array of traditional paisleys, gay stripes, charming moderns* (New Yorker).
—*adj.* made of paisley; having a pattern and colors like paisley: *Old Paisley shawls have been collected from Scotland, Persia, and India* (New Yorker). [< *Paisley,* a city in Scotland]

paisley or **Paisley shawl,** a kind of shawl of paisley fabric, originally made at Paisley, Scotland, in imitation of Indian Cashmere shawls.

Pai·ute (pī yüt′), *n., pl.* **-ute** or **-utes. 1.** a member of a small tribe of Indians of Shoshone stock in southwestern Utah. **2.** this tribe. **3.** the Uto-Aztecan language of this tribe.

pa·ja·maed (pə jä′mid, -jam′id), *adj.* wearing pajamas: *... a rebuilt junk with a crew of black-pajamaed sailors manning the sails* (Atlantic).

pajama party, slumber party.

pa·ja·mas (pə jä′məz, -jam′əz), *n.pl.* **1.** sleeping or lounging garments consisting of a jacket or blouse, and loose trousers: *In the Julius Kayser showrooms, models and salesmen show pajamas to a buyer* (Newsweek). **2.** loose trousers worn especially in Iran and parts of India by Moslem men and women. Also, *especially British,* **pyjamas.** [< Hindustani *pājāmā,* or *paijāmā* < Persian *pāējamah* < *pāi* leg + *jāmah* clothing]

pa·jo (pə jō′), *n. Rare.* the upper part of a pair of pajamas.

pa·ke·ha (pä′kə hä), *n., pl.* **-has** or **ha.** (in New Zealand) a white man, especially a New Zealander of European ancestry. [< Maori *pakeha*]

Pakh·tun (päk tün′), *n.* Pathan: *The term Pathan is the Indian mispronunciation of the name the Pathans give themselves—Pakhtun* (New York Times).

Pak·i·stan·i (pak′ə stan′ē, pä′kə stä′nē), *n., pl.* **-stan·i** or **-stan·is,** *adj.* —*n.* a native or inhabitant of the Republic of Pakistan: *The Pakistani were talking of including Iran too, which like Turkey and Pakistan is Moslem but not Arab* (Time). —*adj.* of or having to do with Pakistan: *Pakistani women are demonstrating against proposals to revive polygamy* (Punch).

pak·tong (pak′tong), *n.* a Chinese alloy having the same ingredients as German silver. [< dialectal variant of Chinese *pai t'ung* (literally) white copper]

pal (pal), *n., v.,* **palled, pal·ling.** *Informal.* —*n.* a close comrade; partner; intimate friend; chum: *I miss you—I've no pal now* (Leonard Merrick). —*v.i.* to associate as pals. [< Gypsy (England) *pal* brother, mate, variant of *pral,* or *plal,* perhaps < Sanskrit *bhrātr* brother] —**Syn.** *n.* buddy.

Pal., Palestine.

PAL (no periods), Phase Alternation Line (a system of color television adopted by many European countries).

P.A.L., Police Athletic League (an organization set up by a police department to provide sports, camping, and other activities for youth).

pa·la·bra (pä lä′brä), *n. Spanish.* **1.** a word. **2.** profuse talk; palaver.

pal·ace (pal′is), *n.* **1. a.** the official residence of a king, queen, bishop, or other exalted personage: *As Her Serene Highness, Princess Grace, she is expected to live in the great 200-room, yellow-stone palace overlooking the Mediterranean* (Newsweek). **b.** *British.* the official residence of an archbishop or bishop within his cathedral city. **2.** a very fine house or building. **3.** a more or less imposing or pretentious place of entertainment: *an old movie palace.* **4.** an official building, especially one of imposing size (often by extension from use in French, Italian, etc.): *the palace of justice.* [< Old French *palais* < Latin *Palātium* (originally) the Palatine Hill in Rome. site of the emperor's palace] —**Syn. 1. a.** castle.

palace car, a luxuriously equipped passenger car on a railroad.

palace revolution, a revolution plotted and carried out by a group of insiders: *A cabal of Appalachian district directors will undertake a palace revolution* (Atlantic).

pal·a·din (pal′ə din), *n.* **1.** one of the twelve knights who comprised, according to legend, the bodyguard and closest companions of Charlemagne. **2.** a knightly defender: *Last summer the paladins of CBS-TV made a fascinating if alarming discovery* (Newsweek). *Let others sing of knights and paladins* (Samuel Daniel). [< Middle French *paladin* < Italian *paladino,* learned borrowing from Latin *Palātinus;* see PALATINE[1]] —**Syn. 2.** champion.

palaeo-, *combining form. Especially British.* a variant form of **paleo-.**

pa·lae·o·an·throp·ic (pā′lē ō an throp′ik, pal′ē-), *adj. Especially British.* paleoanthropic.

pa·lae·o·bot·a·ny (pā′lē ō bot′ə nē, pal′ē-), *n. Especially British.* paleobotany.

pa·lae·o·cli·ma·tol·o·gy (pā′lē ō klī′mə tol′ə jē, pal′ē-), *n. Especially British.* paleoclimatology.

pa·lae·o·mag·net·ic (pā′lē ō mag net′ik, pal′ē-), *adj. Especially British.* paleomagnetic.

pa·lae·o·mag·net·ism (pā′lē ō mag′nə tiz əm, pal′ē-), *n. Especially British.* paleomagnetism: *The new science of palaeomagnetism is reviving the old theory that the world's continents were once joined together like the pieces of a jigsaw puzzle* (New York Times).

pa·laes·tra (pə les′trə), *n., pl.* **-tras, -trae** (-trē). **1.** a public place for physical exercise and training in ancient Greece. **2. a.** a wrestling school. **b.** any gymnasium. Also, **palestra.** [< Latin *palaestra* < Greek *palaístra* < *palaíein* to wrestle]

pal·a·fitte (pal′ə fit), *n.* a prehistoric lake dwelling, supported on piles, especially one in Switzerland or northern Italy. [< French *palafitte* < Italian *palafitta* pile fence < *palo* stake (< Latin *pālus*) + *fitto,* past participle of *figgere* fix < Latin *figere*]

pa·lais de danse (pȧ lā′ də däNs′), *French.* dance hall.

pal·an·quin or **pal·an·keen** (pal′ən kēn′), *n.* a covered couch enclosed by shutters or heavy curtains, carried by poles resting on the shoulders usually of four or six men: *... a procession of highly decorated lacquer palanquins bearing the ladies* (Atlantic). —*v.i.* to travel in a palanquin: *the land of slaves and palankeening* (Thomas Hood). [< Portuguese *palanquim,* or Italian *palanchino;* of Indian origin. Compare Malay *palangki,* Sanskrit *palyanka, paryanka* couch.] —**Syn.** *n.* litter.

Palanquin

pa·las (pa läs′), *n.* the dhak, an East Indian tree of the pea family. [< Hindi *palās*]

pal·at·a·bil·i·ty (pal′ə tə bil′ə tē), *n.* palatable quality or condition: *The palatability of eggs is associated with their size rather than with their coloring* (Scientific American).

pal·at·a·ble (pal′ə tə bəl), *adj.* **1.** agreeable to the taste; pleasing: *That was a most palatable lunch.* **2.** agreeable to the mind or feelings; acceptable: *His eloquence was distinguished by a bold, uncompromising, truth-telling spirit, whether the words might prove palatable or bitter to his audience* (John L. Motley). —**pal′at·a·ble·ness,** *n.* —**Syn. 1.** savory.

pal·at·a·bly (pal′ə tə blē), *adv.* in a palatable manner; agreeably.

pal·a·tal (pal′ə təl), *adj.* **1.** of or having to do with the palate. **2.** *Phonetics.* (of speech sounds) made with the front or middle of the tongue near or touching the hard palate. The *y* in *yet* is a palatal sound. *The palatal nasal, or "n" mouillé, occurs frequently in French* (Simeon Potter). —*n. Phonetics.* a palatal sound. [< French *palatal* < Latin *palātum* palate]

pal·a·tal·i·za·tion (pal′ə tə lə zā′shən), *n.* **1.** the act of palatalizing: *The introduction of a "y" sound before a vowel is called palatalization, because in pronouncing "y" the tongue is humped up toward the palate* (Scientific American). **2.** the state of being palatalized.

pal·a·tal·ize (pal′ə tə līz), *v.t.*, **-ized, -iz·ing.** *Phonetics.* to make palatal; change into a palatal sound.

pal·ate (pal′it), *n.* **1. a.** the roof of the mouth. The bony part in front is the hard palate, formed by parts of the maxillary and palatine bones, and the fleshy part in back is the soft palate, formed by several muscles: *The hard palate or roof of the mouth, in some of the early prehistoric forms, is U-shaped and broad; among modern men, it is narrower and parabolic in outline* (Beals and Hoijer). **b.** the hard palate. **2.** the sense of taste (from the belief, once generally held, that the palate is the organ of taste): *The new flavor pleased his palate.* **3.** a liking: *The lazy girl had no palate for washing dishes. Any subject that was not to their palate they condemned* (Milton). [< Latin *palātum*] —**Syn. 3.** relish.

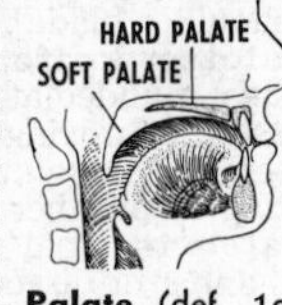

Palate (def. 1a)

pa·la·tial (pə lā′shəl), *adj.* like a palace; fit for a palace; magnificent: *a palatial apartment.* [< Latin *palātium* palace + English *-al*[1]] —**pa·la′tial·ly,** *adv.* —**Syn.** splendid.

pa·lat·i·nate (pə lat′ə nāt, -nit), *n.* the region under the rule of a count palatine.

Pa·lat·i·nate (pə lat′ə nāt, -nit), *n.* a native or inhabitant of the Palatinate, a region in West Germany.

pal·a·tine[1] (pal′ə tīn, -tin), *adj.* **1.** having royal rights in his own territory. A count palatine was subject only to the emperor or king. **2.** of a lord who has royal rights in his own territory. **3.** palatial.
—*n.* **1.** a lord having royal rights in his own territory; palatine lord. **2.** an officer of an imperial palace, originally the chamberlain of a palace. **3.** a fur scarf, cape, etc., formerly worn by women over the shoulders.
[< Latin *Palātīnus* of the *Palātium* or Palatine Hill (palace); a palace official, a chamberlain (in Late Latin, an imperial representative)]

pal·a·tine[2] (pal′ə tīn, -tin), *adj.* **1.** of, having to do with, or in the region of the palate: *In human beings, a palatine tonsil can be seen on each side of the back of the mouth just above the throat and below the roof of the mouth* (World Book Encyclopedia). **2.** designating or having to do with either of the two bones (palatine bones) forming the hard palate.
—*n.* a palatine bone.
[< French *palatine* < Latin *palātum* palate + French *-ine* -ine[1]]

Pal·a·tine (pal′ə tīn, -tin), *adj.* of or having to do with the Palatinate, a region in West Germany west of the Rhine. —*n.* a native or inhabitant of the Palatinate.

pa·lav·er (pə lav′ər, -läv′ər), *n.* **1.** a parley or conference, especially between traders or travelers and uncivilized natives whose customs require the formal exchange of compliments, gifts, etc., before the bringing up of any matter of business. **2.** unnecessary or idle words; mere talk: *After years of futile palaver, Latin America's coffee-producing nations are finally getting together in a hard-boiled cartel to hold up the price of coffee* (Time). **3.** smooth, persuading talk; fluent talk; flattery: *smooth-tongued palaver.*
—*v.i.* **1.** to talk: *Don't stand there palavering all day* (Mark Twain). **2.** to talk fluently or flatteringly, especially so as to persuade or cajole. **3.** to engage in a palaver; parley.
[< Portuguese *palavra* < Latin *parabola* comparison, story, parable. Doublet of PARABLE, PARABOLA, PARABOLE, PAROLE.]
—**Syn.** *n.* **1.** colloquy. **3.** cajolery.

pa·lay (pä′lī), *n.* (in the Philippines) rice in the husk: *To feed this fecund people, [he] must produce 4,600,000 tons of palay in the coming year* (Time). [< Tagalog *palay.* Related to *paddy*[1].]

pa·laz·zo (pä lät′sō), *n., pl.* **-zi** (-sē). *Italian.* **1.** a palace: *She lives in a comfortable apartment carved out of the attic in a princely palace, Palazzo Altieri, in old Rome—a fairy-story palazzo with many courtyards, entrances and exits, porches, and monumental stairways* (Harper's). **2.** a large, substantial mansion in a city, especially in Italy: *What he [Palladio] was called upon to do was almost exclusively the designing of town and country houses, "palazzi" and "ville"* (Nikolaus Pevsner).

pale[1] (pāl), *adj.*, **pal·er, pal·est,** *v.*, **paled, pal·ing.** —*adj.* **1.** without much color; lacking natural color; whitish: *When you have been ill, your face is sometimes pale. Dry sherry is usually pale.* **2.** not bright; dim: *pale blue, a pale glow from the windows.* **3.** lacking vigor; feeble; faint: *a pale policy.*
—*v.i.* to turn pale; lose color or brilliancy: *Helen's face paled at the bad news.* —*v.t.* to cause to become pale; dim: *The glow-worm . . . 'gins to pale his uneffectual fire* (Shakespeare).
[< Old French *pale* < Latin *pallidus* < *pallēre* be pale. Doublet of PALLID.]
—**pale′ly,** *adv.* —**pale′ness,** *n.*
—**Syn.** *adj.* **1. Pale, pallid, wan** mean with little or no color. **Pale,** describing the face of a person, means without much natural or healthy color, and describing things, without much brilliance or depth: *She is pale and tired-looking. The walls are pale green.* **Pallid,** chiefly describing the face, suggests having all color drained away as by sickness or weakness: *Her pallid face shows her suffering.* **Wan** emphasizes the faintness and whiteness coming from a weakened or unhealthy condition: *The starved refugees were wan.* **2.** faint, indistinct. —**Ant.** *adj.* **1.** rosy, ruddy, flushed.

pale[2] (pāl), *n., v.*, **paled, pal·ing.** —*n.* **1.** a long, narrow board, pointed at the top, used for fences; picket: *stakes . . . stuck in one by another like pales* (Daniel Defoe). **2.** boundary; restriction: *The exercise of foreign jurisdiction, within the pale of their own laws* (Thomas Jefferson). **3.** an enclosed place; enclosure: *I brought all my goods into this pale* (Daniel Defoe). **4.** a district or territory within fixed bounds or subject to a particular jurisdiction. **5.** *Archaic.* a fence; barrier: *It is as if a pale had been built round the British Isles* (London Times). **6.** *Heraldry.* an ordinary consisting of a broad vertical stripe in the middle of an escutcheon, usually occupying one third of its breadth. See picture under **invecked.**
beyond (or **outside**) **the pale,** overstepping the bounds; socially unacceptable; improper: *If Agrippa's "De occulta philosophia" is beyond the pale, then Marsilio Ficino and Pico della Mirandola ought also to be hushed up* (New Yorker).
the English Pale, (in French history) the territory of Calais.
the Pale, that part of eastern Ireland (varying in extent at different times) over which English jurisdiction was established.
—*v.t.* to enclose with pales or a fence; fence (in).
[< Old French *pal,* learned borrowing from Latin *pālus* stake. Doublet of PEEL[3], POLE[1].]
—**Syn.** *n.* **2.** limit.

pale-, *combining form.* the form of **paleo-** usually used before vowels, as in *paleethnology.*

pa·le·a (pā′lē ə), *n., pl.* **-le·ae** (-lē ē). *Botany.* **1.** one of the inner, scalelike, usually membranous bracts enclosing the stamens and pistil in the flower of grasses. **2.** one of the bracts at the base of the individual florets in many composite plants. **3.** the scales on the stems of certain ferns. [< Latin *palea* chaff]

pa·le·a·ceous (pā′lē ā′shəs), *adj. Botany.* **1.** furnished or covered with paleae. **2.** of the nature or consistency of chaff; chaffy.

Pa·le·arc·tic (pā′lē ärk′tik, pal′ē-), *adj.* belonging to the northern division of the Old World (Europe, Africa north of the tropic of Cancer, and Asia north of the Himalayas). [< *pale-* + *arctic*]

pa·le·eth·no·log·ic (pā′lē eth′nə loj′ik, pal′ē-), *adj.* of or having to do with paleethnology.

pa·le·eth·no·log·i·cal (pā′lē eth′nə loj′ə kəl, pal′ē-), *adj.* paleethnologic.

pa·le·eth·nol·o·gist (pā′lē eth nol′ə jist, pal′ē-), *n.* a person skilled or engaged in paleethnology.

pa·le·eth·nol·o·gy (pā′lē eth nol′ə jē, pal′ē-), *n.* the branch of ethnology that treats of the earliest or most primitive races of men. [< *pale-* + *ethnology*]

pale·face (pāl′fās′), *n.* a white person. The North American Indians are said to have called white people palefaces. *Where a Paleface comes, a Red man cannot stay* (James Fenimore Cooper).

pale-faced (pāl′fāst′), *adj.* having a pale face; pale: . . . *she found the pale-faced boy still standing there and nothing seemed to have changed* (Heinrich Böll).

pa·le·ich·thy·ol·o·gy (pā′lē ik′thē ol′ə jē, pal′ē-), *n.* the branch of ichthyology that deals with fossil fishes.

paleo-, *combining form.* **1.** old; ancient: *Paleography = ancient writing.*
2. of a relatively early time division: *Paleocene = the earliest epoch of the Tertiary period.* Also, **pale-** before certain vowels. Also, **palaeo-.** [< Greek *palaio-* < *palaiós* ancient]

pa·le·o·an·throp·ic (pā′lē ō an throp′ik, pal′ē-), *adj.* of or belonging to the geological period intermediate between protoanthropic and neanthropic.

pa·le·o·an·thro·pol·o·gist (pā′lē ō an′thrə pol′ə jist, pal′ē-), *n.* an expert in paleoanthropology: *Until the head is thoroughly examined and the proper deductions made, some paleoanthropologists say Dr. Heurzeler's theory is still only a theory* (Wall Street Journal). *By utilizing the logic of structure and the logic of evolutionary development, it has been possible for paleoanthropologists to achieve what seems to the uninitiated almost miracles in reconstructing the characteristics of the earlier, extinct forms of mankind* (Melville J. Herskovits).

pa·le·o·an·thro·pol·o·gy (pā′lē ō an′thrə pol′ə jē, pal′ē-), *n.* the study of the early types of human beings, as represented by their fossils and remains of their cultures: *Plaster casts will be made and sent to all the institutes of paleoanthropology in the world* (New York Times).

pa·le·o·bo·tan·ic (pā′lē ō bə tan′ik, pal′ē-), *adj.* paleobotanical.

pa·le·o·bo·tan·i·cal (pā′lē ō bə tan′ə kəl, pal′ē-), *adj.* of or having to do with paleobotany: *Johannes Iversen is head of the Paleobotanical Laboratory of the Geological Survey of Denmark* (Scientific American). *If the changes were overlooked, the apparent age of every archaeological and paleobotanical specimen would increase by about 2,000 years* (New Science).

pa·le·o·bot·a·nist (pā′lē ō bot′ə nist, pal′ē-), *n.* a person skilled or engaged in paleobotany: *A paleobotanist identified its imprint as a seed pod of the redbud-leaf tree* (Scientific American). *Fossil plants have suffered much alteration and the paleobotanist . . . is from the first concerned with the details of preservation and the use of unpromising material* (Tom M. Harris).

pa·le·o·bot·a·ny (pā′lē ō bot′ə nē, pal′ē-), *n.* the branch of paleontology dealing with fossil plants: *This science [paleontology] in turn is divided into paleozoology, for animals, and paleobotany, for plants* (World Book Encyclopedia). [< *paleo-* + *botany*]

Pa·le·o·cene (pā′lē ə sēn, pal′ē-), *n.* **1.** a geological epoch, the earliest of the Tertiary period of the Cenozoic era, before the Eocene: *Both in Europe and in North America, the Tertiary System is recognized as containing main divisions that in upward order are named "Paleocene," "Eocene," "Oligocene," "Miocene," and "Pliocene"* (Raymond Cecil Moore). **2.** the strata formed during this epoch. —*adj.* of or having to do with this epoch or these strata. [< *paleo-* + Greek *kainós* new]

pa·le·o·cli·ma·tol·o·gy (pā′lē ō klī′mə tol′ə jē, pal′ē-), *n.* the study of the climate of prehistoric times.

pa·le·o·cor·tex (pā′lē ō kôr′teks, pal′ē-), *n.* the older portion of the cortex of the human brain, having to do with the sense of smell: *In general the higher the functions, the higher their seats in the brain—rising through the thalami and their branches, and the basal ganglia, to the paleocortex, which man shares with the higher animals* (Time).

pa·le·o·cos·mic (pā′lē ō koz′mik, pal′ē-), *adj.* belonging to the earliest period of the world to be characterized by human life. [< *paleo-* + *cosmic*]

pa·le·o·crys·tic (pā′lē ō kris′tik, pal′ē-), *adj.* consisting of or containing ice supposed to have remained frozen since early ages. [< *paleo-* + Greek *krýstallos* ice + English *-ic*]

pa·le·o·e·col·o·gy (pā′lē ō ē kol′ə jē, pal′ē-) *n.* the study of the relationship of living things to environment and each other in prehistoric times; the ecology of prehistoric life: *Heinz A. Lowenstam, professor of paleoecology at California Institute of Technology, will discuss skeletal properties and paleoecology* (Science).

pa·le·o·fau·na (pā′lē ō fô′nə, pal′ē-), *n.* the fossil fauna of a geological formation or period. [< *paleo-* + *fauna*]

pa·le·o·flo·ra (pā′lē ō flôr′ə, -flōr′-; pal′ē-), *n.* the fossil flora of a geological formation or period. [< *paleo-* + *flora*]

paleog., paleography.

Pa·le·o·gene (pā′lē ə jēn, pal′ē-), *n.* the lower division of the Tertiary period; Eogene. —*adj.* of or having to do with this division or its rocks. [< *paleo-* + Greek *-genēs* -gen]

pa·le·o·ge·og·ra·phy (pā′lē ō jē og′rə fē, pal′ē-), *n.* the geography of former geological time. [< *paleo-* + *geography*]

pa·le·og·ra·pher (pā′lē og′rə fər, pal′ē-), *n.* a person who is skilled in paleography: *Archaeologists, paleographers, Old and New Testament scholars and language experts had combined forces on deciphering the leather scrolls* (Science News Letter).

pa·le·o·graph·ic (pā′lē ə graf′ik, pal′ē-), *adj.* of or having to do with paleography.

pa·le·o·graph·i·cal (pā′lē ə graf′ə kəl, pal′ē-), *adj.* paleographic: *This fits in with the date assigned by Albright, who, arguing from the paleographical evidence, immediately put the Isaiah scroll at about 100 B.C.* (New Yorker).

pa·le·og·ra·phy (pā′lē og′rə fē, pal′ē-), *n.* **1.** ancient writing or ancient forms of writing. **2.** the study of ancient writings to determine the dates, origins, meanings, etc. [< *paleo-* + *-graphy*]

Pa·le·o-In·di·an (pā′lē ō in′dē ən, pal′ē-), *n.* one of a prehistoric group of people believed to have migrated from Asia to the Americas during the late Ice Age: *Paleo-Indians . . . were big game hunters and preyed on bison and mammoths* (Science News Letter).
—*adj.* of or having to do with Paleo-Indians: *Paleo-Indian artifacts, Paleo-Indian culture.*

pa·le·o·lith (pā′lē ə lith, pal′ē-), *n.* an artifact of paleolithic man; paleolithic tool. [< *paleo-* + Greek *líthos* stone]

pa·le·o·lith·ic or **Pa·le·o·lith·ic** (pā′lē ə lith′ik, pal′ē-), *adj.* of or having to do with the earlier part of the Stone Age: *Paleolithic tools were crudely chipped out of stone. In the Paleolithic period, no animals seem to have been domesticated, and fire was probably unknown* (Emory S. Bogardus). —*n.* this age.

paleolithic man, *Anthropology.* any of the men of the early Stone Age, including, in addition to Homo sapiens, various species now extinct.

pa·le·ol·o·gist (pā′lē ol′ə jist, pal′ē-), *n.* a person skilled in paleology; a student or a writer on antiquity.

pa·le·ol·o·gy (pā′lē ol′ə jē, pal′ē-), *n.* the science of antiquities; archaeology. [< *paleo-* + *-logy*]

pa·le·o·mag·net·ic (pā′lē ō mag net′ik, pal′ē-), *adj.* of or having to do with paleomagnetism.

pa·le·o·mag·net·ism (pā′lē ō mag′nə tiz əm, pal′ē-), *n.* the study of the direction of the residual magnetism in ancient rocks to determine the movement of the magnetic poles or of the rocks.

pa·le·on·to·graph·ic (pā′lē on′tə graf′ik, pal′ē-), *adj.* paleontographical.

pa·le·on·to·graph·i·cal (pā′lē on′tə graf′ə kəl, pal′ē-), *adj.* of or having to do with paleontography.

pa·le·on·tog·ra·phy (pā′lē on tog′rə fē, pal′ē-), *n.* the description of fossil remains. [< *paleo-* + Greek *ōn, óntos* a being + English *-graphy*]

paleontol., paleontology.

pa·le·on·to·log·ic (pā′lē on′tə loj′ik, pal′ē-), *adj.* of or having to do with paleontology. —**pa′le·on′to·log′i·cal·ly,** *adv.*

pa·le·on·to·log·i·cal (pā′lē on′tə loj′ə kəl, pal′ē-), *adj.* paleontologic: *This study was stimulated by the advance of geological and paleontological research, which revealed the considerable age of the earth and suggested that life on earth was a good deal older than had previously been thought* (Beals and Hoijer). *Before embarking on a description of the paleontological stages of man's emergence* (J.S. Weiner).

pa·le·on·tol·o·gist (pā′lē on tol′ə jist, pal′ē-), *n.* a person skilled in paleontology: *The paleontologist is interested in a fossil for hints as to the nature of the organism which caused it* (Science News Letter).

pa·le·on·tol·o·gy (pā′lē on tol′ə jē, pal′ē-), *n.* the science of the forms of life existing long ago, as represented by fossil animals and plants: *Paleontology, the study of indications of prehistoric life, contributes much critical information to the biological sciences even as they, in turn, contribute to paleontology* (Harbaugh and Goodrich). [< *paleo-* + Greek *ōn, óntos* a being + English *-logy*]

pa·le·o·pa·thol·o·gy (pā′lē ō pə thol′ə jē, pal′ē-), *n.* the study of the diseases of historic and prehistoric times: *Paleopathology [studies] . . . the ills of ancient man . . . as deduced from the examination of naturalistic art, old bones, and mummified or otherwise preserved bodies* (New Yorker).

pa·le·o·pe·dol·o·gy (pā′lē ō pi dol′ə jē, pal′ē-), *n.* the branch of geology dealing with the soils of former geological time. [< *paleo-* + Greek *pédon* earth + English *-logy*]

pa·le·o·phy·tol·o·gy (pā′lē ō fī tol′ə jē, pal′ē-), *n.* paleobotany.

pa·le·or·ni·thol·o·gy (pā′lē ôr′nə thol′ə jē, pal′ē-), *n.* the branch of ornithology that deals with fossil birds. [< *pale-* + *ornithology*]

pa·le·o·tech·nic (pā′lē ō tek′nik, pal′ē-), *adj.* having to do with the earlier historical phase of the development of modern industrial machinery, characterized by the use of coal, iron, and the steam engine. The term has become familiar to students of technological history through the writings of Patrick Geddes and Lewis Mumford.

Pa·le·o·trop·i·cal (pā′lē ō trop′ə kəl, pal′ē-), *adj.* belonging to the tropical (and subtropical) regions of the Old World or Eastern Hemisphere. [< *paleo-* + *tropical*]

Pa·le·o·zo·ic (pā′lē ə zō′ik, pal′ē-), *n.* **1.** an early geological era before the Mesozoic, whose fossils represent early forms of life. It was characterized by the development of the first fishes, land plants, amphibians, reptiles, insects, and forests of fernlike trees: *Beginning about 505 million years ago, the Paleozoic is divided into six periods: Cambrian, Ordovician, Silurian, Devonian, Carboniferous, and Permian* (Beals and Hoijer). **2.** the rock strata formed in this era.
—*adj.* of this era or these rock strata: *The Paleozoic rocks are the oldest that contain abundant evidence of life* (Raymond Cecil Moore).
[< *paleo-* + Greek *zōē* life + English *-ic*]

pa·le·o·zo·o·log·i·cal (pā′lē ō zō′ə loj′ə kəl, pal′ē-), *adj.* of or having to do with paleozoology.

pa·le·o·zo·ol·o·gist (pā′lē ō zō ol′ə jist, pal′ē-), *n.* a person skilled in paleozoology.

pa·le·o·zo·ol·o·gy (pā′lē ō zō ol′ə jē, pal′ē-), *n.* the branch of paleontology dealing with fossil animals: *This science [paleontology] in turn is divided into paleozoology, for animals, and paleobotany, for plants* (World Book Encyclopedia). [< *paleo-* + *zoology*]

Pa·ler·mi·tan (pə lėr′mə tən, -lär′-), *adj.* of or having to do with Palermo, the capital of Sicily: *Don Vito was dining, as usual, with an influential member of Palermitan society* (New Yorker). —*n.* a native or inhabitant of Palermo: *. . . the music of this young and extremely gifted Palermitan* (London Times). [< Italian *palermitano*]

Pal·es·tin·i·an (pal′ə stin′ē ən), *adj.* of or having to do with Palestine, or the Holy Land, a region in southwestern Asia: *On the Arab side of the fence the basic difficulty lies in the Palestinian refugees and their state of mind* (Atlantic). —*n.* a native or inhabitant of Palestine: *General Burns said yesterday the crimes connected with infiltration would never be wiped out so long as the problem of the 213,000 former Palestinians in the Gaza strip was unsolved* (New York Times).

pa·les·tra (pə les′trə), *n., pl.* **-tras, -trae** (-trē). palaestra.

pa·let (pā′lit, pal′it), *n. Botany.* a palea. [< *pal(ea)* + *-et*]

pal·e·tot (pal′ə tō, pal′tō), *n.* a loose outer garment, as a coat or cloak, for men or women. [< French *paletot* < Middle French *palletot*, earlier *palletocq*, apparently < Middle English *paltock* a sleeved jacket; origin uncertain]

pal·ette (pal′it), *n.* **1.** a thin board usually oval or oblong, with a thumb hole at one end, used by an artist to lay and mix his colors on. **2.** set of colors on this board. **3.** the selection of colors used by a particular artist: *to use a wide palette.* **4.** Also, **pallette.** a small rounded plate protecting the armpit on a suit of armor. [< French *palette* < Old French (diminutive) < *pale* shovel, oar blade < Latin *pāla* spade, shoulder blade]

Palette

palette knife, a thin flexible blade of steel rounded at one end and set in a handle, used for mixing colors on a palette and to scrape the paint off the canvas before putting on another layer.

pale·wise (pāl′wīz′), *adv. Heraldry.* in the manner or direction of a pale; vertically.

pal·frey (pôl′frē), *n., pl.* **-freys.** *Archaic.* a gentle riding horse, especially one for ladies: *He . . . shook his drowsy squire awake, and cried, "My charger and her palfrey"* (Tennyson). [< Old French *palefreyd* < Late Latin *palafrēdus*, variant of *paraverēdus* a horse for outlying districts < Greek *para-* beside, secondary + Latin *verēdus* light horse < a Celtic word]

Pa·li (pä′lē), *n.* the Middle Indic language, a later form of Sanskrit, used in the sacred writings of the Buddhists and still existing as a literary language in Ceylon, Burma, and Thailand. [< Pali *pāli-bhāsā* language of the canonical texts < Sanskrit *pāli* line, canon + *bhāsā* language]

pa·li·kar (pal′i kär), *n.* a Greek or Albanian militiaman in the war of independence, 1821-1828, against Turkey. Also, **pellekar.** [< New Greek *palikári*, or *pallēkári* < Late Greek *pallikárion* a page (diminutive) < Greek *pállēx*, *pállēkos* a youth]

pal·imp·sest (pal′imp sest), *n.* **1.** parchment or other writing material from which one or more previous writings have been erased to make room for another. **2.** a manuscript with one text written over another. **3.** an oil painting that has lost its original intent by overpainting by another artist: *His weirdest palimpsest . . . had come to him by way of a lawyer* (New Yorker). [< Latin *palimpsestus* < Greek *palímpsēstos* (literally) scraped again < *pálin* again + *psēs-*, stem of *psên* to rub smooth]

pal·in·drome (pal′in drōm), *n.* a word, verse, or sentence which reads the same backward or forward. The sentence "Madam, I'm Adam" is a palindrome that contains (in its first word) another palindrome: *In Classical Latin 'the wolf' was simply* lupus, *in Vulgar Latin* ille lupus *or* lupus ille, *and today the former has become* le loup *in French,* el lobo *in Spanish and* il lupo *in Italian, whereas the latter has produced the palindrome* lupul *in Rumanian* (Simeon Potter). [< Greek *palíndromos* a recurrence; (literally) a running back < *pálin* again, back + *drómos* a running, related to *drameîn* run]

pal·in·drom·ic (pal′in drom′ik), *adj.* having to do with or of the nature of a palindrome.

pal·ing (pā′ling), *n.* **1.** a fence of pales: *I had seen . . . a gap in the paling—one stake broken down* (Charlotte Brontë). **2.** pales collectively, as fencing material: *The fence was only of split paling, but I got my trousers caught on the points* (Geoffrey Household). **3.** a pale in a fence: *The palings round the little gardens were broken and ruinous* (Mrs. Humphry Ward). **4.** the act of making a fence, or of enclosing a place, with pales; fencing. —**Syn. 3.** picket.

pal·in·gen·e·sis (pal′in jen′ə sis), *n.* **1.** rebirth; regeneration; reincarnation. **2.** the reproduction of ancestral features without change. [< Greek *pálin* again + *génesis* birth, genesis]
➤ See **cenogenesis** for usage note.

pal·i·node (pal′ə nōd), *n.* **1.** a poem or song, especially an ode, in which the author retracts something said in a former poem. **2.** (in Scottish Law) a formal retracting; recantation. [< Latin *palinōdia* < Greek *palinōidiā* recantation, retraction < *pálin* again + *ōidē* song, ode]

gathered for food by the natives: *The Atlantic palolo worm . . . when it acquires sexual maturity, annually swarms in June or July, at the time of the third quarter of the moon* (Harbaugh and Goodrich). [< the native name in Samoa]

pal·o·mi·no (pal′ə mē′nō), *n., pl.* **-nos. 1.** a cream-colored or golden-tan horse of Arabian stock. Its mane and tail are usually light colored: *a parade led by a pretty teen-ager riding a palomino* (Newsweek). **2.** a golden-tan or cream color: *The newest mink color is a tawny "palomino" shade, which will appear in quantity for the first time* (New York Times). [American English < Spanish *palomino* a young stock dove < Latin *palumbīnus* (diminutive) < *palumba* ringdove, wood pigeon (because of the color)]

pa·loo·ka (pə lü′kə), *n. Slang.* **1.** a mediocre or inferior boxer or player of any sport or game: *In rubber bridge, a pair of utter palookas could conceivably outscore two experts for an evening simply by holding better cards* (Maclean's). **2.** a stupid, awkward, though frequently muscular lout; especially, such a hoodlum. [origin uncertain]

pa·lo·ver·de (pä′lō vãr′dā), *n.* any of various shrubs or trees of the pea family, found in the arid regions of the southwestern United States and northern Mexico: *Desert wash is traced by ironwood . . . and paloverde . . . plants* (Scientific American).
[< Spanish *paloverde* < *palo* stick, wood (< Latin *pālus* pale[2]) + *verde* green < Latin *viridis*]

palp (palp), *n.* a palpus: *There are a pair of palps on either side of the mouth at the anterior end of the body which sort out edible particles and carry them into the mouth* (A.M. Winchester). [< French *palpe*, learned borrowing from Latin *palpus*]

pal·pa·bil·i·ty (pal′pə bil′ə tē), *n.* the quality of being palpable.

pal·pa·ble (pal′pə bəl), *adj.* **1.** readily seen or heard and recognized; obvious: *a palpable error. For shore it was, and high . . . and palpable to view* (Byron). **2.** that can be touched or felt: *A hit, a very palpable hit* (Shakespeare). **3.** *Medicine.* perceptible by palpation.
[< Late Latin *palpābilis* < Latin *palpāre* to feel, stroke, pat] —**pal′pa·ble·ness,** *n.*
—**Syn. 1.** perceptible, plain, evident, manifest. **2.** tangible.

pal·pa·bly (pal′pə blē), *adv.* **1.** plainly; obviously. **2.** to the touch.

pal·pal (pal′pəl), *adj. Zoology.* having to do with or of the nature of a palpus.

pal·pate[1] (pal′pāt), *v.t.,* **-pat·ed, -pat·ing. 1.** to examine by the sense of touch. **2.** to examine (a bodily organ, growth, etc.) by touching or manipulating with the hands, especially as a preliminary to or in order to confirm a medical diagnosis. [< Latin *palpāre* (with English *-ate*[1]) touch gently, stroke, feel, pat]

pal·pate[2] (pal′pāt), *adj. Zoology.* having a palpus or palpi. [< New Latin *palpus* palpus + English *-ate*[1]]

pal·pa·tion (pal pā′shən), *n.* **1.** the act of touching. **2.** *Medicine.* examination by touch or feeling, as with the hand: *Palpation may disclose the pulse to be fast or slow, regular or irregular, strong or weak, and hard or soft* (Harbaugh and Goodrich).

pal·pa·tor (pal pā′tər), *n.* a person who examines by touching.

pal·pe·bra (pal′pə brə), *n., pl.* **-brae** (-brē). *Anatomy.* an eyelid. [< Latin *palpebrae* eyelids, related to *palpāre* pat gently]

pal·pe·bral (pal′pə brəl), *adj.* of or having to do with an eyelid or the eyelids. [< Late Latin *palpebrālis* < Latin *palpebrae* eyelids; see PALPEBRA]

pal·pi (pal′pī), *n.* the plural of **palpus.**

pal·pi·tant (pal′pə tənt), *adj.* palpitating. [< Latin *palpitāns, -antis,* present participle of *palpitāre* palpitate]

pal·pi·tate (pal′pə tāt), *v.i.,* **-tat·ed, -tat·ing. 1.** to beat very rapidly, irregularly, or strongly, as from emotion, exercise, or disease: *Your heart palpitates when you are excited.* **2.** to quiver; throb; flutter; tremble: *fountains palpitating in the heat* (Tennyson). *His body palpitated with terror.* [< Latin *palpitāre* (with English *-ate*[1]) to throb, flutter (frequentative) < *palpāre* to pat, touch lightly] —**pal′pi·tat′ing·ly,** *adv.*

pal·pi·ta·tion (pal′pə tā′shən), *n.* **1.** a usually rapid beating of the heart. **2.** a quivering; trembling: *I was seized with such a palpitation and trembling that I could not stand* (Tobias Smollett).

pal·pus (pal′pəs), *n., pl.* **-pi.** one of the jointed feelers attached to the mouth of insects, spiders, lobsters, etc. Palpi are organs of touch or taste. [< New Latin *palpus* < Latin, soft palm[1]]

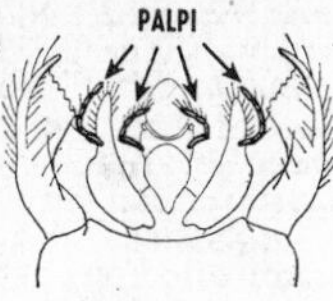

Palpi of an ant

pals·grave (pôlz′grāv, palz′-), *n. Historical.* a German count palatine. [< earlier Dutch *paltsgrave,* adaptation of Middle High German *pfalzgrāve* < Old High German *pfalenzgrâvo* < *pfalenza* palace, palatine[1] + *grâvo* count]

pals·gra·vine (pôlz′grə vēn, palz′-), *n.* the wife or widow of a palsgrave.

pal·ship (pal′ship), *n. U.S. Informal.* **1.** the state of being pals; comradeship: *I do not begrudge the American male the tranquil enjoyment of the locker-room palship which means so much to him* (Harper's). **2.** a liking between pals.

pal·sied (pôl′zid), *adj.* **1.** having the palsy; paralyzed. **2.** shaking; trembling: *old palsied houses* (Robert Louis Stevenson).

pal·staff (pôl′staf, -stäf), *n., pl.* **-staves** (-stāvz). palstave.

pal·stave (pôl′stāv), *n., pl.* **-staves.** *Archaeology.* a form of celt that resembles a chisel, having a tongue that fits directly into a handle. [< Danish *paalstav* < Old Icelandic *pālstafr* < *pāll* hoe + *stafr* stave]

pal·sy (pôl′zi), *n., pl.* **-sies,** *v.,* **-sied, -sy·ing.** —*n.* paralysis; loss of power to feel, to move, or to control motion in any part of the body: *The man had palsy in his arm.*
—*v.t.* **1.** to paralyze. **2.** to make powerless or inert: *Disappointment palsied her heart* (Jane Porter).
[Middle English *palesie, parlesie* < Old French *paralysie,* learned borrowing from unrecorded Medieval Latin *paralysia,* alteration of Latin *paralysis.* Doublet of PARALYSIS.]

pal·sy wal·sy (pal′zē wal′zē), *Slang.* like pals; friendly; closely associated: *. . . in view of the palsy walsy relationship between Roll and Bill Bonelli* (Newsweek).

pal·ter (pôl′tər), *v.i.* **1.** to talk or act insincerely; trifle deceitfully: *Man crouches and blushes . . . he palters and steals* (Emerson). **2.** to act carelessly; trifle: *A hunger for music is one of our noblest appetites, and nothing to be paltered with* (Atlantic). **3.** to haggle; bargain improperly or tiresomely, especially in a matter of duty, honor, etc.: *Who never sold the truth to serve the hour, Nor palter'd with Eternal God for power* (Tennyson). [origin unknown] —**pal′ter·er,** *n.*
—**Syn. 1.** equivocate.

pal·tri·ly (pôl′trə lē), *adv.* in a paltry manner; despicably; meanly.

pal·tri·ness (pôl′trē nis), *n.* the state of being paltry.

pal·try (pôl′trē), *adj.,* **-tri·er, -tri·est. 1.** almost worthless; trifling; petty; mean: *He . . . considered the prize too paltry for the lives it must cost* (John L. Motley). **2.** of no worth; despicable; contemptible: *a paltry trick, a paltry crowd. He is a paltry, imitating pedant* (Jonathan Swift). [perhaps < dialectal *palt,* or *pelt* trash, dirty rag, waste. Compare Low German *paltrig* ragged, torn; Frisian *palt* rag, torn piece.] —**Syn. 1.** insignificant.

pa·lu·dal (pə lü′dəl, pal′yə-), *adj.* **1.** of or having to do with a marsh or fen; marshy. **2.** caused by or arising from a marsh; malarial. [< Latin *palūs, -ūdis* marsh + English *-al*[1]]

pa·lu·da·ment (pə lü′də mənt), *n.* a kind of cloak or mantle worn by an ancient Roman general in war, but later reserved exclusively for the emperor as head of the army. [< Latin *palūdāmentum*]

pa·lu·dic (pə lü′dik), *adj.* paludal.

pa·lu·di·cole (pə lü′də kōl), *adj.* inhabiting or frequenting marshes: *paludicole birds.* [< Latin *palūs, -ūdis* marsh + *colere* inhabit]

pal·u·dic·o·line (pal′yə dik′ə lin), *adj.* paludicole.

pal·u·dic·o·lous (pal′yə dik′ə ləs), *adj.* paludicole.

pal·u·dine (pal′yə din, -dīn), *adj.* paludal.

pal·u·dism (pal′yə diz əm), *n. Medicine.* malaria. [< Latin *palūs, -ūdis* marsh + English *-ism*]

pal·u·dose (pal′yə dōs), *adj.* living or growing in marshes, as animals or plants. [< Latin *palūdōsus* < *palūs, -ūdis* marsh]

Pal·u·drine (pal′yə drēn, -drin), *n. Trademark.* a colorless, synthetic antimalarial drug: *Used in more than 100 cases within six months, paludrine is reported to prevent malarial infection from mosquito bites* (Marguerite Clark). *Formula:* $C_{11}H_{16}ClN_5$

pa·lus·tral (pə lus′trəl), *adj.* of or having to do with marshes; found in or inhabiting marshes; paludal: *In these palustral homes we only croak and wither* (Manchester Guardian). [< Latin *paluster, -tris* (< *pālus* marsh) + English *-al*[1]]

pa·lus·trine (pə lus′trin), *adj.* paludal.

pal·y[1] (pā′lē), *adj.,* **pal·i·er, pal·i·est.** *Archaic.* somewhat pale: *paly locks of gold* (John Greenleaf Whittier).

pal·y[2] (pā′lē), *adj. Heraldry.* (of a shield or a bearing) divided palewise (vertically) into four or more (usually) equal parts of alternate tinctures. [< Old French *palé,* apparently < *pal* a pale[2], stake]

pal·y·nol·o·gist (pal′ə nol′ə jist), *n.* a person skilled in palynology.

pal·y·nol·o·gy (pal′ə nol′ə jē), *n.* the study of plant spores and pollen, especially in fossil form. [< Greek *palýnein* strew + English *-logy*]

pam (pam), *n.* **1.** the jack of clubs in one variety of the game of loo: *Ev'n mighty Pam, that kings and queens o'erthrew* (Alexander Pope). **2.** the variety of loo in which it is the best trump. [apparently abbreviation of French *pamphile* the knave of clubs in loo; the game of loo; (originally) a proper name < Greek *Pámphilos* loved by all]

pam., pamphlet.

pa·ma·quine (pä′mə kwīn), *n.* a yellowish, odorless synthetic drug effective in the treatment of malaria but often toxic to humans. *Formula:* $C_{42}H_{45}N_3O_7$

Pa·mir sheep (pä mir′), Marco Polo sheep. [< the *Pamirs,* a mountain range in Central Asia]

pam·pa (pam′pə), *n.* singular of **pampas:** *Stoneless, soft, immensely fertile, the Argentine pampa stretches sea-flat to the horizon* (Economist).

pam·pas (pam′pəz), *n.pl.* the grass-covered, treeless plains of South America south of the forest-covered belt of the Amazon basin, especially in Argentina: *. . . across the grassy pampas, where wild gauchos tend their restless herds* (New York Times). [< Spanish *pampas,* plural < Quechua (Peru) *pampa* a plain]

pampas grass, an ornamental grass, native in South America but widely cultivated, having large, thick, feathery panicles of a silvery white, borne on stems which sometimes reach a height of 12 feet: *The beautiful pampas grass, throwing out leaves six or eight feet long* (Robert Hogg).

Pampas Grass (to 12 ft. high)

pam·pe·an (pam pē′ən, pam′pē-), *adj.* of or having to do with the pampas.
—*n.* an Indian living on or in the region of the pampas.

pam·per (pam′pər), *v.t.* **1.** to indulge too much; allow too many privileges to: *to pamper a child, to pamper one's appetite.* **2.** *Obsolete.* to cram or glut with food, especially rich food; feed luxuriously. [Middle English *pamperen,* perhaps (frequentative) < obsolete *pampen* to pamper, cram] —**pam′per·er,** *n.* —**Syn. 1.** spoil, humor.

pam·pered (pam′pərd), *adj.* **1.** overindulged; spoiled by luxury: *A pampered body will darken the mind* (Samuel Johnson). **2.** *Obsolete.* overfed.

pam·pe·ro (päm pãr′ō; *Spanish* päm pā′rō), *n., pl.* **-pe·ros** (-pãr′ōz; *Spanish* -pā′rōs). a piercing cold wind that blows from the Andes across the pampas of South America to the Atlantic: *the sudden southwest wind called pampero, almost knocking the breath out of your body, then passing as suddenly away* (W.H. Hudson). [American English < Spanish *pampero* < *pampa;* see PAMPA]

pamph., pamphlet.

pam·phlet (pam′flit), *n.* **1.** a booklet in paper covers. A pamphlet often deals with a question of current interest: *In Europe, the pamphlet is a short piece of writing essentially polemic in nature, concerned with a problem of the moment* (Harper's). **2.** any printed booklet with few pages. [< Medieval Latin

(England) *panfletus*, for Old French *Pamphilet*, popular name for a Latin poem of the 1100's "Pamphilus, seu de Amore" < Greek *Pámphilos* loved by all < *pan-* (see PAN-) + *phílos* loved (one), lover < *phileîn* to love] —**Syn. 1.** tract.

pam·phlet·ar·y (pam′flə ter′ē), *adj.* of, like, or having to do with a pamphlet or pamphleteering.

pam·phlet·eer (pam′flə tir′), *n.* a person who writes pamphlets, especially on controversial subjects: *As a pamphleteer Thomas Paine is without his equal in American literature* (Jones and Leisy). —*v.i.* to write and issue pamphlets.

pam·pro·dac·ty·lous (pam′prō dak′tə ləs), *n. Ornithology.* having all four toes turned forward, as in the coly. [< Greek *pam-* pan- + *pró* before + *dáktylos* finger or toe + English *-ous*]

pan[1] (pan), *n., v.,* **panned, pan·ning.** —*n.* **1.** a dish for cooking and other household uses, usually broad, shallow, and often with no cover: *pots and pans.* **2.** anything like this: **a.** a vessel in which gold, tin, etc., are separated from gravel, crushed quartz, etc., by agitation and washing: *After the car is placed on the dumper, it is clamped in place, elevated and turned over to dump the coal into a pan from which it flows through a telescopic chute into the vessel taking the cargo* (Richmond Times Dispatch). **b.** a relatively broad, shallow vessel, usually of cast iron, in which ores, especially of silver, were formerly ground and amalgamated. **c.** a shallow vessel used for evaporating water from any of various liquid substances, so as to obtain a desired substance, as salt from brine or maple syrup from maple sap. **3.** one of the dishes on a pair of scales. **4.** the contents of a pan; amount that a pan will hold. **5.** (in old-fashioned guns) the hollow part of the lock that held a little gunpowder to set the gun off. **6.** hard subsoil; hardpan. **7.** a hollow or depression in the ground, especially one in which water stands: *A dry pan, or waterhole, which . . . was densely covered with weeds* (H. Rider Haggard). **8.** a natural or artificial basin in which salt is obtained by evaporating sea water. **9.** pan ice: *A boat would be in danger of being carried along with it, and crushed to pieces between the pans* (Newfoundland House Assembly Journal).

—*v.t.* **1.** to cook in a pan. **2. a.** to wash in a pan: *pan gold.* **b.** to wash (gravel, sand, etc.) in a pan to get gold: *Her 800-acre ranch is close to a deserted mining town, where she sometimes pans a little gold out of the old diggings* (Harper's). **3.** *Informal.* to criticize severely: *The drama critic panned the new play.* —*v.i.* **1.** to wash gold-bearing gravel, sand, etc., in a pan in order to separate the gold: *Panning consists merely of segregating by gravity and water the earthy material from the metal in the pan* (White and Renner). **2.** to yield gold when washed in a pan.

pan out, *Informal.* to turn out or work out: *His latest scheme panned out well.*

[Old English *panne*, apparently < Medieval Latin *panna* < Latin *patina*]

pan[2] (pän), *n.* **1.** the betel leaf. **2.** a combination of betel leaf, areca nut, lime, etc., used for chewing like gum in various parts of Asia. [< Hindi *pān* < Sanskrit *parṇa* leaf, feather, betel leaf]

pan[3] (pan), *v.,* **panned, pan·ning.** —*v.i.* (of a motion picture or television camera) to move, either vertically or horizontally, so as to take in a larger scene (panorama) or to follow a moving object, etc.: *to pan from the speaker to the audience.* —*v.t.* to move (a camera) thus. [short for *panorama*]

Pan (pan), *n. Greek Mythology.* the god of forests, pastures, flocks, hunters, and shepherds. Pan is described and pictured as a man with legs like a goat and as playing on musical pipes. The Romans identified him with Faunus.

pan-, *combining form.* all: *Pan-American = of all the Americas. Panacea = a remedy for all diseases.* [< Greek *pân*, neuter of *pâs* all]

pan., panchromatic.

Pan., Panama.

pan·a·ce·a (pan′ə sē′ə), *n.* **1.** a remedy for all diseases or ills; cure-all: *For my panacea . . . let me have a draught of undiluted morning air* (Thoreau). **2.** anything that resembles such a remedy or medicine in the range of virtues claimed for it, as an economic program, political reform, etc.: *There are no panaceas in education. The first panacea for a mis-managed nation is inflation of the currency* (Ernest Hemingway). [< Latin *panacēa* an all-healing herb; also, the goddess of healing < Greek *panákeia* panacea < *panakḗs* all-healing < *pan-* all + *ákos* cure]

pan·a·ce·an (pan′ə sē′ən), *adj.* of the nature of a panacea.

pa·nache (pə nash′, -näsh′), *n.* **1.** a tuft or plume of feathers used ornamentally, especially on a helmet, etc.: *With him came a gallant train . . . decorated with rich surcoats and panaches of feathers* (Washington Irving). **2.** swagger; dash: *With the poise and panache most debs would envy, Catrina Colston wears palest blue organdie* (Sunday Times). [< French *panache*, Middle French *pennache* < Italian *pennaccio*, variant of *pennacchio* < *penna* feather < Latin]

pa·na·da (pə nä′də), *n.* a dish made of bread or crackers boiled in water or milk to a pulp and variously seasoned or flavored. [< Spanish, Portuguese *panada* < Italian *panata* < *pane* bread < Latin *pānis*]

Pan-Af·ri·can (pan af′rə kən), *adj.* of or for all African peoples: *Pan-African movement.*

Pan-Af·ri·can·ism (pan af′rə kə niz′əm), *n.* **1.** the concept of or a movement toward the political union of all African peoples: *It concentrates on exploiting the Africans' . . . resentment against colonialism and even Pan-Africanism to encourage a separatist trade-union movement* (Cape Times). **2.** belief in or support of this concept or movement.

Pan-Af·ri·can·ist (pan af′rə kə nist), *n.* a person who believes in or supports Pan-Africanism: *If Nasser can draw spiritual satisfaction from Egypt's geographical location, why should not Pan-Africanists try to steal a march on him?* (New Yorker). —*adj.* of or having to do with Pan-Africanism: *The most likely prime minister is a veteran and important member of Pan-Africanist councils* (Atlantic).

pan·a·ma (pan′ə mä, -mô), *n.* **1. a.** a fine hat woven from the young leaves of the jipijapa and toquilla plants, especially in Ecuador. **b.** any hat made in imitation of this: *Worsted flannels . . . and cotton and tropical panamas* (Sunday Times). **2.** the leaves, straw, etc., from which the hat is made: *The crowns and underbrims of planters' hats of natural panama are lined with rows of shirred and fluted shrimp ribbon* (New Yorker). [< *Panama*, where they were formerly shipped from]

Panama disease, a common disease of the banana plant, caused by a fungus that attacks the roots and grows on the plant, finally withering it: *Panama disease, a fungus-caused wilt that threatened to wipe out much of the Central American banana industry a few years back, may defy eradication by "hiding out" in wild plants near banana fields* (Science News Letter).

Panama hat, panama (def. 1).

Pan·a·man (pan′ə män′), *adj., n.* Panamanian.

Pan·a·ma·ni·an (pan′ə mā′nē ən), *adj.* of or having to do with Panama: *Panamanian law, though it forbids the death penalty, provides a specially tough maximum sentence of 35 years for presidential assassins* (Time). —*n.* a native or inhabitant of Panama: *They are nevertheless better fed, better housed, better clothed than the Panamanians on the other side of Fourth of July Avenue* (Newsweek).

Pan-A·mer·i·can (pan′ə mer′ə kən), *adj.* **1.** of all Americans; having to do with or involving the people of North, Central, and South America. **2.** including all the countries of North, Central, and South America.

Pan-A·mer·i·can·ism (pan′ə mer′ə kə niz′əm), *n.* **1.** the principle or policy that all the countries in North, Central, and South America should cooperate to promote cultural, commercial, and social progress: *Pan-Americanism rests upon the conviction that there are primary and mutual interests which are peculiar to the republics of this hemisphere and that these can best be conserved by taking counsel together* (Nelson A. Rockefeller). **2.** the advocacy of a political alliance of these countries.

Pan American Union, the former name, 1910-1948, of the Organization of American States, a group of 21 American republics, formed to promote cooperation and further peace.

Pan-An·gli·can (pan ang′glə kən), *adj.* of, having to do with, or including all the churches or church members of the Anglican Communion.

Pan-Ar·ab (pan ar′əb), *adj.* of or for all Arab peoples: *a Pan-Arab empire, a Pan-Arab labor federation.* —*n.* a person who advocates Pan-Arabism: *Extremists of all colorations—Communists, fellow travelers, fanatic Pan-Arabs—won seats* (Newsweek).

Pan-Ar·a·bic (pan ar′ə bik), *adj.* Pan-Arab.

Pan-Ar·ab·ism (pan ar′ə biz əm), *n.* **1.** the concept of or a movement toward the political union of all Arab peoples: *Kurdish opposition to Pan-Arabism is obviously one of the reasons for Kassem's great caution with regard to closer ties to the United Arab Republic* (Atlantic). **2.** belief in or support of this concept or movement.

pan·a·tel·a (pan′ə tel′ə), *n.* panetela: *"Perfecto" or "Panatela" can mean almost anything in length and thickness, depending on which company is doing the labeling* (Harper's).

Pan·ath·e·nae·a (pan′ath ə nē′ə), *n.pl.* the chief national festival of ancient Athens, held annually in honor of Athena, the patroness of the city, the celebration every four years being known, from its special solemnity and magnificence, as the greater Panathenaea, as distinguished from the lesser Panathenaea of other years. [< New Latin *Panathenaea* < Greek *Panathēnaia* < *pan-* all + *Athēnaia* games in honor of *Athena*]

Pan·ath·e·nae·an (pan′ath ə nē′ən), *adj.* of or having to do with the Panathenaea.

Pan·ath·e·na·ic (pan′ath ə nā′ik), *adj.* Panathenaean: *It was also designed to permit a clear view of the Panathenaic Procession that made its way diagonally through the square toward the Acropolis bearing offerings and a new dress to the patron goddess Athena on her birthday* (Scientific American).

Pan·a·vi·sion (pan′ə vizh′ən), *n. Trademark.* a motion-picture medium using 70-millimeter film, a wide screen, and stereophonic sound: *It's an obvious, sentimental story, but extremely well done in Panavision* (Punch).

Pan-Bri·tan·nic (pan′bri tan′ik), *adj.* of, having to do with, or including all the British dominions.

pan·broil (pan′broil′), *v.t.* to cook quickly over a very hot fire in a pan with little or no fat: *The skillet does everything its makers say it will do—panbroils fish and meat, fricassees poultry with dumplings, cooks all kinds of egg dishes, simmers, stews, and so on* (New Yorker).

pan·cake (pan′kāk′), *n., v.,* **-caked, -cak·ing.** —*n.* **1.** a thin, flat cake of batter, fried or baked in a greased pan or on a griddle: *To his lips he raised the buckwheat pancakes, dripping with molasses* (Maurice Thompson). **2.** a quick, almost flat landing made by an aircraft. **3. a.** a facial makeup in the form of a cake, applied as a base for face powder. **b. Pan-Cake,** a trademark for this makeup.

—*v.i.* (of an airplane) to flatten out several feet above the landing surface, stall, and drop to the ground, usually landing heavily. —*v.t.* to cause (an aircraft) to land in this way: *The pilot pancaked his damaged plane onto an open field.*

➤ **Pancake, griddlecake,** though often used as synonyms, are usually differentiated in cookbooks. *Pancake* applies particularly to a relatively light and thin cake, often resembling the *crêpes* of French cookery. *Griddlecake* applies to a somewhat thicker and heavier cake.

Pancake Day, Shrove Tuesday, on which it was formerly customary to eat pancakes: *In Germany it is called Fasnacht, and in England it is called Pancake Day* (World Book Encyclopedia).

pan·cha·ma (pun′chə mə), *n.* (in India) a member of the Scheduled Caste; an untouchable: *Panchamas . . . did the most menial work* (Scientific American). [< Hindi *panchama* < *pañcama* fifth < *pañca* five]

pan·cha·yat (pun chä′yət), *n.* (in India) a council of usually five elders who manage the affairs of a village and represent it before the state government: *The interdependence of the cooperative movement in the rural areas and the role of village panchayats necessitated their grouping into a separate department to be called Cooperation* *and Rural Development Department* (Times of India). [< Hindi *panchayat* < *panch* five < Sanskrit *pañca*]

Pan·chen Lama (pän′chən), one of the two principal lamas of Tibetan Buddhism (the Dalai Lama is the other one). He is doctrinally preeminent in spiritual matters: *They brought back the Panchen Lama, who had been exiled for years in China, to share nominal political power and spiritual rule with the Dalai Lama* (Theodore Hsi-En Chen). [compare Tibetan *Panchen-rinbochi* magnificent, (literally) large-jewel pundit]

pan·chro·mat·ic (pan′krō mat′ik), *adj.* sensitive to light of all colors: *a panchromatic photographic film.*

pan·chro·ma·tism (pan krō′mə tiz əm), *n.* panchromatic quality; panchromatic work.

pan·crat·ic (pan krat′ik), *adj.* having to do with the pancratium.

pan·cra·ti·um (pan krā′shē əm), *n., pl.* **-ti·a** (-shē ə). an athletic contest in ancient Greece, combining wrestling and boxing. [< Latin *pancratium* < Greek *pankrátion* an exercise of all skills < *pan-* all + *krátos* mastery, strength]

pan·cre·as (pan′krē əs, pang′-), *n.* a gland near the stomach that discharges pancreatic juice into the intestine to help digestion. It also produces insulin in the islets of Langerhans. The pancreas of animals when used for food is called sweetbread: *The pancreas is interesting because it is both a duct and a ductless gland at the same time* (A. M. Winchester). [< New Latin *pancreas* < Greek *pánkreas, -atos* sweetbread < *pan-* all + *kréas, -atos* flesh]

pan·cre·at·ic (pan′krē at′ik, pang′-), *adj.* of the pancreas: *The pancreatic juice contains chemicals that help dissolve all three classes of food—fats, carbohydrates, and proteins.*

pan·cre·a·tin (pan′krē ə tin, pang′-), *n.* **1. a.** any of the enzymes of pancreatic juice: *The scientists found that itch enzymes from animal tissues are trypsin, chymotrypsin and pancreatin* (Science News Letter). **b.** a mixture of all these enzymes. **2.** a preparation extracted from the pancreas of animals, used to aid digestion. [< *pancreat*(ic) + *-in*]

pan·cre·a·ti·tis (pan′krē ə tī′tis, pang′-), *n.* inflammation of the pancreas: *American and Canadian alcoholics frequently develop pancreatitis while European alcoholics seldom do* (Science News Letter).

pan·cre·a·tize (pan′krē ə tīz, pang′-), *v.t.*, **-tized, -tiz·ing.** to treat with pancreatin.

pan·cre·a·tot·o·my (pan′krē ə tot′ə mē, pang′-), *n., pl.* **-mies.** surgical incision into the pancreas.

pan·cre·o·zy·min (pan′krē ō zī′min, pang′-), *n.* an intestinal hormone that stimulates secretion of enzymes by the pancreas. [< *pancreas* + *zymin*]

pan·cy·to·pe·ni·a (pan′sī tə pē′nē ə), *n.* aplastic anemia. [< *pan-* + *cyto-* + Greek *peníā* poverty]

pan·da (pan′də), *n.* **1.** the giant panda, a bearlike mammal of Tibet and parts of southern and southwestern China, related to the raccoon, mostly white with black legs. **2.** the lesser panda, a slender, reddish-brown mammal related to and resembling the raccoon, that lives in the Himalayas. [origin uncertain; probably < the native name in Nepal]

Panda (def. 1) (about 6 ft. long)

pan·dal (pan′dəl), *n.* (in India) a shed or arbor constructed for temporary use: *At 3 a.m. the first group were already making their way to the pandal ... set up to accommodate the gathering* (London Times). [< Tamil *pendal*]

pan·da·na·ceous (pan′də nā′shəs), *adj.* belonging to a family of tropical monocotyledonous trees and shrubs, typified by the screw pines. [< New Latin *Pandanaceae* (< Malay *pandan* screw pine) + English *-ous*]

pan·da·nus (pan dā′nəs), *n.* any of a group of tropical trees or shrubs, especially of the islands of the Malay Archipelago and the Indian and the Pacific oceans. The pandanus usually have a palmlike or branched stem, long, narrow leaves, and aerial roots that support the stem or the whole plant. Its edible fruit grows into large heads; screw pine: *There are, for example, the exotic tales of Mr. Maugham, who can deal with blood, thunder, spices and pandanus leaves as well as anybody in the business* (John P. Marquand). [< New Latin *Pandanus* the typical genus < Malay *pandan* screw pine]

Pan·da·rus (pan′dər əs), *n.* a Lycian hero, on the Trojan side in the Trojan War, portrayed by Homer as a great archer and valiant soldier. In medieval romance and by Boccaccio, Chaucer, and Shakespeare, he is portrayed as the go-between in the love affair of Troilus and Cressida.

Pan·de·an (pan dē′ən), *adj.* of or having to do with the god Pan.

Pandean pipes, Panpipe.

pan·dect (pan′dekt), *n.* **1.** a complete body or code of laws. **2.** a comprehensive digest. [< *Pandects*] —**Syn. 2.** compendium.

Pan·dects (pan′dekts), *n.pl.* a digest of Roman civil law in 50 books, made by order of Justinian in the 500's A.D., systematizing the decisions and opinions of jurists. [< Latin *pandectes* < Greek *pandéktēs* encyclopedic book (in plural, the Justinian Code); (literally) all-receiver < *pan-* all + *déchesthai* receive]

pan·dem·ic (pan dem′ik), *adj.* **1.** (of a disease) prevalent throughout an entire country or continent, or the whole world: *Two specifically human diseases usually associated with high mortality rates are pandemic influenza and cholera* (Fenner and Day). **2.** of or having to do with all living people; general; universal. —*n.* a pandemic disease: *The most recent great pandemic of bubonic plague in the world began somewhere in China at the end of the last century* (J.L. Cloudsley-Thompson). [< Greek *pándēmos* pertaining to all the people (< *pan-* all + *dêmos* the populace) + English *-ic*]

pan·de·mo·ni·ac (pan′də mō′nē ak), *adj.* of, having to do with, or characteristic of pandemonium.

pan·de·mon·ic (pan′də mon′ik), *adj.* pandemoniac: *The whole business was so distracted and pandemonic, so haphazard and wasteful of money, that I doubt whether many of [them] really knew what they were doing half the time* (Alan Moorehead).

Pan·de·mo·ni·um (pan′də mō′nē əm), *n.* **1.** the abode of all the demons; hell. **2.** hell's capital. In Milton's *Paradise Lost*, it is the palace built by Satan as the central part of hell. [< New Latin *Pandemonium* (coined by Milton in *Paradise Lost*) < Greek *pan-* all + *daímōn* demon]

pan·de·mo·ni·um (pan′də mō′nē əm), *n.* **1.** a place of wild disorder or lawless confusion: *What kind of a pandemonium that vessel was, I cannot describe, but she was commanded by a lunatic, and might be called a floating Bedlam* (Robert Louis Stevenson). **2.** wild uproar or lawlessness: *McArdle was the only man there who had not been affected by the pandemonium of the factory* (Harper's). [< *Pandemonium*]

pan·der (pan′dər), *n.* **1.** a person who helps other people indulge low desires, passions, or vices. **2.** a male go-between in illicit amours; male bawd; pimp; procurer.
—*v.i.* to act as a pander; supply material or opportunity for vices: *In his quest for popular support he panders to the least responsible elements in the community* (London Times). —*v.t.* to act as a pander to.
[alteration of earlier *pandar* < Middle English *Pandare* Pandarus; influenced by *-er*[1]] —**pan′der·er,** *n.*

pan·der·ess (pan′dər is), *n.* a female pander; procuress.

pan·der·ly (pan′dər lē), *adj.* of the nature of or suitable for a pander.

pan·di·a·ton·ic (pan dī′ə ton′ik), *adj.* completely diatonic: *The slow, sad song about "That Boy," ... is expressively unusual for its lugubrious music, but harmonically it is one of their most intriguing, with its chains of pandiatonic clusters* (London Times).

pan·dic·u·la·tion (pan dik′yə lā′shən), *n.* an instinctive stretching, as on awakening from sleep or while yawning. [< French *pandiculation* < Latin *pandiculārī* stretch oneself < *pandere* to stretch]

P. and L., profit and loss.

pan·door (pan′důr), *n.* pandour.

pan·do·ra (pan dôr′ə, -dōr′-), *n.* bandore; an old musical instrument resembling a guitar or lute, with three, four, or six strings. [< Italian *pandora* < Latin *pandūra* < Greek *pandoûrā* three-stringed lute. Compare BANDORE, MANDOLIN.]

Pan·do·ra (pan dôr′ə, -dōr′-), *n. Greek Mythology.* the first woman, created by the gods to punish mankind for having learned the use of fire. Curiosity led her to open a box and thus let out all sorts of ills into the world. Only Hope remained at the bottom. [< Latin *Pandōra* < Greek *Pandôrā* < *pan-* all + *dôra*, plural of *dôron* gift (because of the gifts that the gods gave her at her creation)]

Pandora's box, 1. *Greek Mythology.* the box containing all human ills. Jupiter gave it to Pandora who opened it and let escape all the human ills which mankind now suffers from. **2.** a source of many troubles: *In 1957 the FCC opened up a skimpy slice of wavelengths for what it projected as "Citizens Radio Service" .... In so doing, the FCC also opened a Pandora's box for itself* (Atlantic).

pan·dore (pan dôr′, -dōr′), *n.* bandore.

pan·dour (pan′důr), *n.* **1.** one of a force of notoriously brutal and rapacious soldiers organized in Croatia in the 1700's, and later incorporated as a regiment in the Austrian Army. **2.** any brutal, plundering soldiers. [< French *pandour* < German *Pandur* < Serbo-Croatian *pàndūr*, earlier *bàndūr* constable, mounted guard, probably < Italian (Venetian) *bandiore* < Medieval Latin *banderius* one who guards; perhaps follower of a *bandum* banner]

pan·dow·dy (pan dou′dē), *n., pl.* **-dies.** *U.S.* a deep-dish apple pie or pudding with a crust on top only, often sweetened with brown sugar or molasses. [American English, perhaps related to obsolete dialectal English *pandoulde* custard < *dowl* mix dough in a hurry]

pan·du·rate (pan′dyə rāt), *adj.* fiddle-shaped, as a leaf. [< Latin *pandūra* pandora, lute + English *-ate*[1]]

pan·du·ri·form (pan dyůr′ə fôrm), *adj.* pandurate. [< Latin *pandūra* pandora, lute + English *-form*]

pan·dy (pan′dē), *n., pl.* **-dies,** *v.,* **-died, -dy·ing.** *Especially Scottish.* —*n.* a stroke on the extended palm with a rod or leather strap, given as a punishment to schoolboys. —*v.t.* to inflict a pandy or pandies on, as a punishment. [supposedly < Latin *pande palmam* hold out (your) hand (the order preceding punishment); *pande*, imperative of *pandere* extend, *palmam*, accusative of *palma* hand]

pane (pān), *n.* **1.** a single sheet of glass in a division of a window, a door, or a sash: *Hailstones as big as eggs broke several panes of glass.* **2.** a panel, as of wainscot, ceiling, door, etc. **3.** *Philately.* **a.** a portion of a full sheet containing a unit of stamps as distributed to post offices. **b.** a page from a booklet of stamps as sold by post offices. **4.** one of the sides of a nut or of the head of a bolt. **5.** one of the sides of the upper surface (table) of a diamond cut as a brilliant. **6.** a piece, portion, or side of anything. **7.** *Obsolete.* a counterpane. [< Old French *pan* < Latin *pannus* piece of cloth (because, earlier, a window was a hole in a wall, covered by flimsy material)]

-paned, *combining form.* having ____ panes: *Diamond-paned = having diamond panes.*

pan·e·gyr·ic (pan′ə jir′ik), *n.* **1.** a speech or writing in praise of a person or thing; formal eulogy: *I profess to write, not his [Johnson's] panegyric ... but his Life* (James Boswell). **2.** enthusiastic or extravagant praise; eulogy. [< Latin *panēgyricus* < Greek *panēgyrikós* < *panēgyris* public assembly < *pan-* all + *ágyris* assembly < *ageírein* gather together] —**Syn. 2.** acclaim.

pan·e·gyr·i·cal (pan′ə jir′ə kəl), *adj.* of the nature of a panegyric; eulogistic; highly laudatory: *She filled a whole page of her diary with panegyrical regrets* (Lytton Strachey). —**pan′e·gyr′i·cal·ly,** *adv.*

pan·e·gyr·ist (pan′ə jir′ist, pan′ə jir′-), *n.* a person who praises enthusiastically or extravagantly; eulogist.

pan·e·gy·rize (pan′ə jə rīz), *v.,* **-rized, -riz·ing.** —*v.t.* to eulogize. —*v.i.* to compose or utter panegyrics.

pan·el (pan′əl), *n., v.,* **-eled, -el·ing** or (*especially British*) **-elled, -el·ling.** —*n.* **1.** a

strip or surface that is different in some way from what is around it. A panel is often sunk below or raised above the rest, and used for a decoration. Panels may be in a door or other woodwork, on large pieces of furniture, or made as parts of a dress. **2.** a small group selected for a special purpose such as discussing or judging: *a panel of experts.* **3. a.** a list of persons called as jurors. **b.** the members of a jury. **4. a.** one section of a switchboard. **b.** the whole, or a section of, an instrument board containing the controls and indicators used in operating an automobile, aircraft, or complex mechanism such as a computer. See picture under **instrument panel. 5.** a panel truck: *There's never been a bigger selection of . . . trucks—panels . . . tandems, 12 pickups to choose from* (Wall Street Journal). **6.** a picture, photograph, or design much longer than wide. **7. a.** a thin wooden board used as a surface for oil painting, sometimes made of several pieces fastened together. **b.** a painting on such a board. **8.** the space in a framework between two posts or struts, as the space in a fence or rail between two posts. **9.** the space between the raised bands on the back of a book. **10.** a compartment or division of a coal mine separated from the rest by thick masses of coal. **11.** a rectangular section of the hull of a rigid airship between two transverse and two longitudinal girders in the frame. **12.** a list of physicians in Great Britain available for the treatment of persons paying for health insurance. **13. a.** a pad, cushion, etc., used as a saddle. **b.** the pad or stuffed lining of a saddle.
—*v.t.* **1.** to furnish or decorate with panels; arrange in panels: *Some one of its former occupants . . . had panelled the walls of this . . . apartment with a dark wood running half way to the low ceiling* (F.H. Smith). **2.** to fit or place as a panel in its frame. **3.** to list for jury duty; select (a jury).
[< Old French *panel* piece < Vulgar Latin *pannellus* (diminutive) < Latin *pannus* piece of cloth. Compare PANE.]
—**Syn.** *n.* **1.** section.

pan·el·beat·er (pan′əl bē′tər), *n. Especially British.* a person who hammers metal panels into shape or does bodywork: *A carrier's van taken from a panelbeater's workshop on Wednesday night was found in the Tamaki River yesterday morning* (New Zealand Herald).

pan·el·board (pan′əl bôrd′, -bōrd′), *n.* **1.** a metal box attached to or set in a wall and containing switches, fuses, and sometimes circuit breakers for a number of electric circuits: *Wilson produces power and lighting distribution panelboards* (Wall Street Journal). **2.** a heavy, hard fiberboard used in the making of luggage, parts of vehicles, etc.: *Hardboard is made by tearing pieces of wood into its basic fibres, then compressing them into panelboards* (Wall Street Journal).

panel discussion, the discussion of a particular issue by a selected group of people, usually before an audience: *A panel discussion on "Radiotelescopes, present and future" will be a feature of the program* (Science).

panel heating, radiant heating.

pan·el·ing (pan′ə ling), *n.* **1.** panels collectively. **2.** the material, as milled lumber, used for panels.

pan·el·ist (pan′ə list), *n.* **1.** a person who takes part in a panel discussion: *Many of the panelists, however, volunteered their own ideas on what to do about the farm problem* (Wall Street Journal). **2.** a member of a panel on a television panel show: *Panelists on "Face the Nation" need not be recognized by the moderator before they put their queries* (Newsweek).

pan·el·ling (pan′ə ling), *n. Especially British.* paneling.

panel show, a television show featuring a group of people, usually celebrities, who take part in a quiz, game, or discussion: *For some, the panel show, in which premeditated questions must be answered spontaneously, is a stiffer test than a prepared speech* (John Lardner).

panel truck, a small, fully enclosed truck, used for delivering groceries or other goods in limited quantities: *. . . a battered old Dodge panel truck, which also served as a maintenance shop and operational headquarters* (New Yorker).

pan·en·do·scope (pan en′də skōp), *n.* a cystoscope which gives a wide view of the urinary bladder. [< *pan-* + *endoscope*]

pan·e·tel·a or **pan·e·tel·la** (pan′ə tel′ə), *n.* a long, slender cigar pointed at the end intended for the mouth. Also, **panatela.** [American English < Spanish *panetela* long, thin cigar, shaped like a thin loaf of bread < *pan* bread < Latin *pānis*]

pan·et·to·ne (pan′ə tō′nē; *Italian* pä′net-tô′ne), *n., pl.* **-ni** (-nē). a Milanese holiday cake made with raisins, candied fruit peels, almonds, etc.: *. . . a formal dress night at the Teatro della Scala in Milan, and panettone, fluffy, raisin and candy-fruit specked cake for breakfast* (Time). [< Italian *panettone* < *panetto* small loaf < *pane* bread < *Latin pānis*]

Pan-Eu·ro·pe·an (pan′yůr ə pē′ən), *adj.* of or having to do with the political union of all Europeans or European countries.

Pan-Eu·ro·pe·an·ism (pan′yůr ə pē′ə-niz əm), *n.* the concept of a political union of all Europeans or European countries.

pan fish, **1.** an edible fish of a size that permits frying whole, as a perch, sunfish, etc. **2.** a king crab.

pan·ful (pan′fůl), *n., pl.* **-fuls.** a quantity sufficient to fill a pan.

pang (pang), *n.* a sudden, short, sharp pain or feeling: *the pangs of a toothache, a pang of pity.* —*v.t.* to cause to suffer pangs. [origin uncertain] —**Syn.** *n.* throe.

pan·ga (päng′gə), *n.* a long, broad-bladed, and sometimes hooked knife resembling a machete, used in Africa, especially by the Mau Mau: *One of the guides took his panga—a broad, hooked blade, about eighteen inches long—and cut me a walking stick* (New Yorker).

pan·gen (pan′jen), *n. Biology.* one of the hypothetical primary constituent units of germ plasm: *As each pangen is characteristic of the cell which produced it, the characteristics of all of the cells of both parents are passed from them to the embryo through the fusion of sperm and egg* (Harbaugh and Goodrich). [< *pan-* + *-gen*]

pan·gen·e·sis (pan jen′ə sis), *n.* the theory, now discredited, advanced by Charles Darwin to explain the phenomena of heredity, that every separate unit or cell of an organism reproduces itself by contributing its share to the germ or bud of the offspring. [< *pan-* + *genesis*]

pan·ge·net·ic (pan′jə net′ik), *adj.* of or having to do with pangenesis.

Pan-Ger·man (pan jėr′mən), *adj.* having to do with all Germans or Pan-Germanism. —*n.* an advocate of Pan-Germanism.

Pan-Ger·man·ic (pan′jėr man′ik), *adj.* Pan-German.

Pan-Ger·man·ism (pan jėr′mə niz əm), *n.* **1.** the idea or principle of a political or cultural union of all German peoples; Pan-Teutonism. **2.** belief in or support of this principle.

Pan-Ger·man·ist (pan jėr′mə nist), *n.* Pan-German.

Pan-Ger·ma·ny (pan jėr′mə nē), *n.* all the German peoples collectively, considered as constituting one political community.

Pan·glos·si·an (pan glos′ē ən), *adj.* characteristic of Doctor Pangloss, a philosopher in Voltaire's satire *Candide,* who maintained that everything is for the best in this best of possible worlds; given to stubborn and undue optimism: *This is not an area in which Panglossian complacency should flourish amid a general hum of self-approval* (London Times). —*n.* a person given to undue optimism: *The Panglossians . . . point out that three of the four U.S. recessions since World War II were due to special causes* (Time).

pan·go·lin (pang gō′lən), *n.* any of an order of scaly toothless mammals of tropical Asia and Africa that roll themselves into a ball when in danger; scaly anteater. [apparently < Malay *pĕng-giling* roller on which tiller-ropes of Malay boats turn, perhaps < *pĕng-* one who + *giling* to roll (because the animal rolls up into a ball when attacked)]

pan·han·dle[1] (pan′han′dəl), *n.* **1.** the handle of a pan. **2.** *U.S.* a narrow strip of land projecting like a handle, as a state or territory extending between two others: *As the uranium fever spread, geological consulting offices opened up in the Texas panhandle.* [< *pan* dish for cooking + *handle*]

pan·han·dle[2] (pan′han′dəl), *v.i., v.t.,* **-dled, -dling.** *Informal.* to beg, especially in the streets: *He prides himself on the fact that he has never panhandled, never visited a soup kitchen, or taken a night's lodging in one of the various hostels maintained by charitable agencies in the city* (Harper's). [American English, probably back formation < *panhandler* < *pan* receptacle used for collecting money + *handler*]

pan·han·dler (pan′han′dlər), *n.* a person who begs, especially in the streets: *A panhandler approached them, and Tony gave him a dollar* (New Yorker).

Pan·hel·len·ic or **pan·hel·len·ic** (pan′-hə len′ik), *adj.* **1.** having to do with all members of the Greek race or Panhellenism. **2.** of or having to do with all college fraternities and sororities.

Pan·hel·len·ism (pan hel′ə niz əm), *n.* **1.** the idea or principle of a political union of all Greeks. **2.** belief in or support of this principle.

Pan·hel·len·ist (pan hel′ə nist), *n.* a person who favors Panhellenism.

pan·ic[1] (pan′ik), *n., adj., v.,* **-icked, -ick·ing.** —*n.* **1.** demoralizing terror, with or without cause, destroying self-control, affecting an individual or sweeping through a whole group of persons or animals. **2.** an outbreak of widespread alarm, as in a community, over financial or commercial matters, which tends to demoralize judgment and lead to hasty, ill-advised measures to avoid loss: *When four banks failed in one day, there was a panic among businessmen.* **3.** *Slang.* a very amusing person or thing: *His costume is a panic.*
—*adj.* caused by panic; showing panic or unreasoning fear: *panic terror, panic fear.*
—*v.t.* **1.** to affect with panic: *Orson Welles, who panicked his fellow Americans with the great Martian invasion broadcast in 1938, has returned to his native heath for good, after nearly ten years abroad* (Newsweek). **2.** *Slang.* to amuse greatly: *His jokes simply panic me.* —*v.i.* to be affected with panic: *Passengers panicked and trampled each other in an effort to break windows or jam their way through exits* (Wall Street Journal).
[< Middle French *panique* < Greek *Pānikós* of Pan (because he was said to cause contagious fear in herds and crowds)]
—**Syn.** *adj.* panicky, frantic.

pan·ic[2] (pan′ik), *n.* **1.** foxtail millet, cultivated in southern Europe for its edible grain. **2.** panic grass. [< Latin *pānicum* foxtail millet < *pānus* ear of millet; (originally) thread. Compare PANICLE.]

Pan·ic (pan′ik), *adj.* of or having to do with Pan or the terror supposed to be caused by him.

pan·i·cal (pan′ə kəl), *adj. Obsolete.* panic.

panic button, *U.S. Informal.* a control button or switch in an aircraft for use in an emergency: *They are not in real danger and can push the panic button and halt the experiment if they really need to* (New York Times).
hit the panic button, *Slang.* to become prematurely or overly excited in the face of a supposed emergency: *Pull yourself together; there's no need to hit the panic button.*

pan ice, *Geology.* blocks or pieces of ice formed along the shore, and afterwards loosened and driven by winds or currents.

panic grass, **1.** any of a group of grasses, many species of which produce edible grain. **2.** the grain of any such grass.

pan·ick·y (pan′ə kē), *adj.* **1.** caused by panic: *panicky haste.* **2.** showing panic: *panicky actions.* **3.** like panic: *panicky feelings.* **4.** liable to lose self-control and have a panic: *a panicky market.*

pan·i·cle (pan′ə kəl), *n. Botany.* **1.** a loose, diversely branching flower cluster. A panicle is produced when a raceme becomes irregularly compound and is a kind of indeterminate inflorescence: *a panicle of oats.* See also picture under **rice. 2.** any loose, diversely branching cluster in which the flowers are borne on pedicels. [< Latin *pānicula* (diminutive) < *pānus* a swelling; thread wound on a bobbin; ear of millet]

Panicle (def. 1)

pan·i·cled (pan′ə kəld), *adj.* having or forming panicles.

pan·ic·mon·ger (pan′ik mung′gər, -mong′-), *n.* a person seeking or inclined to create a panic.

pan·ic-strick·en (pan′ik strik′ən), *adj.* frightened out of one's wits; demoralized by fear: *The Moors, confused and . . . panic-*

stricken, vainly seek to escape (Robert Southey). *Owen and I looked at one another in panic-stricken silence* (W. Wilkie Collins).

pan·ic-struck (pan′ik struk′), *adj.* panic-stricken.

pa·nic·u·late (pə nik′yə lāt, -lit), *adj. Botany.* growing in a panicle; arranged in panicles. [< Latin *pānicula* panicle + English *-ate*[1]] —**pa·nic′u·late′ly,** *adv.*

pa·nic·u·lat·ed (pə nik′yə lā′tid), *adj.* paniculate.

pan·i·er (pan′ē ər), *n.* pannier.

pa·ni·o·lo (pä′nē ō′lō), *n., pl.* **-los.** (in Hawaii) a cowboy: *The saddle base is patterned after those brought to Hawaii by the paniolos, originally Mexican vaqueros who taught Hawaiians to ride, rope, and work with leather* (New York Times). [< Hawaiian *paniolo* < Spanish *español* Spaniard]

Pan-Is·lam (pan is′ləm), *n.* all Islam; all Moslem nations collectively, considered as constituting one political body.

Pan-Is·lam·ic (pan′is lam′ik, -lä′mik), *adj.* having to do with all Islam or with a union of all Moslem nations.

Pan-Is·lam·ism (pan is′lə miz əm), *n.* **1.** the idea or principle of a political union of all Moslem states. **2.** belief in or support of this principle.

Pan·ja·bi (pun jä′bē), *n., pl.* **-bis. 1.** a Punjabi. **2.** the Indo-European language of the Punjab, related to Hindi.

pan·jan·drum (pan jan′drəm), *n.* **1.** a mock title for an imaginary personage of great power or importance: *So he died and she very imprudently married the barber and there were present the Picninnies, and the Joblillies . . . and the grand Panjandrum himself with the little round button at top* (Samuel Foote). **2.** any pretentious personage or official: *There is not space here to describe methods by which the budget officer has become the grand panjandrum of public administration* (New York Times). [coined, probably < Greek *pan-* all + *-jandrum,* a pseudo-Latin ending]

Pan-Ma·lay·an (pan′mā lā′ən), *adj.* of or having to do with all the Malay states or with a union of these states: *a Pan-Malayan Islamic Party, a Pan-Malayan political movement.*

pan·mix·i·a (pan mik′sē ə), *n.* indiscriminate crossing of breeds without selection. [< New Latin *panmixia* < Greek *pan-* all + *mîxis* a mixing]

pan·nage (pan′ij), *n.* **1.** the feeding of swine, etc., in a forest or wood: . . . *herding swine in the forests, in the time of pannage, when acorns and beechmast were on the floor* (Punch). **2.** the right of pasturing swine in a forest. **3.** the payment made to the owner of the forest for this right. [< Old French *panage, pasnage* < Medieval Latin *pasnaticum,* ultimately < Latin *pāscere* to feed]

panne (pan), *n.* a soft, highly lustrous cloth with a long nap, resembling velvet: *We see her in a dress of grey panne* (Westminster Gazette). [< French *panne* downy fabric, fur; Old French, feather, down < Latin *penna* feather]

pan·ni·er (pan′ē ər), *n.* **1.** a basket, especially one of a pair of considerable size to be slung across the shoulders or across the back of a beast of burden: *panniers slung on sturdy horses* (Wordsworth). **2.** a frame of whalebone, wire, etc., formerly used for stretching out the skirt of a woman's dress at the hips. **3.** a puffed drapery about the hips on a woman's skirt. Also, **panier.** [< Old French *panier* < Latin *pānārium* bread basket < *pānis* bread]

Panniers (def. 1)

pan·ni·ered (pan′ē ərd), *adj.* having, or laden with, a pannier or panniers: *panniered skirts, panniered mules.*

pan·ni·kin (pan′ə kin), *n.* **1.** a small pan. **2.** a metal cup or mug, usually shallow.

pan·ning (pan′ing), *n. Slang.* a severe criticism or reprimand: *They were afraid the film would get the same sort of panning as "Peeping Tom" got* (Punch).

pan·nose (pan′ōs), *adj. Botany.* having the appearance or texture of felt or woolen cloth. —**pan′nose·ly,** *adv.*

pa·no·cha (pə nō′chə), *n.* **1.** a coarse grade of dark sugar made in Mexico. **2.** candy made from brown sugar, butter, milk, and nuts. Also, **penuche, penuchi.** [American English < Mexican Spanish *panocha* < Latin *pānucula,* and *pānicula* panicle]

pa·no·che (pə nō′chē), *n.* panocha.

pan·o·plied (pan′ə plid), *adj.* completely armed, equipped, covered, or arrayed: *The large Stratford company manage swordplay and panoplied pageantry with great facility* (Newsweek).

pan·o·ply (pan′ə plē), *n., pl.* **-plies,** *v.,* **-plied, -ply·ing.** —*n.* **1.** a complete suit of armor: *In arms they stood Of golden panoply, refulgent host* (Milton). **2. a.** complete equipment or covering: *armed in the panoply of innocence, an Indian in panoply of paint and feathers. The panoply swells with new weapons which complement the old* (Bulletin of Atomic Scientists). **b.** any splendid array: *That night, the Faery, usually so homely in her attire, appeared in a glittering panoply of enormous uncut jewels* (Lytton Strachey). —*v.t.* to furnish with or as with a panoply: *A rhymed commentary panoplied by snatches or entire choruses of some thirty Irving Berlin songs* (New Yorker). [< Greek *panopliā* the full armor of a hoplite < *pan-* all + *hópla* arms, neuter plural of *hóplon* tool, implement]

pan·op·tic (pan op′tik), *adj.* commanding a full view; seeing everything at once: . . . *his panoptic survey of the American scene called "America as a Civilization"* (Atlantic).

pan·o·ram·a (pan′ə ram′ə, -rä′mə), *n.* **1.** a wide, unbroken view of a surrounding region: *a panorama of beach and sea. At Rio de Janeiro, Sugar Loaf [Mountain] is the centerpiece of a breath-taking panorama* (Newsweek). **2.** a complete survey of some subject: *a panorama of history.* **3. a.** a picture of a landscape or other scene, often shown as if seen from a central point. **b.** such a picture unrolled a part at a time and made to pass continuously before the spectators. **4.** a continuously passing or changing scene: *the panorama of city life.* [< *pan-* + Greek *hórāma* a view < *horân* to see] —**Syn. 1.** prospect.

pan·o·ram·ic (pan′ə ram′ik, -rä′mik), *adj.* of or like a panorama: *a panoramic view.* —**pan′o·ram′i·cal·ly,** *adv.*

panoramic camera, any of various forms of photographic camera for taking panoramic views.

panoramic sight, a periscopic gun sight, usually fitted with a telescopic lens, by which a wide view can be obtained and which may be manipulated to sight in any direction.

pan·o·ram·ist (pan′ə ram′ist, -rä′mist), *n.* a painter of panoramas.

pan-Or·tho·dox (pan ôr′thə doks), *adj.* of, having to do with, or representing all Orthodox churches: *Popular pressure forced the Church of Greece to make a reluctant volte-face about the pan-Orthodox resolution . . . which authorized the Patriarch to resume contacts with the Vatican* (London Times).

pa·nou·chi (pə nü′chē), *n.* panocha.

Pan·pipe (pan′pīp′), *n.* an early musical instrument made of reeds or tubes of different lengths, fastened together side by side, in order of their length. The reeds or tubes were closed at one end and the player blew across their open tops. [< *Pan* + *pipe* (because he played such an instrument)]

Panpipe

pan·psy·chism (pan sī′kiz əm), *n.* the doctrine that the entire universe, or any least particle of it, has a psychic or mental as well as physical side or aspect. [< *pan-* + Greek *psȳchḗ* soul, mind + English *-ism*]

pan·psy·chist (pan sī′kist), *n.* a believer in panpsychism.

pan·sex·u·al (pan sek′shů əl), *adj.* of or having to do with pansexualism: *A fresh crop of pansexual lunacy has sprung full-grown into the headlines* (Punch).

pan·sex·u·al·ism (pan sek′shů ə liz′əm), *n.* the view that the sexual instinct plays a role in all human thought and activity.

pan·sex·u·al·i·ty (pan sek′shů al′ə tē), *n.* pansexualism: *[Freud's] doctrine of pansexuality that originally gave offense has now become a commonplace* (Atlantic).

Pan-Slav (pan släv′, -slav′), *adj.* **1.** of or having to do with all the Slavic races. **2.** of or having to do with Pan-Slavism.

Pan-Slav·ic (pan slä′vik, -slav′ik), *adj.* Pan-Slav.

Pan-Slav·ism (pan′slä′viz əm, -slav′iz-), *n.* **1.** the idea or principle of a political union of all Slavic peoples. **2.** belief in or support of this principle.

Pan-Slav·ist (pan slä′vist, -slav′ist), *n.* an adherent or promoter of Pan-Slavism.

Pan-Sla·von·ic (pan′slə von′ik), *adj.* **1.** of or having to do with all the Slavonian peoples. **2.** Pan-Slavic.

pan·soph·ic (pan sof′ik), *adj.* **1.** having or pretending to have universal knowledge. **2.** relating to universal wisdom or knowledge.

pan·soph·i·cal (pan sof′ə kəl), *adj.* pansophic.

pan·so·phism (pan′sə fiz əm), *n.* the professed possession of universal knowledge.

pan·so·phist (pan′sə fist), *n.* a claimant or pretender to universal knowledge.

pan·so·phy (pan′sə fē), *n.* **1.** universal knowledge; all-embracing wisdom. **2.** the claim or pretension to universal knowledge. [< New Latin *pansophia* < Greek *pánsophos* < *pan-* all + *sophós* clever, wise]

pan·sper·ma·tism (pan spėr′mə tiz əm), *n.* the doctrine that the atmosphere is full of invisible germs ready for development under favorable conditions. [< *pan-* + Greek *spérma, -atos* seed + English *-ism*]

pan·sper·mi·a (pan spėr′mē ə), *n.* panspermatism: *This theory was first suggested in 1908 by the Swedish chemist, Svante Arrhenius, who called it panspermia* (Science News Letter). [< New Latin *panspermia*]

pan·sper·my (pan spėr′mē), *n.* panspermatism. [< New Latin *panspermia*]

Pan's pipes, Panpipe.

pan·sy (pan′zē), *n., pl.* **-sies,** *adj.* —*n.* **1. a.** a variety of violet, that has large flowers with flat, velvety petals, usually of several colors; heartsease. **b.** the flower. **2.** *Slang, used in an unfriendly way.* **a.** a homosexual man or boy. **b.** an effeminate man or boy. —*adj. Slang.* **1.** homosexual. **2.** effeminate: *The Egyptians do not need these fine varieties of . . . cotton for themselves. The fellas . . . don't wear such pansy varieties* (Punch). *He branded American tanks as being "all too pansy"—made for Hollywood, not for fighting* (Newsweek).
[earlier, *pensy,* and *pensee* < French *pensée* pansy; (literally) thought < Old French *penser* to think; see PENSIVE]

pant[1] (pant), *v.i.* **1.** to breathe hard and quickly, as when out of breath: *to pant from the long, steep climb.* **2.** to speak with short, quick breaths. **3.** to long eagerly; yearn: *I am just panting for my turn.* **4.** (of the heart or breast) to throb violently; palpitate; pulsate; beat. **5.** to emit steam or the like in loud puffs: *ships moving, tugs panting, hawsers taut* (H.G. Wells). —*v.t.* to breathe or utter gaspingly: *He has come, I panted* (Robert Louis Stevenson).
—*n.* **1.** a short, quick breath; catching of the breath; gasp. **2.** a puff or cough of an engine. **3.** a throb or heave of the breast.
[perhaps short for Old French *pantoisier,* or *pantiser,* probably < Vulgar Latin *phantasiāre* be oppressed with a nightmare; < Latin *phantasia.* Compare FANTASY.]
—**pant′er,** *n.*
—**Syn.** *v.i.* **1.** gasp, puff.

pant[2] (pant), *n.* a pair of pants.

Pan·tag·ru·el (pan tag′rů el; *French* päɴ tȧ grʏ el′), *n.* (in Rabelais' *Gargantua and Pantagruel*) the last of the giants, son of Gargantua, represented as a coarse and extravagant humorist, dealing satirically with serious subjects.

Pan·ta·gru·el·i·an (pan′tə grů el′ē ən), *adj.* of, having to do with, characteristic of, or appropriate to Pantagruel. —*n.* Pantagruelist.

Pan·ta·gru·el·ism (pan′tə grü′ə liz əm, pan tag′rů-), *n.* Pantagruelian spirit, principles, or practice; coarse humor with satirical intent, often applied to serious subjects.

Pan·ta·gru·el·ist (pan′tə grü′ə list, pan tag′rů-), *n.* an imitator, admirer, or student of Pantagruel or Rabelais.

pan·ta·lets or **pan·ta·lettes** (pan′tə lets′), *n.pl. Especially U.S.* **1.** long, loose drawers with a frill or the like at the bottom of each leg, extending to the ankles and showing beneath the skirt, formerly worn by women and girls. **2.** a pair of trimmed pieces, frills, or the like for attaching to the legs of drawers.

pan·ta·loon (pan′tə lün′), *n.* **1.** a clown. **2.** Also, **Pantaloon. a.** a lean and foolish old

man wearing spectacles, pantaloons, and slippers, who is a comic character in old Italian comedies: *the lean and slipper'd pantaloon* (Shakespeare). **b.** (in modern pantomime) a foolish old man, the butt and abettor of the clown.
pantaloons, *Archaic.* tight-fitting trousers with stockings attached: *I would choose . . . some fashion not so . . . exorbitant as the pantaloons* (John Evelyn).
[< French *pantalon* < Italian *Pantalone,* a character in early Italian comedies who wore full breeches; (originally) a Venetian < *Pantaleone,* a patron saint of Venice]
—**Syn. 1.** buffoon.

pan·ta·looned (pan'tə lünd'), *adj.* wearing pantaloons: *Pantalooned serving girls brought soap, hot water, and towels* (Sunday Express).

pan·tech·ni·con (pan tek'nə kon), *n. British.* **1.** a moving van. **2.** a furniture warehouse. [< name of a building in London, (originally) housing a bazaar of varied craftwork < *pan-* + *technikón,* neuter of Greek *technikós* of the arts < *téchnē* art, skill]

pan·tel·e·graph (pan tel'ə graf, -gräf), *n.* a form of telegraph for transmitting facsimile messages and pictures.

pan·te·leg·ra·phy (pan'tə leg'rə fē), *n.* facsimile telegraphy.

pan·tel·e·phone (pan tel'ə fōn), *n.* a telephonic device for the reproduction at a distance of feeble sounds.

pan·ter·er (pan'tər ər), *n.* pantler; officer in charge of a pantry.

Pan-Teu·ton·ic (pan'tü ton'ik, -tyü-), *adj.* Pan-German.

Pan-Teu·ton·ism (pan'tü'tə niz əm, -tyü'-), *n.* Pan-Germanism.

pan·the·ism (pan'thē iz əm), *n.* **1.** the belief that God and the universe are identical; the doctrine that God does not exist as a personality but is rather the expression of the physical forces of nature: *The author, whose philosophy seems to be a crude but genuinely mystical pantheism, succeeds in communicating the wonder and terror of being alone on a storm-tossed raft in the middle of the world's widest ocean* (New Yorker). **2.** the worship of the gods of all creeds.

pan·the·ist (pan'thē ist), *n.* a believer in pantheism. [< *pan-* + Greek *theós* god + English *-ist*]

pan·the·is·tic (pan'thē is'tik), *adj.* of or having to do with pantheists or pantheism.

pan·the·is·ti·cal (pan'thē is'tə kəl), *adj.* pantheistic.

pan·the·is·ti·cal·ly (pan'thē is'tə klē), *adv.* according to pantheism; from a pantheist's point of view.

Pan·the·on (pan'thē on, pan thē'ən), *n.* **1.** a temple for all the gods built at Rome about 27 B.C., and later used as a Christian church. **2.** a building resembling or compared to the Pantheon at Rome, especially a large public building in Paris containing tombs or memorials of famous French people. [< Latin *Pantheon* < Greek *Pántheion* < *pan-* all + *theós* god + *-ion* place for]

pan·the·on (pan'thē on, pan thē'ən), *n.* **1.** a temple dedicated to all the gods. **2.** a public building containing tombs or memorials of the illustrious dead of a nation. **3.** all the deities of a people, country, culture, etc.: *the ancient Greek pantheon. The teeming pantheon of guided missiles* (Time).

pan·the·on·ic (pan'thē on'ik), *adj.* of the nature of or resembling a pantheon.

pan·ther (pan'thər), *n., pl.* **-thers** or (*collectively*) **-ther. 1.** a puma; cougar; mountain lion. **2.** a leopard, especially the black leopard. **3.** a jaguar. [spelling alteration of Middle English *panter* < Old French *pantere,* learned borrowing from Latin *panthēra* < Greek *pánthēr*] —**pan'ther-like',** *adj.*

pan·ther·ess (pan'thər is), *n.* **1.** a female panther. **2.** a woman thought of as resembling a female panther in manner or temperament.

pan·ther·ine (pan'thər in, -thə rīn), *adj.* pantherlike: *Her pantherine leaps and rapid turns were breathtaking* (New York Times).

pan·ther·ish (pan'thər ish), *adj.* **1.** like a panther. **2.** like that of a panther: *Tosca is a jealous lover, and Callas played the part with pantherish intensity* (Time). —**pan'ther·ish·ly,** *adv.*

pan·tie (pan'tē), *n., pl.* **-ties.** panty.

pan·tile (pan'tīl'), *n.* **1.** a roofing tile made in an S-curve, laid with the concave surface of one overlapped by the concave surface of the next. **2.** a roof tile made with a single curve, laid edge to edge with the next, the junction of two edges being covered by another tile laid with its concave side downward.

pan·tiled (pan'tīld'), *adj.* covered with pantiles: *. . . shimmerings of summer sun upon the pantiled roofs* (Elizabeth Nicholas).

pan·til·ing (pan'tī'ling), *n.* **1.** the covering of a roof with pantiles. **2.** pantiles collectively.

pant·ing (pan'ting), *adj.* that pants; breathing hard and heavily; puffing; gasping; throbbing or heaving: *a panting dog.* —**pant'ing·ly,** *adv.*

pan·ti·soc·ra·cy (pan'tə sok'rə sē), *n., pl.* **-cies. 1.** a scheme of social organization in which all are equal in rank and social position. **2.** a Utopian community in which all the members are equal and all rule. [< Greek *pant-* all + English *isocracy*]

pan·ti·so·crat·ic (pan'tə sō krat'ik), *adj.* having to do with, involving, or upholding pantisocracy.

pant·ler (pant'lər), *n.* (formerly) an officer in a great household who supplied the bread and had charge of the pantry: *A' would have made a good pantler, a' would ha' chipped bread well* (Shakespeare). [alteration of earlier *panter* < Old French *panetier* < Latin *pānis* bread; perhaps influenced by *butler*]

pan·to (pan'tō), *n. British Slang.* pantomime.

Pan·toc·ra·tor (pan tok'rə tər), *n.* the omnipotent ruler (said of Christ): *The range [of artistic themes] was later expanded to include Jesus Christ in his role as Pantocrator* (Harper's). [< Greek *pantokrátōr* < *panto-* all + *krátōr* ruler]

pan·to·fle or **pan·tof·fle** (pan'tə fəl; pan tof'əl, -tü'fəl), *n.* a slipper: *White pantofles with red heels* (Thackeray). [< Middle French *pantoufle;* origin unknown]

pan·to·graph (pan'tə graf, -gräf), *n.* **1.** an instrument for the mechanical copying of plans, drawings, etc., on any scale desired. It consists of a framework of slender, jointed metal rods which simultaneously reproduce a line, circle, etc., drawn by the operator. **2.** an insulated, jointed framework on certain electric locomotives and some other vehicles, for conveying electric current from overhead wires to the motors. [< French *pantographe* < Greek *panto-* all + *graphikḗ* art of drawing or writing]

pan·to·graph·ic (pan'tə graf'ik), *adj.* of, having to do with, or produced by a pantograph. —**pan'to·graph'i·cal·ly,** *adv.*

pan·tog·ra·phy (pan tog'rə fē), *n.* **1.** a general description; entire view of an object. **2.** the process of copying by means of the pantograph.

pan·to·log·ic (pan'tə loj'ik), *adj.* of or having to do with pantology.

pan·to·log·i·cal (pan'tə loj'ə kəl), *adj.* pantologic.

pan·tol·o·gist (pan tol'ə jist), *n.* a person who studies or is versed in universal knowledge.

pan·tol·o·gy (pan tol'ə jē), *n.* a systematic view of all branches of human knowledge; universal knowledge. [< Greek *panto-* all + English *-logy*]

pan·to·mime (pan'tə mīm), *n., v.,* **-mimed, -mim·ing.** —*n.* **1.** a play without words, in which the actors express themselves by gestures. **2.** gestures without words: *As . . . he could not speak a word of French . . . he was obliged to convey this sentiment into pantomime* (Leslie Stephen). **3.** a dramatized tale with broad comedy, music, and dancing, common in England during the Christmas season. **4.** a mime or mimic, especially in the ancient Roman theater: *In come troops of dancers from Lydia, or pantomimes from Alexandria* (Cardinal Newman).
—*v.t.* to express by gestures; represent by dumb show: *Thomas pantomimed infinite perplexity* (H.G. Wells). —*v.i.* to express oneself by dumb show.
[< Latin *pantomīmus* a mime; also, dancer < Greek *pantómīmos* < *panto-* all + *mîmos* mime, mimic]

pan·to·mim·ic (pan'tə mim'ik), *adj.* of, in, or like pantomime: *pantomimic gestures which . . . are substituted for intelligible words* (Macaulay). —**pan'to·mim'i·cal·ly,** *adv.*

pan·to·mim·ic·ry (pan'tə mim'ik rē), *n., pl.* **-ries.** *Obsolete.* pantomime.

pan·to·mim·ist (pan'tə mī'mist), *n.* **1.** an actor in a pantomime. **2.** a person who writes or composes pantomimes.

pan·to·prag·mat·ic (pan'tō prag mat'ik), *adj.* concerned or busied with all things; universally meddlesome. [< Greek *panto-* all + English *pragmatic*]

pan·to·scope (pan'tə skōp), *n.* **1.** a form of photographic lens having a very wide angle, introduced before 1875. **2.** a panoramic camera. [< Greek *panto-* all + English *-scope*]

pan·to·scop·ic (pan'tə skop'ik), *adj.* having a wide range of vision or field of view.

pantoscopic camera, a panoramic camera.

pantoscopic spectacles, bifocals.

pan·to·then·ic acid (pan'tə then'ik), a hydroxy acid, a constituent of the vitamin B complex, that promotes growth, found in plant and animal tissues, especially liver, yeast, bran, and molasses: *The B vitamin they found useful for this detoxifying purpose is pantothenic acid* (Science News Letter). *Formula:* $C_9H_{17}NO_5$ [< Greek *pántothen* from every side (< *panto-* all + *the-,* root of *tithénai* to place, set) + English *-ic*]

pan·toum (pan tüm'), *n.* a French and English adaptation of the Malay pantun, consisting of a series of stanzas of four lines rhyming *abab, bcbc, cdcd,* etc., the last rhyme being *a.* [< French *pantoum* < Malay *pantun*]

pan·trop·ic (pan'trop'ik, -trō'pik), *adj.* drawn to or having an affinity for many kinds of tissues: *a pantropic virus.* [< *pan-* + Greek *tropḗ* a turning + English *-ic*]

pan·try (pan'trē), *n., pl.* **-tries. 1.** a small room in which food, dishes, silverware, table linen, etc., are kept: *A pantry adjoins the kitchen.* **2.** a butler's pantry. [Middle English *panetrie* < Anglo-French *panetrie,* variant of Old French *paneterie* bread room < Medieval Latin *panetaria* < Latin *pānis* bread] —**Syn. 1.** buttery.

pan·try·man (pan'trē mən), *n., pl.* **-men.** a man employed in a pantry.

pants (pants), *n.pl.* **1.** *Especially U.S.* trousers: *I let him have a charge of No. 5 shot in the seat of the pants* (Geoffrey Household). **2.** drawers, especially women's; underpants.
catch with one's pants down, *Slang.* to catch off one's guard or unprepared: *We have realigned our whole sales operations toward the German civilian market so as not to be caught with our pants down in the event of a military pullout* (Wall Street Journal).
wear the pants, *Slang.* play the dominant or masculine role: *Over 90% of the West's nuclear power will remain in American hands, anyway. "Uncle Sam will still wear the pants," stresses a high official* (William Beecher).
[American English, short for *pantaloons*]
➔ **Pants, trousers.** In formal usage the word for men's breeches is *trousers;* on other levels the word is *pants.*

pants suit, a woman's or girl's suit consisting of a jacket and trousers: *Plastic hats, shoes and dresses, pants suits to wear to parties, . . . these are some of the trends* (New York Times).

pan·tun (pan tün'), *n.* a Malay verse form, usually of four lines in which the first and third, and the second and fourth, rhyme. [< Malay *pantun*]

pan·ty (pan'tē), *n., pl.* **-ties.** a kind of undergarment with short legs, fitting around the waist and the lower torso, worn by women and children. Also, **pantie.**

panty girdle, a girdle with short legs, worn as a panty: *If worn tightly, the doctors say, panty girdles . . . may act like tourniquets* (Time).

panty hose, tights made of nylon hosiery material.

pan·ty·waist (pan'tē wāst'), *n.* **1.** an undergarment in two pieces with short pants buttoning to the shirt at the waist, especially worn by children. **2.** *U.S. Slang.* a somewhat effeminate man or boy; sissy: *That pantywaist Gibbs doesn't even like beer* (Time). —*adj. U.S. Slang.* of, having to do with, or like a somewhat effeminate man or boy.

Pan·urge (pan'ėrj; *French* pá nʏrzh'), *n.* (in Rabelais' *Gargantua and Pantagruel*) a clever, likable rogue (although proudly lacking in the traditional virtues); boon companion of Pantagruel. [< French *Panurge* < Greek *panoûrgos* ready to do anything, knavish < *pan-* all + *érgon* work]

pan·zer or **Pan·zer** (pan′zər; *German* pän′tsər), *adj.* armored or mechanized and armored: *A panzer division consists largely of tanks.* —*n.* a mechanized and armored force: *On May 26, 1940, Gort's army was in full retreat from Hitler's Panzers toward the Channel ports* (Time). [< German *Panzer* tank, (literally) armor < Italian *panciera* < *pancia* belly < Latin *pantex*]

pap[1] (pap), *n., v.,* **papped, pap·ping.** —*n.* **1.** very soft food for infants or invalids. **2.** money, favors, etc., from a government official; political patronage. **3.** ideas or facts watered down to a characterless consistency, considered as innocuous and as unsuitable for adults as baby food: *He loathed the pseudoscientific pap which is fed to judges in patent cases and never concocted any of it himself* (Harper's). —*v.t.* to feed with pap. [compare Low German, Middle German *pappe*]

pap[2] (pap), *n.* **1.** *Archaic.* a teat or nipple. **2.** something resembling a teat or nipple in form. [Middle English *pappe,* probably < Scandinavian (compare Swedish *pappe*)]

pa·pa[1] (pä′pə, pə pä′), *n.* father; daddy. [< French *papa* < Late Latin *pāpa*]

pa·pa[2] (pä′pä), *n.* **1.** *Greek Church.* **a.** a parish priest. **b.** the patriarch of Alexandria. **2.** *Rare.* the Pope. [< Medieval Latin *papa* pope < Late Latin *pāpa* bishop; (originally) father]

Pa·pa (pä′pə), *n. U.S.* a code name for the letter *p,* used in transmitting radio messages.

pa·pa·bi·le (pä pä′bē lā), *adj., n., pl.* **-li** (-lē). *Italian.* —*adj.* of papal quality or caliber; capable of being elected Pope: *The cardinals who are "papabile" . . . are well known to the other cardinals* (Xavier Rynne). —*n.* a cardinal regarded as a possible successor to the Pope.

pa·pa·cy (pā′pə sē), *n., pl.* **-cies. 1.** the position, rank, or authority of the Pope. **2.** the time during which a pope rules. **3.** all the popes. **4.** government by the Pope. [< Medieval Latin *papatia,* alteration of *papatus* < Late Latin *pāpa* pope]

Pa·pa·ga·yo (pä′pə gī′ō), *n., pl.* **-yos.** a violent northeast wind with tornadic whirls that descends during October to May from the mountains into the Gulf of Papagayo, at the northwest corner of Costa Rica and the southwest corner of Nicaragua.

pa·pa·in (pə pā′in, pä′pə-), *n.* **1.** a proteolytic enzyme obtained from the half-ripe fruit of the papaya, resembling both pepsin and trypsin in its action. **2.** a preparation of this in the form of a grayish powder, used medicinally to assist digestion.

pa·pal (pā′pəl), *adj.* **1.** of the Pope: *a papal letter.* **2.** of the papacy. **3.** of the Roman Catholic Church: *papal ritual.* [< Medieval Latin *papalis* < Late Latin *pāpa* pope] —**pa′pal·ly,** *adv.* —**Syn. 1.** pontifical.

papal bull, a formal announcement or official order from the Pope: *A 386-year-old Papal Bull calling Queen Elizabeth I a "slave of wickedness" and excommunicating her from the Roman Catholic Church changed hands today* (New York Times).

papal cross, a cross with three transoms; triple cross. See the diagram of **cross.**

papal crown, a tiara.

pa·pal·ism (pā′pə liz əm), *n.* the papal system.

pa·pal·ist (pā′pə list), *n.* an adherent of the papal system or the papacy.

pa·pal·i·za·tion (pā′pə lə zā′shən), *n.* **1.** the act of papalizing. **2.** the state of being papalized.

pa·pal·ize (pā′pə līz), *v.i., v.t.,* **-ized, -iz·ing.** to become or make papal.

Pa·pa·ni·co·laou smear or **test** (pä′pə-nē′kə lou, pap′ə nik′ə-), a test used to diagnose cancer, in which exfoliated cells of organs, such as the stomach or uterus, are obtained, smeared on a glass slide, and stained for microscopic examination. [< George N. *Papanicolaou,* born 1883, a Greek physician in the United States, who developed it]

pa·pas (pä′päs), *n.* a parish priest of the Greek Church; papa: *The papas is a prominent figure . . . because of his long black gown, his tall steeple hat* (Scribner's Magazine). [< Greek *pápas* father]

pa·pav·er·a·ceous (pə pav′ə rā′shəs), *adj.* belonging to the poppy family of plants. [< New Latin *Papaveraceae* the family name (< Latin *papāver* poppy) + English *-ous*]

pa·pav·er·in (pə pav′ər in, -pā′vər-), *n.* papaverine.

pa·pav·er·ine (pə pav′ə rēn, -ər in; -pā′-və rēn, -vər in), *n.* a crystalline alkaloid obtained from opium or made synthetically, used especially in its hydrochloride form. *Formula:* $C_{20}H_{21}NO_4$ [< Latin *papāver* poppy + English *-ine*[2]]

papaverine hydrochloride, a white, slightly bitter powder, a non-habit-forming narcotic, used to relax smooth muscles. *Formula:* $C_{20}H_{21}NO_4.HCl$

pa·paw (pô′pô), *n.* **1.** a small tree of the custard apple family, of the eastern and central United States, bearing oblong, yellowish, edible fruit with many beanlike seeds; fetid shrub. **2.** this fruit. **3.** the papaya. Also, **pawpaw.** [American English, apparently the same word as *papaya*]

pa·pa·ya (pə pä′yə), *n.* **1.** a tropical American herbaceous tree having a straight, palmlike stem with a tuft of large leaves at the top and edible, melonlike fruit with yellowish pulp. **2.** the fruit. [< Spanish *papaya,* probably < Arawak (West Indies) *papaya*]

FRUIT

Papaya Tree and Fruit (12 to 25 ft. high)

pap·a·ya·ceous (pap′ə yā′shəs), *adj.* belonging to the family of tropical and subtropical trees typified by the papaya.

pap boat, a boat-shaped, shallow vessel for holding pap to feed infants and invalids: *Still with this infant (or another) in mind, you might have a look at half dozen or so eighteenth-century pap boats* (New Yorker).

pa·per (pā′pər), *n.* **1. a.** a material, in thin sheets, used for writing, printing, drawing, wrapping packages, and covering walls, etc. Paper is made from wood pulp, rags, etc. **b.** a material like paper, as papyrus. **c.** a material made from paper pulp, as papier-mâché. **2.** a piece or sheet of paper: *his mind was in its original state of white paper* (Charles Lamb). **3.** a piece of paper or sheet with writing or printing on it; document: *Important papers were stolen.* **4.** a wrapper, container, or sheet of paper containing something: *a paper of pins.* **5.** a newspaper; journal: *He bought the morning papers.* **6.** an article; essay: *Professor Smith read a paper on the teaching of English.* **7.** a written examination. **8.** a written promise to pay money or a note, bill of exchange, etc.: *commercial paper. The rapid rise in consumer instalment debt—particularly auto paper—is one of the danger spots in the economy* (Wall Street Journal). **9.** paper money or currency. **10.** wallpaper. **11.** *Slang.* **a.** a free pass to a theater or other entertainment. **b.** persons admitted by free passes.

commit to paper, to write down: *He memorized the message and as soon as he got home committed it to paper.*

on paper, a. in writing or print: *I like your idea. Let's get it down on paper.* **b.** in theory: *The form of their constitution, as it is on paper, admits not of coercion. But necessity introduced it in practice* (American Museum).

papers, a. documents telling who or what one is: *As to my husband's papers I have put them all . . . into Mr. Dale's hands* (Mrs. John Ray). **b.** a ship's papers (the documents of a ship showing where it is registered, who owns it, etc.): *A fine ship named the Redbridge . . . Her papers had been made out for Alicant* (Macaulay).

—*adj.* **1.** made of paper: *paper dolls, a paper napkin or towel.* **2.** having to do with or used for paper: *a paper clip.* **3.** like paper; thin: *almonds with paper shells, paper walls.* **4.** of, consisting of, or carried on by means of letters to newspapers, pamphlets, or books: *paper warfare.* **5.** existing only on paper: *The Western allies are not concerned with any paper arrangement the Soviets may wish to make with a regime of their own creation* (John F. Kennedy). *The proposed . . . Oroville Dam . . . is still a paper dream* (Time).

—*v.t.* **1.** to enclose in or cover with paper. **2.** to cover with wallpaper: *to paper a room.* **3.** to supply with or furnish with paper. **4.** to smooth with sandpaper. **5.** to write or set down on paper. **6.** to write about; describe in writing. **7.** *Slang.* to fill (a place of entertainment) with an audience admitted mostly by free passes: *To get a crowd at the concert, they had to paper the house.*

paper over, to smooth over or cover up (a quarrel, disagreement, etc.): *The talks were called originally to try to paper over the ideological differences between Peking and Moscow* (New York Times).

[< Old French *papier,* learned borrowing from Latin *papȳrus* a paper rush; writing material made from it < Greek *pápȳros* a paper rush. Doublet of PAPYRUS.] —**pa′per·er,** *n.* —**pa′per·like′,** *adj.*

—**Syn.** *adj.* **3.** flimsy, frail.

pa·per·back (pā′pər bak′), *n.* a book with a binding of heavy paper, especially one that is sold or intended to be sold at a relatively low price and to a mass market: *The print is doing for painting what the paperback did for literature* (Time). *Paperbacks are not only cheaper than the hard-cover books but to the students they seem . . . easier to read* (New York Times). —*adj.* **1.** (of books) bound in heavy paper: *A two-volume paperback reissue of a famous work* (Scientific American). **2.** of or having to do with paperback books: *the paperback industry, field, market, etc.*

pa·per·backed (pā′pər bakt′), *adj.* paperback.

pa·per·bark (pā′pər bärk′), *n.* any of various Australian trees, the bark of which peels off in layers.

paper birch, a large North American birch, having a tough, durable white bark used by the Indians in making canoes and tents, and yielding a valuable timber; canoe birch; white birch.

pa·per·board (pā′pər bôrd′, -bōrd′), *n., adj.* pasteboard; cardboard: *Old newspapers, an important ingredient in paperboard, now sell for $20 a ton* (Wall Street Journal).

pa·per·book (pā′pər bu̇k′), *n.* paperback: *. . . a national distributor of magazines and paperbooks* (New York Times).

pa·per·bound (pā′pər bound′), *n., adj.* paperback.

pa·per·boy (pā′pər boi′), *n.* a boy who delivers or sells newspapers; newsboy.

paper chase, the game of hare and hounds when paper is used for the "scent."

paper chromatography, the separation of mixtures of chemical compounds by the use of filter paper as the adsorbing material.

paper clip, a flat, looped piece of wire forming a clip for holding papers together.

paper curtain, *U.S.* an obstacle consisting of red tape and bureaucratic indirection, especially one set up by a governmental body to restrict or prevent the free flow of information and maintain secrecy: *a paper curtain hampering the issue of visitors' permits.*

paper cutter, 1. a machine or device equipped with one or more heavy knifelike blades for cutting, or for trimming the edges of, paper, especially in bulk. **2.** a paper knife.

paper doll, the figure of a person cut out of a sheet of paper or cardboard for use as a child's doll.

paper electrophoresis, a form of paper chromatography in which the mixture to be separated is moved across the filter paper by passing an electric current through the paper.

paper hanger, a person whose business is to cover walls with wallpaper.

paper hanging, the work or business of a paper hanger.

paper hangings, wallpaper.

pa·per·ing (pā′pər ing), *n.* **1.** the act of one who papers, especially the work of a paper hanger. **2.** wallpaper: *a room . . . with such large-figured papering on the walls as inn rooms have* (Charlotte Brontë).

paper knife, 1. a knife with a blade of metal, wood, ivory, etc., used to cut open letters and the pages of books. **2.** a paper cutter.

paper machine, a machine for making paper, consisting of rolls which spread paper pulp into a uniform layer and press it into the final product.

pa·per·mak·er (pā′pər mā′kər), *n.* a person who makes or manufactures paper: *The book is beautifully printed with over eighty illustrations covering Mason's own work and the methods used by primitive papermakers in the Far East* (New Science).

pa·per·mak·ing (pā′pər mā′king), *n.* the science, process, or business of producing paper: *In timber-starved South Africa the eucalyptus is a prime source of pulp for papermaking* (Harper's).

paper mill, a mill in which paper is made: *The paper mill at Hahnemuehle started a monthly delivery of 20,000 sheets of the specially made linen bank note paper* (Harper's).

paper money, 1. money made of paper, not metal, and bearing no interest: *A dollar bill is paper money. The words [In God We Trust] now appear on coins but not on paper money* (New York Times). **2.** negotiable instruments used instead of money, as checks, notes, or drafts.

paper mulberry, a tree of the mulberry family, native to eastern Asia, whose soft inner bark is used in the Far East for making paper and tapa cloth.

paper nautilus, any of a group of eight-armed sea mollusks somewhat like an octopus; argonaut. The female has a very thin, delicate shell in which the young develop. See picture under **nautilus.**

paper profits, profits existing on paper, but not yet realized.

paper pulp, a mass of fibrous material prepared to be made into paper, an intermediate product in the manufacture of paper.

paper rush, the papyrus.

pa·pers (pā′pərz), *n.pl.* See under **paper,** *n.*

Pa·per·tex (pā′pər teks), *n. Trademark.* a strong, synthetic paper made chiefly of nylon. It is highly resistant to tearing and fire, and is used as a fabric in upholstery, garments, tents, etc., or as paper for documents requiring long preservation.

pa·per-thin (pā′pər thin′), *adj.* thin as paper; extremely slender, flimsy, or meager: *a paper-thin blade, paper-thin walls, a paper-thin victory.*

paper tiger, a person or thing that appears to be strong or threatening but is really weak, ineffectual, or cowardly: *Mr. Khrushchev said that those who call imperialism a paper tiger should reflect that the tiger has nuclear teeth* (Manchester Guardian).

paper wasp, any of the social wasps that builds its nest of a papery substance made from dry wood moistened into a paste.

pa·per·weight (pā′pər wāt′), *n.* a small, heavy, often ornamental object put on papers to keep them from being blown away or scattered.

pa·per·work (pā′pər wėrk′), *n.* **1. a.** work done on paper; writing: *There's five hours' paperwork a night for any minister* (Atlantic). **b.** office or clerical work, such as the writing, checking, and sorting of letters, reports, etc.: *In the rear echelon of the corps headquarters, there was only paperwork* (Ralph Ingersoll). **c.** the written work of a student; classroom work; homework: *A four-to-seven-year-old does as much paperwork as any bureaucrat* (New Yorker). **2.** work in paper; work or a structure made of paper.

pa·per·work·er (pā′pər wėr′kər), *n.* a papermaker.

pa·per·works (pā′pər wėrks′), *n.pl. or sing.* an establishment where paper is made.

pa·per·y (pā′pər ē), *adj.* like paper; thin or flimsy.

pap·e·terie (pap′ə trē; *French* påp trē′), *n.* a case or box, usually ornamental, for paper and other writing materials. [< French *papeterie* stationery case; the paper trade < Middle French *papetier* papermaker, or dealer < Old French *papier* paper]

Pa·phi·an (pā′fē ən), *adj.* **1.** of, having to do with, or belonging to Paphos, an ancient city of Cyprus sacred to Aphrodite or Venus, and containing one of her most celebrated temples. **2. a.** having to do with love, especially illicit love or sexual indulgence. **b.** of prostitutes; being a prostitute: *the Paphian sisterhood.* —*n.* a prostitute.

Pa·pi·a·men·to (pä′pē ə men′tō), *n.* a lingua franca spoken in the Dutch West Indies, consisting chiefly of a mixture of Dutch, English, and Spanish. [< Papiamento *Papiamento* < *papia* to speak]

pa·pier col·lé (på pyā′ kô lā′), *pl.* **pa·piers col·lés** (på pyā′ kô lā′). *French.* (in cubism) a collection of pieces of paper or other material arranged to form a design and pasted on a flat surface: *They began simulating reality by pasting it on their pictures in what became known as papiers collés, or collages, collé being the French word for paste* (New Yorker).

pa·pier-mâ·ché (pā′pər mə shā′), *n.* a paper pulp mixed with some stiffener such as glue and molded when moist. It becomes hard and strong when dry, and is used chiefly for decorative objects and for stage properties. *Enormous pieces of group statuary in painted papier-mâché [are] put up by various guilds and other organizations in many parts of the city* (New York Times). —*adj.* made of papier-mâché: *Parents and 5-to-12-year-olds will learn how to make papier-mâché puppets and costumes* (New York Times). *The well-known papier-mâché bedstead in the Victoria and Albert Museum is a metal bedstead with papier-mâché head and foot panels* (London Times). [< French *papier* paper, and *mâché* compressed, mashed < *mâcher* (literally) to chew < Late Latin *masticāre* masticate]

pa·pil·i·o·na·ceous (pə pil′ē ə nā′shəs), *adj.* **1.** *Botany.* **a.** having a zygomorphic corolla somewhat like a butterfly in shape, as most leguminous plants. A papilionaceous flower consists of a large upper petal (vexillum), two lateral petals (alae), and two narrow lower petals below these, forming the carina or keel. **b.** belonging to the pea family of plants; fabaceous. **2.** having to do with or resembling a butterfly. [< Latin *pāpiliō, -ōnis* butterfly + English *-aceous*]

pa·pil·la (pə pil′ə), *n., pl.* **-lae. 1.** a small, nipplelike projection. **2.** a small vascular process at the root of a hair or feather. **3.** one of certain small protuberances concerned with the senses of touch, taste, or smell. **4.** a papule, pimple, or pustule. [< New Latin *papilla* the nipple < Latin *papilla* nipple of the breast, diminutive < *papula* swelling, pimple; see PAPULE]

pa·pil·lae (pə pil′ē), *n.* plural of **papilla:** *the papillae on the tongue.*

pap·il·lar·y (pap′ə ler′ē), *adj.* **1.** of or like a papilla. **2.** having papillae.

pap·il·late (pap′ə lāt), *adj.* covered with papillae.

pa·pil·le·de·ma (pap′ə lə dē′mə), *n.* a swelling or inflammation of the optic nerve due to edema.

pa·pil·lo·e·de·ma (pə pil′ō ə dē′mə), *n.* papilledema.

pa·pil·lo·ma (pap′ə lō′mə), *n., pl.* **-mas, -ma·ta** (-mə tə). a tumor of the skin or mucous membrane, characterized by an overgrown papilla or group of papillae usually covered by a layer of thickened epidermis or epithelium, as a wart or corn: *By condensing the smoke of burning cigarettes and painting the brown gummy condensates or "tar" on the backs of mice, Drs. Evarts Graham and Ernest Wynder and Miss Adele Croninger produced papillomas—benign tumors regarded as precancerous—in 59 per cent of them, and these tumors progressed to true cancer in 44 per cent* (Atlantic). [< New Latin *papilloma* < *papilla* papilla + *-oma* -oma]

pap·il·lon (pap′ə lon), *n.* any of a European breed of toy spaniels, developed from the dwarf spaniels of the 1500's, standing about 11 inches high and having a white silky coat marked with black, red, or tan. [< French, Old French *papillon* (literally) butterfly, learned borrowing from Latin *pāpiliō, -ōnis* (because of their large, curved ears). Doublet of PAVILION.]

pap·il·lose (pap′ə lōs), *adj.* having many papillae. [< *papill*(a) + *-ose*[1]]

pap·il·los·i·ty (pap′ə los′ə tē), *n.* papillose condition.

pap·il·lote (pap′ə lōt), *n.* **1.** a curlpaper. **2.** a ring of paper fringed at one end, put on chops, cutlets, and the like for decoration. [< French, Middle French *papillote* butterfly-like paillette or ornament < Old French *papillon;* see PAPILLON]

pa·pish (pā′pish), *Dialect.* —*adj.* popish. —*n.* a papist.

pa·pism (pā′piz əm), *n.* Roman Catholicism (used in an unfriendly way).

pa·pist (pā′pist), *n., adj.* Roman Catholic (used in an unfriendly way). [< New Latin *papista* < Late Latin *pāpa* pope]

pa·pis·tic (pā pis′tik, pə-), *adj.* papistical.

pa·pis·ti·cal (pā pis′tə kəl, pə-), *adj.* of or having to do with the Pope or the papal system; resembling Roman Catholic usages (used in an unfriendly way). —**pa·pis′ti·cal·ly,** *adv.*

pa·pis·try (pā′pə strē), *n., pl.* **-tries.** the system, doctrines, or usages of the Roman Catholic Church (used in an unfriendly way).

pap·meat (pap′mēt′), *n.* pap or soft food, as for infants or invalids. [< *pap*[1] + *meat*]

pa·poose or **pap·poose** (pa püs′), *n.* a North American Indian baby. [American English < Algonkian (Narragansett) *papoos* child]

pap·pi (pap′ī), *n.* plural of **pappus.**

pap·pose (pap′ōs), *adj. Botany.* **1.** having a pappus. **2.** downy. [< New Latin *papposus* < Latin *pappus* pappus]

pap·pous (pap′əs), *adj.* pappose.

pap·pus (pap′əs), *n., pl.* **pap·pi** (pap′ī). *Botany.* an appendage to a seed, often made of down or bristles: *Dandelion and thistle seeds have pappi.* [< Latin *pappus* down[2] on seeds; (originally) old man, grandfather < Greek *páppos*]

pap·py[1] (pap′ē), *adj.,* **-pi·er, -pi·est.** like pap; watered down: *The demand for pap—pappy plays, pappy views about life, death, and a pappy hereafter—is very much greater than the demand for what requires more energy and guts* (Tyrone Guthrie). [< *pap*[1] + *-y*[1]]

pap·py[2] (pap′ē), *n., pl.* **-pies.** *Dialect.* papa; father.

pap·ri·ka or **pa·pri·ca** (pa prē′kə, pap′rə-), *n.* **1.** the dried fruit of a cultivated variety of the common pepper plant, ground as a condiment; Hungarian pepper. It is much milder than ordinary red pepper. **2.** the plant that produces the fruit from which this is made, grown especially in Hungary and Spain. [< Hungarian *paprika* < Serbo-Croatian < New Greek *pipéri* pepper]

Pap smear or **test** (pap), Papanicolaou smear or test: *The "Pap smear" is effective in spotting potential cancers of the cervix* (Harper's).

Pap·u·an (pap′yů ən), *adj.* of or having to do with Papua, or British New Guinea, part of a large island north of Australia, or with the native negroid race living in Papua. —*n.* **1.** a native or inhabitant of Papua or a person belonging to the racial type that is found there. **2.** any of the native languages or dialects spoken in New Guinea and adjacent islands.
[< *Papua,* the island < Malay *papuwa* frizzled; because of the appearance of the hair of the inhabitants]

pap·u·lar (pap′yə lər), *adj.* of, having to do with, or covered with papillae or pimples.

pap·ule (pap′yül), *n.* a pimple that does not form pus. [< Latin *papula* a swelling, pimple]

pap·y·ra·ceous (pap′ə rā′shəs), *adj.* of the consistency or thinness of paper; papery; paperlike. [< *papyr*(us) + *-aceous*]

pa·py·ro·graph (pə pī′rə graf, -gräf), *n.* any of various devices for producing copies of a writing or the like, especially by a paper stencil. [< Greek *pápȳros* (see PAPYRUS) + English *-graph*]

pap·y·rol·o·gist (pap′ə rol′ə jist), *n.* a person who studies or is an expert in papyrology: *Papyrologists [are] . . . devoted to the care and interpretation of ancient papyri* (New Yorker).

pap·y·rol·o·gy (pap′ə rol′ə jē), *n.* the study of papyri. [< Greek *pápȳros* + English *-logy*]

pa·py·rus (pə pī′rəs), *n., pl.* **-ri** (-rī). **1.** a tall water plant of the sedge family, from which the ancient Egyptians, Greeks, and Romans made a kind of paper to write on. Papyrus has stems 8 to 10 feet high, and is still abundant in Egypt and is also found in Ethiopia, Syria, Sicily, etc. Papyrus is the bulrush of the Bible. **2.** a writing material made from the pith of the papyrus plant, by laying thin slices or strips of it side by side, the whole being then soaked, pressed, and dried: *Letters, written on papyrus in the hieratic character* (Amelia B. Edwards). **3.** an ancient record written on papyrus: *According to papyri found in one of the ancient Negev cities, Nisana, their desert farming produced barley, wheat, legumes, grapes, figs, and dates* (Scientific American). [< Latin *papȳrus* the paper-rush; writing material made from it < Greek *pápȳros* any plant of the paper rush genus. Doublet of PAPER. Compare BIBLE.]

par (pär), *n.* **1.** equality; equal level: *The gains and losses are about on a par. He is quite on a par with his brother.* **2.** an average or normal amount, degree, or condition: *A sick person feels below par.* **3.** the value of a bond, a note, a share of stock, etc., that is printed on it; face value: *That stock is selling above par.* **4.** the established normal value

of the money of one country in terms of the money of another country. **5.** (in golf) the number of strokes required to play a hole or a series of holes without mistakes under normal conditions. On many golf courses 72 is par. *He had hammered out a 5-under par 65 in the second round* (New York Times).
up to par, up to the average, normal, or usual amount, degree, condition, or quality: *Her work is not up to par today because she has a headache.*
—*adj.* **1.** average; normal. **2.** of or at par.
[< Latin *pār, paris,* adjective, equal; noun, a counterpart. Doublet of PEER[1].]

par-, *prefix.* the form of **para-**[1] before vowels and *h,* as in *parenthesis, parhelion.*

par., **1.** paragraph. **2.** parallel. **3.** parenthesis. **4.** parish.

pa·ra[1] (pä rä′), *n., pl.* **-ras** or **-ra.** **1.** 1/40 of a Turkish piaster. **2.** 1/100 of a Yugoslavian dinar. **3.** either of the two coins having these values. [< Turkish *para*]

par·a[2] (par′ə), *n., pl.* **par·as.** *Informal.* a paratrooper: *The Belgian paras sustained only seven casualties in rescuing the hostages* (Time).

Pa·rá (pä rä′), *n.* Pará rubber.

para-[1], *prefix.* **1.** beside; near, as in *paragraph, paradigm, parathyroid.*
2. disordered condition, as in *paranoia.*
3. (in chemical terms) a modification of; an isomer of; a substance related to, as in *paracymene, paradichlorobenzene.* Also, **par-** before vowels and *h.*
[< Greek *pará* beside; near; from]

para-[2], *combining form.* **1.** a defense against; a protection from: *Parachute = a device that protects from falls. Parasol = a device that protects from the sun.*
2. that uses a parachute: *Paratrooper = a soldier that uses a parachute.*
[< French *para-* < Italian < *para,* imperative of *parare* ward off, defend against < Latin *parāre* prepare against]

para., paragraph.

Para., Paraguay.

par·a·a·mi·no·ben·zo·ic acid (par′ə ə mē′nō ben zō′ik, -am′ə nō-), a yellow, crystalline acid, a constituent of the vitamin B complex, present in yeast and in bran. It is used in the manufacture of local anesthetics and in the treatment of rheumatic fever and various skin conditions. *Formula:* $C_7H_7NO_2$ [< *para-*[1] + *aminobenzoic acid*]

par·a·a·mi·no·sal·i·cyl·ic acid (par′ə ə mē′nō sal′ə sil′ik, -am′ə nō-), a synthetic drug used widely in the treatment of tuberculosis, usually in combination with other drugs such as isoniazid and streptomycin. *Formula:* $C_7H_7NO_3$

par·a·bal·loon (par′ə bə lün′), *n.* a mobile radar antenna consisting principally of two paraboloids made of fabric, in part coated thinly with metal, which can be inflated and raised, or lowered and deflated for transportation: *The cameras are mounted in capsules which are equipped with a paraballoon, a combination of a parachute and balloon* (Birmingham Post-Herald).

pa·rab·a·sis (pə rab′ə sis), *n., pl.* **-ses** (-sēz). the chief of the choral parts in ancient Greek comedy, sung by the chorus during an intermission in the action, and consisting of an address from the poet to the audience. [< Greek *parábasis* < *parabaínein* < *pará* beside + *baínein* to go]

par·a·bi·o·sis (par′ə bī ō′sis), *n.* the natural or surgical union of two animals in such a way that there is an exchange of blood. [< *para-*[1] + *-biosis,* as in *anabiosis*]

par·a·bi·ot·ic (par′ə bī ot′ik), *adj.* of or having to do with parabiosis.

par·a·blast (par′ə blast), *n. Embryology.* the nutritive yolk of an ovum or egg. [< *para-*[1] + Greek *blastós* germ, sprout]

par·a·blas·tic (par′ə blas′tik), *adj.* of, having to do with, or derived from the parablast.

par·a·ble (par′ə bəl), *n.* **1.** a brief story, teaching some moral lesson or truth: *Jesus taught in parables. If the story-tellers could ha' got decency and good morals from true stories, who'd have troubled to invent parables?* (Thomas Hardy). **2.** *Archaic.* a comparison or enigmatic saying.
[< Old French *parable,* learned borrowing from Latin *parabola* comparison (in Late Latin, allegory, parable) < Greek *parabolḗ* analogy, comparison; a parabola < *para-* alongside + *bolḗ* a throwing, casting. Doublet of PALAVER, PARABOLA, PARABOLE, PAROLE.]
—**Syn.** **1.** apologue.
➤ See **allegory** for usage note.

pa·rab·o·la (pə rab′ə lə), *n., pl.* **-las.** *Geometry.* a plane curve formed by the intersection of a conical surface with a plane parallel to a side of the cone: *When we throw a ball, it rises for a while and then begins to fall downward; the curve it follows is called a parabola* (John R. Pierce). [< Greek *parabolḗ* parabola; comparison; (literally) putting side by side; see PARABLE. Doublet of PALAVER, PARABLE, PARABOLE, PAROLE.]

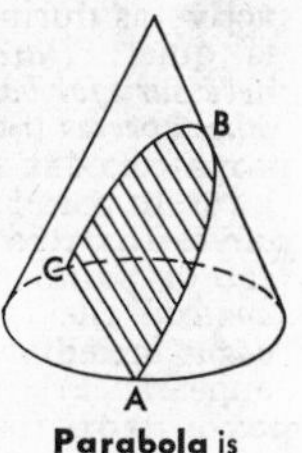

Parabola is curve ABC.

pa·rab·o·le (pə rab′ə lē), *n. Rhetoric.* **1.** a comparison. **2.** a metaphor. [< Greek *parabolḗ.* Doublet of PALAVER, PARABLE, PARABOLA, PAROLE.]

par·a·bol·ic[1] (par′ə bol′ik), *adj. Geometry.* **1.** having the form of a parabola: *a parabolic orbit. He compelled the frothy liquor . . . to spout forth from one glass and descend into the other, in a great parabolic curve* (Hawthorne). **2.** having to do with or resembling a parabola: *a parabolic area.* —**par′a·bol′i·cal·ly,** *adv.*

par·a·bol·ic[2] (par′ə bol′ik), *adj.* of, having to do with, or expressed in a parable. [< *parable* + *-ic*] —**par′a·bol′i·cal·ly,** *adv.*

par·a·bol·i·cal[1] (par′ə bol′ə kəl), *adj.* resembling a parabola in form or outline; parabolic.

par·a·bol·i·cal[2] (par′ə bol′ə kəl), *adj.* of the nature of a parable; parabolic.

parabolic mirror or **reflector,** a concave mirror the reflecting surface of which has the shape of a paraboloid, capable of focusing rays parallel to its axis to a point without spherical aberration: *Parabolic mirrors or reflectors are used in certain telescopes, automobile headlights, searchlights, etc.*

pa·rab·o·lize[1] (pə rab′ə līz), *v.t.,* **-lized, -liz·ing.** to give the form of a parabola or paraboloid to.

pa·rab·o·lize[2] (pə rab′ə līz), *v.t.,* **-lized, -liz·ing.** **1.** to represent in a parable. **2.** to treat as a parable.

pa·rab·o·loid (pə rab′ə loid), *n. Geometry.* **1.** a conoid of which sections made by planes parallel to a given line are parabolas. **2.** Also **paraboloid of revolution.** a solid or surface generated by the revolution of a parabola about its axis. [< Greek *paraboloeidḗs* showing comparison < *parabolḗ* juxtaposition + *eîdos* form]

pa·rab·o·loi·dal (pə rab′ə loi′dəl), *adj.* having to do with or resembling a paraboloid.

paraboloid of revolution, paraboloid (def. 2).

par·a·ca·sein (par′ə kā′sēn, -sē in), *n.* casein obtained from milk by the action of rennet. [< *para*[1]- + *casein*]

Par·a·cel·si·an (par′ə sel′sē ən), *adj.* of or having to do with Paracelsus, a Swiss-German physician and alchemist, or his theories: *We are still close to alchemy, medieval travellers' tales, the Paracelsian twilight zone which lies between magic and science* (Observer). —*n.* a follower or adherent of Paracelsus.

par·a·chute (par′ə shüt), *n., v.,* **-chut·ed, -chut·ing.** —*n.* **1.** an umbrellalike apparatus made of strips of silk or nylon sewn together and used in descending safely through the air from a great height, as from an aircraft: *There are huge parachutes used in guided missile tests, chutes to stabilize torpedoes dropped from airplanes . . . and a parachute that is intended to yank an airplane out of a spin if anything goes wrong in test flights* (Wall Street Journal). **2.** the expansible fold of skin of a flying mammal or reptile, as of the flying squirrel. See picture under **patagium.** **3.** any contrivance, natural or artificial, serving to check a fall through the air.
—*v.i.* to come down by, or as if by, a parachute: *The men in the burning plane parachuted safely to the ground.* —*v.t.* to convey to earth by a parachute.
[< French *parachute* < *para-* para-[2] + *chute* a fall]

Parachute (def. 1)

parachute spinnaker, a type of very large spinnaker used on racing yachts.

par·a·chut·ist (par′ə shü′tist), *n.* **1.** a person who uses a parachute; person skilled in making descents with a parachute: *Parachutists will be dropped to prepare a field for light aircraft* (Science News Letter). **2.** a paratrooper.

Par·a·clete (par′ə klēt), *n.* the Holy Ghost; the Comforter: *It was approaching the third hour, the hour at which the Paraclete originally descended upon the Apostles* (Cardinal Newman). [< Old French *paraclet,* learned borrowing from Latin *paraclētus* < Greek *paráklētos* advocate; (literally) one called to aid < *parakaleîn* to call (in) < *para-* beside + *kaleîn* to call; to comfort, console]

par·a·clete (par′ə klēt), *n.* a friend, advocate, or comforter. [< *Paraclete*]

par·a·com·man·do (par′ə kə man′dō, -män′-), *n., pl.* **-dos** or **-does.** a commando moved by air and landed by parachute in a battle area or behind enemy lines: *The mutiny was put down after Gen. Joseph D. Mobutu, the army commander, led paracommandos into the main police barracks* (New York Times). [< *para-*[2] + *commando*]

par·a·crys·tal·line (par′ə kris′tə lin, -līn), *adj. Chemistry.* having the molecular grouping of a substance just prior to crystallization; resembling the crystalline state. [< *para-*[1] + *crystalline*]

par·a·cy·mene (par′ə sī′mēn), *n. Chemistry.* one of three isomeric forms of cymene.

pa·rade (pə rād′), *n., v.,* **-rad·ed, -rad·ing.** —*n.* **1.** a march for display; procession: *The circus had a parade.* **2.** a group of people walking for display or pleasure. **3.** *British.* a place where people walk for display or pleasure; public promenade. **4.** a great show or display: *A modest man will not make a parade of his wealth.* **5.** a military display or review of troops. **6. a.** a place used for the regular parade of troops. **b.** the level, open space within the walls of a fortification. **7.** *Fencing.* a parry: *He was an admirable swordsman. His parade and riposte were as quick as lightning* (Sir Arthur Conan Doyle).
—*v.t.* **1.** to march through in procession or with display: *The performers and animals paraded the streets.* **2.** to make a great show of: *to parade one's wealth.* **3.** to assemble (troops) for review or inspection. **4.** to march (a person) up and down or through the streets either for show or to expose him to contempt. —*v.i.* **1.** to march in procession; walk proudly as if in a parade. **2.** to come together in military order for review, ceremony, or inspection: *Photographs of the latest Soviet planes were taken when they "paraded" over Moscow* (New York Times).
[< French *parade* (originally) checking (a horse) in maneuvers < Spanish *parada* < *parar* to check; dispose in position < Latin *parāre* prepare; influenced by French *parer* arrange, deck elegantly] —**pa·rad′er,** *n.*
—**Syn.** *v.t.* **2.** display, flaunt.

parade ground, **1.** an extent of open, level ground, usually within or adjacent to a fort, where soldiers are accustomed to parade. **2.** a place for making a great show or display of something.

parade rest, *Military.* a position of rest, especially at parade, in which the soldier stands silent and motionless.

par·a·di·chlor·ben·zene (par′ə dī′klôr ben′zēn, -klōr-; -ben zēn′), *n.* paradichlorobenzene.

par·a·di·chlo·ro·ben·zene (par′ə dī klôr′ō ben′zēn, -klōr′-; -ben zēn′), *n.* a colorless or white, crystalline substance, one of three isomers. used as an insecticide, fumigant, etc. *Formula:* $C_6H_4Cl_2$

par·a·did·dle (par′ə did′əl), *n. Jazz Slang.* a basic drum roll on the snare drum. [imitative]

par·a·digm (par′ə dim, -dīm), *n.* **1.** a pattern; example: *Sir John is impeccable, a paradigm of the gentleman soldier* (Harper's). **2.** *Grammar.* **a.** the set of inflectional forms for a word or class of words: *The final step in morphology is the establishment of paradigms, which can be viewed as sets of grammatical suffixes* (Harold B. Allen). **b.** a part of speech in all its inflectional forms. [< Latin *paradigma* < Greek *parádeigma, -matos* pattern, ultimately < *para-* side by side + *deiknýnai* to show, point out]

par·a·dig·mat·ic (par′ə dig mat′ik), *adj.* **1.** of, having to do with, or consisting of a paradigm. **2.** inflectional, as an affix. —**par′a·dig·mat′i·cal·ly,** *adv.*

par·a·dig·mat·i·cal (par′ə dig mat′ə kəl), *adj.* paradigmatic.

par·a·di·sa·ic (par′ə di sā′ik), *adj.* paradisiacal. —**par′a·di·sa′i·cal·ly,** *adv.*

par·a·di·sa·i·cal (par′ə di sā′ə kəl), *adj.* paradisiacal: *paradisaical ecstasy.*

par·a·di·sal (par′ə dī′səl), *adj.* of or having to do with paradise: . . . *Rio de Janeiro, where thousands of Negroes live in conditions of infernal poverty among scenes of paradisal beauty* (Time).

par·a·dise (par′ə dīs), *n.* **1. a.** the abode of God, the angels, and the righteous; heaven. **b.** an intermediate place spoken of by some theologians, where the souls of the righteous await the Last Judgment. **c.** the Moslem heaven, especially when thought of as a place of hedonistic delight: *The Moors imagined the paradise of their prophet to be situated in that part of the heaven which overhung the kingdom of Granada* (Washington Irving). **2.** a place or condition of great happiness: *This state of things should have been to me a paradise of peace* (Charlotte Brontë). *This sunny island off the Spanish coast has been a smuggler's paradise since time immemorial* (New York Times). **3.** a place of great beauty. **4.** Also, **Paradise.** the Garden of Eden. [partly Old English *paradīs,* partly < Old French *paradis,* learned borrowing from Latin *paradīsus* < Greek *parádeisos* < Iranian (compare Avestan *pairidaēza* enclosed park < *pairi-* around + *daēza* wall)]

par·a·di·se·an (par′ə dī′sē ən, par′ə di-sē′ən), *adj.* **1.** paradisiacal: *After that I see the caravan, . . . winding among hills of a paradisean green shade* (Vladimir Nabokov). **2.** of or belonging to the birds of paradise.

paradise fish, a brilliantly colored East Indian fish, remarkable for the extension of its fins, sometimes kept in aquariums.

par·a·dis·i·ac (par′ə dis′i ak), *adj.* paradisiacal.

par·a·di·si·a·cal (par′ə di sī′ə kəl), *adj.* of, having to do with, or belonging to paradise; like that of paradise: *The Balinese themselves are fully aware of its [Bali's] paradisiacal nature* (New Yorker). [< Late Latin *paradīsiacus* < Greek *paradeisiakós* (originally) like a park < *parádeisos;* see PARADISE; + English *-al*[1]] —**par′a·di·si′a·cal·ly,** *adv.*

pa·ra·dor (pä rä ᴛʜôr′), *n., pl.* **-do·res** (-ᴛʜō′rās). *Spanish.* an inn in Spain, operated by the government.

par·a·dos (par′ə dos), *n.* a mound of earth thrown up behind a trench to prevent its occupants from being silhouetted against the skyline when standing on the firing step and to protect them from shells, bombs, etc., that explode in the rear. [< French *parados* < *para-* para-[2] + *dos* back[1]]

par·a·dox (par′ə doks), *n.* **1.** a statement that may be true but seems to say two opposite things: "*More haste, less speed,*" and "*The child is father to the man*" *are paradoxes.* **2.** a statement that is false because it says two opposite things: *There is that glorious epicurean paradox . . . :* "*give us the luxuries of life, and we will dispense with its necessaries*" (Oliver Wendell Holmes). **3.** a person or thing that seems to be full of contradictions: *Man is an embodied paradox, a bundle of contradictions* (Charles Caleb Colton). **4.** a statement contrary to received opinion or belief. **5.** any inconsistent or contradictory fact, action, or condition: *The Western Allies celebrated the World War II victory over Germany today with the paradox of embracing their old enemy as a new ally* (New York Times). [< Latin *paradoxum* < Greek *parádoxon,* neuter of *parádoxos,* adjective, contrary; noun, paradox < *para-* contrary to, aside + *dóxa* opinion < *dokeîn* to seem]
➔ See **epigram** for usage note.

par·a·dox·i·al (par′ə dok′sē əl), *adj.* paradoxical: *The imprecision of the word "substantial" has a paradoxial advantage in that it would enable the Federal courts to interpret it in accordance with changing attitudes* (Manchester Guardian Weekly).

par·a·dox·i·cal (par′ə dok′sə kəl), *adj.* **1.** of paradoxes; involving a paradox: *Comedians, paradoxical as it may seem, may be too natural* (Charles Lamb). **2.** having the habit of using paradoxes: *He was an eternal talker —brilliant, various, paradoxical, florid* (Edward G. Bulwer-Lytton). —**par′a·dox′i·cal·ly,** *adv.* —**par′a·dox′i·cal·ness,** *n.*

paradoxical sleep, the REM or dreaming period of sleep, when the brain is about as active as during wakefulness but the body is quiet: *Paradoxical sleep seems to be necessary for both humans, cats, and perhaps other species* (Science News Letter).

par·a·dox·ist (par′ə dok′sist), *n.* a person given to paradoxes.

par·a·dox·ure (par′ə doks′yər), *n.* a palm cat or palm civet. [< New Latin *Paradoxurus* the typical genus < Greek *parádoxos* incredible + *ourá* tail (because of its appearance)]

par·a·drop (par′ə drop′), *n., v.,* **-dropped, -drop·ping.** —*n.* an airdrop by means of a parachute: *Carrier crews recently dropped 400 tons of construction vehicles in the first mass paradrop of heavy engineering equipment* (Science News Letter). —*v.t.* to drop (something) by parachute.

par·aes·the·sia (par′əs thē′zhə), *n.* paresthesia.

par·aes·thet·ic (par′əs thet′ik), *adj.* paresthetic.

par·af·fin (par′ə fin), *n.* **1. a.** a colorless or white, almost tasteless substance, like wax, used for making candles, sealing jars, etc.; paraffin wax. Paraffin has no odor and is a solid at ordinary temperatures. It is obtained chiefly from crude petroleum, being chemically a mixture of hydrocarbons. **b.** any of various other mixtures of hydrocarbons. **2.** *Chemistry.* **a.** any member of the methane series. **b.** one of the solid (higher) members of this series, that boils at temperatures over 300 degrees centigrade. Commercial paraffin is made up largely of these hydrocarbons. **3.** paraffin oil.
—*v.t.* to cover or treat with paraffin.
[< German *Paraffin* < Latin *parum* not very, too little (< *parvus* small) + *affinis* associated with, related (because of its low affinity for other substances). Compare AFFINED.]

par·af·fine (par′ə fin, -fēn), *n., v.t.,* **-fined, -fin·ing.** paraffin.

par·af·fin·ic (par′ə fin′ik), *adj.* derived from, related to, or like the paraffins: *The microorganisms are capable of consuming certain paraffinic hydrocarbons found in petroleum* (Scientific American).

paraffin oil, 1. any of various oils associated with paraffin, as oils distilled from bituminous shale, oils obtained from petroleum (especially, heavy or lubricating oils), and oils from which paraffin may be made. **2.** *British.* kerosene.

paraffin series, *Chemistry.* methane series.

paraffin test, a measurement of the amount of gunpowder nitrates contained in a paraffin mold of a person's hand. It is used in criminology to determine whether or not a suspect has recently fired a gun. *Evidence has long been accumulating which shows that the standard "paraffin test" . . . is unreliable* (New Scientist).

paraffin wax, solid paraffin, as distinct from paraffin oil.

par·a·form·al·de·hyde (par′ə fôr mal′də-hīd), *n.* a colorless powder obtained by the polymerization of formaldehyde, used as an antiseptic. *Formula:* $(CH_2O)_n$ [< *para-*[1] + *formaldehyde*]

par·a·ge·ne·si·a (par′ə jə nē′sē ə), *n.* paragenesis.

par·a·gen·e·sis (par′ə jen′ə sis), *n.* the formation of minerals in close contact, so that the development of individual crystals is interfered with, resulting in an interlocked crystalline mass.

par·a·ge·net·ic (par′ə jə net′ik), *adj.* of, having to do with, or originating by paragenesis.

par·a·glid·er (par′ə glī′dər), *n.* a kitelike device with flexible wings, designed to slow down the descent of a space vehicle or serve as an independent reëntry vehicle.

par·a·go·ge (par′ə gō′jē), *n.* the addition of a letter, sound, or syllable at the end of a word, often for ease in pronunciation, without changing the meaning of the word. *Examples:* among-*st,* height-*th* (substandard). [< Late Latin *paragōgē* < Greek *paragōgḗ* (literally) a leading by < *para-* beside, beyond + *agōgḗ* a leading < *ágein* to lead]

par·a·gog·ic (par′ə goj′ik), *adj.* having to do with or of the nature of paragoge.

par·a·gon (par′ə gon), *n., adj., v.,* **-goned, -gon·ing.** —*n.* **1.** a model of excellence or perfection: *a paragon of beauty. Winter, the paragon of art, that kills all forms of life . . . save what is pure and will survive* (Roy Campbell). **2.** a flawless diamond weighing 100 carats or more. **3.** a size of printing type (20 points) twice as large as long primer.

This sentence is set in paragon.

—*adj.* of surpassing excellence: *Those jewels were paragon, without flaw, hair, ice or cloud* (Sir Thomas Browne).
—*v.t.* **1.** *Archaic.* to parallel; compare. **2.** *Archaic.* to match; mate: *Pass to join your peers, paragon charm with charm* (Robert Browning). **3.** *Obsolete.* to excel; surpass: *A maid that paragons description* (Shakespeare). **4.** *Obsolete.* to set forth as a perfect model. **5.** *Obsolete.* to typify; exemplify.
[< Middle French *paragon* comparison; criterion < Italian *parangone* (originally) touchstone < Medieval Greek *parakone* whetstone < Greek *parakonân* to whet, ultimately < *para-* on the side + *akónē* whetstone < *ákaina* point, barb]

pa·rag·o·nite (pə rag′ə nīt), *n.* a kind of mica analogous to muscovite but containing sodium instead of potassium. [< Greek *parágōn,* present participle of *parágein* mislead (because it contains sodium, not potassium) + English *-ite*[1]]

par·a·graph (par′ə graf, -gräf), *n.* **1.** a group of sentences that belong together, usually having some unifying elements, such as meaning or subject, that are not shared with the sentences that come before or follow; distinct part of a chapter, letter, or composition. It is customary to begin a paragraph on a new line and to indent this line, except in some business letters. **2.** a separate note or item of news in a newspaper: *She had been irritated by newspaper paragraphs—nobody could ever find out who wrote them* (H.G. Wells). **3. a.** a sign (‖, ¶) used to show where a paragraph begins or should begin. It is mostly used in correcting written or printed work. **b.** such a sign used to indicate a note or footnote. *Abbr.:* par.
—*v.t.* **1.** to divide into paragraphs. **2.** to write paragraphs about. —*v.i.* to write paragraphs. [< Medieval Latin *paragraphus* < Greek *parágraphos* line (in the margin) marking a break in the continuity of thought < *para-* beside + *gráphein* to write. Doublet of PARAPH.]

par·a·graph·er (par′ə graf′ər, -gräf′-), *n.* a person who writes paragraphs, as for a newspaper: *A gossip paragrapher in the evening newspaper said darkly that the situation had become "intolerable"* (Maclean's).

par·a·graph·i·a (par′ə graf′ē ə), *n.* the writing of words and letters other than those intended, an aphasia associated with certain disorders caused by injury to the brain. [< New Latin *paragraphia* < Greek *para-* beyond + *-graphiā* a writing < *gráphein* to write, draw]

par·a·graph·ic (par′ə graf′ik), *adj.* **1.** of, having to do with, or divided into paragraphs; forming a paragraph. **2.** of or having to do with paragraphia. —**par′a·graph′i·cal·ly,** *adv.*

par·a·graph·i·cal (par′ə graf′ə kəl), *adj.* paragraphic.

par·a·graph·ist (par′ə graf′ist, -gräf′-), *n.* a paragrapher: *It is also a happening which continually piles up those "records" so dear to newspaper paragraphists* (Saturday Review).

Par·a·guay·an (par′ə gwā′ən, -gwī′-), *adj.* of or having to do with Paraguay, a country in central South America, or its inhabitants. —*n.* a native or inhabitant of Paraguay.

Par·a·guay tea (par′ə gwā, -gwī), maté.

par·a·hy·dro·gen (par′ə hī′drə jən), *n.* a form of hydrogen consisting of molecules whose pairs of nuclei have spins in opposite directions.

par·a·in·flu·en·za (par′ə in flü en′zə), *n.* a respiratory illness similar to influenza, caused by any of various myxoviruses that are associated with the common cold and various other respiratory diseases.

par·a·keet (par′ə kēt), *n.* any of various small, brightly colored parrots, most of which have slender bodies and long tails. Also, **paraquet, paroquet, parrakeet, parroket, parroquet.** [< Middle French, Old French *paroquet,* apparently alteration of *perrot* parrot < *Perrot* (diminutive) < *Pierre* Peter]

par·a·ker·a·to·sis (par′ə ker′ə tō′sis), *n.* a relatively mild disease of pigs, marked by dry, scaly, crusted skin.

par·a·kite (par′ə kīt), *n.* a number of kites connected in series and flying tandem, used for sending up meteorological instruments.

par·al·de·hyde (pə ral′də hīd), *n.* a colorless liquid, obtained by the action of sulfuric acid on ordinary acetaldehyde, used as a hypnotic and sedative, as a solvent, in the manufacture of organic compounds, etc. *Formula:* $C_6H_{12}O_3$ [< *par-* + *aldehyde*]

par·a·leip·sis (par′ə līp′sis), *n., pl.* **-ses** (-sēz). paralipsis.

par·a·lep·sis (par′ə lep′sis), *n., pl.* **-ses** (-sēz). paralipsis.

Par·a·li·pom·e·non (par′ə li pom′ə non, -lī-), *n.* either of the books in the Douay Bible known as "Chronicles" in the Protestant Old Testament. [< Latin *paralīpomena* < Greek *paraleipómena* (literally) things omitted, ultimately < *paraleípein* omit < *para-* beside + *leípein* to leave (because it contains details omitted in I, II Kings)]

par·a·lip·sis (par′ə lip′sis), *n., pl.* **-ses** (-sēz). a rhetorical device by which a speaker or writer emphasizes something by pretending to ignore it. *Examples:* "disregarding his other faults," "not to mention his heroism," "to say nothing of his virtues." [< Greek *paráleipsis* omission, passing over < *paraleípein* pass by, leave to the side < *para-* beside + *leípein* leave]

par·al·lac·tic (par′ə lak′tik), *adj.* of or having to do with a parallax.

par·al·lax (par′ə laks), *n.* **1.** the angle between the straight lines that join a heavenly body to two different points of observation, equal to the difference in the directions in which the body is seen from the two points. **2.** apparent shifting of the cross hairs of a telescope, caused by imperfect focusing. [< Greek *parállaxis* change, alternation, < *parallássein* to alter < *para-* beside + *allássein* to change < *állos* other]

S
PARALLAX
A
B
EARTH

Parallax (def. 1) S, star; A, B, points of observation on earth. Seen from A, star S is in direction AS. Seen from B, it is in the direction BS. The parallax is the difference between these 2 directions, or the angle ASB.

par·al·lel (par′ə lel), *adj., n., v.,* **-leled, -leling** or (*especially British*) **-lelled, -lel·ling.** —*adj.* **1.** at or being the same distance apart everywhere like the two rails of a railroad track. In geometry, parallel lines extend alongside one another, always equidistant and (in Euclidean geometry) never meeting however far extended, or (in projective geometry) meeting at infinity. *The Appalachian ridge-and-valley region is the most notable example in the world of parallel ridges and valleys* (Finch and Trewartha). **2.** similar; corresponding: *parallel points in the characters of different men, parallel customs in different countries.* **3.** *Music.* **a.** (of parts) moving so that the interval between them remains the same: *parallel thirds, fifths, etc.* **b.** having to do with major and minor keys having the same tonic, as C major and C minor **4.** having to do with things, especially mechanisms, of which some essential parts are parallel, or which are used to produce parallelism of movement.

Parallel Thirds (def. 3a)

—*n.* **1.** a parallel line or surface. **2.** in geography: **a.** any of the imaginary circles around the earth parallel to the equator, marking degrees of latitude. **b.** the markings on a map or globe that represent these circles. **3.** a person or thing like or similar to another: *We have to go to other centuries to find a parallel to his career* (William Osler). **4.** a comparison to show likeness: *Draw a parallel between this winter and last winter. There is no sort of parallel between the cases* (Joseph Butler). **5.** the condition or relation of being parallel; parallelism: *Niles-Bement-Pond and Bell "would work in parallel" if the transaction is completed* (Wall Street Journal). **6.** an arrangement of the wiring of batteries, lights, etc., in which all the positive poles or terminals are joined to one conductor, and all the negative to the other: *When several devices are connected "in parallel," you can turn on one light or one toaster without having everything else going* (Beauchamp, Mayfield, and West). **7.** a trench dug parallel to the defenses of a fort by an attacking force for its own protection. **parallels,** *Printing.* a reference mark consisting of a pair of vertical parallel lines (‖): *parallels inserted on the margin.*

—*v.t.* **1.** to be at the same distance from throughout the length: *The street parallels the railroad. He had then . . . crossed over a ridge that paralleled their rear* (Rudyard Kipling). **2.** to cause to be or run parallel to. **3.** to find a case that is similar or parallel to; furnish a match for: *Can you parallel that for friendliness?* **4.** to be like; be similar to; correspond or be equivalent to: *Your study closely parallels what he told me.* **5.** to compare in order to show likeness; bring into comparison; liken. **6.** *Obsolete.* to bring into conformity.

[< Latin *parallēlus* < Greek *parállēlos* < *pará allḗlois* beside one another]

—**Syn.** *adj.* **2.** analogous, like. *-n.* **3.** counterpart, match.

parallel bars, a pair of raised bars horizontal to the ground, used in gymnastics to develop the muscles of the arms, chest, etc.

parallel cousin, *Anthropology.* one of two cousins whose parents include two brothers or two sisters; ortho-cousin.

par·al·lel·e·pi·ped (par′ə lel′ə pī′pid, -pip′-id), *n. Geometry.* a solid with three pairs of opposite, parallel faces which are parallelograms. [< Late Latin *parallēlepipedum* < Greek *parallēlepípedon* body with parallel surfaces < *parállēlos* parallel + *epípedon* a plane surface < *epi-* upon + *pédon* ground[1]]

par·al·lel·e·pip·e·don (par′ə lel′ə pip′ə-don), *n.* parallelepiped.

parallel file, a file of uniform section without taper from tang to point.

parallel forces, *Mechanics.* forces that act in parallel lines.

par·al·lel·ism (par′ə lel′iz əm), *n.* **1.** a being parallel. **2.** likeness; similarity; correspondence: *For the first 14 years of life, the schooling of a girl is virtually the same as for a boy. But in high school . . . parallelism is likely to end* (Science News Letter). **3.** parallel statements in writing, expressed in the same grammatical form. *Example:* "He was advised to rise early, to work hard, and to eat heartily." **4.** *Metaphysics.* the doctrine that mental and bodily processes are concomitant, each varying with variation of the other, but that there is no causal relation of interaction between the two series of changes. **5.** *Obsolete.* a simile.

par·al·lel·ist (par′ə lel′ist), *n.* **1.** a person who draws a parallel or comparison. **2.** an advocate of the metaphysical doctrine of parallelism.

par·al·lel·is·tic (par′ə le lis′tik), *adj.* of the nature of or involving parallelism: *This parallelistic development of corbeling differs from that of the true arch, which seems everywhere to be derived from a single original source* (Alfred L. Kroeber).

par·al·lel·i·ty (par′ə lel′ə tē), *n.* parallel arrangement, condition, or character.

par·al·lel·i·za·tion (par′ə lel′ə zā′shən), *n.* **1.** the act of parallelizing: *What America needs now is complete parallelization of the roles of doctor and mechanic, so that each, in an emergency, can do the other's job at a moment's notice* (Punch). **2.** the state of being parallelized.

par·al·lel·ize (par′ə le līz), *v.t.,* **-ized, -izing. 1.** to make parallel; place so as to be parallel, especially for comparison; bring into comparison; compare. **2.** to furnish a parallel for, or form a parallel to; match.

par·al·lel·ly (par′ə lel′lē), *adv.* in a parallel manner.

parallel motion, 1. *Music.* motion involving two parts or voices sounded together and moving in the same direction at the same intervals, usually parallel thirds or sixths. **2.** a mechanism by which the end of a piston rod is caused to move in a straight line in spite of deflecting effort.

parallel of declination, *Astronomy.* any imaginary circle whose plane is parallel to the celestial equator.

parallel of latitude, any imaginary circle on the earth's surface, parallel to the equator, by which degrees of latitude are represented: *Parallels of latitude . . . decrease in size with increasing distance from the equator* (Robert H. Baker).

par·al·lel·o·gram (par′ə lel′ə gram), *n.* **1.** *Geometry.* a four-sided plane figure whose opposite sides are parallel and equal, as a rectangle or diamond. **2.** a thing shaped like this. [< Latin *parallēlogrammus* < Greek *parallēlógrammos* < *parállēlos* parallel + *grammḗ* line[1]]

Parallelograms (def. 1)

par·al·lel·o·pi·ped (par′ə lel′ə pī′pid, -pip′-id), *n.* parallelepiped.

par·al·lels (par′ə lelz), *n.pl.* See under **parallel,** *n.*

parallel sailing, sailing due east or west, as along a parallel of latitude.

par·a·lo·gi·a (par′ə lō′jē ə), *n. Psychology.* a mental disorder characterized by difficulty in expressing ideas or illogicalness and irrelevance in speech. [< New Latin *paralogia* < *para-*[1] + *-logia* -logy]

pa·ral·o·gism (pə ral′ə jiz əm), *n. Logic.* **1.** a piece of false or erroneous reasoning, especially one of which the reasoner himself is unconscious. **2.** reasoning of this kind. [< Late Latin *paralogismus* < Greek *paralogismós* < *paralogízesthai* to reason falsely < *para-* beside + *logízesthai* to reason, argue < *lógos* speech, systematic logic]

pa·ral·o·gist (pə ral′ə jist), *n.* a person who uses paralogisms; a false reasoner.

pa·ral·o·gis·tic (pə ral′ə jis′tik), *adj.* characterized by paralogism or incorrect reasoning; illogical.

pa·ral·o·gize (pə ral′ə jīz), *v.i.,* **-gized, -giz·ing.** to commit a paralogism.

par·a·lyse (par′ə līz), *v.t.,* **-lysed, -lys·ing.** *Especially British.* paralyze.

pa·ral·y·sis (pə ral′ə sis), *n., pl.* **-ses** (-sēz). **1. a.** a lessening or loss of the power of motion or sensation in any part of the body: *The accident left him with paralysis of the legs. To the public "paralysis" means a serious crippling, whereas it may actually be only a barely perceptible and transient loss of muscular control* (New York Times). **b.** a disease characterized by this. **2.** a condition of powerlessness or helpless inactivity; state of being helpless; crippling: *The longshoremen's strike caused a paralysis of shipping.* [< Latin *paralysis* < Greek *parálysis* palsy, disablement; (literally) loosening < *paralýein* loosen from beside < *para-* beside + *lýein* loosen. Doublet of PALSY.]

paralysis ag·i·tans (aj′ə tanz), Parkinson's disease. [< New Latin *paralysis agitans* shaking palsy]

par·a·lyt·ic (par′ə lit′ik), *adj.* of paralysis; having paralysis: *Latest reports showed that there were only forty-nine cases of paralytic polio and two cases of nonparalytic* (New York Times). —*n.* **1.** a person who has paralysis. **2.** a stroke of paralysis.

par·a·ly·za·tion (par′ə lə zā′shən), *n.* **1.** the act of paralyzing. **2.** the state of being paralyzed.

par·a·lyze (par′ə līz), *v.t.,* **-lyzed, -lyzing. 1.** to affect with a lessening or loss of the power of motion or feeling; palsy. **2.** to make powerless or helplessly inactive; make ineffective; cripple: *I overcame the extreme shyness that had formerly paralyzed me in her presence* (Washington Irving). —**par′a·lyz′er,** *n.* —**Syn. 2.** stun, benumb, deaden, stupefy.

par·a·mag·net (par′ə mag′nit), *n.* a paramagnetic body or substance.

par·a·mag·net·ic (par′ə mag net′ik), *adj.* having to do with a class of substances, as liquid oxygen, that have a magnetic permeability slightly greater than that of a vacuum or unity, though much less than that of iron. A paramagnetic substance takes a position parallel to the lines of force in a magnetic field, and is not dependent on the intensity of the magnetic field. —*n.* a paramagnetic substance. [< *para-*[1] + *magnetic*]

par·a·mag·net·ism (par′ə mag′nə tiz əm), *n.* the phenomena exhibited by paramagnetic substances.

par·a·mat·ta (par′ə mat′ə), *n.* a lightweight cloth with a cotton (formerly, silk) warp and a merino wool filling, used for dresses. Also, **parramatta.** [< *Paramatta,* a city in Australia]

par·a·me·ci·um (par′ə mē′shē əm, -sē-), *n., pl.* **-ci·a** (-shē ə, -sē ə). any of a group of one-celled animals shaped like a slender slipper, covered with cilia, and having a groove along one side leading into the gullet. Paramecia are free-swimming ciliates that live in almost all fresh water. *One strain of paramecium—the 'killer' strain—can produce a toxin which destroys another strain—the 'sensitive' strain* (G.M. Wyburn). [< New Latin *Paramecium* the typical genus < Greek *paramḗkēs* oblong < *para-* on one side, against + *mēkos* length]

par·a·med·ic (par′ə med′ik), *n.* a medical corpsman who parachutes from an aircraft: *the rescue plane with paramedics aboard* (Chicago Tribune). [< *para-*² + *medic*¹]

par·a·med·i·cal (par′ə med′ə kəl), *adj.* having to do with medicine in an auxiliary capacity; involving services, studies, etc., that are related to but not part of the medical profession: *The complexity of health problems has given rise to many paramedical callings, from the university physiologist to the hospital aide* (Harper's).

pa·ram·e·ter (pə ram′ə tər), *n.* **1.** *Mathematics.* a quantity that is constant in a particular calculation or case but varies in other cases, especially a constant occurring in the equation of a curve or surface, by the variation of which the equation is made to represent a family of such curves or surfaces. **2.** a factor: *parameters of space and time.* [< New Latin *parametrum* < Greek *para-* beside + *métron* meter]

par·a·met·ric (par′ə met′rik), *adj.* of, having to do with, or in the form of a parameter.

parametric amplifier, a high-frequency amplifier of very low noise that amplifies a signal by varying the capacitance or inductance.

par·a·mil·i·tar·y (par′ə mil′ə ter′ē), *adj.* **1.** organized militarily, but not part of or in cooperation with the official armed forces of a country. **2.** of or having to do with a military force so organized and its tactics: *In the paramilitary arenas of subversion, intimidation, and insurrection, an open and peaceful society is again at a disadvantage* (John F. Kennedy).

par·am·ne·sia (par′am nē′zhə, -zē ə), *n.* **1.** a perversion of the memory characterized by the illusory impression of having previously experienced, seen, heard, etc., that with or in which one is involved at a given moment and for the first time. **2.** a condition, technically a form of aphasia, in which the correct use of words cannot be recalled.

par·am·ne·sic (par′am nē′sik, -zik), *adj.* of, causing, or resembling paramnesia: *The whole place took on a paramnesic air of unreality* (Time).

par·a·mo (par′ə mō; *Spanish* pä′rä mō), *n., pl.* **-mos** (-mōz; *Spanish* -mōs). a high plateau region in tropical South America, especially in the Andes, often bare of all vegetation except mosses, lichens, etc., and swept constantly by strong, cold winds. [< Spanish *páramo;* origin unknown]

par·a·morph (par′ə môrf), *n. Mineralogy.* a pseudomorph formed by a change in molecular structure without a change in chemical composition. [< *para-*¹ + Greek *morphḗ* form]

par·a·mor·phic (par′ə môr′fik), *adj.* of, having to do with, or resembling a paramorph.

par·a·mor·phism (par′ə môr′fiz əm), *n.* the change of one mineral to another having the same chemical composition but a different molecular structure.

par·a·mount (par′ə mount), *adj.* chief in importance; above others; supreme: *to make Britain the paramount power in India* (Macaulay). *Truth is of paramount importance.* —*n.* an overlord; supreme ruler. [< Anglo-French *paramont* above < *par-* by + *amont* up < Latin *ad montem* to the mountain] —**par′a·mount·ly,** *adv.* —**Syn.** *adj.* See **dominant.**

par·a·mount·cy (par′ə mount′sē), *n.* the condition or status of being paramount; supremacy: *We have a duty to them, the duty of recognising the paramountcy of business interests* (Punch).

par·a·mount·ship (par′ə mount′ship), *n.* paramountcy.

par·a·mour (par′ə mu̇r), *n.* **1.** a person who takes the place of a husband or wife illegally. **2.** *Archaic.* a lover. [< Old French *paramour* < *par amour* by (or for) love < Latin *per amorem*]

par·a·nee (par′ə nē′), *n.* the object of a paranoiac's delusions: *Every paranoiac has ... paranees who just can't wait to confirm his delusions of grandeur and even feed on them* (Harper's). [< *paran*(oia) + *-ee*]

par·a·neph·ric (par′ə nef′rik), *adj.* of or having to do with a paranephros.

par·a·neph·ros (par′ə nef′ros), *n.* an adrenal gland. [< New Latin *paranephros* < Greek *para-* beside + *nephrós* kidney]

pa·rang (pä′rang), *n.* a large, heavy knife, somewhat like a machete, used by the Malayans and others as a tool or weapon: *One of Lingard's seamen at once retaliated by striking at the ... savage with his parang — three such choppers brought for the purpose of clearing the bush* (Joseph Conrad). [< Malay *parang*]

par·a·noe·a (par′ə nē′ə), *n.* paranoia.

par·a·noe·ac (par′ə nē′ak), *n., adj.* paranoiac.

par·a·noi·a (par′ə noi′ə), *n. Psychiatry.* a mental disorder characterized by continuing, elaborate delusions of persecution or grandeur that are logically and consistently developed. People suffering from paranoia maintain their intelligence, although paranoia is a chronic form of insanity whose symptoms approach schizophrenia the closer the consciousness comes to realizing the conflicts of personality. *The "Napoleonic complex" disease, paranoia may take the form either of belief that one has unique ability or that all the world is plotting against one* (New York Times). [< New Latin *paranoea* < Greek *paránoia* < *paránoös* distracted < *para-* beside, beyond + *nóos, noûs* mind]

par·a·noi·ac (par′ə noi′ak), *n.* a person afflicted with paranoia. —*adj.* **1.** of or like paranoia. **2.** afflicted with paranoia.

par·a·noid (par′ə noid), *adj.* resembling or tending toward paranoia (used especially of symptoms occurring in many psychoses): *Pure paranoia is rare, but many ill persons exhibit traces of paranoid thinking* (New York Times). *A patient with paranoid psychosis carries to extremes the normal methods of maintaining self-esteem* (Merck Manual). —*n.* a person whose condition tends toward paranoia: ... *the prancing paranoid who planned to rule the world from Berlin* (Time).

paranoid schizophrenia, *Psychiatry.* a mental disease resembling paranoia but also characterized by autistic behavior, hallucinations, and gradual deterioration of the personality.

par·a·nor·mal (par′ə nôr′məl), *adj.* outside normal perception or knowledge; psychic: *paranormal communication.*

Par·an·thro·pus (par′an thrō′pəs, pə-ran′thrə-), *n.* any of an extinct genus of manlike apes characterized by massive jaws and teeth, fossils of which have been discovered in South Africa. [< *par-* + Greek *ánthrōpos* man]

par·a·nu·cle·in (par′ə nü′klē in, -nyü′-), *n. Chemistry.* any of a group of amorphous substances that, unlike true nucleins, do not yield nitrogenous bases on decomposition; pseudonuclein. [< *para-*¹ + *nuclein*]

par·a·nymph (par′ə nimf), *n.* **1.** in ancient Greece: **a.** a friend who went with the bridegroom to bring home the bride. **b.** the bridesmaid who escorted the bride to the bridegroom. **2.** *Poetic.* **a.** a bridesmaid. **b.** a best man. [< Late Latin *paranymphus, paranymphos,* masculine, and *paranýmphē,* feminine < *para-* beside + *nýmphē* bride]

par·a·pet (par′ə pet, -pit), *n.* **1.** a low wall or mound of stone, earth, etc., in front of a walk or platform at the top of a fort, trench, etc., to protect soldiers. See **rampart** for picture. **2.** a low wall or barrier at the edge of a balcony, roof, bridge, or the like: *the parapet of the great dam* (H.G. Wells). [< Middle French *parapet* < Italian *parapetto* < *para* defend! (see PARA-²) + *petto* breast < Latin *pectus*] —**Syn. 1.** rampart.

Parapet (def. 2) on medieval fort

par·a·pet·ed (par′ə pet′id), *adj.* having a parapet or parapets: *a parapeted terrace.*

par·aph (par′əf), *n.* a flourish made after a signature, as in a document, originally as a precaution against forgery and therefore very elaborate. —*v.t.* **1.** to add a paraph to. **2.** to sign, especially with one's initials. [< Middle French *paraphe,* learned borrowing from Medieval Latin *parraffus,* perhaps short for *paragraphum* paragraph mark. Doublet of PARAGRAPH.]

par·a·pher·nal·ia (par′ə fər nāl′yə), *n.pl.* **1.** personal belongings: *trunks containing ... personal property — their sole chattels and paraphernalia on earth* (Arnold Bennett). **2.** equipment; outfit: *the paraphernalia for a chemical experiment. The ample fireplace ... garnished with a crane having various hooks and other paraphernalia* (Harriet Beecher Stowe). *The existence of constructed theories implies deductions, inductions, assumptions and all the paraphernalia of methodology which constitute the philosophy of science* (F.H. George). **3.** *Law.* the articles of personal property which the law formerly allowed a woman to keep during her marriage. [< Medieval Latin *paraphernalia* < Late Latin *parapherna* < Greek *parápherna* a woman's personal property besides her dowry < *para-* besides + *phernḗ* dowry, related to *phérein* to bear]

➔ **Paraphernalia** meaning personal belongings is plural in form and use: *My paraphernalia are ready to be shipped.* When the meaning is equipment, *paraphernalia* is sometimes singular in use: *Military paraphernalia includes guns, rifles, etc.*

➔ See **data, insignia** for related usage notes.

par·a·phil·i·a (par′ə fil′ē ə), *n. Psychology.* anomalous or deviant sexuality. [< New Latin *paraphilia* < *para-*¹ + *-philia*]

par·a·phras·a·ble (par′ə frā′zə bəl), *adj.* that can be paraphrased: *Some sort of paraphrasable meaning could be extracted from every poem* (Listener).

par·a·phrase (par′ə frāz), *v.,* **-phrased, -phras·ing,** *n.* —*v.t.* to state the meaning of (a passage) in other words: *A long-established rule permits reporters to paraphrase everything the President says, but direct quotation must be specifically authorized* (New York Times). —*v.i.* to make a paraphrase. [< noun]

—*n.* **1.** an expression of the meaning of a passage in other words: *I have here given my own paraphrase of this document, which has inspired so much controversy and commentary* (Edmund Wilson). **2.** paraphrasing as a manner of literary treatment or educational technique.

[< Middle French *paraphrase,* learned borrowing from Latin *paraphrasis* < Greek *paráphrasis* < *para-* alongside of + *phrázein* to say] —**par′a·phras′er,** *n.*

par·a·phrast (par′ə frast), *n.* a person who paraphrases; paraphraser.

par·a·phras·tic (par′ə fras′tik), *adj.* **1.** of, having to do with, or of the nature of paraphrase. **2.** given to the use of paraphrase. —**par′a·phras′ti·cal·ly,** *adv.*

par·a·phre·ni·a (par′ə frē′nē ə), *n. Psychiatry.* any paranoid disorder or disease. [< New Latin *paraphrenia* < *para*(*noea*) + Greek *phrḗn, phrenós* mind]

pa·raph·y·sis (pə raf′ə sis), *n., pl.* **-ses** (-sēz). *Botany.* any of the erect, sterile filaments often occurring among the reproductive organs in certain ferns, mosses, fungi, etc. [< New Latin *paraphysis* < Greek *para-* alongside + *phýsis* growth < *phýein* bring forth, produce]

par·a·plasm (par′ə plaz əm), *n.* deutoplasm; the part of the yolk of an egg or ovum that furnishes food for the nourishment of the embryo.

par·a·ple·gi·a (par′ə plē′jē ə), *n.* paralysis of the legs and the lower part of the trunk; paralysis from the chest downward. [< New Latin *paraplegia* < Greek *paraplēgíē* paralysis < *paraplḗssein* to strike at the side; to be paralyzed < *para-* beside + *plḗssein* to strike]

par·a·ple·gic (par′ə plej′ik, -plē′jik), *n.* a person afflicted with paraplegia: *Then there are the paraplegics (both sides paralyzed from the waist down) who can be taught to crutch-walk and wait on themselves* (Marguerite Clark). —*adj.* having to do with, or afflicted with, paraplegia.

par·a·po·di·um (par′ə pō′dē əm), *n., pl.* **-di·a** (-dē ə). one of the paired, jointless metameric processes or rudimentary limbs of annelids, that serve as organs of locomotion, and sometimes of sensation or respiration. [< New Latin *parapodium* < Greek *para-* subsidiary + *poús, podós* foot]

par·a·pro·fes·sion·al (par′ə prə fesh′ə nəl, -fesh′nəl), *n.* a person who assists a teacher or other professional, but does not have the formal training required to be a professional. —*adj.* of or having to do with paraprofessionals: *There is some talk now of using paraprofessional help, trained on the job like interns* (Maclean's).

par·a·psy·chi·cal (par′ə sī′kə kəl), *adj.* parapsychological.

par·a·psy·cho·log·i·cal (par′ə sī′kə loj′ə kəl), *adj.* of or having to do with parapsychology: *Critics often complain about the lack of repeatability of parapsychological experiments* (Harper's).

par·a·psy·chol·o·gist (par′ə sī kol′ə jist), *n.* a person who studies and records parapsychological phenomena.

par·a·psy·chol·o·gy (par′ə sī kol′ə jē), *n.* the branch of psychology having to do with the study of psychic phenomena, as extrasensory perception, telepathy, and clairvoyance; psychical research: *Parapsychology, which is the serious study of . . . occult matters by intelligent and unhysterical people, has become a recognized science* (Wall Street Journal). [< *para-*[1] beyond + *psychology*]

par·a·quat (par′ə kwot), *n.* a herbicide activated by photosynthesis upon contact with weeds. [< *para-*[1] (def. 3) + *quat*(ernary), part of the formula]

par·a·quet (par′ə ket), *n.* parakeet.

par·a·res·cue (par′ə res′kyü), *n.* a rescue by parachutists. [< *para-*[2] + *rescue*]

Pará rubber, **1.** rubber obtained from any of various tropical South American trees of the spurge family. **2.** Also, **Pará rubber tree.** any of these trees, now cultivated in tropical regions throughout the world. [< *Pará,* a city in Brazil, where the rubber is exported]

par·a·sang (par′ə sang), *n.* an ancient Persian measure of length, equal to about 3¼ miles as used by Herodotus and Xenophon, but ranging, according to Pliny and Strabo, to as much as 6½ miles. [< Latin *parasanga* < Greek *parasángēs*]

par·a·se·le·ne (par′ə sə lē′nē), *n., pl.* **-nae** (-nē). a bright moonlike spot on a lunar halo; mock moon: *And all in a moment, reading the very first words of her* [*Edith Sitwell's*] *"English Eccentrics," we are plunged into moonlight* (*albeit paraselene*), *mummies, hocus-pocus itself* (New York Times). [< New Latin *paraselene* < Greek *para-* alongside, subsidiary + *selḗnē* moon < *sélas, -aos* brightness, light]

par·a·se·len·ic (par′ə sə len′ik), *adj.* of or having to do with a paraselene.

par·a·shah (par′ə shä), *n., pl.* **par·a·shoth** (par′ə shōth), **par·a·shi·oth** (par′ə shē′ōth). *Judaism.* **1.** a portion of the Torah (Law) appointed to be read in synagogue services every Sabbath and festival; lesson or reading. **2.** one of the sections into which these lessons are divided. [< Hebrew *pārāshāh* division < *pārash* be separated]

par·a·site (par′ə sīt), *n.* **1.** an animal or plant that lives on, with, or in another organism or host from which it gets its food, always at the expense of the host. It may or may not injure the host, but it is usually unable to exist independently. *Lice, tapeworms, and the mistletoe are parasites.* **2.** a person who lives on others without making any useful and fitting return; hanger-on; toady: *Nine people out of ten looked on him as something of a parasite, with no real work in the world* (John Galsworthy). **3.** a parasite plane. **4.** in ancient Greece: **a.** a person who ate at the table or at the expense of another, earning meals by flattery or wit. **b.** a priest's assistant who was admitted with the priests to the feast after a sacrifice. [< Latin *parasītus* < Greek *parásītos,* adjective, feeding beside < *para-* alongside of + *sîtos* food]

parasite drag, the drag caused by skin friction and the shape of those surfaces of an aircraft which do not contribute lift, as the fuselage, nacelles, ducts, etc.

par·a·sit·e·mi·a (par′ə sī tē′mē ə), *n. Medicine.* the presence of parasites in the blood.

parasite plane, an aircraft designed to be carried aloft by another aircraft and launched in flight.

par·a·sit·ic (par′ə sit′ik), *adj.* **1.** of or like a parasite; living on others: *The white blood cells constitute a gendarmery which is always ready to repel parasitic invasion by engulfing the microscopic invaders and then digesting them* (Scientific American). **2.** (of a disease) caused by parasites. —**par′a·sit′i·cal·ly,** *adv.*

par·a·sit·i·cal (par′ə sit′ə kəl), *adj.* parasitic.

par·a·sit·i·cide (par′ə sit′ə sīd), *adj.* that kills parasites. —*n.* a substance, as a chemical compound or other agent, that kills parasites. [< *parasit*(e) + *-cide*[1]]

parasitic jaeger, the commonest variety of jaeger, a hawklike sea bird of arctic regions with two pointed central tail feathers.

par·a·sit·ism (par′ə sī′tiz əm), *n.* **1. a.** the condition of being a plant or animal parasite; parasitic quality or habits: *Parasitism even goes so far as to destroy the cells of the life form that gives a home to the parasite* (Emory S. Bogardus). **b.** parasitic infestation. **c.** a disease caused by parasites. **2.** the practice of living as a human parasite.

par·a·sit·ize (par′ə sī′tīz), *v.t.,* **-ized, -izing.** to infest as a parasite; be parasitic upon: *Certain bee flies parasitize velvet ants, and robber flies have been observed to capture bee flies* (Scientific American).

par·a·si·to·log·i·cal (par′ə sī′tə loj′ə kəl), *adj.* having to do with parasitology.

par·a·si·tol·o·gist (par′ə sī tol′ə jist), *n.* a person who studies or is skilled in parasitology.

par·a·si·tol·o·gy (par′ə sī tol′ə jē), *n.* the branch of biology, or of medical science, dealing with parasites and parasitism. [< Greek *parásītos* parasite + English *-logy*]

par·a·sit·o·sis (par′ə sī tō′sis), *n.* any parasitic condition or disease; parasitism. [< *parasit*(e) + *-osis*]

par·a·sol (par′ə sôl, -sol), *n.* a small, often brightly colored umbrella, used especially as a protection against the sun; sunshade: *The ladies sat protecting their complexions under large beach umbrellas and small ruffled parasols* (New Yorker). [< French *parasol* < Italian *parasole* < *para-* (see PARA-[2]) + *sole* sun < Latin *sōl, sōlis*]

parasol ant, the leafcutter: *Thousands of people . . . throng through the Bronx Zoo on a sunny day, stopping to look at the parasol ants or the new aardvark* (Harper's).

pa·ras·ti·chy (pə ras′tə kē), *n., pl.* **-chies.** *Botany.* a spiral arrangement of lateral members, such as leaves or scales, where the internodes are short and the members closely crowded, as in the houseleek and pine cone. [< *para-*[1] + Greek *-stichia* < *stíchos* row[1], rank[1] < *steíchein* to walk, go]

par·a·sym·pa·thet·ic (par′ə sim′pə thet′ik), *adj.* of or having to do with the part of the autonomic nervous system that produces such involuntary responses as dilating blood vessels, increasing the activity of digestive and reproductive organs and glands, contracting the pupils of the eyes, slowing down the heart beat, and others, opposed to the action of the sympathetic nervous system. —*n.* a nerve of the parasympathetic nervous system. [< *para-*[1] + *sympathetic*]

par·a·syn·ap·sis (par′ə si nap′sis), *n.* the side-by-side union of chromosomes during synapsis. [< New Latin *parasynapsis* < Greek *para-* para-[1] + *sýnapsis* union. Compare SYNAPSE.]

par·a·syn·the·sis (par′ə sin′thə sis), *n.* the formation of words by adding prefixes or suffixes to a compound or phrase. *Examples: free trade + -er = free-trader; great heart + -ed = great-hearted.* [< New Latin *parasynthesis* < Greek *pára-* alongside + *sýnthesis* composition, synthesis]

par·a·syn·thet·ic (par′ə sin thet′ik), *adj.* having to do with parasynthesis: *Parasynthetic compounds of this same type are dressmaker, innkeeper, . . . and woodpecker* (Simeon Potter).

par·a·tac·tic (par′ə tak′tik), *adj.* of, having to do with, or chracterized by parataxis. —**par′a·tac′ti·cal·ly,** *adv.*

par·a·tac·ti·cal (par′ə tak′tə kəl), *adj.* paratactic.

par·a·tax·is (par′ə tak′sis), *n. Grammar.* the arranging of clauses one after the other without connectives showing the relation between them. *Example:* The rain fell; the river flooded; the house was washed away. [< Greek *parátaxis* placement side by side < *para-* alongside + *táxis* arrangement]

par·a·thi·on (par′ə thī′on), *n.* a yellow or brown liquid, highly toxic to man, that is used to kill mites, aphids, and other insect pests. *Formula:* $C_{10}H_{14}NO_5PS$

par·a·thor·mone (par′ə thôr′mōn), *n.* the hormone produced by the parathyroid glands, which regulates the way the body uses calcium and phosphorus. [< *parath*(yroid) + (h)*ormone*]

par·a·thy·roid (par′ə thī′roid), *adj.* **1.** near the thyroid gland. **2.** of, having to do with, or due to the parathyroid glands: *Parathyroid extract can increase survival following irradiation by more than 50%* (Science News Letter). —*n.* one of the parathyroid glands. [< *para-*[1] + *thyroid*]

parathyroid glands, several (usually four) small endocrine glands near or embedded in the thyroid gland. They secrete a hormone, necessary for life, that enables the body to use calcium and phosphorus.

par·a·troop (par′ə trüp′), *adj.* of or having to do with paratroops: *a paratroop division.*

par·a·troop·er (par′ə trü′pər), *n.* a soldier trained to use a parachute for descent from an aircraft into a battle area or behind enemy lines. [< *para-*[2] + *trooper*]

par·a·troops (par′ə trüps′), *n.pl.* troops moved by air and landed by parachutes in a battle area or behind enemy lines.

par·a·tu·ber·cu·lo·sis (par′ə tü bėr′kyə lō′sis, -tyü-), *n.* a usually fatal, bacterial disease of cattle, sheep, and goats characterized by intestinal infection; Johne's disease.

par·a·ty·phoid (par′ə tī′foid), *adj.* of the nature of or having to do with paratyphoid fever. —*n.* paratyphoid fever. [< *para-*[1] + *typhoid*]

paratyphoid fever, a bacterial disease resembling typhoid fever but usually milder. It occurs in different varieties and with different effects in man, domestic fowl, and other animals.

par a·vance (pȧr ȧ väNs′), *French.* in advance.

par·a·vane (par′ə vān), *n.* **1.** a device shaped somewhat like a torpedo, with sawlike teeth at the front end and sides, towed usually as one of a pair at an angle outward from the stern of a minesweeper, destroyer, etc., so as to cut the mooring cables of mines, causing them to rise to the surface of the water at a safe distance from the ship, where they are exploded or sunk by gunfire. **2.** a somewhat similar device loaded with a heavy explosive charge and linked to the vessel by a cable through which it may be exploded electrically, used against submarines. [< *para-*[1] + *vane*]

par a·vi·on (pȧr ȧ vyôN′), *French.* by airplane (a label for letters, packages, etc., to be sent by air mail).

par·a·xy·lene (par′ə zī′lēn), *n.* one of three isomeric forms of xylene: *Paraxylene is used in the manufacture of polyester fiber and film* (Wall Street Journal).

par·boil (pär′boil′), *v.t.* **1.** to boil till partly cooked: *Mother always parboils the beans before baking them.* **2.** to overheat. —*v.i.* to become overheated: *to parboil in the hot sun.* [< Old French *parboillir* < Late Latin *perbullīre* < *per-* thoroughly + *bullīre* to boil[2]; *par-* later taken as *part*]

par·buck·le (pär′buk′əl), *n., v.,* **-led, -ling.** —*n.* **1.** a device for raising or lowering a heavy object (especially a cylindrical object such as a barrel, naval gun, etc.) vertically or in an inclined plane, consisting of a rope the middle of which is looped around a post at the height to which the object is to be raised, with its two ends passed around the object, and pulled in or let out from above, the object serving as a pulley. **2.** a kind of double sling formed by passing the two ends of a rope, around the object, as a cask, to be raised or lowered. —*v.t.* to raise or lower by means of a parbuckle. [alteration (perhaps influenced by *buckle*) of earlier *parbunkel;* origin unknown]

Par·cae (pär′sē), *n.pl. Roman Mythology.* the Fates.

par·cel (pär′səl), *n., v.,* **-celed, -cel·ing** or (*especially British*) **-celled, -cel·ling,** *adj., adv.* —*n.* **1.** a bundle of things wrapped or packed together; package: *Her arms were filled with gift parcels.* **2.** a container with things packed in it: *Put your shirts in this parcel.* **3.** a piece; tract: *a two-acre parcel fronting on the road, a parcel of land.* **4.** a lot; group of indefinite size; pack: *a parcel of liars.* **5.** *Commerce.* a quantity (sometimes definite) of a commodity dealt with in one transaction, especially in the wholesale market. **6.** *Archaic.* a constituent or component part; item; fragment: *I sent your grace The parcels and particulars of our grief* (Shakespeare).

—*v.t.* **1.** to make into a parcel; put up in parcels. **2.** to wrap strips of canvas around (a rope, etc.) for protection.

parcel out, to divide into, or distribute in, portions: *When I asked why I could not be served by the only other competing distributor . . . I was told that the two companies had parcelled out London between them* (London Times).
—*adj., adv.* in part; partly; partially: (*adj.*) *He was a jester and a parcel poet* (Scott). (*adv.*) *My grandame . . . is parcel blind with age* (Scott).
[< Old French *parcelle* < Vulgar Latin *particella* (diminutive) < Latin *particula* particle]
—**Syn.** *n.* **1.** See **bundle.**

par·cel-gilt (pär′səl gilt′), *adj.* partly gilded: *a parcel-gilt cup, parcel-gilt silver.*

par·cel·ing (pär′sə ling), *n.* **1.** *Nautical.* **a.** the act or process of wrapping strips of canvas, usually tarred, around a rope. **b.** strips of canvas wrapped around a rope for its protection. **2.** a division into parcels or portions; partition.

par·cel·ling (pär′sə ling), *n. Especially British.* parceling.

parcel post or **parcels post,** the branch of the postal service that carries parcels.

par·ce·nar·y (pär′sə ner′ē), *n. Law.* joint heirship.

par·ce·ner (pär′sə nər), *n. Law.* a joint heir; coheir. [earlier, a partaker < Anglo-French *parcener*, Old French *parçonier*, perhaps < *parçon* partition, or < Medieval Latin *partionarius* < Latin *partītiō, -ōnis* partition]

parch (pärch), *v.t.* **1.** to dry by heating; heat to evaporate the water, especially to store without spoiling; roast slightly: *The Indians parched corn.* **2.** to make hot and dry or thirsty: *The fever parched him.* **3.** to dry, shrivel, or wither with cold. —*v.i.* to become dry, hot, or thirsty: *I am parching with the heat. There is a fresh sweet growth of grass in the Spring, but it . . . parches up in the course of the summer* (Washington Irving). [Middle English *parchen*, and *perchen;* origin uncertain] —**Syn.** *v.t.* **1.** scorch, sear, singe, char.

parched (pärcht), *adj.* **1.** dried by heat; roasted. **2.** dried up; scorched. **3.** dry or thirsty, as from heat.

parch·ed·ness (pär′chid nis), *n.* parched condition or quality.

par·chee·si or **par·che·si** (pär chē′zē), *n.* **1.** a game somewhat like backgammon, played by moving pieces according to throws of dice. **2.** pachisi. [see PACHISI]

parch·ment (pärch′mənt), *n.* **1.** the skin of sheep, goats, etc., dried and made into thin sheets for use as a writing material. **2.** a manuscript or document written on parchment: *a parchment with the seal of Caesar* (Shakespeare). **3.** any of various kinds of paper that look like parchment, especially parchment paper. [< Old French *parchemin* (influenced by *parche* bookcover < Latin *parthica* (*pellis*) Parthian leather) < Vulgar Latin *pergamīnum* < Late Greek *pergamēnón* (*mémbrānon*) Pergamene (skin), neuter of Greek *Pergamēnós* of *Pérgamon* Pergamum, the city of its origin] —**parch′ment·like′,** *adj.*

parchment paper, a tough, translucent, glossy paper that looks like parchment, made by soaking ordinary unsized paper in dilute sulfuric acid.

parch·ment·y (pärch′mən tē), *adj.* like parchment: *The lees of the strand traversed, with its trash, parchmenty paper, bottles, bags, and beer tins* (New Yorker).

pard[1] (pärd), *n. Archaic.* a leopard or panther: *a soldier, Full of strange oaths and bearded like the pard* (Shakespeare). *Freckled like a pard* (Keats). [< Old French *parde*, learned borrowing from Latin *pardus* < Greek *párdos* male panther]

pard[2] (pärd), *n. U.S. Slang.* partner; friend; companion: *Thanks, pard, and them's big hopes to live up to* (Alaska Highway News). [short for *pardner*, variant of *partner*]

par·di, par·die, or **par·dy** (pär dē′), *adv., interj. Archaic.* a form of oath formerly much used for emphasis, meaning verily, certainly, or assuredly. Also, **perdie.** [Middle English *pardee*, also *perde* < *par deu* < Old French *par de* by God! < Latin *per* by through, *deus* god]

pard·ner (pärd′nər), *n. Dialect.* partner.

par·don (pär′dən), *n.* **1.** forgiveness; passing over an offense without punishment. **2.** excuse or toleration: *I beg your pardon, but I'm afraid I missed your last remark.* **3. a.** a setting free from punishment. **b.** a legal document setting a person free from punishment. **4.** a papal indulgence. [< Old French *pardon* < *pardoner;* see the verb]
—*v.t.* **1.** to forgive; pass over without punishment or blame: *Grandmother pardons us when we are mischievous.* **2.** to excuse: *Pardon my impatience, but I have a train to catch.* **3.** to set free from punishment; give a legal pardon to: *The governor pardoned the criminal.* **4.** *Obsolete.* to remit (an obligation, debt, etc.).
[< Old French *pardoner*, and *perduner* < Medieval Latin *perdonare* < Latin *per-* thoroughly + *dōnāre* to give < *dōnum* gift]
—**Syn.** *n.* **1.** absolution, amnesty. *-v.t.* **1.** acquit, absolve. See **excuse.** —**Ant.** *v.t.* **3.** convict, condemn.
➔ See **excuse** for a usage note.

par·don·a·ble (pär′də nə bəl), *adj.* that can be pardoned; excusable: *It gives me a feeling of pardonable importance* (George W. Curtis). *I dare say your daughter is pardonable* (Jane Porter). —**par′don·a·ble·ness,** *n.*

par·don·a·bly (pär′də nə blē), *adv.* in a manner admitting of pardon.

par·don·er (pär′də nər, pärd′nər), *n.* **1.** a person who pardons or forgives. **2.** a church official charged with the granting of indulgences in the Middle Ages.

pare (pãr), *v.t.*, **pared, par·ing. 1.** to cut, trim, or shave off the outer part of; peel: *to pare an apple.* **2.** to cut away (an outer part, layer, etc.): *to pare a layer from a corn, to pare one's nails.* **3.** to cut away little by little: *Expenditures by the Federal government have been steadily pared* (Newsweek). [< Old French *parer* arrange, dispose < Latin *parāre* make ready, prepare. Doublet of PARRY.] —**Syn. 1.** skin.

pa·re·cious (pə rē′shəs), *adj. Botany.* paroecious.

par·e·gor·ic (par′ə gôr′ik, -gor′-), *n.* a soothing medicine containing camphor and a very little opium. —*adj.* soothing. [< Late Latin *parēgoricus* < Greek *parēgorikós* soothing < *parēgoreîn* speak soothingly to < *para-* at the side of + *agoreýein* speak in public < *agorá* market place, assembly]

par·e·gor·i·cal (par′ə gôr′ə kəl, -gor′-), *adj. Obsolete.* paregoric.

pa·rei·a·sau·ri·an (pə rī′ə sôr′ē ən), *adj.* belonging to or having to do with an order or group of extinct, heavily built reptiles, known by fossil remains found in South Africa and elsewhere. —*n.* a pareiasaurian reptile. Also, **pariasaurian.** [< New Latin *Pareiasauria* the order name (< Greek *pareiá* cheek + *saûros* lizard) + English *-an*]

pa·rei·ra (pə rãr′ə), *n.* pareira brava.

pareira bra·va (brä′və, brā′-), the root of a South American vine related to the moonseed, formerly used especially in treating disorders of the urinary passages. [< Portuguese *pareira brava* (literally) wild vine]

paren., parenthesis.

pa·ren·chy·ma (pə reng′kə mə), *n.* **1.** the fundamental tissue in plants, composed of living, unspecialized cells from which all other cells are formed. Most of the tissue in the softer parts of leaves, the pulp of fruits, the cortex pith of young stems, etc., is parenchyma. **2.** the essential tissue of an animal organ as contrasted with its connective or supporting tissue. **3. a.** the soft, undifferentiated tissue composing the general substance of the body in some invertebrates, as sponges and flatworms. **b.** the undifferentiated cell substance or endoplasm of a protozoan. [< Greek *parénchyma* anything poured in < *para-* beside + *énchyma* infusion < *en-* in + *chýma* what is poured < *cheîn* to pour]

par·en·chy·mal (pə reng′kə məl), *adj.* parenchymatous: *parenchymal structures.*

par·en·chym·a·tous (par′eng kim′ə təs), *adj.* having to do with or of the nature of parenchyma.

parens., parentheses.

pa·rens pa·tri·ae (pãr′enz pā′trē ē), *n. Latin.* **1.** *Law.* the sovereign power of guardianship over minors and insane or incompetent people as vested in the state or in the monarch: *The Crown, as parens patriae, took under its protection every infant child who was ordinarily resident within the realm* (London Times). **2.** (literally) parent of the country.

par·ent (pãr′ənt), *n.* **1. a.** a father or mother: *A positive means of prompt baby identification brings peace of mind to parents and hospital administrators alike* (Newsweek). **b.** a person who has not produced the offspring but has the legal status of a father or mother, as by adoption. **2.** any animal or plant that produces offspring. **3.** source; cause; origin: *Idleness is the parent of vice* (Herman Melville). *Poverty is the parent of revolution* (Benjamin Jowett). **4.** a parent company: *American Cable asserted it was prepared, "backed by the full resources of its parent,"* [*International Telephone and Telegraph Corp.*] *to establish and operate an overseas cable system* (Wall Street Journal). —*adj.* parental.
[< Old French *parent* < Latin *parēns, -entis*, earlier present participle of *parere* to bring forth]

par·ent·age (pãr′ən tij), *n.* **1.** descent from parents; family line; ancestry. **2.** being a parent; parenthood. —**Syn. 1.** birth.

pa·ren·tal (pə ren′təl), *adj.* **1.** of or having to do with a parent or parents; like a parent's: *parental feelings.* **2.** *Genetics.* of the generation in which hybrids are produced by crossbreeding. *Symbol:* P. —**pa·ren′tal·ly,** *adv.*

Par·en·ta·li·a (par′ən tā′lē ə), *n.pl.* an ancient Roman annual festival in honor of deceased parents and relatives, held from the 13th to the 21st of February, marked by the closing of the temples, the visiting of tombs, and the offering of oblations to the shades of the dead. [< Latin *Parentālia*, neuter plural of *parentālis* parental]

parent company, a business firm which controls one or more subsidiary firms: *A clause in its contract . . . gives the parent company the right to buy up* (*at cost*) *and sell back to the distributor any product that he sells outside his area or to an unauthorized dealer* (Time).

parent element, *Physics.* an element that yields an isotope or daughter element through radioactive decay or nuclear bombardment.

par·en·ter·al (pə ren′tər əl), *adj. Physiology.* not entering by means of or passing through the alimentary canal; not intestinal: *An intravenous injection provides parenteral nourishment.* [< *par-* + *enter*(on) + *-al*[1]] —**par·en′ter·al·ly,** *adv.*

pa·ren·the·ses (pə ren′thə sēz), *n.* plural of **parenthesis.**

pa·ren·the·sis (pə ren′thə sis), *n., pl.* **-ses. 1.** a word, phrase, sentence, etc., inserted within a sentence to explain or qualify something. It is usually marked off by curved lines, square brackets, dashes, or commas. **2.** either or both of two curved lines ( ) used to set off such an expression. **3.** an interval; digression; interlude; hiatus: *I ne'er knew tabacco taken as a parenthesis before* (Ben Jonson). [< Medieval Latin *parenthesis*, Late Latin, addition of a letter (or syllable) in a word < Greek *parénthesis* < *parentithénai* put in beside < *para-* beside + *en-* in + *tithénai* put, place]

pa·ren·the·size (pə ren′thə sīz), *v.t.*, **-sized, -siz·ing. 1.** to insert as or in a parenthesis. **2.** to put between the marks of parenthesis. **3.** to put many parentheses in.

par·en·thet·ic (par′ən thet′ik), *adj.* **1.** qualifying; explanatory. **2.** put in parentheses. **3.** using parentheses.

par·en·thet·i·cal (par′ən thet′ə kəl), *adj.* parenthetic.

par·en·thet·i·cal·ly (par′ən thet′ə klē), *adv.* in a parenthetical manner.

par·ent·hood (pãr′ənt hu̇d), *n.* being a parent; fatherhood or motherhood: *Parenthood begins "officially" with the birth or adoption of an infant, but every girl or boy develops a certain background for motherhood or fatherhood during the years leading to maturity and marriage* (Sidonie M. Gruenberg).

par·ent-in-law (pãr′ənt in lô′), *n., pl.* **par·ents-in-law.** a father-in-law or mother-in-law: *All is well at the end for everybody but the interfering parents-in-law* (Punch).

par·ent·less (pãr′ənt lis), *adj.* **1.** without parents: *He was my own uncle . . . he had taken me when a parentless infant to his house* (Charlotte Brontë). **2.** without known parents, author, or source.

par·er (pãr′ər), *n.* **1.** a person who pares. **2.** an instrument for paring: *an apple parer.*

par·er·gon (pa rėr′gon), *n., pl.* **-er·ga** (-ėr′gə). subordinate or secondary work; by-work: *He and his orchestra played a suite* *of Symphonic Dances from West Side Story, a parergon of the musical show, and a very distinguished one* (London Times).

pa·re·sis (pə rē′sis, par′ə-), *n.* **1.** a partial paralysis that affects the ability to move, but does not affect the ability to feel. **2.** a progressive disease of the brain that gradually causes general paralysis: *General paresis (the result of long-standing syphilitic infection) has yielded spectacularly to treatment with reserpine* (Time). [< New Latin *paresis* < Greek *páresis* loss of strength, paralysis; (literally) a letting go < *pariénai* let pass, fall < *para-* by + *hiénai* let go]

par·es·the·sia (par′əs thē′zhə), *n.* an abnormal sensation of prickling, tingling, or itching of the skin. Also, **paraesthesia.** [< *par-* + *-esthesia* sensation, as in *anesthesia*]

par·es·thet·ic (par′əs thet′ik), *adj.* of, characterized by, or affected with paresthesia. Also, **paraesthetic.**

pa·ret·ic (pə ret′ik, -rē′tik), *adj.* of or having to do with paresis; caused by paresis. —*n.* a person having paresis.

pa·re·u (pä′rā ü), *n. Tahitian.* a rectangular piece of printed cotton cloth worn as a skirt or loincloth by the Polynesians.

par ex·cel·lence (pȧr ek sə läns′; *Anglicized* pär ek′sə läns), *French.* beyond comparison; above all others of the same sort: *Michelangelo on the other hand is always in quest of new motifs, and in this sense he is par excellence the modern artist* (Atlantic).

par ex·em·ple (pȧr eg zän′plə), *French.* for example.

par·fait (pär fā′, pär′fā), *n.* **1.** ice cream with syrup or crushed fruit and whipped cream, served in a tall glass. **2.** a rich ice cream containing eggs and whipped cream frozen unstirred. [< French, Old French *parfait* perfect]

par·fi·lage (pȧr fē lȧzh′), *n. French.* the unraveling of textile fabrics, galloons, etc., especially those containing gold or silver threads, in vogue as a pastime in France and elsewhere in the latter part of the 1700's.

par·fleche (pär′flesh, ˌpär flesh′), *n.* **1.** a kind of very tough rawhide made (originally) by removing the hair from the skin of a buffalo by steeping it in a strong solution of wood ashes (or lye) and water and then drying it in the sun. **2.** an article made of this rawhide: *The Plains Indian parfleche, a large envelope of hide used to store and carry personal possessions, sacred objects, foods, and other objects* (Beals and Hoijer). [American English < Canadian French *parflèche*, apparently < French *parer* to parry, ward off + *flèche* arrow (because it was used as a shield)]

par·get (pär′jit), *n., v.,* **-get·ed, -get·ing** or **-get·ted, -get·ting.** —*n.* **1.** gypsum or other stone for making plaster. **2.** a type of rough plaster consisting of lime, animal hair, and cow dung, formerly used in chimney flues. **3.** plasterwork of an ornamental kind. **4.** whitewash.
—*v.t.* **1.** to coat or plaster with parget. **2.** to plaster with ornamental designs.
[< Old French *pargeter*, and *parjeter* to cast over a surface < *par-* through + *jeter* to throw]

par·get·ing or **par·get·ting** (pär′jə ting), *n.* **1.** the act or process of applying parget or plastering ornamentally. **2.** ornamental plaster or plasterwork.

par·he·li·a·cal (pär′hē lī′ə kəl), *adj.* parhelic.

par·he·lic (pär hē′lik), *adj.* having to do with or resembling a parhelion.

parhelic circle or **ring,** a horizontal halo or circle of light that appears to pass through the sun.

par·he·li·on (pär hē′lē ən, -hēl′yən), *n., pl.* **-he·li·a** (-hē′lē ə, -hēl′yə). a bright circular spot on a solar halo, sometimes seen on either side of the sun and level with it; mock sun; sundog. [< Latin *parēlion* < Greek *parēlion* < *para-* beside + *hēlios* sun]

Pa·ri·ah (pə rī′ə, pä′rē-, par′ē-), *n.* a member of a low caste in southern India and Burma. [< Tamil *paṛaiyar*, plural of *paṛaiyan* drummer (the caste's hereditary duty at festivals) < *paṛai* large festival drum]

pa·ri·ah (pə rī′ə, pä′rē-, par′ē-), *n.* any person or animal generally despised; social outcast: *the juvenile pariah of the village, Huckleberry Finn, son of the town drunkard* (Mark Twain). [< *Pariah*]

pa·ri·ah·dom (pə rī′ə dəm, pä′rē ə-, par′ē-), *n.* the quality or condition of being a pariah; degraded position.

Par·i·an (pãr′ē ən), *adj.* **1.** of Paros, an island in the Aegean Sea: *Parian marble.* **2.** having to do with or made of a type of fine white porcelain resembling Parian marble. —*n.* **1.** a native or inhabitant of Paros. **2.** Parian porcelain.
[< Latin *Parius* of Paros (< Greek *Páros*, proper name) + English *-an*]

pa·ri·a·sau·ri·an (pə rī′ə sôr′ē ən), *adj., n.* pareiasaurian.

par·i·dig·i·tate (par′ə dij′ə tāt), *adj.* having the same number of toes on each foot. [< Latin *pār, paris* + English *digitate*]

pa·ri·es (pãr′ē ēz), *n., pl.* **pa·ri·e·tes.** a wall or structure enclosing, or forming the boundary of, a cavity in an animal or plant body. [< Latin *pariēs, -etis* wall, partition]

pa·ri·e·tal (pə rī′ə təl), *adj.* **1.** *Anatomy.* **a.** of the wall of the body or of one of its cavities. **b.** of or having to do with a parietal bone. **2.** *Botany.* belonging to, connected with, or attached to the wall of a hollow organ or structure, especially of the ovary or of a cell (used especially of ovules). **3.** *U.S.* having to do with or having authority over the residents in the buildings of a college: *a parietal committee.*
—*n.* either of two bones that form part of the sides and top of the skull.
[< Late Latin *parietālis* < Latin *pariēs, -etis* wall]

parietal lobe, *Anatomy.* the middle lobe of each cerebral hemisphere.

pa·ri·e·tes (pə rī′ə tēz), *n.* plural of **paries.**

pa·ril·lin (pə ril′in), *n. Chemistry.* a bitter white crystalline principle obtained from the root of sarsaparilla, used as a flavoring agent. *Formula:* $C_{45}H_{74}O_{17}$ [< (sarsa)-*parilla* + *-in*]

par·i·mu·tu·el (par′i myü′chů əl), *n.* **1.** the system of betting on horse races, dog races, etc., in which those who have bet on the winners divide all the money bet, except for a part withheld for costs, profits, taxes, etc. **2.** a machine for recording such bets; totalizator. —*adj.* of or having to do with this system or machine: *Revenues from pari-mutuel taxes in recent years have been accounting for about 1.5% of the states' total annual tax take* (Wall Street Journal). [< French *parimutuel* mutual wager; *pari* < *parier* to bet < Latin *pariāre* make equal; *mutuel* < Latin *mūtuus* borrowed]

par·i mu·tu·el (par′i myü′chů əl; *French* pȧ rē′ mʏ tʏ el′), *pl.* **par·is mu·tu·els.** pari-mutuel, a system of betting on races.

par·ing (pãr′ing), *n.* **1.** a part pared off; skin; rind: *apple parings.* **2.** the act of paring.

pa·ri pas·su (pãr′ī pas′yü; par′ē pas′ü), *Latin.* at an equal pace or rate; in equal proportion: *The over-all productivity of labor has risen pari passu with this investment* (Atlantic). *Any method which would prevent hemolytic streptococcus infection would, pari passu, prevent further bouts of rheumatic fever* (David Seegal).

par·i·pin·nate (par′i pin′āt), *adj.* (of a leaf) pinnate with an even number of leaflets; pinnate without an odd terminal leaflet. [< Latin *pār, paris* equal + English *pinnate*]

Par·is (par′is), *n. Greek Legend.* a son of Priam, king of Troy. He caused the Trojan War by carrying off Helen, the wife of King Menelaus of Sparta.

Paris or **paris green,** a poisonous, emerald-green powder used as a pigment and in making sprays for killing insects. It is a compound of copper, arsenic, and acetic acid. [< *Paris*, France, where it was formerly made]

par·ish (par′ish), *n.* **1.** a district that has its own church and clergyman. **2.** the people of a parish: *I look upon all the world as my parish* (John Wesley). **3.** (in Louisiana) a county. **4.** a civil district in Great Britain, Northern Ireland, and some other parts of the British Commonwealth.
—*adj.* of or having to do with a parish: *The large and lovely parish church of a country town has now been without a vicar for five months* (Manchester Guardian Weekly).
[< Old French *paroisse*, learned borrowing from Late Latin *parochia*, alteration of *paroecia* < Late Greek *paroikíā* ultimately < Greek *para-* near + *oîkos* a dwelling]

parish house, 1. any building maintained by a parish for its nonreligious functions. **2.** the house of a clergyman.

pa·rish·ion·er (pə rish′ə nər, -rish′nər), *n.* an inhabitant or member of a parish. [< Old French *paroissien* < *paroisse* parish]

par·ish-pump (par′ish pump′), *adj. Especially British.* of local interest or importance; limited in scope or outlook: *Resistance from parish-pump politics is clearly being encountered* (London Times).

parish pump, *Especially British.* local interests; parochial matters: *A regrettable feature of the new policies is a retreat from internationalism towards the parish pump* (Sunday Times).

Pa·ri·sian (pə rizh′ən, -rē′zhən), *adj.* of or having to do with Paris, the capital of France, or with its people. —*n.* a native or inhabitant of Paris.

Pa·ri·si·enne (pə rē′zē en′; *French* pȧ rē-zyen′), *n.* a Parisian woman. —*adj.* Parisian (feminine).

par·is mu·tu·els (par′i myü′chů əlz; *French* pȧ rē′ mʏ tʏ el′), plural of **pari mutuel.**

par·i·syl·lab·ic (par′i sə lab′ik), *adj.* (of Greek and Latin nouns) having the same number of syllables in the oblique cases as in the nominative case. [< Latin *pār, paris* equal + English *syllabic*]

par·i·ty[1] (par′ə tē), *n., pl.* **-ties. 1.** similarity or close correspondence with regard to state, position, condition, value, quality, degree, etc.; equality: *To try to achieve parity in conventional weapons would mean such a regimentation of our industry and manpower ...* (Bulletin of Atomic Scientists). **2.** *U.S.* a balance between the market prices for a farmer's commodities and his own gross expenditures. Parity is calculated to maintain the price of the farmer's product at a level equal in purchasing power to that of a base period, as from 1910 to 1914, or a later ten-year period. *Congress moved in that direction last session when it voted to gradually lower prop floors under cotton, corn, and rice to 65% of parity* (Wall Street Journal). **3.** *Finance.* **a.** equivalence in value in the currency of a foreign country. **b.** equivalence in value at a fixed ratio between moneys of different metals. **4.** (in quantum mechanics) the behavior of a wave function in an atomic or other physical system when it is reflected to form its mirror image. If the sign of the function remains unchanged, parity is even; if the sign is changed, parity is odd. [< Latin *paritās* < *pār, paris* equal]

par·i·ty[2] (par′ə tē), *n. Medicine.* the condition of being parous; fact of having borne children. [< Latin *parere* to give birth + English *-ity*]

parity index, *U.S.* the average prices received by the farmer for his products and the average prices he paid for goods and services in a particular year, each expressed in terms of the equivalent prices during the base period used. It is used to establish the parity ratio.

parity ratio, *U.S.* the ratio between the index of prices received by the farmer and the index of prices he paid in a particular year, used in measuring his purchasing power in that year.

park (pärk), *n.* **1.** land set apart for the pleasure of the public: *Hyde Park is in London. Many cities have beautiful parks.* **2.** land set apart for wild animals. **3.** *British.* a place to leave an automobile, etc., for a time: *Motorists with time on their hands have hunted through parks of two and three hundred cars* (Punch). **4. a.** a space where army vehicles and mules, supplies and artillery pieces, etc., are put when an army camps: *A torch gleamed momentarily in the transport park across the road* (Graham Greene). **b.** the group so assembled. **5.** the grounds around a fine house: *the turrets of an ancient chateau rising out of the trees of its walled park* (Washington Irving). **6.** *U.S.* a high plateaulike valley among mountains. **7.** an open space in a forest or wood. **8.** (in English law) an enclosed tract of land held by royal grant for keeping game. **9.** a place set aside for oyster breeding: *Oysters are obtained chiefly from cultivated parks in Chesapeake Bay* (White and Renner).
—*v.t.* **1.** to leave (an automobile, truck, or other vehicle) for a time in a certain place: *Park your car here.* **2.** to assemble and arrange (army vehicles, artillery, etc.) in a

park. **3.** *Informal.* to place, put, or leave: *to park oneself or one's coat in a chair.* **4.** to enclose in, as in, or as, a park. —*v.i.* to park an automobile, truck, or other vehicle.
[< Old French *parc* < Medieval Latin *parricus* enclosure, probably < Germanic (compare Old English *pearroc* enclosure, paddock)] —**park′er,** *n.* —**park′like′,** *adj.*

par·ka (pär′kə), *n.* **1.** a fur jacket with a hood, worn in Alaska and in northeastern Asia: *The icicles hang down like tusks under the parka hood* (Robert W. Service). **2.** a long woolen or fabric shirt or jacket with a hood. [apparently ultimately < Samoyed (Siberia) *parka* outer garment made of skins]

Parka (def. 1)

Park Avenue, a thoroughfare in New York City along part of which there are very fine, large, expensive office and residential buildings.

park hack, a horse trained and hired for riding in a public park: . . . *park hacks and splendid high-stepping carriage horses* (Thackeray).

par·kin (pär′kin), *n.* a gingerbread cake made with oatmeal and molasses in and near Scotland. [perhaps < the name *Perkin* or *Parkin*]

park·ing (pär′king), *n.* **1.** the act of a person who parks, especially of leaving an automobile, truck, or other vehicle for a time, especially in a public place: *They . . . rely on better control of the traffic . . . and much firmer restrictions on parking* (New Scientist). **2.** ground for or like a park. **3.** turf, with or without trees, in the middle or along the side of a street.

parking light, either of two small lights at the front of a motor vehicle, used in driving at twilight or for parking at night on a thoroughfare.

parking lot, *U.S.* an open area used for parking automobiles and other vehicles, often for a fee. In Great Britain it is called *car park.*

parking meter, *U.S.* a device containing a clock mechanism that is operated by the insertion of coins. It allows an automobile a specified amount of time in a parking area for each coin.

parking orbit, a temporary orbit in which a space vehicle is placed until an increase in its velocity sends it out into space.

parking space, *U.S.* a space in which an automobile or other vehicle may be parked: . . . *U.S. motorists, whose lot it is to dodge potholes, fight traffic jams, and search for nonexistent parking spaces* (Time).

Par·kin·so·ni·an (pär′kin sō′nē ən), *adj.* **1.** of, having to do with, or like Parkinson's disease: *Parkinsonian tremors.* **2.** of, having to do with, or suggesting Parkinson's Law: *The impact of the computer may to some extent be offset by Parkinsonian growth in staffs* (New Scientist).

Par·kin·son·ism (pär′kin sə niz′əm), *n.* Parkinson's disease.

Par·kin·son's disease (pär′kin sənz), a nervous disease, usually occurring late in life, characterized by muscular tremors and weakness, a tendency to walk peculiarly, and a fixity in facial expression: *Antihistamines have been used with moderate success in the treatment of Parkinson's disease* (Beaumont and Dodds). [< James *Parkinson,* 1755-1824, an English physician, who first described it]

Parkinson's Law, any of various humorous tenets satirizing bureaucratic assumptions and practices, propounded by C. Northcote Parkinson (born 1909), a British historian, especially the observations that work expands to fill the time available for its completion and expenditure rises to meet income.

park·land (pärk′land′), *n.* **1.** a grassland area, especially in the temperate zone, with trees in small groups or isolated rather than in forests. **2.** land set aside for use by the public: . . . *New York State's aggressive program to convert the seaway border areas into parkland* (Toronto Daily Star).

park·way (pärk′wā′), *n.* **1.** *U.S.* a broad road with spaces planted with grass, trees, etc., usually restricted to use by cars: *Parkways . . . are great screened corridors, cut off by banks and trees from the sight of urban sprawl and rural mess* (Observer). **2.** a strip along a road planted with grass, shrubs, etc.

parl (pärl), *v.i., v.t., n.* parle.

parl., parliamentary.

Parl., **1.** Parliament. **2.** Parliamentary.

par·lance (pär′ləns), *n.* **1.** way of speaking; talk; language: *common parlance, legal parlance. "I'm satisfied where we be, Sir," said Mrs. Lapham, recurring to the parlance of her youth* (William Dean Howells). **2.** *Archaic.* speech, especially debate; parleying. [< Anglo-French, Old French *parlance* < *parler* to speak; see PARLEY] —**Syn. 1.** idiom.

par·lan·do (pär län′dō), *adj. Music.* **1.** with great freedom (an instrumental direction). **2.** in a speechlike manner (a vocal direction): *Miss Nancy Evans sang . . . too slowly and with too much tone—this is a parlando song* (London Times). [< Italian *parlando,* gerund of *parlare* speak]

par·lan·te (pär län′tā), *adj. Music.* parlando.

par·lay (pär′lā, -lē), *U.S.* —*v.t.* **1.** to risk (an original bet and its winnings) on another bet. **2.** to build up (as a small business, talent, investment, etc.) very successfully or profitably (into): *Since 1933, he has parlayed the proceeds of a small pipe company into a $200 million industrial empire* (New York Times). —*v.i.* to wager an original bet with its winnings on a new race, game, etc.
—*n.* such a wager or a series of such wagers.
[American English < French *paroli* < Italian, the grand cast at dice < *paro* equal < Latin *pār, paris*]

parle (pärl), *v.,* **parled, parl·ing,** *n. Archaic.* —*v.i.* to discuss terms, etc.; parley. —*v.t.* to parley with. —*n.* a parley; talk; discussion. [< Old French *parler;* see PARLEY]

par·le·ment (pär′lə mənt), *n.* **1.** (in France before the Revolution of 1789) the name given to a certain number of supreme courts of justice, in which also the edicts, declarations, and ordinances of the king were registered. **2.** *Obsolete.* parliament. [< Old French *parlement* (literally) speaking; see PARLIAMENT]

par·ley (pär′lē), *n., pl.* **-leys,** *v.,* **-leyed, -ley·ing.** —*n.* **1.** a conference; informal talk: *The Administration's position is that a conference of the Big Four foreign ministers should precede any parley "at the summit"* (New York Times). **2.** an informal discussion with an enemy during a truce about terms of surrender, exchange of prisoners, etc.: *The general held a parley with the enemy about exchanging prisoners.*
—*v.i.* **1.** to discuss terms, especially with an enemy: *We arm to parley* (Sir Winston Churchill). **2.** *Archaic.* to speak; talk: *The housemaids parley at the gate, The scullions on the stair* (Oliver Wendell Holmes).
[< Old French *parlée* < feminine past participle of *parler* to speak < Late Latin *parabolāre* < Latin *parabola* parable]

par·lia·ment (pär′lə mənt), *n.* **1.** a council or congress that is the highest lawmaking body of a country. **2.** the lawmaking body of France, Switzerland, or Italy, or that of Scotland until 1707 or Ireland until 1800, and of certain other countries. **3.** the highest lawmaking body of any political unit: *The illusion has grown up that a "parliament of man" can be assembled under the UN roof* (Wall Street Journal). **4.** *Obsolete.* a formal conference or council for the discussion of some matter or matters of general importance. [< Old French *parlement* < *parler* to speak; see PARLEY]

Par·lia·ment (pär′lə mənt), *n.* **1.** the national lawmaking body of Great Britain and Northern Ireland. It consists of the House of Lords and the House of Commons. *Only then will Parliament be in a position to prescribe for these industries attainable targets* (London Times). **2.** the lawmaking body of certain Commonwealth countries: *In British Columbia we elected the only Indian legislator to sit in a provincial Parliament* (Vancouver Native Voice).

par·lia·men·tar·i·an (pär′lə men tãr′ē ən), *n.* **1.** a person skilled in parliamentary procedure or debate. **2.** a member of a parliament: *A lunch was given . . . for a party of Cabinet Ministers and parliamentarians* (Cape Times).

Par·lia·men·tar·i·an (pär′lə men tãr′ē ən), *n.* (in English history) a person who supported Parliament against Charles I.

par·lia·men·tar·i·an·ism (pär′lə men tãr′ē ə niz′əm), *n.* the parliamentary system of government: *It is necessary to make a distinction between . . . the constant weaknesses of French parliamentarianism and . . . the causes of the present crisis* (Manchester Guardian).

par·lia·men·tar·i·ly (pär′lə men′tə rə lē, -trə lē), *adv.* in a parliamentary manner.

par·lia·men·ta·ri·za·tion (pär′lə men′tər ə zā′shən), *n.* **1.** the act of parliamentarizing. **2.** the state of being parliamentarized.

par·lia·men·ta·rize (pär′lə men′tə rīz), *v.t.,* **-rized, -riz·ing.** to make (a government) parliamentary; subject to the control of a parliament.

par·lia·men·ta·ry (pär′lə men′tər ē, -trē), *adj.* **1.** of a parliament: *parliamentary authority.* **2.** done by a parliament: *parliamentary statutes.* **3.** according to the rules and customs of a parliament or other lawmaking body: *The United States Congress functions in accordance with the rules of parliamentary procedure.* **4.** having a parliament: *a parliamentary form of government.*

parliamentary law, a body of rules recognized for preserving order and regulating debate and procedure in legislative or deliberative bodies.

Parliament Hill, **1.** the hill in Ottawa, capital of Canada, on which the buildings of the Canadian Parliament stand. **2.** the Parliament of Canada: *Old hands on Parliament Hill were shaken to hear the government criticized* (Maclean's).

par·lor (pär′lər), *n.* **1.** a room for receiving or entertaining guests; sitting room: *In what was called the parlor . . . there was a sofa, an uncomfortable couch, . . . our showpiece, much admired* (Arthur H. Tasker). **2.** *U.S.* a decorated room used as a shop: *a beauty parlor.* **3. a.** *British.* a room in an inn more private than the taproom. **b.** a separate and somewhat similar room in a hotel, club, etc.
—*adj.* **1.** used in or suitable for a parlor: *parlor furniture.* **2.** advocating views as if from the safe remoteness of the parlor rather than from a practical contact with the matters involved: *a parlor radical.* Also, *Especially British,* **parlour.**
[< Anglo-French *parlur,* Old French *parleor* < *parler* to speak; see PARLEY]

parlor boarder, *British.* a pupil in a boarding school who lives with the principal's family and has privileges not granted to the ordinary pupils.

parlor car, *U.S.* a railroad passenger car for day travel, more luxurious than a coach and for which a higher fare is charged.

par·lor·maid (pär′lər mād′), *n.* a maidservant who waits on table, answers the door, and performs other duties.

parlor match, a friction match containing little or no sulfur.

parlor pew, *British.* a family pew in a church, furnished like a small parlor, sometimes occupied by the lord of the manor or squire with his household.

par·lour (pär′lər), *n., adj. Especially British.* parlor.

par·lous (pär′ləs), *adj.* **1.** perilous; dangerous: *the parlous state of the European coal industry* (London Times). *Thou art in a parlous state, shepherd* (Shakespeare). **2.** *Dialect or Informal.* very clever; shrewd: *A parlous boy: go to, you are too shrewd* (Shakespeare). —*adv.* extremely; excessively: *You look parlous handsome when you smile* (George J. Whyte-Melville). [short for *perilous*] —**par′lous·ly,** *adv.*

par·ma (pär′mə), *n.* a medium or deep shade of violet. [< *Parma,* a city in Italy]

Par·me·san (pär′mə zan, pär′mə zan′), *n.* Also, **Parmesan cheese.** a hard, dry Italian cheese made from skim milk: *To go with this, there is some of the finest Parmesan we have come across* (New Yorker).
—*adj.* **1.** of or belonging to the city, the province, or the former duchy of Parma in northern Italy. **2.** prepared with Parmesan (cheese): *veal Parmesan.* [probably < Middle French *parmesan,* adaptation of Italian *parmigiano* of *Parma,* a region in Italy]

par·mi·gia·na (pär′mi jä′nə), *adj.* prepared with Parmesan cheese: *veal parmigiana, eggplant parmigiana.* [< Italian *parmigiana,* feminine of *parmigiano* Parmesan]

Par·nas·si·an (pär nas′ē ən), *adj.* **1.** of or having to do with Mount Parnassus, in southern Greece. **2.** of or having to do with a school of French poetry of the latter half of the 1800's, that emphasized metrical form and repression of emotion. —*n.* a French poet of the Parnassian school.

Par·nas·si·an·ism (pär nas′ē ən iz′əm), *n.* the Parnassian style in French poetry.

Par·nas·sus (pär nas′əs), *n.* **1. a.** the fabled mountain of poets, whose summit is their goal. **b.** any gathering place for poets. **2.** a collection of poems, belles lettres, etc.

try or **strive to climb Parnassus,** to try to write poetry: *There is Lowell, who's striving Parnassus to climb With a whole bale of isms tied together with rhyme* (James Russell Lowell).

[< Mount *Parnassus,* in southern Greece, in ancient times sacred to Apollo and the Muses]

pa·ro·chi·al (pə rō′kē əl), *adj.* **1.** of or in a parish: *parochial calls, parochial relief of the poor.* **2.** very limited; narrow: *Some pride or ambition, big or small, imperial or parochial* (Alexander Kinglake). [< Old French *parochial* < Late Latin *parochiālis* < *parochia;* see PARISH] —**pa·ro′chi·al·ly,** *adv.*

pa·ro·chi·al·ism (pə rō′kē ə liz′əm), *n.* parochial character, spirit, or tendency; narrowness of interests or views: *In a journal such as Science News, there is a pressure toward parochialism in the choice of authors which is hard to resist* (Science News).

pa·ro·chi·al·ize (pə rō′kē ə līz), *v.,* **-ized, -iz·ing.** —*v.t.* to make parochial. —*v.i.* to do parish work.

parochial school, a school maintained by a church.

par·o·di·a·ble (par′ə dē ə bəl), *adj.* that can be parodied: *Why is it that nobody has been able to write a successful parody of one who is presumably so supremely parodiable?* (New York Times).

pa·rod·ic (pə rod′ik), *adj.* having to do with or of the nature of a parody: *I am reasonably certain that the author's intentions are not essentially parodic* (Atlantic).

pa·rod·i·cal (pə rod′ə kəl), *adj.* parodic.

par·o·dist (par′ə dist), *n.* a writer of parodies: . . . *Charlotte Rae, a parodist whose target is songbirds that even the Audubon Society wouldn't want to save* (New Yorker).

par·o·dis·tic (par′ə dis′tik), *adj.* of the nature of a parody; that parodies: "*The Hollow Men*" *is in every way a better poem than* "*The Waste Land,*" *though the parodistic style again enforces a poverty of statement and language* (Saturday Review).

par·o·don·tal (par′ə don′təl), *adj.* periodontal.

pa·ro·dos (par′ə dos), *n.* in ancient Greek drama: **1.** the entrance of the chorus into the orchestra. **2.** the song they sang while entering. **3.** the passage by which they entered. [< Greek *párodos*]

par·o·dy (par′ə dē), *n., pl.* **-dies,** *v.,* **-died, -dy·ing.** —*n.* **1.** a humorous imitation of a serious writing. A parody follows the form of the original, but changes its sense to nonsense. *Parodies and caricatures are the most penetrating of criticisms* (Aldous Huxley). *Miss [Phyllis] McGinley does not disdain a single trick of the trade: parody, puns . . . persiflage . . . and epigrams* (Atlantic). **2.** a poor imitation; travesty: *its old pavillion, a little wooden parody of the temple of Vesta at Tibur* (H.G. Wells). **3.** a musical composition making fun of another: *The songs are parodies, or parody-medleys if you're really lucky* (Manchester Guardian Weekly).
—*v.t.* **1.** to make fun of by imitating; make a parody on: *All these peculiarities [of Johnson's style] have been imitated by his admirers and parodied by his assailants* (Macaulay). **2.** to imitate poorly: *Behind him . . . the creature's shadow repeated and parodied his swift gesticulations* (Robert Louis Stevenson).
[< Latin *parōdia* < Greek *parōidíā* < *para-* beside, parallel to + *ōidḗ* song]

parody Mass, (in medieval music) a Mass in which parts of some other composer's chanson or motet were interwoven and alternated with freely invented sections.

pa·roe·cious (pə rē′shəs), *adj. Botany.* having the male and female reproductive organs beside or near each other, as certain mosses; paroicous; parecious. [< Greek *pároikos* (with English *-ous*) dwelling side by side < *para* beside + *oîkos* house. Compare PARISH.]

pa·roe·mi·og·ra·pher (pə rē′mē og′rə fər), *n.* a writer or compiler of proverbs.

pa·roe·mi·og·ra·phy (pə rē′mē og′rə fē), *n., pl.* **-phies. 1.** the writing of proverbs. **2.** a collection of proverbs. [< Greek *paroimíā* proverb + English *-graphy*]

par of exchange, the established normal value of the money of one country in terms of the money of another country using the same metal as a standard of value.

pa·roi·cous (pə roi′kəs), *adj.* paroecious.

pa·rol (pə rōl′, par′əl), *Law.* —*n.* **1.** word of mouth; oral statement. **2.** the pleadings in a suit.
—*adj.* **1.** presented by word of mouth; oral: *parol evidence.* **2.** not under seal.
[earlier *parole;* see PAROLE]

pa·role (pə rōl′), *n., v.,* **-roled, -rol·ing,** *adj.* —*n.* **1. a.** a conditional release from prison or jail before the full term is served. **b.** the state of being paroled or the period of a parole. **2.** conditional freedom allowed in place of imprisonment. **3.** word of honor: *The prisoner of war gave his parole not to try to escape.* **4.** a password given only to officers of the guard and the officer of the day to give them admittance to places otherwise forbidden. **5.** *Law.* parol.
—*v.t.* to put on parole; release on parole: *The judge paroled the boys on condition that they report to him every three months.*
—*adj.* of or having to do with paroles: *a parole officer.*
[< French, Old French *parole* word, speech < Vulgar Latin *parabla* < Latin *parabola* parable; (in Late Latin) a speech, saying. Doublet of PARABLE, PARABOLA, PARABOLE, PALAVER.]

parole board, a group of persons having the authority to parole a prisoner before his sentence has expired, supervise the parolee after his release, and revoke the parole under certain conditons: *Some years ago I had occasion to dedicate a book to the real underdog of the whole prison system: the parole board* (Erle Stanley Gardner).

pa·ro·lee (pə rō′lē′), *n.* a person released on parole.

par·o·no·ma·sia (par′ə nə mā′zhə), *n.* a playing on words that sound alike; punning; pun. [< Latin *paronomasia* < Greek *paronomasíā* < *paronomázein* to alter slightly in naming < *para-* aside + *onomázein* to name < *ónoma* name]

par·o·no·mas·tic (par′ə nə mas′tik), *adj.* having to do with or of the nature of paronomasia; punning. —**par′o·no·mas′ti·cal·ly,** *adv.*

par·o·nych·i·a (par′ə nik′ē ə), *n. Medicine.* an inflammation about the nail; whitlow. [< Latin *parōnychia* < Greek *parōnychíā* < *para-* beside + *ónyx, ónychos* nail]

par·o·nych·i·al (par′ə nik′ē əl), *adj.* having to do with or of the nature of a paronychia.

par·o·nym (par′ə nim), *n.* a paronymous word.

pa·ron·y·mous (pə ron′ə məs), *adj.* **1.** (of words) derived from the same root; cognate. **2.** derived from a word in another language with little or no change in form, as English *canal* for Latin *canalis.* **3.** having the same sound but different spelling and meaning, as *feat* and *feet;* homophonic. [< Greek *parṓnymos* (with English *-ous*) a derivative formed by a slight change < *parōnymeîn* (literally) to alter in naming < *para-* aside, amiss + dialectal *ónyma* name]

pa·ron·y·my (pə ron′ə mē), *n.* **1.** paronymous character. **2.** the transference of a word from one language to another with little or no change in form.

par·o·quet (par′ə ket), *n.* parakeet.

par·o·rex·i·a (par′ə rek′sē ə), *n. Medicine.* perversion of the appetite; a craving to eat articles not suitable for food. [< New Latin *parorexia* < Greek *para-* aside + *órexis* appetite]

pa·ros·mi·a (pə ros′mē ə, -roz′-), *n. Medicine.* disease or perversion of the sense of smell. [< New Latin *parosmia* < Greek *para-* aside + *osmḗ* smell]

pa·rot·ic (pə rot′ik), *adj.* in the region of the ear; parotid.

pa·rot·id (pə rot′id), *adj.* **1.** near the ear. **2.** of the parotid glands, one in front of each ear, that supply saliva to the mouth through the parotid duct. —*n.* either parotid gland. [< Latin *parōtis, -idis* < Greek *parōtís, -ídos* tumor of the parotid gland < *para-* beside + *oûs, ōtós* ear]

pa·rot·i·di·tis (pə rot′ə dī′tis), *n.* parotitis.

par·o·tit·ic (par′ə tit′ik), *adj.* affected with parotitis.

par·o·ti·tis (par′ə tī′tis), *n.* inflammation of the parotid gland, especially as in mumps. [< Latin *parōtis* (see PAROTID)]

pa·ro·toid (pə rō′toid), *adj.* resembling a parotid gland, especially applied to certain cutaneous glands forming the bulge above the eardrum of frogs and toads. —*n.* a parotoid gland.

par·ous (par′əs), *adj.* having borne children. [< Latin *parere* to give birth]

par·ox·ysm (par′ək siz əm), *n.* **1. a.** a severe, sudden attack: *a paroxysm of coughing.* **b.** a sudden attack or increase in the severity of the symptoms of a disease, usually recurring periodically: *a malarial paroxysm.* **2.** a fit; convulsion: *paroxysms of pleasure or rage* (Washington Irving). [< Middle French *paroxysme* < Medieval Latin *paroxysmus* < Greek *paroxysmós* < *paroxýnein* to exasperate, goad < *para-* beyond + *oxýnein* render acute; goad < *oxýs* sharp, pointed]

par·ox·ys·mal (par′ək siz′məl), *adj.* of, like, or having paroxysms: *a paroxysmal frenzy of contending passions* (Shelley). —**par′ox·ys′mal·ly,** *adv.*

par·ox·y·tone (pa rok′sə tōn), *Greek Grammar.* —*adj.* having an acute accent on the next to the last syllable (penult). —*n.* a word so accented. [< Greek *paroxýtonos* < *para-* beside, next to + *oxýtonos* oxytone]

par·quet (pär kā′, -ket′), *n., v.,* **-queted** (-kād′, -ket′id), **-quet·ing** (-kā′ing, -ket′ing) or (*especially British*) **-quet·ted** (-ket′id), **-quet·ting** (-ket′ing). —*n.* **1.** an inlaid wooden flooring composed especially of small blocks of wood. **2.** *U.S.* **a.** the main floor of a theater; the orchestra. **b.** the part of the main floor of a theater from the orchestra pit to the parquet circle. The British term is *stalls.* —*v.t.* to make or put down (an inlaid wooden floor). [< Middle French *parquet,* and *parchet* wooden flooring, compartment; an enclosed portion of a park; (literally) diminutive of *parc* park]

parquet circle, the part of the main floor of a theater that is under the balcony.

par·quet·ry (pär′kə trē), *n., pl.* **-ries.** a mosaic of wood used for floors, wainscoting, etc.; parquet. [< French *parqueterie* < *parquet* parquet]

Parquetry

parr (pär), *n., pl.* **parrs** or (*collectively*) **parr. 1.** a young salmon before it is old enough to go to sea, identifiable by dark bands on its sides. **2.** the young of any of various other fishes, as the coalfish or black cod. [origin unknown]

par·ra·keet (par′ə kēt), *n.* parakeet.

par·ra·mat·ta (par′ə mat′ə), *n.* paramatta.

par·rel or **par·ral** (par′əl), *n.* a sliding ring or collar of rope or iron by which a yard, boom, etc., is attached to a mast and can move up and down on it. [apparently variant of Middle English *parail* equipment, short for *aparail* apparel. Compare Old French *parail* rigging.]

par·ri·cid·al (par′ə sī′dəl), *adj.* of or having to do with parricide.

par·ri·cide[1] (par′ə sīd), *n.* the crime of killing one's parent or parents, or any person for whom one is supposed to have respect or reverence comparable to that traditionally considered owing to a parent: *Oedipus was guilty of parricide.* [< Latin *parricīdium,* earlier *pāricīdium* < unrecorded *pārus* relative + *-cīdium* -cide[2]]

par·ri·cide[2] (par′ə sīd), *n.* a person who kills his parent: *Oedipus was a parricide.* [< Latin *parricīda,* earlier *pāricīda* < unrecorded *pārus* relative + *-cīda* -cide[1]]

par·ridge (pär′ij), *n.* porridge.

par·ritch (pär′ich), *n. Scottish.* porridge.

par·rock (par′ək), *n. Scottish.* a small field or enclosure; paddock. [Old English *pearroc* inclosure, paddock; see PARK]

par·ro·ket or **par·ro·quet** (par′ə ket), *n.* parakeet.

par·rot (par′ət), *n.* **1.** any bird of an order including parakeets, cockatoos, lories, and macaws, with a short hooked bill, and often with bright-colored feathers. Certain larger Old World species, as a gray parrot of West Africa, have fleshy tongues and can be taught to imitate sounds and to repeat words and sentences. **2.** a person who repeats

Yellow-headed Parrot (def. 1) (15 in. long)

words or acts without understanding them. —*v.t.* to repeat without understanding or sense: *On the whole, the students seemed serious and hard-working, but they confined themselves to parroting textbooks* (Atlantic). [perhaps < French *Perrot* (diminutive) < *Pierre* Peter] —**par′rot·like′,** *adj.*

par·rot-cry (par′ət krī′), *n., pl.* **-cries.** a slogan, catch phrase, etc., parroted or repeated over and over without understanding or sense: *The economic writings of today are filled with parrot-cries of "laissez-faire is dead"* (Canada Month).

parrot fever or **disease,** psittacosis.

parrot fish, any of various, mainly tropical, marine fishes having brilliant coloring or a strong hard mouth resembling the bill of a parrot.

par·rot·let (par′ət let), *n.* any of various small, tropical, South American parrots, with green and yellow heads.

par·ry (par′ē), *v.,* **-ried, -ry·ing,** *n., pl.* **-ries.** —*v.t.* to ward off; turn aside; evade (a thrust, stroke, weapon, question, etc.): *He parried the sword with his dagger. She parried our question by asking us one.* —*v.i.* to ward off or turn aside a thrust, blow, question, etc. —*n.* the act of parrying.
[< French *parez,* imperative of *parer* ward off < Italian *parare* ward off, make ready < Latin *parāre* prepare. Doublet of PARE.]

parse (pärs), *v.,* **parsed, pars·ing.** *v.t.* **1.** to analyze (a sentence) grammatically, telling its parts of speech and their uses in the sentence: *Their small world consists in parsing a sentence* (Time). **2.** to describe (a word) grammatically, telling what part of speech it is, its form, and its use in a sentence. —*v.i.* **1.** to analyze a sentence grammatically. **2.** to describe a word grammatically. **3.** to be grammatically or syntactically acceptable: *She is in London . . . wearing exquisite clothes and speaking sentences that parse* (New Yorker).
[perhaps Middle English *pars* parts of speech < Old French *pars* < Latin *pars* (*ōrātiōnis*) part (of speech)] —**pars′er,** *n.*

par·sec (pär′sek), *n.* a unit of distance, used in computing the distances of stars, equal to the distance of a star whose annual parallax is one second of arc, or about 206,265 times the mean distance of the earth from the sun or 3.26 light years, or 19.2 trillion miles. Also, **secpar.** [< *par*(allax of one) *sec*(ond)]

Par·see or **Par·si** (pär′sē, pär sē′), *n.* a member of a Zoroastrian sect in India, especially in western India near Bombay, descended from the Persians who first settled there in the early part of the 700's A.D.: *Parsis, religious exiles from Persia hundreds of years ago, are still Zoroastrians* (Santha Rama Rau). [< Hindustani and Persian *Pārsī* a Persian < *Pārs* Persia]

Par·see·ism or **Par·si·ism** (pär′sē iz əm, pär sē′-), *n.* the religion and customs of the Parsees.

Par·si·fal (pär′sə fəl, -fäl), *n. German Legend.* a knight corresponding to the Percival of Arthurian legend. Also, **Parzival.**

par·si·mo·ni·ous (pär′sə mō′nē əs), *adj.* **1.** too economical; stingy: *parsimonious housekeeping.* **2.** (of things) poor; mean. —**par′si·mo′ni·ous·ly,** *adv.* —**par′si·mo′ni·ous·ness,** *n.* —**Syn. 1.** frugal, stinting, miserly. —**Ant. 1.** generous, liberal, lavish.

par·si·mo·ny (pär′sə mō′nē), *n.* **1.** extreme economy; stinginess: *There is no need to dwell on the other limitations of his character, his jealousy, his parsimony* (Atlantic). **2.** sparingness in the use or expenditure of means: *This is the grand overriding law of the parsimony of nature: every action within a system is executed with the least possible expenditure of energy* (Scientific American). [< Latin *parsimōnia,* ultimately < *parcere* to spare] —**Syn. 1.** niggardliness.

pars·ley (pärs′lē), *n., pl.* **-leys. 1.** a biennial garden herb, a native of the Mediterranean region, with finely divided, often curled, fragrant leaves used to flavor food and to trim platters of meat, etc. **2.** any of certain similar or related plants. [fusion of Old English *petersilie,* and of Middle English *percil* (< Old French *peresil*); both < Vulgar Latin *petrosilium* < Latin *petroselīnum* < Greek *petrosélīnon* < *pétros* rock + *sélīnon* parsley]

parsley family, a group of dicotyledonous plants, chiefly herbs, having alternate, usually compound, and aromatic leaves and small flowers borne in umbels, and bearing a dry fruit consisting of two carpels that split at the base when mature. The family includes the parsley, carrot, celery, caraway, anise, poison hemlock, and angelica.

pars·nip (pärs′nip), *n.* **1.** a biennial vegetable of the parsley family, a native of Europe and part of Asia, having pinnate leaves, yellow flowers, and a long, tapering whitish root that in the cultivated variety is fleshy, sweet, and nutritious. **2.** the root itself. **3.** any of certain allied or similar plants. [alteration of Middle English *passenep* < Old French *pasnaie* < Latin *pastināca;* influenced by Middle English *nep* turnip, neep]

par·son (pär′sən), *n.* **1.** a minister in charge of a parish: *But all the instruction he got . . . was . . . on Sundays, from a parson who taught little effectively* (J.W.R. Scott). **2.** *Informal.* any clergyman; minister; rector. [< Medieval Latin *parsona,* and *persona* parson < Latin *persōna* person, character; actor's mask. Doublet of PERSON.]

par·son·age (pär′sə nij), *n.* **1.** the house provided for a minister by a church: *The country parsonage may now be the most popular literary symbol of England's religious life* (Newsweek). **2.** the benefice of a parson (now used only in ecclesiastical law). [< *parson* + *-age*]

parson bird, a tui.

par·son·ess (pär′sə nis), *n. Informal.* the wife of a parson.

par·son·ic (pär son′ik), *adj.* of, like, or characteristic of a parson: *Others can hardly imagine him as anything else—Broad Church, clean, uplift stuff indeed—no court flunkey he—but every inch of him parsonic* (Punch). —**par·son′i·cal·ly,** *adv.*

par·son·i·cal (pär son′ə kəl), *adj.* parsonic.

part (pärt), *n.* **1.** something less than the whole: *He ate part of an apple. Cowboys live in the western part of the country* **2.** each of several equal quantities into which a whole may be divided; fraction: *A dime is a tenth part of a dollar.* **3.** a thing that helps to make up a whole: *spare parts. A radio has many parts.* **4.** a share: *Everyone must do his part. He had no part in the mischief.* **5.** a side in a dispute or contest: *He always takes his brother's part.* **6. a.** a character in a play; role: *Jane spoke the part of the fairy in our play.* **b.** the words spoken by a character in a play: *to study one's part.* **7.** a role played by a person in real life: *All the world's a stage . . . And one man in his time plays many parts* (Shakespeare). **8.** *U.S.* a dividing line left in combing one's hair. **9. a.** one of the voices or instruments in music: *The four parts in singing are soprano, alto, tenor, and bass.* **b.** the music for it. *Abbr.:* pt.

bear a part, a. to take or sustain a part in a play or in part singing: *He bore a part in the school cantata.* **b.** to have a share in any action, transaction, or other proceeding: *The king himself . . . bore a part in it* (Joseph Priestley).

for one's (own) part, as far as one is concerned: *For my own part, I was indifferent which it might be* (Sir Arthur Conan Doyle).

for the most part, mainly; usually: *The attempts were for the most part unsuccessful.*

in good part, in a friendly or gracious way: *I am sure he will take it in good part* (Anthony Trollope).

in ill or **bad part,** with displeasure or offense: *"People treat us very familiarly," said the Frenchman, "and they do it so innocently that we should be very hard to get on with if we took it in bad part"* (Catherine Drinker Bowen).

in part, in some measure or degree; to some extent; partly: *For we know in part, and we prophesy in part* (I Corinthians 13:9).

on the part of or **on one's part, a.** as far as one is concerned: *He was friendly enough on his part.* **b.** by one: *No objection on my part, I said* (Benjamin Jowett).

part and parcel, an essential part: *It is part and parcel of their whole tradition of duplicity, sham, and subversion* (Wall Street Journal).

parts, a. ability; talent: *He had a strong face, twinkling bright-blue eyes, and a sand-yellow beard, and he seemed a man of parts* (New Yorker). **b.** regions; districts: *He has traveled much in foreign parts.*

take part, to have a share in; participate or be involved in: *No doubt it was true that technically she took no part in public business* (Lytton Strachey). [< Old French *part* < Latin *pars, partis*]
—*v.t.* **1. a.** to divide into two or more pieces. **b.** *Nautical.* to cause (a rope, cable, etc.) to break. **2.** to force apart; divide: *The policeman on horseback parted the crowd.* **3.** to keep apart; form a boundary between. **4.** to separate by a chemical or other technical process. **5.** to brush or comb (the hair) away from a dividing line. **6.** to dissolve or terminate (a connection, etc.) by separation of the parties concerned: *to part company.* **7.** *Archaic.* to divide among a number of persons; distribute as shares; apportion: *They part my garments among them, and cast lots upon my vesture* (Psalms 22:18). —*v.i.* **1.** to be divided into parts; come or go in pieces; break up; break. **2.** to go apart; separate: *The friends parted in anger. We met to part no more* (Tennyson). **3.** *Archaic.* **a.** to die. **b.** to go away; depart.

part from, to go away from; leave: *Our poor boy Thornie parted from us today* (George Eliot).

part with, to give up; let go: *O, that I should part with so much gold* (Christopher Marlowe).
—*adj.* less than the whole: *part time.*
—*adv.* in some measure or degree; partly: *He spoke in words part heard* (Tennyson). [< Old French *partir* divide into parts; depart < Latin *partīre* < *pars, partis* part, noun]
—**Syn.** *n.* **1. Part, portion, piece** mean something less than the whole. **Part** is the general word meaning an element, fraction, or member of the whole, considered apart from the rest: *Save part of the roast for tomorrow night.* **Portion** means a part thought of less in relation to the whole than as an amount or quantity making up a section or share: *Give a portion of each day to recreation.* **Piece** means a separate part, often thought of as complete in itself: *He ate a big piece of cake.* -*v.t.* **1. a.** sever, sunder.
➤ **On the part of** is often a rather long substitute for, *by, among, for,* and the like: *In recent years there has been a noticeable feeling on the part of* (among) *students that education is all-important.*

part., 1. a. participial. **b.** participle. **2.** particular.

part. adj., participial adjective.

par·take (pär tāk′), *v.,* **-took, -tak·en, -tak·ing.** —*v.i.* **1.** to eat or drink some; take some: *Will you partake with us at lunch?* **2.** to take or have a share; participate: *Thou hast provided all things: but with me I see not who partakes . . . who can enjoy alone?* (Milton). —*v.t.* to take a part in; share in: *The soul partakes The season's youth* (Lowell).

partake of, a. to take some of; take of; take: *to partake of food.* **b.** to have to some extent the nature or character of: *Her graciousness partakes of condescension.*
[back formation < earlier *partaker,* or *partaking,* for *part-taker,* or *part-taking*] —**par·tak′er,** *n.* —**Syn.** *v.i.* **2.** See **share.**

par·tak·en (pär tā′kən), *v.* the past participle of **partake.**

par·tan (pär′tən), *n. Scottish.* a crab. [< Gaelic *partan*]

part·ed (pär′tid), *adj.* **1.** divided into parts; severed; cloven. **2.** divided, as the hair, by a parting. **3.** placed or standing apart; separated. **4.** *Botany.* divided into distinct lobes by depressions (sinuses) extending from the margin nearly to the midrib or to the base, as a leaf. **5.** *Heraldry.* party, as a shield. **6.** *Archaic.* deceased.

par·terre (pär tãr′), *n.* **1.** *U.S.* the part of the main floor of a theater under the balcony. The British term is the *pit.* **2.** an ornamental arrangement of flower beds: *They [gardens of Damascus] are not the formal parterres which you might expect from the Oriental taste* (Alexander Kinglake). [< Middle French *parterre* garden space, noun use of *par terre* on the ground[1] < Latin *per* on, *terra* ground]

parterre boxes, a series of boxes in a theater, located just above the back of the main floor: *the parterre boxes of the Metropolitan Opera House.*

par·the·no·car·pic (pär′thə nō kär′pik), *adj.* (of fruit) produced without fertilization: *Of course, such parthenocarpic fruits contain no viable seed* (P.W. Brian). —**par′the·no·car′pi·cal·ly,** *adv.*

par·the·no·car·py (pär′thə nō kär′pē), *n. Botany.* the development of fruit without seeds or fertilization: *Seedless fruits such as the banana and the navel orange are produced by parthenocarpy.* [< Greek *parthénos* virgin + *karpós* fruit + English *-y*[3]]

par·the·no·gen·e·sis (pär′thə nō jen′ə-sis), *n.* **1.** *Biology.* reproduction without any male element, as the development of eggs in certain insects from virgin females without fertilization by union with one of the opposite sex: *Parthenogenesis, or virgin birth, is common among insects but rare among higher forms of life* (Scientific American). **2.** *Botany.* the development of one of the sexual cells of a plant, as an alga or fungus, without previous fusion with a cell of the opposite sex. [< Greek *parthénos* virgin + English *genesis*]

par·the·no·ge·net·ic (pär′thə nō jə net′-ik), *adj.* having to do with or exhibiting the phenomenon of parthenogenesis: *Parthenogenetic development has been induced in the eggs of a number of animals which ordinarily require fertilization* (A.Franklin Shull). —**par′the·no·ge·net′i·cal·ly,** *adv.*

par·the·nog·e·ny (pär′thə noj′ə nē), *n.* parthenogenesis.

Par·the·non (pär′thə non), *n.* the temple of Athena on the Acropolis at Athens, built about 447-438 B.C., regarded as the finest example of Doric architecture. It is equally famous for its decorative sculpture. *The Parthenon with its architectural purity and impressive monumentality* (Atlantic). [< Latin *Parthenōn* < Greek *Parthenṓn* < *hē Parthénos* the virgin goddess (Athena)]

Parthenon

Par·then·o·pe (pär then′ə pē), *n. Greek Legend.* a siren who drowned herself because she failed to lure Ulysses (Odysseus) with her singing.

Par·the·nos (pär′thə nos), *n.* a virgin (a name applied especially to Athena). [< Greek *hē Parthénos* the virgin goddess]

Par·thi·an (pär′thē ən), *adj.* having to do with Parthia, an ancient kingdom of southwestern Asia, southeast of the Caspian Sea, or its inhabitants; of a kind attributed to or associated with the Parthians: *The Moors kept up a Parthian retreat; several times they turned to make battle* (Washington Irving). —*n.* a native or inhabitant of Parthia: *or like the Parthians I shall flying fight* (Shakespeare).

Parthian shot, a sharp parting remark or the like (from the traditional tactic of the mounted archers of ancient Parthia, which was to shoot arrows back at an adversary as they fled or pretended to flee).

par·ti (pär tē′), *n.* a person considered as a matrimonial match: *A girl in our society accepts the best parti which offers itself* (Thackeray). [< French *parti* party, match[2] < Old French, past participle of *partir* to leave]

par·tial (pär′shəl), *adj.* **1.** not complete; not total: *a partial eclipse. Father has made a partial payment on our new car.* **2.** inclined to favor one side more than another; favoring unfairly: *A parent should not be partial to any one of his children.* **3.** *Informal.* favorably inclined: *He is partial to sports.* **4.** *Mathematics.* (of a function of two or more variables) relative to only one of the variables involved, the rest being for the time supposed constant: *Partial product is the result of multiplying a number by one digit of the multiplier* (Richard Madden). —*n.* a partial tone: *the audibility of partials is not only limited by the threshold of frequency sensitivity* (F.A. Kuttner).
[< Old French *parcial,* learned borrowing from Late Latin *partiālis* < Latin *pars, partis* part] —**par′tial·ness,** *n.*
—**Syn.** *adj.* **1.** incomplete, imperfect. **2.** biased, prejudiced, one-sided.

partial determinant, minor determinant.

partial fraction, *Algebra.* one of the fractions into which a given fraction can be resolved, the sum of such simpler fractions being equal to the given fraction.

par·ti·al·i·ty (pär′shē al′ə tē, -shal′-), *n., pl.* **-ties. 1.** a favoring of one more than another or others; favorable prejudice; being partial: *Either I am blinded by the partiality of a parent, or he is a boy of very amiable character* (Tobias Smollett). **2.** a particular liking; fondness: *Children often have a partiality for candy.* —**Syn. 1.** bias, favoritism. **2.** preference, bent.

par·tial·ly (pär′shə lē), *adv.* **1.** in part; not generally or totally; partly: *a school for blind and partially blind children. When stars high in the sky are being studied, the partially closed shutter will serve as a windscreen* (Science News Letter). **2.** in a partial manner; with undue bias. —**Syn. 1.** See **partly.**

partial tone, *Music.* one of the higher or lower tones which sound together with the fundamental tone and form a resulting compound tone. Upper partial tones are also called harmonics on stringed instruments or open tones on wind instruments.

par·ti·bil·i·ty (pär′tə bil′ə tē), *n.* the quality of being partible: *the partibility of an inheritance.*

par·ti·ble (pär′tə bəl), *adj.* that can be divided or distributed among a number; divisible; separable.

par·ti·ceps cri·mi·nis (pär′tə seps krim′-ə nis), *Latin.* a person who shares in a crime; accomplice.

par·tic·i·pance (pär tis′ə pəns), *n.* the fact or quality of participating.

par·tic·i·pan·cy (pär tis′ə pən sē), *n.* participance.

par·tic·i·pant (pär tis′ə pənt), *n.* a person who shares or participates; sharer; participator: *Each correct answer gives the audience participant a right to take [an item] from the girl in the spotlight* (Time). —*adj.* participating; sharing: *It should be of some sociological interest that there are few participant sports which have a greater mass appeal than this flourishing recreation* (Saturday Review). [< Latin *participāns, -antis,* present participle of *participāre* participate]

par·tic·i·pate (pär tis′ə pāt), *v.,* **-pat·ed, -pat·ing.** —*v.i.* to have a share; take part; share in an undertaking: *The teacher participated in the children's games.* —*v.t.* to possess or enjoy in common with others; share; partake: *When I am glowing with the enthusiasm of success, there will be none to participate my joy* (Mary W. Shelley). [< Latin *participāre* (with English *-ate*[1]) < *particeps, -cipis* (one) partaking < *pars, partis* part + *capere* to take] —**Syn.** *v.i.* See **share.**

par·tic·i·pa·tion (pär tis′ə pā′shən), *n.* a taking part; participating: *They wanted more direct participation in the solution of steel production problems* (Newsweek).

par·tic·i·pa·tive (pär tis′ə pā′tiv), *adj.* characterized by participation; participating. —**par·tic′i·pa′tive·ly,** *adv.*

par·tic·i·pa·tor (pär tis′ə pā′tər), *n.* a person who participates: *participators in our misfortune.*

par·tic·i·pa·to·ry (pär tis′ə pə tôr′ē, -tōr′-), *adj.* participative.

par·ti·cip·i·al (pär′tə sip′ē əl), *Grammar.* —*adj.* of or having to do with a participle. *Examples:* a *masked* man, a *becoming* dress (participial adjectives), *cutting* ice, the fatigue of *marching* (participial nouns). —*n.* a verbal derivative of the nature of, or akin to, a participle. [< Latin *participiālis* < *participium* participle]

par·ti·cip·i·al·ly (pär′tə sip′ē ə lē), *adv.* as a participle. In "the girl singing sweetly," *singing* is used participially.

par·ti·ci·ple (pär′tə sip′əl), *n.* a form of a verb used as an adjective or noun. *Abbr.:* part. [< Old French *participle,* variant of *participe,* learned borrowing from Latin *participium* (literally) sharing, partaking < *particeps;* see PARTICIPATE]

➤ A **participle** retains the attributes of a verb, such as tense, voice, power to take an object, and modification by adverbs. *Examples:* the girl *writing* sentences at the blackboard, the recently *stolen* silver, John *having missed* the boat. In these phrases, *writing* is a present participle; *stolen* is a past participle; *having missed* is a perfect participle. See also **dangling participle.**

par·ti·cle (pär′tə kəl), *n.* **1.** a very little bit: *I got a particle of dust in my eye.* **2.** *Physics.* **a.** a minute mass of matter that while still having inertia and attraction is treated as a point without length, breadth, or thickness. **b.** one of the fundamental units of matter, as the electron, neutron, photon, or proton; elementary particle: *[The theory of photons] involves the basic dualism between the continuous and the discontinuous, between wave and particle* (I. Bernard Cohen). **3. a.** a derivational prefix or suffix, as *un-, -ly, -ness.* **b.** a word that cannot be inflected, such as a preposition, conjunction, article, or interjection. *In, if, an,* and *ah* are particles. **c.** the term sometimes applied to all such words collectively when classed together as a single part of speech or form class. **4.** in the Roman Catholic Church: **a.** a fragment of the Eucharistic Host. **b.** the wafer given to each lay communicant. [< Latin *particula* (diminutive) < *pars, partis* part]

particle accelerator, a device used to impart high velocity and hence high energy to atomic or elementary particles, as a betatron or bevatron. By directing the accelerated particles against atomic nuclei, the particle accelerator may be used as an atom smasher. *The monoenergetic neutrons produced by particle accelerators have energies above the displacement threshold* (Science).

particle board, an inexpensive type of fiberboard, made from wood chips and shavings by a gluing and pressing process, and used in construction and as a base for furniture: *Particle board is providing Americans with "mahogany" furniture at low cost* (Science News Letter).

particle physics, the study of elementary particles: *The new particle adds confirmation to . . principles already established in particle physics* (Scientific American).

par·ti·col·ored (pär′tē kul′ərd), *adj.* **1.** colored differently in different parts; variegated in color: *a parti-colored dress.* **2.** diversified; varied: *a parti-colored story.* Also, **party-colored.** [< French *parti* divided, past participle of *partir* to part + English *colored*]

par·ti·col·oured (pär′tē kul′ərd), *adj. Especially British.* parti-colored.

par·tic·u·lar (pər tik′yə lər), *adj.* **1.** apart from others; considered separately; single: *That particular chair is already sold.* **2.** belonging to some one person, thing, group, occasion, etc.: *Jack's particular task is to care for the dog. A particular characteristic of a skunk is his smell.* **3.** different from others; unusual; special: *a particular friend. This vacation was of particular importance to Mary, for she was going to Europe.* **4.** hard to please; wanting everything to be just right; very careful; exact: *She is very particular; nothing but the best will do.* **5.** giving details; full of details: *a particular account of the game.* **6.** *Law.* **a.** having to do with an estate granted to one person for a number of years or for life but ultimately to be the property of someone else. **b.** having to do with the tenant of such an estate. **7.** *Logic.* not referring to the whole extent of a class, but only to some individual or individuals in it; not general: *a particular proposition.* **8.** *Obsolete.* private; personal: *These domestic and particular broils* (Shakespeare). —*n.* **1.** an individual part; item; point: *The work is complete in every particular. All the particulars of the accident are now known.* **2.** *Logic.* **a.** an individual thing in relation to or contrast to the whole class. **b.** a particular proposition.

in particular, especially: *We played around, doing nothing in particular.*

[< Middle French *particuler,* learned borrowing from Latin *particulāris* < *particula* particle] —**Syn.** *adj.* **1.** See **special. 2.** individual, distinctive. **4.** precise, exacting, fastidious. **5.** detailed, minute. -*n.* **1.** See **item.**

par·tic·u·lar·ism (pər tik′yə lə riz′əm), *n.* **1.** exclusive attention or devotion to one's particular party, sect, nation, etc.: *Patriotism and the sense of political unity are not at the root of local particularism, they merely grow out of it and crown it* (Atlantic). **2.** the principle of letting each state of a federation keep its own laws and promote its own interests. **3.** *Theology.* the doctrine, especially in Calvinism, that only those who have been individually predestined to it may achieve salvation.

par·tic·u·lar·ist (pər tik′yə lər ist), *n.* an advocate or adherent of particularism.

par·tic·u·lar·is·tic (pər tik′yə lə ris′tik), *adj.* having to do with, characterized by, or upholding particularism: *Boas and his school do not so much refute evolution as avoid it in favor of particularistic historical researches* (Beals and Hoijer).

par·tic·u·lar·i·ty (pər tik′yə lar′ə tē), *n., pl.* **-ties. 1.** detailed quality; minuteness:

[*The characters in the play*] *are not given that kind of particularity or interior life* (Arthur Miller). **2.** special carefulness. **3.** attentiveness to details: *She had from time to time remarked the Chichester, but never with any particularity* (Arnold Bennett). **4.** a particular feature or trait: *He had a great many other particularities in his character which I will not mention* (Henry Fielding). **5.** the quality of being hard to please. **6.** the quality or fact of being particular. **7.** *Obsolete.* a detail.

par·tic·u·lar·i·za·tion (pər tik′yə lər ə zā′shən), *n.* the act of particularizing.

par·tic·u·lar·ize (pər tik′yə lə rīz), *v.*, **-ized, -iz·ing.** —*v.t.* to mention particularly or individually; treat in detail; specify: *In his family portraits . . . the autobiography becomes particularized and memorable* (Harper's). —*v.i.* to mention individuals; give details: *Stans is more analyst than stylist: "Let me particularize," he is fond of saying* (Time). —**par·tic′u·lar·iz′er,** *n.*

par·tic·u·lar·ly (pər tik′yə lər lē), *adv.* **1.** in a high degree; especially: *The teacher praised Ruth particularly.* **2.** in a particular manner. **3.** in detail; in all of its parts; minutely. —**Syn. 1.** principally, mainly. See **especially.**

par·tic·u·lar·ness (pər tik′yə lər nis), *n.* **1.** the character of being particular; particularity; individuality. **2.** nice attention to detail; fastidiousness; fussiness: *You're getting to be your aunt's own niece, I see, for particularness* (George Eliot).

par·tic·u·late (pär tik′yə lāt), *adj.* of, having to do with, or consisting of separate particles: *Some filters . . . effectively remove particulate matter from gases* (Science News Letter). [< Latin *particula* particle]

par·tie car·rée (pȧr tē′ kȧ rā′), *French.* a party of four: *Parties carrées with the Soviet representative and his wife were a nightmare that was to pursue them to liberated Paris* (Punch).

part·ing (pär′ting), *n.* **1.** a departure; going away; a taking leave: *The friends were sad at parting.* **2.** a division; separation. **3.** a place of division or separation: *to reach the parting of the roads.* **4.** something that parts or separates two things, as a layer of rock, clay, etc., lying between two beds of different formations. **5.** *Archaic.* decease; death. —*adj.* **1.** given, taken, done, etc., at parting: *a parting request, a parting shot.* **2. a.** going away; departing: *The curfew tolls the knell of parting day* (Thomas Gray). **b.** dying. **3.** dividing; separating.

parting cup, a drinking cup having two handles, used by two people in taking a draft of liquor at parting.

parting strip, the strip in each side of a window frame to keep the upper and lower sashes apart.

par·ti pris (pȧr tē′ prē′), *French.* a decision or opinion formed in advance: *They said Nocero had deserved to win, but I think they had a parti pris* (New Yorker).

par·ti·san[1] (pär′tə zən), *n.* **1.** a strong supporter of a person, party, or cause; one whose support is based on feeling rather than on reasoning: *He was a passionate partisan of these people and had organized a Workers' Union* (Edmund Wilson). **2.** a member of a party of light, irregular troops or armed civilians; guerrilla.
—*adj.* of or like a partisan: *Leadership is either partisan or scientific. Partisan leadership takes sides* (Emory S. Bogardus). Also, **partizan.** [< Middle French *partisan*, adaptation of dialectal Italian *partezan*, variant of *partigiano* < *parte* part < Latin *pars, partis* part] —**Syn.** *n.* **1.** follower, adherent, disciple.

par·ti·san[2] (pär′tə zən), *n.* a weapon with a broad blade like a halberd and a long shaft like a pike, carried by foot soldiers in the 1500's and on ceremonial occasions by the bodyguards of a great personage. Also, **partizan.** [< Middle French *partizane* < Italian *partesana*, or *partigiana* < Medieval Latin (Spain) *partesana.* Compare Old High German *parta* halberd.]

par·ti·san·ship (pär′tə zən ship), *n.* **1.** strong loyalty to a party or cause: *Regardless of partisanship, however, one could select in the day-to-day happenings of the past year in Japan many symptoms of the poor health of the body politic* (Atlantic). **2.** a taking sides: *They wanted a President who would stand above petty partisanship* (Newsweek).

par·ti·ta (pär tē′tə), *n.* a series of dance tunes in the same or related keys for one or more instruments. [< Italian *partita* (originally) feminine past participle of *partire* divide < Latin *partīre;* see PARTITE]

par·tite (pär′tīt), *adj.* **1.** divided into parts or portions. **2.** *Botany.* parted. **3.** *Entomology.* divided to the base, as a wing. [< Latin *partītus*, past participle of *partīre* to divide < *pars, partis* part]

par·ti·tion (pär tish′ən), *n.* **1.** a division into parts: *the partition of a man's wealth when he dies.* **2.** a portion; part; section. **3.** something that separates, as a wall between rooms or a septum or other separating membrane in a plant or animal body. **4.** *Mathematics.* a way of expressing a number as a sum of positive whole numbers. **5.** *Logic.* analysis by separation of the integral parts. —*v.t.* **1.** to divide into parts: *to partition a country, partition a building into apartments.* **2.** to separate by a partition. **3.** *Law.* to divide (property) to separate the individual interests. [Middle English *particion* < Old French *particion*, learned borrowing from Latin *partītiō, -ōnis* < *partīre* to part] —**par·ti′tion·er,** *n.* —**Syn.** *n.* **1.** apportionment.

par·ti·tion·ment (pär tish′ən mənt), *n.* the act of dividing; partition.

par·ti·tive (pär′tə tiv), *n.* a word or phrase meaning a part of a collective whole. *Some, few,* and *any* are partitives. —*adj.* expressing a part of a collective whole: *a partitive adjective.* —**par′ti·tive·ly,** *adv.*

par·ti·zan (pär′tə zən), *n., adj.* partisan.

part·let[1] (pärt′lit), *n.* a kind of garment worn around the neck and upper part of the chest, especially by women during the 1500's. [apparently variant of earlier *patelet* < Old French *patelette* band of stuff, diminutive of *patte* flap, paw]

part·let[2] or **Part·let** (pärt′lit), *n.* a hen (especially as a proper name, often in *Dame Partlet*). [< Old French *Pertelote*, a woman's name (from its use as the name of a hen in Chaucer's *Nun's Priest's Tale*)]

part·ly (pärt′lē), *adv.* in part; in some measure or degree: *He is partly to blame.*
—**Syn. Partly, partially** mean in part or to a certain extent, not wholly or totally. **Partly** means not wholly or entirely what is described or stated, with all parts included or in all ways or respects, but only in part or in some measure or degree: *He is partly right.* **Partially** means not totally or generally, with no exceptions and nothing held back, but affecting only one part or to only a limited extent: *He is partially paralyzed.*

part music, music for two or more parts.

part·ner (pärt′nər; *see note below*), *n.* **1.** a person who shares. **2.** a member of a company or firm who shares the risks and profits of the business. **3.** a wife or husband. **4.** a companion in a dance. **5.** a player on the same team or side in a game.
partners, a framework of timber fitted around a hole in a ship's deck: *Our mainmast breaking in the partners of the upper deck, disabled both our pumps* (Alexander Hamilton).
—*v.t.* **1.** to associate as partners. **2.** to be the partner of: *David Blair . . . bears with grace the burden of partnering Miss Fonteyn* (Saturday Review). —*v.i.* to be a partner: *Mr. Adams partnered well and acted with a forthright manner* (London Times).
[Middle English variant of *parcener;* influenced by *part*] —**Syn.** *n.* **1.** sharer, partaker.
➔ The variant **pardner** (pärd′nər) is more common in literature than spoken dialect, although it was recorded in the 1700's as common in Cockney English.

part·ner·ship (pärt′nər ship), *n.* **1.** a being a partner; joint interest; association: *a business partnership, the partnership of marriage.* **2. a.** a company or firm with two or more members who share the risks and profits of the business: *a law partnership.* **b.** the contract that creates such a relation.

part of speech, one of the following groups into which words are divided: noun, pronoun, adjective, verb, adverb, preposition, conjunction, and interjection.
➔ **parts of speech.** One of the fundamental facts of English grammar is that a word may function as more than one part of speech: You may spell a *word* (noun), write a *word* picture (adjective), or *word* a message (verb). This shows that the part of speech to which a word belongs cannot be definitely decided by looking at the word by itself; we need to know how it is used.

par·took (pär tu̇k′), *v.* the past tense of **partake:** *He partook of food and drink.*

par·tridge (pär′trij), *n., pl.* **-tridg·es** or (*collectively*) **-tridge,** *adj.* —*n.* **1.** any of several kinds of game birds belonging to the same group as the quail, pheasant, and grouse. **2.** any of several birds in the United States, that nest on the ground and fly only short distances, as the ruffed grouse and the quail or bobwhite. **3.** any of several tinamous of South America. —*adj.* having a color pattern like that of a partridge, as certain chickens.
[Middle English *partrich* < Old French *perdriz* < Latin *perdix* < Greek *pérdix* partridge < *pérdesthai* to break wind (from the whirring noise of its wings)]

Hungarian Partridge (def. 1) (10 to 12 in. long)

par·tridge·ber·ry (pär′trij ber′ē), *n., pl.* **-ries. 1.** a North American trailing plant of the madder family, having evergreen leaves, fragrant white flowers, and scarlet berries. **2.** the berry.

partridge wood, the hard, beautifully marked, reddish wood of a tropical American tree of the pea family.

parts (pärts), *n.pl.* See under **part,** *n.*

part song, a song with parts in simple harmony for two or more voices especially one to be sung without an accompaniment.

part-time (pärt′tīm′), *adj.* for part of the usual time: *a part-time job.*

part time, part of the time.

part-tim·er (pärt′tī′mər), *n.* a part-time employee or worker: *The part-timer, once the auxiliary, has become the regular—and many part-timers have more than one job* (New York Times).

par·tu·ri·en·cy (pär tu̇r′ē ən sē, -tyu̇r′-), *n.* the state of being parturient.

par·tu·ri·ent (pär tu̇r′ē ənt, -tyu̇r′-), *adj.* **1.** bringing forth young; about to give birth to young. **2.** having to do with childbirth. **3.** ready to bring forth or produce a discovery, idea, principle, etc.

par·tu·ri·fa·cient (pär tu̇r′ə fā′shənt, -tyu̇r′-), *n.* something that hastens childbirth. —*adj.* hastening childbirth. [< Latin *parturīre* be in labor + *faciēns, -entis*, present participle of *facere* to make, do]

par·tu·ri·tion (pär′tu̇ rish′ən, -tyu̇-, -chu̇-), *n.* childbirth. [< Latin *parturītiō, -ōnis* < *parturīre* be in labor < *parere* to bear] —**Syn.** delivery.

part·way (pärt′wā′), *adv.* part of the way; partially; partly: *Mr. Kennedy, going partway back to a proposal he made eight days ago, said . . .* (New York Times).

par·ty (pär′tē), *n., pl.* **-ties,** *adj., v.,* **-tied, -ty·ing.** —*n.* **1.** a group of people doing something together: *a dinner party, a scouting party of three soldiers.* **2.** a gathering for pleasure: *On her birthday she had a party and invited her friends.* **3.** a group of people wanting the same kind of government or action: *the Democratic Party.* **4.** a person who takes part in, aids, or knows about: *He was a party to our plot.* **5.** each of the persons or sides in a contract, lawsuit, etc. **6.** *Informal.* a person: *Your party's on the telephone.* **7.** *Obsolete.* a part.
—*adj.* **1.** of or having to do with a party of people. **2.** of or belonging to a political party: *Bulganin was a party man put in charge of the army* (Wall Street Journal). **3.** *Heraldry.* (of a shield) divided into parts.
—*v.i. Informal.* to give, go to, or take part in a party or parties: *Newsmen . . . keep vigil over the Princess and Townsend partying nearby* (Newsweek).
[< Old French *partie*, (originally) feminine past participle of *partir* to divide < Latin *partīre* < *pars, partis* part]
—**Syn.** *n.* **1.** band. See **company.**
➔ See **person** for usage note.

par·ty-col·ored (pär′tē kul′ərd), *adj.* particolored.

par·ty-col·oured (pär′tē kul′ərd), *adj. Especially British.* parti-colored.

party girl, *U.S.* a prostitute.

par·ty·go·er (pär′tē gō′ər), *n.* a person who goes to parties.

par·ty·go·ing (pär′tē gō′ing), *n.* the activities of a partygoer; partying.

party line, 1. a telephone line by which two or more subscribers are connected with the exchange by one circuit. **2.** a boundary line between adjoining premises. **3.** the officially adopted policies of a political party: *the Administration is insisting on a* *military party line* (New York Times). **4.** the policies advocated and followed by the Communist Party: *The target was anything in books or pictures that didn't carry the party line* (Newsweek).

party liner, 1. a person who follows the policies of a political party. **2.** a person who follows the policies of the Communist Party.

party man, 1. a man belonging to a party. **2.** a man who adheres to his party, regardless of any individual opinion.

party poop·er (pü′pər), *U.S. Slang.* a killjoy; spoilsport; wet blanket.

party wall, *Law.* a wall dividing adjoining properties. Each owner has certain rights in it.

par·u·la (par′ə lə), *n.* an eastern North American warbler of blue, golden-brown, yellow, and white. [< New Latin *Parula* (diminutive) < Latin *pārus* titmouse]

pa·rure (pə rür′), *n.* a set of jewels or other ornaments to be worn together. [< French *parure* < *parer* to arrange < Latin *parāre* to prepare]

par value, the value of a stock, bond, note, etc., printed on it; face value.

par·ve (pär′və, pär vā′), *adj. Yiddish.* (of foods) neither meat nor dairy; neutral, as fish, eggs, and all fruits and vegetables.

par·ve·nu (pär′və nü, -nyü), *n.* **1.** a person who has risen above his class. **2.** a person who has risen to a higher place than he is fit for; upstart. —*adj.* of or like a parvenu. [< French *parvenu,* past participle of *parvenir* to arrive < Latin *pervenīre* < *per-* through + *venīre* to come]

par·ve·nue (pär′və nü, -nyü), *n.* a woman parvenu: *She has often been dismissed as an amoral parvenue, but there is much in her to admire* (Punch). [< French *parvenue,* feminine of *parvenu*]

par·vis (pär′vis), *n.* **1.** the enclosed area in front of a building, especially a cathedral, sometimes surrounded with colonnades: *In the recent production here, the audience sat in stands erected on the parvis in front of Notre Dame* (New Yorker). **2.** a single portico or colonnade in front of a church. **3.** a room over a church porch. [< Old French *parevis,* alteration of *pareïs* paradise < Latin *paradīsus* paradise, (in Medieval Latin, the name given to the atrium of St. Peter's in Rome and to similar courts of churches)]

par·vo·lin (pär′və lin), *n.* parvoline.

par·vo·line (pär′və lēn, -lin), *n.* an oily liquid obtained from certain shales and bituminous coals, or as a ptomaine from decaying mackerel and horse flesh. *Formula:* $C_9H_{13}N$ [< Latin *parvus* little]

Par·zi·val (pär′tsi fäl), *n.* Parsifal.

pas (pä), *n. French.* **1.** a step or movement in dancing. **2.** a kind of dance.

PAS (no periods), para-aminosalicylic acid, a drug used with streptomycin or isoniazid for tuberculosis. *Formula:* $C_7H_7O_3$

Pas·ca·gou·la (pas′kə gü′lə), *n., pl.* **-la** or **-las.** a member of an American Indian tribe that formerly inhabited part of the Gulf Coast of Mississippi.

pas·cal celery (pas′kəl, -kal; pas kal′), celery marketed without bleaching.

Pas·cal's law (pas kalz′, pas′kəlz), (in hydrostatics) the law that in a fluid at rest the pressure is the same in all directions and that, except from the differences of pressure produced by the action of gravity, atmospheric pressure on gas enclosed within a balloon is the same throughout. [< Blaise *Pascal,* 1623-1662, a French physicist and philosopher, who formulated it]

Pasch (pask), *n. Archaic.* **1.** the Jewish feast of the Passover. **2.** the Christian feast of Easter. [< Old French *pasque,* learned borrowing from Late Latin *pascua,* alteration of Latin *pascha* < Greek *páscha* the Passover < Hebrew *pesaḥ*]

pas·chal (pas′kəl), *adj.* **1.** of or having to do with the Passover. **2.** of or having to do with Easter; used in Easter celebrations.

paschal candle or **taper** (in the Roman Catholic Church) a large wax candle placed at the side of the altar, there to remain until Ascension Day.

paschal lamb, (in the Bible) the lamb killed and eaten at Passover, commemorated at the modern Seder by a bone kept on the table with other symbolic foods. Exodus 12:3-14.

Paschal Lamb, Christ or any representation of Him.

paschal moon, the first full moon on or after the vernal equinox. The Roman Catholic Church dates Easter as the first Sunday after the paschal moon.

pas·cu·al (pas′kyů əl), *adj.* growing in pastures. [< Latin *pascuum* pasture]

pas d'ac·tion (pä′ dȧk syôɴ′), *French.* a dance used in ballet as a narrative.

pas de bour·rée (pä′də bü rā′), *French.* a light, rapid ballet movement of one foot in front of or behind the other: *Her footwork proved exemplary, with lightly scurrying pas de bourrées and a notable delicacy in beaten steps* (London Times).

pas de chat (pä′də shä′), *French.* a springing ballet movement in which one foot jumps over the other while moving diagonally across the stage.

pas de deux (pä′ də dœ′), *French.* a dance or figure in ballet for two persons.

pas de trois (pä′ də trwȧ′), *French.* a dance or figure in ballet for three persons.

pas du tout (pä′ dʏ tü′), *French.* not at all; not in the least.

pa·se·ar (pä′sā är′), *n. Southwestern U.S. Slang.* a walk; promenade; airing. [< Spanish *pasear* to promenade]

pa·se·o (pä sā′ō), *n., pl.* **-se·os** (-sā′ōs). *Spanish.* **1.** a place to walk; promenade: *The crowds stroll on the paseo, chattering, laughing, joking, and ogling* (Atlantic). **2.** a stroll.

pash[1] (pash), *Dialect.* —*v.t.* **1.** to smash; shatter. **2.** to strike with a smashing or violent blow. —*v.i.* to dash or strike violently, as waves or rain.
—*n.* **1.** a smashing blow. **2.** a crashing fall.

pash[2] (pash), *n. Dialect.* the head.

pa·sha (pə shä′, pash′ə, pä′shə), *n.* **1.** a former Turkish title of rank. It was put after the name of civil or military officials of high rank. **2.** a person having this title. Also, **pacha.** [< Turkish *paşa,* variant of *başa* < *baş* head]

pa·sha·dom (pə shä′dəm, pash′ə-, pä′shə-), *n.* the office, power, or territory of a pasha: *My own memories of pashadom in its ascendency are disagreeably larded with paunchiness ... and playboy ostentation* (Atlantic).

pa·sha·lik or **pa·sha·lic** (pə shä′lik), *n.* the jurisdiction of a pasha. [< Turkish *paşalık* < *paşa* (see PASHA) + *-lık* -ship]

Pash·to (push′tō), *n., pl.* **-tos. 1.** the language of Afghanistan and of the Pathan tribes of Pakistan: *speaking a language that only a few non-Pathans, usually British, ever learned—Pashto* (New York Times). **2.** a Pathan. [< Persian *pashtō* Afghan]

Pash·tu (push′tü), *n.* Pashto.

Pash·tun (push tün′), *n.* Pathan.

pas·i·graph·ic (pas′ə graf′ik), *adj.* of or having to do with pasigraphy: *The figures of arithmetic are already pasigraphic* (Critical Review).

pas·i·graph·i·cal (pas′ə graf′ə kəl), *adj.* pasigraphic.

pa·sig·ra·phy (pə sig′rə fē), *n.* any of various systems of writing with characters representing ideas instead of words, that may be understood and used by all nations. [< Greek *pâsi* for all, dative plural of *pâs* all + *gráphein* write]

Pa·siph·a·ë (pə sif′ē ē), *n. Greek Legend.* the daughter of Helios, wife of Minos (of Crete), and mother of Ariadne and the Minotaur.

pa·so·do·ble (pä′sō dō′blā), *n. Spanish.* **1.** a brisk march in a quick 2/4 rhythm, frequently played at bullfights. **2.** a one-step dance done to this rhythm.

Pasque (pask), *n.* Pasch.

pasque·flow·er (pask′flou′ər), *n.* any of several anemones with purple or white flowers that bloom early in the spring. [< *pasque* (see PASCH) + *fleur* flower < Old French *flour*]

pas·quil (pas′kwəl), *n.* a pasquinade.

pas·quin·ade (pas′kwə nād′), *n., v.,* **-ad·ed, -ad·ing.** —*n.* a publicly posted satirical writing; lampoon. —*v.t.* to attack by lampoons.
[< French *pasquinade* < Italian *pasquinata* < *Pasquino,* name of a statue where lampoons were posted] —**pas′quin·ad′er,** *n.*

pass[1] (pas, päs), *v.,* **passed, passed** or **past, pass·ing,** *n.* —*v.t.* **1.** to go by; move past; leave behind: *We passed the big truck. Many people pass our house every day.* **2.** to cause to go from one to another; hand around: *The old coin was passed around for everyone to see. The owner passed the business to his partner.* **3.** to get through or by: *We passed the dangerous section of the road successfully.* **4.** to go across or over: *The horse passed the stream.* **5.** to put or direct (a rope, string, etc.): *He passed a rope around his waist for support. Pass your hand over the velvet and feel how soft it is.* **6.** to cause to go, move onward, or proceed: *to pass troops in review, pass dishes under water.* **7.** to discharge from the body. **8.** to be successful in (an examination, a course, etc.): *Jim passed Latin.* **9.** to cause or allow to go through something; sanction or approve: *to pass accounts as correct.* **10.** to ratify or enact: *to pass a bill or law.* **11.** to be approved by (a lawmaking body, etc.): *The new law passed the city council.* **12.** to go beyond; exceed; surpass: *His strange story passes belief.* **13.** to use; spend: *We passed the days happily.* **14.** to cause to go about; circulate: *to pass a counterfeit bill.* **15.** to cause to be accepted or received: *The inspector passed the item after examining it.* **16.** to express; pronounce: *A judge passes sentence on guilty persons. The reviewer passed heavy criticism on the book.* **17.** to let go without action or notice; leave unmentioned: *to pass an insult.* **18.** to leave out; omit, especially payment of (a dividend, etc.). **19. a.** to transfer (the ball, puck, etc.) in football, hockey, and other games. **b.** (in baseball) to pitch four balls to (a batter), forcing him to walk. **20.** to refuse (a hand, chance to bid, etc.) while playing cards. **21.** to thrust. **22.** to promise: *to pass one's word.*
—*v.i.* **1.** to go on; move on; make one's way: *The parade passed. The salesman passed from house to house.* **2.** to go from one to another: *His estate passed to his children.* **3.** to go away; depart: *The time for action has passed. The years pass rapidly.* **4.** to be successful in an examination. **5.** to discharge waste matter from the body. **6.** to be approved by a court, lawmaking body, etc.; be ratified: *The bill passed.* **7.** to come to an end; die: *King Arthur passed in peace. Dynasties pass.* **8. a.** to change: *Water passes from a liquid to a solid state when it freezes.* **b.** to be interchanged or transacted: *Friendly words passed between them.* **9.** to take place; happen: *Tell me all that has passed.* **10.** to be handed about; be in circulation: *Money passes from person to person.* **11.** to be accepted (for or as): *Use silk or a material that will pass for silk. Mr. Crook moved to another city where he passed by the name of Mr. Smith.* **12.** to give a judgment or opinion: *The judges passed on each contestant.* **13.** to go without notice: *He was rude, but let that pass.* **14.** to throw a football, basketball, etc., or shoot a hockey puck from one player to another. **15.** to give up a chance to play a hand, refuse to play a hand, or refuse to bid in playing cards. **16.** (in fencing) to make a thrust.

bring to pass, to cause to be; accomplish: *to bring a miracle to pass.*

come to pass, to take place; happen: *The prophecy came to pass.*

pass away, a. to die: *Mr. Richard Williams ... passed away ... at the great age of ninety years* (Law Times). **b.** to come to an end: *Thus passed the winter away so rapidly* (Frederick Marryat). **c.** to while away: *One day is passed away here very like its defunct predecessor* (Thackeray).

pass by, a. to go or proceed past: *The countrymen ... would all look up When she pass'd by* (Robert Southey). **b.** to disregard; ignore: *His glory is to pass by an offence* (Proverbs 19:11). **c.** to fail to have an effect on: *The ordinary tourist is seen in all his ordinariness in these circumstances. The Romantic Revolution has passed him by* (London Times).

pass off, a. to go away; disappear gradually: *The smell of the paint will pass off in a few days.* **b.** to take place; be done: *In every sense the festival passed off as its promoters must have desired* (London Times). **c.** to get accepted; pretend to be: *He passed himself off as a wealthy man.* **d.** to palm off; impose: *The applicants pass off their goods for those of the Baron de Geer* (Law Times). **e.** to parry: *The young man passed off lightly all such reference* (Algernon Gissing).

pass on, a. to proceed; advance: *Pass on, weak heart, and leave me where I lie* (Tennyson). **b.** to send or hand to the next member of a series: *Please read this and pass it on.* **c.** to die: *Well, how long is it since Fletch passed on?* (John O'Hara). **d.** to pass judgment on; express approval or disapproval of: *"I never bought a dress he didn't pass on," she added* (New York Times).

pass out, a. *Informal.* to faint; lose consciousness: *We carried him home after he passed out.* **b.** *British.* to undergo (a course of instruction) successfully: *At last, I was able to "pass out," and found myself . . . a second lieutenant in the King's Royal Rifle Corps* (Harold Macmillan). **c.** to hand out or distribute: *Librarians . . . are willing to pass out catalogs that have won their confidence* (Publishers' Weekly).

pass over, a. to fail to notice; overlook; disregard: *to pass over a mistake.* **b.** to die: *to pass over early in life.* **c.** to ignore the claims of (a person) to promotion, a post, honor, etc.: *He was passed over by the Army Promotion Board.* **d.** *Informal.* (of Negroes) to be accepted as white: . . . *numerous persons with only a few Negroid traits annually "pass over" and are absorbed into the dominant Caucasoid population* (Beals and Hoijer). **e.** to hand over to another; transfer: *Geology here passes over the continuation of the history of man to Archeology* (James Dwight Dana).

pass up, *U.S.* to fail to take advantage of; give up; refuse: *to pass up the opportunity to go to college, to pass up dessert at dinner.*

—*n.* **1.** the act of passing; passage: *With this arrangement we have a 90 per cent chance of intercepting every pass of a satellite which is higher than 300 miles* (Scientific American). **2.** success in an examination, test, or the like; passing an examination but without honors: *If . . . after the dropping of a pass in Latin as an entrance qualification, Latin would continue to be taught . . . there need be no fears* (New Scientist). **3.** a permission or license to pass: *No one can get into the fort without a pass. The soldier was home on a pass. The officer had a safe-conduct pass through the enemy lines to negotiate the release of U.N. prisoners.* **4.** a state; condition: *Things have come to a pretty pass when such trifles are scrutinized* (John L. Motley). **5.** a free ticket: *a pass to the circus.* **6.** a motion of the hands, as by a hypnotist: *Alexis, after a few passes from Dr. Elliotson, despises pain, reads with the back of his head, sees miles off* (Thackeray). **7.** a sleight-of-hand motion; manipulation; trick: *The magician made passes in the air.* **8.** a throw or transfer of a ball, puck, etc., as in football or hockey. **9.** (in baseball) the pitching of four balls to a batter, forcing him to walk; a walk: *The passes were bad enough but there was no excuse for the wild pitch* (New York Times). **10.** a thrust in fencing. **11.** a refusal of the opportunity to bet, bid, raise, double, etc., in playing cards. **12.** *Informal.* flirt. **13.** *Archaic.* accomplishment; completion. **14.** *Obsolete.* a sally of wit.

make passes at, to attempt to kiss or otherwise flirt with: *Men seldom make passes At girls who wear glasses* (Dorothy Parker).

[< Old French *passer* < Vulgar Latin *passāre* < Latin *passus, -ūs* a step; see PACE[1]]

—**Syn.** *v.t.* **10.** confirm. **12.** transcend. –*v.i.* **1.** proceed, advance. **3.** disappear, vanish.

➔ **passed, past.** The past tense and past participle of *pass* are *passed* (He *passed* the first post. He had *passed*), though *past* is fairly common as the participle. *Past* is the adjective (*past* favors), preposition (*past* the crisis), and adverb (*past* due. They went *past*).

pass[2] (pas, päs), *n.* **1.** a narrow road, path, way, channel, etc.; narrow passage through mountains: *Many passes have become great roads of history. They had reached one of those very narrow passes between two tall stones, which performed the office of stile* (George Eliot). **2.** a navigable channel, as at the mouth or in the delta of a river. [< Old French *pas* step, pace, track < Latin *passus, -ūs.* Doublet of PACE[1].]

pass., **1.** here and there (in a work cited; Latin, *passim*). **2.** passenger. **3.** passive.

pass·a·ble (pas′ə bəl, päs′-), *adj.* **1.** fairly good; moderate: *a passable knowledge of geography.* **2.** that can be passed: *The ford was not passable.* **3.** current; valid: *passable coin.* **4.** that may be enacted: *a passable bill.* [< Old French *passable* < *passer* to pass] —**pass′a·ble·ness,** *n.* —**Syn. 1.** tolerable, mediocre, middling.

pass·a·bly (pas′ə blē, päs′-), *adv.* fairly; moderately: *The passably placed: men and women who work, using some of their old skills, though not on the old level* (Atlantic).

pas·sa·ca·glia (pä′sə käl′yə), *n.* **1.** an old form of dance tune of Spanish origin, constructed on a recurring theme, usually a ground bass, in slow triple rhythm. **2.** the dance performed to this. [< Italian *passacaglia* < Spanish *pasacalle* < *pasar* pass + *calle* street]

pas·sa·caille (pȧ sȧ kä′yə), *n. French.* passacaglia.

pas·sade (pə sād′), *n.* **1.** (in horsemanship) a turn or course of a horse backward or forward on the same ground. **2.** (in fencing) passado. [< Middle French *passade* (originally) action of passing < Italian *passata* < *passare* to pass < Vulgar Latin *passāre*]

pas·sa·do (pə sä′dō), *n., pl.* **-dos** or **-does.** (in fencing) a forward thrust with the sword, one foot being advanced at the same time. [alteration of Middle French *passade,* or Spanish *pasada* < Italian *passata;* see PASSADE]

Passado exhibited by fencer on left

pas·sage[1] (pas′ij), *n., v.,* **-saged, -sag·ing.** —*n.* **1.** a hall or way through a building; passageway: *And face with an undaunted tread the long black passage up to bed* (Robert Louis Stevenson). **2.** a means of passing; way through: *The police opened a passage through the crowd for the governor.* **3.** right, liberty, or leave to pass: *The guard refused us passage.* **4. a.** a passing; a going or moving onward: *the passage of time.* **b.** a passing from one place or state to another: *the passage from sleep to wakefulness.* **5.** a piece from a speech or writing: *a passage from the Bible.* **6.** a going across; voyage: *We had a stormy passage across the Atlantic.* **7.** a ticket that entitles the holder to transportation, especially by boat: *to secure passage for Europe.* **8.** a making into law by a favoring vote of a legislature: *The passage of the bill by both houses of Congress was forecast by the political reporter.* **9.** what passes between persons. **10.** *Archaic.* an occurrence, incident, or event: *It is no act of common passage* (Shakespeare). **11. a.** an exchange of blows or a dispute. **b.** an amorous encounter. **12.** *Music.* a phrase or other division of a piece of music. **13.** a movement of the bowels. **14.** *Obsolete.* death.

—*v.i.* **1.** to make a passage, as in a ship; move across; pass; cross. **2.** to carry on a passage or dispute.

[< Old French *passage* < *passer* to pass]

—**Syn.** *n.* **1.** corridor. **2.** road, path, route.

pas·sage[2] (pas′ij), *v.,* **-saged, -sag·ing,** *n.* —*v.i.* **1.** (of a horse) to move sideways, in obedience to pressure of the rider's leg on the opposite side. **2.** (of a rider) to cause a horse to do this. —*v.t.* to cause (a horse) to passage.

—*n.* a movement of a horse sideways: *She guided Jubilee through . . . such dressage movements as . . . passage* (Newsweek).

[< French *passager,* alteration of *passéger* to promenade < Italian *passeggiare* < Latin *passus;* see PACE[1]]

passage at arms, an exchange of blows; quarrel: . . . *part of the debate was a smart passage at arms between his Grace and Lord Bramwell* (Manchester Examiner).

passage of arms, passage at arms.

pas·sage·way (pas′ij wā′), *n.* a way along which a person or thing can pass; passage: *Halls and alleys are passageways.* —**Syn.** corridor.

pas·sage·work (pas′ij wėrk′), *n.* a musical passage consisting for the most part of flourishes, as arpeggios, double octaves, etc., intended for virtuoso display: *In Chopin's Revolutionary Study he thundered until his tone almost burst and the passagework disintegrated into a meaningless whirr* (London Times).

Pas·sa·ma·quod·dy (pas′ə mə kwod′ē), *n., pl.* **-dy** or **-dies.** **1.** a member of a tribe of the Passamaquoddy Bay region. **2.** the Algonkian language of this tribe.

pas·sant (pas′ənt), *adj. Heraldry.* walking and looking to the right side: *a lion passant.* [< Old French *passant* walking, present participle of *passer* to pass]

passant gardant, *Heraldry.* walking, but with the head turned and looking out from the escutcheon.

passant regardant, *Heraldry.* walking, but with the head turned and looking backward.

pass·back (pas′bak′, päs′-), *n. Sports.* the moving or passing of the ball behind oneself or away from the goal, as in the centering of a football.

pass·band (pas′band′, päs′-), *n. Electronics.* the band of frequencies that will pass through a circuit, filter, or other device without much attenuation.

pass·book (pas′bu̇k′, päs′-), *n.* **1.** a small book in which a bank keeps an account of what a person deposits and withdraws; bankbook. In the United States passbooks are now used chiefly for savings accounts. **2.** a customer's book in which a merchant makes entries of goods sold on credit. **3.** identity papers required of nonwhites by the South African government.

pass degree, *Especially British.* a degree without honors from a college, university, or school.

pas·sé (pa sā′, pas′ā), *adj.* **1.** past. **2.** past its usefulness; out-of-date: *Cloak-and-dagger techniques and mass employment of low-level agents are passé* (Newsweek). [< French *passé,* past participle of *passer* to pass] —**Syn. 2.** antiquated.

passed (past, päst), *adj.* **1.** that has passed or has been passed. **2.** having passed an examination. **3.** qualified for promotion by examination but waiting for a vacancy in the higher grade: *a passed assistant surgeon in the navy.* **4.** (of a dividend) not paid at the proper time.

passed ball, (in baseball) a pitched ball, not touched by the bat, on which a runner or runners advance to the next base or bases because of the catcher's failure to stop the ball.

pas·sel (pas′əl), *n.* a group of indeterminate number; parcel: *A whole passel of people kissed the bride* (Atlantic).

passe·ment (pas′mənt), *Archaic.* —*n.* lace (as of gold or silver), braid, or gimp for trimming. —*v.t.* to trim with passement. [< Middle French *passement* < Old French *passer* to pass]

passe·men·terie (pas men′trē; *French* pȧs mäɴ trē′), *n.* trimming made of beads, braid, cord, gimp, or the like, used for dressmaking, millinery, etc. [< French *passementerie* < Middle French *passementer,* verb < *passement;* see PASSEMENT]

pas·sen·ger (pas′ən jər), *n.* **1.** a traveler in an airplane, car, bus, train, boat, etc. **2.** *Archaic.* **a.** a passer-by. **b.** a traveler; wayfarer: *a foot passenger. The passengers that pass through the land* (Ezekiel 39:15). [alteration of Middle English *passager* < Old French *passagier* < *passage* passage]

pas·sen·ger-mile (pas′ən jər mīl′), *n.* the transportation of one passenger for one mile: *You'll be flying the world's most modern airliner . . . proved by more than a billion passenger-miles* (New Yorker).

passenger pigeon, a kind of wild pigeon of North America, with a long, narrow tail, able to fly for long periods at a time, usually in very large flocks. Although a fairly common item of food in the central United States in the 1800's, the passenger pigeon is now extinct.

passe par·tout (pas′ pär tü′, päs′), **1. a.** a frame for a picture consisting of strips of gummed paper that fasten the glass to the backing. **b.** the paper prepared for this purpose. **2.** that which passes, or by means of which one can pass everywhere, as a master key. [< French *passe-partout* pass everywhere; *passe,* imperative of *passer* to pass; *partout* (literally) through all < *par* (< Latin *per*) + *tout* (< Latin *tōtus*)]

passe·pied (pȧs pyā′), *n. French.* **1.** a lively French dance of the 1600's and 1700's which originated in Brittany and later became a formal and court dance. **2.** the music for this dance: *He ran flawlessly through the gavottes, passepieds, and bourrées . . . that are to be found in Bach's "Overture in the French Manner"* (New Yorker).

pass·er (pas′ər, päs′-), *n.* **1.** a passer-by: *the black-robed priests, who mixed with the passers on the narrow wooden sidewalk* (William Dean Howells). **2.** (in sports) a player who passes.

pass·er-by (pas′ər bī′, päs′-), *n., pl.* **passers-by.** a person that passes by: *That cry is so common . . . that the passers-by never turned their heads* (Rudyard Kipling).

pas·ser·ine (pas′ər in, -ə rīn), *adj.* belonging to or having to do with the very large group of perching birds, including more than half of all birds, such as the warblers, sparrows, chickadees, wrens, thrushes, and swallows: *Among passerine birds the raven has the widest range* (Alfred R. Wallace). —*n.* a perching bird. [< Latin *passerīnus* < *passer, -eris* sparrow]

pas seul (pä sœl′), *French.* a dance movement or dance for one performer; solo dance: *The ferocious pas seul in which Tommy Roll, as the doomed Johnny, expresses his zest for life with the desperation that is the prerogative of the condemned* (New Yorker).

pas·si·bil·i·ty (pas′ə bil′ə tē), *n.* the quality of being passible: *The very truth that came by Jesus Christ may be said to be summed up in the passibility of God* (Andrew M. Fairbairn).

pas·si·ble (pas′ə bəl), *adj.* capable of suffering or feeling; susceptible of sensation or of emotion. [< Old French *passible,* learned borrowing from Latin *passibilis* < *passus,* past participle of *patī* to suffer]

pas·si·flo·ra·ceous (pas′i flô rā′shəs, -flō-), *adj.* belonging to a family of dicotyledonous, herbaceous or woody plants found chiefly in tropical regions, typified by the passionflower. [< New Latin *Passifloraceae* the family name < *Passiflore* the genus name, adapted from *flos passionis* passionflower]

pas·sim (pas′im), *adv. Latin.* here and there; in various places.

➔ **Passim** is used in footnotes in referring to material found in several places in some book or books: "Jespersen, *Language, passim.*"

pass·ing (pas′ing, päs′-), *adj.* **1.** that passes. **2.** transient; fleeting: *a passing smile.* **3.** cursory; incidental: *passing fancy.* **4.** that is now happening: *the passing scene.* **5. a.** allowing a person to pass an examination, test, course, etc.: *75 will be a passing mark.* **b.** in charge of testing and passing candidates; examining. **6.** *Archaic.* surpassing; preëminent: *'Tis a passing shame* (Shakespeare).
—*n.* **1.** act of one that passes; a going by; departure. **2.** a means or place of passing: *A river Runs in three loops about her living-place; And o'er it are three passings* (Tennyson). **3.** death: *The passing of Einstein was a great blow to science.*
in passing, by the way: *It may be remarked, in passing, that . . .* (Charlotte Brontë).
—*adv.* surpassingly; very: *Our love was passing fair and wove a wondrous spell* (Harper's).
—**pass′ing·ly,** *adv.*
—**Syn.** *adj.* **2.** transitory.

passing bell, 1. a bell tolled to announce that a death has just occurred or that a funeral is taking place. **2.** a portent or sign of the passing away of anything: *. . . the passing bell of tyranny* (Shelley).

passing note, passing tone.

passing tone, a musical tone not essential to the harmony, introduced between two successive notes in order to produce a melodic transition.

pas·sion (pash′ən), *n.* **1.** a very strong feeling; emotion: *The opera star sang with great passion. Passions have their root in that which is crippled, blemished, or insecure within us* (Harper's). **2.** a fit or mood of some emotion, especially violent anger; rage: *He flew into a violent passion and abused me mercilessly* (H.G. Wells). *She broke into a passion of tears* (Dickens). **3. a.** love between a man and a woman; sexual desire: *I love thee so, that . . . Nor wit nor reason can my passion hide* (Shakespeare). **b.** a person who is the object of such love or desire. **4. a.** a very strong liking or desire: *She has a passion for music. Her passion for caraway seeds, for instance, was uncontrollable* (Lytton Strachey). **b.** the object of such a passion: *Music is her passion.* **5.** *Archaic.* suffering. **6.** Often, **Passion. a.** the sufferings of Jesus on the cross or after the Last Supper. **b.** the story of these sufferings in the Bible. **c.** a musical setting of this story: *Bach's Passion According to Saint Matthew.* **d.** a representation in art of the sufferings of Christ. **7. a.** the fact or condition of being affected by external force: *The word passion signifies the receiving any action, in a large philosophical sense* (Isaac Watts). **b.** an effect produced by action from without. [< Old French *passiun,* and *passion,* learned borrowing from Latin *passiō, -ōnis* < *patī* to suffer] —**Syn. 1.** See **feeling.**

pas·sion·al (pash′ə nəl), *adj.* of or having to do with passion or the passions: *passional crimes.* —*n.* a book containing accounts of the sufferings (passions) of saints and martyrs, for reading on their festival days.

pas·sion·ar·y (pash′ə ner′ē), *n., pl.* **-ar·ies.** passional.

pas·sion·ate (pash′ə nit), *adj.* **1.** having or showing strong feelings: *The fathers of our country were passionate believers in the rights of man.* **2.** easily moved to a fit or mood of some emotion, especially to anger: *My brother was passionate, and had often beaten me, which I took extremely amiss* (Benjamin Franklin). **3.** resulting from strong feeling: *He made a passionate speech.* **4.** having or showing a very strong love, as of a man for a woman: *a passionate lover.* [< Medieval Latin *passionatus* < Latin *passiō* passion] —**pas′sion·ate·ly,** *adv.* —**pas′sion·ate·ness,** *n.* —**Syn. 2.** quick-tempered, irascible, fiery.

pas·sion·flow·er (pash′ən flou′ər), *n.* **1.** any of a group of mostly American climbing plants with flowers supposed to suggest the crown of thorns, the wounds, the nails, etc., of Christ's crucifixion. Passionflowers are grown for their edible, yellowish or purple fruits and their large, showy flowers. **2.** the flower of any of these plants. [translation of New Latin *flos passionis* flower of the Passion (from the imagined likeness of parts of the flower to the instruments of Christ's Passion)]

Passionflower (def. 2)

pas·sion·fruit (pash′ən früt′), *n.* the fruit of a passionflower, when edible, as the maypop.

pas·sion·ful (pash′ən fəl), *adj.* passionate.

Pas·sion·ist (pash′ə nist), *n.* a member of the Congregation of Discalced (i.e., barefooted) Clerks of the Most Holy Cross and Passion of Our Lord Jesus Christ, a Roman Catholic order founded by St. Paul of the Cross, in Italy, in 1725. The members are pledged to the utmost zeal in keeping fresh the memory of Christ's passion.

pas·sion·less (pash′ən lis), *adj.* without passion; calm: *The Hellenic world emerges . . . half history, half fable. How the great names rise, passionless as marble, bathed in cloudless noon* (Atlantic). —**pas′sion·less·ly,** *adv.* —**pas′sion·less·ness,** *n.*

passion pit, *U.S. Slang.* **1.** a drive-in motion-picture theater. **2.** any motion-picture theater.

Passion Play or **passion play,** a play representing the sufferings and death of Christ. One is given every ten years at Oberammergau, Germany.

Passion Sunday, the second Sunday before Easter Sunday. It is the fifth Sunday in Lent. *Durand tells us, that on Passion Sunday the Church began her public grief, remembering the Mystery of the Cross* (John Brand).

Pas·sion·tide (pash′ən tīd′), *n.* the last two weeks of Lent.

passion vine, the passionflower.

Passion Week, 1. the second week before Easter; fifth week in Lent, between Passion Sunday and Palm Sunday. **2.** (formerly) the week before Easter; Holy Week.

pas·si·vate (pas′ə vāt), *v.t.,* **-vat·ed, -vat·ing.** to make chemically passive.

pas·si·va·tion (pas′ə vā′shən), *n.* **1.** the act or process of passivating. **2.** the state of being passivated.

pas·sive (pas′iv), *adj.* **1.** not acting in return; being acted on without itself acting: *passive disposition.* **2.** not resisting: *the passive obedience of a slave. It would not be a passive condition, but eminently constructive* (London Times). **3.** *Grammar.* showing the subject as acted upon. In "The window was broken by John," *was broken* is in the passive voice. **4.** not readily entering into chemical combination; inert; inactive. **5.** of or having to do with an infection or other abnormal condition of the body, as of an organ in the body, that causes reduced vitality and imperfect muscular reaction. **6.** (of a note, bond, share of stock, etc.) not bearing interest, but entitling the owner or holder to some future benefit or claim.
—*n.* **1.** a verb form or verbal construction that shows the subject as acted on. **2.** the passive voice. *Abbr.:* pass. **3.** a person or thing that is passive.
[< Latin *passīvus* < *patī* to suffer] —**pas′sive·ness,** *n.*
—**Syn.** *adj.* **1.** impassive. **2.** submissive, unresisting, patient.

passive defense, military or civil defense designed to cope with the effects of an attack, as distinguished from one designed to prevent its occurrence: *The second phase of defense is passive defense which Dr. Teller described as defense by shelters and similar means* (Bulletin of Atomic Scientists).

passive immunity, immunity conferred by injecting into one organism antibodies of a serum obtained from another organism.

pas·sive·ly (pas′iv lē), *adv.* **1.** in a passive manner. **2.** as a passive verb. **3.** in the passive voice.

passive resistance, peaceful refusal to comply with, or calculated neglect of, a law or laws, injunction, etc., especially as a form of resistance to a government or other authority. It may take such forms as sit-ins.

passive satellite, an artificial satellite that reflects a signal but does not receive it and transmit it again.

passive voice, a form of transitive verbs or verbal constructions which is regularly used to represent the subject as acted upon, not acting. In "A letter was written by me," *was written* is in the passive voice.

pas·siv·ism (pas′ə viz əm), *n.* **1.** the quality of being passive. **2. a.** passive resistance, as a concept. **b.** the practice of passive resistance.

pas·siv·ist (pas′ə vist), *n.* a person who favors or advocates passivism.

pas·siv·i·ty (pa siv′ə tē), *n.* a being passive; lack of action; nonresistance: *But basic passivity kept him from those heights and depths which the really good writer now and again reaches* (Newsweek).

pass·key (pas′kē′, päs′-), *n., pl.* **-keys. 1.** a key for opening several locks, especially all the locks of a particular set or in a given building; master key. **2.** a private key.

pass law, one of a number of laws in South Africa requiring that all native Africans must carry passes to move about freely: *They were the result of a deliberate act of protest by Africans against oppressive legislation exemplified in the pass laws* (Manchester Guardian).

pass·less (pas′lis, päs′-), *adj.* **1.** impassable. **2.** without a pass, or license to pass.

pass·o·ver (pas′ō′vər, päs′-), *n.* **1.** the paschal lamb, the sacrifice formerly offered in the Temple at Passover time. II Chronicles 30:15. **2.** Christ, the Paschal Lamb: *Christ our passover is sacrificed for us* (I Corinthians 5:7).

Pass·o·ver (pas′ō′vər, päs′-), *n.* an eight-day Jewish festival beginning on the eve of the 15th of Nisan (March-April), commemorating the escape of the Hebrews from Egypt; Feast of Unleavened Bread; Pesach. The festival is marked by the celebration of the Seder service and the eating of matzoth, or unleavened bread. Exodus 12. [< verbal phrase *pass over,* translation of Hebrew *pesaḥ* (in reference to the "passing over" or sparing of the Hebrews in Egypt when God killed the first-born children of the Egyptians). Compare PASCH.]

pass·port (pas′pôrt, -pōrt; päs′-), *n.* **1. a.** a paper or book giving official permission to travel in a certain country, under the protection of one's own government. **b.** a document granted in the 1920's and 1930's by an authority of the League of Nations to various persons who had no national identity, by means of which travel through or residence in certain countries was made possible. **2.** anything that gives one admission or acceptance: *An interest in gardening was a passport to my aunt's favor.* **3.** a document granting a ship, especially a neutral merchant ship in time of war, permission to enter certain waters freely, or requesting such permission for it. **4.** *Archaic.* a safe-conduct, especially one permitting an enemy to leave or pass through a given country or territory.
—*v.t.* to supply or provide with a passport.
[< Middle French *passeport* < *passe,* imperative of Old French *passer* to pass[1] + *port* harbor, port[1]]

pass·port·less (pas′pôrt′lis, -pōrt′-; päs′-), *adj.* without passport: *passportless travelers.*

pass-through (pas′thrü′, päs′-), *n.* **1.** a rectangular opening in the wall between two rooms, as between a kitchen and a dining room or pantry, to permit dishes and food to be passed through upon a shelf or counter space provided there. **2.** the complete transfer of an increase in the cost of a raw material to the ultimate consumer through proportional price increases by the intermediate processors, manufacturers, and dealers.

pas·sus (pas′əs), *n., pl.* **-sus** or **-sus·es.** a section or division of a story, poem, etc.; canto. [< Medieval Latin *passus* < Latin *passus, -ūs* a step; see PACE[1]]

pass·word (pas′wėrd′, päs′-), *n.* a secret word that allows a person speaking it to pass a guard.

past (past, päst), *adj.* **1.** gone by; ended; over: *Our troubles are past.* **2.** just gone by: *The past year was full of trouble.* **3.** having served a term in office: *a past president.* **4.** indicating time gone by, or former action or state: *the past tense, a past participle.*
—*n.* **1. a.** the time gone by; time before: *Life began far back in the past.* **b.** what has happened in the time gone by: *to forget the past. History is a study of the past.* **2.** a past life or history: *Our country has a glorious past.* **3.** a person's past life, especially if hidden or unknown. **4.** the past tense or a verb form in it. *Abbr.:* p.
—*prep.* **1.** farther on than; beyond: *The arrow went past the mark.* **2.** later than; after: *It is past noon.* **3.** beyond in number, amount, age, or degree. **4.** beyond the ability, range, scope, etc., of: *absurd fancies that are past belief.* **5.** no longer capable of: *I was almost past making any exertion* (W. H. Hudson).
—*adv.* so as to pass by or beyond; by: *The cars go past once an hour.*
—*v.* passed; a past participle of **pass**[1].
—**Syn.** *adj.* **2.** bygone, preceding, foregoing.
➔ See **pass** for usage note.

pas·ta (päs′tä), *n. Italian.* any of various foods, as macaroni, spaghetti, etc., made of flour, water, salt, and sometimes milk or eggs, shaped in tubular or other forms and dried.

past absolute, the simple past tense or preterit.

past-due (past′dü′, -dyü′), *adj.* due some time ago; past maturity: *Past-due accounts receivable at the end of 1957 . . . stood at about the same percentage level as a year earlier* (Wall Street Journal).

paste[1] (pāst), *n., v.,* **past·ed, past·ing.** —*n.* **1.** a mixture such as flour and water boiled together, that will stick paper together, stick it to a wall, etc. **2. a.** dough for pastry, made with butter, lard, or other shortening. **b.** noodles, spaghetti, macaroni, etc.; pasta. **c.** any dough. **3.** a soft, doughlike mixture or plastic mass: **a.** a preparation of fish, tomatoes, ground nuts, or some other article of food reduced to a smooth, soft mass: *shrimp paste, almond paste.* **b.** a mixture of clay and water to make earthenware or porcelain. **c.** any of various cleaning materials in the form of a soft mass: *silver-polishing paste.* **4. a.** a hard, brilliant, heavy glass material used in making imitations of precious stones: *shoe buckles of the best paste, sparkling like real diamonds* (Harriet Beecher Stowe). **b.** an artificial gem made of this. **5.** a candy: *fig paste.*
—*v.t.* **1.** to stick with paste: *to paste a label on a box.* **2.** to cover by pasting: *to paste a door over with notices.*
[< Old French *paste* < Late Latin *pasta* pastry, cake < Greek *pastá* (barley) porridge < *pássein* to sprinkle. Compare PASTY[2].]

paste[2] (pāst), *v.,* **past·ed, past·ing,** *n. Slang.* —*v.t.* **1.** to hit with a hard, sharp blow. **2.** to beat; thrash. —*n.* a hard, sharp blow. [probably special use of *paste*[1]]

paste·board (pāst′bôrd′, -bōrd′), *n.* **1.** stiff material made of sheets of paper pasted together or of paper pulp pressed and dried. **2.** *Slang.* a playing card. **3.** *British Slang.* **a.** a visiting card. **b.** a railway ticket.
pasteboards, *Slang.* a deck of playing cards: *I'm that neat with the pasteboards. I can shuffle 'em any way I want* (Benjamin L. Farjeon).
—*adj.* **1.** made of pasteboard. **2.** unsubstantial; counterfeit; sham.

paste·board·y (pāst′bôr′dē, -bōr′-), *adj.* **1.** like pasteboard. **2.** unsubstantial; hollow: *The characters are pasteboardy and the dialogue improbable* (Punch).

paste·down (pāst′doun′), *n.* one of the outer blank leaves of a book that are pasted down on the cover: *A collection of leaves and fragments from manuscripts from the eleventh to the sixteenth centuries . . . had been used as pastedowns in later bindings* (London Times).

pas·tel[1] (pas tel′, pas′tel), *n.* **1. a.** a kind of chalklike crayon used in drawing, made of a dry paste of ground pigments compounded with resin or gum. **b.** this paste. **2.** a drawing made with such crayons. **3.** the art of drawing with pastels. **4.** a soft, pale shade of some color. **5.** a short and slight prose sketch.
—*adj.* soft and pale.
[< French *pastel* < Italian *pastello* (literally) material reduced to a paste < Late Latin *pastellus* a seal or its impression; woad < *pasta* paste[1]]

pas·tel[2] (pas′tel), *n.* **1.** the plant woad. **2.** the blue dye made from woad. [< Middle French *pastel* < Provençal < Late Latin *pastellus;* see PASTEL[1]]

pas·tel·ist or **pas·tel·list** (pas tel′ist, pas′tel ist), *n.* an artist who draws with pastels or colored crayons.

paste·pot (pāst′pot′), *n.* a pot or vessel for holding paste. —*adj. Informal.* hastily or carelessly put together, as if with paste: [*He*] *called the report "a pastepot job" and "pretty sloppy work"* (New York Times).

past·er (pās′tər), *n.* **1.** a slip to paste on or over something. **2.** a person or thing that pastes.

pas·tern (pas′tərn), *n.* **1.** the part of a horse's foot between the fetlock and the hoof. **2.** either of two bones of this part, the upper or great pastern bone and the lower or small pastern bone, connected at a joint, the pastern joint. [Middle English *pastron* < Old French *pasturon* (diminutive) < *pasture* pastern; shackle; pasture]

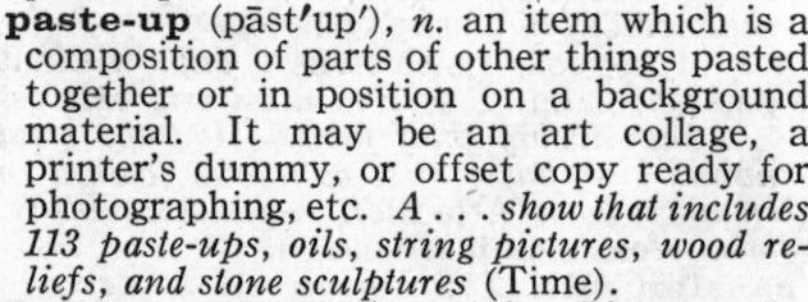

Pastern (def. 1)

paste-up (pāst′up′), *n.* an item which is a composition of parts of other things pasted together or in position on a background material. It may be an art collage, a printer's dummy, or offset copy ready for photographing, etc. *A . . . show that includes 113 paste-ups, oils, string pictures, wood reliefs, and stone sculptures* (Time).

Pas·teur effect (pas tėr′), *Biology.* the shift of primitive organisms from fermentation to respiration in the presence of certain amounts of oxygen. [< Louis *Pasteur;* see PASTEURIZE]

pas·teur·ism (pas′tə riz əm), *n.* the theories, techniques, etc., of Louis Pasteur, the French chemist and bacteriologist, especially the technique of treating or preventing certain diseases, especially hydrophobia (rabies), by inoculation with a virus of gradually increasing strength.

pas·teur·i·za·tion (pas′chər ə zā′shən, -tər-), *n.* **1.** the process of pasteurizing: *The pasteurization of milk is required by law.* **2.** the fact or state of being pasteurized.

pas·teur·ize (pas′chə rīz, -tə-), *v.t.,* **-ized, -iz·ing.** **1.** to heat (milk, wine, beer, etc.) to a high temperature, and then chill it quickly to destroy harmful bacteria. Pasteurizing milk to about 140 degrees Fahrenheit kills the bacteria of undulant fever and bovine tuberculosis. **2.** *Obsolete.* to treat or prevent (rabies) by Pasteur's technique of virus inoculation. [< Louis *Pasteur,* 1822-1895, a French chemist, who invented the process]

pas·teur·iz·er (pas′chə rī′zər, -tə-), *n.* an apparatus for pasteurizing milk, wine, beer, etc.

pas·tic·cio (päs tēt′chō), *n., pl.* **-ci** (-chē). an artistic, musical, or literary work made up of portions of various works; medley, hodgepodge, or potpourri: *What a pasticcio of gauzes, pins, and ribbons go to compound that multifarious thing—a well-dressed woman* (Richard Cumberland). [< Italian *pasticcio;* see PASTICHE]

pas·tiche (pas tēsh′, päs-), *n.* **1.** pasticcio: *The surprise was that they looked like pleasant pastiches of Corot, Pissarro, and Cézanne* (New Yorker). **2.** something done in imitation or ridicule of another artist's style. [< French *pastiche* < Italian *pasticcio* < Vulgar Latin *pastīcium* composed of paste < Late Latin *pasta* pastry; see PASTE[1]]

pas·ti·cheur (pas′tē shėr′, päs′-), *n.* a composer of pastiches. [< French *pasticheur* < *pastiche*]

pas·til (pas′təl), *n.* pastille.

pas·till·age (pas′til ij), *n.* **1.** confectionary work made of sugar paste and formed in imitation of various objects: *The cake is decorated with 46 lb. of marzipan and 25 lb. of royal icing and pastillage* (London Times). **2.** ornamentation in ceramics by means of a surface application of scrolls, flowers, etc., modeled separately in clay. [< French *pastillage* imitation in sugar paste < *pastille;* see PASTILLE]

pas·tille (pas tēl′), *n.* **1.** a flavored or medicated lozenge; troche: *The ancient Egyptians chewed aromatic pastilles* (New Yorker). **2.** a small roll or cone of aromatic paste, burned as a disinfectant, incense, etc. **3.** pastel for crayons. **4.** a crayon made from pastel. [< French *pastille* < Spanish *pastilla* perfume pellet < Latin *pastillus* roll, aromatic lozenge (diminutive) < *pānis, -is* bread]

pas·time (pas′tīm′, päs′-), *n.* a pleasant way of passing time; amusement; recreation, as a game or sport: *Baseball has been called America's national pastime. She also finds time for . . . such normal pastimes as knitting a sweater* (Newsweek). [< *pass*[1] + *time;* perhaps translation of Middle French *passe-temps*] —**Syn.** diversion.

past·i·ness (pās′tē nis), *n.* pasty quality, condition, or consistency.

past·ing (pās′ting), *n. Slang.* a violent and damaging attack; beating: *The Hawks beat the Canadiens 7-1, the worst pasting the Stanley Cup champions took all season* (Maclean's).

pas·tis (pas tēs′), *n.* a strong liqueur with a flavor like absinthe: *No longer the friendly gossip at the pump, no longer the fraternal glass of pastis on the terrace* (London Times). [< French *pastis*]

past master, 1. a person who has filled the office of master in a society, lodge, etc. **2.** a person who has much experience in any profession, art, etc. —**Syn. 2.** adept, expert.

past mistress, a woman well skilled in some accomplishment or study.

past·ness (past′nis, päst′-), *n.* the quality or state of being past.

pas·tor (pas′tər, päs′-), *n.* **1.** a minister in charge of a church; spiritual guide: *A Moses or a David, pastors of their people* (Francis Bacon). **2. a.** a starling of Asia and Europe, whose plumage is partly rose-colored. **b.** any bird of the same group. **3.** *Archaic.* a herdsman or shepherd. [< Anglo-French *pastour,* Old French *pasteur,* < Latin *pāstor* shepherd < *pāscere* to feed]

pas·tor·age (pas′tər ij, päs′-), *n.* a parsonage.

pas·tor·al (pas′tər əl, päs′-), *adj.* **1.** of shepherds or country life: *a pastoral occupation, a pastoral poem. The pastoral peoples, who devote their primary attention to animal husbandry . . . do little or no raising of food plants* (Beals and Hoijer). **2.** simple or naturally beautiful like the country: *a pastoral scene.* **3.** of a pastor, his office, or his duties: *a pastoral visit.*
—*n.* **1. a.** a pastoral play, poem, or picture. **b.** such works as a type or class: *There are some things of an established nature in pastoral, which are essential to it, such as a country scene, innocence, simplicity* (Sir Richard Steele). **2.** a pastoral letter. **3.** a crozier. **4.** pastorale.
[< Latin *pāstōrālis* < *pāstor;* see PASTOR]
—**Syn.** *adj.* **1.** rustic, country, bucolic. See **rural.**

pas·to·ra·le (pas′tə rä′lē, päs′-; pas′tə ral′; *Italian* päs′tô rä′lā), *n., pl.* **-ra·li** (-rä′lē), **-ra·les** (-rä′lēz, -ralz′). *Music.* **1.** an opera, cantata, or other vocal work with a pastoral subject. **2.** an instrumental composition in pastoral or rustic style, usually in 6/8, 9/8, or 12/8 time. [< Italian *pastorale* (originally) pastoral < Latin *pāstōrālis* < *pāstor;* see PASTOR]

Pastoral Epistle, (in the New Testament) one of the Epistles to Timothy or Titus, dealing especially with a pastor's work.

pas·to·ral·ism (pas′tər ə liz′əm, päs′-), *n.* pastoral quality or character.

pas·to·ral·ist (pas′tər ə list, päs′-), *n.* **1.** a keeper of flocks or herds. **2.** a writer of pastorals.

pas·tor·al·ize (pas′tər ə līz, päs′-), *v.t.,* **-ized, -iz·ing.** **1.** to make pastoral or rural: *The* [*Morgenthau*] *plan proposed to destroy* *all German industry and pastoralize the nation* (Time). **2.** to make the subject or theme of a pastoral; celebrate in a pastoral poem.

pastoral letter, 1. a letter from a bishop to his clergy or to the people of his church district: *The call came in a pastoral letter read in all the country's churches* (New York Times). **2.** a letter from a pastor to his people.

pas·tor·al·ly (pas′tər ə lē, päs′-), *adv.* **1.** in a pastoral or rustic manner; in a pastoral. **2.** in the manner of a pastor.

pastoral staff, a crozier.

pas·tor·ate (pas′tər it, päs′-), *n.* **1.** the position or duties of a pastor. **2.** the term of service of a pastor. **3.** pastors as a group. **4.** a pastor's residence; parsonage.

pas·to·ri·um (pas tôr′ē əm, päs-; -tōr′-), *n., pl.* **-to·ri·ums, -to·ri·a** (-tôr′ē ə, -tōr′-). *Southern U.S.* a parsonage. [American English < *pastor* + *-orium,* as in *emporium*]

pas·tor·ship (pas′tər ship, päs′-), *n.* the position or duties of a pastor; pastorate.

past participle, the participle used in forming the English passive (*is stolen*) and perfect (*has stolen*) constructions and as an adjective (*stolen* money). For most verbs the past participle has the same form whether used as an adjective or in a verb phrase; for a few it differs (clean-*shaven* man, had *shaved*). *Abbr.:* pp.

➤ See **participle** for usage note.

past perfect, 1. the verb tense used to show that an event was completed before a given past time. In "He *had learned* to read before he went to school," *had learned* is the past perfect of *learn. Past perfect* and *pluperfect* mean the same. **2.** a verb form or verbal phrase used thus.

past progressive, the verbal tense or tense form that expresses progress, recurrence, or habitual action in the past, as *were running* in the sentence *They were running away from the place.*

pas·tra·mi (pə strä′mē), *n.* a smoked and well-seasoned cut of beef, especially a shoulder cut. [< Yiddish *pastrami* < Rumanian *pastrámă,* ultimately < Turkish *basdırma* dried meat < *basmak* to press]

pas·try (pās′trē), *n., pl.* **-tries. 1.** food made of baked flour paste, made rich with lard, butter, or a vegetable shortening. **2.** pies, tarts, and other foods wholly or partly made of rich flour paste. [< *paste;* probably influenced by Old French *pastaierie* < *pastaier* pasty cook < *paste* paste[1]]

pastry bag, a bag of heavy cloth, rubber, etc., tapering to a small opening to which nozzles of various shapes can be attached. It is used to decorate cakes and pastries by squeezing frosting, whipped cream, etc., through a nozzle.

pastry cook, a person who makes pastry or whose business is making or selling pastry.

pastry tube, a small tube serving the same function as a pastry bag, equipped with a plunger to force out the decorative material.

past tense, 1. the verbal tense commonly used when referring to past time, either without reference to the duration of action (called the *simple past* or *preterit* or *past absolute: He ran a mile yesterday*) or as being in progress, recurring, or habitual (called *past progressive* or *imperfect: He was running a mile when he fell*). **2.** a verb form or verbal phrase used thus.

pas·tur·a·bil·i·ty (pas′chər ə bil′ə tē, päs′-), *n.* the capability of affording pasture.

pas·tur·a·ble (pas′chər ə bəl, päs′-), *adj.* fit for use as pasture; affording pasture.

pas·tur·age (pas′chər ij, päs′-), *n.* **1.** the growing of grass and other plants for cattle, sheep, or horses to feed on. **2.** pastureland. **3.** the act or right of pasturing cattle, sheep, etc.; pasturing. [< Old French *pasturage* < *pasturer,* verb < *pasture* pasture, noun]

pas·tur·al (pas′chər əl, päs′-), *adj.* of or having to do with pasture: *Our most common pastural ornaments, the daisy, buttercup, and primrose* (Pall Mall Gazette).

pas·ture (pas′chər, päs′-), *n., v.,* **-tured, -tur·ing.** —*n.* **1.** a grassy field or hillside; grasslands on which cattle, sheep, or horses can feed: *To-morrow to fresh woods and pastures new* (Milton). **2.** the grass and other plants growing in a field or on a hillside: *These lands afford good pasture.* **3.** any area which serves as a source of food for something: *Drifting plankton pastures are as necessary for good fish nutrition as grasses and vegetation are for land animals* (Science News Letter).

—*v.t.* **1.** to put (cattle, sheep, etc.) out to pasture. **2.** (of cattle, sheep, etc.) to feed on (growing grass, etc.). **3.** (of land) to supply pasturage for. —*v.i.* **1.** (of cattle, sheep, etc.) to graze: *There were smooth areas where sheep had pastured* (W. H. Hudson). **2.** *Obsolete.* to afford pasture.

[< Old French *pasture* < Late Latin *pāstūra* < Latin *pāstus, -ūs* pasture, fodder < *pāscere* to feed] —**pas′tur·er,** *n.*

pas·ture·land (pas′chər land′, päs-), *n.* grassland used or suitable for the grazing of cattle, sheep, or horses; pasturage.

past·y[1] (pās′tē), *adj.,* **past·i·er, past·i·est. 1.** like paste, especially in texture: *a pasty mixture.* **2.** pale; sallow. **3.** flabby: *A little pasty woman with a pinched yellowish face* (John Galsworthy).

pas·ty[2] (pas′tē; *see note below*), *n., pl.* **-ties.** *Especially British.* a pie filled with game, fish, or the like: "*Stary-gazy" is the Cornish word for fish pie or pasty* (Punch). [Middle English *pastei* < Old French *paste* paste, dough < Late Latin *pasta* PASTE[1]. Doublet of PATTY.]

➤ In Great Britain **pasty** is pronounced (pas′tē) or (päs′tē). In the United States the word is read in English literature as (pās′tē), although (pas′tē) is heard in parts of Pennsylvania, Minnesota, etc., where Cornish miners settled in the 1800's.

past·y-faced (pās′tē fāst′), *adj.* having a pale, sallow complexion: *You have been outstripped . . . because you have turned into a nation of pasty-faced stay-at-homes* (Punch).

pat[1] (pat), *v.,* **pat·ted, pat·ting,** *n.* —*v.t.* **1.** to strike or tap lightly with something flat: *his foot patting the ground* (Robert Louis Stevenson). *She patted the dough into a flat cake.* **2.** to tap with the hand as a sign of sympathy, approval, or affection: *to pat a dog.* —*v.i.* **1.** to walk or run with a patting sound. **2.** to strike lightly or gently.

pat on the back, to praise; compliment: "*We have a mission to wake up the country," preaches the bushy-browed editor. "Instead of patting it on the back, we're kicking it*" (Wall Street Journal).

—*n.* **1.** a light stroke or tap with the hand or with something flat: *a fatherly pat o' the cheek* (Robert Browning). **2.** the sound made by patting. **3.** a small mass, especially of butter.

pat on the back, a word of praise; compliment: *Congress gets an awful kicking around. . . . I just wanted to give them a pat on the back* (Hubert H. Humphrey).

[perhaps imitative]

pat[2] (pat), *adj.* to the point; suitable; apt: *When a Keats or an Alexander the Great is the subject, the explanation of his achievement is both too pat and too unenlightening; it is simply genius* (Harper's). —*adv.* aptly; exactly; suitably.

have pat or **know pat,** *Informal.* to have perfectly; know thoroughly: *He . . . had the whole story pat enough* (Mrs. J.H. Riddell).

stand pat, a. *Informal.* to hold to things as they are and refuse to change: *We can't just stand pat on this important issue.* **b.** (in poker) to refuse the opportunity to draw cards; play the cards dealt: *Holding a flush, I stood pat.*

[perhaps special use of *pat*[1]] —**pat′ly,** *adv.* —**pat′ness,** *n.*

—**Syn.** *adj.* appropriate, pertinent, relevant.

Pat (pat), *n.* a nickname for an Irishman.

pat., 1. patent. **2.** patented.

PAT (no periods), (in football) point after touchdown.

pa·ta·ca (pə tä′kə), *n.* **1.** a unit of Portuguese money worth 5.5 escudos or 19 cents, used as local currency in Macao. **2.** a coin having this value. [< Portuguese *pataca*]

pat-a-cake (pat′ə kāk′), *n.* a children's game played by patting the hands together to a nursery rhyme. Also, **patty-cake.**

pa·ta·gi·al (pə tā′jē əl), *adj.* of or having to do with a patagium.

pa·ta·gi·um (pə tā′jē əm), *n., pl.* **-gi·a** (-jē ə). **1.** a wing membrane, as of a bat. **2.** a fold of skin extending along the side of the body of certain gliding mammals and reptiles, as the flying squirrel. **3.** the fold of skin between the upper arm and forearm of birds. **4.** a small, flat sclerite above the wing base of many insects. [< New Latin *patagium* < Latin, gold border of a Roman lady's tunic]

Patagia (def. 2) of a flying squirrel

Pat·a·go·ni·an (pat′ə gō′nē ən), *adj.* of or having to do with Patagonia, a region in the extreme south of South America, or its people. —*n.* **1.** a native or inhabitant of Patagonia. **2.** a member of a very tall Indian race living in Patagonia, known as the Tehuelches.

pat·a·mar (pat′ə mär), *n.* a lateen-rigged vessel with an upward-curving keel and considerable overhang of stern and especially stem, used in the coasting trade of western India. [< Portuguese *patamar* < Marathi *patēmāri* < *patta* tidings + *-māri* a carrier]

pa·tas (pə tä′), *n.* a large, red, terrestrial monkey of western Africa. [< French *patas* < a native word in Senegal]

pat·ball (pat′bôl′), *n.* the game of rounders: *Some . . . want to ginger it up. They dislike seeing cricket turned into pat-ball* (London Daily Express).

patch (pach), *n.* **1.** a piece put on to cover a hole or a tear: *Many a patch of brown and grey variegated the faded scarlet of our uniform* (Charles J. Lever). **2.** a piece of cloth, etc., put over a wound or a sore. **3.** a pad over a hurt eye to protect it: *The man with the patch over his eye turned out to be a musicologist and composer* (New Yorker). **4.** a small bit of black cloth that ladies used to wear on their faces, especially in the 1600's and 1700's, to show off their fair skin. **5.** a small, uneven spot: *a patch of brown on the skin.* **6.** a piece of ground: *a garden patch.* **7.** a scrap or bit of cloth, etc., left over. **8.** a hookup for connecting a telephone line to a short-wave radio transmitter. **9.** *Informal.* a dolt; booby. **10.** *U.S. Slang.* a lawyer.

not a patch on, in no way comparable with; nowhere near: *But what had happened wasn't a patch on what might happen* (Punch).

—*v.t.* **1.** to protect or adorn with a patch or patches; put patches on; mend: *to patch clothes.* **2.** to serve for mending: *O, that that earth . . . Should patch a wall to expel the winter's flaw* (Shakespeare). **3.** to make by joining patches or pieces together: *to patch a quilt; a miscellaneous old gentleman . . . patched together, too, of different epochs, an epitome of times and fashions* (Hawthorne). **4.** to piece together; make hastily. —*v.i.* to mend clothes with patches.

patch up, a. to put an end to; settle: *to patch up a quarrel.* **b.** to make right hastily or for a time: *They bought the aircraft in Australia, patched it up, and flew it to Britain, where it has had a complete overhaul* (London Times). **c.** to put together hastily or poorly: *to patch up a costume for a play.* **d.** to revise; amend: *The first decision that had to be made was whether the existing penal law could be satisfactorily patched up or whether a more basic change in its structure was needed* (New York Times).

[Middle English *pacche;* origin uncertain] —**patch′er,** *n.* —**Syn.** *v.t.* **1.** See **mend.**

patch box, a small box for holding patches for the face, used especially in the 1600's and 1700's.

patch·cord (pach′kôrd′), *n.* an electrical cord with plugs or clips at both ends, used to connect different parts of a sound system, or two different systems.

patch·er·y (pach′ər ē), *n., pl.* **-er·ies. 1.** the act of patching; rough mending; hasty or clumsy patching together; botchery. **2.** something made by patching parts together.

patch·i·ly (pach′ə lē), *adv.* in a patchy manner; irregularly; spasmodically.

patch·i·ness (pach′ē nis), *n.* the condition of being patchy.

patch·ing (pach′ing), *n.* **1.** the act of mending with a patch or patches. **2.** a patch, or patches collectively. **3.** wadding for a rifle.

patch·ou·li or **patch·ou·ly** (pach′ů lē, pə chü′-), *n.* **1.** a penetrating perfume derived from an East Indian plant. **2.** an East Indian plant of the mint family having an essential oil from which the perfume is obtained. [probably < Hindustani *pacholi,* the trade name. Compare Tamil *pachai-*green, and *ilai* leaf.]

patch pocket, a pouchlike pocket made by sewing a piece of material, usually one of which the garment is made, on the outside of a dress, suit, etc.

patch test, *Medicine.* a test for allergy to a particular substance, made by applying the substance to a small area of unbroken skin, usually by means of pads.

patch·up (pach′up′), *adj.* **1.** makeshift: *Usually this is a patch-up kind of job* (Atlantic). **2.** restorative; remedial: *The Administration is now looking to the Senate for some major patch-up work on its housing program* (Wall Street Journal).

patch·work (pach′wėrk′), *n.* **1.** pieces of cloth of various colors or shapes sewed together by the edges: *She made a cover of patchwork for the cushion.* **2.** anything like this: *From the airplane we saw a patchwork of fields and woods.* **3.** anything made of fragments; jumble: *His memoirs were an amateurishly arranged patchwork of reminiscences.*

patch·y (pach′ē), *adj.*, **patch·i·er, patch·i·est.** **1.** abounding in or characterized by patches: *land patchy with rock.* **2.** occurring in, forming, or resembling patches: *a patchy growth of corn.* **3.** made up of fragments, usually put together hurriedly: *a patchy excuse or story. As a critic, Professor Ray is patchy and rather incurious* (Manchester Guardian).

patd., patented.

pate (pāt), *n.* **1. a.** the head: *Let him to the Tower, And chop away that factious pate of his* (Shakespeare). **b.** the top of the head: *He has a bald pate surrounded by a sudsy billow of white hair* (Newsweek). **2.** brains: *a notion fit for an idiot's pate.* **3.** a person with brains: *a shallow pate.* [Middle English *pate;* origin uncertain] —**Syn. 1. b.** crown.

pâte (pät), *n. French.* **1.** paste. **2.** pottery or porcelain paste used in ceramics.

pâ·té (pä tā′), *n. French.* **1.** a paste of finely chopped meat, liver, or the like, with spices and herbs, often served chilled and sliced: *A superb pâté made of saddle of hare, a chicken, a duck, two red partridges . . . and a score of other ingredients* (New York Times). **2.** a case or form of pastry filled with chicken, sweetbreads, oysters, etc.; patty.

-pated, *combining form.* having a ____pate: *Empty-pated = having an empty pate.*

pâ·té de foie gras (pä tā′ də fwä grä′), *French.* a patty or paste made with livers of specially fattened geese: *It was worth its weight in pâté de foie gras* (New York Times).

pa·tel·la (pə tel′ə), *n., pl.* **-tel·las, -tel·lae** (-tel′ē). **1.** the kneecap: *Their report was that Campanella had two spurs on the left patella* (New York Times). **2.** a small pan or shallow vessel. **3.** *Biology.* a structure in the form of a shallow pan or cup, as the spore-bearing structure of certain lichens. [< Latin *patella* (diminutive) < *patina* pan; see PATEN]

pa·tel·lar (pə tel′ər), *adj.* having to do with the kneecap: *Some writers on sciatica have mentioned the absence of the patellar reflex as occurring in this malady* (Arthur S. Eccles).

pa·tel·late (pə tel′āt, -it), *adj.* **1.** having a patella. **2.** patelliform.

pa·tel·li·form (pə tel′ə fôrm), *adj.* having the form of a patella; shaped like a shallow pan, kneecap, or limpet shell. [< Latin *patella* kneecap, shallow pan (see PATELLA) + English *-form*]

pâ·té mai·son (pä tā′ me zôɴ′), *French.* the patty or paste that is the specialty of a particular restaurant.

pat·en (pat′ən), *n.* **1.** the plate on which the bread is placed at the celebration of the Eucharist, or Mass. **2.** a plate or flat piece of metal. Also, **patin, patina, patine.** [< Latin *patena*, or *patina* pan, dish < Greek *patánē* flat dish. Doublet of PATINA[2].]

pa·ten·cy (pā′tən sē, pat′ən-), *n.* **1.** a being patent; obviousness. **2.** *Medicine.* (of a passage, etc.) the condition of being open or unobstructed. **3.** *Phonetics.* openness in varying degrees of the breath passage, characteristic of all sounds but stops.

pat·ent (*n., adj. 1, 4, 6, v.* pat′ənt; *adj. 2, 3, 5* pā′tent, pat′ənt; *especially British* pā′tənt), *n.* **1.** a government grant to a person by which he is the only one allowed to make or sell a new invention for a certain number of years: *Patents . . . are not issued for an idea, but for a specific device, process, or machine that is presumably workable* (Alfred L. Kroeber). **2.** an invention that is patented. **3.** an official document from a government giving a right, privilege, office, etc.: *Alva . . . received an especial patent . . . by which Philip empowered him to proceed against all persons implicated in the troubles* (John L. Motley). **4.** a sign or token indicating a right to something; leave to possess something. **5. a.** the instrument by which public land is granted to a person. **b.** the land so granted: *the 'Patent' . . . the district . . . originally granted to old Major Effingham by the 'king's letters patent'* (James Fenimore Cooper). **6.** a local, minor civil division in Maine.

—*adj.* **1. a.** given or protected by a patent: *a patent stove.* **b.** of or having to do with patents: *patent law.* **2.** open to view or knowledge; evident; plain: *It is patent that cats dislike dogs.* **3. a.** open, as a door, tube, or the passage through which the breath flows. **b.** open to general use; public. **4.** appointed to a right, privilege, office, etc., by a patent. **5.** *Biology.* spreading; expanded, as a plant's petals. **6.** (of flour) of high quality; superior: *Millers blend straight flour from . . . patent, or best-quality flour, and first and second clear flours* (World Book Encyclopedia).

—*v.t.* **1. a.** to get a patent for: *Edison patented many inventions.* **b.** to grant a patent to. **2.** *U.S.* to obtain a patent right to (land). [< Latin *patēns, -entis*, present participle of *patēre* lie open]

—**Syn.** *adj.* **2.** obvious, manifest, palpable.

pat·ent·a·bil·i·ty (pat′ən tə bil′ə tē), *n.* the capability of being patented.

pat·ent·a·ble (pat′ən tə bəl), *adj.* that can be patented.

pa·tente (pȧ tänt′), *n. French.* a license or tax that all business or professional men in France must pay in order to operate legally.

pat·ent·ee (pat′ən tē′), *n.* **1.** a person to whom a patent is granted: *Each Patentee shall be obliged, within three years after the Date of his Patent, to clear and work three acres* (Ontario Bureau of Archives Report). **2.** a person licensed to use another's patent: *a small price to pay for what A.T. and T. spent on teaching its patentees the know-how to use the patents* (Wall Street Journal).

patent insides, newspaper sheets printed on the inside only, and thus sold to publishers of small newspapers, who fill the unprinted side with matter of their own selection.

patent leather, a leather with a finely varnished and very glossy, smooth surface, usually black, made by a process formerly patented.

patent log, one of a variety of patented instruments for recording the speed and distance run by a ship.

pa·tent·ly (pā′tənt lē, pat′ənt-), *adv.* **1.** plainly; clearly; obviously. **2.** openly. —**Syn. 1.** manifestly.

patent medicine, 1. a medicine that is patented. **2.** a medicine that some company owns and sells.

Patent Office, the government office that issues patents and registers trademarks: *If the Patent Office believes a proposed device to be unworkable, it refuses the patent* (Alfred L. Kroeber).

pat·en·tor (pat′ən tər), *n.* **1.** a person who grants a patent. **2.** a patentee.

patent outsides, newspaper sheets printed on the outside only, sold to publishers and filled up by them like patent insides.

patent pool, an agreement between individuals or companies to share the exclusive rights to certain patents, often as a means of limiting the market or preventing normal competition: *Zenith's suit, brought under the antitrust laws, alleged that Hazeltine used "patent pools" to prevent Zenith from selling radios and television sets in Canada, Australia, and Britain* (Wall Street Journal).

pa·ter (pā′tər), *n.* **1.** *British Informal.* father. **2.** the paternoster (being the first word of the Lord's Prayer in Latin). [< Latin *pater* father; (definition 2) short for *paternoster*]

pat·er·a (pat′ər ə), *n., pl.* **-er·ae** (-ər ē). **1.** (in ancient Rome) a broad, shallow, saucerlike dish, used especially in making libations. **2.** *Architecture.* an ornament in bas-relief resembling a round, shallow dish, or having a generally round form. [< Latin *patera* < *patēre* to be open]

Paterae (def. 2)

pa·ter·fa·mil·i·as (pā′tər fə mil′ē əs), *n., pl.* **pa·tres·fa·mil·i·as** (pā′trēz fə mil′ē əs). **1.** a father or head of a family: *According to this account, he was a tender, grousing, home-loving paterfamilias who liked to be with his children when they were young, play with them, and tell them bedtime stories* (New Yorker). **2.** (in Roman law) a male citizen who was the head of a family. [< Latin *paterfamiliās* < *pater, patris* father + Old Latin *familiās*, genitive singular of *familia* a family]

pa·ter·nal (pə tėr′nəl), *adj.* **1.** of or like a father; fatherly: *paternal authority. My position being paternal and protective* (Hawthorne). **2.** related on the father's side of the family: *Everyone has two paternal grandparents and two maternal grandparents.* **3.** received or inherited from one's father: *Mary's blue eyes were a paternal inheritance.* [< Late Latin *paternālis* < Latin *paternus* of a father < *pater, patris* father] —**pa·ter′nal·ly,** *adv.*

pa·ter·nal·ism (pə tėr′nə liz əm), *n.* the principle or practice of managing the affairs of a country or group of employees as a father manages the affairs of children: *In the Congo, paternalism means bread but no votes, good government but no opposition, the best Negro housing in Africa but no real freedom of movement* (Time).

pa·ter·nal·ist (pə tėr′nə list), *n.* a person who believes in or practices paternalism: *. . . paternalists who believe that the human estate is one of perennial childhood* (Saturday Review). —*adj.* paternalistic: *From what General de Gaulle has said, he appears to share these paternalist aspirations* (Economist).

pa·ter·nal·is·tic (pə tėr′nə lis′tik), *adj.* having to do with or characterized by paternalism. —**pa·ter′nal·is′ti·cal·ly,** *adv.*

pa·ter·nal·ize (pə tėr′nə līz), *v.t.*, **-ized, -iz·ing. 1.** to make paternalistic. **2.** to treat in a paternalistic manner.

pa·ter·ni·ty (pə tėr′nə tē), *n.* **1.** state of being a father; fatherhood. **2.** paternal origin or descent: *King Arthur's paternity was unknown. Many of the historical proverbs have a doubtful paternity* (Emerson). [< Late Latin *paternitās* < Latin *paternus* of a father < *pater, patris* father]

pat·er·nos·ter (pat′ər nos′tər, pā′tər-), *n.* **1.** the Lord's Prayer, especially in Latin. **2. a.** one of the beads of a rosary on which the Lord's Prayer is said. **b.** the whole rosary. **3.** an object resembling or strung together like a rosary, especially a fishing line to which hooks and beaded sinkers are attached at regular intervals: *This fish . . . may be caught with a paternoster* (Izaak Walton).

—*v.i.* to fish with a paternoster: *Mr. Such-and-Such of Nuneaton paternostered with a half herring four inches above the river bed . . . and landed a 31 lb. 8 oz. pike* (Punch). [< Latin *pater noster* our father (from the first two words of the Lord's Prayer)]

Pa·ter Pa·tri·ae (pā′tər pā′trē ē), *Latin.* father of his country (applied originally as an epithet to Cicero after his suppression in 63 B.C. of the conspiracy of Catiline against the republic).

pâte-sur-pâte (pät′sər pät′), *n. Ceramics.* decoration by means of slip applied in successive layers to a previously prepared surface so as to produce a very low relief. [< French (literally) paste on paste]

path (path, päth), *n., pl.* **paths** (paᴛʜz, päᴛʜz). **1.** a way made by people or animals walking. It is usually too narrow for automobiles or wagons. *He left the barren-beaten thoroughfare, Chose the green path that show'd the rarer foot* (Tennyson). **2. a.** a walk through a garden or park. **b.** *British.* a track for bicycle or foot racing. **3.** the line along which a person or thing moves; route; track: *The moon has a regular path through the sky.* **4.** a way of acting or behaving: *The paths of glory lead but to the grave* (Thomas Gray).

beat a path to, to hurry to with great enthusiasm, zeal, etc.: *The reporters beat a path to the new candidate's hotel suite for an interview as soon as his nomination was announced.*

cross one's path, a. to meet; encounter: *I greatly enjoyed these early memoirs dating from a time before our paths crossed* (Manchester Guardian Weekly). **b.** to stand in one's way; thwart, oppose, or hinder one's interest, purpose, or designs: *Yet such was his [Cromwell's] genius and resolution that*

he was able to overpower and crush everything crossing his path (Macaulay).
[Old English *pæth*]
—**Syn. 1.** walk, trail, lane. **3.** course.

path., 1. pathological. 2. pathology.

Pa·than (pə tän′, pət hän′), *n.* **1.** a person of Afghan stock dwelling in or near the borderland of Pakistan and Afghanistan, countries in southwestern Asia: *Pathans ... live by their own code of honor ... which knows little middle ground between love for a friend and death for an enemy* (New York Times). **2.** an Afghan (in Afghan use, especially as an ethnic designation). [< Hindustani *Paṭhān* < Afghan *Pēṣ̌tāna* Afghans]

path·break·ing (path′brā′king), *adj.* that prepares or shows the way; innovating: ... *the pathbreaking education bill now on the floor* (Wall Street Journal).

pa·thet·ic (pə thet′ik), *adj.* **1.** arousing pity; pitiful: *the pathetic sight of a crippled child.* **2.** of the emotions; that affects the emotions. **3.** arousing passion or other powerful emotions; stirring: *Thee too, enamour'd of the life I lov'd, Pathetic in its praise ... Ingenious Cowley* (William Cowper). [< Late Latin *pathēticus* < Greek *pathētikós* < *pathētós* liable to suffer < *path-*, stem of *páschein* to suffer] —**Syn. 1.** pitiable, moving, touching, affecting.

pa·thet·i·cal (pə thet′ə kəl), *adj.* pathetic.

pa·thet·i·cal·ly (pə thet′ə klē), *adv.* so as to arouse pity: *She was pathetically ignorant and helpless.*

pathetic fallacy, the attributing of human emotions and characteristics to nature: *The leonine old illustrator never let his pupils fall for the pathetic fallacy, that empty barrels are lonely* (Time).

Pa·thet La·o (pä′thət lä′ō), the communist-supported government and forces in Laos, a country in southeastern Asia, in Indochina.

path·find·er (path′fīn′dər, päth′-), *n.* one that finds a path or way, as through a wilderness: *A hundred years ago science was not yet conceived to be the pathfinder of the practical arts* (Atlantic).

path·find·ing (path′fīn′ding), *n.* the act or process of discovering a path or way; pioneering: *The 593, the first civil engine designed for supersonic flight ... will benefit from three years of pathfinding by TSR-2 before the first prototype ... takes to the air* (London Times). —*adj.* pathbreaking; trailblazing: ... *a pathfinding study which opens up new perspectives in the comparative analysis of Soviet and American political institutions* (Merle Fainsod).

path·ic (path′ik), *n.* **1.** a person who suffers or undergoes something: ... *a mere pathic to thy devilish art* (Philip Massinger). **2.** a catamite.
—*adj.* **1.** undergoing something; passive: ... *the pathic attitude of captive animals towards man* (New Scientist). **2.** having to do with suffering or disease; morbid.
[< Latin *pathicus* < Greek *path-* (stem of *páschein* to suffer) + Latin *-icus* -ic]

path·less (path′lis, päth′-), *adj.* having no path through or across it; untrodden; trackless: *a pathless mountain.* —**path′less·ness,** *n.*

path·o·bi·ol·o·gy (path′ə bī ol′ə jē), *n.* pathology.

path·o·gen (path′ə jən), *n.* any agent capable of producing disease, especially a living microorganism or virus. [< Greek *páthos* suffering + English *-gen*]

path·o·gene (path′ə jēn), *n.* pathogen.

path·o·gen·e·sis (path′ə jen′ə sis), *n.* the production or development of disease.

path·o·ge·net·ic (path′ə jə net′ik), *adj.* pathogenic.

path·o·gen·ic (path′ə jen′ik), *adj.* having to do with pathogenesis; producing disease: [*It*] *turned out to have a much weaker effect upon the dangerous germs, the pathogenic ones* (André Maurois).

path·o·ge·nic·i·ty (path′ə jə nis′ə tē), *n.* the state or quality of being pathogenic.

pa·thog·e·ny (pə thoj′ə nē), *n.* the production of disease; pathogenesis.

pa·thog·no·mon·ic (pə thog′nə mon′ik), *adj.* indicative or characteristic of a particular disease: *And to have their ribs tickled by an oblique pathognomonic reference to homosexuality* (Punch). [< Greek *pathognōmonikós* skilled in diagnosis of diseases, ultimately < *páthos* disease + *gnṓmōn* judge]

pa·thog·no·my (pə thog′nə mē), *n.* **1.** the study of the emotions or the indications of emotions. **2.** the science of the signs or symptoms indicating particular diseases.

pathol., 1. pathological. 2. pathology.

path·o·log·ic (path′ə loj′ik), *adj.* pathological.

path·o·log·i·cal (path′ə loj′ə kəl), *adj.* **1.** of pathology; dealing with diseases or concerned with diseases: *pathological studies.* **2.** due to disease or accompanying disease: *a pathological condition of the blood cells.* —**path′o·log′i·cal·ly,** *adv.* —**Syn. 2.** morbid.

pa·thol·o·gist (pə thol′ə jist), *n.* a person skilled in pathology.

pa·thol·o·gy (pə thol′ə jē), *n., pl.* **-gies. 1.** the study of the causes and nature of diseases. *Abbr.:* path. **2.** the unhealthy conditions and processes caused by a disease. [probably < French *pathologie* < New Latin *pathologia* < Greek *páthos* disease, suffering, emotion + *-logiā* -logy]

path·o·phys·i·o·log·i·cal (path′ə fiz′ē ə loj′ə kəl), *adj.* of or having to do with pathophysiology.

path·o·phys·i·ol·o·gy (path′ə fiz′ē ol′ə jē), *n.* the science dealing with the abnormal functions of organisms and their parts: *Pathophysiology is a comparatively novel course, combining various approaches to the study of disease and its effect on the body* (London Times). [< Greek *páthos* disease + English *physiology*]

pa·thos (pā′thos), *n.* **1.** the quality in speech, writing, music, events, or a scene that arouses a feeling of pity or sadness: *She pleaded for mercy with a touching pathos.* **2.** a pathetic expression or utterance: *As for pathos, I am as provocative of tears as an onion* (Hawthorne). **3.** *Obsolete.* suffering. [< Greek *páthos* suffering; feeling, emotion < *pénthos* grief, sorrow]

path·way (path′wā′, päth′-), *n.* a path.

-pathy, *combining form.* **1.** feeling; the emotions: *Antipathy = a hostile feeling.*
2. disease: *Neuropathy = nervous disease.*
3. treatment of disease in——, or by——: *Osteopathy = treatment of disease in bones. Hydropathy = treatment of disease by the use of water.*
[< Greek *-pátheia* act or quality of suffering feeling < *páthos;* see PATHOS]

pa·tience (pā′shəns), *n.* **1.** willingness to put up with waiting, pain, trouble, etc.; calm endurance without complaining or losing self-control: *The boy needed patience when he was having his teeth filled. The cat showed patience in watching the mousehole.* **2.** long, hard work; steady effort: *to labor with patience.* **3.** a card game played by one person; solitaire. **4.** *Obsolete.* sufferance; indulgence; leave; permission: *I can go no further, sir ... By your patience, I needs must rest me* (Shakespeare). [< Old French *pacience,* learned borrowing from Latin *patientia* < *patiēns* patient]
—**Syn. 1. Patience, forbearance, fortitude** mean power to endure, without complaining, something unpleasant or painful. **Patience** implies calmness and self-control and applies whether one is enduring something unpleasant or merely waiting, or doing something requiring steady effort: *Teachers need patience.* **Forbearance** implies uncommon self-control when greatly tried or provoked: *He endured the many attacks of his political opponents with admirable forbearance.* **Fortitude** implies strength of character and calm courage in facing danger or enduring suffering: *With fortitude, the disabled veteran learned a new trade.*

pa·tient (pā′shənt), *adj.* **1.** willing to put up with waiting, pain, trouble, etc.; enduring calmly without complaining or losing self-control: *patient suffering, patient expectation. Beware the fury of a patient man* (John Dryden). **2.** with steady effort or long, hard work; persistent; constant; diligent: *patient research, patient labor.* **3.** *Archaic.* undergoing the action of another; passive.
patient of, a. able to bear or tolerate: *patient of cold or hunger. Patient of constitutional control, he bears it with meek manliness of soul* (William Cowper). **b.** susceptible to (a particular interpretation): *A way open for them to despise the law which was made patient of such a weak evasion* (Jeremy Taylor).
—*n.* **1.** a person who is being treated by a doctor: *A physician ... may cure the disease and kill the patient* (Francis Bacon). **2.** a person or thing that undergoes some action; recipient: *He that is not free is not an Agent but a Patient* (John Wesley). *Every creature is man's agent or patient* (Emerson). **3.** *Obsolete.* a person who endures or suffers patiently.
[< Old French *pacient,* learned borrowing from Latin *patiēns, -entis,* present participle of *patī* to suffer, endure] —**pa′tient·ly,** *adv.*
—**Syn.** *adj.* **1.** forbearing. **2.** persevering.

pat·in (pat′ən), *n.* paten.

pat·i·na[1] (pat′ə nə), *n.* **1.** a film or incrustation, usually green, on the surface of old bronze or copper, formed by oxidation. **2.** a film or coloring produced in the course of time on wood or other substance. **3.** a surface appearance added to or assumed by anything: *the patina of soft, supple leather, the patina of success.* [< Italian *patina,* perhaps < Latin *patina* pan, patina[2] (because of the incrustation on ancient dishes)]

pat·i·na[2] (pat′ə nə), *n., pl.* **-nae** (-nē). **1.** a broad shallow dish or pan used by the ancient Romans. **2.** paten. [< Latin *patina* shallow pan, dish. Doublet of PATEN.]

pat·i·nate (pat′ə nāt), *v.t.,* **-nat·ed, -nat·ing.** to coat with a patina: *It had taken two thousand years to patinate the urn so beautifully.*

pat·i·nat·ed (pat′ə nā′tid), *adj.* covered with a patina.

pat·i·na·tion (pat′ə nā′shən), *n.* **1.** the process of becoming covered with patina. **2.** the state of being covered with patina: *The superposition of later carvings on earlier ones and differences in patination helped to determine the sequence of execution* (Scientific American).

pat·ine[1] (pat′ən), *n.* paten.

pa·tine[2] (pə tēn′), *n., v.,* **-tined, -tin·ing.** —*n.* patina[1]. —*v.i.* to patinate: *Its foundation was once ivory satin, now patined to a rich oyster colour* (London Times). [< French *patine* < Latin *patina*]

pat·i·nize (pat′ə nīz), *v.t.,* **-nized, -niz·ing.** to patinate.

pat·i·o (pat′ē ō, pä′tē-), *n., pl.* **-i·os. 1.** an inner court or yard open to the sky, found especially in relatively large dwellings of Spanish or Spanish-American design. **2.** *U.S.* a terrace for outdoor eating, lounging, etc. [American English < Spanish *patio,* ultimately < Latin *patēre* to lie open]

Mexican Patio (def. 1)

pâ·tis·se·rie (pə tis′ər ē; *French* pä tēs rē′), *n.* **1.** pastry: *Tante Marie School of Cookery, Pâtisserie and Refresher Courses* (Sunday Times). **2.** a shop that sells pastries: *Lovers have at last the choice between the trees of the park and Danish pâtisseries as a setting for romance* (Manchester Guardian). [< French *pâtisserie* < *pâtissier* pastry cook < Vulgar Latin *pasticium* pasty < Late Latin *pasta;* see PASTE[1]]

pa·to (pä′tō), *n.* a game popular in Argentina played with a ball having six leather handles, and by players mounted on horses. It combines features of polo and basketball.

Pat. Off., Patent Office.

pat·ois (pat′wä), *n., pl.* **pat·ois** (pat′wäz). **1.** a dialect spoken by the common people of a particular district: *the patois of the French Canadians. A scandalous scene ensued, in which all the rude eloquence of the patois and all the pent-up fever of the Midi were released* (London Times). **2.** the cant or jargon of a particular group. **3.** *British.* a provincial dialect or form of speech (sometimes used in an unfriendly way). [< French *patois* < Old French *patoier* handle clumsily < *pate* paw < a Germanic word] —**Syn. 2.** argot.

Pa·tres con·scrip·ti (pā′trēz kən skrip′tī), *Latin.* **1.** the senators of ancient Rome, collectively; the conscript fathers. **2.** a senate, as that of Venice in the late Middle Ages and Renaissance.

pa·tri·a (pā′trē ə), *n. Latin.* a country; native land: *Costa Ricans rallied around their government, placing patria before private political differences* (Newsweek).

pa·tri·al (pā′trē əl), *adj.* **1.** of or having to do with one's native country. **2.** (of nouns and adjectives or their suffixes) indicating nationality or local extraction: "*Rumanian" is a patrial noun and adjective.* [< Old French *patrial* < Latin *patria* fatherland]

pa·tri·a po·tes·tas (pā′trē ə pō tes′tas), **1.** the authority or control of a father. **2.** *Roman Law.* the authority of a male citizen who was the head of a family (paterfamilias), by which technically he controlled the activities and owned the property of his wife and of his children and grandchildren in the male line. [< Latin *patria potestas* (literally) fatherly power]

pa·tri·arch (pā′trē ärk), *n.* **1.** (in the Bible) the father and ruler of a family or tribe: **a.** Abraham, Isaac, or Jacob, as the founders of Israel. **b.** any of the twelve sons of Jacob, supposed to be ancestors of the twelve Israelite tribes. **c.** one of the tribal or family heads living before Noah and the Flood. **2.** a person thought of as the father or founder of something. **3. a.** a venerable old man, especially the oldest man of a village, the oldest member of a profession, company, etc.: *He . . . was reverenced as one of the patriarchs of the village* (Washington Irving). **b.** the head of a flock or herd: *a goat, the patriarch of the flock* (Scott); *the monarch oak, the patriarch of the trees* (John Dryden). **4. a.** a bishop of the highest rank in the early Christian church. **b.** the chief bishop of one of the Eastern non-Orthodox churches. **5.** in the Roman Catholic Church: **a.** the Pope. **b.** a bishop of the highest episcopal rank after the Pope. **6.** (in the Mormon Church) one of the highest dignitaries, who pronounces the blessing of the church; Evangelist. [< Latin *patriarcha* < Greek *patriárchēs* < *patriā* family, clan + *archós* leader]

pa·tri·ar·chal (pā′trē är′kəl), *adj.* **1.** suitable to a patriarch; having to do with a patriarch: *The governor . . . gave a short but truly patriarchal address to his citizens* (Washington Irving). **2.** under the rule of a patriarch: *patriarchal life, a patriarchal church.* **3.** like a patriarch; venerable: *The Selectmen of Boston, plain, patriarchal fathers of the people* (Hawthorne). —**pa′tri·ar′chal·ly,** *adv.*

patriarchal cross, a cross with two transverse pieces, the upper being the shorter, an emblem of the patriarchs of the Greek Church. See the diagram of **cross.**

pa·tri·ar·chal·ism (pā′trē är′kə liz əm), *n.* a patriarchal form of society or government: *Small farms would also be a return to patriarchalism* (Tait's Magazine).

pa·tri·ar·chate (pā′trē är′kit), *n.* **1.** the position, dignity, or authority of a church patriarch. **2.** the church district under a patriarch's authority. **3.** patriarchy.

pa·tri·ar·chic (pā′trē är′kik), *adj.* patriarchal.

pa·tri·ar·chy (pā′trē är′kē), *n., pl.* **-chies. 1.** a form of social organization in which the father is head of the family and in which descent is reckoned in the male line, the children belonging to the father's clan. The joint family of the Hindus and the Roman family are examples. **2.** a family, community, or tribe having this form of organization and governed by a patriarch or by the eldest male.

pat·ri·cen·tric (pat′rə sen′trik), *adj.* having or recognizing the father as the center of the family.

pa·tri·cian (pə trish′ən), *n.* **1.** a noble; aristocrat: *The Prince of Orange, Count Egmont, and many of the leading patricians of the Netherlands* (John L. Motley). **2.** a member of the nobility of ancient Rome or the later Roman Empire and the Byzantine Empire. **3.** a hereditary noble of a medieval Italian republic, as Venice, or citizen of high rank in a German free city.
—*adj.* **1.** of the patricians. **2.** of high social rank; aristocratic. **3.** suitable for an aristocrat: *a patrician air patrician aloofness.*
[< Latin *patricius* belonging to the *patrēs* senators; (literally) fathers (at Rome) + English *-an*] —**pa·tri′cian·ly,** *adv.*

pa·tri·cian·hood (pə trish′ən hu̇d), *n.* **1.** patrician rank or dignity. **2.** patricians as a group.

pa·tri·cian·ism (pə trish′ə niz əm), *n.* patrician rank or spirit.

pa·tri·ci·ate (pə trish′ē āt), *n.* **1.** the position, dignity, or rank of a patrician. **2.** a patrician order or class; aristocracy.

pat·ri·ci·dal (pat′rə sī′dəl), *adj.* relating to patricide.

pat·ri·cide[1] (pat′rə sīd), *n.* the crime of killing one's father. [< Late Latin *patricīdium* < Latin *pater* father + *-cīdium* act of killing, -cide[2]]

pat·ri·cide[2] (pat′rə sīd), *n.* a person who kills his father. [< Medieval Latin *patricida* < Latin *pater* father + *-cīda* killer, -cide[1]]

Pat·rick (pat′rik), *n.* **Saint.** the patron saint of Ireland. He converted Ireland to Christianity.

pat·ri·lat·er·al (pat′rə lat′ər əl), *adj.* paternal.

pat·ri·lin·e·age (pat′rə lin′ē ij), *n.* descent through the male line of a family, clan, tribe, etc.

pat·ri·lin·e·al (pat′rə lin′ē əl), *adj.* **1.** traced through male links only: *"Patrilineal" descent (father to son) was the rule in ancient Rome, China and Israel, and occurs in many primitive societies* (Scientific American). **2.** descending or heritable through male links only: *patrilineal rights.* [< Latin *pater, patris* father + English *lineal*]

pat·ri·lo·cal (pat′rə lō′kəl), *adj.* having its focus in the home of the husband's family: *When the wife comes to live at her husband's home, this is called patrilocal residence* (Melville Herskovits).

pat·ri·lo·cal·i·ty (pat′rə lō kal′ə tē), *n.* residence in or near the home of the husband's family.

pat·ri·mo·ni·al (pat′rə mō′nē əl), *adj.* having to do with a patrimony; inherited from one's father or ancestors. —**pat′ri·mo′ni·al·ly,** *adv.*

pat·ri·mo·ny (pat′rə mō′nē), *n., pl.* **-nies. 1.** property inherited from one's father or ancestors: *Like a man devouring the patrimony of his sons, we have piled up our debts to buy prosperity on credit* (Wall Street Journal). **2.** property belonging to a church, monastery, or convent. **3.** any heritage: *The patrimony of a poor man lies in the strength and dexterity of his hands* (Adam Smith). [< Old French *patremoine* < Latin *patrimōnium* < *pater, patris* father] —**Syn. 1.** inheritance. **3.** legacy.

pat·rin (pat′rin), *n.* leaves, grass, etc., placed as a mark by Gypsies to indicate the course taken. Also, **patteran.** [< Romany *patrin*]

pa·tri·o·fe·lis (pā′trē ə fē′lis, pat′rē-), *n.* a creodont or primitive carnivorous mammal about the size of a jaguar, occurring as fossils in Eocene deposits of Wyoming. [< New Latin *Patriofelis* the genus name < Latin *patrius* of one's father(s) + *fēlis* cat]

pa·tri·ot (pā′trē ət; *especially British* pat′rē ət), *n.* a person who loves and loyally supports his country. [< Late Latin *patriōta* < Greek *patriṓtēs* (fellow) countryman < *patrís, -idos* fatherland < *patḗr, patrós* father]

pa·tri·ot·eer (pā′trē ə tir′; *especially British* pat′rē ə tir′), *n.* a person who makes a parade of his patriotic spirit or service, especially in doing what is for his own profit: *They are quick to detect the phony and they can distinguish a patriot from a patrioteer* (Birmingham News). —*v.i.* to act as a patrioteer; parade as patriotic what is done for one's own profit.

pa·tri·ot·ic (pā′trē ot′ik; *especially British* pat′rē ot′ik), *adj.* **1.** loving one's country. **2.** showing love and loyal support of one's country: *A patriotic mind anxious to be proud of its country even in little things* (H.G. Wells). —**pa′tri·ot′i·cal·ly,** *adv.*

pa·tri·ot·ism (pā′trē ə tiz′əm; *especially British* pat′rē ə tiz′əm), *n.* love and loyal support of one's country: *Patriotism is absolutely essential to national welfare* (Emory S. Bogardus).

Patriot's Day, *U.S.* April 19, the anniversary of the initial skirmishes in the Revolutionary War, at Lexington and Concord, Massachusetts.

pa·tris·tic (pə tris′tik), *adj.* having to do with the early leaders, or fathers, of the Christian Church, or with their writings. [< Latin *pater, patris* father + English *-ist* + *-ic*] —**pa·tris′ti·cal·ly,** *adv.*

pa·tris·ti·cal (pə tris′tə kəl), *adj.* patristic.

pa·tris·tics (pə tris′tiks), *n.* the study of the doctrines, writings, and lives of the fathers of the Christian Church: *Forty-three student ministers quit their jobs . . . to return to their . . . patristics at ten theological seminaries* (Time).

Pa·tro·clus (pə trō′kləs), *n. Greek Legend.* a friend of Achilles who was slain in battle in Achilles' armor by Hector while Achilles sulked in his tent.

pa·trol (pə trōl′), *v.,* **-trolled, -trol·ling,** *n.* —*v.i.* **1.** to go the rounds as a watchman or a policeman does. **2.** to go on patrol; reconnoiter as a patrol. —*v.t.* **1.** to go around (a town, camp, etc.) to watch or guard: *The camp at night [was] sedulously chosen and patrolled* (Robert Louis Stevenson). **2.** to make a patrol of; reconnoiter.
—*n.* **1.** men who patrol: *a police patrol. The patrol was changed at midnight.* **2.** the act of making a repeated circuit of an area to watch or guard. **3.** a small group of soldiers, ships, or airplanes, sent to find out all they can about the enemy. **4.** a unit of usually eight boy scouts. [< French *patrouiller* paddle in mud < Old French *patouiller,* probably < *patte* paw] —**pa·trol′ler,** *n.*

pa·trol·man (pə trōl′mən), *n., pl.* **-men.** *U.S.* **1.** a man who patrols. **2.** a policeman who patrols a certain district.

pat·ro·log·ic (pat′rə loj′ik), *adj.* belonging to patrology.

pat·ro·log·i·cal (pat′rə loj′ə kəl), *adj.* patrologic.

pa·trol·o·gist (pə trol′ə jist), *n.* a person skilled in patrology.

pa·trol·o·gy (pə trol′ə jē), *n., pl.* **-gies. 1. a.** the study of the writings of the fathers of the Christian Church; patristics. **b.** a treatise on these writings. **2.** a collection of the writings of the fathers and other early ecclesiastical writers. [< Greek *patḗr, patrós* father + *-logiā* -logy]

patrol wagon, *U.S.* **1.** a closed wagon or truck used by the police for carrying prisoners. **2.** a light vehicle used by an underwriters' group in reaching fires in order to protect insured goods, etc.

pa·tron[1] (pā′trən), *n.* **1.** a person who buys regularly at a given store or goes regularly to a given restaurant, hotel, etc.: *The enormous demand for military boots was rendering it . . . difficult for him to give to old patrons that . . . attention which he would desire to give* (Arnold Bennett). **2.** a person who gives his approval and support to some person, art, cause, or undertaking: *a renowned patron of learning* (Jonathan Swift). *Books . . . ought to have no patrons but truth and reason* (Francis Bacon). *Patron, Commonly a wretch who supports with insolence and is paid with flattery* (Samuel Johnson). **3.** a guardian saint or god: *St. Crispin, the patron of shoemakers.* **4.** (in ancient Rome) an influential man who took certain persons under his protection, or a master who had freed a slave but retained some claims upon him. **5.** a person who holds the right to present a clergyman to a benefice. **6.** *Obsolete.* **a.** a lord superior. **b.** a founder of a religious order.
—*adj.* guarding; protecting: *a patron saint.*
[< Old French *patroun,* learned borrowing from Latin *patrōnus* patron advocate, protector; person to be respected < *pater, patris* father. Doublet of PADRONE, PATROON[1], PATTERN.]
—**Syn.** *n.* **2.** sponsor, benefactor.

pa·tron[2] (pȧ trôN′), *n. French.* a proprietor.

pa·tron·age (pā′trə nij, pat′rə-), *n.* **1.** regular business given by customers: *to give one's patronage to a local store.* **2.** favor, encouragement, or support given by a patron: *Aided by their patronage and his own abilities, he had arrived at distinguished posts* (John L. Motley). **3.** condescending favor: *an air of patronage.* **4.** the power to give jobs or favors: *the patronage of a governor, mayor, or congressman.* **5.** political jobs or favors. **6.** the right of presentation to an ecclesiastical benefice; advowson.

pa·tron·al (pā′trə nəl), *adj.* acting the part of a patron; protecting; favoring.

pa·tro·nat (pȧ trô nȧ′), *n. French.* a trade association of industrial managers and employers: *[The] patronat has not been doing badly out of the Common Market* (London Times).

pa·tron·ess (pā′trə nis, pat′rə-), *n.* **1.** a woman patron. **2.** a woman who helps some social or charitable affair with her name, money, or presence.

pa·tron·ise (pā′trə nīz, pat′rə-), *v.t.,* **-ised, -is·ing.** *Especially British.* patronize.

pat·ron·ite (pat′rə nīt), *n.* one of the chief ores of vanadium, containing sulfur also.

pa·tron·ize (pā′trə nīz, pat′rə-), *v.t.,* **-ized, -iz·ing. 1.** to be a regular customer of; give regular business to: *We patronize our neighborhood stores.* **2.** to act as a patron toward; support or protect: *to patronize the ballet.* **3.** to treat in a condescending way: *We dislike to have anyone patronize us.* —**pa′tron·iz′er,** *n.* —**pa′tron·iz′ing·ly,** *adv.*

pa·tronne (pȧ trôn′), *n. French.* a proprietress.

patron saint, 1. a saint regarded as the special guardian of a person, church, city, nation, trade, etc.: *St. Christopher is the patron saint of travelers.* **2.** any revered protector, guardian, or leader: *The late John Maynard Keynes . . . is the patron saint of many of the Administration's economists* (New York Times).

pat·ro·nym (pat′rə nim), *n.* a patronymic.

pat·ro·nym·ic (pat′rə nim′ik), *n.* a name derived from the name of a father or ancestor: *Williamson meaning "son of William," and MacDonald meaning "descendant of Donald" are patronymics.* —*adj.* **1.** (of a family name) derived from the name of a father or ancestor. **2.** of or having to do with a suffix or prefix showing such derivation. [< Late Latin *patrōnymicus* < Greek *patrōnymikós*, ultimately < *patḗr, patrós* father + dialectal *ónyma* name]

pa·troon[1] (pə trün′), *n.* a landowner who had certain privileges under the former Dutch governments of New York and New Jersey. A patroon usually owned a large amount of land. [American English < Dutch *patroon* < Latin *patrōnus*. Doublet of PADRONE, PATRON[1], PATTERN.]

pa·troon[2] (pə trün′), *n. Obsolete.* patron[1]. [variant of *patron*[1]]

patroon system, a plan worked out by the Dutch West India Company from 1621 to 1623, based on patroons.

pat·sy (pat′sē), *n., pl.* **-sies.** *Slang.* **1.** an easy mark; victim for a gag or prank: *The Cards stopped being the patsies of the league and zoomed to the championship* (New York Times). **2.** a person to be given the blame for what someone else has done; fall guy: *O'Malley had already picked out his patsy* (Time). [origin uncertain]

pat·tée or **pat·té** (pa tā′, pat′ē), *adj. Heraldry.* (of a cross) having nearly triangular arms that narrow where they meet and widen toward the extremities. Also, **paty.** [< Old French *patte* pawed < earlier *pate* paw]

pat·ten (pat′ən), *n.* **1.** a wooden overshoe with a thick sole. **2.** a kind of wooden sandal or overshoe mounted on an iron ring, to raise the foot above wet ground: *Mrs. Peerybingle . . . clicking over the wet stones in a pair of pattens* (Dickens). [< Old French *patin* < *pate* paw] —**Syn. 1.** clog.

Patten (def. 2)
(19th century)

pat·tened (pat′ənd), *adj.* wearing pattens: *Wherever they went, some pattened girl stopped to courtesy* (Jane Austen).

pat·ter[1] (pat′ər), *v.i.* **1.** to make rapid taps: *The rain patters on a windowpane. Bare feet pattered along the hard floor.* **2.** to move with a rapid tapping sound: *to patter across the room.* —*v.t.* to cause to come or fall with a rapid tapping: *The trees would patter me all over with big drops from the rain of the afternoon* (Robert Louis Stevenson).
—*n.* a series of quick taps or the sound they make: *the patter of sleet.*
[frequentative form < *pat*[1]]

pat·ter[2] (pat′ər), *n.* **1.** rapid and easy talk: *a magician's patter, a salesman's patter.* **2.** the talk of a class or group: *I have more respect for conjurer's patter than for doctor's patter. They are both meant to stupefy* (G.K. Chesterton). **3.** rapid speech, usually for comic effect, introduced into a new song.
—*v.i.* **1.** to talk rapidly, fluently, or glibly: *We take the name of God in vain when we patter through prayers in our worship* (London Times). **2.** *Slang.* to speak or talk some jargon. —*v.t.* to talk or say rapidly and easily, without much thought.
[apparently variant of Middle English *pater*, as in *paternoster*] —**pat′ter·er,** *n.*
—**Syn.** *n.* **2.** jargon, lingo.

pat·ter·an (pat′ər ən), *n.* patrin.

pat·tern (pat′ərn), *n.* **1.** an arrangement of forms and colors; design: *the patterns of wallpaper, rugs, cloth, and jewelry; a pattern of polka dots.* **2.** a model or guide for something to be made: *Mother used a paper pattern in cutting out her new dress.* **3.** a fine example; model to be followed: *Washington was a pattern of manliness.* **4.** form; shape; configuration: *a large, deep cup with a bowl-like pattern.* **5.** the arrangement and use of content in particular forms, styles, etc., in a work of literature, music, etc.: *the regular, easily recognized pattern of a Haydn symphony.* **6.** *Sociology.* the customs, structure, values, etc., of a society arranged to reveal a form that can be studied and compared with other groups: *Ways of behaving abstracted directly from observation of behavior in a given society are called patterns* (Beals and Hoijer). **7. a.** a typical specimen; sample. **b.** something formed after a prototype; copy; likeness. **8.** a model in wood or metal from which a mold is made for casting. **9.** the distribution of shot or shrapnel over or on a target from a shell, bombs, etc. **10.** *Irish.* the festival of a patron saint or the festivities with which it is celebrated: *the occasion of a fair, or a pattern, or market day* (Samuel Lover).
—*v.t.* **1.** to make according to a pattern: *She patterned herself after her mother.* **2.** to work or decorate with a pattern: *The German anti-aircraft guns . . . begin to pattern the sky about them with little balls of black smoke* (H.G. Wells). **3.** *Archaic.* to match, parallel, or equal. **4. a.** *Rare.* to imitate; copy. **b.** *Obsolete.* to be a pattern for; prefigure or foreshadow: *Pattern'd by thy fault, foul sin may say, He learn'd to sin, and thou didst teach the way* (Shakespeare).
[variant of Middle English *patron* < Old French *patron* patron; pattern (from a client's copying his patron) < Latin *patrōnus*. Doublet of PADRONE, PATRON, PATROON[1].]
—**Syn.** *n.* **1.** motif. **2.** See **model. 3.** ideal, exemplar.

pat·terned (pat′ərnd), *adj.* having a pattern or patterns; decorated or worked with a pattern or design: *patterned tiles, a fancy-patterned sofa.*

pat·tern·ing (pat′ər ning), *n.* the formation or arrangement of patterns, as in an artistic creation: *Others . . . have fallen victim to [constructivist sculpture's] dangerous tendency to lead suddenly into intricate but meaningless patternings* (New Yorker).

pat·tern·less (pat′ərn lis), *adj.* without a pattern.

pat·tern·mak·er (pat′ərn mā′kər), *n.* a person who makes patterns, as for castings or clothing.

pat·tern·mak·ing (pat′ərn mā′king), *n.* the act or process of making patterns; the work of a patternmaker.

pat·tern·set·ter (pat′ərn set′ər), *n.* a person or thing that sets or can set a pattern for others to follow: *The plan will not necessarily be a patternsetter for all of the South.*

patter song, a humorous song in which a large number of words are fitted to a few notes and sung rapidly.

pat·tle (pat′əl), *n. Scottish.* a paddle.

pat·ty (pat′ē), *n., pl.* **-ties. 1.** a hollow form of pastry filled with chicken, oysters, etc.; pâté. **2.** a small, round, flat piece of food or candy. [< French *pâté* < Old French *paste*. Doublet of PASTY[2].]

pat·ty-cake (pat′ē kāk′), *n.* pat-a-cake.

patty pan, a small pan for baking little cakes, patties, etc.

patty shell, a pastry case for an individual serving of creamed meat, etc.

pat·u·lous (pach′ə ləs), *adj.* **1.** opening rather widely; expanded. **2.** slightly spreading, as the boughs of a tree. **3.** *Botany.* **a.** spreading slightly, as a calyx. **b.** bearing the flowers loose or dispersed, as a peduncle. [< Latin *patulus* (with English -*ous*) open < *patēre* lie open] —**pat′u·lous·ly,** *adv.* —**pat′u·lous·ness,** *n.*

pat·y (pat′ē), *adj. Heraldry.* pattée.

pau (pou), *adj. Hawaiian.* finished; completed; done.

P.A.U. or **PAU** (no periods), Pan American Union.

pau·ca ver·ba (pô′kə vėr′bə), *Latin.* few words.

pau·cis ver·bis (pô′sis vėr′bis), *Latin.* in few words; with brevity.

pau·ci·ty (pô′sə tē), *n.* **1.** a small number; fewness: *the paucity of the troops* (John L. Motley). **2.** a small amount; scarcity; lack: *Because of the paucity of coonskins, he's using Australian rabbit, skunk, and even American silver fox* (Wall Street Journal). [< Latin *paucitās* < *paucus* few] —**Syn. 2.** dearth, scantiness.

paugh·ty (pô′tē), *adj.,* **-ti·er, -ti·est.** *Scottish.* **1.** haughty; proud. **2.** saucy; impertinent. [origin unknown]

Paul (pôl), *n.* **Saint.** an early Christian missionary, known as the "Apostle of the Gentiles." He started Christian communities in many countries and wrote several of the epistles in the New Testament.

paul·dron (pôl′drən), *n.* a piece of armor for the shoulder. [earlier *pouldron*, alteration of Old French *espauleron* < *espaule* shoulder]

Paul·ine (pô′līn, -lēn), *adj.* **1.** of, having to do with, or written by the Apostle Paul. **2.** of his doctrines or writings, especially the epistles attributed to him in the New Testament.

Pau·li's principle (pou′lēz), *Physics.* the exclusion principle. [< Wolfgang *Pauli*, born 1900, an Austrian physicist, who suggested the principle]

Paul·ist (pô′list), *n.* **1.** (in the Roman Catholic Church) a member of the Congregation of the Missionary Priests of Saint Paul (the Apostle), founded at New York in 1858. **2.** *Obsolete.* (in India) a Jesuit.

Paul·is·ta (pô lis′tə), *n.* an inhabitant of São Paulo, Brazil: *There are more than 13 million Paulistas today, a bustling, proud, predominantly European people contemptuous of the leisured ways of the cariocas of Rio and the country bumpkins to the south* (London Times). [< Brazilian Portuguese *Paulista* < São *Paulo*]

pau·low·ni·a (pô lō′nē ə), *n.* any of a group of Chinese trees of the figwort family, as a species bearing clusters of purplish, trumpet-shaped flowers that bloom in early spring, widely cultivated for ornament. [< New Latin *Paulownia* < Anna *Pavlovna*, daughter of Czar Paul I of Russia]

paunch (pônch, pänch), *n.* **1.** the belly; stomach. **2.** a large, protruding belly: *a short, rosy-cheeked, apoplectic-looking subject, with . . . a paunch like an alderman's* (Charles J. Lever). **3.** the first and largest stomach of a cud-chewing animal. [< Old French *panche* < Latin *pantex*] —**Syn. 1.** abdomen. **2.** potbelly.

paunch·i·ness (pôn′chē nis, pän′-), *n.* a paunchy condition.

paunch·y (pôn′chē, pän′-), *adj.,* **paunch·i·er, paunch·i·est.** having a big paunch: *Now, a little paunchier, a little shorter of wind, they are still successful, but in business, not ball handling* (Newsweek).

pau·per (pô′pər), *n.* **1.** a person supported by charity; person supported by public welfare: *The pauper lives better than the free laborer; the thief better than the pauper* (Emerson). **2.** a very poor person: *On pauper's rations she has made the museum outstanding* (Time). —*adj.* of, relating to, or intended for a pauper or paupers. [< Latin *pauper* poor, related to *paucus* few. Doublet of POOR.]

pau·per·ism (pô′pə riz əm), *n.* **1.** poverty. **2.** paupers as a group. —**Syn. 1.** indigence, destitution.

pau·per·i·za·tion (pô′pər ə zā′shən), *n.* the act or process of pauperizing: *Since Algeria is unable at present to feed more than 3,000,000 people, the result has been mass pauperization* (Time).

pau·per·ize (pô′pə rīz), *v.t.,* **-ized, -iz·ing.** to make a pauper of: *In their search for financial security, they may unwittingly pauperize themselves* (New Yorker). —**pau′per·iz′er,** *n.*

pause (pôz), *v.,* **paused, paus·ing,** *n.* —*v.i.* **1.** to stop for a time; wait: *to pause for lunch. The dog paused when he heard me.* **2.** to dwell; linger: *to pause upon a word.*
[partly < the noun; partly < Late Latin *pausāre* < Latin *pausa*; see the noun]
—*n.* **1.** a moment of silence; rest; stop: *a pause for lunch. It had continued to rain almost without pause all day* (London Times). **2. a.** a brief stop in speaking or reading: *He made a short pause and then went on reading.* **b.** a punctuation mark indicating such a stop. **3.** *Music.* **a.** a sign (𝄐 or 𝄑) above or below a note, meaning that it is to be held for a longer time; fermata. **b.** a rest. **4.** *Prosody.* an interval in a line of verse; caesura.
give pause, to cause to stop or hesitate: *The hazards of the move gave them pause.*
[< Middle French *pause*, learned borrowing from Latin *pausa* < Greek *paûsis* < *paúein* to stop, cease] —**paus′er,** *n.* —**paus′ing·ly,** *adv.*
—**Syn.** *v.i.* **1.** See **stop.**

pause·less (pôz′lis), *adj.* without pause; ceaseless. —**pause′less·ly,** *adv.*

pa·uw (pä′ü, pou), *n.* paauw.

pav·an (pav′ən), *n.* **1.** a grave, stately dance in duple time, introduced into England in the 1500's, performed by couples. **2.**

the music for it, or with the same rhythm. Also, **pavin.** [< Middle French *pavane* < Spanish *pavana* < Italian, feminine of *pavano,* variant of *padovano* having to do with Padua, a city in Italy]

pav·ane (pav′ən; *French* på vån′), *n.* pavan.

pave (pāv), *v.t.,* **paved, pav·ing. 1.** to cover (a street, sidewalk, etc.) with a pavement. **2.** to make smooth or easy; prepare: *He paved the way for me by doing careful work.* [< Old French *paver,* ultimately < Latin *pavīre* to beat, tread down] —**pav′er,** *n.* —**Syn. 2.** facilitate.

pa·vé (på vā′), *n. French.* **1.** pavement. **2.** a setting in which jewels are placed close together, so as to show no metal.

pave·ment (pāv′mənt), *n.* **1.** a covering or surface for streets, sidewalks, etc., made of stones, bricks, wood, asphalt, etc.: *Traffic loads like this are far more than the pavement was designed to bear* (Newsweek). **2.** the material used for paving. **3.** a street, sidewalk, etc., that has been paved. [< Old French *pavement* < *paver* to pave, patterned on Latin *pavīmentum* a beaten-down floor < *pavīre* beat, tread down]

pavement artist, 1. a person who works in the street sketching and selling his drawings, especially portraits of passers-by. **2.** a person who draws figures or scenes on the pavement in order to get money from passers-by.

pav·id (pav′id), *adj.* frightened; fearful; timid: *The pavid matron within the one vehicle . . . shrieked and trembled* (Thackeray). [< Latin *pavidus* fearful, trembling < *pavēre* tremble with fear]

pa·vil·ion (pə vil′yən), *n.* **1.** a light building, usually one somewhat open, used for shelter, pleasure, etc.: *a dance pavilion, a bathing pavilion.* **2.** a large tent raised on posts; tent. **3.** a part of a building, higher and more decorated than the rest. **4.** one of a group of buildings forming a hospital. **5.** the lower part of a gem cut as a brilliant, especially the sloping surfaces between the girdle and the culet, or base. **6.** *Anatomy.* the auricle of the ear. **7.** *Obsolete.* a covering or canopy.
—*v.t.* **1.** to enclose or shelter in a pavilion. **2.** to furnish with a pavilion.
[< Old French *pavillon* < Latin *pāpiliō, -ōnis* tent; (originally) butterfly. Doublet of PAPILLON.]

pav·in (pav′ən), *n.* pavan.

pav·ing (pā′ving), *n.* **1.** material for pavement. **2.** a pavement. **3.** the act or work of a person or thing that paves.

pav·ior (pāv′yər), *n.* a person who lays pavements.

pav·iour (pāv′yər), *n. Especially British.* pavior.

pav·is or **pav·ise** (pav′is), *n.* a large shield used in the Middle Ages, covering the whole body. [< Old French *pavais* < Italian *pavese,* apparently < *Pavia,* a city in Italy, where they were first made]

pav·is·er or **pav·is·or** (pav′ə sər), *n.* a soldier armed with or carrying a pavis.

Pav·lov·i·an (päv lō′vē ən), *adj.* of, having to do with, or characteristic of Ivan Petrovich Pavlov, the physiologist and psychologist, or his research and findings.

PAVN (no periods), People's Army of (North) Vietnam.

Pa·vo (pā′vō), *n., genitive* **Pa·vo·nis.** a southern constellation near Ara; the Peacock.

pav·o·nine (pav′ə nīn, -nin), *adj.* **1.** of, having to do with, or like a peacock. **2.** resembling the plumage of the neck or tail of the peacock in coloring; having an iridescent greenish-blue color. [< Latin *pāvōnīnus* < *pāvō, -ōnis* peacock]

Pa·vo·nis (pə vō′nis), *n.* genitive of **Pavo.**

paw (pô), *n.* **1.** the foot of an animal having claws or nails: *Cats, dogs, monkeys, and bears have paws.* **2.** *Informal.* the hand.
—*v.t.* **1.** to strike or scrape with the paws or feet: *The cat pawed the mouse. The horse pawed the ground, eager to be going again.* **2.** *Informal.* to handle awkwardly, roughly, or in too familiar a manner: *They run their hands over your clothes—they paw you* (H. G. Wells). —*v.i.* **1.** to strike or scrape with the paws or feet: *Neighing steeds, tied to swinging limbs . . . pawed, wheeled, and gazed after their vanished riders* (George Washington Cable). **2.** to use the hands awkwardly, roughly, or in too familiar a manner: *Upstairs the hall was dark, but I found the duke's room and started to paw around it* (Mark Twain).
[< Old French *powe, poue,* or *poe,* perhaps < a Germanic word] —**paw′er,** *n.*

pawk (pôk), *n. British.* a trick or wile. [origin unknown]

pawk·i·ly (pô′kə lē), *adv. British.* in a pawky or arch manner; slyly: *"Indeed!" said Walkinshaw pawkily, "that's a very important circumstance"* (John Galt).

pawk·i·ness (pô′kē nis), *n. British.* pawky quality or state; slyness: *For the pawkiness of this proposal, the man should have been a Scotsman* (Archibald Forbes).

pawk·y (pô′kē), *adj.,* **pawk·i·er, pawk·i·est.** *British.* **1.** tricky; sly; cunning; crafty: *Benjamin Franklin at the court of Louis XVI, with his long hair, his plain clothes, and his pawky manner* (H. G. Wells). **2. a.** saucy. **b.** squeamish. **c.** proud. [< *pawk* + *-y*[1]]

pawl (pôl), *n.* a pivoted bar arranged to catch in the teeth of a ratchet wheel, etc., to prevent movement backward or to impart motion. [perhaps < Dutch *pal,* or < Middle French *pal* stake]

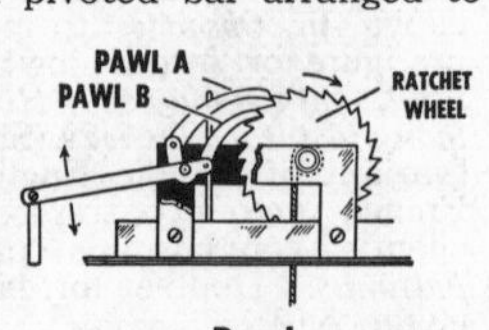

Pawl
The ratchet wheel is moved in the direction of the arrow by pawl A when the lever is moved up, and by pawl B when the lever is moved down.

pawn[1] (pôn), *v.t.* **1.** to leave (something) with another person as security that borrowed money will be repaid: *He pawned his watch to buy food until he could get work.* **2.** to pledge or stake; wager: *Thereon I pawn my credit and mine honour* (Shakespeare). [< noun]
—*n.* **1. a.** something left as security. **b.** a hostage: *He must leave behind, for pawns, His mother, wife and son* (John Dryden). **2.** a pledge. **3.** the act of pawning.
in pawn, in another's possession as security: *His television set is in pawn to pay his room rent.*
[< Old French *pan,* and *pant* piece; pledge, that is, something taken away]

pawn[2] (pôn), *n.* **1.** (in chess) one of the sixteen pieces of lowest value. On reaching the last rank of the board, the pawn acquires the value of any piece its player may desire, except a king. **2.** an unimportant person or thing used by someone for his own purposes: *We have got the poor pawn but the hand which plays the game is still out of our reach* (Sir Arthur Conan Doyle). [< Anglo-French *poun,* Old French *paon,* or *peon* (originally) foot soldier < Late Latin *pedō, -ōnis* splay-footed < Latin *pēs, pedis* foot. Doublet of PEON.]

pawn·a·ble (pô′nə bəl), *adj.* capable of being pawned: *By sundown, when the stores were closing, their pockets were filled with cash and the car was heaped with salable, pawnable wares* (Truman Capote).

pawn·age (pô′nij), *n.* the action or object of pawning.

pawn·bro·ker (pôn′brō′kər), *n.* a man who lends money at interest on articles that are left with him as security for the loan.

pawn·bro·king (pôn′brō′king), *n.* the business of a pawnbroker. —*adj.* that carries on the business of a pawnbroker.

pawn·ee (pô nē′), *n.* the person with whom something is deposited as a pawn or security.

Paw·nee (pô nē′), *n., pl.* **-nee** or **-nees,** *adj.* —*n.* **1.** a member of an American Indian tribe that lived near the forks of the Platte River and belonged to the confederacy of Caddoan linguistic stock. **2.** this confederacy. **3.** their language. —*adj.* of or relating to these Indians. [American English < Caddoan (Pawnee) *parīsu′* hunters]

pawn·er (pô′nər), *n.* the owner of an article or articles in pawn as security.

pawn·or (pô′nər, pô nôr′), *n. Law.* pawner.

pawn·shop (pôn′shop′), *n.* a pawnbroker's shop: *Pawnshops, so often the fences for concealing stolen goods, abound most in the precincts infamous for poverty and crime* (Harper's).

paw·paw (pô′pô), *n.* **1.** papaw. **2.** papaya. See picture under **papaya.** [American English, variant of *papaw*]

pax (paks), *n.* in the Roman Catholic Church: **1.** a kiss of peace given by the celebrant at a High Mass to the members of the clergy in the sanctuary. **2.** a small tablet, bearing a representation of the Crucifixion or some other sacred subject, used, especially during the Middle Ages, as a means of giving the kiss of peace at Mass, being kissed by the celebrant, the clergy, and the congregation. [< Late Latin *pāx, pācis* the kiss of peace < Latin, peace]

Pax (def. 2)

Pax (paks), *n.* the Roman goddess of peace, equivalent to the Greek goddess Irene. [< Latin *Pāx*]

Pax Bri·tan·ni·ca (paks′ bri tan′i kə), the peace of Britain; the public peace established in the realm of Britain.

pax in bel·lo (paks′ in bel′ō), *Latin.* peace in war.

Pax Ro·ma·na (paks′ rō mä′nə), **1.** a period of approximately 200 years (27 B.C.-A.D. 180) which began with the reign of Augustus Caesar, during which there was comparative peace in the then-known civilized world, a peace enforced by the might of Rome: *The barbaric realities of 6th century Britain, with its . . . sheltered relics of the Pax Romana* (Time). **2.** an organization formed by the merger of an Italian students' movement and that of a group of cultural and intellectual leaders. Begun in 1921 and reorganized in 1947, its aims are to spread Catholic charity, activity, and thought through national and international life. **3.** a peace dictated to a conquered nation by its subjugators. [< Latin *pāx Rōmāna* (literally) Roman peace]

pax vo·bis·cum (paks′ vō bis′kəm), *Latin.* peace (be) with you.

pax·wax (paks′waks′), *n.* the tough, elastic ligament, composed of yellow, fibrous tissue, at the back of the neck of various quadruped mammals, by which the head is supported. [apparently variant of Middle English *faxwax,* probably < Old English *feax* hair of the head + *weaxan* to grow]

pay[1] (pā), *v.,* **paid** or (*Obsolete except for def. 10*) **payed, pay·ing,** *n., adj.* —*v.t.* **1.** to give (a person) what is due for things, work, etc.: *He paid the doctor.* **2.** to give (money, etc.) that is due: *to pay $50 for a coat.* **3.** to give money for: *Pay your way.* **4.** to hand over (money owed); hand over the amount of: *to pay a debt, bill, taxes, dividends, or tolls.* **5.** to give; offer; make: *to pay attention, pay compliments, pay a visit.* **6.** to be profitable to; be worth while to: *It pays me to keep that stock. It wouldn't pay me to take that job.* **7.** to yield as a return: *The will to establish a society in which the superior development of some is not paid for by the exploitation, that is, by the deliberate degradation of others* (Edmund Wilson). *That stock pays me four per cent.* **8.** to return for favors or hurts; recompense or requite; reward or punish: *He paid them for their insults by causing them trouble.* **9.** to suffer; undergo: *The one who does wrong must pay the penalty.* **10.** *Nautical.* to let out (a rope, etc.): *As they paid out the chain, we swung clear of them* (Richard Henry Dana). —*v.i.* **1.** to give money; give what is owed: *He owes it and must pay.* **2.** to be profitable or advantageous: *It pays to be polite.*
pay back, a. to return borrowed money: *He paid back the money he borrowed.* **b.** to give the same treatment as received: *I'll pay back the favor by inviting her to dinner.* **c.** to take revenge on: *I'll pay you back yet!*
pay in, a. to make in payment: *He had paid in all the money* (Daniel Defoe). **b.** to make contributions (to a fund): *Men must pay in to the trade society to which they transfer their labour* (Parliamentary Commission Report).
pay off, a. to give all the money that is owed; pay in full: *To enable the directors to pay off pressing liabilities* (Law Reports). **b.** to get even with; get revenge on: *. . . to pay off some grudge* (Julian Hawthorne). **c.** to cause (a ship) to turn leeward: *The Captain paid his vessel off before the wind.* **d.** (of a ship) to fall off to leeward after facing into the wind: *The little vessel 'paid*

off' from the wind (Richard Henry Dana). **e.** *Informal.* to pay money for so-called protection, but actually as a tribute to racketeers, etc.: *I got a phone call from an underworld person . . . who warned me I had to pay off* (Wall Street Journal). **f.** to be profitable or advantageous: *It takes time . . . before overseas processing pays off* (Wall Street Journal).

pay out, to make payment; spend: *I could hardly expect him to pay out a large sum of money for a drawing he knew nothing about* (Listener).

pay up, to pay in full; pay: *The loan has been paid up.*

—*n.* **1. a.** money or the equivalent given for things, service, or work; wages; salary: *Jim gets his pay every Friday.* **b.** return for favors or hurts: *Dislike is the pay for being mean.* **2.** a source of payment. **3.** the act of paying; payment, especially of wages: *rate of pay.* **4.** the condition of being paid, or receiving wages: *workers in a person's pay or employment.* **5.** a person's ability to pay his bills or his record in discharging his debts.

in the pay of, paid by and working for: *Unless we should suppose that the murderers were in the pay of Sparta* (Connop Thirlwall).

—*adj.* **1.** containing a device for receiving money for use: *a pay telephone.* **2.** containing enough metal, oil, etc., to be worth mining, drilling, etc.: *a pay lode.*

[< Old French *paier* < Vulgar Latin *pācāre* pay, satisfy a creditor < Latin, pacify < *pāx, pācis* peace]

—**Syn.** *v.t.* **1. Pay, compensate, remunerate** mean to give money or its equivalent in return for something. **Pay** is the common word meaning to give someone money due for things or services: *He paid the grocer for the things he bought.* **Compensate** suggests making up for time spent, things lost, service given, or the like: *The railroad compensated the farmer for his cow.* **Remunerate** suggests giving a reward in return for services, trouble, etc., and is used especially, as *compensate* also is, as more polite than *pay* and not suggesting crudely that money is expected or due: *The club remunerated the lecturer.* -*n.* **1. a.** compensation, remuneration. ➔ See **paid** for usage note.

pay[2] (pā), *v.t.*, **payed, pay·ing.** to cover (a ship's bottom, seams, rope, etc.) with tar, pitch, or another waterproof substance. [< Old North French *peier*, Old French *poier* < Latin *picāre* (< *pix, picis* pitch]

pay·a·bil·i·ty (pā'ə bil'ə tē), *n.* capability of being profitably worked, as a mine: *Ore of high payability containing a relatively large proportion of high values* (Cape Times).

pay·a·ble (pā'ə bəl), *adj.* **1.** required to be paid; falling due; due: *He must spend $100 soon on bills payable.* **2.** that may be paid. **3.** *Law.* (of a debt) capable of being discharged by delivering the value in money or goods. **4.** capable of yielding profit; commercially profitable: *payable ore deposits.* —**Syn. 1.** unpaid, owing.

pay-as-you-earn (pā'əz yú ėrn'), *n. British.* the withholding of income tax at the time wages or salaries are paid.

pay-as-you-go (pā'əz yú gō'), *U.S.* —*n.* **1.** the withholding of income tax at the time wages or salaries are paid. **2.** the payment or discharge of obligations as they are incurred: *His major emphasis in taking office was to achieve pay-as-you-go* (New York Times). —*adj.* of or having to do with pay-as-you-go: *The proposal to put California taxes on a pay-as-you-go basis is sure to touch off a controversy in the legislature* (Wall Street Journal).

pay-as-you-see (pā'əz yú sē'), *adj.* designating any of several plans for subscription television broadcasting, as one in which the viewer has a direct line to the studio and pays for those programs he wishes to see: *Now there is pending the great question of whether we will have pay-as-you-see TV* (New York Times).

pay·box (pā'boks'), *n. British.* a cashier's booth: *I was having a cup of tea when an old chap came up to the paybox with 6d.* (Cape Times).

pay·check (pā'chek'), *n.*, or **pay check,** a check given in payment of wages or salary: *I took my first paycheck and went out and bought myself what I thought was a genuine Savile Row wardrobe* (New Yorker).

pay claim, 1. a claim for money owed or desired: *These managers voted fat bonuses for themselves before considering the pay claims of the workers* (Wall Street Journal). **2.** a claim for unemployment insurance: *Jobless pay claims dipped for the fifth straight week* (Newsweek).

pay·day (pā'dā'), *n.* the day on which wages are paid: *The following payday Bok found an increase in his weekly envelope* (Edward W. Bok).

pay dirt, 1. *U.S.* earth, ore, etc., containing enough metal to be worth mining: *Two of her officers staked an Indian to search pay dirt* (Maclean's). **2.** *Informal.* something that yields a profit or beneficial result: *Mayor Lee has struck political pay dirt in an unpromising issue* (Harper's).

PAYE (no periods) or **P.A.Y.E., 1.** *British.* pay-as-you-earn: *It has many features comparable to the British income tax system, including P.A.Y.E.* (Manchester Guardian). **2.** pay as you enter.

pay·ee (pā ē'), *n.* a person to whom money is paid or is to be paid, especially a person to whom a bill or check is made payable.

pay envelope, an envelope in which a person's salary or wages are delivered either in cash or by check: *Already this year such clauses have meant fatter pay envelopes for a lot of workers* (Wall Street Journal).

pay·er (pā'ər), *n.* a person who pays; person who is to pay a bill or note.

pay·ing (pā'ing), *adj.* **1.** that pays; giving money or compensation for what is received: *a paying guest.* **2.** yielding a return or profit; remunerative: *a paying business.*

pay·load (pā'lōd'), *n.* **1.** the load carried by an aircraft, train, truck, etc., which is capable of producing a revenue. **2.** the vehicle or satellite, instruments, warhead, etc., which a rocket carries: *The U.S. space program . . . plans to put up bigger payloads before long* (Wall Street Journal). See picture under **intermediate-range ballistic missile.**

pay·mas·ter (pā'mas'tər, -mäs'-), *n.* a person whose job is to pay wages.

paymaster general, the officer at the head of the pay department of an army, navy, or air force.

pay·ment (pā'mənt), *n.* **1.** a paying. **2. a.** the amount paid: *a monthly payment of $10.* **b.** money or other thing paid as wages or a price; pay: *What will he accept as payment?* **3.** reward or punishment.

suspend payments, to declare inability to pay one's debts; become bankrupt; fail: *Because of lagging sales and mounting costs, the corporation had to suspend payments.*

—**Syn. 1.** compensation, remuneration, settlement.

pay·mis·tress (pā'mis'tris), *n.* a woman charged with the payment of wages.

pay·nim or **Pay·nim** (pā'nim), *Archaic.* —*n.* **1.** a pagan; heathen. **2.** a Moslem; Saracen: . . . *the crusader, who had sunk thirty thousand paynims at a blow* (John L. Motley). **3.** pagandom; heathendom.

—*adj.* **1.** pagan; heathen: *A people . . . a remnant that were left Paynim amid their circles, and the stones They pitch up straight to heaven* (Tennyson). **2.** Moslem; Saracen: *Paynim sons of swarthy Spain* (Scott).

[< Old French *paienimme*, earlier *paienisme* < Late Latin *pāgānismus* the religion of the pagans < Latin *pāgānus* rustic; see PAGAN]

pay·off (pā'ôf', -of'), *n.* **1.** a paying of wages. **2.** the time of such payment. **3. a.** the returns from an enterprise, specific action, etc.; result: *You will see the payoff immediately . . . without need for specially trained operators* (Wall Street Journal). *. . . venturing from sixpence up in the football pools—and dreaming of payoffs as high as 300,000 pounds for predicting results* (Maclean's). **b.** *Informal.* a dividing of the returns from some undertaking among those having an interest in it: *the investigation of alleged payoffs by big Government contractors to officials* (New York Times). **c.** *Slang.* anything given or received in reward or punishment. **4.** *Slang.* the climax (of a story, situation, etc.): *Brother, I've heard some dillies in my day, but that's the payoff* (New Yorker). —*adj.* of or having to do with making payment: *payoff schedule.*

—**Syn.** *n.* **4.** culmination.

pay·o·la (pā ō'lə), *n. Slang.* undercover payments or graft, made or given in return for favors, as to disk jockeys for otherwise free promotion of a record, song, or performer.

pay·out (pā'out'), *n.* money paid out; expense.

pay packet, *British.* a pay envelope.

pay pause, *British.* wage freeze: *Because of the pay pause, Service men are to receive only half the increase this year (on April 1), and the rest in a year's time* (Manchester Guardian).

pay·roll (pā'rōl'), *n.*, or **pay roll, 1.** a list of persons to be paid and the amounts that each one is to receive: *He never had to meet a payroll. Payrolls tend to grow and resist pruning and frequently politics substitutes for economics* (Bulletin of Atomic Scientists). **2.** the total amount to be paid to them: *a payroll of $10,000 a month.*

payroll tax, a tax levied on business payrolls, and paid either by the employer or the employee, or both, especially to provide for unemployment insurance.

pay·sage (pā ē zäzh'), *n. French.* a painting or drawing of a rural scene; landscape.

pay scale, range of salaries or wages: *These, then, the highest paid scholars in the land, attain a place on the pay scale equivalent to that of a colonel, at the bottom rank of the military noblesse* (Atlantic).

pay·sheet (pā'shēt'), *n. British.* a list of persons receiving wages with the amounts due to them; payroll.

pay station, a public pay telephone.

payt., payment.

pay television, pay-TV.

pay-TV (pā'tē'vē'), *n.* a system of subscription television in which the user's set is connected directly to the broadcast studio and he pays a monthly charge for an agreed number of special programs: *To theater owners and others, pay-TV was no longer a remote possibility but a distinct threat* (Newsweek).

Pb (no period), lead (chemical element).

P.B., 1. British Pharmacopoeia (Latin *Pharmacopoeia Britannica*). **2.** Prayer Book.

PBA (no periods), Public Buildings Administration.

P.B.A., Patrolmen's Benevolent Association.

PBX (no periods), private branch (telephone) exchange.

pc., 1. piece. **2.** prices.

p.c., 1. per cent. **2.** post card.

PC (no periods), a patrol craft of the U. S. Navy or Coast Guard, a class of fast, small, lightly armed boats used especially for antisubmarine patrolling, reconaissance, etc.

P.C., an abbreviation for the following:
1. Past Commander.
2. Philippine Constabulary.
3. *British.* Police Constable.
4. Post Commander.
5. *British.* **a.** Privy Council. **b.** Privy Councilor.
6. *Canadian.* Progressive Conservative.

p/c, or **P/C, 1.** petty cash. **2.** price or prices current.

PCA (no periods), **1.** Production Code Administration. **2.** Progressive Citizens of America.

pcl., parcel.

pct., 1. per cent. **2.** precinct.

pd., paid.

p.d., 1. per diem. **2.** potential difference.

Pd (no period), palladium (chemical element).

P.D., 1. Per Diem. **2.** Police Department. **3.** Postal District. **4.** Public Defender.

Pd.B., Bachelor of Pedagogy (Latin, *Pedagogiae Baccalaureus*).

Pd.D., Doctor of Pedagogy.

Pd.M., Master of Pedagogy.

p.e., *Statistics.* probable error.

P.E., 1. Presiding Elder. **2.** *Statistics.* probable error. **3.** professional engineer. **4.** Protestant Episcopal.

pea (pē), *n., pl.* **peas,** *Archaic* or *British Dialect* **pease,** *adj.* —*n.* **1.** one of several round seeds in the green pod of an annual plant of the pea family, used as a vegetable. **2.** the plant itself, a vine having pinnate leaves, white flowers, and long dehiscent pods. **3.** any of various similar plants or seeds, especially when used for food, as the cowpea and chickpea. **4.** something small and round like a pea, as the roe of certain fish. **5.** a fragment of iron pyrites from ⅛ to ½ inch in diameter, used in the manufacture of sulfuric acid.

as like as two peas (in a pod), exactly alike: *It has become fashionable among sophisticated European intellectuals, and among some Americans of the same type, to subscribe to*

the theory that the United States and the Soviet Union are almost as like as two peas in a pod (Wall Street Journal).
—*adj.* of the size of a pea: *pea coal.*
[new singular < *pease*[1], taken as a plural]

pea bean, a small, white, nutritious variety of the kidney bean, much used for baking.

pea·ber·ry (pē′ber′ē, -bər-), *n., pl.* **-ries.** a coffee berry with one of its two seeds aborted, the developed seed being round and pealike, not flattened on one side like the ordinary seed.

Pea·bod·y bird (pē′bod′ē, -bə dē), the white-throated sparrow. [probably imitative of its song]

peace (pēs), *n., interj., v.,* **peaced, peac·ing.** —*n.* **1.** freedom from war or strife of any kind: *peace in the family. Peace hath her victories no less renowned than war* (Milton). **2.** public quiet, order, and security. **3.** an agreement between contending parties to end war: *to sign the peace.* **4.** quiet; calm: *peace of mind. We enjoy the peace of the country.* **5.** *Obsolete.* a person who imposes or maintains peace.
at peace, a. not in a state of war: *The United States is at peace with her neighbors.* **b.** not at strife or at variance: *He is at peace with this world and the next* (John W. Warter). **c.** in a state of quietness; quiet; peaceful: *All was at peace in the dead of the night.*
hold or **keep one's peace,** to remain quiet or silent: *Speak not when you should hold your peace* (George Washington).
keep the peace, to refrain, or prevent others, from disturbing the (public) peace; maintain public order: *Dragoons . . . stationed near Berwick, for the purpose of keeping the peace* (Macaulay).
make one's peace, to effect reconciliation for oneself or for someone else: *to make one's peace with an enemy. I will make your peace with him, if I can* (Shakespeare).
make peace, a. to effect a reconciliation between persons or parties at variance: *to make peace between union and management.* **b.** to conclude peace with a nation at the close of a war: *They of Gibeon had made peace with Israel* (Miles Coverdale).
—*interj.* keep still! stay quiet! be silent!
—*v.i. Archaic.* to be or become silent: *When the thunder would not peace at my bidding* (Shakespeare).
[< Old French *pais* < Latin *pāx, pācis,* related to *pangere* to agree upon]
—**Syn.** *n.* **1.** harmony, concord, amity. **4.** tranquility, serenity.

peace·a·ble (pē′sə bəl), *adj.* **1.** liking peace; keeping peace: *Peaceable people keep out of quarrels.* **2.** peaceful: *a peaceable reign.* —**peace′a·ble·ness,** *n.* —**Syn. 1.** pacific, amicable, friendly. **2.** See **peaceful.**

peace·a·bly (pē′sə blē), *adv.* in a peaceable manner: *Peaceably if we can, forcibly if we must* (Henry Clay, quoting Josiah Quincy).

Peace Corps, an agency of the U.S. government, established in 1961 to provide people with technical skill to underdeveloped countries: *For the Peace Corps to succeed . . . its volunteers must have some ideal of life to which they are dedicated* (Saturday Review).

Peace Corpsman, a member of the Peace Corps; volunteer sent by the Peace Corps to help improve conditions in an underdeveloped country.

peace·ful (pēs′fəl), *adj.* **1.** full of peace; quiet; calm: *a peaceful countryside.* **2.** liking peace; keeping peace; peaceable: *peaceful neighbors.* **3.** of or having to do with peace: *to settle a dispute by peaceful means.* —**peace′ful·ly,** *adv.* —**peace′ful·ness,** *n.*
—**Syn. 1. Peaceful, peaceable, placid, serene** mean quiet and calm. **Peaceful** suggests a state of inner quiet, free from disturbance or strife: *These are not peaceful days in which we live.* **Peaceable** suggests a disposition that avoids strife and seeks to maintain peace and order: *Because the chairman remained peaceable, the group calmed down.* **Placid** suggests a disposition that stays undisturbed and undistracted: *Placid cows grazed beside the highway.* **Serene** suggests a disposition that remains quietly and graciously composed even in the midst of confusion: *She is always cool, gracious, and serene.*

peace·keep·ing (pēs′kē′ping), *adj.* maintaining, enforcing, or intervening to achieve a cessation of hostilities between opposing armies, countries, etc.: *a peacekeeping force.*

peace·less (pēs′lis), *adj.* without peace; unquiet. —**peace′less·ness,** *n.*

peace·mak·er (pēs′mā′kər), *n.* a person who makes peace. —**Syn.** mediator.

peace·mak·ing (pēs′mā′king), *n.* the act of making or bringing about peace: *a programme of positive peacemaking* (London Times). —*adj.* that makes or brings about peace: *a peacemaking mission.*

peace marcher, a person who takes part in a march to a government seat, an embassy, etc., to demonstrate for peace: *A group of "peace marchers" . . . will leave Delhi tomorrow on a walk to Peking of some 3,500-4,000 miles* (London Times).

peace·mon·ger (pēs′mung′gər, -mong′-), *n.* a person who persistently advocates peace (used in an unfriendly way): *The peacemongers were ready to have sacrificed the honor of England* (Robert Southey).

peace·nik (pēs′nik), *n. Slang.* a person who demonstrates publicly for peace. [< *peace* + *-nik*]

peace offensive, a determined attempt or campaign by a country to end a state of hostility or to ease strained relations between itself and another country: *The cold war has known many Russian peace offensives for tactical purposes, even under the rigid and belligerent Stalin* (Wall Street Journal).

peace offering, 1. an offering made to obtain peace: *He was not to be sacrificed as a peace offering to revengeful Rome* (John L. Motley). **2.** (in old Jewish custom) an offering of thanksgiving to God, as prescribed in the Levitical law. Leviticus 3: 1-17.

peace officer, a policeman, sheriff, or constable.

peace pipe, a pipe smoked ceremonially by adult male members of certain North American Indian tribes as a token or pledge of peace: *The Professor and Red Cloud . . . were photographed with clasped hands and the peace pipe between them* (J. H. Cook). See picture under **calumet.**

peace·time (pēs′tīm′), *n.* a time of peace: *some of the toughest controls ever imposed on Canadian business in peacetime* (Time). —*adj.* of or having to do with a time of peace: *the peacetime uses of atomic energy.*

peach[1] (pēch), *n.* **1.** a juicy, nearly round fruit of a yellowish-pink color, with downy skin, a sweet pulp, and a rough stone or pit. Peaches are grown in temperate climates, and are clingstones if the pulp sticks to the stone, or freestone if it separates from the stone easily. See picture under **pericarp. 2.** the tree of the rose family that this fruit grows on. **3.** a peach blossom. **4.** any of various similar trees or fruits. **5.** a yellowish pink. **6.** *Slang.* a person or thing especially admired or liked: *Produce dealers here were getting a peach of a price for peaches today* (New York Times).
—*adj.* yellowish-pink.
[< Old French *peche,* earlier *pesche* < Late Latin *persica* < Latin *Persica,* plural of *Persicum* (*mālum*) (literally) Persian apple < Greek *Persikón* (*mâlon*)]

peach[2] (pēch), *v.i. Slang.* to give secret information; turn informer: *No good was to be got by peaching on him* (Henry Kingsley). —*v.t. Obsolete.* to impeach or indict. [short for Middle English *apechen* appeach < Anglo-French *apecher,* Old French *empechier* hinder, impeach < Late Latin *impedicāre*]

peach blossom, the pink flower that blooms on the peach tree just before the leaves in the spring. It is the floral emblem of Delaware.

peach·blow (pēch′blō′), *n.* **1.** a delicate purplish-pink color, like that of a peach blossom. **2.** a ceramic glaze of this color, an identifying feature of some Chinese porcelain.

peaches and cream, *Slang.* splendid; fine; wonderful: *It would be unfair to maintain that all was peaches and cream . . . or to suggest that all city neighborhoods are as filled with goods and services within easy walking distance as our own* (Atlantic).

peach·i·ness (pē′chē nis), *n.* the quality of being peachy.

peach Melba, pêche Melba: *. . . to find peach Melba listed under desserts on a small town menu* (Maclean's).

peach·y (pē′chē), *adj.,* **peach·i·er, peach·i·est. 1.** like a peach; like that of a peach. **2.** *Slang.* fine; wonderful: *Mrs. Stimson came over and said everything looked just peachy* (New Yorker).

pea coat, pea jacket.

pea·cock (pē′kok′), *n., pl.* **-cocks** or (*collectively*) **-cock,** *v.* —*n.* **1.** any of several large birds with beautiful green, blue, and gold feathers. The tail feathers have spots like eyes on them and can be spread out and held upright like a fan. The peacock lives in Asia and Africa, nests on the ground, and can fly only short distances. **2.** any male peacock, especially as contrasted with the *peahen.* **3.** a person who is vain and fond of showing off.

Indian Peacock (def. 1) (not including tail, about 20 in. long)

—*v.i.* to strut like a peacock; make a conceited display; pose. —*v.t.* **1.** to cause to strut or pose like a peacock; make vain. **2.** *Australian Slang.* to pick out the choicest piece of land, so that the adjoining land loses its value to anyone else.
[Middle English *pekok,* also *pakock* < Old English *pēa, pāwa* a peafowl of either sex (< Latin *pāvō, -ōnis*) + *cocc* cock[1]]

Pea·cock (pē′kok′), *n.* the constellation Pavo.

peacock blue, a greenish blue. —**pea′cock-blue′,** *adj.*

pea·cock·ish (pē′kok′ish), *adj.* like a peacock or that of a peacock: *An ardent, almost peacockish vanity* (Spectator).

peacock ore, an iridescent copper ore; bornite.

peacock pheasant, any of various Asiatic pheasants notable for their handsome plumage with eyelike spots and the spurred legs of the male.

pea·cock·y (pē′kok′ē), *adj.* peacocklike; showy; vainglorious.

pea comb, a type of comb on certain breeds of chickens, as the brahmas, made up of three short rows of low serrations.

pea crab, any of certain small crabs that live in the mantle cavities of certain mollusks.

pea family, one of the largest of all plant families, containing dicotyledonous plants of great variety and wide distribution, characterized by having a legume as the fruit. The family includes ornamentals such as the lupine and wisteria, and many plants of great economic importance such as the pea, peanut, bean, indigo, clover, and licorice.

pea·fowl (pē′foul′), *n.* a peacock or peahen.

peag or **peage** (pēg), *n.* wampum. [American English; short for *wampunipeag*]

pea green, a light green. —**pea′-green′,** *adj.*

pea·hen (pē′hen′), *n.* the female of the peacock.

pea jacket, a short, usually dark-blue coat of thick woolen cloth, worn especially by sailors. [American English, perhaps < Frisian *pijekkat*]

Peahen

peak[1] (pēk), *n.* **1.** the pointed top of a mountain or hill: *snowy peaks.* **2.** a mountain or hill that stands alone: *Pike's Peak.* **3.** the highest point: *to reach the peak of one's profession.* **4.** any pointed end or top: *the peak of a roof, the peak of a beard.* **5.** the projecting front part or the brim of a cap. **6.** the narrow part of a ship's hold at the bow or at the stern. **7.** the upper rear corner of a sail that is extended by a gaff, such as a spanker. **8.** the outer end of a gaff: *a full-rigged brig, with the Yankee ensign at her peak* (Richard Henry Dana). **9.** a promontory or point of land; headland. **10.** an advancing or retreating point formed by the hair on the forehead. **11.** *Physics.* **a.** the greatest frequency or highest value of a varying quantity during a given period. **b.** the greatest amount of power used or generated by a unit or group of units during a given period. **12.** *Obsolete.* a beak or bill.
—*adj.* of or having to do with a peak: *peak output. The minister of social affairs infuriated the opposition by hogging a peak viewing-hour* (Economist).
—*v.t.* **1.** to raise straight up; tilt up. **2.** to raise the end of (a yard, gaff, etc.) so that it is as nearly vertical as possible. **3.** to bring to a peak or head. —*v.i.* to come to a peak

or head: *It may develop a typical pattern with appropriations peaking in the first quarter* (Newsweek). [variant of *pick*²]
—**Syn.** *n.* **3.** summit, pinnacle.

peak² (pēk), *v.i.* to droop in health and spirits; waste away: *peaking and pining over what people think of him* (Charles Kingsley). [origin uncertain]

peaked¹ (pēkt, pē′kid), *adj.* having a peak; pointed: *a peaked hat.* [< *peak*¹ + *-ed*²]

peak·ed² (pē′kid), *adj.* sickly in appearance; wan; thin: *He really looked quite peaked and rundown* (John Stephen Strange). [< *peak*² + *-ed*²]

peak-hour (pēk′our′), *adj.* of or having to do with the hour or period of time when something is at its peak: *The Post Office says even peak-hour mail could be speeded up if more of it were properly prepared* (Wall Street Journal).

peak·y (pē′kē), *adj.,* **peak·i·er, peak·i·est.** **1.** peaked or pointed; peaklike. **2.** abounding in peaks.

peal¹ (pēl), *n.* **1.** a loud, long sound: *a peal of thunder, peals of laughter.* **2.** the loud ringing of bells. **3. a.** a set of bells tuned to each other; chimes. **b.** a series of changes rung on a set of bells.
—*v.t.* **1.** to sound out in a peal; ring. *The bells pealed forth their message of Christmas joy.* **2.** *Obsolete.* to overwhelm with noise; assail (the ears, or a person) with loud noise, clamor, etc. —*v.i.* to sound forth in a peal or peals; resound: *an outcry that went pealing through the night* (Hawthorne).
[Middle English *pele;* origin uncertain]
—**Syn.** *n.* **1.** roar.

peal² (pēl), *n. Obsolete.* appeal. [Middle English *pele,* short for *appeal,* noun]

pe·an (pē′ən), *n.* paean.

pea·nut (pē′nut′), *n.* **1.** a plant of the pea family, probably native to South America, whose pods ripen underground and usually contain two large seeds which are used as food and for their oil; groundnut; goober. **2.** one of these pods containing seeds. **3.** one of these seeds, eaten as nuts when roasted. **4.** *Slang.* a small or unimportant person.
peanuts, *Informal.* something of little or no value; a relatively small amount of money: *In terms of cash outlay, the sum is peanuts for an outfit like Krupps* (Montreal Star).
[American English < *pea* + *nut*]

peanut brittle, a candy of caramelized sugar and peanuts.

peanut butter, a food made of peanuts ground until soft and smooth. It is spread on bread, crackers, etc.

peanut gallery, *Slang.* the uppermost balcony of a theater or public hall: *And I can remember sitting high up just like a peanut in the peanut gallery of a great hall in Kansas City* (New Yorker).

peanut oil, oil pressed from peanuts, used especially in cookery and as an ingredient of oleomargarine.

pear (pãr), *n.* **1.** a sweet, juicy, edible fruit rounded at one end and smaller toward the stem end. Pears are pomes and are grown in temperate climates. **2.** the tree of the rose family that this fruit grows on. **3.** any of various similar trees or fruits, as the avocado or the prickly pear. [Old English *pere* < Vulgar Latin *pira,* or *pēra* feminine singular < neuter plural of Latin *pirum*]

pear drop, **1.** a pear-shaped candy, usually flavored with essence of jargonelle. **2.** a pear-shaped jewel used as a pendant.

pearl¹ (pėrl), *n.* **1.** a hard, smooth, white or nearly white gem that has a soft shine like satin. Pearls are formed inside the shell of a kind of oyster or in other similar shellfish. The secretions of carbonate of lime with layers of animal membrane around a grain of sand, parasitic worm, or other foreign matter in the shell produce a pearl. **2.** a thing that looks like a pearl, such as a dewdrop or a tear. **3.** a very fine one of its kind: *She is a pearl among women.* **4.** a very pale, clear, bluish gray; pearl blue. **5.** mother-of-pearl. **6.** a size of printing type (5 point).
This sentence is set in pearl.
cast pearls before swine, to give something very fine to a person who cannot appreciate it: *Oh I do a thankless thing, and cast pearls before swine!* (Dickens).
—*adj.* **1.** very pale, clear bluish-gray. **2.** formed into small, round pieces: *pearl tapioca.*
—*v.i.* to hunt or dive for pearls: *We've pearled on half-shares in the Bay* (Rudyard Kipling). —*v.t.* **1.** to adorn or set with or as with pearls, or with mother-of-pearl. **2.** to make pearly in color or luster. **3.** to convert or reduce to small round pieces, as in making pearl tapioca from the ground root of the cassava.
[< Old French *perle* < Vulgar Latin *perla;* origin uncertain] —**Syn.** *n.* **5.** nacre.

pearl² (pėrl), *v.t., v.i., n.* purl².

pearl·ash (pėrl′ash′), *n.* potassium carbonate, usually made by refining potash.

pearl barley, barley reduced by polishing to small rounded grains, used in soups.

pearl blue, a very pale, clear bluish gray; pearl.

pearl bush, a tall bush of the rose family, native to Asia but cultivated in the western United States as a garden plant, bearing white flowers.

pearl diver, **1.** a person who dives to the ocean bottom to bring up pearl oysters. **2.** *Slang.* a person who washes dishes.

pearl diving, the business of diving for pearls.

pearl·er (pėr′lər), *n.* **1.** a person who fishes for pearls, especially by diving for, or dredging, and opening, oysters. **2.** a boat used in pearl fishing.

pearl·es·cent (pėr les′ənt), *adj.* having a high luster of many colors like a pearl: *We are also told that our swanlike necks should be swathed in pearlescent beads* (New Yorker).

pearl farming, the act or business of cultivating pearl oysters.

pearl·fish (pėrl′fish′), *n., pl.* **-fish·es** or (*collectively*) **-fish.** **1.** any of the small fishes that live in the shells of mollusks and in large holothurians. **2.** any of certain fishes, as a minnow, whose scales are used in the manufacture of artificial pearls.

pearl fisher, a person who fishes for pearls.

pearl-fish·er·y (pėrl′fish′ər ē), *n., pl.* **-er·ies.** **1.** the occupation or industry of fishing for pearls. **2.** the place where this is carried on.

pearl fishing, the occupation of fishing for pearls.

pearl gray, a soft, pale, bluish gray. —**pearl′-gray′,** *adj.*

pearl·i·ness (pėr′lē nis), *n.* the state of being pearly.

pearl·ing (pėr′ling), *n.* the act or industry of seeking for pearls.

pearl·ite (pėr′līt), *n.* **1.** a mixture formed by carbon steels cooling slowly from a high temperature, normally made up of ferrite and cementite in alternate layers. Pearlite contains approximately 0.83 per cent carbon. **2.** perlite.

pearl·ized (pėr′līzd), *adj.* pearlescent: *hats . . . of white pearlized straw* (New Yorker).

pearl millet, a tall grass grown in the southern United States for forage and in India, Africa, and elsewhere for its edible seeds.

pearl oyster, a pearl-bearing oyster.

pearl tapioca, tapioca in the form of small, round grains.

pearl·wort (pėrl′wėrt′), *n.* any of a group of small matted or tufted herbs with threadlike or awl-shaped leaves and minute flowers.

pearl·y (pėr′lē), *adj.,* **pearl·i·er, pearl·i·est.** **1.** like a pearl; having the color or luster of pearls: *pearly teeth.* **2.** like mother-of-pearl, especially in color and luster; nacreous. **3.** adorned with or containing many pearls: *She is wearing a charcoal-gray suit, black pumps, no stockings, a small string of pearls, and square pearly earrings* (New Yorker).

pearly everlasting, a small leafy herb of the composite family, having pearly white bracts about the flowers. It can be dried and kept for winter bouquets.

pearly nautilus, any of several sea mollusks that are somewhat like squids, but have a shell that has a pearly lining and is coiled in a flat spiral composed of a series of chambers. See **nautilus** for picture.

pear·main (pãr′mān), *n.* any of various different varieties of apple. [originally, a type of pear < Old French *permain, parmain,* perhaps < unrecorded Medieval Latin *parmanus* of *Parma,* Italy]

pear-shaped (pãr′shāpt′), *adj.* **1.** in the shape of a pear: *a pear-shaped lamp.* **2.** mellow; resonant; ringing, as if sung with the mouth held open in the shape of a pear: *A handsome man in his mid-forties, who can speak, sing, and write in pear-shaped tones* (New York Times).

peart (pirt, pėrt), *adj. Dialect.* pert. —**peart′ly,** *adv.*

pear·wood (pãr′wu̇d′), *n.* the wood of the pear tree: *This charming handmade table of aged pearwood has 2 pewter wells originally used as wine coolers* (New Yorker).

peas·ant (pez′ənt), *n.* **1.** a farmer of the working class in Europe. **2.** a low fellow; rascal (used in an unfriendly way). —*adj.* of peasants: *peasant labor.* [< Anglo-French *paisant,* Old French *paysant,* earlier *païsenc* < *pays* country < Late Latin *pāgensis* living in a rural district; the territory of a district < Latin *pāgus* rural district]

peas·ant·ry (pez′ən trē), *n.* **1.** peasants as a group: *the British peasantry* (Charlotte Brontë). **2.** the condition of being a peasant. **3.** the conduct or quality of a peasant; rusticity.

pease¹ (pēz), *n., pl.* **peas·es, peas·en, pease.** *Archaic or British Dialect.* a pea. [< Old English *pise* < Late Latin *pisa,* variant of Latin *pīsum* < Greek *píson*]

pease² (pēz), *n. Archaic or British Dialect.* plural of **pea.**

pease·cod or **peas·cod** (pēz′kod′), *n.* the pod of a pea.

pease·cod-bel·lied (pēz′kod′bel′ēd), *adj.* (of a doublet) having the lower front part so shaped and quilted as to project from the body, in a fashion in vogue toward the end of the 1500's.

pease meal, a meal made by grinding peas.

peas·en (pē′zən), *n. Archaic.* a plural of **pease**¹.

pea·shoot·er (pē′shü′tər), *n.* a toy weapon, consisting of a tube, through which one blows peas or similar small objects.

pea·soup·er (pē′sü′pər), *n. Informal.* a pea-soup fog: *The London pea-souper made her homesick for her house in Hollywood* (This Week).

Peasecod-bellied Doublet

pea-soup fog (pē′süp′), *Informal.* a very thick and heavy fog: *The term "pea-soup" has no standing among weathermen, but then most pea-soup fogs—the ones in London, for instance—aren't simply fogs but combinations of fog and smog* (E.B. White).

pea·stick (pē′stik′), *n.* a stake upon which a pea plant is trained: *A generous growth of chickweed et al. around the stems of peas gives support before their tendrils have obtained a firm hold on peasticks* (Punch).

peat¹ (pēt), *n.* **1.** a kind of heavy turf composed of vegetable matter, as a sphagnum moss, partly rotted, used as a fertilizer or especially as fuel in Ireland, Great Britain, and other parts of the world where there are many peat bogs: *Climatic changes may be detected in shifts in the kinds of trees and plants surrounding a bog as reflected in changing pollens in the levels of peat* (Harper's). **2.** a piece of this, usually cut in the shape of a brick, and dried for use as fuel: *The fireplace . . . was fed in winter with sticks and peats brought by the scholars* (Ian Maclaren). [Middle English *pete* < Medieval Latin (England) *peta,* apparently < Scottish; origin uncertain] —**peat′like′,** *adj.*

peat² (pēt), *n. Archaic.* a pet or darling (used of a woman or girl). [probably variant of *pet*]

peat bog, an accumulation of peat or peaty matter: *By the Middle Ages . . . peat bogs were supplying the principal fuel needs of many large towns* (New Scientist).

peat·er·y (pē′tər ē), *n., pl.* **-er·ies.** a place from which peat is dug.

peat hag, broken ground from which peats have been dug: *As the heathery hill rose, it broke into peat hags* (London Times).

peat moor, peat bog.

peat moss, **1.** a peatlike moss, such as sphagnum, used to add humus to garden soil. **2.** peat bog.

peat·y (pē′tē), *adj.,* **peat·i·er, peat·i·est.** of, like, or abounding in peat: *A thin seam of peaty matter . . . along the bottom of a bed of clay* (James Croll).

peau (pō), *n.* **1.** *French.* skin. **2.** any of various fabrics resembling skin: *Celaperm acetate gives brilliant iridescence to this peau, makes its color last longer* (New Yorker).

peau d'ange (pō däNzh′), *French.* angel skin, a smooth, lustrous crepe or satin fabric much used for wedding gowns.

peau-de-cygne (pō′də sē′nyə), *n.* a soft, lustrous, satin-faced silk fabric. [< French *peau-de-cygne* (literally) swan skin]

peau de soie, or **peau-de-soie** (pō′də-swä′), *n.* a soft, silk fabric with little luster, having a satin finish on one or both sides. [< French *peau de soie* (literally) silk skin]

pea·vey (pē′vē), *n., pl.* **-veys.** a strong stick that is tipped with an iron or steel point and has a hinged hook near the end. Lumbermen use peaveys in managing logs. [American English, apparently < J. *Peavey,* who invented it]

Peavey

pea·vy (pē′vē), *n., pl.* **-vies.** peavey.

pe·ba (pē′bə), *n.* the nine-banded armadillo. [apparently < a Tupi word]

peb·ble (peb′əl), *n., v.,* **-bled, -bling.** —*n.* **1.** any small stone, usually worn and rounded, especially by being rolled about by water, by glacial attrition, etc.: *to wake a person by throwing pebbles at his window. So wears the paving pebble in the street* (John Dryden). **2.** a rough, uneven surface on leather, paper, etc. **3.** a substance, especially leather, with a rough, uneven surface. **4. a.** a colorless transparent kind of rock crystal sometimes used instead of glass in spectacles. **b.** a lens made of this. —*v.t.* **1.** to prepare (leather) so that it has a grained surface. **2.** to pelt with pebbles: *The peasants . . . betook themselves to stones, and . . . pebbled the priest* (Scott). **3.** to pave with pebbles: *to pebble a walk.*
[Old English *papolstānas* pebblestones] —**peb′ble·like′,** *adj.*

pebble culture, a stage in the very early culture of prehistoric man in which he used tools crudely fashioned from pebbles: *From its roots in the Oldowan pebble culture in Bed I, the whole development of* [*this*] *hand-axe culture can be traced to its most advanced stage in Bed IV—an evolutionary sequence unequalled anywhere else* (New Scientist).

peb·bled (peb′əld), *adj.* abounding in pebbles; pebbly: *the pebbled shore* (Shakespeare).

peb·ble·dash (peb′əl dash′), *n. British.* mortar with pebbles incorporated into it, used for surfacing or finishing walls or buildings; stucco: *On the left, above a pebbledash bungalow, rolls grassland covered with . . . many barrows* (Punch).

pebble leather, leather with a granulated surface; pebbled leather.

pebble mill, a ball mill used in ceramic work.

pebble tool, a crude tool made by early man by chipping away one side of a pebble to form a rough cutting edge: *Zinianthropus, an Australopithecine discovered at Olduvai in Tanganyika this year . . . was accompanied by pebble tools* (New Scientist).

peb·bly (peb′lē), *adj.,* **-bli·er, -bli·est. 1.** having many pebbles; covered with pebbles: *The pebbly beach hurt our bare feet.* **2.** rough; scratchy: *a pebbly voice.*

pé·brine (pā brēn′), *n.* an epidemic protozoan disease of silkworms, in which small black spots appear. [< French *pébrine* < Provençal *pebrino* < *pebre* pepper < Latin *piper*]

pe·can (pi kän′, -kan′; pē′kan), *n.* **1.** an olive-shaped edible nut with a smooth, thin shell that grows on a kind of hickory tree of the walnut family, common in the southern and central United States. **2.** the tree that it grows on. [American English < Algonkian (compare Cree *pakan* hard-shelled nut)]

Teche Pecan

pec·ca·bil·i·ty (pek′ə-bil′ə tē), *n.* capability of sinning.

pec·ca·ble (pek′ə bəl), *adj.* liable to sin or err: *We hold all mankind to be peccable . . . and errable* (George Berkeley). [< earlier French *peccable* < Latin *peccāre* to sin]

pec·ca·dil·lo (pek′ə dil′ō), *n., pl.* **-loes** or **-los.** a slight sin or fault: *My sins were all peccadilloes* (Henry James). *The artful old man who hides his major offences behind a frank admission of peccadilloes* (London Times). [< Spanish *pecadillo* (diminutive) < *pecado* sin < Latin *peccātum* < *peccāre* to sin]

pec·can·cy (pek′ən sē), *n.* the state or quality of being peccant: *Sins of commission have more of peccancy in them than sins of omission* (Thomas Goodwin).

pec·cant (pek′ənt), *adj.* **1.** guilty of a sin or moral offense; sinning: *a peccant soul* (Milton). **2.** violating some rule or accepted principle of behavior, etc.; not correct: *The peccant officials . . . fell on their knees* (Thomas Carlyle). **3.** *Obsolete.* inducing or that may induce disease; unhealthy. [< Latin *peccāns, -antis,* present participle of *peccāre* to sin] —**pec′cant·ly,** *adv.*

pec·ca·ry (pek′ər ē), *n., pl.* **-ries** or (*collectively*) **-ry.** a kind of wild pig, found in South and Central America, as the collared peccary, extending north to Texas, and the white-lipped peccary of South America; javelina: *Once we found a peccary which, though tame, did not take readily to transport in a canoe and nearly tipped us into the river* (London Times). [< Carib (Guiana or Venezuela) *pakira*]

Collared Peccary (about 3 ft. long)

pec·ca·vi (pe kā′vī, -kä′vē), *n., pl.* **-vis.** an acknowledgment or confession of guilt. [< Latin *peccāvī* I have sinned]

pech (peH), *Scottish.* —*n.* a short, labored breath; pant. —*v.i.* to breathe hard from exertion; pant: *He will tie the burden of them on their own backs, while they groan and pech* (Robert Rollock). [apparently imitative]

pech·an (peH′ən), *n. Scottish.* the stomach: *He puts it in a bad purse that puts it in his pechan* (Richard Heslop).

pêche Mel·ba (pesh′ mel′bə), a dessert of ice cream and peaches, usually flavored with raspberry syrup. [< French *pêche* + Nellie *Melba,* 1861?–1931, an Australian opera star]

peck[1] (pek), *n.* **1.** a unit of dry measure, eight quarts or one fourth of a bushel. *Abbr.:* pk. **2.** a container holding just a peck, to measure with. **3.** a great deal: *a peck of trouble.* [Middle English *pek;* origin uncertain] —**Syn. 3.** heap.

peck[2] (pek), *v.t.* **1.** to strike and pick with the beak or a pointed tool. **2.** to make by striking with the beak or a pointed tool: *Woodpeckers peck holes in trees.* **3.** to strike at and pick up with the beak: *A hen pecks corn.* **4.** *Informal.* to eat only a little, bit by bit. —*v.i.* **1.** to strike with or use the beak. **2.** to aim with a beak; make a pecking motion. **3.** to take food with the beak. **4.** *Informal.* to eat very lightly and daintily. **5.** to find fault.
peck at, a. to try to peck: *It was . . . the greatest of triumph when the birds . . . pecked at the grapes in a picture* (Leslie Stephen). **b.** *Informal.* to eat only a little, bit by bit: *Maud just pecked at her food.* **c.** to keep criticizing: *Miss Watson . . . kept pecking at me, and it got tiresome* (Mark Twain).
peck out, a. to pluck out by or as if by pecking: *She flieth . . . about his eyes and face, and pecketh . . . out his eyes* (John Maplet). **b.** to type on a typewriter with one's forefinger only, slowly and laboriously: *The next step was pecking out stories* (Harper's).
—*n.* **1.** a stroke made with the beak: *The hen gave me a peck.* **2.** a hole or mark made by pecking. **3.** *Informal.* a stiff, unwilling kiss: *a peck on the cheek.* **4.** *British Slang.* food.
[apparently dialectal variant of *pick*[1]]

peck·er (pek′ər), *n.* **1.** a person or thing that pecks. **2.** a woodpecker. **3.** *British Slang.* courage.

peck·er·wood (pek′ər wu̇d′), *n. U.S. Dialect.* **1.** a woodpecker. **2.** a poor white; cracker: *Smith was . . . defeated in 1962 by the usual coalition of peckerwoods, superpatriots, and the* [*White*] *Citizens Councils* (Harper's).

peck horn, althorn.

peck·ing order (pek′ing), **1.** an order of dominance, originally noted among chickens, prescribing which bird can peck another and which bird or birds can, in turn, peck it. The pecking order never changes once it is established at an early age among a flock. **2.** a hierarchy of precedence among any group: *In any modern hospital a pecking order, similar to that seen in bird flocks, may be observed* (Atlantic).

peck·ish (pek′ish), *adj.* **1.** somewhat hungry; disposed to peck or eat: *At forty, admittedly, I rarely feel even peckish* (New Yorker). **2.** impatient; irritable: *I am hungry, thirsty, peckish* (Manchester Guardian). —**peck′ish·ly,** *adv.*

peck order, pecking order.

Peck·snif·fi·an (pek snif′ē ən), *adj.* like Pecksniff; unctuously hypocritical. [< *Pecksniff,* a hypocritical pretender to righteousness in Dickens' *Martin Chuzzlewit*]

Pe·co·ri·no (pā′kə rē′nō), *n.* a sharp-flavored Italian cheese: *Rome's spaghetti all' amatriciana based on Italian salt pork, black peppercorns, tomatoes in profusion, the whole liberally sprinkled with sharp Pecorino cheese* (Atlantic). [< Italian *pecorino* sheep-like]

pec·tase (pek′tās), *n.* an enzyme found in various fruits that has the property of changing pectin into pectic acid and methyl alcohol: *Pectase hydrolyzes the methyl alcohol from soluble pectin to produce pectic acid* (Heber W. Youngken). [< *pect*(in) + *-ase*]

pec·tate (pek′tāt), *n.* a salt or ester of pectic acid.

pec·ten (pek′tən), *n., pl.* **-ti·nes.** a comblike part, especially a membrane in the eyes of most birds and some reptiles and fishes that projects from the choroid coat into the vitreous humor and has parallel folds that suggest the teeth of a comb. [< Latin *pecten, -inis* a comb, rake < *pectere* to comb]

pec·tic (pek′tik), *adj.* of, having to do with, or derived from pectin: *Pectic enzymes from fruits can be made less active if phenolic substances are present* (New Scientist). [< Greek *pēktikós* curdling, congealing < *pektós* < *pēgnýnai* make stiff]

pectic acid, a transparent gelatinous acid, insoluble in water, formed by the hydrolysis of certain esters of pectin. *Formula:* $C_{17}H_{24}O_{16}$

pec·tin (pek′tən), *n.* any of a group of substances, soluble in water, that occur in most fruits and certain vegetables, especially apples and currants. Pectin makes fruit jelly stiff. *Pectin tends to take up water and become gelatinous under certain conditions* (Fred W. Emerson). [< *pect*(ic) (acid) + *-in*]

pec·ti·na·ceous (pek′tə nā′shəs), *adj.* of the nature of or containing pectin.

pec·ti·nate (pek′tə nāt), *adj.* formed like a comb; having straight, narrow, closely set projections or divisions like the teeth of a comb. [< Latin *pectinātus* < *pecten, -inis* a comb]

pec·ti·nat·ed (pek′tə nā′tid), *adj.* pectinate.

pec·ti·na·tion (pek′tə nā′shən), *n.* **1.** the state or condition of being pectinate. **2.** a comblike structure; pecten.

pec·ti·nes (pek′tə nēz), *n.* plural of **pecten.**

pec·to·ral (pek′tər əl), *adj.* **1.** of, in, or on the breast or chest; thoracic: *the pectoral muscles.* **2.** used in treating diseases of the lungs: *a pectoral medicine.* **3.** worn on the breast: *the pectoral cross of a bishop.* **4.** proceeding from the heart or inner consciousness; subjective. **5.** (of a vocal quality) having a full resonance, as if coming from the chest.
—*n.* **1.** a medicine for the lungs. **2.** something worn on the breast for ornament or protection, as a breastplate or a pectoral cross. **3.** a pectoral fin: *The paired fins are the pectorals and the pelvics, or ventrals* (World Book Encyclopedia).
[< Latin *pectorālis* < *pectus, -oris* chest]

pectoral arch or **girdle,** *Anatomy.* the bony or cartilaginous arch supporting the forelimbs of vertebrates, formed in man by the scapulae and clavicles: *In the coelacanth, the pectoral girdle, which in normal teleost fish is a hooplike ring of bones embracing the shoulder blades and so on, has no skeletal connections whatever with the head* (New Scientist).

pectoral fin, either of a pair of fins in fishes that are attached to the body, usually just behind and in line with the gills, and corresponding to the forelimbs of higher vertebrates. See picture under **fin.**

pectoral sandpiper, a reddish-brown sandpiper with a dark biblike marking on the breast, that breeds in the arctic regions of North America and eastern Siberia and winters in South America. The male inflates the throat and breast at mating time.

pec·tose (pek′tōs), *n.* a substance that is contained in the pulp of unripe fleshy fruit, and is readily converted into pectin. [< *pect*(ic) + *-ose*[2]]

pec·u·late (pek′yə lāt), *v.t., v.i.,* **-lat·ed, -lat·ing.** to embezzle; steal (money or goods entrusted to one). [< Latin *pecūlārī* (with English *-ate*[1]) embezzle < *pecūlium* (private) property < *pecū* money; cattle]

pec·u·la·tion (pek′yə lā′shən), *n.* the act of peculating; embezzlement: *But discomfort and alarm were not the only results of the mismanagement of the household; the waste, extravagance, and peculation that also flowed from it were immeasurable* (Lytton Strachey).

pec·u·la·tor (pek′yə lā′tər), *n.* a person who peculates; embezzler.

pe·cul·iar (pi kyül′yər), *adj.* **1.** strange; odd; unusual: *What a peculiar thing to say. It was peculiar that the fish market had no fish last Friday.* **2.** special: *This book has a peculiar value. It belonged to George Washington.* **3.** belonging to one person or thing and not to another: *The Quakers wore a dress peculiar to themselves.*

—*n.* **1.** a property or privilege that is exclusively one's own. **2.** (in English ecclesiastical law) a parish or church exempted from the jurisdiction of the ordinary or bishop in whose diocese it lies.

[< Latin *pecūliāris* of one's own (property) < *pecūlium;* see PECULATE] —**pe·cul′iar·ly,** *adv.*

—**Syn.** *adj.* **1.** eccentric, queer, singular. See **strange. 3.** particular, distinctive.

pe·cu·li·ar·i·ty (pi kyü′lē ar′ə tē), *n., pl.* **-ties. 1.** the condition of being peculiar; strangeness; oddness; unusualness: *We noticed the peculiarity of his manner at once.* **2.** a thing or feature that is strange or odd: *One of his peculiarities is that his eyes are not the same color.* **3.** a peculiar or characteristic quality. **4.** a distinguishing quality or feature. —**Syn. 1.** eccentricity, singularity. **3.** idiosyncrasy.

pe·cul·iar·ize (pi kyül′yə rīz), *v.t.,* **-ized, -iz·ing.** to make peculiar; set apart: *The vestal, peculiarized since childhood, may not have reacted to her ordeal thus* (Harper's).

peculiar people, 1. God's own chosen people, the Jews. Deuteronomy 14:2. **2.** a term applied to themselves by a number of Christian sects.

pe·cu·li·um (pi kyü′lē əm), *n., pl.* **-li·a** (-lē ə). **1.** *Roman Law.* property that a father allowed his wife, child, etc., or a master allowed his slave, to have for his own. **2.** a private possession or appurtenance; private property. [< Latin *pecūlium* (private) property < *pecū* money; cattle]

pe·cu·ni·ar·i·ly (pi kyü′nē er′ə lē), *adv.* in a pecuniary manner; as regards money matters: *I was in moderate circumstances pecuniarily, though I was perhaps better furnished with less fleeting riches than many others* (Charles Dudley Warner).

pe·cu·ni·ar·y (pi kyü′nē er′ē), *adj.* **1.** of or having to do with money: *I pass my whole life, miss, in turning an immense pecuniary mangle* (Dickens). **2.** in the form of money: *pecuniary assistance, a pecuniary compensation.* [< Latin *pecūniārius* < *pecūnia* money < *pecū* money; cattle]

pe·cu·ni·os·i·ty (pi kyü′nē os′ə tē), *n.* the state or fact of being supplied with money: *A Frenchman, whose beringed fingers . . . betokened a certain amount of pecuniosity* (G.A. MacDonnell).

pe·cu·ni·ous (pi kyü′nē əs), *adj.* having much money; wealthy: *But in very truth money is as dirt among those phenomenally pecunious New Yorkers* (Archibald Forbes).

ped., 1. pedal. **2.** pedestal.

ped·a·gese (ped′ə gēz′, -gēs′), *n. U.S. Slang.* the jargon of pedagogues; academese: *With what relief the pedagogues subside into pedagese!* (Time). [< *pedag*(ogue) + *-ese*]

ped·a·gog (ped′ə gog, -gôg), *n.* pedagogue.

ped·a·gog·ic (ped′ə goj′ik, -gō′jik), *adj.* of teachers or teaching; of pedagogy: *. . . at Uppingham, where the redoubtable Dr. Thring, then at the height of his pedagogic fame, was headmaster* (Atlantic). —**ped′a·gog′i·cal·ly,** *adv.*

ped·a·gog·i·cal (ped′ə goj′ə kəl, -gō′jə-), *adj.* pedagogic: *The posing of broad problems which challenge a student's ingenuity and judgment rather than his mere memorization of fact or a formula for solution, was agreed to be an effective pedagogical device* (Science News).

ped·a·gog·ics (ped′ə goj′iks, -gō′jiks), *n.* the science, art, or principles of teaching or education; pedagogy.

ped·a·gog·ism or **ped·a·gogu·ism** (ped′ə gog′iz əm, -gôg′-), *n.* the occupation, character, or ways of a pedagog; system of pedagogy.

ped·a·gog·ist (ped′ə goj′ist, -gō′jist), *n.* a person who is an expert in pedagogy or pedagogics.

ped·a·gogue (ped′ə gog, -gôg), *n.* **1.** a teacher; schoolmaster: *The master, a dryish Scotsman whose reputation as a pedagogue derived from a book he had written* (Scientific American). **2.** a narrow-minded teacher. [< Old French *pedagoge,* learned borrowing from Latin *paedagōgus* < Greek *paidagōgós* < *paîs, paidós* boy + *agōgós* leader < *ágein* to lead] —**Syn. 1.** instructor. **2.** pedant.

ped·a·gogu·ish (ped′ə gog′ish, -gôg′-), *adj.* characteristic of a pedagog; pedantic: *Those narrow and pedagoguish tactics of law . . .* (James Mozley).

ped·a·go·gy (ped′ə gō′jē, -goj′ē), *n.* **1.** teaching. **2.** the art or science of teaching: *The PEA [Progressive Education Association] was formed in 1919 as a protest against the humdrum, the cut and dried, the rote and recitation methods of pedagogy* (Newsweek).

ped·al (ped′əl; pē′dəl *for adj. 1*), *n., v.,* **-aled, -al·ing** or (*especially British*) **-alled, -al·ling,** *adj.* —*n.* **1.** a lever worked by the foot; the part on which the foot is placed to move any kind of machinery. Organs and pianos have pedals for changing the tone The two pedals of a bicycle, pushed down one after the other, make it go. The brake pedal in an automobile is pushed toward the floor to apply the brakes: *As you ride [a bicycle] you push down on the pedals . . that act like spokes of the wheel* (Beauchamp, Mayfield, and West). *Bach had a harpsichord with two rows of keys and pedals* (A.J. Hipkins). See picture under **organ. 2.** pedal point.

—*v.t.* to work or use the pedals of; move by pedals. —*v.i.* to work pedals.

[< Middle French *pedale* foot, trick with the feet < Italian, a footstool < Latin *pedāle* (thing) of the foot, neuter of *pedālis;* see the adjective]

—*adj.* **1.** of or having to do with the foot or feet: *. . . reverse himself laterally some 180 degrees so that his pedal extremities are towards the offending overflow* (New Scientist). **2.** of or having to do with a pedal or pedals; consisting of pedals.

[< Latin *pedālis* of the foot (in size, shape) < *pēs, pedis* foot]

ped·al·board (ped′əl bôrd′, -bōrd′), *n.* the keyboard or set of levers of an organ, played by the feet, and consisting of black and white keys similar in form and arrangement to the manuals, only on a larger scale: *The organ has two full 44-note keyboards and a 13-note pedalboard* (Wall Street Journal).

pe·dal·fer (pə dal′fər), *n.* a type of soil characteristic of humid regions, which has built up under a cover of forest or high grass. It is low in calcium and humus content, rich in iron and aluminum salts. [< Greek *pédon* soil + English *al*(uminum salts) + Latin *ferrum* iron]

ped·al·fer·ic (ped′al fer′ik), *adj.* of, having to do with, or characteristic of pedalfers.

ped·a·lier (ped′ə lir′), *n.* **1.** a pedal keyboard, as of an organ. **2.** a bass pianoforte played, in conjunction with an ordinary pianoforte, by means of a pedal keyboard. [< French *pédalier* < *pédale* pedal]

ped·al·ist (ped′ə list), *n.* a person skilled in the use of the pedals, as of an organ or a bicycle.

pedal point, *Music.* **1.** a tone (usually either tonic or dominant) sustained in one part (usually the bass) through various harmonies, often independent, in the other parts. **2.** the part of a piece containing this.

pedal pushers, a pair of close-fitting calf-length pants for women, originally for bicycle riding, but now in general use as sportswear: *Five pockets down one leg of narrow grey linen pedal pushers lend a gay note with a different hued handkerchief in each pocket* (New York Times).

ped·ant (ped′ənt), *n.* **1.** a person who displays his knowledge in an unnecessary or tiresome way or who puts great stress on minor points of learning: *A man who has been brought up among books, and is able to talk of nothing else, is . . . what we call a pedant* (Joseph Addison). **2.** a dull, narrow-minded teacher or scholar: *He [James I] had the temper of a pedant; and with it a pedant's love of theories, and a pedant's inability to bring his theories into any relation with actual facts* (Richard H. Green). **3.** *Obsolete.* a schoolmaster; teacher. [< Italian *pedante,* perhaps ultimately < Greek *paideúein* educate < *paîs, paidós* boy]

pe·dan·tic (pi dan′tik), *adj.* **1.** displaying one's knowledge more than is necessary: *Coon is learned, but neither stuffy nor pedantic* (Scientific American). **2.** tediously learned; scholarly in a dull and narrow way: *He does not . . . sacrifice sense and spirit to pedantic refinements* (Macaulay). —**pe·dan′ti·cal·ly,** *adv.*

pe·dan·ti·cal (pi dan′tə kəl), *adj.* pedantic.

pe·dan·ti·cism (pi dan′tə siz əm), *n.* a pedantic notion or expression; piece of pedantry.

ped·ant·ism (ped′ən tiz əm), *n.* **1.** pedantry. **2.** a pedanticism: *History books, opulent in nugatory pedantisms* (Thomas Carlyle).

ped·ant·ize (ped′ən tīz), *v.i.,* **-ized, -iz·ing.** to play the pedant, display pedantry: *To vegetate and pedantize on the classics . . .* (Saturday Review).

ped·an·toc·ra·cy (ped′ən tok′rə sē), *n., pl.* **-cies.** government by pedants or a pedant; system of government founded on mere book learning. [< *pedant* + *-ocracy,* as in *democracy*]

pe·dan·to·crat (pi dan′tə krat), *n.* a ruler who governs on pedantic principles.

pe·dan·to·crat·ic (pi dan′tə krat′ik), *adj.* characterized by pedantocracy.

ped·ant·ry (ped′ən trē), *n., pl.* **-ries. 1.** an unnecessary or tiresome display of knowledge: *At the risk of seeming to be pedantic about an art whose most despised enemy is pedantry, let's look briefly at some of the attributes of graphic humor* (Harper's). **2.** overemphasis on book learning: *Pedantry proceeds from much Reading and little Understanding* (Sir Richard Steele). **3.** a pedantic form or expression: *Vanderbilt tends to be impatient with legal pedantries and artificialities* (Harper's).

ped·ate (ped′āt), *adj.* **1. a.** having feet. **b.** having tubular, somewhat footlike organs, as many echinoderms. **2.** footlike. **3.** having divisions like toes: *a pedate leaf.* [< Latin *pedātus,* past participle of *pedāre* to furnish with feet < *pēs, pedis* foot] —**ped′ate·ly,** *adv.*

pe·dat·i·fid (pi dat′ə fid, -dā′tə-), *adj. Botany.* pedately divided, as a leaf. [< Latin *pedātus* (see PEDATE) + *findere* to cleft, split]

pe·dat·i·nerved (pi dat′ə nėrvd′, -dā′tə-), *adj. Botany.* having the nerves or ribs arranged in a pedate manner, as a leaf.

Ped. D., Doctor of Pedagogy.

ped·der (ped′ər), *n. Scottish.* a peddler.

ped·dle (ped′əl), *v.,* **-dled, -dling.** —*v.t.* **1.** to carry from place to place and sell: *Endowed with the build of a light-heavyweight wrestler and the mind of a none-too-scrupulous banker, he had emigrated from Britain to Canada in 1908, made a fortune peddling clothes and real estate in the Chinatowns of the Far West* (Newsweek). **2.** to sell or deal out in small quantities: *to peddle candy, to peddle gossip.* —*v.i.* **1.** to travel about with things to sell. **2.** to occupy oneself with trifles; piddle: *Coteries . . . peddling with the idlest of all literary problems* (John A. Symonds). [apparently < *peddler*]

ped·dler (ped′lər), *n.* a man who travels about selling things that he carries in a pack or in a truck, wagon, or cart. Also, **pedlar, pedler.** [perhaps variant of Middle English *pedder,* apparently < *ped* basket, pannier] —**Syn.** hawker, huckster.

ped·dler·y (ped′lər ē), *n., pl.* **-dler·ies. 1.** the business of a peddler. **2.** peddlers' wares. **3.** trumpery; trash.

ped·dling (ped′ling), *adj.* **1.** engaged in the trade of a peddler. **2.** piddling; trifling; paltry.

ped·er·ast (ped′ə rast, pē′də-), *n.* a person who engages in pederasty.

ped·er·as·tic (ped′ə ras′tik), *adj.* of or having to do with pederasty. —**ped′er·as′ti·cal·ly,** *adv.*

ped·er·as·ty (ped′ə ras′tē, pē′də-), *n.* the unnatural sexual union of males with males, especially of a man with a boy. [< Greek *paiderastíā* < *paiderastḗs* a pederast < *paîs, paidós* boy, child + *erân* to love]

ped·es·tal (ped′ə stəl), *n., v.,* **-taled, -tal·ing** or (*especially British*) **-talled, -tal·ling.** —*n.* **1.** the base on which a column or statue stands. **2.** the base of a tall vase, lamp, etc. **3.** any base; support; foundation. **4.** a place or position of importance, especially one of idolization: *In his eyes, she was always on a pedestal.* —*v.t.* to set on or supply with a pedestal. [< Middle French *piédestall* < Italian *piedestallo* < *piè* foot (< Latin *pēs, pedis*) + *di* of + *stallo* stall[1]]

Pedestal (def. 1) supporting bust

pe·des·tri·an (pə des′trē ən), *n.* a person who goes on foot; walker: *Pedestrians have to watch out for automobiles turning corners.* —*adj.* **1.** going on foot; walking. **2.** for or used by pedestrians: *The pedestrian windows* [*at the bank*] *are proving highly popular with housewives who find it hard to push their baby buggies through a revolving door, or don't feel they are dressed well enough to go into the bank* (Birmingham News). **3.** without imagination; dull; slow: *a pedestrian style in writing. The circumstances and events of his life were anything but pedestrian* (Scientific American). [< Latin *pedester, -tris* on foot; (of writing) commonplace, prosaic (< *pēs, pedis* foot) + English *-ian*] —**Syn.** *adj.* **3.** commonplace, uninspired, prosaic.

pe·des·tri·an·ism (pə des′trē ə niz′əm), *n.* **1.** the practice of traveling on foot; walking: *a large, cheerful street, in which . . . a great deal of pedestrianism went forward* (Henry James). **2.** a commonplace quality or style.

pe·di·ar·chy (pē′dē är′kē), *n., pl.* **-chies.** a society or culture dominated or ruled by children: *Philip Wylie is represented not by "momism" but by "pediarchy" (a society ruled by children, which is what goes on here, according to the gospel of Wylie)* (New York Times). [< Greek *paîs, paidós* child + *árchein* rule]

pe·di·at·ric (pē′dē at′rik, ped′ē-), *adj.* of or having to do with the medical and hygienic care of children. Also, **paediatric.** [< Greek *paîs, paidós* child + English *iatric*]

pe·di·a·tri·cian (pē′dē ə trish′ən, ped′ē-), *n.* a doctor who specializes in pediatrics. Also, **paediatrician.**

pe·di·at·rics (pē′dē at′riks, ped′ē-), *n.* the branch of medicine dealing with children's diseases and the care of babies and children: *Today investigation of the causes of these deformities is laying the basis for a new field of preventive medicine which we might call prenatal pediatrics or prenatal public health—concerned with that part of the population which is in its mother's womb* (Scientific American). Also, **paediatrics.** [< *pediatr*(ic) + *-ics*]

pe·di·at·rist (pē′dē at′rist, ped′ē-), *n.* pediatrician.

pe·di·at·ry (pē′dē at′rē, ped′ē-), *n.* pediatrics.

ped·i·cab (ped′ə cab′), *n.* a vehicle like a jinrikisha built upon a tricycle base and pedaled by the operator: *Pedicab men, as soon as they discovered I was an American, pumped harder, speeding me to my destination* (New Yorker). [< Latin *pēs, pedis* foot + English (taxi)*cab*]

ped·i·cel (ped′ə səl), *n.* **1.** a small stalk or stalklike part, as a main flower stalk when small, a secondary stalk that bears flowers, or each of the secondary or subordinate stalks that immediately bear the flowers in a branched inflorescence (the main stalk being the *peduncle*); an ultimate division of a common peduncle, supporting one flower only: *All those parts—calyx, corolla, stamens, and carpels—are attached to the receptacle, the somewhat specialized summit of the pedicel* (Fred W. Emerson). **2.** any small stalklike structure in an animal. [< New Latin *pedicellus* (diminutive) < Latin *pedīculus* pedicle]

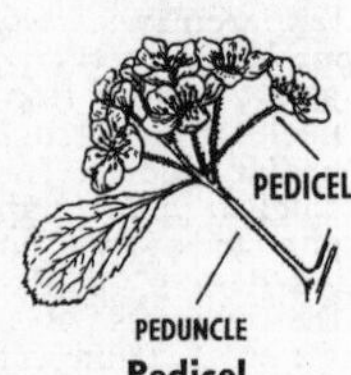

Pedicel

ped·i·cel·lar (ped′ə sel′ər), *adj.* having to do with or of the nature of a pedicel.

ped·i·cel·lar·i·a (ped′ə sə lãr′ē ə), *n., pl.* **-i·ae** (-ē ē). one of many small pinchers which project from the base of the spines of echinoderms and have the functions of warding off foreign matter and seizing food: *In some regions a moplike tangle of threads . . . is dragged across the oyster beds and the starfish that grab onto these with their pedicellariae are removed from the water and destroyed* (Harbaugh and Goodrich). [< New Latin *pedicellaria* < *pedicellus;* see PEDICEL]

ped·i·cel·late (ped′ə sə lit, -lāt), *adj.* having a pedicel or pedicels.

ped·i·cel·lat·ed (ped′ə sə lā′tid), *adj.* pedicellate.

ped·i·cel·la·tion (ped′ə sə lā′shən), *n.* pedicellate condition.

ped·i·cle (ped′ə kəl), *n.* a small stalk; pedicel or peduncle: *A vertebra has a body, and above this a pedicle on either side* (World Book Encyclopedia). [< Latin *pedīculus* footstalk (diminutive) < *pēs, pedis* foot]

pe·dic·u·lar (pi dik′yə lər), *adj.* of or having to do with a louse or lice; lousy. [< Latin *pēdiculāris* < *pēdiculus* louse (diminutive) < *pēdis* louse]

pe·dic·u·late (pi dik′yə lāt, -lit), *adj.* of or belonging to an order of teleost deep-sea fishes characterized by the elongated rays of the dorsal fin, the front one having a bulb on the tip which serves to lure smaller fish. —*n.* a pediculate fish. [< New Latin *Pediculati* the group name < Latin *pedīculus;* see PEDICLE]

ped·i·cule (ped′ə kyül), *n.* pedicle. [< French *pédicule* < Latin *pedīculus;* see PEDICLE]

pe·dic·u·lo·sis (pi dik′yə lō′sis), *n.* the condition of being infested with lice; lousiness; phthiriasis. [< New Latin *pediculosis* < Latin *pēdiculus* louse + New Latin *-osis* -osis]

pe·dic·u·lous (pi dik′yə ləs), *adj.* infested with lice; lousy: *Like a . . . pediculous vermin thou hast but one suit to thy back* (Thomas Dekker).

ped·i·cure (ped′ə kyůr), *n.* **1.** treatment of the feet, as removal of corns, massage, etc. **2.** a person who cares for the feet; chiropodist. [< French *pédicure* < Latin *pēs, pedis* foot + *cūrāre* take care of < *cūra* care]

ped·i·cur·ist (ped′ə kyůr′ist), *n.* a pedicure; chiropodist.

ped·i·form (ped′ə fôrm), *adj.* shaped like a foot. [< Latin *pēs, pedis* foot]

ped·i·gree (ped′ə grē), *n., v.,* **-greed, -gree·ing** —*n.* **1.** a list of ancestors; family tree: *That champion dog has a very fine pedigree.* **2.** line of descent; ancestry: *I can look but a very little way into my pedigree* (Daniel Defoe). *Virtue lieth not in pedigree* (Thomas Hobbes). **3.** derivation, as from a source: *the pedigree of a word.* **4.** distinguished or noble descent: *a man of pedigree.* —*v.t.* **1.** to breed (animals) so as to establish a pedigree. **2.** to obtain a pedigree for (an animal), especially by formal registry of it as the offspring of parents with a pedigree. [apparently < Old French *pied de grue* foot of a crane (because of the clawlike, 3-branched mark used in genealogies to show succession) < Latin *pēs, pedis* foot, *dē* of, and Vulgar Latin *grua,* for Latin *grus* crane] —**Syn.** *n.* **2.** lineage.

ped·i·greed (ped′ə grēd), *adj.* having a known pedigree: *Molly's dog is pedigreed.*

ped·i·ment (ped′ə mənt), *n.* **1.** the low triangular part on the front of buildings in the Greek style. A pediment is like a gable. **2.** a similar decorative part in any building. **3.** a base; foundation. **4.** *Geology.* a gradual slope at the base of a mountainous region in desert or semi-arid areas. It consists of a bedrock foundation covered by a veneer of gravel eroded from the hills. [earlier *periment* and *peremint,* perhaps alteration of *pyramid*]

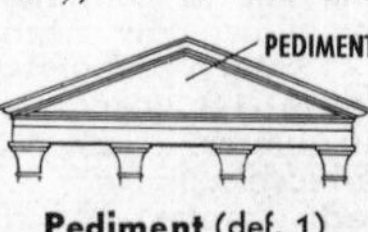

Pediment (def. 1)

ped·i·men·tal (ped′ə men′təl), *adj.* of, on, or like a pediment: *She read off the honorific pedimental letters of a handsome statue, for a sign to herself that she passed it* (George Meredith).

ped·i·ment·ed (ped′ə men′tid), *adj.* having or like a pediment: *The pile confronts us in the form of a large rectangle made by a colonnade of Roman Doric; pedimented and columned porches set off the wings* (Harper's).

ped·i·palp (ped′ə palp), *n., pl.* **ped·i·pal·pi** (ped′ə pal′pī). **1.** one of a pair of short, leglike appendages near the mouth and fangs of spiders, used as aids in feeding and as copulatory organs. **2.** any of an order of arachnids, including the whip scorpions, distinguished by large pedipalpi. [< New Latin *pedipalpus* < Latin *pēs, pedis* foot + New Latin *palpus* palp]

ped·i·pal·pate (ped′ə pal′pāt), *adj.* having pedipalpi.

ped·i·pal·pus (ped′ə pal′pəs), *n., pl.* **-pi** (-pī). pedipalp (def. 1).

ped·lar or **ped·ler** (ped′lər), *n.* peddler.

ped·lar·y or **ped·ler·y** (ped′lər ē), *n., pl.* **-lar·ies** or **-ler·ies.** peddlery.

pedo-, *combining form.* child; children: *Pedodontics = dentistry for children.* [< Greek *paîs, paidós* child]

pe·do·bap·tism (pē′dō bap′tiz əm), *n.* infant baptism.

pe·do·bap·tist (pē′dō bap′tist), *n.* an advocate of the baptism of infants.

ped·o·cal (ped′ə kal), *n.* a type of soil characteristic of arid or semi-arid regions, which has built up under short grass or sparse vegetation. High in calcium and low in iron content, a pedocal is an alkaline soil. [< Greek *pédon* soil + English *cal*(cium)]

ped·o·cal·ic (ped′ə kal′ik), *adj.* of, having to do with, or characteristic of pedocals: *Pedocalic soils evolve in an arid, semiarid or sub-humid climate* (White and Renner).

pe·do·don·tics (pē′də don′tiks), *n.* the branch of dentistry dealing with the prevention of disease in children's teeth and their special care.

pe·do·don·tist (pē′də don′tist), *n.* a dentist who specially practices pedodontics: *The pedodontist pays special attention to the diet of children, especially limiting the use of refined sugars* (World Book Encyclopedia).

pe·do·gen·e·sis (pē′dō jen′ə sis), *n.* reproduction by animals in the larval state: *In this type of reproduction, known as pedogenesis, the young of certain species are produced from non-fertilized eggs while in other species the young are produced only from fertilized eggs* (Harbaugh and Goodrich).

pe·do·log·i·cal[1] (pē′də loj′ə kəl), *adj.* of or having to do with the scientific study of soils: *The soil scientists would study pedological topics and the physical properties of soils in relation to civil engineering demands* (London Times).

pe·do·log·i·cal[2] (pē′də loj′ə kəl), *adj.* of or having to do with the scientific study of the nature of children: *They* [*children*] *need to be individually studied by every pedological method, physical and psychic* (Granville Stanley Hall).

pe·dol·o·gist[1] (pi dol′ə jist), *n.* a student of, or expert in, the scientific study of soils.

pe·dol·o·gist[2] (pi dol′ə jist), *n.* a student of, or expert in, the scientific study of the nature of children.

pe·dol·o·gy[1] (pi dol′ə jē), *n.* the scientific study of the origin and classification of soils. [< Greek *pédon* soil + English *-logy*]

pe·dol·o·gy[2] (pi dol′ə jē), *n.* the scientific study of the nature of children.

pe·dom·e·ter (pi dom′ə tər), *n.* an instrument for recording the number of steps taken and thus measuring the distance traveled. [< French *pédomètre* < Latin *pēs, pedis* foot + Greek *métron* measure]

pe·do·mor·phism (pē′dō môr′fiz əm, ped′ō-), *n.* the retention by an adult organism of infantile or juvenile characteristics.

pe·do·phile (pē′də fīl, -fil), *n.* an adult who is sexually attracted to children.

pe·do·phil·i·a (pē′də fil′ē ə), *n.* sexual attraction in an adult toward children.

pe·do·phil·ic (pē′də fil′ik), *adj.* of, having to do with, or characterized by pedophilia.

ped·rail (ped′rāl), *n.* **1.** a series of flat, round, footlike treads or supporting surfaces fastened around the wheels of a tractor or similar vehicle to enable it to travel over very rough ground. **2.** a tractor or other vehicle fitted with such supports. [< Latin *pēs, pedis* foot + English *rail*]

pe·dre·gal (pā′drə gäl′, ped′rə gəl), *n.* (in Mexico and southwestern United States) a rough and rocky tract, especially in a volcanic region; an old lava field. [< Spanish *pedregal* < *piedra* stone < Latin *petra*]

pe·dro (pē′drō), *n., pl.* **-dros. 1.** the five of trumps in cinch and other card games resembling seven-up. **2.** one of several card games resembling seven-up in which five points are scored for winning the five of trumps in a trick. [American English < Spanish *Sancho-pedro* and *Pedro,* names of card games; trump cards in them < *Pedro*, proper name < Latin *Petrus* Peter]

pe·dun·cle (pi dung′kəl), *n.* a stalk; stem; stalklike part (of a flower, fruit, cluster, or animal body), such as a stalk that bears the fructification in some fungi, the stalk of a lobster's eye, or a white bundle of nerve fibers connecting various parts of the brain. See picture under **pedicel.** [< New Latin *pedunculus* (diminutive) < Latin *pēs, pedis* foot]

pe·dun·cled (pi dung′kəld), *adj.* peduncular.

pe·dun·cu·lar (pi dung′kyə lər), *adj.* of or having to do with a peduncle.

pe·dun·cu·late (pi dung′kyə lit, -lāt), *adj.* **1.** having a peduncle. **2.** growing on a peduncle.

pe·dun·cu·lat·ed (pi dung′kyə lā′tid), *adj.* pedunculate.

peek (pēk), *v.i.* to look quickly and slyly; peep: *You must not peek while you are counting in such games as hide-and-seek.* —*n.* a quick, sly look. [Middle English *piken;* origin uncertain]

peek·a·boo or **peek-a-boo** (pē′kə bü), *n.* a young child's game in which a person's face or body is alternately hidden and revealed to the call of "boo" or "peekaboo"; bo-peep: *When they play peek-a-boo, a father and his baby are sharing an activity* (Sidonie M. Gruenberg). —*adj. Informal.* characterized by a partial revealing, sometimes of a startling nature: *Her peekaboo sheath dress is high-necked forward and slit to the waist astern* (New Yorker). —*interj.* an exclamation, usually used toward a child, intended to startle him.

peel[1] (pēl), *n.* the outer covering or rind of certain fruits, especially citrus fruits. [<verb] —*v.t.* **1.** to strip skin, rind or bark from: *to peel an apple.* **2.** to strip: *The Indians peeled the bark from trees to make canoes.* **3.** *Informal.* to remove (clothing): *to peel off a heavy sweater.* —*v.i.* **1.** to loosen rind, bark, skin, etc. **2.** (of skin, bark, etc.) to come off: *When I was sunburned, my skin peeled.* **3.** *Informal.* to remove clothing, entirely or in part; strip. **4.** *Archaic.* to plunder; despoil: *Is thy land peeled, thy realm marauded?* (Emerson).

peel off, (of an aircraft) to move at an angle, sharply and suddenly away from a group: *They swept the field twice in a tight line of four and then peeled off to land at 5:40* (New York Times).

[variant of *pill*[2], apparently < Old English *pilian* < Latin *pilāre* to strip of hair < *pilus* body hair]

—**Syn.** *n.* skin, bark, husk.

peel[2] (pēl), *n.* a long-handled shovel used to put bread, pies, etc., into an oven or take them out. [< Old French *pele* < Latin *pāla* spade, shovel, baker's peel. Compare PALETTE.]

peel[3] (pēl), *n.* **1.** a small fortified tower or dwelling common in the border counties of England and Scotland in the 1500's, typically having the ground floor vaulted and used as a shelter for cattle, with access to the upper part by a door considerably raised above the ground and reached by a movable stair or the like. **2.** *Obsolete.* **a.** stockade. **b.** a stake. [< Old French *pel,* or *piel* < Latin *pālus* or *pālum* stake. Doublet of PALE[2], POLE[1].]

peel·a·ble (pē′lə bəl), *adj.* that can be peeled.

peeled (pēld), *adj.* stripped of skin, bark, rind, etc.

keep one's eyes peeled, *U.S. Informal.* to be on the alert: *I kept my eyes peeled, but I didn't see her in the afternoon crowd* (Munsey's Magazine).

peel·er[1] (pē′lər), *n.* **1.** a person or thing that peels, strips, or pares. **2.** a log of softwood, as Douglas fir, from which veneer can be taken by cutting around the log. **3.** *U.S. Slang.* a striptease dancer.

peel·er[2] (pē′lər), *n.* *Archaic. British Slang.* a policeman; bobby: *He's gone for a peeler and a search warrant* (Charles Kingsley). [< Sir Robert *Peel,* 1788-1850, a British statesman, who reorganized the London police force]

peel·ing (pē′ling), *n.* a part peeled off or pared off: *a potato peeling.* —**Syn.** paring.

Peel·ite (pē′līt), *n.* (in English history) one of a party of Conservatives who sided with Sir Robert Peel after the repeal of the Corn Laws in 1846. They continued for some years to form a group intermediate between the protectionist Tories and the Liberals, and finally joined the Liberal Party.

peen (pēn), *n.* the part of the head of a hammer (except a claw hammer), sledge, etc., opposite to the face, when rounded, edged, etc., for any of various special uses. —*v.t.* to shape, bend, or make less thick by striking regularly all over with the peen of a hammer: *They divided the heads [of oil drums] into pie-shaped segments, peened them until each segment gave out a separate musical note when struck with padded sticks* (Time). Also, **pein.** [compare dialectal Norwegian *pen* or *pænn* back end of a hammer head, Old Swedish *pæna* beat iron thin with the hammer]

peenge (pēnj), *v.i.,* **peenged, peeng·ing.** *Scottish.* to whine: *That useless peenging thing o' a lassie there at Ellangowan* (Scott). Also, **pinge.**

peep[1] (pēp), *v.i.* **1.** to look through a small or narrow hole or crack: *I shall be upstairs in my room peeping through the window-blinds* (William Dean Howells) **2.** to look when no one knows it: *In the corn opposite to her a rabbit stole along, crouched, and peeped* (John Galsworthy). **3.** to look out as if peeping; come partly out: *Violets peeped among the leaves.* —*v.t.* to cause to stick out a little; show slightly.

—*n.* **1.** a look through a hole or crack; little look; a peek: *to take a peep into the pantry.* **2.** a small hole or crack to look through; peephole. **3.** a secret look. **4.** the first looking or coming out: *at the peep of day.*

[perhaps variant of *peek*]

—**Syn.** *v.i.* **1.** peer, peek.

peep[2] (pēp), *n.* **1.** a short, sharp sound made by a young bird; cheep. **2.** any of various small sandpipers or other shore birds. **3.** a jeep.

—*v.i.* **1.** to make a short, sharp sound: *The bird peeped.* **2.** to speak in a thin, weak voice.

[probably imitative. Compare Danish *pibe,* Swedish *pipa*]

peep·er[1] (pē′pər), *n.* **1.** a person who peeps. **2.** *Informal.* **a.** a mirror. **b.** a spyglass.

peepers, *Informal.* **a.** a pair of spectacles. **b.** the eyes: *a secret . . . invisible . . . to the stupid peepers of that young whiskered prig, Lieutenant Osborne* (Thackeray).

[< *peep*[1] + *-er*[1]]

peep·er[2] (pē′pər), *n.* **1.** a person or thing that peeps or cheeps. **2.** any of certain frogs that make peeping noises. [< *peep*[2] + *-er*[1]]

peep·hole (pēp′hōl′), *n.* a hole through which one may peep.

Peep·ing Tom (pē′ping), **1.** a prying observer, especially a man, who gets pleasure from watching the occupants of a house, room, or other private place without himself being observed. **2.** the tailor who was the only person to look at Lady Godiva as she rode naked through Coventry, for which, according to the legend, he was struck blind.

peep show, an exhibition of objects or pictures viewed through a small opening, usually fitted with a magnifying glass.

peep sight, a rear sight for a gun consisting of a small flat piece of metal, with a tiny hole in the center through which the front sight is aligned with the target.

pee·pul (pē′pəl), *n.* the bo tree of India and China. [< Hindi *pīpal* < Sanskrit *pippala*]

peer[1] (pir), *n.* **1. a.** a person of the same rank, ability, etc., as another; equal: *a jury of one's peers. And drunk delight of battle with my peers* (Tennyson). **b.** anything equal to something else in quality: *a book without a peer.* **2.** a man who has a title; man who is high and great by birth or rank. A duke, marquis, earl, count, viscount, or baron is a peer.

—*v.t.* **1.** to rank with; equal. **2.** *Informal.* to raise to the peerage; ennoble.

[< Old French *per* < Latin *pār, paris* equal. Doublet of PAR.]

peer[2] (pir), *v.i.* **1.** to look closely to see clearly, as a near-sighted person does: *to peer into the night. She peered at the tag to read the price.* **2.** to come out slightly; peep out: *The sun was peering from behind a cloud.* **3.** *Poetic.* to come into sight; appear: *When daffodils begin to peer* (Shakespeare). [probably related to Middle English *piren* < Flemish; influenced by *pear,* variant of *appear*]

peer·age (pir′ij), *n.* **1.** the rank or dignity of a peer: *Five ministers who lost their jobs were consoled with the customary peerages* (Time). **2.** the peers of a country. **3.** a book giving a list of the peers of a country. —**Syn. 2.** nobility.

peer·ess (pir′is), *n.* **1.** the wife or widow of a peer: *The invitations will be restricted to peeresses whose husbands are members of the House of Lords at present* (London Times). **2.** a woman having the rank of a peer in her own right.

peer group, 1. age group: . . . *the happy, easy comfortable adaptation of the child to his peer group* (Max Rafferty). **2.** a group of people of the same background, class, social status, etc.

peer·less (pir′lis), *adj.* without an equal: *His peerless performance won him a prize.* —**peer′less·ly,** *adv.* —**peer′less·ness,** *n.* —**Syn.** unequaled.

peer of the realm or **of the United Kingdom,** a peer entitled as a matter of hereditary right to sit in the House of Lords.

peer·y[1] (pir′ē), *adj.* peering; prying; suspicious: *They engaged a peery servant . . . to watch all her motions* (Samuel Richardson).

peer·y[2] or **peer·ie** (pir′ē), *n., pl.* **peer·ies.** *Scottish.* a peg top, made to spin with a string. [perhaps diminutive form of Scottish *pere* pear (from its shape)]

peet·weet (pēt′wēt), *n.* the spotted sandpiper. [American English; imitative of its cry]

peeve (pēv), *v.,* **peeved, peev·ing,** *n. Informal.* —*v.t., v.i.* to make peevish. —*n. Informal.* an annoyance. [American English; back formation < *peevish*]

pee·vish (pē′vish), *adj.* **1.** cross; fretful; complaining: *A peevish child is unhappy and makes others unhappy.* **2.** *Obsolete.* obstinate. [Middle English *pevysh,* and *pevyeshe;* origin unknown] —**pee′vish·ly,** *adv.* —**pee′vish·ness,** *n.* —**Syn. 1.** petulant, pettish, irritable, querulous.

pee·wee (pē′wē), *n.* **1.** a very small person or thing. **2. a.** pewee. **b.** *Australian.* magpie lark. —*adj.* **1.** small; undersized: *a peewee fighter.* **2.** of, having to do with, or characteristic of younger and smaller players in some sport: *a peewee hockey game, a peewee league.*

pee·wit (pē′wit), *n.* pewit.

peg (peg), *n., v.,* **pegged, peg·ging.** —*n.* **1.** a pin or small bolt of wood, metal, etc., used to fasten parts together, to hang things on, to stop a hole, to make fast a rope or string, to mark the score in a game, etc.: *The head [of a violin] contains pegs, or pins, which are used to tighten or loosen the strings* (World Book Encyclopedia). **2.** a step; degree: *His work is several pegs above yours.* **3.** *U.S. Informal.* a hard throw of a ball, especially in baseball: *Willie Mays saved the Giants a run in the second inning with one of his amazing pegs* (New York Times). **4.** *Informal.* **a.** a wooden leg; peg leg: *The hardest thing about the role was keeping Ahab's wooden peg away from him* (Newsweek). **b.** a leg: *You'll hear about the cannon-ball That carried off his pegs* (Oliver Wendell Holmes). **5.** *British.* a small drink of alcoholic liquor: *I suspected the old fellow was going to cool his wrath with a 'peg'* (F. M. Crawford). **6.** *Dialect.* a tooth, especially a child's tooth. **7.** an implement furnished with a pin, claw, or hook, used for tearing, harpooning, etc. **8.** the price at which a commodity, stock, etc., is pegged.

a peg to hang (something) **on,** an occasion, pretext, excuse, etc., for: *The chief use of a fact is as a peg to hang a thought on* (Lancet).

off the peg, ready-made: *Clothes made in his workrooms are sold off the peg* (Punch).

take down a peg (or two), to lower the pride of; humble: *I must take that proud girl down a peg* (Mrs. Humphry Ward).

—*v.t.* **1.** to fasten or hold with pegs: *to peg down a tent.* **2.** to mark with pegs. **3.** to keep the price of (a commodity, stock, etc.) from going up or down: *to peg wheat at 34¢ a bushel.* **4.** *Informal.* to aim; throw: *to peg the ball to the shortstop.* **5.** to strike or pierce with a peg. —*v.i.* **1.** *Informal.* to work hard; keep on energetically. **2.** to keep score by moving pegs, as in cribbage. **3.** to hit a croquet peg with the ball.

peg out, a. to peg or pitch one's tent: *We are pegging out in a very comfortless spot* (Harper's). **b.** to die: *A fierce little piece bought to console the children after the dog pegged out* (Punch). **c.** to mark the boundary of (a piece of ground, a mining claim, etc.) with pegs: *I . . . pegged out eight square feet, paid the licence fee, and returned to my mates* (W.H. Hall).

[apparently < Middle Dutch *pegge*]

Peg·a·si (peg′ə sī), *n.* genitive of **Pegasus** (the constellation).

Peg·a·sus (peg′ə səs), *n., genitive* (def. 3) **Peg·a·si. 1.** *Greek Mythology.* a horse with wings, the steed of the Muses. **2.** poetic genius; the means by which poets soar in the realms of poetry. **3.** a constellation in the northern sky near Andromeda: *Standing high in the eastern sky, just below Cygnus, we find Pegasus, the winged horse, which contains no stars of the first magnitude although it does have a characteristic figure called the "great square"* (Science News Letter).

Pegasus (def. 1)

peg·board (peg′bôrd′, -bōrd′), *n.* **1.** a board containing evenly spaced holes for pegs, used for scoring games, as cribbage. **2.** a larger board, attached to a wall, having holes for pegs used as hooks to hold tools, utensils, displays, memorandums, etc.

peg·box (peg′boks′), *n.* the head of a stringed instrument containing the pegs to which the strings are attached for tuning.

peg·ger (peg′ər), *n.* **1.** a person or thing that pegs. **2.** a machine for driving pegs in shoemaking.

peg leg, 1. a wooden leg. **2.** *Informal.* a person who has a wooden leg.

peg-leg·ged (peg′leg′id, -legd′), *adj.* having a wooden leg.

peg·ma·tite (peg′mə tīt), *n.* **1.** a coarsely crystallized kind of granite, containing little mica, occurring in veins: *The fossil-bearing sedimentary rocks are sandwiched between younger layers of pegmatite* (Scientific American). **2.** granite with a graphic texture. [< Greek *pêgma, pêgmatos* something joined together or congealed (< *pēgnýnai* to fix in, join, make solid) + English *-ite*[1]]

peg·ma·tit·ic (peg′mə tit′ik), *adj.* consisting of, characteristic of, or resembling pegmatite: *pegmatitic deposits in Norway.*

peg·ma·ti·za·tion (peg′mə tə zā′shən), *n.* the filling of a rock with veins of pegmatite.

peg tankard, a tankard with pegs inserted at regular intervals, formerly used to mark the quantity each person was to drink: *A peg tankard by Cornelius Kierstede with five pegs inside the body in line with the handle; as the tankard was passed around, each bibber drank to his peg but not a drop below* (Time).

peg top, a wooden top spinning on a metal peg.

peg-top (peg′top′), *adj.* shaped like a peg top.

peg tops, trousers wide at the hips and gradually narrowing to the ankles.

peg-top trousers, peg tops.

peh (pā), *n.* the seventeenth letter of the Hebrew alphabet. [< Hebrew *peh*]

Peh·le·vi (pā′lə vē), *n.* Pahlavi.

P.E.I., Prince Edward Island.

peign·oir (pān wär′, pān′wär), *n.* **1.** a loose or very full dressing gown for women, originally worn while the hair was being combed: [*She*] *padded about the palace kitchen in her silken peignoir, serving endless cups of coffee* (Time). **2.** any negligee. [< French *peignoir* < earlier *peignouoir* < *peigner* to comb < Latin *pectināre* < *pecten, -inis* a comb]

pein (pēn), *n., v.* peen.

peine forte et dure (pen fôr′ tā dʏr′), *French.* **1.** very severe and harsh punishment. **2.** a former method of punishment or torture inflicted on a prisoner who refused to plead. It consisted of placing heavy weights on the body of the prisoner until he pleaded or died.

peise (pāz, pēz), *v.t.,* **peised, peis·ing.** *Dialect.* **1.** to weigh or measure the weight of, as in a balance. **2.** to weigh in the mind; consider; ponder. **3.** to weigh down; oppress; burden. [Middle English *peise* < Old French *peser* <Latin *pensāre* to weigh (frequentative) < *pendere*]

pe·jo·rate (pē′jə rāt), *v.,* **-rat·ed, -rat·ing.** —*v.t.* to make worse; cause to deteriorate; disparage. —*v.i.* to become worse. [< Latin *pejorāre* (with English *-ate*[1]) make worse < *pejor* worse]

pe·jo·ra·tive (pē′jə rā′tiv; pi jôr′ə-, -jor′-), *adj.* **1.** tending to make worse; disparaging; depreciatory: *Throughout all the changes of religion, social and political constitution, and rulers, the real mistress of the Greeks has been sophism—sometimes, but not always, in the pejorative sense of the word* (Atlantic). **2.** of or having to do with various disparaging or depreciatory derivative words formed by the addition of a suffix to a root word of neutral or favorable connotations. —*n.* a pejorative word, suffix, or phrase: *What it* [*ingratiatingly*] *actually means is something like 'cringingly anxious to please.' It is a pejorative, and it should be used only as such* (New Yorker). [< *pejorate* + *-ive*] —**pe′jo·ra′tive·ly,** *adv.*

pek·an (pek′ən), *n.* a fisher: *The pekan, or fisher, a subspecies of the American marten, has dark brown or grayish-brown fur* (World Book Encyclopedia). [American English < Canadian French *pécan* < Algonkian (perhaps Abnaki) *pékané*]

Peke (pēk), *n.* a Pekingese (dog): *The breed standard issued by the Kennel Club decrees . . . that the Peke be leonine in shape with massive skull* (Cape Times).

Pe·kin (pē kin′), *n.,* or **Pekin duck,** any of a breed of large white ducks, originally of China, raised primarily for the production of meat: *The Pekin is the most important of all domestic ducks raised in the United States* (World Book Encyclopedia). [< French *Pékin,* spelling of Chinese *Pei-ching* Peking, capital of Chinese People's Republic]

pe·kin (pē kin′), *n.* a silk fabric, originally made only in China, often patterned with broad stripes or figures.

Pe·kin·ese (pē′kə nēz′, -nēs′), *n., pl.* **-ese,** *adj.* Pekingese.

Pe·king (pē king′), *n.,* or **Peking duck,** Pekin.

Pe·king·ese (pē′king ēz′, -ēs′), *n., pl.* **-ese,** *adj.* —*n.* **1.** any of a breed of very small dogs, originally of China, with long silky hair and a pug nose **2.** the form of Chinese used in Peking, the standard form of Mandarin. **3.** a native or inhabitant of Peking, China: *Most Pekingese, men and women alike, now wear a baleful blue dungaree uniform that gives them, and the city streets, a monotonous look* (Time).
—*adj.* of or having to do with Peking or its people.

Pekingese (def. 1)
(6 to 9 in. high at the shoulder)

Peking man, a very early extinct species of man, identified from bones found near Peking in 1929; Sinanthropus pekinensis: *Peking Man, Java man, the Neanderthal—none dates farther back than 600,000 years* (Newsweek).

pekin stripes, 1. lengthwise stripes, especially of uniform width, in textile fabrics. **2.** fabrics with such stripes.

pe·koe (pē′kō; *especially British* pek′ō), *n.* a kind of black tea from Ceylon or India, made from leaves picked while very small. [< Chinese (Amoy dialect) *pek-ho* (literally) white down (because the leaves are picked young with the "down" still on them)]

pel·age (pel′ij), *n.* the hair, fur, wool, or other soft covering of a four-footed mammal. [< French *pelage* the covering of a mammal < Old French *peil,* or *pel* hair < Latin *pilus*]

Pe·la·gi·an (pə lā′jē ən), *n.* a follower of Pelagianism. —*adj.* of or having to do with Pelagius or Pelagianism.

Pe·la·gi·an·ism (pə lā′jē ə niz′əm), *n.* the doctrines of Pelagius who died about 420 A.D., a British monk who denied original sin and maintained that the human will is of itself capable of good without the assistance of divine grace.

pe·lag·ic (pə laj′ik), *adj.* **1.** of the ocean or the open sea: *In the open parts of the ocean, the pelagic region, plants and animals differ considerably from those along the seashore* (Harbaugh and Goodrich). **2.** living on or near the surface of the open sea or ocean, at some distance from land, as certain animals and plants. **3.** of or having to do with a person who hunts seals, or the operation of hunting seals, as a commercial venture on the high seas, using rifles, harpoons, etc.: *pelagic fishery investigations.* [< Latin *pelagicus* < Greek *pelagikós* < *pélagos* sea]

pe·lar·go·nate (pe lär′gə nāt), *n.* a salt of pelargonic acid.

pel·ar·gon·ic acid (pel′är gon′ik, -gō′nik), a colorless or yellowish oily acid, present as an ester in an oil in geranium leaves and produced synthetically. *Formula:* $C_9H_{18}O_2$

pel·ar·go·ni·um (pel′är gō′nē əm), *n.* any of a group of plants of the geranium family, chiefly natives of South Africa, having showy flowers or fragrant leaves; stork's-bill: *The plant that most gardeners in the West —and elsewhere—refer to as a geranium is botanically a pelargonium* (New York Times). [< New Latin *Pelargonium* the genus name < Greek *pelārgós* stork]

Pe·las·gi (pə laz′jī), *n.pl.* the Pelasgians, as a people. [< Latin *Pelasgi* < Greek *Pelasgoí*]

Pe·las·gi·an (pə laz′jē ən), *n.* one of an ancient people (the Pelasgi) of doubtful ethnological affinities, widely spread over the coasts and islands of the eastern Mediterranean and Aegean, and believed to have occupied Greece in prehistoric times. —*adj.* of, having to do with, or characteristic of the Pelasgians: *The Tosks live south of the river, and descend from European Pelasgian tribes* (World Book Encyclopedia).

Pe·las·gic (pə laz′jik), *adj.* Pelasgian.

pe·lec·y·pod (pə les′ə pod), *n.* any lamellibranch or bivalve mollusk.
—*adj.* **1.** having a hatchet-shaped foot, as a bivalve mollusk. **2.** of or having to do with such a mollusk: *Most of what we know about pelecypod digestion is based on studies of marine clams* (Hegner and Stiles). [< Greek *pélekys* hatchet + *poús, podós* foot]

pel·er·ine (pel′ə rēn′), *n.* a kind of cape or mantle worn by women, especially a long narrow silk or lace piece, with ends coming down to a point in the front. [< French *pèlerine,* feminine of *pèlerin* pilgrim < Medieval Latin *pelegrinus*]

Pe·le's hair (pē′lēz, pā′lāz), volcanic glass occurring in fine hairlike threads, as in Hawaii, commonly supposed to have been formed from drops of lava by the wind. [< *Pele,* the Hawaiian goddess of Mount Kilauea, a Hawaiian volcano]

Pe·leus (pē′lyüs, -lē əs), *n. Greek Legend.* a king of the Myrmidons, father of Achilles.

pelf (pelf), *n.* **1.** money or riches, thought of as bad or degrading: *The scholar whom the love of pelf Tempts from his books and from his nobler self* (Longfellow). **2.** *Archaic.* spoil; booty. [< Old French *pelfre* booty, spoils; origin uncertain] —**Syn. 1.** lucre, mammon.

Pel·ham (pel′əm), *n.* a horse's bit combining the snaffle and the curb in one. [< the surname *Pelham*]

Pe·li·as (pē′lē əs, pel′ē-), *n. Greek Legend.* the uncle of Jason, who set as his condition for yielding the throne of Iolcus, in Thessaly, to Jason (its heir) the obtaining of the Golden Fleece, hoping that the quest for this would lead to Jason's death.

pel·i·can (pel′ə kən), *n.* any of a group of very large fish-eating water birds having a huge bill and a pouch on the lower part, used as a scoop to catch small fish. In fable, the pelican was said to feed her young with her own blood. *What, would'st Thou have me turn Pelican and feed thee out of my own vitals* (William Congreve). *Pelicans are large grotesque birds with comical faces and a remarkable talent for fishing* (Science News Letter). [< Late Latin *pelicānus* < Greek *pelekân, -ânos,* perhaps ultimately < *pélekys, -eos* ax (because of the shape of its bill)]

Brown Pelican
(50 in. long)

Pelican State, a nickname of Louisiana.

Pe·li·des (pē lī′dēz), *n. Greek Legend.* **1.** Achilles (as the son of Peleus). **2.** any descendant in the male line of Peleus.

pe·lisse (pə lēs′), *n.* **1.** a coat lined or trimmed with fur. **2.** a long cloak of silk, velvet, etc., with armholes or sleeves, worn by women. [< French *pelisse* < Old French *pelice* < Late Latin *pellīcia* < Latin *pellīcius* of fur < *pellis* skin]

pe·lite (pē′līt), *n.* a rock composed of particles of mud, clay, etc. [< Greek *pēlós* potter's clay, earth + English *-ite*[1]]

pel·la·gra (pə lag′rə, -lā′grə), *n.* a disease marked by eruption on the skin, a nervous condition, and sometimes insanity. It is caused by improper diet, especially one lacking sufficient nicotinic acid (niacin). *Pellagra is a deficiency disease prevalent in districts where maize is one of the staple foodstuffs* (Beaumont and Dodds). [< Italian *pellagra,* apparently < *pelle* (< Latin *pellis* skin) + *agro* rough < Latin *ager;* influenced by *podagra* gout in the feet, podagra]

pel·lag·rous (pə lag′rəs, -lā′grəs), *adj.* of, having to do with, or affected with pellagra.

pel·le·kar (pel′ə kär), *n.* palikar.

Pel·les (pel′ēz), *n.* **Sir,** *Arthurian Legend.* the father of Elaine and grandfather of Galahad, Elaine's son by Lancelot.

pel·let (pel′it), *n.* **1.** a little ball of mud, paper, food, medicine, etc.; pill. **2.** a bullet: *a pellet of birdshot.* **3.** a ball, usually of stone, used as a missile in the 1300's and 1400's. **4.** the undigested and indigestible matter, as bones, feathers, and fur, ejected from the crop by a hawk or other bird of prey. —*v.t.* **1.** to hit with pellets. **2.** to form into pellets: *Researchers are experimenting with a pelleted cattle feed made from newsprint, vitamins, and minerals* (Wall Street Journal). [< Old French *pelote* < Vulgar Latin *pilotta* (diminutive) < Latin *pila* ball] —**pel′let·er,** *n.*

pellet bomb, a fragmentation bomb.

pel·let·i·za·tion (pel′ə tə zā′shən), *n.* the process of forming into pellets: *The increased pelletization of ore also makes it more practical than ever before to ship by rail* (Wall Street Journal).

pel·let·ize (pel′ə tīz), *v.t.,* **-ized, -iz·ing.** to form into pellets: *The results look good enough for a $150,000 pelletizing plant to be built* (Atlantic).

pel·li·cle (pel′ə kəl), *n.* a very thin skin; an external membrane: *The outer covering of Paramecium is called the pellicle, which is a tough, yet flexible material that enables the animal to maintain its definite shape* (A.M. Winchester). [< Latin *pellicula* (diminutive) < *pellis* skin]

pel·lic·u·lar (pə lik′yə lər), *adj.* having the character or quality of a pellicle.

pel·li·to·ry (pel′ə tôr′ē, -tōr′-), *n., pl.* **-ries. 1.** Also, **pellitory of Spain.** a composite plant growing chiefly in Algeria. Its pungent root is used in medicine as a local irritant, sedative, etc. **2.** any of a group of herbs related to the nettle, as the wall pellitory. **3.** any of several similar plants, as the yarrow and feverfew. [fusion of earlier *pelytory,* Middle English *pelestre* < Anglo-French, Old French *piretre,* ultimately < Greek *pyretós* fever, and of earlier *pelletorie,* alteration of Middle English *paritarie* < Anglo-French < Late Latin *parietāria* (*herba*) wall (plant) < *pariēs, -etis* wall]

pell-mell or **pell·mell** (pel′mel′), *adv.* **1.** in a rushing, tumbling mass or crowd: *The children dashed pell-mell down to the beach and into the waves.* **2.** in headlong haste: *She had made her escape that way, and down after her they rushed, pell-mell* (W. H. Hudson). —*adj.* headlong; tumultuous: *The pell-mell rush of industrial activity has started the railroads clicking faster, too* (Newsweek). —*n.* a violent disorder or confusion: *It is the men who are the casualties of this pell-mell* (New Yorker). [< French *pêle-mêle* < Old French *pesle mesle;* latter element apparently < *mesler* mix. Compare MELEE, MEDLEY.]

Pel·lon (pel′on), *n. Trademark.* a nonwoven fabric with a rubber base, used as a stiffener in clothing.

pel·lu·cid (pə lü′sid), *adj.* **1.** transparent; clear: *the pellucid water of a mountain lake, a pellucid sky.* **2.** clearly expressed; easy to understand: *pellucid language, a pellucid style.* [< Latin *pellūcidus* < *perlūcēre* < *per-* through + *lūcēre* to shine. Compare LUCID.]

pel·lu·cid·i·ty (pel′yə sid′ə tē), *n.* pellucid quality; pellucidness.

Pel·man·ism (pel′mə niz əm), *n.* the training system of the Pelman Institute, a British educational organization concerned with the learning and memorizing processes: *Memory, in the popular mind, is equated with knowledge, and the newspapers have never, therefore, been without advertisements for Pelmanism, applied mnemonics, and other variants of You, too, can have a memory like mine* (New Scientist).

pel·met (pel′mit), *n.* a valance or similar covering over a door or window to conceal a curtain rod.

Pel·o·pon·ne·sian (pel′ə pə nē′shən, -zhən), *adj.* of or having to do with the Peloponnesus, a peninsula in Greece, or its people. —*n.* a native or inhabitant of the Peloponnesus.

Pe·lops (pē′lops), *n. Greek Mythology.* a son of Tantalus, and father of Atreus and Thyestes, served to the gods as food, but later restored to life by them.

pe·lo·ri·a (pə lôr′ē ə, -lōr′-), *n. Botany.* regularity or symmetry of structure occurring abnormally in flowers normally irregular or unsymmetrical. [< New Latin *peloria* < Greek *pélōros* monstrous < *pélōr* a prodigy]

pe·lor·ic (pə lôr′ik, -lor′-), *adj.* characterized by peloria.

pel·o·ri·za·tion (pel′ər ə zā′shən), *n.* a becoming affected with peloria.

pel·o·rize (pel′ə rīz), *v.t.,* **-rized, -riz·ing.** to affect with peloria: *The most perfectly pelorized examples had six petals, each marked with black striae like those on the standard petal* (Charles Darwin).

pel·o·ro·vis (pel′ə rō′vis), *n.* an extinct prehistoric giant sheep with a horn spread of twelve feet. [< New Latin *Pelorovis* the genus name < Greek *pélōr* prodigy + Latin *ovis* sheep]

pe·lo·rus (pə lôr′əs, -lōr′-), *n.* a device used on ships for taking bearings, consisting typically of a circular metal plate set in gimbals and having mounted on its surface a compass card and alidade, each of which may be revolved independently of the other. [< *Pelorus,* supposedly Hannibal's navigator on his return from Italy]

pe·lo·ta (pe lō′tə; *Spanish* pā lō′tä), *n.* **1. a.** a game of Basque or Spanish origin played on a walled court with a hard rubber ball. **b.** the ball, caught and slung back with a curved wicker racket strapped over the hand and lower arm: *After the pelota, a rubber-cored ball is smacked against the wall, an opposition player must catch it and fire it back before it has bounced more than once* (Time). **2.** the game of jai alai. [< Spanish *pelota* < *pella* ball < Latin *pila*]

pelt[1] (pelt), *v.t.* **1.** to throw things at; assail: *The boys were pelting the dog with stones. The attorney pelted the witness with angry questions.* **2.** to beat heavily upon: *Hail pelted the roof.* **3.** to throw: *The clouds pelted rain upon us.* —*v.i.* **1.** to beat heavily: *The rain came pelting down.* **2.** to throw. **3.** to hurry. —*n.* **1.** a pelting. **2.** speed: *The horse is coming at full pelt.* [earlier, to strike repeatedly, perhaps variant of Middle English *pilt, pult* thrust; influenced by *pellet*] —**pelt′er,** *n.*

pelt[2] (pelt), *n.* **1.** the skin of a sheep, goat, or small fur-bearing animal, before it is tanned. **2.** the raw skin of a sheep, goat, or other animal stripped of its wool or fur and ready for tanning. **3.** the skin: *his powerful arms folded on the grizzled pelt of his bare breast* (Joseph Conrad). **4. a.** a skin of an animal worn as a garment. **b.** a garment made of a skin. [probably back formation < *peltry*] —**Syn. 1.** See **skin.**

pel·ta (pel′tə), *n., pl.* **-tae** (-tē). a kind of light, small, leather shield used especially by the ancient Greeks. [< Latin *pelta* < Greek *péltē* small leather shield]

pel·tast (pel′tast), *n.* an ancient Greek soldier armed with a pelta. [< Latin *peltasta* < Greek *peltastḗs* < *péltē* small leather shield]

pel·tate (pel′tāt), *adj. Botany.* shield-shaped: **a.** (of a leaf) having the petiole attached to the lower surface of the blade at or near the middle (instead of at the base or end). **b.** (of stalked parts) having a similar attachment. [< Latin *pelta* shield (< Greek *péltē*) + English *-ate*[1]] —**pel′tate·ly,** *adv.*

Pel·tier effect (pel tyā′), a heating or cooling effect produced by the passage of an electric current through the junction of two dissimilar metals, the heating or cooling depending on the direction of the current. [< Jean *Peltier,* 1785-1845, a French physicist, who discovered it]

pelt·ing (pel′ting), *adj. Archaic.* paltry; petty; mean. [probably related to dialectal *palt* or *pelt* thrash; see PALTRY]

Pel·ton wheel (pel′tən), a form of water wheel or turbine having cup-shaped buckets arranged around its circumference, which are struck at a tangent by one or more jets of water moving at a high velocity.

pelt·ry (pel′trē), *n., pl.* **-ries. 1.** pelts; skins; furs. **2.** a pelt: *The traders Touching at times on the coast, to barter and chaffer for peltries* (Longfellow). [< Anglo-French *pelterie,* Old French *peleterie* < *peletier* furrier < *pel* skin < Latin *pellis*]

pe·lure (pə lůr′, -lyůr′), *n.* a crisp, hard, very thin paper. [< French *pelure* < Old French *peleüre* < *peler* to peel]

pel·vic (pel′vik), *adj.* of or having to do with the pelvis.

pelvic arch or **girdle,** the bony or cartilaginous arch supporting the hind limbs of vertebrates, in man formed by the innominate bones and the sacrum: *Each side of the pelvic girdle consists of an ilium, ischium, and pubis* (A. Franklin Shull).

pel·vi·met·ric (pel′və met′rik), *adj.* of or having to do with pelvimetry: *pelvimetric X rays.*

pel·vim·et·ry (pel vim′ə trē), *n.* the measurement of the size of the pelvis, especially of the female, manually, by instrument, or by X rays.

pel·vis (pel′vis), *n., pl.* **-ves** (-vēz). **1.** the basin-shaped cavity formed by the hipbones and the end of the backbone. **2.** the corresponding cavity of any vertebrate. **3.** the bones forming this cavity: *At the hips is the hip girdle, or pelvis, to which the leg bones are attached* (Beauchamp, Mayfield and West). **4.** the expanded upper end of the ureter, forming a basinlike cavity in the kidney. [< Latin *pelvis* basin < Greek *pellís, -idos* basin, pelvis]

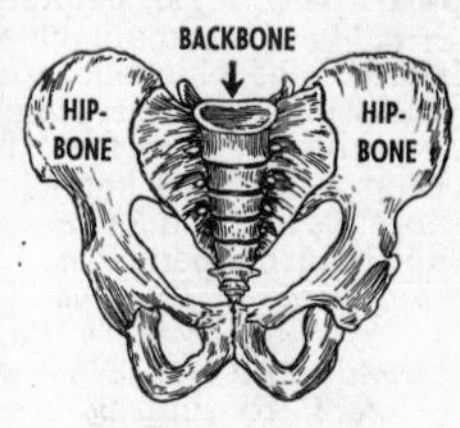

Pelvis (def. 3)

pel·y·co·saur (pel′ə kō sôr), *n.* a prehistoric carnivorous reptile, sometimes more than eight feet in length, which had a tall spiny fin along its back and a few early mammalian characteristics: *Pelycosaurs were ancestors of the mammal-like reptiles called therapsids, and both belong to groups that form links between mammals and reptiles* (Science News Letter). [< New Latin *Pelycosauria* the division name < Greek *pélyx, -ykos* bowl (taken as "pelvis") + *saûros* lizard]

Pelycosaur (about 8 ft. long)

Pem·broke (pem′brůk, -brōk), *n.* one of the two varieties of the Welsh Corgi breed of dogs, characterized by a relatively short tail. See picture under **Welsh corgi.** [< *Pembroke,* a town in Wales]

Pembroke table, a kind of drop-leaf table.

pem·mi·can or **pem·i·can** (pem′ə kən), *n.* **1.** dried meat pounded into a paste with melted fat. It was an important food among certain tribes of North American Indians. **2.** a somewhat similar preparation, usually of beef, plus sugar, currants, etc.: *A Cree Indian word for the conglomerate mixture of dried, shredded, and pounded meats, berries, roots, seeds, and whatever good or bad extraneous object may become trapped in the kneading, pemmican was—and is to this day—the "bread of life" of cold-country explorers* (Wall Street Journal). [American English < Algonkian (Cree) *pimikan* < *pimikew* he makes grease < *pimiy* grease]

pem·phi·goid (pem′fə goid, pem fī′-), *adj.* like or of the nature of pemphigus.

pem·phi·gus (pem′fə gəs, pem fī′-), *n.* a disease of the skin and mucous membranes characterized by eruption of large bubble-like blisters. [< New Latin *pemphigus* < Greek *pémphix, -īgos* pustule, blister; drop of liquid; blast of air]

pen[1] (pen), *n., v.,* **penned, pen·ning.** —*n.* **1. a.** a tool with a point to use in writing with ink. Some pens hold their own ink; others must be dipped into ink: *a ballpoint pen, a fountain pen.* **b.** such a tool fixed to a recording device to make a written record of measurements on a graph. **2. a.** penpoint. **b.** penpoint and holder together. **3. a.** a style of writing; writing: *to use a bitter and ironic pen. The pen is mightier than the sword* (Edward G. Bulwer-Lytton). **b.** a writer; author: [*A book*] *wherein a second Pen had a good share* (Ben Jonson). **4.** a pinfeather. **5.** *Zoology.* the internal, somewhat feather-shaped shell of various cephalopods, as the squids. **6.** a female swan: *The male swan is called a cob, and the female a pen* (World Book Encyclopedia). **7.** *Archaic.* a feather or quill. **8.** *Dialect.* anything similar to or suggesting a feather, as the midrib of a leaf.

dip one's pen in gall, to write with hatred and spite: *Swift dipped his pen in gall when he described the stupidities and vices of mankind in "Gulliver's Travels."*

—*v.t.* **1.** to put into writing; write: *I penned a few words to father today.* **2.** to draw up (a document).

[< Old French *penne* pinion, quill pen < Latin *penna* feather] —**pen′like′,** *adj.*

pen[2] (pen), *n., v.,* **penned** or **pent, pen·ning.** —*n.* **1. a.** a small, closed yard for cows, sheep, pigs, chickens, etc. **b.** any of various enclosures for keeping something, as a portable playpen for a baby, or a place to keep a dog in a kennel. **2.** the number of animals in a pen, or required to fill a pen. **3.** a submarine pen: *Pens for the subs are being completed at Tsingtao,* [*which had been*] *a U. S. Navy Western Pacific HQ after the second world war* (Newsweek).

—*v.t.* **1.** to shut in a pen. **2.** to confine closely; shut in: *John had me penned in a corner where I could not escape.*

[apparently Old English *penn* enclosure] —**pen′like′,** *adj.*

pen[3] (pen), *n. Slang.* penitentiary.

pen., 1. peninsula. **2.** penitentiary.

Pen., Peninsula.

P.E.N., International Association of Poets, Playwrights, Editors, Essayists, and Novelists.

pe·nal (pē′nəl), *adj.* **1.** of, having to do with, or given as punishment: *penal laws, penal labor.* **2.** liable to be punished: *Robbery is a penal offense.* [< Latin *poenālis* < *poena* punishment < Greek *poinē* penalty] —**pe′nal·ly,** *adv.*

penal code, a code of laws dealing with crime and its punishment.

pe·nal·ise (pē′nə līz, pen′ə-), *v.t.,* **-ised, -is·ing.** *Especially British.* penalize.

pe·nal·i·za·tion (pē′nə lə zā′shən), *n.* the act of penalizing: *There must be an incentive to invest capital and no penalization of enterprise and risk-taking* (Wall Street Journal).

pe·nal·ize (pē′nə līz, pen′ə-), *v.t.,* **-ized, -iz·ing. 1.** to declare punishable by law or by rule; set a penalty for: *Speeding on city streets is penalized. Fouls are penalized in many games.* **2.** to inflict a penalty on; punish: *Our team was penalized five yards for being offside. His deafness penalizes him in public life.* —**pe′nal·iz′er,** *n.*

pen·al·ty (pen′əl tē), *n., pl.* **-ties. 1.** a punishment: *The penalty for speeding is a fine of ten dollars.* **2.** a disadvantage imposed on a side or player for breaking rules. **3.** any disadvantage attached to some act or condition: *the penalties of old age.* **4.** a handicap. [alteration of earlier *penality* < Medieval Latin *poenalitas* < Latin *poenālis* having to do with punishment; see PENAL]

penalty box, an enclosure alongside an ice hockey rink where penalized players must stay during the period in which they are barred from play: *The Vees lost a man to the penalty box at 8:10 when McAvoy made a body check against the boards* (Penticton, British Columbia, Herald).

penalty goal, a goal scored upon a penalty kick in either rugby or soccer: *In the 16th minute of the first half T. E. Davies kicked a fine penalty goal for Wales from 35 yards, and wide out* (Sunday Times).

penalty kick, (in soccer and rugby) a free kick, without interference, trying for a goal, awarded to a team because of a major infraction of the rules by their opponents.

pen·ance (pen′əns), *n., v.,* **-anced, -anc·ing.** —*n.* **1.** a punishment borne to show sorrow for sin, to make up for a wrong done, and to obtain pardon: *When the scourge Inexorably, and the torturing hour Calls us to penance* (Milton). **2.** a sacrament of the Roman Catholic, Greek, and other churches, that includes repentance, intention to amend, confession, satisfaction, and absolution.

do penance, to perform some act, or undergo some penalty, in sorrow for sin: *On Sunday the Parish Church of St. Mary, Lambeth, was ... unusually crowded ... to see Mr. John Oliver ... do penance in a White Sheet for ... calling Miss Stephenson ... by an improper name* (London Courier).

—*v.t.* to impose penance on; punish or discipline by requiring a penance.

[< Old French *peneance* < Latin *paenitentia.* Doublet of PENITENCE.]

pe·nang-law·yer (pi nang′lô′yər), *n.* a cane or walking stick made from the stem of a small East Indian palm. [probably alteration of a native name; *lawyer,* with reference to the object's use in settling disputes]

pen·an·nu·lar (pe nan′yə lər), *adj.* almost annular; forming an incomplete ring (with a small portion lacking). [< Latin *pēne, paene* almost + English *annular*]

pe·na·tes or **Pe·na·tes** (pə nā′tēz), *n.pl.* gods of the household and state, worshiped in ancient Rome. [< Latin *Penātēs* < *penes* in, within (a house) < *penus* inner room (sanctuary of a temple); provisions]

pence (pens), *n. British.* a plural of **penny:** *Tobacco and paint shares closed a few pence dearer among the industrial shares* (London Times). *Abbr.:* d.

pen·cel (pen′səl), *n.* **1.** *Archaic.* a small streamer, especially one carried as a banner on a lance. **2.** *Obsolete.* a lady's favor worn or carried by a knight. Also, **pennoncel, pennoncelle, penoncel, pensil, pensile.** [< Anglo-French *pensil,* Old French *penoncel* (diminutive) < *penon,* or *pannon* pennon]

pen·chant (pen′chənt), *n.* a strong taste or liking; inclination: *a penchant for taking long walks.* [< French *penchant,* (literally) present participle of Old French *pencher* to incline < Vulgar Latin *pendicāre* < Latin *pendēre* to hang] —**Syn.** bent.

pen·cil (pen′səl), *n., v.,* **-ciled, -cil·ing** or (*especially British*) **-cilled, -cil·ling.** —*n.* **1.** a pointed tool to write or draw with, usually with a slender strip of lead (graphite) in between two strips of wood or in a metal tube. **2.** any object of like shape: *a styptic pencil.* **3.** a stick of coloring matter: *an eyebrow pencil.* **4. a.** an artist's paintbrush: *Take your pallet ... choose your most delicate camel-hair pencils* (Charlotte Brontë). **b.** the skill or style of an artist. **5.** a set of lines, light rays, or the like coming to a point, or extending in different directions from a point: *The light used for all practical purposes comes from sources of finite area, every point of which emits a pencil* (Hardy and Perrin).

—*v.t.* **1.** to mark or write with a pencil: *to pencil corrections in the margin of a book, to pencil a note.* **2.** to draw or sketch with a pencil: *to pencil an outline of a house.*

[< Old French *pincel,* ultimately < Latin *pēnicillus* painter's brush, pencil (diminutive) < *pēnis* (originally) tail] —**pen′cil·er** or (*especially British*) **pen′cil·ler,** *n.* —**pen′cil·like′,** *adj.*

pencil beam, a narrow, conical radar beam, used for homing in on a target with maximum accuracy.

pen·ciled (pen′səld), *adj.* **1.** marked with or as with a pencil: *her soft, penciled eyebrows* (Harriet Beecher Stowe). **2.** executed, drawn, or written with or as with a pencil: *penciled lines, a penciled note.* **3.** formed into a pencil or pencils, as rays; radiated.

pen·cil·i·form (pen sil′ə fôrm), *adj.* having the form or appearance of a pencil, as of rays, etc.

pen·cil·ing (pen′sə ling), *n.* **1.** the act of one who pencils. **2.** fine coloring or delicate drawing, as may be done with a pencil.

pencil pusher, *Slang.* an office worker; person who works at a desk.

pencil sharpener, a device for sharpening a wooden pencil by shaving it with a blade or series of rotating blades.

pen·craft (pen′kraft′, -kräft′), *n.* writing; penmanship; authorship.

pend[1] (pend), *v.i.* **1.** to remain undecided or unsettled. **2.** *Dialect.* to depend. [back formation < *pending*]

pend[2] (pend), *n. Scottish.* a pendant.

pend·ant (pen′dənt), *n.* **1.** a hanging ornament, such as a locket. **2.** an ornament hanging down from an arch, or a ceiling or roof. **3.** a person or thing forming a parallel or match to another; a match; companion piece. **4.** an additional statement, consideration, etc., that completes or complements another. **5.** an attachment by which something is suspended, as the ring and stem of a pocket watch. **6.** *British, Nautical.* pennant: *I hoisted my pendant on the Irresistible* (Horatio Nelson).

—*adj.* pendent.

[< Old French *pendant,* (originally) present participle *pendre* to hang < Vulgar Latin *pendere* < Latin *pendēre*]

pende·loque (päNd lôk′), *n. French.* a pear-shaped pendant, as a diamond cut in this form.

pend·en·cy (pen′dən sē), *n., pl.* **-cies.** the state or condition of being pending or continuing undecided or awaiting settlement: *The mere pendency of such charges impairs my further service on the commission* (Newsweek).

pend·ent (pen′dənt), *adj.* **1.** hanging: *the pendent branches of a willow.* **2.** overhanging: *a pendent cliff.* **3.** pending. —*n.* pendant. [< Latin *pendēns, -entis,* present participle of *pendēre* to hang] —**pend′ent·ly,** *adv.*

—**Syn.** *adj.* **1.** suspended.

pen·den·te li·te (pen den′tē lī′tē), *Latin.* during litigation; while a lawsuit is pending.

pen·den·tive (pen den′tiv), *n. Architecture.* **1.** the concave, triangular segment of the lower part of a hemispherical dome, between two adjacent penetrating arches: *Builders achieved the transition from a square space to a circular dome by inserting pendentives (spherical triangles) over the four corners* (World Book Encyclopedia). **2.** a similar segment of a groined vault that springs from a single support. [< earlier French *pendentif* < Latin *pendēns;* see PENDENT]

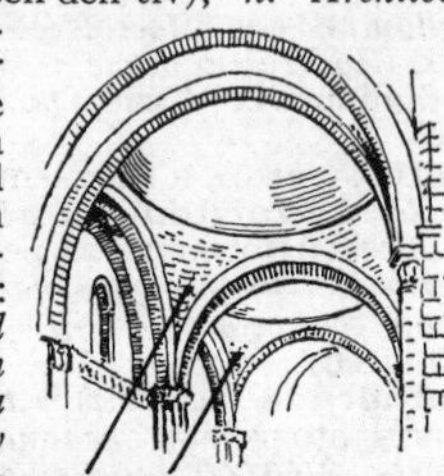

Pendentives (def. 1)

pen·di·cle (pen′də kəl), *n. Scottish.* **1.** a pendant. **2.** an adjunct or appendage. **3.** a small piece of land, a cottage, or the like, attached to an estate. [diminutive form of Latin *pendēre* to hang]

pend·ing (pen′ding), *adj.* **1.** waiting to be decided or settled: *while the agreement was pending.* **2.** overhanging.

—*prep.* **1.** while waiting for; until: *Pending his return, let us get everything ready.* **2.** during: *pending the meeting.*

pen·drag·on or **Pen·drag·on** (pen drag′ən), *n.* chief leader, a title of ancient British chiefs: *the dread Pendragon, Britain's King of kings* (Tennyson). [< Welsh *pendragon* < *pen* chief + *dragon* war leader; dragon standard < Latin *dracō, -ōnis* the dragon emblem of a cohort]

pen·drag·on·ship or **Pen·drag·on·ship** (pen drag′ən ship), *n.* the state, condition, or power of a pendragon.

pen·du·lar (pen′jə lər, -dyə-), *adj.* **1.** of or having to do with a pendulum. **2.** resembling the movement of a pendulum; oscillating: *History may suggest pendular swings, but history has never before seen the breadth of communication and the speed of change (some of it progress) that we have today* (Maclean's).

pen·du·lous (pen′jə ləs, -dyə-), *adj.* **1.** hanging loosely: *The oriole builds a pendulous nest.* **2.** swinging like a pendulum: *pendulous jowls.* [< Latin *pendulus* (with English *-ous*) < *pendēre* hang] —**pen′du·lous·ly,** *adv.* —**pen′du·lous·ness,** *n.*

pen·du·lum (pen′jə ləm, -dyə-), *n.* a weight so hung from a fixed point that it is free to swing to and fro. The movement of the works of a tall clock is often timed by a pendulum. *The utility of the pendulum as a timekeeper is based on the fact that the period is practically independent of the amplitude* (Sears and Zemansky). [< New Latin *pendulum,* (literally) neuter of Latin *pendulus* pendulous]

Pendulum on chime clock

Pe·nel·o·pe (pə nel′ə pē), *n. Greek Legend.* the faithful wife of Odysseus. She waited twenty years for his return in spite of the entreaties of her many suitors.

pe·ne·plain (pē′nə plān′), *n.* a formerly mountainous or hilly area reduced nearly to a plain by erosion: *There is evidence of several peneplains during Cenozoic time in the Appalachians, indicating crustal uplift, renewed uplift, erosion, etc.* (Robert M. Garrels). —*v.t.* to make a peneplain of, as by erosion. [American English < Latin *pēne*, or *paene* almost + English *plain*]

pe·ne·pla·na·tion (pē′nə plə nā′shən), *n.* the forming of a peneplain by erosion: *Peneplanation, especially in a region of much disturbed hard rocks, is judged to demand very prolonged work of erosive processes during time when the land surface was neither raised nor lowered appreciably by earth deformation* (Raymond Cecil Moore).

pe·ne·plane (pē′nə plān′), *n., v.t.,* **-planed, -plan·ing.** peneplain: *That the Lower Pre-Cambrian rocks were peneplaned is indicated by the smooth surface at the base of the Middle Pre-Cambrian* (Raymond Cecil Moore).

pen·e·tra·bil·i·ty (pen′ə trə bil′ə tē), *n.* capability of being penetrated.

pen·e·tra·ble (pen′ə trə bəl), *adj.* that can be penetrated: *It is not penetrable by the eye of man* (Edward Topsell). [< Latin *penetrābilis* < *penetrāre* to penetrate]

pen·e·tra·bly (pen′ə trə blē), *adv.* so as to be penetrable: *... to make their prayers more penetrably enforcing* (Thomas Nashe).

pen·e·tra·li·a (pen′ə trā′lē ə), *n.pl.* **1.** the innermost parts or recesses of a building, especially the sanctuary or inmost shrine of a temple: *Mr. Campbell ... is fain to ... retire into the penetralia of his habitation, in order to avoid this diurnal annoyance* (Tobias Smollett). **2.** innermost parts; secret or hidden recesses: *to disclose the very penetralia of my heart* (Charles J. Lever). [< Latin *penetrālia*, neuter plural of *penetrālis* interior, inmost < *penetrāre* to penetrate]

pen·e·trance (pen′ə trəns), *n.* **1.** the action of penetrating; penetration. **2.** *Genetics.* the measurement, expressed in percentages, of the ability of a gene to manifest itself or its effects: *Penetrance refers to the regularity with which a gene produces a detectable effect* (Hegner and Stiles).

pen·e·trant (pen′ə trənt), *adj.* penetrating.

pen·e·trate (pen′ə trāt), *v.,* **-trat·ed, -trat·ing.** —*v.t.* **1.** to get into or through: *A bullet can penetrate a wall, or two inches into a wall.* **2.** to pierce through: *Our eyes could not penetrate the darkness.* **3.** to soak through; spread through: *The odor penetrated the whole house.* **4.** to see into; understand: *I could not penetrate the mystery.* **5.** to affect or impress very much. —*v.i.* **1.** to make a way: *Even where the trees were thickest, the sunshine penetrated.* **2.** to affect the feelings: *I advised him to give her music o′ mornings; they say it will penetrate* (Shakespeare). [< Latin *penetrāre* (with English *-ate*[1]) < *penitus* deep within, related to *penes* within; see PENATES]

—**Syn.** *v.t.* **1. Penetrate, pierce** mean to go into or through something. **Penetrate** implies going deeply into something, or into it and out the other side, and suggests a driving force or keenness of what goes in: *The bullet penetrated the board.* **Pierce** implies stabbing through the surface, or passing right through, with a sharp-pointed object or something sharp and cutting, as a knife: *The dagger pierced his side.* **3.** pervade, permeate. **4.** discern, comprehend.

pen·e·trat·ing (pen′ə trā′ting), *adj.* **1.** sharp; piercing: *a penetrating sound, a penetrating odor.* **2.** having an acute mind; understanding thoroughly: *penetrating criticism. Nature herself seems ... to write for him with her own bare, sheer, penetrating power* (Matthew Arnold). —**pen′e·trat′ing·ly,** *adv.*

pen·e·tra·tion (pen′ə trā′shən), *n.* **1.** the act or power of penetrating. **2.** the act of entering a country and gaining influence there: *economic penetration.* **3.** sharpness of intellect; insight: *You can pretend to be a man of penetration* (Sir Richard Steele). **4.** the depth to which a projectile will enter a material at a given range. **5. a.** (in a telescope) the power of making distant objects visible or distinct, considered in relation to their distance. **b.** (in a microscope) the power of the objective to give distinct vision for some distance both beyond and within its exact focus. —**Syn. 3.** acumen, acuteness, shrewdness, discernment. See **insight.**

pen·e·tra·tive (pen′ə trā′tiv), *adj.* penetrating; piercing; acute; keen: *the penetrative character of temptations* (Richard C. Trench). *Perhaps one can distinguish between the great scientist and the researcher who is a mere technician largely on the basis of the penetrative logic of the former* (John E. Owen). —**pen′e·tra′tive·ly,** *adv.* —**pen′e·tra′tive·ness,** *n.*

pen·e·tra·tor (pen′ə trā′tər), *n.* a person or thing that penetrates: *He is the perfect penetrator into human vices* (Edward G. Bulwer-Lytton).

pen·e·trom·e·ter (pen′ə trom′ə tər), *n.* an instrument designed to measure the density, compactness, or penetrability of a substance. A marine penetrometer records the firmness of the sediment at the bottom of the ocean. *The penetrometer was designed for use in marine geological and biological research* (Science News Letter).

pen·e·tron (pen′ə tron), *n. Physics.* a meson. [< *penetr*(ate) + *-on*, as in *electron*]

pen·friend or **pen-friend** (pen′frend′), *n. Especially British.* a pen pal: *The teacher asked if I would correspond with one of the islanders who wanted a pen-friend* (Cape Times).

P. Eng., Professional Engineer.

peng·hu·lu (peng hü′lü), *n.* (in the Malay Peninsula, Borneo, etc.) a village or tribal chief: *The elderly penghulu ... of an Iban tribe ... invited [us] to spend a night at his long house before we sailed* (London Times). [< Indonesian *penghulu*]

pen·gö (peng′gœ), *n., pl.* **-gö, -gös** (-gœz). **1.** the standard unit of money of Hungary from 1925 to 1946, worth (usually) about 17 cents, superseded by the forint. **2.** a silver coin or a banknote, representing this unit. [< Hungarian *pengö* (literally) present participle of *peng* to sound, ring; imitative]

pen·guin (pen′gwin, peng′-), *n.* **1.** any of a group of flightless, webfooted marine birds, chiefly of the Antarctic region of the Southern Hemisphere, that have black and white plumage, and short, flipperlike wings with a scaly covering for diving and swimming: *Lady penguins lay only one egg a year and guard it well* (New York Times). **2.** an apparatus for training airplane pilots, having stubby wings, a tail, motor, etc., but capable of being maneuvered only on the ground. **3.** *Slang.* an aviator who does not fly; an administrative officer in the air forces. **4.** *Obsolete.* the great auk. [supposedly < Welsh *pen* head + *gwyn* white]

King Penguin (def. 1) (about 3 ft. tall)

pen·hold·er (pen′hōl′dər), *n.* **1.** the handle by which a pen is held in writing. **2.** a rack for pens.

pen·i·cil (pen′ə sil), *n.* a small bundle or tuft of slightly diverging hairs, resembling a paintbrush, as on a caterpillar. [< Latin *pēnicillus*; see PENCIL]

pen·i·cil·la·mine (pen′ə sil′ə mēn), *n.* an amino acid derived from penicillin, used as a chelating agent. *Formula:* $C_5H_{11}NO_2S$

pen·i·cil·late (pen′ə sil′it, -āt), *adj.* having or forming a small tuft or tufts of hairs, scales, etc.; furnished with a penicil or penicils. [< Latin *pēnicillus* (see PENCIL + English *-ate*[1]] —**pen′i·cil′late·ly,** *adv.*

pen·i·cil·la·tion (pen′ə sə lā′shən), *n.* a growth of hairs, scales, etc., in the form of a penicil.

pen·i·cil·lin (pen′ə sil′in), *n.* an antibacterial substance, the first widely used antibiotic drug, originally obtained from a green mold, used to destroy or sharply check the growth of various harmful bacteria, as some strains of staphylococci, gonococci, pneumococci, etc. Although penicillin can be administered in massive doses to many people, it develops a capacity for a serious allergic reaction in others. *Penicillin is especially effective against the germs of pneumonia and in treating other diseases caused by "round" bacteria* (Sidonie M. Gruenberg). *Formula:* $C_{16}H_{17}N_2O_4SNa$ [< *penicill*(ium) + *-in*]

pen·i·cil·lin·ase (pen′ə sil′ə nās), *n.* an enzyme produced by many forms of bacteria which is used to neutralize allergic reactions to penicillin: *If a person is known to be penicillin sensitive, either a penicillin-free vaccine should be administered or an injection of penicillinase given before the vaccine shot* (Science News Letter).

pen·i·cil·li·um (pen′ə sil′ē əm), *n., pl.* **-cil·li·ums, -cil·li·a** (-sil′ē ə). any of a group of green or bluish-green ascomycetous fungi, including several of the common molds, as two kinds used in ripening cheese, and a kind that forms crusts on jellies and jams. The group also includes species used in the production of penicillin and certain other antibiotic drugs. [< New Latin *Penicillium* the genus name < Latin *pēnicillus* small brush or tail; see PENCIL]

pen·i·cil·lo·ic acid (pen′ə sə lō′ik), the resultant product, no longer antigenic, after the neutralization and breakdown of penicillin by penicillinase: *It acts by rapidly breaking down penicillin to penicilloic acid, which has no antibiotic activity and which does not create sensitivity* (Observer).

pe·nill (pə nil′), *n., pl.* **-nil·lion** (-nil′yən). **1.** a form of improvised verse adapted to an air played on the harp, and sung by the Welsh at an eisteddfod and on other occasions. **2.** a stanza of such verse: *The bards ... struck up a sort of consecutive chorus in a series of penillion or stanzas in praise of Maelgon and his heirship* (Thomas Love Peacock). [< Welsh *pennill* verse, stanza (plural *pennillion, penillion*) < *penn* head]

pen·in·su·la (pə nin′sə lə, -syə-), *n.* a piece of land almost surrounded by water or extending far out into the water: *Florida is a peninsula. His audacious delaying tactics before the Pusan perimeter meant the difference between maintaining a foothold on the peninsula and retreat to Japan* (Newsweek). [< Latin *paeninsula* < *paene* almost + *insula* island]

pen·in·su·lar (pə nin′sə lər, -syə-), *adj.* **1.** like a peninsula. **2.** in or of a peninsula. —*n.* an inhabitant of a peninsula: *The Arabs traded with the far-off peninsulars* (Nation).

pen·in·su·lar·i·ty (pə nin′sə lar′ə tē, -syə-), *n.* **1.** the state of being a peninsula. **2.** the character or habit of mind attributed to those living in a peninsula and having little contact with other people; narrowness of mind; provincialism: *But a tour through Italy at election time ... conveys the tang of a potent peninsularity* (Manchester Guardian).

Peninsular War, the series of military operations carried on from 1808 to 1813 by the British, Spanish, and Portuguese against the French in Spain and Portugal, as a result of which the French were forced to withdraw from the Iberian peninsula.

Peninsula State, a nickname for Florida.

pen·in·su·late (pə nin′sə lāt, -syə-), *v.t.,* **-lat·ed, -lat·ing.** to form into a peninsula or peninsulas: *There are six considerable rivers which, with their numerous branches, peninsulate the whole state* (Jedidiah Morse). [< *peninsul*(a) + *-ate*[1]]

pe·nis (pē′nis), *n., pl.* **-nis·es, -nes** (-nēz). the male organ of copulation. [< Latin *pēnis* penis; (originally) tail]

pen·i·tence (pen′ə təns), *n.* sorrow for sinning or doing wrong; repentance. [< Old French *penitence*, learned borrowing from Latin *paenitentia* < *paenitēns, -entis,* present participle of *paenitēre* repent. Doublet of PENANCE.]

pen·i·tent (pen′ə tənt), *adj.* **1.** sorry for sinning or doing wrong; repenting: *The penitent boy promised never to cheat again.* **2.** expressing repentance: *a low, penitent voice.*

—*n.* **1.** a person who is sorry for sin or wrongdoing. **2.** a person who confesses and does penance for his sins under the direction of the church.

—**Syn.** *adj.* **1.** repentant, contrite, remorseful.

Pen·i·ten·te (pen′ə ten′tā, -tē), *n.* a member of a religious order of flagellants among certain Spanish-American natives of New Mexico and southern Colorado, who practice flagellantism especially during Holy Week. [< American Spanish *Penitente* (literally) penitent, short for *Hermanos Penitentes* Penitent Brothers (the name of the order)]

pen·i·ten·tial (pen′ə ten′shəl), *adj.* **1.** of, showing, or having to do with penitence: *The penitential psalms express remorse for sin. Mr. Benson, on penitential knee, bent to recover her scattered property* (John Stephen Strange). **2.** of or having to do with penance.

—*n.* **1.** a person performing or undergoing penance; penitent. **2.** a book or code of the church canons on penance, its imposition, etc. —**pen′i·ten′tial·ly,** *adv.*

pen·i·ten·tia·ry (pen′ə ten′shər ē), *n., pl.* **-ries,** *adj.* —*n.* **1.** a prison for criminals. **2.** *U.S.* a State or Federal prison: *He had worked as a $600-a-month assistant warden at the Huntsville, Texas, state penitentiary,*

until a convict spotted his picture in an old crime stories magazine (Newsweek). **3.** in the Roman Catholic Church: **a.** a diocesan officer empowered to rule on cases of conscience beyond the scope of the parish priest. **b.** a congregation of the Papal Curia, presided over by a cardinal, that decides questions of penance.
—*adj.* **1.** *U.S.* making one liable to punishment in a prison: *a penitentiary offense.* **2.** used for punishment, discipline, and reformation: *penitentiary measures.* **3.** of penance.
[(definition 1) < Medieval Latin *poenitentiaria;* (definition 3) < Medieval Latin *poenitentiarius,* both noun uses of adjective < Latin *paenitentia* penitence]

pen·i·tent·ly (pen′ə tənt lē), *adv.* in a penitent manner: *He, whom they first pierced and then penitently gazed on, was God* (Edward B. Pusey).

pen·knife (pen′nīf′), *n., pl.* **-knives.** a small pocketknife.

pen·light (pen′līt′), *n.* a small flashlight roughly the size of a fountain pen. —*adj.* of or having to do with a penlight: *penlight batteries.*

pen·man (pen′mən), *n., pl.* **-men. 1.** a writer; author. **2.** a person whose handwriting is good. **3.** *British.* a person whose business is to copy documents, etc.

pen·man·ship (pen′mən ship), *n.* **1.** writing with pen, pencil, etc.; handwriting; calligraphy. **2.** the manner or style of composing a written work; literary composition.

Penn., Pennsylvania.

pen·na (pen′ə), *n., pl.* **pen·nae** (pen′ē). a contour feather of a bird, as distinguished from a down feather, plume, etc. [< Latin *penna* feather]

Penna., Pennsylvania.

pen name, a name used by a writer instead of his real name: *As a way of sloughing off one personality and acquiring a new one, the pen name is not a new idea, nor historically limited to the arts* (Harper's).

pen·nant (pen′ənt), *n.* **1.** a flag, usually long and narrow, used on ships in signaling, as a school banner, etc. **2.** any flag taken as an emblem of superiority or success, especially in an athletic contest: *The mad pace of the Dodgers has most folks believing that Walter Alston's hot-shots have virtually clinched the pennant* (New York Times). **3.** a line at the end of the stem of certain musical notes; hook. [apparently blend of *pendant* ship's rope of various kinds, and of *pennon*]

pen·nate (pen′āt), *adj.* **1.** having wings; having feathers. **2.** *Botany, Obsolete.* pinnate. [< Latin *pennātus* < *penna* feather, wing]

pen·nat·ed (pen′ā tid), *adj.* pennate.

pen·nat·u·la (pə nat′yə lə), *n., pl.* **-las, -lae** (-lē). a sea pen (polyp). [< New Latin *Pennatula* the typical genus, feminine of Late Latin *pennatulus* (diminutive) < Latin *pennātus* winged; see PENNATE]

pen·ni (pen′ē), *n., pl.* **pen·ni·a** (pen′ē ə). **1.** a Finnish unit of money, 1/100 of a markka, now used especially as a money of account. **2.** a coin representing this unit. [< Finnish *penni* < Old Swedish *penninger*]

pen·nied (pen′ēd), *adj.* having a penny or pennies; not penniless: . . . *while you dispensed the fragile chocolate to pennied youngsters* (Westminster Gazette).

pen·ni·less (pen′ē lis), *adj.* without a cent of money; very poor: *The thief snatched my purse and left me penniless in the big city.* —**pen′ni·less·ly,** *adv.* —**pen′ni·less·ness,** *n.*
—**Syn.** destitute, indigent. See **poor.**

pen·non (pen′ən), *n.* **1.** a long, triangular flag originally carried on the lance of a knight. **2.** any flag or banner. **3.** *Nautical.* a pennant. **4.** *Poetic.* a wing; pinion: *Fluttering his pennons vain, plumb down he drops Ten thousand fathom deep* (Milton). [< Old French *penon* < *penne* feather < Latin *penna*]

pen·non·cel or **pen·non·celle** (pen′ən sel), *n.* pencel.

pen·noned (pen′ənd), *adj.* bearing a pennon: *Behind this line we get a glimpse of plumed helmets and pennoned lances of some of the cavalry* (Westminster Gazette).

penn'orth (pen′ərth), *n. British Dialect.* pennyworth.

Penn·sy (pen′sē), *n. U.S. Informal.* a nickname for the Pennsylvania Railroad.

Penn·syl·va·ni·a Dutch or **German** (pen′səl vā′nē ə, -vān′yə), **1.** the descendants of immigrants of the 1600's and 1700's to southeastern Pennsylvania from southern Germany and Switzerland. **2.** a dialect of High German with English intermixed, spoken by them.
➤ See **Dutch** for a usage note.

Penn·syl·va·ni·an (pen′səl vā′nē ən, -vān′yən), *n.* **1.** a native or inhabitant of Pennsylvania. **2.** *Geology.* the second period of Carboniferous time, after the Mississippian and before the Permian, characterized by coal-, oil-, and gas-bearing deposits; Upper Carboniferous (the name used outside of North America). **3.** the strata formed in this period.
—*adj.* **1.** of or having to do with Pennsylvania. **2.** *Geology.* of or having to do with the Pennsylvanian period or its rocks: *The Mississippian and the next following Pennsylvanian Period are the only widely recognized major geologic time divisions that are "made in America"* (Raymond Cecil Moore).

pen·ny (pen′ē), *n., pl.* **pen·nies** or *British* (*collectively for 2*) **pence. 1.** a copper coin of the United States and Canada; cent. 100 pennies = 1 dollar. **2.** a bronze coin, used in England, Australia, New Zealand, equal to 1/12 of a shilling. **3.** a sum of money; money.
turn an honest penny, to earn money honestly: *He turns an honest penny by horse hire* (Augustus Jessopp).
—*adj.* **1.** costing one penny. **2.** cheap.
[Old English *pending,* later *penig*]

penny-a-line (pen′ē ə līn′), *adj.* **1. a.** paid at the rate of a penny a printed line (as many journalists, writers of popular fiction, etc., formerly were). **b.** paid at a low rate and on the basis of space filled (as some writers still are). **2.** carelessly written and with little or no literary merit.

pen·ny-a-lin·er (pen′ē ə lī′nər), *n.* a person who writes, as for a newspaper, at a penny a line or some low rate; hack writer.

penny ante, any variety of poker in which, by agreement between the players, the ante for each hand is set at one cent or some other trifling sum: *A high-school chum of Ike's back in Abilene, Swede spent many an hour at the Belle Springs Creamery playing penny ante poker with Night Foreman Eisenhower during the long, lonely night shift* (Time).

pen·ny-an·te (pen′ē an′tē), *adj.* indicating something of little value or importance; cheap: *a penny-ante salary.*

penny arcade, a place of cheap amusements where the games of chance, pinball machines, etc., originally cost a penny a play.

penny bank, 1. a savings bank at which a sum as low as a penny may be deposited: *A penny bank, for savings of amounts too small to be received at the ordinary savings banks, was opened in Jersey on the 1st of January, 1862* (David T. Ansted). **2.** a small metal, plastic, or ceramic container for saving pennies or small coins: *"I've got the patent on a penny bank—it's a plastic reproduction of an old iron bank"* (New Yorker).

pen·ny·cress (pen′ē kres′), *n.* a cruciferous herb with flat, round pods, found throughout Europe and temperate Asia: *I found a plant of pennycress in a piece of waste ground* (G. Travers).

penny dreadful, *British.* a piece of cheap, sensational fiction, especially a novel or novelette in magazine form or paperback, characterized by violent episodes, maudlin sentiment, etc.: *The country was also flooded with an unprecedented quantity of shilling shockers, penny dreadfuls, and popular magazines* (New Yorker).

pen·ny-far·thing (pen′ē fär′ᴛʜing), *n.* an early form of bicycle having a large front wheel and a small rear one.

penny fee, *Scottish.* small wages paid in money.

penny gaff, *British Slang.* a cheap theater or music hall.

penny paper, a newspaper of the 1800's that sold for a penny.

penny pincher, or **pen·ny-pinch·er** (pen′ē pin′chər), *n. Informal.* a miser; skinflint; person who does not spend or use money freely: *Like so many other men of means, he was a penny pincher* (New Yorker).

pen·ny-pinch·ing (pen′ē pin′ching), *n. Informal.* an exercising of care in the spending of money; being stingy: *Penny-pinching is fine as far as it goes, but it is the whole inflated balloon of Government that really needs to be pinched* (Wall Street Journal). —*adj.* niggardly with money; tight; stingy: *a penny-pinching state legislature.*

pen·ny-plain (pen′ē plān′), *adj.* plain and unpretentious: *"The Wanting Seed" is far less disastrous, but in its penny-plain style, it . . . can be ranked with . . . Orwell and Huxley* (Time).

penny post, the postal system, called such in the days when mail traveled for a penny.

penny press, newspapers produced in the 1800's for the general public rather than for select or literary readers and selling for a penny each: *The penny press dogged the Princess' footsteps, struggling to make significant gossip of every transient expression* (Time).

pen·ny·roy·al (pen′ē roi′əl), *n.* **1.** any of various plants of the mint family, especially a European plant having small aromatic leaves, and a similar American herb that yields a pungent oil formerly much used as a mosquito repellent and medicinally; fleamint. **2.** a fragrant oil made from the American species. [earlier *penneryal,* apparently alteration of *pulyole riall* < Anglo-French *puliol real* < Old French *pouliol,* earlier *pulioel* thyme (ultimately < Latin *pūlejum* pennyroyal), *real* royal]

American Pennyroyal (def. 1) (6 to 18 in. high)

penny stock, stock offered for sale for less than a dollar per share, often for only a few cents: *In a move to eliminate racketeers in penny stocks, the SEC will tighten its small securities regulations* (Time).

pen·ny·weight (pen′ē wāt′), *n.* 24 grains or 1/20 of an ounce in troy weight. *Abbr.:* dwt.

penny wheep, *Scottish.* small beer (formerly sold at a penny a bottle).

pen·ny·whis·tle (pen′ē hwis′əl), *n.* a toy whistle such as children use: *The noise that emerges from some organs of British publicity abroad is more like the peep of a pennywhistle than a fanfare* (Manchester Guardian). —*adj.* of poor quality; inferior: *Since 1949, a million ex-Nazis have been re-enfranchised. A dozen pennywhistle Führers are after their votes* (Time).

pen·ny-wise (pen′ē wīz′), *adj.* saving in regard to small sums: *Franklin was far from being a foxy grandpa benignly counseling homely virtues over the rims of his bifocals or a penny-wise mouther of platitudes* (Wall Street Journal).
penny-wise and pound-foolish, saving in small expenses and wasteful in big ones: *He asserted that dribbling out funds as we are presently doing is penny-wise and pound-foolish* (New York Times).

pen·ny·wort (pen′ē wėrt′), *n.* any of various plants having roundish leaves, as the wall pennywort or navelwort and the marsh pennywort.

pen·ny·worth (pen′ē wėrth′), *n.* **1.** as much as can be bought for a penny. **2.** a small amount: *Give me a pennyworth of advice.* **3.** a bargain (good, bad, etc.): *Many have been ruined by buying good pennyworths* (Benjamin Franklin). **4.** a good bargain.

Pe·nob·scot (pə nob′skot), *n.* **1.** a member of an American Indian tribe of Algonkian stock formerly living near the Penobscot River, Maine. **2.** this tribe. **3.** their language.

pe·no·log·i·cal (pē′nə loj′ə kəl), *adj.* of or having to do with penology: *For eight years I did time in just such a penitentiary, under administrations representing opposite extremes of penological thought* (Atlantic). —**pe′no·log′i·cal·ly,** *adv.*

pe·nol·o·gist (pē nol′ə jist), *n.* a person who is skilled in penology: *On one hand the Senate committee was listening to doctors, penologists, and policemen disagree on how to control drug distribution and handle addicts* (Newsweek).

pe·nol·o·gy (pē nol′ə jē), *n.* **1.** the science of the punishment and rehabilitation of criminals. **2.** the study of the management of prisons. [< Latin *poena* punishment + *-logy*]

pen·on·cel (pen′ən sel), *n.* pencel.

pen pal, a person with whom one corresponds regularly, often in another country

 PRONUNCIATION KEY: hat, āge, cãre, fär; let, ēqual, tėrm; it, īce; hot, ōpen, ôrder; oil, out; cup, pu̇t, rüle;

and without ever being seen personally: *Ellen Roberts, a California teen-ager, was snowed under by an avalanche of Italian pen pals last fall* (Harper's).

pen picture or **portrait,** **1.** a picture drawn with a pen. **2.** a brief written description of a person, event, etc.: *Time [magazine] writers were as flattering with their pen pictures ... as Australia's Dobell was awry with his brushwork* (Time).

pen·point (pen′point′), *n.* **1.** a small metal instrument with a split point, used with a holder for writing in ink; nib. **2.** a point used for writing on any pen, as the ball at the end of a ballpoint pen.

pen-push·er (pen′pu̇sh′ər), *n. Slang.* an office worker; person who works at a desk: *"I take on the paperwork," he said, ... "I'm a pen-pusher"* (New Yorker).

pen·sée (päN sā′), *n., pl.* **pen·sées** (päN-sā′). *French.* a thought or reflection put in literary form: *He expressed this knowledge in a typical Churchillian pensée, under date of April 8, 1945* (Atlantic).

pen·sile[1] (pen′səl), *adj.* **1.** hanging down; pendent. **2.** (of birds) building a hanging nest. [< Latin *pēnsilis* < *pendēre* to hang]

pen·sile[2] or **pen·sil** (pen′səl), *n.* pencil.

pen·sion[1] (pen′shən), *n.* **1.** a regular payment to a person of a specified sum of money which is not wages. Pensions are often paid because of long service, special merit, injuries received, etc. *In V.A. jargon, compensation is paid for a disability suffered in the service, while a pension goes to a low-income veteran who is disabled after discharge* (Wall Street Journal). **2.** a regular payment made to a person not an employee to retain his good will, assistance when needed, etc.; subsidy; fixed allowance. **3.** payment for board and lodging, or for the board and education of a child, etc.: *A full day's pension, if one has a room with bath, will cost about £3* (Atlantic).
—*adj.* of or having to do with a pension: *a pension plan, pension rolls.*
—*v.t.* to give a pension to: *The Army pensioned the soldier for his years of loyal service.*
pension off, to retire from service with a pension: *You have taken it into your head that I mean to pension you off* (Dickens).
[< Old French *pension,* learned borrowing from Latin *pēnsiō, -ōnis* payment, rent < *pendere* to pay, weigh]

pen·sion[2] (päN syôN′), *n. French.* a boarding house or boarding school in France and other parts of Continental Europe: *In the tiny village of Trisenberg, high up on the mountainside, I very much liked a small homely pension run by a friendly, jolly woman, who does all the cooking* (Observer).

pen·sion·a·ble (pen′shə nə bəl), *adj. Especially British.* **1.** qualified for or entitled to a pension. **2.** entitling to a pension: *The Civil Service is to offer pensionable jobs to men and women aged between 40 and 60* (London Times).

pen·sion·ar·y (pen′shə ner′ē), *n., pl.* **-aries,** *adj.* —*n.* **1.** a pensioner. **2.** (formerly, in the Netherlands) the chief magistrate of a city: *Jean Sersanders, the pensionary of Ghent* (J. F. Kirk).
—*adj.* **1.** consisting or of the nature of a pension. **2.** receiving a pension. **3.** mercenary; hireling; venal.

pen·sio·ne (pen syō′nā), *n., pl.* **-ni** (-nē). *Italian.* a boarding house, or pension, in Italy: *"Take it or leave it" is the attitude of the pensione keeper of the better sort when showing a room. As for the inferior pensioni, they have a practice of shanghaiing tourists* (Mary McCarthy).

pen·sion·er (pen′shə nər), *n.* **1.** a person who receives a pension: *In a country that is slowly growing old, there is the overriding problem of the old-age pensioners* (Atlantic). **2.** a hireling; dependent. **3.** a student who pays all his expenses for food, lodging, etc., (commons) at Cambridge University, England, and is not supported by any foundation. **4.** *Obsolete.* **a.** *British.* a gentleman-at-arms. **b.** a member of a bodyguard; attendant; retainer.

pension fund, a fund set up on an actuarial basis to provide pensions for a group at a later date: *This man earned £17 a week, had looked after his money, and contributed about £1 a week to a pension fund that would give him £6 10s a week when he retired at 65* (Manchester Guardian). —**pen′sion-fund′,** *adj.*

pen·sion·naire (päN syô ner′), *n. French.* a person who boards in a pension: *On the fifth floor were the salon, the dining room and kitchen, and some of the rooms occupied by the pensionnaires* (New Yorker).

pension plan, a plan, usually set up on an actuarial basis by an employer alone or by an employer jointly with a union, to provide pensions for retired or disabled employees.

pen·sive (pen′siv), *adj.* **1.** thoughtful in a serious or sad way: *She was in a pensive mood, and sat staring out the window.* **2.** melancholy: ... *the pensive shade of the Italian ruins* (George W. Curtis). [< Old French *pensif* < *penser* to think < Latin *pensāre* weigh, consider (frequentative) < *pendere* to pay, weigh] —**pen′sive·ly,** *adv.* —**pen′sive·ness,** *n.* —**Syn. 1.** meditative, reflective. **2.** sober, grave, sad.

pen·stab (pen′stab′), *n.* an article for a writing desk, commonly a small vessel containing a brush with the bristles turned upward, for thrusting a pen into after using.

pen·stab·ber (pen′stab′ər), *n.* pen-stab.

pen·ste·mon (pen stē′mən), *n.* any of a group of chiefly North American herbs of the figwort family, cultivated for their showy clustered flowers that are usually tubular and two-lipped and of various colors; beardtongue. Also, **pentstemon.** [American English < New Latin *Penstemon* < Greek *penta-* five + *stēmōn* thread, but taken as "stamen"]

pen·ster (pen′stər), *n.* a petty writer.

pen·stock (pen′stok′), *n.* **1. a.** *U.S.* a channel for carrying water to a water wheel. **b.** a pipe for carrying water to a turbine: *Water to drive the turbines drops sixteen times the height of Niagara Falls, through a penstock bored into the mountain and connecting with a huge ten-mile-long tunnel from Tahtsa Lake to the east* (New York Times). **2.** a sluice or floodgate for restraining or regulating the flow from a head of water formed by a weir, dam, etc.: *Apart from the associated damage to penstocks and valves, the large-scale flooding might cause great damage to industrial facilities downstream* (The Effects of Atomic Weapons). [< *pen*[2] + *stock,* in the obsolete sense "trough"]

pent[1] (pent), *adj.* closely confined; penned; shut: *pent in the house all winter.* —*v.* a past tense and a past participle of **pen**[2]: *as if he had in prison long been pent* (Edmund Spenser).

pent[2] (pent), *n.* a sloping roof or covering; penthouse.

pent-, *combining form.* the form of **penta-** before vowels, as in *pentacid.*

penta-, *combining form.* **1.** five: *Pentameter = poetry having five metrical feet to the line.* **2.** having five atoms of a specified substance: *Pentabasic = having five atoms of replaceable hydrogen.*
Also, **pent-** before vowels.
[< Greek *penta-* < *pénte* five]

pen·ta·ba·sic (pen′tə bā′sik), *adj. Chemistry.* (of an acid) having five atoms of hydrogen replaceable by basic atoms or radicals.

pen·ta·car·pel·lar·y (pen′tə kär′pə ler′ē), *adj. Botany.* having five carpels.

pen·ta·chlor·o·phe·nol (pen′tə klôr′ə fē′nōl, -nol; -klōr′-), *n.* a chemical used as a wood preservative and fungicide: *A chemical called pentachlorophenol is sometimes used in swabbing decks of U. S. Navy vessels because it is a wood preservative* (Science News Letter). *Formula:* C_6Cl_5OH

pen·ta·chord (pen′tə kôrd), *n. Music.* **1.** an instrument with five strings. **2.** a diatonic series of five tones.

pent·ac·id (pen tas′id), *adj. Chemistry.* capable of combining with five molecules of a monobasic acid. [< *pent-* + *acid*]

pen·ta·cle (pen′tə kəl), *n.* **1.** a pentagram, or five-pointed star-shaped figure used as a magic or mystic symbol: *He was tracing circles and pentacles in the grass and talking the language of the elves* (G.K. Chesterton). **2.** any of certain other more or less star-shaped figures similarly used, as a hexagram formed by overlapping triangles. [< earlier French *pentacle* or < Medieval Latin *pentaculum,* apparently < Latin *penta-* five + *-culum,* noun suffix]

pen·tad (pen′tad), *n.* **1.** a period of five years. **2.** an element, atom, or radical with a valence of five. **3.** a group or series of five. [< Greek *pentás, -ádos* group of five < *pénte* five]

pen·ta·dac·tyl (pen′tə dak′təl), *adj.* having five toes or fingers: *The limbs are almost typically pentadactyl* (Hegner and Stiles). [< *penta-* + Greek *dáktylos* toe, finger]

pen·ta·e·ryth·ri·tol (pen′tə i rith′rə tōl, -tol), *n.* a white, crystalline compound used for making synthetic lubricants, resins, and paints: *Heydon Newport Chemical Corp. said it is increasing the price on some grades of pentaerythritol, a chemical used in making surface coatings and synthetic resins* (Wall Street Journal). *Formula:* $C_5H_{12}O_4$

pentaerythritol te·tra·ni·trate (tet′rə nī′trāt), a white, crystalline substance derived from the esterification of pentaerythritol with nitric acid, used as an explosive. *Formula:* $C(CH_2ONO_2)_4$ *Abbr.:* PETN (no periods).

pen·ta·gon (pen′tə gon), *n.* a plane figure having five angles and hence five sides. [< Late Latin *pentagōnum* < Greek *pentágōnon* (literally) neuter of *pentágōnos* five-angled < *pénte* five + *gōníā* angle]

Pentagon

Pen·ta·gon (pen′tə gon), *n.* **1.** a building in Arlington, Virginia, that is the headquarters of the U.S. Department of Defense. **2.** the Department of Defense.

pen·tag·o·nal (pen tag′ə nəl), *adj.* having five sides and five angles. —**pen·tag′o·nal·ly,** *adv.*

Pen·ta·gon·ese (pen′tə gon ēz′, -ēs′), *n. U.S. Informal.* military jargon, especially as written or spoken in the Pentagon: *He has been highly successful in translating from the Pentagonese for other members of the Senate* (Time).

Pen·ta·go·ni·an (pen′tə gō′nē ən), *U.S. n.* a person who works in the Pentagon: *The season's dinner parties are invariably dimpled with a dizzying variety of ambassadors, Cabinet members, agency heads, socialites, Pentagonians, and sometimes the President himself* (Time). —*adj.* of or having to do with the Pentagon: *Pentagonian military strategy.*

pen·ta·gram (pen′tə gram), *n.* **1.** a five-pointed star-shaped figure made by extending the sides of a regular pentagon until they meet, used as a mystic or magic symbol; pentacle, pentalpha, or pentangle. **2.** *Mathematics.* a figure of five lines connecting five points. [< Greek *pentágrammon* (literally) a figure of five lines < *pénte* five + *grámma* -gram[1]]

pen·ta·gram·mat·ic (pen′tə grə mat′ik), *adj.* having the figure of a pentagram.

pen·ta·he·dral (pen′tə hē′drəl), *adj.* having five faces.

pen·ta·he·dron (pen′tə hē′drən), *n., pl.* **-drons, -dra** (-drə). a solid figure having five faces. [< *penta-* + Greek *-hedron,* neuter of *-hedros* having bases < *hédra* base[1]]

pen·tail (pen′tāl′), *n.* a variety of tree shrew, a small, squirrellike, insectivorous animal of Borneo, Sumatra, etc., having a long tail naked toward the base, but with the terminal portion fringed on opposite sides with long hairs, so as to look somewhat like a quill pen.

pen·tal·o·gy (pen tal′ə jē), *n., pl.* **-gies.** a combination of five mutually connected parts; pentad: *The story ... forms part of Heinlein's "History of the Future" pentalogy* (Punch).

pen·tal·pha (pen tal′fə), *n.* a pentagram. [< Greek *pentálpha* < *pénte* five + *alpha* alpha (because the figure resembles five Greek *alphas* (A) combined)]

pen·ta·mer (pen′tə mər), *n.* a polymer consisting of five molecules.

pen·tam·er·ous (pen tam′ər əs), *adj.* **1.** *Zoology.* composed or consisting of five parts or organs or five sets of similar parts. **2.** (of a flower) having five members in each whorl (generally written *5-merous*). [< Greek *pentamerḗs* (with English *-ous*) < *pénte* five + *méros* part]

pen·tam·e·ter (pen tam′ə tər), *n.* **1. a.** poetry having five metrical feet or measures in each line. *Example:* "A lít/tle léarn/ing ís/ a dań/g'rous thíng." **b.** iambic pentameter (the measure of *heroic verse,* rhymed or unrhymed, and the *heroic couplet* in English literature). **2.** (in ancient Greek and Latin verse) a line consisting of two feet (either dactyls or spondees), a long syllable, two more dactyls, and another long syllable. When this line is alternated with a hexameter line the resulting form is an elegiac. —*adj.* consisting of five metrical feet or measures. [< Latin *pentameter,* noun < Greek *pentámetros* having five metrical feet < *pénte* five + *métron* measure]

pen·tane (pen′tān), *n.* any of three isomeric hydrocarbons of the methane series, used as an anesthetic, for filling thermometers, etc.: *The light liquids usually used in bubble chambers—liquid hydrogen or pentane—are almost transparent to gamma rays* (Scientific American). *Formula:* C_5H_{12} [< *pent-* + *-ane*]

pen·tan·gle (pen′tang′gəl), *n.* **1.** pentagram. **2.** pentagon.

pen·tan·gu·lar (pen tang′gyə lər), *adj.* having five angles.

pen·tap·o·dy (pen tap′ə dē), *n., pl.* **-dies.** *Prosody.* a measure or series of five feet in a verse. [< Greek *pentápous, -podos* of five feet (< *pénte* five + *poús, podós* foot) + English *-y*[3]]

pen·ta·quine (pen′tə kwēn, -kwin), *n.* a yellowish, crystalline, synthetic drug, used in the treatment of malaria, often in combination with quinine. *Formula:* $C_{18}H_{27}N_3O$

pen·tar·chy (pen′tär kē), *n., pl.* **-chies. 1.** a government by five persons. **2.** a governing body composed of five persons. **3.** a group of five states, each under its own ruler. [< Greek *pentarchíā* rule of five < *pénte* five + *árchein* to rule]

pen·ta·stich (pen′tə stik), *n.* a group of five lines of verse that form a stanza, strophe, or poem. [< Greek *pentástichos* of five lines < *pénte* five + *stíchos* line of verse < *steíchein* to walk, go]

pen·ta·style (pen′tə stīl), *adj.* having five columns in front, as a temple or a portico. —*n.* a pentastyle structure. [< *penta-* + Greek *stŷlos* pillar, column]

pen·ta·syl·lab·ic (pen′tə sə lab′ik), *adj.* having five syllables: *Stress may be measured by instruments precisely, and it is not difficult to perceive the alternating degrees of stress here indicated by numbers in such diverse English pentasyllabic forms as equanimity* (Simeon Potter).

pen·ta·syl·la·ble (pen′tə sil′ə bəl), *n.* a word of five syllables.

Pen·ta·teuch (pen′tə tük, -tyük), *n.* the first five books of the Old Testament: Genesis, Exodus, Leviticus, Numbers, and Deuteronomy: *He dons the traditional black-and-white prayer shawl and straps phylacteries (small leather cases containing texts from the Pentateuch) to his left arm and his forehead* (Time). [< Latin *Pentateuchus* < Greek *pentáteuchos* < *pénte* five + *teûchos* book; (originally) the case for the scrolls < *teúchein* to produce, make]

Pen·ta·teuch·al (pen′tə tü′kəl, -tyü′-), *adj.* of or having to do with the Pentateuch: *I have long regretted that I ... used the Pentateuchal term of "creation"* (Charles Darwin).

pen·tath·lete (pen tath′lēt), *n.* a contestant in a pentathlon. [blend of *pentathlon* and *athlete*]

pen·tath·lon (pen tath′lon), *n.* an athletic contest consisting of five different events. The person having the highest total score wins. [< Greek *péntathlon* < *pénte* five + *âthlon* exercise of skill]

pen·ta·tom·ic (pen′tə tom′ik), *adj. Chemistry.* **1.** having five atoms in the molecule. **2.** containing five replaceable atoms or groups. [< *pent-* + *atomic*]

pen·ta·ton·ic (pen′tə ton′ik), *adj.* (of a musical scale) having five tones: *Melodies are built on varieties of pentatonic and heptatonic scales, and every African society specialized in one of these scales* (Atlantic).

pen·ta·va·lent (pen′tə vā′lənt, pen tav′ə-), *adj. Chemistry.* having a valence of five; quinquevalent: *pentavalent antimony compounds.*

Pen·te·cost (pen′tə kôst, -kost), *n.* **1.** the seventh Sunday after Easter. Pentecost is a Christian festival in memory of the descent of the Holy Ghost upon the Apostles; Whitsunday. Acts 2. **2.** a Jewish religious holiday, observed about seven weeks after the Passover, celebrating the harvest and also the giving of the law to Moses. [< Latin *pentēcostē* < Greek *pentēkostḗ* (*hēméra*) fiftieth (day)]

Pen·te·cos·tal or **pen·te·cos·tal** (pen′-tə kôs′təl, -kos′-; pen′tə kôs′-, -kos′-), *adj.* **1.** of or having to do with Pentecost. **2.** of or having to do with any of various American Protestant religious groups that stress divine inspiration, believing in such manifestations of the Holy Ghost as divine healing, speaking in tongues (glossolalia), and visions. Most Pentecostal groups are fundamentalist. —*n.* a Pentecostalist.

Pen·te·cos·tal·ist (pen′tə kôs′tə list, -kos′-), *n.* a member of a Pentecostal sect or church.

Pen·tel·ic (pen tel′ik), *adj.* of or from Mount Pentelicus, north of Athens, Greece, especially with reference to the famous marble quarried there.

Pentelic marble, a fine-grained white marble much used in ancient Greek sculpture and architecture.

pent·house (pent′hous′), *n.* **1.** an apartment or house built on the top of a building. **2.** a small roofed structure over an elevator shaft, in which the motor, pulley wheels, etc., are housed. **3.** a sloping roof projecting from a building, as to shelter a door. **4.** a shed with a sloping roof, attached to a building. **5.** any of various structures like a sloping roof, as a shed for the protection of besiegers or a covering formed of soldiers' shields held over their heads. [alteration of Middle English *pentis,* apparently short for Old French *apentis* lean-to (influenced by *pente* slope), learned borrowing from Medieval Latin *appendicium* an attached building < Latin *appendere* to append]

Penthouse (def. 3)

pen·tice or **pen·tise** (pen′tis), *n. Obsolete.* penthouse.

pen·ti·men·to (pen′tə men′tō), *n., pl.* **-ti** (-tē). **1.** the emergence of an earlier form in a painting that has been altered and painted over. **2.** such a form before or after its emergence: *Radiographs confirm that the bars cover pentimenti* (New York Times). [< Italian *pentimento* (literally) penitence, reparation]

pent·land·ite (pent′lən dīt), *n.* a mineral found in Ontario, Canada, the chief ore of nickel. It is a combination of nickel, sulfur, and iron. [< a proper name + *-ite*[1]]

pen·to·bar·bi·tal (pen′tə bär′bə tôl, -tal), *n.* a white granular barbiturate used in the preparation of certain medicines, such as pentobarbital sodium. *Formula:* $C_{11}H_{18}O_3N_2$ [< *pent-* (because sodium is attached to the fifth radical of the chain) + *barbital*]

pentobarbital sodium, a white, slightly bitter, soluble crystalline powder used as a sedative and to check convulsions; Nembutal. *Formula:* $C_{11}H_{17}N_2O_3Na$

pent·ode (pen′tōd), *n.* **1.** the vacuum tube most commonly used for amplification in radio and television sets, so-called because it has five electrodes: *Three-grid tubes, or pentodes, are capable of greater amplification than triodes* (Roy F. Allison). **2.** a high-power transistor used for the same purpose, having four wires: *The new transistors ... are equivalent to more complex vacuum tubes called tetrodes and pentodes ... The pentode transistor, now being perfected, has four cat whiskers and can replace three triode transistors for some applications* (Newsweek). [< *pent-* + (electr)*ode*]

pen·to·lin·i·um tartrate (pen′tə lin′ē-əm), a crystalline drug used in the treatment of high blood pressure. *Formula:* $C_{23}H_{42}N_2O_{12}$

pen·to·lite (pen′tə līt), *n.* a high explosive composed of pentaerythritol tetranitrate and TNT.

pen·tom·ic (pen tom′ik), *adj.* five-sided; designating a type of highly mobile army division consisting of five self-supporting units which are equipped for either atomic or conventional warfare: *The United States Army organizes its combat divisions on a pentomic basis* (World Book Encyclopedia).

pen·to·san (pen′tə san), *n.* any of a group of complex carbohydrates (polysaccharides) that yield pentoses when hydrolyzed. Pentosans occur in most plants, in humus, etc.: *Xylose, an example of such a sugar, is found in plants only as a constituent of such complex carbohydrates as pentosans, gums, and hemicelluloses* (Harbaugh and Goodrich).

pen·to·sane (pen′tə sān), *n.* pentosan.

pen·tose (pen′tōs), *n.* any of a class of simple sugars (monosaccharides) that contain five atoms of carbon in each molecule, and are not fermented by yeast. Pentoses are produced in animal tissues, and are obtained from pentosans by hydrolysis. *The nucleus of all cells contains a considerable amount of nucleic acid, a complex molecule containing a pentose sugar, phosphoric acid and a series of organic bases* (John E. Harris). [< *pent-* + *-ose*[2]]

Pen·to·thal Sodium (pen′tə thôl, -thol), *Trademark.* thiopental sodium, a barbiturate used as an anesthetic, a "truth drug," and to treat mental illness.

pent·ox·id (pen tok′sid), *n.* pentoxide.

pent·ox·ide (pen tok′sīd, -sid), *n.* a compound containing five atoms of oxygen combined with another element or radical.

pent roof, a roof sloping in one direction only; shed roof.

pent·ste·mon (pent stē′mən), *n.* penstemon: *"What's pentstemon?" we asked. "A kind of figwort," he said, and we let it ride* (New Yorker). [American English, alteration of New Latin *Penstemon* the genus name < Greek *penta-* five + *stēmōn,* thread, but taken as "stamen"]

pent-up (pent′up′), *adj.* shut up; closely confined: *A relief to perplexed, pent-up emotion* (Justin McCarthy).

pe·nu·che (pə nü′chē), *n.* panocha.

pe·nu·chi (pə nü′chē), *n.* panocha.

pe·nuch·le or **pe·nuck·le** (pē′nuk′əl), *n.* pinochle.

pe·nult (pē′nult, pi nult′), *n.* the next to the last syllable in a word. —*adj.* penultimate. [(originally) abbreviation of earlier *penultima* < Latin *paenultima,* feminine adjective, next-to-last < *paene* almost + *ultimus* last]

pe·nul·ti·ma (pi nul′tə mə), *n.* penult.

pe·nul·ti·mate (pi nul′tə mit), *adj.* **1.** next to the last. **2.** of or having to do with the penult. —*n.* penult.

pe·nul·ti·ma·tum (pi nul′tə mā′təm), *n.* a declaration, demand, or the like, that immediately precedes an ultimatum, or is all but an ultimatum.

pe·num·bra (pi num′brə), *n., pl.* **-brae** (-brē), **-bras. 1.** the partial shadow outside of the complete shadow formed by the sun, moon, etc., during an eclipse: *An observer within the umbra cannot see any part of the source; one within the penumbra can see a portion of the source, while from points outside the penumbra the entire source can be seen* (Sears and Zemansky). **2.** the grayish outer part of a sunspot: *A complete and fully formed spot shows a dark central portion, known as the umbra, surrounded by a not-so-dark area called the penumbra* (Wasley S. Krogdahl). **3.** a partial shade or shadow: *One of the handicaps of poetry is that penumbra of holiness, the legacy of the nineteenth century, which still surrounds it* (Atlantic). [< New Latin *penumbra* < Latin *paene* almost + *umbra* shadow]

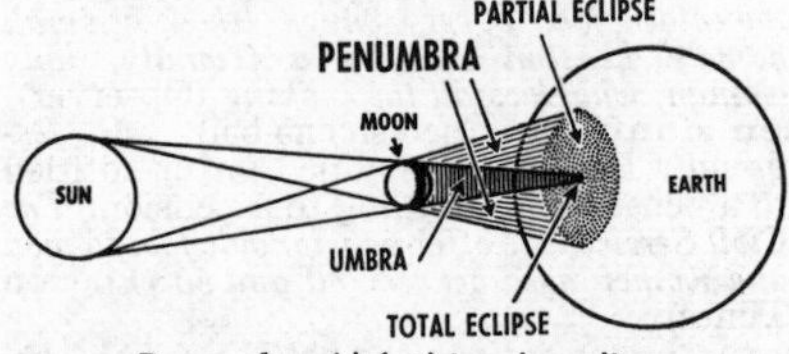

Penumbra (def. 1) in solar eclipse

pe·num·bral (pi num′brəl), *adj.* having to do with or like a penumbra: *This penumbral region of faint partial shadow can scarcely be detected near the beginning of eclipse* (Bernhard, Bennett, and Rice).

pe·nu·ri·ous (pi nůr′ē əs, -nyůr′-), *adj.* **1.** mean about spending or giving money; stingy: *a penurious, accumulating curmudgeon* (Washington Irving). *He lived in the most penurious manner and denied himself every luxury* (William Godwin). **2.** *Obsolete.* **a.** scanty. **b.** not rich or fertile; barren. **c.** indigent; poverty-stricken. [probably < Middle French *penurieux* (with English *-ous*), learned borrowing from Medieval Latin *penuriosus* < Latin *pēnūria* penury] **—pe·nu′ri·ous·ly,** *adv.* **—pe·nu′ri·ous·ness,** *n.* **—Syn. 1.** niggardly.

pen·u·ry (pen′yər ē), *n.* great poverty; extreme want; destitution; indigence: *My scanty purse was exhausted, and ... I experienced the sordid distress of penury* (Washington Irving). [< Latin *pēnūria* want, need, related to *paene* almost]

Pe·nu·ti·an (pə nü′tē ən, -shən), *n.* a grouping of North American Indian languages of the western United States.

pe·on (pē′on, -ən), *n.* **1.** (in Spanish America) a person doing work that requires little skill; unskilled worker. **2.** (in the southwestern United States and Mexico) a worker held for service to work off a debt. **3.** formerly, in India: **a.** a native foot soldier. **b.** a native constable. **c.** a native attendant or orderly. [(definition 1, 2) American English < Mexican Spanish *peón;* (definition 3) < Portuguese *peão* foot soldier; both < Late Latin *pedō, -ōnis* splay-footed. Doublet of PAWN[2].]

pe·on·age (pē′ə nij), *n.* **1.** the condition or service of a peon. **2.** the practice of holding persons to work off debts. **3.** the practice of leasing convict labor on contract to work on farms, in lumber camps, etc.

pe·on·ism (pē′ə niz əm), *n.* peonage.

pe·o·ny (pē′ə nē), *n., pl.* **-nies.** **1.** any of a group of perennial garden plants of the crowfoot family, with large, globular, showy flowers of various shades of red and white, often becoming double under cultivation. **2.** its flower. Also, **paeony.** [< Old French *peoine,* learned borrowing from Latin *paeōnia* < Greek *paiōniā* < *Paiṓn* physician of the gods (supposedly because of its use in medicine)]

Peony (def. 2)

peo·ple (pē′pəl), *n., pl.* **-ple** or (*for def. 2*) **-ples,** *v.,* **-pled, -pling.** —*n.* **1.** men, women, and children; persons: *a street emptied of people. There were ten people present.* **2.** a body of persons composing a community, tribe, race, or nation: *the French people, the peoples of the world.* **3.** the body of citizens of a state; the public: *to seek the support of the people, music that appeals to the people.* **4.** persons of a place, class, or group: *city people, Southern people.* **5.** the common people; lower classes: *The French nobles oppressed the people.* **6.** persons in relation to a superior: *a pastor and his people. A king rules over his people.* **7.** *Informal.* family; relatives: *John has many friends but he likes his own people best.* **8.** a species or other group of animals: *the monkey people.*

be gathered to one's people, to die and be buried: *The patriarch was gathered to his people.*

—*v.t.* **1. a.** to fill with people; populate: *Europe very largely peopled America.* **b.** to fill (with animals, inanimate objects, etc.); stock: *Crystal pools peopled with fish* (Thomas Hood). **2.** to constitute the population of (a country, etc.); inhabit.

[< Anglo-French *people,* Old French *peuple* < Latin *populus.* Doublet of PUEBLO.]

—**Syn.** *n.* **2. People, race, nation** mean a group of persons thought of as a unit larger than a family or community. **People** emphasizes cultural and social unity, applying to a group united by a common culture, common ideals, and a feeling of unity arising from common responsibilities and interests: *the American people, the peoples of the Orient.* **Race** emphasizes biological unity, having common descent and common physical characteristics: *Japanese belong to the Mongolian race.* **Nation** emphasizes political unity, applying to a group united under one government: *Americans are a people and a nation, not a race.* **3.** inhabitants, population.

peo·ple·hood (pē′pəl hu̇d), *n.* the state or fact of being a people, with special emphasis on cultural and social unity, as opposed to political unity: *"These people," says Lodge, "have always had a strong sense of peoplehood. What we are now trying to give them is a strong sense of nationhood"* (Time).

peo·pler (pē′plər), *n.* a person who peoples; inhabitant; colonizer.

people's front, popular front.

People's Party, a political organization formed in the United States in 1891, that advocated increase of currency, state control of railroads, restrictions upon the ownership of land, and an income tax; Populist Party.

People's Republic, any of the Communist states of Europe and Asia: *the Polish People's Republic, the People's Republic of China.*

pep[1] (pep), *n., v.,* **pepped, pep·ping.** *Informal.* —*n.* spirit; energy; vim.

—*v.t.* **pep up,** to fill or inspire with energy, etc.; put new life into: *Besides, Will and I had stuck at home so much that I couldn't help feeling kind of pepped up at the idea of going to any party again* (Frannie Kilbourne).

[American English, short for *pepper*]

pep[2] (pep), *n.* the pip or central part of an artificial flower. [variant of *pip*[3]]

P.E.P., *British.* Political and Economic Planning Organization.

pe·pi·no (pe pē′nō), *n., pl.* **-nos.** **1.** an evergreen shrub of the lily family, a native of the extreme southern part of South America, bearing showy red flowers. **2.** a tropical American plant of the nightshade family, bearing an edible melonlike fruit. [< Spanish *pepino* (diminutive) < Latin *pepō, -ōnis* melon, pumpkin; see PEPO]

pep·los or **pep·lus** (pep′ləs), *n.* a peplum worn by women in ancient Greece. [< Greek *péplos*]

pep·lum (pep′ləm), *n., pl.* **-lums, -la** (-lə). **1.** a short skirt attached about the waist; overskirt. **2.** a full garment worn by women in ancient Greece. [< Latin *peplum,* neuter of *peplus* < Greek *péplos*]

Peplum (def. 2) on caryatid, Erechtheion, Athens

pe·po (pē′pō), *n., pl.* **-pos.** the characteristic fruit of plants of the gourd family, a berry having a fleshy interior with numerous seeds covered by a hard or firm rind that is not easily separated, as the melon, cucumber, and squash. [< New Latin *pepo* < Latin *pepō, -ōnis* pumpkin < Greek *pépōn* (*síkyos*) gourd ripe for eating < *pépōn* ripened, (literally) cooked by the sun < *péptein* to cook]

pep·per (pep′ər), *n.* **1.** a seasoning with a hot taste used for soups, meats, vegetables, etc. Pepper has been used from ancient times for flavoring and acts as a digestive stimulant and carminative. **2.** the plant bearing berries from which pepper is made, a climbing shrub of the pepper family, native to the East Indies, having alternate stalked leaves, with green spikes of hanging flowers, and small berries turning red when ripe. **3. a.** any of several hollow fruits with many seeds and a green, red, or yellow shell, eaten raw, cooked, or pickled. Paprika is made from a variety of pepper. See **septum** for picture. **b.** any of a group of low American herbs or shrubs of the nightshade family, bearing such a fruit, as the sweet pepper, bird pepper, and chili. **4.** a container for pepper: *silver salts and peppers.*

—*v.t.* **1.** to season or sprinkle with pepper. **2.** to sprinkle thickly; dot: *His face is peppered with freckles.* **3.** to hit with small objects, sent thick and fast: *We peppered the enemy's lines with our shot. Members of council peppered him with questions about details of his plan* (Maclean's). **4.** to beat severely; trounce. **5.** to enliven: *Pretty soon he was ... peppering their restrained, unvarying arrangements with exuberant improvisations on his trumpet* (New Yorker).

[Old English *pipor* < Latin *piper* < Greek *píperi,* variant of *péperi.* Compare Sanskrit *pippalī* the long pepper.]

pep·per-and-salt (pep′ər ən sôlt′), *adj.* **1.** black and white finely mixed: *pepper-and-salt hair.* **2.** woven of alternate threads of black and white cotton, wool, etc., so as to have a grayish appearance at a slight distance: *a pepper-and-salt suit.*

pep·per·box (pep′ər boks′), *n.* **1.** a container with holes in the top for sprinkling pepper on food. **2.** *Informal.* a hot-tempered person.

pep·per·corn (pep′ər kôrn′), *n.* **1.** a dried berry or fruit of the pepper plant, ground up to make black pepper. **2. a.** such a berry or fruit paid as a nominal rent: *Manhattan's first art museum building ... was a neoclassic, circular structure, a few steps from City Hall, on ground rented from the city for one peppercorn a year* (Time). **b.** a small tribute or nominal token. [Old English *piporcorn* < *pipor* pepper + *corn* corn, in sense of "seed, fruit"]

pepper family, a group of dicotyledonous aromatic or pungent herbs and shrubs found chiefly in tropical regions. The family includes the pepper and cubeb.

pep·per·grass (pep′ər gras′, -gräs′), *n.* a common weed of the mustard family, with a peppery taste, such as garden cress, used in salads: *"One of the characteristics of peppergrass," the wild-flower book said, "is that its seed pods are as hot as pepper when chewed"* (New Yorker).

pep·per·idge (pep′ər ij), *n.* the black gum: *The black tupelo is sometimes called the black gum tree because of its dark grey bark. This tree is called pepperidge in New England, and many people know it as sour gum because of the sour flavor of its fruit* (World Book Encyclopedia). [American English; origin unknown]

pep·per·i·ness (pep′ər ē nis), *n.* peppery quality.

pepper mill, a device for grinding peppercorns.

pep·per·mint (pep′ər mint), *n.* **1.** a native European herb of the mint family, grown for its aromatic, pungent essential oil that is used in medicine and in candy. **2.** this oil, or a preparation of it. **3.** a candy flavored with oil of peppermint.

peppermint stick, a stick of peppermint-flavored hard candy, usually made in alternating straight or spiral stripes of red and white.

pep·per·mint-stick (pep′ər mint stik′), *adj.* colored like a peppermint stick in red and white stripes. *The peppermint-stick toothpaste is the result of four years of persistent tinkering by Leonard Marraffino, a Mount Vernon, N.Y., printer* (Newsweek).

pepper pot, **1. a.** a West Indian stew of meat, fish, or game and vegetables, made with cassareep, cayenne pepper, and other spices. **b.** any of various somewhat similar highly seasoned stews. **2.** a highly seasoned, rather thick soup made of tripe and vegetables; Philadelphia pepper pot. **3.** *Archaic.* pepperbox.

pepper shaker, a container of metal, glass, etc., usually with a perforated top, from which ground pepper may be shaken on food.

pepper tree or **shrub,** an evergreen tree or shrub of the cashew family, native to tropical America, much grown for its ornamental pinnate leaves, clusters of white flowers, and bunches of small reddish fruit (drupes). One kind is widely grown in California: *When as a child in South Africa the train would pass a wayside station, and I would see a native sitting quietly under a pepper tree, it symbolized permanency to me* (Cape Times).

pepper upper, *Slang.* something that produces pep.

pepper vine, an upright, scarcely twining shrub of the grape family, of the southern United States, with bipinnate leaves and small purplish-black berries.

pep·per·wort (pep′ər wėrt′), *n.* peppergrass.

pep·per·y (pep′ər ē), *adj.* **1.** full of pepper; like pepper: *Some good, strong, peppery doctrine* (Dickens). **2.** hot; sharp. **3. a.** having a hot temper; easily made angry: *Pettingil, whose peppery temper was well known among the boys* (Thomas Bailey Aldrich). **b.** angry and sharp: *a few peppery words and angry jerks of the head* (Elizabeth Gaskell).

pep pill, *Slang.* a stimulating drug, such as amphetamine, put up in pill form and used as a means of combating fatigue, inducing greater effort, etc.: *I began to step up my output, using pep pills and so on to maintain my metabolic rate* (Punch).

pep·pi·ness (pep′ē nis), *n.* *Informal.* the quality or state of being peppy: *The old lady had peppiness and determination beyond her years.*

pep·py (pep′ē), *adj.,* **-pi·er, -pi·est.** *U.S. Informal.* full of pep; energetic; lively: *Scotch terriers are peppy dogs.* [American English, perhaps < *pep*[1] + *-y*[1]]

pep rally, *Informal.* a meeting designed to arouse enthusiasm for a team, political campaign, etc.

pep·sin or **pep·sine** (pep′sin), *n.* **1.** an enzyme that helps to digest meat, eggs, cheese, and other proteins. It is contained in gastric juice: *Pepsin is a digestive enzyme contained in the stomach juices that can bore into tissues and cause ulcers* (Science News Letter). **2.** a medicine containing this enzyme, used to help the digestion of proteins. [< obsolete German *Pepsine* < Greek *pépsis* digestion; (originally) ripening < *péptein* to cook]

pep·sin·ate (pep′sə nāt), *v.t.,* **-at·ed, -at·ing.** to treat, prepare, or mix with pepsin.

pep·sin·o·gen (pep sin′ə jən), *n.* the substance present in the gastric glands from which pepsin is formed during digestion: *Pepsin as it comes from the gastric glands is in an inactive state in which it is called pepsinogen* (A. Franklin Shull). [< *pepsin* + (zym)*ogen*]

pep talk, *Informal.* a speech or short talk designed to fill or inspire with energy, enthusiasm, etc.; exhortation: *Its language is deliberately that of a sales manager giving a pep talk to the boys* (Saturday Review).

pep-talk (pep′tôk′), *v.t. Informal.* to exhort; give a pep talk (to).

pep·tic (pep′tik), *adj.* **1.** promoting digestion; digestive. **2.** able to digest. **3.** of or having to do with pepsin.
—*n.* a substance promoting digestion.
[< Latin *pepticus* < Greek *peptikós* < *peptós* cooked, digested < *péptein* to cook]

peptic ulcer, an ulcer of the mucous membrane (mucosa) of the stomach or of the duodenum, caused entirely or in part by the digestive action of gastric juice: *From their own experience with 32 cases of peptic ulcer in children up to age 15, they conclude that chronic peptic ulcer in children occurs in boys more frequently than girls* (Science News Letter).

pep·tid (pep′tid), *n.* peptide.

pep·tide (pep′tīd, -tid), *n.* any combination of amino acids in which the carboxyl group of one acid is joined with the amino group of another: *The protein of the virus can be broken down by moderate chemical treatment into subunits, each of which is a single peptide chain containing about 150 amino acids* (Scientific American). [< *pept*(one) + *-ide*]

pep·tize (pep′tīz), *v.t.*, **-tized, -tiz·ing.** to change (a gel, etc.) into a colloidal solution or form: *Materials called protective colloids, or peptizing agents, are added to the mixture; and they apparently coat the suspended particles and so prevent their coalescing* (Monroe M. Offner).

pep·to·gen (pep′tə jən), *n.* a substance or preparation that facilitates peptic digestion. [< *pepto*(ne) + *-gen*]

pep·tone (pep′tōn), *n.* any of a class of diffusible and soluble substances into which meat, eggs, cheese, and other proteins are changed by pepsin or trypsin: *A continuation of the process results in the formation of a still more complex peptid called a peptone. Peptones in turn may combine to form proteins* (Harbaugh and Goodrich). [< German *Pepton* < Greek *peptós* cooked, digested (see PEPTIC) + German *-on* -one]

pep·ton·ic (pep ton′ik), *adj.* having to do with or containing peptones.

pep·ton·i·za·tion (pep′tə nə zā′shən), *n.* the process of peptonizing or converting into peptones.

pep·to·nize (pep′tə nīz), *v.t.*, **-nized, -niz·ing. 1.** to convert into a peptone. **2.** to subject (food) to an artificial partial digestion by means of pepsin or pancreatic extract, as an aid to digestion. —**pep′to·niz′er,** *n.*

Pepys·i·an (pēp′sē ən), *adj.* of, written by, or characteristic of Samuel Pepys, English diarist, 1633-1703: *The book as published is not a diary in any spontaneous Pepysian sense* (Atlantic).

Pe·quot (pē′kwot), *n.* **1.** a member of a tribe of American Indians of Algonkian stock, formerly in southern New England. **2.** this tribe. **3.** the language of this tribe. [American English, apparently < Algonkian (some eastern North American language) *Pequatoog* destroyers < *paquatoog* they destroy]

per (pər; *stressed* pėr), *prep.* **1.** for each; for every: *a pint of milk per child, ten cents per pound.* **2.** by; by means of; through: *I send this per my son.* **3.** according to: *per invoice.* [< Latin *per* through, on account of]
➔ **Per** is used chiefly in business or technical English: *per capita, per cent, $50 per week, revolutions per minute.* In general English it is usually avoided: *$50 a week, eight hours a day.*

per-, *prefix.* **1.** through; throughout, as in *perforate, perfume, peruse.*
2. thoroughly; utterly; very, as in *perpendicular, perpetrate, persevere, perfidious.*
3. in chemical terms, the maximum or a large amount of, as in *peroxide.*
[< Latin *per-* < *per*]

per., **1.** period. **2.** person.

per·a·ce·tic acid (pėr′ə sē′tik, -set′ik), a colorless, pungent liquid, related to acetic acid as a peracid, and used as a bleaching agent in textiles, paper, etc., and as a bactericide and fungicide. *Formula:* CH_3-COOOH

per·ac·id (pėr as′id), *n.* an acid containing a greater proportion of oxygen than others made up of the same elements. *Example:* perchloric acid ($HClO_4$) is a peracid in its relation to chloric acid ($HClO_3$).

per·a·cute (pėr′ə kyüt′), *adj.* very acute or severe: *a peracute disease.* [< Latin *peracūtus* < *per-* (intensive) + *acūtus* acute]

per·ad·ven·ture (pėr′əd ven′chər), *Archaic.* —*adv.* maybe; perhaps: *Peradventure I may be an hour later* (Henry Fielding). —*n.* uncertainty; doubt; chance; question: *It was affirmed—and the truth was certainly beyond peradventure—that religious liberty was dead* (John L. Motley). [Middle English alteration of *per-*, or *parauntre*, reduction of *par aventure* < Old French *par aventure* < *par* by + *aventure* chance, adventure; influenced by Latin *adventura*]
—**Syn.** *adv.* possibly.

per·am·bu·late (pə ram′byə lāt), *v.*, **-lat·ed, -lat·ing.** —*v.t.* **1.** to walk through: *Burgomaster Van der Werf . . . ordered the city musicians to perambulate the streets, playing lively melodies and martial airs* (John L. Motley). **2.** to walk through and examine. —*v.i.* to walk or travel about; stroll. [< Latin *perambulāre* (with English *-ate*[1]) < *per-* through + *ambulāre* to walk]

per·am·bu·la·tion (pə ram′byə lā′shən), *n.* a perambulating; journey; tour; survey.

per·am·bu·la·tor (pə ram′byə lā′tər), *n.* **1.** a small carriage in which a baby is pushed about; pram: *She came down into a dark hall where tricycles and perambulators were stored* (New Yorker). **2.** a person who perambulates. **3.** instrument for measuring distances by clocking the number of revolutions of a wheel rolled over the ground, formerly used in surveying.

Perambulator (def. 1)

per·am·bu·la·to·ry (pə ram′byə lə tôr′ē, -tōr′-), *adj.* perambulating; traveling.

per an. or **per ann.,** per annum.

per an·num (pər an′əm), per year; yearly; for each year: *Her salary was $5,000 per annum.* [< Medieval Latin *per* for every (< Latin, through), and Latin *annum*, accusative of *annus* year]

per·bo·rate (pėr bôr′āt, -bōr′-), *n.* a salt of perboric acid, having either the univalent radical $-BO_3$ or the bivalent radical $-B_4O_8$, as perborax (sodium perborate).

per·bo·rax (pėr bôr′aks, -bōr′-), *n.* a crystalline powder, a salt of perboric acid, used in bleaching, as an oxidizing agent, as an antiseptic, etc.; sodium perborate. *Formula:* $NaBO_3.4H_2O$

per·bo·ric acid (pėr bôr′ik, -bōr′-), an acid occurring only in solution or in the form of its salts; peroxyboric acid. *Formula:* HBO_3

per·cale (pər kāl′, -kal′), *n.* a closely woven cotton cloth with a smooth finish, used for dresses, sheets, etc. [< French *percale* < Persian *pergāl*]

per·ca·line (pėr′kə lēn′), *n.* a fine, usually glossy, cotton cloth, often dyed a solid color, used for linings, covering books, etc. [< French *percaline* (diminutive) < *percale*]

per cap., per capita.

per cap·i·ta (pər kap′ə tə), **1.** for each person: *$40 for eight men is $5 per capita.* **2.** *Law.* divided among a number of individuals in equal shares, as an inheritance or estate. [< Medieval Latin *per* by, according to, and Latin *capita*, neuter plural of *caput, -itis* head]

per ca·put (pər kā′pət, kap′ət), per capita: *On a per caput basis, they said, the Soviet agricultural production in 1963 was 10 percent below that of 1958* (London Times).

per·ceiv·a·ble (pər sē′və bəl), *adj.* that can be perceived; perceptible. —**Syn.** intelligible, appreciable.

per·ceiv·a·bly (pər sē′və blē), *adv.* in a perceivable manner. —**Syn.** perceptibly.

per·ceive (pər sēv′), *v.*, **-ceived, -ceiv·ing.** —*v.t.* **1.** to be aware of through the senses; see, hear, taste, smell, or feel: *Did you perceive the colors of that bird? We perceived a little girl coming toward us* (Frederick Marryat). **2.** to take in with the mind; observe: *I perceived that I could not make him change his mind. I plainly perceive some objections remain* (Edmund Burke). —*v.i.* to grasp or take in something with the senses or mind. [< Old North French *perceivre* < Latin *percipere* < *per-* thoroughly + *capere* to grasp] —**per·ceiv′er,** *n.*
—**Syn.** *v.t.* **1, 2.** See **see. 2.** understand, comprehend.

per cent, or **per·cent** (pər sent′), *n.* **1.** hundredths; parts in each hundred. Five per cent is 5 of each 100, or 5/100 of the whole. Five per cent of 40 is the same as 5/100×40, or .05×40. The use of per cent is a convenient way to express many proportions: *shrinkage of less than one per cent. Ten per cent of the children were absent because of illness. Abbr.:* pct. **2.** *Informal.* percentage.
per cents or **percents, a.** (with preceding numeral) securities, especially public ones, bearing the designated rate of interest: *to invest in the three per cents.* **b.** (without preceding numeral) percentages: *The tread of the businessmen who must count their per cents by the paces they take* (Elizabeth Barrett Browning).
[(originally) *per cent.*, abbreviation of Medieval Latin *per centum* by the hundred(s)]
➔ **Per cent** may be written as either two words or one and is not followed by a period. Informally it is used in place of *percentage: A large per cent of the state's apple crop was ruined.*

per·cent·age (pər sen′tij), *n.* **1.** a rate or proportion of each hundred; part of each hundred: *What percentage of children were absent? The French were . . . suffering a lower percentage of casualties than the British* (H. G. Wells). **2.** a part; proportion: *A large percentage of schoolbooks now have pictures. Television attracts a large percentage of the people.* **3.** an allowance, commission, discount, rate of interest, etc., figured by per cent. **4.** *Slang.* advantage or profit.

per·cent·age·wise (pər sen′tij wīz), *adv.* from the standpoint of percentage or percentages: *He estimated sales probably would be off a little more percentagewise for the six months as a whole than the 2 per cent drop suffered in the first quarter* (Wall Street Journal).

per·cen·tile (pər sen′tīl, -təl), *n.* **1.** any value in a series of points on a scale arrived at by dividing a group into a hundred equal parts in order of magnitude. **2.** one of these parts: *A student in the ninetieth percentile of his class on a particular test is in the top ten per cent.* —*adj.* of or having to do with percentiles; being or expressed as a percentage: *a percentile rating.* [apparently < *per cent*, patterned on *quartile, sextile*]

per cen·tum (pər sen′təm), **1.** by the hundred. **2.** for or in every hundred: *[The] senate bill . . . would require all organizations that lend money or give credit to disclose to the customer his cost in interest per centum per annum* (Maclean's).

per·cept (pėr′sept), *n.* **1.** that which is perceived. **2.** the understanding that is the result of perceiving. [< Latin *perceptum* (thing) perceived, neuter past participle of *percipere* to perceive]

per·cep·ti·bil·i·ty (pər sep′tə bil′ə tē), *n.* the fact, quality, or state of being perceptible.

per·cep·ti·ble (pər sep′tə bəl), *adj.* that can be perceived; observable; appreciable: *a perceptible improvement, a perceptible time. The other ship was barely perceptible in the fog.* —**per·cep′ti·ble·ness,** *n.* —**Syn.** palpable, cognizable.

per·cep·ti·bly (pər sep′tə blē), *adv.* in a perceptible way or amount; to a perceptible degree. —**Syn.** visibly.

per·cep·tion (pər sep′shən), *n.* **1.** the act of perceiving: *His perception of the change came in a flash.* **2.** the power of perceiving: *a keen perception. Defect in manners is usually the defect of fine perceptions* (Emerson). **3.** a percept; understanding that is the result of perceiving: *He had a clear perception of what was wrong, and soon fixed it.* [< Latin *perceptiō, -ōnis* < *percipere* perceive]
—**Syn. 1.** insight, apprehension, discernment, comprehension.

per·cep·tion·al (pər sep′shə nəl), *adj.* of or having to do with perception.

per·cep·tive (pər sep′tiv), *adj.* **1.** having to do with perception. **2.** having the power of perceiving; intelligent: *a perceptive reader of poetry, a perceptive audience.* —**per·cep′tive·ly,** *adv.* —**per·cep′tive·ness,** *n.*

per·cep·tiv·i·ty (pėr′sep tiv′ə tē), *n., pl.* **-ties.** perceptive quality; power of perception or thinking.

per·cep·tron (pər sep′tron), *n.* an electronic device that automatically recognizes and identifies shapes or patterns by means of a system of photoelectric cells and electronic-brain units. [< *percep*(tion) + (elec)*tron*]

per·cep·tu·al (pər sep′chü əl), *adj.* of or having to do with perception: *A condition of any satisfactory neurological theory is to recognize and explain perceptual generalization* (George M. Wyburn). —**per·cep′tu·al·ly,** *adv.*

Per·ce·val (pėr′sə vəl), *n.* Percival.

perch[1] (pėrch), *n.* **1.** a bar, branch, or anything else on which a bird can come to rest. **2.** a rather high place or position: *From my perch on the crosstrees, I had nothing below me but the surface of the bay* (Robert Louis Stevenson). *Not making his high place the lawless perch Of wing'd ambitions* (Tennyson). **3.** a measure of length; rod; 5½ yards. **4.** a measure of area; square rod; 30¼ square yards. **5.** a measure of volume in masonry; 24¾ cubic feet. **6.** a pole connecting the front and rear running parts in a wagon. —*v.i.* **1.** to alight and rest; sit: *A robin perched on our porch railing.* **2.** to sit rather high: *He perched on a stool. The little village perches high among the hills* (H. G. Wells). —*v.t.* to place high up: *Mürren is perched precariously on a narrow shelf 5400 feet above sea level* (Newsweek).
[< Old French *perche* < Latin *pertica* pole, measuring rod]

perch[2] (pėrch), *n., pl.* **perch·es** or (*collectively*) **perch. 1.** any of a group of small, edible freshwater fish with a spiny fin, especially the yellow perch of North America. **2.** any of various related fresh- or salt-water fish, as the white perch. [< Old French *perche* < Latin *perca* < Greek *pérkē*, related to *perknós* dark-colored]

Yellow Perch[2] **(def. 1)**
(10 in. long)

per·chance (pər chans′, -chäns′), *adv. Archaic.* **1.** perhaps; it may be; by chance: *To sleep: perchance to dream* (Shakespeare). *The climax would be interesting, if perchance uncomfortable* (Winston Churchill). **2.** by any chance; accidentally: *I counsel thee to stand aloof . . . lest perchance He smite thee with his spear* (William Cullen Bryant).
[< Anglo-French *par chance* < Old French *par* by + *cheance* chance] —**Syn. 1.** peradventure.

perch·er (pėr′chər), *n.* **1.** a person or thing that perches. **2.** a bird with feet adapted for perching.

Per·che·ron (pėr′chə ron, -shə-), *n.* one of a breed of large and strong horses originally raised in Perche, France, as draft animals. [< French *Percheron* < Le *Perche*, a district in France]

per·chlo·rate (pėr klôr′āt, -klōr′-), *n.* a salt of perchloric acid.

per·chlor·eth·yl·ene (pėr′klôr eth′ə lēn, -klōr-), *n.* a colorless, nonflammable liquid, used as a dry-cleaning fluid, degreaser, and solvent, and medically as an anthelmintic agent. *Formula:* $Cl_2C{:}CCl_2$

per·chlo·ric acid (pėr klôr′ik, -klōr′-), a colorless syrupy liquid used as an oxidizing agent, for plating metals, in explosives, etc. It is stable when diluted, but its concentrated form is highly explosive when in contact with oxidizable substances. *Formula:* $HClO_4$

per·chlo·rid (pėr klôr′id, -klōr′-), *n.* perchloride.

per·chlo·ride (pėr klôr′īd, -id; -klōr′-), *n.* a compound of chlorine with another element or radical, containing the maximum proportion of chlorine.

per·chlo·rin·ate (pėr klôr′ə nāt, -klōr′-), *v.t.,* **-at·ed, -at·ing.** to combine or charge with the maximum proportion of chlorine.

per·chlo·rin·a·tion (pėr klôr′ə nā′shən, -klōr′-), *n.* a combining or charging with the maximum proportion of chlorine.

per·chro·mate (pėr krō′māt), *n.* a salt of perchromic acid.

per·chro·mic acid (pėr krō′mik), an unstable, deep-blue crystalline acid. *Possible formula:* $H_3CrO_8.2H_2O$

per·cip·i·ence (pər sip′ē əns), *n.* the act, condition, or power of perceiving; perception; cognizance.

per·cip·i·en·cy (pər sip′ē ən sē), *n., pl.* **-cies.** percipience.

per·cip·i·ent (pər sip′ē ənt), *adj.* **1.** perceiving. **2.** having perception. —*n.* a person or thing which perceives: *Since detectors indicate that no such radiation reaches the percipient from the agent, this is scarcely surprising* (Science). [< Latin *percipiēns, -entis*, present participle of *percipere* perceive] —**per·cip′i·ent·ly,** *adv.*

Per·ci·val or **Per·ci·vale** (pėr′sə vəl), *n.* one of King Arthur's knights, who sought and finally saw the Holy Grail.

per·coid (pėr′koid), *adj.* **1.** resembling a perch. **2.** of or belonging to a group of spiny-finned teleost fishes, including the fresh-water perches, basses, and sunfishes, and certain salt-water fish, such as the mackerels and tunas. —*n.* a percoid fish. [< New Latin *Percoidea* the perch family < Latin *perca* (< Greek *pérkē* perch) + Greek *eîdos* form]

per·coi·de·an (pər koi′dē ən), *adj.* percoid.

per·co·late (pėr′kə lāt), *v.,* **-lat·ed, -lat·ing,** *n.* —*v.i.* to drip or drain through small holes or spaces: *Let the coffee percolate for seven minutes.* —*v.t.* **1.** to filter through; permeate: *Water percolates sand.* **2.** to cause (a liquid or particles) to pass through; filter; sift. **3.** *Slang.* to act efficiently.
—*n.* a liquid that has been percolated.
[< Latin *percōlāre* (with English *-ate*[1]) < *per-* through + *cōlāre* to filter through < *cōlum* strainer]
—**Syn.** *v.t.* **1.** filter, ooze, trickle.

per·co·la·tion (pėr′kə lā′shən), *n.* the act or process of percolating: *Percolation through barley as a new method for separating heavy water from the ordinary kind is reported by three Swedish scientists* (Science News Letter).

per·co·la·tor (pėr′kə lā′tər), *n.* **1.** a kind of coffee pot in which boiling water drains through ground coffee. **2.** a thing that percolates.

per con·tra (pər kon′trə), *Latin.* on the contrary; on the other hand; on the other side: *It is the slogan, not the argument, which rams conviction home. Per contra, the words we stigmatize as offensive goad us to fury* (Atlantic).

per cur·i·am (pėr kyůr′ē am), *Law.* by the court (of an opinion or ruling given jointly by all the judges trying a case, with no signatory author): *It was a brief per curiam decision in a case which involved no contested issue* (Bulletin of Atomic Scientists). [< Latin *per curiăm*]

per·cur·rent (pər kėr′ənt), *adj.* running through the entire length, as the midrib of a leaf.

per·cuss (pər kus′), *v.t., v.i.* to tap or strike gently with the finger or a small hammer, as in medical diagnosis or treatment: *He percusses rapidly over a nerve when the pain is dull or grinding, and percusses slowly when the pain is acute* (T.L. Brunton). [< Latin *percussus*, past participle of *percutere* < *per-* (intensive) + *quatere* strike, beat]

per·cus·sion (pər kush′ən), *n.* **1.** the striking of one body against another with force; stroke; blow. **2.** the shock made by the striking of one body against another with force; impact: *Every part however small which turned over as the result of percussion would suddenly cause another balance to fall* (Science News). **3.** the tapping of a part of the body by a doctor. **4.** *Music.* **a.** the striking of percussion instruments to produce tones: *Dorothy Donegan . . . plays piano with miraculous precision and tremendous percussion* (New Yorker). **b.** the percussion instruments of an orchestra. **c.** their players. **5.** the striking of sound upon the ear. [< Latin *percussiō, -ōnis* < *percussus*; see PERCUSS] —**Syn. 1.** impact.

percussion cap, a small cap containing powder. It explodes when struck by the hammer of the gun and sets off the charge.

percussion instrument, a musical instrument played by striking it, such as a drum, cymbal, tambourine, castanets, or chimes.

per·cus·sion·ist (pər kush′ə nist), *n.* a person who plays a percussion instrument or instruments, especially in an orchestra: *The piece required eight percussionists and two pianists* (New York Times).

percussion lock, a type of gunlock that strikes and fires a percussion cap.

per·cus·sive (pər kus′iv), *adj.* of, having to do with, or characterized by percussion: *His piano Bach is in the approved lighter, percussive, and staccato style* (Edward Tatnall Canby). —*n.* a percussion instrument. —**per·cus′sive·ly,** *adv.* —**per·cus′sive·ness,** *n.*

per·cu·ta·ne·ous (pėr′kyü tā′nē əs), *adj.* made, done, or effected through the skin: *percutaneous absorption.* —**per′cu·ta′ne·ous·ly,** *adv.*

per·die (pər dē′), *adv., interj.* pardi.

per di·em (pər dī′əm, dē′əm), **1.** per day; for each day: *a rate . . . sufficient to cover costs . . . including crew per diem* (Newsweek). **2.** an allowance of so much every day for living expenses, usually while traveling in connection with work: *Petitioner was compensated at a specified per diem rate* (New York Times). [< Medieval Latin *per* to, for every; and Latin *diem*, accusative of *diēs* day]

per·di·tion (pər dish′ən), *n.* **1.** the loss of one's soul or of the joys of heaven; final spiritual ruin; damnation. **2.** hell: *Would you send A soul straight to perdition?* (Robert Browning). **3.** utter loss or destruction; complete ruin: *Nearly eight hundred years were past and gone, since the Arabian invaders had sealed the perdition of Spain* (Washington Irving). **4.** *Obsolete.* diminution; loss: *The perdition of th' athversary hath been very great* (Shakespeare). [< Latin *perditiō, -ōnis* < *perdere* to destroy < *per-* (pejorative) + *dare* give]

per·du (pər dü′, -dyü′), *adj.* hidden away; out of sight; concealed: *James . . . was lying perdu in the lobby* (Scott). —*n. Obsolete.* a soldier in a position of special danger, and hence considered as virtually lost. [< Middle French *perdu*, past participle of *perdre* to lose < Latin *perdere* destroy; see PERDITION]

per·due (pər dü′, -dyü′), *adj.* the feminine of **perdu.**

per·du·ra·bil·i·ty (pər důr′ə bil′ə tē, -dyůr′-), *n.* perdurable quality or state: *The perdurability of the people is manifested in what may be called the physical aspects of the language* (New Yorker).

per·du·ra·ble (pər důr′ə bəl, -dyůr′-), *adj.* everlasting; imperishable; permanent: *cables of perdurable toughness* (Shakespeare); *leaving a name perdurable on earth* (Robert Southey). [< Old French *pardurable* < Late Latin *perdūrābilis* < *perdūrāre* to endure; see PERDURE]

per·du·ra·bly (pər důr′ə blē, -dyůr′-), *adv.* in a perdurable manner; permanently.

per·dure (pər důr′, -dyůr′), *v.i.,* **-dured, -dur·ing.** to endure or continue long or forever. [< Late Latin *perdūrāre* < Latin *per-* (intensive) + *dūrāre* endure, harden < *dūrus* hard]

per·dus (pər düz′, -dyüz′), *n.pl.* a body of soldiers selected for a specially hazardous military duty. [< French *perdus*, plural of *perdu*; see PERDU]

père (per), *n. French.* senior, used after proper names to distinguish a father from his son (*fils*): *Dumas père.*

Père (per), *n. French.* Father, used before the name of a priest: *Père Marquette.*

Père David's deer, a large, grayish-brown deer of northern China: *Some of the rarest deer in the world are the Père David's deer. The 400 survivors exist only in zoos and game parks* (Science News Letter). [< *Père* (Armand) *David*, 1826-1900, a French missionary and naturalist]

per·e·grin (per′ə grin), *n., adj.* peregrine.

per·e·gri·nate (per′ə grə nāt), *v.,* **-nat·ed, -nat·ing,** *adj.* —*v.i.* to travel; journey. —*v.t.* to travel over; traverse. —*adj. Archaic.* foreign: *I perceive . . . that there is something outlandish, peregrinate, and lawless about me* (Edward G. Bulwer-Lytton). [< Latin *peregrīnārī* (with English *-ate*[1]) *peregrīnus* peregrine]

per·e·gri·na·tion (per′ə grə nā′shən), *n.* **1.** a peregrinating; journeying: *The pursuit of the trade meant . . . a regular camping out from month to month, a peregrination among*

farms which could be counted by the hundred (Thomas Hardy). **2.** a journey: *The gray-haired veteran retired, after a long peregrination, to his native town* (George Borrow).
peregrinations, a. travels: *It describes the finding and perilous peregrinations of the Scrolls* (James R. Newman). **b.** a narrative of travels: *to write peregrinations.*

per·e·gri·na·tor (per′ə grə nā′tər), *n.* a person who peregrinates.

per·e·grine (per′ə grin, -grīn, -grēn), *n.* **1.** a large powerful falcon, credited with speeds of 180 miles per hour when diving, formerly much used in Europe for hawking. The American variety is the duck hawk: *Out of the reeds, like an arrow, shot the peregrine* (Charles Kingsley). **2.** a foreign visitor in a country; resident who is not a citizen.
—*adj.* **1.** not native; foreign. **2.** outlandish; strange. **3.** *Astrology.* (of a planet) so situated in the zodiac that it has none of its essential dignities. **4.** being upon a pilgrimage; traveling abroad: *the passage now presents no hindrance To the spirit unappeased and peregrine Between two worlds become much like each other* (T. S. Eliot).
[< Latin *peregrīnus* from foreign parts < *peregrē*, adverb, abroad, or *perager*, noun, one who has gone through (lands) < *per-* outside + *ager* (*Romanus*) the (Roman) territory. Doublet of PILGRIM.]

Peregrine (def. 1) (1 ft. high)

peregrine falcon, peregrine.

peregrine tone, one of the Gregorian tones or chants.

per·e·grin·i·ty (per′ə grin′ə tē), *n.* **1.** the condition of being a foreigner or alien. **2.** *Obsolete.* foreignness; strangeness.

pe·reir·a bark, or **pe·reir·a** (pə rãr′ə), *n.* **1.** the bark of a South American tree of the dogbane family, used in medicine as a source of pereirine. **2.** the tree itself. [< Jonathan *Pereira,* 1804-1853, an English pharmacologist]

pe·rei·rin (pə rãr′in), *n.* pereirine.

pe·rei·rine (pə rãr′ēn, -in), *n.* an alkaloid obtained as a brown powder from pereira bark, formerly used as a substitute for quinine, in tonics, etc. *Formula:* $C_{20}H_{26}N_2O$

per·emp·to·ri·ly (pə remp′tər ə lē; per′əmp tôr′-, -tōr′-), *adv.* in a peremptory manner: *The worship of saints and the doctrine of purgatory were peremptorily rejected as opposed to Scripture* (Philip Schaff).

per·emp·to·ri·ness (pə remp′tər ē nis; per′əmp tôr′-, -tōr′-), *n.* peremptory quality or state: *No peremptoriness, Clary Harlowe: once you declare yourself inflexible, I have done* (Samuel Richardson).

per·emp·to·ry (pə remp′tər ē; per′əmp-tôr′ē, -tōr′-), *adj.* **1.** imperious; positive; dictatorial: *a peremptory teacher. He spoke in a loud and peremptory voice, using the tone of one in authority* (Booth Tarkington). **2.** allowing no denial or refusal: *A peremptory command would have compelled obedience* (Samuel Johnson). **3.** leaving no choice; decisive; final; absolute; conclusive: *a peremptory decree. It is a peremptory point of virtue that a man's independence be secured* (Emerson). [< Latin *perēmptōrius* decisive, deadly; that ends < *perēmptor, -ōris* destroyer < *perimere* destroy < *per-* completely + *emere* (originally) take, buy]
—**Syn. 1.** arbitrary, dogmatic. **3.** definite.

per·en·dure (pėr′en důr′, -dyůr′), *v.i.,* **-dured, -dur·ing.** to endure long or forever.

per·en·ni·al (pə ren′ē əl), *adj.* **1.** lasting through the whole year: *a perennial stream.* **2.** lasting for a very long time; enduring: *the perennial beauty of the hills.* **3.** having underground parts that live more than two years.
—*n.* a perennial plant: *Roses are perennials.* [< Latin *perennis* lasting through the year(s) (< *per-* through + *annus* year) + English *-al*[1]] —**per·en′ni·al·ly,** *adv.*
—**Syn.** *adj.* **2.** abiding, continual, permanent, perpetual, everlasting, eternal.

perf., an abbreviation for the following:
1. perfect.
2. perforated (of stamps).
3. performance.
4. performed.

per·fect (*adj., n.* pėr′fikt; *v.* pər fekt′), *adj.* **1.** without defect; faultless: *a perfect spelling paper, a perfect copy, a perfect circle. Perfect work shows great care.* **2. a.** completely skilled; expert: *a perfect golfer. Our battle is more full of names than yours, Our men more perfect in the use of arms* (Shakespeare). **b.** thoroughly learned or acquired: *The lesson is but plain. And once made perfect, never lost again* (Shakespeare). **3.** having all its parts; complete: *The set was perfect; nothing was missing or broken.* **4.** entire; utter; total: *perfect quiet, a perfect stranger to us.* **5.** pure; unmixed; unalloyed: *perfect blue.* **6.** *Grammar.* **a.** showing action or state completed at a time indicated by another verb in the utterance or by the context. **b.** designating a verb form or verb phrase with such a meaning. Three perfect tenses in English are: perfect (he has done), past perfect (he had done), and future perfect (he will have done). **7.** *Botany.* having both stamens and pistils: *a perfect flower.* **8.** *Music.* having to do with the intervals or original consonances of unison, a fourth, fifth, and octave, as contrasted with the major intervals of a third and sixth. **9.** *Mathematics.* (of a whole number) equal to the sum of its divisors. **10.** *Obsolete.* assured; certain: *Thou art perfect then, our ship hath touch'd upon The deserts of Bohemia?* (Shakespeare). **11.** *Obsolete.* satisfied; contented: *Might we but have that happiness . . . we should think ourselves forever perfect* (Shakespeare).
—*v.t.* **1.** to make perfect; remove all faults from; improve: *to perfect a plan as it is being tried out, to perfect an invention.* **2.** to carry through; complete; finish: . . . *the system of religious persecution commenced by Charles, and perfected by Philip* (John L. Motley). **3.** to make fully skilled: *to perfect oneself in an art.*
—*n. Grammar.* **1.** the perfect tense. **2.** a verb form or verb phrase in the perfect tense. *Have eaten* is the perfect of *eat. Abbr.:* perf.
[alteration (influenced by Latin) of Middle English *parfite* < Old French *parfit* < Latin *perfectus* completed, past participle of *perficere* < *per-* thoroughly + *facere* make, do]
—**per·fect′er,** *n.* —**per′fect·ness,** *n.*
—**Syn.** *adj.* **1.** impeccable. **2. a.** accomplished. **3.** intact.

per·fect·a·bil·i·ty (pər fek′tə bil′ə tē), *n., pl.* **-ties.** perfectibility: *The public imagined that what was intended as a doctrine of perfectability was in fact a statement of American intentions* (Harper's).

perfect cadence, *Music.* a cadence in which the closing chord is the tonic. It can be preceded by the dominant chord (authentic cadence) or the subdominant chord (plagal cadence).

perfect consonance, a unison, octave, fifth, or fourth.

perfect game, 1. a baseball game in which the pitcher allows the opposing team no base hits, no walks, and no runs in nine or more innings: *The Yankees' Larsen . . . pitched the only perfect game in World Series history* (Robert W. Creamer). **2.** a bowling game of twelve consecutive strikes.

per·fect·i·bil·i·ty (pər fek′tə bil′ə tē), *n., pl.* **-ties.** capability of becoming, or being made, perfect: *Patience, he derives from the innermost faith in the perfectibility of man* (Bulletin of Atomic Scientists). *The great majority of those who speak of perfectibility as a dream . . . feel that it . . . would afford them no pleasure if it were realised* (John Stuart Mill).

per·fect·i·ble (pər fek′tə bəl), *adj.* capable of becoming, or being made, perfect: *Man, he thought, was perfectible, and a little calm argument would make him perfect* (Leslie Stephen).

per·fec·tion (pər fek′shən), *n.* **1.** perfect condition; faultless quality; highest excellence: *His work was always perfection.* **2.** a perfect person or thing: *The Empire coach was the perfection of fast travelling* (Charles Lever). **3.** a making complete or perfect: *Perfection of our plans will take another week.* **4.** a quality, trait, accomplishment, etc., of a high degree of excellence. **5.** the highest or most perfect degree of a quality or trait: *the perfection of goodness.*
to perfection, perfectly: *He played the difficult violin concerto to perfection.*
[< Latin *perfectiō, -ōnis* < *perfectus* completed; see PERFECT]
—**Syn. 3.** fulfillment.

per·fec·tion·ism (pər fek′shə niz əm), *n.* **1.** any of various doctrines maintaining that religious, moral, social, or political perfection is attainable: *An anxious perfectionism can . . . destroy those real underpinnings of existence, found in faith, modesty, humor* (Atlantic). **2.** the beliefs or practices of a perfectionist: *Often she has tried to moderate his irritable perfectionism, which can result in his berating other actors* (Time).

per·fec·tion·ist (pər fek′shə nist), *n.* **1.** a person who is not content with anything that is not perfect or nearly perfect: *It is hard to keep house for a perfectionist.* **2.** a person who believes that it is possible to lead a sinless life. —*adj.* of or having to do with perfectionists or perfectionism.

per·fec·tion·is·tic (pər fek′shə nis′tik), *adj.* seeking or demanding perfection, especially to an impractical degree; being a perfectionist: *Juvenile delinquents from wealthy families were found usually to have aggressive, perfectionistic, rigid, or indifferent fathers* (Science News Letter).

per·fec·tive (pər fek′tiv), *adj.* **1.** tending to make perfect or complete. **2.** *Grammar.* (in some languages) designating or having to do with an aspect of the verb that expresses completion of action.
—*n. Grammar.* **1.** the perfective aspect. **2.** a verb form or verb phrase in the perfective aspect. —**per·fec′tive·ly,** *adv.* —**per·fec′tive·ness,** *n.*

per·fect·ly (pėr′fikt lē), *adv.* in a perfect manner or degree; completely or thoroughly; fully; faultlessly; with utmost exactness; entirely: *perfectly new, perfectly clear. I understand the difficulty perfectly, mother* (George Eliot).

perfect number, a number which is equal to the sum of its factors (other than itself). Six, being the sum of its factors 1, 2, and 3, is a perfect number, as is 28 (1, 2, 4, 7, and 14).

per·fec·to (pər fek′tō), *n., pl.* **-tos.** a thick cigar that tapers nearly to a point at both ends. [American English < Spanish *perfecto* perfect < Latin *perfectus*; see PERFECT]

perfect participle, a participle expressing action completed before the time of speaking or acting. In "Having written the letter, she mailed it," *having written* is a perfect participle.
➤ See **participle** for usage note.

perfect pitch, the sense of pitch that enables a person to identify a tone heard and name it as a note on a musical scale.

perfect ream, a package or pile of 516 uniform sheets of printing paper; 21½ quires.

perfect rhyme, rhyme between two words having the same pronunciation but different meanings; rich rhyme. Examples: *bear* (animal), *bear* (carry) *bare* (naked); *sale, sail.*

perfect year, abundant year.

per·fer·vid (pėr fėr′vid), *adj.* very fervid; very ardent: *She was moved by this perfervid letter . . . Its effect—the effect of its passionate flattery—was to lift her nobly to an eminence* (Maurice Hewlett). —**per·fer′vid·ly,** *adv.* —**per·fer′vid·ness,** *n.*

per·fer·vor (pėr fer′vər), *n.* perfervid quality.

per·fid·i·ous (pər fid′ē əs), *adj.* deliberately faithless; treacherous: *Compelled to parley, Bossu resorted to a perfidious stratagem* (John L. Motley). [< Latin *perfidiōsus* (with English *-ous*) < *perfidia* perfidy]
—**per·fid′i·ous·ly,** *adv.* —**per·fid′i·ous·ness,** *n.* —**Syn.** false, traitorous, unfaithful.

per·fi·dy (pėr′fə dē), *n., pl.* **-dies.** a breaking faith; being false to a trust; base treachery: *a forsaken lady . . . bewailing the perfidy of her lover* (Charlotte Brontë). [< Latin *perfidia* < *perfidus* faithless < *per-* (pejorative) + *fidēs, -ēī* faith] —**Syn.** faithlessness, betrayal, disloyalty.

per·fo·li·ate (pər fō′lē it, -āt), *adj.* having the stem apparently passing through the blade: *a perfoliate leaf.* [< New Latin *perfoliatus* < Latin *per-* through + *folium* leaf]

per·fo·li·a·tion (pər fō′lē-ā′shən), *n.* perfoliate condition.

Perfoliate Leaves of bellwort

per·fo·rate (*v.* pėr′fə rāt; *adj.* pėr′fər it, -fə rāt), *v.,* **-rat·ed, -rat·ing,** *adj.* —*v.t.* **1. a.** to make a hole or holes through; pierce: *to perforate a target by bullets.* **b.** to make a hole or holes into; bore into: *trees perforated by woodpeckers.* **2.** to make a row or rows of holes through: *Sheets of postage*

stamps are perforated. The well was perforated from 9,082 to 9,092 feet (Wall Street Journal). —*v.i.* to make its way into or through something; make a perforation.
—*adj.* pierced: *perforate corals.*
[< Latin *perforāre* (with English *-ate*[1]) < *per-* through + *forāre* to bore[1]]
—**Syn.** *v.t.* **1. a.** puncture.

per·fo·rat·ed (pėr′fə rā′tid), *adj.* **1.** pierced with rows of small holes: *a perforated sheet of stamps or coupons.* **2.** full of holes.

per·fo·ra·tion (pėr′fə rā′shən), *n.* **1.** a hole bored or punched through or into something: *the perforations in the top of a salt shaker. Detach the check at the line of perforations.* **2.** a perforating; **3.** a being perforated.

per·fo·ra·tive (pėr′fə rā′tiv), *adj.* tending to perforate; perforating.

per·fo·ra·tor (pėr′fə rā′tər), *n.* **1.** a person or thing that perforates. **2.** an instrument or machine for perforating.

per·force (pər fôrs′, -fōrs′), *adv.* **1.** by necessity; necessarily: *The wind was foul and boisterous, so perforce There must they bide* (William Morris). **2.** *Obsolete.* by force: *to take't again perforce!* (Shakespeare). —*n.* necessity. [< Old French *par force* by force]

per·form (pər fôrm′), *v.t.* **1.** to do: *Perform your duties well. It takes training to perform a swan dive.* **2.** to put into effect; carry out; fulfill: *Perform your promise.* **3.** to go through; render: *to perform the marriage ceremony, to perform a piece of music, to perform the part of Hamlet.* **4.** *Obsolete.* to construct; produce; complete. —*v.i.* **1.** to act, play, sing, or do tricks in public. **2.** to carry out a command, promise, or undertaking: *Wise to resolve, and patient to perform* (Alexander Pope). [< Anglo-French *parfourmer,* variant of Old French *parfournir* accomplish, achieve < *par-* completely + *fournir* to furnish, finish]
—**Syn.** *v.t.* **1.** See **do. 2. Perform, execute, discharge** mean to carry out or put into effect. **Perform** suggests carrying out a process that is long or that requires effort, attention, or skill: *The surgeon performed an operation.* **Execute** suggests carrying out a plan or an order: *The nurse executed the doctor's orders.* **Discharge** suggests carrying out an obligation or duty: *She gave a large party to discharge all her social obligations.*

per·form·a·ble (pər fôr′mə bəl), *adj.* that can be performed.

per·form·ance (pər fôr′məns), *n.* **1.** a performing: *the performance of duty, the efficient performance of an automobile.* **2.** a thing performed; act; deed: *The child's kicks and screams made a disgraceful performance.* **3.** the giving of a play, concert, circus, or other show: *The evening performance is at 8 o'clock.* —**Syn. 1.** execution, accomplishment, achievement.

performance test, *Psychology.* a test in which overt motor reactions are substituted for verbal reactions, used in measuring the intelligence of deaf children, very young children, children speaking only a foreign language, etc.

per·form·a·to·ry (pər fôr′mə tôr′ē, -tōr′-), *adj.* of or having to do with performance.

per·form·er (pər fôr′mər), *n.* a person who performs, especially, one who performs for the entertainment of others: *a talented performer.*

per·form·ing arts (pər fôr′ming), drama, music, and the dance: *Crucial to the projected cultural center is a school of performing arts* (New York Times).

per·fume (*n.* pėr′fyüm, pər fyüm′; *v.* pər fyüm′), *n., v.,* **-fumed, -fum·ing.** —*n.* **1.** a liquid having the sweet smell of flowers, fragrant wood, etc.: *All the perfumes of Arabia will not sweeten this little hand* (Shakespeare). **2.** a sweet smell: *We enjoyed the perfume of the flowers.* [< Middle French *parfum* < *parfumer* to scent; see the verb]
—*v.t.* **1.** to fill with sweet odor: *Flowers perfumed the air. The blue-bells perfume all the air* (Matthew Arnold). **2.** to put a sweet-smelling liquid on: *to perfume one's hair.* [< Middle French *parfumer* < earlier Italian *perfumare* < Latin *per-* through + *fūmāre* to smoke < *fūmus* smoke]
—**Syn.** *n.* **2.** fragrance, scent.

per·fum·er (pər fyü′mər), *n.* **1.** a maker or seller of perfumes. **2.** a person or thing that perfumes.

per·fum·er·y (pər fyü′mər ē, -fyüm′rē), *n., pl.* **-er·ies. 1.** a perfume. **2.** perfumes as a group. **3.** the business of making or selling perfumes. **4.** a perfumer's place of business.

per·func·to·ri·ly (pər fungk′tər ə lē), *adv.* in a perfunctory manner: *She gave some attention to her flowers, but it was perfunctorily bestowed, for they no longer charmed her* (Thomas Hardy).

per·func·to·ri·ness (pər fungk′tər ē nis), *n.* perfunctory quality; carelessness: *The perfunctoriness with which the Government recently rejected the conclusions of the unofficial inquiry ... was disappointing* (London Times).

per·func·to·ry (pər fungk′tər ē), *adj.* **1.** done merely for the sake of getting rid of the duty; mechanical; indifferent: *a perfunctory smile. The little boy gave his face a perfunctory washing. He saw her ... and raised his hat, but in a perfunctory, preoccupied manner* (Arnold Bennett). **2.** acting in a perfunctory way, merely to get rid of a duty or matter: *The new nurse was perfunctory; she did not really care about her work.* [< Latin *perfūnctōrius* (literally) like one who wishes to get through a thing < *perfungī* perform < *per-* completely, or badly + *fungī* execute]
—**Syn. 1.** careless, superficial.

per·fus·ate (pər fyü′zāt), *n.* a substance that is perfused: *The soil perfusate is adequately mixed and aerated and the perfusion is intermittent* (J.H. Quasel).

per·fuse (pər fyüz′), *v.t.,* **-fused, -fus·ing. 1.** to overspread with color, moisture, etc.; suffuse. **2.** to cause to flow or spread through or over; diffuse. **3.** to pass a substance through (an organ or other part of the body), especially by way of the blood stream: *to perfuse the heart with a muscle stimulant.* [< Latin *perfūsus,* past participle of *perfundere* pour out < *per-* (intensive) + *fundere* pour]

per·fu·sion (pər fyü′zhən), *n.* **1.** a perfusing: *The gland might be kept alive by perfusion, and supplied with suitable synthetic substances which it could convert to cortisone* (A.J. Birch). **2.** the condition of being perfused.

per·fu·sive (pər fyü′siv), *adj.* adapted to perfuse; easily perfused.

Per·ga·mene (pėr′gə mēn), *adj.* of or having to do with the ancient city of Pergamum, in Asia Minor, or its famous school of sculpture that flourished in the 100's and 200's B.C.

per·go·la (pėr′gə lə), *n.* an arbor made of a trellis supported by posts, for training vines or other plants: *A trellised arbour (which some years later would have been called a pergola) led from the porch up the hill to an old-fashioned summer-house* (Winston Churchill). [< Italian *pergola* < Latin *pergula* lean-to (roof), arbor (diminutive) < unrecorded *perga* timber work]

Pergola

perh., perhaps.

per·haps (pər haps′, -aps′), *adv.* maybe; possibly; it may be: *Perhaps a letter will come to you today. You may think, perhaps, that this work is unnecessary.* [Middle English *per happes* by chances]

pe·ri (pir′ē), *n., pl.* **-ris. 1.** *Persian Mythology.* a beautiful fairy shut out from paradise until forgiven. **2.** a very beautiful or fairylike being. [< Persian *perī*]

peri-, *prefix.* **1.** around; surrounding, as in *perimeter, peripheral.* **2.** near, as in *perihelion.* [< Greek *peri-* < *perí* around]

per·i·anth (per′ē anth), *n.* the envelope of a flower, including the calyx and the corolla. [< French *périanthe* < Greek *peri-* around + *ánthos* flower]

per·i·apt (per′ē apt), *n.* a charm; amulet: *It is a trafficking with the Evil One. Spells, periapts, and charms, are of his device* (Scott). [< French *périapte* < Greek *períapton* < *periáptein* < *peri-* about + *háptein* to fasten]

per·i·ar·ter·i·tis no·do·sa (per′ē är′tə rī′təs nə dō′sə), polyarteritis.

per·i·as·tron (per′ē as′tron), *n., pl.* **-tra** (-trə). the point in their orbits at which the two components of a double star come closest to each other. [< *peri-* + Greek *ástron* star]

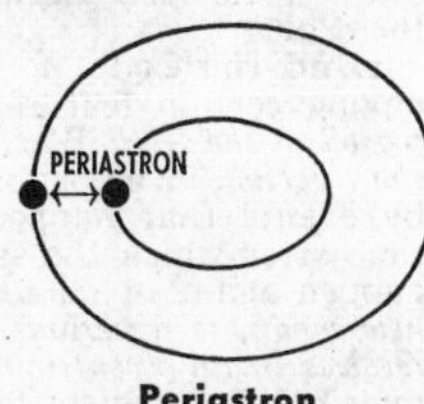

Periastron

per·i·blast (per′ə blast), *n.* the protoplasm surrounding the nucleus of a cell or ovum; cytoplasm. [< Greek *peri-* around + *blastós* germ, sprout]

per·i·blem (per′ə blem), *n.* the layer of meristem in the growing ends of stems and roots of plants from which the cortex develops. [< German *Periblem* < Greek *períblēma* garment; (literally) thing thrown around < *peribállein* throw around, cover with < *peri-* around + *bállein* to throw]

per·i·bran·chi·al (per′ə brang′kē əl), *adj.* of or having to do with the area around the gills of fishes. [< *peri-* + *branchial*]

per·i·car·di·ac (per′ə kär′dē ak), *adj.* pericardial.

per·i·car·di·al (per′ə kär′dē əl), *adj.* **1.** around the heart. **2.** of or having to do with the pericardium: *Blood is taken into the heart from the surrounding pericardial sinus through three pairs of openings in the heart, the ostia* (A. M. Winchester).

per·i·car·di·tis (per′ə kär dī′tis), *n.* inflammation of the pericardium.

per·i·car·di·um (per′ə kär′dē əm), *n., pl.* **-di·a** (-dē ə). the membranous sac enclosing the heart. [< Greek *perikárdion,* neuter of adjective *perikárdios* < *peri-* around + *kardíā* heart]

per·i·carp (per′ə kärp), *n.* **1.** the walls of a ripened ovary or fruit of a flowering plant, sometimes consisting of three layers, the epicarp, mesocarp, and endocarp; seed vessel. **2.** a part that holds the spores in certain algae, such as one surrounding the cystocarp of red algae. [< New Latin *pericarpium* < Greek *perikárpion* pod, husk < *peri-* around + *karpós* fruit]

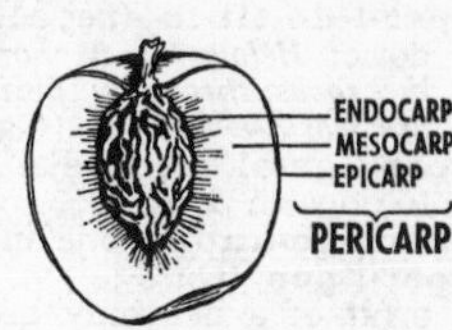

Pericarp (def. 1) of a peach

per·i·car·pi·al (per′ə kär′pē əl), *adj.* of or having to do with a pericarp.

per·i·chon·dri·al (per′ə kon′drē əl), *adj.* of or having to do with the perichondrium.

per·i·chon·dri·um (per′ə kon′drē əm), *n., pl.* **-dri·a** (-drē ə). a membrane of fibrous connective tissue covering the surface of cartilages except at the joints. [< New Latin *perichondrium* < Greek *peri-* around + *chóndros* cartilage]

Per·i·cle·an (per′ə klē′ən), *adj.* of or having to do with Pericles, Athenian statesman and military commander, or the period of his leadership, during which ancient Athens reached its peak of culture, power, and prosperity: *We Greeks are no more descended from the Periclean Greeks than they were from the Mycenaeans* (New Yorker). [< *Pericles,* about 490-429 B.C., a Greek general and statesman + English *-an*]

per·i·cline (per′ə klīn), *n.* a variety of albite found in large, white, opaque crystals. [probably < German *Periklin* < Greek *periklinēs* sloping on all sides < *peri-* around + *klīnein* to slope]

pe·ric·o·pe (pə rik′ə pē), *n., pl.* **-pes, -pae** (-pē). **1.** an extract or selection from a book. **2.** (in ancient Christian churches) a passage of Scripture read on certain Sundays and festive occasions. [< Late Latin *pericopē* < Greek *perikopē* < *perí* around + *kóptein* to cut]

per·i·cra·ni·al (per′ə krā′nē əl), *adj.* of or having to do with the pericranium.

per·i·cra·ni·um (per′ə krā′nē əm), *n., pl.* **-ni·a** (-nē ə). **1.** the membrane covering the bones of the skull; external periosteum of the cranium. **2.** *Humorous.* the brain; skull: *various knotty points which had puzzled his pericranium* (Thomas L. Peacock). [< New Latin *pericranium* < Greek *perikrānion,* neuter of *perikrānios* < *peri-* around + *krānion* skull]

per·i·cy·cle (per′ə sī′kəl), *n. Botany.* the outer portion of the stele lying between the vascular tissues internally and the innermost layer of the cortex externally, and consisting of mainly parenchyma cells. [< Greek *períkyklos* all around, encircling < *peri-* around + *kýklos* a circle]

per·i·cy·clic (per′ə sī′klik, -sik′lik), *adj.* of or having to do with the pericycle.

pericyclic fiber, fiber formed by the rapid division of cells of the pericycle. In certain plants, as flax, the pericyclic fiber contains cellulose and can be used for textiles.

per·i·den·tal (per′ə den′təl), *adj.* periodontal.

per·i·derm (per′ə dėrm), *n.* the cork-producing tissue of stems, together with the cork layers and other tissues derived from it. [< German *Peridermis* < Greek *peri-* + *dérma* skin]

per·i·der·mal (per′ə dėr′məl), *adj.* of or having to do with the periderm.

pe·rid·i·al (pə rid′ē əl), *adj.* of or having to do with a peridium.

pe·rid·i·um (pə rid′ē əm), *n., pl.* **-i·a** (-ē ə). the outer coat or envelope enclosing the sporophore of certain fungi. [< New Latin *peridium* < Greek *pērídion* (diminutive) < *pḗrā* leather bag]

per·i·dot (per′ə dot), *n.* a yellowish-green variety of chrysolite, used as a gem; olivine. [< Old French *peritot,* French *péridot;* origin uncertain]

per·i·dot·ic (per′ə dot′ik), *adj.* of or containing peridot; like peridot.

per·i·do·tite (per′ə dō′tīt), *n.* any of a group of coarse-grained igneous rocks consisting of olivine with an admixture of various other minerals, such as pyroxene, or sometimes mica, chromite, spinel, etc. [< *peridot* + *-ite*[1]]

per·i·do·tit·ic (per′ə də tit′ik), *adj.* peridotic: *Below the Mohorovičic discontinuity, the rocks, probably peridotitic in character, are world-encircling* (Gaskell and Hill).

per·i·ge·al (per′ə jē′əl), *adj.* of or having to do with perigee.

per·i·ge·an (per′ə jē′ən), *adj.* perigeal.

per·i·gee (per′ə jē), *n.* that point in the orbit of a heavenly body where it comes closest to the earth: *The speed is greatest at perigee, when the moon is nearest the earth* (Robert H. Baker). See picture under **apogee.** [< French *périgée* < New Latin *perigeum* < Greek *perígeion* < *peri-* near + *gê* earth]

per·i·gla·cial (per′ə glā′shəl), *adj.* **1.** bordering a glacier or glaciers: *Southern England was largely a periglacial region during the last Ice Age.* **2.** of or characteristic of a periglacial region: *periglacial climate, periglacial deposits.*

Per·i·gor·di·an (per′ə gôr′dē ən), *adj.* of or having to do with the upper paleolithic culture of southern France. [< *Périgord,* region in southern France where remains of this culture were found + *-ian*]

pe·rig·y·nous (pə rij′ə nəs), *adj.* **1.** situated around the pistil on the edge of a cup-like receptacle, as stamens, sepals, and petals. **2.** (of a flower) having its parts so arranged, as the cherry. [< New Latin *perigynus* (with English *-ous*) < Greek *peri-* around + *gynê* female, wife]

pe·rig·y·ny (pə rij′ə nē), *n.* perigynous condition.

per·i·he·li·on (per′ə hē′lē ən, -hēl′yən), *n., pl.* **-he·li·a** (-hē′lē ə, -hēl′yə). that point in the orbit of a heavenly body where it comes closest to the sun. See picture under **aphelion.** [Grecized form of New Latin *perihelium* < Greek *peri-* near + *hḗlios* the sun]

per·il (per′əl), *n., v.,* **-iled, -il·ing** or (*especially British*) **-illed, -il·ling.** —*n.* the chance of harm, loss, or destruction; danger: *The peril of war grew as the negotiations for a settlement of the dispute broke down.*

at one's peril, taking the risk or responsibility of the consequences: *This bridge is not safe; cross it at your peril.*

perils, a case or cause of perils; risks; dangers: *the perils of the sea. To smile at scapes and perils overblown* (Shakespeare).

—*v.t.* to put in danger; imperil. *It threatened to encroach upon our anchorage, and peril the safety of the vessel* (Elisha Kane).

[< Old French *peril,* learned borrowing from Latin *perīculum* trial, risk < unrecorded root *peri-* try]

—**Syn.** *n.* jeopardy, hazard. See **danger.**

pe·ril·la (pə ril′ə), *n.* any of a group of Asiatic herbs of the mint family. Some kinds are grown in gardens for their colorful leaves. [< New Latin *Perilla;* origin unknown]

per·il·ous (per′ə ləs), *adj.* full of peril; dangerous: *a perilous journey. It is always perilous to adopt expediency as a guide* (Benjamin Disraeli). [< Anglo-French *perillous* < Latin *perīculōsus* (with English *-ous*) < *perīculum;* see PERIL] —**per′il·ous·ly,** *adv* —**per′il·ous·ness,** *n.* —**Syn.** hazardous, risky, unsafe. —**Ant.** safe, secure.

peril point, *Commerce.* the rate of duty on an imported product or commodity at or below which the quantity imported from abroad does or probably would do serious damage to the domestic industry producing similar goods: *The bill would provide peril points of 17 cents a pound for lead and 14½ cents for zinc* (Wall Street Journal).

per·i·lune (per′ə lün), *n.* that point in the orbit of a spacecraft where it comes closest to the moon.

per·i·lymph (per′ə limf′), *n.* a fluid between the bony and the membranous labyrinths of the inner ear.

per·i·lym·phat·ic (per′ə lim fat′ik), *adj.* of or having to do with perilymph.

pe·rim·e·ter (pə rim′ə tər), *n.* **1.** the outer boundary of a surface or figure: *the perimeter of a circle, the perimeter of a garden.* **2.** the distance around such a boundary: *The perimeter of a square equals four times the length of one side.* **3.** the outermost line of observation posts, entrenchments, etc., around a military position: *His audacious delaying tactics before the Pusan perimeter meant the difference between maintaining a foothold on the peninsula and retreat to Japan* (Newsweek). **4.** an instrument for measuring the field of vision and determining visual power at different points on the retina. [< Latin *perimetros* < Greek *perímetros* < *peri-* around + *métron* measure] —**Syn. 1.** periphery.

per·i·met·ric (per′ə met′ric), *adj.* of or having to do with the perimeter: *perimetric measurements.* —**per′i·met′ri·cal·ly,** *adv.*

per·i·met·ri·cal (per′ə met′rə kəl), *adj.* perimetric.

per·i·morph (per′ə môrf), *n.* a mineral enclosing another mineral (contrasted with *endomorph*). [< *peri-* + Greek *morphḗ* form]

per·i·mor·phic (per′ə môr′fik), *adj.* of, having to do with, or like perimorph.

per·i·mor·phous (per′ə môr′fəs), *adj.* perimorphic.

per im·pos·si·bi·le (per im′pə sib′ə lē), *Latin.* **1.** as is impossible: *If, per impossibile, profits were equalised throughout our economy, we would have reached a stage of perfect equilibrium* (Punch). **2.** (literally) through the impossible.

per·i·my·si·um (per′ə mizh′ē əm, -miz′-), *n., pl.* **-my·si·a** (-mizh′ē ə, -miz′-). *Anatomy.* the thin connective tissue which surrounds a muscle and also divides its fibers into bundles. [< New Latin *perimysium* < Greek *peri-* around + *mŷs, myós* muscle]

per·i·na·tal (per′ə nā′təl), *adj.* of or having to do with the period of a child's life including the five months preceding birth and the first month after. [< Greek *peri-* around + English *natal*]

per·i·ne·al (per′ə nē′əl), *adj.* of or having to do with the perineum.

per·i·neph·ri·al (per′ə nef′rē əl), *adj.* of or having to do with perinephrium.

per·i·neph·ri·um (per′ə nef′rē əm), *n., pl.* **-ri·a** (-rē ə). the capsule of connective and fatty tissue surrounding a kidney. [< New Latin *perinephrium* < Greek *peri-* around + *nephrós* kidney]

per·i·ne·um (per′ə nē′əm), *n., pl.* **-ne·a** (-nē′ə). **1.** the region of the body between the thighs, especially between the anus and the genitals. **2.** the region included in the opening of the pelvis, containing the roots of the genitals, the anal canal, the urethra, etc. [< Late Latin *perinēum* < Greek *perínaion*]

per·i·neu·ri·al (per′ə nu̇r′ē əl, -nyu̇r′-), *adj.* of or having to do with perineurium.

per·i·neu·ri·tis (per′ə nu̇ rī′tis, -nyu̇-), *n.* inflammation of the perineurium.

per·i·neu·ri·um (per′ə nu̇r′ē əm, -nyu̇r′-), *n., pl.* **-neu·ri·a** (-nu̇r′ē ə, -nyu̇r′-). the sheath of connective tissue surrounding a bundle of nerve fibers. [< New Latin *perineurium* < Greek *peri-* around + *neûron* nerve, sinew]

per·i·oc·u·lar (per′ē ok′yə lər), *adj.* situated about the eye or eyeball. The periocular space is the space between the eyeball and the orbit.

pe·ri·od (pir′ē əd), *n.* **1.** a portion of time having certain features or conditions: *the period of the Civil War. He visited us for a short period.* **2.** a portion of time marked off by events that happen again and again; time after which the same things begin to happen again: *A month, from new moon to new moon, is a period. The seventh satellite revolves in an eccentric orbit with a period of some 200 days* (Scientific American). **3.** one of the subdivisions of a geological era. A period is divided into epochs. **4.** a portion of a game during which there is actual play: *The game was won in the third period.* **5.** one of the portions of time into which a school day is divided. **6.** the time needed for a disease to run its course. **7.** the dot (.) marking the end of most sentences or showing an abbreviation. *Examples:* Mr., Dec., U.S. **8.** the pause at the end of a sentence. **9.** a complete sentence: *The orator spoke in stately periods.* **10.** an end; termination; final stage: *When some well-contested and decisive victory had put a period to the war* (Hawthorne). **11.** the time of menstruating; menstruation. **12.** *Physics.* the interval of time between the recurrence of like phases in a vibration or other periodic motion or phenomenon. **13.** a musical passage, usually a group of eight or sixteen measures divided into two or more complementary or contrasting phrases ending with a cadence. **14.** *Greek Prosody.* a metrical group of two or more cola. **15.** *Obsolete.* a goal: *This is the period of my ambition* (Shakespeare).

—*adj.* characteristic of a certain period of time: *period furniture, a period novel.*

—*interj. Informal.* that's it! that's final! *He said that the bank did not like to lend money for so short a time, and I said the bank didn't like to lend money, period* (Maclean's).

[< Latin *periodus* < Greek *períodos* cycle, circuit; (literally) a going around < *peri-* around + *hodós* a going, a way]

—**Syn.** *n.* **1.** term, interval.

➤ **period.** Whether it logically belongs there or not, a period is generally placed inside the final quotation marks: *"The longer you put it off," he said, "the harder it's going to be."*

per·i·o·date (pėr ī′ə dāt), *n.* a salt of periodic acid. [< *period*(ic acid) + *-ate*[2]]

pe·ri·od·ic (pir′ē od′ik), *adj.* **1.** occurring, appearing, or done again and again at regular intervals: *periodic attacks of malaria.* **2.** happening every now and then: *a periodic fit of clearing up one's desk.* **3.** having to do with a period: *The coming of the new moon is a periodic occurrence.* **4.** expressed in formal sentences whose meanings are not complete without the final words. [< Latin *periodicus* < Greek *periodikós* recurring at stated intervals < *períodos* period]

per·i·od·ic acid (pėr′ī od′ik), a colorless crystalline acid containing iodine with a valence of 7, its highest valence. *Formula:* H_5IO_6 [< *per-* + *iodic*]

pe·ri·od·i·cal (pir′ē od′ə kəl), *n.* a magazine that appears regularly, but less often than daily.

—*adj.* **1.** of or having to do with periodicals. **2.** published at regular intervals, less often than daily. **3.** periodic: *The periodical crises of the system [were becoming] less serious instead of more so* (Edmund Wilson).

periodical cicada, the seventeen-year locust.

pe·ri·od·i·cal·ism (pir′ē od′ə kə liz′əm), *n.* the work of writing for or publishing periodicals: *Her works emerge from the rapid oblivion of periodicalism by virtue of a vital element of power* (Harper's).

pe·ri·od·i·cal·ist (pir′ē od′ə kə list), *n.* a person who writes for or publishes a periodical.

pe·ri·od·i·cal·ly (pir′ē od′ə klē), *adv.* **1.** at regular intervals: *Sections of the track were periodically removed so that . . . hurdlers would have a clear lane to their finish line* (Time). **2.** every now and then. —**Syn. 2.** occasionally.

periodic chart, periodic table.

pe·ri·o·dic·i·ty (pir′ē ə dis′ə tē), *n., pl.* **-ties. 1.** periodic character; tendency to happen at regular intervals: *He would interest himself in the periodicity of the attacks, timing them by his watch* (Arnold Bennett). **2.** *Electricity.* frequency of alternation. **3.** the place occupied by a chemical element in the periodic table: *The Periodic Classification is universally attributed to Mendeléeff, yet the fundamental discovery of periodicity was made by Newlands* (Science News).

periodic law, the law that the properties of chemical elements change at regular intervals when the elements are arranged in the order of their atomic weights.

periodic sentence, a sentence not complete in meaning or grammatical structure without the final words. *Example:* Delighted with the invitation to visit the farm, we prepared to go.

periodic system, a classification of chemical elements based on the periodic law:

The biggest step in the theory of chemistry was the discovery of the periodic system which affords a natural classification of all the elements (H.R. Paneth).

periodic table, a table in which the chemical elements, arranged in the order of their atomic weights, are shown in related groups: *The position of an element in the periodic table determines the complexity of its atom* (Hardy and Perrin).

per·i·o·dide (pėr ī′ə dīd, -did), *n.* an iodide with the maximum proportion of iodine.

pe·ri·od·i·za·tion (pir′ē ə də zā′shən), *n.* the act of periodizing; division into historical periods: *One of Professor Mueller's most obvious examples of wrong-headed periodization is the equating of baroque architecture . . . with baroque music* (Winthrop Sargeant).

pe·ri·od·ize (pir′ē ə dīz), *v.t., v.i.,* **-ized, -iz·ing.** to divide (art, music, etc.) into historical periods: *For a long time, musical historians . . . tended to "periodize" music* (Winthrop Sargeant).

pe·ri·od·o·gram (pir′ē od′ə gram), *n.* a diagram exhibiting the periodic occurrence of certain phenomena.

per·i·o·don·tal (per′ē ə don′təl), *adj.* encasing or surrounding a tooth; peridental: *a periodontal membrane.* [< *peri-* around + Greek *odoús, odóntos* tooth + English *-al*[1]]

per·i·o·don·tia (per′ē ə don′shə, -shē ə), *n.* periodontics. [< New Latin *periodontia*]

per·i·o·don·tics (per′ē ə don′tiks), *n.* the branch of dentistry concerned with the supporting tissues of the teeth.

per·i·o·don·tist (per′ē ə don′tist), *n.* a dentist who specializes in periodontics: *The father had been advised by the dentist that he should see a periodontist for preventive gum and root work* (New York Times).

per·i·o·don·ti·tis (per′ē ō don tī′tis), *n.* inflammation of the supporting tissues of the teeth. [< *periodont*(al) + *-itis*]

per·i·o·don·tol·o·gy (per′ē ō don tol′ə jē), *n.* periodontics.

period piece, an object that belongs to a particular period of the past; a work of art, music, literature, etc., having an antique, archaic, or dated quality: *Perhaps it appealed to her for its Spartan, Victorian qualities or simply as a period piece* (Manchester Guardian Weekly).

per·i·os·te·al (per′ē os′tē əl), *adj.* of, having to do with, or connected with the periosteum.

per·i·os·te·um (per′ē os′tē əm), *n., pl.* **-te·a** (-tē ə). the dense fibrous membrane covering the surface of bones except at the joints. New bone tissue is produced from the inner layer. [< New Latin *periosteum* < Late Latin *periosteon* < Greek *periósteon* < *peri-* around + *ostéon* bone]

per·i·os·tit·ic (per′ē os tit′ik), *adj.* having to do with or affected with periostitis.

per·i·os·ti·tis (per′ē os tī′tis), *n.* inflammation of the periosteum.

per·i·o·tic (per′ē ō′tik, -ot′ik), *adj.* **1.** surrounding the ear. **2.** of or having to do with certain bones or bony elements of the skull that form a protective capsule for the internal ear. [< Greek *peri-* around + *oûs, ōtós* ear + English *-ic*]

per·i·os·tra·cum (per′ē os′trə kəm), *n.* the hard outer layer of the shell of most mollusks. [< New Latin *periostracum* < Greek *peri-* around + *óstrakon* shell]

Per·i·pa·tet·ic (per′ə pə tet′ik), *adj.* having to do with the philosophy of Aristotle, Greek philosopher, who taught while walking; Aristotelian. —*n.* one of Aristotle's disciples. [< Latin *peripatēticus* < Greek *peripatētikós*, ultimately < *peri-* around + *pateîn* to walk]

per·i·pa·tet·ic (per′ə pə tet′ik), *adj.* walking about; traveling from place to place; itinerant: *a peripatetic scissors grinder.* —*n.* a person who wanders or travels about from place to place: *The peripatetic who walked before her was a watchman in that neighbourhood* (Sir Richard Steele). [< *Peripatetic*] —**per′i·pa·tet′i·cal·ly,** *adv.* —**Syn.** *adj.* ambulatory.

per·i·pa·tet·i·cism (per′ə pə tet′ə siz əm), *n.* **1.** the habit or practice of walking about or traveling from place to place. **2.** peripatetic action, exercise, or behavior: *Now 80, she has produced a straightforward autobiography brimful of the peripateticisms of these many years* (New York Times). **3.** Usually, **Peripateticism.** the Peripatetic system of philosophy.

pe·rip·a·tus (pə rip′ə təs), *n.* any of certain primitive, invertebrate, wormlike animals, found in widely separated tropical regions, and having some characteristics of annelid worms and some of arthropods, including a cylindrical, unsegmented body, 15 to 43 pairs of short legs, and tracheae for respiration. They are sometimes classified as arthropods, sometimes as members of a separate phylum. [< New Latin *Peripatus* the genus name < Greek *peripátos* walking about < *peri-* around + *pateîn* to walk]

per·i·pe·te·ia (per′ə pə tē′ə), *n.* a sudden change in circumstances or fortune, as in a play or novel: *He has an absolute control of the peripeteia that Aristotle considered essential to drama* (Sunday Times). [< Greek *peripéteia* < *peri-* around + *píptein* fall]

pe·riph·er·al (pə rif′ər əl), *adj.* **1.** having to do with, situated in, or forming an outside boundary: *More houses and parks were to be seen in the peripheral areas of the city.* **2. a.** of the surface or outer part of a body; external. **b.** perceived or perceiving near the outer edges of the retina: *peripheral vision.* —**pe·riph′er·al·ly,** *adv.*

pe·riph·er·y (pə rif′ər ē), *n., pl.* **-er·ies. 1.** an outside boundary. **2.** *Geometry.* **a.** the circumference of a circle or other closed curve. **b.** the sum of the sides of a polygon. **c.** the length of, or the boundary line of, any closed plane figure. **3.** *Anatomy.* the region in which nerves end. [< Late Latin *periphería* < Greek *periphéreia* < *peri-* around + *phérein* to carry (off)]

per·i·phrase (per′ə frāz), *n., v.,* **-phrased, -phras·ing.** —*n.* a roundabout way of speaking: *"The wife of your father's brother" is a periphrase for "your aunt."* —*v.t.* to express in a roundabout way.

pe·riph·ra·sis (pə rif′rə sis), *n., pl.* **-ses** (-sēz). periphrase, a roundabout way of speaking. [< Latin *periphrasis* < Greek *períphrasis* < *periphrázein* speak in roundabout way < *peri-* around + *phrázein* speak]

per·i·phras·tic (per′ə fras′tik), *adj.* **1.** expressed in a roundabout way: *A periphrastic study in a worn-out poetical fashion* (T.S. Eliot). **2.** *Grammar.* formed by using auxiliaries or particles rather than inflection. *Examples: of John* rather than *John's* (periphrastic genitive); *did run* rather than *ran* (periphrastic conjugation). —**per′i·phras′ti·cal·ly,** *adv.*

per·i·plus (per′ə pləs), *n., pl.* **-pli. 1.** a voyage around a body of land or water. **2.** an account of such a voyage. [< Latin *periplūs* < Greek *períplous* a sailing around < *peri-* around + *plóos* voyage < *pleîn* to sail]

pe·rip·ter·al (pə rip′tər əl), *adj.* surrounded by a single row of columns, as a temple. [< French *périptère* (see PERIPTERY) + English *-al*[1]]

pe·rip·ter·y (pə rip′ter ē), *n., pl.* **-ter·ies.** the air immediately surrounding a flying or falling object, such as a bird, aircraft, or bomb, containing cyclic or vertical air disturbances. [< French *périptère* (ultimately < Greek *peri-* around + *pterón* wing) + English *-y*[3]]

pe·rique (pə rēk′), *n.* a strongly flavored, dark tobacco grown in Louisiana: *Perique, prized because of its rich flavor, is cured by putting the leaves under great pressure* (Roy Flannagan). [American English < Creole French *perique* (supposedly the pseudonym of Pierre Chenet, an Acadian, the first producer)]

per·i·sarc (per′ə särk), *n.* the external horny or chitinous covering of certain hydrozoans. [< Greek *peri-* around + *sárx, sarkós* flesh]

per·i·scope (per′ə skōp), *n.* **1.** an instrument that allows those in a submarine or trench to obtain a view of the surface. It is a tube with an arrangement of prisms or mirrors that reflect light rays down the tube. *The periscope works on the principle that the angle of reflection equals the angle of incidence.* **2.** a periscopic lens. [< Greek *peri-* around + *-scope*]

Periscope (def. 1)

per·i·scop·ic (per′ə skop′ik), *adj.* **1.** giving distinct vision obliquely as well as in a direct line, as a lens. **2.** of or having to do with periscopes.

per·i·scop·i·cal (per′ə skop′ə kəl), *adj.* periscopic.

per·i·se·le·ni·um (per′ə si lē′nē əm), *n.* the point in an elliptical orbit around the moon that is closest to the moon. [< *peri-* near + New Latin *selenium* < Greek *selḗnē* moon]

per·ish (per′ish), *v.i.* **1.** to be destroyed; die: *Soldiers perish in battle. Flowers perish when frost comes. I felt ready to perish with cold.* **2.** to come to ruin morally or spiritually; come to an end: *Except ye repent, ye shall all likewise perish* (Luke 13:3). —*v.t.* **1.** *Dialect.* to injure severely. **2.** *Archaic.* to put an end to; destroy; kill: *We charm man's life and do not perish it* (Thomas Hood). [< Old French *periss-*, stem of *perir* < Latin *perīre* < *per-* (pejorative) + *īre* go] —**Syn.** *v.i.* **1.** See **die.**

per·ish·a·bil·i·ty (per′i shə bil′ə tē), *n.* perishable quality.

per·ish·a·ble (per′i shə bəl), *adj.* **1.** liable to spoil or decay: *Fruit is perishable.* **2.** liable to perish; that perishes: *the perishable enthusiasm of youth.*
—*n.* **perishables,** something perishable.
—**per′ish·a·ble·ness,** *n.*

per·ish·er (per′ish ər), *n.* *British Slang.* annoying fellow; rascal.

per·ish·ing (per′ish ing), *adj.* **1.** that perishes. **2.** deadly. **3.** *British Informal.* beastly; darned: *Hold this perishing split pin* (Punch).
—*adv.* excessively; extremely: *a perishing cold morning.* —**per′ish·ing·ly,** *adv.*

per·i·sphere (per′ə sfir), *n.* a large steel structure in the shape of a sphere, a feature of several world's fairs.

per·i·spore (per′ə spôr, -spōr), *n.* the outer membrane or covering of a spore. [< *peri-* around + *spore*]

pe·ris·sad (pə ris′ad), *n.* an atom or element whose valence is expressed by an odd number. —*adj.* having the valence expressed by an odd number. [< Greek *perissós* odd, uneven]

pe·ris·so·dac·tyl or **pe·ris·so·dac·tyle** (pə ris′ə dak′təl), *Zoology.* —*adj.* having an uneven number of toes. —*n.* any of a large group of quadruped mammals including the horses, tapirs, and rhinoceroses, characterized by an uneven number of hoofed toes, the third being the largest and sometimes the only functional one. [< New Latin *Perissodactyla* the order name < Greek *perissós* uneven + *dáktylos* a toe]

pe·ris·so·dac·ty·lous (pə ris′ə dak′tə ləs). *adj.* perissodactyl.

per·i·stal·sis (per′ə stal′sis), *n., pl.* **-ses** (-sēz). a movement in the wall of a hollow organ by which it propels its contents onward, as the wavelike, circular contractions of the alimentary canal. [< New Latin *peristalsis* < Greek *peristaltikós*; see PERISTALTIC]

per·i·stal·tic (per′ə stal′tik), *adj.* of or having to do with peristalsis: *As the struggling fly reaches the throat, the muscles carry it down to the esophagus, which carries it on to the stomach by means of peristaltic contractions* (A.M. Winchester). [< Greek *peristaltikós* contracting around < *peristéllein* to compress; (originally) wrap around < *peri-* around + *stéllein* to wrap, bind, compress] —**per′i·stal′ti·cal·ly,** *adv.*

pe·ris·te·ron·ic (pə ris′tə ron′ik), *adj.* of or having to do with pigeons. [< Greek *peristerṓn* dove-cote (< *peristerá* pigeon) + English *-ic*]

per·i·stome (per′ə stōm), *n.* **1.** *Botany.* the one or two rings or fringes of toothlike appendages around the mouth of the capsule or theca in mosses. **2.** *Zoology.* any special structure or set of parts around the mouth or oral opening in various invertebrates. [< New Latin *peristoma* < Greek *peristómion* the region around the mouth (of anything); epiglottis < *peri-* around + *stóma* mouth]

per·i·streph·ic (per′ə stref′ik), *adj.* turning; rotating.

per·i·sty·lar (per′ə stī′lər), *adj.* of, having to do with, or like a peristyle.

per·i·style (per′ə stīl), *n.* **1.** a row of columns surrounding a building, court, or the like. **2.** a space or court so enclosed. [<

French *péristyle,* learned borrowing from Latin *peristȳlon,* ultimately < Greek *peri-* around + *stȳlos* pillar] —**Syn. 1.** colonnade.

per·i·the·ci·al (per′ə thē′shē əl, -sē-), *adj.* of or having to do with the perithecium.

per·i·the·ci·um (per′ə thē′shē əm, -sē-), *n., pl.* **-ci·a** (-sē ə). the fruit of certain fungi, usually a rounded or flask-shaped receptacle with a narrow opening, enclosing the asci or spore sacs. [< New Latin *perithecium* Greek *peri-* around + *thēkē* case, receptacle]

per·i·to·nae·um (per′ə tə nē′əm), *n., pl.* **-naea** (-nē′ə). peritoneum.

per·i·to·ne·al or **per·i·to·nae·al** (per′ə-tə nē′əl), *adj.* of the peritoneum.

per·i·to·ne·um (per′ə tə nē′əm), *n., pl.* **-ne·a** (-nē′ə). the thin membrane that lines the walls of the abdomen and covers the organs in it. The peritoneum is a transparent structure with many folds, such as the omentum and mesentery. [< Late Latin *peritonaeum* < Greek *peritónaion* stretched over < *peri-* around + *teínein* to stretch]

per·i·to·ni·tis (per′ə tə nī′tis), *n.* inflammation of the peritoneum. [< Greek *peritónaion* (see PERITONEUM) + English *-itis*]

pe·rit·ri·cha (pə rit′rə kə), *n.pl.* bacteria with the cilia (organs of locomotion) around the entire body. [< New Latin *Peritricha* the order name < Greek *peri-* around + *thríx, trichós* hair]

pe·rit·ri·chous (pə rit′rə kəs), *adj.* **1.** having a band of cilia around the body. **2.** of or having to do with peritricha.

pe·ri·tus (pe rē′tůs), *n., pl.* **-ti** (-tē). *Latin.* (in the Roman Catholic Church) a theological advisor or consultant: *Karl Rahner, the celebrated Austrian theologian . . . served as a Council peritus during the first session of the Council* (Xavier Rynne).

per·i·vas·cu·lar (per′ə vas′kyə lər), *adj.* surrounding a blood vessel: *perivascular areas of the heart.*

per·i·vis·cer·al (per′ə vis′ər əl), *adj.* surrounding and containing viscera. The perivisceral cavity is the general body cavity containing the alimentary canal and its appendages.

per·i·wig (per′ə wig), *n., v.,* **-wigged, wigging.** —*n.* a wig: *To church; and with my mourning, very handsome, and new periwig, make a great show* (Samuel Pepys). —*v.t.* to dress or cover with a wig: *the periwigged . . . gentleman of the artist's legend* (Hawthorne) [< earlier *perewyke* < French *perruque;* influenced by *wig.* Doublet of PERUKE.] —**Syn.** *n.* peruke.

per·i·win·kle[1] (per′ə wing′kəl), *n.* **1.** any of a group of usually low, trailing evergreen plants of the dogbane family, with blue, white, or purplish flowers. The American periwinkle is called myrtle. **2.** a light-blue color: *Navy, periwinkle, and beige are the most-sought-after colors in dress and coat ensembles* (New York Times). [alteration of Middle English *perwynke,* Old English *pervince* < Latin *pervinca* < *pervincīre* fasten around < *peri-* around + *vincīre* to bind; influenced by *periwinkle*[2]]

per·i·win·kle[2] (per′ə wing′kəl), *n.* **1.** a sea snail with a thick, cone-shaped, spiral shell, used for food in Europe. **2.** the shell of this snail or of certain other marine univalve mollusks. **3.** a winkle. [origin uncertain. Compare Old English *pīnewincle* < Latin *pīna* mussel < Greek *pīnē.*]

Common Periwinkle[2] (def. 1) (diameter, ¾ in.)

per·jink (pər jingk′), *adj. Scottish.* exact or precise; neat or trim. [origin unknown]

per·jure (pėr′jər), *v.t.,* **-jured, -jur·ing.** to make (oneself) guilty of perjury.

perjure oneself, to lie under oath; swear falsely; swear that something is true which one knows to be false: *A person who has . . . perjured himself [is] the bane of society* (Joseph Priestley).

[Middle English *parjuren* < Old French *parjurer,* learned borrowing from Latin *perjūrāre* < *per-* (pejorative) + *jūrāre* to swear < *jūs, jūris* right, justice]

per·jured (pėr′jərd), *adj.* **1.** guilty of perjury: *a perjured witness.* **2.** characterized by or involving perjury: *perjured evidence.*

be perjured, to be guilty or proven guilty of perjury: *Keep you that ye be not perjured and let truth be always in your mouth* (Earl Rivers). —**Syn. 1.** forsworn.

per·jur·er (pėr′jər ər), *n.* a person who commits perjury.

per·ju·ri·ous (pər jůr′ē əs), *adj.* perjured. —**per·ju′ri·ous·ly,** *adv.*

per·ju·ry (pėr′jər ē), *n., pl.* **-ries. 1.** the act of swearing that something is true which one knows to be false. **2.** a violation of a promise made on oath to do or not to do something: *If thou swear'st, Thou mayst prove false; at lovers' perjuries, They say, Jove laughs* (Shakespeare). [< Anglo-French *perjurie* < Latin *perjūrium* < *perjūrāre* perjure]

perk[1] (pėrk), *v.i.* **1.** to move, lift the head, or act briskly or saucily: *. . . their round, little-eyed meek faces perking sidewise* (William Hone). **2.** to put oneself forward briskly or assertively. **3.** *British.* to preen, as before a mirror: *You'd be perking at the glass the next minute* (George Eliot). —*v.t.* to raise smartly or briskly: *The squirrel, flippant, pert . . . whisks his brush, And perks his ears* (William Cowper).

perk out, to make trim or smart: *She is all perked out in her Sunday clothes.*

perk up, a. to raise the spirits; brighten up: *The sick girl perked up when she received the flowers.* **b.** to make trim or smart: *You are not quite a woman yourself—though you perk yourself up so daintily* (J.P. Kennedy). **c.** to liven up; become brisk: *Demand for lead has perked up amid reports that the price might move up again* (Wall Street Journal).

—*adj.* **1.** saucy; pert; cocky. **2.** in good spirits. **3.** spruce; smart.

[Middle English *perken;* origin uncertain]

perk[2] (pėrk), *v.t., v.i. Informal.* to percolate (coffee): *Pour cold water, add coffee, plug in: Perk automatically* (Wall Street Journal). [short for *percolate*]

perk[3] (pėrk), *n. British Informal.* perquisite: "*perks for workers regardless of cost*" *has put many firms out of business* (Sydney Morning Herald).

perk·i·ly (pėr′kə lē), *adv.* in a perky manner: *Indeed, the minute words fail, author [Gore] Vidal perkily rushes in with a new sound effect* (Time).

perk·i·ness (pėr′kē nis), *n.* perky quality.

perk·y (pėr′kē), *adj.,* **perk·i·er, perk·i·est.** smart; brisk; saucy; pert: *The suits include a perky one of gray flannel with a nipped-in jacket* (New Yorker). —**Syn.** jaunty.

per·lite (pėr′līt), *n.* a form of obsidian or other vitreous rock broken up by minute spherical cracks; pearlite. [< French *perlite* < German *Perlit* < *Perle* pearl + *-it* -ite[1]]

per·lit·ic (pėr lit′ik), *adj.* of or having to do with perlite.

Per·lon (pėr′lon), *n. Trademark,* a synthetic fiber similar to but tougher than nylon, manufactured in Germany.

per·lus·trate (pėr lus′trāt), *v.t.,* **-trat·ed, -trat·ing.** to travel through and view; survey or inspect thoroughly: *Mr. Asterias perlustrated the sea-coast for several days* (Thomas L. Peacock). [< Latin *perlūstrāre* (with English *-ate*[1]) < *per-* through + *lūstrāre* to travel, survey]

per·lus·tra·tion (pėr′lus trā′shən), *n.* the act of perlustrating; survey; inspection.

perm (pėrm), *British Informal.* —*n.* a permanent wave: *They arrived in the morning with scarves tied over their perms* (Sunday Times). —*v.t.* to give a permanent wave to: *Have you just had your hair permed, dear?* (Punch).

perm., permanent.

per M, per thousand.

perm·a·frost (pėr′mə frôst′, -frost′), *n.* a layer of permanently frozen soil and other deposits, sometimes reaching a depth of a thousand feet or more, found near the surface throughout most of the arctic regions: *There, well preserved by the cold of the permafrost, they store all their perishable foods* (Edmonton Journal). [apparently < *perma-* (nent) + *frost*]

Perm·al·loy (pėr′mə loi), *n. Trademark.* any of a group of alloys consisting of iron and nickel with small amounts of various other metals, noted for high magnetic permeability. [apparently < *perm*(anent) + *alloy*]

per·ma·nence (pėr′mə nəns), *n.* a being permanent; lasting quality or condition: *the permanence of the sun.* —**Syn.** durability.

per·ma·nen·cy (pėr′mə nən sē), *n., pl.* **-cies. 1.** permanence: *the just announced permanency of several big military establishments* (Wall Street Journal). **2.** a permanent person, thing, or position: *Inspectors of police [are] required by the government of Kenya for one tour of three years with possibility of permanency* (London News Chronicle).

per·ma·nent (pėr′mə nənt), *adj.* **1.** lasting; intended to last; not for a short time only: *a permanent filling in a tooth. After doing odd jobs for a week, he got a permanent position as office boy.* **2.** *Botany.* persistent. —*n. Informal.* a permanent wave. [< Latin *permanēns, -entis* staying to the end, present participle of *permanēre* < *per-* through + *manēre* to stay] —**per′ma·nent·ly,** *adv.* —**Syn.** *adj.* **1.** abiding, enduring. See **lasting.** —**Ant.** *adj.* **1.** temporary.

permanent magnet, a magnet whose property continues after the magnetizing current has ceased to pass through it: *Permanent magnets are used in thermostats, television sets, and guided missiles* (Wall Street Journal).

permanent magnetism, magnetism which continues after the magnetizing influence has been withdrawn.

permanent wave, a wave lasting several months, put in the hair by any of a number of special processes: *Permanent waves have become almost as accepted a part of American beauty routine as lipstick* (Sidonie M. Gruenberg).

permanent way, the roadbed, track, etc., of a railroad, as distinguished from a temporary way used in construction, etc.: *We had only to walk up the permanent way between the two trains and get in from the wrong side* (Geoffrey Household).

per·man·ga·nate (pər mang′gə nāt), *n.* a salt of an acid containing manganese. A solution of potassium permanganate is used as an antiseptic.

per·man·gan·ic acid (pėr′man gan′ik), an acid that is unstable except in dilute solutions. Its aqueous solution is used as an oxidizing agent. *Formula:* $HMnO_4$

per·me·a·bil·i·ty (pėr′mē ə bil′ə tē), *n.* **1.** state of being permeable: *The damage may be in the form of changing the permeability of cell walls* (Science News Letter). **2.** *Physics.* the ratio of magnetic induction to the intensity of the magnetic field: *The permeability depends on the past history (magnetically speaking) of the iron* (Sears and Zemansky). **3.** the amount of gas diffused through the fabric of an airship in a given period of time.

per·me·a·ble (pėr′mē ə bəl), *adj.* that can be permeated: *A sponge is permeable by water.* [< Latin *permeābilis* < *permeāre;* see PERMEATE] —**Syn.** pervious.

per·me·ance (pėr′mē əns), *n.* **1.** a permeating. **2.** *Physics.* the reciprocal of the reluctance of a magnetic circuit.

per·me·ant (pėr′mē ənt), *adj.* permeating.

per·me·ate (pėr′mē āt), *v.,* **-at·ed, -at·ing.** —*v.t.* **1.** to spread through the whole of; pass through; soak through: *The odor of smoke permeated the house.* **2.** to penetrate: *Water will easily permeate a cotton dress.* —*v.i.* to diffuse itself. [< Latin *permeāre* (with English *-ate*[1]) < *per-* through + *meāre* to pass] —**Syn.** *v.t.* **1.** pervade, saturate.

per·me·a·tion (pėr′mē ā′shən), *n.* a permeating; penetration; diffusion through; saturation.

per·me·a·tive (pėr′mē ā′tiv), *adj.* tending to permeate.

per men·sem (pər men′sem), *Latin.* by the month.

Per·mi·an (pėr′mē ən), *n.* **1.** a geological period, the last of the Paleozoic era, after the Pennsylvanian and before the Triassic. It was characterized by the end of the trilobites, the spread of the reptiles, and the occurrence of ice-sheet glaciation in Australia, India, and South Africa. **2.** the rocks formed in this period. —*adj.* of this period or these rocks. [< *Perm,* a former province in Russia, where such strata are found + *-ian*]

per mill or **per mil** (pər mil′), by the thousand; in thousands.

per·mil·lage (pər mil′ij), *n.* rate per thousand.

per·mis·si·bil·i·ty (pər mis′ə bil′ə tē), *n.* the quality of being permissible; allowableness.

per·mis·si·ble (pər mis′ə bəl), *adj.* that can be permitted; allowable. —**Syn.** admissible.

per·mis·si·bly (pər mis′ə blē), *adv.* in a permissible way; as may be permitted; allowably.

per·mis·sion (pər mish′ən), *n.* a permitting; consent; leave: *He asked the teacher's permission to go home early.* [< Latin *per-*

missiō, -ōnis < *permittere* to permit] —**Syn.** sufferance, authorization, sanction. —**Ant.** prohibition.

per·mis·sive (pər mis′iv), *adj.* **1.** permitting; allowing; not forbidding: *Not a positive, but a permissive command* (Henry More). *Permissive fathers in the group were . . . persuasive and efficient* (Newsweek). *A discussion of pragmatism was naturally related to their own anxieties about permissive education* (Harper's). **2.** that may or may not be done; permitted; allowed; optional: *Mr. Harriman . . . emphasized that the legislation was "permissive" and not binding upon the city* (New York Times). —**per·mis′sive·ly,** *adv.* —**per·mis′sive·ness,** *n.*

per·mit (*v.* pər mit′; *n.* pėr′mit, pər mit′), *v.*, **-mit·ted, -mit·ting,** *n.* —*v.t.* **1. a.** to allow (a person, etc.) to do something; give leave to: *Permit me to explain. Mr. Nash permitted us to swim in his pond.* **b.** to provide opportunity for; allow: *vents permitting the escape of gases, conditions permitting no delay.* **2.** to let (something) be done or occur; authorize: *The law permits smoking in this store. It is not permitted unto them to speak* (I Corinthians 14:34). **3.** *Obsolete.* to hand over or give up. —*v.i.* to give leave or opportunity; allow: *I will go on Monday, the weather permitting.*

permit of, to admit of: *rules that permit of no exceptions.*

—*n.* **1.** a formal written order giving permission to do something: *a permit to fish or hunt.* **2.** permission.

[< Latin *permittere* to allow < *per-* through + *mittere* send]

—**Syn.** *v.t.* **1. a. Permit, allow** mean to let someone or something do something. **Permit** implies willingness or consent: *His parents permitted him to enlist when he was seventeen.* **Allow** means not to forbid or prevent, without necessarily giving permission or approval: *That teacher allows too much noise in the room.*

per·mit·tee (pėr′mə tē′), *n.* a person to whom a permit is granted.

per·mit·ter (pər mit′ər), *n.* a person who permits.

per·mit·tiv·i·ty (per′mə tiv′ə tē), *n. Electricity.* dielectric constant or coefficient.

Permo-, *combining form.* Permian; Permian and ____: *Permo-Carboniferous glaciation = Permian and Carboniferous glaciation.*

per·mut·a·ble (pər myü′tə bəl), *adj.* **1.** interchangeable. **2.** liable to change; changeable.

per·mu·tate (pėr′myə tāt, pər myü′-), *v.*, **-tat·ed, -tat·ing.** —*v.t.* **1.** to change; alter. **2.** to exchange; change the order of; go through the permutations of. —*v.i.* to be changed; be altered. [< Latin *permūtātus,* past participle of *permūtāre* permute]

per·mu·ta·tion (pėr′myə tā′shən), *n.* **1.** a change from one state, position, order, etc., to another; alteration: *A good deal of the score of "Wonderful Town" . . . is based on various permutations of the simple interval of a fifth* (New Yorker). *After trying hundreds of permutations of nutrient media we hit on several which suited the microorganisms* (Hutner and McLaughlin). **2.** *Mathematics.* **a.** a changing of the order of a set of things; arranging in different orders. **b.** such an arrangement or group: *The permutations of a, b, and c are abc, acb, bac, bca, cab, cba.* [< Latin *permūtātiō, -ōnis* < *permūtāre* permute] —**Syn. 1.** mutation, modification.

per·mute (pər myüt′), *v.t.*, **-mut·ed, -mut·ing. 1.** to change; alter. **2.** *Mathematics.* to change the order of (numbers, letters, etc.); subject to permutation. [< Latin *permūtāre* < *per-* throughout + *mūtāre* to change] —**per·mut′er,** *n.*

pern (pėrn), *n.* any of various Old World hawks of moderate size that eat chiefly insects. [< New Latin *Pernis* the genus name, adaptation of Greek *ptérnis* a kind of hawk]

Common Pern or honey buzzard (2 ft. long)

per·ni·cious (pər nish′əs), *adj.* **1.** that will destroy or ruin; causing great harm or damage: *Gambling is a pernicious habit.* **2.** fatal; deadly. **3.** wicked; villainous: *O most pernicious woman!* (Shakespeare). [< Middle French *pernicieux* (with English *-ous*) destructive, learned borrowing from Latin *perniciōsus* < *perniciēs* destruction < *per-* completely + *necāre* to kill < *nex, necis* death] —**per·ni′cious·ly,** *adv.* —**per·ni′cious·ness,** *n.* —**Syn. 1.** injurious, noxious.

pernicious anemia, a very severe form of anemia in which the number of red corpuscles in the blood decreases. It is accompanied by paleness, fatigue, and digestive and nervous disturbances.

per·nick·e·ti·ness (pər nik′ə tē nis), *n. Informal.* fastidiousness; fussiness.

per·nick·e·ty (pər nik′ə tē), *adj. Informal.* **1.** overly fastidious; fussy: *It is clear that the planning, no matter how grandiose, is also much too pernickety* (London Times). **2.** requiring precise and careful handling; ticklish; persnickety. [extension of Scottish *pernicky;* origin uncertain]

Per·nod or **per·nod** (per nō′), *n.* a green absinthe made in France: *I went in, sat at an unset table that stood by itself, and ordered a Pernod* (New Yorker).

per·o·ne (per′ə nē), *n. Anatomy.* the fibula. [< New Latin *perone* < Greek *perónē* fibula; (originally) buckle, brooch < *peírein* to pierce]

per·o·ne·al (per′ə nē′əl), *adj. Anatomy.* **1.** of or having to do with the fibula. **2.** in the region of the fibula. [< *perone* + *-al*[1]]

Pe·ron·ism (pə rō′niz əm), *n.* the beliefs, policies, and government of, or typical of, Juan Perón, former president of Argentina: *The threat of Peronism to the Western Hemisphere apparently has ended* (New York Times).

Pe·ro·nis·mo (pe′rō nēz′mō), *n. Spanish.* Peronism: *The schools . . . must teach the child the mysticism, the soul and the sentiment of Peronismo* (Time).

Pe·ron·ist (pə rō′nist), *adj., n.* Peronista.

Pe·ro·nis·ta (pe′rō nēs′tä), *Spanish.* —*adj.* of or having to do with Juan Perón or Peronism: *the Peronista Party, Peronista leaders. The Argentine tradition until the Peronista experiment was a long one of economic liberalism* (Atlantic). —*n.* a supporter of Perón or Peronism: *About an equal number of Churchmen lined up . . . confronting the jeering Peronistas* (New York Times).

per·o·rate (per′ə rāt), *v.i.*, **-rat·ed, -rat·ing. 1.** to make a formal conclusion to a speech. **2.** to speak at length; make a speech; harangue.

[< Latin *perōrāre* (with English *-ate*[1]) < *per-* completely + *ōrāre* speak formally] —**Syn. 2.** descant, expatiate.

per·o·ra·tion (per′ə rā′shən), *n.* **1.** the last part of an oration or discussion. It sums up what has been said and is usually delivered with considerable force. **2.** a rhetorical outburst: *a fiery peroration.* **3.** a discourse. [< Latin *perōrātiō, -ōnis* < *perōrāre* perorate]

per·o·ra·tion·al (per′ə rā′shə nəl), *adj.* of or having to do with a peroration.

per·ox·id (pə rok′sid), *n.* peroxide.

per·ox·i·dase (pə rok′sə dās, -dāz), *n.* an enzyme found in many plants, leucocytes, and bacteria, which catalyzes the transfer of oxygen from organic peroxides to another substance which is able to receive it: *Iodine is liberated from iodides in the presence of peroxidase, manganese, and oxygen* (Beaumont and Dodds).

per·ox·ide (pə rok′sīd), *n., v.*, **-id·ed, -id·ing.** —*n.* **1.** an oxide of a given element or radical that contains the greatest, or an unusual, amount of oxygen. **2.** hydrogen peroxide. —*v.t.* to bleach (hair) by applying hydrogen peroxide. [< *per-* + *oxide*]

per·ox·y·ac·id (pə rok′sē as′id), *n.* an acid in which the -OH group has been replaced by the -OOH group. [< *per-* + *oxy*(gen) + *acid*]

per·ox·y·bo·rate (pə rok′sē bôr′āt, -bōr′-), *n.* a salt of peroxyboric acid; perborate.

per·ox·y·bo·ric acid (pə rok′sē bôr′ik, -bōr′-), perboric acid.

per·pend[1] (pėr′pənd), *n.* a large stone passing entirely through a wall so as to face on both sides and form a border. [Middle English *parpend* < Old French *parpein, perpein* < Vulgar Latin *perpetāneus* continuous < Latin *perpes;* see PERPETUAL]

per·pend[2] (pər pend′), *Archaic.* —*v.t.* to weigh mentally; ponder; consider: *Perpend my words* (Shakespeare). —*v.i.* to ponder; reflect: *Therefore perpend, my princess, and give ear* (Shakespeare). [< Latin *perpendere* < *per-* thoroughly + *pendere* ponder; (literally) to weigh. Compare PENSIVE.]

per·pen·dic·u·lar (pėr′pən dik′yə lər), *adj.* **1.** standing straight up; upright. **2.** very steep; precipitous: *a perpendicular cliff.* **3.** *Geometry.* at right angles. **4.** having to do with the English Gothic style of architecture, characterized by emphasis on vertical lines, especially in window tracery.

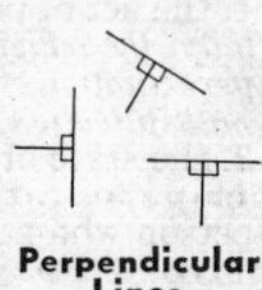

Perpendicular Lines (def. 3)

—*n.* **1.** a perpendicular line or plane. **2. a.** a perpendicular position: *Springing to her accustomed perpendicular like a bowed sapling* (Thomas Hardy). **b.** a steep or precipitous slope. **3.** moral uprightness; rectitude. **4.** an instrument or appliance for indicating the vertical line from any point, as a plumb rule.

[< Old French *perpendiculer,* learned borrowing from Latin *perpendiculāris* < *perpendiculum* plumb line, ultimately < *per-* through + *pendēre* to hang] —**per′pen·dic′u·lar·ly,** *adv.*

—**Syn.** *adj.* **1.** erect.

per·pen·dic·u·lar·i·ty (pėr′pən dik′yə lar′ə tē), *n.* **1.** a vertical or upright position; verticality. **2.** an upright attitude or posture. **3.** *Geometry.* the position or direction at right angles to a given line, surface, or plane.

per·pent (pėr′pənt), *n.* perpend[1].

per·pe·trate (pėr′pə trāt), *v.*, **-trat·ed, -trat·ing,** *adj.* —*v.t.* **1.** to do or commit (a crime, fraud, trick, or anything bad or foolish): *The king's brother perpetrated the cruel murder of the prince.* **2.** *Informal.* to do or make (something implied to be bad or atrocious): *to perpetrate a pun. Sir Philip induced two of his sisters to perpetrate a duet* (Charlotte Brontë). —*adj. Obsolete.* perpetrated.

[< Latin *perpetrāre* (with English *-ate*[1]) < *per-* (intensive) + *patrāre* perform, accomplish]

per·pe·tra·tion (pėr′pə trā′shən), *n.* **1.** the act of perpetrating. **2.** something perpetrated; an evil action; atrocity.

per·pe·tra·tor (pėr′pə trā′tər), *n.* a person who perpetrates or commits an evil deed.

per·pet·u·a·ble (pər pech′ů ə bəl), *adj.* that can be perpetuated.

per·pet·u·al (pər pech′ů əl), *adj.* **1.** lasting forever; eternal: *the perpetual hills.* **2.** lasting throughout life; ceasing only at death: *a perpetual income.* **3.** never ceasing; continuous: *a perpetual stream of visitors. He moved in an atmosphere of perpetual ambush* (Rudyard Kipling). **4.** *Horticulture.* being in bloom more or less continuously throughout the year or the season.

—*n.* **1.** any of several continuously-blooming hybrid varieties of rose. **2.** a perennial. **3.** a perpetual bond.

[< Old French *perpetuel,* learned borrowing from Latin *perpetuālis* < *perpetuus* continuous < *perpes, -etis* lasting < *per-* through + root of *petere* seek] —**per·pet′u·al·ness,** *n.*

—**Syn.** *adj.* **1.** permanent, enduring, everlasting. **3.** constant.

perpetual bond, a bond in which the debtor agrees to pay a certain annual interest without time limit, and assumes no obligation to repay the principal at a maturity date.

perpetual calendar, a calendar to show the day of the week on which a date will fall in any given year.

per·pet·u·al·ly (pər pech′ů ə lē), *adv.* forever.

perpetual motion, the motion of a hypothetical machine which being once set in motion should go on forever by creating its own energy, unless it were stopped by some external force or the wearing out of the machine: *Only in the nineteenth century was science able to frame an indictment of perpetual motion and to pronounce it an impossibility* (Science News).

per·pet·u·ance (pər pech′ů əns), *n.* perpetuation.

per·pet·u·ate (*v.* pər pech′ů āt; *adj.* pər pech′ů it), *v.*, **-at·ed, -at·ing,** *adj.* —*v.t.* to make perpetual; keep from being forgotten: *The Washington Monument was built to perpetuate the memory of a great man.* —*adj.* made perpetual.

[< Latin *perpetuāre* (with English *-ate*[1]) < *perpetuus;* see PERPETUAL]

per·pet·u·a·tion (pər pech′ü ā′shən), *n.* **1.** the act of perpetuating: *While fundamentally the chief role of reproduction is the perpetuation of the species, it also accomplishes multiplication* (Harbaugh and Goodrich). **2.** the state of being perpetuated.

per·pet·u·a·tor (pər pech′ü ā′tər), *n.* a person who perpetuates.

per·pe·tu·i·ty (pėr′pə tü′ə tē, -tyü′-), *n., pl.* **-ties. 1.** a being perpetual; existence forever: *A third attribute of the king's majesty is his perpetuity . . . The king never dies* (William Blackstone). **2.** a perpetual possession, tenure, or position. **3.** *Law.* **a.** (of an estate) the quality or condition of being inalienable perpetually or longer than the legal time limit. **b.** the estate so restricted: *A perpetuity can spend only the income from its assets* (World Book Encyclopedia). **4.** a perpetual annuity.

in perpetuity, forever: *The idea was not for the United States to subsidize their armed forces in perpetuity* (Wall Street Journal).

[< Old French *perpetuite,* learned borrowing from Latin *perpetuitās* < *perpetuus;* see PERPETUAL]

—**Syn. 1.** endlessness, eternity.

per·pe·tu·um mo·bi·le (pər pet′yu̇ əm mob′ə lē), perpetual motion: *George Balanchine has set three of his most enchanting ballerinas to moving in a kind of perpetuum mobile* (New York Times).

per·plex (pər pleks′), *v.t.* **1.** to trouble with doubt; puzzle; bewilder: *This problem is hard enough to perplex even the teacher.* **2.** to make difficult to understand or settle; confuse: *difficulties that must have perplexed the engagement and retarded the marriage* (Jane Austen).

[originally, adjective < Latin *perplexus* confused, involved < *per-* completely + *plexus* entangled, past participle of *plectere* to intertwine] —**Syn. 1.** mystify, nonplus. See **puzzle. 2.** complicate, muddle.

per·plexed (pər plekst′), *adj.* **1.** bewildered; puzzled. **2.** intricate; involved; complicated: *He had engaged Dominie Sampson's assistance to disentangle some perplexed accounts* (Scott).

per·plex·ed·ly (pər plek′sid lē), *adv.* in a perplexed manner.

per·plex·ing (pər plek′sing), *adj.* that perplexes; causing perplexity. —**per·plex′ing·ly,** *adv.*

per·plex·i·ty (pər plek′sə tē), *n., pl.* **-ties. 1.** a not knowing what to do or how to act; perplexed condition; confusion; being puzzled: *John's perplexity was so great that he asked many persons for advice.* **2.** something that perplexes: *My mind is disturbed with a thousand perplexities of doubt* (Samuel Johnson). [< Late Latin *perplexitās* < Latin *perplexus* perplex] —**Syn. 1.** bewilderment, distraction.

per·qui·site (pėr′kwə zit), *n.* **1. a.** anything received for work besides the regular pay: *The maid had the old dresses of her mistress as a perquisite.* **b.** a tip expected as a matter of course for doing one's job. **2.** the income from any job, office, etc.; pay; wages. **3.** casual profits that come to the lord of a manor, in addition to his regular annual revenue. **4.** something advantageous specially belonging: *perquisites of trade. Undergraduate elections are important events . . . and the winners enjoy many lucrative perquisites* (New Yorker). **5.** *Obsolete.* an adjunct: *My wife [is] very fine today in her new suit of laced cuffs and perquisites* (Samuel Pepys).

[< Medieval Latin *perquisitum* a thing gained; profit < Latin *perquīsītum* a thing sought after, neuter past participle of *perquīrere* to seek, ask for < *per-* (intensive) + *quaerere* to seek]

—**Syn. 1. a.** bonus.

per·qui·si·tion (pėr′kwə zish′ən), *n.* a diligent or thorough search or inquiry.

per·ron (per′ən), *n. Architecture.* **1.** a flight of steps ascending to a platform, as at an entrance, or to a terrace. **2.** a platform at the entrance of a large building, with steps to the ground. **3.** a large block of stone used as a platform. [< Old French *perron,* perhaps < Vulgar Latin *petrō, -onis* (augmentative) < Latin *petra* rock < Greek *pétrā* stone]

Perron (def. 1) at Palace of Fontainebleau, France

per·ro·quet (per′ə ket), *n.* parrakeet.

per·ruque (pə rük′), *n.* peruke: *But his only costly gift was a sixty-thousand-franc Paris wig, perruques having just come into style* (New Yorker). [< Middle French *perruque;* see PERUKE]

per·ru·quier (pe rʏ kyā′; *Anglicized* pə rü′kē ər), *n. French.* a wigmaker.

per·ry (per′ē), *n., pl.* **-ries.** *British.* a beverage somewhat resembling hard cider, made from fermented pear juice. [Middle English *pereye* < Old French *pere,* ultimately Latin *pirum* pear]

pers., 1. person. **2.** personal.

Pers., 1. Persia. **2.** Persian.

per·salt (pėr′sôlt′), *n. Chemistry.* a salt formed by the combination of an acid with the peroxide of a metal; salt of a peracid.

perse (pėrs), *adj., n.* **1.** dark blue; purplish-black. **2.** *Archaic.* blue; bluish; blue-gray. [< Old French *perse,* perhaps < Late Latin *persus* blue]

per se (pėr sē′, sā′), *Latin.* by itself; in itself; intrinsically: *Disarmament, per se, will not prevent war* (Bertrand Russell).

➔ The first pronunciation is the traditional one in English-speaking use; the second, now very common, imitates in part the present school pronunciation of Latin.

per second per second, during one second, of a series of seconds (in connection with a constant acceleration measured in intervals of 1 second each). *Example:* the acceleration of gravity is about 32 feet per second per second, which means that the velocity of a freely falling body increases by 32 feet per second during each successive second of fall.

per·se·cute (pėr′sə kyüt), *v.t.,* **-cut·ed, -cut·ing. 1.** to treat badly; do harm to again and again; oppress: *The cruel boy persecuted the kitten by throwing stones at it whenever it came near.* **2.** to punish for religious reasons: *Blessed are they which are persecuted for righteousness' sake* (Matthew 5:10). **3.** to annoy; harass: *persecuted by silly questions. We sat in the shade . . . persecuted by small stinging flies* (W. H. Hudson). [< Middle French *persécuter,* back formation < Old French *persecuteur,* learned borrowing from Latin *persecūtor* < *persequī;* see PURSUE]

—**Syn. 1.** wrong, torment. **3.** worry, vex.

per·se·cut·ee (pėr′sə kyü tē′), *n.* a person, especially a refugee, who has suffered persecution: *The truly unfortunate were . . . "persecutees" who dared not return home for fear of further persecution* (Dwight D. Eisenhower).

per·se·cu·tion (pėr′sə kyü′shən), *n.* **1.** a persecuting: *the boy's persecution of the kitten.* **2.** a being persecuted: *The kitten's persecution by the boy made it run away.* **3.** *Obsolete.* prosecution. [< Latin *persecūtiō, -ōnis* < *persequī;* see PURSUE]

per·se·cu·tion·al (pėr′sə kyü′shə nəl), *adj.* of or relating to persecution.

per·se·cu·tive (pėr′sə kyü′tiv), *adj.* of a persecuting character; tending or addicted to persecution.

per·se·cu·tor (pėr′sə kyü′tər), *n.* a person who persecutes.

per·se·cu·to·ry (pėr′sə kyü′tər ē, pėr′sə-kyü′-), *adj.* persecutive.

Per·se·i (pėr′sē ī), *n.* genitive of **Perseus** (the constellation).

Per·se·id (pėr′sē id), *n.* any of a shower of meteors seeming to radiate from the constellation Perseus and reappearing each August. [< New Latin *Perseïdes,* plural of *Perseïs* daughter of Perseus < *Perseus*]

Per·seph·o·ne (pər sef′ə nē), *n. Greek Mythology.* the daughter of Zeus and Demeter, who was carried off by Haees, the king of the lower world, and made his queen, but allowed to spend part of each year on the earth. Her return to earth brings greenness and spring and summer, and her departure, fall and winter. The Romans called her Proserpina, often Anglicized as Proserpine.

Per·se·us (pėr′sē əs, -syüs), *n., genitive* (def. 2) **Per·se·i. 1.** *Greek Mythology.* a hero, the son of Zeus and Danaë, who slew Medusa and rescued Andromeda from a sea monster. **2.** a northern constellation near Cassiopeia. It contains the famous variable star, Algol.

per·se·ver·ance (pėr′sə vir′əns), *n.* **1.** a sticking to a purpose or aim; never giving up what one has set out to do: *By perseverance the crippled boy learned how to swim. 'Tis known by the name of perseverance in a good cause — and of obstinacy in a bad one* (Laurence Sterne). **2.** *Theology.* continuance in a state of grace leading finally to eternal salvation: *the perseverance of God's grace.* —**Syn. 1.** tenacity, diligence. See **persistence.**

per·se·ver·ant (pėr′sə vir′ənt), *adj.* persevering: *Such women as were not only devout, but sedulous, diligent, constant, perseverant in their devotion* (John Donne).

per·sev·er·a·tion (pər sev′ə rā′shən), *n.* **1.** *Psychology.* the spontaneous repetition of past experiences. **2.** *Obsolete.* a persevering; perseverance.

per·se·vere (pėr′sə vir′), *v.i.,* **-vered, -vering.** to continue steadily in doing something hard; persist: *in our opposed paths to persevere* (Coventry Patmore). [Middle English *perseveren* < Old French *perseverer,* learned borrowing from Latin *persevērāre* < *persevērus,* adjective < *per-* very + *sevērus* strict]

per·se·ver·ing (pėr′sə vir′ing), *adj.* that perseveres; stubbornly persistent. —**per′se·ver′ing·ly,** *adv.*

Per·sian (pėr′zhən; *especially British* pėr′shən), *adj.* of or having to do with ancient Persia or modern Iran, a country in southwestern Asia south of the Caspian Sea, its people, or their language.

—*n.* **1.** a native or inhabitant of ancient Persia or modern Iran. **2.** the Iranian language of Persia; Farsi. **3.** Pahlavi. **4.** *Obsolete.* a thin, soft silk fabric, used for linings.

Persians, Persian blinds: *He raised the Persians to admit some light into the store.*

Persian apple, citron.

Persian blinds, window shutters made with adjustable slats like Venetian blinds, but hung outside rather than inside; persiennes.

Persian carpet, a Persian rug.

Persian cat, a long-haired cat originally from Persia (Iran) and Afghanistan.

Persian lamb, 1. a very curly fur from lambs of Persia (Iran) and some parts of central Asia; karakul. **2.** a lamb having this fur.

Persian rug, an Oriental rug or carpet made in Persia.

Persian walnut, the English walnut.

Persian wheel, a water-lifting wheel, as one with buckets at the rim, or one with radial or curved partitions for dipping the water near the rim and discharging it near the axle; noria.

per·si·car·y (pėr′sə ker′ē), *n.* any of various plants of the buckwheat family, as some of the smartweeds, whose leaves resemble those of the peach. [< New Latin *persicaria* the species name < Medieval Latin *persicarius* peachwort; (originally) peach tree < Latin *persicum* peach]

per·si·ennes (pėr′zē enz′; *French* per syen′), *n.pl.* Persian blinds. [< French *persiennes*]

per·si·flage (pėr′sə fläzh), *n.* light, joking talk or writing: *King was . . . full of airy persiflage . . . and . . . danced dialectical rings round Prout* (Rudyard Kipling). *She could see, behind the screen of persiflage, that John was worried* (New Yorker). [< French *persiflage* < *persifler* to banter, apparently < *per-* through + Old French *siffler* to whistle, hiss < Latin *sīfilāre,* variant of *sībilāre.* Compare SIBILANT.]

—**Syn.** banter, raillery.

per·sim·mon (pər sim′ən), *n.* **1.** any of a group of trees, as a North American tree with a plumlike fruit containing one to ten seeds, and a Japanese and Chinese variety bearing a large red fruit. **2.** the fruit of any of these trees, as the fruit of the North American tree which is very astringent when green but sweet and edible when very ripe: *In latitudes further north the persimmon usually awaits the first frost to become edible* (Clarke County Democrat). [American English < Algonkian (Powhatan) *pasimenan* fruit dried artificially < *pasimeneu* he dries fruit]

Persimmon (def. 2)

per·sist (pər sist′, -zist′), *v.i.* **1.** to continue firmly; refuse to stop or be changed: *Jane persists in reading in bed.* **2.** to remain in existence; last; stay; endure: *On the tops of very high mountains, snow persists throughout the year.* **3.** to say again and again; maintain: *He persisted that he was innocent of the crime.* **4.** *Archaic.* to continue to be; remain: *They persisted deaf . . .* (Milton). [< Latin *persistere* < *per-* thoroughly + *sistere* to stand] —**per·sist′er,** *n.* —**Syn. 1.** persevere.

per·sist·ence (pər sis′təns, -zis′-), *n.* **1.** a persisting. **2.** a being persistent; doggedness: *the persistence of a fly buzzing around one's head.* **3.** a continuing existence: *the stubborn persistence of a cough.*

—**Syn. 1. Persistence, perseverance** mean a holding fast to a purpose or course of action. **Persistence,** having a good or bad sense according to one's attitude toward what is done, emphasizes holding stubbornly or obstinately to one's purpose and continuing firmly and often annoyingly against disapproval, opposition, advice, etc.: *By persistence many people won religious freedom.* **Perseverance,** always in a good sense, emphasizes refusing to be discouraged by obstacles or difficulties, but continuing steadily with courage and patience: *Perseverance leads to success.*

per·sist·en·cy (pər sis′tən sē, -zis′-), *n.* persistence.

per·sist·ent (pər sis′tənt, -zis′-), *adj.* **1.** having lasting qualities, especially in the face of disapproval, dislike, or difficulties; persisting: *a persistent worker, a persistent beggar.* **2.** going on; continuing; lasting: *a persistent headache.* **3.** constantly repeated; recurring. **4.** *Botany.* continuing without withering, as a calyx which remains after the corolla has withered; permanent. **5.** *Zoology.* permanent; not lost or altered during development: *persistent horns.* —**per·sist′ent·ly,** *adv.* —**Syn. 1.** persevering, untiring, insistent.

per·snick·e·ty (pər snik′ə tē), *adj. Informal.* pernickety; fussy: *In contrast to the selfish, pontifical, persnickety skinflints who dominate our literature of millionaires* (New York Times).

per·son (pėr′sən), *n.* **1.** a man, woman, or child; human being: *Any person who wishes may come. If that person calls again, tell him I refuse to see him.* **2.** a human body, distinct from the mind or soul: *The king's person was sacred. Beelzebub arose, With care his sweet person adorning* (Shelley). **3.** bodily appearance: *He has a fine person.* **4.** *Grammar.* **a.** a change in a pronoun or verb to show the person speaking (first person), the person spoken to (second person), or the person or thing spoken of (third person). *I* and *we* are used for the first person; *thou* and *you,* for the second person; *he, she, it,* and *they,* for the third person. **b.** a form of a pronoun or verb giving such indication. *Comes* is the third person singular of *come. Abbr.:* pers. **5.** *Theology.* any of the three modes of being in the Trinity (Father, Son, and Holy Ghost). **6.** a character assumed in a drama or in actual life viewed as a drama; part played: *I must take upon me the person of a philosopher, and make them a present of my advice* (Sir Richard Steele). **7.** *Law.* a human being, or an entity such as a corporation, a partnership, or occasionally a collection of property, as the estate of a dead person, recognized by the law as capable of having legal rights and duties. A corporation is sometimes called an artificial person. **8.** *Obsolete.* a mask anciently worn by actors; disguise: *Certain it is that no man can long put on a person and act a part* (Jeremy Taylor).

in person, a. personally; with or by one's own action or bodily presence: *to appear in person. Charlemagne excused the bishops from serving in person* (Joseph Priestley). **b.** on the stage, as opposed to a motion picture or television: *The star will be featured in person in the forthcoming production.*

in the person of, in the character or guise of: *. . . persecuting Horace and Virgil in the persons of their successors* (John Dryden).

[Middle English *persone* < Old French < Latin *persōna* person, personality; (originally) character in a drama; actor; mask worn by an actor. Doublet of PARSON.]

➤ **Person** is the ordinary word for referring to a human being. *Individual* has the same meaning (though it is applied to single objects and animals as well) but emphasizes the person's singleness, aloneness, and is slightly heavy or pretentious unless that emphasis is needed. *Party* is legal or substandard.

Per·son (pėr′sən), *n. Theology.* person.

per·so·na (pər sō′nə), *n., pl.* **-nae.** *Latin.* **1.** a person. **2.** the voice of the author or the author's creation in a literary work: *Reilly seems to be partly a persona of the poet* (Manchester Guardian Weekly).

per·son·a·ble (pėr′sə nə bəl), *adj.* having a pleasing appearance; good-looking; attractive: *Miss Ingamells . . . a personable if somewhat heavy creature of twenty-eight* (Arnold Bennett). —**per′son·a·ble·ness,** *n.* —**Syn.** comely, presentable.

per·so·nae (pər sō′nē), *n.pl. Latin.* persons or characters in a book, play, etc.

per·son·age (pėr′sə nij), *n.* **1.** a person of importance: *Who am I indeed? Perhaps a personage in disguise* (Charlotte Brontë). **2.** a person: *a grandfatherly sort of personage* (Hawthorne). **3.** a character in a book, play, etc., or in history. **4.** the impersonation of such a character; part: *to assume the personage of Caesar, Hamlet, etc.* **5.** *Archaic.* the body; bodily frame. [< Old French *personage* < *persone* person + *-age* -age. Doublet of PARSONAGE.]

per·so·na gra·ta (pər sō′nə grā′tə), *pl.* **perso·nae gra·tae** (pər sō′nē grā′tē). *Latin.* **1.** an acceptable person: *If it were published, he would no longer be persona grata at Stanbrook* (Atlantic). **2.** a diplomatic representative personally acceptable to the government to which he is accredited: *Premier Diem . . . insisted that France name an ambassador to Vietnam after ascertaining if the envoy was persona grata* (New York Times).

per·son·al (pėr′sə nəl, pėrs′nəl), *adj.* **1.** of or having to do with a person in his private life; individual; private: *a personal matter, a personal call, a personal letter.* **2.** done in person; directly by oneself, not through others or by letter: *a personal visit.* **3.** of the body or bodily appearance: *personal cleanliness, personal beauty.* **4.** about or against a person or persons: *personal abuse, a personal question.* **5.** inclined to make remarks or ask questions about the private affairs of others: *Don't be too personal.* **6.** *Grammar.* showing person. *I, we, thou, you, he, she, it* and *they* are personal pronouns. **7.** *Law.* **a.** of or having to do with possessions that can be moved, not land or buildings. **b.** of or having to do with persons rather than things: *a personal action.* **8.** having the nature of a person; that is a person, not a thing or abstraction.

—*n. U.S.* a short paragraph in a newspaper about a particular person or persons: *Put a personal in the Baltimore Sun* (Mark Twain). [< Latin *persōnālis* < *persōna* person] —**Syn.** *adj.* **3.** physical, corporeal.

personal equation, an individual tendency for which allowance should be made.

per·son·a·li·a (pėr′sə nā′lē ə, -nāl′yə), *n. pl.* personal items, anecdotes, etc.: *The wife . . . talked . . . about people in the neighborhood . . . My aunt received these personalia cheerfully* (H.G. Wells). [< New Latin *personalia,* neuter plural of Latin *persōnālis* personal]

per·son·al·ise (pėr′sə nə līz, pėrs′nə-), *v.t.,* **-ised, -is·ing.** *Especially British.* personalize.

per·son·al·ism (pėr′sə nə liz′əm, pėrs′nə-liz-), *n.* **1.** the quality or character of being personal: *In Texas . . . personalism is the curse of politics* (Harper's). **2.** a theory, doctrine, method, system, or the like, in which personal feelings and relationships rather than impersonal or universal standards or axioms are stressed: *Loyalty . . . is practised in a small, concentrated circle of personalism* (London Times).

per·son·al·ist (pėr′sə nə list, pėrs′nə-), *adj.* of, having to do with, or characteristic of personalism; stressing personal rather than impersonal aspects: *A Christian social philosophy must be personalist, challenging any suggestion that the individual human being may be regarded as an instrument of the state's policies and purposes* (London Times). —*n.* a believer in or advocate of personalism.

per·son·al·is·tic (pėr′sə nə lis′tik), *adj.* personalist: *Yet this same generation—because it is so personalistic—has made civil rights its overriding issue* (Time).

per·son·al·i·ty (pėr′sə nal′ə tē), *n., pl.* **-ties. 1.** the personal or individual quality that makes one person be different and act differently from another. In psychology, personality is the total physical, intellectual, and emotional structure of an individual, including abilities, interests, and attitudes. *A baby two weeks old does not have much personality. Many psychologists are inclined to attribute the formation of personality entirely to the operation of the cultural and physical environment* (Beals and Hoijer). **2.** the qualities of a person; distinctive personal character: *The boy is developing a fine personality.* **3.** a person; personage: *personalities of stage and screen.* **4.** the quality of being a person, not a thing. **5.** *Law.* personal estate or property; personalty.

personalities, personal remarks made about or against some person: *Personalities are not in good taste in general conversation.*

—**Syn. 1.** See **character.**

personality cult, 1. great or excessive devotion to a person or a type of personality which binds a group of people together. **2.** cult of personality: *The personality cult, as exemplified by Stalin, became a term of derision and scorn* (Charles B. McLane).

per·son·al·i·za·tion (pėr′sə nə lə zā′shən, pėrs′nə-), *n.* **1.** a personalizing. **2.** a being personalized. **3.** an instance of this: *[The] style . . . is full of . . . personalizations which belong to the author* (Sean O'Faolain).

per·son·al·ize (pėr′sə nə līz, pėrs′nə-), *v.t.,* **-ized, -iz·ing. 1.** to make personal: *personalized stationery.* **2.** to personify. **3.** to take as personal.

per·son·al·ly (pėr′sə nə lē, pėrs′nə-), *adv.* **1.** in person; not by the aid of others: *to deal personally with one's customers. She saw to the comforts of her guests personally.* **2.** as far as oneself is concerned: *Personally, I like apples better than oranges.* **3.** as a person: *We like him personally, but dislike his way of living.* —**Syn. 1.** individually. **2.** subjectively.

personal property, property that is not land, buildings, mines, or forests; possessions that can be moved.

per·son·al·ty (pėr′sə nəl tē), *n., pl.* **-ties.** *Law.* personal property; movables as contrasted with real estate: *Towns whose citizens owned a lot of "personalty" actually voted to reject the document* (Wall Street Journal).

per·so·na non gra·ta (pər sō′nə non grā′tə), *pl.* **per·so·nae non gra·tae** (per sō′nē non grā′tē). *Latin.* **1.** a person who is not acceptable: *Some men, would-be customers but apparently personae non gratae, never got in the café* (New Yorker). **2.** a diplomatic representative who is not acceptable to the government to which he is accredited: *They also point out that a properly accredited ambassador may be declared persona non grata, while a high commissioner may not* (New York Times).

per·son·ate[1] (pėr′sə nāt), *v.,* **-at·ed, -at·ing.** —*v.t.* **1.** to act the part of (a character in a play, etc.); impersonate. **2.** (in literature, art, etc.) to represent as a person; personify. **3.** *Law.* to pretend to be (someone else), usually for purposes of fraud. —*v.i.* to act; play a part: *An actor's first duty . . . is . . . to personate* (Sir Henry Irving). [< Late Latin *persōnāre* (with English *-ate*[1]) represent < Latin *persōna,* see PERSON]

per·son·ate[2] (pėr′sə nit, -nāt), *adj. Botany.* (of a labiate corolla) having the lower lip pushed upward so as to close the opening between the lips, as in the snapdragon; masked. [< Latin *persōnātus* masked < *persōna* mask; see PERSON]

per·son·a·tion (pėr′sə nā′shən), *n.* **1.** a personating. **2.** a personifying. **3.** a person embodying a quality, etc.: *Mr. Pickwick was the very personation of kindness and humanity* (Dickens).

per·son·a·tive (pėr′sə nā′tiv), *adj.* having the quality of personating; involving dramatic representation.

per·son·a·tor (pėr′sə nā′tər), *n.* a person who personates.

per·son·i·fi·ca·tion (pər son′ə fə kā′shən), *n.* **1.** a striking example; type: *She is the very personification of selfishness.* **2.** a representing as a person, such as speaking of the sun as *he* and the moon as *she: Poetry written in the 1700's used many personifications of abstract qualities.* **3.** a person or creature imagined as representing a thing or idea: *Satan is the personification of evil.* **4.** a figure of speech in which a lifeless thing or quality is spoken of as if alive. *Example:* There Honour comes, a pilgrim grey (William Collins).

—**Syn. 1.** exemplification.

per·son·i·fi·er (pər son′ə fī′ər), *n.* a person who personifies.

per·son·i·fy (pər son′ə fī), *v.t.*, **-fied, -fy·ing.** **1.** to be a type of; embody: *Satan personifies evil.* **2.** to regard or represent as a person. We often personify the sun and moon, referring to the sun as *he* and the moon as *she: Greek philosophy has a tendency to personify ideas* (Benjamin Jowett). [probably patterned on French *personnifier* < *personne* person + *-fier* -fy] —**Syn. 1.** exemplify.

per·son·nel (pėr′sə nel′), *n.* the persons employed in any work, business, or service: *to issue an order to all personnel, the personnel of a hospital.*
—*adj.* **1.** of or having to do with personnel: *Reorganize the 34 agencies concerned with overseas economic operations, eliminating personnel duplications and other waste* (Newsweek). **2.** used by personnel. **3.** in charge of personnel.
[< French *personnel*, adjective, personal]

personnel director, a personnel manager.

personnel manager, an executive whose duties are to manage the hiring, position, pay, and discharge or retirement of employees, to keep records concerning them, and to maintain or improve the relationship existing between them and management.

personnel officer, an officer, especially a military officer, in charge of personnel: *He had told his personnel officer that he could take only one boxful of the division's records when they sailed* (Ralph Ingersoll).

per·son-to-per·son (pėr′sən tə pėr′sən), *adj.* between persons; between individuals; personal: *a person-to-person telephone call. The Yurok had a good many person-to-person quarrels and enmities, but few class or communal clashes* (Alfred L. Kroeber).

per·spec·tive (pər spek′tiv), *n.* **1. a.** the art of picturing objects on a flat surface so as to give the appearance of distance: *[Fauvism] had discarded perspective, the sublime technical triumph of the Renaissance* (New Yorker). **b.** a drawing or picture in perspective. **2.** the effect of distance on the appearance of objects: *Railroad tracks seem to meet at the horizon because of perspective.* **3.** the effect of the distance of events upon the mind: *Greater perspective makes happenings of last year seem less important.* **4.** a view of things or facts in which they are in the right relations: *We have endeavoured ... to observe a kind of perspective, that one part may cast light upon another* (Francis Bacon). **5.** a view in front; distant view: *a perspective of lakes and hills.* **6.** a mental view, outlook, or prospect: *Sleeping or waking, I beheld the same black perspective of approaching ruin* (Robert Louis Stevenson). **7.** *Obsolete.* an optical glass, as a magnifying glass.
in perspective, a. drawn or viewed in accordance with the rules or principles of perspective: *The engraver said he must ... "put it in proper perspective"* (London Daily Chronicle). **b.** from a particular mental point of view: *to examine an issue in perspective.*
[< Medieval Latin *perspectiva* (*ars*) (science) of optics, feminine of *perspectivus;* see the adjective]
—*adj.* **1.** of perspective. **2.** drawn so as to show the proper perspective: *a perspective drawing.* **3.** *Obsolete.* **a.** optical. **b.** assisting the sight, as an optical instrument: *a perspective glass.*
[< Medieval Latin *perspectivus* < Latin *perspicere* look through; inspect < *per-* through + *specere* to look] —**per·spec′tive·ly,** *adv.* —**Syn.** *n.* **5.** vista.

per·spec·tiv·ism (pər spek′tə viz əm), *n.* **1.** *Philosophy.* the theory or view that everything is seen or known only from particular perspectives. **2.** the use of perspective in art, literature, etc.

per·spec·tiv·ist (pər spek′tə vist), *adj.* of, having to do with, or characteristic of perspectivism. —*n.* a person who believes in perspectivism.

per·spec·to·graph (pər spek′tə graf, -gräf), *n.* an instrument used in drawing objects in perspective.

Per·spex (pėr′speks), *n. British, Trademark.* a transparent acrylic resin, similar to Lucite.

per·spi·ca·cious (pėr′spə kā′shəs), *adj.* **1.** keen in observing and understanding; discerning: *Your perspicacious wit, and solid judgment, together with your acquired learning render [you] ... a most accomplish'd and desirable patron* (Ralph Cudworth). **2.** *Archaic.* clear-sighted. [< Latin *perspicāx, -ācis* (with English *-ous*) sharp-sighted < *perspicere* to see through < *per-* through + *specere* to look] —**per′spi·ca′cious·ly,** *adv.* —**Syn. 1.** shrewd, acute.
➤ **Perspicacious** and **perspicuous** are not synonymous; the former means "discerning," the latter "lucid": *a perspicacious critic, a perspicuous argument.*

per·spi·cac·i·ty (pėr′spə kas′ə tē), *n.* **1.** wisdom and understanding in dealing with people or with facts; keen perception; discernment: *Unbelievable artistic perspicacity and integrity mingle with childlike humor and credulity* (Wall Street Journal). *A royal commission was about to be formed ... and Peel, with great perspicacity, asked the Prince to preside over it* (Lytton Strachey). **2.** *Archaic.* keenness of eyesight. —**Syn. 1.** penetration.

per·spi·cu·i·ty (pėr′spə kyü′ə tē), *n.* clearness in expression; ease in being understood: *There is nothing more desirable in composition than perspicuity; and in perspicuity precision is included* (Robert Southey). —**Syn.** plainness, lucidity.

per·spic·u·ous (pər spik′yů əs), *adj.* easily understood; clear; lucid: *His manner of telling a story, or explaining his thoughts, was forcible, perspicuous and original* (William Godwin). [< Latin *perspicuus* (with English *-ous*) transparent, clear < *perspicere* < *per-* through + *specere* to look] —**per·spic′u·ous·ly,** *adv.* —**per·spic′u·ous·ness,** *n.* —**Syn.** intelligible.
➤ See **perspicacious** for usage note.

per·spir·a·ble (pər spīr′ə bəl), *adj.* **1.** capable of sweating. **2.** that can be sweated (out).

per·spi·ra·tion (pėr′spə rā′shən), *n.* **1.** sweat. **2.** sweating: *Genius is one per cent inspiration and ninety nine per cent perspiration* (Thomas A. Edison). —**Syn. 1.** See **sweat.**

per·spir·a·to·ry (pər spīr′ə tôr′ē, -tōr′-), *adj.* **1.** of sweat. **2.** causing sweat.

per·spire (pər spīr′), *v.*, **-spired, -spir·ing.** —*v.i., v.t.* to sweat. [< Latin *perspīrāre* to blow or breathe constantly (said of the wind) < *per-* through + *spīrāre* to breathe, blow] —**per·spir′ing·ly,** *adv.*

per stir·pes (pər stėr′pēz), *Law.* by stocks or families (used of succession to property in which the descendants of one heir share the portion which would have come to that heir if living): *to divide an estate per stirpes.* [< Medieval Latin *per* by, according to, and Latin *stirpes*, plural of *stirps, stirpis* stock; family; (originally) stem, stalk]

per·suad·a·ble (pər swā′də bəl), *adj.* that can be persuaded; easy to persuade.

per·suade (pər swād′), *v.t.*, **-suad·ed, -suad·ing. 1.** to win over to do or believe; make willing or sure by urging, arguing, etc.: *He persuaded me to go. We persuaded Harry that he was wrong.* **2.** to convince: *For I am persuaded, that neither death, nor life ... nor things present, nor things to come ... shall be able to separate us from the love of God, which is in Christ Jesus our Lord* (Romans 8:38-39). **3.** *Archaic.* to urge, plead with, or counsel strongly: *Hadst thou thy wits, and didst persuade revenge, It could not move thus* (Shakespeare). [< Latin *persuādēre* < *per-* (intensive) + *suādēre* to urge, related to *suāvis* sweet, agreeable]
—**Syn. 1. Persuade, convince** mean to get someone to do or believe something. **Persuade** emphasizes winning a person over to a desired belief or action by strong urging, arguing, advising, and appealing to his feelings as well as to his mind: *I knew I should study, but he persuaded me to go to the movies.* **Convince** emphasizes overcoming a person's objections or disbelief by proof or arguments appealing to his reason and understanding: *I have convinced her that she needs a vacation, but cannot persuade her to take one.*

per·suad·er (pər swā′dər), *n.* **1.** a person or thing that persuades. **2.** *Slang.* a spur, weapon, or other thing used to induce effort or obedience: *He never appeared on deck without his "persuader", which was three rattans twisted into one* (Frederick Marryat).

per·sua·si·bil·i·ty (pər swā′sə bil′ə tē), *n.* the quality of being persuasible; capability of being, or readiness to be, persuaded.

per·sua·si·ble (pər swā′sə bəl), *adj.* that can be persuaded; open to persuasion; persuadable.

per·sua·sion (pər swā′zhən), *n.* **1.** a persuading: *All our persuasion was of no use; she would not come.* **2.** the power of persuading: *Is 't possible that my deserts to you can lack persuasion?* (Shakespeare). **3.** a firm belief: *He had a strong persuasion that Likeman was wrong* (H. G. Wells). **4. a.** a religious belief; creed: *All Christians are not of the same persuasion.* **b.** a body of persons holding a particular religious belief; sect; denomination: *The Quakers have been called the "friendly persuasion."* **5.** *Humorous.* kind; sort; description: *a house filled with pets of every persuasion.*
persuasions, beliefs: *to cling tenaciously to persuasions.*
[< Latin *persuāsiō, -ōnis* < *persuādēre* persuade] —**Syn. 3.** assurance, conviction.

per·sua·sive (pər swā′siv, -ziv), *adj.* able, intended, or fitted to persuade: *The salesman had a very persuasive way of talking.* —*n.* something adapted or intended to persuade.
—**per·sua′sive·ly,** *adv.* —**per·sua′sive·ness,** *n.* —**Syn.** *adj.* moving, winning.

per·sul·fate (pėr sul′fāt), *n.* a salt of persulfuric acid.

per·sul·fu·ric acid (pėr′sul fyůr′ik), **1.** a highly unstable, crystalline acid used as an oxidizing agent. *Formula:* H_2SO_5 **2.** a crystalline acid containing a high proportion of sulfur and oxygen, used as an oxidizing agent. *Formula:* $H_2S_2O_8$

pert (pėrt), *adj.* **1.** too forward or free in speech or action; saucy; bold: *a pert girl, a pert reply. The boy was very pert.* **2.** *Informal.* in good health or spirits; lively: *a very pert old woman.* **3.** *Obsolete.* **a.** expert; skilled. **b.** sharp; adroit; clever. [short for Middle English *apert* open, frank < Old French *apert* < Latin *apertus*, past participle of *aperīre* to open] —**pert′ly,** *adv.* —**pert′ness,** *n.* —**Syn. 1.** impudent, impertinent. —**Ant. 1.** modest, retiring.

PERT (no periods), Program Evaluation Review Technique (a computerized management system for handling complex programs, such as the production of missile systems).

pert., pertaining.

per·tain (pər tān′), *v.i.* **1.** to belong or be connected as a part, possession, etc.: *We own the house and the land pertaining to it.* **2.** to have to do with; be related; refer: *documents pertaining to the case.* **3.** to be appropriate: *We had a turkey and everything else that pertains to Thanksgiving Day.* **4.** *Archaic.* to belong as one's care or concern. [Middle English *perteynen* < Old French *partenir* < Latin *pertinēre* to reach, concern < *per-* (intensive) + *tenēre* to hold]

per·ti·na·cious (pėr′tə nā′shəs), *adj.* **1.** holding firmly to a purpose, action, or opinion; very persistent; resolute: *a pertinacious beggar. A bulldog is a pertinacious fighter.* **2.** stubborn to excess; obstinate. **3.** obstinately or persistently continuing; not yielding to treatment: *a pertinacious cough.* [< Latin *pertināx, -ācis* firm (with English *-ous*) < *per-* (intensive) + *tenāx, -ācis* tenacious] —**per′ti·na′cious·ly,** *adv.* —**per′ti·na′cious·ness,** *n.* —**Syn. 1.** determined, dogged, stubborn.

per·ti·nac·i·ty (pėr′tə nas′ə tē), *n.* great persistence; holding firmly to a purpose, action, or opinion: *Again and again ... with the inexorable pertinacity of a child intent upon some object important to itself, did he renew his efforts* (Hawthorne). —**Syn.** tenacity.

per·ti·nence (pėr′tə nəns), *n.* the quality of being to the point; fitness; relevance: *The pertinence of the boy's replies showed that he was not stupid.*

per·ti·nen·cy (pėr′tə nən sē), *n.* pertinence: *It seems entirely arbitrary to exclude social implications from the realm of "pertinency"* (Bulletin of Atomic Scientists).

per·ti·nent (pėr′tə nənt), *adj.* having to do with what is being considered; relating to the matter in hand; to the point; relevant: *If your question is pertinent, I will answer it.* [< Latin *pertinēns, -entis*, present participle of *pertinēre;* see PERTAIN] —**per′ti·nent·ly,** *adv.*
—**Syn. Pertinent, relevant** mean relating to the matter in hand. **Pertinent** means directly to the point of the matter, belonging properly and fittingly to what is being considered and helping to explain or solve it: *A summary of the events leading up to this situation would be pertinent information.* **Relevant** means having some bearing on the problem or enough connection with it to have some meaning or importance: *Even incidents seeming unimportant in themselves might be relevant.*

per·turb (pər tėrb′), *v.t.* **1.** to disturb greatly; make uneasy or troubled; upset:

Highly perturbed, he wondered what was coming next (Arnold Bennett). **2.** to cause disorder or irregularity in; agitate: *perturbed waters.* **3.** *Astronomy.* to cause perturbation in. [< Latin *perturbāre* < *per-* thoroughly + *turbāre* to confuse < *turba* turmoil, disorder] —**per·turb′er,** *n.* —**Syn. 1.** excite, trouble, distress.

per·turb·a·bil·i·ty (pər tėr′bə bil′ə tē), *n.* the quality of being perturbable; capability of being, or readiness to be, perturbed: *In addition, he had the assistance of his opponent's unfortunate perturbability* (New Yorker).

per·turb·a·ble (pər tėr′bə bəl), *adj.* that can be perturbed; liable to be disquieted or agitated.

per·tur·ba·tion (pėr′tər bā′shən), *n.* **1.** a perturbing. **2.** a perturbed condition: *Though the violence of her perturbations gradually subsided, her cheerfulness did not return* (Lytton Strachey). **3.** a thing, act, or event that causes disturbance or agitation: *The crown ... O polish'd perturbation! golden care!* (Shakespeare). **4.** *Astronomy.* a disturbance in the motion of a planet or other heavenly body in orbit caused by the attraction of a body or bodies other than its primary: *Perturbations, or disturbances in the motions, of the planets Neptune and Plato first led ... astronomers to hunt for a distant planet beyond Neptune* (Science News Letter).

per·tur·ba·tor (pėr′tər bā′tər), *n.* a person who perturbs; disturber: *All these perturbators must yield pride of blindness, surely, to the Englishman* (Sunday Times).

per·turb·ed·ly (pər tėr′bid lē), *adv.* in a perturbed manner; confusedly; distractedly.

per·tuse (pər tüs′, -tyüs′), *adj. Botany.* having holes or slits, as a leaf. [< Latin *pertūsus,* past participle of *pertundere* perforate < *per-* through + *tundere* to beat]

per·tus·sal (pər tus′əl), *adj.* of or having to do with whooping cough.

per·tus·sis (pər tus′is), *n.* whooping cough. [< New Latin *pertussis* < Latin *per-* (intensive) + *tussis* a cough]

pe·ruke (pə rük′), *n.* a wig, especially of the kind worn by men in the 1600's and 1700's; periwig. [< Middle French *perruque* (originally) head of hair, hairdress < Italian *perrucca;* origin uncertain. Doublet of PERIWIG.]

Peruke

pe·ruked (pə rükt′), *adj.* wearing a peruke: *a peruked barrister in trailing robes* (Time).

pe·rus·a·ble (pə rü′zə bəl), *adj.* that can be perused.

pe·ru·sal (pə rü′zəl), *n.* a perusing, especially a reading through or over.

pe·ruse (pə rüz′), *v.t.,* **-rused, -rus·ing. 1.** to read through carefully: *I will show you what to turn over unread and what to peruse* (Sir Richard Steele). *She perused "Middlemarch"; she was disappointed* (Lytton Strachey). **2.** to read, now often hastily or more or less casually: *to peruse the paper at breakfast.* **3.** to examine, inspect, or consider in detail: *The Stranger ... with a curious eye Perused the Arab youth* (Robert Southey). [earlier, use up < *per-* completely + *use,* verb] —**pe·rus′er,** *n.*

Peruv., Peruvian.

Pe·ru·vi·an (pə rü′vē ən), *adj.* of or having to do with Peru, a country on the west coast of South America, or its people: *The Peruvian representative in the O.A.S. denied the charge* (London Times). —*n.* a native or inhabitant of Peru: *Peruvians ... rank third in the world in the number of specialists sent to the United States for training* (New York Times).

Peruvian bark, bark from which quinine is obtained; cinchona.

per·vade (pər vād′), *v.t.,* **-vad·ed, -vad·ing. 1.** to go or spread throughout; be throughout: *The odor of pines pervades the air. He worked so hard that weariness pervaded his whole body.* **2.** to be found throughout (the body of a work, etc.), so as to characterize, flavor unmistakably, etc.: *a broad generosity pervaded his life* (Baron Charnwood). **3.** to pass through; traverse. [< Latin *pervādere* < *per-* through + *vādere* to go] —**per·vad′er,** *n.* —**Syn. 1.** penetrate, permeate, impregnate.

per·va·sion (pər vā′zhən), *n.* **1.** the act of pervading. **2.** the state of being pervaded; permeation.

per·va·sive (pər vā′siv), *adj.* **1.** tending to pervade. **2.** having power to pervade. —**per·va′sive·ly,** *adv.* —**per·va′sive·ness,** *n.*

per·verse (pər vėrs′), *adj.* **1. a.** contrary and willful; stubborn: *The perverse child did just what we told him not to do.* **b.** that is contrary to what is wanted, reasonable, or required: *perverse weather.* **2.** persistent in wrong: *What is more likely, considering our perverse nature, than that we should neglect the duties, while we wish to retain the privileges, of our Christian profession?* (Cardinal Newman). **3.** turned away from what is right or good; wicked: *blameless ... in the midst of a crooked and perverse nation* (Philippians 2:15). **4.** not correct; wrong: *perverse reasoning.* [< Latin *perversus* turned away, past participle of *pervertere* pervert] —**per·verse′ly,** *adv.* —**per·verse′ness,** *n.* —**Syn. 1. a.** wayward, obstinate.

per·ver·sion (pər vėr′zhən, -shən), *n.* **1.** a turning or being turned to what is wrong; change to what is unnatural, abnormal, or wrong: *A tendency to eat sand is a perversion of appetite.* **2.** a perverted form.

per·ver·si·ty (pər vėr′sə tē), *n., pl.* **-ties. 1.** the quality of being perverse. **2.** perverse character or conduct. **3.** a perverse act.

per·ver·sive (pər vėr′siv), *adj.* that perverts or tends to pervert.

per·vert (*v.* pər vėrt′; *n.* pėr′vėrt), *v.t.* **1.** to lead or turn from the right way or from the truth; lead astray: *Reading silly stories perverts our taste for good books.* **2.** to give a wrong meaning to; misconstrue: *His enemies perverted his friendly remark and made it into an insult. Ye have perverted the words of the living God* (Jeremiah 23:36). **3.** to use for wrong purposes or in a wrong way; misapply: *A clever criminal perverts his talents.* **4.** to change from what is natural or normal, now especially what is generally accepted or defined by law as natural or normal in sexual behavior.
—*n.* a perverted person, now especially one who practices sexual perversion.
[< Latin *pervertere* < *per-* (pejorative) + *vertere* to turn] —**per·vert′er,** *n.*
—**Syn.** *v.t.* **1.** corrupt, debase, deprave. **2.** misinterpret, distort, falsify.

per·vert·ed (pər vėr′tid), *adj.* **1.** turned from the right or usual way; misguided; misapplied: *a perverted enthusiasm for coarse and vulgar literature.* **2.** distorted: *a perverted meaning.* **3.** vicious by nature or habit; wicked. **4.** of or having to do with a sexual pervert. **5.** being a sexual pervert. —**per·vert′ed·ly,** *adv.* —**per·vert′ed·ness,** *n.*

per·vert·i·ble (pər vėr′tə bəl), *adj.* that can be perverted.

per·vi·ca·cious (pėr′və kā′shəs), *adj.* headstrong; willful. [< Latin *pervicāx, -cācis* (with English *-ous*) stubborn < *pervic-,* stem of *pervincere* < *per-* (intensive) + *vincere* conquer]

per·vi·ous (pėr′vē əs), *adj.* **1.** giving passage or entrance; permeable: *Sand is easily pervious to water.* **2.** open to influence, argument, etc. **3.** having the quality of penetrating or permeating; pervasive. [< Latin *pervius* (with English *-ous*) < *per-* through + *via* way] —**per′vi·ous·ness,** *n.*

Pe·sah or **Pe·sach** (pā′säн), *n.* the Passover festival. [< Hebrew *pesaḥ* a passing over; see PASCH]

pe·se·ta (pə sā′tə), *n.* **1.** the unit of money of Spain, worth about 1⅔ cents. **2.** a coin or bank note equal to one peseta. [< Spanish *peseta* (diminutive) < *pesa* weight; see PESO]

pe·se·wa (pə se′wə), *n.* a unit of money in Ghana. The pesewa replaced and is equivalent to the British penny. [< Fanti *pesawa*]

Pe·shi·to or **Pe·shit·to** (pə shē′tō), *n.* Peshitta.

Pe·shit·ta (pə shēt′tä), *n.* the chief Syriac version of the Bible. [< Syriac *pshīṭto* simple]

pes·ki·ness (pes′kē nis), *n.* the quality or condition of being pesky: *The analogy would be complete if the might of the U.S. lion should prove less effective than the peskiness of Ho Chi Minh, the mosquito* (Time).

pes·ky (pes′kē), *adj.,* **-ki·er, -ki·est.** *U.S. Informal.* troublesome; annoying: *a pesky cold, pesky mosquitoes.* [alteration of *pesty* < *pest*]

pe·so (pā′sō), *n., pl.* **-sos. 1.** the unit of money in Mexico, worth about 8 cents. **2.** any of the monetary units worth varying amounts used in Argentina, Bolivia, Colombia, the Philippines, and Uruguay. **3.** either of the monetary units in Cuba or the Dominican Republic worth one dollar. **4.** a coin or bank note equal to a peso in any of these countries. **5.** a former gold or silver coin used in Spain and in the Spanish colonies worth eight reals; a piece of eight. **6.** *U.S. Slang.* an American dollar. [< Spanish *peso* a coin of a certain weight; weight < Latin *pēnsum,* past participle of *pendere* to weigh. Compare POISE[1].]

pes·sa·ry (pes′ər ē), *n., pl.* **-ries.** *Medicine.* **1.** a device worn in the vagina to prevent or remedy various displacements of the uterus. **2.** a device worn in the vagina or cervical canal to prevent conception. **3.** a vaginal suppository. [< Late Latin *pessārium* < *pessum* or *-us* pessary, medicated tampon of wool or lint < Greek *pessós* oval stone]

pes·si·mism (pes′ə miz əm), *n.* **1.** the tendency to look on the dark side of things or to see difficulties and disadvantages: *Pessimism, when you get used to it, is just as agreeable as optimism* (Arnold Bennett). **2. a.** the belief that things naturally tend to evil, or that life is not worth while. **b.** the belief or doctrine that goodness, happiness, etc., are necessarily and always outweighed in human life by badness, grief, etc. [< Latin *pessimus,* superlative of *malus* bad, worst + English *-ism;* patterned on *optimism*]

pes·si·mist (pes′ə mist), *n.* **1.** a person inclined to see all the difficulties and disadvantages or to look on the dark side of things: *The optimist proclaims that we live in the best of all possible worlds; and the pessimist fears this is true* (James Branch Cabell). **2.** a person who thinks that life holds more evil than good, and so is not worth living.

pes·si·mis·tic (pes′ə mis′tik), *adj.* **1.** disposed to take a gloomy view of things and to see the dark side of life. **2.** believing that life holds more evil than good, and so is not worth while. —**pes′si·mis′ti·cal·ly,** *adv.* —**Syn. 1.** See **cynical.**

pes·si·mize (pes′ə mīz), *v.,* **-mized, -miz·ing.** —*v.i.* to hold or express pessimistic views. —*v.t.* to make the worst (rather than the best) of; take the least hopeful view of.

pes·si·mum (pes′ə məm), *n., pl.* **-mums, -ma** (-mə), *adj.* —*n.* **1.** the least favorable or worst point, degree, amount, etc., for the purpose. **2.** *Biology.* the degree or amount of heat, light, food, moisture, etc., least favorable for the reproduction or other vital processes of an organism. —*adj.* least favorable or worst: *There is no reason why, so far as possible, we should not try to avoid a "pessimum" population* (New York Times). [< Latin *pessimum,* neuter of *pessimus;* see PESSIMISM]

pest (pest), *n.* **1.** any person or thing that causes trouble, injuries, or destruction; nuisance: *Mosquitoes are pests. I was a nuisance, an incumbrance, and a pest* (Dickens). **2.** *Archaic.* a pestilence, especially an outbreak of the plague. [< Latin *pestis* plague] —**Syn. 1.** annoyance.

Pes·ta·loz·zi·an (pes′tə lot′sē ən), *adj.* of or having to do with the Swiss educational reformer Johann Heinrich Pestalozzi (1746-1827), or his system of elementary instruction, of which teaching by object lessons adapted to the judged capacity of each child was the principal feature.

pes·ter (pes′tər), *v.t.* **1.** to trouble persistently; annoy; vex: *Flies pester us. Don't pester me with foolish questions.* **2.** *Obsolete.* to crowd to excess; overcrowd. [apparently short for obsolete *empester* encumber < Old French *empestrer* to hobble an animal at pasture; influenced by *pest*] —**pes′ter·er,** *n.* —**pes′ter·ing·ly,** *adv.* —**Syn. 1.** See **tease.**

pest·hole (pest′hōl′), *n.* a place that breeds or is likely to have epidemic disease.

pest·house (pest′hous′), *n.* a hospital for persons ill with highly infectious diseases.

pes·ti·cide (pes′tə sīd), *n.* any of various substances used to kill harmful insects (insecticide), fungi (fungicide), vermin, or other living organisms that destroy or inhibit plant growth, carry disease, etc.: *A pesticide that kills injurious plant mites, but leaves beneficial honeybees and other insects alive has been developed* (Science News Letter). [< Latin *pestis* plague, pest + English *-cide*[1]; probably patterned on *insecticide*]

pes·tif·er·ous (pes tif′ər əs), *adj.* **1.** bringing disease or infection; pestilential: *Rats* *are pestiferous.* **2.** bringing moral evil; pernicious: *the pestiferous influence of a bad example.* **3.** *Informal.* troublesome; annoying. **4.** *Archaic.* stricken with a dangerous, very contagious disease, especially the plague. [< Latin *pestiferus* (with English *-ous*) < *pestis* plague + *ferre* bring] —**pes·tif′er·ous·ly,** *adv.*

pes·ti·lence (pes′tə ləns), *n.* **1.** any disease that spreads rapidly causing many deaths. Smallpox, yellow fever, and the plague are pestilences. **2.** something morally pestilent; wickedness. —**Syn. 1.** epidemic, pest.

pes·ti·lent (pes′tə lənt), *adj.* **1.** often causing death: *Smallpox is a pestilent disease.* **2.** very harmful to morals; destroying peace; noxious; pernicious: *a pestilent den of vice, the pestilent effects of war.* **3.** troublesome; annoying: *a few pestilent agitators* (Gaspard D. Coligny). **4.** having to do with a pestilence. [< Latin *pestilēns, -entis* pestilent < *pestis* plague] —**pes′ti·lent·ly,** *adv.*

pes·ti·len·tial (pes′tə len′shəl), *adj.* **1.** like a pestilence; having to do with pestilences. **2.** carrying infection: *pestilential vapors* (Longfellow). **3.** harmful; dangerous; pernicious: *So pestilential, so infectious a thing is sin* (Jeremy Taylor). —**pes′ti·len′tial·ly,** *adv.*

pes·tle (pes′əl, -təl), *n., v.,* **-tled, -tling.** —*n.* **1.** a tool, usually club-shaped, for pounding or crushing substances into a powder in a mortar. See picture under **mortar. 2.** any of various mechanical appliances for pounding, stamping, pressing, etc., as a vertically moving or pounding part in a machine.
—*v.t., v.i.* to pound or crush with a pestle.
[< Old French *pestel,* learned borrowing from Medieval Latin *pestillum,* variant of Latin *pistillum* < *pīnsere* to pound. Doublet of PISTIL.]

pes·to·log·i·cal (pes′tə loj′ə kəl), *adj.* of or having to do with pestology.

pes·tol·o·gy (pes tol′ə jē), *n.* the scientific study of insect pests.

pest·y (pes′tē), *adj.* **1.** like a pest; pestiferous: *Ants were particularly pesty last year* (New York Times). **2.** full of pests.

pet[1] (pet), *n., adj., v.,* **pet·ted, pet·ting.** —*n.* **1.** any animal kept as a favorite and treated with affection. **2.** any person who is treated with special kindness or favor; a darling; a favorite: *teacher's pet; the spoiled pet of a wealthy family* (Charlotte Brontë).
—*adj.* **1.** treated or kept as a pet: *a pet rabbit.* **2.** showing affection; expressing fondness: *a pet name.* **3.** especially cherished; darling; favorite: *a pet chair.* **4.** *Informal.* particular; special: *a pet aversion, a pet theory, a pet phrase.*
—*v.t.* **1.** to treat as a pet; stroke; pat; touch lovingly and gently: *Helen is petting the kitten.* **2.** to yield to the wishes of; indulge: *She enjoyed being fêted and petted as much as a cat enjoys being stroked* (Harriet Beecher Stowe). —*v.i. U.S. Informal.* to indulge in petting.
[< Scottish Gaelic *peata*]
—**Syn.** *v.t.* **1, 2.** coddle, pamper.

pet[2] (pet), *n., v.,* **pet·ted, pet·ting.** —*n.* a fit of peevishness; fretful discontent: *He tossed the tidbit angrily in his cart, and drove off in a pet* (Hawthorne). —*v.i.* to be in a pet; sulk. [origin uncertain; perhaps influenced by *petulant*]

Pet., Peter (2 books of the New Testament).

pet·al (pet′əl), *n.* one of the parts of a flower that is usually colored; one of the leaves of a corolla: *A rose has many petals.* See **corolla** for picture. [< New Latin *petalum* (in Latin, metal plate) < Greek *pétalon* leaf, thin plate < *petannýnai* to spread open] —**pet′al·like′,** *adj.*

-petaled, *combining form.* having —— petals: *Six-petaled = having six petals.*

pet·al·if·er·ous (pet′ə lif′ər əs), *adj.* bearing petals. [< *petal* + *-ferous*]

pet·al·ine (pet′ə lin, -līn), *adj.* **1.** having to do with a petal. **2.** attached to a petal. **3.** resembling a petal. [< *petal* + *-ine*[1]]

pet·a·lism (pet′ə liz əm), *n.* (in ancient Syracuse) a mode of banishing citizens for five years by popular vote, with olive leaves for ballots. [< Greek *petalismós* < *pétalon* petal]

pet·al·ite (pət′ə līt), *n.* a mineral composed of a silicate of aluminum and lithium, occurring in white masses, often tinged with gray, red, or green. [< Greek *pétalon* leaf + English *-ite*[1]]

pet·alled (pet′əld), *adj.* having petals; adorned with petals or petallike objects: *... a petalled headdress* (London Times).

-petalled, *combining form. Especially British.* -petaled.

pet·a·lo·dy (pet′ə lō′dē), *n.* a condition in flowers in which other organs assume the appearance of petals, as the stamens in most double flowers. [< Greek *petalṓdēs* leaflike (< *pétalon* petal) + English *-y*[3]]

pet·al·oid (pet′ə loid), *adj.* having the form of a petal; resembling petals in texture and color, as certain bracts.

pet·al·ous (pet′ə ləs), *adj.* having petals.

pé·tanque (pā tänk′), *n. French.* a game somewhat resembling bowls: *Pétanque is ... played normally within a span of fifteen to thirty-five feet* (New Yorker).

pe·tard (pi tärd′), *n.* **1.** an explosive device formerly used in warfare to break doors or gates or to breach a wall. **2.** *Especially British.* a kind of firecracker.
hoist with (or **on**) **one's own petard,** injured or destroyed by one's own scheme or device for the ruin of others: *Almost every British proposal for self-government to date has been similarly hoist on its own petard* (Harper's).
[< Middle French *pétard* < *péter* break wind < Old French *pet* a breaking of wind, ultimately < Latin *pēdere* to break wind]

Petard (def. 1)

pet·a·sus or **pet·a·sos** (pet′ə səs), *n.* **1.** a low-crowned, broad-brimmed hat worn by the ancient Greeks. **2.** the winged hat worn by Hermes (Mercury). [< Greek *pétasos* < root of *petannýnai* to spread out]

pe·tau·rist (pə tôr′ist), *n.* any of the flying phalangers. [< Latin *petaurista* < Greek *petauristḗs* leaper < *pétauron* springboard]

pet·cock (pet′kok′), *n.* a small faucet inserted in a pipe or cylinder for draining liquids, testing or reducing pressure, etc. [< *pet,* in an uncertain sense + *cock*[1] faucet]

pe·tech·i·a (pə tek′ē ə, -tē′kē-), *n., pl.* **-tech·i·ae** (-tek′ē ē, -tē′kē-). any of the small reddish or purplish spots occurring on the skin or on mucous or serous membranes, caused by minute hemorrhages in connection with certain infectious diseases, asphyxia, or radiation sickness. [< New Latin *petechiae* < Italian *petecchia,* singular, speck]

pe·tech·i·al (pə tek′ē əl, -tē′kē-), *adj.* having to do with or accompanied by petechiae: *petechial hemorrhages.*

petechial fever, 1. typhus fever. **2.** epidemic cerebrospinal meningitis.

pe·tech·i·ate (pə tek′ē āt, -it; -tē′kē-), *adj.* having petechiae.

pete·man (pēt′mən), *n., pl.* **-men.** *Slang.* a safecracker. [< *pete*(r), in obsolete slang sense of "safe" + *man*]

pe·ter[1] (pē′tər), *v.i. U.S. Informal.*
peter out, to come to an end gradually; give out; fail: *The worst blizzard since 1949 lashed the upper Midwest, then petered out in Canada* (Wall Street Journal).
[American English; origin unknown]

pe·ter[2] (pē′tər), *n.* blue peter, a flag hoisted as a signal of sailing.

pe·ter[3] (pē′tər), *v.i.* to play an unnecessarily high card in bridge as a signal for one's partner to continue leading or to return a card of the same suit: *North began by laying down the heart king on which South petered, so that the suit was continued* (London Times). —*n.* the play of petering: *He was quick to realise that this might be the beginning of a peter* (Manchester Guardian Weekly). [< *peter*[2]]

Pe·ter (pē′tər), *n.* **1. Saint,** one of the twelve disciples chosen by Jesus as His Apostles. He was also called Simon or Simon Peter and assumed the leadership of the disciples after Christ's death. **2.** either of two books in the New Testament that bear his name. *Abbr.:* Pet.
rob Peter to pay Paul, to take something away from one to pay, satisfy, or advance another: *... those that rob Peter, as we say, to pay Paul, and take the bread out of their masters' mouths to give it to strangers* (Roger L'Estrange).

pe·ter·man (pē′tər mən), *n., pl.* **-men.** *Slang.* **1.** a thief who steals travelers' bags, etc. **2.** a thief who uses knockout drops as an aid to robbery. **3.** a safe cracker; peteman. [< *peter,* obsolete slang sense "trunk, luggage" + *man.* Compare PETEMAN.]

Peter Pan, 1. a play by Sir James Barrie, produced in 1904. **2.** the hero of this play and of several stories by Barrie, a little boy who refused to grow up.

Peter Pan collar, a small, round collar which can close at the front.

pe·ter·sham (pē′tər shəm), *n.* **1.** a heavy, rough woolen fabric. **2.** a garment made of this, especially a type of overcoat or breeches fashionable in the early 1800's. [< Viscount *Petersham,* 1780-1851, a famous dandy]

Peter's pence or **Peter pence, 1.** a tax of one penny from every householder in England (and certain countries of Europe) having land of a certain value, paid annually before the Reformation to the papal see. **2.** a voluntary contribution to the papal treasury, made since 1860 by Roman Catholics of various countries. [< St. *Peter,* traditionally, the first bishop of Rome]

peth·i·din (peth′ə din), *n.* pethidine.

peth·i·dine (peth′ə dēn, -din), *n.* meperidine hydrochloride, a synthetic narcotic.

pé·til·lant (pā tē yäN′), *adj. French.* slightly effervescent: *a pétillant wine.*

pet·i·o·lar (pet′ē ə lər), *adj.* **1.** of or having to do with a petiole. **2.** proceeding from a petiole; supported by a petiole.

pet·i·o·late (pet′ē ə lāt), *adj.* having a petiole: *a petiolate leaf, a petiolate insect.*

pet·i·o·lat·ed (pet′ē ə lā′tid), *adj.* petiolate.

pet·i·ole (pet′ē ōl), *n.* **1.** *Botany.* the slender stalk by which a leaf is attached to the stem. **2.** *Zoology.* a stalklike part, as that connecting the abdomen and thorax in wasps, ants, etc., or the eyestalk in lobsters, crabs, etc. [< New Latin *petiole* < Latin *petiolus* stalk; (literally, diminutive) < *pēs, pedis* foot]

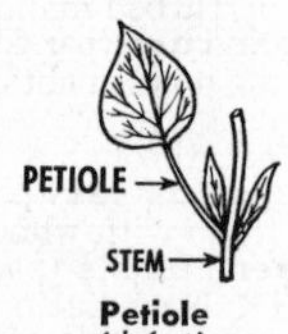

Petiole (def. 1)

pet·i·o·lule (pet′ē ə lül, pet′ē ol′yül), *n. Botany.* a small or partial petiole, such as belongs to the leaflets of compound leaves. [< New Latin *petiolulus* (diminutive) < *petiolus* petiole]

pet·it (pet′ē; *French* pə tē′), *adj. Law.* minor; small; petty; trivial: *petit larceny.* [< Old French *petit,* ultimately < Late Latin *pitinnus* very small (child). Doublet of PETTY.]

pe·tit bour·geois (pə tē′ bür zhwä′), *pl.* **pe·tits bour·geois** (pə tē′ bür zhwä′). *French.* **1.** a member of the petite bourgeoisie, or lower middle class: *This mass of essentially conservative petit bourgeois* (New York Times). **2.** the petite bourgeoisie, or lower middle class: *French peasants and the petit bourgeois have hoarded more than 15 times as much gold as there is in the Bank of France* (Time).

pe·tit-bour·geois (pə tē′bür zhwä′), *adj. French.* of, having to do with, or characteristic of the lower middle class or a member of it: *... succumbs to a callow young piano player and follows him to his petit-bourgeois home* (Time). *There was something shabby, something petit-bourgeois, about taking meals in the stuffy cubicle in which you were also to sleep* (New Yorker). Also, **petty-bourgeois.**

pe·tite (pə tēt′), *adj.* of small size; little; tiny (used especially with reference to a woman or girl). [< Old French *petite,* feminine of *petit* little] —**pe·tite′ness,** *n.*

pe·tite bour·geoise (pə tēt′ bür zhwäz′), *pl.* **pe·tites bour·geoises** (pə tēt′bür zhwäz′). *French.* the feminine of **petit bourgeois:** *petite bourgeoise housewives ... very bustling and gossipy, good mothers and housekeepers* (Katherine Gauss Jackson).

pe·tite bour·geoi·sie (pə tēt′ bür zhwä-zē′), *French.* the class of small businessmen and white-collar workers, in general belonging to the lower middle class.

pet·it four (pet′ē fôr′, fōr′; *French* pə tē für′), *pl.* **pet·its fours** (pet′ē fôrz′, fōrz′; *French* pə tē für′), a small fancy cake or cooky with decorative frosting. [< French *petit four* little oven; *four* < Latin *furnus.* Compare FURNACE.]

pe·ti·tion (pə tish′ən), *n.* **1. a.** a formal request to a superior or to one in authority for some privilege, right, benefit, etc.: *The peo-*

ple signed a petition asking the city council for a new sidewalk. **b.** the document containing such a request, and usually the signatures of the persons making it. **2.** *Law.* a written application for an order of court or for some action by a judge: *Mr. P. G. Wodehouse . . . filed a naturalization petition as a first step towards obtaining United States citizenship* (London Times). **3. a.** a prayer. **b.** one of the clauses of a prayer, as of the Lord's Prayer. **4.** that which is requested or prayed for: *If it please the king to grant my petition, and to perform my request* (Esther 5:8). **5.** the act of formally asking or humbly requesting. **6.** *English History.* the form in which Parliament formerly presented a measure to be granted by the king (now represented by the passing of a bill for the royal assent).
make (a) petition, to ask; supplicate: *to make petition for clemency.*
—v.t., v.i. **1.** to ask earnestly; make a petition to: *They petitioned the mayor to use his influence with the city council.* **2.** to pray.
[< Old French *peticion,* learned borrowing from Latin *petītiō, -ōnis* < *petere* to seek] **—pe·ti′tion·er,** *n.* **—Syn.** *n.* **1. a.** suit, entreaty, supplication. *-v.t., v.i.* **1.** entreat, beg.

pe·ti·tion·ar·y (pə tish′ə ner′ē), *adj.* **1.** of a petition. **2.** containing a petition. **3.** *Archaic.* suppliant; entreating: *To say no to a poor petitionary rogue* (Charles Lamb).

pe·ti·tion·ee (pə tish′ə nē′), *n.* the person against whom a petition is made.

Petition of Right, a parliamentary declaration of the rights and liberties of the English people, assented to in 1628 by Charles I (though later ignored by him). It is one of the fundamental features of the present British constitution.

pe·ti·ti·o prin·ci·pi·i (pə tish′ē ō prin-sip′ē ī), *Logic.* **1.** a begging the question; a fallacy of reasoning in which what is to be proved is assumed to be true in the premise. **2.** a fallacy of reasoning arising from the assumption of a premise which no opponent will admit to be true. *Example:* Since all students are of the same faith, therefore religion ought to be taught in the public schools. This begs the question as to whether all students are, in fact, of the same faith. [< Latin *petītiō principiī* (literally) a begging of the beginning (or first premise)]

pet·it juror (pet′ē), a juror on a petit jury.

pet·it jury (pet′ē), a jury consisting usually of 12 persons, chosen to decide a case in court; trial jury. Also, **petty jury.**

pet·it larceny (pet′ē), petty larceny.

pe·tit-maî·tre (pə tē me′trə), *n., pl.* **pe·tits-maî·tres** (pə tē me′trə). *French.* a fop; dandy: *Every clerk, apprentice, and even waiter . . . assumes the air and apparel of a petit-maître* (Tobias Smollett).

pe·tit mal (pə tē mäl′), a mild form of epilepsy characterized by short lapses of consciousness without warning and without violent convulsions, with slight muscular tremors, etc.

pe·tit point (pet′ē point′), embroidery made on canvas by short, slanting parallel stitches suggesting tents. [< French *petit* small, *point* stitch]

pe·tits pois (pə tē pwä′), *French.* very small green peas.

PETN (no periods), pentaerythritol tetranitrate.

pe·to (pā′tō), *n.* any of various large marine food fishes of tropical seas. [< American Spanish *peto* < Spanish, breastplate]

Pe·trar·chan sonnet (pi trär′kən), the Italian sonnet, composed of an octave and a sestet. [< *Petrarch* (Francesco Petrarca), 1304-1374, an Italian sonneteer]

pet·rel (pet′rəl), *n.* any of a group of small sea birds, as a small black-and-white bird with long, pointed wings. Petrels breed especially on oceanic islands and fly far out to sea, often following ships. The smaller kinds are also called Mother Carey's chickens. [supposedly a diminutive of Saint *Peter,* from his walking on the sea]

Stormy Petrel
(about 5½ in. long)

Pe·tri or **pe·tri dish** (pā′trē, pē′-), a shallow, circular glass dish with a loose cover, used in the preparation of bacteriological cultures: *About a month or two after I had started working with him he was busy one evening cleaning up several Petri dishes* (André Maurois). [< Julius *Petri,* 1852-1922, a German bacteriologist, who invented it]

pet·ri·fac·tion (pet′rə fak′shən), *n.* **1.** a petrifying or being petrified. **2.** something petrified.

pet·ri·fac·tive (pet′rə fak′tiv), *adj.* causing petrifaction.

pet·ri·fi·ca·tion (pet′rə fə kā′shən), *n.* petrifaction.

pet·ri·fy (pet′rə fī), *v.,* **-fied, -fy·ing.** *—v.t.* **1.** to turn into stone; change (plant or animal matter) into a substance like stone: *There is a petrified forest in Arizona.* **2.** to make hard as stone; stiffen; deaden: *I don't learn much from our senators . . . Policy seems to petrify their minds* (George Meredith). **3.** to paralyze with fear, horror, or surprise; stupefy: *The bird was petrified with terror as the snake came near.*
—v.i. **1.** to become stone or a substance like stone: *Cement like that of the Ancients, which petrified* (Alexander Gordon). **2.** to become rigid like stone; harden: *Like Niobe we marble grow, and petrify with grief* (John Dryden).
[< French *pétrifier* < Latin *petra* stone (< Greek *pétra*) + French *-fier* -fy]

Pe·trine (pē′trīn, -trin), *adj.* of or having to do with the apostle Peter or the two New Testament Epistles bearing his name.

petro-, *combining form.* **1.** rock; rocks: *Petroglyph = a rock carving. Petrology = the science of rocks.*
2. petroleum: *Petrochemistry = the chemistry of petroleum.*
[< Greek *pétra* rock]

pet·ro·chem·i·cal (pet′rō kem′ə kəl), *n.* a chemical made or derived from petroleum: *Within 10 years, petrochemicals are expected to account for half the industry's production* (World Book Annual). *—adj.* of or having to do with petrochemicals or petrochemistry: [*Their*] *record growth . . . is an indication of their success in cutting investment costs of petroleum and petrochemical units* (Economist).

pet·ro·chem·is·try (pet′rō kem′ə strē), *n.* **1.** the study or science of the chemical properties and derivatives of petroleum; the chemistry of petroleum. **2.** the manufacture of chemicals from petroleum and natural gas: *Petrochemistry supplies close to 25 per cent of our national chemical needs* (Wall Street Journal). [< *petro-* + *chemistry*]

pet·ro·drome (pet′rə drōm), *n.* an East African elephant shrew having hind feet with only four toes, and frequenting rocky hills. [< New Latin *Petrodomus* the genus name < Greek *pétra* rock + *drómos* course, related to *dramein* to run]

petrog., petrography.

pet·ro·gen·e·sis (pet′rə jen′ə sis), *n.* the genesis or origin of rocks, especially as a subject of scientific study. [< *petro-* + *genesis*]

pet·ro·ge·net·ic (pet′rō jə net′ik), *adj.* of or having to do with petrogenesis.

pet·ro·gen·ic (pet′rə jen′ik), *adj.* petrogenetic.

pe·trog·e·ny (pi troj′ə nē), *n.* petrogenesis.

pet·ro·glyph (pet′rə glif), *n.* a rock carving (usually prehistoric), especially a pictograph or the like incised or carved in rock: *The crescent is not a common figure among petroglyphs and pictographs of northern Arizona* (Science News Letter). [< French *pétroglyphe* < Greek *pétra* rock + *-glyphē* a carving, glyph]

pet·ro·glyph·ic (pet′rə glif′ik), *adj.* **1.** belonging to a petroglyph. **2.** like a petroglyph.

pe·trog·ly·phy (pi trog′lə fē), *n.* the art or process of carving upon rocks.

pet·ro·gram (pet′rə gram), *n.* a drawing or painting on stone, usually found in prehistoric caves. [< *petro-* + *-gram*]

pe·trog·ra·pher (pi trog′rə fər), *n.* an expert in petrography.

pet·ro·graph·ic (pet′rə graf′ik), *adj.* of or having to do with petrography. **—pet′ro·graph′i·cal·ly,** *adv.*

pet·ro·graph·i·cal (pet′rə graf′ə kəl), *adj.* petrographic.

petrographic microscope, a microscope equipped with two Nicol prisms for polarizing light, used for studying and identifying rocks and minerals.

pe·trog·ra·phy (pi trog′rə fē), *n.* the branch of geology that deals with the scientific description and classification of rocks.

pet·rol (pet′rəl), *n.* **1.** *British.* gasoline: *a petrol filling station* (London Times). *We inspected the charred remains of an experimental farm set on fire two nights before with straw soaked in petrol* (Manchester Guardian). **2.** *Obsolete.* petroleum. [< Old French *petrole,* learned borrowing from Medieval Latin *petroleum* mineral oil. Doublet of PETROLEUM.]

petrol., petrology.

pet·ro·la·tum (pet′rə lā′təm), *n.* **1.** a white or light-yellow salve or ointment made from petroleum. **2.** mineral oil; liquid petrolatum. [American English < New Latin *petrolatum* < English *petrol* + New Latin *-atum,* -ate[1]]

pe·tro·le·ous (pə trō′lē əs), *adj.* containing petroleum: *In the sweltering reaches of the petroleous Persian Gulf . . . Britain maintains some of the last outposts of Empire* (Time).

pe·tro·le·um (pə trō′lē əm), *n.* an oily, inflammable liquid found in the earth, consisting mainly of a mixture of various hydrocarbons. Gasoline, kerosene, fuel oil, paraffin, and lubricants are made from petroleum. *Petroleum . . . is nature's composite of the hydrocarbon-remains of many forms of marine life* (P.V. Smith). [< Medieval Latin *petroleum* < Greek *pétra* rock + Latin *oleum* oil. Doublet of PETROL.]

petroleum coke, a substance composed of almost pure carbon, derived as a by-product of the distillation of heavy crude oil. Petroleum coke is used in electrodes, in the refining of certain metals such as aluminum, and for other purposes.

petroleum ether, ligroin.

petroleum fly, a fly found near pools of crude petroleum in which it breeds.

petroleum geologist, an expert in or a student of the branch of geology dealing with petroleum deposits in the earth.

petroleum jelly, petrolatum.

petroleum naphtha, naphtha.

pé·tro·leur (pā trô lœr′), *n. French.* **1.** an arsonist. **2.** a supporter of the Commune of Paris who, in May, 1871, tried to destroy important structures by fire.

pé·tro·leuse (pā trô lœz′), *n. French.* the feminine of **pétroleur.**

pe·trol·ic (pə trol′ik), *adj.* **1.** of petroleum. **2.** like petroleum. **3.** obtained from petroleum.

pet·rol·i·za·tion (pet′rə lə zā′shən), *n.* the act or process of petrolizing.

pet·rol·ize (pet′rə līz), *v.t.,* **-ized, -iz·ing.** **1.** to treat with petroleum; spread petroleum on (water) to destroy mosquito larvae. **2.** to set on fire by means of petroleum.

pet·ro·log·ic (pet′rə loj′ik), *adj.* having to do with or relating to petrology. **—pet′ro·log′i·cal·ly,** *adv.*

pet·ro·log·i·cal (pet′rə loj′ə kəl), *adj.* petrologic.

pe·trol·o·gist (pi trol′ə jist), *n.* an expert in petrology.

pe·trol·o·gy (pi trol′ə jē), *n.* the branch of geology that deals with rocks, including their origin, structure, changes, etc.

pet·ro·nel (pet′rə nəl), *n.* a large pistol or carbine fired with the butt held against the chest, used in the 1500's and the 1600's, especially by cavalry. [< Middle French *petrinal,* dialectal variant of *poitrinal* < *poitrine* breast, chest < Vulgar Latin *pectorina* < Latin *pectus, pectoris*]

pe·tro·sal (pi trō′səl), *adj.* petrous. *—n.* a petrous bone or part. [< Latin *petrōsus* + English *-al*]

pet·rous (pet′rəs, pē′trəs), *adj.* **1.** *Anatomy.* designating or having to do with the very dense, hard portion of the temporal bone (or, in certain animals, an analogous separate bone) which forms a protective case for the internal ear. **2.** of the nature of stone; stony; rocky. [< Latin *petrōsus* (with English *-ous*) < *petra* rock, stone < Greek *pétra*]

pet·ta·ble (pet′ə bəl), *adj.* that can be petted: . . . *as pettable as a kitten* (Atlantic).

pet·ti·coat (pet′ē kōt), *n.* **1.** a skirt that hangs from the waist or from the shoulders, worn beneath the dress by women, girls, and babies. **2.** a skirt, trimmed and sometimes stiffened. **3.** *Informal.* a woman or girl: *There was nobody knew better how to make his way among the petticoats than my grandfather* (Washington Irving). **4.** a dressing-table cover reaching down to the floor. **5.** a sheeting hung around a yacht while being launched, to hide its outlines. **6. a.** a skirt or flared part of a petticoat insulator. **b.** a petticoat insulator.

petticoats, a. women and girls: *Ignorance is pardonable only in petticoats* (Lord Chesterfield). **b.** *Archaic.* skirts worn typically by women or children collectively: *A mouse . . . took shelter under Dolly's petticoats* (Jonathan Swift).

—*adj.* **1.** of a woman; female; feminine: *A kind of petticoat council was forthwith held . . . at which the governor's lady presided* (Washington Irving). **2.** womanish.

[Middle English *pety coote* little coat; see PETTY]

petticoat breeches, a kind of loose breeches not gathered at the bottom of each leg but hanging somewhat like petticoats, worn by men in the middle 1600's.

pet·ti·coat·ed (pet′ē kō′tid), *adj.* wearing petticoats.

petticoat government, the undue rule or predominance of women in the home or in politics.

petticoat insulator, an inverted cup-shaped insulator of porcelain or the like, as for supporting a telegraph or telephone wire, having one or more flared parts suggesting skirts.

pet·ti·fog (pet′ē fog, -fôg), *v.i.,* **-fogged, -fog·ging. 1.** to plead or conduct a petty case in a minor court of law. **2.** to use petty, mean, or cheating methods in law. **3.** to wrangle or quibble about small petty points. [back formation < *pettifogger*]

pet·ti·fog·ger (pet′ē fog′ər, -fôg′-), *n.* **1.** an inferior lawyer who uses petty, mean, cheating methods: *He carried home with him all the knavish chicanery of the lowest pettifogger* (Tobias Smollett). **2.** any inferior person who uses petty, mean, cheating methods: *appointing as ambassador some political pettifogger skilled in delays, sophisms, and misapprehensions* (Washington Irving). [apparently < *petty* + *fogger,* probably < the *Fugger* family, German merchants in the 1400's and 1500's]

pet·ti·fog·ger·y (pet′ē fog′ər ē, -fôg′-), *n., pl.* **-ger·ies. 1.** the practice of a pettifogger: *Players are apt to fall victims to . . . pettifoggery on a huge scale* (New Yorker). **2.** an act characteristic of a pettifogger.

pet·ti·fog·ging (pet′ē fog′ing, -fôg′-), *adj.* shifty; tricky; quibbling: *Some men . . . retain through life . . . a pettifogging and disputatious spirit* (London Times). —*n.* trickery; chicanery.

pet·ti·ly (pet′ə lē), *adv.* in a petty manner.

pet·ti·ness (pet′ē nis), *n.* **1.** the quality of being petty; triviality; insignificance. **2.** an instance of this; a petty trait.

pet·ting (pet′ing), *n. U.S. Informal.* hugging, kissing, and other amorous play.

pet·tish (pet′ish), *adj.* peevish; cross; petulant: *a pettish reply.* [< *pet*[2] + *-ish*] —**pet′tish·ly,** *adv.* —**pet′tish·ness,** *n.*

pet·ti·toes (pet′ē tōz′), *n.pl.* **1.** the feet of a pig, especially when used as food: *a present of pigs' pettitoes* (George Eliot). **2.** the feet or toes of a human being, especially of a child. [apparently < *petty* + *toes*]

pet·tle[1] (pet′əl), *v.t.,* **-tled, -tling.** *Scottish.* to pet; fondle; indulge. [(frequentative) < *pet*[1]]

pet·tle[2] (pet′əl), *n. British.* paddle[1] (def. 8).

pet·to (pet′tō), *n., pl.* **-ti** (-tē). *Italian.* the breast.

pet·ty (pet′ē), *adj.,* **-ti·er, -ti·est. 1. a.** having little importance or value; small: *She insisted on telling me all her petty troubles.* **b.** on a small scale: *a petty shopkeeper, petty theft, petty animosities.* **2.** mean; narrow-minded: *A gossip has a petty mind.* **3.** of lower rank or importance; subordinate: *a petty official.* **4.** *Obsolete.* small in size or stature. [spelling variant of *petit* < later English pronunciation of Old French *petit.* Doublet of PETIT.] —**Syn. 1. a.** trifling, slight, paltry, trivial, insignificant. **3.** minor.

pet·ty-bour·geois (pet′ē bůr zhwä′), *adj.* petit-bourgeois.

petty cash, 1. small sums of money spent or received. **2.** a sum of money kept on hand to pay small expenses.

petty juror, petit juror.

petty jury, petit jury.

petty larceny, theft in which the value of the property taken is less than a certain amount.

petty officer, 1. a noncommissioned officer in the U.S. or British navy. *Abbr.:* P.O. **2.** *Obsolete.* a minor official; inferior officer.

petty sessions, *British.* a court with summary jurisdiction over minor offenses in a given district.

pet·u·lance (pech′ə ləns), *n.* **1.** bad humor; condition of being irritated by trifles; peevishness. **2.** *Obsolete.* **a.** immodesty. **b.** sauciness; rudeness.

pet·u·lan·cy (pech′ə lən sē), *n.* petulance.

pet·u·lant (pech′ə lənt), *adj.* **1.** peevish; subject to little fits of bad temper; irritable over trifles: *His temper was acid, petulant and harsh* (William Godwin). **2.** *Obsolete.* **a.** forward or immodest; wanton. **b.** saucy; insolent: *a young petulant jackanapes* (Tobias Smollett). [< Latin *petulāns, -antis* mischievous, petulant < *pet-,* root of *petere* seek, aim at] —**pet′u·lant·ly,** *adv.*

pe·tu·ni·a (pə tü′nē ə, -tyü′-; -tün′yə, -tyün′-), *n.* **1.** any of a group of low, straggling plants with funnel-shaped flowers of white, pink, and shades of red and purple. The petunia was originally native to South America and is a member of the nightshade family. **2.** the flower of any of these plants. **3.** a dark violet or purple. [< New Latin *Petunia* the genus name < French *petun* tobacco < Guarani (Paraguay) *petȳ* (the *ȳ* is a nasal sound)]

Petunia (def. 2)

pe·tun·se (pe tůn′se), *n.* petuntse.

pe·tun·tse or **pe·tun·tze** (pe tůn′tse; *Chinese* bī′důn′dzə), *n.* a white earth made by pulverizing partially decomposed granite, used especially in China in the manufacture of porcelain. [< Chinese *pai* white + *tuntzŭ* briquettes (because the pulverized granite is transported in this form)]

peu à peu (pœ′ ȧ pœ′), *French.* little by little; a little or few at a time.

peu de chose (pœd′ shōz′), *French.* a small thing; not much of a thing (or person); trivial matter.

Peul or **Peuhl** (pyül, pül), *n.* a Fulani, especially one living in Guinea, Senegal, or Chad.

pew (pyü), *n.* a bench in a church for people to sit on, fastened to the floor and provided with a back. In some churches the pews are separated by partitions and are reserved for the use of certain worshipers, as the members of a family: *One of the senior boys ushered them into a pew at the rear of the chapel* (New Yorker). [Middle English *puwe* pew, pulpit < Old French *puie,* or *puy* balcony, < Latin *podia,* plural of *podium* balcony (in Medieval Latin, raised lectern or pulpit)]

pew·age (pyü′ij), *n.* **1.** the pews in a church collectively. **2.** the arrangement of pews. **3.** the rent paid for pews.

pe·wee (pē′wē), *n.* any of certain small American birds with an olive-colored or gray back, as the wood pewee, phoebe, or certain other American flycatchers. [American English, variant of *pewit*]

pew·ful (pyü′fůl), *n., pl.* **-fuls. 1.** the amount that a pew can hold. **2.** the contents of a pew.

pe·wit (pē′wit, pyü′it), *n.* **1.** the lapwing. **2.** the black-headed gull. **3.** the pewee. [imitative. Compare Flemish *piewit-voghel* pewit bird.]

pew rent, the payment for use of a pew in church.

pew·ter (pyü′tər), *n.* **1.** an alloy of tin with lead, copper, or other metals. **2.** dishes or other utensils made of this alloy: *rows of resplendent pewter ranged on a long dresser* (Washington Irving). —*adj.* made of pewter: *a pewter mug.* [< Old French *peaultre,* perhaps < Italian *peltro,* perhaps < Latin *peltrum*]

pew·ter·er (pyü′tər ər), *n.* a worker in pewter; person who makes pewter utensils.

pew·ter·y (pyü′tər ē), *n., pl.* **-ter·ies. 1.** pewter utensils collectively. **2.** a room or place in which pewter utensils are kept.

Pey·e·ri·an (pī ir′ē ən), *adj.* having to do with or named after Johann Konrad Peyer (1653-1712), a Swiss anatomist.

Peyerian glands or **patches,** patchlike aggregations of follicles composed of lymphoid tissue which are situated in the walls of the small intestine, and undergo lesion in typhoid fever.

pe·yo·te (pā ō′tē; *Spanish* pā yō′tā), *n.* **1.** the mescal or any of several other cacti. **2.** a stimulating drug contained in the small buttonlike tops of the mescal, used by Indians in Mexico and the southwest United States; mescaline: *That's what's so bad about peyote. It can make sick people well, and that's how it gets converts* (New Yorker). [American English < Mexican Spanish *peyote* < Nahuatl *peyotl*]

pe·yo·tism (pā ō′tiz əm), *n.* **1.** use of or addiction to peyote: *Peyotism . . . spread to the Comanches and Kiowas* (Scientific American). **2.** Also, **Peyotism.** the form of religion of the Native American Church.

pe·yo·tl (pā ō′təl), *n.* peyote.

pf (no period), *Music.* a little louder (as a direction; Italian, *più forte*).

pf., 1. pfennig. **2.** preferred.

Pfc. or **Pfc** (no period), private first class.

pfd., preferred.

PFDA (no periods), Pure Food and Drug Administration (an agency of the United States government); officially, the Food and Drug Administration, FDA (no periods).

Pfeif·fer's bacillus (fī′fərz), a bacillus found in the respiratory tract and thought to be the cause of influenzal meningitis and conjunctivitis. [< Richard *Pfeiffer,* 1858-1945, a German bacteriologist]

pfen·nig (pfen′ig), *n., pl.* **pfen·nigs, pfen·ni·ge** (pfen′i gə). a German coin, worth 1/100 of a Deutsche mark in West Germany. [< German *Pfennig.* Related to PENNY.]

pfg., pfennig.

pfu·i (pfü′ē), *interj. German.* an exclamation of disgust or impatience.

Pg., 1. Portugal. **2.** Portuguese.

p.g., paying guest.

P.G., 1. postgraduate. **2.** Past Grand (Master, etc.). **3.** paying guest.

PGA (no periods) or **P.G.A.,** Professional Golfers' Association.

pH, a symbol used (with a number) to express acidity or alkalinity in testing soils for suitability to specific crops, in analyzing body secretions, in various industrial applications, etc. It represents the logarithm of the reciprocal (or negative logarithm) of the hydrogen-ion concentration (in gram atoms per liter) in a given solution, usually determined by the use of a substance (indicator) known to change color at a certain concentration. The *p*H scale in common use ranges from 0 to 14, *p*H7 (the hydrogen-ion concentration, 10^{-7} or .0000001, in pure water) being taken as neutral, 6 to 0 increasingly acid, and 8 to 14 increasingly alkaline. Most soils are in the range between *p*H3 and *p*H10. *The soil with its pH6.5, the most preferable for growing roses, is ideal* (New York Times).

ph., 1. phase. **2.** phone. **3.** phosphor.

Ph (no period), *Chemistry.* phenyl.

P.H., Purple Heart.

PHA (no periods) or **P.H.A.,** Public Housing Administration.

Phae·a·cia (fē ā′shə), *n. Greek Legend.* an island visited by Ulysses (Odysseus) during his voyage.

Phae·dra (fē′drə), *n. Greek Legend.* the daughter of Minos and Pasiphaë, and wife of Theseus, king of Athens. She loved her stepson Hippolytus, but caused his death by falsely accusing him.

phae·no·gam (fē′nə gam), *n.* phanerogam.

phae·nog·a·mous (fi nog′ə məs), *adj.* phanerogamous.

Pha·ë·thon (fā′ə thon), *n. Greek and Roman Mythology.* the son of Helios and Clymene, who tried for one day to drive the sun, his father's chariot. He so nearly set the earth on fire that Zeus had to strike him dead with a thunderbolt. [< Latin *Phaëthon* < Greek *Phaethōn* (literally) shining, related to *phainein* show forth, shine]

pha·e·ton (fā′ə tən), *n.* **1.** a lightweight, four-wheeled carriage with or without a top, pulled by one or two horses, and having one or two seats. **2.** an open automobile similar to a touring car. **3.** the body of such an automobile. [< French *phaéton* < *Phaëton* Phaëthon]

Phaeton (def. 1)

phage (fāj), *n.* a bacteriophage: *Although phages had been observed for most types of bacteria, they had only once before been noticed attacking lactic streptococci* (J.A. Barnett). [short for *bacteriophage*]

-phage, *combining form.* that eats or devours: *Bacteriophage = that devours bacteria.* [< Greek *phageîn* eat]

phag·e·de·na or **phag·e·dae·na** (faj′ə-dē′nə), *n. Medicine.* **1.** an ulcer or ulceration that spreads rapidly and destroys the surrounding parts. **2.** gangrene. [< Latin *phagedaena* < Greek *phagédaina* an "eating" sore or ulcer < *phageîn* eat]

phag·e·den·ic or **phag·e·daen·ic** (faj′ə-den′ik, -dē′nik), *adj. Medicine.* **1.** like phagedena. **2.** characterized by phagedena. **3.** affected with phagedena.

phag·o·cyte (fag′ə sīt), *n.* a leucocyte or white blood cell capable of absorbing and destroying waste or harmful material, such as disease-producing bacteria: *All through [Fleming's] life he never abandoned the search for a substance which would kill the microbes without weakening the phagocytes* (André Maurois). [< German *Phagocyten,* plural < Greek *phageîn* eat + *kýtos* hollow vessel; body]

phag·o·cyt·ic (fag′ə sit′ik), *adj.* **1.** having to do with a phagocyte. **2.** having the nature or function of a phagocyte: *The [small] filariae were daily destroyed by large phagocytic cells of the body* (F. Hawking).

phagocytic index, the average number of bacteria destroyed by each phagocyte during an incubation of phagocytes, bacteria, and serum.

phag·o·cyt·ize (fag′ə sī′tīz), *v.t.,* **-ized, -iz·ing.** (of phagocytes) to absorb or destroy (foreign matter, bacteria, etc.): *Necrotic cells often fuse together and are phagocytized* (John W. Saunders, Jr.).

phag·o·cy·to·sis (fag′ə sī tō′sis), *n.* the absorption or destruction of foreign matter, bacteria, etc., by a phagocyte or phagocytes. [< *phagocyt*(e) + *-osis*]

pha·gol·y·sis (fə gol′ə sis), *n.* the dissolution or destruction of phagocytes. [< Greek *phageîn* eat + *lýsis* a loosening]

pha·i·no·pep·la (fā ī′nō pep′lə, fā′ə-), *n.* a bird of the southwestern United States and Mexico, related to the waxwings. It has shiny black plumage and a pointed crest. [< New Latin *Phainopepla* the genus name < Greek *phaínein* to shine + *péplos* robe]

pha·lae·nid moth (fə lē′nid), any of a large group of dull-colored moths, including the underwing moth and many varieties whose larvae are very destructive to crops; noctuid moth.

phal·ae·nop·sis (fal′ə nop′sis), *n.* any of a group of orchids native to India, Malaya, and the Philippines, used in bridal bouquets and for other decorative purposes. [< New Latin *Phalaenopsis* the genus name < Greek *phálaina* moth + *ópsis* appearance]

pha·lan·gal (fə lang′gəl), *adj.* phalangeal.

phal·ange (fal′ənj, fə lanj′), *n.* **1.** *Anatomy.* any bone of the fingers or toes; phalanx. **2.** *Botany.* a bundle of stamens united by their filaments; phalanx. [< Old French *phalange,* learned borrowing from Latin *phalanx;* see PHALANX]

pha·lan·ge·al (fə lan′jē əl), *adj. Anatomy.* **1.** of or having to do with a phalanx or phalanges. **2.** like a phalanx or phalanges.

pha·lan·ger (fə lan′jər), *n.* any of a group of comparatively small, tree-climbing mammals of Australasia. They hunt chiefly at night, carry their young in a pouch, and have long tails. [< New Latin *phalanger* < Greek *phalángion* venomous spider < *phálanx, -angos;* see PHALANX (because the phalanger has webbed hind toes)]

pha·lan·ges (fə lan′jēz), *n.* a plural of **phalanx.**

pha·lan·gid (phə lan′jid), *n.* daddy-longlegs. [< New Latin *Phalangium* the genus name < Greek *phalángion* venomous spider; see PHALANGER]

phal·an·ste·ri·an (fal′ən stir′ē ən), *adj.* **1.** of or having to do with a phalanstery. **2.** of or having to do with phalansterianism.
—*n.* **1.** a member of a phalanstery. **2.** a supporter of phalansterianism; Fourierist.

phal·an·ste·ri·an·ism (fal′ən stir′ē ə niz′-əm), *n.* the system of phalansteries; Fourierism.

phal·an·ster·ism (fal′ən stə riz′əm), *n.* phalansterianism.

phal·an·ster·y (fal′ən ster′ē), *n., pl.* **-ster·ies. 1.** in Fourierism: **a.** the building or set of buildings occupied by a phalanx. **b.** a socialistic community; phalanx. **2. a.** any similar association of persons. **b.** the building or buildings occupied by them. [< French *phalanstère* (coined by Fourier) < *phalange* a community in Fourier's system (< Greek *phálanx, -angos;* see PHALANX), with ending < *monastère* monastery]

pha·lanx (fā′langks, fal′angks), *n., pl.* **-lanx·es** or **-lan·ges. 1. a.** (in ancient Greece), a special battle formation of infantry fighting in close ranks with their shields joined and long spears overlapping each other. **b.** any body of troops in close array: *Anon they [the demons] move in perfect phalanx* (Milton). **2.** a compact or closely massed body of persons, animals, or things: *A phalanx of sheep blocked the road.* **3.** a number of persons united for a common purpose. **4.** *Anatomy.* any bone in the fingers or toes. **5.** *Botany.* a bundle of stamens united by their filaments in plants with two or more groups of stamens. **6.** (in Fourierism) a community of about 1,800 persons living in a phalanstery as one family, with property held in common.
in phalanx, in combination; unitedly; solidly: *On this occasion, the crown lawyers opposed in phalanx* (James Mill).
[< Latin *phalanx, -angis* < Greek *phálanx, -angos* line of battle; finger bone; (originally) round bar or leg]

phal·a·rope (fal′ə rōp), *n.* any of three varieties of small swimming and wading birds that breed in the Northern Hemisphere, resembling the sandpipers but with lobate toes. The females are larger and more brightly colored than the males, which brood the eggs. [< French *phalarope* < New Latin *Phalaropus* < Greek *phalārís* coot (< *phálāros* white-spotted) bald white head) + *poús, podós* foot]

phal·lic (fal′ik), *adj.* of or having to do with a phallus or phallicism; symbolic of male generative power. [< Greek *phallikós* < *phallós* penis, phallus]

phal·li·cal (fal′ə kəl), *adj.* phallic.

phal·li·cism (fal′ə siz əm), *n.* worship of the phallus or of the organs of sex as symbols of the generative power in nature.

phal·li·cist (fal′ə sist), *n.* a person who studies, or is an expert in, phallicism.

phal·lism (fal′iz əm), *n.* phallicism.

phal·lus (fal′əs), *n., pl.* **phal·li** (fal′ī). **1.** an image or model of the penis, symbolizing the generative power of nature, venerated and carried in solemn procession in Bacchic and other ceremonies, and commonly worn as part of his costume by any actor in the Old Comedy, in ancient Greece. **2.** *Anatomy.* **a.** the penis or clitoris. **b.** the embryonic structure from which either develops. [< Latin *phallus* < Greek *phallós* penis, phallus]

Pha·nar·i·ot (fə nar′ē ət), *n.* one of a class of Greeks in Constantinople who, after the Turkish conquest, held important official positions under the Turks. —*adj.* **1.** of or having to do with the Phanariots. **2.** characteristic of the Phanariots. [< New Greek *phanariṓtēs* < Turkish *Fanar* a district of Constantinople in which many Greeks lived]

Pha·nar·i·ote (fə nar′ē ōt), *n., adj.* Phanariot.

phan·er·o·gam (fan′ər ə gam), *n. Archaic.* any of a large division of the vegetable kingdom comprising those seed-producing plants which have their organs of reproduction (stamens and pistils) developed and distinctly apparent; a flowering plant. Also, **phaenogam, phenogam.** [< French *phanérogame* < Greek *phanerós* visible (< *phaínein* to show, appear) + *gámos* marriage]

phan·er·o·gam·ic (fan′ər ə gam′ik), *adj.* of or having to do with the phanerogams.

phan·er·og·a·mous (fan′ə rog′ə məs), *adj.* having the characters of the phanerogams; having stamens and pistils; flowering.

Phan·er·o·zo·ic (fan′ər ə zō′ik), *adj.* of or having to do with the geological eon comprising the Paleozoic, Mesozoic, and Cenozoic eras. —*n.* the Phanerozoic eon: *At most times during the Phanerozoic, the sea covered much more of the continents than it does at present* (New Scientist). [< Greek *phanerós* visible (see PHANEROGRAM) + *zōḗ* life + English *-ic*]

phan·tasm (fan′taz əm), *n.* **1.** a thing seen only in one's imagination; unreal fancy, as a ghost: *the phantasms of a dream.* **2.** a supposed appearance of an absent person, living or dead. **3.** a deceiving likeness (of something): *a phantasm of hope.* **4.** *Philosophy.* a mental image or representation of a real object. **5.** *Archaic.* deceptive appearance: *'Tis all phantasm* (Emerson). [< Old French *fantasme,* learned borrowing from Latin *phantasma* < Greek *phántasma* image < *phantázein* make visible, ultimately < *phaínein* to show. Doublet of PHANTASMA, PHANTOM.]

phan·tas·ma (fan taz′mə), *n., pl.* **-ma·ta. 1.** an illusion; vision; dream: *Like a phantasma or a hideous dream* (Shakespeare). **2.** an apparition; specter. [< Latin *phantasma.* Doublet of PHANTASM, PHANTOM.]

phan·tas·ma·go·ri·a (fan taz′mə gôr′ē ə, -gōr′-), *n.* **1.** a shifting scene of real things, illusions, imaginary fancies, deceptions, and the like: *the phantasmagoria of a dream. . . . a phantasmagoria of symbolic persons and animals, divine and diabolical beings, celestial and infernal phenomena* (New Yorker). *Instead of a turreted town crammed with phantasmagoria, it now appeared before him as a plain, ordinary, workaday city* (Harper's). **2.** a show of optical illusions in which figures increase or decrease in size, fade away, and pass into each other, etc. [coined < Greek *phántasma* image, perhaps + *ágorā* assembly]

phan·tas·ma·go·ri·al (fan taz′mə gôr′ē əl, -gōr′-), *adj.* **1.** of a phantasmagoria. **2. a.** like a phantasmagoria. **b.** visionary; phantasmal.

phan·tas·ma·gor·ic (fan taz′mə gôr′ik, -gor′-), *adj.* phantasmagorial: *The lanterns gave a phantasmagoric quality to the funeral procession* (Jorge Amado).

phan·tas·ma·gor·i·cal (fan taz′mə gôr′ə-kəl, -gor′-), *adj.* phantasmagorial: *Mr. Gaddis's manner . . . brings to mind the phantasmagorical canvases of Hieronymus Bosch* (Atlantic).

phan·tas·ma·go·rist (fan taz′mə gôr′ist, -gōr′-), *n.* a person who exhibits or produces a phantasmagoria.

phan·tas·ma·go·ry (fan taz′mə gôr′ē, -gōr′-), *n., pl.* **-ries.** a phantasmagoria.

phan·tas·mal (fan taz′məl), *adj.* of a phantasm; unreal; imaginary. —**phan·tas′mal·ly,** *adv.*

phan·tas·ma·ta (fan taz′mə tə), *n.* the plural of **phantasma.**

phan·tas·mic (fan taz′mik), *adj.* phantasmal.

phan·ta·sy (fan′tə sē, -zē), *n., pl.* **-sies. 1.** fantasy. **2.** *Music.* fantasia.

phan·tom (fan′təm), *n.* **1.** an image of the mind: *the phantoms of a dream. His fevered brain filled the room with phantoms from the past. The phantom of starvation drove him to theft. She was a phantom of delight When first she gleamed upon my sight* (Wordsworth). **2.** a vague, dim, or shadowy appearance; ghost: *The forms Of which these are the phantoms* (Shelley). **3.** mere show; appearance without material substance: *a phantom of a government, the phantom of a once flourishing town.* **4.** *Obsolete.* **a.** unreality; deception. **b.** an instance of this; a delusion or deception.
—*adj.* like a ghost; unreal; merely apparent: *a phantom ship, phantom prosperity. I retire, impenetrable to ridicule, under the phantom cloud of Elia* (Charles Lamb).
[< Old French *fantosme* < Vulgar Latin *phantagma,* variant of Latin *phantasma.* Doublet of PHANTASM, PHANTASMA.]
—**phan′tom·like′,** *adj.*
—**Syn.** *n.* **2.** apparition, specter.

phantom freight, a charge for shipping from a distant plant a product, as an automobile, actually delivered from a plant close by: *The National Automobile Dealers Assn. told investigation senators . . . the charging of "phantom freight" by automobile manufacturers should be ended* (Birmingham News).

phan·tom·ic (fan tom′ik), *adj.* phantomlike; unreal.

phantom limb pain, pain felt in a limb that has been amputated: *Phantom limb pains . . . can be relieved in many cases by ultrasound treatment* (Science News Letter).

phantom order, a standing order for materials, especially weapons, airplanes, etc., placed by the United States government with a firm, but not acted upon until an official signal for proceeding is given.

Phar. or **phar., 1.** pharmaceutic. **2.** pharmacopoeia. **3.** pharmacy.

Phar·aoh or **phar·aoh** (fãr′ō, -ē ō), *n.* the title given to the kings of ancient Egypt.

[Old English *Pharaon* < Late Latin *Pharaō, -ōnis* < Greek *Pharaṓ* < Hebrew *par'oh* < an Egyptian word meaning literally "great house"]

Pharaoh's ant, a very tiny reddish or pale ant. It is a common house pest that is attracted by greasy food.

Pharaoh's hen or **chicken,** a vulture of the Mediterranean region and southern Asia, about two feet long, with mostly white plumage. It is frequently represented in ancient Egyptian art.

Pharaoh's rat, the ichneumon.

Phar·a·on·ic (fãr′ē on′ik), *adj.* **1.** of or having to do with a Pharaoh or the Pharaohs. **2.** like or characteristic of a Pharaoh or the Pharaohs.

Phar.B., *U.S.* Bachelor of Pharmacy.

Phar.D., *U.S.* Doctor of Pharmacy.

phare (fãr), *n.* pharos.

Phar·i·sa·ic (far′ə sā′ik), *adj.* of or having to do with the Pharisees. [< Late Latin *Pharisaicus* < Greek *pharisaïkós*]

phar·i·sa·ic (far′ə sā′ik), *adj.* **1.** making an outward show of religion or morality without the real spirit. **2.** thinking oneself more moral than others; hypocritical; self-righteous: *smug and pharisaic fools* (John Galsworthy). [< *Pharisaic*] **—phar′i·sa′i·cal·ly,** *adv.* **—phar′i·sa′i·cal·ness,** *n.*

phar·i·sa·i·cal (far′ə sā′ə kəl), *adj.* pharisaic.

Phar·i·sa·ism (far′ə sā iz′əm), *n.* the doctrine and practice of the Pharisees.

phar·i·sa·ism (far′ə sā iz′əm), *n.* **1.** rigid observance of the external forms of religion without genuine piety. **2.** self-righteousness; hypocrisy.

Phar·i·see (far′ə sē), *n.* a member of an ancient Jewish sect that was very strict in keeping to tradition and the laws of its religion. [< Old French *pharise*, and Old English *fariseos*, plural, both learned borrowings from Latin *pharisaeus* < Greek *pharisaîos* < Aramaic *pərishayyā*]

phar·i·see (far′ə sē), *n.* **1.** a person who makes a show of religion rather than following its spirit; formalist; hypocrite. **2.** a person who considers himself much better than other persons. [< *Pharisee*]

Phar·i·see·ism (far′ə sē iz′əm), *n.* Pharisaism.

phar·i·see·ism (far′ə sē iz′əm), *n.* pharisaism.

Pharm. or **pharm., 1.** pharmaceutic. **2.** pharmacopoeia. **3.** pharmacy.

Phar.M., *U.S.* Master of Pharmacy.

phar·ma·cal (fär′mə kəl), *adj.* pharmaceutic.

phar·ma·ceu·tic (fär′mə sü′tik), *adj.* **1.** having to do with pharmacy. **2.** engaged in pharmacy. —*n.* a pharmaceutic preparation; medicinal drug. [< Late Latin *pharmaceuticus* < Greek *pharmakeutikós* < *pharmakân* be in need of drugs < *phármakon* drug, poison] **—phar′ma·ceu′ti·cal·ly,** *adv.*

phar·ma·ceu·ti·cal (fär′mə sü′tə kəl), *adj.* pharmaceutic. —*n.* a medicinal drug; pharmaceutic.

phar·ma·ceu·tics (fär′mə sü′tiks), *n.* pharmacy.

phar·ma·ceu·tist (fär′mə sü′tist), *n.* a pharmacist.

phar·ma·cist (fär′mə sist), *n.* a druggist; chemist who prepares medicines.

phar·ma·co·dy·nam·ic (fär′mə kō dī nam′ik), *adj.* relating to the powers or effects of drugs.

phar·ma·co·dy·nam·ics (fär′mə kō dī nam′iks), *n.* the branch of pharmacology dealing with the powers or effects of drugs in an organism. [< Greek *phármakon* drug, poison + English *dynamics*]

phar·ma·cog·no·sist (fär′mə kog′nə sist), *n.* a person skilled in pharmacognosy.

phar·ma·cog·nos·tic (fär′mə kog nos′tik), *adj.* having to do with pharmacognosy.

phar·ma·cog·no·sy (fär′mə kog′nə sē), *n.* the branch of pharmacy dealing with medicinal substances in their natural or unprepared state; the knowledge of drugs. [< Greek *phármakon* drug, poison + *gnōsis* knowledge (< *gignṓskein* to know) + English *-y*[3]]

pharmacol., pharmacology.

phar·ma·co·log·ic (fär′mə kə loj′ik), *adj.* pharmacological.

phar·ma·co·log·i·cal (fär′mə kə loj′ə kəl), *adj.* having to do with or relating to pharmacology.**—phar′ma·co·log′i·cal·ly,** *adv.*

phar·ma·col·o·gist (fär′mə kol′ə jist), *n.* a person skilled in the science of drugs: *Sooner or later, the pharmacologist will supply the physician with the means of affecting, in any desired sense, the functions of any physiological element of the body* (Thomas Huxley).

phar·ma·col·o·gy (fär′mə kol′ə jē), *n.* the science of drugs, their preparation, uses, and particularly their effects. [< New Latin *pharmacologia* < Greek *phármakon* drug, poison + *-logiā* -logy]

phar·ma·co·poe·ia or **phar·ma·co·pe·ia** (fär′mə kə pē′ə), *n., pl.* **-ias. 1.** a book containing an official list and description of drugs and medicines. **2.** a stock or collection of drugs, medicines, or remedies. [< New Latin *pharmacopoeia* < Greek *pharmakopoiíā* < *pharmakopoiós*, adjective, preparing drugs < *phármakon* drug, poison + *poieîn* to make]

phar·ma·co·poe·ial or **phar·ma·co·pe·ial** (fär′mə kə pē′əl), *adj.* **1.** having to do with a pharmacopoeia. **2.** recognized in, or prepared, administered, etc., according to the directions of the official pharmacopoeia.

phar·ma·co·poe·ist or **phar·ma·co·pe·ist** (fär′mə kə pē′ist), *n.* a compiler of a pharmacopoeia.

phar·ma·co·ther·a·peu·tic (fär′mə kō ther′ə pyü′tik), *adj.* of or having to do with pharmacotherapeutics.

phar·ma·co·ther·a·peu·tics (fär′mə kō ther′ə pyü′tiks), *n.* the scientific study of the treatment of disease by means of drugs.

phar·ma·co·ther·a·py (fär′mə kō ther′ə pē), *n.* treatment of disease by means of drugs.

phar·ma·cy (fär′mə sē), *n., pl.* **-cies. 1.** the preparation and dispensing of drugs and medicines; occupation of a druggist. **2.** a place where drugs and medicines are prepared or sold; drugstore. **3.** a pharmacopoeial collection. [Middle English *fermocie* a medicine; the use of medicines < Old French *farmacie*, learned borrowing from Medieval Latin *pharmacia* < Greek *pharmakeíā* < *pharmakeús* preparer of drugs < *phármakon* drug, poison]

Pharm.D., *U.S.* Doctor of Pharmacy.

phar·mic (fär′mik), *adj.* of or having to do with pharmacy or drugs.

Pharm.M., *U.S.* Master of Pharmacy.

phar·os (fãr′os), *n.* a lighthouse, beacon, or other guiding light: *a steep . . . mount, on the top of which . . . had been a pharos or lighthouse* (Washington Irving). [< Latin *pharos* < Greek *pháros* lighthouse < *Pháros* Pharos (of Alexandria)]

Phar·os of Alexandria (fãr′os), one of the seven wonders of the ancient world, a celebrated lighthouse on the island of Pharos, now a small peninsula in Northern Egypt.

pha·ryn·gal (fə ring′gəl), *adj.* **1.** *Phonetics.* articulated in the pharynx. **2.** pharyngeal.

pha·ryn·ge·al (fə rin′jē əl, far′in jē′-), *adj.* **1.** having to do with the pharynx. **2.** connected with the pharynx.

pharyngeal tonsil, a mass of lymphoid glandular tissue at the back of the upper part of the pharynx, especially in children, the abnormal enlargement of which is called adenoids.

phar·yn·gec·to·my (far′in jek′tə mē), *n., pl.* **-mies.** the removal of part or all of the pharynx. [< Greek *phárynx, -yngos* pharynx + *ektomḗ* a cutting out]

pha·ryn·ges (fə rin′jēz), *n.* a plural of **pharynx.**

phar·yn·gi·tis (far′in jī′tis), *n.* inflammation of the mucous membrane of the pharynx. [< New Latin *pharyngitis* < Greek *phárynx, -yngos* pharynx + *-îtis* -itis]

phar·yn·gol·o·gy (far′ing gol′ə jē), *n.* the branch of medicine dealing with the structure, functions, and diseases of the pharynx. [< Greek *phárynx, -yngos* pharynx + English *-logy*]

pha·ryn·go·na·sal (fə ring′gō nā′zəl), *adj.* having to do with the pharynx and nose. [< Greek *phárynx, -yngos* pharynx + English *nasal*]

pha·ryn·go·scope (fə ring′gə skōp), *n.* an instrument for examining the pharynx. [< Greek *phárynx, -yngos* pharynx + English *-scope*]

phar·yn·gos·co·py (far′ing gos′kə pē), *n.* inspection of the pharynx.

phar·yn·got·o·my (far′ing got′ə mē), *n., pl.* **-mies.** surgical incision into the pharynx. [< Greek *phárynx, -yngos* pharynx + *-tomiā* a cutting]

phar·ynx (far′ingks), *n., pl.* **phar·ynx·es** or **pha·ryn·ges.** the tube or cavity that connects the mouth and nasal passages with the esophagus. In mammals, the pharynx contains the opening from the mouth, the opening of the esophagus, of the larynx, and of the passages from the nose. *The length of the pharynx varies slightly as the larynx is raised or lowered in speech* (C. K. Thomas). [< New Latin *pharynx* < Greek *phárynx, -yngos* pharynx, windpipe, throat]

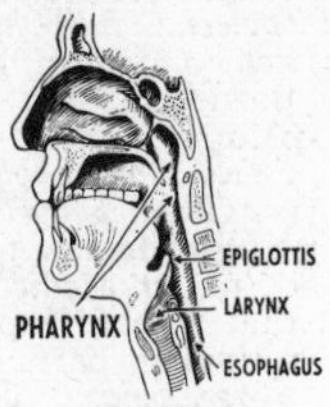

Pharynx of a human being

phase (fāz), *n., v.,* **phased, phas·ing.** —*n.* **1.** one of the changing states or stages of development of a person or thing: *A phase of my life was closing tonight, a new one opening tomorrow* (Charlotte Brontë). **2.** one side, part, or view (of a subject): *What phase of mathematics are you studying now?* **3.** the apparent shape of the illuminated part of the disk of the moon or of a planet as viewed from the earth. The new moon, first quarter, full moon, and last quarter, are four phases of the moon. See picture under **moon. 4.** *Physics.* a particular stage or point in a recurring sequence of movements or changes, considered in relation to a starting point of normal position (used with reference to circular motion, simple harmonic motion, or an alternating current, sound vibration, etc.): *The current in all parts of a series circuit is in the same phase.* **5.** one of the states, especially of coloration, of fur, plumage, etc., characteristic of certain animals at certain seasons or ages; color phase: *Ermine is the fur of a weasel in its winter phase.* **6.** *Biology.* one of the distinct stages in meiosis or mitosis. See picture under **mitosis. 7.** *Physical Chemistry.* a homogeneous part of a heterogeneous system, separated from other parts by definite boundaries, as ice in water. *Abbr.:* ph.

in phase, *Physics.* in the same phase: *They are in phase with each other, both reaching maximum values at the same instant* (J.A. Ratcliffe).

out of phase, a. *Physics.* in a different phase, or in different phases: *voltages that are out of phase.* **b.** out of step: *He was childlike and foolish, totally out of phase with all other Dominicans, a stranger in a foreign land* (Atlantic).

—*v.t.* **1.** to plan, execute, time, or adjust (an action, operation, program, etc.) according to definite phases: *to phase an army's withdrawal.* **2.** to bring or put (something) into an operation, program, etc., as a phase or in phases.

phase in, to develop or integrate as a phase or in phases: *It is hoped that seven to nine additional units will be "phased in" yearly until the planned total is reached* (New York Times).

phase out, to discontinue or eliminate as a phase or in phases: *During the last few years the service has been phasing out its aircraft of World War II vintage* (New York Times).

[probably back formation < *phases*, plural of *phasis*]

phase angle, 1. *Astronomy.* the angle formed by the earth and the sun as seen from a planet, such as the moon: *The phase angle is greatest when the planet is near quadrature* (Robert H. Baker). **2.** *Physics.* an angle representing two quantities which show differences in phase: *The current is said to lag behind the voltage by ⅓π rad, or by a phase angle of 60 electrical degrees* (Shortley and Williams).

phase-con·trast microscope (fāz′kon′trast), a microscope which uses the differences in phase of light passing through or reflected by the object under examination, to form distinct and contrastive images of different parts of the object: *The phase-contrast microscope . . . has made it possible to observe in living cells structures which previously could be seen only if the cells were killed and stained* (Scientific American).

phase modulation, a means of electronic modulation in which the phase of the carrier wave is varied in order to transmit the amplitude and pitch of the signal.

phase-out (fāz′out′), *n.* the discontinuation of an operation, production, program, etc., by stages: *The British government would plan a gradual phase-out of the British strategic nuclear forces* (Harper's).

phase rule, *Physical Chemistry.* F = C − P + 2, where F represents the freedom of a substance, C its components, and P its phases.

pha·sis (fā′sis), *n., pl.* **-ses** (-sēz). phase, especially: **a.** any one aspect of a thing of varying appearances. **b.** a state or stage of change or development. [< New Latin *phasis* < Greek *phásis* phase, appearance < *phaínein* to show, appear]

phas·mid (faz′mid), *n.* a walking stick, or stick insect. [< New Latin *Phasma* the genus name < Greek *phásma* apparition < *phaínein* to appear]

Ph.B., *U.S.* Bachelor of Philosophy (Latin, *Philosophiae Baccalaureus*).

Ph.C., Pharmaceutical Chemist.

Ph.D., Doctor of Philosophy (Latin, *Philosophiae Doctor*).

pheas·ant (fez′ənt), *n., pl.* **-ants** or (*collectively*) **-ant. 1.** any of a group of large game birds with bright plumage in the male, and long pointed tail feathers, that nest on the ground and fly only short distances. Pheasants are native to Asia but are now established in Europe and America. **2.** any of various similar birds, as the ruffed grouse. [< Anglo-French *fesant,* Old French *fesan,* learned borrowing from Latin *phāsiānus* < Greek *phāsiānós* (literally) Phasian (bird) < *Phâsis,* the river Phasis in Colchis]

Ring-necked Pheasant (def. 1) (including tail, about 3 ft. long)

pheas·ant·ry (fez′ən trē), *n., pl.* **-ries.** a place where pheasants are bred and kept.

pheas·ant's-eye (fez′ənts ī′), *n.* any of certain plants, as an herb of the crowfoot family grown for its scarlet or crimson flowers, or a variety of common garden pink.

phe·be (fē′bē), *n.* phoebe.

phel·lem (fel′əm), *n. Botany.* cork. [< Greek *phellós* cork + English *-em,* as in *phloem*]

phel·lo·derm (fel′ə dėrm), *n. Botany.* a layer of parenchymatous cells often containing chlorophyll, formed in the stems and roots of some plants from the inner cells of the phellogen. [< Greek *phellós* cork + *dérma* skin]

phel·lo·der·mal (fel′ə dėr′məl), *adj.* of or having to do with the phelloderm.

phel·lo·gen (fel′ə jən), *n.* a layer of cellular tissue or secondary meristem forming cork cells toward the outside and phelloderm toward the inside of the stem and root of many plants; cork cambium. [< Greek *phellós* cork + English *-gen*]

phel·lo·ge·net·ic (fel′ə jə net′ik), *adj.* **1.** producing cork. **2.** like phellogen.

phel·lo·gen·ic (fel′ə jen′ik), *adj.* **1.** like phellogen. **2.** having to do with phellogen.

phen-, *combining form.* a benzene derivative, as in *phenacetin, phenyl.* Also, **pheno-** before consonants. [< French *phén-* < Greek *phaínein* show forth (because such early substances were by-products from the making of illuminating gas)]

phe·na·caine hydrochloride, or **phe·na·caine** (fē′nə kān, fen′ə-), *n.* a white, soluble crystalline powder used as a local anesthetic, especially for the eye; Holocaine hydrochloride. *Formula:* $C_{18}H_{22}N_2O_2.HCl.H_2O$

phe·nac·e·tin or **phe·nac·e·tine** (fə nas′ə tin), *n.* a white, soluble crystalline powder, used to relieve fever and pain. *Formula:* $C_{10}H_{13}NO_2$

phen·a·cite (fen′ə sīt), *n.* a mineral, a colorless, yellow, or brown silicate of beryllium, sometimes used as a gem, occurring in quartzlike transparent or translucent crystals. *Formula:* Be_2SiO_4 [< Greek *phénāx, -ākos* a cheat + English *-ite*[1] (because it was mistaken for quartz)]

phe·nac·o·mys (fə nak′ə mis), *n.* any of a group of small voles or mice with, usually, long, silky fur, found in Canada, Alaska, and mountains of western United States. [< New Latin *Phenacomys* the genus name < Greek *phénāx, -akos* deceiver + New Latin *-mys* mouse]

phen·a·kis·to·scope (fen′ə kis′tə skōp), *n.* a scientific toy consisting of a disk with figures upon it arranged radially, representing a moving object in successive positions. When the disk is turned around rapidly and the viewer sees the figures through a fixed slit (or their reflections in a mirror through radial slits in the disk itself) in quick succession the eye receives the impression of actual motion. [< Greek *phenakistḗs* cheater + English *-scope* (because the viewer sees only a representation of motion)]

phe·nan·threne (fə nan′thrēn), *n.* a colorless hydrocarbon crystallizing in shining scales, found in association with anthracene (with which it is isomeric) and used in making dyes, drugs, and explosives. *Formula:* $C_{14}H_{10}$

phen·a·zin (fen′ə zin), *n.* phenazine.

phen·a·zine (fen′ə zēn, -zin), *n.* a basic chemical compound crystallizing in long yellowish needles. It is a source of many important dyes. *Formula:* $C_{12}H_8N_2$

phe·na·zone (fē′nə zōn), *n.* **1.** antipyrine, a white crystalline powder. **2.** a yellowish, crystalline compound isomeric with phenazine.

phen·el·zine (fen′əl zēn), *n.* a synthetic drug that helps to relieve mental depression.

Phen·er·gan (fen′ər gan), *n. Trademark.* a tranquilizing drug used in treating allergies and motion sickness and as a light anesthetic. *Formula:* $C_{17}H_{20}N_2S$

phe·net·i·din (fə net′ə din), *n.* phenetidine.

phe·net·i·dine (fə net′ə dēn, -din), *n.* a colorless liquid base found in three isomeric forms. It is derived from phenetole, and is used in making phenacetin and dyes. *Formula:* $C_8H_{11}ON$

phen·e·tol (fen′ə tol), *n.* phenetole.

phen·e·tole (fen′ə tōl, -tol), *n.* a colorless volatile, aromatic liquid. *Formula:* $C_8H_{10}O$ [< *phen*(o)- + *et*(hyl) + *-ol*[1]]

phen·for·min (fen′fər min), *n.* DBI; a drug used against diabetes.

Phe·ni·cian (fə nish′ən, -nē′shən), *adj., n.* Phoenician.

phe·nix (fē′niks), *n.* phoenix.

pheno-, *combining form.* the form of **phen-** before consonants, as in *phenobarbital.*

phe·no·bar·bi·tal (fē′nō bär′bə tōl, -tal; fen′ə-), *n.* a white powder, used chiefly in the form of phenobarbital sodium as a hypnotic or sedative. It is a crystalline barbiturate. *Formula:* $C_{12}H_{12}N_2O_3$

phenobarbital sodium, a bitter, white soluble powder, used as a hypnotic or sedative. *Formula:* $C_{12}H_{11}N_2O_3Na$

phe·no·bar·bi·tone (fē′nō bär′bə tōn), *n. Especially British.* phenobarbital: *Treatment with phenobarbitone for a few weeks apparently terminated both the addiction and its unpleasant result* (New Scientist).

phe·no·cop·y (fē′nə kop′ē), *n., pl.* **-cop·ies.** a phenotype that simulates the traits characteristic of another genotype: . . . *chemically induced phenocopy of a tomato mutant* (Science).

phe·no·cryst (fē′nə krist, fen′ə-), *n.* any of the large or conspicuous crystals in a porphyritic rock. [< French *phénocryste* < Greek *phaínein* to show, appear + *krýstallos* crystal]

phe·no·gam (fē′nə gam), *n.* phanerogam.

phe·no·gam·ic (fē′nə gam′ik), *adj.* phanerogamic.

phe·nog·a·mous (fi nog′ə məs), *adj.* phanerogamous.

phe·nol (fē′nol, -nōl), *n.* **1.** carbolic acid. **2.** any of a series of aromatic hydroxyl derivatives of benzene, of which phenol is the first member.

phe·no·late (fē′nə lāt), *n.* a salt of phenol; phenoxide.

phe·no·lic (fi nō′lik, -nol′ik), *adj.* **1.** of the nature of phenol. **2.** belonging to phenol. —*n.* any of a group of thermosetting synthetic resins, obtained chiefly by the reaction of a phenol with an aldehyde, used for molding, in varnishes, etc.

phenolic resin, phenolic.

phe·no·lize (fē′nə līz), *v.t.,* **-lized, -liz·ing.** to treat with phenol: *Phenolized vaccine gives better protection than the alcoholized type* (Science News Letter).

phe·no·log·i·cal (fē′nə log′ə kəl), *adj.* of or having to do with phenology or the objects of its study.

phe·nol·o·gist (fi nol′ə jist), *n.* a person who studies phenology.

phe·nol·o·gy (fi nol′ə jē), *n.* the study of periodic occurrences in nature, as the migration of birds, the ripening of fruit, etc., and their relation to climate.

phe·nol·phthal·ein (fē′nōl thal′ēn, -fthal′-), *n.* a white or pale-yellow powder used in testing acidity, making dyes, medicines, etc. Its solution is red when basic, colorless when acid. *Formula:* $C_{20}H_{14}O_4$

phe·nom·e·na (fə nom′ə nə), *n.* a plural of **phenomenon:** *It is expected to obtain data on solar radiation, sky brightness and other important phenomena* (New York Times).

➤ **Phenomena** is sometimes taken to be a singular and so used, but this construction is not current in standard English.

phe·nom·e·nal (fə nom′ə nəl), *adj.* **1.** of or having to do with a phenomenon or phenomena. **2.** having the nature of a phenomenon; apparent; sensible; perceptible: *Seen in the light of thought, the world always is phenomenal* (Emerson). **3.** very notable or remarkable; extraordinary; exceptional: *a phenomenal memory.* **4.** based on or dealing entirely in terms of things that are or have been observed; not using or containing hypotheses: *phenomenal geology.*
—*n.* **the phenomenal,** things that are known by the senses: *The ideal is the subjective, the phenomenal the objective* (John Grote).
—**phe·nom′e·nal·ly,** *adv.*

phe·nom·e·nal·ism (fə nom′ə nə liz′əm), *n.* **1.** any of various theories that knowledge is attainable only through careful observation of phenomena; doctrine that knowledge consists solely in the accumulation and manipulation of observed data. **2.** *Philosophy.* the doctrine that phenomena are the realities and therefore the only possible objects of knowledge; absolute externalism.

phe·nom·e·nal·ist (fə nom′ə nə list), *n.* a supporter of phenomenalism.

phe·nom·e·nal·is·tic (fə nom′ə nə lis′tik), *adj.* of or having to do with phenomenalism.

phe·nom·e·nal·i·ty (fə nom′ə nal′ə tē), *n., pl.* **-ties. 1.** the quality or state of being phenomenal. **2.** a phenomenal act, feat, etc.: *Among de Gaulle's phenomenalities would now appear to be the possession of supernormal mental and physical detachment from personal events* (New Yorker).

phe·nom·e·no·log·i·cal (fə nom′ə nə log′ə kəl), *adj.* of or having to do with phenomenology. —**phe·nom′e·no·log′i·cal·ly,** *adv.*

phe·nom·e·nol·o·gist (fə nom′ə nol′ə jist), *n.* a person engaged in phenomenology.

phe·nom·e·nol·o·gy (fə nom′ə nol′ə jē), *n.* **1.** the science of phenomena, as distinct from ontology or the science of being. **2.** that division of any science which describes and classifies its phenomena.

phe·nom·e·non (fə nom′ə non), *n., pl.* **-na** or (*especially for def. 2*) **-nons. 1.** a fact, event, or circumstance that can be observed: *Lightning is an electrical phenomenon. Fever and inflammation are phenomena of disease.* **2.** something or someone extraordinary or remarkable: *You might have thought a goose the rarest of all birds — a feathered phenomenon* (Dickens). **3.** *Philosophy.* something that the senses or the mind directly takes note of; an immediate object of perception, as distinguished from a thing in itself. [< Late Latin *phaenomenon* appearance < Greek *phainómenon,* ultimately < *phaínein* show forth]

phe·no·thi·a·zin (fē′nō thī′ə zin), *n.* phenothiazine.

phe·no·thi·a·zine (fē′nō thī′ə zēn, -zin), *n.* a yellowish crystalline substance used in making dyes, as an insecticide, and as a vermifuge for cattle, sheep, etc. *Formula:* $C_{12}H_9NS$

phe·no·type (fē′nə tīp), *n. Biology.* **1.** a character or individual organism defined by its appearance and not by its genetic constitution or hereditary potentialities. **2.** a group of animals or plants having one or more such characters in common. **3.** the visible result of the interaction between a genotype and its environment.

phe·no·typ·ic (fē′nə tip′ik), *adj.* of or having to do with phenotypes: *Flowering is an apparent or phenotypic response of the genotype to its environment* (Science News Letter). —**phe′no·typ′i·cal·ly,** *adv.*

phe·no·typ·i·cal (fē′nə tip′ə kəl), *adj.* phenotypic.

phe·nox·ide (fi nok′sīd), *n.* phenolate.

phen·yl (fen′əl, fē′nəl), *n.* a univalent radical ($-C_6H_5$) occurring in benzene, phenol, and an extensive series of aromatic compounds, formed by removing one hydrogen atom from a benzene molecule. *Abbr.:* Ph (no period). [< French *phényle* < *phène* benzene + *-yle* -yl]

phen·yl·al·a·nine (fen′ə lal′ə nēn, fē′nə-), *n.* an amino acid which results from the hydrolysis of protein and is normally converted to tyrosine in the body. When, as a result of a hereditary defect, the conversion does not take place properly, phenylketonuria results. *Formula:* $C_9H_{11}NO_2$

phen·yl·a·mine (fen′ə lə mēn′, fē′nə lam′-in), *n.* the systematic name for aniline.

phen·yl·bu·ta·zone (fen′əl byü′tə zōn, fē′nəl-), *n.* a synthetic drug derived from coal tar and used to treat rheumatism and arthritis. *Formula:* $C_{19}H_{20}N_2O_2$

phen·yl·ene (fen′ə lēn, fē′nə-), *n.* a bivalent radical ($-C_6H_4-$) formed by removing two hydrogen atoms from a benzene molecule.

phe·nyl·ic (fi nil′ik), *adj.* **1.** of phenyl. **2.** derived from phenyl.

phen·yl·ke·to·nu·ri·a (fen′əl kē′tə nyůr′ē-ə, fē′nəl-; -nůr′-), *n.* a hereditary disease caused by an inability to metabolize phenylalanine properly in the body, resulting in mental deficiency and poor physical development.

phen·yl·ke·to·nu·ric (fen′əl kē′tə nyůr′-ik, fē′nəl-; -nůr′-), *adj.* of, having to do with, or affected with phenylketonuria: *It will be possible to perform experiments with these animals that cannot be performed with phenylketonuric children* (Science News Letter). —*n.* a person affected with phenylketonuria: *The mental defect of phenylketonurics is graded, and a few of them are stupid but not sufficiently so to be classed as feeble-minded* (J.B.S. Haldane).

phen·yl·thi·o·car·bam·id (fen′əl thī′ō-kär bam′id, -id; fē′nəl-), *n.* phenylthiourea.

phen·yl·thi·o·u·re·a (fen′əl thī′ō yů rē′ə, -yůr′ē-; fē′nəl-), *n.* a crystalline substance that is either bitter, slightly sweet, or tasteless, depending on the heredity of the taster, used in various genetic tests. *Formula:* $C_7H_8N_2S$

phe·on (fē′on), *n.* **1.** *Heraldry.* the barbed head of an arrow or spear, with the point directed downward. **2.** a barbed javelin formerly carried by a royal sergeant at arms. [origin unknown]

Pher·e·cra·te·an (fer′ə krə tē′ən), *Ancient Prosody.* —*adj.* noting or having to do with a logaoedic tripody, catalectic or acatalectic, whose first or second foot is a dactyl, the others being trochees. —*n.* a Pherecratean tripody or verse. [< *Pherecrates,* a Greek comic poet of the 400's B.C. + *-an*]

Pher·e·crat·ic (fer′ə krat′ik), *adj., n.* Pherecratean.

pher·o·mone (fer′ə mōn), *n.* a substance secreted externally by certain animal species, especially insects, to affect the behavior or development of other members of the species: *The queen substance of honeybees, which inhibits ovary development . . . in workers, is a pheromone* (New Scientist). [< *phero-* (< Greek *phérein* carry) + (hor)*mone*]

phew (fyü, pfyü), *interj.* an exclamation of disgust, impatience, surprise, etc. [imitative of blowing outward with the lips. Compare POOF.]

Ph.G., *U.S.* Graduate in Pharmacy.

phi (fī, fē), *n.* the 21st letter of the Greek alphabet (Φ, φ), corresponding phonetically to English *f,* but usually transliterated by *ph.* [< Greek *phî*]

phi·al (fī′əl), *n.* a small bottle; vial. [Middle English *fiole* < Old French *fiole,* apparently learned borrowing from Medieval Latin *phiola,* variant of Latin *phiala* < Greek *phiálē* broad, flat drinking vessel]

Phi Be·ta Kap·pa (fī′ bā′tə kap′ə, bē′tə), **1.** an honorary society composed of American college students and graduates in liberal arts and science who have ranked high in scholarship: *The bride was graduated summa cum laude in 1947 from Barnard College, where she was elected to Phi Beta Kappa* (New York Times). **2.** a member of this society. [< the initial letters of the Greek phrase *ph*(*ilosophíā*) *b*(*íou*) *k*(*ybernḗtēs*) philosophy the guide of life]

Phi Bete (fī′bāt′), *U.S. Informal.* a member of Phi Beta Kappa: *A Phi Bete* (*Chicago '41*), *Lorenz is a finance-trained protégé of former Ford President Robert McNamara* (Time).

Phid·i·an (fid′ē ən), *adj.* **1.** of or having to do with the sculpture of Phidias. **2.** like the work of Phidias. [< *Phidias,* about 490-420 B.C., a Greek sculptor + English *-an*]

phil-, *combining form.* the form of **philo-** before vowels, as in *philanthropy.*

-phil, *combining form.* variant of **-phile,** as in *eosinophil.*

phil., philosophy.

Phil., an abbreviation for the following:
1. Philemon (book of the New Testament)
2. Philip.
3. Philippians (book of the New Testament).
4. a. Philippine. **b.** Philippines.

Phila., Philadelphia.

phil·a·beg (fil′ə beg), *n.* filibeg; kilt.

Phil·a·del·phi·a lawyer (fil′ə del′fē ə, -fyə), *U.S.* **1.** a very shrewd, able lawyer (as many in Philadelphia, Pennsylvania, were, and all were popularly believed to be, during the 1700's). **2.** a very shrewd lawyer of dubious scruples, enormously skilled in the niceties and technicalities of legal language, tactics, etc. (as many in Philadelphia were popularly believed to be during the 1800's).

phil·a·del·phi·an (fil′ə del′fē ən, -fyən), *adj.* having or showing brotherly love, especially for one's fellow beings. —*n.* a person imbued with brotherly love, especially for his fellow beings. [< Greek *philadelphiā* (< *philádelphos* having brotherly love < *phílos* loving + *adelphós* brother) + English *-an*]

Phil·a·del·phi·an (fil′ə del′fē ən, -fyən), *adj.* of or having to do with Philadelphia, Pennsylvania. —*n.* a native or inhabitant of Philadelphia.

Philadelphia pepper pot, pepper pot.

Philadelphia vireo, a North American vireo with a light yellowish breast.

Phi·lan·der (fə lan′dər), *n.* a name given to a lover in old romance, poetry, etc. [< Greek *phílandros,* adjective < *phílos* loving, fond of + *anḗr, andrós* man]

phi·lan·der (fə lan′dər), *v.i.* (of a man) to make love without serious intentions; flirt. [< *Philander*] —**phi·lan′der·er,** *n.*

phil·an·thrope (fil′ən thrōp), *n.* a philanthropist. [< French *philanthrope* < Greek *philánthrōpos* loving mankind < *phílos* loving + *ánthrōpos* mankind]

phil·an·throp·ic (fil′ən throp′ik), *adj.* **1. a.** having to do with or characterized by philanthropy. **b.** engaged in philanthropy: *a philanthropic foundation.* **2.** charitable; benevolent; kindly: *a philanthropic nature.* —**phil′an·throp′i·cal·ly,** *adv.*

phil·an·throp·i·cal (fil′ən throp′ə kəl), *adj.* philanthropic.

phi·lan·thro·pist (fə lan′thrə pist), *n.* a person who shows his love for mankind by practical kindness and helpfulness to humanity.

phi·lan·thro·pize (fə lan′thrə pīz), *v.t.,* **-pized, -piz·ing.** to treat philanthropically.

phi·lan·thro·poid (fə lan′thrə poid), *n.* a person who is in charge of disbursing the money of a philanthropist or philanthropic foundation: *The big foundations assembled a great bureaucracy of philanthropoids, who hatched projects and scattered them over the nation* (Newsweek). [< *philanthrop*(ist) + *-oid*]

phi·lan·thro·py (fə lan′thrə pē), *n., pl.* **-pies. 1.** love of mankind shown by practical kindness and helpfulness to humanity: *The Red Cross appeals to philanthropy.* **2.** a thing that benefits humanity; philanthropic agency, enterprise, gift, etc.: *A hospital is a useful philanthropy.* [< Late Latin *philanthrōpia* < Greek *philanthrōpiā* < *philánthrōpos;* see PHILANTHROPE] —**Syn. 1.** benevolence, charity.

phil·a·tel·ic (fil′ə tel′ik), *adj.* of or having to do with philately: *Last Thursday marked the end of the first year of stamp-issuing by the United Nations—a philatelic development which was widely opposed, in advance, by American and British collectors* (New York Times). —**phil′a·tel′i·cal·ly,** *adv.*

phil·a·tel·i·cal (fil′ə tel′ə kəl), *adj.* philatelic.

phi·lat·e·list (fə lat′ə list), *n.* a collector of postage stamps, postmarks, etc.: *A philatelist applied for room for a stamp display* (Wall Street Journal).

phi·lat·e·ly (fə lat′ə lē), *n.* the collecting, arranging, and study of postage stamps, stamped envelopes, post cards, etc. [< French *philatélie,* ultimately < Greek *phílos* loving + *atéleia* exemption from public assessments (since a postage stamp shows prepayment of postal tax)]

Phi·la·the·a (fə lā′thē ə), *n.* an international, interdenominational organization of Bible classes for young women. [< Greek *phílos* loving + *theós* god]

-phile, *combining form.* a lover of ——; a person who is fond of ——: *Aelurophile = a lover of cats.* Also, **-phil.** [< French *-phile,* ultimately < Greek *phílos* loving]

Philem., Philemon (book of New Testament).

Phi·le·mon (fə lē′mən), *n.* **1.** one of the shortest books of the New Testament, a letter from Paul to a convert of his who lived in Colossae. *Abbr.:* Philem. **2.** *Greek Mythology.* a poor man who, with his wife Baucis, showed hospitality to Zeus and Hermes in disguise.

phi·le·nor (fə lē′nər), *n.* a handsome North American swallow-tailed butterfly, having black forewings and steel-blue hindwings, all with greenish reflections. [< New Latin *philenor* < Greek *philḗnōr* loving one's husband < *phílos* loving + *anḗr* man]

phil·har·mon·ic (fil′här mon′ik, fil′ər-), *adj.* **1.** devoted to music; loving music: *A musical club is often called a philharmonic society.* **2.** given by a philharmonic society: *a philharmonic concert.* —*n.* a philharmonic society or concert. [< French *philharmonique* < Italian *filarmonico* < Greek *phílos* loving + *tà harmoniká* the (theory of) music. Compare HARMONIC.]

Phil·har·mon·ic (fil′här mon′ik, fil′ər-), *n.* a particular symphony orchestra: *the Vienna Philharmonic, New York Philharmonic, etc.*

phil·hel·lene (fil hel′ēn), *n.* a friend or supporter of the Greeks, especially in their struggle against the Turks for independence. [< Greek *philéllēn* loving the Greeks < *phílos* loving + *Héllēn* Greek, Hellene]

phil·hel·len·ic (fil′hə len′ik, -lē′nik), *adj.* loving, friendly to, or supporting the cause of Greece or the Greeks, especially relating to national independence.

phil·hel·len·ism (fil hel′ə niz əm), *n.* philhellene spirit or principles.

phil·hel·len·ist (fil hel′ə-nist, fil′hə lē′-), *n.* philhellene.

Phil. I. or **Phil. Is.,** Philippine Islands.

-philia, *combining form.* a fondness or craving for: *Aelurophilia = a fondness for cats.* [< Greek *philía* affection < *phílos* loving]

phil·i·beg (fil′ə beg), *n.* filibeg; kilt.

Phil·ip (fil′əp), *n.* **1.** one of the twelve disciples chosen by Jesus as His Apostles. John 1:44. **2.** (in the New Testament) one of the seven overseers of charitable works at Jerusalem, and afterwards a missionary; Philip the Evangelist. Acts 6:5; 8:5–40; 21:8–9.

Phi·lip·pi·an (fə lip′ē ən), *adj.* of or having to do with Philippi, a city of ancient Macedonia. —*n.* a native or inhabitant of Philippi.

Phi·lip·pi·ans (fə lip′ē ənz), *n.pl.* (*singular in use*) one of the books of the New Testament, a letter from Paul to the early Christians of Philippi. *Abbr.:* Phil.

Phi·lip·pic (fə lip′ik), *n.* **1.** any of several orations by Demosthenes denouncing King Philip II of Macedonia and attempting to arouse the Athenians to resist Philip's growing power. **2.** any of several orations by Cicero denouncing Mark Antony. [< Latin *Philippicus* < Greek *Philippikós* having to do with *Phílippos* Philip (here, Philip of Macedonia)]

phi·lip·pic (fə lip′ik), *n.* a bitter attack in words: *With what satisfaction did I remember all Miss Debby Kittery's philippics against Ellery Davenport* (Harriet Beecher Stowe).

Phil·ip·pine (fil′ə pēn), *adj.* of or having to do with the Philippines, a country of more than 7,100 islands in the western Pacific, southeast of Asia and north of Australia, or their inhabitants. Also, **Filipine, Filipino.**

Philippine Spanish, the dialect of Spanish spoken by Spanish speakers in the Philippines.

Philip the Evangelist, Philip, one of the seven overseers of charitable works.

Phi·lis·ti·a (fə lis′tē ə), *n.* **1.** a place where uncultured, commonplace people live. **2.** the land of the ancient Philistines. [< Medieval Latin *Philistia;* see PHILISTINE]

Phi·lis·tine (fə lis′tin; fil′ə stēn, -stīn), *n.* **1.** (in the Bible) one of the warlike, people in southwest Palestine who attacked the Israelites many times: *He shall begin to deliver Israel out of the hand of the Philistines* (Judges 13:5). **2.** a person who is common-

place in ideas and tastes; one who is indifferent to or contemptuous of poetry, music, the fine arts, etc.: *You are a Philistine, Henry: you have no romance in you* (George Bernard Shaw).
—*adj.* **1.** of the Philistines: *Goliath, the Philistine champion.* **2.** lacking culture; commonplace: *Byron ... had in him a cross of the true Philistine breed* (Algernon Charles Swinburne).
[(definition 1) < Late Latin *Philistīnī*, plural < Greek *Philistînoi* < Hebrew *pəlishtīm;* (definition 2) < German *Philister*, adapted by Matthew Arnold]

Phi·lis·tin·ism or **phi·lis·tin·ism** (fə lis′tə niz əm, fil′ə stə niz′-), *n.* the character or views of uncultured, commonplace persons: *Philistinism! We have not the expression in English ... perhaps ... because we have so much of the thing* (Matthew Arnold).

Phil·lis (fil′is), *n.* Phyllis.

philo-, *combining form.* loving; having an affection for: *Philoprogenitive = loving one's progeny.* Also, **phil-** before vowels. [< Greek *philo-* < *phílos* loving]

phil·o·bib·lic (fil′ə bib′lik), *adj.* fond of books; bibliophilous. [< Greek *philóbiblos* (< *phílos* loving + *bíblos* book) + English *-ic*]

phil·o·bib·list (fil′ə bib′list), *n.* a lover of books; bibliophile.

Phil·oc·te·tes (fil′ok tē′tēz), *n. Greek Mythology.* a Greek archer, hero in the Trojan War. He inherited the bow and arrow of Hercules from his father; only by means of this could Paris be shot and Troy destroyed. Bitten by a serpent on the way to the war, and obnoxious to his companions because of his wound, he was for some years abandoned on the uninhabited island of Lemnos, but later brought to Troy.

phil·o·den·dron (fil′ə den′drən), *n.* **1.** any of a group of tropical American climbing evergreen plants of the arum family, often grown as house plants for their variously-shaped, smooth (but tough), shiny leaves. **2.** any of certain related or similar plants. [< New Latin *Philodendron* the genus name < Greek *philódendron*, neuter of *philódendros* < *phílos* fond of + *déndron* tree (because it clings to trees)]

Black Gold Philodendron (def. 1) (to 3 ft. long)

phi·log·y·nist (fə loj′ə nist), *n.* a lover or admirer of women.

phi·log·y·nous (fə loj′ə nəs), *adj.* loving women.

phi·log·y·ny (fə loj′ə nē), *n.* love of women. [< Greek *philogyniā* < *philogýnēs* loving women < *phílos* loving + *gynḗ* woman]

philol., philology.

phi·lol·o·ger (fə lol′ə jər), *n. Archaic.* a philologist.

phil·o·lo·gi·an (fil′ə lō′jē ən), *n.* a philologist.

phil·o·log·ic (fil′ə loj′ik), *adj.* of or having to do with philology; concerned with the study of language.

phil·o·log·i·cal (fil′ə loj′ə kəl), *adj.* philologic. —**phil′o·log′i·cal·ly,** *adv.*

phi·lol·o·gist (fə lol′ə jist), *n.* a person skilled in philology: *The philologists of the nineteenth century succeeded in promoting the autonomy of linguistics as an independent discipline* (Simeon Potter). *Learn'd philologists, who chase A panting syllable through time and space, Start it at home, and hunt it in the dark, to Gaul, to Greece, and into Noah's ark* (William Cowper).

phil·o·logue (fil′ə log, -lôg), *n.* a philologist.

phi·lol·o·gy (fə lol′ə jē), *n.* **1.** an older name for linguistics. **2.** the study of literary and other records. **3.** (formerly) literary or classical scholarship; the study of literature, including grammar, criticism, etymology, etc. [< Latin *philologia* < Greek *philologiā* < *philólogos* fond of words or discourse < *phílos* loving + *lógos* word, speech]

phil·o·math (fil′ə math), *n.* **1. a.** a lover of learning. **b.** a student, especially of mathematics or science. **2.** *Obsolete.* an astrologer. [< Greek *philomathḗs* fond of learning < *phílos* loving + *manthánein* learn]

phil·o·math·ic (fil′ə math′ik), *adj.* **1.** devoted to learning. **2.** *Obsolete.* astrological.

phi·lom·a·thy (fə lom′ə thē), *n.* love of learning.

phil·o·mel or **Phil·o·mel** (fil′ə mel), *n. Poetic.* the nightingale: *All night long sweet Philomel pours forth her ravishing, delightful song* (Tobias Smollett). [< Latin *philomela* < Greek *Philomêla* Philomela; nightingale < *phílos* loving + *mêlon* apple, fruit]

Phil·o·me·la (fil′ə mē′lə), *n.* **1.** *Greek Mythology.* a princess who was turned into a nightingale and as a bird continued to lament the tragedy of her life. **2.** *Poetic.* the nightingale.

phil·o·pe·na (fil′ə pē′nə), *n.* **1.** a game involving the sharing of a nut with two kernels between two people, with the agreement that the one failing to keep some stated condition shall pay a forfeit. **2.** the nut. **3.** the forfeit. [American English < French, or Dutch *Philippine*, half-translation of *Philippchen*, mispronunciation of German *Vielliebchen* (literally) very dear[1]]

phil·o·pro·ge·ne·i·ty (fil′ə prō′jə nē′ə tē), *n.* love of one's offspring; philoprogenitiveness.

phil·o·pro·gen·i·tive (fil′ō prō jen′ə tiv), *adj.* **1.** loving one's offspring; having to do with love of offspring. **2.** inclined to produce many offspring; prolific. [< *philo-* + Latin *progenitus*, past participle of *progignere* to beget + English *-ive*] —**phil′o·pro·gen′i·tive·ness,** *n.*

philos., philosophy.

phil·o·sophe (fil′ə zof′), *n.* **1.** one of a group of French rationalist, humanistic, deistic, and often revolutionary philosophers of the 1700's, typified by Denis Diderot: *The intellectual life of Paris centered on ... the philosophes, who were presently to compile a great encyclopedia of human knowledge* (Atlantic). **2.** a philosopher: *Madison was the last of the Virginia philosophes, the ultimate innocent who could seriously consult the Cabbala for the principles of good government* (Manchester Guardian). [< Old French *philosophe;* see PHILOSOPHER]

phi·los·o·pher (fə los′ə fər), *n.* **1.** a person who studies philosophy a great deal: *Our philosophers have not been slow to go beyond the ... dogma that all utterances other than statements of fact ... are literally meaningless* (London Times). **2.** a person who has a system of philosophy. **3. a.** a person who shows the calmness of philosophy under hard conditions, accepting life and making the best of it: *There was never yet philosopher That could endure the toothache patiently* (Shakespeare). **b.** a person who is guided in his life by principles which relate to man as a rational and social being: *To be a philosopher is not merely to have subtle thoughts, nor even to found a school, but so to love wisdom as to live according to its dictates, a life of simplicity, independence, magnanimity, and trust* (Thoreau). **4.** *Obsolete.* **a.** an alchemist. **b.** an expert in some other occult science. [< Anglo-French *philosofre*, Old French *philosophe*, learned borrowing from Latin *philosophus* < Greek *philósophos* lover of wisdom < *phílos* loving + *sophós* wise]

philosophers' stone, a substance believed by alchemists to have the power to change baser metals into gold or silver. It had, according to some, the power of prolonging life indefinitely and of curing all wounds and diseases.

phil·o·soph·ic (fil′ə sof′ik), *adj.* **1.** of philosophy or philosophers: *Some scientian prejudices need superseding when applied without discrimination to problems essentially philosophic* (A. T. Macqueen). **2.** knowing much about philosophy. **3.** devoted to philosophy. **4.** wise; calm; reasonable: *to be philosophic in defeat. They were mostly scholarly, quiet men, of calm and philosophic temperament* (Harriet Beecher Stowe).

phil·o·soph·i·cal (fil′ə sof′ə kəl), *adj.* philosophic; like a philosopher. —**phil′o·soph′i·cal·ly,** *adv.*

phi·los·o·phise (fə los′ə fīz), *v.i., v.t.,* **-phised, -phis·ing.** *Especially British.* philosophize.

phi·los·o·phism (fə los′ə fiz əm), *n.* **1.** the affectation of philosophy, especially sophistry. **2.** a sophism.

phi·los·o·phist (fə los′ə fist), *n.* a person who philosophizes or speculates erroneously.

phi·los·o·phize (fə los′ə fīz), *v.,* **-phized, -phiz·ing.** —*v.i.* to think or reason as a philosopher does; try to understand and explain things: *to philosophize about life, death, mind, matter, God, etc.* —*v.t.* to explain or treat philosophically. —**phi·los′o·phiz′er,** *n.*

phi·los·o·phy (fə los′ə fē), *n., pl.* **-phies. 1.** the study of the truth or principles underlying all knowledge; study of the most general causes and principles of the universe. **2.** an explanation or theory of the universe, especially an explanation or particular system arranged by a philosopher: *the philosophy of Plato.* **3.** a system for guiding life, as a body of principles of conduct, religious beliefs, or traditions: *the philosophy of a New England Puritan.* **4.** the broad general principles of a particular subject or field of activity: *the philosophy of history, the army's military philosophy, a design philosophy for aircraft.* **5.** a reasonable attitude; accepting things as they are and making the best of them; calmness. **6.** (originally) the love or pursuit of wisdom, in its broadest sense. [< Latin *philosophia* < Greek *philosophiā* love of wisdom < *philósophos* philosopher]

Phil. Soc., 1. Philological Society (of London). **2.** Philosophical Society (of America).

phil·ter or **phil·tre** (fil′tər), *n.* **1.** a drug or potion used to make a person fall in love; love potion: *He is a veritable necromancer, equipped with philters and elixirs of wondrous potency* (Harper's). **2.** a magic drink; magic potion: *Tell me now, fairy ... can't you give me a charm, or a philtre, or something of that sort, to make me a handsome man?* (Charlotte Brontë). [< French *philtre*, learned borrowing from Latin *philtrum* < Greek *phíltron* love charm < *phileîn* to love]

Phil. Trans., Philosophical Transactions (of the Royal Society of London).

phi phenomenon, *Psychology.* **1. a.** the perception of movement in a moving object. **b.** the movement perceived in such an object. **2.** the apparent movement perceived when several pictures or other stationary visual stimuli are presented successively at very brief intervals.

phiz (fiz), *n., pl.* **phiz·es.** *Slang.* face; countenance: *There was no mistaking that tanned, genial phiz of his* (Thomas Bailey Aldrich) [short for *physiognomy*]

phle·bi·tis (fli bī′tis), *n.* inflammation of a vein. [< Greek *phléps, phlebós* vein + English *-itis*]

phleb·o·scle·ro·sis (fleb′ō skli rō′sis), *n.* a thickening and hardening of the wall of a vein. [< Greek *phléps, phlebós* vein + English *sclerosis*]

phleb·o·scle·rot·ic (fleb′ō skli rot′ik), *adj.* having to do with phlebosclerosis.

phle·bot·o·mist (fli bot′ə mist), *n.* a person who treats patients by phlebotomy.

phle·bot·o·mize (fli bot′ə mīz), *v.t., v.i.,* **-mized, -miz·ing.** to practice phlebotomy; bleed.

phle·bot·o·my (fli bot′ə mē), *n., pl.* **-mies.** the opening of a vein to let blood; bleeding as a therapeutic device. [< Late Latin *phlebotomia* < Greek *phlebotomiā*, ultimately < *phléps, phlebós* blood vessel + *témnein* to cut]

Phleg·e·thon (fleg′ə thon, flej′-), *n. Greek Mythology.* the river of fire, one of the five rivers of Hades. [< Latin *Phlegethon* < Greek *Phlegéthōn*, present participle of *phlegéthein* to burn, blaze]

phlegm (flem), *n.* **1.** the thick discharge from the nose and throat that accompanies a cold. It is often an abnormally heavy discharge and is composed of mucus secreted by the mucous membranes of the respiratory passages. **2.** sluggish disposition or temperament; indifference: *Michael Redgrave as the air marshal is just the right mixture of phlegm and haw* (Time). **3.** coolness; calmness: *The French government's only sustainers of phlegm and order appear to be the Foreign Legion* (New Yorker). *The patience of the people was creditable to their phlegm* (George Meredith). **4.** (in ancient and medieval times) one of the four humors, supposedly a somewhat cold, viscous substance in the body, thought to cause sluggishness. [< Old French *fleugme*, learned borrowing from Late Latin *phlegma* < Greek *phlégma* moist humor (resulting from heat) < *phlégein* to burn]

phleg·mat·ic (fleg mat′ik), *adj.* **1.** sluggish; indifferent; not easily aroused to enthusiasm; apathetic. **2.** not easily excited; cool; calm: *John is phlegmatic; he never seems to get excited about anything.* **3.** *Obsolete.* **a.** of the nature of phlegm considered as one of the four humors. **b.** abounding in phlegm. **c.** producing phlegm. [< Late Latin *phlegmaticus* < Greek *phlegmatikós* full of phlegm < *phlégma* phlegm] —**phleg·mat′i·cal·ly,** *adv.*

phleg·mat·i·cal (fleg mat′ə kəl), *adj.* phlegmatic.

phleg·mon (fleg′mon), *n. Medicine.* inflammation of the connective tissue, especially the subcutaneous connective tissue. [< Latin *phlegmon* < Greek *phlegmonē* inflammation < *phlégein* to burn]

phleg·mo·nous (fleg′mə nəs), *adj.* **1.** having to do with a phlegmon. **2.** like a phlegmon.

phlegm·y (flem′ē), *adj.* **1.** like phlegm. **2.** characterized by phlegm. **3.** phlegmatic.

phlob·a·phene (flob′ə fēn), *n. Chemistry.* any of various reddish-brown substances found in the bark of the oak or in other material containing tannin. [< Greek *phlóos* bark + *baphē* dyeing, dye + English *-ene*]

phlo·em or **phlo·ëm** (flō′em), *n.* the tissue in a plant or tree through which dissolved food materials manufactured in the leaves pass downward to the stems and roots; bast: *. . . the phloem carries away the sugars and proteins which are synthesized there* (Fred W. Emerson). [< German *Phloem* < Greek *phlóos* bark, (human) skin; (originally) a swelling, growth < *phleîn* be full of, abound (in)]

phlo·gis·tic (flō jis′tik), *adj.* **1.** *Medicine.* inflammatory. **2.** *Old Chemistry.* having to do with or relating to phlogiston. **3.** *Obsolete.* **a.** burning; fiery. **b.** expressive of passionate anger; very heated.

phlo·gis·ton (flō jis′tən; *British, also* flō-gis′tən), *n.* a supposed element causing inflammability, once thought to exist in all things that burn. [< New Latin *phlogiston*, adjective < Greek *phlogistón*, neuter of *phlogistós* inflammable, ultimately < *phlóx*, *phlogós* flame]

phlog·o·pite (flog′ə pīt), *n. Mineralogy.* a magnesium mica, usually of a brownish-yellow or brownish-red color. [< German *Phlogopit* < Greek *phlogōpós* fiery (< *phlóx, phlogós* flame + *ōps, ōpós* face, look) + German *-it* -ite[1]]

phlo·go·sis (flə gō′sis), *n. Medicine.* inflammation, especially of external parts of the body. [< New Latin *phlogosis* < Greek *phlógōsis* < *phlóx, phlogós* flame]

phlo·rhi·zin (flə rē′zin), *n.* phlorizin.

phlo·rid·zin (flə rid′zin), *n.* phlorizin.

phlor·i·zin (flôr′ə zin, flor′-; flə rī′-), *n.* a bitter glucoside crystallizing in silky white needles, obtained from the bark of the root of the apple, pear, plum, and cherry, formerly used medicinally as a tonic and antimalarial. *Formula:* $C_{21}H_{24}O_{10}$. [< Greek *phlóos* bark (see PHLOEM) + *rhiza* root + English *-in*]

phlox (floks), *n.* **1.** any of a group of plants with clusters of showy flowers in various colors. It is one of several North American herbs that either spreads by creeping or stands erect to a height of about five feet. *By and large, however, phlox is one of the most satisfactory garden plants* (New York Times). **2.** the flower of any of these plants. [< New Latin *Phlox* the genus name < Latin *phlox* < Greek *phlóx* a kind of plant; (literally) flame]

Phlox (def. 1)

phlox·in (flok′sin), *n.* a purple coal-tar dye, resembling eosin. [< Greek *phlóx* flame + English *-in*]

phlyc·te·na or **phlyc·tae·na** (flik tē′nə), *n., pl.* **-nae** (-nē). *Medicine.* a small vesicle or blister. [< New Latin *phlyctaena* < Greek *phlýktaina* blister < *phlýein* to swell]

Ph.M., Master of Philosophy.

-phobe, *combining form.* a person who has fear, aversion, or hatred toward ——: *Aelurophobe = a person who has a fear or hatred of cats. Francophobe = a person who fears or hates the French or France.* [< French *-phobe*, learned borrowing from Latin *-phobus* < Greek *-phóbos* fearing < *phóbos* panic, fear]

pho·bi·a (fō′bē ə), *n.* a persistent, morbid, or insane fear of a specific thing or group of things: *In the phobias . . . two stages in the neurotic process are clearly discernible* (Sigmund Freud). [< *-phobia*]

-phobia, *combining form.* fear, hatred, or dread of ——: *Francophobia = fear of the French or France. Claustrophobia = fear of enclosed rooms or narrow places.* [< Greek *-phobiā* < *phóbos* panic, fear]

pho·bic (fō′bik), *adj.* **1.** having or characterized by a morbid or insane fear. **2.** of or having to do with a morbid or insane fear.

Pho·bos (fō′bəs, fob′əs), *n.* the inner satellite of Mars, about twelve miles in diameter. It is the only satellite yet discovered that revolves around its planet faster than the planet rotates. [< New Latin *Phobos* < Greek *Phóbos* a son of Mars < *phóbos* fear]

Pho·cian (fō′shən), *adj.* of or having to do with Phocis, a region in central Greece. —*n.* a native or inhabitant of Phocis.

pho·cine (fō′sīn, -sin), *adj.* **1.** of or having to do with seals. **2.** of or belonging to the subfamily comprising the typical seals. [< New Latin *Phocinae* the subfamily name < Latin *phōca* < Greek *phṓkē* seal]

pho·co·me·li·a (fō′kə mē′lē ə), *n.* absence or incomplete development of the arms or legs, the hands or feet being attached close to the body; seal limb. [< Greek *phṓkē* seal + *mélos* limb]

Phoe·be (fē′bē), *n.* **1.** *Greek Mythology.* the goddess of the moon. Phoebe was also called Artemis by the Greeks and Diana by the Romans. **2.** *Poetic.* the moon. [< Latin *Phoebe* < Greek *Phoíbē*, feminine of *Phoîbos* Phoebus]

phoe·be (fē′bē), *n.* any of various small American birds, especially a flycatcher of eastern North America, having a grayish-olive back, a whitish breast, and a low crest on the head. [American English; earlier, *phebe*, imitative of the bird's song; spelling later adapted to *Phoebe*, proper name]

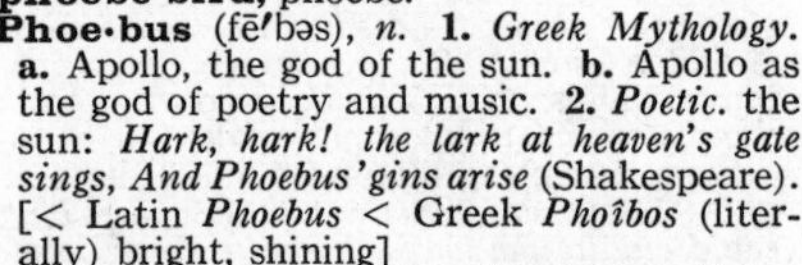

Phoebe (7 in. long)

Phoe·be·an (fi bē′ən), *adj.* **1.** of or having to do with Phoebus or Apollo as the god of poetry. **2.** characteristic of Phoebus or Apollo as the god of poetry.

phoebe bird, phoebe.

Phoe·bus (fē′bəs), *n.* **1.** *Greek Mythology.* **a.** Apollo, the god of the sun. **b.** Apollo as the god of poetry and music. **2.** *Poetic.* the sun: *Hark, hark! the lark at heaven's gate sings, And Phoebus' gins arise* (Shakespeare). [< Latin *Phoebus* < Greek *Phoîbos* (literally) bright, shining]

phoe·ni·ca·ceous (fē′nə kā′shəs), *adj.* belonging to the palm family of plants. [< New Latin *Phoenix, -icis* the genus name (< Greek *phoînix, -īkos* date-palm) + English *-aceous*]

Phoe·ni·cian (fə nish′ən, -nē′shən), *adj.* of or having to do with Phoenicia, an ancient kingdom in the eastern Mediterranean, its people, or their language. —*n.* **1.** a native or inhabitant of Phoenicia or of a Phoenician colony: *The invention of the alphabet by the Phoenicians more than three thousand years ago was one of the greatest single contributions to the cultural development of mankind* (New York Times). **2.** the extinct Semitic language of Phoenicia.

Phoe·ni·cis (fi nī′sis), *n.* genitive of **Phoenix.**

phoe·nix (fē′niks), *n.* **1.** a mythical bird, the only one of its kind, said to live 500 or 600 years, to burn itself on a funeral nest of herbs and to rise again from a small worm in the ashes, fresh and beautiful, for another long life. It is often used as a symbol of immortality. **2.** that which rises from the ashes of its predecessor. Also, **phenix.** [Old English *fenix* < unrecorded Medieval Latin *phenix*, variant of Latin *phoenix, -īcis* < Greek *phoînix, -īkos*]

Phoe·nix (fē′niks), *n., genitive* **Phoe·ni·cis.** a southern constellation near Piscis Austrinus.

phon (fon), *n.* the unit for measuring the level of loudness of sound, especially of complex sound: *A 60-decibel sound with a frequency of 1,000 vibrations a second has a loudness of 60 phons* (World Book Encyclopedia). [< Greek *phōnḗ* a sound]

phon-, *combining form.* the form of **phono-** before vowels, as in *phonate.*

phon., phonetics.

pho·nas·the·ni·a (fō′nəs thē′nē ə), *n.* weakness of the voice from fatigue.

pho·nate (fō′nāt), *v.t., v.i.,* **-nat·ed, -nat·ing.** to utter (vocal sound); sound vocally. [< *phon-* + *-ate*[1]]

pho·na·tion (fō nā′shən), *n.* **1.** the production or utterance of vocal sound, usually as distinguished from articulation. **2.** vocal utterance; voice production.

phon·au·to·graph (fōn ô′tə graf, -gräf), *n.* an early automatic apparatus for indicating the vibrations of sound graphically, having a membrane set in vibration by sound waves and having a stylus attached which makes a tracing on a revolving cylinder.

phon·au·to·graph·ic (fōn ô′tə graf′ik), *adj.* of or having to do with a phonautograph.

phone[1] (fōn), *n., v.t., v.i.,* **phoned, phon·ing.** *Informal.* telephone: *My tenant phoned me at 10 a.m. that Sunday* (Newsweek). [American English; short for *telephone*]

phone[2] (fōn), *n. Phonetics.* a speech sound: *. . . [the linguistic scientist] begins by breaking up the flow of speech into minimum sound-units, or phones* (W. Nelson Francis). [< Greek *phōnḗ* voice, sound]

-phone, *combining form.* sound, as in *megaphone, microphone, saxophone, xylophone.* [< Greek *phōnḗ* a sound]

pho·neme (fō′nēm), *n.* **1.** *Phonetics.* one of a group of distinctive sounds that make up the words of a language. The words *cat* and *bat* are distinguished by their initial phonemes /k/ and /b/. A phoneme comprises several slightly different sounds (allophones) the differences between which are not meaningful. The *p* in *pit* and the *p* in *ship*, though differing slightly in pronunciation, belong to the one phoneme /p/. *And one contrast anywhere in the language is enough to establish separate phonemes elsewhere in the language* (George P. Faust). **2.** *Obsolete.* phone[2]. [< French *phonème* < Greek *phṓnēma* a sound < *phōneîn* to sound < *phōnḗ* a sound]

pho·ne·mic (fō nē′mik, fə-), *adj. Phonetics.* **1.** of or having to do with phonemes: *a phonemic analysis of a language.* **2.** involving the distinguishing of meanings; distinctive: *The difference between "p" and "b" is phonemic in English.* —**pho·ne′mi·cal·ly,** *adv.*

pho·ne·mics (fō nē′miks, fə-), *n.* the branch of linguistics dealing with phonemes: *. . . phonemics is phonetics systematized* (Simeon Potter).

phonet., phonetics.

pho·net·ic (fō net′ik, fə-), *adj.* **1.** of or having to do with speech sounds: *phonetic laws, a phonetic description of a language.* **2. a.** representing speech sounds; indicating pronunciation: *phonetic symbols, phonetic spelling.* **b.** (of a system of spelling) having each sound represented by one letter and each letter represent one sound: *a phonetic alphabet.* [< New Latin *phoneticus* < Greek *phōnētikós* vocal < *phōnētós* utterable < *phōneîn* to speak < *phōnḗ* a sound]

pho·net·i·cal (fō net′ə kəl, fə-), *adj.* phonetic.

pho·net·i·cal·ly (fō net′ə klē, fə-), *adv.* in a phonetic manner; as regards the sound and not the spelling of words.

pho·ne·ti·cian (fō′nə tish′ən), *n.* a person skilled in phonetics.

pho·net·i·cist (fō net′ə sist), *n.* a phonetician.

pho·net·i·cize (fō net′ə sīz), *v.t.,* **-cized, -ciz·ing.** to represent or spell phonetically: *Mr. Ernest Bean had made a pleasant speech to the company carefully phoneticized in Russian* (London Times).

pho·net·ics (fō net′iks, fə-), *n.* **1.** the branch of linguistics dealing with speech sounds and the art of pronunciation. Phonetics is concerned with the production of these speech sounds by the articulating organs of the speaker, the sound waves in which they result, and the auditory effect they produce on the hearer. **2.** the body of speech sounds of any one language, their manner of articulation, and their relation to one another. **3.** the application of the science of speech sounds to the learning of languages.

pho·ne·tism (fō′nə tiz əm), *n.* the use of a phonetic system of writing or spelling.

pho·ne·tist (fō′nə tist), *n.* **1.** a phonetician. **2.** a supporter or user of phonetic spelling.

Phone·vi·sion (fōn′vizh′ən), *n. Trademark.* a form of subscription television which uses telephone lines to transmit a scrambled picture and sound, and provides its subscribers with a decoding device by which they can be unscrambled. [< (tele)*phone* + (tele)*vision*]

pho·ney (fō′nē), *adj.,* **-ni·er, -ni·est,** *n., pl.* **-neys,** *v.t.,* **-neyed, -ney·ing.** *Slang.* phony: *Even the Birmingham accents were phoney* (Kenneth Tynan).

pho·ney·ness (fō′nē nis), *n. Slang.* phoniness: *The common purpose running through* *most of present-day drama and literature is the demolition of phoneyness* (Observer).

phon·gyi (pōn′jē, pun′-), *n.* pongyi: *As soon as day breaks, the phongyis in the village monastery take their early morning meal* (London Times).

pho·ni·at·rics (fō′nē at′riks), *n.* the treatment of speech defects.

phon·ic (fon′ik, fō′nik), *adj.* **1.** of or having to do with sound. **2.** of speech sounds; phonetic: *The phonic system of the language he speaks is quite different from the system . . . which the reading primers use* (Harper's). **3.** voiced. [< Greek *phōnikós,* for *phōnētikós* vocal, ultimately < *phōnḗ* a sound]

phon·ics (fon′iks, fō′niks), *n.* **1.** simplified phonetics for teaching reading. **2.** the science of sound in general; acoustics. **3.** *Obsolete.* phonetics. [< Greek *phōnḗ* a sound + English *-ics*]

pho·ni·ness (fō′nē nis), *n. Slang.* phony quality or character; sham.

phono-, *combining form.* sound; sounds: *Phonometer = an instrument that measures sound. Phonology = the system of sounds (used in a language).* Also, **phon-** before vowels. [< Greek *phōnḗ* sound]

pho·no·car·di·o·gram (fō′nō kär′dē ə-gram), *n.* the record made by a phonocardiograph.

pho·no·car·di·o·graph (fō′nō kär′dē ə-graf, -gräf), *n.* a device that graphically represents on a photographic film the sounds of the heart: *Working with the electrocardiograph, . . . the phonocardiograph is of particular value in detecting types of heart disease curable by surgery* (Family Weekly).

pho·no·car·di·og·ra·phy (fō′nō kär′dē-og′rə fē), *n.* the graphic recording of the sounds of the heart by means of a phonocardiograph: *His problem was to find a way of quietening pregnant women so that the technique of phonocardiography could be used to record the heart-beats of the unborn child* (New Scientist).

Pho·no·film (fō′nə film′), *n. Trademark.* an early form of sound track invented by Lee de Forest, an American inventor.

pho·no·gram (fō′nə gram), *n.* **1.** a character or symbol representing a single speech sound, syllable, or word. **2.** *Obsolete.* a phonograph record.

pho·no·gram·ic or **pho·no·gram·mic** (fō′nə gram′ik), *adj.* **1.** like a phonogram. **2.** *Obsolete.* consisting of phonograph records.

pho·no·graph (fō′nə graf, -gräf), *n.* **1.** an instrument that reproduces the sounds transcribed on a phonograph record. **2.** *Obsolete.* an instrument that records and reproduces sounds, usually on a wax cylinder or disk. [American English < *phono-* + *graph*]

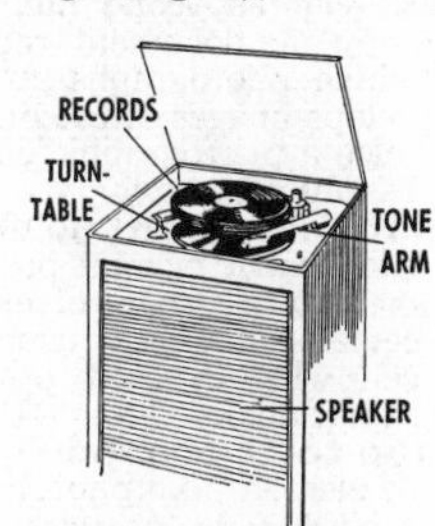

Phonograph (def. 1)

pho·nog·ra·pher (fō nog′rə fər), *n.* **1.** a person who uses phonography; a shorthand writer (in Pitman's system). **2.** a phonetist.

pho·no·graph·ic (fō′nə graf′ik), *adj.* **1.** of a phonograph. **2.** produced by a phonograph. **3.** of phonography. **4.** of phonograms. —**pho′no·graph′i·cal·ly,** *adv.*

phonograph needle, the small, pointed piece of metal, sapphire, diamond, or other material in a phonograph which receives and transmits the vibrations from the record.

phonograph record, a thin disk, now usually of vinyl or other plastic, on the surface of which sound is transcribed in narrow grooves. The pitch of the sound picked up by the needle is controlled by microscopic variations in the grooves.

pho·nog·ra·phy (fō nog′rə fē), *n.* **1.** the art of writing according to sound; phonetic spelling: *Writing becomes the vehicle of language, the "graphic counterpart of speech" (phonography)* (Scientific American). **2.** phonetic shorthand, especially the phonetic shorthand devised by Sir Isaac Pitman in 1837. **3.** *Obsolete.* the study of speech sounds and their phonetic transcription.

pho·no·lite (fō′nə līt), *n.* any of various volcanic rocks which ring when struck, composed of orthoclase, nephelite, and certain other minerals; clinkstone.

pho·no·lit·ic (fō′nə lit′ik), *adj.* **1.** having to do with phonolite. **2.** consisting of phonolite.

pho·no·log·ic (fō′nə loj′ik), *adj.* of, having to do with, or relating to phonology; phonetic: *A phonologic study of language, no matter how detailed, can tell us nothing about meaning, because the phonemes themselves have no direct connection with content* (H.A. Gleason, Jr.). —**pho′no·log′i·cal·ly,** *adv.*

pho·no·log·i·cal (fō′nə loj′ə kəl), *adj.* phonologic.

pho·nol·o·gist (fō nol′ə jist), *n.* an expert in phonology: *The phonologist will begin his task by making numerous phonetic transcriptions . . . before attempting to construct his phonemic pattern* (Simeon Potter).

pho·nol·o·gy (fō nol′ə jē), *n.* **1.** the system of sounds used in a language: *A linguist examining the phonology of a language can identify the points at which divergences of interpretation can be expected* (H.A. Gleason, Jr.). **2.** the study of sounds of a language, their history and changes: *Phonology deals with the phonemes and sequences of phonemes* (H.A. Gleason, Jr.).

phon·o·ma·ni·a (fon′ə mā′nē ə), *n.* a mania for murder or killing. [< New Latin *phonomania* < Greek *phónos* murder, slaughter + English *mania*]

pho·nom·e·ter (fō nom′ə tər), *n.* an instrument for measuring the pitch (frequency) or volume (intensity) of sound.

pho·no·met·ric (fō′nə met′rik), *adj.* **1.** having to do with a phonometer. **2.** having to do with the measurement of sound.

pho·nom·e·try (fō nom′ə trē), *n.* the measurement of sound with a phonometer.

pho·non (fō′non), *n.* a particle or quantum of thermal energy in a crystal lattice, analogous to the photon.

pho·no·phore (fō′nə fôr, -fōr), *n.* **1.** an apparatus which permits telephoning over a telegraph wire without interfering with the current by which telegraph messages are simultaneously transmitted. **2.** a system using such an apparatus.

pho·no·pore (fō′nə pôr, -pōr), *n.* phonophore.

pho·no·scope (fō′nə skōp), *n.* **1.** an instrument for indicating or representing sound vibrations in a visible form. **2.** an instrument for testing the quality of musical strings.

pho·no·type (fō′nə tīp), *n.* **1.** a character or letter of a phonetic alphabet adapted for printing. **2.** phonetic print or type.

pho·no·typ·ic (fō′nə tip′ik), *adj.* having to do with or relating to phonotype or phonotypy. —**pho′no·typ′i·cal·ly,** *adv.*

pho·no·typ·i·cal (fō′nə tip′ə kəl), *adj.* phonotypic.

pho·no·typ·ist (fō′nə tī′pist), *n.* an advocate or user of phonotypy.

pho·no·ty·py (fō′nə tī′pē), *n.* a system of phonetic shorthand, devised by Sir Isaac Pitman; phonography.

pho·ny (fō′nē), *adj.,* **-ni·er, -ni·est,** *n., pl.* **-nies,** *v.,* **-nied, -ny·ing.** *U.S. Slang.* —*adj.* not genuine; counterfeit; fake: *I . . . gave the sucker my name and address (both phony of course) and promised to send two hundred dollars as soon as I got home* (Saturday Evening Post). —*n.* a fake; pretender: *He says he is a very important man but he is nothing but a phony. The twenty-dollar bill was a phony.* —*v.t.* to make phony; counterfeit; fake; pretend: *But when they talk like McCarthy, Republicans do not merely exaggerate their case, they phony it* (Life). Also, **phoney.** [American English; apparently, earlier *fawney* a gilt brass ring used by swindlers, perhaps < Irish *fáinne* ring] —**Syn.** *adj.* sham, false, bogus, spurious.

pho·ny·ness (fō′nē nis), *n.* phoniness.

phoo·ey (fü′ē), *interj. U.S. Slang.* an exclamation of scorn or contempt; bah; pfui: *Ruben and I are pals. All those stories about a fight—phooey* (New York Times).

-phore, *combining form.* a thing that bears, or carries_____: *Oophore = a structure that bears eggs. Semaphore = an apparatus that carries signaling devices.* [< Greek *-phóros* < *phérein* to bear, carry]

phor·e·sy (fôr′ə sē), *n. Zoology.* the nonparasitic transportation of one species by another, especially among arthropods: *This mode of travel, known as phoresy, seems to be a response to specific conditions of the environment* (Scientific American). [< New Latin *phoresia* < Greek *phórēsis* a carrying < *phérein* to carry]

phos·gene (fos′jēn), *n.* a colorless poisonous liquid or gas with a suffocating odor, used in chemical warfare and also in organic synthesis; carbonyl chloride: *The main war gases available toward the end of the last war were phosgene, mustard gas, and lewisite* (James P. Baxter). *Formula:* $COCl_2$ [< Greek *phôs, phōtós* light[1] + *-genēs* -gen (because originally obtained by action of sunlight on chlorine and carbonic oxide)]

phos·ge·nite (fos′jə nīt), *n.* a mineral, a chloride and carbonate of lead, occurring in white or yellowish tetragonal crystals, and playing a role in bone formation. *Formula:* $Pb_2Cl_2CO_3$

phos·pha·gen (fos′fə jən), *n.* phosphocreatine.

phos·pha·tase (fos′fə tās), *n.* an enzyme which splits carbohydrate and phosphate compounds.

phos·phate (fos′fāt), *n.* **1.** a salt or ester of an acid containing phosphorus. It is present in rocks and in plant and animal remains. Phosphates are necessary to the growth of plants and animals and have extensive use as fertilizers. **2.** a fertilizer containing such salts. **3.** a drink of carbonated water flavored with fruit syrup, and containing a little phosphoric acid. [< French *phosphate* < *phosph(ore)* phosphorus + *-ate* -ate[1]]

phosphate rock, a sedimentary rock that contains calcium phosphate. It is, when crushed, a primary source of phosphorus in agriculture.

phos·phat·ic (fos fat′ik), *adj.* **1.** of the nature of phosphoric acid or phosphates. **2.** characterized by phosphoric acid or phosphates. **3.** containing phosphoric acid or phosphates.

phos·pha·tide (fos′fə tīd, -tid), *n.* any of a group of fatty substances present in cellular tissue and consisting of esters of phosphoric acid; phospholipid.

phos·pha·ti·za·tion (fos′fə tə zā′shən), *n.* **1.** the act of phosphatizing. **2.** the fact or condition of being phosphatized.

phos·pha·tize (fos′fə tīz), *v.t.,* **-tized, -tiz·ing.** **1.** to treat with phosphates. **2.** to reduce to the form of a phosphate or phosphates.

phos·pha·tu·ri·a (fos′fə tůr′ē ə, -tyůr′-), *n. Medicine.* an abnormal condition indicated by an excess of phosphates in the urine.

phos·pha·tu·ric (fos′fə tůr′ik, -tyůr′-), *adj. Medicine.* of or having to do with phosphaturia.

phos·phene (fos′fēn), *n.* a luminous image, as of rings of light, produced by mechanical excitation of the retina, as by pressing the eyeball when the lid is closed. [< French *phosphène* < Greek *phôs, phōtós* light[1] + *phaínein* to shine, make appear]

phos·phid (fos′fid), *n.* phosphide.

phos·phide (fos′fīd, -fid), *n.* a compound of phosphorus with a basic element or radical.

phos·phin (fos′fin), *n.* phosphine.

phos·phine (fos′fēn, -fin), *n.* **1.** a colorless, extremely poisonous gas, a phosphorus hydride, with an odor like that of garlic or decaying fish. It is spontaneously inflammable in air. *Formula:* PH_3 **2.** any of various organic compounds derived from this gas. **3.** an acridine dye.

phos·phin·ic (fos fin′ik), *adj.* **1.** of or having to do with phosphine. **2.** derived from phosphine.

phos·phite (fos′fīt), *n.* a salt or ester of phosphorous acid. [< *phosph*(orus) + *-ite*]

phos·pho·cre·a·tin (fos′fō krē′ə tin), *n.* phosphocreatine.

phos·pho·cre·a·tine (fos′fō krē′ə tēn, -tin), *n.* an energy-giving substance in muscle tissue, consisting of creatine and phosphoric acid. *Formula:* $C_4H_{10}N_3O_5P$

phos·pho·lip·id (fos′fō lip′id, -lī′pid), *n.* phospholipide: *Disturbances in the relative amount of cholesterol, fatty proteins, and phospholipids in the blood have already been named by cardiovascular experts as the possible cause of artery degeneration* (Newsweek).

phos·pho·lip·ide (fos′fō lip′īd, -id; -lī′pīd, -lī′pid), *n.* phosphatide.

phos·pho·ni·um (fos fō′nē əm), *n.* a univalent radical (PH_4-), analogous to ammonium.

phos·pho·pro·tein (fos′fō prō′tēn, -tē in), *n.* any of a group of proteins, as caseinogen, consisting of a simple protein combined with some phosphorus compound other than nucleic acid or lecithin.

phos·phor (fos′fər), *n.* **1.** a substance which gives off light when exposed to certain types of energy, such as ultraviolet rays or X rays, widely used in fluorescent lamps, television tubes, etc. **2.** *Obsolete.* phosphorus. —*adj. Obsolete.* phosphorescent. [< New Latin *phosphorus* phosphorus]

Phos·phor (fos′fər), *n. Poetic.* the morning star; Venus (when appearing at or just before sunrise). [< Latin *phōsphorus;* see PHOSPHORUS]

phos·pho·rate (fos′fə rāt), *v.t.,* **-rat·ed, -rat·ing.** to combine or impregnate with phosphorus.

phosphor bronze, a hard, tough bronze containing less than one per cent of phosphorus, used especially in marine fittings.

phos·pho·resce (fos′fə res′), *v.i.,* **-resced, -resc·ing.** to be luminous without noticeable heat.

phos·pho·res·cence (fos′fə res′əns), *n.* **1.** a giving off light without burning or by very slow burning without noticeable heat: *the phosphorescence of fireflies.* **2.** the light given off in this way. **3.** the property of a substance that causes this. **4.** *Physics.* light given off by a substance as a result of the absorption of certain rays, as X rays or ultraviolet rays, and continuing for a period of time after the substance has ceased to be exposed to these rays.

phos·pho·res·cent (fos′fə res′ənt), *adj.* showing phosphorescence: *A phosphorescent jewel gives off its glow and color in the dark and loses its beauty in the light of day* (Atlantic). —**phos′pho·res′cent·ly,** *adv.*

phos·pho·ret·ed or **phos·pho·ret·ted** (fos′fə ret′id), *adj.* phosphureted.

phos·phor·ic (fos fôr′ik, -for′-), *adj.* having to do with or containing phosphorus, especially in its higher valence.

phosphoric acid, 1. a colorless, odorless acid containing phosphorus, obtained chiefly by the decomposition of phosphates, and used in many chemcial processes, in making fertilizers, as a reagent, etc.; orthophosphoric acid. *Formula:* H_3PO_4 **2.** metaphosphoric acid. *Formula:* HPO_3 **3.** pyrophosphoric acid. *Formula:* $H_4P_2O_7$

phos·pho·rism (fos′fə riz əm), *n.* chronic phosphorus poisoning.

phos·pho·rite (fos′fə rīt), *n.* **1.** a mineral, a noncrystallized variety of apatite. **2.** any variety of phosphate rock.

phos·pho·rit·ic (fos′fə rit′ik), *adj.* of or having to do with phosphorite: *Significantly he included "other phosphoritic substances" in his patent, indicating that he foresaw the role of minerals as sources of phosphate* (Scientific American).

phos·phor·o·scope (fos fôr′ə skōp, -for′-), *n.* an apparatus for observing and measuring the duration of phosphorescence caused by rays of light or other energy.

phos·pho·rous (fos′fər əs; fos fôr′-, -for′-), *adj.* **1.** having to do with or containing phosphorus, especially in its lower valence. **2.** phosphorescent.

phosphorous acid, a white or yellowish, unstable, crystalline acid obtained from phosphorus by oxidation and by other methods. Its salts are phosphites. *Formula:* H_3PO_3

phos·pho·rus (fos′fər əs), *n.* **1.** a solid nonmetallic chemical element of the nitrogen group, existing in several forms different in physical and chemical properties but not in kind of atoms. The two common forms are a yellow, poisonous, inflammable substance, which undergoes slow combustion at ordinary temperatures and appears luminous in the dark, and a reddish-brown powder, nonluminous, nonpoisonous, and less inflammable. *No animal or plant can exist without phosphorus, and of all the substances necessary for plant growth, compounds containing available phosphorus are the most likely to be deficient* (W.R. Jones). *Symbol:* P; *at. wt.:* (C^{12}) 30.9738 or (O^{16}) 30.975; *at. no.:* 15; *valence:* 1, 3, 4, 5. **2.** a phosphorescent substance. [< New Latin *phosphorus* < Latin *phōsphorus* morning star, torchbearer < Greek *phōsphóros* morning star, torchbearer < *phôs, phōtós* light[1] + *-phóros* -phore < *phérein* to bear]

phos·pho·rus 32 (fos′fər əs thėr′tē tü′), *n.* a radioisotope of phosphorus used in biological research and medical therapy. It has been applied to the study of bone metabolism, employed as a radioactive tracer to measure the distribution and absorption of phosphorus in plant growth, and used in the diagnosis and treatment of cancer. [its mass number is 32]

phos·phor·y·lase (fos fôr′ə lās, -for′-), *n.* an enzyme which assists in the formation of glucose (in the form of a phosphate) from glycogen and a phosphate: *Use of muscle to do work and its recovery depends upon the chemical action of . . . phosphorylase* (Science News Letter).

phos·pho·ryl·ate (fos′fər ə lāt), *v.t.,* **-at·ed, -at·ing.** to convert into a phosphorus compound.

phos·pho·ryl·a·tion (fos′fər ə lā′shən), *n.* conversion into a phosphorus compound: *The mitochondria are the site of oxidative phosphorylation, which is the main mechanism by which the energy of respiration is stored* (Scientific American).

phos·phu·ret·ed or **phos·phu·ret·ted** (fos′fyə ret′id), *adj.* combined with phosphorus. [< earlier *phosphuret* phosphide, alteration of earlier *phosphur* < French *phosphure*]

phosphureted hydrogen, phosphine.

phos·sy jaw (fos′ē), necrosis of the jawbone or teeth, caused by continued inhalation of phosphorus vapors.

phos·vi·tin (fos′vī′tən), *n.* a phosphoprotein contained in the yolk of eggs. [< *phos*(phorus) + Latin *vit*(*ellus*) egg yolk + English *-in*]

phot (fōt, fot), *n.* a C.G.S. unit of illumination, equivalent to one lumen to a square centimeter. [< Greek *phôs, phōtós* light[1]]

phot., 1. photograph. 2. photography.

pho·tic (fō′tik), *adj.* **1.** of or having to do with light. **2.** relating to the production of light by organisms, or to their stimulation under the influence of light. [< Greek *phôs, phōtós* light[1] + English *-ic*]

pho·tics (fō′tiks), *n.* the science of light and its intrinsic properties (sometimes used instead of *optics,* when optics is restricted to the science of light as affecting vision).

pho·to (fō′tō), *n., pl.* **-tos,** *v.t., v.i. Informal.* photograph.

photo-, *combining form.* **1.** light: *Photobiotic = needing light to thrive.* **2.** photographic or photograph: *Photoengraving = photographic engraving.* [< Greek *phōto-* < *phôs, phōtós* light[1]]

pho·to·ac·tin·ic (fō′tō ak tin′ik), *adj.* giving off rays which produce chemical changes in the objects irradiated, especially blue light or ultraviolet rays.

pho·to·ac·ti·vate (fō′tō ak′tə vāt), *v.t.,* **-vat·ed, -vat·ing.** to activate by photocatalysis.

pho·to·ac·ti·va·tion (fō′tō ak′tə vā′shən), *n.* activation through photocatalysis.

pho·to·au·to·troph·ic (fō′tō ô′tə trof′ik), *adj.* providing its own nourishment and obtaining energy from light: *With the exception of the colorless forms, most algae are photoautotrophic* (Osmund Holm-Hansen). [< *photo-* + *autotrophic*]

pho·to·bi·o·log·i·cal (fō′tō bī′ə loj′ə kəl), *adj.* of or having to do with photobiology or biological processes, such as photosynthesis, using radiant energy. —**pho′to·bi′o·log′i·cal·ly,** *adv.*

pho·to·bi·ol·o·gy (fō′tō bī ol′ə jē), *n.* the branch of biology dealing with the relation of light or radiant energy to biological processes.

pho·to·bi·ot·ic (fō′tō bī ot′ik), *adj.* (of an organism) needing light, especially sunlight, to live or thrive.

pho·to·ca·tal·y·sis (fō′tō kə tal′ə sis), *n.* catalysis depending upon radiant energy.

pho·to·cat·a·lyst (fō′tō kat′ə list), *n.* a catalyst activated by radiant energy.

pho·to·cath·ode (fō′tō kath′ōd), *n.* a cathode which emits electrons when stimulated by radiant energy.

pho·to·cell (fō′tə sel′), *n.* a photoelectric cell: *The photocell . . . makes possible certain precise measurements . . . that were impossible with photographic emulsions* (New Astronomy).

pho·to·chem·i·cal (fō′tō kem′ə kəl), *adj.* of or having to do with the chemical action of light: *Night sky glow not caused by moonlight and starlight is due to photochemical reactions in the upper air* (Science News Letter). —**pho′to·chem′i·cal·ly,** *adv.*

pho·to·chem·is·try (fō′tō kem′ə strē), *n.* the branch of chemistry dealing with the chemical action of light, as in photography.

pho·to·chrome (fō′tə krōm), *n.* a photograph in colors; a colored picture produced by photochromy.

pho·to·chro·mic (fō′tə krō′mik), *adj.* **1.** sensitive to changes in light: *A reversible photochromic glass—one that darkens on exposure to light and clears again when the light fades—has been invented* (Scientific American). **2.** having to do with photochromes.

pho·to·chro·my (fō′tə krō′mē), *n. Obsolete.* color photography.

pho·to·chron·o·graph (fō′tō kron′ə graf, -gräf), *n.* **1.** a device for photographing a moving object at regular, brief intervals. **2.** a photograph so taken. **3.** an instrument for photographing the transit of a star. **4.** a device for measuring and recording small time intervals.

pho·to·com·pose (fō′tō kəm pōz′), *v.t.,* **-posed, -pos·ing.** to prepare (printing plates) by photocomposition; compose on a photocomposing machine.

pho·to·com·pos·ing (fō′tō kəm pō′zing), *adj.* of or having to do with photocomposition.

pho·to·com·po·si·tion (fō′tō kom′pə zish′ən), *n.* a method of typesetting in which negatives and positives of type are made on film or photosensitive paper and then transferred to metal printing plates.

pho·to·con·duct·ance (fō′tō kən duk′təns), *n. Electricity.* conductance varying with illumination.

pho·to·con·duct·ing (fō′tō kən duk′ting), *adj.* conducting electricity only upon exposure to light: *photoconducting materials.*

pho·to·con·duc·tion or **pho·to·con·duc·tion** (fō′tō kən duk′shən), *n.* the ability of an electrical conductor to conduct electricity upon exposure to light.

pho·to·con·duc·tive (fō′tō kən duk′tiv), *adj.* of or having to do with photoconduction; photoconducting: *photoconductive detectors, photoconductive properties.*

pho·to·con·duc·tiv·i·ty (fō′tō kon′duk tiv′ə tē), *n. Electricity.* conductivity varying with illumination.

pho·to·con·duc·tor (fō′tō kən duk′tər), *n.* a conductor whose ability to conduct electricity improves notably upon exposure to light.

pho·to·cop·i·er (fō′tō kop′ē ər), *n.* a device or machine that produces photocopies.

pho·to·cop·y (fō′tō kop′ē), *n., pl.* **-cop·ies,** *v.,* **-cop·ied, -cop·y·ing.** —*n.* a photographic copy of a document, reproduced by a device which photographs and automatically develops images of the original. —*v.t.* to produce a photographic copy of (a document) by this process.

pho·to·cur·rent (fō′tō kėr′ənt), *n. Physics.* the electric current produced by the movement of a stream of electrons given off by certain substances, usually in a photoelectric cell, when exposed to light or certain other radiations.

pho·to·de·com·po·si·tion (fō′tō dē′kom pə zish′ən), *n.* photolysis: *The reaction of excited ions provides the mechanism for photodecomposition* (New Scientist).

pho·to·de·tec·tor (fō′tō di tek′tər), *n.* a semiconductor device that detects radiant energy, especially infrared radiation, by photoconductive or photovoltaic action, used in electronic equipment to detect changes in temperature, in solar telescopes, etc.

pho·to·dis·in·te·gra·tion (fō′tō dis in′tə grā′shən), *n. Physics.* the breaking down of the nucleus of an atom caused by bombardment with high-energy gamma rays.

pho·to·dis·so·ci·a·tion (fō′tō di sō′sē ā′shən, -shē-), *n.* dissociation of a chemical compound by the absorption of radiant energy, such as light, ultraviolet rays, etc.

pho·to·dra·ma (fō′tə drä′mə, -dram′ə), *n.* a motion picture; photoplay.

pho·to·dra·mat·ic (fō′tə drə mat′ik), *adj.* **1.** of or having to do with a photodrama. **2.** like a photodrama.

pho·to·dram·a·tist (fō′tə dram′ə tist, -dram′ə-), *n.* a writer of photodramas.

pho·to·dy·nam·ic (fō′tō dī nam′ik, -di-), *adj.* having to do with the energy of light.

pho·to·dy·nam·ics (fō′tō dī nam′iks, -di-), *n.* the science dealing with the energy of light, especially in relation to growth or movement in plants.

pho·to·e·las·tic (fō′tō i las′tik), *adj.* of or having to do with photoelasticity.

pho·to·e·las·tic·i·ty (fō′tō i las′tis′ə tē, -ē′las-), *n. Physics.* optical changes in a transparent dielectric, such as glass, due to compression or other stresses.

pho·to·e·lec·tric (fō′tō i lek′trik), *adj.* **1.** having to do with the electricity or the electrical effects produced by light or other radiation: *The photoelectric measurement of starlight has become . . . a major instrument for studying the universe* (New Astronomy). **2.** of or having to do with an apparatus for taking photographs by electric light. —**pho′to·e·lec′tri·cal·ly,** *adv.*

pho·to·e·lec·tri·cal (fō′tō i lek′trə kəl), *adj.* photoelectric.

photoelectric cell, 1. any cell or vacuum tube used for the detection and measurement of light, which produces variations in the resistance or electromotive force of part of an electric current in accordance with variations in the light, or similar radiation, falling upon it; electric eye: *This light falls on a photoelectric cell which produces an electric current corresponding to the intensity of the light* (John R. Pierce). **2.** a phototube.

photoelectric effect, the transfer of the kinetic energy of a photon in light or gamma radiation to an electron of a metal it strikes, causing the emission or escape of the electron.

photoelectric exposure meter, *Photography.* a type of exposure meter in which the amount of light on a subject is measured by a photoelectric cell.

pho·to·e·lec·tric·i·ty (fō′tō i lek′tris′ə tē, -ē′lek-), *n.* **1.** electricity produced or affected by light. **2.** the science dealing with electricity or electrical effects produced by light.

pho·to·e·lec·tron (fō′tō i lek′tron), *n.* an electron liberated from a substance by the photoelectric effect: *Experiments by Millikan showed that the kinetic energies of photoelectrons were in exact agreement with the formula proposed by Einstein* (Sears and Zemansky).

pho·to·e·lec·tron·ic (fō′tō i lek′tron′ik, -ē′lek-), *adj.* of or having to do with the relationships between electricity and light.

pho·to·e·lec·tron·ics (fō′tō i lek′tron′iks, -ē′lek-), *n.* the study and application of the effects of electricity and light upon each other.

pho·to·e·lec·tro·type (fō′tō i lek′trə tīp), *n.* an electrotype made by photography.

pho·to·e·mis·sive (fō′tō i mis′iv), *adj. Physics.* giving out, or capable of giving out, electrons when subjected to the action of light or other suitable radiation.

pho·to·en·grave (fō′tō en grāv′), *v.t.,* **-graved, -grav·ing.** to make a photoengraving of. —**pho′to·en·grav′er,** *n.*

pho·to·en·grav·ing (fō′tō en grā′ving), *n.* **1.** a process by which plates to print from are produced with the aid of photography. **2.** the plate so produced. **3.** a picture printed from it.

pho·to·etch (fō′tō ech′), *v.t.* to etch with the aid of photography; make a photoetching of.

pho·to·etch·ing (fō′tō ech′ing), *n.* **1.** any process of photoengraving in which the plate is etched by acid, etc. **2.** a plate or print so produced.

photo finish, 1. (in racing) a finish so close that a photograph is required to decide the winner. **2.** any contest decided by a narrow margin of victory: *While the verdict went against him, it was very much a photo finish with no clear vote of confidence for the* [*victor*] *either* (Sunday Times).

pho·to·fin·ish·er (fō′tō fin′i shər), *n.* **1.** a person who does photofinishing: *One major photofinisher went so far as to import qualified help from abroad* (Jacob Deschin). **2.** one of two or more contestants in a photo finish: *He was third, three-quarters of a length back of the photofinishers* (New York Times).

pho·to·fin·ish·ing (fō′tō fin′i shing), *n.* the developing, printing, enlarging, etc., of exposed photographic films or plates, especially by a commercial establishment.

pho·to·flash lamp (fō′tə flash′), *Photography.* a flash bulb.

photoflash photography, photography with the aid of flash bulbs.

pho·to·flood lamp (fō′tə flud′), an electric light bulb of high wattage that gives very bright, sustained light for taking pictures.

photog., 1. photographic. **2.** photography

pho·to·gel·a·tin (fō′tō jel′ə tin), *adj.* **1.** designating or having to do with a photographic process using gelatin. **2.** made by a photographic process using gelatin.

pho·to·gen (fō′tə jen), *n.* **1.** a substance, organ, or organism that emits light, as the firefly. **2.** *Obsolete.* kerosene.

pho·to·gene (fō′tə jēn), *n.* **1.** a visual afterimage. **2.** *Obsolete.* a photograph.

pho·to·gen·ic (fō′tə jen′ik), *adj.* **1.** photographing very well, especially in motion pictures: *a photogenic face.* **2.** *Biology.* phosphorescent; luminescent: *Certain bacteria are photogenic.* **3.** produced or caused by light. [< *photo-* + Greek *-gen* producing, produced (by) + *-ic*] —**pho′to·gen′i·cal·ly,** *adv.*

pho·to·ge·o·log·ic (fō′tō jē′ə loj′ik), *adj.* photogeological: *The maps and a table . . . represent the first known photogeologic study of the moon* (Science News Letter).

pho·to·ge·o·log·i·cal (fō′tō jē′ə loj′ə kəl), *adj.* of or having to do with photogeology: *SOEKOR has also carried out seven photogeological surveys covering about 120,000 square miles* (Sunday Times). —**pho′to·ge′o·log′i·cal·ly,** *adv.*

pho·to·ge·ol·o·gy (fō′tō jē ol′ə jē), *n.* the study of aerial photographs to identify and map geological formations.

pho·to·gram·met·ric (fō′tō grə met′rik), *adj.* of or having to do with photogrammetry.

pho·to·gram·me·try (fō′tō gram′ə trē), *n.* the art or science of making surveys or maps with the help of photographs, especially aerial photographs. [< *photogram,* obsolete variant of *photograph* + *-metry;* probably influenced by German *Photogrammetrie*]

pho·to·graph (fō′tə graf, -gräf), *n.* a picture made with a camera. A photograph is made by the action of the light rays from the thing pictured coming through the lens of the camera onto a film spread over a surface of glass, paper, celluloid, or metal. —*v.t.* to take a photograph of. —*v.i.* **1.** to take photographs. **2.** to look (clear, unnatural, etc.) in a photograph: *She does not photograph well.*

pho·to·graph·a·ble (fō′tə graf′ə bəl), *adj.* that can be photographed: *The most distant photographable galaxies are so faint that they are not visible to the eye through the telescope* (Scientific American).

pho·tog·ra·pher (fə tog′rə fər), *n.* **1.** a person who takes photographs. **2.** a person whose business is taking photographs.

pho·to·graph·ic (fō′tə graf′ik), *adj.* **1.** of or like photography: *photographic accuracy.* **2.** used in or produced by photography: *photographic plates, a photographic process.* —**pho′to·graph′i·cal·ly,** *adv.*

pho·to·graph·i·cal (fō′tə graf′ə kəl), *adj.* photographic.

pho·tog·ra·phy (fə tog′rə fē), *n.* the taking of photographs: *Photography is the marvelous, anonymous folk-art of our time* (New York Times). *Photography is, above all, reporting* (Helmut Gernsheim).

pho·to·gra·vure (fō′tə grə vyůr′, -grā′vyər), *n.* **1.** photoengraving. **2.** a picture printed from a metal plate on which a photograph has been engraved. [< French *photogravure* < *photo*(*graphie*) (ultimately < English *photograph*) + *gravure* process or art of engraving]

pho·to·he·li·o·graph (fō′tə hē′lē ə graf, -gräf), *n.* a telescope adapted for making photographs of the sun.

photo interpretation, the study of photographs to describe or identify the things contained in them, used especially in military intelligence: *The old World War II intelligence techniques of photo interpretation have now been largely supplanted by the use of complex, interlinked tape-recorder and computer apparatus* (Harper's).

pho·to·i·on·i·za·tion (fō′tō ī′ə nə zā′shən), *n.* ionization by the action or energy supplied by light or other radiation: *Because an atom which has lost an electron is called an ion, the process is known as photoionization* (Harrie Massey).

pho·to·jour·nal·ism (fō′tō jėr′nə liz əm), *n.* journalism which uses photographic rather than written material as the basis of a story: *Photojournalism has a powerful immediate impact upon millions of people, for the impact of the visual image is far greater than that of words* (Harper's).

pho·to·jour·nal·ist (fō′tō jėr′nə list), *n.* a photographer who specializes in photojournalistic work: *Mr. de Vincent combines the eye of the artist with the reportorial sense of the competent photojournalist* (New York Times).

pho·to·jour·nal·is·tic (fō′tō jėr′nə lis′tik), *adj.* of or having to do with photojournalism: *He* [*Brady*] *pioneered the full-scale photojournalistic reporting of war, setting the ground rules for photography in the field from his day on* (Saturday Review).

pho·to·ki·ne·sis (fō′tə ki nē′sis, -kī-), *n. Physiology.* movement caused by light. [< *photo-* + Greek *kínēsis* motion, a setting in motion < *kīneîn* to set in motion, move]

pho·to·ki·net·ic (fō′tə ki net′ik, -kī-), *adj.* of or having to do with photokinesis.

pho·to·lith (fō′tə lith), *adj.* photolithographic.

pho·to·lith·o (fō′tə lith′ō), *n., pl.* **-lith·os.** a photolithograph.

pho·to·lith·o·graph (fō′tə lith′ə graf, -gräf), *n.* a print produced by photolithography. —*v.t.* to produce or copy by photolithography.

pho·to·lith·o·graph·ic (fō′tə lith′ə graf′ik), *adj.* **1.** having to do with photolithography. **2.** produced by photolithography.

pho·to·li·thog·ra·phy (fō′tə li thog′rə fē), *n.* a process of producing, by photography, designs upon lithographic stone or metal plates, from which prints may be taken as in ordinary lithography or by offset.

pho·to·log·i·cal (fō′tə loj′ə kəl), *adj.* having to do with photology; optical. —**pho′to·log′i·cal·ly,** *adv.*

pho·tol·o·gist (fō tol′ə jist), *n.* an expert in photology.

pho·tol·o·gy (fō tol′ə jē), *n.* the science of light.

pho·to·lu·mi·nes·cence (fō′tō lü′mə nes′əns), *n.* luminescence caused by the absorption of radiant energy in the form of visible or nonvisible light.

pho·tol·y·sis (fō tol′ə sis), *n.* **1.** chemical decomposition of a substance resulting from the action of light: *Further tests with the dye-reducing extracts showed that they caused photolysis, producing oxygen* (Science News Letter). **2.** the movements of protoplasm, especially protoplasm containing chlorophyll granules, under the influence of light: *In photolysis the energy necessary to perform the split comes from light through the mediation of chlorophyll* (H. Lees). [< *photo-* + Greek *lýsis* a loosening]

pho·to·lyt·ic (fō′tə lit′ik), *adj.* having to do with or producing photolysis: *The intense photolytic flash is replaced by a pulse of microwave energy* (New Scientist).

photom., photometry.

pho·to·mac·ro·graph (fō′tō mak′rə graf, -gräf), *n.* macrophotograph: *A photograph of a coin at twice life-size is a photomacrograph* (Kodak Handbook News).

pho·to·ma·crog·ra·phy (fō′tō mə krog′rə fē), *n.* macrophotography.

pho·to·mag·net·ic (fō′tō mag net′ik), *adj.* designating certain rays of the spectrum having, or supposed to have, a magnetic influence.

pho·to·mag·net·ism (fō′tō mag′nə tiz əm), *n.* the science dealing with the relation of magnetism to light.

pho·to·map (fō′tō map′), *n., v.,* **-mapped, -map·ping.** —*n.* a map made from an aerial photograph or photographs, now usually one in which a number of photographs made from a given altitude are matched and given, by means of an overlay, such conventional characteristics of a map as a grid, lines of contour, etc.: *When the atlas is completed . . . it will include 1,758 . . . "photomaps"* (London Times). —*v.t.* to prepare maps or surveys of (an area, stars, etc.) with aerial photographs: *to photomap the skies by using a telescopic camera.*

pho·to·me·chan·i·cal (fō′tō mə kan′ə kəl), *adj.* having to do with or designating any method of printing in which the plate or other printing surface is prepared by means of a photographic and a mechanical process, as photoengraving, photogravure, or photo-offset. —**pho′to·me·chan′i·cal·ly,** *adv.*

pho·tom·e·ter (fō tom′ə tər), *n.* an instrument for measuring the intensity of light or the relative illuminating power of different lights: *The photometer is used to measure, simultaneously, the luminosities and diameters of galaxies lying beyond those in our own neighborhood of the universe* (Science News Letter).

pho·to·met·ric (fō′tō met′rik), *adj.* having to do with photometry or a photometer. —**pho′to·met′ri·cal·ly,** *adv.*

pho·to·met·ri·cal (fō′tō met′rə kəl), *adj.* photometric.

pho·tom·e·trist (fō tom′ə trist), *n.* a person who practices photometry.

pho·tom·e·try (fō tom′ə trē), *n.* **1.** the branch of physics dealing with measurements of the intensity of light. **2.** the measurement of light, especially with the aid of the photometer.

pho·to·mi·cro·graph (fō′tō mī′krə graf, -gräf), *n.* an enlarged photograph of a microscopic object, taken through a microscope; microphotograph: *The photomicrograph . . . shows a single crystal of cadmium iodide glowing in a water solution* (Scientific American).

pho·to·mi·cro·graph·ic (fō′tō mī′krə-graf′ik), *adj.* **1.** of, having to do with, or used in photomicrography: *photomicrographic apparatus.* **2.** obtained or made by photomicrography.

pho·to·mi·crog·ra·phy (fō′tō mī krog′-rə fē), *n.* the art of obtaining photographs of microscopic objects on a magnified scale.

pho·to·mi·cro·scope (fō′tō mī′krə skōp), *n.* an apparatus consisting of a microscope, a camera, and a light source, all mounted on a stable base, and used to photograph microscopic objects.

pho·to·mon·tage (fō′tō mon täzh′, -môn-), *n.* **1.** the process of combining several photographs, or parts of them, into a single picture. **2.** the resulting picture.

pho·to·mo·sa·ic (fō′tō mō zā′ik), *n.* a group of aerial photographs put together to form a continuous photograph of an area: *This global photomosaic—the first complete view of the world's weather—was assembled from 450 pictures taken by Tiros 9 during a 24-hour period in 1965* (Science News Letter).

pho·to·mul·ti·pli·er (fō′tō mul′tə plī′ər), *n.* or **photomultiplier tube,** a vacuum tube having a series of supplementary electrodes between the photocathode and the anode. When light strikes the photoemissive cathode a cascade of electrons is emitted and amplified at each supplementary electrode: *. . . photomultipliers . . . have greatly aided in the discovery and study of this light production by green plants, especially since this light is of low intensity* (Some Applications of Atomic Energy in Plant Science).

pho·to·mu·ral (fō′tō myůr′əl), *n.* a mural consisting of a greatly enlarged photograph or group of matched photographs: *Latin American architecture since 1945 comprises large-scale photomurals* (New Yorker).

pho·ton (fō′ton), *n.* a unit particle of light, an element of radiant energy, according to the quantum theory; a light quantum. It has a momentum equal to its energy divided by the velocity of light, and moves as a unit with the velocity of light. *[Einstein] said that light, in spite of its wave nature, must be composed of energy particles, or photons* (World Book Encyclopedia).

pho·to·nas·ty (fō′tō nas′tē), *n. Biology.* response to diffuse light or to variations in the intensity of light, as in the growth of a plant organ.

pho·to·nu·cle·ar (fō′tō nü′klē ər, -nyü′-), *adj.* of or having to do with the action or effect of photons upon atomic nuclei: *The accelerator . . . is designed to be particularly suitable for looking at photonuclear processes over a wide range of conditions* (New Scientist).

pho·to-off·set (fō′tō ôf′set, -of′-), *n., v.,* **-set, -set·ting** *—n.* a process of printing in which a page of type, a picture, etc., is photographed and the image then transferred to a specially sensitized lithographic plate and printed by offset; offset lithography. *—v.t.* to print or reproduce by photo-offset; offset.

pho·to·ox·i·da·tion (fō′tō ok′sə dā′shən), *n.* oxidation induced by the chemical action of light: *Cellulose is a prey to all four of the major museum enemies: photooxidation, humidity change, air pollution, and biological attack* (New Scientist).

pho·to·pe·ri·od (fō′tō pir′ē əd), *n.* the length of time during which a plant or animal is exposed to light each day, considered especially with reference to the effect of the light on growth and development.

pho·to·pe·ri·od·ic (fō′tō pir′ē od′ik), *adj.* of or having to do with a photoperiod: *photoperiodic behavior* (W.W. Schwabe). **—pho′to·pe′ri·od′i·cal·ly,** *adv.*

pho·to·pe·ri·od·i·cal (fō′tō pir′ē od′ə-kəl), *adj.* photoperiodic: *There is some kind of photoperiodical response in every higher plant* (Science News Letter).

pho·to·pe·ri·od·ism (fō′tō pir′ē ə diz′əm), *n. Physiology.* the response of a plant or animal to the length of its daily exposure to light, especially as shown by changes in vital processes: *Photoperiodism . . . is largely responsible for the separation of many wild flowers into spring, summer, and fall blooming classes* (Science News Letter). *Biologists have wondered whether photoperiodism also controls the reproductive life of animals . . . They are now able to report that the quail is indeed photoperiodic* (Scientific American).

pho·toph·i·lous (fō tof′ə ləs), *adj.* (of an organism) flourishing in strong light, especially sunlight; light-loving.

pho·toph·i·ly (fō tof′ə lē), *n.* the quality or condition of living or flourishing in light.

pho·to·pho·bi·a (fō′tō fō′bē ə), *n.* an abnormal dread of, or shrinking from, light.

pho·to·phone (fō′tō fōn), *n.* a telephone in which sound vibrations are conveyed by means of a beam of reflected light. [American English < *photo-* + (tele)*phone*]

pho·to·phore (fō′tō fôr, -fōr), *n.* a luminous, cup-shaped organ on the bellies of certain deep-sea crustaceans and fishes.

pho·to·pho·re·sis (fō′tō fə rē′sis), *n.* the unidirectional movement of small particles, suspended in gas or falling in a vacuum, produced by a beam of light. [< *photo-* + Greek *phórēsis* a carrying < *phérein* carry]

pho·to·phos·pho·ryl·a·tion (fō′tō fos′-fər ə lā′shən), *n.* phosphorylation induced by the presence of radiant energy in the form of visible or nonvisible light: *Cyclic photophosphorylation . . . provides a mechanism for the utilization of light energy without the consumption of water* (Science).

pho·to·pi·a (fō tō′pē ə), *n.* the ability to see in light, especially sunlight, of a sufficient intensity to permit color differentiation. [< New Latin *photopia* < Greek *phôs, phōtós* light[1] + *ōps* eye]

pho·top·ic (fō top′ik, -tō′pik), *adj.* able to see in light of a sufficient intensity to permit color differentiation.

pho·to·play (fō′tə plā′), *n.* **1.** a motion-picture play. **2.** a script or scenario for a motion-picture play: *It is a good deal better than either the photoplay or the novel which were its cause* (Atlantic).

pho·to·print (fō′tə print′), *n.* a print produced by a photomechanical process.

pho·to·re·ac·tion (fō′tō rē ak′shən), *n.* any chemical reaction induced by the presence of light.

pho·to·re·cep·tion (fō′tō ri sep′shən), *n.* the reception of and response to light by plant or animal cells having pigments sensitive to radiant energy. Photoreception is essential to photosynthesis and phototropism in plants, and to vision in animals. *The collective evidence in favor of photoreception by some form of riboflavin conjugate is also sufficiently impressive* (Scientific American).

pho·to·re·cep·tive (fō′tō ri sep′tiv), *adj.* of or having to do with photoreception.

pho·to·re·cep·tor (fō′tō ri sep′tər), *n.* a nerve ending which is sensitive to light: *Rod photoreceptors of the eye are responsible for colourless vision of low intensities* (New Scientist).

pho·to·re·con·nais·sance (fō′tō ri kon′-ə səns), *n.* aerial reconnaissance during which information is gathered by taking aerial photographs: *Photo-reconnaissance indicated that the enemy had installed a hundred or more sites for launching flying bombs and perhaps half a dozen sites for a larger type of rocket* (James Phinney Baxter).

pho·to·sen·si·tive (fō′tō sen′sə tiv), *adj.* readily stimulated to action by light or other radiant energy.

photosensitive glass, a special glass which, upon exposure to a photographic negative, develops a print when heated. It is used for making ornaments, permanent records, etc.

pho·to·sen·si·tiv·i·ty (fō′tō sen′sə tiv′ə-tē), *n* the quality of being readily stimulated to action by light or other radiant energy.

pho·to·spec·tro·scope (fō′tō spek′trə-skōp), *n.* a spectroscope with an attached camera, used for photographing and recording spectra.

pho·to·spec·tro·scop·ic (fō′tō spek′trə-skop′ik), *adj.* having to do with photographing and recording spectra with a spectroscope.

pho·to·sphere (fō′tə sfir), *n.* **1.** the brilliant gaseous surface or envelope of the sun, surrounded by the atmosphere: *While the particles in the corona move at a far higher speed than those in the photosphere, they are so much more thinly dispersed that radiating collisions are relatively infrequent* (Fred Hoyle). **2.** a sphere of light, radiance, or glory: *Her hopes mingled with the sunshine in an ideal photosphere* (Thomas Hardy).

pho·to·spher·ic (fō′tə sfer′ik), *adj.* **1.** of or having to do with the photosphere or a photosphere. **2.** characteristic of the photosphere or a photosphere.

pho·to·stat (fō′tə stat), *n., v.,* **-stat·ed, -stat·ing** or **-stat·ted, -stat·ting.** *—n.* **1.** a photograph made with a special camera for making photographic copies of documents, maps, drawings, pages of books, etc., directly on specially prepared paper. **2. Photostat,** *Trademark.* a name for a camera of this kind. *—v.t.* to make a photostat of. **—pho′to·stat′er,** *n.*

pho·to·stat·ic (fō′tə stat′ik), *adj.* **1.** of or having to do with a photostat. **2.** produced by a photostat.

pho·to·syn·the·sis (fō′tə sin′thə sis), *n.* **1.** the process by which plant cells make carbohydrates from carbon dioxide and water in the presence of chlorophyll and light: *Photosynthesis, called by some the most important chemical reaction occurring in nature, takes place only in plants containing certain pigments, principally chlorophyll* (Harbaugh and Goodrich). **2.** the process by which chemical compounds are synthesized by means of light or other forms of radiant energy.

pho·to·syn·the·size (fō′tə sin′thə sīz), *v.,* **-sized, -siz·ing** *—v.i.* to carry on photosynthesis: *A red alga is best adapted to photosynthesize in the bluish-green light of deep water* (G.E. Fogg). *—v.t.* to produce by photosynthesis: *Plants photosynthesize protein as well as carbohydrates directly under light* (Time).

pho·to·syn·thet·ic (fō′tə sin thet′ik), *adj.* **1.** of or relating to photosynthesis: *The crux of the whole photosynthetic process was the conversion of light energy into chemical energy* (Harper's). **2.** promoting photosynthesis: *The photosynthetic function is accomplished by the green stems* (Fred W. Emerson). **—pho′to·syn·thet′i·cal·ly,** *adv.*

pho·to·tac·tic (fō′tō tak′tik), *adj.* (of cells or organisms) characterized by arranging themselves in some particular way in response to light: *A phototropic or phototactic response might become dependent on the oxygen supplied by photosynthesis* (Scientific American).

pho·to·tax·is (fō′tō tak′sis), *n.* the tendency of an organism to move in response to light: *Several workers have found negative phototaxis (movement away from light) in a number of species* (E.B.Edney). [< German *Phototaxis* < Greek *phôs, phōtós* light[1] + *táxis* arrangement]

pho·to·tax·y (fō′tō tak′sē), *n.* phototaxis.

pho·to·tel·e·graph (fō′tō tel′ə graf, -gräf), *v.t., v.i.* to send by phototelegraphy. *—n.* a picture, message, etc., thus sent.

pho·to·tel·e·graph·ic (fō′tō tel′ə graf′ik), *adj.* of or having to do with phototelegraphy. **—pho′to·tel′e·graph′i·cal·ly,** *adv.*

pho·to·tel·e·graph·i·cal (fō′tō tel′ə graf′-ə kəl), *adj.* phototelegraphic.

pho·to·te·leg·ra·phy (fō′tō tə leg′rə fē), *n.* **1.** telegraphy by means of light, as with a heliograph. **2.** the electric transmission of photographs; telephotography.

pho·to·tel·e·scope (fō′tō tel′ə skōp), *n.* a telescope with a photographic apparatus, used for photographing heavenly bodies.

pho·to·tel·e·scop·ic (fō′tō tel′ə skop′ik), *adj.* of or having to do with a phototelescope.

pho·to·the·od·o·lite (fō′tō thē od′ə lit), *n.* a camera with the movability of a theodolite, used for tracking space vehicles or for photographing very large objects.

pho·to·ther·a·peu·tic (fō′tō ther′ə pyü′-tik), *adj.* having to do with phototherapy.

pho·to·ther·a·peu·tics (fō′tō ther′ə pyü′-tiks), *n.* phototherapy.

pho·to·ther·a·py (fō′tō ther′ə pē), *n.* therapy in which light rays are used, as in treating certain skin diseases.

pho·to·ther·mic (fō′tō thėr′mik), *adj.* **1.** having to do with the heating effects of light. **2.** of or relating to both light and heat.

pho·to·ton·ic (fō'tō ton'ik), *adj.* exhibiting phototonus in the normal way; sensitive to light.

pho·tot·o·nus (fō tot'ə nəs), *n.* **1.** the normal condition of sensitiveness to light in leaves, etc., maintained by regular exposure to light, as opposed to the rigidity induced by long exposure to darkness. **2.** the irritability exhibited by protoplasm when exposed to light of a certain intensity. [< New Latin *phototonus* < Greek *phôs, phōtós* light[1] + *tónos* tension]

pho·to·top·o·graph·ic (fō'tō top'ə graf'ik), *adj.* photogrammetric.

pho·to·to·pog·ra·phy (fō'tō tə pog'rə fē), *n.* photogrammetry.

pho·to·tran·sis·tor (fō'tō tran zis'tər), *n.* a semiconductor device that is sensitive to light, usually consisting of a small disk of germanium which generates photoelectric currents when light is focused upon it: *The principle is similar to the light-sensitive effect used in phototransistors, and has been known for some time* (New Scientist).

pho·to·trop·ic (fō'tō trop'ik), *adj.* **1.** *Botany.* bending or turning in response to light: *Most plants are phototropic.* **2.** sensitive to changes in amount of radiation: *phototropic glass.* —**pho'to·trop'i·cal·ly,** *adv.*

pho·tot·ro·pism (fō tot'rə piz əm, fō'tō-trō'piz əm), *n. Botany.* **1.** a tendency to turn in response to light. **2.** growth in a certain direction in response to light.

pho·to·tube (fō'tō tüb', -tyüb'), *n.* **1.** a vacuum tube in which electrons are emitted as a direct result of light or other radiation falling on the cathode: *The currents obtainable with vacuum phototubes are extremely small . . .* (Sears and Zemansky). **2.** a photoelectric cell.

pho·to·type (fō'tə tīp), *n.* **1.** a block on which a photograph is reproduced so that it can be printed. **2.** the process used in making such a block. **3.** a picture, etc., printed from such a block.

pho·to·type·set·ting (fō'tō tīp'set'ing), *n.* any of several typesetting processes in which negatives of type are produced on photographic film and transferred to metal printing plates.

pho·to·typ·ic (fō'tō tip'ik), *adj.* **1.** of or like a phototype. **2.** produced by phototypy.

pho·to·ty·po·graph·ic (fō'tō tī'pə graf'ik), *adj.* **1.** of or having to do with phototypography. **2.** like phototypography.

pho·to·ty·pog·ra·phy (fō'tō tī pog'rə fē), *n.* any of various methods of making printing surfaces by a photographic or photomechanical process.

pho·to·ty·py (fō'tō tī'pē, fō tot'ə-), *n.* the art or process of making phototypes.

pho·to·vol·ta·ic (fō'tō vol tā'ik), *adj.* **1.** generating an electric current when acted on by light or a similar form of radiant energy, as a photoelectric cell: *The photovoltaic cell is even more sluggish than selenium, and it therefore does not lend itself to use with rapidly varying light sources* (Hardy and Perrin). **2.** photoelectric.

phr., phrase.

phrag·mo·cone (frag'mə kōn), *n.* the conical, chambered or septate, internal skeleton of a belemnite (a fossil). [< Greek *phragmós* fence + *kônos* cone]

phras·al (frā'zəl), *adj.* **1.** of or consisting of a phrase or phrases. **2.** like a phrase or phrases.

phrase (frāz), *n., v.,* **phrased, phras·ing.** —*n.* **1.** a combination of words: *He spoke in simple phrases so that the children understood him.* **2.** an expression often used: *"Call up" is the common phrase for "get a telephone connection." In the old phrase, it is six of the one and half a dozen of the other* (Robert Louis Stevenson). **3.** a short, striking expression. *Examples:* A Fair Deal. A war to end wars. Liberty or death. **4.** *Grammar.* a group of words not containing a subject and predicate and functioning as a subject, object, verb, modifier, or other syntactic unit. **5.** *Music.* a short part of a piece of music, usually containing four measures, ending with a cadence, and either independent or forming part of a period: *To establish the mood of a phrase, . . . to convey what we believe to be the precise meaning the composer wishes to express, is one of the greatest problems facing a pianist* (Ruth Slenczynska). **6.** a series of movements that make up a dance pattern. **7.** manner or style of expression; diction; phraseology; language: *the lady who was, in chivalrous phrase, empress of his thoughts and commander of his actions* (Scott). **8.** a group of words spoken as a unit and separated by pauses: *His short phrases made his speech sound jerky.*

—*v.t.* **1.** to express in a particular way; find expression for: *She phrased her excuse politely.* **2.** to mark off into phrases. **3.** to bring out the phrases of (a piece of music). —*v.i.* **1.** to use a phrase or phrases. **2.** to indicate or make phrases, as in music.

[< Latin *phrasis* < Greek *phrásis* speech, way of speaking < *phrázein* to express, tell]

phrase·book (frāz'bu̇k'), *n.* a book containing a collection of idiomatic phrases used in a language, with their explanations or translations: *I started mugging up my handy phrasebook, which tells you in six languages how to cope with the emergencies that arise* (Manchester Guardian).

phrase·mak·er (frāz'mā'kər), *n.* person skilled in making up unusual or striking phrases: *Above all, there is Churchill the phrasemaker, who could beat even Bernard Shaw to the verbal draw* (Time).

phrase·mak·ing (frāz'mā'king), *n.* skill in making up unusual or striking phrases: *In his outline of radio's fiscal woes, Minow again showed his penchant for colorful phrasemaking, which a year ago had pinned the "vast wasteland" tag on television* (Sam Chase).

phrase·mon·ger (frāz'mung'gər, -mong'-), *n.* a person who deals in phrases; person given to fine but often empty phrases: *If Robespierre had been a statesman instead of a phrasemonger . . .* (John Morley).

phra·se·o·gram (frā'zē ə gram), *n.* a written symbol representing a phrase, especially in shorthand.

phra·se·o·graph (frā'zē ə graf, -gräf), *n.* **1.** a phrase represented by a phraseogram. **2.** a phraseogram.

phra·se·o·graph·ic (frā'zē ə graf'ik), *adj.* **1.** of phraseograms; like a phraseogram. **2.** written in phraseograms.

phra·se·og·ra·phy (frā'zē og'rə fē), *n.* **1.** the representation of phrases or sentences by abbreviated, written characters or symbols, especially in shorthand; the use of phraseograms. **2.** written phraseology.

phra·se·o·log·i·cal (frā'zē ə loj'ə kəl), *adj.* **1.** of or having to do with phraseology: *He was at every moment in complete command . . . of every phraseological subtlety* (New Yorker). **2.** characterized by a particular phraseology, or by the use of phrases or peculiar expressions. —**phra'se·o·log'i·cal·ly,** *adv.*

phra·se·ol·o·gist (frā'zē ol'ə jist), *n.* **1.** a person who deals with phraseology. **2.** a skillful inventor or user of phrases; phrasemaker: *All that could come out of any new conference is what cold-war phraseologists term an "easing of tensions"* (Newsweek).

phra·se·ol·o·gy (frā'zē ol'ə jē), *n., pl.* **-gies.** the selection or arrangement of words; particular way in which a person expresses himself in language: *scientific phraseology.* [< *phrase* + *-logy*] —**Syn.** See **diction.**

phras·er (frā'zər), *n.* **1.** a person who uses or makes phrases. **2.** a person given to fine phrases; phrasemonger.

phras·ing (frā'zing), *n.* **1. a.** the manner or style of verbal expression; phraseology; wording: *Milton . . . mixes the extremest vernacular with the most exquisite and scholarly phrasing* (George Saintsbury). **b.** the grouping of spoken words by pauses. **2.** *Music.* **a.** a marking off or dividing into phrases. **b.** the playing of phrases. **c.** the manner in which a composition is phrased.

phra·tric (frā'trik), *adj.* **1.** of or having to do with a phratry or clan. **2.** consisting of phratries.

phra·try (frā'trē), *n., pl.* **-tries.** **1.** each of the larger subdivisions of a tribe in ancient Athens. Members of a phratry regarded one another as "brothers." **2.** a similar tribal unit, usually comprising two or more clans: *. . . the head woman then notifies the chief of all the clans in her phratry* (Beals and Hoijer). [< Greek *phrātríā* < *phrātēr* fellow clansman. Compare FRATERNITY.]

phre·at·ic (frē at'ik), *adj.* **1.** of or having to do with a well or wells. **2.** having to do with or characteristic of water in the saturated area just below the water table. [< Greek *phréat-, phréar* well + English *-ic*]

phre·at·o·phyte (frē at'ə fīt), *n.* any plant that obtains water by the deep penetration of its roots into the water table: *It is almost impossible to get rid of phreatophytes by any means other than denying them water* (Roscoe Fleming). [< Greek *phréat-, phréar* well + English *-phyte*]

phren., phrenology.

phre·net·ic (fri net'ik), *adj.* **1.** frenzied; frantic: *He would . . . make them even more phrenetic than they had been originally* (New Yorker). **2.** insane. —*n.* a madman. Also, **frenetic.** [< Old French *frenetique,* learned borrowing from Latin *phrenēticus.* Doublet of FRANTIC.] —**phre·net'i·cal·ly,** *adv.*

phre·net·i·cal (fri net'ə kəl), *adj.* phrenetic.

phren·ic (fren'ik), *adj.* **1.** *Anatomy.* of or having to do with the diaphragm: *The lung may be put to rest by cutting the phrenic nerve* (Marguerite Clark). **2.** *Obsolete.* of or having to do with the mind, especially as distinguished from the soul. [< New Latin *phrenicus* < Greek *phrēn* the diaphragm, midriff; also, mind, spirit]

phre·nit·ic (fri nit'ik), *adj.* affected with or suffering from phrenitis; subject to fits of delirium or madness.

phre·ni·tis (fri nī'tis), *n. Obsolete.* **1.** inflammation of the diaphragm. **2.** inflammation of the brain; encephalitis. **3.** delirium. [< Greek *phrenîtis* inflammation of the brain. Compare FRANTIC.]

phrenol., phrenology.

phren·o·log·ic (fren'ə loj'ik), *adj.* phrenological.

phren·o·log·i·cal (fren'ə loj'ə kəl), *adj.* of or having to do with phrenology.

phre·nol·o·gist (fri nol'ə jist), *n.* a person who professes to tell a person's character from the shape of his skull.

phre·nol·o·gy (fri nol'ə jē), *n.* **1.** the theory that the shape of the skull shows what sort of mind and character a person has. **2.** the practice of reading character from the shape of the skull. [American English < Greek *phrēn, phrēnos* (see PHRENIC) + English *-logy*]

phren·sy (fren'zē), *n., pl.* **-sies,** *v.t.,* **-sied, -sy·ing.** frenzy.

Phryg·i·an (frij'ē ən), *adj.* of or having to do with Phrygia, an ancient country in central and northwestern Asia Minor, its people, or their language. —*n.* **1.** a native or inhabitant of Phrygia. **2.** the Indo-European language of the ancient Phrygians.

Phrygian cap, a conical cap with its apex turned over toward the front, worn by the ancient Phrygians and in modern times adopted as a symbol of liberty.

Phrygian Cap
on statue of Paris in Vatican Museum

PHS (no periods), Public Health Service.

phthal·ate (thal'āt, fthal'-), *n.* a salt of phthalic acid.

phthal·ein (thal'ēn, -ē in; fthal'-), *n.* any of a series of organic dyes, as eosin, produced by combining phthalic anhydride with phenols.

phthal·ic acid (thal'ik, fthal'-), one of three isomeric acids formed from certain benzene derivatives, especially a colorless crystalline substance prepared from phthalic anhydride and used in making dyes and various synthetics. *Formula:* $C_8H_6O_4$ [short for *naphthalic* < *naphthal(ene)* + *-ic*]

phthalic anhydride, a white crystalline substance prepared from naphthalene, used in making various resins, dyes, insecticides, etc.: *The new fireproof plastic is made from phthalic anhydride by addition of four chlorine atoms* (Science News Letter). *Formula:* $C_8H_4O_3$

phthal·in (thal'in, fthal'-), *n.* any of a series of colorless chemical compounds produced by the reduction of phthaleins.

phthi·o·col (thī'ə kōl, -kol), *n. Biochemistry.* a yellow pigment having certain properties of vitamin K. *Formula:* $C_{11}H_8O_3$

phthi·ri·a·sis (thi rī'ə sis, fthi-), *n. Medicine.* the state of being infested with lice, with the resulting irritation or other effects; pediculosis. [< Latin *phthīriasis* < Greek *phtheiriasis* < *phtheiriân* be full of lice < *phtheír* louse]

phthis·ic (tiz′ik), *Archaic.* —*n.* phthisis. —*adj.* phthisical.
[< Latin *phthisica,* feminine of *phthisicus* < Greek *phthisikós,* adjective, consumptive < *phthísis* phthisis]

phthis·i·cal (tiz′ə kəl), *adj.* having to do with, like, or affected with phthisis.

phthis·ick·y (tiz′ə kē), *adj. Archaic.* **1.** tubercular. **2.** asthmatic.

phthi·sis (thī′sis), *n.* **1.** a tuberculous disease, especially pulmonary tuberculosis of the lungs; consumption. **2.** any progressive, wasting disease, especially a disease of the lungs. [< Latin *phthisis* < Greek *phthísis* any wasting disease < *phthíein* to waste away]

phy·co·cy·a·nin (fī′kō sī′ə nin), *n.* a blue pigment found in association with chlorophyll, especially in the cells of the blue-green algae: *Phycocyanin was found to be the key to why plants blossom in accordance with the length of daylight and darkness* (Science News Letter). [< Greek *phŷkos* seaweed + *kýanos* blue + English *-in*]

phy·co·e·ryth·rin (fī′kō ə rith′rin), *n.* a red pigment found in the red algae and, in association with phycocyanin, in the blue-green algae. [< Greek *phŷkos* seaweed + *erythrós* red + English *-in*]

phy·col·o·gist (fī kol′ə jist), *n.* a student of phycology; algologist.

phy·col·o·gy (fī kol′ə jē), *n.* the branch of botany dealing with seaweeds or algae; algology. [< Greek *phŷkos* seaweed + English *-logy*]

phy·co·my·cete (fī′kō mī sēt′), *n.* a phycomycetous fungus.

phy·co·my·ce·tous (fī′kō mī sē′təs), *adj.* of or belonging to the lowest class or group of fungi, whose members live as parasites or saprophytes and resemble algae. [< New Latin *Phycomyceteae* a division of fungi (< Greek *phŷkos* seaweed + *mýkēs, -ētos* fungus, mushroom) + English *-ous*]

phy·la (fī′lə), *n.* **1.** the plural of **phylum.** **2.** the plural of **phylon.**

phy·lac·ter·y (fə lak′tər ē), *n., pl.* **-ter·ies.** **1.** either of two small leather cases containing texts from the Jewish law, worn by orthodox Jews during weekday morning prayers, to remind them to keep the Law. One is strapped to the forehead, the other to the left arm: *Herr Löwenthal put his sample case out of the way . . . put on his phylacteries, and climbed into the upper berth and said his prayers* (Katherine Anne Porter). **2.** a reminder: *Trust not to thy remembrance in things which need phylacteries* (Sir Thomas Browne). **3.** a charm worn as a protection; amulet. **4.** an ostentatious or hypocritical display of righteousness; mark of pharisaism. [< Late Latin *phylactērium* < Greek *phylaktḗrion* safeguard; guardpost < *phylaktḗr* guard, watchman]

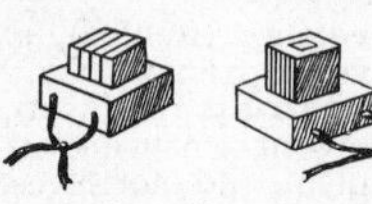
Phylacteries (def. 1)

phy·le (fī′lē), *n., pl.* **-lae** (-lē). **1.** (in ancient Greece) a tribe or clan, based on supposed kinship. **2.** (in Attica) a political, administrative, and military subdivision, made chiefly on a geographical basis. [< Greek *phȳlḗ* tribe, clan, related to *phýein* beget]

phy·let·ic (fī let′ik), *adj.* of or having to do with a biological phylum, or a line of descent: . . . *a special terminology arising from the experimental and natural observation of animals at their own phyletic level* (New Scientist). [< Greek *phȳletikós* tribal < *phȳlétēs* tribesman < *phȳlḗ* tribe; with meaning from English *phylum*]

Phyl·lis (fil′is), *n.* a name in pastoral poetry for a comely rustic maiden or sweetheart. Also, **Phillis.**
[< Latin *Phyllis,* a girl's name in Virgil and Horace < Greek *Phyllís* (literally) foliage < *phýllon* leaf]

phyl·lite (fil′īt), *n.* a rock consisting of an argillaceous schist or slate, containing scales or flakes of mica. [< Greek *phýllon* leaf + English *-ite*[1]]

phyl·lo·clad (fil′ə klad), *n.* phylloclade.

phyl·lo·clade (fil′ə klād), *n.* **1.** a flattened or enlarged stem or branch, resembling or performing the function of a leaf, as in the cactus. **2.** a cladophyll. [< New Latin *phyllocladium* < Greek *phýllon* leaf + *kládos* branch, sprout]

phyl·lode (fil′ōd), *n.* an expanded and, usually, flattened petiole resembling and having the functions of a leaf, the true leaf blade being absent or much reduced in size, as in many acacias. [< French *phyllode* < New Latin *phyllodium* < Greek *phyllṓdēs* leaflike < *phýllon* leaf + *eîdos* form]

PHYLLODE

Phyllode of South African acacia

phyl·lo·dy (fil′ə dē), *n.* **1.** the condition in which parts of a flower are transformed into ordinary leaves. **2.** the condition in which a leaf stalk is changed into a phyllode. [< *phyllode* + *-y*[3]]

phyl·loid (fil′oid), *adj.* resembling a leaf.

phyl·lome (fil′ōm), *n.* **1.** a leaf of a plant or any organ homologous with a leaf, or regarded as a modified leaf (as a sepal, petal, stamen, etc.). **2.** all the leaves of a plant, taken as a whole; foliage. [< German *Phyllome* < New Latin *phylloma* < Greek *phýllōma* foliage < *phýllon* leaf]

phyl·lom·ic (fə lom′ik, -lō′mik), *adj.* of or like a phyllome.

phyl·loph·a·gous (fə lof′ə gəs), *adj.* leaf-eating, as certain beetles and chafers. [< Greek *phýllon* leaf + *phageîn* eat + English *-ous*]

phyl·lo·phore (fil′ə fôr, -fōr), *n. Botany.* the terminal leaf-producing bud or growing point of a stem (used especially with reference to palms). [< Greek *phýllon* leaf + English *-phore*]

phyl·lo·pod (fil′ə pod), *adj.* of or belonging to a group of small crustaceans with four or more pairs of leaflike appendages which function as both swimming feet and gills. —*n.* a phyllopod crustacean. [< New Latin *Phyllopoda* the group name < Greek *phýllon* leaf + *poús, podós* foot]

phyl·lop·o·dan (fə lop′ə dən), *adj., n.* phyllopod.

phyl·lo·tax·is (fil′ə tak′sis), *n.* **1.** the distribution or arrangement of leaves on a stem. **2.** the laws collectively which govern such distribution. [< New Latin *phyllotaxis* < Greek *phýllon* leaf + *táxis* arrangement]

phyl·lo·tax·y (fil′ə tak′sē), *n.* phyllotaxis.

phyl·lox·e·ra (fil′ok sir′ə, fə lok′sər-), *n., pl.* **phyl·lox·e·rae** (fil′ok-sir′ē, fə lok′sə rē). any of a group of plant lice. The grape phylloxera destroys grapevines by infesting the leaves and roots. [< New Latin *Phylloxera* the genus name < Greek *phýllon* leaf + *xērós* dry (because the lice "dry up the foliage")]

Phylloxera or vine pest (Lines show actual lengths.)

phyl·lox·e·ral (fə lok′sər əl), *adj.* of or having to do with the phylloxera.

phyl·lox·e·rat·ed (fə-lok′sə rā′tid), *adj.* infested with phylloxerae.

phyl·lox·er·ic (fil′ok ser′ik), *adj.* phylloxeral.

phyl·lox·e·rized (fə lok′sə rīzd), *adj.* phylloxerated.

phy·lo·gen·e·sis (fī′lə jen′ə sis), *n.* phylogeny.

phy·lo·ge·net·ic (fī′lə jə net′ik), *adj.* of or having to do with phylogeny. —**phy′lo·ge·net′i·cal·ly,** *adv.*

phy·lo·gen·ic (fī′lə jen′ik), *adj.* phylogenetic.

phy·log·e·nist (fī loj′ə nist), *n.* a student of or expert in phylogeny: *As phylogenists, Whitman and Heinroth both sought to develop in detail the relationship between families and species of birds* (Scientific American).

phy·log·e·ny (fī loj′ə nē), *n., pl.* **-nies.** the origin and development of a kind of animal or plant; racial history: *Ontogeny recapitulates phylogeny* (Henry E. Crampton). [< German *Phylogenie* < Greek *phŷlon* race[2] + *-geneia* origin]

phy·lon (fī′lon), *n., pl.* **-la.** *Biology.* a tribe; a genetically related subdivision; phylum. [< Greek *phŷlon* race[2]]

phy·lum (fī′ləm), *n., pl.* **-la.** **1.** *Biology.* a primary division of the animal or vegetable kingdom, usually equivalent to a subkingdom, as the thallophytes, protozoa, or arthropoda. The animals or plants in a phylum are considered to be related by descent from a common ancestral form: *Since all animal phyla with the exception of the vertebrates are present in early Cambrian rocks, it is evident that much of the evolutionary sequence has not yet been examined* (Willard Bascom). **2.** a group of languages that includes two or more linguistic families or stocks: . . . *Haida and Tlingit, apparently related to the Athabascan family, with which they form the Na-Dené phylum, are immediately adjacent* (H.A. Gleason, Jr.). [< New Latin *phylum* < Greek *phŷlon* race[2], stock]

phys., **1.** physical. **2.** physician. **3.** physics.

phys. ed., physical education.

phys·i·at·rics (fiz′ē at′riks), *n.* physical medicine.

phys·i·at·rist (fiz′ē at′rist), *n.* a person skilled in physiatrics.

phys·ic (fiz′ik), *n., v.,* **-icked, -ick·ing.** —*n.* **1.** a medicine, especially one that moves the bowels; cathartic. **2.** the art of healing; science and practice of medicine: *Throw physic to the dogs; I'll none of it* (Shakespeare). **3.** *Archaic.* natural science. —*v.t.* **1.** to move the bowels of. **2.** to give medicine to; dose; treat. **3.** to act like a medicine on; cure: *The labor we delight in physics pain* (Shakespeare). [< Latin *physica* < Greek *physikḗ* (*epistḗmē*) (knowledge) of nature < *phýsis* nature < *phýein* to produce] —**Syn.** *v.t.* **3.** relieve, alleviate.

phys·i·cal (fiz′ə kəl), *adj.* **1.** of the body: *physical exercise, a physical disability.* **2.** of matter; material: *The tide is a physical force.* **3.** according to the laws of nature. **4.** of the science of physics.
—*n. Informal.* a physical examination.
—**phys′i·cal·ly,** *adv.* —**phys′i·cal·ness,** *n.*
—**Syn.** *adj.* **1.** bodily.

physical anthropologist, a student of or expert in physical anthropology: *The physical anthropologist is, in one sense, a biologist who concentrates his attention on man* (Beals and Hoijer).

physical anthropology, the branch of anthropology that deals with the development of man's personal characteristics, including his bodily formation and mental traits.

physical chemistry, the branch of chemistry that deals with the basic laws of the properties of substances as formulated by physics and their relations to chemical composition and changes.

physical culture, the development of the body by appropriate exercise.

physical education, instruction in how to exercise and take care of the body, especially as part of a school or college curriculum.

physical examination, an examination of the various parts of a person's body to determine the state of health, especially as made by a physician.

physical geography, the branch of geography that deals with the natural features of the earth's surface, such as land forms, climate, winds, ocean currents, and all other physical features of the earth.

physical inventory, an inventory made by a count of stock or equipment instead of by checking books of account.

physical medicine, the branch of medicine that deals with curing disease and improving health by physical means, especially physical therapy or physiotherapy.

physical metallurgy, the science and technology of the production and compounding of metals and alloys: *Physical metallurgy is the branch of metallurgy which adapts metals to human use* (A.E. Adami).

physical production, production measured by quantities of goods produced, rather than by money values. An index of physical production reflects changes in output, not changes in price.

physical science, **1.** physics. **2.** physics, chemistry, geology, astronomy, and other sciences dealing with inanimate matter.

physical therapist, physiotherapist.

physical therapy, physiotherapy.

phy·si·cian (fə zish′ən), *n.* **1.** a doctor of medicine. **2.** any practitioner of the healing art: *More needs she the divine than the physician* (Shakespeare). **3.** a person who cures any of various maladies or infirmities, as of the soul; healer. [Middle English *fisicien* < Old French, learned borrowing from Medieval Latin *physicus* doctor, or *physica* medical science (in Latin, natural science); see PHYSIC]

➔ **Physician,** in the sense of def. 1, is subject to strict definition under law throughout most of the world today. The usual prerequisites are a successfully completed course of study in an accredited school of medicine, normally followed by a period of internship and oftentimes further examination by some governmental or other official authority preliminary to the granting of a license to engage in the practice of medicine. In Great Britain, the physician is one who practices medicine as distinguished from one who practices surgery (a surgeon). Today, all surgeons in the United States hold degrees as doctors of medicine, although one who specializes in surgery is usually referred to as a "surgeon," just as one who specializes in gynecology is referred to as a "gynecologist," one who specializes in psychiatry is referred to as a "psychiatrist," etc.

phys·i·cist (fiz′ə sist), *n.* **1.** a person who studies or is skilled in physics; expert in physics: *In studying these phenomena, the classical aerodynamicist must learn from the physicist who has some knowledge of spectroscopy* (Louis N. Ridenour). **2.** *Archaic.* a natural philosopher.

phys·i·co·chem·i·cal (fiz′i kō kem′ə kəl), *adj.* of or having to do with both physics and chemistry: *physicochemical research.* —**phys′i·co·chem′i·cal·ly,** *adv.*

phys·ics (fiz′iks), *n.* **1.** the science that deals with the properties and interrelationships of matter and energy, excluding chemical and biological change. Physics studies mechanics, heat, light, sound, electricity, magnetism, radiation, and atomic structure: *The aim of theoretical physics must be to find a complete set of mutually consistent postulates or axioms from which the properties of nature ... can be deduced in the form of a number of theorems* (H.J. Bhaba). **2.** a textbook or treatise on physics. **3.** *Archaic.* natural science. [< Latin *physica,* or Greek *tà physiká* the natural things. Compare METAPHYSICS.]

phys·i·o·chem·i·cal (fiz′ē ō kem′ə kəl), *adj.* of or having to do with the chemistry of living animals and plants.

phys·i·oc·ra·cy (fiz′ē ok′rə sē), *n., pl.* **-cies. 1.** the economic doctrines and system advocated by the physiocrats. **2.** government by, or in accordance with, nature.

phys·i·o·crat (fiz′ē ə krat), *n.* a follower of the school of economic thought founded by the French economist François Quesnay, in the 1700's, who believed that land was the only real source of wealth and the only proper source of taxation, maintained that society should be governed by an inherent natural order, and advocated free trade. [< French *physiocrate* < *physiocratie* physiocracy < Greek *phýsis* nature + *krátos* rule]

phys·i·o·crat·ic (fiz′ē ə krat′ik), *adj.* **1.** of or having to do with government according to nature. **2.** of or having to do with the physiocrats or their doctrines.

phys·i·og·nom·ic (fiz′ē og nom′ik, -ə-nom′-), *adj.* of or having to do with physiognomy. —**phys′i·og·nom′i·cal·ly,** *adv.*

phys·i·og·nom·i·cal (fiz′ē og nom′ə kəl, -ə nom′-), *adj.* physiognomic.

phys·i·og·no·mist (fiz′ē og′nə mist, -on′-ə-), *n.* a person skilled in physiognomy.

phys·i·og·no·my (fiz′ē og′nə mē, -on′ə-), *n., pl.* **-mies. 1.** the kind of features or type of face one has; one's face: *a ruddy physiognomy, a kindly physiognomy. His physiognomy indicated the inanity of character which pervaded his life* (Scott). **2.** the art of estimating character from the features of the face or the form of the body. **3.** the general aspect or looks of a countryside, a situation, etc.: *the rugged physiognomy of northern Scotland.* [< Late Latin *physiognōmia* < a variant of Greek *physiognōmoníā* < *phýsis* nature + *gnṓmōn, -onos* a judge] —**Syn. 1.** countenance.

phys·i·og·ra·pher (fiz′ē og′rə fər), *n.* a person skilled in physiography.

phys·i·o·graph·ic (fiz′ē ə graf′ik), *adj.* of or having to do with physiography.

phys·i·o·graph·i·cal (fiz′ē ə graf′ə kəl), *adj.* physiographic.

phys·i·og·ra·phy (fiz′ē og′rə fē), *n.* **1.** physical geography. **2.** geomorphology. **3.** (formerly) the science of nature or of natural phenomena in general. [< Greek *phýsis* nature + English *-graphy*]

physiol., 1. physiological. **2.** physiologist. **3.** physiology.

phys·i·ol·a·ter (fiz′ē ol′ə tər), *n.* a person who worships nature.

phys·i·ol·a·try (fiz′ē ol′ə trē), *n.* the worship of nature. [< Greek *phýsis* nature + *latreíā* worship]

phys·i·o·log·ic (fiz′ē ə loj′ik), *adj.* physiological.

phys·i·o·log·i·cal (fiz′ē ə loj′ə kəl), *adj.* **1.** having to do with physiology: *Digestion is a physiological process.* **2.** having to do with the normal or healthy functioning of an organism: *Food and sleep are physiological needs.* —**phys′i·o·log′i·cal·ly,** *adv.*

phys·i·ol·o·gist (fiz′ē ol′ə jist), *n.* a person who studies or is skilled in physiology; an expert in physiology.

phys·i·ol·o·gy (fiz′ē ol′ə jē), *n., pl.* **-gies. 1.** the science dealing with the normal functions of living things or their organs: *animal physiology, plant physiology, the physiology of the blood.* **2.** a textbook or treatise on this science. **3.** all the functions and activities of a living thing or of one of its organs. [< Latin *physiologia* < Greek *physiologíā* natural science < *physiólogos* one discoursing on nature < *phýsis* nature + *-lógos* treating of < *légein* speak]

phys·i·o·pa·thol·o·gy (fiz′ē ō pə thol′ə-jē), *n.* the science dealing with the physiological aspects of disease.

phys·i·o·sorp·tion (fiz′ē ō sôrp′shən, -zôrp′-), *n.* adsorption in which one or more layers of molecules are held weakly to a surface by physical forces. [< Greek *phýsis* nature + English (ad)*sorption*]

phys·i·o·ther·a·peu·tic (fiz′ē ō ther′ə-pyü′tik), *adj.* of or having to do with physiotherapy.

phys·i·o·ther·a·pist (fiz′ē ō ther′ə pist), *n.* a person skilled in physiotherapy.

phys·i·o·ther·a·py (fiz′ē ō ther′ə pē), *n.* the treatment of diseases and defects by physical remedies, such as massage or electricity, rather than by drugs; physical therapy. [< Greek *phýsis* nature + English *therapy*]

phy·sique (fə zēk′), *n.* bodily structure, organization, or development; physical appearance; body: *Samson was a man of strong physique.* [< French *physique,* noun use of adjective, physical < Old French *fusique* a physic < Latin *physicus* < Greek *physikós;* see PHYSIC]

phy·so·clis·tous (fī′sō klis′təs), *adj.* (of fishes) having no duct joining the air bladder with the alimentary canal, as perches. [< Greek *phŷsa* bladder + *-kleistos* (with English *-ous*) closed, shut]

phy·so·stig·min (fī′sō stig′min), *n.* physostigmine.

phy·so·stig·mine (fī′sō stig′mēn, -min), *n.* a highly potent, crystalline alkaloid, constituting the active principle of the calabar bean; eserine. It is used in medicine to stimulate the parasympathetic nerves, to contract the pupil of the eye, to treat myasthenia gravis, etc. *Formula:* $C_{15}H_{21}N_3O_2$ [< German *Physostigmin* < New Latin *Physostigma* the Calabar bean genus (< Greek *phŷsa* bladder, bellows + New Latin *stigma* stigma, part of a pistil of a plant) + German *-in* -ine[2]]

phy·sos·to·mous (fī sos′tə məs), *adj.* (of fishes) having the air bladder connected with the alimentary canal by an air duct. [< New Latin *Physostomi* the group name (< Greek *phŷsa* bladder + *stóma* mouth)]

phyt-, *combining form.* the form of **phyto-** before vowels, as in *phytin.*

-phyte, *combining form.* a growth; a plant: *Aerophyte = a plant nourished by the air.* [< Greek *phytón* a plant, shoot < *phýein* grow, beget]

phy·tic acid (fī′tik), an acid found in cereal seeds. It is a constituent of Phytin and other salts, and is used as a rust inhibitor, metal cleaner, etc. *Formula:* $C_6H_{18}O_{24}P_6$

Phy·tin (fī′tin), *n. Trademark.* a calcium and magnesium salt containing phosphorus, present as a reserve material in seeds, tubers, and rhizomes. Phytin is used as a dietary supplement, providing calcium, organic phosphorus, and inositol. [< *phyt-* + *-in*]

phyto-, *combining form.* a plant; plants: *Phytochemistry = the chemistry of plants. Phytology = the science of plants.* Also, **phyt-** before vowels. [< Greek *phytón* plant]

phy·to·bi·ol·o·gy (fī′tō bī ol′ə jē), *n.* the branch of biology which deals with plants.

phy·to·chem·is·try (fī′tō kem′ə strē), *n.* the chemistry of plants.

phy·to·chrome (fī′tə krōm), *n.* a bluish, light-sensitive pigment in plants which absorbs red or infrared rays and acts as an enzyme in controlling growth and other photoperiodic responses.

phy·to·cid·al (fī′tō sī′dəl), *adj.* able to kill plants. [< *phyto-* + *-cid*(e)[2] + *-al*[1]]

phy·to·gen·e·sis (fī′tō jen′ə sis), *n.* the development or evolution of plants.

phy·to·ge·net·ic (fī′tō jə net′ik), *adj.* **1.** of or having to do with phytogenesis. **2.** of vegetable or plant origin. —**phy′to·ge·net′i·cal·ly,** *adv.*

phy·to·ge·net·i·cal (fī′tō jə net′ə kəl), *adj.* phytogenetic.

phy·to·gen·ic (fī′tō jen′ik), *adj.* phytogenetic.

phy·tog·e·nous (fī toj′ə nəs), *adj.* phytogenic.

phy·tog·e·ny (fī toj′ə nē), *n.* phytogenesis.

phy·to·ge·o·graph·i·cal (fī′tō jē′ə graf′ə-kəl), *adj.* of or having to do with phytogeography: *Botanists have always regarded the British Isles as a phytogeographical whole* (New Scientist). —**phy′to·ge′o·graph′i·cal·ly,** *adv.*

phy·to·ge·og·ra·phy (fī′tō jē og′rə fē), *n.* the science that deals with the geographical distribution of plants: *What bearing had the phytogeography of the past on the evolution and dispersal of major groups like the flowering plants?* (London Times).

phy·tog·ra·phy (fī tog′rə fē), *n.* the branch of botany that deals with the description, naming, and classifying of plants; descriptive botany; plant taxonomy. [< New Latin *phytographia* < Greek *phytón* plant + English *-graphy*]

phy·to·hor·mone (fī′tō hôr′mōn), *n. Botany, Chemistry.* an auxin.

phy·toid (fī′toid), *adj.* of or like a plant.

phy·tol (fī′tōl, -tol), *n.* a colorless, oily, unsaturated alcohol, derived from chlorophyll, used in making vitamins E and K. *Formula:* $C_{20}H_{40}O$

phy·to·lac·ca·ceous (fī′tō la kā′shəs), *adj.* belonging to a family of chiefly tropical dicotyledonous trees, shrubs, and herbs, typified by the pokeweed. [< New Latin *Phytolacca* the genus name (< Greek *phytón* plant + New Latin *lacca* lake[2]) + English *-aceous* (because of the red juice of the berries]

phy·to·log·ic (fī′tə loj′ik), *adj.* of or having to do with phytology; botanical.

phy·to·log·i·cal (fī′tə loj′ə kəl), *adj.* phytologic.

phy·tol·o·gist (fī tol′ə jist), *n.* a person skilled in phytology; botanist.

phy·tol·o·gy (fī tol′ə jē), *n.* the science of plants; botany.

phy·ton (fī′ton), *n.* the smallest part of a plant; plant unit.

phy·to·pa·le·on·tol·o·gy (fī′tō pā′lē on-tol′ə jē), *n.* geologic botany.

phy·to·pa·thol·o·gist (fī′tō pə thol′ə-jist), *n.* a person skilled in phytopathology; mycologist.

phy·to·pa·thol·o·gy (fī′tō pə thol′ə jē), *n.* **1.** the science that deals with the diseases of plants: *The control of banana leaf disease probably represents one of the greatest achievements in the history of phytopathology* (C.W. Wardlaw). **2.** *Medicine.* the study of diseases caused by plant parasites, fungi, etc.; mycology.

phy·toph·a·gous (fī tof′ə gəs), *adj.* feeding on plants; herbivorous: *A wide variety of animals, including most carnivorous and phytophagous vertebrates and invertebrates, might be classed as predators* (Harbaugh and Goodrich). [< *phyto-* + Greek *phageîn* eat + English *-ous*]

phy·to·plank·ton (fī′tō plangk′tən), *n.* the part of the plankton of any body of water which consists of plants, usually algae: *The phytoplankton serves as food for tiny sea animals ... which in turn are eaten by fish, birds or other sea-going animals* (Science News Letter).

phy·to·so·ci·ol·o·gy (fī′tō sō′sē ol′ə jē, -shē-), *n.* the branch of plant ecology dealing with the interrelations among the plants of various areas. [< *phyto-* + *sociology*]

phy·tos·ter·ol (fī tos′tə rōl, -rol), *n.* any of several plant alcohols, as ergosterol, that have the properties of sterols.

phy·to·tox·ic (fī′tō tok′sik), *adj.* toxic or injurious to plants: *A fungicide must have no damaging effect on the plant, that is, it should not be phytotoxic* (R.L. Wain).

phy·to·tox·ic·i·ty (fī′tō tok sis′ə tē), *n.* a toxic or poisonous quality injurious to plants: *There are available a number of excellent protective fungicides which, although* *not entirely free from phytotoxicity, are playing an important part in controlling plant diseases* (New Scientist).

phy·to·tron (fī′tə tron), *n.* a structure or laboratory apparatus in which climatic conditions are simulated for the study of plants in a controlled environment. [< *phyto-* + *-tron,* probably suggested by *cyclotron*]

pi[1] (pī), *n., pl.* **pis. 1.** the ratio of the circumference of any circle to its diameter, usually written as π and equal to 3.14159+. **2.** the 16th letter of the Greek alphabet (Π, π), equivalent to English *P, p.* [(definition 1) < name of Greek letter π, used as abbreviation of Greek *periphéreia* periphery]

pi[2] (pī), *n., pl.* **pis,** *v.,* **pied, pi·ing.** —*n.* **1.** printing types all mixed up. **2.** any confused mixture. —*v.t.* to mix up (type). Also, **pie.** [origin uncertain; perhaps < *pie*[1] (because of its miscellaneous contents)]

pi., piaster.

PI (no periods), programed instruction.

P. I., Philippine Islands.

pi·a[1] (pī′ə), *n.* pia mater.

pi·a[2] (pē′ə), *n.* a perennial herb of Polynesia, the East Indies, etc., with a tuberous root that yields a nutritious starch, the so-called South Sea arrowroot. [< the Polynesian name]

pi·ac·u·lar (pī ak′yə lər), *adj.* **1.** making expiation; expiatory. **2.** needing expiation; sinful; wicked. [< Latin *piāculāris* expiatory < *piāculum* expiation < *piāre* to appease < *pius* devout]

pi·ac·u·la·tive (pī ak′yə lə tiv), *adj.* piacular: *The young are red and pustular Clutching piaculative pence* (T.S. Eliot).

piaffe (pyaf), *v.i.,* **piaffed, piaf·fing.** in horsemanship: **1.** to move the diagonally opposite legs, as in the trot, but without going forward, backward, or sideways. **2.** to move at a very slow trotting pace forward, backward, or sideways. [< French *piaffer* to strut; see PIAFFER]

piaf·fer (pyaf′ər), *n.* the act of piaffing. [< French *piaffer,* noun use of infinitive, to strut < obsolete *piaffe* outward show, parade; origin uncertain]

pi·al (pī′əl), *adj.* of or having to do with the pia mater: *the pial surface.*

pi·a ma·ter (pī′ə mā′tər), *Anatomy.* the innermost of three membranes enveloping the brain and spinal cord. [< Medieval Latin *pia mater* pious mother, mistranslation of Arabic *'umm raqīqah* thin (or tender) mother]

pi·a·nette (pē′ə net′), *n. British.* **1.** a small upright piano. **2.** a street piano. [< *pian*(o) + *-ette*]

pi·an·ism (pē an′iz əm, pē′ə niz-), *n.* performance on the piano; technique or skill in playing the piano: *His pianism has refined, and he achieved beautiful tone coloring in the fourth poetical variation of the slow movement* (New York Times).

pi·a·nis·si·mo (pē′ə nis′ə mō), *adj., adv., n., pl.* **-mos, -mi** (-mē). *Music.* —*adj.* very soft (used as a direction). —*adv.* very softly: *We simply paid closer attention to the score. When it said pianissimo, we played pianissimo* (Time). —*n.* a very soft passage or movement: *I especially admired the orchestra's dry, understated pianissimos* (New Yorker). [< Italian *pianissimo,* superlative of *piano;* see PIANO[2]]

pi·an·ist (pē an′ist, pē′ə nist), *n.* a person who plays the piano: *a concert pianist.*

pia·niste (pyä nēst′), *n. French.* a pianist.

pi·a·nis·tic (pē′ə nis′tik), *adj.* of, having to do with, or characteristic of a pianist: *pianistic artistry.*

pi·an·o[1] (pē an′ō), *n., pl.* **-os.** a large musical instrument whose tones range over several octaves and come from many wires. The wires are sounded by hammers that are worked by striking keys on a keyboard. *Although the piano is the only true solo instrument among our standard concert instruments, it is the exception, rather than the rule, to find it unaccompanied in modern jazz* (New Yorker). [< Italian *piano,* short for *pianoforte*]

pi·a·no[2] (pē ä′nō), *adj., adv., n., pl.* **-nos.** *Music.* —*adj.* soft; low (used as a direction): *In piano singing her tone remains pure* (London Times). —*adv.* softly. —*n.* a soft passage or movement. [< Italian *piano* < Latin *plānus* plain, flat (in Late Latin, smooth, graceful). Doublet of PLAIN[1], PLANE[1], PLAN.]

pi·an·o·for·te (pē an′ə fôr′tē, -fōr′-; -an′ə-fôrt, -fōrt), *n. Archaic.* a piano[1]: . . . *the two young men . . . sitting down at the pianoforte, would escape from the present and the future in the sweet familiar gaiety of a Haydn duet* (Lytton Strachey). [< Italian *pianoforte* < *piano* soft (see PIANO[2]) + *forte* loud < Latin *fortis* strong (because of its greater capability of gradation in dynamics)]

pia·no no·bi·le (pyä′nō nô′bē lā), *n., pl.* **pia·ni no·bi·li** (pyä′nē nô′bē lē). *Italian.* the main floor of a palazzo: *The first floor of her palace on the Tiber had been converted into shops, and she lived on the piano nobile* (John Cheever).

pi·as·sa·ba or **pi·a·sa·ba** (pē′ə sä′bə), *n.* piassava.

pi·as·sa·va or **pi·a·sa·va** (pē′ə sä′və), *n.* **1.** a stout woody fiber obtained from the leafstalks of two Brazilian palms, one of which also yields the coquilla nut, used in making coarse brooms, brushes, etc., and ropes. **2.** a stiff, coarse fiber obtained from an African palm. **3.** one of these palms. [< Portuguese *piassaba,* also *piassava* < Tupi (Brazil) *piaçába*]

pi·as·ter or **pi·as·tre** (pē as′tər), *n.* **1.** any of the various coins worth 1/100 of a pound, used in Egypt, Lebanon, Libya, Sudan, Syria, and Turkey. **2.** the monetary unit of South Vietnam, worth about 3 cents. **3.** a former Spanish silver coin worth about a dollar; peso. [< French *piastre* < Italian *piastra* (literally) metal plate < Medieval Latin *plastra* < Latin *emplastra* plaster, salve. Doublet of PLASTER.]

pi·az·za (pē az′ə; *Italian* pyät′tsä), *n., pl.* **-zas,** *Italian* **-ze** (-tsä). **1.** *Especially U.S.* a large porch along one or more sides of a house; veranda: *the low projecting eaves forming a piazza along the front, capable of being closed up in bad weather* (Washington Irving). **2.** an open public square in Italian cities and towns: *Rome's Il Tempo suggests that "statutes be built to him and piazzas named in his honor"* (Time). **3.** *Especially British.* an exterior covered walk with columns. [< Italian *piazza* < Vulgar Latin *plattia,* for Latin *platēa* courtyard, broad street. Doublet of PLACE[1], PLAZA.]

Piazza (def. 1)

Piazza (def. 2)
St. Marks, Venice

pi·broch (pē′brok), *n.* a kind of musical piece performed on the bagpipe, generally of either a warlike or sad character: *Some pipe of war Sends the bold pibroch from afar* (Scott). [< Scottish Gaelic *piobaireachd* art of pipe-playing < *piobair* piper < *piob* pipe, probably ultimately < Latin *pīpa*]

pi·ca[1] (pī′kə), *n.* **1.** *Printing.* **a.** a size of type (12 point).

This sentence is set in pica.

b. a unit of linear measure used in typesetting and printing, the height of the block of a type of pica, 12 points or 1/6 inch. **2.** a size of typewriter type, larger than elite, having 10 characters to the inch (the equivalent of 12-point printing type). [< Medieval Latin (England) *pica* name of a book of rules for determining dates of holy days, supposed to have been printed in pica]

pi·ca[2] (pī′kə), *n.* a craving for inedible substances as food, especially mineral substances such as chalk, clay, etc. It is a form of geophagy, sometimes occurring during pregnancy. [< Medieval Latin *pica* < Latin *pīca* magpie (because the bird appears to be omnivorous)]

pic·a·dor (pik′ə dôr), *n.* **1.** one of the horsemen who open a bullfight by irritating the bull with pricks of their lances. **2.** an agile debater; witty person. [< Spanish *picador* (literally) one who pricks < *picar* to pierce < *pica* pike[1]]

PICAO (no periods), Provisional International Civil Aviation Organization.

Pic·ard (pik′ərd), *n.* the dialect of French spoken in Picardy.

Pic·ar·dy third (pik′ər dē), *Music.* **1.** the major third in the final chord of a passage composed in the minor key. **2.** the effect that it produces. [translation of French *tierce de Picardie* < *Picardie* Picardy, France, where it is used in church compositions]

pic·a·resque (pik′ə resk′), *adj.* dealing with rogues and their adventures: *"Gil Blas," "Moll Flanders,"* and *"Anthony Adverse" are picaresque works.* [< Spanish *picaresco* < *pícaro* rogue; see PICARO]

pic·a·ro (pik′ə rō), *n., pl.* **-ros.** a rogue; knave. [< Spanish *pícaro* a rogue, roguelike; origin uncertain; perhaps < *picar* to prick < *pica* pike[1]]

pic·a·roon (pik′ə rün′), *n.* **1.** a rogue; thief; brigand: *I see in thy countenance something of the pedlar—something of the picaroon* (Scott). **2.** a pirate: *He was somewhat of a trader, something more of a smuggler, with a considerable dash of the picaroon* (Washington Irving). **3.** a piratical or privateering ship: *Kennelled in the picaroon a weary band were we* (Rudyard Kipling).
—*v.i.* to act or cruise as a brigand or pirate. [< Spanish *picarón* (augmentative) < *pícaro* rogue; see PICARO]

pic·a·yune (pik′ə yün′), *U.S.* —*adj.* small; petty; mean; paltry: *picayune criticism. My accent was excellent, but my vocabulary picayune* (Atlantic).
—*n.* **1.** an insignificant person or thing; trifle. **2.** any coin of small value, especially the 5-cent piece. **3.** the Spanish half real (formerly used in Florida, Louisiana, etc.). [American English, apparently < Creole *picaillon* coin worth 5 cents < Provençal *picaioun* a coin, perhaps related to *picar* to sound, clink]

pic·a·yun·ish (pik′ə yü′nish), *adj.* picayune.

Pic·ca·dil·ly (pik′ə dil′ē), *n.* one of the main business streets in London.

Piccadilly Circus, an open space formed by the convergence of several streets in western London.

pic·ca·lil·li (pik′ə lil′ē), *n., pl.* **-lis.** a relish of East Indian origin made of chopped pickles, onions, tomatoes, etc., with hot spices. [origin uncertain; perhaps a fanciful derivative of *pickle*]

pic·ca·nin·ny (pik′ə nin′ē), *n., pl.* **-nies.** pickaninny.

pic·co·lo (pik′ə lō), *n., pl.* **-los.** a small, shrill flute sounding an octave higher than the ordinary flute: *The best suspense music is supplied by muted brasses, and combinations like the piccolo, harp and xylophone* (Time). [< Italian *piccolo* < (*flauto*) *piccolo* small (flute). Compare Italian *picca* point.]

pic·co·lo·ist (pik′ə lō′ist), *n.* a player on the piccolo.

pice (pīs), *n., pl.* **pice.** a former bronze coin of India and Pakistan worth ¼ of an anna, replaced in India in 1957 and in Pakistan in 1961 by the paisa. [< Hindi *paisā* a copper coin, perhaps < *pāī* < Sanskrit *pad, pāda* one quarter; (originally) foot]

pic·e·ous (pis′ē əs, pī′sē-), *adj.* of, having to do with, or resembling pitch: **a.** inflammable; combustible. **b.** *Zoology.* of the color of pitch; pitch-black. [< Latin *piceus* (with English *-ous*) < *pix, picis* pitch[2]]

pi·ces·cent (pi ses′ənt), *adj.* nearly piceous or pitch-black in color. [< *pice*(ous) + *-escent*]

pich·i·ci·a·go (pich′ə sē ä′gō, -ā′gō), *n., pl.* **-gos** or (*collectively*) **-go.** a small armadillo of South America, about 5 inches long, with a pinkish shell covering its back. [< Spanish *pichiciego* < *pichey* the little armadillo, perhaps from a native name + Spanish *ciego* blind (< Latin *caecus*)]

pich·u·rim (pich′ər im, pish′-), *n.* a South American tree of the laurel family, with seeds having thick aromatic cotyledons (pichurim beans) that are used medicinally and as a substitute for nutmegs. [apparently < a native word]

pi·cine (pī′sīn, -sin), *adj.* of, belonging to, or having to do with woodpeckers. [< Latin *pīcus* woodpecker + English *-ine*[1]]

pick[1] (pik), *v.t.* **1.** to choose; select: *to pick the right words. I picked a winning horse at the races.* **2.** to pull away with the fingers, beak, etc.; gather; pluck: *to pick flowers, to pick a caterpillar from a leaf.* **3.** to pierce, dig into, or break up with something pointed: *to pick a road, ground, or rocks.* **4.** to use something pointed to remove things from: *to pick one's teeth.* **5. a.** to open with a pointed instrument, wire, etc., or by manipulation of the mechanism: *to pick a lock or safe.* **b.** to steal the contents of: *to pick a pocket or purse.* **6.** to prepare for use by removing feathers, waste parts, etc.: *to pick a chicken, to pick a bone clean.* **7.** to pull apart: *The hair in the pillow needs to be picked, as it has matted.* **8.** *U.S.* **a.** to use the fingers on (the strings of a musical instrument) with a plucking motion: *to play a banjo by picking its strings.* **b.** to play thus: *He could pick the banjo in a way no one has ever heard it picked since.* **9.** to seek and find occasion for; seek and find: *Whatever she had, she seemed to survey only to pick flaws in it* (Harriet Beecher Stowe). *He did not lack courage but he never picked a quarrel and very seldom fought* (Atlantic). **10. a.** to take up (seeds, small pieces of food, etc.) with the bill or teeth, as a bird or squirrel. **b.** to eat (food) in small pieces, slowly, or without appetite: *I picked a meal in fear and trembling* (Robert Louis Stevenson).

—*v.i.* **1.** to use or work with a pick, pickax, etc. **2.** to eat with small bites or daintily. **3.** to make a careful choice or selection. **4.** to gather fruit, etc. **5.** to pilfer: *to pick and steal.*

pick and choose, to select fastidiously: *As matters stand, the army is an employer that can pick and choose* (Maclean's).

pick at, a. to pull on with the fingers, etc.: *The sick man picked at the blankets.* **b.** to eat only a little at a time: *to pick at one's supper.* **c.** *Informal.* to find fault with; nag: *I'm always being picked at. I wish I was dead* (Cosmopolitan).

pick in, (in a painting or drawing) to work in or fill in: *Then the shadows are "picked in" by assistants* (George A. Sala).

pick off, a. to bring down one by one, by or as by shooting: *to pick off a few disorganized opponents. The rifleman picked off the enemy.* **b.** (in baseball) to catch (a runner) off base and throw him out: *The catcher handles bunts and pop-ups, picks off runners who stray from base* (Atlantic).

pick on, a. *Informal.* to find fault with; nag at: *Why pick on me?* **b.** *Informal.* to annoy; tease: *The larger boys picked on him during recess.* **c.** to choose; select: *Why did he pick on you first?*

pick out, a. to choose with care; select: *He picked out for this purpose a Pole whom he believed to be a genuine revolutionary* (Edmund Wilson). **b.** to distinguish from the surroundings: *Can you pick me out in this group picture?* **c.** to make out (the sense or meaning): *Goethe ... did not know Greek well and had to pick out its meaning by the help of a Latin translation* (Matthew Arnold). **d.** to select the notes of (a tune) one by one, especially laboriously, on a keyboard, etc., and so play it: *She picked it out upon the keyboard, and ... enriched the same with well-sounding chords* (Robert Louis Stevenson). **e.** to embellish, especially by lines or spots of contrasting color following outlines, etc.: *The ceiling ... was richly gilt and picked out in violet* (Benjamin Disraeli). **f.** to remove or extract by picking: *to pick mussels out of the shells, to pick out loose threads from a hem.*

pick over, a. to look over carefully: *to pick over vegetables before buying.* **b.** to prepare for use: *Pick over and hull the strawberries.*

pick up, a. to take up: *The boy picked up a stone. The bird picked up a worm.* **b.** to summon or recover (courage, hope, etc.): *to pick up one's spirits.* **c.** to recover after an illness or after any check or depression; improve: *Unless demand picks up, mill men fear the cutbacks may spread throughout synthetics* (Wall Street Journal). **d.** to give (a person) fresh energy, courage, etc.: *A good dinner will pick you up.* **e.** to get by chance: *to pick up a bargain.* **f.** to acquire or attain (a skill, etc.) by chance or opportunity: *The ... child ... is not so quick in picking up parlour tricks* (Mary Kingsley). **g.** to pay for: *The London casino offered to pick up the $35,000 bill for a charter flight from New York* (New York Times). **h.** to take into a vehicle or ship: *to pick up passengers.* **i.** to take along with one: *to pick up a coat at the cleaner's.* **j.** to find again; regain: *Here we picked up the trail.* **k.** to succeed in seeing, hearing, etc.: *to pick up four of Jupiter's moons with a telescope, to pick up a radio program from Paris.* **l.** to go faster; increase in speed: *Other rivers picked up speed, boiled out of gorges* (Time). **m.** to pack; prepare to move out: *What will happen when we pick up and leave in a year or so?* (New Yorker). **n.** to arrest: *Many colleges have long intervened with police when their students had been picked up for such apolitical offenses as brawling or disturbing the peace* (Saturday Review). **o.** *Informal.* to become acquainted with without being introduced: *The only girls I knew were the ones I picked up* (New Yorker). **p.** *U.S.* to tidy up; put in order: *to pick up a room or one's desk.* **q.** *Golf.* to pick up one's ball: *He [Bobby Jones] "picked up" during the 1921 British Open in a fit of pique* (New Yorker).

—*n.* **1.** the act of choosing; choice; selection: *He let me have the first pick.* **2.** a person or thing selected from among others: *That book is my first pick.* **3.** the best or most desirable specimen or specimens, part, etc.: *We got a high price for the pick of our peaches.* **4.** the total amount of a crop gathered at one time. **5.** a plectrum.

[Middle English *picken*, perhaps < Scandinavian (compare Old Icelandic *pikka* pick, peck)]

—**Syn.** *v.t.* **1.** See **choose.**

pick[2] (pik), *n.* **1** a tool with a heavy, sharp-pointed iron or steel bar, attached through an eye in the center to a wooden handle, used for breaking earth, rock, etc.; pickax. **2.** any of various pointed or pronged tools or instruments. Ice is broken into pieces with a pick. [Middle English *pik*, variant of *pike* pike[2], Old English *pīc*. Probably related to PICK[1].]

pick[3] (pik), *v.t.* **1.** to throw (the shuttle) across the loom. **2.** *British Dialect.* **a.** to throw; hurl. **b.** to pitch (hay, grain, etc.). —*n.* **1.** a cast or throw of the shuttle in weaving. **2.** a single thread of the woof in cloth, especially as a measure of its fineness: *20 picks per inch.* **3.** *British Dialect.* a pitch; throw.

[variant of *pitch*[1]]

pick·a·back (pik′ə bak′), *adv.* on the back or shoulders: *Some had to be carried pickaback or on improvised stretchers* (Newsweek). —*adj.* of or having to do with transporting of loaded truck trailers on flatcars; piggyback: *a pickaback flatcar, pickaback service.* Also, **piggyback.** [origin uncertain]

pickaback plane, an aircraft that carries a fuel load too large to permit a takeoff in the normal fashion, and must be launched in the air from the top of a larger aircraft.

pick·a·nin·ny (pik′ə nin′ē), *n., pl.* **-nies. 1.** a small Negro child (now usually used in an unfriendly way in the United States). **2.** any small child. [perhaps American English, ultimately < Portuguese *pequenino* very small or perhaps < Spanish *pequeñin* < *pequeño* small + *niño* boy]

➔ **Pickaninny.** In the United States and the West Indies, this word is normally applied only to a Negro child; in Australia, it is applied to a child belonging to any of the various dark-skinned aboriginal tribes. In some areas, as in parts of Africa, the term has become part of a native dialect, or the lingua franca of the region, and is used, without any implication of contempt, simply to mean "a small child."

pick·a·pack (pik′ə pak′), *adv.* pickaback.

pick·ax or **pick·axe** (pik′aks′), *n., v.,* **-axed, -ax·ing.** —*n.* a heavy tool with a sharp point at one end and a chisel-like blade of equal length at the other, for breaking up dirt, rocks, etc.; pick. —*v.t.* to break, clear, etc., with a pickax. —*v.i.* to work with or use a pickax. [alteration of Middle English *picois*, and *pikeis* < Old French *picois*, related to *pic*, or *pik* pick[2]; influenced by English *ax*]

Pickax

picked[1] (pikt), *adj.* **1.** with waste parts removed and ready for use: *a freshly picked chicken.* **2.** with produce, fruit, grain, etc., removed; stripped: *a clean picked field.* **3.** specially selected for merit: *The crew of the lugger ... all of whom were picked men, remarkable for their strength and activity* (Frederick Marryat). [< *pick*[1] + *-ed*[2]] —**Syn. 1.** plucked. **3.** choice, excellent.

picked[2] (pikt), *adj. Archaic.* **1.** having a sharp point; pointed; spiked. **2.** covered with sharp points; prickly. [< *pick*[2] + *-ed*[2]]

pick·eer (pi kir′), *v.i. Archaic.* to reconnoiter; scout. [apparently < French *picorer* maraud, steal cattle, ultimately < Latin *pecus* cattle]

Pick·el·hau·be (pik′əl hou′bə), *n. German.* the spiked helmet formerly worn by German soldiers.

pick·er[1] (pik′ər), *n.* **1.** a person who gathers, picks, or collects: *an apple picker, a rag picker.* **2.** a tool or machine for picking anything: *Mr. Alleman showed ... the corn picker with which he can pick twenty acres of corn in a ten-hour day* (New York Times). **3. a.** a machine for separating and cleaning the fibers of cotton, wool, and the like. **b.** a person who runs such a machine.

pick·er[2] (pik′ər), *n.* the small piece in a loom, usually of leather, that drives the shuttle back and forth through the warp.

pick·er·el (pik′ər əl, pik′rəl), *n., pl.* **-els** or (*collectively*) **-el. 1.** (in the United States and Canada) any of certain of the smaller species of pike. **2.** (in Great Britain) a pike not yet full grown, but of a size large enough to catch. **3.** the pike perch. [Middle English *pykerel* (diminutive) < *pike*[3]]

pickerel frog, a common, spotted, green or brown frog of eastern North America. See picture under **frog.**

pick·er·el·weed (pik′ər əl wēd′, pik′rəl-), *n.* any of a group of North American herbs with spikes of blue flowers and heart-shaped leaves, growing in shallow, usually quiet, water.

pick·er-up (pik′ər up), *n., pl.* **pick·ers-up. 1.** a person who picks up: *a picker-up of words, a picker-up of trifles.* **2.** a person employed to collect the game shot by a shooting party.

pick·et (pik′it), *n.* **1.** a pointed stake or peg driven into the ground to make a fence, to tie a horse to, etc. **2.** a small body of troops posted around a larger body to watch for the enemy and guard against surprise. **3.** a person stationed by a labor union near a factory, store, etc., where there is a strike, to try to prevent employees from working or customers from buying: *Pickets had been removed and workers had returned to their jobs at twelve different plants where they had been on strike* (New York Times). **4.** a person who takes part in a public demonstration or boycott to support a cause; demonstrator: *500 pickets marched around City Hall ... protesting the treatment of Negroes in Birmingham* (Wall Street Journal).

—*v.t.* **1.** to enclose with pickets; fence. **2.** to tie to a picket: *There was a stake driven down where an animal had been picketed for the night* (Owen Wister). **3.** to post as a picket; guard with or as if with pickets. **4.** to station pickets at or near: *to picket a factory.* —*v.i.* to act as a picket.

[< French *piquet* (diminutive) < *pic* pick[2]; see PIKE[1]] —**pick′et·er,** *n.*

—**Syn.** *n.* **2.** sentry, sentinel.

picket fence, a fence made of pickets.

picket line, 1. a line of persons acting as pickets at or near a factory, store, etc.: *When the skeleton crew showed up for work ... they were met by a sullen, hostile picket line of several hundred strikers* (Newsweek). **2.** a military position held by an advance guard of men stationed at intervals: *The picket line of Minitrack stations across their expected path is strung out in a north-south line* (Scientific American). **3.** a rope to which cavalry and artillery horses are tied while being groomed.

picket pin, a long iron pin with a swivel link at the top, to which a picket rope is tied.

picket ship, a ship used as a radar picket.

pick·ing (pik′ing), *n.* the act of a person or thing that picks.

pickings, a. amount picked: *The final pickings may bring the crop closer to 15 million bales* (Wall Street Journal). **b.** perquisites; profits; returns: *The time was 1930 and interior designers in that lean year were having slim pickings indeed* (New York Times). **c.** things left over; scraps: *The vultures had then but small pickings* (Milton). **d.** things stolen or received dishonestly: *It must be confessed that the pickings of the office [of Paymaster General] were enormous* (W.P. Courtney).

pick·le[1] (pik′əl), *n., v.,* **-led, -ling.** —*n.* **1.** salt water (brine), vinegar, or other liquid in which meats, fish, vegetables, etc., can be preserved: *to put ham in pickle before smok-*

ing it. **2.** a cucumber preserved in pickle: *a dill pickle.* **3.** any other vegetable preserved in pickle. **4.** *Informal.* trouble; difficulty: *I could see no way out of the pickle I was in* (Robert Louis Stevenson). **5.** an acid solution or other chemical preparation, used for cleaning metal castings, etc.

in pickle, kept prepared for use: *to have a rod in pickle to punish a naughty child.*

—*v.t.* **1.** to preserve in pickle: *to pickle onions, eggs, or beets.* **2.** to clean with an acid solution or other chemical preparation: *The cold-rolling firms take steel from the rerollers and "pickle" it to clean off scale* (London Times).

[< Middle Dutch *pekel*]

—**Syn.** *n.* **4.** plight, predicament.

pick·le² (pik′əl), *n. Scottish.* **1.** a grain of wheat, barley, or oats; kernel. **2.** a very small quantity; a very little; trifle. [origin unknown]

pick·led (pik′əld), *adj.* **1.** preserved in or treated with a pickle. **2.** *U.S. Slang.* intoxicated; drunk.

pick·ler (pik′lər), *n.* a person who pickles.

pick·le·worm (pik′əl wėrm′), *n.* the larva of a pyralid moth of North and South America that lays its eggs on young cucumbers and other plants of the gourd family, the larva boring into the fruit and spoiling it.

pick·lock (pik′lok′), *n.* **1.** a person who picks a lock or locks, especially in order to steal; thief; burglar. **2.** an instrument for picking locks.

pick-me-up (pik′mē up′), *n. Informal.* a stimulating or bracing drink, food, or medicine: *When his spirits flag, he takes an egg as a pick-me-up* (New Yorker).

pick·off (pik′ôf′, -of′), *n.* **1.** a baseball play in which a runner is caught off base by a sudden throw from the pitcher or catcher: *They proved that a perfect pickoff at first could be foozled not once but again* (New York Times). **2.** an offensive play in basketball in which one player blocks a defensive man in order to free another player, guarded by that man, for a pass.

pick·pack (pik′pak′), *adv.* pickaback.

pick·pock·et (pik′pok′it), *n.* a person who steals from people's pockets: *Pickpockets often work in crowds of people.*

pick·purse (pik′pėrs′), *n.* a person who steals purses or their contents.

pick·some (pik′səm), *adj.* given to picking and choosing; fastidious; particular. —**pick′some·ness,** *n.*

pick·thank (pik′thangk′), *n. Dialect.* a flatterer; talebearer: *He takes to sulking at home and dining a crew of worthless pickthanks who . . . tell him what he wants to hear* (Time).

pick·up (pik′up′), *n.* **1.** a picking up: *He went out and dropped the envelope in the mail for the midnight pickup* (New Yorker). **2.** *Informal.* a getting better; improvement: *a pickup in his health, a pickup in business.* **3.** a going faster; increase in speed; acceleration: *People who must drive a lot know the big difference a gasoline can make in pickup, economy and all around smooth operation* (Maclean's). **4.** *Informal.* an acquaintance made without an introduction, especially an acquaintance of the opposite sex. **5.** something obtained or secured when or as chance offers, as a bargain or a hurried meal: *While we were having our pickup . . . the children came down and settled around the table* (New Yorker). **6.** *Sports.* a catching (or sometimes hitting) of a ball very soon after it has bounced on the ground: *Two snappy double-plays, the first that started with a dazzling pickup by Sam Dente, helped the youngster* (New York Times). **7.** *Radio.* **a.** the reception of sound waves in the transmitter and their conversion into electrical waves for broadcasting: *The short-wave pickups . . . lost a good deal of their value when nobody had anything very special to say* (New York Times). **b.** the apparatus for such reception. **c.** the place from which a broadcast is transmitted: *The network said the program would originate at thirteen pickup points from the Atlantic to the Pacific* (New York Times). **d.** the electrical system for connecting a program originating outside the studio to the broadcasting station. **8.** *Television.* **a.** the reception of images in the transmitter and their conversion into electrical waves for broadcasting: *A new measuring circuit . . . simplifies range changing and reduces stray pickup* (Scientific American). **b.** the apparatus that does this. **9.** a device that transforms into electric current the sound impulse communicated to the needle by the groove of a phonograph record, the current being typically very weak, capable in itself only of serving as a signal to the amplifier: *We must have stereo pickups . . . [but] at this moment you cannot go and buy one in any shop* (Saturday Review). **10.** a pickup truck.

—*adj.* of or having to do with an informal game or group that is assembled on the spot or for one time only: *Small groups of correspondents—seldom more than enough for a pickup baseball game* (A.J. Liebling).

pickup arm, a tone arm.

pickup truck, a small, light truck with an open back, used for light hauling.

pickup tube, an electron beam tube for conversion of an optical image into an electric signal: *In the modern pickup tube, scanning takes place as the beam of electrons from the electron gun is guided by a series of electromagnets* (Kenneth Harwood).

Pick·wick·i·an (pik wik′ē ən), *adj.* **1.** of, having to do with, or characteristic of Mr. Pickwick or his club. **2.** given a special meaning for the occasion, regardless of the real meaning: *words used in a Pickwickian sense.*

pick·y (pik′ē), *adj.,* **pick·i·er, pick·i·est.** *U.S. Informal.* **1.** choosy; particular: *People are very picky this year in buying new cars.* **2.** finding fault about trifles; nagging: *If I hear one more picky, cavilling, unconstructive word out of you . . . you and I are finished* (New Yorker).

pic·nic (pik′nik), *n., v.,* **-nicked, -nick·ing,** *adj.* —*n.* **1. a.** a pleasure trip with a meal in the open air: *a picnic at the beach.* **b.** any outdoor meal: *to have a picnic in one's yard.* **2.** *Slang.* a pleasant time or experience; very easy job. **3.** picnic ham.

—*v.i.* **1.** to go on or take part in a picnic. **2.** to eat in picnic style.

—*adj.* for or at a picnic: *a picnic lunch.*

[< French *piquenique,* perhaps a rhyming reduplication of French *pique*]

picnic ham, a smoked shoulder of pork, cut to look like a ham; picnic.

pic·nick·er (pik′nik ər), *n.* a person who picnics.

pico-, *combining form.* one trillionth of a _____: *Picofarad = one trillionth of a farad.*

pi·co·cu·rie (pī′kō kyůr′ē, pī′kō kyů rē′), *n.* one trillionth of a curie; micromicrocurie.

pi·co·far·ad (pī′kō far′əd, -ad), *n.* one trillionth of a farad; micromicrofarad.

pic·o·lin (pik′ə lin), *n.* picoline.

pic·o·line (pik′ə lēn, -lin), *n.* a colorless liquid obtained in three isomeric forms by the distillation of bones and coal, used as a solvent for waterproofing fabrics, etc. *Formula:* C_6H_7N [< Latin *pix, picis* pitch²]

pi·co·sec·ond (pī′kō sek′ənd), *n.* a trillionth of a second: *Laser pulses lasting about . . . one picosecond, can now be measured accurately for the first time* (Science News).

pi·cot (pē′kō), *n., pl.* **-cots** (-kōz), *v.,* **-coted** (-kōd), **-cot·ing** (-kō ing). —*n.* one of a number of fancy loops in embroidery, tatting, etc., or along the edge of lace, ribbon, etc.: *A hard-twisted yarn is used to add to the beauty of the small picots* (World Book Encyclopedia). —*v.t., v.i.* to trim with picots. [< French *picot* (diminutive) *pic* a point, pick³; see PIKE¹]

pic·o·tee (pik′ə tē′), *n.* a variety of carnation having white or yellow petals edged with a darker color, usually red. [< French *picotée,* past participle of *picoter* mark with pricks or points < Old French *picot* little peak; see PICOT]

picot stitch, a chain stitch; stitch consisting of a loop of thread held in place with a small stitch.

pic·rate (pik′rāt), *n.* a salt or ester of picric acid. [< *picr*(ic acid) + *-ate*²]

pic·ric acid (pik′rik), a poisonous, yellow, crystalline, intensely bitter acid, used in explosives and in dyeing; trinitrophenol. *Formula:* $C_6H_3N_3O_7$ [< Greek *pikrós* bitter, sharp + English *-ic*]

pic·rite (pik′rīt), *n.* any of a group of igneous rocks of granular texture, composed chiefly of olivine and augite. [< Greek *pikrós* bitter + English *-ite*¹ (because of the bitter taste of the magnesium it contains)]

pic·rol (pik′rōl, -rol), *n.* a bitter, odorless, colorless, crystalline antiseptic, used as a substitute for iodoform. [< *picr*(ic acid)]

pic·ro·tox·ic (pik′rō tok′sik), *adj.* of or derived from picrotoxin; having picrotoxin as the base.

pic·ro·tox·in (pik′rō tok′sin), *n.* a bitter, very poisonous, crystalline, chemical compound obtained from the seeds of several plants, similar to strychnine in action: *He was promptly put on the standard treatment for such cases: an injection of picrotoxin to stimulate the nervous system* (Time). *Formula:* $C_{30}H_{34}O_{13}$ [< Greek *pikrós* bitter, sharp + English *toxin*]

Pict (pikt), *n.* a member of an ancient people who formerly lived in the northern part of Great Britain. [< Late Latin *Pictī,* plural]

Pict·ish (pik′tish), *adj.* of or having to do with the Picts. —*n.* the language of the Picts.

pic·to·gram (pik′tə gram), *n.* pictograph.

pic·to·graph (pik′tə graf, -gräf), *n.* **1.** a picture used as a sign or symbol, especially in a system of picture writing. **2.** a writing or record in such symbols: *Discovery was made of pictographs in Arizona indicating that the brilliant supernova of July 4, 1054, was observed and recorded by prehistoric American Indians* (Science News Letter). **3.** a diagram or chart presenting statistical data by using pictures of different colors, sizes, or numbers. [< Latin *pictus,* past participle of *pingere* to paint + English *-graph*]

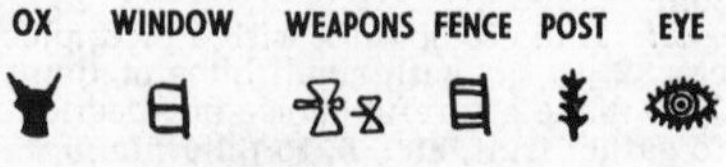

OX WINDOW WEAPONS FENCE POST EYE

East Mediterranean Pictographs (def. 1)

pic·to·graph·ic (pik′tə graf′ik), *adj.* **1.** of or having to do with pictography. **2.** like, of the nature of, or consisting of pictographs.

pic·tog·ra·phy (pik tog′rə fē), *n.* the use of pictographs; picture writing.

Pic·tor (pik′tər), *n., genitive* **Pic·to·ris.** a southern constellation near the star Canopus.

pic·to·ri·al (pik tôr′ē əl, -tōr′-), *adj.* **1.** having to do with, consisting of, or expressed in a picture or pictures: *pictorial writing or symbols.* **2.** making a picture for the mind; vivid. **3.** illustrated by pictures: *a pictorial history, a pictorial magazine.* **4.** of, belonging to, or produced by a painter; having to do with painting or drawing: *Pictorial skill being so rare in the colonies, the painter became an object of general curiosity* (Hawthorne).

—*n.* a magazine or part of a newspaper in which pictures are an important part.

[< Latin *pictōrius* (< *pictor, -ōris* painter < *pingere* to make pictures, paint, color) + English *-al*¹] —**pic·to′ri·al·ly,** *adv.*

—**Syn.** *adj.* **2.** graphic.

pic·to·ri·al·ist (pik tôr′ē ə list, -tōr′-), *n.* a person who uses a pictorial style, especially a photographer whose purpose is artistic rather than commercial, documentary, etc.

Pic·to·ris (pik tôr′is, -tōr′-), *n.* genitive of **Pictor.**

pic·tur·a·ble (pik′chər ə bəl), *adj.* that can be or is suitable for being pictured: *Nor did her gift for such picturable phrases ever leave her* (Atlantic).

pic·tur·al (pik′chər əl), *adj.* having to do with or of the nature of a picture or pictures; pictorial: *pictural incarnations of the fiend* (Edgar Allan Poe).

pic·ture (pik′chər), *n., v.,* **-tured, -tur·ing.** —*n.* **1.** a drawing, painting, portrait, or photograph, or a print of any of these: *This book contains a good picture of Lee.* **2.** a scene: *The trees and brook make a lovely picture.* **3.** a mental image; a visualized conception; idea: *to have a clear picture of the problem.* **4.** something beautiful: *What a picture you are in those furs* (Winston Churchill). **5.** an exact likeness; image: *He is the picture of his father.* **6.** an example; embodiment: *Old Balthus van Tassel was a perfect picture of a thriving, contented, liberal-hearted farmer* (Washington Irving). **7.** a vivid description or account: *Gibbon's picture of the latter days of ancient Rome.* **8.** a motion picture: *It is more often the director, not the star, who makes a picture great, or even good* (Newsweek). **9.** a tableau, as in the theater. **10.** a visible image of something formed by physical means, as by a lens. **11.** *Informal.* state of affairs; condition; situation: *The employment picture is much brighter than it was a year ago* (New York Times).

pictures, *Informal.* **a.** a motion picture.

During his very successful career in pictures he has appeared in some . . . thrilling productions (Kinematograph and Lantern Weekly). **b.** a motion picture theater: *Charlotte is coming to the Zoo with me this afternoon. Alone. And later on to the pictures* (P.G. Wodehouse).

—*v.t.* **1. a.** to draw, paint, etc.; make into a picture: *The artist pictured the saints.* **b.** to reflect, as a mirror. **2.** to form a picture of in the mind; imagine: *He was older than she had been picturing him* (Arnold Bennett). **3.** to depict in words; describe graphically and vividly: *The speaker pictured the suffering of the poor. I think this last sentence pictures him exactly* (Madame D'Arblay).

[< Latin *pictūra* < *pingere* to make pictures, paint]

picture book, a book consisting largely or wholly of pictures, especially for children: *a picture book of animals.*

pic·tured (pik′chərd), *adj.* **1.** illustrated or adorned with pictures. **2.** represented in a picture. **3.** having the appearance of something in a picture.

picture gallery, 1. a hall or building containing a collection of pictures. **2.** the collection itself.

picture hat, a woman's wide-brimmed hat, originally often black and trimmed with ostrich feathers.

pic·ture·less (pik′chər lis), *adj.* without a picture or pictures: *a pictureless book.*

picture molding, a molded strip of wood high on a wall, as to hang pictures from. Picture hooks fit over one of the members of the molding.

Pic·ture·phone (pik′chər fōn′) *n. Trademark.* a telephone set equipped with a small television camera tube, picture tube, and screen, designed to permit persons to see one another as they talk on the telephone.

picture postcard, a postcard with a picture on one side.

picture rail or **rod,** a rod placed and used like a picture molding: *The immediate remedy would be to discard the mediocre bronze and lower the Gainsborough to the picture rail* (Atlantic).

pic·tures (pik′chərz), *n.pl.* See under **picture,** *n.*

picture show, *U.S. Informal.* **1. a.** a motion picture. **b.** a motion picture theater. **2.** an exhibition of paintings or photographs.

pic·tur·esque (pik′chə resk′), *adj.* **1.** quaint or interesting enough to be used as the subject of a picture: *a picturesque old mill. An experienced, industrious, ambitious, and often quite picturesque liar* (Mark Twain). **2.** making a picture for the mind; vivid: *picturesque language.*

—*n.* **the picturesque,** something picturesque; the picturesque principle, element, or quality in art, nature, or language: *Multitudinous lovers of the merely quaint and picturesque* (Newsweek).

[< *pictur*(e) + *-esque*, perhaps patterned on French *pittoresque* < Italian *pittoresco* pictorial < *pittore* painter (< Latin *pictor, -ōris*) + *-esco* -esque] —**pic′tur·esque′ly,** *adv.* —**pic′tur·esque′ness,** *n.*

—**Syn.** *adj.* **2.** graphic, pictorial.

picture tube, a cathode ray tube which reproduces a transmitted picture on the screen of a television set; Kinescope.

GLASS BULB
ELECTRON GUN
BEAM
YOKE
PATH
SENSITIZED SCREEN

Picture Tube
Electron gun bombards sensitized screen with electrons, and yoke deflects them to scan screen in horizontal lines, recreating light and dark areas of the picture.

picture window, a large window in the living room of a house or apartment, giving a sweeping view of the outside: *Will that architectural pet the "picture" window succumb to the rising desire for personal privacy?* (Sunday Times).

picture writing, 1. the recording of events or expressing of ideas by pictures or drawings that literally or figuratively represent things and actions. **2.** pictures used to record events or express ideas: *All the various receipts and disbursements were set down in the picture writing of the country* (William H. Prescott).

pic·tur·i·za·tion (pik′chər ə zā′shən), *n.* **1.** the act of picturizing: *The molecules are represented by cubes instead of spheres or some other shape for ease of picturization* (W. K. Burton). **2.** the state of being picturized. **3.** a picturized form of a novel or the like.

pic·tur·ize (pik′chə rīz), *v.t.,* **-ized, -iz·ing. 1.** to represent in a picture or pictures. **2.** to put (a novel, drama, etc.) into the form of a motion picture.

pic·ul (pik′əl), *n., pl.* **-ul** or **-uls.** a unit of weight equal to 100 catties, or about 135 pounds, long used in commerce in various parts of southern and southeastern Asia. [< Malay, or Javanese *pikul* a man's load]

pic·u·let (pik′yə lit), *n.* any of a group of small, soft-tailed birds of tropical regions, related to and resembling the woodpeckers. [< obsolete *picule* (< Latin *pīcus* woodpecker) + *-et*]

pid·dle (pid′əl), *v.i.,* **-dled, -dling. 1.** to do anything in a trifling or ineffective way. **2.** to pick at one's food. [origin uncertain. Compare Low German *pudeln* to splash, make an error, miss the mark.] —**Syn. 1.** dabble.

pid·dler (pid′lər), *n.* **1.** a mere trifler. **2.** a person who picks at his food.

pid·dling (pid′ling), *adj.* trifling; petty: *It's too piddling, she thought, to worry about curling your eyelashes* (New Yorker). —**Syn.** paltry.

pid·dock (pid′ək), *n.* any of a group of bivalve mollusks with a long egg-shaped shell, that burrow into clay, wood, soft rock, etc. [origin uncertain; perhaps Old English *puduc* wart]

pidg·in (pij′ən), *n.* **1.** *Chinese pidgin English.* business. **2.** pidgin English. **3.** any language spoken with a reduced grammar and vocabulary as a trade or communications jargon: *a French pidgin. The men keep calling to the team in a sort of pidgin Eskimo language* (New Yorker). Also, **pigeon.**

➤ **pidgin, pigeon.** The latter form, sometimes occurring in popular use but without currency among linguists, derives from the more familiar homonym.

pidgin English, one of several forms of English, with reduced grammatical structure and vocabulary, used in western Africa, Australia, Melanesia, and formerly in China, as a trade or communication jargon: *A good deal of amusement, too, was to be had in the exchanges of pidgin English* (London Times). [*pidgin*, alteration of pronunciation of *business*]

pidg·in·ize (pij′ə nīz), *v.t.,* **-ized, -iz·ing.** to form or develop into pidgin or any mixture of languages such as pidgin: *Pidginized varieties of French are found in North Africa and New Caledonia* (Robert A. Hall, Jr.).

pi-dog (pī′dôg′, -dog′), *n.* pye-dog: *Pi-dogs yapped perpetual background alarum* (London Times).

pie¹ (pī), *n.* **1.** fruit, meat, vegetables, etc., enclosed partially or wholly by a crust of pastry and baked: *apple pie, chicken pie.* **2.** a round layer cake with a filling of cream, custard, jelly, etc.: *Boston cream pie.* **3.** *U.S.* the sum total of income, costs, etc., with reference to the portions into which it may be divided, as on a pie chart: *Transportation is that slice of the cost pie often overlooked by management when it wants to cut costs* (Wall Street Journal). **4.** *U.S. Slang.* something quite easy or desirable: *easy as pie.* [Middle English *pye*, origin uncertain] —**pie′-like′,** *adj.*

pie² (pī), *n.* a magpie. [< Old French *pie* < Latin *pīca*]

pie³ (pī), *n., v.t.,* **pied, pie·ing.** pi²

pie⁴ (pī), *n.* a book of rules for finding the particulars of the service for the day, as used in England before the Reformation. Also, **pye.** [Middle English *pye*, perhaps abbreviation of Medieval Latin *pica* pica¹]

pie⁵ (pī), *n.* a bronze coin of India, equal to 1/12 of an anna. [Anglo-Indian (probably originally equal to *pice*) < Hindi and Marathi *pāī* < Sanskrit *padī*, or *pad* quarter]

pie·bald (pī′bôld′), *adj.* **1.** spotted in two colors, especially white and black, or another dark color: *a piebald horse.* **2.** mixed or mongrel: *Here we are, a society and a nation . . . a vast and piebald congregation* (Maurice Hewlett). —*n.* a piebald animal, especially a horse. [apparently < *pie*² + *bald*, with the meanings "spotted," or "white" (because of the magpie's pied plumage)]

piece (pēs), *n., adj., v.,* **pieced, piec·ing.** —*n.* **1.** one of the parts into which a thing is divided or broken: *to fall or cut to pieces. The cup broke into pieces.* **2.** a small quantity; portion; part: *a piece of land containing two acres, a piece of bread, a piece of paper.* **3.** a single thing of a set or class: *a piece of furniture, a piece of luggage. This set of china has 144 pieces.* **4.** a coin: *pieces of eight. A nickel is a five-cent piece.* **5.** an example or instance of an action, function, quality, etc.: *Sleeping with the light on is a piece of nonsense.* **6.** a single composition in an art: *a new piece at a theater, a piece of music, a piece of poetry, to recite a piece. His pieces went over so well that he was offered sixty rubles a month to become a regular contributor* (Edmund Wilson). **7.** a gun; cannon: *a fowling piece. Clean the piece after firing.* **8.** a more or less definite quantity in which various industrial products are made, sold, or used: *cloth, ribbon, or lace sold only by the piece.* **9. a.** any of the disks, cubes, figures, stones, etc., used in playing checkers, chess, and other games; a man. **b.** (in chess) a superior man, as distinguished from a pawn; a king, queen, bishop, knight, or rook. **10.** the amount of work done or to be done at any one time: *to work by the piece.* **11.** *Dialect.* **a.** a short period of time; while: *to sit and rest for a piece.* **b.** a short distance: *down the road a piece.* **12.** *Obsolete.* an individual; person.

go to pieces, a. to break into fragments; break up: *Another ship had gone to pieces on the rocks.* **b.** to become shattered; break down physically or mentally; collapse: *Bankruptcy and the loss of his friends caused the ruined man to go to pieces.* **c.** to become disorganized or confused; fall apart: *Where the book goes to pieces is in its economic, social, and political history* (New Scientist).

of a piece, of the same kind or quality; in keeping; uniform: *His rusty and worn suit . . . was of a piece with his uncarpeted room* (Charles Reade). *His face and body look all of a piece like some fabulous Humpty Dumpty* (Harper's).

piece of one's mind, *Informal.* **a.** a candid opinion: *He gave them a piece of his mind on the subject.* **b.** a scolding: *His mother gave Philip a piece of her mind.*

speak one's piece, to voice one's opinions: *I feel better after speaking my piece.*

to pieces, a. to bits or fragments: *to break a dish to pieces.* **b.** to a state of separation of the constituent parts, or apart: *to take a clock to pieces. Given these facts, his argument falls to pieces.*

—*adj.* **1.** composed of pieces. **2.** having to do with piecework.

—*v.t.* **1.** to make or repair by adding or joining pieces: *to piece a dress.* **2.** to join, unite, or put together in one piece: *to piece a patchwork quilt, to piece together a story.*

[< Old French *piece* < Vulgar Latin *pettia* fragment, probably < Celtic, or Gaulish (compare Welsh *peth*, Breton *pez*)]

—**Syn.** *n.* **1.** scrap, fragment. **2.** See **part.**

piece bag, a bag for holding scraps of cloth: *My piece bag gave her great delight, and for the rest of the holiday she designed and made a complete* [*doll's*] *wardrobe, from a christening robe to a sunsuit* (Observer).

pièce de ré·sis·tance (pyes də rā zēs-täɴs′), *French.* **1.** the chief dish of a meal. **2.** the most important or outstanding article, person, subject, event, etc., in any collection, group, or series: *A table service for a party of four in the nursery is made of pliable, unbreakable plastic, and includes, as the pièce de résistance, a Lazy Susan* (New Yorker).

pièce d'oc·ca·sion (pyes dô kȧ zyôɴ′), *French.* **1.** a piece or work for a special occasion: *The work . . . is certainly a pièce d'occasion for this orchestra, who played it with tremendous verve and finish* (London Times). **2.** a bargain.

piece-dyed (pēs′dīd′), *adj.* (of cloth) dyed in the piece, or after it is woven or knitted.

piece goods, yard goods, usually of a fixed width: *Quietly steady conditions prevailed in the cotton piece goods market last week* (Times of India).

piece·meal (pēs′mēl′), *adv.* **1.** piece by piece; a little at a time: *In reality he has treated such problems piecemeal in various segments of the book* (Bulletin of Atomic Scientists). **2.** piece from piece; to pieces; into fragments: *The lamb was torn piecemeal by the wolves.*

—*adj.* done piece by piece; fragmentary.

—*v.t.* to divide piecemeal; dismember: *They moved in slowly and gave the* [*enemy*] *a chance to piecemeal them* (Time).

[Middle English *pece mele* < *pece* piece +

-mele, obsolete suffix meaning "by small measures"]
—**Syn.** *adv.* **1.** gradually.

piece of eight, a former Spanish peso, worth 8 reals. It corresponded to the American dollar.

piec·er (pē′sər), *n.* a person who pieces or patches, especially one who joins broken threads together in a spinning mill.

piece rate, the rate of payment for piecework; payment by the amount done, not by the time worked: *The men allege that the piece rate schedules are out of date and demand a revision* (London Times).

piece·work (pēs′wėrk′), *n.* work paid for by the amount done, not by the time it takes: *Since the employes are paid on a piecework basis the worker was managing to pad his income substantially* (Wall Street Journal).

piece·work·er (pēs′wėr′kər), *n.* a person who does piecework.

pie chart, a graph in the form of a circle divided into sectors that resemble pieces of a pie, drawn to show the percentages into which any total sum is divided: *The Company provided a pie chart in the report, showing how it spent the $7,627,000,000 total income* (Wall Street Journal).

pie crust, pastry used for the bottom and often the top of a pie: *Friendships, like pie crusts, are easily broken* (New Yorker).

pie crust table, a table having an ornamental edge suggesting the crust of a pie.

pied (pīd), *adj.* **1.** having patches of two or more colors; many-colored; parti-colored. **2.** spotted: *Daisies pied and violets blue* (Shakespeare). **3.** wearing a costume of two or more colors: *The Pied Piper.* [< *pie*^{2} + *-ed*^{2} (because of the variegation in a magpie's plumage)] —**Syn. 2.** dappled.

pied-à-terre (pyā tȧ ter′), *n., pl.* **pieds-à-terre** (pyā tȧ ter′). *French.* **1.** a temporary lodging: *In England most of the noblemen and nearly all the squires still regarded their London houses only as pieds-à-terre, and looked on their seats in the country as their real homes* (Nikolaus Pevsner). **2.** a foothold. **3.** (literally) foot on the ground.

pied-billed grebe (pīd′bild′), a small North American grebe with a rounded bill, that lives in ponds, swamps, etc.

pied·fort (pē ā′fôr′, pyā′-), *n.* a coin struck on a blank of unusual thickness. [< French *piedfort* < *pied* foot + *fort* strong]

pied·mont (pēd′mont), *n.* a district lying along or near the foot of a mountain range. —*adj.* lying along or near the foot of a mountain range: *a piedmont plain, a piedmont glacier.* [American English < Italian *Piemonte,* Old Italian *Piedmont,* a region in Italy, (literally) foot of the mountain (< Latin *Pedimontium* < *pēs, pedis* foot + *mons, montis* mountain)]

Pied·mon·tese (pēd′mon tēz′, -tēs′), *adj., n., pl.* **-tese.** —*adj.* of or having to do with Piedmont, a region in northwestern Italy bordering on Switzerland and France, or its people. —*n.* a native or inhabitant of Piedmont.

pied noir (pyā nwȧr′), *pl.* **pieds noirs** (pyā nwȧr′). *French.* **1.** a North African, especially an Algerian, of European descent (used in an unfriendly way). **2.** (literally) black foot.

Pied Piper, or **Pied Piper of Ham·e·lin** (ham′ə lin), (in medieval legend) a magician who freed the town of Hamelin in Prussia from a plague of rats in 1284 by playing on his pipe. When refused his promised reward, he led its children away.

pie·fort (pē ā′fôr′, pyā′-), *n.* piedfort.

pie in the sky, *Slang.* something pleasant but unattainable; an impractical ideal: *Talk of economic growth to support a higher budget seems like pie in the sky to this Administration* (Atlantic).

pie·man (pī′mən), *n., pl.* **-men.** a man who makes or sells pies.

pie·plant (pī′plant′, -plänt′), *n. U.S.* the common garden rhubarb, so called from its use in pies.

pie plate, a baking dish or pan for pies.

pier (pir), *n.* **1.** a structure supported on columns or piles extending into the water, used as a walk or a landing place for ships: *The Chelsea* [*a ferry boat*] *was found nosed against a pier a block away from where she was supposed to be* (Newsweek). **2.** a breakwater. **3.** one of the solid supports on which the arches of a bridge rest. **4. a.** the solid part of a wall between windows, doors, etc. **b.** a support larger than a column, especially (in medieval vaulting) a member resembling a cluster of columns, or a square pillar. **c.** the support on which a door, etc., is hung. **d.** any solid support, especially of masonry, that bears pressure or thrust from above, as the pillar, portion of wall, etc., from which an arch springs, or a buttress. [Middle English *per* < Medieval Latin *pera,* perhaps Latinization of Old North French *pire, piere* a breakwater, related to Old French *pierre* stone < Latin *petra*]

Piers (def. 3)

pierce (pirs), *v.,* **pierced, pierc·ing.** —*v.t.* **1.** to go into; go through: *A tunnel pierces the mountain.* **2.** to make a hole in; bore into or through: *to pierce leather with an awl. A nail pierced the tire of our car.* **3.** to force a way through or into; force a way: *to pierce a line of defense. A sharp cry pierced the air.* **4.** to make a way through or into with the eye or the mind: *to pierce a disguise, to pierce a mystery.* **5.** to affect sharply: *Can no prayers pierce thee?* (Shakespeare). —*v.i.* to force or make a way into or through something: *a chill that pierced into the marrow* (Robert Louis Stevenson). [Middle English *percen* < Old French *percier* < Vulgar Latin *pertūsiāre* to bore, or press through < Latin *pertundere* < *per-* through + *tundere* to beat] —**pierc′er,** *n.* —**Syn.** *v.t.* **1.** See **penetrate. 2.** prick, perforate.

pierce·a·ble (pir′sə bəl), *adj.* that can be pierced.

pierc·ing (pir′sing), *adj.* that pierces; penetrating; sharp; keen: *piercing cold, a piercing look; . . . eyes, blue and piercing, truly eagle-like . . . perhaps staring into his own fierce spirit* (Edmund Wilson). —**pierc′ing·ly,** *adv.* —**pierc′ing·ness,** *n.*

pier glass, a tall mirror, originally one designed to fill the pier or space between two windows.

pier·head (pir′hed′), *n.* the outward or seaward end of a pier: *The ship came too close to the pierhead, however, and the master . . . reversed his engines just quickly enough to avoid brushing the pier* (New York Times).

Pi·e·ri·an (pī ir′ē ən), *adj.* **1.** of or having to do with the Muses or with poetry. **2.** of or having to do with Pieria, a district in ancient Thessaly, the fabled home of the Muses.

Pierian spring, the fountain of knowledge and poetic inspiration (now always in a figurative sense, but believed by the ancient Greeks to have actual existence): *A little learning is a dangerous thing; Drink deep, or taste not the Pierian spring* (Alexander Pope).

pi·er·id (pī er′əd), *adj.* pieridine: *He published a paper on the pigment in the wings of pierid butterflies* (London Times). —*n.* a pieridine butterfly.

pi·er·i·dine (pī er′ə dīn, -din), *adj.* of or belonging to a family of butterflies that includes the cabbage white and the sulphurs. [< New Latin *Pieridinae* the subfamily name < *Pieris, -idis* the typical genus < Greek *Pīerídes* the Muses; (literally) ones inhabiting Pieria]

Pier·rette (pi ret′; *French* pye ret′), *n.* a female character corresponding to Pierrot. [< French *Pierrette,* feminine of *Pierrot* Pierrot]

Pi·er·rot (pē′ə rō; *French* pye rō′), *n.* a clown who is a frequent character in French pantomime, derived from the traditional Italian comedy. He has his face whitened and wears loose white pantaloons and a jacket, with big buttons and a ruff. [< French, Old French *Pierrot* (diminutive) < *Pierre* Peter < Late Latin *Petrus* < Greek *Pétros,* as a common noun, "stone"]

pier table, a table or low bracket intended to occupy the pier or space between two windows, often used under a pier glass.

pi·et (pī′ət), *n. Scottish.* **1.** a magpie. **2.** a water ouzel. Also, **pyet.** [apparently < *pie*^{2}]

pie·tà or **Pie·tà** (pyā tä′), *n.* a representation in painting or sculpture of the Virgin Mary seated and holding the body of the dead Christ on her lap or in her arms: *By the light of this candle, he was engaged in making a Pietà, to serve, like Titian's, for his own tomb* (New Yorker). [< Italian *pietà* piety, pity < Latin *pietās*]

Pi·e·tism (pī′ə tiz əm), *n.* **1.** a movement, beginning in the late 1600's in Germany, to revive personal piety in the Lutheran Church. **2.** the principles and practices of the Pietists. [< German *Pietismus* < New Latin *collegia pietatis* unions for religious education (*pietatis,* genitive of Latin *pietās* piety) + German *-ismus* -ism]

pi·e·tism (pī′ə tiz əm), *n.* **1.** deep piety. **2.** exaggerated or pretended piety. [< *Pietism*]

Pi·e·tist (pī′ə tist), *n.* a believer in Pietism.

pi·e·tist (pī′ə tist), *n.* a person conspicuous for pietism. —**Syn.** devotee.

Pi·e·tis·tic (pī′ə tis′tik), *adj.* of or having to do with Pietism or the Pietists.

pi·e·tis·tic (pī′ə tis′tik), *adj.* **1.** conspicuous for pietism; very pious. **2.** too pious; pious with exaggeration or affectation: . . . *within the framework of pietistic moralism* (Time). —**pi′e·tis′ti·cal·ly,** *adv.*

pie·tra du·ra (pyā′trä dü′rä), *pl.* **pie·tre du·re** (pyā′trā dü′rā). *Italian.* a mosaic in a hard stone, such as agate or jasper.

pi·e·ty (pī′ə tē), *n., pl.* **-ties. 1.** a being pious; reverence for God (or the gods); devotion to religion: *True piety is cheerful as the day* (William Cowper). **2.** dutiful regard for one's parents. **3.** a pious act, remark, belief, etc.: *the small pieties with which they larded their discourse* (Samuel Butler). **4.** *Obsolete.* pity. [Middle English *piete* pity < Old French *piete,* learned borrowing from Latin *pietās, -ātis* piety < *pīus* pious. Doublet of PITY.] —**Syn. 1.** godliness, devoutness.

pi·e·zo·e·lec·tric (pī ē′zō i lek′trik), *adj.* of or having to do with piezoelectricity: *A cunning investigation has revealed piezoelectric effects in two compounds previously thought innocent* (New Scientist). —**pi·e′zo·e·lec′tri·cal·ly,** *adv.*

pi·e·zo·e·lec·tric·i·ty (pī ē′zō i lek′tris′ə tē, -ē′lek-), *n.* electricity induced by pressure, as that of certain crystals vibrating in an alternating electrical field. [< Greek *piézein* to press, squeeze + English *electricity*]

pi·e·zom·e·ter (pī′ə zom′ə tər), *n.* any of several instruments for measuring pressure, or something connected with pressure, as one for showing the compressibility of water or other liquids under varying pressures. [< Greek *piézein* to press + English *-meter*]

pi·e·zo·met·ric (pī ē′zə met′rik), *adj.* of, having to do with, or done by piezometry.

pi·e·zo·met·ri·cal (pī ē′zə met′rə kəl), *adj.* piezometric.

pi·e·zom·e·try (pī′ə zom′ə trē), *n.* the measurement of pressure or something connected with pressure; use of the piezometer.

pif·fle (pif′əl), *n., v.,* **-fled, -fling.** *Informal.* —*n.* silly talk or behavior; nonsense. —*v.i.* to talk or act in a weakly foolish, ineffective manner: *They piddled and piffled with iron. I'd given my orders for steel!* (Rudyard Kipling). [probably imitative]

pif·fler (pif′lər), *n. Informal.* a trifler; piddler.

pif·fling (pif′ling), *adj. Informal.* that piffles; weakly ineffective; trifling.

pig^1 (pig), *n., v.,* **pigged, pig·ging.** —*n.* **1.** a swine or hog, a domestic animal raised for its meat. **2.** a young swine or hog. **3.** pork (used humorously, except in reference to young or suckling pigs). **4.** *Informal.* a person who seems or acts like a pig; greedy or dirty person. **5. a.** an oblong mass of metal, especially of iron or lead, obtained from the smelting furnace and run into a mold, usually of sand, while still hot so that it is of a size and shape convenient for storage, etc.: *The first actual tap of the metal for casting into pigs occurred yesterday* (Wall Street Journal). **b.** a mold or channel in a pig bed. **c.** metal in such masses; pig iron or pig lead.

in pig, (of a sow) pregnant: *The September pig sample on farms in England and Wales shows a slight increase in the breeding herd compared with July, but little difference between the numbers of sows and gilts in pig* (London Times).

—*v.i.* **1.** to bring forth pigs; farrow. **2.** to herd, lodge, or sleep together like pigs, especially in filth: *a dozen felons, pigging together on bare bricks in a hole fifteen feet square* (Macaulay).

pig it, to herd, lodge, or sleep together like pigs: *You'd have to pig it with the goats and the cattle* (Grant Allen).

[Middle English *pigge*, perhaps unrecorded Old English *picga*, implied in *pic-bred* acorn, mast; (literally) pig-bread]

pig[2] (pig), *n. Scottish.* an earthenware pot, pitcher, jar, etc.; crock. [origin unknown]

pig bed, the bed or series of sand molds in which pigs of iron are cast.

pig·boat (pig′bōt′), *n. U.S. Navy Slang.* a submarine: *Captain Alvis had one answer known to any man who ever underwent pig-boat training: all submariners are volunteers, and not every volunteer becomes a submariner* (Time).

pig deer, the babirusa.

pi·geon[1] (pij′ən), *n., pl.* **-geons** or (*collectively*) **-geon. 1.** any of a family of birds with a plump body and short legs, comprising numerous species found throughout the world, and including the rock pigeon, the passenger pigeon (now extinct), and the white crowned pigeon, and many varieties of domestic pigeons; dove. **2.** *Slang.* a person who is, or lets himself be, easily tricked, especially in gambling: *This living and moving Moggs is a pigeon for the plucking if ever there was one* (Punch). *He was a famous pigeon for the play-men; they lived upon him* (Thackeray). [Middle English *pejoun* < Old French *pijon* young dove < Vulgar Latin *pībiō*, alteration of Late Latin *pīpiō, -ōnis* squab, a young piping bird. Compare Latin *pīpiāre*, or *pīpīre* to cheep.] —**Syn. 2.** simpleton, dupe, gull.

Band-tailed Pigeon[1] **(def. 1— 15 in. long)**

pi·geon[2] (pij′ən), *n.* pidgin.
➔ See **pidgin** for usage note.

pigeon breast, chicken breast.

pi·geon-breast·ed (pij′ən bres′tid), *adj.* chicken-breasted; having a deformity in the form of a sharply protruded sternum. —**pi′geon-breast′ed·ness,** *n.*

pigeon English, pidgin English.

pi·geon·gram (pij′ən gram), *n.* a message carried by pigeon: *To remind us that aeroplanes were not the only means of transport, there is a rare pigeongram flown from Cape Town during the 1919 peace celebrations* (Scotsman). [< *pigeon*[1] + *-gram*[1]]

pigeon hawk, a pigeon-sized falcon which breeds in northern North America; merlin. See picture under **merlin.**

pi·geon-heart·ed (pij′ən här′tid), *adj.* very timid or cowardly; faint-hearted; chicken-hearted.

pi·geon·hole (pij′ən hōl′), *n., v.,* **-holed, -hol·ing.** —*n.* **1. a.** a small place built, usually as one of a series, for domestic pigeons to nest in. **b.** a small hole in a wall for pigeons to pass in and out. **2.** one of a set of boxlike compartments for holding papers and other articles in a desk, a cabinet, etc.: *A frivolous little Chinese pagoda at each side of a compartment of pigeonholes* (New Yorker).
—*v.t.* **1.** to put in a pigeonhole; put away. **2.** to classify and lay aside in memory where one can refer to it. **3.** to put aside with the idea of dismissing, forgetting, or neglecting. **4.** to furnish with pigeonholes.

pi·geon-liv·ered (pij′ən liv′ərd), *adj. Archaic.* meek; gentle: *But I am pigeon-livered, and lack gall To make oppression bitter* (Shakespeare).

pigeon pea, 1. the small, nutritious seed of an East Indian shrub of the pea family, now widely cultivated in tropical areas. **2.** the plant itself.

pigeon post, the conveyance of letters or dispatches by pigeon: *The Caliphs made the pigeon post a regular institution in the Nile delta* (London Daily News).

pigeon pox, an infectious, viral disease of pigeons, marked chiefly by the breaking out of small yellow nodules on the head.

pi·geon·ry (pij′ən rē), *n., pl.* **-ries.** a place where pigeons are kept.

pi·geon's-blood (pij′ənz blud′), *n.* a deep-red color, the color most esteemed in the ruby.

pigeon's or **pigeon milk,** a whitish liquid containing solid, cheeselike bits, which is formed in the crop of the adult pigeon and regurgitated to feed its young.

pi·geon-toe (pij′ən tō′), *v.t., v.i.,* **-toed, -toe·ing.** to walk with the toes turned inward: *He pigeon-toed his way across the rug* (Harper's).

pi·geon-toed (pij′ən tōd′), *adj.* having the toes or feet turned inward.

pi·geon·wing (pij′ən wing′), *n. U.S.* **1.** a figure in skating, in which the skater makes the outline of a bird's wing. **2.** a dance step performed by jumping and hitting the heels together in the air.

pig-eyed (pig′īd′), *adj.* having small, deep-set eyes: *There was the same ruddy pig-eyed visage, topped by a fringe of white hair* (Wall Street Journal).

pig·fish (pig′fish′), *n., pl.* **-fish·es** or (*collectively*) **-fish.** any of certain fishes, as a grunt of the Atlantic Coast of North America, or the sailor's-choice.

pig·ger·y (pig′ər ē), *n., pl.* **-ger·ies.** *Especially British.* **1.** a place where pigs are kept or raised. **2.** pigs as a group; swine.

pig·gie (pig′ē), *n., pl.* **-gies.** piggy.

pig·gin (pig′in), *n. Especially Dialect.* a small wooden pail with one stave longer than the rest and serving as a handle; pipkin. [perhaps related to PIG[2]]

pig·gish (pig′ish), *adj.* of, having to do with, or like a pig; greedy; filthy. —**pig′gish·ly,** *adv.* —**pig′gish·ness,** *n.*

pig·gy (pig′ē), *adj.,* **-gi·er, -gi·est,** *n., pl.* **-gies.** —*adj.* like a pig; piggish: *Henry VIII . . . is even piggier* (Punch). —*n.* a little pig.

pig·gy·back (pig′ē bak′), *adv.* pickaback: *a father carrying a baby piggyback.*
—*adj.* of or having to do with the transporting of loaded truck trailers on flatcars: *Piggyback traffic, hauling loaded trucks to the terminal nearest their destination, went up . . . to more than 250,000 carloads during the year* (World Book Annual).
—*n.* the transporting of loaded truck trailers on flatcars to the point nearest the place where the freight is to be delivered: *Trucks often offer lower rates, too; rails fight back with piggyback* (Wall Street Journal).
—*v.t., v.i.* to carry or move by piggyback: *The New Haven Railroad has been piggybacking trucks for several years on a limited basis in New England* (Wall Street Journal).

piggy bank, 1. a small receptacle, of metal, china, etc., in the shape of a pig, with a slot in the back through which money, especially coins, can be dropped: *Taxes and inflation have cracked more of their piggy banks than wild spending* (Harper's). **2.** any similar receptacle.

pig·head·ed (pig′hed′id), *adj.* stupidly obstinate or stubborn: *The nasty old men, debauched and selfish, pig-headed and ridiculous, with their perpetual burden of debts, confusions, and disreputabilities* (Lytton Strachey). —**pig′-head′ed·ness,** *n.*

pig in a poke, something that a person buys or accepts without seeing it or knowing its value.

pig iron, 1. crude iron as it first comes from the blast furnace or smelter, formerly usually cast into oblong masses called pigs, but now often transferred in molten form to the next process, used to make steel, cast iron, and wrought iron. **2.** this iron as a material, molten or in pigs.

pig Latin, a children's slang consisting of English pronounced with the initial consonant of each word placed at the end and with a nonsense syllable (usually "ay") added. *Example:* Oodgay orningmay = Good morning. *Stella had just got on to pig Latin and never shut her mouth for a minute* (New Yorker).

pig lead, lead in the form of pigs.

pig·let (pig′lit), *n.* a little pig: *the squealing of many little piglets* (W. H. Hudson).

pig·like (pig′līk′), *adj., adv.* in the manner or like that of a pig: *Little piglike eyes stared from her face* (*adj.*). *They bolted down their food piglike* (*adv.*).

pig·ling (pig′ling), *n.* a little pig.

pig·man (pig′mən), *n., pl.* **-men.** a person who tends pigs: *A pigman is a skilled worker deserving good wages* (London Times).

pig·ment (pig′mənt), *n.* **1.** a coloring matter, especially a powder or some easily pulverized dry substance, that, when mixed with oil, water, or other liquid vehicle, constitutes a paint: *A remarkably white pigment, titanium dioxide, makes possible the sparkling beauty of your refrigerator, the enduring whiteness of your home, the pastel shades for your car* (Newsweek). **2.** *Biology.* any organic substance occurring in and coloring any part of an animal or plant; the natural coloring matter of a cell or tissue. [< Latin *pigmentum* < root of *pingere* to paint, color. Doublet of PIMENTO.]

pig·men·tal (pig men′təl), *adj.* pigmentary.

pig·men·tar·y (pig′mən ter′ē), *adj.* **1.** of, having to do with, containing, or consisting of pigment. **2.** *Biology.* characterized by the formation or presence of pigment.

pig·men·ta·tion (pig′mən tā′shən), *n.* **1.** the deposit of pigment in the tissue of a living animal or plant, causing coloration or discoloration. **2.** the coloration of an animal or plant.

pig·ment·ed (pig′mən tid), *adj.* charged with pigment; colored.

pig·my (pig′mē), *n., pl.* **-mies,** *adj.* pygmy.

Pig·my (pig′mē), *n., pl.* **-mies,** *adj.* Pygmy.

pigmy sperm whale, a rare black and grayish whale of warm seas, 9 to 13 feet long with a small dorsal fin.

pi·gno·lia nut (pi nōl′yə, pig-), pine nut.

pig·no·rate (pig′nə rāt), *v.t.,* **-rat·ed, -rat·ing. 1.** to pledge, mortgage, or pawn. **2.** to take in pawn. [< Medieval Latin *pignorare* (with English *-ate*[1]) < Latin *pignerāre* < *pignus* pledge]

pig·no·ra·tion (pig′nə rā′shən), *n.* the act of pledging or pawning.

pig·nus (pig′nəs), *n., pl.* **-no·ra** (-nər ə). *Roman and Civil Law.* **1.** property pledged or pawned. **2.** a contract for pawning property. [< Latin *pignus, -eris* pledge, security]

pig·nut (pig′nut′), *n.* **1. a.** a thin-shelled, oily, bitterish nut, the fruit of a hickory of North America. **b.** the tree itself. **2. a.** the tuber of a European earthnut. **b.** the plant itself. Also, **hognut.** [< *pig*[1] + *nut*]

pig·pen (pig′pen′), *n.* **1.** a pen where pigs are kept. **2.** a filthy place.

pigs in blankets, 1. small frankfurters or sausages baked or broiled in a casing of dough. **2.** broiled or sautéed oysters, chicken livers, etc., wrapped in slices of bacon.

pig·skin (pig′skin′), *n.* **1.** the skin or hide of a pig. **2.** leather made from it. **3.** *Informal.* a football. **4.** *Informal.* a saddle.

pig·stick (pig′stik′), *v.i.,* **-stuck, -stick·ing.** to hunt wild boar on horseback, with a spear.

pig·stick·er (pig′stik′ər), *n.* **1.** a person who hunts wild boar. **2.** *Informal.* a large pocketknife.

pig·stick·ing (pig′stik′ing), *n.* the sport of hunting wild boar on horseback, with a spear.

pig·sty (pig′stī′), *n., pl.* **-sties.** a pigpen.

pig·tail (pig′tāl′), *n.* **1.** a braid of hair hanging from the back of the head: *Marley in his pigtail, usual waistcoat, tights and boots* (Dickens). *Her abundant hair hung over her shoulder in two tight pigtails* (Arnold Bennett). **2.** tobacco in a thin twisted roll or rope.

pig·tailed (pig′tāld′), *adj.* **1.** having a tail like a pig's. **2.** wearing a pigtail or pigtails.

pig·weed (pig′wēd′), *n.* **1.** any goosefoot, especially the white pigweed, a coarse weed with narrow, notched leaves. **2.** any of certain weedy amaranths, especially the red-root.

pi·ka (pī′kə), *n.* any of certain small mammals, related to the rabbit but having short ears, and inhabiting rocky mountain slopes in the Northern Hemisphere; cony; rock rabbit. [< Tungus (Siberia) *piika*, probably imitative of its cry]

pike[1] (pīk), *n., v.,* **piked, pik·ing.** —*n.* a long wooden shaft with a sharp-pointed head of iron or steel, used especially by foot soldiers before the invention (in the 1700's) of the bayonet; spear: *He wanted pikes to set before his archers* (Shakespeare). See picture under **pikeman.** —*v.t.* to pierce, wound, or kill with or as with a pike. [< French *pique* < *piquer* pierce < *pic* pick[2], probably through Vulgar Latin *piccus*, ultimately < Germanic (compare Old English *pīc*)]

pike[2] (pīk), *n.* a sharp point or pointed tip, as the head of an arrow or spear or the spike in the center of a buckler. [Old English *pīc* pick[2]; probably influenced by French *pique* pike[1]]

pike[3] (pīk), *n., pl.* **pikes** or (*collectively*) **pike. 1.** any of a group of large, slender, predatory, fresh-water fishes of the Northern Hemisphere, having spiny fins and a long, narrow, pointed head, as the northern pike and the pickerel: *And pikes, the tyrants of the watery plains* (Alexander Pope). **2.** any of certain similar fishes, as the gar pike and the pike perch. [apparently < *pike*[2] + *fish* (because of the shape of its snout)]

pike[4] (pīk), *n. U.S.* **1.** a turnpike. **2.** any main highway, especially one on which toll is paid. **3.** the toll paid at a turnpike gate. [short for *turnpike*]

pike[5] (pīk), *n.* in Northern England: **1.** a pointed summit. **2.** a mountain or hill with a pointed summit (widely used in the names of mountains and hills, especially in Cumberland, Westmorland, and Lancashire). [perhaps extended use of *pike*[2] (compare Old English *hornpīc* pinnacle), or < dialectal Norwegian *pîk* peaked mountain]

pike[6] (pīk), *v.i.*, **piked, pik•ing.** *Informal.* **1.** to depart. **2.** to die. [Middle English *pyken* (perhaps originally) to furnish oneself with a walking stick (see PIKE[2]); origin uncertain]

pike[7] (pīk), *v.i.*, **piked, pik•ing.** to gamble or do anything in a small, cautious way; be a piker. [origin uncertain; perhaps back formation < *piker*]

piked (pīkt), *adj.* pointed; spiked; peaked.

piked dogfish, a small shark of the North American coast.

piked whale, a small baleen whale with a gray and white band across the flipper.

pike•man (pīk′mən), *n., pl.* **-men.** a soldier armed with a pike.

pike perch, either of two large varieties of North American perches, the walleyed pike and the sauger, that resemble a pike, especially in the shape of the head: *The government finally stocked the waters with pike perch and gambusia, both of whom are fond of mosquito eggs* (New Yorker).

pik•er (pī′kər), *n. U.S. Slang.* **1.** a person who does things in a small or cheap way. **2.** a cautious or timid gambler who makes only small bets. [American English < *Pike* a migrant to California, (originally) from Pike County, Missouri. Compare English *piker* a tramp.]

Pikeman

pike•staff (pīk′staf′, -stäf′), *n., pl.* **-staves** (-stāvz). **1.** the wooden shaft of a pike or spear. **2.** *Scottish.* a staff or walking stick with a metal point or spike at the lower end like an alpenstock. [< *pike*[1] + *staff*]

pi•laf or **pi•laff** (pi läf′), *n.* pilau.

pi•lar (pī′lər), *adj.* having to do with the hair. [< Latin *pilus* hair + English *-ar*]

pi•la•ry (pī′lər ē), *adj.* pilar.

pi•las•ter (pə las′tər), *n.* a flat rectangular pillar, with capital and base, forming part of a wall (and projecting somewhat from it) and serving as a supporting member like a pier, or built against a wall as a decorative accent. [< Middle French *pilastre* < Italian *pilastro* < *pila* pilaster, pillar < Latin *pīla* pillar]

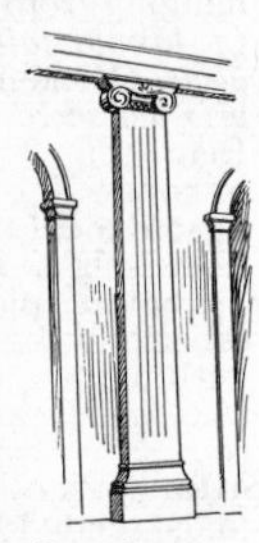

pi•las•tered (pə las′tərd), *adj.* furnished with pilasters: *One of the handsomest public buildings ever put up in this country . . . gracefully pillared and pilastered, garlanded with stone leaves . . .* (New Yorker).

Renaissance Pilaster

pil•as•trade (pil′ə sträd′), *n.* a row of pilasters. [< Italian *pilastrata* < *pila* pilaster + *strata* row[1]]

pil•as•trad•ed (pil′ə strā′did), *adj.* having a pilastrade.

pi•lau or **pi•law** (pi lô′), *n.* an Oriental dish consisting of rice or cracked wheat boiled with mutton, fowl, or fish, and flavored with spices, raisins, etc. [< Persian *pilāw*, or Turkish *pilâv*]

pil•chard (pil′chərd), *n.* **1.** a small European marine food fish, the sardine, related to the herring, but smaller and rounder. **2.** any of certain similar fishes, as a variety found off the California coast: *In the Mediterranean and off California considerably larger "sardines" are caught, more correctly called pilchards* (Wall Street Journal). [alteration of earlier *pilcher;* origin uncertain]

pile[1] (pīl), *n., v.*, **piled, pil•ing.** —*n.* **1.** many or several things lying one upon another in a more or less orderly way: *a pile of stones, packages, lumber, or firewood.* **2.** a mass like a hill or mound: *a pile of dirt, snow, or sand.* **3.** a heap of wood on which a dead body or sacrifice is burned; funeral pile. **4.** a large structure or mass of buildings; massive edifice: *The cathedral is a huge, gloomy pile* (Tobias Smollett). **5.** Also, **piles.** *Informal.* a large amount: *I have a pile of work to do. We took piles of pictures.* **6.** *Informal.* a very large amount of money; fortune: *to make one's pile.* **7.** *Nuclear Physics.* the former name of a reactor: *Fissionable material to fuel the pile will be obtained from the AEC on an extended loan basis* (Science News Letter). **8.** *Electricity.* **a.** a series of plates of different metals, arranged alternately with cloth or paper wet with acid between them, for producing an electric current; galvanic pile. **b.** any similar apparatus for producing an electric current; battery. **9.** a fagot.
—*v.t.* **1. a.** to make into a pile; heap evenly; heap up: *The boys piled the blankets in the corner.* **b.** to amass; accumulate: *to pile up a fortune.* **2.** to cover with large amounts: *to pile a plate with food.* **3.** to place (an object) above something else. —*v.i.* **1.** to gather or rise in piles: *Snow piled against the fences. No doubt, at slightly lower artificial price props, surpluses may pile up at a less appalling rate than otherwise; but they will pile up* (Newsweek). **2.** to go in a confused, rushing crowd: *to pile out into the street.* **3.** to join together in a group to attack someone.
[< Middle French, Old French *pile* < Latin *pīla* pillar] —**pil′er,** *n.*
—**Syn.** *n.* **1.** stack, heap.

pile[2] (pīl), *n., v.*, **piled, pil•ing.** —*n.* **1.** a large, heavy beam or post of timber, usually sharpened at the lower end, or a similar post of steel or concrete, driven or set into the earth, often under water, to help support a bridge, wharf, building, etc.: *He could see on the shore . . . bamboo huts perched upon piles* (Joseph Conrad). **2.** the heavy javelin used in the ancient Roman army by foot soldiers. **3.** a pointed blade of grass. **4.** (in heraldry) a wedge-shaped bearing, usually extending from the top or upper third (chief) of the escutcheon, with point downward.
—*v.t.* to furnish, strengthen, or support with piles; drive piles into.
[Old English *pīl* stake[1], shaft < Latin *pīlum* heavy javelin]

pile[3] (pīl), *n.* **1.** the nap of a fabric, especially a soft, thick nap such as that on velvet, plush, and many carpets: *The pile of that Chinese rug is almost half an inch long.* **2.** one of the projecting threads or loops of such a nap. **3.** a soft fine hair or down, as the fine short hair of cattle and the wool of sheep. [< Latin *pilus* hair]
➔ **Pile** in the sense of def. 1 is commonly thought of as a special kind of *nap*, but in strict technical use *nap* is limited to the short fibers of certain yarns, raised by brushing, etc., and forming a less dense and regular surface, as on wool or flannel. *Shag*, originally any long, rough nap, is now used chiefly of woven loops, cut or uncut, that are longer and coarser than *pile*, as on certain kinds of rugs.

pi•le•a (pī′lē ə, pil′ē-), *n.* the plural of **pileum.**

pi•le•ate (pī′lē it, -āt; pil′ē-), *adj.* **1.** *Botany.* having a pileus or cap, as certain fungi. **2.** pileated. [< Latin *pīleātus*, variant of *pilleātus* having a *pilleus* a felt skullcap, related to *pilus* hair]

pi•le•at•ed (pī′lē ā′tid, pil′ē-), *adj.* **1.** (of a bird) having the feathers on the top of the head (pileum) conspicuous; crested. **2.** *Botany.* pileate.

pileated woodpecker, a very large woodpecker of North America, black with white markings on face, neck, and wings, and a prominent bright-red crest.

piled (pīld), *adj.* having a soft, thick nap, as velvet and similar woven (textile) fabrics.

pile driver or **engine,** a machine for driving piles or stakes into the ground, usually consisting of a heavy block of iron (the ram or monkey or pile hammer) suspended in a frame between two guide posts, that is alternately let fall upon the pile head and raised to a height by steam or other power.

pile dwelling, a lake dwelling; palafitte: *Their predecessors of the Neolithic age whose pile dwellings . . . have yielded wheat and coral* (Archibald H. Sayce).

pi•le•ous (pī′lē əs), *adj.* of or having to do with hair; pilose; hairy.

piles (pīlz), *n.pl.* a swelling of blood vessels at the anus, often painful; hemorrhoids. [Middle English *pyles;* origin uncertain. Compare Latin *pila* ball[1].]

pi•le•um (pī′lē əm, pil′ē-), *n., pl.* **pi•le•a** (pī′lē ə, pil′ē-). the top of a bird's head between the bill and the nape; the forehead and crown. [< New Latin *pileum* < Latin *pīleum*, neuter of *pīleus*, skullcap, variant of *pilleus*]

pile-up (pīl′up′), *n.* **1.** a piling up; accumulation. **2.** a massive collision involving a number of speeding vehicles, etc.: *a pile-up of cars.*

pi•le•us (pī′lē əs, pil′ē-), *n., pl.* **pi•le•i** (pī′lē ī, pil′ē-). **1.** *Botany.* the broad umbrellalike structure forming the top of a mushroom; the cap. It is supported by a stalk or stem (the stipe) and bears radiating plates (gills) on the under side. **2.** a kind of felt skullcap worn by the ancient Romans and Greeks. [< New Latin *pileus* a fungus cap; < Latin *pīleus*, variant of *pilleus* skullcap]

pile•wort (pīl′wėrt′), *n.* **1.** a European herb of the crowfoot family, with bright-yellow, starry flowers and tuberous roots, formerly used in poultices; celandine; lesser celandine. **2.** the fireweed. **3.** the prince's feather.

pil•fer (pil′fər), *v.i., v.t.* to steal in small quantities: *to pilfer from a petty-cash box, to pilfer stamps. And not a year but pilfers as he goes Some youthful grace that age would gladly keep* (William Cowper). [< Old French *pelfrer* to rob, or < Middle English *pilfre* booty, both from Old French *pelfre* booty, pelf] —**pil′fer•er,** *n.* —**Syn.** filch. See **steal.**

pil•fer•age (pil′fər ij), *n.* **1.** the act or practice of pilfering; petty theft: *A new type of lock for fire exits is designed to give . . . protection from pilferage through unguarded or unlocked emergency exit doors* (New York Times). **2.** that which is pilfered; stolen goods.

pil•fer•ing (pil′fər ing), *n.* pilferage.

pil•gar•lic (pil gär′lik), *n. Dialect.* **1.** a poor creature; wretch: *And so poor pilgarlic came home alone* (Jonathan Swift). **2. a.** a bald head. **b.** a baldheaded man.

pil•grim (pil′grəm), *n.* **1.** a person who journeys to a sacred or holy place, especially a distant shrine, as an act of religious devotion: *Pilgrimes were they alle That toward Canterbury wolden ryde* (Chaucer). **2.** a person on a journey; traveler; wanderer: *Like pilgrims to th' appointed place we tend; The world's an inn and death the journey's end* (John Dryden). [< unrecorded Anglo-French *pelegrin*, Old French *pelerin* < Medieval Latin *peregrinus* pilgrim < Latin *peregrīnus* foreigner. Doublet of PEREGRINE, PELERINE.] —**Syn. 2.** wayfarer, sojourner.

Pil•grim (pil′grəm), *n.* one of the Puritan settlers of Plymouth Colony in New England in 1620.

pil•grim•age (pil′grə mij), *n., v.*, **-aged, -ag•ing.** —*n.* **1.** a pilgrim's journey; journey to some sacred place as an act of religious devotion: *Than longen folk to goen on pilgrimages* (Chaucer). *Give me my scallop-shell . . . My staff of faith . . . My scrip of joy . . . and thus I'll take my pilgrimage* (Sir Walter Raleigh). **2.** a journey, especially a long one. **3.** life thought of as a journey: *My sword I give to him that shall succeed me in my pilgrimage, and my courage and skill to him that can get it* (John Bunyan).
—*v.i.* to make a pilgrimage; go on a pilgrimage: *They pilgrimaged to the Holy Land.*
[< unrecorded Anglo-French *pelgrimage*, Old French *pelrimage* < *pelegriner* go as a pilgrim < *pelerin* pilgrim]
—**Syn.** *n.* **2.** peregrination, wayfaring.

pilgrim bottle, a flat bottle having rings for the insertion of a cord by which it may be carried; costrel.

Pilgrim Fathers, any of the early settlers of New England, especially the English separatist leaders of the first group to come in the *Mayflower*, who founded the first colony in New England, at Plymouth, Massachusetts, in 1620.

pi•li (pē lē′), *n.* **1.** the edible nut or seed of a Philippine tree; pili nut. **2.** the tree itself. [< Tagalog *pili*]

pi•lif•er•ous (pī lif′ər əs), *adj.* bearing or having hair, hairs, or hairlike processes. [< Latin *pilus* hair + English *-ferous*]

pil•i•form (pil′ə fôrm), *adj.* having the form of a hair; hairlike. [< Latin *pilus* hair + English *-form*]

pi•lig•er•ous (pī lij′ər əs), *adj.* bearing hair. [< Latin *pilus* hair + *gerere* to bear + English *-ous*]

pi·li·ki·a (pē lē kē′ä), *n. Hawaiian.* trouble; bother.

pil·ing (pī′ling), *n.* **1.** piles or heavy beams driven into the ground, often under water: *. . . with the buildings frailly poised on the oaken pilings that are their principal foundations* (New Yorker). **2.** a structure made of piles. **3.** the placing and driving of piles into position.

pili nut, a pili.

pill[1] (pil), *n.* **1.** medicine made up into a small, solid mass to be swallowed whole, now usually round and flattened or in capsule form. **2.** something disagreeable that has to be endured: *This is a bitter pill for him to swallow.* **3.** a very small ball or mass of anything; pellet. **4.** *Slang.* a ball, especially a golf ball or baseball. **5.** *Slang.* an unpleasant, objectionable, or boring person. **6.** *Slang.* a cigarette.
pills, *British Slang.* billiards: *We can play pills then till lunch, you know* (Westminster Gazette).
sugar or **sweeten the pill,** to cause the unpleasant to seem more agreeable: *Although the decision may be a disappointment, the pill is sweetened by the forecast of a higher dividend for next year* (London Times).
the pill, an oral contraceptive for women: *85 per cent of all the patients had shifted to using the two most effective family planning methods—the pill and the intrauterine device* (New York Times).
—*v.t.* **1.** to treat or dose with pills. **2.** *Slang.* to reject by ballot; blackball. —*v.i.* to form small fuzzy balls of fibers on certain knitted fabrics, especially fabrics made from spun nylon yarn: *a sweater that pills.*
[Middle English *pille* < Middle Dutch, or Middle Low German *pille,* ultimately < Latin *pilula* (diminutive) < *pila* ball[1]]

pill[2] (pil), *v.t.* **1.** *Archaic.* to rob, plunder, or pillage (a person or country). **2.** *Archaic or Dialect.* to peel. **3.** *Obsolete.* **a.** to remove the hair from; make bald. **b.** to remove (hair). —*v.i. Obsolete.* to pillage; rob; plunder. [Middle English *pilien,* Old English *pilian* to peel off; to pluck, probably < Latin *pilāre* take off hair (and hide[2]) < *pilus* hair]

pil·lage (pil′ij), *v.,* **-laged, -lag·ing,** *n.* —*v.t.* **1.** to rob with violence; plunder: *Pirates pillaged the towns along the coast.* **2.** to take possession of or carry off as booty. —*v.i.* to take booty; plunder: *The soldiers were allowed to pillage.*
—*n.* **1.** the act of plundering or taking as spoil; plunder, especially that practiced in war. **2.** goods forcibly taken from another, especially from an enemy in war; booty.
[< Old French *pillage* < *piller* to plunder; origin uncertain] —**pil′lag·er,** *n.*
—**Syn.** *v.t.* **1.** sack, strip, rifle. -*n.* **1.** robbery, spoliation.

pil·lar (pil′ər), *n.* **1.** a strong, slender, upright structure; column. Pillars are usually made of stone, wood, or metal, and used as supports or ornaments for a building. Sometimes a pillar stands alone as a monument. **2.** any upright support of a structure, such as a bedpost, one of the posts in a framed truss in a roof, or the single central support or pedestal of a table, a machine, etc. **3.** anything slender and upright like a pillar, as an upright mass of cloud or stone: *The Lord went before them by day in a pillar of a cloud . . . and by night in a pillar of fire* (Exodus 13:21). **4.** a main supporter or support, as of a state, institution, or principle: *He . . . was a deacon and a pillar of the church* (Maurice Hewlett).
from pillar to post, from one thing or place to another without any definite purpose: *He seems to have dragged his family from pillar to post in Tennessee, Alabama, and Georgia* (New Yorker).
—*v.t.* to provide with or as with a pillar or pillars for support, ornament, etc.; buttress; strengthen.
[< Old French *piler,* noun < Vulgar Latin *pīlāre* (in Medieval Latin, *pīlārius* pillar) < Latin *pīla* pillar, pile[1]]
—**Syn.** *n.* **4.** mainstay.
➤ **Pillar** in sense of def. 1 is a word of wider application than *column* (which is properly a pillar of particular shape and proportions), and may be applied to a structure composed of several columns or shafts, built around a central core.

pillar box, *British.* a hollow pillar about five feet high, erected in a public place, containing a receptacle for posting letters; mailbox.

pillar dollar, an old silver coin of Spain, with a figure of the Pillars of Hercules, coined especially for use in the former Spanish colonies in America; piece of eight.

pil·lared (pil′ərd), *adj.* **1.** provided with pillars: *We walked up a ramp, under a huge version of the pillared gateway that marks all Shinto shrines, and into a forest of stone lanterns* (New Yorker). **2.** built in the form of pillars.

pillar of society, a person of strong character or important position.

pillar post, *British.* pillar box.

Pil·lars of Hercules (pil′ərz), the two high points of land at the eastern end of the Strait of Gibraltar, one on either side of the strait. The one on the European side is the Rock of Gibraltar; the one on the African side is Jebel Musa. They were (according to Greek legend) the points at which Hercules supported the world as part of his legendary labors.

pill·box (pil′boks′), *n.* **1.** a small box, usually shallow and often round, for holding pills. **2.** a small, low fortress, especially a round one, with thick, strong walls and roof of reinforced concrete, armed with machine guns, antitank weapons, etc.: *Close beside us, a grim-looking pillbox was half buried in the sand, and the edge of a mine field was marked by a few fluttering patches of white cloth strung on a strand of wire* (Atlantic). **3.** a woman's brimless hat of felt, straw, etc., fashioned like a shallow cylinder.

pill bug, a small, terrestrial, isopod crustacean similar to the sow bug, that rolls into a ball when disturbed.

pil·lion (pil′yən), *n.* **1.** a pad or cushion attached behind a saddle, especially as a seat for a woman, or to carry something on, as a piece of luggage: *I proposed that Jack . . . should ride on my Aunt Gainor's horse, with Miss Peniston on the pillion behind him* (Weir Mitchell). **2.** a seat behind the ordinary saddle of a motorcycle, on which a second person may ride. **3.** *Obsolete.* a kind of saddle, especially a woman's light saddle.
—*adv.* on a pillion: *Princess Margaret, week-ending privately on a country estate, rides pillion on a motorcycle* (Maclean's).
[< Scottish Gaelic *pillin,* or *pillean* (diminutive) < *pell* cushion < Latin *pellis* skin]

pil·li·winks (pil′ə wingks′), *n.pl.* an old instrument of torture for squeezing the fingers. [origin unknown]

pil·lo·ry (pil′ər ē), *n., pl.* **-ries,** *v.,* **-ried, -ry·ing.** —*n.* **1.** a wooden framework erected on a post, with holes through which a person's head and hands were put. The pillory was formerly used as a punishment, being set up in a public place where the crowd could make fun of the offender. **2.** any means or instance of exposing a person, or some act, condition, etc., to public ridicule.

Pillory (def. 1)

—*v.t.* **1.** to put (a person) in the pillory; punish by exposure in a pillory. **2.** to expose to public ridicule, contempt, or abuse.
[< Old French *pellori;* origin uncertain]

pil·low (pil′ō), *n.* **1. a.** a bag or case, usually of ticking or other cloth, filled with feathers, down, or other soft material, used to support the head (or, sometimes, other parts) when resting or sleeping. **b.** any object improvised for the same purpose: *to use one's coat for a pillow.* **2.** a pillion. **3.** a pad on which bobbin (or pillow) lace is made. **4.** a supporting piece or part, such as the block on which the inner end of a bowsprit rests.
—*v.t.* **1.** to rest or place on or as on a pillow: *to pillow a child on one's lap.* **2.** to be a pillow for: *He lay with his arm pillowing his head.* —*v.i.* to rest the head on or as on a pillow: *Thou shalt pillow on my breast* (Joseph Rodman Drake).
[Old English *pyle,* and *pilu,* ultimately < Latin *pulvīnus* cushion] —**pil′low·like′,** *adj.*

pillow bar, **1.** one of the bars or brides connecting parts of the pattern of pillow lace. **2.** the ground or filling formed by such threads.

pil·low·bere or **pil·low·beer** (pil′ō bir′), *n. Archaic or Dialect.* a pillowcase. [< *pillow* + Middle English *bere* a covering, case. Compare Old English *hlēor-bera* cheek-cover.]

pillow block, a block or cradle, similar to a bearing, that supports a shaft or roller.

pil·low·case (pil′ō kās′), *n.* a washable cover, usually of white or colored cotton or linen, pulled over a pillow.

pil·lowed (pil′ōd), *adj.* furnished with a pillow or pillows.

pillow lace, bobbin lace.

pillow lava, lava, usually of a basaltic kind, found in the form of round, closely packed masses, believed to have hardened under water.

pillow sham, a decorative covering, separate from but often matching the bedspread, laid over the pillow of a bed.

pil·low·slip (pil′ō slip′), *n.* a pillowcase.

pil·low·y (pil′ō ē), *adj.* pillowlike; soft; yielding.

pill pusher, *Slang.* **1.** a doctor. **2.** a druggist.

pills (pilz), *n.pl.* See under **pill,** *n.*

pi·lo·car·pin (pī′lō kär′pin, pil′ō-), *n.* pilocarpine.

pi·lo·car·pine (pī′lō kär′pēn, -pin; pil′ō-), *n.* an alkaloid obtained from the leaves of the jaborandi. It is used to stimulate perspiration and the secretion of urine, as an antidote for atropine poisoning, and as a myotic. *The drug pilocarpine, which causes a profuse flow of saliva, does not greatly lessen a dehydrated person's desire for water* (Scientific American). *Formula:* $C_{11}H_{16}N_2O_2$
[< New Latin *Pilocarpus* the jaborandi genus (< Greek *pîlos* hair; ball + *karpós* fruit) + English *-ine*[2] (the fruit is ball-shaped)]

pi·lo·ni·dal cyst (pī′lə nī′dəl), a cyst of congenital origin which has an opening at the base of the spine, and usually contains a wad of hair. [< Latin *pilus* hair + *nīdus* nest + English *-al*[1]]

pilonidal sinus, pilonidal cyst.

pi·lose (pī′lōs), *adj.* covered with hair, especially with fine soft hair; hairy; pilous. [< Latin *pilōsus* < *pilus* hair. Doublet of PILOUS.] —**Syn.** villous.

pi·los·i·ty (pī los′ə tē), *n.* the state of being pilose or pilous; hairiness.

pi·lot (pī′lət), *n.* **1.** a person who steers a ship or boat; steersman; helmsman. **2.** a person trained and licensed to steer ships in or out of a harbor or through dangerous waters: *A ship takes on a pilot before coming into a large harbor.* **3.** a person who operates the controls of an airplane, airship, or other aircraft in flight, especially one qualified and licensed to do this. **4.** a guide; leader. **5.** a device that controls the action of one part of a machine, motor, etc., especially a small or simple part that guides or activates a larger or more complex one. **6.** *U.S.* the cowcatcher of a locomotive, streetcar, etc. **7.** a pilot film, study, etc.: *A pilot is now being filmed* (New York Times).
—*v.t.* **1.** to act as the pilot of; steer: *The aviator pilots his airplane. The Finance Minister was obviously unhappy while piloting the Bill* (London Times). **2.** to guide; lead: *The manager piloted us through the big factory.*
—*adj.* **1.** of or having to do with a pilot or pilots: *a pilot launch.* **2.** that acts as a pilot or in any way as a guide: *a pilot star.* **3. a.** that guides, controls, or indicates the operation of another, usually a larger and more complex, part: *a pilot switch.* **b.** that serves as an advance, preliminary, or experimental version of some action, operation, etc., to be carried out on a larger or more elaborate scale: *a pilot study.*
[< Middle French *pilot* < Italian *piloto,* alteration of unrecorded Late Greek *pēdōtēs* < Greek *pēdón* steering oar]

pi·lot·age (pī′lə tij), *n.* **1.** the act or practice of piloting. **2.** the art or duties of a pilot. **3.** the fee paid for the service of a pilot. [< Middle French *pilotage* < *pilot* pilot + *-age* -age]

pilot balloon, a small, free balloon sent aloft and observed to determine the direction or force of winds or air currents.

pilot biscuit or **bread,** a large, flat cracker; ship biscuit; hardtack.

pilot boat, a boat in which pilots cruise offshore in order to meet incoming ships: *A note [was] sent onshore by a pilot boat* (Frederick Marryat).

pilot burner, a pilot light.

pilot cloth, a heavy, woolen cloth used especially for pea jackets.

pilot coat, a pea jacket: *my travelling wear of country velveteen, pilot coat, and knitted spencer* (Robert Louis Stevenson).

pilot engine, a locomotive sent on ahead of a railroad train to see that the way is clear.

pilot film, one of a projected series of filmed television programs, used by the producer as a sample in selling the series to a network or sponsor.

pilot fish, a small fish, bluish with dark vertical bars, found in warm seas, often accompanying sharks.

pilot house, a cabin raised above the upper deck of a ship, sheltering the steering gear or helm and other instruments used by the helmsman; wheel house.

pi·lot·ing (pī′lə ting), *n.* **1.** the work or profession of a pilot; pilotage. **2.** air or marine navigation by reference to known landmarks, such as mountain peaks, railroad tracks, or beacons, often with the aid of a map or chart.

pi·lo·tis (pē lô tē′), *n.pl. French.* a row of massive, wedge-shaped stilts of concrete used as the foundation of a building.

pilot jack, a flag hoisted by a vessel as the signal flag for the letter "G" (in the International Code of Signals), meaning "I require a pilot," or that for the letter "H," meaning "I have a pilot on board."

pilot lamp, a small electric light used as an indicator, as on many machines, appliances, etc., often mounted behind red glass, lighting up when the electric or other power is turned on, or burning continuously to show the location of a switch or the like.

pi·lot·less (pī′lət lis), *adj.* **1.** without a pilot. **2.** designed or adapted to fly by means of a preset, self-reacting, or radar-controlled unit rather than a human pilot: *a pilotless airplane, a pilotless bomber.*

pilot light, 1. a small light kept burning all the time and used to light a main light whenever desired, as the little flame in a gas stove, gas water heater, etc., that ignites the gas in a main burner when the jet is opened. **2.** a pilot lamp.

pilot plant, the equipment necessary to carry out on a small scale for test purposes, for eliminating production problems, etc., a process for which full-scale operations are planned: *While serving as student training grounds, field centers in India and Thailand in effect double as Point Four pilot plants* (Newsweek).

pilot snake, 1. a copperhead. **2.** a harmless black snake or rat snake of the eastern United States.

pilot study, a preliminary study to determine factors requiring analysis, as a tentative analysis, often of sociological data.

pilot truck, an assembly of two or four wheels on a locomotive, forward of the driving wheels.

pilot whale, any of several varieties of dolphins; blackfish: *Kritzler at once recognized the helpless cetacea as blackfish or pilot whales and counted forty-eight, one dead but all the rest still alive and blowing* (Atlantic).

pi·lous (pī′ləs), *adj.* **1.** pilose; hairy. **2.** consisting of hair; hairlike. [< Latin *pilōsus* (with English *-ous*). Doublet of PILOSE.]

pil·pul (pil′pül), *n.* subtle or searching debate on a Talmudic subject among Jewish scholars; scholarly or critical argumentation: *One is reminded . . . of the technique of Jewish pilpul, that purely intellectual exercise which consists in explaining some passage from Scripture in a fantastically far-fetched way* (Edmund Wilson). [< Aramaic *pilpūl* discussion, controversy]

pil·pul·ist (pil′pü list), *n.* a person who is skilled in pilpul or pilpulistic debate.

pil·pul·is·tic (pil′pü lis′tik), *adj.* having to do with or of the nature of pilpul: *pilpulistic arguments.*

Pil·sen·er (pil′zə nər, -sə-; -znər, -snər), *n.* **1.** a pale lager beer made in or near Pilsen. **2.** any superior lager beer. [< German *Pilsener* < *Pilsen,* a city in Czechoslovakia]

Pilt·down Man (pilt′doun′), an alleged prehistoric man identified from bones found at Piltdown, Sussex, England, proved in 1953 to be a hoax.

pil·u·lar (pil′yə lər), *adj.* of, having to do with, or like a pill: *medicine in pilular form.* [< Latin *pilula* pilule + English *-ar*]

pil·ule (pil′yül), *n.* a pill, especially a small pill. [< Middle French *pilule,* learned borrowing from Latin *pilula* (diminutive) < *pila* ball[1], globe]

pil·u·lous (pil′yə ləs), *adj.* pilular.

Pi·ma[1] (pē′mə), *n.,* or **Pima cotton, 1.** a cotton, originally raised in Arizona by crossing native and Egyptian cotton, used in rain wear, tires, shirt fabrics, etc. **2.** a strong, smooth fabric made of this cotton: *Our own B. H. Wragge does a play suit of pistachio Pima cotton and a Maypole skirt* (New Yorker). [< *Pima,* a county in Arizona]

Pi·ma[2] (pē′mə), *n., pl.* **-ma** or **-mas. 1.** a member of an agricultural tribe of Pimans living in southern Arizona and northwestern Mexico. **2.** this tribe. **3.** their Piman language.

Pi·man (pē′mən), *n., pl.* **-mans** or **-man. 1.** an American Indian linguistic family of southern Arizona and northwestern Mexico, a branch of Uto-Aztecan. **2.** a member of a tribe speaking a language of this family. *—adj.* of or having to do with this linguistic family or the tribes that speak a language of this family.

pi·men·to (pə men′tō), *n., pl.* **-tos. 1.** kind of sweet red pepper, used as a vegetable, relish, and a stuffing for green olives, etc. **2.** allspice. **3.** the tropical American tree of the myrtle family that produces allspice. [< Spanish *pimienta* black pepper, or *pimiento* green or red pepper, capsicum < Medieval Latin *pigmentum* spice < Late Latin, vegetable juice; a drug < Latin, pigment. Doublet of PIGMENT.]

Pimento (def. 1)

pimento cheese, a processed cheese, used sliced or as a spread, etc., made by mixing chopped pimentos (sweet red peppers) with a smooth cheese, especially Neufchatel.

pi·mes·on (pī′mes′ən, -mē′sən), *n.,* or **pi meson,** a meson having a mass from 264 to 273 times that of an electron. Charged pi-mesons decay into neutrinos and mu-mesons; neutral pi-mesons decay into quanta of light or radiation: *These are pi-mesons, or pions, which are the field quanta of nuclear forces* (Scientific American). Also, **pion.**

pi·mien·to (pi myen′tō), *n., pl.* **-tos.** pimento. [< Spanish *pimiento* pimento]

pi·mo·la (pi mō′lə), *n.* an olive stuffed with pimento (sweet red pepper). [perhaps < *pim*(ento) + Latin *olea* olive]

pimp (pimp), *n., v.i., v.t.* pander. [origin uncertain]

pim·per·nel (pim′pər nel), *n.* **1.** any of a group of small herbs of the primrose family, especially the scarlet pimpernel, with bright scarlet flowers (varying to purple, white, or blue) that close when cloudy or rainy weather approaches. **2.** the flower of any of these plants. [< Old French *pimprenele,* learned borrowing from Medieval Latin *pimpinella* perhaps related to Latin *piper* pepper]

pimp·er·y (pim′pər ē), *n., pl.* **-er·ies.** the act or occupation of a pimp.

pimp·ing (pim′ping), *adj. Informal.* **1.** trifling; paltry; petty. **2.** weak; sickly. [origin uncertain]

pim·ple (pim′pəl), *n.* a small, inflamed swelling on the skin that may or may not contain pus; papule or pustule: *Mr. Lely . . . remark all these roughnesses, pimples, warts, and everything as you see me, otherwise I will never pay a farthing for it* [*his portrait*] (Oliver Cromwell).
[origin uncertain. Compare Old English *piplian* to grow pimply.]

pim·pled (pim′pəld), *adj.* having pimples: *a pimpled adolescent.*

pim·ply (pim′plē), *adj.,* **-pli·er, -pli·est.** pimpled.

pin (pin), *n., v.,* **pinned, pin·ning.** *—n.* **1.** a short, slender piece of wire with a point at one end and a head at the other, for fastening things together. **2.** any of various fastenings consisting essentially or in part of a pointed penetrating bar: *She took the pins out of her hair.* **3.** a badge with a pin or clasp, usually concealed at the back, to fasten it to the clothing: *She wore her class pin.* **4.** an ornament that has a pin or clasp; brooch. **5.** a peg made of wood or metal, used to fasten things or parts together, hold something, hang things on, etc. **6. a.** a thole or tholepin. **b.** a belaying pin. **7.** each of the pegs in a stringed musical instrument around which the strings are fastened at one end, and by turning which they are tuned. **8.** one of a set of bottle-shaped wooden objects used in the game of ninepins, tenpins, etc. **9.** (in golf) a stick with a numbered flag at the top, placed in a hole to mark it. **10.** the part of a key which enters the lock, especially if solid instead of hollow. **11. a.** a linchpin. **b.** a rolling pin. **c.** a clothespin. **12.** something small or worthless: *not worth a pin, not to care a pin.* **13.** *Obsolete.* a peg, nail, or stud marking the center of a target.

on pins and needles, very anxious or uneasy: *It does mean that a particular American industry is on pins and needles for many months and that the manufacturers can't make many plans ahead* (Wall Street Journal).

pins, *Informal.* legs: *Who ventures this road better be firm on his pins* (Richard H. Barham).

—v.t. **1.** to fasten with a pin or pins; put a pin through. **2.** to fasten or attach firmly to or on; tack; fasten as if with pins: *A couple of professed wits, who . . . had thought to pin themselves upon a gentleman* (Tatler). **3.** to hold fast in one position: *When the tree fell, it pinned him to the ground.* **4.** (in wrestling) to cause (an opponent) to have a fall and to hold both his shoulders on the ground: *The Penn State wrestler pinned his man, the first bout of the day to end with a fall* (New York Times). **5.** *Slang.* to give a fraternity pin to, as an indication of interest in becoming engaged.

pin down, a. to hold or bind to an undertaking or pledge: *one of those pestilent fellows that pin a man down to facts* (Washington Irving). **b.** to fix firmly; determine with accuracy; establish: *We have pinned down the important principle* (New York Times).

pin on, a. to fix (blame, responsibility, etc.) on: *Police could pin no crimes on Signor Russo* (Manchester Guardian Weekly). **b.** to place (one's trust, hope, etc.) entirely on: *I now pin my hopes on a meeting at Dieppe* (Harriet Granville).

[Old English *pinn* peg, perhaps ultimately < Latin *pinna* wing, pinion] **—pin′like′,** *adj.*

pi·ña (pē′nyä), *n., pl.* **-ñas.** in Latin America: **1.** the pineapple. **2.** a beverage flavored with pineapple. [< American Spanish *piña,* earlier *pinna* pineapple; (originally) pine cone, pine nut < Latin *pīnea* < *pīnus* pine tree]

pi·na·ceous (pī nā′shəs), *adj.* of or belonging to the pine family of trees and shrubs. [< New Latin *Pinaceae* the pine family (< Latin *pīnus* pine tree) + English *-ous*]

piña cloth, a fine, sheer fabric made in the Philippines and elsewhere from the fibers of the leaves of the pineapple plant.

pin·a·coid (pin′ə koid), *n.* a form of crystal consisting of two parallel faces. [< Greek *pinax, -akos* slab + English *-oid*]

pin·a·co·the·ca (pin′ə kō thē′kə), *n., pl.,* **-cas.** a picture gallery; art gallery. [< Latin *pinacothēca* < Greek *pinakothēkē* < *pínax, -akos* slab, tablet + *thēkē* chest, repository]

pin·a·fore (pin′ə fôr, -fōr), *n.* **1.** a child's apron that covers most of the dress. **2.** a kind of light apronlike dress without sleeves, worn by women and girls. [< *pin,* verb + *afore* (because it was originally pinned to the dress-front)]

pin·a·fored (pin′ə fôrd, -fōrd), *adj.* wearing a pinafore.

Pi·na·ko·thek (pē′nä kō tāk′), *n. German.* pinacotheca.

pi·nas·ter (pī nas′tər, pə-), *n.* a pine of southern Europe, having stout leaves set in dense whorls and cones arranged around the branches in radiating clusters of from four to eight; maritime pine. [< Latin *pīnāster* wild pine < *pīnus* pine tree]

pi·ña·ta (pē nyä′tä), *n., pl.* **-tas.** *Spanish.* a papier-mâché or clay pot shaped like a person, animal, etc., and filled with candy, fruit, etc., which is hung above the heads of children at Christmas time in Mexico and other Latin-American countries. The children are blindfolded and given chances to break the piñata with a stick to obtain the candy. *Households that don't mind a minor rumpus might like to try hanging a piñata* (New Yorker).

pin·ball (pin′bôl′), *n.* a game played on a slanted board in which a ball or marble is hit with a hammer on a spring so that it rolls up a groove, then down the board, striking bumpers, pins, or pegs, or rolling into numbered compartments or through alleys to score points.

pinball machine, a device on which pinball is played: *A sales manager caught a youthful salesman playing a pinball machine during selling time and fired him* (Wall Street Journal).

pin borer, any of various small beetles of Europe and North America that make minute holes through the bark of infested trees.

pin boy, a boy or man who sets up the pins in a bowling alley.

pince-nez (pans′nā′, pins′-), *n.* a pair of eyeglasses kept in place by a spring that clips onto the bridge of the nose. [< French *pince-nez* (literally) pinch-nose]

pin·cer (pin′sər), *adj.* of or like pincers or their actions. —*n.* pincers.

pin·cers (pin′sərz), *n., pl.* **-cers. 1.** a tool for gripping and holding tight, made like scissors but with jaws instead of blades: *They also tried a piece of rubber tubing and a pair of pincers, but . . . they had trouble with high-velocity jets of gas* (Alban Charnley). **2.** an organ or pair of organs of various animals resembling this tool, as the large claw (chela) of a lobster, crab, etc. **3.** a military operation in which the enemy is surrounded and crushed by the meeting of columns driven on each side of him. [Middle English *pynceours,* apparently < Anglo-French < Old French *pincier* to pinch]

Pincers (def. 1)

pinch (pinch), *v.t.* **1.** to squeeze between the thumb and forefinger, with the teeth or claws, or with any instrument having two jaws or parts between which something may be grasped: *to pinch a child's cheek playfully.* **2.** to press so as to hurt; squeeze: *His shoes pinch his feet* **3.** to cause sharp discomfort or distress to, as cold, hunger, or want does. **4.** to cause to shrink or become thin: *a face pinched by hunger.* **5.** to cause (a plant) to shrivel or wither up, as by frost. **6.** to bring into difficulty or trouble; afflict: *The king finding his affairs pinch him at home* (Daniel Defoe). **7. a.** to limit closely; stint: *to be pinched for space or time. With earnings pinched by disappointing demand, the oil companies would like to cut their reliance on domestic oil* (Wall Street Journal). **b.** *Dialect.* to limit or restrict closely the supply of (anything). **8.** to put in or add by pinches or small quantities: *The cook pinched more salt into the soup each time she sampled it.* **9.** *Slang.* to arrest. **10.** *Slang.* to steal; purloin. **11.** to sail (a vessel) close to the wind to such a degree that the sails shake. **12.** to move (something heavy) by a succession of small heaves with a pinch bar.
—*v.i.* **1.** to exert a squeezing pressure or force; compress: *Where does that shoe pinch?* **2.** to cause discomfort, distress, etc.: *Here's the pang that pinches* (Shakespeare). **3.** to be sparing, parsimonious, or stingy; stint oneself: *Her father and sister were obliged to pinch, in order to allow her the small luxuries* (Elizabeth Gaskell). **4.** (of a vein or deposit of ore, etc.) to become narrower or smaller; give out altogether.
—*n.* **1.** the act of pinching; a squeeze between two hard edges; nip. **2.** a sharp pressure that hurts; squeeze: *the pinch of tight shoes.* **3. a.** as much as can be taken up with the tip of the finger and thumb: *a pinch of salt or snuff.* **b.** a very small quantity. **4.** sharp discomfort or distress: *the pinch of poverty, the pinch of hunger.* **5.** a time or occasion of special need; emergency: *I will help you in a pinch.* **6.** *Slang.* an arrest. **7.** *Slang.* a stealing. **8.** a pinch bar.
with a pinch of salt, with some reservation or allowance: *It was necessary to take all his statistics with a pinch of salt* (Peter Ustinov).
[perhaps < Old North French *pinchier,* variant of Old French *pincier;* origin uncertain. Compare Vulgar Latin *pīccāre* to pierce, Flemish *pinssen.*] —**pinch′er,** *n.*
—**Syn.** *v.t.* **1.** nip, tweak. —*n.* **3. b.** bit. **5.** hardship, strait.

pinch bar, a kind of crowbar or lever with a projection that serves as a fulcrum, used for moving heavy objects or loosening coal.

pinch·beck (pinch′bek), *n.* **1.** an alloy of zinc and copper, used in imitation of gold. **2.** something not genuine; imitation.
—*adj.* **1.** made of pinchbeck. **2.** not genuine; sham: *pinchbeck patriotism, pinchbeck heroism.*
[< Christopher *Pinchbeck,* about 1670-1732, an English watchmaker, inventor of the alloy]
—**Syn.** *adj.* **2.** spurious.

pinch·bot·tle (pinch′bot′əl), *n.* a bottle with pinched or concave sides: *We made it clean smelling and gutsy and put it up in hefty glass pinchbottles* (New Yorker).

pinch·cock (pinch′kok′), *n.* a clamp used to compress a flexible or elastic tube so as to regulate or stop the flow of a liquid. [< *pinch* + *cock*[1] faucet]

pin·check (pin′chek′), *n.* **1.** a fine check smaller than a shepherd's check, used as part of a regular pattern in certain worsteds, rayons, and other fabrics: *Bonwit's slender spring worsted dress in dapper pinchecks succinctly tailored for business in town* (New Yorker). **2.** a garment or fabric having such checks.

pinched (pincht), *adj.* **1.** compressed, as between the finger and thumb. **2.** contracted, as if by pinching; shrunken, or thin and drawn, as the face or features: *In the biting easterly wind her face looked small and pinched, and cold* (John Galsworthy). **3.** distressed; straitened: *Apparently not too badly pinched, the smallest producer is not, however, turning out cars at anything like its pace of a year earlier* (Wall Street Journal).

pinch·ed·ness (pin′chid nis), *n.* the state of being pinched.

pinch effect, *Nuclear Physics.* the constriction of an electric current sent through a highly ionized gas or molten conductor and resulting from the current's own magnetic field. It is useful in thermonuclear research, especially in experiments for controlling thermonuclear fusion.

pin cherry, a wild cherry that has light-red, sour fruit.

pinch·ers (pin′chərz), *n., pl.* **-ers.** pincers.

pinch-hit (pinch′hit′), *v.i.,* **-hit, -hit·ting. 1.** *Baseball.* to bat for the officially listed batter, especially when a hit is badly needed. **2.** to take another's place in an emergency: *Wild signals of distress from the Chief Whip called on some back-bencher to rise and pinch-hit until the Prime Minister was ready* (Punch). [American English, back formation < *pinch hitter*]

pinch hitter, a person who pinch-hits for another.

pinch·ing (pin′ching), *adj.* **1.** that pinches; nipping; sharp. **2.** distressing; causing straits. **3.** sparing, parsimonious, or niggardly. —**pinch′ing·ly,** *adv.*

pinch·pen·ny (pinch′pen′ē), *adj., n., pl.* **-nies.** *Informal.* —*adj.* too economical; frugal; miserly: *a pinchpenny management. The company was now specializing in macaroni, which Philip regarded as both prosaic and pinchpenny* (New Yorker). —*n.* a niggardly person; skinflint; miser.

pinch runner, *Baseball.* a player who is substituted for a base runner: *Casey then took Hook out for a pinch runner, Rod Kanehl* (New York Times).

pinc·pinc (pingk′pingk′), *n.* any of a group of South African warblers.

pin curl, a curl of hair kept in place by a bobby pin or clip.

pin-curl (pin′kėrl′), *v.t.* to curl (hair) by keeping the locks in place with bobby pins.

pin·cush·ion (pin′ku̇sh′ən), *n.* a small cushion to stick pins (and sometimes needles) in until needed

pincushion flower, **1.** guelder-rose. **2.** scabious.

Pin·dar·ic (pin dar′ik), *adj.* **1.** of, having to do with, or in the style of Pindar, a Greek lyric poet: *The Rector of Exeter in my day was a Pindaric scholar* (New Yorker). **2.** of elaborate or irregular metrical structure. —*n.* an ode in irregular or constantly changing meter. [< *Pindar,* about 522-443 B.C., a Greek lyric poet + *-ic*]

Pindaric ode, an ode or other form of verse with an elaborate or irregular metrical structure.

Pin·dar·ics (pin dar′iks), *n.pl.* a Pindaric ode.

pin·dling (pin′dling), *adj. U.S. Informal.* puny; sickly; delicate. [origin uncertain; perhaps variant of *piddling*]

pine[1] (pīn), *n.* **1. a.** any of a group of coniferous evergreen trees, ranging in size from that of a low bush up to a height of nearly 250 feet, and bearing woody cones and clusters of needle-shaped leaves that grow out from temporary scalelike leaves. Many kinds are valuable for timber, turpentine, resin, tar, etc. *It is usually easy to distinguish the pines from other evergreen conifers by the arrangement of their leaves (needles) in groups of two, three, or five* (Fred W. Emerson). **b.** any of various coniferous trees resembling pines, especially in areas where true pines do not occur. **2.** the wood of one of these trees, much used in construction. **3.** *Informal.* the pineapple. [Old English *pīn* < Latin *pīnus, -ūs*] —**pine′like′,** *adj.*

pine[2] (pīn), *v.,* **pined, pin·ing,** *n.* —*v.i.* **1.** to long eagerly; yearn: *to pine for home. The mother was pining to see her son.* **2.** to waste away with pain, hunger, grief, or desire, *to pine with homesickness, to pine away with longing.* —*v.t. Archaic.* to repine at; lament; mourn.
—*n.* **1.** *Archaic or Scottish.* pain, suffering, or misery: *heavy-dragg'd wi' pine an' grievin'* (Robert Burns). **2.** *Obsolete.* effort; pains.
[Old English *pīnian* cause to suffer; later, suffer < *pīn* torture, punishment < Vulgar Latin *pēna,* variant of Latin *poena* penalty < Greek *poinḗ.* Compare PAIN.]
—**Syn.** *v.i.* **2.** languish.

pin·e·al (pin′ē əl), *adj.* **1.** having to do with a pine cone or resembling it in shape. **2.** of or having to do with the pineal body. [< French *pinéal* < Latin *pīnea* pine cone < *pīnus* pine tree]

pineal body or **gland,** a small, somewhat conical gland of unknown function (perhaps a vestigial sense organ), in the brain of all vertebrates that have a cranium.

pineal eye, the projection of the pineal gland on the head of some reptiles, that resembles an eye in structure.

pine·ap·ple (pī′nap′əl), *n.* **1.** the edible, juicy fruit of a tropical South American plant Somewhat like a large pine cone in appearance, it is a large, seedless, multiple fruit developed from a conical spike of flowers, and surmounted by a crown of small leaves. **2.** the plant itself, widely cultivated in tropical regions. It has a short stem and bears a dense cluster of small flowers, rising from a cluster of rigid, recurved leaves which are edged with spines. **3.** some other plant of the same family, as the wild pineapple. **4.** *Slang.* a hand grenade or bomb (so called from the crisscross pattern on some kinds). [Middle English *pīnappel* pine cone]

pineapple cloth, piña cloth.

pineapple family, a large group of monocotyledonous tropical American herbs, mostly epiphytic plants with stiff leaves. The family includes the pineapple, Spanish or black moss, and billbergia.

pine barren, *Especially U.S.* a level, sandy tract covered sparsely with pine trees: *the Georgia pine barrens.*

pine cone, the cone or fruit (strobile) of a pine tree. The cone of the white pine cone with a tassel of needles is the emblem of Maine.

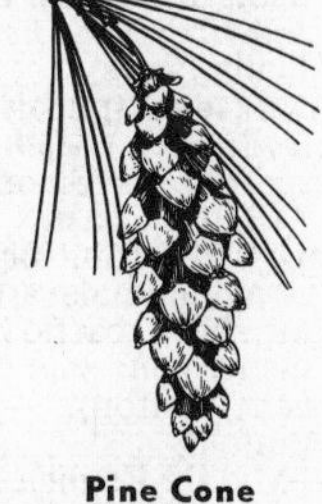
Pine Cone of white pine

pine·drops (pīn′drops′), *n., pl.* **-drops. 1.** a slender, purplish, leafless, North American plant related to the Indian pipe, with nodding white to red flowers. It is parasitic on the roots of pine trees. **2.** beechdrops.

pine family, a large group of coniferous trees and shrubs that have resinous sap, including the pine, fir, spruce, hemlock, larch, and cedar of Lebanon.

pine finch, pine siskin.

pine grosbeak, a finch about the size of a robin, living in the northern and mountainous regions of Europe and North America. The male has rosy plumage.

pine·land (pīn′land′, -lənd), *n.* land covered with pine trees: *Mr. Stark's grandfather . . . founded the family fortune by setting up a sawmill and buying vast tracts of East Texas and Southwest Louisiana pinelands* (New York Times).

pine linnet, pine siskin.

pine marten, the marten.

pi·nene (pī′nēn), *n.* a terpene found in oil of turpentine and other essential oils, occurring in two isomeric forms, and used in making resins, as a solvent, etc. *Formula:* $C_{10}H_{16}$ [< *pin*(e)[1] + *-ene*]

pine needle, the very slender, needle-shaped leaf of a pine tree.

pine nut, 1. the edible seed or kernel found in the cone of any of various pines, as the piñon; pignolia nut. 2. a pine cone, especially one containing edible seeds.

pin·er·y (pī′nər ē), *n., pl.* **-er·ies.** 1. a forest or plantation of pine trees. 2. a place where pineapples are grown. [< *pin*(e)¹ + *-ery*]

pine·sap (pīn′sap′), *n.* a leafless, yellowish or reddish plant of the Northern Hemisphere, similar and related to the Indian pipe, and parasitic on pine roots or growing in decaying organic matter.

pine siskin, a small, streaked, brownish North American finch, that has yellow patches on the wings and tail.

pine snake, a harmless, burrowing, bull snake of the eastern United States.

pine tar, tar obtained by destructive distillation of pine wood, used in making certain soaps, in medicine for the treatment of certain skin diseases, as an expectorant, and for tar paints.

Pine·tree Chain or **Line** (pīn′trē′), a chain of radar stations built as a joint undertaking by Canada and the United States along the Canadian-American border.

pine tree shilling, a silver coin bearing the figure of a pine tree, minted by the Massachusetts Bay Colony in the 1600's, and having the legal value of an English shilling but a slightly smaller silver content.

Pine Tree State, a nickname of Maine.

pi·ne·tum (pī nē′təm), *n., pl.* **-tums, -ta** (-tə). 1. a plantation or collection of growing pine trees of various species, especially for scientific or ornamental purposes. 2. a treatise on pines. [< Latin *pīnētum* pine grove < *pīnus* pine tree]

pine warbler, a grayish-green, yellow-breasted warbler, inhabiting the pine forests of eastern North America.

pine woods sparrow, a brownish sparrow with a buff breast, found in the southern United States and Mexico, especially in pine woods.

pine·y (pī′nē), *adj.,* **pin·i·er, pin·i·est.** piny: *There is . . . a poet's feeling for the piney Carolina country, in the small, quiet, graceful tale he tells* (Newsweek).

pin·feath·er (pin′feᴛʜ′ər), *n.* an undeveloped feather, especially one just breaking through the skin, that looks like a small stub: *Remove all the pinfeathers from the chicken before cooking it.*

pin-fire (pin′fīr′), *adj.* 1. having to do with an early type of cartridge fitted with a pin which, when struck by the hammer of the firearm, is driven into and explodes a percussion cap in the cartridge. 2. having to do with a firearm using such a cartridge.
—*n.* 1. a pin-fire cartridge. 2. a firearm using a pin-fire cartridge: *The weapon is a pin-fire, and has six chambers* (London Daily News).

pin·fish (pin′fish′), *n., pl.* **-fish·es** or (*collectively*) **-fish.** either of two elongated sparoid fishes or porgies of the southern Atlantic Coast.

pin·fold (pin′fōld′), *n.* 1. a. a place where stray animals are kept; pound. b. a fold for sheep, cattle, etc. 2. a place of confinement; pen: *men . . . pester'd in this pinfold here* (Milton). —*v.t.* to shut up in or as in a pinfold.
[Middle English *pynfold,* variant (probably influenced by Old English *pyndan* empound, pen up) of Old English *pundfald* < *pund* pound³ + *fald* fold²]
—**Syn.** *v.t.* impound.

ping (ping), *n.* a sound like that of a rifle bullet whistling through the air or striking an object. —*v.i.* to make such a sound; produce a ping: *After her marriage, she installed a range in the cellar of her own city house and spent hours pinging away at the target* (New Yorker). —*v.t.* to strike with such a sound; cause to ping. [imitative]

pinge (pinj), *v.i.,* **pinged, ping·ing.** peenge.

pin·go (ping′gō), *n., pl.* **ping·os** or **ping·oes.** an arctic mound or hill shaped like a volcano, consisting of an outer layer of soil covering a core of solid ice: *The Mackenzie flows away from everything useful, away from civilization itself into a region where pingos pop out of the permafrost and builders drill holes through glare ice with steam hoses* (Maclean's). [< an Eskimo word]

Ping-pong (ping′pong′, -pông′), *n. Trademark.* a game like tennis, played on a table with small wooden paddles and a light, hollow celluloid ball; table tennis. [imitative reduplication]

Ping-pong

pin·guid (ping′gwid), *adj.* 1. unctuous; greasy; oily. 2. (of soil) rich; fertile. [< Latin *pinguere* + English *-id,* as in *liquid*]

pin·guid·i·ty (ping gwid′ə tē), *n.* fatness; fatty matter.

pin·head (pin′hed′), *n.* 1. the head of a pin. 2. something very small or worthless. 3. a small minnow. 4. *Slang.* a person of little intelligence; nitwit.

pin·head·ed (pin′hed′id), *adj.* 1. having a head like that of a pin. 2. *Slang.* having little intelligence; stupid: *Left-wing editorialists seized on Monty's remarks to create a picture of pinheaded generals eager to trigger the world into war* (Time).

pin·hole (pin′hōl′), *n.* 1. a small hole made by or as by a pin. 2. a hole for a pin or peg to go in.

pinhole camera, a simple camera, such as a box camera, having a small opening in place of a lens, through which light enters when uncovered. At any normal distance, it renders a sharp image of the photographed objects, but it requires very bright light and long exposure time.

pin·ing (pī′ning), *adj.* that pines; languishing; wasting; failing with grief or longing. —*n.* a disease of progressive weakness and emaciation in sheep or cattle, resulting from a cobalt deficiency in the diet: *Pining is most common where the underlying bedrock is granite* (New Scientist). [< *pin*(e)² + *-ing*²] —**pin′ing·ly,** *adv.*

pin·ion¹ (pin′yən), *n.* 1. the outermost segment of a bird's wing, the bones of which correspond to those of the human wrist and hand and on which the flight feathers grow. 2. *Poetic.* the wing of a bird, as used for flight; flying feathers: *First a speck, and then a vulture, Till the air is dark with pinions* (Longfellow). 3. any one of the stiff flying feathers of a bird's wing; quill: *He is pluck'd, when hither He sends so poor a pinion of his wing* (Shakespeare). 4. the anterior border of an insect's wing, especially in reference to its color, markings, etc.
—*v.t.* 1. a. to cut off or tie the pinions of (a bird) to prevent it from flying. b. to cut or bind (a wing) thus. 2. a. to bind the arms of (a person) so as to deprive him of their use: *Finding us all prostrate upon our faces . . . they pinioned us with strong ropes* (Jonathan Swift). b. to bind (the arms) thus: *The captive's arms were pinioned to his sides.*
[< Middle French *pignon* < Old French *pennon* < *penne* < Latin *penna* feather, also *pinna* wing, pinion]

pin·ion² (pin′yən), *n.* 1. a small bevel or spur gear with teeth that fit into those of a larger gear or rack; planetary gear. See pictures under **gear** and **planetary.** 2. a spindle, arbor, or axle having teeth that engage with the teeth of a wheel. [< Middle French *pignon* < Old French, crenelation, battlement < Vulgar Latin *pinniō, -ōnis* < Latin *pinna* pinnacle, battlement; (originally) pinion¹, feather]

pin·ioned (pin′yənd), *adj.* having pinions; winged. [< *pinion*¹ + *-ed*²]

pin·ite¹ (pin′īt, pī′nīt), *n.* a mineral consisting essentially of a silicate of aluminum and potassium. [< German *Pinit* < *Pini,* a mine at Aue, East Germany, where it is found + *-it* -ite¹]

pi·nite² (pī′nīt, pin′īt), *n.* a sweetish, white, crystalline substance obtained from the resin of a species of pine, and from certain other plants. *Formula:* $C_7H_{14}O_6$ [< French *pinite* < Latin *pīnus* pine tree + French *-ite* -ite¹]

pi·ni·tol (pī′nə tōl, pin′ə tol), *n.* pinite, a sweetish, crystalline substance. [< *pinit*(e)² + *-ol*²]

pink¹ (pingk), *n.* 1. a color obtained by mixing red with white; a light or pale red, often with a slight purple tinge. 2. Also, **Pink.** *Informal.* a person with somewhat radical political opinions: *He can hardly be called a pink, much less a Red* (Time). 3. a. the highest degree or condition; height: *By exercising every day he kept himself in the pink of health. Even near the soft spots, the economy seems to be in the pink of condition* (Time). b. the highest type or example of excellence: *He is the pink of courtesy. My fellow motorists were the pink of consideration* (News Chronicle). 4. any of a group of herbs widely grown for their showy flowers of various colors, mostly white, pink, and red, often variegated, as the sweet william and the clove pink or carnation. 5. the flower of any of these plants. 6. scarlet cloth, as worn by fox hunters: *an English country gentleman, hunting in pink* (Francis M. Crawford). 7. a fox hunter. 8. *Obsolete.* a fop or dandy.
—*adj.* 1. pale-red, often with a slight purple tinge: *a pink carnation, pink ribbon, pink cheeks.* 2. *Informal.* moderately radical: *Many of them speak . . . in the mildly indulgent tone . . . used when speaking of a son at college whose politics were faintly pink* (New Yorker). 3. *Informal.* over-refined; exquisite; smart: *a pink tea.*
—*v.i. Informal.* to turn pink; flush; blush.
[origin uncertain] —**pink′ly,** *adv.* —**pink′ness,** *n.*

pink² (pingk), *v.t.* 1. to prick or pierce with a sword, spear, or dagger: *The épée wielder can score by pinking his opponent anywhere on the body* (Time). *By my hand, I will pink your flesh full of holes with my rapier for this* (Ben Jonson). 2. to cut the edge of (cloth) in small scallops or notches, to prevent the edge from raveling or to make a decorative finish. 3. to ornament (cloth, leather, or the like) by cutting or punching a pattern of small, round holes, often in order to show a material or color beneath. 4. *British Dialect.* to adorn; beautify; deck. [Middle English *pynken,* perhaps Old English *pyngan* to prick. Compare Old English *pynca* point.]

pink³ (pingk), *n.* any of various sailing vessels or boats with a narrow stern. [apparently < Middle Dutch *pincke* small ship, fishing boat]

pink⁴ (pingk), *Dialect.* —*v.i.* 1. (of the eyes) to be half shut; blink. 2. to look or peer with contracted eyes: *A hungry fox lay winking and pinking as if he had sore eyes* (Sir Roger L'Estrange).
pink in, *Dialect.* (of daylight, etc.) to diminish: *I'll be with ye as soon as daylight begins to pink in* (Thomas Hardy).
—*adj.* (especially of the eye) contracted or winking; half-shut.
[probably < Middle Dutch *pincken* to blink, glimmer; origin unknown]

pink bollworm, a small, pinkish moth larva which feeds on seeds of the cotton plant and on cotton bolls. It is a serious pest of cotton throughout the world.

pink disease, 1. acrodynia. 2. a fungous disease that attacks the bark of trees and is characterized by a pink growth on their branches.

pink elephants, visions or hallucinations caused by prolonged and excessive drinking of alcoholic liquor: *Now those legendary pink elephants are under scientific scrutiny. Medical researchers have been tracking them down by studying the victims of delirium tremens* (Maclean's).

pink·er (ping′kər), *n.* 1. a person or thing that pinks. 2. a pinking iron.

Pin·ker·ton (ping′kər tən), *n. U.S. Slang.* a private detective, especially one employed by the company founded by Allan Pinkerton, 1819-1884, an American detective born in Scotland.

pink·eye (pingk′ī′), *n.* 1. an acute, very contagious form of conjunctivitis, characterized by inflammation and soreness of the membrane that lines the eyelids and covers the eyeball. 2. any form of conjunctivitis. [American English, taken as < *pink*¹. Compare earlier *pink-yied,* and *pinkenye* small eyed < *pink*⁴ to blink.]

pink family, a group of dicotyledonous herbs found chiefly in temperate and subarctic regions. The family includes the pink, campion, lychnis, babies'-breath, and chickweed.

pink gin, an alcoholic drink consisting of gin and Angostura Bitters, often with water or ice added.

pink·ie¹ (ping′kē), *n.* the smallest finger of the human hand; little finger: *She keeps her pinkie raised when holding a teacup* (Time). Also, **pinky.**
[origin uncertain; probably < Dutch *pink* little finger]

pink·ie² (ping′kē), *n. U.S.* a type of fishing boat with a very narrow stern, used along the Atlantic Coast. Also, **pinky.** [perhaps American English < *pink*³ + *-ie*]

pink·ing iron (ping′king), a tool of iron or steel with a specially shaped end for pinking cloth, etc., being driven through the material by blows of a hammer on the other end.

pinking shears, shears for pinking cloth.

pink·ish (ping′kish), *adj.* somewhat pink. —**pink′ish·ness,** *n.* —**Syn.** rosy.

Pink Lady, *U.S.* a cocktail made with gin and brandy, mixed with fruit juices and egg white.

pink·o (ping′kō), *n., pl.* **pink·os** or **pink·oes,** *adj. U.S. Slang.* —*n.* a suspected Communist sympathizer; leftist: *People simply mark him down as a pinko and file him away in their minds to be dealt with later* (New Yorker). —*adj.* suspected of sympathizing with the Communists; leftist; radical: *There are those who regard 1928 as practically a pinko compromise* (Harper's). [< *pink*¹, as close to *Red*]

pink rhododendron, a rhododendron of the western United States, with pink flowers; California rosebay.

pink·root (pingk′rüt′, -rủt′), *n.* **1.** the root of any of a group of herbs, especially a variety of the southern United States with showy red and yellow, funnel-shaped flowers, used as a vermifuge. **2.** any of these plants.

pink salmon, humpback (def. 4).

pink slip, *U.S. Slang.* a notification to an employee that he has been discharged.

Pink·ster (pingk′stər), *n. U.S. Dialect, now Archaic.* Whitsuntide. Also, **Pinxter.** [American English < Dutch *Pinkster* Pentecost. Compare Old Saxon *pincostôn.*]

pinkster flower, pinxter flower.

pink·y¹ (ping′kē), *adj.* somewhat pink; pinkish. [< *pink*¹ + *-y*¹]

pink·y² (ping′kē), *n., pl.* **pink·ies.** *U.S.* pinkie; the little finger.

pink·y³ (ping′kē), *n., pl.* **pink·ies.** a fishing boat of the Atlantic Coast; pinkie. [< *pink*³ + *-y*²]

pin·lev·er watch or **clock** (pin′lev′ər, -lē′vər), a timepiece having all or most of its holes fitted with metals in place of jewels. Pin-lever watches and clocks are less reliable and durable and less costly than jeweled timepieces.

pin mark, a small depression in the shank of a printing type, sometimes containing an identifying number or symbol.

pin money, 1. an allowance of money made by a man to his wife or daughter for her own use: *What pin money, what jewels, what carriages you will have!* (Jane Austen). **2.** a small amount of money used to buy extra things for one's own use and often earned through part-time activities.

pin·na (pin′ə), *n., pl.* **pin·nae** (pin′ē), **pin·nas. 1.** *Zoology.* **a.** a feather, wing, or winglike part. **b.** a fin, flipper, or similar part. **2.** *Anatomy.* the auricle of the ear; external ear. **3.** *Botany.* one of the primary divisions of a pinnate leaf, especially in ferns; leaflet. [< Latin *pinna* feather, wing]

pin·nace (pin′is) *n.* **1.** a ship's boat: *He used ... to take the ship's pinnace and go out into the road a-fishing* (Daniel Defoe). **2.** *Poetic.* any light sailing vessel: *The winged pinnace shot along the sea* (Alexander Pope). [< Middle French *pinace* < Italian *pinaccia,* or Spanish *pinaza* < Spanish *pina* pine¹ < Latin *pīnus* pine tree]

pin·na·cle (pin′ə kəl), *n., v.,* **-cled, -cling.** —*n.* **1.** a high peak or point of rock: *Far off, three mountain-tops, Three silent pinnacles of aged snow, Stood sunset-flush'd* (Tennyson). **2.** the highest point: *at the pinnacle of his fame.* **3.** a slender ornamental turret or spire, usually terminating in a pyramid or cone, crowning a buttress, or rising above the roof or coping of a building. —*v.t.* **1.** to put on or as on a pinnacle. **2.** to furnish with a pinnacle or pinnacles. **3.** to form the pinnacle of; crown. [< Old French *pinacle,* learned borrowing from Latin *pinnāculum* (diminutive) < *pinna* peak, point; pinion¹] —**Syn.** *n.* **2.** apex, top, zenith, acme.

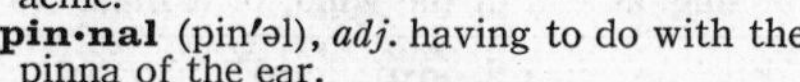

Pinnacle (def. 3)

pin·nal (pin′əl), *adj.* having to do with the pinna of the ear.

pin·nate (pin′āt, -it), *adj.* **1.** like a feather; having lateral parts or branches arranged on each side of a common axis, like the vanes of a feather. **2.** *Botany.* (of a compound leaf) having a series of leaflets arranged on each side of a common petiole, the leaflets being usually opposite, sometimes alternate. [< Latin *pinnātus* (with English *-ate*¹) < *pinna* point, pinion, feather] —**pin′nate·ly,** *adv.*

Pinnate Leaf (def. 2) of walnut

pin·nat·ed (pin′ā tid), *adj.* pinnate.

pin·nat·i·fid (pi nat′ə fid), *adj. Botany.* (of a leaf) divided or cleft in a pinnate manner, with the divisions extending halfway down to the midrib, or somewhat further, and the divisions or lobes narrow or acute. [< New Latin *pinnatifidus* < Latin *pinnātus* winged, feathered + a root of *findere* to cleave, divide]

pin·nat·i·lo·bate (pi nat′ə lō′bāt), *adj. Botany.* (of a leaf) lobed in a pinnate manner. [< Latin *pinnātus* pinnate + *lobate*]

pin·nat·i·lobed (pi nat′ə lōbd), *adj.* pinnatilobate.

pin·na·tion (pi nā′shən), *n. Botany.* a pinnate condition or formation.

pin·nat·i·par·tite (pi nat′ə pär′tīt), *adj. Botany.* (of a leaf) parted in a pinnate manner.

pin·nat·i·ped (pi nat′ə ped), *adj.* (of a bird) having lobate toes. [< Latin *pinnātus* pinnate + *pēs, pedis* foot]

pin·nat·i·sect (pi nat′ə sekt), *adj. Botany.* (of a leaf) divided in a pinnate manner; cut down to the midrib, but with the divisions not articulated so as to form separate leaflets. [< Latin *pinnātus* pinnate + *secāre* to cut]

pin·nat·i·sect·ed (pi nat′ə sek′tid), *adj.* pinnatisect.

pin·ner (pin′ər), *n.* **1.** a person or thing that pins. **2.** Also, **pinners.** a kind of headdress with two long flaps, pinned on and hanging down, one on each side, worn especially by noblewomen in the 1600's and 1700's: *the mistress of the family ... dressed in her coif and pinners* (Scott).

pin·ni·grade (pin′ə grād), *adj.* moving on land by means of finlike parts or flippers, as seals and walruses. —*n.* a pinnigrade animal. [< Latin *pinna* feather, wing + *gradus, -ūs* step < *gradī* to walk]

pin·ni·ped (pin′ə ped), *adj.* **1.** of or belonging to a suborder of carnivorous mammals that includes seals and walruses. **2.** having finlike feet. —*n.* a pinniped animal. [< New Latin *Pinnipedia* the suborder name; (literally) fin-footed ones < *penna,* or Latin *pinna* wing, fin + *pēs, pedis* foot]

pin·ni·pe·di·an (pin′ə pē′dē ən), *adj., n.* pinniped.

pin·nu·la (pin′yə lə), *n., pl.* **-lae** (-lē). **1.** pinnule. **2.** a barb of a feather. [< Latin *pinnula* (diminutive) < *pinna* pinna]

pin·nu·lar (pin′yə lər), *adj.* of or having to do with a pinnule.

pin·nu·late (pin′yə lāt), *adj.* having pinnules.

pin·nu·lat·ed (pin′yə lā′tid), *adj.* pinnulate.

pin·nule (pin′yül), *n.* **1.** *Zoology.* a part or organ resembling a small wing or fin, or a barb of a feather: **a.** a small, finlike appendage or short, detached fin-ray in certain fishes, as the mackerel. **b.** each of the lateral branches of the arms in crinoids. **2.** *Botany.* one of the secondary or ultimate divisions of a pinnate leaf, especially in ferns; a subdivision of a pinna. [< Latin *pinnula* pinnula]

pin·ny (pin′ē), *n., pl.* **-nies.** *Informal.* a pinafore: *Harassed mum, waving from the pavement in her pinny and old slippers* (Punch).

pin oak, an oak native to the eastern United States but widely distributed, whose dead branches resemble pins driven into the trunk; swamp oak: *The pin oaks are suffering from a fungus induced disease called leaf blister* (New Yorker).

pi·noch·le or **pi·noc·le** (pē′nuk′əl, -nok′-), *n.* **1.** a card game resembling bezique, played with a double deck of all cards above the eight (totaling 48). The object is to score points by melding certain combinations and by taking cards in tricks. **2.** a combination of the jack of diamonds and the queen of spades in this game. [American English; origin uncertain]

pi·no·cy·to·sis (pi′nō sī tō′sis, pi′-), *n.* the process by which cells take in fluids: *... glucose, which amoebae normally absorb only in trace amounts, enters freely by means of pinocytosis* (Scientific American). [< Greek *pinein* to drink + English *cyt-* + *-osis*]

pi·no·le (pi nō′lā), *n.* a coarse meal made from parched corn (or, occasionally, wheat), usually slightly sweetened with the flour of mesquite beans, used as a foodstuff in the southwestern United States. [American English < Mexican Spanish *pinole* < Nahuatl *pinolli*]

pi·ñon (pin′yən, pēn′yōn), *n.* **1.** any of various low pines, especially of the southern Rocky Mountain region, southwestern United States, and Mexico, producing large, edible seeds. **2.** the seed. Also, **pinyon.** [American English < Spanish *piñón* pine nut; a pine bearing edible seed < *piña* pine cone; see PIÑA]

pin·point (pin′point′), *v.t.* **1.** to mark the exact geographical position of, by sticking a pin or similar pointer into the spot on a map where coordinates intersect: *to pinpoint a field on a military map, to pinpoint a topographical feature, etc.* **2.** to ascertain the exact nature, extent, etc., of: *A Midwest machine tool maker foresees industry entering a period of uncertainty until it can better pinpoint the consequences of a Democratic victory* (Wall Street Journal). **3.** to locate, determine, or establish (anything) with accuracy and precision: *His refusal to help simply pinpoints his cowardice.* **4.** to make a particular and specific target of; seek not to hit anything other than, as in dropping bombs, firing missiles, artillery, etc.: *They were Israeli planes, picking off objectives pinpointed by ground-to-air radio* (Newsweek). —*adj.* **1.** accurate and precise: *pinpoint bombing.* **2.** of the size of a pinpoint; very small; minute: *pinpoint areas, pinpoint perforations, pinpoint particles.* —*n.* **1.** the point of a pin. **2.** something extremely small: *What diamonds you'll see are mostly tiny things, used to add a pinpoint of a sparkle to a watch face* (New Yorker). **3.** the exact location of something, as a target that has been pinpointed: *The bombs hit the pinpoints at which they were aimed.*

pin·prick (pin′prik′), *n.* **1.** the prick of a pin; a minute puncture such as that made by the point of a pin: *Its destination was a pinprick in the map* (Harper's). **2.** a petty annoyance; minute irritation: *The action was viewed in Allied circles as another pinprick in the "cold blockade" of the city* (New York Times).

pins (pinz), *n.pl.* See under **pin,** *n.*

pin·scher (pin′shər), *n.* a Doberman pinscher. [< German *Pinscher,* earlier *Pinsch,* apparently < English *pinch* (because its ears are usually clipped)]

pin·seal (pin′sēl′), *n.* **1.** sealskin tanned into high-grade leather for making wallets, shoes, etc. **2.** the skin of the fur seal: *Pinseal (the fur, not what you use for wallets) comes in a brown ... and makes ... a pillbox with a slight peak at the top* (New Yorker).

pin·set·ter (pin′set′ər), *n. U.S.* a pinspotter.

pin·spot·ter (pin′spot′ər), *n. U.S.* a machine that automatically sets up the pins in a bowling alley.

pin·stripe (pin′strīp′), *n.* **1.** a fine stripe. **2.** a garment made of cloth having fine stripes: *The King snarled, flicking ashes off his blue pinstripe* (New Yorker).

pin·striped (pin′strīpt′), *adj.* having pinstripes; marked with fine stripes: *He had on a double-breasted, pinstriped brown jacket* (New Yorker).

pint (pīnt), *n.* **1.** a unit of liquid or dry measure, equal to half a quart or one-eighth of a gallon; 16 fluid ounces (in liquid measure) or 33.6 cu.in. (in U.S. dry measure). *Abbr.:* pt. **2. a.** a container holding a pint. **b.** such a container with its contents: *a pint of milk, a pint of strawberries.* **c.** the contents: *to drink two pints of milk.* [< Old French *pinte,* perhaps < Middle Dutch *pinte* (originally) a plug]

pin·ta (pin′tə), *n.* a skin disease prevalent especially in tropical America and parts of the Caribbean, characterized by roughness, blotches, and ulceration of the skin. It is caused by a spirochete which appears to be identical to the one causing syphilis.

Pinta spots the skin white, brown, blue, yellow or violet (Science News Letter). [< Spanish *pinta* (literally) colored spot < Vulgar Latin *pincta,* for Latin *picta* < *pingere* to paint]

pin table, *British.* a pinball machine: *Signor Taviani, the Italian Minister of the Interior, has declared war on pin tables and slot machines* (London Times).

pin·ta·do (pin tä′dō), *n., pl.* **-dos, -does,** or (*collectively*) **-do.** the cero, a food and game fish found along the Atlantic coast of America. [< Spanish *pintado* (literally) painted, past participle of *pintar* to paint]

pin·tail (pin′tāl′), *n., pl.* **-tails** or (*collectively*) **-tail. 1.** the ruddy duck of North America. **2.** the sharp-tailed grouse of North America. **3.** the pin-tailed sand grouse. **4.** the pintail duck.

pintail duck, a fresh-water duck of the Northern Hemisphere, with a pointed tail, the two middle feathers being longer than the rest; pintail.

pin-tailed sand grouse (pin′tāld′), a sand grouse of Asia, Africa, and southern Europe, having its central tail feathers elongated.

pin·ta·no (pin tä′nō), *n., pl.* **-nos** or (*collectively*) **-no.** a small tropical American fish, green with dark stripes, found especially in the relatively shallow water over or near coral reefs; sergeant major. [origin uncertain; compare Spanish *pinta* spot]

pin·tle (pin′təl), *n.* **1.** a pin or bolt, especially one on which some other part turns, as in a hinge. **2.** a sturdy metal pin on the back of a powered towing vehicle by which it is attached to a towed vehicle. [Old English *pintel* penis]

Pintle (def. 1) in a hinge

pin·tle-hook (pin′təl hu̇k′), *n.* the hook of a gun limber by which the eye of the gun carriage is engaged; pintle.

pin·to (pin′tō), *adj., n., pl.* **-tos.** —*adj.* spotted in two colors; piebald. —*n.* **1.** a pinto horse or pony: *Mr. Roe also demolishes the idea that the Indian pony, or pinto, came about as the accidental mating of two strays* (New York Times). **2.** the pinto bean: *All sorts of beans turn up there—navy beans, yellow-eyes, pintos . . .* (New Yorker). [American English < Spanish *pinto* painted]

pinto bean, *Western U.S.* a field or shell variety of the common bean, whose edible seeds are spotted or mottled.

Pintsch gas (pinch), an illuminating gas obtained by distilling oil, formerly much used in railroad passenger cars, and still used in certain types of buoys. [< Richard *Pintsch,* 1840-1919, a German inventor]

pint-size (pīnt′sīz′), *adj. Informal.* pint-sized: *The pint-size jeep will operate on pavements or rugs, and will even climb grades* (Science News Letter).

pint-sized (pīnt′sīzd′), *adj. Informal.* relatively small in size; smaller than the standard size of its kind; small: *a pint-sized tractor. They also developed a pint-sized gas turbine delivering 5 to 10 horsepower* (World Book Encyclopedia).

pin tuck, a very narrow tuck, as made in cloth by sewing.

pin-up (pin′up′), *n. Informal.* **1.** a picture of a very attractive girl pinned up on a wall, as in a barracks, usually by admirers who have not met the girl. **2.** a very attractive girl, especially one considered attractive enough to be the subject of such a picture.
—*adj.* **1.** very attractive: *a pin-up queen.* **2.** of or consisting of pin-ups: *pin-up art.*

pin·wale corduroy (pin′wāl′), a corduroy with very fine, narrow ridges.

pin·weed (pin′wēd′), *n.* **1.** any of a group of low North American herbs related to the rockrose, with slender stems and leaves. **2.** the alfileria.

pin·wheel (pin′hwēl′), *n.* **1.** a kind of firework that revolves rapidly when lighted. **2.** a toy made of a revolving wheel of paper, usually of contrasting colors, twisted into vanes that catch the wind, and fastened to a stick by a pin. **3.** *Machinery.* a wheel in which pins are fixed as cogs.
—*v i.* to turn around rapidly as a pinwheel does: *While Woodhouse was hauling frantically on the reins, the saddle slipped, and the jockey went pinwheeling into the dirt* (New York Times).

pin·work (pin′wėrk′), *n.* the small, fine, raised parts of a design in needle-point lace.

pin·worm (pin′wėrm′), *n.* a small, threadlike, nematode worm infesting the small intestine, colon, and rectum, especially of children.

pin wrench, a wrench that has a pin or pins to fit into holes in nuts, etc., to be turned.

pinx., pinxit.

pinx·it (pingk′sit), *Latin.* he (or she) painted (it, or this). It is inscribed on some paintings after the name of the painter.

Pinx·ter (pingk′stər), *n.* Pinkster.

pinxter flower, a wild azalea common in swamps and woods from Canada to Texas, having pink or whitish flowers. Also, **pinkster flower.** [< Dutch *Pinkster* Pinkster, Pentecost]

pin·y (pī′nē), *adj.,* **pin·i·er, pin·i·est. 1.** abounding in, covered with, or consisting of pine trees: *piny mountains.* **2.** having to do with or suggesting pines: *the piny odors in the night air* (Longfellow). Also, **piney.**

pin·yon (pin′yən, pēn′yōn), *n.* piñon.

pinyon jay, a grayish-blue jay, having no crest, found especially in the Rocky Mountains or their foothills.

PIO (no periods), **1.** public information office. **2.** public information officer.

piob·aireachd (pē′brok), *n.* pibroch: *One of the greatest exhibitions of piping is the traditional piobaireachd, . . . a complicated and elaborate set of variations* (New York Times).

pi·on (pī′on), *n.* pi-meson: *Today the proton is no longer considered a simple particle. Given enough energy it can turn itself into a neutron and a positive pion (brief for pi-meson) and according to the quantum theory it will make frequent brief forays into that state even if no energy is supplied* (New Scientist). [< *pi*-(mes)*on*]

pi·o·neer (pī′ə nir′), *n.* **1.** a person who settles in a part of the country that has not been occupied before except by primitive tribes: *restless and intrepid pioneers whose axes and rifles have opened a path from the Alleghanies to the western prairies* (Francis Parkman). **2.** a person who goes first, or does something first, and so prepares a way for others: *Florence Nightingale was a pioneer in hospital reform.* **3.** *Especially British.* one of a group of soldiers in a unit, especially of military engineers, who make roads, build bridges, dig trenches, etc. **4.** *Obsolete.* a person who digs a trench, pit, etc.; digger; miner.
—*v.t.* **1.** to prepare, clear, or open up (a way, road, etc.): *I will pioneer a new way, explore unknown powers* (Mary Shelley). **2.** to prepare the way for: *It was the first airline to use X rays for inspecting equipment, and pioneered "package" summer vacations in cooperation with Miami hotels* (Newsweek). —*v.i.* to act as pioneer; open or prepare the way as a pioneer.
—*adj.* **1.** that is a pioneer: *a pioneer settler.* **2.** that goes ahead so that others may follow; exploratory: *pioneer research in nuclear physics.*
[< Middle French *pionnier,* Old French *paonier* < *peon* foot soldier < Medieval Latin *pedo, -onis* < Latin *pēs, pedis* foot. Related to PAWN², PEON.]

piou·piou (pyü pyü′), *n. Informal.* a French common soldier. [< French *pioupiou*]

pi·ous (pī′əs), *adj.* **1.** having or showing reverence for God; religious. **2.** done or used from real or pretended religious motives, or for some good object: *a pious fraud, a pious deception.* **3.** *Archaic.* dutiful to parents. **4.** sacred, as distinguished from secular. [< Latin *pīus* (with English *-ous*) dutiful] —**pi′ous·ly,** *adv.* —**pi′ous·ness,** *n.*
—**Syn. 1. Pious, devout** mean religious. **Pious** emphasizes showing religion or reverence for God by carefully observing religious duties and practices, such as going to church, and sometimes suggests that more religion is shown than felt: *She is pious at church in the morning and gossips all afternoon.* **Devout** emphasizes feeling true reverence that usually is expressed in prayer or devotion to religious observances, but may not be shown at all: *He is a devout Christian and a good man.* —**Ant. 1.** impious, irreligious, irreverent.

pip¹ (pip), *n.* **1.** the seed of a fleshy fruit, as of an apple or orange. **2.** *Slang.* a person or thing that is very attractive, admirable, or extraordinary; pippin: *Wait till you meet her —she's really a pip!* [apparently short for *pippin*]

pip² (pip), *n.* **1. a.** a contagious disease of poultry and other birds, characterized by the secretion of thick mucus in the mouth and throat and sometimes by white scale on the tongue. **b.** the scale itself. **2.** *Informal.* a slight illness (used in a humorous way). [apparently < Middle Dutch *pippe* < Vulgar Latin *pippīta,* and *pīpīta,* ultimately < Latin *pītuīta* (literally) phlegm]

pip³ (pip), *n.* **1.** one of the spots or symbols on playing cards, dominoes, or dice: *The object is to draw cards to get a higher number of pips . . . than the dealer without going over 21* (Scientific American). **2.** the starlike shoulder insigne worn by second lieutenants (one pip), lieutenants (two pips), and captains (three pips) in the British Army, or the armies of any of the countries in the British Commonwealth. **3. a.** the individual rhizome of the lily of the valley. **b.** the dormant rhizome or root of any of several other plants, as the peony and anemone. **4.** one of the diamond-shaped segments of the surface of a pineapple. **5.** the central part of an artificial flower; pep. [origin uncertain]

pip⁴ (pip), *v.,* **pipped, pip·ping.** —*v.i.* to peep; chirp. —*v.t.* (of a young bird) to break through (the shell) when hatching. [probably variant of *peep²*]

pip⁵ (pip), *n.* a luminous spot or irregularity on a radar screen; blip: *These pulses were recorded as pips on a cathode ray screen* (Scientific American). [perhaps < *pip³*]

pip·age (pī′pij), *n.* **1.** the conveyance of water, gas, petroleum, etc., by means of pipes. **2.** the charge made for this. **3.** a system or network of such pipes. [< *pip*(e) + *-age*]

pi·pal (pē′pəl), *n.,* or **pipal tree,** a fig tree of India, resembling the banyan but lacking prop roots; Bo tree. Also, **peepul, pipul.** [< Hindi *pīpal* < Sanskrit *pippala*]

pipe (pīp), *n., v.,* **piped, pip·ing.** —*n.* **1.** a tube through which a liquid or gas can flow: *A stove or furnace must have a pipe and a chimney to carry away the gases and smoke.* **2. a.** a tube with a bowl of clay, wood, or other material at one end, for smoking tobacco, opium, etc. **b.** the quantity of tobacco, opium, etc., a pipe will hold: *Sir Jeoffrey . . . gave me a pipe of his own tobacco* (Sir Richard Steele). **3.** a musical wind instrument consisting of a single tube of reed, straw, etc., or especially wood, into which a player blows, as a flute, oboe, or clarinet. **4.** any tube by which the sounds are produced in a musical instrument, especially each of the wooden or metal tubes (organ pipes) in an organ; flue pipe or reed pipe: *An organ pipe sounds only one note, and the larger the pipe the lower its pitch* (New Yorker). **5.** a small kind of flute, formerly played with one hand while the other hand beat a drum or tabor. **6.** a shrill sound, voice, or song: *the pipe of a lark.* **7. a.** a boatswain's whistle. **b.** the signal or call made by blowing it. **8. a.** a cask, varying in size, for wine, etc. **b.** as much as such a cask holds, now usually reckoned as four barrels or 126 (wine) gallons. **c.** such a cask with its contents. **9. a.** any of various tubular or cylindrical natural formations, as the stem of a plant, etc. **b.** a tubular organ, passage, canal, or vessel in an animal body. **10. a.** a vein of ore of a more or less cylindrical form. **b.** a mass, more or less cylindrical and often extending far into the ground, of bluish, volcanic rock within which diamonds are embedded, found especially in parts of South Africa. **11.** any of various tubular or cylindrical objects, contrivances, or parts.
pipes, a. a set of musical tubes or pipes; syrinx: *the pipes of Pan.* See picture under **panpipe. b.** a bagpipe: *The pipes resumed their clamorous strain* (Scott). **c.** *Slang.* the vocal apparatus, especially of a singer: *A strange orator straining his pipes, to persuade strange people* (Richard Mulcaster). **d.** *Informal.* the respiratory passages: *Depth of girth he [the horse] must have, or his pipes and heart have no room to play* (Joseph Addison) **e.** *Obsolete.* any wind instrument, as a woodwind: *. . . the pipes that baseborn minds dance after* (Francis Quarles).
—*v.i.* **1.** to play on a pipe. **2.** to whistle or sing, as a bird, the wind, or a man: *No*

more they ... heard the steady wind pipe boisterously Through the strained rigging (William Morris). **3.** to speak or talk loudly and shrilly. **4.** to give orders, signals, etc., with or as with a boatswain's whistle. **5.** *Metallurgy.* to form cylindrical cavities, as steel ingots or castings when solidifying. **6.** *Mining.* to carve so as to form a cylindrical hole. —*v.t.* **1.** to convey (water, gas, oil, etc.) through or by means of a pipe or pipes. **2.** to transmit (a recording, television program, conversation, etc.) by means of radio-frequency, telephone, or other types of transmission lines: *Current motion pictures and sport events will be among the initial programs piped into the Telemeter-equipped homes* (Wall Street Journal). **3.** to furnish or supply with pipes: *Our street is being piped for gas.* **4.** to play (a tune, music) on a pipe. **5.** to utter in a loud, shrill or clear voice, as a bird, a singer, or a speaker. **6.** to give orders, signals, calls, etc., to with a boatswain's whistle. **7.** to lead or summon by the sound of a pipe: *Pipe all hands on deck.* **8.** to trim or ornament (a dress, etc.) with piping.

pipe down, *U.S. Slang.* to be quiet; shut up: *Listen, if you don't pipe down about TV and programming and keep quiet, you won't be able to sell a show in Sheboygan* (New Yorker).

pipe one's (or **the**) **eye.** See under **eye,** *n.*

pipe up, a. to begin to play or sing (music); strike up: *Once he piped up to a different air, a kind of country love song* (Robert Louis Stevenson). **b.** *Slang.* to speak: *As the guard laid a hand upon me, she piped up* (Mark Twain). **c.** to rise or increase: *The wind is heading me and piping up, so I shall be lucky if I don't start losing some of my advantage now* (Observer).

[Old English *pīpe* < Vulgar Latin *pīppa,* for Latin *pīpa* < *pīpāre* to chirp; probably (originally) imitative] —**pipe′like′,** *adj.*

—**Syn.** *n.* **1.** conduit, duct.

pipe band, a group of musicians all of whom play on bagpipes.

pipe clay, a fine white kind of clay, that forms a ductile paste with water. Pipe clay is used for making tobacco pipes, whitening shoes, etc.

pipe-clay (pīp′klā′), *v.t.* to whiten with pipe clay.

pipe dream, *Informal.* **1.** a dream produced by smoking opium. **2.** an impractical, groundless, or fantastic idea, scheme, etc.: *The best that can be said about the prospects for gold is that pipe dreams and rumours about an increase in its dollar price are a little less improbable than they were* (Economist).

pipe·fish (pīp′fish′), *n., pl.* **-fish·es** or (*collectively*) **-fish.** any of a group of marine fish commonly having a long snout and a long, slender, angular body covered with armorlike plates.

pipe fitter, a person specially trained or experienced in the installing and repairing of pipes.

pipe·ful (pīp′fu̇l), *n., pl.* **-fuls.** a quantity sufficient to fill the bowl of a pipe.

pipe·lay·er (pīp′lā′ər), *n.* **1.** a person who lays pipes for the conveyance of water, gas, etc. **2.** a person, especially a politician, who lays plans for the promotion of some scheme or purpose.

pipe·lay·ing (pīp′lā′ing), *n.* **1.** the act of laying down pipes for gas, water, and other purposes. **2.** a laying of plans for the accomplishment of some scheme or purpose, especially a political one.

pipe·line (pīp′līn′), *n., v.,* **-lined, lin·ing.** —*n.* **1.** a line of pipes for carrying oil, natural gas, water, etc., now usually over a considerable distance and often (especially in the case of oil) with pumps at intervals to maintain the rate of flow: *The pipeline is the low-cost, efficient transporter of fuel for any distance* (Harper's). **2.** *Informal.* a source of information, usually secret: *a pipeline into the White House. His pipeline this time was a seat next to a Dutch diplomat at a luncheon* (Newsweek). **3.** a flow of materials through a series of productive processes: *How fast civilian pipelines fill up ... depends on government rationing of the output of steel mills* (Newsweek). —*v.t.* **1.** to carry by a pipeline. **2.** to provide with a pipeline.

Oil Pipeline (def. 1) in process of being laid

pipe of peace, peace pipe; calumet.

pipe organ, an organ with pipes of different lengths sounded by air blown through them, as distinguished from a reed or electronic organ.

pip·er (pī′pər), *n.* a person who plays on a pipe or bagpipe, especially one who goes about the country playing at different places.

pay the piper, a. to defray the cost: *In the commercial theatre the cheerfully amoral majority pays the piper—and calls the tune* (London Times). **b.** to bear the consequences: *Which of you two comes down ...? Who pays the piper?* (J.S. LeFanu).

pip·er·a·ceous (pip′ə rā′shəs), *adj.* belonging to the pepper family of plants. [< Latin *piper, -eris* pepper + English *-aceous*]

pi·per·a·zin (pi per′ə zin), *n.* piperazine.

pi·per·a·zine (pi per′ə zin, -zēn), *n.* a basic, crystalline compound obtained by the action of ammonia on ethylene bromide or chloride, used medicinally in treating roundworm infestation, and, formerly, rheumatism: *A new type of drug, related to piperazine, has been found which specifically inhibits anaerobic organisms (organisms which will not grow in the presence of oxygen)* (New Scientist). *Formula:* $C_4H_{10}N_2$ [< Latin *piper* pepper + English *azine*]

pi·per·i·dine (pi per′ə din, -dēn), *n.* a volatile liquid base, having a pepperlike odor, obtained from pyridine or piperine. It is a vasodilator. *Formula:* $C_5H_{22}N$ [< *piper*(ine) + *-ide* + *-ine*²]

pip·er·in (pip′ər in), *n.* piperine.

pip·er·ine (pip′ər in, -ə rēn), *n.* a white, crystalline alkaloid, obtained from a species of pepper or prepared synthetically, used as an antipyretic and insecticide. *Formula:* $C_{17}H_{19}NO_3$ [< Latin *piper* pepper + English *-ine*²]

pip·er·o·nal (pip′ər ə nal), *n.* a white, crystalline aldehyde, a benzene derivative, with an odor like that of heliotrope, used in making perfumes, suntan lotions, etc. *Formula:* $C_8H_6O_3$ [< *piper*(ine) + *-on*(e) + *-al*¹]

pipes (pīps), *n.pl.* See under **pipe,** *n.*

pipe·stem (pīp′stem′), *n.* **1.** the rigid tube (stem) of a tobacco pipe, through which the smoke is drawn from the bowl by sucking. **2.** something thin.

pipe·stone (pīp′stōn′), *n.* a hard red clay or soft stone used by the North American Indians for peace pipes: *The only large deposit of pipestone in the United States is in Pipestone County* (World Book Encyclopedia).

pi·pette or **pi·pet** (pī pet′, pi-), *n., v.,* **-pet·ted, -pet·ting.** —*n.* a slender pipe or tube used to transfer or measure small quantities of a liquid or gas. The most common type is a small glass tube that widens into a bulb at the middle, into which liquid may be sucked, and in which it may be retained by closing the top end with a stopper, thumb, etc. *The buret and the pipet are both calibrated to deliver a certain volume rather than to contain a certain volume* (W.N. Jones). —*v.t.* to pour, transfer, or draw off or out by means of a pipette: *With a medicine dropper he catches the animal in a drop of water, pipettes the drop on a glass slide and places the slide under his microscope* (Scientific American). [< French *pipette* (diminutive) < Old French *pipe* pipe]

pipe·work (pīp′wėrk′), *n.* pipes; piping: *Fuels affected by heat may give rise to deposits which foul the pipework* (New Scientist).

pipe·wort (pīp′wėrt′), *n.* any of a family of chiefly tropical aquatic or marsh herbs, stemless or nearly so, with fibrous roots, linear leaves, and naked scapes bearing dense heads of minute flowers.

pip·ing (pī′ping), *n.* **1.** the act of a person or thing that pipes. **2.** pipes: *a house equipped with copper piping.* **3.** material for pipes; a pipe: *three feet of piping.* **4.** a shrill sound: *the piping of frogs in the spring.* **5.** the music of pipes. **6.** a narrow band of material, sometimes containing a cord, used for trimming along edges and seams: *A two-piece dress of black-and-taupe striped wool jersey has piping of black leather on the collar* (New Yorker). **7.** ornamental lines of icing, frosting, meringue, etc.

—*adj.* **1.** sounding shrilly; shrill: *a high, piping voice. Taglioni came, to give grace and dignity to the figure, and Lablache, to train the piping treble upon his own rich bass* (Lytton Strachey). **2.** *Archaic.* **a.** characterized by or appropriate to the music of the pastoral pipe: *In this weak piping time of Peace* (Shakespeare). **b.** that plays a musical pipe: *Lowing herds, and piping swains* (Jonathan Swift).

piping hot, so as to hiss; very hot: *The coffee is piping hot.*

piping crow, any of various birds related to the shrikes and found in and around Australia and New Guinea, such as a species with black and white plumage, that is often domesticated and can be taught to speak words.

piping plover, a small white and sand-colored plover of eastern North America.

pip·is·trel or **pip·is·trelle** (pip′ə strel′), *n.* any of a group of small brown or grayish bats, as the eastern pipistrel of North America.

[< French *pipistrelle* < Italian *pipistrello,* variant of *vespertilio* < Latin *vespertīliō;* see VESPERTILIONINE]

pip·it (pip′it), *n.* any of a group of small brownish birds, similar to the lark, that sing while flying; titlark. [imitative. Compare French *pitpit.*]

pip·kin (pip′kin), *n.* **1.** *British.* a small earthenware pot, used chiefly in cookery. **2.** *Dialect.* a piggin. [perhaps < *pip*(e) + *-kin*]

pip·less (pip′lis), *adj.* without pips or seeds, as an orange.

pip·per (pip′ər), *n.* a small hole in the reticle of an optical sight or computing sight: *I seek only to stay on his tail, to track him with the pipper in the gunsight and pull the trigger* (Harper's). [< *pip*³ + *-er*¹]

pip·pin (pip′in), *n.* **1.** any of several kinds of apple, ripening in the fall, that are roundish in form, yellowish-green in color, and have firm flesh of excellent flavor: *I will make an end of my dinner, there's pippins and cheese to come* (Shakespeare). *Is not old wine wholesomest, old pippins toothsomest?* (John Webster). **2.** *Obsolete or Dialect.* the seed (pip) of a fruit. **3.** *Slang.* someone or something especially attractive. [< Old French *pepin;* origin uncertain]

pip·ra·dol (pip′rə dol), *n.* a drug used to stimulate the central nervous system in cases of emotional depression or fatigue; Meratran. *Formula:* $C_{18}H_{21}NO$

pip·sis·se·wa (pip sis′ə wə), *n.* any of a group of low, creeping evergreen plants related to the shinleaf, especially a kind whose leaves are used in medicine as a tonic, astringent, and diuretic; wintergreen. [American English < Algonkian (Cree) name < *pipisisikweu* it reduces (stone in the bladder) to fine particles]

pip·squeak (pip′skwēk′), *n. Slang.* **1.** an insignificant person; a petty object: *Her notion is that he could be a big wheel on Madison Avenue instead of a publicity pipsqueak in a charitable foundation if he would just show a little get-up-and-go* (New Yorker). **2.** a small type of high-velocity shell distinguished by the sound of its flight. It was used during World War I.

pi·pul (pē′pəl), *n.* pipal.

pip·y (pī′pē), *adj.,* **pip·i·er, pip·i·est. 1.** pipelike; tubular. **2.** piping; shrill.

pi·quan·cy (pē′kən sē), *n.* piquant quality: *To his piquancy and richness of characterization he was able to add the deepest spiritual dimensions* (Wall Street Journal).

pi·quant (pē′kənt), *adj.* **1.** stimulating to the mind, interest, etc.: *a piquant bit of news. Sir Robert's pre-eminence is piquant in many respects* (Observer). **2.** interestingly attractive: *a piquant smile.* **3.** pleasantly sharp; stimulating to the taste; appetizing: *piquant pickles, a piquant sauce.* **4.** *Archaic.* unpleasantly sharp or biting; stinging. [< Old French *piquant,* present participle of *piquer* to prick, sting; see PIQUE] —**pi′quant·ly,** *adv.* —**pi′quant·ness,** *n.*

pi·quante (pē känt′), *adj.* piquant: *a piquante girl, a piquante sauce.* [< French *piquante,* feminine of *piquant* piquant]

pique (pēk), *n., v.,* **piqued, pi·quing.** —*n.* **1.** a feeling of anger at being slighted; wounded pride: *In a pique, she left the party. It should comfort no one that a group of men are powerful enough to legislate by pique* (Wall Street Journal). **2.** *Archaic.* a fit of ill feeling between persons; personal quarrel: *Her sudden freak ... must have been*

caused by some little pique or misunderstanding between them (George Eliot). [< Middle French *pique* < Old French *piquer* to prick; see the verb]
—*v.t.* **1.** to cause a feeling of anger in; wound the pride of: *It piqued her that they should have a secret she did not share.* **2.** to arouse; stir up: *The curiosity of the boys was piqued by the locked trunk.* **3.** *Aeronautics, Obsolete.* to dive at in an attack.

pique oneself on or **upon,** to feel proud about; take pride in: *Men who are thought to pique themselves upon their wit* (Alexander Pope).
[< French, Old French *piquer* to prick, sting < *pic* a pick[2], perhaps < Germanic (compare Old English *pīc*)]
—**Syn.** *n.* **1.** umbrage.

pi·qué (pi kā′), *n.* a fabric, usually cotton, but sometimes rayon or silk, woven commonly with narrow ribs or raised stripes: *For either day or evening, there's a princesse dress of navy honeycomb silk piqué* (New Yorker). [< French *piqué* (literally) quilted, past participle of *piquer* to backstitch < Old French, to prick; see PIQUE, verb]

pi·quet (pi ket′), *n.* a complicated card game for two, played with a deck of 32 cards, all below the seven being discarded: *Piquet she held the best game at the cards for two persons, though she would ridicule the pedantry of the terms* (Charles Lamb). [< French *piquet*, earlier *picquet*, perhaps < *pic* a score in the game, or < *piquer* pique, verb]

pi·ra·cy (pī′rə sē), *n., pl.* **-cies. 1.** robbery on the sea. **2.** the act of publishing or using a book, play, musical composition, etc., without the author's or publisher's permission. [< Medieval Latin *piratia*, earlier *pirata* < unrecorded Medieval Greek *peirateia* < Greek *peirātḗs* pirate]

pi·ra·gua (pə rä′gwə, -rag′wə), *n.* pirogue. [< Spanish *piragua* < a Carib (South America) word meaning a large dug-out canoe. Doublet of PIROGUE.]

Pi·ran·del·li·an (pir′ən del′ē ən), *adj.* of, having to do with, or in the style of Luigi Pirandello, 1867–1936, Italian playwright, poet, and novelist.

pi·ra·nha (pi rän′yə), *n., pl.* **-nhas** or (*collectively*) **-nha.** any of a group of small South American fish that attack man and other large mammals in the water; caribe. [< Portuguese *piranha* < Tupi (Brazil) *pira nya*, variant of *pira'ya* (literally) scissors]

pi·ra·ru·cu (pə rä′rə kü), *n.* the arapaima, a very large South American fish. [< Tupi *pirarucu*]

pi·rate (pī′rit), *n., v.,* **-rat·ed, -rat·ing.** —*n.* **1.** a person who attacks and robs ships: *Along the middle of the eighteenth century, it served as a handy spot for hanging pirates* (New Yorker). **2.** a ship used by pirates: *Squadrons of pirates hung yet about the smaller islands* (James A. Froude). **3.** anyone who roves about in quest of plunder; marauder: *Pirates of the desert . . .* (Washington Irving).
—*v.i.* to commit an act of piracy or be a pirate. —*v.t.* **1.** to practice piracy upon; plunder as a pirate. **2.** to rob; plunder. **3.** to publish or use without the author's permission. **4.** to appropriate or use (something, the exclusive rights to which have been assigned to another): *to pirate a wave length. Rather than investing millions of dollars in research, development and testing, they . . . pirate drugs from the West* (Science News Letter).
[< Latin *pīrata* < Greek *peirātḗs* < *peirân* to attack; (originally) to try, make a hostile attempt on] —**pi′rate·like′,** *adj.*

pirate perch, a small, voracious fish of a dark-olive to pinkish color profusely dotted with black, found in sluggish waters of the eastern United States and the Mississippi basin.

pi·rate·ry or **pi·rat·ry** (pī′rə trē), *n., pl.* **-ries.** piracy; piratical depredation.

pi·rat·ic (pī rat′ik), *adj.* piratical.

pi·rat·i·cal (pī rat′ə kəl), *adj.* **1.** of or like pirates. **2.** like piracy. —**pi·rat′i·cal·ly,** *adv.*

Pi·rith·o·us (pī rith′ō əs), *n. Greek Legend.* a king of the Lapithae, who accompanied Theseus on his journey to Hades in order to abduct Persephone, but was imprisoned forever by Pluto.

pirn (pėrn), *n. Scottish.* **1.** a weaver's bobbin, spool, or reel. **2.** a fishing reel. [Middle English *pyrne*; origin uncertain]

pi·ro·gen (pi rō′gən), *n.pl.* piroshki. [< Yiddish *pirogen*, plural of *pirog* stuffed pastry < Russian; see PIROSHKI]

pi·ro·gi (pi rō′gē), *n.pl.* piroshki. [< Russian *pirogi*, plural of *pirog*; see PIROSHKI]

pi·rogue (pə rōg′), *n.* **1.** a canoe hollowed from the trunk of a tree; dugout. **2.** any of various relatively heavy canoes or small boats that somewhat resemble this, made in various parts of the world. **3.** a two-masted, flat-bottomed sailing barge, used especially in the Caribbean and in the Atlantic coastal waters southward to Brazil. [< French *pirogue* < Spanish *piragua*. Doublet of PIRAGUA.]

pir·o·plasm (pir′ə plaz′əm), *n., pl.* **-plasms, -plas·ma·ta** (-plaz′mə tə). the parasitic protozoan that infects the red blood cells of animals and causes piroplasmosis. [< *Piroplasma*, the genus name; see PIROPLASMOSIS]

pir·o·plas·mo·sis (pir′ə plaz mō′sis), *n.* any of various infectious diseases of cattle, sheep, horses, etc., caused by a protozoan parasite and transmitted by ticks. [< *Piroplasma*, the genus name of the protozoan (< Latin *pirum* pear + New Latin *plasma* plasma) + *-osis*]

pi·rosh·ki (pi rôsh′kē, -rosh′-), *n.pl.* small turnovers stuffed with meat, fish, chicken, or egg and vegetables. [< Russian *pirozhki*, plural of *pirozhok* (diminutive) < *pirog* stuffed pastry]

pir·ou·ette (pir′ů et′), *n., v.,* **-et·ted, -et·ting.** —*n.* (in ballet, etc.) the act of spinning around on one foot or on the point of the toe: *A rotation which would put to shame the most finished pirouettes of the opera-dancer* (Robert Patterson). —*v.i.* to spin around on the toe; move with a whirling motion: *I can see myself chasing about the barn . . . while the Guernsey gaily pirouettes from manger to door and back again* (Harper's). [< Middle French *pirouette* (originally) a spinning top, whirligig < Italian *piruolo* whirligig + French *-ouette*, a diminutive suffix] —**pir′ou·et′ter,** *n.*

pis al·ler (pē zȧ lā′), *French.* **1.** the least of possible evils; last resource; makeshift. **2.** (literally) to go worse.

Pi·san (pē′zən), *adj.* of or having to do with Pisa, Italy: *Pisan architecture. Wherever the Pisan influence reached in Tuscany, the black and white stripes appear* (New Yorker). —*n.* a native or inhabitant of Pisa.

pis·ca·ry (pis′kər ē), *n., pl.* **-ries. 1.** *Law.* the right or privilege to fish in a body of water owned by another. **2.** a place for catching fish; fishery. [< Late Latin *piscaria* < Latin, a fish market, feminine of *piscārius* having to do with fishing or to fish < *piscis* fish]

pis·ca·tol·o·gy (pis′kə tol′ə jē), *n.* **1.** the science of fishing; the methods of fishermen, the nature and habits of fish, etc., as the object of systematic study. **2.** *Obsolete.* ichthyology. [< Latin *piscātus* a fishing + English *-logy*]

pis·ca·tor (pis kā′tər), *n.* a fisherman; angler. [< Latin *piscātor* < *piscis* fish]

pis·ca·to·ri·al (pis′kə tôr′ē əl, -tōr′-), *adj.* **1.** of or having to do with fishermen or fishing. **2.** characteristic of fishermen or fishing. **3.** employed in or addicted to fishing. [< Latin *piscātōrius* (< *piscātor, -ōris* fisherman < *piscis* fish) + English *-al*[1]] —**pis′ca·to′ri·al·ly,** *adv.*

pis·ca·to·ry (pis′kə tôr′ē, -tōr′-), *adj.* piscatorial.

Pis·ces (pis′ēz, pī′sēz), *n.pl., genitive* (*def. 1*) **Pis·ci·um. 1.** a northern constellation between Aquarius and Aries, originally considered to have the shape of fishes; the Fishes: *In modern times, the sun is seen against the background of Pisces, the Fishes, when it crosses the equator about March 21* (Bernhard, Bennett, and Rice). **2.** the twelfth sign of the zodiac, which the sun enters about February 19; the Fishes. *Symbol:* ♓. **3.** a superclass of vertebrate animals comprising all the fishes. [< Latin *Piscēs*, plural of *piscis* a fish]

pis·ci·cap·ture (pis′i kap′chər), *n.* the catching of fish. [< Latin *piscis* fish + English *capture*]

pis·ci·cul·tur·al (pis′i kul′chər əl), *adj.* of or having to do with pisciculture.

pis·ci·cul·ture (pis′i kul′chər), *n.* the breeding, rearing, conservation, etc., of fish by means that supplement or replace those normally available in nature. [< Latin *piscis* fish + English *culture*]

pis·ci·cul·tur·ist (pis′i kul′chər ist), *n.* a person engaged or interested in pisciculture.

pis·ci·form (pis′ə fôrm), *adj.* fish-shaped. [< Latin *piscis* fish + English *-form*]

pis·ci·na (pi sī′nə, -sē′-), *n., pl.* **-nae** (-nē). a basin with a drain to carry away the water, used in churches in ritual ablutions, now usually placed in the sacristy. [< Medieval Latin *piscina* basin in a church < Latin *piscīna* pool, fish pond < *piscis* a fish]

pis·ci·nal (pis′ə nəl), *adj.* having to do with a piscina.

pis·cine (pis′īn, -in), *adj.* **1.** of or having to do with a fish or fishes. **2.** characteristic of a fish or fishes. [< Latin *piscis* a fish + English *-ine*[1]]

Pis·ci·um (pis′ē əm), *n.* genitive of **Pisces.**

pis·civ·o·rous (pi siv′ər əs), *adj.* feeding solely or chiefly on fish; fish-eating. [< Latin *piscis* fish + *vorāre* devour]

pis·co (pis′kō, pēs′-), *n.* a Peruvian brandy made from the dregs left in a wine press. [< *Pisco*, a city in Peru]

Pis·gah (piz′gə), *n.* **Mount,** a mountain range in what is now Jordan, northeast of the Dead Sea. From its summit, Mount Nebo, Moses viewed the Promised Land of Canaan. Deuteronomy 34:1–4.

pish (pish, psh), *interj., n.* a sound made to express mild contempt or impatience. —*v.i.* to make such a sound: *The Captain kept Pishing and Tushing and presently . . . swearing* (H. G. Wells). —*v.t.* to say "pish" to. [imitative]

pi·si·form (pī′sə fôrm), *adj.* **1.** of small globular form; pea-shaped. **2.** designating or having to do with the pisiform bone. —*n.* the pisiform bone. [< New Latin *pisiformis* < Latin *pisum* pea (probably < Greek *písos*) + *forma* shape, form]

pisiform bone, a pea-shaped bone of the human wrist (carpus) in the proximal row of carpal bones.

pis·mire (pis′mīr′), *n. Archaic.* an ant: *The spider's skill,—The pismire's care to garner up his wheat* (Thomas Hood). [Middle English *pissemire* < *piss* urine (because of the acrid smell of an anthill) + *mire* ant < Germanic (compare Norwegian *myre*, Middle Dutch *miere*)]

pi·so·lite (pī′sə līt), *n.* a variety of limestone consisting of rounded grains about the size of small peas. [adaptation of New Latin *pisolithus* < Greek *písos* pea + *líthos* -lite]

pi·so·lit·ic (pī′sə lit′ik), *adj.* **1.** having to do with pisolite. **2.** characteristic of pisolite. **3.** having the structure of pisolite.

pis·tache (pis tash′), *n.* pistachio.

pis·ta·chi·o (pis tä′shē ō, -tash′ē-), *n., pl.* **-chi·os. 1.** the nut of the fruit of a small tree of the cashew family, having an edible greenish kernel with a flavor that suggests almond. **2.** the kernel, used for flavoring. **3.** the flavor. **4.** the tree itself, a native of western Asia, much grown in southern Europe. **5.** a light-green color with a tinge of yellow. [< Old French *pistache* the tree, and Italian *pistacchio* the nut, both learned borrowings from Latin *pistācium* < Greek *pistákion* < *pistákē* the pistachio tree]

NUTS
Pistachio
Left, branch; right, nuts

pis·ta·reen (pis tə rēn′), *n.* the former Spanish peseta, nominally worth two reals, used especially in the Spanish colonies in America. —*adj.* petty; paltry. [American English, apparently < a diminutive form of Spanish *peseta* peseta]

piste (pēst), *n.* **1.** the track of a race course or training ground: *The downhill was run on the Tofana Canalone piste which was hard, occasionally icy and very fast* (Sunday Times). **2.** the beaten track of a horse or other animal. [< French *piste* < Latin *pista* (*via*) beaten track < *pīnsere* to pound[2]]

pis·til (pis′təl), *n.* **1.** the part of a flower that produces seeds, consisting, when complete, of an ovary, a style, and a stigma: *The pistils of the columbine and pea are made up of single carpels* (Heber W. Youngken). See picture under **style. 2.** such organs taken collectively, when there are more than one; gynoecium. [< French *pistile* < New Latin *pistillum* pistil < Latin *pistillum* pestle. Doublet of PESTLE.]

pis·til·lar·y (pis′tə ler′ē), *adj.* of or having to do with a pistil.

pis·til·late (pis′tə lāt, -lit), *adj.* **1.** having a pistil or pistils and no stamens: *If one or more pistils are present and stamens wanting, the flower is called pistillate or female* (Heber W. Youngken). **2.** having a pistil or pistils. [< *pistil* + *-ate*[1]]

pis·til·lo·dy (pis′tə lō′dē), *n.* the metamorphosis of other organs of a flower, as the perianth, sepals, or stamens, into pistils or carpels. [< New Latin *pistillodium* < *pistillum* pistil]

pis·tol (pis′təl), *n., v.,* **-toled, -tol·ing** or (*especially British*) **-tolled, -tol·ling.** —*n.* any of various small, short guns intended to be held and fired with one hand. The two chief classes of pistols in modern use are revolvers and automatics. —*v.t.* to kill or wound by shooting with a pistol: *This varlet ... threatened to pistol me* (John Evelyn). [< obsolete French *pistole* < German *Pistole* < Czech *píšťala* firearm; (originally) pipe]

pis·tole (pis tōl′), *n.* **1.** a former Spanish gold coin, worth $4. **2.** any of various former European gold coins, worth about the same amount. [< French *pistole* coin; (originally) pistol. Compare ÉCU.]

pis·to·leer or **pis·to·lier** (pis tə lir′), *n. Archaic.* **1.** a person who uses or is skilled in the use of a pistol. **2.** a soldier armed with a pistol. [< *pistol* + *-eer,* or < obsolete French *pistolier* < *pistole* pistol]

pis·to·le·ro (pis′tə lãr′ō), *n., pl.* **-ros.** a Latin-American gunman: *He ran away to Mexico and grew up a pistolero in the service of a provincial dictator* (Time). [American English < Spanish *pistolero* gunman < *pistola* pistol]

pistol grip, a grip or handle resembling the butt of a pistol, on the under side of the stock of a rifle or gun, to afford a better hold for the hand.

pis·tol-whip (pis′təl hwip′), *v.t.,* **-whipped, -whip·ping.** to beat (a person) with a pistol, usually with the barrel of the pistol.

pis·ton (pis′tən), *n.* **1.** a disk or short cylinder of wood or metal, fitting closely inside a hollow cylinder or tube in which it is moved back and forth by some force, often the pressure of steam. On one side it is attached to a piston rod or connecting rod by which it imparts motion to machinery, as in an engine, or by which motion is imparted to it, as in a pump. **2.** (in the cornet and other brass wind instruments) a sliding valve which moves in a cylinder by finger pressure, opening the air passage into additional tubings (crooks) which extend the effective length of the air passage and lower the pitch (a half step, whole step, or one and a half steps lower). [< earlier French *piston* < Italian *pistone* < *pistare* to pound[2] < Late Latin *pistāre* (frequentative) < *pīnsere* to pound[2]]

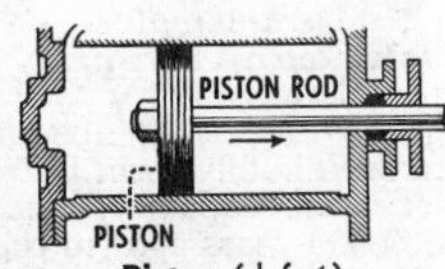

Piston (def. 1)

pis·ton·head (pis′tən hed′), *n.* the movable disk or cylinder to which the piston rod is attached; piston.

pis·ton·like (pis′tən līk′), *adj., adv.* in the manner of or like the movements of a piston: *He runs with a peculiar, pistonlike gait* (*adj.*). *Their arms moved pistonlike at their sides* (*adv.*).

piston pin, (in automobile engines) a shaft connecting the piston to the connecting rod.

piston ring, a metal packing ring, usually split so it can expand, fitted in a groove around a piston to insure a tight fit.

piston rod, a rod by which a piston imparts motion, or by which motion is imparted to it: **a.** the rod connecting the piston to the crosshead and connecting rod of a double-acting engine. **b.** a connecting rod.

pit[1] (pit), *n., v.,* **pit·ted, pit·ting.** —*n.* **1.** a hole or cavity in the ground, formed either by digging or by some natural process. **2.** *Mining.* **a.** an open hole or excavation made in digging for some mineral deposit. **b.** an excavation made for obtaining coal; the shaft of a coal mine. **c.** the mine as a whole: *They were playing havoc with legitimate union demands, and acting in a manner prejudicial to others at the pit and contrary to the spirit of trade unionism* (London Times). **3.** a covered or otherwise hidden hole, used as a trap for wild animals; pitfall. **4.** an unsuspected danger or trap. **5.** a deep place; gulf; abyss. **6.** hell, or some part of it, conceived as a sunken place, or as a dungeon or place of confinement. **7.** a large grave for many bodies. **8.** a hollow on the surface of anything; hole. **9.** a natural hollow or depression in the body: *to be hit in the pit of the stomach.* **10.** a small depressed scar, as one left on the skin after smallpox; pockmark. **11.** an enclosure in which animals, as gamecocks or terriers, are set to fight. **12.** *British.* **a.** (before about 1850) the parquet or orchestra section of a theater. **b.** (after about 1850) the rear part of the main floor of a theater, where the seats are cheaper. **c.** the people who sit there. **13.** *U.S.* that portion of the floor of an exchange, especially a commodity exchange, devoted to trade in a particular item: *the wheat pit. An early sinking spell was overcome in most pits by short covering and replacement demand* (Wall Street Journal). **14. a.** the portion of a garage used for greasing cars. **b.** an area at the side of an automobile race track for repairing or refueling cars. **15.** the enclosure at the end of a bowling alley where the pins fall. **16.** an area at a sports track filled with sawdust, etc., to soften the impact of landing after a pole vault or other jump. **17.** the part of a casino containing the gambling tables.

the pits, a place for the repair, refueling, inspection, etc., of motor vehicles beside the track of an automobile racing course: *The second Vanwall ... stopped at the pits on the seventh lap for carburetor adjustment* (London Times).

—*v.t.* **1.** to mark with small depressed scars or pits: *a little swarthy young man ... much pitted with the smallpox* (George Du Maurier). **2.** to set (gamecocks, terriers, etc.) to fight for sport. **3.** to set to fight or compete; match: *The little man pitted his brains against the big man's strength. She had pitted herself against Fate* (John Galsworthy). *The game will pit civilian all-stars against military all-stars of the Midnight Sun League* (New York Times). **4.** to put or cast into a pit.

—*v.i.* **1.** to become marked with pits or small depressions. **2.** *Medicine.* (of skin or tissue) to retain for a time the mark of pressure made by a finger, etc.

[Old English *pytt,* ultimately < Latin *puteus* well[2]] —**Syn.** *n.* **3.** snare.

pit[2] (pit), *n., v.,* **pit·ted, pit·ting.** *U.S.* —*n.* the stone of a fruit, as of the cherry, peach, plum, date, etc. —*v.t.* to remove the pit from. [American English < Dutch *pit* kernel, marrow. Related to PITH.] —**pit′ter,** *n.*

pi·ta (pē′tə), *n.* **1.** a tough fiber obtained from the leaves of the century plant and certain other agaves, used for cordage, etc. **2.** any of these plants. **3.** a similar fiber obtained from other plants, as varieties of yucca. **4.** any of these plants. [< Spanish *pita* < Quechua (Peru), fine thread made of bast[1]]

pit·a·pat or **pit-a-pat** (pit′ə pat′), *adv., n., v.,* **-pat·ted, -pat·ting.** —*adv.* with a quick succession of beats or taps; flutteringly; patteringly. —*n.* the movement or sound of something going pitapat; palpitation; pattering: *'Tis but the pit-a-pat of two young hearts* (John Dryden). *He hopes to adapt this to catch the pit-a-pat of the first stout heart to ride a satellite* (Time). —*v.i.* to go pitapat; palpitate; patter. Also, **pitpat, pittypat.** [reduplication of *pat*[1]]

pit band, *U.S.* an orchestra playing immediately in front of and below the stage of a theater: *Every now and then one hears of musicians from the pit bands of Broadway musicals getting together to play symphonic works* (New York Times).

pit boss, the supervisor of the gambling tables in a casino: *The prosecution will prove that the cashiers and the pit bosses, working in collusion, altered the figures* (London Times).

pitch[1] (pich), *v.t.* **1.** to throw; fling; hurl; toss: *to pitch a stone into a lake, to pitch the debris over a cliff. The men were pitching horseshoes.* **2.** to pick up and fling (hay, straw, etc.) in a mass with a pitchfork onto a vehicle, into a barn, etc. **3. a.** to throw (the ball) to the batter in a game of baseball: *to pitch curves and fast balls.* **b.** to loft (a golf ball) so that it alights with little roll. **4.** *U.S. Slang.* to sell or try to sell (a product, service, etc.), often by high-pressure means. **5.** to erect (a tent, etc.) or establish (a camp, etc.); set up as a temporary shelter or abode. **6.** to fix firmly, as in the ground: *In this half-circle I pitched two rows of strong stakes, driving them into the ground till they stood very firm like piles* (Daniel Defoe). **7.** to put, set, or plant in a fixed or definite place or position: *Here is a place to build a breastwork; here ye can pitch a fort* (Rudyard Kipling). **8.** to set at a particular value, level, point, or degree: *to pitch one's hopes too high.* **9.** to determine the musical key of (a tune, instrument, the voice, etc.): *He ... pitched the tunes with his pitchpipe* (Harriet Beecher Stowe). **10.** in card games: **a.** to indicate one's choice of trump by an opening lead of (a card of the suit chosen). **b.** to settle (the trump suit) thus. **11.** *Archaic.* to put in due order; set in array.

—*v.i.* **1.** to throw; toss; hurl: *He nearly always pitches too far.* **2. a.** to throw the ball to the batter in a game of baseball. **b.** to act as pitcher for a team. **c.** to strike a golf ball with a lofted club so that it goes up in the air and alights with little roll: *Cary then pitched to within a yard of the flag, before tapping in a putt for a birdie* (New York Times). **3.** *U.S. Slang.* to sell or try to sell something, often by high-pressure means: *Before I got on radio and television ... I pitched at state fairs and in hotels* (New York Times). **4.** to set up a tent, shelter, etc.; establish a camp; encamp. **5.** to take up a position; settle; alight. **6.** to plunge or fall forward; fall headlong: *The man lost his balance and pitched down the cliff.* **7.** (of a ship) to plunge with the bow rising and then falling: *The ship pitched about in the storm.* **8.** to slope downward; incline; dip.

in there pitching, *Slang.* putting forth one's best efforts; working hard, busily, or steadily: *I don't know which came first, the dishonest customer or the dishonest dealer, but they're both in there pitching* (Maclean's).

pitch in, *Informal.* to work or begin to work vigorously: *I took hold with Dan and pitched right in* (Rudyard Kipling).

pitch into, *Informal.* to attack: *If any man had told me, then ... I should have pitched into him* (Dickens).

pitch on or **upon,** to fix or settle on; select; choose: *If one holy place was desecrated, the monks pitched upon another* (Cardinal Newman).

—*n.* **1.** a throw; fling; hurl; toss: *It's more than one maybe will get a bloody head on him with the pitch of my stone* (John M. Synge). **2.** a point or position on a scale; degree; stage; level: *The poor man has reached the lowest pitch of bad fortune.* **3.** *Music.* **a.** the highness or lowness of a tone or sound, which depends upon the frequency of the vibrations producing it. The slower the rate of vibrations per second the lower the pitch. **b.** a particular standard of pitch for voices and instruments, never internationally standardized, but now generally accepted as 440 vibrations per second for a′ (the first *a* above the middle *c*): *East and West met in perfect harmony here today and agreed on a different pitch, not political but musical* (New York Times). **4.** height, especially of an arch or roof. **5.** the highest point or degree; acme; climax: *happy to the pitch of ecstasy* (H.G. Wells). **6.** *Sports.* **a.** the act of pitching or throwing a ball. **b.** the manner of doing this: *He is starting a fast pitch.* **7.** something pitched. **8.** *U.S. Slang.* **a.** a talk, argument, offer, plan, etc., used to persuade, as in selling, or to promote an idea, product, etc.: *He's ... been sending letters to foreign airlines making a pitch to represent them on the West Coast* (Wall Street Journal). *It will be packaged in an economy-size tube and, as a new pitch, he will also sell it in the form of candy* (Harper's). **b.** a television or radio commercial: *Any blame for lengthy commercials belongs to the broadcasters and sponsors. The FCC has no jurisdiction over the length of pitches* (Newsweek). **9. a.** a place of pitching or encamping or taking up a position: *It was a pleasant little island of green they chose for their midday pitch* (H. G. Wells). **b.** a spot in a street or market place where a peddler, street performer, etc., regularly stations himself; stand: *When he arrived at the market, the best pitches were gone* (Atlantic). **10.** the quantity of hay, straw, etc., raised with a pitchfork at one time. **11.** a steep place; declivity. **12.** the amount of slope: *Some roads in the Rocky Mountains have a very steep pitch.* **13.** the slope or steepness of a roof: *The roof had a sharp pitch.* **14.** *Mining.* the inclination of a vein of ore, seam of coal, etc., from the horizontal; dip or rise. **15.** the distance between the centers of two successive teeth of a cogwheel, gearwheel, etc. **16.** the distance between two successive lines or points, especially in screw threads, where it is measured parallel to the axis and indicates the distance the screw moves forward in one turn. **17.** the distance which an aircraft propeller would move forward in one revolution if turning in a semisolid. **18.** the movement of the longitudinal axis of an aircraft up or down from the horizontal plane. **19.** a plunge forward or headlong; lurch. **20.** a downward plunging of the fore part of a ship in a rough sea. **21.** *Cricket.* the ground between and around the wickets. **22.** the act of pitching on or choosing a place to live in, etc.: *Perhaps I could not have made a better pitch than I have done.* **23.** a variety of seven-up, in which the trump is settled by the first card played.

make a pitch, *Informal.* to make a persuasive request; make a bid: *Madison Avenue took a poke at—and made a pitch to—Wall Street* (New York Times).

[Middle English *picchen,* perhaps Old English *pīcian* pick[1]]

—**Syn.** *v.t.* **1.** cast, heave.

pitch[2] (pich), *n.* **1.** a black, sticky substance made from tar or turpentine, used to cover the seams of ships, to cover roofs, to make pavements, etc.: *Though pitch is a solid at ordinary temperatures, it is classed by science as a liquid with a viscosity many billions of times greater than that of water* (Scientific American). **2.** the resin or crude turpentine which exudes from pine and fir trees. **3.** any of several other resins.

—*v.t.* to cover, coat, or smear with pitch.

[Old English *pic* < Latin *pix, picis*]

pitch-and-putt (pich′ən put′), *adj.* of or having to do with golf played on a small course, usually consisting of nine holes: *a pitch-and-putt player.* —*n.* **1.** the game of golf played on a pitch-and-putt course. **2.** a pitch-and-putt course.

pitch-and-run (pich′ən run′), *n. Golf.* a chip shot that rolls a distance after being lofted in the air.

pitch-and-toss (pich′ən tôs′, -tos′), *n.* a game in which coins are thrown at a mark, and the player whose coin comes closest to the mark tosses all the coins played and keeps those which land heads up.

pitch-black (pich′blak′), *adj.* intensely black or dark; pitch-dark: *He groped along the pitch-black street for the remembered outline of the house* (Edith Wharton). [< *pitch*[2] + *black*]

pitch·blende (pich′blend′), *n.* a native oxide of uranium, found usually in blackish, pitchlike masses. It is a source of uranium, radium, and actinium. *The incidence of lung cancer in miners of uranium ore (pitchblende) is high* (New York Times). [translation of German *Pechblende* < *Pech* pitch[2] + *Blende* blende]

pitch circle, the pitch line of a gearwheel.

pitch-dark (pich′därk′), *adj.* as dark as pitch; intensely dark; pitch-black. [< *pitch*[2] + *dark*]

pitched (picht), *adj.* prepared with a proper array of troops, as a battle.

-pitched, *combining form.* **1.** having a ____ pitch: *A high-pitched voice = a voice having a high pitch.*
2. having a ____ pitch or slope: *A single-pitched roof = a roof having a single pitch.*

pitched battle, a battle, especially a major battle, with troops properly arranged and tactics planned on both sides: *Eight persons were wounded in a pitched battle in which a part of the mob stormed the gates of one plant* (Wall Street Journal).

pitch·er[1] (pich′ər), *n.* **1.** a container for holding and pouring liquids, with a lip on one side and a handle on the other: *The water in the pitcher was frozen.* **2.** the amount a pitcher holds: *to drink a pitcher of milk.* **3.** a leaf, or a part of one, modified into the form of a pitcher; ascidium. [< Old French *pichier, picher,* alteration of *bichier* < Vulgar Latin *bicārium,* perhaps < Greek *bîkos* earthen jar. Doublet of BEAKER.] —**pitch′er·like′,** *adj.* —**Syn. 1.** ewer, jug.

pitch·er[2] (pich′ər), *n.* **1.** the player on a baseball team who throws the ball for the batter to try and hit. **2.** a person who pitches hay, straw, etc. **3.** a golf club with a metal head that slopes at a relatively flat angle, so as to give loft to the ball when it is hit; number 7 iron. [< *pitch*[1] + *-er*[1]]

pitch·er·ful (pich′ər fůl), *n., pl.* **-fuls.** the quantity sufficient to fill a pitcher.

pitcher plant, any of various plants which have the leaves, or some of them, modified into the form of a pitcher (ascidium), as the huntsman's-cup. The pitcher often contains a liquid secretion in which insects are captured and digested by the plant.

Pitcher Plant (1 to 2 ft. high)

pitch·fork (pich′fôrk′), *n.* a large fork having two to four long, slightly curved steel prongs or tines and a long wooden handle, used in pitching hay, straw, etc.; hayfork. —*v.t.* **1.** to lift and throw with or as with a pitchfork: *A workman . . . was pitchforking lavender into one of a battery of cylindrical copper stills that lined the wall* (New Yorker). **2.** to thrust (a person) forcibly or unsuitably into some position or office: *Here he was . . . pitchforked into a coil of scandal* (Edith Wharton).

pitch·i·ness (pich′ē nis), *n.* the state or quality of being pitchy; blackness; darkness.

pitch·ing niblick (pich′ing), a golf club with a metal head that slopes at an angle flatter than that of a pitcher, but less than that of a niblick; number 8 iron.

pitch line, an imaginary line passing through the teeth of a gearwheel, pinion, rack, etc., so as to touch or coincide with the corresponding line in another gearwheel, etc., when the two are geared together.

Pitchfork

pitch·man (pich′man′), *n., pl.* **-men. 1.** *U.S. Informal.* a person who sells small articles on the street or at fairs, carnivals, etc.: *His right-hand men double as soldiers . . . and pitchmen, selling postcards and knickknacks to tourists* (Wall Street Journal). **2.** *U.S. Slang.* a person who sells or promotes a product, cause, idea, etc., especially by high-pressure means: *a television pitchman. An adept pitchman, however, can get his customer half-hooked by telephone* (New York Times).

pitch·out (pich′out′), *n.* **1.** (in baseball) a wide pitch thrown to prevent the batter from hitting the ball, and to give the catcher a chance to catch a runner off base. **2.** (in football) a lateral pass behind the line of scrimmage: *Dick Jones ran 30 yards to the Rutgers 3 and scored two plays later on a pitchout* (New York Times).

pitch pine, a pine tree which yields pitch or turpentine, especially a pine of eastern North America with reddish-brown bark, needles in groups of three, and persistent cones.

pitch pipe, a small musical pipe having a fixed tone or tones, blown to set the pitch for singing or tuning an instrument.

pitch·stone (pich′stōn′), *n.* obsidian or other vitreous rock that looks like hardened pitch. [translation of German *Pechstein* < *Pech* pitch[2] + *Stein* stone]

pitch·un·der (pich′un′dər), *n.* a marked tendency in an aircraft, especially one moving at high speed, to pitch downward.

pitch·up (pich′up′), *n.* a marked tendency in an aircraft, especially one moving at high speed, to pitch upward: *We are somewhat plagued by pitchup in the control of supersonic aircraft* (Atlantic).

pitch·y (pich′ē), *adj.,* **pitch·i·er, pitch·i·est. 1.** full of pitch; bituminous or resinous. **2.** coated, smeared, or sticky with pitch. **3.** of the nature or consistency of pitch; sticky. **4.** as black as pitch; pitch-black: *thick pitchy smoke* (Nicholas Wiseman). **5.** (of darkness) intense; pitch-dark: *Hans Sachse . . . in describing Chaos, said it was so pitchy dark, that even the very cats ran against each other* (Samuel Taylor Coleridge).

pit·e·ous (pit′ē əs), *adj.* **1.** to be pitied; moving the heart; deserving pity: *The starving children were a piteous sight.* **2.** *Archaic.* full of pity; compassionate; merciful. **3.** *Obsolete.* paltry; mean. [< Anglo-French *pitous,* variant of Old French *pitos* < Medieval Latin *pietosus* pitiful, dutiful < Latin *pietās* pity, piety < *pius* pious] —**pit′e·ous·ly,** *adv.* —**pit′e·ous·ness,** *n.* —**Syn. 1.** pathetic, pitiable. See **pitiful.**

pit·fall (pit′fôl′), *n.* **1.** a hidden pit in which to catch animals or men. **2.** any trap or hidden danger: *The road to conquest of poliomyelitis, or infantile paralysis, has been long and full of pitfalls* (Science News Letter).

pith (pith), *n.* **1.** *Botany.* **a.** the central column of spongy cellular tissue in the stems and branches of dicotyledonous plants; medulla: *The roots of most dicotyledonous plants lack a pith, the xylem extending to the center* (Harbaugh and Goodrich). **b.** the internal parenchymatous tissue of certain other stems, as palms, rushes, etc. **c.** a similar tissue occurring in other parts of plants, as that lining the rind of the orange and certain other fruits. **2.** the soft inner substance or marrow of a spinal column, bone, feather, etc. **3.** the important or essential part; essence; substance: *the pith of a speech. It's his abominable pride, that's the pith of the matter* (Cardinal Newman). **4.** strength; vigor; energy: *his look of native pith and genuine power* (Charlotte Brontë).

—*v.t.* **1.** to remove or extract the pith from (plants, etc.). **2.** to pierce or sever the spinal cord of (an animal) so as to kill it or render it insensible.

[Old English *pitha*]

—**Syn.** *n.* **3.** gist. **4.** force.

pit·head (pit′hed′), *n.* **1.** the entrance to a mine: *Wives and children . . . gathered at the pithead to talk by phone to their men below on Mine Level 13* (Time). **2.** the ground surrounding it. [< *pit*[1] + *head*]

pith·e·can·thrope (pith′ə kan′thrōp), *n.* Pithecanthropus.

pith·e·can·throp·ic (pith′ə kan throp′ik), *adj.* pithecanthropoid.

pith·e·can·thro·pine (pith′ə kan′thrə pīn), *adj.* pithecanthropoid.

pith·e·can·thro·poid (pith′ə kan′thrə poid), *adj.* **1.** resembling a Pithecanthropus. **2.** related to a Pithecanthropus. [< *pithecanthrop*(us) + *-oid*]

Pith·e·can·thro·pus (pith′ə kan thrō′pəs, -kan′thrə-), *n., pl.* **-pi** (-pī). one of a group of extinct ape men, approximating man in bodily form but with a much smaller brain capacity, whose existence about 500,000 years ago (in the Pleistocene) is assumed from remains first found in Java in 1891; Java man. The group has been viewed by some as a link between apes and men, and by others as a kind of man, and is considered to have been related to Peking man. *The earliest known ancestor of man, the famous Pithecanthropus, of whom several new specimens have been found, had a brain case that ranged from 775 to 935 cubic centimeters, some 75 per cent larger than the brain of the gorilla* (Ogburn and Nimkoff). [< New Latin *Pithecanthropus* < Greek *píthēkos* ape + *ánthrōpos* man]

pi·the·coid (pi thē′koid, pith′ə-), *adj.* **1.** resembling the apes, especially the anthropoid apes; simian. **2.** having to do with the apes. [< French *pithécoïde* < Greek *píthēkos* ape + *eîdos* form]

pith helmet, a helmet-shaped sun hat made originally of the dried pith of the spongewood of Bengal, but now made of various substances.

pi·thi·a·tism (pi thī′ə tiz əm), *n. Medicine.* **1.** a disorder caused by suggestion, such as forms of hysteria. **2.** the cure of mental disorders by persuasion. [< Greek *peíthein* persuade + *iatós* curable + English *-ism*]

pith·i·ly (pith′ə lē), *adv.* in a pithy manner; tersely and forcibly.

pith·i·ness (pith′ē nis), *n.* the quality or character of being pithy.

pith·less (pith′lis), *adj.* without pith; wanting strength; weak. —**pith′less·ly,** *adv.*

pith·os (pith′os), *n.* (in ancient Greece) a very large, wide-mouthed, earthenware jar of spheroidal form, used for storing wine, oil, grain, etc. It was in a pithos, commonly spoken of as a tub, that Diogenes, the Cynic philosopher, is said to have taken up his abode. *At one entrance to this building was a "lustral area" . . . it was surrounded by tall "pithos" jars for water* (Scientific American). [< Greek *píthos*]

pith·y (pith′ē), *adj.,* **pith·i·er, pith·i·est. 1.** full of substance, meaning, force, or vigor;

crisply concise and to the point: *pithy phrases, a pithy speaker.* **2.** of or like pith. **3.** full of pith: *a pithy orange.* —**Syn. 1.** pointed.

pit·i·a·ble (pit′ē ə bəl), *adj.* **1.** deserving pity; moving the heart; to be pitied. **2.** deserving contempt or scorn; mean; contemptible; miserable. —**pit′i·a·ble·ness,** *n.* —**Syn. 1.** lamentable, deplorable. See **pitiful.**

pit·i·a·bly (pit′ē ə blē), *adv.* in a pitiable manner.

pit·i·er (pit′ē ər), *n.* a person who pities.

pit·i·ful (pit′i fəl), *adj.* **1.** deserving pity; moving the heart: *a pitiful story, a pitiful sight.* **2.** feeling or showing pity; tender: *The Lord is very pitiful, and of tender mercy* (James 5:11). **3.** deserving contempt; to be scorned; mean. —**pit′i·ful·ly,** *adv.* —**pit′i·ful·ness,** *n.*

—**Syn. 1. Pitiful, piteous, pitiable** mean arousing pity or to be pitied. **Pitiful** emphasizes the effect on others, that of arousing pity, made by someone or something felt to be touching or pathetic: *The deserted children were pitiful.* **Piteous** emphasizes the quality in the thing itself that makes it appeal for pity and move the heart: *Their sad faces were piteous.* **Pitiable** emphasizes arousing sorrow or regret, often mixed with contempt, for what deserves or needs to be pitied: *Their bodies and clothes were in a pitiable condition.* **2.** compassionate, merciful.

pit·i·less (pit′ə lis), *adj.* without pity or mercy; merciless: *Ruffians, pitiless as proud* (William Cowper). *The pelting of this pitiless storm* (Shakespeare). —**pit′i·less·ly,** *adv.* —**pit′i·less·ness,** *n.* —**Syn.** ruthless. See **cruel.**

pit·man (pit′mən), *n., pl.* **-men** or (*for def. 3*) **-mans. 1.** a man who works in a pit or mine, especially a coal mine. **2.** a sawyer's helper who stands in a pit below the timber to be sawed and works the lower end of a pitsaw. **3.** a connecting rod. [< *pit*[1] + *man*]

pi·ton (pē′ton), *n.* **1.** an iron bar or spike with a ring in one end to which a rope can be secured, used in mountain climbing: *Unable to move or risk driving a piton into the rock, Bonatti hung motionless for an hour* (Time). **2.** a mountain peak or peaklike formation of rock that rises sharply and abruptly to a point. [< Frence *piton* point, peak]

Pi·tot-stat·ic tube (pē tō′stat′ik), *Aeronautics.* a device for determining the speed of the air by measuring the difference in pressure between moving and still air.

Pi·tot tube (pē tō′), *Aeronautics.* a bent tube with an open end pointed against the flow of a gas or liquid, used for determining the velocity of fluids: *The Pitot tube is kept accurately headed with the direction of travel of the airplane by means of an attached wind vane* (Harold E. Baughman). See picture under **air-speed indicator.** [< Henri *Pitot,* 1695-1771, a French physicist]

pit·pat (pit′pat′), *adv., n., v.,* **-pat·ted, -pat·ting.** pitapat.

pit pony, *British.* a pony employed in coal mines: *There is a waiting list of fifty families seeking retired pit ponies for their children* (London Times).

pit·prop (pit′prop′), *n.* a beam or other heavy prop used to support the roof of a mine: *The wall along the coal seam collapsed with a roar, and a gale-force gust of wind tossed men, machinery, and pitprops like feathers in its wake* (Time).

Pit·res·sin (pi tres′in), *n. Trademark.* vasopressin, a pituitary hormone: *About 25 per cent of the patients also require another hormone, Pitressin, to regulate the body's water balance* (New York Times).

pits (pits), *n.pl.* See under **pit**[1], *n.*

pit·saw (pit′sô′), *n.* a large saw with handles for two men, one working on the log and the other beneath it in a sawpit.

pit·ta (pit′ə), *n.* **1.** any of various plump, short-tailed, brightly colored perching birds, inhabiting forest floors of southeastern Asia, Australia, and Africa. **2.** the ant thrush of South America. [< New Latin *Pitta* the typical genus < Telugu *piṭṭa* anything small; a pet]

pit·tance (pit′əns), *n.* **1.** a small allowance of money; very scanty wage or stipend: *a widow's pittance. She . . . contrived to earn a pittance scarcely sufficient to support life* (Mary Shelley). **2.** a small amount or portion: *to retain at least a pittance of hope.* [Middle English *pitaunce* < Old French *pitance* piety, pity; later, portion of food allowed a monk < Vulgar Latin *pīetantia* < Latin *pīetās* pity, piety]

pit·ter-pat·ter (pit′ər pat′ər), *n.* a rapid succession of light beats or taps, as of rain, a child's steps, etc. —*adv.* with a rapid succession of beats or taps. [Compare PITAPAT.]

pit·ty-pat (pit′ē pat′), *adv., n., v.,* **-pat·ted, -pat·ting.** pitapat.

pi·tu·i·tar·y (pi tü′ə ter′ē, -tyü′-), *adj., n., pl.* **-tar·ies.** —*adj.* **1.** designating or having to do with the pituitary gland. **2.** designating a type of physique, obese and with large bone structure, thought to be caused by excessive secretion of the pituitary gland. **3.** *Obsolete.* **a.** of or having to do with mucus. **b.** secreting mucus.

—*n.* **1.** the pituitary gland: *The pituitary is both the smallest and the most important of the ductless glands* (New Yorker). **2.** any of various extracts made from the pituitary gland and used in medical preparations.

[< New Latin *pituitarius* < Latin *pītuītārius* relating to phlegm, mucus < *pītuīta* phlegm (because it was believed that the gland channeled mucus to the nose)]

pituitary gland or **body,** a small, oval endocrine gland situated beneath the brain, in a cavity of the sphenoid bone; hypophysis; master gland. It secretes hormones that promote growth, stimulate and regulate other glands, raise blood pressure, promote milk secretion, etc. *The pituitary gland, a pea-sized object cannily concealed in the middle of the skull, was once believed to be the soul's abiding place* (Time).

pi·tu·i·tous (pi tü′ə təs, -tyü′-), *adj.* **1.** caused by or discharging an excess of mucus. **2.** *Obsolete.* **a.** consisting of mucus. **b.** resembling mucus. **c.** having to do with mucus. [< Latin *pītuītōsus* (with English *-ous*) < *pītuīta* phlegm]

Pi·tu·i·trin (pi tü′ə trin, -tyü′-), *n. Trademark.* a preparation or extract from the posterior lobe of the pituitary gland of cattle, used in treating diabetes insipidus shock, to aid in uterine contraction during childbirth, etc. [< *pituit*(ary) + *-in*]

pit viper, any of a group of venomous snakes of America, the East Indies, Europe east of the lower Volga River, and Asia, having perforated fangs and a pit between the eye and nostril. Rattlesnakes, water moccasins, copperheads, fer-de-lances, and bushmasters are pit vipers.

pit·y (pit′ē), *n., pl.* **pit·ies,** *v.,* **pit·ied, pit·y·ing.** —*n.* **1.** a tender or sorrowful feeling or emotion aroused by the suffering, distress, or misfortune of another; compassion; sympathy: *A beggar that is dumb . . . May challenge double pity* (Sir Walter Raleigh). *Grief for the calamity of another is pity* (Thomas Hobbes). **2.** a ground or cause for pity or regret; thing to be sorry for: *It is a pity to be kept in the house in good weather.*

for pity's sake, an exclamation of surprise or protest: *But for pity's sake, spare us that indignity!* (Time).

have or **take pity on,** to show pity for: *He that hath pity upon the poor lendeth unto the Lord* (Proverbs 19:17).

—*v.t.* to feel pity for; be sorry for: *I pity those who are out in the cold tonight.* —*v.i.* to feel pity; be compassionate.

[< Old French *pite* < Latin *pīetās* piety, pity < *pīus* pious. Doublet of PIETY.] —**pit′y·ing·ly,** *adv.*

—**Syn.** *n.* **1. Pity, compassion, sympathy** mean a feeling for the sorrows or sufferings of others. **Pity** means a feeling of sorrow for someone who is suffering or in sorrow or distress, and often felt to be weak or unfortunate: *Nobody wants pity from his friends.* **Compassion** adds the idea of tenderness and a strong desire to help or protect: *He had compassion on the sobbing child.* **Sympathy** means a feeling with another in his sorrow and sharing and understanding it: *He expects sympathy from his brother.*

pit·y·ri·a·sis (pit′ə rī′ə sis), *n.* **1.** any of various skin conditions characterized by the formation and eventual peeling off of small scales of skin. **2.** a dry, scaly skin condition in domestic animals, occurring during the course of certain fungoid or filarial diseases. [< Greek *pityríāsis* scurf, dandruff < *pítyron* bran + *-íāsis* -iasis]

piu (pyü), *adv. Music.* more (as part of a direction): *piu andante.* [< Italian *più*]

Pi·ute (pī üt′), *n.* Paiute.

piv·ot (piv′ət), *n.* **1.** a short shaft or pin, usually of metal and often pointed, on which something turns, as the pin of a hinge or the end of an axle or spindle. **2.** that on which something turns, hinges, or depends; central point: *the pivot of our hopes. A permanent pivot in the center of one's inner life is also a stake beyond which one cannot range* (Edmund Wilson).

—*v.t.* to furnish with, mount on, or attach by means of a pivot or pivots. —*v.i.* **1.** to turn on or as if on a pivot: *to pivot on one's heel. There is a recess, and the board at the back pivots; a very simple hiding place* (Joseph Conrad). **2.** to execute a dance figure suggesting pivoting. **3.** to change seats, as at a bridge table, when one player remains in his place, so that the partnerships change.

—*adj.* pivotal.

[< Old French *pivot;* origin uncertain]

piv·ot·al (piv′ə təl), *adj.* **1.** of or having to do with a pivot. **2.** like a pivot; serving as a pivot on which something turns or depends; very important: *The Berlin problem is a pivotal issue between the United States and Soviet Russia.* —**piv′ot·al·ly,** *adv.* —**Syn. 2.** central, cardinal, vital.

pivot gun, a gun mounted on a pivot or a rotating carriage, a setting which makes it possible to point the gun in any direction.

pivot joint, a joint in which a bony pivot fits into a corresponding cavity or ring in another bone, permitting only rotating movement.

pix[1] (piks), *n.* pyx.

pix[2] (piks), *n.pl. Slang.* pictures. [probably short for *pictures*]

pix·i·lat·ed (pik′sə lā′tid), *adj. U.S. Informal.* **1.** slightly crazy: *The poor woman has been pixilated for years.* **2.** foolish and amusing: *as pixilated as a cat filled with catnip.* [perhaps < *pixy,* perhaps patterned on *titillated*]

pix·y or **pix·ie** (pik′sē), *n., pl.* **pix·ies.** a fairy or elf. [origin uncertain] —**Syn.** sprite.

pix·y·ish or **pix·ie·ish** (pik′sē ish), *adj.* like that of a pixy; mischievous: *a pixyish look.*

pix·y-led (pik′sē led′), *adj.* **1.** led astray by pixies. **2.** lost; bewildered.

pi·zazz (pə zaz′), *n. U.S. Slang.* **1.** liveliness; pep. **2.** flashy style or quality; ornateness: *. . . the U.S. driver's growing fondness for pizazz* (Time).

pizz., *Music.* pizzicato.

piz·za (pēt′sə; *Italian* pēt′tsä), *n.,* or **pizza pie,** a spicy, pielike, Italian dish consisting of a large flat cake of bread dough covered with cheese, tomato sauce, herbs, and often with anchovies, bits of sausage, or the like and then baked: *At the Italian pavilion, hungry people sat down and ate spaghetti and pizza pies while a mandolin band plunked tunefully away* (Cape Times). [< Italian *pizza,* perhaps < *pesta* (thing) pounded, ultimately < Latin *pista,* feminine past participle of *pīnsere* to pound[2], beat]

piz·ze·ri·a (pēt′sə rē′ə; *Italian* pēt′tsä-rē′ä), *n.* a restaurant or bakery where pizzas are baked and sold. [< Italian *pizzeria* < *pizza;* see PIZZA]

piz·zi·ca·to (pit′sə kä′tō), *adj., n., pl.* **-ti** (-tē). *Music.* —*adj.* (of a tone or passage) played on a violin, cello, etc., by plucking or pinching the string with the finger instead of using the bow. —*n.* a tone or passage played in this way. [< Italian *pizzicato* picked, pinched]

P.J., **1.** Presiding Judge. **2.** Probate Judge.

p·js (pē′jāz′), *n.pl.,* or **p.j.'s,** *Slang.* pajamas.

pk., **1.** pack. **2.** park. **3.** peak. **4.** peck.

PK (no periods), psychokinesis.

pkg., package or packages.

pks., **1.** packs. **2.** parks. **3.** peaks. **4.** pecks.

pkt., packet.

PKU (no periods), phenylketonuria.

pkwy., parkway.

pl., **1.** place. **2.** plate or plates. **3.** plural.

Pl., Place.

P.L., **1.** Poet Laureate. **2.** public law.

P.L.A., Port of London Authority.

pla·ca·bil·i·ty (plā′kə bil′ə tē), *n.* the quality or character of being placable; readiness to be appeased or to forgive; mildness of disposition.

pla·ca·ble (plā′kə bəl), *adj.* that may be appeased or pacified; easily quieted; forgiving: *Methought I saw him placable and* *mild* (Milton). [< Latin *plācābilis* < *plācāre* placate] —**pla′ca·ble·ness,** *n.* —**Syn.** conciliatory.

pla·ca·bly (plā′kə blē), *adv.* in a placable manner. "*Ay, ay," said Dunstan, very placably, "you do me justice, I see*" (George Eliot).

plac·ard (*n.* plak′ärd; *v.* plə kärd′, plak′ärd), *n.* a notice printed or written on one side of a single sheet, to be posted in a public place; poster: *There were also placards calling for men on nearly all the taxicabs* (H. G. Wells).
—*v.t.* **1.** to put placards on or in: *The circus placarded the city with advertisements.* **2.** to give public notice of with a placard or placards: *to placard a reward offered.* **3.** to post or display as a placard: *to placard a bill or notice.*
[earlier, "sealed" document, plate of armor, an undergarment < Middle French *placard* < Old French *plaquier* to piece together, stick, plaster < Middle Dutch *placken.* Compare PLAQUE.] —**pla·card′er,** *n.*

pla·cate (plā′kāt, plak′āt), *v.t.,* **-cat·ed, -cat·ing.** to soothe or satisfy the anger of; make peaceful; pacify; conciliate: *A victory so complete . . . failed to placate the indignant young actress* (Joseph Knight). [< Latin *plācāre* (with English *-ate*[1]) be pleasing, soothe] —**pla′cat·er,** *n.* —**pla′cat·ing·ly,** *adv.* —**Syn.** appease, propitiate.

pla·ca·tion (plā kā′shən), *n.* the act of placating; an appeasing; pacifying. —**Syn.** conciliation, propitiation.

pla·ca·tive (plā′kə tiv, plak′ə-), *adj.* placatory.

pla·ca·to·ry (plā′kə tôr′ē, -tōr′-; plak′ə-), *adj.* tending or calculated to placate; conciliatory. [< Latin *plācātōrius* < *plācāre* placate]

place[1] (plās), *n., v.,* **placed, plac·ing.** —*n.* **1.** the part of space occupied by a particular person or object; position in space or with reference to other bodies: *In the world I fill up a place, which may be better supplied when I have made it empty* (Shakespeare). **2.** a particular portion of space or of the earth's surface, of a definite or indefinite size, but of definite position; location: *We leave the well-loved place, where first we gazed upon the sky* (Tennyson). **3.** a city, town, village, district, etc.: *What is the name of this place?* **4.** a building or spot used for a specified purpose: *A church is a place of worship. A store or office is a place of business.* **5.** a house, house and grounds, etc.; dwelling: *to keep a place in the city. The Smiths have a small place in the country.* **6.** a part or spot in a body, surface, etc.: *The dentist filled the decayed place in the tooth.* **7.** a particular page or other point in a book or other writing: *to mark one's place. This is the place where the story gets most exciting.* **8.** a fitting or reasonable ground or occasion: *A funeral is not the place for humor. There is a time and place for everything.* **9.** the proper or natural position or situation for a person or thing: *The country is not a place for a person of my temper* (Richard Addison). **10.** position or rank in any order of merit; standing: *We have not attempted to ascertain his place among historians* (William Gladstone). **11.** social position; rank in society; station: *In ancient times, a master and a slave had very different places in life.* **12.** position in time: *The performance went too slowly in several places.* **13.** space or a seat for a person, as in a theater, train, coach, etc.: *Try to save me a place if you board the train before I do. We took our places at the table. Many of the boys . . . will be found places at their nearest grammar schools* (Sunday Times). **14.** a situation, job, post, or office: *to get a place in a store. I know my price, I am worth no worse a place* (Shakespeare). **15.** official position; political power: *Nought's permanent among the human race, except the Whigs not getting into place* (Byron). **16.** official function; duty; business: *It's not the place of a newspaper to print rumors. It's not my place to find fault.* **17.** a step or point in any order of proceeding: *In the first place, the room is too small; in the second place, it is too dirty.* **18.** *Mathematics.* the position of a figure in a number or series, in decimal or any other notation: *in the third decimal place.* **19.** the position of a competitor or team at the end of or during a race or contest: *last place. The team was still in seventh place on July 4.* **20.** a ranking position, especially one of the first three, at the end of a race: *John outran his rival for a place.* **21.** the second position at the end of a horse race. **22.** a short street, court, etc. (now usually as part of a name): *Waverley Place. Abbr.:* Pl. **23.** an open space or square in a city, town, etc. **24.** space in general; extension in three dimensions (especially as contrasted with *time*): *He passed the flaming bounds of Place and Time* (Thomas Gray). **25.** *Astronomy.* the position of a heavenly body at any instant. **26.** in falconry: **a.** the pitch of a falcon or any other bird. **b.** the greatest elevation which it attains in its flight: *a falcon, towering in her pride of place* (Shakespeare). **27.** *Archaic.* space or room: *Place, nobles for the Falcon-Knight!* (Scott).

give or **make place, a.** to make room; step aside: *Make place! bear back there!* (Ben Jonson). **b.** to yield; give in: *The stern expression of his eye gradually gave place to a look of softness* (James Fenimore Cooper).

go places, *U.S. Slang.* to advance rapidly toward success; achieve success: *The young assistant manager is going places in his company.*

in place, a. in the proper or usual place; in the original place: *books in place on shelves.* **b.** fitting, appropriate, or timely; seasonable: *If Mr. Manss were not a successful pastor, he would be very much in place as a journalist* (Chicago Advance).

in the first place, first; firstly; before anything else: *Two thousand . . . lost their lives, and the priests in the first place* (Francis Brooke).

in (the) place of, instead of: *to use water in the place of milk, to receive extra pay in place of a vacation.*

know one's place, to be aware of and act according to one's position in life: *She was very uppity and could not be made to know her place.*

out of place, a. not in the proper or usual place: *The second volume seems to be out of place; I cannot find it on the shelf.* **b.** inappropriate or ill-timed; unsuitable: *Talk about the depths of being . . . is not always out of place, but it is mostly idle chatter* (J. M. Cameron).

places, *Mathematics.* the number of figures in a number or series, especially after the decimal point in a decimal: *to mark off three places.*

put (a person) in his place, to lower a person's dignity, as by a rebuke; humble or degrade: *The liberals had expected the Kennedy administration to put Franco sharply in his place* (Alastair Reid).

take place, a. to happen; occur: *Mr. Wilson reminded the House that the exploratory talks had been taking place* (Manchester Guardian Weekly). **b.** *Obsolete.* to take precedence: *Though Miss Crawford is in a manner at home at the Parsonage, you are not to be taking place of her* (Jane Austen).

—*v.t.* **1.** to put in a particular place; set in a specified position; station: *Guards had been placed at all the exits. The orphan was placed in a good home.* **2.** to put in the proper order or position; arrange; dispose: *He had fewer troops than his enemy, but he placed them with more skill.* **3.** to identify by connecting with the proper place, circumstances, etc.: *I am sure I have met you before, but I cannot place you.* **4.** to determine the date of; assign to an age, etc.: *Homer is usually placed about the 800's B.C.* **5.** to appoint (a person) to a position or office; install. **6.** to find a place or situation for (a person): *He had resolved to place me happily in the world* (Samuel Johnson). **7.** to entrust to an appropriate person, firm, etc., for action, treatment, disposal, or the like: *Orders for next year's Christmas cards have already been placed.* **8.** to attribute or ascribe: *She . . . places her disappointment . . . to her being . . . less affluent than many of her acquaintance* (Jane Austen). **9.** to decide or state the position of (a horse) at the end of a race, especially of the first three: *The favorite was not even placed.* **10.** to produce (sounds of song or speech) with emphasis upon resonance assisted by the body organs involved; pitch.

—*v.i.* **1.** to finish among the first three, or other stated number, in a race or competition: *The favorite failed to place in the first heat and was eliminated.* **2.** to finish second in a horse race.

[< Old French *place* < Vulgar Latin *plattia,* for Latin *platēa* courtyard; earlier, street < Greek *plateîa* (*hodós*) broad (way) < *platýs* broad. Doublet of PLAZA, PIAZZA.]

—**Syn.** *n.* **2. Place, position, location** mean a particular portion of space, or of the earth's surface. **Place** is the general term: *a quiet place, a strange place for storing books.* **Position** is place with respect to another place or places or within a framework or reference: *a lower position, the position of a star with regard to a ship's course. The enemy is in a good position to attack.* **Location** may be used for either *place* or *position,* but it stresses a little more than either of these the uniqueness or isolation of a place in relation to anything or everything outside it: *a good location for a housing project. The Crocker Ridge location also should give fine views of the peaks of the northern Yosemite* (Sierra Club Bulletin). **13.** room. *-v.t.* **1.** locate. See **put.**

place[2] (plȧs), *n. French.* a public square in a city or town; plaza.

place·a·ble (plā′sə bəl), *adj.* that can be placed.

place aux dames (plȧs ō dȧm′), *French.* (make) way for the ladies.

pla·ce·bo (plə sē′bō), *n., pl.* **-bos** or **-boes. 1.** (in the Roman Catholic Church) the vespers of the office for the dead, from the beginning of the opening antiphon with the word *placebo* (Psalms 114:9 of the Vulgate; Psalms 116:9 of the Authorized Version). **2.** a pill, preparation, etc., given to a person as medicine, but actually containing no active ingredients. Placebos are sometimes given for psychological effect, especially to satisfy or please a patient who actually needs no additional medicine. They are also used to establish the basis for a statistical control in testing the effectiveness of new medicines. *The bottle, as the doctor had reason to know, contained a placebo—sugar pills* (Time). **3.** a thing said merely to flatter, please, or mollify: *So arbitrary a substance seems more a placebo to quiet the disturbed mind than a valid explanation of a physical phenomenon* (John R. Pierce). [< Latin *placēbō* I shall please]

place card, a small card with a person's name on it, marking his place at a table.

place in the sun, a favorable position; as favorable a position as any occupied by others.

place kick, the kicking of a ball placed on or held near the ground in football, soccer, etc.

place-kick (plās′kik′), *v.i.* to make a place kick: *From specialist Ben Agajanian, who only place-kicks, to versatile Frank Gifford . . . the Giants were unstoppable* (Newsweek). —*v.t.* **1.** to kick (a ball) as a place kick. **2.** to score (points, a goal, etc.) by means of a place kick: *Tackle Bill Miller place-kicked four conversions* (New York Times). —**place′-kick′er,** *n.*

place·less (plās′lis), *adj.* **1.** having no place or locality; not local: *Combining abstract and representational elements in a vague, placeless locality, the Chilean Matta . . . presents a strange world of fantasy* (New York Times). **2.** having no employment or public office.

place·man (plās′mən), *n., pl.* **-men.** a person who holds or aspires to an appointment or office, especially public office, without regard to his fitness for it: *a Cabinet which contains, not placemen alone, but independent and popular noblemen and gentlemen* (Macaulay).

place mat, a mat of linen, plastic, paper, etc., put under each person's plate or table setting: *The milk poured out over the place mat and then traced little white rivulets over the dark surface of the table* (New Yorker).

place·ment (plās′mənt), *n.* **1.** a placing: *Representatives of the social agencies that really do the work of child placement answered* (New York Times). **2.** a being placed; location; arrangement. **3.** the finding of work or a job for a person. **4.** *Football.* **a.** a placing and holding of the ball on the ground for an attempt to kick a goal by a place kick. **b.** the position of the ball thus placed.

place name, a name of a place or locality; any geographical name. *Examples:* Athens, Asia, Samoa, Niagara Falls, Rio Grande, Black Sea, Arctic Ocean. *The place names in the struggle have become household words half across the world* (Punch).

pla·cen·ta (plə sen′tə), *n., pl.* **-tae** (-tē), **-tas. 1.** the organ by which the fetus is attached to the inner wall of the uterus and nourished: *Until the moment of birth a developing baby is entirely dependent upon the placenta* (Scientific American). **2.** the part of the ovary of flowering plants that bears the ovules, usually the enlarged or modified margins of the carpellary leaves. **3.** a structure that bears the sporangia in ferns. [< New Latin *placenta (uterina)* (uterine) cake < Latin *placenta* flat cake < Greek *plakoûs, -oûntos* placenta; flat seed of the mallow, short for *plakóeis* flat < *pláx, plakós* flat surface]

pla·cen·tal (plə sen′təl), *adj.* **1.** of or having to do with the placenta. **2.** having a placenta. —*n.* a placental mammal.

plac·en·tar·y (plas′ən ter′ē, plə sen′tər-), *adj., n., pl.* **-tar·ies.** —*adj.* **1.** of or having to do with the placenta; placental. **2.** made or done with reference to the placenta or to placentation: *a placentary classification.* —*n.* a placental mammal.

pla·cen·tate (plə sen′tāt), *adj.* placental.

plac·en·ta·tion (plas′ən tā′shən), *n.* **1.** the formation and disposition of the placenta in the uterus. **2.** the structure of the placenta. **3.** *Botany.* the disposition or arrangement of the placenta or placentae in the ovary.

pla·cen·ti·form (plə sen′tə fôrm), *adj.* having the form of a placenta.

plac·er[1] (plas′ər), *n.* **1.** a place where gold or other minerals can be washed out of loose sand or gravel. **2.** a deposit of sand, gravel, or earth in the bed of a stream, containing particles of gold or other valuable minerals. [American English < Spanish *placer,* variant of *placel* sandbank < *plaza;* see PLAZA]

plac·er[2] (plā′sər), *n.* a person or thing that places, locates, or sets.

placer mining, the washing of loose sand or gravel for gold or other minerals.

plac·es (plā′siz), *n.pl.* See under **place**[1], *n.*

pla·cet (plā′sit), *n.* an expression of assent or sanction; permission. [< Latin *placet* it pleases]

place value, the value of a digit as determined by its place in a whole number. In the number 1963 the place value of 1 is 1,000; of 9, 900; of 6, 60; and of 3, 3.

plac·id (plas′id), *adj.* pleasantly calm or peaceful; quiet: *The small restaurant had an intimate and placid atmosphere. I think I could . . . live with animals, they are so placid and self-contained* (Walt Whitman). [< Latin *placidus* < *placēre* to please]
—**Syn.** unruffled, tranquil, serene. See **peaceful.**

pla·cid·i·ty (plə sid′ə tē), *n.* calmness; tranquility; peacefulness. —**Syn.** serenity.

plac·id·ly (plas′id lē), *adv.* in a placid manner; quietly; without disturbance or passion.

plac·id·ness (plas′id nis), *n.* the state or character of being placid; calmness.

plack (plak), *n.* **1.** a small coin of little value, formerly current in Scotland. **2.** *Scottish.* a bit; scarcely anything: *His offer isn't worth a plack.* [origin uncertain. Compare Middle Dutch *placke,* Old French *plaque* a coin.]

plack·et (plak′it), *n.* **1.** an opening or slit in a garment, especially at the top of a skirt, to make it easy to put on. **2.** a pocket in a skirt. **3.** *Archaic.* **a.** an apron. **b.** a petticoat. **c.** a woman. [perhaps (originally) *placcat* a kind of undergarment or armor, apparently variant of *placard*]

placket hole, 1. an opening to give access to a pocket in a skirt. **2.** a placket.

plack·less (plak′lis), *adj. Scottish.* without a plack; penniless.

plac·o·derm (plak′ə dėrm), *n.* any of a class of extinct sharklike fishes having primitive jaws, and hard, bony plates covering the body. The placoderms were the marine counterparts of the armored dinosaurs. *During the Devonian Period . . . [the agnatha] gradually disappeared and were replaced by the placoderms, which retained the armor and acquired primitive jaws and paired fins* (Scientific American). [< Greek *pláx, plakós* flat surface + *dérma* skin]

Silurian Placoderm

plac·oid (plak′oid), *adj.* **1.** platelike, as the hard, spiny scales of a shark. **2.** having platelike scales. —*n.* any fish having placoid scales. [< New Latin *Placoidei* the group name < Greek *pláx, plakós* flat surface + *eîdos* form]

pla·fond (plȧ fôN′), *n. Architecture.* a ceiling, either flat or vaulted, especially one of a decorative character: *There I entered the Wine House, a restaurant with a painted ceiling—all cupids, like the plafond of a municipal theatre in a small French city* (New Yorker). [< earlier French *plafond* ceiling < *plat* flat (see PLAT[1]) + *fond* bottom. Compare FOND[2], FUND.]

pla·gal (plā′gəl), *adj. Music.* **1.** designating a cadence in which the chord of the subdominant immediately precedes that of the tonic. **2.** (in Gregorian music) designating a mode that has its compass a fourth below that of the corresponding authentic mode. The keynote (final tone) is the same as in the authentic mode (the fourth tone of the plagal mode). [< Medieval Latin *plagalis* < *plaga* plagal mode, apparently alteration of *plagius* plagal < Medieval Greek *plagios* < Greek, oblique < *plágos* side]

plage[1] (plāj), *n.* a bright and intensely hot cloud in the sun's chromosphere, usually, but not always, accompanying and surrounding a sunspot. Plages are primarily composed of calcium and hydrogen and emit very short ultraviolet rays. *We see also the bright clouds, called plages or faculae that accompany sunspots, floating low in the atmosphere* (Scientific American). [< French *plage* region, zone, learned borrowing from Latin *plaga*]

plage[2] (plȧzh), *n. French.* a beach; seaside resort: *Along the lake front . . . a plage that is dotted during the day with bright-hued parasols* (New Yorker).

pla·gia·rism (plā′jə riz əm), *n.* **1.** the act of plagiarizing: *If an author is once detected in borrowing, he will be suspected of plagiarism ever after* (William Hazlitt). **2.** an idea, expression, plot, etc., taken from another and used as one's own. [< Latin *plagiārius* literary thief, kidnaper; earlier, plunderer (< *plaga* snare, net) + English *-ism*]

pla·gia·rist (plā′jər ist), *n.* a person who plagiarizes: *We then spoke of Newton's controversy with Leibnitz . . . and how Newton attempted to prove that his German contemporary was a plagiarist* (Scientific American).

pla·gia·ris·tic (plā′jə ris′tik), *adj.* **1.** like a plagiarist. **2.** having to do with or like plagiarism. —**pla′gia·ris′ti·cal·ly,** *adv.*

pla·gia·rize (plā′jə rīz), *v.,* **-rized, -riz·ing.** —*v.t.* to take (the thoughts, writings, inventions, etc., of another) and use as one's own, especially, to take and use (a passage, plot, etc., from the work of another writer): *I could not help plagiarizing Miss Hannah More's first line* (Harriet Beecher Stowe). —*v.i.* to take ideas, passages, etc., and represent them as one's own: *He even had doubts whether in 'The Silent Places,' he had been plagiarizing, more or less unconsciously, from Henry James's 'Great Good Place'* (H. G. Wells). —**pla′gia·riz′er,** *n.*

pla·gia·ry (plā′jər ē), *n., pl.* **-ries. 1.** plagiarism: *Such kind of borrowing . . . if it be not bettered by the borrower, among good authors is accounted plagiary* (Milton). **2.** a plagiarist. [< Latin *plagiārius* literary thief; see PLAGIARISM]

pla·gi·o·clase (plā′jē ə klās), *n.* triclinic feldspar having its two prominent cleavage directions oblique to one another. [< German *Plagioklas* < Greek *plágios* oblique + *klásis* cleavage]

pla·gi·o·clas·tic (plā′jē ə klas′tik), *adj. Mineralogy.* characterized by two different cleavage directions oblique to each other, as certain feldspars.

pla·gi·o·trop·ic (plā′jē ə trop′ik), *adj.* **1.** of or having to do with plagiotropism. **2.** exhibiting plagiotropism; growing in a position which is more or less divergent from the vertical, as many lateral branches and roots. —**pla′gi·o·trop′i·cal·ly,** *adv.*

pla·gi·o·tro·pism (plā′jē ot′rə piz əm), *n.* a turning by which the organs of certain plants take up an oblique position more or less divergent from the vertical, as the result of reacting differently to the influences of light, gravitation, and other external forces. [< Greek *plágios* oblique, slanting + English *tropism*]

plague (plāg), *n., v.,* **plagued, pla·guing.** —*n.* **1.** a very dangerous disease that spreads rapidly and often causes many deaths. It occurs in several forms, one of which is bubonic plague. The plague is common in Asia and has several times swept through Europe. *Plague, the dreaded "Black Death" of the Middle Ages, may exist in non-fatal chronic form, contrary to long-standing assumptions of medical science* (Science News Letter). **2.** a thing or person that torments, vexes, annoys, troubles, offends, or is disagreeable: *a plague of counterfeit money.* **3.** *Informal.* trouble. **4.** a punishment thought to be sent from God: *the ten plagues of Egypt.*

plague on or **plague take,** may a plague, or mischief of some kind, befall (a thing, person, etc.): *Plague take the fellow!*
—*v.t.* **1. a.** to cause to suffer from a plague: *The Lord plagued Pharaoh and his house with great plagues* (Genesis 12:17). **b.** to trouble or torment in any manner: *God save thee, ancient Mariner! From the fiends, that plague thee thus!* (Samuel Taylor Coleridge). **2.** to vex; annoy; bother: *The little boy plagued his father with questions.*
[Middle English *plage* < Middle French *plague,* learned borrowing from Late Latin *plāga* pestilence, < Latin, blow[1], wound[1], probably related to *plangere* to strike]
—**pla′guer,** *n.* —**Syn.** *v.t.* **2.** trouble, worry, pester, harass. See **tease.**

plague spot, 1. a spot on the body which is due to a plague or pestilence. **2.** a locality where there is a plague. **3.** a seat of some grave or foul evil: *a plague spot of vice. The town was a plague spot of rebellion.*

plague-strick·en (plāg′strik′ən), *adj.* stricken with a plague or pestilence.

pla·gui·ly (plā′gə lē), *adv. Informal.* plaguy.

pla·guy or **pla·guey** (plā′gē), *Informal.* —*adj.* **1.** troublesome; annoying. **2.** excessive; very great. —*adv.* vexatiously; exceedingly: *It was plaguy hard on a fellow . . . to be gulled that way* (Harriet Beecher Stowe).

plaice (plās), *n., pl.* **plaice** or (*occasionally*) **plaic·es. 1.** a large European flatfish, sometimes weighing more than ten pounds, much used for food in Great Britain and parts of Europe. **2.** any of certain related American flatfishes or flounders. [< Old French *plaïs* < Late Latin *platessa* flatfish < Greek *platýs* flat[1]]

plaid (plad), *n.* **1.** any cloth with a pattern of checks or crisscross stripes, in various colors. **2.** a pattern of this kind; tartan. **3.** a long piece of twilled woolen cloth, usually having a pattern of checks or stripes in many colors, worn about the shoulders by the Scottish Highlanders: *The Gael around him threw His graceful plaid of varied hue* (Scott).
—*adj.* having a pattern of checks or crisscross stripes: *a plaid dress.*
[< Scottish Gaelic *plaide* blanket, mantle]
—**Syn.** *adj.* checkered.

Plaid (def. 3)

plaid·ed (plad′id), *adj.* **1.** made of plaid. **2.** having a plaid pattern. **3.** wearing a plaid.

plaid·o·yer (pled′wə yā′), *n. Law.* the speech of an advocate; a pleading; plea: *Legally, the testimony of these witnesses was immaterial—Mr. Hauser did not mention one of them in his last plaidoyer* (Hannah Arendt). [< French, noun use of *plaidoyer* to plead < *plaid* plea; see PLEA]

plain[1] (plān), *adj.* **1.** easily seen or heard; evident; obvious; manifest: *The meaning is plain. It was plain he was offended.* **2.** not very hard; easy: *Tell me what you want in a few plain words.* **3.** that is clearly what the name expresses; unmistakable; downright; absolute: *plain foolishness.* **4.** not intricate; uncomplicated: *plain sewing.* **5.** straightforward; direct: *to give a plain answer to a question.* **6.** outspoken; candid; frank: *plain speech. I will sing a song if anybody will sing another; else, to be plain with you, I will sing none* (Izaak Walton). **7.** without ornament, decoration, or bright color; simple: *a plain dress.* **8.** without figured pattern, varied weave, or variegated colors: *a plain blue dress.* **9.** not rich or highly seasoned: *plain cake, a plain diet.* **10.** simple in manner; not distinguished by rank, culture, position, etc.; common; ordinary: *I preached to several hundred of plain people* (John Wesley). **11.** not beautiful; homely: *Eliza and Maria . . . were neither exactly pretty nor exactly plain* (Samuel Butler). **12.** flat; level; smooth: *plain ground. The crooked shall be made straight, and the rough places plain* (Isaiah 40:4). **13.** without obstructions; open; clear: *in plain sight or view.* **14.** in cards: **a.** not a court card or an ace. **b.** not trumps.
—*adv.* in a plain manner; clearly.
—*n.* **1.** a flat stretch of land; tract of level or

nearly level land. **2.** a broad, level expanse, as a lunar sea: *Whether or not the maria were ever seas—now at least, they are and for millions of years have been what we call plains* (Bernhard, Bennet, and Rice).
plains, (especially in North America) a level, treeless, or almost treeless, tract of country; prairie: *the Great Plains. Cattle and horses wandered over the plains.*
the Plain, (in French history) a moderate party in the Legislative Assembly and the National Convention of the French Revolution (so called from its occupying seats on the main floor).
[< Old French *plain* < Latin *plānus* flat[1], level. Doublet of PIANO[2], PLAN, PLANE[1].]
—**Syn.** *adj.* **1.** apparent. **2.** intelligible, simple. **3.** undisguised, sheer. **6.** unaffected. **7.** unembellished.

plain[2] (plān), *v.i. Archaic and Dialect.* to complain. [< Old French *plaign-*, stem of *plaindre*, earlier *plaingre* < Latin *plangere* lament, (literally) beat the breast]

plain chant, plain song.

plain·clothes (plān′klōz′, -klōᴛʜz′), *adj.* not in uniform when on duty.

plain clothes, the ordinary dress of civil life; nonofficial dress.

plain·clothes·man (plān′klōz′mən, -klōᴛʜz′-), *n., pl.* **-men.** a policeman or detective wearing ordinary clothes, not a uniform, when on duty: *In come the neighbors, the police are called, plainclothesmen arrive, along with a reporter and photographer* (New Yorker).

plain dealer, a person who deals frankly and honestly with others.

plain dealing, frank, honest dealing with others.

plain·er (plā′nər), *n. Dialect.* a complainer.

plain Jane, a girl or woman who is ordinary, homely, or unsophisticated: *[She] was a plain Jane with weird endearing ways* (Time).

plain-Jane (plān′jān′), *adj. Informal.* homely; simple; ordinary: *From these plain-Jane foundations, the author builds a fascinating and terrifying tale* (New Yorker).

plain-laid (plān′lād′), *adj.* (of a rope) made by twisting three strands together from left to right or clockwise with the ends held away.

plain·ly (plān′lē), *adv.* in a plain manner; clearly; manifestly; frankly; simply.

plain·ness (plān′nis), *n.* the state or quality of being plain.

Plain People, any of several religious groups, including the Amish and the Mennonites, who stress simplicity in clothing and in living: *The Amish are the strictest group of the Pennsylvania Dutch or Plain People, who settled in Lancaster County in 1727* (London Times).

plains (plānz), *n.pl.* See under **plain**[1], *n.*

plain sail, 1. the sails used in ordinary sailing, collectively, as distinguished from flying sails, etc. **2.** any one of these sails.

plain sailing, 1. sailing on a smooth, easy course, free of difficulty or obstruction. **2.** a simple or easy course of action; clear path or line of progress: *Albert had foreseen that his married life would not be all plain sailing* (Lytton Strachey).

Plains Indian (plānz), a member of any of the tribes of North American Indians which formerly inhabited the Great Plains. They were of various linguistic stocks (Algonkian, Athapascan, Caddoan, Kiowan, Siouan, Uto-Aztecan), but shared a culture based on their nomadic following of the buffalo.

plains·man (plānz′mən), *n., pl.* **-men.** a man who lives on the plains; inhabitant or native of flat country: *The coolies . . . fled up the hill as fast as plainsmen run across the level* (Rudyard Kipling).

plain song, 1. vocal music used in the Christian church from the earliest times. Plain song is sung in unison. It is rhythmical although the beats are not regular. **2.** a melody taken as the theme for a contrapuntal treatment. **3.** any simple melody or musical theme.

plain-spo·ken (plān′spō′kən), *adj.* plain or frank in speech: *He is athletic, pugnacious, and plain-spoken and the very opposite of retiring* (New York Times). —**plain′-spo′ken·ness,** *n.* —**Syn.** blunt, outspoken, candid.

plain·stones (plān′stōnz′), *n.pl. Scottish.* flagstones.

plaint (plānt), *n.* **1.** a complaint. **2.** *Law.* an oral or written statement of the cause for an action. **3.** *Archaic.* a lament. [< Old French *plaint* < Latin *plānctus, -ūs* lamentation < *plangere* to lament, beat the breast]

plain·text (plān′tekst′), *n.* **1.** the text of any message that conveys an intelligible meaning in the language in which it is written, having no hidden meaning. **2.** the intelligible text intended for, or derived from, a cryptogram: *Cryptography aims at making the message unintelligible to outsiders by various transformations of the plaintext* (Scientific American).

plain·tiff (plān′tif), *n. Law.* a person who begins a lawsuit: *The plaintiff accused the defendant of fraud.* [< Anglo-French *plaintiff,* noun use of Old French *plaintif* complaining; see PLAINTIVE]

plain·tive (plān′tiv), *adj.* mournful; sad: *a plaintive song, the plaintive cry of a bird.* [< Old French *plaintif, plaintive* < *plaint* plaint] —**plain′tive·ly,** *adv.* —**plain′tive·ness,** *n.* —**Syn.** melancholy, doleful, sorrowful.

plain tripe, the walls of the first stomach or rumen of a ruminant animal, especially of a steer or cow, used as food.

plain-wo·ven (plān′wō′vən), *adj.* woven with a plain or simple weave, without twill, figure, or the like.

plai·sance (plā zäns′; *French* ple zäɴs′), *n.* a pleasure ground, or place of amusements: *the Midway Plaisance at Chicago in 1893.* [< Old French *plaisance* pleasure. Doublet of PLEASANCE.]

plais·ter (plās′tər), *n., v.t. Obsolete.* plaster.

plait (plāt, plat *for n., v. 1;* plāt, plēt *for n., v. 2*), *n.* **1.** *Especially British.* a braid: *She wore her hair in a plait.* **2.** a pleat.
—*v.t.* **1.** to braid: *She plaits her hair.* **2.** to pleat: *[He] wore his shirt plaited and puffed out* (Washington Irving).
[< Old French *pleit* fold[1], way of folding < Latin *plicitum,* variant of *plicātum,* neuter past participle of *plicāre* to fold. Doublet of PLEAT, PLIGHT[1].]

plan (plan), *n., v.,* **planned, plan·ning.** —*n.* **1.** a way of making or doing something that has been worked out beforehand; scheme of action: *Our summer plans were upset by Mother's illness.* **2.** a way of proceeding; method: *The good old rule . . . the simple plan, That they should take, who have the power, And they should keep who can* (Wordsworth). **3.** a drawing or diagram to show how a garden, a floor of a house, a park, etc., is arranged. **4.** a drawing or diagram of any object, made by projection upon a flat surface, usually a horizontal plane.
—*v.t.* **1.** to think out beforehand how (something) is to be made or done; design; scheme; devise: *I plan to reach New York by train on Tuesday and stay two days.* **2.** to make a plan of; prepare a drawing or diagram of. —*v.i.* to make a plan or plans.
[< earlier French *plan* ground plan; plane surface, learned borrowing from Latin *plānus* flat[1]. Doublet of PIANO[2], PLAIN[1], PLANE[1].]
—**Syn.** *n.* **1. Plan, design, project** mean a proposed way of doing or making something. **Plan** is the general term: *He has a plan for increasing production.* **Design** applies to a plan carefully contrived to achieve a given effect, purpose, or goal: *They have a design for a rich, full life.* **Project** applies to a plan proposed for trial or experiment, often on a grand scale and sometimes impracticable: *He introduced a project for slum clearance.*

pla·nar (plā′nər), *adj.* of, having to do with, or situated in a plane.

pla·nar·i·an (plə när′ē ən), *n.* any of a group of fresh-water, turbellarian flatworms, characterized by an intestine divided into three main branches: *A flatworm known as the planarian can even grow a new head to replace one that it has lost* (World Book Encyclopedia).
—*adj.* belonging to the planarians.
[< New Latin *Planaria* the earlier genus name (< feminine of Late Latin *plānārius* level, as ground < Latin *plānus* flat[1], level) + English *-an*]

pla·nar·i·ty (plə nar′ə tē), *n.* the quality or state of being planar; flatness: *the planarity of the molecular structure.*

pla·na·tion (plā nā′shən), *n. Geology.* the process of erosion and deposition by which a stream produces a nearly level land surface. [< Latin *plānum* plane[1] + English *-ation*]

planch or **planche** (planch, plänch), *n.* **1.** a slab or flat piece or metal, stone, baked clay, etc. **2.** *Dialect.* **a.** a plank; board. **b.** a floor. [< Old French *planche* < Late Latin *planca* board, slab. Doublet of PLANK.]

plan·chet (plan′chit), *n.* a flat piece of metal to be stamped to form a coin. [< *planch* + *-et;* see PLANCH]

plan·chette (plan shet′), *n.* a small board supported on two casters and a vertical pencil. The pencil is supposed to write words, sentences, etc., when a person rests his fingers lightly on the planchette. [earlier, small plank < French *planchette* (diminutive) < Old French *planche* plank; see PLANCH]

Planck's constant (plangks), *Physics.* a universal constant having the value of the ratio of the energy of a quantum to its frequency, that is, energy equals Planck's constant times frequency: *The basic unit of angular momentum is Planck's constant divided by 4π, that is h/4π* (H. J. Bhaba). *Symbol:* h; *Value:* 6.624×10^{-27} erg-sec. [< Max *Planck,* 1858-1947, a German physicist, who first recognized it]

plane[1] (plān), *n., adj., v.,* **planed, plan·ing.** —*n.* **1.** a flat or level surface of a material body. **2.** a level; grade: *Try to keep your work on a high plane.* **3.** a thin, flat, or curved supporting surface of an airplane. **4.** an airplane: *Despite the $4 billion a year being spent, the kill-rate against even a flight of relatively slow propeller-driven planes would be well below 100 per cent* (Newsweek). **5.** *Geometry.* a surface such that if any two points on it are joined by a straight line, the line will be contained wholly in the surface.
—*adj.* **1.** flat; level; not convex or concave. **2.** having a flat or level surface. **3.** being wholly in a plane: *a plane figure.* **4.** of or having to do with figures wholly in a plane: *plane geometry*
—*v.i.* **1.** to travel by airplane: *The President's son planed in from Washington* (Time). **2.** to glide or soar, as an airplane does. **3.** (of a boat, etc.) to rise slightly out of the water while moving at great speed.
[< Latin *plānum* level surface, and *plānus,* adjective, level. Doublet of PIANO[2], PLAIN[1], PLAN.]

plane[2] (plān), *n., v.,* **planed, plan·ing.** —*n.* **1.** a carpenter's tool with an adjustable, chisel-like blade for smoothing or shaping wood. **2.** a machine for smoothing or removing metal. **3.** a mason's tool resembling a large wooden trowel, used to smooth or level the surface of clay, of sand in a mold, etc.

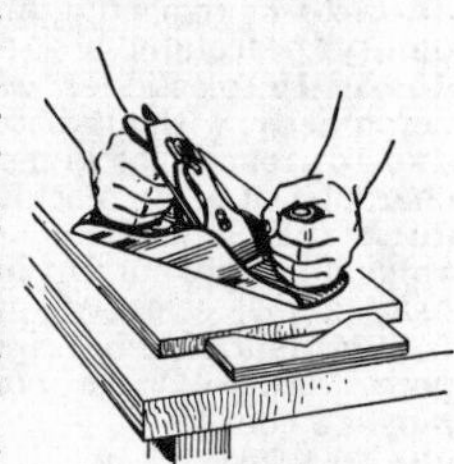
Plane[2] (def. 1)

—*v.t.* **1.** to smooth or level with a plane; use a plane on. **2.** to remove or shave with a plane. —*v.i.* **1.** to work with or use a plane: *a rosy-cheeked Englishman . . . up to his knees in shavings, and planing away at a bench* (Herman Melville). **2.** to function or be intended to function as a plane.
[< Old French *plane* < Latin *plāna* < *plānāre* make level < *plānus* plain[1]]

plane[3] (plān), *n. British.* the plane tree; sycamore. [< Middle French *plane* < Latin *platanus* < Greek *plátanos* < *platýs* broad (because of the shape of its leaf). Doublet of PLANTAIN[1].]

plane angle, an angle formed by the intersection of two straight lines in the same plane.

plane geometry, the branch of geometry that deals with figures lying in one plane.

plane iron, the cutting blade of a plane.

plane·load (plān′lōd′), *n.* a full load of passengers or freight in an aircraft: *a planeload of heavy machinery or weapons.*

plane·mak·er (plān′mā′kər), *n. U.S.* an aircraft manufacturer: *To survive, many a planemaker has diversified to other fields* (Time).

plane·ness (plān′nis), *n.* the condition of being plane, or of having a plane surface.

plane-po·lar·ized (plān′pō′lər īzd), *adj.* (of light) polarized so that all the vibrations of the waves take place in one plane.

plane-post (plān′pōst′), *v.t. British.* to send or convey (letters, etc.) by plane post.
plane post, *British.* a postal service conducted by airplane; an air post.
plan·er (plā′nər), *n.* a person or thing that planes, especially a machine for planing wood or for finishing flat surfaces on metal.
planer tree, a small tree of the elm family, of the southeastern United States, producing a small, oval, nutlike fruit and having a hard, light-brown wood. [< New Latin *Planera* the genus name < Johann J. *Planer,* 1743-1789, a German botanist]
plane sailing, the navigation of a vessel in which courses are plotted and distances estimated as if the earth's surface were a plane.
plane-shear (plān′shir′), *n.* plank-sheer; gunwale.
plane spotter, a person, usually a civilian volunteer, who watches for and reports the presence of enemy, or any unidentified, aircraft in an area of the sky.
plan·et (plan′it), *n.* **1.** one of the heavenly bodies (except comets or meteors) that revolve around the sun. Mercury, Venus, Earth, Mars, Jupiter, Saturn, Uranus, Neptune, and Pluto are planets. Other planets are the asteroids or planetoids between Mars and Jupiter. *What one realizes first about the planets is their appearance and disappearance in the nightly sky, their stations and retrogradations* (Science). *Observe how system into system runs, What other planets circle other suns* (Alexander Pope). **2.** (in astrology) a heavenly body supposed to influence people's lives and events. **3.** anything thought to exert such influence. **4.** *Obsolete.* one of the seven heavenly bodies (the sun, the moon, Mercury, Venus, Mars, Jupiter, and Saturn) known since ancient times and distinguished by ancient peoples from the fixed stars in that they seem to move among the fixed stars, when viewed from Earth. [< Old French *planete,* learned borrowing from Late Latin *planētēs,* plural < Greek *planêtes* (*astéres*) wandering stars < *planâsthai* to wander]
plane table, an instrument used in the field for surveying, plotting maps, etc., consisting of a drawing board mounted on a tripod, and having an alidade pivoted over its center.
plan·e·tar·i·um (plan′ə tãr′ē əm), *n., pl.* **-tar·i·a** (-tãr′ē ə), **-tar·i·ums. 1.** an apparatus that shows the movements of the sun, moon, planets, and stars by projecting lights on the inside of a dome shaped like a hemisphere. **2.** a room or building with such an apparatus. **3.** any plan, model, or structure representing the planetary system, such as the orrery: *Designed primarily as a planetarium for the astronomical instruction of the emperor's children, it also banged on gongs every quarter hour* (Newsweek). [< New Latin *planetarium* < Latin *planētārius* astrologer; (literally) having to do with planets < *planētēs;* see PLANET]
plan·e·tar·y (plan′ə ter′ē), *adj.* **1.** of a planet; having to do with planets: *Planetary satellites turn only fast enough to present the same face to their planet* (Time). **2.** wandering; erratic. **3.** of or belonging to the earth; terrestrial; mundane. **4.** having to do with a form of transmission for varying the speed transmitted from an engine: *the planetary gears of an automobile.* **5.** moving in an orbit. **6.** (in astrology) having to do with a planet or the planets as exerting influence on mankind and events.

PLANETARY GEAR
SUN GEAR

Planetary Gears (def. 4) of an automobile (pinions) each turn on their own axes while rotating around the central sun gear.

planetary nebula, a nebula consisting of an envelope of gas many billions of miles in diameter surrounding a very hot star. The famous Ring Nebula in Lyra is a planetary nebula.
planetary wave, *Meteorology.* a strong current of air, 30,000 to 40,000 feet above the earth's surface, that circles the earth in the Northern Hemisphere, flowing generally from west to east: *Meteorologists call this great meandering current, which circles the earth, the planetary wave* (Science News Letter).
planetary wind, planetary wave.
plan·e·tes·i·mal (plan′ə tes′ə məl), *adj.* of or having to do with the planetesimal hypothesis. —*n.* one of the minute bodies of the planetesimal hypothesis: *The mass of gas eventually cooled, congealing into small solid lumps, the planetesimals* (Atlantic). [< *planet* + *-esimal,* as in *infinitesimal*]
planetesimal hypothesis or **theory,** the hypothesis that minute bodies in space move in planetary orbits and gradually unite to form the planets of a given planetary system.
plan·et·oid (plan′ə toid), *n.* a very small planet; asteroid: *Scientists like to think that these planetoids may be pieces of a big planet that once upon a time traveled around the sun between Mars and Jupiter* (Beauchamp, Mayfield, and West). [< *planet* + *-oid*]
plan·et·oi·dal (plan′ə toi′dəl), *adj.* of, having to do with, or like a planetoid.
plan·et·ol·o·gy (plan′ə tol′ə jē), *n.* the scientific study of the planets: *General planetology [is] ... a branch of astronomy that deals with the study and interpretation of the physical and chemical properties of planets* (New Scientist).
plane tree, any of a group of tall, spreading trees, with broad, angular, palmately lobed leaves and bark that scales off in irregular patches, as one kind, a native of Iran and the Levant, commonly planted as an ornamental tree in Europe; platan. In the United States, plane trees are usually called buttonwood, sycamore, or buttonball.
plan·et-strick·en (plan′it strik′ən), *adj.* planet-struck.
plan·et-struck (plan′it struk′), *adj.* **1.** stricken by the supposed influence of a planet; blasted. **2.** panic-stricken.
planet wheel, any of the cogwheels, gears, etc., in an epicyclic train, whose axes revolve around the common center, or central gear.
plan·form (plan′fôrm′), *n.* the form or shape of an object, as an airfoil, as seen from above: *A greater proportion of the planform might be filled with passengers* (New Scientist).
plan·gen·cy (plan′jən sē), *n.* the state or quality of being plangent.
plan·gent (plan′jənt), *adj.* **1.** making the noise of waves breaking or beating on the shore: *the weltering of the plangent wave* (Sir Henry Taylor). **2.** resounding loudly: *St. Margaret's bells ... Hark! how those plangent comforters call and cry* (William Ernest Henley). [< Latin *plangēns, -entis,* present participle of *plangere* to beat the breast, lament] —**plan′gent·ly,** *adv.*
plan·gor·ous (plang′gər əs), *adj.* characterized by loud lamentation; wailing. [< Latin *plangor* (< *plangere* to lament) + English *-ous*]
plan·i·fi·ca·tion (plan′ə fə kā′shən), *n.* the act or process of planning: *economic planification.* [< French *planification* < *plan;* see PLAN]
pla·nim·e·ter (plə nim′ə tər), *n.* an instrument for measuring mechanically the area of plane figures by tracing their boundaries with a pointer. [< Latin *plānus* level + English *-meter*]
plan·i·met·ric (plan′ə met′rik), *adj.* having to do with planimetry or the measurement of plane surfaces.
plan·i·met·ri·cal (plan′ə met′rə kəl), *adj.* planimetric.
pla·nim·e·try (plə nim′ə trē), *n.* the measurement of plane surfaces.
pla·ni·ros·tral (plā′nə ros′trəl), *adj.* having a broad, flat beak. [< Latin *plānus* flat + English *rostral*]
plan·ish (plan′ish), *v.t.* to flatten, smooth, or toughen (metal) by hammering lightly, rolling, etc. [< obsolete French *planiss-,* stem of *planir* to smooth < *plan* plain[1], level]
plan·i·sphere (plan′ə sfir), *n.* a projection or representation of the whole or a part of a sphere on a plane, especially a map of half or more of the celestial sphere with an adjustable device to show the part of the heavens visible at a given time. [< Medieval Latin *planisphaerium* < Latin *plānus* plain[1], flat + *sphaera* sphere < Greek *sphaîra*]
pla·ni·spi·ral (plā′nə spī′rəl), *adj.* planospiral.
plank (plangk), *n.* **1.** a long, flat piece of sawed timber, especially one more than two inches thick and four inches wide. **2.** timber consisting of such pieces; planking. **3.** a flat timber forming part of the outer side of a ship's hull. **4.** *U.S.* an article or feature of the platform of a political party: *State's rights ... a major plank in his election campaign* (New York Times). **5.** anything that supports or saves in time of need (with allusion to the use of a plank to save a shipwrecked man from drowning).
walk the plank, a. to walk off a plank extending from a ship's side over the water. Pirates used to make their prisoners do this: *It would have been necessary for Howe and Nelson to make every French sailor whom they took walk the plank* (Macaulay). **b.** to be dismissed from one's job: *His work was unsatisfactory and it was not long before he walked the plank.*
—*v.t.* **1.** to furnish, lay, floor, or cover with planks. **2.** to cook and serve on a board, often with a decorative border of vegetables and potatoes: *planked steak, fish, etc.* **3.** *Informal.* to put or set with force: *He planked down the package. He finished the glass and planked it down firmly on the table* (Arnold Bennett). **4.** *Informal.* to pay at once: *She planked out her money.*
[< Old North French, Old French *planche* < Late Latin *planca* board, marble slab. Doublet of PLANCH.]
plank·ing (plang′king), *n.* **1.** the act or process of laying or covering with planks. **2.** planks collectively. **3.** the outer side of a ship's hull.
plank-sheer (plangk′shir′), *n.* one of the planks laid across the tops of the ribs or the frame of the hull of a ship at the line of the deck; gunwale.
plank·ton (plangk′tən), *n.* the small animal and plant organisms that float or drift in water, especially at or near the surface at night. It includes small crustaceans, algae, protozoans, etc., and serves as an important source of food for larger animals, such as fish. *Fine mesh nets are towed from a ship to bring up hundreds of kinds of microscopic sea life, lumped under the general name of plankton* (Science News Letter). [< German *Plankton* < Greek *planktón,* neuter of *planktós* wandering, drifting < *plázesthai* to wander]
plank·ton·ic (plangk ton′ik), *adj.* **1.** of or having to do with plankton. **2.** characteristic of plankton.
plan·less (plan′lis), *adj.* without a plan or design; haphazard; unsystematic: *Like the U.S. itself, ... Britain in 1960 is a victim of "urban sprawl," the planless mushrooming of cities* (Time). *She made me feel more planless and incidental than ever* (H.G. Wells). —**plan′less·ly,** *adv.* —**plan′less·ness,** *n.* —**Syn.** disorderly.
planned parenthood, birth control.
plan·ner (plan′ər), *n.* a person who plans or makes a plan; deviser; arranger: *Secret intelligence reports on the Soviet Army have given U.S. planners an unexpected jolt* (Newsweek).
plan·o·blast (plan′ə blast), *n.* the free-swimming form of certain hydrozoans. [< Greek *plános* wandering + *blastós* germ, sprout]
pla·no-con·cave (plā′nō kon′kāv, -kong′-), *adj.* flat on one side and concave on the other. [< Latin *plānus* flat + English *concave*]
pla·no-con·vex (plā′nō kon′veks), *adj.* flat on one side and convex on the other. [< Latin *plānus* flat + English *convex*]
pla·no-cy·lin·dri·cal (plā′nō sə lin′drə kəl), *adj.* flat on one side and cylindrical on the other. [< Latin *plānus* flat]
pla·no·graph (plā′nə graf, -gräf), *v.t.* to print from a plane surface. —*n.* a print, etc., made by planography.
plan·o·graph·ic (plan′ə graf′ik), *adj.* **1.** having to do with planography. **2.** used in planography. **3.** produced by planography: *Offset is a planographic technique.*
plan·og·ra·phist (pla nog′rə fist), *n.* a person who prints by means of planography.
plan·og·ra·phy (pla nog′rə fē), *n.* printing done from plane surfaces, as in lithography, collotype, and offset, in contrast to intaglio or relief work. [< Latin *plānus* level + English *-graphy*]
pla·nom·e·ter (plə nom′ə tər), *n.* a flat plate, usually of iron, used as a standard gauge for plane surfaces. [< Latin *plānus* flat + English *-meter*]

pla·no·spi·ral (plā′nō spī′rəl), *adj.* coiled in one plane: *The shell of the nautilus is planospiral.* [< Latin *plānus* flat + English *spiral*]

plant (plant, plänt), *n.* **1.** a member of the lower of the two series of organized living beings, the vegetable kingdom; a vegetable, in the widest sense. A plant is generally distinguished from an animal by the absence of locomotion and of special organs of sensation and digestion, and by its power of living wholly upon inorganic substances. Trees, shrubs, herbs, fungi, algae, etc., are plants. *Some animals . . . spend their entire adult lives in a fixed position while many plants are able to move freely from place to place* (Scientific American). **2.** an herb or other small vegetable growth, in contrast with a tree or a shrub: *a tomato plant, a house plant.* **3.** a shoot or slip recently sprouted from seed, or rooted as a cutting or layer. **4.** such a slip ready for transplanting. **5.** the fixtures, implements, machinery, apparatus, and often the buildings used in carrying on any industrial process, as manufacturing some article, producing power, etc.: *an aircraft plant, a power plant.* **6.** the workmen employed at a plant: *The whole plant is on strike.* **7.** the complete apparatus used for a specific mechanical operation or process: *the heating plant on a ship.* **8.** the complete equipment for any purpose: *a plant of a few hundred aeroplanes . . . armed with machine guns, and the motor repair vans and so forth needed to go with the aeroplanes* (H.G. Wells). **9.** the buildings, equipment, or any other material resources belonging to, or needed to maintain, an institution: *No one knows the total cost of bringing the U.S. educational plant up to the size required to handle expected enrollments* (Wall Street Journal). **10.** *Slang.* a scheme or plot to swindle or defraud a person: "*It's a conspiracy,*" *said Ben Allen.* "*A regular plant,*" *added Mr. Bob Sawyer* (Dickens). **11.** *Slang.* a person or thing so placed or a plan so devised as to trap, trick, lure, or deceive criminals or wrongdoers. **12.** a person, supposedly a member of the audience, who assists a performer on the stage: *a magician's plant.*
—*v.t.* **1.** to put or set in the ground to take root and grow, as seeds, young trees, shoots, cuttings, etc.: *to plant potatoes.* **2.** to lay out and prepare by putting or setting seed, etc., in the ground; furnish with plants: *to plant a garden, an orchard, or a crop, to plant a field with trees. Growers are expected to plant 17,443,000 acres to cotton this year* (New York Times). **3.** to set or place firmly; put or fix in position: *The boy planted his feet far apart. Columbus planted the Spanish flag firmly in the soil of the new continent he had found for his rulers.* **4.** to post; station: *to plant guards at an entrance.* **5.** to establish or found (a colony, city, etc.). **6.** to establish (a person) as a settler or colonist. **7.** to colonize or settle (an area); stock with inhabitants, cattle, etc. **8.** to locate or situate: *a town planted at the mouth of a river.* **9.** to implant (an idea, sentiment, etc.); introduce and establish firmly (a doctrine, religion, principle, practice, etc.): *That noble thirst of fame and reputation which is planted in the hearts of all men* (Sir Richard Steele). **10.** to introduce (a breed of animals) into a country. **11.** to deposit (young fish, spawn, oysters) in a river, tidal water, etc. **12.** *Slang.* to deliver (a blow, etc.) with a definite aim. **13.** *Slang.* to hide (something stolen, etc.). **14.** *Slang.* to place (a person or thing) as a plant, trap, or trick: *Mr. Leviero denied that the story had been "planted" with him by a Government source* (New York Times). **15.** *Slang.* to salt (a mine, claim, etc.).
[partly Old English *plante* young plant, sprout, cutting (< Latin *planta* sprout), and partly < Old French *plante* plant < Medieval Latin *planta* plant < Latin] —**plant′like′,** *adj.*

Plan·tag·e·net (plan taj′ə nit), *n.* a member of the royal family that ruled England from 1154 to 1485. The English kings from Henry II through Richard III were Plantagenets.

plan·ta·gi·na·ceous (plan′tə jə nā′shəs), *adj.* belonging to the family of plants typified by the plantain. [< New Latin *Plantaginaceae* the family name (< Latin *plantāgo* plaintain[2]) + English *-ous*]

plan·tain[1] (plan′tən), *n.* **1.** a treelike, tropical, herbaceous plant closely related to the banana. **2.** its fruit, longer and more starchy than the banana, and usually eaten cooked. [< Spanish *plátano,* learned borrowing from Latin *platanus* < Greek *plátanos* < *platýs* broad (because of the shape of its leaf). Doublet of PLANE[3].]

plan·tain[2] (plan′tən), *n.* any of a group of herbs, especially a common weed with broad, flat leaves spread out close to the ground, and long, slender spikes carrying flowers and seeds. [< Old French *plantain* < Vulgar Latin *plantanus* < Latin *plantāgo, -inis* < *planta* sole of the foot (because of its flat leaves)]

Common Plantain[2]
(1 to 2 ft. high)

plantain lily, any of a group of lilies native to China and Japan, grown for their attractive ribbed foliage and tubular white or bluish flowers.

plant-an·i·mal (plant′an′ə məl), *n.* a zoophyte.

plan·tar (plan′tər), *adj.* of or having to do with the sole of the foot: *a plantar wart.* [< Latin *plantāris* < *planta* sole of the foot]

plan·ta·tion (plan tā′shən), *n.* **1.** an estate or farm in a tropical or semitropical climate, on which cotton, tobacco, sugar cane, coffee, or other crops are raised. The work on a plantation is done by laborers who live there. **2.** a large group of trees or other plants which have been planted: *a rubber plantation. From its palm plantations comes much of the oil for Britons' soap and margarine* (Newsweek). **3.** a colony: *the Virginia plantation.* **4.** a local, minor civil division in Maine: *Local government is administered by the state's three classes of municipalities—towns, cities, and plantations* (World Book Encyclopedia). **5.** the act of planting. [< Latin *plantātiō, -ōnis* a planting < *plantāre* to plant < *planta* a sprout] —**Syn. 3.** settlement.

plant bug, any of various hemipterous insects that attack the flowers, leaves, and fruit of many plants.

plant caterpillar, a caterpillar, the larva of any of several Australasian moths, within which a parasitic fungus is growing, killing the caterpillar and sending up a long shoot from the head.

plant·er (plan′tər, plän′-), *n.* **1.** a man who owns or runs a plantation: *a cotton planter. One of the most considerable planters in the Brazils* (Daniel Defoe). **2.** an implement or machine for planting: *a corn planter.* **3.** a person who plants. **4.** a box, stand, or other holder, usually decorative, for house plants: *Hand-crafted, copper bound redwood planters in three smart shapes* (Wall Street Journal). **5.** an early settler; colonist.

plant hopper, lantern fly.

plan·ti·grade (plan′tə grād), *adj.* walking on the whole sole of the foot, as bears, raccoons, man, etc.: *Humans and those with a humanlike, or plantigrade foot . . . walk on the sole of the foot with the heel touching the ground* (Science News Letter). —*n.* a plantigrade animal. [< French *plantigrade* < Latin *planta* sole of the foot + *gradus, -ūs* step, degree, related to *gradī* walk]

plant·let (plant′lit, plänt′-), *n.* **1.** an undeveloped or rudimentary plant. **2.** a small plant. [< *plant* + *-let*]

plant louse, an aphid or related insect which sucks juices from plants.

plan·toc·ra·cy (plan tok′rə sē), *n., pl.* **-cies. 1.** government by planters. **2.** plantation owners as a class: *From sugar, rum, coffee, and slavery, a rich plantocracy grew* (Newsweek). [< *plant*(er) + *-ocracy,* as in *democracy*]

plant pathologist, an expert in plant pathology.

plant pathology, the study of plant diseases and their treatment.

plant physiology, the scientific study of the life processes or functions of plants: *The study of how plants grow and how they manufacture food lies in the province of plant physiology.*

plants·man (plants′mən), *n., pl.* **-men.** a nurseryman; florist.

plan·u·la (plan′yə lə), *n., pl.* **-lae** (-lē). the flat, ciliated, free-swimming larva of a coelenterate: *The fertilized egg, after fertilization, produces a larva or planula* (A. Franklin Shull). [< New Latin *planula* (diminutive) < Latin *plānus* flat, level; see PLAIN[1]]

plan·u·lar (plan′yə lər), *adj.* **1.** of flattened form. **2.** having to do with a planula or like a planula.

plan·u·late (plan′yə lit), *adj.* planular.

plap (plap), *v.i.,* **plapped, plap·ping.** *British.* to plop. [imitative]

plaque (plak), *n.* **1.** an ornamental tablet of metal, porcelain, etc., intended to be hung up as a wall decoration, to be inserted in a piece of furniture, etc.: *Gregory Jackson . . . presented to the Cardinal a plaque* (New York Times). **2.** a platelike ornament or badge, as a badge of high rank in an honorary order. **3.** *Anatomy.* a small, flat discoidal formation, as a blood platelet: *The accumulation of cholesterol in the blood vessels forms plaques which may eventually restrict the flow of blood* (New York Times). **4.** a gelatinous deposit formed on the surface of teeth by food debris and bacteria: *Tartar begins as plaque, a film on your teeth that quickly hardens into this tough, cementlike substance* (Time). [< Middle French *plaque* < Middle Dutch *plak* flat board]

pla·quette (pla ket′), *n.* a small plaque.

plash[1] (plash), *v.t., v.i.* to splash: *Far below him plashed the waters* (Longfellow).
—*n.* **1.** a splash: *the plash and murmur of the waves* (Hawthorne). **2.** a shallow piece of standing water; puddle: *As he that leaves A shallow plash to plunge him in the deep* (Shakespeare). **3.** *Scottish.* a heavy fall of rain.
[probably imitative]

plash[2] (plash), *v.t.* **1.** to bend and interweave (stems, branches, and twigs, sometimes partly cut) to form a hedge. **2.** to make or repair (a hedge) in this way. [< Old French *plaissier,* and *plessier* < *plaisse,* and *plesse* hedge < Vulgar Latin *plectia,* variant of Latin *plecta* wickerwork, trellis < *plectere* to interweave] —**plash′er,** *n.*

plash·y (plash′ē), *adj.* **1.** abounding in pools of water; marshy; wet: *Seek'st thou the plashy brink Of weedy lake?* (William Cullen Bryant). **2.** plashing or splashing. **3.** marked as if splashed with color: *a serpent's plashy neck* (Keats). [< *plash*[1] + *-y*[1]]

plasm (plaz′əm), *n.* plasma.

plas·ma (plaz′mə), *n.* **1.** the liquid part of blood or lymph, in which the corpuscles or blood cells float. Plasma can be kept indefinitely by freezing or drying and is often used in transfusions in place of whole blood. *In the capillaries some of the liquid part of the blood, the plasma, oozes through the walls into the spaces surrounding the cells* (Beauchamp, Mayfield, and West). **2.** *Physiology.* the fluid contained in muscle tissue; muscle plasma. **3.** the watery part of milk, as distinguished from the globules of fat. **4.** *Physics.* a highly ionized gas, consisting of almost equal numbers of free electrons and positive ions (atomic nuclei lacking their electron shells). **5.** *Biology.* protoplasm, especially the general body of protoplasm as distinct from the nucleus. **6.** a faintly translucent, green variety of quartz, much used in ancient times for ornaments. [< New Latin *plasma* (in Late Latin, something molded, created) < Greek *plásma* < *plássein* to form, mold]

plas·ma·blast (plaz′mə blast), *n.* the parent or stem cell of a plasma cell: *After she had injected a vaccine intravenously into an experimental animal, plasmablasts began to appear in its spleen* (Scientific American). [< *plasma* + Greek *blastós* germ]

plasma cell, a mononuclear cell that produces antibodies in chronically inflamed connective tissue.

plas·ma·cyte (plaz′mə sīt), *n.* a plasma cell.

plas·ma·gene (plaz′mə jēn), *n.* a minute particle or element found in the cytoplasm of certain microorganisms, insects, and plants. It is regarded as being a hereditary factor corresponding in function to the genes found in the chromosome. *There are many different kinds of plasmagenes in Paramecium, each self-reproducing and capable of mutation* (Laurence H. Snyder).

plas·ma·lem·ma (plaz′mə lem′ə), *n.* plasma membrane.

plasma membrane, the thin membrane that forms the outer surface of the protoplasm of a cell; cell membrane. See picture under **cell.**

plas·ma·pher·e·sis (plaz′mə fer′ə sis), *n.* the removal of blood from the body and the separation, by centrifugation, of the plasma from the cells, which are then washed in a saline solution and returned to the blood stream. This process is used to obtain plasma, as well as to treat certain pathological conditions. [< New Latin *plasmapheresis* < *plasma* + Greek *aphaíresis* a taking away; see APHERESIS]

plasma physics, the branch of physics which studies the behavior of highly ionized gases.

plas·mat·ic (plaz mat′ik), *adj.* of plasma; containing plasma; like plasma.

plas·mic (plaz′mik), *adj.* plasmatic.

plas·min (plaz′min), *n.* an enzyme in the blood which can dissolve blood clots; fibrinolysin.

plas·min·o·gen (plaz min′ə jən), *n.* the inactive form of plasmin; profibrinolysin.

Plas·mo·chin (plaz′mə kin), *n. Trademark.* an antimalarial drug; pamaquine.

plas·mo·di·um (plaz mō′dē əm), *n., pl.* **-di·a** (-dē ə). **1.** a mass or sheet of naked protoplasm formed by the fusion, or by the aggregation, of a number of amoebalike bodies, as in the slime molds. **2.** any of a group of parasitic protozoans, including the organisms which cause malaria. [< German *Plasmodium* < New Latin *plasmodium* < *plasma* plasma + *-odium,* a noun suffix]

plas·mo·gen (plaz′mə jən), *n.* (used formerly in biology) formative protoplasm; the highest stage of protoplasm from which tissue and organs are formed. [< Greek *plásma* something molded + English *-gen*]

plas·moid (plaz′moid), *n.* a tightly packed, luminous pellet of plasma ions, formed when plasma moves across a magnetic field: *Some recent experiments which have generated remarkable bodies that we call plasmoids* (Scientific American).

plas·mol·y·sis (plaz mol′ə sis), *n. Botany.* the contraction of protoplasm in a living cell, caused by the withdrawal of liquid when the cell is placed in a liquid of greater density than the cell sap: *Plasmolysis can be seen with the microscope if pieces of water plants are mounted in a 5 to 10 per cent solution of table salt* (Fred W. Emerson). [< Greek *plásma* something molded + *lýsis* a loosening]

plas·mo·lyt·ic (plaz′mə lit′ik), *adj.* **1.** having to do with plasmolysis. **2.** showing plasmolysis. **3.** causing plasmolysis.

plas·mo·lyze (plaz′mə līz), *v.t., v.i.,* **-lyzed, -lyz·ing.** to contract by plasmolysis.

Plas·mon (plaz′mon), *n. Trademark.* an almost odorless and tasteless, flourlike food preparation obtained from milk, consisting essentially of the protein of milk. [coined from *plasma*]

plas·mo·quine (plaz′mə kwīn), *n.* pamaquine.

plas·mo·some (plaz′mə sōm), *n. Biology.* a true nucleolus, as distinguished from a karyosome. [< Greek *plásma* something molded + *sôma* body]

plas·ome (plas′ōm), *n.* (formerly) one of the smallest theoretical units of living substance; pangen; biophore; gemmule. [< German *Plasom,* earlier *Plasmatosom* < Greek *plásma* something created + *sôma* body]

plas·ter (plas′tər, pläs′-), *n.* **1.** a soft, sticky mixture, consisting mainly of lime, sand, and water, that hardens on drying, used for covering walls, ceilings, etc.: *Ordinary plaster is very similar to mortar save that it usually contains hair or other fibers to help hold it in place* (W.N. Jones). **2.** plaster of Paris. **3.** a medical preparation, consisting of some substance spread on cloth, that will stick to the body and protect cuts, relieve pain, aches, etc.: *mustard plaster.* **4.** a healing or soothing means or measure.
—*v.t.* **1.** to cover (walls, ceilings, etc.) with plaster. **2.** to smear, bedaub, or fill in with plaster; apply plaster to. **3.** to use plaster of Paris on or in making. **4.** to spread with anything thickly: *Dick's shoes were plastered with mud. Smee plastered his sitters with adulation as methodically as he covered his canvas* (Thackeray). **5.** to make smooth and flat: *He plastered his hair down.* **6.** to apply a plaster to. **7.** to apply like a plaster. **8.** *U.S. Slang.* to punish, injure, or attack violently; wreak havoc, ruin, destruction, etc., upon.
[noun (definition 1) < Old French *plastre,* learned borrowing from Medieval Latin *plastrum* a medical plaster, builder's plaster < Latin *emplastrum* < Greek *émplastron,* salve, plaster, ultimately < *en-* on + *plastós* molded < *plássein* to mold; (noun definition 3) Old English *plaster* < Medieval Latin *plastrum.* Doublet of PIASTER.] —**plas′ter·like′,** *adj.*
—**Syn.** *n.* **1.** stucco. **3.** poultice. *-v.t.* **5.** slick.

plas·ter·board (plas′tər bôrd′, -bōrd′; pläs′-), *n.* a thin board made of a layer of plaster between pressed felt, covered with paper and used for walls, partitions, etc.

plaster cast, 1. a mold, as of a piece of sculpture, made with plaster of Paris. **2.** *Medicine.* a mold made from a bandage of gauze and plaster of Paris to hold a broken or dislocated bone in place.

plas·tered (plas′tərd, pläs′-), *adj. Slang.* drunk.

plas·ter·er (plas′tər ər, pläs′-), *n.* a person who plasters walls, etc.

plas·ter·ing (plas′tər ing, pläs′-), *n.* a covering of plaster on walls, etc.

plaster of Paris, calcined gypsum, a white powdery substance which, when mixed with water, swells and hardens quickly and can be made into molds, casts, etc., by pouring, shaping, carving, turning, etc.: *Plaster of Paris expands slightly when it sets—a requisite for any material that is to find use as a mold or a casting* (Monroe M. Offner).

plaster saint, lifeless embodiment of moral perfection: *Single men in barracks don't grow into plaster saints* (Rudyard Kipling).

plas·ter·work (plas′tər wėrk′, -pläs-′), *n.* work done with or in plaster, especially on walls, ceilings, etc.

plas·ter·y (plas′tər ē, pläs′-), *adj.* like plaster; resembling plaster.

plas·tic (plas′tik), *adj.* **1.** made of a plastic: *a plastic hose, plastic cup, etc.* **2.** molding or giving shape to material. **3.** having to do with or involving molding or modeling; that expresses itself in three dimensions: *Sculpture is a plastic art.* **4.** easily modeled or shaped: *Clay, wax, and plaster are plastic substances.* **5.** easily influenced; impressionable; pliable: *the plastic mind of a child.* **6.** *Biology.* capable of forming, or being organized into, living tissue. **7.** *Physics.* (of a substance) able to be deformed in any direction and to retain its deformed condition permanently without rupture. **8.** *Archaic.* producing natural forms, especially living organisms; formative; procreative.
—*n.* **1.** any of various substances that harden and retain their shape after being molded or shaped when softened by heat, pressure, etc., as glass and rubber. **2.** any of a large group of synthetic organic compounds made from such basic raw materials as coal, water, and limestone, especially by polymerization. Plastics are molded, laminated, extruded, etc., into various forms, such as sheets, fibers, and bottles. *Bakelite, polyethylene, and Lucite are plastics.*
[< Latin *plasticus* < Greek *plastikós* able to be molded < *plastós* molded < *plássein* to form, mold] —**plas′ti·cal·ly,** *adv.*

plastic bomb, a puttylike mixture of two or more explosives used especially by terrorists or irregular forces.

plastic deformation or **flow,** *Physics.* the alteration of the shape of a solid by the application of a sufficient and sustained stress: *Plastic deformation of solids is brought about when planes of atoms in the component crystals slip along adjacent planes, in a few directions favored by the crystalline atomic arrangement* (Alan Holden).

plastic foam, a plastic having a soft, spongy texture, suitable for use in furniture cushions, mattresses, upholstery, etc.: *Plastic foam is being used increasingly for insulating linings in clothing in addition to its cushioning application* (Wall Street Journal).

Plas·ti·cine (plas′tə sēn), *n. Trademark.* a composition that remains plastic for a long time, used by children and sculptors instead of modeling clay. [< *plastic* + *-ine*[1]]

plas·ti·cise (plas′tə sīz), *v.t., v.i.,* **-cised, -cis·ing.** *Especially British.* plasticize. —**plas′ti·cis′er,** *n.*

plas·ti·cism (plas′tə siz əm), *n.* plastic quality; plasticity.

plas·tic·i·ty (plas tis′ə tē), *n.* **1.** the quality of being plastic: *Yet it is this graphic weakness that gives his Hesiod etchings their strong plasticity and complicated charm* (New Yorker). **2.** the capability of being molded, formed, or modeled. **3.** *Physics.* the capability of being deformed permanently. **4.** *Chemistry.* the property of particles of being displaced without removal from the sphere of attraction.

plas·ti·ci·za·tion (plas′tə sə zā′shən), *n.* **1.** the act of plasticizing; a making or becoming plastic. **2.** the state of being plasticized.

plas·ti·cize (plas′tə sīz), *v.,* **-cized, -ciz·ing.** —*v.t.* to make plastic. —*v.i.* to become plastic.

plas·ti·ciz·er (plas′tə sī′zər), *n.* something that causes a substance to become or remain soft, flexible, or viscous, especially any of various chemicals: *The new product has potentialities as both a good emulsifier and a paint plasticizer* (Wall Street Journal).

plastic operation, an operation involving plastic surgery.

plastic surgeon, a surgeon who specializes in plastic surgery: *Creating new skulls, or large parts of them, from rib bones is being done by plastic surgeons in Cincinnati* (Science News Letter).

plastic surgery, surgery that restores, remedies, or improves the outer appearance of the body, replaces or repairs lost or deformed parts, etc.

plas·tid (plas′tid), *n. Biology.* **1.** an individual mass or unit of protoplasm, as a cell or one-celled organism. **2.** any of various small differentiated masses of protoplasm present in various cells, as a chromoplast, chloroplast, etc.: *The cells of most plants contain protoplasmic bodies called plastids, which multiply by fission* (Harbaugh and Goodrich). [< German *Plastiden,* plural < Greek *plástides,* feminine plural of *plástēs* one who molds < *plastós* molded]

plas·tique (plas tēk′), *n.* **1.** controlled movement and statuelike posing in ballet. **2.** a plastic bomb. [< French *plastique* plastic]

plas·ti·queur (plas′ti kœr′), *n.* a person who throws plastic bombs: *Plastiqueurs have blown up two flats in the next street* (Punch). [< French *plastiqueur* < *plastique*]

plas·ti·sol (plas′tə sol, -sōl), *n.* a plasticized liquid dispersion of resin particles, used for coating steel, for padding, and in the manufacture of toys. [< *plasti*(c) + *sol*[4] solution]

plas·tom·e·ter (plas tom′ə tər), *n.* a device used to measure the plasticity of materials.

plas·tral (plas′trəl), *adj. Zoology.* of, having to do with, or like a plastron.

plas·tron (plas′trən), *n.* **1.** a breastplate, especially of steel, worn under a coat of mail. **2.** a leather guard worn over the chest by a fencer. **3.** an ornamental, detachable front of a woman's bodice: *One in navy wool rivets eyes on a chest-high square plastron, which unbuttons to show beneath still another plastron of white piqué* (Sunday Times). **4.** the starched front of a man's shirt. **5.** the ventral part of the shell of a turtle or tortoise; breastplate. [< Middle French *plastron* breastplate, shirt front adaptation of Italian *piastrone* (augmentative) < *piastra* plate of metal, piastre < Medieval Latin *plastrum* plaster]

plas·trum (plas′trəm), *n.* plastron.

plat[1] (plat), *n., v.,* **plat·ted, plat·ting.** —*n.* **1.** *U.S.* a map or diagram, especially of a town or other group of buildings proposed to be built; chart; plan. **2.** a tract of land divided into house lots; a small piece of ground; plot: *smooth plats of fruitful ground* (Tennyson). —*v.t.* to map out in detail; chart; plan. [apparently variant of *plot;* influenced by obsolete *plat* flat surface < Old French *plat* < Vulgar Latin *plattus* < Greek *platýs* broad, flat]

plat[2] (plat), *n., v.,* **plat·ted, plat·ting.** *Especially Dialect.* —*n.* a braid; plait. —*v.t.* to braid; plait: *And they clothed him with purple, and platted a crown of thorns, and put it about his head* (Mark 15:17). [variant of *plait*]

plat[3] (plá), *n. French.* **1.** a plate or dish. **2.** a dish of food, as served at the table.

plat., platoon.

plat·an or **plat·ane** (plat′ən), *n.* a plane tree: *three tall platanes . . . very poor as to foliage* (Joseph Conrad). [< Latin *platanus* plane tree]

plat·a·na·ceous (plat′ə nā′shəs), *adj.* belonging to or having to do with the family of plants typified by the plane tree. [< New Latin *Platanaceae* the family name (< Latin *platanus* plane tree) + English *-ous*]

pla·ta·no (plä′tä nō, -tə-), *n., pl.* **-nos.** in Latin America: **1.** the fruit of the tropical plantain. **2.** a banana. [< Spanish *plátano;* see PLANTAIN¹]

plat·band (plat′band′), *n. Architecture.* **1.** a flat, rectangular molding with a projection much less than the width. **2.** a fillet between the flutings of a column. [< Middle French *platebande* < *plate* flat + *bande* band]

plat du jour (plä′ dy zhür′), *pl.* **plats du jour** (plä′ dy zhür′). *French.* **1.** the specialty of the day in a restaurant: *On Thursdays the plat du jour will be paella (which the Spanish dictionaries define as a savoury dish of rice with meat, shellfish, etc.)* (Manchester Guardian). **2.** (literally) dish of the day.

plate (plāt), *n., v.,* **plat·ed, plat·ing.** —*n.* **1.** a dish, usually round, that is almost flat: *a china dinner plate, a pie plate. Our food is served on plates.* **2.** the contents of such a dish: *a small plate of stew.* **3.** a plateful. **4.** something having the shape of a plate: *A plate is passed in church to receive the collection.* **5.** a part of a meal, served on or in a separate dish; course. **6.** the dishes and food served to a person at a meal. **7. a.** dishes or other utensils of gold or silver: *a salt-cellar of silver . . . one of the neatest pieces of plate that ever I saw* (Samuel Pepys). **b.** dishes and utensils covered with a thin layer of silver or gold; plated ware. **8.** a thin, flat sheet or piece of metal: *The warship was covered with steel plates.* **9.** one of the pieces of steel welded together or riveted to form the hull of a ship: *to damage the bow plates in a collision.* **10.** armor composed of thin pieces of iron or steel fastened together, or upon leather, heavy cloth, etc.; plate armor. **11.** metal hammered, rolled, or cast as a sheet or sheets, as a material: *Plate has been running a close second to cold-rolled sheets as the tightest item on the steel list* (New York Times). **12.** *Anatomy, Zoology.* a platelike part, organ, or structure, as a lamina: *Some reptiles and fishes have a covering of horny or bony plates.* **13.** a smooth or polished piece of metal, etc., for writing or engraving on, for printing from, etc. **14.** such a piece when engraved. **15.** a printed impression obtained from such an engraved piece of metal, or from a woodcut, especially a full-page illustration printed on special paper: *a color plate.* **16.** any sheet of metal, plastic, etc., engraved or otherwise treated so as to be printed from, as an engraved or etched copperplate, the zinc or other surface used in offset, a stereotype or electrotype, etc. **17.** any full-page inserted illustration forming part of a book. **18.** a thin sheet of glass, metal, etc., coated with chemicals that are sensitive to light: *A photographic plate because of its lightness and simplicity, commends itself strongly as apparatus for use at a height of 100,000 feet or more* (E. P. George). **19.** (in baseball) home plate: *Another Braves' run crossed the plate in the seventh* (New York Times). **20.** *Dentistry.* a piece of metal, plastic, or other firm material shaped to the mouth, with false teeth set into it. **21.** a thin cut of beef from the lower end of the ribs, used especially to make corned beef. **22.** *Electronics.* (in a vacuum tube) the electrode toward which the electrons flow, originally made in the form of a flat plate, but now usually cylindrical. **23.** *Architecture.* a beam that supports the ends of rafters, etc., usually running horizontally between corner posts. **24.** plate glass. **25.** *Especially British.* **a.** a gold or silver cup or other prize given to the winner of a race, especially a horse race. **b.** a contest in which the prize is (or was originally) such an object. **26. a.** *British Dialect.* a railroad rail. **b.** Also, **plate rail.** a primitive type of rail with a raised flange along the outer edge. **27.** *Historical.* precious metal; bullion. **28.** *Obsolete.* a piece of silver money; silver coin. **29.** *Slang.* a fashionably dressed person. *Abbr.:* pl.
—*v.t.* **1.** to cover (a less valuable or more easily corroded metal) with a thin layer of gold, silver, or other metal by mechanical, electrical, or chemical means. **2.** to overlay with protective metal plates; cover with armor plate. **3.** to make a stereotype or electrotype plate of (type) for printing. **4.** *Papermaking.* to treat (paper) with polished metal plates or rollers to give it a glossy finish.
[< Old French *plate,* feminine of *plat,* adjective, thin plate, leaf of metal < Vulgar Latin *plattus* flat < Greek *platýs*] —**plate′like′**, *adj.*

plate armor, plate; thin pieces of armor.

pla·teau (pla tō′), *n., pl.* **-teaus** or **-teaux** (-tōz′). **1.** a plain in the mountains or at a height above the sea; large, high plain: *They found that chinchilla fur was ideal wear in the intense cold of the high mountain plateaux* (New Scientist). **2.** *Psychology.* a temporary halt in the learning progress of an individual, depicted by a level stretch on the curve or chart showing the rate of learning. **3.** a level, especially the level at which something is stabilized for a period, as would be shown on a graph by a horizontal line: *Some predicted a continued slow rise in economic activity, some a "plateau" for a while before a new rise* (Wall Street Journal). [< French *plateau* < Old French *platel* (diminutive) < *plat* flat; see PLATE] —**Syn. 1.** tableland, mesa.

Plateaus (def. 1)

plat·ed (plā′tid), *adj.* **1.** (of a fabric) having one yarn on the face and another kind on the back. **2.** overlaid with plates, as of metal, for protection or ornament. **3.** overlaid with a coating or surface of a material more valuable than the body, especially with a thin film of gold or silver.

plate·ful (plāt′fu̇l), *n., pl.* **-fuls.** as much as a plate will hold.

plate glass, thick, very clear glass made in smooth, polished sheets and used for large windowpanes, mirrors, etc.: *Plate glass is made from higher grade ingredients than those used for ordinary window glass* (Monroe M. Offner).

plate·hold·er (plāt′hōl′dər), *n. Photography.* a receptacle impervious to light, for holding a sensitized plate, used for exposing the plate within the camera by the removal of a slide, and for carrying the plate before and after using: *Baade closed the plateholder, removed it and inserted another* (Scientific American).

plate·lay·er (plāt′lā′ər), *n. British.* a person who lays, keeps in order, and replaces the rails on a tramway or railway; tracklayer: *The first train . . . set off at 7 A.M. packed with the line's toughest platelayers under the command of the company secretary* (Manchester Guardian).

plate·let (plāt′lit), *n.* **1.** a small body occurring in great numbers in blood and essential to coagulation; one of the three cellular elements of blood: *Platelets are colorless cells in the blood and are involved in blood clotting* (Science News Letter). **2.** a small or minute plate. [< *plate* + *-let*]

plat·en (plat′ən), *n.* **1.** a flat metal plate in a printing press, that presses the paper against the inked type so as to secure an impression. **2.** a cylinder serving the same purpose. **3.** the roller against which the paper rests in a typewriter. **4.** a heated plate placed between wood fiber mats to consolidate them into hardboard. [< Old French *platine* < *plat* flat; see PLATE]

plate paper, **1.** a heavy, spongy, unsized paper with a smooth, dull finish, used for taking impressions from engraved plates. **2.** a similar heavy paper, as that used for books. **3.** a paper finished with a high gloss, as by supercalendering.

plate proof, *Printing.* a proof taken from an electrotype or stereotype plate.

plat·er (plā′tər), *n.* **1.** a person or thing that plates. **2.** an inferior race horse, especially one that changes owners frequently or may be presumed to be usually for sale; selling-plater. **3.** *Obsolete.* a horse that runs mostly in plate races.

plate race, *Especially British.* a horse race with a plate as the prize.

plate rail, **1.** a rail or narrow shelf attached to a wall to hold ornamental plates, etc. **2.** plate, an early type of flanged railroad rail.

plat·er·esque (plat′ə resk′), *adj.* in or resembling a style of architecture, especially of Spain, characterized by rich, excessively ornamented forms suggestive of silver work. [< Spanish *plateresco* < *platero* silversmith, goldsmith (< *plata* silver) + *-esco* -esque]

plate tracery, *Architecture.* tracery formed by cutting openings through stone, rather than by assembling pieces.

plat·form (plat′fôrm), *n.* **1.** a raised level surface or structure formed with planks, boards, or the like. **2.** the walk between or beside the tracks of a railroad station. **3.** *U.S.* the floor beyond the inside doors at either end of a railroad passenger car; vestibule. **4.** a piece of raised flooring, in a hall or in the open air, from which a speaker addresses his audience. **5.** a plan of action or statement of principles adopted by a political group, especially a political party at a convention where candidates are nominated: *The platform of the new political party demands lower taxes. But it is, in a sense, ratified by this far-ranging message which is intended to be a platform for the campaign* (Newsweek). **6.** a draft or scheme of principles or doctrines, made by or on behalf of a religious party, church, or sect. **7. a.** a slightly raised level area on which a piece of artillery is mounted in a fortification. **b.** a terrace; flat piece of ground: *Grove nods at grove, each alley has a brother, And half the platform just reflects the other* (Alexander Pope). **8.** a kind of outer sole of cork, etc., one half inch or more in thickness, on a woman's shoe. **9.** *Obsolete.* a scheme; design.
—*adj.* of or having to do with a platform used by public speakers: *platform oratory.*
[< Middle French *plateforme,* earlier *platte fourme* (literally) flat form]
—**Syn.** *n.* **5.** policy, program.

platform car, a railroad car having no top or enclosing sides; flatcar.

plat·form·er (plat′fôr′mər), *n.* (in petroleum refining) a reformer in which the process of platforming is carried out: *A . . . petroleum marketing subsidiary, added a 5,000 barrel-per-day platformer to its New Orleans refinery* (Wall Street Journal). [< *plat*(inum) + (re)*former*]

plat·form·ing (plat′fôr′ming), *n.* the process in petroleum refining in which platinum is used as a catalyst in the presence of hydrogen to raise gasoline octane ratings. [< *plat*(inum) + (re)*forming*]

platform shoe, a woman's cloglike shoe having a thick outer sole that usually extends solidly the length of the shoe, becoming thicker under the heel: *They wore wooden platform shoes because there was no leather* (New Yorker).

platform ticket, *British.* a ticket permitting a person other than a passenger to enter upon a railroad platform.

plat·i·na (plat′ə nə, plə tē′-), *n.* platinum. [< earlier Spanish *platina* < *plata* silver (because it resembles silver)]

plat·i·nate (plat′ə nāt), *n. Chemistry.* a salt of platinic acid. [< *platin*(ic acid) + *-ate*²]

plat·ing (plā′ting), *n.* **1.** a thin layer of silver, gold, or other metal. **2.** a covering of metal plates. **3.** the act of a person or thing that plates.

pla·tin·ic (plə tin′ik), *adj. Chemistry.* **1.** of platinum. **2.** containing platinum, especially with a valence of four.

plat·i·nif·er·ous (plat′ə nif′ər əs), *adj.* bearing or yielding platinum. [< *platin*(um) + *-ferous*]

plat·in·i·rid·i·um (plat′ən i rid′ē əm), *n.* a native alloy of platinum and iridium, occurring in whitish grains or cubes.

plat·i·nize (plat′ə nīz), *v.t.,* **-nized, -niz·ing.** to coat or treat with platinum.

plat·i·no·cy·an·ic acid (plat′ə nō sī an′ik), an acid of platinum and cyanide, formed by the decomposition of its salts in solution. *Formula:* $H_2Pt(CN)_4$

plat·i·no·cy·a·nid (plat′ə nō sī′ə nid), *n.* platinocyanide.

plat·i·no·cy·a·nide (plat′ə nō sī′ə nīd), *n.* a salt of platinocyanic acid: *Röntgen observed a bright fluorescence among some nearby crystals of platinocyanide* (Scientific American). [< *platinum* + *cyanide*]

plat·i·noid (plat′ə noid), *adj.* resembling platinum. —*n.* **1.** any of a group of metals commonly found in association with platinum and resembling it in several properties, as palladium, iridium, and osmium. **2.** a platinumlike alloy consisting essentially of copper, nickel, zinc, and tungsten, used especially for electrical resistance coils.

plat·i·no·type (plat′ə nə tīp), *n.* **1.** a process of photographic printing using a platinum salt and producing a print in platinum black. **2.** a print made by this process.

plat·i·nous (plat′ə nəs), *adj. Chemistry.* **1.** of platinum. **2.** containing platinum, especially with a valence of two.

plat·i·num (plat′ə nəm), *n.* **1.** a rare, precious, metallic chemical element of a white color like silver but less bright, very heavy, ductile, and malleable. It is used as a catalyst, for chemical and industrial equipment, in dentistry, for jewelry, etc. *Besides in jewelry, platinum is used as a catalyst in the petroleum industry* (Wall Street Journal). *Symbol:* Pt; *at.wt.:* (C^{12}) 195.09 or (O^{16}) 195.09; *at.no.:* 78; *valence:* 1,2,3,4,6; *specific gravity:* 21.37 to 21.447; *melting point:* 3,224°F. **2.** a light-gray color, less bright than silver and having a faint bluish tinge. [< New Latin *platinum,* alteration of *platina* platina]

platinum black, a dull-black powder consisting of very finely divided metallic platinum. It is used as an oxidizing agent because it can condense large amounts of oxygen upon its surface.

platinum blonde or **blond,** a person, especially a woman, having silvery blond hair.

plat·i·tude (plat′ə tüd, -tyüd), *n.* **1.** a dull or commonplace remark, especially one spoken or written solemnly as if it were fresh and important: *"Better late than never" is a platitude.* **2.** flatness; triteness; dullness; insipidity (as a quality of speech or writing): *Her utterly unliterary style has at least the merit of being a vehicle exactly suited to her thoughts and feelings; and even the platitude of her phraseology carries with it a curiously personal flavour* (Lytton Strachey). [< French *platitude* < *plat* flat (saying); see PLATE] —**Syn. 2.** commonplaceness.

plat·i·tu·di·nar·i·an (plat′ə tü′də när′ē ən, -tyü′-), *n.* a person given to platitudes.

plat·i·tu·di·nize (plat′ə tü′də nīz, -tyü′-), *v.i.,* **-nized, -niz·ing.** to utter platitudes.

plat·i·tu·di·nous (plat′ə tü′də nəs, -tyü′-), *adj.* **1.** characterized by platitudes; using platitudes: *The fantastic Lorca imagery, mixture of the bizarre and the platitudinous, comes through particularly well in the translation* (Harper's). **2.** being a platitude. —**plat′i·tu′di·nous·ly,** *adv.* —**plat′i·tu′di·nous·ness,** *n.*

Pla·ton·ic (plə ton′ik), *adj.* **1.** of or having to do with Plato or his doctrines: *the Platonic philosophy.* **2.** Also, **platonic. a.** designating love or affection, especially for one of the opposite sex, of a purely spiritual character, and free from sensual desire: *without admission that their love could not remain platonic* (John Galsworthy). **b.** feeling or professing such love. **3.** idealistic; not practical: *The League of Nations seemed a Platonic scheme to many people.* [< *Plato,* about 427-347 B.C., a Greek philosopher] —**pla·ton′i·cal·ly,** *adv.* —**Syn. 3.** visionary, utopian.

Pla·ton·i·cal (plə ton′ə kəl), *adj.* Platonic.

Platonic year, *Astronomy.* a period in which sun, moon, planets, and stars were supposed to complete their movements; great year.

Pla·to·nism (plā′tə niz əm), *n.* **1.** the philosophy or doctrines of Plato or his followers; academism. **2.** a Platonic doctrine or saying. **3.** the doctrine or practice of Platonic love.

Pla·to·nist (plā′tə nist), *n.* a follower of Plato; a person who believes in Plato's philosophy.

Pla·to·nis·tic (plā′tə nis′tik), *adj.* **1.** having to do with the Platonists or Platonism. **2.** characteristic of the Platonists or Platonism.

Pla·to·nize (plā′tə nīz), *v.,* **-nized, -niz·ing.** —*v.t.* to make Platonic; give a Platonic character to; explain in accordance with Platonic principles. —*v.i.* to follow the opinions or doctrines of Plato; reason like Plato: *The gentlemen and the maids Platonizing and singing madrigals had nothing else to do* (New Yorker).

pla·toon (plə tün′), *n.* **1.** a tactical unit of infantry or other ground forces, usually consisting of two or more sub-units and commanded by a lieutenant. There are usually four platoons in a company. **2.** a subdivision of a police force. **3.** *U.S.* a football team that specializes in either offensive or defensive play: *He has shifted Frank Gifford, his most versatile backfield man, from the defensive to the offensive platoon* (New York Times). **4.** a small group or company of people: *If you speak of the age, you mean your own platoon of people* (Emerson). [< French *peloton* platoon, group of persons < Middle French, little ball (diminutive) < *pelote* ball; see PELOTE]

Platt·deutsch (plät′doich′), *n.* Low German, the speech of North Germany, now often considered a nonstandard dialect. [< German *Plattdeutsch* < *platt* of the lowlands, (literally) flat (ultimately < Vulgar Latin *plattus;* see PLAT[1]) + *Deutsch* the German language]

platte·land (plät′land′), *n.* (in South Africa) a country district; rural area; hinterland: *The Africans reacted like lightning crackling across the platteland sky* (Time). [< Afrikaans *platteland* < Dutch < *platte* flat + *land* land]

plat·ter[1] (plat′ər), *n.* **1.** a large, shallow dish for holding or serving food, especially meat and fish. **2.** *Slang.* a phonograph record: *The long-play, 33⅓ r.p.m. platters, commonly known as albums* (Wall Street Journal). **3.** *Slang.* home plate.

on a (silver) platter, without requiring any effort; very lightly or easily: *A former Army major . . . charged that six years before, Mr. Hopkins had "handed" the Russians the A-bomb on a platter* (New York Times).

[< Anglo-French *plater* < Old French *plat* plate, dish, flat surface; see PLATE]

—**Syn. 1.** trencher.

plat·ter[2] (plat′ər), *n.* a person who plats or plaits. [< *plat*[2] + *-er*[1]]

platter pull, a type of ski tow in which the skier is pulled up the slope by a disk attached to a towing cable. The skier straddles the extension so that the disk presses against him.

plat·ting (plat′ing), *n.* **1.** the act or work of a person who plats. **2.** straw, grass, or the like, platted into braid, or into some other form, as for hats, etc. [< *plat*[2] + *-ing*[1]]

plat·y (plā′tē), *adj.* consisting of or easily separating into plates, as mica; flaky.

plat·y·fish (plat′ə fish′), *n., pl.* **-fish·es** or (*collectively*) **-fish.** a tropical fresh-water fish inhabiting waters of British Honduras, Guatemala, and southern Mexico. It has a large variety of color patterns, grows to a length of just over two inches, and is a favorite of tropical-fish collectors. [< Greek *platýs* flat + English *fish*]

plat·y·hel·minth (plat′ə hel′minth), *n.* any of a phylum of worms, including the tapeworms, flukes, planarians, etc., characterized by soft, usually flat, bilaterally symmetrical bodies; flatworm. [< New Latin *Platyhelmintha* the group name < Greek *platýs* flat + *hélmins, -inthos* worm, helminth]

plat·y·pus (plat′ə pəs), *n., pl.* **-pus·es, -pi** (-pī). the duckbill, an egg-laying mammal of Australia and Tasmania: *The male platypus is as venomous as a poisonous snake* (Scientific American). [< Greek *platýpous* flat-footed < *platýs* flat + *poûs* foot]

Platypus (including tail, 2 ft. long)

plat·y·pus·ar·y (plat′ə pə ser′ē), *n., pl.* **-ar·ies.** an artificial habitat designed for platypuses kept in captivity, including a water tank and burrowing bank.

plat·y·rhyn·chous (plat′ə ring′kəs), *adj.* having a broad, flat bill, as certain flycatchers. [< Greek *platýs* broad, flat + *rhýnchos* beak, bill + English *-ous*]

plat·yr·rhine (plat′ə rīn, -ər in), *adj.* having a broad, flat nose or a nasal index of from 51 to 58. —*n.* a platyrrhine person, monkey, ape, or skull. [< New Latin *Platyrrhini* name of a division of apes < Greek *platýs* flat + *rhīs, rhīnós* nose]

plat·yr·rhin·i·an (plat′ə rin′ē ən), *adj.* platyrrhine.

plau·dit (plô′dit), *n.* any hearty or enthusiastic expression of approval; acclaim.

plaudits, a round of applause; clapping, or cheering, as an enthusiastic expression of approval or praise: *The actress bowed in response to the plaudits of the audience.*

[short for earlier *plaudite!* actor's request for applause < Latin, imperative of *plaudere* to applaud] —**Syn.** acclamation.

plau·di·to·ry (plô′də tôr′ē, -tōr′-), *adj.* applauding; laudatory.

plau·si·bil·i·ty (plô′zə bil′ə tē), *n.* the appearance of being true or reasonable; plausible quality: *The last excuse . . . was allowed . . . to have more plausibility but less truth* (Jonathan Swift). *The persuasiveness and plausibility of the book, however, are due to the author's ability* (Wall Street Journal).

plau·si·ble (plô′zə bəl), *adj.* **1.** appearing true, reasonable, or fair: *For my own sake I've told a plausible lie at the club* (Joseph Conrad). **2.** (of persons) apparently worthy of confidence but often not really so: *a plausible liar.* [< Latin *plausibilis* deserving applause, pleasing < *plaudere* to applaud] —**plau′si·ble·ness,** *n.*

plau·si·bly (plô′zə blē), *adv.* with an appearance of truth or trustworthiness; in a way that seems true or right; with fair show: *The story was plausibly told — whether it was true or not remains to be seen.*

plau·sive (plô′siv), *adj.* **1.** having the quality of applauding; applausive. **2.** *Obsolete.* plausible.

plaus·tral (plôs′trəl), *adj.* having to do with a wagon or cart. [< Latin *plaustrum* wagon, cart + English *-al*[1]]

Plau·tine (plô′tīn), *adj.* of or having to do with Plautus, 254?-184 B.C., Roman writer of comedies, or his works: *There is Plautine merriment at the Strand Theatre* (London Times).

play (plā), *n.* **1.** something done to amuse oneself; fun; sport; recreation: *to watch children at play. Play consists of those activities which are not consciously performed for the sake of any reward beyond themselves* (Emory S. Bogardus). *All work and no play makes Jack a dull boy.* **2.** the carrying on or playing of a game: *Play was slow in the first half of the game.* **3.** the manner or style of carrying on or playing a game: *Both sides showed great play.* **4.** an act or maneuver in carrying on or playing a game: *Tom made a clever play at checkers.* **5.** turn to play: *It is your play next.* **6.** a literary composition in the form of dialogue, adapted for performance on the stage with appropriate action, costume, and scenery; dramatic piece; drama: *"Peter Pan" is a charming play. Mr. Eliot is saying that a play, as we conceive of it . . . is something which, by its nature, demands prose wherever prose will serve* (Atlantic). **7.** a dramatic or theatrical performance, as on the stage. **8.** action or dealing of a specified kind (now used only in *fair play* and *foul play*). **9.** action; activity; operation; working: *the lively play of fancy. There was an engine in the room which was in full play.* **10.** gambling: *to lose vast sums at play.* **11.** the act of lightly or briskly wielding or plying (used especially in combinations): *swordplay.* **12.** light, quick movement: *the play of sunlight on leaves.* **13.** elusive change or transition (of light or color): *the play of light in a diamond.* **14.** freedom or opportunity for action; scope for activity: *to give free play to one's faculties. The boy gave his fancy full play in telling what he could do with a million dollars.* **15.** free or unimpeded movement; the proper motion of a piece of mechanism, or a part of the living body: *the play of muscles.* **16.** the space in or through which anything, especially a piece of mechanism, can or does move: *the play of a wheel on an axle.* **17.** *Obsolete.* a particular amusement; game: *The plays of children are nonsense but very educative nonsense* (Emerson).

bring or **call into play,** to begin to exercise; bring into action; make active: *The intelligence and judgment of Mr. Ruskin . . . are brought into play* (Matthew Arnold). *There is . . . hardly a decision on such an issue that does not call into play an entire range of political and legal activities* (Saturday Review).

in play, a. (of a ball, etc.) being used in the course of the game; in or during legitimate play: *Walton tried another big kick, but the ball fell in play, and was well returned by Strand-Jones* (Westminster Gazette). **b.** as a joke: *He said it merely in play.*

out of play, (of a ball, etc.) not being used; not in or during legitimate play: *A runner cannot be tagged while the ball is out of play.*

[Old English *plega* exercise]

—*v.t.* **1.** to represent or act (a part) in a dramatic performance or in real life: *to play one's part well.* **2.** to act or behave as or like; perform the duties or characteristic actions of: *to play the host, to play the fool. Nor did the shift . . . release a love of power for its own sake or an impulse to play the great man* (Edmund Wilson). **3.** to represent (a person or character) in a dramatic performance: *to play Hamlet. Mary Martin played Peter Pan.* **4.** to perform or act (a drama, pageant, etc.) on or as on the stage: *to play a tragedy.* **5.** to give dramatic performances in: *to play the best theaters, to play the largest cities.* **6.** to engage in (a game or definite form of amusement): *to play golf. Children play tag and ball.* **7.** to perform, do, or execute: *to play a trick on someone.* **8.** to represent or imitate, especially for amusement: *to play spacemen, to play store.* **9.** to perform (music or a piece of music) on an instrument: *to play a symphony.* **10.** to perform on (a musical instrument): *to play a piano.* **11.** to keep in continuous motion or exercise; operate; work (any instrument): *to play a hose on a burning building.* **12.** to cause to move or pass lightly: *The ship played its light along the coast.* **13.** to stake or wager in a game: *to play five dollars.* **14.** to lay a stake or wager on: *to play the horses.* **15.** to contend against in a game or as in a game: *New York played Boston for the championship.* **16.** to use (a person) in a game; include in a team, etc. **17.** to allow (a hooked fish) to exhaust itself by pulling on the line: *M.A. Norden . . . is shown playing a 137-lb. tarpon in a recent Alabama Deep Sea Fishing Rodeo* (Time). **18.** to put into action in a game: *to play the king of hearts.*

—*v.i.* **1.** to have fun; do something in sport; amuse or divert oneself: *The children played in the yard.* **2.** to do something which is not to be taken seriously, but merely as done in sport. **3.** to make believe; pretend in fun. **4.** to dally; trifle; toy: *to play with a new idea, to play with matches. He played with his watch-chain wearily* (Dickens). **5.** to engage or take part in a game: *to play with skill.* **6.** to gamble. **7.** to act, behave, or conduct oneself in some specified way: *to play fair, to play false, to play sick.* **8.** to perform on a musical instrument: *to play in an orchestra.* **9.** (of the instrument or the music) to sound: *The music began to play.* **10.** to act on or as on a stage; perform: *to play in a tragedy.* **11.** to move briskly or lightly, especially with alternating or irregular motion: *Leaves play in the wind. A breeze played on the waters.* **12.** to change or alternate rapidly, as colors in iridescence: *the firelight playing on her red frock* (John Galsworthy). **13.** to move or revolve freely, usually within a definite space, as a part of any mechanism: *The wheel plays in a track.* **14.** to operate or act continuously or with repeated action: *that fine Elizabethan hall, where the fountain plays* (Charles Lamb). *The guns played on the enemy.*

play down, a. to make light of; de-emphasize; understate: *They want to play down politics, play up "good government" and "responsible leadership"* (Newsweek). **b.** to lower one's standards to suit the demands of others; condescend: *Miss Holliday had won "a kind of immortality" with an art that never "played down"* (New York Times).

play off, a. to play an additional game or match in order to decide a draw or tie: *We're going to play off for the Wolcott cup* (Munsey's Magazine). **b.** to pit (one person or thing) against another, especially for one's own advantage: *to play off one party against another.*

play on or **upon,** to take advantage of; make use of: *to play upon a person's fears.*

play out, a. to perform to the end; bring to an end: *to play out a tragedy.* **b.** to exhaust; wear out: *The endless war was playing out both the men and the supplies.* **c.** to diminish; wear off: *When their initial lure had played out, the pioneers of the West found other attractions to induce them to stay on* (Ernest Gruening).

play up, *U.S.* to make the most of; exploit: *Happy customers and favorable reviews are quoted, successful promotions of the firm's books are played up* (Time).

play up to, *Slang.* to try to get into the favor of; flatter: *to play up to a celebrity.*

play with, a. to touch or finger lightly, by way of amusement: *The Commissioner moved his legs, playing with a penknife* (Graham Greene). **b.** to treat frivolously: *Montaigne . . . could thus afford to play with life, and the abysses into which it leads us* (Cardinal Newman).

[Old English *plegian* to exercise, busy oneself with]

—**Syn.** *n.* **1. Play, sport, game** mean activity or exercise of mind or body engaged in for recreation or fun. **Play** is the general word: *Play is as necessary as work.* **Sport** applies to any form of athletics or an outdoor pastime, whether it requires much or little activity or is merely watched for pleasure: *Fencing, swimming, fishing, and horse racing are his favorite sports.* **Game** applies especially to an activity in the form of a contest, mental or physical, played by certain rules: *Tennis and chess are games.* –*v.i.* **1.** frolic, revel.

pla·ya (plä′yə), *n.* **1.** *Southwestern U.S.* a plain of silt or mud, covered with water during the wet season. **2.** *Geology.* the basin floor of an undrained desert which contains water at irregular periods. [American English < Spanish *playa* beach, strand < Late Latin *plagia* coast, side < Latin *plaga* place, region, something spread out]

play·a·bil·i·ty (plā′ə bil′ə tē), *n.* the quality of being playable: *He continued to study each of the eighteen holes, to see what could be done to improve its playability* (New Yorker).

play·a·ble (plā′ə bəl), *adj.* **1.** that can be played. **2.** fit to be played on.

play-act (plā′akt′), *v.i.* **1.** to perform in a dramatic production. **2.** to make believe; pretend. —*v.t.* to act (a part, etc.); portray: *. . . just play-acting the bohemian* (Punch).

play-act·ing (plā′ak′ting), *n.* the acting of plays; dramatic performance.

play·ac·tor (plā′ak′tər), *n.* an actor of plays; dramatic performer.

play·back (plā′bak′), *n.* the replaying of a sound recording, especially a tape recording, or of videotape, usually just after it has been made.

play·bill (plā′bil′), *n.* **1.** a handbill or placard announcing a play. **2.** a program of a play.

play·boy (plā′boi′), *n.* **1.** *Informal.* a man, usually wealthy, whose chief interest is having a good time: *This takes me back to the Algonquin where over cocktails I met two playboys from Dallas, Texas* (Punch). **2.** *Irish.* a man who seeks to play a role to his own advantage; clever or tricky pretender: *The Playboy of the Western World* (J.M. Synge).

play-by-play (plā′bī plā′), *adj. U.S.* denoting a running commentary, especially on a sports event.

play·clothes (plā′klōz′, -klōᴛʜz′), *n.pl.* comfortable clothes worn for play or recreation.

play·day (plā′dā′), *n.* a day given to pastime or diversion; holiday.

play doctor, *U.S.* a writer employed to revise a playscript prior to production.

play·down (plā′doun′), *n.* (in Canada) a play-off.

played-out (plād′out′), *adj.* suffering from overuse so as to be worn-out, worthless, or hackneyed: *played-out jokes.*

play·er (plā′ər), *n.* **1.** a person who plays, or is qualified to play, in some game: *a ball player, a card player, a tennis player.* **2.** a person who plays for stakes; gambler. **3.** an actor: *All the world's a stage, And all the men and women merely players* (Shakespeare). **4.** a musician. **5.** a mechanical device enabling a musical instrument, especially a piano, to be played automatically; piano player. **6.** a person who plays rather than works; idler.

player piano, a piano played by machinery.

Player Piano

play·fel·low (plā′fel′ō), *n.* a playmate.

play field, a playing field.

play·ful (plā′fəl), *adj.* **1.** full of fun; fond of playing; frolicsome: *a playful puppy. The playful children just let loose from school* (Oliver Goldsmith). **2.** not serious; joking: *a playful remark.* —**play′ful·ly,** *adv.* —**play′ful·ness,** *n.* —**Syn.** **1.** sportive. **2.** bantering, jesting, humorous, jocular.

play·girl (plā′gėrl′), *n. Informal.* a woman or girl, usually wealthy, whose chief interest is having a good time.

play·go·er (plā′gō′ər), *n.* a person who goes often to the theater: *I'm in favor of introducing as many changes as possible to make the playgoer happy* (New York Times).

play·go·ing (plā′gō′ing), *adj.,* going often to the theater. —*n.* the practice or habit of going often to the theater: *His dapper discourses range from playgoing and Einstein's theory . . . to the top hat* (Newsweek).

play·ground (plā′ground′), *n.* **1.** a piece of ground used for outdoor play, especially by children, often containing equipment for games and sports. **2.** a recreation or resort area: *Over the past decade fashionable low-tax playgrounds such as Bermuda and Monte Carlo have been challenged* (London Times).

play·house (plā′hous′), *n.* **1.** a small house for a child to play in. **2.** a small building separate from a main building, for the recreation of people of any age. **3.** a toy house for a child; doll house. **4.** a theater: *Successful periods in the playhouse do owe something to what is going on outside the playhouse* (Harper's).

play·ing card (plā′ing), one of a set of cards used for playing such games as poker, bridge, euchre, rummy, etc.; one of a pack of 52 cards arranged in four suits (spades, hearts, diamonds, and clubs) of 13 cards each.

playing field, 1. a field or piece of ground for games or a game: *It is being performed each night by floodlight on the playing fields beside the Avon* (London Times). **2.** *U.S.* an area marked off as comprising that within which the play of a particular game may, according to the rules, take place; field of play.

play·land (plā′land′), *n.* an amusement park.

play·let (plā′lit), *n.* a short dramatic play: *The three playlets are almost identical in form and spirit* (New Yorker).

play·mak·er (plā′mā′kər), *n.* an offensive player, as in basketball, who sets up plays in which his teammates can score: *Cousy, having become the Celtics' acknowledged playmaker, began to direct their attack with a confidence that . . . bordered on audacity* (New Yorker).

play·mate (plā′māt′), *n.* a person, especially a child, who plays regularly with another. —**Syn.** playfellow.

play-off (plā′ôf′, -of′), *n.* an extra game or round played off to settle a tie.

play on or **upon words,** a pun.

play·pen (plā′pen′) *n.* a portable, usually folding, enclosure, with sides consisting of wooden bars or netting, used for keeping a child confined while playing.

play·room (plā′rüm′, -rům′), *n. U.S.* a room in which people, especially children, may play.

play·script (plā′skript′), *n.* the script of a play: *He's merely learning a part. There's the playscript in his hand* (New Yorker).

play·some (plā′səm), *adj.* playful

play street, a street temporarily or permanently closed to traffic to enable children to play outdoors safely.

play suit, 1. a matching outfit, usually consisting of shorts, a blouse and sometimes a skirt or jacket for women and girls. It is worn at the beach, on picnics, for tennis, etc. *Here's the perfect play suit in luxurious white terry* (New Yorker). **2.** playclothes for children.

play therapy, the therapeutic use of play, in the presence of a therapist, as a means of reducing a child's tensions and of promoting the child's emotional growth and health.

play·thing (plā′thing′), *n.* **1.** a thing to play with; toy: *Some livelier plaything gives his youth delight* (Alexander Pope). **2.** something treated as a thing to play with.

play·time (plā′tīm′), *n.* time for play or recreation

play·wright (plā′rīt′) *n.* a writer of plays; dramatist.

play·writ·ing (plā′rī′ting), *n.* the writing of plays; occupation of a playwright: *[The critic] points angrily . . . at what has gone wrong today, particularly in American playwriting* (New York Times).

pla·za (plä′zə, plaz′ə), *n.* a public square in a city or town; place. [American English < Spanish *plaza,* learned borrowing from Latin *platēa* courtyard, broad street < Greek *plateîa* (*hodós*) broad (way). Doublet of PIAZZA, PLACE[1].]

pla·za de to·ros (plä′thä dā tō′rōs, -sä), *Spanish.* a bull ring: *He was young, but he knew a lot about the injuries that occur in a plaza de toros* (Barnaby Conrad).

plea (plē), *n.* **1.** a request, especially one made prayerfully or pleadingly; appeal: *a plea for pity.* **2.** an argument or claim in defense; excuse: *The man's plea was that he did not see the signal.* **3.** *Law.* **a.** the answer made by a defendant to a charge against him in a court of law. **b.** an argument or allegation of fact made in support of one side in a lawsuit. **c.** a plea which alleges some new fact on the basis of which the suit should be dismissed, delayed, or barred, but does not answer the charge; special plea. **4.** *British, Law.* an action at law; lawsuit.
[Middle English *plai, plaid* < Old French *plaid* lawsuit, decision plea < Late Latin *placitum* < Latin, (that) which pleases < *placēre* to please]
—**Syn. 1.** entreaty, prayer.

pleach (plēch), *v.t.* to interweave (growing branches, vines, etc.); intertwine or entwine: *Walking in a thick-pleached alley in mine orchard* (Shakespeare). [earlier form of *plash*[2], probably < dialectal Old French *plechier,* variant of *plessier*]

plead (plēd), *v.,* **plead·ed** or (*Informal*) **pled, plead·ing.** —*v.t.* **1.** to offer reasons for or against (a cause, proposal, etc.); argue. **2.** to offer as an excuse: *The woman who stole pleaded poverty.* **3. a.** to argue for or against in a court of law: *He had a good lawyer to plead his case.* **b.** to answer to a charge in a law court; make a plea of: *The prisoner pleaded guilty.* —*v.i.* **1.** to ask earnestly; make an earnest appeal; beg; implore: *When the rent was due, the poor man pleaded for more time.* **2. a.** to conduct a case in a court of law. **b.** to make any allegation as part of an action at law, especially to present an answer or objection on the part of a defendant. **c.** *Obsoleie.* to go to law; litigate.
[Middle English *plaiden* < Old French *plaidier* < Vulgar Latin *placitāre* < Late Latin *placitum* plea < Latin *placēre* to please] —**Syn.** *v.i.* **1.** entreat, supplicate, beseech.

plead·a·ble (plē′də bəl), *adj.* that can be alleged, urged, or claimed in behalf of something.

plead·er (plē′dər), *n.* **1.** a person who pleads, especially in a court of law. **2.** a person who entreats or intercedes.

plead·ing (plē′ding), *n.* **1.** earnest entreaty; intercession; advocacy; supplication. **2. a.** the advocating of a case in a court of law. **b.** the art or science of preparing or presenting pleas in legal cases. **c.** a formal, usually written, allegation setting forth the cause of action or defense.
pleadings, the formal charges or claims by the plaintiff and answers by the defendant in a lawsuit, made alternately until the issue is submitted for decision: *The Court is entitled to look at the pleadings in the Irish action* (Law Reports).
—*adj.* that pleads; entreating; beseeching; imploring. —**plead′ing·ly,** *adv.*

pleas·ance (plez′əns), *n.* **1.** a pleasant place, usually with trees, fountains, and flowers, and maintained as part of the grounds of a country estate. **2.** *Archaic and Poetic.* delight; pleasure: *a feeling of solace and pleasance* (Scott). [< Old French *plaisance* pleasure < *plaisant* pleasant. Doublet of PLAISANCE.]

pleas·ant (plez′ənt), *adj.* **1.** giving pleasure; pleasing; agreeable: *a pleasant outing in the country, a pleasant swim on a hot day.* **2.** easy to get along with; agreeable; friendly: *a pleasant young man.* **3.** fair; not stormy: *pleasant weather.* [< Old French *plaisant,* present participle of *plaisir* to please] —**pleas′ant·ly,** *adv.* —**pleas′ant·ness,** *n.*
—**Syn. 1. Pleasant, pleasing, agreeable** mean giving pleasure or satisfaction to the mind, feelings, or senses. **Pleasant** applies to the person or thing that gives pleasure: *We spent a pleasant evening.* **Pleasing** applies to the person who receives pleasure: *It was pleasing to me because I wanted to see them.* **Agreeable** suggests being to a person's own taste or liking: *I think this cough medicine has an agreeable flavor.* **2.** congenial, amiable.

pleas·ant·ry (plez′ən trē), *n., pl.* **-ries. 1.** a good-natured joke; jesting action or witty remark: *He . . . made him the butt of his pleasantries* (Washington Irving). **2.** fun; joking. —**Syn. 1.** witticism, jest. **2.** drollery, banter, raillery.

please (plēz), *v.,* **pleased, pleas·ing.** —*v.t.* **1.** to be agreeable to; cause to be happy or glad: *Toys please children.* **2.** to be the will of (used impersonally): *May it please the court to show mercy.*
—*v.i.* **1.** to be agreeable; make happy or glad: *Such a fine meal cannot fail to please. For we that live to please must please to live* (Samuel Johnson). **2.** to wish; like; think fit: *Do what you please.* **3.** may it please you (now used merely as a polite addition to requests or commands): *Come here, please. Over the piano was printed a notice: Please do not shoot the pianist. He is doing his best* (Oscar Wilde).
be pleased, a. to be moved to pleasure: *I was pleased with the quality of his work.* **b.** to be disposed; like; choose: *The governor is pleased to doubt our having such letters as we mentioned* (Benjamin Franklin).
if you please, if you like; with your permission: *Pray sir, put your sword up if you please* (Shakespeare). *Will you take another cup? If you please* (Hugh Binning).
please oneself, a. to gratify or satisfy oneself: *I purposed not so much to please myself, and a few, as to be beneficial* (Thomas Granger). **b.** *Informal.* to do as one likes: *Since he didn't accept my advice, I told him to please himself.*
[Middle English *plesen* < Old French *plesir,* and *plaisir* < Latin *placēre*] —**pleas′er,** *n.*
—**Syn.** *v.t.* **1.** gratify, delight, content, suit.
➤ **Pleased** is followed by *with,* not *at: His boss was very pleased with his work.*

pleas·ing (plē′zing), *adj.* that gives pleasure or satisfaction; agreeable: *a pleasing smile, a very well-mannered and pleasing young man.* —**pleas′ing·ly,** *adv.* —**pleas′ing·ness,** *n.* —**Syn.** See **pleasant.**

pleas of the Crown, 1. (originally, in England) pleas or legal actions over which the Crown claimed exclusive jurisdiction. **2.** (later, in England) all criminal actions or proceedings. **3.** (in Scotland) the actions for robbery, rape, murder, and arson.

pleas·ur·a·ble (plezh′ər ə bəl, plā′zhər-), *adj.* pleasant; agreeable. —**pleas′ur·a·ble·ness,** *n.* —**Syn.** gratifying.

pleas·ur·a·bly (plezh′ər ə blē, plā′zhər-), *adv.* in a pleasurable manner; with pleasure.

pleas·ure (plezh′ər, plā′zhər), *n., v.,* **-ured, -ur·ing.** —*n.* **1.** a feeling of being pleased; enjoyment; delight: *The boy's pleasure in the gift was good to see. Pleasure, not gold, is now the quest* (New Yorker). **2.** something that pleases; cause of joy or delight: *It would be a pleasure to see you again.* **3.** worldly or frivolous enjoyment: sensuous gratification. **4.** one's will, desire, or choice: *What is your pleasure in this matter?*
at one's pleasure, as or when one pleases; at will; at discretion: *. . . whom the housekeeper . . . huffed about at her pleasure* (Scott).
during one's pleasure, while one pleases: *. . . a Secretary . . . who shall hold office during Her Majesty's pleasure* (Acts of Parliament).
take pleasure, to be pleased; delight: *I take pleasure in introducing the next speaker.*
—*v.t.* to give pleasure to; please; gratify.
—*v.i.* **1.** to take pleasure; delight. **2.** *Informal.* to go out for pleasure.
[Middle English *plesir,* or *plesere* < Old French *plesir,* and *plaisir,* noun use of infinitive; see PLEASE; English spelling influenced by *measure*]
—**Syn.** *n.* **1. Pleasure, delight, joy** mean a feeling of satisfaction and happiness coming from having, experiencing, or expecting something good or to one's liking. **Pleasure** is the general word applying to this feeling, whether or not it is shown in any way: *The compliment gave her pleasure.* **Delight** means great pleasure, usually shown or expressed in a lively way: *The child clapped her hands in delight.* **Joy** implies intense delight and happiness, often expressing itself in rejoicing: *Success brought him joy.*

pleasure boat, a boat designed or used for pleasure.

pleas·ure-dome (plezh′ər dōm′, plā′zhər-), *n.* a large and stately mansion, estate, hotel, etc. [allusion to Samuel Taylor Coleridge's *Kubla Khan*]

pleasure ground, a piece of ground or land appropriated to pleasure or enjoyment.

pleas·ure-house (plezh′ər hous′, plā′zhər-), *n.* a house for purposes of pleasure or enjoyment.

pleas·ure·less (plezh′ər lis, plā′zhər-), *adj.* without pleasure; joyless.

pleat (plēt), *n.* a flat, usually narrow fold made in a fabric by doubling it on itself, especially one of a series of folds by which the edge of a garment or drapery is symmetrically taken in. Pleats are arranged in many different fashions. *Twenty years ago it would have been possible to market all-wool fabrics with pleats of great durability, if only the pleater had been aware of research* (London Times). —*v.t.* to fold or arrange (garments, draperies, etc.) in pleats: *a pleated skirt.* [variant of *plait*] —**pleat′er,** *n.*

pleat·less (plēt′lis), *adj.* having no pleats: *The trends to . . . two-button suits and pleatless trousers are expected to continue* (Wall Street Journal).

pleb[1] (pleb), *n. Slang.* a plebeian.

pleb[2] (pleb), *n. Slang.* a plebe at a military or naval academy.

plebe[1] (plēb), *n. U.S.* a member of the lowest class at a military or naval academy, especially the United States Military Academy at West Point, the Naval Academy at Annapolis, or the Air Force Academy at Colorado Springs. [American English, perhaps short for *plebeian*]

plebe[2] (plēb), *n. Obsolete.* the common people of ancient Rome; the plebs. [< Middle French *plèbe,* learned borrowing from Latin *plēbs* plebs]

ple·be·ian (pli bē′ən), *n.* **1.** one of the common people of ancient Rome. **2.** one of the common people. **3.** a common, vulgar person: *To the brave, there is but one sort of plebeian, and that is the coward* (Edward G. Bulwer-Lytton).
—*adj.* **1.** of the plebeians. **2.** belonging or having to do with the common people: *the craftsmen and other plebeian inhabitants of the town* (Hawthorne). **3.** common; vulgar. [< Latin *plēbēius* (< *plēbēs,* variant of *plēbs* the common people) + English *-an*]
—**Syn.** *n.* **2.** commoner. **3.** cad. *-adj.* **3.** coarse.

ple·be·ian·ism (pli bē′ə niz əm), *n.* plebeian character or ways: *The young fellow was dressed very genteelly, with a sword, and carried no marks of plebeianism about him* (Laurence Sterne).

ple·bis·ci·tar·y (plə bis′ə ter′ē, -tər-), *adj.* **1.** relating to or of the nature of a plebiscite. **2.** based on or favoring a plebiscite: *Swiss democracy is unique, for it is not parliamentary but plebiscitary democracy* (Manchester Guardian).

pleb·i·scite (pleb′ə sīt, -sit), *n.* a direct vote by the qualified voters of a state on some important question: *The plebiscite in Kashmir desired by the U.N. has never taken place* (Wall Street Journal). [< French, Middle French *plébiscite,* learned borrowing from Latin *plēbiscītum* < *plēbēī,* genitive of *plēbs* the common people + *scītum* decree, ultimately < *scīre* to know]

pleb·is·ci·tum (pleb′ə sī′təm), *n., pl.* **-ta** (-tə). **1.** a law enacted by the ancient Roman plebeians. **2.** a plebiscite: *Physical force is not all on the side of the tyrants, nor does a plebiscitum invariably sanction only a crime* (Spectator). [< Latin *plēbiscītum* plebiscite]

plebs (plebz), *n., pl.* **ple·bes** (plē′bēz). **1.** the common people of ancient Rome. **2.** the common people; the populace. [< Latin *plēbs, plēbis*] —**Syn. 2.** hoi polloi.

plec·tog·nath (plek′təg nath), *adj.* of or belonging to an order of teleost fishes having powerful jaws and teeth and (typically) bony or spiny scales, as the triggerfish, puffer, and filefish. —*n.* a plectognath fish. [< New Latin *Plectognathi* the order name < Greek *plektós* plaited, twisted (< *plékein* to twist) + *gnáthos* jaw]

plec·tog·na·thous (plek tog′nə thəs), *adj.* plectognath.

plec·tron (plek′tron, -trən), *n., pl.* **-trons, -tra** (-trə). plectrum.

plec·trop·ter·us (plek trop′tər əs), *n.* any of a group of spur-winged geese of Africa. [< New Latin *Plectropterus* the genus name < Greek *plêktron* cockspur + *pterón* wing]

plec·trum (plek′trəm), *n., pl.* **-trums, -tra** (-trə). a small piece of ivory, horn, metal, etc., used for plucking the strings of a mandolin, lyre, zither, or other wire-strung instrument. [< Latin *plēctrum* < Greek *plêktron* (literally) thing to strike with < *plēssein* to strike]

pled (pled), *v. Informal.* pleaded; a past

tense and past participle of **plead:** *The man pled for mercy.*

pledge (plej), *n., v.,* **pledged, pledg·ing.** —*n.* **1.** a solemn promise: *a pledge to support a candidate. The drunkard signed a pledge never to drink again.* **2.** something that secures or makes safe; security: *The knight left a jewel as pledge for the borrowed horse.* **3.** the condition of being held as security: *to put bonds in pledge for a loan.* **4.** *U.S.* a person who has promised to join an organization but is serving a probationary period before membership: *Postcards sent out to undergraduates, pledges, and alumni of . . . an academic fraternity* (Newsweek). **5.** something given to show favor or love or as a promise of something to come; sign; token: *Bear her this jewel, pledge of my affection* (Shakespeare). **6.** the drinking of a health or toast. **7.** *Law.* **a.** the act of delivering something to another as security for the repayment of a debt or performance of a contract. **b.** the contract by which such a delivery is formally made. **8.** *Obsolete.* **a.** a person who acts as surety for another. **b.** a hostage.

take or **sign the pledge,** to promise not to drink alcoholic liquor: *Once, the mere picture of a ragged urchin crouched outside a snowbound inn waiting for her father to emerge drunk with the comforts of beer . . . was enough to make strong men sign the pledge* (Manchester Guardian Weekly).

—*v.t.* **1.** to undertake to give; promise solemnly: *to pledge allegiance to the flag, to pledge $100 to a charity.* **2.** to cause to promise solemnly; bind by a promise: *to pledge hearers to secrecy.* **3.** to give as security: *to pledge one's honor, to pledge land for a loan.* **4.** to drink a health to; drink in honor of (someone) and wish (him) well; toast: *The knights rose from the banquet table to pledge the king. Drink to me only with thine eyes, And I will pledge with mine* (Ben Jonson). [< Anglo-French, Old French *plege* < Medieval Latin *plegium, plevium* < *plevire* to incur risk for, go bail for; to warrant, apparently < a Germanic word. Related to PLIGHT[2].]

—**Syn.** *n.* **1.** covenant, vow. **2.** surety, guarantee. *-v.t.* **3.** pawn.

pledg·ee (ple jē′), *n.* **1.** *Law.* a person with whom something is deposited as a pledge. **2.** a person to whom a pledge is made.

pledg·er (plej′ər), *n.* **1.** a person who pledges. **2.** *Law.* pledgor: *This . . . may be said to rest on the assent of the pledger . . . which empowered the pledgee to sell in default of payment* (Edward Poste).

pledg·et (plej′it), *n.* a small, absorbent compress of gauze, cotton, or the like, for use on a wound, sore, etc.: *He drew a pledget of linen . . . through the wound* (John Henry). [origin uncertain]

pledg·or or **pledge·or** (ple jôr′), *n. Law.* a person who deposits something as a pledge; pledger.

Ple·iad (plē′ad, plī′-), *n.* any of the Pleiades.

ple·iad (plē′ad, plī′-), *n.* a brilliant cluster or group of persons or things, especially of seven: *Donne, Chillingworth, Sir T. Browne, Jeremy Taylor, Milton, South, Barrow, form a pleiad, a constellation of seven stars, such as no literature can match* (Thomas De Quincey). [< *Pleiad*]

Ple·ia·des (plē′ə dēz, plī′-), *n.pl.* **1.** a group of hundreds of stars in the constellation Taurus, commonly spoken of as seven, though only six can normally be seen with the naked eye: *On the Bull's shoulder is the famous group of the Pleiades, often called the Seven Sisters, sometimes the Seven Brothers* (Bernhard, Bennett, and Rice). **2.** *Greek Mythology.* seven of the daughters of Atlas and Pleione who were transformed by the gods into this group of stars.

plein-air (plān′ãr′), *adj.* of or having to do with certain impressionist schools and styles of painting that originated in France about 1870 and aimed at the representation of effects of atmosphere and light that cannot be observed in the studio; open-air. [< French *en plein air* in open air]

plein-air·ism (plān′ãr′iz əm), *n.* the principles or methods of the plein-air painters.

plein-air·ist (plān′ãr′ist), *n.* an artist of the plein-air school: *For plein-airist Monet this meant capturing al fresco the bluish sunshine of the Ile-de-France* (New Yorker).

Plei·o·cene (plī′ə sēn), *n., adj.* Pliocene.

plei·o·trop·ic (plī′ə trop′ik), *adj. Genetics.* controlling or effecting change in more than one character: *The mutation was pleiotropic* (Scientific American). *Frequently, and mysteriously, the streptomycin resistance is "pleiotropic"—it brings about simultaneously one or more metabolically unrelated nutritional requirements* (New Scientist). [< Greek *pleiōn* more, comparative of *polýs* much, many + *trópos* a turning]

Pleis·to·cene (plīs′tə sēn), *n.* **1.** the geological epoch before the present period; ice age. It was characterized by vast glaciers and the presence of man in Europe. *Within the Quaternary most of the time is taken up by the Pleistocene, estimated at 980,000 years, while the Holocene or Recent has lasted only 20,000 years* (Beals and Hoijer). **2.** the deposits of gravel, etc., made in this epoch.

—*adj.* of this epoch or these deposits: *the great Pleistocene glaciers of Europe and North America.* [< Greek *pleîstos* most, superlative of *polýs* much, many + *kainós* recent]

plen., plenipotentiary.

ple·na (plē′nə), *n.* plenums; a plural of **plenum.**

ple·na·ri·ly (plē′nər ə lē, plen′ər-), *adv.* in a plenary manner; fully; completely: *The priest employed . . . may not be plenarily inspired* (Manchester Examiner).

ple·na·ry (plē′nər ē, plen′ər-), *adj.* **1.** full; complete; entire; absolute: *to invest an ambassador with plenary power.* **2.** attended by all of its qualified members; fully constituted: *a plenary session of a committee.* [< Late Latin *plēnārius* < Latin *plēnus* full]

plenary indulgence, (in the Roman Catholic Church) complete remission of temporal penalty for sin.

ple·ni·lune (plē′nə lün, plen′ə-), *n. Poetic.* **1.** a full moon. **2.** the time of the full moon. [< Latin *plēnilūnium* < *plēnus* full + *lūna* moon]

ple·nip·o·tence (plə nip′ə təns), *n.* a fullness or completeness of power: . . . *the plenipotence of a free nation* (Milton).

ple·nip·o·tent (plə nip′ə tənt), *Rare.* —*adj.* invested with or possessing full power or authority; plenipotentiary. —*n.* a plenipotent person; plenipotentiary. [< Late Latin *plēnipotēns, -entis* < Latin *plēnus* full + *potēns* potent, empowered]

plen·i·po·ten·ti·ar·y (plen′ə pə ten′shē-er′ē, -shər-), *n., pl.* **-ar·ies,** *adj.* —*n.* a diplomatic agent having full power or authority: *Each municipality was, as it were, a little sovereign, sending envoys to a congress to vote and to sign as plenipotentiaries* (John L. Motley).

—*adj.* having or giving full power and authority.

[< Medieval Latin *plenipotentiarius* < Late Latin *plēnipotēns* plenipotent]

plen·ish (plen′ish), *v.t. Especially Scottish.* to fill up; furnish; supply; stock. [< Old French *pleniss-,* stem of *plenir* < Latin *plēnus* full]

plen·ish·ing (plen′i shing), *n. Especially Scottish.* **1.** the act of filling up or furnishing. **2. a.** that with which anything is furnished; equipment. **b.** household furniture. **3.** the outfit contributed by a bride for setting up housekeeping.

ple·nism (plē′niz əm), *n.* the theory that all space is a plenum and that there is no such thing as a vacuum.

ple·nist (plē′nist), *n.* a person who maintains that all space is full of matter and denies the possibility of a vacuum: *Neither rarefied air nor mercury vapor, as the "plenists" desperately asserted, was to be found in the vacant space* (Scientific American). [< *plen*(um) + *-ist*]

plen·i·tude (plen′ə tüd, -tyüd), *n.* **1.** fullness; completeness: *Her force of character, emerging at length in all its plenitude, imposed itself absolutely upon its environment* (Lytton Strachey). **2.** plentifulness; abundance: *Its present deer population varies . . . depending on the season and the plenitude of available forage* (Atlantic). [< Latin *plēnitūdō, -inis* completeness, fullness < *plēnus* full] —**Syn. 2.** copiousness.

plen·i·tu·di·nous (plen′ə tü′də nəs, -tyü′-), *adj.* stout; portly.

plen·te·ous (plen′tē əs), *adj.* **1.** present or existing in full supply; abundant; plentiful; copious: *rich, plenteous tresses* (Charlotte Brontë). **2.** bearing or yielding abundantly (of); prolific (in); fertile: *The seasons had been plenteous in corn* (George Eliot). —**plen′te·ous·ly,** *adv.* —**plen′te·ous·ness,** *n.*

plen·ti·ful (plen′ti fəl), *adj.* **1.** more than enough; ample; abundant: *Ten gallons of gasoline is a plentiful supply for a seventy-mile trip. Apples are cheap now they are plentiful.* **2.** furnished with or yielding abundance: *to set a plentiful table.* —**plen′ti·ful·ly,** *adv.* —**plen′ti·ful·ness,** *n.*

—**Syn. 1.** copious, profuse. **2.** bountiful, generous. —**Ant. 1.** scarce, insufficient. **1, 2.** scant.

plen·ty (plen′tē), *n., pl.* **-ties,** *adj., adv.* —*n.* **1.** a full supply; all that a person needs; large enough number or quantity: *You have plenty of time to catch the train.* **2.** the quality or condition of being plentiful; abundance: *years of peace and plenty.*

—*adj.* enough; plentiful; abundant: *Six potatoes will be plenty.*

—*adv. Informal.* quite; fully: *plenty good enough.*

[Middle English *pleynte,* also *plenteth* < Old French *plente,* earlier *plentet* < Latin *plēnitās* fullness < *plēnus* full]

—**Syn.** *n.* **1.** profusion, copiousness.

ple·num (plē′nəm), *n., pl.* **-nums** or **-na,** *adj.* —*n.* **1. a.** an enclosed quantity of air or other gas under greater pressure than the outside atmosphere. **b.** such a condition of pressure. **2.** a space that is filled, or conceived as being filled, with matter. **3.** the whole of space regarded as being filled with matter. **4.** a full assembly, as a joint assembly of the upper and lower houses of a legislature. **5. a.** a condition of fullness. **b.** a full place, thing, etc.

—*adj.* of or having to do with a plenum. [< Latin *plēnum* (*spatium*) full (space), (literally) neuter of *plēnus* full]

plenum chamber, a chamber above the furnace in a hot-air heating system, into which the warm air from the furnace goes before it is carried off by ducts.

plenum method or **system,** a system in which fresh air is forced by artificial means into a space to be ventilated, and the used air driven out by displacement.

ple·o·chro·ic (plē′ə krō′ik), *adj.* showing different colors because of selective absorption of light when viewed in two or three different directions, as certain double-refracting crystals. [< Greek *pléōn* more, comparative of *polýs* much, many + *chróā* color + English *-ic*]

ple·och·ro·ism (plē ok′rō iz əm), *n.* the quality of being pleochroic, as exhibited by certain crystals.

ple·o·chro·ma·tism (plē′ə krō′mə tiz əm), *n.* pleochroism.

ple·o·mor·phic (plē′ə môr′fik), *adj.* exhibiting different forms at different stages of the life cycle, as certain bacteria and fungi. [< Greek *pléōn* more, comparative of *polýs* much, many + *morphḗ* form + English *-ic*]

ple·o·mor·phism (plē′ə môr′fiz əm), *n. Biology.* **1.** the existence of different forms or types in a species, genus, etc. **2.** the occurrence of more than one independent stage in the life cycle of a species.

ple·o·nasm (plē′ə naz əm), *n.* **1.** the use of more words than are necessary to express an idea: "*The two twins*" *is a pleonasm.* **2.** the unnecessary word, phrase, or expression. [< Late Latin *pleonasmos* < Greek *pleonasmós* < *pleonázein* to be redundant < *pléōn* more, comparative of *polýs* much]

ple·o·nas·tic (plē′ə nas′tik), *adj.* using more words than are needed; superfluous; redundant. —**ple′o·nas′ti·cal·ly,** *adv.*

ple·o·nas·ti·cal (plē′ə nas′tə kəl), *adj.* pleonastic.

ple·o·nec·tic (plē′ə nek′tik), *adj.* of or having to do with pleonexia.

ple·o·nex·i·a (plē′ə nek′sē ə), *n.* **1.** greed or grasping selfishness, especially as an indication of mental disorder. **2.** a condition in which the hemoglobin of the blood releases less oxygen than normal to body tissues. [< New Latin *pleonexia* < Greek *pleonexíā* < *pléōn* more, comparative of *polýs* much + *échein* to have]

ple·o·pod (plē′ə pod), *n.* a swimmeret: *The abdominal swimmerets (pleopods) . . . and the wide uropods, with the telson, form a broad terminal paddle for swimming* (Tracy I. Storer). [< Greek *pleîn* to swim + *poûs, podós* foot]

ple·ro·ma (plə rō′mə), *n.* (in Gnosticism) the spiritual universe as the abode of God and of the totality of divine powers and emanations. [< Greek *plḗrōma* a filling; see PLEROME]

ple·rome (plir′ōm), *n. Botany.* the innermost region of an apical meristem, composed of actively dividing cells: *Procambium or plerome originates the primary or first vascular bundles, the cambium, and sometimes the pith* (Heber W. Youngken). [< German *Plerom* < Greek *plērōma* a filling < *plēroûn* to fill < *plērēs* full]

Ple·si·an·thro·pus (plē′sē an′thrə pəs), *n.* an early manlike ape, considered to be one of the Australopithecines, whose bones have been found in South Africa: *By comparing sections of the snout of Telanthropus with those of the two established apemen, Paranthropus and Plesianthropus ... he found that Telanthropus approached the human stock "very closely"* (New York Times). [< New Latin *Plesianthropus* the genus name < Greek *plēsíos* near + *ánthrōpos* man]

ple·si·o·saur (plē′sē ə sôr), *n.* any of a group of large sea reptiles, now extinct, that had a long neck, small head, short tail, and four large flippers instead of legs. Plesiosaurs were common in the early Mesozoic era. *Four main groups of Mesozoic marine reptiles are recognized: icthyosaurs, mosasaurs, plesiosaurs, and turtles* (Raymond Cecil Moore). [< New Latin *Plesiosaurus* the genus name < Greek *plēsíos* near + *saûros* lizard]

Plesiosaur (about 40 ft. long)

ple·si·o·sau·rus (plē′sē ə sôr′əs), *n., pl.* **-sau·ri** (-sôr′ī). plesiosaur.

ples·sor or **ples·ser** (ples′ər), *n.* plexor.

pleth·o·ra (pleth′ər ə), *n.* **1.** excessive fullness; too much; superabundance: *a plethora of words, a plethora of food. This being the big Paris season, there is such a plethora of local and foreign attractions to look at and listen to that the real problem is to try and pick out the hundred best* (New Yorker). **2.** a disease caused by an excess of red corpuscles in the blood or an increase in the quantity of blood in the body: *Your character is like a person in a plethora, absolutely dying from too much health* (Richard Brinsley Sheridan). [< Late Latin *plēthōra* < Greek *plēthṓrā* fullness of humors < *plḗthein* be full < *plêthos* multitude, mass] —**Syn. 1.** superfluity, oversupply.

ple·thor·ic (ple thôr′ik, -thor′-; pleth′ər-), *adj.* **1.** too full; inflated: *a plethoric style of writing, plethoric opulence.* **2.** having too much blood or too many red corpuscles in the blood; afflicted with plethora: *a plethoric condition, a plethoric person.* —**ple·thor′i·cal·ly,** *adv.*

ple·thor·i·cal (ple thôr′ə kəl, -thor′-), *adj.* plethoric.

ple·thys·mo·graph (plə thiz′mə graf, -gräf), *n.* a device for measuring and recording the variation in the size or volume of a part of the body, as altered by the flow of blood in it: *The test is made by measuring the blood flow in a finger tip with an instrument called a plethysmograph while a brief electric shock is given at regular intervals to the back of the foot* (Science News Letter). [< Greek *plēthysmós* enlargement (< *plēthýs* fullness) + English *-graph*]

pleth·ys·mog·raph·y (pleth′iz mog′rə fē), *n.* the use of a plethysmograph: *Electrical Impedance Plethysmography. The electrical resistive measurement of the blood pulse volume, peripheral and central blood flow* (Science).

pleu·ra[1] (plůr′ə), *n., pl.* **pleu·rae** (plůr′ē). a thin membrane in the body of a mammal, covering the lungs and folded back to make a lining for the thorax or chest cavity. [< New Latin *pleura* < Greek *pleurā́* the side, rib, or *pleurá* side, plural of *pleurón* rib]

pleu·ra[2] (plůr′ə), *n.* plural of **pleuron.**

pleu·ral (plůr′əl), *adj.* of the pleura: ... *pleural inflammation ... affecting the base of the left lung* (Morell Mackenzie).

pleural cavity, the space between the two layers of the pleura: *The space between the body wall and the lungs is designated the pleural cavity* (Harbaugh and Goodrich).

pleu·rec·to·my (plů rek′tə mē), *n., pl.* **-mies.** the surgical removal of part of the pleura. [< Greek *pleurā́* the side + *ektomḗ* a cutting out]

pleu·ri·sy (plůr′ə sē), *n.* inflammation of the thin membrane covering the lungs and lining the thorax: *Pleurisy usually occurs as a complication of pneumonia, tuberculosis, and other infectious diseases* (World Book Encyclopedia). [< Old French *pleursie,* alteration of Late Latin *pleurisis* lung trouble, for Latin *pleurītis* pleurisy, pain in the side < Greek *pleurîtis* < *pleurā́* the side, rib; see PLEURA]

pleurisy root, 1. the butterfly weed, whose root has been used as a popular remedy for pleurisy. **2.** the root.

pleu·rit·ic (plů rit′ik), *adj.* **1.** having pleurisy. **2.** of pleurisy. **3.** causing pleurisy.

pleu·ri·tis (plů rī′tis), *n.* pleurisy.

pleu·ro·dont (plůr′ə dont), *adj.* **1.** (of a tooth) not in a socket but issuing directly from and fixed to the upper or lower jawbone at the side or front. **2.** having such teeth, as certain lizards. —*n.* a pleurodont animal. [< Greek *pleurón* side + *odoús, odóntos* tooth]

pleu·ro·dyn·i·a (plůr′ə din′ē ə, -dī′nē-), *n.* a virus infection causing painful inflammation of the muscles of the diaphragm and the chest and many symptoms similar to those of poliomyelitis; devil's grip: *An alert pediatrician recognized the ... painful but noncrippling disease also known as pleurodynia* (Newsweek). [< New Latin *pleurodynia* < Greek *pleurón* side + *odýnē* pain]

pleu·ro·dyn·ic (plůr′ə din′ik), *adj.* of or having to do with pleurodynia.

pleu·ron (plůr′on), *n., pl.* **pleu·ra.** a lateral part of the body of an arthropod, especially of a thoracic segment of an insect. [< New Latin *pleuron* < Greek *pleurón* rib, side]

pleu·ro·per·i·car·di·al (plůr′ō per′ə kär′dē əl), *adj.* having to do with the pleura and pericardium (applied to a friction sound heard in auscultation in cases of pleurisy). [< Greek *pleurā́* the side + English *pericardial*]

pleu·ro·per·i·to·ne·al (plůr′ō per′ə tə nē′əl), *adj.* having to do with the pleura, or pleurae, and the peritoneum.

pleu·ro·pneu·mo·nia (plůr′ō nü mōn′yə, -mō′nē ə; -nyü-), *n.* pneumonia complicated with pleurisy: *The nomadic Fulani herdsmen of Nigeria had developed for themselves a crude form of inoculation against pleuropneumonia which is surely, if true, one of the most remarkable examples of preliterate science* (S. H. Waddington).

pleu·rot·o·my (plů rot′ə mē), *n., pl.* **-mies.** a surgical incision into the pleura. [< Greek *pleurā́* the side + *-tomíā* a cutting]

plex·i·form (plek′sə fôrm), *adj.* shaped like or resembling a plexus: *Its papilla is covered with a plexiform mesh of dilated vessels* (British Medical Journal). [< Latin *plexus* braid + English *-form*]

Plex·i·glas (plek′sə glas′, -gläs′), *n. Trademark.* plexiglass.

plex·i·glass (plek′sə glas′, -gläs′), *n.* a light, transparent thermoplastic, often used in place of glass. [< *pl*(astic) + (fl)*exi*(ble) + *glass*]

plex·im·e·ter (plek sim′ə tər), *n.* a small, thin plate, as of ivory, designed to be placed in contact with the body and struck with a plexor in diagnosis, examination, etc., by percussion. [< Greek *plêxis* stroke, percussion (< *plḗssein* to strike) + English *-meter*]

plex·or (plek′sər), *n.* a small hammer used for tapping the body (percussion) in diagnosis, examination, etc. Also, **plessor, plesser.** [< Greek *plêxis* a stroke (< *plḗssein* to strike) + English *-or,* as in *flexor*]

plex·us (plek′səs), *n., pl.* **-us·es** or **-us. 1.** a network of nerve fibers, blood vessels, lymphatics, etc.: *The solar plexus is a collection of nerves behind the stomach.* **2.** any intertwined or interwoven mass; web; network. [< New Latin *plexus* < Latin *plexus, -ūs* a braid < *plectere* to twine, braid]

plf., plaintiff.

pli·a·bil·i·ty (plī′ə bil′ə tē), *n.* a being pliable; flexibility: *Pliability in politics, if accompanied by honesty, is a virtue* (Henry Adams).

pli·a·ble (plī′ə bəl), *adj.* **1.** easily bent; flexible; supple: *Willow twigs are pliable.* **2.** easily influenced; yielding: *He is too pliable to be a good leader.* [< Middle French *pliable* < *plier* to bend; see PLY[2]] —**pli′a·ble·ness,** *n.*

pli·a·bly (plī′ə blē), *adv.* in a pliable manner; yieldingly; compliantly: *I come into the hands of my God as pliably ... as that first clod of earth of which he made me in Adam* (John Donne).

pli·an·cy (plī′ən sē), *n.* a being easily bent or influenced; being pliant: *To be overlooked for want of political pliancy, is a circumstance I need not blush to own* (Richard Watson). —**Syn.** flexibility, pliability.

pli·ant (plī′ənt), *adj.* **1.** bending easily; flexible; supple. **2.** easily influenced; yielding: *It was his wish that Lord Granville, a young man whom he believed to be pliant to his influence, should be Palmerston's successor* (Lytton Strachey). [< Old French *pliant* bending, present participle of *plier;* see PLY[2]] —**pli′ant·ly,** *adv.* —**pli′ant·ness,** *n.* —**Syn. 1.** pliable, limber. See **flexible.** —**Ant. 1.** rigid.

pliant hour, a moment that lends itself to some purpose; suitable time (from Shakespeare's use of it in *Othello*).

pli·ca (plī′kə), *n., pl.* **-cae** (-sē). **1.** a fold or folding of skin, membrane, etc.: *The mucous membrane lining of the intestinal wall has many plicae* (Carl C. Francis). **2.** a matted, filthy condition of the hair caused by disease. [< Medieval Latin *plica* < Latin *plicāre* to fold, interweave]

plica po·lon·i·ca (pə lon′ə kə), plica, caused by disease. [< New Latin *plica polonica*]

pli·cate (plī′kāt), *adj.* **1.** folded like a fan; pleated. **2.** (of a leaf) folded along its ribs like a closed fan: *Thus birch leaves are plicate, folded several times lengthwise, like a fan* (New York Times). [< Latin *plicātus* folded, past participle of *plicāre* to fold] —**pli′cate·ly,** *adv.* —**pli′cate·ness,** *n.*

pli·cat·ed (plī′kā tid), *adj.* plicate.

pli·ca·tion (plī kā′shən), *n.* **1.** a folding or fold. **2.** plicate form or condition: *An artist of the Chinese school ... may accentuate folds of drapery by a kind of shadow beneath the plication* (W. Anderson).

plic·a·ture (plik′ə chər), *n.* plication.

pli·é (plē ā′), *n. French.* **1.** (in ballet) a position with both knees bent but with the feet remaining on the floor and the back straight. **2.** (literally) bent.

plied (plīd), *v.* the past tense and past participle of **ply**[1] and **ply**[2].

pli·er (plī′ər), *n.* **1.** a person or thing that plies. **2.** pliers.

pli·ers (plī′ərz), *n., pl.* **-ers.** small pincers with long jaws for bending wire, holding small objects, etc. [< *ply*[2], verb]

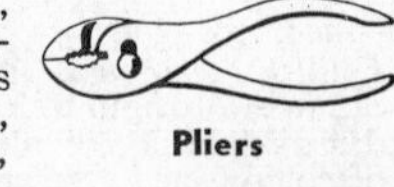
Pliers

plight[1] (plīt), *n.* a condition or state, now usually bad: *He was in a sad plight when he became ill and had no money. I think myself in better plight for a lender than you are* (Shakespeare). [< Anglo-French *plit* (originally) manner of folding, for unrecorded *pleit;* confused with *plight*[2]. Doublet of PLAIT.] —**Syn.** dilemma, scrape, fix. See **predicament.**

plight[2] (plīt), *v.t.* to pledge; promise: *to plight one's faith.*
[Old English *plihtan* < *pliht,* noun]
—*n.* a solemn promise; pledge: *a mutual plight of faith* (George Meredith).
[Old English *pliht* (originally) danger; (later) the incurring of risk in warranting; pledge] —**plight′er,** *n.*

plim·soles (plim′səlz), *n.pl.* plimsolls.

Plim·soll mark or **line** (plim′səl, -sol), a mark or line on the hull of a ship that shows how deep it may ride in the water after loading. A Plimsoll mark is required on British merchant ships and now appears on most other merchant ships. [< Samuel *Plimsoll,* 1824-1898, a member of Parliament who succeeded in having the law against overloading passed]

plim·solls (plim′səlz), *n.pl. British.* light canvas shoes with rubber soles; sneakers.

Plimsoll's mark or **line,** Plimsoll mark or line.

plink (plingk), *v.t.* **1.** to produce a tinkling sound on (a musical instrument, etc.). **2.** to shoot or throw at a target, especially in a more or less casual way: *The neighborhood youngsters had gathered to plink tin cans off our yard fence* (Time). —*v.i.* **1.** to play on a musical instrument, etc., in a tinkling fashion: *So far he has done everything from Chinese-style plinking to jittering rock 'n' roll* (Newsweek). **2.** to shoot or throw something at a target. [imitative] —**plink′er,** *n.*

plinth (plinth), *n.* **1.** the lower, square part of the base of a column. **2.** a square base of a pedestal, as for a statue, bust, or vase. **3.** the squared base of a piece of furniture. **4.** a projecting part of a wall immediately above the ground, often consisting of a course (plinth course) or courses of bricks or stones. [< Latin *plinthus* < Greek *plínthos*]

Pli·o·cene (plī′ə sēn), *n.* **1.** a geological epoch marked by the rising of mountains in western America and the migration of mammals between continents. The Pliocene is the last epoch of the Tertiary period of the Cenozoic era, after the Miocene. *We must of course have had direct ancestors during the Pliocene* (Alfred L. Kroeber). **2.** the rock strata formed in this epoch. —*adj.* of this epoch or these rock strata: *Pliocene beds—deposits some millions of years old—in East Africa are promising sites for future explorations* (Science News Letter). Also, **Pleiocene.** [< Greek *pleíōn* more, comparative of *polýs* much + *kainós* recent]

Pli·o·film (plī′ə film), *n. Trademark.* a clear, flexible plastic, a rubber hydrochloride, used to make raincoats and various kinds of moistureproof or protective bags, wrappings, etc.

Pli·o·hip·pus (plī′ə hip′əs), *n.* any of a group of extinct mammals of the horse family, living about 12,000,000 years ago. It is a direct ancestor of the modern horse and is the first horselike animal with a hoof having only one toe. *Pliohippus had a shoulder height of some 40 inches* (Hegner and Stiles). [< *Plio*(cene) + Greek *híppos* horse]

pli·o·saur (plī′ə sôr), *n.* any of a group of large Mesozoic sea reptiles related and similar to the plesiosaurs, but with a shorter neck, larger head, and stronger jaws and teeth: *The large-headed, bull-necked pliosaurs must have had considerable hydrostatic problems* (New Scientist). [< New Latin *Pliosaurus* the genus name < Greek *pleíon* more + *saûros* lizard]

Pli·o·tron (plī′ə tron), *n. Trademark.* a type of vacuum tube, used in wireless apparatus, with an exceptionally high degree of vacuum, and containing a filament, plate, and grid. [< Greek *pleíōn* more, comparative of *polýs* much + English (elec)*tron*]

plis·ky or **plis·kie** (plis′kē), *n., pl.* **-kies,** *adj. Scottish.* —*n.* a mischievous trick. —*adj.* mischievous: *Auld Habkin o' the Pethfit, who was a plisky body* (John Service). [origin unknown]

plis·sé (plē sā′), *n.* a fabric like crepe, made of cotton, acetate, or rayon, which has the appearance of seersucker caused by a chemical shrinking with caustic soda. [< French *plissé*, (originally) past participle of *plisser* pleat < *pli;* see PLY², noun]

plod (plod), *v.,* **plod·ded, plod·ding,** *n.* —*v.i.* **1.** to walk heavily; trudge: *The old man plods wearily along the road.* **2.** to proceed in a slow or dull way; work patiently with effort: *The secret of good work—to plod on and still keep the passion fresh* (George Meredith). —*v.t.* to walk slowly or heavily along or through: *The plowman homeward plods his weary way* (Thomas Gray).
—*n.* **1.** the act or course of plodding. **2.** a sound of heavy tread.
[perhaps imitative]
—**Syn.** *v.i.* **1.** See **walk.**

plod·der (plod′ər), *n.* **1.** a person who plods: *Small have continual plodders ever won, Save base authority from others' books* (Shakespeare). **2.** a dull, laborious person.

plod·ding (plod′ing), *adj.* patiently laborious: *a man of plodding habits.* —**plod′ding·ly,** *adv.*

plonk¹ (plongk), *v., n., adv.* plunk.

plonk² (plongk), *n. Australian Slang.* cheap wine.

plop (plop), *n., v.,* **plopped, plop·ping,** *adv.* —*n.* **1.** a sound like that of a flat object striking water without a splash. **2.** a falling with a plop.
—*v.i.* **1.** to make a sound like that of a flat object striking water without a splash. **2.** to fall with such a sound. —*v.t.* to cause (something) to plop, or fall with a plop.
—*adv.* with a plop: *The old ship went down all on a sudden with a lurch to starboard—plop* (Joseph Conrad).
[imitative]

plosh (plosh), *n.* a splash: *... the rhythmic groan and plosh of these giant wheels turning slowly in the current* (Atlantic). [variant of *plash*¹]

plo·sion (plō′zhən), *n. Phonetics.* explosion: *In plosive sounds the organs are separated with great rapidity and the plosion itself is thus heard as an instantaneous noise* (Simeon Potter). [< (ex)*plosion*]

plo·sive (plō′siv), *adj., n. Phonetics.* explosive: *We know that, of all the various vowels, plosives, fricatives and other sounds of speech, certain ones occur very often and others less so* (Colin Cherry). [< (ex)*plosive*]

plot (plot), *n., v.,* **plot·ted, plot·ting.** —*n.* **1.** a secret plan, especially to do something wrong: *Two men formed a plot to rob the bank.* **2.** the plan or main story of a play, novel, poem, etc.: *Boys like plots dealing with adventure.* **3.** a small piece of ground: *a garden plot.* **4.** a map; diagram. **5.** *Nautical.* the course or position of a ship, aircraft, etc., drawn on a chart.
—*v.t.* **1.** to plan secretly with others; plan: *to plot mischief or revenge.* **2.** to divide (land) into plots: *The farm was plotted out into house lots.* **3.** to make a map or diagram of. **4.** to mark the position of (something) on a map or diagram. **5.** *Mathematics.* **a.** to determine the location of (a point) by means of its coordinates; mark (a point) on graph paper. **b.** to make (a curve) by connecting points marked out on a graph. **c.** to represent (an equation, etc.) by means of a curve drawn through points on a graph. —*v.i.* to contrive a plot; conspire.
[perhaps Old English *plot* patch of ground. Compare PLAT¹, COMPLOT.]
—**Syn.** *n.* **1.** intrigue, conspiracy. —*v.t.* **1.,** *v.i.* **Plot, conspire, scheme** mean to plan secretly. **Plot** implies forming secretly, alone or together with others, a carefully designed plan, usually harmful or treacherous, against a person, group, or country: *Enemy agents plotted to blow up the plant.* **Conspire** implies combining with others to carry out an illegal act, especially treachery or treason: *They conspired to overthrow the government.* **Scheme** implies careful planning, often in a crafty or underhand way, to gain one's own ends: *He schemed to become president.*

plot·less (plot′lis), *adj.* without a plot or story; having no plot: *It is just as true that most Balanchine ballets are "abstract" in the sense that they are plotless* (Harper's). —**plot′less·ness,** *n.*

plot·line (plot′līn′), *n.* the line or course along which the plot of a play, novel, etc., moves or develops: *a poorly constructed plotline.*

plot·tage (plot′ij), *n.* the area of a plot or plat (of land): *Improvement of adjoining plottage will add a ten-story and penthouse building to the thirty-seven-story skyscraper* (New York Times). [< *plot* + *-age*]

plot·ter (plot′ər), *n.* a person or thing that plots: *A suspected plotter was shot to death* (New York Times). [*The*] *plotter* [*is*] *a device combining a protractor with a ruler* (P.V.H. Weems).

plot·ting board (plot′ing), a large board on which the positions of missiles, aircraft, ships, etc., are plotted.

plotting paper, ruled paper on which curves, diagrams, etc., can be plotted; graph paper.

plot·ty (plot′ē), *adj.,* **-ti·er, -ti·est.** *Informal.* characterized by an elaborate plot: *We don't want it to get plotty, do we? We want a flow of feeling, don't we?* (Listener).

plough (plou), *Especially British.* —*n.* a plow.
—*v.i.* to plow. —*v.t.* **1.** to plow (land). **2.** *Slang.* to fail (a student); flunk; pluck: *A Greek classmate of mine at Exeter was ploughed in preliminary Greek* (Joel Sayre). —**plough′er,** *n.*

plough·a·ble (plou′ə bəl), *adj. Especially British.* plowable.

plough·back (plou′bak′), *n. Especially British.* plowback: *Companies will prefer to let their retained profits run down rather than cut their dividend to increase ploughback* (Manchester Guardian Weekly).

plough·boy (plou′boi′), *n. Especially British.* plowboy.

plough·land (plou′land′), *n. Especially British.* plowland.

plough·man (plou′mən), *n., pl.* **-men.** *Especially British.* plowman: *But pity the poor ploughman—if he does not ride a tractor, his working day amounts to plodding his weary way up and down 25 miles of fields* (News Chronicle).

plough·share (plou′shãr′), *n. Especially British.* plowshare.

plounce (plouns), *v.,* **plounced, plounc·ing.** *Dialect.* —*v.t.* to plunge, especially into water or liquid mud; duck. —*v.i.* to plunge; flounder. [origin uncertain]

plov·er (pluv′ər, plō′vər), *n., pl.* **-ers** or (*collectively*) **-er. 1.** any of a group of several shore birds similar to the sandpipers, with a short bill and tail like that of a pigeon, and rounded body, as the killdeer and the golden plover. **2.** any of several related birds of the same family, as the turnstones. **3.** any of various snipes and sandpipers. [< Anglo-French *plover*, Old French *plouvier* < Vulgar Latin *plovārius* (perhaps literally) rain bird < *plovĕre* to rain, for Latin *pluere* < *pluvia* rain]

Golden Plover (def. 1) (about 11 in. long)

plow (plou), *n.* **1.** a big, heavy, farm implement for cutting the soil and turning it over: *The plow bottom lifts, turns, and breaks up the soil* (World Book Encyclopedia). **2.** a machine for removing snow; snowplow. **3.** any of various instruments, parts of machinery, etc., resembling a plow in shape or action.

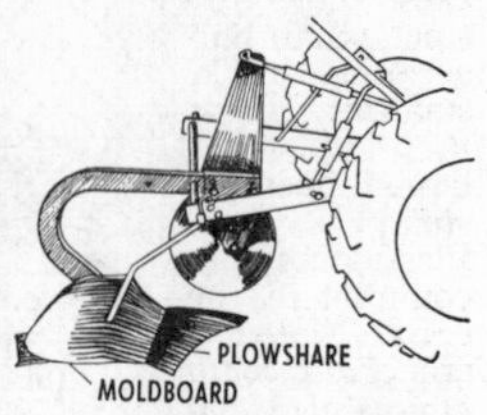

Plow (def. 1)

—*v.t.* **1.** to turn up (soil) with a plow; till: *to plow a straight furrow.* **2.** to remove with a plow or as if with a plow: *to plow snow, to plow up old roots.* **3.** to furrow: *to plow a field, wrinkles plowed in one's face by time.* **4. a.** to cut the surface of (water). **b.** to travel (a course) in this manner. **5.** *British.* to fail (a student); plough. —*v.i.* **1.** to use a plow: *The farmer prefers to plow in the fall, so that he can begin seeding in the spring as soon as weather permits* (Colby and Foster). **2.** to move as a plow does; advance slowly and with effort: *the ... horse-dealer whose caravans plowed through their fastnesses belly deep in snow* (Rudyard Kipling). **3.** to move through water by cutting the surface: *The ship plowed through the waves.* **4.** to bear or admit of plowing: *the soil plows well.*
plow back, to reinvest (the profits of a business) in the same business: *Nearly 40 per cent of all the profits United States Steel has earned during this period has been plowed back into this program* (New York Times).
plow into, to invest: *In the last ten years Imperial Oil has plowed a billion dollars into the Canadian economy* (Maclean's).
plow out, a. to dig or thrust out (of the ground) with a plow: *to plow out roots or weeds.* **b.** to remove; cast out; hollow out: *channels plowed out by a river. God loves not to plow out the heart of our endeavours with ... sad tasks* (Milton).
plow under, a. to bury in the soil by plowing (any grass, legume, etc.) as a form of green manure: *This crop furnishes hay and perhaps some pasturage before it is plowed under* (Fred W. Emerson). **b.** *U.S.* to reduce overproduction by plowing up (a crop): *to plow under acres of wheat.* **c.** *Informal.* to defeat; destroy; overcome: *The nation's educators are particularly worried about the possible "plowing under" of smaller colleges with lower standards* (Science News Letter).
plow up, a. to break up (ground) by plowing: *The wild boar plows it* [*the earth*] *up like a furrow, and does irreparable damage in the cultivated lands* (Oliver Goldsmith). **b.** to dig or thrust out (of the ground) by plowing: *to plow up crops.* **c.** to cut up; scratch deeply; bruise: *For he ... hath plowed up my heart* (William Barlow).
Also, *especially British,* **plough.**
[Middle English *plow*, Old English *plōh*] —**plow′er,** *n.*

Plow (plou), *n.* **1.** the Big Dipper; Charles's Wain. **2.** the entire constellation Ursa Major. [< *plow*]

plow·a·ble (plou′ə bəl), *adj.* that can be plowed; capable of cultivation; arable: *These regions have favorable geographical location ... generous rainfall, plowable land, and deposits of coal and iron* (Ogburn and Nimkoff). Also, *especially British,* **ploughable.**

plow·back (plou′bak′), *n.* **1.** a reinvestment of profits of a business in the same business.

2. the sum that has been reinvested. Also, *especially British,* **ploughback.**

plow·boy (plou′boi′), *n.* **1.** a boy who guides the horses drawing a plow. **2.** a country boy. Also, *especially British,* **ploughboy.**

plow·land (plou′land′, -lənd), *n.* **1.** an old English measure of land, usually 120 acres, considered as the area capable of being tilled with a team of eight oxen. **2.** arable land: *The plowlands of the Eastern states were cleared and plowed mainly by oxen, because oxen move more slowly than horses and have more patience with all that happens while breaking in stumpland* (Harper's). Also, *especially British,* **ploughland.**

plow·man (plou′mən), *n., pl.* **-men. 1.** a man who guides a plow. **2.** a farm worker: *A twentieth-century plowman in mud-caked boots plodding homeward down a puddled lane in springtime twilight* (Carlos Baker). Also, *especially British,* **ploughman.**

plow·share (plou′shãr′), *n.* the blade of a plow, the part that cuts the soil; share: . . . *Countries by future Plowshares to be torn, and Cities raised by Nations yet unborn* (Matthew Prior). Also, *especially British,* **ploughshare.** [< *plow* + *share*²]

plow·tail (plou′tāl′), *n.* the handle or handles of a plow.

plow·wright (plou′rīt′), *n.* a person who makes and repairs plows.

ploy¹ (ploi), *n.* **1.** *Informal.* a remark or action by which the advantage is or may be gained over another; gambit. **2.** *British Informal.* an action or proceeding, especially one in which a person amuses himself: *Their "ploy" of that week happened to be rabbit-shooting with saloon-pistols* (Rudyard Kipling). [perhaps short for *employ,* noun, in obsolete meaning "use"]

ploy² (ploi), *v.i.* (of troops) to move from formation in a line to formation in a column: *There . . . they acquire the art of ploying and deploying their troops* (Sir Charles Napier). [back formation < *deploy*]

ploy·ment (ploi′mənt), *n. Military.* the formation of a column from a line.

plu., plural.

pluck (pluk), *v.t.* **1.** to pull off; pick: *to pluck a person out of bed. She plucked flowers in the garden.* **2.** to pull at; pull; tug; jerk: *to pluck a person by the sleeve.* **3.** to pull on (the strings of a musical instrument). **4.** to pull off the feathers or hair from: *to pluck a chicken, to pluck one's eyebrows.* **5.** *Slang.* to rob; swindle; fleece. **6.** *British Informal.* to reject (a candidate) in an examination. *—v.i.* to pull sharply or forcibly; tug (at): *Do not pluck at his rein* (William Butler Yeats).

pluck up, a. to get new courage; cheer up: *Even those passengers who were most distrustful of themselves plucked up amazingly* (Dickens). **b.** *Rare.* to uproot; demolish: *I plucked up her social fiction* (Elizabeth Barrett Browning).

—n. **1.** the act of picking or pulling. **2.** courage; boldness; spirit: *the pluck, daring, and admirable work of our aviators* (H. G. Wells). *The one thing the English value is pluck* (Emerson). **3.** the heart, liver, and lungs of an animal, used for food.

[Old English *ploccian, pluccian* to pull off, cull; later, to draw, snatch] **—pluck′er,** *n.*

—Syn. *v.t.* **2.** tweak. *-n.* **2.** resolution, stamina.

pluck·a·ble (pluk′ə bəl), *adj.* that can be plucked: *There are about three and a half ounces of pluckable leaf on each plant* (New York Times).

pluck·i·ly (pluk′ə lē), *adv.* in a plucky manner; with courage or spirit: *"No," said Frank, pluckily, as he put his horse into a faster trot* (Anthony Trollope).

pluck·i·ness (pluk′ē nis), *n.* the character of being plucky; pluck; courage: *Her quaint, queer expression, in which curiosity, pluckiness, and a foretaste of amusement mingled* (Adeline Whitney).

pluck·y (pluk′ē), *adj.,* **pluck·i·er, pluck·i·est.** having or showing courage: *a plucky dog.*

—Syn. brave, mettlesome, spirited.

plug (plug), *n., v.,* **plugged, plug·ging.** *—n.* **1.** a piece of wood, etc., used to stop up a hole. **2.** a device to make an electrical connection. **3.** a place where a hose can be attached; hydrant. **4. a.** a cake of pressed tobacco. **b.** a piece of this cut off for chewing. **5.** a spark plug. **6.** *Informal.* an advertisement, especially one put in a radio or television program: *Mr. Harper reported the Democratic convention . . . but . . . has not mentioned it since last month and I want to put in a plug for it* (Bernard De Voto). **7.** a worn-out or inferior horse: *An old plug named Snowball kept getting in the way* (Time). **8.** *U.S. Informal.* a shopworn or unsalable article. **9.** *Slang.* a blow of the fist; punch. **10.** *U.S. Slang.* a plug hat. **11.** a fishing lure made of wood, metal, or plastic, and imitating the action or appearance of some natural food of a fish: *Some fishermen are taking fish on a jointed eel plug* (New York Times). **12.** an iron wedge which is driven between two other wedges (feathers) to split rock. **13.** a small clump of sod, especially sod sold to restore a lawn: *As the name implies, plugs are clumps of grass plants* (New York Times). **14.** *Geology.* **a.** a cylindrical mass of igneous rock formed in the crater of an extinct volcano. **b.** a cylindrical mass of rock salt that has pushed its way upward through overlying rock and formed a dome, often containing quantities of oil and natural gas: *The plugs are cylindrical masses of rock salt, vertical-sided, circular, or elliptical in cross section, and 1 or 2 miles in diameter* (Raymond Cecil Moore).

—v.t. **1.** to stop up or fill with a plug: *Opinion was sadly split as to how the air-defense gap could be plugged* (Newsweek). **2.** *Informal.* to recommend or advertise, especially on a radio or television program: *to plug a new product.* **3.** *Slang.* to put a bullet into; shoot. **4.** *Slang.* to strike with the fist; punch. **5.** to cut a small tapering piece from (a watermelon) in testing ripeness. *—v.i.* **1.** *Informal.* to work steadily; plod: *Mary plugged away at the typewriter.* **2.** *Slang.* to hit; shoot.

plug in, to make an electrical connection by inserting a plug: *On a "background" visit to John Foster Dulles early last month, James Shepley . . . brought a tape recorder into the Secretary's office, plugged it in, and asked a number of questions about Administration foreign policy* (Newsweek).

[apparently < Dutch, Middle Dutch *plugge* a bung, stopper]

—Syn. *n.* **1.** stopper, stopple. **3.** cock. **6.** endorsement. *-v.t.* **1.** close.

plug·board (plug′bôrd′, -bōrd′), *n.* **1.** a switchboard in which the connections are made by inserting plugs. **2.** a removable panel with hundreds of electric terminals into which connecting wire cords may be plugged to control a program or other process in a computer or punch-card machine: *The instructions are programmed on the experimental equipment through a plugboard* (New Scientist).

plug·ger (plug′ər), *n.* **1.** a person or thing that plugs: *Any place and every place where crowds congregated were targets for the pluggers' enthusiasms* (Newsweek). **2.** a dentist's instrument, of various forms, for driving and packing a filling material into a hole in a decayed tooth.

plug hat, *U.S. Informal.* a man's high silk hat.

plug-in (plug′in′), *adj.* needing only to be plugged in to an electrical outlet to operate: *Plug-in fryers and griddles, and a built-in rotisserie were new additions* (New York Times). *—n.* a place where a piece of plug-in equipment can be connected.

plug·o·la (plə gō′lə), *n. U.S. Slang.* undercover payment for mentioning or displaying a product on another sponsor's radio or television program: . . . *the Congressional investigation into the plugola and payola radio scandals* (Harper's). [< *plug* (def. 6) + (pay)*ola*]

plug-ug·ly (plug′ug′lē), *n., pl.* **-lies.** *Slang.* a ruffian; rowdy; tough: *In one Harrigan play, a plug-ugly enters, sneaking along menacingly and brandishing a club* (New Yorker).

plum¹ (plum), *n.* **1.** a roundish, juicy fruit with a smooth skin of purple, blue, red, green, or yellow, and a stone or pit. **2.** any tree that it grows on. The plum is a member of the rose family and is closely related to the cherry. **3. a.** any of several unrelated trees bearing a similar edible fruit. **b.** the fruit itself. **4.** a raisin, currant, etc., in a pudding, cake, etc., especially in a plum pudding: *He stuck in his thumb, and pulled out a plum* (nursery rhyme). **5.** a sugarplum. **6.** something very good or desirable: *His new job is a fine plum.* **7.** a dark purple varying from bluish to reddish. **8.** *British Slang.* **a.** the sum of £100,000: *a stockbroker in the city, who died worth a plum* (Frederick Marryat). **b.** a person who has £100,000.

—adj. dark bluish- or reddish-purple.

[Old English *plūme,* ultimately < Vulgar Latin *prūna* < Latin *prūnum* < Greek *proûnon,* variant of *proúmnon.* Doublet of PRUNE.] **—plum′like′,** *adj.*

—Syn. *n.* **6.** prize.

plum² (plum), *adj., adv.* plumb.

plum·age (plü′mij), *n.* the feathers of a bird: *A parrot has bright plumage.* [< Old French *plumage* < *plume;* see PLUME]

plu·maged (plü′mijd), *adj.* furnished with or having plumage: *some common dull-plumaged little bird* (W. H. Hudson).

plu·mate (plü′māt, -mit), *adj. Zoology.* resembling a feather, as a hair or bristle that bears smaller hairs, or an insect's antenna covered with fine hairs. [< Latin *plūmātus,* past participle of *plūmāre* to provide with feathers < *plūma* feather]

plumb (plum), *n.* a small weight used on the end of a line to find the depth of water or to see if a wall is vertical.

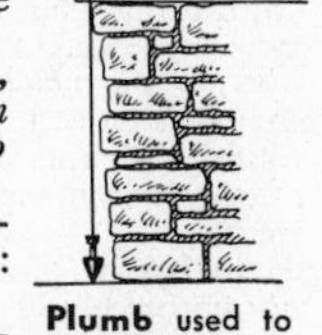

Plumb used to test vertical line of wall

out of plumb or **off plumb,** not vertical: *The column is seriously off plumb* (Pall Mall Gazette).

—adj. **1.** vertical. **2.** *Informal.* complete; thorough: *plumb foolishness.*

—adv. **1.** vertically. **2.** *Informal.* completely; thoroughly: *That horse is plumb worn out.*

—v.t. **1.** to test or adjust by a plumb line; test; sound: *Our line was not long enough to plumb the depths of the lake.* **2.** to get to the bottom of; fathom: *No one could plumb the mystery.* **3.** to close with a lead seal. **4.** *Informal.* to supply or repair the plumbing of.

—v.i. **1.** to be vertical; hang vertically. **2.** *Informal.* to be employed as a plumber.

[Middle English *plum,* or *plumbe* < Old French *plom,* and *plomb* < Latin *plumbum* the element lead] **—plumb′ness,** *n.*

—Syn. *n.* plummet. *-adj.* **1.** perpendicular. **2.** absolute.

plumb·a·ble (plum′ə bəl), *adj.* that can be plumbed.

plum·bag·i·na·ceous (plum baj′ə nā′shəs), *adj.* belonging to a family of dicotyledonous herbs and shrubs typified by the plumbago (leadwort). [< New Latin *Plumbaginaceae* the family name (< Latin *plumbāgō, -inis* plumbago) + English *-ous*]

plum·bag·i·nous (plum baj′ə nəs), *adj.* of the nature of, having to do with, or containing graphite (plumbago): *It . . . considerably resembles the plumbaginous powder . . . obtained by the action of acid on cast iron* (Michael Faraday).

plum·ba·go (plum bā′gō), *n., pl.* **-gos. 1.** graphite: *The other crystalline form of carbon is called graphite (plumbago, black lead)* (Monroe M. Offner). **2.** any of a group of herbaceous plants of warm regions, grown for their spikes of showy blue, white, or scarlet flowers; leadwort. [< Latin *plumbāgō, -inis* lead ore; leadwort < *plumbum* the element lead]

plumb bob, the weight at the end of a plumb line: *Today, just as did our ancestors, we use a plumb bob in all surveying, in the construction of buildings . . . and in measuring the size and shape of the earth* (Robert M. Garrels).

plum·be·ous (plum′bē əs), *adj.* made of or resembling lead; leaden. [< Latin *plumbeus* (with English *-ous*) leaden, dull < *plumbum* the element lead]

plumb·er (plum′ər), *n.* **1.** a man whose work is putting in and repairing water pipes and fixtures in buildings: *When the water pipe froze we sent for a plumber.* **2.** (originally) a man who dealt and worked in lead. [< Old French *plombier* < Latin (*artifex*) *plumbārius* (worker) in lead < *plumbum* the element lead]

plumber's friend or **helper,** a rubber suction cup at the end of a stick; plunger.

plumb·er·y (plum′ər ē), *n., pl.* **-er·ies. 1.** the shop or workplace of a plumber. **2.** the work of a plumber; plumbing.

plum·bic (plum′bik), *adj.* **1.** of or having to do with lead. **2.** containing lead, especially with a valence of four. [< Latin *plumbum* the element lead + English *-ic*]

plum·bif·er·ous (plum bif′ər əs), *adj.* containing or yielding lead. [< Latin *plumbum* the element lead + English *-ferous*]

plumb·ing (plum′ing), *n.* **1.** the work or trade of a plumber. **2.** the water pipes and fixtures in a building: *bathroom plumbing.* **3.** the act of using a plumb line.

plumb·ing·ware (plum′ing wãr′), *n.* the plumbing fixtures for a bathroom, kitchen, etc.

plum·bism (plum′biz əm), *n.* lead poisoning: *It is the solubility of lead when taken into the system that causes plumbism* (The Speaker).

plumb·less (plum′lis), *adj.* that cannot be plumbed or sounded; unfathomable: *The moment shot away into the plumbless depths of the past* (Dickens).

plumb line, 1. a line with a plumb at the end, used to find the depth of water or to test the straightness of a wall. **2.** a line that is vertical, as one formed by the surface of a wall.

plum·bous (plum′bəs), *adj.* **1.** of lead. **2.** containing lead, especially with a valence of two. [< Latin *plumbōsus* (with English *-ous*) < *plumbum*]

plumb rule, a narrow board fitted with a plumb line and bob, used by carpenters and masons for measuring angles from the vertical.

plum·bum (plum′bəm), *n.* lead. [< Latin *plumbum*]

plum cake, a cake containing raisins, currants, and often other fruits.

plum·col·or (plum′kul′ər), *n.* a dark purple; plum.

plum·col·ored (plum′kul′ərd), *adj.* dark-purple; plum.

plum·cot (plum′kot), *n.* a hybrid between the plum and the apricot. [< *plum*[1] + (apri)*cot*]

plum duff, a heavy pudding of flour, water, suet, and raisins or currants, boiled in a cloth or bag.

plume (plüm), *n., v.,* **plumed, plum·ing.** —*n.* **1.** a large, long feather; feather. **2.** a feather, bunch of feathers, or tuft of hair worn as an ornament on a hat, helmet, etc.: *Her photograph . . . showed her stiff in her glories of plumes and satin* (Maurice H. Hewlett). **3.** plumage. **4.** any plumose part or formation, as of an insect, seed, leaf, etc. **5.** something resembling a plume. **6.** an ornament or token of distinction or honor: *medals and other plumes of rank.* **7.** the hollow cylinder of spray thrown up by an underwater atomic explosion. **8.** the spray thrown up by a vessel moving at high speed.
—*v.t.* **1.** to furnish with plumes. **2.** to smooth or arrange the feathers of: *The eagle plumed its wing.*
—*v.i.* to form a plumelike cloud, as spray, vapor, smoke, etc.: *In the sub-zero weather, their exhausts pluming white in the gray streets . . .* (Newsweek).
plume oneself on, to be proud of; show pride concerning: *Grace plumed herself on her skill in dancing.*
[< Old French *plume* < Latin *plūma* pinfeather, down] —**plume′like′,** *adj.*
—**Syn.** *v.t.* **2.** preen.

plume·bird (plüm′bėrd′), *n.* any of a group of birds of New Guinea, notable for the luxuriance and brilliance of their plumage.

plumed (plümd), *adj.* **1.** having plumes or plumelike parts. **2.** adorned with or as with a plume or plumes: *plumed steeds gorgeously caparisoned* (Amelia B. Edwards).

plume·less (plüm′lis), *adj.* without plumes or feathers: *Her dragons . . . fold their plumeless wings* (John A. Symonds).

plume·let (plüm′lit), *n.* a small plume.

plume poppy, a showy plant of the poppy family, native to China and Japan, often cultivated in garden borders; tree celandine. It grows to a height of six feet or more and its panicles of yellowish-white flowers may reach one foot in length.

plu·mi·corn (plü′mə kôrn), *n.* one of a pair of hornlike or earlike tufts of feathers on the head of certain owls, as the horned owls. [< Latin *plūma* feather + *cornū* horn]

plum·met (plum′it), *n.* **1.** a weight fastened to a line; plumb. **2.** something that weighs down or depresses: *Ignorance itself is a plummet o'er me* (Shakespeare).
—*v.i.* to plunge; drop: *to plummet into the sea.* [< Old French *plommet* (diminutive) < *plom,* and *plomb* the element lead; see PLUMB]

plum·mi·ly (plum′ə lē), *adv. Informal.* in a plummy way: [*She was*] *plummily sedate* (London Times).

plum·mi·ness (plum′ē nis), *n.* plummy quality or condition: *The creamy richness—free from all "plumminess"—of her contralto voice is a constant delight* (London Times).

plum·my (plum′ē), *adj.,* **-mi·er, -mi·est. 1.** full of or resembling plums: *a plummy crimson.* **2.** *Informal.* good; desirable: *Signing one's self over to wickedness for the sake of getting something plummy* (George Eliot). **3.** *Informal.* rich and too refined: *a plummy, Lady Bountiful voice* (New Yorker).

plu·mose (plü′mōs), *adj.* **1.** having feathers or plumes; feathered: *In wind-pollinated flowers such as the grasses, the stigmata are the numerous feathery hairs which cover the ends of the styles and are intended to catch flying pollen grains. Such stigmata are called plumose* (Heber W. Youngken). **2.** like a plume; feathery. [< Latin *plūmōsus* < *plūma* pinfeather] —**plu′mose·ly,** *adv.*

plu·mos·i·ty (plü mos′ə tē), *n.* the state of being plumose.

plump[1] (plump), *adj.* rounded out; chubby: *A healthy baby has plump cheeks.* —*v.t., v.i.* to make plump; become plump: *Plump the pillows on your bed.* [origin uncertain. Compare Middle Dutch *plomp,* Middle Low German *plump* blunt, thick, clumsy.] —**plump′ly,** *adv.* —**plump′ness,** *n.*

plump[2] (plump), *v.i.* **1.** to fall or drop heavily or suddenly: *All out of breath, she plumped down on a chair.* **2.** *Informal.* to burst or plunge: *to plump out of a room, to plump into the water.* **3.** to vote at an election for one candidate alone: *I'll plump or I'll split for them as treat me the handsomest and are the most of what I call gentlemen* (George Eliot). —*v.t.* **1. a.** to drop, let fall, etc.: *to plump down one's bags at the station.* **b.** to pay at once and in one lot: *to plump down $10.* **2.** *Informal.* to utter abruptly; blurt: *If it ain't a liberty to plump it out . . . what do you do for your living?* (Dickens).
plump for, to give one's complete support to; support wholeheartedly, unanimously, etc.: *to plump for lower taxes. The New Jersey delegation plumped for Jones.*
—*n. Informal.* **1.** a sudden plunge; heavy fall. **2.** the sound made by a plunge or fall.
—*adv.* **1.** heavily or suddenly: *He ran plump into me.* **2.** directly or bluntly, as in speaking.
—*adj.* direct; downright; blunt: *I hate qualifying arguers—plump assertion or plump denial for me* (Maria Edgeworth).
[imitative; probably < Middle Dutch *plompen,* or Middle Low German *plumpen* plunge abruptly into water, make a sound of hitting water. Perhaps related to PLUMP[1].]

plump[3] (plump), *n. Archaic.* a compact group of persons, animals, or things; clump; bunch: *A whole plump of rogues* (Beaumont and Fletcher). [Middle English *plumpe*]

plump·er[1] (plum′pər), *n.* **1.** something that plumps or makes plump. **2.** a small, light ball formerly sometimes carried in the mouth by women to fill out hollow cheeks: *. . . vamped up for show with paint, patches, plumpers, and every external ornament that art can suggest* (The Connoisseur). [< *plump*[1] + *-er*[1]]

plump·er[2] (plum′pər), *n.* **1.** the act of plumping or falling heavily. **2. a.** a voter who plumps. **b.** the vote of such a person. **3.** *Slang.* a downright lie; whopper. [< *plump*[2] + *-er*[5]]

plump·ish (plum′pish), *adj.* somewhat plump; roundish: *a plumpish figure.*

plum pudding, a rich boiled or steamed pudding containing raisins, currants, spices, etc.

plump·y (plum′pē), *adj.* plump, as in body or form: *plumpy Bacchus* (Shakespeare).

plu·mule (plü′myül), *n.* **1.** a small, soft feather. **2.** the rudimentary terminal bud of the embryo of a seed, sometimes containing immature leaves. It is situated at the end of the hypocotyl, and is either within or enclosed by the cotyledon or cotyledons. [< Latin *plūmula* (diminutive) < *plūma* feather]

Plumule (def. 2) in bean seed

plum·y (plü′mē), *adj.* **1.** having plumes or feathers: *a flock of white plumy birds* (Charlotte Brontë). **2.** adorned with a plume or plumes: *a plumy helmet.* **3.** like a plume; feathery: *the plumy palms of Memphis* (Amelia B. Edwards).

plun·der (plun′dər), *v.t.* **1.** to rob by force; rob: *to plunder a bank. The Greeks plundered Troy and destroyed the city.* **2.** to take (goods, valuables, etc.) by illegal force or as an enemy: *The law of self-preservation had now obliged the fugitive Tartars to plunder provisions* (Thomas DeQuincey). —*v.i.* to commit a robbery or robberies, especially by force; loot.
—*n.* **1.** things taken in plundering; booty; loot: *They carried off the plunder in their ships.* **2.** the act of robbing by force: *In olden times soldiers often gained great wealth by plunder of a conquered city.* **3.** *U.S. Dialect.* **a.** personal belongings or household goods. **b.** luggage; baggage.
[probably ultimately < Middle Low German *plundern* < *plunder* household goods]
—**plun′der·er,** *n.*
—**Syn.** *v.t.* **1.** loot, sack. *-n.* **1. Plunder, booty, loot** mean things taken by force. **Plunder** applies to things carried off by invading soldiers during a war or by bandits and other robbers: *Much plunder from Europe reached America after World War II.* **Booty** applies particularly to things carried off and shared later by a band of robbers: *The bandits fought over their booty.* **Loot** applies particularly to things carried off from bodies and buildings in a city destroyed in war or the scene of a fire, wreck, etc., but is used also of anything taken by robbery or other crime: *Much loot was sold after the great earthquake.*

plun·der·age (plun′dər ij), *n.* **1.** the act of plundering; pillage; spoliation. **2.** *Maritime Law.* **a.** the embezzlement of goods on board a ship. **b.** the goods embezzled. [< *plunder* + *-age*]

plun·der·bund (plun′dər bund), *n. U.S. Informal.* a league or organized body of plunderers, especially plunderers of the public. [American English < *plunder* + *Bund*]

plun·der·ous (plun′dər əs), *adj.* given to plundering: *I think it very likely . . . that the owner of this little hoard buried his money on the approach of the king's army and Rupert's plunderous troopers* (Arthur Henfrey).

plunge (plunj), *v.,* **plunged, plung·ing,** *n.* —*v.t.* to throw or thrust with force into a liquid, place, or condition: *to plunge one's hand into water, to plunge the world into war.* —*v.i.* **1.** to throw oneself (into water, danger, a fight, etc.): *to plunge into debt, to plunge feverishly into study. A stone dropped . . . plunges into water deep enough to float a skiff* (Scott). **2.** to rush; dash: *to plunge into a burning building.* **3.** to pitch suddenly and violently: *The ship plunged about in the storm.* **4.** *Informal.* to gamble heavily.
—*n.* **1.** the act of plunging: *The fullback made a 2-yard plunge for a first down.* **2.** a dive into the water. **3.** a place for diving.
take the plunge, to plunge into a new course of action, in spite of fear, reluctance, or risk: *Mr. Shonfield, brave man that he is, has taken the plunge and stated the fact in bald language* (New Yorker).
[< Old French *plungier* < Vulgar Latin *plumbicāre* to heave the sounding lead < Latin *plumbum* the element lead]
—**Syn.** *v.t.* immerse, submerge. See **dip.** *-v.i.* **1.** leap, dive.

plunge bath, a bath which is large enough for the bather to be completely immersed in it: *About A.D. 115-120 at least four new heated rooms were added, and an unusually large plunge bath, 44 ft. long by 11 ft. wide* (London Times).

plunge pool, the deep pool at the base of a waterfall which often cuts back under the falls, causing the overhanging rock face to collapse and moving the location of the falls further upstream.

plung·er (plun′jər), *n.* **1.** a person, animal, or thing that plunges: *Essentially, Dwight Eisenhower is no plunger, and he believed that there were other aspects to his job that had to be settled before he got around to politics* (Time). **2. a.** a part of a machine that works with a plunging motion; piston; ram. **b.** a concave, rubber suction cup at the end of a stick, used to free clogged pipes or drains by air pressure; plumber's helper. **3.** a small pistonlike device in the valve of an automobile tire.

plung·ing fire (plun′jing), gunfire, especially artillery fire, in which the projectiles descend on the target at an angle approaching the perpendicular, as by a battery firing from a higher elevation or in a high, looping trajectory.

plunk (plungk), *v.t.* **1.** to pluck (a banjo, guitar, etc.). **2.** to play with a sound like the plucking of a banjo, etc.; twang: *It was cranked out by scores of organ-grinders and plunked out on a thousand parlor pianofortes* (New Yorker). **3.** to throw, push, put, drop, etc., heavily or suddenly. —*v.i.* **1.** to make a sharp, twanging sound. **2.** to fall or drop down abruptly; plump.

plunk down, to hand over payment: *He plunked down four thousand dollars for the car.*

plunk for, *Informal.* to plump for: *He'll plunk for more public housing, federal aid for schools, hospitals, health measures* (Wall Street Journal).

—*n. Informal.* **1.** the act or sound of plunking: *They played in such magnificent time that every high-stepping foot in all the line came down with the same jubilant plunk* (Booth Tarkington). **2.** a direct, forcible blow. **3.** *U.S. Slang.* a dollar: *I'll sell you the Candersen place for three thousand plunks* (Sinclair Lewis).

—*adv.* with a plunk.

[imitative] —**Syn.** *v.t.* **1.** pick.

plu·per·fect (plü′pėr′fikt), *n.* past perfect. —*adj.* **1.** of, in, or having to do with the past perfect. **2.** more than perfect; very excellent. [short for Latin (*tempus praeteritum*) *plūs* (*quam*) *perfectum* (past tense) more (than) perfect] —**plu′per′fect·ly,** *adv.*

plu·per·fec·tion (plü′pər fek′shən), *n.* the quality or state of being pluperfect: *The eye of the average elephant . . . is of such rich green pluperfection that it looks like nothing more than a cardboard imitation from a decorator's window* (Time).

plupf., pluperfect.

plur., **1.** plural. **2.** plurality.

plu·ral (plůr′əl), *adj.* **1.** more than one. **2.** *Grammar.* indicating or implying more than one. **3.** having to do with or involving a plurality of persons or things; being one of such a plurality: *Better have none than plural faith* (Shakespeare).

—*n. Grammar.* **1.** a form of a word to show it means more than one. *Books* is the plural of *book; men* of *man; are* of *is; we* of *I; these* of *this.* **2.** a form or class of forms used to show more than one. *Abbr.:* pl.

[< Latin *plūrālis* < *plūs, plūris* more, comparative of *multus* much]

plu·ral·ism (plůr′ə liz əm), *n.* **1.** the character, condition, or an instance of being plural. **2.** *Ecclesiastical.* the system or practice by which one person holds two or more offices, especially benefices, at the same time. **3.** the theory or belief, incorporated in or essential to various systems of philosophy, that reality has its essence or ultimate being in several or many principles or substances: *Philosophically this is neither pluralism nor out-and-out monism. It is not the former because ultimately no other source of being but God, no principle of life but the Divine, is recognized* (Contemporary Review).

plu·ral·ist (plůr′ə list), *n.* **1.** a person who holds two or more offices, especially ecclesiastical benefices, at the same time. **2.** *Philosophy.* an adherent of pluralism. —*adj.* pluralistic: *Only similar nongovernmental, nonnational, pluralist organizations of scientists could effectively control the weapons* (Harper's).

plu·ral·is·tic (plůr′ə lis′tik), *adj.* of or having to do with pluralism: *The later Eleatics were pluralistic—holding to the distinction of matter and spirit* (Alexander Winchell). —**plu′ral·is′ti·cal·ly,** *adv.*

plu·ral·i·ty (plů ral′ə tē), *n., pl.* **-ties.** **1.** *U.S.* the difference between the largest number of votes and the next largest in an election. **2.** the greater number; the majority. **3. a.** the fact of being numerous; vastness; greatness: *The plurality of effort, which has been effective in finding the oil the nation needs, thus is also useful in developing methods to prevent its waste* (Atlantic). **b.** a large number or quantity; multitude. **4.** the state or fact of being plural. **5.** *Ecclesiastical.* **a.** the simultaneous holding of two or more offices or benefices; pluralism. **b.** any of the offices held under pluralism.

plu·ral·i·za·tion (plůr′ə lə zā′shən), *n.* a pluralizing: *Many people are saying that there has been a pluralization of power, a change from the time when the world was dominated by Russia and the United States* (Harper's).

plu·ral·ize (plůr′ə līz), *v.t., v.i.,* **-ized, -iz·ing.** to make or become plural; express in the plural form: *Those words which we have adopted from Latin or Greek . . . unaltered, have usually been pluralized according to Greek or Latin grammar* (John Earle).

plural livings, two or more ecclesiastical benefices held by one person at the same time.

plu·ral·ly (plůr′ə lē), *adv.* in the plural number; so as to express or imply more than one: *The "heavens" when used plurally . . . remained expressive of the starry space beyond* (John Ruskin).

plural marriage, the marriage of a man to two or more women at the same time; polygamy, especially with reference to the Mormons.

plural wife, any of the wives of a polygamist, or in a plural marriage.

pluri-, *combining form.* having more than one ——; having many ——: *Pluriaxial* = *having more than one axis.* [< Latin *plūs, plūris* more]

plu·ri·ax·i·al (plůr′ē ak′sē əl), *adj.* **1.** having more than one axis. **2.** *Botany.* having flowers growing on secondary shoots. [< *pluri-* + *axial*]

plu·ri·cel·lu·lar (plůr′ə sel′yə lər), *adj.* having several cells; multicellular. [< *pluri-* + *cellular*]

plu·ri·lit·er·al (plůr′ə lit′ər əl), *adj.* consisting of more than three letters as a Hebrew root. —*n.* a pluriliteral root. [< Latin *pluri-* + *littera* letter of the alphabet + English *-al*[1]]

plu·rip·o·tent (plů rip′ə tənt), *adj.* capable of developing, growing, or producing in a number of ways: *pluripotent cells.* [< *pluri-* + Latin *potēns* potent]

plu·ri·se·ri·al (plůr′ə sir′ē əl), *adj.* consisting of several series. [< *pluri-* + *seri*(es) + *-al*[1]]

plu·ri·syl·lab·ic (plůr′ə sə lab′ik), *adj.* having more than one syllable.

plu·ri·syl·la·ble (plůr′ə sil′ə bəl), *n.* a word of more than one syllable. [< *pluri-* + *syllable*]

plus (plus), *prep., adj., n.,* **plus·es** or **plus·ses,** *v.,* **plussed, plus·sing.** —*prep.* **1.** added to: *3 plus 2 equals 5.* **2.** and also: *The work of an engineer requires intelligence plus experience.*

—*adj.* **1. a.** and more: *His mark was B plus.* **b.** *Informal.* additional; extra: *a plus value.* **2. a.** showing addition: *the plus sign.* **b.** more than zero; positive: *a plus quantity.* **3.** positively electrified; positive. **4.** *Botany.* of or having to do with the strain of heterothallic fungi that acts as the male in reproduction.

be plus, *Informal.* to have in addition: *Since his niece married he is plus a nephew.*

—*n.* **1.** the plus sign (+). **2.** an added quantity; something extra; gain: *The pluses of his new job outweigh the disadvantages of having to move.* **3.** a positive quantity.

—*v.t. Informal.* **1.** to add; gain: *He plussed two more points in the game.* **2.** to add to; augment: *to plus a score.*

[< Medieval Latin *plus* < Latin *plūs* more, comparative of *multus* much]

—**Syn.** *n.* **2.** addition, increase.

plus fours, loose, baggy knickers that come down below the knee, worn especially by men for golf. [apparently because they were originally four inches longer than ordinary knickers]

plush (plush), *n.* a fabric of silk, cotton, wool, rayon, etc., like velvet but having a longer and softer pile.

—*adj. Slang.* luxurious; expensive, stylish; fashionable: *Thomas is so busy on the road making money to keep his family in plush surroundings that he is a stranger in his own house* (Time).

[< French *pluche,* short for *peluche* (literally) hairy fabric < Vulgar Latin *pilūcea,* adjective < Latin *pilus* hair] —**plush′like′,** *adj.*

plush·y (plush′ē), *adj.,* **plush·i·er, plush·i·est.** of or like plush: *Then followed a long gaze out of the window, across the damp gravel and plushy lawn* (Henry Kingsley).

Plu·tar·chan (plü tär′kən), *adj.* **1.** of or having to do with Plutarch, a Greek biographer of the century ending in 100 A.D. **2.** of or like the group of famous Greeks and Romans whose lives were written by Plutarch.

Plu·tar·chi·an (plü tär′kē ən), *adj.* Plutarchan: *Plutarchian heroes were they, in their virtues* (London Daily News).

Plu·to (plü′tō), *n.* **1.** in Greek and Roman Mythology: **a.** the god of the lower world and husband of Persephone. He was also called Hades by the Greeks and Dis by the Romans. **b.** a nymph who was the mother of Tantalus. **2.** the planet of the solar system that is farthest from the sun. It was discovered in 1930, and revolves about the sun once every 248.4 years, at an average distance from the sun of about 3,700,000,000 miles.

plu·toc·ra·cy (plü tok′rə sē), *n., pl.* **-cies.** **1.** a government in which the rich rule: *Public spirit in the masses was dead or sleeping; the Commonwealth was a plutocracy* (James A. Froude). **2.** a ruling class of wealthy people. [< Greek *plutokratíā* < *ploûtos* wealth (related to *polýs* much, many) + *krátos* power]

plu·to·crat (plü′tə krat), *n.* **1.** a person who has power or influence because of his wealth. **2.** a wealthy person. —**Syn. 2.** nabob, Croesus.

plu·to·crat·ic (plü′tə krat′ik), *adj.* **1.** having power or influence because of wealth. **2.** of or having to do with plutocrats or plutocracy. —**plu′to·crat′i·cal·ly,** *adv.*

plu·to·crat·i·cal (plü′tə krat′ə kəl), *adj.* plutocratic.

plu·to·de·moc·ra·cy (plü′tō də mok′rə sē), *n., pl.* **-cies.** a democracy dominated by plutocrats: *. . . the classic line of Fascist propaganda against plutodemocracy* (New Yorker). [< Greek *ploûtos* wealth + English *democracy*]

plu·tol·a·try (plü tol′ə trē), *n.* the worship of wealth: *. . . this barbarizing plutolatry which seems to be so rapidly supplanting the worship of what alone is lovely and enduring* (James Russell Lowell). [< Greek *ploûtos* wealth + *latreíā* worship]

plu·tol·o·gist (plü tol′ə jist), *n.* a person skilled in plutology.

plu·tol·o·gy (plü tol′ə jē), *n.* the science of wealth; political economy. [< Greek *ploûtos* wealth + English *-logy*]

plu·ton (plü′ton), *n.* a plutonic rock. [back formation < *plutonic*]

Plu·to·ni·an (plü tō′nē ən), *adj.* of or having to do with Pluto or the lower world: *He . . . from the door of that Plutonian hall, invisible ascended his high throne* (Milton).

plu·ton·ic (plü ton′ik), *adj.* noting a class of igneous rocks that have solidified far below the earth's surface. [< Latin *Plūtōn, -ōnis,* variant of *Plūtō* (< Greek *Ploútōn, -ōnos* god of the lower world, perhaps < *ploûtos* wealth) + English *-ic*]

Plu·ton·ic (plü ton′ik), *adj.* **1.** Plutonian; infernal. **2.** of or having to do with the theory that the present condition of the earth's crust is mainly due to igneous action. [< *Plūtō, -ōnis* Pluto + English *-ic*]

Plu·to·nism (plü′tə niz əm), *n.* the Plutonic theory.

Plu·to·nist (plü′tə nist), *n.* an adherent of the Plutonic theory: *In the geological contest . . . between the Neptunists and the Plutonists, the two great battle cries were, on the one side, Water, on the other, Fire* (Archibald Geikie).

plu·to·ni·um (plü tō′nē əm), *n.* a radioactive chemical element derived from neptunium, important in atomic fission. Plutonium is also a product of uranium by chain reaction. *Symbol:* Pu; *at.no.:* 94; *at.wt.:* (C^{12}) 242 or (O^{16}) 242; *valence:* 3,4,5,6. [< New Latin *plutonium* < Latin *plūtōnium,* adjective, relating to Pluto; patterned on *neptunium,* and *uranium*]

plu·to·nom·ic (plü′tə nom′ik), *adj.* of or having to do with plutonomy: *. . . those plutonomic doctrines which are erected into a faith for states or for individuals, and which tend to supplant everywhere duty by interest* (Macmillan's Magazine).

plu·ton·o·mist (plü ton′ə mist), *n.* a person skilled in plutonomy; political economist.

plu·ton·o·my (plü ton′ə mē), *n.* the science of the production and distribution of wealth; political economy. [< Greek *ploûtos* wealth + *nómos* law]

Plu·tus (plü′təs), *n. Greek Mythology.* the god of riches and son of Demeter, blinded by Jupiter. [< Latin *Plūtus* < Greek *Ploûtos* (literally) wealth]

plu·vi·al (plü′vē əl), *adj.* **1.** of or having to do with rain. **2.** *Geology.* caused by rain. —*n.* a period of geological change in an area as a result of prolonged rainfall: *With the onset of the last pluvial, man was able to penetrate the deserts once more* (A.J. Arkell). [< Latin *pluviālis* < *pluvia* rain]

plu·vi·o·graph (plü′vē ə graf, -gräf), *n.* a self-recording rain gauge. [< Latin *pluvia* rain + English *-graph*]

plu·vi·o·graph·ic (plü′vē ə graf′ik), *adj.* **1.** of or having to do with a pluviograph. **2.** given by or derived from a pluviograph: *a pluviographic record.*

plu·vi·og·ra·phy (plü′vē og′rə fē), *n.* the method of recording rainfall by a pluviograph.

plu·vi·om·e·ter (plü′vē om′ə tər), *n.* an instrument for measuring the amount of rainfall. [< Latin *pluvia* rain + English *-meter*]

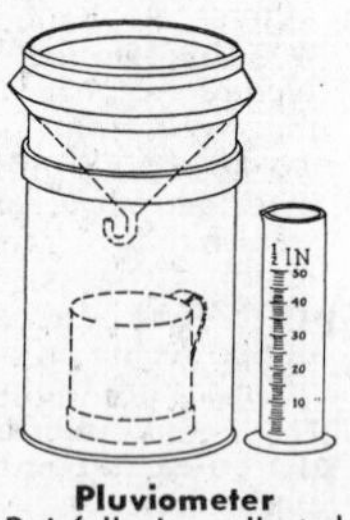

Pluviometer
Rainfall is collected through brass funnel into cup, then transferred to graduated measure.

plu·vi·o·met·ric (plü′vē ə met′rik), *adj.* made by means of a pulviometer: *pluviometric observations.* —**plu′vi·o·met′ri·cal·ly,** *adv.*

plu·vi·o·met·ri·cal (plü′vē ə met′rə kəl), *adj.* pluviometric.

plu·vi·om·e·try (plü′vē om′ə trē), *n.* the use of the pluviometer.

Plu·vi·ôse (plü′vē ōs; *French* ply vyōz′), *n.* the fifth month of the French Revolutionary calendar, extending from January 20 to February 18. [< French *Pluviôse* < Latin *pluviōsus* pluvious]

plu·vi·ose (plü′vē ōs), *adj.* pluvious.

plu·vi·ous (plü′vē əs), *adj.* rainy; of rain. [< Latin *pluviōsus* (with English *-ous*) < *pluvia* rain]

ply[1] (plī), *v.*, **plied, ply·ing.** —*v.t.* **1.** to work with; use: *The dressmaker plies her needle.* **2.** to keep up work on; work away at or on: *to ply one's trade. We plied the water with our oars.* **3.** to urge again and again: *The enemy plied our messenger with questions to make him tell his errand.* **4.** to supply with in a pressing manner: *to ply a person with food or drink.* **5.** to go back and forth regularly on: *Boats ply the river.* —*v.i.* **1.** to work busily or steadily: *Soon all the boats . . . were dropped . . . all the paddles plying* (Herman Melville). **2.** to go back and forth regularly between certain places: *A bus plies between the station and the hotel.* **3.** to travel; go; move: *Thither he plies* (Milton). **4.** *Nautical.* to turn a sailing ship to windward.
[Middle English *plyen*, probably short for *aplien* apply] —**Syn.** *v.t.* **1.** employ. **3.** importune.

ply[2] (plī), *n.*, *pl.* **plies,** *v.*, **plied, ply·ing.** —*n.* **1.** thickness; fold. **2.** a strand or twist of cord, yarn, or thread: *Three-ply rope is made of three twists.* **3.** an inclination of mind; a tendency of character. [< French *pli* a fold < Old French *plier* to fold; see the verb]
—*v.t. Dialect.* **1.** to bend, fold, or shape. **2.** *Obsolete.* to adapt. —*v.i. Obsolete.* to bend or yield.
[< Old French *plier*, alteration of *pleiier*, and *ployer* < Latin *plicāre* to fold. Compare PLIANT.]
—**Syn.** *n.* **1.** layer.

ply·er (plī′ər), *n.* plier.

ply·ers (plī′ərz), *n.,pl.* **-ers.** pliers.

Plym·outh Brethren (plim′əth), a Protestant religious sect recognizing no official order of ministers and having no formal creed, that came into existence about 1830 at Plymouth, England.

Plymouth cloak, a staff; cudgel: *Shall I walk in a Plymouth Cloak (that's to say) like a rogue, in my hose and doublet, and a crabtree cudgel in my hand* (Thomas Dekker).

Plymouth Rock, any of an American breed of gray-and-black domestic poultry kept for the production of both meat and eggs.

ply·wood (plī′wu̇d′), *n.* a board or boards, made of several thin layers of wood glued together. [< *ply*[2] + *wood*]

p.m., an abbreviation for the following:
1. a. after noon (Latin, *post meridiem*). **b.** the time from noon to midnight.
2. post-mortem.

Pm (no period), promethium (chemical element).

P.M., an abbreviation for the following:
1. a. after noon (Latin, *post meridiem*). **b.** the time from noon to midnight.
2. Past Master.
3. Paymaster.
4. Police Magistrate.
5. Postmaster.
6. post-mortem.
7. Prime Minister.
8. Provost Marshal.

PMA (no periods), Production and Marketing Administration.

P.M.G., **1.** Paymaster General. **2.** Postmaster General.

pmk (no period), postmark.

pmkd (no period), postmarked.

PMLA (no periods), Publications of the Modern Language Association of America.

p.n. or **P/N,** promissory note.

pneum., **1.** pneumatic. **2.** pneumatics.

pneu·ma (nü′mə, nyü′-), *n.* spirit or soul: *Hippocrates taught the existence of an "intermediate nature," which though distinct from the mortal Soul or pneuma, was the source of vital activity* (William Grant Stevenson). [< Greek *pneûma* spirit, breath, a wind < *pneîn* to blow, breathe]

pneu·mat·ic (nü mat′ik, nyü-), *adj.* **1.** filled with air; containing air, especially air under pressure: *a pneumatic tire.* **2.** worked by air, especially air under pressure: *a pneumatic drill.* **3.** having to do with air and other gases. **4.** containing or connected with air cavities, as the bones of birds or the swim bladder of fishes. **5.** *Theology.* of or having to do with the spirit; spiritual.
—*n.* a pneumatic tire.
[< Latin *pneumaticus* < Greek *pneumatikós* of (the nature of) wind, spirit < *pneûma* a wind; see PNEUMA] —**pneu·mat′i·cal·ly,** *adv.*

pneu·ma·tic·i·ty (nü′mə tis′ə tē, nyü′-), *n.* the fact or condition of being pneumatic.

pneu·mat·ics (nü mat′iks, nyü-), *n.* the branch of physics that deals with the pressure, elasticity, weight, and other mechanical properties of air and other gases; pneumodynamics.

pneumatic tube, a tube for sending through notes, letters, etc., by means of air pressure.

pneu·ma·to·cyst (nü mat′ə sist, nyü-), *n.* an air sac, as in a hydrozoan. [< Greek *pneûma, -atos* breath, wind + English *cyst*]

pneu·ma·tol·o·gy (nü′mə tol′ə jē, nyü′-), *n.* **1.** *Theology.* the doctrine of the Holy Spirit. **2.** the doctrine of spirits or spiritual beings, in the 1600's considered a branch of metaphysics. **3.** pneumatics. **4.** *Obsolete.* psychology. [< Greek *pneûma, -atos* spirit, breath + English *-logy*]

pneu·ma·tol·y·sis (nü′mə tol′ə sis, nyü′-), *n. Geology.* the process by which minerals and ores are formed by the action of vapors given off from igneous magmas. [< Greek *pneûma, -atos* breath, wind + *lýsis* a loosening]

pneu·ma·to·lyt·ic or **pneu·ma·to·lit·ic** (nü′mə tō lit′ik, nyü′-), *adj. Geology.* of, having to do with, or formed by pneumatolysis.

pneu·ma·tom·e·ter (nü′mə tom′ə tər, nyü′-), *n.* an instrument for measuring the amount of air breathed in and out at each inspiration or expiration, or the force of inspiration or expiration. [< Greek *pneûma, -atos* breath + English *-meter*]

pneu·ma·to·phore (nü′mə tō fôr, nyü′-; -fōr; nü mat′ə-, nyü-), *n.* **1.** a structure supposed to serve as a channel for air, arising from the roots of various trees that grow in swampy places in the tropics. **2.** a hollow structure containing gas in certain hydrozoans, serving as a float. [< Greek *pneûma, -atos* wind, breath + English *-phore*]

pneu·ma·to·ther·a·py (nü′mə tō ther′ə pē, nyü′-), *n.* therapy in which the inhalation of compressed or rarefied air is used. [< Greek *pneûma, -atos* breath, wind + English *therapy*]

pneu·mec·to·my (nü mek′tə mē, nyü-), *n.*, *pl.* **-mies.** the surgical removal of part of a lung. [< Greek *pneúmōn* lung + *ektomḗ* a cutting out]

pneu·mo·ba·cil·lus (nü′mō bə sil′əs, nyü′-), *n.*, *pl.* **-cil·li** (-sil′ī). a bacillus commonly present in cases of pneumonia, pleurisy, etc., but considered almost certainly not the causative agent of the disease. [< New Latin *pneumobacillus* < Greek *pneúmōn* lung + Late Latin *bacillus* bacillus]

pneu·mo·coc·cal (nü′mə kok′əl, nyü′-), *adj.* having to do with or caused by a pneumococcus.

pneu·mo·coc·cic (nü′mə kok′sik, nyü′-), *adj.* pneumococcal.

pneu·mo·coc·cous (nü′mə kok′əs, nyü′-), *adj.* pneumococcal.

pneu·mo·coc·cus (nü′mə kok′əs, nyü′-), *n.*, *pl.* **-coc·ci** (-kok′sī). the bacterium that causes lobar pneumonia. [< New Latin *pneumococcus* < Greek *pneúmōn* lung + New Latin *coccus* coccus]

pneu·mo·co·ni·o·sis (nü′mə kō′nē ō′sis, nyü′-), *n.* chronic inflammation of the lungs, produced by the inhalation of mineral dust; pneumonoconiosis. [< New Latin *pneumoconiosis* < Greek *pneúmōn* lung + *kónis* dust + New Latin *-osis* -osis]

pneu·mo·dy·nam·ics (nü′mō dī nam′iks, nyü′-), *n.* pneumatics.

pneu·mo·gas·tric (nü′mə gas′trik, nyü′-), *adj.* **1.** of or having to do with the lungs and the stomach or abdomen. **2.** of or having to do with a vagus nerve.
—*n.* a vagus nerve.
[< Greek *pneúmōn* lung + English *gastric*]

pneumogastric nerve, either of the vagus nerves, a pair of cranial nerves that supply the respiratory organs, the stomach, etc.

pneu·mo·gram (nü′mə gram, nyü′-), *n.* a diagram or tracing made by a pneumograph.

pneu·mo·graph (nü′mə graf, -gräf; nyü′-), *n.* an instrument for automatically recording the movements of the human chest in respiration. [< Greek *pneúmōn* lung + English *-graph*]

pneu·mog·ra·phy (nü mog′rə fē, nyü-), *n.* **1.** a description of the lungs. **2.** the recording of respiratory movement, especially by a pneumograph. **3.** a method of X-raying tissues by introducing air into them.

pneu·mo·nec·to·my (nü′mə nek′tə mē, nyü′-), *n.*, *pl.* **-mies.** the surgical removal of a lung. [< Greek *pneúmōn* lung + *ektomḗ* a cutting out]

pneu·mo·nia (nü mōn′yə, -mō′nē ə; nyü-), *n.* a disease in which the lungs are inflamed, often an acute infection of the lung accompanied by fever, pain, and a severe cough. [< New Latin *pneumonia* < Greek *pneumoniā* < *pneúmōn* lung < *pneûma* breath, spirit < *pneîn* to breathe, blow]

pneu·mon·ic (nü mon′ik, nyü-), *adj.* **1.** of the nature of or resembling pneumonia (applied especially to certain forms or stages of pulmonary tuberculosis) **2.** having to do with, characterized by, or affected with pneumonia. **3.** of, having to do with, or affecting the lungs; pulmonary.

pneumonic plague, a usually fatal, contagious disease, characterized by fever, chills, prostration, and infection of the lungs, usually transmitted by a flea that has bitten a rat infected with the plague bacillus.

pneu·mo·ni·tis (nü′mə nī′təs, nyü′-), *n.* any of various acute inflammations of the lungs; pneumonia. [< Greek *pneúmōn* lung + English *-itis*]

pneu·mo·no·co·ni·o·sis (nü′mə nō kō′nē ō′sis, nyü′-), *n.* pneumoconiosis.

pneu·mo·noph·thi·sis (nü′mə nof thī′sis, nyü′-), *n.* tuberculosis of the lungs; pulmonary tuberculosis. [< Greek *pneúmōn, -onos* lung + English *phthisis*]

pneu·mo·per·i·to·ne·um (nü′mə per′ə tə nē′um, nyü′-), *n.*, *pl.* **-ne·a** (-nē′ə). **1.** the presence of air or other gas in the peritoneal cavity. **2.** the introduction of air into the peritoneal area for diagnosis or to rest and relax the lungs and permit faster healing of lesions in tubercular patients. [< Greek *pneûma* breath, wind + English *peritoneum*]

pneu·mo·stome (nü′mə stōm, nyü′-), *n.* a small opening through which air passes to and from the mantle or respiratory cavity of gastropods. [< Greek *pneûma* wind + *stóma* mouth]

pneu·mo·tho·rax (nü′mō thôr′aks, -thōr′-; nyü′-), *n.* the presence of air or gas in the pleural cavity, as produced by the introduction of a needle into the cavity so as to collapse a lung in the treatment of pulmonary tuberculosis (artificial pneumothorax), or as produced by other than outside causes (spontaneous pneumothorax). [< Greek *pneûma* wind, spirit + English *thorax*]

PNG (no periods) or **P.N.G.,** persona non grata.

p-n junction (pē′en′), **1.** a junction between a p-type region and an n-type region in a semiconducting crystal. **2.** such a crystal, used as a rectifier or in transistors.

pnxt., pinxit.

PNYA (no periods), Port of New York Authority.

po., (in baseball) putout or putouts.

p.o., 1. post office. 2. (in baseball) putout or putouts.
Po (no period), polonium (chemical element).
P.O., an abbreviation for the following:
1. Peninsular and Oriental (Steam Navigation Company).
2. petty officer.
3. pilot officer (in the Royal Air Force).
4. postal order.
5. post office.
po·a·ceous (pō ā′shəs), *adj.* of or belonging to the grass family of plants; gramineous. [< New Latin *Poa* the genus name (< Greek *póā* grass) + English *-aceous*]
poach[1] (pōch), *v.t.* **1.** to trespass on (another's land), especially to hunt or fish. **2.** to take (game or fish) without any right. **3.** to steal or lure away by unfair methods: *The rebel stevedores union ... was suspended from the congress for having poached members from the transport union* (New York Times). **4.** to trample (soft ground) into muddy holes. **5. a.** to mix with water and reduce to a uniform consistency. **b.** to mix thoroughly (paper pulp) with the bleach liquor. *—v.i.* **1.** to trespass on the lands or rights of another, especially to hunt or fish. **2.** to take game or fish illegally or by unsportsmanlike means. **3.** (of land) to become soft, miry, and full of holes by being trampled. **4.** to sink into wet, heavy ground in walking. [< Middle French *pocher* < Old French *pochier* poke out, gouge < Germanic (compare Low German *pōken*). Related to POKE[1].] **—poach′er,** *n.* **—Syn.** *v.i.* **1.** encroach.
poach[2] (pōch), *v.t.* **1.** to cook (an egg) by breaking it into water that is simmering. **2.** to cook (any of various foods, especially fish) by simmering for a short time in a liquid. [< Old French *pochier* (literally) to put in a bag (because the yolk is thought of as enclosed in the white of the egg) < *poche* cooking spoon < Late Latin *popia,* perhaps < a Gaulish word]
P.O.B. or **POB** (no periods), Post Office Box.
po·chard (pō′chərd), *n., pl.* **-chards** or (*collectively*) **-chard. 1.** a European diving duck that has a reddish-brown head and neck. **2.** any of various related ducks, as the redhead (American pochard) of North America. [origin uncertain]
po·chette (pô shet′), *n. French.* a small violin; kit: *I recognized a tiny pochette—one of those miniature fiddles that dancing masters in the eighteenth century carried around tucked in the capacious flapped pockets of their coats* (New Yorker).
pock[1] (pok), *n.* a pimple, mark, or pit on the skin, caused by smallpox and certain other diseases.
—v.t. **1.** to pit, scar, or mark as if with pocks: *The tens of thousands of craters that pock the face of the moon* (Scientific American). **2.** to scatter over (an area) like pocks.
[Old English *pocc* a pustule. Related to POKE[2].]
pock[2] (pok), *n. Scottish.* a poke; bag.
pock·et (pok′it), *n.* **1.** a small bag sewed into clothing for carrying a purse or other small articles. **2.** a hollow place; enclosed place. **3.** a small bag or pouch: *Lucy Locket lost her pocket* (nursery rhyme). **4.** a bag at the corner or side of a pool or billiard table. **5. a.** a hole in the earth containing gold or other ore: *The miner struck a pocket of silver.* **b.** a single lump of ore; small mass of ore. **c.** a bin in which ore or rock may be stored. **d.** a hole in a mine shaft, tunnel, etc., containing poisonous or explosive gas. **6.** *Aeronautics.* a condition in the air that causes an aircraft to drop suddenly; air pocket. **7.** a pouch in an animal body, especially the abdominal pouch of a marsupial or the cheek pouch of a squirrel, chipmunk, etc. **8.** an isolated group or collection of things: *a pocket of resistance in a recently occupied city. Pockets of unsold vehicles remain unobtrusively in fields and yards* (London Times). **9.** (in racing) a position in which one is blocked or hemmed in by others. **10.** a strip of cloth with open ends, sewed to a sail. A thin wooden spar is passed through it to stiffen the leech or side. **11.** a space between certain pins at which a bowler aims: ... *while a left-handed bowler tries to hit the pocket between the 1 and 2 pins* (World Book Encyclopedia).
in one's (hip) pocket, under one's control or influence: *Even before he plunges into his program, ... Mr. Aznavour has his audience in his pocket* (Howard Taubman). *Britain, on the key issues, remained in America's pocket* (Drew Middleton).
in pocket, having or gaining money: *At the end of their peregrination, they are above a hundred crowns in pocket* (Tobias Smollett).
line one's pocket, to make a large profit, especially in an unscrupulous manner: *Some people had gained control of a "handful of banks" to line their own pockets* (New York Times).
out of pocket, spending or losing money: *Apart from his sacrifice of time, he'll be out of pocket $21,480* (Maclean's).
—v.t. **1.** to put in one's pocket: *He pocketed the letter* (Thomas Hardy). *He held out a pound to her and she pocketed it ...* (Graham Greene). **2.** to shut in; hem in; confine as in a pocket: *A voice pocketed deep in the throat, granular ... complaining* (Modern Writing No. 2). **3.** to hold back; suppress; hide: *He pocketed his pride and said nothing.* **4.** to take and endure, without doing anything about it: *He pocketed the insult.* **5.** to take secretly or dishonestly: *One partner pocketed all the profits.* **6.** to force or drive into a pocket, as a billiard ball or contestant in a race. **7.** *U.S.* to refrain from signing (a bill or other legislation) to keep it from becoming law.
—adj. **1.** meant to be carried in a pocket: *a pocket handkerchief.* **2. a.** small enough to go in a pocket: *a pocket camera.* **b.** small for its kind.
[< Anglo-French *pokete* (diminutive) < Old North French *poke,* or *poque* poke[2]] **—pock′et·like′,** *adj.*
—Syn. *n.* **2.** enclosure. **3.** reticule. *-v.t.* **3.** stifle. **5.** steal.
pock·et·a·ble (pok′ə tə bəl), *adj.* that can be carried or put in a pocket: *He has also written two easily pocketable books* (Harper's).
pocket battleship, a warship smaller than a cruiser but carrying much larger guns.
pocket billiards, pool.
pock·et·book (pok′it bu̇k′), *n.* **1.** a woman's purse. **2.** a case for carrying money, papers, etc., in a pocket. **3.** supply of money; finances; funds: *a vacation easy on the pocketbook. They [foreign countries] lack the right to intervene in our national pocketbook for aid* (Wall Street Journal). **4.** a soft-covered or paper-bound book of such size that it is easily carried in the pocket. **—Syn. 1.** handbag. **2.** wallet.
pocket borough, (formerly, in Great Britain) a borough whose parliamentary representation was controlled by a single person or family: *His father had him elected to Parliament in 1754 from a "pocket borough" owned by the family* (World Book Encyclopedia).
pocket chamber, a device, about the size and shape of a fountain pen, to measure radioactivity. It consists of two charged electrodes which lose potential as the air inside the device becomes ionized, the loss of potential being measured to determine the amount of exposure to radiation.
pock·et·ful (pok′it fu̇l), *n., pl.* **-fuls.** as much as a pocket will hold: ... *a whole pocketful of money* (Thackeray).
pocket gopher, any of a group of burrowing rodents with large cheek pouches; gopher. See picture under **gopher.**
pock·et-hand·ker·chief (pok′it hang′kər chif), *n.* **1.** a handkerchief carried in the pocket. **2.** something very small; a pocket-size thing: *The white pocket-handkerchiefs of Davidia involucrata are there, with lilacs, laburnums, shrub roses* (London Times).
pock·et·knife (pok′it nīf′), *n., pl.* **-knives.** a small knife with one or more blades that fold into the handle.
pock·et·less (pok′it lis), *adj.* without a pocket: ... *a charming billiard room with a long pocketless table* (The Month).
pocket money, money for spending.
pocket mouse, any of various small, mouselike American rodents with external cheek pouches, found in western North America, especially in desert areas or areas of sandy soil.
pocket piece, a coin, often one not current, carried habitually in the pocket, as for luck or for its associations.
pock·et-size (pok′it sīz′), *adj.* **1.** small enough to go in a pocket: *a pocket-size radio, camera, etc.* **2.** *Informal.* small for its kind: *a pocket-size field. The pocket-size market of Switzerland, with a total population smaller than London ...* (London Times).
pock·et-sized (pok′it sīzd′), *adj.* pocket-size.
pocket veto, *U.S.* **1.** a method of vetoing a bill that can be used by the President of the United States on a bill presented to him at the end of a session. If the President does not sign the bill within ten days after Congress adjourns, it does not become a law. **2.** a similar method used by the governor of a State.
pock·et-ve·to (pok′it vē′tō), *v.t.,* **-toed, -to·ing.** *U.S.* to veto (a bill) by means of the pocket veto.
pock·mark (pok′märk′), *n.* a mark or pit on the skin; pock. *—v.t.* to disfigure or mark as if with pockmarks; pock: *Bomb craters ... pockmark surrounding rice paddies and hillsides* (New York Times). *The field of inquiry is ... pockmarked with anomalies* (Manchester Guardian Weekly).
pock-marked (pok′märkt′), *adj.* marked with or as if with pocks: *a pock-marked face, a pock-marked field.* **—Syn.** pitted.
pock·y (pok′ē), *adj.,* **pock·i·er, pock·i·est. 1.** marked with pocks. **2.** *Archaic.* of, having to do with, or like pocks or the pox.
po·co (pō′kō), *adv., adj. Music.* little; somewhat (used in directions to qualify other expressions). [< Italian *poco* < Latin *paucus* little, few]
po·co a po·co (pō′kō ä pō′kō), *Music.* little by little; gradually. [< Italian *poco a poco*]
po·co·cu·ran·te (pō′kō kü ran′tē; *Italian* pō′kō kü rän′tā), *adj.* caring little; careless; indifferent. *—n.* a careless, indifferent person. [< Italian *pococurante* < *poco* little (< Latin *paucus*) + *curante* caring, present participle of *curare* to care < Latin *cūrāre*]
po·co·cu·ran·te·ism (pō′kō kü ran′tē izəm, -rän′-), *n.* pococurantism: *His great and fatal fault ... his affectation of scepticism and pococuranteism* (Harriet Martineau).
po·co·cu·ran·tism (pō′kō kü ran′tiz əm, -rän′-), *n.* the character, disposition, or habits of a pococurante.
po·co·sin (pə kō′sin), *n.* a tract of swampy land; dismal. [American English < Algonkian (language uncertain) *páquesen* or *poquosin* the land is in a watery state]
pod[1] (pod), *n., v.,* **pod·ded, pod·ding.** *—n.* **1.** a case or shell in two parts hinged together, in which the seeds of beans, peas, and similar plants develop; legume or silicle. **2.** any dry, dehiscent pericarp, usually having several seeds, whether of one carpel or of several. **3.** a streamlined cover over anything carried externally, especially on the wings or fuselage of an aircraft: *a gun pod or missile pod. Lockheed said the swept-wing craft will be powered by two Bristol-Orpheus engines mounted in pods at the rear of the fuselage* (Wall Street Journal). *—v.i.* **1.** to bear or produce pods. **2.** to fill out into a pod. *—v.t.* to empty out of the pods; shell (peas, etc.).
[origin uncertain. Compare earlier *podder,* variant of *podware* food crops.] **—pod′like′,** *adj.*

Pod[1] (def. 1) of peas

pod[2] (pod), *n.* **1.** a small herd of seals, whales, etc. **2.** a small flock of birds.
pod[3] (pod), *n.* **1.** the straight groove in the body of certain augers and bits. **2.** the socket in a brace in which the bit is inserted. [origin uncertain. Compare Old English *pād* a covering, and PAD[1].]
p.o.d., pay on delivery.
P.O.D., Post Office Department.
po·dag·ra (pə dag′rə), *n.* **1.** gout in the foot. **2.** gout generally. [< Latin *podagra* < Greek *podágrā* (literally) a foot trap < *poús, podós* foot + *ágrā* a catching, hunting]
po·dag·ric (pə dag′rik), *adj.* having to do with gout; gouty.
pod auger, the straight groove in the body of certain augers and bits; pod.
pod corn, a variety of corn in which each grain or kernel is enclosed in an individual pod or husk, the whole ear being also in a husk, thought to approach nearest to the primitive ancestor of all corn.
Pod. D., Doctor of Podiatry.
pod·ded (pod′id), *adj.* **1.** bearing pods; leguminous. **2.** enclosed within a pod. **3.** swollen like a pod. [< *pod*[1] + *-ed*[2]]
pod·dy (pod′ē), *n. Australian.* a young calf, lamb, etc., taken from its mother and fed by hand.

po·des·ta (pō des′tə; *Italian* pō′de stä′), *n.* in Italy: **1.** a chief government official in medieval towns and republics. **2.** a subordinate municipal judge in certain modern cities. **3.** (under the Fascists) a city official or municipal judge. [< Italian *podestà* < Old Italian *podestate* < Latin *potestās, -ātis* power; public official, perhaps < *potest* he has power < *posse* to be able]

po·de·ti·um (pō dē′shē əm), *n., pl.* **-ti·a** (-shē ə). *Botany.* **1.** a stalklike or shrubby outgrowth of the thallus of certain lichens, bearing the apothecium or fruiting body. **2.** any stalklike elevation. [< New Latin *podetium* < Greek *poús, podós* foot]

podge (poj), *n.* a podgy person, animal, or thing.

podg·i·ly (poj′ə lē), *adv.* in a podgy way: *He stood, podgily square . . .* (Punch).

podg·i·ness (poj′ē nis), *n.* pudginess: *His . . . ancestor had long subsided into whiskered podginess and flaccid inertia* (Glasgow Herald).

podg·y (poj′ē), *adj.,* **podg·i·er, podg·i·est.** short and fat; pudgy: *I wish I had had a shake of that trembling, podgy hand* (Thackeray). [variant of *pudgy*] —**Syn.** dumpy.

po·di·a·trist (pə dī′ə trist), *n.* a person who treats disorders of the human foot.

po·di·a·try (pə dī′ə trē), *n.* the study and treatment of ailments of the human foot. [< Greek *poús, podós* foot + *iātreiā* a healing]

pod·ite (pod′īt), *n.* a segment of the limb of a crustacean or other arthropod.

po·dit·ti (pə dit′ē), *n.* an Australian kingfisher. [< an Australian native word]

po·di·um (pō′dē əm), *n., pl.* **-di·a** (-dē ə). **1.** a raised platform. **2.** a raised platform surrounding the arena in an ancient amphitheater. **3.** a continuous projecting base or pedestal. **4.** a continuous bench around a room. **5. a.** *Zoology.* an animal structure that serves as a foot. **b.** *Botany.* a footstalk or other supporting part.

take the podium, *U.S.* to begin to address an audience or conduct an orchestra: *The conductor took the podium.*

[< Latin *podium* parapet, balcony < Greek *pódion* foot of a vase (diminutive) < *poús, podós* foot]

pod·o·car·pus (pod′ə kär′pəs), *n.* any of a group of evergreen trees or shrubs of the Southern Hemisphere with a fleshy, drupelike fruit and a valuable wood, widely used in construction, cabinets, carving, etc. [< New Latin *Podocarpus* the genus name < Greek *poús, podós* foot + *karpós* fruit]

pod·o·phyl·lin (pod′ə fil′in), *n.* a yellow, bitter resin from the dried rhizome of the May apple, used as a cathartic. [< *podophyll*(um) + *-in*]

pod·o·phyl·lum (pod′ə fil′əm), *n.* the dried rhizome of the May apple. [< New Latin *Podophyllum* the genus name < Greek *poús, podós* foot + *phýllon* leaf]

pod·sol (pod′sol), *n.* podzol.

pod·sol·ic (pod sol′ik), *adj.* podzolic.

Po·dunk (pō′dungk), *n. U.S.* **1.** the name of an imaginary town noted for its small size, dullness, and lack of progress. **2.** *Slang.* any small or insignificant town or village: *All such sufferers could well reflect upon the example set by the Mayo brothers, who converted Rochester, Minnesota, from a Podunk into a world center* (Harper's). [< Algonkian (Mohegan, or Massachusetts) *Potunk,* a place name, perhaps a corruption of *plukohke,* a neck or corner of land]

pod·zol (pod′zol), *n.* a white or gray soil that is highly leached, found in certain cool, moist climates, especially northern Russia. Also, **podsol.** [< Russian *podzol* < *pod-* under + *zola* ashes]

pod·zol·ic (pod zol′ik), *adj.* of or having to do with podzol. Also, **podsolic.**

pod·zo·li·za·tion (pod′zə lə zā′shən), *n.* the process of development of a podzolic soil.

P.O.E. or **POE** (no periods), **1.** port of embarkation. **2.** port of entry.

po·em (pō′əm), *n.* **1.** an arrangement of words in lines usually with a regularly repeated accent and often with rhyme; composition in verse: *a lyric poem, a pastoral poem.* **2.** a composition showing great beauty or nobility of language or thought: *a prose poem.* **3.** something beautiful often likened to a poem: *a tone poem, a face that is a poem.* [< Old French *poeme,* learned borrowing from Latin *poēma* < Greek *póēma,* variant of *poíēma* < *poeîn,* variant of *poieîn* to make, compose]

po·e·sy (pō′ə sē, -zē), *n., pl.* **-sies. 1.** *Archaic.* **a.** poetry. **b.** a poem. **2.** *Obsolete.* a motto or short inscription (often metrical, and usually in patterned or formal language). [< Old French *poësie,* learned borrowing from Latin *poēsis* < Greek *póēsis,* variant of *poíēsis* composition < *poieîn;* see POEM]

po·et (pō′it), *n.* **1.** a person who writes poetry. **2.** a person who has great ability to feel and express beauty: *Herr Wieland is a poet with color* (New Yorker). [< Latin *poēta* < Greek *poētḗs,* variant of *poiētḗs* maker, author < *poieîn;* see POEM] —**Syn. 1.** bard.

poet., 1. a. poetic. **b.** poetical. **2.** poetry.

po·et·as·ter (pō′it as′tər), *n.* a writer of rather poor poetry. [< New Latin *poetaster* < Latin *poēta* poet + *-aster,* a diminutive suffix] —**Syn.** rhymester.

po·et·as·ter·y (pō′it as′tər ē, -trē), *n.* the work of a poetaster; poor poetry or versification: *Fitzgerald is insulted as much for his politics as for his poetastery* (Fraser's Magazine).

po·et·ess (pō′ə tis), *n.* a woman poet.

po·et·ic (pō et′ik), *adj.* **1.** having to do with poems or poets: *the ranks of the poetic tribe* (William Cowper). **2.** suitable for poems or poets: *"Alas," "o'er," "plenteous," and "blithe" are poetic words.* **3.** consisting of verse or poems: *a poetic translation.* **4.** showing beautiful or imaginative language, imagery, or thought: *poetic movement.*

—*n.* poetics.

—**po·et′i·cal·ly,** *adv.,* —**po·et′i·cal·ness,** *n.*

—**Syn.** *adj.* **4.** lyrical.

po·et·i·cal (pō et′ə kəl), *adj.* poetic: *. . . the poetical manner in which you paint some of the scenes about you* (Alexander Pope).

po·et·i·cise (pō et′ə sīz), *v.t., v.i.,* **-cised, -cis·ing.** *Especially British.* poeticize: *Neil Currie's new translation is clear and exciting to listen to—and with none of that fustian poeticising* (Punch).

po·et·i·cism (pō et′ə siz əm), *n.* **1.** overly poetic character or practice; overly poetic diction. **2.** a banal or stereotyped expression in a poem: *But except for one or two poeticisms sprinkled here and there, these earlier poems stand up well* (Atlantic).

po·et·i·cize (pō et′ə sīz), *v.,* **-cized, -ciz·ing.** —*v.t.* to make poetic; treat poetically; put into poetry: *The working class was . . . idealized and poeticized by wayward genius* (Contemporary Review). —*v.i.* to write or speak as a poet.

poetic or **poetical justice,** ideal justice with virtue being suitably rewarded and vice properly punished, as exemplified often in poetry and fiction.

poetic license, variation from regular usages and facts allowed in poetry.

po·et·ics (pō et′iks), *n.* **1.** the part of literary criticism that deals with the nature and laws of poetry. **2.** a formal or systematic study on poetry: *Aristotle's "Poetics."*

po·et·i·cule (pō et′ə kyül), *n.* a petty or insignificant poet; poetaster: *The Elizabethans were, with the exception of Shakespeare, a gaggle of turgid poeticules* (New Yorker). [diminutive form < Latin *poēta* poet]

po·et·ize (pō′ə tīz), *v.,* **-ized, -iz·ing.** —*v.i.* to write poetry. —*v.t.* **1.** to write poetry about. **2.** to make poetic: *All the activities of newspaper production were poetized by her fervour* (Arnold Bennett). —**po′et·iz′er,** *n.*

poet laureate, *pl.* **poets laureate. 1.** (in Great Britain) a poet appointed by the king or queen to write poems in celebration of court and national events. **2.** the official poet of any country, State, etc. **3.** any poet distinguished for excellence.

po·et·ry (pō′ə trē), *n.* **1.** poems: *a collection of poetry.* **2.** the art of writing poems: *Shakespeare and Milton were masters of English poetry.* **3.** poetic quality; poetic spirit or feeling: *the poetry of nature. Poetry is the material out of which poems are made* (Atlantic).

[< Old French *poetrie,* learned borrowing from Medieval Latin *poētria* < Latin *poēta* poet]

Poets' Corner, the space in Westminster Abbey containing memorials of illustrious English writers.

po-faced (pō′fāst′), *adj. British Informal.* poker-faced: *Several times . . . that rather po-faced aspect of his raises a smile* (Manchester Guardian Weekly).

P. of H., Patrons of Husbandry.

pog·a·mog·gan (pog′ə mog′ən), *n.* a war club of American Indians of the Great Lakes region and the Plains, having a slender handle and a heavy, knobbed head, used as a weapon and in ceremonies. [American English < Algonkian (Ojibwa) *pägämâgan* (literally) something used for striking]

POGO (no periods), Polar Orbiting Geophysical Observatory.

po·go·ni·a (pə gō′nē ə, -gōn′yə), *n.* any of a group of North American orchids that grow on the ground, as the snakemouth. [< New Latin *Pogonia* the genus name < Greek *pōgon, pṓgōnos* beard]

pog·o·nip (pog′ə nip), *n. U.S.* a cold winter fog containing ice particles, that sometimes occurs in valleys in the Sierra Nevada Mountains. [American English < a Shoshonean word]

po·go stick (pō′gō), a toy consisting of a stick that contains a spring, and has footrests near the bottom and a handle at the top. A person stands on it and works the spring by jumping on the steps for the feet. *His income has bounced up and down like a man on a pogo stick* (Wall Street Journal).

po·grom (pō grom′, pō′grəm), *n.* an organized attack, especially against the Jews: *The only means of combating the pogroms is armed resistance* (London Daily News). [< Russian *pogrom* devastation]

po·grom·ist (pō grom′ist, pō′grə mist), *n.* an organizer of or a participant in a pogrom: *. . . a country where hatemongers and pogromists enjoyed immunity and where the murderers of Jews were treated leniently* (Manchester Guardian Weekly).

po·gy (pō′gē), *n., pl.* **-gies** or (*collectively*) **-gy. 1.** a perch of the western coast of the United States that bears live young. **2.** the menhaden. [American English, apparently short for earlier *pauhagen, paughaden* the menhaden, perhaps < Algonkian (Abnaki) *pookagan* < a verb, meaning "one manures the land" (apparently the fish was used as fertilizer)]

poh (pō), *interj.* pooh.

poi (poi), *n.* a Hawaiian food made of the root of the taro, baked, pounded, moistened, and fermented. [< Hawaiian *poi*]

poign·ance (poi′nəns, poin′yəns), *n.* poignancy: *Everything that surrounded me . . . lent poignance to my uneasiness* (A.L. Haddon).

poign·an·cy (poi′nən sē, poin′yən-), *n.* a being poignant; piercing quality; sharpness: *poignancy of flavor, poignancy of delight.*

poign·ant (poi′nənt, poin′yənt), *adj.* **1.** very painful; piercing: *poignant suffering, a poignant reminder of one's failures.* **2.** keen; intense: *a subject of poignant interest.* **3.** sharp to the taste or smell: *poignant sauces.* [< Old French *poignant,* present participle of *poindre* to prick < Latin *pungere*] —**poign′ant·ly,** *adv.* —**Syn. 1.** severe.

poi·ki·lo·therm (poi′kə lə thėrm′), *n.* a poikilothermal animal.

poi·ki·lo·ther·mal (poi′kə lō thėr′məl), *adj.* (of animals) having a body temperature that varies with that of the environment; cold-blooded. [< Greek *poikílos* various, variegated + *thérmē* heat + English *-al*[1]]

poi·ki·lo·ther·mic (poi′kə lō thėr′mik), *adj.* poikilothermal.

poi·ki·lo·ther·mous (poi′kə lō thėr′məs), *adj.* poikilothermal.

poi·lu (pwä′lü), *n.* a nickname for a French soldier: *France of September, 1914, which had the spunk and imagination to taxi its reinforcements of poilus to the Marne* (New Yorker).

[< French *poilu* a French soldier in World War I; earlier, strong man; (literally) virile, hairy < Old French *pelu* < *peil, poil* hair < Latin *pilus*]

poin·ci·an·a (poin′sē an′ə), *n.* **1.** any of a group of tropical trees or shrubs of the pea family, having showy scarlet, orange, or yellow flowers. **2.** the royal poinciana. [< New Latin *Poinciana* the genus name < de *Poinci,* a governor of the Antilles in the 1600's, who wrote a natural history of the islands]

poind (poind, pʏnd, pind), *Scottish.* —*v.t.* **1.** to seize and sell under warrant (the goods of a debtor). **2.** to impound (stray cattle, contraband goods, etc.). —*n.* the act of poinding. [Old English *pyndan* to impound, pen up]

poin·set·ti·a (poin set′ē ə, -set′ə), *n.* a plant having a small flower surrounded by large scarlet leaves that look like petals. The poinsettia is a perennial Mexican plant of the spurge family, widely used for Christmas decoration in the United States. [American English < New Latin *poinsettia* < Joel R. *Poinsett*, 1779-1851, discoverer of the plant]

Poinsettia (2 to 10 ft. tall)

point (point), *n.* **1.** a sharp end; something having a sharp end: *the point of a needle, a point of rock.* **2. a.** a tiny round mark; dot: *A period is a point. Use a point to set off decimals. Commas and points they set exactly right* (Alexander Pope). **b.** a diacritical mark used in Semitic languages. **3.** *Mathematics.* something that has position but not extension. Two lines meet or cross at a point. **4.** a place; spot: *Stop at this point.* **5.** any particular or definite position, condition, or time; degree; stage: *the boiling point, the point of death. When it came to the point of shooting, he could not.* **6.** an item; detail: *He answered my questions point by point.* **7.** a distinguishing mark or quality: *Honesty is not her strong point.* **8.** a physical characteristic or feature of an animal, as one used to judge excellence or purity of breed: *The good points in a cow aren't necessarily features of beauty* (Winston Churchill). **9.** the main idea or purpose; important or essential thing: *to miss the point of a joke. I missed the point of your talk.* **10.** force; effectiveness: *He writes with point.* **11.** a particular aim, end, or purpose: *to carry one's point.* **12. a.** each of the 32 positions indicating direction marked at the circumference of the card of a compass. **b.** the interval between any two adjacent points of a compass; 11 degrees 15 minutes. **13.** a piece of land with a sharp end sticking out into the water; cape. **14.** a unit of credit, scoring, or measuring: *Our team won the game by ten points. The university credited him with five points for the semester's work. That stock has gone up a point. During the war meat was rationed by points per pound. Abbr.:* pt. **15.** (in printing) a unit for measuring type; about 1/72 inch. **16.** *Informal.* a hint; suggestion: *to get some points on farming.* **17.** lace made with a needle; needle point. **18. a.** *British.* a railroad switch. **b.** the tip of the angle formed by two rails of a frog in a railroad switch. **19. a.** the position of one of the players in cricket, lacrosse, etc. **b.** the player in this position. **20.** (in boxing) the tip of the chin. **21.** (in hunting) the attitude, usually with muzzle pointing and one foreleg raised, assumed by a pointer or setter on finding game. **22.** one of the 24 long pointed spaces of a backgammon board. **23. a.** a tungsten or platinum piece, especially in the distributor of an automobile engine, for making or breaking the flow of current. **b.** *Especially British.* an outlet; socket. **24.** a short, musical strain, especially one sounded as a signal. **25.** a small body of troops that patrols ahead of the advance guard or behind the rear guard to reconnoiter, as for obstacles or enemy forces. **26.** a stroke with the bayonet. **27.** *Phonetics.* the tip of the tongue. **28.** *Archaic.* a tagged lace or cord used in the Middle Ages to lace or fasten various parts of the clothes: *Their points being broken — Down fell their hose* (Shakespeare). **29.** *Obsolete.* **a.** conclusion; culmination. **b.** condition; plight. **c.** determination; resolution.

at the point of, in the act of; very near to: *at the point of leaving.*

beside the point, unimportant; irrelevant: *He did what the others wanted; his own wishes were beside the point to them.*

in point, pertinent; apt: *a case in point.*

in point of, as regards: *States were too busy with their laws and too negligent in point of education* (Alexander Hamilton).

make a point of, to insist upon: *to make a point of arriving on time.*

on the point of, just about; on the verge of: *She was on the point of going out when a neighbor dropped in.*

strain or **stretch a point, a.** to exceed one's usual limit of procedure; go further than one is entitled to go: *We've not quite so much proof as I could wish. It would be straining a point to arrest him, as it stands* (G.A. Lawrence). **b.** to do more than one is bound to do; make a special exception: *I am not likely, I think, to ask anything very unreasonable, and if I did, they might have stretched a point* (Scott).

to the point, pertinent, apt: *His speech was brief and to the point.*

—*v.t.* **1.** to sharpen: *to point a pencil.* **2. a.** to mark with dots; punctuate. **b.** to indicate decimals. **c.** to mark points in (the writing of Semitic languages, shorthand, etc.). **3.** to give force to (speech, action, etc.): *to point one's remarks. The preacher told a story to point his advice.* **4.** to show with the finger; call attention to. **5.** to direct (a finger, weapon, etc.): *to point a gun at a person.* **6.** to fill joints of (brickwork) with mortar or cement. **7.** (of a dog) to show (game) by standing rigid looking toward it.

—*v.i.* **1.** to indicate position or direction, or direct attention with, or as if with, the finger: *to point at a house.* **2.** to tend; aim. **3.** to have a specified direction: *The signboard points north. The ship pointed east.* **4.** (of a dog) to show the presence of game by standing rigid and looking toward it. **5.** (of an abscess) to come to a head.

point off, to mark off with points or dots: *To divide by 100 is done by only pointing off two figures for decimals* (Charles Hutton).

point out, to show or call attention to: *Please point out my mistakes.*

point up, to put emphasis on; call or give special attention to: *The report of the discussions points up the responsibility of teachers, school librarians, and all agencies . . . to coordinate their efforts* (Saturday Review).

[< Old French *point,* and *pointe* a prick, mark, sharp point; a small measure of space or time < Latin *pūnctum,* neuter, and *pūncta,* feminine, past participles of *pungere* to pierce]

—**Syn.** *n.* **6.** particular. **7.** trait, characteristic. **9.** object. *-v.t.* **5.** aim, level.

point after touchdown, (in football) a point scored for a successful conversion.

point-blank (*adj.* point′blangk′; *adv.* point′blangk′), *adj.* **1. a.** fired straight at the mark, especially without the need to aim because a target is so close: *a point-blank salvo.* **b.** that permits firing in this fashion: *point-blank range.* **2.** plain and blunt; direct: *a point-blank question.*

—*adv.* **1.** straight at the mark: *to fire point-blank.* **2.** plainly and bluntly; directly: *One boy gave excuses, but the other refused point-blank.*

[apparently < *point,* verb + *blank* the white mark in the center of a target]

point-by-point (point′bī point′), *adj.* minutely itemized or detailed: *You are of course entitled to a point-by-point refutation of these articles* (New York Times).

point count, (in bridge) a system of bidding based upon point values given to the honor cards.

point d'ap·pui (pwaN′ dȧ pwē′), *French.* **1.** a secure position serving as a base for operations, as in war or diplomacy. **2.** (literally) point of support.

point d'es·prit (pwaN′ des prē′), *French.* **1.** a net fabric with dots woven into it singly or in groups. **2.** (literally) point of spirit.

point-de·vice, point-de·vise or **point-de·vyse** (point′di vīs′), *Archaic.* —*adj.* **1.** perfect; precise. **2.** scrupulously nice or neat. —*adv.* completely; perfectly; exactly. [Middle English *at poynt devys;* origin uncertain]

point duty, the duty of a policeman assigned to a road crossing, or other particular point in a thoroughfare, to regulate the traffic.

pointe (*French* pwaNt; *Anglicized* point), *n.* *Ballet.* **1.** the toe, especially (as a dancing position) the tip of the toe. **2.** the reinforced toe of the ballet slipper. [< French *pointe,* feminine of *point* point]

point·ed (poin′tid), *adj.* **1.** having a point or points: *a pointed roof.* **2.** sharp; piercing: *a pointed wit.* **3.** directed; aimed: *a pointed remark.* **4.** emphatic: *He showed her pointed attention.* —**point′ed·ly,** *adv.* —**point′ed·ness,** *n.* —**Syn. 1.** peaked. **2.** keen. **3.** leveled. **4.** marked.

pointed arch, an arch that forms a point at the top, characteristic of the Gothic style of architecture.

pointed fox, the fur of red fox made to imitate that of silver fox, by dyeing it black and adding white or white-tipped hairs.

pointed style, the Gothic style of architecture, characterized by pointed arches.

point·er (poin′tər), *n.* **1.** a person or thing that points. **2.** a long, tapering stick used in pointing things out, as on a map or blackboard. **3.** the hand of a clock, meter, etc. **4.** any of a breed of short-haired hunting dogs with a smooth coat and trained to point at game. **5.** any of various other hunting dogs that point at game, as the German short-haired pointer and the German wire-haired pointer. **6.** *Informal.* a hint; suggestion: *Dick gave Tom some pointers on improving his tennis.* —**Syn. 6.** tip.

Pointer (def. 4—24 to 25 in. high at the shoulder)

Point·ers (poin′tərz), *n.* the two stars forming the outer line of the bowl of the Big Dipper. A line connecting them points approximately to the North Star.

Point Four, the fourth point in a United States government program, instituted by President Truman, which granted aid to economically undeveloped countries.

point·ful (point′fəl), *adj.* full of point; meaningful; pertinent; apt: *. . . vivid and pointful in its portrayal of character* (Manchester Guardian Weekly). —**point′ful·ly,** *adv.* —**point′ful·ness,** *n.*

poin·til·lism (pwan′tə liz əm), *n.* a method of painting introduced by French impressionists, producing luminous effects by laying on the colors in points or dots of unmixed color that are blended by the eye. [< French *pointillisme* < *pointiller* to mark with little dots or points < *point* point]

poin·til·lisme (pwaN tē yēz′mə), *n.* *French.* pointillism.

poin·til·list (pwan′tə list), *n.* an artist who follows the style of pointillism. —*adj.* of, having to do with, or characteristic of pointillism.

poin·til·liste (pwaN tē yēst′), *n. French.* pointillist.

poin·til·lis·tic (pwan′tə lis′tik), *adj.* pointillist.

point lace, lace made with a needle.

point-laced (point′lāst′), *adj.* trimmed with point lace.

point·less (point′lis), *adj.* **1.** without a point: *a pointless sword, a pointless pencil.* **2.** without force or meaning: *a pointless story, a pointless question.* —**point′less·ly,** *adv.* —**point′less·ness,** *n.* —**Syn. 1.** blunt. **2.** meaningless.

point of honor, a matter that affects a person's honor, principles, sense of duty, etc.

point of no return, 1. the point in the flight of an aircraft at which it is safer to proceed than to turn back: *We also figure out the point of no return—the point beyond which we wouldn't have enough gas to turn around and get back* (New Yorker). **2.** the point in any course of action at which one can no longer safely turn back: *Now that the proletariat has turned against its leaders, the dictators have no choice but to yield. They have passed the point of no return to Stalinism* (Newsweek).

point of order, a question raised as to whether proceedings are according to the rules.

point-of-pur·chase (point′əv pėr′chəs), *adj.* designating a type of advertising aimed at a purchaser when he is in a store or market ready to buy.

point-of-sale (point′əv sāl′), *adj.* point-of-purchase.

point of view, 1. the position from which objects are considered: *a distant point of view.* **2.** an attitude of mind: *a stubborn point of view. Farmers and campers have different points of view toward rain.*

points of the compass, the 32 directions marked on a compass. North, south, east, and west are the four main, or cardinal, points of the compass.

point source, a source of light which is so highly concentrated that it can be considered to come from a single point.

point system, 1. a system of promoting students by credits for individual subjects, rather than by the completion of a set program for each term. **2.** a system of penalizing motorists for infractions of traffic rules and laws, each type of infraction carrying a certain number of penalty points. **3.** *Printing.* a system of measuring type and leads, in which the pica body equals 12 points. **4.** any of various systems of printing for the blind, as Braille, using raised dots in various combinations as symbols for letters.

point target, a structure or object selected for direct bombing or gunfire.

point-to-point (point′tə point′), *n.* a cross-country or steeplechase horse race over a course marked by flags at the salient points: [*His*] *youngest daughter had taken a tumble at a local point-to-point and broken a leg* (Punch). —*adj.* made, reckoned, etc., from one point or place to another in a direct line: *a point-to-point steeplechase: The Scouts blazed a trail by marching with point-to-point compass readings. Because the transmission must be directional, its usefulness apparently will be limited to point-to-point communication* (Scientific American).

point·y (poin′tē), *adj.*, **point·i·er, point·i·est.** pointed: *a small, merry-looking man with a pointy nose* (New Yorker).

poise[1] (poiz), *n., v.*, **poised, pois·ing.** —*n.* **1.** mental balance, composure, or self-possession: *She has perfect poise and never seems embarrassed.* **2.** the way in which the body, head, etc., are held; carriage: *the gladiator-like poise of his small round head on his big neck and shoulders* (George Du Maurier). **3.** a pause between two periods of motion or change; suspense of movement: *At the poise of the flying year* (Richard Watson Gilder). **4.** the condition of being equally balanced between alternatives; state of indecision; suspense. **5.** *Obsolete.* **a.** a being heavy. **b.** gravity; importance: *Occasions . . . of some poise, Wherein we must have use of your advice* (Shakespeare).
[< Old French *pois,* variant of *peis* < Vulgar Latin *pēsum,* for Latin *pēnsum* weight < *pendere* to weigh]
—*v.t.* **1.** to balance: *to poise yourself on your toes.* **2.** to hold or carry evenly or steadily: *The athlete poised the weight in the air before throwing it.* **3.** to consider; ponder: *a thousand resolutions . . . weighed, poised and perpended* (Laurence Sterne). **4.** *Obsolete.* to make stable, as by adding weight; ballast. **5.** *Obsolete.* to weigh.
—*v.i.* **1.** to be balanced or held in equilibrium. **2.** to hang supported or suspended. **3.** to hover, as a bird in air: *A hummingbird can poise for several moments over a single flower.*
[< Anglo-French *poiser* < Old French *pois-*, stem of *peser* to weigh < Vulgar Latin *pēsare,* for Latin *pēnsāre* (intensive) < *pendere* to weigh]
—**Syn.** *n.* **1.** equanimity.

poise[2] (poiz), *n.* a unit of measurement of viscosity in the C.G.S. system. [< Jean Marie *Poiseuille,* 1797-1869, a French physiologist]

poi·son (poi′zən), *n.* **1.** a drug or other substance very dangerous to life and health: *Strychnine and opium are poisons.* **2.** anything dangerous or deadly: *Avoid hatreds—they are poison* (John Galsworthy). **3.** a substance that stops or weakens the action of a catalyst or enzyme.
—*v.t.* **1.** to kill or harm by poison: *Farmers poison thousands of rats every year.* **2.** to put poison in or on: *to poison food, to poison arrows.* **3.** to have a dangerous or harmful effect on: *Lies poison the mind. Whispering tongues can poison truth* (Samuel Taylor Coleridge). **4.** to stop or weaken the action of (a catalyst or enzyme).
—*adj.* poisonous; toxic: *the poison waters of our polluted streams.*
[< Old French *poison,* earlier *puisun* < Latin *pōtiō, -ōnis.* Doublet of POTION.]
—**poi′son·er,** *n.* —**Syn.** *n.* **1.** venom.

poison dogwood or **elder,** poison sumac.

poison gas, a poisonous gas, especially any of various deadly gases for use against an enemy in time of warfare.

poison hemlock, the common hemlock.

poi·son·ing (poi′zə ning), *n.* **1.** the administering of a poison: *a case of murder by poisoning.* **2.** the ingestion of a poison: *Death occurred by poisoning.* **3.** the condition produced by ingesting a poison or poisonous substance: *An overdose of the drug resulted in poisoning.*

poison ivy, any of several plants with white, berrylike fruit and glossy, green, compound leaves of three leaflets each that cause a painful rash on most people if they touch them. Poison ivy is a North American climbing shrub of the cashew family.

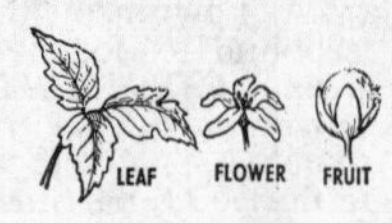

Poison Ivy

poison oak, 1. any of several varieties of poison ivy, especially of western United States, which tend to grow in a bushy rather than twining form. **2.** poison sumac.

poi·son·ous (poi′zə nəs), *adj.* **1.** containing poison; very harmful to life and health; venomous: *The rattlesnake's bite is poisonous.* **2.** having a dangerous or harmful effect: *a poisonous lie.* —**poi′son·ous·ly,** *adv.* —**poi′son·ous·ness,** *n.* —**Syn. 2.** malevolent, malignant.

poi·son-pen (poi′zən pen′), *adj.* designating vicious, slanderous, defamatory and (usually) anonymous writings to or about a person: *"The Raven" was a story about the devastation wreaked upon a French village by a series of poison-pen letters* (New York Times).

poison sumac, a plant growing in swamps that has a white, berrylike fruit and leaves composed of seven to thirteen leaflets that become brilliantly red in the autumn and cause a very severe rash on most people if they touch them. Poison sumac is a tall North American shrub of the cashew family.

Pois·son distribution (pwä sôN′), *Statistics.* a distribution differing from the normal curve that can be applied to distributions that are not continuous, as when the variable cannot have all values but is limited to particular values. Poisson's distribution is often used in bacteriological experiments when the variable is limited to the number of cells in an area. [< Denis *Poisson,* 1781-1840, a French mathematician and physicist, who devised it]

po·kal (pō käl′), *n.* an ornamental drinking cup or goblet, of silver, glass, or other material, especially one of German make. [< German *Pokal,* ultimately < Late Latin *baucalis* earthen wine cup < Greek *baúkalis*]

poke[1] (pōk), *v.*, **poked, pok·ing,** *n.* —*v.t.* **1. a.** to push against with something pointed: *to poke the ashes of a fire. He poked me in the ribs with his elbow.* **b.** *Informal.* to hit with the fist: *He poked me in the nose.* **2.** to thrust; push: *The old gossip was always poking her nose into other people's business.* **3.** to make by poking: *He poked a hole in the paper.* —*v.i.* **1.** to make a thrust with the arm, fist, a stick, or the like. **2.** to pry. **3.** to go lazily; loiter: *They . . . dig out a canoe from a cotton-wood tree, and in this poke along shore silently* (Washington Irving). **4.** to thrust itself or stick (out): *Pens and pencils poked out over the top of his coat pocket.*
—*n.* **1. a.** a poking; thrust; push. **b.** *Informal.* a blow with the fist. **2.** a slow, lazy person. **3.** a device fastened on cattle, pigs, etc., to prevent them from breaking through fences.
[Middle English *poken.* Compare Middle Dutch, Middle Low German *pōken.* Perhaps related to POACH[1].]
—**Syn.** *v.t.* **1. a.** prod, nudge. *-v.i.* **2.** search, grope. **3.** dawdle, potter. *-n.* **1. a.** nudge.

poke[2] (pōk), *n.* **1.** *Dialect.* a bag; sack. **2.** *Archaic.* a pocket: *not a penny in poke* (Robert Browning). **3.** *Scottish.* the bag or wallet of a roving beggar. **4.** *Slang.* **a.** money: *The panorama is . . . contrived and . . . its purpose is to mesmerize the tourist so that later he may be easily relieved of his poke* (Maclean's). **b.** a wallet; purse. [probably < Old North French *poke,* or *poque* < Germanic (compare Old English *pocca,* or *pohha* bag, pocket)]

poke[3] (pōk), *n.* **1.** a bonnet or hat with a large brim in front. **2.** the brim: *The close poke of her little black bonnet hid her face from him* (George Eliot). [(originally) brim of a bonnet; perhaps noun use of *poke*[1]]

poke[4] (pōk), *n.* pokeweed. [American English, short for Algonkian (Virginia) *puccoon* any plant used for dyeing]

poke·ber·ry (pōk′ber′ē), *n., pl.* **-ries. 1.** the deep-purple berry of the pokeweed. **2.** the pokeweed. [American English < *poke*[4], or *poke*(weed) + *berry*]

poke bonnet, a bonnet with a projecting brim.

poke check, a quick poke with a hockey stick attempting to steal or push the puck from another player.

pok·er[1] (pō′kər), *n.* **1.** a person or thing that pokes. **2.** a metal rod for stirring a fire. [< *pok*(e)[1] + *-er*[1]]

pok·er[2] (pō′kər), *n.* a card game in which the players bet on the value of the cards that they hold in their hands, the winner taking the pool. [American English; origin uncertain. Compare Middle Low German, Middle Dutch *poken* to brag, also, to play]

po·ker[3] (pō′kər), *n. Obsolete.* a hobgoblin or demon; bugbear: *As if old poker was coming to take them away* (Horace Walpole). [origin uncertain. Compare Swedish *pocker,* Danish *pokker* the devil. Perhaps related to PUCK[1].]

poker back, an arthritic condition or disease characterized by stiffening of the spine.

poker face, *Informal.* a face that does not show one's thoughts or feelings.

po·ker-faced (pō′kər fāst′), *adj.* of or like a poker face; having a poker face; expressionless: *The manager tried to look poker-faced but succeeded only in looking miserable* (New Yorker).

po·ker·ish (pō′kər ish), *adj. U.S. Informal.* mysteriously fearsome; eerie; uncanny: *There is something pokerish about a deserted dwelling, even in broad daylight* (James Russell Lowell). [< *poker*[3] + *-ish*]

poke·root (pōk′rüt, -rủt), *n.* pokeweed.

poker spine, poker back.

pok·er·work (pō′kər wėrk′), *n.* ornamental work executed by burning designs on wood, leather, etc., with a hot instrument, originally a poker; pyrography.

poke·weed (pōk′wēd′), *n.* any of a group of tropical or subtropical plants, especially a tall weed of North America with juicy, purple berries and poisonous roots sometimes called the inkberry; inkberry. The pokeweed is used in medicine and its young shoots, somewhat like asparagus, are sometimes boiled and eaten. [American English < *poke*[4] + *weed*]

pok·ey[1] (pō′kē), *n. U.S. Slang.* a jail: *After all, if he'd said those things to the cop he'd have had a night in the pokey as well as the $25 fine* (Wall Street Journal). [origin uncertain]

pok·y or **pok·ey**[2] (pō′kē), *adj.*, **pok·i·er, pok·i·est. 1.** puttering; dull; stupid: *I wouldn't have your pokey old husband* (Sinclair Lewis). **2.** moving, acting, etc., slowly; slow: *The firemen . . . complained that the Russians had been too poky about reporting the fire* (New Yorker). **3.** small; confined; cramped; mean: *Do you suppose I gave up my position at school in order to live in a poky little hole . . . ?* (Arnold Bennett). **4.** shabby; dowdy. [< *pok*(e)[1] + *-y*[1]]

pol (pol), *n. Informal.* a politician: *Our committee offices used to be full of old pols and cigar smoke* (Maclean's).

pol., 1. polar. **2.** political. **3.** politics.

POL (no periods), *Military.* petroleum, oil, and lubricants: *On the march the bulk is devoted to gasoline and lubricants, called, in the language of the supply officer, POL* (Dwight D. Eisenhower).

Pol., 1. Poland. **2.** Polish.

Po·la·bi·an (pō lā′bē ən), *adj.* of or having to do with a Slavic people who formerly lived in the basin of the Elbe river and on the Baltic coast of northern Germany and who became completely Germanized. —*n.* **1.** one of this people. **2.** the Slavic language of this people, extinct since the 1700's. [< Czech *Polabe* a Polabian (< *po* near, on + *Labe* the Elbe) + English *-ian*]

po·lac·ca[1] (pō läk′kä), *n. Italian.* polonaise (sometimes used in musical directions).

po·lac·ca[2] (pə lak′ə), *n.* a merchant vessel with two or three masts, used on the Mediterranean. [< Italian *polacca*]

Po·lack (pō′läk *for 1;* pō′lak *for 2*), *n.* **1.** *Slang.* a person of Polish descent (used in an unfriendly way). **2.** *Obsolete.* **a.** a native or inhabitant of Poland; Pole. **b.** the king of Poland: *. . . he sent out to suppress His nephew's levies; which to him appear'd To be a preparation 'gainst the Polack* (Shakespeare). [< Polish *Polak*]

Po·la·col·or (pō′lə kul′ər), *n. Trademark.* a special color film with its own developing and printing agents, from which a finished positive color print may be obtained in less than a minute after exposure. [< *Pola*(roid) + *color*]

po·la·cre (pə lä′kər), *n.* a two- or three-masted ship; polacca. [< French *polacre*]

Po·land China hog (pō′lənd), any of an American breed of large black-and-white hogs.

po·lar (pō′lər), *adj.* **1.** of or near the North or South Pole: *a polar wind. It is very cold in the polar regions.* **2.** having to do with a pole or poles. **3.** of the poles of a magnet, electric battery, etc. **4.** opposite in character, like the poles of a magnet: *Love and hatred are polar feelings or attitudes.* **5.** *Geometry.* having to do with or reciprocal to a pole. **6.** *Chemistry.* ionizing when dissolved or fused; ionic. [< Medieval Latin *polaris* < Latin *polus* pole[2]] —**Syn. 4.** contrary.

Po·lar·a·mine (pō′lər ə mēn′), *n. Trademark.* a powerful antihistamine drug used to treat various allergies.

polar axis, the axis in the mounting of an equatorial telescope that is parallel to the earth's axis.

polar bear, a large white bear of the arctic regions.

polar body or **cell,** *Biology.* one of the tiny cells that arise by a very unequal meiotic division of the ovum at or near the time of fertilization.

Polar Bear (about 4 ft. high at the shoulder)

polar cap, *Astronomy.* a white area at each pole of the planet Mars, resembling ice or snow, which increases and decreases with the changes of the planet's seasons.

polar circle, either of two circles of the earth parallel to the equator, one of which is everywhere distant 23 degrees 28 minutes from the North Pole and the other equally distant from the South Pole; Arctic or Antarctic Circle.

polar coordinates, *Mathematics.* coordinates defining a point in a plane, being the length of the straight line drawn to it from a fixed point and the angle which this line makes with a fixed initial line or axis.

polar distance, *Astronomy.* the complement of the declination of a heavenly body; codeclination.

polar easterly, a prevailing wind which blows from east to west between each of the poles and 60 degrees north or south latitude.

polar front, the boundary or boundary region between the cold polar winds and the warmer winds of tropical origin.

po·lar·im·e·ter (pō′lə rim′ə tər), *n.* **1.** an instrument used to measure the amount of polarized light received from a given source. **2.** a form of polariscope for measuring the amount of rotation of the plane of polarization. [< *polari*(ze) + *-meter*]

po·lar·i·met·ric (pō′lər ə met′rik), *adj.* of or having to do with a polarimeter or polarimetry.

po·lar·im·e·try (pō′lə rim′ə trē), *n.* the use of a polarimeter; art or process of measuring or analyzing the polarization of light.

Po·lar·is (pō lãr′is), *n.* the North Star; polestar. See picture under **Dipper.** [< Medieval Latin *Polaris* < Latin *polus;* see POLE[2]]

po·lar·i·scope (pō lar′ə skōp), *n.* an instrument for showing the polarization of light, or for examining substances in polarized light.

po·lar·ise (pō′lə rīz), *v.t.,* **-ised, -is·ing.** *Especially British.* polarize. —**po′lar·is·er,** *n.*

po·lar·i·ty (pō lar′ə tē), *n., pl.* **-ties. 1.** the possession of an axis with reference to which certain physical properties are determined. A magnet or battery has polarity. **2.** a positive or negative polar condition, as in electricity: *Reversing the polarity of an applied voltage, for instance, means interchanging the positive and negative conditions of the terminals to which it is applied* (Roy F. Allison). **3.** the possession or exhibition of two opposite or contrasted principles or tendencies: *Many psychologists view polarity as an obvious factor in human behavior.*

po·lar·iz·a·ble (pō′lə rī′zə bəl), *adj.* that can be polarized.

po·lar·iz·a·bil·i·ty (pō′lə rī′zə bil′ə tē), *n.* the quality of being polarizable.

po·lar·i·za·tion (pō′lər ə zā′shən), *n.* **1.** the production or acquisition of polarity. **2.** the process by which gases produced during electrolysis are deposited on electrodes of a cell, giving rise to a reverse electromotive force. **3.** *Optics.* a state, or the production of a state, in which rays of light exhibit different properties in different directions, as when they are reflected from glass in a particular way, or when they are passed through a crystal of tourmaline that confines the light vibrations to a single plane

po·lar·ize (pō′lə rīz), *v.,* **-ized, -iz·ing.** —*v.t.* **1.** to give polarity to; cause polarization in. **2.** to give an arbitrary direction, or a special meaning or application, to: *to polarize a discussion.* —*v.i.* to acquire polarity. [< French *polariser* < *pôle* pole] —**po′lar·iz·er,** *n.*

po·lar·iz·ing angle (pō′lə rī′zing), *Optics.* the angle of incidence at which the maximum polarization of incident light takes place.

polar lights, the aurora borealis or aurora australis.

po·lar·o·gram (pō lar′ə gram), *n.* a record made by a polarograph.

po·lar·o·graph (pō lar′ə graf, -gräf), *n.* a device for measuring and making records (polarograms) of changes in the strength of a current in an electrolytic solution between a very large and a very small electrode as a result of changing the voltage difference between the electrodes, used in the qualitative and quantitative analysis of chemical mixtures. [< *polar*(ity) + *-graph*]

po·lar·o·graph·ic (pō lar′ə graf′ik), *adj.* of or having to do with a polarograph.

po·lar·og·ra·phy (pō′lə rog′rə fē), *n.* the analysis of chemicals with the polarograph.

Po·la·roid (pō′lə roid), *n. Trademark.* a thin, transparent material that polarizes light, used in lamps, eyeglasses, etc., to reduce glare.

Polaroid Land Camera, *Trademark.* a type of camera whose special film contains its own developing and printing agents so that a finished positive print is available within a half minute after exposure.

polar orbit, an orbit in which an earth satellite passes over or near the earth's poles instead of the equator.

polar valence, *Chemistry.* electrovalence.

Polar Year, either of two years, 1882-83 and 1932-33, the First and Second International Polar Years, when the nations of the world jointly conducted experiments and collected data in geophysics. The International Geophysical Year of 1957-58 was an outgrowth from and follow-up of the Polar Years.

pol·der (pōl′dər), *n.* a tract of low land reclaimed from the sea, or other body of water and protected by dikes: *The asparagus . . . is grown in the polders reclaimed from the sea near Mont St. Michel* (Westminster Gazette). [< Dutch *Polder*]

pole[1] (pōl), *n., v.,* **poled, pol·ing.** —*n.* **1.** a long, slender piece of wood, steel, etc.: *a telephone pole, a flagpole.* **2.** the tapered wooden shaft of a vehicle; tongue. **3.** a measure of length; rod; 5½ yards. **4.** a measure of area; square rod; 30¼ square yards. **5. a.** a ship's mast: *We were scudding before a heavy gale, under bare poles* (Frederick Marryat). **b.** any spar, especially a light spar. **6.** the starting position nearest the inner rail or boundary fence of a race track: *to have the pole.*
—*v.t.* **1.** to make (a boat) go with a pole: *Barges . . . floated and sailed from the upper rivers to New Orleans . . . and were tediously . . . poled back by hand* (Mark Twain). **2.** to stir (molten metal or glass) with a pole of green wood, so as to reduce the oxygen in the mass by introducing carbon that reacts with the oxygen. **3.** *Slang.* (in baseball) to hit (a long drive, especially a home run): *Long, the second batter to face Jim Davis, poled his fourth homer of the season into the right-field stands* (New York Times).
—*v.i.* to pole a boat: *And poling upstream in white water, unassisted by a motor, is an art not easily acquired* (Atlantic).
[Old English *pāl,* ultimately < Latin *pālus* stake. Doublet of PALE[2].]

pole[2] (pōl), *n.* **1.** either end of the earth's axis. The North Pole and South Pole are opposite each other. **2.** either of two parts where opposite forces are strongest. A magnet or battery has both a positive pole and a negative pole. **3.** *Geometry.* **a.** either end of the axis of any sphere. **b.** the origin or fixed point in a system of coordinates. **4.** either celestial pole. **5.** *Biology.* **a.** each extremity of the main axis of a nucleus or cell, especially an egg cell. **b.** each extremity of the spindle formed in a cell during mitosis. **c.** the point on a nerve cell where a process originates. **6.** each of two opposed or complementary principles.

poles apart, very different from one another; at opposite poles: *Mr. McKay and Mr. Lessing are poles apart in many of their views and judgments* (Wall Street Journal).
[< Latin *polus* end of an axis; the sky < Greek *pólos* axis, the sky < *pélein* to come into being, be]

Pole (pōl), *n.* a native or inhabitant of Poland, a country in central Europe between Germany and Russia. [< German *Pole,* singular of *Polen* the Poles < Middle High German *Polâne* < obsolete Polish *polanie* (literally) field dwellers < *pole* field]

pole·ax or **pole·axe** (pōl′aks′), *n., v.,* **-axed, -ax·ing.** —*n.* **1.** an ax with a long handle and a hook or spike opposite the blade. **2.** a kind of battle-ax; halberd. —*v.t.* to fell with or as if with a poleax. [Middle English *pollax* < *polle* poll, head + *ax* ax; spelling influenced by *pole*[1]]

pole bean, any of various varieties of beans with long stems, grown by planting next to poles, wire, etc., up which they may climb.

pole·cat (pōl′kat′), *n., pl.* **-cats** or (*collectively*) **-cat. 1.** a small, dark-brown, carnivorous, European mammal related to the weasel, with a very disagreeable odor; fitchew. The domesticated ferret is closely related to it. **2.** the North American skunk. **3.** *U.S. Informal.* a mean or contemptible person. [Middle English *polcat* < Old French *poule* fowl, hen (see PULLET) + Middle English *cat* cat (perhaps because it preys on poultry)]

Polecat (def. 1—including tail, 2½ ft. long)

pol. econ., political economy.

pole horse, a horse harnessed beside the pole of a vehicle; poler.

pole·jump (pōl′jump′), *v.i.* to polevault. —**pole′jump′er,** *n.*

pole jump, pole vault.

pole·man (pōl′man′), *n., pl.* **-men.** a man using a pole in surveying, logging, construction work, etc.

po·lem·ic (pə lem′ik), *n.* **1.** argument; dispute; controversy: *Writing polemics against a czar in a candlelit cellar could be dangerous* (Newsweek). **2.** a vigorous controversialist. —*adj.* of controversy or disagreement; of dispute: *My father's little library consisted chiefly of books in polemic divinity* (Benjamin Franklin). [< Greek *polemikós* belligerent < *pólemos* war] —**po·lem′i·cal·ly,** *adv.* —**Syn.** *adj.* controversial.

po·lem·i·cal (pə lem′ə kəl), *adj.* polemic: *the polemical philanthropists of the age* (Hawthorne).

po·lem·i·cist (pə lem′ə sist), *n.* a writer of polemics: *The Church has had . . . able ecclesiastics, effective polemicists and apologists* (Andrew M. Fairbairn).

po·lem·i·cize (pə lem′ə sīz), *v.i.,* **-cized, -ciz·ing.** polemize: *Skeptics have long theorized and polemicized about the phenomenon without producing a fully convincing natural explanation* (Time).

po·lem·ics (pə lem′iks), *n.* **1.** the art or practice of disputation or controversy. **2.** *Theology.* the branch of theology that deals with the history or conduct of ecclesiastical controversy. —**Syn. 1.** argumentation.

pol·e·mist (pol′ə mist), *n.* polemicist.

pol·e·mize (pol′ə mīz), *v.i.,* **-mized, -miz·ing.** to engage in polemics; carry on a controversy.

pol·e·mo·ni·a·ceous (pol′ə mō′nē ā′shəs), *adj.* belonging to a family of dicotyledonous herbs including many ornamental flowers, as the phlox and Jacob's ladder. [< New Latin *Polemoniaceae* the family name (< Greek *polemōnion* Greek valerian < *pólemos* war) + English *-ous*]

po·len·ta (pō len′tə), *n.* a thick porridge made of corn meal, commonly eaten in Italy. [< Italian *polenta* < Latin, peeled barley]

pole of cold, the place in either polar region where the lowest winter temperature occurs, as Verkhoyansk in northern central Asia.

pole of inaccessibility, the point on the Antarctic continent which is the geographic center, being the point farthest from the coast in every direction.

pole·piece (pōl′pēs′), *n.* a piece of iron forming the end of an electromagnet, through which the lines of magnetic force are concentrated and directed: *The distribu-*

tion of the electromotive force in the various sections of the coils on the armature depends very greatly on the shape of the polepieces (Paget E. Higgs).

pole plate, a horizontal timber (plate) laid across the tie beams and supporting the ends of rafters in a roof.

pol·er (pō′lər), *n.* **1.** a person who poles a boat. **2.** an animal harnessed beside the pole of a vehicle; pole horse.

pole·star (pōl′stär′), *n.* **1.** the North Star, formerly much used as a guide by sailors. **2.** a guiding principle; guide. **3.** the center of attraction, interest, or attention. —**Syn. 1.** Polaris.

pole trap, a circular steel trap set on the top of a post: *Golden eagles ... are found crippled in forbidden pole traps* (New Scientist).

pole vault, a vault over a high, horizontal bar between uprights, by using a long pole.

Pole Vault

pole·vault (pōl′vôlt′), *v.i.* to vault over a horizontal bar, by using a long pole. —**pole′-vault′er,** *n.*

pole·vault·ing (pōl′vôl′ting), *n.* the act or practice of vaulting with the aid of a pole.

pole·ward (pōl′wərd), *adj., adv.* toward the North or the South Pole: *The air about the equator rises, and flows poleward in both directions* (J.W. Powell).

pole·wards (pōl′wərdz), *adv.* poleward.

po·ley (pō′lē), *adj. Australian.* hornless; polled: *a poley cow.*

po·lice (pə lēs′), *n., v.,* **-liced, -lic·ing.** —*n.* **1.** persons whose duty is keeping order and arresting people who break the law: *It is the function of the police to be on the watch for antisocial conduct and to apprehend the offender as soon as possible* (Emory S. Bogardus). **2.** the department of a government that keeps order and arrests persons who break the law. **3.** regulation and control of a community, especially with reference to matters of public order, safety, health, morals, etc.; public order. **4.** *U.S.* **a.** the cleaning, and keeping clean, of a military camp, area, etc. **b.** the soldiers detailed to do this.

—*v.t.* **1.** to keep order in: *to police the streets, to police the seas.* **2.** to control, regulate, or administer (a law, operation, program, etc.) to discover or prevent the breaking of a law, rule, or agreement: *... authority to police prescription-drug advertising* (Wall Street Journal). **3.** *U.S.* to keep (a military camp) clean and in order. **4.** *Obsolete.* to regulate (a state or country).

[< Middle French *police,* learned borrowing from Medieval Latin *politia* the state, settled order of government < Late Latin *polītīa.* Doublet of POLICY[1], POLITY.]

—**Syn.** *n.* **1.** constabulary, gendarmery.

police action, a peacekeeping military action or campaign carried out against insurgent or aggressive forces in the interest of world peace: *The Korean war was not a war between sovereign nations, but a United Nations police action* (Bulletin of Atomic Scientists).

police constable, *British.* a policeman of the lowest rank; patrolman.

police court, a court for settling minor charges brought by the police. It has the power to hold people charged with serious offenses for trial in higher courts.

police dog, 1. a kind of large, strong dog that looks like a wolf; German shepherd. See picture under **German shepherd. 2.** any dog trained to work with policemen, guards, etc., such as the Doberman pinscher or bull terrier.

police force, 1. a body of policemen. **2.** the police department of a city, town, etc.: *If you can identify the murderer ..., you probably belong on the police force yourself* (New Yorker). **3.** a peacekeeping force: *The UN police force would stay in the Middle East indefinitely* (Harper's).

police jury, the central governing body of a county (parish) in Louisiana.

police justice or **magistrate,** a justice who presides at a police court.

po·lice·man (pə lēs′mən), *n., pl.* **-men.** a member of the police.

police officer, 1. an officer in a police force. **2.** a policeman.

police power, the power of the state to protect the public welfare, safety, and order by controlling under law the actions of persons.

police reporter, a newspaper reporter who covers the police department.

police state, a state strictly policed by governmental authority, thus having only a minimum of social, economic, and political liberty.

police station, the headquarters of a police force for a particular precinct; station house.

po·lice·wom·an (pə lēs′wu̇m′ən), *n., pl.* **-wom·en.** a woman who is a member of the police.

pol·i·clin·ic (pol′i klin′ik), *n.* a department of a hospital at which outpatients are treated. [< German *Poliklinik* < Greek *pólis* city + German *Klinik* bedside instruction (because the instruction was originally done in the patient's home instead of at the hospital). Compare CLINIC.]

pol·i·cy[1] (pol′ə sē), *n., pl.* **-cies. 1.** a plan of action; way of management: *It is a poor policy to promise more than you can do. The tight-money policy was also reducing the pressure on prices* (Time). **2.** practical wisdom; prudence: *In this ... he was actuated by policy rather than sentiment* (Edward A. Freeman). **3.** political skill or shrewdness: *Never did base and rotten policy Colour her working* (Shakespeare). **4.** *Obsolete.* the conduct of public affairs; government. [< Old French *policie,* learned borrowing from Late Latin *polītīa* state organization < Latin, citizenship < Greek *polīteiā* citizenship, polity < *polī́tēs* citizen < *pólis* city-state. Doublet of POLICE, POLITY.]

pol·i·cy[2] (pol′ə sē), *n., pl.* **-cies. 1.** a written agreement about insurance: *My fire insurance policy states that I shall receive $10,000 if my house burns down.* **2.** *U.S.* a method of gambling by betting on numbers drawn in a lottery. [< Middle French *police* < Italian *polizza* written evidence of a transaction, ultimately < Latin *apodīxis* proof < Greek *apódeixis* proof, publication, declaration]

pol·i·cy·hold·er (pol′ə sē hōl′dər), *n.* a person who holds an insurance policy.

pol·i·cy·mak·er (pol′ə sē mā′kər), *n.* a person who is qualified or authorized to devise policies; high official.

policy racket, numbers pool. [American English, probably < (*wagering*) *policy*]

policy shop, *U.S.* a place where bets are made in policy gambling.

po·li·o (pō′lē ō), *n.* infantile paralysis.

po·li·o·my·e·li·tis (pō′lē ō mī′ə lī′tis, pol′ē-), *n.* **1.** infantile paralysis. **2.** any inflammation of the gray matter of the spinal cord. [< New Latin *poliomyelitis* < Greek *poliós* gray + *myelós* marrow + English *-itis*]

polio vaccine, a vaccine given to prevent poliomyelitis, prepared from a killed poliovirus that has been grown in monkeys, as the Salk vaccine, or from a weakened live virus, as the Sabin vaccine.

po·li·o·vi·rus (pō′lē ō vī′rəs), *n.* the virus which causes infantile paralysis: *Polioviruses are primarily parasites of the human gut* (New Scientist).

pol·ish (pol′ish), *v.t.* **1.** to make smooth and shiny: *to polish shoes.* **2.** to remove by smoothing. **3.** to put into a better condition; improve: *to polish a manuscript.* **4.** to make elegant; refine: *to polish manners. Arts that polish life* (Milton). —*v.i.* **1.** to become smooth and shiny. **2.** to become improved or more refined.

polish off, *Informal.* **a.** to get rid of summarily; finish: *We nearly polished off the Licensing Bill in the Commons* (Punch). **b.** to defeat: *Northampton Town failed to polish off their rivals* (London Times). **c.** to eat up or drink up: *An hour and a half before he was to walk on stage, he unconcernedly primed himself by heartily polishing off a steak and playing pingpong* (Time).

polish up, to get into a better condition; improve: *... to dot his i's and cross his t's and polish up his manuscript* (Manchester Examiner).

—*n.* **1.** a substance used to give smoothness or shine: *silver polish.* **2.** a polished condition; smoothness: *The polish of the furniture reflected our faces like a mirror.* **3.** a polishing. **4.** a being polished. **5.** culture; elegance; refinement. **6.** the outer hulls of rice, as removed by the milling process, used as a livestock feed.

[Middle English *polisen* < Old French *poliss-,* stem of *polir* < Latin *polīre*] —**pol′ish·er,** *n.*

—**Syn.** *v.t.* **1.** burnish, brighten. -*n.* **2. Polish, luster, sheen** mean the shine of a surface. **Polish** suggests the shine given a surface by rubbing: *Rain spoiled the car's bright polish.* **Luster** suggests the shine of reflecting light, often of shifting colors: *Furniture that has been waxed has a luster.* **Sheen** suggests a more steady gleam or brilliance: *Highly polished metal has a sheen.*

Pol·ish (pō′lish), *adj.* of or having to do with Poland, a country in central Europe between Germany and Russia, its people, or their language. —*n.* **1.** the West Slavic language of Poland. **2.** any of a breed of light, European chicken, with a drooping crest of feathers on its head and, in some varieties, a beard.

pol·ished (pol′isht), *adj.* **1.** that has been polished; glossy and smooth. **2.** having naturally a smooth, glossy surface. **3.** refined; cultured; elegant: *I consider it as one of the first refinements of polished societies* (Jane Austen).

polit., 1. political. **2.** politics.

Po·lit·bu·ro (pə lit′byu̇r′ō), *n.* **1.** the Communist Party executive committee which examines and controls policy and matters of state in the Soviet Union. It was known as the Presidium from 1952 until 1966. **2.** a similar executive committee in any of various countries, as Hungary or Bulgaria. **3.** any political group which controls state policy in the manner of a Communist Politburo. [< Russian *Politbjuro* Political Bureau]

po·lite (pə līt′), *adj.* **1.** having or showing good manners; behaving properly: *a polite person, a polite reply.* **2.** refined; elegant: *Helen wished to learn all the customs of polite society.* [< Latin *polītus* refined; (literally) polished, past participle of *polīre* to polish] —**po·lite′ly,** *adv.* —**po·lite′ness,** *n.*

—**Syn. 1. Polite, civil, courteous** mean having the manners necessary in social relations. **Polite** means having and showing good manners at all times: *That polite boy gave me his seat.* **Civil** means being just polite enough not to be rude: *Anyone should be able to give a civil answer.* **Courteous** adds to *polite* the idea of showing thoughtful attention to the feelings and wishes of others: *I go to that store because the clerks are courteous.* **2.** polished, cultured.

pol·i·tesse (pol′i tes′; *French* pô lē tes′), *n.* politeness: *Diplomatic politesse has been thrown aside; that happens during war* (New York Times). [< French *politesse* < Italian *politezza* courtliness, cleanliness < *polito* polite < Latin *polītus*]

pol·i·tic (pol′ə tik), *adj.* **1.** wise in looking out for one's own interests; prudent: *A politic person tries not to offend people.* **2.** scheming; crafty. **3.** political: *The state is a body politic.* [< Latin *polīticus* < Greek *polītikós* an official; having to do with citizens < *polī́tēs* citizen < *pólis* city] —**pol′i·tic·ly,** *adv.* —**Syn. 1.** shrewd, astute.

po·lit·i·cal (pə lit′ə kəl), *adj.* **1.** of or concerned with politics: *political wisdom. The whirlpool of political vicissitude which makes the tenure of office generally so fragile* (Hawthorne). **2.** having to do with citizens or government: *Treason is a political offense.* **3.** of politicians or their methods: *a political slogan, political parties.* **4.** having a definite system of government: *Modern man is a political animal.* —**po·lit′i·cal·ly,** *adv.* —**Syn. 2.** civil, civic.

political asylum, the granting of protection and the right of residence and freedom of movement to a national of another country who has fled his own country: [*He*] *identified himself as an Estonian, begged political asylum* (Time).

political economist, a person skilled in political economy.

political economy, economics.

political geography, the branch of geography that deals with the political divisions or states of the earth, their boundaries, possessions, and centers of population.

po·lit·i·cal·ize (pə lit′ə kə līz), *v.*, **-ized, -iz·ing.** —*v.t.* to make political: *Both are political institutions which necessarily politicalize foreign trade and investment* (Newsweek). —*v.i.* to practice or discourse on politics.

political science, the science of the development, principles, and conduct of government.

political scientist, a person skilled in political science.

po·lit·i·cas·ter (pə lit′ə kas′tər), *n.* a petty politician. [< *politic*(ian) + Latin *-aster*, a diminutive suffix]

pol·i·ti·cian (pol′ə tish′ən), *n.* **1.** a person who gives much time to political affairs; a person who is experienced in politics. **2.** a person active in politics chiefly for his own profit or that of his party. **3.** a person holding political office: *The shallow politicians who now labour at the helm of administration* (Tobias Smollett). **4.** an expert in the theory or science of government and the art of governing; person skilled in statecraft.

—**Syn. 1. Politician, statesman** mean someone active or skilled in public or governmental affairs. **Politician** especially suggests ability to deal with people and accomplish things for the good of the people and the country, but in America often is used slightingly or contemptuously to suggest a man without principles scheming for his own or his party's good: *All office-holders are politicians.* **Statesman,** always in a good sense, emphasizes sound judgment, shrewdness, farsightedness, and skill in dealing with public problems and managing national affairs: *Lincoln was a statesman.*

po·lit·i·ci·za·tion (pə lit′ə sə zā′shən), *n.* the act or process of politicizing: *As a young man he saw the crude politicization that reduced Wagner to a mere prophet of German racialism* (Observer).

po·lit·i·cize (pə lit′ə sīz), *v.*, **-cized, -ciz·ing.** —*v.t.* to give a political character to: *Like America, Great Britain is a modern, large-scale society with a politicized population* (Bulletin of Atomic Scientists). —*v.i.* to participate in or discuss politics: *We talk and squabble and politicize about education as a vote-catching agency* (Pall Mall Gazette).

pol·i·tick (pol′ə tik), *v.i.* to practice politics; indulge in political activity: *It is his natural way of speaking and of politicking* (New York Times). *The President put in a busy day of politicking* (Wall Street Journal).

po·lit·i·co (pə lit′ə kō), *n.*, *pl.* **-cos.** a politician. [< Italian *politico*, or Spanish *político* (literally) politic < Latin *politicus*]

po·lit·i·co-e·co·nom·ic (pə lit′ə kō ē′kə-nom′ik, -ek′ə-), *adj.* having to do with political economy: *His arguments ... concentrate on the aspects of politico-economic reality which are concealed from the public by official propaganda* (Manchester Guardian).

po·lit·i·co-e·co·nom·i·cal (pə lit′ə kō-ē′kə nom′ə kəl, -ek′ə-), *adj.* politico-economic.

po·lit·i·co-ge·o·graph·i·cal (pə lit′ə kō-jē′ə graf′ə kəl), *adj.* having to do with political geography.

po·lit·i·co-mil·i·tar·y (pə lit′ə kō mil′ə-ter′ē), *adj.* having to do with politics and military activity: *In his new post ...* [*he*] *is expected to fill ... the role of White House politico-military adviser* (Atlantic).

po·lit·i·co-re·li·gious (pə lit′ə kō ri lij′-əs), *adj.* political and religious.

po·lit·i·co-sci·en·tif·ic (pə lit′ə kō sī′-ən tif′ik), *adj.* political and scientific.

po·lit·i·co-so·cial (pə lit′ə kō sō′shəl), *adj.* political and social.

pol·i·tics (pol′ə tiks), *n.* **1.** the science and art of government, concerned with the form, organization, and administration of a state or states and the relationship between states. **2.** the management of political affairs: *Theodore Roosevelt was engaged in politics for many years.* **3.** political principles or opinions: *A man's politics are his own affair.* **4.** political methods or maneuvers: *the politics of the last election.* **5.** political science.

play politics, to use a political issue or issues for some gain or advantage without regard to what is just or right: *All this provides ammunition for those in both parties who want to play politics with the issue* (New York Times).

➤ **Politics** is used as either singular or plural: *Politics is a good topic for discussion. His politics were a matter of great concern to his friends.*

pol·i·ty (pol′ə tē), *n.*, *pl.* **-ties. 1.** government. **2.** a particular form of government: *that the true historical polity of the Netherlands was a representative, constitutional government* (John L. Motley). **3.** a community with a government; state: *The Jewish polity was utterly destroyed, and the nation dispersed over the face of the earth* (Joseph Butler). *The former student, now a voting member of the polity, is again confused* (Bulletin of Atomic Scientists). **4.** the condition of having a government or civil organization: *races without polity.* [< Middle French *politie*, learned borrowing from Late Latin *polītia* government < Latin, citizenship < Greek *polīteíā* < *polítēs* citizen; of one's city < *pólis* city. Doublet of POLICE, POLICY[1].]

pol·ka (pōl′kə, pō′kə), *n.*, *v.*, **-kaed, -ka·ing.** —*n.* **1.** a kind of lively dance. It is performed usually by couples, in duple time. **2.** music for it. —*v.i.* to dance a polka. [< French *polka*, German *Polka*, apparently < Czech *polka* (a name given in Prague in 1831 in tribute to the Poles who revolted unsuccessfully against Russia in 1830)]

pol·ka dot (pō′kə), **1.** a dot or round spot repeated to form a pattern on cloth. **2.** a pattern or fabric with such dots. [< *polka* (because of the popularity of the dance in the 1800's)] —**pol′ka-dot′**, *adj.*

pol·ka-dot·ted (pō′kə dot′id), *adj.* covered with polka dots.

polka mazurka, 1. a modification of a mazurka to the movement of a polka, with music in triple time. **2.** a piece of music for this dance or in its rhythm.

poll[1] (pōl), *n.* **1.** a collection of votes; voting: *to decide a question by a poll, to exclude women from the poll.* **2.** the number of votes cast: *a heavy or light poll.* **3.** the result of these votes: *He was returned at the head of the poll* (James A. Froude). **4. a.** a list of persons, especially a list of voters. **b.** a person or individual in a number or list. **5.** poll tax. **6.** a survey of public opinion concerning a particular subject: *The Governors reported that thirty-seven of thirty-nine Governors answering a telegraph poll ...* (New York Times). **7.** the head, especially the part of it on which the hair grows: *The arrow pierced his neck from throat to poll* (Thomas Hobbes). **8.** the blunt end of a pick, hammer, or other tool, used to pound or crush.

polls, the place where votes are cast and counted: *The polls will close at four. 26 million Frenchmen were to go to the polls and with their ballots reveal what the politicians called "tomorrow's secret"* (Time).

—*v.t.* **1.** to receive (as votes): *He polled 25,000 votes.* **2.** to cast (a vote); vote: *A large vote was polled. Sir Anthony Eden ... said: "We must poll every vote"* (London Times). **3.** to take or register the votes of: *to poll a village on the matter of building a new school.* **4.** to enter in a list or roll, as for the purpose of levying a poll tax. **5.** to question or canvass in a public-opinion poll: *For production materials, four out of five purchasing agents polled are buying in the 60-day and under range* (Wall Street Journal). **6.** to cut off or cut short the hair, wool, horns, branches, etc., of: *Avenues of peculiarly polled plane trees* (New Yorker). —*v.i.* to vote at a poll; give one's vote.

—*adj. Especially British.* polled; hornless: *So far three of the bulls bred have proved pure* (*homozygous*) *for the poll character, and produce brown and white poll calves* (London Times).

[origin uncertain. Compare Middle Dutch *polle* top of the head, Middle Low German *pol* head]

poll[2] (pol), *n.* **the poll,** *British Slang.* (at Cambridge University) those students who obtain a pass degree or degree without honors. [apparently < Greek *hoi polloí* plural, the many]

Poll (pol), *n.* a common name for a parrot. [< *Poll*, variant of *Moll*, a woman's name]

pol·lack (pol′ək), *n.*, *pl.* **-lacks** or (*collectively*) **-lack.** any of several salt-water food fishes related to the haddock and the cod, as a variety of the northern Pacific. [origin uncertain. Compare Gaelic *pollag* the fresh-water herring]

pol·lard (pol′ərd), *n.* **1.** a tree that has had its branches cut back nearly to the trunk, so as to produce a thick, close growth of young branches. **2.** an animal, as a stag, ox, sheep, or goat without horns. —*v.t.* to make a pollard of, as a tree; poll.
[< *poll*[1] to cut off + *-ard*, an obsolete suffix]

polled (pōld), *adj.* **1.** hornless: *How long will it be before a naturally polled Ayrshire bull wins at the Royal Show?* (London Times). **2.** shorn; shaven. **3.** bald.

poll·ee (pō lē′), *n.* a person who is questioned in a public-opinion poll.

pol·len (pol′ən), *n.* a fine, yellowish powder formed in the anthers of flowers. Grains of pollen carried to the pistils of flowers fertilize them. *Ideas for clothes fly through the air like ragweed pollen* (New Yorker). [< New Latin *pollen* < Latin, mill dust, fine flour]

pollen count, the number of grains of pollen to be found at a specified time and place in a cubic yard of air: *Hay fever sufferers will profit more from a forecast of wind speed and direction than from local pollen counts* (Science News Letter).

pol·le·no·sis (pol′ə nō′sis), *n.* pollinosis.

pol·ler·a (pə yãr′ə), *n.* a colorful, embroidered costume for women which is traditional at Latin-American fiestas, having a full skirt and a flaring blouse worn off the shoulder. [< American Spanish *pollera* (literally) hooped petticoat < Spanish *pollera* chicken coop < *pollo* chicken < Latin *pullus;* see POULTRY]

poll evil (pōl), an inflamed or ulcerous sore in horses between the ligament of the neck and the first bone of the neck, caused by bruising followed by infection.

pol·lex (pol′eks), *n.*, *pl.* **pol·li·ces** (pol′ə-sēz). the innermost digit of the forelimb; the thumb or a part corresponding to it. [< Latin *pollex, -icis* the thumb; big toe]

pol·li·cal (pol′ə kəl), *adj.* of or having to do with the pollex: *the pollical muscles.*

pol·li·ce ver·so (pol′ə sē vėr′sō), *Latin.* with thumb turned downward or reversed (a sign used by the ancient Romans to indicate death for a gladiator who had been defeated).

pol·li·nate (pol′ə nāt), *v.t.*, **-nat·ed, -nat·ing.** to carry pollen from stamens to pistils of; shed pollen on: *Many flowers are pollinated by bees.* [< New Latin *pollen, -inis* pollen + English *-ate*[1]]

pol·li·na·tion (pol′ə nā′shən), *n.* the transfer of pollen from the stamens to the pistils for fertilization, as by insects or the wind: *A considerable time, occasionally even months, often elapses between pollination and fertilization; but commonly only a few days or hours* (Bennett and Dyer).

pol·li·na·tor (pol′ə nā′tər), *n.* any insect or other agent that pollinates plants.

poll·ing (pō′ling), *adj.* **1.** that polls. **2.** of, for, or having to do with the registering or casting of votes: *polling day, a polling place.*

pol·lin·ic (po lin′ik), *adj.* of or having to do with pollen.

pol·li·nif·er·ous (pol′ə nif′ər əs), *adj.* **1.** producing or bearing pollen. **2.** carrying or adapted for carrying pollen, as certain organs of bees. [< New Latin *pollen, -inis* pollen + English *-ferous*]

pol·lin·i·um (pə lin′ē əm), *n.*, *pl.* **-i·a** (-ē ə). an agglutinated or coherent mass or body of pollen grains, characteristic of plants of the milkweed and orchid families. [< New Latin *pollinium* < *pollen, -inis* pollen + *-ium*, a diminutive suffix]

pol·li·nize (pol′ə nīz), *v.t.*, **-nized, -niz·ing.** pollinate.

pol·li·no·sis (pol′ə nō′sis), *n.* hay fever. Also, **pollenosis.** [< New Latin *pollinosis* < *pollen, -inis* pollen + *-osis* -osis]

pol·li·wog (pol′ē wog), *n.* **1.** a tadpole. **2.** a person who has not crossed the equator on shipboard. [apparent alteration of Middle English *polwygle* < *polle* poll, head + *wiglen* to wiggle. Compare TADPOLE.]

pol·lock (pol′ək), *n.*, *pl.* **-locks** or (*collectively*) **-lock.** pollack.

poll parrot (pol), a parrot.

polls (pōlz), *n.pl.* See under **poll,** *n.*

poll·ster (pōl′stər), *n.* **1.** a person who takes a public-opinion poll. **2.** a person who takes, or evaluates the results of, public-opinion polls, as a trade or profession: *The pollsters assume that what is true of a sample of a few hundred is true of everybody* (Harper's).

poll·tak·er (pōl′tā′kər), *n.* pollster: *We have a nationwide network of some five thousand polltakers* (Harper's).

poll tax (pōl), a tax on every person, or on every person of a specified class, especially as a prerequisite to the right to vote in public elections in some states.

poll-tax·er (pōl′tak′sər), *n. U.S. Informal.* person supporting the levy of a poll tax.

pol·lu·tant (pə lü′tənt), *n.* a polluting agent or medium: *Two other auto exhaust pollutants . . . play a much larger role in the formation of smog* (Atlantic).

pol·lute (pə lüt′), *v.t.,* **-lut·ed, -lut·ing. 1.** to make physically impure, foul, or dirty; contaminate: *The water at the bathing beach was polluted by refuse from the factory. Nature, as well as man, pollutes the air in myriad ways* (Scientific American). **2.** to make ceremonially or morally impure; defile; sully: *an ancient temple . . . which having been polluted some years before by an unnatural murder, was . . . looked upon as profane* (Jonathan Swift). [< Latin *pollūtus,* past participle of *polluere* to soil, defile] **—pol·lut′er,** *n.*

pol·lut·ed (pə lü′tid), *adj.* **1. a.** contaminated by smoke particles, fuel exhaust, gases, etc.: *polluted air.* **b.** contaminated by waste matter: *polluted water.* **2.** impure; unclean: *Leave them to their polluted ways* (Milton). **3.** *Slang.* drunk. **—pol·lut′ed·ness,** *n.*

pol·lu·tion (pə lü′shən), *n.* **1.** a polluting; defiling; uncleanness: *One of the principal difficulties of freeing the river from pollution was that certain persons had prescriptive rights to pass their sewage into the Thames* (London Daily News). **2.** air pollution.

Pol·lux (pol′əks), *n.* **1.** *Greek and Roman Mythology.* one of the twin sons of Zeus and Leda. Pollux was immortal; his brother, Castor, was mortal. **2.** the brighter of the two brightest stars in the constellation Gemini.

Pol·ly (pol′ē), *n.* a common name for a parrot.

Pol·ly·an·na (pol′ē an′ə), *n.* a person, especially a girl or woman, who is untiringly cheerful and optimistic, usually to excess or to the point of foolishness in the face of difficulty, trouble, or disaster: *Now it would take a veritable Pollyanna to believe that it makes no difference to the governing of a country whether a President is sick or well* (Wall Street Journal). [< *Pollyanna,* the heroine of several novels by Eleanor Porter]

Pol·ly·an·na·ish (pol′ē an′ə ish), *adj.* characteristic of a Pollyanna; untiringly cheerful and optimistic.

pol·ly·wog (pol′ē wog), *n.* polliwog.

po·lo (pō′lō), *n.* **1.** a game like hockey, played by men on horseback with long-handled mallets and a wooden ball. **2.** water polo. [Anglo-Indian < a native word of Northern India]

Polo Player (def. 1) about to strike ball

polo coat, a tailored, double-breasted topcoat of camel's hair or a similar, usually soft fabric.

po·lo·ist (pō′lō ist), *n.* a player of polo.

pol·o·naise (pol′ə nāz′, pō′lə-), *n.* **1.** a slow, stately dance, in three-quarter time. It consists chiefly of a march or promenade of couples. **2.** music for it. **3.** a one-piece woman's overdress with a waist and an open skirt, popular especially in the 1700's and 1800's. [< French *polonaise,* feminine adjective, (literally) Polish]

po·lo·ni·um (pə lō′nē əm), *n.* a radioactive chemical element that occurs in pitchblende; radium F. *Symbol:* Po; *at.wt.:* (C^{12}) 210 or (O^{16}) 210; *at.no.:* 84. [< New Latin *polonium* < medieval Latin *Polonia* Poland (because Poland was the homeland of Marie Curie)]

Polonaise (def 3.)

Po·lo·ni·us (pə lō′nē əs), *n.* a pompous old man, the father of Ophelia in Shakespeare's *Hamlet.*

Po·lo·ni·za·tion (pō′lə nə zā′shən), *n.* **1.** the act of Polonizing. **2.** the condition of being Polonized.

Po·lo·nize (pō′lə nīz), *v.t.,* **-nized, -niz·ing.** to make Polish in customs, language, etc.: *Their residence there tends to Polonize the districts in which they live* (Contemporary Review). [< *Polonia,* Latinized form of *Poland* + English *-ize*]

po·lo·ny (pə lō′nē), *n., pl.* **-nies.** *Especially British.* a sausage made of partly cooked pork: *I've chickens and conies, and pretty polonies, And excellent peppermint drops* (W. S. Gilbert). [origin uncertain]

polo shirt, a close-fitting shirt of knitted cotton, jersey, etc., with short sleeves, with or without a collar, pulled on over the head, worn by men and women for sports.

pol·ter·geist (pōl′tər gīst), *n.* a spirit or ghost that is supposed to make its presence known by tappings, the slamming of doors, or other happenings that cannot be explained. [< German *Poltergeist* < *poltern* make a noise + *Geist* spirit, ghost]

pol·troon (pol trün′), *n.* a wretched coward: *What a miserable little poltroon had fear . . . made of me* (Charlotte Brontë). *—adj.* base; cowardly; contemptible. [< Middle French *poltrôn* < Italian *poltrone* (originally) colt, coward (because of a colt's habit of taking fright and running), or perhaps < *poltro* lazy]

pol·troon·er·y (pol trü′nər ē), *n.* the behavior of a poltroon; cowardice: *. . . counsels that had hitherto resulted in a concert of miserable poltroonery* (William Gladstone).

pol·troon·ish (pol trü′nish), *adj.* like a poltroon; cowardly: *Patience may be very Christian in you, but it is very poltroonish in me* (Catherine Sedgwick).

Pol·warth (pōl′wərth), *n.* any of a breed of sheep found in Australia, a cross between the Merino and the Lincoln.

poly-, *combining form.* more than one; many; extensive, as in *polyangular, polyethylene, polynomial.* [< Greek *polýs* much, many]

pol·y·ac·id (pol′ē as′id), *adj. Chemistry.* equivalent in combining capacity to an acid radical of valence greater than unity as a base.

pol·y·a·cryl·ic acid (pol′ē ə kril′ik), a polymer of acrylic acid, used in manufacturing nylon.

pol·y·ac·ry·lo·ni·trile (pol′ē ak′rə lō nī′trəl, -trĭl, -trēl; -ə kril′ō nī′-), *n.* a polymer of acrylonitrile used in manufacturing synthetic fibers, such as Orlon.

pol·y·a·del·phous (pol′ē ə del′fəs), *adj. Botany.* having the stamens united in three or more bundles or groups. [< *poly-* + Greek *adelphós* (with English *-ous*) brother]

pol·y·aes·the·sia (pol′ē əs thē′zhə), *n. Medicine.* a morbid condition of the sense of touch, as in locomotor ataxia, in which a single stimulus, as the prick of a pin, is felt at two or more places.

pol·y·am·id (pol′ē am′id), *n.* polyamide.

pol·y·am·ide (pol′ē am′īd, -id), *n.* a chemical compound containing two or more amide (-NH_2) radicals, especially a polymeric amide.

pol·y·a·mine (pol′ē ə mēn′, -am′in), *n.* a chemical compound containing more than one amino group.

pol·y·an·drous (pol′ē an′drəs), *adj.* **1.** having more than one husband at the same time: *Polyandrous families, for instance, need not be restricted to one wife but may have two or more; in other words, they may practice polyandry and polygamy at once* (New Yorker). **2.** *Botany.* having numerous stamens, of an indefinite number.

pol·y·an·dry (pol′ē an′drē, pol′ē an′-), *n.* **1.** the practice or condition of having more than one husband at the same time. **2.** *Botany.* the condition of being polyandrous. [< Greek *polyandríā* < *polyándros* having many men or mates < *polýs* much, many + *anḗr, andrós* man, husband]

pol·y·an·gu·lar (pol′ē ang′gyə lər), *adj.* having many angles; polygonal.

pol·y·an·tha rose (pol′ē an′thə), one of a group of hybrid roses bearing large clumps of flowers on low, bushy plants, obtained by crossing several species of the rose. [< Greek *polýanthos;* see POLYANTHUS]

pol·y·an·thus (pol′ē an′thəs), *n.* **1.** the oxlip. **2.** a kind of narcissus bearing clusters of small yellow or white flowers. **3.** a hybrid primrose bearing flowers of many colors in umbels. [< New Latin *polyanthus* < Greek *polýanthos,* variant of *polyanthḗs* blooming prolifically < *polýs* many + *ánthos* flower]

pol·y·ar·chy (pol′ē är′kē), *n., pl.* **-chies.** government of a state or city by many. [< Greek *polyarchíā* < *polýs* many + *archós* ruler]

pol·y·ar·te·ri·tis (pol′ē är′tə rī′təs), *n.* a disease characterized by inflammation and lesions of the external walls of the smaller arteries and by the formation of nodules within the arteries, resulting in a weakening and damaging of the surrounding tissues and organs.

pol·y·ar·thrit·ic (pol′ē är thrit′ik), *adj.* having to do with or suffering from polyarthritis.

pol·y·ar·thri·tis (pol′ē är thrī′tis), *n.* an inflammation of several or many joints.

pol·y·ar·tic·u·lar (pol′ē är tik′yə lər), *adj.* **1.** having many joints. **2.** affecting many joints.

pol·y·a·tom·ic (pol′ē ə tom′ik), *adj.* containing or consisting of many atoms, especially having many replaceable hydrogen atoms.

pol·y·ba·sic (pol′ē bā′sik), *adj.* (of an acid) having two or more hydrogen atoms that can be replaced by basic atoms or radicals.

po·lyb·a·site (pə lib′ə sīt), *n.* a blackish mineral with a metallic luster, consisting essentially of silver, sulfur, and antimony. It is a valuable silver ore. [< German *Polybasit* < *poly-* poly- + *Base* (< Latin *basis*) base + *-it* -ite[1] (apparently because of its high proportion of basic sulfide of silver)]

pol·y·but·a·di·ene (pol′ē byü′tə dī′ēn, -dī-ēn′), *n.* an improved type of synthetic rubber produced from butadiene and occurring in several polymeric forms.

pol·y·car·bo·nate (pol′ē kär′bə nāt), *n.* any of a group of plastic resins, derived from phosgene and a phenol, resistant to impact and heat softening.

pol·y·car·pel·lar·y (pol′ē kär′pə ler′ē), *adj. Botany.* having or consisting of many or several carpels.

pol·y·car·pous (pol′ē kär′pəs), *adj. Botany.* consisting of many or several carpels. [< Greek *polýkarpos* fruitful < *polýs* much + *karpós* fruit, seed]

pol·y·cen·tric (pol′ē sen′trik), *adj.* **1.** having several centers or central parts: *polycentric chromosomes.* **2.** of or characterized by polycentrism.

pol·y·cen·trism (pol′ē sen′triz əm), *n.* a principle of communism that permits moderately independent leadership and variations in political dogma among the communist parties of the world.

pol·y·cen·trist (pol′ē sen′trist), *n.* one who advocates or practices polycentrism. *—adj.* of or characterized by polycentrism; polycentric: *Rumania would not take sides in the dispute, but preferred the "polycentrist" approach* (Time).

pol·y·chaete (pol′ē kēt), *n.* any of a class of annelid worms, including most of the common marine worms, having a series of unsegmented appendages or parapodia covered with many bristles or setae. *—adj.* of or belonging to the polychaetes. [< New Latin *Polychaeta* the class name < Greek *polychaítēs* having much hair < *polýs* much + *chaítē* mane, bristle]

pol·y·chae·tous (pol′ē kē′təs), *adj.* polychaete.

pol·y·cha·si·al (pol′ē kā′zē əl), *adj.* of or having to do with a polychasium.

pol·y·cha·si·um (pol′ē kā′zē əm), *n., pl.* **-si·a** (-zē ə). *Botany.* a form of cymose inflorescence in which each axis produces more than two lateral axes. [< New Latin *polychasium* < Greek *polýs* much + *chásis* division < *cháskein* to yawn, gape. Compare CHASM.]

pol·y·chro·mat·ic (pol′ē krō mat′ik), *adj.* polychrome.

pol·y·chrome (pol′ē krōm), *adj., n., v.t.,* **-chromed, -chrom·ing.** *—adj.* having many or various colors; decorated in many colors. *—n.* **1.** a work of art in several colors, as a colored statue. **2.** a combination of many colors.
—v.t. to decorate in several colors; paint by using polychromy: *to polychrome statuary.* [< French *polychrome* < Greek *polýchrōmos* < *polýs* many + *chrôma, -atos* color]

pol·y·chrom·ic (pol′ē krō′mik), *adj.* polychrome.

pol·y·chro·my (pol′ē krō′mē), *n.* **1.** polychrome coloring. **2.** the art of painting or decorating in several colors, especially as anciently used in pottery and architecture.

Pol·y·cle·tan (pol′i klē′tən), *adj.* Polyclitan.

pol·y·clin·ic (pol′ē klin′ik), *n.* a clinic or hospital dealing with many different diseases.

Pol·y·cli·tan (pol′i klī′tən), *adj.* **1.** of or having to do with Polyclitus, or Polycletus, of Argos, a celebrated Greek sculptor, whose statue of the Doryphorus (spear bearer) long served as a standard of the perfect human proportions. **2.** having to do with or observing the principles of art laid down by Polyclitus.

pol·y·con·ic (pol′ē kon′ik), *adj.* having to do with or based upon many cones.

polyconic projection, a system of map projection in which each parallel of latitude is represented as if projected on a cone touching the earth's surface along that parallel.

pol·y·cot·y·le·don (pol′ē kot′ə lē′dən), *n.* a plant of which the seed contains more than two cotyledons.

pol·y·cot·y·le·don·ous (pol′ē kot′ə lē′də nəs, -led′ə-), *adj.* having more than two cotyledons in the seed, as many gymnosperms.

po·ly·crys·tal·line (pol′ē kris′tə lin, -līn), *adj.* **1.** composed of many crystals: *Most solids are polycrystalline* (Scientific American). **2.** composed of crystals with different space lattices: *a polycrystalline metal.*

pol·y·cy·clic (pol′ē sī′klik, -sik′lik), *adj.* **1.** having many rounds, turns, or whorls, as a shell: *Some populations go through several such cycles in a year, and to these the term polycyclic is applied* (J. Green). **2.** *Electricity.* having many cycles or circuits. **3.** *Chemistry.* having more than one ring in a molecule.

pol·y·cyst·ic (pol′ē sis′tik), *adj.* having or consisting of several cysts: *a polycystic tumor.*

pol·y·cy·the·mi·a or **pol·y·cy·thae·mi·a** (pol′ē sī thē′mē ə), *n.* a disease caused by overactivity of the bone marrow, producing an excessive number of red blood corpuscles and a hemoglobin count that is too high. [< *poly-* + *cyt-* + *-emia*]

pol·y·dac·tyl or **pol·y·dac·tyle** (pol′ē dak′təl), *adj.* having many or several fingers or toes, especially more than the normal number. —*n.* a polydactyl animal. [< French *polydactyle* < Greek *polydáktylos* < *polýs* many + *dáktylos* finger, toe]

pol·y·dac·tyl·ism (pol′ē dak′tə liz əm), *n.* the condition or state of being polydactyl.

pol·y·dac·tyl·ous (pol′ē dak′tə ləs), *adj.* polydactyl.

pol·y·dac·tyl·y (pol′ē dak′tə lē), *n.* polydactylism.

pol·y·de·mon·ism or **pol·y·dae·mon·ism** (pol′ē dē′mə niz əm), *n.* the belief in many supernatural powers or evil spirits.

pol·y·de·mon·is·tic or **pol·y·dae·mon·is·tic** (pol′ē dē′mə nis′tik), *adj.* having to do with or characterized by polydemonism.

pol·y·dip·si·a (pol′ē dip′sē ə), *n.* abnormally excessive thirst. [< New Latin *polydipsia* < Greek *polýs* much + *dípsa* thirst]

Pol·y·do·rus (pol′i dôr′əs, -dōr′-), *n. Greek Legend.* the youngest son of Priam, killed by Achilles.

pol·y·e·lec·tro·lyte (pol′ē i lek′trə līt), *n.* an electrolyte of high molecular weight that dissociates unevenly in solution, leaving positive or negative ions joined to the polymer structure. Polyelectrolytes are used as soil conditioners and flocculating agents.

pol·y·em·bry·o·ny (pol′ē em′brē ō′nē, -brē ə-), *n. Botany.* the formation or presence of more than one embryo in a seed. [< *poly-* + Greek *émbryon* embryo + English *-y*[3]]

pol·y·ene (pol′ē ēn), *n.* any of a group of chemical compounds characterized by a number of coupled double bonds.

pol·y·es·ter (pol′ē es′tər), *n.* one of a large group of synthetic polymeric resins made by changing various acids into esters with alcohols, glycerine, or glycols. Polyesters are used in the manufacture of paints, synthetic fibers, films, and reinforced plastics for construction.

polyester fiber, a synthetic, wrinkle- and abrasion-resistant fiber made by the condensation of terephthalic acid and glycol, used alone or in combination with other fibers in shirts, suits, etc.

pol·y·eth·nic (pol′ē eth′nik), *adj.* belonging to or containing many nations or races.

pol·y·eth·y·lene (pol′ē eth′ə lēn), *n.* any of several thermoplastic synthetic resins produced by the polymerization of ethylene, used for containers, insulation, tubing, etc. *Formula:* $(C_2H_4)_n$

polyethylene glycol, any of various colorless and odorless polymers of ethylene glycol, ranging from viscous liquids, with molecular weights of about 200, to waxy solids, with molecular weights of about 6000. Polyethylene glycols are used as lubricants, solvents, intermediates, bases for cosmetics, etc. *Formula:* $HOCH_2(CH_2OCH_2)_nCH_2OH$

pol·y·foil (pol′ē foil′), *Architecture.* —*adj.* consisting of or decorated with more than five foils; multifoil: *a polyfoil window, a polyfoil arch.* —*n.* a polyfoil opening or ornament; multifoil.

po·lyg·a·la (pə lig′ə lə), *n.* any of a large group of herbs and shrubs, commonly known as milkworts, as the fringed polygala of North America. [< New Latin *Polygala* the typical genus < Latin *polygala* the milkwort < Greek *polýgalon* < *polýs* much + *gála* milk]

pol·y·ga·la·ceous (pol′ē gə lā′shəs, pə lig′ə-), *adj.* belonging to the milkwort family of plants typified by the milkwort or polygala.

po·lyg·a·mist (pə lig′ə mist), *n.* a person who practices or favors polygamy.

po·lyg·a·mous (pə lig′ə məs), *adj.* **1.** having more than one wife at the same time. **2.** *Botany.* bearing both unisexual and hermaphrodite flowers on the same plant or on different plants of the same species. **3.** *Zoology.* **a.** (of an animal) having several mates: *The war is, perhaps, severest between the males of polygamous animals* (Charles Darwin). **b.** (of a species) characterized by polygamy. —**po·lyg′a·mous·ly,** *adv.*

po·lyg·a·my (pə lig′ə mē), *n.* **1.** the practice or condition of having more than one wife at the same time. The Moslem religion permits polygamy. **2.** *Zoology.* the practice of mating with several individuals of the opposite sex, usually one male with several females. [< Greek *polygamíā* < *polýgamos* often married < *polýs* many + *gámos* marriage]

pol·y·gen·e·sis (pol′ē jen′ə sis), *n. Biology.* the theory of the origination of a race or species from several independent ancestors or germ cells.

pol·y·ge·net·ic (pol′ē jə net′ik), *adj.* **1.** *Biology.* of or having to do with polygenesis. **2.** having more than one origin; formed in several different ways or at several different times.

pol·y·gen·ic (pol′ē jen′ik), *adj.* of or having to do with polygeny.

polygenic inheritance, the presence of complex hereditary characters that have developed from a relatively large number of genes.

po·lyg·e·ny (pə lij′ə nē), *n.* the theoretical origination of mankind or a human race from several separate and independent pairs of ancestors.

pol·y·glot (pol′ē glot), *adj.* **1.** knowing several languages: *The new school had a large and polyglot student body* (Atlantic). **2.** written in several languages: *a polyglot Bible.* —*n.* **1.** a person who knows several languages. **2.** a book written in several languages: *commentaries and polyglots.* **3.** a mixture or confusion of several languages. [< Greek *polýglōttos* < *polýs* many + *glôtta* tongue, variant of *glôssa*]

pol·y·glot·tal (pol′ē glot′əl), *adj.* speaking several languages.

pol·y·glot·tic (pol′ē glot′ik), *adj.* polyglottal.

pol·y·gon (pol′ē gon), *n.* a closed plane figure with straight sides. Polygons usually have more than three sides and angles. [< Latin *polygōnum* < Greek *polýgōnon* (originally) neuter of *polýgōnos* polygonal < *polýs* many + *gōníā* angle]

pol·y·go·na·ceous (pol′ē gə nā′shəs), *adj.* belonging to the buckwheat family of plants, including the knotgrass, jointweed, and dock. [< New Latin *Polygonaceae* the family name (< Latin *polygonon* polygonum) + English *-ous*]

po·lyg·o·nal (pə lig′ə nəl), *adj.* having more than four angles and four sides. —**po·lyg′o·nal·ly,** *adv.*

po·lyg·o·no·met·ric (pə lig′ə nə met′rik), *adj.* of or having to do with polygonometry.

pol·y·go·nom·e·try (pol′ē gə nom′ə trē), *n.* a branch of mathematics dealing with the measurement and properties of polygons.

po·lyg·o·num (pə lig′ə nəm), *n.* any of a large and widely distributed group of plants of the buckwheat family, consisting mainly of herbs, characterized by a stem with swollen joints sheathed by the stipules, as the knotgrass, bistort, and smartweed. [< New Latin *Polygonum* the genus name < Latin *polygonon* knotgrass < Greek *polýgonon* < *polýs* many + *góny* knee, joint (because it has many joints)]

po·lyg·o·ny (pə lig′ə nē), *n.* polygonum.

pol·y·graph (pol′ē graf, -gräf), *n.* **1.** an apparatus resembling a pantograph, used for making two or more identical drawings or writings simultaneously. **2.** a prolific or versatile author. **3.** *Medicine.* an instrument for recording several pulsations, as of an artery, a vein, and the heart, all at once. **4.** a lie detector: *An upward swing of the record of a lie detector, or polygraph, may point to innocence, not guilt* (Science News Letter). [probably < *poly-* + *-graph.* Compare French *polygraphe* instrument that makes simultaneous drawings, Greek *polygráphos* one that writes much.]

pol·y·graph·ic (pol′ē graf′ik), *adj.* **1.** having to do with multiplication of copies of a drawing or writing: *a polygraphic instrument.* **2.** done with a polygraph: *a polygraphic copy or writing.*

pol·y·graph·i·cal (pol′ē graf′ə kəl), *adj.* polygraphic.

po·lyg·y·nous (pə lij′ə nəs), *adj.* **1.** having more than one wife or concubine, or both, at the same time. **2.** of, having to do with, or involving polygyny. **3.** *Botany.* having many pistils or styles.

po·lyg·y·ny (pə lij′ə nē), *n.* **1.** the practice or condition of having more than one wife or concubine, or both, at the same time. **2.** the practice of a male animal of having several mates. **3.** *Botany.* the state of having many pistils or styles. [< *poly-* + Greek *gynḗ* woman, wife; patterned on *polygamy, polyandry*]

pol·y·hal·ite (pol′ē hal′īt), *n.* a mineral consisting essentially of a hydrous sulphate of calcium, magnesium, and potassium, occurring usually in fibrous masses, and of a brick-red color caused by the presence of iron. [< German *Polyhalit* < *poly-* poly- + Greek *háls* salt + German *-it* -ite[1]]

pol·y·he·dral (pol′ē hē′drəl), *adj.* **1.** of or having to do with a polyhedron. **2.** having many faces.

pol·y·he·dron (pol′ē hē′drən), *n., pl.* **-drons, -dra** (-drə). a solid figure having many faces, especially more than six. [< New Latin *polyhedron* < Greek *polýedron,* neuter of *polýedros* < *polýs* many + *hédra* side, base]

pol·y·his·tor (pol′ē his′tər), *n.* a person of great or varied learning; polymath. [< Greek *polyístōr* < *polýs* much + *hístōr* one who learns by enquiry or study. Compare HISTORY.]

pol·y·his·to·ri·an (pol′ē his tôr′ē ən, -tōr′-), *n.* a polyhistor.

pol·y·his·tor·ic (pol′ē his tôr′ik, -tor′-), *adj.* of, having to do with, or exhibiting polyhistory or wide and varied knowledge.

pol·y·his·to·ry (pol′ē his′tər ē, -his′trē), *n.* great or varied learning.

pol·y·hy·dric (pol′ē hī′drik), *adj.* polyhydroxy: *polyhydric alcohols.*

pol·y·hy·drox·y (pol′ē hī drok′sē), *adj. Chemistry.* having several hydroxyl (-OH) radicals. [< *poly-* + *hydrox*(yl) + *-y*[3]]

Pol·y·hym·ni·a (pol′ē him′nē ə), *n. Greek Mythology.* the Muse of religious poetry. [< Latin *Polyhymnia* < Greek *Polýmnia,* short for *Polyýmnia* < *polýs* many + *hýmnos* song]

pol·y·i·so·bu·ty·lene (pol′ē ī′sə byü′tə lēn), *n.* any of a group of polymers derived from petroleum hydrocarbons catalyzed at low temperatures, ranging from oils to solids much like rubber.

pol·y·i·so·cy·an·ate (pol′ē ī′sə sī′ə nit, -nāt), *n.* polyurethane.

pol·y·i·so·prene (pol′ē ī′sə prēn), *n.* one of the chief constituents of natural rubber. Polyisoprene can also be made synthetically from isoprene and used as a substitute for natural rubber.

pol·y·lin·gual (pol′ē ling′gwəl), *adj.* **1.** speaking, reading, or writing many languages: *The polylingual, much-traveled son of a wealthy Swedish banker* (Time). **2.** written in many languages: *He transferred to the new house his vast polylingual library* (New Yorker).

pol·y·lin·guist (pol′ē ling′gwist), *n.* a person learned in many languages.

pol·y·lith (pol′i lith), *n.* a structure, as a monument or column, built up of many or several stones. [< *poly-* + Greek *líthos* stone]

pol·y·lith·ic (pol′ē lith′ik), *adj.* consisting of many stones; built up of several blocks, as a shaft or column.

pol·y·math (pol′ē math), *n.* a man of much or varied learning; polyhistor: *Even a lifetime of sixty-seven years is hardly sufficient to become a serious polymath* (Atlantic). —*adj.* having great or varied learning: *These would need to be collated by polymath historians, who command the language and literature and science of the period* (New Scientist). [< Greek *polymathḗs* having learned much < *polýs* much + *manthánein* learn]

pol·y·math·ic (pol′ē math′ik), *adj.* having to do with or characterized by polymathy.

po·lym·a·thy (pə lim′ə thē), *n.* great learning: *Aristotle . . . exhibits . . . much of that polymathy which he transmitted to the Peripatetics generally* (George Grote).

pol·y·mer (pol′i mər), *n.* a chemical compound in which the molecules are formed by two or more simpler molecules, all of the same kind, combining with each other, usually with no loss of any components: *Like cellulose, lignin is a polymer, that is, a giant molecule built up from identical or similar smaller molecular units* (Scientific American). [back formation < *polymeric*]

pol·y·mer·ase (pol′i mə rās), *n.* an enzyme that polymerizes nucleotides to form nucleic acid. [< *polymer* + *-ase*]

pol·y·mer·ic (pol′ē mer′ik), *adj.* having the same elements combined in the same proportions by weight, but differing in molecular weight and in chemical properties. Acetylene, C_2H_2, and benzene, C_6H_6, are polymeric compounds. [< German *polymerisch* < Greek *polymerḗs* (< *polýs* many + *méros* part, section) + German *-isch* -ic]

pol·y·mer·ise (pol′i mə rīz, pə lim′ə-), *v.t., v.i.,* **-ised, -is·ing.** *Especially British.* polymerize.

po·lym·er·ism (pə lim′ə riz əm, pol′i mə-), *n.* **1.** *Chemistry.* the condition of being polymeric. **2.** *Botany.* the condition of being polymerous.

pol·y·mer·i·za·tion (pol′i mər ə zā′shən, pə lim′ər ə-) *n. Chemistry.* **1.** the act or process of forming a polymer or polymeric compound. **2.** a reaction in which two or more molecules of the same kind unite, forming a more complex molecule with a higher molecular weight and different chemical and physical properties (the new molecule retaining the same elements in the same proportion as the parent substance), as $CH_3CHO = (CH_3CHO)_3$, by which is indicated the formation of paraldehyde from acetaldehyde. **3.** the conversion of one compound into another by such a process: *the polymerization of acetylene to benzene.*

pol·y·mer·ize (pol′i mə rīz, pə lim′ə-), *v.t., v.i.,* **-ized, -iz·ing. 1.** to make or become polymeric; form a polymer. **2.** to undergo or cause to undergo polymerization.

po·lym·er·ous (pə lim′ər əs), *adj.* **1.** *Biology.* composed of many parts, members, or segments. **2.** *Botany.* (of a flower) having many members in each whorl. [< *poly-* + Greek *méros* (with English *-ous*) part, section]

pol·y·mix·in (pol′ē mik′sin), *n.* polymyxin.

Po·lym·ni·a (pō lim′nē ə), *n.* Polyhymnia.

pol·y·morph (pol′ē môrf), *n.* **1.** a polymorphous organism, or one of its different forms, characters, etc. **2. a.** a substance that crystallizes in two or more different forms. **b.** one of these forms.

pol·y·mor·phic (pol′ē môr′fik), *adj.* polymorphous.

pol·y·mor·phism (pol′ē môr′fiz əm), *n.* a polymorphous state or condition.

pol·y·mor·pho·nu·cle·ar (pol′ē môr′fō-nü′klē ər, -nyü′-), *adj.* having nuclei of various shapes, especially nuclei that have lobes, as certain leucocytes.

pol·y·mor·phous (pol′ē môr′fəs), *adj.* **1.** having, assuming, or passing through many or various stages, as the honey bee. **2.** crystallizing in two or more forms, especially in forms belonging to different systems. [< Greek *polýmorphos* (with English *-ous*) < *polýs* many + *morphḗ* form]

pol·y·myx·in (pol′ē mik′sin), *n.* any of a group of antibiotic substances produced by certain bacilli, used against infections caused by gram-negative bacteria. [< New Latin *polymyxa* a species of bacteria + English *-in*]

Pol·y·ne·sian (pol′ə nē′zhən, -shən), *n.* **1.** a member of any of the brown races that live in Polynesia, a group of islands in the Pacific, east of Australia and the Phillippines. **2.** the Austronesian languages of Polynesia, including Maori, Hawaiian, etc. —*adj.* of or having to do with Polynesia, its people, or their languages.

pol·y·neu·ri·tis (pol′ē nů rī′tis, -nyů-), *n.* multiple neuritis.

po·lyn·ia or **po·lyn·ya** (pə lin′yə, pol′ən-yä′), *n.* a space of open water in the midst of ice, especially in the arctic seas. [< Russian *polyn′ja*]

Pol·y·ni·ces (pol′ə nī′sēz), *n. Greek Legend.* a son of Oedipus, slain by his brother Eteocles in the expedition of the Seven Against Thebes, and buried by his sister Antigone at the cost of her own life.

pol·y·no·mi·al (pol′ē nō′mē əl), *n.* **1.** an algebraic expression consisting of two or more rational and integral terms. *Examples:* ab, x^2y, and 3npq are monomials; $ab+x^2y$ and $pq-p^2+q$ are polynomials. **2.** *Biology.* a name of a variety, species, etc., consisting of two or more terms. —*adj.* consisting of two or more terms: "*Homo sapiens*" *is a polynomial expression.* [< *poly-* + *-nomial,* as in *binomial*]

pol·y·nu·cle·ar (pol′ē nü′klē ər, -nyü′-), *adj.* having several nuclei.

pol·y·nu·cle·o·tide (pol′ē nü′klē ə tīd, -nyü′-), *n.* a substance composed of a number of nucleotides, as nucleic acid.

pol·y·ol (pol′ē ōl, -ol), *n.* any of various alcohols, such as sorbitol, that contain many hydroxyl radicals. Polyols are used as surfactants, in plastics, etc. [< *poly-* + (alcoh)*ol*]

pol·y·o·le·fin (pol′ē ō′lə fin), *n.* any of a large group of olefins, including polyethylene and polystyrene, produced by polymerization with catalysts at low pressure.

pol·y·o·ma (pol′ē ō′mə), *n.,* or **polyoma virus,** a virus isolated from leukemic mice that has been shown to produce cancerous tumors in several species of rodents and has stimulated the search for more evidence of the presence of viruses in human cancer. [< *poly-* + *-oma*]

pol·y·ox·y·meth·y·lene (pol′ē ok′sə meth′-ə lēn), *n.* a polymerized form of formaldehyde. It is a thermoplastic resin.

pol·yp (pol′ip), *n.* **1.** a rather simple form of water animal, having a saclike body with fingerlike tentacles around the edge to gather in food, as the hydra, coral, and sea anemone. Polyps are coelenterates and often grow in colonies with their bases connected. Some polyps produce a swimming stage called a medusa. **2.** a tumor arising from a mucous or serous surface, as in the nose or stomach: *In some cases, signs of cancer can be seen . . . when the gross appearance of the polyps is not cancerous* (Science News Letter). [< French *polype,* learned borrowing from Latin *polypus* < Greek *polýpous* < *polýs* many + *poús, podós* foot]

pol·y·par·y (pol′ē per′ē), *n., pl.* **-par·ies.** the common stem, stock, or supporting structure of a colony of polyps, as corals. [< New Latin *polyparium* < Latin *polypus* + *-ārium* -ary]

pol·y·pep·tid (pol′ē pep′tid), *n.* polypeptide.

pol·y·pep·tide (pol′ē pep′tīd, -tid), *n.* any of a group of compounds containing two or more molecules of amino acids and one or more peptide (-CO.NH-) groups.

pol·y·pet·a·lous (pol′ē pet′ə ləs), *adj.* **1.** having the petals distinct or separate; choripetalous. **2.** having many petals.

pol·y·phage (pol′i fāj), *n.* a person that eats much or to excess.

pol·y·pha·gi·a (pol′ē fā′jē ə), *n.* **1.** *Medicine.* **a.** excessive eating. **b.** excessive appetite; bulimia. **2.** *Zoology.* the habit of feeding on many different kinds of food. [< New Latin *polyphagia* < Greek *polyphagía* < *polyphágos* voracious < *polýs* much + *phageîn* to eat]

po·lyph·a·gous (pə lif′ə gəs), *adj.* eating many different kinds of food.

po·lyph·a·gy (pə lif′ə jē), *n. Medicine, Zoology.* polyphagia.

pol·y·phar·ma·cy (pol′ē fär′mə sē), *n.* the use of many different drugs or medicines, usually indiscriminately, in the treatment of a disease: *. . . an example of polypharmacy that may do serious harm, such as neurological damage in unsuspected pernicious anemia* (Harper's).

pol·y·phase (pol′ē fāz), *adj.* having different phases; of or having to do with a system combining two or more alternating electric currents of identical frequency but differing from one another in phase.

Pol·y·phe·mus (pol′ē fē′məs), *n. Greek Mythology.* the Cyclops who captured Odysseus and his companions and ate two of them every day. Odysseus blinded him and escaped with his remaining men.

Polyphemus moth, a large, tan American silkworm moth, that has an eyespot on each hind wing.

pol·y·phone (pol′ē fōn), *n. Phonetics.* a polyphonic symbol.

pol·y·phon·ic (pol′ē fon′ik), *adj.* **1.** *Music.* having two or more voices or parts, each with an independent melody but all harmonizing; contrapuntal. **2.** that can produce more than one tone at a time, as a piano or harp. **3.** producing many sounds; many-voiced. **4.** *Phonetics.* representing more than one sound, as English *oo* in *food, good.*

polyphonic prose, writing printed like prose but incorporating a definite rhythmic pattern, rhyme, etc., so as to give the effect of verse when read, especially when read aloud.

po·lyph·o·nist (pə lif′ə nist), *n.* a polyphonic composer or theorist; contrapuntist: *. . . the motets of pre-Bach polyphonists* (Time).

po·lyph·o·nous (pə lif′ə nəs), *adj.* polyphonic.

po·lyph·o·ny (pə lif′ə nē), *n.* **1.** *Music.* polyphonic composition; counterpoint. **2.** a multiplicity of sounds. **3.** *Phonetics.* the representation of more than one sound by the same letter or symbol. [< Greek *polyphōnía* < *polýphōnos* having many sounds or voices < *polýs* many + *phōnḗ* sound]

pol·y·phy·let·ic (pol′ē fī let′ik), *adj.* developed from more than one ancestral type, as a group of animals. [< German *polyphyletisch* < Greek *polýs* many + *phŷlḗ, -etos* clan, tribe + German *-isch* -ic] —**pol′y·phy·let′i·cal·ly,** *adv.*

pol·y·phyl·lous (pol′ē fil′əs), *adj. Botany.* **1.** having distinct or separate leaves. **2.** having or consisting of many leaves. [< Greek *polýphyllos* (with English *-ous*) having many leaves < *polýs* many + *phýllon* leaf]

po·lyp·i·dom (pə lip′ə dəm), *n.* polypary.

pol·y·pite (pol′i pīt), *n.* an individual zooid of a compound polyp.

pol·y·ploid (pol′ē ploid), *adj.* having a chromosome number that is three or more times the haploid number. —*n.* an organism or cell having three or more times the haploid number of chromosomes. [< *poly-* + *-ploid,* as in *haploid*]

pol·y·ploi·dic (pol′ē ploi′dik), *adj.* polyploid.

pol·y·ploi·dy (pol′ē ploi′dē), *n.* **1.** the natural condition of being polyploid. **2.** a polyploid condition brought about by use of chemicals, hormones, or other special means, in order to develop new species of plants.

pol·y·po·di·a·ceous (pol′ē pō′dē ā′shəs), *adj.* belonging to the chief family of ferns, including the polypody, spleenwort, walking-fern, maidenhair, brake, and certain tree ferns. [< New Latin *Polypodiaceae* the family name (< Latin *polypodium* polypody) + English *-ous*]

pol·y·po·dy (pol′ē pō′dē), *n., pl.* **-dies.** any of a group of ferns, especially a widely distributed species that grows on moist rocks, old walls, and trees, and has naked, round spore cases, deeply pinnate fronds, and creeping stems. [< Latin *polypodium* < Greek *polypódion* a kind of fern; (literally, diminutive) < *polýpous, -podos* many-footed < *polýs* many + *poús, podós* foot (because its rootstock has many branches)]

Polypody (wall fern—fronds, 4 to 10 in. long)

pol·y·poid (pol′ē poid), *adj.* resembling a polyp (animal).

pol·y·po·sis (pol′ē pō′sis), *n.* the forming of many tumors or polyps on a part of the body.

pol·y·pous (pol′ə pəs), *adj.* of, having to do with, or like a polyp.

pol·y·prag·mat·ic (pol′ē prag mat′ik), *adj.* busy about many affairs; officious; meddlesome.

pol·y·pro·py·lene (pol′ē prō′pə lēn), *n.* a lightweight thermoplastic resin, similar in appearance to polyethylene but harder and having a higher melting point, used for films, insulating material, piping, baby bottles, and other molded plastics. It is a polymerized form of propylene gas. *Formula:* $(C_3H_6)_n$

pol·yp·tych (pol′ip tik), *n.* a combination of more than three panels or frames folded or hinged together, bearing pictures, carvings, or the like, as a picture or an altarpiece: *The Goldene Tafeln, four painted panels from a polyptych, are parts of an altar which was put together . . . in 1410* (London Times). [< Late Latin *polyptycha,* neuter plural, account books, ledgers < Greek *polýptychos* manifold < *polýs* many + *ptychê* a fold]

pol·y·pus (pol′ə pəs), *n., pl.* **-pi** (-pī). polyp. [< Latin *polypus* polyp]

pol·y·rhythm (pol′ē riᴛʜ′əm), *n.* a complex of different rhythms used simultaneously in a musical piece or rendition: *Music styles are found where polyrhythms are the counterpart of the polyphony of* [*European and American*] *music, where drums are more important than singers* (Melville J. Herskovits).

pol·y·rhyth·mic (pol′ē riᴛʜ′mik), *adj.* having or using different rhythms simultaneously.

pol·y·sac·cha·rid (pol′ē sak′ər id), *n.* polysaccharide.

pol·y·sac·cha·ride (pol′ē sak′ə rīd, -ər id), *n.* any of a class of carbohydrates, as starch, dextrin, and insulin, that can be decomposed into two or more simple sugars by hydrolysis: *When many molecules of simple sugar are combined . . . a polysaccharide is produced* (A. Franklin Shull).

pol·y·sep·a·lous (pol′ē sep′ə ləs), *adj. Botany.* **1.** having the sepals distinct or separate; chorisepalous. **2.** having numerous sepals.

pol·y·sper·mous (pol′ē spėr′məs), *adj. Botany.* containing or producing many seeds.

pol·y·sty·rene (pol′ē stī′rēn, -stir′ən), *n.* a colorless, transparent plastic used for insulation and in making toys, household appliances, luggage, reeds for musical instruments, synthetic rubber, dishes, tile, implements, etc. It is a polymerized form of styrene. *Dow Chemical Co. said it is introducing a new, heat resistant general purpose polystyrene with improved toughness* (Wall Street Journal). *Formula:* $(C_8H_8)_n$

pol·y·sul·fide or **pol·y·sul·phide** (pol′ē-sul′fīd, -fid), *n.* a chemical compound containing more than one atom of sulfur combined with another atom or radical.

pol·y·syl·lab·ic (pol′ē sə lab′ik), *adj.* **1.** of more than three syllables: *Unlike Ancient Greek and Modern French, Latin at no period bore the chief stress on the final syllable of a polysyllabic word* (Simeon Potter). **2.** having words of more than three syllables, as a language. —**pol′y·syl·lab′i·cal·ly,** *adv.*

pol·y·syl·lab·i·cal (pol′ē sə lab′ə kəl), *adj.* polysyllabic.

pol·y·syl·la·ble (pol′ē sil′ə bəl), *n.* a word of more than three syllables. *Politician* and *possibility* are polysyllables. [adaptation of Medieval Latin *polysyllaba* (*vox*) many-syllabled (word), feminine of *polysyllabus* < Greek *polysýllabos* < *polýs* many + *syllabê* syllable]

pol·y·syn·de·ton (pol′ē sin′də ton), *n. Rhetoric.* the use of several conjunctions in close succession. *Example: And* the rain descended, *and* the floods came, *and* the winds blew, *and* beat upon that house; *and* it fell; *and* great was the fall of it (Matthew 7:27). [< New Latin *polysyndeton* < *poly-* poly- + *syndeton* < Greek *sýndetos* connected < *syndeîn* bind together < *syn-* together + *deîn* to bind. Compare ASYNDETON, SYNDETIC.]

pol·y·syn·the·sis (pol′ē sin′thə sis), *n., pl.* **-ses** (-sēz). **1.** the synthesis of many elements. **2.** the combination of several words of a sentence into one word, as in the languages of the North American Indians. In the North American Indian language, Oneida, *g-nagla′-sl-i-zak-s,* means "I search for a village."

pol·y·syn·thet·ic (pol′ē sin thet′ik), *adj.* characterized by polysynthesis.

pol·y·tech·nic (pol′ē tek′nik), *adj.* having to do with or dealing with many arts or sciences: *a polytechnic school.* —*n.* a technical school. [< French *polytechnique* < Greek *polýtechnos* skilled in many arts < *polýs* many + *téchnē* art, skill]

pol·y·tech·ni·cal (pol′ē tek′nə kəl), *adj.* polytechnic.

pol·y·tet·ra·flu·or·o·eth·y·lene (pol′ē-tet′rə flü′ər ə eth′ə lēn), *n.* a slippery, acid-resistant plastic resin that is easily shaped and can be cut with a knife, even at extreme temperatures, used for replacing surfaces of diseased joints, coating frying pans and other utensils, and as a dry lubricant, substituting for oil in some machinery. It is a polymerized form of tetrafluoroethylene. *Formula:* $(C_2F_4)_n$

pol·y·the·ism (pol′ē thē′iz əm), *n.* the belief in more than one god: *A number of advanced groups like the Egyptians, Greeks, and Romans had polytheism, a hierarchy of gods* (Ogburn and Nimkoff). [< French *polythéisme* < Greek *polýtheos* of many gods (< *polýs* many + *theós* god) + French *-isme* -ism]

pol·y·the·ist (pol′ē thē′ist), *n.* a person who believes in more than one god. —*adj.* polytheistic.

pol·y·the·is·tic (pol′ē thē is′tik), *adj.* having to do with or characterized by belief in many gods. —**pol′y·the·is′ti·cal·ly,** *adv.*

pol·y·the·is·ti·cal (pol′ē thē is′tə kəl), *adj.* polytheistic.

pol·y·thene (pol′ē thēn), *n.* polyethylene.

pol·y·to·nal (pol′ē tō′nəl), *adj. Music.* having or using different harmonic keys simultaneously. —**pol′y·to′nal·ly,** *adv.*

pol·y·to·nal·i·ty (pol′ē tō nal′ə tē), *n. Music.* **1.** the use of different harmonic keys simultaneously. **2.** the sounds produced by using different harmonic keys simultaneously.

pol·y·tone (pol′ē tōn), *n.* variance of tone, especially in ordinary speech.

pol·y·troph·ic (pol′ē trof′ik), *adj.* subsisting on a variety of organic substances, as pathogenic bacteria. [< Greek *polýtrophos* highly nourished (< *polýs* much + *tréphein* nourish) + English *-ic*]

pol·y·type (pol′ē tīp′), *n.* **1.** a cast produced by pressing a woodcut or other plate into semi-fluid metal. **2.** a copy of an engraving or of printed matter made from a cast thus produced.

pol·y·typ·ic (pol′ē tip′ik), *adj.* having or involving many or several different types.

pol·y·typ·i·cal (pol′ē tip′ə kəl), *adj.* polytypic.

pol·y·un·sat·u·rate (pol′ē un sach′ə rāt), *n.* a polyunsaturated substance: *The unsaturated fats, including so-called polyunsaturates, generally are found in vegetable oils* (Wall Street Journal).

pol·y·un·sat·u·rat·ed (pol′ē un sach′ə rā′-tid), *adj.* having many double or triple bonds and free valences, as a vegetable oil or fatty acid.

pol·y·u·re·than (pol′ē yůr′ə than), *n.* polyurethane.

pol·y·u·re·thane (pol′ē yůr′ə thān), *n.* a strong plastic resin that resists fire, the effects of weather, and the corrosive action of acids and oxygen, made in the form of rigid or flexible foams or solids. The wide variations of density and form make polyurethane's uses varied, and it is now used as a substitute for foam rubber in the form of a flexible foam, as a binder, filler, and strengthener for fractured bones in the form of a rigid solid, and as insulation in building construction or as a stiffener for sheet-metal structures in the form of a rigid foam.

pol·y·u·ri·a (pol′ē yůr′ē ə), *n. Medicine.* an excessive excretion of urine, as in diabetes and certain nervous diseases. [< New Latin *polyuria* < *poly-* poly- + *-uria* -uria]

pol·y·u·ric (pol′ē yůr′ik), *adj.* of, having to do with, or affected with polyuria.

pol·y·u·ro·nide (pol′ē yůr′ə nīd), *n.* a natural gum or resin found in humus or decaying vegetation which improves soil condition by binding the particles together.

pol·y·va·lence (pol′ē vā′ləns, pə liv′ə-), *n. Chemistry.* multivalence.

pol·y·va·lent (pol′ē vā′lənt, pə liv′ə-), *adj.* **1.** *Chemistry.* multivalent. **2.** containing the proper antibodies or antigens to resist more than one species or strain of disease organisms, as a serum.

pol·y·vi·nyl (pol′ē vī′nəl), *adj.* of or having to do with any of a group of chemical compounds formed by the polymerization of one or more compounds that have the vinyl (CH_2:CH-) group. Many polyvinyl compounds are important as thermoplastic resins.

polyvinyl acetate, a transparent thermoplastic resin formed by the polymerization of vinyl acetate, used in making adhesives, paints, lacquers, and plastics.

polyvinyl alcohol, a resin made from polyvinyl acetate, used as an adhesive, for coating materials, in molding, etc.

polyvinyl chloride, a thermoplastic synthetic resin formed by the polymerization of vinyl chloride, used especially in fabrics, pipes, floor coverings, etc., for its hardness and resistance to chemicals. *Abbr.:* PVC (no periods).

pol·y·vi·nyl·i·dene chloride (pol′ē vī-nil′ə dēn), a thermoplastic synthetic resin formed by the polymerization of vinylidene chloride, used for moldings and filaments.

polyvinylidene resin, vinylidene resin.

polyvinyl pyr·ro·li·done (pi rō′lə dōn), a substance made from formaldehyde and acetylene, used chiefly with iodine and other antiseptics as an effective agent against bacteria, fungus, and virus, as a substitute for blood plasma in a time of shortage, and also in cosmetics, detergents, etc. *Formula:* $(C_6H_9NO)_n$

polyvinyl resin, vinyl resin.

Po·lyx·e·na (pə lik′sə nə), *n. Greek Legend.* a daughter of Priam and Hecuba, and the bride of Achilles. At her wedding Achilles was slain by Paris, and Polyxena was later sacrificed by the Greeks on his funeral pyre.

pol·y·zo·an (pol′ē zō′ən), *n., adj.* bryozoan. [< New Latin *Polyzoa* (< Greek *polýs* many + *zôion* animal) + English *-an*]

pol·y·zo·ar·i·al (pol′ē zō ãr′ē əl), *adj.* of or having to do with a polyzoarium.

pol·y·zo·ar·i·um (pol′ē zō ãr′ē əm), *n., pl.* **-ar·i·a** (-ãr′ē ə). a colony of bryozoans or its supporting skeleton. [< New Latin *polyzoarium* < *Polyzoa* polyzoan + *-arium* -ary]

pol·y·zo·ic (pol′ē zō′ik), *adj. Zoology.* **1.** of or like the bryozoans. **2.** composed of a number of individual zooids existing in the form of a colony. **3.** of or having to do with a spore that produces many sporozoites.

pol·y·zon·al (pol′ē zō′nəl), *adj.* having several or many zones (applied especially to a type of lens composed of a number of annular segments).

pol·y·zo·on (pol′ē zō′on), *n., pl.* **-zo·a** (-zō′ə). a bryozoan or polyzoan. [< New Latin *polyzoön* < Greek *polýs* many + *zôion* animal]

pom·ace (pum′is), *n.* **1.** apple pulp or similar fruit pulp before or after the juice has been pressed out. **2.** what is left after oil has been pressed out of something, as the substance of certain fish. [< Medieval Latin *pomacium* cider < Latin *pōmum* apple]

pomace fly, any of a group of several flies whose larvae live in decaying fruit; fruit fly.

po·ma·ceous (pə mā′shəs), *adj.* **1.** belonging to a group of plants of the rose family bearing pomes or pomelike fruits, as the apple and hawthorn; malaceous. **2.** of, having to do with, or consisting of apples. **3.** of the nature of a pome or apple. [< New Latin *pomaceus* (with English *-ous*) < Latin *pōmum* fruit; apple]

po·made (pə mād′, -mäd′), *n., v.,* **-mad·ed, -mad·ing.** —*n.* a perfumed ointment for the scalp and hair. —*v.t.* to dress (the scalp and hair) with pomade. [< Middle French *pommade* < Italian *pomata* < *pomo* apple < Latin *pōmum;* see POME (because it originally contained apple pulp)]

Po·mak (pō mäk′), *n.* any of a group of Bulgarian Moslems living near the border with Greece.

po·man·der (pə man′dər, pō′man-), *n.* **1.** ball of mixed aromatic substances formerly carried for perfume or as a guard against infection. **2.** the case in which this was carried, usually a hollow ball of gold, silver, etc., in the shape of an apple or orange. [alteration of Old French *pome d'ambre* < *pome* apple (see POME) + *d'ambre* of amber]

po·ma·rine jaeger (pō′mə rīn), a hawk-like sea bird, a variety of jaeger with broad, blunt, elongated central tail feathers.

po·ma·tum (pō mā′təm, -mä′-), *n., v.t.* pomade. [< New Latin *pomatum* < Italian *pomata* pomade]

pome (pōm), *n.* a fruit consisting of firm, juicy flesh surrounding a core that contains several seeds. Apples, pears, and quinces are pomes. [earlier, ball, apple < Old French *pome* < Vulgar Latin *pōma* < Latin *pōmum* fruit; apple] —**pome′like′,** *adj.*

pome·gran·ate (pom′gran′it, pum′-; pom-gran′-), *n.* **1.** the edible fruit of a tropical Asiatic and African tree, widely cultivated in subtropical regions. It is a large, roundish, many-celled berry, enclosed in a tough, leathery, reddish-yellow rind, and contains many seeds, each enveloped in a pleasantly acid, juicy, reddish pulp. **2.** the tree it grows on. **3.** *Australian Slang.* a British immigrant; pommy. [alteration of Old French *pome grenate* < *pome* (see POME) + *grenate* having grains, ultimately < Latin *grānāta,* feminine < *grānum* grain. Compare GRENADE.]

Pomegranate (def. 1) Above, whole fruit; below, cross section of it

pom·e·lo (pom′ə lō), *n., pl.* **-los. 1.** the grapefruit. **2.** the shaddock. Also, **pummelo.** [origin uncertain]

Pom·er·a·ni·an (pom′ə rā′nē ən), *adj.* of or having to do with Pomerania, on the south coast of the Baltic Sea, or its people. —*n.* **1.** a native or inhabitant of Pomerania. **2.** any of a breed of small dogs, weighing from 3 to 7 pounds, with a sharp nose, pointed ears and long, thick, silky hair.

Pomeranian (def. 2—about 7 in. high at the shoulder)

pom·fret (pom′frit, pum′-), *n.* **1.** a fish of the Indian and Pacific oceans, used as food, as the black pomfret or the white pomfret, sometimes known as the silver pomfret when young: *Pomfret that tastes rather like Dover sole* (Santha Rama Rau). **2.** a kind of sea bream found near Bermuda; hen fish. [apparently earlier *pamplee* < French *pample*]

po·mi·cul·ture (pō′mə kul′chər), *n.* the cultivation or growing of fruit. [< Latin *pōmum* fruit, apple + *cultūra* culture]

po·mi·cul·tur·ist (pō′mə kul′chər ist), *n.* a person who cultivates or raises fruit.

po·mif·er·ous (pō mif′ər əs), *adj.* bearing pomes or pomelike fruits. [< Latin *pōmifer* < *pōmum* fruit + *ferre* to bear + English *-ous*]

pom·mé or **pom·mée** (pô mā′), *adj. Heraldry.* (of a cross) having arms that terminate in knobs, globes, or balls. [< French *pomme,* past participle of *pommer* to end in a round head < *pomme* apple]

pom·mel (pum′əl, pom′-), *n., v.,* **-meled, -mel·ing** or (*especially British*) **-melled, -mel·ling.** —*n.* **1.** the part of a saddle that sticks up at the front. **2.** a rounded knob on the end of the hilt of a sword, dagger, etc. —*v.t.* to beat with the fists; strike; beat: *My cousin defied me to . . . fight him . . . I agreed, for I felt the strength of a giant in me, and I longed to pommel him soundly* (Washington Irving). Also, **pummel.** [< Old French *pomel* a rounded knob < *pom* hilt of a sword, (originally) variant of *pome;* see POME] —**pom′mel·er,** *n.*

Pommel (def. 1)

pom·my (pom′ē), *n., pl.* **-mies.** *Australian Slang.* a British immigrant who has recently come to Australia; pomegranate.

po·mo·log·i·cal (pō′mə loj′ə kəl), *adj.* of or having to do with pomology.

po·mol·o·gist (pō mol′ə jist), *n.* a person who is skilled in pomology.

po·mol·o·gy (pō mol′ə jē), *n.* the branch of science that deals with fruits and fruit growing. [< New Latin *pomologia* < Latin *pōmum* fruit; apple + *-logia* -logy]

Po·mo·na (pə mō′nə), *n. Roman Mythology.* the goddess of fruits and fruit trees, wooed and wedded by Vertumnus, the god of the seasons. [< Latin *Pōmōna* < *pōmum* fruit; apple]

pomp (pomp), *n.* **1.** a stately display; splendor; magnificence: *The king was crowned with great pomp.* **2.** a showy display; boastful show: *the pomps and vanities of the world.* **3.** *Archaic.* a triumphal or ceremonial procession or pageant: *The heavens . . . rung . . . While the bright pomp ascended jubilant* (Milton). [< Old French *pompe* < Latin *pompa* < Greek *pompḗ* procession display; (literally) a sending, ultimately < *pémpein* to send] —**Syn. 1.** flourish, grandeur.

Pom·pa·dour (pom′pə dôr, -dōr, -dúr), *adj.* having to do with or named after the Marquise de Pompadour, the mistress of Louis XV of France: *Pompadour ribbons.*

pom·pa·dour (pom′pə dôr, -dōr, -dúr), *n.* **1.** an arrangement of a woman's hair, in which it is puffed high over the forehead. **2.** an arrangement of a man's hair in which it is brushed straight up and back from the forehead. **3.** the hair so arranged. **4.** a shade of crimson or pink. **5.** a fabric with small floral designs of bright colors, especially crimson. [< *Pompadour*]

Pompadour (def. 1)

pom·pa·no (pom′pə nō), *n., pl.* **-nos** or (*collectively*) **-no. 1.** any of a group of food fishes of the West Indies and the coasts of southern North America. **2.** a similar fish of the California coast. [American English < American Spanish *pámpano* any of various fish < Spanish, a vine tendril, or scion]

Pom·pei·an (pom pā′ən, -pē′-), *adj.* of or having to do with Pompeii, an ancient city of southeastern Italy, or its people. Pompeii was buried by an eruption of Mount Vesuvius in 79 A.D. —*n.* a native or inhabitant of Pompeii.

Pompeian red, a dull red color of the shade found on the walls of many houses in Pompeii.

pom·pier (pôN pyā′), *French.* —*n.* **1.** a fireman. **2.** a thoroughly conventional and uninspired artist. —*adj.* thoroughly conventional; unimaginative; hackneyed: *a pompier artist, pompier band music.*

pom·pi·on (pum′pē ən), *n. Dialect.* a pumpkin.

pom-pom (pom′pom′), *n.* **1.** an automatic anti-aircraft gun used especially on shipboard during World War II. It usually consisted of four gun barrels mounted as a unit, each with its own magazine of explosive shells. **2.** any of various other automatic weapons, as the Maxim one-pounder used in the Boer War or the Hotchkiss heavy machine gun used in World War I. [imitative of the sound of its firing]

pom·pon (pom′pon), *n.* **1.** an ornamental tuft or ball of feathers, silk, or the like, worn on a hat or dress, on the shoes, etc. **2.** a ball of wool, worn on the front or top of a certain kind of soldier's or sailor's hat, etc. **3.** a kind of chrysanthemum or dahlia with very small, rounded flowers. [< French *pompon,* perhaps < Old French *pompe* pomp]

pom·poned (pom′pond), *adj.* having a pompon or pompons: *a pomponed cap.*

pom·pos·i·ty (pom pos′ə tē), *n., pl.* **-ties. 1.** a pompous quality. **2.** a pompous show of self-importance. [< Late Latin *pompōsitās* ostentation < *pompōsus* pompous]

pom·pous (pom′pəs), *adj.* **1. a.** trying to seem magnificent; fond of display; acting proudly; self-important: *The leader of the band bowed in a pompous manner.* **b.** (of language) ostentatious; lofty. **2.** characterized by pomp; splendid; magnificent; stately: *It was a glorious spectacle . . . to behold this pompous pageant issuing forth . . . the pennons and devices . . . fluttering above a sea of crests and plumes* (Washington Irving). [< Late Latin *pompōsus* (with English *-ous*) < Latin *pompa* pomp] —**pom′pous·ly,** *adv.* —**pom′pous·ness,** *n.*
—**Syn. 1. a.** pretentious, inflated, grandiose, vainglorious.

Pomp·tine (pomp′tin), *adj.* Pontine.

ponce (pons), *n. Especially British Slang.* a pimp; procurer. [perhaps < *pounce*[1], verb]

pon·ceau (pon sō′), *n.* **1.** the bright red color of the corn poppy; coquelicot. **2.** any of several red coal-tar dyes. [< French *ponceau* < Old French *pouncel* poppy]

ponce·let (pons′lit), *n. Physics.* a unit of power equivalent to 100 kilogrammeters per second. [< Jean-Victor *Poncelet,* 1788-1867, a French mathematician and engineer]

pon·cho (pon′chō), *n., pl.* **-chos.** a large piece of cloth, often waterproof, with a slit in the middle for the head to go through. Ponchos are worn in South America as cloaks. Waterproof ponchos are used in the army and navy and by hikers and campers. [< American Spanish *poncho* < Araucanian (Chile) *pontho* woolen fabric]

pond (pond), *n.* a body of still water, smaller than a lake: *In New Hampshire and beyond They like to call a lake a pond* (New Yorker). [probably (originally) variant of *pound*[3]]

pond·age (pon′dij), *n.* the capacity of a pond.

pond·ed (pon′did), *adj.* confined in a pond; dammed up: *The storm water remained ponded for weeks* (Harper's).

pon·der (pon′dər), *v.i.* to consider carefully; think over: *pondering on his unhappy lot* (Dickens). —*v.t.* to weigh (a matter, words, etc.); meditate upon: *to ponder a problem.* [< Old French *ponderer* to weigh, balance < Latin *ponderāre* to weigh < *pondus, -eris* weight, related to *pendĕre* to hang] —**pon′der·er,** *n.* —**pon′der·ing·ly,** *adv.*

pon·der·a·bil·i·ty (pon′dər ə bil′ə tē), *n.* the property of being ponderable or having weight.

pon·der·a·ble (pon′dər ə bəl), *adj.* that can be weighed; having perceptible weight; appreciable: *Not all the advantages of a good education are ponderable.*

pon·der·a·tion (pon′də rā′shən), *n.* the act of weighing.

pon·de·ro·sa pine (pon′də rō′sə), a pine tree of western North America that grows to great size, valuable as a lumber source; western yellow pine. [< New Latin *ponderosa* the species name < Latin *ponderōsus* ponderous]

pon·der·os·i·ty (pon′də ros′ə tē), *n., pl.* **-ties.** a ponderous character or quality.

pon·der·ous (pon′dər əs), *adj.* **1.** very heavy: *a ponderous mass of iron.* **2.** heavy and clumsy: *A hippopotamus is ponderous.* **3.** dull; tiresome: *The speaker talked in a ponderous way.* [< Latin *ponderōsus* (with English *-ous*) < *pondus, -eris* weight; see PONDER] —**pon′der·ous·ly,** *adv.* —**pon′der·ous·ness,** *n.*
—**Syn. 1.** weighty, massive. **2.** unwieldy, cumbersome.

pond fish, any of various fishes found in ponds, especially any of numerous small American fresh-water sunfishes.

pond lily, water lily.

pon·dok (pon′dok), *n. Afrikaans.* a shanty or hovel, often at least partly of mud.

pon·dok·kie (pon dok′ē), *n. Afrikaans.* a pondok: *Thousands of shanties and pondokkies grew overnight with the swiftness of a malignant fungus in the bush* (Harper's).

pond scum, 1. any free-floating, fresh-water alga that forms a green scum on stagnant water, as a spirogyra or related alga. **2.** the green film formed by these algae.

pond·weed (pond′wēd′), *n.* any of a large group of water plants, with submerged and sometimes floating leaves, that grow in quiet water.

pone[1] (pōn), *n. Southern U.S.* **1.** bread made of corn meal. **2.** a loaf or cake of this bread. [American English, earlier *ponap,* and *appone* < Algonkian (Powhatan) *äpan* something baked < *äpen* she bakes]

pone[2] (pōn), *n.* the player at the dealer's right in certain card games. [< Latin *pōnere* place]

po·nent (pō′nənt), *n. Obsolete.* the west. —*adj. Archaic.* western; west: *Forth rush the Levant and the Ponent winds* (Milton). [< Italian *ponente* < Medieval Latin *ponens, -entis* the west; (literally) setting sun < Latin *pōnere* to put, set down]

pong[1] (pong), *n.* the sound of a ringing blow; bang. —*v.i.* to make such a sound.

pong[2] (pong), *n. British Slang.* a very bad smell; stink: *When . . . rotting in the sun it [seaweed] gives off a pong that attracts flies and drives holidaymakers into the next county* (New Scientist).

pon·gee (pon jē′), *n.* **1.** a soft silk, usually left in natural brownish-yellow color. The thread for it is obtained from the cocoon of a silkworm native to China. **2.** a similar cloth of cotton or rayon, or of dyed silk. [< Chinese (Mandarin) *pen-chi* one's own machine; loom]

pon·gid (pon′jid), *adj.* of or having to do with the anthropoid apes most closely related to man, as the chimpanzee. [< New Latin *Pongidae* the ape family < *Pongo* the typical genus < a native name in Africa]

pon·gyi (pōn′jē, pun′-), *n.* (in Burma) a Buddhist priest or monk. Also, **phongyi.** [< Burmese *hpōngyī* < *hpōn* glory + *kyī* great]

pon·iard (pon′yərd), *n.* a dagger: *She speaks poniards and every word stabs* (Shakespeare). *—v.t.* to kill or wound by stabbing with a poniard: *We could have poniarded these geese by touch, but we could not pistol them* (Atlantic). [< Middle French *poignard* < Old French *poing* fist < Latin *pūgnus*, related to *pugil* pugilist]

pons (ponz), *n., pl.* **pon·tes** (pon′tēz). *Anatomy.* **1.** a part that connects two parts, as if bridging the space between them. **2.** pons Varolii. [< Latin *pōns* bridge]

pons as·i·no·rum (as′ə nôr′əm, -nōr′-), **1.** asses' bridge; a reference to the fifth proposition in the first book of Euclid which was difficult to "get over" for beginners. **2.** any problem that is difficult for beginners. [< New Latin *pons asinorum* < Latin *pōns* bridge, *asinōrum*, genitive plural of *asinus* ass]

pons Va·ro·li·i (və rō′lē ī), a band of nerve fibers in the brain, just above the medulla oblongata, consisting of transverse fibers connecting the two lobes of the cerebellum, and longitudinal fibers connecting the medulla with the cerebrum. See picture under **brain.** [< New Latin *pons Varolii* < Costanzo *Varoli*, about 1543-1575, an Italian anatomist]

pon·tal (pon′təl), *adj.* of or having to do with a bridge or bridges. [< Latin *pōns, pontis* bridge + English *-al*[1]]

Pon·tic (pon′tik), *adj.* of or having to do with Pontus or the Black sea, or with Pontus, an ancient country south of it. [< Latin *Ponticus* < Greek *Pontikós* < *póntos* sea, especially, the Black Sea]

pon·ti·cel·lo (pon′tə chel′ō), *n., pl.* **-los.** the bridge of a stringed musical instrument. [< Italian *ponticello* (diminutive) < *ponte* bridge < Latin *pōns, pontis*]

pon·ti·fex (pon′tə feks), *n., pl.* **-tif·i·ces. 1.** (in ancient Rome) a member of the principal college of priests, not assigned to the service of any particular god. The chief pontifex (Pontifex Maximus) was the highest religious authority of the state. **2.** the Pope; pontiff. [< Latin *pontifex, -ficis* a high priest of Rome, perhaps < *pōns, pontis* bridge + *facere* make. Doublet of PONTIFF.]

pon·tiff (pon′tif), *n.* **1.** the Pope. **2.** a bishop. **3.** a chief priest or high priest. **4.** a member of the principal college of priests in ancient Rome; pontifex. [< Middle French *pontife*, learned borrowing from Latin *pontifex.* Doublet of PONTIFEX.]

pon·tif·i·cal (pon tif′ə kəl), *adj.* **1.** of or having to do with the Pope; papal. **2.** of or having to do with a bishop. **3.** befitting or characteristic of a pontiff; stately; dignified. **4.** dogmatic.
—n. a book containing the forms for sacraments and other rites and ceremonies to be performed by bishops.
pontificals, the vestments and marks of dignity used by cardinals and bishops at certain ecclesiastical functions or ceremonies: *For a bishop to ride on hunting in his pontificals ... is against public honesty* (Jeremy Taylor).
—pon·tif′i·cal·ly, *adv.*

Pontifical College, the highest organization of priests in ancient Rome.

pon·tif·i·cate (*n.* pon tif′ə kit, -kāt; *v.* pon tif′ə kāt), *n., v.,* **-cat·ed, -cat·ing.** *—n.* the office or term of office of a pontiff. *—v.i.* **1.** to behave or speak pompously. **2.** to officiate as a pontiff, especially as a bishop. [< Latin *pontificātus, -ūs* office of a pontifex (< *pontifex, -ficis*) + English *-ate*[3]]

pon·tif·i·ca·tion (pon tif′ə kā′shən), *n.* **1.** the act of pontificating: *[A] study of a question that has recently been a subject for much pontification but very little analysis* (Economist). **2.** something said or written in a pompous manner: *After these pontifications it is truly startling to turn to twelve pages of epilogue* (Economist).

pon·tif·i·ces (pon tif′ə sēz), *n.* the plural of **pontifex.**

pon·til (pon′təl), *n.* punty.

Pon·tine (pon′tīn, -tin), *adj.* of or having to do with the Pontine Marshes, in central Italy, on the Mediterranean.

Pont l'É·vêque or **pont l'é·vêque** (pôɴ′ lā vek′), a soft cheddar cheese made of cream thickened by heat. [< *Pont l'Évêque*, a region in France where this cheese was first made]

pont·lev·is (pont lev′is), *n.* a drawbridge. [< French *pont-levis* < *pont* bridge (see PONTOON[1]) + *levis* movable (up and down), ultimately < Latin *levāre* raise]

Pon·to·caine (pon′tə kān), *n. Trademark.* a local anesthetic; tetracaine hydrochloride.

pon·ton (pon′tən), *n. U.S. Army.* pontoon boat. [< French *ponton;* see PONTOON[1]]

pon·to·nier (pon′tə nir′), *n.* a soldier or officer in charge of bridge equipment or the building of pontoon bridges. [< French *pontonnier* < *ponton;* see PONTOON[1]]

pon·toon[1] (pon tün′), *n.* **1.** a low, flat-bottomed boat. **2.** such a boat, or some other floating structure, used as one of the supports of a bridge. **3.** either of the two boat-shaped parts of an airplane, for landing on or taking off from water. **4.** a caisson, especially a caisson used in salvage work at sea, as in raising a sunken ship, removing wreckage, etc. [< French, Middle French *ponton* < Latin *pontō, -ōnis* < *pōns, pontis* bridge]

pon·toon[2] (pon tün′), *n. British.* a card game; twenty-one. [origin uncertain]

pontoon bridge, a bridge supported by low, flat-bottomed boats or other floating structures.

pontoon train, *Military.* a train of vehicles carrying pontoons and other bridge equipment.

po·ny (pō′nē), *n., pl.* **-nies,** *v.,* **-nied, -ny·ing.** *—n.* **1.** a young horse. **2.** a horse of a small breed, especially one not over 14 hands high. **3.** *U.S. Slang.* a translation of a book, which a pupil uses instead of translating the book himself; trot. **4.** *Informal.* **a.** a small glass, usually holding less than two ounces of alcoholic liquor. **b.** the amount such a glass will hold: *to drink a pony of brandy.* **5.** something small of its kind. **6.** *British Slang.* the sum of 25 pounds sterling.
—v.t., v.i. U.S. Slang. to translate with the aid of a pony.
pony up, *U.S. Slang.* **a.** to pay (money), as in settling an account (up): *I wish you'd pony up your end of the legal fee to Swineforth* (New Yorker). **b.** to come up with; produce: *The man of doubtful social habits and temperamental vagaries cannot pony up the required quota of references* (Harper's).
[< French *poulenet* a little foal (diminutive) < *poulain* foal, ultimately < Latin *pullus* young animal]

pony edition, an edition of a newspaper or magazine that is smaller than the main edition, often through omission of advertising, local news items, etc., designed especially for shipment by air to overseas subscribers.

pony engine, a small locomotive for shunting.

pony express, *U.S.* a system of carrying letters and very small packages in the western United States in 1860 and 1861 by relays of men mounted on fast ponies or horses.

Pony League, 1. a group of baseball clubs for boys thirteen and fourteen years old. **2.** one of these clubs: *In Little League, players perform on a half-sized diamond ... Pony Leagues use a diamond three-quarters the regulation size* (Wall Street Journal).

po·ny·skin (pō′nē skin′), *n.* **1.** the skin of a pony with the hair left on. **2.** a fabric made like this in markings and texture: *slacks of black-and-white plush cotton ponyskin* (New Yorker).

po·ny·tail (pō′nē tāl′), *n.* an arrangement of a woman's hair in which it is pulled back and bound, with the ends falling free from where the hair is gathered, close to the crown of the head: *She turned and twisted, picking off a few pieces of fluff, patting the shining ponytail of hair* (New Yorker).

po·ny·tailed (pō′nē tāld′), *adj.* wearing a ponytail.

po·ny·trek·king (pō′nē trek′ing), *n. Especially British.* travel by pony.

pony truck, a two- or four-wheeled leading or trailing truck, on some locomotives.

pooch (püch), *n. Slang.* a dog: *Dog Food makers vie keenly to feed a U.S. pooch population that's growing faster than the human one* (Wall Street Journal). [American English; origin unknown]

pood (püd), *n.* a Russian weight, equal to 36.113 pounds.
[< Russian *pud* < Scandinavian (compare Norwegian, Old Icelandic *pund*), ultimately < Latin *pondus* weight]

poo·dle (pü′dəl), *n.* any of a breed of intelligent dogs, originally bred for use as gun dogs but now virtually always kept as pets. There are standard, miniature, and toy varieties, all with long curling hair, usually black, brown, gray, or white, that is often clipped and shaved in an elaborate manner. [< German *Pudel*, short for *Pudelhund* < dialectal German *pudeln* to splash water] **—poo′dle·like′,** *adj.*

Poodle (standard size, 15 in. or over at the shoulder)

poodle cloth, a woolly cloth with a nubby texture caused by the large knots in the weaving.

poodle cut, an arrangement of a woman's hair in short, small, close ringlets resembling a poodle's fur.

poof (püf), *n.* a sound imitating a short sharp puff of the breath as in blowing out a candle. *—interj.* an expression of contemptuous rejection. Also, **pouf.** [imitative]

pooh (pü), *interj., n.* an exclamation of contempt: *"Pooh! pooh" cries the squire; "all stuff and nonsense"* (Henry Fielding).

Pooh-Bah (pü′bä′), *n.* **1.** a person holding many offices or positions, especially many small offices without much authority. **2.** a very pompous person: *The Federal government didn't want to be a big "Pooh-Bah" but instead to count on the medical profession to do the right thing* (Newsweek). [< *Pooh-Bah*, a character in *The Mikado*, by Gilbert and Sullivan, who fills many insignificant offices]

pooh-pooh (pü′pü′), *v.t.* to express contempt for; make light of: *An authority on nutrition pooh-poohed the idea that we are better off with less fat in hot weather* (New York Times). *—v.i.* to pooh-pooh someone or something. *—interj.* an exclamation of contempt.

poo·ka (pü′kə), *n.* (in Irish legend) an evil spirit, sometimes in the form of an animal, as a horse or rabbit: *Ireland's Celtic saints built Christian shrines of turf and mud to fend off pixies, pookas, hobgoblins and leprechauns* (Time). [Old English *pūca*]

pool[1] (pül), *n.* **1.** a small body of still water; small pond. **2.** a still, deep place in a stream. **3.** a puddle: *a pool of grease under a car.* **4.** a tank of water to swim or bathe in: *a swimming pool.* **5.** a section of an oil field in which petroleum is accumulated in the pores of sedimentary rock; oil pool. **6.** *Medicine.* a collection of an abnormal quantity of blood in some part of the circulatory system of the body. [Old English *pōl*]

pool[2] (pül), *n.* **1.** a game played on a special table with six pockets. The players try to drive balls into the pockets with long sticks called cues. **2. a.** things or money put together by different persons for common advantage: *The hikers put all their food and money in a pool.* **b.** a group of people, usually having the same skills, who are drawn upon as needed: *the labor pool. The secretaries laid off for the most part were members of studio secretarial pools with low seniority* (Wall Street Journal). **3.** an arrangement between several companies, groups, etc., to prevent competition by controlling prices. **4.** the persons who form a pool. **5. a.** a fund raised by a group of persons for purposes of speculation, as in the stock market, commodities, etc. **b.** the members of such a group. **6. a.** the total of the stakes of all participants in some races, card games, etc., that may be won or from which winnings are taken; pot. **b.** the total staked by a group of players, who will share proportionately in the event of winning. **c.** the participant in such a game, race, etc., or the members of such a group. **7.** *Fencing.* a contest in which each member of one team fights each member of the other.
—v.t. to put (things or money) together for common advantage: *The three boys pooled their savings for a year to buy a boat. They work as a team, pooling their knowledge and their talents* (New Yorker). *—v.i.* to enter into or form a pool.

[< French *poule* booty, hen, perhaps < Old French *poule* hen, young fowl < Late Latin *pulla* chick < Latin *pullus;* meaning influenced by *pool*[1]]

pool hall, a poolroom.

pool reactor, an atomic reactor submerged in a tank of water that acts as a coolant and radiation shield; swimming pool reactor.

pool·room (pül′rüm′, -rům′), *n.* **1.** *U.S.* a room or place for playing pool or billiards. **2.** a place where people bet on races, games, etc. [American English < *pool*[2] + *room*]

pool·side (pül′sīd′), *n.* the area beside a swimming pool. *—adj.* at the poolside; beside a swimming pool: *a poolside party.*

pool table, a billiard table with six pockets, on which pool is played: *A pool table has been installed in the billiard parlor* (Time).

poon (pün), *n.* **1.** any of a group of large East Indian trees, whose light, hard wood is used for masts and spars. **2.** the wood of any of these trees. [< Singhalese *pūna,* or Tamil *punnai*]

poop[1] (püp), *n.* **1.** a deck at the stern above the ordinary deck, often forming the roof of a cabin. **2.** the stern of a ship.
—v.t. **1.** (of a wave) to break over the stern of (a ship): *The frigate was pooped by a tremendous sea* (Frederick Marryat). **2.** (of a ship) to receive (a wave) over the stern. [< Old French *poupe,* earlier *pope* < Italian *poppa* < Latin *puppis, -is* stern]

poop[2] (püp), *v.i. Slang.* to become exhausted; be worn out, as by overexertion, etc.
poop out, *Slang.* to become exhausted, lose vigor: *This ivy was green at a time when other ivies had pooped out* (New Yorker).

poop[3] (püp), *n. U.S. Slang.* information; gossip: *The current astronomical poop is that canals are . . . optical illusions* (New Yorker).

poop[4] (püp), *n.* nincompoop.

pooped (püpt), *adj. Slang.* tired; exhausted: *I'm too pooped to think any more* (New Yorker).

-pooped, *combining form.* having a —— poop: *High-pooped = having a high poop.*

poor (půr), *adj.* **1.** having few things or nothing; needy: *The poor man had nothing, save one little ewe lamb* (II Samuel 12:3). **2.** not good in quality; lacking something needed: *poor soil, a poor crop, a poor cook, poor health, a poor head for figures.* **3.** small in amount; scanty: *Upon this discovery the treasure-seekers, already reduced to a poor half dozen . . . fled outright* (Robert Louis Stevenson). **4.** needing pity; unfortunate: *This poor child has hurt himself. The voter who seems likely to be commiserated with most . . . is the poor taxpayer* (Newsweek). **5.** not favorable: *a poor chance for recovery.* **6.** shabby; worn-out: *a poor, threadbare coat.*
—n. **the poor,** persons who are needy: *The destruction of the poor is their poverty* (Proverbs 10:15).
[Middle English *pore,* short for *pouere* < Old French *povre* < Latin *pauper, -eris,* related to *paucus* few. Doublet of PAUPER.]
—poor′ness, *n.*
—Syn. adj. **1. Poor, penniless, impoverished** mean with little or no money or property. **Poor** has a rather wide range of meaning, from having no money or property at all and being dependent on charity for the necessities of life, to having no money to buy comforts or luxuries: *She is a poor widow.* **Penniless** means without any money at all, but sometimes only temporarily: *She found herself penniless in a strange city.* **Impoverished** means reduced to poverty from comfortable circumstances, even wealth: *Many stars of silent movies are now impoverished.* **3.** insufficient, inadequate.

poor box, a box for receiving contributions of money for the relief of the poor, usually set at the entrance of a church: [*He*] *became miserly to the point of putting trouser buttons in the parish poor box* (Atlantic).

poor boy, *U.S. Slang.* a hero sandwich.

poor boy sweater, a kind of close-fitting, knitted pullover: *The poor boy sweater, a skimpy, clinging, ribbed knit, was also popular with the younger ladies* (Oleg Cassini).

Poor Clare (klãr), (in the Roman Catholic Church) one of an order of Franciscan nuns founded by St. Clare at Assisi in 1212. They live under varying rules of poverty, at one time being absolutely dependent upon alms.

poor farm, *U.S.* a farm maintained at public expense by a government, especially a county government, as a place in which very poor people may live and work.

poor·house (půr′hous′), *n.* a house in which paupers live at public expense; almshouse; workhouse.

poor·ish (půr′ish), *adj.* somewhat poor; of rather poor quality: *Nobody else can tell a poorish story so masterfully* (Punch).

poor law, a law providing for the relief or support of the poor: *The Rev. E. F. is a gentleman, a keen Poor Law guardian, and a theological author* (J. W. R. Scott).

poor·ly (půr′lē), *adv.* in a poor manner; not enough; badly; meanly: *A desert is poorly supplied with water. Tom did poorly in the test.* *—adj. Informal.* in bad health.

poor man's, that is a smaller, cheaper, easier, lighter, etc., version of something or someone: *. . . Spengler, the poor man's Nietzsche* (New Statesman). *Blue Scout Junior* [*is*] *called the "poor man's rocket" because of its low cost* (New York Times).

poor mouth, *Dialect or Informal.* **1.** a claim or complaint of poverty, especially when exaggerated: *We read the news article . . . accusing us of making a poor mouth about Princess Margaret's bills* (New York Times). **2.** a person who makes such a claim or complaint: *Roblin* [*was*] *castigating his opponents as "poor mouths" . . . who had no faith in Manitoba's future* (Canadian Saturday Night).

poor-mouth (půr′mouᴛʜ′), *v.i. Informal.* to complain of one's economic or other circumstances; speak belittlingly or apologetically of oneself or one's position: *Players from 28 nations . . . whizzed in on a chartered plane . . . poor-mouthing in many tongues that they were used to clay courts and expected to play miserably on the grass* (Time).

poor relation, **1.** a relative in humble circumstances: *A Poor Relation . . . is a preposterous shadow, lengthening in the noontide of your prosperity* (Charles Lamb). **2.** a person or thing of inferior circumstances, secondary importance, etc.: *Until a short time ago sculpture in Canada was a poor relation,* [*for*] *sculptors found little sponsorship and a small market* (Atlantic).

Poor Richard, Richard Saunders, the pen name used by Benjamin Franklin in *Poor Richard's Almanac: Poor Richard's counsels concerning the shortest route to honest riches became the very "voice and oracle of the bourgeoisie" everywhere* (Harper's).

poor-spir·it·ed (půr′spir′ə tid), *adj.* having or showing a poor, cowardly, or abject spirit.

poort (pürt), *n.* (in South Africa) a narrow pass between rocks or hills: *It was an old, infallible trap in the narrowest neck of the poort where the rock walls came close* (Harper's). [< Afrikaans *poort* < Dutch]

poor·tith (pôr′tith, pōr′-), *n. Scottish.* condition of being poor; poverty. [< Old French *povretet* < Latin *paupertās;* see POVERTY]

poor white, a white person (especially in the southern United States) having little or no money and low social position (often used in an unfriendly way).

poor·will (půr′wil), *n.* a bird of western North America that feeds on insects and closely resembles the whip-poor-will. It is definitely proved that the poorwill hibernates. [imitative of its note]

pop[1] (pop), *v.,* **popped, pop·ping,** *n., adv.*
—v.i. **1.** to make a short, quick, explosive sound: *The firecrackers popped in bunches.* **2.** to move, go, or come suddenly or unexpectedly: *Our neighbor popped in for a short call.* **3.** *Informal.* to shoot. **4.** to burst open with a pop: *The chestnuts were popping in the fire.* **5.** to bulge; protrude: *Surprise made her eyes pop out.* **6.** *Informal.* to give birth: *Our mammals are popping all the time. Our Bengal tigers had four cubs last year; most of the deer present us with young* (New Yorker). **7.** (in baseball) to hit a short, high ball over the infield. *—v.t.* **1.** to thrust or put suddenly: *She popped her head through the window.* **2.** to put (a question) suddenly. **3.** to cause to make a sudden explosion; burst with a pop: *to pop a balloon.* **4.** *U.S.* to heat or roast (popcorn) until it bursts with a pop.
pop off, *Slang.* **a.** to fall asleep: *All I need to do is lie down, and I can pop right off.* **b.** to die: *I am afraid I shall pop off just when my mind is able to run alone* (Keats). **c.** to state loudly as a complaint: *Many of his older colleagues, observing him sourly and listening to him pop off . . . thought he was at least partly insane* (New Yorker).
pop out, (in baseball) to hit a fly ball which is caught by a fielder: *to pop out to left field.*
—n. **1.** a short, quick, explosive sound: *the pop of a cork.* **2.** a shot from a gun, etc. **3.** a nonalcoholic carbonated drink: *strawberry pop.* **4.** (in baseball) a fly ball that can easily be caught; pop fly.
—adv. with a pop; suddenly.
[imitative]

pop[2] (pop), *adj.* **1.** *Informal.* popular: *The entertainment sheet Variety each week decrees which pop songs are hits on the basis of surveys and polls* (Time). **2.** having to do with pop art: *a pop artist, pop paintings.* *—n.* **1.** a popular song or tune. **2.** pop art: *The artists of pop . . . have not the rankest whisper of radical politics about them* (Atlantic). [(originally) abbreviation of *popular*]

pop[3] (pop), *n. U.S. Informal.* papa; father.

pop., **1. a.** popular. **b.** popularly. **2.** population.

P.O.P., point-of-purchase: *the P.O.P. medium* (New York Times).

pop art, a contemporary form of painting and sculpture which partly imitates and partly satirizes the style, content, and subject matter of popular advertisements, comic strips, and other products of commercial art and design.

pop artist, a painter or sculptor who produces pop art: *The pop artists, a cool and casual lot, could not have cared less about their critics* (Time).

pop·corn (pop′kôrn′), *n.* **1.** a kind of Indian corn, the kernels of which burst open and puff out when heated. **2.** the white, puffed-out kernels. [American English < *pop*[1] + *corn*[1]]

Pope or **pope**[1] (pōp), *n.* **1.** the supreme head of the Roman Catholic Church: *the Pope, the last three popes.* **2.** a person who assumes, or is considered to have, a position or authority like that of the Pope. [Old English *pāpa* < Late Latin *pāpa,* and *pappa* pope < Latin *pāpa* bishop, tutor, in these senses < Greek *páppa,* or *páppas* patriarch, bishop; (originally) father]

pope[2] (pōp), *n.* (in the Greek Church) a parish priest; papa. [< Slavic (compare Russian *pop′*) < Greek *pappâs*]

pope·dom (pōp′dəm), *n.* **1.** the office or dignity of a pope. **2.** the tenure of office of a pope. **3.** the papal government; papacy. **4.** a system resembling the papacy.

Pope Joan, a card game resembling stops.

pop·er·y (pō′pər ē), *n.* the doctrines, customs, and ceremonies of the Roman Catholic Church (used in an unfriendly way).

pope's nose, *Slang.* the projecting, terminal portion of a bird's body from which the tail feathers spring.

pop·eye (pop′ī′), *n.* a bulging, prominent eye.

pop·eyed (pop′īd′), *adj.* having a popeye or popeyes: *a popeyed, squatting frog.*

pop fly, (in baseball) a short, high fly ball which can be caught quite easily.

pop·gun (pop′gun′), *n.* a toy gun that shoots with a popping sound.

pop·in·jay (pop′in jā), *n.* **1.** a vain, overtalkative person; conceited, silly person: *as pert and as proud as any popinjay* (Scott). **2.** the figure of a parrot, formerly used as a mark to shoot at: *He had . . . on several occasions, carried off the prize from the Duke in shooting at the popinjay* (John L. Motley). **3.** *Obsolete.* a parrot. **4.** *British.* the green woodpecker. [< Old French *papingay, papegay* < Spanish *papagayo* < Arabic *babaghā′* < Persian *babghā*]

pop·ish (pō′pish), *adj.* of or having to do with the Roman Catholic Church (used in an unfriendly way). **—pop′ish·ly,** *adv.* **—pop′ish·ness,** *n.*

pop·lar (pop′lər), *n.* **1. a.** any of several trees that grow very rapidly and produce light, soft wood, as the Lombardy poplar, the cottonwood, and the aspen. Poplars belong to the willow family and are native to temperate regions. **b.** the wood of such a tree. **2. a.** a tree of another group resembling these in some way, especially the tulip tree. **b.** the wood of any of these trees. [< Old French *poplier,* extended < *pouple* poplar < Latin *pōpulus*]

pop·lin (pop′lin), *n.* a ribbed fabric, made of silk and wool, cotton and wool, or cotton, and used for making dresses and other clothing, tents, etc. [< French *popeline,* or *papeline* < Italian *papalina,* feminine (literally) papal, perhaps < the papal capital of Avignon]

pop·lit·e·al (pop lit′ē əl, pop′lə tē′-), *adj. Anatomy.* of, having to do with, or in the region of the ham (the hollow part of the leg back of the knee). [< New Latin *popliteus* (*musculus*) (muscle) of the ham (< Latin *poples, -itis* ham, back of the knee) + English *-al*[1]]

pop·off (pop′ôf′, -of′), *n. U.S. Informal.* a person who expresses complaints, opinions, etc., in a noisy, pretentious, or irresponsible way: [*He*] *has seemed irritable, withdrawn . . . a reckless popoff in his informal pronouncements, and a wooden soldier while reading his formal speeches* (Time).

pop·o·ver (pop′ō′vər) *n. U.S.* a very light and hollow muffin made from a batter similar to that used for Yorkshire pudding. [American English < *pop*[1] + *over*]

pop·pa (pop′ə), *n. U.S. Informal.* **1.** father. **2.** any elderly man.

pop·per (pop′ər), *n.* **1.** a person or thing that pops. **2.** *U.S.* a wire basket or metal pan used for popping popcorn.

pop·pet (pop′it), *n.* **1.** a valve that controls the flow of water, gas, etc., by moving straight up and down instead of being hinged. **2. a.** one of the small pieces of wood on the gunwale of a boat forming the rowlocks. **b.** a timber placed beneath a ship's hull to support the ship in launching: *The workers then build strong supports called poppets on the launching timbers at the bow and the stern* (World Book Encyclopedia). **3.** a bead that can be attached to other beads by a snap coupling to form a chain. Poppets are used especially to make necklaces, bracelets, etc., adjustable in length. **4.** *Especially British.* a small or dainty person, especially a pretty child, girl, etc.; pet: "*Little poppet!*" *she murmured to herself, maternally reflecting upon Florence's tender youth* (Arnold Bennett). **5.** *Obsolete.* **a.** a doll. **b.** a puppet.
[Middle English variant of *puppet*]

pop·pet·head (pop′it hed′), *n.* the tailstock or the headstock of a lathe.

pop·pied (pop′ēd), *adj.* **1.** covered or adorned with poppies. **2.** affected by or as by opium; listless.

pop·ping crease (pop′ing), (in cricket) a line parallel to the wicket, marking the batsman's position.

pop·ple[1] (pop′əl), *v.,* **-pled, -pling,** *n.* —*v.i.* to move in a tumbling, irregular manner, as boiling water. —*n.* a rolling or tossing of water in choppy tumultuous waves. [probably imitative. Compare Middle Dutch *popelen* to murmur, babble.]

pop·ple[2] (pop′əl), *n. Dialect.* a poplar.

pop·py (pop′ē), *n., pl.* **-pies. 1.** any of a group of herbs of the poppy family with showy, delicate flowers of various colors, and roundish capsules containing many small seeds. The juice from the capsule of one variety is used to make opium. **2.** any of various related plants, as the California poppy. **3.** the flower of any of these plants. **4.** a bright red; poppy red. **5.** *U.S.* an artificial flower resembling a poppy sold in an annual drive by the American Legion and several other veterans' groups as a means of raising funds for their charitable activities. [Old English *popig,* earlier *popaeg,* perhaps ultimately < Latin *papāver*]

pop·py·cock (pop′ē kok′), *n., interj. Informal.* nonsense; bosh: *All this profit-sharing and welfare work and insurance . . . is simply poppycock* (Sinclair Lewis). [American English, perhaps < Dutch *poppekak* (literally) soft dung]

Poppy Day, the Saturday nearest to November 11, when artificial poppies are sold to help disabled veterans.

poppy family, a group of dicotyledonous herbs, widely distributed in North Temperate regions, having a milky juice and flowers of various colors. The family includes the poppy, bloodroot, celandine, and California poppy.

pop·py·head (pop′ē hed′), *n. Architecture.* an ornamental finial, often richly carved, as at the top of the upright end of a bench or pew.

poppy red, poppy (def. 4).

poppy seed, seed of the poppy, used in baking to flavor rolls, bread, cookies, etc., especially by scattering over the top, and as a filling in cakes and pastries.

pops (pops), *adj. Slang.* having to do with or performing musical pieces of general or popular appeal: *a pops concert.* [< plural of *pop*[2]]

Pop·si·cle (pop′sə kəl), *n. Trademark.* molded ice cream or fruit-flavored ice on a stick.

pop·skull (pop′skul), *n. U.S. Slang.* bootleg whiskey or other liquor.

pop·sy (pop′sē), *n., pl.* **-sies.** *Slang.* an affectionate name for a girl; a pretty girl. [< dialectal *pop* (< *poppet*) + *-sy,* as in *fubsy*]

pop-top (pop′top′), *adj.* provided with a tab or other device for opening without a can opener or bottle opener: *a pop-top beer can.* —*n.* a pop-top container.

pop·u·lace (pop′yə lis), *n.* the common people: *The populace, who hated Pompey, threw flowers upon the tribune as he passed* (James A. Froude). [< French *populace* < Italian *popolaccio* < *popolo* people < Latin *populus*]

pop·u·lar (pop′yə lər), *adj.* **1.** liked by acquaintances or associates: *the most popular girl in school.* **2.** liked by most people: *a popular song.* **3.** of the people; by the people; representing the people. **4.** widespread among many people; common: *It is a popular belief that black cats bring bad luck.* **5.** suited to or intended for ordinary people: *popular science, popular prices.* [< Latin *populāris* < *populus* people] —**Syn. 3.** See **general. 4.** prevailing, current.

popular front or **Popular Front,** a coalition of communist, socialist, and moderate political parties against fascism, especially in France: *France is not the only country where the Popular Front strategy may bear fruit* (Wall Street Journal).

pop·u·lar·ise (pop′yə lə rīz), *v.t.,* **-ised, -is·ing.** *Especially British.* popularize.

pop·u·lar·i·ty (pop′yə lar′ə tē), *n.* a being liked generally: . . . *in spite of the steady march of repression his* [*Dr. Nkrumah's*] *popularity has remained* (Manchester Guardian).

pop·u·lar·i·za·tion (pop′yə lər ə zā′shən), *n.* **1.** the act of popularizing: *The Bulletin, therefore, thinks it proper to devote its pages once again to a task of scientific popularization* (Bulletin of Atomic Scientists). **2.** the state of being popularized.

pop·u·lar·ize (pop′yə lə rīz), *v.t.,* **-ized, -iz·ing.** to make popular, especially by writing about (a subject) in a way that is understandable to most people. —**pop′u·lar·iz′er,** *n.*

pop·u·lar·ly (pop′yə lər lē), *adv.* **1.** in a popular manner: *The book is popularly written . . . and contains only a modest amount of technical information* (Bulletin of Atomic Scientists). **2.** by the people; in general: [*He was*] *seeking to be the first popularly elected Democratic Senator in the history of this usually rock-ribbed Republican state* (Wall Street Journal).

popular vote, the vote of the entire electorate, thought of as including all the people.

pop·u·late (pop′yə lāt), *v.t.,* **-lat·ed, -lat·ing. 1.** to inhabit: *This city is densely populated. The novels were populated with people who . . . were fated . . . to be baulked of the success they deserved* (London Times). **2.** to furnish with inhabitants: *Immigrants largely from Europe populated America.* [< Medieval Latin *populare* (with English *-ate*[1]) < < Latin *populus* people] —**Syn. 2.** people.

pop·u·la·tion (pop′yə lā′shən), *n.* **1.** the people of a city or a country: *The impending overpopulation of the earth can be prevented only by a policy of stabilizing the population of every country* (F. S. Bodenheimer). *Population . . . increases in a geometrical ratio, subsistence in an arithmetical ratio* (Thomas R. Malthus). **2.** the number of people: *a population of 1,000,000, an increasing population.* **3.** a part of the inhabitants distinguished in any way from the rest: *the native-born population.* **4.** the act or process of furnishing with inhabitants. **5.** *Statistics.* the entire group of items or individuals from which the samples under consideration are presumed to come. **6.** *Biology.* **a.** the aggregate of organisms that inhabit a particular locality or region. **b.** a (specified) portion of this aggregate: *the deer population of North America.* **7.** Also, **Population.** *Astronomy.* one of two numbered groups (Population I and II) into which the stars of the various galaxies have been divided for classification, on the basis of color, position, etc.: *The type I population . . . is represented by our region of the galaxy and was accordingly the first to be recognized* (Robert H. Baker).

pop·u·la·tion·al (pop′yə lā′shə nəl), *adj.* of or having to do with population: *Speech tends to be one of the most persistent populational characters* (A. L. Kroeber).

population explosion, a rapid increase in population caused by a rise in the birth rate, usually accompanied by a decline in the death rate, because of advances in medicine, agricultural output, etc.: *There was growing understanding of the danger of the population explosion that threatens the world* (Science News Letter).

population parameter, *Statistics.* a quantity that is constant for a particular distribution of a population but varies for other distributions.

pop·u·la·tor (pop′yə lā′tər), *n.* a person or thing that populates or peoples.

Pop·u·lism (pop′yə liz əm), *n.* the principles and policies of the Populists.

Pop·u·list (pop′yə list), *U.S.* —*n.* a member or supporter of the People's Party, a political party formed in the United States in 1891. The Populists advocated government control of the railroads, limitation of private ownership of land, an increase in currency, an income tax, etc. —*adj.* Populistic. [American English < Latin *populus* people + English *-ist*]

Pop·u·lis·tic (pop′yə lis′tik), *adj.* of or having to do with Populism or Populists.

Populist Party, the People's Party.

pop·u·lous (pop′yə ləs), *adj.* **1.** full of people; having many people per square mile: *The Pays de Caux, the most fertile and populous region in all France* (John F. Kirk). **2.** plentiful; abundant: *Mormon crickets, on the other hand, will be less populous this year* (Science News Letter). [< Latin *populōsus* < *populus* people] —**pop′u·lous·ly,** *adv.* —**pop′u·lous·ness,** *n.*

pop-up (pop′up′), *n.* **1.** (in baseball) a pop fly: *A full swing might produce a useless strike-out or pop-up* (New Yorker). **2.** a part of a book, greeting card, child's game, etc., that springs up when a cover or thing it is attached to is opened. —*adj.* of or having to do with something that pops up: *a pop-up book. Instead of using the pop-up toaster, I bend over and make toast in the broiler of the kitchen stove* (Wall Street Journal).

p.o.r., pay on return.

por·bea·gle (pôr′bē′gəl), *n.* a voracious shark of northern waters, that attains a length of from 10 to 12 feet. [< a dialectal Cornish word]

por·ce·lain (pôr′sə lin, pōr′-; pôrs′lən, pōrs′-), *n.* **1.** a very fine earthenware, usually having a translucent white body and a transparent glaze; china: *Teacups are often made of porcelain. The precious porcelain of human clay* (Byron). **2.** a dish or other object made of this material. [< French *pourcelaine* < Italian *porcellana* a cowrie shell; chinaware < *porcella* young sow < Latin *porcus* hog (because the shell is shaped like a pig's back)]

por·ce·lained (pôr′sə lind, pōr′-; pôrs′lənd, pōrs′-), *adj.* covered or lined with porcelain.

por·ce·lain·ize (pôr′sə lə nīz, pōr′-; pôrs′lə-, pōrs′-), *v.t.,* **-ized, -iz·ing.** to coat (a surface) with something hard like porcelain.

por·ce·la·ne·ous or **por·cel·la·ne·ous** (pôr′sə lā′nē əs, pōr′-), *adj.* resembling porcelain.

por·cel·la·nite (pôr′sə lə nīt, pōr′-; pôr-sel′ə nīt, pōr-), *n.* a clay hardened by natural baking, somewhat resembling porcelain or jasper.

porch (pôrch, pōrch), *n.* **1.** a covered entrance to a building. **2.** *U.S.* **a.** a veranda. **b.** a room open to the outside air, often having no walls, or walls of screen or glass: *a sleeping or dining porch.* **3.** a portico. [< Old French *porche* < Latin *porticus, -ūs.* Doublet of PORTICO.]

Porch (pôrch, pōrch), *n.* **the,** the Stoic school of philosophy. [translation of Greek *stoá* porch (because of the public covered walk in ancient Athens where the philosopher Zeno taught)]

porch climber, *Informal.* a thief who gains entrance to a house by climbing a porch or veranda.

por·cine (pôr′sīn, -sin), *adj.* **1.** of pigs or hogs. **2.** like or characteristic of pigs or hogs; swinish: *The porcine head of the churchwarden was not on his shoulders by accident* (George MacDonald). [< Latin *porcīnus* < *porcus* hog]

por·cu·pine (pôr′kyə pīn), *n., pl.* **-pines** or (*collectively*) **-pine.** any of several rodents covered with quills or spines growing in their coarse hair, as the North American porcupine with short quills or the European porcupine with long quills: *The porcupine, which normally feeds to a considerable extent on small plants such as shrubs and grasses is driven by hunger to a diet largely of bark* (Fred W. Emerson). [< Old French *porc-espin* < Latin *porcus* hog, pig + *spīna* thorn, spine]

[Porcupine (including tail, about 3 ft. long)

porcupine anteater, echidna.

porcupine fish, sea porcupine.

pore[1] (pôr, pōr), *v.i.,* **pored, por·ing. 1.** to gaze earnestly or steadily. **2.** to study long and steadily: *He would rather pore over a book than play. I explained my dilemma, and he produced a map of the mountains, and together we pored over it* (Harper's). **3.** to meditate or ponder intently: *to pore over a problem.* [Middle English *pouren;* origin uncertain] —**por′er,** *n.*

pore[2] (pôr, pōr), *n.* **1.** a very small opening. Sweat comes through the pores in the human skin and pores in leaves allow for the passage of water and carbon dioxide. The surface of pottery and lumber has pores. *Like human skin, soil has holes that are called pores* (Science News Letter). See picture under **epidermis. 2.** *Astronomy.* one of many dark spots on the surface of the sun. [< Old French *pore,* learned borrowing from Latin *porus* < Greek *póros* (literally) passage < *perân* to penetrate, pass]

por·gy (pôr′gē), *n., pl.* **-gies** or (*collectively*) **-gy.** any of various salt-water food fishes, such as the scup of the eastern coast of the United States and the sea bream or red porgy of Mediterranean and Atlantic waters. [American English; origin uncertain]

po·rif·er·an (pô rif′ər ən, pō-), *n.* any of the large group comprising the sponges. [< New Latin *Porifera* the phylum (< Late Latin *porus* hole, passage; see PORE[2]; + Latin *ferre* to bear) + English *-an*]

po·rif·er·ous (pô rif′ər əs, pō-), *adj.* **1.** having pores. **2.** of or having to do with the sponges.

po·rism (pôr′iz əm, pōr′-), *n. Geometry.* any of various differently defined propositions of the ancient Greek mathematicians, especially as an extra proposition or corollary inserted by Euclid's commentators, or as a proposition affirming the possibility of finding such conditions as will make a certain problem indeterminate, or capable of innumerable solutions. [< Late Latin *porisma* < Greek *pórisma* a deduction, a corollary < *porízein* to deduce, carry < *póros* way, path, ford]

pork (pôrk, pōrk), *n.* **1.** the meat of a pig or hog, used for food: *salt pork, a roast of pork.* **2.** *U.S. Slang.* money from Federal or State appropriations, taxes, licenses, etc., spent to confer local benefits for political reasons. [< Old French *porc* < Latin *porcus* hog, pig]

pork barrel, *U.S. Slang.* a Federal appropriation for a project that will benefit or appeal to a particular body of constituents, although it may not fulfill a need: *Democrats are counting, too, on the traditional election-year pork barrel to help a troubled candidate here and there* (Wall Street Journal). —**pork′-bar′rel,** *adj.*

pork-bar·rel·ing (pôrk′bar′ə ling, pōrk′-), *U.S. Slang.* —*n.* the use of Federal appropriations for private advantage. —*adj.* given to or engaged in pork-barreling: *pork-barreling politicians.*

pork·er (pôr′kər, pōr′-), *n.* a pig, especially one fattened to eat: *Beechmast is very good feeding for swine to make them porkers, and for bacon* (Captain John Smith).

pork·fish (pôrk′fish′, pōrk′-), *n., pl.* **-fish·es** or (*collectively*) **-fish.** a fish of the Atlantic coast from Florida to Brazil, resembling a sea bream.

pork·ling (pôrk′ling, pōrk′-), *n.* a young pig.

pork·pie (pôrk′pī′, pōrk′-), *n.,* or **pork pie, 1.** a hat with a low, round crown, flat on top, and resembling the meat pie in shape: *The flat-top looks like a cross between the saucy porkpies of the college crowd and the more fashionable felts of the snap-brim set* (Wall Street Journal). **2.** *British.* a deep, circular pie of pastry enclosing minced pork: *He would buy a bun or . . . cold porkpie and munch it while he watched the film* (Scientific American).

porkpie or **pork-pie hat,** porkpie.

pork·y (pôr′kē, pōr′-), *adj.,* **pork·i·er, pork·i·est. 1.** of or like pork: *a porky taste.* **2.** fat: *a porky face.*

por·nog·ra·pher (pôr nog′rə fər), *n.* a person who writes, sells, or distributes pornography.

por·no·graph·ic (pôr′nə graf′ik), *adj.* obscene.

por·nog·ra·phy (pôr nog′rə fē), *n.* obscene writings or pictures: *Local penalties against possession and distribution of pornography are small and not enforced effectively* (Newsweek). [ultimately < Greek *pórnē* harlot + English *-graphy*]

po·ro·mer·ic (pô′rə mer′ik, pō′-), *adj.* (of a plastic) having a very high degree of porosity; consisting of millions of microscopic pores: *poromeric shoe material.* [< *poro*(us) + (poly)*meric*]

po·ros·i·ty (pô ros′ə tē, pō-), *n., pl.* **-ties. 1.** a porous quality or condition. **2.** a porous part or structure. **3.** the ratio of the number of pores of a substance to the volume of its mass.

po·rous (pôr′əs, pōr′-), *adj.* full of pores or tiny holes; permeable by water, air, light, etc.: *the soil retains or even improves its desirable porous structure* (K.S. Spiegler). *Cloth, blotting paper, and ordinary flowerpots are porous.* —**po′rous·ness,** *n.*

por·phyr·i·a (pôr fir′ē ə), *n.* a metabolic disorder marked by the presence of porphyrin in the blood. [< New Latin *porphyria* < *porphyrin*]

por·phy·rin (pôr′fər in), *n. Biochemistry.* any of a group of derivatives of pyrrole, especially an iron-free decomposition product of hematin or a magnesium-free decomposition product of chlorophyll. They occur in body tissue, urine, etc., but their function is unknown. [< Greek *porphýrā* purple + English *-in*]

por·phy·rite (pôr′fə rīt), *n.* a kind of porphyry containing triclinic feldspar and no quartz. [< Latin *porphyrītēs* < Greek *porphyrítēs* like purple < *porphýros* purple]

por·phy·rit·ic (pôr′fə rit′ik), *adj.* **1.** of, having to do with, containing, or resembling porphyry. **2.** of the nature or structure characteristic of porphyry; containing distinct crystals embedded in a compact groundmass. —**por′phy·rit′i·cal·ly,** *adv.*

por·phy·roid (pôr′fə roid), *n.* a rock resembling porphyry or of porphyritic structure, especially a sedimentary or igneous rock that has been altered by some metamorphic agency and has taken on a more or less perfectly developed porphyritic structure.

por·phy·ry (pôr′fər ē), *n., pl.* **-ries. 1.** a hard red or purplish rock of ancient Egypt containing white crystals. **2.** any igneous rock in which crystals are scattered through a mass of finely-grained minerals. [< Old French *porphyre, porfire* < Italian *porfiro,* ultimately < Greek *porphýros* purple]

por·poise (pôr′pəs), *n., pl.* **-pois·es** or (*collectively*) **-poise,** *v.,* **-poised, -pois·ing.** —*n.* **1.** a sea animal from 4 to 8 feet long, somewhat like a small whale. Porpoises are mammals, related to the whale, and live in groups in the northern Atlantic and Pacific oceans. They are blackish in color with a somewhat paler belly and a blunt, rounded snout. *The porpoise is a superior animal with a sense of humor, curiosity, and imagination more highly developed than that of a dog* (Atlantic). **2.** any of several other small sea mammals, especially the common dolphin or the bottle-nosed dolphin. —*v.i.* to move, travel, or dive in the manner of a porpoise; make a series of bumps or plunges: *The Coroner asked . . . if it was usual for a machine . . . to porpoise when taking off on a perfectly smooth sea* (London Times). [< Old French *porpeis,* also *porpois,* ultimately < Latin *porcus* hog + *piscis* fish]

Porpoise (def. 1—about 4 to 8 ft. long

por·ra·ceous (pə rā′shəs), *adj.* leek-green. [< Latin *porrāceus* (with English *-ous*) < *porrum* leek]

por·ridge (pôr′ij, por′-), *n.* a food made of oatmeal or other cereal boiled in water or milk until it thickens: *oatmeal porridge.* [apparently variant of *pottage*]

por·ridg·y (pôr′ij ē, pōr′-), *adj.* resembling porridge.

por·rin·ger (pôr′ən jər, por′-), *n.* **1.** a small dish, deeper than a plate or saucer, from which soup, porridge, bread and milk, etc., can be eaten. **2.** a small bowl, mug, etc., especially one intended to be used by a child. [Middle English *pottinger,* alteration of earlier *potager* < Old French < *potage* pottage, porridge]

port[1] (pôrt, pōrt), *n.* **1.** a place where ships and boats can be sheltered from storms; harbor. **2.** a place where ships and boats can load and unload; city or town with a harbor: *New York and San Francisco are important ports.* **3.** a port of entry. **4.** a place, position, or condition in which one takes or may take refuge; haven.
[Old English *port* < Latin *portus*] —**Syn. 1, 2.** See **harbor.**

port[2] (pôrt, pōrt), *n.* **1.** an opening in the side of a ship to let in light and air or for loading and unloading: *a cargo port.* **2.** an opening in the side of a ship through which to shoot. **3.** a cover for such an opening. **4.** an opening in machinery for steam, air, water, etc., to pass through. **5.** a gate, especially that of a city. [< Old French *porte* < Latin *porta* gate]

port[3] (pôrt, pōrt), *n.* the left side of a ship when facing the bow.
—*adj.* **1.** on the left side of a ship: *the port side of the main deck* (Joseph Conrad). **2.** on the left: *Southpaws customarily are reserved for rivals whose principal thumpers swing from the port side* (New York Times).
—*adv.* to or toward the left side of a ship or boat.
—*v.t., v.i.* to turn or shift to the left side: *to port the helm.*
[origin uncertain; perhaps < *port*[1]]

port[4] (pôrt, pōrt), *n.* **1.** the way of holding one's head and body; bearing: *regal port. She dressed well, and had a presence and port calculated to set off handsome attire* (Charlotte Brontë). **2.** the position of a weapon when ported. —*v.t.* to bring, hold, or carry (a rifle or sword) across and close to the body with the barrel or blade near the left shoulder.
[< Old French *port* < *porter* to carry < Latin *portāre*]
—**Syn.** *n.* **1.** carriage, mien.

port[5] (pôrt, pōrt), *n.* a strong, sweet wine, that is dark red or tawny, or occasionally white, originally from Portugal. [short for *Oporto* (in Portuguese *O Porto* the Port), a city in Portugal, from which it was shipped]

port[6] (pôrt, pōrt), *n. Australian.* a traveling bag; portmanteau.

Port., 1. Portugal. 2. Portuguese.

port·a·bil·i·ty (pôr′tə bil′ə tē, pōr′-), *n.* the state of being portable; portableness.

port·a·ble (pôr′tə bəl, pōr′-), *adj.* **1.** that can be carried; easily carried: *a portable typewriter, portable phonograph, etc.* **2.** *Obsolete.* that can be borne or tolerated; bearable: *How light and portable my pain seems now!* (Shakespeare). —*n.* something designed to be carried or readily moved, as a typewriter or radio: *My sister's TV is a portable.*
[< Late Latin *portābilis* < Latin *portāre* to carry] —**port′a·ble·ness,** *n.*

por·ta·ca·val (pôr′tə kā′vəl, pōr′-), *adj. Anatomy.* having to do with the portal vein and the vena cava.

por·tage (pôr′tij, pōr′-), *n., v.,* **-taged, -tag·ing.** —*n.* **1.** a carrying of boats, provisions, etc., overland from one river, lake, etc., to another. **2.** the place over which this is done: *As we were carrying the canoe upon a rocky portage, she fell, and was entirely bilged* (Robert Louis Stevenson). **3.** the act of carrying. **4.** the cost of carrying.
—*v.t., v.i.* **1.** to carry (boats, goods, etc.) over land between navigable waters. **2.** to make a portage over (a place) or around (rapids, a cataract, etc.).
[< Old French *portage* < *porter* to carry]

por·tal[1] (pôr′təl, pōr′-), *n.* a door, gate, or entrance, usually an imposing one, as in a cathedral. [< Medieval Latin *portale,* noun use of neuter adjective *portalis* portal < Latin *porta* gate]

por·tal[2] (pôr′təl, pōr′-), *adj.* **1.** of or having to do with the transverse fissure of the liver, through which the blood vessels enter. **2.** of or having to do with the portal vein. —*n.* the portal vein.
[< Medieval Latin *portale,* neuter adjective < Latin *porta* gate]

por·tal-to-por·tal pay (pôr′təl tə pôr′təl, pōr′təl tə pōr′təl), wages paid to an employee for the time he spends going to, and coming from, his actual place of work after having arrived on the grounds of the employer: ... *left standing, a decision barring portal-to-portal pay for employes required to change clothes before reporting to work and shower afterwards* (Wall Street Journal).

por·ta·men·to (pôr′tə men′tō, pōr′-; *Italian* pôr′tä men′tō), *n., pl.* **-ti** (-tē). *Music.* a gliding continuously without break from one pitch or note to another, as in singing or in playing a stringed instrument. [< Italian *portamento* (literally) a carrying < *portare* to carry < Latin *portāre*]

por·tance (pôr′təns, pōr′-), *n. Archaic.* **1.** carriage; bearing. **2.** conduct; behavior. [< Middle French *portance* action of carrying, favor < Old French *porter;* see PORT[4]]

port arms, 1. the command to bring or hold a rifle or other weapon in front of and diagonally across the body with the barrel up, while standing at attention. **2.** the position in which a weapon is thus held: *His eye caught the recruiting poster, which displayed a clean-shaven young man ... holding a rifle at port arms* (Atlantic).

por·ta·tive (pôr′tə tiv, pōr′-), *adj.* **1.** easily carried; portable. **2.** of, or having the power or function of carrying. [< Old French *portatif, portative* < *porter* to carry; see PORT[4]]

port authority, a commission appointed to manage a port.

port·cray·on (pôrt′krā′ən, pōrt′-), *n.* a holder or handle for a drawing crayon. [< French *portecrayon* (literally) carry crayon]

port·cul·lis (pôrt kul′is, pōrt-), *n.* a strong gate or grating of iron sliding up and down in grooves, used to close or open the gateway of an ancient castle or fortress: *Up drawbridge, grooms—what, Warder, ho! Let the portcullis fall!* (Scott). [< Old French *porte coleïce* sliding gate, ultimately < Latin *porta* gate, *cōlāre* to filter through < *cōlum* colander]

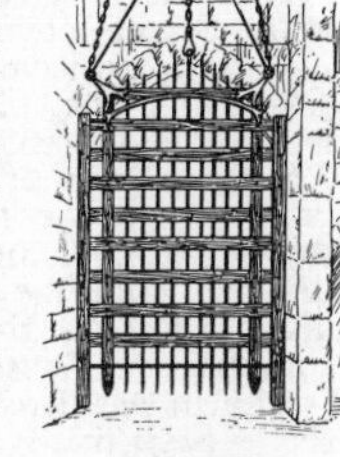

Portcullis

port de bras (pôr də brä′), *pl.* **ports de bras** (pôr də brä′). *French.* **1.** (in ballet) the technique of moving the arms. **2.** an exercise or figure through which this technique is developed or displayed: *Her ... warmly expansive ports de bras ... seem to enfold the whole audience in their embrace* (London Times).

Port du Sa·lut (pôr′ dʏ sȧ lʏ′), a cheese with a hard rind and a soft interior that tastes much like Swiss cheese. [< *Port du Salut,* a Trappist monastery in Bayonne, France]

Porte (pôrt, pōrt), *n.* the Turkish government before 1923. [< Middle French *porte,* short for *la Sublime Porte* (literally) High Gate, translation of the Turkish official title, with reference to the palace gate at which justice was administered]

porte-co·chere or **porte-co·chère** (pôrt′kō shãr′, pōrt′-), *n.* **1.** a porch at the door of a building under which carriages and automobiles stop so that persons getting in or out are sheltered: *They alighted under a porte-cochère with a glass roof* (Winston Churchill). **2.** *Archaic.* an entrance for carriages, leading into a courtyard. [< French *porte-cochère* coach gate]

porte-mon·naie (pôrt′mun′ē, pōrt′-; *French* pôrt′mô ne′), *n.* a purse; pocketbook. [< French *porte-monnaie* (literally) carry money < *porter* carry + *monnaie* money]

por·tend (pôr tend′, pōr-), *v.t.* **1.** to indicate beforehand; be a portent of: *Black clouds portend a storm.* **2.** *Obsolete.* to signify; mean. [< Latin *portendere* < *por-* before + *tendere* to extend] —**Syn. 1.** foreshadow, betoken, forebode.

por·te·ño (pôr tān′yō), *n.* a native or resident of Buenos Aires, Argentina. [< American Spanish *porteño* (literally) a port dweller]

por·tent (pôr′tent, pōr′-), *n.* **1.** a warning of coming evil; sign; omen: *The black clouds were a portent of bad weather.* **2.** the fact or quality of portending: *an occurrence of dire portent.* **3.** a prodigy; wonder; marvel: *There have been great captains ... But Frederic was not one of those brilliant portents* (Macaulay).
[< Latin *portentum,* (originally) neuter past participle of *portendere* to portend] —**Syn. 1.** token, presage.

por·ten·tous (pôr ten′təs, pōr-), *adj.* **1.** indicating evil to come; ominous; threatening: *direful omens and portentous sights and sounds in the air* (Washington Irving). **2.** amazing; extraordinary: *The cause of that celestial anger—the gay, portentous Palmerston* (Lytton Strachey). *What must have been the sensations of the Aztecs themselves, as they looked on the portentous pageant!* (William H. Prescott). —**por·ten′tous·ly,** *adv.* —**por·ten′tous·ness,** *n.*
—**Syn. 1.** foreboding, warning. **2.** wonderful, marvelous.

por·ter[1] (pôr′tər, pōr′-), *n.* **1.** a man employed to carry burdens or baggage: *Give your bags to the porter.* **2.** *U.S.* an attendant in a parlor car or sleeping car. —*v.t.* to carry as a porter: *Enough drink had been portered on the big trays to inflame an army* (New Yorker). [< Old French *porteour* < Late Latin *portātor* < Latin *portāre* to carry]

por·ter[2] (pôr′tər, pōr′-), *n. Archaic or British.* **1.** a doorkeeper; gatekeeper: *The porter let them in.* **2.** a janitor: *It was the hour when cooks and doormen walk dogs, and when porters scrub the lobby floor mats with soap and water* (New Yorker). [< Anglo-French *porter,* Old French *portier* < Late Latin *portārius* < Latin *porta* gate]

por·ter[3] (pôr′tər, pōr′-), *n.* **1.** a heavy, dark-brown beer: *The only genuine and wholesome beverage in England is London porter* (Tobias Smollett). **2.** *Obsolete.* a mixture of light beer, or ale, and stout, resembling this in flavor and color. [short for *porter's ale,* apparently < *porter*[2] (the original consumers)]

por·ter·age (pôr′tər ij, pōr′-), *n.* **1.** the act or work of a porter. **2.** the charge for this.

por·ter·ess (pôr′tər is, pōr′-), *n.* portress.

por·ter·house (pôr′tər hous′, pōr′-), *n.* **1.** *Especially U.S.* a choice beefsteak containing the tenderloin. **2.** *Archaic.* **a.** an establishment at which porter and other malt liquors are sold. **b.** a chophouse. [(definition 1) because this cut was allegedly popularized about 1814 by the keeper of a New York porterhouse]

porterhouse steak, porterhouse.

port·fo·li·o (pôrt fō′lē ō, pōrt-), *n., pl.* **-li·os. 1.** a portable case for loose papers, drawings, etc.; brief case: *adding to the many notes and tentative essays which had already accumulated in his portfolios* (Samuel Butler). **2.** the position and duties of a cabinet member, diplomat, or minister of state: *The Secretary of Defense resigned his portfolio.* **3.** holdings in the form of stocks, bonds, etc.: *There has been increased buying ... by the managers of larger investment portfolios* (Wall Street Journal). [alteration of earlier *porto folio* < Italian *portafoglia* < *portare* to carry (< Latin *portāre*) + *foglio* sheet, leaf < Latin *folium*]

port·hole (pôrt′hōl′, pōrt′-), *n.* **1.** an opening in the side of a ship to let in light and air. **2.** an opening in a fort, pillbox, side of a tank, ship, wall, etc., through which to shoot. **3.** a port or opening for the passage of steam, air, etc.

Por·tia (pôr′shə, pōr′-), *n.* a woman lawyer: *Mary is the daughter of a ... dentist who would have preferred a Portia to a naiad* (Time). [< *Portia,* the heroine of Shakespeare's *Merchant of Venice* who disguises herself as a lawyer]

por·ti·co (pôr′tə kō, pōr′-), *n., pl.* **-coes** or **-cos.** a roof supported by columns, forming a porch or a covered walk. [< Italian *portico* < Latin *porticus, -ūs* < *porta* gate. Doublet of PORCH.]

Portico

por·ti·coed (pôr′tə kōd, pōr′-), *adj.* having a portico or porticoes.

por·tiere or **por·tière** (pôr tyãr′, pōr-), *n.* a curtain hung at a doorway. [< Middle French *portière* < Old French *porte* door, port[2]]

por·tion (pôr′shən, pōr′-), *n.* **1.** a part; share: *A portion of each school day is devoted to arithmetic.* **2.** a quantity of food served for one person: *Each child ate his portion.* **3.** the part of an estate that goes to an heir; property inherited. **4.** a dowry: *I married Mrs. Mary Burton ... with whom I received four hundred pounds for a portion* (Jonathan Swift). **5.** one's lot; fate: *This is the portion of a wicked man from God and the heritage appointed unto him by God* (Job 20:29).
—*v.t.* **1.** to divide into parts or shares: *After his death, his money was portioned out among his children. The country was portioned out among the captains of the invaders* (Macaulay). **2.** to give (a thing to a person) as share; give a portion, inheritance, dowry, etc., to: *When I marry with their consent they will portion me most handsomely* (Dickens). **3.** to provide with a lot or fate.
[< Old French *porcioun, portion,* learned borrowing from Latin *portiō, -ōnis,* related to *pars, partis* part] —**por′tion·er,** *n.*
—**Syn.** *n.* **1.** See **part. 5.** destiny. *-v.t.* **1, 2.** apportion.

por·tion·less (pôr′shən lis, pōr′-), *adj.* **1.** having no portion or share. **2.** having no dowry: *a portionless maid.*

port·land cement (pôrt′lənd, pōrt′-), a kind of cement, made by burning limestone and clay in a kiln and then grinding this product to a very fine powder. It is used in making mortar and concrete. [< the Isle of *Portland,* a peninsula in Dorset, England]

Portland stone, a white limestone used in building, quarried in the Isle of Portland, a peninsula in Dorset, England: *Viewed with a shaft of sunlight on it, the Portland stone is startlingly white* (London Times).

port·li·ness (pôrt′lē nis, pōrt′-), *n.* the character or state of being portly in manner, appearance, or person.

port·ly (pôrt′lē, pōrt′-), *adj.,* **-li·er, -li·est,** *n., pl.* **-lies.** —*adj.* **1.** stout; corpulent: *a portly, rubicund man of middle age* (Winston Churchill). **2.** stately; dignified.
—*n.* **1.** a stout man: *Portlies have always had a propensity for double-breasted suits* (Newsweek). **2.** a suit made for a stout man: *Only a few stores carry portlies.* [< *port*[4]]
—**Syn.** *adj.* **1.** See **fat.**

port·man·teau (pôrt man′tō, pōrt-), *n., pl.* **-teaus** or **-teaux** (-tōz), *adj.* —*n. Especially British.* a stiff, oblong traveling bag with two compartments opening like a book. —*adj.* combining two or more different things of the same kind: *The portmanteau revue here brings to light an unfamiliar humorist and an unfamiliar ballerina* (New Yorker). [< Middle French *portmanteau* < *porter* to carry (see PORT[4]) + *manteau* mantle]

portmanteau word, a word made by combining parts of two words; blend.

port of call, a port at which a vessel is scheduled to stop to discharge and receive cargo and passengers, take on supplies, etc.: *Manila is a port of call for practically all ships plying between India and Eastern Asia* (Colby and Foster).

port of entry, a city with a custom house, through which persons or merchandise may enter legally into a country; port.

Port Or·ford cedar (ôr′fərd), **1.** a tall tree of the cypress family, native to Oregon and northern California. **2.** the beautiful spotty-grained wood of this tree.

Por·to Ri·can (pôr′tə rē′kən, pōr′-), Puerto Rican.

por·trait (pôr′trit, -trāt; pōr′-), *n.* **1.** a picture of a person, especially of the face. **2.** a picture in words; description: *That character ... is almost the only exact portrait in the whole book* (Charles Kingsley). **3.** a drawing, painting, etc., of any object: *The most ancient extant portrait anyways purporting to be the whale's* (Herman Melville). [< Old French *portrait,* (originally) past participle of Old French *portraire* to portray]

por·trait·ist (pôr′trā tist, pōr′-), *n.* a person who paints portraits: *As a portraitist, Sargent was a prodigious worker* (Newsweek).

por·trai·ture (pôr′trə chůr, -chər; pōr′-), *n.* **1.** the act of portraying: *the portraitures of insignificant people by ordinary painters* (Sir Richard Steele). **2.** a portrait or portraits. **3.** a picture in words. [< Old French *portraiture* < *portrait* portrait]

por·tray (pôr trā′, pōr-), *v.t.* **1.** to picture in words; describe: *The book portrays life long ago.* **2.** to make a picture of: *to portray a historical scene.* **3.** to represent on the stage. [< Old French *pourtraire* < Latin *prōtrahere* reveal, prolong (in Medieval Latin, to draw, paint) < *prō-* forth + *trahere* draw] —**por·tray′er,** *n.* —**Syn. 1.** depict. **3.** impersonate, act.

por·tray·a·ble (pôr trā′ə bəl, pōr-), *adj.* that can be portrayed.

por·tray·al (pôr trā′əl, pōr-), *n.* **1.** a portraying by drawing or in words. **2.** a picture; description. **3.** the acting of a rôle in a play.

por·tress (pôr′tris, pōr′-), *n.* a female porter; woman who acts as a porter.

port·side[1] (pôrt′sīd′, pōrt′-), *n.* the left side of a ship when facing the bow; port: *[The] motor whaleboat approached the trawler's starboard quarter, was waved to the portside where a ladder was lowered* (Time). —*adj.* on the left side; port: *The manager took out his next batter, replaced him with a portside swinger as a pinch hitter.* —*adv.* to or toward the left side: *The S.S. Champlain slid through morning mist, and, portside, Staten Island dimly floated past* (Atlantic).

port·side[2] (pôrt′sīd′, pōrt′-), *n.* the water front of a port. —*adj.* waterfront: *portside docks.*

port·sid·er (pôrt′sī′dər, pōrt′-), *n. Slang.* a left-handed person, especially a baseball pitcher.

Por·tu·guese (pôr′chə gēz′, -gēs′; pōr′-), *n., pl.* **-guese,** *adj.* —*n.* **1.** a native or inhabitant of Portugal. **2.** the Romance language of Portugal. Portuguese is also the chief language of Brazil. —*adj.* of or having to do with Portugal, its people, or their language.

Portuguese cabbage, a plant related to the cabbage, having thick, broad, edible leaves like those of the cabbage, originally cultivated by the Portuguese of Bermuda.

Portuguese man-of-war, any of several large marine hydrozoans, having a large air sac that acts as a float, and many long thin tentacles, remarkable for brilliant coloring and great power of stinging.

por·tu·lac·a (pôr′chə lak′ə, pōr′-), *n.* a low-growing plant with thick, fleshy leaves and variously colored flowers. It is an herb of the purslane family. [< Latin *portulāca*]

por·tu·la·ca·ceous (pôr′chə lə kā′shəs, pōr′-), *adj.* belonging to the purslane family of plants.

port·wide (pôrt′wīd′, pōrt′-), *adj.* of or having to do with an entire port: *The threat of a portwide strike by longshoremen receded yesterday* (New York Times).

port-wine mark (pôrt′wīn′, pōrt′-), a deep-purple or dark-red birthmark composed of capillaries, usually on the face.

pos., 1. positive. 2. possessive.

po·sa·da (pō sä′də; *Spanish* pō sä′ᴛʜä), *n.* **1.** an inn. **2.** a religious ceremony held in many Mexican homes on the nine nights before Christmas. [< Spanish *posada* < *posar* to lodge < Latin *pausāre;* see POSE[1]]

pose[1] (pōz), *n., v.,* **posed, pos·ing.** —*n.* **1.** position of the body; way of holding the body: *She too got up . . . Her pose had a kind of defiance in it* (Mrs. Humphry Ward). **2.** an attitude assumed for effect; pretense; affectation: *His anger is not a pose.* —*v.i.* **1.** to hold a position: *to pose for a portrait.* **2.** to put on an attitude for effect; make a false pretense: *He posed as a rich man though he owed more than he owned.* —*v.t.* **1.** to put in a certain position: *The artist posed him before painting his picture.* **2.** to put forward for discussion; state: *to pose a question.* [< Old French *poser* < Late Latin *pausāre* to pause < Latin *pausa* a pause; in Romance languages, influenced by *pos-,* the perfect stem of Latin *pōnere* to place (from the meaning "cause to pause, set down"); this influence spread to many English compounds, such as *compose, dispose, oppose*]

pose[2] (pōz), *v.t.,* **posed, pos·ing. 1.** to puzzle completely; perplex; nonplus: *Kolory himself would be effectually posed were he called upon to draw up the articles of his faith* (Herman Melville). **2.** *Obsolete.* to examine by questioning; interrogate. [variant of *oppose,* or perhaps of *appose*]

Po·sei·don (pə sī′dən), *n. Greek Mythology.* the god of the sea and of horses, son of Cronus and Rhea, equivalent of the Roman god Neptune. His weapon and attribute is the trident.

Poseidon

pos·er[1] (pō′zər), *n.* a person who poses, especially a poseur. [< *pos*(e)[1] + *-er*[1]]

pos·er[2] (pō′zər), *n.* **1.** a very puzzling problem or question. **2.** *Archaic.* a person who examines by questions. [< *pos*(e)[2] + *-er*[1]]

po·seur (pō zœr′), *n.* an affected person; one who poses to impress others: *I was . . . a little of a prig and poseur in those days* (H.G. Wells). [< French *poseur* < *poser* pose[1]]

po·seuse (pō zoez′), *n.* a woman poseur.

posh (posh), *adj. Informal.* elegant or fine in appearance; stylish; luxurious: *When I was a kid I used to look forward to the time when I could afford to eat in posh restaurants* (Maclean's). [origin unknown]

po·sied (pō′zēd), *adj.* **1.** furnished with posies or nosegays. **2.** *Archaic.* inscribed with a posy or motto: *Many a ring of posied gold* (Shakespeare).

pos·i·grade (poz′ə grād), *adj. Aerospace.* having positive acceleration; going or thrusting forward: *posigrade motion. The thrust of the small, posigrade rockets . . . gives the spacecraft a gentle separation push away from the booster* (John H. Glenn, Jr.). [< *posi*(tive) + (retro) *grade*]

pos·it (poz′it), *v.t.* **1.** to lay down or assume as a fact or principle; affirm. **2.** to place, put, or set. [< Latin *positus,* past participle of *pōnere* to set, place]

po·si·tion (pə zish′ən), *n.* **1.** the place where a thing or person is: *The house is in a sheltered position. Your careless remark put me in an awkward position.* **2.** a way of being placed: *Sit in a more comfortable position.* **3.** proper place: *Is every man in his position?* **4.** a condition with reference to place or circumstances: *The army maneuvered for position before attacking.* **5.** a job: *He lost his position because he was not honest.* **6.** standing, especially high standing; rank: *He was raised to the position of captain in the navy.* **7.** a way of thinking; set of opinions: *What is your position on this question?* **8.** *Greek and Latin Prosody.* the situation of a short vowel before two or more consonants or their equivalent, making the syllable metrically long. —*v.t.* **1.** to put in a particular position; place: *By adjusting the controls, the nails are fed out of slotted storage banks and positioned as desired* (Wall Street Journal). **2.** to determine the position of; locate. [< Latin *positiō, -ōnis* < *pōnere* to set] —**Syn.** *n.* **1.** situation, site, location. See **place. 5. Position, job, situation** mean employment. **Position** is somewhat formal and usually suggests white-collar work: *He has a position in a bank.* **Situation** is chiefly used in employment advertising: *situations available.* **Job** is the informal word for employment of any kind, but emphasizes the idea of work to do: *He has a job on a ranch this summer. I don't envy the President his job.* **6.** status.

po·si·tion·al (pə zish′ə nəl), *adj.* of, having to do with, or depending on position.

po·si·tion·er (pə zish′ə nər), *n.* a person or thing that puts another in a certain position.

position paper, a formal statement defining the position of a person or group on a particular issue: *Great stress was laid on agreed position papers . . . by the staff of the National Security Council* (Harper's).

pos·i·tive (poz′ə tiv), *adj.* **1.** admitting of no question; without doubt; sure: *We have positive knowledge that the earth moves around the sun. Nor is Socrates positive of anything but the duty of enquiry* (Benjamin Jowett). **2.** too sure; too confident: *Her positive manner annoys people. He was a very positive man—the embodiment of authority* (Harper's). **3. a.** definite; emphatic: *"No. I will not," was his positive refusal.* **b.** *Informal.* downright; out-and-out: *Most of the luxuries . . . are positive hindrances to the elevation of mankind* (Thoreau). **4.** that can be thought of as real and present: *Light is a positive thing; darkness is only the absence of light.* **5.** showing that a particular disease, condition, germ, etc., is present. **6.** that definitely does something or adds something; practical: *Don't just make criticisms; give us some positive help. The children's constant thought of one another constitutes a positive value* (Saturday Review). **7.** tending in the direction thought of as that of increase or progress: *Motion in the direction that the hands of the clock move is positive.* **8.** counting up from zero; plus: *Five above zero is a positive quantity. We must say that the product of two negative numbers is a positive number* (John R. Pierce). **9. a.** of the kind of electricity produced by rubbing glass with silk; lacking electrons. **b.** characterized by the presence or production of such electricity. **10.** *Photography.* having the lines and shadows in the same position as in the original: *the positive image on a print.* **11.** *Grammar.* of the simple form of an adjective or adverb. **12.** *Biology.* moving or turning toward light, the earth, or any other stimulus: *If a plant organ reacts by turning toward the source of a stimulus, it exhibits a positive tropism* (Fred W. Emerson). **13.** having a tendency to lose electrons, and thus to become charged with positive electricity, as a chemical element or radical. **14.** arbitrarily laid down or imposed; determined by enactment or convention: *positive law.* **15.** *Philosophy.* concerned with or based on matters of experience; not speculative or theoretical; empirical. **16.** having no relation to or comparison with other things; absolute; unconditional. **17.** in machinery: **a.** dependable because determined by a firm structure or by exactly controlled forces or movements: *a positive stroke.* **b.** functioning for the special purpose required: *positive lubrication.* **18.** *U.S.* of or having to do with commodities which cannot be shipped to other countries without an individual export license: *The Commerce Department added several scientific items to its positive list and eased restrictions on others* (Wall Street Journal). —*n.* **1.** a positive degree or quantity. **2.** *Electricity.* the plate in a battery from which the current flows into the wire. **3.** *Photography.* a print made from a photographic film or plate. **4.** *Grammar.* the simple form of an adjective or adverb as distinct from the comparative and superlative. *Fast* is the positive; *faster* is the comparative; *fastest* is the superlative. [< Latin *positīvus,* ultimately < *pōnere* to set] —**pos′i·tive·ly,** *adv.* —**pos′i·tive·ness,** *n.* —**Syn.** *adj.* **1.** unquestionable, unmistakable, indisputable. **2.** dogmatic. **3. a.** imperative, express.

positive acceleration, an increase in velocity.

positive electricity, electricity in which the proton is the elementary unit.

positive lens, a convex lens that converges light rays.

pos·i·tiv·ism (poz′ə tə viz′əm), *n.* **1.** a philosophical system founded by Auguste Comte, a French philosopher and sociologist, that deals only with positive facts and phenomena, rejecting abstract speculation. **2.** a being positive; definiteness; assurance; dogmatism. [< French *positivisme* (coined by Comte) < *positif* positive + *-isme* -ism]

pos·i·tiv·ist (poz′ə tə vist), *n.* a person who maintains the doctrines of positivism.

pos·i·tiv·is·tic (poz′ə tə vis′tik), *adj.* of or having to do with the positivists or positivism.

pos·i·tiv·i·ty (poz′ə tiv′ə tē), *n.* the state or character of being positive.

pos·i·tron (poz′ə tron), *n.* a particle having the same magnitude of mass and charge as an electron, but exhibiting a positive charge, present in cosmic rays and also emitted in beta decay; positive electron: *Beta rays of opposite charge have been detected and identified as positrons* (Scientific American).

pos·i·tro·ni·um (poz′ə trō′nē əm), *n. Physics.* an electrically neutral atom consisting of an electron and a positron which destroy each other in less than a millionth of a second: *The source is positronium, a short-lived stuff made of the simplest atom yet discovered* (Science News Letter).

pos·net (pos′net), *n. Archaic.* a metal pot or vessel for use in cooking. [< Old French *poçonnet* (diminutive) < *poçon* pot, vessel]

po·sol·o·gy (pə sol′ə jē), *n.* the branch of medical science that is concerned with the doses in which medicines should be administered. [< Greek *pósos* how much + English *-logy*]

poss., **1.** possession. **2.** possessive. **3. a.** possible. **b.** possibly.

pos·se (pos′ē), *n.* **1.** a group of men summoned by a sheriff to help him: *The posse pursued the thief.* **2.** all the male citizens from which the sheriff may pick a police force; posse comitatus. **3.** a band, company, or assemblage: *a small posse of helpers and spectators* (London Times). *A posse of children came down for the summer holidays* (Leonard Merrick). [< Medieval Latin *posse* body of men, power < Latin *posse* to be able]

pos·se com·i·ta·tus (pos′ē kom′ə tā′təs), **1.** the entire body of male citizens, as the body from which a sheriff is authorized to call for aid in keeping the peace and carrying out certain of his other duties as an officer of the law: *It was his auxiliary duty to muster a posse comitatus or call upon the law-abiding members of the county to set up a "hue and cry" and join the chase* (New Yorker). **2.** a group of men summoned by a sheriff to help him; posse. [< Medieval Latin (England) *posse comitatus* force of the county]

pos·sess (pə zes′), *v.t.* **1.** to own; have: *Washington possessed great wisdom.* **2. a.** to hold as property; hold; occupy. **b.** to hold as a tenant. **3.** to influence strongly; control: *a naturally taciturn man possessed by an idea* (Joseph Conrad). **4.** to control by an evil spirit: *He fought like one possessed. Frank Carney's drama about a young Irish girl who is supernaturally possessed is exciting* (New Yorker). **5.** to maintain; keep: *Possess your soul in patience.* **6.** *Archaic.* to take; win. **7.** *Obsolete.* to put in possession of; give to. [probably back formation < *possession*]

pos·sessed (pə zest′), *adj.* **1.** dominated by or as by an evil spirit or influence; demoniac; lunatic; mad; crazy: *He upset the table . . . and rushed through the coffee-room like one possessed* (Charles J. Lever). **2.** having or owning as property or a quality: *a man possessed of more wealth than brains.* **3.** remaining calm or steady; composed; self-possessed.

pos·ses·sion (pə zesh′ən), *n.* **1.** a possessing; holding: *Our soldiers fought hard for the possession of the hilltop.* **2. a.** ownership: *At his father's death he came into possession of a million dollars.* **b.** the holding or control of a thing as a tenant. **3.** a thing possessed; property. **4.** a territory under the rule of a country: *Guam is a possession of the United States.* **5.** domination by a particular feeling, idea, etc. **6.** self-control; composure. **7.** domination by a demon or spirit: *Under states of possession, devotees experience a change in their customary behavior, even the timbre and pitch of their voice may alter* (Melville J. Herskovits).
[< Latin *possessiō, -ōnis* < *possidēre* to possess]
—**Syn. 1.** tenure. **3.** belonging.

pos·ses·sive (pə zes′iv), *adj.* **1.** of possession. **2.** showing possession. *My, your, his,* and *our* are in the possessive case. **3.** desirous of ownership: *a possessive nature.* **4.** asserting or claiming ownership: *a possessive manner.*
—*n.* **1. a.** the possessive case. **b.** a word in this case. In "the boy's books," *boy's* is a possessive. **2. a.** a group of words having the meaning or function of the possessive case. *Example:* of the boy, of the boy's, etc. **b.** a possessive pronoun or adjective. —**pos·ses′sive·ly,** *adv.* —**pos·ses′sive·ness,** *n.*

possessive adjective, an adjective that shows possession. It is formed from a personal pronoun: *My, your, his, etc., are possessive adjectives.*

possessive case, *Grammar.* the case that expresses possession, origin, or various other relationships; genitive case. It is regularly formed in singular nouns by the addition of *'s,* as in the *boy's book, James's money, Socrates's wife* (the *s* being sometimes omitted, as in for *conscience' sake, Socrates' wife, Moses' mandates,* either by a natural contraction of two sibilant sounds into one or in order to avoid an unpleasant sequence of sibilants), and in plural nouns ending in *s* by the addition of the apostrophe alone, as in *the boys' books,* and in other plural nouns by the addition of *'s,* as in *men's wear.*

possessive pronoun, a pronoun that shows possession. There are two kinds, the substantive form (*mine, yours,* etc.), and the attributive form (*my, your,* etc.). The latter is also called a possessive adjective.

pos·ses·sor (pə zes′ər), *n.* a person who possesses: *This charm was too dangerous to its possessor* (Ann Radcliffe).

pos·ses·sor·ship (pə zes′ər ship), *n.* the condition of a possessor; holding something as owner.

pos·ses·so·ry (pə zes′ər ē), *adj.* **1.** having to do with a possessor or possession. **2.** arising from possession: *a possessory interest.* **3.** having possession.

pos·set (pos′it), *n., v.,* **-set·ed, -set·ing** or (*sometimes*) **-set·ted, -set·ting.** —*n.* a hot drink made of milk, alcoholic liquor, and spices. It was formerly widely used as a remedy for colds. —*v.t.* **1.** to give or administer a posset to: *As she laid him in bed and possetted him, how frail and fragile he looked* (Arnold Bennett). **2.** *Obsolete.* to curdle like a posset. [Middle English *possot*]

posset cup, a cup, often with two or more handles, used in drinking posset.

pos·si·bil·i·ty (pos′ə bil′ə tē), *n., pl.* **-ties. 1.** a being possible: *There is a possibility that the train may be late.* **2.** a possible thing, circumstance, or person: *Her clearer intellect saw possibilities which did not occur to him* (Anthony Trollope).

pos·si·ble (pos′ə bəl), *adj.* **1.** that can be; that can be done; that can happen: *Come if possible.* **2.** that can be true or a fact: *It is possible that he went.* **3.** that can be done, chosen, etc., properly: *the only possible action, the only possible candidate.*
—*n.* a possible candidate, winner, etc.: *The President and party leaders considered two dozen possibles* (Time).
[< Latin *possibilis* < *posse* be able]
—**Syn.** *adj.* **1. Possible, practicable, feasible** mean capable of happening or being done. **Possible** means that with suitable conditions and methods something may exist, happen, or be done: *It is possible to cure tuberculosis.* **Practicable** means that under present circumstances or by available means something (a plan, method, invention) can easily or effectively be carried out, done, or used: *The X-ray is a practicable way of discovering unsuspected diseases.* **Feasible** suggests something not yet tried, but seeming likely to be practicable: *Would compulsory X-rays, like compulsory vaccination, be feasible?*

pos·si·bly (pos′ə blē), *adv.* **1.** by any possibility; no matter what happens: *I cannot possibly go.* **2.** perhaps: *Possibly you are right.*

pos·sie (pos′ē), *n. Australian Slang.* position. Also, **possy.**

pos·sum (pos′əm), *n.* **1.** *U.S.* an opossum. **2.** (in Australia) any of various phalangers.
play possum, to put on a false appearance; pretend ignorance or illness.
[American English, short for *opossum* (which pretends to be dead when attacked)]

pos·sum·haw (pos′əm hô′), *n.* **1.** a shrub or small tree, a variety of holly, having small, red or orange fruit and growing in the southeastern United States; bearberry. **2.** a shrub of the honeysuckle family found in wet areas of the southeastern United States; withe rod.

pos·sy (pos′ē), *n.* possie.

post[1] (pōst), *n.* **1.** a piece of timber, metal, or the like, set upright, usually as a support: *the posts of a door, gate, or bed; a hitching post.* **2.** a post, line, etc., where a race starts or ends: *She kept switching her tail while she was being saddled and all during the parade to the post* (New Yorker).
—*v.t.* **1.** to fasten (a notice) up in a place where it can easily be seen: *The list of winners will be posted soon.* **2.** to make known by or as if by a posted notice; make public: *to post a reward.* **3.** to put (a name) in a list that is published or posted up: *to post three ships as missing.* **4.** to cover (a wall, etc.) with notices or bills. **5.** to put up notices warning people to keep out of: *That farmer posts his land.*
[Old English *post* < Latin *postis, -is* post, (apparently, originally) projecting, perhaps < *por-* forth (for *per-*) + *stāre* to stand]

post[2] (pōst), *n.* **1.** the place where a soldier, policeman, etc., is stationed; place where one is supposed to be when on duty: *When the fire alarm sounds, each man rushes to his post. Men like soldiers may not quit the post Allotted by the Gods* (Tennyson). **2.** a place where soldiers are stationed; military station; fort: *One southern post commander called out his troops and seized a Tunisian road block* (Wall Street Journal). **3.** the soldiers occupying a military station. **4.** *U.S.* a local branch of a veterans' organization, as of the American Legion or the Veterans of Foreign Wars. **5.** a job or position: *the post of secretary, a diplomatic post.* **6.** a trading station, especially in an uncivilized or unsettled country: *Fort Laramie is one of the posts established by the American fur company . . . Here . . . the arm of the United States has little force* (Francis Parkman). **7.** a place on the floor of a stock exchange for trading in certain securities. **8.** (in the British Army) either of two bugle calls (first post and last post) calling soldiers to their quarters for the night.
take post, a. (formerly in the British Navy) to be commissioned as captain of a ship of not less than 20 guns: *Sir William Sanderson [and others] take post by a general order* (John Chamberlayne). **b.** *Military.* to occupy a position: *A body of two thousand men . . . were directed to take post at the bridge of Alcantara* (William F.P. Napier).
—*v.t.* **1.** to station at a post; place (troops, etc.) at a particular point: *The captain posted guards at the door. Kim felt sure that the boy had been posted to guide him* (Rudyard Kipling). **2.** to appoint to a post of command in the armed forces.
[< Middle French *poste* < Italian *posto* < Latin *positus,* past participle of *pōnere* to station, place, put]

post[3] (pōst), *n.* **1.** an established system for carrying letters, papers, packages, etc.; the mail: *to send a package by post.* **2.** *Especially British.* a single mail; the letters, etc., thus delivered: *this morning's post.* **3.** *Archaic.* a postman. **4.** *Archaic.* a person, vehicle, or ship that carries mail. **5.** a post office. **6.** a letter box. **7. a.** one of a series of fixed stations along a route for furnishing relays of men and horses for carrying letters, etc., and supplying service to travelers by post horse, post chaise, etc.: *The town began as a Pony Express post and later grew into an important mining center.* **b.** the distance between one post or station and the next; a stage. **8.** a size of paper, about 16x20 inches. **9.** a newspaper or magazine: *the Saturday Evening Post.* **10.** *Obsolete.* a courier; postrider.
—*v.t.* **1.** to send by post; mail: *to post a letter.* **2.** *Informal.* to supply with information up to date; inform: *to be well posted on current events. Baseball fans always post themselves as to the standing of the teams.* **3.** *Bookkeeping.* **a.** to transfer (an entry) from journal to ledger. **b.** to enter (an item) in due place and form. **c.** to make all requisite entries in (a ledger, etc.). —*v.i.* **1.** to travel with post horses or by post chaise: *His father and mother were with him, having posted from home in their carriage* (Samuel Butler). **2.** to travel with speed; hasten: *He posted upstairs, taking three steps at once* (Scott). **3.** to rise and fall in the saddle in rhythm with the horse's trot.
—*adv.* by post; speedily.
[< Middle French *poste* (originally) relay of horses for couriers < Italian *posta* < Latin, variant of *posita,* feminine past participle of *pōnere* to place]

post-, *prefix.* **1.** after in time; later, as in *postgraduate, post-mortem, postscript.*
2. after in space; behind, as in *postnasal, postposition, postorbital.*
3. after and more or less caused by, as in *postoperative, posttraumatic.*
[< Latin *post-* < *post* after, behind]

post·age (pōs′tij), *n.* **1.** the amount paid for sending anything by mail. **2.** the stamp or stamps used to send a letter or package.

postage currency, a fractional paper currency issued by the United States in 1862-63, during the Civil War, resembling the postage stamps that had previously been used instead of coins.

postage meter, a machine that stamps postage on a letter or package and postmarks it.

postage stamp, an official stamp placed on mail to show that postage has been paid.

post·al (pōs′təl), *adj.* having to do with mail and post offices: *postal regulations, a postal clerk, etc.* —*n. U.S.* a post card. —**post′al·ly,** *adv.*

postal card, a post card.

postal note, a type of money order formerly issued by U.S. post offices for amounts up to $10. It was abolished in 1951.

postal order, *British.* a type of money order issued by a post office for one of a number of fixed sums: *I have sent the postal order back to him because he was too late in paying* (London Times).

post·au·dit (pōst ô′dit), *n.* an audit conducted after a transaction has been settled or completed: *The postaudit . . . is conducted under the auspices of the Indian Auditor General* [*and*] *is not confined to financial accounting* (Atlantic).

post·ax·i·al (pōst ak′sē əl), *adj.* **1.** behind the axis. **2.** of, having to do with, or on the posterior side of the limb of a vertebrate.

post·bag (pōst′bag′), *n. British.* **1.** a mailbag. **2.** mail: *My postbag has brightened up a lot this last week with many interesting letters* (Punch).

post beetle, any of various beetles whose larvae bore into posts and other timber.

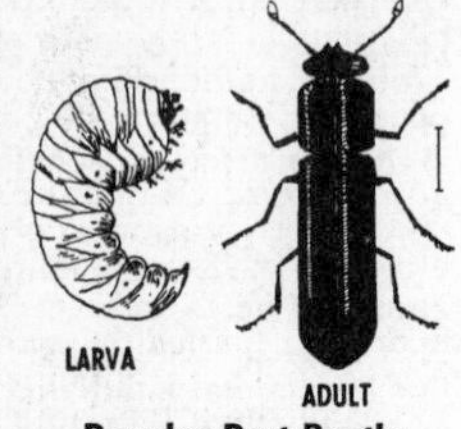

Powder Post Beetle
(Line shows actual length.)

post - bellum (pōst′bel′əm), *adj.* **1.** after the war. **2.** *Especially U.S.* after the American Civil War: *The cowboy migrations westward were a post-bellum phenomenon* (Horace Gregory). [American English < Latin *post bellum* after the war]

post·box (pōst′boks′), *n.* a box in which letters are mailed or deposited for dispatch; letter box; mailbox.

post·boy (pōst′boi′), *n.* **1.** a boy or man who carries mail. **2.** a man who rides one of the horses drawing a carriage; postilion.

post·ca·non·i·cal (pōst′kə non′ə kəl), *adj.* of later date than the canon; written later than the canon of Scripture.

post card, or **post·card** (pōst′kärd′), *n.* **1.** a card with a government postage stamp printed on it. **2.** any card, especially one with a picture on one side, for sending a message by mail.

post chaise, a hired carriage that was used for traveling before there were railroads.

post chariot, a carriage for posting or traveling, used especially in the 1700's.

post·clas·sic (pōst klas′ik), *adj.* postclassical.

post·clas·si·cal (pōst klas′ə kəl), *adj.* existing or occurring after the classic or classical period, especially of Greek and Latin literature or art.

post·coach (pōst′kōch′), *n.* a stagecoach used for carrying mail; mail coach: *In 1803 a postcoach service was opened between Bristol and Holyhead* (Manchester Guardian Weekly).

post·co·lo·ni·al (pōst′kə lō′nē əl), *adj.* after a state of colonialism: *postcolonial Africa, a postcolonial regime. The post-colonial* [*British*] *Commonwealth is the greatest multiracial association in the world* (Atlantic).

post·date (pōst′dāt′), *v.t.*, **-dat·ed, -dat·ing.** **1.** to give a later date than the true date to (a letter, check, etc.): *Many of the Berlin newspapers which are published in the evening are postdated by a day* (Charles Lowe). **2.** to follow in time.

post·deb (pōst deb′), *n. Informal.* a post-debutante: *Dede Hickingbotham, another postdeb, getting a rush from the stag line* (Frances Moffat).

post·deb·u·tante (pōst deb′yə tänt, -tant; pōst′deb yə tänt′), *n.* a girl who is past her first formal appearance in society: *Baltimore's annual Spinsters' Ball* [*is*] *a white tie affair in which passed-over postdebutantes in their late 20s take another try at meeting the right sort of man* (Time).

post·di·lu·vi·an (pōst′də lü′vē ən, -dī-), *adj.* existing or occurring after the Flood. —*n.* a person who has lived since the Flood.

post·doc·tor·al (pōst dok′tər əl), *adj.* having to do with advanced academic work after the doctorate: *postdoctoral fellowships, postdoctoral research.*

post·doc·tor·ate (pōst dok′tər it), *adj.* postdoctoral: *Specialization requires two to five years in formal postdoctorate training* (T.B. Eveleth).

post·ed (pōs′tid), *adj.* **1.** having posts: *a four-posted bed.* **2.** *Informal.* informed. **3.** forbidden by signs to trespassers: *posted land.*

post·er[1] (pōs′tər), *n.* **1.** a large printed sheet or notice put up in some public place: *He . . . noted . . . the glare of the recruiting posters on every vacant piece of wall* (H. G. Wells). **2.** a person who posts notices, etc. —*adj. Informal.* having posts: *a four-poster bed.*

post·er[2] (pōs′tər), *n.* **1.** a post horse. **2.** *Obsolete.* a person who travels swiftly.

poste res·tante (pōst′ res tänt′), **1.** a direction written on mail which is to remain at the post office till called for: *Six hundred and eighty-one addresses of women were traced through poste restantes and letters undelivered* (Keith Simpson). **2.** a post-office department in charge of such mail. [< French *poste restante* < *poste* post[3], *restante* remaining < Old French *rester* to rest]

pos·te·ri·or (pos tir′ē ər), *adj.* **1.** situated behind; back; rear; hind: *It has been known for some years that the output of the posterior lobe hormones was controlled by the brain in some way* (Bernard Donovan). **2.** later; coming after. **3.** *Botany.* situated on the side nearest the axis; superior.
—*n.* **posteriors,** the buttocks: *He drops upon his knees or posteriors* (Edward Ward).
[< Latin *posterior*, comparative of *posterus* subsequent < *post* after] —**pos·te′ri·or·ly,** *adv.*
—**Syn.** *adj.* **2.** subsequent, succeeding, following.

pos·te·ri·or·i·ty (pos tir′ē ôr′ə tē, -or′-), *n., pl.* **-or·i·ties.** **1.** the state or quality of being posterior. **2.** a posterior position or date.

pos·ter·i·ty (pos ter′ə tē), *n.* **1.** generations of the future: *If we burn up all the coal and oil in the world, what will posterity do? Posterity would remember him as the author of many fine poems* (Atlantic). *Methinks the truth should live from age to age, As 'twere retail'd to all posterity* (Shakespeare). **2.** all of a person's descendants: *that the inheritance of the king should be to his posterity alone* (Ecclesiasticus 45:25). [< Latin *posteritās* < *posterus;* see POSTERIOR] —**Syn. 2.** progeny.

pos·tern (pōs′tərn, pos′-), *n.* **1.** a back door or gate. **2.** any small door or gate: *We slipped out of the side postern into a night of darkness* (Robert Louis Stevenson).
—*adj.* **1.** of or like a postern. **2.** rear; lesser: *The castle had a postern door.*
[< Old French *posterne*, ultimately < Latin *posterus* behind; see POSTERIOR]

West Postern (def. 2) in walls of Troy

pos·te·ro·lat·er·al (pos′tər ō lat′ər əl), *adj.* situated at the back and toward one side; both posterior and lateral. [< *posterior* + *lateral*]

Post Exchange or **post exchange,** a general store at a military post that sells cigarettes, candy, etc., to military personnel and their dependents: *Military employees are paid from post exchange revenue if they work in exchanges of their own* (New York Times). *Abbr.:* PX (no periods).

post·ex·il·i·an (pōst′eg zil′ē ən, -ek sil′-), *adj.* following the Babylonian exile or captivity of the Jews in the early 500's B.C.

post·ex·il·ic (pōst′eg zil′ik, -ek sil′-), *adj.* postexilian.

post·face (pōst′fis), *n.* an explanatory note following the body of a text; afterword: *In the postface we were faced with a problem, since "On Wisconsin" would have little meaning to Spanish-speaking readers* (Scientific American). [< *post-* + *-face*, as in *preface*]

post·fix (*v.* pōst fiks′; *n.* pōst′fiks), *v.t.* to affix at the end of something; append; suffix. —*n.* a word, syllable, or letter added to the end of a word; suffix. [< *post-* + *fix*, verb; patterned on *prefix*]

post·free (pōst′frē′), *adj.* **1.** free from postage charge, as the official mail of a government department or of certain government officials. **2.** with the postage prepaid; postpaid.

post·fron·tal (pōst frun′təl), *adj.* **1.** behind the forehead. **2.** toward the rear of the frontal lobe of the cerebrum.

post·gan·gli·on·ic (pōst′gang lē on′ik), *adj.* (of nerve fibers) lying within or behind an autonomic ganglion.

post·gla·cial (pōst glā′shəl), *adj.* coming after the glacial period or ice age; Recent: *The Colorado plateau . . . has been pushed upward some 2,000 feet in the present postglacial period* (Scientific American).

post·grad (pōst grad′), *n., adj. Informal.* postgraduate: *"I've got a B.A. from Toronto and I've done a year of postgrad work"* (Maclean's).

post·grad·u·ate (pōst graj′ů it), *n.* a student who continues studying in college or at school after graduation; graduate student.
—*adj.* **1.** taking a course of study after graduation. **2.** of or for postgraduates: *Some 20,000 family doctors . . . spend at least 150 hours every three years in postgraduate medical study* (Newsweek).

post·haste (pōst′hāst′), *adv.* very speedily; in great haste: *This . . . brought Mr. Beaulieu Plummer post-haste from the estate office up to the house* (H. G. Wells).
—*n. Archaic.* haste or speed like that of a messenger: *Norfolk and myself, In haste, post-haste, are come to join with you* (Shakespeare).
[apparently < *post*[3] courier + *haste*, noun; perhaps influenced by former letter directions, *haste post! haste*]

post hoc (pōst′ hok′), *Latin.* after this; subsequent: *Though all this has been post hoc to the formation of CND, it is of course by no means certain that it has been in any way propter hoc* (Punch).

post hoc, er·go prop·ter hoc (pōst′ hok ėr′gō prop′tər hok), *Latin.* after this, therefore as a result of this (a common logical fallacy that what comes before another must also be its cause): *But no cancer-causing agent was known in tobacco smoke, so medical researchers were careful not to fall into the arguing post hoc, ergo propter hoc* (Time).

post·hole (pōst′hōl′), *n.* a hole dug in the ground to receive the end of a post: *At the bottom of the trench are the excavated postholes of an ancient Indian house* (Scientific American).

post·horn (pōst′hôrn′), *n.* a small horn similar to a bugle, formerly used by a post-rider or the guard of a mail coach to announce arrival, and now sometimes used on coaches. [< *post*[3] + *horn*]

post horse, a horse hired by travelers.

post·house (pōst′hous′), *n.* (formerly) a house where relays of post horses were kept for the convenience of travelers: *There was also a separate chain of posthouses, maintained for the royal messengers* (Scientific American).

post·hu·mous (pos′chů məs), *adj.* **1.** born after the death of the father: *a posthumous child.* **2.** published after the death of the author: *a posthumous book.* **3.** happening after death: *posthumous fame.* [< Late Latin *posthumus*, (with English *-ous*) variant of Latin *postumus* last born; (originally) superlative of *post* after; the *h* appeared because it was erroneously taken as < *post* after + *humus* earth; the grave]

post·hu·mous·ly (pos′chů məs lē), *adv.* after death: *He was posthumously restored to his former rank in the U.S. Army Air Corps* (Newsweek).

post·hyp·not·ic (pōst′hip not′ik), *adj.* **1.** after hypnosis: *a posthypnotic trance.* **2.** (of a suggestion given during hypnosis) intended to be carried out after the subject has emerged from hypnosis: *Scientists used posthypnotic suggestion to induce people to . . . dream about certain subjects* (Morris Fishbein). —**post′hyp·not′i·cal·ly,** *adv.*

pos·tiche (pôs tēsh′), *adj.* **1.** added inappropriately, as ornament. **2.** false; counterfeit.
—*n.* **1.** an imitation or substitute: *Fastidiousness, at any rate, is very good postiche for modesty* (Ouida). **2.** a pretense. **3.** a false hairpiece.
[< French *postiche* < Italian *appositiccio* < Late Latin *appositīcius* additional < Latin *appōnere* to add to. Compare APPOSITE.]

pos·ti·cous (pos tī′kəs), *adj. Botany.* **1.**

posterior; turning outward. **2.** placed on the outer side of a stamen. [< Latin *postīcus* (with English *-ous*) posterior < *post* behind]

pos·til·ion or **pos·til·lion** (pōs til′yən, pos-), *n.* a man who rides one of the horses drawing a carriage [< French *postillon* < Italian *postiglione* < *posta* post, mail]

post·im·pres·sion·ism (pōst′im presh′ə niz əm), *n.* the doctrines and methods of a school of modern art which maintains that art must be complete self-expression untrammeled by rules, tradition, or reality. Cubism and expressionism are later developments of the postimpressionist movement. *Gauguin had just discovered a new way of painting flat areas with brilliant, arbitrary colors that marked the beginning of postimpressionism* (Time).

post·im·pres·sion·ist (pōst′im presh′ə nist), *n.* an artist who practices postimpressionism: *With the postimpressionists, the Louvre . . . bought not a single Cézanne, Van Gogh or Seurat before World War II* (Time). —*adj.* postimpressionistic: *His canvases are vigorous postimpressionist efforts* (Anthony Lewis).

post·im·pres·sion·is·tic (pōst′im presh′ə nis′tik), *adj.* of or having to do with postimpressionism.

post·ing[1] (pōs′ting), *n.* an assignment to a post, station, or position: *the posting of a soldier or policeman.* [< *post*[2] + *-ing*[1]]

post·ing[2] (pōs′ting), *n. Bookkeeping.* **1.** the transferring of an entry from journal to ledger. **2.** the entry of an item in due place and form. **3.** the bringing of account books up to date: *The posting of the totals of special columns is best performed at the end of each month* (Schmidt and Bergstrom). [< *post*[3] + *-ing*[1]]

post·lim·i·nar·y (pōst lim′ə ner′ē), *adj.* of or having to do with the right of postliminy.

post·li·min·i·um (pōst′li min′ē əm), *n.* postliminy.

post·lim·i·ny (pōst lim′ə nē), *n.* (in international law) the right by which persons or things taken in war are restored to their former status when coming again under the control of the nation to which they belonged. [< Latin *postlīminium* a return behind one's own threshold < *post* behind + *līmen, -inis* threshold]

post·lude (pōst′lüd), *n.* **1.** a concluding musical piece or movement. **2.** music played at the end of a church service. [< *post-* + *-lude*, as in *prelude*]

post·man (pōst′mən), *n., pl.* **-men. 1.** a man who carries and delivers mail for the government; mailman. **2.** *Obsolete.* a mounted courier; postrider.

postman's knock, *British.* post office, a children's game.

post·mark (pōst′märk′), *n.* an official mark stamped on mail to cancel the postage stamp and record the place and date of mailing. —*v.t.* to stamp with a postmark: *The New York Stock Exchange recently received a letter postmarked Birmingham, Ala., inquiring about the purchase of two seats* (Wall Street Journal)

post·mas·ter (pōst′mas′tər, -mäs′-), *n.* **1.** a person in charge of a post office: *Postmasters furnished their own printed stamps, known as "Postmaster's Provisionals"* (New Yorker). **2.** *Obsolete.* the master of a station for supplying post horses to travelers.

postmaster general, *pl.* **postmasters general.** the person at the head of the postal system of a country.

post·mas·ter·ship (pōst′mas′tər ship, -mäs′-), *n.* the office or term of office of a postmaster.

post·me·rid·i·an (pōst′mə rid′ē ən), *adj.* occurring after noon; of or having to do with the afternoon: *the postmeridian sun.* [< Latin *postmerīdiānus* < *post merīdiem* post meridiem]

post me·rid·i·em (mə rid′ē əm), after noon. *Abbr.:* p.m., P.M. [< Latin *post merīdiem* after midday; *merīdiem*, accusative of *merīdiēs* < *medius* middle + *diēs* day. Compare MERIDIAN.]

post·mil·le·nar·i·an (pōst′mil ə nãr′ē ən), *n.* a postmillennialist.

post·mil·le·nar·i·an·ism (pōst′mil ə nãr′ē ə niz′əm), *n.* postmillennialism.

post·mil·len·ni·al (pōst′mə len′ē əl), *adj.* of or having to do with the period following the millennium.

post·mil·len·ni·al·ism (pōst′mə len′ē ə liz′əm), *n.* the doctrine or belief that the second coming of Christ will follow the millennium.

post·mil·len·ni·al·ist (pōst′mə len′ē ə list), *n.* a believer in postmillennialism.

post·mis·tress (pōst′mis′tris), *n.* a woman in charge of a post office.

post·mor·tem (pōst môr′təm), *adj.* **1.** after death: *A post-mortem examination showed that the man had been poisoned.* **2.** of or used in an autopsy or autopsies. **3.** *Slang.* following, and concerned with, some difficult or unpleasant event: *a post-mortem debate or discussion.*
—*n.* **1.** an examination after death; autopsy: *He carried out a post-mortem on the body . . . the first he had carried out on a death caused by a blow* (London Times). **2.** *Slang.* a discussion following, and concerned with, some difficult or unpleasant event, such as the loss of an election or the failure of a new play: *After the final exams, we all gathered in the local coffee shop for a post-mortem.*
—*v.t.* to make an autopsy on.
—*v.i.* to perform an autopsy.
[< Latin *post* after, *mortem*, accusative of *mors, mortis* death]

post·na·sal (pōst nā′zəl), *adj.* behind the nose or nasal cavity.

post·na·tal (pōst nā′təl), *adj.* after birth: *I . . . had . . . hopes, therefore, that his son's blunders might be due to postnatal, rather than congenital misfortunes* (Samuel Butler). —**post·na′tal·ly,** *adv.*

post·nup·tial (pōst nup′shəl), *adj.* after marriage: *a postnuptial gift to a wife.* —**post·nup′tial·ly,** *adv.*

post·o·bit (pōst ō′bit, -ob′it), *n.* a written agreement signed by a borrower promising to pay a certain sum of money to the lender on the death of a person whose heir the borrower expects to be. —*adj.* effective after a person's death. [short for Late Latin *post obitum* after death < Latin *post* after, *obitum*, accusative of *obitus, -ūs* destruction, death; (literally) an approach to anything < *ob-* to + *īre* to go]

post ob·i·tum (pōst ob′ə təm), *Latin.* after death.

post office, 1. a place where mail is handled and postage stamps are sold. **2.** Often, **Post Office.** the government department that takes charge of mail: *The Post Office has mechanized the handling of paper work* (Newsweek). **3.** a children's game in which players are called to another room (the post office) to be kissed (to get mail). Each player calls for the next. *Often at children's parties, someone's rather showily broad-minded mother would suggest a game of Spin the Bottle or Post Office* (New Yorker).

post-of·fice box (pōst′ôf′is, -of′-), Also, **Post Office Box.** a rented box or pigeonhole at a post office, in which all the letters and papers for a private person, firm, or organization are put and kept till called for. *Abbr.:* P.O.B.

post-office order, *British.* a type of money order issued by a post office for a sum payable to a person whose name is given in an accompanying official letter.

post·op·er·a·tive (post op′ə rā′tiv, -ər ə-), *adj* occurring after a surgical operation: *postoperative pains.* —**post·op′er·a′tive·ly,** *adv.*

post·or·bit·al (pōst ôr′bə təl), *adj.* situated behind the socket or orbit of the eye.

post·paid (pōst′pād′), *adj.* with the postage paid for.

post·par·tum (pōst pär′təm), *adj.* taking place after the birth of a child: *postpartum hemorrhage. Postpartum mental illness hits from one out of 300 to one out of 750 mothers* (Science News Letter). [< Latin *post* after + *partum*, accusative of *partus, -ūs* a giving birth < *parere* to bring forth]

post·plane (pōst′plān′), *n.* an airplane employed in the postal service; mailplane.

post·pon·a·ble (pōst pō′nə bəl), *adj.* that can be postponed: *A drop in egg prices shows up quickly in postponable purchases in country stores* (Wall Street Journal).

post·pone (pōst pōn′), *v.,* **-poned, -pon·ing.** —*v.t.* **1.** to put off till later; put off to a later time: *The ball game was postponed because of rain. He postponed his departure until after supper* (H. G. Wells). **2.** to place after in order of importance or estimation; subordinate: *to postpone private gain to the public welfare.* —*v.i.* **1.** to delay. **2.** *Medicine.* to be later in coming on or recurring, as an attack of malaria, etc. [< Latin *postpōnere* < *post-* after + *pōnere* to put, place] —**post·pon′er,** *n.* —**Syn.** *v.t., v.i.* **1.** defer. See **delay.**

post·pone·ment (pōst pōn′mənt), *n.* a putting off till later; delay: *There was no need for the postponement of our marriage* (Mary E. Braddon). —**Syn.** deferment.

post·po·si·tion (pōst′pə zish′ən), *n.* **1.** the act of placing after. **2.** the state of being placed after. **3.** *Grammar.* a word or particle placed after or at the end of a word, as a modifier or to show syntactical relationship. *Example:* In *postmaster general* the adjective *general* is a postposition. [< Late Latin *postpositiō, -ōnis* < Latin *postpōnere* postpone]

post·pos·i·tive (pōst poz′ə tiv), *Grammar.* —*adj.* placed after or at the end of a word; enclitic. —*n.* a postpositive word or particle. —**post·pos′i·tive·ly,** *adv.*

post·pran·di·al (pōst pran′dē əl), *adj.* after-dinner: *a postprandial nap.* [< Latin *post* after + *prandium* luncheon, meal + English *-al*[1]] —**post·pran′di·al·ly,** *adv.*

post·rid·er (pōst′rī′dər), *n.* a man who carries mail or dispatches on horseback.

post road, 1. a road or route over which mail is or was carried: *It was in Westport, Connecticut, in a cottage not far from the old post road, that Van Wyck Brooks settled down* (Edward Weeks). **2.** a road with stations which furnish horses.

pos·trorse (pos trôrs′), *adj. Biology.* retrorse. [< New Latin *postrorsus* < Latin *posterior* posterior + (*ve*)*rsus* turned]

post·script (pōst′skript), *n.* **1.** an addition to a letter, written after the writer's name has been signed: *Sir Gervaise, like a woman, had written his mind in his postscript* (James Fenimore Cooper). *Abbr.:* P.S. **2.** a supplementary part appended to any composition or literary work: *Lazarsfeld . . . touches the nerve of the matter in his postscript to the study* (Saturday Review). [short for earlier *postscriptum* < Medieval Latin, (originally) neuter past participle of *postscribere* < Latin *post-* after + *scrībere* to write] —**Syn. 2.** addendum, appendix.

post·script·al (pōst skrip′təl), *adj.* of or like a postscript.

post·syn·ap·tic (pōst′si nap′tik), *adj.* occurring after a synapse: *In the chapter on synaptic transmission, major emphasis is placed on postsynaptic events* (Science).

post ten·e·bras lux (pōst ten′ə bras luks), *Latin.* after darkness light.

post time, the time set for the start of a horse race: *Post time for the first race is 10:30 A.M.* (New Yorker).

post town, *British.* a town where the main post office of a given area is located: *. . . a stored list of the 2200 GPO post towns* (New Scientist).

post·trau·mat·ic (pōst′trô mat′ik), *adj.* occurring after a wound: *a posttraumatic disorder.*

pos·tu·lant (pos′chə lənt), *n.* **1.** a candidate, especially for admission to a religious order: *Each year some 75 young women between the ages of 16 and 30 are accepted as postulants* (Time). **2.** a person who asks or applies for something; petitioner. [< Latin *postulāns, -antis*, present participle of *postulāre* to demand]

pos·tu·late (*n.* pos′chə lit; *v.* pos′chə lāt), *n., v.,* **-lat·ed, -lat·ing.** —*n.* something taken for granted or assumed as a basis for reasoning; a fundamental principle; necessary condition: *One postulate in geometry is that a straight line may be drawn between any two points. The underlying postulate . . . was that knowledge is good and that those who advance knowledge need no further justification for their existence* (Bertrand Russell). —*v.t.* **1.** to take for granted; assume without proof as a basis of reasoning; require as a fundamental principle or necessary condition: *Geometry postulates many things as a basis for its reasoning.* **2.** to require; demand; claim. [< New Latin *postulatum* < Latin *postulāre* to demand] —**Syn.** *n.* hypothesis.

pos·tu·la·tion (pos′chə lā′shən), *n.* **1.** a postulating: *Professor Einstein's postulation of the equivalence of mass and energy through the concept of relativity* (Bulletin of Atomic Scientists). **2.** the thing postulated.

pos·tu·la·tion·al (pos′chə lā′shə nəl), *adj.* of or having to do with a postulation.

pos·tu·la·tor (pos′chə lā′tər), *n.* a person who postulates.

pos·tur·al (pos′chər əl), *adj.* of or having to do with posture: *exercises to correct a postural defect.*

pos·ture (pos′chər), *n., v.,* **-tured, -tur·ing.** —*n.* **1.** the position of the body; way of

holding the body: *Good posture is important for health.* **2.** a condition; situation; state: *In the present posture of public affairs it is difficult to invest money without good advice.* **3.** a mental or spiritual attitude: *A firm policy is likely to be lacking until the President determines what should be the total American posture toward Russia* (Atlantic). **4.** a pose, as of an artist's model; the attitude of a figure in a painting, etc. **5.** an affected or unnatural attitude; contortion of the body: *He would . . . dance about him, and make a thousand antic postures and gestures* (Daniel Defoe).
—*v.i.* **1.** to take a certain posture: *The dancer postured before the mirror, bending and twisting her body.* **2.** to pose for effect.
—*v.t.* to put in a certain posture: *Alice had been playing with the mirror's reflections—posturing her arms . . . clasping her hands behind her neck* (Booth Tarkington).
[< French *posture* < Italian *postura* < Latin *positūra* < *pōnere* to place] —**pos'tur·er,** *n.*
—**Syn.** *n.* **1.** carriage, bearing, stance. **2.** phase. **3.** outlook.

posture master, *Archaic.* **1.** a contortionist or acrobat: *throwing himself into all the attitudes of a posture master* (Herman Melville). **2.** a teacher of postures.

pos·tur·ize (pos'chə rīz), *v.t., v.i.,* **-ized, -iz·ing.** to pose; posture.

post·vo·cal·ic (pōst'vō kal'ik), *adj.* following immediately after a vowel: *The lack of constriction of post-vocalic -r . . . in burn, barn, beard occurs mostly in eastern New England, New York City, and the South Atlantic States* (Raven I. McDavid, Jr.).

post·war (pōst'wôr'), *adj.* after the war: *postwar economy.*

post·wom·an (pōst'wům'ən), *n., pl.* **-wom·en.** a woman who carries and delivers mail for the government.

po·sy (pō'zē), *n., pl.* **-sies. 1.** a flower. **2.** a bunch of flowers; bouquet. **3.** a motto or line of poetry engraved within a ring, etc. [variant of *poesy*] —**Syn. 2.** nosegay.

pot[1] (pot), *n., v.,* **pot·ted, pot·ting.** —*n.* **1.** a round, deep container made of metal or earthenware. There are many different kinds of pots. **2. a.** a pot and what is in it. **b.** the amount a pot can hold: *He had a pot of beans.* **3.** alcoholic liquor: *He carries her into a public-house to give her a pot and a cake* (Daniel Defoe). **4.** a basket used to catch fish, lobsters, etc. **5.** *Informal.* a large sum of money: *If a man brings in a big new client, his share of the pot can be upped in a single partnership meeting* (Harper's). **6.** *Informal.* all the money bet at one time. **7. a.** a chamber pot. **b.** a chimney pot. **c.** a flower pot. **8.** a potshot. **9.** *Slang.* a potbelly. **10.** *British Slang.* a person of importance: *one of the principal men out there—a big pot* (Joseph Conrad). **11.** *U.S. Slang.* marijuana: *On the tour,* [*he*] *was introduced not only to modern jazz but to . . . "pot," as the musicians call it* (New Yorker).

go to pot, to go to ruin: *After losing his job he took to drinking and went to pot. We went by sea . . . and, coming back, had like to have gone to pot in a storm* (Tobias Smollett).

in one's pots, drunk: *In their pots* [*they*] *will promise anything* (Fynes Moryson).

keep the pot boiling, *Informal.* **a.** to make a living: *He doesn't earn much money—just enough to keep the pot boiling.* **b.** to keep things going in a lively way: *His lieutenants keep the rebellion pot boiling in . . . Ireland* (London Times).
—*v.t.* **1.** to put into a pot: *to pot young tomato plants.* **2.** to cook and preserve in a pot. **3.** to cook (meat) thoroughly by simmering or braising in a pot. **4.** to take a potshot at; shoot: *We had got to within sixty yards' range . . . and were just about to sit down comfortably to "pot" them* [*two lions*], *when they suddenly surprised us by . . . bolting off* (J. H. Patterson). **5.** *Informal.* to seize; win; secure. —*v.i.* **1.** to take a potshot; shoot: *These "townies" pot at game birds and animals* (Manchester Guardian Weekly). **2.** *Obsolete.* to drink liquor: *I learned it in England, where indeed they are most potent in potting* (Shakespeare).
[Old English *pott*] —**pot'like',** *adj.*

pot[2] (pot), *n. Scottish.* a deep hole in the ground; pit. [Middle English *pot;* perhaps special use of *pot*[1]. Compare dialectal Swedish *pott,* or *putt* pit, water hole.]

pot., potential.

po·ta·bil·i·ty (pō'tə bil'ə tē), *n.* potable quality: *the potability of sea water.*

po·ta·ble (pō'tə bəl), *adj.* fit for drinking; drinkable: *In dozens of places where the water was not potable, they set up purifying systems* (Newsweek).
—*n.* **potables, a.** anything drinkable: *He bought eatables and potables.* **b.** alcoholic liquor.
[< Late Latin *pōtābilis* < Latin *pōtāre* to drink]

po·tage (pô täzh'), *n. French.* soup: *As a base for homemade potages, the chicken broths put up in vacuum packed jars . . . are an enormous help . . . to the hurried soup maker* (New Yorker).

po·tam·ic (pə tam'ik), *adj.* having to do with rivers. [< Greek *potamós* river + English *-ic*]

pot·a·mo·log·i·cal (pot'ə mə loj'ə kəl), *adj.* of or having to do with potamology.

pot·a·mol·o·gist (pot'ə mol'ə jist), *n.* a person skilled in potamology.

pot·a·mol·o·gy (pot'ə mol'ə jē), *n.* the scientific study of rivers. [< Greek *potamós* river + English *-logy*]

pot·ash (pot'ash'), *n.* **1.** any of several substances made from various minerals, wood ashes, blast furnace dust, etc., and used in soap, fertilizers, and glass making. It is mainly impure potassium carbonate. When purified, it is known as pearlash. **2.** potassium. **3.** caustic potash; potassium hydroxide. **4.** potassium oxide. [< earlier *pot-ashes,* translation of Dutch *potasschen* (literally) pot ashes]

potash alum, alum; a mineral salt used in medicine, dyeing, etc.

potash bulbs, a combination of glass bulbs for holding a solution of caustic potash, used in chemical analysis of organic substances.

potash feldspar, orthoclase.

po·tass (pō tas'), *n.* **1.** potash. **2.** potassium.

po·tas·sa (pō tas'ə), *n.* potass; potash.

po·tas·sic (pə tas'ik), *adj.* **1.** of or having to do with potassium. **2.** containing potassium.

po·tas·si·um (pə tas'ē əm), *n.* a soft, silver-white, metallic chemical element, occurring in nature only in compounds, as in saltpeter. It is an alkali metal and oxidizes rapidly when exposed to the air. Potassium is the lightest element known except lithium. *Symbol:* K; *at. wt.:* (C^{12}) 39.102 or (O^{16}) 39.100; *at. no.:* 19; *valence:* 1. [earlier *potass* (< French *potasse* < New Latin *potassa*) + *-ium,* as in *sodium*]

po·tas·si·um-ar·gon dating (pə tas'ē əm är'gon), a method of dating organic, geological, or archaeological specimens by measuring in the rock in which a specimen is found the amount of argon accumulated through the decay of radioactive potassium: *By means of potassium-argon dating, the age of the African man, Zinjanthropus, has been determined to be 1,750,000 years in the past* (Science News Letter).

potassium bicarbonate, a colorless, odorless substance with a slightly salty taste, obtained by passing carbon dioxide into a solution of potassium carbonate in water, and used in baking in place of baking powder or yeast, in medicine, and as a fire-extinguishing agent. *Formula:* $KHCO_3$

potassium bisulfate, a colorless salt, used in fusing metals and converting tartrates into potassium bitartrate. *Formula:* $KHSO_4$

potassium bitartrate, cream of tartar.

potassium bromide, a white, crystalline substance with a pungent, salty taste, used in medicine as a sedative, in photography, etc. *Formula:* KBr

potassium carbonate, a white, alkaline salt obtained from wood ashes, etc., used in making glass, soft soaps, fertilizers, etc. *Formula:* K_2CO_3

potassium chlorate, a colorless, poisonous, crystalline substance used as an oxidizing agent in explosives, matches, etc. *Formula:* $KClO_3$

potassium chloride, a colorless or white, crystalline compound obtained chiefly from carnallite, used in fertilizers, explosives, etc. *Formula:* KCl

potassium citrate, a white, crystalline substance used in medicine as a diuretic, expectorant, and antacid. In certain heart operations, potassium citrate is introduced into the coronary blood vessels to arrest heart beat. *Formula:* $K_3C_6H_5O_7.H_2O$

potassium cyanate, a white crystal or powder used in the manufacture of drugs, in organic synthesis, and to kill weeds, crabgrass, etc. *Formula:* KCNO

potassium cyanide, a very poisonous, white, crystalline compound used for removing gold from ore, in electroplating, as an insecticide, in photography, etc. *Formula:* KCN

potassium dichromate, a poisonous, yellowish-red, crystalline salt used in dyeing, in photography, as an oxidizing agent, etc. *Formula:* $K_2Cr_2O_7$

potassium fluoride, a white, crystalline, poisonous powder, used as a preservative and a disinfectant, in insecticides, and in etching glass. *Formula:* KF

potassium hydroxide, a very strong alkali used in making soft soap and as a reagent; caustic potash. *Formula:* KOH

potassium iodide, a colorless or white, crystalline compound, used in manufacturing photographic emulsions, as an additive in iodized table salt, and in medicine as an expectorant. *Formula:* KI

potassium nitrate, a colorless or white, crystalline salt used as an oxidizing agent, in gunpowder, explosives, and fertilizers, in preserving meat, and in medicine; niter; saltpeter. *Formula:* KNO_3

potassium permanganate, a dark purple crystalline compound used as an oxidizing agent, disinfectant, etc. *Formula:* $KMnO_4$

potassium sodium tartrate, Rochelle salt.

potassium sulfate, a colorless or white, crystalline salt used as a reagent, in fertilizers, in medicine as a cathartic, in making glass, etc. *Formula:* K_2SO_4

po·ta·tion (pō tā'shən), *n.* **1.** the act of drinking. **2.** a drink, especially of alcoholic liquor. [< Old French *potacion,* or *potation,* learned borrowing from Latin *pōtātiō, -ōnis* < *pōtāre* to drink]

po·ta·to (pə tā'tō), *n., pl.* **-toes. 1.** a starchy tuber of a cultivated plant of the nightshade family, the vegetable most widely used in Europe and America; white potato; Irish potato. **2.** the plant producing these tubers, originating in South America. Potatoes have trumpet-shaped flowers that are white, bluish or purplish. **3.** the sweet potato. [< Spanish *patata* < Carib (perhaps Taino) *batata* sweet potato]

potato beetle, a black-and-yellow striped beetle that damages potato plants; Colorado potato beetle.

EGGS LARVA ADULT ADULT

Potato Beetle
(Line shows actual length.)

potato blight, a destructive disease of the potato in which the leaves and stem develop yellow, brown, and black spots, caused by a parasitic fungus; late blight: *About 20,000 acres in Lincolnshire are now being sprayed with liquid chemical to combat the threatening potato blight* (New Scientist).

potato bug, a potato beetle.

potato chip, *U.S.* a thin slice of raw potato fried in deep fat: *Our "potato chips" are their* [*British*] *"crisps"* (Holiday).

potato crisp, *British.* a potato chip: *I subsided gratefully on to a ravaged packet of potato crisps* (Punch).

potato family, a name occasionally used for the nightshade family.

potato psyl·lid (sil'id), an insect related to the aphids that attacks potato plants, transmitting a viral disease which causes extensive damage to the leaves. [< New Latin *Psyllidae* the family name < Greek *psýlla* flea]

potato race, a race in which each runner picks up and carries to a receptacle, one at a time, potatoes placed at intervals along the course. The potato is often carried with a spoon or knife.

potato ring, a ring or decorated circular band of silver, used as a stand for a bowl in Ireland in the 1700's, and mistakenly believed to have held potatoes together on a table.

po·ta·to·ry (pō'tə tôr'ē, -tōr'-), *adj.* **1.** of, having to do with, or given to drinking. **2.** drinkable. [< Late Latin *pōtātōrius* < Latin *pōtāre* to drink]

potato vine, 1. the potato plant, especially the part above ground. **2.** a North American vine of the morning-glory family, having large, white and purplish, funnel-shaped flowers and a large root; man-of-the-earth.

potato worm, the larva of a sphinx or hawk moth which attacks potatoes, tomatoes, tobacco, and related plants.

pot-au-feu (pô′tō fœ′), *n. French.* **1.** beef and vegetables cooked together as a stew: *Finally, to have done with our rich man, seldom does he see . . . the pot-au-feu itself —the foundation glory of French cooking* (New Yorker). **2.** (literally) pot on the fire.

Pot·a·wat·o·mi (pot′ə wot′ə mē), *n., pl.* **-mi** or **-mis. 1.** a tribe of North American Indians inhabiting the area of Lakes Michigan and Superior. **2.** a member of this tribe. **3.** the Algonkian language of this tribe.

pot·bank (pot′bangk′), *n. British.* a building in which pottery is made: *One contemporary account describes such a potbank in the 1840's* (London Times).

pot·bel·lied (pot′bel′ēd), *adj.* having a potbelly: *The Firebee is an ugly little pilotless airplane, built like a potbellied bug* (Time).

pot·bel·ly (pot′bel′ē), *n., pl.* **-lies.** a distended or protuberant belly. —**Syn.** paunch.

potbelly or **potbellied stove,** a round, squat, wood- or coal-burning stove used for heating.

pot·boil (pot′boil′), *v.t., v.i.* to write or otherwise produce (a potboiler): *For ten years, hopeful author [Marjorie] Rawlings worked on newspapers, potboiled syndicated verse, wrote (but seldom sold) short stories* (Time).

pot·boil·er (pot′boi′lər), *n.* a work of literature or art produced merely to make a living: *In this magnolia-scented potboiler of the Civil War era, he has little to offer his readers* (Time). [the "boiling pot" is symbolic of the necessities of life]

pot·bound (pot′bound′), *adj.* (of plants) having roots that have grown practically to fill the pot, so the plant cannot grow more without repotting.

pot·boy (pot′boi′), *n.* a man or boy who works in a tavern, serving customers, washing glasses, etc.

pot cheese, *U.S.* cottage cheese, usually in large curds: *Cottage cheese and pot cheese are the only cheeses suitable to a low-calorie diet* (Consumer Reports).

pot companion, a drinking companion; boon companion.

po·teen (pō tēn′), *n.* (in Ireland) illicitly distilled whiskey: *You may drink your poteen hot from the still, or, if you are a man of continence, you may wait till it cools* (New Yorker). Also, **potheen.** [< Irish *poitīn,* short for *uisge poitīn* poteen whiskey, (literally, diminutive) < *pota* pot, vessel, probably < English *pot*[1]]

pot egg, an artificial nest egg: *Inside, the nest is made of well-patted, hollowed out earth with some straw on top and a few pot eggs* (Susan Egerton-Jones).

Po·tem·kin Village (pō tem′kin), a false façade intended to cover up a bad situation, activity, etc.: *The Party's myth of a bright future might seem to Russian poets like the biggest Potemkin Village of them all* (New Yorker). [< Prince Grigori *Potemkin,* 1739-1791, a Russian statesman and governor of the Crimea, who is said to have fooled Catherine the Great during her tour of the Crimea in 1787 by building sham villages to hide the area's actual poverty]

po·tence (pō′təns), *n.* potency, power, or strength.

po·ten·cy (pō′tən sē), *n., pl.* **-cies. 1.** power; strength: *the potency of an argument, the potency of a drug.* **2.** power to develop: *Books . . . do contain a potency of life in them to be as active as that soul was whose progeny they are* (Milton). [< Latin *potentia* < *potēns, -entis;* see POTENT] —**Syn. 1.** force, efficacy. **2.** potentiality.

po·tent (pō′tənt), *adj.* **1.** having great power; powerful: *a potent remedy for a disease, potent reasons.* **2.** exercising great moral influence: *if bravery be the most potent charm to win the favor of the fair* (Francis Parkman). *His good deeds had a potent effect on his comrades.* **3.** having sexual power. **4.** *Heraldry.* (of a cross) having arms that end in a form like the head of a crutch. [< Latin *potēns, -entis,* present participle of unrecorded Old Latin *potēre* be powerful, able < *potis* powerful] —**po′tent·ly,** *adv.* —**po′tent·ness,** *n.* —**Syn. 1.** mighty, strong.

po·ten·tate (pō′tən tāt), *n.* **1.** a person having great power: *In the base camps of the Big Four, a panoply of potentates and elected chieftains made ready for the fateful journey* (Time). **2.** a ruler: *Kings, queens, and emperors are potentates.* **3.** a powerful city, state, or the like. [< Late Latin *potentātus, -ūs* potentate < Latin, power, dominion < *potēns;* see POTENT] —**Syn. 1.** autocrat. **2.** monarch, sovereign.

po·ten·tial (pə ten′shəl), *adj.* **1.** possible as opposed to actual; capable of coming into being or action: *The potential efficiency of modern chemical weapons is generally comparable to that of atomic weapons* (Bulletin of Atomic Scientists). **2.** *Grammar.* expressing possibility, as by the use of *may, might, can, could,* etc.: *the potential subjunctive or potential mood.* **3.** *Physics.* existing in a positional form, not as motion. **4.** having to do with voltage.

—*n.* **1.** something potential; possibility: *Many markets of massive potential await American wares abroad* (Wall Street Journal). **2.** *Grammar.* **a.** the potential subjunctive or potential mood. **b.** a verb form or verbal phrase used thus. **3.** the amount of electrification of a point with reference to some standard; electromotive force expressed in volts: *A current of high potential is used in transmitting electric power over long distances. When the ends of a wire are connected to two points . . . such as the terminals of a cell or generator, there will be a current in the wire but the potential of each point of the wire remains constant in time* (Sears and Zemansky). **4.** *Physics.* a function or quantity that expresses force, as electromotive force.

[< Late Latin *potentiālis* < Latin *potentia* potency < *potēns* potent]

—**Syn.** *adj.* **1.** See **latent.**

potential energy, energy that is due to position or the like, not to motion: *A tightly coiled spring or a raised weight has potential energy. The potential energy stored up in a pair of attracting bodies is equal to the work that would be necessary to pull them infinitely apart* (Scientific American).

po·ten·ti·al·i·ty (pə ten′shē al′ə tē), *n., pl.* **-ties. 1.** potential state or quality; possibility as opposed to actuality; latent power or capacity: *We feel that the potentialities of the human brain are inexhaustible* (Scientific American). **2.** something potential; a possibility.

po·ten·tial·ize (pə ten′shə līz), *v.t.,* **-ized, -iz·ing.** to make potential; give potentiality to.

po·ten·tial·ly (pə ten′shə lē), *adv.* possibly, but not yet actually.

po·ten·ti·ate (pə ten′shē āt), *v.t.,* **-at·ed, -at·ing.** to give power or potency to; make more active; strengthen: *Miltown didn't potentiate the effects of alcohol—a very important thing for some drivers to know* (New Yorker).

—**Syn.** increase, intensify.

po·ten·ti·a·tion (pə ten′shē ā′shən), *n.* a making more active; a strengthening; increase; intensification.

po·ten·ti·a·tor (pə ten′shē ā′tər), *n.* something that potentiates: *MSG is known to the trade as a flavor potentiator* (New Yorker).

po·ten·til·la (pō′tən til′ə), *n.* any of a large group of low plants of the rose family that have mainly pinnate or palmate compound leaves, and are widely found in temperate regions; cinquefoil. [< New Latin *Potentilla* the genus name < Medieval Latin *potentilla* garden valerian < Latin *potēns, -entis* potent + *-illa,* a diminutive suffix]

po·ten·ti·om·e·ter (pə ten′shē om′ə tər), *n.* **1.** an instrument for measuring electromotive force: *The potentiometer . . . is a device for accurately measuring the ratio of two voltages. Since one of these is usually the accurately known voltage of a standard cell, the potentiometer serves for precision measurement of the other, unknown, voltage* (Shortley and Williams). **2.** an instrument for changing or controlling electromotive force.

po·ten·ti·o·met·ric (pə ten′shē ə met′rik), *adj.* of or by means of a potentiometer.

po·tent·i·za·tion (pō′tən tə zā′shən), *n.* **1.** a making potent. **2.** a being made potent.

po·tent·ize (pō′tən tīz), *v.t.,* **-ized, -iz·ing. 1.** to make potent. **2.** to develop the power of (a drug) by attenuation.

pot·ful (pot′fu̇l), *n., pl.* **-fuls.** as much as a pot can hold.

pot furnace, a furnace in which there are pots for melting small amounts of glass: *For low-volume special glass products, pot furnaces and day tanks are used* (George J. Bair).

pot·hang·er (pot′hang′ər), *n.* **1.** a rack, bar, etc., for hanging a pothook or a pot at different heights over an open fire. **2.** a stroke in writing like a pothook; any irregular written character: *When I started doing pothooks and pothangers . . ., the teacher transferred the pencil firmly from my left hand to my right* (London Times).

poth·e·car·y (poth′ə kãr′ē), *n., pl.* **-car·ies.** *Archaic.* apothecary.

po·theen (pō thēn′), *n.* poteen.

poth·er (poᴛʜ′ər), *n.* **1.** confusion; disturbance; fuss: *The children are making a great pother about the picnic.* **2.** a choking cloud of dust or smoke. **3.** mental disturbance.

—*v.t.* to bother; worry. —*v.i.* to fuss.

[earlier *puther;* origin uncertain; pronunciation influenced by *bother*] —**Syn.** *n.* **1.** commotion, flurry. *-v.t.* harass.

pot·herb (pot′ėrb′, -hėrb′), *n.* **1.** any plant whose leaves and stems are boiled as a vegetable, such as spinach. **2.** a plant used as seasoning in cooking, such as sage or parsley.

pot·hold·er (pot′hōl′dər), *n.* a thick pad of cloth or other material for handling hot pots, lids, etc.

pot·hole (pot′hōl′), *n.* **1.** a deep, round hole, especially one made in rock by stones and gravel being spun around in the current of a river: *In one Saskatchewan area, four-fifths of all sloughs and potholes normally filled with water are dry* (Maclean's). **2.** a depression or hollow part forming a defect in the surface of a street or road: *They need frequent wheel alignment because they drive up on curbs and don't bother to steer around potholes* (Maclean's).

pot·holed (pot′hōld′), *adj.* having many potholes: *potholed streets.*

pot·hol·er (pot′hō′lər), *n. Informal.* a speleologist: *Neither paleolithic men, nor the potholers of today had ever been here before us* (Time).

pot·hook (pot′hu̇k′), *n.* **1.** a hook for hanging a pot or kettle over an open fire. **2.** a rod with a hook for lifting hot pots, etc. **3.** an S-shaped stroke in writing, especially one made by children in learning to write.

po·thos (pō′thos), *n.* any of a genus of climbing shrubs of the arum family, with glossy, heart-shaped leaves, native to tropical areas of the Old World. Some kinds are cultivated as foliage plants. [< New Latin *Pothos* the genus name < Singhalese *pōtha*]

pot·house (pot′hous′), *n.* a tavern or alehouse.

pot·hunt·er (pot′hun′tər), *n.* **1.** a person who shoots anything he comes upon regardless of the rules of sport: *flocks [of birds] that have escaped the murderous gun of the pothunter* (George W. Cable). **2.** a person who takes part in contests merely to win prizes. **3.** a person who hunts for food or for profit. **4.** a person who digs up or hunts for archaeological objects as a hobby; an amateur archaeologist: *The Southwestern archaeologist looks upon the Sunday digger as a . . . reckless despoiler of irreplaceable antiquities. To him "pothunter" is a swearword* (Harper's).

pot·hunt·ing (pot′hun′ting), *n., adj.* hunting as a pothunter.

po·tiche (pō tēsh′), *n., pl.* **-tiches** (-tēsh′). a vase or jar of Chinese or Japanese style with a rounded or polygonal body narrowing at the top. [< French *potiche* an Oriental porcelain vase < *pot* pot, vessel < Vulgar Latin *pottus*]

Potiche

po·ti·cho·ma·ni·a (pō′tə-shō mā′nē ə), *n.* the art or process of imitating Japanese or other painted porcelain by coating the inner surface of glass vessels with designs painted on paper or linen: *Charlotte Yonge more than once mentions the art of potichomania in her novels* (London Times). [< French *potichomanie* < *potiche* (see POTICHE) + *manie* mania]

po·tion (pō′shən), *n.* **1.** a drink, especially one that is used as a medicine or poison, or in magic: *a pitch-like potion of gin and molasses . . . a sovereign cure for all colds and catarrhs* (Herman Melville). *You promised me that your charms and potions would secure me her acceptance* (Nicholas P.S. Wiseman). **2.** a kind of drink or beverage: *As to the intoxicating potion sold for wine, it is a vile, unpalatable, and pernicious sophistication* (Tobias Smollett). [< Old French *pocion,* or *potion* < Latin *pōtiō, -ōnis.* Doublet of POISON.]

Pot·i·phar (pot′ə fər), *n.* (in the Bible) an officer of Pharaoh, who owned Joseph as a slave. Potiphar's wife tried to seduce Joseph. Genesis 39:1-23.

pot·latch (pot′lach′), *n.* **1.** a gift or present among certain American Indians of the northern Pacific coast: *They [Indians] . . . expressed the friendliest sentiments, perhaps with a view to a liberal "potlatch" of trinkets* (Theodore Winthrop). **2.** Also, **Potlatch.** a ceremonial festival among these Indians at which gifts are bestowed on the guests: *A Northwest Coast tribe [was] famous for their potlatches . . ., [at which] rich chiefs gave away or destroyed enormous quantities of valuable property . . . in order to display their wealth* (Melville Jacobs). **3.** *U.S. Informal.* a feast at which presents are given and received: *That night there was a grand wedding and a potlatch* (Jack London). [American English < Chinook jargon *potlatch* < Wakashan (Nootka) *patshatl* giving, or a gift]

pot·lead (pot′led′), *n.* a form of graphite or black lead, used to coat the bottom of a racing boat to reduce the friction of the water. —*v.t.* to treat (a boat) with potlead.

pot·lick·er or **pot·lik·ker** (pot′lik′ər), *n.* pot liquor.

pot·line (pot′līn′), *n.* a series of electrolytic cells in which aluminum is produced from alumina dissolved in a cryolite solution.

pot liquor, the liquid in which meat, vegetables, etc., have been cooked, used as broth, for gravy, etc.

pot·luck (pot′luk′), *n.* whatever food happens to be ready or on hand for a meal: *Lapham's idea of hospitality was still to bring a heavy-buying customer home to potluck* (William D. Howells).

take potluck, a. to be a guest and eat whatever food is ready or on hand: *Do, pray, stop and dine . . . take . . . potluck* (Richard H. Barham). **b.** to accept whatever is available: *I went to the auction to buy a lamp, but took potluck and came home with a candlestick.*

pot·man (pot′mən), *n., pl.* **-men.** *British.* a man who works as a potboy.

pot marigold, a common marigold, the flower heads of which were used for seasoning; calendula: *The marigold often mentioned in literature is the pot marigold* (World Book Encyclopedia).

po·too (pō tü′), *n.* a large goatsucker of the West Indies and Central America: *Mrs. Fry showed color movies of rare and brilliant birds like the weird potoo* (New York Times). [imitative of its cry]

po·to·roo (pō′tə rü′), *n., pl.* **-roos** or (*collectively*) **-roo.** a kangaroo rat. [< an Australian native word]

pot·pie (pot′pī′), *n. U.S.* **1.** a baked meat pie. **2.** a stew with dumplings.

pot·pour·ri (pō′pu̇ rē′, pot pu̇r′ē), *n., pl.* **-ris. 1.** a musical or literary medley: *The orchestra played a potpourri of Italian, French, and Austrian folksongs.* **2.** a fragrant mixture of dried flower petals and spices. [earlier, a mixed stew < French *pot pourri,* translation of Spanish *olla podrida* rotten pot. Compare OLLA PODRIDA.]

pot roast, beef browned in a pot and cooked slowly with only a little water.

pots (pots), *n.pl.* See under **pot**[1], *n.*

pot·sherd (pot′shėrd′), *n.* a broken piece of earthenware: *Some of the potsherds could be fitted together into graceful drinking vessels* (Time). [< *pot*[1] + *sherd,* variant of *shard*]

pot·shot (pot′shot′), *n.* **1.** a shot taken at game merely to provide a meal, with little regard to the rules of sport. **2.** a shot at or attack against something within easy reach, as from close range or from ambush: *Chinese Reds and their Nationalist enemies are taking potshots at each other between China's mainland and Quemoy* (Wall Street Journal).

pot still, a still in which heat is applied directly to a pot which contains the mash: *Irish whiskey is made in a pot still, which is simply a pot surrounded by Irish anthracite coal from Kilkenny* (Brendan Behan).

pot·stone (pot′stōn′), *n.* a kind of soapstone formerly used to make household utensils.

pot·sy (pot′sē), *n., pl.* **-sies. 1.** hopscotch: *Two girls were playing potsy, and the gaming area, on the sidewalk, had been marked out with yellow chalk* (New Yorker). **2.** the pebble used in hopscotch. [origin unknown]

pot·tage (pot′ij), *n.* a thick soup. [Middle English *potage* < Old French < *pot* pot (< Vulgar Latin *pottus*) + *-age* -age]

pot·ted (pot′id), *adj.* **1.** put into a pot: *In every corner and in front of the windows, ferns and potted plants squatted* (New Yorker). **2.** cooked and preserved in pots or cans: *potted beef.* **3.** *Slang.* drunk; intoxicated. **4.** *British Slang.* **a.** shortened; condensed: *a potted biography. For his potted tale of the unflappable Aeneas, Ovid plundered Virgil ruthlessly* (London Times). **b.** recorded; canned: *potted music.*

pot·ter[1] (pot′ər), *n.* a person who makes pots, dishes, vases, etc., out of clay. [Old English *pottere* < *pott* pot + *-ere* -er[1]]

pot·ter[2] (pot′ər), *v.i., v.t. Especially British.* to keep busy in a rather useless way; putter: *She potters about the house all day, but gets little done. But when one party has pottered along in power for ten years and more, the other is likely to be short of candidates* (H.F. Ellis). [(apparently frequentative) < obsolete *pote,* Old English *potian* to push, poke. Related to PUT[1], PUTTER[1].] —**pot′ter·er,** *n.* —**pot′ter·ing·ly,** *adv.*

potter's clay, clay that is free or nearly free from iron, suitable for making pottery.

potter's field, 1. a piece of ground for burying people who have no friends or money. **2.** (in the Bible) a field supposed to have been bought by Judas with his bribe for betraying Jesus, used as a burial place for strangers. Matthew 27:7-8.

Potter's Wheel

potter's wheel, a rotating horizontal disk upon which clay is molded into dishes, etc.

potter wasp, any of various solitary wasps that make vaselike mounds of mud and sand for their young. See the picture under **nest.**

pot·ter·y (pot′ər ē), *n., pl.* **-ter·ies. 1.** pots, dishes, vases, etc., made from clay and hardened by heat. **2.** the art or business of making them; ceramics. **3.** a place where they are made. [< Old French *poterie* < *potier* potter < *pot* pot < Vulgar Latin *pottus*]

Indian Pottery (def. 1)

pot·ting shed (pot′ing), a shed used by a gardener to plant or transplant flowers into pots, or to store equipment, etc.

pot·tle (pot′əl), *n.* **1.** a former liquid measure equal to two quarts. **2.** a pot or tankard holding two quarts. **3.** the liquid in it. **4.** alcoholic liquor. **5.** a small wicker basket: *a pottle of fine strawberries* (Tobias Smollett). [< Old French *potel* (diminutive) < *pot* pot < Vulgar Latin *pottus*]

pot·to (pot′ō), *n., pl.* **-tos. 1.** a small, sluggish, West African mammal resembling a lemur. It spends most of its time in trees, and is unique in having the spines of its vertebrae exposed. **2.** the kinkajou. [< a West African word]

Pott's disease (pots), tuberculosis of the spinal column, often resulting in a marked curvature of the spine caused by the destruction of affected vertebrae. [< Percival *Pott,* 1713-1788, a British surgeon who described the condition resulting from this disease]

pot·ty[1] (pot′ē), *adj.,* **-ti·er, -ti·est.** *British Informal.* **1.** petty; insignificant. **2.** foolish; crazy: *The pottier their ideas the better I like them* (Listener). [origin uncertain]

pot·ty[2] (pot′ē), *n., pl.* **-ties.** *Informal.* a small chamber pot.

pot-val·iant (pot′val′yənt), *adj.* brave through drink: *a man who has drunk himself pot-valiant* (Tobias Smollett).

pot-wal·lop·er (pot′wol′ə pər), *n.* **1.** (formerly in some British boroughs) a man who qualified as a voter by having a separate fireplace over which his own pots boiled. **2.** *U.S. Slang.* a kitchen worker of low grade, especially a dishwasher. [alteration of earlier *potwaller* < *pot*[1] + *waller* < *wall* to boil, Old English *weallan;* influenced by dialectal *wallop* boil hard]

pouch (pouch), *n.* **1.** a bag; sack: *a postman's pouch, a pouch of tobacco. A great leather pouch which held about a pound and a half of powder . . . and another with shot* (Daniel Defoe). **2.** a baglike fold of skin: *A kangaroo carries its young in a pouch. His lips were parted and pale, and there were deep pouches under the eyes* (Rudyard Kipling). **3. a.** a baglike cavity or cyst in a plant; silicle. **b.** any pocketlike space in the body: *the pharyngeal pouch, ileocecal pouch.* **4.** *Especially Scottish.* a pocket in a garment. **5.** a small bag to hold money: *a poor devil without penny in pouch* (Washington Irving).
—*v.t.* **1.** to put into a pouch or pocket; pocket. **2.** (of a fish or bird) to swallow. **3.** to submit to without protest: *I will pouch up no such affront* (Scott). **4.** *Informal.* to provide with money; give a present of money to: *Coningsby . . . had been pouched in a manner worthy of a Marquess* (Benjamin Disraeli). —*v.i.* to form a pouch or pouchlike cavity.
[< Old North French *pouche,* Old French *poche* < a Germanic word. Related to POKE[2].] —**pouch′like′,** *adj.*

pouched (poucht), *adj.* having a pouch, as pelicans, gophers, and kangaroos: *The common ancestor of all the kangaroos [probably] resembled the present-day tiny pouched mice* (New Scientist).

pouched rat, 1. the pocket gopher. See picture under **gopher. 2.** the kangaroo rat. **3.** any of various pouched rodents of Africa.

pouch·y (pou′chē), *adj.,* **pouch·i·er, pouch·i·est.** having pouches; like a pouch; baggy: *White hair abristle, pouchy eyes aflame, he tirelessly took the floor of the House to shrill the rebel yell of "white supremacy"* (Time).

pou·dreuse (pü drœz′), *n.* a small dressing table or vanity: *A Louis XV kingwood poudreuse [went] for £300* (London Times). [< French *poudreuse* < *poudre* powder]

pouf (püf), *n.* **1.** a kind of women's headdress fashionable at the end of the 1700's. It has reappeared in a modified form called bouffant. **2.** a high roll or pad of hair worn by women. **3.** any part of a dress gathered up in a bunch: *There are folds around it to the hips; below, in back, great butterfly-wing poufs spread outward* (New Yorker). **4.** a very soft, stuffed, backless ottoman or couch: *Here, in the tree house, they sat on brocaded poufs around a low, round table* (New Yorker). **5.** poof.
—*interj.* poof: *One moment they wring their dossiers inside out for you, and then—pouf!—they shut up like a clam* (New Yorker).
[< French *pouf* < Middle French; (originally) imitative of a sound; later extended to objects that appeared inflated, or puffed out. Compare PUFF.]

pouff or **pouffe** (püf), *n. Especially British.* pouf: *Fezes, sheepskins, and leather drawing room pouffes were recklessly bought from Arab peddlers at their asking price* (Punch).

Pou·jad·ism (pü zhä′diz əm), *n.* **1.** the movement, principles, and practices of the Poujadists: *Poujadism and serious tax reform are contradictions in terms, [since] the essence of M. Poujade's contribution to fiscal theory has been the vague notion that taxes should be paid at "the source"* (Harper's). **2.** any similar movement advocating drastic tax reduction: *It was an intellectual Poujadism with overtones of the Ku Klux Klan and prefigurations of Nazism* (A. J. Liebling).

Pou·jad·ist (pü zhä′dist), *n.* a member of a right-wing French political movement or party composed chiefly of small businessmen, that favors drastic reduction in taxation: *The Poujadists demanded abrogation of all penalties on tax fraud, and amnesties on all pending cases of tax evasion* (New York Times). —*adj.* of the Poujadists or Poujadism: *The Poujadist symbol, an enameled red cock crowing, flared from every lapel* (Time). [< French *Poujadiste* < Pierre *Poujade,* a store owner in central France who started the movement in 1953 + French *-iste* -ist]

pou·laine (pü lān′), *n.* **1.** a long, tapering point into which the toe of a shoe, etc., was prolonged, in a fashion of the 1300's and 1400's. **2.** a shoe or the like with such a point: *An extreme version of this Renaissance* *shoe, called the . . . poulaine, had bells or pompons attached to the high peak* (Wall Street Journal). [< Old French *poulaine, Poulaine* Poland (because this kind of shoe was worn there)]

pou·lard (pü lärd′), *n.* a young hen spayed to improve the flesh for use as food; a fattened hen. [< Middle French *poularde* < *poule* hen + *-arde,* a noun suffix; see POULTRY]

poule (pül), *n. French.* **1.** a prostitute. **2.** (literally) a hen.

poult (pōlt), *n.* a young turkey, pheasant, or other domestic fowl: *Agricultural scientists have shown that a number of different antibiotics make turkey poults and piglets grow faster* (H. O. J. Collier). [Middle English *poult,* short for *poullet* pullet < Old French *poulet;* see POULTRY]

poult-de-soie (pü′də swä′), *n. French.* a soft, rich, corded silk fabric of the grosgrain type; peau de soie: . . . *a full-length dress of white poult-de-soie* (New Yorker).

poul·ter (pōl′tər), *n. Obsolete.* a poulterer.

poul·ter·er (pōl′tər ər), *n.* a dealer in poultry. [< obsolete *poulter* dealer in poultry < Old French *pouletier* < *poulet* pullet; see POULTRY]

poul·tice (pōl′tis), *n., v.,* **-ticed, -tic·ing.** —*n.* a soft, moist mass of mustard, herbs, etc., applied hot to the body for therapy. —*v.t.* **1.** to put a poultice on. **2.** to soothe; salve: *I am not willing to spend . . . hours listening to someone denounce me in an effort to poultice his private wounds* (Harper's). [alteration of earlier *pultes* < Latin *pultēs,* plural of *puls, pultis* mush < Greek *póltos* porridge. Compare PULSE[2].]

poul·try (pōl′trē), *n.* chickens, turkeys, ducks, geese, etc.: *These aging birds provide much of the meat for firms that can poultry and turn out frozen chicken pies* (Wall Street Journal). [< Old French *pouleterie* < *poulet* pullet (diminutive) < *poule* hen < Vulgar Latin *pulla* < Latin *pullus* young fowl; young of animals in general]

poul·try·man (pōl′trē mən), *n., pl.* **-men.** **1.** a man who raises poultry commercially: *Many of us—fruit growers, livestock men, poultrymen, to name a few—receive none of the subsidies you talk about* (Wall Street Journal). **2.** a man who sells poultry, eggs, etc.

pounce[1] (pouns), *v.,* **pounced, pounc·ing,** *n.* —*v.i.* **1.** to come down with a rush and seize: *The cat pounced upon the mouse. His mother would pounce . . . on his remarks as a barn-owl pounces upon a mouse* (Samuel Butler). **2.** to dash, come, or jump suddenly: *to pounce onto the stage.* —*v.t.* to swoop down upon and seize suddenly: *As if an eagle . . . Stoop'd from his highest pitch to pounce a wren* (William Cowper). [< noun] —*n.* **1.** a sudden swoop or pouncing. **2.** the claw or talon of a bird of prey.
[apparently contraction of Middle English *ponchoun* an instrument for punching < Old French *poinchon;* see PUNCHEON[2]. Related to PUNCH[1].]

pounce[2] (pouns), *n., v.,* **pounced, pounc·ing.** —*n.* **1.** a fine powder formerly used to prevent ink from spreading in writing, or to prepare parchment for writing. **2.** a fine powder used for transferring a design through a stencil.
—*v.t.* **1.** to trace (a design) with pounce rubbed through perforations. **2.** to sprinkle, smooth, or prepare with pounce.
[< French, Old French *ponce* < Late Latin *pōmex,* for Latin *pūmex, -icis.* Doublet of PUMICE.] —**pounc′er,** *n.*

pounce[3] (pouns), *v.t.,* **pounced, pounc·ing.** *Obsolete.* **1.** to emboss (metal) with repoussé work. **2.** to ornament (a garment) with eyelets or figures cut out. [Middle English *pounsen,* variant of *pounsonen* to prick, pink < Old French *ponchonner,* apparently related to *poinchon;* see PUNCHEON[2]. Related to POUNCE[1].]

pounce box, a box with a perforated lid for sprinkling or spraying pounce: *These [items] included an inkwell, plenty of quill pens, penknife, . . . pounce box and pounce* (London Times). [< *pounce*[2]]

poun·cet box (poun′sit), *Archaic.* a small box, with a perforated lid, for holding perfumes. [perhaps for *pounced box* (that is, perforated)]

pound[1] (pound), *n., pl.* **pounds** or (*collectively*) **pound. 1.** a unit of weight. 1 pound avoirdupois = 16 ounces. 1 pound troy = 12 ounces. *A jet plane traveling 1,500 mph hits the rain drops with a force of 70,000 pounds per square inch* (Newsweek) *Abbr.:* lb. **2. a.** a unit of money of Great Britain, worth about $2.40. 1 pound = 20 shillings. *Symbol:* £. **b.** a unit of money of Bermuda, Nigeria, and certain other members of the British Commonwealth. **3.** a gold coin and monetary unit of Egypt, Israel, Peru, Turkey, etc., about equal to a British pound. **4.** a former Scottish money of account. **5.** (in the New Testament) a mina (a Semitic money unit). [Old English *pund* < Latin *pondō,* adverb, (originally) for *lībra pondō* a pound by weight, ultimately < *pondus, -eris* weight, related to *pendēre* hang, and to *pendere* to weigh]

pound[2] (pound), *v.t.* **1.** to hit hard again and again; hit heavily: *He pounded the door with his fist. The Germans suddenly got the range . . . and began to pound us with high explosive* (H. G. Wells). **2.** to make into a powder or pulp by pounding: *to pound drugs with a pestle in a mortar.* **3.** to produce (sound) by pounding or as if by pounding: *to pound out a tune on a piano.* **4.** to make solid or firm by beating. —*v.i.* **1.** to beat hard; throb: *After running fast you can feel your heart pound.* **2.** to move with a pounding sound: *He pounded down the hill to catch the bus.* **3.** to produce sound by pounding or as if by pounding: *We could hear drums pounding in the distance.* **4.** (of a ship) to force its way through heavy waves.
—*n.* **1.** the act of pounding. **2.** a heavy or forcible blow; thump. **3.** the sound of a blow; thud.
[Old English *pūnian;* the *-d* is a later addition. Compare SOUND[1].]
—**Syn.** *v.t.* **1.** thump. See **beat.** **2.** pulverize, triturate.

pound[3] (pound), *n.* **1.** an enclosed place in which to keep stray animals: *a dog pound.* **2.** an enclosure for keeping, confining, or trapping animals. **3.** a place of confinement, as a prison, or water enclosed by nets to catch fish, etc.: *In his opinion, the nine-mile pound could be adequately provided with water* (London Times).
—*v.t.* to shut up in or as if in a pound; impound; imprison.
[Old English *pund,* in *pund-fald* pinfold. Compare *pyndan* to enclose.]

pound·age[1] (poun′dij), *n.* **1.** a tax, commission, rate, etc., of so much per pound of British money or per pound of weight. **2.** the weight of a person, product, etc., in pounds: *Extra poundage often goes hand in hand with a beautiful glowing complexion* (New York Times). *The poundage sold in one year has determined how much selling time the Board will allow a warehouse in the following year* (Wall Street Journal). [< *pound*[1] + *-age*]

pound·age[2] (poun′dij), *n.* **1.** a putting in a pound. **2.** the fee for release from a pound.

pound·al (poun′dəl), *n.* the amount of force that, acting for one second on a mass of one pound, gives it a velocity of one foot per second. 1 poundal = 13,825 dynes.

pound cake, 1. a cake, usually made with a pound of sugar and a pound of butter for each pound of flour, and plenty of eggs. **2.** a rich, sweet cake somewhat like this.

pound·er (poun′dər), *n.* a person or thing that pounds, pulverizes, or beats. [Old English *punere.* See POUND[2].]

-pounder, *combining form.* **1.** a person or thing weighing a specified number of pounds: *The baby was a nine-pounder. The bass was a fine seven-pounder.*
2. a gun firing a shell that weighs a specified number of pounds: *fine cannon, eighteen-pounders, with their carriages* (Benjamin Franklin).
3. a bank note, jewel, etc., worth a specified number of pounds sterling: *I pocketed the little donation—it was a ten-pounder* (F. Marryat).

pound-fool·ish (pound′fü′lish), *adj.* foolish or careless in regard to large sums: . . . *resigned rather than supervise what he considered a badly organized, penny-wise, pound-foolish effort* (Newsweek).

pound net, fish nets arranged to form an enclosed space with a narrow opening.

pound of flesh, the full payment of a debt demanded by the person to whom it is due regardless of the consequences to the debtor. [in allusion to Shylock's bargain with Antonio in Shakespeare's *The Merchant of Venice*]

pound sterling, a unit of money of Great Britain. 1 pound = 20 shillings. One pound sterling was worth about five dollars in 1900, and is worth about $2.40 now.

pour (pôr, pōr), *v.t.* **1.** to cause to flow in a steady stream: *to pour milk from a bottle, to pour coal on a fire, to pour shells into the enemy trenches, to pour money into undeveloped areas.* **2.** to make known freely or without reserve: *The melancholy poet poured forth his sorrow in a poem. I could pour out to her all my little worries* (Samuel Butler). —*v.i.* to flow in a steady stream: *The crowd poured out of the church. The rain poured down. The cold blasts poured down from the mountains* (James Fenimore Cooper).

pour it on, *U.S. Informal.* **a.** to do or express something with great vigor and enthusiasm, especially in advancing one's interest, using persuasion, etc.: *The salesman poured it on so well that the customers believed they really wanted to buy. On his first night in Manhattan he went before the United Nations General Assembly and poured it on—5,500 words* (Time). **b.** to keep increasing one's score or advantage in a game, even when victory is no longer at issue: *Our team was leading 60-0, but the crowd kept yelling, "Pour it on!"*
—*n.* **1.** a pouring. **2.** a heavy rain; downpour. **3.** amount of molten metal poured at a time. **4.** *Scottish.* a great quantity.
[Middle English *pouren;* origin uncertain]
—**pour′er,** *n.* —**pour′ing·ly,** *adv.*
—**Syn.** *n.* **1.** outpouring, effluence.

pour·a·ble (pôr′ə bəl, pōr′-), *adj.* that can be poured; flowing easily.

pour ac·quit (pür à kē′), *French.* **1.** received payment. **2.** (literally) for receipt.

pour·boire (pür bwàr′), *n. French.* **1.** a small present of money; tip. **2.** (literally) (money) for drinking.

pour le mé·rite (pür lə mā rēt′), *French.* for merit.

pour le sport (pür lə spôr′), *French.* for sport: . . . *all beautifully dressed pour le sport* (Harper's). *A Buddhist . . . would never dream of hunting animals pour le sport* (New Yorker).

pour·par·ler (pür pàr lā′), *n.* an informal conference; preliminary discussion: . . . *the end of the opening pourparlers between the French and Algerian diplomats* (New Yorker). [< French *pourparler,* noun use of infinitive, to discuss, plot < *pour-* before + *parler* to talk; see PARLEY]

pour·point (pu̇r′point′), *n.* a stuffed and quilted doublet worn by men in the 1300's and 1400's. [< Old French *pourpoint,* quilt, (literally) past participle of *pourpoindre* to quilt, embroider < *pour-* through + *poindre* to prick < Latin *pungere*]

pour point depressant (pôr, pōr), a chemical substance added to engine oil to enable it to flow freely at low temperatures.

pousse-ca·fé (püs′kä fā′), *n., pl.* **-fés** (-fā′). **1.** a small glass of liqueur served with or after coffee. **2.** *U.S.* a small glass of various liqueurs arranged in layers. [< French *pousse-café* (literally) push coffee]

pousse-pousse (püs′püs′), *n. French.* a jinrikisha.

pous·sette (pü set′), *n., v.,* **-set·ted, -set·ting.** —*n.* a dancing round and round with hands joined, as of a couple in a country dance. —*v.i.* to dance in this way: *The turf-cutter seized old Olly Dowden, and . . . poussetted with her* (Thomas Hardy). [< French *poussette* (literally) little push < Middle French *pousse* a push < Old French *pousser* to push < Latin *pulsāre*]

pous·sie (pü′sē), *n. Scottish.* pussy; a hare.

pou sto (pü stō′, pou), a place to stand on; basis of operations: *She . . . Who learns the one pou sto whence after-hands May move the world* (Tennyson). [< Greek *poû stô* (a place) where I may stand; from the saying (about the lever principle) attributed to Archimedes, "Give me a place where I may stand and I will move the world"]

pout[1] (pout), *v.i.* **1.** to thrust or push out the lips, as a displeased or sulky child does. **2.** to show displeasure. **3.** to swell out; protrude. —*v.t.* **1.** to push out (the lips). **2.** to say with a pout: *"That's the reason," pouted Louisa* (Dickens).
—*n.* **1.** a pushing out of the lips when displeased or sulky. **2.** a fit of sullenness: *There ensued a puerile tussle that put me in a precious pout, that I should be kept waiting by such things* (George W. Cable).

in the pouts, in a pouting mood; sulky: *Panurge somewhat vexed Friar John, and put him in the pouts* (Peter A. Motteux).

[Middle English *pouten,* probably imitative of pursing the lips. Compare POOH.]

pout[2] (pout), *n., pl.* **pouts** or (*collectively*) **pout. 1.** any of various freshwater catfishes, such as the horned pout. **2.** eelpout. [Old English *-pūte,* in *ǣlepūte* eelpout]

Horned Pout[2] (def. 1) (to 1 ft. long)

pout·er (pou′tər), *n.* **1.** a person who pouts. **2.** any of a breed of domestic pigeons that puff out their chests.

pout·y (pou′tē), *adj.,* **pout·i·er, pout·i·est.** *Informal.* inclined to pout: . . . *a thin, pouty, platinum-blond teenage girl* (New Yorker). [American English < *pout*[1] + *-y*[1]]

English Pouter (def. 2)

pov·er·ty (pov′ər tē), *n.* **1.** the condition of being poor: *Being out of work usually causes poverty.* **2.** lack of what is needed; poor quality: *The poverty of the soil makes the crops small.* **3.** a small amount: *A dull person's talk shows poverty of ideas.* [< Old French *pouerte* < Latin *paupertās* < *pauper* poor]

—**Syn. 1. Poverty, want, destitution** mean the condition of being poor. **Poverty** emphasizes, more strongly than *poorness* does, owning nothing at all or having not enough for all the necessities of life: *Their tattered clothing and broken furniture indicated their poverty.* **Want** emphasizes extreme need, having too little to live on: *Welfare agencies help those in want.* **Destitution** emphasizes complete lack even of food and shelter, and often suggests having been deprived of possessions once had: *The Red Cross relieved the destitution following the floods.* **2.** deficiency.

poverty line, the minimum yearly income that a family needs for subsistence, as determined by the U.S. government. A family whose income falls below the poverty line is classified as poor.

pov·er·ty-strick·en (pov′ər tē strik′ən), *adj.* extremely poor: *The poverty-stricken exiles contributed far more, in proportion . . . than the wealthy merchants* (John L. Motley). —**Syn.** indigent, destitute, penniless.

pow[1] (pou), *n.* a sudden explosive sound; bang: *I heard a "pow" over my head* (Jim Bentley). *Pow! . . . flashbulbs popped* (Time). [imitative]

pow[2] (pō, pou), *n. Scottish.* poll; a head.

POW (no periods) or **P.O.W.,** prisoner of war.

pow·der (pou′dər), *n.* **1.** a solid reduced to dust by pounding, crushing, or grinding. **2.** some special kind of powder: *face powder.* **3.** gunpowder or any similar explosive.

take a powder, *U.S. Slang.* to go or run away; disappear; vanish: *When the police arrived, the burglars took a powder over the back fence.*

—*v.t.* **1.** to make into powder; pulverize. **2.** to sprinkle or cover with powder. **3.** to apply powder to (the face, etc.): *to powder one's nose.* **4.** to sprinkle: *The ground was lightly powdered with snow.* —*v.i.* **1.** to become powder: *The soil powdered in the heat.* **2.** to use powder as a cosmetic: *She saw herself going down the years, powdering a little more, painting a little more* (John Galsworthy). **3.** *British Informal.* to rush; hurry.

[Middle English *poudre* < Old French, earlier *poldre* < Latin *pulvis,* and *pulver* dust] —**pow′der·er,** *n.*

powder blue, a light blue. —**pow′der-blue′,** *adj.*

powder chest, a chest for holding gunpowder.

powder down, downy feathers that grow indefinitely and continually crumble at their ends into a kind of powder. They are found especially in the herons.

pow·dered milk (pou′dərd), dried milk.

powdered sugar, a sugar produced by grinding granulated sugar: *Confectioners' sugar is very fine powdered sugar.*

powder flask, a flask or case of horn, metal, or leather for carrying gunpowder.

powder horn, a powder flask made of an animal's horn.

Powder Horn

powder keg, 1. a small barrel for storing gunpowder: *When their powder kegs were empty, they surrendered* (Atlantic). **2.** something that threatens to explode suddenly or without warning: *It is part of the whole development which makes the Middle East the powder keg that it is today* (Atlantic).

powder magazine, a place where gunpowder is stored.

powder metallurgy, the technique or process of making metallic articles by shaping and coalescing powdered metals and alloys under heat and pressure.

powder mill, a mill for making gunpowder.

powder monkey, 1. a boy formerly employed on warships, etc., to carry powder to the guns: *Ellangowan had him placed as cabin-boy or powder monkey on board an armed sloop or yacht belonging to the revenue* (Scott). **2.** a person skilled in the use of dynamite and other explosives, especially as used in construction work.

powder post, wood decayed to powder or eaten by worms which burrow through it and convert it into powder.

powder puff, a soft puff or pad for applying powder to the skin.

powder room, a small dressing room or lavatory, especially one having a dressing table.

pow·der·y (pou′dər ē), *adj.* **1.** of powder. **2.** like powder; in the form of powder; dusty: *The snow was too dry and powdery to make good snowballs.* **3.** easily made into powder. **4.** sprinkled or covered with powder. —**Syn. 2.** mealy.

powdery mildew, 1. any of various fungi that attack many plants such as the pea, peach, rose, apple, grape, and cereal grains. It produces a light, powdery coat of conidia on the leaves. **2.** the diseased condition produced by these fungi.

pow·er (pou′ər), *n.* **1.** strength; might; force: *the power of Samson. In a world of power, diplomacy cannot afford sentimentality* (Newsweek). **2.** the ability to do or act: *I will give you all the help in my power.* **3.** a particular ability: *He has great powers of concentration.* **4.** control; authority; influence; right: *Congress has the power to declare war.* **5.** a person, thing, body, or nation having authority or influence: *Five powers held a peace conference. Dr. Adenauer declared that the establishment of the unity of Germany constitutes an obligation arising for the four Powers* (London Times). **6.** energy or force that can do work: *Running water produces power to run mills. Man is feeling his way gingerly toward harnessing thermonuclear power* (Scientific American). **7.** a simple machine. **8.** the capacity for exerting mechanical force, as measured by the rate at which it is exerted or at which the work is done. Power is expressed in foot-pounds per minute, ergs per second, horsepower, watts, etc. . . . *the power is equal to the product of the current and the potential difference* (Sears and Zemansky). **9.** *Mathematics.* the product of a number multiplied by itself: *16 is the 4th power of 2.* **10.** the capacity of an instrument to magnify. The higher the power of a telescope or microscope, the more details you can see: *Magnifying power of a given objective varies with the ocular (eyepiece) used* (Bernhard, Bennett, and Rice). **11.** a seizure of uncontrollable religious enthusiasm. **12.** *Archaic.* a military or naval force: *Brutus and Cassius are levying powers* (Shakespeare). **13.** *Dialect.* a large number or amount: *I've heard a power of queer things of yourself* (J. M. Synge).

in power, having control or authority: *He* [*Pitt*] *had often declared that, while he was in power, England should never make a peace of Utrecht* (Macaulay).

powers, a. deity; divinity: *Then adore the woodland pow'rs with pray'r* (John Dryden). **b.** the sixth of the nine orders of angels in medieval theology: . . . *the powers and thrones above* (John Keble).

the powers that be, those who have control or authority: *Participation in the Hungarian rising was a criminal act from the point of view of the powers that be in Hungary* (Economist).

to the nth power. See under **nth.**

—*v.t.* to supply (something) with power: *Spun by hot gases from the combustion chamber, the turbine or "windmill" powers the turbocar* (Maclean's). —*v.i.* to move by means of power or force: *The young* [*contestant*] *powered his way into the run-off* (Wall Street Journal).

[Middle English *pouer* < Anglo-French *poër, pouair,* variants of Old French *poeir,* noun use of infinitive < Vulgar Latin *potere,* for Latin *posse* to be able]

—**Syn.** *n.* **1. Power, strength, force** mean ability to do something or capacity for something. **Power** is the general word applying to any physical, mental, or moral ability or capacity, whether used or not: *Every normal, healthy person has power to think.* **Strength** means a power within the person or thing, belonging to it as a quality, to do, bear, or resist much: *He has strength of character.* **Force** means active use of power or strength to get something done or bring something about: *We had to use force to get into the house.* **3.** faculty. **4.** command, sway, dominion.

power amplifier, an amplifier which has a relatively high output of current, as in a radio.

pow·er·boat (pou′ər bōt′), *n.* a boat propelled by an inboard engine; motorboat.

pow·er·boat·ing (pou′ər bō′ting), *n.* motorboating.

power brake, a brake for an automobile, truck, etc., that uses the vacuum produced by the engine to force hydraulic fluid or compressed air to the brake shoes of the wheel, requiring very little pressure on the brake pedal to stop the vehicle.

power cable, a heavy, insulated wire or group of wires for carrying electricity to an electric motor, piece of electronic equipment, etc.

power dive, a dive made by an airplane at or nearly at peak power, especially as a maneuver in bombing or aerial fighting.

pow·er-dive (pou′ər dīv′), *v.,* **-dived** or (*U.S. Informal and British Dialect*) **-dove, -dived, -div·ing.** —*v.i.* to make a power dive. —*v.t.* to cause (an airplane) to make a power dive.

power drill, a drill worked by a motor, not by hand.

pow·ered (pou′ərd), *adj.* **1.** having power: *a powered lawn mower.* **2.** using power of a specific kind or degree: *a high-powered racing car, a gasoline-powered engine.*

pow·er·ful (pou′ər fəl), *adj.* **1.** having great power or force; mighty; strong: *a powerful nation, a powerful opponent, a powerful argument.* **2.** *Dialect.* great in quantity or number: *a powerful deal o' trouble* (Harriet Beecher Stowe).

—*adv. Dialect.* very; exceedingly: *powerful weary, a powerful cold day.* —**pow′er·ful·ness,** *n.*

—**Syn.** *adj.* **1.** potent. See **mighty.**

pow·er·ful·ly (pou′ər fə lē, -flē), *adv.* with power; strongly.

pow·er·house (pou′ər hous′), *n.* **1.** a building containing boilers, engines, dynamos, etc., for generating electric power. **2.** *Informal.* a powerful, energetic, or highly effective person or group: *A powerhouse of physical energy, he bounces and bounds with swift, long strides* (Time).

pow·er·less (pou′ər lis), *adj.* without power; helpless: *a powerless hand* (Shakespeare). *The mouse was powerless in the cat's claws. I now felt powerless to escape* (W.H. Hudson). —**pow′er·less·ly,** *adv.* —**pow′er·less·ness,** *n.* —**Syn.** weak, impotent.

power line, a power cable or other wire for carrying electricity: *Every light in the district . . . blinked out—somebody had hit the power line* (Time).

power loading, the gross weight of a propeller-driven aircraft divided by the horsepower of its engines.

power loom, a loom worked by steam, electricity, water power, etc.,

power of appointment, authority given to one person over the property of another.

power of attorney, a written statement giving one person legal power to act for another.

power pack, *Radio.* an assemblage of electrical units used to change the voltage of a power line or battery to the necessary voltage for plate, screen, and filament circuits: *It requires no cumbersome power pack because it operates at very low voltage* (Science News Letter).

power plant, 1. a building with machinery for generating power: *These new turbine-electric giants will be the biggest power plants on any of this country's rail lines* (Wall Street Journal). 2. a motor; engine: *the power plant of an automobile. Which kind of nuclear power plant will be used in the first plane has not been determined* (Science News Letter).

power play, 1. *Sports.* a play in which members of the offensive team converge at a given point to exert mass force or pressure on the defense: *a five-man power play in ice hockey.* 2. any action, move, or play in which strong force or pressure is used to attain a goal: *Russia's squeeze on West Berlin now had become a subtle power play* (Newsweek).

power politics, (in international affairs) diplomacy which uses the threat of superior military power: *People stand appalled at the revelation of a horrible political fraud conceived for the sake of power politics* (London Times).

power press, a printing press worked by a motor or engine, not by hand.

power rail, the rail that carries the current for an electric railroad.

power reactor, any of several types of nuclear reactors used to produce power for generating heat or electricity, operating a ship or plane, etc.: *Adequate shielding must be engineered into power reactors and other sources of radiation* (Scientific American).

pow·ers (pou′ərz), *n.pl.* See under **power,** *n.*

power shovel, a machine for digging, operated by steam power or, more usually, by a diesel or gasoline engine: *Siberia's great shallow coal seams can be mined with power shovels* (Newsweek).

power station, a powerhouse.

power steering, a steering mechanism in an automobile, truck, etc., in which a mechanical, hydraulic, or pneumatic device enables the wheels to be turned with very little effort: *Passenger car drivers . . . like . . . power steering because it makes parking and turning around so much easier* (Newsweek).

Pow·ha·tan (pou′ə tan′), *n.* an American Indian language of the Algonkian linguistic stock.

pow·wow (pou′wou′), *n.* 1. an American Indian ceremony, usually accompanied by magic, feasting, and dancing, performed for the cure of disease, success in hunting, etc. 2. a council or conference of or with American Indians. 3. *U.S. Informal.* any conference or meeting: *I'll be back early, for a last powwow on the terrace* (Edith Wharton). *India's top nuclear physicist had something to say at the Geneva atoms-for-peace powwow that could hold real meaning* (Newsweek). 4. an American Indian priest or medicine man.

—*v.i.* 1. to hold an Indian powwow. 2. *U.S. Informal.* to confer: *We would go to the cave and powwow over what we had done* (Mark Twain).

[American English < Algonkian (probably Narragansett) *powwow* shaman, medicine man < a verb meaning "use divination"; (literally) "to dream"]

pox (poks), *n.* 1. any disease that covers the body or parts of the body with sores, such as smallpox. 2. syphilis. [spelling alteration of *pocks,* plural of *pock*]

poz·zo·la·na (pot′sō lä′nə), *n.* pozzuolana.

poz·zo·la·nic (pot′sō lä′nik), *adj.* pozzuolanic.

poz·zuo·la·na (pot′swō lä′nə), *n.* a volcanic rock or ash used in making hydraulic cement. It contains silica, alumina, lime, etc. *The aqueducts of ancient times were generally built of stone, brick, or pozzuolana* (World Book Encyclopedia). [< Italian *pozzuolana,* noun use of feminine adjective < *Pozzuoli,* Italy, where it was first found]

poz·zuo·la·nic (pot′swō lä′nik), *adj.* consisting of or resembling pozzuolana.

pp (no period), pianissimo.

pp., 1. pages. 2. past participle. 3. pianissimo. 4. privately printed.

p.p., 1. parcel post. 2. parish priest. 3. past participle. 4. postpaid.

P.P., 1. Parcel Post. 2. Parish Priest. 3. past participle. 4. postpaid.

ppd., 1. postpaid. 2. prepaid.

PP factor, pellagra-preventive factor; nicotinic acid.

pph., pamphlet.

p.p.i., policy proof of interest.

PPI (no periods), plan position indicator: *The PPI screen shows a flat map of the circular region above the radar* (Scientific American).

PPLO (no periods), pleuropneumonia-like organism (a filterable microorganism, such as the Eaton agent, that resembles both viruses and bacteria).

p.p.m. or **ppm** (no periods), parts per million.

ppr. or **p.pr.,** present participle.

P.P.S. or **p.p.s.,** 1. a second postscript (Latin, *post postscriptum*). 2. *British.* Parliamentary Private Secretary.

p.q., previous question.

P.Q., 1. previous question. 2. Province of Quebec.

pr., an abbreviation for the following:
1. pair or pairs.
2. paper.
3. power.
4. preferred (stock).
5. present.
6. price.
7. priest.
8. printing.
9. pronoun.

Pr (no period), praseodymium (chemical element).

Pr., 1. preferred (stock). 2. Provençal.

PR (no periods), public relations: *To hire a PR firm to manage an entire major campaign would involve an unthinkable degree of abdication for a self-respecting political leader* (Harper's).

P.R., 1. proportional representation. 2. Puerto Rico.

PRA (no periods), Public Roads Administration.

prac·tic (prak′tik), *Archaic.* —*adj.* practical. —*n.* practice, not theory. [probably < Old French *practique*; see PRACTICAL]

prac·ti·ca·bil·i·ty (prak′tə kə bil′ə tē), *n., pl.* **-ties.** the quality of being practicable; capability of being done, effected, or used: *Both the practicability and the wisdom of dispersion have lately been questioned, and certainly the problem of "fall-out" raises entirely new questions* (Bulletin of Atomic Scientists).

prac·ti·ca·ble (prak′tə kə bəl), *adj.* 1. that can be done; capable of being put into practice: *a practicable idea.* 2. that can be used or crossed over: *a practicable road. The moat had been rendered practicable in many places by the heaps of rubbish* (John L. Motley). [< French *praticable* < *pratiquer* to practice (see PRACTICAL); English spelling influenced by *practic*] —**prac′ti·ca·ble·ness,** *n.* —**Syn. 1.** feasible. See **possible.**

prac·ti·ca·bly (prak′tə kə blē), *adv.* in a practicable manner.

prac·ti·cal (prak′tə kəl), *adj.* 1. having to do with action or practice rather than thought or theory: *Earning a living is a practical matter.* 2. fit for actual practice: *a practical plan. My scheme . . . was so much more practical . . . than the one hatched by those three simple-minded conspirators* (W. H. Hudson). 3. useful. 4. having good sense; using common sense. 5. engaged in actual practice or work: *A practical farmer runs a farm.* 6. being such in effect; virtual: *So many of our soldiers were killed that our victory was a practical defeat.* 7. matter-of-fact; prosaic: *A common-place, practical reply . . . was, I was sure, the best* (Charlotte Brontë). [extension of *practic* < Old French *practique,* learned borrowing from Late Latin *practicus* < Greek *prāktikós* < *prāktós* < *prāttein,* variant of *prāssein* do, act] —**prac′ti·cal·ness,** *n.* —**Syn. 1.** See **sensible.**

prac·ti·cal·i·ty (prak′tə kal′ə tē), *n., pl.* **-ties.** 1. the quality of being practical; practical habit of mind: *Company officials believe they can prove the practicality of an increased number of machines* (Wall Street Journal). 2. a practical matter.

prac·ti·cal·ize (prak′tə kə līz), *v.t.,* **-ized, -iz·ing.** to make practical or workable: *Some [color measurements] may serve better, if modified or practicalized* (Matthew Luckiesh).

practical joke, a trick played on a person to have a laugh at him: *brutal practical jokes.*

practical joker, a person who plays practical jokes: *They became notorious practical jokers and offenders of the orthodox* (Newsweek).

prac·ti·cal·ly (prak′tə klē), *adv.* 1. really; in effect. 2. *Informal.* almost; nearly: *I lived in the slums until I was practically a man* (Time). 3. in a practical way; in a useful way. 4. by actual practice. —**Syn. 1.** virtually.

practical nurse, a woman whose occupation is to care for the sick, but who lacks the hospital training or diploma of a registered nurse.

prac·ti·cant (prak′tə kənt), *n.* a practitioner: *The faith became virtually moribund in the North with perhaps 100,000 practicants* (C.L. Sulzberger).

prac·tice (prak′tis), *n., v.,* **-ticed, -tic·ing.** —*n.* 1. action done many times over for skill: *Practice makes perfect. Practice is as essential to the great writer as it is to the great violinist* (Atlantic). 2. skill gained by experience or exercise: *He was out of practice at batting.* 3. the action or process of doing or being something: *His plan is good in theory, but not in actual practice.* 4. the usual way; custom: *It is the practice in our town to blow the whistles at noon.* 5. the working at or following of a profession or occupation: *engaged in the practice of law.* 6. the business of a lawyer or doctor: *Dr. Adams sold his practice.* 7. *Law.* the established method of conducting legal proceedings. 8. a. *Archaic.* a scheme; plot. b. plotting; trickery.

practices, actions; acts (usually in a bad sense): *the practices of criminals.*

[< verb]

—*v.t.* 1. to do (some act) again and again to learn to do it well: *to practice playing the piano.* 2. to make a custom of; do usually: *Practice what you preach.* 3. to follow, observe, or use day after day: *to practice moderation. We practised republican principles long before a republic was thought of* (Joseph Conrad). 4. to work at or follow as a profession, art, or occupation: *to practice medicine.* 5. to give training to; drill. 6. to take advantage of. 7. to carry out; do: *lest some treachery should be suddenly practised by the enemies* (II Maccabees 14:22). 8. *Obsolete.* to plot: *I doubt My uncle practises more harm to me* (Shakespeare). —*v.i.* 1. to do something again and again to learn to do it well: *to practice with the rifle.* 2. to do something as a habit or practice: *to practice as well as preach.* 3. to practice a profession: *That young lawyer is just starting to practice.* 4. *Archaic.* to scheme; plot.

[< Old French *practiser,* earlier *practiquer* < Medieval Latin *practicare* < Late Latin *prācticus* practical] —**prac′tic·er,** *n.*

—**Syn.** *n.* 1. drill, exercise. 4. habit. See **custom.** *-v.t.* 1. See **exercise.** 5. train.

➔ **practice, practise.** The noun is always spelled *practice*; the verb is either *practice* or *practise.* Noun: *Practice makes perfect.* Verb: *We must practice* (or *practise*) *what we preach.*

prac·ticed (prak′tist), *adj.* 1. experienced; skilled; expert; proficient: *a practiced musician.* 2. acquired or perfected through practice: *practiced charm.* —**Syn. 1.** versed, accomplished.

prac·tic·es (prak′tə siz), *n.pl.* See under **practice,** *n.*

prac·ti·cum (prak′tə kəm), *n., pl.* **-cums, -ca** (-kə). (in colleges and schools) a course in practical work or in independent research, or an exercise of a practical nature, as in laboratory or field work. [< German *Praktikum* < New Latin (*collegium*) *practicum* practical (course) < Medieval Latin *practicare* to practice]

prac·tise (prak′tis), *n., v.t., v.i.,* **-tised, -tis·ing.** practice. —**prac′tis·er,** *n.*

prac·ti·tion·er (prak tish′ə nər, -tish′nər), *n.* 1. a person engaged in the practice of a profession: *He was a medical practitioner for ten years; later he taught medicine. Science enriches . . . the lives of its practitioners* (Polykarp Kusch). 2. a person who makes a practice of anything: *To these simple practitioners of the open-air life the settled populations seemed corrupt, crowded, vicious* (H. G. Wells). 3. a person authorized as a Christian Science healer. [earlier *practician* (< Old French *practicien* < *practique*; see PRACTICAL + *-er*[1])

prad (prad), *n. Especially British Slang.* a horse: *The black and white prads—to use circus argot—of the Stefan Frankordis, working more in the Viennese style, are breathtaking* (London Times). [by metathesis < Dutch *paard* < Late Latin *paraverēdus* a horse for outlying districts; see PALFREY]

pra·do (prä′dō), *n., pl.* **-dos.** a fashionable

boulevard or promenade, especially in a Spanish-speaking country. [< Spanish *prado* (originally) field, pasture < Latin *prātum* meadow]

prae·co·cial (pri kō′shəl), *adj.* precocial.

prae·di·al (prē′dē əl), *adj.* predial.

prae·fect (prē′fekt), *n.* prefect.

prae·lect (pri lekt′), *v.i.* prelect.

prae·lec·tion (pri lek′shən), *n.* prelection.

prae·lec·tor (pri lek′tər), *n.* prelector.

prae·mu·ni·re (prē′myů nī′rē), *n.* in English law: **1.** a writ of summons on the charge of resorting to a foreign court or authority, such as that of the Pope, and so disregarding the supremacy of the sovereign. **2.** this offense. **3.** the penalty of forfeiture, imprisonment, outlawry, etc., incurred for it. [short for *praemunire facias* (words occurring in the writ), (literally) that thou do warn; *praemunire* warn < Medieval Latin confusion of Latin *praemunīre* to fortify, and *praemonēre* to warn]

prae·no·men (prē nō′mən), *n. pl.* **-no·mens** or **-nom·i·na** (-nom′ə nə). the first or personal name of a person, especially of a Roman citizen, as *Marcus* in *Marcus Tullius Cicero*. Also, **prenomen.** [< Latin *praenōmen* forename < *prae-* before + *nōmen* name]

prae·nom·i·nal (prē nom′ə nəl,) *adj.* of or having to do with a praenomen.

prae·pos·i·tor (prē poz′ə tər), *n.* prepositor.

prae·pos·tor (prē pos′tər), *n.* prepositor.

Prae·sid·i·um (pri sid′ē əm), *n.* Presidium: *Mr. Khrushchev ... is going as a member of the Praesidium of the Supreme Soviet* (London Times).

prae·tex·ta (prē teks′tə), *n., pl.* **-tex·tae** (-teks′tē). (in ancient Rome) a white toga with a purple border worn by boys until they were entitled to wear the toga of manhood and by girls until they were married: *the usual youth's garment, the short praetexta, reaching below the knee* (Nicholas P.S. Wiseman). [< Latin *praetexta*, short for *toga praetexta* toga fringed in front; *praetexta* < *praetexere* to weave, or border at the front < *prae-* before + *texere* to weave, or border]

prae·tor (prē′tər, -tôr), *n.* **1.** a magistrate or judge in ancient Rome. A praetor ranked next below a consul. **2.** a consul as leader of the ancient Roman army. Also, **pretor.** [< Latin *praetor, -ōris* < unrecorded *prae-itor* one who goes before < *prae-* before + stem of *īre* to go]

prae·to·ri·al (prē tôr′ē əl, -tōr′-), *adj.* of or having to do with a Roman praetor. Also, **pretorial.**

prae·to·ri·an (prē tôr′ē ən, -tōr′-), *adj.* **1.** of or having to do with a praetor. **2.** having to do with the bodyguard of a Roman commander or emperor.
—*n.* **1.** a man having the rank of a praetor. **2.** a soldier of the bodyguard of a Roman commander or emperor. Also, **pretorian.**

Praetorian Guard, the bodyguard of a Roman emperor.

prae·to·ri·an·ism (prē tôr′ē ə niz əm, -tōr′-), *n.* **1.** any system like that of the Roman praetorian organization. **2.** military despotism, especially when corrupt: *The actions of the Peruvian military ... giving rise to fears that praetorianism would spread through others of the politically "soft" republic* (K.H. Silvert).

prae·to·ri·um (prē tôr′ē əm, -tōr′-), *n., pl.* **-to·ri·a** (-tôr′ē ə, -tōr′-). **1.** the commander's headquarters in an ancient Roman camp. **2.** the official residence of the governor of an ancient Roman province: *The praetorium can be reasonably identified as in the palace of Herod* (Atlantic). Also, **pretorium.** [< Latin *praetorium* < *praetor* praetor]

prae·tor·ship (prē′tər ship), *n.* the office, dignity, or term of office of a praetor. Also, **pretorship.**

prag·mat·ic (prag mat′ik), *adj.* **1.** concerned with practical results or values; of or having to do with pragmatism: *a pragmatic philosophy.* **2.** having to do with the affairs of a state or community. **3.** busy; active. **4.** meddlesome; interfering. **5.** conceited; opinionated. **6.** matter-of-fact: *Their pragmatic ... approach increasingly fits the apolitical mood of the workers* (Economist). **7.** treating the facts of history systematically, with special reference to their causes and effects.
—*n.* **1.** a pragmatic sanction. **2.** a busybody. **3.** a conceited person.
[< Latin *prāgmaticus* < Greek *prāgmatikós* efficient, one skilled in business or civil affairs < *prâgma, -atos* civil business; deed, act < *prâssein* to do, act. Compare PRACTICAL.] —**prag·mat′i·cal·ly,** *adv.* —**prag·mat′i·cal·ness,** *n.*
—**Syn.** *adj.* **4.** officious.

prag·mat·i·cal (prag mat′ə kəl), *adj.* pragmatic: *a pair of ... prating, pragmatical rascals* (Rudyard Kipling).

prag·mat·ics (prag mat′iks), *n.* a division of semiotics which studies the relations between signs and their users.

pragmatic sanction, any of various imperial decrees issued as fundamental law by former European emperors or monarchs.

Pragmatic Sanction, a compact by which Charles VI, who had no sons, tried to maintain the succession to the throne of Austria in his line, through his daughter Maria Theresa.

prag·ma·tism (prag′mə tiz əm), *n.* **1.** the philosophy that tests the value and truth of ideas by their practical consequences. **2.** pragmatic quality or condition. **3.** officiousness. **4.** dogmatism. **5.** a matter-of-fact way of viewing things.

prag·ma·tist (prag′mə tist), *n.* **1.** a person who believes in pragmatism: *If the individual was to be justified by the pragmatist's idea that "a thing is true if it works," it could only be done in terms of the outer ... world, where things can be seen, tested, and measured* (Wall Street Journal). **2.** a busybody.
—*adj.* pragmatistic.

prag·ma·tis·tic (prag′mə tis′tik), *adj.* of or having to do with pragmatism or pragmatists.

prag·ma·tize (prag′mə tīz), *v.t.,* **-tized, -tiz·ing.** to represent as real or material. —**prag′ma·tiz′er,** *n.*

pra·hu (prä′hü, -ü), *n.* a proa.

Prai·rial (pre ryȧl′), *n.* the ninth month of the French Revolutionary calendar, extending from May 20 to June 18. [< French *Prairial* < *prairie* meadow, prairie]

prai·rie (prãr′ē), *n.* **1.** a large area of level or rolling land with grass but no trees: *We saw the green, oceanlike expanse of prairie, stretching swell over swell to the horizon* (Francis Parkman). **2.** *U.S. Dialect.* a small open space in a forest. [American English < French *prairie* < Old French *praerie* < Vulgar Latin *prātaria* < Latin *prātum* meadow]

Prai·rie (prãr′ē), *adj.* of or having to do with the Prairie Provinces (Manitoba, Saskatchewan, and Alberta) of western Canada. —*n.* a Prairie Province: *The rural-urban split in Canada is greater than ever; and the Prairies are as solidly conservative as in 1962* (John Meisel).

prairie chicken, 1. a variety of grouse that lives on the prairies of North America, noted for its elaborate courtship. **2.** the sharp-tailed grouse.

Prairie Chicken (def. 1) (about 1½ ft. long)

prairie clover, any of various herbs of the pea family with small, pink, purple, or white flowers in dense heads or spikes.

prai·ried (prãr′ēd), *adj.* having many prairies; bordered by prairies.

prairie dog, a burrowing animal like a woodchuck but smaller, found on the Great Plains and in the Rocky Mountain region. Prairie dogs sometimes live in large colonies and make a yipping, bark-like noise. *Prairie dogs live in a "dog society" highly organized with respect to economic needs, social behavior and population control* (Science News Letter).

Prairie Dog (about 1 ft. long)

prairie falcon, a brownish falcon about the size of the duck hawk, found in the prairies and open areas of western North America.

prairie oyster, *Slang.* a raw egg, peppered and salted, and drunk in vinegar or brandy: *Turtle eggs are delicious swallowed as prairie oysters* (New Yorker).

prairie rattlesnake, a rather small variety of rattlesnake of western North America, having a maximum length of about five feet.

prairie schooner, a large covered wagon used by emigrants in crossing the plains of North America before the railroads were built.

Prairie Schooner

prairie squirrel, any of various burrowing rodents of western North America; gopher.

Prairie State, a nickname of Illinois.

prairie warbler, a warbler of eastern United States having yellow under parts with black stripes on the sides and face.

prairie wolf, the coyote.

praise (prāz), *n., v.,* **praised, prais·ing.** —*n.* **1.** saying that a thing or person is good; words that tell the worth or value of a thing or person. **2.** words or song setting forth the glory and goodness of God. **3.** *Archaic.* a ground for praise or merit: *A restless crowd ... Whose highest praise is that they live in vain* (William Cowper).
damn with faint praise, to praise with so little enthusiasm as to condemn: *Damn with faint praise, assent with civil leer* (Alexander Pope).
sing the praise or **praises of,** to praise with enthusiasm: *He sang the praises of his home town.*
[< verb]
—*v.t.* **1.** to express approval or admiration of: *She was enthusiastically praising the beauties of Gothic architecture* (F. Marion Crawford). **2.** to worship in words or song: *to praise God.* —*v.i.* to give praise.
[< Old French *preisier* < Late Latin *pretiāre* to value, prize < Latin *pretium* a prize, price. Doublet of PRIZE³.] —**prais′er,** *n.*
—**Syn.** *n.* **1.** commendation, acclaim. *-v.t.* **1. Praise, approve, commend** mean to think or speak well of. **Praise** means to express heartily a high opinion or admiration of someone or something: *The coach praised the team for its fine playing.* **Approve** means to have or express a favorable opinion of: *Everyone approved his idea.* **Commend** suggests a formal expression of favorable opinion: *The mayor commended the boys for their quick thinking at the disaster.*

praise·ful (prāz′fəl), *adj.* **1.** giving praise: *praiseful words.* **2.** *Obsolete.* praiseworthy.

praise·wor·thi·ly (prāz′wėr′ᴛʜə lē), *adv.* in a manner that deserves praise.

praise·wor·thi·ness (prāz′wėr′ᴛʜē nis), *n.* praiseworthy character or quality: *Where ... is the praiseworthiness of obedience if it only be paid in instances where we give up nothing?* (Samuel Richardson).

praise·wor·thy (prāz′wėr′ᴛʜē), *adj.,* **-thi·er, -thi·est.** worthy of praise; deserving approval; commendable; laudable: *He does not ask what is allowable, but what is commendable and praiseworthy* (William Law).
—**Syn.** meritorious.

Pra·krit (prä′krit), *n.* any of the Indo-European vernacular languages or dialects of northern and central India, especially those of the ancient and medieval periods. [< Sanskrit *prākṛta* natural, common, vulgar. Compare SANSKRIT.]

pra·line (prä′lēn), *n.* a small cake of candy made of brown sugar and nuts, usually pecans or almonds: *You will find Marcel confronting you with an owlish eye and nibbling a meditative praline* (New Yorker). [American English < French *praline* < Marshal Duplessis-*Praslin*, 1598-1675, whose cook invented them]

prall·tril·ler (präl′tril′ər), *n. Music.* a melodic embellishment consisting of the rapid alternation of a principal tone with one usually a step above it; an inverted mordent. [< German *Pralltriller* < *Prall* recoil + *Triller* a trill]

pram¹ (pram), *n. British Informal.* perambulator; baby carriage: *They accept air travel as something normal and unmagical like being pushed around in a pram* (Punch).

pram² (pram), *n.* a small rowboat with a flat bottom and a rectangular bow: *Harbors from Maine to California swarm with new thousands of prams, skiffs and small sailing craft* (Time). [< Dutch *praam*, ultimately < a Slavic word]

prance (prans, präns), *v.,* **pranced, pranc·ing,** *n.* —*v.i.* **1.** to spring about on the hind legs: *Horses prance when they feel lively.* **2.** to ride on a horse doing this: *The insulting tyrant, prancing o'er the field ... His horse's hoofs wet with patrician blood* (Joseph Addison). **3.** to move gaily or proudly;

swagger. **4.** to dance; caper. —*v.t.* to cause to prance.
—*n.* a prancing.
[Middle English *prancen,* and *prauncen;* origin uncertain] —**pranc′er,** *n.* —**pranc′ing·ly,** *adv.*

pranc·y (pran′sē, prän′-), *adj.,* **pranc·i·er, pranc·i·est.** that prances; characterized by prancing: *The trumpeting band of Emil Coleman and the prancy one of Mark Monte* . . . (New Yorker).

pran·di·al (pran′dē əl), *adj.* of or having to do with a meal, especially dinner. [< Latin *prandium* luncheon; meal + English *-al*[1]]

Prandt·l number (prän′təl), *Physics.* the specific heat of a fluid at constant pressure multiplied by its viscosity, and the product divided by its thermal conductivity. [< Ludwig *Prandtl,* 1875-1953, a German physicist]

prang (prang), *Slang.* —*n.* a crash of or in an aircraft. —*v.t., v.i.* **1.** to crash (an airplane, etc.): *Suppose I start cornering a little too fast . . . and I prang the crate?* (New Yorker). **2.** to destroy (a target, enemy airplane, etc.). [imitative]

prank[1] (prangk), *n.* a piece of mischief; playful trick: *On April Fools' Day people play pranks on each other. They . . . played all manner of mischievous pranks* (Herman Melville). —*v.i.* to indulge in a prank or pranks.
[origin uncertain] —**Syn.** *n.* antic.

prank[2] (prangk), *v.t.* to dress in a showy way; adorn: *when violets pranked the turf with blue* (Oliver Wendell Holmes). —*v.i.* to make a show or display; show off: *White houses prank where once were huts* (Matthew Arnold).
[origin uncertain. Compare Middle Low German *prank* showiness, Dutch *pronken* to show off, strut.]

prank·ish (prang′kish), *adj.* **1.** full of pranks; fond of pranks: *Philip's headmaster wrote this report of his athletic, prankish and unbookish pupil* (Newsweek). **2.** like a prank. —**prank′ish·ly,** *adv.* —**prank′ish·ness,** *n.*

prank·some (prangk′səm), *adj.* prankish.

prank·ster (prangk′stər), *n.* a person who plays practical jokes or other pranks: *Halloween pranksters sometimes do real damage with their tricks.*

prank·y (prang′kē), *adj.,* **prank·i·er, prank·i·est.** fond of pranks; prankish: *Who can believe that young Randolph would be as . . . conventionally pranky as he here makes out?* (New York Times).

prao (prou), *n.* a proa.

prase (prāz), *n.* an indistinctly crystalline variety of green quartz. [< French *prase,* learned borrowing from Latin *prasius* < Greek *prásios* (*líthos*) leek-green (stone) < *práson* leek]

pra·se·o·dym·i·um (prā′zē ō dim′ē əm, -sē-), *n.* a silvery-white, rare-earth metallic chemical element forming green salts. It is present in cerite, didymium, and various other substances. *Symbol:* Pr; *at.wt.:* (C^{12}) 140.907 or (O^{16}) 140.92; *at.no.:* 59; *valence:* 3,4.
[< New Latin *praseodymium* < Greek *prásios* leek-green (see PRASE) + New Latin *didymium* < Greek *dídymos* twin < *dýo* double, twofold, two]

prat (prat), *n. Slang.* the rump: *Everybody's against sin but you're not going to get off your prat to do anything about it* (Harper's). [origin unknown]

prate (prāt), *v.,* **prat·ed, prat·ing,** *n.* —*v.i.* to talk a great deal in a foolish way: *to prate without ceasing.* —*v.t.* to say in empty or foolish talk.
—*n.* a prating; empty or foolish talk: *Hold your prate* (Samuel Lover).
[Middle English *praten;* origin uncertain. Compare Middle Dutch *praeten,* Middle Low German *praten.*] —**prat′er,** *n.* —**prat′ing·ly,** *adv.*
—**Syn.** *n.* chatter, prattle.

prat·fall (prat′fôl′), *n. U.S. Slang.* **1.** a fall on the backside taken as part of a comic, roughhouse, or slapstick routine: *There is not a person alive who can suppress a guffaw at a perfectly timed pratfall* (Time). **2.** any laughable mischance. [< earlier *prat* buttocks + *fall*]

pra·tie (prā′tē), *n. Dialect.* potato: *His praties will surely rot in the soil and his hens lay addled eggs for ever more* (Manchester Guardian Weekly).

prat·in·cole (prat′ing kōl, prā′tin-), *n.* any of a group of swallowlike shore birds of the Eastern Hemisphere, related to the plovers. [< New Latin *pratincola* the species name < Latin *prātum* meadow + *incola* inhabitant, resident < *incolere* < *in-* in + *colere* to dwell; also, cultivate]

pra·tique (pra tēk′, prat′ik), *n.* permission or license granted to a ship to carry on commerce with a port after passing quarantine or showing a clean bill of health. [< Old French *pratique,* earlier *practique* usage, practice; see PRACTIC]

prat·tle (prat′əl), *v.,* **-tled, -tling,** *n.* —*v.i.* **1.** to talk as a child does; talk freely and carelessly. **2.** to talk in a foolish way; chatter. **3.** to sound like baby talk; babble: *the prattling of a brook or of leaves.* —*v.t.* **1.** to say in a childish way. **2.** to say by chattering or babbling: *prattling scandal as he goes* (William Cowper).
—*n.* **1.** simple, artless talk: *The child had plenty of prattle in him* (Samuel Butler). **2.** baby talk; foolish talk. **3.** a sound like baby talk; babble: *the prattle of a brook.*
[(frequentative) < *prate.* Compare Middle Low German *pratelen.*] —**prat′tler,** *n.* —**prat′tling·ly,** *adv.*

pra·u (prä′ü, prou), *n.* a proa: *For centuries, native praus flashed out from inlets and rivers* (Time).

prav·i·ty (prav′ə tē), *n., pl.* **-ties.** bad or corrupt state; moral perversion or corruption; depravity: *The punishment . . . was proportioned to the apprehended and intended consequences of the crime, not to the pravity of the offender* (Robert Southey). [< Latin *prāvitās* < *prāvus* crooked, perverse. Compare DEPRAVITY.]

prawn (prôn), *n.* any of several edible shellfish much like shrimp but larger. —*v.i.* to fish for or catch prawns. [Middle English *prayne,* and *prane;* origin uncertain]
—**prawn′er,** *n.*

Prawn (to 6 in. long)

prax·is (prak′sis), *n.* **1.** practice, especially as contrasted with theory. **2.** custom; use. **3.** an example or group of examples for practice. [< Medieval Latin *praxis* < Greek *prâxis* a doing, acting < *prâssein* to do, act. Compare PRACTICAL.]

Prax·it·e·le·an (prak sit′ə lē′ən), *adj.* having to do with or characteristic of Praxiteles, a Greek sculptor who lived about 350 B.C., or of his sculpture: *Leonardo, habitually obsessed with the generalized form of Praxitelean sculpture . . .* (London Times).

pray (prā), *v.i.* **1.** to speak to God in worship; enter into spiritual communion with God; offer worship. **2.** to make earnest request to God or to any other object of worship: *to pray for help, to pray for one's family.* —*v.t.* **1.** to ask earnestly: *There is nothing that we can do now but pray God to help.* **2.** to ask earnestly for: *I know not how to pray your patience* (Shakespeare). **3.** to bring or get by praying: *to pray souls out of purgatory.* **4.** please: *Pray come with me.* **5.** to offer (a prayer).
[< Old French *preier,* and *prier* < Late Latin *precāre* to pray for < Latin *precārī* < *prex, precis* prayer]
—**Syn.** *v.t.* **1.** entreat, implore, beseech, beg. **2.** crave.

prayer[1] (prãr), *n.* **1.** the act of praying: *Prayer as communion with the deity is not characteristic of Japanese Buddhism* (Atlantic). **2.** the thing prayed for: *Their prayer was for peace.* **3.** a form of words to be used in praying: *The Lord's Prayer begins, "Our Father, which art in heaven." The farmers offered prayers for rain.* **4.** a form of worship; religious service consisting mainly of prayers: *Prayer is one of the principal categories of worship* (Melville J. Herskovits). **5.** an earnest or humble request. **6.** the part of a pleading in a court proceeding or in a petition to a public body that states the action or relief desired. **7.** *U.S. Slang.* a chance: *The other candidate didn't have a prayer* (New Yorker). [Middle English *praiere* < Old French *preiere* < Vulgar Latin *precāria* < Latin *precārius* (literally) things obtained by entreaty < *precārī* to pray, entreat]

pray·er[2] (prā′ər), *n.* a person who prays. [< *pray* + *-er*[1]]

prayer beads (prãr), a rosary: *I left Mr. Filfil passing his prayer beads of yellow amber through his fingers* (New Yorker).

prayer book (prãr), a book of prayers.

Prayer Book, the Book of Common Prayer.

prayer·ful (prãr′fəl), *adj.* having the habit of praying often; devout: *the prayerful life of monks. A prayerful silence filled the church.* —**prayer′ful·ly,** *adv.* —**prayer′ful·ness,** *n.* —**Syn.** pious, reverent.

prayer·less (prãr′lis), *adj.* without prayer or the habit of praying; not having the blessing or protection of prayer: *The mayor of the village spoke a few words, and in prayerless silence the coffin of Albert Camus was lowered* (Time). —**prayer′less·ly,** *adv.* —**prayer′less·ness,** *n.*

prayer meeting (prãr), a meeting for prayer and worship: . . . *a protest march and prayer meeting at the Capitol* (Time).

Prayer of Manasses (prãr), an apocryphal book of the Protestant Bible.

prayer rug (prãr), a rug to kneel on during prayer, used especially by Moslems: *He rises every morning at 4 to read the Koran, prays five times a day in the mosque or on a prayer rug* (Time).

prayer shawl (prãr), a tallith: *In his prayer shawl and phylacteries, he rose to ask her what had happened* (Isaac Bashevis Singer).

prayer stick (prãr), a decorated stick used by Pueblo Indians in their religious ceremonies: *He . . . stumbled upon the shrine, with fresh prayer sticks around it* (New Yorker).

prayer wheel (prãr), a cylinder inscribed with or containing prayers, used by the Buddhists of Tibet. When it is rotated each turn counts as an uttered prayer. *Prayer wheels abound, from small, hand-operated ones to huge structures weighing tons and turned by water power* (New Yorker).

Prayer Wheel in Buddhist Temple, Japan

pray·ing mantis (prā′ing), a mantis.

pre-, *prefix.* before in place, time, order, rank, or importance, as in *precursor, predominate, preface, prehistoric, prepay, prewar.* [< Latin *prae-* < *prae* before]
➔ When **pre-** is joined to a root with initial *e,* the latter is spelled with *ë* or preceded by the hyphen: *preëmpt, pre-empt.* The hyphen is also used before roots with an initial capital letter: *pre-Cambrian, pre-Christian.* Otherwise prefix and root are joined directly without any mark: *preoccupy, prescription.*

Words not separately defined in this dictionary appear in the following listing:

pre·ab′do·men
pre′ac·cept′
pre′ac·cept′ance
pre·ac′cess
pre′ac·ces′si·ble
pre′ac·cord′
pre′ac·count′
pre′ac·count′ing
pre′ac·cu′mu·late
pre′ac·cu′mu·la′tion
pre′ac·cu·sa′tion
pre′ac·cuse′
pre′ac·e·tab′u·lar
pre′ac·knowl′edge
pre′ac·knowl′edg·ment
pre′ac·quaint′
pre′ac·quaint′ance
pre′ac·quaint′ed
pre′ac·quire′
pre′ac·quired′
pre′ac·quit′
pre′ac·quit′tal
pre·act′
pre·ac′tion
pre′a·dapt′
pre′a·dapt′a·ble
pre′ad·ap·ta′tion
pre′ad·just′
pre′ad·just′a·ble
pre′ad·just′ment
pre′ad·min′is·tra′tion
pre′ad·min′is·tra′tive
pre′ad·min′is·tra′tor
pre′ad·mis′sion
pre′ad·mit′
pre′ad·mon′ish
pre′ad·mo·ni′tion
pre′ad·o·les′cent
pre′a·dopt′
pre′a·dop′tion
pre′a·dult′
pre′a·dult′hood
pre′ad·vert′en·cy
pre′ad·vert′ent
pre·ad′ver·tise
pre·ad′ver·tise′ment
pre·ad′ver·tis′er
pre·ad′ver·tis′ing
pre′ad·vice′
pre′ad·vis′a·ble
pre′ad·vise′
pre′ad·vis′er
pre′ad·vi′so·ry
pre′af·fect′
pre′af·fec′tion
pre′af·fil′i·a′tion
pre′af·fir·ma′tion
pre′af·ter·noon′
pre′ag·gres′sion
pre′ag·gres′sive
pre′a·gree′ment
pre′ag·ri·cul′tur·al
pre′a·larm′
pre′al·co·hol′ic
pre′al·le·ga′tion
pre′al·lege′
pre′al·li′ance

pre′al·lied′
pre′al·lot′
pre′al·lot′ment
pre′al·low′
pre′al·ly′
pre·al′pha·bet
pre·al′tar
pre′al·ter·a′tion
pre′a·mal′ga·ma′tion
pre·am′bu·lar
pre·a′nal
pre′a·naph′o·ral
pre′an·es·thet′ic
pre′an·nex′
pre′an·nounce′
pre′an·nounce′ment
pre′an·nounc′er
pre′an·te·pe′nult
pre′an·te·pe·nul′ti-
mate
pre′an·tiq′ui·ty
pre′a·or′tic
pre′ap·pear′ance
pre′ap·per·cep′tion
pre′ap·point′
pre′ap·point′ment
pre′ap·pre·hen′sion
pre′ap·prise′
pre′ap·pro·ba′tion
pre′ap·prov′al
pre′ap·prove′
pre·ap′ti·tude
pre′ar·range′
pre′ar·range′ment
pre′ar·rest′
pre′ar·rest′ment
pre′-Ar·thu′ri·an
pre′ar·tis′tic
pre-Ar′y·an
pre′as·cer·tain′
pre′as·cer·tain′ment
pre′as·sem′ble
pre′as·sign′
pre′as·signed′
pre′as·sume′
pre′as·sur′ance
pre′as·sure′
pre′-As·syr′i·an
pre′at·tach′ment
pre′at·tune′
pre·au′di·to′ry
pre-Au′gus·tine
pre′a·ver′
pre′a·vow′al
pre·ax′i·ad
pre′-Bab·y·lo′ni·an
pre·bach′e·lor
pre·bac′il·lar′y
pre′-Ba·co′ni·an
pre′bap·tis′mal
pre·bap′tize
pre·bar′gain
pre·bas′al
pre·bas′i·lar
pre′be·a·tif′ic
pre′ben·e·dic′tion
pre′be·troth′al
pre′block·ade′
pre·bod′ing
pre·boil′
pre·boy′hood
pre·break′fast
pre·breathe′
pre-Brit′ish
pre′bro·mid′ic
pre·bron′chi·al
pre·buc′cal
pre-Bud′dhist
pre·budg′et
pre·budg′et·ar′y
pre-Byz′an·tine
pre·cal′cu·la·ble
pre·cal′cu·late
pre′cal·cu·la′tion
pre-Cam′bridge
pre′cam·paign′
pre·can′di·da·cy
pre·can′vass
pre·cap′il·lar′y
pre·cap′i·tal·ist
pre′cap·i·tal·is′tic
pre·cap′ture
pre′-Car·bon·if′er-
ous
pre·car′di·ac
pre·car′ni·val
pre′-Car·o·lin′gi·an
pre′car·ti·lag′i·nous
pre-Cath′o·lic
pre·cau′dal
pre·cau′tious
pre-Celt′ic
pre·cen′sure
pre·cen′sus
pre′-Cen·ten′ni·al
pre·cen′tral
pre′cer·e·bel′lar
pre·cer′e·bral
pre′cer·ti·fi·ca′tion
pre·cer′ti·fy
pre·charge′
pre′-Chau·ce′ri·an
pre·check′
pre·child′hood
pre′-Chi·nese′
pre·chlo′ro·form
pre·choose′
pre·cho′roid
pre′-Chris·ti·an′ic
pre-Christ′mas
pre′cir·cu·la′tion
pre′ci·ta′tion
pre·cit′ed
pre′civ·i·li·za′tion
pre·claim′
pre·claim′ant
pre·clas′sic
pre·clas′si·cal
pre′clas·si·fi·ca′tion
pre·clas′si·fied
pre·clas′si·fy
pre·cler′i·cal
pre′coc·cyg′e·al
pre′cog·i·ta′tion
pre·cog′ni·za·ble
pre·cog′ni·zant
pre·cog′nize
pre·coil′
pre′col·laps′i·ble
pre′col·lect′
pre′col·lect′a·ble
pre′col·lec′tion
pre′col·lec′tor
pre·col′lege
pre′col·le′gi·ate
pre′com·bus′tion
pre′com·mend′
pre·com′ment
pre′com·mer′cial
pre′com·mit′
pre′com·mun′ion
pre′com·pli′ance
pre·com′pli·cate
pre′com·pose′
pre′com·pre·hend′
pre′com·pre·hen′-
sion
pre′com·pre·hen′sive
pre′com·press′
pre′com·pute′
pre′con·ceal′
pre′con·cede′
pre′con·ceiv′a·ble
pre·con′cen·trat′ed
pre·con′cen·trat′ed·ly
pre′con·cen·tra′tion
pre′con·cep′tion·al
pre′con·ces′sion
pre′con·clude′
pre′con·clu′sion
pre′con·cur′
pre′con·cur′rence
pre′con·cur′rent
pre′con·demn′
pre′con·dem·na′tion
pre′con·den·sa′tion
pre′con·dense′
pre′con·duct′
pre′con·duc′tor
pre′con·fer′
pre·con′fer·ence
pre′con·fess′
pre′con·fes′sion
pre′con·fide′
pre′con·fig′ure
pre′con·fine′
pre′con·fine′ment
pre′con·firm′
pre′con·fir·ma′tion
pre′con·form′
pre′con·form′i·ty
pre′con·ges′tion
pre-Con′gress
pre′con·gres′sion·al
pre′con·jec′ture
pre′con·nu′bi·al
pre·con′se·crate
pre′con·se·cra′tion
pre′con·sent′
pre′con·sid′er
pre′con·sid′er·a′tion
pre′con·sol′i·date
pre′con·sol′i·dat′ed
pre′con·sol′i·da′tion
pre′con·so·nan′tal
pre′con·stit′u·ent
pre·con′sti·tute
pre′con·struct′
pre′con·struc′tion
pre′con·sul·ta′tion
pre′con·sume′
pre′con·tained′
pre·con′tem·plate
pre′con·tem·pla′tion
pre′con·ti·nen′tal
pre′con·tract′
pre′con·trac′tive
pre′con·trac′tu·al
pre′con·triv′ance
pre′con·trive′
pre′con·ven′tion
pre′con·ver′sion
pre′con·vert′
pre′con·vey′
pre′con·vey′ance
pre′con·vict′
pre′con·vic′tion
pre·cook′
pre·cook′er
pre′-Co·per′ni·can
pre·cop′y
pre′cor·o·na′tion
pre′cor·rec′tion
pre′cor·res·pond′ent
pre·cor′ri·dor
pre′cor·rupt′
pre′cor·rup′tion
pre·cos′mic
pre·cos′mi·cal
pre·cos′tal
pre·coun′sel
pre·coun′sel·lor
pre′cre·ate′
pre′cre·a′tion
pre′cre·a′tive
pre·crit′i·cism
pre·cru′cial
pre′-Cru·sade′
pre·crys′tal·line
pre·cul′ti·vate
pre′cul·ti·va′tion
pre·cul′tur·al
pre·cul′ture
pre·cure′
pre′cur·ric′u·lar
pre′cur·ric′u·lum
pre·cut′
pre·cyst′ic
pre·damn′
pre′dam·na′tion
pre′-Dar·win′i·an
pre·day′light′
pre·day′time′
pre′de·cease′
pre′de·cide′
pre′de·ci′sion
pre′de·ci′sive
pre′dec·la·ra′tion
pre′de·clare′
pre′dec·li·na′tion
pre′de·cline′
pre·ded′i·cate
pre′ded·i·ca′tion
pre′de·fine′
pre′def·i·ni′tion
pre·del′e·gate
pre′del·e·ga′tion
pre′de·lib′er·a′tion
pre′de·lin′quen·cy
pre′de·lin′quent
pre·dem′on·strate
pre′dem·on·stra′tion
pre·den′tal
pre′de·part·men′tal
pre′de·pres′sion
pre′de·scribe′
pre′de·scrip′tion
pre′de·sert′, *n.*
pre′de·sert′, *v.t.*
pre′de·sert′er
pre′de·ser′tion
pre′de·sign′
pre′de·tain′
pre′de·tain′er
pre′de·ten′tion
pre′de·ter′mi·nate
pre′de·vel′op
pre′de·vel′op·ment
pre′de·vise′
pre′di·ag·no′sis
pre′di·ag·nos′tic
pre′di·as·tol′ic
pre′-Dick·en′si·an
pre·di′e·tar′y
pre·dig′i·tal
pre·din′ner
pre′dip·lo·mat′ic
pre′di·rect′
pre′di·rec′tion
pre′di·rec′tor
pre′dis·a·gree′ment
pre·dis′ci·pline
pre′dis·clo′sure
pre·dis′count
pre′dis·cour′age
pre′dis·cour′age-
ment
pre·dis′course
pre′dis·cov′er
pre′dis·cov′er·er
pre′dis·cov′er·y
pre′dis·cus′sion
pre′dis·perse′
pre′dis·per′sion
pre′dis·pos′a·ble
pre′dis·pos′al
pre′dis·rupt′
pre′dis·rup′tion
pre′dis·so·lu′tion
pre′dis·solve′
pre′dis·suade′
pre′dis·tin′guish
pre·doc′tor·al
pre·doc′tor·ate
pre′doc·u·men′ta·ry
pre′do·mes′tic
pre·doom′
pre-Dor′ic
pre·dor′sal
pre·draft′
Pre′-Dra·vid′i·an
pre·draw′
pre·drill′
pre·dry′
pre·dusk′
pre-Dutch′
pre-East′er
pre′ë·co·nom′ic
pre′ë·co·nom′i·cal
pre·ëd′it
pre′ë·di′tion
pre′ëd·i·to′ri·al
pre·ëd′u·cate
pre′ëd·u·ca′tion
pre′ëd·u·ca′tion·al
pre′ë·lec′tric
pre′ë·lec′tri·cal
pre′ël·e·men′tal
pre′ël·e·men′ta·ry
pre′-E·liz′a·be′than
pre′ë·man′ci·pa′tion
pre′ëm·bar′rass
pre′ëm·bar′rass·ment
pre′ëm·bod′i·ment
pre′ëm·bod′y
pre′ë·mer′gen·cy
pre′ë·mo′tion
pre′ë·mo′tion·al
pre-Em′pire
pre′ëm·ploy′
pre′ëm·ploy′ment
pre′ën·a′ble
pre′ën·act′
pre′ën·ac′tion
pre′ën·close′
pre′ën·clo′sure
pre′ën·coun′ter
pre′ën·deav′or
pre′ën·dorse′
pre′ën·dorse′ment
pre′ën·force′
pre′ën·force′ment
pre′ën·gage′
pre′ën·gage′ment
pre′ën·gi·neered′
pre′ën·gi·neer′ing
pre′ën·large′
pre′ën·large′ment
pre′ën·light′en
pre′ën·light′en·ing
pre′ën·light′en·ment
pre′ën·list′
pre′ën·list′ment
pre′ën·roll′
pre′ën·roll′ment
pre·ën′ter
pre′ën·ter·tain′
pre′ën·ter·tain′er
pre′ën·ter·tain′ment
pre·ën′trance
pre·ën′try
pre′ë·nu′mer·ate
pre′ë·nu′mer·a′tion
pre′ën·vel′op
pre′ën·vel′op·ment
pre′ën·vi′ron·men′tal
pre′ëp·i·dem′ic
pre·ëp′och·al
pre′ë·quip′
pre′ë·quip′ment
pre′ë·rect′
pre′ë·rec′tion
pre′ë·rupt′
pre′ë·rup′tion
pre′ë·rup′tive
pre′ës·sen′tial
pre′ës·tab′lish
pre′ës·tab′lish·ment
pre·ës′ti·mate
pre′ës·ti·ma′tion
pre′ë·vap′o·rate
pre′ë·vap′o·ra′tion
pre′ëv·o·lu′tion·al
pre′ëv·o·lu′tion·ar′y
pre′ëx·act′
pre′ëx·ac′tion
pre′ëx·am′i·na′tion
pre′ëx·am′ine
pre′ëx·am′in·er
pre′ëx·change′
pre′ëx·clude′
pre′ëx·clu′sion
pre′ëx·clu′sive
pre′ëx·cuse′
pre·ëx′e·cute
pre′ëx·e·cu′tion
pre′ëx·empt′
pre′ëx·emp′tion
pre′ëx·haust′
pre′ëx·haus′tion
pre′ëx·hib′it
pre′ëx·hi·bi′tion
pre′ëx·hib′i·tor
pre′ëx·ist′
pre′ëx·ist′ence
pre′ëx·ist′ent
pre′ëx·pe·di′tion
pre′ëx·pe·di′tion·ar′y
pre′ëx·per′i·men′tal
pre′ëx·pose′
pre′ëx·po·si′tion
pre′ëx·tin′guish
pre′ëx·tin′guish·ment
pre·fab′u·lous
pre·fash′ion
pre·fed′er·al
pre·fes′ti·val
pre·feu′dal
pre·feu′dal·ism
pre·flight′
pre·flow′er·ing
pre′foun·da′tion
pre′fra·ter′nal
pre′fra·ter′nal·ly
pre·freeze′
pre-French′
pre·fresh′man
pre·fur′lough
pre·fur′nish
pre·gain′
pre′-Gal·i·le′an
pre·gal′va·nize
pre′game
pre·gath′er
pre·gath′er·ing
pre′ge·o·log′i·cal
pre-Geor′gian
pre-Ger′man
pre′-Ger·man′ic
pre·girl′hood
pre·gla′cial
pre-Goth′ic
pre′grad·u·a′tion
pre′grat·i·fi·ca′tion
pre·grat′i·fy
pre-Greek′
pre′guar·an·tee′
pre·hard′en
pre·har′vest
pre·haunt′
pre·hear′ing
pre·heat′ed
pre-He′brew
pre′-Hel·len′ic
pre′-His·pan′ic
pre·hol′i·day
pre′-Ho·mer′ic
pre·hu′man
pre·im′age
pre′i·mag′i·nar′y
pre′i·mag′i·na′tion
pre′i·mag′ine
pre′im·bibe′
pre′im·bue′
pre·im′i·tate
pre′im·i·ta′tion
pre·im′i·ta′tive
pre′im·pe′ri·al
pre′im·press′
pre′im·pres′sion
pre′im·pres′sive
pre′in·au′gu·ral
pre′in·au′gu·rate
pre-In′ca
pre′in·car·na′tion
pre′in·cen′tive
pre′in·cli·na′tion
pre′in·cline′
pre′in·cor′po·rate
pre′in·cor′po·ra′tion
pre′in·de·pend′ence
pre′in·de·pend′ent
pre-In′di·an
pre·in′di·cate
pre′in·di·ca′tion
pre′in·dis·pose′
pre′in·dis′po·si′tion
pre′in·duc′tion
pre′in·duc′tive
pre′in·flec′tion·al
pre′in·flict′
pre′in·flic′tion
pre′in·form′
pre′in·for·ma′tion
pre′in·hab′it
pre′in·hab′it·ant
pre′in·hab′i·ta′tion
pre′in·here′
pre′in·her′it
pre′in·her′it·ance
pre′in·i′tial
pre′in·i′ti·ate
pre′in·i′ti·a′tion
pre′in·qui·si′tion
pre′in·scribe′
pre′in·scrip′tion
pre′in·sert′
pre′in·ser′tion
pre′in·spect′
pre′in·spec′tion
pre′in·stall′
pre′in·stal·la′tion
pre′in·still′
pre′in·stil·la′tion
pre′in·struct′
pre·in′su·late
pre′in·su·la′tion
pre′in·sur′ance
pre′in·sure′
pre′in·tend′
pre′in·ten′tion
pre′in·ter·change′
pre·in′ter·est
pre′in·ter′pret
pre′in·ter′pre·ta′tion
pre·in′ter·view
pre·in′ti·mate
pre′in·ti·ma′tion
pre′in·ven·to′ry
pre′in·vest′ment
pre′in·volve′
pre′in·volve′ment
pre-I′rish
pre-Is′lam
pre′-Is·lam′ic
pre-Is′lam·ite
pre·is′sue
pre-Jew′ish
pre′-John·so′ni·an
pre·jun′ior
pre′jus·ti·fi·ca′tion
pre·jus′ti·fy
pre·kin′der·gar′ten
pre·kin′dle
pre·know′
pre·knowl′edge
pre′-Ko·ran′ic
pre·la′bel
pre·lac′te·al
pre-Lat′in
pre·launch′
pre·law′
pre·law′ful
pre·le′gal
pre·leg′is·la′tive
pre·li′cense
pre·lim′it
pre′lin·guis′tic
pre′-Lin·nae′an
pre·lit′er·ar′y
pre·lit′er·ate
pre·lit′er·a·ture
pre·load′
pre·loan′
pre·lo′cate
pre·log′i·cal
pre·lu′bri·cate
pre·lum′bar

 PRONUNCIATION KEY: hat, āge, cãre, fär; let, ēqual, tėrm; it, īce; hot, ōpen, ôrder; oil, out; cup, pu̇t, rüle;

pre-Lu′ther·an
pre·ma·chine′
pre·mad′ness
pre·make′
pre·mak′er
pre′-Ma·lay′an
pre′ma·lig′nant
pre′man·dib′u·lar
pre′ma·ni′a·cal
pre′man·u·fac′ture
pre·mar′i·tal
pre·mar′riage
pre·mar′ry
pre-Marx′i·an
pre·match′
pre′ma·te′ri·al
pre′mat·ri·mo′ni·al
pre·meas′ure
pre·meas′ure·ment
pre·med′i·cate
pre′med·i·ca′tion
pre′me·di·e′val
pre′mem·o·ran′dum
pre′me·mo′ri·al
pre′men·o·pau′sal
pre·merg′er
pre′-Mes·si·an′ic
pre-Meth′od·ist
pre·mid′night′
pre·mid′sum′mer
pre·min′is·ter
pre·mix′ture
pre·mod′el
pre·mod′ern
pre′-Mo·ham′me·dan
pre·mold′
pre′mo·nar′chi·cal
pre·mon′e·tar′y
pre′-Mon·go′li·an
pre′mon·u·men′tal
pre·mor′al
pre′mo·ral′i·ty
pre·mor′al·ly
pre·morn′ing
pre·mor′tal
pre′mo·sa′ic
pre′-Mo·sa′ic
pre-Mos′lem
pre·mourn′
pre·move′
pre′mu·nic′i·pal
pre·mu′si·cal
pre·mus′ter
pre′-My·ce·nae′an
pre·myth′i·cal
pre′-Na·po′le·on′ic
pre·na′tion·al
pre·na′tive
pre·nat′u·ral
pre·na′val
pre·neb′u·lar
pre′ne·go′ti·ate
pre′ne·go′ti·a′tion
pre′ne·o·lith′ic
pre′ne·phrit′ic
pre′-New·to′ni·an
pre-Nor′man
pre-Norse′
pre·num′ber
pre·num′ber·ing
pre·nup′tial
pre·nurs′er·y
pre′ob·jec′tion
pre′ob·li·ga′tion
pre′ob·serv′ance
pre′ob·ser·va′tion
pre′ob·ser·va′tion·al
pre′ob·serve′
pre′ob·tain′
pre′ob·tain′a·ble
pre′oc·cip′i·tal
pre′oc·clu′sion
pre·oc′cu·pant
pre·of′fer
pre·o′pen
pre·o′pen·ing
pre·op′er·at′ing
pre·op′er·a′tive
pre·op′tic
pre′or·dain′
pre′or·dained′
pre′or·dain′ment
pre·or′der
pre′or·gan′ic
pre′o·rig′i·nal
pre′o·rig′i·nal·ly
pre′-Pa·le·o·zo′ic
pre′par·lia·men′ta·ry
pre′par·oc·cip′i·tal
pre·par′ti·san
pre′par·ti′tion
pre·part′ner·ship
pre·pat′ent
pre-Paul′ine
pre·pen′e·trate
pre′pen·e·tra′tion
pre·peo′ple
pre′per·cep′tion
pre′per·i·to·ne′al
pre-Per′mi·an
pre-Pe′trine
pre′pig·men′tal
pre·pi′ous
pre′pi·tu′i·tar′y
pre·place′
pre′pla·cen′tal
pre·planned′
pre·plant′
pre·plot′
pre·pol′ish
pre-Pol′ish
pre·pol′i·tic
pre′po·lit′i·cal
pre′por·tray′
pre′por·tray′al
pre′po·ten′tial
pre·pran′di·al
pre′prep·a·ra′tion
pre·price′
pre·pri′ma′ry
pre·prim′er
pre′pro·duc′tion
pre′pro·fess′
pre′pro·hi·bi′tion
pre′pro·nounce′
pre′pro·nounce′ment
pre′pro·phet′ic
pre·prove′
pre′pro·vide′
pre′psy·chol′o·gy
pre·pu′ber·tal
pre′pub·li·ca′tion
pre·pub′lish
pre′qual·i·fi·ca′tion
pre·qual′i·fy
pre·quar′an·tine
pre·ques′tion
pre·rail′road′
pre·rail′way′
pre-Raph′a·el
pre·ra′tion·al
pre·read′i·ness
pre′re·ceipt′
pre′re·ceive′
pre′re·ceiv′er
pre′re·ces′sion
pre′rec·og·ni′tion
pre′rec·om·mend′
pre·rec′on·cile
pre·rec′on·cile′ment
pre′-Re·con·struc′-tion
pre·rec′tal
pre′re·deem′
pre′re·demp′tion
pre·ref′er·ence
pre′re·fine′ment
pre′re·form′
pre′ref·or·ma′tion
pre′-Ref·or·ma′tion
pre′re·form′a·to′ry
pre·reg′is·ter
pre′reg·is·tra′tion
pre′reg·u·la′tion
pre′re·lease′
pre′re·li′gious
pre′re·mit′tance
pre′re·morse′
pre-Ren′ais·sance
pre·re′nal
pre′rep·re·sent′
pre′rep·re·sen·ta′tion
pre′re·quire′
pre′re·quire′ment
pre′re·sem′blance
pre′re·sem′ble
pre′re·solve′
pre′res·pi·ra′tion
pre′re·spire′
pre′-Res·to·ra′tion
pre′re·stric′tion
pre′re·veal′
pre′rev·e·la′tion
pre′re·view′
pre′re·vi′sion
pre′re·viv′al
pre′-Rev·o·lu′tion
pre′rev·o·lu′tion·ar′y
pre-Ro′man
pre′ro·man′tic
pre′ro·man′ti·cism
pre·roy′al
pre·sa′cral
pre′sal·va′tion
pre·san′i·tar′y
pre′sar·to·ri′al
pre·sav′age
pre·sav′age·ry
pre-Sax′on
pre′scho·las′tic
pre′sci·en·tif′ic
pre·scout′
pre·seal′
pre·search′
pre·sea′son
pre·sea′son·al
pre·sec′u·lar
pre′se·cure′
pre′se·lect′
pre′se·lec′tion
pre·sell′
pre·sem′i·nar′y
pre′-Se·mit′ic
pre·se′nile
pre·sen′ior
pre·sen′si·tize
pre·sen′tence
pre·serv′ice
pre·ses′sion
pre·set′tle
pre·set′tle·ment
pre·shad′ow
pre-Shake′speare
pre′-Shake·spear′i·an
pre·shape′
pre·sharp′en
pre·ship′
pre·ship′ment
pre·show′
pre·shrink′
pre·sift′
pre·sig′nal
pre′-Si·lu′ri·an
pre·slav′er·y
pre·so′cial
pre′-So·crat′ic
pre·so′lar
pre·soph′o·more
pre·space′
pre-Span′ish
pre·spi′nal
pre·sput′nik
pre·stamp′
pre′stand·ard·i·za′-tion
pre·stand′ard·ize
pre·steam′
pre·stim′u·lus
pre·stock′
pre·strength′en
pre·stretch′
pre′strike′
pre·stud′y
pre′sub·sist′ence
pre′sub·sist′ent
pre′suc·cess′
pre′suc·cess′ful
pre′sup·ple·men′-ta·ry
pre·sur′ger·y
pre·sur′gi·cal
pre′sus·pect′
pre·symp′tom
pre′syn·ap′tic
pre-Syr′i·an
pre′sys·tol′ic
pre·taste′
pre·tast′er
pre·tax′
pre′tax·a′tion
pre·tel′e·graph
pre′tel·e·graph′ic
pre·tel′e·phone
pre′tel·e·phon′ic
pre·tem′po·ral
pre′ter·res′tri·al
pre-Ter′ti·ar′y
pre′-Thanks·giv′ing
pre′tho·rac′ic
pre·tib′i·al
pre·tinc′ture
pre·tour′na·ment
pre·tra′che·al
pre′tra·di′tion·al
pre·train′
pre·trea′ty
pre·trib′al
pre-Tu′dor
pre′un·der·stand′
pre·un′ion
pre′u·nite′
pre·vac′ci·nate
pre′vac·ci·na′tion
pre′val·u·a′tion
pre·val′ue
pre·ver′bal
pre′-Ver·gil′i·an
pre·ver′nal
pre·ver′te·bral
pre·ves′i·cle
pre′-Vic·to′ri·an
pre·vis′it
pre·vis′i·tor
pre·vo′cal
pre·vo′cal·ly
pre′vo·li′tion·al
pre-Vol′stead
pre·vote′
pre·warn′
pre·weigh′
pre·wire′
pre·wrap′

preach (prēch), *v.i.* **1.** to speak publicly on a religious subject: *Who is going to preach at the Christmas Service?* **2.** to give earnest advice. **3.** to give advice earnestly, usually in a meddling or tiresome way: *Great-Aunt Lucy is forever preaching about good manners.*
—*v.t.* **1.** to deliver (a sermon): *Dr. Clark preached a very eloquent sermon.* **2.** to make known by preaching; proclaim: *to preach the Gospel.* **3.** to recommend strongly; urge: *The coach was always preaching exercise and fresh air. Practice what you preach.*
preach down, a. to condemn by preaching; speak against: *to preach down war and violence.* **b.** to suppress or silence by preaching: *to preach down criticism.*
preach up, to commend by preaching; speak in favor of: *Philosophy and Christianity both preach up forgiveness of injuries* (Henry Fielding).
—*n. Informal.* a sermon; religious discourse: [< Old French *preche,* French *prêche* a preaching; from the verb]
[< Old French *prechier,* short for *preëchier* < *predichier,* learned borrowing from Latin *praedicāre* declare publicly (in Late Latin, to preach). Doublet of PREDICATE.]
—**Syn.** *v.t.* **3.** advocate.

preach·er (prē′chər), *n.* a person who preaches; clergyman; minister: *I think they come under the heading of what the old preacher called vanity* (New Yorker).
the Preacher, a title given to the author or narrator of the book of Ecclesiastes; the Ecclesiast: *These are the words of the Preacher, the son of David, King of Jerusalem* (Miles Coverdale).

preach·er·ship (prē′chər ship), *n.* the office of a preacher.

preach·i·fy (prē′chə fī), *v.i.,* **-fied, -fy·ing.** *Informal.* to preach or moralize too much.

preach·ing (prē′ching), *n.* **1. a.** what is preached; sermon. **b.** a public religious service with a sermon. **2.** the act or practice of a person who preaches: *France combines an imperishable structure with the perpetual preaching of insurrection* (Newsweek). —**preach′ing·ly,** *adv.*

preaching cross, a cross formerly erected to mark a place for open-air preaching, as by monks.

Preaching Cross at Inveraray, Scotland

preach·ment (prēch′mənt), *n.* **1.** a preaching: . . . *those, who, mistaken because of insidious and unhealthy preachments, may have followed improper conduct for free and calm men* (New York Times). **2.** a long, tiresome sermon or speech: *Most parents tend to rely on preachments to impart their values to their children* (Sidonie M. Gruenberg).

preach·y (prē′chē), *adj.,* **preach·i·er, preach·i·est.** *Informal.* **1.** inclined to preach: *Of the 1,400-odd books . . . many, of course, are teachy, preachy pills of moralism* (Newsweek). **2.** suggestive of preaching. —**Syn. 1.** didactic.

pre·a·dam·ic (prē′ə dam′ik), *adj.* before Adam.

pre·ad·a·mite (prē ad′ə mīt), *n.* **1.** a person believed to have lived before Adam. **2.** a person who holds that there were men in existence before Adam.
—*adj.* **1.** that existed before Adam: *detached broken fossils of preadamite whales* (Herman Melville). **2.** having to do with the preadamites.
[< New Latin *Praeadamitae,* plural < Latin *prae-* before + *Adam* Adam + *-itae* -ite[1]]

pre·ad·am·it·ic (prē′ad əm it′ik), *adj.* preadamite.

pre·ad·o·les·cence (prē′ad ə les′əns), *n.* **1.** the period of life between childhood and adolescence: *Almost all little girls, caught in the special exaltations of preadolescence, . . . long to be some kind of heroine* (Maclean's). **2.** prepuberty.

pre·al·bu·mi·nu·ric (prē al byü′mə nůr′ik), *adj.* preceding the occurrence of albuminuria: *the prealbuminuric stage of Bright's disease.*

pre·am·ble (prē′am′bəl), *n.* **1.** a preliminary statement; introduction to a speech or a writing: *The reasons for a law and its general purpose are often stated in a preamble. This is a long preamble of a tale* (Chaucer). **2.** a preliminary or introductory fact or circumstance: *This was the preamble of the great troubles that . . . followed* (Robert Blair). [< Old French *preambule,* learned borrowing from Medieval Latin *praeambulum,* noun use of adjective, preliminary (in Late Latin, walking before) < Late Latin *praeambulāre* < Latin *prae-* before + *ambulāre* to walk]

pre·amp (prē amp′), *n.* a preamplifier.

pre·am·pli·fi·er (prē am′plə fī′ər), *n.* a unit that gives preliminary amplification to very weak impulses, bringing them to a level suitable for further amplification: *Everybody has taken to being an expert and hooking up his separately purchased tuner, amplifier, preamplifier* (New Yorker).

pre·a·tom·ic (prē′ə tom′ik), *adj.* before August 6, 1945, the first military use of the atom bomb, at Hiroshima: *Preatomic age radioactivity was caused by naturally occurring radioisotopes and cosmic radiation* (Science News Letter).

pre·au·dit (prē ô′dit), *n.* an audit conducted before a transaction has been settled or completed: *The shipping agency would then submit the figures for domestic and foreign construction to the Controller General for a legal ruling and preaudit by the General Accounting Office before committing itself to a construction subsidy figure* (New York Times).

pre·ax·i·al (prē′ak′sē əl), *adj.* **1.** in front of the body. **2.** of or having to do with the inner side of the arm or of the leg.

preb·end (preb′ənd), *n. British.* **1.** the salary given to a clergyman connected with a cathedral or a collegiate church. **2.** the particular property or church tax from which the money comes for this salary. **3.** a prebendary. [< Old French *prebende,* learned borrowing from Late Latin *praebenda* allowance < Latin, (literally) things to be furnished < *praebēre* to furnish, offer, short for *praehibēre* < *prae-* before + *habēre* to hold. Doublet of PROVENDER.]

pre·ben·dal (pri ben′dəl), *adj.* having to do with a prebend or a prebendary.

preb·en·dar·y (preb′ən der′ē), *n., pl.* **-dar·ies.** *British.* a clergyman who has a prebend.

prec., preceding.

pre·cal·cic (prē kal′sik), *adj.* (of certain minerals) mostly calcic.

Pre-Cam·bri·an (prē kam′brē ən), *n.* **1.** the geological period that includes all the time before the Cambrian: *The Pre-Cambrian includes all the history of the earth from its supposed origin until the invasion of the Cambrian seas over the eroded continents. This span of time involved is at least a billion and a half years* (Robert M. Garrels). **2.** the rocks formed in this period. *—adj.* of this period or these rocks.

Pre-Cambrian shield, a large area over which Pre-Cambrian rocks are exposed at the surface. Most of eastern Canada and the Adirondack Mountains in New York State is a Pre-Cambrian shield.

pre·can·cel (prē kan′səl), *v.,* **-celed, -cel·ing** or (*especially British*) **-celled, -cel·ling,** *n.* *—v.t.* to put a mark of cancellation on (a postage stamp) before sale for use on bulk mail or parcel post. *—n.* a precanceled postage stamp.

pre·can·cer·ous (prē kan′sər əs), *adj.* of or having to do with a condition of the tissues which, while not now cancerous, may develop into cancer, as certain skin growths: *Examination of the lungs of cigarette smokers under the microscope reveals precancerous changes* (Atlantic).

pre·car·i·ous (pri kãr′ē əs), *adj.* **1.** dependent on the will or pleasure of another. **2.** not safe or secure; uncertain; dangerous; risky: *A soldier leads a precarious life. His power was more precarious than ... he was willing to admit* (Scott). **3.** poorly founded; doubtful; assumed: *a precarious opinion or conclusion.* [< Latin *precārius* (with English *-ous*) obtainable by entreaty; dependent on another's will, uncertain < *prex, precis* prayer] **—pre·car′i·ous·ly,** *adv.* **—pre·car′i·ous·ness,** *n.*

—**Syn. 2.** perilous, hazardous. —**Ant. 2.** certain, secure, safe, sure.

pre·cast (prē kast′, -käst′), *v.t.,* **-cast, -cast·ing.** to cast (a building material) into blocks before using it for building.

prec·a·tive (prek′ə tiv), *adj.* expressing entreaty or desire; supplicatory. [< Late Latin *precātīvus* < Latin *precārī* entreat]

prec·a·to·ry (prek′ə tôr′ē, -tōr′-), *adj.* of, like, or expressing entreaty or supplication. [< Late Latin *precātōrius* < Latin *precātor, -ōris* entreater < *precārī* to entreat, pray]

pre·cau·tion (pri kô′shən), *n.* **1.** a taking care beforehand: *Proper precaution is prudent.* **2.** care taken beforehand; thing done beforehand to ward off evil or secure good results: *Locking doors is a precaution.* [< Late Latin *praecautiō, -ōnis* < Latin *praecavēre* guard against beforehand < *prae-* before + *cavēre* be on one's guard] —**Syn. 1.** forethought, foresight. **2.** safeguard.

pre·cau·tion·al (pri kô′shə nəl), *adj.* precautionary.

pre·cau·tion·ar·y (pri kô′shə ner′ē), *adj.* of or using precaution: *throwing a precautionary glance around, as if to assure himself that we were not alone* (Charles Lever).

pre·cau·tious (pri kô′shəs), *adj.* using or showing precaution: *This precautious way of reasoning and acting has proved ... an uninterrupted source of felicity* (Sir Richard Steele). **—pre·cau′tious·ly,** *adv.*

pre·cede (prē sēd′), *v.,* **-ced·ed, -ced·ing.** *—v.t.* **1.** to go before; come before: *A precedes B in the alphabet. Mr. Eisenhower preceded Mr. Kennedy as President.* **2.** to be higher than in rank or importance: *A major precedes a captain.* **3.** to introduce by something preliminary; preface.

—v.i. to go or come before, as in rank, order, place, or time.

[< Latin *praecēdere* < *prae-* before + *cēdere* to go. Compare PRECESSION.]

prec·e·dence (pres′ə dəns, pri sē′-), *n.* **1.** the act or fact of preceding. **2.** higher position or rank; greater importance: *This work takes precedence over all other work.* **3.** the right to precede others in ceremonies or social affairs; social superiority: *A Senator takes precedence over a Representative.* —**Syn. 1.** antecedence. **2.** priority.

prec·e·den·cy (pres′ə dən sē, pri sē′-), *n., pl.* **-cies.** precedence.

prec·e·dent (*n.* pres′ə dənt; *adj.* pri sē′dənt, pres′ə-), *n.* **1.** a case that may serve as an example or reason for a later case: *There was no precedent for Roosevelt's election to a third term as President.* **2.** *Law.* a judicial decision, case, proceeding, etc., that serves as a guide or pattern in future similar or analogous situations: *A decision of a court often serves as a precedent in another court. Precedent to a court is what past performances are to sports and the theater* (Wall Street Journal). [< adjective]

—adj. preceding. [< Latin *praecēdēns, -entis,* present participle of *praecēdere* precede] **—pre·ced′ent·ly,** *adv.*

prec·e·dent·ed (pres′ə den′tid), *adj.* justified by precedent.

prec·e·den·tial (pres′ə den′shəl), *adj.* **1.** of, being, or like a precedent: *If he is appointed, any applicant ... can claim ... appointment on the strength of this precedential case* (New York Independent). **2.** having precedence; preceding: *It becomes necessary to distinguish the several precedential or introductory facts ... from the ultimate principal fact* (Jeremy Bentham). **3.** having to do with social precedence: *Charles the Fifth settled a precedential hubbub between two dames of high degree* (Fraser's Magazine).

pre·ced·ing (prē sē′ding), *adj.* going before; coming before; previous: *The preceding winter weeks had been dull and gloomy so that today's spring sunshine was a welcome change.*

—**Syn.** See **previous.**

pre·cent (pri sent′), *v.t., v.i.* to act as precentor. [perhaps back formation < *precentor*]

pre·cen·tor (pri sen′tər), *n.* a person who leads and directs the singing of a church choir or congregation: *Observe a bevy of them ... joining in tiny chorus to the directing melody of an elder precentor* (Cowden Clarke). [< Latin *praecentor, -ōris* < *praecinere* sing before < *prae-* before + *canere* sing]

pre·cen·to·ri·al (prē′sen tôr′ē əl, -tōr′-), *adj.* of or having to do with a precentor.

pre·cen·tor·ship (pri sen′tər ship), *n.* the office, position, or function of a precentor.

pre·cept (prē′sept), *n.* **1.** a rule of action or behavior; maxim: *"If at first you don't succeed, try, try again" is a familiar precept. His high-school science course covered many of the basic precepts of modern physics.* **2.** *Law.* a writ; warrant; a written order issued pursuant to law. [< Anglo-French *precep,* and *precept,* learned borrowing from Latin *praeceptum* (originally) neuter past participle of *praecipere* to order, advise, anticipate < *prae-* before + *capere* to take] —**Syn. 1.** teaching, adage, axiom.

pre·cep·tive (pri sep′tiv), *adj.* of the nature of or expressing a precept; instructive. **—pre·cep′tive·ly,** *adv.*

pre·cep·tor (pri sep′tər), *n.* **1.** an instructor; teacher; tutor. **2.** the head of a preceptory. [< Latin *praeceptor, -ōris* < *praecipere;* see PRECEPT] —**Syn. 1.** schoolmaster.

pre·cep·to·ral (pri sep′tər əl), *adj.* preceptorial.

pre·cep·tor·ate (pri sep′tər it), *n.* the office of a preceptor.

pre·cep·to·ri·al (prē′sep tôr′ē əl, -tōr′-), *adj.* **1.** of a preceptor; like that of a preceptor: *Wilson immediately proposed the preceptorial system to supplement the stultifying lectures of the day* (Newsweek). **2.** using preceptors.

pre·cep·tor·ship (pri sep′tər ship), *n.* the office or position of a preceptor.

pre·cep·to·ry (pri sep′tər ē), *n., pl.* **-ries,** *adj.* *—n.* **1.** a subordinate house or community of the Knights Templars. **2.** the estate or manor of such a community. *—adj.* preceptive.

[< Medieval Latin *praeceptoria* (literally) having to do with a preceptor, or instructor]

pre·cep·tress (pri sep′tris), *n.* a woman preceptor.

pre·ce·ram·ic (prē′sə ram′ik), *adj.* of, having to do with, or belonging to a period or culture that existed before the making of pottery: *Associated human artifacts indicated occupation by preceramic Basket Makers estimated to date between 1500 and 2500 years ago* (Science).

pre·cess (prē ses′), *v.i.* to undergo precession: *When a steady twist is applied to a top ... the top wobbles or precesses slowly at right angles to the direction of the disturbing forces* (J. Little).

pre·ces·sion (prē sesh′ən), *n.* **1.** the act or fact of going first; precedence. **2.** the rotation of a spinning rigid body that has been tipped from its vertical axis by external torques acting on it. This phenomenon is illustrated by the wobble of a top and the gyration of the earth's axis. *The cross has shifted southward in the sky due to the earth's precession* (World Book Encyclopedia). **3.** the precession of the equinoxes. [< Late Latin *praecessiō, -ōnis* < Latin *praecēdere* precede]

pre·ces·sion·al (prē sesh′ə nəl), *adj.* of or caused by the precession of the equinoxes: *Now the axis points to a part of the sky close to our Polaris, but during this period, known as the "precessional" cycle, it points to a number of other stars* (Science News Letter).

precession of the equinoxes, 1. the earlier occurrence of the equinoxes in each successive sidereal year. This is the result of a slow westward movement of the equinoxes along the ecliptic caused by a gradual change in the direction of the earth's axis because of the combined action of the sun, moon, and planets on the mass of matter accumulated about the earth's equator. **2.** this motion of the equinoctial points. **3.** this change in the direction of the earth's axis.

pre·chor·dal (prē′kôr′dəl), *adj.* situated in front of the notochord, especially of the embryos of higher vertebrates.

pre-Chris·tian (prē kris′chən), *adj.* **1.** of or having to do with the times before the birth of Christ; before Christ. **2.** before the introduction of Christianity: *The Yule log and the holly wreath are only two of the many Christmas symbols that originated in pre-Christian times.*

pré·cieuse (prā syœz′), *n. French.* **1.** a woman who affects too much refinement of taste, language, etc. **2.** (literally) too refined; precious.

—adj. overrefined; precious: *Her conversation is natural and reasonable, not précieuse and affected* (Horace Walpole).

pré·cieux (prā syœ′), *n. French.* a man who is overly refined and usually affects overly developed taste or has affectations of language.

pre·cinct (prē′singkt), *n.* **1.** a district within certain boundaries, for governmental, administrative, or other purposes: *an election precinct, a police precinct.* **2.** the space within a boundary: *Do not leave the school precincts during school hours. The slightest invasion of the precincts which had been assigned to another tribe produced desperate skirmishes* (Scott). **3.** the ground immediately surrounding a church, temple, etc.: *They reached the precinct of the God, And on the hallowed turf their feet now trod* (William Morris).

precincts, a boundary; limit: *The whole population of the valley seemed to be gathered within the precincts of the grove* (Herman Melville).

[< Medieval Latin *praecinctum,* (originally) neuter past participle of Latin *praecingere* enclose < *prae-* before + *cingere* to gird, surround]

pre·ci·os·i·ty (presh′ē os′ə tē), *n., pl.* **-ties. 1.** too much refinement; affectation: *Her work was sick, he told her—cramped with preciosity and mannerisms* (New Yorker). **2.** the persons showing such refinement: *All London had indeed been present ... The entire preciosity of the metropolis* (Arnold Bennett).

preciosities, precious things; articles of value: *five invaluable trunks, full of preciosities* (Arnold Bennett).

[< Old French *preciosite* < *precieux,* earlier *precios* precious]

—**Syn. 1.** fastidiousness.

pre·cious (presh′əs), *adj.* **1.** worth much; valuable; of great importance: *Gold, silver, and platinum are often called the precious metals. They were folk to whom sleep was precious* (John Galsworthy). **2.** much loved; dear: *a precious child.* **3.** too nice; overrefined: *His poetry is flowery, effeminate, almost precious in tone.* **4.** *Informal.* very great: *He's put things in a precious mess!* **5.** of great moral or spiritual worth: *the precious blood of Christ* (I Peter 1:19). **6.** choice; fine:

Did you ever see such a precious set of villains? (Frederick Marryat). **7.** gross; arrant: *Here, Mr. Speaker, is a precious mockery* (Edmund Burke).
—*adv. Informal.* very; extremely: *precious little money. I'll take precious good care never to sing in a theatre again* (George Du Maurier).
[< Old French *precios* (with English *-ous*), learned borrowing from Latin *pretiōsus* < *pretium* value, price] —**pre′cious·ness,** *n.*
—**Syn.** *adj.* **1.** See **valuable.**

precious garnet, a variety of garnet sometimes used as a gem; pyrope.

pre·cious·ly (presh′əs lē), *adv.* **1.** at great cost: *Some preciously by shattered porcelain fall, And some by aromatic splinters die* (John Dryden). **2.** *Rare.* in a valuable manner or degree: *The time 'twixt six and now Must by us both be spent most preciously* (Shakespeare). **3.** extremely: *Captain Tagrag was my opponent, and preciously we poked each other* (Thackeray). **4.** with extreme care in matters of detail: *Your art of painting from nature is not yet quite perfectly and preciously imitative* (Philip G. Hamerton).

precious stone, a jewel; gem: *Diamonds, rubies, and sapphires are precious stones.*

prec·i·pice (pres′ə pis), *n.* **1.** a very steep cliff; almost vertical slope: *A few steps more, and I was standing on the very edge of a bank, a precipice not less than fifty feet deep* (W. H. Hudson). **2.** a situation of great peril; critical position: *By giving the nation the feeling of hanging on a precipice, they succeeded in mobilizing public opinion behind them* (Newsweek). [< French *précipice,* learned borrowing from Latin *praecipitium* < *praeceps, -cipitis* steep; (literally) headlong < *prae-* forth, ahead + *caput, capitis* head]
—**Syn. 1.** escarpment, crag.

pre·cip·i·ta·bil·i·ty (pri sip′ə tə bil′ə tē), *n.* the quality of being precipitable: *The authors have examined the precipitability and precipitation of . . . sulphates* (Nature).

pre·cip·i·ta·ble (pri sip′ə tə bəl), *adj.* that can be precipitated, as from solution: *The amount of precipitable water contained in the world's atmosphere is only equivalent to 1 in. of rainfall . . .* (J. D. Ovington).

pre·cip·i·tance (pri sip′ə təns), *n.* headlong haste; rashness: *The youth expects to force his way by genius, vigour, and precipitance* (Samuel Johnson).

pre·cip·i·tan·cy (pri sip′ə tən sē), *n., pl.* **-cies.** precipitance: *hurried on by the precipitancy of youth* (Jonathan Swift).

pre·cip·i·tant (pri sip′ə tənt), *adj.* **1.** very sudden or abrupt. **2.** acting in a hasty or rash manner. **3.** falling or rushing headlong; directed straight downward: *Our men put the enemy to precipitant flight. He . . . Downright into the world's first region throws His flight precipitant* (Milton). **4.** falling to the bottom as a precipitate.
—*n.* a substance that causes another substance in solution in a liquid to be deposited in solid form.
[< Latin *praecipitāns, -antis,* present participle of *praecipitāre;* see PRECIPITATE] —**pre·cip′i·tant·ly,** *adv.*

pre·cip·i·tate (*v.* pri sip′ə tāt; *adj., n.* pri sip′ə tāt, -tit), *v.,* **-tat·ed, -tat·ing,** *adj., n.* —*v.t.* **1.** to hasten the beginning of; bring about suddenly: *to precipitate a war; . . . the depression of the forties which had precipitated the events of '48 . . .* (Edmund Wilson). **2.** to throw headlong; hurl: *to precipitate a rock down a cliff, to precipitate oneself into a struggle.* **3.** to separate (a substance) out from a solution as a solid: *The plate was prepared by the all but impossible process of precipitating silver chloride from solution . . .* (A.W. Haslett). **4.** to condense from vapor in the form of rain, dew, etc.
—*v.i.* **1.** to be deposited from solution as a solid. **2.** to be condensed as rain, dew, etc. **3.** to rush headlong; **4.** *Obsolete.* to fall headlong. [< Latin *praecipitāre* (with English *-ate*[1]) < *praeceps, -cipitis* headlong; see PRECIPICE]
—*adj.* **1.** very hurried; sudden: *A cool breeze caused a precipitate drop in the temperature.* **2.** with great haste and force; plunging or rushing; headlong: *Through the Sweet-water Valley precipitate leaps the Nebraska* (Longfellow). **3.** hasty; rash: *Any precipitate speech, or hasty action, would be a crime* (Mrs. Humphry Ward).
—*n.* **1.** a substance, usually crystalline, separated out from a solution as a solid. **2.** moisture condensed from vapor by cooling and deposited in drops as rain, dew, etc. [< New Latin *praecipitatum,* neuter noun, < Latin *praecipitāre;* see the verb] —**pre·cip′i·tate′ly,** *adv.* —**pre·cip′i·tate′ness,** *n.*

pre·cip·i·ta·tion (pri sip′ə tā′shən), *n.* **1.** the act or state of precipitating; throwing down or falling headlong. **2.** a hastening or hurrying. **3.** a sudden bringing on: *the precipitation of a quarrel, the precipitation of a war without warning.* **4.** unwise or rash rapidity; sudden haste. **5. a.** the separating of a substance from a solution as a solid. **b.** the substance separated out from a solution as a solid; precipitate. **6. a.** the depositing of moisture in the form of rain, hail, snow, sleet, ice, etc.: *In steppe lands and arid regions, evaporation is greater than precipitation* (R. N. Elston). **b.** the substance that is thus precipitated. **c.** the amount that is precipitated. **7.** (in spiritualism) materialization.

pre·cip·i·ta·tive (pri sip′ə tā′tiv), *adj.* having to do with precipitation; tending to precipitate.

pre·cip·i·ta·tor (pri sip′ə tā′tər), *n.* a person or thing that precipitates: *The slopes of elevations towards the sea are great precipitators of rain* (American).

pre·cip·i·tin (pri sip′ə tin), *n.* an antibody formed in blood serum as a result of inoculating with a foreign protein; coagulin. When the antibody is brought into contact with its soluble antigen, a precipitate forms: *Since this is a precipitation reaction, the particular type of antibody involved is known as a precipitin* (Harbaugh and Goodrich).

pre·cip·i·tous (pri sip′ə təs), *adj.* **1.** like a precipice; very steep: *precipitous cliffs. Access was gained by precipitous stone steps carved into the walls of rock* (Newsweek). **2.** hasty; rash. **3.** rushing headlong; very rapid: *The sweep Of some precipitous rivulet to the wave* (Tennyson).
[< Latin *praeceps, -cipitis* (see PRECIPICE) + English *-ous*] —**pre·cip′i·tous·ly,** *adv.* —**pre·cip′i·tous·ness,** *n.*
—**Syn. 1.** See **steep.**

pré·cis (prā′sē, prā sē′), *n., pl.* **-cis.** an abstract; summary: *Morton trotted up to the Capitol with the President's précis of the proposal to brief the Senate's leaders* (Time).
[< French, Middle French *précis,* noun use of adjective, condensed, precise < Latin *praecīsus.* See PRECISE.]
—**Syn.** compendium.

pre·cise (pri sīs′), *adj.* **1.** exact; accurate; definite: *a precise instrument. The precise sum was 34 cents. The essential criterion must always be that the information sought is reducible to a precise formula . . .* (Anthony H. Richmond). **2.** careful; particular: *precise handwriting.* **3.** strict; scrupulous; fastidious: *We had precise orders to come home by nine o'clock.* [< Middle French *précis, précise,* learned borrowings from Latin *praecīsus* abridged, cut off < *praecīdere* to cut short < *prae-* in front + *caedere* to cut] —**pre·cise′ness,** *n.*
—**Syn. 1.** correct.

pre·cise·ly (pri sīs′lē), *adv.* in a precise manner; exactly: *Do precisely as the directions say. Precisely in this respect, we seem to have fallen short of what was expected of us* (Bulletin of Atomic Scientists).

pre·ci·sian (pri sizh′ən), *n.* **1.** a person who is rigidly precise in the observance of rules or forms: *A profane person calls a man of piety a precisian* (Isaac Watts). **2.** a person who is precise in religious observance, such as an English Puritan of the 1500's and 1600's. —*adj.* of or having to do with a precisian or precisians: *A martyr to the political strategy of a precisian government* (Saturday Review). [< *precis*(e) + *-ian*]

pre·ci·sian·ism (pri sizh′ə niz əm), *n.* **1.** the quality or state of being a precisian. **2.** the doctrine or conduct of precisians.

pre·ci·sion (pri sizh′ən), *n.* **1.** accuracy; exactness; definiteness: *to speak with precision. A weapon of precision is one that can be delivered precisely where it is wanted* (Bulletin of Atomic Scientists). **2.** careful exactness: *to dress with precision.*
—*adj.* having to do with or characterized by precision: *The rendezvous was an extraordinary demonstration of precision control* (New York Times).
—**Syn.** *n.* **1.** correctness, preciseness.

precision bombing, the dropping of bombs from an aircraft on a specific building, group of buildings, or other narrowly defined target, usually with the aid of a special bombsight or from a relatively low altitude.

pre·ci·sion·ism (pri sizh′ə niz əm), *n.* **1.** the practice of precision; insistence on precision. **2.** the art or methods of the American school of purism: *Charles Sheeler, whose crystalline visions of locomotive-driving wheels . . . created the 1920's style called precisionism* (Time).

pre·ci·sion·ist (pri sizh′ə nist), *n.* a person who insists on or affects precision, especially in expression or language; purist. —*adj.* of or having to do with precisionism or the precisionists.

pre·clin·i·cal (prē klin′ə kəl), *adj.* **1.** coming or occurring before clinical use: *a preclinical test of a new drug.* **2.** preceding or preparing for clinical studies or aspects of medicine: *preclinical students.*

pre·clude (pri klüd′), *v.t.,* **-clud·ed, -clud·ing.** to shut out; make impossible; prevent: *Constant vigilance precludes surprise. The heavy thunderstorm precluded our going to the beach.*
[< Latin *praeclūdere* < *prae-* before, ahead + *claudere* to shut]
—**Syn.** exclude, hinder.

pre·clu·sion (pri klü′zhən), *n.* a precluding or being precluded: *The preclusion of disturbance and indecorum in Christian assemblies* (Samuel Taylor Coleridge). [< Latin *praeclūsiō, -ōnis* < *praeclūdere* preclude]

pre·clu·sive (pri klü′siv), *adj.* tending or serving to preclude. [< Latin *praeclūsus,* past participle of *praeclūdere* + English *-ive*] —**pre·clu′sive·ly,** *adv.*

pre·co·cial (pri kō′shəl), *adj.* of or having to do with birds, such as grouse, whose chicks are downy when hatched and able to run about: *The common song birds are all altricial, while domestic fowls, partridges, most wading birds, and the various ducks are precocial* (A. Franklin Shul). Also, **praecocial.**
[< Latin *praecox, -cocis* precocious + English *-al*[1]]

pre·co·cious (pri kō′shəs), *adj.* **1.** developed earlier than usual: *This very precocious child could read well at the age of four.* **2.** developed too early; occurring before the natural time: *a precocious taste for beer.* [*The*] *furniture, too, shows precocious dilapidation* (New Statesman). **3.** of, having to do with, or indicating premature development: *Her imperfect articulation was the least precocious thing she had about her* (Charlotte Brontë). **4.** flowering or fruiting early, as before the appearance of leaves.
[< Latin *praecox, -cocis* (with English *-ous*) maturing early < *praecoquere* to ripen fully < *prae-* before its time + *coquere* to ripen; (literally) to cook] —**pre·co′cious·ly,** *adv.* —**pre·co′cious·ness,** *n.*

pre·coc·i·ty (pri kos′ə tē), *n.* precocious development; early maturity: *Their* [*dramatic*] *productions . . . bear the marks of precocity and premature decay* (William Hazlitt).

pre·cog·ni·tion (prē′kog nish′ən), *n.* **1.** previous cognition or knowledge; foreknowledge: *He further claims the laboratory proof of precognition* (*as in preguessing the order of a pack of cards which is to be mechanically shuffled*) (Newsweek). **2.** in Scots law: **a.** a preliminary examination, as of witnesses. **b.** the evidence taken at it.

pre·cog·ni·tive (prē kog′nə tiv), *adj.* of the nature of or giving foreknowledge: *a precognitive dream.*

pre-Co·lum·bi·an (prē′kə lum′bē ən), *adj.* of or belonging to the period before the arrival of Columbus in America; representative of American culture during or before the 1400's: *pre-Columbian Mexican sculpture.* [*There*] *is a selection of pre-Columbian figurines, mainly from terra cotta and dating from around 1000 B.C. to 900 A.D.* (New Yorker).

pre·con·ceive (prē′kən sēv′), *v.t.,* **-ceived, -ceiv·ing.** to form an idea or opinion of beforehand: *The Coliseum was very much what I had preconceived it* (Nathaniel Hawthorne).

pre·con·cep·tion (prē′kən sep′shən), *n.* **1.** an idea or opinion formed beforehand: *the incapacity of actual objects for satisfying our preconceptions of them* (Charles Lamb). **2.** the act of preconceiving. —**Syn. 1.** prejudgment.

pre·con·cert (prē'kən sėrt'), *v.t.* to arrange beforehand: *acting in concert by the aid of preconcerted signals* (Washington Irving). —*n.* a previous arrangement; preconcerted agreement or action: *We arose, as if by preconcert, to make examination of our treasure* (Edgar Allan Poe).

pre·con·di·tion (prē'kən dish'ən), *n.* a condition required to be fulfilled beforehand; prerequisite: *Nonconformity is the basic precondition of art, as it is the precondition of good thinking ...* (Ben Shahn). —*v.t.* to condition beforehand: *For a weekend trip, the pilot will be preconditioned by eating a low residue diet* (Time).

pre·co·nize (prē'kə nīz), *v.t.*, **-nized, -niz·ing.** **1. a.** to proclaim; announce publicly. **b.** to commend publicly. **2.** (of the Pope) to confirm publicly and officially the appointment of (a bishop, etc.). [< Medieval Latin *praeconizare* < Latin *praecō, -ōnis* public crier, herald]

pre·con·quest (prē kon'kwest, -kong'-), *adj.* existing or occurring before the conquest of a nation.

Pre-Con·quest (prē kon'kwest, -kong'-), *adj.* of or belonging to the period before the Conquest; of the times before the conquest of England by William the Conqueror: *pre-Conquest churches, the pre-Conquest English.*

pre·con·scious (prē kon'shəs), *adj.* **1.** before or preceding consciousness. **2.** not in the conscious mind but readily recalled; foreconscious: *preconscious memories. Now it was time to discover whether humans could make use of preconscious information* (Wall Street Journal).
—*n.* the part of the mind between the conscious and the subconscious; foreconscious: *Being repressed ... means being unable to pass out of the unconscious system because of the doorkeeper's refusal of admittance into the preconscious* (Sigmund Freud).

pre·cool (prē kül'), *v.t.* to cool ahead of time; cool (produce, meat, etc.) by artificial means before shipping: *It [Tasmania] will need greater facilities for storing and precooling its export apples* (Gordon Greenwood). —**pre·cool'er,** *n.*

pre·curse (pri kėrs'), *v.t.*, **-cursed, -curs·ing.** to run or go before; forerun, precede, and indicate the approach of. [< Latin *praecursus,* past participle of *praecurrere;* see PRECURSOR]

pre·cur·sive (pri kėr'siv), *adj.* precursory: *He hints that our present world-wide area of breakdown may be the precursive symptom of a mutation of Christianity* (Stephen Spender).

pre·cur·sor (pri kėr'sər), *n.* a forerunner: *A severe cold may be the precursor of pneumonia.* [< Latin *praecursor, -ōris* < *praecurrere* < *prae-* before, ahead + *currere* to run] —**Syn.** predecessor, herald, harbinger.

pre·cur·so·ry (pri kėr'sər ē), *adj.* indicative of something to follow; introductory. —**Syn.** prefatory, preliminary.

pred., 1. predicate. **2. a.** predicative. **b.** predicatively.

pre·da·cious or **pre·da·ceous** (pri dā'shəs), *adj.* living by prey; predatory: *Gaudy, fast on the wing and deadly to its prey, the dragonfly ... is highly predacious* (Science News Letter). [< Latin *praedārī* to rob (< *praeda* prey) + English *-aceous*] —**pre·da'cious·ness, pre·da'ceous·ness,** *n.*

pre·dac·i·ty (pri das'ə tē), *n.* the fact or quality of being predacious: *He has inherited the predacity of that somewhat older and until now better known member of his race, Genghis Khan* (Saturday Review).

pre·date (prē dāt'), *v.t.*, **-dat·ed, -dat·ing.** **1.** to date before the actual time: *to predate a check.* **2.** to precede in date; antedate: *The younger ones had troubles of their own, predating the controversy* (Joseph Hitrec).

pre·da·tion (prē dā'shən), *n.* **1.** the act of preying on another animal or animals: *Any food chain, after the first plant-eating animal, is a succession of predations* (Tracy I. Storer). **2.** *Obsolete.* the act of plundering or pillaging; depredation. [< Latin *praedātiō, -ōnis* < *praedārī;* see PREDATOR]

predation pressure, the impact of predatory animals on a given environment, constituting a continuing factor in the ecological balance between predator and prey.

pred·a·tism (pred'ə tiz əm), *n.* the state of being predatory.

pred·a·tor (pred'ə tər), *n.* an animal or other organism that preys upon another or others: *Predators must be nocturnal if their prey comes out only at night* (Cloudsley and Thompson).
[< Latin *praedātor, -ōris* < *praedārī* to plunder < *praeda* prey, booty]

pred·a·to·ri·ly (pred'ə tôr'ə lē, -tōr'-), *adv.* in a predatory manner.

pred·a·to·ri·ness (pred'ə tôr'ē nis, -tōr'-), *n.* predatory quality or character: *The techniques of power [and] ... the predatoriness of officialdom, become even more insidiously efficient* (London Times).

pred·a·to·ry (pred'ə tôr'ē, -tōr'-), *adj.* **1.** of or inclined to plundering or robbery: *predatory border warfare. Predatory tramps infested the highways.* **2. a.** preying upon other animals: *Hawks and owls are predatory birds. Field trials were then set up in semi-arid bush country ... under completely natural conditions, which included the presence of foxes and other predatory animals* (Fenner and Day). **b.** feeding upon and destructive to crops, trees, buildings, etc.: *predatory insects.* **3.** intentionally destructive: *Predatory price-cutting is sometimes used to destroy competing firms.*
[< Latin *praedātōrius* < *praedātor* predator]
—**Syn. 1.** marauding, thieving, rapacious.

pre·dawn (prē dôn', prē'dôn), *n.* the part of the day just before the dawn: *The predawn's copper haze ...* (Robert Irwin). —*adj.* of the time preceding the dawn: *The ring of the telephone shattered the predawn stillness* (New York Times).

pred·e·ces·sor (pred'ə ses'ər), *n.* **1.** a person holding an office or position before another: *John Adams was Jefferson's predecessor as President.* **2.** a thing that came before another. **3.** an ancestor; forefather. [< Late Latin *praedēcessor* < Latin *prae-* before + *dēcessor, -ōris* retiring official (of a province) < *dēcēdere* go away]

pre·del·la (pri del'ə), *n.* **1.** the platform on which an altar is placed: *The step or base (predella) on which the altar stands often is considered a part of the altar* (James Chillman). **2.** a raised shelf at the back of an altar. **3.** a painting or sculpture on the front of this, often forming an appendage to an altarpiece: *The small scenes Fra Angelico painted in translucent colors for the predella ... are each in themselves small hymns of praise* (Time). **4.** any painting forming a similar appendage to another painting.
[< Italian *predella* stool, probably < Old High German *pret* board + Italian *-ella,* a diminutive suffix]

Predella (def. 1)
Altar of Notre Dame, Paris

pre·des·ig·nate (prē dez'ig nāt), *v.t.*, **-nat·ed, -nat·ing.** **1.** to designate beforehand; specify in advance. **2.** *Logic.* to designate the range of (the predicate) by annexing to the subject a quantitative particle such as "one," "alone," or "nothing but."

pre·des·ig·na·tion (prē'dez ig nā'shən), *n.* **1.** a designating beforehand. **2.** *Logic.* a sign, symbol, or word expressing logical quantity.

pre·des·ti·nar·i·an (prē des'tə nãr'ē ən), *adj.* of, having to do with, or believing in predestination.
—*n.* a person who believes in or upholds the doctrine of predestination.

pre·des·ti·nar·i·an·ism (prē des'tə nãr'ē ə niz'əm), *n.* the system or doctrines of the predestinarians.

pre·des·ti·nate (*v.* prē des'tə nāt; *adj.* prē des'tə nit, -nāt), *v.*, **-nat·ed, -nat·ing,** *adj.* —*v.t.* **1.** to decree or ordain beforehand. **2.** *Theology.* to foreordain by divine purpose.
—*adj. Archaic.* predestined.
[< Latin *praedēstināre* (with English *-ate*[1]) appoint beforehand < *prae-* before + *dēstināre* establish, make fast, apparently ultimately < *dē-* (intensive) + *stāre* to stand]

pre·des·ti·na·tion (prē'des tə nā'shən), *n.* **1.** an ordaining beforehand; destiny; fate: *a kind of moral predestination, or overruling principle which cannot be resisted* (Samuel Johnson). **2.** the action of God in deciding beforehand what shall happen. **3.** the doctrine that by God's decree certain souls will be saved and others lost: *... one of the most disastrous of human ideas, the doctrine of predestination!* (New Yorker).

pre·des·ti·na·tor (prē des'tə nā'tər), *n.* **1.** a person who predestinates or foreordains. **2.** a person who believes in predestination; predestinarian.

pre·des·tine (prē des'tən), *v.t.*, **-tined, -tin·ing.** to determine or settle beforehand; foreordain. [< Old French *predestiner,* learned borrowing from Latin *praedēstināre* to predestinate]

pre·de·ter·mi·na·tion (prē'di tėr'mə nā'shən), *n.* a predetermining or being predetermined.

pre·de·ter·mi·na·tive (prē'di tėr'mə nā'tiv), *adj.* having the quality of predetermining.

pre·de·ter·mine (prē'di tėr'mən), *v.t.*, **-mined, -min·ing.** **1.** to determine or decide beforehand: *The time for the meeting was predetermined.* **2.** to direct or impel beforehand (to something): *Two world wars predetermined the henceforth inevitable symbiosis of scientific activity and political decision* (Bulletin of Atomic Scientists).

pre·di·al (prē'dē əl), *adj.* **1.** consisting of land. **2.** having to do with, arising from, or attached to land: *predial tithes, predial serfs.* Also, **praedial.** [< Medieval Latin *praedialis* < Latin *praedium* farm, estate]

pred·i·ca·bil·i·ty (pred'ə kə bil'ə tē), *n.* the quality of being predicable.

pred·i·ca·ble (pred'ə kə bəl), *adj.* that can be predicated or affirmed; assertable. —*n.* **1.** a thing that can be predicated; attribute. **2.** *Logic.* any of the various kinds of predicate that can be used of a subject. According to Aristotle they were genus, definition, difference, property, and accident, but subsequently definition was omitted and species added.

pred·i·ca·bly (pred'ə kə blē), *adv.* in a predicable manner.

pre·dic·a·ment (pri dik'ə mənt), *n.* **1.** an unpleasant, difficult, or dangerous situation: *She was in a predicament when she missed the last train home.* **2.** any condition, state, or situation. **3.** that which can be predicated; attribute. **4.** *Logic.* one of the categories or classes of predication. [< Late Latin *praedicāmentum* quality, category; (literally) something predicated < Latin *praedicāre;* see PREDICATE]
—**Syn. 1. Predicament, plight, dilemma** mean a bad situation. **Predicament** implies that it is perplexing or difficult to get out of it: *The world is in a dangerous predicament.* **Plight** implies that it is unfortunate or even hopeless: *He is worried by the plight of his relatives who are in territory conquered by the enemy.* **Dilemma** implies that it involves a choice between two things, both disagreeable: *He is faced with the dilemma of telling a lie or betraying his friend.*

pre·dic·a·men·tal (pri dik'ə men'təl), *adj.* of or having to do with predicaments.

pred·i·cant (pred'ə kənt), *adj.* given to or characterized by preaching. —*n.* a preacher, especially a member of a predicant religious order. [< Late Latin *praedicāns, -antis,* present participle of Latin *praedicāre;* see PREDICATE]

pred·i·cate (*n., adj.* pred'ə kit; *v.* pred'ə kāt), *n., adj., v.*, **-cat·ed, -cat·ing.** —*n.* **1.** the word or words expressing what is said about the subject. *Examples:* Men *work.* The men *dug wells.* The men *are soldiers.* **2.** *Logic.* that which is said of the subject in a proposition; the second term of a proposition. *Examples:* All men are *mortal.* That man is not *my father.* [< Late Latin *praedicātum* (originally) neuter past participle of Latin *praedicāre;* see the verb]
—*adj.* **1.** *Grammar.* belonging to the predicate. In "Horses are strong," *strong* is a predicate adjective: *When the predicate tells more than one thing about the subject, it is called a compound predicate* (Harold B. Allen). **2.** predicated.
—*v.t.* **1.** to found or base (a statement, action, etc.) on something. **2.** to declare, assert, or affirm to be real or true: *Most religions predicate life after death.* **3.** to connote; imply. **4.** to declare to be an attribute or quality (of some person or thing): *We predicate goodness and mercy of God.* **5.** *Logic.* **a.** to state or assert (something) about

the subject of a proposition. **b.** to make (a term) the predicate in a proposition. **6.** *Informal.* to predict.
—*v.i.* to make a statement; assert; affirm: *Your mentality, too, is bully, as we all predicate* (Max Beerbohm).
[< Latin *praedicāre* (with English *-ate*[1]) declare publicly < *prae-* before + *dicāre* consecrate, dedicate. Doublet of PREACH.]

➔ **predicate.** A predicate of a clause or sentence, in grammar, is the verb with its modifiers, objects, complements, etc. It may be a simple verb of complete meaning (The big bell *tolled*), a verb and its modifier (The sun *sank quickly*), a transitive verb and its object (He finally *landed the big fish*), a linking verb and a complement, either a predicate adjective (The man *was sick*) or a predicate noun (The man *was a thief*).

pred·i·ca·tion (pred′ə kā′shən), *n.* **1.** a predicating; affirming; assertion: *It may confidently be assumed that predication is common to all Indo-European languages* (Simeon Potter). **2.** *Logic.* the assertion of something about or of a subject.

pred·i·ca·tive (pred′ə kā′tiv), *adj.* **1.** predicating; expressing predication. **2.** acting as a predicate.

pred·i·ca·tive·ly (pred′ə kā′tiv lē), *adv.* as a predicate.

pred·i·ca·to·ry (pred′ə kə tôr′ē, -tōr′-), *adj.* **1.** of or having to do with a preacher; preaching. **2.** characterized by being proclaimed or preached.

pre·dict (pri dikt′), *v.t.* to tell beforehand; prophesy: *The weather bureau predicts rain for tomorrow.* —*v.i.* to utter prediction; prophesy. [< Latin *praedictus* < *praedīcere* < *prae-* before + *dīcere* to say] —**Syn.** *v.t.* foretell, presage.

pre·dict·a·bil·i·ty (pri dik′tə bil′ə tē), *n.* the quality of being predictable: *The happy thing about Westerns . . . is their gentle predictability* (Newsweek).

pre·dict·a·ble (pri dik′tə bəl), *adj.* that can be predicted: *Every generation demonstrates some events to be regular and predictable, which the preceding generation had declared to be irregular and unpredictable* (Henry T. Buckle).

pre·dict·a·bly (pri dik′tə blē), *adv.* in a predictable manner: *Predictably, congressional reaction ranged from sympathetic understanding to outrage* (Time).

pre·dict·ed-log race (pri dik′tid lôg′, -log′), a boat race between cruisers or yachts in which each contestant submits in advance his log predicting the time he will pass check points and the finish of a course. All clocks, radios, and communications are barred, and the winner is the one who sticks closest to his estimated time schedule: *A predicted-log race is really not a race but a test of navigation* (New York Times).

pre·dic·tion (pri dik′shən), *n.* **1.** the act of predicting. **2.** a thing predicted; prophecy: *The official predictions about the weather often come true. Many authorities . . . insist economists should never make precise predictions* (Newsweek). —**Syn. 2.** augury, prognostication.

pre·dic·tive (pri dik′tiv), *adj.* foretelling; prophetic: *There is probably more interest in their methodological approach than in the predictive powers of their theories* (F.H. George). —**pre·dic′tive·ly,** *adv.*

pre·dic·tor (pri dik′tər), *n.* **1.** a person or thing that predicts or foretells. **2.** an instrument that calculates fire data on moving targets, especially aircraft, and by which a weapon or battery of weapons is automatically aimed, so that a shell fired at a given moment will intercept the target at a given point (assuming the rate and direction of movement of the target do not alter in the meantime): *anti-aircraft predictors.*

pre·di·gest (prē′di jest′, -dī-), *v.t.* **1.** to digest beforehand: *Everything is predigested for us* (Time). *Foods are pre-mixed, pre-breaded, pre-fried—everything but predigested* (Harper's). **2.** to treat (food) by an artificial process similar to digestion, in order to make it more digestible.

pre·di·ges·tion (prē′di jes′chən, -dī-), *n.* the digestion (of food) by artificial means before introduction into the stomach.

pre·di·kant (prā′di känt′), *n.* a clergyman of the Dutch Reformed Church in South Africa: *The predikant, who had unfortunately lent himself to the oppressions of the Company, now plied them with religious advice* (Cape of Good Hope Literary Gazette). [< Afrikaans *predikant* < Dutch < Late Latin *praedicāns;* see PREDICANT]

pre·di·lec·tion (prē′də lek′shən, pred′ə-), *n.* a liking; preference: *In spite of her predilection for my powerful rival, she liked to flirt with me* (Washington Irving). [< Middle French *prédilection* < Medieval Latin *praedilectus* well beloved, (literally) past participle of *praediligere* prefer before others < Latin *prae-* before + *dīligere* choose. Compare DILIGENT.] —**Syn.** partiality, predisposition.

pre·dis·pose (prē′dis pōz′), *v.t.,* **-posed, -pos·ing. 1.** to give an inclination or tendency to; make liable or susceptible: *A cold predisposes a person to other diseases.* **2.** to put into a favorable or suitable frame of mind, emotional condition, etc.: *He is predisposed to be generous to his friends.* **3.** to dispose of, give away, or bequeath before the usual or specified time.

pre·dis·po·si·tion (prē′dis pə zish′ən), *n.* a previous inclination or tendency; susceptibility or liability: *a predisposition to look on the dark side of things, a predisposition to colds.*

pred·nis·o·lone (pred nis′ə lōn), *n.* a powerful steroid hormone, used in treating arthritis, inflammatory diseases, asthma, and certain allergies. It does not upset the water balance of the body and has fewer unpleasant side effects than cortisone. *Formula:* $C_{21}H_{28}O_5$

pred·ni·sone (pred′nə sōn), *n.* a drug very similar to prednisolone, usually administered orally. *Formula:* $C_{21}H_{26}O_5$

pre·dom·i·nance (pri dom′ə nəns), *n.* **1.** a being predominant; prevalence: *the predominance of weeds in the deserted garden.* **2.** *Astrology.* superior influence; ascendancy.

pre·dom·i·nan·cy (pri dom′ə nən sē), *n.* predominance.

pre·dom·i·nant (pri dom′ə nənt), *adj.* **1.** having more power, influence, or authority than others; superior. **2.** most noticeable; prevailing: *Green was the predominant color in the forest.* —**pre·dom′i·nant·ly,** *adv.* —**Syn. 1.** controlling, ruling. See **dominant.** —**Ant. 1.** subordinate, secondary.

pre·dom·i·nate (pri dom′ə nāt), *v.,* **-nat·ed, -nat·ing.** —*v.i.* to be greater in power, strength, influence, or numbers: *In this character of the Americans, a love of freedom is the predominating feature* (Edmund Burke). *Life is made up of sobs, sniffles, and smiles, with sniffles predominating* (O. Henry). *Knowledge will always predominate over ignorance, as man governs the other animals* (Samuel Johnson). —*v.t.* to dominate; control: *Let your close fire predominate his smoke* (Shakespeare). —**pre·dom′i·nat′ing·ly,** *adv.*

pre·dom·i·na·tion (pri dom′ə nā′shən), *n.* the act of predominating; superior power or influence; prevalence: *You would not trust to the predomination of right, which, you believe, is in your opinions* (Samuel Johnson).

pre·dom·i·na·tor (pri dom′ə nā′tər), *n.* a person or thing that predominates.

pre·dy·nas·tic (prē′dī nas′tik), *adj.* existing before the recognized dynasties, especially of Egypt before 3500 B.C.: *M. Perrot found an ivory female statuette very similar to predynastic figures from El Amrah in Egypt* (New Scientist).

pree (prē), *v.,* **preed, pree·ing,** *n. Scottish.* —*v.t.* to make proof or trial of, especially by tasting.
pree the mouth of, to kiss.
—*n.* a trial; taste. [short for obsolete *preve, prieve,* variants of *prove*]

pre·ech·o (prē ek′ō), *n., pl.* **-ech·oes,** *v.,* **-ech·oed, -ech·o·ing.** —*n.* **1.** an echo heard on a phonograph record before hearing the sound that causes it, due to a defect in the record: *A new and exciting Leinsdorf is marred by pre-echo* (Atlantic). **2.** a foreshadowing. —*v.t.* to show or hint at beforehand; prefigure; foreshadow: *Fittingly, the disturbance pre-echoed a scene in the play* (Time). *One after another his familiar devices are pre-echoed—the cello obbligato, the divided cellos, the flutter of the woodwind . .* (London Times).

pre·ë·lect or **pre-e·lect** (prē′i lekt′), *v.t.* to elect or choose beforehand.

pre·ë·lec·tion or **pre-e·lec·tion** (prē′i-lek′shən), *n.* an anticipatory election; previous choice. —*adj.* before an election: *a preëlection campaign. The pollsters took a pre-election look at 1960 presidential preference* (Time).

pre·ë·mer·gence or **pre-e·mer·gence** (prē′i mėr′jəns), *adj.* before emerging or appearing: *A preëmergence herbicide kills weeds before the plants push up through the soil.*

pree·mie (prē′mē), *n. Informal.* a premature baby: *To examine the eyes of these very small "preemies," the doctors must use special techniques* (Newsweek).

pre·ëm·i·nence or **pre-em·i·nence** (prē-em′ə nəns), *n.* superiority; excellence: *the preëminence of Edison among the inventors of his day.*

pre·ëm·i·nent or **pre-em·i·nent** (prē-em′ə nənt), *adj.* standing out above all others; superior to others. [< Latin *praeēminēns, -entis,* present participle of *praeēminēre* excel; rise above < *prae-* before + *ēminēre* stand out] —**pre·ëm′i·nent·ly, pre-em′i·nent·ly,** *adv.*

pre·ëmpt or **pre-empt** (prē empt′), *v.t.* **1.** to secure before someone else can; acquire or take possession of beforehand: *The cat had preëmpted the comfortable chair. When Istanbul's mayor raised a feeble protest, the Premier, it was said, suggested he take a long vacation and promptly pre-empted his office* (Time). **2.** *U.S.* to settle on (land) with the right to buy it before others: *He preëmpted the land by occupying it.* **3.** *Cards.* to shut out (other bids) by making an opening bid at a high level. —*v.i.* **1.** to preëmpt a thing, place, etc. **2.** *Cards.* to bid at a high level to prevent one's opponents from bidding or exchanging informational bids, or to keep one's partner from changing the declaration at whist, bridge, etc.
—*n. Cards.* the act or practice of preëmpting: *It is amazing how often pre-empts induce the most cautious bidders to make risky bids* (Manchester Guardian Weekly).
[American English, back formation < *preëmption*]

pre·ëmp·tion or **pre-emp·tion** (prē-emp′shən), *n.* the act or right of purchasing before others or in preference to others: *It is neither right nor legal that Mr. Hardy's preëmption should gobble up over 250 acres of hay lands* (Regina Journal). [< *pre-* + Latin *ēmptiō, -ōnis* buying < *emere* to buy]

pre·ëmp·tive or **pre-emp·tive** (prē emp′-tiv), *adj.* having to do with or like preëmption; preëmpting: *It demands an instant response and therefore tempts pre-emptive action* (Bulletin of Atomic Scientists).

pre·ëmp·tor or **pre-emp·tor** (prē emp′-tər), *n.* a person who preëmpts, especially one who takes up land with the privilege of preëmption.

pre·ëmp·to·ry or **pre-emp·to·ry** (prē-emp′tər ē), *adj.* preëmptive.

preen[1] (prēn), *v.t., v.i.* **1.** to smooth or arrange (the feathers) with the beak, as a bird does: *Past the Ryemeadow's lonely woodland nook Where many a stubble gray goose preens her wing* (John Masefield). **2.** to dress (oneself) carefully; primp. **3.** to pride or please (oneself): *Prince, we may preen ourselves on gain, but is there not some tinge of loss . . . ?* (New Yorker). [perhaps variant of *prune*[3] to preen, dress carefully; influenced by dialectal *preen* to pin up, sew up < *preen*[2]. Compare PRUNE[3].] —**preen′er,** *n.*

preen[2] (prēn), *n. Scottish.* a pin; brooch. [Old English *prēon* a pin, brooch]

preen gland, the uropygial gland: *Most birds have a pair of preen glands over the tail . . . that secretes a preening ointment* (Scientific American).

pre-Eng·lish (prē ing′lish), *n.* the ancient continental West Germanic dialect which later became English. —*adj.* **1.** having to do with this dialect. **2.** of or having to do with Britain or its peoples or languages before the Anglo-Saxon conquest.

pre·ëx·il·i·an or **pre-ex·il·i·an** (prē′eg-zil′ē ən, -ek sil′-), *adj.* **1.** before the Babylonian Captivity or Exile of the Jews; before the 600's B.C. **2.** before exile.

pre·ëx·il·ic or **pre-ex·il·ic** (prē′eg zil′ik), *adj.* preëxilian.

pref., 1. preface. **2.** preference. **3.** preferred. **4. a.** prefix. **b.** prefixed.

pre·fab (prē′fab′), *n., v.,* **-fabbed, -fab·bing,** *adj. Informal.* —*n.* a prefabricated house: *Its scattering of prefabs and trailers and barracks, indeed gave the appearance of being at the edge of the civilized world* (New Yorker). —*v.t.* to prefabricate. —*adj.* prefabricated: *The company had rented four prefab buildings*

(Maclean's). [American English, short for *prefabricate*]

pre·fab·ri·cate (prē fab′rə kāt), *v.t.*, **-cat·ed, -cat·ing.** **1.** to make all standardized parts of (a house, etc.): *The erection of a prefabricated house requires merely the assembling of the various sections.* **2.** to prepare in advance: *Secretary of State Dulles says he has brought no prefabricated American plan to the London conference on German rearmament* (Wall Street Journal).

pre·fab·ri·ca·tion (prē′fab rə kā′shən), *n.* the construction or manufacture of prefabricated houses, etc.: *In prefabrication, builders use assembly-line methods to manufacture the parts of the house separately. These parts can be assembled with great speed at the buyer's site* (Arthur R. Carr).

pre·fab·ri·ca·tor (prē fab′rə kā′tər), *n.* a person or company that prefabricates: *The low-cost house is the prefabricator's specialty, of course* (Wall Street Journal).

pref·ace (pref′is), *n., v.*, **-aced, -ac·ing.** —*n.* **1.** an introduction to a book, writing, or speech: *This book has a preface written by the author.* **2.** something preliminary or introductory: *He . . . seemed to look upon a certain mass of disappointment as the natural preface to all realizations* (Thomas Hardy). **3.** Also, **Preface.** the introduction to the Canon of the Mass, ending with the Sanctus.
—*v.t.* **1.** to introduce by written or spoken remarks; give a preface to. **2.** to be a preface to; begin: *A depressing and difficult passage has prefaced every new page I have turned in life* (Charlotte Brontë).
[< Old French *preface*, ultimately < Latin *praefātiō* < *praefārī* to preface, foretell < *prae-* before + *fārī* speak]
—**Syn.** *n.* **1.** See **introduction.**

pref·a·to·ri·ly (pref′ə tôr′ə lē, -tōr′-), *adv.* by way of preface.

pref·a·to·ry (pref′ə tôr′ē, -tōr′-), *adj.* like a preface; given as a preface; introductory; preliminary: *The issue also contains a prefatory note assuring the reader . . . that it is possible for a magazine to take advertising and still be honest* (New Yorker).

pre·fect (prē′fekt), *n.* **1.** (in ancient Rome) the title of various military and civil officers, as the chief official of a city, the civil governor of a province, or the commander of the Praetorian Guard. **2.** the chief administrative official of a department of France: *. . . addressed a meeting in Paris of the "super prefects" of different regions of France* (London Times). **3.** (in modern Europe) a chief officer, chief magistrate, etc. **4.** (in certain schools, especially English schools) a senior student who has some authority over other students; monitor; prepositor: *Her face . . . regarded him as she must have learned, ten years ago, when she was a school prefect, to regard one of the girls* (Harper's). **5.** (in Jesuit schools, colleges, etc.) a dean. Also, **praefect.** [< Old French *prefect*, learned borrowing from Latin *praefectus* public overseer, (originally) one put in charge; (literally) past participle of *praeficere* < *prae-* in front, before + *facere* to make]

pre·fec·to·ri·al (prē′fek tôr′ē əl, -tōr′-), *adj.* having to do with a prefect or a prefecture: *A massive grey building typical of the "prefectorial baroque" . . .* (London Times).

pre·fec·tur·al (pri fek′chər əl), *adj.* of or belonging to a prefecture: *He makes weekly trips to Shizuoka, the prefectural capital, and to Tokyo on occasion for official business* (Wall Street Journal).

pre·fec·ture (prē′fek chər), *n.* the office, jurisdiction, territory, or official residence of a prefect: *The country [Morocco] is divided into 19 provinces and 5 urban prefectures* (James S. Coleman). [< Latin *praefectūra* < *praefectus* prefect]

pre·fer (pri fėr′), *v.t.*, **-ferred, -fer·ring.** **1.** to choose rather; like better: *I will come later, if you prefer.* **2.** to put forward; present: *to prefer a claim to property.* **3.** to advance; promote: *He was preferred to the rank of major.* **4.** *Law.* to give preference to, as a creditor. [< Old French *preferer*, learned borrowing from Latin *praeferre* < *prae-* before + *ferre* to carry] —**pre·fer′rer,** *n.*

pref·er·a·bil·i·ty (pref′ər ə bil′ə tē, pref′rə-), *n.* the state or quality of being preferable.

pref·er·a·ble (pref′ər ə bəl, pref′rə-), *adj.* to be preferred; more desirable. —**pref′er·a·ble·ness,** *n.*

pref·er·a·bly (pref′ər ə blē, pref′rə-), *adv.* by choice: *He wants a secretary, preferably one who is a college graduate.*

pref·er·ence (pref′ər əns, pref′rəns), *n.* **1.** the act or attitude of liking better: *My preference is for beef rather than lamb. A teacher should not show preference for any one of her pupils.* **2.** a thing preferred; first choice: *Her preference in reading is a novel.* **3.** the favoring of one country or group of countries in international trade by admitting their products at a lower import duty than that levied on others. **4.** *Law.* priority of payment given to a certain debt or class of debts. **5.** a type of card game for three players, using a deck of 32 cards. [< Middle French *preference*, learned borrowing from Medieval Latin *praeferentia* < Latin *praeferēns, -entis*, present participle of *praeferre* prefer] —**Syn. 1.** selection, election. See **choice.**

preference share or **stock,** *British.* a share which has priority over other classes of shares as to payment of dividends and distribution of assets.

pref·er·en·tial (pref′ə ren′shəl), *adj.* **1.** of, giving, or receiving preference: *Workers who lose their jobs to an automatic device should be given preferential hiring status* (Wall Street Journal). *We should give preferential treatment to the countries who are bearing their share of the burden of collective defense* (Newsweek). **2.** having import duties favoring particular countries: *a preferential tariff.* **3.** (of votes, voting, etc.) indicating or permitting indication of the order of one's preference: *Both . . . were unopposed in the preferential portion of the primary—a sort of popularity poll* (Wall Street Journal). —**pref′er·en′tial·ly,** *adv.*

pref·er·en·tial·ism (pref′ə ren′shə liz əm), *n.* the system of giving preference in the fixing of a tariff: *The old-fashioned protectionism, which is now popping up again under the guise of Colonial preferentialism* (Liberty Review).

pref·er·en·tial·ist (pref′ə ren′shə list), *n.* a supporter of preference in tariff relations.

preferential shop, a shop giving preference to union members in hiring, promotion, etc.

preferential voting, a system of voting in which the voter indicates the order of his choice of candidates for an office, so that if no candidate has a majority of first choices, the election may be determined by totaling the first-choice, second-choice, etc., votes cast for each contestant (usually on the basis of so many points per vote, decreasing from first to second choice, and so on, the winner being the one whose point score is highest).

pre·fer·ment (pri fėr′mənt), *n.* **1.** advancement; promotion: *Captain White seeks preferment in the army.* **2.** a position or office giving social or financial advancement, especially one in the church: *their hunger for lands and office and preferment* (James A. Froude).

pre·ferred stock (pri fėrd′), stock on which dividends must be paid at a predetermined rate before any can be paid on the common stock.

pre·fig·ur·a·tion (prē′fig yə rā′shən), *n.* **1.** a prefiguring; representation beforehand by a figure or type. **2.** that in which something is prefigured; prototype.

pre·fig·ur·a·tive (prē fig′yər ə tiv), *adj.* showing by previous figures, types, or similarity.

pre·fig·ure (prē fig′yər), *v.t.*, **-ured, -ur·ing.** **1.** to represent beforehand by a figure or type: *In one painting of Christ, His shadow is that of a cross, prefiguring the Crucifixion.* **2.** to imagine to oneself beforehand: *My first sensations . . . were far from being so flattering as I had prefigured them* (Laurence Sterne). [< Latin *praefigūrāre* < *prae-* before + *figūrāre* to form, shape < *figūra* a form]

pre·fig·ure·ment (prē fig′yər mənt), *n.* the act of prefiguring.

pre·fin·ish (prē fin′ish), *v.t.* to finish (a panel, window, wall section, etc.) prior to installation in a building: *The window is to be prefinished and pre-glazed* (Harper's).

pre·fix (*n.* prē′fiks; *v.* prē fiks′), *n.* a syllable, syllables, or word put at the beginning of a word to change its meaning or to form a new word, as in *pre*paid, *under*line, *dis*appear, *un*like: *Prefixes are affixes which precede the root with which they are most closely associated* (H.A. Gleason). [< New Latin *praefixum*, noun use of neuter of Latin *praefixus* < *praefigere* < *prae-* in front + *fīgere* to fix in, establish]
—*v.t.* **1.** to put before: *We prefix "Mr." to a man's name.* **2.** to place (a word or particle) before a word, especially in combination with it. **3.** to fix beforehand. **4.** *Obsolete.* to fix in one's mind beforehand. [perhaps < Middle French *prefixer* < *pre-* before + *fixer* to fix, place; or < Middle French *prefix*, learned borrowing from Latin *praefixus*; see noun]

pre·fix·al (prē′fik səl, prē fik′-), *adj.* **1.** of the nature of a prefix. **2.** characterized by prefixes. —**pre′fix·al·ly,** *adv.*

pre·fix·a·tion (prē′fik sā′shən), *n.* the use or forming of prefixes.

pre·fix·ion (prē fik′shən), *n.* the act of prefixing.

pre·form (prē fôrm′), *v.t.* to form beforehand; determine beforehand the form or shape of.

pre·for·ma·tion (prē′fôr mā′shən), *n.* **1.** a shaping beforehand. **2.** an old theory of generation according to which the individual exists complete in the germ cell, further development being merely in size.

pre·for·ma·tion·ist (prē′fôr mā′shə nist), *n.* a person who accepts the theory of preformation: *By the 17th century the sway of the preformationists was almost unchallenged, and the concept was pushed to the most absurd extremes* (Scientific American).

pre·for·ma·tive (prē fôr′mə tiv), *adj.* determining form beforehand; preforming.

pre·fron·tal (prē frun′təl), *n.* a bone in the anterior part of the skull of certain vertebrates, especially in amphibia and reptiles. —*adj.* designating this bone or region.

prefrontal leucotomy, prefrontal lobotomy.

prefrontal lobotomy, a brain operation in which the nerves between the hypothalamic region and the cerebral cortex are cut to relieve the symptoms of mental illness: *Some patients who have had the prefrontal lobotomy operation still hear voices or strange sounds that do not really exist* (Science News Letter).

preg·na·bil·i·ty (preg′nə bil′ə tē), *n.* capability of being attacked; vulnerability.

preg·na·ble (preg′nə bəl), *adj.* open to attack; assailable; vulnerable. [< Old French *prenable*, and *pregnable* < stem of *prendre* < Latin *prendere*, short for *prehendere* to seize, take]

preg·nan·cy (preg′nən sē), *n., pl.* **-cies.** pregnant quality or condition: *to go through the last months of pregnancy, a remark of obvious pregnancy.*

pregnancy disease, a disease of ewes caused by carbohydrate deficiency and occurring in the last month of pregnancy, most often in older ewes carrying twins or triplets; twin lamb disease: *Animals affected with pregnancy disease . . . may lie . . . flat on the side for days. Usually there is no fever. The disease lasts from 1 to 10 days, and death results in more than 90% of the cases* (M.S. Shahan).

preg·nant[1] (preg′nənt), *adj.* **1.** having an embryo or embryos developing in the uterus; being with child or young. **2.** filled; loaded: *The silence was pregnant with tragedy* (Harper's). **3.** fertile; rich; abounding: *a mind pregnant with ideas.* **4.** filled with meaning; significant: *Most proverbs are pregnant sayings. Historians will one day record our country's successes and failures in world affairs during these pregnant middle years of the twentieth century* (Atlantic). [< Latin *praegnāns, -antis*, variant of *praegnās, -ātis* < *prae-* before + unrecorded *gna-* to bear young] —**preg′nant·ly,** *adv.*

preg·nant[2] (preg′nənt), *adj. Archaic.* (of an argument, evidence, etc.) urgent; weighty; compelling: *One of the constables, besides the pregnant proof already produced, offers to make oath* (Scott). [< Old French *pregnant*, and *preignant* violent, pressing; (literally) present participle of *preindre* < Latin *premere* to press] —**Syn.** cogent.

pregnant mare's serum, a serum containing a hormone taken from pregnant mares and injected into ewes or cows to control ovulation.

preg·nen·o·lone (preg nen′ə lōn), *n.* a drug obtained from stigmasterol and other steroids, used in the treatment of extreme fatigue, arthritis, and certain diseases. *Formula:* $C_{21}H_{32}O_2$

pre·hal·lux (prē hal′əks), *n.* a rudimentary structure found on the inner side of the tarsus of some mammals, reptiles, and amphibians, supposed to represent an additional digit. [< *pre-* + *hallux*]

pre·heat (prē hēt′), *v.t.* to heat before using.

pre·heat·er (prē hē′tər), *n.* a furnace, hot chamber, or the like, in which something is placed, or through which something is passed, in order to be preheated.

pre·hen·sile (prē hen′səl), *adj.* adapted for seizing, grasping, or holding on: *Many monkeys of the New World have prehensile tails.* [< French *préhensile* < Latin *prehēnsus* < *prehendere* to grasp]

Prehensile Tail of a spider monkey

pre·hen·sil·i·ty (prē′hen sil′ə tē), *n.* the character of being prehensile.

pre·hen·sion (prē hen′shən), *n.* **1.** the act of taking hold physically; grasping; seizing. **2.** grasping with the mind; mental apprehension. [< Latin *prehēnsiō, -ōnis* < *prehendere* to grasp]

pre·hen·sive (prē hen′siv), *adj.* **1.** seizing or laying hold of. **2.** (of the mind) apprehending.

pre·hen·so·ry (prē hen′sər ē), *adj.* prehensive.

pre·his·to·ri·an (prē′his tôr′ē ən, -tōr′-), *n.* a person who studies the remains, customs, and conditions of prehistoric times: *Prehistorians had recovered coarse (but recognizable) stone tools from the strata which yield the bones of . . . the Australopithecine fossils* (Robert J. Braidwood).

pre·his·tor·ic (prē′his tôr′ik, -tor′-), *adj.* of or belonging to periods before recorded history: *Some prehistoric people lived in caves. Prehistoric men and animals are known from skeletal materials found in the crust of the earth* (Beals and Hoijer).

pre·his·tor·i·cal (prē′his tôr′ə kəl, -tor′-), *adj.* prehistoric.

pre·his·tor·i·cal·ly (prē′his tôr′ə klē, -tor′-), *adv.* before recorded history.

pre·his·to·ry or **pre-his·to·ry** (prē his′tər ē, -trē), *n.* history before recorded history; prehistoric matters or times: *A team of archeologists led by Sr. B'han Bollek has discovered in that unexplored waste traces of a lost people of pre-history* (Harper's).

prehn·ite (prā′nīt, pren′īt), *n.* a mineral consisting of a hydrous silicate of aluminum and calcium, occurring in crystalline aggregates, and usually of a pale-green color. *Formula:* $Ca_2Al_2Si_3O_{10}(OH)_2$ [< German *Prehnit* < Colonel van *Prehn*, a Dutch governor of Cape Colony, who brought it to Europe in the late 1700's]

pre·hom·i·nid (prē hom′ə nid), *adj.* of or having to do with a group of extinct, manlike primates regarded as immediate ancestors of the hominids. —*n.* a prehominid animal: *Walking upright was initiated by prehominids* (New Yorker).

pre·ig·ni·tion (prē′ig nish′ən), *n.* the ignition of the explosive mixture in an internal-combustion engine before the piston is in a position to begin its working stroke, especially before the inlet valve has closed or before full compression of the mixture is reached in the cylinder.

pre·in·dus·tri·al (prē′in dus′trē əl), *adj.* existing or occurring before industrialization: *It would take . . . 500 years for Lake Michigan to return to its preindustrial purity* (Atlantic).

pre·judge (prē juj′), *v.*, **-judged, -judg·ing.** —*v.t.* to pass judgment on (a person, opinion, action, etc.) beforehand; judge without due consideration: *The jury was reminded to keep an open mind during the trial and not to prejudge the case.* —*v.i.* to judge beforehand; judge without knowing all the facts. [< French *préjuger*, alteration (influenced by earlier *juger*) of Latin *praejūdicāre* to prejudge, prejudice < *prae-* before + *jūdicāre* to judicate < *jūdex, -icis* a judge] —**pre·judg′er,** *n.*

pre·judge·ment (prē juj′mənt), *n. Especially British.* prejudgment.

pre·judg·ment (prē juj′mənt), *n.* the act of prejudging; judgment before full knowledge or examination of the case; decision or condemnation in advance: *I listen that I may know, without prejudgment* (George Eliot).

prej·u·dice (prej′ə dis), *n., v.*, **-diced, -dic·ing.** —*n.* **1.** an opinion formed without taking time and care to judge fairly: *My grandfather had a strong prejudice against doctors. I am . . . a bundle of prejudices—made up of likings and dislikings* (Charles Lamb). **2.** harm; injury: *I will do nothing to the prejudice of my cousin in this matter.*

to the or **in prejudice of,** to the detriment or injury of: *A material error, which I have committed in another place, to the prejudice of the Empress* (Thomas Jefferson).

without prejudice, without damaging or lessening an existing right or claim, especially one's legal right, claim, interest, etc.: *The above I offer without prejudice, in case it is not agreed to* (Manning and Granger).

—*v.t.* **1.** to cause a prejudice in; fill with prejudice: *One unfortunate experience prejudiced him against all lawyers.* **2.** to damage; harm; injure, as by some action that weakens (a right, claim, statement, etc.): *His bravado carried him too far and prejudiced his case* (Robert Louis Stevenson).

[< Old French *prejudice*, learned borrowing from Latin *praejūdicium* < *prae-* before + *jūdicium* judgment < *jūdex, -icis* a judge]

—**Syn.** *n.* **1. Prejudice, bias** mean an opinion or judgment without a good basis. **Prejudice** applies to an opinion, usually unfavorable, formed beforehand with no basis except personal feelings: *She has a prejudice against modern furniture.* **Bias** applies to an opinion or judgment that is slanted against or in favor of someone or something because of personal liking or a fixed idea: *He often does foolish things because of his bias in favor of the underdog.*

prej·u·di·cial (prej′ə dish′əl), *adj.* causing prejudice or disadvantage; hurtful: *They were playing havoc with legitimate union demands, and acting in a manner prejudicial to others at the pit and contrary to the spirit of trade unionism* (London Times). —**Syn.** detrimental, damaging.

prej·u·di·cial·ly (prej′ə dish′ə lē), *adv.* in a prejudiced manner; with prejudice.

prel·a·cy (prel′ə sē), *n., pl.* **-cies. 1.** the position or rank of a prelate. **2.** prelates as a group. **3.** church government by prelates. [< Anglo-French *prelacie*, learned borrowing from Medieval Latin *praelatia* < *praelatus* prelate]

pre·lap·sar·i·an (prē′lap sãr′ē ən), *adj.* of the time or condition before a fall, especially the fall of man: *The monks and hermits were trying . . . to re-create the life of prelapsarian Adam* (Manchester Guardian). [< *pre-* + Latin *lapsus* fall + English *-arian*, as in *infralapsarian*]

prel·ate (prel′it), *n.* a clergyman of high rank, such as a bishop: *Dr. Ramsey, many have remarked, looks more like a Rugby forward than a prelate of England's dignified church* (Newsweek). [< Medieval Latin *praelatus* prelate (in Late Latin, noble) < Latin, (literally) one that is preferred, past participle of *praeferre* prefer]

prel·ate·ship (prel′it ship), *n.* the office or rank of a prelate.

pre·lat·ic (pri lat′ik), *adj.* **1.** of or having to do with a prelate. **2.** of the nature of a prelate. **3.** supporting prelacy (often used in an unfriendly way).

pre·lat·i·cal (pri lat′ə kəl), *adj.* prelatic.

prel·at·ism (prel′ə tiz əm), *n.* **1.** prelacy; episcopacy. **2.** the support of prelacy (often used in an unfriendly way).

prel·at·ist (prel′ə tist), *n.* a supporter of prelacy (often used in an unfriendly way).

prel·at·ize (prel′ə tīz), *v.t.*, **-ized, -iz·ing.** to make prelatical; bring under the influence and power of prelacy.

prel·a·ture (prel′ə chər), *n.* prelacy. [< Medieval Latin *praelatura* < *praelatus* prelate]

pre·lect (pri lekt′), *v.i.* to discourse publicly; deliver a lecture. Also, **praelect.** [< Latin *praelēctus*, past participle of *praelegere* read to others, lecture upon < *prae-* before + *legere* read]

pre·lec·tion (pri lek′shən), *n.* a public lecture or discourse. Also, **praelection.**

pre·lec·tor (pri lek′tər), *n.* a public reader of lectures or discourses; a lecturer, as in a university. Also, **praelector.**

pre·li·ba·tion (prē′lī bā′shən), *n.* a tasting beforehand; foretaste. [< Latin *praelībātiō, -ōnis* anticipation, a taste < *praelībāre* < *prae-* before + *lībāre* to taste]

pre·lim (pri lim′), *n. Informal.* a preliminary examination. Prelims are also given to some candidates for the doctorate before writing the dissertation. *He was miserably lonely, failed his "prelims" and had to leave at the end of his first year* (Sunday Times).

prelim., preliminary.

pre·lim·i·nar·i·ly (pri lim′ə ner′ə lē), *adv.* in a preliminary manner; as a preliminary; previously.

pre·lim·i·nar·y (pri lim′ə ner′ē), *adj., n., pl.* **-nar·ies.** —*adj.* coming before the main business; leading to something more important: *After the preliminary exercises of prayer and song, the speaker of the day gave an address.* —*n.* **1.** a preliminary step; something preparatory: *The ambassadors dispensed with formal preliminaries and opened their discussions immediately.* **2.** a preliminary examination. [< New Latin *praeliminaris* < Latin *prae-* before + *līmen, -inis* threshold] —**Syn.** *adj.* prefatory, introductory.

prel·ude (prel′yüd, prē′lüd), *n., v.*, **-ud·ed, -ud·ing.** —*n.* **1.** anything serving as an introduction; preliminary performance: *the organ prelude to a church service. The treaty is regarded as a prelude to such a conference* (New York Times). **2. a.** a piece of music, or part of it, that introduces another piece or part: *But remember that the preludes and fugues were first of all reverie pieces used in the church service* (Atlantic). **b.** a short, independent instrumental movement or piece of an imaginative, improvised nature, following no special form.

—*v.t.* **1.** to be a prelude or introduction to: *When the gray of morn preludes the splendour of the day* (John Dryden). **2.** to introduce with a prelude: *He preluded his address with a sonorous blast of the nose* (Washington Irving). **3.** *Music.* to play as a prelude.

—*v.i.* **1.** to give a prelude or introductory performance. **2.** *Music.* to play a prelude.

[< Middle French *prélude*, learned borrowing from Medieval Latin *praeludium* < Latin *praelūdere* to preface < *prae-* before + *lūdere* to play]

pre·lud·er (pri lü′dər, prel′yə-), *n.* **1.** a person who preludes. **2.** a person who plays a musical prelude.

pre·lu·di·al (pri lü′dē əl), *adj.* of or like a prelude; introductory: *a preludial dinner.*

pre·lu·sion (pri lü′zhən), *n.* a prelude or introduction. [< Latin *praelūsiō, -ōnis* a prefacing < *praelūdere* to perform before; see PRELUDE]

pre·lu·sive (pri lü′siv), *adj.* serving as a prelude; preliminary; introductory. —**pre·lu′sive·ly,** *adv.*

pre·lu·so·ri·ly (pri lü′sər ə lē), *adv.* by way of introduction or prelude.

pre·lu·so·ry (pri lü′sər ē), *adj.* prelusive.

pre·man (prē′man′), *n., pl.* **-men.** a prehistoric man: *arboreal premen.*

pre·ma·ture (prē′mə chůr′, -tůr′, -tyůr′), *adj.* **1.** before the proper time; too soon: *A premature baby is one born more than two weeks early or weighing less than 5½ pounds. He was already decrepit with premature old age* (John L. Motley). **2.** hasty; rash, as in action: *I had been a little too premature in coming to this conclusion* (Herman Melville). [< Latin *praemātūrus* < *prae-* beforehand, early + *mātūrus* ripe] —**pre′ma·ture′ness,** *n.*

pre·ma·ture·ly (prē′mə chůr′lē, -tůr′-, -tyůr′-), *adv.* before the proper time: *prematurely gray.*

pre·ma·tu·ri·ty (prē′mə chůr′ə tē, -tůr′-, -tyůr′-), *n.* the quality or state of being premature: *For most of the deaths of babies under one month, prematurity is the chief cause* (Newsweek).

pre·max·il·la (prē′mak sil′ə), *n., pl.* **-max·il·lae** (-mak sil′ē). one of a pair of bones of the upper jaw of vertebrates, situated in front of and between the maxillary bones. [< New Latin *praemaxilla* < Latin *prae-* before, forward + *maxilla* maxilla]

pre·max·il·lar·y (prē mak′sə ler′ē), *adj., n., pl.* **-lar·ies.** —*adj.* **1.** in front of the maxillary bones. **2.** of or having to do with premaxillae. —*n.* a premaxilla.

pre·med (prē′med, prē med′), *Informal.* —*n.* a premedical student: *As far as the liberal arts are concerned, says the report, the premed is short-changed* (Time). —*adj.* premedical.

pre·med·ic (prē med′ik), *n.* a premed.

pre·med·i·cal (prē med′ə kəl), *adj.* preparing for the study of medicine: *a premedical student, a premedical curriculum.*

pre·med·i·tate (prē med′ə tāt), *v.t., v.i.,*

-tat·ed, -tat·ing. to consider or plan beforehand: *The murder was premeditated.* [< Latin *praemeditārī* (with English *-ate*[1]) < *prae-* before + *meditārī* to meditate]

pre·med·i·tat·ed·ly (prē med′ə tā′tid lē), *adv.* with premeditation; deliberately.

pre·med·i·ta·tion (prē′med ə tā′shən), *n.* previous deliberation or planning.

pre·med·i·ta·tive (prē med′ə tā′tiv), *adj.* characterized by premeditation.

pre·med·i·ta·tor (prē med′ə tā′tər), *n.* a person who premeditates.

pre·men·stru·al (prē men′strü əl), *adj.* occurring before menstruation.

pre·mier (*n.* pri mir′, prē′mē ər; *adj.* prē′mē ər, prem′yər), *n.* a prime minister: *It has been my aim to get the premiers of the four provinces working closer together than ever before* (Maclean's).
[short for *premier minister* (literally) first minister]
—*adj.* **1.** first in rank; chief: *The show directors, faced with rising costs . . . to stage Scotland's premier agricultural event, were disappointed* (London Times). **2.** first in time; earliest.
[< Old French *premier* first < Latin *prīmārius* < *prīmus* first. Doublet of PRIMARY.]

pre·mier dan·seur (prə myā′ däɴ sœr′), *French.* the leading male dancer in a ballet or ballet company: *Serge Golovine, premier danseur of the de Cuevas Ballet . . . possesses this muscular animation to an extraordinary degree* (New Statesman).

pre·mière (pri mir′, prə myãr′), *n., adj., v.,* **-mièred, -mièr·ing.** —*n.* **1.** a first public performance: *the première of a new play.* **2.** the leading woman (in a play or the like).
—*adj.* premier.
—*v.t.* to give the first public performance of (a play, etc.): *The romantic opera "Louise" was premièred in 1900* (Time).
[< French *première,* (originally) feminine of *premier* first; see PREMIER]

pre·mière dan·seuse (prə myer′ däɴ-sœz′), *French.* the leading woman dancer in a ballet or ballet company: *Miss Fonteyn, première danseuse of the Sadler's Wells Ballet, was made a Dame of the British Empire* (Newsweek).

pre·mier·ship (pri mir′ship, prē′mē ər-), *n.* **1.** the office or rank of a prime minister: *Andre Tardieu, perhaps the most brilliant politician of the years between the two world wars, abandoned politics after two premierships* (Wall Street Journal). **2.** the state of being first or foremost.

pre·mil·le·nar·i·an (prē′mil ə nãr′ē ən), *n.* a supporter of premillennialism. —*adj.* premillennial.

pre·mil·le·nar·i·an·ism (prē′mil ə nãr′ē-ə niz′əm), *n.* premillennialism.

pre·mil·len·ni·al (prē′mə len′ē əl), *adj. Theology.* preceding the millenium; having to do with the world as it now is.

pre·mil·len·ni·al·ism (prē′mə len′ē ə liz′-əm), *n.* the belief that Christ will come again before the millennium and reign a thousand years upon a righteous, happy earth.

pre·mil·len·ni·al·ist (prē′mə len′ē ə list), *n.* a premillenarian.

prem·ise (*n.* prem′is; *v.* pri mīz′), *n., v.,* **-ised, -is·ing.** —*n. Logic.* a statement assumed to be true and used to draw a conclusion. *Example:* Major premise: All men are mortal. Minor premise: He is a man. Conclusion: He is mortal.
premises, a. a house or building with its grounds: *Each had entered the Brink's premises several times at night to study the layout* (Newsweek). **b.** *Law.* things mentioned previously, such as the names of the parties concerned, a description of the property, the price, grounds for complaint, etc.: *The court having considered the premises are of the opinion . . .* (Bloomfield's American Law Reports). **c.** *Law.* the property forming the subject of a document: *Alice Higgins devised the premises, being a term for 999 years, to trustees, in trust to herself for life, remainder to H. Higgins, her son, and Mary, his wife* (William Cruise).
—*v.t.* **1.** to set forth as an introduction or explanation; mention beforehand: *Having premised these circumstances, I will now let the nervous gentleman proceed with his stories* (Washington Irving). **2.** *Obsolete.* to imply beforehand; presuppose. —*v.i.* to make a premise.
[< Old French *premisse,* learned borrowing from Latin *praemissa* (*propositiō*) (the proposition) put before; (originally) feminine past participle of *praemittere* < Latin *prae-* before + *mittere* to send]

prem·iss (prem′is), *n. Logic.* premise.

pre·mi·um (prē′mē əm), *n., pl.* **-ums,** *adj.* —*n.* **1.** a reward, especially given as an incentive to buy; prize: *Some magazines give premiums for obtaining new subscriptions.* **2.** something more than the ordinary price or wages: *Mr. Brown has to pay 6 per cent interest on his loan, and also a premium of two hundred dollars.* **3.** the amount of money paid for insurance: *He pays premiums on his life insurance four times a year.* **4.** the excess value of one form of money over another of the same nominal value, as of gold or silver coins over paper currency. **5.** an unusual or unfair value: *Giving money to beggars may put a premium on idleness.* **6.** a fee paid for instruction in some occupation.
at a premium, a. at more than the usual value or price: . . . *entitled to extra seats for every football game, which could be sold to lesser fry at a handsome premium* (New Yorker). **b.** in high esteem; much wanted: *John Lyon put their charms at a premium* (Harrovian).
—*adj.* of a higher grade or quality: . . . *introduced a new . . . nylon cord premium tire which . . . will give up to 40 per cent more mileage* (Wall Street Journal).
[< Latin *praemium* reward, booty < *prae-* before + *emere* to buy]

premium pay, wages at more than the basic rate for overtime work or for work on holidays or weekends: *The union retains six paid holidays, with provision for premium pay if a worker was required to work on those days* (New York Times).

pre·mix (prē′miks′), *n.* any product mixed beforehand: *Bottlers like the premix because it gives them complete quality control over the product* (Wall Street Journal). —*adj.* of a premix. —*v.t.* to prepare by mixing beforehand: *premixed cement. Kitchens are entering the push-button stage; foods are premixed, pre-breaded, pre-fried* (Harper's).

pre·mo·lar (prē mō′lər), *n.* **1.** one of the permanent teeth between the canine teeth and the molars; bicuspid: *In mammals, the teeth are specialized to accomplish specific functions. Premolars and molars* [*are*] *for grinding* (A.M. Winchester). **2.** one of the molars of the milk teeth, preceding the permanent molars. —*adj.* of the premolars.

pre·mon·ish (prē mon′ish), *v.t.* to advise; caution; forewarn. —*v.i.* to give warning beforehand. [< *pre-* + (ad)*monish*]

pre·mo·ni·tion (prē′mə nish′ən, prem′ə-), *n.* notification or warning of what is to come; forewarning: *a vague premonition of disaster.* [< Middle French *premonicion,* learned borrowing from Latin *praemonitiō, -ōnis* < *praemonēre* < *prae-* before + *monēre* to warn]

pre·mon·i·to·ri·ly (pri mon′ə tôr′ə lē, -tōr′-), *adv.* by way of premonition.

pre·mon·i·to·ry (pri mon′ə tôr′ē, -tōr′-), *adj.* giving warning beforehand: *It is established practice in this country to get anyone showing premonitory symptoms of major drama away from the theatre* (Observer).

Pre·mon·strant (prē mon′strənt), *n., adj.* Premonstratensian.

Pre·mon·stra·ten·sian (prē mon′strə-ten′shən), *adj.* of or having to do with a Roman Catholic religious order founded by Saint Norbert at Prémontré, near Laon, France, in 1120. —*n.* a member of the Premonstratensian order; white canon. [< Medieval Latin *Premonstratensis* (< *Prémontré,* a city in France) + English *-ian*]

pre·morse (pri môrs′), *n. Botany.* having the end abruptly truncate, as if bitten or broken off, as certain roots. [< Latin *praemorsus,* past participle of *praemordēre* to bite in front < *prae-* before + *mordēre* to bite]

pre·mun·dane (prē mun′dān), *adj.* existing or occurring before the creation of the world; antemundane.

pre·na·tal (prē nā′təl), *adj.* previous to birth: *prenatal damage to the skull. Investigation . . . is laying the basis for a new field of preventive medicine which we might call prenatal pediatrics* (Scientific American). —**pre·na′tal·ly,** *adv.*

pre·no·men (prē nō′mən), *n., pl.* **-no·mens** or **-nom·i·na** (-nom′ə nə). praenomen.

pre·nom·i·nate (pri nom′ə nāt), *adj., v.,* **-nat·ed, -nat·ing.** *Obsolete.* —*adj.* named before; named above. —*v.t.* to name beforehand; mention or specify in advance. [< Latin *praenōminātus* < *praenōmināre* to name in the first place]

pre·no·tion (prē nō′shən), *n.* a previous notion; preconceived idea; preconception. [< Latin *praenōtiō, -ōnis* preconception < *prae-* before + *nōtiō, -ōnis* concept, definition < *nōscere* become acquainted]

pren·tice (pren′tis), *Archaic.* —*n.* an apprentice. —*adj.* of or like an apprentice; inexperienced; unskilled.

pre·oc·cu·pan·cy (prē ok′yə pən sē), *n., pl.* **-cies.** the fact of occupying previously; earlier occupancy.

pre·oc·cu·pa·tion (prē ok′yə pā′shən), *n.* **1.** the act of preoccupying. **2.** the condition of being preoccupied; absorption.

pre·oc·cu·pied (prē ok′yə pīd), *adj.* **1.** absorbed in thought; abstracted. **2.** occupied previously. **3.** *Biology.* (of a generic or specific name) already used for something else and therefore unavailable as a name for another group.

pre·oc·cu·py (prē ok′yə pī), *v.t.,* **-pied, -py·ing. 1.** to take up all the attention of: *The question of getting to New York preoccupied her mind.* **2.** to occupy beforehand; take possession of before others: *Our favorite seats had been preoccupied.* **3.** *Obsolete.* to prepossess; bias.

pre·o·ral (prē ôr′əl, -ōr′-), *adj. Zoology.* situated in front of the mouth. —**pre·o′ral·ly,** *adv.*

pre·or·di·na·tion (prē′or də nā′shən), *n.* a preordaining or being preordained.

prep (prep), *adj., v.,* **prepped, prep·ping,** *n.* —*adj. U.S. Informal.* preparatory: *a good prep course in business English.*
—*v.i. U.S. Informal.* **1.** to attend preparatory school: *And then there are all of the guys who are left out of things because they went to high schools instead of prepping* (Harper's). **2.** to study; prepare: *She prepped for the real thing in a succession of out-of-town productions, from Munich, Germany to Pocatello, Idaho* (Time).
—*n.* **1.** Often, **Prep.** *U.S. Informal.* a preparatory school: *He goes to Poly Prep.* **2.** *British Slang.* preparation of lessons; homework: *It is necessary to devote the long winter evenings to long weary hours of prep* (Punch).

prep., 1. preparation. **2.** preparatory. **3.** preposition.

pre·pack (prē pak′), *v.t.* to prepackage: *Portions of cheese for the customer are being prepacked in plastic bags duly sealed* (New Scientist).

pre·pack·age (prē pak′ij), *v.t.,* **-aged, -aging.** to package beforehand in certain weights, sizes, or grades, usually with the price attached: *Most meat now sold in such self-service departments is prepackaged in the store rather than by packers* (Wall Street Journal).

pre·paid (prē pād′), *v.* the past tense and past participle of **prepay:** *Send this shipment prepaid.*

prep·a·ra·tion (prep′ə rā′shən), *n.* **1.** a preparing. **2.** a being prepared. **3.** a thing done to prepare for something: *to make preparations for a journey.* **4.** a medicine, food, or other substance made by a special process. **5.** an animal body or part of one prepared for dissection, or preserved for examination. **6.** *Music.* **a.** the leading up to a discord by sounding the dissonant tone in it as a consonant tone in the preceding chord. **b.** the consonance which becomes dissonance (usually the suspension) in the next chord. [< Old French *preparacion,* learned borrowing from Latin *praeparātiō, -ōnis* < *praeparāre;* see PREPARE]

pre·par·a·tive (pri par′ə tiv), *adj.* preparatory. —*n.* something that prepares, or helps to prepare; preliminary; preparation: *if discontent and misery are preparatives for liberty* (Charles Kingsley). —**pre·par′a·tive·ly,** *adv.*

pre·par·a·tor (pri par′ə tər), *n.* a person who prepares food or medicine by a special process or prepares animals for dissection.

pre·par·a·to·ri·ly (pri par′ə tôr′ə lē, -tōr′-), *adv.* in a preparatory manner.

pre·par·a·to·ry (pri par′ə tôr′ē, -tōr′-), *adj.* **1.** of or for preparation; preparing: *Preparatory schools fit pupils for college.* **2.** as an introduction; preliminary: *preparatory remarks.*

preparatory command, the first part of a military command in two parts.

preparatory school, 1. *U.S.* a private school, usually from grades 9 through 12, that prepares boys or girls for college. 2. *British.* a private school that prepares boys of 6 to 14 for the public schools.

pre·pare (pri pãr′), *v.,* **-pared, -par·ing.** —*v.t.* 1. to make ready; put in condition for something: *to prepare a meal, to prepare a room for a guest, to prepare a lesson, to prepare a boy for college.* 2. to make by a special process: *to prepare the medicine prescribed, to prepare aluminum from bauxite.* 3. *Music.* to lead up to (a discord) by sounding the dissonant tone as a consonant tone in the preceding chord. 4. *Archaic.* to provide; furnish. —*v.i.* to put oneself, or things, in readiness; get ready: *The thunderbolt Hangs silent; but prepare. I speak, it falls* (Tennyson). [< Latin *praeparāre* < *prae-* before + *parāre* make ready] —**pre·par′er,** *n.* —**Syn.** *v.t.* 2. devise, contrive.

pre·par·ed·ly (pri pãr′id lē), *adv.* with suitable preparation.

pre·par·ed·ness (pri pãr′id nis, -pãrd′nis), *n.* 1. a being prepared; readiness. 2. the possession of adequate military forces and defenses to meet threats or outbreaks of war: *Constant preparedness is the price of peace, the President maintains.*

prepared piano, 1. a piano that has had its timbre altered to produce unconventional sounds by attaching various objects to the strings. 2. the method of playing such a piano: *... a method pioneered by composer John Cage, who called it "prepared piano"* (Time).

pre·pay (prē pā′), *v.t.,* **-paid, -pay·ing.** 1. to pay in advance. 2. to pay for in advance.

pre·pay·a·ble (prē pā′ə bəl), *adj.* that can be or is to be prepaid.

pre·pay·ment (prē pā′mənt), *n.* the act of paying beforehand; payment in advance.

pre·pense (pri pens′), *adj.* planned beforehand; premeditated; deliberate. [alteration of Middle English *purpense* < Old French *purpenser* < *pour-* forward + *penser* to think; see PENSIVE] —**pre·pense′ly,** *adv.*

pre·plan (prē plan′), *v.t.,* **-planned, -planning.** to plan beforehand; plan ahead: *The academic curriculum must be preplanned at different levels of difficulty* (Atlantic).

pre·pol·lex (prē pol′eks), *n., pl.* **-pol·li·ces** (-pol′ə sēz). a rudimentary structure found in some animals on the radial edge of the hand or forefoot, supposed to represent an additional digit. [< *pre-* + *pollex*]

pre·pon·der·ance (prē pon′dər əns), *n.* 1. a greater number; greater weight; greater power or influence: *In July the hot days have the preponderance.* 2. a being the chief or most important element: *the preponderance of oaks in these woods.*

pre·pon·der·an·cy (prē pon′dər ən sē), *n., pl.* **-cies.** preponderance.

pre·pon·der·ant (prē pon′dər ənt), *adj.* 1. weighing more; being stronger or more numerous; having more power. 2. chief; most important; predominant: *Faithfulness is one of the preponderant characteristics of dogs.* [< Latin *praeponderāns, -antis,* present participle of *praeponderāre* preponderate] —**pre·pon′der·ant·ly,** *adv.*

pre·pon·der·ate (prē pon′də rāt), *v.,* **-at·ed, -at·ing.** —*v.i.* 1. to be greater than something else in weight, power, force, influence, number, amount, etc.: *Oaks and maples preponderate in our woods. The good in this state of existence preponderates over the bad* (Dickens). 2. to be chief; be most important; predominate. —*v.t.* to be greater than; outweigh. [< Latin *praeponderāre* (with English *-ate*[1]) outweigh < *prae-* before + *ponderāre* to weigh < *pondus, -eris* weight] —**pre·pon′der·at′ing·ly,** *adv.*

pre·pon·der·a·tion (prē pon′də rā′shən), *n.* the act or fact of preponderating; superiority in weight, force, number, etc.

pre·pon·der·ous (prē pon′dər əs), *adj.* preponderant. —**pre·pon′der·ous·ly,** *adv.*

prep·o·si·tion (prep′ə zish′ən), *n.* a word that shows certain relations between other words. *With, for, by,* and *in* are prepositions in the sentence "A man *with* rugs *for* sale walked *by* our house *in* the morning." [< Latin *praepositiō, -ōnis* < *praepōnere* < *prae-* before + *pōnere* put]

➤ **preposition at end of sentence.** Though formerly sometimes censured in textbooks, the use of a preposition at the end of a sentence is not always objectionable or easily avoidable (*What did you do it for?*). The effort to avoid it (*Tell me what you object to*) sometimes produces a clumsy (*Tell me to what you object*) or fussy effect (*Tell me what it is to which you object*).

prep·o·si·tion·al (prep′ə zish′ə nəl), *adj.* 1. having to do with a preposition: *a prepositional phrase.* 2. having the nature or function of a preposition. —**prep′o·si′tion·al·ly,** *adv.*

pre·pos·i·tive (prē poz′ə tiv), *Grammar.* —*adj.* put before; prefixed. —*n.* prepositive word or particle. —**pre·pos′i·tive·ly,** *adv.*

pre·pos·i·tor (prē poz′ə tər), *n.* (at some English public schools) any of the senior boys who discipline the younger students, especially out of the classroom; monitor. Also, **praepositor, praepostor, preposter.** [< Latin *praepositus* chief, head; (literally) one placed in authority, (originally) past participle of *praepōnere* (see PREPOSITION) + English *-or*]

pre·pos·i·to·ri·al (prē poz′ə tôr′ē əl, -tōr′-), *adj.* of or having to do with prepositors.

pre·pos·sess (prē′pə zes′), *v.t.* 1. to fill with a favorable feeling or opinion: *We were prepossessed by the boy's modest behavior.* 2. to fill with a feeling or opinion: *The teacher ... did not prepossess me in favour of his pursuits* (Mary Shelley). 3. to take or get possession of beforehand.

pre·pos·sess·ing (prē′pə zes′ing), *adj.* making a favorable first impression; attractive; pleasing: *a most prepossessing young man. Clean clothes and good manners are prepossessing.* —**pre′pos·sess′ing·ly,** *adv.* —**pre′pos·sess′ing·ness,** *n.*

pre·pos·ses·sion (prē′pə zesh′ən), *n.* 1. a favorable feeling or opinion formed beforehand; prejudice; bias: *A well-written letter applying for a position will create a prepossession in the writer's favor.* 2. prior possession or occupancy.

pre·pos·ter·ous (pri pos′tər əs, -trəs), *adj.* contrary to nature, reason, or common sense; absurd; senseless: *It would be preposterous to shovel coal with a teaspoon.* [< Latin *praeposterus* (with English *-ous*) absurd; (originally) in reverse order < *prae-* before + *posterus* coming after < *post* after] —**pre·pos′ter·ous·ly,** *adv.* —**pre·pos′ter·ous·ness,** *n.* —**Syn.** foolish, nonsensical. See **ridiculous.**

pre·pos·tor (prē pos′tər), *n.* prepositor.

pre·po·tence (prē pō′təns), *n.* prepotency.

pre·po·ten·cy (prē pō′tən sē), *n., pl.* **-cies.** 1. superior power or influence; predominance: *The "prepotency" of pain [is seen in] ... its ability to suffuse the entire field of consciousness with distress and to crowd out all other thoughts* (Martin E. Spencer). 2. *Genetics.* the marked power of one parent, variety, etc., to transmit a special character or characters to the progeny.

pre·po·tent (prē pō′tənt), *adj.* 1. having greater power or influence than others; predominant: *An ambiguous, prepotent figure had come to disturb the ... jealously guarded balance of the English constitution* (Lytton Strachey). 2. *Genetics.* **a.** of prepotency. **b.** exhibiting prepotency. [< Latin *praepotens, -entis,* present participle of *praeposse* be superior, very powerful < *prae-* before + *posse* be able] —**pre·po′tent·ly,** *adv.*

pre·pri·ma·ry school (prē prī′mer′ē, -mər-), a school for very young children; a combination of nursery school and kindergarten.

pre·print (prē′print′), *n.* a printing in advance, especially a portion of a work issued before publication of the whole. —*v.t.* to print in advance of publication: *The ads are preprinted by gravure in a continuous roll* (Sunday Times).

prep school, *Informal.* a preparatory school: *The same sort of tension has been going on for years and years round prep school scholarships* (Punch).

pre·psy·chot·ic (prē′sī kot′ik), *adj.* showing indications of psychosis; occurring before or leading to psychosis: *In psychotic and prepsychotic subjects they [hallucinogenic drugs] may induce an acute psychotic reaction* (Walter Modell).

pre·pu·ber·ty (prē pyü′bər tē), *n.* the period of life just prior to puberty: *Estrogen ..., given over a prolonged period in prepuberty, has been used clinically to cut down the ultimate height of tall girls* (Nathan Dreskin).

pre·pu·bes·cent (prē′pyü bes′ənt), *adj.* having to do with prepuberty; immature: *It relies for its climax on an offstage sound effect of prepubescent ... humor* (Time).

pre·puce (prē′pyüs), *n.* 1. the fold of skin covering the end of the penis; foreskin. 2. a similar fold of skin covering the end of the clitoris. [< Middle French, Old French *prepuce,* learned borrowing from Latin *praepūtium*]

pre·pu·pa (prē pyü′pə), *n., pl.* **-pae** (-pē), **-pas.** 1. the inactive stage before pupation in the development of many insects. 2. the form of an insect in this stage: *We inject hemolymph from these prepupae into young larvae* (Scientific American).

pre·pu·pal (prē pyü′pəl), *adj.* of, having to do with, or in the form of a prepupa.

pre·pu·tial (prē pyü′shəl), *adj.* of or having to do with the prepuce.

Pre-Raph·a·el·ite (prē raf′ē ə līt, -rā′fē-), *n.* 1. any Italian painter preceding Raphael. 2. one of a group of English artists formed in 1848, including John Everett Millais and Dante Gabriel Rossetti, who aimed to work in the spirit that prevailed before the time of Raphael. 3. any modern artist having similar aims or methods.
—*adj.* 1. existing before Raphael. 2. of or belonging to the Pre-Raphaelites: *Of the many forces which exerted an influence upon the young Picasso, ... one was the Pre-Raphaelite movement* (Listener). 3. characteristic of or resembling the Pre-Raphaelites or their principles and style: *[He was] the husband of an indifferent one whose Pre-Raphaelite ecstasies and graces he found laughable, though lovable* (New Yorker).

Pre-Raph·a·el·it·ism (prē raf′ē ə līt′iz-əm, -rā′fē-), *n.* 1. the style of painting in vogue from the time of Giotto to that of Raphael. 2. the revival of this style by the Pre-Raphaelites.

pre·re·cord (prē′ri kôrd′), *v.t.* to record in advance for later use: *"Parts of this program were prerecorded on video tape," says the announcer triumphantly* (Atlantic).

pre·req·ui·site (prē rek′wə zit), *n.* something required beforehand: *A high-school course is the usual prerequisite to college work.* —*adj.* required beforehand.

pre·rog·a·tive (pri rog′ə tiv), *n.* 1. a right or privilege that nobody else has: *The government has the prerogative of coining money.* 2. special superiority of right or privilege, such as may derive from an official position, office, etc.; precedence.
the Royal Prerogative, the original nonstatutory powers of the British sovereign recognized by common law, now constitutionally exercised by, or on the advice of, ministers responsible to Parliament: *In his opinion, the very lowest claim of the Royal Prerogative should include "a right on the part of the King to be the permanent President of his Ministerial Council"* (Lytton Strachey).
—*adj.* 1. having or exercising a prerogative. 2. *Law.* of or having to do with a prerogative court.
[< Latin *praerogātīva* privilege, favoring token; (originally) feminine adjective, allotted to vote first < *praerogāre* ask for a vote first < *prae-* before + *rogāre* ask]
—**Syn.** *n.* 1. See **privilege.**

prerogative court, 1. (in Great Britain) a former ecclesiastical court for the trial of certain testamentary cases. 2. (in the state of New Jersey) the probate court.

pres., 1. present. 2. presidency. 3. president.

Pres., 1. Presbyterian. 2. President.

pre·sa (prā′sä), *n., pl.* **-se** (-sā). a notation in music used in a canon to show where the successive voice parts are to take up the theme. It is variously represented as :S:, +, or ※.
[< Italian *presa* a taking]

pres·age (*n.* pres′ij; *v.* pri sāj′), *n., v.,* **presaged, pre·sag·ing.** —*n.* 1. a sign felt as a warning; omen. 2. a feeling that something is about to happen: *She could not sleep at night and was haunted by a presage of disaster* (Samuel Butler). 3. a prediction; prognostication.
—*v.t.* 1. to give warning of; predict: *Some people think that a circle round the moon presages a storm.* 2. to have or give a prophetic impression of. —*v.i.* to form or utter a presage or prediction.
[< Latin *praesāgium* < *praesāgīre* to forebode < *praesāgus* foreboding, adjective < *prae-* before + *sāgus* prophetic] —**pre·sag′er,** *n.* —**pre·sag′ing·ly,** *adv.*

pre·sage·ful (pri sāj′fəl), *adj.* **1.** full of presage; foreboding. **2.** ominous.

Presb., Presbyterian.

pres·by·cu·sis (prez′bə kyü′sis), *n.* hearing impairment due to aging. [< Greek *présbys* old man + *ákousis* hearing]

pres·by·o·pi·a (prez′bē ō′pē ə), *n.* a condition of the eye accompanying old age, in which only distant objects may be seen distinctly, unless glasses with corrective lenses are worn: *If they cannot see fine print and are having trouble with telephone books . . . it may be that presbyopia is developing* (Science News Letter).
[< New Latin *presbyopia* < Greek *présbys* old man + New Latin *-opia* < Greek *ṓps* eye]

pres·by·op·ic (prez′bē op′ik), *adj.* **1.** having to do with presbyopia. **2.** affected with presbyopia.

pres·by·ter (prez′bə tər, pres′-), *n.* **1.** an elder in the early Christian Church. **2.** a minister or a lay elder in the Presbyterian Church. **3.** a minister or a priest in the Episcopal Church. [< Latin *presbyter* an elder < Greek *presbýteros,* (originally) comparative of *présbys* old (man). Doublet of PRIEST.]

pres·byt·er·al (prez bit′ər əl, pres-), *adj.* presbyterial.

pres·byt·er·ate (prez bit′ə rāt, pres-), *n.* **1.** the office of presbyter. **2.** a body of presbyters; presbytery.

pres·by·te·ri·al (prez′bə tir′ē əl, pres′-), *adj.* **1.** of or having to do with presbyters or a presbytery. **2.** presbyterian.

Pres·by·te·ri·an (prez′bə tir′ē ən, pres′-), *adj.* **1.** being or naming a Protestant denomination or church governed by elected presbyters or elders, all of equal rank: *The Presbyterian Church in the U.S.* (*Southern*) *has taken a revamped stand on the question of marriage of divorced persons* (Newsweek). **2.** of the Presbyterian Church.
—*n.* **1.** a member of the Presbyterian Church. **2.** a supporter of Presbyterianism.
[< Latin *presbyterium* presbytery + English *-an*]

pres·by·te·ri·an (prez′bə tir′ē ən, pres′-), *adj.* having to do with or based on the principle of ecclesiastical government by presbyters or presbyteries.

Pres·by·te·ri·an·ism (prez′bə tir′ē ə niz′-əm, pres′-), *n.* **1.** the system of church government by elders all (including ministers) of equal rank. **2.** the beliefs and organizational system characterizing Presbyterian churches: *The prime suggestion about taking Episcopacy into the system of Presbyterianism . . .* (Manchester Guardian).

pres·by·ter·y (prez′bə ter′ē, pres′-), *n., pl.* **-ter·ies. 1.** a meeting or court of all the ministers and certain of the elders within a district of a Presbyterian church. **2.** the district under the jurisdiction of such a meeting or court: *The 900 commissioners, or delegates, agreed to put the proposition up to the church's 256 Presbyteries, or local units, for ratification* (New York Times). **3.** the part of a church set aside for the clergy. **4.** a priest's house in the Roman Catholic Church; rectory. **5.** a body of presbyters or elders.
[< Latin *presbyterium* < Greek *presbytérion* council of elders; also, its meeting place < *presbýteros* presbyter]

APSE
PRESBYTERY
CHOIR
NAVE

Presbytery (def. 3) in Wells Cathedral, England

pre·school (prē′skül′), *adj.* before the age of going to regular school: *preschool training. Of the preschool children who are most susceptible to the disease, nearly one-third have not been inoculated at all* (Maclean's).
—*n.* a school for the observation or training of young children, usually under five years of age, sometimes divided in groups according to age.

pre·school·er (prē′skü′lər), *n. Informal.* a young child in or eligible for preschool: *It is not easy to fit the restless, busy, curious preschooler into a smooth-running household* (Sidonie M. Gruenberg).

pre·sci·ence (prē′shē əns, presh′ē-), *n.* knowledge of things before they exist or happen; foreknowledge; foresight: *a man of considerable prescience. The day Archduke Franz Ferdinand was assassinated at Sarajevo, Mussolini, with quite a bit of prescience, remarked . . . that it looked like the start of a major European war* (New Yorker). [< Old French *prescience,* learned borrowing from Latin *praescientia* < Latin *praesciēns, -entis,* present participle of *praescīre* to foreknow < *prae-* before + *scīre* to know]

pre·sci·ent (prē′shē ənt, presh′ē-), *adj.* knowing beforehand; foreseeing: *the sharks . . . following them in the same prescient way that vultures hover over the banners of marching regiments* (Herman Melville). —**pre′sci·ent·ly,** *adv.*

pre·scind (pri sind′), *v.t.* to cut off, detach, or separate from. [< Latin *praescindere* < *prae-* in front + *scindere* to cut]

pre·scribe (pri skrīb′), *v.,* **-scribed, -scrib·ing.** —*v.t.* **1.** to lay down as a rule to be followed; order; direct: *Good citizens do what the laws prescribe.* **2.** to order as a remedy or treatment: *The doctor prescribed quinine.* **3.** *Law.* to make invalid or outlawed because of the passage of time. —*v.i.* **1.** to lay down a rule or rules; dictate; direct: *to do as the law prescribes.* **2.** to give medical advice; issue a prescription. **3.** *Law.* to claim a right or title to something by virtue of long use and enjoyment of it. **4.** (in Scots law) to become invalid because of the passage of time. [< Latin *praescrībere* < *prae-* before + *scrībere* to write] —**pre·scrib′er,** *n.* —**Syn.** *v.t., v.i.* **1.** command, assign, set, appoint, ordain, enjoin.

pre·script (*n.* prē′skript; *adj.* pri skript′, prē′skript), *n.* a rule; order; direction. —*adj.* prescribed; ordained; appointed. [< Latin *praescriptum,* neuter past participle of *praescrībere* prescribe]

pre·scrip·ti·ble (pri skrip′tə bəl), *adj.* **1.** liable to prescription. **2.** derived from or founded on prescription.

pre·scrip·tion (pri skrip′shən), *n.* **1.** the act of prescribing. **2.** something prescribed; order; direction: *He was carrying no "prescription" for peace in the Far East in his mission to Peiping* (New York Times). **3.** a written direction for preparing and using a medicine: *a prescription for a cough. Their task . . . is to make a quick diagnosis—take a case history, make a physical examination, write a prescription* (Time). **4.** the medicine. **5.** *Law.* **a.** possession or use of a thing long enough to give a right or title to it: *to claim a right by prescription, to acquire a thing by prescription.* **b.** the right or title so established. **c.** the process of so establishing a right or title. **d.** a limitation of the time within which a claim may be made or an action brought; negative prescription.

pre·scrip·tive (pri skrip′tiv), *adj.* **1.** prescribing: *a prescriptive system of grammar. In his* [*Johnson's*] *concept of a descriptive rather than prescriptive dictionary he discovered what the twentieth century takes for granted* (Saturday Review). **2.** depending on legal prescription: *a prescriptive title.* **3.** established by long use or custom: *the prescriptive respectability of a family with a mural monument and venerable tankards* (George Eliot). —**pre·scrip′tive·ly,** *adv.* —**pre·scrip′tive·ness,** *n.*

pres·ence (prez′əns), *n.* **1.** the fact or condition of being present in a place: *I just learned of his presence in the city. The French are determined to make a deal . . . for the preservation of . . . France's "economic and cultural presence" in North Vietnam* (Newsweek). **2.** the place where a person is: *The messenger was admitted to my grandfather's presence.* **3.** formal attendance upon a person of very high rank: *The knight retired from the royal presence.* **4.** appearance; bearing: *a man of noble presence.* **5.** something present, especially a ghost, spirit, or the like: *She really felt drawn to worship him, as if he were the shrine . . . of that Presence to which he bore such solemn witness* (Cardinal Newman). **6.** the feeling or illusion of being in the place in which sound originated rather than listening to a recording of it: *They have the benefit of the latest techniques . . . mostly in the intangible matter of "projection," or "presence"* (Musical America). **7.** a living person, especially one of very high rank: *Slowly passed that august Presence Down the thronged and shouting street* (John Greenleaf Whittier). **8.** *Obsolete.* an assembly, especially of people of high rank; company: *Here is like to be a good presence of Worthies* (Shakespeare). **9.** *Obsolete.* a presence chamber.
in the presence of, in the sight or company of: *in the presence of danger. He signed his name in the presence of two witnesses.*
saving your presence, with an apology for doing or saying this in your presence: *Some of the members of your organization are unscrupulous schemers, saving your presence.*
[< Old French *presence* < Latin *praesentia* < *praesēns* present, beside. See PRESENT[1].]

presence chamber, the room in which a king or some very important person receives guests.

presence of mind, the ability to think calmly and quickly when taken by surprise.

presence room, a presence chamber.

pres·ent[1] (prez′ənt), *adj.* **1.** being in the place or thing in question; at hand, not absent: *Every member of the class was present. Oxygen is present in the air.* **2.** at this time; being or occurring now; current: *present prices. Let this great truth be present night and day* (Alexander Pope). **3.** *Grammar.* denoting action now going on or a state now existing. *Go* is the present tense; *went* is the past tense. *Abbr.:* pr. **4.** *Obsolete.* **a.** attentive. **b.** having presence of mind; self-possessed. **c.** prompt to act; ready: *God is our refuge and strength, a very present help in trouble* (Psalms 46:1). **5.** *Obsolete.* immediate.
—*n.* **1.** the present time: *At present people need courage.* **2.** *Grammar.* **a.** the present tense. **b.** a verb form or verbal phrase in that tense. **3.** *Obsolete.* the thing or person that is present; affair in hand; present occasion.
by these presents, by these words; by this document: *know all men by these presents.*
for the present, for this time; for now: *That will be enough for the present.*
[< Latin *praesēns, -entis* present, (originally) present participle of *praeësse* to be before a thing, to rule over < *prae-* before + *esse* to be] —**Syn.** *adj.* **2.** See **current.**

pre·sent[2] (*v.* pri zent′; *n.* prez′ənt), *v.t.* **1.** to give: *to present a book as a prize to the winner. They presented flowers to their teacher.* **2.** to offer; offer formally: *She presented the tray of sandwiches to each guest.* **3.** to bring before the mind; offer for consideration: *He presented reasons for his action. Augustin Thierry . . . had presented the Norman Conquest in terms of a class struggle between the conquerors and the Saxons* (Edmund Wilson). **4.** to offer to view or notice: *The new library presents a fine appearance.* **5.** to bring before the public; give a public performance of: *Our school presented a play.* **6.** to set forth in words: *The speaker presented arguments for his side.* **7.** to hand in; send in: *The grocer presented his bill.* **8.** to introduce (one person to another); introduce formally: *to be presented at court. May I present my sister?* **9.** to direct; point; turn: *The soldier presented his face to the enemy.* **10.** to aim (a weapon). **11.** to recommend (a clergyman) for a benefice. **12.** *Law.* **a.** to bring a formal charge against (a person, etc.). **b.** to bring (an offense, etc.) to the notice of a court, magistrate, or person in authority. **13.** *Archaic.* to represent (a character) on the stage.
—*v.i.* **1.** to point, face, or project in a particular direction. **2.** to aim or level a weapon. **3.** to present a clergyman for a benefice.
present with, to furnish with (something as a gift): *Our class presented the school with a picture.*
[< Old French *presenter* < Latin *praesentāre* + *praesēns* present[1], beside]
—*n.* a thing given; gift: *I can make no marriage present; Little can I give my wife* (Tennyson).
[< Old French *present,* in *en present* (to offer) in the presence of] —**pre·sent′er,** *n.*
—**Syn.** *v.t.* **1.** See **give. 8.** See **introduce.** -*n.* See **gift.**

pre·sent·a·bil·i·ty (pri zen′tə bil′ə tē), *n.* presentable state or quality.

pre·sent·a·ble (pri zen′tə bəl), *adj.* **1.** fit to be seen: *to make a house presentable for company.* **2.** suitable in appearance, dress, manners, etc., for being introduced into society or company: *a very presentable young man.* **3.** suitable to be offered or given. —**pre·sent′a·ble·ness,** *n.*

pre·sent·a·bly (pri zen′tə blē), *adv.* in a presentable manner; so as to have a decent appearance.

pre·sent arms (pri zent′), **1.** to bring a rifle, etc., to a vertical position in front of the body. **2.** this position.

pres·en·ta·tion (prez′ən tā′shən, prē′zən-), *n.* **1.** a giving: *the presentation of a gift.* **2.** a gift. **3.** a bringing forward; offering to be considered: *the presentation of a plan. The subject matter of all science is essentially the same: systematic observation and systematic presentation of the observations in communicable form* (F.H. George). **4.** an offering to be seen; showing: *the presentation of a play.* **5.** a formal introduction: *the presentation of a lady to the queen.* **6.** the act or right of presenting a clergyman to the bishop as a candidate for a benefice. **7.** the presenting of a bill, draft, note, etc., as for payment or acceptance. **8.** the position taken by the fetus during labor: *shoulder presentation.* **9.** *Psychology.* an idea; cognition.

pres·en·ta·tion·al (prez′ən tā′shə nəl, prē′zən-), *adj.* **1.** of or having to do with presentation. **2.** (of words) presentive; notional.

pres·en·ta·tion·ism (prez′ən tā′shə nizəm, prē′zən-), *n.* the theory that perception by the senses gives knowledge of reality.

pres·en·ta·tion·ist (prez′ən tā′shə nist, prē′zən-), *n.* a supporter of the theory of presentationism. —*adj.* having to do with presentationism.

pre·sen·ta·tive (pri zen′tə tiv), *adj.* **1.** knowable by perception. **2.** being capable of or having to do with ecclesiastical presentation.

pres·ent-day (prez′ənt dā′), *adj.* of the present time: *All five of these men, Darwin perhaps excepted, . . . would be regarded as misfits in present-day society* (New York Times).

pres·en·tee (prez′ən tē′), *n.* **1.** a person to whom something is presented. **2.** a person who is presented. **3.** a clergyman presented for institution to a benefice.

pre·sen·tient (pri sen′shənt), *adj.* feeling beforehand; having a presentiment.

pre·sen·ti·ment (pri zen′tə mənt), *n.* a feeling or impression that something is about to happen; vague sense of approaching misfortune; foreboding: *a presentiment of death.* [< Middle French *presentiment* < *pre-* before + *sentiment* impression, sentiment]

pre·sen·ti·men·tal (pri zen′tə men′təl), *adj.* relating to a presentiment.

pre·sen·tive (pri zen′tiv), *adj.* (of words) presenting an object or conception directly to the mind. —*n.* a presentive word. —**pre·sen′tive·ly,** *adv.* —**pre·sen′tive·ness,** *n.*

pres·ent·ly (prez′ənt lē), *adv.* **1.** before long; soon: *The clock will strike presently. Love was the wish to understand, and presently with constant failure the wish died* (Graham Greene). **2.** at the present time; at this time: *The vessel is presently in the Government's mothball fleet* (Wall Street Journal). **3.** *Archaic.* at once. —**Syn. 1.** shortly. See **immediately. 2.** now, currently.

pre·sent·ment (pri zent′mənt), *n.* **1.** a bringing forward; offering to be considered. **2.** a showing; offering to be seen. **3.** a representation on the stage or by a portrait. **4.** a statement by a grand jury of an offense from their own knowledge: *In its presentment, regarded as one of the most bitter ever handed up in the county, the grand jury asserted that the men had misled the taxpayers* (New York Times). **5.** the presenting of a bill, note, etc., as for payment or acceptance. **6.** a bringing to mind; suggestion. [< Old French *presentement* < *presenter* to present, bestow]

pres·en·toir (prez′ən twär′), *n.* **1.** a tray or salver on which things are presented. **2.** a kind of stand or holder for a bowl, cup, or the like. **3.** *Obsolete.* a shallow bowl or cup with a tall supporting stem, for holding fruit or flowers. [< *present*², verb + French *-oir,* a noun suffix]

Japanese Presentoir (def. 2)

present participle, the participle used in forming the English progressive tense or aspect (*is running, was running,* etc.) and as an adjective (the *running* horse). When used adjectivally, neither the present nor the past participle indicates time, which must be deduced from the context: *Singing merrily, we left* (or *shall leave,* etc.).

➔ See **participle** for usage note.

present perfect, perfect.

present tense, the verbal tense commonly used when referring to present time, either without reference to the duration of the action (as "He *runs,*" sometimes called *simple present*) or as being in progress, recurring, or habitual (as "He *is running,*" called *present progressive*).

present value or **worth,** (of a sum payable at a given future date) an amount which, plus the interest upon it for the time from the actual date to the given future date, will equal the sum then due: *The present value of $1,060 due one year from date, interest being allowed at 6 per cent, is $1,000.*

pre·se·pio (prā ze′pyō), *n., pl.* **-pios.** a representation of the Nativity; crèche: *The magnificent 18th-century crèche . . . is one of the famous Neopolitan presepios that delighted King Charles III* (Time). [< Italian *presepio* (literally) stable, manger < Latin *praesaepium*]

pre·serv·a·ble (pri zėr′və bəl), *adj.* that can be preserved.

pres·er·va·tion (prez′ər vā′shən), *n.* **1.** a preserving; keeping safe: *Doctors work for the preservation of our health.* **2.** a being preserved; being kept safe: *They* [*the villas*] *contain frescoes . . . worthy of preservation* (Newsweek).

pres·er·va·tion·ist (prez′ər vā′shə nist), *n.* a person who believes in and advocates preservation of traditional things: *Then there are the total preservationists who would permanently maintain these significant examples even if they impede a sound new development* (New Yorker).

pre·serv·a·tive (pri zėr′və tiv), *n.* any substance that will prevent decay or injury: *Paint is a preservative for wood surfaces. Salt is a preservative for meat.* —*adj.* that preserves.

pre·serv·a·to·ry (pri zėr′və tôr′ē, -tōr′-), *adj., n., pl.* **-ries.** —*adj.* preservative. —*n.* **1.** a preservative. **2.** an apparatus for preserving substances for food. **3.** a place where the preserving of food products is carried on.

pre·serve (pri zėrv′), *v.,* **-served, -serv·ing,** *n.* —*v.t.* **1.** to keep from harm or change; keep safe; protect: *those who wish to preserve the present order of society* (Charles Kingsley). **2.** to keep up; maintain: *Mr. Travers preserved an immobility which struck D'Alcacer as obviously affected* (Joseph Conrad). **3.** to keep from spoiling: *Ice helps to preserve food.* **4.** to prepare (food) to keep it from spoiling: *Boiling with sugar, salting, smoking, and pickling are different ways of preserving food.* **5.** to protect (game or fish) for personal use. **6.** *Archaic.* to keep alive. —*v.i.* **1.** to make preserves, especially of fruit. **2.** to raise and protect game for special use.

—*n.* a place where wild animals or fish are protected: *People are not allowed to hunt on the preserve.*

preserves, fruit or the like cooked with sugar and sealed from the air: *She made plum preserves.*

[< Old French *preserver* < Late Latin *praeservāre* to preserve, observe a custom < Latin *prae-* before + *servāre* keep]

—**Syn.** *v.t.* **1.** save, shield, guard.

pre·serv·er (pri zėr′vər), *n.* a person or thing that saves and protects from danger.

pre·set (prē set′), *v.t.,* **-set, -set·ting.** to set in advance: *If it is known in advance which elements are to be watched for, the instrument can be preset so that only relevant wavelengths are scanned* (A. Haslett).

pre·side (pri zīd′), *v.i.,* **-sid·ed, -sid·ing. 1.** to hold the place of authority; have charge of a meeting. **2.** to have authority; have control: *The manager presides over the business of this store.* [< Middle French *présider,* learned borrowing from *praesidēre* preside over, guard < *prae-* before, ahead + *sedēre* to sit] —**pre·sid′er,** *n.*

pres·i·dence (prez′ə dəns, prez′dəns), *n.* **1.** the act or function of presiding. **2.** the office of president.

pres·i·den·cy (prez′ə dən sē, prez′dən-), *n., pl.* **-cies. 1.** the office of president: *Helen was elected to the presidency of the Junior Club.* **2.** the time during which a president is in office. **3.** a local administrative board in the Mormon Church. **4.** Often, **Presidency.** one of three former administrative divisions (Madras, Bombay, and, originally, Bengal) of British India.

Pres·i·den·cy (prez′ə dən sē, prez′dən-), *n., pl.* **-cies. 1.** the office of President of the United States: *to seek the Presidency. As Mr. Eisenhower completed his third year in the Presidency, his intimates ticked off the changes that had taken place in the man* (Newsweek). **2.** the time of office of a President: *The United States entered World War II in the Presidency of Franklin D. Roosevelt.*

pres·i·dent (prez′ə dənt, prez′dənt), *n.* **1.** the chief officer of a company, college, society, club, etc. **2.** the highest executive officer of a republic: *The president of the national council . . . has followed up his resignation from the council by resigning from the council of the Crown* (London Times). **3.** the chief officer of the Mormon hierarchy. **4.** (in Mexico) the mayor of a town or city.

[< Latin *praesidēns, -entis* (literally) one presiding, present participle of *praesidēre* to preside]

Pres·i·dent (prez′ə dənt, prez′dənt), *n.* **1.** the highest executive officer of the United States: *They wanted a President who would stand above petty partisanship, who would be a President of all the people* (Newsweek). **2.** the highest executive officer of any republic, especially in South America, Italy, and France.

pres·i·dent-e·lect (prez′ə dənt i lekt′, prez′dənt-), *n.* a president elected but not yet inaugurated. [American English < *president* + *elect*]

pres·i·den·tial (prez′ə den′shəl), *adj.* of or belonging to a president or presidency: *a presidential election. The steel price rises . . . brought presidential wrath on the industry* (New York Times). —**pres′i·den′tial·ly,** *adv.*

Presidential Medal of Freedom, a decoration given by the United States to a civilian, or to a member of the armed forces of a friendly nation.

presidential primary, a direct primary that allows voters to express their preference for presidential candidates by voting for the presidential nominees or for delegates to party conventions pledged to particular nominees.

pres·i·dent·ship (prez′ə dənt ship, prez′dənt-), *n.* **1.** the office or function of a president; presidency: *In accepting the Presidentship . . . Mrs. Bandaranaike becomes the first woman in Ceylon to take up the leadership of a major political group* (Times of India). **2.** the term of office of a president.

pre·sid·i·al (pri sid′ē əl), *adj.* **1.** of or having to do with a garrison. **2.** of or having to do with a presidio.

pre·sid·i·ar·y (pri sid′ē er′ē), *adj.* presidial.

pre·sid·ing elder (pri zī′ding), a former title of a district superintendent in the Methodist Church, a clergyman who supervises a number of churches and makes recommendations to the bishop.

pre·sid·i·o (pri sid′ē ō), *n., pl.* **-i·os. 1. a.** (in Spanish America) a garrisoned fort; military post. **b.** (in southwestern United States and California) a fort during the period of Spanish or Mexican control: *An expedition led by Captain Gaspar de Portolá . . . established presidios, or military forts, at the site of San Diego* (World Book Encyclopedia). **2.** a Spanish penal settlement in a colony or other Spanish possession. [American English < Spanish *presidio* < Latin *praesidium* presidium]

pre·sid·i·um (pri sid′ē əm), *n.* **1.** a governmental administrative committee in the Soviet Union. **2.** Also, **Presidium.** (from 1952-1966) the chief executive and policy-making body of the Communist Party of the Soviet Union, led by the premier or party secretary. It is now officially known as the Politburo. [< Latin *praesidium* a presiding over < *praesidēre* to preside]

pre·sig·ni·fy (prē sig′nə fī), *v.t.,* **-fied, -fy·ing.** to signify beforehand; foreshow. [< Latin *praesignificāre* < *prae-* before + *significāre* signify]

press[1] (pres), *v.t.* **1.** to use force or weight steadily against; push with steady force: *Press the button to ring the bell.* **2.** to squeeze; squeeze out: *to press apples for cider, to press cotton into bales.* **3.** to clasp; hug: *He pressed my hand in greeting.* **4.** to make smooth; flatten: *to press clothes with an iron; . . . real butterflies and vari-colored leaves, pressed between layers of vinyl plastic* (New Yorker). **5.** to move by pushing steadily (up, down, against, etc.). **6.** to shape by force, often over a form; stamp: *to press*

phonograph records, to press steel. **7.** to urge onward; cause to hurry. **8.** to urge (a person); keep asking; entreat: *Because it was so stormy, we pressed our guest to stay all night.* **9.** to lay stress upon; insist on: *We now agree on two of the three major principles for which we have pressed* (Wall Street Journal). **10.** to constrain; compel; force. **11.** to urge for acceptance: *to press the need for vigilance.* **12.** to weigh heavily upon (the mind, a person, etc.). **13.** (in weight lifting) to lift (a bar) in the press. **14.** *Archaic.* to crowd upon; throng.
—*v.i.* **1.** to use force steadily. **2.** to push forward; keep pushing: *The boy pressed on in spite of the wind.* **3.** to crowd; throng: *The crowd pressed about a famous actor. A great roar of a cheer went up from a crowd that was pressing all around* (Edmund Wilson). **4.** to iron clothes. **5.** to ask insistently; refer to something often and with emphasis: *Don't press for an answer yet.* **6.** to harass; oppress; trouble: *The reflection that he had wasted his time . . . pressed upon his mind* (Maria Edgeworth). **7.** to be urgent; demand prompt attention: *We must be up and away at once; the hour presses.*
—*n.* **1.** a pressing; pressure; push: *the press of ambition. The press of many duties keeps the President very busy.* **2.** a pressed condition: *These trousers will hold a press.* **3.** any of various instruments or machines for exerting pressure: *a tie press, a cider press, a steel press.* **4.** a machine for printing; printing press. **5.** an establishment for printing books, etc. **6.** the process or art of printing. **7.** newspapers and periodicals and those who write for them: *to release a story to the press, the freedom of the press.* **8.** notice given in newspapers or magazines: *The Senator's remarks got a good press.* **9.** a crowd; throng: *The little boy was lost in the press.* **10.** a pressing forward or together; crowding: *the press of memories into his mind.* **11.** urgency; hurry: *There is no press about answering my note.* **12.** a cupboard or closet for clothes, books, etc. **13.** (in weight lifting) the lifting of a bar off the floor to the chest, holding it there a few seconds, and then putting it up over the head.

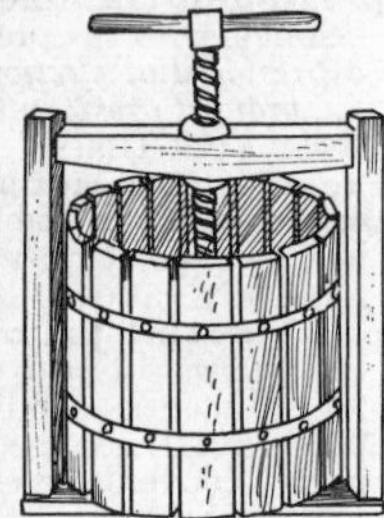
Cider Press[1] (def. 3)

Pilgrim Press[1] (def. 12)

go to press, to begin to be printed: *The newspaper goes to press at midnight.*
[< Old French *presser* < Latin *pressāre* (frequentative) < *premere* to press]

press² (pres), *v.t.* **1. a.** to force into service, often for which a person is not trained, or a thing is not designed: *Several mothers were pressed into service as kindergarten teachers.* **b.** to force into naval or military service. **2.** to seize and use, as land or a building.
—*n.* **1.** an impressment into service, usually naval or military. **2.** an order for such impressment.
[< obsolete *prest* to engage by loan, to pay in advance. Compare PREST¹.]

press., pressure.

press agent, an agent in charge of publicity for a person, organization, etc.: *There are no press agents any more. They are all public relations counselors* (New York Times).

press·a·gent (pres′ā′jənt), *v.t. Informal.* to give publicity to or advertise, as a press agent does, or through a press agent: *"Monty" has not press-agented himself as an expert on schooling* (Tuscaloosa News).

press·a·gen·try (pres′ā′jən trē), *n. Informal.* the profession or activities of a press agent: *Many companies also fail to realize the difference between press-agentry and public relations* (Time).

press association, an agency subscribed to by newspapers, that gathers and distributes news (other than local) to them.

press·board (pres′bôrd′, -bōrd′), *n.* a smooth pasteboard or heavy paper used in a press, as for finishing cloth.

press box, *U.S.* an enclosed space in a sports arena, usually high above the playing field, set aside for reporters: *Women are barred from the press box in all major-league baseball parks, and from many a football press box as well* (Newsweek).

press bureau, an office or department that does the work of a press agent.

press·but·ton (pres′but′ən), *n. Especially British.* push button: *The pressbutton marks a code on the underside of the tray* (New Scientist).

press·cake (pres′kāk′), *n.* a cake of compressed material: *Low cost protein foods have been developed from such indigenous resources as oilseed meals and presscakes* (Rose and Sherman).

press clipping, a piece, usually a paragraph, article, or notice, cut out from a newspaper: *A selection of press clippings . . . shows that 46 were hostile* (Harper's).

press conference, a news conference: *The President gave the press conference a strong speech in defense of the foreign aid in general* (Wall Street Journal).

press corps, a group of newsmen from various publications and news agencies who regularly report news from a particular place.

press correspondent, a newspaper correspondent.

press·er (pres′ər), *n.* a person or thing that presses: *Pressers iron the wrinkles out of the completed garments and press the inside edges of seams flat* (World Book Encyclopedia).

presser foot, the part of a sewing machine that holds the cloth firmly in position; foot.

press·forge (pres′fôrj′), *v.t.,* **-forged, -forging.** to forge by means of a forging press: *Automobile crankshafts could be press-forged at 150 per hour, compared with one-third that number for drop-forging* (Burnham Finney).

press gallery, a gallery for reporters: *I closely watched Senator Symington for years from the press gallery as a Senate correspondent* (Harper's).

press gang, a group of men formerly employed to impress other men for service, especially in the British navy or army in the 1700's: *A press gang, that was in need of men for a man-of-war, came aboard and pressed poor Charles* (John Galt).

press-gang (pres′gang′), *v.t. Especially British.* **1.** to force into naval or military service; press: *The greater the efforts to press-gang conscripts, the more recruits the Viet-cong get* (Manchester Guardian Weekly). **2.** to force, impress, or lure into any activity: *East Germans are press-ganged to the polls* (Manchester Guardian Weekly).

press·ing (pres′ing), *adj.* requiring immediate action or attention; urgent: *The danger now became too pressing to admit of longer delay* (James Fenimore Cooper).
—*n.* **1.** a phonograph record: *The stereo pressings have the prefix SXL* (London Times). **2.** all the phonograph records pressed at one time: . . . *RCA Victor recording of the Tchaikovsky concerts (first pressing: 150,000 copies)* (Time).
—**press′ing·ly,** *adv.* —**press′ing·ness,** *n.*

press·man (pres′mən), *n., pl.* **-men. 1.** a man who operates or has charge of a printing press. **2.** a reporter: *When I learned at the press conference that stories of this kind were on the censored list I at once revoked the order and told the pressmen to write as they pleased* . . . (Dwight D. Eisenhower).

press·mark (pres′märk′), *n.* a mark put on a book or other volume to indicate its location in a library.

press money, money paid to a soldier or sailor on enlistment.

press of sail or **canvas,** all the sail the wind allows: *The British fleet was just out of sight with the exception of one or two stragglers, under a press of canvas* (Joseph Conrad).

pres·sor (pres′ər), *adj. Physiology.* increasing pressure; stimulating: *A pressor nerve is one whose stimulation causes an increase of blood pressure.*

press release, a news story, item, or piece of publicity issued by or on behalf of the individual or group involved to a newspaper or newspapers for publication.

press·room (pres′rüm′, -rům′), *n.* a room containing printing presses.

press·run (pres′run′), *n.* **1.** the run of a printing press for a specific number of copies: *As TIME's pressrun begins in Chicago* . . . (Time). **2.** the number of copies run off: *El Diario . . . doubled its regular 75,000 copy pressrun* (Newsweek).

press secretary, a secretary who handles the public relations and arranges press conferences of a politician, etc.: *At 47, he is the most influential Presidential press secretary in U.S. history* (Newsweek).

pres·sur·al (presh′ər əl), *adj.* of the nature of mechanical pressure.

pres·sure (presh′ər), *n., v.,* **-sured, -sur·ing.**
—*n.* **1.** the continued action of a weight or force: *The pressure of the wind filled the sails of the boat.* **2.** the force per unit of area: *There is a pressure of 20 pounds to the square inch on this tire. At sea level, air exerts a pressure in all directions of about 14.7 pounds per square inch* (Thomas A. Blair). **3.** a state of trouble or strain: *the pressure of poverty, working under pressure.* **4.** a compelling force or influence: *He changed his mind under pressure from others. Society was constantly changing under the pressure of economic necessities* (Edmund Wilson). **5.** the need for prompt or decisive action; urgency: *the unceasing pressure of business affairs.* **6.** electromotive force. **7.** *Obsolete.* an impression; image; stamp.
—*v.t., v.i.* to force or urge by exerting pressure; press (for): *Legislators cannot be pressured into voting for something that is unconstitutional* (New York Times).
[< Old French *pressure,* learned borrowing from Latin *pressūra* < *premere* to press]

pressure cabin, an airplane cabin that can be pressurized.

pres·sure-cook (presh′ər kůk′), *v.t.* to cook in a pressure cooker: *These exotic ingredients were pressure-cooked on location* (Time).

pressure cooker, an airtight apparatus for cooking with steam under pressure.

pressure flaking, a flaking of flint tools by applying pressure with a hard point: *Finds of projectile points shaped by pressure flaking accompanied by a variety of skin-scraping tools* . . . (Science News Letter).

pressure gauge, 1. a device for measuring pressure, as an attachment for indicating the pressure of steam in a boiler: *Pressure gauges will tell what portions of the foundations bear the most weight* (Science News Letter). **2.** a device used in gunnery to measure the pressure in the bore or chamber of a gun when the charge explodes.

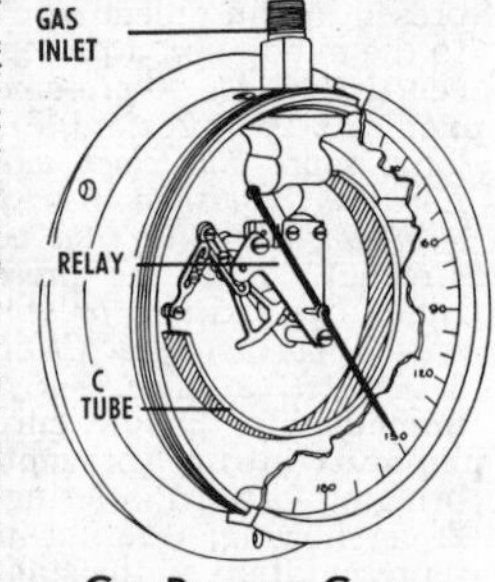

Gas Pressure Gauge (def. 1)
As pressure mounts, expanding gas forces the hollow, C-shaped tube to assume a progressively greater radius. Motion of tube is relayed to indicator needle.

pressure gradient, the rate at which atmospheric pressure decreases by units of horizontal distance along the line in which the pressure decreases most rapidly.

pressure group, any business, professional, or labor group, etc., which attempts to further its own interests by exerting pressure on legislative bodies or administrative departments or agencies: *The guild helps its members in many other ways, by bargaining energetically with local councils and by forming a pressure group for showmen's interests in Parliament* (Economist).

pressure head, *Physics.* the pressure of a liquid, as at a given point in a pipe, expressed in terms of the height of a column of the liquid that would exert an equivalent pressure.

pressure hull, the hull, or part of the hull, of a submarine designed to withstand the pressure of the sea when submerged: . . . *ricocheting at wild angles off the pressure hull of U-94* (Maclean's).

pressure ice, ice forced together by tides of arctic waters, forming a kind of ridge: *The pregnant female bear . . . builds her den in snow, drifted deep around pressure ice* (Harper's).

pressure jump, a sudden, slight increase in barometric pressure, occurring along an atmospheric front and preceding a tornado or other storm.

pressure ridge, a ridge of ice in arctic waters caused by lateral pressure.

pres·sure-sen·si·tive (presh′ər sen′sə tiv), *adj.* (of tapes, cements, etc.) sealing when pressure is applied: *Pressure-sensitive adhesive tape used to cover underground pipelines* (Wall Street Journal).

pressure suit, a garment that provides pressure upon the body so that respiration and circulation can continue normally, or nearly so, under low-pressure conditions, such as occur at high altitudes: . . . *struggled into a silver-tinted pressure suit that had been tailored to a skintight fit* (Time). See picture under **space suit.**

pressure tank, a tank which holds air, fuel, etc., under greater pressure than is normal in open atmospheric conditions: *Present launching sites of liquid-propelled missiles require . . . heavily shielded bunkers of caves, containing corrosion-resistant pressure tanks for the dangerous liquids* (Scientific American).

pres·sur·i·za·tion (presh′ər ə zā′shən), *n.* the act or process of pressurizing: *Pressurization in the cockpit can be lost as a result of a break in the canopy or otherwise* (Atlantic).

pres·sur·ize (presh′ə rīz), *v.t.,* **-ized, -iz·ing. 1.** to keep the atmospheric pressure inside of (the cabin of an airplane) at a normal level in spite of the altitude: *The pilot will have to be provided with air, presumably by pressurizing his cabin* (Time). **2.** to place under high pressure: *If in some way hydrogen can be heated and pressurized, and it alone be the rocket propellant, we would realize a large gain in the velocity of the propellant* (Scientific American). *The reactor coolant system does not have to be pressurized* (New York Times).

pres·sur·ized water reactor (presh′ə-rīzd), an atomic reactor using a slightly enriched natural uranium as fuel, in which water under high pressure carries the heat from the reactor to make steam for turbines that produce electric power: . . . *pressurized water reactors, the most advanced of several potential nuclear power reactors* (Wall Street Journal).

pres·sur·iz·er (presh′ə rī′zər), *n.* a device that regulates air pressure in an enclosure: *The cab includes features such as a . . . pressurizer that keeps the cab free of dust, dirt, and pollen* (London Times).

press·work (pres′wėrk′), *n.* **1.** the working or management of a printing press. **2.** the work done by a printing press.

prest[1] (prest), *Obsolete.* —*n.* **1.** a loan. **2.** advance payment to a soldier or sailor at enlistment. —*v.t.* to enlist. [< Old French *prest* a loan, advance pay; (literally) action of preparing < *prester* furnish, lend < Late Latin *praestāre* lend < Latin, to furnish, offer, vouch for]

prest[2] (prest), *adj. Obsolete.* ready. [< Old French *prest* < Late Latin *praestus* < Latin *praestō (esse)* (to be) at hand]

pres·ta·tion (pres tā′shən), *n.* a payment, as of money or service, made or exacted as a feudal or customary duty.

pres·ter (pres′tər), *n. Obsolete.* a priest. [< Old French *prestre* priest; see PRIEST]

Prester John, a legendary Christian priest and king of the Middle Ages, said to have ruled a kingdom somewhere in Asia or Africa.

pres·ti·dig·i·ta·tion (pres′tə dij′ə tā′-shən), *n.* sleight of hand; legerdemain. [< French *prestidigitation* < *prestidigitateur* prestidigitator]

pres·ti·dig·i·ta·tor (pres′tə dij′ə tā′tər), *n.* a person skilled in sleight of hand; conjurer: [*They are*] *watching a prestidigitator, and waiting to see what cute little animal will pop out of his hat next* (Howard Taubman). [< French *prestidigitateur,* apparently coined < *preste* nimble (< Italian *presto* presto) + Latin *digitus* finger + French *-ateur,* an agent suffix < Latin *-ator*]

pres·tige (pres tēzh′, pres′tij), *n.* reputation, influence, or distinction based on what is known of one's abilities, achievements, opportunities, associations, etc.: *After Napoleon's first battles, prestige did half his work for him* (George Meredith). *Thus it happened that while by the end of the reign the power of the sovereign had appreciably diminished, the prestige of the sovereign had enormously grown* (Lytton Strachey). —*adj.* prestigious: *Founding a prestige college is almost like trying for artificially aged wine* (New York Times). [< Middle French *prestige* illusion, magic spell, (in plural) juggler's tricks, learned borrowing from Latin *praestīgiae,* plural]

pres·tig·i·a·tion (pres tij′ē ā′shən), *n.* prestidigitation. [< Latin *praestigiāre* to deceive with juggling tricks]

pres·tig·i·a·tor (pres tij′ē ā′tər), *n.* prestidigitator.

pres·ti·gious (pres tij′əs), *adj.* **1.** having prestige: *The holder of the most prestigious job in journalism today is . . . the TV critic* (Newsweek). **2.** *Obsolete.* practicing or involving magic or jugglery; deceptive.

pres·tis·si·mo (pres tis′ə mō), *adv., adj., n., pl.* **-mos.** *Music.* —*adv., adj.* very quick (used as a direction). —*n.* a very quick part. [< Italian *prestissimo,* superlative of *presto* presto]

pres·to (pres′tō), *adv., adj., n., pl.* **-tos,** *interj.* —*adv.* quickly (used especially as a musical direction).
—*adj.* quick.
—*n.* a quick part in a piece of music.
—*interj.* right away; at once: *Drive several miles down the turnpike, around a cloverleaf, under an overpass, over an underpass, across a throughway, through a crossway, and presto! there we are* (Atlantic).
[< Italian *presto* < Latin *praestus* ready < Latin *praestō,* adverb, ready]

presto chan·go (chān′jō), *Slang.* change immediately or suddenly, as if by magic (used as an interjection): *Presto chango, it is now a low table* (New York Times).

pre·stress (prē stres′), *v.t.* to subject (a material) to heavy internal stress in making or casting to help withstand subsequent external loads or stresses. Bricks, concrete, and structural steel are prestressed by embedding steel wires or rods that are under tension: *It was found that prestressing doubled the ability of one aluminum alloy, used in the aircraft industry, to carry an external load* (Science News Letter). *Consulting engineers said that prestressed concrete might lead to the solution of these pavement problems* (New York Times).

pre·sum·a·ble (pri zü′mə bəl), *adj.* that can be presumed or taken for granted; probable; likely: *the presumable time of their arrival.*

pre·sum·a·bly (pri zü′mə blē), *adv.* as may be reasonably supposed; probably.

pre·sume (pri züm′), *v.,* **-sumed, -sum·ing.** —*v.t.* **1.** to take for granted without proving; suppose: *The law presumes innocence until guilt is proved.* **2.** to take upon oneself; venture; dare: *May I presume to tell you you are wrong? The plan which I shall presume to suggest* (Edmund Burke). —*v.i.* **1.** to take something for granted; assume. **2.** to take an unfair advantage (on, upon): *Don't presume on a person's good nature by borrowing from him every week.* **3.** to act with improper boldness; take liberties. [< Latin *praesūmere* anticipate, be arrogant (in Late Latin, take for granted) < *prae-* before + *sūmere* take] —**pre·sum′er,** *n.* —**pre·sum′-ing·ly,** *adv.*

pre·sum·ed·ly (pri zü′mid lē), *adv.* as is or may be supposed.

pre·sump·tion (pri zump′shən), *n.* **1.** the act of presuming: *This is a matter that concerns myself only, and it is presumption on his part to interfere in it* (W. H. Hudson). **2. a.** a thing taken for granted; assumption: supposition: *The innocence of the accused is a necessary presumption under American law.* **b.** *Law.* an inference that something not known to be true is a fact, based on the proved existence of some other fact. **3.** a cause or reason for presuming; probability: *The more he disliked a thing the greater the presumption that it was right* (Samuel Butler). **4.** unpleasant boldness: *It is presumption to go to a party when one has not been invited.* [< Latin *praesumptiō, -ōnis* < *praesūmere* presume] —**Syn. 4.** forwardness, effrontery.

pre·sump·tive (pri zump′tiv), *adj.* **1.** based on likelihood; presumed: *a presumptive title to an estate.* **2.** giving ground for presumption or belief: *The man's running away was regarded as presumptive evidence of his guilt.*

presumptive heir, heir presumptive.

pre·sump·tive·ly (pri zump′tiv lē), *adv.* by presumption; presumably: *The most disparate social personalities combined* [*here*] *without explosion. The reason was, presumptively, that . . . the guests . . . had the tradition of good breeding* (Samuel H. Adams).

pre·sump·tu·ous (pri zump′chü əs), *adj.* **1.** acting without permission or right; too bold; forward: *But it is presumptuous and untrue to insist that God must back us up whatever we do* (Atlantic). **2.** *Obsolete.* presumptive. [< Late Latin *praesumptuōsus* < Latin *praesumptiō, -ōnis* audacity, presumption; patterned on *sumptuōsus* expensive < *sumptus, -ūs* expense] —**pre·sump′tu·ous·ly,** *adv.* —**pre·sump′tu·ous·ness,** *n.* —**Syn. 1.** overbold, impudent, arrogant, presuming, impertinent.

pre·sup·pose (prē′sə pōz′), *v.t.,* **-posed, -pos·ing. 1.** to take for granted in advance; assume beforehand: *Let us presuppose that he wants more money.* **2.** to require as a necessary condition; imply: *A fight presupposes fighters.*

pre·sup·po·si·tion (prē′sup ə zish′ən), *n.* **1.** a presupposing: *Acting on the presupposition that a flu epidemic will break out this winter, the Department of Health is issuing a vaccine.* **2.** the thing presupposed: *Professor Sidarov outlined the fundamental presupposition of all Soviet historical works* (London Times).

pre·sur·mise (prē′sėr mīz′), *v.,* **-mised, -mis·ing,** *n.* —*v.t.* to surmise beforehand. —*n.* a surmise previously formed.

pret., preterit.

pre·tence (pri tens′, prē′tens), *n. Especially British.* pretense.

pre·tend (pri tend′), *v.t.* **1.** to claim falsely: *She pretends to like you, but talks about you behind your back.* **2.** to claim falsely to have: *to pretend illness.* **3.** to claim: *I don't pretend to be a musician. Speak in honest language and say the minority will be in danger from the majority. And is there an assembly on earth where this danger may not be equally pretended?* (Thomas Jefferson). **4.** to venture; attempt; presume: *I cannot pretend to judge between them.* **5.** *Obsolete.* to extend or hold (something) in front of or over, as a concealment, defense, etc. —*v.i.* **1.** to make believe: *Let's pretend that we are soldiers. Some of their lives are not so saintly as they pretend* (Francis A. Gasquet). **2.** to lay claim: *James Stuart pretended to the English throne.* **3.** to make pretensions (to): *a square white house pretending neither to beauty nor state* (Mrs. Humphry Ward). **4.** to aspire (to), as a candidate or suitor: *A . . . fellow . . . might pretend surely to his kinswoman's hand* (Thackeray).
—*adj.* pretended; feigned: *It is a pretend meal this evening, with nothing whatever on the table* (James M. Barrie).
[< Latin *praetendere* < *prae-* before + *tendere* to stretch]
—**Syn.** *v.t.* **1,2. Pretend, affect, assume** mean to give a false impression by word, manner, or deed. **Pretend** implies a conscious intent to deceive: *She pretends ignorance of the whole affair.* **Affect** suggests using a false manner, more for effect than to deceive: *When she applied for a job, she affected simplicity.* **Assume** suggests putting on an appearance which, though not really genuine, is not wholly false: *She assumed a look of sorrow.*

pre·tend·ed (pri ten′did), *adj.* **1.** claimed falsely; asserted falsely. **2.** fictitious; counterfeit; feigned. —**pre·tend′ed·ly,** *adv.*

pre·tend·er (pri ten′dər), *n.* **1.** a person who pretends. **2.** a person who makes claims to a throne, often without just right.

pre·tense (pri tens′, prē′tens), *n.* **1.** a pretending; make-believe: *My anger was all pretense.* **2.** a false appearance: *Under pretense of picking up the handkerchief, she took the money. In this great barrage against the pretensions and pretenses of his contemporaries, Lewis . . . by no means exhausted his creative energies* (New Yorker). **3.** a false claim: *The girls made a pretense of knowing the boys' secret.* **4.** a claim: *He makes no pretense to special knowledge.* **5.** a showing off; display: *Her manner is free from pretense.* **6.** anything done to show off. **7.** *Obsolete.* an expressed aim, intention, etc. Also, *especially British,* **pretence.** [< Anglo-French *pretensse,* ultimately < Latin *praetendere* pretend] —**Syn. 5.** ostentation.

pre·ten·sion (pri ten′shən), *n.* **1.** a claim: *The young prince has pretensions to the throne.*

He makes no pretensions to special wisdom. **2.** a putting forward of a claim; demand. **3.** a pretentious display. **4.** an intention; design; aim.

pre·ten·tious (pri ten′shəs), *adj.* **1.** making claims to excellence or importance: *a pretentious person, book, or speech.* **2.** doing things for show or to make a fine appearance: *a pretentious style of entertaining guests.* [< French *prétentieux* (with English *-ous*), ultimately < Latin *praetendere* pretend] —**pre·ten′tious·ly,** *adv.* —**pre·ten′tious·ness,** *n.*

pre·ter·hu·man (prē′tər hyü′mən), *adj.* beyond what is human. [< Latin *praeter* beyond + English *human*]

pret·er·it or **pret·er·ite** (pret′ər it), *n.* *Grammar.* a tense (preterit tense) or verb form used when referring to past time. *Examples: Obeyed* is the preterit of *obey; spoke,* of *speak;* and *saw,* of *see.* See also **past tense.** —*adj.* **1.** *Grammar.* expressing past time. **2.** *Obsolete.* bygone; past. [< Latin *praeteritus* < *praeter-* beyond + *īre* go]

preterit or **preterite present,** *Grammar.* **1.** preterit form with present meaning (applied specifically to certain Germanic or Old English verbs). **2.** a preterit present verb or verb form.

pre·ter·i·tion (pret′ə rish′ən), *n.* **1. a.** omission; neglect. **b.** an instance of this. **2.** the passing over by a testator of someone who would normally be an heir, as a son. **3.** the passing over by God of those not elected to salvation. [< Late Latin *praeteritiō, -ōnis* < Latin *praeteritus;* see PRETERIT]

pre·ter·i·tive (pri ter′ə tiv), *adj. Grammar.* **1.** expressing past time. **2.** (of certain verbs) limited to past tenses.

pre·ter·le·gal (prē′tər lē′gəl), *adj.* beyond what is legal; not according to law. [< Latin *praeter* beyond + English *legal*]

pre·ter·mis·sion (prē′tər mish′ən), *n.* an omission; neglect.

pre·ter·mit (prē′tər mit′), *v.t.,* **-mit·ted, -mit·ting. 1.** to leave out; omit. **2.** to let pass without notice; overlook intentionally. [< Latin *praetermittere* < *praeter-* past, beyond + *mittere* let go, send]

pre·ter·nat·u·ral (prē′tər nach′ər əl, -nach′rəl), *adj.* **1.** out of the ordinary course of nature; abnormal; exceptional; unusual: *preternatural keenness of sight* (W. H. Hudson). **2.** due to something above or beyond nature; supernatural: *Eglinton Wood—a place well noted from ancient times for preternatural appearances* (John Galt). [< Medieval Latin *praeternaturalis* < Latin *praeter nātūram* (*praeterque fātum*) beyond nature (and beyond fate) < *praeter-* beyond + *nātūra* nature] —**pre′ter·nat′u·ral·ly,** *adv.* —**pre′ter·nat′u·ral·ness,** *n.*

pre·ter·nat·u·ral·ism (prē′tər nach′ər ə-liz′əm, -nach′rə liz-), *n.* **1.** preternatural character or condition. **2.** the recognition of the preternatural.

pre·ter·nor·mal (prē′tər nôr′məl), *adj.* beyond what is normal. [< Latin *praeter* beyond + English *normal*]

pre·test (*v.* prē test′; *n.* prē′test′), *v.t.* **1.** to test (a product, method, object, etc.) in advance of regular use or application: *Aircraft builders and designers . . . pretest structural parts and whole aircraft in simulated flights* (J.J. Jaklitsch). **2.** to subject (students) to a preliminary test. —*n.* a pretesting; preliminary test.

pre·text (prē′tekst), *n.* a false reason concealing the real reason; pretense; excuse: *He used his sore finger as a pretext for not going to school.* [< Latin *praetextus* < *praetexere* to disguise, cover < *prae-* in front + *texere* to weave]

pre·ti·um la·bo·rum non vi·le (prē′shē-əm lə bôr′əm non vī′lē, -bōr′-), *Latin.* no mean reward for labor (the motto of the Order of the Golden Fleece).

pre·tor (prē′tər), *n.* praetor.

pre·to·ri·al (prē tôr′ē əl, -tōr′-), *adj.* praetorial.

pre·to·ri·an (prē tôr′ē ən, -tōr′-), *adj., n.* praetorian.

pre·to·ri·um (prē tôr′ē əm, -tōr′-), *n., pl.* **-to·ri·a** (-tôr′ē ə, -tōr′-). praetorium.

pre·tor·ship (prē′tər ship), *n.* praetorship.

pre·treat (prē trēt′), *v.t.* to treat beforehand: *. . . techniques for pretreating sewage and industrial waste so that it need not pollute the nation's waters* (Time).

pre·treat·ment (prē trēt′mənt), *n.* a treatment beforehand: *Phosphate fertilizers could be produced by pretreatment of seawater with phosphoric acid* (Atlantic).

pre·tri·al (prē′trī′əl), *n.* a meeting held by a judge or other arbitrator before a trial to clarify the issues so as to save time and costs at the trial: *There is nothing wrong with pressure to settle the case at pretrial rather than years later* (New York Times). —*adj.* **1.** having to do with such a meeting. **2.** occurring or existing before a trial: *Pretrial publicity had prejudiced the jury.*

pret·ti·fi·ca·tion (prit′ə fə kā′shən), *n.* the fact or process of prettifying: *Fortunately, for all their painstaking prettification of their product, English apple-growers have not prettified the taste out of the fruit* (Sylvia Haymon).

pret·ti·fi·er (prit′ə fī′ər), *n.* a person or thing that prettifies: *. . . the work of the spoiler and prettifier in Cornwall* (W.T. Oliver).

pret·ti·fy (prit′ə fī), *v.t.,* **-fied, -fy·ing.** to make artificially pretty: *Until the last few decades, "restorers" hid more pictures, under new and falsely prettifying layers of paint and varnish, than they cleaned* (Time).

pret·ti·ly (prit′ə lē), *adv.* in a pretty manner; pleasingly; gracefully; nicely.

pret·ti·ness (prit′ē nis), *n.* **1.** the state or quality of being pretty: *Prettiness may be considered a superficial or surface quality* (Matthew Luckiesh). **2.** a pretty thing or person, generally suggesting triteness: *Surburban villas, Belgrave terraces, and other such prettinesses* (Hawthorne).

pret·ty (prit′ē), *adj.,* **-ti·er, -ti·est,** *n., pl.* **-ties,** *adv., v.,* **-tied, -ty·ing.** —*adj.* **1.** pleasing (used to describe people and things that are good-looking in a feminine or childish way, dainty, sweet, charming, etc., but not stately, grand, elegant, or very important): *a very pretty girl, a pretty piece of verse, a pretty tune, pretty manners.* **2.** not at all pleasing: *This is a pretty mess, indeed.* **3.** too dainty or delicate; foppish: *He talks well, but can the pretty little man fight?* **4.** *Archaic.* brave; bold; fine: *Robin Hood was a pretty fellow.* **5.** *Informal.* considerable in amount or extent: *He paid a pretty sum.*

sitting pretty, *Slang.* well off: *His uncle died and left him enough to be sitting pretty.*

—*n.* **1.** a pretty person or thing. **2.** *Archaic.* a brave, bold man or boy: *Back to back, my pretties* (Oliver Goldsmith).

—*adv.* fairly; rather; quite: *It is pretty late. It is pretty difficult to legislate against frenzy or against fools* (Time).

—*v.t.* to make pretty: *. . . prettied by formal bouquets of red and white carnations* (Maclean's).

pretty up, to prettify: *The administrative budget pretties up the picture of Government cost and power* (Wall Street Journal).

[Old English *prættig* cunning, skillful, artful < *prætt* trick, wile, craft]

pret·ty·ish (prit′ē ish), *adj. Informal.* rather pretty.

pretty penny, *Informal.* a large sum of money: *Highways, already costing states a pretty penny, are going to eat into state treasuries at a faster pace* (Wall Street Journal).

pret·ty-pret·ty (prit′ē prit′ē), *adj., n., pl.* **-ties.** —*adj.* pretty in an overdone or mawkish way: *pretty-pretty pictures or verse. [The] make-up was softly feminine without being pretty-pretty* (London Times). —*n.* knickknack.

pretty-pretties, pretty things; ornaments: *This room contains a small fortune in pretty-pretties* (Bow Bells Weekly).

pre·typ·i·fy (prē tip′ə fī), *v.t.,* **-fied, -fy·ing.** to typify beforehand; prefigure; foreshadow.

pret·zel (pret′səl), *n.* a hard biscuit, usually in the form of a knot, salted on the outside: *The order of the evening is beer, pretzels, and pristine jazz* (New Yorker). [American English < German *Brezel, Bretzel* < Old High German *brezitella* < a diminutive form of unrecorded Medieval Latin *brachitum* a kind of biscuit baked in the shape of folded arms < Latin *brachium* arm < Greek *brachīōn* upper arm]

pre·vail (pri vāl′), *v.i.* **1.** to exist in many places; be in general use: *The custom still prevails of hanging up stockings the night before Christmas.* **2.** to be the most usual or strongest: *Sadness prevailed in our minds.* **3.** to be the stronger; win the victory; succeed: *I decline to accept the end of man . . . I believe that man will not merely endure: he will prevail* (William Faulkner). **4.** to be effective: *But why Prevail'd not thy pure prayers?* (Tennyson).

prevail on, upon, or **with,** to persuade: *Can't I prevail upon you to stay for dinner? The governor prevailed with me to take charge of our Northwestern frontier* (Benjamin Franklin).

[< Latin *praevalēre* < *prae-* before + *valēre* have power]

pre·vail·ing (pri vā′ling), *adj.* **1.** that prevails; having superior force or influence; victorious: *Yellow is the prevailing color in her room.* **2.** in general use; common: *a prevailing style. The prevailing summer winds here are from the west.* —**pre·vail′ing·ly,** *adv.* —**pre·vail′ing·ness,** *n.* —**Syn. 2.** See **current.**

prevailing westerlies, the usual westerly winds that blow between 30 degrees and 60 degrees latitude, both north and south of the equator.

prev·a·lence (prev′ə ləns), *n.* widespread occurrence; general use: *the prevalence of complaints about the weather.*

prev·a·lent (prev′ə lent), *adj.* **1.** widespread; in general use; common: *Colds are prevalent in the winter.* **2.** predominant; victorious. [< Latin *praevalēns, -entis,* present participle of *prevalēre* prevail] —**prev′a·lent·ly,** *adv.* —**Syn. 1.** usual, ordinary, prevailing.

pre·var·i·cate (prē var′ə kāt), *v.i.,* **-cat·ed, -cat·ing. 1.** to turn aside from the truth in speech or act; lie. **2.** to speak evasively; equivocate. [< Latin *praevāricārī* make a sham accusation, deviate; (literally) walk crookedly < *prae-* before + *vāricāre* to straddle < *vāricus* straddling < *vārus* knockkneed, crooked]

pre·var·i·ca·tion (prē var′ə kā′shən), *n.* a prevaricating; departure from the truth.

pre·var·i·ca·tor (prē var′ə kā′tər), *n.* a person who prevaricates.

pre·ve·nance (prē′və nəns), *n.* anticipation, especially of the wants of others. [< French *prévenance*]

pre·ven·ience (prē vēn′yəns), *n.* **1.** antecedence. **2.** anticipation.

pre·ven·ient (prē vēn′yənt), *adj.* **1.** coming before. **2.** anticipatory. **3.** tending to prevent. [< Latin *praeveniēns, -entis,* present participle of *praevenīre* to anticipate, come before; see PREVENT] —**pre·ve′nient·ly,** *adv.*

prevenient grace, *Theology.* divine grace turning the heart toward God.

pre·vent (pri vent′), *v.t.* **1.** to stop or keep (from): *Illness prevented him from doing his work.* **2.** to keep from happening: *Rain prevented the game.* **3.** *Archaic.* to come before; go before; do before. —*v.i.* to hinder: *I will meet you at six if nothing prevents.* [< Latin *praeventus,* past participle of *praevenīre* < *prae-* before + *venīre* to come] —**pre·vent′er,** *n.*

—**Syn.** *v.t.* 1,2, *v.i.* **Prevent, hinder, impede** mean to get in the way of action or progress. **Prevent** means to keep a person or thing from doing something or making progress, acting or setting up an obstacle to stop him or it: *Business prevented his going.* **Hinder** means to hold back, so that making, starting, going ahead, or finishing is late, difficult, or impossible: *The wrong food hinders growth.* **Impede** means to slow up movement and progress by putting something binding, fouling, etc., on or in the way: *Mud impedes the advance of troops.*

pre·vent·a·ble (pri ven′tə bəl), *adj.* that can be prevented: *In those regions of the world where work for the blind is in its infancy, . . . 50% to 60% of the cases of blindness result from preventable infectious diseases* (F.E. Davis).

pre·vent·a·tive (pri ven′tə tiv), *adj., n.* preventive.

pre·vent·i·ble (pri ven′tə bəl), *adj.* preventable.

pre·ven·tion (pri ven′shən), *n.* **1.** a preventing: *the prevention of fire.* **2.** something that prevents.

pre·ven·tive (pri ven′tiv), *adj.* that prevents: *preventive measures against disease.* —*n.* something that prevents: *Vaccination is a preventive against smallpox.* —**pre·ven′tive·ly,** *adv.* —**pre·ven′tive·ness,** *n.*

preventive detention, *British Law.* the imprisonment of persistent offenders, usually for a period of from 5 to 10 years, to prevent them from committing more offenses.

preventive medicine, the branch of medicine concerned with the prevention of disease.

preventive war, an aggressive war waged against another nation, supposedly started in anticipation of attack by that nation: *The Turks have no nervous apprehension of an attack from Syria which might provoke them into a preventive war* (Wall Street Journal).

pre·ven·to·ri·um (prē′ven tôr′ē əm, -tōr′-), *n., pl.* **-to·ri·ums, -to·ri·a** (-tôr′ē ə, -tōr′-). an institution for preventing the spread of a disease, especially tuberculosis, as by the treatment of persons in an incipient stage of the disease or in danger of the disease: *"Preventoria" flourished [as] summer camps where youngsters exposed to TB were fed milk, eggs, and other nourishing foods and given plenty of fresh air and sunlight* (Jonathan Spivak). [< *prevent* + *-orium* as in *sanatorium*]

pre·view (prē′vyü′), *n.* **1.** a previous view, inspection, survey, etc.: *a preview of things to come.* **2.** an advance showing of a motion picture or scenes from a motion picture, or television program, or a display of a new product: *The previews . . . turned out to be, for the most part, regular concerts with explanatory remarks by Mr. Bernstein* (Francis D. Perkins). —*v.t.* to view beforehand.

pre·vi·ous (prē′vē əs), *adj.* **1.** coming or going before; that came before; earlier. **2.** *Informal.* quick; hasty; premature. *Don't be too previous about refusing.*

previous to, before; preceding: *Previous to her departure she gave a party.*

[< Latin *praevius* (with English *-ous*) leading the way < *prae-* before + *via* road] —**pre′vi·ous·ness,** *n.*

—**Syn. 1. Previous, preceding, prior** mean coming before something. **Previous** means earlier: *I cannot go, for I have a previous engagement* (one made before). **Preceding** means coming immediately before: *Check the preceding statement.* **Prior** adds to *previous* the idea of coming first in order of importance: *I have a prior engagement* (one that has first call).

Previous Examination, *British.* the first examination for the degree of B.A. at Cambridge University.

pre·vi·ous·ly (prē′vē əs lē), *adv.* at a previous time.

previous question, the question whether a vote shall be taken on the main question without further debate. *Abbr.:* p.q.

pre·vise (pri vīz′), *v.t.,* **-vised, -vis·ing. 1.** to foresee; forecast. **2.** to forewarn. [< Latin *praevīsus,* past participle of *praevidēre* < *prae-* before + *vidēre* to see]

pre·vi·sion (pri vizh′ən), *n.* **1.** foresight; foreknowledge: *She knew by prevision what most women learn only by experience* (Thomas Hardy). **2.** a prophetic vision or perception: *Some prevision warned the explorer of trouble.* [< *pre-* + *vision*]

pre·vi·sion·al (pri vizh′ə nəl), *adj.* of or having to do with prevision; foreseeing; forecasting. —**pre·vi′sion·al·ly,** *adv.*

pre·vo·cal·ic (prē′vō kal′ik), *adj.* immediately preceding a vowel.

pre·vo·ca·tion·al (prē′vō kā′shə nəl), *adj.* designating, having to do with, or consisting of training taken before entering a vocational school.

pre·voy·ance (pri voi′əns), *n.* foresight; forethought. [< French *prévoyance* < *prévoir* < Latin *praevidēre* to foresee; see PREVISE]

pre·vue (prē′vyü′), *n. U.S.* preview.

pre·war (prē′wôr′), *adj.* before the war: *. . . so security-conscious a regime as the one that ruled prewar and wartime Japan* (New Yorker).

prex (preks), *n. U.S. Slang.* prexy.

prex·y (prek′sē), *n., pl.* **prex·ies.** *U.S. Slang.* a president, as of a college: *The gentleman . . . is still prexy of one of the land's snootiest colleges* (Saturday Review).

prey (prā), *n.* **1.** any animal hunted or seized for food, especially by another animal: *Mice and birds are the prey of cats. The relative number of predatory fish . . . increased significantly compared with their prey* (F.S. Bodenheimer). **2.** the habit of hunting and killing other animals for food: *Hawks are birds of prey.* **3.** a person or thing injured; victim: *to be a prey to fear or disease. Meanwhile, Victoria, in growing agitation, was a prey to temper and to nerves* (Lytton Strachey). **4.** *Archaic.* booty; spoil; plunder.

—*v.i.* **prey on** or **upon, a.** to hunt or kill for food: *Cats prey upon mice.* **b.** to be a strain upon; injure; irritate: *Worry preys on her mind.* **c.** to rob; plunder: *A succession of ferocious invaders descended through the western passes, to prey on the defenceless wealth of Hindostan* (Macaulay).

[< Old French *preie* < Vulgar Latin *prēda,* for Latin *praeda*] —**prey′er,** *n.*

P.R.I. or **PRI** (no periods), Party of Revolutionary Institutions, a major political party of Mexico.

pri·a·can·thid (prī′ə kan′thid), *n.* any of various small, carnivorous, acanthopterygian fish of tropical seas, occasionally found off the coast of the United States. —*adj.* belonging or having to do with these fish. [< New Latin *Priacanthidae* the family name < Greek *príōn* saw, tool + *ákantha* thorn]

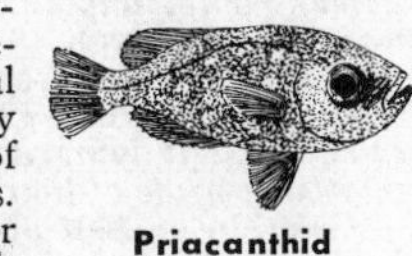

Priacanthid
(14 in. long)

Pri·am (prī′əm), *n. Greek Legend.* the king of Troy at the time of the Trojan War. He was the father of Hector, Paris, and Cassandra.

Pri·a·pe·an (prī′ə pē′ən), *adj.* Priapic.

Pri·ap·ic or **pri·ap·ic** (prī ap′ik, -ā′pik), *adj.* **1.** of or having to do with Priapus and his worship. **2.** phallic. —**Pri·ap′i·cal·ly, pri·ap′i·cal·ly,** *adv.*

pri·a·pism (prī′ə piz əm), *n.* licentiousness; intentional indecency.

Pri·a·pus (prī ā′pəs), *n. Greek and Roman Mythology.* the Greek and Roman god of procreation. He protected gardens, vineyards, flocks, etc.

pri·a·pus (prī ā′pəs), *n.* a phallus.

price (prīs), *n., v.,* **priced, pric·ing.** —*n.* **1.** the amount for which a thing is sold or can be bought; cost to the buyer: *That car has a price of nearly $4,000.* **2.** a reward offered for the capture of a person alive or dead: *Every member of the gang has a price on his head.* **3.** what must be given, done, undergone, etc., to obtain a thing: *to secure wealth at the price of health. We paid a heavy price for the victory, for we lost ten thousand soldiers.* **4.** value; worth: *a diamond of great price.*

at any price, at any cost, no matter how great: *to buy victory at any price.*

beyond or **without price,** so valuable that it cannot be bought: *A robe of samite without price . . . clung about her lissome limbs* (Tennyson).

—*v.t.* **1.** to put a price on; set the price of: *The hat was priced at $5.00.* **2.** *Informal.* to ask the price of; find out the price of: *to price a rug.*

[Middle English *pris* (originally) honor, praise, reward < Old French < Latin *pretium.* Compare PRIZE[1], PRAISE.] —**pric′er,** *n.*

—**Syn.** *n.* **1. Price, charge, cost** mean the amount asked or paid for something. **Price** is used mainly of goods, and applies especially to what the seller asks for them: *The price of meat is high now.* **Charge** is used mainly of services rather than goods: *There is no charge for delivery.* **Cost** is used of either goods or services, and applies to whatever is spent, whether money, effort, etc.: *The cost of the house was high.*

price control, the fixing of prices, usually by a government agency, especially by establishing maximum or minimum prices for commodities and rents: *Rationing and price controls locked up the excess purchasing power in savings and staved off the worst of the inflation until the end of the war* (Bulletin of Atomic Scientists).

price cutting, a sharp lowering of prices, especially because of competitive pressure: *As to stabilizing the industry, minimum prices did tend to diminish price cutting, to bolster profits and labor standards and to reduce labor disturbances* (New York Times). —**price′-cut′ting,** *adj.*

price-earn·ings ratio (prīs′ėr′ningz), the ratio between the market price of a stock and its dollar earnings per share. A price of $64 with earnings of $8 per share has a ratio of 8 to 1. *The price-earnings ratios of many blue-chip stocks, which had swollen far out of proportion, were settling back* (Newsweek).

price fixing, 1. the practice of setting and maintaining a retail price for one's products. **2.** the practice of agreeing among several manufacturers to set a noncompetitive price on a product which they all make: *It was the first large-scale criminal price fixing case against the industry in more than 20 years* (Time). **3.** the control of prices by a governmental agency.

price index, consumer price index: *The price index is designed to show the month-to-month change in prices of goods and services bought by urban wage earners and clerical worker families* (Wall Street Journal).

price·less (prīs′lis), *adj.* **1.** beyond price; extremely valuable. **2.** *Informal.* very amusing, absurd, etc.; delightful: *Send me some of your priceless little sketches for my rummage sale on the 26th* (Punch). —**price′less·ness,** *n.*

price level, 1. the general level of prices, as may be shown by a price index: *But until the public shows strong and definite hostility toward inflationary wage settlements, we must expect rising labor costs to push the price level slowly upward* (Sumner H. Slichter). **2.** the average price of any product during a certain period: *The whole TV price level slid downhill with General Electric's introduction of portable sets priced substantially below table or console models* (Time).

price packing, the practice on the part of certain dealers, as some sellers of automobiles, of raising unpublicized retail prices so as to appear to offer attractive discounts or allowances without reducing their margin of profit: *Finally, there is so much razzle-dazzle and price packing in the auto salesman's spiel that list price is a joke* (Time).

price prop, price support.

price ring, *Especially British.* a number of manufacturers who act together to set a noncompetitive price on a product which they all make: *If necessary the maintenance of price rings and gross restrictive practices should be made criminal offences* (London Times).

price support, artificial support, generally provided by a government, to keep prices of products or commodities or foreign exchange rates from falling below certain stipulated levels. It commonly takes the form of direct subsidy to the producer, government purchase at the level of support when the price in the open market falls below that level, or loans to permit producers to hold back their production in storage pending a rise in price in the open market or an increase in protective tariffs. *The five-year program calls for price supports on specified amounts of these two metals plus tungsten and acid-grade fluorspar* (Wall Street Journal).

price-sup·port·ed (prīs′sə pôr′tid, -pōr′-), *adj.* that is given price support: *As with other price-supported agricultural commodities, overproduction is encouraged because the farmer does not have to suffer the consequences of a glutted market* (Wall Street Journal).

price tag, 1. a tag or ticket marked with the price of the article to which it is attached. **2.** *Informal.* an estimated worth or cost; value: *To answer these questions means putting a price tag on events which are obviously incalculable* (Newsweek).

price war, a competitive struggle between sellers of a product in which the price is progressively slashed until it may drop below cost: *At consumer levels a rash of price wars . . . cut service station prices as low as 14.9¢ per gal. before taxes* (Time).

price·wise (prīs′wīz), *adv.* with respect to price or prices: *Shipping men say that Swedish pulp isn't able to compete pricewise with the Canadian product* (Wall Street Journal).

pric·ey (prī′sē), *adj. British Informal.* expensive: *When we travel we go the cheapest comfortable way we can. We don't hire aeroplanes, we avoid the pricey hotels* (Sunday Times).

prick (prik), *n.* **1.** a puncture. **2.** a little hole or mark made by a sharp point. **3.** a pricking. **4.** a sharp pain. **5.** that which pricks or pierces, as a goad for oxen. **6.** stinging compunction; remorse: *the prick of conscience.*

kick against the pricks, to make useless resistance that only hurts oneself: *He found it hard to kick against the pricks, yet, for that reason, kicked every day the harder* (London Times).

—*v.t.* **1.** to make a little hole in with a sharp point: *The cat pricked me with its claws.* **2.** to mark with a sharp point: *I pricked the map with a pin to show our route.* **3.** to cause sharp pain to: *His conscience pricked him suddenly* (John Galsworthy). **4.** to raise or erect: *The dog pricked his ears at the sound* of footsteps. **5.** *Archaic.* to spur; urge on: *My duty pricks me on to utter that Which else no worldly good should draw from me* (Shakespeare). **6.** to transplant (seedlings). **7.** to shoe (a horse) improperly, by driving a nail into the quick. *—v.i.* **1.** to pierce a little hole in something. **2.** to cause or feel a sharp pain. **3.** *Archaic.* to ride fast.

prick up, a. to point upward; stand erect: *The spires of churches are to be seen pricking up through the greenery* (Blackwood's Magazine). **b.** *Nautical.* to chart with dividers: *The captain ordered the ship's course to be pricked up.*

[Old English *prica* a point, puncture, particle] **—prick′ing·ly,** *adv.*

—**Syn.** *v.t.* **1.** puncture. *-v.i.* **2.** sting.

prick-eared (prik′ird′), *adj.* **1.** having erect ears (used especially of dogs). **2.** having the hair cut short so that the ears are prominent (used originally in England in the 1640's of the Roundheads by the Cavaliers).

prick·er (prik′ər), *n.* **1.** a person or thing that pricks. **2.** any sharp-pointed instrument. **3.** *Archaic.* a horseman.

prick·et[1] (prik′it), *n.* **1.** a sharp metal point on which to stick a candle. **2.** a candlestick with such a point or points. [Middle English *pryket,* perhaps < *pryk* prick + *-et* -et. Compare Medieval Latin (England) *priket-tum.*]

prick·et[2] (prik′it), *n.* a buck in his second year, with straight, still unbranched horns. [perhaps < *pricket*[1]. Perhaps related to BROCKET.]

prick·le (prik′əl), *n., v.,* **-led, -ling.** *—n.* **1. a.** a small, sharp point; thorn; spine. **b.** *Botany.* a sharp point growing from the bark of a plant like a thorn but able to be peeled off: *A prickle is a sharp outgrowth from the superficial tissues of a stem or a leaf* (Fred W. Emerson). **2.** a prickly or smarting sensation: *I feel the old, familiar prickle of excitement* (Punch).

—v.i. to feel a prickly or smarting sensation: *Her skin prickled when she saw the big snake.* *—v.t.* **1.** to cause such a sensation in: *I . . . Felt a horror over me creep, Prickle my skin and catch my breath* (Tennyson). **2.** to goad; prod.

[Old English *pricel,* variant of *pricels* thing to prick with < *prician* to prick; later fused with *prickle* (diminutive) < *prick,* noun]

prick·li·ness (prik′lē nis), *n.* a prickly quality: *In Whistler the pride of an American went with the pugnacity of an Englishman and the prickliness of an alien* (Harper's).

prick·ly (prik′lē), *adj.,* **-li·er, -li·est. 1.** having many sharp points like thorns: *a prickly rosebush, the prickly porcupine.* **2.** sharp and stinging; itching: *Heat sometimes causes a prickly rash on the skin.* **3.** hard to deal with: *a prickly question.*

prickly ash, a shrub or small tree of the rue family, with ashlike leaves and strong prickles. Its bark is used in medicine.

prickly heat, a red, itching rash on the skin, caused by inflammation of the sweat glands; miliaria: *Known as prickly heat, this rash seems to bother babies less than it does mothers* (Sidonie M. Gruenberg).

prickly pear, 1. the round or pear-shaped, usually prickly fruit of a certain group of cactus. The edible kinds, called tunas, are raised as food for people and livestock. **2.** any of the group of cactus, with flat, fleshy, jointed stems, bearing this fruit and growing from several inches to over 20 feet high.

prickly poppy, any of a group of plants of the poppy family, of the southwestern United States, Mexico, and South America, with prickly foliage and orange, yellow, or white flowers, as the Mexican poppy.

prick song, *Obsolete.* **1.** written music. **2.** a descant; counterpoint. [(originally) *prikked song* < *prick* (because of the points and dots found in a manuscript or musical score)]

prick·spur (prik′spėr′), *n.* an early form of horseman's spur with a single pricking point. It was in general use before the 1300's, when it was superseded by the spur with a rowel.

pride (prīd), *n., v.,* **prid·ed, prid·ing.** *—n.* **1.** a high opinion of one's own worth or possessions: *He left Temple's protection only to learn that pride is a luxury to the poor* (Time). **2.** pleasure or satisfaction in something concerned with oneself: *to take pride in a hard job well done.* **3.** something that a person is proud of: *Her youngest child is her great pride. Glasgow is the pride of Scotland* (Tobias Smollett). **4.** too high an opinion of oneself; conceit: *Pride goes before a fall.* **5.** acting as if better than others; scorn of others. **6.** the best part; most flourishing period; prime: *in the pride of manhood. The bees humming round the gay roses Proclaim it the pride of the year* (Robert Burns). **7.** *Archaic.* splendor; pomp: . . . *all Quality, Pride, Pomp, and Circumstance of glorious war* (Shakespeare). **8.** *Archaic.* high spirit; mettle. **9.** *Obsolete.* sexual desire in a female animal; heat. **10.** a group (of lions): *They came upon it lying down, surrounded by a very large pride of lions* (New Yorker).

—v.t. **pride oneself on,** to be proud of: *We pride ourselves on our clean streets.*

[Old English *prȳde* < *prūd* proud]

—**Syn.** *n.* **1. Pride, conceit** mean a high opinion of oneself. **Pride** implies pleased satisfaction with what one is, has, or has done, and suggests either proper self-respect and personal dignity because of real worth or excessive self-love and arrogance because of imagined superiority: *A man without pride deserves contempt.* **Conceit** implies much too high an opinion of one's own abilities and accomplishments, and often suggests an unpleasantly assertive manner: *Conceit makes the criminal think he is too clever to be caught.* **4.** vanity, arrogance.

pride·ful (prīd′fəl), *adj.* proud: *"Depart," he cried, "perverse and prideful nymph"* (William Richardson). **—pride′ful·ly,** *adv.* **—pride′ful·ness,** *n.*

pride·less (prīd′lis), *adj.* without pride.

pride of China or **India,** the chinaberry: *As I reached the big pride of India bush . . . I paused to eavesdrop* (New Yorker).

pride of place, *Especially British.* the highest position; the honor, pride, or distinction of first place: *Of the many versions of The Magic Flute which I have heard, I must give this one pride of place* (Listener).

prie-dieu (prē dyœ′), *n.* a small desk for a prayer book or the like, with a piece on which to kneel: *a dark-red prie-dieu, furnished duly with rich missal and ebon rosary* (Charlotte Brontë). [< French *prie-dieu* (literally) pray God; *prie,* imperative of *prier* pray; *Dieu* God < Latin *deus*]

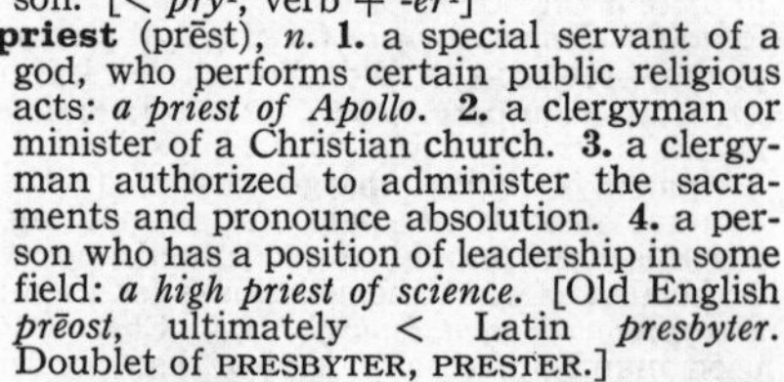
Prie-dieu

pri·er (prī′ər), *n.* a person who pries; inquisitive person. [< *pry*[1], verb + *-er*[1]]

priest (prēst), *n.* **1.** a special servant of a god, who performs certain public religious acts: *a priest of Apollo.* **2.** a clergyman or minister of a Christian church. **3.** a clergyman authorized to administer the sacraments and pronounce absolution. **4.** a person who has a position of leadership in some field: *a high priest of science.* [Old English *prēost,* ultimately < Latin *presbyter.* Doublet of PRESBYTER, PRESTER.]

priest·craft (prēst′kraft′, -kräft′), *n.* the skills, methods, etc., of priests, especially when applied to worldly ends: *It is better that men should be governed by priestcraft than by brute violence* (Macaulay).

priest·ess (prēs′tis), *n.* a woman who serves at an altar or in sacred rites: *a priestess of Diana, a priestess of beauty.*

priest·fish (prēst′fish′), *n.* a rockfish of a slaty-black color, abundant along the Pacific Coast of the United States.

priest·hood (prēst′hu̇d), *n.* **1.** the position or rank of priest: *He was admitted to the priesthood.* **2.** priests as a group: *the priesthood of Spain.* [Old English *prēosthād* < *prēost* priest + *-hād* hood]

priest-king (prēst′king′), *n.* a temporal ruler regarded as the direct representative of a god.

priest·like (prēst′līk′), *adj.* priestly: *The moving waters at their priestlike task Of pure ablution around earth's human shores* (Keats).

priest·li·ness (prēst′lē nis), *n.* the quality of being priestly; the appearance and manner of a priest: *The real pastoral character is but an expression, in outward life, of priestliness* (R.C. Moberly).

priest·ly (prēst′lē), *adj.,* **-li·er, -li·est. 1.** of or having to do with a priest: *the priestly office.* **2.** like a priest; suitable for a priest: *priestly sobriety.* —**Syn. 1.** sacerdotal.

priest-rid·den (prēst′rid′ən), *adj.* dominated by priests (used in an unfriendly way).

priest's crown, the dandelion (so called because of the bald appearance of the seed after the pappus has blown off).

priest's hole, a secret chamber in some English houses for hiding a Roman Catholic priest during a raid by a sheriff or soldiers when the penal laws were being enforced, especially against the Jesuits in the reigns of Elizabeth I and James I.

prig[1] (prig), *n.* a person who is too particular about speech and manners, and prides himself on being better than others: *A prig is a fellow who is always making you a present of his opinions* (George Eliot). [origin uncertain]

prig[2] (prig), *v.,* **prigged, prig·ging,** *n.* *—v.i. Scottish.* **1.** to quarrel or haggle about a price, terms, etc. **2.** to beg; importune. *—v.t.* to pilfer or steal: *I think we'd find that Mr. Beeton has been prigging little things out of the rooms here and there* (Rudyard Kipling).

prig down, *Slang.* to try to beat down: *He'll be sure to prig down your price* (Joseph Wright).

—n. a petty thief. [origin uncertain]

prig·ger (prig′ər), *n. Archaic.* a thief: *Horse thieves were [called] priggers of prancers* (London Times). [< *prig*[2] + *-er*[1]]

prig·ger·y (prig′ər ē), *n., pl.* **-ger·ies.** the conduct or character of a prig.

prig·gish (prig′ish), *adj.* too particular about doing right in things that show outwardly; priding oneself on being better than others. **—prig′gish·ly,** *adv.* **—prig′gish·ness,** *n.*

prig·gism (prig′iz əm), *n.* priggishness.

prill (pril), *n.* a small ball or pellet roughly the size of small shot. *—v.t.* to form (balls or pellets) of metal, chemicals, etc.

prim (prim), *adj.,* **prim·mer, prim·mest,** *v.,* **primmed, prim·ming.** *—adj.* stiffly precise, neat, proper, or formal: *friends . . . staid and prim, of evangelical tendencies* (Samuel Butler).

—v.t. **1.** to form (the face or mouth) into an expression of stiff demureness. **2.** to make (a person, thing, etc.) prim. *—v.i.* to draw up the mouth in an affectedly nice way: *They mince and prim and pout, and are sigh-away* (George Meredith). [origin uncertain] **—prim′ly,** *adv.* **—prim′ness,** *n.*

prim., 1. primary. **2.** primate. **3.** primitive.

pri·ma bal·le·ri·na (prē′mə bal′ə rē′nə), *pl.* **pri·ma bal·le·ri·nas.** the principal woman dancer in a ballet company. [< Italian *prima ballerina* first ballerina, ultimately < Latin *prīma,* feminine, first + Late Latin *ballāre* to dance]

pri·ma·cy (prī′mə sē), *n., pl.* **-cies. 1.** being first in order, rank, importance, etc. **2.** the position or rank of a church primate. **3.** (in the Roman Catholic Church) the supreme power of the Pope. [< Old French *primacie,* learned borrowing from Medieval Latin (England) *primatia,* for Latin *prīmātus, -ūs* < *prīmās, -ātis* of first rank; see PRIMATE] —**Syn. 1.** preëminence.

pri·ma don·na (prē′mə don′ə, prim′ə), *pl.* **pri·ma don·nas. 1.** the principal woman singer in an opera, operatic company, or concert group. **2.** anyone who is or can be as temperamental as a prima donna: *[His] genius was for making men work as a team. He had to handle the prima donnas of a dozen different nations* (Newsweek). [< Italian *prima donna* first lady < Latin *prīma domina.* Compare PRIME[1], noun, DONNA.] —**Syn. 1.** diva.

pri·ma fa·ci·e (prī′mə fā′shē ē, fā′shē), at first view; before investigation. [< Latin *prīmā faciē,* ablative of *prīma faciēs* first appearance. Compare PRIME[1], noun, FACE.] **—pri′ma-fa′ci·e,** *adj.*

prima-facie case, *Law.* a case supported by prima-facie evidence.

prima-facie evidence, *Law.* evidence sufficient to establish a fact, or raise a presumption of fact, unless rebutted: *Opposition . . . is usually taken as prima-facie evidence of disloyalty* (Atlantic).

pri·mage (prī′mij), *n.* a small allowance formerly paid by a shipper to the master and crew of a vessel for the loading and care of goods. [origin uncertain. Compare Medieval Latin (England) *primagium* primage, allowance for loading.]

pri·ma in·ter pa·res (prī′mə in′tər pãr′ēz), *Latin.* first among her peers.

pri·mal (prī′məl), *adj.* **1.** of early times; first; primeval: *It hath the primal eldest curse*

 PRONUNCIATION KEY: hat, āge, cãre, fär; let, ēqual, tėrm; it, īce; hot, ōpen, ôrder; oil, out; cup, pu̇t, rüle;

upon it, A brother's murder (Shakespeare). **2.** chief; fundamental. [< Medieval Latin *primalis* < Latin *prīmus* first] **—pri′mal·ly,** *adv.* **—Syn. 1.** original.

pri·ma·quine (prī′mə kwin), *n.* a synthetic drug used to cure some forms of malaria. *Formula:* $C_{15}H_{21}N_3O$

pri·ma·ri·ly (prī′mer′ə lē, -mər-; prī mãr′-), *adv.* **1.** chiefly; principally: *Napoleon was primarily a general.* **2.** at first; originally. **—Syn. 1.** preëminently.

pri·ma·ri·ness (prī′mer′ē nis, -mər-), *n.* the state of being primary, or first, in time, act, or intention.

pri·ma·ry (prī′mer′ē, -mər-), *adj., n., pl.* **-ries.** *—adj.* **1.** first in time; first in order. **2.** from which others have come; original; fundamental. **3.** first in importance; chief. **4.** of or having to do with the inducing circuit, coil, or current in an induction coil or the like: *If there were 110 volts in the primary coil, the voltage of the secondary coil would be 2200* (Beauchamp, Mayfield, and West). **5.** of or having to do with one of the large flight feathers growing on the distal section of a bird's wing. **6.** *Chemistry.* **a.** characterized by the replacement of a single atom or group. **b.** formed by replacing a single atom or group. **7.** *Geology.* **a.** formed or developed directly from magma, as a rock or ore. **b.** *Obsolete.* Archeozoic. **8.** *Grammar.* **a.** (of word structure) consisting of a single free morpheme (*boy*) or of two or more bound morphemes (*receive*). **b.** (of suffixes) added directly to an unanalyzable root. **c.** (of tenses in certain older Indo-European languages) expressing present or future time. **9.** utilizing the crude products of nature as raw materials, as an industry: *Some industries also are classed as primary because they use only the crude products of the soil, forest, or mine as their raw materials* (Finch and Trewartha). **10.** *Metallurgy.* derived from ore rather than from a combination of ore and scrap or from scrap alone.
—*n.* **1.** anything that is first in order, rank, or importance. **2.** *U.S.* a meeting or gathering of the voters of a political party in an election district to choose candidates for office. **3.** a primary color. **4.** a primary coil or circuit. **5.** a heavenly body around which another revolves. **6.** a primary feather. **7.** a positively charged atomic nucleus traveling at high velocity that is commonly stopped on entering the earth's atmosphere by collision with an atom of other matter, the collision resulting in the formation of a number of secondary particles.
[< Latin *prīmārius* of the first rank, chief < *prīmus* first. Doublet of PREMIER.]
—Syn. *adj.* **1.** See **elementary. 3.** principal, prime.

primary accent, 1. the strongest accent in the pronunciation of a word. **2.** a mark (′) used to show this.

primary atypical pneumonia, a form of pneumonia, rarely fatal, that is caused by the Eaton agent and associated viruses.

primary carbon atom, a carbon atom joined to only one other carbon atom.

primary colors, pigments or colors that are, or are thought to be, fundamental. Red, yellow, and blue are the primary colors in pigments. In psychology, yellow, blue, green, and red are primary colors.

primary election, an election to choose candidates for office from a certain political party: *The letter recommended that Mr. Eisenhower enter his name in all Presidential primary elections* (Newsweek).

primary grades, *U.S.* the first three grades of elementary school.

primary group, *Sociology.* a group whose members have direct, intimate contact with each other: *By primary groups I mean those characterized by intimate face-to-face association and co-operation* (Ogburn and Nimkoff).

primary root, *Botany.* the single root which develops from the embryo itself.

primary school, the first three or four grades of the elementary school.

primary stress, the strongest stress in the pronunciation of a word.

primary syphilis, the first stage of syphilis, indicated by a painless chancre, usually on the genitals.

primary wave, an earthquake wave traveling through solids faster than the secondary wave, and causing rocks to vibrate parallel with the wave.

pri·ma·tal (prī mā′təl), *n.* a primate of a church or country.

pri·mate (prī′mit, -māt), *n.* **1.** an archbishop or bishop ranking above all other bishops in a church, country, or province. **2.** any of the highest order of mammals, including human beings, apes, and monkeys. **3.** a person who is first in rank or importance; chief; leader. [(definition 1) < Latin *prīmās, -ātis* of first rank (in Medieval Latin, a superior bishop or archbishop) < *prīmus* first; probably influenced by Old French *primat;* (definition 2) < New Latin *Primates,* the order name; (literally) plural of Latin *prīmās* first] **—Syn. 1.** metropolitan.

Primate of All England, the Archbishop of Canterbury.

Primate of England, the Archbishop of York.

pri·mate·ship (prī′mit ship, -māt-), *n.* the position or rank of a church primate.

pri·ma·tial (prī mā′shəl), *adj.* of, having to do with, or characteristic of a primate or primateship: *primatial duties.*

pri·ma·tol·o·gist (prī′mə tol′ə jist), *n.* a person skilled in primatology: *Primatologists more than anybody else realize how little is known about the gorilla* (New Scientist).

pri·ma·tol·o·gy (prī′mə tol′ə jē), *n.* the study of the origin, structure, development, and behavior of primates.

pri·ma·ver·a (prē′mə vãr′ə), *n.* **1.** a tall tree of Mexico and Central America whose bright yellow flowers appear in the early spring. **2.** its wood, used in cabinetmaking. [< Spanish *primavera* springtime]

pri·ma·ver·al (prē′mə vir′əl), *adj.* of or having to do with the early springtime: *. . . an aspect of morning brightness and primaveral gaiety* (London Daily Telegraph). [< Spanish *primavera* springtime + English *-al*[1]]

prime[1] (prīm), *adj.* **1.** first in rank; chief: *His prime object was to lower the tax rate.* **2.** first in time or order; fundamental; original: *the prime causes of war.* **3.** first in quality; first-rate; excellent: *prime ribs of beef.* **4.** that cannot be divided without a remainder by any whole number except itself and 1: *7, 11, and 13 are prime numbers.* **5.** having no common divisor but 1: *2 is prime to 9.* **6.** ranking high in credit: *Interest on short-term loans to prime . . . private borrowers also dropped a little more than 1 per cent* (World Book Annual).
[partly < Latin *prīmus* first, partly < Old French *prime,* learned borrowing from Latin]
—*n.* **1.** the best time; best condition: *A man of forty is in the prime of life.* **2.** the best part. **3.** the first part; beginning: *We see how quickly sundry arts mechanical were found out, in the very prime of the world* (Richard Hooker). **4.** springtime: *And brought him presents, flowers, if it were prime, Or mellow fruit if it were harvest time* (Edmund Spenser). **5.** early manhood or womanhood; youth: *They were now in the happy prime of youth* (Hawthorne). **6.** the second of the seven canonical hours, or the service for it, originally fixed for the first hour of the day (beginning at 6 A.M.). **7.** a prime number. **8. a.** one of the sixty minutes in a degree. **b.** the mark (′) indicating such a part. B′ is read "B prime." **9.** *Music.* **a.** the same tone or note in another octave. **b.** the octave or octaves between two such tones or notes. **c.** the tonic or keynote. **10.** *Fencing.* the first defensive position in fencing.
[Old English *prīm* (noun definition 6); later, the first period (of the day) < Late Latin *prīma* the first service < Latin *prīma* (*hōra*) first hour (of the Roman day)]
—prime′ness, *n.*
—Syn. *adj.* **1.** principal. **2.** primordial. **3.** choice.

prime[2] (prīm), *v.,* **primed, prim·ing,** *n.* —*v.t.* **1.** to prepare by putting something in or on, as gasoline into a carburetor or cylinder, to facilitate starting the engine. **2.** to supply (a gun) with powder, especially to set off the main charge: *Our two combatants had taken the ground, and were priming their pistols* (Tobias Smollett). **3.** to cover (a surface) with a first coat of paint or oil, so that paint will not soak in. **4.** to equip (a person) with information, words, etc.: *to prime a person with a speech.* **5.** to pour water into (a pump) to start action. —*v.i.* **1.** to prime a firearm, charge, pump, etc. **2.** (of a boiler or steam engine) to let water pass to the cylinder in the form of spray along with the steam.
—*n.* something that primes; priming.
[origin uncertain. Perhaps related to PRIME[1] as a "first operation" or to PRIMAGE as a "loading."]

prime conductor, a conductor that collects and retains positive electricity.

prime cost, the cost of the labor and material in production.

prime·ly (prīm′lē), *adv.* **1.** *Informal.* exceedingly well; excellently: *primely cooked venison.* **2.** *Obsolete.* at first; originally. **3.** *Obsolete.* chiefly; principally.

prime meridian, a meridian from which the longitude east and west is measured. It passes through Greenwich, England and its longitude is 0 degrees.

prime minister, the chief minister of a government. He is the head of the cabinet and the chief of state. **—Syn.** premier.

prime-min·is·te·ri·al (prīm′min′ə stir′ē-əl), *adj.* of or having to do with a prime minister: *Official black Citroëns shuttled to and from the beige stone prime-ministerial residence on the Rue de Varenne* (Time).

prime ministership, the office of a prime minister; prime ministry: *The contenders for the prime ministership are not all out-of-office politicians* (Maclean's).

prime ministry, the office or position of prime minister.

prime mover, 1. the first agent that puts a machine in motion, such as wind or electricity. **2.** a machine, such as a water wheel or steam engine, that receives and modifies energy supplied by some natural source: *To obtain more electrical energy from a generator, the prime mover must supply more mechanical energy* (World Book Encyclopedia). **3.** a person or thing that starts or does the most for any enterprise. **4.** *Philosophy.* that from which all movement derives, but which itself neither moves nor intervenes in the later action.

prime number, a whole number that cannot be divided without a remainder by any whole number except itself and 1: *2, 3, 5, 7, 11, and 13 are prime numbers.*

prime paper, the commercial paper issued to large corporations and other big borrowers with excellent credit ratings, frequently without the need for security.

prim·er[1] (prim′ər; *British for 1, 2, 4* prī′mər), *n.* **1.** a first book in reading. **2.** a first book; beginner's book: *a primer of statistics.* **3.** either of two sizes of printing type, great primer, 18-point type, or long primer, 10-point type. **4.** *Archaic.* a prayer book used to teach children to read. [< Medieval Latin *primarius* (originally) a simplified collection of prayers and services < Latin *prīmārius* adjective, first in rank; see PRIMARY]

prim·er[2] (prī′mər), *n.* **1.** a person or thing that primes. **2.** a cap or cylinder containing a little gunpowder, used for firing a charge. [apparently < *prim*(e)[2] + *-er*[1]]

prime rate, the lowest rate of interest charged by banks to large commercial customers with very high credit ratings: *Rates for all other customers are scaled upward from the prime rate* (Wall Street Journal).

pri·me·ro (pri mãr′ō), *n.* a card game, popular in England in the 1500's and 1600's. [apparently alteration of Spanish *primera,* (literally) feminine of *primero* first < Latin *prīmārius;* see PRIMARY]

prime time, the peak hours of television viewing (in the United States, approximately 6 to 11 p.m.): *The network was . . . gambling on soap opera in prime time* (Time). **—prime′-time′,** *adj.*

pri·meur (prē mœr′), *n. French.* **1.** a fruit or vegetable before its ordinary season: *The Queen is particularly fond of what the French call primeurs, baby carrots, new peas, very young spinach, and tiny new potatoes* (Sunday Telegraph). **2.** anything new or early.

pri·me·val (prī mē′vəl), *adj.* **1.** of or having to do with the first age or ages, especially of the world: *In its primeval state the earth was a fiery glowing ball. A semi-mystical attitude is that not only space but also time itself began with the primeval atom* (Time). **2.** ancient: *primeval forests untouched by the ax.* [< Latin *prīmaevus* early in life (< *prīmus* first + *aevum* age) + English *-al*[1]) —**pri·me′val·ly,** *adv.* —**Syn. 2.** prehistoric.

pri·mi·ge·ni·al (prī′mə jē′nē əl), *adj.* **1.** of a primitive type: *the primigenial elephant.* **2.** *Obsolete.* first generated or produced; primary; original. [< Latin *prīmigenius* first of its kind (< *prīmus* first + *genus* kind, or *gen-*, root of *gignere* to beget) + English *-al*[1]]

pri·mi·grav·i·da (prī′mə grav′ə də), *n., pl.* **-i·dae** (-ə dē). a woman pregnant for the first time. [< New Latin *primigravida* < Latin *prīmus* first + *gravidus* gravid]

pri·mine (prī′min), *n. Botany.* the outer integument of an ovule. [< French *primine* (originally) the outer coat < Latin *prīmus* first + French *-ine* -ine[1]]

prim·ing (prī′ming), *n.* **1.** powder or other material used to set fire to an explosive. **2.** a first coat of paint, sizing, etc.

pri·mip·a·ra (prī mip′ər ə), *n., pl.* **-a·ras, -a·rae** (-ə rē). **1.** a woman who has borne only one child. **2.** a woman who is having her first baby. [< Latin *prīmipara* < *prīmus* first + *-para*, feminine of *-parus* < *parere* to bear young]

pri·mi·par·i·ty (prī′mə par′ə tē), *n.* primiparous condition.

pri·mip·a·rous (prī mip′ər əs), *adj.* bearing a child, or young, for the first time.

prim·i·tive (prim′ə tiv), *adj.* **1.** of early times; of long ago: *Primitive people often lived in caves.* **2.** first of the kind: *primitive Christians.* **3.** very simple; such as people had early in human history: *A primitive way of making a fire is by rubbing two sticks together. A trip to Africa opened their eyes to primitive art* (Time). **4.** original; primary: *a primitive word.* **5.** *Biology.* **a.** primordial. **b.** representing or related to an ancient group or species.
—*n.* **1.** an artist belonging to an early period, especially before the Renaissance. **2.** an artist who does not use the techniques of perspective, shading, or the like in painting. **3.** a picture painted by such an artist: *The focus this week is again on the Europeans, for the shows include an exhibition of modern French and Dutch primitives at the Kleemann Galleries* (New Yorker). **4.** a person living in a primitive society or in primitive times. **5.** an algebraic or geometrical expression from which another is derived. **6.** a word from which another is derived.
[< Latin *prīmitīvus* < *prīmitiae* first things, first fruits < *prīmus* first] —**prim′i·tive·ly,** *adv.* —**prim′i·tive·ness,** *n.*
—**Syn.** *adj.* **1.** prehistoric.

Primitive Methodist, a member of a Methodist sect formed in the early 1800's in England.

prim·i·tiv·ism (prim′ə tə viz′əm), *n.* preference for the primitive, especially in art or religion: *Primitivism, for example, as illustrated by Picasso's concern with Negro art, . . . was much less artificial* [*in Spain*] (Atlantic).

prim·i·tiv·ist (prim′ə tə vist), *n.* a person who believes in primitivism.

prim·i·tiv·is·tic (prim′ə tə vis′tik), *adj.* of or characteristic of primitivism or primitivists.

prim·i·tiv·i·ty (prim′ə tiv′ə tē), *n.* primitive quality, character, or condition: *Polygamy . . . is conditioned not by primitivity in culture, but by particular conditions affecting the ratio of men to women in a given society* (Beals and Hoijer).

pri·mo (prē′mō), *n. Italian.* the first or principal part in a musical duet or trio.

pri·mo·gen·i·tor (prī′mə jen′ə tər), *n.* **1.** an ancestor; forefather. **2.** the earliest ancestor. [< Late Latin *prīmōgenitor* < Latin *prīmō* at first + *genitor* begetter; patterned on *prīmōgenitus;* see PRIMOGENITURE]

pri·mo·gen·i·ture (prī′mə jen′ə chür, -chər), *n.* **1.** the state, condition, or fact of being the first-born of the children of the same parents. **2.** the right or principle of inheritance or succession by the first-born, especially the inheritance of a family estate by the eldest son. [< Medieval Latin *primogenitura* < Latin *prīmōgenitus* first-born < *prīmō* at first (< *prīmus* first) + *gignere* to beget, produce]

pri·mor·di·al (prī môr′dē əl), *adj.* **1.** existing at the very beginning: *primordial rock. Primordial man could have had little or no tradition before the development of speech* (H. G. Wells). **2.** original; elementary: *primordial laws.* [< Latin *prīmōrdiālis* < *prīmōrdium* the beginning; see PRIMORDIUM]

pri·mor·di·al·ism (prī môr′dē ə liz′əm), *n.* a continuance of or adherence to what is primordial; preference for the primitive.

pri·mor·di·al·ly (prī môr′dē ə lē), *adv.* under original conditions; at the beginning.

primordial meristem, *Botany.* the actively dividing cells lying behind the root cap.

pri·mor·di·um (prī môr′dē əm), *n., pl.* **-di·a** (-dē ə). **1.** the very beginning; earliest stage. **2.** *Embryology.* the first cells in the earliest stages of the development of an organ or structure. [< Latin *prīmōrdium,* (literally) neuter of *prīmōrdius* original < *prīmus* first + *ōrdīrī* to begin]

primp (primp), *v.t.* to dress (oneself) for show; prink: *to primp oneself for a party, to primp up the hair.* —*v.i.* to dress carefully. [apparently variation of *prim,* verb]

prim·rose (prim′rōz′), *n.* **1.** any of a large group of perennial plants of the primrose family with flowers of various colors, growing chiefly in the north temperate regions of Europe and Asia. The common primrose of Europe is pale yellow. **2.** the evening primrose. **3.** the flower of any of these plants. **4.** a pale yellow. —*adj.* **1.** pale-yellow. **2.** of or like a primrose; gay; pleasant.
[< Old French *primerose,* adaptation of Medieval Latin *prima rose* primula; (literally) first rose]
—**Syn.** *adj.* **2.** flowery.

Chinese Primrose (def. 1)

primrose family, a group of dicotyledonous herbs found chiefly in northern temperate regions, grown for their showy flowers. The family includes the primrose, cyclamen, shooting star, brookweed, and pimpernel.

primrose path, **1.** a pleasant way. **2.** a path of pleasure: *He also can try to wheedle his way out of the arms of the anxious lady who has led him down the primrose path* (New York Times).

primrose yellow, pale yellow.

prim·sie (prim′sē), *adj. Scottish.* artificially formal. [< *prim* + *-sie,* a diminutive suffix]

prim·u·la (prim′yə lə), *n.* a primrose. [< New Latin *Primula* the typical genus < Medieval Latin *primula veris* cowslip; later, daisy; (literally) firstling of spring < Latin *prīmulus* first (< *prīmus* first); *vēris,* genitive of *vēr* spring]

prim·u·la·ceous (prim′yə lā′shəs), *adj.* belonging to the primrose family. [< New Latin *Primulaceae* the order name < *Primula* primula + English *-ous*]

pri·mum mo·bi·le (prī′məm mob′ə lē), **1.** a prime mover: *Man may be unique . . . in a way that has nothing to do with our being the wound-up and running-down toy of some ancient god or primum mobile* (New Yorker). **2.** (in medieval astronomy) the sphere of the fixed stars. [< Medieval Latin *primum mobile,* noun use of neuter of Latin *prīmus* first + *mobilis* moving; translation of Arabic *al-muḥarrik al-awwal* the first mover]

pri·mus (prī′məs), *n., pl.* **-mus·es.** the senior bishop of the Scottish Episcopal Church. He is chosen by the other bishops, presides at all their meetings, and has ceremonial privileges, but no metropolitan authority. [< Latin *prīmus* first]

Pri·mus (prī′məs), *n. Trademark.* a portable stove which burns vaporized oil.

pri·mus in·ter pa·res (prī′məs in′tər pâr′ēz), *Latin.* first among his peers: *The idea of the Soviet Communist Party as primus inter pares was not abandoned for ten years* (Atlantic).

prim·y (prī′mē), *adj.* at the prime or best stage: *a violet in the youth of primy nature* (Shakespeare). [< *prim*(e)[1] + *-y*[1]]

prin., **1. a.** principal. **b.** principally. **2.** principle.

prince (prins), *n.* **1. a.** a male member of a royal family. **b.** a son or grandson of a king or queen; son of a king's or queen's son. **2.** a sovereign. **3.** the ruler of a small state subordinate to a king or emperor. **4.** the English equivalent of certain titles of nobility of varying importance or rank in other countries. **5.** the greatest or best of a group; chief: *a merchant prince. That prince of pioneers* [*Daniel Boone*] (Francis Parkman). **6.** *Obsolete.* a queen ruling in her own right. [< Old French *prince* < Latin *prīnceps, -cipis* chief < *prīmus* first + *-cip,* stem related to *capere* to take]

Prince Al·bert (al′bərt), a long, double-breasted coat, worn by men. [American English, probably < *Prince Albert* of England, husband of Queen Victoria]

Prince Albert (mid-19th century)

prince-bish·op (prins′bish′əp), *n.* a bishop who is also a prince, especially formerly a German bishop who had the temporal authority and possessions of a bishopric. [translation of German *Fürstbischof*]

Prince Charles spaniel (chärlz), a black, tan, and white variety of the English toy spaniel.

Prince Charming, **1.** the fairy-tale prince who marries Cinderella. **2.** an ideal type of man; a perfect lover: *. . . a dance palace where young Cinderellas could meet their Prince Charmings* (New York Times).

prince consort, a prince who is the husband of a queen or empress ruling in her own right; one who is a prince in his own right or (occasionally) one granted princely status by the marriage.

prince·dom (prins′dəm), *n.* **1.** the territory ruled by a prince. **2.** the position, rank, or dignity of a prince.
princedoms, principalities, an order of angels: *The angelic hosts, the archangelic pomps, thrones, dominations, princedoms, rank on rank* (Elizabeth Barrett Browning).

prince imperial, the eldest son of an emperor or empress.

prince·kin (prins′kin), *n.* a princeling.

prince·let (prins′lit), *n.* a princeling.

prince·li·ness (prins′lē nis), *n.* princely quality.

prince·ling (prins′ling), *n.* a young, little, or petty prince: *the younger son of a German princeling* (Lytton Strachey). [< *prince* + *-ling*]

prince·ly (prins′lē), *adj.,* **-li·er, -li·est,** *adv.* —*adj.* **1.** of a prince or his rank; royal: *princely power, the princely families of Europe.* **2.** like a prince; noble; stately: *a princely manner.* **3.** fit for a prince; magnificent; sumptuous: *a princely gift.*
—*adv.* in the manner of a prince; royally.
—**Syn.** *adj.* **2.** courtly.

Prince of Darkness, the Devil; Satan.

Prince of Peace, Jesus Christ.

prince of the blood, a prince of a royal family.

Prince of Wales, the title conferred on the eldest son, or heir apparent, of the British sovereign.

prince regent, a prince who acts as the regent of a country, especially an uncle or cousin of the lawful heir or sovereign during his minority or incapacity.

prince royal, the oldest son of a king or queen.

Prince Ru·pert's drop (rü′pėrts), a small glass bulb that is cooled quickly, becoming subjected to unequal strains of contraction. If a portion of its tail is broken off, the bulb flies into pieces. [< *Prince Rupert,* 1619-1682, British soldier and inventor, grandson of James I of England]

prince's-feath·er (prin′siz feᴛʜ′ər), *n.* a tall, handsome annual garden plant of the amaranth family with thick, feathery red or greenish spikes.

Prince's metal, an alloy of about three parts of copper and one of zinc, resembling gold in color and once used in cheap jewelry. [< *Prince* Rupert; see PRINCE RUPERT'S DROP]

prin·cess (prin′ses, -sis), *n.* **1.** a daughter or granddaughter of a king or queen; daughter of a king's or queen's son. **2.** the wife or widow of a prince. **3.** a woman having the rank of a prince.
—*adj.* princesse.
[< Old French *princesse,* feminine of *prince* prince]

prin·cesse (prin ses′; prin′ses, -sis), *adj.* (of a woman's clothing) one-piece and close-fitting with a flaring skirt and vertical seams: *Her dress was white linen, cut princesse over the hips, long and full-skirted* (New Yorker). [< French *princesse*]

prin·cess·ly (prin′ses lē, -sis-), *adj.* of, like, or befitting a princess: *She is handsome . . . and her manners are princessly* (Byron).

princess marble, sodalite.

princess of the blood, a princess of a royal family.
princess royal, the oldest daughter of a king or queen.
princess tree, a Chinese tree of medium height, with downy leaves and fragrant violet flowers, which has become naturalized in the eastern coastal United States.
Prince·to·ni·an (prins tō′nē ən), *n.* a student or graduate of Princeton University.
prin·ci·pal (prin′sə pəl), *adj.* most important; main; chief: *Chicago is the principal city of Illinois.*
—*n.* **1.** a chief person; one who gives orders: *She is one of the principals of the Royal Ballet* (Maclean's). **2. a.** the head, or one of the heads, of an elementary or secondary school. **b.** (especially in Great Britain) the head of a college. **3.** a sum of money on which interest is paid. **4.** money or property from which income is received. **5.** a person who hires or authorizes another person to act for him: *Mr. Smith does the business of renting the houses for Mr. Jones, his principal.* **6.** a person directly responsible for a crime. **7.** a person responsible for the payment of a debt that another person has endorsed. **8.** *Music.* an organ stop whose tones are of the same quality as the open diapason but an octave higher. **9.** anything of chief importance, as a main truss or rafter in a building: *Our lodgings . . . Shook as the earth did quake; the very principals did seem to rend, And all to topple* (Shakespeare). **10.** each of the combatants in a duel.
[< Old French *principal,* learned borrowing from Latin *prīncipālis* first; later, princely (in Late Latin, noun, overseer) < *prīnceps* chief; see PRINCE]
—**Syn.** *adj.* cardinal, foremost, prime, leading, prominent. —**Ant.** *adj.* minor, secondary.
principal boy, *British.* a female player who takes the leading male part in a pantomime: *Clarice Mayne, soon to become one of the best-loved principal boys in the north, made her first appearance as Prince Charming in "Cinderella"* (London Times).
prin·ci·pal·i·ty (prin′sə pal′ə tē), *n., pl.* **-ties. 1.** a small state or country ruled by a prince: *In that province [Normandy] they found a mighty state, which gradually extended its influence over the neighbouring principalities of Brittany and Maine* (Macaulay). **2.** the country from which a prince gets his title. **3.** supreme power: *Josephus . . . calls the Commonwealth of the Hebrews a Theocracy, because the principality was in God only* (Milton). **4.** chief place or rank: *Christ hath the primacy of order and the principality of influence* (Thomas Manton).
principalities, the order of angels next above the powers: *For we wrestle not against flesh and blood, but against principalities* (Ephesians 6:12).
prin·ci·pal·ly (prin′sə pə lē, -sə plē), *adv.* for the most part; above all; chiefly: *What I principally insist on, is due execution* (Jonathan Swift). —**Syn.** See **especially.**
principal parts, a set of verb forms from which all the other forms of the verb can usually be inferred. In Modern English the principal parts are the infinitive, past tense, and past participle. *Examples:* go, went, gone; do, did, done; drive, drove, driven; push, pushed, pushed.
prin·ci·pal·ship (prin′sə pəl ship), *n.* the position or office of a principal.
prin·ci·pate (prin′sə pāt), *n.* **1.** a chief place or authority: *Under two metaphors the principate of the whole church was promised* (Isaac Barrow). **2.** a principality. [< Latin *prīncipātus, -ūs* the first place (in an army or state) < *prīnceps, -cipis* chief + *-ātus* -ate³; see PRINCE]
prin·ci·pe (*Italian* prēn′chē pā; *Spanish* prēn′thē pā, -sē-; *Portuguese* prēN′si pə), *n., pl. Italian* **-pi** (-pē); *Spanish* **-pes** (-pās); *Portuguese* **-pes** (-pəs). *Italian, Spanish, Portuguese.* a prince.
prin·ci·pes·sa (prēn′chē pās′sä), *n., pl.* **-se** (-sā). *Italian.* a princess.
prin·cip·i·a (prin sip′ē ə), *n.* plural of **principium.**
Prin·cip·i·a (prin sip′ē ə), *n.pl.* **1.** Sir Isaac Newton's famous treatise on mathematical physics, published in 1686. **2.** first principles or elements.
prin·cip·i·um (prin sip′ē əm), *n., pl.* **-i·a** (-ē ə). a principle, especially a first principle or element. [< Latin *prīncipium* beginning, origin < *prīnceps, -cipis* first, chief; see PRINCE]
prin·ci·ple (prin′sə pəl), *n., v.,* **-pled, -pling.** —*n.* **1.** a truth that is a foundation for other truths: *the principles of democratic government.* **2.** a fundamental belief: *religious principles.* **3.** a rule of action or conduct: *I make it a principle to save some money each week.* **4.** uprightness; honor: *Washington was a man of principle. Not only was it right as a matter of principle to bring the question . . . out into the open, they said; it also was good politics* (Newsweek). **5.** a rule of science explaining how things act: *the principle of the lever. A jet engine is based on a principle known since ancient times.* **6.** the method of operation. **7.** a source; origin; first cause or force: *Thales said that the first principle of all things was water* (John Stuart Blackie). **8.** one of the elements that compose a substance, especially one that gives some special quality or effect: *the bitter principle in a drug.* **9. Principle.** (in the belief of Christian Scientists) God.
in principle, as regards the general truth or rule: *Early last year Parliament approved, in principle, pay hikes for all of them, from judges to tug-boat skippers* (Newsweek).
on principle, a. according to a certain principle: *There was a time when I could not read Pope, but disliked him on principle* (James Russell Lowell). **b.** for reasons of right conduct: *Outward acts, done on principle, create inward habits* (Cardinal Newman).
—*v.t. Obsolete.* to teach the basic facts of a subject; impress; indoctrinate.
[< Old French *principe,* learned borrowing from Latin *principium* principium; patterned on *participle*]
—**Syn.** *n.* **2.** tenet. **3.** precept. **4.** integrity. **8.** constituent, ingredient, component.
prin·ci·pled (prin′sə pəld), *adj.* having principles; that is so or such on principle: *She was firm, and fiery, and high principled* (John Ruskin).
-principled, *combining form.* having a ____ principle or principles: *High-principled = having high principles.*
principle of relativity, relativity (def. 4): *The new idea that Einstein introduced in 1905 . . . was the principle of relativity* (Scientific American).
prin·cock (prin′kok), *n. Obsolete.* a pert or conceited young fellow. [origin uncertain]
prin·cox (prin′koks), *n. Obsolete.* princock.
prink (pringk), *v.t.* to dress for show; decorate: *A sixteen-storey tower packed with families and nattily prinked out in rectangles of daffodil and grey* (Punch). —*v.i.* to fuss over one's appearance. [origin uncertain. Perhaps related to PRANK². Compare German *prangen.*] —**prink′er,** *n.*
print (print), *v.t.* **1.** to use type, blocks, plates, etc., and ink or dye to stamp (words, pictures, designs, etc.) on paper or the like. **2.** to stamp letters, words, etc., on with type, etc., and ink: *Some presses print rolls rather than sheets of paper.* **3.** to cause to be printed; publish. **4.** to make with words or letters the way they look in print instead of in writing: *Print your name clearly.* **5.** to stamp with designs, patterns, pictures, etc.: *Machines print wallpaper, cloth, etc.* **6. a.** to make (marks), stamp. **b.** to make marks on; produce marks or figures on by pressure; impress: *Little footsteps lightly print the ground* (Thomas Gray). **7.** to fix (in the heart, mind, or memory): *The scene is printed in my memory.* **8.** to produce a photograph by transmission of light through (a negative).
—*v.i.* **1.** to produce books, newspapers, etc., by a printing press. **2.** to make letters or words the way they look in print instead of in writing. **3.** to be a printer; use a press in printing. **4.** to take an impression from type, etc. **5.** (of type, a block, etc.) to give an impression on paper, etc.
print out, to produce (information or output) in printed or readable form: *The computer quickly prints out which defects a patient might have, in order of probability* (Atlantic).
—*n.* **1.** printed words, letters, etc.: *This book has clear print.* **2.** printed condition: *Here is one fundamental reason why freelance articles so rarely see print* (Science News Letter). **3.** a printed publication; newspaper or magazine: *the story they had read . . . in the public prints* (Booth Tarkington). **4.** an edition or impression of a book, etc., made at one time. **5.** a picture or design printed from a block or plate: *prints of racehorses* (John Galsworthy). **6. a.** cloth with a pattern printed on it: *She has two dresses made of print.* **b.** a dress made of such cloth: *She wore a cotton print.* **7.** the pattern or design so printed. **8.** a mark made by pressing or stamping: *the print of a foot in the ground.* **9.** something that prints; stamp; die. **10.** something that has been marked or shaped by pressing or stamping. **11.** a photograph produced from a negative.
in print, a. in printed form: *'Tis pleasant, sure, to see one's name in print* (Byron). **b.** (of books, etc.) still available for purchase from the publisher: *Author and Title Entries of Books in Print and for Sale* (The American Catalogue).
out of print, no longer sold by the publisher: *Many books that are out of print are reissued in paperback form.*
[< Old French *priente* an impression < *preindre* to press]
print., printing.
print·a·bil·i·ty (prin′tə bil′ə tē), *n.* **1.** the ability to take printing: *New chemicals brighten paper and improve its printability.* **2.** the ability to make an imprint. **3.** fitness to be printed; suitableness for print: *Lawyers, even private detectives are called to check facts for their authenticity and printability* (Wall Street Journal).
print·a·ble (prin′tə bəl), *adj.* **1.** that can be printed. **2.** that can be printed from or on. **3.** fit to be printed: *Lemaire . . . called him names not printable in these prim days* (Temple Bar).
prin·ta·nier (praN tá nyā′), *adj. French.* **1.** prepared with chopped vegetables: *To his mind life without . . . gigot printanier was worse than death* (Punch). **2.** (literally) of spring.
print·ed circuit (prin′tid), an electrical circuit which utilizes paths of silver or silver oxide printed on a chassis or panel to conduct the current: *Handcrafted chassis uses no printed circuits, gives you dependability with less service headaches* (Maclean's).
print·er (prin′tər), *n.* **1.** a person whose business or work is printing or setting type. **2.** an instrument or appliance used for printing.
printer's devil, a young helper or errand boy in a printing shop.
printer's ream, a package or pile of 516 uniform sheets of writing or typewriter paper; perfect ream.
print·er·y (prin′tər ē), *n., pl.* **-er·ies. 1.** a shop with printing presses. **2.** a factory, etc., where cloth is printed; printworks.
print·ing (prin′ting), *n.* **1.** the producing of books, newspapers, etc., by impression from movable types, plates, etc.: *The printing of the city's newspapers is not considered a part of the printing industry proper, since the big newspapers set their own type and have their own presses* (New York Times). **2.** printed words, letters, etc. **3.** all the copies printed at one time: *The first printing was swallowed up before publication* (New Yorker). **4.** letters made like those in print.
printing ink, ink used in typographic printing.
printing out, *Photography.* the act of printing an image on a kind of sensitized paper so that it is visible and complete in detail, and need not be brought out by developing.
printing press, a machine for printing from types, plates, etc.
print·less (print′lis), *adj.* making, leaving, or showing no print or trace.
print·mak·er (print′mā′kər), *n.* a person who makes a picture or design printed from a block or plate.
print·mak·ing (print′mā′king), *n.* the art or process of printing pictures or designs from a block or plate.
print·out (print′out′), *n.* **1. a.** the printed output of an electronic computer. **b.** the act of producing such an output. **2.** printing out.
print paper, paper of a kind or class used for printing on.
print seller, a person who sells prints or engravings.
print shop, 1. a shop where printing is done. **2.** a shop where printed pictures are sold.
print·works (print′wėrks′), *n.* an establishment for printing textiles, as calico.
pri·on (prī′on), *n.* any of four similar petrels of the Southern Hemisphere whose

bills are edged with projections resembling the teeth of a saw. [< Greek *priōn* a saw]

pri·or[1] (prī′ər), *adj.* coming before; earlier: *prior generations of man.*
prior to, coming before in time, order, or importance; earlier than; before: *The thought is always prior to the fact* (Emerson). *An agreement was reached prior to the outbreak of the war.*
[< Latin *prior, -ōris* former, earlier, superior]
—**Syn.** See **previous.**

pri·or[2] (prī′ər), *n.* **1.** the head of a priory or monastery for men. Priors usually rank below abbots. **2.** the superior of a house of canons regular or of friars. **3.** a chief magistrate, as in the medieval republic of Florence. [Old English *prior* < Medieval Latin, noun use of Latin *prior, -ōris* prior, superior]

prior art, the earlier patents or inventions that bar a proposed invention from becoming patentable.

pri·or·ate (prī′ər it), *n.* **1.** the office, rank, or time of service of a prior. **2.** a priory.

pri·or·ess (prī′ər is), *n.* the head of a convent or priory for women. Prioresses usually rank below abbesses.

pri·or·i·ty (prī ôr′ə tē, -or′-), *n., pl.* **-ties.** **1.** a being earlier in time. **2.** a coming before in order or importance: *Fire engines and ambulances have priority over other traffic.* **3.** *U.S.* a rating entitling the holder to first, or early, claim on money, facilities, materials, transportation, etc., given to persons or things in order of importance: *A system of priorities for spending on weapons and equipment in the next decade has been sketched by the defence department* (Vancouver Sun). **4.** a preferential position allotted to any project, research, development, etc., which gives it first claim to the necessary resources.
—**Syn. 2.** precedence.

pri·or·ship (prī′ər ship), *n.* the office, rank, or time of service of a prior.

pri·o·ry (prī′ər ē), *n., pl.* **-ries.** **1.** a religious house governed by a prior or prioress. A priory is often, but not necessarily, dependent on an abbey. **2.** a priorate. [Middle English *priorie* < Anglo-French, apparently learned borrowing from Medieval Latin *prioria* < *prior* prior, officer of a monastery]

pris·can (pris′kən), *adj.* primitive. [< Latin *priscus* old + English *-an*]

Pris·ci·an (prish′ē ən, prish′ən), *n.*
break Priscian's head, to violate the rules of grammar: [*They*] *hold no sin so deeply red, As that of breaking Priscian's head* (Samuel Butler).
[< *Priscian,* about 500-530, an author of a Latin grammar]

Pris·co·line (pris′kə lēn, -lin), *n. Trademark.* a drug used to relax or dilate blood vessels and as a heart stimulant in the treatment of high blood pressure and related conditions: *Victims of painful bursitis are being relieved by Priscoline, a powerful dilator of tiny blood vessels* (Newsweek). *Formula:* $C_{10}H_{12}N_2$

prise (prīz), *v.t.,* **prised, pris·ing,** *n. Especially British.* prize[4].

pris·iad·ka (pris yäd′kə), *n.* a step of Slavic folk dancing, in which the legs are alternately kicked out and retracted, and the weight is supported on the retracted leg in a squatting position: *Silver statuettes of men dancing the prisiadka . . . were made near Kiev in the sixth century* (Listener). [< Russian *prisyadka*]

prism (priz′əm), *n.* **1.** a solid whose bases or ends have the same size and shape and are parallel to one another, and each of whose sides has two pairs of parallel edges: *A six-sided pencil before it is sharpened has the shape of one kind of prism.* **2.** a transparent prism, usually with three-sided ends, that separates white light passing through it into the colors of the rainbow. See also picture under **spectroscope.** **3.** a crystal form consisting of three or more planes parallel to the vertical axis of the crystal.
[< Late Latin *prisma* < Greek *prîsma, -atos* (originally) a thing sawed off < *prízein* to saw, earlier *prī́ein*]

Prisms
Left, (def. 1); right, (def. 2)

pris·mat·ic (priz mat′ik), *adj.* **1.** of or like a prism: *These hoods were fitted with prismatic lenses having their broad bases outward* (Scientific American). **2.** formed by a transparent prism. **3.** varied in color. [< Greek *prîsma, -atos* prism + English *-ic*]
—**Syn. 3.** polychrome.

pris·mat·i·cal (priz mat′ə kəl), *adj.* prismatic.

pris·mat·i·cal·ly (priz mat′ə klē), *adv.* by, or as if by, a prism: *His colour changed almost prismatically* (Thomas Medwin).

prismatic colors, the colors formed when white light is passed through a prism; red, orange, yellow, green, blue, indigo, and violet. These are the colors of the rainbow.

prismatic layer, the middle layer of the shell of most mollusks.

prism binoculars, binoculars in which two pairs of triangular prisms are introduced to shorten the length of the apparatus and form an erect image: *It takes additional lenses* (*or prisms*) *to form an erected field as in a spyglass or prism binoculars . . .* (Bernhard, Bennett, and Rice).

pris·moid (priz′moid), *n.* a solid like a prism except that one end is smaller than the other. [< *prism* + *-oid*]

pris·moi·dal (priz moi′dəl), *adj.* of or having to do with the form of a prismoid.

pris·my (priz′mē), *adj.* prismatic: *They saw the prismy hues in thin spray showers* (John Greenleaf Whittier).

pris·on (priz′ən), *n.* **1.** a public building in which criminals are confined: *In a Boise courtroom last week, five more men were sentenced to prison* (Time). **2.** any place where a person or animal is shut up against his will: *The small apartment was a prison to the big dog, and he longed to be back on the farm.*
—*v.t.* to imprison.
[Middle English *prisun,* alteration of Old French *preson* (originally) act of detaining < Latin *prehēnsiō, -ōnis* a seizing, arrest < *prehendere* seize] —**pris′on·like′,** *adj.*
—**Syn.** *n.* **1.** penitentiary.

prison breach or **breaking,** *Law.* a prison break.

prison break, a breaking and going out of prison by one lawfully confined therein.

prison camp, a camp used for the confinement of prisoners, especially prisoners of war or political prisoners.

pris·on·er (priz′ə nər, priz′nər), *n.* **1.** a person who is kept shut up against his will or who is not free to move: *An untimely ague stay'd me a prisoner in my chamber* (Shakespeare). **2.** a prisoner of war: *The enemy prisoners were interned in prison camps.* **3.** a person arrested and held for trial.

prisoner of war, a person captured by the enemy in war: *Relations between West Germany and the Soviet Union could never be genuinely normal unless Germans still held as prisoners of war by Communist countries were returned* (London Times). *Abbr.:* POW (no periods).

prisoners' base, an old game for children, a form of tag.

prison house, **1.** a house or place of imprisonment; prison. **2.** imprisonment; confinement: *. . . to escape from the prison house of London streets and factories* (London Daily Chronicle).

pris·si·ly (pris′ə lē), *adv. U.S. Informal.* in a prissy manner: *He dies . . . of what the picture prissily describes as "an incurable disease"* (Time).

pris·si·ness (pris′ē nis), *n. U.S. Informal.* a sissified, fussy primness.

pris·sy (pris′ē), *adj.,* **-si·er, -si·est.** *U.S. Informal.* **1.** too precise and fussy: *For nearly three hours Burdett—poised, precise, prissy—detailed his secret career as a Communist and a spy* (Time). **2.** too easily shocked; overnice: *a prissy mama's boy.* [American English, perhaps humorous alteration of *precise,* or *precious*]

pris·tine (pris′tēn, -tin, -tīn), *adj.* as it was in its earliest time or state; original; primitive: *The colors of the paintings inside the pyramid had kept their pristine freshness in spite of their age. Much of Congress' effort in the security field since 1946 has been spent in the endeavor to retain the pristine secrecy of atomic energy information* (Bulletin of Atomic Scientists). [< Latin *pristinus* < *prīs-,* stem related to *prīmus* first]
—**Syn.** primeval, primordial.

prith·ee (priᴛʜ′ē), *interj. Archaic.* I pray thee: *Prithee, come hither. Prithee, young one, who art thou?* (Hawthorne). [earlier *preythe* (literally) reduction of (*I*) *pray thee*]

prit·tle-prat·tle (prit′əl prat′əl), *n. Archaic.* empty, trifling talk; chatter. [varied reduplication of *prattle*]

priv., privative.

pri·va·cy (prī′və sē; *British also* priv′ə sē), *n., pl.* **-cies.** **1.** the condition of being private; being away from others; seclusion: *in the privacy of one's home.* **2.** the absence of publicity; secrecy: *He told me his reasons in strict privacy.* **3.** a private matter: *So few of the new generation seemed aware that there were any privacies left to respect* (Edith Wharton).
privacies, private places; places of retreat: *Beautiful glooms . . . Wildwood privacies* (Sidney Lanier).
—**Syn. 1.** solitude. **2.** concealment.

Pri·vat·do·cent or **pri·vat·do·cent** (prē vät′dō tsent′), *n., pl.* **-do·cen·ten** (-dō tsen′tən). (in German universities) a teacher or lecturer recognized by the university, but paid by students' fees: *For 12 years he was on the staff of the Hamburg Observatory and towards the end of that period was also privatdocent at the University of Hamburg* (Scientific American). [< German *Privatdocent* < *privat* private (because he was not on the state payroll) + *Docent,* or *Dozent* teacher < Latin *docēns, -entis,* present participle of *docēre* to teach]

Pri·vat·do·zent (prē vät′dō tsent′), *n., pl.* **-do·zen·ten** (-dō tsen′tən). Privatdocent.

pri·vate (prī′vit), *adj.* **1.** not for the public; for just a few special people or for one: *a private car, a private house, a private letter.* **2.** not public; individual; personal: *the private life of a king, my private opinion.* **3.** confidential; secret: *News which reached him through private channels* (Macaulay). *Placing the purse . . . in a private pocket, our traveller strode gallantly on through the wood* (Scott). **4.** secluded: *some private corner.* **5.** alone: *He wishes to be private.* **6.** having no public office: *a private citizen.*
—*n.* **1.** a common soldier, not an officer; a soldier or marine of the lowest rank: *to be promoted from private to corporal. Abbr.:* Pvt. **2.** *Obsolete.* a private citizen. **3.** *Obsolete.* a private or personal matter.
in private, a. not publicly: *They do desire some speech with you in private* (Ben Jonson). **b.** secretly: *Confess they do, but not greatly in private* (George Sandys).
[< Latin *prīvātus* apart from the public life, private, past participle of *prīvāre* deprive, free, release from < *prīvus* one's own, single, individual. Doublet of PRIVY.] —**pri′vate·ness,** *n.*
—**Syn.** *adj.* **4.** isolated. **5.** solitary.

private bank, a bank conducted by an individual or group of individuals on an unincorporated basis.

private bill, (in the House of Representatives and the House of Commons) a bill or act affecting the interests of a particular individual or corporation only: *He will also take immediate charge of a large engineering section whose duties will include . . . matters arising from Private Bills in Parliament* (Sunday Times).

private detective, a detective who is employed by private citizens for certain specified lawful purposes; detective not on the public payroll.

private enterprise, **1.** the business of a person, company, etc., of making and selling things, as contrasted with government control: *And there are those of us who feel the Government has already eaten too much of the pie of private enterprise—to the point of indigestion* (Wall Street Journal). **2.** an economic system based on such individual enterprise.

pri·va·teer (prī′və tir′), *n.* **1.** an armed ship owned by private persons and holding a government commission to attack and capture enemy ships: *There were perhaps 3,700 scattered privateers serving as the great bulk of the American Navy* (Newsweek). **2.** the commander or one of the crew of a privateer. —*v.i.* to cruise as a privateer. [< *privat*(e) + *-eer*]

pri·va·teers·man (prī′və tirz′mən), *n., pl.* **-men.** an officer or sailor of a privateer.

private eye, *Slang.* a private detective: *The "private eye" of fiction is a lean and dashing type* (New York Times).

private first class, *U.S.* the higher of the two grades of private in the Marine

Corps and the Army, having an insigne of one chevron. *Abbr.:* Pfc.

pri·vate-la·bel (prī′vit lā′bəl), *adj.* (of merchandise) bearing the brand or label of the company offering it for retail sale rather than the brand of the manufacturer or processor.

private law, that branch of the law which deals with the rights and duties of persons in their relations with one another as private individuals.

pri·vate·ly (prī′vit lē), *adv.* in a private manner; not publicly; secretly: *She had been privately married to him above a fortnight* (Joseph Addison).

private member, *British.* a member of the House of Commons who is not a member of the Ministry or an active leader of the opposition party; back-bencher: *The Speaker ruled that an issue of this sort, except when it concerned the police in London, could only be raised in a bill or on a private member's motion* (Economist).

private of the army, *U.S.* an enlisted man in the Army below private first class and above recruit.

Private Res., *U.S.* private resolution (used with a number).

private school, **1.** *U.S.* an educational institution, as a preparatory school or parochial school, owned and operated by other than a government authority. **2.** *British.* a school owned and operated by a person or persons for private profit.

➤ **Private school, public school** mean very different things in the United States and Great Britain. In Great Britain, a "public school" is one of the schools such as Eton, Harrow, and Winchester, that operates under a royal charter as a private foundation; such schools would be called "private schools" in the United States. The British equivalent of the American "public school" is the "council school" or any of various other institutions owned and operated by a public authority and supported by public funds.

pri·vate-wire system (prī′vit wīr′), a telephone or teletype system privately operated.

pri·va·tion (prī vā′shən), *n.* **1.** a lack of the comforts or of the necessities of life: *Many people died because of privation during the war. The Parisians had had five months of siege, were reduced to the direst privation, and saw France . . . now bound over to the Germans by the Republic* (Edmund Wilson). **2.** loss; absence; being deprived: *Privation of the company of all other human beings is a serious hardship.* **3.** *Logic.* the loss or absence of a quality; negative quality. [< Latin *prīvātiō, -ōnis* < *prīvāre* to deprive; see PRIVATE]

—**Syn. 1.** need, destitution.

pri·vat·ism (prī′və tiz əm), *n. U.S.* avoidance of involvement in matters outside of one's own private life; retreat into privacy.

priv·a·tive (priv′ə tiv), *adj.* **1.** *Grammar and Logic.* expressing deprivation or denial of something. *Un-* is a privative prefix; *never* is a privative word. **2.** *Obsolete.* having the quality of depriving. —*n. Grammar.* a privative prefix or suffix. [< Latin *prīvātīvus* < *prīvāre* to deprive; see PRIVATE] —**priv′a·tive·ly,** *adv.*

priv·et (priv′it), *n.* **1.** either of two bushy evergreen shrubs of the olive family, native to Japan and the Mediterranean region, having smooth, dark-green leaves, and clusters of small, white flowers, succeeded by small, shining black berries. They are much used for hedges. **2.** any of several other related plants, also planted for hedges. **3.** a related shrub, of swamps of the southern United States. [origin unknown]

Privet (def. 1)

priv·i·lege (priv′ə lij, priv′lij), *n., v.,* **-leged, -leg·ing.** —*n.* **1.** a special right, advantage, or favor: *Mr. Jones has given us the privilege of using his television set. Immunity from most laws is the privilege of an ambassador to another country.* **2.** a contract containing an option to buy, sell, or both buy and sell.

—*v.t.* to give a privilege to.

[< Old French *privilege,* learned borrowing from Latin *prīvilēgum* law applying to one individual < *prīvus* individual, single + *lex, lēgis* law]

—**Syn.** *n.* **1. Privilege, prerogative** mean a special right. **Privilege** means a special right given to a person as a favor or due him because of his position, age, sex, citizenship, etc., that often gives him an advantage over others: *Alumni have the privilege of buying football tickets at special rates.* **Prerogative** means a privilege or legal right belonging to a person by birth, office, position, etc., which always places him before or above others: *Changing her mind is often jokingly called a woman's prerogative.*

priv·i·leged (priv′ə lijd, priv′lijd), *adj.* **1.** having some privilege or privileges: *The nobility in Europe was a privileged class.* **2.** not subject to court action, as for slander: *Words spoken by a Senator on the Senate floor are privileged.*

privileged communication, *Law.* a communication which a witness cannot legally be compelled to disclose.

priv·i·ly (priv′ə lē), *adv.* in a private manner; secretly: *He took him aside, and told him the news privily and briefly* (Edward A. Freeman). —**Syn.** confidentially.

priv·i·ty (priv′ə tē), *n., pl.* **-ties. 1.** private knowledge: *There had been five . . . attempts to assassinate the Prince, all of them with the privity of the Spanish government* (John L. Motley). **2.** complicity. **3.** a legally recognized relation between two people, as that of owner and tenant or employer and servant. [< Old French *privite,* and *privete* < *prive* privy]

priv·y (priv′ē), *adj., n., pl.* **priv·ies.** —*adj.* **1.** private: *What I may do . . . must remain privy* (Punch). **2.** *Archaic.* hidden; secret. **privy to,** having secret or private knowledge of: *At that time the Vice President was not privy to whatever reasoning formulated White House decisions* (Wall Street Journal).

—*n.* **1.** a small outhouse used as a toilet: *He introduced soakage pits and compost heaps, improved wells, and privies* (Atlantic). **2.** a person who has a legal interest or part in any action or is directly affected by it.

[< Old French *prive* < Latin *prīvātus* private; as noun, a private friend or place. Doublet of PRIVATE.]

privy chamber, **1.** a private apartment in a royal residence, as in Great Britain. **2.** *Archaic.* a room reserved for the private or exclusive use of some particular person or persons.

privy council, a group of personal advisers to a ruler or other person of high rank or authority.

Privy Council, **1.** (in Great Britain) the body of persons acting as personal advisers to the sovereign in matters of state, the welfare of the Crown, or the security of the realm. Most of its duties are now performed by the cabinet or committees of Parliament. **2.** a similar body of advisers, as in certain British Commonwealth nations or colonies and in Japan until it was abolished in 1947. [< *privy council*]

privy councillor, *Especially British.* privy councilor.

privy councilor, a member of a privy council.

privy purse, an allowance for the private expenses of the British sovereign.

privy seal, (in Great Britain) the seal affixed to grants, etc., that were afterwards to receive the great seal, and to documents that did not require the great seal.

prix (prē), *n. French.* prize; price.

Prix de Rome (prē′ də rōm′), an annual prize awarded by the French government to a student in the fine arts for four years' study in Rome. [< French *Prix de Rome* (literally) prize of Rome]

prix fixe (prē′ fēks′), *French.* **1.** a meal served at a fixed price; table d'hôte: *For the three-thousand-franc prix fixe, the lobster was succulent, the champagne dry . . . the gossip unbridled* (New Yorker). **2.** the price of such a meal. **3.** (literally) fixed price.

prize[1] (prīz), *n.* **1.** a reward won after trying against other people: *Prizes will be given for the three best stories.* **2.** any reward worth working for: *The beautiful Miss Mannering, of high family, with an Indian fortune, was a prize worth looking after* (Scott). **3.** *Archaic.* an advantage; privilege: *It is war's prize to take all vantages* (Shakespeare).

—*adj.* **1.** given as a prize: *All the prize ribbons handed out at shows held in accordance with the A.K.C.'s regulations . . . must bear the facsimile of its corporate seal* (New Yorker). **2.** that has won a prize. **3.** worthy of a prize: *prize vegetables.*

[alteration of Middle English *pris;* see PRICE[1]]

—**Syn.** *n.* **1.** award, premium.

prize[2] (prīz), *n., v.,* **prized, priz·ing.** —*n.* a thing or person that is taken or captured, especially an enemy's ship and its cargo taken at sea.

—*v.t.* to capture as a prize.

[Middle English *prise* < Old French, seizure, alteration of Vulgar Latin *prēsa,* ultimately < Latin *prehendere* to seize]

prize[3] (prīz), *v.t.,* **prized, priz·ing. 1.** to value highly; think much of: *She prizes her best china.* **2.** to estimate the value of; appraise.

[Middle English *prisen* < Old French *prisier,* variant of *preisier* < Late Latin *pretiāre* < Latin *pretium* prize, reward, price. Doublet of PRAISE.]

—**Syn. 1.** esteem. **2.** rate.

prize[4] (prīz), *v.,* **prized, priz·ing,** *n.* —*v.t. Especially British.* to raise or move by force; pry.

—*n.* **1.** the act of prizing; leverage. **2.** *Dialect.* an instrument used for prizing; lever. Also, *especially British,* **prise.**

[Middle English *prize* a lever < Old French *prise* a taking hold, grasp; see PRIZE[2]]

prize court, a court that makes decisions concerning ships and other property captured at sea during a war.

prize fight, a boxing match that people pay money to see.

prize fighter, a man who boxes for money.

prize fighting, boxing for pay.

prize·giv·ing (prīz′giv′ing), *n. British.* a ceremony at which prizes are awarded: *We were crowded up rather in the manner of a school prizegiving* (London Times).

prize·man (prīz′mən), *n., pl.* **-men.** *Especially British.* the winner of a prize, especially in a college or school: *a prizeman in classics.*

prize money, money obtained by the sale of ships and other property captured at sea in the course of a war. Prize money is sometimes divided among those who made the capture.

priz·er (prī′zər), *n. Archaic.* a person who competes for a prize.

prize ring, **1.** a square space enclosed by ropes, used for prize fights. **2.** prize fighting.

prize·win·ner (prīz′win′ər), *n.* a person or thing that wins a prize: *A biochemist and Nobel prizewinner . . . he said he was optimistic about man's adaptability to a changing environment* (London Times).

prize·win·ning (prīz′win′ing), *adj.* that has won a prize: *a prizewinning novel, a prizewinning cake at a fair.*

prize·wor·thy (prīz′wėr′ᴛʜē), *adj.* deserving of a prize: *Their desk is similarly prizeworthy and suitable for home use* (New Yorker).

pro[1] (prō), *adv., n., pl.* **pros.** —*adv.* in favor of; for. —*n.* **1.** a reason in favor of. The pros and cons of a question are the arguments for and against it. **2. a.** a person who votes in favor of something. **b.** an affirmative vote.

[abstracted from *pro and con,* or independent use of *pro-*[1]]

pro[2] (prō), *n., pl.* **pros,** *adj. Slang.* professional: *Television also has its circus of seasoned pros whom one sees week after week* (Listener). *Early in his pro career Moore had difficulty getting fights in this country* (New York Times).

pro[3] (prō), *prep. Latin.* before; for; forth.

pro-[1], *prefix.* **1.** forward, as in *proceed, project.*

2. forth; out, as in *prolong, proclaim.*

3. on the side of; in favor of; in behalf of, as in *pro-British, proclerical.*

4. in place of; acting as, as in *pronoun, proconsul.*

[< Latin *prō-,* prefix, and *prō,* preposition, or adverb]

pro-[2], *prefix* before; in front of, as in *prologue, proscenium.*

[< Greek *pro-* < *pró,* preposition, before, forward]

PRO (no periods) or **P.R.O.,** (in the armed forces) Public Relations Officer: *Those who get in his way . . . end up as small-time P.R.O.s at remote Engineer Corps posts* (New Yorker).

pro·a (prō′ə), *n.* a swift Malay sailing boat built with one side flat and balanced by an outrigger. [earlier *parao* < Malay *parahu;* spelling influenced by English *prow* and Portuguese *proa* prow]

Proa

pro-Al·ly (prō′-al′ī, -ə lī′), *adj.* supporting the Allies in either World War I or World War II.

prob., 1. a. probable. **b.** probably. **2.** probate. **3.** problem.

prob·a·bi·lism (prob′ə bə liz′əm), *n.* **1.** the philosophical doctrine that certainty is impossible and that probability suffices to govern faith and practice. **2.** (in the Roman Catholic Church) the doctrine that where authorities differ as to the lawfulness of an action, either opinion may be followed.

prob·a·bi·list (prob′ə bə list), *n.* a person who holds the doctrine of probabilism.

prob·a·bi·lis·tic (prob′ə bə lis′tik), *adj.* **1.** of probabilists or probabilism in theology. **2.** likely and useful; practical although not completely provable: *Clausius, Maxwell, and Boltzmann showed how to derive the laws of gases from probabilistic assumptions about the behavior of individual molecules* (Scientific American).

prob·a·bil·i·ty (prob′ə bil′ə tē), *n., pl.* **-ties. 1.** the quality or fact of being likely or probable; chance: *There is a probability that school will close a week earlier than usual.* **2.** something likely to happen: *A storm is one of the probabilities for tomorrow.* **3.** the ratio $\frac{p}{p+q}$ where p is the probable number of occurrences and q is the probable number of nonoccurrences: *But this process proved to be one that was regulated by chance and the laws of probability rather than by the causal or determinative principles* (Atlantic).

in all probability, probably: . . . *these cliffs corresponding in all probability to ancient lines of fault* (Samuel Haughton).

probability curve, *Statistics.* a bell-shaped curve; normal curve. See **normal curve** for picture.

prob·a·ble (prob′ə bəl), *adj.* **1.** likely to happen: *Cooler weather is probable after this shower.* **2.** likely to be true: *Something he ate is the probable cause of his pain.* **3.** affording ground for belief: *probable evidence.* [< Latin *probābilis* < *probāre* to try, test; see PROVE]

probable cause, *Law.* good reason for assuming that a charge has sufficient evidence.

probable error, *Statistics.* the amount by which the arithmetical mean of a sample is expected to vary because of chance alone: *The probable error means that in sampling data some error is bound to occur* (Emory S. Bogardus).

prob·a·bly (prob′ə blē), *adv.* more likely than not: *He will probably refuse the offer.* —**Syn.** presumably.

pro·bang (prō′bang), *n. Medicine.* a slender, elastic rod tipped with a sponge, ball, or the like, used to remove foreign bodies from the esophagus, etc. [earlier *provang;* influenced by *probe*]

pro·bate (prō′bāt), *n., adj., v.,* **-bat·ed, -bat·ing.** *Law.* —*n.* **1.** the official proving of a will as genuine. **2.** a true copy of a will with a certificate that it has been proved genuine.
—*adj.* of or concerned with the probating of wills or a probate court: *a probate judge.*
—*v.t.* to prove by legal process the genuineness of (a will).
[< Latin *probātum,* neuter past participle of *probāre* prove, test, consider good]

probate court, a court concerned with the probate of wills, settlement of estates, etc.

pro·ba·tion (prō bā′shən), *n.* **1.** a trial or testing of conduct, character, qualifications, etc.: *the general doctrine of religion, that our present life is a state of probation for a future one* (Joseph Butler). *After a period of probation a novice becomes a nun.* **2.** any act or process of testing. **3.** the system of letting young offenders against the law, or first offenders, go free without receiving the punishment which they are sentenced to, unless there is a further offense: *The person on probation makes monthly reports, pays the fine . . ., and makes restitution . . . to the person or persons injured by him* (Emory S. Bogardus). **4.** (in some colleges, universities, etc.) a status or period of trial for students who have failing marks, have broken rules, etc. **5.** proof; demonstration. [< Latin *probātiō, -ōnis* a proving < *probāre* prove, test, consider good]

pro·ba·tion·al (prō bā′shə nəl), *adj.* probationary.

pro·ba·tion·ar·y (prō bā′shə ner′ē), *adj.* **1.** of or having to do with probation: *Pythagoras . . . required from those he instructed in philosophy a probationary silence of five years* (Samuel Johnson). **2.** on probation: *The College elected him probationary Fellow* (W.J. Courthope).

pro·ba·tion·er (prō bā′shə nər), *n.* a person who is on probation. —**Syn.** novice, novitiate.

pro·ba·tion·er·ship (prō bā′shə nər ship), *n.* the condition or period of a probationer.

probation officer, *Law.* an officer appointed to supervise offenders who have been placed on probation.

pro·ba·tive (prō′bə tiv, prob′ə-), *adj.* **1.** giving proof or evidence: . . . *the probative fact* (Jeremy Bentham). **2.** for a trial or test: *Some are only probative, and designed to . . . stir up those virtues which before lay dormant in the soul* (Robert South). —**Syn. 1.** demonstrative.

pro·ba·to·ry (prō′bə tôr′ē, -tōr′-), *adj.* probative: . . . *probatory chastisements* (John Bramhall).

probe (prōb), *v.,* **probed, prob·ing,** *n.* —*v.t.* **1.** to search into; examine thoroughly; investigate: *to probe a person's thoughts or feelings to find out why he acted as he did. Man in his unquenchable thirst for oil has probed ever deeper into the desert wastes of the Middle East* (Newsweek). **2.** to examine with a probe. **3.** *Military.* to test the strength or defenses of (the enemy), as by a raid, etc.: *An enemy unit of undetermined strength briefly probed a central sector position* (New York Times). —*v.i.* to search; penetrate: *to probe into the causes of crime. We searched our minds in long discussions late each night and didn't spare each other as we probed for answers* (Norman Cousins). [< noun]
—*n.* **1.** a thorough examination; investigation: *a probe into juvenile delinquency.* **2.** *U.S.* an investigation, usually by a legislative body or a committee of its members in an effort to discover evidences of law violation: *An energetic, youthful trustbuster will guide the Senate probe* (Wall Street Journal). **3.** a slender instrument with a rounded end for exploring the depth or direction of a wound, a cavity in the body, etc. **4.** a rocket, satellite, etc., carrying scientific instruments, to record or report back information about space, other planets, etc.: *Probes which will pass in the vicinity of either Venus or Mars . . . are now well within the reach of rocket technology* (Harper's). **5.** *Military.* a testing of the strength or defenses of the enemy: *Light enemy probes and scattered patrol contacts have been reported* (New York Times). **6.** a projecting pipelike device on an airplane which receives the fuel from a tanker plane when refueling in flight.
[< Late Latin *proba* a proof < Latin *probāre* prove. Doublet of PROOF.] —**prob′er,** *n.* —**prob′ing·ly,** *adv.*
—**Syn.** *v.t.* **1.** scrutinize.

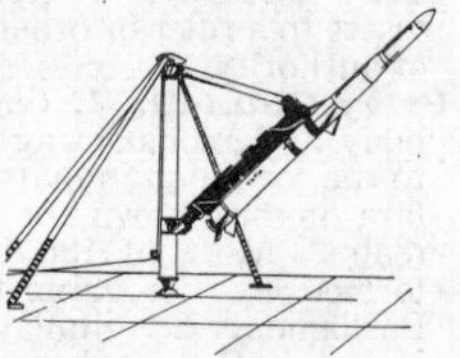
Probe (def. 4)
U.S.A.F.'s Blue Scout Jr. tests launch techniques.

probe-and-drogue (prōb′ən drōg′), *n.* a method of refueling planes in flight. The plane to be refueled sends out a flexible hose (probe) into a funnel-shaped device (drogue) of a tanker plane to receive fuel.

pro·ben·e·cid (prō ben′ə sid), *n.* a drug stimulating the excretion of uric acid, used in treating gouty arthritis and other conditions. *Formula:* $C_{13}H_{19}NO_4S$

pro·bi·ty (prō′bə tē, prob′ə-), *n.* high principle; uprightness; honesty: *a man of unquestioned probity.* [< Latin *probitās* < *probus* righteous, proper, worthy] —**Syn.** integrity, rectitude.

prob·lem (prob′ləm), *n.* **1.** a question; difficult question: *In biology there is still the problem of the basic chemistry of life* (Atlantic). **2.** a matter of doubt or difficulty: *This important constitutional problem* [*must not*] *remain clouded in doubt* (Newsweek). **3.** something to be worked out: *a problem in arithmetic.*
—*adj.* **1.** that causes difficulty: *a problem child.* **2.** having a plot based on a problem, especially a problem of social conduct, relationship, or responsibility: *a problem novel.* [< Latin *problēma* < Greek *próblēma, -atos* < *probállein* propose, put forth < *pro-* forward + *bállein* to throw]

prob·lem·at·ic (prob′lə mat′ik), *adj.* having the nature of a problem; doubtful; uncertain; questionable: *What the weather will be is often problematic.* [< Late Latin *problematicus* < Greek *problēmatikós* < *próblēma, -atos* problem] —**prob′lem·at′i·cal·ly,** *adv.* —**Syn.** dubious, disputable.

prob·lem·at·i·cal (prob′lə mat′ə kəl), *adj.* problematic.

prob·lem·ist (prob′lə mist), *n.* a person who makes up or solves problems in chess, mathematics, etc.

pro bo·no pu·bli·co (prō bō′nō pub′lə kō), *Latin.* for the public welfare: *Unfortunately, children can be neither fed nor educated . . . by man's prestige or gratification in doing something pro bono publico* (Harper's).

pro·bos·cid·e·an or **pro·bos·cid·i·an** (prō′bə sid′ē ən), *adj.* **1.** belonging to or having to do with the order consisting of the elephants and similar animals now extinct. **2. a.** having a proboscis. **b.** having to do with or like a proboscis. —*n.* an elephant, mammoth, etc. [< New Latin *Proboscidea* the order name (< Latin *proboscis, -idis* proboscis) + English *-an*]

pro·bos·cis (prō bos′is), *n., pl.* **-bos·cis·es, -bos·ci·des** (-bos′ə dēz). **1.** an elephant's trunk. **2.** a long, flexible snout, as of the tapir or certain monkeys. **3.** the mouth parts of some insects developed to great length for sucking: *the proboscis of a fly or a mosquito.* **4.** any similar organ, as: **a.** an organ of many worms, as annelids and nemerteans, usually eversible and opening above the mouth. **b.** the tongue of certain gastropods. **5.** *Humorous.* a person's nose. [< Latin *proboscis, -idis* < Greek *proboskís, -ídos* (literally) a means for taking in food < *pró* forth + *bóskein* to feed, nourish]

proboscis monkey, a large, long-tailed monkey of Borneo, having a long nose.

Head of Proboscis Monkey

proc., 1. proceedings. **2.** process.

pro·ca·cious (prō kā′shəs), *adj.* bold; forward; pert: . . . *a vain, proud, procacious, tempting mind* (Richard Baxter). [< Latin *procāx, -cācis* (with English *-ous*) < *procāre* ask]

pro·cac·i·ty (prō kas′ə tē), *n.* impudence; petulance.

pro·caine amide (prō kān′, prō′kān), a compound related to procaine hydrochloride, used in the treatment of arrhythmia. *Formula:* $C_{13}H_{21}ON_3$

procaine hydrochloride, a local anesthetic, similar to, but much less toxic than, cocaine; Novocaine. *Formula:* $C_{13}H_{20}N_2O_2 \cdot HCl$

pro·cam·bi·al (prō kam′bē əl), *adj.* of the procambium.

pro·cam·bi·um (prō kam′bē əm), *n. Botany.* any undifferentiated tissue from which the vascular bundles are developed. [< New Latin *procambium* < *pro-* pro-[1] + *cambium* cambium]

pro·carp (prō′kärp), *n.* the female sex organ of certain algae and fungi. [< New Latin *procarpium* < Greek *pró* pro-[2] + *karpós* fruit]

pro·ca·the·dral (prō′kə thē′drəl), *n.* a church used temporarily as a cathedral.

pro·ce·den·do (prō′sə den′dō), *n., pl.* **-dos.** *Law.* a writ of a superior court commanding a subordinate court to proceed to judgment. [< Latin *prōcēdendo (ad jūdicium)* (literally) proceeding (to judgment) < *prōcēdere* to proceed]

pro·ce·dur·al (prə sē′jər əl), *adj.* of or having to do with procedure: *The recommendations the Commission made . . . were purely procedural ones* (New Yorker). —**pro·ce′dur·al·ly,** *adv.*

pro·ce·dure (prə sē′jər), *n.* **1.** a way of proceeding; method of doing things: *What is your procedure in making bread?* **2.** the customary manners or ways of conducting some business: *parliamentary procedure, legal procedure.* **3.** *Obsolete.* the going on of an action; progress; course. [< Middle French *procédure* < Old French *proceder* to proceed, learned borrowing from Latin *prōcēdere*]

pro·ceed (*v.* prə sēd′; *n.* prō′sēd), *v.i.* **1.** to go on after having stopped; move forward: *Please proceed with your story.* **2.** to be carried on; take place: *The trial may proceed.* **3.** to carry on any activity: *He proceeded to light his pipe.* **4.** to come forth; issue; go out: *Heat proceeds from fire.* **5.** to advance to a higher status: *to proceed to master of arts.* **6.** to begin and carry on an action at law: *Though rebellion is declared, it is not proceeded against as such* (Edmund Burke).

—*n.* **proceeds,** money obtained from a sale, etc.: *The proceeds from the school play will be used to buy a new curtain for the stage.*

[< Latin *prōcēdere* < *prō-* forward + *cēdere* to move] —**pro·ceed′er,** *n.*

—**Syn.** *v.i.* **1.** progress. See **advance. 4.** emanate. —**Ant.** *v.i.* **1.** stop, halt, pause.

pro·ceed·ing (prə sē′ding), *n.* action; conduct; what is done; performance: *He wrote a memorandum, pointing out the unconstitutional nature of Lord Melbourne's proceedings . . .* (Lytton Strachey).

proceedings, a. the action in a case in a law court: *Having already as much law proceedings on his hands as he could manage . . .* (James H. Monk). **b.** a record of what was done at the meetings of a society, club, etc.; minutes: *Proceedings of the Philological Society* (a title). *Abbr.:* proc.

—**Syn.** dealing, doing.

proc·e·leus·mat·ic (pros′ə lüs mat′ik), *adj.* **1.** inciting; inspiring: *a proceleusmatic song.* **2.** of, having to do with, or consisting of a metrical foot of four short syllables, or verse containing such feet. —*n.* a metrical foot of four short syllables. [< Late Latin *proceleusmaticus* < Greek *prokeleusmatikós* < *prokeleúein* rouse to action beforehand < *pró* before + *keleúein* to urge]

proc·el·lar·i·an (pros′ə lãr′ē ən), *adj.* of or having to do with a group of sea birds that includes the petrels and related birds. [< New Latin *Procellaria* the genus name (< Latin *procella* storm) + English *-an*]

pro·ce·phal·ic (prō′sə fal′ik), *adj.* having to do with or forming the forepart of the head: *procephalic processes, the procephalic lobe.* [< *pro-*² + Greek *kephalḗ* head + English *-ic*]

proc·ess¹ (pros′es; *especially British* prō′ses), *n.* **1.** a set of actions or changes in a special order: *the process of reading, a process of decay. By what process or processes is cloth made from wool?* **2.** a part that grows out or sticks out: *the process of a bone.* **3.** a written command or summons to appear in a law court. **4.** the proceedings in a legal case or action. **5.** forward movement; progress; course: *Saturnian Juno now, with double care, Attends the fatal process of the war* (John Dryden).

in process, a. in the course or condition: *In process of time the house will be finished.* **b.** in the course or condition of being done: *The author has just finished one book and has another in process.*

—*v.t.* **1.** to treat, prepare, or handle by some special method: *to process fruit and vegetables for market. Computing machines process information very quickly. [Fort] Dix . . . processes men for overseas duty and on their return to this country* (New York Times). **2.** to start legal action against, especially by serving a process on.

—*adj.* treated or prepared by some special method.

[< Old French *proces* a journey, going < Latin *prōcessus, -ūs* progress < *prōcēdere* to proceed] —**Syn.** *n.* **1.** procedure, operation.

➔ The plural of **process** is regular and pronounced (pros′e siz). The pronunciation (pros′ə sēz), apparently on the analogy of *indices, analyses,* etc., is not in established use.

pro·cess² (prə ses′), *v.i. British.* to go, walk, or march in procession: *The pilgrims process energetically around the courtyard with their candles . . . led by jolly bearded monks* (Manchester Guardian Weekly). [back formation < *procession*]

process cheese, a cheese mixture prepared by melting various hard cheeses, especially cheddars, emulsifying them, and mixing them with whey, water, tartrate and phosphate salts, or other ingredients.

proc·essed cheese (pros′est), process cheese.

process heat, heat produced for industrial or commercial use: *The reactors can take over the job of supplying process heat . . . and space heat which account for half the energy consumed in the U.S.* (Time).

proc·ess·ing tax (pros′əs ing), a federal tax placed on processes involved in handling certain commodities, especially agricultural commodities.

pro·ces·sion (prə sesh′ən), *n.* **1.** something that moves forward; persons marching or riding: *a procession of ants. A funeral procession filled the street.* **2.** an orderly moving forward: *We formed lines to march in procession onto the platform.* —*v.i.* to move in procession. [< Late Latin *prōcessiō, -ōnis* a ceremonial marching (in Latin, a marching onwards) < Latin *prōcēdere* to proceed] —**Syn.** *n.* **1.** cortege.

pro·ces·sion·al (prə sesh′ə nəl), *adj.* **1.** of a procession: *Crowds . . . lining the processional route* (Punch). **2.** used or sung in a procession: . . . *the great processional elephant* (B.M. Croker).

—*n.* **1.** processional music: *The choir and clergy marched into the church singing the processional.* **2.** a book containing hymns, litanies, etc., for use in religious processions.

pro·ces·sion·ar·y (prə sesh′ə ner′ē), *adj.* **1.** consisting of a formal or solemn procession. **2.** forming and moving in a procession: *processionary caterpillars.*

proc·es·sor (pros′əs ər; *Especially British* prō′səs ər), *n.* a person who processes, as agricultural produce into marketable condition by cleaning, culling, etc.

process patent, a patent on the method of producing a product.

process printing, a method of printing pictures in color, by which almost any shade can be reproduced from a combination of half-tone plates in red, yellow, blue, and, usually, black.

process server, a person who serves summonses, subpoenas, etc.

pro·cès-ver·bal (prō sā′ver bäl′; *French* prô se′ver bȧl′), *n., pl.* **-baux** (-bō′). **1.** a report of proceedings, as of an assembly; minutes: . . . *when French and American experts would also meet to draw up the procès-verbal of the talks* (London Times). **2.** (in French law) a written account of facts in a criminal or other charge. [< French *procès-verbal* < *procès* process, report of proceedings + *verbal* verbal]

pro·chain (prô shaɴ′), *adj. French.* prochein.

pro·chan·cel·lor (prō chan′sə lər), *n.* a deputy or assistant of the vice-chancellor in certain British universities.

pro·chein (prō′shen), *adj. Law.* nearest; closest; next. [< Anglo-French, Old French *prochain,* or *prucein* < Vulgar Latin *propiānus* < Latin *prope* near to]

pro·cho·os (prō′kō os), *n., pl.* **-cho·oi** (-kō-oi). (in ancient Greece) a pitcherlike vessel, resembling the oinochoe but usually more slender, used for pouring out wine and for pouring water on the hands before a meal. [< Greek *próchoos* < *procheîn* pour forth < *pro-* before + *cheîn* to pour]

pro·chro·nism (prō′krə niz əm), *n.* the assigning of an event to a period earlier than its actual date: *It is a prochronism to talk of the May fly, for . . . the first ten days of June usually constitute the May-fly season* (J.A. Gibbs). [< *pro-*² + Greek *chrónos* time + English *-ism*]

pro·claim (prə klām′, prō-), *v.t.* **1.** to make known publicly and officially; declare publicly: *War was proclaimed. The people proclaimed him king. His actions proclaim his love.* **2. a.** to declare (a person) to be an outlaw; denounce: *I heard myself proclaim'd; And by the happy hollow of a tree escaped the hunt* (Shakespeare). **b.** to subject (a place) to legal restrictions. [< Latin *prōclāmāre* < *prō-* forth + *clāmāre* to shout; spelling influenced by *claim,* verb] —**pro·claim′er,** *n.*

—**Syn. 1.** publish. See **announce.**

proc·la·ma·tion (prok′lə mā′shən), *n.* an official announcement; public declaration: *the President's annual Thanksgiving proclamation. The revolution broke out in France in February, 1848 . . . with the immediate fall of Louis-Philippe and the proclamation of the French Republic* (Edmund Wilson).

—**Syn. Proclamation, edict** mean a notice or order issued by authority. **Proclamation** means an official public announcement by an executive or administrative officer, such as a president, governor, or mayor: *The governor issued a proclamation declaring martial law in the disaster area.* **Edict** means a public order or law proclaimed by the highest authority, usually a decree of a ruler or court with supreme or absolute authority: *The dictator issued an edict seizing the mines.*

pro·clam·a·to·ry (prō klam′ə tôr′ē, -tōr′-), *adj.* in the manner of making a proclamation: *proclamatory style, a proclamatory voice.*

pro·clit·ic (prō klit′ik), *adj.* (of a word) so closely connected with a following word as to have no independent accent. —*n.* a proclitic word. In the following example *to* is a proclitic word: *to see and to do.* [< New Latin *procliticus* < Greek *proklī́nein* bend forward; patterned on Greek *enklitikós* enclitic] —**pro·clit′i·cal·ly,** *adv.*

pro·cliv·i·ty (prō kliv′ə tē), *n., pl.* **-ties.** tendency; inclination; predisposition; leaning; propensity: *The old woman had a proclivity for finding fault. There are many spots in Florida that attract people with a proclivity for uncrowded but urbane resort life* (New Yorker). [< Latin *prōclīvitās* < *prōclīvis* prone to; (literally) sloping, inclining < *prō-* forward + *clīvus* a slope, related to *clīnāre* to bend. Compare ACCLIVITY.] —**Syn.** bias, bent.

pro·clor·per·a·zine (prō′klôr per′ə zēn), *n.* a synthetic drug used as a tranquilizer and to stop vomiting. *Formula:* $C_{20}H_{24}ClN_3S$

Proc·ne (prok′nē), *n. Greek Mythology.* Philomela's sister, who was turned into a swallow.

proc·ni·as (prok′nē as), *n.* any of several cotingas of tropical America, as a variety of northern South America noted for its penetrating, bell-like voice. [< New Latin *procnias* < Latin *Procne* Procne < Greek *Próknē*]

Procnias (7¾ in. long)

pro-Com·mu·nist (prō-kom′yə nist), *adj.* favoring, aligned with, or committed to the Communists or Communism: . . . *the pro-Communist Pathet Lao* (Wall Street Journal). —*n.* a member of a pro-Communist armed forces or political group: *Malaya proposes to prevent pro-Communists among the Singapore Chinese from penetrating the Borneo territories* (New York Times).

pro·con·sul (prō kon′səl), *n.* **1.** a governor or military commander of an ancient Roman province, with duties and powers like a consul's. **2.** the governor of a British or French colony. [< Latin *prōcōnsul,* probably < *prō cōnsule* in place of a consul]

Pro·con·sul (prō kon′səl), *n.* a manlike ape of the Miocene period, which lived in Africa approximately 25,000,000 years ago and is considered by some anthropologists to be an ancestor of man.

pro·con·su·lar (prō kon′sə lər), *adj.* of, having to do with, or governed by a proconsul: *proconsular rule.*

pro·con·su·late (prō kon′sə lit), *n.* the position or term of a proconsul.

pro·con·sul·ship (prō kon′səl ship), *n.* proconsulate.

pro·cras·ti·nate (prō kras′tə nāt), *v.,* **-nat·ed, -nat·ing.** —*v.i., v.t.* to put things off until later; delay; delay repeatedly: *to procrastinate until an opportunity is lost.* [< Latin *prōcrāstināre* (with English *-ate*¹) < *prō-* forward + *crāstinus* belonging to tomorrow < *crās* tomorrow] —**Syn.** defer, postpone.

pro·cras·ti·na·tion (prō kras′tə nā′shən), *n.* the act or habit of putting things off till later; delay: *Procrastination is the thief of time* (Edward Young). —**Syn.** dilatoriness, postponement.

pro·cras·ti·na·tive (prō kras′tə nā′tiv), *adj.* procrastinating; dilatory: *I was too procrastinative and inert while you were still in my neighborhood* (The Critic).

pro·cras·ti·na·tor (prō kras′tə nā′tər), *n.* a person who procrastinates.

pro·cras·ti·na·to·ry (prō kras′tə nə tôr′ē, -tōr′-), *adj.* procrastinative.

pro·cre·ant (prō′krē ənt), *adj.* generating; having to do with procreation: *procreant*

cause. Always the procreant urge of the world (Walt Whitman). [< Latin *prōcreāns, -antis,* present participle of *prōcreāre* to procreate]

pro·cre·ate (prō′krē āt), *v.,* **-at·ed, -at·ing.** —*v.t.* **1.** to become father to; beget. **2.** to bring into being; produce: *Only two on an average survive to procreate their kind* (Charles Darwin). —*v.i.* to produce offspring. [< Latin *prōcreāre* (with English *-ate*[1]) < *prō-* forth + *creāre* to create, bring forth, beget]

pro·cre·a·tion (prō′krē ā′shən), *n.* **1.** a begetting; becoming a father. **2.** production.

pro·cre·a·tive (prō′krē ā′tiv), *adj.* **1.** begetting; bringing into being. **2.** concerned with or having to do with procreation: *the procreative faculty.* —**pro′cre·a′tive·ness,** *n.*

pro·cre·a·tor (prō′krē ā′tər), *n.* a person who begets; parent.

proc·ris (prok′ris), *n.* any moth of a widespread group (found in Europe, Africa, Australia, and both Americas) having blue forewings and brown hindwings. [< New Latin *Procris* the genus name < Latin < Greek *Prókris* Procris, a princess in Greek mythology]

Pro·crus·te·an (prō krus′tē ən), *adj.* **1.** of or having to do with Procrustes or his bed. **2.** tending to produce conformity by violent and arbitrary means: *The Federal statutes of constitutionality now applicable to the states [are] not so strict as to be "Procrustean"* (New York Times).

Pro·crus·tes (prō krus′tēz), *n. Greek Legend.* a robber who stretched his victims or cut short their legs to make them fit the length of his bed. [< Latin *Procrustes* < Greek *Prokroústēs* (literally) one who stretches < *prokroúein* to stretch or hammer out < *pró* forth, out + *kroúein* to strike, beat]

Procrustes' bed, anything with which people or things are forced to conform, especially by violent and arbitrary means: *It is becoming increasingly necessary to find some way of breaking out of the Procrustes' bed that the British press has got itself clamped into . . . as a result of its excessive dependence on advertising subsidies* (Francis Williams).

proc·tec·to·my (prok tek′tə mē), *n., pl.* **-mies.** the surgical removal of all or part of the rectum. [< Greek *prōktós* anus + *ektomē* a cutting out]

proc·ti·tis (prok tī′təs), *n.* inflammation of the rectum and anus.

proc·to·de·um or **proc·to·dae·um** (prok′tə dē′əm), *n.* an invagination of ectodermal tissue in the embryo which forms part of the anal passage. [< Greek *prōktós* anus + *odaîos* (thing) that is on the way + New Latin *-um,* a noun suffix]

proc·to·log·ic (prok′tə loj′ik), *adj.* of or having to do with proctology.

proc·to·log·i·cal (prok′tə loj′ə kəl), *adj.* proctologic.

proc·tol·o·gist (prok tol′ə jist), *n.* a person skilled in proctology.

proc·tol·o·gy (prok tol′ə jē), *n.* the branch of medicine dealing with the rectum and anus. [< Greek *prōktós* anus + English *-logy*]

proc·tor (prok′tər), *n.* **1. a.** an official in a college, university, or school who keeps order. **b.** a person who supervises students during an examination. **2.** a person employed to manage another's case in a law court. —*v.t.* to serve as a proctor at (an examination): *Goudsmit was proctoring an examination one suffocating August afternoon* (New Yorker). [reduction of *procurator*] —**Syn. 2.** attorney, counselor.

proc·to·ri·al (prok tôr′ē əl, -tōr′-), *adj.* of or having to do with a proctor. —**proc·to′ri·al·ly,** *adv.*

proc·tor·ship (prok′tər ship), *n.* the position of a proctor.

proc·to·scope (prok′tə skōp), *n.* an instrument for inspecting the rectum. [< Greek *prōktós* anus + English *-scope*]

proc·to·scop·ic (prok′tə skop′ik), *adj.* of or having to do with a proctoscope.

proc·tos·to·my (prok tos′tə mē), *n., pl.* **-mies.** the making of a new permanent opening in the rectum. [< Greek *prōktós* anus + *stóma* mouth, opening + English *-y*[3]]

proc·tot·o·my (prok tot′ə mē), *n., pl.* **-mies.** a surgical incision into the rectum. [< Greek *prōktós* anus + *-tomiā* a cutting]

pro·cum·bent (prō kum′bənt), *adj.* **1.** lying face down; prone; prostrate. **2.** (of a plant or stem) lying along the ground but not sending down roots. [< Latin *prōcumbēns, -entis,* present participle of *prōcumbere* lean or fall forward < *prō-* forward + *cubāre* to lie, recline] —**Syn. 2.** trailing.

pro·cur·a·ble (prə kyůr′ə bəl), *adj.* that can be procured or obtained: . . . *no wine or spirits being procurable on the premises* (Annie Brassey).

proc·u·ra·cy (prok′yər ə sē), *n., pl.* **-cies.** the office or service of a procurator; management of an affair for another.

pro·cur·ance (prə kyůr′əns), *n.* the act of procuring.

proc·u·ra·tion (prok′yə rā′shən), *n.* **1.** the act of procuring. **2.** management for another; agency. **3. a.** the appointment of an agent. **b.** the authority given; power of attorney.

proc·u·ra·tor (prok′yə rā′tər), *n.* **1.** a person employed to manage the affairs of another; person authorized to act for another; agent. **2.** a financial agent or administrator of an imperial Roman province. **3.** any of the chief law-enforcement officers of the Soviet Union; prosecutor; attorney general. [< Latin *prōcūrātor, -ōris* < *prōcūrāre;* see PROCURE. Doublet of PROCUREUR.]

Procurator Fiscal, the public prosecutor of a county in Scotland. He initiates investigations of suspicious deaths and sometimes acts as coroner.

proc·u·ra·to·ri·al (prok′yər ə tôr′ē əl, -tōr′-), *adj.* of or having to do with a procurator.

proc·u·ra·tor·ship (prok′yə rā′tər ship), *n.* the office, function, or term of a procurator: . . . *during the procuratorship of the luckless Pilate (26-36 A.D.)* (Harper's).

proc·u·ra·to·ry (prok′yər ə tôr′ē, -tōr′-), *adj.* having to do with a procurator or with procuration.

pro·cure (prə kyůr′), *v.,* **-cured, -cur·ing.** —*v.t.* **1.** to obtain by care or effort; get: *It is hard to procure water in the desert. A friend procured a position in the bank for my brother.* **2.** to bring about; cause: *The traitors procured the death of the prince.* **3.** to obtain (women) for the gratification of lust. —*v.i.* to act as a procurer or procuress: *How doth my dear morsel, thy mistress? Procures she still?* (Shakespeare). [< Latin *prōcūrāre* manage, take care of < *prō-* on behalf of + *cūrāre* take care about < *cūra* care] —**Syn.** *v.t.* **1.** acquire, gain, win, secure.

pro·cure·ment (prə kyůr′mənt), *n.* a procuring: *It was by . . . the procurement of my uncle, that I was kidnapped* (Robert Louis Stevenson).

pro·cur·er (prə kyůr′ər), *n.* **1.** a person who procures. **2.** a pander; pimp.

pro·cur·ess (prə kyůr′is), *n.* a woman procurer; bawd.

pro·cu·reur (prô kʏ rœr′), *n.* **1.** an attorney; procurator. **2.** a public prosecutor. [< French *procureur* < Latin *prōcūrātor* < *prōcūrāre;* see PROCURE. Doublet of PROCURATOR.]

Pro·cy·on (prō′sē on), *n.* a star of the first magnitude in the constellation Canis Minor: *Above Canis Major is Canis Minor, with Procyon, another first magnitude star* (Science News Letter). [< Latin *Procyōn* < Greek *Prokýōn* < *pró* before + *kýōn* dog (because it rises before the Dog Star, Sirius)]

prod (prod), *v.,* **prod·ded, prod·ding,** *n.* —*v.t.* **1.** to poke or jab with something pointed: *to prod an animal with a stick.* **2.** to stir up; urge on: *to prod a lazy boy to action by threats and entreaties. I have vitality enough to kick when prodded* (Thomas Huxley). **3.** to make by poking: *The lady has prodded little spirting holes in the damp sand . . . with her parasol* (Dickens).
—*n.* **1.** a poke; thrust: *a prod in the ribs.* **2.** a sharp-pointed stick; goad: *a cattle prod.* **3.** words, actions, or feelings that prod: *Weekends I call my salesmen on the phone and give them a prod* (New Yorker).
[origin uncertain] —**Syn.** *v.t.* **2.** incite.

prod., produced.

prod·der (prod′ər), *n.* a person or thing that prods.

pro·de·ni·a (prō dē′nē ə), *n.* any of a group of noctuid moths, common in the United States, whose larvae feed on various succulent vegetables. [< New Latin *Prodenia* the genus name]

prod·i·gal (prod′ə gəl), *adj.* **1.** spending too much; wasting money or other resources; wasteful: *to be prodigal of affection. America has been prodigal of its forests.* **2.** abundant; lavish; giving or yielding lavishly or profusely: *Of these things I shall be very prodigal in my discourse* (Henry Neville).
—*n.* a person who is wasteful or extravagant; spendthrift: *The father welcomed the prodigal back home.* [< Latin *prōdigus* (see PRODIGALITY) + English *-al*[1]] —**prod′i·gal·ly,** *adv.* —**Syn.** *adj.* **1.** extravagant. —**Ant.** *adj.* **1.** frugal, saving, stingy.

prod·i·gal·i·ty (prod′ə gal′ə tē), *n., pl.* **-ties. 1.** wasteful or reckless extravagance: *It is often surprising how men begin to curb their prodigality when convinced they must pay for it* (Wall Street Journal). **2.** rich abundance; profuseness: *the prodigality of jungle growth. In face of this prodigality, the bare islet with its severe outline seems still more of a desert* (Atlantic). [< Late Latin *prōdigālitās* < Latin *prōdigus* wasteful < *prōdigere* to squander, (literally) drive forth < *prōd-,* variant of *prō-* forth + *agere* to drive] —**Syn. 2.** profusion.

pro·dig·i·o·sin (prō dij′ē ō′sin), *n.* an antibiotic used against coccidiodomycosis. *Formula:* $C_{20}H_{25}N_3O$ [< New Latin (*Chromobacterium*) *Prodigiosum,* the name of the bacteria which produce it + English *-in*]

pro·di·gious (prə dij′əs), *adj.* **1.** very great; vast; huge: *The ocean contains a prodigious amount of water.* **2.** wonderful; marvelous; amazing: *a prodigious feat.* **3.** out of the ordinary; abnormal; monstrous: *Nature breeds, Perverse, all monstrous, all prodigious things* (Milton). **4.** *Obsolete.* being a portent. [< Latin *prōdigiōsus* < *prōdigium* prodigy, omen] —**pro·di′gious·ly,** *adv.* —**pro·di′gious·ness,** *n.* —**Syn. 1.** immense. **2.** astonishing.

prod·i·gy (prod′ə jē), *n., pl.* **-gies. 1.** a marvel; wonder; surprise: *An infant prodigy is a child remarkably brilliant in some respect.* **2.** a marvelous example: *The warriors performed prodigies of valor.* **3.** a wonderful sign or omen: *An eclipse of the sun seemed a prodigy to early man. The old men paid careful attention to omens and prodigies, and especially to their dreams* (Francis Parkman). **4.** something out of the ordinary; abnormality; monstrosity. [< Latin *prōdigium* omen < *prōd-,* variant of *prō-* forth + *-igium,* related to *aiō* I speak]

pro·do·mos (prō dō′mos), *n., pl.* **-moi** (-moi). a roofed, open space with pillars on one side; pillared portico. [< Greek *pró* before + *dómos* house]

prod·ro·mal (prod′rə məl), *adj.* (of disease symptoms) preliminary; premonitory.

pro·drome (prō′drōm), *n.* a symptom giving warning of illness. [< Middle French *prodrome,* learned borrowing from New Latin *prodromus* < Greek *pródromos* (one) going before < *pro-* forward + *drómos* a running, related to *dramein* to run]

pro·drom·ic (prə drom′ik), *adj.* prodromal.

prod·ro·mous (prod′rə məs), *adj.* prodromal.

pro·duce (*v.* prə düs′, -dyüs′; *n.* prod′üs, -yüs; prō′düs, -dyüs), *v.,* **-duced, -duc·ing,** *n.* —*v.t.* **1.** to bring into existence; make: *to produce a work of art. This factory produces stoves.* **2.** to bring about; cause: *His hard work produced success.* **3.** to bring forth; supply; create: *Hens produce eggs. His business produced a large profit.* **4.** to bring forward; show: *Produce your proof.* **5.** to bring (a play, etc.) before the public. **6.** to extend (a line or plane); continue. **7.** *Obsolete.* to prolong; lengthen. —*v.i.* to yield offspring, crops, products, dividends, interest, etc.
—*n.* **1.** what is produced; yield: *Vegetables are a garden's produce.* **2.** offspring; progeny.
[< Latin *prōdūcere* < *prō-* forth + *dūcere* to bring, lead]
—**Syn.** *v.t.* **1.** manufacture. **2.** effect. **3.** yield.

pro·duce·a·ble (prə dü′sə bəl, -dyü′-), *adj.* producible.

pro·duc·er (prə dü′sər, -dyü′-), *n.* **1.** a person or thing that produces. **2.** a person who grows or makes things that are to be used or consumed by others. **3. a.** a person who has general charge of the production of a motion picture, television show, play, etc. **b.** *British.* a director of a motion picture, play, etc. **4.** a furnace for manufacturing producer gas. **5.** a producing oil well: *During the past three months the Company participated in completing 8 producers and 7 dry holes* (Wall Street Journal).

producer gas, a gas produced by the incomplete combustion of coke or coal, or by passing air and steam over burning coke or coal. It is used mainly as an industrial fuel: *For many industrial purposes producer gas with its low calorific value . . . is quite satisfactory* (Monroe M. Offner).

producers' goods, articles used in the production of other articles, such as machinery, tools, timber, and ore.

pro·duc·i·bil·i·ty (prə dü'sə bil'ə tē, -dyü'-), *n.* the quality of being producible; capability of producing: *The U.S. it is estimated has an excess producibility of between 1,000,000 and 2,000,000 barrels daily* (Wall Street Journal).

pro·duc·i·ble (prə dü'sə bəl, -dyü'-), *adj.* that can be produced: *. . . wealth being no more producible without painful toil than any other crop* (Spectator).

prod·uct (prod'əkt, -ukt), *n.* **1.** that which is produced; result of work or of growth: *factory products, farm products. The products of respiration help indirectly to make certain soil minerals available to plants* (Fred W. Emerson). **2.** a number or quantity resulting from multiplying: *$40 is the product of $8 by 5.* **3.** *Chemistry.* a substance obtained from another substance through chemical change. [< Latin *prōductum,* noun use of neuter past participle of *prōdūcere* to produce]

pro·duc·tion (prə duk'shən), *n.* **1. a.** the act of producing; creation; manufacture: *His business is the production of automobiles.* **b.** *Slang.* the act of exaggerating something out of proportion to its importance: *to make a production out of taking snapshots.* **2.** something that is produced: *That worthless book is the production of an ignorant author.*

production car, *Especially British.* an automobile that is a standard model made by a manufacturer, as contrasted with a custom-made car or one which has been altered; stock car: *Production-car races and rallies have shown that the performance and handling of these cars can be vastly improved* (Punch).

production line, a line in a factory along which a product is assembled part by part in a certain order and at a certain speed by workers, each of whom is responsible for a single operation. The production line is the basis of mass production and the standardization of products. *No production line now exists for the Jupiter; those fired so far were "hand-tooled," i.e., individually assembled* (Time).

production model, a standard product; product as it comes from regular production.

production number, a portion of a musical play, motion picture, television show, etc., which is an extravaganza in itself, requiring elaborate costumes and scenery and many performers.

production well, a well drilled in a proven area to extract oil or gas.

pro·duc·tion·wise (prə duk'shən wīz'), *adv.* from the standpoint of production: *Productionwise, the company's plant is up to date and capable of increase* (London Times).

pro·duc·tive (prə duk'tiv), *adj.* **1.** bringing forth; producing: *fields now productive only of weeds, hasty words productive of quarrels.* **2.** producing food or other articles of commerce: *Farming is productive labor.* **3.** producing abundantly; fertile: *a productive farm, a productive writer.* —**pro·duc'tive·ly,** *adv.* —**pro·duc'tive·ness,** *n.* —**Syn. 3.** See **fertile.**

pro·duc·tiv·i·ty (prō'duk tiv'ə tē), *n.* the power to produce; productiveness: *There is only one effective way to control long-range inflationary pressures, and that is increased productivity* (Harper's).

product mix, the diverse forms of a product manufactured by a company: *[It] usually operates at a higher percentage of capacity than the industry average because of the company's product mix—the types of steel it produces* (Wall Street Journal).

pro·em (prō'em), *n.* an introduction; preface; preamble: *Thus much may serve by way of proem, Proceed we therefore to our poem* (Jonathan Swift). [Middle English *proheme* < Old French, learned borrowing from Latin *prœmium* < Greek *prooímion* < *pro-* before + *oîmos* melodic line of a song; (literally) course, way, road] —**Syn.** foreword, exordium.

pro·e·mi·al (prō ē'mē əl), *adj.* introductory; prefatory; preliminary.

pro·en·zyme (prō en'zīm), *n.* a protein formed in the cells of an organism, the inactive forerunner of an enzyme, which is converted into an active enzyme by a further reaction; zymogen: *The key enzyme, fibrinolysin, exists normally in the blood in the form of an inactive proenzyme, profibrinolysin* (Saturday Review).

prof (prof), *n. Informal.* professor.

Prof. or **prof.,** professor.

pro·face (prō fās'), *interj. Obsolete.* May it do you good! (a courteous expression used at a dinner or other meal). [< Middle French *prou fasse; prou* profit < Vulgar Latin *prōs, prōdis; fasse,* subjunctive of *faire* do < Latin *facere*]

prof·a·na·tion (prof'ə nā'shən), *n.* the act of showing contempt or disregard toward something holy; mistreatment of something sacred: *Reverence forbids quotation, for the profanation of divine names and ideas becomes revolting and unbearable* (Atlantic). —**Syn.** desecration, defilement.

pro·fan·a·to·ry (prə fan'ə tôr'ē, -tōr'-), *adj.* profaning.

pro·fane (prə fān'), *adj., v.,* **-faned, -fan·ing.** —*adj.* **1.** not sacred; worldly: *profane literature.* **2.** with contempt or disregard for God or holy things: *a profane man using profane language.* **3.** not initiated into religious rites or mysteries. **4.** common; vulgar: *the profane rites of savages.*

—*v.t.* **1.** to treat (holy things) with contempt or disregard: *Soldiers profaned the church when they stabled their horses in it.* **2.** to put to wrong or unworthy use: *I feel me much to blame, So idly to profane the precious time* (Shakespeare).

[< Old French *prophane,* learned borrowing from Latin *profānus* (literally) not consecrated < *prō-* outside of + *fānum* shrine] —**pro·fane'ly,** *adv.* —**pro·fane'ness,** *n.* —**pro·fan'er,** *n.*

—**Syn.** *adj.* **1.** secular. **2.** irreverent, blasphemous. *-v.t.* **1.** desecrate, violate.

pro·fan·i·ty (prə fan'ə tē), *n., pl.* **-ties. 1.** the use of profane language; swearing. **2.** a being profane; lack of reverence.

pro·fa·num vul·gus (prō fā'nəm vul'gəs), *Latin.* the common herd.

pro·fert (prō'fərt), *n. Law.* an exhibition of a record or paper in open court, or a formal allegation that it is so exhibited. [< Latin *prōfert (in cūriā)* he produces (in court), third person present of *prōferre* bring forward < *prō-* forth + *ferre* to bear]

pro·fess (prə fes'), *v.t.* **1.** to lay claim to; claim: *He professed the greatest respect for the law. I don't profess to be an expert.* **2.** to declare openly: *He professed his loyalty to the United States. We profess Ourselves to be the slaves of chance* (Shakespeare). **3.** to declare one's belief in: *Christians profess Christ and the Christian religion.* **4.** to have as one's profession or business: *to profess law.* **5.** to receive or admit into a religious order. —*v.i.* to make a profession or professions. [back formation < (to be) *professed*] —**Syn.** *v.t.* **1.** assume, pretend. **2.** own, aver, acknowledge.

pro·fessed (prə fest'), *adj.* **1.** alleged; pretended: *How hast thou the heart, Being . . . my friend profess'd, To mangle me with that word "banished"?* (Shakespeare). **2.** avowed or acknowledged; openly declared: *a professed liar.* **3.** having taken the vows of, or been received into, a religious order: *a professed nun.* [Middle English *professed,* earlier *profess* < Old French *profes,* or *professe,* ultimately < Latin *prōfitērī* < *prō-* forth + *fatērī* confess]

pro·fess·ed·ly (prə fes'id lē), *adv.* **1.** avowedly: *Many there are, who openly and almost professedly regulate all their conduct by their love of money* (Samuel Johnson). **2.** ostensibly: *That, it seems, is not the view held in certain professedly liberal quarters* (Wall Street Journal).

pro·fes·sion (prə fesh'ən), *n.* **1.** an occupation requiring an education, especially law, medicine, teaching, or the ministry. **2.** the people engaged in such an occupation. **3.** the act of professing; open declaration: *Professions of friendliness have alternated somewhat bewilderingly with activities which are far from friendly* (Wall Street Journal). **4.** a declaration of belief in a religion. **5.** the religion or faith professed. **6.** taking the vows and entering a religious order.

pro·fes·sion·al (prə fesh'ə nəl, -fesh'nəl), *adj.* **1.** of or having to do with a profession: *Dr. Smith has a professional gravity very unlike his ordinary joking manner.* **2.** engaged in a profession: *A lawyer or a doctor is a professional man.* **3.** making a business or trade of something that others do for pleasure: *a professional musician, a professional ballplayer.* **4.** undertaken or engaged in by professionals rather than amateurs: *a professional ball game.* **5.** making a business of something not properly to be regarded as a business: *a professional politician. The Government should change some of its witnesses and put an end to what The New York Times called "the repeated use of totally unreliable paid professional informers"* (New York Times). *In that strange crew he was unique: he was the only professional criminal in the lot* (Harper's).

—*n.* **1.** a person who makes a business or trade of something that others do for pleasure, as singing or dancing. **2.** a person who belongs to a recognized profession; professional man.

pro·fes·sion·al·ism (prə fesh'ə nə liz'əm, -fesh'nə liz-), *n.* **1.** professional character, spirit, or methods: *The production is marked by an assured professionalism* (Wall Street Journal). **2.** the standing, practice, or methods of a professional, as distinguished from those of an amateur.

pro·fes·sion·al·ist (prə fesh'ə nə list, -fesh'nə-), *n.* a person whose work, character, etc., is marked by professionalism.

pro·fes·sion·al·i·za·tion (prə fesh'ə nə lə zā'shən, -fesh'nə-), *n.* a making or becoming professional: *The effect of all this is narrowness, intellectual pallor, professionalization—the very antithesis of the goals of liberal education* (Harper's).

pro·fes·sion·al·ize (prə fesh'ə nə līz, -fesh'nə-), *v.t., v.i.,* **-ized, -iz·ing.** to make or become professional.

pro·fes·sion·al·ly (prə fesh'ə nə lē, -fesh'nə-), *adv.* **1.** in a professional manner. **2.** in professional matters; because of one's profession: *Do you wish to consult me professionally?* (Mary E. Braddon).

pro·fes·sor (prə fes'ər), *n.* **1.** a teacher of the highest rank in a college or university. *Abbr.:* Prof. **2.** *Informal.* **a.** a teacher. **b.** a person who claims special knowledge of or proficiency in any field: *The old professor tried to sell his snake oil at the fair but the crowd only laughed at his claims.* **3.** a person who professes: *a professor of religion. There is no error . . . which has not had its professors* (John Locke). **4.** a person who declares his belief in a religion. **5.** *U.S. Slang.* a piano player in a cheap saloon, theater, brothel, etc. [< Latin *prōfessor, -ōris* < *prōfitērī* to profess, declare publicly; see PROFESSED]

pro·fes·sor·ate (prə fes'ər it), *n.* **1.** the office or term of service of a professor. **2.** a group of professors. [< *professor* + *-ate*[3]]

pro·fes·so·ri·al (prō'fe sôr'ē əl, -sōr'-; prof'ə-), *adj.* of, having to do with, or characteristic of a professor: *[His] speeches are grave and professorial, not rabble-rousing* (Harper's). —**pro'fes·so'ri·al·ly,** *adv.*

pro·fes·so·ri·ate (prō'fe sôr'ē it, -sōr'-; prof'ə-), *n.* **1.** a group of professors. **2.** a professorship.

pro·fes·sor·ship (prə fes'ər ship), *n.* the position or rank of a professor: *Most of the great American historians of the nineteenth century held no professorships* (Atlantic).

prof·fer (prof'ər), *v.t.* to offer for acceptance; offer: *We proffered regrets at having to leave so early.* —*n.* an offer made: *His proffer of advice was accepted. Hoping that the enemy . . . would make a proffer of peace* (Edmund Burke). [Middle English *proffren* < Anglo-French *proffrir* < earlier Old French *poroffrir* < *pour-* forth (< Latin *prō-* pro-[1]) + *offrir* offer < Latin *offerre*] —**Syn.** *v.t.* tender. See **offer.**

pro·fi·bri·no·ly·sin (prō fī'brə nō lī'sin, -nol'ə-), *n.* an inactive proenzyme in the blood from which fibrinolysin is formed by certain blood activators.

pro·fi·cien·cy (prə fish'ən sē), *n., pl.* **-cies.** a being proficient; knowledge; skill; expertness: *Don Geronimo had been educated in England . . . which . . . accounted for his pro-*

ficiency in the English language (George H. Borrow).

pro·fi·cient (prə fish′ənt), *adj.* advanced in any art, science, or subject; skilled; expert: *She was very proficient in music.* —*n.* an expert: *He was a proficient in golf.* [< Latin *prōficiēns, -entis* accomplish, make progress, be useful; (literally) present participle of *prōficere* < *prō-* forward + *facere* to make] —**pro·fi′cient·ly,** *adv.* —**Syn.** *adj.* versed, qualified, adept, competent. See **expert.**

pro·file (prō′fīl), *n., v.,* **-filed, -fil·ing.** —*n.* **1.** a side view, especially of the human face. **2.** an outline. **3.** a drawing of a transverse vertical section of a building, bridge, etc. **4.** a concise description of a person's abilities, personality, or career: *In a lengthy profile a few years ago, the Harvard Law Record called him "A scholar on the Bench"* (New York Times). **5.** *Psychology.* a diagram showing a person's abilities or traits. **6.** a diagram of collected data or measurements, as of a natural phenomenon or other scientific data: *If we took gravity readings all over the earth and corrected them to sea level, we would have a gravity profile of the geoid* (Scientific American).
—*v.t.* **1.** to draw a profile of. **2.** to write a profile of: *Who will The Observer profile next Sunday?* (New Scientist).
[< earlier Italian *profile* < *profilare* to draw in outline < Latin *prō-* forth + *fīlum* thread]
—**Syn.** *n.* **2.** See **outline.**

Profile (def. 1) of John Adams

pro·fil·er (prō′fī lər), *n.* a writer of journalistic or literary profiles: *Lillian Ross, crack profiler for The New Yorker magazine, is in Switzerland working up a series on Charlie Chaplin* (Newsweek).

pro·fil·ist (prō′fī list), *n.* a person who makes profile portraits, especially silhouettes.

prof·it (prof′it), *n.* **1.** Often, **profits.** gain from a business; what is left when the cost of goods and of carrying on the business is subtracted from the amount of money taken in: *The profits in this business are not large.* **2.** the gain from any transaction: *to make a profit from the sale of stock.* **3.** advantage; benefit: *What profit is there in worrying?*
—*v.i.* **1.** to make a gain from a business; make a profit. **2.** to get advantage; gain; benefit: *A wise person profits by his mistakes.* **3.** *Obsolete.* to make progress; advance. —*v.t.* to be an advantage or benefit to: *For what shall it profit a man, if he shall gain the whole world, and lose his own soul?* (Mark 8:36).
[< Old French *profit* < Latin *prōfectus, -ūs* an advance < *prōficere;* see PROFICIENT]
—**prof′it·er,** *n.*
—**Syn.** *n.* **1.** revenue, returns, proceeds. **3.** See **advantage.**

prof·it·a·bil·i·ty (prof′ə tə bil′ə tē), *n.* the quality or state of being profitable: *Profitability and the growth of the firm are the criteria of success in a business* (Scientific American).

prof·it·a·ble (prof′ə tə bəl), *adj.* **1.** yielding a financial profit; lucrative; gainful: *The sale held by the Girl Scouts was very profitable.* **2.** giving a gain or benefit; useful: *We spent a profitable afternoon in the library.* —**prof′it·a·ble·ness,** *n.* —**Syn. 2.** beneficial, fruitful.

prof·it·a·bly (prof′ə tə blē), *adv.* with profit: *I think it may be profitably taught in the Universities* (Thomas Hobbes).

profit and loss, an accounting record to show net profit or loss. —**prof′it-and-loss′,** *adj.*

prof·it·eer (prof′ə tir′), *n.* a person who makes an unfair profit by taking advantage of public necessity: *Profiteers made much money in World War I.* —*v.i.* to seek or make excessive profits by taking advantage of public necessity. [< *profit* + *-eer*]

prof·it·eer·ing (prof′ə tir′ing), *n.* the act of a person who profiteers: *There were harsh laws against profiteering in France in 1793* (H.G. Wells).

pro·fit·e·role (prə fit′ə rōl′), *n.* a small, light puff of pastry or an hors d'oeuvre, filled with ice cream, whipped cream, fruit, creamed meat or fish, etc. [< Middle French *profiterole* < Old French *profit* (see PROFIT) + *-erole,* a diminutive suffix]

prof·it·less (prof′it lis), *adj.* without profit, gain, or advantage; unprofitable: . . . *hours of utterly profitless talk* (Manchester Examiner). —**prof′it·less·ly,** *adv.*

prof·it-mak·ing (prof′it mā′king), *adj.* that makes a profit: *the only profit-making political organization in the world* (Harper's).

profit margin, the amount by which selling price exceeds costs: *Business has tended to become more competitive and profit margins have been reduced* (London Times).

profit sharing, the sharing of profits between employer and employees: *"Co-ownership" is something other than profit sharing, though the two may be combined in a single scheme* (London Times). —**prof′it-shar′ing,** *adj.*

profit squeeze, a narrow or narrowing profit margin: *Retail concerns are confronted with a "profit squeeze from rising expenses"* (Wall Street Journal).

profit taking, the selling of stocks, etc., to take a profit: *Frequently in the new year there is profit taking by those who, for tax reasons, have not wanted to sell stocks in the year just passed* (Wall Street Journal).

prof·it·wise (prof′it wīz′), *adv.* with respect to profits: *Far from being in dire straits, profitwise, the steel corporations . . . have been showing a . . . profit rate . . . higher than last year* (New York Times).

prof·li·ga·cy (prof′lə gə sē), *n.* **1.** great wickedness; vice. **2.** reckless extravagance.

prof·li·gate (prof′lə git), *adj.* **1.** very wicked; shamelessly bad: *a profligate wretch without any sense of principle, morality, or religion* (Tobias Smollett). **2.** recklessly extravagant. —*n.* a person who is very wicked or extravagant. [< Latin *prōflīgātus* (literally) ruined, past participle of *prōflīgāre* < *prō-* down, forth + *flīgere* to strike, dash] —**prof′li·gate·ly,** *adv.* —**prof′li·gate·ness,** *n.*

prof·lu·ent (prof′lü ənt), *adj.* **1.** flowing forth or along: *the profluent stream* (Milton). **2.** *Obsolete.* running out of the main body. [< Latin *prōfluēns, -entis,* present participle of *prōfluere* flow forth or onward < *prō-* forth + *fluere* to flow]

pro for·ma (prō fôr′mə), *Latin.* for the sake of form; as a matter of form: *Later, after a pro forma floor debate, they dropped the signboard ban* (Time).

pro·found (prə found′), *adj.* **1.** very deep: *a profound sigh, a profound sleep.* **2.** deeply felt; very great: *profound despair, profound sympathy.* **3. a.** going far deeper than what is easily understood: *a profound book.* **b.** having or showing great knowledge or understanding: *a profound thinker. Could this conflict of attachments be resolved by a profounder understanding of the principle of loyalty?* (Atlantic). **4.** carried far down; going far down; low: *a profound bow.*
—*n. Poetic.* **1.** the deep; the sea; the ocean. **2.** an immeasurable abyss, as of space or time.
[Middle English *profound* < Old French *parfond,* and *profond,* learned borrowing from Latin *profundus* < *prō* forth + *fundus* bottom] —**pro·found′ly,** *adv.* —**pro·found′ness,** *n.*
—**Syn.** *adj.* **3.** abstruse, recondite.

pro·fun·di·ty (prə fun′də tē), *n., pl.* **-ties.** **1.** a being profound; great depth. **2.** a very deep thing or place; an abyss: *through the vast profundity obscure* (Milton).
profundities, profound or deep matters: *I am . . . not able to dive into these profundities . . . not able to understand, much less to discuss* (Robert Burton).
[< Latin *profunditās* < *profundus* profound]

pro·fuse (prə fyüs′), *adj.* **1.** very abundant: *profuse thanks.* **2.** spending or giving freely; lavish; extravagant: *a profuse spender.* [< Latin *profūsus* poured forth, past participle of *profundere* < *prō-* forth + *fundere* to pour]
—**pro·fuse′ly,** *adv.* —**pro·fuse′ness,** *n.*
—**Syn. 1, 2. Profuse, lavish** mean occurring, spending, or giving freely. **Profuse** suggests great generosity, often excessive or insincere: *They were profuse in their praise.* **Lavish** suggests unstinting generosity but not necessarily extravagance: *It was a lavish display of gifts.*

pro·fu·sion (prə fyü′zhən), *n.* **1.** great abundance: *a certain fruit which grew in profusion there* (Joseph Conrad). **2.** extravagance; lavishness.

pro·fu·sive (prə fyü′siv), *adj.* profuse; lavish; prodigal: . . . *a profusive variety of spring flowers* (Harper's). —**pro·fu′sive·ly,** *adv.* —**pro·fu′sive·ness,** *n.*

prog (prog), *v.,* **progged, prog·ging,** *n. Dialect.* —*v.i.* **1.** to search or prowl about, especially for food. **2.** to beg. —*n.* food, especially for a journey. [origin uncertain]

prog., progressive.

pro·gen·i·tive (prō jen′ə tiv), *adj.* producing offspring; reproductive.

pro·gen·i·tor (prō jen′ə tər), *n.* an ancestor in the direct line; forefather. [< Latin *prōgenitor, -ōris* < *prōgignere* < *prō-* forth + *gignere* to produce]

pro·gen·i·to·ri·al (prō jen′ə tôr′ē əl, -tōr′-), *adj.* having to do with or being a progenitor.

pro·gen·i·tor·ship (prō jen′ə tər ship), *n.* the position or fact of being a progenitor: *Cicero would [disown] the intellectual progenitorship of a cicerone* (Blackwood's Magazine).

pro·gen·i·tress (prō jen′ə tris), *n.* a woman progenitor.

pro·gen·i·ture (prō jen′ə chər), *n.* **1.** a begetting; birth. **2.** offspring; progeny.

prog·e·ny (proj′ə nē), *n., pl.* **-nies.** **1.** children; offspring; descendants: *Kittens are a cat's progeny.* **2.** something that is produced by or originates from something: *Around this fort a progeny of little Dutch-built houses . . . soon sprang up* (Washington Irving). [< Old French *progenie,* learned borrowing from Latin *prōgeniēs* < *prōgignere* to beget; see PROGENITOR]

pro·ge·ri·a (prō jir′ē ə), *n.* **1.** a being prematurely old. **2.** a children's disease characterized by mental maturity and a high susceptibility to diseases of old people. A child having progeria develops a wrinkled skin and loses his hair. [< New Latin *progeria* < Greek *progḗrōs* prematurely old < *pró* before + *gêras* old age]

pro·ges·ta·gen (prō jes′tə jən), *n.* any of various synthetic hormones similar to progesterone in action, as norethindrone.

pro·ges·ta·tion·al (prō′jes tā′shə nəl), *adj.* of or characteristic of the part of the menstrual cycle immediately before menstruation.

pro·ges·ter·one (prō jes′tə rōn), *n.* a hormone secreted by the corpus luteum and placenta that makes the lining of the uterus more ready to receive a fertilized ovum. It is used medically to treat disorders of the uterus, arthritis, etc. *Formula:* $C_{21}H_{30}O_2$ [< *proge*(stin) + *ster*(ol) + *-one*]

pro·ges·tin (prō jes′tin), *n.* any substance that makes the lining of the uterus readier to receive a fertilized ovum, as progesterone. [< *pro-*[1] + Latin *gestāre* to bear + English *-in*]

pro·ges·to·gen (prō jes′tə jən), *n.* progestagen.

pro·glot·tic (prō glot′ik), *adj.* of or having to do with the proglottis.

pro·glot·tid (prō glot′id), *n.* the proglottis.

pro·glot·tis (prō glot′is), *n., pl.* **-glot·ti·des** (-glot′ə dēz). one of the segments or joints of a tapeworm, containing both male and female sexual organs. [< New Latin *proglottis, -idis* < Greek *pro-* before + *glôtta* tongue (because of its shape)]

prog·nath·ic (prog nath′ik), *adj.* prognathous.

prog·na·thism (prog′nə thiz əm), *n.* a prognathous condition.

prog·na·thous (prog′nə thəs, prog nā′-), *adj.* **1.** (of a skull or a person) having the jaws protruding beyond the upper part of the face. **2.** (of the jaws) protruding. [< *pro-*[2] forward + Greek *gnáthos* jaw + English *-ous*]

prog·na·thy (prog′nə thē), *n.* prognathism.

prog·no·sis (prog nō′sis), *n., pl.* **-ses** (-sēz). **1.** a forecast of the probable course of a disease. **2.** an estimate of what will probably happen: *The prognosis, on this practical level, does not appear favorable* (New Yorker). [< Late Latin *prognōsis* < Greek *prógnōsis* < *progignṓskein* know beforehand < *pro-* before + *gignṓskein* to recognize]

prog·nos·tic (prog nos′tik), *adj.* indicating something in the future. —*n.* **1.** an indication; sign. **2.** a forecast; prediction: *Philosophers . . . awaited in anxious impatience the fulfilment of their prognostics* (Washington

Irving). [< Latin *prognōsticum* < Greek *prognōstikón* omen < *prognōstikein*, related to *progignṓskein;* see PROGNOSIS]

prog·nos·ti·cate (prog nos′tə kāt), *v.t.*, **-cat·ed, -cat·ing.** **1.** to predict from facts; forecast: *He did prognosticate . . . that on the eighteenth of April a storm should burst over this land* (Jane Porter). **2.** (of things) to indicate beforehand.

prog·nos·ti·ca·tion (prog nos′tə kā′shən), *n.* **1.** a forecast; prediction: *The Doctor's prognostication in reference to the weather was speedily verified* (Dickens). **2.** the act of foretelling.

prog·nos·ti·ca·tive (prog nos′tə kā′tiv), *adj.* having the character of a prognostic; predictive: *The comet . . . was thought prognosticative of the fall of Islamism* (John C. Hobhouse).

prog·nos·ti·ca·tor (prog nos′tə kā′tər), *n.* a person or thing that prognosticates.

pro·gram (prō′gram, -grəm), *n., v.,* **-gramed, -gram·ing** or **-grammed, -gram·ming.** —*n.* **1.** a list of items or events; list of performers, etc.: *a theater program.* **2.** the items composing an entertainment: *The entire program was delightful.* **3.** a plan of what is to be done: *a school program. On top of a big military program they have piled a large capital investment program* (Newsweek). **4. a.** a set of instructions fed into a computer outlining the steps to be performed by the machine in a specific operation. **b.** a set of instructions arranged for any automatic machine to follow: *An automatic screw machine obeys the program determined by the setup of the tools on the turrets.* **5.** (in programed instruction) a series of statements and questions to each of which a student is required to respond. **6.** *Obsolete.* a public notice. **7.** *Obsolete.* a prospectus; syllabus.

—*v.t.* **1.** to arrange or enter in a program. **2.** to draw up a program or plan for: *Today's farmer has numerous choices in programming his year's activities* (Wall Street Journal). **3.** to prepare a set of instructions for (a computer or other automatic machine): *General-purpose computers now on the market can be programmed to do translation* (Scientific American). **4.** to arrange (information) in sequential units for use in programmed instruction.

[< Late Latin *programma* < Greek *prógramma, -atos* proclamation < *prográphein* write publicly < *pro-* forth + *gráphein* to write] —**pro′gram·mer,** *n.*

pro·gram·mat·ic (prō′grə mat′ik), *n.* **1.** having to do with or of the nature of a program: *One wishes freedom for the individual investigator, yet programmatic research is the essence of applied research* (James B. Conant). **2.** of the nature of program music. —**pro′gram·mat′i·cal·ly,** *adv.*

pro·gramme (prō′gram, -grəm), *n., v.,* **-grammed, -gram·ming.** *Especially British.* program.

programmed instruction, a progressive sequence of written material presented in small units which a student must learn before being allowed to read the next unit, as used in teaching machines or programmed textbooks.

programmed learning, programmed instruction.

pro·gram·ming (prō′gram ing, -grə ming), *n.* **1.** the planning and arranging of a program or programs, especially for radio and television. **2.** the technique or process of preparing instructions for a computer or other automatic machine.

program music, music intended to convey impressions of images, scenes, or events.

program picture, a motion picture forming part of a program but not constituting the main feature of it.

prog·ress (*n.* prog′res; *especially British* prō′gres; *v.* prə gres′), *n.* **1.** an advance; growth; development; improvement: *the progress of science, the progress of a disease.* **2.** a moving forward; going ahead: *to make rapid progress on a journey, the progress of the earth around the sun.* **3.** a journey or official tour, especially by a ruler or a judge: *How Summer's royal progress shall be wrought* (John Masefield). **4.** *Sociology.* the development of mankind, a group, or an individual toward an objective recognized as desirable. **5.** *Biology.* increasing specialization and adaptation to environment, ultimate function, etc., during development or evolution.

in progress, being carried out or on; taking place: *work in progress.*

—*v.i.* **1.** to get better; advance; develop: *Our country . . . is fast progressing in its political importance and social happiness* (George Washington). **2.** to move forward; go ahead: *The nation's economy has progressed some time without a recession.* —*v.t.* to cause to move onward or advance; push forward: *Pending litigation will be progressed* (New York Times).

[< Latin *prōgressus, -ūs* < *prōgredī* go forward < *prō-* forward + *gradī* to walk]

—**Syn.** *v.i.* **1.** improve, grow.

pro·gres·sion (prə gresh′ən), *n.* **1.** a moving forward; going ahead: *Creeping is a slow method of progression.* **2.** *Mathematics.* a succession of quantities in which there is always the same relation between each quantity and the one succeeding it: *2, 4, 6, 8, 10 are in arithmetical progression. 2, 4, 8, 16 are in geometrical progression.* **3.** the apparent or actual motion of a planet from west to east. **4.** *Music.* **a.** the act of passing from one tone to another in melody, or from one chord to another in harmony. **b.** a sequence.

pro·gres·sion·al (prə gresh′ə nəl), *adj.* having to do with progression, advance, or improvement: *. . . the progressional force of civilization* (American Anthropologist).

pro·gres·sion·ism (prə gresh′ə niz əm), *n.* progress; evolutionary progress.

pro·gres·sion·ist (prə gresh′ə nist), *n.* **1.** a person who favors or believes in progress, as in politics: *These two [antagonistic] parties were named by the Japanese the progressionists and the seclusionists* (Atlantic). **2.** a person who believes that living organisms have progressed from simple to complex forms.

prog·ress·ist (prog′res ist, prō′gres-), *n.* a person who favors progress; progressive.

pro·gres·sive (prə gres′iv), *adj.* **1.** making progress; advancing to something better; improving: *a progressive nation.* **2.** favoring progress; wanting improvement or reform in government, business, etc.: *He is blamed . . . for helping to keep the Administration on a progressive course* (Time). **3.** moving forward; going ahead: *a progressive disease.* **4.** going from one to the next; involving shifts of players or guests from one table to another: *progressive bridge.* **5.** of, following, or based on the theories and practices of progressive education: *a progressive school; a progressive curriculum which includes regular courses* (Newsweek). **6.** *Grammar.* showing the action as going on. *Is reading, was reading,* and *has been reading* are progressive forms of *read.* **7.** *Phonetics.* (of assimilation) in which a preceding sound influences one that follows. **8.** increasing in proportion to the increase of something else: *a progressive income tax increase as a person's earnings increase.*

—*n.* a person who favors progress or reform, especially in political or social matters: *He is a progressive in his beliefs.* —**pro·gres′sive·ly,** *adv.* —**pro·gres′sive·ness,** *n.*

Pro·gres·sive (prə gres′iv), *adj.* of a Progressive Party. —*n.* a member of a Progressive Party.

Progressive Conservative, **1.** a member of the Progressive Conservative Party. **2.** of or having to do with the Progressive Conservative Party.

Progressive Conservative Party, the former Conservative Party of Canada.

progressive education, a system of education based on the principles of John Dewey and his followers, characterized by emphasis on fitting a course of study to the abilities and interests of the pupils rather than fitting the pupils to a given curriculum.

progressive jazz, a jazz style closely resembling bebop, but technically more elaborate and experimental.

Progressive Party, **1.** a political party formed in 1912 under the leadership of Theodore Roosevelt, advocating direct primaries, the initiative, the referendum, the recall, woman suffrage, etc. **2.** a similar political party organized in 1924 and led by Senator Robert M. La Follette. **3.** a political party formed in 1948 by Henry A. Wallace.

pro·gres·siv·ism (prə gres′ə viz əm), *n.* the principles and practices of progressives: *When the New Deal came along, [H.L. Mencken] could not keep abreast of its "progressivism" and its "new ideas"* (Newsweek).

Pro·gres·siv·ism (prə gres′ə viz əm), *n.* *U.S.* the doctrines of a Progressive Party.

pro·gres·siv·ist (prə gres′ə vist), *n.* **1.** a person who believes in progressive education. **2.** a progressive.

prog·res·siv·i·ty (prog′rə siv′ə tē, prō′grə-), *n.* progressive quality; progressiveness.

pro·gym·no·sperm (prō jim′nə spėrm), *n.* any of the fossil plants believed to be progenitors of the gymnosperms: *A specimen . . . from Devonian deposits . . . provided C.B. Beck with evidence that this form was a fernlike progymnosperm* (Charles Heiser).

pro·hib·it (prō hib′it), *v.t.* **1.** to forbid by law or authority: *to prohibit the sale of alcoholic beverages. Picking flowers in this park is prohibited.* **2.** to prevent; hinder: *Bad weather prohibited flying. Good manners prohibit me from so rude an answer.* [< Latin *prohibitus,* past participle of *prohibēre* < *prō-* away, forth + *habēre* to keep] —**Syn.** **1.** See **forbid.** **2.** preclude, debar.

➔ **Prohibited** is followed by *from,* not *against: We are prohibited from smoking on school grounds.* The noun *prohibition* is followed by *against: The prohibition against smoking on school grounds is strictly enforced.*

pro·hi·bi·tion (prō′ə bish′ən), *n.* **1.** the act of prohibiting or forbidding: *The prohibition against swimming in the city's reservoirs is sensible.* **2.** a law or order that prohibits. **3.** a law or laws against making or selling alcoholic liquors.

➔ See **prohibit** for usage note.

pro·hi·bi·tion·ism (prō′ə bish′ə niz əm), *n.* the principles and practices of prohibitionists: *The bad saloon did more harm to the liquor trade than prohibitionism* (North American Review).

pro·hi·bi·tion·ist (prō′ə bish′ə nist), *n.* a person who favors laws against the manufacture and sale of alcoholic liquors.

Pro·hi·bi·tion·ist (prō′ə bish′ə nist), *n.* a member of the Prohibition Party.

Prohibition Party, a political party, organized in 1869, advocating the prohibition by law of the manufacture and sale of alcoholic liquor.

pro·hib·i·tive (prō hib′ə tiv), *adj.* prohibiting; preventing: *a prohibitive cost.* —**pro·hib′i·tive·ly,** *adv.* —**pro·hib′i·tive·ness,** *n.*

pro·hib·i·tor (prō hib′ə tər), *n.* a person who prohibits.

pro·hib·i·to·ri·ly (prō hib′ə tôr′ə lē, -tōr′-), *adv.* in a prohibitory way; with prohibitory effect.

pro·hib·i·to·ry (prō hib′ə tôr′ē, -tōr′-), *adj.* prohibitive.

proj·ect (*n.* proj′ekt; *v.* prə jekt′), *n.* **1.** a plan; scheme: *Flying in a heavy machine was once thought an impossible project.* **2.** an undertaking; enterprise: *to grant funds for a research project.* **3.** *Education.* a special assignment planned and carried out by an entire class. **4.** *U.S.* a housing project: *Lucretia . . . lives in the same project, one flight up* (New Yorker). [< Latin *prōjectum* < *prōjicere;* see the verb]

—*v.t.* **1.** to plan; scheme: *a projected tax decrease, to project a population increase of 20 per cent in ten years. I projected and drew up a plan for the union* (Benjamin Franklin). **2.** to cause to stick out or protrude: *to project a pier out into the lake.* **3.** to throw or cast forward: *to project a missile into space. A cannon projects shot.* **4.** to cause to fall on a surface or into space: *Motion pictures are projected on the screen. The tree projects a shadow on the grass.* **5.** to draw lines through (a point, line, figure, etc.), and reproduce it on a surface. **6.** *Psychology.* to treat as objective and external (what is essentially subjective). —*v.i.* **1.** to stick out: *The rocky point projects far into the water.* **2.** *U.S. Dialect.* to make plans, especially in an ineffective way.

[< Latin *prōjectus,* past participle of *prōjicere* stretch out, expel < *prō-* forward + *jacere* to throw]

—**Syn.** *n.* **1.** See **plan.** *-v.t.* **1.** devise, contrive. *-v.i.* **1.** protrude.

pro·ject·a·ble (prə jek′tə bəl), *adj.* that can be projected.

pro·ject·ed (prə jek′tid), *adj.* put forward as a project; planned: *He was favourable to the projected marriage* (Lytton Strachey). *The unions proposed that the new commission look into past, present, and projected manpower requirements* (Wall Street Journal).

pro·jec·tile (prə jek′təl), *n.* an object that can be thrown, hurled, or shot, such as a stone, spear, or bullet: *In this chapter we shall discuss the motion of a projectile, such as a baseball or golf ball, a bomb released from a plane, a rifle bullet, or the shell of a gun* (Sears and Zemansky).
—*adj.* **1.** that can be thrown, hurled, or shot: *Bullets and arrows are projectile weapons.* **2.** forcing forward; impelling: *a projectile force.* **3.** that can be thrust forward: *the projectile jaws of a fish.*
[< New Latin *projectilis* < Latin *prōjicere;* see PROJECT]

pro·jec·tion (prə jek′shən), *n.* **1.** a part that projects or sticks out: *rocky projections on the face of a cliff.* **2.** a sticking out. **3.** a throwing or casting forward: *the projection of a cannon ball from a cannon, the projection of motion pictures on a screen.* **4.** *Geometry.* the projecting of a figure, etc., upon a surface. **5.** the representation, upon a flat surface, of all or part of the surface of the earth or the celestial sphere. **6.** a forming of projects or plans. **7.** *Psychology, Psychiatry.* the treating of what is essentially subjective as objective and external. **8.** *Alchemy.* the casting of the powder of the philosophers' stone upon metal in fusion in order to transmute it into gold or silver.

pro·jec·tion·al (prə jek′shə nəl), *adj.* of or having to do with projection.

pro·jec·tion·ist (prə jek′shə nist), *n.* **1.** the operator of a motion-picture projector: *Nobody wants to see a multitude of technicians and cameramen and projectionists and ushers thrown out of work* (Punch). **2.** the operator of a television camera. **3.** a person who draws a representation, such as a Mercator's projection, of a curved surface upon a plane.

projection print, a photographic enlargement made by projecting an image onto a sensitized surface: *The two common types of photographs are contact prints and projection prints.*

projection room, a room for the projection of motion pictures: *The light in the projection room went on . . . and there was a pause while the operator loaded a new reel* (New Yorker).

pro·jec·tive (prə jek′tiv), *adj.* of or having to do with projection; produced by projection. —**pro·jec′tive·ly,** *adv.*

projective geometry, the branch of geometry that deals with those properties of geometric figures that are unchanged after projection.

projective technique, *Psychology.* a method of evaluating personality factors by having the individual explain pictures and ink dots, supply dialogue, etc.

pro·jec·tiv·i·ty (prō′jek tiv′ə tē), *n.* the character of being projective, as two plane figures.

pro·jec·tor (prə jek′tər), *n.* **1.** an apparatus for projecting a picture on a screen: *a motion-picture projector, a slide projector.* **2.** a person who forms projects; schemer: *The women . . . think us still either projectors or conjurers* (Robert Boyle).

pro·jet (prô zhe′), *n. French.* **1.** a plan; project. **2.** a draft of a proposed treaty.

prol., prologue.

pro·la·bor (prō lā′bər), *adj.* supporting organized labor: *a prolabor congressman. The A.F.L.-C.I.O. is toning down its clamor for prolabor changes in the Taft-Hartley Law* (Wall Street Journal).

pro·lac·tin (prō lak′tin), *n.* a hormone from the anterior part of the pituitary gland that induces the mammary glands to give milk and affects the activity of the corpus luteum. [< *pro-*[1] + Latin *lac, lactis* milk + English *-in*]

pro·lam·in (prō lam′in, prō′lə min), *n.* any of a group of simple proteins that are soluble in dilute alcohol but insoluble in water and absolute alcohol, as gliadin. The prolamins are present in cereals. [< *pr*(otein) + *-ol*[1] + *amin*(e)]

pro·lam·ine (prō lam′in, -ēn; prō′lə min, -mēn), *n.* prolamin.

pro·lan (prō′lan), *n.* either of two hormones secreted by the pituitary gland that influence the activity of the gonads. They are present in urine during pregnancy. [< German *Prolan* < Latin *prōlēs* offspring]

pro·lapse (prō laps′), *n., v.,* **-lapsed, -laps·ing.** —*n.* the misplacement of an organ of the body: *a prolapse of the uterus.* —*v.i.* (of an organ) to fall; slip out of place. [< Late Latin *prōlapsus, -ūs* < Latin *prolābī* slip forward or down < *prō-* forth + *lābī* to slip, slide]

pro·lap·sus (prō lap′səs), *n., pl.* **-sus.** a prolapse.

pro·late (prō′lāt), *adj.* **1.** elongated in the direction of the polar diameter: *A prolate spheroid is generated by the revolution of an ellipse about its longer axis.* **2.** extended or extending in width. [< Latin *prōlātus*, past participle of *prōferre* extend, bring forward < *prō-* forth + *ferre* bring, bear]

Prolate Spheroid (def. 1)

prole (prōl), *n. Slang.* a proletarian: *The proles are not human beings* (George Orwell). *The boatswain, a "good prole" who doesn't believe in unions or democracy, is afraid to take the helm* (Observer).

pro·leg (prō′leg′), *n.* an abdominal leg of a caterpillar or other larva.

pro·le·gom·e·na (prō′lə gom′ə nə), *n., pl.* of **pro·le·gom·e·non** (prō′lə gom′ə non). preliminary materials in a book, treatise, etc.; preface; introduction. [< Greek *prolegómenon* anything said beforehand < *prolégein* say beforehand < *pró-* before + *légein* to say]

pro·le·gom·e·nar·y (prō′lə gom′ə ner′ē), *adj.* prolegomenous: *. . . a mass of prolegomenary notes* (London Daily Chronicle).

pro·le·gom·e·nous (prō′lə gom′ə nəs), *adj.* of or having to do with prolegomena: *It may not be amiss in the prolegomenous or introductory chapter, to say something of that species of writing* (Henry Fielding).

pro·lep·sis (prō lep′sis), *n., pl.* **-ses** (-sēz). **1.** anticipation. **2.** anticipation of objections in order to answer them in advance. **3.** an epithet in anticipation of its becoming applicable. *Example:* "The murdered king falls by a traitor's hand." **4.** an anachronism. [< Latin *prolepsis* < Greek *prólēpsis* (rhetorical) anticipation; preconception < *prolambánein* anticipate < *pró-* before + *lambánein* show forth, seize; grasp with the senses or mind]

pro·lep·tic (prō lep′tik), *adj.* **1.** anticipative: *A proleptic instinct made him look forward* (Eden Philpotts). **2.** involving prolepsis. —**pro·lep′ti·cal·ly,** *adv.*

pro·lé·taire (prô lā ter′), *n. French.* a proletarian.

pro·le·tar·i·an (prō′lə tãr′ē ən), *adj.* **1.** of or belonging to the proletariat: *. . . irreverent proletarian humor* (Newsweek). **2.** of or belonging to the proletary of ancient Rome. **3.** *Obsolete.* low; vulgar.
—*n.* a person belonging to the proletariat: *The proletarians had not come from their factories at this hour* (Booth Tarkington).
[< Latin *prōlētārius* furnishing the state only with children (< *prōlēs* offspring < *prō-* forth + *alere* nourish, sustain) + English *-an*] —**pro′le·tar′i·an·ly,** *adv.*

pro·le·tar·i·an·ism (prō′lə tãr′ē ə niz′əm), *n.* the condition of being proletarian: *They had overturned feudalism, and now they had created proletarianism* (John Rae).

pro·le·tar·i·an·i·za·tion (prō′lə tãr′ē ə nə zā′shən), *n.* the act or process of proletarianizing: *The simple fact is that the political élites which put Hitler in power have vanished, and so have the social strata—most notably the "petty bourgeoisie" struggling against proletarianization* (Manchester Guardian Weekly).

pro·le·tar·i·an·ize (prō′lə tãr′ē ə nīz), *v.t.,* **-ized, -iz·ing.** to make a proletarian of; cause to become proletarian.

pro·le·tar·i·at (prō′lə tãr′ē ət), *n.* **1.** the lowest class in economic and social status. The proletariat includes unskilled laborers, casual laborers, and tramps: *The West has faced the task of absorbing its proletariat . . . and of giving it the feeling of fully belonging* (Saturday Review). **2.** (in Europe) the laboring class, especially as contrasted by the socialists formerly with slaves and serfs, and now with the middle class: *The dictatorship of the proletariat* (Karl Marx). **3.** the proletaries in ancient Rome. [< French *prolétariat* < Latin *prōlētārius* proletarian + French *-at* -ate[3]]

pro·le·tar·i·ate (prō′lə tãr′ē it), *n.* proletariat.

pro·le·tar·y (prō′lə ter′ē), *n., pl.* **-tar·ies,** *adj.* —*n.* a person of the poorest class in ancient Rome, regarded as contributing nothing but children to the state. —*adj.* belonging to the lowest or poorest class. [< Latin *prōlētārius;* see PROLETARIAN]

pro·li·cide[1] (prō′lə sīd), *n.* the crime of killing one's offspring either before or soon after birth. [< Latin *prōlēs* offspring + English *-cide*[2]]

pro·li·cide[2] (prō′lə sīd), *n.* a person who kills his offspring before or soon after birth. [< Latin *prōlēs* offspring + English *-cide*[1]]

pro·lif·er·ate (prō lif′ə rāt), *v.i., v.t.,* **-at·ed, -at·ing.** **1.** to grow or produce by multiplication of parts, as in budding or cell division. **2.** to multiply; spread; propagate: *These conferences proliferate like measles spots* (Harper's). [back formation < *proliferation*]

pro·lif·er·a·tion (prō lif′ə rā′shən), *n.* **1.** reproduction by budding. **2.** a spreading; propagation. [< French *prolifération* < *prolifère* < Medieval Latin *prolifer;* see PROLIFEROUS]

pro·lif·er·ous (prō lif′ər əs), *adj.* **1.** producing new individuals by budding, cell division, etc. **2.** producing an addition from a part that is normally ultimate, as a shoot or a new flower from the midst of a flower. [< Medieval Latin *prolifer* < Latin *prōlēs* offspring (see PROLETARIAN) + *-fer* bearing + English *-ous*]

pro·lif·ic (prə lif′ik), *adj.* **1.** producing offspring abundantly: *Rabbits are prolific animals.* **2.** producing much: *a prolific tree, garden, imagination, or writer.* **3.** characterized by abundant production: *a garden prolific of weeds.* [< Medieval Latin *prolificus* < Latin *prōlēs* offspring (see PROLETARIAN) + *facere* to make] —**pro·lif′ic·ly,** *adv.* —**pro·lif′ic·ness,** *n.*

pro·lif·i·ca·cy (prə lif′ə kə sē), *n.* the quality or state of being prolific: *The only feature which keeps oysters from extinction is their prolificacy* (Hegner and Stiles).

pro·lif·i·cal·ly (prə lif′ə klē), *adv.* in a prolific manner: *Organisms multiply prolifically in some parts of the ocean and not in others* (Scientific American).

pro·lig·er·ous (prō lij′ər əs), *adj.* **1.** producing progeny; generative; germinative. **2.** *Botany.* proliferous. [< Latin *prōlēs* offspring (see PROLETARIAN) + *gerere* to bear + English *-ous*]

pro·lin (prō′lin), *n.* proline.

pro·line (prō′lēn, -lin), *n.* an amino acid, a product of the decomposition of certain proteins. *Formula:* $C_5H_9NO_2$ [< German *Prolin*]

pro·lix (prō liks′, prō′liks), *adj.* using too many words; too long; tedious: *Conscious dullness has little right to be prolix* (Samuel Johnson). [< Latin *prōlixus* (literally) poured out < *prō-* forth + *lix-*, a root related to *liquēre* to flow, be liquid] —**pro·lix′ly,** *adv.* —**pro·lix′ness,** *n.* —**Syn.** wordy, verbose.

pro·lix·i·ty (prō lik′sə tē), *n., pl.* **-ties.** too great length; tedious length of speech or writing: *the insufferable prolixity of the most prolix of hosts* (Charles J. Lever).

pro·loc·u·tor (prō lok′yə tər), *n.* **1.** a chairman. **2.** a spokesman. [< Latin *prōlocūtor* pleader, advocate < *prōloquī* speak out < *prō-* forth + *loquī* to speak]

Pro·loc·u·tor (prō lok′yə tər), *n.* the Lord Chancellor, as chairman of the House of Lords.

pro·loc·u·tor·ship (prō lok′yə tər ship), *n.* the office or position of a prolocutor.

pro·logue or **pro·log** (prō′lôg, -log), *n.* **1.** a speech or poem addressed to the audience by one of the actors at the beginning of a play. **2.** an introduction to a novel, poem, or other literary work. **3.** any introductory act or event: *The conference . . . had a prologue and epilogue of arrivals and departures* (New Yorker). **4.** the actor who speaks the prologue to a play. [< Latin *prōlogus* < Greek *prólogos* < *pro-* before + *lógos* speech]

pro·logu·ize or **pro·log·ize** (prō′lô gīz, -lo-), *v.i.,* **-ized, -iz·ing.** **1.** to compose a prologue. **2.** to deliver a prologue: *There may prologuize the spirit of Philip* (Milton). —**pro′logu·iz′er** or **pro′log·iz′er,** *n.*

pro·long (prə lông′, -long′), *v.t.* **1.** to make longer; extend: *It was useless to prolong the discussion* (Edith Wharton). **2.** *Obsolete.* to put off in time; postpone: *This wedding-day Perhaps is but prolong'd: have patience* (Shakespeare). [< Late Latin *prōlongāre* < *prō-* forth + *longus* long. Compare PURLOIN.] —**pro·long′er,** *n.* —**Syn. 1.** stretch, protract. See **lengthen.**

pro·long·a·ble (prə lông′ə bəl, -long′-), *adj.* that can be prolonged: *Had the rod been really indefinitely prolongable . . .* (Philosophical Magazine).

pro·lon·gate (prə lông′gāt, -long′-), *v.t.*, **-gat·ed, -gat·ing.** to prolong.

pro·lon·ga·tion (prō′lông gā′shən, -long-), *n.* **1.** a lengthening in time or space; extension: *the sofas resembling a prolongation of uneasy chairs* (George Eliot). **2.** an added part: *The mountains formed a prolongation of the range.*

pro·longe (prō lonj′; *French* prô lôNzh′), *n.* a strong rope with a hook at one end and a toggle at the other, formerly used in moving unlimbered guns, etc. [< French *prolonge* < *prolonger* to prolong]

pro·longed (prə lôngd′, -longd′), *adj.* **1.** lengthened; extended: *the last guest who had made a prolonged stay in his hotel* (Joseph Conrad). **2.** beyond the ordinary, especially in length: *a lean, lank, dark, young man with . . . irregular, rather prolonged features* (H. G. Wells).

pro·long·ment (prə lông′mənt, -long′-), *n.* **1.** the act of prolonging. **2.** the state of being prolonged: *. . . the prolongment of a few earthly days* (Thomas Nashe).

pro·lu·sion (prō lü′zhən), *n.* **1.** a preliminary: *But why such long prolusion and display, Such turning and adjustment of the harp?* (Robert Browning). **2.** an introductory exercise, performance, essay, etc.: *All this tiresome prolusion is only to enable you to understand* (W.H. Hudson). [< Latin *prōlūsiō, -ōnis* < *prōlūdere* to play or practice beforehand < *prō-* before + *lūdere* to play]

pro·lu·so·ry (prō lü′sər ē), *adj.* serving for prolusion; introductory.

prom[1] (prom), *n. U.S. Informal.* a dance or ball given by a college or high-school class. [American English; short for *promenade*]

prom[2] or **Prom** (prom), *n. British Informal.* a promenade concert: *There was a sense of occasion about Saturday evening's Prom, such as normally only attends first and last nights* (London Times).

prom., 1. promontory. 2. promoted.

prom·a·chos (prom′ə kos), *n., pl.* **-choi** (-koi). (in ancient Greece) a person who fights before or for others; champion or defender (used especially of Athene or Apollo). [< Greek *prómachos* < *pró* before + *máchesthai* to fight]

pro·ma·zine (prō′mə zēn, -zin), *n.* a tranquilizing drug used to relieve anxiety and tension in mental illness, alcoholism, and drug addiction. *Formula:* $C_{17}H_{20}N_2S$

pro me·mo·ri·a (prō mə môr′ē ə, -mōr′-), *Latin.* for remembrance; for a memorial.

prom·e·nade (prom′ə nād′, -näd′), *n., v.,* **-nad·ed, -nad·ing.** —*n.* **1.** a walk for pleasure or display: *The Easter promenade is well known as a fashion show.* **2.** a public place for such a walk: *The boardwalk at Atlantic City is a famous promenade.* **3.** a dance; ball; prom. **4.** a march of all the guests at the opening of a formal dance. **5.** a ride, drive, or excursion in a boat: *What do you think of a little promenade at sea?* (Joseph Conrad). **6.** a square-dancing figure in which a couple or, usually, all the couples of a set march once around the square, circle, etc.
—*v.i.* to walk about or up and down for exercise, pleasure, or display. —*v.t.* **1.** to walk through; walk about. **2.** to take on a promenade.
[< earlier French *promenade* < *promener* take for a walk, for Old French *pourmener* < Latin *prōmināre* drive (a beast) on < *prō-* forward + *mināre* drive with shouts < *minae* threats] —**prom′e·nad′er,** *n.*

promenade concert, *British.* a concert at which the audience stands instead of being seated.

promenade deck, a space, usually enclosed, on an upper deck of a ship where passengers can walk about without being exposed to the weather.

prom·er·ops (prom′ə rops), *n.* **1.** any of several nectar-eating South African birds with a slender, curved bill and a very long tail. **2.** any of various other slender-billed birds. [< New Latin *Promerops* the genus name < Greek *pró* before + *mérops* bee eater]

pro·met·a·phase (prō met′ə fāz), *n.* a stage of mitosis occurring between the prophase and the metaphase. [< *pro-*[2] + *metaphase*]

pro·meth·a·zine (prō meth′ə zēn), *n.* Phenergan: *Promethazine . . . is also one of the safest drugs for light anesthesia* (Newsweek). [< *pro*(pyl) + *meth*(yl) + (thi)*azine*]

Pro·me·the·an (prə mē′thē ən), *adj.* of, having to do with, or suggestive of Prometheus: *Andrews is drawn to whatever in architecture is boldly marked with personality, whatever is Promethean and existential* (Harper's).

Pro·me·the·us (prə mē′thē əs, -thüs), *n. Greek Mythology.* one of the Titans. He stole fire from heaven and taught men its use. Zeus punished him by chaining him to a rock.

pro·me·thi·um (prə mē′thē əm), *n.* a rare-earth metallic chemical element whose radioactive isotopes were discovered as a fission product of uranium; (formerly) illinium: *The only rare earth not found in nature is promethium* (Science News Letter). *Symbol:* Pm; *at.no.:* 61; *at.wt.:* (C^{12}) 147 or (O^{16}) 147. [< *Prometheus* + New Latin *-ium,* a suffix meaning "element"]

Pro·min (prō′min), *n. Trademark.* a drug derived from sulfone, used in the treatment of leprosy and tuberculosis. *Formula:* $C_{24}H_{34}N_2Na_2O_{18}S_3$

pro·mine (prō mēn′), *n.* a growth-promoting hormone first isolated from the thymus gland of calves. [< *prom*(ote) + *-ine*]

prom·i·nence (prom′ə nəns), *n.* **1.** the quality or fact of being prominent, distinguished, or conspicuous: *the prominence of Washington as a leader, the prominence of football as a sport, the prominence of athletics in some schools.* **2.** something that juts out or projects, especially upward: *A hill is a prominence.* **3.** a projecting cloud of gas above the atmosphere of the sun: *Spectacular upsurgings of gases in the chromosphere, known as prominences, are sometimes seen: these may shoot out to distances of the order of a few hundred thousand miles* (A.J. Higgs).

prom·i·nent (prom′ə nənt), *adj.* **1.** well-known; important: *a prominent citizen.* **2.** easy to see: *A single tree in a field is prominent.* **3.** standing out; projecting: *Some insects have prominent eyes.* [< Latin *prōminēns, -entis,* present participle of *prōminēre* to jut or stand out < *prō-* forward + *minēre* to jut < *minae, -ārum* projecting points (of mountains); threats] —**prom′i·nent·ly,** *adv.*
—**Syn. 1.** leading. See **eminent. 2. Prominent, conspicuous** mean attracting attention and easily seen. **Prominent** applies to something that stands out from its surroundings or background so that it attracts attention and is easy to see: *He put her picture in a prominent position on his desk.* **Conspicuous** applies to something so plain that it is impossible not to see it, or so unusual, odd, loud, colorful, etc., that it attracts attention: *Bright sweaters are conspicuous in an office.*

prom·is·cu·i·ty (prom′is kyü′ə tē, prō′-mis-), *n., pl.* **-ties.** the fact, state, or condition of being promiscuous.

pro·mis·cu·ous (prə mis′kyu̇ əs), *adj.* **1.** mixed and in disorder: *a promiscuous heap of clothing on a closet floor.* **2.** making no distinctions, especially in sexual relationships. **3.** *Informal.* casual. [< Latin *prōmiscuus* (with English *-ous*) mixed < *prō miscuō* as common < *miscēre* to mix] —**pro·mis′cu·ous·ly,** *adv.* —**pro·mis′cu·ous·ness,** *n.* —**Syn. 1.** miscellaneous.

prom·ise (prom′is), *n., v.,* **-ised, -is·ing.** —*n.* **1.** words said or written, binding a person to do or not to do something: *words of promise* (Tennyson). *A man of honor always keeps his promise.* **2.** an indication of what may be expected: *The clouds give promise of rain. In each dewdrop of the morning lies the promise of a day* (Thoreau). **3.** indication of future excellence; something that gives hope of success: *a young scholar who shows promise.*
—*v.t.* **1.** to make a promise of (something) to (a person, etc.): *to promise help to a friend.* **2.** to give indication of; give hope of; give ground for expectation of: *dark skies that promise snow, a young man who promises much.* **3.** to assure: *Good manners are never out of place, I promise you.* —*v.i.* **1.** to give one's word; make a promise. **2.** to give ground for expectation: *He thought that voyage promised very fair, and that there was a great prospect of advantage* (Daniel Defoe).
[< Latin *prōmissum* < *prōmittere* send forth, foretell; promise < *prō-* before + *mittere* to put, send] —**prom′is·er,** *n.*
—**Syn.** *n.* **1.** vow, pledge, covenant.

Prom·ised Land (prom′ist), **1.** (in the Bible) the country promised by God to Abraham and his descendants; Canaan. Genesis 15:18; 17:1-8. **2.** heaven.

promised land, a place or condition of expected happiness: *America has been a promised land for many immigrants.*

prom·is·ee (prom′ə sē′), *n.* a person to whom a promise is made.

prom·is·ing (prom′ə sing), *adj.* likely to turn out well; hopeful: *a promising beginning, a promising young writer.* —**prom′is·ing·ly,** *adv.*

prom·i·sor (prom′ə sôr, prom′ə sôr′), *n.* a person who makes a promise.

prom·is·so·ry (prom′ə sôr′ē, -sōr′-), *adj.* containing or implying a promise: *promissory oaths.*

promissory note, a written promise to pay a stated sum of money to a certain person at a certain time.

Pro·mi·zole (prō′mə zōl), *n. Trademark.* a drug used in the treatment of leprosy and, combined with streptomycin, in the treatment of tubercular diseases. *Formula:* $C_9H_9N_3O_2S_2$

pro·mo (prō′mō), *n. U.S. Informal.* a television announcement of a forthcoming program on the same network. [short for *promotion*]

prom·on·to·ry (prom′ən tôr′ē, -tōr′-), *n., pl.* **-ries. 1.** a high point of land extending from the coast into the water; headland: *that bold green promontory, known to seamen as Java Head* (Herman Melville). **2.** *Anatomy.* a part that bulges out. [< Medieval Latin *promontorium,* variation (influenced by Latin *mōns* mount) of Latin *prōmunturium*]

Promontory (def. 1)

pro·mor·pho·log·i·cal (prō′môr fə loj′ə-kəl), *adj.* having to do with promorphology.

pro·mor·phol·o·gist (prō′môr fol′ə jist), *n.* a person who is skilled in promorphology.

pro·mor·phol·o·gy (prō′môr fol′ə jē), *n.* the branch of morphology which deals with organic forms from the point of view of geometry or mathematical law. [< German *Promorphologie* < *pro-* pro-[2] + *Morphologie* morphology]

pro·mote (prə mōt′), *v.t.,* **-mot·ed, -mot·ing. 1.** to raise in rank, condition, or importance: *Those who pass the test will be promoted to the next higher grade.* **2.** to help to grow or develop; help to success: *A kindly feeling toward other countries will promote peace.* **3.** to help to organize; start: *Several bankers promoted the new company.* **4.** to further the sale of (an article) by advertising. [< Latin *prōmōtus,* past participle of *prōmovēre* < *prō-* forward + *movēre* to move]
—**Syn. 1.** advance, elevate, exalt. **2. Promote, further** mean to help something move toward a desired end. **Promote** applies to any phase or stage of development, including the initial one: *a fair designed to promote the sale of goods. The teacher strove to promote the students' interest in Shakespeare.* **Further** applies especially to any stage beyond the initial one: *Getting a scholarship will further his education.*

pro·mot·er (prə mō′tər), *n.* **1.** a person or thing that promotes, encourages, or furthers: *Good humor is a promoter of friendship.* **2.** a person who organizes new companies and secures capital for them.

Promoter of the Faith, devil's advocate.

pro·mo·tion (prə mō′shən), *n.* **1.** an advance in rank or importance: *The clerk was given a promotion and an increase in salary.* **2.** a helping to grow or develop; helping along to success: *The local doctors were busy in the promotion of a health campaign.* **3.** a helping to organize; starting: *It took much time and money for the promotion of the new company.*

pro·mo·tion·al (prə mō′shə nəl), *adj.* of, having to do with, or used in the promotion of a person, product, or enterprise: *The firm mails out around three and a half million . . . promotional pamphlets, and so on—in the course of a year* (New Yorker).

pro·mo·tive (prə mō′tiv), *adj.* tending to promote: *promotive of business interests.*

Pro·mo·tor Fi·de·i (prō mō′tər fī′dē ī), *pl.* **Pro·mo·to·res Fidei** (prō′mō tō′rēz). Promoter of the Faith. [< New Latin *Promotor Fidei*]

prompt (prompt), *adj.* **1.** ready and willing; on time; quick: *Be prompt to obey. But he learns to tell time much earlier than he learns to be prompt* (Sidonie M. Gruenberg). **2.** done at once; made without delay: *I expect a prompt answer.* **3.** *Especially British.* of a prompter; used in prompting: *a prompt box on a stage.*
—*v.t.* **1.** to cause (someone) to do something: *His curiosity prompted him to ask questions.* **2.** to give rise to; suggest; inspire: *A kind thought prompted the gift.* **3.** to remind (a learner, speaker, actor, etc.) of the words or actions needed: *Do you know your part in the play, or shall I prompt you?*
—*v.i.* to act as prompter.
—*n.* **1.** an act of prompting. **2.** something that prompts. **3.** *Commerce.* **a.** a limit of time allowed for payment of goods purchased. **b.** the contract determining this limit of time.
[< Latin *promptus* ready, at hand; (originally) past participle of *prōmere* bring to light < *prō-* forward + *emere* buy, (originally) take. Doublet of PRONTO.] —**prompt′ly,** *adv.* —**prompt′ness,** *n.*
—**Syn.** *adj.* **1.** punctual. See **ready. 2.** immediate, swift. *-v.t.* **1.** incite, impel, induce.

prompt·book (prompt′buk′), *n.* a copy of a play prepared for the prompter's use, containing the text as it is to be spoken and directions for the performance.

prompt·er (promp′tər), *n.* a person who tells actors, speakers, etc., what to say when they forget.

promp·ti·tude (promp′tə tüd, -tyüd), *n.* readiness in acting or deciding; promptness: *Our borrowers generally have met the repayment installments on their loans with a commendable promptitude* (London Times).

prompt note, a note reminding a person of the date a loan is due.

promp·ture (promp′chər), *n. Archaic.* prompting; suggestion; instigation.

pro·mul·gate (prō mul′gāt; *especially British* prom′əl gāt), *v.t.*, **-gat·ed, -gat·ing. 1.** to announce officially; proclaim formally: *The constitution probably will soon be promulgated and elections are promised within a year* (Newsweek). **2.** to spread far and wide: *Schools try to promulgate knowledge and good habits.* [< Latin *prōmulgāre*]

pro·mul·ga·tion (prō′mul gā′shən; *especially British* prom′əl gā′shən), *n.* **1.** a promulgating: . . . *the very promulgation of the gospel* (Richard Hooker). **2.** a being promulgated. **3.** the official publication of a new law or decree.

pro·mul·ga·tor (prō mul′gā tər; *especially British* prom′əl gā′tər), *n.* a person who promulgates: *Christ . . . the promulgator . . . of a new spiritual economy* (John Goodwin).

pro·mulge (prō mulj′), *v.t.*, **mulged, -mulg·ing.** *Archaic.* to promulgate.

pro·my·ce·li·al (prō′mī sē′lē əl), *adj.* of or having to do with the promycelium.

pro·my·ce·li·um (prō′mī sē′lē əm), *n., pl.* **-li·a** (-lē ə). *Botany.* the filamentous product of the germination of a spore. [< *pro-*[2] + *mycelium*]

prom·y·shlen·nik (prom′ə shlen′ik), *n., pl.* **-shlen·ni·ki** (-shlen′ə kē). a Russian frontiersman of Siberia, the Aleutian Islands, or Alaska: *The promyshlenniki, the gangs of Russian fur hunters . . ., were a tough lot* (New Scientist). [< Russian *promyshlennik*]

pron., **1. a.** pronominal. **b.** pronoun. **2. a.** pronounced. **b.** pronunciation.

pro·na·os (prō nā′os), *n., pl.* **-na·oi** (-nā′oi). the porch or vestibule in front of the cella of a temple: *The chapel has an atrium, or pronaos, supported by slender Corinthian columns* (New Yorker). [< Latin *pronāos* < Greek *prónāos* < *pró* before + *nāós* temple]

Pronaos
Troad, Greece

pro·na·tal·ist (prō nā′tə list), *adj.* favoring a high rate of birth: . . . *a reluctance to develop pronatalist policies* (London Times).

pro·nate (prō′nāt), *v.*, **-nat·ed, -nat·ing.** —*v.t.* **1.** to hold (the hand or forelimb) with the palm down. **2.** to make prone. —*v.i.* to be pronated. [< Late Latin *prōnāre* (with English *-ate*[1]) throw (oneself) face down, bow to the ground < *prōnus* prone]

pro·na·tion (prō nā′shən), *n.* **1. a.** a rotation of the hand or forelimb so that the palm turns down. **b.** a similar movement of the foot, hind limb, shoulder, etc. **2.** such a position. **3.** a making prone.

pro·na·tor (prō nā′tər), *n.* a muscle that effects or assists in pronation.

prone (prōn), *adj.* **1.** inclined; liable: *We are prone to think evil of people we dislike.* **2.** lying face down. **3.** lying flat: *Ancient towers . . . Fall prone* (William Cowper). **4.** *Poetic.* having a downward slope or direction: *The sun . . . was hasting now with prone career To the ocean isles* (Milton). **5.** abject; base. [< Latin *prōnus* bent forward; inclined to < *prō-* forward] —**prone′ly,** *adv.*
—**Syn. 1.** disposed, apt. **3.** recumbent, prostrate.

prone·ness (prōn′nis), *n.* **1.** inclination; tendency; preference. **2.** prone position.

pro·neph·ric (prō nef′rik), *adj.* of or having to do with the pronephros: *the pronephric duct.*

pro·neph·ros (prō nef′ros), *n., pl.* **-roi** (-roi). *Embryology.* the most anterior part of the renal organ of vertebrate embryos. [< New Latin *pronephros* < Greek *pró* pro-[2] + *nephrós* kidney]

prong (prông, prong), *n.* **1.** one of the pointed ends of a fork, antler, etc. **2.** a branch or fork of a small stream: *Carpenter's Creek, a branch of Jackson's, which is the principal prong of the James River* (George Washington). **3.** any branch, fork, division, or section: *200 guerrillas . . . struck in three prongs* (New York Times).
—*v.t.* **1.** to pierce or stab with a prong. **2.** to supply with prongs. **3.** to turn up the soil with a fork; fork.
[origin uncertain]

-pronged, *combining form.* having —— prongs, sections, aspects, etc.: . . . *a three-pronged thrust consisting of sabotage, infiltration, and ultimate invasion* (New York Times).

prong·horn (prông′hôrn′, prong′-), *n., pl.* **-horns** or (*collectively*) **-horn.** a mammal like an antelope, living on the plains of western North America. Both sexes have bony horns with one short branch or prong jutting forward and with a black covering which is shed annually. [American English; short for earlier *pronghorn*(ed antelope)]

Pronghorn
(about 3 ft. high at the shoulder)

pronghorn antelope, the pronghorn.

pro·nom·i·nal (prō nom′ə nəl), *adj.* of or having to do with pronouns; having the nature of a pronoun. [< Late Latin *prōnōminālis* < Latin *prōnōmen, -inis* pronoun]

pro·nom·i·nal·ly (prō nom′ə nə lē), *adv.* like a pronoun.

pro·noun (prō′noun), *n. Grammar.* **1.** a word used to indicate without naming; word used instead of a noun. **2.** the part of speech or form class to which such words belong. *Examples: I, we, you, he, it,* and *they* are personal pronouns; *my, mine, your, yours, his, our, ours, their, theirs,* etc., are possessive pronouns; *who, whose, which, this, mine,* and *whatever* are interrogative pronouns; *who, that, which,* and *what* are also relative pronouns. *Abbr.:* pron. [< *pro-*[1] in place of + *noun,* as translation of Latin *prōnōmen* < *prō-* in place of + *nōmen* name]

pro·nounce (prə nouns′), *v.*, **-nounced, -nounc·ing.** —*v.t.* **1.** to make the sounds of; speak: *Pronounce your words clearly. In the word "dumb" you don't pronounce the "b."* **2.** to declare (a person or thing) to be: *The doctor pronounced her cured.* **3.** to declare formally or solemnly: *The judge pronounced sentence on the criminal.* —*v.i.* **1.** to pronounce words: *In speaking, they pronounce through the nose and throat* (Jonathan Swift). **2.** to give an opinion or decision: *Only an expert should pronounce on this case.* [< Old French *pronuncier,* learned borrowing from Latin *prōnūntiāre* < *prō-* forth + *nūntiāre* announce < *nūntius* messenger; information, report] —**pro·nounc′er,** *n.*

pro·nounce·a·ble (prə noun′sə bəl), *adj.* that can be pronounced: *There is no Name pronounceable by Men or Angels, which can define God as He is* (George Wither).

pro·nounced (prə nounst′), *adj.* strongly marked; decided: *She has very pronounced likes and dislikes.*

pro·nounc·ed·ly (prə noun′sid lē), *adv.* in a pronounced manner; to a pronounced degree: *This was not air he was breathing, he felt, but a denser, hot fluid with a pronouncedly sweet taste* (Atlantic).

pro·nounce·ment (prə nouns′mənt), *n.* **1.** a formal statement; a declaration. **2.** an opinion; decision.

pro·nounc·ing alphabet (prə noun′sing), *Military.* a list of short, easily distinguished words used to identify letters in a radio or telephonic message; alphabet code: *"Alfa" and "Bravo" have replaced the former "Able" and "Baker" in the authorized pronouncing alphabet.*

pron·to (pron′tō), *adv. U.S. Informal.* promptly; quickly; right away: *Immigration authorities had him arrested and deported pronto* (Liberty). [American English < Spanish *pronto* < Latin *promptus.* Doublet of PROMPT.]

Pron·to·sil (pron′tə səl), *n. Trademark.* a dye product formerly used in the treatment of streptococcal infections. It was found in 1932 to contain sulfanilamide, the first of the sulfa drugs to be widely used. *Formula:* $C_{12}H_{13}N_5O_2S.HCl$

pro·nu·cle·us (prō nü′klē əs, -nyü′-), *n., pl.* **-cle·i** (-klē ī). *Biology.* the nucleus of a sperm or of an ovum, just before these unite in fertilization to form the nucleus (synkaryon) of the zygote. [< New Latin *pronucleus* < Greek *pró* pro-[2], earlier + New Latin *nucleus* nucleus]

pro·nun·ci·a·men·to (prə nun′sē ə men′tō, -shē-), *n., pl.* **-tos.** a formal announcement; proclamation; manifesto. [American English < Spanish *pronunciamiento* < *pronunciar* to pronounce < Latin *prōnūntiāre*]

pro·nun·ci·a·tion (prə nun′sē ā′shən), *n.* **1.** a way of pronouncing: *This book gives the pronunciation of each main word.* **2.** a pronouncing. [< Latin *prōnūntiātiō, -ōnis* < *prōnūntiāre* to pronounce]

pro·oe·mi·on (prō ē′mē on), *n., pl.* **-mi·a** (-mē ə). proem.

pro·oe·mi·um (prō ē′mē əm), *n., pl.* **-mi·a** (-mē ə). proem.

proof (prüf), *n.* **1.** a way or means of showing beyond doubt the truth of something: *Is what you say a guess, or have you proof?* **2.** the establishment of the truth of anything; demonstration: *In proof of this theory, I shall make certain studies.* **3.** an act of testing; trial: *to put a theory to the proof.* **4.** the condition of having been tested and approved. **5.** a trial impression from type. A book is first printed in proof so that errors can be corrected and additions made: *Did the author correct the proofs?* (G. B. Williams). **6.** a trial print of an etching, photographic negative, etc. **7. a.** the standard strength of alcoholic liquors. **b.** strength with reference to this standard: *This brandy is 84 proof.*
—*adj.* **1.** of tested value against something: *proof against being taken by surprise.* **2.** used to test or prove; serving for a trial. **3.** (of an alcoholic liquor) of standard strength.
—*v.t.* **1.** to render proof against something; make resistant to something. **2. a.** to proofread. **b.** to make a proof of.
[< Old French *prouve,* alteration (influenced by *prouver* to prove) of earlier *prueve* < Late Latin *proba* < Latin *probāre* prove. Doublet of PROBE.] —**proof′er,** *n.*
—**Syn.** *n.* **1.** See **evidence. 2.** confirmation, corroboration. **3.** experiment.

-proof, *suffix.* protected against ——; safe from ——: *Fireproof = safe from fire. Waterproof = protected against water.*

proof coin, 1. a coin struck as a test of a new die. **2.** one of a limited number of early impressions, especially struck by a mint for dealers and collectors.

proof gallon, a gallon of proof spirit.

proof·ing (prü′fing), *n.* the treating of something to make it resistant: *"Pigeon proofing" of buildings . . . involves the use of screens and spikes* (Wall Street Journal).

proof·less (prüf′lis), *adj.* without proof.

proof of loss, a written statement from an insured person claiming payment of loss under an insurance policy: *Nor did he* *remember that in order to collect fully on a fire insurance policy, proof of loss must be supplied within sixty days* (New Yorker).

proof positive, incontrovertible proof: *He had won ascendancy again, and it was all a tribute to his dreams, proof positive of his skill in making his myths come true* (Listener).

proof·read (prüf′rēd′), *v.t., v.i.,* **-read** (-red′), **-read·ing.** to read (printers' proofs, etc.) and mark errors to be corrected. [American English; probably back formation < *proofreading,* or *proofreader*] —**proof′-read′er,** *n.*

proof·read·ing (prüf′rē′ding), *n.* the act of reading printers' proofs.

proof sheet, a printers' proof.

proof spirit, **1.** *U.S.* an alcoholic liquor, or mixture of alcohol and water, with a specific gravity of .93353 and with half of its volume consisting of alcohol of a specific gravity of .7939 at 60 degrees Fahrenheit. **2.** (in Great Britain) a similar alcoholic liquor with a specific gravity of .91984.

proof-test (prüf′test′), *v.t.* to subject (a weapon) to a conclusive test of its capacities or condition.

proof text, a passage of Scripture brought forward to prove a special doctrine or belief: *The story of Peter and the "rock" in Matthew 16 can now be traced to one particular passage of Isaiah, used elsewhere in the New Testament and in the Scrolls as a proof text for the founding of the community* (Harper's).

prop[1] (prop), *v.,* **propped, prop·ping,** *n.* —*v.t.* **1.** to hold up by placing a support under or against: *Prop the clothesline with a stick She sat silent, her head still propped by the arm that rested on the back of the sofa* (Edith Wharton). **2.** to support; sustain: *to prop a failing cause. Justice should not be propped up by injustice* (Edward Miall). —*v.i. Australian.* (of a horse) to stop suddenly. [< noun] —*n.* a thing or person used to support another: *The boys used two sticks as props for the sagging tent. Advertising is an indispensable prop to the women's clothing business.* [origin uncertain. Compare Middle Dutch *proppe.*] —**Syn.** *n.* support, brace, stay.

prop[2] (prop), *n. Informal.* **1.** an object, such as a weapon or chair, used in a play. **2.** a property man. [short for *property*]

prop[3] (prop), *n. Slang.* an airplane propeller. [short for *propeller*]

prop., **1.** properly. **2.** property. **3.** proposition. **4.** proprietor.

pro·pae·deu·tic (prō′pi dü′tik, -dyü′-), *adj.* of, having to do with, or of the nature of preliminary instruction; introductory to some art or science. —*n.* a propaedeutic subject or study. [< Greek *propaideúein* teach beforehand (< *pró* before + *paideúein* teach, bring up) + inserted English *-t* + *-ic*]

pro·pae·deu·ti·cal (prō′pi dü′tə kəl, -dyü′-), *adj.* propaedeutic.

pro·pae·deu·tics (prō′pə dü′tiks, -dyü′-), *n.* the preliminary rules or principles necessary for the study of some art or science.

prop·a·ga·bil·i·ty (prop′ə gə bil′ə tē), *n.* propagable quality: . . . *the propagability of the micrococcus of tubercle by the milk of cows affected with tuberculosis* (William B. Carpenter).

prop·a·ga·ble (prop′ə gə bəl), *adj.* that can be propagated: . . . *the olive not being successfully propagable by seed* (Thomas Browne).

prop·a·gan·da (prop′ə gan′də), *n.* **1.** systematic efforts to spread opinions or beliefs; any plan or method for spreading opinions or beliefs. **2.** the opinions or beliefs thus spread: *None the less, national propaganda in its historical forms has been resisted* (London Times). [< New Latin (*congregatio de*) *propaganda* (*fide*) (congregation for) propagating (the faith); *propaganda,* ablative feminine gerundive of Latin *prōpāgāre* to propagate]

Prop·a·gan·da (prop′ə gan′də), *n.* a committee of cardinals established by Pope Gregory XV in 1622 to supervise foreign missions.

prop·a·gan·dism (prop′ə gan′diz əm), *n.* the use of propaganda.

prop·a·gan·dist (prop′ə gan′dist), *n.* a person who gives time or effort to the spreading of some opinion, belief, or principle: *The monks . . . were the chief propagandists of Christianity in Palestine* (Alexander W. Kinglake). —*adj.* of propaganda or propagandists.

prop·a·gan·dist·ic (prop′ə gan dis′tik), *adj.* of or having to do with propagandists or the use of propaganda: *There are obvious propagandistic advantages in popularizing English art abroad* (New Yorker). —**prop′-a·gan·dist′i·cal·ly,** *adv.*

prop·a·gan·dize (prop′ə gan′dīz), *v.,* **-dized, -diz·ing.** —*v.t.* **1.** to propagate or spread (doctrines, etc.) by propaganda. **2.** to subject to propaganda: *to propagandize voters. Officially, of course, she is doing her job of propagandizing the workers* (Harper's). —*v.i.* to carry on propaganda: *The Ministry of Health, in propagandizing, is not so far forward as the Ministry of Agriculture* (J.W.R. Scott). —**prop′a·gan′diz·er,** *n.*

prop·a·gate (prop′ə gāt), *v.,* **-gat·ed, -gat·ing.** —*v.i.* **1.** to produce offspring. **2.** to reproduce. —*v.t.* **1.** to increase in number or intensity: *Trees propagate themselves by seeds.* **2.** to cause to increase in number by the production of young: *Cows and sheep are propagated on farms.* **3.** to spread (news, knowledge, etc.): *Don't propagate unkind reports.* **4.** to pass on; send further: *Sound is propagated by vibrations.* [< Latin *prōpāgāre* (with English *-ate*[1]) to multiply plants by slips or layers < *prō-* forth + *pag-,* root of *pangere* make fast, pin down] —**Syn.** *-v.t.* **1.** multiply. **3.** extend, diffuse.

prop·a·ga·tion (prop′ə gā′shən), *n.* **1.** the breeding of plants or animals: *Our propagation of poppies is by seed, and of roses by cuttings.* **2.** a making more widely known; getting more widely believed; spreading: *the propagation of the principles of science.* **3.** a passing on; sending further; spreading or extending: *the propagation of the shock of an earthquake, the propagation of a family trait from father to son.* **4.** the travel of electromagnetic or sound waves through a medium such as air or water.

prop·a·ga·tion·al (prop′ə gā′shə nəl), *adj.* of or having to do with propagation: . . . *atmospheric and propagational disturbances* (New Scientist).

prop·a·ga·tive (prop′ə gā′tiv), *adj.* serving or tending to propagate: *A church without propagative power . . . cannot be other than a calamity* (Henry Drummond).

prop·a·ga·tor (prop′ə gā′tər), *n.* a person or thing that propagates: *A zealous propagator of Christianity* (Edward A. Freeman).

prop·a·gule (prop′ə gyül), *n. Botany.* a bud or other offshoot able to develop into a new plant.

pro·pane (prō′pān), *n.* a heavy, colorless, gaseous hydrocarbon of the methane series, present in crude petroleum, used as a fuel, refrigerant, solvent, etc. *Formula:* C_3H_8

pro·pa·nol (prō′pə nōl, -nol), *n.* propyl alcohol. [< *propan*(e) + *-ol*[1]]

pro·par·ox·y·tone (prō′par ok′sə tōn), *adj., n., v.,* **-toned, -ton·ing.** *Greek Grammar.* —*adj.* having an acute accent on the antepenult. —*n.* a proparoxytone word. —*v.t.* to accent on the antepenult. [< Greek *proparoxýtonos* < *pro-* before + *paroxýtonos* paroxytone]

pro·par·ox·y·ton·ic (prō′par ok′sə ton′ik), *adj.* proparoxytone.

pro pa·tri·a (prō pā′trē ə, pat′rē ə), *Latin.* for one's country or native land.

pro·pel (prə pel′), *v.t.,* **-pelled, -pel·ling.** to drive forward; force ahead: *to propel a boat by oars, a person propelled by ambition.* [< Latin *prōpellere* < *prō-* forward + *pellere* to push]

pro·pel·la·ble (prə pel′ə bəl), *adj.* that can be propelled: *Some* [*barges*] *are propellable by oars* (Hawthorne).

pro·pel·lant (prə pel′ənt), *n.* a propelling agent, as an explosive that propels a projectile, or a fuel and an oxidizer that propel a rocket: *In a rocket, the propellant is some material carried along in tanks* (Christian Science Monitor). See picture under **rocket.** [alteration of earlier *propellent*]

pro·pel·lent (prə pel′ənt), *adj.* propelling; driving forward: *The mayor was the propellent force for new street lights.* —*n.* a thing or person that propels. [< Latin *prōpellēns, -entis,* present participle of *prōpellere* propel]

pro·pel·ler (prə pel′ər), *n.* **1.** a device consisting of a revolving hub with blades, for propelling boats, airships, and airplanes: *However, a propeller is still far more effective than a jet at low flying speed* (J.M. Stephenson). See **angular velocity** for picture. **2.** a person or thing that propels.

pro·pend (prō pend′), *v.i. Archaic.* to incline; tend: *My thinking all propended to the ancient world of herdsmen and warriors* (Alexander W. Kinglake). [< Latin *prōpendēre* incline to; see PROPENSITY.]

pro·pense (prō pens′), *adj. Archaic.* inclined; disposed.

pro·pen·sion (prō pen′shən), *n. Archaic.* inclination; tendency: *There seemed to be something fatal in that propension of nature tending directly to the life of misery which was to befall me* (Daniel Defoe).

pro·pen·si·ty (prə pen′sə tē), *n., pl.* **-ties.** a natural inclination or bent; inclination: *the natural propensity to find fault* (James Fenimore Cooper). *Most boys have a propensity for playing with machinery.* [< Latin *prōpēnsus,* past participle of *prōpendēre* incline to; weigh over (< *prō-* forward + *pendēre* hang) + English *-ity*]

pro·pe·nyl (prō′pə nəl), *n.* any of certain hydrocarbon radicals of the formula C_3H_5

prop·er (prop′ər), *adj.* **1.** correct; right; fitting: *soil in proper condition for planting, to use a word in its proper sense. Night is the proper time to sleep, and bed the proper place.* **2.** strictly so called; in the strict sense of the word: *England proper does not include Wales.* **3.** decent; respectable: *proper conduct.* **4.** *Grammar.* designating a particular person, place, etc. *France* is a proper noun, *French* a proper adjective. **5.** *Informal.* complete; thorough; fine; excellent: *a proper jest, and never heard before* (Shakespeare). **6.** *Archaic.* good-looking; handsome: *By St. Anne! but he is a proper youth* (Scott). **7.** belonging exclusively or distinctively: *qualities proper to a substance.* **8.** (of a heraldic bearing) represented in its natural colors: *an eagle proper.* **9.** *Archaic.* belonging to oneself; own: *to shroud me from my proper scorn* (Tennyson). —*adv. Informal.* properly; completely; thoroughly: *Had 'em that time—had 'em proper!* (Sir Arthur Conan Doyle).
[< Old French *propre,* learned borrowing from Latin *proprius* one's own]
—**Syn.** *adj.* **1.** suitable, becoming, appropriate. **3.** seemly, decorous.

➔ **Proper adjectives.** Proper nouns used as adjectives and adjectives directly derived from proper names are regularly capitalized. When their reference to a particular person, place, etc., has been weakened or lost, they become simple adjectives and are usually not capitalized: *the French language, Roman ruins* (but *roman type*).

prop·er·din (prop′ər din), *n.* a protein substance present in blood plasma, held to be capable of inactivating or killing various bacteria and viruses and of reducing the effects of radiation. [< *pro-*[1] + Latin *perdere* to destroy + English *-in*]

proper fraction, a fraction less than 1: *2/3, 1/8, 3/4, and 199/200 are proper fractions.*

prop·er·ly (prop′ər lē), *adv.* **1.** in a proper, correct, or fitting manner: *to eat properly, to be dressed properly for cold weather.* **2.** rightly; justly: *to be properly indignant at the offer of a bribe.* **3.** strictly: *Properly speaking, a whale is not a fish.* **4.** *Informal.* thoroughly; completely; excellently.

proper motion, *Astronomy.* the apparent angular motion of a star across the sky after allowing for precession, nutation, and aberration, due to real motions of the star itself: *It is extremely improbable that two unconnected stars will have the same proper motion, and so the components of an optical double will be found to be moving independently* (W.H. Marshall).

proper noun, a noun naming a particular person, place, or thing, written with an initial capital letter. *John, Chicago,* and *World War* are proper nouns.

prop·er·tied (prop′ər tēd), *adj.* owning property: *the propertied classes.*

prop·er·ty (prop′ər tē), *n., pl.* **-ties.** **1.** a thing or things owned; possession or possessions: *This house is Mr. Bell's property. When the main forms of property are intangible the difficulty of defining rights and duties is much greater* (Atlantic). **2.** ownership; the right of ownership. **3.** a piece of land or real estate: *a property on Main Street.* **4.** a quality or power belonging specially to something: *Soap has the property of removing dirt. All bodies when placed in a suitably large magnetic field develop magnetic properties* (W.D. Corner). **5.** *Logic.* a quality that is common to all the members of a class, but does not necessarily distinguish that class from other classes.

properties, furniture, weapons, etc. (everything except scenery and clothes), used in staging a play: *I will draw a bill of properties such as our play needs* (Shakespeare). [Middle English *proprete* < Old French *propriete* < Latin *proprietās* < *proprius* one's own, proper. Doublet of PROPRIETY.] —**prop′er·ty·less,** *adj.*

—**Syn. 1. Property, goods, effects** mean what someone owns. **Property** means whatever someone legally owns, including land, buildings, animals, money, stocks, documents, objects, and rights: *Property is taxable.* **Goods** means movable personal property, as distinguished from land, buildings, etc., but applies chiefly to things of use in the house or on the land, such as furniture, furnishings, implements, never to money or papers, etc.: *Professional movers packed our goods.* **Effects** means personal possessions, including goods, clothing, jewelry, personal belongings, and papers: *I packed our other effects.* **4.** See **quality.**

property man, a man employed in a theater to look after the stage properties.

pro·phage (prō′fāj), *n.* a provirus; a fusion of the genetic material of a virus with that of a host bacterium, capable under certain circumstances of becoming a group of viral particles. [< *pro-*[2] + Greek *phageîn* eat]

pro·phase (prō′fāz′), *n. Biology.* the first stage in mitosis, that includes the formation of the spindle and the lengthwise splitting of the chromosomes: *It is also highly probable that the chromosomes are more liable to break . . . at a stage called prophase, prior to cell formation* (Bulletin of Atomic Scientists). See **mitosis** for picture. [< *pro-*[2] + *phase*]

proph·e·cy (prof′ə sē), *n., pl.* **-cies. 1.** telling what will happen; foretelling future events. **2.** something told about the future; indication of something to come: *A laughing face . . . where scarce appeared The uncertain prophecy of beard* (John Greenleaf Whittier). **3.** a divinely inspired utterance, revelation, writing, etc. **4.** a book of prophecies: *the prophecy of Isaiah.* [< Old French *prophecie,* learned borrowing from Latin *prophētīa* < Greek *prophēteiā* < *prophḗtēs* prophet]

proph·e·si·a·ble (prof′ə sī′ə bəl), *adj.* capable of being prophesied: *. . . the forseeable, or at least reasonably prophesiable, conditions over the next 20 years* (Scientific American).

proph·e·si·er (prof′ə sī′ər), *n.* a person who prophesies or predicts: *. . . has deceived me, like a double-meaning prophesier* (Shakespeare).

proph·e·sy (prof′ə sī), *v.,* **-sied, -sy·ing.** —*v.i.* **1.** to tell what will happen. **2.** to speak when or as if divinely inspired. **3.** *Obsolete.* to interpret or expound the Scriptures. —*v.t.* **1.** to foretell; predict: *The sailor prophesied a severe storm.* **2.** to utter in prophecy: *The prophets prophesy lies in my name* (Jeremiah 14:14). [(originally) spelling variant of Middle English *prophecy,* verb]

proph·et (prof′it), *n.* **1.** a person who tells what will happen. **2.** a person who preaches what he believes has been revealed to him: *Every religion has its prophets.* **3.** a spokesman of some cause, doctrine, etc.: *Nothing could have been further from [Theodore] Roosevelt's intentions than to set up as the prophet of some great Reformation* (Baron Charnwood).

the Prophet, a. Mohammed: *If but the Vine and Love-abjuring Band Are in the Prophet's Paradise to stand* (Edward FitzGerald). **b.** Joseph Smith, the founder of the Mormon religion: *The Prophet, his brother Hyram, and other leading Mormons were seized* (John H. Blunt).

the Prophets, books of the Old Testament written by prophets: *The Prophets are divided into the Major Prophets and Minor Prophets.*

[< Latin *prophēta,* or *prophētes* < Greek *prophḗtēs,* ultimately < *pro-* before + *phánai* to speak]

proph·et·ess (prof′ə tis), *n.* a woman prophet.

proph·et·hood (prof′it hu̇d), *n.* the character or office of a prophet.

pro·phet·ic (prə fet′ik), *adj.* **1.** belonging to a prophet; such as a prophet has: *prophetic power.* **2.** containing prophecy: *a prophetic saying.* **3.** giving warning of what is to happen; foretelling: *Thunder is prophetic of showers. It seem'd to those within the wall A cry prophetic of their fall* (Byron).

pro·phet·i·cal (prə fet′ə kəl), *adj.* prophetic.

pro·phet·i·cal·ly (prə fet′ə klē), *adv.* in a prophetic manner.

proph·et·ism (prof′ə tiz əm), *n.* the action or practice of a prophet or prophets, especially the system or principles of the Hebrew prophets: *Prophetism attained its apogee among the Semites of Palestine* (Thomas Huxley).

pro·phy·lac·tic (prō′fə lak′tik, prof′ə-), *adj.* **1.** protecting from disease: *vaccination and other prophylactic measures. Hope of preventing tuberculosis by daily prophylactic doses of the drug isoniazid is now seen* (Science News Letter). **2.** protective; preservative; precautionary.

—*n.* **1.** a medicine, treatment, or device that protects against disease. **2.** a precaution: *To keep the mind engrossed was the great prophylactic against fear* (John Buchan).

[< Greek *prophylaktikós* < *prophylássein* take precautions against < *pro-* before + *phylássein,* dialectal variant of *phyláttein* to guard < *phýlax, -akos* a guard] —**pro′phy·lac′ti·cal·ly,** *adv.*

pro·phy·lax·is (prō′fə lak′sis, prof′ə-), *n.* **1.** a protection from disease. **2.** the treatment to prevent disease. [< New Latin *prophylaxis* < Greek *pro-* before + *phýlaxis* protection < *prophylássein;* see PROPHYLACTIC]

pro·pine (prō pēn′, -pīn′), *n., v.,* **-pined, -pin·ing.** *Scottish.* —*n.* a gift. [< Middle French *propine* < *propiner;* see the verb] —*v.t.* **1.** to offer (something) to one to drink. **2.** to give; present. [< Middle French *propiner,* learned borrowing from Latin *propīnāre* supply with food or water; (originally) drink one's health < Greek *propieîn,* reduction of *propínein* drink a toast < *pró* forth + *pínein* to drink]

pro·pin·qui·ty (prō ping′kwə tē), *n.* **1.** nearness in place, especially personal nearness. **2.** nearness of blood; kinship. [< Latin *propinquitās* < *propinquus* near < *prope* near]

pro·pi·ol·ic acid (prō′pē ol′ik), a liquid organic acid with an odor resembling that of acetic acid. *Formula:* $C_3H_2O_2$ [< *propi*(onic) + *-ol*[1] + *-ic*]

pro·pi·o·nate (prō′pē ə nāt), *n.* a salt or ester of propionic acid.

pro·pi·on·ic acid (prō′pē on′ik, -ō′nik), a fatty acid with a pungent odor, found in perspiration and produced synthetically from ethyl alcohol and carbon monoxide, used in the form of its propionates to inhibit mold in bread, as an ingredient in perfumes, etc. *Formula:* $C_3H_6O_2$ [< French *propionique* < *pro*(to)- first + Greek *píon* fat + French *-ique* -ic (because it is the first of the true carboxylic acids)]

pro·pi·o·nyl (prō′pē ə nəl), *n.* a univalent radical (C_3H_5O) contained in propionic acid, etc. [< *propion*(ic) + *-yl*]

pro·pi·ti·a·ble (prə pish′ē ə bəl), *adj.* that may be propitiated.

pro·pi·ti·ate (prə pish′ē āt), *v.t.,* **-at·ed, -at·ing.** to prevent or reduce the anger of; win the favor of; appease or conciliate: *Let fierce Achilles . . . The god propitiate, and the pest assuage* (Alexander Pope). [< Latin *propitiāre* (with English *-ate*[1]) < *propitius* propitious] —**pro·pi′ti·at′ing·ly,** *adv.*

pro·pi·ti·a·tion (prə pish′ē ā′shən), *n.* **1.** the act of propitiating. **2.** that which propitiates. **3.** *Theology.* Christ, and His life and death, as the means by which reconciliation of God and mankind is attained.

pro·pi·ti·a·tive (prə pish′ē ā′tiv), *adj.* serving or tending to propitiate.

pro·pi·ti·a·tor (prə pish′ē ā′tər), *n.* a person who propitiates.

pro·pi·ti·a·to·ry (prə pish′ē ə tôr′ē, -tōr′-), *adj., n., pl.* **-ries.** —*adj.* intended to propitiate; making propitiation; conciliatory: *a propitiatory offering.* —*n.* the mercy seat.

pro·pi·tious (prə pish′əs), *adj.* **1.** favorable: *propitious weather for our trip, a propitious reception. The seed of pessimism, once lodged within him, flourished in a propitious soil* (Lytton Strachey). **2.** favorably inclined; gracious. [< Old French *propicius,* learned borrowing from Latin *propitius* (originally) falling forward < *prō-* forward + *petere* go toward] —**pro·pi′tious·ly,** *adv.* —**pro·pi′tious·ness,** *n.* —**Syn. 1.** auspicious, promising.

prop·jet (prop′jet′), *n.* a turboprop: *The propjet has propellers driven by jet engines* (Wall Street Journal).

prop man, *Informal.* property man; a man in charge of stage properties at a theater who furnishes them as needed

prop·o·lis (prop′ə lis), *n.* a reddish, resinous substance collected by bees from the buds of trees, used to stop up crevices in the hives, to strengthen the cells, etc. [< Latin *propolis* < Greek *própolis* bee glue; (originally) suburb < *pró* before + *pólis* city (because it is used to line the outer part of the hive)]

pro·pone (prə pōn′), *v.t.,* **-poned, -pon·ing.** *Scottish.* to propose; propound. [< Latin *prōpōnere* < *prō-* before + *pōnere* to put, place]

pro·po·nent (prə pō′nənt), *n.* **1.** a person who makes a proposal or proposition. **2.** a favorer; supporter: *Proponents of the bill argued that Federal regulation of natural-gas production . . . was discriminatory* (Newsweek). **3.** *Law.* a person who submits a will for probate. [< Latin *prōpōnēns, -entis,* present participle of *prōpōnere;* see PROPONE]

pro·por·tion (prə pôr′shən, -pōr′-), *n.* **1.** the relation in size, number, amount, or degree of one thing compared to another: *Each man's pay will be in proportion to his work. Mix water and orange juice in the proportions of three to one by taking three measures of water to every measure of orange juice.* **2.** a proper relation between parts; balance; harmony: *His short legs were not in proportion to his long body. The commerce of your colonies is out of all proportion beyond the numbers of the people* (Edmund Burke). **3.** a part; share: *A large proportion of Nevada is desert.* **4.** *Mathematics.* **a.** an equality of ratios. *Example:* 4 is to 2 as 10 is to 5. **b.** a method of finding the fourth term of such a proportion when three are known.

proportions, a. size; extent: *He left an art collection of considerable proportions.* **b.** dimensions: *He has the proportions of a dwarf.*

—*v.t.* **1.** to fit (one thing to another) so that they go together suitably: *The designs in that rug are well proportioned.* **2.** to adjust in proper proportion or relation: *The punishment should be proportioned to the offence* (John Stuart Mill).

[< Latin *prōportiō, -ōnis* < unrecorded *prō portiōne* in relation to the part —**pro·por′tion·er,** *n.*

pro·por·tion·a·ble (prə pôr′shə nə bəl, -pōr′-), *adj.* being in due proportion; proportional: *For us to levy power Proportionable to the enemy Is all impossible* (Shakespeare).

pro·por·tion·al (prə pôr′shə nəl, -pōr′-), *adj.* **1.** in the proper proportion; corresponding: *The increase in price is proportional to the improvement in the car.* **2.** *Mathematics.* having the same or a constant ratio: *The corresponding sides of mutually equiangular triangles are proportional.* —*n.* one of the terms of a proportion in mathematics.

proportional counter, a radiation counter similar to the Geiger-Muller counter, in which the amplitude of the pulse produced by the particle being counted is proportional to the amount of ionization it discharges. It is used in identifying various types of charged particles.

pro·por·tion·al·ism (prə pôr′shə nə liz′əm), *n.* the theory or practice of proportional representation: *Proportionalism still rules in Austria and neither party wishes to be the first to disrupt it* (London Times).

pro·por·tion·al·i·ty (prə pôr′shə nal′ə tē, -pōr′-), *n.* the quality or state of being in proportion.

pro·por·tion·al·ly (prə pôr′shə nə lē, -pōr′-), *adv.* in proportion: *The seats are then divided proportionally among the victorious group* (Time).

proportional representation, representation in an elected legislature in proportion to the number of voters in a district, city, state, etc.

pro·por·tion·ate (*adj.* prə pôr′shə nit, -pōr′-; *v.* prə pôr′shə nāt, -pōr′-), *adj., v.,* **-at·ed, -at·ing.** —*adj.* in the proper proportion; proportioned; proportional: *The money obtained by the fair was really not proportionate to the effort we put into it.* —*v.t.* to make proportionate; proportion. [< Latin *prōportiōnātus* < *prōportiō;* see PROPORTION] —**pro·por′tion·ate·ness,** *n.*

pro·por·tion·ate·ly (prə pôr′shə nit lē, -pōr′-), *adv.* in proportion: *The money the boys earned was divided proportionately to the time each worked.*

pro·por·tioned (prə pôr′shənd, -pōr′-), *adj.* **1.** adjusted in proportion; proportionate: *proportioned returns.* **2.** formed with proportions: *Another apartment, proportioned like the first* (Ann Radcliffe).

pro·por·tion·ment (prə pôr′shən mənt, -pōr′-), *n.* **1.** a proportioning. **2.** a being proportioned.

pro·por·tions (prə pôr′shənz, -pōr′-), *n.pl.* See under **proportion,** *n.*

pro·pos·al (prə pō′zəl), *n.* **1.** what is proposed; plan; scheme; suggestion: *a proposal to reduce taxes, constitutional proposals. The club will now hear this member's proposal.* **2.** an offer of marriage. **3.** the act of proposing: *Proposal is easier than performance.*

—**Syn. 1. Proposal, proposition** mean something put forward for consideration. **Proposal,** the more general term, applies to any suggestion, offer, plan, etc., however it may be stated: *The young people made a proposal to the City Council.* **Proposition** applies to a proposal stated in precise and specific terms: *The Council approved the idea, but not the proposition set forth.*

pro·pose (prə pōz′), *v.,* **-posed, -pos·ing** —*v.t.* **1.** to put forward for consideration, discussion, acceptance, etc.; suggest: *to propose a theory or explanation. Men must be taught as if you taught them not, And things unknown proposed as things forgot* (Alexander Pope). **2.** to present (the name of someone) for office, membership, etc. **3.** to present as a toast to be drunk. **4.** to intend; plan: *She proposes to save half of all she earns.* —*v.i.* **1.** to make an offer of marriage. **2.** to form a design or purpose: *Man proposes, God disposes.*

[< Middle French, Old French *proposer* (< *pro-* forth + *poser;* see POSE[1]) adaptation of Latin *prōpōnere;* see PROPONE] —**pro·pos′er,** *n.*

—**Syn.** *v.t.* **1.** offer. **2.** nominate. **4.** design, purpose.

prop·o·si·tion (prop′ə zish′ən), *n.* **1.** what is offered to be considered; proposal: *The tailor made a proposition to buy out his rival's business. To this rational proposition no objection could be raised* (James Fenimore Cooper). **2.** a statement; assertion. *Example:* "All men are created equal." A proposition in logic is a statement to be proved either true or false. **3.** a statement that is to be proved true, as in a debate. *Example:* Resolved: that our school should have a bank. **4.** a problem to be solved: *a proposition in geometry.* **5.** *U.S. Informal.* a business enterprise; an affair to be dealt with; an undertaking: *a tough proposition, a paying proposition.* **6.** *U.S. Informal.* a person or thing to be dealt with: *He's a cool proposition. The expense is a serious proposition.*

—*v.t. U.S. Informal.* to propose a scheme, plan, or action to, often an improper one.

[< Latin *prōpositiō, -ōnis* a setting forth < *prōpōnere;* see PROPONE]

—**Syn.** *n.* **1.** See **proposal.**

➤ **Proposition** as a synonym for *offer, plan, proposal* is largely confined to commercial jargon: *I have a proposition* (standard English *a plan*) *that may interest you.*

prop·o·si·tion·al (prop′ə zish′ə nəl), *adj.* **1.** having to do with or constituting a proposition. **2.** considered as a proposition. —**prop′o·si′tion·al·ly,** *adv.*

pro·pos·i·tus (prō poz′ə təs), *n. Law.* a person from whom descent or genealogical relationships are traced. [< Latin *prōpositus,* past participle of *prōpōnere;* see PROPONE]

pro·pound (prə pound′), *v.t.* to put forward; propose: *to propound a theory, to propound a question, to propound a riddle.* [alteration of *propone*] —**pro·pound′er,** *n.*

pro·pox·y·phene hydrochloride (prə pok′sə fēn), a chemical compound used to relieve pain, as a sedative, etc. It is a crystalline drug held to be as effective as codeine. *Formula:* $C_{22}H_{29}NO_2.HCl$ [< *prop*(ionic) + *oxy*(gen) + *phen*(yl)]

prop·per (prop′ər), *n.* a person or thing that props or supports.

pro·prae·tor or **pro·pre·tor** (prō prē′tər, -tôr), *n.* an officer who, after having served as praetor in ancient Rome, was sent to govern a province: *In 92 Sulla went as propraetor to Asia* (James A. Froude). [< Latin *prōpraetor* (literally) in place of the praetor < *prō* pro-[1] + *praetor* praetor]

pro·pri·e·tar·y (prə prī′ə ter′ē), *adj., n., pl.* **-tar·ies.** —*adj.* **1.** belonging to a proprietor: *a proprietary right, a proprietary interest.* **2.** holding property: *a proprietary class.* **3.** *U.S.* owned by a private person or company; belonging to or controlled by a private person or company as property: *A proprietary medicine is a patent medicine.* [< noun]

—*n.* **1.** an owner; proprietor. **2.** a group of owners: *The proprietary desired certain modifications in the existing policy* (Arnold Bennett). **3.** the holding of property; ownership. **4.** a proprietary medicine. **5.** the owner or owners of a proprietary colony.

[< Late Latin *proprietārius* < Latin *proprietās* ownership; see PROPRIETY]

proprietary colony, (in American history) a colony granted by the British government to some person or persons who had complete control, such as Maryland.

pro·pri·e·ties (prə prī′ə tēz), *n.pl.* See under **propriety.**

pro·pri·e·tor (prə prī′ə tər), *n.* **1.** an owner: *A number of boarding house proprietors are converting their rooms into flatlets* (London Times). **2.** (in American history) the owner of a proprietary colony. [American English, probably alteration of *proprietary*]

pro·pri·e·to·ri·al (prə prī′ə tôr′ē əl, -tōr′-), *adj.* of or having to do with a proprietor: *proprietorial pride.*

pro·pri·e·tor·ship (prə prī′ə tər ship), *n.* ownership.

pro·pri·e·to·ry (prə prī′ə tôr′ē, -tōr′-), *adj.* proprietary.

pro·pri·e·tress (prə prī′ə tris), *n.* a woman owner or manager.

pro·pri·e·ty (prə prī′ə tē), *n., pl.* **-ties. 1.** the quality of being proper; fitness: *a remark of doubtful propriety.* **2.** proper behavior: *Propriety demands that a boy tip his hat to a lady whom he knows.* **3.** *Archaic.* proper or peculiar character: *Silence that dreadful bell; it frights the isle from her propriety* (Shakespeare). **4.** *Obsolete.* property.

proprieties, conventional standards or requirements of proper behavior: *The proprieties . . . and even the graces, as far as they are simple, pure, and honest, would follow as an almost inevitable consequence* (Hannah More).

[< Old French *propriete,* learned borrowing from Latin *proprietās* appropriateness, peculiar nature < *proprius* one's own, proper. Doublet of PROPERTY.]

—**Syn. 1.** aptness, suitability. **2.** etiquette, decorum, decency.

pro·pri·o·cep·tion (prō′prē ə sep′shən), *n.* a proprioceptive sense; the perception of internal bodily conditions, such as the state of muscular contraction: *Most complex of the additional senses, with more paraphernalia in the brain than even the sense of sight, is . . . proprioception or position sense* (Time).

pro·pri·o·cep·tive (prō′prē ə sep′tiv), *adj.* **1.** receiving stimuli from within the body. **2.** of or having to do with such stimuli. [coined < Latin *proprius* one's own + *-ceptus* taken (< *capere* to take) + English *-ive*]

pro·pri·o·cep·tor (prō′prē ə sep′tər), *n.* a sense organ that receives stimuli from within the body.

pro·pri·o mo·tu (prō′prē ō mō′tü, mō′tyü), *Latin.* of one's own accord.

pro·proc·tor (prō prok′tər), *n.* an assistant or deputy proctor in a British university.

prop root, a root that supports a plant by growing downward into the ground from above the soil, as in corn and the mangrove: *The root hairs absorb nourishment from the soil, the green leaves build up carbohydrates, prop roots make their appearance at the first node (joint) above ground, and the seedling grows larger* (Heber W. Youngken).

Prop Roots of mangrove

prop·ter hoc (prop′tər hok′), *Latin.* because of this: *Nevertheless, it is fair to admit that, perhaps not propter hoc, the situation has radically changed in Italy since the Luces arrived* (Harper's).

prop·to·sis (prop tō′sis), *n.* an abnormal protrusion, especially of the eyeball. [< Greek *próptōsis* a falling forward < *pro-* forward + *ptōsis* ptosis]

pro·pug·nac·u·lum (prō′pug nak′yə ləm), *n., pl.* **-la** (-lə). a bulwark; defense. [< Latin *prōpugnāculum* < *prōpugnāre* defend < *prō-* before + *pugnāre* to fight]

pro·pul·sion (prə pul′shən), *n.* **1.** a driving forward or onward: *propulsion by jet engines.* **2.** a propelling force or impulse. [< Latin *prōpulsus,* past participle of *prōpellere* to propel + English *-ion*]

pro·pul·sive (prə pul′siv), *adj.* driving forward or onward; propelling.

pro·pul·sor (prə pul′sər), *n.* something intended to provide propulsion: *A propulsor for hydrofoil boats . . . combines hot exhaust gases with cold water* (New York Times).

pro·pul·so·ry (prə pul′sər ē), *adj.* propulsive.

prop wash, slip stream: *Four helicopters flew low overhead, and their prop wash parted the reeds and kept the running North Koreans in sight* (Time).

prop word, a substantive which adds little or no meaning to that of the adjective modifying it. In the sentence *Which car will you take, the old or the new one,* "one" is a prop word.

pro·pyl (prō′pəl), *n.* the univalent radical, C_3H_7, of propane. [< *prop*(ionic) + *-yl*]

prop·y·lae·um (prop′ə lē′əm), *n., pl.* **-lae·a** (-lē′ə). a vestibule or entrance to a temple or other enclosure, especially when elaborate or of architectural importance. [< Latin *propylaeum* < Greek *propýlaion* entrance, gateway; (literally) neuter of *propýlaios,* adjective < *pró* before + *pýlē* gate]

Prop·y·lae·um (prop′ə lē′əm), *n.* the monumental gateway to the Acropolis at Athens. Once in ruins, it has been partly restored.

propyl alcohol, a colorless liquid used as a solvent for waxes, oils, resins, etc. *Formula:* C_3H_8O

pro·pyl·ene (prō′pə lēn), *n.* a colorless, gaseous hydrocarbon homologous with ethylene, used in organic synthesis. *Formula:* C_3H_6 [< *propyl* + *-ene*]

propylene glycol, a colorless, viscous, liquid compound of propylene, used as an antifreeze, as a solvent, in organic synthesis, etc. *Formula:* $C_3H_8O_2$

pro·pyl·ic (prō pil′ik), *adj.* of, having to do with, or containing propyl.

prop·y·lite (prop′ə lit), *n.* a volcanic rock with triclinic feldspars greatly altered by hydrothermal action, occurring in regions of silver deposits. [American English < Greek *própylon,* variant of *propýlaion* gateway (see PROPYLAEUM) + English *-ite*[1] (because it was created at the start of the Tertiary period)]

prop·y·lit·ic (prop′ə lit′ik), *adj.* of or like propylite: *These rocks . . . exhibiting interesting examples of the so-called propylitic modification* (Geological Society Quarterly).

prop·y·lon (prop′ə lon), *n., pl.* **-lons, -la** (-lə). a monumental gateway standing before the actual entrance, or pylon, of a temple,etc.,in ancient Egypt: *The main gateway, or propylon, was a covered, H-shaped passage with the doorway in the center of the crossbar* (Scientific American). [< Greek *própylon,* variant of *propýlaion* gateway; see PROPYLAEUM]

Propylon at Karnak, Egypt

pro·pyl·thi·o·u·ra·cil (prō′pəl thī′ō yůr′ə səl), *n.* a white, crystalline compound which inhibits thyroid activity, used to control hyperthyroidism. *Formula:* $C_7H_{10}N_2OS$

pro ra·ta (prō rā′tə, rä′tə), in proportion; according to the share, interest, etc., of each: *The preference issues will be offered pro rata to shareholders at 115* (London Daily Telegraph). [< Latin *prō ratā* (*parte*) according to (the portion) figured for each; *ratā,* ablative < *rērī* to count, figure]

pro·rat·a·ble (prō rā′tə bəl), *adj.* that can be prorated.

pro·rate (prō rāt′, prō′rāt′), *v.t., v.i.*, **-rat·ed, -rat·ing.** to distribute or assess proportionally: *We prorated the money according to the number of days each had worked. He is perfectly willing to prorate the special assessment* (Sinclair Lewis). [American English < *pro rata*]

pro·ra·tion (prō rā′shən), *n.* a prorating, especially a restriction, by law, of oil and gas production, limiting each producer to a set proportion of his total productive capacity. [< *prorat*(e) + *-ion*]

prore (prôr, prōr), *n. Poetic.* the prow of a ship: *The tall ship whose lofty prore Shall never stem the billows more* (Scott). [< Middle French *prore* < Latin *prōra*]

pro re na·ta (prō rē nā′tə), *Latin.* as the occasion requires; to meet the emergency.

pro·ro·ga·tion (prō′rə gā′shən), *n.* the discontinuance of the meetings of a lawmaking body without dissolving it. [< Latin *prōrogātiō, -ōnis* < *prōrogāre* to prolong, defer; see PROROGUE]

pro·rogue (prō rōg′), *v.t.*, **-rogued, -rogu·ing. 1.** to discontinue the regular meetings of (a lawmaking body) for a time: *King Charles I prorogued the English Parliament.* **2.** *Obsolete.* to defer; postpone. [< Middle French *proroguer*, learned borrowing from Latin *prōrogāre* to defer, prolong < *prō-* forward + *rogāre* to ask for]

pros., prosody.

pro·sa·ic (prō zā′ik), *adj.* **1.** like prose; matter-of-fact; ordinary; not exciting: *a prosaic mind or style, to lead a prosaic life. No product is too prosaic or too mundane to profit greatly by attractive packaging* (Wall Street Journal). **2.** of, in, or having to do with prose. [< Late Latin *prōsaicus* < Latin *prōsa* prose] —**pro·sa′ic·ness,** *n.* —**Syn. 1.** commonplace, humdrum, dull, tedious.

pro·sa·i·cal·ly (prō zā′ə klē), *adv.* in a prosaic manner: *Good advice to mothers . . . very prosaically delivered* (Henry Hallam).

pro·sa·i·cism (prō zā′ə siz əm), *n.* prosaism: *It is the prosaicism of these two writers to which is owing their especial quotability* (Edgar Allan Poe).

pro·sa·ism (prō′zā iz əm), *n.* **1.** prosaic character. **2.** a prosaic remark or expression.

pro·sce·ni·um (prō sē′nē əm), *n., pl.* **-ni·a** (-nē ə). **1.** the part of the stage in front of the curtain. **2.** the curtain and the framework that holds it. **3.** the stage of an ancient theater. [< Latin *proscaenium* < Greek *proskēnion* < *pró-* in front of + *skēnḗ* stage, (originally) tent. Compare SCENE.]

proscenium arch, an arch or archway or equivalent opening in the wall between the stage and the auditorium of a theatre.

pro·sciut·to (prō shü′tō), *n., pl.* **-ti** (-tē), **-tos.** dry-cured, spiced, and often smoked ham, sliced very thin and frequently served with melon or figs. [< Italian *prosciutto*]

pro·scribe (prō skrīb′), *v.t.*, **-scribed, -scrib·ing. 1.** to prohibit as wrong or dangerous; condemn: *In earlier days, the church proscribed dancing and cardplaying. It is difficult to proscribe a party without infringing on the right of the individual to dissent* (Bulletin of Atomic Scientists). **2.** to put outside of the protection of the law; outlaw: *In ancient Rome, a proscribed person's property belonged to the state, and anyone might kill him.* **3.** to forbid to come into a certain place; banish. [< Latin *prōscrībere* < *prō-* before (the public) + *scrībere* to write] —**pro·scrib′er,** *n.* —**Syn. 1.** forbid, interdict. **3.** exile.

pro·script (prō′skript), *n.* a proscribed person: *As each proscript rose and stood From kneeling in the ashen dust* (Dante Gabriel Rossetti).

pro·scrip·tion (prō skrip′shən), *n.* **1.** a proscribing: *No one would raise a hand against the proscription of spinach from the national diet* (Atlantic). **2.** a being proscribed. [< Latin *prōscrīptiō, -ōnis* < *prōscrībere* proscribe]

pro·scrip·tive (prō skrip′tiv), *adj.* proscribing; tending to proscribe: *The Imperial ministers pursued with proscriptive laws, and ineffectual arms, the rebels whom they had made* (Edward Gibbon). —**pro·scrip′tive·ly,** *adv.*

prose (prōz), *n., adj., v.,* **prosed, pros·ing.** —*n.* **1.** the ordinary form of spoken or written language; plain language not arranged in verses: *The definition of good prose is—proper words in their proper places* (Samuel Taylor Coleridge). *Prose is a magnificent instrument of communication* (Atlantic). **2.** dull, ordinary talk.
—*adj.* **1.** of prose; in prose. **2.** lacking imagination; matter-of-fact; commonplace.
—*v.i.* **1.** to talk or write in a dull, commonplace way. **2.** to compose or write prose.
—*v.t.* to write in prose; turn into prose.
[< Old French *prose*, learned borrowing from Latin *prōsa* (*ōrātiō*) straightforward (speech); (literally) feminine of *prōs* < *prōrsus*, for unrecorded *prōversus* straightway, direct < *prō-* forth, forward + *vertere* to turn]

pro·sec·tor (prō sek′tər), *n.* a person who dissects bodies as demonstrations for classes in anatomy. [< Latin *prōsector* anatomist < *prōsecāre* to cut up < *prō-* before + *secāre* to cut]

pros·e·cut·a·ble (pros′ə kyü′tə bəl), *adj.* that can be prosecuted; liable to prosecution: *. . . the dearth of prosecutable crime* (New Yorker).

pros·e·cute (pros′ə kyüt), *v.*, **-cut·ed, -cut·ing.** —*v.t.* **1.** to bring before a court of law: *Reckless drivers will be prosecuted.* **2.** to carry out; follow up; pursue: *He prosecuted an inquiry into reasons for the company's failure.* **3.** to carry on (a business or occupation); practice: *Those polar fisheries could only be prosecuted in the short summer of that climate* (Herman Melville). —*v.i.* **1.** to bring a case before a law court. **2.** to act as prosecuting attorney. [< Latin *prōsecūtus*, past participle of *prōsequī* to pursue < *prō-* forth + *sequī* follow. Related to PURSUE.]

pros·e·cut·ing attorney (pros′ə kyü′ting), an attorney for the government; public prosecutor.

pros·e·cu·tion (pros′ə kyü′shən), *n.* **1.** the carrying on of a lawsuit: *The prosecution will be abandoned if the stolen money is returned.* **2.** the side that starts action against another in a law court. The prosecution makes certain charges against the defense. **3.** a carrying out; following up: *In the prosecution of his plan, he stored away a supply of food.*

pros·e·cu·tor (pros′ə kyü′tər), *n.* **1.** the lawyer in charge of the government's side of a case against an accused person. **2.** a person who starts legal proceedings against another person: *Who is the prosecutor in this case?* **3.** a person who follows up or carries out any action, project, or business.

pros·e·cu·to·ry (pros′ə kyə tôr′ē, -tōr′-), *adj.* of or having to do with prosecution: *. . . fixed rules of law by which police, prosecutory, and judicial agencies . . . must abide* (Atlantic).

pros·e·lyte (pros′ə līt), *n., v.,* **-lyt·ed, -lyt·ing.** —*n.* a person who has been converted from one opinion, religious belief, etc., to another: *These proselytes of the gate are as welcome as the true Hebrews* (Charles Lamb).
—*v.t.* **1.** to convert from one opinion, religious belief, etc., to another: *I have no wish to proselyte any reluctant mind* (Emerson). **2.** to induce to join; enlist; solicit: *to proselyte high-school athletes for a college.* —*v.i.* to make proselytes.
[< Latin *prosēlytus* < Greek *prosḗlytos* one who has come over (to a faith); (literally) having arrived < *prós* toward + *ely-*, stem of *érchesthai* to come] —**pros′e·lyt′er,** *n.*

pros·e·lyt·ism (pros′ə lī tiz′əm, -lə-), *n.* **1.** the act or fact of proselyting: *The spirit of proselytism attends this spirit of fanaticism* (Edmund Burke). **2.** the condition of being a proselyte.

pros·e·lyt·ist (pros′ə lī′tist, -lə-), *n.* a person who proselytes; proselytizer: *The Mormon proselytists report unusual success in their missionary work* (New York Evangelist).

pros·e·lyt·i·za·tion (pros′ə lī′tə zā′shən), *n.* the act or work of proselytizing: *The society was able to adopt a method of proselytization that quickly turned out to be very effective* (New Yorker).

pros·e·lyt·ize (pros′ə lī tīz, -lə-), *v.*, **-ized, -iz·ing.** —*v.i.* to make converts; make proselytes. —*v.t.* to make a proselyte of; convert: *One of these whom they endeavour to proselytize* (Edmund Burke). —**pros′e·lyt·iz′er,** *n.*

pros·en·ce·phal·ic (pros′en sə fal′ik), *adj.* of or having to do with the prosencephalon.

pros·en·ceph·a·lon (pros′en sef′ə lon), *n., pl.* **-la** (-lə). the anterior segment of the brain, consisting of the cerebral hemispheres, or their equivalent, and certain adjacent parts; forebrain; diencephalon and telencephalon. [< French *prosencéphalon* forebrain < Greek *prós* forward + *enképhalon* (literally) within the head < *en* in + *kephalḗ* head]

pros·en·chy·ma (pros eng′ki mə), *n.* a type of tissue characteristic of the woody and bast portions of plants, consisting of long, narrow cells with pointed ends that sometimes form ducts or vessels. [< Greek *prós* toward + English (par)*enchyma*]

pros·en·chym·a·tous (pros′eng kim′ə-təs), *adj.* consisting of or having to do with prosenchyma.

prose poem, a work printed as prose but having elements of poetry in it, such as rhythms, poetic imagery, etc.; composition in polyphonic prose.

prose poet, a person who writes prose poems.

prose poetry, polyphonic prose.

pros·er (prō′zər), *n.* **1.** a person who talks or writes in a dull, commonplace way. **2.** a writer of prose.

Pro·ser·pi·na (prō sėr′pə nə), *n. Roman Mythology.* the daughter of Jupiter and Ceres. Pluto carried her off and made her queen of the Lower World. Because she was allowed to spend part of each year on the earth, she symbolized the changes in the seasons. The Greeks called her Persephone.

Pro·ser·pi·ne (pros′ər pīn, prō sėr′pə nē), *n.* Proserpina.

pros·i·ly (prō′zə lē), *adv.* in a prosy manner; prosaically; tediously.

pro·sim·i·an (prō sim′ē ən), *n.* a primate belonging to the more primitive of the two divisions of primates, including all early fossil primates and modern lemurs, lorises, tarsiers, and tree shrews. [< *pro-*[2] + *simian*]

pros·i·ness (prō′zē nis), *n.* prosy character or quality: *. . . settling down again to the prosiness of their everyday life* (G. Jackson).

pro·sit (prō′sit; *German* prō′zēt), *interj.* to your health!: *The man behind the counter poured us out a little something—and we murmured prosit!* (London Times). [< German *Prosit* < Latin *prōsit* (literally) may it be to your good (health), third person subjunctive of *prodesse* be good for]

pro·slav·er·y (prō slā′vər ē, -slāv′rē), *adj.* favoring slavery. [< *pro*[1] + *slavery*]

pro·so·di·ac (prō sō′dē ak), *adj.* prosodic.

pros·o·di·a·cal (pros′ə dī′ə kəl), *adj.* prosodic.

pro·sod·ic (prō sod′ik), *adj.* of or having to do with prosody: *. . . prosodic features of the language—stress, transition, and pitch* (Harold Whitehall). —**pro·sod′i·cal·ly,** *adv.*

pro·sod·i·cal (prō sod′ə kəl), *adj.* prosodic.

pros·o·dist (pros′ə dist), *n.* a person skilled in the technique of versification.

pros·o·dy (pros′ə dē), *n.* the science of poetic meters and versification: *Latin prosody. Japanese prosody came to be based upon syllable-count because the language has no stress accent, as in English, or quantity, as in Latin* (Atlantic). [< Latin *prosōdia* < Greek *prosōidíā* accent, modulation and all the other features that characterize speech < *prós* in addition to + *ōidḗ* song, poem, ode]

pro·so·po·poe·ia (prō sō′pə pē′ə), *n.* **1.** personification. **2.** the representation of an imaginary or absent person as speaking or acting. [< Latin *prosōpopoeia* < *prosōpopiīā* < *prósōpon* a person, face (< *prós* toward + *ōps, ōpós* face, countenance) + *poieîn* to make]

pros·pect (pros′pekt), *n.* **1.** a thing expected or looked forward to. **2.** the act of looking forward; expectation: *The prospect of a vacation is pleasant.* **3.** outlook for the future: *Is there any prospect of rain?* **4.** a person who may become a customer, candidate, etc.; prospective customer: *the fortnightly form-letter, to be mimeographed and sent out to a thousand "prospects"* (Sinclair Lewis). **5. a.** a view; scene: *The prospect from the mountain was grand.* **b.** the direction in which a building, room, etc., faces; exposure; view: *the gate whose prospect is toward the east* (Ezekiel 42:15). **6.** *Mining.* **a.** an apparent indication of a metal, mineral deposit, etc. **b.** a spot giving such indications. **c.** a mine in an early stage.

in prospect, looked forward to; expected: *Everything in prospect appears to me so very gloomy* (Edmund Burke).

prospects, probabilities of success, profit, etc.: *good prospects in business, a young man's prospects in life. With the death of Francis, the prospects of the Huguenots brightened* (Walter Besant).

—*v.i.* to explore a region for oil, gold, or

other minerals: *to prospect for uranium.* —*v.t.* to search: *to prospect a region for silver.* [< Latin *prōspectus, -ūs* < *prōspicere* to look out, on; foresee < *prō-* forward + *specere* to look. Doublet of PROSPECTUS.]
—**Syn.** *n.* **2.** anticipation.

pros·pec·tion (prə spek′shən), *n.* **1.** a looking forward; foresight. **2.** a prospecting, as for gold or the like: *Its object is to make an immediate, thorough archaeological prospection of the territory, for much certainly remains unknown* (Manchester Guardian).

pro·spec·tive (prə spek′tiv), *adj.* **1.** probable; expected: *I won't have a prospective guest discussed* (Winston Churchill). **2.** looking forward to the future.

pro·spec·tive·ly (prə spek′tiv lē), *adv.* in prospect or expectation; in the future.

pros·pec·tor (pros′pek tər, prə spek′-), *n.* a person who explores or examines a region for gold, silver, oil, uranium, etc. [American English < *prospect,* verb + *-or*]

pros·pects (pros′pekts), *n.pl.* See under **prospect,** *n.*

pro·spec·tus (prə spek′təs), *n.* **1.** a printed statement describing and advertising something: *the prospectus of a new company or issue of stock. He wanted his son to learn how little confidence was to be placed in glowing prospectuses and flaming articles* (Samuel Butler). **2.** *British.* a university or college catalogue. [< Latin *prōspectus.* Doublet of PROSPECT.]

pros·per (pros′pər), *v.i.* to be successful; have good fortune; flourish: *Whatsoever he doeth shall prosper* (Psalms 1:3). *Well may you prosper!* (Shakespeare). —*v.t.* to make successful; cause to flourish: *Let everyone of you lay by him in store, as God hath prospered him* (I Corinthians 16:2). [< Middle French *prosperer,* learned borrowing from Latin *prosperāre* < *prosperus* prosperous < *prō-* for, according to + *spēs* hope]

pros·per·i·ty (pros per′ə tē), *n., pl.* **-ties.** a prosperous condition; good fortune; success: *the comforts and prosperities of his middle age* (H.G. Wells).

Pros·per·o (pros′pə rō), *n.* the exiled duke in Shakespeare's play *The Tempest,* who, by magic, restores himself and his daughter to their rank and wealth.

pros·per·ous (pros′pər əs), *adj.* **1.** successful; thriving; doing well; fortunate: *a prosperous merchant.* **2.** favorable; helpful: *prosperous weather for growing wheat.* [< Latin *prosperus* (with English *-ous*); see PROSPER] —**pros′per·ous·ly,** *adv.* —**pros′per·ous·ness,** *n.* —**Syn. 1.** flourishing, rich, wealthy. —**Ant. 1.** unsuccessful, needy, poor.

prost (prōst), *interj.* prosit.

pros·tate (pros′tāt), *n.* a large gland surrounding the male urethra in front of the bladder. —*adj.* designating or having to do with this gland. [< Medieval Latin *prostata* < Greek *prostátēs* one standing in front, ultimately < *pro-* before + *sténai* to stand]

pros·ta·tec·to·my (pros′tə tek′tə mē), *n., pl.* **-mies.** surgical removal of all or part of the prostate. [< *prostat*(e) + Greek *ektomē* a cutting out]

pros·tat·ic (pros tat′ik), *adj.* of or having to do with the prostate gland: *There is no doubt that Freud suffered while in the U.S. both from chronic appendicitis and prostatic discomfort* (Time).

pros·ta·ti·tis (pros′tə tī′tis), *n.* inflammation of the prostate gland.

pros·ta·tot·o·my (pros′tə tot′ə mē), *n., pl.* **-mies.** surgical incision into the prostate. [< *prostat*(e) + Greek *-tomíā* a cutting]

pros·the·sis (pros′thə sis), *n., pl.* **-the·ses** (-thə sēz). **1.** the addition of a false tooth, artificial leg, etc., to the body. **2.** the part itself: *In the basement Dr. Michiels has established a modern dental laboratory, turning out expertly made prostheses and gold inlays* (Newsweek). **3.** the art of making lifelike artificial parts of the human body. **4.** the addition of a letter or syllable to a word, especially at the beginning, as "be-" in "beknownst." [< Late Latin *prosthesis* (definition 4) < Greek *prósthesis* addition, ultimately < *prós* in addition to + *thésis* a placing or setting down < *tithénai* to put]

pros·thet·ic (pros thet′ik), *adj.* of or having to do with prosthesis: *prosthetic dentistry.*

pros·thet·ics (pros thet′iks), *n.* the branch of surgery or dentistry dealing with prosthetic devices.

pros·the·tist (pros′thə tist), *n.* **1.** a specialist in the prosthesis of limbs, etc. **2.** a prosthodontist.

pros·thi·on (pros′thē on), *n.* the middle point of the anterior surface of the upper jaw. [< Greek *prósthion,* neuter of *prósthios* foremost, front]

pros·tho·don·ti·a (pros′thə don′shē ə, -don′shə), *n.* the branch of dentistry dealing with the making of crowns, bridges, or artificial teeth. [< *prosth*(etic) + *-odontia,* as in *orthodontia*]

pros·tho·don·tics (pros′thə don′tiks), *n.* prosthodontia.

pros·tho·don·tist (pros′thə don′tist), *n.* a dentist who makes artificial teeth.

Pro·stig·mine (prō stig′min), *n. Trademark.* neostigmine.

pros·ti·tute (pros′tə tüt, -tyüt), *n., v.,* **-tut·ed, -tut·ing,** *adj.* —*n.* **1.** a woman who gets money for immoral behavior with men, especially for indiscriminate sexual intercourse. **2.** a person who does base things for money.
—*v.t.* **1.** to put to an unworthy or base use: *to prostitute artistic skills. The soup—alas! that I should so far prostitute the word* (Charles Lever). **2.** to submit to immoral or unworthy behavior for money.
—*adj.* debased or debasing; corrupt: *I found how the world had been misled by prostitute writers* (Jonathan Swift).
[< Latin *prōstitūtus,* or *prōstitūta,* feminine, past participle of *prōstituere* to prostitute < *prō-* before (the public) + *statuere* cause to stand]
—**Syn.** *n.* **1.** harlot, whore. *-v.t.* **1.** defile, debase.

pros·ti·tu·tion (pros′tə tü′shən, -tyü′-), *n.* the use of one's body, honor, talents, etc., in a base way.

pros·ti·tu·tor (pros′tə tü′tər, -tyü′-), *n.* a person or thing that prostitutes: . . . *prostitutors of the ballot* (New York Voice).

pro·sto·mi·um (prō stō′mē əm), *n.* the part of the body in front of the mouth of mollusks, worms, and certain other invertebrates. [< New Latin *prostomium* < Greek *prostómion* (literally) something in front of the mouth < *pró* before + *stóma* mouth]

pros·trate (pros′trāt), *v.,* **-trat·ed, -trat·ing,** *adj.* —*v.t.* **1.** to lay down flat; cast down: *The captives prostrated themselves before the conqueror.* **2.** to make very weak or helpless; exhaust: *Sickness often prostrates people. In prostrating one enemy, he had mortified a hundred* (Scott).
—*adj.* **1.** lying flat with face downward. **2.** lying flat. **3. a.** overcome; helpless: *a prostrate enemy, to be prostrate with grief.* **b.** submissive: *prostrate humility.* **4.** *Botany.* lying along the ground: *a prostrate stem or plant.*
[< Latin *prōstrātus,* past participle of *prōsternere* < *prō-* forth + *sternere* to strew]
—**Syn.** *adj.* **1, 2.** prone.

pros·tra·tion (pros trā′shən), *n.* **1.** the act of prostrating; bowing down low or lying face down in submission, respect, or worship. **2.** a being very much worn out or used up in body or mind; exhaustion; dejection.

pro·style (prō′stīl), *adj.* having a portico in front, standing out from the walls of the building: *a prostyle Greek temple.* —*n.* a prostyle portico or building. [< Latin *prostȳlos* having pillars in front < unrecorded Greek *próstȳlos* < Greek *pro-* before + *stŷlos* pillar, column]

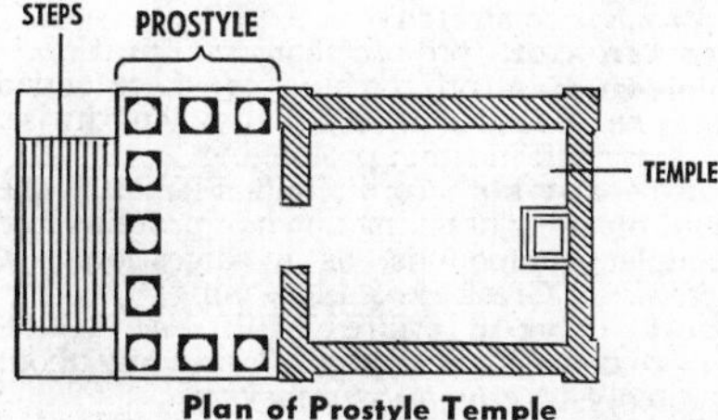

Plan of Prostyle Temple

pros·y (prō′zē), *adj.,* **pros·i·er, pros·i·est.** like prose; commonplace; dull; tiresome: *an argument that was so prosy that many a head by and by began to nod* (Mark Twain).

prot-, *combining form.* the form of **proto-** before vowels, as in *protamine.*

Prot., Protestant.

pro·tac·tin·i·um (prō′tak tin′ē əm), *n.* a very rare, heavy, radioactive metallic chemical element. On emission of an alpha particle, it yields actinium. *Symbol:* Pa; *at. wt.:* (C^{12}) 231 or (O^{16}) 231; *at.no.:* 91; *valence:* 4,5. Formerly, **protoactinium.** [< *prot-* + *actinium*]

pro·tag·o·nist (prō tag′ə nist), *n.* **1.** the main character in a play, story, or novel. **2.** a person who takes a leading part; active supporter; champion: *A new scene opened; and new protagonists—Mr. Gladstone and Mr. Disraeli—struggled together in the limelight* (Lytton Strachey). [< Greek *prōtagōnistḗs* < *prôtos* first + *agōnistḗs* actor < *agṓn* a contest, struggle < *ágein* to do]

pro·ta·min (prō′tə min), *n.* protamine.

pro·ta·mine (prō′tə mēn, -min), *n.* any of a group of basic proteins that are not coagulated by heat, are soluble in water, and form amino acids when hydrolyzed: *Nucleoproteins are formed by a salt-like union of a nucleic acid and a basic protein such as protamine or histone* (G.M. Wyburn). [< *prot-* + *amine*]

pro·tan·dric (prō tan′drik), *adj.* proterandrous: *The European oyster [is] protandric, the gonad of an individual first producing sperm and then eggs, in rhythmic alternation* (Tracy I. Storer).

pro·tan·drous (prō tan′drəs), *adj.* proterandrous.

pro·tan·dry (prō tan′drē), *n.* proterandry.

pro·ta·nope (prō′tə nōp), *n.* a person suffering from protanopia, having little or no perception of the red end of the spectrum: *A protanope confuses red and bluish green with gray, and, indeed, with each other* (Deane B. Judd).

pro·ta·no·pi·a (prō′tə nō′pē ə), *n.* a form of color blindness probably due to a lack of receptors sensitive to red light, which appears indistinguishable from dim green or yellow light, or may not be seen at all. [< New Latin *protanopia* < Greek *prôtos* first + *an-* not + *ṓps* eye]

pro·ta·no·pic (prō′tə nō′pik), *adj.* affected with protanopia: *One per cent of men is protanopic* (New Scientist).

pro tan·to (prō tan′tō), *Latin.* for so much; to that extent.

prot·a·sis (prot′ə sis), *n., pl.* **-ses** (-sēz). **1.** *Grammar.* the clause expressing the condition in a conditional sentence. **2.** the introduction of the characters and subject in the first part of a classical drama. [< Latin *protasis* < Greek *prótasis* < *proteínein* stretch ahead < *pro-* before + *teínein* to stretch]

pro·te·a (prō′tē ə), *n.* any of a group of chiefly South African trees and shrubs with large cone-shaped heads of red or purple flowers that have no petals: *Note the proteas and silver trees that grew in profusion on what is now a built-up area* (Cape Times). [< New Latin *Protea* the genus name, alteration of *Proteus* (because there are many different forms of the plant)]

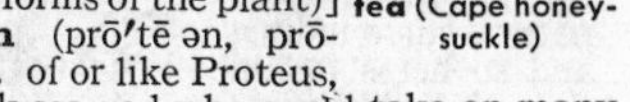
Branch of Protea (Cape honeysuckle)

Pro·te·an (prō′tē ən, prō tē′-), *adj.* of or like Proteus, the Greek sea god who could take on many forms.

pro·te·an[1] (prō′tē ən, prō tē′-), *adj.* readily assuming different forms or characters; exceedingly variable: *He is, of course, one of our most protean artists* (New Yorker). [< *Proteus* + *-an*]

pro·te·an[2] (prō′tē ən), *n.* any of a group of insoluble compounds derived from protein by the action of water or enzymes. [< *prote*(in) + *-an*]

pro·te·ase (prō′tē ās), *n.* any of various proteolytic enzymes, such as pepsin. [< *prote*(olysis) + *-ase*]

pro·tect (prə tekt′), *v.t.* **1.** to shield from harm or danger; shelter; defend; guard: *Protect yourself from danger. Protect the baby's eyes from the sun.* **2.** to guard (home industry) against foreign goods by taxing any which are brought into the country. **3.** to provide money for the payment of (a draft, bond, or other obligation) when it falls due.
[< Latin *prōtectus,* past participle of *prōtegere* < *prō-* in front + *tegere* to cover] —**Syn. 1.** secure. See **guard.**

pro·tect·ant (prə tek′tənt), *n.* a substance that provides protection: *A new silicone metal protectant . . . is the answer to many problems in corrosion* (Scientific American).

pro·tect·ed cruiser (prə tek′tid), a former type of light cruiser with armored decks but no armor on its sides.

protected state, a state or nation under the protectorate of a stronger power.

pro·tect·ing (prə tek′ting), *adj.* that protects: *To thy wings protecting shade My self I carry will* (Mary Herbert Pembroke).

pro·tect·ing·ly (prə tek′ting lē), *adv.* so as to protect.

pro·tec·tion (prə tek′shən), *n.* **1.** the act of protecting, or condition of being kept from harm; defense: *We have policemen for our protection.* **2.** a thing or person that prevents damage: *An apron is a protection when doing dirty work.* **3.** the system of taxing foreign goods so that people are more likely to buy goods made in their own country; the opposite of free trade. **4.** something that assures safe passage through a region; passport. **5.** *Informal.* the payment of money to racketeers or gangsters as a form of tribute in order not to be molested. **6.** *U.S.* a certificate of nationality issued to seamen who are citizens: *the out-ward-bound sailor in quest of a protection* (Hawthorne). —**Syn. 1.** guard, security. **2.** shield, safeguard, bulwark.

pro·tec·tion·al (prə tek′shə nəl), *adj.* having to do with, characterized by, or fostered by protection: *the protectional expansion of national commerce* (Henry Morley).

pro·tec·tion·ism (prə tek′shə niz əm), *n.* the economic system or theory of protection, in which high tariffs on imported goods give domestic producers encouragement and advantage: *The new upsurge of economic nationalism known in this country as protectionism* . . . (New York Times).

pro·tec·tion·ist (prə tek′shə nist), *n.* a person who favors protectionism: *The protectionists, who are usually protectionists for individual industries and areas, are vociferous as always* (Wall Street Journal). —*adj.* of protectionism or protectionists.

pro·tec·tive (prə tek′tiv), *adj.* **1.** being a defense; protecting: *the hard protective shell of a turtle. Marathon came up with protective packaging that made frozen food specialties practical* (Newsweek). **2.** preventing injury to those around: *a protective device on a machine.* **3.** guarding against foreign-made goods by putting a high tax or duty on them: *protective legislation.* —**pro·tec′tive·ly,** *adv.* —**pro·tec′tive·ness,** *n.*

protective colloid, a substance added to a colloidal suspension to keep the particles from coming together: *Gelatin and gum arabic are protective colloids in ice cream and India ink. Materials called protective colloids, or peptizing agents, are added to the mixture; and they apparently coat the suspended particles and so prevent their coalescing* (Offner).

protective coloring or **coloration,** a coloring some animals have that makes them hard to distinguish from their natural surroundings, and so helps to hide them from their enemies.

LEAF

BUTTERFLY

Protective Coloration of the leaf butterfly

protective covenant, an agreement among property owners in an area not to sell or rent property to members of certain specified ethnic or religious groups; a restrictive covenant.

protective cover, 1. the presence of fighter aircraft flying above friendly ships, troops, bombers, etc., to repel enemy air attack on them: *Flying protective cover for these bombers, Sabre jets destroyed several enemy aircraft in air battles* (New York Times). **2.** the aircraft giving this protection.

protective mimicry, a close resemblance of a defenseless animal to some different animal, which is less susceptible to attack from predators. For example, the viceroy butterfly closely resembles the monarch, which is not eaten by birds, etc., because of its disagreeable taste.

protective tariff, a tariff chiefly to protect home industry against foreign competition, not to produce revenue: *Heavy revenue duties . . . have the same effect as protective tariffs in obstructing free trade* (Time).

pro·tec·tor (prə tek′tər), *n.* **1. a.** a person who protects; defender. **b.** a thing that protects: *The catcher in baseball wears a chest protector.* **2.** the head of a kingdom when the king or queen cannot rule: *Oliver Cromwell was Lord Protector of England from 1653 to 1658.* —**Syn. 1. a.** guardian. **2.** regent.

Pro·tec·tor·ate (prə tek′tər it), *n.* the period (1653-1659) during which Oliver and Richard Cromwell were Lord Protectors of England. [< *protector* + *-ate*[3]]

pro·tec·tor·ate (prə tek′tər it), *n.* **1.** a weak country under the protection and partial control of a strong country: *Some parts of Africa and Asia are still European protectorates.* **2.** such protection and control. **3.** the position or term of a protector. **4.** government by a protector.

pro·tec·tor·ship (prə tek′tər ship), *n.* **1.** the position or term of a protector. **2.** the period during which a protector governs.

pro·tec·to·ry (prə tek′tər ē), *n., pl.* **-ries.** an institution for the care and training of homeless or delinquent children.

pro·tec·tress (prə tek′tris), *n.* a woman protector.

pro·té·gé (prō′tə zhā), *n.* **1.** a person or group under the protection or kindly care of another, especially of a person of superior position, influence, skill, etc.: *The young pianist was a protégé of the celebrated composer.* **2.** something under the care and protection of another: . . . *with Formosa becoming a United Nations protégé and the people of Formosa, by plebiscite or otherwise, deciding their future* (London Times). [< French *protégé,* past participle of *protéger,* learned borrowing from Latin *prōtegere* protect]

pro·té·gée (prō′tə zhā), *n.* a woman protégé.

pro·te·id (prō′tē id), *n.* protein. —*adj.* containing much protein.

pro·te·ide (prō′tē īd, -id), *n., adj.* protein.

pro·tein (prō′tēn, -tē in), *n.* **1.** a complex compound containing nitrogen that is a necessary part of the cells of animals and plants: *Meat, milk, cheese, eggs, and beans contain protein. Proteins are built up of amino acids, which unite, with a loss of water, to form peptide chains* (Scientific American). **2.** (formerly) the nitrogenous substances once thought to be the essential constituents of all animals and plants. —*adj.* of or containing protein.
[< German *Protein* < Greek *prōteîos* of the first quality (< *prôtos* first) + German *-in* -in]

pro·te·in·a·ceous (prō′tē ə nā′shəs), *adj.* of or like protein: *A rather starchy seed like the wheat grain will imbibe relatively little water, while a proteinaceous one like the pea will absorb a great deal* (Science News Letter).

pro·te·in·ase (prō′tē ə nās, -tē nās), *n.* any of various proteases that change proteins to polypeptides.

pro·tein·ic (prō tēn′ik, -tē in′-), *adj.* proteinaceous: *Secretin . . . is proteinic in nature, a polypeptide* (Science News Letter).

pro·te·in·u·ri·a (prō tē′ə nůr′ē ə), *n.* the presence of protein in the urine.

pro tem (prō tem′), pro tempore.

pro tem·po·re (prō tem′pə rē), *Latin.* for the time being; temporarily: *to appoint someone to an office pro tempore.* —**pro-tem′po·re,** *adj.*

pro·tend (prō tend′), *v.t.* **1.** to stretch forth; hold out before oneself. **2.** to extend in one dimension, especially lengthwise: *His staff protending like a hunter's spear* (Wordsworth). **3.** to extend in duration; prolong. [< Latin *prōtendere* < *prō-* before + *tendere* to stretch]

pro·ten·sion (prō ten′shən), *n.* duration.

pro·ten·sive (prō ten′siv), *adj.* **1.** extended in one dimension, especially lengthwise. **2.** extended in time; prolonging.

pro·te·ol·y·sis (prō′tē ol′ə sis), *n.* the hydrolysis or breaking down of proteins into simpler compounds, as in digestion. [< *protein* + Greek *lýsis* a loosening]

pro·te·o·lyt·ic (prō′tē ə lit′ik), *adj.* **1.** having to do with proteolysis. **2.** bringing about proteolysis: *a proteolytic enzyme.*

pro·te·ose (prō′tē ōs), *n.* any of a class of soluble compounds derived from proteins by the action of the gastric and pancreatic juices.

pro·ter·an·drous (prō′tə ran′drəs, prot′ə-), *adj.* exhibiting proterandry.

pro·ter·an·dry (prō′tə ran′drē, prot′ə-), *n.* **1.** *Botany.* the maturation of the stamens and the discharge of the pollen before the pistils of the flower are mature. **2.** *Zoology.* the maturation of the male organs or individuals of a hermaphroditic animal or a zooid colony before the female. [< Greek *próteros* prior (< *pró* before) + *anḗr, andrós* man, male + English *-y*[3]]

prot·er·og·y·nous (prot′ə roj′ə nəs), *adj.* exhibiting proterogyny.

prot·er·og·y·ny (prot′ə roj′ə nē), *n.* **1.** *Botany.* the maturation of the pistils in a flower before the stamens have matured their pollen. **2.** *Zoology.* the maturation of the female organs or individuals of a hermaphroditic animal or a zooid colony before the male. [< Greek *próteros* prior (< *pró* before) + *gynḗ* woman, female]

Prot·er·o·zo·ic (prot′ər ə zō′ik), *n.* **1.** a very old geological era, following the Archeozoic, in which sponges, sea worms, and other forms of sea life appeared: *The Archeozoic probably began about 1,500 million years ago, and the Proterozoic 925 million years ago* (Beals and Hoijer). **2.** the group of rocks formed in this era. —*adj.* of this era or these rocks. [< Greek *próteros* prior + *zōḗ* life + English *-ic*]

pro·ter·vi·ty (prə tėr′və tē), *n., pl.* **-ties. 1.** wantonness; petulance: . . . *the peevishness and protervity of age* (Caleb D'Anvers). **2.** an instance or show of this. [< Old French *protervite* < Latin *protervitās* < *protervus* violent, bold]

Pro·tes·i·la·us (prə tes′ə lā′əs), *n. Greek Legend.* the first Greek killed in the Trojan War.

pro·test (*n., adj.* prō′test; *v.* prə test′), *n.* **1.** a statement that denies or objects strongly: *They yielded only after protest. A written protest, couched in the strongest terms, was dispatched . . . for delivery* (London Times). **2.** a solemn declaration: *The accused man was judged guilty in spite of his protest of innocence.* **3.** a written statement by a notary public that a bill, note, check, etc., has been presented to someone who has refused to pay it or accept it. **4.** an attested declaration by the master of a ship in regard to some accident, injury, etc., during a voyage. **5.** *Sports.* an objection to a player or a play as illegal.
under protest, unwillingly; objecting: *The husband appeared under protest, and prayed to be dismissed* (J. Haggard).
—*adj.* characterized by protest; organized or conducted to protest against injustice, discrimination, etc.: *a protest meeting, a protest movement. In the protest parade . . . were businessmen, farmers, and housewives* (Wall Street Journal).
—*v.i.* **1.** to make objections; object: *The boys protested against having girls in the game.* **2.** to make a solemn declaration or affirmation: *The lady doth protest too much, methinks* (Shakespeare). —*v.t.* **1.** to object to: *to protest a decision.* **2.** to declare solemnly; assert: *The accused man protested his innocence.* **3.** to state that (a check, note, bill, etc.) has not been paid. **4.** to say in protest: *"Oh no, you didn't!" she protested, firmly* (Arnold Bennett). **5.** *Obsolete.* to make known: *Do me right, or I will protest your cowardice* (Shakespeare). **6.** *Obsolete.* to promise solemnly: *On Diana's altar to protest For aye austerity and single life* (Shakespeare). **7.** *Obsolete.* to call to witness.
[< Middle French *protester* to protest; say publicly, learned borrowing from Latin *prōtestārī* < *prō-* forth, before + *testis* witness] —**pro·test′er,** *n.*

Prot·es·tant (prot′ə stənt), *n.* **1.** a member of any of certain Christian churches that have split off from the Roman Catholic Church since the 1500's: *Lutherans, Baptists, Presbyterians, Methodists, Unitarians, Quakers, and many others are Protestants.* **2.** (in the 1600's) a Lutheran or an Anglican, as contrasted with a Calvinist, Presbyterian, Quaker, or other dissenter. **3.** one of the German princes who protested the decision of the Diet of Spires in 1529, which had denounced the Reformation.
—*adj.* of Protestants or their religion.
[< German or French *Protestant* one who protests < Latin *prōtestans, -antis,* present participle of *prōtestārī;* see PROTEST]

pro·tes·tant (prə tes′tənt), *n.* a person who protests; protester: *One of the protestants, though his first reaction was milder than most, was Abraham Lincoln* (Atlantic). —*adj.* protesting. [noun use of French *protestant,* present participle of *protester;* see PROTEST]

Protestant Episcopal Church, a church in the United States that has about the same principles and beliefs as the Church of England.

Prot·es·tant·ism (prot′ə stən tiz′əm), *n.* **1.** the religion of Protestants. **2.** their prin-

 PRONUNCIATION KEY: hat, āge, cãre, fär; let, ēqual, tėrm; it, īce; hot, ōpen, ôrder; oil, out; cup, půt, rüle;

ciples and beliefs. **3.** Protestants or Protestant churches as a group.

prot·es·tant·ism (prot′ə stən tiz′əm), *n.* the condition of protesting; an attitude of protest. [< *Protestantism*]

Prot·es·tant·ize (prot′ə stən tīz), *v.t.,* **-ized, -iz·ing.** to make Protestant; change to Protestantism: *The introduction of a vernacular liturgy and congregational singing stirred many ... Catholics to feel that their church was being "Protestantized"* (Time).

prot·es·ta·tion (prot′ə stā′shən), *n.* **1.** a solemn declaration; a protesting: *The Duke was ... vehement ... in his protestations of loyalty* (John L. Motley). **2.** a protest; a formal dissent or disapproval.

pro·tes·ta·to·ry (prə tes′tə tôr′ē, -tōr′-), *adj.* making protestation; expressing a protest.

pro·test·ing (prə tes′ting), *adj.* that protests; making a protest. —**pro·test′ing·ly,** *adv.*

pro·tes·tor (prə tes′tər), *n.* a person who makes a protest; protester.

Pro·te·us (prō′tē əs, -tyüs), *n.* **1.** *Greek Mythology.* a sea god who had the power of assuming many different forms. **2.** any person or thing capable of taking on various aspects or characters.

pro·te·us (prō′tē əs, -tyüs), *n.* **1.** a blind salamander living in the subterranean waters of limestone caves in eastern Europe. It is related to the menobranch of North America. **2.** any of a group of microorganisms or bacteria, some of which are saprophytic and some pathogenic in man and fowl. [< New Latin *Proteus* the genus name < *Proteus*]

pro·te·van·gel (prō′ti van′jəl), *n.* the protevangelium.

pro·te·van·gel·i·um (prō′ti van jel′ē əm), *n.* the promise concerning the seed of the woman, regarded as the earliest announcement of the gospel. Genesis 3:15. [< New Latin *protevangelium* < Greek *prôtos* first + Latin *evangelium* evangel]

pro·tha·la·mi·on (prō′thə lā′mē on), *n., pl.* **-mi·a** (-mē ə). a song or poem to celebrate a marriage. [< Greek *pró* before + *thálamos* bridal chamber; probably patterned on *epithalamium*]

pro·tha·la·mi·um (prō′thə lā′mē əm), *n., pl.* **-mi·a** (-mē ə). prothalamion.

pro·thal·li·al (prō thal′ē əl), *adj.* of a prothallium.

pro·thal·line (prō thal′īn, -in), *adj.* of, like, or belonging to a prothallium.

pro·thal·li·um (prō thal′ē əm), *n., pl.* **-thal·li·a** (-thal′ē ə). **1.** the gametophyte of ferns, etc. **2.** the analogous rudimentary gametophyte in gymnosperms. [< New Latin *prothallium* < Greek *pró* before + New Latin *thallus* thallus + *-ium,* a diminutive suffix]

PROTHALLIUM

Prothallium (def. 1) of a fern

pro·thal·lus (prō thal′əs) *n., pl.* **-thal·li** (-thal′ī). prothallium.

proth·e·sis (proth′ə sis), *n.* **1. a.** the preparation of the Eucharistic elements in the Greek Church. **b.** the table on which this is done. **c.** the part of the sanctuary where this table stands. **2.** prosthesis of a word or the human body.
[< Greek *próthesis* a setting forth in public < *protithénai* < *pro-* before + *tithénai* to set, put]

pro·thet·ic (prō thet′ik), *adj.* having to do with or exhibiting prothesis. —**pro·thet′i·cal·ly,** *adv.*

pro·thon·o·tar·i·al (prō thon′ə târ′ē əl), *adj.* of or belonging to a prothonotary.

pro·thon·o·tar·y (prō thon′ə ter′ē), *n., pl.* **-tar·ies. 1.** a chief clerk, secretary, or registrar, especially of a court of law. **2.** the Roman Catholic official in charge of the registry of pontifical acts, canonizations, etc. **3.** the chief secretary of the patriarch of Constantinople in the Greek Church. **4.** a prothonotary warbler. Also, **protonotary.** [< Medieval Latin *prothonotarius* < Medieval Greek *prōtonōtários* < *prôtos* first + Late Greek *nōtários* clerk, notary]

pro·thon·o·tar·y·ship (prō thon′ə ter′ē-ship), *n.* the office of a prothonotary.

prothonotary warbler, a golden-yellow warbler of the central and eastern United States that has an olive back and bluish-gray wings and tail.

pro·tho·rac·ic (prō′thə ras′ik), *adj.* of or having to do with the prothorax.

pro·tho·rax (prō thôr′aks, -thōr′-), *n., pl.* **-tho·rax·es, -tho·ra·ces** (-thôr′ə sēz, -thōr′-). the anterior division of an insect's thorax, bearing the first pair of legs. [< French *prothorax* < *pro-* pro-[1] + New Latin *thorax* thorax < Greek *thōrāx* chest]

pro·throm·base (prō throm′bās), *n.* the proenzyme of thrombase.

pro·throm·bin (prō throm′bin), *n.* a substance in the blood plasma, essential to clotting, from which thrombin is derived; thrombogen. [< *pro-*[2] + *thrombin*]

pro·tist (prō′tist), *n., pl.* **-tis·ta** (-tis′tə). any single-celled animal or plant. [< German *Protista,* plural < Greek *prṓtistos* the very first, superlative of *prôtos* first (< *pró* before)]

pro·tis·tan (prō tis′tən), *adj.* of or having to do with single-celled animals or plants. —*n.* a single-celled animal or plant.

pro·tis·tic (prō tis′tik), *adj.* protistan.

pro·ti·um (prō′tē əm, -shē-), *n.* the ordinary isotope of hydrogen, having a mass number of 1.0 *Symbol:* H^1 (no period). [< *prot*(on) + New Latin *-ium,* a noun suffix meaning "element" (because the nucleus contains one proton only)]

proto-, *combining form.* **1.** first in time: *Protomartyr = the first martyr.*
2. first in importance; chief; primary, as in *protopope.*
Also, **prot-** before vowels.
[< Greek *prōto-* < *prôtos* first, superlative of *prôteros* < *pró,* preposition, before; see PRO-[2]]

pro·to·ac·tin·i·um (prō′tō ak tin′ē əm), *n. Obsolete.* protactinium.

pro·to·an·throp·ic (prō′tō an throp′ik), *adj.* of or belonging to the earliest period of the existence of man.

pro·to·ca·non·i·cal (prō′tō kə non′ə kəl), *adj.* of or forming a first or original canon.

protocanonical books, the books of the Bible whose canonicity has always been universally acknowledged in the church.

pro·to·cat·e·chu·ic acid (prō′tō kat′ə-chü′ik, -shü′-), a crystalline compound derived from vanillin or produced synthetically, occurring naturally in various plants. *Formula:* $C_7H_6O_4$

pro·toc·er·as (prō tos′ər əs), *n.* an extinct ungulate mammal of North America, about the size of a sheep and distantly related to the chevrotains, with two or three pairs of horns on the head of the male. [< New Latin *Protoceras* the genus name < Greek *prôtos* first + *kéras* horn]

pro·to·cer·a·tops (prō′tō ser′ə tops), *n.* a species of hornless, plant-eating dinosaur, about six feet long, that lived during the late Cretaceous period in Asia and North America. [< New Latin *Protoceratops* < Greek *prôtos* first + *kéras, -atos* horn + *ôps* eye]

pro·to·col (prō′tə kol, -kôl), *n., v.,* **-colled, -col·ling.** —*n.* **1.** a first draft or record from which a document, especially a treaty, is prepared. **2.** the rules of etiquette of the diplomatic corps. **3.** rules for any procedure. **4.** a formal or official statement of a proceeding or transaction, as a clinical report, or a report on a scientific experiment or on the preparation and testing of a drug. **5.** *U.S.* the original record of a Spanish land grant made in parts of the Southwest and West.
—*v.i.* to draw up protocols. —*v.t.* to embody in a protocol.
[< Old French *protocolle* minutes of a document, learned borrowing from Medieval Latin *protocollum* < Greek *prōtókollon* a first leaf (with date and contents) glued onto a papyrus roll < *prôtos* first + *kólla* glue]

pro·to·col·ar (prō′tə kol′ər), *adj.* protocolary.

pro·to·col·a·ry (prō′tə kol′ər ē), *adj.* of or having to do with protocol or a protocol: *After these protocolary preliminaries, I got down to the main purpose of my visit* (New Yorker).

pro·to·derm (prō′tə dėrm), *n.* dermatogen.

pro·to·dy·nas·tic (prō′tō dī nas′tik), *adj.* of or having to do with the earliest royal dynasties of a country: *... fine stone vessels from protodynastic Egypt* (Joseph Alsop).

pro·to·fas·cism (prō′tō fash′iz əm), *n.* a movement or ideology characterized by fascist tendencies and ideas and usually associated with a political party of the far right.

pro·to·fas·cist (prō′tō fash′ist), *n.* **1.** a member of a protofascist party. **2.** a person who favors or supports protofascism. —*adj.* of or having to do with protofascism or protofascists: *... the protofascist wing of the Syrian political spectrum* (Dwight J. Simpson).

pro·to·gal·ax·y (prō′tō gal′ək sē), *n., pl.* **-ax·ies. 1.** a hypothetical mass of contracting gas in space from which the galaxies were formed as the result of a cosmic explosion of hydrogen. **2.** a galaxy in the earliest stage or process of formation.

Pro·to-Ger·man·ic (prō′tə jėr man′ik), *adj.* of or having to do with the hypothetical language that was the ancestor of the Germanic languages. —*n.* this language; primitive or original Germanic.

pro·to·gine (prō′tə jin, -jēn), *n.* a fine-grained variety of granite, occurring chiefly in the Alps. [< French *protogine,* ultimately < Greek *prôtos* first + *gígnesthai* be born]

pro·tog·y·nous (prō toj′ə nəs), *adj.* proterogynous.

pro·tog·y·ny (prō toj′ə nē), *n.* proterogyny.

pro·to·his·tor·ic (prō′tō his tôr′ik, -tor′-), *adj.* of or belonging to the beginnings of recorded history.

pro·to·his·to·ry (prō′tō his′tər ē, -trē), *n.* history at the dawn or beginnings of recorded history; protohistoric matters or times.

pro·to·hu·man (prō′tō hyü′mən), *adj.* resembling or preceding the earliest human; prehominid.

pro·to·lan·guage (prō′tō lang′gwij), *n.* a hypothetical, reconstructed language assumed to be the ancestor of one or more recorded or existing languages.

pro·to·lith·ic (prō′tə lith′ik), *adj.* of or having to do with the earliest Stone Age; eolithic. [< *proto-* + *lithic*[1]]

pro·to·mar·tyr (prō′tō mär′tər), *n.* **1.** the first martyr in any cause: *The small city of St. Albans ... with its Roman theater, its place where a protomartyr was executed ...* (London Times). **2.** Stephen, the first Christian martyr. Acts 7. [< Late Latin *prōtomartyr* < Greek *prōtómartys* < *prôtos* first + *mártys* martyr]

pro·to·morph (prō′tə môrf), *n.* a primitive form.

pro·to·mor·phic (prō′tə môr′fik), *adj.* primitive. [< *proto-* + Greek *morphḗ* form + English *-ic*]

pro·ton (prō′ton), *n.* a tiny particle carrying one unit of positive electricity. All atoms are built up of electrons and protons. The number of protons in an atom is the atomic number of the element. [< Greek *prôtos* first + *-on,* as in *electron*]

proton accelerator, a device, such as a bevatron, to increase the velocity of protons and other atomic particles, thereby increasing their energy.

proton beam, a beam of high-energy protons as developed by a proton accelerator.

pro·to·ne·ma (prō′tə nē′mə), *n., pl.* **-ma·ta** (-mə tə). a filamentous structure in mosses from which the more visible, leafy portion grows. [< Greek *prôtos* first + *nêma, -atos* thread < *neîn* to spin]

pro·ton·o·tar·y (prō ton′ə ter′ē), *n., pl.* **-tar·ies.** prothonotary.

pro·ton-pro·ton chain (prō′ton prō′ton), a nuclear reaction believed to be the source of energy of the sun and other hydrogen-rich stars. It begins with the fusion of two protons to form a deuteron, the nucleus of a heavy hydrogen atom, which then changes in two stages into helium, releasing two protons to join the chain again. The reaction liberates tremendous energy.

proton synchrotron, a proton accelerator.

pro·to·path·ic (prō′tə path′ik), *adj. Biology, Psychology.* **1.** having only primitive sense powers. **2.** of or having to do with primitive receptors. [< *proto-* + Greek *páthos* a suffering, disease + English *-ic*]

pro·to·phlo·em (prō′tō flō′em), *n.* the first phloem tissue to develop, lying closest to the outer part of the stem; the primitive phloem of a vascular bundle. [< German

Protophloem < Greek *prôtos* first + German *Phloem* phloem]

pro·to·plan·et (prō′tə plan′it), *n.* an earlier form of planet believed to have its origin in the condensation of solar gases and dust. The sun, moon, earth, and other planets are thought to have originated in this way.

pro·to·plasm (prō′tə plaz′əm), *n.* **1.** living matter; the substance that is the physical basis of life; the living substance of all plant and animal cells. Protoplasm is a colorless matter somewhat like soft jelly or white of egg. **2.** (formerly) cytoplasm. [< German *Protoplasma* < Greek *prôtos* first + *plásma* something molded < *plássein* to mold]

pro·to·plas·mic (prō′tə plaz′mik), *adj.* of protoplasm; having to do with protoplasm: *Beneath the water was an intricate pattern of teeming protoplasmic life* (Time).

pro·to·plast (prō′tə plast), *n.* **1.** a mass of protoplasm. **2. a.** the first formed; the original. **b.** the hypothetical first man. [< Middle French *protoplaste*, learned borrowing from Latin *prōtoplastus* the first man < Greek *prōtóplastos* < *prôtos* first + *plastós* < *plássein* to form, mold]

pro·to·plas·tic (prō′tə plas′tik), *adj.* of or having to do with a protoplast.

pro·top·o·dite (prō top′ə dīt), *n.* the section or joint of an appendage which attaches to the body of a crustacean. [< *proto-* + Greek *poús, podós* foot + English *-ite*[1]]

pro·to·pope (prō′tə pōp), *n.* a priest of superior rank in the Greek Church; chief priest. [< *proto-* + *pope*]

pro·to·por·phy·rin (prō′tə pôr′fər in), *n.* a porphyrin or pigment occurring in cells and produced synthetically that is a basic part of hemoglobin in red blood and chlorophyll in green plants. *Formula:* $C_{34}H_{34}N_4O_4$

pro·to·pro·te·ose (prō′tō prō′tē ōs), *n.* any of various primary proteoses formed by the breakdown of proteins.

pro·to·stele (prō′tə stēl, -stē′lē), *n. Botany.* the solid stele of most roots, and of the first-formed portion of some primitive stems.

pro·to·ste·lic (prō′tə stē′lik), *adj.* of or having to do with protostele.

pro·to·troph·ic (prō′tə trof′ik), *adj.* getting nourishment from inorganic substances, as the nitrobacteria. [< *proto-* + Greek *trophē* nourishment + English *-ic*]

pro·to·typ·al (prō′tə tī′pəl), *adj.* of, having to do with, or forming a prototype.

pro·to·type (prō′tə tīp), *n.* the first or primary type of anything; the original or model: *A modern ship has its prototype in the hollowed log used by savages. The prototype of the foreign agent is the spy* (Bulletin of Atomic Scientists). [< Middle French *prototype* < New Latin *prototypon* < Greek *prōtótypon*, (originally) neuter of *prōtótypos* original, primitive < *prôtos* first + *týpos* type, model < *týptein* to strike]

pro·to·typ·ic (prō′tə tip′ik), *adj.* prototypal.

pro·to·typ·i·cal (prō′tə tip′ə kəl), *adj.* prototypal.

pro·to·ver·a·trine (prō′tō ver′ə trēn, -trin), *n.* an alkaloid drug obtained from the rhizomes of several false hellebores, used in treating hypertension.

pro·tox·id (prō tok′sid), *n.* protoxide.

pro·tox·ide (prō tok′sīd, -sid), *n.* that member of a series of oxides which has the smallest proportion of oxygen. [< *prot-* + *oxide*]

pro·to·xy·lem (prō′tə zī′lem), *n.* the first xylem tissue to develop, lying closest to the pith; the primitive xylem of a vascular bundle. [< *proto-* + *xylem*]

pro·to·zo·a (prō′tə zō′ə), *n.pl.* protozoans. [< New Latin *Protozoa* the phylum name < Greek *prôtos* first + *zôa*, plural of *zôion* animal]

pro·to·zo·al (prō′tə zō′əl), *adj.* protozoan.

pro·to·zo·an (prō′tə zō′ən), *n.* a microscopic animal that consists of a single cell. Protozoans, such as the amoeba or the paramecium, are found in water or soil and reproduce by fission, budding, or dividing into spores. *The protozoans are the lowliest and simplest forms of animal life* (White and Renner). —*adj.* belonging or having to do with, or caused by, protozoans. [< *protozo*(a) + *-an*]

pro·to·zo·ic (prō′tə zō′ik), *adj.* protozoan.

pro·to·zo·o·log·i·cal (prō′tə zō′ə loj′ə kəl), *adj.* of or having to do with protozoology.

pro·to·zo·ol·o·gist (prō′tə zō ol′ə jist), *n.* a person skilled in protozoology.

pro·to·zo·ol·o·gy (prō′tə zō ol′ə jē), *n.* the branch of zoology or of pathology that deals with protozoans.

pro·to·zo·on (prō′tə zō′on), *n., pl.* **-zo·a** (-zō′ə). a protozoan.

pro·tract (prō trakt′), *v.t.* **1.** to draw out; lengthen in time: *to protract a visit. He attempted . . . to prevent, or at least to protract, his ruin* (Edward Gibbon). **2.** to slide out; thrust out; extend. **3.** to draw by means of a scale and protractor; plot: *to protract a piece of land in surveying.* [< Latin *prōtractus*, past participle of *prōtrahere* < *prō-* forward + *trahere* to drag]

pro·tract·ed (prō trak′tid), *adj.* lengthened. —**pro·tract′ed·ness,** *n.*

pro·tract·ed·ly (prō trak′tid lē), *adv.* in a protracted or drawn-out fashion: *His older brother, Ben, who dies somewhat protractedly of pneumonia in the second act* . . . (New Yorker).

pro·trac·tile (prō trak′təl), *adj.* capable of being lengthened out, or of being thrust forth: *The turtle has a protractile head.*

pro·trac·tion (prō trak′shən), *n.* **1.** the act of drawing out; extension. **2.** a drawing that has exactly the same proportions as the thing it represents. **3.** something that is protracted or plotted; plot.

pro·trac·tive (prō trak′tiv), *adj.* protracting; prolonging.

pro·trac·tor (prō trak′tər), *n.* **1.** an instrument in the form of a semicircle for drawing or measuring angles. **2.** a person or thing that protracts, as a muscle that extends a part of the body.

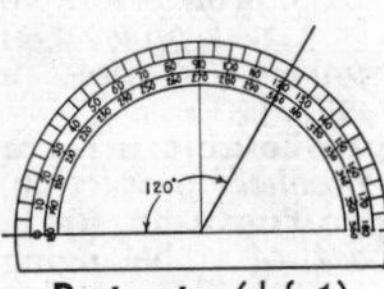

Protractor (def. 1) measuring a 120-degree angle

pro·trud·a·ble (prō trü′də bəl), *adj.* protrusile.

pro·trude (prō trüd′), *v.,* **-trud·ed, -trud·ing.** —*v.t.* to thrust forth; stick out: *The saucy child protruded her tongue.* —*v.i.* to be thrust forth; project: *Her teeth protrude too far.* [< Latin *prōtrūdere* < *prō-* forward + *trūdere* to thrust]

pro·trud·ent (prō trü′dənt), *adj.* protruding.

pro·tru·si·ble (prō trü′sə bəl), *adj.* protrusile.

pro·tru·sile (prō trü′səl), *adj.* capable of being protruded: *An elephant's trunk is protrusile.*

pro·tru·sion (prō trü′zhən), *n.* **1.** a protruding or being protruded: *Starvation caused the protrusion of the poor cat's bones.* **2.** something that sticks out; projection: *A protrusion of rock gave us shelter from the storm.* [< Latin *prōtrūsus*, past participle of *prōtrūdere* protrude + English *-ion*]

pro·tru·sive (prō trü′siv), *adj.* sticking out; projecting. —**pro·tru′sive·ly,** *adv.*

pro·tu·ber·ance (prō tü′bər əns, -tyü′-), *n.* **1.** a part that sticks out; bulge; swelling: *From the protuberance in their father's coat pocket, the children guessed that he had brought them candy.* **2.** a protuberant quality or condition.

pro·tu·ber·an·cy (prō tü′bər ən sē, -tyü′-), *n., pl.* **-cies.** protuberance.

pro·tu·ber·ant (prō tü′bər ənt, -tyü′-), *adj.* bulging out; sticking out; prominent. [< Latin *prōtūberāns, -antis* bulging, present participle of *prōtūberāre* grow forth < *prō-* forward + *tūber, -eris* lump, tuber] —**pro·tu′ber·ant·ly,** *adv.*

pro·tu·ber·ate (prō tü′bə rāt, -tyü′-), *v.i.,* **-at·ed, -at·ing.** to bulge. [< Latin *prōtūberāre* (with English *-ate*[1]); see PROTUBERANT]

pro·tu·ran (prō tyůr′ən), *n.* any of a group of tiny primitive insects that live under bark and in damp places. Proturans are blind and wingless and are believed to represent a very early stage in the evolution of insects. *A new species of proturan, one of earth's most primitive insects, has been found in South America* (Science News Letter). —*adj.* of or having to do with the proturans. [< New Latin *Protura* the class name (< Greek *prôtos* first + *ourá* tail) + English *-an*]

pro·tyl (prō′təl), *n.* protyle.

pro·tyle (prō′tīl, -təl), *n.* the hypothetical, undifferentiated matter from which the chemical elements may have been derived. [< *prot-* + Greek *hýlē* matter]

proud (proud), *adj.* **1.** thinking well of oneself: *The vile are only vain; the great are proud* (Byron). **2.** feeling or showing great pleasure or satisfaction: *I am proud to call him my friend.* **3.** having a becoming sense of what is due oneself, or one's position or character: *too proud to ask for charity.* **4.** thinking too well of oneself; haughty; arrogant: *a proud, insolent man. This proud fellow . . . who scorns us all* (Tennyson). **5.** such as to make a person proud; highly honorable, creditable, or gratifying: *It was a proud moment for Tom when he shook hands with the President.* **6.** proceeding from pride; due to pride: *a proud smile, a father's proud look at his child.* **7.** imposing; stately; majestic; magnificent: *proud cities. The big ship was a proud sight.* **8.** (of persons) of exalted rank or station: *proud nobles.* **9.** full of spirit or mettle: *a proud war horse.* **10.** *Obsolete.* valiant; brave.

do one proud, *Informal.* to make proud; do very well; gratify highly: *They haven't done you very proud, have they?* (Graham Greene).

proud of, thinking well of; being well satisfied with; proud because of: *to be proud of oneself, to be proud of one's family.*

[Old English *prūd*, and *prūt*, probably < Old French *prod*, and *prud* valiant < Late Latin *prōde* profitable, of use, ultimately < Latin *prōdesse* be useful, profitable < *prō-* for + *esse* to be]

—**Syn. 1. Proud, overbearing, supercilious** mean having or showing a high opinion of oneself. **Proud** suggests either being above anything low, mean, or contemptible, or thinking oneself better than others: *He has a strong, proud face.* **Overbearing** suggests being rudely dictating or haughtily insulting in behavior and speech: *Promoted too quickly, the conceited youth became overbearing.* **Supercilious** suggests being conceited, and revealing it in a coolly scornful attitude: *With a supercilious smile, he refused our invitation.* —**Ant. 4.** humble.

proud flesh, formation of too many grainlike particles of flesh on, or around the edges of, a healing wound.

proud·ly (proud′lē), *adv.* in a proud manner; with pride; with a good opinion of oneself.

proud·ness (proud′nis), *n.* the condition or quality of being proud; pride.

Proust·i·an (prüs′tē ən), *adj.* of, having to do with, or suggestive of the novelist Marcel Proust or his works: *The salutes, the flag being lowered at sunset, the bugler sounding recall—I found myself remembering every detail with an almost Proustian clarity* (New Yorker). *Best, perhaps, are the evocations of childhood, which reveal a Proustian sensibility* (Punch). —*n.* a student or admirer of the works of Proust: *I have heard Durrell fans celebrating the enchantments of Justine and Balthazar with the fervor one encounters among pious Proustians* (Atlantic). *Proustians will recognize their man everywhere* (Newsweek).

proust·ite (prüs′tīt), *n.* a mineral consisting of a sulfide of arsenic and silver, occurring in crystals or masses of a red color: *The ruby silver minerals, proustite and pyrargyrite, are of minor importance as sources of silver* (W. R. Jones). [< French *proustite* < Joseph-Louis *Proust*, 1754-1826, a French chemist, who discovered it + *-ite* -ite[1]]

prov., 1. provident. **2.** province. **3.** provincial. **4.** provincialism. **5.** provisional. **6.** provost.

Prov., 1. Provençal. **2.** Provence. **3.** Proverbs (book of the Old Testament). **4.** Province. **5.** Provost.

prov·a·ble (prü′və bəl), *adj.* that can be proved. Also, **proveable.**

prov·a·ble·ness (prü′və bəl nis), *n.* the state or quality of being provable; capability of being proved.

prov·a·bly (prü′və blē), *adv.* in a manner capable of proof: *U.S. Federal income taxes do not apply in Puerto Rico, and any new business not provably running away from U.S. taxes or unions was freed from the island income tax for ten years* (Time).

prov·and (prov′ənd), *n. Archaic.* provender; provisions, especially food and fodder for an army. [apparently < Old French *provende;* see PROVENDER]

prov·ant (prov′ənt), *n. Archaic.* provand.

prove (prüv), *v.,* **proved, proved** or **prov·en, prov·ing.** —*v.t.* **1.** to establish (a thing) as true; make certain; demonstrate the truth of by evidence or argument: *to prove that one is right, to prove a point.* **2.** to give demonstration or proof of by action: *to* *prove one's skill. Ev'ry knight is proud to prove his worth* (John Dryden). **3.** to establish the genuineness or validity of: *One [executor] alone is competent to prove a will and carry out its provisions* (Whitaker's Almanac). **4.** to subject to some testing process; try out; test: *to prove a new gun.* **5.** to test the correctness of (a mathematical calculation): *Multiplication can be proved by division.* **6.** *Law.* to obtain probate of (a will). **7.** *Archaic.* to put to the test; try the qualities of: *Prove all things: hold fast that which is good* (I Thessalonians 5:21). *The exception proves the rule.* **8.** *Archaic.* to find out by experience; have experience of; experience: *They only shall His mercy prove* (John Wesley). **9.** *Printing.* to take a proof of (type, a plate, etc.). *—v.i.* **1.** to be found to be; turn out: *This book proved interesting. He has proved to be a capable administrator.* **2.** *Obsolete.* to make a trial (of something).

prove out, to show or be shown, by means of a testing process, as ready and safe for use: *The . . . irrigation project, a vast complex, can't prove out until a great deal more money is spent on it* (Wall Street Journal).

prove up, *U.S.* **a.** to show that the requirements of the law for taking up (government land, mineral rights, etc.) have been fulfilled, so that a patent may be issued: *A number of promising discoveries had also been made and were now being proved up* (North Star). **b.** to adduce the proof of right: *My wife proved up on her Cherokee blood* (J.H. Beadle).

[< Old French *prover* < Latin *probāre* < *probus* worthy]

—**Syn.** *v.t.* **1.** corroborate, verify, confirm.

➤ **proved, proven.** *Proved* is the usual verbal form, *proven* the usual adjectival form: *He had proved his ability. His proven ability could not be doubted.*

prove·a·ble (prü'və bəl), *adj.* provable.

prove·a·bly (prü'və blē), *adv.* provably.

pro·vec·tion (prō vek'shən), *n. Linguistics.* the carrying of a terminal letter of a word to the beginning of the succeeding word, as in *a newt* for *an ewt.* [< Late Latin *prōvectiō, -ōnis* < Latin *prōvehere* < *prō-* forth + *vehere* carry]

pro·ved·i·tor (prō ved'ə tər), *n. Obsolete.* **1.** a purveyor; steward. **2.** an overseer. [< earlier Italian *proveditore* < *provedere* to provide < Latin *prōvidēre;* see PROVIDE]

prov·en (prü'vən), *v.* proved; a past participle of **prove:** *We do not wish guilty persons to get away. Neither do we wish innocent persons or persons not yet proven guilty to be subjected to unlawful and unconstitutional procedures* (New York Times).

➤ See **prove** for usage note.

prov·e·nance (prov'ə nəns), *n.* source; origin: *If a specimen fluoresces with a different color from that of a genuine specimen of the same provenance and period, the chances are that it is spurious* (George Savage). *They are . . . men dissolved "into an anonymous mass" because they are "without an authentic world, without provenance or roots" —without, that is to say, belief and faith that they can live by* (Atlantic).

[< French *provenance* < Middle French *provenant,* present participle of *provenir* come forth, learned borrowing from Latin *prōvenīre*]

Pro·ven·çal (prō'vən säl', prov'ən-), *n.* **1.** a native or inhabitant of Provence, a region in southeastern France bordering the Mediterranean. **2.** the Romance language spoken in Provence; langue d'oc. In its medieval form, Old Provençal, it was widely known in Europe as one of the principal languages used by the troubadours. *—adj.* of or having to do with Provence, its people, or their language.

prov·en·der (prov'ən dər), *n.* **1.** dry food for animals, such as hay or corn. **2.** *Informal.* food. [< Old French *provendre,* variant of *provende;* alteration of Vulgar Latin *prōbenda* < Latin *praebenda.* Doublet of PREBEND.]

pro·ve·ni·ence (prō vē'nē əns, -vēn'yəns), *n.* source; origin. [probably alteration of *provenance*]

pro·ven·tric·u·lus (prō'ven trik'yə ləs), *n., pl.* **-li** (-lī). **1.** the soft first (true or glandular) stomach of a bird, which secretes gastric juices. It lies between the crop and gizzard. **2.** the digestive chamber between the crop and stomach (midgut) in insects. **3.** (in worms) a muscular crop. [< New Latin *proventriculus* < Latin *prō-* before + *ventriculus* (originally) a pouch]

prov·er (prü'vər), *n.* **1.** a person or thing that proves or tries. **2.** a skilled workman employed to strike off proofs from engraved plates.

prov·erb (prov'ėrb), *n.* **1.** a short wise saying used for a long time by many people: *"Haste makes waste" is a proverb. Fast bind, fast find; A proverb never stale in thrifty mind* (Shakespeare). **2.** a well-known case: *He is a proverb for carelessness. This house . . . will I cast out of my sight: and Israel shall be a proverb and a byword among all people* (I Kings 9:7).

—v.t. **1.** to say in the form of a proverb; speak of proverbially. **2.** to make a byword of: *Am I not sung and proverbed for a fool in every street?* (Milton).

[Middle English *proverbe* < Old French, learned borrowing from Latin *prōverbium* < *prō-* forth + *verbum* word, (originally) a speaking, speech]

—**Syn.** *n.* **1.** adage, maxim, saw.

➤ See **epigram** for usage note.

pro·ver·bi·al (prə vėr'bē əl), *adj.* **1. a.** of a proverb. **b.** expressed in a proverb: *proverbial wisdom.* **c.** like a proverb: *proverbial brevity, a proverbial saying.* **2.** that has become a proverb: *the proverbial stitch in time.* **3.** well-known: *the proverbial loyalty of dogs, the proverbial London fog.* —**Syn. 3.** unquestioned, familiar.

pro·ver·bi·al·ist (prə vėr'bē ə list), *n.* a person who originates, collects, or uses proverbs.

pro·ver·bi·al·ly (prə vėr'bē ə lē), *adv.* in a proverbial manner; according to a proverb or proverbs: *The ant is proverbially industrious.*

Prov·erbs (prov'ėrbz), *n.pl.* a book of the Old Testament made up of sayings of the wise men of Israel, including Solomon. *Abbr.:* Prov.

pro·vide (prə vīd'), *v.,* **-vid·ed, -vid·ing.** *—v.t.* **1.** to supply; furnish: *The garden provides vegetables for the family. Sheep provide us with wool.* **2.** to state as a condition beforehand: *Our club's rules provide that dues must be paid monthly.* **3.** to get ready; prepare beforehand: *Mother provides a good dinner. The wise ant her wintry store provides* (John Dryden). *—v.i.* **1.** to supply means of support; arrange to supply means of support: *A father provides for his family.* **2.** to take care for the future: *to provide against accident, to provide for old age.* [< Latin *prōvidēre* look after; (literally) foresee < *prō-* ahead + *vidēre* to see. Doublet of PURVEY.] —**Syn.** *v.t.* **2.** stipulate.

pro·vid·ed (prə vī'did), *conj.* on the condition that; if: *She will go provided her friends can go also. I will tell you the real story, provided you won't quote me.* —**Syn.** providing.

prov·i·dence (prov'ə dəns), *n.,* **1.** God's care and help: *Trusting in providence, the Pilgrims sailed for the unknown world.* **2.** an instance of God's care and help: *There's a special providence in the fall of a sparrow* (Shakespeare). **3.** care for the future; good management. **4.** *Dialect.* the act of providing (for).

make providence, *Dialect.* to make provision: *Sudden death came to the fathers, and no providence made for the daughters* (John B. Berners).

—**Syn. 3.** foresight, prudence.

Prov·i·dence (prov'ə dəns), *n.* God: *Vigilant over all that he has made, Kind Providence attends with gracious aid* (William Cowper).

prov·i·dent (prov'ə dənt), *adj.* **1.** having or showing foresight; careful in providing for the future: *Provident men lay aside money for their families. He had been provident enough to take with him some of his best working tools* (Cardinal Newman). **2.** economical; frugal: *We had tried to be reasonably provident in joint planning and management* (Atlantic). [< Latin *prōvidēns, -entis,* present participle of *prōvidēre;* see PROVIDE] **—prov'i·dent·ly,** *adv.* —**Syn. 1.** foreseeing, prudent.

prov·i·den·tial (prov'ə den'shəl), *adj.* **1.** fortunate: *Our delay seemed providential, for the train we planned to take was wrecked.* **2.** of or proceeding from divine power or influence: *the providential nature of the universe.* **—prov'i·den'tial·ly,** *adv.* —**Syn. 1.** lucky, opportune.

pro·vid·er (prə vī'dər), *n.* a person who provides, furnishes, or supplies.

pro·vid·ing (prə vī'ding), *conj.* on the condition that: *I shall go providing it doesn't rain.*

prov·ince (prov'əns), *n.* **1.** one of the main divisions of a country: *Canada is made up of provinces instead of states.* **2.** a part of a country outside the capital or the largest cities: *The government brought four army regiments and 500 navy personnel from the provinces to swell Santiago's military strength to 30,000* (Newsweek). **3.** proper work or activity: *Teaching spelling is not within the province of a college. The enforcement of law is not within the doctor's province.* **4.** division; department: *the province of science, the province of literature.* **5.** an ancient Roman territory outside Italy, ruled by a Roman governor. **6.** any of certain North American British colonies, some of which became states of the United States and the others of which became provinces of Canada. **7.** a large church district governed by an archbishop.

[< Old French *province,* learned borrowing from Latin *prōvincia*]

—**Syn. 3.** sphere, domain. **4.** branch.

pro·vin·cial (prə vin'shəl), *adj.* **1.** of a province: *a provincial government.* **2.** belonging or peculiar to some particular province or provinces rather than to the whole country; local: *provincial English, provincial customs. This Tuscan speech was not a provincial dialect but . . . it was essentially the speech of the educated society of one city, namely Florence* (Simeon Potter). **3.** having the manners, speech, dress, point of view, etc., of people living in a province. **4.** lacking refinement or polish; narrow: *a provincial point of view. [Thoreau] was worse than provincial—he was parochial* (Henry James). *—n.* **1.** a person born or living in a province. **2.** a provincial person. **3.** *Ecclesiastical.* **a.** the head of a province. **b.** a superior in some religious orders superintending his fraternity in a given district.

—**Syn.** *adj.* **2.** regional, sectional. **3.** rural, rustic.

pro·vin·cial·ise (prə vin'shə līz), *v.t.,* **-ised, -is·ing.** *Especially British.* provincialize: *Ever since schools under the control of local bodies were "provincialised" two years ago a variety of conflicting statements have been made regarding the possibility of de-provincialising them and assigning them to the State* (Times of India).

pro·vin·cial·ism (prə vin'shə liz əm), *n.* **1.** provincial manners, habit of thought, etc.: *Neither "provincialism" nor "sectionalism" holds the South together but something deeper than these and essential to our system* (Harper's). **2.** narrow-mindedness. **3.** a word, expression, or way of pronunciation peculiar to a district or a country: *Seldom has he sung an aria — never, perhaps, a complete role — without provincialisms; by which I mean an excessive or inappropriate use of aspirates, sobs, gulps, portamenti and the like* (New York Times). —**Syn. 3.** patois.

pro·vin·cial·ist (prə vin'shə list), *n.* **1.** a supporter or advocate of the rights and claims of a province: *The "provincialists" are incapable of providing the Quebec wing of a Canadian party* (Canadian Forum). **2.** a native or inhabitant of a province; provincial: *Such practical skill comes of itself in condensed masses of population, and it is this which gives the Londoner his advantage over the provincialist* (William Taylor).

pro·vin·ci·al·i·ty (prə vin'shē al'ə tē), *n., pl.* **-ties. 1.** provincial quality or character. **2.** a provincial characteristic or trait.

pro·vin·cial·ize (prə vin'shə līz), *v.t.,* **-ized, -iz·ing. 1.** to make provincial; give a provincial character or name to. **2.** to bring under the jurisdiction of a province: *Lesage wants to provincialize such federally administered plans as unemployment insurance and old-age pensions* (Maclean's).

pro·vin·cial·ly (prə vin'shə lē), *adv.* in a provincial manner or capacity.

prov·ing ground (prü'ving), **1.** a place, usually a large tract of land, for testing equipment, especially military equipment, vehicles, etc.: *The island is studded with the hallmark of the proving ground: towers* (Newsweek). **2.** any place that affords the possibility of testing an idea, invention, skill, etc.: *The whole southern portion of the southern hemisphere is an excellent proving ground for many large-scale meteorological theories* (E. F. Roots). *Ellington himself, who has always used his orchestra as a proving ground for his compositions, has begun to write large, ambitious pieces again* (New Yorker).

pro·vi·rus (prō vī′rəs), *n.* a latent form of a virus, created by the fusion of the genetic material of a virus with that of the host bacterium: *The provirus may suddenly develop into virus and the bacterium give rise to a group of virus particles* (Scientific American).

pro·vi·sion (prə vizh′ən), *n.* **1.** a statement making a condition: *The rules of our library include a provision that hands must be clean before books are taken out. A provision of the lease is that the rent must be paid promptly.* **2.** a taking care for the future. **3.** care taken for the future; arrangement made beforehand: *There is a provision for making the building larger if necessary.* **4.** that which is made ready; supply; stock, especially of food; food: *Even the provision shops are closed, which seems to me the only reason why French housewives have refrigerators* (Punch). **5.** appointment to an ecclesiastical office, especially by the Pope to an office not yet vacant.

make provision, to take care for the future; make arrangements beforehand: *Mr. Arch made provision for his children's education.*

provisions, supply of food and drinks: *The English for want of provisions were forced to break up siege* (Philemon Holland).

—*v.t.* to supply with provisions: *The cave was well provisioned; they had bread, oil, figs, dried grapes, and wine* (Cardinal Newman).

[< Latin *prōvīsiō, -ōnis* < *prōvidēre;* see PROVIDE]

—**Syn.** *n.* See **food.**

pro·vi·sion·al (prə vizh′ə nəl), *adj.* for the time being; temporary: *a provisional agreement, a provisional governor.* —*n.* a postage stamp issued for use until the regular issue is available. —**Syn.** *adj.* provisory.

pro·vi·sion·al·ly (prə vizh′ə nə lē), *adv.* **1.** for the time being; temporarily. **2.** conditionally.

pro·vi·sion·ar·y (prə vizh′ə ner′ē), *adj.* **1.** provisional. **2.** of or having to do with a provision.

pro·vi·sion·er (prə vizh′ə nər), *n.* a person who furnishes, or deals in, provisions.

pro·vi·sions (prə vizh′ənz), *n.pl.* See under **provision,** *n.*

pro·vi·so (prə vī′zō), *n., pl.* **-sos** or **-soes.** a sentence or part of a sentence in a contract, or other agreement, that states a condition; condition: *Tom was admitted to the eighth grade with the proviso that he was to be put back if he failed any subject. They would accept a six-day conference, with the proviso . . . that its duration be fixed in advance* (New York Times). [< Medieval Latin *proviso quod* it being provided that < Latin *prōvīsō,* ablative < *prōvidēre* provide] —**Syn.** stipulation, provision.

pro·vi·sor (prə vī′zər), *n.* **1.** *Ecclesiastical.* the holder of a papal provision. **2.** *Obsolete.* **a.** a purveyor. **b.** a supervisor. [< Anglo-French *provisour,* Old French *proviseur* < Latin *prōvīsor* < *prōvidēre* provide]

pro·vi·so·ri·ly (prə vī′zər ə lē), *adv.* in a provisory way; provisionally; conditionally.

pro·vi·so·ry (prə vī′zər ē), *adj.* **1.** containing a proviso; conditional. **2.** provisional.

pro·vi·ta·min (prō vī′tə min), *n.* a compound, such as carotene, that can be converted into a vitamin by chemical change within the body: *The one important qualification is that the animals get enough protein, minerals and carotene (provitamin A) to keep them healthy* (Science News Letter). [< *pro-*[2] before + *vitamin*]

pro·vo·ca·teur (prô vô kȧ tœr′), *n. French.* a person who provokes trouble or incites to violence, riot, etc.: *We shall combat ruthlessly provocateurs . . . and all those who disturb public order, threaten, or commit lynching* (Time).

prov·o·ca·tion (prov′ə kā′shən), *n.* **1.** the act of provoking: *Ankara radio said yesterday that the Turkish authorities had arrested 2,124 persons "suspected of acts of provocation" in connexion with Tuesday's anti-Greek riots* (London Times). **2.** something that stirs one up; cause of anger: *Though the other boys' remarks were a provocation, John kept his temper.* **3.** *Obsolete.* a challenge. [< Latin *prōvocātiō, -ōnis* < *prōvocāre;* see PROVOKE] —**Syn. 1.** incitement. **2.** affront.

pro·voc·a·tive (prə vok′ə tiv), *adj.* **1.** irritating; vexing: *Do not think I want to be provocative if I say it is inconceivable to establish normal relations between our States as long as this question is unsolved* (London Times). **2.** tending or serving to call forth action, thought, laughter, etc.: *a remark provocative of mirth. A Falstaff, almost as provocative of laughter as his prototype* (Hawthorne). —*n.* something that rouses or irritates. —**pro·voc′a·tive·ly,** *adv.* —**pro·voc′a·tive·ness,** *n.*

pro·voc·a·to·ry (prə vok′ə tôr′ē, -tōr′-), *adj.* provocative.

pro·voke (prə vōk′), *v.t.,* **-voked, -vok·ing.** **1.** to make angry; vex: *She provoked him by her teasing.* **2.** to stir up; excite: *An insult provokes a person to anger.* **3.** to bring about; start into action; cause: *The President's speech provoked much discussion.* **4.** to induce (a physical condition, etc.): *a drug which provokes a rise in temperature.* **5.** *Obsolete.* to call forth; summon. [< Old French *provoker,* and *provoquer,* learned borrowings from Latin *prōvocāre* to appeal, challenge < *prō-* forth + *vocāre* to call]

—**Syn. 1.** exasperate, nettle. See **irritate. 2.** rouse, kindle.

pro·vok·er (prə vō′kər), *n.* **1.** a person or thing that provokes, excites, promotes, or stirs up. **2.** a person or thing that stirs up anger or other passion.

pro·vok·ing (prə vō′king), *adj.* that provokes; irritating: *"It's very provoking," Humpty Dumpty said, "to be called an egg—very!"* (Lewis Carroll). —**pro·vok′ing·ly,** *adv.*

pro·vo·lo·ne (prô′vō lō′nā), *n.* a hard Italian cheese with a sharp, smoky flavor. [< Italian *provolone*]

prov·ost (prov′əst; *especially Military* prō′vō), *n.* **1.** a person appointed to superintend or preside, such as the head of certain colleges or churches: *The title of the head of a college at Oxford depends on which college he is head of; at some colleges he is known as the Master, and at others as the Warden, the Provost . . .* (New Yorker). **2.** the chief magistrate of a Scottish town. **3.** *Obsolete.* a sheriff.

[partly Old English *profost;* partly < Old French *provost,* both < Medieval Latin *propositus,* alteration of Latin *praepositus* a chief, prefect; (literally) placed in charge of; (originally) past participle of *praepōnere* < *prae-* at the head of, before + *pōnere* to place]

provost court, a military court set up within occupied enemy territory to try minor offenses committed by soldiers or civilians.

provost guard, a detail of soldiers under the provost marshal, especially a detail assigned for some special occasion, emergency, etc.

provost marshal, 1. (in the army) an officer acting as head of police in a camp or district, and charged with the maintenance of order, etc. **2.** (in the navy) an officer charged with the safekeeping of prisoners until their trial by court-martial.

prov·ost·ship (prov′əst ship), *n.* the position or authority of a provost.

prow[1] (prou), *n.* **1.** the pointed front part of a ship or boat; bow. **2.** something like it: *the prow of an airship.* **3.** *Poetic.* a ship. [< Old French *proue* < dialectal Italian *prua* < Latin *prōra* < Greek *prôira*]

POOP

PROW

Prow[1] (def. 1) and poop of the Mayflower

prow[2] (prou), *adj. Archaic.* valiant; brave; gallant. [< Old French *pru,* and *prou,* earlier *prud,* and *prod* valiant. Related to PROUD.]

prow·ess (prou′is), *n.* **1.** bravery; daring. **2.** brave or daring acts. **3.** unusual skill or ability: *The knights of old were famous for their prowess with the spear.* [< Old French *proece* < *prod* valiant, proud] —**Syn. 1.** courage, valor. —**Ant. 1.** cowardice, timidity.

prow·ess·ful (prou′is fəl), *adj.* full of prowess; valorous; valiant.

pro-West·ern (prō wes′tərn), *adj.* on the side of the West; favoring the anti-Communist countries or their policies: *Most papers, basing their foreign coverage on dispatches from the West, have a pro-Western coloring* (Atlantic).

prowl (proul), *v.i.* **1.** to go about slowly and secretly, hunting for something to eat or steal: *Many wild animals prowl at night.* **2.** to wander: *He got up and prowled about his room, blundering against chairs and tables in the darkness* (H. G. Wells). —*v.t.* to go across (a place or region) by prowling: *Lunt prowls the aisles in white tie and tails, picking up objects* (Newsweek).

—*n.* the act of prowling: *Some wild animal in its nightly prowl* (Jane Porter). *An evocative, semi-autobiographical prowl among the littered streets and crumbling tenements* (Time).

on the prowl, prowling about: *The patronage seekers are still on the prowl* (Harry S. Truman).

[Middle English *prollen;* origin uncertain] —**prowl′er,** *n.* —**prowl′ing·ly,** *adv.*

—**Syn.** *v.i.* **1.** slink.

prowl car, a police car connected with headquarters by radio telephone; squad car.

prox., proximo.

Prox·i·ma Centauri (prok′sə mə), one of the three stars that constitute Alpha Centauri. It is closer to the earth than any other star except the sun, being 4.3 light years away. *In the heavens, it was discovered that Proxima Centauri, star nearest the solar system, shoots out terrific geysers of flaming gases to double its brightness in a few minutes* (Science News Letter). [< New Latin *Proxima Centauri* (literally) nearest of *Centauri,* the star group *Alpha Centauri*]

prox·i·mad (prok′sə mad), *adv. Anatomy.* toward the point of origin, or proximal part. [< *proxim*(al) + Latin *ad* toward]

prox·i·mal (prok′sə məl), *adj.* **1.** nearest. **2.** situated toward the point of origin or attachment, especially of a limb, bone, or other structure. [< Latin *proximus* nearest + English *-al*[1]] —**prox′i·mal·ly,** *adv.*

prox·i·mate (prok′sə mit), *adj.* **1.** next; nearest: *The proximate cause offers the greater promise of rewarding investigation* (Observer). **2.** near the exact amount; approximate. [< Latin *proximātus,* past participle of *proximāre* come near < *proximus* nearest] —**Syn. 1.** immediate, contiguous.

proximate analysis, *Chemistry.* a form of analysis in which the constituent compounds of a complex mixture are determined.

prox·i·mate·ly (prok′sə mit lē), *adv.* next; very nearly; approximately.

prox·im·i·ty (prok sim′ə tē), *n.* nearness; closeness: *Marriages in proximity of blood are amongst us forbidden* (John Florio). [< Latin *proximitās* < *proximus* nearest] —**Syn.** propinquity, vicinity.

proximity fuse, a tiny radio device set in the nose of a projectile that makes the shell explode when it comes within a certain distance of the target: *The proximity fuse played a major part . . . in halting the German breakthrough in the Ardennes* (New Scientist).

prox·i·mo (prok′sə mō), *adv.* in or of the coming month: *on the 1st proximo.* [short for Latin *proximō mēnse* during next month; ablative singular of *proximus* near, *mēnsis* month]

prox·y (prok′sē), *n., pl.* **prox·ies.** **1.** the action of a deputy or substitute: *In marriage by proxy, someone is substituted for the absent bridegroom at the marriage service.* **2.** an agent; deputy; substitute, as one appointed to vote for others at a stockholders' meeting: *A month long proxy fight between management of the . . . corporation and a group of dissident stockholders moved to the annual meeting . . . yesterday* (Wall Street Journal). **3.** a writing authorizing a proxy to act or vote for a person: *A proxy is a sort of power of attorney.* **4.** a vote so given: *The proxy with the most recent date is the one that's counted.* [Middle English *prockesye* < *procracie,* alteration of *procuracy* procuracy, the office of proctor] —**Syn. 2.** delegate, representative.

prs., pairs.

prude (prüd), *n.* a person who is too proper or too modest about sex; a person who puts on extremely proper or modest airs. [< French *prude* < *prudefemme* excellent woman < Old French *preudefemme,* and *prodfemme* < feminine of *prou* excellent, brave, earlier *prod* + *femme* woman. Compare PROUD.]

pru·dence (prü′dəns), *n.* **1.** wise thought before acting; good judgment: *All the virtues* *range themselves on the side of prudence, on the art of securing a present well-being* (Emerson). **2.** good management; economy. —**Syn. 1. Prudence, foresight** mean thought in acting and planning. **Prudence** emphasizes common sense in directing oneself and one's affairs, giving thought to one's actions and their consequences, and usually suggests caution, watchfulness, and saving: *Prudence is wisdom in everyday life.* **Foresight** emphasizes ability to see what is likely to happen, and giving thought to being prepared: *He had the foresight to carry fire insurance.*

pru·dent (prü′dənt), *adj.* planning carefully ahead of time; sensible; discreet: *A prudent man saves part of his wages. I thought it prudent not to exacerbate the growing moodiness of his temper by any comment* (Edgar Allan Poe). [< Latin *prūdēns, -entis,* short for *prōvidēns* provident] —**pru′dent·ly,** *adv.* —**Syn.** judicious, wise, cautious. —**Ant.** foolish, rash, thoughtless, indiscreet.

pru·den·tial (prü den′shəl), *adj.* **1.** of, marked by, or showing prudence. **2.** that may make decisions or give advice: *a prudential committee.* —**pru·den′tial·ly,** *adv.*

prud·er·y (prü′dər ē), *n., pl.* **-er·ies. 1.** extreme modesty or regard for the proprieties of speech and behavior, especially when not genuine. **2.** a prudish act or remark.

prud'·homme (prʏ dôm′), *n.* a member of a French tribunal appointed to arbitrate labor disputes. [< French *prud'homme* < Old French *prodhome* < *prod* brave, excellent + *ome, home* man]

prud·ish (prü′dish), *adj.* like a prude; excessively proper or modest; too modest about sex. —**prud′ish·ly,** *adv.* —**prud′ish·ness,** *n.* —**Syn.** priggish, prim.

pru·i·nose (prü′ə nōs), *adj. Biology.* covered with a frostlike bloom or powdery secretion. [< Latin *pruīnōsus* frosty < *pruīna* hoarfrost]

prune[1] (prün), *n.* **1.** a kind of dried sweet plum: *We had stewed prunes for breakfast.* **2.** a plum suitable for drying. **3.** *Slang.* a person thought to be unattractive, stupid, or unpleasant.

prunes and prism or **prisms,** a mincing or affectedly nice manner of speaking or behaving: *Papa, potatoes, poultry, prunes, and prism, are all very good words for the lips: especially prunes and prism* (Dickens).

[Middle English *prunne* < Old French *prune* a plum < Vulgar Latin *prūna.* Doublet of PLUM[1].]

prune[2] (prün), *v.,* **pruned, prun·ing.** —*v.t.* **1.** to cut out useless or undesirable parts from. **2.** to cut superfluous or undesirable branches or twigs from (a bush, tree, etc.): *to prune fruit trees or grape vines.* **3.** to cut off or out: *The editor pruned the needless words from the writer's manuscript. Undoubtedly, these will be pruned out in the next edition* (Bulletin of Atomic Scientists). —*v.i.* to cut off superfluous twigs or branches: *Very often pruning brings about the introduction of fungus spores to the freshly cut or broken tissues* (Fred W. Emerson). [Middle English *prouynen* < Old French *proignier,* and *proöignier* < Latin *pro-* for + *roöignier* clip, (originally) round off, ultimately < Latin *rotundus* round] —**Syn.** *v.t.* **1.** trim.

prune[3] (prün), *v.t., v.i.,* **pruned, prun·ing.** to dress carefully; preen. [Middle English *proynen,* and *pruynen;* origin uncertain. Apparently related to PREEN[1].]

pru·nel·la (prü nel′ə), *n.* **1.** a strong, smooth fabric formerly used for the uppers of shoes. **2.** a similar fabric, used for women's dresses. [probably < French, Old French *prunelle* sloe, wild plum (perhaps because of its color)]

pru·nelle (prü nel′), *n.* a small, yellow plum dried for the market, both skin and stone being removed. [earlier *prunella* < obsolete Italian, a small kind of plum, (diminutive) < *pruna* plum < Vulgar Latin *prūna;* spelling influenced by French *prunelle.* Compare PLUM.]

prun·er (prü′nər), *n.* a person or thing that prunes, or removes what is superfluous.

prun·ing hook (prü′ning), a long-handled tool with a hooked blade, used for pruning fruit trees, brambles, etc. [*pruning* < *prune*[2] + *-ing*[2]]

pruning knife, a knife, often with a curved blade, used for pruning.

pruning shears, strong, heavy shears used to prune vines, shrubs, etc.

prunt (prunt), *n.* **1.** an ornamental stud or shaped piece of glass fixed on a glass vessel. **2.** a tool with which such pieces are formed. [origin uncertain; perhaps dialectal variant of *print*]

prunt·ed (prun′tid), *adj.* ornamented with prunts.

pru·ri·ence (průr′ē əns), *n.* a being prurient.

pru·ri·en·cy (průr′ē ən sē), *n., pl.* **-cies.** prurience.

pru·ri·ent (průr′ē ənt), *adj.* **1.** having lustful thoughts or wishes: *Parkhurst's motives were prurient rather than public-spirited* (New Yorker). *King discoursed acridly . . . of boys with prurient minds who perverted their few and baleful talents to sap discipline . . . and destroy reverence* (Rudyard Kipling). **2.** being uneasy, as with desire, longing, curiosity, etc.: *Prurient curiosity is presumably as old as the race and has a very rich American history* (Newsweek). **3.** itching: *In filthy sloughs they roll a prurient skin* (Tennyson).

—*n.* a prurient person.

[< Latin *prūriēns, -entis,* present participle of *prūrīre* to itch; be wanton] —**pru′ri·ent·ly,** *adv.*

—**Syn.** *adj.* **1.** lewd, lascivious.

pru·rig·i·nous (prů rij′ə nəs), *adj.* **1.** of, like, causing, or caused by prurigo. **2.** uneasy. [< Latin *prūrīginōsus* < Latin *prūrīgō* prurigo]

pru·ri·go (prů rī′gō), *n.* a skin disease with violent itching and an eruption. [< Latin *prūrīgō* itching, lasciviousness < *prūrīre* to itch; perhaps influenced by *porrīgō* dandruff, scurvy]

pru·rit·ic (prů rit′ik), *adj.* of, having to do with, or like pruritus.

pru·ri·tus (prů rī′təs), *n.* itching, especially without visible eruption. [< Latin *prūrītus, -ūs* an itching < *prūrīre* to itch (for), be wanton]

Prus. or **Pruss., 1.** Prussia. **2.** Prussian.

Prus·sian (prush′ən), *adj.* of or having to do with Prussia, its people, or their language: *He leaned out of the window with a Prussian thrust, waving a bill and bellowing* (Atlantic).

—*n.* **1.** a native or inhabitant of Prussia. **2.** the dialect of German spoken in modern Prussia. **3.** Old Prussian.

Prussian blue, a deep-blue pigment, a ferrocyanide of iron: *Prussian blue, another common pigment, can be identified by its stainlike character and tendency to bleach in the presence of alkalis* (Scientific American). *Formula:* $C_{18}Fe_7N_{18}$ [< *Prussia* (because it was discovered in 1704 in Berlin, the capital) + *-an*]

Prus·sian·ism (prush′ə niz əm), *n.* the spirit, system, policy, or methods of the Prussians, especially authoritarian methods associated with Bismarck (used in an unfriendly way): *Von Salomon's unreconstructed Prussianism and his violent hatred for the United States* (Harper's).

Prus·sian·ize (prush′ə nīz), *v.t.,* **-ized, -iz·ing.** to make Prussian or like Prussia in organization or character.

prus·si·ate (prush′ē it, prus′-), *n.* **1.** a salt of prussic acid; cyanide. **2.** ferricyanide: *treated with a solution of red prussiate of potash, a beautiful red picture will be obtained* (Scientific American). **3.** ferrocyanide. [< French *prussiate* < (*acide*) *prussique* prussic (acid) + *-ate* -ate[2]]

prus·sic (prus′ik), *adj.* hydrocyanic.

prussic acid, a deadly poison that smells like bitter almonds; hydrocyanic acid. [< French *acide prussique* < *bleu de Prusse* Prussian blue]

pru·ta (prü′tä), *n., pl.* **pru·toth** (prü tōt′, -tōs′), **pru·ta** or **pru·tas.** a coin of Israel worth one-thousandth of an Israeli pound: *The 50th anniversary stamp will have a face value of 120 pruta . . . and the design shows a number of Tel Aviv public buildings* (Sunday Times). [< Hebrew *pərūṭāh*]

pry[1] (prī), *v.,* **pried, pry·ing,** *n., pl.* **pries.** —*v.i.* to look with curiosity; peep: *She likes to pry into the private affairs of others. They ask questions, dig and pry and dig again to find out what and why and where and who and how* (New Yorker). —*n.* **1.** an inquisitive person. **2.** an inquisitive and rudely personal glance, question, etc. [Middle English *prien;* origin uncertain] —**Syn.** *n.* **1.** busybody.

pry[2] (prī), *v.,* **pried, pry·ing,** *n., pl.* **pries.** —*v.t.* **1.** to raise or move by force: *to pry the top off a bottle. Run . . . and fetch something to pry open the door* (Herman Melville). **2.** to get with much effort: *We finally pried the secret out of him.* [< noun]

—*n.* **1.** a lever for prying. **2.** the act of prying. [< dialectal *prize* a lever, taken as a plural. See PRIZE[4].]

pry·er (prī′ər), *n.* prier.

pry·ing (prī′ing), *adj.* looking or searching curiously; inquisitive. [< *pry*[1] + *-ing*[2]] —**pry′ing·ly,** *adv.* —**Syn.** See **curious.**

pryt·a·ne·um (prit′ə nē′əm), *n., pl.* **-ne·a** (-nē′ə). a public hall in ancient Greek states or cities housing the official hearth of the community, especially that of Athens, in which the hospitality of the city was extended to honored citizens, ambassadors, etc. [< Latin *prytanēum* < Greek *prytaneîon* < *prýtanis;* see PRYTANIS]

pryt·a·nis (prit′ə nis), *n., pl.* **-nes** (-nēz). **1.** a chief magistrate in certain ancient Greek states. **2.** a member in ancient Athens of any of the ten sections of the council or senate during the presidency of that section, each section presiding for a period of five weeks. [< Latin *prytanis* < Greek *prýtanis,* probably ultimately < *pró* before]

pryt·a·ny (prit′ə nē), *n., pl.* **-nies. 1.** the office or dignity of a prytanis. **2.** each of the ten sections of the ancient Athenian council or senate during the presidency of that section. **3.** the period of five weeks during which each section presided. [< Greek *prytaneíā* < *prýtanis* prytanis]

pryth·ee (priᴛʜ′ i), *interj.* prithee.

Prze·wal·ski's horse (pər zhe väl′skiz), a wild pony native to the Mongolian Plains. It is about four feet high and has a brushlike mane. [< *Przewalski,* a Russian explorer of the 1800's]

ps., pieces.

p.s., postscript (Latin, *post scriptum*).

Ps., 1. Psalm. **2.** Psalms (a book of the Bible).

P.S., an abbreviation for the following:
1. passenger steamer.
2. permanent secretary.
3. postscript (Latin, *post scriptum*).
4. private secretary.
5. Privy Seal.
6. *Theater.* prompt side.
7. Public School.

Psa., 1. Psalm. **2.** Psalms (a book of the Bible).

P.S.A., Photographic Society of America.

psalm (säm, sälm), *n.* a sacred song or poem: *Hymns devout and holy psalms, Singing everlastingly* (Milton). —*v.t.* to sing or celebrate in psalms: *The word is psalmed like a litany around the long table* (Manchester Guardian). [Old English *sealm,* also *psealm* < Latin *psalmus* < Greek *psalmós* (originally) performance on a stringed instrument < *psállein* to pluck]

Psalm (säm, sälm), *n.* any of the 150 sacred songs or hymns that together form a book of the Old Testament. [< *psalm*]

psalm·book (säm′bůk′, sälm′-), *n.* a collection of metrical translations of the Psalms prepared for public worship. —**Syn.** Psalter.

psalm·ist (sä′mist, säl′-), *n.* the author of a psalm or psalms.

Psalm·ist (sä′mist, säl′-), *n.* **the,** King David, to whom many of the Psalms are ascribed.

psal·mod·ic (sal mod′ik), *adj.* **1.** of or having to do with psalmody. **2.** having the style or character of psalmody.

psal·mo·dist (sä′mə dist, säl′-, sal′-), *n.* a person who composes or sings psalms or hymns.

psal·mo·dy (sä′mə dē, säl′-, sal′-), *n., pl.* **-dies. 1.** the act, practice, or art of singing psalms or hymns, especially in public worship: *All of them joined in the psalmody with strong marks of devotion* (Tobias Smollett). **2.** psalms or hymns. **3.** the arrangement of psalms for singing: *No wonder the Church of Scotland resisted the introduction of an adequate psalmody for centuries if this emasculated kind of singing was what they foresaw and feared* (London Times). [< Late Latin *psalmōdia* < Greek *psalmōidiā* < *psalmós* psalm + *ōidē* song, ode]

Psalms (sämz, sälmz), *n.* a book of the Old Testament consisting of 150 psalms; Psalter. Psalms is a part of the Hagiographa. *Abbr.:* Ps.

Psal·ter (sôl′tər), *n.* **1.** the Book of Psalms. **2.** a version of the Psalms for liturgical or devotional use. **3.** a prayer book containing such a version: *Each pew contained several hymn books and psalters.* [Old English *saltere* < Late Latin *psaltērium* (in Latin, certain liturgical songs); (originally) a psaltery < Greek *psaltḗrion.* Doublet of PSALTERY.]

psal·te·ri·an (sôl tir′ē ən), *adj.* **1.** having to do with the Psalter. **2.** having the style of the Psalter.

psal·te·ri·on (sôl tir′ē on, sal-), *n.* psaltery.

psal·te·ri·um (sôl tir′ē əm, sal-), *n., pl.* **-te·ri·a** (-tir′ē ə). the third stomach of a cow, deer, or other ruminant; omasum: *On the second swallowing it passes into the psalterium and on to the abomasum* (A.M. Winchester). [< Late Latin *psaltērium* a psalter book (because its folds are like leaves of a book)]

psal·ter·y (sôl′tər ē, -trē), *n., pl.* **-ter·ies.** an ancient musical instrument, played by plucking the strings: *Reciting poems to the psaltery or a bamboo flute, and verse playlets for dancers, are madly unchic* (New Yorker). [Middle English *sautree* < Latin *psaltērium* < Greek *psaltḗrion* stringed instrument < *psállein* to pluck. Compare Old English *saltere* and Anglo-French *saltere, sautere.* Doublet of PSALTER.]

Psaltery

Psal·ter·y (sôl′tər ē, -trē), *n.* the Book of Psalms. [< *psaltery*]

psal·tress (sôl′tris), *n. Rare.* a woman who plays on the psaltery.

psam·mite (sam′īt), *n.* sandstone. [< French *psammite* < Greek *psámmos* sand + French *-ite* -ite[1]]

psam·mit·ic (sa mit′ik), *adj.* of, having to do with, or resembling psammite.

PSC (no periods) or **P.S.C.,** Public Service Commission.

pschent (psʜent), *n.* the sovereign crown of all ancient Egypt, composed of the white crown or tall, pointed miter of southern Egypt combined with the red crown, square in front and rising to a point behind, of northern Egypt. [< Greek *pschént* < Egyptian *p-skhent* the double crown]

pse·phite (sē′fīt), *n.* any coarse fragmental rock. [< German *Psephit,* or French *pséphite* < Greek *psêphos* pebble + French *-ite* -ite[1]]

pse·pho·log·i·cal (sē′fə loj′ə kəl), *adj.* of or having to do with psephology: *As the first results of the Truman-Dewey contest for the Presidency were coming in, a UNIVAC computer in Washington was processing the data . . . in strict accordance with the psephological rules prepared for it* (New Scientist).

pse·phol·o·gist (sē fol′ə jist), *n.* an expert in psephology.

pse·phol·o·gy (sē fol′ə jē), *n.* the study of electoral systems and trends and of patterns of behavior in voting: *Kendall will also be able, incidentally, to test the cube law of psephology, which says that if the ratio of the votes cast for two parties is A/B the ratio of parliamentary seats will be A^3/B^3* (New Scientist). [< Greek *psêphos* pebble used in voting + English *-logy*]

pseud-, *combining form.* a form of **pseudo-** sometimes used before vowels, as in *pseudaxis.*

pseud., pseudonym.

pseu·dax·is (sü dak′sis), *n. Botany.* a sympodium. [< *pseud-* + *axis*[1]]

pseu·de·pig·ra·pha (sü′də pig′rə fə), *n.pl.* spurious writings, especially certain writings professing to be Biblical in character, but not considered canonical, inspired, or worthy of a place in religious use. [< New Latin *pseudepigrapha,* ultimately < Greek *pseudepígraphos* falsely ascribed < *pseudḗs* false + *epigraphḗ* ascription; (originally) inscription. Compare EPIGRAPH.]

pseu·de·pig·ra·phal (sü′də pig′rə fəl), *adj.* pseudepigraphic.

pseu·dep·i·graph·ic (sü′dep ə graf′ik), *adj.* of or having to do with pseudepigrapha; spurious.

pseu·dep·i·graph·i·cal (sü′dep ə graf′ə kəl), *adj.* pseudepigraphic.

pseu·de·pig·ra·phous (sü′də pig′rə fəs), *adj.* pseudepigraphic.

pseu·do (sü′dō), *adj.* **1.** false; sham; pretended: *pseudo religion, pseudo anger.* **2.** having only the appearance of: *Luxuries . . . when long gratified, become a sort of pseudo necessaries* (Scott). [< Greek *pseudḗs* false; see PSEUDO-] —**Syn. 1.** spurious, counterfeit.

pseudo-, *combining form.* **1.** pseudo: *Pseudomorph = a false form. Pseudonym = a name used by an author. Pseudoscience = pretended science.*
2. (in chemical terms) resembling; related to; isomeric with, as in *pseudonuclein.* Also, **pseud-** before vowels.
[< Greek *pseudo-* < *pseûdos* falsehood, fallacy, or < *pseudḗs* false < *pseúdein* deceive]

pseu·do·a·quat·ic (sü′dō ə kwat′ik, -kwot′-), *adj.* not really aquatic, but growing in wet places.

pseu·do·ar·cha·ic (sü′dō är kā′ik), *adj.* not genuinely archaic.

pseu·do·carp (sü′də kärp), *n.* a fruit that includes other parts in addition to the mature ovary and its contents, as the apple, pineapple, or pear. [< *pseudo-* + Greek *karpós* fruit]

pseu·do·car·pous (sü′də kär′pəs), *adj.* of or having to do with a pseudocarp.

pseu·do·clas·sic (sü′də klas′ik), *adj.* pretending to be classic; falsely supposed to be classic. —*n.* a pseudoclassic work of art or literature.

pseu·do·clas·si·cal (sü′dō klas′ə kəl), *adj.* pseudoclassic.

pseu·do·clas·si·cism (sü′dō klas′ə siz əm) *n.* a false, spurious, or sham classicism.

pseu·do·coel (sü′də sēl), *n.* a body cavity in some primitive animals, similar to the coelom except that it is unlined: *In roundworms . . . a cavity termed the pseudocoel, existing between the digestive tract and muscles, contains a body fluid which is set in circulation by the wriggling movements characteristic of such animals* (Harbaugh and Goodrich). [< *pseudo-* + Greek *koîlos* hollow]

pseu·do·coe·lom (sü′dō sē′ləm), *n.* pseudocoel.

pseu·do·cy·e·sis (sü′dō sī ē′sis), *n.* illness in which the patient thinks herself pregnant and displays some of the appropriate symptoms: *Rarely in medical annals has the poignant phenomenon of false pregnancy—pseudocyesis—survived such odds of matter over mind* (Time). [< *pseudo-* + Greek *kýēsis* conception]

pseu·do·dox (sü′də doks), *n.* an erroneous or false opinion. [< *pseudo-* + Greek *dóxa* opinion]

pseu·do·glob·u·lin (sü′dō glob′yə lin), *n.* any globulin that is soluble in pure water.

pseu·do·he·mo·phil·i·a (sü′dō hē′mə fil′ē ə, -hem′ə-), *n.* an abnormal condition of the blood platelets in which there is extensive bleeding from a cut or wound but faster clotting of the blood than in hemophilia.

pseu·do·her·maph·ro·dite (sü′dō hėr maf′rə dīt), *n.* a person affected by pseudohermaphroditism: *Pseudohermaphrodites . . . can be helped by surgery to become normal men and women* (Time). —*adj.* pseudohermaphroditic.

pseu·do·her·maph·ro·dit·ic (sü′dō hėr maf′rə dit′ik), *adj.* affected by pseudohermaphroditism.

pseu·do·her·maph·ro·dit·ism (sü′dō hėr maf′rə dī tiz′əm), *n.* an appearance of hermaphroditism, as that due to a malformation of the external genitals: *When the glandular upset takes place after birth, progressive changes are noted . . . and before long, the child presents the picture of pseudohermaphroditism, in which a boy or girl has the external sex characteristics of the opposite sex* (Newsweek).

pseu·do·hex·ag·o·nal (sü′dō hek sag′ə nəl), *adj.* falsely hexagonal; appearing to be hexagonal, though not really so: *The chromic acid in the . . . stain distorts the spheroidal pollen grains to a pseudohexagonal shape* (Scientific American).

pseu·do·hy·per·troph·ic (sü′dō hī′pər trof′ik), *adj.* **1.** producing or affected with pseudohypertrophy. **2.** characterized by pseudohypertrophy: *Surgical sterilization . . . should certainly be considered in the case of persons with a history of such hereditary afflictions as pseudohypertrophic muscular dystrophy* (Harper's).

pseu·do·hy·per·tro·phy (sü′dō hī pėr′trə fē), *n., pl.* **-phies.** an enlargement of an organ by growth of fat or connective tissue as in hypertrophy, but with atrophy of the organ itself.

pseu·do·log·i·cal (sü′də loj′ə kəl), *adj.* having to do with or relating to pseudology. —**pseu′do·log′i·cal·ly,** *adv.*

pseu·dol·o·gist (sü dol′ə jist), *n.* a creator of falsehoods; systematic liar.

pseu·dol·o·gy (sü dol′ə jē), *n.* lying, especially as an art or a subject of study. [< Greek *pseudologíā* < *pseudológos* speaking falsely < *pseudḗs* false + *lógos* speech]

pseu·do·mon·as (sü′də mon′as, -mō′nas), *n., pl.* **-mon·a·des** (-mon′ə dēz). any of a group of motile microorganisms or bacteria, some of which are pathogenic: *Urinary tract infections caused by pseudomonas include everything from the serious kidney disease to cystitis* (Science News Letter). [< New Latin *Pseudomonas* the genus name < *pseudo-* + *monas*]

pseu·do·morph (sü′də môrf), *n.* **1.** a false or deceptive form. **2.** a mineral which has the form of another mineral. [< Medieval Greek *pseudómorphos* < Greek *pseudḗs* false + *morphḗ* form]

pseu·do·mor·phic (sü′də môr′fik), *adj.* **1.** of or having to do with a pseudomorph. **2.** like a pseudomorph.

pseu·do·mor·phism (sü′də môr′fiz əm), *n.* **1.** the state of being a pseudomorph. **2.** the process by which this is brought about.

pseu·do·mor·phous (sü′də môr′fəs), *adj.* having a false form, or a form proper to something else; characterized by pseudomorphism.

pseu·do·nu·cle·in (sü′də nü′klē in), *n.* paranuclein.

pseu·do·nym (sü′də nim), *n.* a name used by an author instead of his real name: *Mark Twain is a pseudonym for Samuel Langhorne Clemens. Moravia was then forbidden to write under his own name, and he adopted the pseudonym of Pseudo* (Atlantic). [< Greek *pseudṓnymon,* neuter of *pseudṓnymos* falsely named < *pseudḗs* false + dialectal *ónyma* name] —**Syn.** pen name, nom de plume.

pseu·do·nym·i·ty (sü′də nim′ə tē), *n., pl.* **-ties.** the use of a pseudonym or false name; pseudonymous character.

pseu·don·y·mous (sü don′ə məs), *adj.* **1.** bearing a false name: *The pseudonymous author (the name means "jailbird") was in a Nazi concentration camp* (New York Times). **2.** writing or written under an assumed or fictitious name. —**pseu·don′y·mous·ly,** *adv.*

pseu·do·pod (sü′də pod), *n.* pseudopodium.

pseu·dop·o·dal (sü dop′ə dəl), *adj.* pseudopodial.

pseu·do·po·di·al (sü′də pō′dē əl), *adj.* **1.** having to do with pseudopodia. **2.** forming or formed by pseudopodia: *a pseudopodial process, pseudopodial movement.*

pseu·do·po·di·um (sü′də pō′dē əm), *n., pl.* **-di·a** (-dē ə). **1.** a temporary protrusion of the protoplasm of a protozoan, serving as a means of locomotion, and a way of surrounding and thereby absorbing food: *As the finger-like pseudopodium (the "false foot") of the amoeba advances, one sees the cytoplasm* (Scientific American). See picture under **amoeba. 2.** the posterior extremity of a rotifer, serving as a swimming organ, etc. [< New Latin *pseudopodium* < Greek *pseudḗs* false + *pódion* (diminutive) < *poús, podós* foot]

pseu·do·preg·nan·cy (sü′dō preg′nən sē), *n., pl.* **-cies. 1.** a condition similar to pregnancy, found among dogs, rabbits, etc., after a sterile mating. **2.** pseudocyesis.

pseu·do·ra·bies (sü′dō rā′bēz), *n.* an abnormal dread of rabies, sometimes causing symptoms much like those of actual rabies; lyssophobia.

pseu·do·sci·ence (sü′dō sī′əns), *n.* false or pretended science: *The experience of other countries shows that secrecy in science and the domination of ideological motives very often bring, among other negative consequences . . . a flowering of pseudoscience and very costly research and construction projects* (Bulletin of Atomic Scientists).

pseu·do·sci·en·tif·ic (sü′dō sī′ən tif′ik), *adj.* of or having to do with pseudoscience; falsely scientific: *. . . a classical case of a man of genius who ventures into a branch of science for which he is ill prepared and dissipates his great energies on pseudoscientific nonsense* (Scientific American).

pseu·do·sci·en·tist (sü′dō sī′ən tist), *n.* a person who is engaged in pseudoscience or pseudoscientific pursuits.

pseu·do·scope (sü′də skōp), *n.* an optical instrument that makes concave parts appear convex, and convex parts concave: *It is possible to investigate some of the limits within which the mind will accept misinformation from the eyes by means of an instrument called the pseudoscope, a binocular-like device* (Scientific American).

pseu·do·scop·ic (sü′də skop′ik), *adj.* of or having to do with the pseudoscope or with pseudoscopy. —**pseu′do·scop′i·cal·ly,** *adv.*

pseu·dos·co·py (sü dos′kə pē), *n.* **1.** the use of the pseudoscope. **2.** the production of optical illusions similar to those caused by the pseudoscope: *"Pseudoscopy"—that is to say, the effects of the left eye seeing what the right eye ought to have seen, and vice versa . . .* (New Scientist).

pseu·do·scor·pi·on (sü′dō skôr′pē ən), *n.* an arachnid resembling the true scorpion but without tail or poison glands; book scorpion.

p.s.f. or **psf** (no periods), pounds per square foot.

pshaw (shô), *interj., n.* an exclamation expressing contempt, impatience, etc.: *She writhed with impatience more than pain, and uttered "pshaws!" and "pishes!"* (Thomas Hood). —*v.t., v.i.* to say "pshaw": *He fretted, pished, and pshawed* (Charlotte Brontë). [< imitative]

psi[1] (sī, psē), *n.* the 23rd letter of the Greek alphabet (Ψ, ψ) corresponding to the sound *s* or sometimes *ps* in English. [< Greek *psî*]

psi[2] (sī, psē), *n.* the group of psychological or nonphysical phenomena, including extrasensory perception, telepathy, and clairvoyance, that forms the subject matter of parapsychology: *Nonphysical though psi appears to be as judged by the familiar criteria of space and time, it is, nonetheless, a natural function of the normal personality* (Science). [< Greek *psî,* first letter of *psȳchḗ* breath, life, soul]

p.s.i. or **psi** (no periods), pounds per square inch: *It takes quite a sophisticated shelter to withstand 100 psi overpressure* (Harper's).

p.s.i.a., pounds per square inch absolute.

p.s.i.g., pounds per square inch gauge.

psi·lan·thro·pism (sī lan′thrə piz əm), *n.* the doctrine or belief that Jesus was a mere man. [< Greek *psīlós* bare, mere + *ánthrōpos* a man + English *-ism*]

psi·lan·thro·pist (sī lan′thrə pist), *n.* a person who believes that Jesus was a mere man.

psi·lan·thro·py (sī lan′thrə pē), *n.* psilanthropism.

psi·lo·cy·bin or **psi·lo·cy·bine** (sī′lə sī′bin, -bēn), *n.* a hallucinogenic substance extracted from a Mexican mushroom and since synthesized, used experimentally to induce certain delusional and psychotic states. [< *Psilocybe* (*mexicana*) the mushroom + English *-in, -ine*[2]]

psi·lom·e·lane (sī lom′ə lān), *n.* a common ore of manganese, a hydrated oxide, occurring in smooth, black, amorphous masses, or in botryoidal or stalactitic shapes. [< Greek *psīlós* bare, mere + *mélās, -anos* black]

psi·lo·sis (sī lō′sis), *n.* **1.** the falling out of the hair. **2.** sprue, a chronic disease of tropical regions. [< New Latin *psilosis* < Late Latin *psīlōsis* stripping of flesh < Greek *psīlōsis* a stripping bare < *psīlós* bare]

psit·ta·cine (sit′ə sēn), *adj.* **1.** of or having to do with a parrot or parrots: *Parrots and birds of the psittacine family, such as parakeets, may give psittacosis to their owners* (Science News Letter). **2.** like a parrot. [< Greek *psittakós* parrot + English *-ine*[1]]

psit·ta·cism (sit′ə siz əm), *n.* a parrotlike use or repetition of words without awareness or understanding of their meaning: *A complicating factor in this whole business was an indiscriminate psittacism . . .* [*which*] *inevitably immobilizes and stultifies doctrinal dynamism* (New Yorker). [< Greek *psittakós* parrot + English *-ism*]

psit·ta·co·sis (sit′ə kō′sis), *n.* a contagious virus disease occurring especially in parrots and related birds, communicable to people; parrot fever. [< New Latin *psittacosis* < Greek *psittakós* parrot + New Latin *-osis* -osis]

pso·ad·ic (sō ad′ik), *adj.* of or having to do with the psoas muscles.

pso·as (sō′əs), *n.* either of two muscles of the loin. [< New Latin *psoas,* plural < Greek *psóa* loin muscle]

pso·ra (sôr′ə, sōr′-), *n.* **1.** scabies. **2.** psoriasis. [< Greek *psṓrā* itch, mange, scurvy < *psên* to rub]

pso·ra·le·a (sə rā′lē ə), *n.* any of a group of herbs of the pea family, usually covered with glandular dots, as the breadroot. [< New Latin *Psoralea* the genus name < Greek *psōraléos* scabby < *psṓrā;* see PSORA]

pso·ri·a·sis (sə rī′ə sis), *n.* a chronic inflammatory skin disease characterized by dry, scaling patches and a reddened skin. [< New Latin *psoriasis* < Late Latin *psōriāsis* mange, scurvy < Greek *psōríāsis* a being itchy < *psōriân* have the itch < *psṓrā;* see PSORA]

pso·ri·at·ic (sôr′ē at′ik, sōr′-), *adj.* **1.** of the nature of psoriasis. **2.** having psoriasis.

P.SS. or **p.ss.,** postscripts (Latin, *postscripta*).

P.S.T., P.s.t., or **PST** (no periods), Pacific Standard Time.

psych (sīk), *n. Informal.* psychology: *to major in psych, to take a psych course.* —*v.t. Slang.* **1.** to psychoanalyze. **2.** to use psychology on; psychologize: *Westrum . . . plans to "psych" the Mets with inspiration, optimism, and appeals to the spirit* (New York Times). **3.** to trick, defeat, etc., by the use of psychology: *It looked as if they had been "psyched" out of a vulnerable slam* (Scotsman).

psych-, *combining form.* a form of **psycho-** in some cases used before vowels, as in *psychics.*

psych., **1.** psychological. **2.** psychology.

psy·chal (sī′kəl), *adj.* of or having to do with the soul; spiritual; psychic.

psy·cha·nal·y·sis (sī′kə nal′ə sis), *n.* psychoanalysis.

psy·chas·the·ni·a (sī′kas thē′nē ə, -thənī′-), *n.* mental exhaustion; mental weakness shown by fears, unreasonable ideas, etc. [probably < French *psychasthénie* < *psych-* psych- + *asthénie* weakness, asthenia < Greek *asthéneia*]

psy·chas·then·ic (sī′kas then′ik), *adj.* **1.** of or having to do with psychasthenia. **2.** having psychasthenia.
—*n.* a person suffering from psychasthenia.

psy·che (sī′kē), *n.* **1.** the human soul or spirit. **2.** the mind: *We need to know more about the interrelationship of the psyche and the soma, the mind and the body* (William C. Menninger). [< Latin *psȳchē* < Greek *psȳchḗ* breath; life < *psýchein* breathe; blow]

Psy·che (sī′kē), *n. Greek and Roman Mythology.* the human soul or spirit pictured as a beautiful young girl, usually with butterfly wings. Psyche was loved by Cupid and was made immortal by Jupiter. [< Latin *Psȳchē* < Greek *Psȳchḗ* (literally) breath; life]

psy·che·del·i·a (sī′kə del′ē ə), *n.pl.* books, music, artifacts, etc., that emphasize psychedelic activities: *Shops that sell the lawful artifacts of psychedelia—skin jewels, bells, water pipes, glow-in-the-dark posters and body paint—are springing up faster than marijuana plants* (New York Times).

psy·che·del·ic (sī′kə del′ik), *adj.* revealing the mind or psyche; producing a mental state of extremely intensified perception; consciousness-expanding: *Even a single dose of such psychedelic drugs as LSD may result in . . . depression and suicidal or homicidal impulses* (New York Times).
—*n.* a psychedelic drug or substance: *LSD and the other psychedelics including marijuana, present a serious social problem* (Maclean's). Also, **psychodelic.** [< *psyche* + Greek *dêlos* visible + English *-ic*]

Psyche knot, an arrangement of hair in a twist which projects from the back of the head, such as classic Greek statues have.

psy·chi·a·ter (sī kī′ə tər, si-), *n. Obsolete.* a psychiatrist. [< Greek *psȳchḗ* soul, mind + *īātḗr,* variant of *īātrós* physician]

psy·chi·at·ric (sī′kē at′rik), *adj.* of or having to do with the treatment of mental disorders: *Psychiatric case work is helping other persons to make adjustments* (Emory S. Bogardus). —**psy′chi·at′ri·cal·ly,** *adv.*

psy·chi·at·ri·cal (sī′kē at′rə kəl), *adj.* psychiatric.

psy·chi·a·trist (sī kī′ə trist, si-), *n.* a doctor who treats mental disorders: *The psychiatrist is concerned with minds that stray from the normal* (Science News Letter).

psy·chi·a·try (sī kī′ə trē, si-), *n.* the study and treatment of mental disorders: *Psychiatry does not employ the technical methods of psychoanalysis* (Sigmund Freud). [probably < French *psychiatrie* < *psych-* psych- + Greek *īātreíā* cure < *īātrós* physician < *īâsthai* to heal]

psy·chic (sī′kik), *adj.* **1.** of the soul or mind; mental: *illness due to psychic causes. Let us now consider the major categories under which psychic . . . disorders are conveniently classified* (Sunday Times). **2.** outside the known laws of physics; supernatural. A psychic force or influence is believed by spiritualists to explain second sight, telepathy, table moving, and tappings, etc. **3.** especially susceptible to psychic influences.
—*n.* **1.** a person supposed to be specially sensitive or responsive to psychic force or spiritual influences; medium. **2.** things that are psychic; the realm of parapsychology. **3.** a psychic bid.
[< Greek *psȳchikós* < *psȳchḗ* soul, mind]
—**psy′chi·cal·ly,** *adv.*
—**Syn.** *adj.* **2.** telepathic.

psy·chi·cal (sī′kə kəl), *adj.* psychic.

psychic bid, (in contract bridge) a bid made to mislead the opponents, on a hand lacking the values normally indicated by the bid.

psychic energizer, an antidepressant; energizer.

psy·chics (sī′kiks), *n.* **1.** psychology. **2.** the study of psychic phenomena.

psy·cho (sī′kō), *n., pl.* **-chos,** *adj. Slang.* —*n.* a psychopath: *It turns upon getting rid of a bully by making out that he is a "psycho"* (Sunday Times). —*adj.* psychopathic: *He had been through the D.T.s, jails and psycho wards before getting cured* (Time).

psycho-, *combining form.* mind; spirit; soul: *Psychoanalysis = examination of the mind. Psychology = science of the mind.* Also, **psych-** before vowels.
[< Greek *psycho-* < *psȳchḗ* soul, mind, life, breath]

psy·cho·a·cous·tics (sī′kō ə küs′tiks, -kous′-), *n.* the branch of acoustics that deals with the mental and auditory aspects of sound communication.

psy·cho·a·nal·y·sis (sī′kō ə nal′ə sis), *n.* **1. a.** the minute examination of a mind or minds to discover the underlying mental causes producing certain mental and nervous disorders: *Psychoanalysis aims at and achieves nothing more than the discovery of the unconscious in mental life* (Sigmund Freud). **b.** analysis of mind or personality. **2.** the body of theory originated and first developed by Freud.

psy·cho·an·a·lyst (sī′kō an′ə list), *n.* a person who is skilled in or practices psychoanalysis: *In the psychoanalyst's room the patient is first induced to talk about the subjects that he feels unable to discuss with anyone* (Listener).

psy·cho·an·a·lyt·ic (sī′kō an′ə lit′ik), *adj.* having to do with or of the nature of psychoanalysis. —**psy′cho·an′a·lyt′i·cal·ly,** *adv.*

psy·cho·an·a·lyt·i·cal (sī′kō an′ə lit′ə kəl), *adj.* psychoanalytic.

psy·cho·an·a·lyze (sī′kō an′ə līz), *v.t.,* **-lyzed, -lyz·ing.** to examine by psychoanalysis. —**psy′cho·an′a·lyz′er,** *n.*

psy·cho·bi·o·log·ic (sī′kō bī′ə loj′ik), *adj.* psychobiological.

psy·cho·bi·o·log·i·cal (sī′kō bī′ə loj′ə kəl), *adj.* dealing with the interrelationship of mental and biological functions: *A behavioristic social psychology which understands human actions as those of a psychobiological organism . . .* (George Simpson).

psy·cho·bi·ol·o·gist (sī′kō bī ol′ə jist), *n.* a person who studies the interrelationship of mental and biological functions.

psy·cho·bi·ol·o·gy (sī′kō bī ol′ə jē), *n.* the branch of biology which deals with the interrelationship of mental and biological functions as affecting personality.

psy·cho·chem·i·cal (sī′kō kem′ə kəl), *adj.* (of chemicals used in warfare) producing temporary psychological or psychosomatic disorders: *a psychochemical agent, gas, etc.* —*n.* a chemical producing such disorders.

psy·cho·del·ic (sī′kō del′ik), *adj., n.* psychedelic.

psy·cho·dra·ma (sī′kō drä′mə, -dram′ə), *n.* the acting out of a personal situation by a patient with the help of an audience or other actors, used in psychotherapy to reveal to the patient the social significance of his problems and aid in emotional adjustment: *Two patients volunteered to stage a psychodrama, one acting the submissive wife . . . the other playing the domineering husband* (Time).

psy·cho·dra·mat·ic (sī′kō drə mat′ik), *adj.* of or having to do with psychodrama.

psy·cho·dy·nam·ic (sī′kō dī nam′ik), *adj.*

of or having to do with mental powers or activities that relate to or derive from motivation, impulse, etc.: *I find them, in general, contradictory, puzzling, and confusing from a psychodynamic point of view* (New Yorker).

psy·cho·dy·nam·i·cal·ly (sī′kō dī nam′ə klē), *adv.* according to psychodynamics.

psy·cho·dy·nam·ics (sī′kō dī nam′iks), *n.* the science, usually classified as a branch of psychology, that deals with psychodynamic phenomena: [*The history of science*] *is the psychodynamics of the intellectual reaction between people, books, and nature* (Edwin G. Boring).

psy·cho·gal·van·ic (sī′kō gal van′ik), *adj.* of or having to do with the electrical responses of the body to mental or emotional stimuli: *They are now using, . . . scientific devices like the psychogalvanic skin response test to see how people like television programs* (Maclean's).

psy·cho·gal·va·nom·e·ter (sī′kō gal′və nom′ə tər), *n.* a galvanometer that records and measures decreases in the electrical resistance of the skin in response to emotional stimuli involved in selected questions, pictures, etc.

psy·cho·gen·e·sis (sī′kō jen′ə sis), *n.* **1.** the origin or development of the mind or soul. **2.** animal evolution due to mental activity rather than to natural selection. [< *psycho-* + *genesis*]

psy·cho·ge·net·ic (sī′kō jə net′ik), *adj.* having to do with the formation of the mind by development. **—psy′cho·ge·net′i·cal·ly,** *adv.*

psy·cho·gen·ic (sī′kō jen′ik), *adj.* of psychic origin: *psychogenic symptoms of a disorder.*

psy·chog·no·sis (sī kog′nə sis), *n.* the study of the mind or soul. [< *psycho-* + Greek *gnôsis* knowledge]

psy·cho·gon·ic (sī′kō gon′ik), *adj.* psychogenetic.

psy·chog·o·ny (sī kog′ə nē), *n.* the origin and development of the soul or mind.

psy·cho·gram (sī′kə gram), *n.* **1.** *Psychology.* a chart or record of a person's mental makeup. **2.** a writing or message supposedly sent by a disembodied spirit or produced by a psychic agency: *The term "psychogram" . . . rather mystically suggests a quasi-letter form which is the product of the subconscious mind* (London Times).

psy·cho·graph (sī′kə graf, -gräf), *n. Psychology.* a chart or biographical sketch indicating the various factors in a particular individual's personality.

psy·cho·graph·ic (sī′kō graf′ik), *adj.* of or having to do with psychography.

psy·chog·ra·phy (sī kog′rə fē), *n.* **1.** the history or description of a person's mental processes: *You aim, then, at a sort of spiritual biography of your subject — what has recently been called a psychography* (London Daily Chronicle). **2.** writing supposed to be due to a disembodied spirit. [< *psycho-* + *-graphy*]

psy·cho·ki·ne·sis (sī′kō ki nē′sis), *n.* the supposed ability of a person to exert influence upon the movement of inanimate objects, such as the rolling of dice or the turning of cards: *Psychokinesis* (*the "mind over matter" effect*) *is not yet a scientifically proven effect* (New Scientist).

psychol., 1. psychological. 2. psychology.

psy·cho·lin·guis·tic (sī′kō ling gwis′tik), *adj.* of or having to do with psycholinguistics: *psycholinguistic phenomena.*

psy·cho·lin·guis·tics (sī′kō ling gwis′tiks), *n.* a branch of linguistics that deals with the mental states and processes in language and speech.

psy·cho·log·ic (sī′kə loj′ik), *adj.* psychological.

psy·cho·log·i·cal (sī′kə loj′ə kəl), *adj.* **1.** of the mind: *For three days the fathers faced a barrage of psychological tests, interviews, and group activities* (Newsweek). **2.** of psychology or psychologists: *It sought also to restore economic health, psychological self-confidence and military vigor* (New York Times). **3.** like psychology..

psy·cho·log·i·cal·ly (sī′kə loj′ə klē), *adv.* **1.** in a psychological manner. **2.** in psychological respects: *It takes art to persuade us that psychologically we are all of us, in T.S. Eliot's phrase, eaten by the same worm* (Wall Street Journal).

psychological moment, 1. the very moment to get the desired effect in the mind. **2.** the critical moment.

psychological warfare, the systematic efforts to affect morale, loyalty, etc., especially of large national groups: *In West Germany the Russians were waging psychological warfare with a skill that was dangerous to underrate* (London Times).

psy·chol·o·gist (sī kol′ə jist), *n.* a person skilled or trained in psychology: *A psychologist . . . is trained to understand the mind and its activities* (Marguerite Clark).

psy·chol·o·gize (sī kol′ə jīz), *v.i., v.t.,* **-gized, -giz·ing.** to investigate by psychological methods: *A man about town does not psychologize himself, he accepts his condition with touching simplicity* (John Galsworthy).

psy·cho·logue (sī′kə lôg, -log), *n.* a psychologist.

psy·chol·o·gy (sī kol′ə jē), *n., pl.* **-gies. 1.** the science of the mind. Psychology examines the reasons why people act, think, and feel as they do: *As psychology analyzes mental processes, so sociology analyzes social processes* (Emory S. Bogardus). **2.** a textbook or handbook of psychology. **3.** the mental states and processes of a person or persons; mental nature and behavior: *Mrs. Jones knew her husband's psychology. Symptoms appear immediately on withdrawal, often with the saddest effects on the psychology of the patient* (A.J.Birch). [< New Latin *psychologia* < Greek *psȳchḗ* soul, mind + New Latin *-logia* -logy]

psy·cho·man·cy (sī′kō man′sē), *n.* **1.** occult communication between souls or with spirits. **2.** *Obsolete.* necromancy. [< *psycho-* + Greek *manteíā* divination]

psy·cho·man·tic (sī′kō man′tik), *adj.* of or having to do with psychomancy.

psy·chom·e·ter (sī kom′ə tər), *n.* **1.** an instrument used in psychometry. **2.** a person supposed to possess the faculty of psychometry.

psy·cho·met·ric (sī′kō met′rik), *adj.* **1.** having to do with psychometry. **2.** of the nature of psychometry. **—psy′cho·met′ri·cal·ly,** *adv.*

psy·cho·met·ri·cal (sī′kō met′rə kəl), *adj.* psychometric.

psy·cho·me·tri·cian (sī′kō me trish′ən), *n.* psychometrist.

psy·cho·met·rics (sī′kō met′riks), *n.* the measurement of mental facts and relations; psychometry.

psy·chom·e·trist (sī kom′ə trist), *n.* **1.** a person skilled in psychometry. **2.** a person supposed to possess the faculty of psychometry.

psy·chom·e·trize (sī kom′ə trīz), *v.t.,* **-trized, -triz·ing.** to practice the art of psychometry upon (an object).

psy·chom·e·try (sī kom′ə trē), *n.* **1.** the measurement of mental facts and relations. **2.** the alleged art or power of divining facts about an object or its owner through contact with it or proximity to it.

psy·cho·mo·tor (sī′kō mō′tər), *adj.* of or designating muscular activity directly related to mental processes.

psy·cho·neu·ro·sis (sī′kō nů rō′sis, -nyů-), *n., pl.* **-ses** (-sēz). a mental disorder with physical symptoms but without apparent organic disease: *In both the actual neuroses and the psychoneuroses the symptoms proceed from the libido* (Sigmund Freud). [< New Latin *psychoneurosis* < *psycho-* psycho + *neurosis* neurosis]

psy·cho·neu·rot·ic (sī′kō nů rot′ik, -nyů-), *adj.* of or having to do with psychoneurosis. —*n.* a person suffering from psychoneurosis.

psy·cho·nom·ic (sī′kə nom′ik), *adj.* of or having to do with psychonomics.

psy·cho·nom·ics (sī′kə nom′iks), *n.* the branch of psychology that deals with the laws of mental action, especially the relations of the individual mind to its environment. [< *psycho-* + Greek *nómos* law + English *-ics*]

psy·cho·path (sī′kə path), *n.* a person suffering from mental disease.

psy·cho·path·ic (sī′kə path′ik), *adj.* **1.** of or having to do with mental diseases. **2.** having a mental disease. **3.** likely to become insane.
—*n.* a psychopath. **—psy′cho·path′i·cal·ly,** *adv.*

psy·chop·a·thist (sī kop′ə thist), *n. Obsolete.* a person who studies or treats mental disease.

psy·cho·path·o·log·i·cal (sī′kō path′ə loj′ə kəl), *adj.* of or having to do with psychopathology. **—psy′cho·path′o·log′i·cal·ly,** *adv.*

psy·cho·pa·thol·o·gist (sī′kō pə thol′ə jist), *n.* a student of or expert in psychopathology.

psy·cho·pa·thol·o·gy (sī′kō pə thol′ə jē), *n.* the science of disease of the mind.

psy·chop·a·thy (sī kop′ə thē), *n.* **1.** mental disease. **2.** mental eccentricity or instability so extreme as to border on insanity. **3.** the treatment of disease by psychic means.

psy·cho·phar·ma·co·log·i·cal (sī′kō fär′mə kə loj′ə kəl), *adj.* of or having to do with psychopharmacology.

psy·cho·phar·ma·col·o·gy (sī′kō fär′mə kol′ə jē), *n.* a branch of pharmacology concerned with the effects of drugs on mental disturbances.

psy·cho·phys·i·cal (sī′kō fiz′ə kəl), *adj.* of or having to do with psychophysics: *The psychophysical methods . . . generally aim to connect stimulus and response, or stimulus and sensation* (F.H.George).

psy·cho·phys·i·cist (sī′kō fiz′ə sist), *n.* a student of psychophysics.

psy·cho·phys·ics (sī′kō fiz′iks), *n.* the branch of psychology that deals with the physical relations of mental phenomena, especially the relations between physical stimuli and sensations.

psy·cho·phys·i·o·log·ic (sī′kō fiz′ē ə loj′ik), *adj.* psychophysiological.

psy·cho·phys·i·o·log·i·cal (sī′kō fiz′ē ə loj′ə kəl), *adj.* of or having to do with psychophysiology.

psy·cho·phys·i·ol·o·gist (sī′kō fiz′ē ol′ə jist), *n.* a student of or expert in psychophysiology.

psy·cho·phys·i·ol·o·gy (sī′kō fiz′ē ol′ə jē), *n.* the branch of physiology which deals with mental phenomena.

psy·cho·pomp (sī′kō pomp), *n. Greek and Roman Mythology.* a conductor of souls to the place of the dead, especially Charon, Hermes, or Apollo. [< Greek *psȳchopompós* < *psȳchḗ* soul, spirit + *pompós* conductor < *pémpein* to send]

psy·cho·sen·so·ry (sī′kō sen′sər ē), *adj.* having to do with percepts or impulses that do not originate in the sense organs.

psy·cho·sex·u·al (sī′kə sek′shů əl), *adj.* of or having to do with the psychological aspects of sex or both the mental and sexual processes: *psychosexual development, growth, maturity, etc.* **—psy′cho·sex′u·al·ly,** *adv.*

psy·cho·sis (sī kō′sis), *n., pl.* **-ses** (-sēz). any severe form of mental disturbance or disease, with deep and far-reaching disorders of behavior: *Alcoholism may be a symptom of . . . psychosis, or may bring to notice an already existing psychosis* (Strecker, Ebaugh, and Ewalt). [< New Latin *psychosis* < Greek *psȳchḗ* soul, mind + New Latin *-osis* -osis]

psy·cho·so·cial (sī′kō sō′shəl), *adj.* of or having to do with the interrelationship of psychological and social processes, disciplines, services, etc.: *a psychosocial study, psychosocial assistance, etc.* **—psy′cho·so′cial·ly,** *adv.*

psy·cho·so·ci·o·log·i·cal (sī′kō sō′sē ə loj′ə kəl, -shē-), *adj.* psychosocial.

psy·cho·so·ci·ol·o·gist (sī′kō sō′sē ol′ə jist, -shē-), *n.* a person skilled in the interrelationships of psychology and sociology.

psy·cho·so·mat·ic (sī′kō sō mat′ik), *adj.* of or having to do with both mind and body: *This is part of the growing belief of the psychosomatic* (*mind-body*) *experts that high blood pressure . . .* [*is*] *aided and abetted by upset emotions* (Marguerite Clark). [< *psycho-* + Greek *sōmătikós* somatic < *sôma* body] **—psy′cho·so·mat′i·cal·ly,** *adv.*

psychosomatic medicine, the use of the methods and principles of psychology in the treatment of physical ailments.

psy·cho·sur·ger·y (sī′kō sėr′jər ē), *n.* brain surgery used in the treatment of certain psychoses.

psy·cho·tech·nol·o·gy (sī′kō tek nol′ə jē), *n.* a branch of technology that deals with the application of psychology as a guide in handling practical problems.

psy·cho·ther·a·peu·tic (sī′kō ther′ə pyü′tik), *adj.* mentally healing.

psy·cho·ther·a·peu·tics (sī′kō ther′ə pyü′tiks), *n.* the scientific basis of psychotherapy.

psy·cho·ther·a·peu·tist (sī′kō ther′ə pyü′tist), *n.* a psychotherapist.

psy·cho·ther·a·pist (sī′kō ther′ə pist), *n.* a person, as a psychiatrist, psychoanalyst, etc., who practices psychotherapy.

psy·cho·ther·a·py (sī′kō ther′ə pē), *n.* the treatment of mental or nervous disorder by psychological means, especially those involving intercommunication, as by psychoanalysis, hypnotism, etc.

psy·chot·ic (sī kot′ik), *adj.* of, having to do with, or caused by serious mental disease; insane: *How absurd, I never heard of Communism, this is a witch hunt, my accuser is psychotic* (Eric Bentley). —*n.* an insane person: *For the most part psychotics are aware of their disturbance—either because it itself makes them suffer or because others make them suffer for it* (Harper's). —**psy·chot′i·cal·ly,** *adv.*

psy·chot·o·mi·met·ic (sī kot′ō mi met′ik, -mī-), *adj.* producing a state akin to or symptomatic of psychosis: *They were conducting experiments with LSD and other psychotomimetic drugs* (Harper's). —*n.* a psychotomimetic drug or substance. [< *psychot*(ic) + connective *-o-* + *mimetic*]

psy·cho·tox·ic (sī′kō tok′sik), *adj.* affecting the mind in a toxic or harmful manner: *He asked for laws to control the production and sale of such drugs as barbiturates, amphetamines, and other psychotoxic drugs* (New York Times).

psy·cho·trop·ic (sī′ko trop′ik), *adj.* affecting the mental processes: *a psychotropic drug.*

psy·cho·zo·ic (sī′kō zō′ik), *adj.* of or belonging to the geological period of living creatures having minds or intelligence: *Our interest, . . . is in planets that may have intelligent life now, not in planets . . . whose "psychozoic era" has passed* (Scientific American).

psy·chrom·e·ter (sī krom′ə tər), *n.* a kind of hygrometer having wet and dry bulb thermometers. It is used to determine the relative humidity. [< Greek *psȳchrós* cold + English *-meter*]

psy·chro·met·ric (sī′krə met′rik), *adj.* of or having to do with psychrometry.

psy·chrom·e·try (sī krom′ə trē), *n.* the branch of physics that deals with the measurement of the relative humidity in the air.

psy·chro·phil·ic (sī′krə fil′ik), *adj.* (of certain bacteria) requiring low temperatures for development. [< Greek *psȳchrós* cold + English *-phil* + *-ic*]

psy·war (sī′wôr′), *n. Informal.* psychological warfare: *In the local bureaucratic jargon, this can come under the heading of "civic action" . . . or "psywar"* (Wall Street Journal).

pt., an abbreviation for the following:
1. part.
2. past tense.
3. payment.
4. pint or pints.
5. point.
6. port.
7. preterit.

p.t., **1.** pro tempore. **2.** *British.* purchase tax.

Pt (no period), platinum (chemical element).

P.t., Pacific time.

P.T., **1.** physical training. **2.** *British.* purchase tax.

P.T.A. or **PTA** (no periods), Parent-Teacher Association, an organization of the parents and teachers of a school, established to improve the environment of the community for children, especially by supporting the activities of the school.

Ptah (ptä, ptäн), *n.* (in ancient Egypt) the chief god of Memphis, father of men and gods and ruler of the world.

ptar·mi·gan (tär′mə gən), *n., pl.* **-gans** or (*collectively*) **-gan.** any of several kinds of grouse that have feathered feet and are found in mountainous and northern regions. The plumage of most varieties is brownish in summer, white in winter. [< Scottish Gaelic *tàrmachan*]

Rock Ptarmigan
in winter plumage
(about 14 in. long)

PT boat, (in the United States) a small, fast motorboat which carries torpedoes, depth bombs, etc.: *Kennedy was hospitalized for an old injury, suffered when he was a wartime PT boat commander* (Newsweek). [< *P*(atrol) *T*(orpedo) boat]

PTC (no periods), phenylthiocarbamide.

Pte., Private (in the British Army): *And you with the Etruscan look not Pte. Maecenas by any chance?* (Listener).

pter·an·o·don (ter an′ə don), *n.* a large, toothless pterodactyl with a hornlike crest projecting from its head. [< New Latin *Pteranodon* the genus name < Greek *pterón* wing + *an-* without + *odoús, odóntos* tooth]

pter·i·do·log·i·cal (ter′ə də loj′ə kəl), *adj.* having to do with pteridology.

pter·i·dol·o·gist (ter′ə dol′ə jist), *n.* an expert in the study of ferns.

pter·i·dol·o·gy (ter′ə dol′ə jē), *n.* the branch of botany that deals with ferns. [< Greek *pterís, -ídos* fern (< *pterón* feather) + English *-logy*]

pter·i·do·phyte (ter′ə də fīt), *n.* any of the highest group of seedless plants having roots, stems, and leaves: *Ferns, horsetails, and club mosses are pteridophytes. The tissues of seed plants and pteridophytes are all derived from a fertilized egg* (*zygote*) *which has undergone repeated divisions* (Heber W. Youngken). [< Greek *pterís, -ídos* fern (< *pterón* feather) + English *-phyte*]

pter·i·do·phyt·ic (ter′ə də fit′ik), *adj.* of or having to do with pteridophytes.

pter·i·doph·y·tous (ter′ə dof′ə təs), *adj.* pteridophytic.

pter·i·do·sperm (ter′ə də spėrm), *n.* any of a group of fossil plants having the external aspect of ferns, but bearing true seeds: *. . . fernlike pteridosperms are the earliest to start protecting their seeds* (New Scientist). [< Greek *pterís, -ídos* fern + English *sperm*]

pter·o·dac·tyl (ter′ə dak′təl), *n.* any of various extinct flying reptiles that had wings somewhat like a bat's. [< Greek *pterón* wing + *dáktylos* finger, toe]

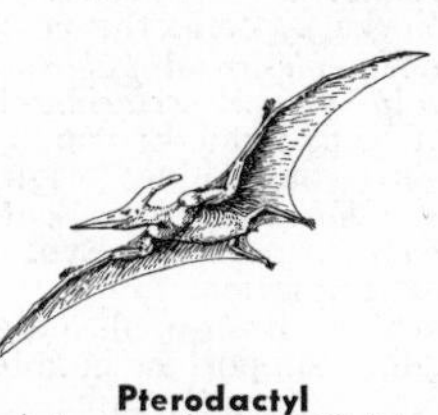

Pterodactyl
(wingspread, about 20 ft.)

pte·ron (ter′on), *n. Architecture.* a side row of columns in a classical temple. [< Greek *pterón* wing]

pter·o·pod (ter′ə pod), *adj.* of or belonging to a group of mollusks with lateral portions of the foot expanded into winglike lobes used in swimming. —*n.* a pteropod mollusk. [< New Latin *Pteropoda* a group or class name < Greek *pterópous, -podos* wingfooted < *pterón* wing, feather + *poús, podós* foot]

pte·rop·o·dan (tə rop′ə dən), *adj., n.* pteropod.

pte·rop·o·dous (tə rop′ə dəs), *adj.* **1.** pteropod. **2.** characteristic of a pteropod.

pter·o·saur (ter′ə sôr), *n.* an extinct flying reptile; pterodactyl: *On the land were the dinosaurs, in the sea the ichthyosaurs . . . in the air the pterosaurs* (A. Franklin Shull). [< New Latin *Pterosauria* the order name < Greek *pterón* wing + *saûros* lizard]

pter·o·sau·ri·an (ter′ə sôr′ē ən), *adj.* **1.** of or belonging to the same order as the pterodactyl. **2.** like a pterodactyl. —*n.* a pterodactyl.

pte·ryg·i·um (tə rij′ē əm), *n., pl.* **-i·ums, -i·a** (-ē ə). a triangular patch of thickened conjunctiva growing over the cornea that obscures vision: *Recent scientific studies . . . did not take into consideration whether or not those people with pterygium wore any kind of eyeglasses or sunglasses* (New Scientist). [< Greek *pterýgion* little wing, fin]

pter·y·goid (ter′ə goid), *adj.* **1.** winglike. **2.** of or having to do with either of two processes of the sphenoid bone. —*n.* a pterygoid muscle, nerve, etc. [< Greek *pterygoeidēs* winglike < *ptéryx, -ygos* wing (< *pterón* wing, feather) + *eîdos* form, shape]

pterygoid plate, either of the two sections, the lateral section or the medial section, that make up a pterygoid process.

pterygoid process, **1.** either of two processes descending, one on each side, from the point of juncture of the main body and the great wing of the sphenoid bone of the skull. Each process consists of a lateral and a medial section. **2.** any of the four pterygoid plates.

pter·y·la (ter′ə lə), *n., pl.* **-lae** (-lē). one of the definite tracts or areas on the skin of a bird, on which feathers grow. [< New Latin *pteryla* < Greek *pterón* feather + *hýlē* wood]

pter·y·log·ra·phy (ter′ə log′rə fē), *n., pl.* **-phies.** **1.** the description of pterylae. **2.** a treatise on pterylosis. [< *pteryla* + *-graphy*]

pter·y·lo·sis (ter′ə lō′sis), *n.* the arrangement or disposition of the feathers of a bird in definite tracts, or pterylae. [< *pteryl*(a) + *-osis*]

ptg., printing.

ptis·an (tiz′ən, ti zan′), *n.* a nourishing decoction often having a slight medicinal quality, originally one made from barley. [spelling alteration (influenced by Latin *ptisana*) of Middle English *tisane* < Old French *tisane*, learned borrowing from Late Latin *tisana*, variant of Latin *ptisana* crushed barley < Greek *ptisánē*]

p.t.o. or **P.T.O.,** *Especially British.* please turn over.

Ptol·e·ma·ic (tol′ə mā′ik), *adj.* **1.** of or having to do with the astronomer Ptolemy: *The Ptolemaic constellations of the Horse, the Bird, and the Kneeler became respectively Pegasus, Cygnus, and Hercules* (Robert H. Baker). **2.** of or having to do with the Ptolemies, who were rulers of Egypt from 323 B.C. to 30 B.C.

Ptolemaic system, the system of astronomy developed by the astronomer Ptolemy. It stated that the earth was the fixed center of the universe and that the heavenly bodies moved around the earth: *The outstanding solution of the problem, on the basis of the central, motionless earth, was the Ptolemaic system* (Robert H. Baker).

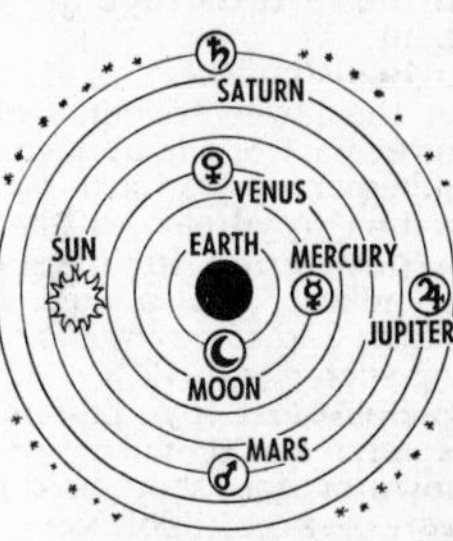

Ptolemaic System

Ptol·e·ma·ist (tol′ə mā′ist), *n.* a supporter of the Ptolemaic system of astronomy.

pto·maine or **pto·main** (tō′mān, tō-mān′), *n.* a substance, often poisonous, produced in decaying matter. Improperly canned foods may contain ptomaines. Ptomaines are a group of basic, nitrogenous, organic compounds. [< Italian *ptomaina* < Greek *ptôma* corpse, (literally) a fall; fallen thing < *píptein* to fall]

ptomaine poisoning, **1.** poisoning caused by ptomaines. **2.** food poisoning.

pto·sis (tō′sis), *n.* a slipping down of an organ, especially the drooping of the upper eyelid, caused by paralysis of the muscle that causes it to open. [< Greek *ptôsis* a falling < *píptein* to fall]

pto·tic (tō′tik), *adj.* **1.** having to do with or like ptosis. **2.** affected with ptosis.

pts., **1.** parts. **2.** pints. **3.** points.

Pty., Pty (no period), or **pty.,** proprietary: *The commentary is sponsored by Ford Motor Company of South Africa (Pty.), Limited* (Cape Times).

pty·a·lin (tī′ə lin), *n.* an enzyme contained in the saliva of man and of certain other animals. It possesses the property of converting starch into dextrin and maltose, thus aiding digestion. [< Greek *ptýalon* saliva (< *ptýein* to spit) + English *-in*]

pty·a·lism (tī′ə liz əm), *n.* excessive secretion of saliva: *This may go down in recent baseball history as the year of ptyalism, which is a $3.95 word for excess salivation* (Scientific American). [< Greek *ptýalon* saliva + English *-ism*]

p-type (pē′tīp′), *adj.* (of a semiconductor or its conductivity) positive type; having as the carrier of an electrical charge positive holes rather than negative electrons: *The wandering hole gives the aluminum-doped region positive* (*p-type*) *conductivity* (Scientific American). [< *p*(ositive) *type*]

Pu (no period), plutonium (chemical element).

pub (pub), *n., v.,* **pubbed, pub·bing.** *British Informal and U.S. Slang.* —*n.* a saloon; tavern; public house: *I drove on and lunched very late at a remote pub overlooking the Blackmoor Vale.* —*v.i.* to visit or frequent pubs: *I was about to ask him to go pubbing with us when I noticed that he was carrying a* *book by T.S. Eliot* (H. Allen Smith). [< *pub*(lic)]

pub., **1.** public. **2.** publication. **3.** published. **4.** publisher. **5.** publishing.

pub-crawl (pub′krôl′), *Slang.* —*v.i.* to go from one pub or bar to another: *I'd rather pub-crawl than visit Whitehall* (Saturday Review). —*n.* a round of several pubs made by one or more persons: *The oil wealth of neighboring Arab countries has often been squandered on Cadillacs, harems and princely pub-crawls* (Time). —**pub′-crawl′er,** *n.*

pu·ber·al (pyü′bər əl), *adj.* of or at the age of puberty: *Two papers relate physique and puberal status to leadership and personality characteristics in junior high school boys* (Dale B. Harris). [< Late Latin *pūberālis* < Latin *pūber* a youth]

pu·ber·ty (pyü′bər tē), *n.* the physical beginning of manhood and womanhood. Puberty comes at about 14 in boys and about 12 in girls. *The onset of puberty and adolescence is accompanied by numerous changes in both personality and behavior* (Beals and Hoijer). [< Latin *pūbertās* < *pūbēs, -eris* adult, full grown, manly]

pu·ber·u·lent (pyü ber′yə lənt), *adj. Botany.* covered with fine, short down; minutely pubescent. [< Latin *pūber* downy + *-ulent*, on the analogy of *pulverulent*]

pu·ber·u·lous (pyü ber′yə ləs), *adj.* puberulent.

pu·bes[1] (pyü′bēz), *n.* **1.** the hair appearing on the lower abdomen at puberty. **2.** the lower part of the hypogastrium. **3.** *Botany.* pubescence. [< Latin *pūbēs*]

pu·bes[2] (pyü′bēz), *n.* the plural of **pubis.**

pu·bes·cence (pyü bes′əns), *n.* **1.** arrival at puberty. **2.** a soft, downy growth on plants and some insects. **3.** the fact of having such a growth.

pu·bes·cent (pyü bes′ənt), *adj.* **1.** arriving or arrived at puberty. **2.** covered with down or fine, short hair: *a pubescent stem or leaf.* —*n.* an adolescent at the age of puberty: *Among other figures introduced are some Italian pubescents who are gone on the lingo of jazz* (New Yorker). [< Latin *pūbēscēns, -entis* reaching puberty, present participle of *pūbēscere* < *pūbēs, -eris* mature, adult]

pu·bic (pyü′bik), *adj.* **1.** having to do with the pubis. **2.** in the region of the pubis.

pubic symphysis, the place at the front of the pelvis where the pubis of one side is joined to the other.

pu·bis (pyü′bis), *n., pl.* **-bes.** the part of either hipbone that, with the corresponding part of the other, forms the front of the pelvis: *The pelvic structure is made up of three sets of paired bones, the ilium, the ischium and the pubis* (Scientific American). [< New Latin *os pūbis* bone of the groin < Latin *os* bone, *pūbis*, genitive of *pūbēs* the genital area]

pub·keep·er (pub′kē′pər), *n. Especially British.* a person who owns, manages, or keeps a public house.

publ., **1.** published. **2.** publisher.

pub·lic (pub′lik), *adj.* **1.** of, belonging to, or concerning the people as a whole: *public affairs. The Restrictive Practices Court's ruling that the yarn spinners agreement is contrary to the public interest is a bitter pill for the cotton industry* (Manchester Guardian). **2.** done, made, acting, etc., for the people as a whole: *a public relief.* **3.** open to all the people; serving all the people: *a public park, a public meeting.* **4.** of or engaged in the affairs or service of the people: *a public official. Public employment does bring with it certain obligations beyond those required of citizens in private life* (Bulletin of Atomic Scientists). **5.** known to many or all; not private: *The fact became public.* **6.** international: *public law.*

go public, to offer stocks or bonds for sale to the public for the first time: *To raise the money, family-owned Lykes went public in 1958, though the family still owns 64% of the stock* (Time).

—*n.* **1.** the people in general; all the people: *to inform the public.* **2.** a particular section of the people: *There is a separate public for every picture and every book* (John Ruskin). *At the other pole are the more stable groups called publics, characterized by deliberate discussion of issues confronting the group* (Ogburn and Nimkoff). **3.** *British Informal.* a public house.

in public, not in private or secretly; publicly; openly: *to stand up in public for what you believe.*

[< Latin *pūblicus*, earlier *poplicus* (influenced by *pūbēs* adult male population) < *populus* the people]

public accountant, **1.** an accountant who makes his services available to anyone for a fee or on a contract basis: *Auditing is one of the chief jobs of public accountants* (R.K. Mautz). **2.** certified public accountant.

pub·lic-ad·dress system (pub′lik ə dres′), an apparatus consisting of one or more microphones, amplifiers, and loudspeakers, by which speeches, announcements, music, etc., may be made audible to a large audience, as on a public street or square, in a stadium for athletics, in the various rooms of a building, etc.: *He was not quite equal to the hazards of public-address systems ... the emotional impact of facing a vast crowd, the split-minute timing* (Time). *Abbr.:* P.A.

pub·li·can (pub′lə kən), *n.* **1.** *British.* the keeper of a public house: *The publican took the opportunity to present my hero with a bill ... for bottles of spirits supplied to his wife* (Samuel Butler). **2. a.** a tax collector of ancient Rome. **b.** any collector of tolls, tribute, etc. [< Latin *pūblicānus* < *pūblicum* public revenue, (originally) neuter of *pūblicus* public]

pub·li·ca·tion (pub′lə kā′shən), *n.* **1.** a book, newspaper, or magazine; anything that is published: *"Boy's Life" is a publication of the Boy Scouts. Abbr.:* pub. **2.** the printing and selling of books, newspapers, magazines, etc. **3.** the first public sale of a book, magazine, etc.: *The first printing was swallowed up before publication* (New Yorker). **4. a.** the act of making known: *The widespread publication of traffic laws helps prevent accidents.* **b.** the fact or state of being made known. [< Latin *pūblicātiō, -ōnis* a publishing; (originally) a confiscation < *pūblicāre* to confiscate for public use < *pūblicus* public] —**Syn. 4. a.** promulgation, dissemination.

public charge, an indigent person who requires support or maintenance from public funds: *Since the wife ... had no way to support herself, it was her husband's job to see that she did not become a public charge* (Harper's).

public defender, a person designated by a court or other governmental agency as an attorney to defend persons involved in litigation or legal difficulties who do not have the means to hire their own attorney: *Ohio will consider creating an office of public defender to protect consumers from utility rate-gouging* (New York Times).

public domain, lands belonging to the State or the Federal government.

in the public domain, (of works, material, inventions, etc.) available for unrestricted use because unprotected by copyright or patent: *I had to use material in the public domain or be imitative.*

public enemy, a person or thing that is a menace to the public.

public funds, *British.* the stock of the national debt, considered as a mode of investment.

public health, **1.** the health of the community taken as a whole. **2.** measures taken to maintain and improve the general level of health, as by preventive medicine, immunization, sanitation, and the organization of medical and hospital facilities: *No longer does public health concern itself solely with environmental hygiene* (J.L.Burn).

public house, **1.** *British.* a place where alcoholic liquor is sold to be drunk; saloon. **2.** an inn; hotel.

public housing, *U.S.* housing owned or operated by a municipality or other public body, usually through Federal aid, designed especially for families with low income: *A neighborhood that we remembered as an appalling slum ... is now abloom with public housing* (New Yorker).

pub·li·cise (pub′lə sīz), *v.t.,* **-cised, -cising.** *Especially British.* publicize.

pub·li·cist (pub′lə sist), *n.* **1.** a person skilled or trained in law or in public affairs: *Still others are articulate publicists, professional lobbyists associated with America's biggest industry—war* (Atlantic). **2.** a writer on law, politics, or public affairs: *Dr. Tsuru is a leading publicist for the neutralist view of world affairs* (Atlantic).

pub·lic·i·ty (pub lis′ə tē), *n.* **1.** public notice: *the publicity that actors desire.* **2.** measures used for getting, or the process of getting, public notice: *a campaign of publicity for a new automobile.* **3.** a being public; being seen by or known to everybody: *in the publicity of the streets.* —**Syn. 2.** advertising, propaganda.

pub·li·cize (pub′lə sīz), *v.t.,* **-cized, -cizing.** to give publicity to: *The means of picking the fights and publicizing them will be the classic device of Congressional inquiry* (New York Times).

pub·lic·ly (pub′lə klē), *adv.* **1.** in a public manner; openly. **2.** by the public.

pub·lic·ness (pub′lik nis), *n.* the quality or character of being public.

public opinion, the opinion of the people in a country, community, etc.: *to make a survey of public opinion. Public opinion can be wrong, misguided, mistaken* (Wall Street Journal).

public policy, the policy or general purpose of the law that protects the public from acts contrary to its welfare even when there is no positive statutory prohibition: *A clue as to the direction in which the rail carriers are headed will be the public policy decisions on the bankrupt New Haven Railroad's Boston-New York passenger service* (New York Times).

public prosecutor, a district attorney: *Antisocial behavior and the resultant social disorganization have made necessary the public prosecutor* (Emory S. Bogardus).

public relations, **1.** the activities of an organization that is concerned with giving the general public a better understanding of its policies and purposes, by giving out news through the newspapers, magazines, radio, television, motion pictures, etc. **2.** the attitude of the public toward which these activities are directed: *to have good public relations.* **3.** the business of such activities: *to take up public relations as a career.*

Public Res., Public Resolution (used with a number).

public school, **1.** *U.S.* a free school maintained by taxes, especially an elementary or secondary school: *The chances of a private school graduate's making Who's Who are 6 to 1 over the public school man* (Newsweek). **2.** *British.* an endowed, private, boarding school: *A young man of 24, [graduate of a] public school, and with school certificate, seeks an active and interesting position* (London Times). —**pub′lic-school′,** *adj.*

➤ See **private school** for usage note.

public servant, **1.** a person who works for the government: *It is the function of every policeman to be an extremely valuable public servant* (Emory S. Bogardus). **2.** *U.S.* a public-service corporation.

public service, **1.** government service: *His career, apart from public service sojourns in Washington, has been ... closely identified with Boston* (New York Times). **2.** *U.S.* a service performed to promote the public welfare, as the supplying of gas, electricity, water, transportation, etc. **3.** something done for the general good: *The Citizens Union's annual award for public service will be presented tomorrow* (New York Times).

pub·lic-serv·ice corporation (pub′lik sėr′vis), a corporation formed or chartered to give service to the general public, as by furnishing gas or electricity, bus or railroad transportation, etc.

pub·lic-spir·it·ed (pub′lik spir′ə tid), *adj.* having or showing an unselfish desire for the public good: *A committee of 342 public-spirited men and women leaders ... has been organized* (New York Times). —**pub′lic-spir′it·ed·ly,** *adv.* —**pub′lic-spir′it·ed·ness,** *n.*

public utilities, shares of stock or other securities issued by public utilities.

public utility, a company or corporation formed or chartered to render any of certain essential services to the public, as furnishing gas, electricity, water, transportation, etc., often having a monopoly on its particular service within an area or areas, and subject to special governmental control or regulation; utility: *Natural gas, they said, was not a public utility since the field was highly competitive* (Newsweek). —**pub′lic-u·til′i·ty,** *adj.*

public works, highways, dams, docks, canals, etc., built by the government at public expense and for public use.

pub·lish (pub′lish), *v.t.* **1.** to prepare and offer (a book, paper, map, piece of music, etc.) for sale or distribution: *Professor*

Jaroslav Pelikan . . . is general editor for the volumes being published (Time). **2.** to bring out the book or books of: *Some American writers are published abroad before they achieve publication in this country.* **3.** to make publicly or generally known: *Don't publish the faults of your friends. Publish it that she is dead* (Shakespeare). **4.** to announce formally or officially. —*v.i.* **1.** to come into circulation; be published: *The newspapers here publish every single day.* **2.** to prepare a work for publication and distribution: *We have been publishing for many authors for many years.* [< Old French *publiss-*, stem of *publier*, learned borrowing from Latin *pūblicāre* < *pūblicus* (see PUBLIC); spelling influenced by *cherish, astonish,* etc.] —**Syn.** *v.t.* **3.** divulge, reveal, disclose. —**Ant.** *v.t.* **3.** hide.

pub·lish·a·ble (pub′li shə bəl), *adj.* that can be published: *A couple of years on the analytical couch might help him to mature but nothing will ever make him publishable* (Harper's).

pub·lish·er (pub′li shər), *n.* **1.** a person or company whose business is to publish books, newspapers, magazines, etc.: *The publishers dropped more than $8 million in advertising revenue* (Newsweek). *Abbr.:* pub. **2.** a person who makes something public.

pub·lish·ing house (pub′li shing), a company which publishes books, magazines, etc.; publisher: *Gide had long felt the need for . . . a publishing house which would afford a hearing to young authors* (Atlantic).

pub·lish·ment (pub′lish mənt), *n.* publication.

PUC (no periods) or **P.U.C.,** Public Utilities Commission, a commission set up at various government levels to regulate public utilities: *The PUC may decide on a general decrease in rates* (British Columbia Daily News).

puc·coon (pə kün′), *n.* **1.** any of various plants yielding a red dye, especially the bloodroot, and certain American plants of the borage family. See picture under **bloodroot. 2.** the pigment or dye obtained from any of these plants. [American English < Algonkian (Powhatan) *păhkan*, a plant whose juice was used for dyeing < an Algonkian root meaning "blood." Related to POKE[4].]

puce (pyüs), *n., adj.* purplish brown. [< French *puce* (literally) a flea < Old French *pulce* < Latin *pūlex, -icis*]

puck[1] (puk), *n.* a malicious or mischievous spirit; goblin. [Old English *pūca;* origin uncertain]

puck[2] (puk), *n.* a hard rubber disk used in the game of ice hockey: *A home-team player . . . banged his stick into Richard's scalp while tangling with him over the puck* (Newsweek). [probably < dialectal *puck* to strike or hit. Related to POKE[1].]

Puck (puk), *n.* a mischievous fairy in English folklore, who appears in Shakespeare's *A Midsummer Night's Dream.* [< *puck*[1]]

puck·a (puk′ə), *adj. Anglo-Indian.* **1.** reliable; good. **2.** solid; substantial. **3.** permanent. Also, **pukka.** [< Hindi *pakkā* substantial, solid; cooked, ripe]

puck·er (puk′ər), *v.t., v.i.* to draw into wrinkles or irregular folds: *to pucker one's brow, pucker cloth in sewing. The baby's lips puckered just before he began to cry. Trabert till that moment had looked tense and puckered up* (London Times). —*n.* an irregular fold; wrinkle: *There are puckers in the shoulders of this ill-fitting coat.* [apparently related to POKE[2].] —**Syn.** *v.t., v.i.* crease, purse.

puck·er·y (puk′ər ē), *adj.* puckered; puckering; tending to pucker.

puck·ish (puk′ish), *adj.* mischievous; impish: *a puckish twinkle of the eyes. He got a puckish delight out of teasing his sister.* —**puck′ish·ly,** *adv.* —**puck′ish·ness,** *n.*

puc·ras (puk′rəs), *n.* any of various pheasants of the Himalaya region and parts of India and China, distinguished by the long crests and ear tufts of the males. Also, **pukras.** [< a native name]

pud[1] (püd), *n.* a pood.

pud[2] (pud), *n. British Slang.* pudding.

pud[3] (pud), *n. Informal.* fist; hand. [origin unknown]

pud·der (pud′ər), *v.i.* **1.** to go poking about; potter; dabble (in). **2.** to poke or stir about, as with the hand or a stick.

pud·ding (pu̇d′ing), *n.* **1.** a soft cooked food, usually sweet: *plum pudding. Rice pudding is nourishing.* **2.** anything soft like a pudding. **3.** *Scottish.* a kind of sausage. [origin uncertain. Compare French *boudin* stuffed sausage, Old English *puduc* wart, *puddewurst* black pudding.]

pud·ding·head (pu̇d′ing hed′, pu̇d′ən-), *n. Informal.* a stupid person.

pud·ding·head·ed (pu̇d′ing hed′id, pu̇d′ən-), *adj. Informal.* stupid.

pudding stone, a rock composed of pebbles held together by cementlike stone; conglomerate: *The church . . . is made of rocks, carefully selected to give a variegated, pudding stone effect* (New Yorker).

pud·ding·y (pu̇d′ing ē), *adj. Especially British.* having the appearance, shape, or consistency of a pudding: *The textures were puddingy when they should have been crisp* (London Times).

pud·dle (pud′əl), *n., v.,* **-dled, -dling.** —*n.* **1.** a small pool of water, especially dirty water: *a puddle of rain.* **2.** a small pool of any liquid: *a puddle of ink.* **3.** wet clay and sand stirred into a paste, used as a watertight lining for embankments, canals, etc. **4.** the molten metal that flows before the flame of a welding torch and forms the weld when cooled: *Move the flame across the surface of the sheet metal, carrying the puddle along the surface* (Purvis and Toboldt).

—*v.t.* **1.** to make wet or muddy. **2.** to mix up (wet clay and sand) into a thick paste. **3.** to use a mixture of wet clay and sand to stop water from running through: *Puddle up that hole in the wall.* **4.** to stir (melted iron) along with an oxidizing agent to make wrought iron. **5.** to prepare (soil) for planting while wet, as in a rice paddy. **6.** to damage the texture of (soil, especially a heavy soil) by plowing, harrowing, etc., before excess water has drained.

[Middle English *puddel*, apparently (diminutive) < Old English *pudd* ditch]

pud·dle-jump (pud′əl jump′), *v.t., v.i. Informal.* to fly a light airplane for short trips: *[He] has done some syndicated drawing and free-lance writing, puddle-jumped in his private plane* (Time).

pud·dle-jump·er (pud′əl jum′pər), *n.* **1.** *Informal.* a lightweight airplane or helicopter: *We consider all types . . . big and little transports or puddle-jumpers* (Newsweek). **2.** *Slang.* an old or dilapidated automobile.

pud·dler (pud′lər), *n.* **1.** a person or thing that puddles. **2.** a person employed in the process of converting cast iron into wrought iron.

pud·dling (pud′ling), *n.* **1.** the act or process of converting pig iron into wrought iron by stirring the molten metal along with an oxidizing agent. **2.** the process of converting clay and sand into puddle. **3.** the process of lining or filling something with puddle. **4.** the clay and sand used in puddling; a puddle.

puddling furnace, a furnace for converting pig iron into wrought iron.

pud·dly (pud′lē), *adj.* **1.** full of puddles. **2.** like a puddle.

pud·dock (pud′ək), *n. Dialect.* a paddock; toad.

pu·den·cy (pyü′dən sē), *n.* modesty. [< Latin *pudentia* < *pudēns, -entis*, present participle of *pudēre* to make or be ashamed]

pu·den·dal (pyü den′dəl), *adj.* of or having to do with the pudenda: *The chemical was put into the pain-killing solution used for pudendal block anesthesia* (Science News Letter).

pu·den·dum (pyü den′dəm), *n., pl.* **-da** (-də). the external genitals, especially of the female. [< Latin *pudendum* (literally) thing to be ashamed of, neuter gerundive of *pudēre* be ashamed]

pudge (puj), *n.* a pudgy person.

pudg·i·ly (puj′ə lē), *adv.* in a pudgy manner.

pudg·i·ness (puj′ē nis), *n.* **1.** shortness; fatness; thickness. **2.** plumpness.

pudg·y (puj′ē), *adj.,* **pudg·i·er, pudg·i·est.** short and fat or thick: *pudgy fingers.* —**Syn.** dumpy.

pu·di·bund (pyü′də bund), *adj.* shamefaced; modest; prudish. [< Latin *pudibundus* < *pudēre* be ashamed]

pu·dic·i·ty (pyü dis′ə tē), *n.* modesty; chastity. [< Middle French *pudicité*, ultimately < Latin *pudīcus* modest; chaste]

pu·du (pü′dü), *n.* the smallest deer known, about a foot high and weighing about 20 pounds; rabbit deer. Pudus live in the forests of western South America and have short, spikelike antlers and rough, brown or gray fur. [< American Spanish *pudu*]

pueb·lo (pweb′lō), *n., pl.* **-los.** *U.S.* an Indian village built of adobe and stone. Pueblos were common in the southwestern United States, and some are still in use. [American English < Spanish *pueblo* a people, community < Latin *populus.* Doublet of PEOPLE.]

Pueb·lo (pweb′lō), *n., pl.* **-los.** a member of any of a group of Indian tribes in the southwestern United States and northern Mexico, of several linguistic stocks but sharing the culture typified by the pueblo. Pueblos were and are agricultural and known for such handicrafts as textiles and decorated earthenware. [< *pueblo*]

pu·er·ile (pyü′ər əl; *especially British* pyü′ə rīl), *adj.* foolish for a grown person to say or do; childish: *Such ravings, if invented by the pen of fiction, would seem puerile caricature* (John L. Motley). [< Latin *puerīlis* < *puer* boy, child] —**pu′er·ile·ly,** *adv.* —**pu′er·ile·ness,** *n.* —**Syn.** juvenile, immature.

pu·er·il·ism (pyü′ər ə liz′əm), *n.* childishness, especially that due to mental illness.

pu·er·il·i·ty (pyü′ə ril′ə tē), *n., pl.* **-ties. 1.** childishness; foolishness. **2.** a foolish act, idea, or statement.

pu·er·pe·ra (pyü ėr′pər ə), *n.* a woman in childbirth, or in the period immediately following parturition. [< Latin *puerpera* woman in childbirth < *puer* child, boy + *parere* to bear children]

pu·er·per·al (pyü ėr′pər əl), *adj.* of or having to do with childbirth: *puerperal pain.* [< New Latin *puerperalis* < Latin *puerpera*; see PUERPERA] —**pu·er′per·al·ly,** *adv.*

puerperal fever, a dangerous infection of the placenta occurring after childbirth; childbed fever.

pu·er·pe·ri·um (pyü′ər pir′ē əm), *n.* the state of a woman at and immediately following childbirth. [< Latin *puerperium* childbirth, childbed < *puerpera;* see PUERPERA]

Puer·to Ri·can (pwer′tə rē′kən), *adj.* of or having to do with Puerto Rico or its inhabitants. —*n.* a native or inhabitant of Puerto Rico: *Taxation without representation is still tyranny, hence Puerto Ricans pay no income tax* (Newsweek).

Puerto Rican cherry, acerola.

puff (puf), *v.i.* **1.** to blow with short, quick blasts: *The bellows puffed on the fire.* **2.** to breathe quick and hard: *She puffed as she climbed the stairs.* **3.** to give out puffs; move with puffs: *The engine puffed out of the station.* **4.** to move or come in puffs: *Smoke puffed out of the chimney.* **5.** to smoke: *to puff away at a pipe.* **6.** to become swollen or distended; swell: *A stung lip puffs up.* —*v.t.* **1.** to blow (air, vapor, etc.) in short, quick blasts; drive by puffing. **2.** to put out with a puff of breath. **3.** to smoke (a cigarette, pipe, cigar, etc.). **4.** to swell with air or pride: *He puffed out his cheeks. He puffed out his chest when the teacher praised his work.* **5.** to praise in exaggerated language: *They puffed him to the skies.* **6.** to arrange in soft, round masses.

—*n.* **1.** a short, quick blast: *a puff of wind.* **2.** a small quantity (of air, smoke, etc.) blown out in short, quick blasts: *a puff of smoke. The puffs depend on the presence of vapor in the atmosphere before the passage of the aircraft* (G.N. Lance). **3.** a quick, hard breath. **4.** the act or process of swelling. **5.** a soft, round mass: *a puff of hair.* **6.** a small pad for putting powder on the skin, etc. **7.** a light pastry filled with whipped cream, jam, etc.: *a cream puff.* **8.** extravagant praise: *Writing puffs for a fan magazine is a useful spur to the editorial imagination* (Newsweek). **9.** a portion of material gathered and held down at the edges but left full in the middle in dresses, etc. **10.** a quilted bed coverlet filled with cotton, wool, down, or similar material. **11.** *Dialect.* a puffball.

—*adj.* inflated with praise or commendation: *Does anybody claim that . . . press junkets, and puff blurbs are confined to the securities business?* (Harper's).

[Middle English *puffen*, Old English *pyffan;* perhaps (originally) imitative. Compare Middle Dutch *puffen.*]

—**Syn.** *n.* **4.** distension. **8.** flattery.

puff adder, 1. a large and very poisonous African snake that puffs up the upper part of its body when excited. **2.** a harmless North American snake which puffs out its body; hognose snake: *Puff adders, if irritated,* *will roll over belly-side up, with tongue comically protruding and play dead* (Science News Letter).

puff·ball (puf′bôl′), *n.* any of a group of ball-shaped mushrooms, edible while immature, which, when mature, give off a dark cloud of tiny spores if suddenly broken: *The young puffball is firm and white throughout but . . . the tissues darken* (Fred W. Emerson).

Pasture Puffball (diameter, 3 to 5 in.)

puff·bird (puf′bėrd′), *n.* any of a group of usually plain-colored, tropical American birds, so called from their habit of puffing out their feathers.

puffed-up (puft′up′), *adj.* **1.** inflated with or as if with air. **2.** swollen; distended: *Influenza left her with eyes too puffed-up to read.* **3.** overweening; conceited; pretentious.

puff·er (puf′ər), *n.* **1.** a person or thing that puffs, as a steam locomotive or steamboat: . . . *there were literally hundreds of little fishing smacks and small puffers* (Lord Louis Mountbatten). *A puffer is a boat that has to be seen to be adequately disbelieved* (Time). **2.** any of various fishes capable of inflating the body by swallowing water or air; a blowfish, globefish, toadfish, or swellfish.

puff·er·y (puf′ər ē), *n., pl.* **-er·ies. 1.** exaggerated praise: *publicity puffery.* **2.** a puff in a dress or other garment.

puff·i·ly (puf′ə lē), *adv.* in a puffy manner.

puf·fin (puf′ən), *n.* any of certain sea birds of arctic regions, with a high, narrow, furrowed, parti-colored bill and vermilion feet: *Large colonies of Manx shearwaters, puffins, and gulls . . . are unusually accessible to students* (A.W. Haslett). [Middle English *poffin;* origin uncertain]

Horned Puffin (12½ in. long)

puff·i·ness (puf′ē nis), *n.* puffy condition: *A coat . . . with wide revers shirred inside for extra puffiness* (New Yorker).

puff·ing adder (puf′ing), a small, harmless snake; hognose snake.

puff paste, a very light, flaky, rich dough for making pies, tarts, etc.

puff·y (puf′ē), *adj.,* **puff·i·er, puff·i·est. 1.** puffed out; swollen: *Her eyes are puffy from crying.* **2.** puffed-up; vain. **3.** coming in puffs. **4.** fat; corpulent: *a very stout, puffy man* (Thackeray). —**Syn. 2.** conceited.

pug[1] (pug), *n.* **1.** any of a breed of small, tan dogs, having a curly tail and a short, upturned nose. **2.** a pug nose. **3.** a fox. [origin uncertain]

Pug[1] (def. 1) (10 to 11 in. high at the shoulder)

pug[2] (pug), *v.,* **pugged, pug·ging,** *n.* —*v.t.* **1.** to mix (clay, etc.) with water, as in brickmaking. **2.** to stop or fill in with clay or the like. **3.** to pack or cover with mortar to deaden sound.
—*n.* pugged clay.
[origin uncertain; perhaps imitative of the sound of the pounding of clay]

pug[3] (pug), *n. Slang.* a boxer; pugilist. [short for *pugilist*]

pug[4] (pug), *n., v.,* **pugged, pug·ging.** *Anglo-Indian.* —*n.* the footprint (of an animal). —*v.t.* to track (game) by footprints. [< Hindi *pag* footprint]

pug·dog (pug′dôg′, -dog′), *n.* a small dog with a curly tail and a pug nose; pug.

pug·ga·ree or **pug·a·ree** (pug′ə rē), *n.* puggree.

pug·gree (pug′rē), *n.* **1.** a light turban worn in India. **2.** a scarf wound around a hat or helmet and falling down behind, serving as protection against the sun: *He put on a new flannel suit, freshly waxed boots, and a chalked helmet with a new puggree around it* (New Yorker). [< Hindustani *pagrī* turban]

pug·gry (pug′rē), *n., pl.* **-gries.** puggree.

pugh (pü, pů), *interj.* an exclamation of contempt or disgust. [variant of *pooh*]

pu·gil·ism (pyü′jə liz əm), *n.* the art of fighting with the fists; boxing. [< Latin *pugil, -ilis* boxer, related to *pūgnus* fist, and *pūgna* a fight + English *-ism*]

pu·gil·ist (pyü′jə list), *n.* a person who fights with the fists; boxer.

pu·gil·is·tic (pyü′jə lis′tik), *adj.* of or having to do with pugilism or pugilists. —**pu′gil·is′ti·cal·ly,** *adv.*

pug·mark (pug′märk′), *n.* the footprint of an animal: *Within 10 minutes we were kneeling over the pugmarks of a tiger . . .* (London Times). [< *pug*[4] + *mark*[1]]

pug mill, a mill which grinds, mixes, and works clays and similar substances to make them plastic for use in making brick or pottery, in dressing ore, etc.

pug·na·cious (pug nā′shəs), *adj.* having the habit of fighting; fond of fighting; quarrelsome: *a young cuckoo . . . very fierce and pugnacious* (Gilbert White). [< Latin *pugnāx, -ācis* (with English *-ous*) < *pugnāre* to fight] —**pug·na′cious·ly,** *adv.* —**pug·na′cious·ness,** *n.* —**Syn.** combative.

pug·nac·i·ty (pug nas′ə tē), *n.* a fondness for fighting; quarrelsomeness: *One must make some allowance for the critic's pugnacity and desire to shock* (Atlantic). —**Syn.** belligerency.

pug nose, a short, turned-up nose.

pug-nosed (pug′nōzd′), *adj.* having a pug nose. —**Syn.** snub-nosed.

pug·ree (pug′rē), *n.* puggree.

puir (pyr), *adj., n. Scottish.* poor.

puis·ne (pyü′nē), *adj. Law.* **1.** inferior in rank; younger; junior: *The Lord Chief Justice can take direct responsibility rather than accept it on behalf of a puisne judge* (Manchester Guardian). **2.** later: *a puisne mortgage.*
—*n.* **1.** *Law.* a junior judge. **2.** *Obsolete.* a junior.
[early variant of *puny* < Old French *puisne*]

pu·is·sance (pyü′ə səns; pyü is′əns, pwis′-), *n.* power; might; force; strength: *to prove his puissance in battle brave* (Edmund Spenser). *My performance as an arm taker and door closer took on an even more thoroughly bogus puissance* (New Yorker). —**Syn.** potency.

pu·is·sant (pyü′ə sənt; pyü is′ənt, pwis′-), *adj.* powerful; mighty; strong: *The star attraction was . . . Rajpramukh of Rajasthan, descendant of the sun gods and a most puissant poloist* (Time). *I see in my mind a noble and puissant nation rousing herself like a strong man after sleep* (Milton). [< Old French *puissant* being powerful < Vulgar Latin *possēns, -entis,* for Latin *potēns, -entis;* see POTENT] —**pu′is·sant·ly,** *adv.* —**pu′is·sant·ness,** *n.* —**Syn.** vigorous, forceful.

pu·ja (pü′jä), *n.* **1.** any Hindu religious ceremony or rite. **2.** rites performed in Hindu worship of idols: *Who will perform puja [ritual prayer] before the gods when the temple priests are having their day off?* (Time). [< Sanskrit *pūjā*]

puke (pyük), *n., v.i., v.t.,* **puked, puk·ing.** vomit: . . . *the infant, Mewling and puking in the nurse's arms* (Shakespeare).

➔ **Puke** was accepted in standard English from the time of Shakespeare, as shown by his use of it in *As You Like It,* until the middle of the 1800's, but is now generally avoided in polite speech or writing.

Pukh·tan (puн′tən), *n.* Pathan.

puk·ka (puk′ə), *adj.* pucka.

pukka sahib, *Anglo-Indian.* a good man; real gentleman: *His father was a pukka sahib in His Majesty's civil service* (Time).

puk·ras (puk′rəs), *n.* pucras.

pul (pül), *n.* a copper coin of Afghanistan, worth 1/100 of an afghani. [< Persian *pūl*]

pul·chri·tude (pul′krə tüd, -tyüd), *n.* beauty: *feminine pulchritude.* [< Latin *pulchritūdō, -dinis* < *pulcher* beautiful] —**Syn.** loveliness.

pul·chri·tu·di·nous (pul′krə tü′də nəs, -tyü′-), *adj.* physically beautiful (often used as a humorous affectation).

pule (pyül), *v.i.,* **puled, pul·ing.** to cry in a thin voice, as a sick child does; whimper; whine. [perhaps imitative. Compare Old French *piauler.*]

pul·er (pyü′lər), *n.* a whiner; a sickly, complaining person.

pu·li (pü′lē), *n., pl.* **-lik** (-lēk). any of a breed of medium-sized, long-haired sheep dogs originally bred in Hungary and having a solid, usually gray or dull-black coat: *The Puli is frequently the Hungarian shepherd's only companion* (New Yorker). [< Hungarian *puli*]

pul·ing (pyü′ling), *adj.* whining; weakly querulous. —**pul′ing·ly,** *adv.*

Pu·lit·zer Prize (pyü′lit sər, půl′it-), *U.S.* any one of various prizes given each year for the best American drama, novel, biography, history, book of verse, editorial, and cartoon, established by Joseph Pulitzer and first awarded in 1917: *Fifteen Times reporters have won the Pulitzer Prize for outstanding achievement in covering the news* (New Yorker). [< Joseph *Pulitzer,* 1847-1911, an American journalist]

pulk (pulk), *n.* a boatlike traveling sledge drawn by a single reindeer, used in Lapland. [< Finnish *pulkka*]

pul·ka (pul′kə), *n.* a pulk.

pull (pů1), *v.t.* **1.** to move with the fingers, claws, teeth, etc., in such a way that the thing moved follows the fingers, etc.: *to pull a trigger, to pull a sled uphill.* **2.** to tug at (something) with the fingers, etc.: *to pull a person's hair, to pull a rope.* **3.** to pick; pluck: *to pull flowers.* **4.** to draw out; extract: *to pull a tooth.* **5.** to tear, rend, or separate into parts by pulling: *to pull a book into shreds, to pull a house down, to pull an argument to pieces.* **6.** to stretch too far; strain: *The football player pulled a ligament in his leg.* **7.** *U.S.* to draw out (a gun, knife, etc.) in a threatening manner. **8. a.** to be provided or rowed with: *The boat pulls eight oars.* **b.** to operate (an oar) in rowing. **c.** to move (a boat) by rowing. **9.** *Slang.* to carry through; perform: *Don't try to pull that trick on me again.* **10.** *Golf.* to hit (a ball) so that it curves to the left; hook: *He pulled his tee shot slightly and the ball seemed to be bound for a bunker* (News Chronicle). **11.** *Baseball.* to hit (a ball) along or near the foul line on the same side of the plate as that on which the batter stands: *to pull the ball into right field.* **12.** *Cricket.* to hit (a ball pitched on the wicket or on the off side) to the on side. **13.** to hold back, especially to keep from winning: *to pull a horse in a race, to pull punches in a fight.* **14.** *Printing.* to take (an impression, proof, or copy) by printing: *Proofs of editorial and advertising matter are pulled on glossy enamel paper* (Time).
—*v.i.* **1.** to tug with the fingers: *He pulled at his tie nervously.* **2.** to move, usually with effort or force: *I pulled ahead of my brother in the race.* **3.** to row: *Pull for the shore.* **4.** to suck: *to pull on a cigar.* **5.** to drink, especially heartily or thirstily.

pull apart, a. to separate into pieces by pulling: *The children pulled the flowers apart.* **b.** to be severely critical of: *to pull apart a term paper.*

pull down, a. to demolish; destroy: *Desirous of pulling the house down and building a new one on its site* (Law Reports). **b.** to lower: *He should pull down the blind* (Dickens). **c.** to depose or dethrone (a ruler); overthrow (a government) by force: *In such times a sovereign like Louis the Fifteenth . . . would have been pulled down before his misgovernment had lasted for a month* (Macaulay). **d.** to depress in health, spirits, etc.: *I did pull down myself, fasting* (Philip Sidney). **e.** to seize; overcome: *You weren't within half a field of the fair unknown when they pulled the fox down* (Hawley Smart). **f.** to earn: *For all the money they demand and pull down, Brazilian dockers get precious little work done* (Time).

pull for, *Slang.* **a.** to give help to: *to pull for the underdog.* **b.** to support enthusiastically: *The final, official word on the international grand prizes had gone out, . . . and nothing could dampen the enthusiasm of those who had been pulling for Rauschenberg from the start* (Harper's).

pull in, a. *Slang.* to arrest (a person): *to pull in every known gambler in town.* **b.** to stop; check: *I must pull in, or my letter will never end* (Thomas Twining). **c.** to arrive: *He pulled in this morning.*

pull off, a. to remove by or as if by stripping: *to pull off the bark of a sycamore branch. I could bash his head against the corner of the dock before the RCMP guard could pull me off* (Maclean's). **b.** *Slang.* to do successfully; succeed in: *It is an exceptionally difficult trick, but they see no reason why*

 PRONUNCIATION KEY: hat, āge, cãre, fär; let, ēqual, tėrm; it, īce; hot, ōpen, ôrder; oil, out; cup, půt, rüle;

with practice they should not pull it off (Manchester Guardian).
pull oneself together, to gather one's faculties, energy, etc.: *Then she pulled herself together to write to Lord Melbourne* (Lytton Strachey).
pull out, *Especially U.S.* **a.** to leave; move away from: *The train pulled out of the station.* **b.** to withdraw from a venture, undertaking, etc.: *He was pulling out of the Pike County project while there was still plenty of work* (Harper's).
pull over, to bring a vehicle to the side of the road or street: *I considered that I had not time to pull over to my near side* (Morning Post).
pull through, to overcome a difficult or dangerous situation, especially by recovering one's health: *They think she'll pull through—and the boy too* (Graham Greene).
pull together, to work in harmony; get on together: *Let . . . danger appear . . . then they all pulled together* (Frederick Marryat). *Where tenants for life and trustees did not pull together, sales could not in such cases be effected* (Law Times).
pull up, a. to tear up; uproot: *The weeds themselves must be pulled up by the root* (Adam Dickson). **b.** to cause to stop; stop: *to pull up . . . a post chaise on the highway* (J.H. Vaux). **c.** to check oneself in a course of action: *But it is a dangerous slope we are on, and unless we pull up now it may be hard to stop at the point we want* (Manchester Guardian). **d.** to reprimand; rebuke: [*He*] *avowed his unalterable determination to "pull up" the cabman in the morning* (Dickens). **e.** to move ahead: *At forty yards Harding invariably led by a yard or more, but from this onward Cary pulled up, passing him at about sixty yards* (Outing). **f.** to jolt; startle: *The reader is pulled up more smartly when the general* [*MacArthur*] *records how he listened, then aged 70, to the cautious advice of a military conference on the Korean War* (London Times).
—*n.* **1.** the act or effort of pulling: *The boy gave a pull at the rope.* **2.** a difficult climb, journey, or other effort: *It was a hard pull to get up the hill.* **3.** a handle, rope, ring, or other thing to pull by: *a bell pull, a curtain pull.* **4.** a drink. **5.** a suck: *a long pull at a cigar.* **6.** a pulling of the ball in golf, baseball, cricket, etc. **7.** *U.S. Slang.* influence; advantage: *to use political pull to get a job. They used their . . . "pull" in Italian banking to favour German enterprises* (H.G. Wells).
[Old English *pullian*] —**pull'er,** *n.*
—**Syn.** *v.t., v.i.* **1. Pull, tug, jerk** mean to draw toward oneself. **Pull** is the general word meaning to draw (or try to draw) toward or after oneself or in a specified or implied direction: *Pull the curtains across.* **Tug** means to pull hard or long, but does not always mean causing the thing or person to move: *The dog tugged at the tablecloth.* **Jerk** means to pull, push, or twist quickly and suddenly: *She jerked her hand away. He jerked his hat off.*
pull·back (pu̇l'bak'), *n.* **1.** a withdrawal: *Washington hopes that the Kremlin may conceive it to be in its own interest to make further pullbacks* (Atlantic). **2.** a retrenchment.
pull·down (pu̇l'doun'), *adj.* that can be pulled down or lowered: *pulldown table legs.*
pulled wool (pu̇ld), wool removed from the pelts of slaughtered sheep.
pul·let (pu̇l'it), *n.* a young hen, usually less than a year old. [< Old French *poulet* young fowl, or *poulette* young hen (diminutives) < *poule* hen; see POULTRY]
pul·ley (pu̇l'ē), *n., pl.* **-leys. 1.** a wheel with a grooved rim in which a rope can run, and so change the direction of the pull: *Our flag is raised to the top of a pole by a rope and two pulleys.* **2.** a set of such wheels, used to increase the power applied. **3.** a wheel used to transfer power by driving a belt or being driven by a belt that moves some other part of the machine. [< Old French *poulie,* perhaps < Medieval Latin *poleia,* ultimately < Greek *polídion* (diminutive) < *pólos* axle, pole < *poleîn* to revolve]

Pulley (def. 1)

pull hitter, a batter who consistently pulls the ball: *With a left-handed pull hitter coming to bat, the outfield was shifted to right.*
pull-in (pu̇l'in'), *n. British.* a place to obtain refreshments by the roadside; drive-in: *Many motorists, when . . . they realize that they have no* [*help*] *of any kind but a board saying "Good Pull-In 300 Yds," take to foul language* (Punch).
Pull·man car (pu̇l'mən), *U.S.* **1.** a railroad car with berths or small rooms for passengers to sleep in; sleeping car. **2.** a railroad car with especially comfortable seats. [American English < George M. *Pullman,* 1831-1897, an American inventor, who designed it]
pullman slipper, a soft slipper that can be folded compactly for traveling.
pull-on (pu̇l'on', -ôn'), *adj.* that is pulled on to be worn, as a garment having no fastenings: *a pull-on blouse or sweater.* —*n.* a pull-on garment: *Dotted black and white pull-ons match stretch nylon gloves* (New Yorker).
pul·lo·rum disease (pə lôr'əm, -lōr'-), a disease of chickens, turkeys, ducks, and some other birds, often fatal to the very young, caused by a toxin-forming bacterium. It affects the reproductive organs of hens with the consequence that chicks may have a well-developed infection when they are hatched. [< Latin *pullōrum,* genitive plural of *pullus* young fowl]
pull·out (pu̇l'out'), *n.* **1.** a withdrawal, especially of troops: *The pullout may start this week; Gaza troops will exit by the overland motor route* (Wall Street Journal). **2.** (of aircraft) the action of recovering from a dive and returning to level flight: *Engineers and metallurgists worked for years to develop these planes that will withstand the centrifugal forces of high-speed turns and pullouts* (James Phinney Baxter III). —*adj.* that pulls out: *a pullout shelf of a desk.*
pull·o·ver (pu̇l'ō'vər), *adj.* (of a garment) put on by pulling it over the head: *Among them are pullover dresses with fairly high round necks* (New Yorker). —*n.* a sweater put on by pulling it over the head: *We hunted out an ancient pullover of her husband's* (Punch).
pull strap, a small strap attached to the top of a shoe or boot to assist in pulling it on easily: *They . . . had the Presidential seal on each boot and the initials LBJ on the pull straps* (New York Times).
pull-toy (pu̇l'toi'), *n.* a toy that is intended to be pulled about on wheels by a child: *Nine bright-painted wooden soldiers . . . ride around in a pull-toy* (New Yorker).
pul·lu·late (pul'yə lāt), *v.i.,* **-lat·ed, -lat·ing. 1.** (of a seed) to sprout; germinate. **2.** (of a plant or animal) to breed; multiply. **3.** to be developed or produced abundantly. **4.** to teem; swarm: *Patrons were assailed with . . . mashed potatoes pullulating with marshmallow whip* (New Yorker). [< Latin *pullulāre* (with English *-ate*[1]) to sprout out and spread < *pullulus* a sprout or bud (diminutive) < *pullus* the young of any animal; sprout of a plant]
pul·lu·la·tion (pul'yə lā'shən), *n.* **1.** sprouting; germination; generation; production. **2.** offspring; progeny. **3.** *Botany.* generation or reproduction by budding.
pull-up (pu̇l'up'), *n.* **1.** (in calisthenics) the action of chinning oneself: *I've done push-ups and pull-ups and sit-ups until my muscles twitched like a thoroughbred's flanks* (Maclean's). **2.** *British.* a pull-in: *a favourite pull-up for cyclists* (London Chronicle).
pul·mo·cu·ta·ne·ous (pul'mō kyü tā'nē əs), *adj.* having to do with or supplying the lungs and skin: *pulmocutaneous arteries, pulmocutaneous vessels.* [< Latin *pulmō, -ōnis* lung + English *cutaneous*]
pul·mom·e·ter (pul mom'ə tər), *n.* an instrument for measuring the capacity of the lungs; spirometer.
pul·mom·e·try (pul mom'ə trē), *n.* the measurement of the capacity of the lungs; spirometry.
pul·mo·nar·y (pul'mə ner'ē), *adj.* **1.** of or having to do with the lungs. Pneumonia is a pulmonary disease. **2.** having lungs or similar organs. [< Latin *pulmōnārius* < *pulmō, -ōnis* lung. Related to Greek *pleúmōn,* or *pneúmōn* lung.]
pulmonary anthrax, woolsorters' disease.
pulmonary artery, the artery which carries venous blood directly from the right ventricle of the heart to the lungs: *As it forks again, we take the pulmonary artery to the lungs* (A. M. Winchester).
pulmonary tuberculosis, tuberculosis of the lungs.
pulmonary valve, a set of three crescent-shaped flaps at the opening of the pulmonary artery; the semilunar valves: *When the ventricle contracts . . . the pulmonary valve is opened and blood flows through* (Scientific American).
pulmonary vein, one of the four veins which carry oxygenated blood directly from the lungs to the left auricle of the heart.
pul·mo·nate (pul'mə nāt, -nit), *adj.* **1.** having lungs or lunglike organs. **2.** of or belonging to a group of gastropod mollusks that have lunglike sacs and include most land snails and slugs, and some aquatic snails. —*n.* a pulmonate gastropod. [< Latin *pulmō, -ōnis* lung + English *-ate*[1]]
pul·mon·ic (pul mon'ik), *adj.* **1.** pulmonary. **2.** pneumonic. [< French *pulmonique* < Latin *pulmō, -ōnis* lung + French *-ique* -ic]
Pul·mo·tor (pu̇l'mō'tər, pul'-), *n. Trademark.* a mechanical apparatus for producing artificial respiration which pumps air or oxygen in and out of the lungs, used in cases of drowning, asphyxiation, etc.; respirator. [< Latin *pulmō* lung + English *motor*]
pulp (pulp), *n.* **1.** the soft part of any fruit or vegetable: *the pulp of an orange.* **2.** the soft inner part of a tooth, containing blood vessels and nerves: *Even teeth in which the pulps had been removed or destroyed were found to have some traces of radiophosphorus* (Shirley Hughes). **3.** any soft, wet mass: *Paper is made from wood pulp.* **4.** *Slang.* a magazine printed on cheap paper, and usually containing matter of a cheap sensational nature: *Commercial writers who once filled the pulps and slicks with short stories have arrived here* (Maclean's). **5.** *Mining.* **a.** pulverized ore mixed with water. **b.** dry pulverized ore.
—*v.t.* **1.** to reduce to pulp: *Extracts from the various organs must then be removed and pulped and . . . injected into the patient* (Punch). **2.** to remove the pulp from. —*v.i.* to become pulpy.
[< Latin *pulpa*]
pul·pal (pul'pəl), *adj.* of or having to do with pulp.
pulp·board (pulp'bôrd', -bōrd'), *n.* a kind of millboard made directly from paper pulp instead of sheets of paper.
pulp·er (pul'pər), *n.* a machine for reducing fruit, wood, etc., to pulp.
pulp·i·fi·ca·tion (pul'pə fə kā'shən), *n.* the act or process of converting into pulp.
pulp·i·fi·er (pul'pə fī'ər), *n.* a pulper.
pulp·i·fy (pul'pə fī), *v.t.,* **-fied, -fy·ing.** to reduce to pulp.
pulp·i·ness (pul'pē nis), *n.* the quality or state of being pulpy; softness; flabbiness.
pul·pit (pu̇l'pit), *n.* **1.** a platform or raised structure in a church from which a clergyman preaches: *This eloquent and ornate carving on a church pulpit was done by Indian hands* (Newsweek). **2. a.** preachers or preachings: *The pulpit is against horse racing on Sunday.* **b.** the Christian ministry. **3.** a safety rail, usually of iron, lashed to the end of the bowsprit of a whaling vessel to insure the safety of the harpooner. [< Late Latin *pulpitum* < Latin, scaffold, platform]

Pulpit (def. 1)

pul·pit·eer (pu̇l'pə tir'), *n.* a preacher by profession (used in an unfriendly way): *These words came from no Sunday pulpiteer, but from the assistant to the president* (Time). [< *pulpit* + *-eer*]
pul·pit·er (pu̇l'pə tər), *n.* a pulpiteer.
pulp·less (pulp'lis), *adj.* lacking pulp.
pulp mill, a mill to convert wood into pulp for making paper and other products: *Every corn stalk and bit of straw will be grist for Israel's new pulp mill* (Science News Letter).
pul·pous (pul'pəs), *adj.* pulpy.
pulp·wood (pulp'wu̇d'), *n.* **1.** wood reduced to pulp for making paper. **2.** wood suitable for making paper.

pulp·y (pul′pē), *adj.*, **pulp·i·er, pulp·i·est.** of pulp; like pulp; soft.

pul·que (pu̇l′kē; *Spanish* pül′kā), *n.* an alcoholic beverage made from the fermented juice of certain agaves. Pulque is much used in Mexico and Central America. [American English < Mexican Spanish *pulque*, apparently < a Nahuatl word]

pul·sant (pul′sənt), *adj.* pulsating; throbbing.

pul·sar (pul′sər), *n.* a radio star that emits pulsed radio waves; a pulsating radio source: *Dr. Shklovskiy figures the distance of this pulsar at about 1,000 light years. In his opinion pulsars should be powerful cosmic ray sources* (Science News). [< *pulse* + *-ar*, as in *quasar*]

pul·sate (pul′sāt), *v.i.*, **-sat·ed, -sat·ing. 1.** to beat; throb. **2.** to vibrate; quiver. [< Latin *pulsāre* (with English *-ate*[1]) (frequentative) < *pellere* to beat]

pul·sa·tile (pul′sə təl), *adj.* **1.** pulsating; throbbing. **2.** played by striking.

pul·sa·til·la (pul′sə til′ə), *n.* **1.** any of various perennial herbs of the crowfoot family with white or purplish flowers, certain kinds of which are used medicinally; pasqueflower. **2.** an extract or preparation obtained from such a plant. [< New Latin *Pulsatilla* the genus name < Medieval Latin *pulsatilla* (diminutive) < Latin *pulsāta* driven about < *pulsāre* to pulsate (because the flower is easily driven about by the wind)]

pul·sa·tion (pul sā′shən), *n.* **1.** beating; throbbing: *This would suggest some slow pulsation taking place in the sun which gradually alters the strength of these solar streamers* (E.F. George). **2.** a beat; throb. **3.** vibration; quiver.

pul·sa·tive (pul′sə tiv), *adj.* pulsating. —**pul′sa·tive·ly,** *adv.*

pul·sa·tor (pul sā′tər), *n.* **1.** a machine that pulsates, especially a kind of pump. **2.** a device for separating diamonds from dirt. [< Latin *pulsātor, -ōris* a beater, knocker < *pulsāre* to pulsate]

pul·sa·to·ry (pul′sə tôr′ē, -tōr′-), *adj.* pulsating; throbbing.

pulse[1] (puls), *n., v.,* **pulsed, puls·ing.** —*n.* **1.** the beating of the heart; changing flow of blood in the arteries caused by the beating of the heart: *A wave of distention, the pulse, travels along the arteries* (Harbaugh and Goodrich). **2.** any regular, measured beat: *the pulse in music, the pulse of an engine.* **3.** feeling; sentiment: *the pulse of the nation.* **4.** *Electronics.* an electromagnetic wave, or a modulation of an electromagnetic wave, which lasts a short time: *In radar, for instance, the signals used are pulses, which rise and fall in amplitude over a short time* (John Pierce).

pulses, each successive beat or throb of the arteries or heart: *This means that pulses, to be counted, must be analyzed by both detectors simultaneously* (Science).

[< Latin *pulsus, -ūs* < *pellere* to beat]

—*v.i.* to beat; throb; vibrate: *His heart pulsed with excitement. Theodore Dreiser could make a page pulse with life* (Newsweek).

[< Latin *pulsāre* (frequentative < *pellere* to beat. Doublet of PUSH.] —**pulse′like′,** *adj.*

pulse[2] (puls), *n.* **1.** peas, beans, and lentils, used as food. **2.** a plant which yields such seeds. [< Old French *pols,* and *pouls* < Latin *puls, pultis* porridge; see POULTICE]

pulse·beat (puls′bēt′), *n.* **1.** a beat or pulsation of an artery: *The doctors noted irregular breathing movements and a possible heartbeat, although they could not detect a pulsebeat* (The Warren Report). **2.** a sign or suggestion of feeling, sentiment, etc.: *Instead of capturing the hypnotic quality of Marquand's even-tempered prose, the writer may find he has only reproduced Marquand's low emotional pulsebeat* (Time).

pulse-code modulation (puls′kōd′), a system of radio transmission in which successive electromagnetic waves of short duration are sampled periodically, quantized, and transmitted by code: *Pulse Code Modulation . . . is being used experimentally in the United Kingdom for sending telephone calls* (London Times).

pulsed (pulst), *adj.* that come in pulses; having pulsations: *The natural mode of communication with or between machines is by means of pulsed electrical signals* (John R. Pierce).

pulse·jet (puls′jet′), *n.* a type of jet engine into which the air necessary for the burning of the fuel is admitted by valves in spurts: *This helicopter was powered with pulsejets, which is what the Nazi V-1 buzz bombs were* (Harper's).

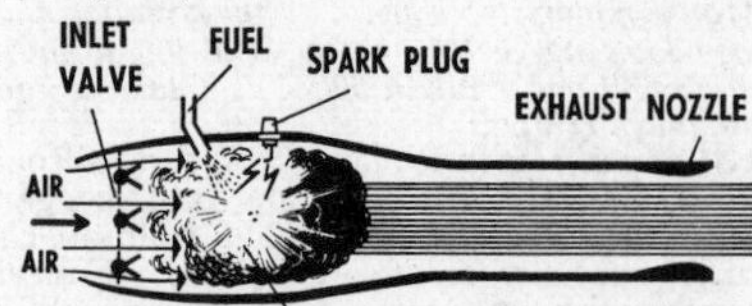

Pulsejet Engine creates thrust by ejecting high velocity gases rearward through an exhaust nozzle.

pulse·less (puls′lis), *adj.* **1.** having no pulse or pulsation; motionless; lifeless: *It has even been able to monitor the heart rate during profound shock when the patient was clinically pulseless* (Science News Letter). **2.** without feeling or pity.

pulse-po·si·tion modulation (puls′pə-zish′ən), pulse-time modulation.

puls·er (pul′sər), *n. Electronics.* an instrument that produces recurring high voltage pulses of short duration: *The voltage required . . . is provided by an electronic pulser, which removes the voltage from the crystal in less than 10 nanoseconds* (New Scientist).

puls·es (pul′siz), *n.pl.* See under **pulse**[1], *n.*

pulse-tak·er (puls′tā′kər), *n. Informal.* a person who seeks to find out what views, sentiments, etc., are held and by what proportion of the people, or any particular segment of the people: *Farm pulse-takers now predict a similar outcome in votes late this year* (Wall Street Journal).

pulse-tak·ing (puls′tā′king), *n. Informal.* the conducting of a survey to find out or check what views, sentiments, etc., are popular in respect to a subject.

pulse-time modulation (puls′tīm′), a system of radio transmission in which successive electromagnetic waves of short duration, timed to transmit the amplitude and pitch of the signal, are produced by modulation of the carrier.

pulse warmer, a covering for the wrist to protect against cold; wristlet.

pulse wave, the wave of raised tension and arterial expansion which starts from the aorta with each ventricular systole and travels to the capillaries.

pul·sim·e·ter (pul sim′ə tər), *n.* an instrument for measuring and recording the strength or quickness of the pulse. [< Latin *pulsus* pulse, beat + English *-meter*]

pul·sion (pul′shən), *n.* the act of driving or pushing forward. [< Latin *pulsiō, -ōnis* < *pulsāre;* see PULSE[1], verb]

pul·som·e·ter (pul som′ə tər), *n.* **1.** a pump operated by steam but having no piston. **2.** a pulsimeter. [< *pulse*[1] + *-meter*]

pul·ta·ceous (pul tā′shəs), *adj.* resembling pap; semifluid; pulpy. [< Latin *puls, pultis* pottage, mush + English *-aceous*]

pu·lu (pü′lü), *n.* a yellowish, silky, vegetable wool obtained from the base of the leafstalks of the Hawaiian tree ferns, formerly used for stuffing pillows and mattresses. [< Hawaiian *pulu* (literally) wet, soaked]

pul·ver·a·ble (pul′vər ə bəl), *adj.* that can be reduced to dust or powder.

pul·ver·ise (pul′və rīz), *v.t., v.i.,* **-ised, -is·ing.** *Especially British.* pulverize.

pul·ver·iz·a·ble (pul′və rī′zə bəl), *adj.* pulverable.

pul·ver·i·za·tion (pul′vər ə zā′shən), *n.* the act of pulverizing, or reducing to dust or powder.

pul·ver·ize (pul′və rīz), *v.,* **-ized, -iz·ing.** —*v.t.* **1.** to grind to powder or dust. **2.** to break to pieces; demolish: *to pulverize an enemy force by bombardment, to pulverize the hopes of the people.* —*v.i.* to become dust: *The stern old faiths have all pulverized* (Emerson). [< Late Latin *pulverizāre* < Latin *pulvis, -eris* dust]

pul·ver·iz·er (pul′və rī′zər), *n.* **1.** a person or thing that pulverizes. **2.** a machine for breaking the soil, crushing stone, grinding grain, etc. **3.** a bird that habitually rolls or wallows in the dust or takes sand baths.

pul·ver·u·lence (pul ver′yə ləns, -ver′ə-), *n.* dustiness; powder.

pul·ver·u·lent (pul ver′yə lənt, -ə-), *adj.* **1.** consisting of fine powder. **2.** crumbling to dust: *pulverulent rock.* **3.** covered with dust or powder. [< Latin *pulverulentus* full of dust < *pulvis, -eris* dust]

pul·vil·lus (pul vil′əs), *n., pl.* **-vil·li** (-vil′ī). a cushionlike pad or process on the foot of an insect, as the fly, by which it can adhere to walls, ceilings, etc. [< Latin *pulvillus* small pillow (diminutive) < *pulvīnus* cushion]

pul·vi·nate (pul′və nāt), *adj.* cushion-shaped; cushionlike. [< Latin *pulvīnātus* cushionlike < *pulvīnus* cushion, bulge]

pul·vi·nat·ed (pul′və nā′tid), *adj.* pulvinate.

pul·vi·nus (pul vī′nəs), *n., pl.* **-ni** (-nī). any cushionlike swelling at the base of a leaf or leaflet at the point of junction with the axis: *The pulvinus is sensitive to environal stimuli* (Heber W. Youngken). [< Latin *pulvīnus* cushion, bulge]

pu·ma (pyü′mə), *n., pl.* **-mas** or (*collectively*) **-ma. 1.** the cougar, a large American wildcat; mountain lion. See **cougar** for picture. **2.** its fur. [< Spanish *puma* < Quechua (Peru)]

pum·ice (pum′is), *n., v.,* **-iced, -ic·ing.** —*n.* a light, spongy stone thrown up from volcanoes, used for cleaning, smoothing, and polishing: *Rub your hands with pumice to remove the ink. Most of the fragments are . . . in microscopic slivers or in frothy bits of pumice* (Gilluly, and others). —*v.t.* to clean, smooth, or polish with pumice: *to pumice one's skin. The slab is then pumiced to reduce it to a level surface* (Ernest Spon). [Middle English *pomice* < Old French *pomis,* learned borrowing from Late Latin *pōmex,* for Latin *pūmex, -icis.* Doublet of POUNCE[2].]

pu·mi·ceous (pyü mish′əs), *adj.* consisting of or resembling pumice.

pumice stone, pumice.

pum·mel (pum′əl), *v.,* **-meled, -mel·ing** or (*especially British*) **-melled, -mel·ling,** *n.* —*v.t., v.i.* to beat; beat with the fists; pommel. —*n.* a pommel. [variant of *pommel*]

pum·me·lo (pum′ə lō), *n., pl.* **-los.** pomelo: *No one is sure just how [the grapefruit] originated from its ancestors, variously called the pummelo or shaddock* (Science News Letter).

pump[1] (pump), *n.* an apparatus or machine for forcing liquids, air, or gas into or out of things: *a water pump, an oil pump. The design of rocket pumps again demands careful choice of materials* (D. Hurden). See also **well**[2] for picture.

—*v.t.* **1.** to move (liquids, air, etc.) by a pump: *Pump water from the well into a pail.* **2.** to blow air into. **3.** to remove water, etc., from by a pump: *to pump out a flooded cellar. Pump the well dry.* **4.** to move by, or as if by, a pump handle: *Eager greeters pumped his hands and bussed his glowing pink cheeks* (Time). **5.** to draw, force, etc., as if from a pump: *to pump air into one's lungs. Bill purchases by the Federal Reserve naturally have the opposite effect of pumping money into the banks* (Wall Street Journal). **6.** to shoot or fire in a stream: *to pump shells into the enemy lines.* **7.** to get information out of; try to get information out of: *Don't let him pump you.* —*v.i.* **1.** to work a pump. **2.** to work as a pump does: *to pump for words.* **3.** to move up and down like a pump handle.

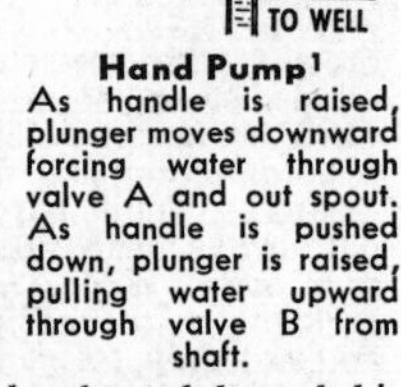

Hand Pump[1] As handle is raised, plunger moves downward forcing water through valve A and out spout. As handle is pushed down, plunger is raised, pulling water upward through valve B from shaft.

pump up, to inflate (an automobile tire, a football, etc.) by pumping air into it: *to pump up the tire on a bicycle.*

[Middle English *pompe,* perhaps < Germanic (compare earlier Dutch *pompe* a conduit)] —**pump′er,** *n.*

pump[2] (pump), *n.* a low-cut shoe with no fasteners: *black patent-leather dancing pumps.* [origin uncertain]

pump·a·ble (pum′pə bəl), *adj.* that can be pumped: *It is a major problem to maintain a low-viscosity, readily pumpable mud at a high specific gravity* (New Scientist).

pump-ac·tion (pump′ak′shən), *adj.* (of a shotgun or rifle) having a mechanism that ejects the used shell, reloads, and cocks the piece, by pushing a slide forward and back on the underside of the barrel.

pump·age (pum′pij), *n.* **1.** the work done in pumping. **2.** the quantity pumped: *Maximum pumpage rate of all stations totals 215,000,000 gallons daily* (Wall Street Journal).

pum·per·nick·el (pum′pər nik′əl), *n.* a

coarse, slightly sour bread made of unbolted rye: *There was also a large plate of cold cuts, real German pumpernickel . . . and a bowl of fruit and nuts* (New Yorker). [American English < German *Pumpernickel* (originally) bumpkin; perhaps (literally) lumbering Nicholas]

pump gun, a rifle or shotgun from which a used shell may be ejected and a fresh one placed in firing position from a magazine by pushing a slide on the under side of the barrel forward and back.

pump house, the place where a pump or pumps are installed and operate.

pump·ing station (pum′ping), an installation of pumps used to propel water, oil, or gas, etc., through a pipeline, an irrigation canal, etc.: *The pumpline had to be shut down last November when Syrian political enthusiasts blew up pumping stations* (New Yorker).

pum·pi·on (pum′pē ən), *n. Obsolete.* a pumpkin.

pump·kin (pump′kin, pung′-), *n.* **1.** a large, roundish, orange-yellow fruit of a trailing vine of the gourd family, used for making pies, as a vegetable, and as food for stock. **2.** the vine that it grows on. **3.** any of certain large squashes.

some pumpkins or **punkins,** *U.S. Informal.* a person or thing of considerable consequence: *She is some punkins, that I wun't deny, For ain't she some related to you 'n' I?* (James Russell Lowell). *A man whose sneer can do all that is clearly some pumpkins* (New Yorker).

[alteration of earlier *pumpion* < earlier French *pompon,* for *pepon,* learned borrowing from Latin *pepō, -ōnis* melon, pumpkin < Greek *pépōn, -onos* (originally) cooked by the sun, ripe]

pumpkin pine, a variety of white pine noted for the fine grain of its wood: . . . *an antique dining table carved from pumpkin pine* (New York Times).

pump·kin·seed (pump′kin sēd′, pung′-), *n.* **1.** the flattish, oval seed of a pumpkin. **2.** any of certain small fresh-water sunfishes of North America.

pump-ox·y·gen·a·tor (pump′ok′sə jə nā′-tər), *n.* a mechanical device which oxygenates the blood and circulates it throughout the body, taking over the functions of the heart and lungs during major chest surgery; heart-lung machine: *The successful development of pump-oxygenators . . . has opened up a new field of direct-vision cardiac surgery* (New Scientist).

pump priming, government expenditure, especially on public works, intended to stimulate business and thus to relieve depression and unemployment: *The Administration balked at the hysterical demands for unlimited pump priming and boondoggles* (Wall Street Journal). —**pump′-prim′ing,** *adj.*

pump rod, the piston rod of a pump.

pump room, 1. a room or building where a pump is worked. **2.** a room or place at a spa or mineral spring where the water is dispensed for drinking, etc.: *I was yesterday at the pump room, and drank about a pint of the water* (Tobias Smollett).

pump well, 1. a well having a pump. **2.** a compartment containing the pumps of a ship.

pun[1] (pun), *n., v.,* **punned, pun·ning.** —*n.* the use of a word where it can have two or more different meanings; a play on words: *"We must all hang together, or we shall all hang separately" is a famous pun by Benjamin Franklin.* —*v.i., v.t.* to make puns. [origin uncertain. Compare Italian *puntiglio* fine point]

pun[2] (pun), *v.t.,* **punned, pun·ning.** *Especially British Dialect.* to pound; reduce to powder by beating; beat. [variant of *pound*[2]]

pu·na (pü′nä), *n.* **1.** a high, arid plateau, in the Peruvian Andes. **2.** sickness due to high altitude. [< Spanish *puna* < Quechua (Peru)]

punch[1] (punch), *v.t.* **1.** to hit with the fist: *They punched each other like boxers. You punch the ball too hard.* **2.** *Informal.* to deliver with force or effectiveness: . . . *heroines and villains who punched home Verdi's galloping melodies with tremendous gusto* (New York Times). **3.** *U.S.* to herd or drive (cattle): *"When I got out of school I really wasn't sure what I wanted to do," he recalls. "So I went back to punching cows"* (Wall Street Journal). —*v.i.* to give a punch or punches; hit; strike: *Boys punch; girls sometimes slap.* [Middle English *punchen* goad (cattle); stab. Apparently related to POUNCE[1], POUNCE[3], PUNCH[2], PUNCHEON[2].]

—*n.* **1.** a quick thrust or blow: *Patterson has a punch, exceptional poise for his age* (Newsweek). **2.** *Informal.* vigorous force or effectiveness: *United States satellites, although smaller than the Russian sputniks, will pack as much scientific punch* (Science News Letter).

beat to the punch, to do anything sooner than (one's opponent): *There was no claim that Soviet scientists had beaten their American counterparts to the punch* (New York Times).

pull (one's) punches, to act or speak with fear, caution, or hesitation; be overly restrained: *The company is pulling its punches because of monopoly fears* (Wall Street Journal).

[perhaps contraction of *puncheon*[2]] —**punch′less,** *adj.*

—**Syn.** *v.t., v.i.* **1.** strike, poke, cuff.

punch[2] (punch), *v.t.* **1.** to pierce, cut, stamp, force, or drive with a punch: *The train conductor punched our tickets.* **2.** to make (a hole) with a punch or any pointed instrument. —*v.i.* to insert a card in a time clock to have the time of one's arrival or departure recorded on it: *He punched in and out regularly but when Personnel checked up later they were aghast to discover the new man was unknown* (Maclean's).

—*n.* **1.** a tool or apparatus for piercing, perforating, or stamping materials, impressing a design, forcing nails beneath a surface, driving bolts out of holes, and the like. **2.** a tool for making holes. [apparently contraction of *puncheon*[2]. Apparently related to PUNCH[1].]

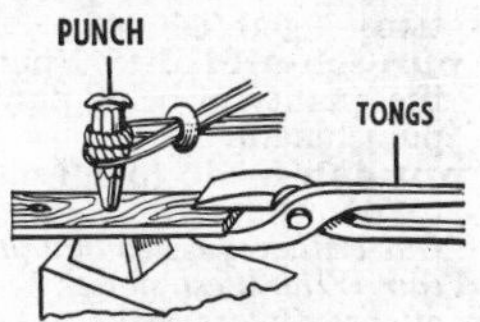

Punch[2] (def. 1)
A hole is punched in the board by striking the punch with a hammer. Tongs hold the board in place.

—**Syn.** *v.t.* **1.** puncture, perforate.

punch[3] (punch), *n.* a drink made of different liquids mixed together. [probably < Hindustani *pãnch* five < Sanskrit *pañca* (because of the number of ingredients in the drink)]

Punch (punch), *n.* the principal character in a Punch-and-Judy show, a hook-nosed, humpbacked little puppet.

pleased as Punch, very much pleased: *She was pleased as Punch with all her birthday presents.*

[contraction of *punchinello*]

Punch-and-Ju·dy show (punch′ ən jü′-dē), a traditional English puppet show in which Punch quarrels violently with his wife Judy.

punch·ball (punch′bôl′), *n.* a variation of baseball, usually played in city streets, in which a rubber ball is punched with the fist instead of being hit with a bat.

punch·board (punch′bôrd′, -bōrd′), *n.* a gambling device consisting of a board containing many holes in which are rolled slips of paper to be punched out by a player who pays for the privilege, a few of which reward him with a prize.

punch bowl, a large bowl for serving punch.

punch card, a card on which data are recorded by means of holes punched in positions determined by a prearranged code, for use in data processing by machine, machine bookkeeping, etc.: *Information . . . is fed into the computer that turns out navigational data on punch cards* (Scientific American).

punch-drunk (punch′drungk′), *adj.* (of a boxer) afflicted with a condition resulting from a cerebral concussion, or small hemorrhage in the brain, the symptoms of which include a marked loss of muscular coordination and the ability to orient oneself in time or place, resembling drunkenness to some extent: *I executed a nervous, almost dance-like step that characterized a punch-drunk boxer out of Hemingway* (New Yorker).

punch-drunk·en·ness (punch′drung′kən-nis), *n.* the condition of being punch-drunk.

punched card (puncht), a punch card.

punched tape, paper tape punched for processing in various machines in the same fashion and for the same purposes as punch cards: *The punched tape may then be processed into the vital records and reports you need, either through your own electronic computer or at a computer service center* (Maclean's).

pun·cheon[1] (pun′chən), *n.* **1.** a large cask for liquor. **2.** the amount that it holds. [< Old French *poinchon, poinçon,* and *ponson;* origin uncertain. The Old French forms are identical with those of *puncheon*[2], but there seems to be no connection between the words.]

pun·cheon[2] (pun′chən), *n.* **1.** a slab of timber or a piece of a split log, with the face roughly smoothed: *She did it by boiling lye soap out of skillet grease and wood ashes, scrubbing puncheon floors . . .* (Harper's). **2.** a short, upright piece of wood in the frame of a building. **3.** *Obsolete.* an instrument for punching; punch. [< Old French *poinchon,* and *poinçon* < Vulgar Latin *pūnctiō, -ōnis* a punch, awl (in Latin, a pricking) < Latin *pungere* to pierce]

punch·er (pun′chər), *n.* **1.** a person or thing that punches. **2.** *Western U.S.* a cowpuncher: *Judge Henry gave me charge of him and some other punchers taking cattle* (Owen Wister). [American English < *punch*[1] + *-er*[1]]

Pun·chi·nel·lo (pun′chə nel′ō), *n.* **1.** the principal character in a traditional Italian puppet show, the prototype of Punch. **2.** punchinello. [earlier *polichinello* < dialectal Italian *Pulcinella,* probably (originally) < diminutive form of *pulcino* chick < Latin *pullus* chick]

pun·chi·nel·lo (pun′chə nel′ō), *n., pl.* **-los** or **-loes. 1.** a clown. **2.** any grotesque or absurd person or thing.

punch·ing bag (pun′ching), a leather bag filled with air or stuffed, to be hung up and punched with the fists for exercise.

punch line, the line or sentence in a story, play, or drama which makes or enforces the point: *When you find five-year-old kids giving you the punch lines to classic jokes, it seems as though everybody's hep* (New Yorker).

punch mark, a mark punched on metal, a coin, etc., for identification or checking purposes.

punch press, a press used to cut, indent, or shape metals.

punch-up (punch′up′), *n. British Informal.* a fight: *Enter the headmaster into a classroom punch-up* (London Times).

punch·y (pun′chē), *adj.,* **punch·i·er, punch·i·est.** *Informal.* **1.** having lots of punch; terse; hard-hitting: *His ideas were ingenious, naïve, droll, and punchy* (New Yorker). **2.** punch-drunk: *It's about a punchy ex-fighter whom a criminal employs as a murder weapon* (New York Times).

punc·tate (pungk′tāt), *adj.* dotted; spotted. [< Latin *punctum* a point, prick; (originally) neuter past participle of *pungere*]

punc·tat·ed (pungk′tā tid), *adj.* punctate.

punc·ta·tim (pungk tā′tim), *adv. Latin.* point for point.

punc·ta·tion (pungk tā′shən), *n.* **1.** a spotted condition or marking. **2.** one of the spots or marks.

punc·til·i·o (pungk til′ē ō), *n., pl.* **-i·os. 1.** a detail of honor, conduct, ceremony, etc.: *The newcomers were not accustomed to give much regard to the punctilios of law, and consequently ran frequently afoul of the elaborate Mexican codes* (Atlantic). **2.** care in attending to such details. [probably patterned (influenced by Latin *punctum*) on Spanish *puntillo,* or Italian *puntiglio* < *punto* point < Latin *punctum;* see PUNCTATE]

punc·til·i·ous (pungk til′ē əs), *adj.* **1.** very careful and exact: *A nurse should be punctilious in following the doctor's orders.* **2.** paying strict attention to details of conduct and ceremony: *From being reserved and punctilious, he is become easy and obliging* (Tobias Smollett). —**punc·til′i·ous·ly,** *adv.* —**punc·til′i·ous·ness,** *n.* —**Syn. 1.** particular, meticulous. See **scrupulous. 2.** fastidious, ceremonious. —**Ant. 1.** negligent.

punc·tu·al (pungk′chü əl), *adj.* **1.** prompt; on time: *He is punctual to the minute.* **2.** being a point; resembling a point. **3.** *Mathematics.* of or having to do with a point: *punctual coordinates.* **4.** *Archaic.* punctilious. [< Medieval Latin *punctualis* pertaining to a point < Latin *punctus, -ūs* point < *pungere* to pierce] —**punc′tu·al·ness,** *n.*

punc·tu·al·i·ty (pungk′chü al′ə tē), *n.* a being on time; promptness: *Punctuality at meals was rigidly enforced at Gateshead Hall* (Charlotte Brontë).

punc·tu·al·ly (pungk′chü ə lē), *adv.* promptly; on time.

punc·tu·ate (pungk′chü āt), *v.*, **-at·ed, -at·ing.** —*v.i.* to use periods, commas, and other marks to help make the meaning clear. —*v.t.* **1.** to put punctuation marks in. **2.** to interrupt now and then: *His speech was punctuated with cheers. Three and a half years of continual internal strife punctuated at increasingly frequent intervals by the efforts of the party leaders to restore order* (London Times). **3.** to give point or emphasis to; emphasize: *He punctuated his remarks with gestures.* [< Medieval Latin *punctuare* (with English *-ate*[1]) < Latin *punctus, -ūs* point < *pungere* to pierce] —**Syn.** *v.t.* **3.** accentuate.

punc·tu·a·tion (pungk′chü ā′shən), *n.* the use of periods, commas, and other marks to help make the meaning clear. Punctuation does for writing and printing what pauses and changes of voice do for speech.

punctuation marks, marks used in writing or printing to help make the meaning clear: *Periods, commas, question marks, colons, etc., are punctuation marks. The punctuation marks, however, are not conceived of as representing features of speech* (Henry A. Gleason).

punc·tu·a·tive (pungk′chü ā′tiv), *adj.* serving to punctuate.

punc·tu·a·tor (pungk′chü ā′tər), *n.* a person who punctuates writing or printing.

punc·tu·late (pungk′chə lāt), *adj.* marked with small points, dots, or depressions. [< New Latin *punctulatus* < Latin *punctulum* (diminutive) < *punctum* point; see PUNCTATE]

punc·tu·lat·ed (pungk′chə lā′tid), *adj.* punctulate.

punc·tu·la·tion (pungk′chə lā′shən), *n.* punctulate condition or marking.

punc·tur·a·ble (pungk′chər ə bəl), *adj.* that can be punctured.

punc·ture (pungk′chər), *n.*, *v.*, **-tured, -turing.** —*n.* **1.** a hole made by something pointed. **2.** the act or process of puncturing. **3.** *Zoology.* a minute, rounded pit or depression.
—*v.t.* **1.** to make a hole in with something pointed: *If the nails fail, puncture their tires with a bullet* (George Bernard Shaw). **2.** to reduce, spoil, or destroy as if by a puncture: *His ego was punctured by the criticism.*
—*v.i.* to have or get a puncture.
[< Latin *punctūra* < *pungere* to prick, pierce]
—**Syn.** *v.t.* **1.** pierce, prick, perforate.

pun·dit (pun′dit), *n.* **1.** a very learned person; expert; authority: *Perhaps some clever pundit will be able to tell me what these words mean* (William H. Hudson). **2.** a very learned Hindu. [< Hindi *paṇḍit* < Sanskrit *paṇḍita*, adjective, learned]

pun·dit·i·cal (pun dit′ə kəl), *adj.* of or having to do with a pundit or punditry: *A prodigious amount of punditical energy is used in trying to describe the difference between a Supreme Court liberal and a Supreme Court conservative* (Time).

pun·dit·ry (pun′də trē), *n.* **1.** pundits collectively: *A resourceful thinker ... who is assuredly in the avant garde of social-economic punditry* (Sunday Times). **2.** the characteristics of a pundit; opinions or actions befitting a pundit: *When the President stuck by his policy of talking softly and backing the U.N., a new spate of punditry and radio-TV commentary bewailed his disappointing stand* (Time).

pung (pung), *n.* a sleigh with a boxlike body: *I have trouble in resisting the notion that I was somehow a son of pioneers, whose neighbors traveled in pungs* (Atlantic). [earlier *tom pung*, supposedly a variant of *toboggan*]

pun·gen·cy (pun′jən sē), *n.* pungent quality: *the pungency of pepper. In high-level conferences he expresses his views with pungency and vigor* (Harper's).

pun·gent (pun′jənt), *adj.* **1.** sharply affecting the organs of taste and smell: *a pungent pickle, the pungent smell of burning leaves.* **2.** sharp; biting: *pungent criticism.* **3.** stimulating to the mind; keen; lively: *a pungent wit.* **4.** *Biology.* piercing; sharp-pointed. [< Latin *pungēns, -entis*, present participle of *pungere* to prick, pierce] —**pun′gent·ly,** *adv.* —**pun′gent·ness,** *n.* —**Syn. 1.** piquant, spicy. **2.** caustic. **3.** poignant.

pung·ey (pun′jē), *n.*, *pl.* **-eys.** *U.S.* a kind of fast-sailing schooner used for oyster fishing and dredging in Chesapeake Bay. [origin unknown]

pun·gi stick or **stake** (pun′jē), a sharpened bamboo stick two or three feet high and often dipped in dung to infect the tip, stuck into the ground at an angle so as to puncture the foot of an enemy soldier: *Pungi sticks ... with which the Viet Cong sow government trails* (Time). Also, **punji stick** or **stake.** [< Annamese *pungi*]

pung·y (pun′jē), *n.*, *pl.* **pung·ies.** pungey.

Pu·nic (pyü′nik), *adj.* **1.** of or having to do with ancient Carthage or its inhabitants. **2.** treacherous; faithless. —*n.* the Semitic language of ancient Carthage. [< Latin *Pūnicus* < *Poenus* a Carthaginian]

Pu·ni·ca fi·des (pyü′nə kə fī′dēz), *Latin.* Punic faith; perfidy or treachery.

pu·ni·ly (pyü′nə lē), *adv.* in a puny manner; weakly.

pu·ni·ness (pyü′nē nis), *n.* the state of being puny; weakness.

pun·ish (pun′ish), *v.t.* **1.** to cause pain, loss, or discomfort to for some fault or offense: *The government punishes criminals.* **2.** to cause pain, loss, or discomfort for: *The law punishes crimes.* **3.** to deal with severely, roughly, or greedily: *to punish a car by very fast driving. He punished my champagne* (Thackeray). —*v.i.* to subject to punishment. [< Old French *puniss-*, stem of *punir* < Latin *pūnīre*, related to *poena* a penalty < Greek *poinḗ* penalty, satisfaction] —**pun′ish·er,** *n.*

pun·ish·a·bil·i·ty (pun′i shə bil′ə tē), *n.* the quality of being punishable; liability to punishment.

pun·ish·a·ble (pun′i shə bəl), *adj.* **1.** liable to punishment. **2.** deserving punishment: *One critic requested that the reading of American Wild West stories be made a punishable offense* (Newsweek). —**pun′ish·a·ble·ness,** *n.*

pun·ish·a·bly (pun′i shə blē), *adv.* in a punishable manner.

pun·ish·ment (pun′ish mənt), *n.* **1.** a punishing or being punished. **2.** pain, suffering, or loss. **3.** *Informal.* severe or rough treatment: *Only the finest ... oils can withstand the punishment a tractor engine receives* (London Times).

pu·ni·tive (pyü′nə tiv), *adj.* **1.** concerned with punishment: *Julius Caesar's first invasion of Britain was a punitive military expedition.* **2.** inflicting punishment: *He had no comment on whether possible punitive action against the Teamsters will be discussed* (Wall Street Journal). *Where it is established that a defendant was inspired by actual malice ... the jury may award ... punitive damages ... or "spite money"* (Time). [< Medieval Latin *punitivus* < Latin *pūnīre* to punish] —**pu′ni·tive·ly,** *adv.* —**pu′ni·tive·ness,** *n.*

pu·ni·to·ry (pyü′nə tôr′ē, -tōr′-), *adj.* punitive.

Pun·ja·bi (pun jä′bē), *n.* **1.** a native or inhabitant of the Punjab: *They were afraid the Punjabis would vote for somebody else* (Atlantic). **2.** Panjabi; a dialect or language spoken in the Punjab. —*adj.* of, having to do with, or characteristic of the Punjab or its people: *Eight little Pakistani girls did a Punjabi folk dance* (Time). [< Hindi *pañjābī* < *Pañjāb* the Punjab < *pānj-*, and *pānch* five (< Sanskrit *pañca*) + *āb* waters]

pun·ji stick or **stake** (pun′jē), pungi stick or stake.

punk (pungk), *n.* **1.** a preparation that burns very slowly, usually of a light-brown color and made from fungus. A stick of punk is used to light fireworks: *To celebrate Fourth of July we all got an allotment of firecrackers, a stick of punk and half a dozen sparklers* (Guy Endore). **2.** decayed wood used as tinder. **3.** *Slang.* a young, inexperienced, or worthless person: *The alderman is a young punk without enough brains to come in out of the rain* (Toronto Flash). *Four air cadets ... were attacked ... by a carload of these warped punks* (Vancouver Province). **4.** *Obsolete.* anything worthless. [American English < Algonkian (Delaware) *ponk;* see PUNKIE]
—*adj. U.S. Slang.* **1.** poor or bad in quality: *a punk day, a punk argument.* **2.** not well; miserable: *to feel punk.*
[American English, perhaps < *punk*, noun, in sense of "rotten"]

pun·kah or **pun·ka** (pung′kə), *n.* (in India and Indonesia) a fan, especially a large swinging fan hung from the ceiling and kept in motion by a servant or by machinery: *The courtroom was sombre ... High up ... the punkahs were swaying short to and fro* (Joseph Conrad). [< Hindi *pankhā* < *pankh* feather < Sanskrit *pakṣa* wing]

punk·ie or **punk·y**[1] (pung′kē), *n.*, *pl.* **punkies.** any of various midges of the northern United States, which bite severely; no-see-um. [American English < Dutch (of New York, New Jersey) *ponki* < Algonkian (Delaware) *ponk* (literally) living ashes (because of the painful bites of the insects)]

punk·y[2] (pung′kē), *adj.*, **punk·i·er, punk·i·est.** **1.** containing, or of the nature of, punk or touchwood; spongy: *Sometimes a flame once kindled is stubborn. It might lie dormant and unseen, smoldering slowly away within the punky wood of some rotting windfall* (Maclean's). *The words of the Charter are soft and punky* (New Yorker). **2.** (of fire) smoldering; burning slowly without flame.

pun·ner (pun′ər), *n.* a person who makes puns; punster.

pun·net (pun′it), *n.* a small, round, shallow chip basket, used chiefly for fruits and vegetables: *... for the sake of making it quite impossible for the most moronic shopper to be misled by the big strawberries on top of the punnet* (Economist). [origin uncertain]

pun·ster (pun′stər), *n.* a person fond of making puns: *The punsters are making it tough for the sane folk around here* (New York Times). [< *pun*[1] + *-ster*]

punt[1] (punt), *n.* a kick given to a football released from the hands but not allowed to drop to the ground: *Tailback Jim Sears raced a punt back 69 yards* (New York Times). —*v.t.* to kick (a football) released from the hands but not allowed to drop to the ground. [origin uncertain]

punt[2] (punt), *n.* a shallow, flat-bottomed boat having square ends, usually moved by pushing with a pole against the bottom of a river, etc.
—*v.t.* **1.** to propel (a boat) by pushing with a pole against the bottom of a river, pond, etc. **2.** to carry in a punt. —*v.i.* to use a punt; travel by punt: *A woman who punts well—and there are such—can steer rings around many men* (London Times).
[Old English *punt* < Latin *pontō, -ōnis* punt, a kind of ship; also, a floating bridge, pontoon < *pōns, pontis* bridge]

Punt[2]

punt[3] (punt), *v.i.* **1.** to bet against the banker in a card game. **2.** to gamble.
—*n.* **1.** a player betting against the banker; punter. **2.** a point in certain card games.
[< French *ponter* < Spanish *puntar*, ultimately < Latin *punctum* a point (originally) neuter past participle of *pungere* to pierce, prick]

punt·er[1] (pun′tər), *n.* a person who punts a boat: *To watch the punter in his pride, you have to catch him in an aquatic traffic jam* (London Times).

punt·er[2] (pun′tər), *n.* a person who punts a football.

punt·er[3] (pun′tər), *n.* a person who punts at faro, etc.: *Every punter [bettor] is entitled to outsmart his bookmaker if he can, and good luck to him* (Time).

pun·to (pun′tō), *n.,pl.* **-tos.** *Obsolete.* a thrust or pass in fencing. [< Italian *punto* point < Latin *punctum;* see PUNT[3]]

pun·ty (pun′tē), *n.*, *pl.* **-ties.** an iron or steel rod used in glass making for handling the hot glass. [< French *pontil*, or Italian *pontello* (diminutive) < *punto* point < Latin *punctum;* see PUNCTATE]

pu·ny (pyü′nē), *adj.*, **-ni·er, -ni·est.** **1.** of less than usual size and strength; weak: *My uncle was a thin, puny little man* (Washington Irving). **2.** petty; not important: *this bloodstained rubbish of the ancient world, these puny kings and tawdry emperors* (H.G. Wells). *Over eighty per cent of the voting population went to the polls—a figure that makes American election intensities look puny* (New Yorker). **3.** *Obsolete.* inferior in rank; younger. [< Middle French *puîné* < Old French *puisne* born later < *puis* afterwards (ultimately < Latin *postea*) + *ne* born < Latin *nāscī* be born] —**Syn. 1.** undeveloped, stunted, small, feeble. **2.** trivial, insignificant. —**Ant. 1.** robust.

pup (pup), *n.*, *v.*, **pupped, pup·ping.** —*n.* **1.** a young dog; puppy. **2.** a young fox, wolf, seal, etc. **3.** a silly, conceited young man:

Baker loathed going to this red-haired young pup for supplies (Atlantic).
—*v.i.* to bring forth pups.
[short for *puppy*]

pu·pa (pyü′pə), *n., pl.* **-pae** (-pē), **-pas. 1.** the stage between the larva and the adult in the development of many insects: *Finally, the larva seems to have eaten its fill and goes into a quiescent stage called the pupa* (A.M. Winchester). **2.** the form of an insect in this stage. Most pupae are inactive and some, such as those of many moths, are enclosed in a tough case or cocoon. *A somewhat different rhythm is seen in the moulting of insects, the hatching of their eggs and emergence of pupae* (Cloudsley and Thompson). [< New Latin *pupa* < Latin *pūpa* girl, doll]

Pupa of a ladybug (Lines show actual lengths.)

pu·pal (pyü′pəl), *adj.* of, having to do with, or in the form of a pupa: *They were ready to emerge from their pupal shucks* (New Scientist).

pu·par·i·um (pyü pãr′ē əm), *n., pl.* **-i·a** (-ē ə). the hard pupal case formed, especially by certain dipterous insects, from the outermost larval skin. [< New Latin *puparium* < *pupa* pupa + *-arium* -ary]

pu·pate (pyü′pāt), *v.i.,* **-pat·ed, -pat·ing.** to become a pupa: *There is an increase in number after the majority of larvae have pupated* (F.S. Bodenheimer). [< *pup*(a) + *-ate*[1]]

pu·pa·tion (pyü pā′shən), *n.* **1.** the act of pupating: *Materials secreted by a gland-like mass associated with the brain of these insects have a controlling influence upon the process of pupation* (Harbaugh and Goodrich). **2.** the state of being a pupa; pupal condition. **3.** the time during which an insect is a pupa.

pu·pi·form (pyü′pə fôrm), *adj.* having the form of a pupa. [< *pupa* + *-form*]

pu·pil[1] (pyü′pəl), *n.* **1.** a person who is learning in school or being taught by someone: *The music teacher takes private pupils.* **2.** *Law.* a boy or girl under the care of a guardian. [Middle English *pupille* a minor ward < Old French *pupille* < Latin *pūpillus,* and *pūpilla* ward (diminutives) < *pūpus* boy, and *pūpa* girl] —**Syn. 1.** scholar, learner. See **student.**

pu·pil[2] (pyü′pəl), *n.* the black spot in the center of the iris of the eye. The pupil, which is the only place where light can enter the eye, is an opening that expands and contracts, thus controlling the amount of light that strikes the retina. *The diameter of the pupil is changed automatically by the expansion or contraction of the iris* (Shortley and Williams). [< Latin *pūpilla* (originally) little doll, (diminutive) < *pūpa* girl, doll]

pu·pil·age or **pu·pil·lage** (pyü′pə lij), *n.* the state or condition of being a pupil, scholar, or ward: *One learnt what was and was not cricket during the period of pupilage* (London Times). [< *pupil*[1] + *-age*]

pu·pil·lar·i·ty or **pu·pi·lar·i·ty** (pyü′pə-lar′ə tē), *n. Law.* the period between birth and puberty. [< Middle French *pupillarité,* ultimately < Latin *pūpillāris* having to do with an orphan or minor]

pu·pil·lar·y[1] (pyü′pə ler′ē), *adj.* belonging to a pupil, scholar, or ward. [perhaps < Middle French *pupillaire,* learned borrowing from Latin *pūpillāris* < *pūpillus* pupil]

pu·pil·lar·y[2] (pyü′pə ler′ē), *adj.* of or having to do with the pupil of the eye. [< New Latin *pupilla* pupil (of the eye) + English *-ary*]

pu·pil·lom·e·ter (pyü′pə lom′ə tər), *n.* an instrument for measuring the size of the pupil of the eye. [< New Latin *pupilla* pupil (of the eye) + English *-meter*]

pu·pip·a·rous (pyü pip′ər əs), *adj.* bringing forth young that are already pupae: *Many ticks are pupiparous.* [< New Latin *pupa* pupa + Latin *parere* to bear offspring + English *-ous*]

pup·pet (pup′it), *n.* **1.** a small doll: *... the motherly airs of my little daughters when they are playing with their puppets* (Joseph Addison). **2.** a figure made to look like a person or animal, and moved by wires, strings, or the hands: *Come ... let us shut up the box and the puppets, for our play is played out* (Thackeray). **3.** anybody who is not independent, waits to be told how to act, and does what somebody else says: *She had ... acted but as a puppet in the hands of others* (Maria Edgeworth). *Chancellor Adenauer has always held that a neutralized Germany would inevitably become a Soviet puppet* (New York Times). [earlier *poppet* < Old French *poupette* < a diminutive form of Vulgar Latin *puppa,* for Latin *pūpa* girl, doll] —**pup′pet·like′,** *adj.*

pup·pet·eer (pup′ə tir′), *n.* a person who manipulates puppets: *... as ... an adroit puppeteer has put his marionettes through their paces* (Saturday Review).

pup·pet·mas·ter (pup′it mas′tər, -mäs′-), *n.* a person in charge of the performance in a puppet show: *The most complete and authoritative work is "The History of the English Puppet Theatre," by George Speaight, himself a puppetmaster* (Edmund Wilson).

pup·pet·ry (pup′ə trē), *n., pl.* **-ries. 1.** the action of puppets. **2.** artificial action like that of a puppet. **3.** the art or craft of making puppets, putting on puppet shows, etc. **4.** puppets collectively.

puppet show, a display or exhibition of puppets, especially a dramatic performance with or of puppets.

Puppet Show

Pup·pis (pup′is), *n. Astronomy.* a constellation now considered as separate but formerly held to be a part of the larger constellation Argo: *Next to Canis Major, to the left, is the constellation of Puppis, the poop, or stern, of the ship, Argo Navis* (Science News Letter). [< Latin *puppis* poop, stern]

pup·py (pup′ē), *n., pl.* **-pies. 1.** a young dog. **2.** a young fox, wolf, etc. **3.** a silly, conceited young man: *"You are an insolent puppy" Sir George stated* (Arnold Bennett). [probably < Old French *poupee* doll, toy < Vulgar Latin *puppa;* see PUPPET] —**pup′py-like′,** *adj.*

pup·py·hood (pup′ē hůd), *n.* the state or period of being a puppy.

pup·py·ish (pup′ē ish), *adj.* of the nature or character of a puppy; proper to a puppy: *What began as an undergraduate romp, with all the puppyish vitality and touching bravura of adolescence, has declined into schoolboy humor* (Sunday Times).

pup·py·ism (pup′ē iz əm), *n.* the character or conduct of a puppy.

puppy love, the clumsy, short-lived romantic affection that exists between adolescent boys and girls; calf love: *A pretty little redhead to whom he plighted his puppy love when he was a schoolboy* (Time).

pup tent, a small, low tent, usually for one or two persons: *One burly lot of Yugoslav Communists pitched their U.S. Army pup tents beside the road ...* (Time).

pur (pėr), *n., v.,* **purred, pur·ring.** purr.

pur., purchasing.

pu·ra·na or **Pu·ra·na** (pů rä′nə), *n.* (in Sanskrit literature) one of a class of sacred writings, of relatively late date, composed almost entirely in the epic couplet, and consisting of partly legendary and partly speculative histories of the universe, together with the genealogy and deeds of gods and heroes, etc. There are eighteen principal puranas. *His thorough knowledge of the Vedas, the Sutras and Puranas ... earned him ... admiration* (Time). [< Sanskrit *purāná* belonging to former times < *purā* formerly]

pur·blind (pėr′blīnd′), *adj.* **1.** nearly blind: *The deep joy we take in the company of people with whom we have just recently fallen in love is undisguisable, even to a purblind waiter* (New Yorker). **2.** slow to discern or understand: *O purblind race of miserable men* (Tennyson). **3.** *Obsolete.* totally blind. [Middle English (originally) *pur blind* pure, in earlier sense "entirely," blind] —**pur′-blind′ly,** *adv.* —**pur′blind′ness,** *n.* —**Syn. 2.** dull, obtuse.

pur·chas·a·bil·i·ty (pėr′chə sə bil′ə tē), *n.* the quality of being purchasable.

pur·chas·a·ble (pėr′chə sə bəl), *adj.* **1.** that can be bought. **2.** venal.

pur·chase (pėr′chəs), *v.,* **-chased, -chas·ing,** *n.* —*v.t.* **1.** to get by paying a price; buy. **2.** to get in return for something: *to purchase safety at the cost of happiness.* **3.** *Law.* to acquire other than by inheritance. **4.** to hoist, haul, or draw by the aid of some mechanical device. **5.** *Obsolete.* to go after and get possession of.
—*n.* **1.** the act of buying: *the purchase of a new car.* **2.** the thing bought: *Next year's economic push will have to come from a combination of bigger business investment and rising government purchases* (Newsweek). **3.** a firm hold to help move something or to keep from slipping: *Wind the rope twice around the tree to get a better purchase.* **4.** a device for obtaining such a hold. **5.** the annual income, as rent, from land. **6.** *Law.* an acquiring of property other than by inheritance. **7.** *Obsolete.* booty. **8.** *Obsolete.* acquisition; gain.
[< Anglo-French *purchacer* to pursue < *pur-* forth (< Latin *prō-* pro-[1]) + *chacer,* Old French *chacier* to chase, pursue]
—**Syn.** *n.* **1.** See **buy.**

pur·chase·a·ble (pėr′chə sə bəl), *adj.* purchasable.

purchase journal, (in accounting) a book of original entry for recording purchases.

pur·chas·er (pėr′chə sər), *n.* a buyer.

purchase tax, *British.* a tax on retail sales of consumer goods, except food, fuel, and books, differing from the American sales tax in that the rate for each class of goods is based inversely on its estimated necessity in daily life: *It is suggested that the Government should sweep away all direct taxes, including turnover and purchase tax* (Sunday Times).

pur·chas·ing agent (pėr′chə sing), a buyer for a company who evaluates competitive bids on services or products needed, awards contracts, and orders new products.

purchasing power, 1. the ability to buy things, as measured by the amount of money one earns or has available: *For the workers who did not share in the new round of raises, the higher prices would mean a decrease in real purchasing power* (Time). **2.** the value of a unit of currency, as measured by the amount of things one can buy with it in a given period in comparison with some earlier period: *With a drop in purchasing power of the dollar, the depreciation allowances ... fall far short of the current cost of the needed replacement items* (Wall Street Journal).

pur·dah (pėr′də), *n.* in India: **1.** a curtain serving to screen women from the sight of men or strangers: *The purdah hung, Crimson and blue ... Across a portal carved in sandalwood* (Edwin Arnold). *In Peshawar is the university and a college for women, where there are mixed debates with a purdah curtain dividing the sexes* (London Times). **2.** the condition of being kept hidden from men or strangers: *He met and talked with everybody of any importance except for a few Moslem sultanas in purdah* (Harper's). [< Hindustani *pardah* < Persian, veil, curtain]

pur·do·ni·an or **pur·do·ni·on** (pėr dō′nē ən), *n. British.* purdonium.

pur·do·ni·um (pėr dō′nē əm), *n. British.* a coal scuttle for indoor use: *That a coal scuttle is more salable when called a purdonium appears to hold in all sections of society* (London Times). [< *Purdon,* name of the designer of the box]

pure (pyůr), *adj.,* **pur·er, pur·est,** *n.* —*adj.* **1.** not mixed with anything else; unadulterated; genuine: *pure gold. If a material contains only one element or only one compound, the chemist calls the material pure.* **2.** perfectly clean; spotless: *pure hands.* **3.** without defects; perfect; correct: *to speak pure French. One would imagine that the words already in the English dictionary were all pure* (Guy Endore). **4.** nothing else than; mere; sheer: *pure accident. His method of stating ideas ... contains a large element of pure incantation* (Edmund Wilson). **5.** with no evil; without sin; chaste: *a pure mind.* **6.** abstract or theoretical: *pure mathematics. If one insists that there are two kinds of science, pure and applied, then there are two kinds of scientific research, pure and applied* (Thomas M. Rivers). **7.** keeping the same qualities, characteristics, etc., from generation to generation; of unmixed descent: *I saw that he was not a pure Indian, for ... he wore a beard and moustache* (William H. Hudson). **8.** *Genetics.* homozygous, and therefore breeding true for at least one hereditary character: *Research mice ... which have been kept very close to "pure" through 275 generations by means of brother-sister mating* (Newsweek). **9.** *Phonetics.* (of a vowel) constant in sound; not diphthongal. **10. a.** *Logic.* (of a proposition or syllogism) not modal. **b.** *Philosophy.* independent of sense or experience: *pure knowledge, pure intuition.*

pure and simple, nothing else but; plainly and simply: *China . . . declared that the Kremlin leaders were "accomplices of the U.S. imperialists, pure and simple"* (New York Times).

—*n.* that which is pure.

[< Old French *pur* < Latin *pūrus*] —**pure′ness,** *n.*

—**Syn.** *adj.* **1.** unalloyed. **2.** immaculate. **3.** faultless. **4.** utter. **5.** virtuous.

pure-blood·ed (pyůr′blud′id), *adj.* **1.** descended through a long line of unmixed ethnic or racial stock: *In Central America, Guatemala is 50 per cent pure-blooded Indian, the remainder Spanish or mestizo* (Newsweek). **2.** purebred.

pure·bred (pyůr′bred′), *adj.* bred from good stock: *purebred Holstein cows. Many new seed varieties are the result of painstaking crossing of two purebred plants to produce a hybrid* (Wall Street Journal). —*n.* a thoroughbred.

pure culture, *Bacteriology.* a culture containing only a single species of organism.

pu·rée (pyů rā′, pyůr′ā), *n., v.,* **-réed, -ré·ing.** —*n.* **1.** food boiled until soft and pushed through a sieve. **2.** a thick dessert, entree, or soup. —*v.t.* to make into a purée. [< French *purée,* (originally) past participle of Old French *purer* to strain; suppurate < Late Latin *pūrāre* < Latin *pūs, pūris* pus]

pure-heart·ed (pyůr′här′tid), *adj.* free from evil or guilt; guileless; sincere: *He has written about it, and revealed the pure-hearted ache for a better life that lies behind it* (Sunday Times). —**pure′-heart′ed·ness,** *n.*

Pure Land, 1. the paradise that awaits the believers in Amida, the Buddha of Amidism. **2.** the sect that practices Amidism; Jodo. **3.** the form of Mahayana Buddhism practiced by this sect; Amidism.

pure line, *Genetics.* a strain of plants or animals that breeds true for one or more characters, obtained by continued inbreeding and selection or by self-fertilization: *the increased vigor of "hybrid" offspring as compared to the parental "pure lines"* (Bulletin of Atomic Scientists).

pure·ly (pyůr′lē), *adv.* **1.** in a pure manner. **2.** exclusively; entirely. **3.** merely. **4.** innocently; chastely.

pur·fle (pėr′fəl), *v.,* **-fled, -fling,** *n.* —*v.t.* to finish with an ornamental border: *a robe purfled with embroidery, a violin purfled with inlaid work.* —*n.* an ornamental border. [< Old French *pourfiler* < *pour-* (< Latin *prō-,* or *per-*) + *fil* thread < Latin *fīlum*]

pur·fling (pėr′fling), *n.* ornamental bordering. [< *purfl*(e) + *-ing*¹]

pur·ga·tion (pėr gā′shən), *n.* a purging; cleansing: *a thorough purgation of the mind* (Henry Hallam).

pur·ga·tive (pėr′gə tiv), *n.* a medicine that empties the bowels: *Castor oil is a purgative.* —*adj.* purging: *The coarse or macabre joke, on the part of the early Western writers, had often a purgative function* (New Yorker). [< Late Latin *pūrgātīvus* < Latin *pūrgāre;* see PURGE] —**pur′ga·tive·ly,** *adv.* —**pur′ga·tive·ness,** *n.*

pur·ga·to·ri·al (pėr′gə tôr′ē əl, -tōr′-), *adj.* of, like, or having to do with purgatory: *to enter into the purgatorial state of matrimony* (W. H. Hudson). *It has been a period of complete satisfaction, and it came at the tail end of a long purgatorial experience* (Atlantic).

pur·ga·to·ri·an (pėr′gə tôr′ē ən, -tōr′-), *adj.* purgatorial.

pur·ga·to·ry (pėr′gə tôr′ē, -tōr′-), *n., pl.* **-ries,** *adj.* —*n.* **1.** (in the belief of Roman Catholics) a temporary condition or place in which the souls of those who have died penitent are purified from venial sin or the effects of sin, by punishment: *England is like the paradise of women, the purgatory of men, and the hell of horses* (John Florio). **2.** any condition or place of temporary suffering or punishment: *I shuddered at the thought of spending another night in such a purgatory* (W. H. Hudson). *She wondered how long this purgatory was to last* (Thomas Hardy). —*adj.* purgative. [< Medieval Latin *purgatorium,* (originally) neuter adjective, purging < Latin *pūrgāre;* see PURGE]

purge (pėrj), *v.,* **purged, purg·ing,** *n.* —*v.t.* **1.** to wash away all that is not clean from; make clean: *King Arthur tried to purge his land of sin.* **2.** to clear of any undesired thing or person, such as air in a water pipe or opponents in a nation. **3.** to empty (the bowels). **4.** to clear of defilement or imputed guilt. —*v.i.* **1.** to become clean. **2.** to undergo or cause emptying of the bowels. [< Old French *purgier* < Latin *pūrgāre,* earlier *pūrigāre* to cleanse, purify < *pūrus* pure + *agere* to drive, make]

—*n.* **1.** the act of purging. **2.** a medicine that purges; purgative. **3.** the elimination of undesired persons from a nation or party: *His career was helped somewhat by his ruthless execution of party purges in the satellites* (Newsweek).

[(definition 3) loan translation < Russian *chistka* cleaning, political purge < *chistit′* to clean, purge]

purge·a·ble (pėr′jə bəl), *adj.* that can be purged.

purg·ee (pėr jē′), *n.* a person who is purged, as from a country or political party: *The six purgees bellowed their protests from the convention podium* (Time).

purg·er (pėr′jər), *n.* **1.** a person or thing that purges or cleanses. **2.** a cathartic.

purg·ing flax (pėr′jing), an Old-World species of flax, a decoction of which is used as a cathartic and diuretic.

pu·ri·fi·ca·tion (pyůr′ə fə kā′shən), *n.* **1.** a purifying. **2.** the state of being purified.

Pu·ri·fi·ca·tion (pyůr′ə fə kā′shən), *n.* a Christian festival, observed on February 2, commemorating the purifying of the Virgin Mary after the birth of Christ.

pu·ri·fi·ca·tor (pyůr′ə fə kā′tər), *n. Ecclesiastical.* a cloth used at Communion for wiping the chalice, etc.

pu·ri·fi·ca·to·ry (pyů rif′ə kə tôr′ē, -tōr′-), *adj.* serving to purify.

pu·ri·fi·er (pyůr′ə fī′ər), *n.* **1.** a person or thing that purifies or cleans: *Some 99,000 gallons of drinkable water were produced and distributed by the Army's new mobile purifier* (Science). **2.** a purificator.

pu·ri·form (pyůr′ə fôrm), *adj.* having the form of pus; puslike. [< Latin *pūs, pūris* pus + English *-form*]

pu·ri·fy (pyůr′ə fī), *v.,* **-fied, -fy·ing.** —*v.t.* **1.** to make pure: *Filters are used to purify water.* **2.** to free from whatever is evil: *to purify the heart.* **3.** to make ceremonially clean: *And the Jews' passover was nigh at hand; and many went out of the country up to Jerusalem before the passover, to purify themselves* (John 11:55). **4.** to free of objectionable characteristics: *to purify a language.* **5.** to clear or purge (of or from). —*v.i.* to become pure. [< Old French *purifier* < Latin *pūrificāre* < *pūrus* pure + *facere* to make]

Pu·rim (půr′im, pyůr′-; *Hebrew* pü rēm′), *n.* a Jewish religious holiday, celebrated each year in February or March, commemorating the deliverance of the Jews from being massacred by Haman (Esther 9:20-32): *Purim is a time of rejoicing over events of 2,400 years ago* (New York Times). [< Hebrew *purim,* plural of *pur* lot, chance]

pu·rin (pyůr′in), *n.* purine.

pu·rine (pyůr′ēn, -in), *n.* **1.** a colorless, crystalline compound regarded as a parent substance of a group that includes uric acid, xanthine, caffeine, theobromine, etc. **2.** any of the compounds of this group: *The purines and pterines contribute a major source of colour to the wings of butterflies* (B. Nickerson). [< German *Purin* < Latin *pūrus* pure + New Latin *ūricus* uric acid + German *-in* -ine²]

Pu·rin·e·thol (pyů rin′ə thol), *n. Trademark.* a drug used in the treatment of leukemia. *Formula:* $C_5H_4N_4S$

pur·ism (pyůr′iz əm), *n.* **1.** the avoidance of all words and expressions that are judged unacceptable. **2.** the insistence that others do this. **3.** the theory or methods of a group of French artists who, about 1918, revolted against cubism and stressed the portrayal of recognizable objects, using stylization and precise drawing to express the spirit of the machine age: *In 1918, with Amédée Ozenfant, [Le Corbusier] founded the painting movement called Purism* (New Yorker).

pur·ist (pyůr′ist), *n.* a person who is very careful or too careful about purity in language. A purist dislikes slang and all expressions that are not formally correct. *Even purists do not hesitate to say bedlam (Bethlehem)* (Scientific American). [< French *puriste* < Latin *pūrus* pure + French *-iste* -ist]

pu·ris·tic (pyů ris′tik), *adj.* very careful or too careful about purity in language: *Many linguists are as puristic as one could wish, turning quite pale in the presence of "the reason is because"* (Paul Roberts).

Pu·ri·tan (pyůr′ə tən), *n.* a member of a group in the Church of England during the 1500's and 1600's who wanted simpler forms of worship and stricter morals. —*adj.* of the Puritans: *Singing the Hundredth Psalm, the grand old Puritan anthem* (Longfellow). [< *purit*(y) + *-an*]

pu·ri·tan (pyůr′ə tən), *n.* a person who is very strict in morals and religion. —*adj.* very strict in morals and religion. [< *Puritan*]

pu·ri·tan·ic (pyůr′ə tan′ik), *adj.* puritanical.

Pu·ri·tan·i·cal (pyůr′ə tan′ə kəl), *adj.* having to do with or like the Puritans.

pu·ri·tan·i·cal (pyůr′ə tan′ə kəl), *adj.* of or like a puritan; very strict or too strict in morals or religion. [< *Puritanical*] —**pu′ri·tan′i·cal·ly,** *adv.* —**pu′ri·tan′i·cal·ness,** *n.* —**Syn.** austere.

Pu·ri·tan·ism (pyůr′ə tə niz′əm), *n.* the principles and practices of the Puritans.

pu·ri·tan·ism (pyůr′ə tə niz′əm), *n.* puritanical behavior or principles. [< *Puritanism*]

pu·ri·tan·ize (pyůr′ə tə nīz), *v.,* **-ized, -iz·ing.** —*v.i.* to practice puritanism. —*v.t.* to make puritan.

pu·ri·ty (pyůr′ə tē), *n.* **1.** freedom from dirt or mixture; clearness; cleanness: *the purity of drinking water.* **2.** freedom from moral corruption or evil; innocence: *No one doubts the purity of Joan of Arc's motives. Claude's agonizing longing for purity struggles against a sensuality that is wholly animal* (Saturday Review). **3.** freedom from foreign or inappropriate elements; correctness: *purity of style.* **4.** saturation: *The purity of color is its amount of difference from gray of the same brightness. The purity of any spectrum color is of course 100%, and the purity of white is zero* (Sears and Zemansky). [< Old French *purete,* learned borrowings from Late Latin *pūritās* < Latin *pūrus* pure]

Pur·kin·je cell (pėr kin′jē), any of the large branching cells, with cone-shaped bodies, that make up the intermediate layer of the cerebellar cortex: *Each Purkinje cell sends its message out of the cerebellum through a long threadlike axon* (Scientific American). [< Johannes E. *Purkinje,* 1787-1869, a Bohemian physiologist]

purl¹ (pėrl), *v.i.* **1.** to flow with rippling motions and a murmuring sound: *A shallow brook purls.* **2.** to pass with a sound like this: *The words . . . purled out of Miss Foster's mouth like a bright spring out of moss* (Arnold Bennett).

—*n.* **1.** a purling motion or sound. **2.** the act of purling.

[perhaps < Scandinavian (compare Norwegian *purla* to ripple)]

purl² (pėrl), *v.t., v.i.* **1.** to knit with inverted stitches. **2.** to border (material) with small loops. **3.** *Archaic.* to embroider with gold or silver thread.

—*n.* **1.** an inversion of stitches in knitting, producing a ribbed appearance. **2.** a loop, or chain of small loops, along the edge of lace, braid, ribbon, etc. **3.** a thread of twisted gold or silver wire. **4.** *Obsolete.* the pleat or fold of a ruff or neckband.

[apparently variant of earlier *pirl* to twist; origin uncertain]

purl³ (pėrl), *n.* **1.** a medicated or spiced malt liquor. **2.** a mixture of hot beer with gin and sometimes also sugar and ginger. [origin unknown]

pur·li·cue (pėr′lə kyü), *n.* the space enclosed by the extended forefinger and thumb: *Mr. Russet made a triangle of his purlicues and peered through it at his antagonist* (New Yorker). [origin uncertain]

pur·lieu (pėr′lü), *n.* **1.** a piece of land on the border of a forest, especially one formerly included in the forest and still subject in part to the forest laws. **2.** one's haunt or resort; one's bounds. **3.** any bordering, neighboring, or outlying region or district. [alteration (influenced by French *lieu* place) of Anglo-French *puralee* (originally) a perambulation < *poraler* to go through < Old French *por-* forth, pro-¹ + *aler* to go]

pur·lin or **pur·line** (pėr′lən), *n.* a horizontal beam running the length of a roof and supporting the top rafters of the roof. [Middle English *purlyn;* origin uncertain]

pur·loin (pėr loin′), *v.t., v.i.* to steal: *A certain document of the last importance has been purloined from the royal apartments*

(Edgar Allan Poe). [< Anglo-French *purloigner* to remove < *pur-* forth, pro-[1] + *loin* afar < Latin *longē*, adverb < *longus* long. Related to PROLONG.] —**pur·loin′er,** *n.*

pu·ro·my·cin (pyůr′ō mī′sin), *n.* an antibiotic drug produced from a soil actinomycete, used to treat certain protozoan diseases and to retard tumor growth. *Formula:* $C_{22}H_{29}N_7O_5$

pur·ple (pėr′pəl), *n., adj., v.,* **-pled, -pling.** —*n.* **1.** a dark color made by mixing red and blue. **2.** crimson. This was the ancient meaning of purple. **3.** purple cloth or clothing, especially as worn by emperors, kings, etc., to indicate high rank. **4.** imperial, royal, or high rank: *A prince is born to the purple.* **5.** the rank or position of a cardinal. **6.** any of a group of gastropods having a gland that secretes a purplish fluid. One kind is common on both shores of the Atlantic.
—*adj.* **1.** of the color of purple. **2.** crimson. **3.** imperial; royal. **4.** brilliant; gorgeous. **5.** very ornate in style: *He has a taste for purple prose that is, to say the least, unfashionable* (Listener).
—*v.t., v.i.* to make or become purple.
[Old English *purple*, variant of *purpure* < Latin *purpura* < Greek *porphýrā* a shell fish; the purple dye obtained from it. Doublet of PORPHYRY.]

purple finch, a sparrow-sized finch of eastern North America, the male of which has a rose-colored breast, head, and rump.

pur·ple-fringed orchid (pėr′pəl frinjd′), one of two North American orchids, with fringed, purplish flowers.

purple gallinule, a brilliantly colored gallinule, of the warmer regions of America, having bluish-purple head, neck, and under parts.

purple grackle, a large, purplish, iridescent blackbird found along the Atlantic coastal belt from southern New England and New York to Florida and Louisiana.

pur·ple·heart (pėr′pəl härt′), *n.* **1.** a tree growing in tropical America whose wood is used for fine furniture and intricate inlaid work. **2.** the wood itself, purple in color, and noted for its durability.

purple heart, *British Slang.* a narcotic drug sold in the form of a purple tablet; drinamyl: . . . *the danger to teen-agers through the ease of getting purple hearts and pep pills* (Scotsman).

Purple Heart, *U.S.* a medal awarded to members of the armed forces for wounds received in action against an enemy or as a result of enemy action.

purple heron, a European heron resembling the common heron, but darker in coloration and in some places purplish: *The purple heron, with its angular wing and gorgeous body, kept us close company* (London Times).

purple loosestrife, a variety of loosestrife three feet or more in height with spikes of purple flowers, found in north temperate regions and Australia.

purple martin, a large, blue-black swallow of temperate North America, except the Pacific Coast region. See picture under **martin.**

purple medic, lucerne; alfalfa.

purple patch or **passage,** a part or passage of a written work that is very ornate in style: *His narrative is robust, but it falls easily into the purple patches of a boys' magazine* (Punch).

purple sandpiper, a sandpiper with black or grayish head and back, found in arctic regions and, in the winter, south into the northern United States.

purple vetch, a weak-stemmed plant of the pea family with purple and white flowers, extensively grown in the Pacific Coast states for cattle feed and as ground cover.

pur·plish (pėr′plish), *adj.* somewhat purple.

pur·ply (pėr′plē), *adj.* purplish.

pur·port (*v.* pər pôrt′, -pōrt′; pėr′pôrt, -pōrt; *n.* pėr′pôrt, -pōrt), *v.t.* **1.** to claim; profess: *The document purported to be official. The recommendations . . . were purely procedural ones—or, at any rate, that is what they were intended to be and purported to be* (New Yorker). **2.** to have as its main idea; mean: *a statement purporting certain facts.*
—*n.* the main idea; meaning: *The purport of her letter was that she could not come.* [< Anglo-French *purporter* < *pur-* forth, pro-[1] + *porter* to carry < Latin *portāre*] —**pur·port′ed·ly,** *adv.* —**Syn.** *n.* sense, gist, signification. See **meaning.**

pur·port·less (pėr′pôrt lis, -pōrt-), *adj.* without purport or meaning.

pur·pose (pėr′pəs), *n., v.,* **-posed, -pos·ing.** —*n.* **1.** something one has in mind to get or do; plan; aim; intention: *His purpose was to discover how long these guests intended to stay* (Joseph Conrad). **2.** object or end for which a thing is made, done, used, etc.: *The purpose of government he conceived to be the execution of justice* (James A. Froude).
on purpose, with a purpose; not by accident: *It was merely a mistake, but her Ladyship was convinced that it was done on purpose* (Maria Edgeworth).
to good purpose, with good results: *His letter may . . . be made public to good purpose* (Free-thinker).
to little or **no purpose,** with few or no results: *I used to insist on this . . . but . . . to no purpose* (Harriet Martineau).
—*v.t., v.i.* to plan; aim; intend: *my next experiment . . . which I purpose to describe more at length* (Thoreau). *I purposed writing a little comment on each virtue* (Benjamin Franklin).
[< Old French *pourpos* < *pourposer* to propose < *pour-* forth + *poser;* see POSE[1]]
—**Syn.** *n.* **1.** See **intention.**

pur·pose·ful (pėr′pəs fəl), *adj.* having a purpose: *It has been my natural disposition to see this war as something purposeful* (H. G. Wells). —**pur′pose·ful·ly,** *adv.* —**pur′pose·ful·ness,** *n.*

pur·pose·less (pėr′pəs lis), *adj.* lacking a purpose. —**pur′pose·less·ly,** *adv.* —**pur′pose·less·ness,** *n.*

pur·pose·ly (pėr′pəs lē), *adv.* on purpose; intentionally.

pur·pos·ive (pėr′pə siv), *adj.* **1.** acting with, having, or serving some purpose: *a purposive organ, a purposive structure.* **2.** resolute: *His mental processes were abnormally purposive* (Harper's). **3.** of or having to do with purpose: *The purposive approach . . . sees man as a composite body and mind whose controlling force is drive, motivation or purpose* (Scientific American). —**pur′pos·ive·ly,** *adv.* —**pur′pos·ive·ness,** *n.*

pur·pres·ture (pėr pres′chər), *n. Law.* an illegal enclosure of or encroachment upon property that belongs to the public or, formerly, to another person, as the shutting up or obstruction of a highway or of navigable waters. [< Old French *purpresture* < *purprendre* usurp, occupy < *pur-* (< Latin *prō* before, for) + *prendre* < Latin *prehendere* seize, take]

pur·pu·ra (pėr′pyůr ə), *n.* any of various diseases characterized by purple or livid spots on the skin or mucous membrane, caused by hemorrhages underneath the skin. [< Latin *purpura;* see PURPLE]

pur·pu·rate (pėr′pyə rāt), *n. Chemical.* a salt of purpuric acid. [< *purpur*(ic acid) + *-ate*[2]]

pur·pure (pėr′pyůr), *n. Heraldry.* the purple color in coats of arms, in engraving represented by diagonal lines from the sinister chief to the dexter base. [Old English *purpure;* see PURPLE]

pur·pu·re·al (pėr pyůr′ē əl), *adj. Poetic.* purple: *fields invested with purpureal gleams* (Wordsworth). [< Latin *purpureus* purple + English *-al*]

pur·pu·ric (pər pyůr′ik), *adj.* **1.** having or producing a purple color. **2.** of or like the disease purpura. **3.** *Chemistry.* having to do with or derived from purpuric acid.

purpuric acid, a nitrogen-containing, organic acid, yielding salts which form purple or red solutions. *Formula:* $C_8H_5N_5O_6$

pur·pu·rin (pėr′pyər in), *n.* a red or orange, crystalline organic compound, originally obtained from madder, but now also prepared from alizarin, used in dyeing. *Formula:* $C_{14}H_8O_5$ [< Latin *purpura* purple dye + English *-in*]

purr (pėr), *n.* a low, murmuring sound such as a cat makes when pleased. —*v.i., v.t.* to make a low murmuring sound: *It [a young leopard] . . . purred like a cat when we stroked it with our hands* (Daniel Defoe). . . . *His engine purring almost inaudibly along the level road* (H. G. Wells). *The little girl purred content.* Also, **pur.** [imitative]

pur sang (pyr säN′), *French.* **1.** true-born; thoroughbred: *Why . . . did a mathematician pur sang, as Boole certainly was, feel drawn to logic* (New Scientist). **2.** (literally) pure blood.

purse (pėrs), *n., v.,* **pursed, purs·ing.** —*n.* **1.** a bag or case for carrying money around with one. **2.** a small bag or container to hold

small change, usually carried in a handbag or a pocket. **3.** money; resources; treasury: *He . . . had no resources save the purse of his stepfather* (Arnold Bennett). **4.** a sum of money: *A purse was made up for the victims of the fire.* **5.** any baglike receptacle, as an animal's pouch, a seed capsule, or a covering for a golf club: *Then he fitted the golden head of his club with a chamois purse* (New Yorker).
—*v.t.* **1.** to draw together; press into folds or wrinkles: *She pursed her lips and frowned.* **2.** to put in a purse.
[Old English *purs* < Late Latin *bursa* < Greek *býrsa* hide, skin. Doublet of BOURSE, BURSA, BURSE.]

purse crab, coconut crab.

purse·ful (pėrs′fůl), *n., pl.* **-fuls.** as much as a purse contains: . . . *a purseful of profits* (Time).

purse net, purse seine.

purse-proud (pėrs′proud′), *adj.* proud of being rich.

purs·er (pėr′sər), *n.* the officer who keeps the accounts of a ship or airplane, pays wages, and attends to other matters of business.

purse seine, a fishing net or seine which is pulled around a school of fish until the ends are brought together, the bottom then being drawn in under the fish to close as a bag.

purse seiner, a boat used in fishing with a purse seine: *I had meant to get a job fishing on a purse seiner at Vancouver* (Canada Month).

purse strings, 1. the strings pulled to close a purse. **2.** control of the money.
control or **hold the purse strings,** to control the expenditure of money: *Congress controls the purse strings* (New York Times). *The politicians hold the purse strings and therefore can enact the detailed regulations which the scientist must obey* (Science News Letter).
loosen the purse strings, to be generous in spending money: *Widespread loosening of the buying public's purse strings is bringing better business* (Wall Street Journal).
tighten the purse strings, to be sparing in spending money: *to tighten the purse strings after taking a cut in salary.*

pur·si·ness (pėr′sē nis), *n.* a pursy condition; shortness of breath.

purs·lane (pėrs′lān, -lən), *n.* **1.** a common plant that has small, yellow flowers and small, thick leaves. It is an herb and is sometimes used for salads, for flavoring, or as a potherb. *Purslane, a common garden weed, is flourishing this season despite the hot, dry weather* (New York Times). **2.** any of several plants like it that belong to the purslane family. [< Old French *porcelaine*, alteration of Latin *porcilāca*, variant of *portulāca* portulaca < *portula* small door (diminutive) < *porta* gate (because of the open seed capsules which cover it)]

Purslane (def. 1)

purslane family, a group of dicotyledonous herbs found chiefly in warm, arid regions. The family includes the purslane, claytonia, and bitterroot.

pur·su·a·ble (pər sü′ə bəl), *adj.* that can be pursued.

pur·su·al (pər sü′əl), *n.* the act of pursuing; pursuit: *From hawks to seas, To galaxies All Nature is pursual* (New Yorker). [< *pursu*(e) + *-al*[2]]

pur·su·ance (pər sü′əns), *n.* a following; carrying out; pursuit: *In pursuance of his duty, the policeman risked his life.*

pur·su·ant (pər sü′ənt), *adj.* following; carrying out.
pursuant to, acting according to; in accordance with; following.

pur·su·ant·ly (pər sü′ənt lē), *adv.* pursuant.

pur·sue (pər sü′), *v.,* **-sued, -su·ing.** —*v.t.* **1.** to follow to catch or kill; chase: *to pursue game. The policeman pursued the robbers.* **2.** to proceed along; follow in action; follow: *He pursued a wise course by taking no chances.* **3.** to strive for; try to get; seek: *to pursue pleasure. Depart from evil, and do good; Seek peace and pursue it* (Psalms 34:14). **4.** to carry on; keep on with: *She pursued the study of French for four years. At Harvard he had the leisure to pursue his*

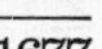

studies. **5.** to continue to annoy or trouble; torment: *to pursue a teacher with questions.* —*v.i.* to follow in pursuit: *The wicked flee when no man pursueth* (Proverbs 28:1). [< Anglo-French *pursuer,* Old French *persuire,* or *poursuivre* < Latin *prōsequī;* see PROSECUTE] —**pur·su′ing·ly,** *adv.* —**Syn.** *v.t.* **1.** hunt, track.

pur·su·er (pər sü′ər), *n.* one who pursues; one who follows in haste with the purpose of overtaking.

pur·suit (pər süt′), *n.* **1.** the act of pursuing: *the pursuit of game, the pursuit of pleasure, in the pursuit of science. Man's aims are seen as pursuit of satisfaction (biological) and pursuit of security (cultural)* (Time). **2.** an occupation: *Fishing is his favorite pursuit; reading is mine.* [< Anglo-French *purseute,* Old French *poursuite* < *persuire* to pursue]

pursuit plane, a fighter aircraft that has high speed and a high rate of climb, and can be maneuvered with ease.

pur·sui·vant (pėr′swə vənt), *n.* **1.** an assistant to a herald; officer below a herald in rank. **2.** a follower; attendant: *sleep, the gracious pursuivant of toil* (Robert Bridges). **3.** *Poetic.* a herald or messenger: *these grey locks, the pursuivants of death* (Shakespeare). [< Old French *poursuivant,* (originally) present participle of *poursuivre* to pursue]

pur·sy[1] (pėr′sē), *adj.,* **-si·er, -si·est.** **1.** short-winded or puffy. **2.** fat: *figures of little pursy cupids* (Washington Irving). [< Anglo-French *pursif,* variant of Old French *polsif* < *poulser* to pant < Latin *pulsāre* to beat; see PULSE[1]]

pur·sy[2] (pėr′sē), *adj.,* **-si·er, -si·est.** **1.** having puckers; puckered. **2.** rich; purse-proud: *The pursy man means by freedom the right to do as he pleases* (Emerson).

pur·te·nance (pėr′tə nəns), *n. Archaic.* the heart, liver, lungs, and windpipe of an animal. [perhaps < unrecorded Anglo-French *purtinaunce,* for Old French *pertinence* pertinence]

pu·ru·lence (pyůr′ə ləns, -yə-), *n.* formation or discharge of pus; suppuration.

pu·ru·len·cy (pyůr′ə lən sē, -yə-), *n.* purulence.

pu·ru·lent (pyůr′ə lənt, -yə-), *adj.* **1.** full of pus; discharging pus; like pus: *a purulent sore, a purulent discharge from the nose during a cold.* **2.** corrupt; rotten; cheap: *It is an unintermitted eyesore of drive-ins, diners, souvenir stands, purulent amusement parks* (Harper's). [< Latin *pūrulentus* < *pūs, pūris* pus] —**pu′ru·lent·ly,** *adv.*

pur·vey (pər vā′), *v.t., v.i.* to supply (food or provisions); provide; furnish: *to purvey meat for an army, to purvey for a royal household.* [< Anglo-French *porveier,* or *purveier* < Latin *prōvidēre.* Doublet of PROVIDE.]

pur·vey·ance (pər vā′əns), *n.* **1.** a purveying. **2.** provisions; supplies. **3.** (formerly, in England) the right of the king or queen to supplies, use of horses, and personal service, especially when traveling.

pur·vey·or (pər vā′ər), *n.* **1.** a person who supplies provisions: *a purveyor of fine foods and meats.* **2.** a person who supplies anything: *a purveyor of gossip. He . . . considered "fellows who wrote" as the mere paid purveyors of rich men's pleasures* (Edith Wharton). **3.** (formerly, in England) an officer who provided or exacted food, etc., in accordance with the right of purveyance.

pur·view (pėr′vyü), *n.* **1.** the range of operation, activity, concern, etc.; scope; extent: *matters within the purview of the government.* **2.** the outlook. **3.** the main part of a statute, following the preamble. [< Anglo-French *purveu* (originally) past participle of *porveier* to purvey]

pus (pus), *n.* the liquid formed by inflammation of infected tissue in the body, that consists of white blood cells, bacteria, serum, etc. [< Latin *pūs, pūris*]

Pu·sey·ism (pyü′zē iz əm), *n.* the Oxford movement of the 1800's; Tractarianism. [< Edward B. *Pusey,* 1800-1882, one of the leaders of the Oxford movement]

Pu·sey·ist (pyü′zē ist), *n.* an adherent of Puseyism; Tractarianist.

Pu·sey·ite (pyü′zē īt), *n.* an adherent of Puseyism; Tractarianist.

push (půsh), *v.t.* **1.** to move (something) away by pressing against it: *Push the door; don't pull.* **2.** to move up, down, back, forward, etc., by pressing: *Push him outdoors.* **3.** to thrust: *Trees push their roots down into the ground.* **4.** to force (one's way): *We had to push our way through the crowd.* **5.** to make go forward; urge: *He pushed his plans cleverly.* **6.** to continue with; follow up: *to push a claim.* **7.** to extend: *Alexander pushed his conquests still farther east.* **8.** to urge the use, practice, sale, etc., of: *They could also compel the chemists to "push" the sale of certain articles* (Cape Times). —*v.i.* **1.** to move from shore: *We pushed off in the boat.* **2.** to press hard: *to push with all one's might.* **3.** to go forward by force: *I pushed into the next wigwam upon my hands and knees* (Byron). **4.** to sit at an oar and row a boat with forward strokes: *to push down a stream.*

push around, *Informal.* to treat roughly or with contempt; bully; harass: *The British people are tired of being pushed around* (Manchester Guardian).

push off, to depart; leave: *The corporation didn't want men who came to get rich quickly and then push off* (Manchester Guardian Weekly).

push on, to keep going; proceed: *So we pushed on. We pushed on for miles* (Punch).

—*n.* **1.** *Informal.* force; energy: *The seaway means push and purpose for the community* (Newsweek). **2.** an act of pushing: *Give the door a push.* **3.** a hard effort; determined advance. **4.** (in Australia) a gang of larrikins.

[< Old French *pousser,* earlier *poulser* < Latin *pulsāre* to beat. Doublet of PULSE[1].]

—**Syn.** *v.t.* **1. Push, shove** mean to move someone or something by pressing against it. **Push** emphasizes pressing against the person or thing in order to move it ahead, aside, etc., away from oneself or something else: *She pushed the drawer closed.* **Shove** emphasizes moving someone or something out of the way by pushing roughly, or something hard to move or heavy by pushing it along with force and effort: *He shoved his way through the crowd. He shoved the piano across the room.*

push·ball (půsh′bôl′), *n.* **1.** a game played with a large, heavy ball, usually about six feet in diameter. Two sides of players try to push it toward opposite goals. **2.** the ball used: *Certain Congressmen may follow the Senate's lead in making this most serious matter a political pushball* (New York Times).

push·bar (půsh′bär′), *n.* a bar which transmits a thrust or pushing force: *In no time the sled had more speed than we could keep up with . . . without changing my grip on the pushbar I pivoted in behind him* (Canada Month).

push bike, *Especially British.* a bicycle operated by pedals rather than by a motor: *I was on a three-thousand-mile push bike ride through India with four Indian students* (Punch).

push broom, a long-handled, wide brush that is pushed like a mop to clean floors: *. . . mechanized sweeper that does the work of 5 man-powered push brooms* (Wall Street Journal).

push button, a small button or knob pushed to turn an electric current on or off.

push-but·ton (půsh′but′ən), *adj.* of or having to do with actions carried out by automatic or remote-controlled mechanisms: *push-button warfare, the push-button era.*

push·cart (půsh′kärt′), *n.* a light cart pushed by hand.

push·chair (push′chãr′), *n. British.* a light baby carriage; stroller: *Tired, wonderful mothers bump pushchairs down . . . staircases to get their babies into the light and air* (Manchester Guardian).

push·er (půsh′ər), *n.* **1.** a person or thing that pushes. **2.** an airplane with propeller or propellers behind instead of in front: *In France the great early pioneers . . . had tractor-type monoplanes, although Farman and Voisin also used pushers* (Atlantic). **3.** *Informal.* an unlawful peddler of narcotics: *"Pushers" could be eliminated if the clinics made narcotics available legally under strict supervision* (New York Times).

push·ful (půsh′fəl), *adj. Informal.* full of push; self-assertive; active and energetic in prosecuting one's affairs: *He was pushful and jittery under the most innocent circumstances* (Maclean's). —**push′ful·ly,** *adv.* —**push′ful·ness,** *n.*

push·i·ness (půsh′ē nis), *n.* forwardness; self-assertiveness.

push·ing (půsh′ing), *adj.* **1.** that pushes. **2.** enterprising: *We . . . are pleased with his pushing and persevering spirit* (Washington Irving). **3.** forward; aggressive: *the cocksureness of pushing vulgarity and self-conceit* (Samuel Butler). —**push′ing·ly,** *adv.* —**push′ing·ness,** *n.*

push-o·ver (půsh′ō′vər), *n. Slang.* **1.** something very easy to do: *It was a push-over, he added, with five days off a week* (Sunday Times). **2.** a person very easy to beat in a contest: *He must have been the proverbial push-over* (Cape Times). **3.** a person easily influenced or swayed or unable to resist a particular appeal: *I am not usually a push-over for newsreel shots or telecasts of races* (New Yorker). **4.** the beginning of a dive in an airplane as the stick is pushed forward.

push-over try, *British.* (in Rugby football) a try scored in the midst of or as the direct result of a scrummage: *Two scrums followed, and from the second the visitors achieved a push-over try* (Sunday Times).

push·pin (půsh′pin′), *n.* **1.** a thin tack with a glass head, that can be pushed into a wall, etc., without leaving a noticeable mark. **2.** a children's game played with pins. **3.** child's play; triviality.

push-pull (půsh′půl′), *adj. Radio.* of or having such an arrangement of two circuit elements that the effect of one supplements the other: *a push-pull circuit or amplifier.*

push·rod (půsh′rod′), *n.* a rod, as in an internal-combustion engine, that acts with a cam or cams to open and close the valves of the cylinders.

Push·tu (push′tü), *n.* Pashto: *Afghanistan champions the Pathan cause because . . . Pushtu, the Pathan tongue, is spoken widely in Afghanistan* (London Times).

push·up (půsh′up′), *n.* a calisthenic exercise in which a person, lying prone, raises his body, held stiff, with the toes as pivot, by pushing downward with his hands: *A few brisk pushups and you're in fine fettle for a chummy joust with Customs* (New Yorker). —*adj.* (of sleeves) that can be worn pushed up from the wrist.

push·y (půsh′ē), *adj.,* **push·i·er, push·i·est.** forward; aggressive: *But what in the son was smirking and pushy was in the father shrewd and masterful* (New Yorker).

pu·sil·la·nim·i·ty (pyü′sə lə nim′ə tē), *n.* cowardliness; timidity.

pu·sil·lan·i·mous (pyü′sə lan′ə məs), *adj.* cowardly; faint-hearted; mean-spirited: *an indignity which no prince, how inconsiderable or pusillanimous soever, could tamely endure* (Thomas W. Robertson). *One cannot contemplate this pusillanimous conduct of Montezuma without mingled feelings of pity and contempt* (William H. Prescott). [< Latin *pusillanimis* (with English *-ous*) < *pusillus* little + *animus* courage] —**pu′sil·lan′i·mous·ly,** *adv.* —**pu′sil·lan′i·mous·ness,** *n.* —**Syn.** timorous, spiritless. —**Ant.** brave, courageous.

pus·ley (pus′lē), *n.* pussley.

puss (půs), *n.* **1.** a cat. **2.** a hare. **3.** a girl: *The little puss seems already to have airs enough to make a husband . . . miserable* (George Eliot). **4.** *Slang.* the face; mouth: *[She] owns a deadpan puss and a willing set of lungs, all of which she puts to good use demolishing Tin Pan Alley tearjerkers* (New Yorker). [< Germanic (compare Dutch *poes,* Low German *puus, puus-katte*)]

puss-in-the-cor·ner (půs′in ᴛʜə kôr′nər), *n.* a game for children, of whom one stands in the center and tries to capture one of the bases as the other players change places.

puss·ley or **puss·ly** (pus′lē), *n. U.S.* purslane: *Miss Alexander was up and helping weed pussley out of the garden* (New Yorker).

puss moth, a large European moth, having the forewings of a whitish or light-gray color with darker markings and spots: *When searching poplars and willows, there is also a good chance of finding the button-shaped eggs of the puss moth* (New Scientist).

puss·y[1] (půs′ē), *n., pl.* **puss·ies.** **1.** a cat: *Pussy is most often a southpaw when she is not ambidextrous* (Science News Letter). **2.** a catkin, as of a willow. **3.** a hare. **4. a.** the game of tipcat. **b.** the cat used in this game. [< *puss* + *-y*[2]]

pus·sy[2] (pus′ē), *adj.,* **-si·er, -si·est.** full of pus. [< *pus* + *-y*[1]]

puss·y·cat (půs′ē kat′), *n.* a cat; pussy: *Whether I paint a skyscraper or a pussycat I want to make it more interesting* (Time).

puss·y·foot (půs′ē fůt′), *v., n., pl.* **-foots.** *Slang.* —*v.i. U.S.* **1.** to move softly and cautiously to avoid being seen. **2.** to be cautious and timid about revealing one's opinions or committing oneself: *We have pussyfooted around on this boycott long enough and it has come time to be frank and honest* (Time). —*n.* a person who pussyfoots.

pussy willow, 1. *U.S.* a small North American willow with silky catkins. **2.** any of various similar willows.

Pussy Willow Sprig (def. 1)

pus·tu·lant (pus′chə lənt), *adj.* causing pustules. —*n.* an irritant that causes pustules. [< Latin *pustulāns, -antis,* present participle of *pustulāre;* see PUSTULATE]

pus·tu·lar (pus′chə lər), *adj.* **1.** of, like, or having to do with pustules. **2.** characterized by pustules.

pus·tu·late (*v.* pus′chə lāt; *adj.* pus′chə lit), *v.,* **-lat·ed, -lat·ing,** *adj.* —*v.t., v.i.* to form pustules. —*adj.* having pustules. [< Latin *pustulāre* (with English *ate*[1]) < *pustula* pustule]

pus·tu·la·tion (pus′chə lā′shən), *n.* **1.** the formation of pustules. **2.** a pustule.

pus·tule (pus′chül), *n.* **1.** a pimple containing pus. **2.** any swelling like a pimple or blister, such as the pustules of chicken pox. [< Latin *pustula*]

pus·tu·lous (pus′chə ləs), *adj.* pustular.

pusz·ta (pu̇s′tä), *n.* the Hungarian steppe: *They saw the infinite horizons of the ... puszta* (New Yorker). [< Hungarian *puszta* (literally) barren, empty]

put[1] (pu̇t), *v.,* **put, put·ting,** *n.* —*v.t.* **1.** to cause to be in some place or position; place; lay: *I put sugar in my tea. Put away your toys.* **2.** to cause to be in some state, condition, position, relation, etc.: *to put a room in order, to put oneself under the care of a doctor. We put the house on the market.* **3.** to express: *to put one's thoughts in writing, to put a French poem in English. The teacher puts things clearly.* **4.** to propose or submit for answer, consideration, deliberation, etc.: *He put several questions before me.* **5.** to throw or cast (a 16-pound ball, etc.) from the hand placed close to the shoulder. **6.** to set at a particular place, point, amount, etc., in a scale of estimation; appraise: *He puts the distance at five miles.* **7.** to apply: *A doctor puts his skill to good use.* **8.** to impose: *C. suspected ... that he was putting a joke upon him* (Hawthorne). **9.** to assign; attribute: *He put a wrong construction on my action.*
—*v.i.* **1.** to take one's course; go; turn; proceed: *The ship put out to sea.* **2.** *U.S. Informal.* to make off; be off: *to put for work.* **3.** *Dialect.* (of a plant) to send forth shoots.
put about, a. *Nautical.* to put (a ship) on the opposite tack: *The Stella was then put about, and the other broadside given* (Frederick Marryat). **b.** *Nautical.* to turn on to the other tack; change direction: *Down with the helm, and let us put about* (John Wilson). **c.** to circulate: *Who has put this lie about?* (Mrs. Lynn Linton).
put across, *Informal.* **a.** to carry out successfully: *And, gentlemen, we'll put it across! We'll do it by working!* (H.L. Foster). **b.** to cause to be understood or appreciated; get across: *He could not put his point of view across to the audience.*
put aside, a. to save for future use: *to put aside a dollar a week.* **b.** to lay aside out of use: *A curious kind of egalitarian, humanitarian attitude has let us quickly put aside vice as a proposition, and go to misery* (Daniel P. Moynihan).
put away, a. to save for future use: *The fruit should be ... carefully put away in bins* (Journal of the Royal Agricultural Society). **b.** *Informal.* to consume as food or drink: *to put away a meal.* **c.** *Informal.* to put in jail; imprison: *They never had enough on Duncan to make an actual arrest, but cops hear things ... and they were anxious to put him away* (John O'Hara). **d.** *Informal.* to commit to a mental institution: *You knew their daughter had to be put away? It was a tragic thing ... she cut her wrists* (New Yorker). **e.** *Informal.* to kill: *A reward, I should have greatly valued ... were he [a dog] not now in danger of being put away* (Anne Brontë).
put by, a. to save for future use: *The old gentleman had put by a little money* (Dickens). **b.** to turn aside; reject: *There is no putting by that crown; queens you must always be* (John Ruskin). **c.** to evade: *The chancellor ... smiling, put the question by* (Tennyson).
put down, a. to put an end to; suppress; crush: *Sir Peter is such an enemy to scandal, I believe he would have it put down by parliament* (Richard Brinsley Sheridan). **b.** to write down: *I have put you down in my will for a ring* (New Monthly Magazine). **c.** to pay as a down payment: *to put down a deposit of $10 on a typewriter.* **d.** *Informal.* to lower in importance; slight or belittle; snub: *They sensed that even some of Mr. Johnson's normally solid supporters thought he should be put down a bit* (Atlantic). **e.** *Informal.* to kill: *If unwanted babies, why not "put down" our elderly parents, too?* (Manchester Guardian Weekly). **f.** to land: *We put down in Murmansk, but soon our stewardess jubilantly announced that our pilot had talked Vnukovo airport in Moscow into letting us come in* (Time).
put forth, a. to send out; sprout: *to put forth buds.* **b.** to exert: *to put forth effort.* **c.** to start, especially to sea: *to put forth on a voyage.* **d.** to issue; publish: *to put forth an edict.* **e.** to stretch forth or out: *He put forth his staff that he had in his hand* (Miles Coverdale).
put forward, to advance for consideration or acceptance; propound; suggest: *His conclusions are hasty and the broad proposals which he puts forward contain no evidence that they could ever be successfully applied* (New Yorker).
put in, *Informal.* **a.** to spend (time, etc.) as specified: *I try and put in three miles before lunch* (Graham Greene). **b.** to enter port: *The ship put in at Singapore.* **c.** to enter; go in: *The ladies ... were busy at the bridge tables just off the center of the lobby on the afternoon I put in* (Saturday Review). **d.** to sow; plant: *to put in crops.* **e.** to get in (a word); interpose: *Baxter himself attempted to put in a word* (Macaulay). **f.** to furnish in addition: *The Lords put in amendments which the Commons would not accept* (T.G. Tout).
put in for, to make a claim, plea, or offer for: *He put in for a grant to fight City Hall* (Harper's).
put off, a. to lay aside; postpone: *All things are now in readiness, and must not be put off* (John Dryden). **b.** to bid or cause to wait: *We made up our minds we were not going to be put off any longer with such excuses.* **c.** to hold back or stop from: *Don't let the formidable get-up ... put you off some extremely fine music-making* (Harper's). **d.** to get rid of; dispose of: *As to oxen, I put off two lots in the year* (Journal of the Royal Agricultural Society).
put on, a. to take on oneself: *He loved primitive people like Indians and trappers ... who were not trying to put on airs* (New York Times). **b.** to pretend: *It was all put on that I might hear and rave* (John Dryden). **c.** to impose; inflict: *The fines were not fixed sums; the king could put on just what he liked* (M.J. Guest). **d.** to don; clothe with: *Mrs. Venn ... is going away to put on her things* (Thomas Hardy). **e.** to add: *to put on weight.* **f.** to apply; exert: *to put on speed, put on pressure.* **g.** to set to work: *to put men on to clean up a job.* **h.** to direct, stage, or sponsor (a play, lecture, etc.): *The Foundation for Integrative Education was putting on the last in a six-evening series of discussions* (New York Times). **i.** *Slang.* to play a trick on; tease playfully; poke fun at: *Are you putting me on?*
put (one) over on, to impose (something false or deceptive) on: *The discovery ... served to exacerbate the situation, confirming the eternal Cornish suspicion that Englishmen live only for the chance to put one over on them* (Punch).
put out, a. to extinguish: *to put out a candle, light, or fire.* **b.** to embarrass; disconcert: *You must not be at all surprised or put out at feeling the difficulties you describe* (Cardinal Newman). **c.** to annoy; irritate: *Sir Dene [was] ... thoroughly put out with the captain* (Mrs. Henry Wood). **d.** to destroy the sight of: *Will you put out mine eyes?* (Shakespeare). **e.** to inconvenience: *Please don't put yourself out; I'll look for the book myself.* **f.** to eject: *He is ... put out by the constables* (Benjamin Jowett). **g.** to publish: *In its fourth communiqué put out in November of last year, the liaison office made an obvious effort ...* (New Yorker). **h.** to cause to be out in a game or sport: *to put out a batter at first base.* **i.** to set out on a voyage: *Dozens of Chinese would "cheerfully" put out in small boats to sell food to their enemies* (Punch). **j.** to invest: *The syndicate in Toronto isn't interested in marijuana because the profits aren't high enough. Most of the people who put out are independent operators* (Maclean's).
put over, *Informal.* **a.** to carry out successfully; put across: *You don't go into any business ... and put it over without running the risk of being shot* (Gertrude Atherton). **b.** to postpone; defer: *I wanted to put [the meeting] over until Sunday, so as not to interfere with my work* (New Yorker).
put through, a. to cause to pass through any process: *We saw an ancient instructor putting his class of girls through what looked like early ballet exercises* (Maclean's). **b.** to carry out successfully: *Taking prompt action ... to "put through" a certain nefarious design* (Longman's Magazine). **c.** to send or pass between points, as a telegram, a telephone call, or a person: *to put a call through to London. Will you put me through to Chicago?*
put to it, to force to a course; put in difficulty: *Commission houses are put to it to keep up with the clerical work involved* (Wall Street Journal).
put up, a. to raise; lift: *Shopkeepers had hastily put up their shutters* (Maxwell Gray). **b.** to offer; give; show: *to put up a prayer, put up a brave front.* **c.** to propose for election or adoption: *He took a solemn vow that he would never permit his name to be put up for president of the club* (New Yorker). **d.** to offer for sale by auction: *Oughtn't the post ... to have been put up for public competition?* (Chambers's Journal). **e.** to lay aside: *I have put my complaint up again, for to my foes my bill I dare not show* (Chaucer). **f.** to pay; deposit: *A wealthy Bostonian ... put up the money* (Boston Journal). **g.** to take up or give lodging or food: *He ... put up at the New Southern Hotel in Jackson* (New Yorker). *Can you put us up for the night?* (Rolf Boldrewood). **h.** to build: *to put up a house.* **i.** to preserve (fruit, etc.): *to put up six jars of blackberries.* **j.** to make up: *Prussia, together with the remaining states, puts up sixteen army corps* (Harper's Magazine). **k.** to dress (hair): *to put up one's hair before a party.* **l.** to cause (game) to rise from cover: *He noticed some teal and mallard in a stubble field and walking across, he put them up* (London Times). **m.** to raise in amount: *Making preparations to put up the price still higher* (Saturday Review).
put upon, to impose upon; take advantage of; victimize: *However frustrated, distracted, and put upon the great press corps was, out of its agony came reading matter* (Newsweek).
put up to, a. to inform of; make aware of: *He put me up to one or two things worth knowing* (Cornhill Magazine). **b.** to stir up to; incite to: *Mr. Lasky ... in an act of admirable self-restraint ... does not suggest that Joe Kennedy actually put Mr. Khrushchev up to it* (Wall Street Journal).
put up with, to bear with patience; tolerate: *to put up with hot weather, put up with scorn.*
—*n.* **1.** a throw or cast. **2.** *Commerce.* the privilege of delivering a certain amount of stock, etc., at a specified price within a certain period of time: *Puts, like calls, chiefly are bought by speculators* (Wall Street Journal).
[< Old English *putian*]
—**Syn.** *v.t.* **1, 2. Put, place, set** mean to cause someone or something to be in some place, position, condition, relation, etc. **Put** emphasizes the action of moving something into or out of a place or position or bringing it into some condition, state, or relation: *Put your hand in mine.* **Place** emphasizes the idea of a definite spot, condition, etc., more than action: *Place your hands behind your head.* **Set** emphasizes causing to be in a stated or certain position, etc.: *Set the box down over there.*

put[2] (put), *n. Dialect.* a stupid or silly fellow; bumpkin. [origin unknown]

put[3] (put), *v.,* **put·ted, put·ting,** *n.* putt.

put[4] (put), *n.* a short, explosive sound, as that made by an outboard motor.

pu·ta·men (pyü tā′mən), *n., pl.* **-tam·i·na** (-tam′ə nə). **1.** a hard or stony endocarp, such as the stone of a peach. **2.** the outer zone of the extraventricular portion of the gray matter of the brain, thought by some to be the area of the brain reacting to sensations of pleasure. [< Latin *putāmen, -inis* < *putāre;* see PUTATIVE]

put-and-take (pu̇t′ən tāk′), *n.* any gambling game played with a six-sided top or teetotum, in which all the players contribute to the pool from which winnings are taken: *It has been a game of put-and-take with all the accent on take* (New York Times).

pu·ta·tive (pyü′tə tiv), *adj.* supposed; reputed: *the putative author of a book.* [< Latin *putātīvus* < *putāre* to cleanse, trim, to prune trees; reckon, think] —**pu′ta·tive·ly,** *adv.*

put-down (pu̇t′doun′), *n. Informal.* **1.** a slighting or belittling of a person or thing: *The early church fathers would have examined Adam Ogilvy carefully for horns . . . if they had heard his contemptuous put-down of patience, a paramount Christian virtue* (Time). **2.** a comment, reply, etc., intended to snub or belittle.

put·log (pu̇t′lôg, -log; put′-), *n.* one of the short horizontal members that support the flooring of a scaffold. [earlier *putlock,* perhaps < *put*[1]]

put-off (pu̇t′ôf′, -of′), *n.* **1.** a putting off or postponing; postponement. **2.** a getting rid of by evasion or the like: *I would have asked farther, but Alan gave me the put-off* (Robert Louis Stevenson). **3.** an evasion.

put-on (pu̇t′on′, -ôn′), *adj.* assumed; affected; pretended: . . . *the put-on atheism of Left Bank beatniks* (Time). —*n.* **1.** a pretension or affectation. **2.** *Slang.* a mischievous joke or trick played for fun; practical joke; hoax: *"Pop Art" is . . . possibly a "put-on"* (New York Times).

put·out (pu̇t′out′), *n.* the act of putting a player out, as in baseball or cricket: *Mantle made all three putouts in his lone inning at short* (New York Times).

put-put (put′put′), *n., v.,* **-put·ted, -put·ting.** —*n.* **1.** the succession of sharp, explosive noises made by a small gasoline engine. **2.** *Slang.* a boat or vehicle operated by such an engine. —*v.i.* to go or travel by means of such an engine.

pu·tre·fa·cient (pyü′trə fā′shənt), *adj.* putrefying; putrefactive. —*n.* an agent or substance that produces putrefaction.

pu·tre·fac·tion (pyü′trə fak′shən), *n.* a decay; rotting.

pu·tre·fac·tive (pyü′trə fak′tiv), *adj.* **1.** causing putrefaction. **2.** characterized by or having to do with putrefaction. —**pu′tre·fac′tive·ness,** *n.*

pu·tre·fi·a·ble (pyü′trə fī′ə bəl), *adj.* likely to become putrefied.

pu·tre·fi·er (pyü′trə fī′ər), *n.* a putrefacient.

pu·tre·fy (pyü′trə fī), *v.i., v.t.,* **-fied, -fy·ing.** **1.** to rot; decay; decompose. **2.** to become or cause to be gangrenous. [< Middle French *putrefier,* learned borrowing from Latin *putrefierī,* and *putrefacere* < *puter* rotten (see PUTRESCENT) + *fierī* become, passive of *facere* make]

pu·tresce (pyü tres′), *v.i.,* **-tresced, -tresc·ing.** to begin to putrefy; become putrid.

pu·tres·cence (pyü tres′əns), *n.* **1.** a putrescent condition. **2.** putrescent matter.

pu·tres·cent (pyü tres′ənt), *adj.* **1.** becoming putrid; rotting. **2.** having to do with putrefaction. [< Latin *pūtrēscēns, -entis,* present participle of *pūtrēscere* grow rotten < *pūtēre* to stink < *puter* rotten, related to *pūs, pūris* pus]

pu·tres·ci·ble (pyü tres′ə bəl), *adj.* likely to rot. —*n.* a substance that will rot.

pu·tres·cine (pyü tres′ēn, -in), *n.* a colorless, evil-smelling ptomaine, formed during the decay of animal tissue. *Formula:* $C_4H_{12}N_2$ [< Latin *pūtrēscere* (see PUTRESCENT) + English *-ine*[2]]

pu·trid (pyü′trid), *adj.* **1.** rotten; foul: *a putrid odor, putrid meat.* **2. a.** thoroughly corrupt or depraved. **b.** extremely bad. **3.** gangrenous: *putrid flesh.* [< Latin *pūtridus* < *puter,* rotten; see PUTRESCENT] —**pu′trid·ly,** *adv.* —**pu′trid·ness,** *n.*

pu·trid·i·ty (pyü trid′ə tē), *n.* **1.** putrid condition. **2.** putrid matter.

putsch (pu̇ch), *n.* an uprising; insurrection: *The common political experience of Eastern Europe between wars was the putsch and persecution at home, jealousy and chauvinism abroad* (Newsweek). [< German *Putsch* (literally) push, thrust]

putsch·ist (pu̇ch′ist), *n.* a person who advocates or takes part in a putsch: *When he first began his guerrilla fight, . . . Rodriguez himself laughed off Castro as a petty putschist* (Time).

putt (put), *v.t., v.i.* to strike (a golf ball) gently and carefully in an effort to make it roll into the hole. —*n.* **1.** the stroke made in putting: *Bayliss had single putts on the first four greens coming back* (London Times). **2.** the act of putting. [variant of *put*[1]]

put·tee (put′ē, pu tē′), *n.* **1.** a long, narrow strip of cloth wound around the leg from ankle to knee, worn by sportsmen, soldiers, etc.: *He wore the . . . short-sleeved tunic, boots and puttees of the Force Publique* (London Times). **2.** a gaiter of cloth or leather reaching from ankle to knee, worn by soldiers, riders, etc. Also, **puttie, putty.** [< Hindi *paṭṭī* a bandage, strip < Sanskrit *paṭī* cloth]

Puttees
Left, (def. 1); right, (def. 2)

put·ter[1] (put′ər), *v.i.* to keep busy in a rather useless way: *Mary likes to spend the afternoon puttering in the garden.* Also, *especially British,* **potter.** [variant of *potter*[2]] —**put′ter·er,** *n.*

putt·er[2] (put′ər), *n.* **1.** a golf player who putts. **2.** a golf club used in putting. [< *putt* + *-er*[1]]

put·ter[3] (pu̇t′ər), *n.* a person or thing that puts. [< *put*[1] + *-er*[1]]

put·ti (püt′ē), *n., pl.* of **put·to** (püt′ō). *Italian.* representations of cupidlike children used in art, especially during the Renaissance: *Two oil sketches of putti with swags of fruit . . . were sold for £420* (London Times).

put·tie (put′ē), *n.* puttee.

put·ti·er (put′ē ər), *n.* a person who putties, as a glazier. [< *putty*[1] + *-er*[1]]

putt·ing green (put′ing), **1.** that part of a golf course within 20 yards of the hole, except the hazards; the smooth turf or sand around a golf hole. **2.** a similar area off the course, used to practice putting: *He put in another four and a half hours on the putting green.* [< *putt* + *-ing*[2]]

put·tock (put′ək), *n. Dialect.* any of certain birds of prey, especially a kite or a buzzard. [Middle English *puttok*]

putt-putt (put′put′), *n., v.i.* put-put.

put·ty[1] (put′ē), *n., pl.* **-ties,** *v.,* **-tied, -ty·ing.** —*n.* **1.** a soft mixture of whiting and linseed oil, used for sealing the edges of panes of glass, etc. **2.** a pipe-joint compound. **3.** a very smooth mortar of lime and water mixed, used in plastering. **4.** putty powder. **5.** putty color.
—*v.t.* to stop up or cover with putty: *He puttied up the holes in the woodwork before painting it.*
[< French *potée* (originally) potful < Old French *pot* pot, container < Vulgar Latin *pottus*]

put·ty[2] (put′ē), *n., pl.* **-ties.** puttee.

putty color, a light gray. [< *putty*[1]]

put·ty-col·ored (put′ē kul′ərd), *adj.* light-gray.

putty powder, fine, abrasive powder, especially tin oxide, used to polish glass, stone, or metal.

put·ty·root (put′ē rüt′, -ru̇t′), *n.* a North American orchid, with racemes of brownish flowers; Adam-and-Eve. The corm it produces contains a glutinous matter that has been used as a cement.

put-up (pu̇t′up′), *adj. Informal.* planned beforehand, or deliberately, in a secret or crafty manner: *His election was a put-up job by the party bosses.*

put-up·on (pu̇t′ə pon′, -pôn′), *adj.* imposed upon; taken advantage of; victimized: . . . *a rich, overbearing builder and his put-upon, endlessly complaining family* (New Yorker).

puy (pwē), *n.* a small volcanic cone of a type common in Auvergne, central France. [< French *puy* hill < Old French, balcony, elevation. Doublet of PEW.]

puz·zle (puz′əl), *n., v.,* **-zled, -zling.** —*n.* **1.** a hard problem: *How to get all my clothes into one suitcase was a puzzle.* **2.** a problem or task to be done for fun: *A famous Chinese puzzle has seven pieces of wood to fit together.* **3.** a puzzled condition: *The new student was in a puzzle about where to go.*
—*v.t.* to make unable to answer, solve, or understand something; perplex: *How the dog got out of the house puzzled us.* —*v.i.* **1.** to be perplexed. **2.** to exercise one's mind on something hard.
puzzle out, to find out by thinking or trying hard: *to puzzle out the meaning of a sentence.*
puzzle over, to think hard about; try hard to do or work out: *He puzzled over his homework for an hour.*
[origin uncertain] —**puz′zling·ly,** *adv.* —**puz′zling·ness,** *n.*
—**Syn.** *n.* **3.** bewilderment, quandary. *-v.t.* **Puzzle, perplex, bewilder** mean to make a person uncertain what to think, say, or do. **Puzzle** suggests a problem having so many parts or sides and being so mixed up or involved that it is hard to understand or solve: *My friend's behavior puzzles me.* **Perplex** in addition adds the idea of troubling with doubt about how to decide or act: *They were worried and perplexed by their son's behavior.* **Bewilder** adds and emphasizes the idea of confusing and causing one to feel lost among all the various possibilities: *City traffic bewilders him.*

puzzle box, a box or pen from which an animal may learn to release itself by clawing a string, pressing a lever, etc., used in experiments dealing with animal behavior or intelligence: *He* [*E.L. Thorndike*] *invented the puzzle box to investigate how such animals as cats and dogs solve problems* (B.F. Skinner).

puz·zled·ly (puz′əld lē), *adv.* in a puzzled manner.

puz·zle·head (puz′əl hed′), *n.* a person of confused ideas.

puz·zle·head·ed (puz′əl hed′id), *adj.* having or showing confused ideas.

puzzle jug, a jug with perforated sides from which one can drink without spilling only by closing a certain airhole with the finger: *He made . . . the traditional instruments of rustic amusement, puzzle jugs which deluged the unwary with ale* (London Times).

puz·zle·ment (puz′əl mənt), *n.* a puzzled condition: *He was just talking in a tone of sheer, hopeless . . . puzzlement—bafflement* (A. S. M. Hutchinson).

puz·zle-mug (puz′əl mug′), *n.* a drinking-vessel of pottery with perforated sides, several small spouts, and an inner tube through which the liquid contents may be drawn up to the mouth when a particular hole is closed with the finger.

puz·zler (puz′lər), *n.* **1.** a person or thing that puzzles. **2.** a person who occupies himself with puzzles.

puz·zlist (puz′ə list, puz′list), *n.* an inventor of puzzles.

PVA (no periods), polyvinyl alcohol.

PVC (no periods), polyvinyl chloride: *The PVC coating protects it against ultraviolet radiation* (New Scientist).

PVP (no periods), polyvinyl pyrrolidone.

Pvt., private: *Pvt. John E. Martin.*

PW (no periods) or **P.W.,** prisoner of war: *Captured airmen were separated from other P.W.s and taken to a place near Pyongyang* (Time).

PWA (no periods), Public Works Administration.

P wave, a primary wave: *When an earthquake occurs under the Indian Ocean, its P waves pass through the core of the earth to recording stations in the United States, on the opposite side of the world* (Walter Sullivan).

P.W.D. or **PWD** (no periods), Public Works Department.

pwe (pwe), *n.* a Burmese festival in which groups of actors, singers, and dancers perform on outdoor stages: *A pwe . . ., compounded of classical Burmese drama and dance and comic routines that are likely to dwell suggestively on either sex or politics* (New York Times). [< Burmese *pwe*]

pwt., pennyweight.

PX (no periods) or **P.X.,** post exchange: *Her colleagues delighted in baked beans from the PX* (New Yorker).

pxt., pinxit.

py-, *combining form.* the form of **pyo-** before vowels, as in *pyoid.*

pya (pyä), *n.* a monetary unit of Burma, one hundredth of a kyat. [< Burmese *pya*]

py·ae·mi·a (pī ē′mē ə), *n.* pyemia.

py·ae·mic (pī ē′mik), *adj.* pyemic.

pyc·nid·i·um (pik nid′ē əm), *n., pl.* **-i·a** (-ē ə). a spore fruit in some fungi. Typically it is a rounded or flask-shaped receptacle enclosing conidia borne on conidiophores. [< New Latin *pycnidium* < Greek *pyknós* thick, dense + New Latin *-idium,* a diminutive suffix]

pyc·ni·o·spore (pik′nē ə spôr, -spōr), *n. Botany.* a spermatium. [< Greek *pyknós* thick, dense + English *spore*]

pyc·ni·um (pik′nē əm), *n., pl.* **-ni·a** (-nē ə). *Botany.* **1.** a spermogonium, especially of certain rust fungi. **2.** a pycnidium. [< New Latin *pycnium* < Greek *pyknós* thick, dense + New Latin *-ium*, a noun suffix]

pyc·nom·e·ter (pik nom′ə tər), *n.* an instrument, consisting usually of a glass flask with a thermometer, for determining the relative density or specific gravity of liquids. [< Greek *pyknós* thick, dense]

pyc·no·style (pik′nə stīl), *Architecture.* —*adj.* of or having to do with an arrangement of columns in which the intercolumniation measures one and a half diameters. —*n.* a pycnostyle colonnade. [< Latin *pycnostȳlos* < Greek *pyknóstȳlos* < *pyknós* thick, dense + *stŷlos* column]

pye (pī), *n.* a book of rules for finding the ecclesiastical service of the day; pie.

pye-dog (pī′dôg′, -dog′), *n.* an ownerless dog of low breed found in towns and villages of India and other parts of Asia. [< Hindi *pāhī* outsider + English *dog*]

py·e·li·tis (pī′ə lī′tis), *n.* inflammation of the pelvis of the kidney. [< New Latin *pyelitis* < Greek *pýelos* basin + New Latin *-itis* -itis]

py·e·lo·gram (pī′ə lə gram), *n.* an X-ray photograph of the kidney and ureter. [< Greek *pýelos* basin + English *-gram*]

py·e·lo·graph (pī′ə lə graf, -gräf), *n.* a pyelogram.

py·e·lo·graph·ic (pī′ə lə graf′ik), *adj.* of, having to do with, or obtained by pyelography.

py·e·log·ra·phy (pī′ə log′rə fē), *n.* the art of making X-ray pictures of the kidneys and ureters, after the injection of an opaque solution. [< Greek *pýelos* basin + English *-graphy*]

py·e·lo·ne·phri·tis (pī′ə lō nē frī′tis), *n.* an inflammation of the kidney and the pelvis: *Pyelonephritis as a cause of hypertension continues to be overlooked by many physicians* (Morris Fishbein). [< Greek *pýelos* basin + English *nephritis*]

py·e·los·co·py (pī′ə los′kə pē), *n.* fluoroscopic observation of the kidney, usually after injection of an opaque medium.

py·e·mi·a (pī ē′mē ə), *n.* a form of blood poisoning, caused by bacteria that produce pus, and characterized by multiple abscesses in different parts of the body. Also, **pyaemia.** [< New Latin *pyaemia,* perhaps < French *pyohémie* < Greek *pýon* pus + *haîma* blood]

py·e·mic (pī ē′mik), *adj.* **1.** of or having to do with pyemia. **2.** affected with pyemia. Also, **pyaemic.**

py·et (pī′ət), *n. Scottish.* piet.

py·garg (pī′gärg), *n.* (in the Bible) a kind of antelope, perhaps the addax. Deuteronomy 14:5. [< Latin *pȳgargus* < Greek *pȳ́gargos* < *pȳgḗ* rump + *argós* white]

py·gid·i·al (pī jid′ē əl), *adj.* of or having to do with the pygidium.

py·gid·i·um (pī jid′ē əm), *n., pl.* **-i·a** (-ē ə). the caudal part or terminal segment of the body in insects, crustaceans, and other invertebrates.
[< New Latin *pygidium* < Greek *pȳgídion* diminutive) < *pȳgḗ* rump]

pyg·mae·an or **pyg·me·an** (pig mē′ən), *adj.* very small in size, ability, capacity, etc.; pygmy.

Pyg·ma·li·on (pig mā′lē ən, -māl′yən), *n. Greek Legend.* a sculptor who fell in love with a statue he had made. Aphrodite gave it life, and it became Galatea.

pyg·moid (pig′moid), *adj.* of the form of of resembling Pygmies: *The pygmoid Twa ... are rarely seen, being hunters and forest dwellers* (Atlantic).

Pyg·my (pig′mē), *n., pl.* **-mies,** *adj.* —*n.* **1.** one of a group of dark-skinned people native to equatorial Africa who are less than five feet in height. **2.** one of a race of very small humans supposed to exist in parts of Africa and Asia.
—*adj.* of or having to do with the Pygmies. Also, **Pigmy.**
[< Middle English *Pigmei* < Latin *pygmaei* < Greek *pygmaîoi* (originally) plural, adjective, dwarfish < *pygmḗ* cubit, fist < *pýx,* adverb, with the fist]

pyg·my (pig′mē), *n., pl.* **-mies,** *adj.* —*n.* **1.** a very small person; dwarf: *... rumors of South American pygmies* (Science News Letter). **2.** any very small animal or thing, especially when compared with something else or with a certain standard: *He proceeded to the 50,000-bird colony of Adélie Penguins (18-inch pygmies compared to the 40-inch Emperors)* (Newsweek).
—*adj.* **1.** very small: *Pygmy marmosets live along the Amazon River in South America.* **2.** of very small capacity or power: *a pygmy mind.* Also, **pigmy.**

pyg·my·ish (pig′mē ish), *adj.* like a pygmy; dwarfish: *Compared with its giant kin ... the white [marlin] seems almost pygmyish* (Time).

pyg·my·ism (pig′mē iz əm), *n.* the condition or character of being a pygmy.

pygmy nuthatch, a small nuthatch inhabiting the coniferous forests of western North America.

pygmy owl, either of two small, grayish or reddish brown owls of western North America and South America, that often hunt during the day.

py·ic (pī′ik), *adj.* suppurating. [< *py-* + *-ic*]

py·in (pī′in), *n.* an albuminous substance found in pus.

py·ja·mas (pə jä′məz, -jam′əz), *n.pl. Especially British.* pajamas.

pyk·nic (pik′nik), *Anthropology.* —*adj.* characterized by rounded contours and a stocky form; plump and squat: *His pyknic Priestleyan features puckered in concentration* (Sunday Times).
—*n.* a person of this type: *When they go insane, pyknics are more likely to be manic-depressives* (Alfred L. Kroeber).
[< Greek *pyknós* thick, dense + English *-ic*]

pyk·no·sis (pik nō′sis), *n., pl.* **-ses** (-sēz). **1.** a condition in which the nucleus of a cell stains more deeply than usual in microscopic study. This condition is thought to be a precursor of necrosis. **2.** the thickening of a fluid or semisolid substance. [< Greek *pyknós* thick, dense + English *-osis*]

pyk·not·ic (pik not′ik), *adj.* having to do with or characterized by pyknosis: *pyknotic cells.*

pyk·rete (pī′krēt), *n.* a frozen slurry of water and wood pulp for use as building material in arctic regions. [< *Pyke,* the name of the inventor + (conc)*rete*]

py·lon (pī′lon), *n.* **1.** a tall steel framework used to carry high-tension wires across country: *The caption ... implies that overhead lines in Borrowdale are to be erected on lattice towers — commonly referred to as "pylons"* (London Times). **2.** a post or tower for guiding aviators as a marker for the course in an air race. **3.** a horizontal structure attached to the underside of an airplane's wing, containing reserve fuel or weapons: *These devices, known as pylons, are part of the underbelly of F-84 Thunderjets* (Science News Letter). **4.** one of a pair of high structures of masonry that marks an entrance at either side of a bridge. **5.** a gateway, particularly of an Egyptian temple. See **propylon** for picture. [< Greek *pylṓn* gateway < *pýlē* gate]

py·lo·rec·to·my (pī′lə rek′tə mē), *n., pl.* **-mies. 1.** the surgical removal of the pylorus. **2.** the surgical removal of part of the stomach. [< *pylor*(us) + Greek *ektomē* a cutting out]

py·lor·ic (pī lôr′ik, -lor′-; pi-), *adj.* of or having to do with the pylorus: *pyloric glands, pyloric sphincter.*

py·lor·o·spasm (pī lôr′ə spaz əm, -lor′-; pi-), *n.* a closing of the pylorus; spasm of the pylorus or of the part of the stomach close to the pylorus: *Heavy drinking may also produce in some people the condition called pylorospasm* (Scientific American).

py·lo·rus (pī lôr′əs, -lor′-; pi-), *n., pl.* **-lo·ri** (-lôr′ī, -lor′-). the opening that leads from the stomach into the intestine. [< Late Latin *pylōrus* < Greek *pylōrós* (originally) gatekeeper < *pýlē* gate + *oûros* watcher < *horân* to see]

pyo-, *combining form.* pus: *Pyogenesis = the formation of pus.* Also, **py-** before vowels. [< Greek *pýon* pus]

py·o·der·ma (pī′ə dėr′mə), *n.* any disease of the skin characterized by the formation of pus. [< *pyo-* + *derma*]

py·o·der·mi·a (pī′ə dėr′mē ə), *adj.* pyoderma.

py·o·gen·e·sis (pī′ə jen′ə sis), *n.* the formation of pus; suppuration. [< *pyo-* + *genesis*]

py·o·gen·ic (pī′ə jen′ik), *adj.* producing or generating pus; attended with or having to do with the formation of pus.

py·og·e·nous (pī oj′ə nəs), *adj.* pyogenic.

py·oid (pī′oid), *adj.* of the nature of or resembling pus; purulent. [< *py-* + *-oid*]

py·o·ne·phri·tis (pī′ō ni frī′tis), *n.* suppurative inflammation of a kidney. [< *pyo-* + *nephritis*]

py·o·per·i·car·di·um (pī′ō per′ə kär′dē əm), *n.* the presence, or a collection, of pus in the pericardium.

py·oph·thal·mi·a (pī′of thal′mē ə), *n.* an inflammation of the eye that causes pus to form. [< *py-* + *ophthalmia*]

py·o·pneu·mo·tho·rax (pī′ō nü′mō thôr′aks, -nyü′-; -thōr′-), *n.* the presence of pus and air in the pleural cavities.

py·or·rhe·a or **py·or·rhoe·a** (pī′ə rē′ə), *n.* a disease of the gums in which pockets of pus form about the teeth, the gums shrink, and the teeth become loose: *The quantities of the two vitamins in body fluids of people with parodontal lesions, or pyorrhea, [are] lower than normal* (Science News Letter). [< New Latin *pyorrhoea* < Greek *pýon* pus + *rhoiā́* a flow < *rheîn* to flow]

py·or·rhe·al or **py·or·rhoe·al** (pī′ə rē′əl), *adj.* of or having to do with pyorrhea.

py·o·sis (pī ō′sis), *n.* the formation of pus; suppuration. [< New Latin *pyosis* < Greek *pýōsis* < *pýon* pus + New Latin *-osis* -osis]

py·o·tho·rax (pī′ō thôr′aks, -thōr′-), *n.* the collection of pus in the pleural cavities.

py·o·u·re·ter (pī′ō yů rē′tər, -yůr′ə-), *n.* the collection of pus in a ureter. [< *pyo-* + *ureter*]

pyr-, the form of **pyro-** that appears before *h,* and sometimes before vowels, as in *pyrene, pyrheliometer.*

py·ra·can·tha (pī′rə kan′thə, pir′ə-), *n.* any of a group of thorny, evergreen shrubs; firethorn: *Pyracantha in the North has long since been denuded of its berries* (New York Times). [< Latin *pyracantha* < Greek *pyrákantha* < *pŷr* fire + *ákantha* thorn]

pyr·a·lid (pir′ə lid), *n.* any of a large family of plain-colored moths with slender bodies, as the meal moth.
—*adj.* belonging to or having to do with this family.
[< New Latin *Pyralidae* the family name < Latin *pyralis* a winged insect that supposedly lived in fire < Greek *pyralís* < *pŷr* fire]

py·ral·i·dan (pī ral′ə dən), *n., adj.* pyralid.

py·ral·i·did (pī ral′ə did), *n., adj.* pyralid.

Py·ra·lin (pī′rə lin), *n. Trademark.* a substance composed essentially of pyroxylin and camphor, variously colored to imitate ivory, amber, tortoise shell, ebony, etc., and used in the manufacture of many products, as combs and other toilet articles, knife handles, and trays. [apparently contraction of *pyroxylin*]

pyr·a·mid (pir′ə mid), *n.* **1.** a solid having triangular sides meeting in a point. **2.** a thing or things having the form of a pyramid: *a pyramid of stones.* **3.** a crystal each of whose faces intersects the vertical axis and one or two of the lateral axes.

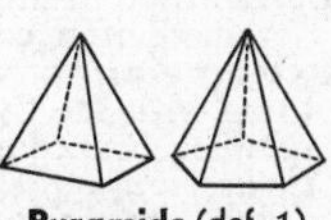

Pyramids (def. 1)
Left, square base; right, pentagon base

—*v.i.* to be in the form of a pyramid. —*v.t.* **1.** to put in the form of a pyramid. **2.** to raise or increase (costs, wages, etc.) gradually: *They are pyramiding their costs in their pricing, just as steel is doing* (Wall Street Journal). **3.** to increase (one's operations, holdings, etc.) in buying or selling stock on margin by using the profits to buy or sell more: *He pyramided his winnings and piled gold on gold ... and finally saw himself a millionaire three times over* (Percy Marks). [< Latin *pȳramis, -idis* < Greek *pȳramís, -ídos*]

py·ram·i·dal (pə ram′ə dəl), *adj.* **1.** shaped like a pyramid: *the pyramidal structures of ancient Egypt* (William H. Prescott). *The pyramidal cells in one hemisphere of the brain may activate the symmetrical region of the other hemisphere* (Scientific American). **2.** colossal; huge; extraordinarily great (a French use): *a pyramidal success.* —**py·ram′i·dal·ly,** *adv.*

pyr·a·mid·ic (pir′ə mid′ik), *adj.* pyramidal: *The enormous gate which rose O'er them in almost pyramidic pride* (Byron).

pyr·a·mid·i·cal (pir′ə mid′ə kəl), *adj.* pyramidal: *This bounding line [of a building] from top to bottom may either be inclined inwards, and the mass therefore pyramidical; or vertical, and the mass form one grand cliff* (John Ruskin). [< Greek *pȳramidikós* pyramidic (< *pȳramís, -ídos* pyramid) + English *-al*[1]] —**pyr′a·mid′i·cal·ly,** *adv.* —**pyr′a·mid′i·cal·ness,** *n.*

pyr·a·mid·i·on (pir′ə mid′ē on), *n., pl.* **-i·ons, -i·a** (-ē ə). **1.** a small pyramid forming the apex of an obelisk. **2.** any small pyramid. [< New Latin *pyramidion*]

Pyr·a·mids (pir′ə midz), *n.pl.* the huge, massive stone pyramids, serving as royal tombs, built by the ancient Egyptians.

Egyptian Pyramids at Giza

Pyr·a·mus (pir′ə- məs), *n. Greek Legend.* a young man who loved Thisbe and killed himself because he thought that she had been devoured by a lion.

py·ran (pī′ran, pī ran′), *n.* one of two isomeric compounds, each having a ring of five carbon atoms and one oxygen atom. *Formula:* C_5H_6O [< *pyr*(one) + *-an,* variant of *-ane*]

py·rar·gy·rite (pī rär′jə rīt), *n.* a dark-colored mineral consisting of a sulfide of silver and antimony, and showing, when transparent, a deep ruby-red color by transmitted light. *Formula:* Ag_3SbS_3 [probably < German *Pyrargyrit* < Greek *pŷr* fire + *árgyros* silver + German *-it* -ite[1] (probably because of its dark-red color)]

py·ra·zin·a·mid (pī′rə zin′ə mid), *n.* pyrazinamide.

py·ra·zin·a·mide (pī′rə zin′ə mīd), *n.* a drug sometimes used in the treatment of tuberculosis, especially in conjunction with isoniazid or streptomycin, in persons who are resistant to or sensitive to other drugs. *Formula:* $C_5H_5N_3O$

pyr·a·zine (pir′ə zēn, -zin), *n. Chemistry.* **1.** a feebly basic, crystalline organic compound, with an odor like heliotrope. *Formula:* $C_4H_4N_2$ **2.** any of various compounds derived from it: *The new TB medicine is a pyrazine chemical* (Science News Letter). [< *pyr-* + *azine*]

pyre (pīr), *n.* **1.** a pile of wood for burning a dead body as a funeral rite: *Only within the past century have grieving widows been restrained from throwing themselves on their husbands' funeral pyres* (Newsweek). **2.** any large pile or heap of burnable material. [< Latin *pyra* < Greek *pyrā́* < *pŷr* fire]

py·rene[1] (pī′rēn), *n.* **1.** a stone of a fruit, especially when there are several in one fruit. **2.** a nutlet. [probably < New Latin *pyrena* < Greek *pȳrḗn* stone of a fruit]

py·rene[2] (pī′rēn), *n.* a solid hydrocarbon, obtained from coal tar. *Formula:* $C_{16}H_{10}$

Pyr·e·ne·an (pir′ə nē′ən), *adj.* of or having to do with the Pyrenees, a mountain range between France and Spain: *Swarms of butterflies, dragonflies and other insects fly southwards over the Pyrenean passes* (Observer). —*n.* **1.** a native or inhabitant of the Pyrenees. **2.** the Great Pyrenees dog: *Pyreneans, puppies for sale* (London Times).

Pyr·e·nees (pir′ə nēz), *n.* the Great Pyrenees dog.

py·re·thrin (pī rē′thrən, -reth′rən), *n.* one of the constituents or active principles of pyrethrum: *Insects cannot build resistance to pyrethrins because they are a natural insecticide* (Cape Times). [< *pyrethr*(um) + *-in*]

py·re·thrum (pī rē′thrəm, -reth′rəm), *n., pl.* **-thrums. 1.** any of various chrysanthemums, much cultivated for their showy white, lilac, or red flowers: *The rich "white highlands" whence comes most of Kenya's lucrative coffee, tea, sisal and pyrethrum* (Time). **2.** an insecticide made of the powdered flower heads of any of certain of these: *With the appearance of the scientists on the field of battle, the old stand-bys of pyrethrum, oils and arsenic compounds were developed* (Science News Letter). [< Latin *pyrethrum* feverfew, pellitory < Greek *pýrethron,* probably < *pŷr* fire]

py·ret·ic (pī ret′ik), *adj.* **1.** of or having to do with fever. **2.** producing fever: *Whenever the bodily temperature falls below normal, pyretic treatment is demanded* (H.C. Wood). **3.** feverish.
[< New Latin *pyreticus* < Greek *pyretós* fever < *pŷr* fire]

pyr·e·tol·o·gy (pir′ə tol′ə jē, pī′rə-), *n.* the science of, or accumulated knowledge of, fevers. [perhaps < New Latin *pyretologia* < Greek *pyretós* fever (< *pŷr* fire) + New Latin *-logia* -logy]

pyr·e·to·ther·a·py (pir′ə tə ther′ə pē, pī′rə-), *n.* therapy in which fever is induced in the patient. [< Greek *pyretós* fever + English *therapy*]

Py·rex (pī′reks), *n. Trademark.* a kind of glassware that will not break when heated: *One of the newest glasses is borosilicate glass, widely advertised under the trade name "Pyrex"* (Monroe M. Offner).
[perhaps < Greek *pŷr* fire + Latin (*sil*)*ex* silica]

py·rex·i·a (pī rek′sē ə), *n.* a fever: *A patient's chart is occasionally labeled PUO, meaning pyrexia (fever) of unknown origin* (Scientific American). [< New Latin *pyrexia* < Greek *pyréssein* be feverish < *pyretós* fever; see PYRETIC]

py·rex·i·al (pī rek′sē əl), *adj.* of or having to do with a fever.

py·rex·ic (pī rek′sik), *adj.* feverish.

pyr·ge·om·e·ter (pīr′jē om′ə tər, pir′-), *n.* an instrument for measuring the heat radiated outward into space from the earth's surface. [< *pyr-* + *geo-* + *-meter*]

pyr·he·li·om·e·ter (pīr hē′li om′ə tər, pir-), *n.* an instrument for measuring the intensity of the sun's heat.

Pyr·i·ben·za·mine (pir′ə ben′zə mēn, -min), *n. Trademark.* an antihistamine used especially in treating allergies. *Formula:* $C_{16}H_{21}N_3$ [< *pyri*(dine) + *benz*(ene) + *amine*]

py·rid·ic (pī rid′ik), *adj.* of or related to pyridine.

pyr·i·din (pir′ə din), *n.* pyridine.

pyr·i·dine (pir′ə dēn, -din), *n.* a liquid organic base with a pungent odor, occurring in coal tar, etc., and serving as the parent substance of many compounds. It is used as a solvent and waterproofing agent, and in making various drugs and vitamins. *Formula:* C_5H_5N
[< *pyr*(role) + *-id* + *-ine*[2]]

pyr·i·dox·in (pir′ə dok′sin), *n.* pyridoxine: *Pyridoxin appears to be widespread in the animal and vegetable kingdoms* (Beaumont and Dodds).

pyr·i·dox·ine (pir′ə dok′sēn, -sin), *n.* vitamin B_6, essential to human nutrition, found in wheat germ, yeast, fish, liver, etc. *Formula:* $C_8H_{11}NO_3$ [< *pyrid*(ine) + *ox*(ygen) + *-ine*[2]]

pyr·i·form (pir′ə fôrm), *adj.* pear-shaped. [< Medieval Latin *pyrum,* for Latin *pirum* pear + English *-form*]

py·rim·i·dine (pī rim′ə dēn, pir′ə mə-; -din), *n.* **1.** a liquid or crystalline compound with a strong odor, whose molecular arrangement is a six-membered ring containing atoms of nitrogen. It is found in living matter and is a constituent of nucleic acid. *Formula:* $C_4H_4N_2$ **2.** any of a group of compounds having similar structure, as uracil and sulfadiazine. [< German *Pyrimidin* < *Pyridin* pyridine]

py·rite (pī′rīt), *n., pl.* **-rites** (-rīts). a yellow mineral with a metallic luster, a native iron disulfide; iron pyrites; fool's gold. It is used in making sulfuric acid. *Pyrite, in mistake for gold, was the first mineral shipped from America to England* (W. R. Jones). *Formula:* FeS_2 [< Latin *pyrītēs;* see PYRITES]

py·ri·tes (pī rī′tēz, pi-; pī′rīts), *n.* **1.** pyrite; iron pyrites. **2.** any of various compounds of sulfur and a metal, as tin pyrites, an ore of tin, or copper pyrites. [< Latin *pyrītēs* < Greek *pyrī́tēs* (*líthos*) flint, (stone, or ore) of fire < *pŷr* fire]

py·rit·ic (pī rit′ik, pi-), *adj.* **1.** having to do with pyrites. **2.** consisting of or resembling pyrites.

py·rit·i·cal (pī rit′ə kəl, pi-), *adj.* pyritic.

py·ro (pī′rō), *n.* pyrogallol or pyrogallic acid.

pyro-, *combining form.* **1.** of, having to do with, using, or caused by fire: *Pyromania = an obsession with fire. Pyrotechnics = the making of fireworks.*
2. heat; high temperatures: *Pyrometer = an instrument that measures high temperatures.*
3. formed by heat: *Pyroacid = an acid formed by heat.* Also, **pyr-** before *h* and some vowels. [< Greek *pyro-* < *pŷr, pyrós*]

py·ro·ac·id (pī′rō as′id, pir′ō-), *n.* any of various acids obtained by subjecting other acids to heat. [< *pyr-* + *acid*]

py·ro·cat·e·chin (pī′rə kat′ə chin, -kin), *n.* pyrocatechol.

py·ro·cat·e·chol (pī′rə kat′ə kōl, -chōl, -kol; pir′ə-), *n.* a colorless, crystalline benzene derivative, occurring in certain plants, etc., and prepared from phenol by distillation of catechol. It is used in photography as a developer and medicinally as an antiseptic. *Formula:* $C_6H_6O_2$

Py·ro·cer·am (pī′rə ser′əm, -sə ram′; pir′ə-), *n. Trademark.* a light, crystalline ceramic made from glass that can withstand sudden and extreme temperature and heat changes: *Pyroceram can be used to make items ranging from cooking pans to airplane skins* (Wall Street Journal). [< *pyro-* + *ceram*(ic)]

py·ro·chem·i·cal (pī′rə kem′ə kəl, pir′ə-), *adj.* having to do with or producing chemical changes at high temperatures. —**py′ro·chem′i·cal·ly,** *adv.*

py·ro·clas·tic (pī′rə klas′tik, pir′ə-), *adj.* composed chiefly of fragments of volcanic origin: *pyroclastic flows, pyroclastic texture. Agglomerate and tuff are pyroclastic rocks.* [< *pyro-* + *clastic*]

py·ro·con·duc·tiv·i·ty (pī′rō kon′duk-tiv′ə tē, pir′ō-), *n.* electrical conductivity induced by heat.

py·ro·crys·tal·line (pī′rə kris′tə lin, -līn; pir′ə-), *adj.* crystallized from a molten magma or highly heated solution.

py·ro·e·lec·tric (pī′rō i lek′trik, pir′ō-), *adj.* of, having to do with, or having pyroelectricity. —*n.* a pyroelectric crystal.

py·ro·e·lec·tric·i·ty (pī′rō i lek′tris′ə tē, pir′ō-; -ē′lek-), *n.* **1.** the electrified state or electric polarity produced in certain crystals by a change in temperature. **2.** the part of physics dealing with such phenomena.

py·ro·gal·late (pī′rə gal′āt, pir′ə-), *n.* an ether of pyrogallol. [< *pyro-* + *gall*(ic acid) + *-ate*[2]]

py·ro·gal·lic (pī′rə gal′ik, pir′ə-), *adj.* obtained from gallic acid by the action of heat.

pyrogallic acid, pyrogallol.

py·ro·gal·lol (pī′rə gal′ōl, -ol; -gə lōl′; pir′ə-), *n.* a white, crystalline compound obtained by heating gallic acid with water, used as a photographic developer, in medicine, and as a reagent. Pyrogallol is a phenol but can also be regarded as an acid. *Formula:* $C_6H_6O_3$ [< *pyro-* + *gall*(ic acid) + *-ol*[1]]

py·ro·gen (pī′rə jən, pir′ə-), *n.* a substance that, when introduced into the blood, produces fever: *Pyrogens in pure form can, with advantage, replace the older materials and methods for producing a general stimulation of the defense mechanisms of the body* (London Times). [< *pyro-* + *-gen*]

py·ro·gen·ic (pī′rə jen′ik, pir′ə-), *adj.* **1.** producing heat or fever. **2.** produced by fire: *Volcanic rock is pyrogenic.*

py·rog·e·nous (pī roj′ə nəs, pi-), *adj.* pyrogenic.

py·rog·nos·tics (pī′rəg nos′tiks, pir′əg-), *n.pl.* the characteristics of a mineral shown by the use of a blowpipe. [< *pyro-* fire + Greek *gnōstikós* having to do with knowledge]

py·rog·ra·pher (pī rog′rə fər, pi-), *n.* a person who is skilled in pyrography.

py·ro·graph·ic (pī′rə graf′ik, pir′ə-), *adj.* of, having to do with, or used in pyrography: *a pyrographic decoration.*

Py·ro·graph·ite (pī′rə graf′īt), *n. Trademark.* a strong graphite able to resist the effect of very high temperatures, used in missiles and other manufacture: *Pyrographite, a material it claims will solve the high-heat problems in the missile, nuclear reactor and industrial fields* (Wall Street Journal).

py·rog·ra·phy (pī rog′rə fē, pi-), *n., pl.* **-phies. 1.** the art of burning designs on wood, leather, etc. **2.** objects decorated by pyrography. **3.** a design or figure used in pyrography.

py·ro·gra·vure (pī′rō grə vyůr′, -grā′vyůr; pir′ō-), *n.* pyrography.

py·rol·a·ter (pī rol′ə tər), *n.* a fire worshiper.

py·rol·a·try (pī rol′ə trē), *n.* the worship of fire: *Anything like pyrolatry or worship of fire, as a mere element, is foreign to the character of the Greeks* (Max Müller). [< *pyro-* + Greek *latreíā* worship]

py·ro·lig·ne·ous (pī′rə lig′nē əs, pir′ə-), *adj.* produced by the distillation of wood. [< French *pyroligneux* (with English *-ous*) < Greek *pŷr, pyrós* fire + Latin *ligneus* of wood, ligneous]

pyroligneous acid, a crude acetic acid obtained by the destructive distillation of wood, and used in smoking meats; wood vinegar: *A portion of the distillate is converted to an acidic, watery fluid known as pyroligneous acid* (W.N. Jones).

pyroligneous alcohol or **spirit,** methyl alcohol.

py·ro·lig·nic (pī′rə lig′nik, pir′ə-), *adj.* pyroligneous.

py·ro·log·i·cal (pī′rə loj′ə kəl, pir′ə-), *adj.* having to do with or involving pyrology.

py·rol·o·gist (pī rol′ə jist, pi-), *n.* a person skilled in pyrology.

py·rol·o·gy (pī rol′ə jē, pi-), *n.* **1.** the science of heat. **2.** chemical or mineralogical analysis by the use of fire or the blowpipe. [< New Latin *pyrologia* < *pyro-* pyro- + *-logia* -logy]

py·ro·lu·site (pī′rə lü′sīt, pir′ə-; pī rol′yə-, pi-), *n.* native manganese dioxide, used as a source of manganese in glassmaking, and in making various chemicals, as chlorine and oxygen. *Formula:* MnO_2 [< German *Pyrolusit* < Greek *pŷr, pyrós* fire + *loúein* to wash + German *-it* -ite[1]]

py·rol·y·sis (pī rol′ə sis, pi-), *n.* chemical decomposition produced by exposure to high temperatures: *He established by pyrolysis that the strength of binding varies considerably in hydrocarbons* (New Scientist). [< *pyro-* + *lysis*]

py·ro·lyt·ic (pī′rə lit′ik, pir′ə-), *adj.* of, like, or by pyrolysis.

py·ro·mag·net·ic (pī′rō mag net′ik, pir′ō-), *adj.* **1.** having to do with magnetism as modified by heat. **2.** of or depending upon the combined action of heat and magnetism.

py·ro·man·cy (pī′rə man′sē, pir′ə-), *n.* divination by fire, or by forms appearing in fire. [< Old French *pyromancie,* and *piromance,* learned borrowings from Medieval Latin *piromancia, pyromanteia* < Greek *pŷr, pyrós* fire + *manteiā* divination]

py·ro·ma·ni·a (pī′rə mā′nē ə, pir′ə-), *n.* an obsession showing an unusual concern with fire and often involving a compulsion to start fires; incendiarism.

py·ro·ma·ni·ac (pī′rə mā′nē ak, pir′ə), *n.* a person with a mania for setting fires.

py·ro·ma·ni·a·cal (pī′rō mə nī′ə kəl, pir′ō-), *adj.* **1.** affected with or having a tendency toward pyromania. **2.** caused by a pyromaniac: *a pyromaniacal fire.*

Py·ro·men (pī′rə mən), *n. Trademark.* a polysaccharide derived from certain bacteria, used to induce fever and treat allergies and skin diseases. It has been used on animals and a small number of humans to prevent the formation of scar tissue at the ends of a severed spine so as to permit nerve fibers to grow across and thus regain ability to function. *Pyromen helps virus-ravaged nerves to rebuild themselves so that they can again assert control over the muscles* (Time).

py·ro·met·al·lur·gi·cal (pī′rō met′ə lėr′jə kəl, pir′ō-), *adj.* of or having to do with pyrometallurgy: *The work is part of an experimental investigation of pyrometallurgical processing for nuclear fuel* (Scientific American).

py·ro·met·al·lur·gy (pī′rō met′ə lėr′jē, pir′ō-), *n.* the use of heat in refining ores, in order to hasten reactions, melt the metal, etc.

py·rom·e·ter (pī rom′ə tər, pi-), *n.* **1.** an instrument for measuring very high temperatures: *An optical pyrometer . . . tells the temperature of a substance, within five degrees, by its intensity of radiation* (New Yorker). **2.** an instrument for measuring the expansion of solids by heat.

py·ro·met·ric (pī′rə met′rik, pir′ə-), *adj.* of or having to do with pyrometry or a pyrometer. —**py′ro·met′ri·cal·ly,** *adv.*

py·ro·met·ri·cal (pī′rə met′rə kəl, pir′ə-), *adj.* pyrometric.

pyrometric cone, any of a series of cones, each melting at different temperatures, used to measure the several degrees of heat in pottery kilns.

py·rom·e·try (pī rom′ə trē, pi-), *n.* **1.** the measurement of very high temperatures. **2.** the science of measuring very high temperatures.

py·ro·mor·phite (pī′rə môr′fīt, pir′ə-), *n.* a mineral consisting of chloride and phosphate of lead, occurring both in crystals and masses, green, yellow, brown, or whitish in color; green lead ore. [< German *Pyromorphit* < Greek *pŷr, pyrós* fire + *morphḗ* form + German *-it* -ite[1]]

py·rone (pī′rōn, pī rōn′), *n.* either of two isomeric compounds, one of which is the source of various natural yellow dyes. *Formula:* $C_5H_4O_2$ [< German *Pyron,* probably < Greek *pŷr* fire + German *-on* -one]

py·rope (pī′rōp), *n.* a deep-red variety of garnet, frequently used as a gem; precious garnet. [< Old French *pirope,* learned borrowing from Latin *pyrōpus* < Greek *pyrōpós* gold-colored bronze (literally) fire-eyed < *pŷr, pyrós* fire + *ṓps, ōpós* eye, face]

py·ro·pho·bi·a (pī′rə fō′bē ə, pir′ə-), *n.* a morbid dread of fire. [< *pyro-* + *-phobia*]

py·ro·pho·bic (pī′rə fō′bik, pir′ə-), *adj.* of, having to do with, or affected with pyrophobia.

py·ro·phor·ic (pī′rə fôr′ik, -for′-; pir′ə-), *adj.* **1.** having the property of taking fire simply through exposure to air; that catches fire spontaneously, as certain compounds of phosphorus: *Many of the metals used in nuclear technology, notably uranium, plutonium, thorium and zirconium, are pyrophoric* (Scientific American). **2.** (of an insect, marine organism, etc.) that is, or is like, a firefly; giving off light. [< New Latin *pyrophorus* (< Greek *pyrophóros* (literally) fire-bearing < *pŷr, pyrós* fire + *phórein* carry) + English *-ic*]

py·ro·phor·ic·i·ty (pī′rə fə ris′ə tē, pir′ə-), *n.* **1.** spontaneous combustion upon exposure to air. **2.** the tendency to react in this way; pyrophoric nature or quality.

py·ro·phos·phate (pī′rō fos′fāt, pir′ō-), *n.* a salt of pyrophosphoric acid.

py·ro·phos·phor·ic acid (pī′rō fos fôr′ik, -for′-; pir′ō-), a tetrabasic acid of phosphorus. *Formula:* $H_4P_2O_7$

py·ro·pho·tom·e·ter (pī′rō fō tom′ə tər, pir′ō-), *n.* a form of pyrometer, that measures temperatures by optical means.

py·ro·phyl·lite (pī′rə fil′īt, pir′ə-), *n.* a hydrous silicate of aluminum, usually of a whitish or greenish color. It is used as a filler and polisher, and in making slate pencils, lubricants, and cosmetics. *Pyrophyllite . . . is for commercial purposes generally included in the statistics relating to talc* (W. R. Jones). *Formula:* $Al_2O_3.4SiO_2.H_2O$ [< German *Pyrophyllite* < Greek *pŷr, pyrós* fire + *phýllon* leaf + German *-it* -ite[1] (because it leafs out under heat)]

py·ro·sis (pī rō′sis, pi-), *n.* heartburn; a burning sensation in the stomach and throat with acrid eructation: *The preparation of bismuth is used in pyrosis* (R.J. Graves). [< New Latin *pyrosis* < Greek *pýrōsis* < *pŷr, pyrós* fire + New Latin *-osis* -osis]

py·ro·stat (pī′rə stat, pir′ə-), *n.* a thermostat for high temperature. Pyrostats are used to give warning of fire or to activate a sprinkler system. [< *pyro-* + (thermo)*stat*]

py·ro·stilp·nite (pī′rō stilp′nīt), *n.* a mineral, a sulfide of arsenic and silver, occurring in minute, bright-red, monoclinic crystals; fireblende. [< *pyro-* + Greek *stilpnós* shining + English *-ite*[1]]

py·ro·sul·fate (pī′rə sul′fāt, pir′ə-), *n.* a salt of pyrosulfuric acid.

py·ro·sul·fu·ric acid (pī′rō sul fyůr′ik, pir′ō-), a thick, fuming liquid acid, a powerful oxidizing and dehydrating agent; disulfuric acid. *Formula:* $H_2S_2O_7$

py·ro·tech·nic (pī′rə tek′nik, pir′ə-), *adj.* **1.** of or having to do with fireworks: *a pyrotechnic display.* **2.** resembling fireworks; brilliant; sensational: *pyrotechnic eloquence, pyrotechnic dancing.* —**py′ro·tech′ni·cal·ly,** *adv.*

py·ro·tech·ni·cal (pī′rə tek′nə kəl, pir′ə-), *adj.* pyrotechnic: *All the warmth of her nature was exhausted by her manner: there was a sort of pyrotechnical blaze, without any real heat* (English Life).

py·ro·tech·ni·cian (pī′rə tek nish′ən, pir′ə-), *n.* pyrotechnist.

py·ro·tech·nics (pī′rə tek′niks, pir′ə-), *n.* **1.** the making of fireworks. **2.** the use of fireworks. **3.** a display of fireworks. **4.** a brilliant or sensational display, as of anger, wit, or lightning: *The meanings of the prose are sacrificed to the mechanics of . . . pyrotechnics* (Newsweek).

py·ro·tech·nist (pī′rə tek′nist, pir′ə-), *n.* a person skilled in pyrotechnics: *The whole skill of the pyrotechnists . . . was employed to produce a display of fireworks which might vie with any that had been seen in the gardens of Versailles* (Macaulay).

py·ro·tech·ny (pī′rə tek′nē, pir′ə-), *n., pl.* **-nies.** pyrotechnics: [*They*] *make such a noise in the world . . . with artificial volcanoes and puerile pyrotechny of all kinds* (Blackwood's Magazine). [< French *pyrotechnie* < Greek *pŷr, pyrós* fire + *téchnē* art, skill]

py·ro·tox·in (pī′rə tok′sin, pir′ə-), *n.* a toxin that causes fever.

py·rox·ene (pī′rok sēn), *n.* a common mineral, usually calcium and magnesium silicate, but occurring in many varieties, often found in igneous rock, as granites and lavas. [< French *pyroxène* < Greek *pŷr, pyrós* fire + *xénos* stranger (because it was not considered to be native to igneous rocks)]

py·rox·en·ic (pī′rok sen′ik), *adj.* of, having to do with, or containing a pyroxene or pyroxenes.

py·rox·e·nite (pī rok′sə nīt), *n.* any rock composed essentially, or in large part, of pyroxene of any kind.

py·rox·y·lin or **py·rox·y·line** (pī rok′sə-lin), *n.* any of various substances made by nitrating certain forms of cellulose: *Guncotton and the soluble cellulose nitrates used in making celluloid, collodion, etc., are pyroxylins.* [< *pyro-* + Greek *xýlon* wood + English *-ine*[2]]

Pyr·rha (pir′ə), *n. Greek Mythology.* the wife of Deucalion. She and her husband were the only ones to survive a great flood sent by Zeus to destroy mankind.

pyr·rhic[1] (pir′ik), *n.* an ancient Greek dance: *A thrilling weapon dance, the pyrrhic, was performed by warriors* (World Book Encyclopedia). —*adj.* of or having to do with a war dance.
[< Greek *pyrrhíchē* (*órchēsis*) perhaps (dance) of *Pýrrhichos,* supposedly the creator of the dance, or perhaps (as Aristotle says) < *pyrá* pyre (because it was first used at the funeral, that is, burning, of Patroclus)]

pyr·rhic[2] (pir′ik), *n.* a measure in poetry consisting of two short syllables or two unaccented syllables: *They intended to vary the ordinary rhythm by introducing an accentual pyrrhic* (English Metre).
—*adj.* consisting of or having to do with pyrrhics.
[< Latin *pyrrhichius* < Greek *pyrrhíchios* (*poús*) pyrrhic (foot) < *pyrrhíchē*; see PYRRHIC[1] (because the meter was used in that dance)]

Pyr·rhic (pir′ik), *adj.* of or having to do with Pyrrhus, a king of Epirus in Greece.

Pyrrhic victory, a victory won at too great a cost: *Out of the wreckage he salvaged a Pyrrhic victory, an amendment to get rid of the onerous provision for a two-thirds approval of tax bills* (Newsweek). [< *Pyrrhus,* king of Epirus in Greece, who defeated Roman armies in 280 B.C., but lost so many men in doing so that he could not attack Rome itself + English *-ic*]

Pyr·rho·nism (pir′ə niz əm), *n.* skepticism; the philosophy of the Greek Pyrrho of Elis. Its central doctrine concerns the impossibility of attaining certainty of knowledge. *The Pyrrhonism of my opinions has at all times rendered me notorious* (Edgar Allan Poe).

Pyr·rho·nist (pir′ə nist), *n.* **1.** an adherent of Pyrrhonism. **2.** a person who doubts everything.

Pyr·rho·nis·tic (pir′ə nis′tik), *adj.* of or having to do with Pyrrhonists or Pyrrhonism: *These manners are brought together in a Pyrrhonistic unity which expresses perfectly the ambivalence of any East-West attitude* (Manchester Guardian Weekly).

pyr·rho·tine (pir′ə tēn, -tin), *n.* pyrrhotite.

pyr·rho·tite (pir′ə tīt), *n.* a native iron sulfide having a bronze color and a metallic luster, occurring in crystals and masses. It often contains nickel and is usually slightly magnetic. *The dominant mineral being pyrrhotite, in which most of the pentlandite occurs as scattered grains* (W. R. Jones). [< Greek *pyrrhótēs* redness < *pyrrhós* fiery red < *pŷr* fire (because of its color) + English *-ite*[1]]

pyr·rho·tit·ic (pir′ə tit′ik), *adj.* of, having to do with, or containing pyrrhotite.

pyr·rhu·lox·i·a (pir′ə lok′sē ə), *n.* a gray finch with a reddish crest and tail, of the southwestern United States and Mexico, resembling and related to the cardinal. [< New Latin *Pyrrhuloxia* the genus name, perhaps < Greek *pyrrhós* fiery red]

Pyr·rhus (pir′əs), *n. Greek Legend.* a son of Achilles, who slew Priam and married Andromache.

pyr·rol (pir′ol, -ōl), *n.* pyrrole.

pyr·role (pi rōl′, pī-; pir′ōl, pī′rōl), *n.* a colorless liquid, that smells like chloroform, obtained mostly from coal tar. It is the parent compound of chlorophyll, hemin, various proteins, and other important natural substances. *If in place of the hydrogens we attach to the nitrogen a ring made up of four carbon atoms, we get a compound called pyrrole* (Scientific American). *Formula:* C_4H_5N
[< German *Pyrrol* < Greek *pyrrhós* fiery red + German *-ol* -ole]

pyr·ro·li·dine (pi rō′lə dēn, -din; -rol′ə-), *n.* a colorless liquid, forming the base of proline and various alkaloids. *Formula:* C_4H_9N [< *pyrrol*(e) + *-id* + *-ine*[2]]

py·ru·vate (pī rü′vāt, pi-), *n.* a salt or ester of pyruvic acid.

py·ru·vic acid (pī rü′vik, pi-), a colorless acid that smells like acetic acid, produced by the dry distillation of racemic acid or tartaric acid. It is an important intermediate product in carbohydrate and protein metabolism. ***A severe thiamine deficiency state . . . is characterized by the accumulation of pyruvic and lactic acids*** (Time). *Formula:* $C_3H_4O_3$ [< *pyr-* + Latin *ūva* grape + English *-ic*]

pyruvic aldehyde, a substance, containing both an aldehyde and a ketone, used in organic synthesis and tanning. *Formula:* $C_3H_4O_2$

pyruvic oxidase, an enzyme which changes pyruvic acid to acetic acid. It is a factor in converting carbon dioxide and water into sugars and starches.

Py·thag·o·re·an (pi thag′ə rē′ən), *adj.* of or having to do with Pythagoras, a Greek philosopher, religious teacher, and mathematician, his teachings, or his followers. —*n.* a follower of Pythagoras.

Py·thag·o·re·an·ism (pi thag′ə rē′ə nizəm), *n.* the doctrines of philosophy originated by Pythagoras, often especially with reference to the doctrine of transmigration of souls.

Pythagorean Theorem or **theorem,** the theorem that the square of the hypotenuse of a right triangle equals the sum of the squares of the other two sides: ***Many Greek discoveries, such as the Pythagorean theorem . . . were known long, long before to the Babylonians*** (Science).

Pyth·i·a (pith′ē ə), *n.* the priestess of Apollo at Delphi, who delivered the divine responses to questions.

Pyth·i·ad (pith′ē ad), *n.* the period of four years intervening between two successive celebrations of the Pythian games.

Pyth·i·an (pith′ē ən), *adj.* **1.** of or having to do with Apollo or the oracle at Delphi. **2.** of or having to do with Pythian games. [< Latin *Pȳthius* < Greek *Pȳ́thios* of Delphi (earlier called Pytho), or the Delphic Apollo, + English *-an*]

Pythian games, one of the great national festivals of ancient Greece, held every four years at Delphi in honor of Apollo.

Pyth·i·as (pith′ē əs), *n. Roman Legend.* a man famous for his devoted friendship with Damon.

Pyth·ic (pith′ik), *adj.* Pythian.

py·tho·gen·ic (pī′thə jen′ik, pith′ə-), *adj.* produced by putrefaction or filth (used especially of diseases, as typhoid fever). [< Greek *pȳ́thein* to rot + English *-gen* + *-ic*]

Py·thon (pī′thon, -thən), *n. Greek Mythology.* the huge serpent or monster that was hatched from the mud left after the deluge that only Deucalion and Pyrrha survived. It was slain by Apollo.

py·thon (pī′thon, -thən), *n.* **1.** any of several large snakes of the Old World that are related to the boas, and kill their prey by crushing. Pythons usually live in wet, forested areas. ***The female python, on the other hand, coils around her eggs and incubates them with body heat*** (New Yorker). **2.** any large boa. **3.** a spirit or demon that possesses some person. **4.** a person so possessed. [< Python]

py·tho·ness (pī′thə nis), *n.* **1.** the priestess of Apollo at Delphi, who gave out the answers of the oracle. **2.** a prophetess. [earlier *pytoness* < Old French *phitonise,* learned borrowing from Late Latin *phȳthōnissa* < *Pȳthō, -ōnis* a familiar spirit, demon possessing a soothsayer < Greek *Pȳ́thō* region in which Delphi is]

py·thon·ic (pī thon′ik, pi-), *adj.* **1.** having to do with the Python or with pythons. **2.** snakelike. **3.** oracular.

py·u·ri·a (pī yůr′ē ə), *n.* the presence of pus in discharged urine. [< New Latin *pyuria*]

pyx (piks), *n.* **1.** the box in which the consecrated Host is kept or carried. **2.** the box at the British mint in which specimen coins are kept to be tested for weight and purity. **trial of the pyx,** the final official trial of the purity and weight of British coins. Also, **pix.** [< Latin *pyxis, -idis* box < Greek *pyxis, -ídos* < *pýxos* boxwood]

Pyx·i·dis (pik′sə dis), *n.* genitive of **Pyxis.**

pyx·id·i·um (pik sid′ē əm), *n., pl.* **-i·a** (-ē ə). a seed vessel that bursts open transversely into a top and bottom part, the top part acting as a lid. [< New Latin *pyxidium* < Greek *pyxídion* (diminutive) < *pyxís, -ídos* box; see PYX]

Pyxidium

pyx·ie (pik′sē), *n.* **1.** a very small, trailing evergreen shrub that has numerous small, white, star-shaped blossoms, found in pine barrens of the eastern United States. **2.** *Botany.* a pyxidium. [American English, contraction of New Latin *Pyxidanthera* the genus name < Latin *pyxis* (see PYX) + *anthēra* anther (because its anthers open like a box lid)]

pyx·is (pik′sis), *n., pl.* **pyx·i·des** (pik′sə dēz). **1.** a boxlike vase; casket. **2.** *Botany.* pyxidium. [< Latin *pyxis, -idis* < Greek *pyxís, -ídos* a box; see PYX]

Greek Pyxis (def. 1—about 450 B.C.)

Pyx·is (pik′sis), *n., genitive* **Pyx·i·dis.** a small southern constellation, one of the four parts into which Argo was divided: ***Near the Hydra's head lie Puppis and Pyxis, part of the old ship Argo*** (Bernhard, Bennett, and Rice). [< New Latin *Pyxis nautica* the mariner's compass]

Q Roman 100's A.D. — Greek 600's B.C. — Phoenician 1000's B.C. — Egyptian 3000's B.C.

Qq Qq *Qq* *Qq*

Q or **q** (kyü), *n., pl.* **Q's** or **Qs, q's** or **qs. 1.** the 17th letter of the English alphabet. **2.** the sound represented by this letter. In modern English spelling, *q* is generally used in combination with *u* to stand for the sound *kw,* as in *quiet* (kwī′ət), or *k,* as in *antique* (an tēk′). **3.** the seventeenth, or more usually the sixteenth of a series (with *I* or *J* omitted). **4.** something like the letter Q in shape.

q., an abbreviation for the following:
1. farthing (Latin, *quadrans*).
2. quart or quarts.
3. quarter; one fourth of a hundredweight.
4. quarterly.
5. quarto.
6. quasi.
7. queen.
8. query.
9. question.
10. quintal.
11. quire.

Q (no period), quetzal (a monetary unit).

Q., an abbreviation for the following:
1. quarto.
2. Quebec.
3. Queen.
4. Queensland.
5. query.
6. question.
7. quire.

qa., farthing (Latin, *quadrans*).

qa·di (kä′dē), *n., pl.* **-dis.** cadi.

qa·id (kä ēd′), *n.* caid.

Q. and A., question and answer: *Three busloads of foreign students got coffee, cocoa, cookies, and an hour of Q. and A.* (Newsweek).

Qash·qai (käsh′kī), *n.* one of the nomadic tribes of the mountains of Iran, a kingdom in southwestern Asia, speaking a Turkic language: *The planes were already gassed up and armed for a reconnaissance sweep over the remote province of Fars, where 150,000 Qashqai tribesmen are revolting against the Shah and his new Premier* (Time).

qat (kät), *n. Arabic.* kat, a shrub of the staff-tree family native to Arabia and Africa: *There will have to be food on the mat, and money for qat, to take the place of promises from the north* (Economist).

q.b., *Football.* quarterback.

QB (no periods), *Chess.* queen's bishop.

Q.B., Queen's Bench.

Q boat, a Q ship.

Q.C. or **QC** (no periods), Queen's Counsel.

Q-clear·ance (kyü′klir′əns), *n. U.S.* a certification of a person's loyalty and reliability issued by the government only after the most thorough and searching investigation, required by the Atomic Energy Commission before allowing access to secret information: *As an employee of an AEC contractor, he could not reveal restricted data to individuals not having a Q-clearance* (Bulletin of Atomic Scientists).

q.d., 1. as if one should say (Latin, *quasi dicat*). **2.** as if said (Latin, *quasi dictum*).

Q.E.D., which was to be proved (Latin, *quod erat demonstrandum*).

Q.E.F., which was to be done (Latin, *quod erat faciendum*).

Q.E.I., which was to be found out (Latin, *quod erat inveniendum*).

Q fever, a rickettsial disease somewhat like influenza, usually lasting a short time, characterized by fever, headache, and chills: *In recent years many other odd infections have cropped up in the United States, among them rickettsial pox, Q fever . . .* (Scientific American). [< short for *Queensland* fever (where it was first described), or for *query fever,* as it was first called]

qiv·i·ut (kiv′ē üt), *n.* the soft, silky under wool of the arctic musk ox, used as a textile fiber: *Teal feels that he has made progress toward his goal of showing that the oxen can support Northern man. His conviction hinges on the quality of their wool, called by the Eskimos "qiviut," a term that he translates as "golden fleece of the arctic"* (New Yorker). [< Eskimo]

Qkt (no periods), *Chess.* queen's knight.

ql., quintal.

q.l. or **q.lib.,** as much as you please (Latin, *quantum libet*).

Q.M. or **QM** (no periods), quartermaster.

Q.M.C. or **QMC** (no periods), Quartermaster Corps.

Q.M.G., QMG (no periods), or **Q.M.Gen.,** quartermaster-general.

Q.M.Sgt., quartermaster sergeant.

qoph (kōf), *n.* koph.

q. p. or **q.pl.,** as much as you please (Latin, *quantum placet*).

qq., questions.

Qq (no period), quartos.

qq.v., which see (Latin, *quae vide;* used in referring to more than one item).

qr., an abbreviation for the following:
1. farthing (Latin, *quadrans*).
2. quarter; one fourth of a hundredweight.
3. quire.

QR (no periods), *Chess.* queen's rook.

qrs., an abbreviation for the following:
1. farthings (Latin, *quadrantes*).
2. quarters.
3. quires.

q.s., 1. as much as suffices (Latin, *quantum sufficit*). **2.** quarter section.

QSG (no periods), quasi-stellar galaxy: *. . . many of what were believed to be faint blue stars, occurring by the thousands, are QSG's* (Roy K. Marshall).

Q ship, (in World War I) a merchant ship fitted with concealed guns and manned by a naval crew disguised as ordinary seamen, designed to decoy and destroy enemy submarines: *In 1916 as a young naval lieutenant, Campbell conceived (and executed) the idea of the top-secret Q ships—armed submarine hunters camouflaged as tramp steamers* (Newsweek).

QSO (no periods), quasi-stellar object: *The objects known variously as superstars, quasars, quasi-stellar objects or (for short), QSO's . . .* (New Scientist).

qt., 1. quantity. **2.** quart or quarts.

q.t., *Slang.* quiet.

on the q.t., very quietly; secretly: *to do something on the q.t.*

qto., quarto.

qts., quarts.

qu., 1. quart. **2.** quarter. **3.** quarterly. **4.** queen. **5.** query. **6.** question.

qua (kwā, kwä), *adv.* as being; as; in the character or capacity of: *Qua father, he pitied the boy; qua judge, he condemned him.* [< Latin *quā* by what way, how, where, adverb to *quī* who]

quack[1] (kwak), *n.* **1.** the sound a duck makes. **2.** a sound resembling or imitating this. *—v.i.* to make the sound of a duck, or one resembling it. [probably imitative]

quack[2] (kwak), *n.* **1.** a person who dishonestly pretends to be a doctor: *Running after quacks and mountebanks . . . for medicines and remedies* (Daniel Defoe). **2.** an ignorant pretender to knowledge or skill of any sort: *Don't pay a quack to tell your fortune. In painting . . . Fortunato . . . was a quack* (Edgar Allan Poe).
—adj. **1.** used by quacks: *The doctors of medicine . . . offered me quack cures for imaginary diseases* (George Bernard Shaw). **2.** not genuine: *a quack doctor.*
—v.i. **1.** to be a quack. **2.** to advertise or urge as a quack does. *—v.t.* to treat by quack methods or medicines.
[*quacksalver*] **—Syn.** *n.* **2.** charlatan.

quack[3] (kwak), *n.* quack grass: *He who sets out to subdue a piece of quack must resolve on no half-way measures* (Report of Vermont Board of Agriculture).

quack·er·y (kwak′ərē), *n., pl.* **-er·ies.** the practices or methods of a quack: *He warned against reaching into the medicine chest of economic quackery every time the slightest quiver runs through production and employment* (New York Times). **—Syn.** charlatanry.

quack grass, a perennial, coarse, weedy grass which grows wild on sandy or gravelly soil; couch grass. [American English, perhaps variant of *quick grass*]

quack·ish (kwak′ish), *adj.* like a quack or charlatan; dealing in quackery: *Last week Dr. Aslan's purported cure for the ravages of age was exposed as merely the latest in an armlong list of quackish remedies* (Time).

quack·sal·ver (kwak′sal vər), *n.* **1.** a quack doctor. **2.** a charlatan: *Brother Zeal-of-the-land is no vulgar impostor, no mere religious quacksalver* (Algernon Charles Swinburne). [< earlier Dutch *quacksalver* (literally) a hawker of salve < *quacken, kwakken* boast of, quack + *salf* salve]

quack·y[1] (kwak′ē), *adj.* (of the voice) having a flat, metallic quality, resembling the quack of a duck: *Our women's voices are, on the whole, ungentle . . . they are pitched unpleasantly high and hardened by throat contractions into an habitual "quacky" or metallic quality* (F. Osgood).

quack·y[2] (kwak′ē), *adj.* suited to a quack; quackish; using the methods of quackery: *Who although a little quacky per se has . . . a whole legion of active quacks at his control* (Edgar Allan Poe). [< *quack*[2] + *-y*[1]]

quad[1] (kwod), *n. Informal.* the quadrangle of a college.

quad[2] (kwod), *n. Informal.* a quadruplet.

quad[3] (kwod), *n., v.,* **quad·ded, quad·ding.** *Printing. —n.* a quadrat. *—v.t.* to fill (a line) with quads, in typesetting.

quad[4] (kwod), *n. British Slang.* quod; prison.

quad., 1. quadrangle. **2.** quadrant.

quadr-, *combining form.* the form of **quadri-** before vowels, as in *quadrant.*

quad·ra (kwod′rə), *n., pl.* **-rae** (-rē). **1.** a square frame or border for enclosing a bas-relief. **2.** any frame or border. [< Latin *quadra*]

quad·ra·ble (kwod′rə bəl), *adj.* that can be squared. [< Latin *quadrāre* to square + English *-able*]

quad·ra·ge·nar·i·an (kwod′rə jə nãr′ē ən), *adj.* **1.** forty years old. **2.** between forty and fifty.
—n. **1.** a person who is forty years old. **2.** a person between forty and fifty years old.
[< Latin *quadrāgēnārius* (literally) having forty (< *quadrāgēnī* forty each < *quadrāginta* forty, related to *quattuor* four)]

Quad·ra·ges·i·ma (kwod′rə jes′ə mə), *n.* **1.** the first Sunday in Lent. **2.** the forty days of Lent. [< Late Latin *Quadrāgēsima* (in Latin, fortieth) < *quadrāgēnī;* see QUADRAGENARIAN]

Quad·ra·ges·i·mal (kwod′rə jes′ə məl), *adj.* **1.** of or during Lent; suitable for Lent; Lenten. **2.** Also, **quadragesimal.** lasting forty days, as the fast of Lent.

Quadragesima Sunday, the first Sunday in Lent.

quad·ran·gle (kwod′rang′gəl), *n.* **1.** a four-sided space or court wholly or nearly surrounded by buildings: *the quadrangle of a palace, a college quadrangle.* **2.** the buildings around a quadrangle: *There was a square court behind, round which the house, huts, and store formed a quadrangle* (Henry Kingsley). **3.** a quadrilateral. **4.** the rectangular area represented by one of the United States Geological Survey topographic maps. The two common sizes are tracts about 13 miles wide by 17 miles north to south and 6½ miles wide by 8½ miles. [< Late Latin *quadrangulum,* neuter of Latin adjective *quadriangulus* < *quadri-* four- + *angulus* angle]

quad·ran·gled (kwod′rang′gəld), *adj.* **1.** quadrangular. **2.** containing a quadrangle.

quad·ran·gu·lar (kwod rang′gyə lər), *adj.* like a quadrangle; having four corners or angles: *a quadrangular-shaped house.*

quad·ran·gu·lar·ly (kwod rang′gyə lər lē), *adv.* in the form of a quadrangle.

quad·rant (kwod′rənt), *n.* **1. a.** a quarter of a circle or of its circumference; arc of 90 degrees. **b.** the area contained by such an arc and two radii drawn one to each end. **2.** a thing or part shaped like a quarter circle. **3.** an instrument with a graduated quarter of a circle, used in astronomy, surveying,

Quadrants
Left, (def. 1a); right, (def. 1b)

Q R

and navigation for measuring altitudes. **4.** *Geometry.* one of the four parts into which a plane is divided by two straight lines crossing at right angles. The upper right-hand section is the first quadrant, and, in a counterclockwise direction, the others are the second, third, and fourth quadrants respectively. **5.** *Embryology.* one of the four blastomeres in the four-cell stage of the ovum.
[< Latin *quadrāns, -antis* a fourth, related to *quattuor* four]

quad·ran·tal (kwod ran′təl), *adj.* of or having to do with a quadrant; included in the fourth part of the surface of a circle.

quadrantal deviation, a compass error.

quadrant of safety, the region toward which it is best for a person to run when he sees a tornado approaching.

quad·rat (kwod′rət), *n.* **1.** *Printing.* a piece of metal used for wide spaces in setting type; quad. **2.** (in experimental agriculture) a square area of convenient size laid off for the purpose of accurate planting. **3.** (in phytogeography) a similar square laid off for close study of the relative abundance of species or of other questions. [apparently variant of *quadrate,* noun]

quad·rate (*adj., n.* kwod′rit, -rāt; *v.* kwod′rāt), *adj., n., v.,* **-rat·ed, -rat·ing.** *—adj.* **1.** square; rectangular. **2.** of or designating the quadrate bone. **3.** *Heraldry.* (of a cross) having arms which expand into a square at their junction. **4.** *Astrology.* (of two heavenly bodies) 90 degrees distant from each other.
—n. **1.** something square or rectangular; square; rectangle: *His person was a quadrate, his step massy and elephantine* (Charles Lamb). **2.** a quadrate bone.
—v.t., v.i. **1.** to square; agree. **2.** to conform.
[< Latin *quadrātus* < *quadrus* square, related to *quattuor* four]

quadrate bone, (in birds and reptiles) one of the pair of bones joining the lower jaw to the skull.

quad·rat·ic (kwod rat′ik), *adj.* **1.** *Algebra.* involving a square or squares, but no higher powers. **2.** square. *—n.* a quadratic equation.

quad·rat·i·cal (kwod rat′ə kəl), *adj.* quadratic.

quad·rat·i·cal·ly (kwod rat′ə klē), *adv.* to the second degree.

quadratic equation, an equation involving a square or squares, but no higher powers, of the unknown quantity or quantities: $X^2 + 3X + 2 = 12$ *is a quadratic equation.*

quad·rat·ics (kwod rat′iks), *n.* the branch of algebra that deals with quadratic equations.

quad·ra·trix (kwod rā′triks), *n.* a curve used for finding a square equivalent in area to the figure bounded by a given curve, or for finding a straight line equal to a circle, arc, or the like. [< New Latin *quadratrix* < Latin *quadrāre* to square]

quad·ra·ture (kwod′rə chər), *n.* **1.** the act of squaring. **2.** the finding of a square equal in area to a given surface, especially one bounded by a curve. **3.** *Astronomy.* **a.** the position of a heavenly body that is 90 degrees away from another. **b.** either of the two points in the orbit of a heavenly body halfway between the points of conjunction and opposition: *A half moon is visible at the quadratures of the moon.* [< Latin *quadrātūra* < *quadrātus* quadrate]

quadrature of the circle, the problem, insoluble by geometric methods alone, of squaring the circle, that is of finding a square whose area equals that of a given circle.

quad·ren·ni·al (kwod ren′ē əl), *adj.* **1.** occurring every four years: *The United States has a quadrennial presidential election.* **2.** of or for four years.
—n. **1.** something that occurs every four years. **2.** a fourth anniversary.
[< Latin *quadriennium* period of four years (see QUADRENNIUM) + English *-al*[1]]

quad·ren·ni·al·ly (kwod ren′ē ə lē), *adv.* once in four years.

quad·ren·ni·um (kwod ren′ē əm), *n., pl.* **-ren·ni·ums, -ren·ni·a** (-ren′ē ə). a period of four years. [alteration of Latin *quadriennium* period of four years < *quadri-* four + *-enn-* < *annus* year]

quadri-, *combining form.* four; having four ——; four times: *Quadrilateral = having four sides (and four angles).* Also **quadr-** before vowels; **quadru-.** [< Latin *quadri-,* related to *quattuor* four]

quad·ri·ad (kwod′rē ad), *n.* a series of four; a group of four.

quad·ric (kwod′rik), *Mathematics.* *—adj.* of the second degree (applied especially to functions or equations with more than two variables). *—n.* an expression or surface of the second degree.

quad·ri·cen·ten·ni·al (kwod′rə sen ten′ē əl), *adj.* **1.** of or having to do with 400 years or a 400th anniversary. **2.** 400 years old.
—n. **1.** a 400th anniversary. **2.** its celebration.

quad·ri·ceps (kwod′rə seps), *n.* the great muscle of the front of the thigh, which extends the leg, and is considered as having four heads or origins. [< New Latin *quadriceps* < Latin *quadri-* four + *caput* head]

quad·ri·cip·i·tal (kwod′rə sip′ə təl), *adj.* having to do with the quadriceps.

quad·ri·corn (kwod′rə kôrn), *adj.* having four horns or hornlike parts: *quadricorn sheep.* *—n.* a quadricorn animal. [< New Latin *quadricornis* < Latin *quadri-* four + *cornū* horn]

quad·ri·cor·nous (kwod′rə kôr′nəs), *adj.* quadricorn.

quad·ri·cy·cle (kwod′rə sī′kəl), *n.* a four-wheeled vehicle like a bicycle or tricycle. [< *quadri-* + *-cycle,* as in *bicycle*]

quad·ri·en·ni·al (kwod rē en′ē əl), *adj.* quadrennial.

quad·ri·en·ni·al·ly (kwod rē en′ē ə lē), *adv.* quadrennially.

quad·ri·en·ni·um (kwod rē en′ē əm), *n., pl.* **-en·ni·ums, -en·ni·a** (-en′ē ə). quadrennium.

quad·ri·far·i·ous (kwod′rə fãr′ē əs), *adj.* **1.** set or arranged in four rows or series. **2.** having four parts; fourfold. [< Late Latin *quadrifarius* (with English *-ous*) fourfold < Latin *quadri-* four + *fārī* to speak]

quad·ri·fid (kwod′rə fid), *adj.* cleft or divided into four parts or lobes. [< Latin *quadrifīdus* < *quadri-* four + *fīd-,* a root of *findere* to split, divide]

quad·ri·fo·li·ate (kwod′rə fō′lē it), *adj.* having four leaves; having leaves in whorls of four. [< Latin *quadri-* four + *folium* leaf + English *-ate*[1]]

quad·ri·fo·li·o·late (kwod′ri fō′lē ə lāt, -fō lī′ə lit), *adj.* (of a compound leaf) having four leaflets.

quad·ri·form (kwod′rə fôrm), *adj.* having or combining four forms. [< Late Latin *quadriformis* < Latin *quadri-* four + *forma* form]

quad·ri·fron·tal (kwod′rə frun′təl), *adj.* having four fronts or faces.

quad·ri·ga (kwod rī′gə), *n., pl.* **-gae** (-jē). (in ancient Rome) a two-wheeled chariot pulled by four horses harnessed abreast. [< Latin *quadrīga* a team of four horses < *quadri-* four + *jugum* yoke, span]

quad·ri·lat·er·al (kwod′rə lat′ər əl), *adj.* having four sides and four angles.
—n. **1. a.** a plane figure having four sides and four angles. **b.** something having this form. **2.** a figure formed by four straight lines which, if extended, intersect at six points; complete quadrilateral. **3.** an area lying defended by four fortresses, one at each corner.
[< Latin *quadrilaterus* (< *quadri-* four + *latus, -eris* side) + English *-al*[1]]

Quadrilaterals
(def. 1a)

quad·ri·lin·gual (kwod′rə ling′gwəl), *adj.* using or involving four languages: *A few blocks away . . . petite Eartha Kitt took her listeners on a quadrilingual (English, French, Spanish, Turkish) tour* (Time). [< Latin *quadri-* four + *lingua* speech, tongue + English *-al*[1]]

quad·ri·lit·er·al (kwod′rə lit′ər əl), *adj.* consisting of four letters or of four consonants. *—n.* a quadriliteral word or root. [< Latin *quadri-* four + *lītera* letter + English *-al*[1]]

quad·ril·lage (kȧ drē lȧzh′), *n. French.* a system of defense in which an area is divided into small squares, and each square guarded by a small detachment of troops, sometimes used to protect the local population against guerrilla attacks.

qua·drille[1] (kwə dril′), *n.* **1.** a square dance for four couples that usually has five parts or movements. **2.** the music for it. [< French *cuadrille* < Spanish *cuadrilla* troop of horsemen < *cuadro* square (in battle) < Latin *quadrus* square]

qua·drille[2] (kwə dril′), *n.* a card game for four persons, popular in the 1700's: *Improving hourly in her Skill, To cheat and wrangle at Quadrille* (Jonathan Swift). [< French *cuadrille,* alteration of Spanish *cuartillo* (diminutive) < *cuarto* fourth < Latin *quartus*]

quad·ril·lion (kwod ril′yən), *n., adj.* **1.** (in the United States and France) 1 followed by 15 zeros. **2.** (in Great Britain, Germany, etc.) 1 followed by 24 zeros. [alteration of French *quadrillon* < *quadri-* four + *million* million]

quad·ril·lionth (kwod ril′yənth), *n.* **1.** the last in a series of a quadrillion. **2.** one of a quadrillion equal parts. *—adj.* last in a series of a quadrillion.

quad·ri·nate (kwod′rə nāt), *adj.* **1.** quadruple. **2.** *Botany.* having four leaflets to a petiole; quadrifoliate. [< Latin *quadrīni* four each + English *-ate*[1]]

quad·ri·no·dal (kwod′rə nō′dəl), *adj.* having four nodes, as a vibrating string or organ pipe, or the oscillating surface of a seiche.

quad·ri·no·mi·al (kwod′rə nō′mē əl), *Algebra.* *—adj.* consisting of four terms. *—n.* an expression consisting of four terms, such as $a^2 - ab + 4a - b^2$. [< *quadri-* + *-nomial,* as in *binomial*]

quad·ri·par·tite (kwod′rə pär′tīt), *adj.* divided into or consisting of four parts. [< Latin *quadripartītus,* past participle of *quadripartīre* divide into four parts < *quadri-* four + *partīre* to divide < *pars, partis* part]

quad·ri·par·ti·tion (kwod′rə pär tish′ən), *n.* a dividing by four or into four parts. [< *quadri-* + *partition*]

quad·ri·ple·gi·a (kwod′rə plē′jē ə), *n.* paralysis of both arms and both legs. [< New Latin *quadriplegia* < Latin *quadri-* four + Greek *plēgē* a stroke]

quad·ri·pleg·ic (kwod′rə plej′ik, -plē′jik), *n.* a person afflicted with quadriplegia.

quad·ri·reme (kwod′rə rēm), *n.* an ancient ship with four rows of oars on each side, one above the other. [< Latin *quadrirēmis* < *quadri-* four + *rēmus* oar]

quad·ri·sect (kwod′rə sekt), *v.t.* to divide into four equal parts. [< *quadri-* + *-sect,* as in *bisect*]

quad·ri·syl·lab·ic (kwod′rə sə lab′ik), *adj.* **1.** of or having to do with quadrisyllables. **2.** consisting of four syllables.

quad·ri·syl·la·ble (kwod′rə sil′ə bəl), *n.* a word of four syllables. [< *quadri-* + *syllable*]

quad·ri·va·lence (kwod′rə vā′ləns, kwod-riv′ə-), *n.* the quality of being quadrivalent.

quad·ri·va·len·cy (kwod′rə vā′lən sē, kwod riv′ə-), *n.* quadrivalence.

quad·ri·va·lent (kwod′rə vā′lənt, kwod-riv′ə-), *Chemistry.* *—adj.* **1.** having a valence of four; tetravalent. **2.** having four different valences. *—n.* a quadrivalent atom or element. **—quad′ri·va′lent·ly,** *adv.*

quad·riv·i·al (kwod riv′ē əl), *adj.* **1. a.** having four ways meeting in a point. **b.** (of roads) leading in four directions. **2.** belonging to the quadrivium. *—n.* one of the four arts constituting the quadrivium. [< Medieval Latin *quadrivialis* < Latin *quadrivium* the meeting of four roads; see QUADRIVIUM]

quad·riv·i·um (kwod riv′ē əm), *n., pl.* **-i·ums, -i·a** (-ē ə). **1.** (in ancient Rome and in the Middle Ages) arithmetic, geometry, astronomy, and music, the more advanced four of the seven liberal arts. **2.** a place where four ways meet. [< Late Latin *quadrivium* < Latin, crossroads, meeting of four roads < *quadri-* four + *via* way]

quad·roon (kwod rün′), *n.* a person having one fourth Negro blood; child of a white person and a mulatto. [alteration of earlier *quarteron* < Spanish *cuarterón* < *cuarto* fourth < Latin *quartus*]

quadru-, *combining form.* a variant of **quadri-,** as in *quadrumanous, quadruplane.*

quad·ru·mane (kwod′rü mān), *n.* a quadrumanous animal.

quad·ru·ma·nous (kwod rü′mə nəs), *adj.* **1.** four-handed; using all four feet as hands, as monkeys do. **2.** of or belonging to a former grouping of animals that included monkeys, apes, and lemurs. [< New Latin *quadrumanus* < Latin *quadru-*, variant of *quadri-* four + *manus* hand]

quad·rum·vi·rate (kwod rum′vər it), *n.* **1.** a group of four men. **2.** any association of four in office or authority. [< *quadr-* four + *-umvirate*, as in *triumvirate*]

quad·ru·ped (kwod′rú ped), *n.* an animal that has four feet: *a hairy quadruped . . . with a tail and pointed ears, probably arboreal in its habits* (Charles R. Darwin). —*adj.* having four feet. [< Latin *quadrupēs, -pedis* < *quadru-*, variant of *quadri-* four + *pēs, pedis* foot]

quad·ru·pe·dal (kwod rü′pə dəl, kwod′rú-ped′əl), *adj.* **1.** of, having to do with, or like a quadruped; four-footed. **2.** on the hands and knees: *Seeing him just quadrupedal in the grass, the priest raised his eyebrows rather sadly* (Gilbert K. Chesterton).

quad·ru·plane (kwod′rú plān), *n.* an airplane with four supporting surfaces, one above another. [< *quadru-* + *plane*]

quad·ru·ple (kwod′rú pəl, kwod rü′-), *adj., adv., n., v.,* **-pled, -pling.** —*adj.* **1.** consisting of four parts; including four parts or parties; fourfold: *a quadruple agreement.* **2.** four times; four times as great. **3.** *Music.* having four beats to each measure, with the first and third beats accented.
—*adv.* four times; four times as great.
—*n.* a number or amount four times as great as another: *80 is the quadruple of 20.*
—*v.t., v.i.* to make or become four times as great or as numerous: *The mail quadrupled in size.*
[< Latin *quadruplus* < *quadru-*, variant of *quadri-* four + *-plus* -fold]

quadruple alliance, an alliance of four powers, especially the alliance of Great Britain, France, the Netherlands, and Austria in 1718, and that of Great Britain, France, Spain, and Portugal in 1834.

quadruple measure or **time, 1.** a musical measure of four beats with an accent on the first and third. **2.** this rhythm.

quad·ru·plet (kwod′rú plit, kwod rü′-), *n.* **1.** one of four children born at the same time from the same mother. **2.** any group or combination of four. **3.** a group of four notes to be played in the time of three.

quad·ru·plex (kwod′rú pleks), *adj.* **1.** fourfold. **2.** of or designating a system of telegraphy by which four messages, two in each direction, may be sent over one wire at the same time. [< Latin *quadruplex* fourfold < *quadru-*, variant of *quadri-* four + *-plex, -plicis*, related to *plaga* flat(ness), surroundings]

quad·ru·pli·cate (*adj., n.* kwod rü′plə kit; *v.* kwod rü′plə kāt), *adj., v.,* **-cat·ed, -cat·ing,** *n.* —*adj.* **1.** fourfold; quadruple. **2.** *Mathematics.* raised to the fourth power.
—*v.t.* to make fourfold; quadruple.
—*n.* one of four things, especially four copies of a document, exactly alike.
in quadruplicate, in four copies exactly alike: *The student filled out the form in quadruplicate for the registrar, bursar, dean, and academic adviser.*
[< Latin *quadruplicātus*, past participle of *quadruplicāre* < *quadruplex, -icis;* see QUADRUPLEX]

quad·ru·pli·ca·tion (kwod rü′plə kā′shən), *n.* **1.** the act of making fourfold: *Of the current defense situation he says: "We have had quadruplication instead of unification"* (Newsweek). **2.** something quadruplicated.

quad·ru·ply (kwod′rú plē), *adv.* in a fourfold manner or degree; to a fourfold extent or amount: *When the reconciliation did take place . . . it was so doubly, trebly, quadruply sweet* (Atlantic).

quae·re (kwir′ē), *v. imperative.* query; ask (used to introduce or suggest a question): *Quaere, is this point fully proved? Quaere, whether the contrary is not more probable?*
—*n.* a query or question: *I wondered a little at your quaere who Cheselden was?* (Jonathan Swift). [< Latin *quaere* (literally) ask, imperative of *quaerere* to seek, ask for]

quae·re ver·um (kwir′ē vir′əm), *Latin.* seek the truth.

quaes·tor (kwes′tər, kwēs′-), *n.* **1.** an official of ancient Rome in charge of the public funds; treasurer: *During the next 20 years, Caesar climbed nimbly up the ladder of state offices — quaestor, aedile, praetor, consul* (Time). **2.** a public prosecutor in certain criminal cases in ancient Rome. Also, **questor.** [< Latin *quaestor*, variant of *quaesītor* an investigator < *quaerere* ask for]

quaes·to·ri·al (kwes tôr′ē əl, -tōr′-; kwēs-), *adj.* of or having to do with a quaestor or his position. Also, **questorial.**

quaes·tor·ship (kwes′tər ship, kwēs′-), *n.* the position or term of office of a quaestor. Also, **questorship.**

quaff (kwäf, kwaf, kwôf), *v.i., v.t.* to drink in large drafts; drink freely: *Last night among his fellow roughs he jested, quaffed and swore* (Francis H. C. Doyle). *Felicity . . . is quaffed out of a golden cup in every latitude* (Joseph Conrad). —*n.* **1.** the act of quaffing. **2.** something quaffed; deep drink. [earlier *quaft;* origin uncertain]

quaff·er (kwäf′ər, kwaf′-, kwôf′-), *n.* a person who quaffs or drinks deeply.

quag[1] (kwag, kwog), *n.* a quagmire; bog: *Let me get off the bridge . . . that firm bit by the quag will do* (John Masefield).

quag[2] (kwag, kwog), *v.i.,* **quagged, quagging.** *British Dialect.* to shake, as boggy ground or soft, flabby flesh: *Many a poor head will ache, and many a poor belly quag, if it is so bad as they tell me* (Richard Blackmore). [perhaps imitative. Compare QUAKE.]

quag·ga (kwag′ə), *n.* a South African zebra closely related to Burchell's zebra but having stripes only on the front part of the body. It became extinct in the 1870's. *The poor quagga . . . is a timid animal with a gait and figure much resembling those of an ass* (T. Pringle). [apparently < a Hottentot name]

quag·ge·ry (kwag′ər ē, kwog′-), *n., pl.* **-ries.** a bog or marsh.

quag·gy (kwag′ē, kwog′-), *adj.,* **-gi·er, -gi·est. 1.** soft and muddy; boggy; miry; swampy: *Some dismal rood of quaggy land about the river's edge* (William Morris). **2.** soft and flabby: *quaggy flesh.* —**Syn. 1.** marshy.

quag·mire (kwag′mīr′, kwog′-), *n.* **1.** soft, muddy ground; boggy or miry place: *Many streets are unpaved and unlighted; in heavy rain they turn to quagmires* (Time). **2.** a difficult situation: *I have followed Cupid's Jack-a-lantern, and find myself in a quagmire at last* (Richard Brinsley Sheridan).

qua·hog or **qua·haug** (kwô′hog, -hôg; kwə hog′, -hôg′), *n.* an almost circular, edible American clam; hard clam. Its shell was one of the main sources of wampum. *We were able to make a more detailed study of how amino acids are preserved in the edible clam, or quahog, of the Atlantic coast* (Scientific American). [American English < Algonkian (probably Pequot) *p'quaghhaug* hard clam]

quai (kā), *n., pl.* **quais** (kā). *French.* a quay.

quaich or **quaigh** (kwāʜ), *n. Scottish.* a shallow drinking cup with two handles. [< Scottish Gaelic *cuach* cup]

Quai d'Or·say (kā′ dôr sā′), **1.** the French foreign office. **2.** the French government. **3.** a street in Paris along the left bank of the Seine River.

quail[1] (kwāl), *n., pl.* **quails** or (*collectively*) **quail. 1.** any of various game birds about ten inches long, belonging to the same family as chickens and pheasants, as the Gambel's quail and the bobwhite: *If you were to ask whether the bobwhite is a quail or a partridge, the answer would depend on the part of the country you were in. In the East, the name quail is used interchangeably with bobwhite: bobwhite is quail and quail is bobwhite. In the South bobwhite is called partridge* (Science News Letter). **2.** *U.S. Slang.* a good-looking young woman. **3.** *Archaic.* a courtesan: *Here's Agamemnon —an honest fellow enough, and one that loves quails* (Shakespeare). [< Old French *quaille* < Germanic (compare Old High German *quatala*, and *wahtala*)]

Quail[1] **or bobwhite (def. 1) (about 10 in. long)**

quail[2] (kwāl), *v.i.* **1.** to be afraid; lose courage; shrink back in fear: *looking at me with a rigidity of aspect under which I absolutely quailed* (Herman Melville). *They . . . felt their hearts quailing under their multiplied hardships* (Washington Irving). *She made Barnes quail before her by the shafts of contempt which she flashed at him* (Thackeray). **2.** to bend or shake as if in fear: *trees that quail before a blast of wind.* [apparently < Old French *coaillier* to coagulate < Latin *coāgulāre*] —**Syn. 1.** quake, cower, flinch.

quaint (kwānt), *adj.* **1. a.** strange or odd in an interesting, pleasing, or amusing way: *Old photographs seem quaint to us today.* **b.** old-fashioned but picturesque or attractive: *a quaint old house.* **2.** *Obsolete.* wise; skilled; clever: *to show how quaint an orator you are* (Shakespeare). **3.** *Obsolete.* skillfully made; pretty; elegant; fine: *I never saw a better-fashion'd gown, More quaint, more pleasing* (Shakespeare). **4.** *Obsolete.* strange; odd; singular: *In his wizard habit strange, Came forth, —a quaint and fearful sight* (Scott). [< Old French *cointe*, and *queinte* pretty, clever, knowing < Latin *cognitus* known, past participle of *cognōscere* to know] —**quaint′ly,** *adv.* —**quaint′ness,** *n.*

quake (kwāk), *v.,* **quaked, quak·ing,** *n.* —*v.i.* to shake; tremble: *She quaked with fear. Quake in the present winter's state and wish That warmer days would come* (Shakespeare). *The mountains quake [illegible] Him, and the hills melt, and the earth [illegible]ned at His presence* (Nahum 1:5).
—*n.* **1.** a shaking; tremb[illegible]. **2.** an earthquake. [Old English *cwa[illegible]an*]
—**Syn.** *v.i.* See **shiver.**

quake grass, quaking grass.

quak·er (kwā′kər), *n.* **1.** a person or thing that quakes. **2.** any of various plain-colored birds and moths.
quakers, *British Dialect.* quaking grass: *It's this green all along this valley, . . . the quakers on the slopes, and the pines up there on the crests* (Berton Roueché).
—*adj.* of or having to do with a quaker or Quaker.

Quak·er (kwā′kər), *n.* a member of a Christian group called the Society of Friends, founded by George Fox in the mid-1600's; Friend. Traditionally Quakers have refused to go to war or to take oaths; their clothes, manners, and religious services are ordinarily very plain and simple. *What a balm and a solace it is . . . to . . . seat yourself for a quiet half hour . . . among the gentle Quakers* (Charles Lamb). [< *quake*, verb; reputedly from the fact that George Fox, the founder, told his followers to "tremble at the word of the Lord"; earlier used also of a foreign sect]

Quaker City, *U.S.* Philadelphia.

Quak·er·ess (kwā′kər is), *n.* a Quaker woman or girl.

quaker grass, quaking grass.

Quaker gun, a dummy gun, as in a ship or fort. [from the opposition of Quakers to all warfare]

Quak·er·ish (kwā′kər ish), *adj.* like the Quakers; suitable for Quakers: *Don't address me as if I were a beauty; I am your plain Quakerish governess* (Charlotte Brontë).

Quak·er·ism (kwā′kə riz əm), *n.* the principles and customs of the Quakers: *He has once or twice referred to Quakerism as the wellspring of his beliefs* (Harper's).

quak·er·la·dy (kwā′kər lā′dē), *n., pl.* **-dies.** a small, delicate plant with bluish flowers; innocence or bluet.

Quak·er·ly (kwā′kər lē), *adj.* like or suitable for a Quaker. —*adv.* after the fashion of the Quakers.

Quaker meeting, 1. a religious service of Quakers, during which there may be long periods of silence. **2.** *Informal.* a silent group.

quak·ers (kwā′kərz), *n.pl.* See under **quaker,** *n.*

Quaker State, a nickname of Pennsylvania.

quak·i·ly (kwā′kə lē), *adv.* quakingly.

quak·i·ness (kwā′kē nis), *n.* the condition of being quaky or shaking: *the quakiness of a bog.*

quak·ing (kwā′king), *adj.* that quakes; shaking; trembling. —**quak′ing·ly,** *adv.*

quaking aspen, an American poplar tree with flat, delicate stems and leaves that tremble in the slightest breeze.

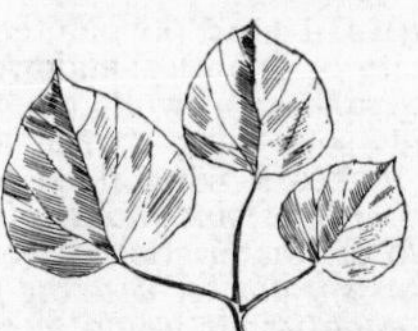

Quaking Aspen Leaves

quaking grass, any of various grasses having spikelets on the slender branches of the panicle that move at the slightest breeze.

quak·y (kwā′kē), *adj.*, **quak·i·er, quak·i·est.** inclined to quake; quaking; trembling.

qual·i·fi·a·ble (kwol′ə fī′ə bəl), *adj.* that can be qualified or modified.

qual·i·fi·ca·tion (kwol′ə fə kā′shən), *n.* **1.** that which makes a person fit for a job, task, office, etc.: *To know the way is one qualification for a guide.* **2.** that which limits, changes, or makes less free and full: *His pleasure had one qualification; his friends could not enjoy it, too.* **3.** modification; limitation; restriction: *The statement was made without any qualification.*

qual·i·fi·ca·tive (kwol′ə fə kā′tiv), *adj.* serving to qualify or modify. —*n.* something serving to qualify, as a qualifying term or expression: *These pedagogical reflections were interrupted by a fellow farther along the bar, who was using qualificatives that the bartender on duty . . . couldn't go along with* (New Yorker).

qual·i·fi·ca·tor (kwol′ə fə kā′tər), *n.* (in the Roman Catholic Church) an officer whose business it is to examine causes and prepare them for trial.

qual·i·fied (kwol′ə fīd), *adj.* **1.** having the desirable or required qualifications; fitted: *a qualified pilot, a vessel qualified for use at sea, a qualified voter.* **2.** modified, limited, or restricted in some way: *qualified acceptance.* **3.** *British Slang.* a euphemism for various oaths: *He was . . . told not to make a qualified fool of himself* (Rudyard Kipling). —**qual′i·fied′ly,** *adv.* —**qual′i·fied′ness,** *n.* —**Syn. 1.** adapted, competent.

qualified endorsement, (in business) an endorsement with the words "without recourse" added.

qual·i·fi·er (kwol′ə fī′ər), *n.* **1.** a person, animal, or thing that qualifies: *Other qualifiers with their four-lap average speeds* (New York Times). **2.** a word that qualifies or modifies another word: *Adjectives and adverbs are qualifiers.* —**Syn. 2.** modifier.

qual·i·fy (kwol′ə fī), *v.*, **-fied, -fy·ing.** —*v.t.* **1.** to make fit or competent: *Can you qualify yourself for the job?* **2.** to furnish with legal power; make legally capable: *No one but a landholder was qualified to be elected into that body* (George Bancroft). **3.** to make less strong; change somewhat; limit: *Qualify your statement that dogs are loyal by adding "usually."* **4.** to characterize by attributing some quality to; give a descriptive name to; characterize: *The "Devil's drawing-room," As some have qualified that wondrous place* (Byron). **5.** *Grammar.* to limit or modify the meaning of: *Adverbs qualify verbs.* **6.** to modify the strength or flavor of (a liquid): *Tea which he drank . . . qualified with brandy* (Tobias Smollett). —*v.i.* **1.** to become fit; show oneself fit: *Can you qualify for the Boy Scouts?* **2.** to become legally capable: *to qualify as a voter.* **3.** *Sports.* to gain the right to compete in a race, contest, or tournament. [< Medieval Latin *qualificare* < Latin *quālis* of what sort + *facere* to make] —**Syn.** *v.t.* **1.** prepare, equip. **3.** moderate, temper, adapt. —**qual′i·fy′ing·ly,** *adv.*

qual·i·ta·tive (kwol′ə tā′tiv), *adj.* concerned with quality or qualities: *Both the qualitative and the quantitative facts about foods are important. How the strength of the winds is related to the intensity of the differential heating is still a mystery. The qualitative working of the atmospheric heat is understood, but not its quantitative operation* (Science News Letter). [< Late Latin *quālitātīvus* < Latin *quālitās, -ātis* quality] —**qual′i·ta′tive·ly,** *adv.*

qualitative analysis, a testing of something to find out what chemical substances are in it: *It is, rather, a physicochemical treatment of the principles of chemical equilibrium as applied to aqueous solutions and a fundamental exposition of the theoretical principles of qualitative and quantitative analysis* (Science).

qual·i·tied (kwol′ə tēd), *adj.* having a quality or qualities; endowed.

qual·i·ty (kwol′ə tē), *n., pl.* **-ties,** *adj.* —*n.* **1.** something special about an object that makes it what it is: *One quality of iron is hardness; one quality of sugar is sweetness.* **2.** a characteristic; attribute: *I chose my wife, as she did her wedding gown . . . for . . . such qualities as would wear well* (Oliver Goldsmith). **3.** the kind that anything is: *That is a poor quality of cloth.* **4.** nature; disposition; temper: *Trials often test a man's quality. You know the fiery quality of the duke* (Shakespeare). **5.** character; position; relation: *Dr. Smith was present, but in quality of friend, not physician.* **6.** fineness; merit; excellence: *There is more difference in the quality of our pleasures than the amount* (Emerson). **7.** an accomplishment; attainment: *A just deportment, manners grac'd with ease, Elegant phrase . . . Are qualities that . . .* (William Cowper). **8.** *Archaic.* high rank; good or high social position: *The house . . . is frequented by gentry of the best quality* (Henry Fielding). **9.** *Dialect.* people of high rank: *It was "baker's bread"—what the quality eat; none of your low-down corn-pone* (Mark Twain). **10.** *Acoustics.* the character of sounds aside from pitch and volume or intensity; timbre: *The quality of a sound is determined by the number of overtones present and their respective intensities* (Sears and Zemansky). **11.** *Logic.* the character of a proposition as affirmative or negative. **12.** *Phonetics.* the sound of a vowel as determined by the shape of the oral resonance chamber, especially by the position of the tongue and lips.

—*adj.* of good or high quality: *quality merchandise. The Superintendent declared: "Educational excellence for every child in this city means quality integrated education"* (Leonard Buder).

[< Old French *qualite,* learned borrowing from Latin *quālitās* (coined by Cicero) < *quālis* of what sort]

—**Syn.** *n.* **1. Quality, property** mean a distinguishing mark or characteristic of a thing. **Quality,** the more general term, applies to any distinctive or characteristic feature: *Strength is a quality of steel.* **Property** applies to a quality essential to the nature of a thing or always manifested by it: *Heaviness is a property of lead.* **2.** trait, feature.

quality control, the inspection of manufactured products from the raw materials that go into them to their finished form to insure that they meet the standards of quality set by the manufacturer.

qualm (kwäm, kwälm), *n.* **1.** a disturbing feeling in the mind; uneasiness; misgiving; doubt: *At the haunted house I felt a sudden qualm of apprehension and terror. I tried the test with some qualms.* **2.** a disturbance or scruple of conscience: *. . . an ignorant ruffianly gaucho, who . . . would . . . fight, steal, and do other naughty things without a qualm* (W.H. Hudson). *She had no qualms, no foreboding, no dubious sensation of weakness* (Arnold Bennett). **3.** a feeling of faintness or sickness, especially of nausea, that lasts for just a moment. **4.** a sudden fit of anything: *Immediately after one of these fits of extravagance he will be taken with violent qualms of economy* (Washington Irving). [origin uncertain] —**Syn. 2.** compunction.

qualm·ish (kwä′mish, kwäl′-), *adj.* **1.** inclined to have qualms: *Elizabeth was not desirous of peace. She was qualmish at the very suggestion* (John L. Motley). **2.** having qualms. **3.** apt to cause qualms. —**qualm′ish·ly,** *adv.* —**qualm′ish·ness,** *n.*

qualm·less (kwäm′lis, kwälm′-), *adj.* having or feeling no qualms: *Any qualms that she may have suffered in the beginning disappeared . . . By the end of January she was qualmless* (Warwick Deeping).

qualm·y (kwä′mē, kwäl′-), *adj.* qualmish.

quam·ash (kwom′ash, kwə mash′), *n.* camass, a plant of the lily family.

quan·da·ry (kwon′dər ē, -drē), *n., pl.* **-ries.** a state of perplexity or uncertainty; dilemma: *Having captured our men, we were in a quandary how to keep them* (Theodore Roosevelt). [origin unknown] —**Syn.** predicament, difficulty, puzzle.

quand même (käN mem′), *French.* even though; notwithstanding; come what may.

quan·dong or **quan·dang** (kwon′dong′), *n.* **1.** an Australian tree related to the sandalwood, that has an edible fruit and a nutlike seed with an edible kernel. **2.** the fruit of this tree. **3.** the seed or kernel. [< the native Australian name]

quant (kwant, kwont), *British.* —*n.* Also, **quant pole.** a pole with a flat board or cap at one end to prevent it from sinking into the mud, used to propel a boat: *No quant pole ever enters the water at the point planned* (Punch). —*v.t., v.i.* to propel (a boat) with a quant. [perhaps < Latin *contus* boat pole < Greek *kontós* < *kenteîn* to goad]

quan·ta (kwon′tə), *n.* plural of **quantum:** *This theory states that energy is not released continuously, but in units, or bundles, called quanta* (World Book Encyclopedia).

quan·tal (kwon′təl), *adj.* having to do with quanta or the quantum theory.

quan·tic (kwon′tik), *n. Mathematics.* a homogeneous function of two or more variables. [< Latin *quantus* how much + English *-ic;* probably patterned on *cubic*]

quan·ti·fi·a·ble (kwon′tə fī′ə bəl), *adj.* that can be counted or measured.

quan·ti·fi·ca·tion (kwon′tə fə kā′shən), *n.* a quantifying: *The economist is inclined to overlook the fact that the basic data of economics are not sales-inventory ratios or the wholesale commodity index but human values and choices, hardly subject to quantification, or chart-reading* (Wall Street Journal).

quan·ti·fi·ca·tion·al (kwon′tə fə kā′shə nəl), *adj.* of or having to do with quantification: *Those arguments must be recast in a "suitably formalized language that provides for quantificational notation"* (Stephen Toulmin).

quan·ti·fy (kwon′tə fī), *v.t.*, **-fied, -fy·ing.** **1.** to determine the quantity of; measure: *Anything that can be quantified ought to be quantified, everything that will submit to scientific measure ought to be measured* (Saturday Review). **2.** to express or indicate the quantity of: *to quantify a syllable or verse.* **3.** *Logic.* to make explicit the quantity or extent of: *We quantify the assertion "Men are sinners," by putting "all," "some," "most," "many," etc., before "men."* [< Medieval Latin *quantificare* < Latin *quantus* how much + *facere* to make]

quan·tise (kwon′tīz), *v.t.*, **-tised, -tis·ing.** *Especially British.* quantize: *Quantising a theory is a process of reformulating the mathematics so that the quantities that enter have discrete values* (C.W. Kilmister). —**quan′tis·er,** *n.*

quan·ti·tate (kwon′tə tāt), *v.t.*, **-tat·ed, -tat·ing.** to determine the quantity of; measure: *Attempts . . . are made to quantitate the output of those faculty members who have not gained tenure* (Bulletin of Atomic Scientists).

quan·ti·ta·tive (kwon′tə tā′tiv), *adj.* **1.** concerned with quantity: *a quantitative change, quantitative superiority. Quantitative research during the first half of the present century on the numerical fluctuations of wild animal populations led to the flowering of the science of animal ecology and formed a solid foundation for a theory of animal populations* (Science News Letter). **2.** that can be measured. **3.** (of verse) having feet consisting of long and short, rather than stressed and unstressed, syllables: *Perhaps the best quantitative verses in our language . . . are to be found in Mother Goose . . .* (Lowell). **4.** *Phonetics.* of or having to do with the quantity or duration of a speech sound. [< Medieval Latin *quantitativus* < Latin *quantitās, -ātis* quantity] —**quan′ti·ta′tive·ly,** *adv.*

quantitative analysis, the testing of something to find out not only what chemical substances are in it, but also just how much there is of each substance.

quan·ti·ty (kwon′tə tē), *n., pl.* **-ties.** **1.** an amount: *Use equal quantities of nuts and raisins in the cake.* **2.** a large amount; large number: *The baker buys flour in quantity. The professor owns quantities of books.* **3.** something that is measurable. **4.** *Music.* the length or duration of a note. **5.** the length or duration of a sound or syllable in speech or poetry: *Who, for false quantities, was whipt at school* (John Dryden). **6.** *Mathematics.* **a.** something having magnitude, or size, extent, amount, etc. **b.** a figure or symbol representing this. **7.** *Logic.* **a.** the character of a proposition as universal or particular. **b.** how far a term or concept in a proposition is supposed to extend, as indicated by words like *all, some,* or *no.* [< Old French *quantite,* learned borrowing from Latin *quantitās* < *quantus* how much]

quantity surveyor, a surveyor who estimates or determines the quantities of work and materials needed for a job: *The plans of the buildings . . . will be now submitted to the quantity surveyor, with a view to the quantities being taken out* (London Daily News).

quan·ti·za·tion (kwon′tə zā′shən), *n.* the fact or process of quantizing.

quan·tize (kwon′tīz), *v.t.*, **-tized, -tiz·ing.** **1.** to apply quantum mechanics or the quantum theory to; measure (energy) in quanta: *He assumed that the processes are quantized not only in space but in time; that is, we have cycles during which all action takes place* (Scientific American). *Much of the behavior of atoms and electrons could be ex-*

plained only on the assumption that the field in the atom is quantized (Scientific American). **2.** to restrict the magnitude of (an observable quantity) in all or some of its range to a set of distinct values, especially to multiples of a definite unit: . . . *rotatory energy is limited to certain discrete values, or, as the physicist says, is "quantized"* (Scientific American).

quan·tiz·er (kwon′tī zər), *n.* a person or thing that quantizes.

quan·tong (kwon′tong′), *n.* quandong, an Australian tree or its fruit.

quan·tum (kwon′təm), *n., pl.* **-ta. 1.** *Physics.* **a.** the smallest amount of energy capable of existing independently: *One radiation quantum can modify the nucleus of a germ cell sufficiently to cause a mutation, an inheritable change of character; but only one in many million quanta will score that kind of bull's eye* (Atlantic). **b.** this amount of energy regarded as a unit. **2.** a sum; amount; quantity; share or portion: *Every member pressing forward to throw on his quantum of wisdom, the subject was quickly buried under a mountain of words* (Washington Irving). [< Latin *quantum,* neuter adjective, how(ever) much]

quantum electrodynamics, the quantum theory as applied to electrodynamics: *Quantum electrodynamics . . . is concerned with the interaction of the electron, the particle of electricity, with radiation* (Science News Letter).

quantum jump, 1. *Physics.* the change in the orbit of an electron in an atom accompanying the loss or gain of a quantum of energy: *The action of the solid-state maser also depends on quantum jumps, but they are jumps of electrons within individual atoms rather than energy transitions of whole molecules* (Scientific American). **2.** a sharply defined, considerable development or improvement of a process, instrument, machine, weapon, etc.: *The birth of the Nautilus literally added a new dimension to undersea warfare . . . Some admirals go so far as to call it a "quantum jump" comparable to the shift from sail to steam* (Newsweek).

quan·tum-me·chan·i·cal (kwon′təm mə kan′ə kəl), *adj.* of, having to do with, or characteristic of quantum mechanics.

quantum mechanics, the quantum theory as applied to the physical measurement of atomic structures and related phenomena.

quan·tum me·ru·it (kwon′təm mer′ů it), *Latin.* as much as one has merited or deserved.

quan·tum mu·ta·tus ab il·lo (kwon′təm myü tā′təs ab il′ō), *Latin.* how greatly changed from what he was!

quantum number, one of a set of numbers assigned to an atomic system, specifying the number of quanta or units of energy, angular momentum, etc., in the system.

quan·tum suf·fi·cit (kwon′təm suf′ə sit), *Latin.* as much as is sufficient.

quantum theory, the theory introduced by Max Planck, the German physicist, that whenever radiant energy is transferred, the transfer occurs in pulsations or stages rather than continuously, and that the amount transferred during each stage is a definite quantity: *What the quantum theory explains is the distinctiveness and the individuality of the 90-odd elements of which the world is made. What a long way for a theory to have come, that started out as a theory of the recondite subject of black-body radiation* (Scientific American).

quan·tum va·le·bat (kwon′təm və lē′bat), *Latin.* as much as it was worth.

qua·qua·ver·sal (kwā′kwə vėr′səl), *adj.* turned, pointing, or dipping in all directions. —*n. Geology.* a domed structure with the strata dipping away in all directions from a center. [< Late Latin *quāquāversus* (< *quāquā* where + *versus* toward)]

qua·qua·ver·sal·ly (kwā′kwə vėr′sə lē), *adv.* in all directions from a central point or area.

quar., 1. quarter. **2.** quarterly.

quar·an·tin·a·ble (kwôr′ən tē′nə bəl, kwor′-), *adj.* **1.** subject or liable to quarantine. **2.** requiring or giving grounds for quarantine. **3.** that quarantine can prevent from spreading: *A drug company official notes flu isn't a quarantinable disease* (Wall Street Journal).

quar·an·tine (kwôr′ən tēn, kwor′-), *v.,* **-tined, -tin·ing,** *n.* —*v.t.* **1.** to keep away from others for a time to prevent the spread of an infectious disease: *My brother was quarantined for three weeks when he had scarlet fever.* **2.** to isolate for a time for any reason. [< noun]

—*n.* **1.** the state of being quarantined: *The house was in quarantine for three weeks when the child had scarlet fever.* **2.** detention, isolation, and other measures taken to prevent the spread of an infectious disease. **3.** a place where people, animals, plants, ships, etc., are held until it is sure that they have no infectious diseases, insect pests, etc. **4.** a period of detention or isolation imposed on ships, persons, etc., when liable or suspected to be bringing some infectious disease. **5.** isolation, exclusion, and similar measures taken against an undesirable person, group, etc.: *Nothing we know of at present justifies departure from the well-tried policy of vigilance and quarantine eschewing alarmism* (Jewish Chronicle).

[< Italian *quarantina* < *quaranta* forty < Latin *quadrāgintā,* related to *quattuor* four (from the 40 days of the original period of isolation)]

quare (kwãr, kwär), *adj.* **1.** *Dialect.* queer. **2.** *Prison Slang.* condemned: . . . *wait tensely for a reprieve to arrive for the quare fellow* (Time). [variant of *queer*]

quark (kwôrk), *n. Nuclear Physics.* one of a hypothetical set of three elementary particles, each with an electric charge less than that of the electron, whose existence and properties were predicted by the eightfold way. [< the phrase "three *quarks*" in *Finnegans Wake,* a novel by James Joyce]

quar·rel[1] (kwôr′əl, kwor′-), *n., v.,* **-reled, -rel·ing** or (*especially British*) **-relled, -rel·ling.** —*n.* **1.** an angry dispute or disagreement; breaking off of friendly relations: *They have had a quarrel and don't speak to each other. Love quarrels are easily made up, but of money quarrels there is no end* (Maria Edgeworth). **2.** a cause for a dispute or disagreement; reason for breaking off friendly relations: *An honest man has no quarrel with the laws.* **3.** one's cause or side in a dispute or contest: *The knight took up the poor man's quarrel and fought his oppressor.*

—*v.i.* **1.** to dispute or disagree angrily; break off friendly relations; stop being friends: *The sisters quarrelled among themselves as all sisters will* (Winston Churchill). **2.** to find fault; complain: *It is useless for a girl to quarrel with fate because she is not a boy.*

[< Old French *quarrel,* or *querele* < Latin *querella, querēla* complaint < *querī* complain]

—**Syn.** *n.* **1. Quarrel, feud** mean an angry disagreement or unfriendly relation between two people or groups. **Quarrel** applies to an angry dispute, soon over or ending in a fight or in severed relations: *The children had a quarrel over the division of the candy.* **Feud** applies to a long-lasting quarrel, marked by violence and revenge when between two groups, by bitterness and repeated verbal attacks when between individuals: *The senator and the columnist carried on a feud. -v.i.* **1.** bicker, wrangle, squabble. **2.** cavil.

quar·rel[2] (kwôr′əl, kwor′-), *n.* **1.** a bolt or arrow with a square head, used with a crossbow. **2.** a small, square or diamond-shaped pane of glass, used in latticed windows. **3.** a stonemason's chisel. **4.** quarry. [< Old French *quarrel* < Medieval Latin *quadrellus* (diminutive) < Latin *quadrus* square]

quar·rel·er (kwôr′ə lər, kwor′-), *n.* a person who quarrels.

quar·rel·ler (kwôr′ə lər, kwor′-), *n. Especially British.* quarreler.

quar·rel·some (kwôr′əl səm, kwor′-), *adj.* too ready to quarrel; fond of fighting and disputing: *A quarrelsome child has few friends. On our idle days they were mutinous and quarrelsome, finding fault with their pork, the bread, etc., and in continual ill humor* (Benjamin Franklin). —**quar′rel·some·ly,** *adv.* —**quar′rel·some·ness,** *n.*

—**Syn.** choleric, irascible, disputatious.

quar·ri·er (kwôr′ē ər, kwor′-), *n.* a worker who quarries stone, slate, etc.

quar·ry[1] (kwôr′ē, kwor′-), *n., pl.* **-ries,** *v.,* **-ried, -ry·ing.** —*n.* a place where stone, slate, etc., is dug, cut, or blasted out for use in building: *an ancient quarry from which the stone has been cut out in smooth masses* (Amelia B. Edwards).

—*v.t.* **1.** to obtain from a quarry: *We watched the workmen quarry out a huge block of stone.* **2.** to dig out by hard work, as if from a quarry: *This is the story of Sandburg's boyhood quarried with deftness and tact out of the rich profusion of "Always the Young Strangers"* (Saturday Review). **3.** to make a quarry in.

[< Medieval Latin *quareia* < *quareria* < *quadraria* < Latin *quadrus* a square]

quar·ry[2] (kwôr′ē, kwor′-), *n., pl.* **-ries. 1.** an animal chased in a hunt; game; prey: *a falcon swooping on its quarry* (Herbert Spencer). *The fox hunters chased their quarry for hours.* **2.** anything hunted or eagerly pursued: *Hunter and quarry under the same roof, all unbeknownst to one another* (New Yorker). [< Old French *cuiree* < *cuir* skin, hide < Latin *corium*]

quar·ry[3] (kwôr′ē, kwor′-), *n., pl.* **-ries,** *adj.* —*n.* **1.** a small, square or diamond-shaped pane of glass, used in latticed windows; quarrel: *This window was filled with old painted glass in . . . quarries* (Margaret O. W. Oliphant). **2.** a tile or stone that is square or diamond-shaped: *What ground remains . . . is flagged with large quarries of white marble* (Sir Richard Steele). —*adj.* square or diamond-shaped: *quarry tile.* [< *quarrel*[2]]

quar·ry-faced (kwôr′ē fāst′, kwor′-), *adj.* **1.** (of building stone) rough-faced, as taken from the quarry. **2.** built of such stone, as masonry.

quar·ry·man (kwôr′ē mən, kwor′-), *n., pl.* **-men.** a person who works in a quarry: *The fragmentation of the broken rock is a further factor which the miner and quarryman have to consider* (New Scientist).

quarry sap, quarry water.

quarry water, the moisture contained in newly quarried stone.

quart[1] (kwôrt), *n.* **1.** a measure for liquids, equal to 1/4 of a gallon; 32 fluid ounces, or in Britain, 40 fluid ounces. *Abbr.:* qt. **2.** a measure for dry things, equal to 1/8 of a peck; 67.2 cubic inches, or in Britain, 69.35 cubic inches. **3. a.** a container holding a quart. **b.** the contents of such a container: *to drink a quart of milk.* **4.** *Music.* the interval of a fourth. [< Old French *quarte* < Latin *quarta,* feminine adjective, fourth]

quart[2] (kärt), *n.* **1.** a sequence of four cards in a suit: *Quart major means the sequence of the four highest cards of a suit.* **2.** *Fencing.* the fourth in a series of eight parries; carte. [< Old French *quarte* (literally) fourth; see QUART[1]]

quart., 1. quarter. **2.** quarterly.

quar·tal (kwôr′təl), *adj. Music.* of or having to do with a quart: *Quartal harmony is built in fourths, and clusters are built in seconds* (World Book Encyclopedia).

quar·tan (kwôr′tən), *adj.* recurring every fourth day, by inclusive counting. —*n.* a fever or ague with two days between attacks. [< Old French *quartaine (fievre)* < Latin *(febris) quartāna* quartan (fever), feminine adjective < *quartus* fourth]

quartan malaria, a mild, persistent form of malaria in which the attacks occur every 72 hours.

quarte (kärt), *n. Fencing.* the fourth in a series of eight parries; carte. [< French *quarte* < Old French; see QUART[1]]

quar·ter (kwôr′tər), *n.* **1.** one of four equal or corresponding parts; half of a half; one fourth: *Each of the four boys had a quarter of an apple.* **2. a.** one fourth of a dollar; 25 cents: *These peaches are one pound for a quarter.* **b.** a coin of the United States, worth 25 cents, made of copper and nickel and formerly of silver: *Do you have change for a quarter?* **c.** a silver coin of Canada, worth 25 cents. **3. a.** one fourth of an hour; 15 minutes: *I've scarcely been ten minutes . . . at least a quarter it can hardly be* (Byron). **b.** the moment marking this period: *"The quarter's gone!" cried Mr. Tapley* (Dickens). **4. a.** one fourth of a year; 3 months: *Many savings banks pay interest every quarter.* **b.** one fourth of a school year: *He had withdrawn Miss Mannering from the school at the end of the first quarter* (Scott). **c.** one of four equal periods of play in football, basketball, soccer, etc. **5.** one of the four periods of the moon, lasting about 7 days each. **6. a.** one fourth of a yard; 9 inches. **b.** one fourth of a mile; 440 yards: *He runs a fast quarter for a youngster.* **7. a.** one fourth of a hundredweight; 25 pounds in the United States or 28 pounds in Great Britain. **b.** one fourth of a pound; 4 ounces avoirdupois or 3 ounces troy. **c.** *British.* one fourth of a cartload of grain, about 8 bushels: *a quarter of oats.* **8.** a region; place: *It was the opinion of Mark Lescarbot . . . that* *the immediate descendants of Noah peopled this quarter of the globe* (Washington Irving). **9.** a district: *the almost unmapped quarter inhabited by artists, musicians, and "people who wrote"* (Edith Wharton). **10.** a certain part of a community, group, etc.: *The bankers' theory was not accepted in other quarters.* **11. a.** a point of the compass; direction: *In what quarter is the wind?* **b.** one fourth of the distance between any two adjacent points of the 32 marked on a compass; 2 degrees 48 minutes 45 seconds. **12. a.** mercy shown a defeated enemy in sparing his life: *The Indians gave no quarter when they attacked the pioneer settlement.* **b.** kindly or merciful treatment; indulgence: *Mr. Molinari-Pradelli gave no quarter to his singers and extracted every ounce of power out of the orchestra* (London Times). **13. a.** one of the four parts into which an animal's carcass is divided in butchering: *a quarter of lamb.* **b.** a leg and its adjoining parts: *The cattle were so small that a stout native could walk off with an entire quarter* (Herman Melville). **c.** either side of a horse's hoof, between heel and toe. **14.** the part of a ship's side near the stern: *All the stern and quarter of her was beaten to pieces with the sea* (Daniel Defoe). **15.** *Heraldry.* **a.** one of the four (or more) parts into which a shield is divided by lines at right angles. **b.** an emblem occupying the upper right fourth of a shield. **16.** the part of a boot or shoe above the heel and below the top of either side of the foot from the middle of the back to the vamp. **17.** *Architecture.* an upright post in partitions, to which the laths are nailed. **18.** *Music.* a quarter note: *That tone is held for two quarters.* **19.** a quarterback. **20.** *Archaic.* treatment; terms: *They will give thee fair quarter* (Scott).

at close quarters, very close together; almost touching: *Living at close quarters, the father and mother quarreled constantly, and the boy had to witness these quarrels* (Edmund Wilson).

cry (for) quarter, to call for mercy: *Cry For quarter, or for victory* (Byron).

quarters, a. a place to live or stay: *The baseball team has winter quarters in the South. The servants have quarters in a cottage.* **b.** a proper position or station: *Call the drummer . . . and let him beat to quarters* (Frederick Marryat).

—*v.t.* **1. a.** to divide into quarters: *Mother quartered the apple for the four boys.* **b.** to divide into parts: *to quarter a chicken for frying.* **2. a.** to give a place to live in; station; lodge: *Coligny . . . quartered all the women in the cathedral and other churches* (John L. Motley). **b.** to impose (soldiers) on a household or community for food and lodging; billet: *Soldiers were quartered on recalcitrant boroughs* (John R. Green). **3.** to cut the body of (a person) into quarters, as a sign of disgrace after hanging. **4.** to place or bear (coats of arms, etc.) in quarters of a shield: *The royal banner of England, quartering the lion, the leopard, and the harp* (Hawthorne). **5.** to range over (ground) in every direction in search of game: *You could see the owls abroad . . . before sunset, in quest of prey, quartering the ground like harriers* (W.H. Hudson).

—*v.i.* **1.** to live or stay in a place: *the village where he proposed to quarter for the night* (Scott). **2.** *Nautical.* (of the wind) to blow on a ship's quarter: *She [a ship] came down upon us with the wind quartering* (Daniel Defoe). **3. a.** to range in every direction: *The dogs quartered, seeking game.* **b.** to move in a slanting direction: *The swimmer quartered because of the strong current.* **4.** to enter a new quarter: *The new moon's quartered in with foul weather* (Frederick Marryat).

—*adj.* being one of four equal parts; being equal to only about one fourth of full measure: *a quarter inch, reduced to quarter rations.*

[< Old French *quartier* < Latin *quartārius* a fourth < *quartus* fourth]

—**Syn.** *n.* **5.** phase. **8.** locality.

quar·ter·age (kwôr′tər ij), *n.* **1.** a quarterly payment, charge, or allowance: *A half-starved Clerk, eked out his lean quarterage, by these merry perquisites* (Benjamin Disraeli). **2. a.** the quartering of troops. **b.** quarters for troops. [< Old French *quarterage* < *quarter* quarter + *-age* -age]

quar·ter·back (kwôr′tər bak′), *n.* **1.** *Football.* **a.** one of four players behind the line. The quarterback usually calls the plays on offense, and in certain formations he receives the ball directly from the center. **b.** the position of quarterback. **2.** a person who directs any group or activity: *The third-base coach is the quarterback of the team; he calls the signals on a relay from the manager* (New York Times).

—*v.t.* to direct the activities of: *Fullback dad is the provider, mother quarterbacks the housekeeping* (Maclean's). *A less wishful and probably sounder conjecture is that Ho has gone back to his old trick of standing behind the lines and quarterbacking Communist strategy for all Southeast Asia* (Time). —*v.i.* to serve as a quarterback: *So at the very least you would expect the Republican followers to show some interest, if no more than the Monday morning quarterbacking of indignation and disgust* (Wall Street Journal).

[American English, probably patterned on *halfback, fullback*]

quarterback sneak, *Football.* a play in which the quarterback does not hand off the ball, but keeps it and charges forward: *It was Lalla, on a quarterback sneak, who took the ball over from 1 foot out* (New York Times).

quarter boat, any boat hung on davits over a ship's quarter: *We . . . lowered away the quarter boats, and went ashore* (Richard H. Dana).

quarter crack, a crack in the side wall of a horse's hoof resulting in lameness.

quarter day, a day beginning or ending a quarter of the year, especially for dating rents, salaries, etc. In England, the quarter days are March 25 (Lady Day), June 24 (Midsummer Day), September 29 (Michaelmas), and December 25 (Christmas).

quar·ter·deck (kwôr′tər dek′), *n.* **1.** (on a sailing vessel) the part of the upper deck between the mainmast and the stern, used especially by the officers of a ship: *Following as best they might, the newsmen could expect only rudeness or a quarterdeck tongue-lashing when they got close* (Time). **2.** (on a steam naval vessel) a deck area designated as the ceremonial post of the commanding officer. —*v.i.* to walk up and down as on a quarterdeck: *He continued quarterdecking about the room for a few times in silence, and his annoyance subsided* (E. F. Benson).

quar·ter·deck·er (kwôr′tər dek′ər), *n.* *Informal.* a person, especially a ship's officer, who is looked upon more as a stickler for small points of etiquette than as a thorough master of his job.

quarter eagle, *U.S.* a former gold coin worth $2.50.

quar·tered (kwôr′tərd), *adj.* **1.** divided into quarters: *yon cloudless, quartered moon* (Oliver Wendell Holmes). **2.** furnished with rooms or lodging. **3.** quartersawed. **4.** having quarters as specified: *a short-quartered horse, low-quartered shoes.* **5.** *Heraldry.* **a.** (of a coat of arms) divided or arranged in quarters. **b.** (of a cross) having a square piece missing in the center.

Quartered Arms (def. 5a)

quar·ter·fi·nal (kwôr′tər fī′nəl), *n.* the round just before the semifinals in a tournament. —*adj.* of or having to do with this round.

quar·ter·fi·nal·ist (kwôr′tər fī′nə list), *n.* a contestant or team in a quarterfinal.

quarter grain, the grain of wood shown when a log is quartered.

quarter horse, *U.S.* a breed of horses derived from thoroughbred stock, originally bred for racing on quarter-mile tracks, now widely bred in the West for working cattle, playing polo, and riding: *The average racing quarter horse can dash over 20 seconds, often faster at this distance than some thoroughbreds* (Wall Street Journal). *Cowboys usually ride quarter horses . . . for cutting, or sorting out, cattle from a herd . . . Many polo ponies have quarter horse blood* (World Book Encyclopedia).

quar·ter-hour (kwôr′tər our′), *n.* **1.** fifteen minutes. **2.** a point one fourth or three fourths of the way in an hour.

quarter ill, blackleg in cattle and sheep.

quar·ter·ing (kwôr′tər ing), *n.* **1.** the act of dividing into fourths. **2.** the act of assigning quarters, as for soldiers: *For an average of about $100 a month, a sum equal to the quartering allowance he gets from Uncle Sam, an Abilene airman will be able to rent a fully-furnished three-bedroom home complete with picture windows and carport* (Wall Street Journal). **3.** *Heraldry.* **a.** the division of a shield into quarters or parts. **b.** one of such parts. **c.** the coat of arms on it.

quarterings, the various coats of arms arranged on a shield: *a fat duchess, with fourteen quarterings* (Charles Lever).

—*adj.* **1.** (of a wind or sea) blowing on a ship's side near the stern: *Rolling and surging along, as we were now, through quartering seas, with an occasional shower of spray coming aboard as a whitecap slapped the guardrail* (Atlantic). **2.** that quarters.

quarter light, 1. a window in the side of a carriage, as distinguished from the windows in the doors. **2.** *Especially British.* a small window in the side of an automobile which usually turns on a swivel, as distinguished from the ordinary windows.

quar·ter·ly (kwôr′tər lē), *adj., adv., n., pl.* **-lies.** —*adj.* **1.** happening or done four times a year: *to make quarterly payments on one's insurance.* **2.** having to do with or covering a quarter of a year.

—*adv.* **1.** once each quarter of a year: *Father pays his income tax quarterly.* **2.** *Heraldry.* **a.** in the quarters of a shield. **b.** with division into quarters. **3.** in or by quarters.

—*n.* a magazine published every three months. *Abbr.:* quart.

quar·ter·mas·ter (kwôr′tər mas′tər, -mäs′-), *n.* **1.** (in the army) an officer who has charge of providing quarters, clothing, fuel, transportation, etc., for troops. **2.** (in the navy or merchant marine) a petty officer on a ship who has charge of the steering, the compasses, and signals: *Deep water merchant mariners sailing into the Great Lakes via the St. Lawrence Seaway will find the fresh-water lingo quite different from ocean-going language . . . Speed is reckoned in miles per hour not in knots, while the sailor steering the boat is a "wheelsman," not a "quartermaster"* (Wall Street Journal).

Quartermaster Corps, the department of the United States Army that provides for the quarters, equipment, etc., of troops: *The Quartermaster Corps is a gigantic department store with thousands of branches . . . the largest service organization in the army* (Ralph Ingersoll).

quar·ter·mas·ter-gen·er·al (kwôr′tər-mas′tər jen′ər əl, -mäs′-; -jen′rəl), *n., pl.* **-als. 1.** *U.S. Military.* the staff officer in charge of the Quartermaster Corps. **2.** *British Military.* a staff officer whose department is charged with all orders relating to the marching, embarking, billeting, quartering, etc., of troops. *Abbr.:* Q.M. Gen.

quar·ter-mi·ler (kwôr′tər mī′lər), *n.* runner or racer who runs a quarter of a mile.

quar·tern (kwôr′tərn), *n.* **1.** *British.* **a.** a quarter; fourth part. **b.** one fourth of a pint; gill. **c.** one fourth of a peck or of a stone. **d.** a quarter of a pound. **2.** a quartern loaf. [Middle English *quartron* < Old French *quarteron* < *quart* fourth < Latin *quartus*]

quartern loaf, a large, round loaf of bread weighing about four pounds.

quarter note, a musical note equal to one fourth of a whole note; crotchet.

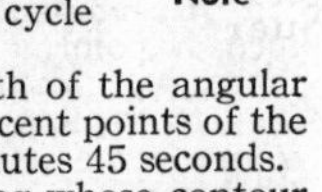

Quarter Note

quar·ter-phase (kwôr′tər-fāz′), *adj.* combining, producing, or carrying two alternating electric currents which differ in phase by one quarter of a cycle (90 degrees); diphase.

quarter point, one fourth of the angular distance between two adjacent points of the compass; 2 degrees 48 minutes 45 seconds.

quarter round, a molding whose contour is exactly or approximately a quadrant; ovolo.

quar·ters (kwôr′tərz), *n.pl.* See under **quarter,** *n.*

quar·ter·saw (kwôr′tər sô′), *v.t.,* **-sawed, -sawed** or **-sawn, -saw·ing.** to saw (a log) lengthwise into quarters and then into boards. Logs are quartersawed to show the grain of the wood.

quarter section, *U.S. and Canada.* a piece of land, usually square, containing 160 acres.

quarter sessions, 1. an English court,

held quarterly, that has limited criminal jurisdiction and certain other powers. **2.** any of various other courts held quarterly.

quar·ter·staff (kwôr′tər staf′, -stäf′), *n., pl.* **-staves. 1.** an old English weapon consisting of a stout pole 6 to 8 feet long, tipped with iron. **2.** exercise or fighting with this weapon: *He was famous throughout the province for strength of arm and skill at quarterstaff* (Washington Irving).

quar·ter·staves (kwôr′tər stāvz′), *n.* the plural of **quarterstaff.**

quarter step, a quarter tone in music.

quarter tone, half of a half-tone in music.

quar·tet or **quar·tette** (kwôr tet′), *n.* **1.** a group of four musicians (singers or players). **2.** a piece of music for four voices or instruments. **3.** any group of four; set of four. [< French *quartette* < Italian *quartetto* < *quarto* fourth < Latin *quartus*]

quar·tic (kwôr′tik), *Mathematics. —adj.* of the fourth degree. *—n.* an expression or surface of the fourth degree. [< Latin *quartus* fourth + English *-ic*]

quar·tier (kȧr tyā′), *n. French.* a section of a town or city; quarter.

quar·tile (kwôr′tīl, -təl), *n.* **1.** one of the points on a scale of the frequency distribution of data which divide the data into four parts, each having the same frequency: *The upper quartile is the point reached or exceeded by 25 per cent of the cases plotted on the frequency scale.* **2.** *Astrology.* the aspect of two heavenly bodies when their longitudes differ by 90 degrees. *—adj.* of or having to do with quartiles; being a quartile. [< Medieval Latin *quartilis* < Latin *quartus* fourth]

quart major, (in cards) a sequence of ace, king, queen, and jack of a suit.

quar·to (kwôr′tō), *n., pl.* **-tos,** *adj. —n.* **1.** the page size (usually about 9 by 12 inches) resulting when a sheet is folded twice, forming four leaves or eight pages. *Abbr.:* 4to, 4°, q., Q., qto. **2.** a book having such pages. *—adj.* of this size; having pages of this size. [< Medieval Latin *in quarto* in the fourth (of a sheet)]

quartz (kwôrts), *n.* a very hard mineral composed of silica. Common quartz crystals are colorless and transparent, but amethyst, jasper, and many other colored stones are quartz. It forms the rocks quartzite and sandstone, and is an important constituent in granite, gneiss, and other rocks. *Formula:* SiO_2 [< German *Quarz*] **—quartz′like′,** *adj.*

quartz clock, an electric clock in which the frequency of current supplied to the clock motor is controlled by the vibrations of a quartz crystal: *The highly accurate standard quartz clocks at the Royal Greenwich Observatory and ... at the United States Naval Observatory, keep time to better than one part in ten thousand million* (New Scientist).

quartz-di·o·rite (kwôrts′dī′ə rīt), *n.* a variety of diorite having quartz as one of its main components.

quartz glass, a clear, vitreous solid, or glass, produced by fusion of a very pure form of quartz or rock crystal, and said to be the clearest solid known. It is remarkably transparent to the infrared, visible, and ultraviolet radiations, and is used to transmit ultraviolet rays to diseased parts of the body.

quartz·if·er·ous (kwôrt sif′ər əs), *adj.* consisting of quartz; containing quartz.

quartz·ite (kwôrt′sīt), *n.* a granular rock consisting mostly of quartz: *Frank L. Hess reported uranium in quartzite of pre-Cambrian age very early in the century* (Bulletin of Atomic Scientists).

quartz·it·ic (kwôrt sit′ik), *adj.* of the nature of or consisting of quartzite.

quartz lamp, a mercury vapor lamp that has a quartz vacuum tube, allowing ultraviolet rays to pass through: *The big advantage in using the quartz lamps to cook food is that their intense heat and rapid cooking cut down the moisture loss* (Wall Street Journal).

quartz·ose (kwôrt′sōs), *adj.* consisting mainly or wholly of quartz; quartzlike.

quartz plate, a quartz crystal cut so as to have electric polarity.

qua·sar (kwā′sär, kwä′-; -zär), *n.* a quasi-stellar object or body: *It takes about a year for the heat from the central core of quasars ... to be transferred to the surface as radio waves and light* (Science News Letter). [< *quas*(i)-(stell)*ar*]

quash[1] (kwosh), *v.t.* to put down completely; crush: *I wanted to scream, but the physical weariness had quashed down that nonsense* (Jane Carlyle). [< Old French *quasser*, and *casser* < Latin *quassāre* shatter < *quatere* to shake] **—Syn.** suppress, quell.

quash[2] (kwosh), *v.t. Law.* to make void; annul: *The judge quashed the charges against the prisoner.* [< Old French *quasser* < Late Latin *cassāre* < Latin *cassus* null; influenced in Old French by *quasser* quash[1]] **—Syn.** nullify, invalidate.

qua·si (kwā′sī, -zī; kwä′sē, -zē), *adj.* seeming; not real; halfway: *The party was also said to have suggested that seven elected members should sit on the Executive Council as quasi Ministers* (London Times). *—adv.* seemingly; not really; partly; almost: *a quasi humorous remark.* [< Latin *quasi* as if; as it were]

quasi-, *prefix.* quasi; partly: *Quasi-judicial = judicial to some degree.* [< *quasi*]

quasi contract, a legal obligation similar to a contract.

qua·si-ju·di·cial (kwā′sī jü dish′əl, -zī-; kwä′sē-, -zē-), *adj.* **1.** having in some degree, or within a specified area, such authority as belongs to the judiciary: *Where so grave a matter as loyalty is involved, the defendant cannot constitutionally be condemned in a "quasi-judicial" procedure which denies him the right to confront his accusers* (New York Times). **2.** judicial in nature but not under the authority or within the power of a judiciary: *quasi-judicial problems.*

qua·si-leg·is·la·tive (kwā′sī lej′is lā′tiv, -zī-; kwä′sē-, -zē-), *adj.* **1.** having in some degree, or within a specified area, such authority as belongs to the legislature: *a quasi-legislative body.* **2.** legislative in nature but not under the authority or within the power of the legislature: *... quasi-legislative questions brought by citizens seeking to vindicate the public good rather than with a concrete dispute* (Irving R. Kaufman).

qua·si-mil·i·tar·y (kwā′sī mil′ə ter ē, -zī-; kwä′sē-, -zē-), *adj.* partly military; semimilitary: *The history of the world shows that republics and democracies have generally lost their liberties by way of passing from civilian to quasi-military status* (Newsweek).

qua·si-pub·lic (kwā′sī pub′lik, -zī-; kwä′sē-, -zē-), *adj.* public in nature, function, or concern, but privately owned or controlled: *These institutions represent the unselfish cooperation of private, quasi-public, and foundations groups with public officials* (New York Times).

qua·si-stel·lar (kwā′sī stel′ər, -zī-; kwä′sē-, -zē-), *adj.* having to do with or designating an extragalactic object or body that appears to be larger than a star but smaller than a nebula and that is the source of powerful emissions of electromagnetic waves.

quass (kväs), *n.* kvass, a kind of sour Russian beer.

quas·sia (kwosh′ə), *n.* **1.** a bitter drug obtained from the wood of a tropical American tree, used as a tonic, a purge, and a substitute for hops. **2.** the wood. **3.** the tree. [< New Latin *Quassia* the genus name of the trees < *Quassi*, a Surinam Negro who first used the bark as a fever remedy]

quassia family, a group of dicotyledonous trees and shrubs of warm regions, having bitter bark and flowers in panicles or racemes. The family includes the quassia, mountain damson, and tree of heaven.

quas·sin (kwos′in), *n.* the bitter principle of quassia, obtained as a white, crystalline substance. *Formula:* $C_{22}H_{30}O_6$ [< *quass*(ia) + *-in*]

qua·ter·cen·te·nar·y (kwā′tər sen′tə ner′ē), *adj., n., pl.* **-nar·ies.** *—adj.* of, comprising, or having to do with a period of 400 years. *—n.* the 400th anniversary of some event, or its celebration. [< Latin *quater* four times + English *centenary*]

qua·ter·na·ry (kwə tėr′nər ē), *n., pl.* **-ries,** *adj. —n.* **1.** a group of four. **2.** the number four; 4.

—adj. **1.** consisting of four. **2.** arranged in fours.

[< Latin *quaternārius* < *quaternī* four each < *quater* four times, related to *quattuor* four]

Qua·ter·na·ry (kwə tėr′nər ē), *n., pl.* **-ries,** *adj. —n.* **1.** the geological period including the Pleistocene and Recent. **2.** the deposits made in this period. *—adj.* of this period or these deposits.

qua·ter·nate (kwə tėr′nit), *adj.* **1.** consisting of four; arranged in fours. **2.** *Botany.* consisting of four leaflets.

qua·ter·ni·on (kwə tėr′nē ən), *n.* **1.** a group or set of four: *four quaternions of soldiers* (Acts 12:4). **2.** *Mathematics.* the quotient of two vectors considered as depending on four geometrical elements and as expressible by an algebraic quadrinomial.

quaternions, the calculus of vectors in which a quaternion is employed: *... the value of quaternions for pursuing researches in physics* (Herbert Spencer).

[< Late Latin *quaterniō, -ōnis* < Latin *quaternī*; see QUATERNARY]

qua·ter·ni·ty (kwə tėr′nə tē), *n., pl.* **-ties. 1.** a group or set of four persons or things: *A remarkable quaternity of great-grandmamma, grandmamma, mamma, and little daughter* (Saturday Review). **2.** the state of being four. [< Late Latin *quaternitās* < *quaternī*; see QUATERNARY]

Qua·ter·ni·ty (kwə tėr′nə tē), *n.* the union of four persons in one godhead.

qua·ter·nize (kwə tėr′nīz), *v.t.,* **-nized, -niz·ing.** to divide into four parts or components: *These amine groups are then quaternized by a chemical treatment ...* (Science News Letter).

qua·tor·zain (kə tôr′zān, kat′ər-), *n.* **1.** a poem of fourteen lines resembling a sonnet but not in strict sonnet form. **2.** a sonnet. [< Middle French *quatorzaine* a set of 14 < *quatorze* quatorze]

qua·torze (kə tôrz′), *n.* (in piquet) 4 aces, kings, queens, or jacks, counting for 14 points. [< French *quatorze* fourteen < Latin *quattuordecim*]

quat·rain (kwot′rān), *n.* a stanza or poem of four lines, usually with alternate rhymes: *Who but Landor could have written the faultless and pathetic quatrain? I strove with none, for none was worth my strife; Nature I loved, and, next to Nature, Art; I warmed both hands before the fire of life; It sinks, and I am ready to depart* (Edmund C. Stedman). [< Middle French *quatrain* < Old French *quatre* four < Latin *quattuor*]

qua·tre (kä′tər; *French* kȧ′trə), *n.* a four in cards, dice, dominoes, or the like. [< Old French *quatre* four < Latin *quattuor*]

quat·re·foil (kat′ər foil′, -rə-), *n.* **1.** a leaf or flower composed of four leaflets or petals: *The four-leaf clover is a quatrefoil.* **2.** *Architecture.* an ornament having four lobes: *Another Longton Hall piece, a jug of lobed quatrefoil shape and baluster outline ... was sold to Messrs. Amor for £150* (London Times). [< Old French *quatre* four (see QUATRE) + *feuil* leaf < Latin *folium*]

Quatrefoils (def. 2)

quat·tro·cen·tist (kwät′trō chen′tist), *n.* an Italian artist of the 1400's, of the style of art called quattrocento.

quat·tro·cen·to (kwät′trō chen′tō), *n.* the 1400's considered as an epoch of art or literature, especially in Italy.

—adj. of this epoch, especially in art or architecture: *The settings were purely quattrocento, very scholarly, and very pretty, with enchanting processions, festivals, and dances* (London Times).

[< Italian *quattrocento*, short for *mille quattrocento* one thousand and four hundred; *quattro* < Latin *quattuor* four]

quat·tu·or·de·cil·lion (kwät′yü ôr də sil′yən), *n.* **1.** (in the United States and France) 1 followed by 45 zeros. **2.** (in Great Britain, Germany, etc.) 1 followed by 84 zeros. [< Latin *quattuordecim* fourteen + English *-illion*, as in *million*]

qua·ver (kwā′vər), *v.i.* **1.** to shake; tremble: *The old man's voice quavered. Like rivers over reeds Which quaver in the current* (Philip J. Bailey). **2.** to trill in singing or in playing on an instrument. *—v.t.* **1.** to sound, speak, or sing in trembling tones. **2.** to sing with trills.

—n. **1.** a shaking or trembling, especially of the voice: *His voice ... had nothing of the tremulous quaver and cackle of an old man's utterance* (Hawthorne). **2.** a trill in singing or in playing on an instrument. **3.** *Music.* an eighth note.

[frequentative form of earlier *quave* shake] **—qua′ver·ing·ly,** *adv.*

qua·ver·er (kwā′vər ər), *n.* a person or thing that quavers.

qua·ver·y (kwā′vər ē), *adj.* that quavers; trembling.

quay (kē), *n.* a solid landing place where ships load and unload, often built of stone: *to assign proper wharfs and quays in each port, for the exclusive landing and loading of merchandise* (William Ewart Blackstone). *Other stewards walked off and discussed on the quay whether they should return to the ship* (London Times). —*v.t.* to furnish with a quay or quays. [< Old North French *cai, caie,* and *kay* < a Celtic word] —**Syn.** *n.* pier, wharf.

Quay

quay·age (kē′ij), *n.* **1.** a fee or charge for use of a quay: *docking quayage.* **2.** quays collectively. **3.** space on a quay or occupied by a quay. [< French *quayage* < Old French *cai* quay]

quay·side (kē′sīd′), *n.* the area immediately adjacent to a quay: *The great liner rises high above the quayside, a floating representative of the United States* (Manchester Guardian).

Que., Quebec.

quean (kwēn), *n.* **1.** a bold, impudent girl or woman; hussy: *Such is the sprinkling, which some careless quean Flirts on you from her mop* (Jonathan Swift). **2.** a prostitute. **3.** *Scottish.* a girl or young woman: *Queans, O' plump and strapping in their teens* (Robert Burns). [Old English *cwene*]

quea·si·ly (kwē′zə lē), *adv.* in a queasy manner; with squeamishness.

quea·si·ness (kwē′zē nis), *n.* **1.** nausea. **2.** disgust. **3.** squeamishness.

quea·sy (kwē′zē), *adj.,* **-si·er, -si·est.** **1.** inclined to nausea; easily upset: *a queasy stomach. Travelers who sit on the left side of a plane, particularly in the seats immediately aft of the wing, are more apt to be queasy, the doctors suggest* (Newsweek). **2.** tending to unsettle the stomach. **3.** uneasy; uncomfortable: *But more and more observers are beginning to get queasy about the soaring consumer debt* (Wall Street Journal). **4.** squeamish; fastidious. **5.** *Archaic.* uncertain; hazardous.
[origin uncertain] —**Syn. 4.** finical.

Que·bec (kwi bek′), *n. U.S.* a code name for the letter *q*, used in transmitting radio messages.

Que·bec·er or **Que·beck·er** (kwi bek′ər), *n.* a native or inhabitant of Quebec, a province and city in Canada: *Quebeckers resent the lack of adequate, senior representation in the federal cabinet* (Maclean's).

Quebec heater, (in Canada) a potbelly stove: . . . *with the living room warm from both the Quebec heater and the fireplace* (Maclean's).

Que·be·cois (kā be kwä′), *n., pl.* **-cois.** *French.* a Quebecer: *There were many Quebecois who voted Liberal* [*between*] *1917–58* (Canadian Forum).

que·bra·cho (kā brä′chō), *n., pl.* **-chos.** **1.** any of several South American trees with very hard wood and a bark used in tanning and dyeing and in medicine. The white quebracho belongs to the dogbane family. The red quebracho is of the cashew family. **2.** the wood or bark of any of these trees: *Thinning agents presently in use are derived mostly from quebracho, an imported wood chemical product, or substitutes of it* (Wall Street Journal). [< Spanish *quebracho* (literally) break-ax < *quebrar* to break (< Latin *crepāre*) + *hacha* axe]

Quech·ua (kech′wä), *n.* **1.** an Indian of the dominant tribal group in the Inca empire. **2.** the language of the Quechuas. Certain dialects are still spoken in parts of Peru and Ecuador. *An alphabet for writing Quechua, ancient language of the Incas still in common use, was devised and agreed upon by experts in the field* (Science News Letter). [< Spanish *Quechua* < the native Quechua (Peru) name]

Quech·uan (kech′wən), *adj.* of or having to do with the Quechuas, their civilization, or their language. —*n.* an Indian of the dominant tribal group in the Inca empire; Quechua.

queen (kwēn), *n.* **1.** the wife of a king. **2.** a woman ruler. **3.** a woman who is very stately or beautiful: *the queen of the May.* **4.** a woman who is very important: *the queen of society.* **5.** the fully developed female in a colony of bees, ants, etc., that lays eggs. There is usually only one queen in a hive of bees. See picture under **bee. 6.** a playing card with a picture of a queen. **7.** the piece in chess that can move any number of squares in any straight or diagonal direction. **8.** the chief, best, finest, etc.: *the rose, queen of flowers.* **9.** *Slang.* a male homosexual.
—*v.i.* to reign as queen. —*v.t.* to make a queen of.
queen it, to act like a queen: *She's a fine girl . . . fit to queen it in any drawing-room* (George Meredith).
[Old English *cwēn*]

Queen Anne Style Chair (def. 2)

Queen Anne (an), **1.** of or having to do with a style of English domestic architecture of the early 1700's, characterized by roomy and dignified buildings and by the use of red brick. **2.** of or having to do with a style of furniture in England in the early 1700's, characterized by an increase in comfort and in the use of upholstery. [< *Queen Anne* of Great Britain and Ireland, who reigned from 1702 to 1714]

Queen Anne cottage, a kind of ornamental wooden cottage developed in England and the United States in the late 1800's.

Queen Anne's lace, the wild carrot (so called from the clusters of lacy white flowers).

queen bee, queen (def. 5): *The United States Government is inquiring whether the advertising and sale of royal jelly, the queen bee food, is a "racket"* (Science News Letter).

queen butterfly, a chocolate-brown and black butterfly of the southwestern United States and Mexico.

queen consort, the wife of a reigning king.

queen·dom (kwēn′dəm), *n.* **1.** the realm of a queen. **2.** the position or dignity of a queen.

queen dowager, the widow of a king.

queen·fish (kwēn′fish′), *n., pl.* **-fish·es** or (*collectively*) **-fish.** a small food fish with large scales, found on the coast of southern California.

queen·hood (kwēn′hu̇d), *n.* the rank or dignity of a queen: *She* [*Queen Guinevere*] . . . *with all grace of womanhood and queenhood, answer'd him* (Tennyson).

queen·ing (kwē′ning), *n.* **1.** any of several varieties of apples. **2.** (in chess) the promotion of a pawn which has reached the eighth rank to become a queen. [apparently < *queen* + *-ing*[1]]

queen·less (kwēn′lis), *adj.* without a queen: *Queenless worker bees will even desert young larvae to join in a group with a queen* (New Scientist).

queen·let (kwēn′lit), *n.* a petty queen.

queen·like (kwēn′līk′), *adj.* resembling a queen.

queen·li·ness (kwēn′lē nis), *n.* the condition or quality of being queenly.

queen·ly (kwēn′lē), *adj.,* **-li·er, -li·est,** *adv.* —*adj.* **1.** of a queen: *queenly rank or majesty.* **2.** like that of a queen: *a queenly bearing or presence, queenly dignity.* **3.** like a queen: *You are a queenly creature, not to be treated as any puny trollop of a handmaid* (George Meredith).
—*adv.* in a queenly manner; as a queen does: *Queenly responsive when the loyal hand Rose from the clay it work'd in as she past* (Tennyson).

Queen Mab (mab), a fairy queen in English folklore, who delivers dreams to men when she drives over their sleeping bodies in her chariot: *Even so dazzling a figure of romance as Maeve, the warrior queen of Connacht, survived only as the fragile Queen Mab of the English poets* (Scientific American).

queen mother, the widow of a former king and mother of a reigning king or queen.

queen of the prairie, a tall American perennial of the rose family with large clusters of pink flowers, growing in meadows and prairies.

queen olive, a large olive with a small pit.

queen·pin (kwēn′pin′), *n. Slang.* the most important woman in a group: *In the working classes the oldest woman was the queenpin of the extended family, ruling over her daughters and their children* (Michael Young). [patterned after *kingpin*]

queen post, one of a pair of timbers extending vertically upward from the tie beam of a roof truss or the like. The queen post supports the rafter or rafters of the truss.

Queen Posts

queen regent,
1. a queen ruling in place of an absent or unfit king. **2.** a queen ruling in her own right.

queen regnant, a queen ruling in her own right.

queen·root (kwēn′rüt′, -ru̇t′), *n.* queen's root, an herb of the spurge family.

Queen's Bench (kwēnz), *British.* a former court of record and the highest common-law court in England. *Abbr.:* Q.B.

Queensberry Rules, Marquis of Queensberry Rules: *The clash in Commons today will be fought under Queensberry Rules* (Philip Rawstorne).

Queen's Birthday, a holiday observed in the British Commonwealth on the actual or arbitrarily set birthday of the ruler.

Queen's Colour, the Union Jack as an emblem of, or carried with the colors of, a British regiment: *In brilliant sunshine on Saturday the Queen's Colour of the 2nd Battalion, Grenadier Guards, was trooped in the presence of the Queen in the Horse Guards Parade* (London Times).

queen's counsel, *British.* a barrister or the body of barristers appointed counsel to the Crown. *Abbr.:* Q.C.

queen's English, accepted English, especially correct British usage in speech and writing.

queen's evidence, *British.* state's evidence.

Queen's Gambit, a conventional series of moves, starting with the advance of the pawn in front of the queen, as the opening of a game of chess.

queen·ship (kwēn′ship), *n.* the dignity or office of a queen.

Queens·land·er (kwēnz′lən dər), *n.* a native or inhabitant of Queensland, Australia: . . . *Baulch, a 23-year-old Queenslander, who is playing in his first British tournament* (David Gray).

Queens·land hemp (kwēnz′lənd), a tropical plant of the mallow family, a species of sida, that yields a useful fiber.

Queensland nut, the macadamia.

queen's proctor, (in British law) an officer representing the Crown who has the right to intervene in certain divorce and nullity cases.

queen's root, an herb of the spurge family of the southern United States, having a thick, woody root with alterative, emetic, and purgative properties.

Queen's Scout, **1.** the highest rating in the British Boy Scouts. **2.** a boy who has attained this rating: *The . . . boys chosen to attend the Jamboree will all be Queen's Scouts* (Manitoulin Expositor).

Queen's shilling, (in the British Army) a shilling formerly paid a recruit to make his enlistment binding.
take the queen's shilling, to enlist: . . . *the dirtiest private that ever took the queen's shilling* (George Newby).

Queen's speech, a speech read by the queen at the opening of the British Parliament, prepared by the ministers of the government to explain domestic and foreign policy.

queens·ware (kwēnz′wãr′), *n.* cream-colored Wedgewood pottery: *His earthenware so impressed Queen Charlotte I that she made Wedgewood her court potter and ordered that pearly pottery be called queensware* (Time).

queen truss, the truss within queen posts.

queer (kwir), *adj.* **1.** strange; odd; peculiar: *That was a queer remark for her to make. The old three-cornered hat, And the breeches, and all that, Are so queer!* (Oliver Wendell Holmes). *I don't mind your queer opinions one little bit* (George Bernard Shaw). **2.** *Informal.* probably bad; causing doubt or suspicion: *There is something very queer about her. All the world is queer but thee and me, and even thou art a little queer* (Robert Owen). **3.** not well; faint; giddy: *They had given him brandy, rather a lot—that perhaps was the reason he felt so queer* (John Galsworthy). **4.** *Slang.* bad; counterfeit: *queer money.* **5.** mentally unbalanced: *He . . .*

wondered if Zeena were also turning "queer" (Edith Wharton). **6.** homosexual.
—*n.* **1.** an odd or eccentric person. **2.** a homosexual.
—*v.t. Slang.* to spoil; ruin: *to queer one's chances of success. To-morrow when Mr. Nehru slides into friendship with Pakistan, closer relations with America ... there will be nobody to queer his pitch* (Manchester Guardian).
[origin uncertain; perhaps < Low German *queer* across]
—**Syn.** *adj.* **1.** singular, curious, unusual.

queer·ish (kwir′ish), *adj.* rather queer: *I still feel queerish* (New Yorker).

queer·ly (kwir′lē), *adv.* in a queer manner.

queer·ness (kwir′nis), *n.* **1.** queer nature or behavior. **2.** something strange or odd; peculiarity. —**Syn. 2.** oddity.

Queer Street, an imaginary street in which people in financial or other difficulties, or shady characters generally, are supposed to live: *Look out, fellow Christians, particularly you that lodge in Queer Street!* (Dickens).

queest (kwēst), *n.* the wood pigeon or ringdove: *The queest ... has had to put up with a certain indifference on the part of naturalists because it is so common* (Robert Nye). [Middle English *quisht, quysht* cushat; see CUSHAT]

que·le·a (kwē′lē ə), *n.* a red-billed weaver-bird of Africa: *Sections of East Africa suffered greatly from the depredations of birds known as queleas* (E.I. Farrington). [< New Latin *quelea,* probably < an African word]

quell (kwel), *v.t.* **1.** to put down (disorder, rebellion, etc.); quash: *to quell a riot. The tumult ... was not quelled until several had fallen on both sides* (Francis Parkman). **2.** to put an end to; overcome: *to quell one's fears.* [Middle English *quellen* quell, Old English *cwellan* to kill] —**Syn. 2.** allay.

quell·er (kwel′ər), *n.* a person that quells or suppresses.

que·ma·de·ro (kā′mä dăr′ō), *n., pl.* **-dos.** a place of execution by fire: *And this is the quemadero, where criminals were burned to death* (Henry Roth). [< Spanish *quemadero* < *quemado,* past participle of *quemar* to burn]

quench (kwench), *v.t.* **1.** to put an end to; stop: *to quench a thirst.* **2.** to drown out; put out: *Water quenched the fire. Not all its snow could quench our hearthfire's ruddy glow* (John Greenleaf Whittier). *Hope seemed almost quenched in utter gloom* (W. H. Hudson). **3.** to cool suddenly by plunging into water or other liquid: *Hot steel is quenched to harden it.* —*v.i.* to become quenched; be extinguished.
—*n.* **1.** the act of quenching. **2.** the state or fact of being quenched.
[Old English *-cwencan,* as in *ācwencan* quench, put out]
—**Syn.** *v.t.* **1.** allay, slake. **2.** extinguish, stifle.

quench·a·ble (kwen′chə bəl), *adj.* that can be quenched.

quench·er (kwen′chər), *n.* a person or thing that quenches.

quench-hard·en (kwench′här′dən), *v.t.* to harden (an iron alloy) by heating it to a point above the temperature range where austenite forms and then cooling it.

quench·less (kwench′lis), *adj.* that cannot be quenched; inextinguishable: *quenchless thirst.*

que·nelle (kə nel′), *n.* a ball of seasoned meat paste. [< French *quenelle* < German *Knödel* dumpling < *knoten* to knot]

quer·cet·ic (kwər set′ik, -sē′tik), *adj.* of or having to do with quercetin.

quer·ce·tin (kwėr′sə tin), *n.* a yellow, crystalline dye prepared from quercitrin. *Formula:* $C_{15}H_{10}O_7$ [< Latin *quercētum* an oak wood + English *-in*]

quer·cine (kwėr′sin, -sīn), *adj.* **1.** of or having to do with the oak. **2.** made of oak; oaken. [< Latin *quercīnus* < *quercus, -ūs* oak]

quer·cit·rin (kwėr′sit′rin), *n.* a yellow, crystalline powder extracted from the bark of the black oak. *Formula:* $C_{21}H_{20}O_{11}$

quer·cit·ron (kwėr′sit′rən), *n.* **1.** the black oak of North America. **2.** its inner bark, used in tanning, which yields a yellow dye. **3.** the dye itself. [earlier *quereicitron* < Latin *quercus, -ūs* oak + English *citron* (probably because of the color)]

quer·cus (kwer′kəs), *n.* the oak: *British or American, quercus is a noble tree* (London Times). [< Latin *quercus, -ūs* oak]

que·ri·da (kā rē′də), *n. Southwestern U.S.* darling; sweetheart: *In every* [*court*] *in the Pecos some little señorita was proud to be known as his querida* (Walter N. Burns). [< Spanish *querida,* feminine past participle of *querer* to love, want < Latin *quaerere* seek]

quer·i·mo·ni·ous (kwir′i mō′nē əs), *adj.* complaining much.

quer·i·mo·ny (kwir′i mō′nē), *n., pl.* **-nies.** **1.** the act of complaining. **2.** a complaint. [< Latin *querimōnia* < *querī* to complain]

que·rist (kwir′ist), *n.* a person who asks or inquires; questioner. [< Medieval Latin *quere* (< Latin *quaere* ask; see QUAERE) + English *-ist*]

quern (kwėrn), *n.* **1.** a simple hand mill for grinding grain, consisting commonly of two circular stones: *a quern in its place, The grains it ground beside it — barley, wheat* (Atlantic). **2.** a small hand mill used to grind pepper or other spices. [Old English *cweorn*]

quer·u·lous (kwer′ə ləs, -yə-), *adj.* **1.** complaining; faultfinding; fretful; peevish: *Mrs. Henry was that day ailing and querulous* (Robert Louis Stevenson). **2.** producing sounds as of complaining, or sounding as if uttered in complaint: *The brown-clad maidens ... Dance to the querulous pipe and shrill* (William Morris). *One querulous rook, unable to sleep, protested now and then* (Dickens). [< Late Latin *querulōsus* < Latin *querulus* < *querī* to complain] —**Syn. 1.** petulant.

quer·u·lous·ly (kwer′ə ləs lē, -yə-), *adv.* in a complaining or querulous manner.

quer·u·lous·ness (kwer′ə ləs nis, -yə-), *n.* **1.** the state of being querulous; disposition to complain. **2.** the habit of murmuring.

que·ry (kwir′ē), *n., pl.* **-ries,** *v.,* **-ried, -ry·ing.** —*n.* **1.** a question; inquiry. **2.** a doubt. **3.** the sign (?) put after a question or used to express doubt about something written or printed; question mark.
—*v.t.* **1.** to ask; ask about; inquire into. **2.** to ask questions of. **3.** to express doubt about. **4.** to mark (a word, etc.) in a printer's proof with a question mark to indicate doubt of its correctness.
—*v.i.* to ask questions: *prompt to query, answer, and debate* (Alexander Pope).
[< Medieval Latin *quere* < Latin *quaere* ask; see QUAERE] —**Syn.** *n.* **1.** See **question.**

ques., question.

quest (kwest), *n.* **1.** a search; hunt: *Mary went to the library in quest of something to read.* **2. a.** an expedition of knights: *There sat Arthur on the dais-throne, And those that had gone out upon the quest, Wasted and worn ... stood before the King* (Tennyson). **b.** the knights in such an expedition. **c.** the object sought for. **3. a.** an inquest. **b.** a jury of inquest.
—*v.t.* to search for; hunt. —*v.i.* **1.** to go about in search of something; search or seek: *This sense of man's balanced greatness and fallibility in the search for truth has made ours a profoundly questing civilization* (Adlai Stevenson). **2.** of hunting dogs: **a.** to search for game. **b.** to bark when in sight of game; bay: *Who cry out for him yet as hounds that quest, And roar as on their quarry* (Algernon Charles Swinburne).
[< Old French *queste* < Vulgar Latin *quaesita* < Latin *quaerere* seek]
—**Syn.** *n.* **1.** pursuit.

quest·er (kwes′tər), *n.* **1.** a seeker or searcher. **2.** a dog used to find game.

ques·tion (kwes′chən), *n.* **1.** the act of asking: *to examine by question and answer.* **2.** the thing asked; a sentence, in interrogative form, addressed to someone to get information; inquiry. **3.** a matter of doubt or dispute; controversy: *A question arose about the ownership of the property.* **4. a.** a matter to be talked over, investigated, considered, etc.: *the question of prohibition. What is the question you have raised?* **b.** a problem: *He could neither buy nor sell as well as his father. It was not a question of brains; it was a question of individuality* (Arnold Bennett). **5. a.** a proposal to be debated or voted on: *The president asked if the club members were ready for the question. When the Clerk at the Table called the question I should of course have asked the indulgence of the House and begged that the question be put down a week later* (Sunday Times). **b.** the taking of a vote on such a proposal. **6.** a judicial examination or trial; interrogation. **7.** a dispute or issue to be decided by a judicial or official body.

beg the question, to take for granted the very thing argued about: *Is this a work of history, or is it a beautifully packaged literary newsreel? Perhaps the "or" begs the question, for there is no reason why history cannot be vivid ... as well as reflective* (Telford Taylor).

beside the question, off the subject: *So many of the speaker's comments were beside the question the audience got bored.*

beyond question or **beyond all question, a.** without doubt: [*Alexander Pope's*] *The Dunciad ... is beyond all question full of coarse abuse* (Leslie Stephen). **b.** inevitable; certain to happen: *Sometimes, when defeat is beyond question, nothing matters but the style of going down* (New Yorker).

call in (or **into**) **question,** to dispute; challenge: *a person who was jealous lest his courage should be called in question* (Jonathan Swift).

in question, a. under consideration or discussion: *His father ... had* (*besides this gentleman in question*) *Two other sons* (Shakespeare). **b.** in dispute: *What is not in question is the difficulty of making good color plates* (John Shearman).

out of the question, impossible: *He began by agreeing ... that war now seemed out of the question* (New York Times).

pop the question, *Informal.* to propose marriage: *She agreed to marry him as soon as he popped the question.*

without question, without a doubt; not to be disputed: *The architecture of the Old Quarter* [*of New Orleans*] *is a blend of Spanish and French ... and is without question the most fascinating bit of city housing in the United States* (David McReynolds).

—*v.t.* **1.** to ask a question or questions of; seek information from. **2.** to ask or inquire about: *We questioned the long delay. 'Tis safer to Avoid what's grown than question how 'tis born* (Shakespeare). **3.** to doubt; dispute: *I question the truth of his story. No man can question whether wounds and sickness are not really painful* (Samuel Johnson). *The best English lawyers questioned ... the legality of a government by royal instructions* (George Bancroft). —*v.i.* to ask a question or questions: *He that questioneth much shall learn much* (Francis Bacon).
[< Anglo-French *questiun,* Old French *question* legal inquest; torture, learned borrowing from Latin *quaestiō, -ōnis* a seeking < *quaerere* to seek]
—**Syn.** *n.* **2. Question, query** mean something asked. **Question** applies to any request for information: *I have some questions about today's lesson.* **Query** applies particularly to a question raised as a matter of doubt or objection and seeking a specific or authoritative answer: *He put several queries concerning items in the budget.*
—*v.t.* **1. Question, ask, interrogate** mean to seek information from someone. **Ask** is the general word, and suggests nothing more: *I asked him why he did it.* **Question** often implies asking repeatedly or persistently: *I questioned the boy until he told all he knew.* **Interrogate** implies questioning formally and methodically: *The committee interrogated the candidates for the position.* **3.** challenge.

ques·tion·a·ble (kwes′chə nə bəl), *adj.* **1.** open to question or dispute; doubtful; uncertain: *Whether your statement is true is questionable. The facts respecting him* [*Governor Van Twiller*] *were so scattered and vague, and divers of them so questionable in point of authenticity, that I have had to give up the search* (Washington Irving). **2.** of doubtful propriety, honesty, morality, respectability, or the like: *the questionable associates of a gambler.* **3.** *Obsolete.* (of a person) open to questioning: *Thou comest in such a questionable shape That I will speak to thee* (Shakespeare). —**Syn. 1.** debatable, disputable. **2.** dubious.

ques·tion·a·ble·ness (kwes′chə nə bəl nis), *n.* doubtful character; suspicious state.

ques·tion·a·bly (kwes′chə nə blē), *adv.* in a questionable manner; doubtfully.

ques·tion·ar·y (kwes′chə ner′ē), *n., pl.* **-ar·ies,** *adj.* —*n.* a questionnaire. —*adj.* questioning; interrogatory.

ques·tion-beg·ging (kwes′chən beg′ing), *n.* a taking for granted the very thing argued about: *There is some question-begging here, but no matter ...* (Renata Adler).

ques·tion·er (kwes′chə nər), *n.* a person who questions: *Frequently the question is asked, "What use are cosmic rays?" By use-*

fulness the questioner means usually the conversion of their inflowing energy into some controllable form of power (Science News Letter).

ques·tion·ing (kwes′chə ning), *n.* the asking of questions; inquiry; interrogation: *The committee members' questioning clearly suggested that few of them view favorably the Administration's tactics on the gold problem* (Wall Street Journal). —*adj.* **1.** that questions: *Like a ghost that is speechless, Till some questioning voice dissolves the spell of its silence* (Longfellow). **2.** inquisitive: *Under . . . the questioning eye of his father* (Charlotte Smith).

ques·tion·ing·ly (kwes′chə ning lē), *adv.* interrogatively; as one who questions.

ques·tion·ist (kwes′chə nist), *n.* a questioner; inquirer.

ques·tion·less (kwes′chən lis), *adj.* **1.** without question; beyond doubt. **2.** unquestioning. —*adv.* without question; beyond doubt: *a young man . . . who can questionless write a good hand and keep books* (George Eliot).

question mark, 1. a mark (?) put after a question in writing or printing; mark of interrogation; query. **2.** *Informal.* a difficult or debatable question; problem: *These are question marks that the next 48 hours will resolve one way or another* (London Times).

ques·tion·naire (kwes′chə nãr′), *n., v.,* **-naired, -nair·ing.** —*n.* a list of questions, usually a written or printed list. Questionnaires are used to gather statistical data, to obtain a sampling of opinion, etc. *Upon Edmont alone Gilliéron relied for all his investigations, furnishing him with a questionnaire of some 1,920 words, including phrases, clauses and sentences* (Simeon Potter). *The unguided interview may be considered as something between the free association technique of the psychiatrist and the use of a questionnaire* (Science News Letter). —*v.t.* to submit a list of questions to: *What kind of man . . . becomes an outstanding scientist? To answer his question, Bello interviewed or questionnaired 107 young . . . scientists* (Time). [< French *questionnaire*]

question time, 1. a period of about 45 minutes, usually four times a week, in which Ministers answer appropriate questions submitted in advance by Members of the British House of Commons. A Member submitting a question may also ask supplementary questions arising from the Minister's answer to the original question. **2.** a similar period in a similar parliamentary body.

ques·tor (kwes′tər, kwēs′-), *n.* quaestor.

ques·to·ri·al (kwes tôr′ē əl, -tōr′-; kwēs-), *adj.* quaestorial.

ques·tor·ship (kwes′tər ship, kwēs′-), *n.* quaestorship.

quet·zal (ket säl′), *n.* **1.** a Central American bird having brilliant golden-green and scarlet plumage. The adult male has long, flowing tail feathers. **2.** the basic unit of money of Guatemala, worth about one dollar. Also, **quezal.** [< Mexican Spanish *quetzal*, earlier *quetzale* < Nahuatl *quetzalli* brilliant, resplendent (because of the bird's plumage)]

Quet·zal·co·a·tl (ket säl′kō ä′təl), *n.* a chief deity of the Aztecs and Toltecs in Mexico before the Spanish conquest, typically represented in sculpture as a plumed or feathered serpent: *And among the Aztecs of Yucatan the first Spanish explorers discovered a strong tradition of earlier European visitors. Was the blue-eyed god Quetzalcoatl perhaps a European?* (New York Times). [< Nahuatl *Quetzalcoatl* < *Quetzalli* (see QUETZAL) + *coatl* snake]

queue (kyü), *n., v.,* **queued, queu·ing** or **queue·ing.** —*n.* **1.** a braid of hair hanging down from the back of the head: *His long, powdered locks hung in a well-tended queue down his back* (Harriet Beecher Stowe). **2.** *Especially British.* a long line of people, automobiles, etc.: *There are those who do not wish to make a lifetime career outside the United Kingdom but who would be prepared to go abroad for a short time provided they would not lose their place in the queue for a more permanent post in this country* (London Times). **3.** a container for wine: *In Champagne it's called a queue and contains 216 liters* (Atlantic).
—*v.i. Especially British.* to form or stand in a long line; take one's place in a queue: *Thirty-three vessels are queueing at the Mersey Bar 20 miles from port waiting to dock* (London Times). —*v.t. Especially British.* to arrange (persons) in or as if in a queue or queues.

Chinese Queue (def. 1)

queue up, *Especially British.* to queue: *Queuing up is a symbol of British fair play* (Time).
[< French *queue* < Old French *coue* < Latin *cōda*, variant of *cauda* tail]

queue-jump (kyü′jump′), *v.i. British.* to go out of turn; go ahead of those who have been waiting: *To acknowledge that patients can queue-jump on any grounds other than medical is to open an enormous moral fester* (Linda Blandford). —**queue′-jump′er,** *n.*

queu·er (kyü′ər), *n.* a person who stands in line: *The queuers were hoping for standing room. Reserved seats had been gone since July* (Time).

quey (kwā), *n. Scottish.* a heifer. [< Old Icelandic *kwīga*, apparently < *kū* cow]

que·zal (ke säl′), *n.* quetzal.

quib·ble (kwib′əl), *n., v.,* **-bled, -bling.** —*n.* **1.** an unfair and petty evasion of the real point or truth by using words with a double meaning: *The fairest court of justice is a naval court-martial — no brow-beating of witnesses . . . and no legal quibbles attended to* (Frederick Marryat). *To a plain understanding his objections seem to be mere quibbles* (Macaulay). **2.** a play upon words; pun: *It was very natural . . . that the common people, by a quibble . . . should call the proposed "Moderation" the "Murderation"* (John L. Motley). —*v.i.* to evade the real point or the truth by twisting the meaning of words: *He was not averse to quibbling with Posey Kime, Department of Justice attorney, over whether an associate in the rights congress was known as Marjorie Robinson or Margaret Robinson* (New York Times). *Oh, Miss Lucretia, who pride yourself on your plain speaking, that you should be caught quibbling!* (Winston Churchill). [apparently, diminutive < obsolete *quib* quip < Latin *quibus*, dative and ablative plural of *quī* who, which (because it was much used in legal jargon)] —**quib′bling·ly,** *adv.* —**Syn.** *n.* **1.** equivocation.

quib·bler (kwib′lər), *n.* a person who evades plain truth by twisting the meaning of words.

quib·ble·some (kwib′əl səm), *adj.* tending to evade or confuse the real point or truth in petty ways: *Strauss can be evasive, quibblesome and not above beclouding a point with big handfuls of debater's dust* (Time).

quiche lor·raine (kēsh lô ren′), *French.* a cheese pie baked in a rich crust and often containing minced ham or bacon: *Two years ago, a whole cityful of people who up until then may not have been quite sure how to spell quiche lorraine would have thought shame upon themselves if this stylish cheese pie had not regularly lent its high-toned elegance to their cocktail trays* (New Yorker).

quick (kwik), *adj.* **1.** fast and sudden; swift: *With a quick turn he avoided hitting the other car. Use an instant cake mix if you want a quick way to make a cake.* **2.** begun and ended in a very short time: *a quick visit, a quick glance at the paper.* **3.** coming soon; prompt: *a quick answer.* **4.** not patient; hasty: *a quick temper.* **5.** acting quickly; ready; lively: *a quick wit. Most dogs have a quick ear.* **6.** understanding or learning quickly: *a child who is quick in school.* **7.** brisk: *a quick fire.* **8.** sharp: *a quick curve.* **9.** productive: *a quick vein of ore.* **10.** readily convertible into cash. **11.** having some quality or feature suggesting a living thing. **12.** *Archaic.* living; alive.
—*n.* **1.** the tender, sensitive flesh under a fingernail or toenail: *to bite one's nails to the quick.* **2.** the tender, sensitive part of one's feelings: *The boy's pride was cut to the quick by the words of blame.* **3.** living persons: *But the quick are frequently as much of a problem as the dead* (Wall Street Journal). **4.** *Especially British.* quickset.
—*adv.* quickly.
[Old English *cwic* alive]
—**Syn.** *adj.* **1. Quick, fast, rapid** mean done, happening, moving, or acting with speed. **Quick** especially describes something done or made or happening with speed or without delay: *You made a quick trip.* **Fast** especially describes something moving or acting, and emphasizes the swiftness with which it acts or moves: *I took a fast plane.* **Rapid** emphasizes the rate of speed, the swiftness of the action or movement, or series of movements, performed: *I had to do some rapid maneuvering.* **4.** impatient, irascible. **5.** nimble, agile. —**Ant.** *adj.* **1.** slow, sluggish.

quick assets, *Accounting.* cash or things that can be sold quickly, without appreciable loss.

quick bread, biscuits, or corn bread, muffins, etc., that do not rise before baking: *Of the 600 women questioned, 500 said that they used packaged cake mixes most often, then puddings, pastries and quick breads* (New York Times).

quick-change (kwik′chānj′), *adj.* **1.** very quick in changing one's mind, costume, appearance, etc.: *She seems to be a very mousy character, and at the museum where she works nobody suspects that she is a mental quick-change artist* (New Yorker). **2.** capable of being changed rapidly: *While engaged on the development of new types of quick-change cutting tools . . .* (New Scientist).

quick·en (kwik′ən), *v.i.* **1.** to move more quickly; become faster: *His pulse quickened.* **2.** to become more active or alive: *Edwardian sportsmen were at their prime after the Press had quickened just enough to make them household names when they deserved it* (London Times). **3.** to become living: *Summer flies . . . that quicken even with blowing* (Shakespeare). **4.** to grow bright or brighter: *The river, the mountain, the quickening east, swam before his eyes* (Bret Harte). **5. a.** (of a child in the womb) to show life by movements: *The baby's muscular activity as first felt by the mother is called quickening or "feeling life"* (Sidonie M. Gruenberg). **b.** (of the mother) to enter that stage of pregnancy in which the movements of the child are felt. —*v.t.* **1.** to cause to move more quickly; hasten: *Quicken your pace.* **2.** to stir up; make alive: *Reading adventure stories quickened his imagination. British shipbuilding needed to be streamlined, modernized, quickened up* (London Times). **3.** to kindle: *He quickened the hot ashes into flames.* **4.** to give or restore life to. —**Syn.** *v.t.* **1.** hurry, expedite, accelerate. **2.** inspire, rouse, stimulate, animate. —**Ant.** *v.t.* **1.** slacken.

quick·en·er (kwik′ə nər), *n.* **1.** a person or thing that quickens. **2.** something that reinvigorates.

quick fire, a rapid succession of shots.

quick-fire (kwik′fīr′), *adj.* rapid-fire.

quick-fir·ing (kwik′fīr′ing), *adj.* rapid-fire.

quick-freeze (kwik′frēz′), *v.t.,* **-froze, -fro·zen, -freez·ing.** to subject (food) to rapid freezing to prepare it for storing at freezing temperatures: *You can quick-freeze a month's supply of food, and keep it safely in your zero-zone freezer for up to one year* (Maclean's).

quick-freez·ing (kwik′frē′zing), *n.* the process whereby food is subjected to rapid freezing as preparation for storage at freezing temperatures.

quick-fro·zen (kwik′frō′zən), *adj.* (of food) prepared for storage by very rapid freezing: *Mr. Birdseye gave the world its first packaged quick-frozen foods and laid the foundation for today's frozen food industry* (New York Herald Tribune). —*v.* the past participle of **quick-freeze.**

quick grass, a western North American couch grass, ranging from Nebraska to British Columbia and south to Texas and Arizona. [< Middle English *quike*, variant of *quitch* (grass). Compare COUCH GRASS, QUACK GRASS.]

quick·hatch (kwik′hach′), *n.* the wolverine. [alteration by folk etymology of Cree *kwekwuhakao*]

quick·ie (kwik′ē), *Slang.* —*n.* **1.** a motion picture, novel, or the like, produced cheaply and in haste: *But his book remains, somehow, for all its basic honesty, a sort of journalistic quickie in blackface* (New York Times). **2.** a short drink of alcoholic liquor. **3.** anything done very hastily: *Election year brought the usual flutter of campaign quickies* (Time).
—*adj.* **1.** fast; quick; requiring little preparation: *a quickie training course for Directors, mostly on non-controversial matters* (Wall Street Journal). **2.** giving little warn-

ing: *The turbulence that expressed itself in the early sit-down strikes and in hundreds of quickie shutdowns has yielded to a more co-operative relationship* (New York Times).

quick·ish (kwik′ish), *adj.* rather quick: *Neame and Parker, for Harrow, made steady progress against Sinclair and Douglas Pennant, a quickish left-hander* (London Times).

quick kick, *Football.* a punt kicked on one of the first three downs and not from the formation usual for kicking, intended to surprise the opponents and catch them out of position.

quick-kick·er (kwik′kik′ər), *n.* a football player skilled in kicking surprise punts over the other team's safety man: *His most famous pupil: North Carolina's All-American Charlie Justice, one of the game's finest quick-kickers* (Time).

quick·lime (kwik′līm′), *n.* a white, alkaline substance obtained by burning limestone and used for making mortar, glass, insecticides, etc.; lime; calcium oxide.

quick·ly (kwik′lē), *adv.* rapidly; with haste; very soon: *Slum boys are tempted by dreams of "easy money" and quickly-won esteem* (Scientific American). *Leave the sickroom quickly and come into it quickly, not suddenly, nor with a rush* (Florence Nightingale). *Retaliation and vengeance quickly followed* (Leopold von Ranke).

quick march, a march in quick time.

quick-mix (kwik′miks′), *n.* any of various food products offered for sale with most of the ingredients already mixed, usually requiring only the addition of a final ingredient and cooking: *Sales of quick-mix drinking chocolate in particular were so successful that they outstripped our supplies* (London Times).

quick·ness (kwik′nis), *n.* **1.** speed: *the quickness of motion.* **2.** briskness; promptness: *the quickness of the imagination or wit.* **3.** acuteness; keenness: *Would not quickness of sensation be an inconvenience to an animal that must lie still?* (John Locke). **4.** sharpness; pungency.

quick·sand (kwik′sand′), *n.* **1.** wet sand that will not support one's weight. Quicksand may engulf men and animals. **2.** a condition resembling that of animals or persons perishing in quicksand: *The roots of conflict, he believes, lie buried in the quicksands of human nature* (Newsweek). *It would have the great merit of eliciting information and perhaps revealing the location of any financial quicksands* (Wall Street Journal). *It is my duty ... to see that he is properly mated —not wrecked upon the quicksands of marriage* (George Meredith).

quick·sand·y (kwik′san′dē), *adj.*, **-sand·i·er, -sand·i·est.** of, like, or containing quicksand: *a quicksandy spot* (Vladimir Nabokov).

quick·set (kwik′set′), *Especially British.* —*n.* **1.** a plant or cutting, especially of hawthorn, set to grow in a hedge: *I am afraid I shall see great neglects among my quicksets* (Jonathan Swift). **2.** a hedge of such plants. —*adj.* formed of such plants.

quick-sight·ed (kwik′sī′tid), *adj.* quick to see or discern: *a wonderfully active and quick-sighted person ... able to see what is going on all round* (W. H. Hudson). —**quick′-sight′ed·ness,** *n.*

quick·sil·ver (kwik′sil′vər), *n.* **1.** mercury, the metallic chemical element. **2.** something as shining, quick-moving, and elusive as mercury: *Emmett by contrast is a piece of quicksilver, brilliant but unpredictable* (London Times).
—*v.t.* to coat, treat, or mix with mercury.
—*adj.* quicksilvery: *Dr. Pringle ... speaks swiftly, with quicksilver linking of thought and expression* (London Times).
[Old English *cwicseolfor,* translation of Latin *argentum vīvum* living silver; *vīvum,* neuter of *vīvus* living]

quick·sil·ver·y (kwik′sil′vər ē), *adj.*, **-ver·i·er, -ver·i·est.** resembling quicksilver; bright and quick-moving: *The quicksilvery score, with its pastoral interludes and lavish descriptive effects, is a delight* (Time).

quick·step (kwik′step′), *n., v.,* **-stepped, -step·ping.** —*n.* **1.** a step used in marching in quick time: *The Grand Army starts off to war with a rousing quickstep, soon changes its tune to fit a war for which ... hardly any of the soldiers were prepared* (Time). **2.** music in a brisk march rhythm. **3.** a lively dance step.
—*v.i.* **1.** to march or progress at a lively pace: *But for all the explanations of the [ticker] tape-watchers there was one that underlay them all: The growing belief ... that the whole economy ... was once again quick-stepping to new peaks* (Newsweek). **2.** to dance the quickstep.

quick study, a person who memorizes rapidly: *Until a fortnight ago, [he] had never had Ravel's score in his hands, but he is what is known in the theatre as a quick study* (Time).

quick-tem·pered (kwik′tem′pərd), *adj.* easily angered. —**Syn.** irascible, peppery

quick time, a fast speed of marching. In quick time, soldiers march four miles an hour.

quick trick, (in bridge) a card (as an ace) or combination of cards (as a king and queen in the same suit) that may be counted upon to win a trick the first or second time a suit is played, unless trumped.

quick-trig·gered (kwik′trig′ərd), *adj.* **1.** that shoots fast: *He had made his way, by jeep and on foot, into the wild, roadless fastness of Cuba's Sierra Maestra ... dodging quick-triggered army patrols* (Newsweek). **2.** quickly put in action or set in motion: *Igaya knows that only quick-triggered reflexes and a good memory stand between him and death* (Newsweek). *Actually the quick-triggered Seawolf got away before Mrs. Cole could strike her hard with the metal protected champagne bottle* (New York Times).

quick-wit·ted (kwik′wit′id), *adj.* having a quick mind; mentally alert. —**Syn.** keen, sharp.

quick-wit·ted·ly (kwik′wit′id lē), *adv.* cleverly; acutely.

quick-wit·ted·ness (kwik′wit′id nis), *n.* readiness of wit; cleverness.

quid[1] (kwid), *n.* **1.** a piece to be chewed. **2.** a bite of chewing tobacco: *A large roll of tobacco was presented ... and every individual took a comfortable quid* (Tobias Smollett). [Old English *cwidu* cud]

quid[2] (kwid), *n., pl.* **quid.** *Especially British Slang.* one pound. [origin uncertain]

quid·dit (kwid′it), *n. Archaic.* quiddity. [short for *quiddity*]

quid·di·ty (kwid′ə tē), *n., pl.* **-ties. 1.** that which makes a thing what it is; essence: *The quiddity ... of poetry as distinguished from prose* (Thomas De Quincey). **2.** a distinction of no importance; quibble: *How now, how now, mad wag! What, in thy quips and thy quiddities?* (Shakespeare). *His stylized manner and his quips and quiddities will grow stale* (Newsweek). [< Medieval Latin *quidditas* < Latin *quid* what, neuter of *quis* who]

quid·dle (kwid′əl), *v.,* **-dled, -dling,** *n. Dialect.* —*v.i.* to trifle; fiddle; fuss: *I should like to know who's a going to stop to quiddle with young uns?* (Harriet Beecher Stowe). —*n.* a person given to fussing: *The Englishman is ... a quiddle about his toast and his chop* (Emerson). [origin uncertain. Perhaps related to TWIDDLE, or FIDDLE.]

quid·nunc (kwid′nungk′), *n.* an inquisitive person; gossip: *the crowd of village idlers, quidnuncs, tattlers and newsmongers* (Arnold Bennett). *At week's end the Russians themselves provided an unexpectedly fast answer for the quidnuncs* (Time). [< Latin *quid nunc* what now?; *quid,* neuter of *quis* who]

quid pro quo (kwid′ prō kwō′), *Latin.* **1.** one thing in return for another; compensation: *A laughable quid pro quo ... occurred to him in a conversation* (Thackeray). *We must cease thinking of economic aid as a short-run political tool which calls for a military quid pro quo* (W. Averell Harriman). **2.** (literally) something for something.

quids (kwidz), *n.pl. Especially British Slang.* money; cash: *"If only you boffins," (R.A.F. slang for a scientist) said Collins, "would give us a cheap way of locating an aircraft, then we'd be quids in"* (Time). [plural of *quid*[2]]

¿quién sa·be? (kyen sä′bā), *Spanish.* who knows?: *All climbed out carrying suitcases. "What are you going to do, rob the Treasury?" joshed a guard. "¿Quién sabe?" replied baby-faced José Alemán* (Time).

qui·esce (kwī es′), *v.i.,* **-esced, -esc·ing.** to become quiet or calm.

qui·es·cence (kwī es′əns), *n.* absence of activity; quietness; stillness: *Movement, not quiescence, is the irrevocable lot of the inhabitants of a globe spinning at nineteen miles a second* (J.W.R. Scott). —**Syn.** calmness, passivity.

qui·es·cen·cy (kwī es′ən sē), *n.* quiescence.

qui·es·cent (kwī es′ənt), *adj.* quiet and motionless; inactive; still: *For a time he [a whale] lay quiescent* (Herman Melville). *And the debate, which had been relatively quiescent, became hotter than ever* (Newsweek). [< Latin *quiēscēns, -entis,* present participle of *quiēscere* to rest < *quiēs* rest, quiet] —**Syn.** passive.

qui·es·cent·ly (kwī es′ənt lē), *adv.* in a quiescent manner; calmly; quietly.

qui·et[1] (kwī′ət), *adj.* **1.** moving very little; still; calm: *a quiet lake, a quiet river.* **2.** with no or little noise; silent; hushed: *quiet footsteps, a quiet street. The holy time is quiet as a nun Breathless with adoration* (Wordsworth). **3.** saying little: *During dinner ... we were unusually quiet, even to gravity* (W.H. Hudson). **4.** peaceful: *a quiet person, a quiet night's sleep. Anything for a quiet life! All had been quiet since the news of the capitulation at Lerida* (James A. Froude). **5.** gentle. **6.** unobtrusive; inconspicuous: *quiet manners.* **7.** not showy or bright: *Gray is a quiet color.* **8.** not active: *a quiet life in the country; a quiet trading on the stock exchange. The snow was piling up on the north side of the hogans and there was no smoke from the holes in the domeshaped roofs. All the chimneys were quiet* (Harper's).
—*v.t.* to make quiet: *The mother quieted her frightened child. In trying to quiet one set of malcontents, he had created another* (Macaulay). —*v.i.* to become quiet: *The wind quieted down.*
—*adv.* in a quiet manner; quietly.
[< Latin *quiētus* resting, past participle of *quiēscere* to rest < *quiēs, -ētis* rest. Doublet of COY, QUIT, adjective.]
—**Syn.** *adj.* **1.** See **still.**

qui·et[2] (kwī′ət), *n.* **1.** absence of motion or noise; stillness: *The first indications came in late June when orders began to improve after a long spell of quiet* (Wall Street Journal). **2.** freedom from disturbance: *Go to the library to read in quiet. His small force would be large enough to overawe them in times of quiet* (William H. Prescott). [< Latin *quiēs, -ētis* rest]

qui·et·en (kwī′ə tən), *Especially British.* —*v.t.* to make quiet: *At last ... to quieten them, I promised to ... write a short story* (Arnold Bennett). —*v.i.* to become quiet: *Her heart had quietened down while she rested* (Joseph Conrad). *The situation will somehow quieten down one day, and the old order will be able to survive* (London Times).

qui·et·er (kwī′ə tər), *n.* a person or thing that quiets.

qui·et·ish (kwī′ə tish), *adj.* somewhat quiet: *After a quietish spell in the first fortnight of August, Elsey's horses have come back to form in no hesitant manner* (London Times).

qui·et·ism (kwī′ə tiz əm), *n.* **1.** a form of religious mysticism requiring abandonment of the will, withdrawal from worldly interests, and passive meditation on God and divine things. **2.** quietness of mind or life: *Dissent and deviation are treason, and quietism is sacrilege* (Atlantic). [< Italian *quietismo* < Latin *quiētus* quiet + Italian *-ismo* -ism]

qui·et·ist (kwī′ə tist), *n.* **1.** a person who believes in or practices quietism. **2.** a person who seeks quietness. —*adj.* quietistic: *He accused Tolstoy of helping to bring about the failure of the 1905 Revolution because of his quietist influence on the peasantry* (Ernest J. Simmons).

qui·et·is·tic (kwī′ə tis′tik), *adj.* of or having to do with quietists or quietism: *Though the element of realism in this almost quietistic manifestation of the Baroque spirit is apparently derived from Caravaggio and the Spaniards, its essential characteristics are the peculiar result of the climate of independent thought in the France of Louis XIII* (London Times).

qui·et·ly (kwī′it lē), *adv.* **1.** in a quiet manner; peacefully; calmly. **2.** without motion. **3.** without noise.

qui·et·ness (kwī′it nis), *n.* the state of being quiet; stillness; calmness: *In quietness and in confidence shall be your strength* (Isaiah 30:15).

qui·et-spo·ken (kwī′ət spō′kən), *adj.* **1.** speaking in a quiet, calm manner: *Wiesner, a reflective, quiet-spoken man, is able to deal with it quite calmly* (Daniel Lang). **2.** spoken quietly: ... *a terse, quiet-spoken,* *but vigorous and very effective attack on M. Debrés' statements* (Manchester Guardian Weekly).

qui·e·tude (kwī′ə tüd, -tyüd), *n.* quietness; stillness; calmness: *That suave master of many roles . . . whom the masters of Shangri-La have selected as the man to carry on their great tradition of quietude and culture* (Wall Street Journal). [< Late Latin *quiētūdō* < Latin *quiētus* quiet, adjective] —**Syn.** placidity, tranquillity.

qui·e·tus (kwī ē′təs), *n.* **1.** a final getting rid of anything; finishing stroke; anything that ends or settles: *At his press conference . . . President Eisenhower rightly tried to put the quietus on the war talk of some in the Administration and Congress* (Wall Street Journal). **2.** something that quiets: *The nurse ran to give its accustomed quietus to the little screaming infant* (Thackeray). **3.** a receipt. [< Medieval Latin *quietus est* he is discharged < Latin *quiētus est* he is at rest; *quiētus* quiet, adjective]

quiff (kwif), *n.* **1.** *British Slang.* a curl or lock of hair worn on the forehead: *Our eye was . . . [on] that famous quiff of rebellious hair ritualistically uncovered three times as Lord Morrison took off his medieval hat and bowed to the Woolsack* (Manchester Guardian). **2.** *Slang.* a cheap woman; a prostitute. [perhaps < Italian *cuffia* coif]

quill (kwil), *n.* **1.** a large, strong flight feather. **2.** the hollow stem of a feather: *Each main shaft or quill sprouts forth some 600 dowls or barbs on either side to form the familiar vane of the feather* (Atlantic). **3.** a thing made from the hollow stem of a feather: **a.** a pen. **b.** a toothpick. **c.** an instrument used for plucking the strings of a mandolin, lute, etc. **4.** the stiff, sharp hollow spine of a porcupine or hedgehog. **5.** a spool, bobbin, or spindle. **6.** a piece of cinnamon or cinchona bark curled up in the form of a tube.

Quill (def. 3a)

—*v.t.* to pleat (fabric, garments, etc.) into small, cylindrical folds resembling quills. —*v.i.* to wind thread or yarn on a quill: *The big textile machinery maker is boosting the loom winders as equipment which brings an "entirely new concept" to fabric production — integration of the quilling process with the loom* (Wall Street Journal). [Middle English *quil* stiff hollow stalk, a reed; origin uncertain]

quil·lai (ki lī′), *n.* **1.** a tree of Chile; soapbark. **2.** its bark; soapbark. [< Spanish *quillái* < Araucanian (Chile) < *quillcan* to wash]

quil·lai·a bark (ki lī′ə, kwi lā′-), the bark of the quillai.

quill driver, a writer; clerk (used in a contemptuous way).

quill driving, working with a pen; writing (used in a contemptuous way).

quilled (kwild), *adj.* **1.** having quills: *a quilled mammal.* **2.** having the form of a quill: *quilled bark.*

quil·let (kwil′it), *n.* a nicety; subtlety; quibble. [perhaps short for a variant of *quiddity*]

quill feather, one of the large feathers of the wing or tail of a bird.

quill·ing (kwil′ing), *n.* quilled strip of silk, lace, etc.; a fluted or pleated edging.

quil·lon (kē yôN′), *n. French.* either arm of a transverse piece forming a guard for the hand between the hilt and the blade of a sword: *The sword that went with the harness had a blade made in the Rhineland, a splendid gold and garnet pommel, two gold filigree mounts on the grip, gold quillons and two jeweled gold scabbard-bosses* (Scientific American).

quill·wort (kwil′wėrt′), *n.* any of a group of grasslike pteridophytic plants with quill-like leaves, growing especially in or near water.

quilt (kwilt), *n.* **1.** a bedcover made of two pieces of cloth with a soft pad between, held in place by lines of stitching. The top of a quilt often consists of bits and pieces of cloth sewed together in a design. **2.** anything resembling a quilt: *a quilt of clouds.*

—*v.i. U.S.* to make quilts; do quilted work.

—*v.t.* **1.** to stitch together with a soft lining: *to quilt a bathrobe. Whether dressed for palace or law court, Coke was always well turned out in handsome gown or doublet, quilted sleeves* . . . (Atlantic). **2.** to sew in lines or patterns: *The bedcover was quilted in a flower design.* **3.** to sew up between pieces of material: *Secret papers were quilted in her belt.*

[< Old French *cuilte,* and *coultre* < Latin *culcita* cushion]

—**Syn.** *n.* **1.** comforter.

quilt·er (kwil′tər), *n.* **1.** a person who quilts: *Seventeen-year-old Jane could tell the old time quilters the results of adding alum, chrome, tin, copper and iron to natural dyes such as great-great-grandmother used* (Science News Letter). **2.** a sewing-machine attachment for quilting fabrics.

quilt·ing (kwil′ting), *n.* **1.** quilted work. **2.** material for making quilts. **3.** a stout fabric woven so as to appear quilted. **4.** a quilting bee.

quilting bee, *U.S.* a friendly gathering of women to make a quilt: *Quilting bees and threshings were community occasions* (Maclean's).

quilting frame, a frame to stretch and hold the fabrics and padding of a quilt in place while it is being sewed.

quin (kwin), *n. Informal.* a quintuplet: *For a man, producing a book provides rather the same kind of fulfillment . . . as childbirth does for a woman, but the author . . . can go on having quins . . . every other year for a lifetime* (James Morris).

qui·na (kē′nə, kwī′-), *n.* **1.** cinchona bark. **2.** quinine. [< Spanish *quina* < Quechua (Peru) *kina* cinchona bark]

quin·a·crine hydrochloride, or **quin·a·crine** (kwin′ə krēn, -krin), *n.* Atabrine, a drug used in the treatment of malaria: *Atabrine is the trade name given this drug by the Germans and has been so commonly used that it is employed here. The official name in this country is quinacrine, in England mepacrine* (James Phinney Baxter III). [< *quin*(ine) + *acr*(id)*ine*]

qui·nal·dine (kwi nal′din), *n. Chemistry.* a colorless, liquid compound occurring in coal tar and also obtained by synthetic methods, used in the preparation of certain dyes. *Formula:* $C_{10}H_9N$ [< *quin*(oline) + *al-d*(ehyde) + (anil)*ine*]

qui·na·ry (kwī′nər ē), *adj., n., pl.* **-ries.** —*adj.* **1.** having to do with the number five. **2.** based on the number five. **3.** consisting of five (things or parts).

—*n.* a group of five.

[< Latin *quīnārius* < *quīnī* five each < *quīnque* five]

qui·nate (kwī′nāt, -nit), *adj.* (of a leaf) composed of five leaflets; quinquefoliolate. [< New Latin *quinatus* < Latin *quīnī* five each < *quīnque* five]

quin·az·o·lin (kwi naz′ə lin), *n.* quinazoline.

quin·az·o·line (kwi naz′ə lēn, -lin), *n.* **1.** a colorless, crystalline substance generally considered as a quinoline derivative. *Formula:* $C_8H_6N_2$ **2.** any of various substances derived from this compound. [< *quin*(oline) + *azol*(e) + *-ine*[2]]

quince (kwins), *n.* **1.** the hard, yellowish, acid, pear-shaped fruit of a small Asiatic tree of the rose family, used for preserves and jelly. **2.** the tree it grows on. **3.** any of certain similar shrubs or trees grown for their blossoms, as the Japanese quince. [(originally) plural of Middle English *quyne* < Old French *cooin* < Latin *cotōneum* (*mālum*), variant of *Cydōnium* < Greek *kydōnion* (*málon*) (apple) of or from Cydonia, a town in Crete]

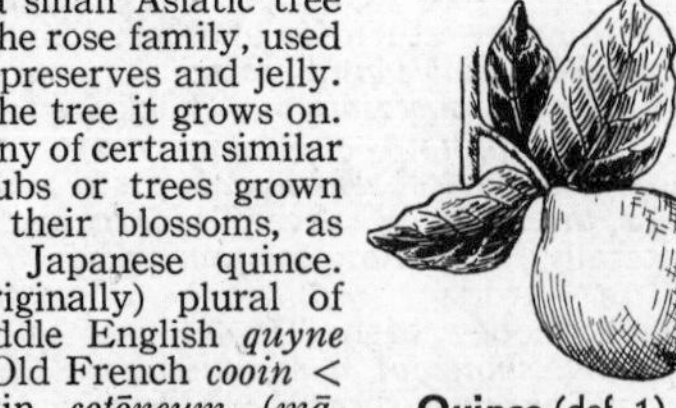
Quince (def. 1)

quin·cen·te·nar·y (kwin sen′tə ner′ē), *adj., n., pl.* **-nar·ies.** —*adj.* having to do with five hundred or a period of five hundred years; marking the completion of five hundred years. —*n.* a five-hundredth anniversary, or its celebration.

quin·cen·ten·ni·al (kwin′sen ten′ē əl), *adj., n.* quincentenary.

quin·cun·cial (kwin kun′shəl), *adj.* of, having to do with, or consisting of a quincunx.

quin·cun·cial·ly (kwin kun′shə lē), *adv.* in a quincuncial manner or order.

quin·cunx (kwin′kungks), *n., pl.* (*for defs. 1 and 2*) **-cunx·es.** **1.** an arrangement of five things in a square or rectangle, one at each corner and one in the middle. **2.** an overlapping arrangement of five petals or leaves, in which two are interior, two are exterior, and one is partly interior and partly exterior. **3.** *Astrology.* an aspect of planets in which they are at a distance of five signs or 150 degrees from each other: *But the quincunx of heaven runs low, and 'tis time to close the five ports of knowledge* (Sir Thomas Browne). [< Latin *quīncūnx, -uncis* (literally) five-twelfths < *quīnque* five + *uncia* an ounce, a twelfth]

quin·dec·a·gon (kwin dek′ə gon), *n. Geometry.* a plane figure with 15 angles and 15 sides. [< Latin *quīndecim* fifteen < *quīnque* five + *decem* ten; patterned on English *decagon*]

quin·de·cem·vir (kwin′di sem′vər), *n., pl.* **-vi·ri** (-və rī). in ancient Rome: **1.** one of a body of fifteen men. **2.** one of a body of fifteen priests who, at the close of the republic, had charge of the Sibylline Books. [< Latin *quīndecemvir* < *quīndecim* (see QUINDECAGON) + *vir* man]

quin·de·cen·ni·al (kwin′di sen′ē əl), *adj.* of or having to do with fifteen years or a fifteenth anniversary. —*n.* a fifteenth anniversary. [< Latin *quīndecim* (see QUINDECAGON); patterned on English *biennial*]

quin·el·la (kwi nel′ə), *n.* a bet on a sporting event, especially horse racing, in which one picks the first two finishers but not necessarily in order of finish: *The usual totalizator facilities operate on all races with quinellas on the first three and last races* (Cape Times). [origin uncertain]

quin·gen·te·nar·y (kwin jen′tə ner′ē), *adj., n., pl.* **-nar·ies.** quincentenary. [< Latin *quīngentī* five hundred; patterned on *centenary*]

quin·i·a (kwin′ē ə), *n.* quinine.

quin·ic acid (kwin′ik), a white, crystalline, organic acid, obtained from cinchona bark, coffee beans, etc. *Formula:* $C_7H_{12}O_6$

quin·i·din (kwin′ə din), *n.* quinidine.

quin·i·dine (kwin′ə dēn, -din), *n. Chemistry.* an alkaloid isomeric with quinine, and associated with it in certain species of cinchona: *Balm for some cases of disordered heart rhythm is quinidine. This chemical is a relative of the old anti-malaria drug, quinine* (Science News Letter). *Formula:* $C_{20}H_{24}N_2O_2$ [< *quin*(a) + *-id* + *-ine*[2]]

quin·ie·la (kwin yel′ə), *n.* a quinella: . . . *an old betting gimmick—the quiniela* (Audax Minor).

quin·in (kwin′in), *n.* quinine.

qui·ni·na (ki nē′nə), *n.* quinine.

qui·nine (kwī′nīn; *especially British* kwi-nēn′), *n.* **1.** a bitter, crystalline alkaloid made from the bark of a cinchona tree, used for colds, malaria, and fevers, as a muscle relaxant, etc. *Formula:* $C_{20}H_{24}N_2O_2.3H_2O$ **2.** any of various compounds of quinine used as medicine. [< *quin*(a) + *-ine*[2]]

quinine water, a carbonated drink containing a small amount of quinine and a little lemon and lime juice: *Sales of quinine water, a rising star on the fizz-water horizon, have moved up from about 100,000 cases in 1949 to about 1.2 million cases last year* (Wall Street Journal).

quin·nat salmon, or **quin·nat** (kwin′-at), *n.* the chinook salmon, a large salmon of the Pacific Coast. [American English < Salishan *t'kwinnat*]

qui·no·a (kē′nō ä), *n.* **1.** an annual plant of the amaranth family, found on the Pacific slopes of the Andes, cultivated in Chile and Peru as a grain. **2.** an herb of the goosefoot family, also grown since early times by the natives of the Andean region, used to make bread, soup, a beverage, etc. **3.** the seed of either of these plants. [American Spanish *quínoa*]

quin·oid (kwin′oid), *n.* a chemical compound having a structure like that of quinone. —*adj.* like quinone in structure.

qui·noi·din (kwi noi′din), *n.* quinoidine.

qui·noi·dine (kwi noi′dēn, -din), *n. Pharmacy.* a brownish-black, resinous substance consisting of amorphous alkaloids. It is obtained as a by-product in the manufacture of quinine, and used as a cheap substitute for it. [< *quin*(a) + *-oid* + *-ine*[2]]

quin·ol (kwin′ol, -ōl), *n.* hydroquinone: *The cage in which the aloof and volatile molecules on the inert gases are trapped is made up of ordinary quinol, a photographic developing material, also known as hydroquinone* (Science News Letter). [< *quin*(a) + *-ol*[2]]

quin·o·lin (kwin′ə lin), *n.* quinoline.

quin·o·line (kwin′ə lēn, -lin), *n.* a nitrogenous organic base, a colorless, oily liquid with a pungent odor, occurring in coal tar and obtained from aniline. It is used as an antiseptic, as a solvent, and in the preparation of other compounds. *Some of the products already evolving are new types of phenolic plastics, new pharmaceuticals based on quinoline (nicotinic acid) and on picoline (tuberculosis drugs), and new rocket fuels* (Scientific American). *Formula:* C_9H_7N [< *quinol* + *-ine*[2]]

qui·none (kwi nōn′, kwin′ōn), *n.* **1.** a yellowish, crystalline compound with an irritating odor, obtained by the oxidation of aniline and regarded as a benzene with two hydrogen atoms replaced by two oxygen atoms. It is used in tanning and making dyes. *Quinone will, for example, oxidise another material and be itself reduced to hydroquinone* (New Scientist). *Woodward's synthesis starts with the simple coal-tar derivative quinone, proceeds directly and yields an abundance of reserpine* (Scientific American). *Formula:* $C_6H_4O_2$ **2.** any of a group of compounds, of which this is the type. [< *quin*(ic acid) + *-one*]

qui·non·i·mine (kwi non′ə mēn, -min), *n.* **1.** a compound derived from quinone by the substitution of an -NH radical for one atom of oxygen. *Formula:* C_6H_5NO **2.** any compound similarly derived from quinone. [< *quinon*(e) + *imine*]

quin·o·noid (kwin′ənoid, kwinō′-), *adj.* like quinone in structure. [< *quinon*(e) + *-oid*]

quin·ox·a·lin (kwi nok′sə lin), *n.* quinoxaline.

quin·ox·a·line (kwi nok′sə lēn, -lin), *n.* a colorless, crystalline compound, used in organic synthesis. *Formula:* $C_8H_6N_2$ [< *quin*(oline) + (gly)*oxal*(in) + *-ine*[2]]

quinqu-, *combining form.* the form of **quinque-** before vowels, as in *quinquangular.*

quin·qua·ge·nar·i·an (kwin′kwə jə när′ē ən), *n.* a person 50 years old or between 50 and 60. —*adj.* **1.** 50 years old or between 50 and 60. **2.** characteristic of one who is 50 years old. [< Latin *quīnquāgēnārius* having fifty (< *quīnquāgēnī* fifty each < *quīnquāginta* fifty < *quīnque* five) + English *-an*]

Quin·qua·ges·i·ma (kwin′kwə jes′ə mə), *n.*, or **Quinquagesima Sunday,** the Sunday before the beginning of Lent; Shrove Sunday. [< Latin *quīnquāgēsima,* feminine adjective, fiftieth (in Late Latin, the period from Easter to Whitsunday)]

quin·quan·gu·lar (kwin kwang′gyə lər), *adj.* having five angles. [< Late Latin *quīnquangulus* (< Latin *quīnque* five + *angulus* angle) + English *-ar*]

quinque-, *combining form.* five; having five; five times ____: *Quinquefoliate = having five leaves. Quinquennium = a period of five years.* Also, **quinqu-** before vowels. [< Latin *quīnque-* < *quīnque*]

quin·que·far·i·ous (kwin′kwə fãr′ē əs), *adj.* fivefold; in five rows. [< *quinque-* + Latin *-farius* (with English *-ous*), an adjective suffix expressing quantity]

quin·que·fid (kwin′kwə fid), *adj.* split into five parts or lobes. [< *quinque-* + Latin *-fidus* cleft < *findere* to cleave, divide]

quin·que·fo·li·ate (kwin′kwə fō′lē it), *adj.* having five leaves or leaflets.

quin·que·fo·li·o·late (kwin′kwə fō′lē ə-lāt, -fə lī′ə lit), *adj.* having five leaflets; quinate.

quin·que·loc·u·lar (kwin′kwə lok′yə-lər), *adj.* having five compartments.

quin·quen·ni·ad (kwin kwen′ē ad), *n.* a period of five years; quinquennium.

quin·quen·ni·al (kwin kwen′ē əl), *adj.* **1.** occurring every five years: *A number of the permanent commissions of the congress, bodies whose work goes on in between the quinquennial meetings, read and debated separately* (London Times). **2.** of or for five years.
—*n.* **1.** something that occurs every five years. **2.** something lasting five years. [< Latin *quīnquennis* (< *quīnque* five + *annus* year) + English *-al*[1]]

quin·quen·ni·al·ly (kwin kwen′ē ə lē), *adv.* **1.** once in five years. **2.** during a period of five years.

quin·quen·ni·um (kwin kwen′ē əm), *n., pl.* **-quen·ni·a** (-kwen′ē ə). a period of five years. [< Latin *quīnquennium* < *quīnque* five + *annus* year]

quin·que·par·tite (kwin′kwə pär′tīt), *adj.* divided into or consisting of five parts. [< Latin *quīnquepartītus* < *quīnque* five + *partīrī* to divide < *pars, partis* past]

quin·que·reme (kwin′kwə rēm), *n.* a galley with five tiers of oars: *It is unlikely that triremes and quinqueremes were three- or five-story vessels, as is often asserted; instead, the terms probably refer to the number of men employed on each oar* (Scientific American). [< Latin *quīnquerēmis* < *quīnque* five + *rēmus* oar. Compare TRIREME.]

quin·que·va·lence (kwin′kwə vā′ləns, kwing kwev′ə-), *n.* **1.** the condition of having a valence of five; pentavalence. **2.** the condition of having five different valences.

quin·que·va·len·cy (kwin′kwə vā′lən sē, kwing kwev′ə-), *n.* quinquevalence.

quin·que·va·lent (kwin′kwə vā′lənt, kwing kwev′ə-), *adj.* **1.** having a valence of five; pentavalent. **2.** having five different valences.

quin·qui·va·lent (kwin′kwə vā′lənt, kwing kwiv′ə-), *adj.* quinquevalent.

quin·sy (kwin′zē), *n.* tonsillitis with pus; very sore throat with an abscess in the tonsils. [Middle English *quinacy* < Medieval Latin *quinancia* < Greek *kynánchē* (originally) dog's collar < *kýōn, kynós* dog + *ánchein* to choke]

quint[1] (kwint), *n. Informal.* a quintuplet.

quint[2] (kwint, kint), *n.* **1.** a set or sequence of five, as in piquet. **2.** *Music.* a fifth. [< French, Old French *quint,* or *quinte,* feminine < Latin *quīntus* and *quīnta* a fifth, related to *quīnque* five]

quin·ta (kin′tə), *n.* (in Spain, Latin America, etc.) a country house or villa: . . . *his presidential quinta in suburban Olivos* (Time). [< Spanish and Portuguese *quinta*]

quin·tain (kwin′tin), *n.* in the Middle Ages: **1.** a post set up as a mark to be tilted at. **2.** the exercise of tilting at a target. [< Old French *quintaine* < Medieval Latin *quintana,* apparently < Latin *quīntāna* market place of a Roman camp, (originally) placed between the stations of the fifth and sixth maniples < *quīntus* fifth (maniple)]

quin·tal (kwin′təl), *n.* **1.** a hundredweight. In the United States, a quintal equals 100 pounds; in Great Britain, 112 pounds. **2.** (in the metric system) a unit of weight equal to 100 kilograms or 220.46 pounds avoirdupois: *A million quintals of wheat . . . and unspecified quantities of sugar and potatoes will be distributed* (New York Times). *Abbr.:* ql. [< Medieval Latin *quintale* < Arabic *qinṭār* weight of a hundred pounds, probably ultimately < Latin *centēnārius* < *centum* hundred. Compare KANTAR.]

quin·tan (kwin′tən), *adj.* recurring every fifth day by inclusive count. —*n.* a fever or ague with three days between attacks. [< Latin *quīntāna* (*febris*) (literally) (fever) of the fifth (day, by Roman count) < *quīntus* fifth, related to *quīnque* five]

quinte (kaNt), *n. Fencing.* the fifth in a series of eight parries. [< French *quinte,* feminine of *quint;* see QUINT[2]]

quin·tes·sence (kwin tes′əns), *n.* **1.** the purest form of some quality; pure essence. **2.** the most perfect example of something: *Her costume was the quintessence of good taste and style.* **3.** (in medieval philosophy) the ether of Aristotle, a fifth element (added to earth, water, fire, and air) permeating all things and forming the substance of the heavenly bodies. [< Middle French *quinte essence,* learned borrowing from Medieval Latin *quinta essentia* fifth essence, translation of Greek *pémptē ousíā* Aristotle's "fifth substance"] —**Syn. 1.** pith.

quin·tes·sen·tial (kwin′tə sen′shəl), *adj.* having the nature of a quintessence; of the purest or most perfect kind: *Costain has created what amounts to a quintessential recapture of the English novel, from Smollett to Dickens* (Wall Street Journal). *They don't pay sufficient attention to the quintessential requirement: that it be easy for the reader to find what he is looking for* (Atlantic).

quin·tes·sen·tial·ize (kwin′tə sen′shə-līz), *v.t.*, **-ized, -iz·ing.** to make quintessential; reduce or refine to a quintessence.

quin·tes·sen·tial·ly (kwin′tə sen′shə lē), *adv.* in a quintessential manner: *He is, quintessentially, the non-organization man . . .* (Harper's).

quin·tet or **quin·tette** (kwin tet′), *n.* **1. a.** a group of five musicians (singers or players). **b.** a piece of music for five voices or instruments. **2.** any group of five; set of five. **3.** *Informal.* a men's basketball team. [probably < French *quintette* < Italian *quintetto* (diminutive) < *quinto* fifth < Latin *quīntus;* see QUINTAN]

quin·tile (kwin′təl, -tīl), *adj. Astrology.* of or designating the aspect of two heavenly bodies distant from each other by 72 degrees, or a fifth part of the zodiac. —*n.* **1. a.** one of the points or marks dividing a frequency distribution into five parts, each containing one fifth of the total number of observations, etc. **b.** any of the five parts thus formed. **2.** *Astrology.* a quintile aspect. [probably < New Latin *quintus* fifth < Latin *quīntus;* patterned on English *quartile*]

quin·til·lion (kwin til′yən), *n., adj.* **1.** (in the United States and France) 1 followed by 18 zeros. **2.** (in Great Britain) 1 followed by 30 zeros. [< Latin *quīntus* fifth; patterned on English *million*]

quin·til·lionth (kwin til′yənth), *adj.* last in a series of a quintillion. —*n.* **1.** the last in a series of a quintillion. **2.** one of a quintillion equal parts.

quin·troon (kwin trün′), *n.* a person having one sixteenth Negro blood. [alteration of Spanish *quinterón* < *quinto* fifth < Latin *quīntus* (because the person is fifth in descent from a Negro); after *quadroon*]

quin·tu·ple (kwin′tu̇ pəl, -tyu̇-; kwin tü′-, -tyü′-), *adj., v.,* **-pled, -pling,** *n.* —*adj.* **1.** fivefold; consisting of five parts. **2.** five times as great.
—*v.t.* to make five times as great: *He had quintupled a fortune already considerable* (Henry James). *He has in seventeen years of pin-wheeling brilliance quintupled the magazine's circulation* (Newsweek). —*v.i.* to become five times as great.
—*n.* a number, amount, etc., five times as great as another.
[< French *quintuple* < Late Latin *quīntuplex* < Latin *quīntus* fifth + *-plex;* see QUADUPLEX]

quin·tu·plet (kwin′tu̇ plit, -tyu̇-; kwin-tü′-, -tyü′-), *n.* **1.** one of five children born at the same time from the same mother: *Many people have heard of the Dionne quintuplets of Canada.* **2.** any group or combination of five; set of five.

quin·tu·pli·cate (*adj., n.* kwin tü′plə kit, -tyü′-; *v.* kwin tü′plə kāt, -tyü′-), *adj., v.,* **-cat·ed, -cat·ing,** *n.* —*adj.* five old; quintuple. —*v.t.* to make fivefold; quintuple. —*n.* one of a set of five.

in quintuplicate, in five copies exactly alike: *Such a person must fill out fifteen forms in quintuplicate . . . showing just why he should be allowed a British bicycle* (New Yorker).

quinze (kwinz; *French* kaNz), *n.* a card game somewhat similar to twenty-one, in which the object is to score fifteen, or as near as possible to that number, without exceeding it. [< French *quinze* < Latin *quīndecim;* see QUINDECAGON]

quip (kwip), *n., v.,* **quipped, quip·ping.** —*n.* **1.** a clever or witty saying: *I am generally known as a discouragingly slow man with a quip* (New Yorker). **2.** a sharp, cutting remark: *If I sent him word again it was not well cut, he would send me word he cut it to please himself. This is called the Quip Modest* (Shakespeare). **3.** a quibble: *tricks of controversy and quips of law* (Benjamin Jowett). **4.** something odd or strange. **5.** a knickknack.
—*v.i.* to make quips. —*v.t.* to sneer at.
[perhaps for earlier *quippy* < Latin *quippe* indeed! I dare say]
—**Syn.** *n.* **1.** witticism. **2.** sarcasm.

quip·pish (kwip′ish), *adj.* **1.** clever; witty. **2.** sarcastic; cutting: *The dialogue is more quippish than witty* (Time).

quip·ster (kwip′stər), *n.* a person who often makes quips.

qui·pu (kē′pü, kwip′ü), *n., pl.* **-pus.** a device consisting of a cord with knotted strings or threads of various colors, used by the ancient Peruvians for recording events, keeping accounts, sending messages, etc. [earlier *quipo* < Spanish < Quechua (Peru) *quipu* knot]

quire[1] (kwīr), *n., v.,* **quired, quir·ing.** —*n.* **1.** 24 or 25 sheets of paper of the same size and quality. **2. a.** (in bookbinding) a set of four sheets folded to make eight leaves. **b.** any similar set of sheets in proper order, but before binding.

in quires, in sheets and not bound, as a book: *I gave my book . . . to the Heralds Office in quires* (Anthony Wood).
—*v.t.* to arrange in quires; fold in quires.
[< Old French *quaier,* earlier *quaer* < Late Latin *quaternus* < Latin *quaternī* four each, related to *quattuor* four. Doublet of CAHIER, CASERN.]

quire[2] (kwīr), *n. Archaic.* choir.

Quir·i·nal (kwir′ə nəl), *n.* **1.** one of the seven hills upon which Rome was built. **2.** a palace built there, formerly the royal palace, now the official residence of the president of Italy: *Gronchi, unlike Einaudi, refuses to live in the Quirinal, explaining "I don't want my children to develop crown-prince complexes"* (Newsweek). **3.** the Italian government, as distinguished from the Vatican (representing the papacy).
—*adj.* **1.** of or having to do with the Quirinal hill, the palace on it, or the Italian government. **2.** of, relating to, or like Quirinus.
[< Latin *Quirīnālis* < *Quirīnus* Quirinus]

Qui·ri·nus (kwi rī′nəs), *n. Roman Mythology.* a god of war. Romulus was identified with him in early mythology. Later, Quirinus was viewed as the son of Mars.

Qui·ri·tes (kwi rī′tēz), *n.pl.* the citizens of ancient Rome considered in their civil capacity. [< Latin *Quirītēs,* plural of *Quirīs* (originally) citizens of the Sabine town of Cures]

quirk (kwėrk), *n.* **1.** a peculiar way of acting: *Every man had his own quirks and twists* (Harriet Beecher Stowe). **2.** a clever or witty saying; quip: *Your rhymes . . . your quirks and your conundrums* (William Godwin). **3.** a quibble. **4.** a quibbling; equivocation. **5.** a sudden twist or turn: *a quirk in the road.* **6.** a flourish in writing. **7.** a sudden turn or flourish in a musical air: *light quirks of music, broken and uneven* (Alexander Pope). **8.** *Architecture.* an acute angle or recess; a deep indentation.
—*adj.* having a quirk.
—*v.t.* to form with a quirk.
—**Syn.** *n.* **3.** shift, evasion.

quirked (kwėrkt), *adj.* formed with a quirk or channel: *a quirked molding.*

quirk·i·ly (kwėr′kə lē), *adv.* in a quirky manner.

quirk·i·ness (kwėr′kē nis), *n.* the state or quality of being quirky: *Some jazz highbrows . . . attribute Armstrong's fondness for Lombardo to the same inexplicable quirkiness that occasionally moves a thoroughbred race horse to pal around with a goat* (New Yorker).

quirk·ish (kwėr′kish), *adj.* having the character of a quirk; full of quirks, quibbles, or artful evasions.

quirk·y (kwėr′kē), *adj.,* **quirk·i·er, quirk·i·est.** full of quirks, twists, or shifts: *The writing has a quirky, personal quality that gives it an uncommon flavor* (New Yorker).

quir·ley or **quir·ly** (kwėr′lē), *n., pl.* **-leys** or **-lies.** *U.S. Slang.* a hand-rolled cigarette: *A cigarette is best called a quirly; it is seldom rolled or made, it is fashioned, shaped, spun, or built; it is not lit, fire is put to it* (Harper's).

quirt (kwėrt), *n.* a riding whip with a short, stout handle and a lash of braided leather: *Our horses were lathered with sweat and it was use of quirt on rump rather than kindness in the voice that urged the horses on* (Maclean's).
—*v.t.* to strike with a quirt. [American English < American Spanish *cuarta* < Spanish, a whip long enough to reach the *cuarta,* or guide mule, of a team of four < Latin *quarta,* feminine of *quartus* fourth]

quis cus·to·di·et ip·sos cus·to·des? (kwis kus tō′dē et ip′sos kus tō′dēz), *Latin.* who shall guard the guardians?

qui s'ex·cuse s'ac·cuse (kē seks kyz′ sȧ kyz′), *French.* who excuses himself accuses himself.

quis·le (kwiz′əl), *v.i.,* **-led, -ling.** *Slang.* to act as a quisling.

quis·ling (kwiz′ling), *n.* any person who treacherously helps to prepare the way for enemy occupation of his own country; traitor. [< Norwegian *quisling* < Vidkun *Quisling,* 1887-1945, a Norwegian Nazi, who was the premier of the puppet government during the German occupation of Norway in World War II]

quis se·pa·ra·bit? (kwis sep′ə rā′bit), *Latin.* who shall separate (us)?

quit[1] (kwit), *v.,* **quit** or **quit·ted, quit·ting,** *adj.* —*v.t.* **1.** *Especially U.S.* to stop: *The men quit work when the whistle blew.* **2.** to leave: *He quit his room in anger. His big brother is quitting school this June.* **3.** to give up; let go: *to quit a job.* **4.** to pay back; pay off (a debt): *A thousand marks . . . To quit the penalty and to ransom him* (Shakespeare). **5.** to free; clear; rid: *to quit oneself of a nuisance.* **6.** *Archaic.* to behave or conduct (oneself); acquit: *Quit yourselves like men, and fight* (I Samuel 4:9). —*v.i.* **1.** to stop working. **2.** to leave: *If he doesn't pay his rent, he will receive notice to quit.* **3.** *Informal.* to leave a position, job, etc.; resign. [< Old French *quiter,* learned borrowing from Medieval Latin *quietare* to discharge debts < Latin *quiētus;* see QUIET[1]]
—*adj.* free; clear; rid: *I gave him money to be quit of him.*
[< Old French *quite,* learned borrowing from Medieval Latin *quittus,* alteration of Latin *quiētus.* Doublet of QUIET[1], COY.]
—**Syn.** *v.t.* **4.** repay.

quit[2] (kwit), *n.* any of various small perching birds of the West Indies, etc., as the banana quit. [apparently imitative]

quitch (kwich), *n.,* or **quitch grass,** couch grass, a kind of spreading grass that is a common weed in gardens. [Old English *cwice,* related to *cwic* quick. Compare QUICK GRASS, COUCH GRASS.]

quit·claim (kwit′klām′), *n.* **1.** the giving up of a claim or right of action. **2.** a quitclaim deed. [< Anglo-French *quiteclame* < *quiteclamer;* see the verb] —*v.t.* to give up claim to (a possession, right of action, etc.). [< Anglo-French *quiteclamer* < *quite* free, quit, clear + *clamer* to claim]

quitclaim deed, a document in which a person gives up his claim, title, or interest in a piece of property to someone else but does not guarantee that the title is valid.

quite (kwīt), *adv.* **1.** completely; wholly; entirely: *a hat quite out of fashion. I am quite alone. Are you quite satisfied?* **2.** actually; really; positively: *quite the thing, quite a change in the weather.* **3.** *Informal.* to a considerable extent or degree: *quite pretty. It is quite hot.* **4.** absolutely; definitely (as an answer to a question or remark). [Middle English *quite,* (originally) variant of *quit*[1], adjective, clear, free] —**Syn. 1.** totally. **3.** somewhat.

➔ **quite.** The formal meaning of *quite* is "entirely, wholly." In informal English, it is generally used with the reduced meaning of "to a considerable extent or degree": Formal: *The fox was quite exhausted when we reached it.* Informal: *He is quite worried. We hiked quite a distance.* A number of convenient phrases with *quite* are good informal usage: *quite a few* people, *quite a little* time, etc.

qui trans·tu·lit sus·ti·net (kwī trans′tyü lit sus′tə net, -tü-), *Latin.* he who transplanted (still) sustains (the motto of Connecticut, alluding to God's guidance of the first settlers and their descendants).

quit·rent (kwit′rent′), *n.* a fixed rent paid in money, instead of services rendered under a feudal system: *The courtly Laureate pays his quitrent ode, his peppercorn of praise* (William Cowper).

quits (kwits), *adj.* on even terms by repayment or retaliation: *Simply knock him off his horse, and then you will be quits* (William H. Hudson).
call it quits, *U.S.* to break off or abandon an attempt to do something; stop for a time or permanently: *Disarmament negotiators in London called it quits for now* (Wall Street Journal). *Mrs. Robinson retired at the age of 65. But she wasn't ready to call it quits* (New York Times).
cry quits, to admit that things are now even: *I should have fired at you, so we may cry quits on that score* (Frederick Marryat).
[< *quit*[1], adjective + *-s,* perhaps plural (because *quit* was taken as a noun)]

quit·tance (kwit′əns), *n.* **1.** a release from debt or obligation. **2.** the paper certifying this; a receipt: *He then folded the quittance, and put it under his cap* (Scott). **3.** repayment; reprisal. [< Old French *quitance* < *quiter;* see QUIT[1], verb] —**Syn. 3.** recompense, requital.

quit·ter (kwit′ər), *n. U.S. Informal.* **1.** one who gives up easily. **2.** one who gives up too easily; coward. [American English < *quit*[1], verb + *-er*[1]] —**Syn. 1.** shirker.

quit·tor (kwit′ər), *n.* an ulcer on a horse's foot. [earlier *quittor-bone,* apparently < Middle English *quiture* pus, a discharge from a sore < Old French *cuiture* (literally) cooking < Latin *coctūra* < *coquere* to cook]

qui va là? (kē vȧ lȧ′), *French.* who goes there?

quiv·er[1] (kwiv′ər), *v.i.* to shake; shiver; tremble: *The dog quivered with excitement. Her lip quivered like that of a child about to cry* (Booth Tarkington). —*v.t.* to cause to quiver: *Impotent as a bird with both wings broken, it still quivered its shattered pinions* (Charlotte Brontë). —*n.* an act of quivering: *Her face was whiter even than his, though not a quiver of mouth or eyelash betrayed emotion* (Francis Marion Crawford). [probably variant of *quaver;* perhaps influenced by *shiver*[1], *quiver*[3]] —**Syn.** *v.i.* See **shake.**

quiv·er[2] (kwiv′ər), *n.* **1.** a case to hold arrows: *a quiver of dogskin at his back, and a . . . bow in his hand* (Francis Parkman). **2.** the supply of arrows in such a case. [< Anglo-French *quiveir,* Old French *quivre,* probably < Germanic (compare Old High German *chohhāri*)]

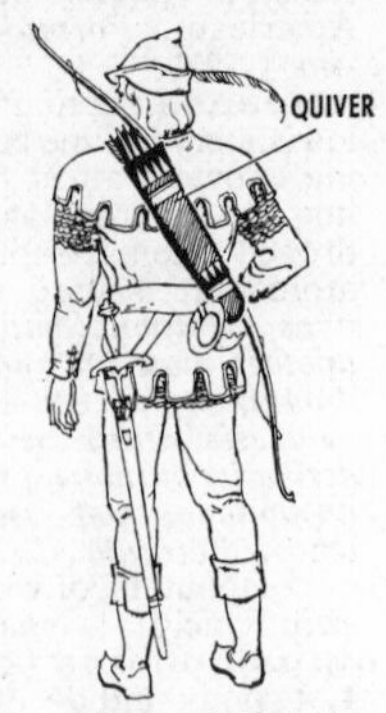

Quiver[2] **(def. 1)**

quiv·er[3] (kwiv′ər), *adj. Dialect.* nimble; quick. [Middle English *cwiver,* Old English *cwiferlīce* actively]

quiv·ered (kwiv′ərd), *adj.* **1.** furnished with a quiver. **2.** held in, or as if in, a quiver.

quiv·er·ful (kwiv′ər fůl), *n., pl.* **-fuls. 1.** as much or as many as a quiver can hold. **2.** a sizable number or quantity: *Armed with a bad temper and a quiverful of sarcastic rejoinders . . .* (Atlantic).

quiv·er·y (kwiv′ər ē), *adj.* shivery; tremulous: *She clung to him in the dances . . . and afterwards hinted of a mood which made Clyde a little quivery and erratic* (Theodore Dreiser).

qui vive? (kē vēv′), *French.* who goes there?
on the qui vive, watchful; alert: *She looked quite stunning as she walked across the dining room to the table, not at all unlike a girl on the qui vive appropriate to a big college weekend* (J. D. Salinger). *Riled water is prized by fishermen, here as elsewhere, because their quarry is thought to be on the qui vive in it, looking for worms and other things that freshets wash their way* (New Yorker).
[< French *qui vive?* a sentinel's challenge (literally) (long) live who?; expecting such a reply as *Vive le roi!* Long live the King!]

Qui·xo·te (kē hō′tē, kwik′sət), *n.* **Don,** a chivalrous, romantic, and very impractical knight who is the hero of a famous romance by Cervantes: *But he is no Quixote, for he recognizes a windmill when he sees one* (New York Times).

quix·ot·ic (kwik sot′ik), *adj.* **1.** resembling Don Quixote; extravagantly chivalrous or romantic: *But, truly Irish to the last, they have declared with Quixotic bravado that they will never participate in the proceedings of a British Parliament which claims to exercise jurisdiction over any part of Ireland* (London Times). **2.** visionary; not practical.
—**Syn. 2.** utopian, impractical.

quix·ot·i·cal (kwik sot′ə kəl), *adj.* quixotic.

quix·ot·i·cal·ly (kwik sot′ə klē), *adv.* after the manner of Don Quixote; in an absurdly romantic manner: *We even ran into . . . a fellow customer in a tobacco shop at Reading, who quixotically favored the Tories but intended to vote for Labor* (Wall Street Journal).

quix·ot·ism (kwik′sə tiz əm), *n.* quixotic character or behavior.

quix·ot·ry (kwik′sə trē), *n.* quixotism: *The tower, in faultless local style, harmonizes with the several that have survived in this majestic panorama from the Middle Ages, but the quixotry of the action was complicated by the fact that it was inadvertently built on someone else's land* (New Yorker).

quiz (kwiz), *v.,* **quizzed, quiz·zing,** *n., pl.* **quiz·zes.** —*v.t.* **1.** to examine informally by questions; question; interrogate: *In its annual pulse-taking, the NRDGA quizzed 312 stores, with a volume of $2.5 billion* (Newsweek). **2.** *U.S.* to test the knowledge of; examine (a student or class) orally or in a brief written exercise. **3.** to make fun of; mock: *Then let us walk about and quiz people* (Jane Austen).
—*n.* **1.** *U.S.* an informal written or oral examination; test: *to have a quiz in history.* **2.** an act of quizzing or questioning: *My first lesson should be in the form of a quiz* (J.W. Brown). **3.** a person who makes fun of others. **4.** a practical joke. **5.** an odd or ec-

centric person: *Young ladies have a remarkable way of letting you know that they think you a "quiz," without actually saying the words* (Charlotte Brontë).
—**Syn.** *v.t.* **3.** ridicule.

quiz game, a game, as on a quiz show, in which contestants compete in answering questions.

quiz kid, *U.S. Slang.* a child prodigy; whiz kid: *. . . being put on show to answer questions on baseball like some . . . quiz kid* (Patrick Ryan).

quiz·mas·ter (kwiz′mas′tər, -mäs′), *n.* the master of ceremonies who conducts a quiz show and asks the questions: *What Moscow television's Sunday "Evening of Merry Questions" really needed, its quizmaster decided last week, was giveaway prizes, just like in America* (Newsweek).

quiz program, a quiz show: *So much of life is in question-and-answer form these days: the radio quiz programs, the loyalty investigations . . .* (New Yorker).

quiz show, a radio or television show in which a panel of experts or of celebrities, or contestants for prizes, try to answer questions, usually receiving a reward if they succeed: *All three networks . . . offer much the same fare: frivolous entertainment, consisting of Westerns, vaudeville, quiz shows, and an occasional detective story* (Harper's).

quiz·zer (kwiz′ər), *n.* a person who quizzes.

quiz·zi·cal (kwiz′ə kəl), *adj.* **1.** odd; queer; comical. **2.** that suggests making fun of others; teasing: *a quizzical smile. A little quizzical wrinkle of the brow that suggested a faintly amused attempt to follow my uncle's mental operations* (H. G. Wells).

quiz·zi·cal·i·ty (kwiz′ə kal′ə tē), *n.* a quizzical quality or expression: *There was a touch of quizzicality in one of her lifted eyebrows* (John Galsworthy).

quiz·zi·cal·ly (kwiz′ə klē), *adv.* in a quizzical manner; with playful slyness.

quiz·zing glass (kwiz′ing), a single eyeglass; monocle: *There was a wee young man with a mop of black ringlets and a quizzing glass* (Max Beerbohm).

Qum·ran Community (kům′rän), a community of Jews located, about 100 years before Christ, at Qumran, an area near the western shore of the Dead Sea, and described in the Dead Sea Scrolls, which were recently discovered in the vicinity of Qumran. Some authorities identify them as Essenes, members of an ascetic sect.

quo' (kwō), *v.* quoth.

quo·ad (kwō′ad), *prep. Latin.* so far as; as to.

quo·ad hoc (kwō′ad hok′), *Latin.* as far as this; to this extent.

quo a·ni·mo (kwō an′ə mō), *Latin.* with what mind; with what intention.

quod (kwod), *n. British Slang.* prison: *a vagrant oft in quod* (Rudyard Kipling). Also, **quad.** [origin uncertain]

quod·dy (kwod′ē), *n., pl.* **-dies.** a double-ended sailboat formerly used for fishing along the Maine coast. [< (Passama)-*quoddy* Bay, an inlet between Maine and New Brunswick]

quod e·rat de·mon·stran·dum (kwod er′at dem′ən stran′dəm), *Latin.* which was to be proved. *Abbr.:* Q.E.D.

quod e·rat fa·ci·en·dum (kwod er′at fā′shē en′dəm), *Latin.* which was to be done. *Abbr.:* Q.E.F.

quod·li·bet (kwod′li bet), *n.* **1.** *Music.* **a.** a fanciful harmonic combination of two or more melodies: *Singing several popular songs together creates a quodlibet* (World Book Encyclopedia). **b.** a medley. **2.** a scholastic argumentation upon a subject chosen at will, but almost always theological. [< Latin *quodlibet* < *quod* what + *libet* it pleases (one)]

quod·li·bet·i·cal (kwod′li bet′ə kəl), *adj.* of, having to do with, or like a quodlibet or quodlibets: *I must say that my question was disputatious as well as quodlibetical* (Harper's). —**quod′li·bet′i·cal·ly,** *adv.*

quod vi·de (kwod vī′dē), *Latin.* which see. *Abbr.:* q.v.
➔ See **q.v.** for usage note.

quoin (koin, kwoin), *n.* **1.** an external angle or corner of a wall or building. **2.** a stone forming an outside angle of a wall; cornerstone. **3.** a wedge-shaped block of wood, metal, stone, etc., used in building, especially one of the stones in the curve of an arch. **4.** *Printing.* a short wedge used to lock up a form.
—*v.t.* **1.** to provide or construct with quoins. **2.** to secure or raise with quoins.
[variant of *coin.* Compare COIGN.]

quoit (kwoit), *n.* a heavy, flattish, iron or rope ring thrown to encircle a peg stuck in the ground or to come as close to it as possible.
quoits, a game, somewhat like horseshoes, played by tossing a heavy ring so that it will encircle a peg: *The game of quoits . . . does not depend so much upon superior strength as upon superior skill* (Joseph Strutt).
—*v.t.* to toss like a quoit. [perhaps < Old French *coite* cushion; flat stone]
➔ **Quoits,** meaning the game, is plural in form and singular in use: *Quoits is often played with horseshoes.*

Quoit

quoit·er (kwoi′tər), *n.* a person who plays at quoits; a quoit thrower.

quo·mo·do (kwō′mə dō, kwō mō′-), *n.* the manner, way, or means: *Mr. Northerton was desirous of departing that evening, and nothing remained for him but to contrive the quomodo* (Henry Fielding). [< Latin *quō modō* in what way?]

quon·dam (kwon′dəm), *adj.* that once was; former: *English law may come to be assessed by historians as the most valuable and lasting benefit conferred by this country on its quondam empire* (London Times). [< Latin *quondam* at one time, formerly]

Quon·set hut (kwon′sit), *U.S.* a prefabricated metal building, shaped like a half-cylinder: *Steel Quonset huts are winning wide acceptance as an important "working tool" on the farm* (Time). [< *Quonset* Point, Naval Air Station, Rhode Island]

quo·rum (kwôr′əm, kwōr′-), *n.* **1.** the number of members of any society or assembly that must be present if the business done is to be legal or binding. More than one half the membership usually constitutes a quorum if no special rule exists. **2.** *British.* **a.** (originally) certain justices of the peace whose presence was necessary to make a session of court legal. **b.** (later) all justices of the peace. [< Latin *quōrum* of whom, genitive plural of *quī* (from the use of the word in commissions written in Latin)]

quo·rum pars mag·na fu·i (kwôr′əm pärz mag′nə fū′ī, kwōr′əm), *Latin.* **1.** in which I had a large share. **2.** (literally) of which I was a great part.

quot., quotation.

quo·ta (kwō′tə), *n., v.,* **-taed, -ta·ing.** —*n.* **1.** the share of a total due from or to a particular district, state, person, etc.: *Each member of the club was given his quota of tickets to sell for the party. Each state in the United States was assigned its quota of soldiers during the first World War.* **2.** the number of immigrants of any specific nationality who are legally allowed to enter the United States in any year. —*v.t.* to assign or divide in shares; allot: *Every floor in every office building would have to have its quotaed shade of color* (New York Times). [< Medieval Latin *quota* < Latin *quota* (*pars*) how large a part; *quota,* feminine of *quotus* how many, how much]

quot·a·bil·i·ty (kwō′tə bil′ə tē), *n.* fitness for being quoted.

quot·a·ble (kwō′tə bəl), *adj.* **1.** that can be quoted: *And he gave them, as he often does, a quotable comment* (Harper's). **2.** that can be quoted with propriety. **3.** suitable for quoting: *His Senate prayers were pithy and quotable* (Newsweek).

quot·a·ble·ness (kwō′tə bəl nis), *n.* quotability.

quo·ta·tion (kwō tā′shən), *n.* **1.** somebody's words repeated exactly by another person; passage quoted from a book, speech, etc.: *From what author does this quotation come? When the quotation is not only apt, but has in it a term of wit or satire, it is still the better qualified for a medal, as it has a double capacity of pleasing* (Joseph Addison). **2.** the act of quoting; practice of citing: *Quotation is a habit of some preachers. Classical quotation is the parole of literary men all over the world* (Samuel Johnson). *Emerson . . . believed in quotation, and borrowed from everybody . . . not in any stealthy or shamefaced way, but proudly* (Oliver Wendell Holmes). **3. a.** the stating of the current price of a stock, commodity, etc. **b.** the price stated: *What was today's market quotation on wheat?*

quotation mark, one of a pair of marks used to indicate the beginning and end of a quotation. For an ordinary quotation, use these marks (" "). For a quotation within another quotation, use these (' '). In Great Britain this practice is commonly reversed.

quote (kwōt), *v.,* **quot·ed, quot·ing,** *n.* —*v.t.* **1.** to repeat the exact words of; give words or passages from: *to quote Shakespeare or one of his plays, to quote chapter and verse from the Bible.* **2.** to bring forward as an example or authority: *The judge quoted various cases in support of his opinion.* **3.** to give (a price): *The real-estate agent quoted a price on the house that we could not afford.* **4.** to state the current price of (a stock, commodity, etc.). **5.** to enclose within quotation marks: *The dialogue in old books is not quoted.* —*v.i.* to repeat exactly the words of another or a passage from a book: *The minister quoted from the Bible.*
—*n.* **1.** a quotation: *American reporters abroad incessantly mine The Economist's pages for handy exportable quotes* (Newsweek). **2.** a quotation mark.
[Middle English *coten* to mark in the margin < Medieval Latin *quotare* to number chapters < Latin *quotus* which or what number (in a sequence) < *quot* how many]
—**Syn.** *v.t.* **2. Quote, cite** mean to bring forward as authority or evidence. **Quote** means to use the words of another (either repeated exactly or given in a summary) and to identify the speaker: *The Commissioner was quoted as saying action will be taken.* **Cite** means to name as evidence or authority, but not to quote, a passage, author, or book, with exact title, page, etc.: *To support his argument he cited Article 68, Chapter 10, of the Charter of the United Nations.*

quot·er (kwō′tər), *n.* a person who quotes or cites the words of an author or a speaker: *Next to the originator of a good sentence is the first quoter of it* (Emerson). *Mr. Roughead, a great reader and quoter of Dickens, is a little like another most kind-hearted man whose business lay with criminals, dear Mr. Wemmick in Great Expectations* (London Times).

quoth (kwōth), *v.t. Archaic.* said: *Quoth the raven, "Nevermore"* (Edgar Allan Poe). [Middle English *quoth,* past tense of *quethen,* Old English *cwethan.* Related to BEQUEATH.]

quoth·a (kwō′thə), *interj. Archaic.* quoth he! indeed! (used ironically or contemptuously in repeating the words of another): *Here are ye clavering about the Duke of Argyle, and this man Martingale gaun to break on our hands, and lose us gude sixty pounds — I wonder what duke will pay that, quotha* (Scott). [< earlier *quoth'a* said he < *quoth* (see QUOTH) + *'a,* reduction of *he*]

quo·tid·i·an (kwō tid′ē ən), *adj.* reappearing daily; daily: *In quotidian matters this is not a smooth-running country — certainly not for the visitor who wants to make every day count; a travel agent, therefore, is worth his fee* (Atlantic).
—*n.* a fever or ague that occurs daily.
[< Latin *quotīdiānus,* variant of *cottīdiānus* < *cottīdiē* daily < *quotus* which or what number (in a sequence) + *diēs* day]

quo·tient (kwō′shənt), *n.* a number obtained by dividing one number by another: *In 26 ÷ 2=13, 13 is the quotient.* [< Latin *quotiēns* how many times < *quot* how many]

quo war·ran·to (kwō wə ran′tō), *Law.* **1.** a writ commanding a person to show by what authority he holds a public office or exercises a public privilege or franchise. It is a remedy for usurpation of office or of corporate franchises. **2.** the legal proceedings taken against such a person. [< Medieval Latin *quo warranto* by what warrant < Latin *quō,* ablative of *quī* what + Medieval Latin *warrantō,* ablative of *warrantus.* Compare WARRANT.]

Qu·r'an (ků rän′, -ran′), *n.* the Koran. [< Arabic *qur'ān*]

q.v., which see (Latin *quod vide;* used in referring to a single item).
➔ The abbreviation **q.v.** is used in scholarly writing as a reference to another book, article, or the like, already mentioned, and indicates that further information will be found there. It has now been generally replaced in reference works by the English word *see.*

qy., query.

R Roman 100's A.D. **P** Greek 600's B.C. Phoenician 1000's B.C. Semitic 1500's B.C. Egyptian 3000's B.C.

Rr Rr *Rr* *Rr*

R or **r** (är), *n., pl.* **R's** or **Rs, r's** or **rs. 1.** the 18th letter of the English alphabet. **2.** any sound represented by this letter. **3.** the eighteenth, or more usually the seventeenth, of a series (either *I* or *J* being omitted).

the three R's, Reading, (W)riting, (A)rithmetic: *Middle-class schools, in which education is pushed beyond the three R's* (The Reader).

r (no period), an abbreviation or symbol for the following:
1. *Electricity.* resistance.
2. roentgen or roentgens.
3. ruble.
4. *Statistics.* correlation coefficient.

r., an abbreviation for the following:
1. king (Latin, *rex*).
2. queen (Latin, *regina*).
3. rabbi.
4. radium (dosage).
5. radius.
6. a. railroad. **b.** railway.
7. rain.
8. rare.
9. *Commerce.* received.
10. recipe.
11. rector.
12. a. residence. **b.** resides.
13. retired.
14. right.
15. rises.
16. river.
17. road.
18. rod or rods.
19. *Chess.* rook.
20. royal.
21. rubber.
22. ruble or rubles.
23. (in scoring baseball and cricket) run or runs.
24. rupee or rupees.

R (no period), an abbreviation or symbol for the following:
1. *Physics, Chemistry.* gas constant.
2. *Chemistry.* radical.
3. radius.
4. Rand.
5. ratio.
6. Réaumur.
7. *Electricity.* resistance.
8. Restricted (a symbol for motion pictures restricted to an adult audience).
9. *Chess.* rook.
10. ruble or rubles.

R., an abbreviation for the following:
1. King (Latin, *rex*).
2. Queen (Latin, *regina*).
3. rabbi.
4. a. railroad. **b.** railway.
5. range.
6. Réaumur.
7. rector.
8. redactor.
9. Republican.
10. respond or response (in church services).
11. right (especially in stage directions).
12. River.
13. road.
14. roentgen.
15. Royal.
16. rupee or rupees.

Ra (rä), *n.* the ancient Egyptian sun god and supreme deity, typically represented as a hawk-headed man bearing the sun on his head. Also, **Re.** [< Egyptian *r'* the sun]

Ra (no period), radium (chemical element).

RA (no periods), Regular Army.

R.A., an abbreviation for the following:
1. rear admiral.
2. Regular Army.
3. *Astronomy.* right ascension.
4. a. Royal Academician (member of the Royal Academy). **b.** Royal Academy (of Great Britain).
5. Royal Artillery (of Great Britain).

R.A.A.F. or **RAAF** (no periods), Royal Australian Air Force.

ra·bat (rȧ bȧ′, rə bat′), *n.* a breast cover, usually black, worn by certain clergymen, attached to a collar and hanging down over the breast, especially in the form of two flat or plaited bands: *The different varieties of bishop . . . could be distinguished from non-bishops by their scarlet rabats* (New Yorker). [< French *rabat* collar, turned-down collar < Old French *rabattre;* see REBATE]

ra·ba·to (rə bä′tō, -bā′-), *n., pl.* **-toes.** rebato, a stiff collar of lace.

rab·bet (rab′it), *n., v.,* **-bet·ed, -bet·ing.** —*n.* **1.** a cut, groove, or slot made on the edge or surface of a board or the like, to receive the end or edge of another piece of wood shaped to fit it. **2.** a joint so made.

Rabbets (def. 2)

—*v.t.* **1.** to cut or form a rabbet in. **2.** to join with a rabbet. —*v.i.* to form a joint or bring pieces together with a rabbet. Also, **rebate.**
[< Old French *rabat* a beating down < *rabattre;* see REBATE]

rabbet joint, a joint formed by a rabbet.

rab·bi (rab′ī), *n., pl.* **-bis** or **-bies. 1.** a teacher of the Jewish religion, leader of a Jewish congregation. **2.** a Jewish title for a doctor or expounder of the law: *They said unto him, Rabbi, (which is to say, being interpreted, Master)* (John 1:38). [Old English *rabbi* (originally) a term of address < Medieval Latin < Greek *rabbí* < Aramaic *rabbī* my master]

rab·bin (rab′in), *n.* a rabbi. [perhaps < Middle French *rabbin,* learned borrowing from Medieval Latin *rabbinus;* probably (originally) formed as plural of *rabbi* rabbi]

rab·bin·ate (rab′ə nit, -nāt), *n.* **1.** the office or position of a rabbi: *Yeshiva, which is in New York, trains students for the orthodox rabbinate* (New York Times). **2.** the period during which one is a rabbi. **3.** rabbis as a group: *Today the only tourists who brave Cyprus are young Israelis who come over for civil marriages—prohibited at home by Israel's rabbinate* (Atlantic).

rab·bin·ic (rə bin′ik), *adj.* rabbinical.

Rab·bin·ic (rə bin′ik), *n.* the Hebrew language or dialect as used by the rabbis in writings; the later Hebrew language.

rab·bin·i·cal (rə bin′ə kəl), *adj.* of or having to do with rabbis, their learning, writings, etc.: *The complete Isaiah scroll . . . showed every evidence of having been executed in strict conformity with rabbinical rules* (New Yorker).

rab·bin·i·cal·ly (rə bin′ə klē), *adv.* in a rabbinical manner; by or like a rabbi: *Its slaughter must be rabbinically supervised and conducted according to a set ritual pattern that stresses humaneness* (Time).

rab·bin·ism (rab′ə niz əm), *n.* **1.** a rabbinical expression or phrase. **2.** the teachings or traditions of the rabbis.

rab·bin·ist (rab′ə nist), *n.* a Jewish person who accepts the Talmud and the traditions of the rabbis: *Those who stood up for the Talmud and its traditions were chiefly the rabbins and their followers, from whence the party had the name of rabbinists* (Thomas Stackhouse).

rab·bin·is·tic (rab′ə nis′tik), *adj.* **1.** of or having to do with a rabbinist. **2.** accepting the Talmud and the traditions of the Talmud.

rab·bin·is·ti·cal (rab′ə nis′tə kəl), *adj.* rabbinistic.

rab·bit (rab′it), *n.* **1. a.** a burrowing animal about as big as a cat, with soft fur, a short, fluffy tail, and long ears. Rabbits are rodentlike mammals similar to the hare, and include the gray European species and the American cottontails. *The . . . European rabbit is the animal that has devastated large areas of Australia and New Zealand, necessitating extreme control methods* (New York Times). **b.** a hare. **2.** the fur of a rabbit or hare. **3.** Welsh rabbit.
—*v.i.* to hunt or catch rabbits.
[Middle English *rabet*]

rabbit ball, *Baseball Slang.* a very lively or bouncy baseball: *Even then the old-timers were complaining about the rabbit ball, so called — supposedly the ball had been made more elastic . . .* (Atlantic).

rabbit brush or **bush,** a desert plant of the aster family, common in western North America.

rabbit deer, pudu.

rabbit ear antenna, *Informal.* a small, portable television receiving antenna, with two adjustable upright or diagonal rods resembling the ears of a rabbit.

rabbit ears, *U.S. Slang.* **1.** too much attention by an umpire, referee, or player to the reactions or attitudes of the spectators at a sporting event: *Rabbit ears in a boxing judge or referee . . . affected more than one decision in the days before television* (New York Times). **2.** the umpire, referee, or player at a sporting event characterized by this.

rab·bit·er (rab′ə tər), *n.* **1.** a person who hunts or traps rabbits: *There won't be a lot of rabbiters on hand* (New Yorker). **2.** a person hired to protect land or property from damage by rabbits.

rabbit fever, tularemia, a disease of rodents and some other animals, communicable to people and transmitted chiefly by insects: *Beware of soft-shelled ticks. They can be carriers of a serious disease that most often strikes at hunters, rabbit fever* (Science News Letter).

rabbit food, *Slang.* green salads or raw vegetables.

rab·bit·like (rab′it līk′), *adj.* **1.** like a rabbit; timid or afraid. **2.** prolific: *Mankind had been rabbitlike in the unplanned breeding of itself* (London Times).

rabbit punch, a sharp blow on the back of the neck, at or near the base of the skull: *He denounced the rabbit punch, and low blows* (Newsweek). [because this is the typical method of stunning rabbits before butchering them]

rab·bit·ry (rab′ə trē), *n., pl.* **-ries. 1.** a place where rabbits are kept. **2.** a collection of rabbits.

rabbit's foot, 1. the hind foot of a rabbit or hare, kept as a token of good luck. **2.** a common species of clover.

rab·bit·wood (rab′it wu̇d′), *n.* a parasitic North American shrub related to the sandalwood, with oblong leaves, greenish-white flowers, and drupaceous fruit; buffalo nut.

rab·bit·y (rab′ə tē), *adj.,* **-bit·i·er, -bit·i·est. 1.** somewhat like a rabbit or rabbits: *a rabbity look, rabbity creatures.* **2.** of or full of rabbits: *I remember the smell of sea and seaweed . . . the warm smell as of a rabbity field after rain* (Atlantic).

rab·ble[1] (rab′əl), *n., v.,* **-bled, -bling,** *adj.* —*n.* a disorderly crowd; mob: *A rabble of angry citizens stormed the embassy.*
the rabble, the lower classes (used in an unfriendly way): *Theognis complains that the rabble rule the state with monstrous laws* (John Addington Symonds).
—*v.t.* to attack (a person or his property) as a rabble does; mob.
—*adj.* disorderly; rude; low.
[Middle English *rabel.* Perhaps related to RABBLE[3].]

rab·ble[2] (rab′əl), *n., v.,* **-bled, -bling.** —*n.* **1.** an iron bar bent at one end, used for stirring, skimming, or gathering molten metal in puddling: *The slag is now drawn with a rabble into molds prepared for it* (Rossiter Raymond). **2.** any similar instrument. —*v.t.* to stir, skim, or gather with a rabble: *The molten metal is thoroughly stirred, or rabbled, to make it uniform* (Harper's). [< French, Middle French *râble* < Old French *roable* < Latin *rutābulum* oven rake; fire shovel < *ruere* to fall; dig up]

rab·ble[3] (rab′əl), *v.t., v.i.,* **-bled, -bling.** *Obsolete.* to speak in a rapid, confused manner; gabble. [Middle English *rablen.* Compare Dutch *rabbelen.*]

rab·ble·ment (rab′əl mənt), *n. Archaic.* **1.** a mob; rabble. **2.** disorder; tumult.

rab·bler (rab′lər), *n.* a person who works with or uses a rabble in puddling.

rab·ble-rous·er (rab′əl rou′zər), *n.* a person who tries to stir up groups of people with speeches tending to arouse them to acts of violence against some existing condition, usually to serve his own ends; an agitator: *Hitler, although half-educated, was . . . an eminently successful rabble-rouser* (Wall Street Journal).

rab·ble-rous·ing (rab′əl rou′zing), *adj.* inciting or agitating as or like a rabble-rouser;

demagogic: *a rabble-rousing speech or speaker.* —*n.* the actions or methods of a rabble-rouser; demagoguery: *The Southern press is full of slanting, suppression, and rabble-rousing against integration* (Time).

rab·bo·ni (rä bō′nī, -nē), *n.* master, a Jewish title of honor (applied especially to religious teachers and learned persons). John 20:16. [< Hebrew *rabbōnī*]

Rab·e·lai·si·an (rab′ə lā′zē ən, -zhən), *adj.* **1.** of or having to do with the French writer François Rabelais, 1494?-1553: *For most English readers Rabelais has taken the very form and pressure of his eccentric, full-blooded translator, and doubtless he would have smiled upon the joyous excess to which Urquhart, with the aid of Cotgrave's lustily Rabelaisian Dictionary (1611), carried his verbal gymnastics* (Douglas Bush). **2.** characterized by broad, coarse humor: *Miss Wallace sermonized about ... "tight-pants contests" and Rabelaisian drinking parties* (Maclean's).

Rab·e·lai·si·an·ism (rab′ə lā′zē ə niz′əm, -zhə niz-), *n.* broad, coarse humor.

ra·bi (rab′ē), *n.* (in India) the spring crop, sown in autumn: *Where indigo is grown in the kharif, barley is its usual accompaniment in the rabi* (Arthur H. Church). [< Arabic *rabī*ʻ spring]

rab·id (rab′id), *adj.* **1.** unreasonably extreme; fanatical; violent: *You know by temper we are rabid idealists* (George R. Gissing). **2.** furious; raging: *to be rabid with anger.* **3. a.** having rabies; mad: *a rabid dog.* **b.** of rabies. [< Latin *rabidus* < *rabere* be mad < *rabiēs* madness] —**Syn. 1.** impassioned. **2.** frantic, raving.

ra·bid·i·ty (rə bid′ə tē), *n.* rabidness.

rab·id·ly (rab′id lē), *adv.* in a rabid manner; madly; furiously.

rab·id·ness (rab′id nis), *n.* a rabid madness; unreasonableness.

ra·bies (rā′bēz, -bē ēz), *n.* a virus disease, usually fatal, that causes mental disturbance, muscular spasms, and paralysis in dogs and other infected animals; hydrophobia: *Rabies is almost sure death to both man and animals unless serum is given before symptoms of the disease appear* (Science News Letter). [< Latin *rabiēs*, related to *rabere* be mad. Doublet of RAGE.]

R.A.C., Royal Automobile Club (of Great Britain): *The R.A.C. advised drivers to avoid main roads where possible* (Sunday Times).

ra·ca (rä′kə, rā′-), *adj.* worthless (an ancient Jewish expression of contempt). Matthew 5:22. [< Late Latin *raca* foolish; empty < Greek *rakā* < Aramaic *rēkā*]

rac·coon (ra kün′), *n.* **1.** a small, grayish-brown, flesh-eating mammal of North America, with a bushy, ringed tail. It lives in wooded areas near water and is active at night. **2.** its fur. Also, **racoon.** [American English < Algonkian (Powhatan) *ärähkun* < *ärähkunĕm* he scratches with the hands (because of the animal's habit of leaving long scratches on the trees he climbs)]

Raccoon (def. 1) (including tail, about 32 in. long)

raccoon dog, a small Asiatic wild dog, somewhat like a raccoon.

race[1] (rās), *n., v.,* **raced, rac·ing.** —*n.* **1.** a contest of speed, as in running, driving, riding, sailing, etc.: *Often the races were run in foul weather, and often Dave ran barefoot* (Time). **2.** Often, **races.** a series of horse races run at a set time over a regular course. **3.** any contest that suggests a race: *a political race.* **4.** onward movement: *the race of life.* **5.** a strong or fast current of water: *This evening the Talbot weighed and went back to the Cowes, because her anchor would not hold here, the tide set with so strong a race* (John Winthrop). **6.** the channel of a stream: *The race, ... a canal 20 to 30 feet wide, ... carried ... through rocks and hills* (Jedidiah Morse). **7.** a channel leading water to or from a place where its energy is utilized: *The water, brought through races by miles of fluming, spouted clear and strong over heaps of auriferous earth* (Rolf Boldrewood). **8.** a track, groove, etc., for a sliding or rolling part of a machine, as a channel for ball bearings: *... a split bushing was pressed in place between the main journal and the inner race of the ball bearings* (Purvis and Toboldt). **9.** the current of air driven back by a propeller of an aircraft. **10.** *Scottish.* the act of running; run: *The noble stag ... Held westward with unwearied race* (Scott). **11.** (in Australia) a fenced path used to separate sheep from a fold.
—*v.i.* **1.** to engage in a contest of speed. **2.** to run, move, or go swiftly: *Race to the doctor for help.* **3.** (of a motor, wheel, etc.) to run too fast, as when load or resistance is lessened without corresponding lessening of power: *The motor engine raced before it was shut off* (Sinclair Lewis). —*v.t.* **1.** to try to beat in a contest of speed; run a race with. **2.** to cause to run in a race. **3.** to cause to run, move, or go swiftly. **4.** to cause (a motor, wheel, etc.) to run too fast with reduced load: *Don't race your engine while it's cold.*
[Middle English *ras* < Scandinavian (compare Old Icelandic *rās* strong current). Related to Old English *rǣs* a rush, running.]
—**Syn.** *n.* **3.** rivalry. **4.** progress. **7.** sluice, conduit, canal. *-v.i.* **2.** dash, rush.

race[2] (rās), *n.* **1.** a group of persons connected by common descent or origin: *We were two daughters of one race* (Tennyson). *Troy's whole race thou wouldst confound* (Alexander Pope). **2.** a great division of mankind having certain physical peculiarities in common: *the white race, the yellow race. The whole concept of race, as it is traditionally defined, may be profoundly modified or even dropped altogether, once the genetic approach has been fully exploited* (Beals and Hoijer). **3.** human beings, as a group: *the human race, to which so many of my readers belong* (Gilbert K. Chesterton). *That ev'ry tribe ... Might feel themselves allied to all the race* (William Cowper). **4.** a group of animals or plants having the same ancestry: *the race of fishes.* **5.** a group, class, or kind, especially of people: *the brave race of seamen.* **6. a.** the condition of belonging to a particular stock: *Race was of importance to Hitler. Good-bye to the Anglo-Saxon race, Farewell to the Norman blood!* (A. L. Gordon). *Our earth is but a small star in the great universe. Yet of it we can make, if we choose, a planet unvexed by war, untroubled by hunger or fear, undivided by senseless distinctions of race, color, or theory* (Stephen Vincent Benét). **b.** qualities due to this. **7.** stock of high quality: *The look of race, which had been hers since childhood* (Winston Churchill). **8.** a lively or stimulating quality. **9.** the characteristic taste of a particular type of wine. **10.** *Zoology.* a variety characteristic of a given area: *The plains ... bred a generous race of horses* (Edward Gibbon). **11.** *Botany.* any group whose characters continue from one generation to another: *A race, in this technical sense of the term, is a variety which is perpetuated with considerable certainty by sexual propagation* (Asa Gray). [< Middle French *race*, earlier *rasse* < Italian *razza;* origin uncertain]
—**Syn. 1, 2.** See **people.**

race[3] (rās), *n.* a rhizome: *a race or two of ginger* (Shakespeare). [< Old French *rais*, or *raiz* < Latin *rādīx, -īcis* root]

race·a·bout (rās′ə bout′), *n.* **1.** a type of racing yacht with a short bowsprit and a rig like that of a sloop. **2.** a type of automobile built or remodeled for racing: *a fully restored 1910 Simplex raceabout.*

race-bait·er (rās′bā′tər), *n.* a person given to race-baiting: *Charlie Miller's new home was smeared and smashed by race-baiters* (Time).

race-bait·ing (rās′bā′ting), *n.* the persecution of people of a different race or races: *As the Negroes begin to vote in ever larger numbers, race-baiting in Southern politics should decrease* (Atlantic).

race card, *British.* a form sheet: *When I walk through the gate there on the first day and buy my race card, then I know that Ascot has really started* (Roger Angell).

race course, ground laid out for racing; race track: *The results of chance happenings on the race course are drastic enough to tempt the most literal-minded to consult astrologists* (Atlantic).

race·go·er (rās′gō′ər), *n.* a person who frequently goes to horse races, automobile races, or the like: *Still, as any racegoer can tell you, the best horses don't always win* (New Yorker).

race horse, a horse bred, trained, or kept for racing: *English race horses have come to surpass in fleetness and size the parent Arabs* (Charles Darwin).

race knife, a knife with a bent lip for marking, numbering, etc. [< *race*, variant of *raze* + *knife*]

ra·ceme (rā sēm′, rə-), *n.* a simple flower cluster having its flowers on nearly equal stalks along a stem, the lower flowers blooming first: *The lily of the valley, currant, and chokecherry have racemes.* [< Latin *racēmus* cluster (of grapes or berries). Doublet of RAISIN.]

Raceme of lily of the valley

ra·cemed (rā sēmd′, rə-), *adj.* arranged in racemes.

race meeting, *British.* a number of horse races held at the same time on one day or successive days.

ra·ce·mic (rā sē′mik, -sem′ik; rə-), *adj. Chemistry.* of or designating an optically inactive compound formed by the combination of dextrorotatory and levorotatory forms in equal molecular proportions: *Total synthesis of racemic aldosterone, said to be the most potent hormone of the adrenal glands ...* (Science News Letter). [< Latin *racēmus* cluster (of grapes or berries) + English *-ic*]

racemic acid, an optically inactive form of tartaric acid, occurring in the juice of grapes along with ordinary tartaric acid. *Formula:* $C_4H_6O_6$

rac·e·mif·er·ous (ras′ə mif′ər əs), *adj.* bearing racemes: *The vine its racemiferous branches spread* (Hans Busk).

rac·e·mism (ras′ə miz əm, rə sē′-), *n.* the joining of dextrorotatory and levorotatory molecules in an optically inactive substance.

rac·e·mi·za·tion (ras′ə mə zā′shən), *n. Chemistry.* the act or process of producing a racemic compound.

rac·e·mize (ras′ə mīz, rə sē′-), *v.t., v.i.,* **-mized, -miz·ing.** to make or become optically inactive through racemism.

rac·e·mose (ras′ə mōs), *adj.* **1.** in the form of a raceme; characteristic of racemes: *... shining and smoking among the ghosts of racemose bird cherries in scumbled bloom* (New Yorker). **2.** arranged in racemes. [< Latin *racēmōsus* full of clusters < *racēmus* cluster (of grapes or berries); meaning influenced by English *raceme*]

racemose gland, a gland formed of a system of ducts which branch into sacs and resemble clusters of grapes, as the pancreas.

rac·er (rā′sər), *n.* **1.** a person, animal, boat, automobile, airplane, or bicycle that takes part in races. **2.** any of various North American snakes that are able to move very rapidly, as the blacksnake, blue racer, etc.

race relations, the way in which people of different racial groups live or work together or treat one another: *Race relations are a question of major significance, not only between white and coloured, but equally as important between Indians and Fijians* (Manchester Guardian).

race riot, *U.S.* a violent clash between people of different racial groups within the same community, especially between whites and Negroes, usually over some real or imagined affront: *In studies of race riots it has been found that they sometimes begin in the aggressiveness resulting from the frustrations of repressed minority groups* (Emory S. Bogardus).

race suicide, the extinction of a people that tends to result when, by deliberate limitation of the number of children, the birth rate falls below the death rate.

race track, ground laid out for racing; race course.

race·track·er (rās′trak′ər), *n.* a racegoer: *To some racetrackers, old Belmont is a dearly beloved horse park* (New York Times).

race·way (rās′wā′), *n.* **1.** a passage or channel for water, especially for a mill: *From No. 1 the water is carried through a raceway into tank No. 2* (Rossiter Raymond). **2.** a metal pipe enclosing electric wiring inside a building: *The strong, weight-saving cellular steel subflooring system that provides quick, efficient construction and continuous raceways for all types of wiring* (Wall Street Journal). **3.** a track used for harness racing: *What started out as a routine investigation of labor racketeering at the harness raceways ...* (Newsweek).

Ra·chel (rā′chəl), *n.* (in the Bible) the favorite wife of Jacob, and the mother of Joseph and Benjamin. Genesis 29-35.

rach·et (rach′it), *n. Especially British.* ratchet.

ra·chis (rā′kis), *n., pl.* **ra·chis·es, rach·i·des** (rak′ə dēz, rā′kə-). **1.** *Botany.* **a.** a stem, as in grasses: *A spike is a cluster of flowers, sessile or nearly so, borne in the axils of bracts on an elongated rachis* (Heber W. Youngken). **b.** a stalk, as of a pinnately compound leaf or frond: *In contrast, leaves are pinnately compound . . . if the leaflets arise along an axis or rachis as in the walnuts, hickories . . .* (Fred W. Emerson). **2.** the shaft of a feather: *In Casuarius each primitive feather consists of a long and slender rachis bearing two series of rami* (Alfred Newton). **3.** the spinal column: *The separation of the rachis into skull and vertebral column is not completely effected in Amphioxus* (Francis J. Bell). [< New Latin *rachis* < Greek *rháchis* backbone]

ra·chit·ic (rə kit′ik), *adj.* **1.** having to do with rickets. **2.** suffering from rickets: *A series of infantile diseases had left Gwen so rachitic and knock-kneed that she could barely walk* (Time).

ra·chi·tis (rə kī′tis), *n.* rickets: *In rachitis, the bones may be bent in any direction* (Robert B. Todd). [< New Latin *rachitis* < Greek *rhachîtis* a disease of the spine < *rháchis* spine + *-ītis* -itis]

Rach·man·ism (rak′mə niz əm, räk′-), *n. British.* unscrupulous practices by landlords, as the extortion of high rents in rundown properties: *When we talk of Rachmanism, we are not talking so much of houses in bad condition, or overcrowded, as of those cases where landlords get rid of tenants by intimidation where they cannot do so by lawful means* (Lord Silkin). [< Peter *Rachman*, a speculator in London slum properties who died in 1962 + *-ism*]

ra·cial (rā′shəl), *adj.* having to do with a race; characteristic of a race; among a race or races: *racial traits, racial dislikes, racial equality. The Commonwealth's outstanding characteristic is that it is a multi-racial association, and that its whole future depends on the absence of racial discrimination* (Manchester Guardian Weekly). —**Syn.** ethnic.

ra·cial·ism (rā′shə liz əm), *n.* unreasonable race prejudice: *The Prime Minister spoke on race relations, commenting that . . . there had been less racialism in debate and more moderation* (London Times).

ra·cial·ist (rā′shə list), *n.* a person who supports racialism.

ra·cial·is·tic (rā′shə lis′tik), *adj.* of or having to do with racialism or racialists.

ra·cial·ly (rā′shə lē), *adv.* in respect to race; as influenced by race or lineage: *[They] were . . . probably racially connected with the complex group of peoples embracing the Tatar-Mongolians* (Edward Clodd).

rac·i·ly (rā′sə lē), *adv.* in a racy manner or style; piquantly; spicily: *An ex-reporter for U.P. and a magazine writer, Sack employs a racily frenetic style* (Time).

rac·i·ness (rā′sē nis), *n.* the quality or condition of being racy: *His [Milton's] images and descriptions . . . do not seem . . . to have the freshness, raciness, and energy of immediate observation* (Samuel Johnson).

rac·ing (rā′sing), *n.* **1.** the act of engaging in a race. **2.** the business of arranging for or carrying on races, especially between horses.

racing form, form sheet.

rac·ism (rā′siz əm), *n.* **1.** the exaggeration of inherent racial differences: . . . *the biological racism which furnished a fraudulent scientific sanction for the atrocities committed in Hitler's Germany and elsewhere* (Science). **2.** prejudice in favor of certain races: *Racism, which by definition involves a form of subjection of one race by another, is evil. "Apartheid" cannot succeed* (New York Times). **3.** a political or social policy or system based on racism: *Racial determinism . . . easily slips into the political field, where this approach is called racism* (Melville J. Herskovits).

rac·ist (rā′sist), *n.* a person who believes in or supports racism. —*adj.* of or having to do with racism: *a racist attitude or speech.*

rack[1] (rak), *n.* **1.** a frame with bars, shelves, or pegs to hold, arrange, or keep things on: *a hat rack, a tool rack, a baggage rack.* **2.** a frame of bars to hold hay and other food for cattle, horses, etc. **3.** a framework set on a wagon for carrying hay, straw, etc. **4.** an instrument once used for torturing people by stretching them between rollers at each end of a frame: *During the troubles of the fifteenth century, a rack was introduced into the Tower, and was occasionally used* (Macaulay). **5.** a cause or condition of great suffering in body or mind: *Little knew they the rack of pain which had driven Lucy almost into a fever* (Charlotte Brontë). **6.** a stretch; strain. **7.** a bar with pegs or teeth on one edge into which teeth on the rim of a bevel wheel, pinion, etc., can fit. **8.** a framework in a printing shop for storing type in galleys, cases, etc. **9.** the frame used in a game of pool. **10.** the antlers of a deer, elk, etc., especially when large and spreading.

Rack[1] **and Pinion** (def. 7)

on or **upon the rack,** in great pain; suffering very much: *Let me choose, For as I am, I live upon the rack* (Shakespeare).

—*v.t.* **1.** to hurt very much: *to be racked with grief. A toothache racked his jaw.* **2.** to stretch; strain. **3.** to torture on the rack. **4. a.** to raise (rent) above a fair or normal amount: *He racked no rents to maintain the expenses of his establishment* (Quarterly Review). **b.** to oppress (a person) with high rents or other demands for money: *Here are no hard landlords to rack us with high rents* (Captain John Smith). **5.** to put (a thing) on a rack.

rack up, *U.S. Informal.* to accumulate: *More than a fourth of the nation's annual retail sales volume is racked up in November and December* (Wall Street Journal).

[Middle English *rakke;* origin uncertain]

—**Syn.** *n.* **5.** agony. *-v.t.* **1.** agonize.

rack[2] (rak), *n.* wreck; destruction (archaic except in *to go to rack and ruin*). [variant of *wrack*[1]. Compare RACK[4].]

rack[3] (rak), *n.* **1.** a horse's gait in which the forefeet move as in a slow gallop while the hind feet move as in a trot or pace; single-foot. **2.** a pace.

—*v.i.* **1.** to go at a rack: *No one ever saw him trotting or galloping; he only racks* (Frederick Marryat). **2.** to pace.

rack[4] (rak), *n.* flying, broken clouds driven by the wind: *Across the sky the driving rack of the rain cloud Grows for a moment then* (Longfellow). *And, like this insubstantial pageant faded, Leave not a rack behind* (Shakespeare). —*v.i.* (of clouds or fog) to be driven before the wind: *I looked up . . . and saw the clouds rack at an unusual rate* (John Bunyan). [Middle English *rak*, perhaps < Scandinavian (compare Old Icelandic *rek* jetsam, wreckage). Related to WRECK, WRACK[1].]

rack[5] (rak), *n.* the neck part of a forequarter of mutton, pork, or veal, especially when made into a roast for cooking: *a rack of lamb.* [origin uncertain]

rack[6] (rak), *v.t.* to draw off (wine or cider) from the lees: *At the end of fermentation the beer is run to tanks from which it may be "racked" into casks . . .* (H. J. Bunker). [< Middle French *raqué* pressed from marc of grapes. Compare Provençal *arracar* to rack, *raca* dregs.]

rack[7] (rak), *n.* **1.** the track or trail made by an animal, especially that of a deer, as marked by gaps in hedges, etc. **2.** *Dialect.* a narrow path or track. [Middle English *rakke*, perhaps < Scandinavian (compare Old Icelandic *rāk* stripe)]

rack car, a railroad car with racks for carrying objects, such as automobiles or timber: . . . *three-tiered rack cars, which carry up to 18 autos* (Wall Street Journal).

rack·er[1] (rak′ər), *n.* a person or thing that racks or tortures, strains, etc. [< *rack*[1] + *-er*[1]]

rack·er[2] (rak′ər), *n.* a racking horse. [< *rack*[3] + *-er*[1]]

rack·er[3] (rak′ər), *n.* **1.** a person who racks wine or cider. **2.** a device for racking. [< *rack*[6] + *-er*[1]]

rack·et[1] (rak′it), *n.* **1.** *U.S.* a loud and confused noise; loud talk; din: *Don't make a racket when others are reading. Imagine the thunderous racket made by . . . these carts . . . returning empty* (W.H. Hudson). **2.** a time of gay parties and social excitement. **3.** *U.S. Informal.* **a.** a dishonest scheme for getting money from people by threatening violence or damage. **b.** any dishonest scheme: *Everyone wants the illegal drug racket broken and crime by addicts stopped* (Harper's). **4.** *U.S. Slang.* an occupation. **5.** strain or other adverse consequences.

stand the racket, to hold out against strain or wear and tear: *I like a quiet life . . . Don't believe I could stand the racket* (Anthony Hope).

—*v.i.* **1.** to make a racket; move about in a noisy way: *I . . . sometimes spent further hours a day racketing along underground in a thunderous, crowded, and filthy Bronx express* (Manchester Guardian). **2.** to live a gay life; take part in social excitement: *He racketed round 'mong them nabobs* (Harriet Beecher Stowe).

[probably < earlier British slang *racket* a type of fraud, scheme]

—**Syn.** *n.* **1.** uproar, clamor, hubbub. **2.** revelry.

rack·et[2] (rak′it), *n.* **1. a.** a light, long-handled, wide bat made of a network of catgut, cord, or nylon stretched across a frame, used for games like tennis or badminton: *The main object of modern lawn tennis is to meet the ball with a full racket* (Charles G. Heathcote). **b.** a small, short-handled, wooden implement, commonly surfaced with sandpaper, cork, or dimpled rubber, used to strike the ball in table tennis; paddle. **2.** a snowshoe that resembles a tennis racket. Also, **racquet.**

rackets, a game played in a walled court with a ball and rackets: *Rackets . . . is, like any other athletic game, very much a thing of skill and practice* (William Hazlitt).

[< French *raquette*, perhaps < Spanish *raqueta* < Arabic *rāḥa* palm of the hand]

➔ **Rackets,** the game, is plural in form and singular in use: *Rackets is played in a walled court.*

rack·et·eer (rak′ə tir′), *U.S. Informal.* —*n.* a person who extorts money by threatening violence or damage: *They are convinced the crackdown is scaring off the racketeers* (Wall Street Journal). —*v.i.* to extort money by threatening violence or damage. [American English < *racket*[1] (definition 3) + *-eer*]

rack·et·eer·ing (rak′ə tir′ing), *n. U.S. Informal.* the business of a racketeer.

rack·ets (rak′its), *n.pl.* See under **racket**[2].

racket store, *Southwestern U.S.* a dime store.

rack·et·tail (rak′it tāl′), *n.* a hummingbird having two very long tail feathers with the ends shaped like rackets.

rack·et·y (rak′ə tē), *adj.*, **-et·i·er, -et·i·est.** **1.** noisy: *This rackety music from America brought delight for two reasons* (Punch). **2.** characterized by social excitement or dissipation. [< *racket*[1] + *-y*[1]]

rack·ing·ly (rak′ing lē), *adv.* in a racking or disturbing manner; torturingly.

rack jobber, a wholesale distributor who provides notions, housewares, etc., and such services as price marking and display material to supermarkets, drug stores, and other retail outlets: *Supermarket operators and the rack jobbers . . . are out to capture a greater share of the soft goods market* (New York Times).

rack·le (rak′əl), *adj. Scottish.* hasty; rash; impetuous; headstrong. [origin uncertain. Perhaps related to RECK.]

rack rail, a rail in an inclined-plane railway, having cogs or teeth with which the cogwheel of the locomotive engages.

rack railway, a railway using a rack rail.

rack-rent (rak′rent′), *n.* an unreasonably high rent, nearly equal to the value of the holding: *Agriculture cannot be expected to flourish where . . . the husbandman begins on a rack-rent* (Tobias Smollett). —*v.t.* to exact rack-rent from (a tenant) or for (land): *It was a maxim with his family . . . never to rack-rent old tenants or their descendants* (Samuel Richardson). [< *rack*[1] to stretch + *rent*[1]]

rack-rent·er (rak′ren′tər), *n.* **1.** a person subjected to rack-rent. **2.** a person who exacts rack-rent.

rack·work (rak′wėrk′), *n.* **1.** a mechanism in which a rack is used. **2.** a rack and pinion, or the like.

ra·con (rā′kon), *n. Especially U.S.* radar beacon. [< *ra*(dar) (bea)*con*]

rac·on·teur (rak′on tėr′), *n.* a person clever at telling stories, anecdotes, etc.: *There never was, in my opinion, a raconteur, from Charles Lamb or Theodore Hook down to Gilbert à Beckett or H.J. Byron, . . . who spoke and told anecdotes at a dinner-table, . . . that was not conscious that he was going to be funny* (Lester Wallack). [< French *raconteur* < Old French *raconter* relate, recount < *re-* again, re- + *aconter* recount]

ra·con·teuse (rak′on tœz′), *n. French.* woman raconteur.

ra·coon (ra kün′), *n.* raccoon.

racoon dog, raccoon dog.

rac·quet (rak′it), *n.* a racket used in tennis and similar games.

racquets, the game of rackets: *Racquets is played in a walled court.*

rac·y (rā′sē), *adj.,* **rac·i·er, rac·i·est. 1.** vigorous; lively: *In Whitman and Melville letters again became as racy as the jabber of a waterside saloon* (Lewis Mumford). **2.** having an agreeably peculiar taste or flavor: *a racy apple.* **3.** somewhat improper; risqué: *a racy story, a racy dress.* **4.** fresh; unspoiled; pure. [< *race*[2] (definition 9) + *-y*[1]] —**Syn. 1.** spirited. **2.** piquant, spicy.

rad (rad), *n.* a unit for measuring absorbed doses of radiation, equal to 100 ergs of energy per gram: *The quantity of total body radiation that is fatal in almost all cases is close to 800 rads* (Arnold L. Bachman). [< *rad*(iation)]

rad., 1. radical; the mathematical sign √‾. **2.** radio. **3.** radius. **4.** radix (root).

RADA (no periods) or **R.A.D.A.,** Royal Academy of Dramatic Art.

ra·dar (rā′där), *n.* **1.** an instrument for determining the distance and direction of unseen objects by the reflection of radio waves: *Three radars, plus computers and other equipment, guide it to its target* (New York Times). **2.** this and other instruments and techniques which have developed from it, as a field of electronics: *to study radar.* **3.** a process by which the reflection of radio waves is measured: *The miracle underlying all radar is that men have learned . . . to measure time in such infinitesimal amounts that radio echo ranges of objects miles away can be read with accuracy in yards* (James Phinney Baxter). [American English < *ra*(dio) *d*(etecting) *a*(nd) *r*(anging)]

radar beacon, a beacon that transmits radar waves to aid navigators to determine a plane's position.

radar fence or **screen,** a protective chain of radar posts so placed around an area that their field is continuous: *The defense of North America involves radar screens, military airplanes, and defense against submarines* (Bulletin of Atomic Scientists).

ra·dar·man (rā′där man′, -mən), *n., pl.* **-men.** a technician in a branch of the armed forces, who operates or services radar equipment: *The radarmen travel by aerial tramway from base camp in the foreground to the dome* (New York Times).

radar picket, a ship or aircraft with radar, stationed near the outside boundary of some area to detect approaching aircraft: *The third, designed as a radar picket . . . will displace an estimated 4,000 tons, and will undoubtedly be the world's largest submarine* (New York Times).

ra·dar·scope (rā′där skōp), *n.* a screen or oscilloscope which displays visually the signals received in a radar set; scope: *Even in bad weather the radarscope or radio and radar navigational aids were available to the crew* (United States Air Force Report on the Ballistic Missile).

rad·dle[1] (rad′əl), *n., v.,* **-dled, -dling.** —*n.* **1.** one of the many slender sticks fastened to or woven between upright stakes to form a fence, etc. **2.** such sticks. **3.** a fence made of them.
—*v.t.* to interweave.
[< Anglo-French *reidele* a stick, Old French *reddalle*]

rad·dle[2] (rad′əl), *n., v.,* **-dled, -dling.** —*n.* red ocher; hematite: *He would whistle the sheep into the ancient fold, marking them with his raddle* (Walter S. Landor). —*v.t.* **1.** to paint with red ocher. **2.** to color heavily with rouge: *The second hussy . . . being raddled with red paint* (George J. Whyte-Melville). Also, **reddle, ruddle.** [variant of *ruddle*]

rad·dled (rad′əld), *adj.* coarsely streaked with red, as if painted with raddle: *raddled cheeks.* Also, **reddled, ruddled.**

rad·dle·man (rad′əl mən), *n., pl.* **-men.** a person who digs or sells red ocher. Also, **reddleman, ruddleman.**

Ra·dha (rä′dä), *n. Hindu Mythology.* a shepherdess who was the consort of Krishna: *Radha and Krishna are the archetypal lovers of Hindu India* (Manchester Guardian Weekly).

ra·di·ac (rā′dē ak), *n.* a device for detecting and measuring radioactivity. [< *r*(adio) *a*(ctivity) *d*(etection) *i*(dentification) *a*(nd) *c*(omputation)]

ra·di·al (rā′dē əl), *adj.* **1.** arranged like or in radii or rays: *At a little distance from the center the wind is probably nearly radial* (Science). **2.** of the radius of a circle: *. . . the placing of a large fraction of the total mass at the radial distance assigned to the phosphorus atoms* (A. W. Haslett). **3.** of or near the radius (a bone of the forearm): *a radial nerve; . . . palpating the radial pulse at the wrist* (Time). **4.** of or having to do with the arm of a starfish or other echinoderm.

Radial Pattern (def. 1)

radial engine, an internal-combustion engine for an airplane, having radially arranged cylinders.

ra·di·al·ly (rā′dē ə lē), *adv.* like the spokes of a wheel; in rays; like radii or rays: *. . . most of the adult echinoderms are radially symmetrical* (Hegner and Stiles).

ra·di·al-ply (rā′dē əl plī′), *adj.* of or having to do with a kind of tire with cords at right angles to the center line of the tread: *Radial-ply tires, standard in Europe for many years, made their debut in the United States* (Science News Letter).

radial symmetry, *Zoology.* a condition in which like parts are arranged about an axis, from which they radiate like the parts of a flower, as in many echinoderms.

radial velocity, the velocity of a star along the line of sight of an observer, determined by measuring the positions of lines in the star's spectrum, usually with a spectroscope.

ra·di·an (rā′dē ən), *n.* the angle at the center of a circle, that subtends an arc of the circle equal in length to the radius; an angle of 57.2958+ degrees. [< *radi*(us) + *-an*]

ra·di·ance (rā′dē əns), *n.* **1.** vivid brightness; brilliance: *the radiance of the sun, of electric lights, of a smile.* **2.** radiation.

ra·di·an·cy (rā′dē ən sē), *n.* radiance.

ra·di·ant (rā′dē ənt), *adj.* **1.** shining; bright; beaming: *radiant sunshine, a radiant smile.* **2.** sending out rays of light or heat: *The sun is a radiant body.* **3.** bright with light: *The new house was radiant with light* (Arnold Bennett). **4.** sent off in rays from some source; radiated: *radiant heat. We get radiant energy from the sun.* **5.** strikingly fine or splendid, as looks, beauty, etc., or the person: *He delighted in the radiant good looks of his betrothed* (Edith Wharton).
—*n.* **1.** *Physics.* a point or object from which light or heat radiates. **2.** the point in the heavens from which the meteors in a shower seem to have come: *The radiant of a meteoric shower is the vanishing point in the perspective of the parallel trails* (Robert H. Baker).
[< Latin *radiāns, -antis,* present participle of *radiāre* to beam < *radius* beam, ray]
—**Syn.** *adj.* **1.** See **bright.**

radiant energy, *Physics.* rays or waves of heat, light, or electricity (and, formerly, sound), that are sent out through space: *The physicist recognizes these various forms of light as manifestations of radiant energy* (Fred W. Emerson).

radiant heating, a system of heating in which a network of hot-water or steam pipes is enclosed within walls, floors, etc., instead of using radiators: *The best place to put panels for radiant heating is in the ceiling, not the floor* (Science News Letter).

ra·di·ant·ly (rā′dē ənt lē), *adv.* with radiant brightness or glittering splendor.

ra·di·ate (rā′dē āt), *v.,* **-at·ed, -at·ing,** *adj., n.* —*v.t.* **1.** to give out rays of: *The sun radiates light and heat.* **2.** to give out; send forth: *Her face radiates joy.* —*v.i.* **1.** to give out rays; shine: *Many giant red stars are known to be radiating* (New Astronomy). **2.** to issue in rays: *Heat radiates from those hot steam pipes.* **3.** to spread out from a center: *Roads radiate from the city in every direction.*
—*adj.* **1.** having rays: *A daisy is a radiate flower.* **2.** radiating from a center. **3.** of an animal with a radial structure.
—*n.* any invertebrate animal having a radial structure.
[< Latin *radiāre* (with English *-ate*[1]); see RADIANT]
—**Syn.** *v.i.* **1.** glow. **3.** diverge.

ra·di·ate·ly (rā′dē it lē), *adv.* radially.

ra·di·a·tion (rā′dē ā′shən), *n.* **1.** the act or process of giving out and transmitting light, heat, or other radiant energy: *If you hold your hand in the beam of heat from a reflector-type electric heater, your hand is heated by radiation* (John R. Pierce). **2.** the energy radiated: *The steam pipes do not afford sufficient radiation for so large a room. The masses of the stars vary only from about a tenth of the solar mass to about 50 times that mass, while the total radiation emitted increases about 500,000 times* (W.H. Marshall). **3. a.** the giving forth of radioactive rays by molecules and atoms of a radioactive substance, as a result of internal changes: *In the high-temperature air of the shock wave . . . ionization and radiation are taking place* (Atlantic). **b.** the ray or rays given forth: *Other radiations from nuclei are alpha particles, beta particles, and neutrons.* **4.** divergence from a central point; radial arrangement or structure: *The beauty of a crest or bird's wing consists . . . in the radiation of the plumes* (John Ruskin). **5.** *Informal.* the radiators of a central heating system referred to collectively, or their capacity: *The plumbing contractor will figure out how much radiation you need.*

radiation belt, 1. either of two broad bands of radiation around the earth and centered on the earth's magnetic equator; Van Allen radiation belt. **2.** any similar belt near either of these: *The satellite's radiation counters have revealed a radiation belt beneath the two Van Allen belts; the new belt consists of energetic protons* (Scientific American).

radiation chemistry, the branch of chemistry that studies the chemical influence of radiation on matter: *Chemical concerns continue to expand their research of radiation chemistry* (Wall Street Journal).

radiation counter, any device for detecting and counting radioactive rays in a given area, as a Geiger counter.

radiation fog, a fog that forms when air near or along the ground at night loses warmth through outward radiation: *London is known for its dense, dark radiation fogs. Radiation fog reaches its greatest depth and density at sunrise, i.e., at the end of the nightly cooling period* (Neuberger and Stephens).

radiation sickness, a disease resulting from an overdose of radiation from radioactive materials, and usually characterized by internal bleeding and changes in tissue structure: *Following ten years of research . . . the treatment of radiation sickness with bone-marrow cells is finding a place in medicine* (New Scientist).

ra·di·a·tive (rā′dē ā′tiv), *adj.* having to do with radiation; radiating: *With unfailing intuition Einstein was led to the introduction of the idea of the photon as the carrier of momentum and energy in individual radiative processes* (Scientific American).

ra·di·a·tor (rā′dē ā′tər), *n.* **1.** a heating device consisting of a set of pipes through which steam or hot water passes. **2.** a device for cooling circulating water: *The radiator of an automobile gives off heat very fast and so cools the water inside.* **3.** a person or thing that radiates: *Once their enormous distances are appreciated, it becomes clear that [stars] are radiators of vast power* (Bondi and Bondi). [< *radiat*(e) + *-or*]

rad·i·cal (rad′ə kəl), *adj.* **1.** going to the root; fundamental; basic: *Cruelty is a radical fault. If she wants to reduce, she must make a radical change in her diet.* **2.** favoring extreme social changes or reforms; extreme: *A global ideology . . . has the power to capture radical revolutionary minds* (Newsweek). *I never dared be radical when young For fear it would make me conservative when old* (Robert Frost). **3.** of or from the root or roots: *Since book is a simple word consisting of one morpheme, it may be said to contain one and only one root or radical element* (Simeon Potter). **4.** *Botany.* arising from the root or the base of the stem; basal. **5.** *Mathematics.* having to do with or forming the root of a number or quantity. [< Late Latin *rādīcālis* < Latin *rādīx, -īcis* root]
—*n.* **1.** a person who favors extreme changes or reforms; person with extreme opinions: *It was clear that he had awakened deep currents of resentment, and of hope, among young radicals in France* (Newsweek). *A radical is a man with both feet firmly planted in the air* (Franklin D. Roosevelt). **2.** an atom or

group of atoms acting as a unit in chemical reactions. Ammonium (NH_4) is a radical in NH_4OH and NH_4Cl. *Such radicals may be produced by the high-temperature decomposition of hydrocarbons such as methane, CH_4, which forms the methyl radical, CH_3* (M.P. Barnett). **3.** the mathematical sign ($\sqrt{\ }$) put before an expression to show that some root of it is to be extracted. **4.** any of a number of Chinese written characters common to many written words: *Chinese characters are classified in a dictionary under 214 radicals, or meaning indicators* (World Book Encyclopedia). **5.** *Linguistics, Grammar.* a word or a part of a word serving as a root on which other words are formed: *Love* is the radical of *lovely, loveliness,* and *loving.* **6.** anything fundamental or basic.
[< adjective; (definition 1) < French *radical* < Middle French, adjective, learned borrowing from Late Latin *rādīcālis;* see the adjective] —**Syn.** *adj.* **3.** original, primary.

radical axis, *Geometry.* the straight line joining the points of intersection of two circles, or between two circles that do not intersect, from which tangents at any point to both circles will be of equal length.

radical empiricism, the philosophical theory proposed by William James that experience is the sole basis of and only norm for the perception and investigation of reality.

radical empiricist, a person who maintains the doctrines of radical empiricism.

radical expression, *Algebra.* an expression, especially an irrational number or quantity, involving a radical sign.

rad·i·cal·ism (rad′ə kə liz′əm), *n.* **1.** the principles or practices of radicals; the advocacy of sudden, violent, or thoroughgoing social change. **2.** the state or condition of being radical: *They are gravely hampered in carrying it out by current fears of radicalism* (Atlantic).

rad·i·cal·i·za·tion (rad′ə kə lə zā′shən), *n.* **1.** the process of making radical. **2.** the process of becoming radical: *There were, the author finds, three reasons for the radicalization of scientists* (Bulletin of Atomic Scientists).

rad·i·cal·ize (rad′ə kə līz), *v.,* **-ized, -iz·ing.** —*v.t.* to make radical: *It is inferred . . . that Lord Salisbury means to radicalize his land program for England* (New York Tribune). —*v.i.* to become radical: *When it [the Reform Bill] and the Catholic question were both carried . . . Herbert Grimstone radicalized* (Lady Lytton).

rad·i·cal·ly (rad′ə klē), *adv.* **1.** by root or origin; primitively; originally; naturally: *The language, which is called the Manx, is radically Erse, or Irish* (Jedidiah Morse). **2.** in a radical manner; at the origin or root; fundamentally; essentially: *a radically defective system.*

rad·i·cal·ness (rad′ə kəl nis), *n.* the condition of being radical.

radical right, a reactionary or right-wing element in a country, political party, etc., that advocates radical or extremist policies: *The tough-talking militarist has been a standardbearer for the so-called "radical right"* (Wall Street Journal).

radical sign, the mathematical sign ($\sqrt{\ }$) put before an expression to show that some root of it is to be extracted, as in $\sqrt{a}$, $\sqrt[3]{926}$, $\sqrt[4]{m}$.

rad·i·cand (rad′ə kand′), *n.* the quantity placed under a radical sign. [< Latin *rādīcandus,* gerundive of *rādīcāre* take root]

rad·i·cant (rad′ə kənt), *adj. Botany.* producing roots from stems or leaves. [< Latin *rādīcans, -antis,* present participle of *rādīcāre;* see RADICATE]

rad·i·cate (rad′ə kāt), *v.,* **-cat·ed, -cat·ing,** *adj.* —*v.i.* to take root; produce roots: *Trees began . . . to radicate where but lately a shrub wanted moisture* (Thomas Blount). —*v.t.* to cause to take root; plant firmly: *Radicate Thy Love within me, O my God, Let it be rooted deep* (Richard Welton). —*adj. Biology.* rooted. [< Latin *rādīcāre* (with English *-ate*[1]) < *rādīx, -īcis* root]

rad·i·ca·tion (rad′ə kā′shən), *n.* the manner of rooting; fixation as by roots; rooting.

rad·i·cel (rad′ə səl), *n.* a little root; a rootlet or radicle. [< New Latin *radicella* (diminutive) < Latin *rādīcula* radicle]

rad·i·ces (rad′ə sēz, rā′də-), *n.* a plural of **radix.**

rad·i·cle (rad′ə kəl), *n.* **1.** the part of a seed that develops into the main root. **2.** a little root. **3.** *Anatomy.* a rootlike part, as one of the fibrils of a nerve fiber. **4.** *Chemistry.* a radical: *[Positive ions] are first adsorbed on to acid radicles at the surface of the protoplast in exchange for hydrogen ions* (J.F. Sutcliffe).
[< Latin *rādīcula* (diminutive) < *rādīx, -īcis* root]

ra·di·i (rā′dē ī), *n.* a plural of **radius.**

ra·di·o (rā′dē ō), *n., pl.* **-di·os,** *adj., v.,* **-di·oed, -di·o·ing.** —*n.* **1.** the way of sending and receiving words, music, etc., by electric waves, without connecting wires. **2.** an apparatus for receiving and making audible the words so sent; a radio receiver. **3.** *Informal.* a message sent by radio. **4.** the business of radiobroadcasting: *He left the movies and got a job in radio.* **5.** the branch of physics dealing with electromagnetic waves as used in communication.
—*adj.* **1.** of or having to do with radio: *Seventeen minutes after launching, its first radio signals beeped to the tracking station* (Time). **2.** used in radio: *a radio transmitter.* **3.** of or having to do with electric frequencies higher than 15,000 cycles per second.
—*v.t.* **1.** to transmit or send out by radio: *The ship radioed a call for help.* **2.** to communicate with by radio. —*v.i.* to transmit or send out a message, news, music, etc., by radio: *Word that the proclamation had been signed was radioed ahead from the speeding Presidential limousine* (New York Times).
[< *radio-,* abstracted from *radiotelegraphy*]

radio-, *combining form.* **1.** radio: *Radiotelegraphy = radio telegraphy.*
2. radial; radially: *Radiosymmetrical = radially symmetrical.*
3. radiant energy: *Radiometer = an instrument that measures radiant energy.*
4. radioactive: *Radioisotope = a radioactive isotope.*
[< Latin *radius* (originally) ray, beam]

ra·di·o·ac·ti·vate (rā′dē ō ak′tə vāt), *v.t.,* **-vat·ed, -vat·ing.** to make radioactive. [< *radioactive + -ate*[1]]

ra·di·o·ac·tive (rā′dē ō ak′tiv), *adj.* **1.** giving off radiant energy in the form of alpha, beta, or gamma rays by the breaking up of atoms: *Radium, uranium, and thorium are radioactive metallic elements. It takes some time for air currents to distribute radioactive dust across the world* (New Scientist). **2.** of or relating to this property: *Further disposal studies showed that the 55-gallon oil drum containers, used to package radioactive wastes were very rugged* (Science News Letter).

radioactive decay, the spontaneous disintegration of a radioactive substance, at the characteristic rate of the particular radioisotope, and accompanied by the emission of nuclear radiation: *The spontaneous change taking place in an unstable atomic nucleus is known as radioactive decay* (The Effects of Atomic Weapons).

Radioactive Decay of an Atom. An alpha particle (+), a beta particle (−) and a gamma ray (X ray) are emitted.

ra·di·o·ac·tive·ly (rā′dē ō ak′tiv lē), *adv.* **1.** in a radioactive manner: *When cosmic-ray particles disrupt the nuclei of atoms in the earth's atmosphere, some of the neutrons . . . splash upward and decay radioactively into a belt of protons and electrons* (Scientific American). **2.** by or with radioactivity: *Kuiper believes that the moon is radioactively contaminated to a depth of 30 ft. below the surface* (Time). *Radioactively labeled organic compounds, now expensive, should be widely distributed at reasonable prices* (Scientific American). **3.** from the standpoint of radioactivity: *Radioactively speaking, L.A. had thus lived two days in one* (Time).

radioactive series, one of several series of isotopes of certain elements representing various stages of disintegration of a radioactive substance. Three of these series occur naturally (the actinium, thorium, and uranium series) and others, such as the neptunium series, are artificially produced.

ra·di·o·ac·tiv·i·ty (rā′dē ō ak tiv′ə tē), *n.* **1.** the property of being radioactive: *We'll have to learn to control radioactivity just as we learned to control fire* (Bulletin of Atomic Scientists). **2.** the radiation given off: *How much liability insurance should a plant have against the not inconceivable possibility that it overheat and spew its radioactivity around the neighborhood?* (Newsweek).

radio altimeter, an altimeter which uses radio signals to measure height from the ground at low altitudes: *A radio altimeter . . . tells airplane pilots to within a few inches how high they are above the airstrip* (Science News Letter).

radio astronomer, an expert in radio astronomy: *Radio astronomers have just succeeded in measuring some of the radio stars* (Scientific American).

ra·di·o·as·tro·nom·i·cal (rā′dē ō as′trə nom′ə kəl), *adj.* of or having to do with radio astronomy: *Observations, particularly radio-astronomical observations, have established that any lunar atmosphere cannot exceed 10^{-13} of the Earth's atmosphere* (New Scientist).

radio astronomy, the branch of astronomy dealing with the detection and interpretation of objects in space by means of radio waves that these objects give off. It enables observers to study heavenly bodies beyond the range of ordinary telescopes. *Radio astronomy today is in about the same stage of infancy as visual astronomy was soon after Galileo invented the first optical telescope* (Scientific American).

ra·di·o·au·to·graph (rā′dē ō ô′tə graf, -gräf), *n.* a picture of an object produced on a sensitized surface, as of photographic film, rays from some radioactive substance etc.; autoradiograph: *Radioautographs showed that the new growing leaves drew on mature leaves for [phosphorus] until the old leaves were depleted and died* (Some Applications of Atomic Energy in Plant Science).

ra·di·o·au·tog·ra·phy (rā′dē ō ô tog′rə fē), *n.* the process of producing radioautographs; autoradiography: *An account of radioautography is followed by consideration of hazards and precautions in radioisotope work* (New Scientist).

radio beacon, a radio station for sending special signals so that ships, airplanes, etc., can determine their position.

radio beam, a continuous signal by radio to show the proper course for an airplane, especially one giving the course to a certain airport: *Improved radio beam landing aid . . . will provide pilots with a better radio highway to their landing strips* (Science News Letter).

ra·di·o·bi·o·log·i·cal (rā′dē ō bī′ə loj′ə kəl), *adj.* **1.** of or having to do with radiobiology: *radiobiological phenomena or studies.* **2.** caused by radiation: *Removal of oxygen before irradiation was found to protect cells against many kinds of radiobiological damage* (Science News Letter).

ra·di·o·bi·ol·o·gist (rā′dē ō bī ol′ə jist), *n.* an expert in radiobiology: *Radiobiologists guessed that constant exposure to internal radiation somehow diminished the beagle's natural resistance to stress* (Time).

ra·di·o·bi·ol·o·gy (rā′dē ō bī ol′ə jē), *n.* the branch of biology dealing with the effects of radiation on animal bodies: *He began to use viruses and bacteria as material for radiobiology* (Scientific American).

ra·di·o·broad·cast (rā′dē ō brôd′kast′, -käst′), *n., v.,* **-cast** or **-cast·ed, -cast·ing.** —*n.* a broadcasting by radio. —*v.t., v.i.* to broadcast by radio. —**ra′di·o·broad′cast′er,** *n.*

radio car, an automobile, such as a squad car, equipped with a two-way radio: *Several radio cars responded* (New York Times).

ra·di·o·car·bon (rā′dē ō kär′bən), *adj.* having to do with a method of determining the age of a substance, as a fossil, by measuring its radioactive carbon content: *With the temperature cycles thus established, the next step was to date them by radiocarbon analysis* (Scientific American). —*n.* a radioactive isotope of carbon having a mass of 14; carbon 14.

ra·di·o·cast (rā′dē ō kast′, -käst′), *v.,* **-cast** or **-cast·ed, -cast·ing,** *n.* —*v.t., v.i.* to broadcast by radio. —*n.* a radiobroadcast: *In the rich voice with which he dominated the radiocast of the coronation, the archbishop was ranging through the state of Christianity around the world* (Time). —**ra′di·o·cast′er,** *n.*

ra·di·o·ce·si·um or **ra·di·o·cae·si·um** (rā′dē ō sē′zē əm), *n.* a radioisotope of cesium, used in radiotherapy.

ra·di·o·chem·i·cal (rā′dē ō kem′ə kəl), *adj.* of or having to do with radiochemistry: *radiochemical studies.* —*n.* a chemical to which radioactive isotopes have been added: *It is offering a full range of radiochemicals* *with the addition of radioisotopes to its line of laboratory reagents* (New York Times).

ra·di·o·chem·ist (rā′dē ō kem′ist), *n.* an expert in radiochemistry: *The radiochemist has many questions in common with the radiobiologist* (Scientific American).

ra·di·o·chem·is·try (rā′dē ō kem′ə strē), *n.* the branch of chemistry dealing with radioactive substances.

ra·di·o·co·balt (rā′dē ō kō′bôlt), *n.* a radioactive isotope of cobalt, used in radiology and radiotherapy: *A piece of radiocobalt, as big as a pea, can replace an X-ray set weighing several hundred pounds* (Atlantic).

ra·di·o·com·pass (rā′dē ō kum′pəs), *n.* a device for finding the direction from which radio messages are received, used to determine position, as of an aircraft or a ship at sea; radio direction finder: *The abandoned B-24's radiocompass was still in perfect working order despite the crash* (Science News Letter).

ra·di·o·con·duc·tor (rā′dē ō kən duk′tər), *n.* a device that detects electric waves, as a coherer in wireless telegraphy.

ra·di·o·di·ag·no·sis (rā′dē ō dī′əg nō′sis), *n.* medical diagnosis by means of X rays, radiographs, etc.

radio direction finder, a radiocompass.

ra·di·o·el·e·ment (rā′dē ō el′ə mənt), *n.* a radioactive element, especially one produced artificially: *Weathering effects beyond two years will depend very critically upon the nature of the radioelements which then predominate in the fallout debris* (Bulletin of Atomic Scientists).

radio emission, the emission of radio waves by objects in space: *Giant antennae forming radio telescopes allow the observation of radio emissions of heavenly bodies* (Science News Letter).

Radio Free Europe, an unofficial, independent radio station established in 1950 which broadcasts programs concerning the West to the Soviet satellite countries, chiefly to counteract Soviet Communist broadcasts.

radio frequency, **1.** a frequency of electrical vibrations above 15,000 cycles per second: *Techniques using radio frequencies are therefore the method par excellence for studying low-energy transitions in atoms and molecules* (J. Little). *Abbr.:* RF (no periods). **2.** the frequency of the waves which transmit a particular radio broadcast, etc. —**ra′di·o-fre′quen·cy,** *adj.*

radio galaxy, a galaxy that emits radio waves: *It seemed likely . . . that most radio sources in space . . were remote radio galaxies which emitted vast amounts of energy by unknown mechanisms* (London Times).

ra·di·o·gen·ic (rā′dē ō jen′ik), *adj.* **1.** formed as a product of radioactivity: *The data on three purely radiogenic rocks whose ages have been measured . . .* (Scientific American). **2.** *Slang.* suitable for radiobroadcasting.
[< *radio-* + *-gen* + *-ic*]

ra·di·o·ge·ol·o·gy (rā′dē ō jē ol′ə jē), *n.* the branch of geology dealing with the relation of radioactivity to geology.

ra·di·o·gold (rā′dē ō gōld′), *n.* a radioisotope of gold, used in the treatment of cancer: *Radiogold, which was almost unknown in 1950, is now being distributed at the rate of more than 50,000 millicuries each month* (Science).

ra·di·o·go·ni·om·e·ter (rā′dē ō gō′nē om′ə tər), *n.* a radiocompass.

ra·di·o·go·ni·o·met·ric (rā′dē ō gō′nē ə met′rik), *adj.* **1.** of or having to do with a radiogoniometer. **2.** used in radiogoniometry.

ra·di·o·go·ni·o·met·ri·cal (rā′dē ō gō′nē ə met′rə kəl), *adj.* radiogoniometric.

ra·di·o·go·ni·om·e·try (rā′dē ō gō′nē om′ə trē), *n.* the art of using a radiogoniometer.

ra·di·o·gram[1] (rā′dē ō gram), *n.* **1.** a message transmitted by radio: *In the next twelve years [the secret code-cracking center] was to decipher some 45,000 intercepted cables, radiograms, and other messages* (Newsweek). **2.** a radiograph.

ra·di·o·gram[2] (rā′dē ō gram), *n. British.* a radiogramophone: *With the saving on the radiogram I bought some records* (Sunday Times).

ra·di·o·gram·o·phone (rā′dē ō gram′ə fōn), *n. British.* a radio and phonograph combined in a single unit.

ra·di·o·graph (rā′dē ō graf, -gräf), *n.* a picture produced by X rays or other rays on a photographic plate, commonly called an X-ray picture: *The radiograph was taken at the surgeon's request . . . and two days later it was decided to operate* (Science News). —*v.t.* to make a radiograph of: *At this plant the company manufactures projectors for radiographing metals* (Newsweek).

ra·di·og·ra·pher (rā′dē og′rə fər), *n.* a person skilled in radiography.

ra·di·o·graph·ic (rā′dē ō graf′ik), *adj.* of or having to do with radiographs or radiography: *There were those patients who for a special radiographic examination . . .* (Bulletin of Atomic Scientists).

ra·di·o·graph·i·cal (rā′dē ō graf′ə kəl), *adj.* radiographic.

ra·di·o·graph·i·cal·ly (rā′dē ō graf′ə klē), *adv.* by radiography.

ra·di·og·ra·phy (rā′dē og′rə fē), *n.* the production of images on sensitized plates by means of X rays: *A field in which radium and its daughter product radon have been used for some time is industrial radiography* (Crammer and Peierls).

ra·di·o·i·o·dine (rā′dē ō ī′ə dīn, -din, -dēn), *n.* a radioisotope of iodine, used in the treatment of thyroid disorders: *A given amount of radioiodine ingested appears to deliver considerably more radiation to infant thyroids than to those of adults* (Scientific American).

ra·di·o·i·ron (rā′dē ō ī′ərn), *n.* a radioisotope of iron, used in studying hemoglobin and red blood cells, and various kinds of anemia characterized by iron deficiency.

ra·di·o·i·so·tope (rā′dē ō ī′sə tōp), *n.* a radioactive isotope, especially one produced artificially: *A million medical patients are being diagnosed or treated with radioisotopes each year* (Bulletin of Atomic Scientists).

ra·di·o·i·so·top·ic (rā′dē ō ī′sə top′ik), *adj.* of or having to do with radioisotopes: *One satellite of each group had a radioisotopic nuclear generator* (New Scientist).

ra·di·o·lar·i·an (rā′dē ō lãr′ē ən), *n.* any of a large group of minute marine protozoans having an amoebiform body with numerous, fine, radiating pseudopods. —*adj.* of or belonging to the radiolarians. [< New Latin *Radiolaria* the order name < Late Latin *radiolus* (diminutive) < Latin *radius* ray]

radio link, the part of a communication system which transmits messages by radio waves rather than by cables or wires: *Changes in a capacitance vary the frequency of a signal transmitted by radio link to the shore* (New Scientist).

ra·di·o·lo·ca·tion (rā′dē ō lō kā′shən), *n. British.* the use of radar, sonar, etc., to determine the position and course of an object: *He appreciated, long in advance of anyone else, the possibilities of using radiolocation in Fighter Defense* (New Yorker).

ra·di·o·lo·ca·tor (rā′dē ō lō′kā tər, -lō-kā′-), *n. British, Obsolete.* radar.

ra·di·o·log·ic (rā′dē ō loj′ik), *adj.* radiological.

ra·di·o·log·i·cal (rā′dē ō loj′ə kəl), *adj.* **1.** of or having to do with radiology. **2.** of or having to do with the rays from radioactive substances: *A British physicist speculates on the composition and possible radiological effects of the superbomb tested in the Pacific last spring* (Bulletin of Atomic Scientists). —**ra′di·o·log′i·cal·ly,** *adv.*

ra·di·ol·o·gist (rā′dē ol′ə jist), *n.* a person skilled in radiology: *Radiologists die, on the average, five years younger than physicians having no contact with radiation* (Time).

ra·di·ol·o·gy (rā′dē ol′ə jē), *n.* **1.** the science dealing with X rays or the rays from radioactive substances, especially for medical diagnosis or treatment. **2.** the art of using X rays to examine, photograph, or treat bones, organs, etc.

ra·di·o·lu·cent (rā′dē ō lü′sənt), *adj.* roentgenolucent.

ra·di·ol·y·sis (rā′dē ol′ə sis), *n.* the chemical decomposition of a substance resulting from the action of radiation: *Organic fluids in the radioactive environment of a reactor are subject to radiolysis* (Bulletin of Atomic Scientists). [< *radio-* + Greek *lýsis* a loosening]

ra·di·o·man (rā′dē ō man′), *n., pl.* **-men. 1.** a member of the crew of a ship, airplane, etc., in charge of sending and receiving radio messages: *At dawn, Captain Faeste and the two radiomen jumped and were picked up by a waiting lifeboat* (Newsweek). **2.** a person who works in radiobroadcasting: *A group of radiomen fearfully hired Alfred Politz Research, Inc. to find out if anyone was still listening to radio in the nation's TV areas* (Time).

ra·di·o·me·te·or·o·graph (rā′dē ō mē′tē-ər ə graf, -gräf; -mē′tē or′-), *n.* a radiosonde.

ra·di·om·e·ter (rā′dē om′ə tər), *n.* **1.** an instrument used for indicating the transformation of radiant energy into mechanical force, consisting of an exhausted glass vessel containing vanes which revolve on an axis when exposed to light. **2.** an instrument based on the same principle, but used for detecting and measuring small amounts of radiant energy.

Radiometer (def. 1)

ra·di·o·met·ric (rā′dē ō met′rik), *adj.* having to do with the radiometer or with radiometry: *Radiometric methods may be divided into two classes, depending upon whether the detector of radiation employed is selective or nonselective with respect to wave length* (Hardy and Perrin).

ra·di·o·met·ri·cal·ly (rā′dē ō met′rə klē), *adv.* by using radiometry.

ra·di·om·e·try (rā′dē om′ə trē), *n.* the measurement of radiant energy.

ra·di·o·mi·crom·e·ter (rā′dē ō mī krom′ə tər), *n.* a thermoelectric device for measuring minute changes in temperature. [< *radio-* + *micrometer*]

ra·di·o·mi·met·ic (rā′dē ō mi met′ik), *adj.* having an effect on living tissue almost identical with that of radiation: *a radiomimetic chemical, drug, or agent. The knowledge that substances can be "radiomimetic" is largely a product of World War II research in poison gases* (Scientific American).

ra·di·o·ne·cro·sis (rā′dē ō nə krō′sis), *n., pl.* **-ses** (-sēz). necrosis brought about by irradiation.

radio noise, atmospheric sound picked up by radio: *Terrestrial magnetism is concerned with the study of celestial objects as radio sources. One of its earliest discoveries was that the planet Jupiter is a source of radio noise* (New Yorker).

ra·di·o·nu·clide (rā′dē ō nü′klīd, -nyü′-), *n.* a nuclide that is radioactive: *The synthetic radioactive fallout is produced in a "hot" laboratory by processing the radionuclide, lanthanum 140* (Science News Letter).

ra·di·o·paque (rā′dē ō pāk′), *adj.* not transparent to X rays or other radioactive substances: *The velocity of blood flow—is easily determined by injecting a radiopaque substance into the bloodstream and measuring the rate of travel of its shadow on a film* (Scientific American).

ra·di·o·phare (rā′dē ō fãr), *n.* a radio station for determining the position of ships at sea. [< *radio-* + Greek *phâros* lighthouse]

ra·di·o·phar·ma·ceu·ti·cal (rā′dē ō fär′mə sü′tə kəl), *n.* a radioactive drug used especially for the treatment of tumors and for diagnostic purposes.

ra·di·o·phone (rā′dē ō fōn), *n.* a radiotelephone. [< *radio-* + *-phone*]

ra·di·o·phon·ic (rā′dē ō fon′ik), *adj.* having to do with the radiophone or radiophony.

radio phonograph, an appliance including both a radio receiver and a phonograph.

ra·di·oph·o·ny (rā′dē of′ə nē), *n.* the science or process of producing sound by the action of radiant energy.

ra·di·o·phos·pho·rus (rā′dē ō fos′fər əs), *n.* a radioisotope of phosphorus, used in the treatment of leukemia and other diseases of the blood: *Radiophosphorus is being used to treat the means whereby cells make inorganic phosphate available to play its part in the fermentation of sugar* (New Scientist).

ra·di·o·pho·to (rā′dē ō fō′tō), *n., pl.* **-tos.** a radiophotograph: *Still pictures taken a mere nine minutes before in London would be upon us in a moment having been miraculously transmitted by radiophoto across the broad stretches of the Atlantic* (New Yorker).

ra·di·o·pho·to·graph (rā′dē ō fō′tə graf, -gräf), *n.* a photograph transmitted by radio.

ra·di·o·pho·to·graph·ic (rā′dē ō fō′tə-graf′ik), *adj.* of or by radio photography.

ra·di·o·pho·tog·ra·phy (rā′dē ō fə tog′rə fē), *n.* the transmission of a photograph by radio.

ra·di·o·phys·ics (rā′dē ō fiz′iks), *n.* the branch of physics dealing with radioactive substances: *My own subject of radiophysics has, on many occasions, been advanced by the observations of the gifted and enthusiastic amateur* (Bulletin of Atomic Scientists).

radio pill, a miniaturized radio transmitter enclosed in a plastic capsule that can be swallowed and used to transmit signals on gastrointestinal and other conditions as it passes through the body.

ra·di·o·scope (rā′dē ō skōp), *n.* **1.** an instrument for studying and applying X rays. **2.** a form of spinthariscope.

ra·di·o·scop·ic (rā′dē ō skop′ik), *adj.* of or having to do with the radioscope or radioscopy.

ra·di·o·scop·i·cal (rā′dē ō skop′ə kəl), *adj.* radioscopic.

ra·di·os·co·py (rā′dē os′kə pē), *n.* the examination of opaque objects by means of X rays or other radioactive substances.

ra·di·o·sen·si·tive (rā′dē ō sen′sə tiv), *adj.* sensitive to X rays or other radioactivity: *a radiosensitive tumor. Another weed, Anisantha sterilis, was found remarkably radiosensitive since only 5,000 rad was lethal* (Science News Letter).

ra·di·o·sen·si·tiv·i·ty (rā′dē ō sen′sə tiv′ə tē), *n.* the sensitivity of tissues, organisms, etc., to X rays or other radioactivity: *The increased radiosensitivity of a child's body must be considered in contrast to that of the adult* (Bulletin of Atomic Scientists).

ra·di·o·so·di·um (rā′dē ō sō′dē əm), *n.* a radioisotope of sodium, used in studying blood circulation and water metabolism, and in the treatment of kidney and other diseases: *Perley used radiosodium (Na^{24}) to study exchangeable sodium in healthy young adults and children* (Morris Fishbein).

ra·di·o·sonde (rā′dē ō sond), *n.* an instrument carried into the stratosphere by means of a balloon to altitudes upwards of 15 miles (depending on the information desired), from which it descends by parachute, automatically reporting data on atmospheric temperature, pressure, and humidity to ground observers by means of a tiny radio transmitter. [< *radio-* + French *sonde* depth sounding]

radio source, radio star: *The accurate location of these radio sources in the universe . . . has led to new discoveries of great astronomical interest* (Bulletin of Atomic Scientists).

radio spectrum, the entire range of radio waves, from 3 centimeters to 30,000 meters.

radio star, a powerful mass of energy in space that emits radio waves instead of light waves. Radio stars are studied by radio astronomers. *There seem to be a great number of these radio stars: more than 200 are now known, and it is likely that vastly greater numbers will be found as radio telescopes are improved* (A.C.B. Lovell).

radio station, 1. an installation consisting of radio-transmitting devices, broadcasting studios, and all other equipment necessary for radiobroadcasting. **2.** an organization or department in the business of commercial broadcasting.

ra·di·o·stron·ti·um (rā′dē ō stron′shē əm, -tē əm), *n.* a radioisotope of strontium that forms part of the fall-out of a hydrogen bomb explosion; strontium 90: *Radiostrontium . . . is the principal radioactive hazard to the farms and forests if atomic war comes* (Science News Letter).

radio studio, a room, usually with special acoustic properties, from which a radiobroadcast can be made.

ra·di·o·sur·ger·y (rā′dē ō sėr′jər ē), *n.* surgery combined with the use of radium: *Radiosurgery on the brain without opening the skull was reported by Swedish and American neurosurgeons speaking at the Second International Congress of Neurological Surgery in Washington, D.C.* (Science News Letter).

ra·di·o·sym·met·ri·cal (rā′dē ō si met′rə kəl), *adj.* radially symmetrical; actinomorphic.

ra·di·o·tel·e·gram (rā′dē ō tel′ə gram), *n.* a message transmitted by radiotelegraphy; radiogram.

ra·di·o·tel·e·graph (rā′dē ō tel′ə graf, -gräf), *n.* a telegraph worked by radio. —*v.t., v.i.* to telegraph by radio.

ra·di·o·tel·e·graph·ic (rā′dē ō tel′ə graf′ik), *adj.* of or having to do with radiotelegraphy.

ra·di·o·te·leg·ra·phy (rā′dē ō tə leg′rə fē), *n.* a telegraphing by radio.

radio telemetry, the automatic taking of measurements at distant or inaccessible points, as within a nuclear reactor, and the transmission of the data to a receiving point by means specifically of radio.

ra·di·o·tel·e·phone (rā′dē ō tel′ə fōn), *n., v.,* **-phoned, -phon·ing.** —*n.* a radio transmitter using voice communication: *[The skiff] is also fitted out with a radiotelephone, a radio compass . . .* (New Yorker). —*v.t., v.i.* to telephone by radio: *Dulles radiotelephoned to the White House a request to report to the nation on the crisis* (Time).

ra·di·o·tel·e·phon·ic (rā′dē ō tel′ə fon′ik), *adj.* of or having to do with a radiotelephone: *Sputnik IV is in radiotelephonic contact with the earth* (Times of India).

ra·di·o·te·leph·o·ny (rā′dē ō tə lef′ə nē), *n.* radio communication by means of voice signals.

radio telescope, a device for detecting and recording radio waves coming from stars and other objects in outer space: *A great advantage of the radio telescope is that it can "see" much farther than optical instruments* (Scientific American).

Radio Telescope with reflector 250 ft. wide

ra·di·o·ther·a·peu·tic (rā′dē ō ther′ə pyü′tik), *adj.* of or having to do with the treatment of disease by means of X rays or radioactive agencies: *Safety measures are employed by those specially educated in radiographic and radiotherapeutic techniques* (Arnold L. Bachman).

ra·di·o·ther·a·peu·tics (rā′dē ō ther′ə pyü′tiks), *n.* the branch of therapeutics that deals with the use of X rays or radioactive substances such as radium in the treatment of disease.

ra·di·o·ther·a·pist (rā′dē ō ther′ə pist), *n.* a person skilled in radiotherapy: *By dividing and spreading the dose radiotherapists can treat cancerous tissue with thousands of rads without excessive damage to the patient* (Scientific American).

ra·di·o·ther·a·py (rā′dē ō ther′ə pē), *n.* the treatment of disease by means of X rays or radioactive agencies: *. . . kilocurie sources of radiocaesium for use in radiotherapy* (Bulletin of Atomic Scientists).

ra·di·o·ther·my (rā′dē ō thėr′mē), *n.* diathermy by a short-wave radio apparatus. [< *radio-* + Greek *thérmē* heat]

ra·di·o·tho·ri·um (rā′dē ō thôr′ē əm, -thōr′-), *n.* a radioactive isotope of thorium, having a mass number of 228. It is a disintegration product of mesothorium II. [< New Latin *radiothorium* < *radio-* radio- + *thorium* thorium]

ra·di·o·trac·er (rā′dē ō trā′sər), *n.* a radioisotopic tracer: *The key to the technique is the addition of isotopes . . . called intrinsic radiotracers* (New Scientist).

ra·di·o·trans·par·ent (rā′dē ō trans pãr′ənt), *adj.* transparent to X rays and other radioactive substances; not radiopaque: *The X rays would show exactly . . . how deep the radiotransparent layers go* (Science News Letter).

radio tube, a vacuum tube used in a radio set.

ra·di·o·ul·nar (rā′dē ō ul′nər), *adj. Anatomy.* of the radius and the ulna (bones of the forearm). [< *radius* + *uln*(a) + *-ar*]

ra·di·o·vi·sion (rā′dē ō vizh′ən), *n.* television by means of radio.

radio wave, an electromagnetic wave within the radio frequencies: *Radio waves travel at the speed of light: 186,282 miles a second* (World Book Encyclopedia).

rad·ish (rad′ish), *n.* **1.** the small, crisp, root of a plant of the mustard family, with a red, white, or blackish skin, used as a relish and in salads: *And under an old oak's domestic shade, Enjoy'd, spare feast! a radish and an egg* (William Cowper). **2.** the plant. [< Middle French *radis* < Italian *radice* < Latin *rādīx, -īcis* root. Doublet of RADIX.]

ra·di·um (rā′dē əm), *n.* a metallic, radioactive chemical element found in very small amounts in uranium ores such as pitchblende, used in treating cancer and in making luminous paint. Radium atoms are constantly giving off alpha, beta, and gamma rays, and break down in successive forms finally into lead. *Radium is never found free, but it is found combined in almost all rocks in extremely minute quantities* (Monroe M. Offner). *Symbol:* Ra; *at.wt.:* (C^{12}) 226 or (O^{16}) 226.05; *at.no.:* 88; *valence:* 2. See **disintegration** for diagram. [< New Latin *radium* < Latin *radius* ray, beam]

radium emanation, radon, a gaseous chemical element, a product of radioactive disintegration.

ra·di·um·i·za·tion (rā′dē ə mə zā′shən), *n.* treatment with radium or the radium emanation.

ra·di·um·ize (rā′dē ə mīz), *v.t.,* **-ized, -iz·ing.** to treat with radium or the radium emanation; subject to the rays emitted by radium or its compounds or products.

ra·di·um·ther·a·py (rā′dē əm ther′ə pē), *n.* the treatment of disease by means of radium.

ra·di·us (rā′dē əs), *n., pl.* **-di·i** or **-di·us·es. 1.** any line going straight from the center to the outside of a circle or sphere. **2.** a circular area measured by the length of its radius: *The explosion could be heard within a radius of ten miles.* **3. a.** the distance an airplane, ship, etc., can travel and still have enough fuel to return: *a submarine with a cruising radius of 4,000 miles.* **b.** the field of operation or range of influence of anything. **4.** any radial or radiating part: **a.** that one of the two bones of the forearm, which is on the thumb side. **b.** a corresponding bone in the forelimb of other vertebrates. **c.** a rod, bar, etc., forming one of a set extending in several directions from one point, as a wheel spoke. **5.** a line thought of as dividing an animal having radial symmetry into like parts. **6.** the distance between the center and the axis of rotation in an eccentric; eccentricity. [< Latin *radius* ray, spoke of a wheel, radius bone. Doublet of RAY[1].]

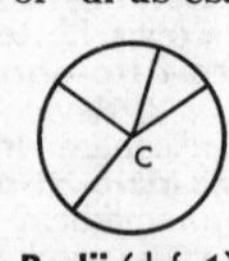

Radii (def. 1) are the lines from C.

radius rod, a rod flexibly connected, at one end to the chassis or underframe of an automobile, and at the other end to an axle.

radius vector, *pl.* **radii vectores** or **radius vectors. 1.** a straight line, or its length, joining a fixed point and a variable point. **2.** *Astronomy.* such a line, or distance, with the sun or other central body taken as a fixed point, and a planet, comet, etc., as the variable point. [< New Latin *radius vector* < *radius* radius, *vector* vector]

ra·dix (rā′diks), *n., pl.* **rad·i·ces** or **ra·dix·es. 1.** a root; radical; source or origin. **2.** *Mathematics.* a number taken as the base of a system of numbers, logarithms, or the like: *The radix of the decimal system is ten.* **3.** *Linguistics.* a root or etymon. **4.** the root of a plant, especially a plant used in the preparation of a medicine. [< Latin *rādīx, -īcis* root. Doublet of RADISH.]

ra·dome (rā′dōm), *n.* a domelike structure, usually a hemisphere of plastic, used to shelter a radar antenna that might otherwise suffer damage from the elements, as on an aircraft or in an arctic installation: *Manned by a crew of four, the WF-2 is equipped with a long-range antenna housed in its saucer-shaped top which is the largest radome ever designed for a carrier-based plane* (Science News Letter). [< *ra*(dar) + *dome*]

ra·don (rā′don), *n.* a heavy, radioactive gas. It is a rare chemical element, formed by the radioactive decay of radium. *Radon, an alpha-emitting daughter of radium, is easily measured by its radioactivity* (Scientific American). *Symbol:* Rn; *at.wt.:* (C^{12}) 222 or (O^{16}) 222; *at.no.:* 86. Formerly, **niton.** See **disintegration** for diagram. [< *radium*]

rad·u·la (raj′ů lə), *n., pl.* **-lae** (-lē). a horny band in the mouth of a mollusk, set with tiny teeth: *[The limpet] gathers food into its mouth with a long tongue, or radula, which looks like a ribbon and is covered with rows of teeth* (World Book Encyclopedia). [< Latin *rādula* a scraper < *rādere* to scrape]

rad·u·lar (raj′ů lər), *adj.* of a radula; like a radula: *radular teeth.*

R.A.F. or **RAF** (no periods), Royal Air Force (of Great Britain).

ra·fale (rä fäl′), *n. French, Military.* a sudden, brief, violent burst of artillery fire, repeated at intervals. [< French *rafale* (literally) squall]

raff (raf), *n.* **1.** a quantity; heap. **2.** the riffraff: *jostling with . . . coal whippers, brazen women, ragged children, and the raff*

 PRONUNCIATION KEY: hat, āge, cãre, fär; let, ēqual, tėrm; it, īce; hot, ōpen, ôrder; oil, out; cup, pu̇t, rüle;

and refuse of the river (Dickens). 3. *British Dialect.* rubbish. [apparently abstracted from Middle English *riffe and raff* one and all; see RIFFRAFF]

raf·fi·a (raf′ē ə), *n.* **1.** the soft fiber from the leafstalks of a kind of palm tree growing in the Malagasy Republic, used in making baskets, mats, etc. **2. a.** Also, **raffia palm.** a palm tree with long, plumelike, pinnate leaves whose leafstalks yield this fiber. **b.** any other palm of this group. Also, **raphia.** [< Malagasy *rafia*]

raf·fi·nose (raf′ə nōs), *n.* a colorless, crystalline sugar, present in sugar beets, cottonseed, etc. It yields fructose, glucose, and galactose when hydrolyzed. *Formula:* $C_{18}H_{32}O_{16}\cdot 5H_2O$ [< French *raffiner* refine + English *-ose*[2]]

raff·ish (raf′ish), *adj.* rowdy; disreputable; dissipated.

raff·ish·ly (raf′ish lē), *adv.* in a raffish manner.

raff·ish·ness (raf′ish nis), *n.* a raffish quality or condition: *The people of Agra manage to combine a leisurely grace with a certain manner of raffishness* (London Times).

raf·fle[1] (raf′əl), *n., v.,* **-fled, -fling.** —*n.* a sale in which people each pay a small sum for a chance of getting an article: *She wore a cloth coat, preferring it to a mink stole she won in a raffle a year ago* (Newsweek). —*v.t.* to sell (an article) by a raffle. —*v.i.* to hold a raffle. [Middle English *rafle* a dice game < Old French *rafle* plundering, stripping, ultimately < Germanic (compare Dutch *rafelen* ravel, pluck)] —**raf′fler,** *n.*

raf·fle[2] (raf′əl), *n.* **1.** rubbish. **2.** a tangle, especially of ropes, rags, and canvas: *The top-men clear the raffle with their clasp-knives in their teeth* (Rudyard Kipling). [< *raff* trash + *-le,* a diminutive suffix]

raf·fle·sia (ra flē′zhə), *n.* any of a group of parasitic Malaysian plants without stems or leaves, and with a single large flower, sometimes 3 feet in diameter. [< New Latin *Rafflesia* the genus name < T. Stamford *Raffles,* 1781-1826, a British governor of Sumatra, who discovered the plant]

raf·fle·si·a·ceous (ra flē′zē ā′shəs), *adj.* of or belonging to the family of plants typified by the rafflesia.

raft[1] (raft, räft), *n.* **1.** logs or boards fastened together to make a floating platform: *When our friends had been told in English and Spanish that the raft was named after the Incas' great . . . sun king . . . Gerd Vold christened the raft Kon-tiki* (Thor Heyerdahl). **2.** any floating platform, as used by swimmers, or for life rafts, etc.
—*v.t.* **1.** to send by raft; carry on a raft: *We crossed it [a river] . . . rafting over our horses and equipage* (Francis Parkman). **2.** to make into a raft. —*v.i.* to use a raft; work on or guide a raft.
[Middle English *rafte* < Scandinavian (compare Old Icelandic *raptr* log, rafter)]

raft[2] (raft, räft), *n. Informal.* a large number; abundance: *a raft of troubles.* [variant of Middle English *raff* heap]

raft·er[1] (raf′tər, räf′-), *n.* a slanting beam of a roof: *He held the ridgepole up, and spiked again The rafters of the Home* (Edwin Markham). [Old English *ræfter*]

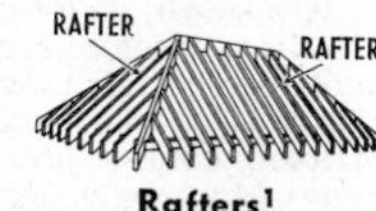

Rafters[1]

raft·er[2] (raf′tər, räf′-), *n.* a person who rafts timber.

raft·ered (raf′tərd, räf′-), *adj.* built with rafters; with rafters left exposed on a ceiling.

rafts·man (rafts′mən, räfts′-), *n., pl.* **-men.** a man who manages, or works on, a raft.

rag[1] (rag), *n., adj., v.,* **ragged, rag·ging.** —*n.* **1.** a torn or waste piece of cloth. **2.** a small piece of cloth. **3.** a small piece of anything of no value. **4.** a shred, scrap, or fragmentary bit of anything. **5.** a contemptuous or humorous term for some article of clothing, a flag, a theater curtain, a piece of paper money, etc. **6.** a beggarly, worthless, or wretched person. **7.** a rough projection; jag. **8.** the white, stringy core of an orange, etc. **9.** *Informal.* a piece of ragtime music.
chew the rag, *Slang.* to talk at length; chat: *The way as that Sam chewed the rag was just jammy* (Punch).
rags, a. clothing that is much torn or worn; tatters: *The base degree to which I now am fallen, These rags, this grinding . . .* (Milton). **b.** *Slang.* clothing: *I stood up and shook my rags off and jumped into the river* (Mark Twain). **c.** extreme poverty: *We seem to have moved from rags to riches overnight* (New York Times).
—*adj.* made from rags: *rag paper, a rag rug.*
—*v.t.* to make ragged. —*v.i.* **1.** to become ragged. **2.** *U.S. Slang.* to dress in fine clothes.
[Middle English *ragge,* perhaps < Scandinavian (compare Old Icelandic *rögg* shaggy tuft), or perhaps unrecorded Old English *ragg,* implied in *raggig* raglike]

rag[2] (rag), *v.,* **ragged, rag·ging,** *n. Slang.* —*v.t.* **1.** to play jokes on: *In a series of rough charades it rags with slapstick humour an oaf who tries to rise in society by a bourgeois marriage* (Punch). **2.** to tease: *I remember some kids were ragging me and they told me we were poor and I couldn't understand it* (Maclean's). **3.** to scold.
—*n.* **1.** a ragging. **2.** *Especially British.* a boisterous public demonstration.
[origin uncertain]

rag[3] (rag), *n.* **1.** a large roofing slate. **2.** any of various coarse rocks used in building: *Of shale and hornblende, rag and trap and tuff* (Tennyson). [Middle English *ragge;* origin unknown]

ra·ga (rä′gə), *n., pl.* **-gas.** a traditional Hindu melodic form, consisting of certain prescribed combinations of notes with regular ascending and descending patterns. [< Sanskrit *raga* (literally) color, mood]

rag·a·muf·fin (rag′ə muf′ən), *n.* **1.** a ragged, disreputable fellow. **2.** a ragged child. [probably < *rag*[1] + *muffin,* in an uncertain sense]

rag·a·muf·fin·ly (rag′ə muf′ən lē), *adj.* like a ragamuffin; ragged; slovenly.

rag-and-bone man (rag′ən bōn′), *Especially British.* a ragman: *When I was a small boy a rag-and-bone man, as he would then be called, would carry away virtually anything (and would take the knocker off the door as well)* (New Scientist).

rag baby, a rag doll.

rag·bag (rag′bag′), *n.* **1.** a bag for storing rags, scraps of cloth, etc. **2.** a motley collection: *The book is a ragbag of philosophical odds and ends.*

rag bolt, a bolt having the shank barbed so as to resist withdrawal. [< *rag*[1], in rare sense of "jagged projection" + *bolt*[1]]

rag doll, a limp doll made of rags or scraps of cloth: *Rag dolls are the most popular of all homemade dolls* (Nina R. Jordan).

rage (rāj), *n., v.,* **raged, rag·ing.** —*n.* **1.** violent anger: *a voice quivering with rage. Mad with rage, Dick dashed into the fight.* **2.** a fit of violent anger: *to be in a rage.* **3.** violence: *the rage of a savage tiger, the rage of a storm.* **4.** great enthusiasm. **5.** a violent feeling, appetite, etc.; frenzy: *Dinmont . . . said little . . . till the rage of thirst and hunger was appeased* (Scott). **6.** *Obsolete.* madness; insanity: *The great rage, You see is kill'd in him* (Shakespeare).
the rage, what everybody wants for a short time; the fashion: *Rocking chairs became the rage* (Carol L. Thompson).
—*v.i.* **1.** to be furious with anger. **2.** to speak or move with furious anger: *Keep your temper; don't rage.* **3.** to act violently; move, proceed, or continue with great violence: *The fire raged. A heavy gulf thunderstorm was raging* (Joseph Conrad).
[< Old French *rage* < Vulgar Latin *rabia* < Latin *rabiēs* madness. Doublet of RABIES.]
—**Syn.** *n.* **1. Rage, fury** mean violent anger. **Rage** means anger so great and strong that a person or animal loses control over his feelings or good judgment and acts or speaks violently or coldly turns his mind to finding a way to get even: *In his rage at being publicly punished, he broke the teacher's favorite vase.* **Fury** means rage so wild and fierce that it destroys common sense and makes a person into an enraged wild animal, wanting to harm and destroy: *In its fury the mob went through the streets wrecking cars.*

rage·ful (rāj′fəl), *adj.* full of rage: *Nor thou be rageful, like a handled bee* (Tennyson).

rage·ful·ly (rāj′fə lē), *adv.* in a raging manner; violently; tempestuously: *ragefully tempested with storms of persecution* (John Donne).

rag·ged (rag′id), *adj.* **1.** worn or torn into rags; tattered: *ragged trousers.* **2.** wearing torn or badly worn-out clothing: *a ragged urchin of the streets.* **3.** not straight and tidy; rough: *an Airedale's ragged coat, a ragged garden.* **4.** having loose shreds or bits: *a ragged wound.* **5.** having rough or sharp points; uneven; jagged: *ragged rocks.* **6.** harsh: *a ragged voice.* **7.** faulty; imperfect; irregular: *ragged rhyme.* —**rag′ged·ly,** *adv.* —**rag′ged·ness,** *n.* —**Syn. 1.** rent, frayed.

ragged edge, the very edge; brink: *on the ragged edge of mental collapse.*

ragged robin, a perennial plant, a lychnis with ragged-looking, pink or white petals; cuckooflower.

rag·ged·y (rag′ə dē), *adj.,* **-ged·i·er, -ged·i·est. 1.** ragged: *a raggedy coat.* **2.** that looks ragged: *Oh, the Raggedy Man he works for Pa* (James Whitcomb Riley).

rag·gee or **rag·gi** (rag′ē), *n.* an East Indian cereal grass, grown in Asia for its grain. [< Hindustani *rāgī*]

rag·get·y (rag′ə tē), *adj.,* **-get·i·er, -get·i·est.** *Especially British.* raggedy: *When I drove into LaPaz, an armed if raggety civilian was doing official guard duty at the city gate* (Manchester Guardian Weekly).

rag·gle-tag·gle (rag′əl tag′əl), *adj. Informal or Dialect.* slipshod; slovenly; raggedy: *Next came the pedlars, a genial, raggle-taggle, clownish company, all around the church* (Manchester Guardian). [< *ragtag*]

rag·gy (rag′ē), *adj.,* **-gi·er, -gi·est.** *Dialect.* ragged: *if it's raggy and dirty you are* (John Millington Synge).

rag·i (rag′ē), *n.* raggee.

rag·ing (rā′jing), *adj.* that rages; violent, as a tempest, or as disease or pain; furious: *a raging fever, raging anger.*

rag·ing·ly (rā′jing lē), *adv.* in a raging manner; with fury; with violent impetuosity.

rag·lan (rag′lən), *n.* a loose topcoat or overcoat with sleeves cut so as to continue up to the collar. [< Baron *Raglan,* 1788-1855, a British field marshal]

raglan sleeve, a sleeve cut so as to continue up to the collar.

rag·like (rag′līk′), *adj.* like a rag.

rag·man (rag′man′), *n., pl.* **-men.** a man who gathers, buys, or sells rags, old newspapers, magazines, etc.

Rag·na·rok (räg′nə rok′), *n. Norse Mythology.* the destruction of the world in the war between the gods and the forces of evil led by Loki; Twilight of the Gods. [< Old Icelandic *Ragnarøk* < *ragna,* genitive plural of *røgn* god; (gods and the world) + *røk* reckoning, history, origin]

Rag·na·rök (räg′nə rœk′), *n.* Ragnarok.

ra·gout (ra gü′), *n., v.,* **-gouted** (-güd′), **-gout·ing** (-gü′ing). —*n.* a highly seasoned stew of meat and vegetables: *When he found her prefer a plain dish to a ragout, [he] had nothing to say to her* (Jane Austen). —*v.t.* to make into a ragout [< French *ragoût* < Middle French *ragoûter* restore the appetite < *re-* back, re- + *à* to (< Latin *ad*) + *goût* < Latin *gustus, -ūs* taste]

rag·pick·er (rag′pik′ər), *n.* a person who picks up rags and other waste material from the streets, rubbish heaps, etc.: *One building is filled with the families of 900 ragpickers who pay $1 a month in rent* (Time).

rags (ragz), *n.pl.* See under **rag**[1], *n.*

rag·stone (rag′stōn′), *n. British.* rag, a roofing slate or building stone; a coarse sandstone.

rag·tag (rag′tag′), *n.* the riffraff; rabble. —*adj. U.S. Informal.* characteristic or consisting of riffraff: *His forces had been whittled down to a ragtag band* (Newsweek).

ragtag and bobtail, ragtag.

rag·time (rag′tīm′), *n.* **1.** a musical rhythm with accents falling at unusual places. **2.** music with accents falling at unusual places; jazz. [American English; perhaps earlier *ragged time* (because of the rhythm)]

rag·weed (rag′wēd′), *n.* **1.** any of several coarse weeds of the composite family whose pollen is one of the most common causes of hay fever. **2.** *U.S. Dialect.* the marsh elder. **3.** *British.* ragwort.

rag·worm (rag′wėrm′), *n.* any of various nereid worms of the European coast, much used as bait.

rag·wort (rag′wėrt′), *n.* any of various composite plants with irregularly lobed leaves and yellow flowers.

rah (rä), *interj., n.* hurrah. [American English, short for *hurrah*]

rah-rah (rä′rä′), *interj., n.* hurrah. —*adj. Informal.* characteristic of college cheering, college life, etc.; collegiate: *rah-rah spectator sports.*

ra·ia (rä′yə), *n. Obsolete.* rayah.

raid (rād), *n.* **1.** an attack; sudden attack: *Each venture Is a new beginning, a raid on the inarticulate With shabby equipment always deteriorating* (T.S. Eliot). **2.** a sudden attack, usually by a small force having no intention of holding the territory invaded: *an Indian raid.* **3.** an entering and seizing what is inside. **4.** a deliberate attempt by speculators to force down prices on stock exchanges. **5.** a predatory, often unscrupulous incursion into the domain of another for the purpose of securing something: *a raid by one union on the membership of another, a raid by a college on the faculty of another.*
—*v.t.* **1.** to attack suddenly. **2.** to force a way into; enter and seize what is in: *The police raided the gambling house.* **3.** to make a raid upon: [*The university*] *is out to raid faculties from coast to coast* (Time). —*v.i.* to engage in a raid.
[Northern English form of Old English *rād* a riding. Compare ROAD.] —**raid′er,** *n.*

rail[1] (rāl), *n.* **1.** a bar of wood or of metal: *There are stair rails, fence rails, rails protecting monuments, etc. Bars laid along the ground for a car or railroad track are called rails.* **2.** railroad: *to ship by rail.* **3.** a fence enclosing a race track: *to ride a horse near the rail.* **4.** the upper part of the bulwarks of a ship. **5.** a horizontal board or piece in a framework or paneling: *a chair rail.*
off the rails, *Especially British.* out of the proper or normal condition; out of control; haywire: *At that time it seemed to me the national government was going seriously off the rails* (Walter Gordon).
—*v.t.* **1.** to furnish with rails. **2.** to enclose with bars.
rail in, to enclose within a fence: *A space was railed in for the reception of the . . . jurors* (Maria Edgeworth).
rail off, to separate by a fence: *The footpaths were railed off along the whole distance* (James A. Froude).
[< Old French *reille* < Latin *rēgula* straight rod, related to *regere* to straighten. Doublet of RULE.]

rail[2] (rāl), *v.i.* to complain bitterly; use violent and reproachful language: *He railed at his hard luck. Poets, like disputants, when reasons fail, Have one sure refuge left, and that's to rail* (John Dryden). *Why rail at fate? The mischief is your own* (John G. Whittier). —*v.t.* to bring or force by railing. [< Middle French *railler* < Old Provençal *ralhar,* probably < Vulgar Latin *ragulāre,* for Late Latin *ragere* to bray, brawl. Doublet of RALLY[2].] —**rail′er,** *n.* —**Syn.** *v.i., v.t.* scold, revile, upbraid.

rail[3] (rāl), *n., pl.* **rails** or (*collectively*) **rail.** any of a group of small, dull-colored wading birds with short wings, plump bodies, long toes, and a harsh cry, that live in marshes and swamps. [< Old French *raale,* perhaps < *raler* to rattle; perhaps imitative]

Virginia Rail[3]
(about 10 in. long)

rail[4] (rāl), *n. Archaic.* **1.** a garment; cloak. **2.** a kerchief. [Old English *hrægl*]

rail·bird[1] (rāl′bėrd′), *n. U.S. Slang.* a person fond of watching horse races and workouts from a position at the rail of the track.

rail·bird[2] (rāl′bėrd′), *n. U.S.* a rail, especially the Carolina rail.

rail·car (rāl′kär′), *n. Especially British.* any railroad car other than an engine and tender that is used to transport passengers or freight: *Frankel's lorries and railcars are scouring half of Scotland for timber* (Keith Richardson).

rail·head (rāl′hed′), *n.* **1.** the farthest point to which the rails of a railroad have been laid: *The Indian Government pays for the long, expensive haul from Pathankot, the railhead on the plains* (London Times). **2.** a place on a railroad where supplies for troops are unloaded: *There a huge wall chart showed the whereabouts of fifty-three aircraft in motion between railheads, advance bases, and radar sites* (Harper's). **3.** the upper part of a steel rail with which the cars, etc., come in contact. **4.** a farthest point: *somewhere beyond the railheads Of reason, south or north, Lies a magnetic mountain Riveting sky to earth* (C. Day Lewis).

rail·ing (rā′ling), *n.* **1.** a barrier made of rails, rails and supports, or the like. **2.** material for rails. **3.** rails. —**Syn. 1.** balustrade.

rail·ler·y (rā′lər ē), *n., pl.* **-ler·ies. 1.** good-humored ridicule; teasing; joking. **2.** a bantering remark. [< French *raillerie* < Middle French *railler;* see RAIL[2]] —**Syn. 1.** badinage, persiflage.

rail·man (rāl′man′), *n., pl.* **-men.** an owner or executive of a railroad company.

rail·road (rāl′rōd′), *n. Especially U.S.* **1.** a road or track with parallel steel rails on which the wheels of the cars go. **2. a.** the tracks, stations, trains, and other property of a system of transportation that uses rails, together with the people who manage them: *The Columbia was a turbulent river . . . It had its era of steamboats, which gave way in time to the railroads* (Newsweek). **b.** the company or corporation which owns and operates this. *Abbr.:* R.R. **3.** *Bowling.* a split, especially one that leaves the 7 and 10 pins standing.
—*v.t. U.S.* **1.** to send by railroad; carry on a railroad. **2.** *Informal.* to send along or force through quickly or too quickly to be fair: *His enemies tried to railroad him to prison without a fair trial.* —*v.i. U.S.* to work on a railroad.

rail·road·er (rāl′rō′dər), *n. U.S.* **1.** a person who works on a railroad: *Memphis railroaders were known to fight with strangers who sang the slanderous lines* (Time). **2.** a person who owns or operates a railroad: *I happened to be one of a committee of railroaders appointed to study the ability of the railroads to meet anticipated transportation demands of World War II* (Wall Street Journal).

railroad flat, an apartment in which the rooms are lined up in a row like boxcars: *In some of the row houses, railroad flats run from front to back* (Harper's).

rail·road·i·a·na (rāl′rō dē ä′nə, -an′ə, -ā′nə), *n.pl.* a collection of books, documents, facts, etc., about railroads.

rail·road·ing (rāl′rō′ding), *n. U.S.* **1.** the construction or operation of railroads: *Mr. Walker has served the Canadian Pacific for more than 65 years, a record believed to be unique in Canadian railroading* (Banff, Crag, and Canyon). **2.** *Informal.* the act or process of hurrying (a thing or person) along.

rail·road·man (rāl′rōd′man′, -mən), *n., pl.* **-men.** *Especially U.S.* a railroader: *Many railroadmen believe that a merger . . . would create a behemoth that could hardly be run efficiently* (Time).

rail·split·ter (rāl′split′ər), *n. U.S.* a person who splits logs into fence rails.
the railsplitter, Abraham Lincoln: *The railsplitter had defeated the man full of words . . . Truth gave the victory to Lincoln; a trick bestowed the Senatorship upon Douglas* (Margaret L. Coit).

rail tongs, tracklayers' tongs for lifting rails.

rail·way (rāl′wā′), *n.* **1.** *Especially British.* a railroad: *With the development of these two industries* [*of rubber and tin in Malaya*] *came the building of railways and roads* (Atlantic). *Abbr.:* Ry. **2.** any track made of rails: *a cog railway.* **3.** a streetcar line.

rail·wayed (rāl′wād′), *adj.* having railways: *not foreseeing restless and railwayed generations* (Arthur S. M. Hutchinson).

rail·way·man (rāl′wā′man′, -mən), *n., pl.* **-men.** *Especially British.* a railroader: *Railwaymen on duty at stations . . . are being trained to give artificial respiration in cases of electrocution* (Cape Times).

railway stitch, an embroidery stitch consisting of a loop of thread held in place by a small stitch.

rail·work·er (rāl′wėr′kər), *n.* a person who works for a railroad: *In recent weeks some 200,000 railworkers have been granted wage increases* (Wall Street Journal).

rai·ment (rā′mənt), *n.* clothing; garments. [Middle English *raiment,* short for *arraiment* < *array,* verb]

rain (rān), *n.* **1.** water falling in drops from the clouds. **2.** the fall of such drops: *a hard rain.* **3.** a thick, fast fall of anything: *a rain of bullets.*
the rains, the rainy season; the seasonal rainfalls: *The heavy tropical rains are usually confined to definite periods* (Thomas Henry Huxley).
—*v.i.* **1.** to fall in drops of water: *It is raining.* **2.** to fall like rain: *Sparks rained down from the burning roof.* **3.** to pour down rain.
—*v.t.* **1.** to send down (rain): *I will rain upon him . . . an overflowing rain, and great hailstones* (Ezekiel 38:22). **2.** to send like rain: *The children rained flowers on their queen.*
it never rains but it pours, events of a kind, especially misfortunes, come all together or not at all: *As it never rains but it pours, news of another disaster was rife in the city in the evening* (Earl Dunmore).
rain off, *British.* to rain out: *An open-air meeting was rained off, but pickets patrolled the dock entrances* (London Times).
rain out, to cancel because of rain: *The second game of the scheduled double-header was rained out in the third inning with Cincinnati leading* (New York Times).
[Old English *regn*]
—**Syn.** *v.t.* **2.** shower.

rain·band (rān′band′), *n.* a dark band in the solar spectrum, due to the water vapor in the atmosphere.

rain·bar·rel (rān′bar′əl), *n.* a barrel used to collect rain water for drinking or washing.

rain·bird (rān′bėrd′), *n.* any of several kinds of birds, as the green woodpecker or the Jamaican cuckoo, supposed to foretell rain by its cries or actions: *From a group of trees came the liquid call of the rainbird* (Cape Times).

rain·bow (rān′bō′), *n.* **1.** a bow or arch of seven colors seen sometimes in the sky, or in mist or spray when the sun shines on it from behind the observer. The colors are violet, indigo, blue, green, yellow, orange, and red. *The rainbow, one of the most beautiful of natural phenomena, is a spectrum produced by the dispersion of sunlight by spherical raindrops* (John Charles Duncan). [*There was*] *a rainbow round about the throne* (Revelation 4:3). **2.** anything similar, as a lunar rainbow or moonbow. **3.** a rainbow trout: *. . . to stock rainbows where the water is suitable for them* (London Times).
—*adj.* **1.** having to do with a rainbow. **2.** like or suggesting a rainbow: *the endless parrot-tribe with their rainbow hues* (William H. Prescott).
—*v.t.* to brighten or span with, or as with, a rainbow: *The great bridge rainbows the skyline* (Manchester Guardian Weekly).
—*v.i.* to take the form or color pattern of a rainbow: *The sails . . . rainbowed with small signalling flags* (London Times).
[Old English *regnboga* < *regn* rain + *boga* bow, curve, arch]

rainbow snake, a burrowing snake of the southeastern United States which has a red belly and red or yellow striped back; hoop snake.

rainbow trout, a kind of trout which is native to western North America and has been introduced in other areas, named for its bright pinkish coloring: *A rainbow trout that has entered or returned from the sea is called a steelhead.*

rain·bow·y (rān′bō′ē), *adj.* of or like a rainbow: *a brilliant splash of rainbowy colors.*

rain·cape (rān′kāp′), *n.* a waterproof cape for protection from rain: *Easier to slip on than a raincoat, the polyethylene plastic raincape is full enough to be worn over suits or bulky outerwear* (Science News Letter).

rain check, 1. a ticket for future use, given to the spectators at a baseball game or other outdoor performance stopped by rain. **2.** a promise to offer again an invitation which a person cannot now accept: *I can't accept your luncheon invitation today, but I'll gladly take a rain check on it.*

rain cloud, a cloud from which rain falls.

rain·coat (rān′kōt′), *n.* a waterproof coat for protection from rain: *I had decided to go incognito, in an old raincoat and with a cloth cap pulled over my eyes* (New Yorker). [American English < *rain* + *coat*]

rain·coat·ed (rān′kō′tid), *adj.* wearing a raincoat: *In the shadows, raincoated gunmen . . . wait in ambush* (Newsweek).

rain dance, a ritual dance, performed by many primitive peoples, to bring rain: *Against the terra-cotta house walls of the plaza, the katcinas are dancing the summer rain dance* (Ruth Benedict).

rain·drop (rān′drop′), *n.* a drop of rain: *Raindrops fall at a speed of about 500 to 1,000 feet a minute* (Science News Letter).

rain·fall (rān′fôl′), *n.* **1.** a shower of rain: *The existence of both crystals and droplets within one cloud will always greatly facilitate rainfall* (Eric Kraus). **2.** the amount of water in the form of rain, snow, etc., falling within a given time and area: *The yearly rainfall in New York is much greater than that in Arizona.*

rain forest, a large, very dense forest in a region where rain is very heavy throughout the year, usually in tropical areas, but sometimes in northern areas, as in southeastern Alaska: *The brush turkeys live in dense, steamy rain forests of Australia and New Guinea, where the sun seldom penetrates* (Scientific American).

rain·fowl (rān′foul′), *n.* a bird supposed to foretell rain by its cries or actions, especially by being noisy or uneasy.

rain gauge, an instrument for measuring rainfall. See **pluviometer** for picture.

rain·i·ly (rā′nə lē), *adv.* in a rainy manner; with rain falling.

rain·i·ness (rā′nē nis), *n.* a rainy state.

rain·less (rān′lis), *adj.* without rain: *a rainless region or season.* —**rain′less·ness,** *n.*

rain·mak·er (rān′mā′kər), *n.* a person who tries to produce rain, especially by supernatural or artificial means: *At least two states—Massachusetts and Maryland—are turning to professional rainmakers in an effort to get the farmers some moisture* (Wall Street Journal).

rain·mak·ing (rān′mā′king), *n.* the producing of rain by artificial or supernatural means. One method is to seed a cloud with crystals of silver iodide or dry ice. As the crystals heat up and expand they collect particles of moisture and build up a heavy moisture concentration within the cloud. When this becomes too heavy to hold, the cloud releases it as rain. *When scientific rainmaking was invented in the U.S. in the late 1940's, it seemed that at last man could do something about the weather* (Time). —*adj.* producing or attempting to produce rain: *The land of Mr. [Saul] Bellow's anticipation is a remarkable place . . . rainmaking ceremonies infallibly succeed . . .* (New Yorker).

rain·out (rān′out′), *n.* **1. a.** the postponement or cancellation of an outdoor event, as a ball game, concert, etc., because of rain: *In case of a rainout, the next two nights are available* (New York Times). **b.** an event that is rained out. **2.** precipitation of radioactive water droplets due to an underwater nuclear explosion or unfavorable atmospheric conditions: *It was evident that the extent of the rainout was much greater than that . . . from any previous nuclear detonation* (A.W. Haslett).

rain·proof (rān′prüf′), *adj.* that will not let rain through; impervious to rain. —*v.t.* to make impervious to rain.

rains (rānz), *n.pl.* See under **rain,** *n.*

rain·show·er (rān′shou′ər), *n.* a shower of rain: *The Weather Bureau described it as "a good rainshower," but said only .02 inches had been measured* (New York Times).

rain·storm (rān′stôrm′), *n.* a storm with much rain.

rain·wash (rān′wosh′, -wôsh′), *n.* **1.** a washing along or away by the force of rain: *Rainwash on hill slopes marks the initial stage in the movement of the surface waters that are gathered later into well-defined streams and rivers* (Gilluly, Waters, and Woodford). **2.** displacement of soil, sand, etc., brought about by rainfall: *Shells were also found in pre-Roman rainwash at Northfleet* (London Times).

rain water, water that has fallen as rain: *Rain water poured in the holes, spoiling additional grain* (Wall Street Journal).

rain·wear (rān′wãr′), *n.* clothes made to be worn in the rain, such as raincoats, rubbers, etc.: *He observed . . . "Good thing I brought my rainwear from the Coast." He plunged into the closet and emerged with an armful of mackintoshes, trench coats, and waterproofs of various weights* (S. J. Perelman).

rain·y (rā′nē), *adj.,* **rain·i·er, rain·i·est. 1.** having rain; having much rain: *When the wind was easterly, the weather was gloomy, dark, and rainy* (John H. Moore). **2.** bringing rain: *The sky is filled with dark, rainy clouds.* **3.** wet with rain: *rainy streets.*

rainy day, a possible time of greater need in the future: *to save money for a rainy day.*

rais·a·ble (rā′zə bəl), *adj.* that can be raised.

raise (rāz), *v.,* **raised, rais·ing,** *n.* —*v.t.* **1.** to lift up: *Children in school raise their hands to answer.* **2.** to set upright: *Raise the overturned lamp.* **3.** to cause to rise: *to raise a cloud of dust.* **4.** to put or take into a higher position; make higher or nobler; elevate: *to raise a salesman to manager. The boy raised himself by hard study to be a great lawyer.* **5.** to increase in amount, price, pay, etc.: *to raise the rent.* **6.** to increase in degree, intensity, or force, etc.: *I cannot hear you; please raise your voice.* **7.** to make of higher pitch. **8.** (in games) to bet or bid more than. **9.** to gather together; collect; manage to get: *The leader raised an army.* **10.** to breed; grow: *The farmer raises crops and cattle.* **11.** to bring into being. **12.** to cause to appear: *to raise the ghost of Napoleon.* **13.** to bring about; cause: *A funny remark raises a laugh.* **14.** to utter: *to raise a shout.* **15.** to build; create; produce; start; set up: *People raise monuments to soldiers who have died for their country.* **16.** to rouse; stir up: *to raise prejudice. The dog raised a rabbit from the underbrush.* **17.** *Informal.* to bring up; rear: *Parents raise their children.* **18.** to cause to become light: *Yeast raises bread.* **19.** to bring back to life: *to raise the dead.* **20. a.** to put an end to: *Our soldiers raised the siege of the fort by driving away the enemy.* **b.** to break up and remove: *Captain Bonneville and his confederate Indians raised their camp* (Washington Irving). **21.** to come in sight of: *After a long voyage the ship raised land.* **22.** to falsify the value of (a check, note, etc.) by making the sum larger.

—*v.i.* **1.** *U.S.* to rise to the top; attain a higher level or position: *The water having raised . . . I could form no accurate judgment of the progress* (George Washington). **2.** (at an auction or in games) to increase one's bid or bet.

—*n.* **1.** a raised place. **2.** *U.S.* an increase in amount, price, pay, etc. **3.** the amount of such an increase. **4.** *Mining.* a passage or shaft driven upward to connect one level with a higher one.

[Middle English *reisen* < Scandinavian (compare Old Icelandic *reisa,* related to Old English *rǣran*). Related to REAR².]

—**Syn.** *v.t.* **1, 2. Raise, lift, elevate** mean to move something to a higher position. **Raise** is the most general term, but applies especially to putting an object in an upright or proper position: *to raise a ladder or a windowshade.* **Lift** applies to moving an object bodily: *He could raise the ladder but not lift it.* **Elevate** applies especially to raising something to a higher rank or nobler state: *Good reading elevates the mind.* **4.** promote, advance, exalt. **9.** muster.

➔ **raise, rear.** *Raise* is good informal usage in the sense of bring up: *He was born and raised in Oregon. Rear* is formal in this sense: *He was reared in the South. Bring up* in this sense is used in all levels: *He was brought up by his grandparents.*

raised (rāzd), *adj.* **1.** made light with yeast, not with baking powder: *raised doughnuts.* **2.** embossed: *the raised figure of a horse.*

rais·er (rā′zər), *n.* a person who grows or raises things: *a cattle raiser.*

rai·sin (rā′zən), *n.* **1.** a sweet, dried grape, used especially in cooking and baking. **2.** a dark-purple color with a bluish tinge. [< Old French *raizin* < Latin *racēmus* cluster (of grapes or berries). Doublet of RACEME.]

rais·ing (rā′zing), *n.* **1.** the act of lifting up. **2.** a raised place. **3.** the process of bringing up the nap of cloth by carding with teasels. **4.** the process of embossing or ornamenting sheet metal by hammering, spinning, or stamping.

rai·son d'é·tat (re zôɴ′ dā tȧ′), *French.* political reason; reason of state: *Neither the Moscow display nor the one in Merion has been open to the public for years, the former for obvious raisons d'état* (New Yorker).

rai·son d'ê·tre (re zôɴ′ de′trə), *French.* reason for being; justification: *The raison d'être for a strategic weapon is to deter* (Bulletin of Atomic Scientists).

rai·son·né (re zô nā′), *adj. French.* systematic; logical.

raj (räj), *n.* (in India) rule; dominion: *the British raj.* [< Hindi *rāj*]

ra·jah or **ra·ja** (rä′jə), *n.* **1.** a ruler or chief in India, Java, Borneo, etc.: *The Nizam of Hyderabad . . . receives the equivalent of a million dollars a year . . . while other rajas and princes of small and poor states may receive only a couple of thousand* (Santha Rama Rau). **2.** a title given to important Hindus in India. [< Hindi *rājā* < Sanskrit, nominative of *rājan* king]

ra·jah·ship or **ra·ja·ship** (rä′jə ship), *n.* **1.** the office, rank, or authority of a rajah. **2.** the territory ruled by a rajah.

Ra·jas·tha·ni (rä′jə stä′nē), *n.* a dialect of Hindi spoken in northwest central India.

Raj·put (räj′püt), *n.* a member of a Hindu military, landowning, and ruling caste. [< Hindi *rājpūt* < Sanskrit *rājaputra* king's son]

rake¹ (rāk), *n., v.,* **raked, rak·ing.** —*n.* **1.** a long-handled tool having a bar at one end with teeth in it. A rake is used for smoothing the soil or gathering together loose leaves, hay, straw, etc. **2.** any of various tools or instruments similar to a rake.

—*v.t.* **1.** to move with a rake: *Rake the leaves off the grass.* **2.** to gather; gather together. **3.** to search carefully: *He raked the newspapers for descriptions of the accident.* **4.** to fire guns along the length of (a ship, line of soldiers, etc.). **5.** to bring up (something) forgotten or unknown: *to rake up an old scandal.* —*v.i.* **1.** to use a rake: *I like to rake.* **2.** to search with a rake. **3.** to scrape or sweep: *The sea rakes against the shore.*

[Old English *raca*] —**rak′er,** *n.*

rake² (rāk), *n.* a profligate or dissolute person: *gambling half the day with the rakes and dandies of the fashionable club* (Edith Wharton). [short for *rakehell*]

rake³ (rāk), *n., v.,* **raked, rak·ing.** —*n.* **1.** a slant; slope: *A ship's smokestacks have a slight backward rake.* **2.** the inward slant between the leading and trailing edges on the wing tip of an airplane. **3.** the angle between a cutting tool and the surface of the work.

—*v.t.* to cause to incline or slope. —*v.i.* to incline from the perpendicular, as masts or funnels. [origin uncertain]

rake⁴ (rāk), *v.i.,* **raked, rak·ing. 1.** (of a hawk) to fly along after the game or to fly wide of it. **2.** (of a dog) to hunt with the nose close to the ground. [probably Old English *racian*]

ra·kee (rä kē′, rak′ē), *n.* raki.

rake·hell (rāk′hel′), *n., adj.* profligate: *[This] man of the world and Broadway rakehell, makes his true confession . . .* (New York Times). [probably alteration of Middle English *rakel,* also *rackle* rough, hasty (perhaps influenced by *rake*¹ to search) + *hell*]

rake·hell·y (rāk′hel′ē), *adj.* profligate; dissolute; recklessly extravagant: *some idle squire, debauched page, or rakehelly archer from foreign parts* (Scott).

rake-off (rāk′ôf′, -of′), *n. U.S. Slang.* a share or portion, often an amount taken or received illicitly: *Her husband testified earlier that he was getting a rake-off on a dice game* (New York Times).

rak·er·y (rā′kər ē), *n., pl.* **-er·ies.** rakish conduct or practices; immorality: *He . . . instructed his Lordship in all the rakery and intrigues of the lewd town* (Roger North).

rake's progress, a downhill course: *Compared with my rake's progress of the first three weeks, this week has been exasperatingly slow* (Observer). [< *The Rake's Progress,* a series of engravings by the English artist William Hogarth, 1697-1764, showing the progressive deterioration of a rake]

ra·ki (rä kē′, rak′ē), *n.* an alcoholic liquor distilled from grain, or from grapes, plums, etc., flavored with anise, in southeastern Europe and the Near East: *By this time Uncle had raised his glass of raki and was heatedly toasting the officer and the United States of America* (Atlantic). [< Turkish *raki* brandy, spirits]

rak·ing (rā′king), *adj.* **1.** that rakes. **2.** sweeping lengthwise or from end to end.

rak·ish¹ (rā′kish), *adj.* **1.** smart; jaunty; dashing: *a hat set at a rakish angle.* **2.** suggesting dash and speed: *He owns a rakish boat.* —**rak′ish·ness,** *n.*

rak·ish² (rā′kish), *adj.* like a rake; immoral; dissolute. —**rak′ish·ness,** *n.* —**Syn.** licentious.

rak·ish·ly¹ (rā′kish lē), *adv.* jauntily.

rak·ish·ly² (rā′kish lē), *adv.* in a rakish or dissolute manner.

râle (räl), *n.* an abnormal crackling, whistling, or other sound accompanying the normal sounds of breathing, a symptom of certain pulmonary diseases: *Rehearsing over and over with strangled râle His latest breath* (New Yorker). [< French *râle* (originally) death rattle < *râler* to rattle < Old French *raler.* Compare RAIL³.]

rall., *Music.* rallentando.

ral·len·tan·do (räl′len tän′dō), *adj., n., pl.* **-dos.** *Music.* —*adj.* slackening; becoming slower. —*n.* a phrase or passage played or to be played in this manner: *He made a rather dubious rallentando in his solo* (London Times). [< Italian *rallentando* a slowing down, < *rallentare* to slow down < *lento* slow]

ral·li·er (ral′ē ər), *n.* a person who rallies.

ral·li·form (ral′ə fôrm), *adj.* (of birds) resembling the rails. [< New Latin *Rallus* the genus name + English *-form*]

ral·line (ral′īn, -in), *adj.* related to or resembling the rails. [< New Latin *Rallus* the genus name + English *-ine*[1]]

ral·ly[1] (ral′ē), *v.,* **-lied, -ly·ing,** *n., pl.* **-lies.** —*v.t.* **1.** to bring together; bring together again; get in order again: *The commander was able to rally the fleeing troops.* **2.** to pull together; revive: *He rallied all his energy for one last effort.* —*v.i.* **1.** to come together again; reassemble: *There is Jackson standing like a stone wall. Rally behind the Virginians* (Bernard E. Bee). **2.** to come together in a body for a common purpose or action: *The girls at the camp rallied to do the housework when the servants were sick.* **3.** to come to help a person, party, or cause: *He rallied to the side of his injured friend.* **4.** to recover health and strength: *The sick man may rally now.* **5.** to recover more or less from a drop in prices. **6.** to take part in a rally in tennis and similar games.

—*n.* **1.** the act of rallying; recovery. **2.** a coming together; mass meeting: *a political rally.* **3. a.** the act of hitting the ball back and forth several times in tennis and similar games: *Kershaw was now increasing his own pace of stroke which led to many long rallies* (London Times). **b.** an exchange or flurry of blows in a boxing match. **4.** a rise following a drop in prices: *a sudden rally in the grain market.* **5.** an automobile race: *The form of the rally has been altered since last year, in deference to the increasing restrictions placed on public-road motoring events by the authorities* (Sunday Times).

[< French *rallier* < *re-* again, re- + *allier* to ally]

—**Syn.** *v.t.* **2.** summon. *-n.* **1.** recuperation.

ral·ly[2] (ral′ē), *v.,* **-lied, -ly·ing.** —*v.t.* to make fun of; tease: *The boys rallied John on his short haircut.* —*v.i.* to indulge in teasing banter. [< French, Middle French *railler.* Doublet of RAIL[2].] —**ral′ly·ing·ly,** *adv.*

ral·ly·ing cry (ral′ē ing), a battle cry; war cry: *His voice was the rallying cry for thousands of workers-turned-saboteurs* (Harper's).

rallying point, a point or place at which to rally strength or resources: *She reached a rallying point in her fight against the disease.*

ral·ly·ist (ral′ē ist), *n.* a contestant in an automobile race.

ram (ram), *n., v.,* **rammed, ram·ming.** —*n.* **1.** a male sheep. **2.** a machine or part of a machine that strikes heavy blows, as the plunger of a force pump, the weight of a pile driver, or the piston of a hydraulic press: *The central part of the ram of the press (the "mandrel") pushes downwards and forces a hole right through the billet* (F. A. Fox). **3.** a beak at the bow of a warship, used to break through the sides of enemy ships. **4.** a ship with such a beak. **5.** a pump in which the force of a descending column of water raises some of the water above its original level. **6.** a battering ram: *The walls were forty feet in thickness and could neither be burnt nor driven in with the ram* (James A. Froude). [Old English *ramm*]

—*v.t.* **1.** to butt against; strike head on; strike violently: *One ship rammed the other ship. I rammed my head against the door in the dark.* **2.** to push hard; drive down or in by heavy blows as piles, etc. **3.** to cram, stuff, or thrust. **4.** to push (a charge) into a firearm or cannon, especially through the muzzle with a ramrod.

[Middle English *rammen* to tamp down earth, perhaps < *ram,* noun]

Ram (ram), *n.* Aries, a constellation and the first sign of the zodiac. [< *ram*]

R.A.M., **1.** Royal Academy of Music. **2.** Royal Arch Mason.

Ra·ma (rä′mə), *n.* the sixth, seventh, and eighth incarnations of Vishnu, as Balarama, Parashurama, and Ramachandra. [< Sanskrit *Rāma*]

Ra·ma·chan·dra (rä′mə chun′drə), *n.* the eighth incarnation of Vishnu. [< Sanskrit *Rāmacandra*]

Ram·a·dan (ram′ə dän′), *n.* **1.** the ninth month of the Moslem year, during which fasting is rigidly practiced daily from dawn until sunset. Because the Islamic calendar is based on lunar months Ramadan comes at different seasons. *The first two days of Ramadan are the hardest, Moslems say; after that, all-day fasting becomes a habit* (New Yorker). **2.** the fasting itself. [< Arabic *Ramaḍān* (originally) the hot month < *ramiḍa* he burnt, scorched]

ra·mal (rā′məl), *adj.* **1.** of or having to do with a branch or ramus: *A ramal leaf is one which is affixed directly to a branch* (Heber W. Youngken). **2.** like a branch or ramus.

Ra·man effect (rä′mən), the scattering of incident light by the molecules of a transparent substance, in such a way that the wavelengths of the scattered light are lengthened or shortened. [< Sir Chandrasekhara V. *Raman,* born 1888, an Indian physicist, who discovered it]

Ra·ma·pi·the·cus (rä′mə pith′ə kəs), *n.* a manlike primate, similar to Kenyapithecus, originally discovered in the Siwalik Hills of northwestern India. [< *Rama* + Greek *píthēkos* ape]

Ra·ma·ya·na (rä mä′yə nə), *n.* the second of the two great ancient epics of Hinduism with Ramachandra as its hero, written in Sanskrit probably early in the Christian era. [< Sanskrit *Rāmāyaṇa*]

Ram·a·zan (ram′ə zän′), *n.* Ramadan.

ram·ble (ram′bəl), *v.,* **-bled, -bling,** *n.* —*v.i.* **1.** to wander about: *We rambled here and there through the woods.* **2.** to talk or write about first one thing and then another with no useful connections. **3.** to spread irregularly in various directions: *Vines rambled over the wall.*

—*n.* a walk for pleasure, not to go to any special place: *One day . . . being on my rambles, I entered a green lane which I had never seen before* (George Borrow).

[origin uncertain. Apparently related to Middle English *romblen* to roam.]

—**Syn.** *v.i.* **1.** rove, range, meander. See **roam.**

ram·bler (ram′blər), *n.* **1.** a person or thing that rambles: *a rambler in the wood* (Thoreau). **2.** any of various climbing roses, especially the crimson rambler, an ornamental plant with clusters of bright-red flowers. **3.** *Informal.* a bungalow or ranch house.

ram·bling (ram′bling), *adj.* **1.** that rambles; wandering: *rambling roses.* **2.** straying from one subject to another: *a rambling speech.* **3.** that is a ramble: *a rambling walk.*

ram·bling·ly (ram′bling lē), *adv.* in a rambling manner: *. . . written in the author's characteristic, ramblingly effusive style, that sometimes seems like Ruskin and sherbet* (Manchester Guardian).

Ram·bouil·let (ram′bu̇ lā; *French* räN-bü ye′), *n.* a French merino sheep raised for wool and meat. [< *Rambouillet,* a town in France, famous for its sheep and wool]

ram·bunc·tious (ram bungk′shəs), *adj. U.S. Informal.* **1.** wild and uncontrollable; unruly: *Ever since she got out of college she's been too rambunctious to live with* (Sinclair Lewis). **2.** noisy and violent; boisterous: *The gay rambunctious story revolves around a happy-go-lucky boy and two pretty girls on a spree* (Times of India). [American English, earlier *rambustious,* perhaps < *ram,* verb + *robustious,* or variant of *bumptious*] —**ram·bunc′tious·ly,** *adv.* —**ram·bunc′tious·ness,** *n.*

ram·bu·tan (ram bü′tən), *n.* **1.** the bright-red, spiny, edible fruit of a Malayan tree of the soapberry family, having a pulp of a subacid flavor. **2.** the tree itself. [< Malay *rambutan* < *rambut* hair (because of its appearance) + *-an,* a derivative suffix]

ram·e·kin or **ram·e·quin** (ram′ə kin), *n.* **1.** a small, separately cooked portion of some food, especially one topped with cheese and bread crumbs. **2.** a small baking dish holding enough for one portion. [< French *ramequin,* perhaps < obsolete Dutch *rammeken* toasted bread, or < German *Rahm* cream]

ram·head (ram′hed′), *n.* **1.** part of the arm of a crane. **2.** a block for guiding the halyards of a ship.

ra·mi (rā′mī), *n.* plural of **ramus.**

ram·ie (ram′ē), *n.* **1.** a perennial, urticaceous Asiatic herb that yields a strong, lustrous fiber used in making textiles, etc. **2.** this fiber. [< Malay *rami* plant]

ram·i·fi·ca·tion (ram′ə fə kā′shən), *n.* **1.** a dividing or spreading out into branches or parts. **2.** an offshoot; branch; subdivision.

ram·i·form (ram′ə fôrm), *adj.* **1.** branchlike. **2.** branched: *a ramiform plant.* [< Latin *rāmus* branch + English *-form*]

ram·i·fy (ram′ə fī), *v.,* **-fied, -fy·ing.** —*v.i.* to divide or spread out into branchlike parts: *Quartz veins ramify through the rock in all directions* (F. Kingdon-Ward). —*v.t.* to cause to branch out. [< French, Old French *ramifier* < Medieval Latin *ramificari* < Latin *rāmus* branch + *facere* make]

ram·jet (ram′jet′), *n.* a type of jet engine in which the fuel is fed into air compressed by the speed of the airplane, guided missile, etc., in which it is contained. A ramjet must reach a speed of at least 300 miles an hour to operate efficiently. *The ramjet . . . is considered ideal for missiles or man-carrying planes operating at speeds between two and five times the speed of sound* (New York Times). [< *ram,* verb + *jet* (engine)]

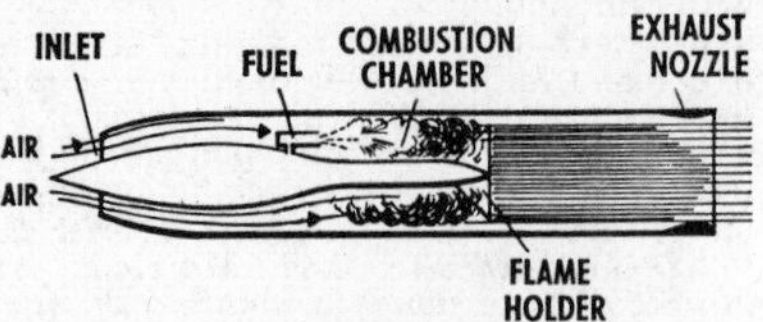

Ramjet
Air entering engine through inlet is compressed in combustion chamber by high forward speed. Fuel is fed into chamber and mixture is ignited, producing hot gases which expand through nozzle creating forward thrust.

ram·mer (ram′ər), *n.* a person or thing that rams.

ram·mish (ram′ish), *adj.* **1.** like a ram; rank in smell or taste. **2.** lustful.

ra·mose (rā′mōs, rə mōs′), *adj.* having many branches; branching. [< Latin *rāmōsus* < *rāmus* a branch]

ra·mous (rā′məs), *adj.* **1.** ramose. **2.** of or like a branch.

ramp[1] (ramp), *n.* a sloping way connecting two different levels of a building, road, etc.; slope. [< Middle French *rampe* < Old French *ramper;* see RAMP[2]]

Ramp[1]

ramp[2] (ramp), *v.i.* **1.** to rush wildly about; behave violently: *It is one thing to hear a lion in captivity . . . quite another . . . when he is ramping around . . . one's fragile tent* (J. H. Patterson). **2.** to jump or rush with fury. **3.** to stand on the hind legs; raise the forepaws in the air, as a lion in coats of arms. **4.** to take a threatening posture. —*n.* an act of ramping. [< Old French *ramper* to creep, climb < Germanic (compare Middle High German *rimpfen,* related to *rampf* cramp)]

ramp[3] (ramp), *n.* **1.** a kind of wild onion of eastern North America, related to the ramson, and having a strongly-flavored edible root: *Mountain folk traditionally gather ramps for festive occasions [in late April]* (New York Times). **2.** the ramson. [< earlier *ramps,* variant of *rams,* Old English *hramsa*]

ram·page (*n.* ram′pāj; *v.* ram pāj′, ram′pāj), *n., v.,* **-paged, -pag·ing.** —*n.* a fit of rushing wildly about; spell of violent behavior; wild outbreak: *The mad elephant went on a rampage and killed its keeper.* —*v.i.* to rush wildly about; behave violently; rage: *He could not lie still, but . . . raged and rampaged up and down his . . . bedroom* (George Du Maurier).

ram·pa·geous (ram pā′jəs), *adj.* violent; unruly; boisterous: *It is a dignified spectacle, and we shudder to think of the rampageous free for all* (Listener).

ram·pa·geous·ly (ram pā′jəs lē), *adv.* in a rampageous manner; wildly; violently.

ram·pa·geous·ness (ram pā′jəs nis), *n.* a rampageous manner.

ram·pag·ing (ram pā′jing, ram′pā-), *adj.* violent; rampageous: *These developments make an interesting counterpoint to the rampaging attacks on U.S. facilities* (Wall Street Journal).

ramp·an·cy (ram′pən sē), *n.* a being rampant.

ramp·ant (ram′pənt), *adj.* **1.** growing without any check: *The vines ran rampant over the fence.* **2.** passing beyond restraint or usual limits; unchecked: *Anarchy was rampant after the dictator died.* **3.** angry; excited; violent. **4.** *Heraldry.* standing up on the hind legs. **5.** (of animals) rearing. **6.** *Architecture.* (of an arch or vault) having

Rampant Lion (def. 4)

different levels of support for the two sides. [< Old French *rampant,* present participle of *ramper;* see RAMP[2]] —**Syn. 3.** furious, raging.

ramp·ant·ly (ram′pənt lē), *adv.* in a rampant manner.

ram·part (ram′pärt), *n.* **1.** a wide bank of earth, often with a wall on top, built around a fort to help defend it: *O'er the ramparts we watched . . .* (Francis Scott Key). **2.** anything that defends; defense; protection: *to strengthen the ramparts of freedom.* —*v.t.* to fortify or surround with, or as if with, a rampart: *Against our ramparted gates* (Shakespeare). [< Middle French *rempart* < *remparer* to fortify < *re-* (< Latin *re-* back) + *emparer* fortify, ultimately < Latin *ante* before + *parāre* to prepare] —**Syn.** *n.* **1.** embankment. **2.** bastion, bulwark.

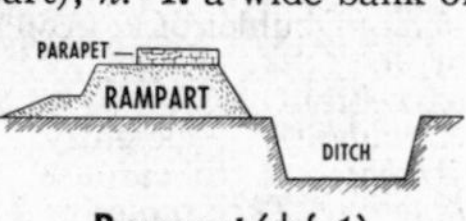

Rampart (def. 1)

ram·pi·on (ram′pē ən), *n.* **1.** a European bellflower, whose white, tuberous roots are sometimes used for salad. **2.** any of a group of blue-flowered plants of the bellflower family, native to Europe and parts of Asia [probably < a Romance form (ultimately diminutive) < Latin *rāpa* turnip]

ram·pire (ram′pīr), *n., v.t.,* **-pired, -pir·ing.** *Archaic.* rampart. [< Middle French *rampar,* variant of *rempart;* see RAMPART]

ram·rod (ram′rod′), *n., adj., v.,* **-rod·ded, -rod·ding.** —*n.* **1.** a rod for ramming down the charge in a gun that is loaded from the muzzle. **2.** a rod for cleaning the barrel of a gun. **3.** a stiff, unbending person. —*adj.* stiff; rigid; unbending: *He . . . walked ten times with ramrod dignity from the wings and bowed misty-eyed to the packed hall* (Time). —*v.t. Informal.* to push forward vigorously; ram (through): *to ramrod a bill through Congress.*

Ramrod (def. 1) used with Civil War gun

ram·shack·le (ram′shak′əl), *adj.* **1.** loose and shaky; likely to come apart: *With rare exceptions the buildings were old and ramshackle, and some were worse* (Time). **2.** weak; feeble: *. . . the whole ramshackle structure of federal taxes* (Theodore H. White). **3.** decadent: *He had also become an expert on the ramshackle politics of the Turkish empire* (Punch). [earlier *ramshackled,* variant of *ransackled* (ultimately frequentative) < *ransack*] —**Syn. 1.** rickety, dilapidated.

ram's horn, the shophar.

ram·son (ram′zən, -sən), *n.* a kind of garlic with broad leaves.
ramsons, the bulbous root of this plant, used as a relish: *There were little glass dishes of pickles, olives, and ramsons on the cocktail table.*
[Old English *hramsan* (originally) plural of *hramsa*]

ram·stam (ram′stam′), *Scottish.* —*adj.* impetuous; reckless: *The hairumscairum, ramstam boys* (Robert Burns). —*adv.* in a rush; precipitately: *The least we'll get, if we gang ramstam in on them will be a broken head* (Scott). [perhaps < *ram* + dialectal *stam* to stamp]

ram·til (ram′təl), *n.* a composite African plant cultivated in India and parts of Africa for the oil produced from its seeds. [< Hindi *rāmtīl* < Sanskrit *Rāma* Rama + *tila* sesame seed]

ram·u·lose (ram′yə lōs), *adj.* having many small branches. [< Latin *rāmulōsus* < *rāmulus* (diminutive) < *rāmus* branch]

ram·u·lous (ram′yə ləs), *adj.* ramulose.

ra·mus (rā′məs), *n., pl.* **-mi** (-mī). a branch, as of a plant, a vein, or a bone. [< Latin *rāmus* branch]

ran (ran), *v.* the past tense of **run.**

Ran (rän), *n. Norse Mythology.* a sea goddess who caught drowning men in her net.

rance (rans), *n.* a red Belgian marble with blue and white veins. [probably < Middle French *rance*]

ranch (ranch), *n.* **1.** a very large farm and its buildings. Many ranches are for raising cattle. **2.** a farm: *a chicken ranch, a fruit ranch.* **3.** the persons working or living on a ranch: *The entire ranch was at the party.*
—*v.i.* to work on a ranch; manage a ranch.
[American English < American Spanish *rancho* small farm, group of farm huts < Spanish, (originally) group of persons who eat together < Old High German *hring* circle, assembly]

ranch·er (ran′chər), *n.* a person who owns, manages, or works on a ranch.

ran·che·ri·a (ran′chə rē′ə), *n.* (in Spanish America and southwestern U.S.) a group of ranchos or rude huts for Indians or rancheros. [American English < Spanish *ranchería* < *rancho;* see RANCH]

ran·che·ro (ran chãr′ō, rän-), *n., pl.* **-ros. 1.** a rancher. **2.** a herdsman on a ranch. [American English < American Spanish *ranchero* < *rancho;* see RANCH]

ranch house, 1. the main house on a ranch, in which the owner or manager and his family live. **2.** a one-story dwelling, like most houses on a ranch, having a low roof.

ranch·man (ranch′man′), *n., pl.* **-men.** a rancher.

ran·cho (ran′chō, rän′-), *n., pl.* **-chos.** in Spanish America: **1.** a ranch. **2.** a rude hut or group of huts for herdsmen or laborers: *I put up for the night at the solitary mud rancho of an old herdsman* (W.H. Hudson). [American English < American Spanish *rancho;* see RANCH]

ran·cid (ran′sid), *adj.* **1.** stale; spoiled: *rancid fat.* **2.** tasting or smelling like stale fat or butter: *rancid fumes.* **3.** nasty; disagreeable; odious: *He's a rancid fellow* (Robert Louis Stevenson). [< Latin *rancidus* < *rancēre* be rank]

ran·cid·i·ty (ran sid′ə tē), *n.* rancid quality.

ran·cid·ly (ran′sid lē), *adv.* with a rancid odor; mustily.

ran·cid·ness (ran′sid nis), *n.* rancid quality or condition.

ran·cor (rang′kər), *n.* bitter resentment or ill will; extreme hatred or spite: *This silly affair . . . greatly increased his rancor against me* (Benjamin Franklin). [< Old French *rancour,* and *rancor,* learned borrowings < Late Latin *rancor* rankness < Latin *rancēre* be rank] —**Syn.** malice, animosity.

ran·cor·ous (rang′kər əs), *adj.* spiteful; bitterly malicious: *a rancorous old man.*

ran·cor·ous·ly (rang′kər əs lē), *adv.* with spiteful malice or vindictiveness.

ran·cor·ous·ness (rang′kər əs nis), *n.* spitefulness; vindictiveness.

ran·cour (rang′kər), *n. Especially British.* rancor.

rand[1] (rand), *n.* **1.** a strip of leather for leveling, set in a shoe at the heel before the lifts are attached. **2.** *British Dialect.* **a.** a border or margin, as of unplowed land around a field. **b.** a strip of meat. [Old English *rand* border, margin]

Rand or **rand**[2] (rand), *n.* a South African unit of money, worth about $1.40. [< Afrikaans *rand* < Dutch, field border]

ran·dan[1] (ran′dan, ran dan′), *n. British Dialect.* disorderly behavior; a spree. [perhaps variant of Middle English *randun;* see RANDOM]

ran·dan[2] (ran′dan, ran dan′), *n.* **1.** a style of rowing in which the middle one of three rowers in a boat uses a pair of sculls and the other two use one oar each. **2.** a boat for such rowing. [origin uncertain]

R & B or **R and B** (no periods), rhythm and blues.

R & D (no periods), research and development.

ran·dem (ran′dəm), *adv.* with three horses harnessed tandem. —*n.* a carriage or a team driven randem. [probably < *tandem;* form influenced by *random*]

ran·dom (ran′dəm), *adj.* by chance; with no plan; casual: *random sampling. John was not listening and made a random answer to the teacher's question. Cancer is brought about through a random mutation or change in the character of body cells* (Observer).
—*n.* **at random,** by chance; with no plan or purpose: *Alice took a book at random from the shelf. Laurence had chosen these illustrations . . . quite at random* (William H. Mallock).
[Middle English *randun* impetuosity, speed < Old French *randon* rapid rush, disorder, perhaps < Germanic (compare Old High German *rant*)]
—**Syn.** *adj.* **Random, haphazard** mean made, done, happening, or coming by chance, not plan. **Random** implies being without definite aim, direction, purpose, or plan: *His random guess at the number of beans in the jar won the prize.* **Haphazard** implies being determined by chance, not by plan or aim: *Because of her haphazard way of buying clothes, she never looks well dressed.*

random access, access to the memory of a computer in which each successive source of information is chosen at random and independent of the location of previous sources.

ran·dom·i·za·tion (ran′də mə zā′shən), *n.* **1.** the act or process of randomizing: *If the cards are dealt at random, any further randomization through the use of mixed strategies by the players is superfluous* (Scientific American). **2.** the state of being randomized.

ran·dom·ize (ran′də mīz), *v.t.,* **-ized, -iz·ing.** to put, take, or perform at random to eliminate or lessen bias or other subjective limitations, or to control the variables of a scientific experiment, statistical procedure, etc.

ran·dom·ly (ran′dəm lē), *adv.* in a random manner: *We moved on randomly, befuddled by a dim nostalgia for Old Meldrum and kindred spots* (New Yorker).

ran·dom·ness (ran′dəm nis), *n.* random quality or condition: [*Einstein*] *declared that randomness rather than lawfulness is the fundamental characteristic of natural events* (Saturday Review).

random sample, *Statistics.* a sample consisting of items drawn independently from the total group and therefore likely to have the various elements in the same proportion as in the total group: *In economic and social studies it is difficult to apply the mechanical methods necessary to obtain a random sample* (Croxton and Cowden). *In theory, a random sample gives each case in the universe an equal chance of being included* (World Book Encyclopedia).

R and R (no periods), *U.S. Military.* rest and recreation: *The two . . . doughboys were flown to Tokyo together for a few unworried, unregimented . . . days of R and R* (Newsweek).

rand·y (ran′dē), *adj., n., pl.* **rand·ies.** *Scottish.* —*adj.* boisterous; coarse; disorderly: *Maire John herself was a randy old lady who would have delighted Apuleius in the days of silver Latin* (New Yorker). —*n.* **1.** a rude beggar; rough tramp. **2.** a virago. [probably < dialectal *rand,* variant of *rant* + *-y*[1]]

ra·nee (rä′nē), *n.* **1.** the wife of a rajah. **2.** a ruling Hindu queen or princess. Also, **rani.** [< Hindi *rāṇī* < Sanskrit *rājñī*]

rang (rang), *v.* a past tense of **ring**[2]: *The telephone rang.*

ran·ga·ti·ra (ran′gə tir′ə), *n.* **1.** a Maori chief. **2.** a Maori master or mistress. [< Maori *rangatira*]

range (rānj), *n., v.,* **ranged, rang·ing,** *adj.* —*n.* **1.** the distance between certain limits; extent: *a range of prices from 5 cents to 25 dollars, range of vision, a limited range of ideas.* **2. a.** the distance a gun, projectile, etc., can operate: *to be within range of the enemy.* **b.** the distance from a gun, etc., of an object aimed at: *to set the sights of a cannon for a range of 1,000 yards.* **3.** the greatest distance an aircraft, rocket, or the like, can travel on a single load of fuel. **4.** a place to practice shooting, bombing, etc.: *a rifle range, a missile range.* **5.** land for grazing. **6.** the act of wandering or moving about. **7.** a row or line of mountains: *the Green Mountain range of the Applachian system.* **8.** a row; line: *. . . ranges of books in perfect order* (George Eliot). **9.** a line of direction: *The two barns are in direct range with the house.* **10.** rank, class, or order: *The cohesion of the nation was greatest in the lowest ranges* (William Stubbs). **11.** the district in which certain plants or animals live: *the reindeer, who is even less Arctic in his range than the musk ox* (Elisha K. Kane). **12.** a stove for cooking: *a gas range, a coal range.* **13.** *Statistics.* the difference between the smallest and the greatest values which a variable bears in frequency distribution: *The range of this variation is unusually small.* **14.** *U.S.* a row of townships, each six miles square, between two meridians six miles apart: *A real ghost roams about township 14, range 15* (Neepawa, Manitoba, Star). **15.** *Surveying.* a line extended so as to intersect a transit line. **16.** the part of an animal hide near the tail. [probably < verb]

—*v.i.* **1.** to vary within certain limits: *prices ranging from $5 to $10.* **2.** to wander; rove; roam: *to range through the woods. Their talk ranged over matters of mutual interest.* **3.** to run in a line; extend: *a boundary ranging from east to west.* **4.** to be found; occur: *a plant ranging from Canada to Mexico.* **5.** to have a particular range. **6.** to find the distance or direction of something. **7.** to search an area: *The eye ranged over an immense extent of wilderness* (Washington Irving).

—*v.t.* **1.** to wander over: *Buffalo once ranged these plains.* **2.** to put in a row or rows: *Range the books by size.* **3.** to put in groups or classes; classify. **4.** to put in a line on someone's side: *Loyal citizens ranged themselves with the government.* **5.** to make straight or even: *to range lines of type.* **6.** to direct (a telescope) upon an object; train. **7. a.** to find the proper elevation for (a gun). **b.** to give the proper elevation to (a gun).

—*adj.* of or on land for grazing: *a range pony, range cattle.*

[< Old French *ranger* to array < *rang;* see RANK[1]]

—**Syn.** *n.* **1. Range, scope, compass** mean the extent of what something can do or take in. **Range** emphasizes the extent (and variety) that can be covered or taken in by something in operation or action, such as the mind, the eye, a machine, or a force: *The car was out of his range of vision.* **Scope** emphasizes the limits beyond which the understanding, view, application, etc., cannot extend: *Some technical terms are beyond the scope of this dictionary.* **Compass** emphasizes the limits within which something can act or operate: *Geographical names are within the compass of many dictionaries.* **8.** series.

range finder, an instrument for estimating the range or distance of an object: *This superb 35mm camera has lens-coupled range finder combined with view finder* (Time).

range·find·ing (rānj′fīn′ding), *n.* the act or process of estimating the range or distance of an object, as by a range finder: *There has been a great deal of speculation in the USA about the possibilities of using the laser for rangefinding, particularly in space* (New Scientist).

range·land (rānj′land′), *n.* land for grazing; range: *Less than five percent of the rain running off southwestern rangelands ever reaches a point downstream where it can be put to use* (Science News Letter).

rang·er (rān′jər), *n.* **1.** a person employed to guard a tract of forest: *Rangers also patrol roads in remote ranges towing a horse trailer so that they can take to horseback if necessary* (Newsweek). **2.** Also, **Ranger.** one of a body of armed men employed in ranging over a region to police it: *. . . the [Texas] Rangers, the oldest police force in the U.S. with statewide jurisdiction* (Newsweek). **3.** Also, **Ranger.** a soldier in the United States Army in World War II trained for raids and surprise attacks; commando. **4.** a person or thing that ranges; rover. **5.** *British.* the official title of the keeper of a royal park or forest: *The Ancient Order of Foresters Friendly Society has elected Mr. G. S. Bridger, of Southsea, as high chief ranger for the coming year* (London Times).

rang·er·ship (rān′jər ship), *n.* the office of ranger or keeper of a forest or park.

rang·i·ness (rān′jē nis), *n.* the quality or condition of being rangy.

rang·y (rān′jē), *adj.,* **rang·i·er, rang·i·est. 1.** fitted for ranging or moving about: *The ponies . . . used for circle-riding in the morning have need to be strong and rangy* (Theodore Roosevelt). **2.** slender and long-limbed: *a rangy horse.* **3.** (in Australia) mountainous.

ra·ni (rä′nē), *n.* ranee.

rank[1] (rangk), *n.* **1.** a row or line, especially of soldiers, placed side by side: *The Tuscan army . . . Rank behind rank* (Macaulay). **2.** position; grade; class: *the rank of colonel. Los Angeles is a city of high rank. A zoo contains animals of all ranks.* **3.** high position: *Dukes and generals are men of rank.* **4.** orderly arrangement or array: *to break rank.* **5.** (in chess and checkers) a straight line of squares parallel to the king row.

pull rank, *Especially U.S.* to use one's position to gain something: *The young lieutenant was bossy and always pulling rank.*

ranks, a. an army; soldiers: *An advance party of 26 officers and 144 other ranks would sail from Sydney to Penang* (London Times). **b.** the rank and file: *He regarded himself as a man in the ranks, the member of an awkward squad* (Graham Greene).

—*v.t.* **1.** to arrange in a row or line. **2.** to put in some special order in a list; classify: *Rank the States in the order of size.* **3.** *U.S.* to be more important than; outrank: *A major ranks a captain.* —*v.i.* **1.** to take or have a certain rank or position: *Bill ranked low in the test. New York State ranks first in wealth.* **2.** to form a rank or ranks; stand in rank. **3.** *U.S.* to be the highest in rank or standing.

[< Old French *rang,* earlier *reng* < Germanic (compare Old High German *hring* circle, ring). Compare RANCH.]

—**Syn.** *n.* **2.** standing, status, station. **3.** eminence, distinction.

rank[2] (rangk), *adj.* **1.** large and coarse: *rank grass.* **2.** growing richly: *a rank growth of weeds.* **3.** producing a dense but coarse growth: *rank swampland.* **4.** having a strong, bad smell or taste: *rank meat. A rank cigar of the sort that they sell to students* (Rudyard Kipling). **5.** strongly marked; extreme: *rank ingratitude, rank nonsense.* **6.** coarse; indecent. **7.** *Especially Law.* high or excessive in amount. [Middle English *ranke* luxuriant, vigorous, Old English *ranc* proud, overweening; full grown] —**rank′ly,** *adv.* —**rank′ness,** *n.* —**Syn. 4.** rancid. **5.** flagrant, absolute. **6.** obscene.

rank and file, 1. a. common soldiers, not officers. **b.** the people in a business, labor union, political party, etc., who are not a part of the management: *This sudden flurry of costly strikes points to a weakness in Britain's labor union structure which so often finds the leaders being flouted by the rank and file* (New York Times). **2.** the common people. —**rank′-and-file′,** *adj.*

rank and filer, a member of the rank and file: *Management and union rank and filers alike had hoped Congress would act swiftly* (Newsweek).

rank·er (rang′kər), *n.* **1.** *Informal.* a person who ranks. **2.** a soldier in the ranks: *Gentlemen-rankers out on the spree, Damned from hell to Eternity* (Rudyard Kipling). **3.** an officer promoted from the ranks. [< *rank*[1] + *-er*[1]]

Ran·kine cycle (rang′kən), *Thermodynamics.* a kind of Carnot cycle, used as a standard of thermal efficiency. It comprises the introduction of water by pump, evaporation, adiabatic expansion, and condensation. [< William J.M. *Rankine,* 1820-1872, a Scottish scientist and engineer]

Rankine scale, a scale in which temperatures are measured as 460 degrees plus the Fahrenheit value, absolute zero being minus 460 degrees Fahrenheit.

rank·ing (rang′king), *n.* a standing: *He has a poor ranking in his class. Stirling Moss, No. 2 driver in the world rankings . . .* (Atlantic). —*adj.* leading; foremost: *He was the ranking U.S. Senator, and as the Senate's president pro tem he stood fourth in line of succession to the presidency* (Time). [< *rank*[1] + *-ing*[1]]

ran·kle (rang′kəl), *v.,* **-kled, -kling.** —*v.i.* to be sore; cause soreness; continue to give pain: *The memory of the insult rankled in his mind. The blister rankled as he walked.* —*v.t.* to cause pain or soreness in or to. [< Old French *rancler,* also *draoncler* < *draoncle* a festering sore, learned borrowing from Medieval Latin *dracunculus* sore, ulcer, apparently (diminutive) < Latin *dracō, -ōnis* serpent, dragon < Greek *drákōn, -ontos*]

ranks (rangks), *n.pl.* See under **rank**[1], *n.*

ran·sack (ran′sak), *v.t.* **1.** to search thoroughly through: *The thief ransacked the house for jewelry.* **2.** to rob; plunder: *to ransack a defeated country of works of art.* [< Scandinavian (compare Old Icelandic *rannsaka* search a house < *rann* house + *-saka* search)] —**ran′sack·er,** *n.* —**Syn. 1.** rummage. **2.** pillage.

ran·som (ran′səm), *n.* **1.** the redemption of a prisoner, slave, captured goods, etc., for a price. **2.** the price paid or demanded before a captive is set free: *The robber chief held the travelers prisoners for ransom.* **3.** a means of delivering or rescuing, as from sin or its consequences: *Even the Son of man came . . . to give his life for a ransom for many* (Mark 10:45).

—*v.t.* **1.** to obtain the release of (a captive) by paying a price: *O come, O come, Emmanuel, And ransom captive Israel* (J.M. Neale). **2.** to redeem or deliver, especially from sin or ignorance: *Poor sick people, richer in His eyes who ransomed us . . . than I* (Tennyson). **3.** to release upon payment. **4.** to hold for ransom; demand a ransom for.

[Middle English *ranscun* < Old French *rançon,* earlier *raençon* < Latin *redemptiō, -ōnis.* Doublet of REDEMPTION.] —**ran′som·er,** *n.*

rant (rant), *v.i.* **1.** to speak wildly, extravagantly, violently, or noisily. **2.** *Archaic.* **a.** to carouse: *Wi' quaffing and laughing, They ranted and they sang* (Robert Burns). **b.** to lead a dissolute life.

rant and rave, to scold violently: *Rant and rave as he might, the children blithely went on with their playing.*

—*n.* **1. a.** an extravagant, violent, or noisy speech: *Madly enough he preached . . . with imperfect utterance, amid much frothy rant* (Thomas Carlyle). **b.** ranting words: *He sometimes . . . in his rants talked with Norman haughtiness of the Celtic barbarians* (Macaulay). **2.** *Scottish.* a noisy spree.

[< earlier Dutch *ranten*] —**rant′er,** *n.* —**rant′ing·ly,** *adv.*

—**Syn.** *v.i.* **1.** declaim, rave.

rant·i·pole (ran′tə pōl), *n., adj., v.,* **-poled, -pol·ing.** —*n.* **1.** a rude, romping boy or girl. **2.** a boisterous, wild fellow. **3.** a termagant. —*adj.* boisterous; riotous; wild: *This rantipole hero had . . . singled out the blooming Katrina for the object of his uncouth gallantries* (Washington Irving).

—*v.i.* to romp rudely; act in a boisterous, wild fashion.

[apparently < *ranty* + *poll*[1] head]

rant·y (ran′tē), *adj. British Dialect.* **1.** raving or wild with passion, anger, pain, etc. **2.** lively, boisterous, or riotous. [< *rant* + *-y*[1]]

ra·nun·cu·la·ceous (rə nung′kyə lā′shəs), *adj.* belonging to the crowfoot family: *Aconite, anemone, hepatica, columbine, larkspur, and peony are ranunculaceous plants.* [< New Latin *Ranunculaceae* the family name (< Latin *rānunculus* ranunculus) + English *-ous*]

ra·nun·cu·lus (rə nung′kyə ləs), *n., pl.* **-lus·es, -li** (-lī). any plant of a large and widely distributed group of herbs, with divided leaves and five-petaled flowers; buttercup. [< Latin *rānunculus* a medicinal plant; (originally) small frog < *rāna* frog (because of the shape)]

Ranunculus (buttercup)

ranz des vaches (räNz′ dā vâsh′, räN′), *French, Music.* a Swiss herdsman's call to lead cattle to higher pastures.

R.A.O.C., Royal Army Ordnance Corps (of Great Britain).

Ra·oult's law (rä üls′), *Chemistry.* the statement or principle that the vapor pressure of a substance in solution is proportional to the molecular weight of the substance expressed in grams. [< François M. *Raoult,* 1830-1901, a French chemist]

rap[1] (rap), *n., v.,* **rapped, rap·ping.** —*n.* **1.** a quick, light blow: *a rap on the head.* **2.** a light, sharp knock: *Did I just hear a rap on the door?* **3.** a sound, as of knocking, ascribed to spirits. **4.** *U.S. Slang.* **a.** blame; rebuke: *He who has the bad taste to meddle with the caprices of believers . . . gets the rap and the orders of dismissal* (Atlantic). **b.** conviction; prison sentence: *He was either a big-shot bootlegger or a crook whom the government had had to prosecute for income-tax evasion because it could not hang a murder rap on him* (Harper's).

beat the rap, *U.S. Slang.* to escape conviction or prison sentence: *He almost beat the conspiracy rap when he was charged with forgery.*

take the rap, *U.S. Slang.* to pay the penalty; take the blame: *History shows when the economy is down, the party in power takes the rap* (Wall Street Journal).

—*v.i.* to knock sharply; tap: *to rap on a door. The chairman rapped on the table for order.*

—*v.t.* **1.** to strike sharply on: *She rapped him over the knuckles with her fan* (Tobias Smollett). **2.** *U.S. Slang.* to rebuke; criticize; condemn: *The chairman rapped the Cuban delegate for naming names* (Newsweek). **3.** to answer (a spiritual medium) by raps. **4.** *Obsolete.* to affect with joy: *What, dear sir, Thus raps you* (Shakespeare).

rap out, to say sharply: *Adams then rapped out a hundred Greek verses* (Henry Fielding). [probably imitative]

rap[2] (rap), *n.* **1.** *Informal.* the least bit: *I don't care a rap.* **2. a.** a counterfeit coin, formerly used in Ireland for a halfpenny. **b.** a coin of the smallest value, or the smallest amount of money: *Here is my hand to you with all my heart; but of money, not one rap* (Robert Louis Stevenson). [origin uncertain. Compare obsolete German *Rappen* a coin.]

rap[3] (rap), *v.t.,* **rapped** or **rapt, rap·ping.** *Archaic.* **1.** to enrapture. **2.** to carry off. **3.** to seize; steal. [(definition 1) < *rapt,* adjective; (definition 2) perhaps related to dialectal German *rappen* to hasten]

ra·pa·cious (rə pā′shəs), *adj.* **1.** seizing by force; plundering: *rapacious pirates.* **2.** grasping; greedy: *a rapacious miser.* **3.** (of animals) living by the capture of prey. [< Latin *rapāx, -ācis* (with English *-ous*) grasping < *rapere* to seize] **—ra·pa′cious·ly,** *adv.* **—ra·pa′cious·ness,** *n.* **—Syn. 2.** avaricious. **3.** predatory.

ra·pac·i·ty (rə pas′ə tē), *n.* a rapacious spirit, action, or practice; greed: *the rapacity of the great claimants of lands who held seats in the council* (George Bancroft). **—Syn.** voracity, cupidity, covetousness.

rape[1] (rāp), *n., v.,* **raped, rap·ing.** **—*n.*** **1.** a seizing and carrying off by force. **2.** the crime of having sexual intercourse with a woman or girl forcibly and against her will. **3.** any violent seizure or hostile action against a weaker opponent: *The Rape of the Lock* (Alexander Pope). *Hitherto our attitude to this illegality has been unpleasantly reminiscent of Mr. Neville Chamberlain's comment on Hitler's rape of Czechoslovakia* (London Times). [< verb]
—*v.t., v.i.* **1.** to seize and carry off by force. **2.** to force (a woman or girl) to have sexual intercourse against her will. **3.** to rob or plunder: *I raped your richest roadstead, I plundered Singapore* (Rudyard Kipling).
[< Latin *rapere* to seize, lift]

rape[2] (rāp), *n.* a small European plant of the mustard family, whose leaves are used as food for sheep and hogs. The seeds of the rape yield an oil that is used as a lubricant, etc. [< Latin *rāpa,* and *rāpum* turnip]

rape[3] (rāp), *n.* the refuse of grapes after the juice has been pressed out. [< French *râpe* < Old French, grater < Medieval Latin *raspa,* perhaps < Germanic (compare Old High German *raspōn* to grate)]

rape[4] (rāp), *n.* one of the six divisions of the county of Sussex, England, intermediate between a hundred and the shire. [Middle English *rape;* origin unknown]

rape oil, a brownish-yellow oil obtained from the rapeseed, used chiefly as a lubricant and in the manufacture of soap and rubber; colza oil. [< *rape*[2]]

rape·seed (rāp′sēd′), *n.* **1.** the seed of rape. **2.** the plant.

rapeseed oil, rape oil.

Raph·a·el (raf′ē əl, rā′fē-), *n.* (in Hebrew and Christian tradition) one of the archangels; the healing angel. [ultimately < Greek *Rhaphaēl* < Hebrew *Rәfā'ēl* (literally) God healed]

ra·phe (rā′fē), *n.* **1.** *Anatomy.* a seamlike union between two parts of an organ of the body. **2.** *Botany.* **a.** (in certain ovules) the vascular tissue connecting the hilum with the chalaza. **b.** a median line or rib on a valve of a diatom. [< New Latin *raphe* < Greek *rhaphḗ* suture, seam; thing sewn < *rhaphís, -ídos* needle < *rháptein* to stitch, sew. Compare RHAPSODY.]

ra·phi·a (rā′fē ə), *n.* raffia.

raph·i·des (raf′ə dēz), *n. pl. of* **raphis.** minute needle-shaped crystals of calcium oxalate, that occur in the cells of many plants. [< New Latin *raphides* < Greek *rhaphís, -idos* a needle; see RAPHE]

raph·is (raf′is), *n.* one of the raphides.

rap·id (rap′id), *adj.* **1.** moving, acting, or doing with speed; quick; swift: *a rapid walk, a rapid worker.* **2.** going on or forward at a fast rate: *rapid growth, rapid development.* **3.** fairly steep: *a rapid slope.* **4.** arranged for brief exposures to light: *a rapid film.*
—*n.* **rapids,** a part of a river's course where the water rushes quickly: *Most hair-raising future project: A trip on the rapids of the Colorado River* (Newsweek).
[< Latin *rapidus* < *rapere* to hurry away; seize]
—Syn. *adj.* **1.** fleet, speedy. See **quick.**

rap·id-fire (rap′id fīr′), *adj.* **1.** firing shots in quick succession. **2.** ready and quick; occurring in quick succession: *rapid-fire remarks, rapid-fire commands, rapid-fire wit.*

rap·id-fir·er (rap′id fīr′ər), *n.* a rapid-fire gun.

rap·id-fir·ing (rap′id fīr′ing), *adj.* rapidfire.

ra·pid·i·ty (rə pid′ə tē), *n.* quickness; swiftness; speed.

rap·id·ly (rap′id lē), *adv.* swiftly; quickly.

rap·id·ness (rap′id nis), *n.* rapid condition; a rapid action.

ra·pi·do (rä′pē dō), *n., pl.* **-dos.** (in Italy, Spain, and Latin America) an express train. [< Italian *rapido,* Spanish *rápido* (literally) rapid]

rap·ids (rap′idz), *n.pl.* See under **rapid,** *n.*

rapid transit, 1. subway or elevated railroad, in or near a city. **2.** lightning chess.

ra·pi·er (rā′pē ər), *n.* a light sword used for thrusting. [< Middle French *rapière* < Old French *rapiere,* adjective < *râpe* a grater, rasp (because of its perforated guard)]

Rapier

ra·pi·er·like (rā′pē ər līk′), *adj.* sharp; keen: *a rapierlike edge, rapierlike wit.*

rap·ine (rap′in), *n.* a robbing by force and carrying off; plundering: *The soldiers in the enemy's land got their food by rapine.* [< Latin *rapīna* < *rapere* to seize, hurry off]

rap·ist (rā′pist), *n.* a person who is guilty of rape.

rap·loch (rap′lōʜ), *Scottish.* **—*n.*** a coarse, undyed, homespun woolen. **—*adj.*** coarse; rough; homely: *Tho' rough an' raploch be her measure, She's seldom lazy* (Robert Burns).

rap·pa·ree (rap′ə rē′), *n.* **1.** an Irish freebooter, especially of the late 1600's. **2.** a robber. [< Irish *rapaire* (originally) short pike; later, the wielder of the pike]

rap·pee (ra pē′), *n.* a strong snuff made from the darker and ranker kinds of tobacco leaves. [< French *(tabac) râpé* (literally) grated (tobacco) < Old French *râpe;* see RAPE[3]]

rap·pel[1] (ra pel′), *n.* the roll or beat of the drum to call soldiers to arms. [< French *rappel* < *rappeler* to recall; see REPEAL]

rap·pel[2] (ra pel′), *v.i.,* **-pelled, -pel·ling.** (in mountain climbing) to descend a very steep cliff on a rope by means of short, swinging drops, the rope being secured at the summit, passed between the legs, across the chest, and over the shoulder of the person, the other end hanging free. [< French *rappeler;* see REPEAL]

rap·pen (rap′ən), *n., pl.* **-pen. 1.** the Swiss centime. **2.** a coin worth one rappen: *As a boy, my father earned a few rappen by carrying hot lunches to workers in a nearby factory* (New Yorker). [< German *rappen* < Middle High German *rappe* a coin with the head of a bird on it < *rappe, rabe* raven]

rap·per (rap′ər), *n.* **1.** a person who raps, especially as a means of communication, in a séance. **2.** a door knocker. [< *rap*[1] + *-er*[1]]

Rapp·ite (rap′īt), *n.* a member of the Harmonists. [< George *Rapp,* 1757-1847, the leader of the Harmonists + *-ite*[1]]

rap·port (ra pôrt′, -pōrt′; *French* rȧ pôr′), *n.* **1.** relation; connection: *Some time might be necessary before sufficient rapport ... is built up between observer and observed* (Anthony H. Richmond). **2.** agreement; harmony: *the rapport of close friends.* [< French *rapport* < *rapporter* bring back < *re-* again, re- + *apporter* < Latin *adportāre* bring < *ad-* to + *portāre* carry]

rap·por·tage (rȧ pôr täzh′), *n. French.* reportage: *Sometimes the article is analytical; sometimes ... it can best be described as rapportage with comment* (London Times).

rap·por·teur (rȧ pôr tœr′), *n. French.* **1.** a reporter; recorder: *Mr. Goullart is a most delightful rapporteur and the reader remains spellbound* (Saturday Review). **2.** a member of a legislative, military, or other official group, appointed to make or draw up a report: *Three rapporteurs were appointed to summarize the work of the conference and look into the possibility of a second meeting* (Bulletin of Atomic Scientists).

rap·proche·ment (rȧ prôsh mäɴ′), *n.* the establishment or renewal of friendly relations: *Such a rapprochement of the reformed and evangelical churches would carry one stage farther the cause of Christian unity* (London Times). [< French *rapprochement* < *rapprocher* bring near < *re-* re- + Old French *aprochier* to approach] **—Syn.** reconciliation.

rap·scal·lion (rap skal′yən), *n.* a rascal; rogue; scamp: *A set of ferocious-looking rapscallions had boarded the steamer* (James Runciman). Also, **rascallion.** [earlier *rascallion* < *rascal*]

rapt (rapt), *adj.* **1.** lost in delight: *rapt with joy.* **2.** so busy thinking of or enjoying one thing that one does not know what else is happening: *Rapt in his task he did not hear the footsteps approaching.* **3.** carried away in body or spirit from earth, life, or ordinary affairs: *Rapt into future times, the bard begun* (Alexander Pope). **4.** showing a rapt condition; caused by a rapt condition: *a rapt smile. The girls listened to the story with rapt attention.*
—*v.* a past tense and past participle of **rap**[3].
[< Latin *raptus,* past participle of *rapere* seize]
—Syn. *adj.* **1.** enraptured, ecstatic. **2.** engrossed, spellbound, absorbed. **3.** transported.

rapt·ly (rapt′lē), *adv.* rapturously: *At this point, even now, the narrator's eyes strain toward the screen as he raptly awaits once again the great moment* (New Yorker).

rapt·ness (rapt′nis), *n.* rapt condition.

rap·tor (rap′tər, -tôr), *n.* any raptorial bird; a bird of prey: *Some raptors never attack birds, others only occasionally* (W.H. Hudson). [< Latin *raptor;* see RAPTORIAL]

rap·to·ri·al (rap tôr′ē əl, -tōr′-), *adj.* **1.** adapted for seizing prey; having a hooked beak and sharp claws suited for seizing prey. **2.** belonging to or having to do with birds of prey, such as the eagles, hawks, etc. [< Latin *raptor, -ōris* robber (< *rapere* to seize) + English *-al*[1]]

rap·ture (rap′chər), *n., v.,* **-tured, -tur·ing.** **—*n.*** **1.** a strong feeling that absorbs the mind; very great joy: *The mother gazed with rapture at her long-lost son.* **2.** Often, **raptures.** an expression of great joy. **3.** *Obsolete.* a carrying or transporting.
—*v.t.* to enrapture.
[< *rapt;* patterned on *capture*]
—Syn. *n.* **1. Rapture, ecstasy** mean a feeling of being lifted high in mind and spirits. **Rapture** implies great happiness and perfect joy, but often suggests being filled with it rather than being excited by it: *In rapture the child listened to the talking doll.* **Ecstasy** implies being overwhelmed or carried away in almost a trance by great joy (or sometimes another strong emotion): *Sue's ecstasy was unbounded when Bob asked to marry her.*

rapture of the deep, nitrogen narcosis: *Skin divers are subject to everything from cramps to rapture of the deep* (New Yorker).

rapture of the depths, rapture of the deep: *Scuba divers, breathing oxygen at great depths beneath the sea, have experienced ... rapture of the depths* (New York Times).

rap·tur·ous (rap′chər əs), *adj.* full of rapture; expressing or feeling rapture. **—Syn.** ecstatic, blissful, transported.

rap·tur·ous·ly (rap′chər əs lē), *adv.* with rapture; ecstatically.

rap·tur·ous·ness (rap′chər əs nis), *n.* the state of being rapturous.

rap·tus (rap′təs), *n.* rapturous emotion; ecstatic feeling: *He respected the state of raptus in which all these poems were written* (Atlantic). [< Latin *raptus;* see RAPT]

ra·ra a·vis (rãr′ə ā′vis), *pl.* **ra·rae a·ves** (rãr′ē ā′vēz). *Latin.* **1.** a person or thing seldom met: *The once familiar village iceman is now rara avis* (Atlantic). **2.** (literally) a rare bird.

rare[1] (rãr), *adj.,* **rar·er, rar·est. 1.** seldom seen or found: *Peacocks and storks are rare birds in the United States. The three-o'clock in the morning courage which Bonaparte thought was the rarest* (Thoreau). **2.** not happening often; unusual: *a rare event.* **3.** unusually excellent, admirable, or desirable: *rare beauty. Edison had rare powers as an inventor.* **4.** not dense; thin: *The higher you go, the rarer the air is.* [< Latin *rārus*]
—Syn. 1. Rare, scarce mean not often or easily found. **Rare** applies to something uncommon or unusual at any time, and often suggests excellence or value above the ordinary: *The Gutenberg Bible is a rare book.* **Scarce** applies to something usually or formerly common or plentiful but not existing or produced in large enough numbers or quantities at the present time: *Water is becoming scarce in some parts of the country.* **2.** infrequent, uncommon.

rare[2] (rãr), *adj.,* **rar·er, rar·est.** not cooked much: *a rare steak.* [variant of *rear*[3], Old

English *hrēr* lightly cooked] —**Syn.** underdone.

rare bird, a rarity; rara avis: *Prokofiev's opera . . . first saw production in Chicago and is a rare bird in England* (Manchester Guardian Weekly).

rare·bit (rãr′bit), *n.* Welsh rabbit. [alteration of (Welsh) *rabbit*]

rare earth, an oxide of a rare-earth element: *Rare earths can be used in control rods for nuclear reactors, and also as a radiation shielding ingredient in concrete* (Science News Letter).

rare-earth (rãr′ėrth′), *adj.* of or having to do with rare earth.

rare-earth element or **metal,** any of the rare metallic elements having atomic numbers 57 to 71 of the periodic system, as cerium and erbium; lanthanide: *Relatively large proportions of the rare-earth elements are formed in fission and their separation was the subject of intense study as a part of the "Manhattan Project"* (K.S. Spiegler).

rar·ee show (rãr′ē), **1.** a show carried about in a box; peep show. **2.** any show or spectacle. [probably alteration of earlier *rare show*]

rar·e·fac·tion (rãr′ə fak′shən), *n.* **1.** a rarefying. **2.** a being rarefied.

rar·e·fac·tive (rãr′ə fak′tiv), *adj.* causing, attended with, or characterized by rarefaction. [< Latin *rārēfactum,* past participle of *rārēfacere* rarefy + English *-ive*]

rar·e·fi·ca·tion (rãr′ə fə kā′shən), *n.* rarefaction.

rar·e·fy (rãr′ə fī), *v.,* **-fied, -fy·ing.** —*v.t.* **1.** to make less dense: *The air on high mountains is rarefied.* **2.** to refine; purify. —*v.i.* to become less dense. [< Latin *rārēfacere* < *rārē,* adverb, rare (< *rārus,* adjective) + *facere* make, -fy]

rare·ly (rãr′lē), *adv.* **1.** not often or commonly; infrequently; seldom: *a sight rarely seen. He is rarely late.* **2.** unusually; unusually well.

rarely ever, *Informal.* seldom: *I rarely ever go.*

rare·ness[1] (rãr′nis), *n.* rare quality or condition.

rare·ness[2] (rãr′nis), *n.* the state of being rare or underdone, as in cooking.

rare·ripe (rãr′rīp′), *adj.* (of fruits, grains, etc.) coming early to maturity; ripening early in the year; early ripe. —*n.* a fruit or vegetable that is ripe early, especially a variety of peach. [< *rare,* obsolete form of *rathe* + *ripe*]

rar·i·fy (rãr′ə fī), *v.t., v.i.* **-fied, -fy·ing.** rarefy.

rar·ing (rãr′ing), *adj. Informal.* full of desire; very eager: *Members had come back to Westminster raring for a fight* (Punch). [< present participle of *rare,* dialectal variant of *rear*[2]]

rar·i·ty (rãr′ə tē), *n., pl.* **-ties. 1.** something rare: *He was that priceless rarity, an intuitive thinker who was able to assemble and grasp great generalities* (Atlantic). **2.** fewness; scarcity. **3.** lack of density; thinness: *The rarity of the air in the mountains is bad for people with weak hearts.* —**Syn. 1.** exception. **2.** paucity, infrequency. **3.** tenuity.

ras (ras), *n.* **1.** a headland, promontory, or cape (used in many place names on the Arabian and African coasts, etc.). **2.** (in Ethiopia) a prince, governor, or chief. [< Arabic *rās* head]

ras·cal (ras′kəl), *n.* **1.** a bad, dishonest person. **2.** a mischievous person, child, or animal; scamp: *He's a lucky young rascal. Come here, you little rascal.* **3.** *Obsolete.* one of the rabble.

—*adj.* **1.** low; mean; dishonest: *My days spent in rascal enterprises and rubbish selling* (H. G. Wells). **2.** *Obsolete.* of low birth; baseborn; base.

[< Old French *rascaille* < *rasque* scurvy, filth < Vulgar Latin *rāsicāre* to scrape < Latin *rādere* to scrape, scratch]

ras·cal·i·ty (ras kal′ə tē), *n., pl.* **-ties. 1.** rascally character or conduct: *. . . a harlequin playing a clarinet and presumably representing the spirit of pure Gallic rascality* (New Yorker). **2.** a rascally act or practice: *I don't want to be told about any of his rascalities* (Joseph Conrad). **3.** rascals as a group.

ras·cal·lion (ras kal′yən), *n.* a rapscallion.

ras·cal·ly (ras′kə lē), *adj.* mean; dishonest; bad: *There was none of any quality, but poor and rascally people* (Samuel Pepys). —*adv.* in a rascally manner.

ras·casse (ras kas′), *n.* a scorpionfish of the Mediterranean, used in preparing bouillabaisse. [< French *rascasse* < Provençal *rascasso*]

rase (rāz), *v.t.,* **rased, ras·ing.** raze: *cities rased to the ground* (Macaulay). [< Old French *raser* < Vulgar Latin *rāsāre* < Latin *rādere* to scrape, scratch, shave]

rash[1] (rash), *adj.* **1.** too hasty; careless; reckless; taking too much risk: *a rash remark. It is rash to cross the street without looking both ways.* **2.** *Obsolete.* quick and strong in action: *rash gunpowder* (Shakespeare). [Middle English *rasch* quick, probably < Middle Dutch, or Middle Low German, fast, quick, nimble]

—**Syn. 1. Rash, reckless** mean acting or speaking without due care or thought. **Rash** emphasizes being in too great a rush, speaking hastily or plunging into action without stopping to think: *You should never make rash promises.* **Reckless** emphasizes being without caution, acting carelessly without paying attention to possible consequences: *The dog was killed by a reckless driver.*

rash[2] (rash), *n.* **1.** a breaking out with many small red spots on the skin: *Scarlet fever causes a rash.* **2.** *Informal.* an outbreak: *a rash of investigations, a rash of letters. A few years ago the popular press broke out with a . . . rash of editorials scolding American novelists for the way they were portraying their native country* (Harper's). [< Old French *rasche,* and *rasque* scurf, scurvy; see RASCAL]

rash[3] (rash), *n. Scottish.* rush (the plant).

rash·er (rash′ər), *n.* a thin slice of bacon or ham for frying or broiling: *great rashers of broiled ham . . . done to a turn, and smoking hot* (Dickens). [origin uncertain; perhaps < obsolete *rash* to cut, slash]

rash·ly (rash′lē), *adv.* hastily; presumptuously.

rash·ness (rash′nis), *n.* an unwise boldness; a recklessness. —**Syn.** temerity, foolhardiness.

Ras·kol·nik (räs kôl′nik), *n., pl.* **-niks, -ni·ki** (-nə kē). (in Russia) a dissenter from the Orthodox Church. [< Russian *Raskol'nik* < *raskolot'* split < *raskol* split < *raz-* apart + *kolot'* to split]

ra·so·ri·al (rə sôr′ē əl, -sōr′-), *adj.* of or having to do with birds that scratch the ground for food, as the chicken. [< New Latin *Rasores,* the order name (< Latin *rādere* to scratch) + English *-ial*]

ra·sor·ite (rā′zər īt), *n.* kernite. [< *Rasor,* a proper name + *-ite*[1]]

rasp (rasp, räsp), *v.i.* **1.** to produce a harsh, grating sound: *The file rasped as he worked.* **2.** to produce a harsh effect; grate: *The sound rasped on his ears.* —*v.t.* **1.** to utter with a grating sound: *to rasp out a command.* **2.** to have a harsh, grating effect on. **3.** to scrape with a rough instrument.

—*n.* **1.** a harsh, grating sound: *the rasp of crickets, the rasp in a person's voice.* **2.** a coarse file with point-like teeth. **3.** the act of rasping, or rubbing with something like a rasp. [< Old French *rasper,* related to *râpe;* see RAPE[3]]

Rasp (def. 2)

rasp·ber·ry (raz′ber′ē, -brē; räz′-), *n., pl.* **-ries. 1.** a small, hollow, cone-shaped fruit that grows on bushes of the rose family. It is usually red or black, but some kinds are white or yellow. **2.** any of the bushes that it grows on. **3.** a reddish purple. **4.** *U.S. Slang.* a sound of disapproval or derision made with the tongue and lips. —*adj.* reddish-purple.

[earlier *raspis* raspberry (origin uncertain) + *berry*]

raspberry sawfly, a sawfly, whose pale-green larvae attack the raspberry, blackberry, etc.

rasped (raspt, räspt), *adj.* **1.** raspy. **2.** (of book edges) roughened to imitate a deckle edge, but left uncut.

rasp·er (ras′pər, räs′-), *n.* **1.** a person or thing that rasps. **2.** a machine for scraping sugar cane.

rasp·ing (ras′ping, räs′-), *adj.* raspy: *a rasping sound, a rasping tool.*

rasp·ing·ly (ras′ping lē, räs′-), *adv.* with a harsh, rasping sound or effect; gratingly: *He spoke so often, so raspingly . . . that he became perhaps the most colossal gadfly in political history* (Newsweek).

rasp·y (ras′pē, räs′-), *adj.,* **rasp·i·er, rasp·i·est. 1.** grating; harsh; rough. **2.** irritable: *a raspy disposition.*

ras·se (ras′ə, ras), *n.* a small civet cat, widely distributed from Malaya, China, India, etc., to Madagascar, and often kept in captivity for the civet that it yields. [< Javanese *rase*]

ras·sle (ras′əl), *v.t., v.i.,* **-sled, -sling.** *Dialect.* wrestle.

Ras·ta·far·i·an (ras′tə fãr′ē ən), *n.* a member of a West Indian cult advocating the supremacy of the Emperor of Ethiopia and seeking to come under his jurisdiction. —*adj.* of or having to do with this cult. [< *Ras Tafari,* original name of Haile Selassie, emperor of Ethiopia + *-an*]

ras·ter (ras′tər), *n.* (in a television receiving set) a pattern of close parallel lines in the cathode-ray tube on which the image is formed. [< German *Raster* screen, ultimately < Latin *rādere* to scratch]

ra·sure (rā′zhər), *n.* erasure; obliteration; effacement. [< Latin *rāsūra* < *rādere* to scrape, scratch]

rat (rat), *n., interj., v.,* **rat·ted, rat·ting.** —*n.* **1.** any of a large group of various long-tailed rodents native to the Old World, like a mouse but larger. Rats are found in almost any place inhabited by man, are frequent spreaders of disease, and cause great damage, especially the brown rat and black rat. **2.** any of several groups of similar rodents of the New World, as the wood rats, cotton rats, and kangaroo rats. **3.** any of various other mammals, as the muskrat. **4.** *Slang.* a low, mean, disloyal person who abandons his party or associates, especially in time of trouble. **5.** *Informal.* a scab (workman). **6.** *U.S. Informal.* a roll of hair or other material worn to puff out a woman's hair.

smell a rat, to suspect a trick or scheme: *He'll be sure to smell a rat if I'm with you* (William Dean Howells).

—*interj.* **rats,** *Slang.* an exclamation used to indicate scornful impatience or disbelief: *"We are alone at last," repeated Miss Vavasour . . . "Oh rapture!" "Oh rats!" said the manager of the theater* (Leonard Merrick).

—*v.i.* **1.** to hunt for rats; catch rats. **2.** *Informal.* to behave in a low, mean, disloyal way. **3.** *Informal.* to act as a rat or scab. **4.** *U.S. Slang.* to turn informer.

rat on, *Slang.* to go back on; welsh (as on an obligation or promise): *. . . if the Russians rat on the agreement* (Manchester Guardian).

[Old English *ræt,* apparently < Vulgar Latin *rattus*] —**rat′like′,** *adj.*

ra·ta (rä′tə), *n.* **1.** a large forest tree of New Zealand with dark red flowers and a hard, red wood: *The venerable rata, often measuring forty feet in circumference, [is] covered with scarlet flowers* (Ernst Dieffenbach). **2.** a parasitic climbing vine of the same species. [< Maori *rata*]

rat·a·bil·i·ty (rā′tə bil′ə tē), *n.* the quality of being ratable. Also, **rateability.**

rat·a·ble (rā′tə bəl), *adj.* **1.** that can be rated. **2.** proportional. **3.** *British.* taxable. Also, **rateable.**

rat·a·bly (rā′tə blē), *adv.* in a ratable manner; proportionately. Also, **rateably.**

rat·a·fee (rat′ə fē′), *n.* ratafia.

rat·a·fi·a (rat′ə fē′ə), *n.* **1.** a cordial flavored with fruit kernels or almonds. **2.** a sweet biscuit similarly flavored. [< French *ratafia* < Creole, also *tafia,* name for rum; origin uncertain]

rat·al (rā′təl), *n. British.* the amount on which rates or taxes are assessed.

ra·tan (ra tan′), *n.* rattan.

rat·a·plan (rat′ə plan′), *n.* the sound of a drum; tattoo. [< French *rataplan;* imitative]

rat-a-tat (rat′ə tat′), *n.* rat-tat, as in the beating of a drum.

rat·bag (rat′bag′), *n. Australian Slang.* a queer person; crank; creep: *A senior police officer said the letters "probably come from ratbags, . . . but we can't take a chance"* (Manchester Guardian).

rat·bite fever or **disease** (rat′bīt′), a disease, formerly common in Japan, characterized by fever, ulceration, and a purplish rash, caused by the bite of a rat or other infected animal.

rat·catch·er (rat′kach′ər), *n.* a person or animal that catches rats; ratter.

rat·catch·ing (rat′kach′ing), *n.* the catching of rats.

ratch (rach), *n.* a ratchet. [perhaps < German *Rätsche,* or *Ratsche*]

rat cheese, Cheddar cheese: *It is also known, . . . after one of its biggest fans,* [*as*] *rat cheese* (New York Times).

ratch·et (rach′it), *n.* **1.** a wheel or bar with teeth that come against a catch so that motion is permitted in one direction but not in the other. **2.** the catch. **3.** the entire device, wheel and catch or bar and catch.
—*v.t.* to operate or move by means of a ratchet: *One crew attached the chain, . . . secured the cable, . . . and ratcheted the lever with verve* (Punch).
—*v.i.* to move in the manner of a ratchet: *The angular borer turning clear around without stopping to ratchet* (Thomas Young).
[< French *rochet* < Italian *rocchetto* bobbin, spindle, (diminutive) < *rocca* distaff < Germanic (compare Old High German *roccho* distaff, spindle)]

Ratchet (def. 3)

ratchet bar, a bar with pegs or teeth to hold against a ratchet wheel; rack.

ratchet brace, a carpenters' brace in which, by means of a ratchet, a reciprocating motion of the handle is converted into a rotary motion of the bit.

ratchet drill, a drill rotated by a ratchet wheel moved by a pawl and lever.

ratchet wheel, a wheel with teeth and a catch that permits motion in only one direction.

ratch·et·y (rach′ə tē), *adj.* resembling the movement of a ratchet; jerky; clipping: *By dawn the little Long Island village was noisily abustle. By 6 a.m. ratchety Coopers, purring Allards, and roaring Ferraris were already turning up* (Time).

rate[1] (rāt), *n., v.,* **rat·ed, rat·ing.** —*n.* **1.** quantity, amount, or degree measured in proportion to something else: *The rate of interest is 6 cents on the dollar. The railroad rate is 4 cents a mile. Parcel post rates depend on weight and distance.* **2.** the degree of speed, progress, etc.: *The car was going at the rate of 40 miles an hour. The General posted along at a great rate* (Dickens). **3.** a price: *the rates for a long-distance telephone call. We pay the regular rate.* **4.** class; grade; rating. **5.** *British.* a tax on property for some local purpose. **6.** *Obsolete.* a style of living: *Nor do I now make moan to be abridged From such a noble rate* (Shakespeare).
at any rate, in any case; under any circumstances: *Commercially the arrangement was not a success, at any rate for the firm* (Joseph Conrad).
at that or **this rate,** in that or this case; under such circumstances: *At this rate, overspeculation will be followed by declines, but there is a vast difference between a speculative reaction and a panic* (Boston Transcript).
—*v.t.* **1.** to put a value on: *We rated the house as worth $15,000.* **2.** to consider; regard: *He was rated one of the richest men in town.* **3.** to subject to a certain tax. **4.** to fix at a certain rate. **5.** to put in a certain class or grade: *I should be rated ship's boy* (Robert Louis Stevenson). **6.** to arrange for transporting (goods) at a certain rate. **7.** *Informal.* to be worthy of: *She rates the best seat in the house.* **8.** to design for a certain speed. **9.** to determine the speed of.
—*v.i.* to be regarded; be classed; rank: *The orchestra's conductor rates high as a musician.*
[< Old French *rate* < Medieval Latin *rata* (*pars*) fixed (amount); *rata* < Latin *rērī* to reckon. Compare PRORATE.]
—**Syn.** *n.* **4.** rank, order.

rate[2] (rāt), *v.t., v.i.,* **rat·ed, rat·ing.** to scold: [*Elizabeth I*] *rated great nobles as if they were schoolboys* (John R. Green). [Middle English *räten;* origin uncertain. Compare Swedish *rata* to reject, find fault with.]

ra·té (rä tā′), *n. French.* a failure; bungler: *This cousin, a typical Chekhovian raté, has slipped out of painting into architecture, out of architecture into working for a lithographer, and has never been effectual at anything* (New Yorker).

rate·a·bil·i·ty (rā′tə bil′ə tē), *n.* ratability.

rate·a·ble (rā′tə bəl), *adj.* ratable: *In my own county, which has a very moderate rateable value, the yearly expenditure . . . is close on a million* (J. W. R. Scott).

rate·a·bly (rā′tə blē), *adv.* ratably.

rate card, a card listing rates for advertising.

ra·tel (rā′təl, rä′-), *n.* either of two badger-like, carnivorous mammals, one found in South and East Africa and the other in southern Asia, having a gray back and black underside. [< Afrikaans *ratel* < German *Ratel-Maus* (literally) rattle-mouse]

rate meter, a device in a radiation counter which indicates the rate at which ions are absorbed: *The whole soft-landing operation is a complex manoeuvre involving feedback from a . . . radar rate meter* (New Scientist).

rate of exchange, the rate or price per unit at which the currency of one country may be exchanged for the currency of another.

rate·pay·er (rāt′pā′ər), *n. British.* a taxpayer: *As one of many over-taxed ratepayers I can well understand the local feeling* (London Times).

rate·pay·ing (rāt′pā′ing), *adj. British.* paying a tax.

rat·er[1] (rā′tər), *n.* a person or thing that rates, estimates, measures, etc.: *His surveys had also uncovered a rather disquieting fact for TV raters who assumed everyone tuned in is watching* (Newsweek).

rat·er[2] (rā′tər), *n.* a person who scolds.

rat·fink (rat′fingk′), *n. U.S. Slang.* a fink: *I can't fake it; if I do I look like the ratfink of the century* (Time).

rat·fish (rat′fish′), *n., pl.* **-fish·es** or (*collectively*) **-fish.** a cartilaginous fish with a long, thin tail and large crushing plates instead of teeth; chimaera: *Liver oil from ratfish is the richest source of butyl alcohol* (Science News Letter).

rat flea, any of several species of fleas that infest rats and are carriers of diseases such as bubonic plague and typhus.

rat·guard (rat′gärd′), *n.* a sheet metal disk attached to the moorings of a vessel to keep rats from boarding it: *Ships calling at Canton began swapping rum and ratguards for labor and litchi nuts* (Time).

rath[1] (rath, räth), *adj., adv. Archaic.* rathe.

rath[2] (räth), *n.* a fortified dwelling of an ancient Irish chief: *Away to the northeast, near Sligo, was the hillside fortification, called a rath, where the hero-king Eoghan Bel had been buried* (T. H. White). [< Irish *rath*]

rat·haus (rät′hous), *n.* a town hall: *His body lay on a catafalque in front of his beloved rathaus* (Time). [< German *Rathaus* < *Rat* council, assembly + *Haus* house]

rathe (rāᴛʜ), *adj., adv. Archaic.* early; growing or blooming early: *the rathe primrose* (Milton); *men of rathe and riper years* (Tennyson). [Old English *hræth* quick]

rath·er (raᴛʜ′ər, räᴛʜ′-), *adv.* **1.** more readily; more willingly: *I would rather go today than tomorrow. She would rather play than rest.* **2.** more properly or justly; with better reason: *This is rather for your father to decide than for you.* **3.** more truly: *It was late Monday night or, rather, early Tuesday morning.* **4.** (with verbs) in some degree: *He rather felt that this was unwise.* **5.** to some extent; more than a little; somewhat: *After working so long he was rather tired.* **6.** on the contrary: *The sick man is no better today; rather, he is worse.* **7.** *Dialect.* earlier; sooner.
had rather, would more willingly; prefer to: *I had rather err with Plato than be right with Horace* (Shelley).
—*interj. British Informal.* yes, indeed! certainly! very much so!
[Old English *hrathor,* comparative of *hrathe* quickly]
➔ See **had** for usage note.

rat·hole (rat′hōl′), *n.* **1.** a hole gnawed in woodwork, etc., by a rat or rats. **2.** a disreputable place or condition: *Who routed you from a rathole . . . to perch you in a palace?* (H. and J. Smith).
down the rathole, to nothing; down the drain: *His last pile of money—thirty-five thousand dollars—went down the rathole when he tried to save an old friend from bankruptcy* (New Yorker).

raths·kel·ler (räts′kel′ər, raths′-), *n.* a restaurant selling alcoholic drinks. It is usually below street level. [American English < German *Rathskeller* < *Rathaus* town hall (< *Rat* town council) + *Keller* cellar (because it was originally a wineshop in the town hall)]

rat·i·cide (rat′ə sīd), *n.* a poisonous substance for killing rats; rodenticide. [< *rat* + *-cide*[1]]

rat·i·fi·ca·tion (rat′ə fə kā′shən), *n.* confirmation; approval: *the ratification of a treaty by the Senate.*

rat·i·fi·er (rat′ə fī′ər), *n.* a person or thing that ratifies or sanctions.

rat·i·fy (rat′ə fī), *v.t.,* **-fied, -fy·ing.** to confirm; approve: *The two countries will ratify the agreement made by their representatives.* [< Old French *ratifier,* learned borrowing from Medieval Latin *ratificare* < Latin *rērī* to reckon + *facere* make] —**Syn.** sanction, authorize. See **approve.**

ra·tine (ra tēn′), *n.* ratiné.

rat·i·né (rat′ə nā′), *n.* any of various fabrics, of wool or cotton, with a curled or tufted nap or a looped or rough surface: *Bouclé, ratiné, and éponge are all similar in character, made from a special three-ply yarn producing a curly surface and spongy cloth* (Bernice G. Chambers). [< French *ratiné,* past participle of *ratiner* < Old French *ratine,* earlier *rastin* cloth of frizzed wool; origin uncertain. Related to RATTEEN.]

rat·ing[1] (rā′ting), *n.* **1.** a class; grade. **2. a.** the position in a class or grade: *the rating of a seaman, the rating of a ship according to tonnage.* **b.** an enlisted man in the Royal Navy, British merchant navy, etc.: *The Eagle . . . will embark 400 relatives of officers and ratings for a day at sea* (Sunday Times). **3.** an amount fixed as a rate: *a rating of 80 per cent in English.* **4.** a credit rating. **5.** *British.* the fixing of the amount of a tax. **6.** the operating characteristics of a machine, such as voltage or horsepower. **7.** *U.S.* an evaluation of the percentage of listeners or viewers of a particular radio or television program, usually based on surveys taken to determine the extent of a program's popularity: *After a fortnight of low ratings and blows from the reviewers, an emergency meeting of network bigwigs was held to try to pep up the show* (Newsweek).

rat·ing[2] (rā′ting), *n.* a scolding; reproving.

ra·ti·o (rā′shē ō, -shō), *n., pl.* **-ti·os.** **1.** relative magnitude: "*He has sheep and cows in the ratio of 10 to 3" means that he has ten sheep for every three cows, or 3⅓ times as many sheep as cows.* **2.** a quotient. The ratio between two quantities is the number of times one contains the other. *The ratio of 6 to 10 is 6/10. The ratio of 10 to 6 is 10/6.* **3.** proportional relation; rate, as of gold to silver. [< Latin *ratiō, -ōnis* reckoning < *rērī* to reckon. Doublet of RATION, REASON.]

ra·ti·oc·i·nate (rash′ē os′ə nāt), *v.i.,* **-nat·ed, -nat·ing.** to carry on a process of reasoning; reason: *Besides (I ratiocinated) I was not the first rogue male to fall for the charms of a young thing only five-sixths his age* (Punch). [< Latin *ratiōcinārī* (with English *-ate*[1]) < *ratiō, -ōnis;* see RATIO]

ra·ti·oc·i·na·tion (rash′ē os′ə nā′shən), *n.* **1.** reasoning; process of reasoning: *On the way home, I tried to envision the rival patterns of ratiocination* (New Yorker). **2.** a conclusion arrived at by reasoning: *subtle definitions, or intricate ratiocinations* (Samuel Johnson).

ra·ti·oc·i·na·tive (rash′ē os′ə nā′tiv), *adj.* of or characterized by reasoning: *Hoyle's book abounds in theories which make Sherlock Holmes's ratiocinative high jinks look as unexciting as an old calabash pipe* (Scientific American).

ra·ti·oc·i·na·tor (rash′ē os′ə nā′tər), *n.* a person who reasons.

ra·ti·oc·i·na·to·ry (rash′ē os′ə nə tôr′ē, -tōr′-), *adj.* of, having to do with, or characterized by ratiocination: *He was far from sympathising with Croly's ratiocinatory warnings to do something* (Atlantic).

ra·tion (rash′ən, rā′shən), *n.* **1.** a fixed allowance of food; daily allowance of food for a person or animal: *Rations of rice have been provided for those engaged on this work, and its distribution arranged by the village* (Science News). **2.** a portion of anything dealt out: *rations of sugar, rations of coal.*
—*v.t.* **1.** to supply with rations: *to ration an army.* **2.** to allow only certain amounts to: *to ration citizens when supplies are scarce.* **3.** to distribute in limited amounts: *to ration food to the public in wartime.*
[< French, Middle French *ration,* learned borrowing from Latin *ratiō, -ōnis* (in Medieval Latin, share, proportion). Doublet of RATIO, REASON.]
—**Syn.** *n.* **1.** See **food.** **2.** share, allotment.

ra·tion·al (rash′ə nəl, rash′nəl), *adj.* **1.** sensible; reasonable; reasoned out: *When* *very angry, people seldom act in a rational way.* **2.** able to think and reason clearly: *As children grow older, they become more rational. The patient appeared perfectly rational.* **3.** of reason; based on reasoning: *a rational explanation.* **4.** *Mathematics.* **a.** expressible as a whole number or a fraction composed of whole numbers. **b.** involving no root that cannot be extracted. **5.** *Prosody.* of or having to do with a syllable in Greek or Latin verse that has the metrical value needed to fit the pattern.

—*n.* that which is rational or reasonable.

[< Latin *ratiōnālis* < *ratiō;* see RATIO] —**ra′tion·al·ness,** *n.*

—**Syn.** *adj.* **1.** sound, wise, judicious, sane.

—**Ant.** *adj.* **1.** unreasonable.

ra·tion·ale (rash′ə nal′; -nä′lē, -nā′-), *n.* **1.** the whys and wherefores; the fundamental reason: *We must examine the rationale of the rule* (Edgar Allan Poe). **2.** a statement of reasons; reasoned principles: *The rationale of this policy was spelled out in letters written by Stalin and published in "Bolshevik" on October 2, 1952* (W. Averell Harriman). [< Latin *ratiōnāle,* neuter of *ratiōnālis* rational < *ratiō;* see RATIO]

ra·tion·al·ise (rash′ə nə līz, rash′nə-), *v.t., v.i.,* **-ised, -is·ing.** *Especially British.* rationalize.

ra·tion·al·ism (rash′ə nə liz′əm, rash′nə-liz-), *n.* **1.** the principle or habit of accepting reason as the supreme authority in matters of opinion, belief, or conduct. **2.** the philosophical doctrine that reason is in itself a source of knowledge, independent of the senses. **3.** *Theology.* the examination of dogma or the explanation of the supernatural by reason.

ra·tion·al·ist (rash′ə nə list, rash′nə-), *n.* **1.** a person who accepts reason as the supreme authority in matters of opinion, belief, or conduct. **2.** an adherent of the philosophical theory of rationalism. **3.** a believer in the theological doctrine of rationalism.

—*adj.* rationalistic: *a liberal and rationalist reaction against Calvinist rigour* (Henry Morley).

ra·tion·al·is·tic (rash′ə nə lis′tik, rash′-nə-), *adj.* of rationalists or rationalism: *Modern man has become so rationalistic in his attitude that his tendency is toward a non-recognition and denial of the unconscious* (New Yorker). —**ra′tion·al·is′ti·cal·ly,** *adv.*

ra·tion·al·is·ti·cal (rash′ə nə lis′tə kəl, rash′nə-), *adj.* rationalistic.

ra·tion·al·i·ty (rash′ə nal′ə tē), *n., pl.* **-ties.** **1.** the possession of reason; reasonableness: *Mr. Smith is a visionary, but no one doubts his rationality.* **2.** a rational or reasonable view, practice, etc.

ra·tion·al·i·za·tion (rash′ə nə lə zā′shən, rash′nə-), *n.* **1.** the act of rationalizing: *Thus, what Taylor did for rationalization of physical work, the psychologists do for the mental and emotional aspect of the worker* (Erich Fromm). **2.** the fact or state of being rationalized.

ra·tion·al·ize (rash′ə nə līz, rash′nə-), *v.,* **-ized, -iz·ing.** —*v.t.* **1.** to make rational or conformable to reason: *When life has been duly rationalized by science, it will be seen that among a man's duties, care of the body is imperative* (Herbert Spencer). **2.** to treat or explain in a rational manner. **3.** to find (often unconsciously) an explanation or excuse for: *She rationalizes her gluttony by saying, "I must eat enough to keep up my strength."* **4.** to explain (myth, legend, etc.) in terms of contemporary scientific knowledge. **5.** to organize or run (a business, industry, operation, etc.) on economically sound or proven methods of administration and production: *He wanted the six hundred-odd societies to rationalize themselves and offer better terms* (Punch). **6.** *Mathematics.* to clear from irrational quantities. —*v.i.* to find excuses (often unconsciously) for one's desires. —**ra′tion·al·iz′er,** *n.*

ra·tion·al·ly (rash′ə nə lē, rash′nə-), *adv.* in a rational manner; reasonably; sensibly.

rational number, a real number.

rat·ite (rat′īt), *adj.* **1.** having a flat breastbone with no keel: *Ostriches and emus are ratite birds.* **2.** of or having to do with ratite birds. —*n.* a ratite bird. [< New Latin *Ratitae* the class name < Latin *ratis* raft, timber; spelling influenced by English *-ite*[1]]

rat kangaroo, any of certain small kangaroos about the size of a rabbit, found in Australia and Tasmania.

rat·line or **rat·lin** (rat′lin), *n.* **1.** one of the small ropes that cross the shrouds of a ship, used as steps for going aloft. **2.** the small, tarred rope from which these are made. [Middle English *ratling,* and *radelyng;* origin uncertain; spelling influenced by English *line*[1]]

Ratlines (def. 1) (R)

RA·TO or **ra·to** (rā′tō), *n. Aeronautics.* a unit of one or more rockets, providing extra power to speed up an airplane during take-off. [< *r*(ocket) *a*(ssisted) *t*(ake)-*o*(ff)]

ra·toon (ra tün′), *n.* a shoot springing up from the root of a plant after it has been cropped: *ratoons of sugar cane.* —*v.i., v.t.* to send up or cause to send up new shoots after being cropped. Also, **rattoon.** [< Spanish *retoño* < *retoñar* to sprout < *otoño* autumn < Latin *autumnus*]

rat·proof (rat′prüf′), *adj.* so made that rats cannot enter. —*v.t.* to make ratproof: *The modern farmsteading is ratproofed, to deny food to rats; the modern town warehouse is ratproofed, to deny water to rats* (Sunday Times).

rat race, *Informal.* an endless scramble and confusion; tiring but inescapable routine: *M.K. and I, only half-consciously, were entering the rat race of preposterously expensive dances, clothes-buying, and date-collecting that eventually turns schoolgirls into New York debutantes* (New Yorker).

rats (rats). See under **rat,** *interj.*

rats·bane (rats′bān′), *n.* any poison for rats: *God forgive her! . . . it might have been ratsbane and two men of God dying in agonies* (New Yorker). [< *rats* + *bane*]

rat snake, any of various snakes such as the corn snake and the chicken snake of North America, that kill rats and other rodents and are sometimes domesticated for this purpose: *The [Davis Mountain] rat snake immediately seized one of the mice in his mouth and constricted it with a single loop of its body* (Science News Letter).

rat·tail (rat′tāl′), *adj.* having a tail or tail-like part like that of a rat; long and slender: *Everything in the house, down to the last rat-tail hinge and hickory floor-peg, is historically accurate* (Atlantic).

rat-tailed (rat′tāld′), *adj.* rattail: *Silver used in the Revolutionary Period is recognized by the rat-tailed spoon and the pistol-handled knife* (New York Times).

rat·tan (ra tan′), *n.* **1.** Also, **rattan palm.** any of several East Indian and African climbing palms with very long, thin, jointed stems. **2.** the stems of such palm trees, used for wickerwork, canes, etc. **3.** a cane, switch, or stick, especially a walking stick, made from a piece of such stems. Also, **ratan.** [ultimately < Malay *rōtan*]

rat-tat (rat′tat′), *n.* a sound as of rapping: *Then came a sharp rat-tat at the door* (George Gissing). Also, **rat-a-tat.**

rat·teen (ra tēn′), *n.* any of various fabrics with tufted, looped, or rough surfaces. [< French *ratine;* origin uncertain. Related to RATINÉ.]

rat·ten (rat′ən), *v.t.* **1.** to damage or destroy (work, tools, machinery). **2.** to frighten or coerce an employer or workman. —*v.i.* to practice rattening. [perhaps related to RAT (because of the rodent's frequent destructive habits)] —**rat′ten·er,** *n.*

rat·ter (rat′ər), *n.* **1.** a person or animal that catches rats; ratcatcher: *Our terrier is a good ratter.* **2.** a person who informs on, betrays, or deserts his associates.

rat·tish (rat′ish), *adj.* **1.** of, having to do with, or resembling a rat. **2.** infested with rats.

rat·tle[1] (rat′əl), *v.,* **-tled, -tling,** *n.* —*v.i.* **1.** to make a number of short, sharp sounds: *The window rattled in the wind.* **2.** to move with short, sharp sounds: *The old car rattled down the street.* **3.** to talk quickly, on and on: *They . . . rattled on in a free, wild, racy talk* (William Dean Howells). —*v.t.* **1.** to cause to rattle: *The door did not yield . . . he rattled the handle violently* (Edith Wharton). **2.** to say or do quickly: *He rattled off the dates without a moment's hesitation. He sat down to the piano, and rattled a lively piece of music* (Harriet Beecher Stowe). **3.** *Informal.* to confuse; upset. **4.** *Informal.* to stir up; rouse. **5.** to chase (game) vigorously.

—*n.* **1.** a number of short, sharp sounds: *the rattle of empty bottles.* **2.** a sound in the throat occurring in some diseases of the lungs and also often just before death. **3.** a racket; uproar. **4.** a toy, instrument, etc., that makes a noise when it is shaken: *The baby shakes his rattle.* **5.** the series of horny pieces at the end of a rattlesnake's tail. **6.** any of certain plants whose ripe seeds rattle in their cases, as the yellow rattle. **7.** trivial talk; chatter: *People look her rattle for wit* (George Meredith).

[Middle English *ratelen;* probably ultimately imitative. Compare Low German *ratelen.*]

rat·tle[2] (rat′əl), *v.t.,* **-tled, -tling.** to furnish with ratlines on: *to rattle the rigging down.* [back formation < *ratline,* taken as verbal noun *ratlin'*]

rat·tle·box (rat′əl boks′), *n.* **1.** a boxlike toy for making a rattling sound; rattle. **2.** any of various plants of the pea family whose ripened seeds rattle in the inflated pod.

rat·tle·brain (rat′əl brān′), *n.* a giddy, thoughtless person.

rat·tle·brained (rat′əl brānd′), *adj.* like a rattlebrain; giddy; whimsical; foolish: *Churchill feels that he can boil up into excitement over the most rattlebrained military excursion* (New Yorker).

rat·tle·head (rat′əl hed′), *n.* a rattlebrain.

rat·tle·head·ed (rat′əl hed′id), *adj.* rattlebrained.

rat·tle·pate (rat′əl pāt′), *n.* a rattlebrain: *Alice was endlessly patient with her brother, though he was a rattlepate and never in time for anything* (New Yorker).

rat·tle·pat·ed (rat′əl pā′tid), *adj.* like a rattlepate.

rat·tler (rat′lər), *n. Informal.* **1.** *U.S.* a rattlesnake: *A rattler bit me once though* (Bush News [St. Catherines, Ontario]). **2.** a machine or vehicle that rattles when used, especially because of age, hard use, etc.

rat·tle·root (rat′əl rüt′, -rút′), *n.* **1.** any of various plants whose roots have been considered a remedy for snake bite. **2.** Seneca snake root. [< *rattle*(snake) *root*]

rat·tle·snake (rat′əl snāk′), *n.* any of various poisonous American snakes (pit vipers) with a thick body and a broad, triangular head, that make a rattling noise with the tail, including the timber rattlesnake and the diamondback rattlesnake: *The rattlesnake is by far the most abundant and important of the poisonous snakes in the United States* (A. M. Winchester). [American English < *rattle*[1] + *snake*]

rattlesnake plantain, any of various low terrestrial orchids with spotted leaves and whitish flowers, found in north temperate regions. [American English (because of its spotted leaves)]

rattlesnake root, **1. a.** any of various composite plants whose roots have been considered a remedy for snake bites. **b.** the root of any of these plants. **2. a.** the senega or Seneca snakeroot. **b.** its root. [American English < *rattlesnake* + *root*[1] (because of its reputed value in cases of snake bite)]

rattlesnake weed, **1.** a North American hawkweed, having leaves marked with purple veins. Its leaves and root are thought to be medicinal. **2.** a weed of the parsley family, found in southern and western North America. **3.** a marsh plant of the same family, found in the southeast United States. **4.** a rattlesnake plantain. [American English (because of its coloration, or its reputation as a remedy for snake bites)]

rat·tle·trap (rat′əl trap′), *n.* **1.** a rattling, rickety wagon or other vehicle: *Rattletraps have been a big cause of accidents on other turnpikes* (Wall Street Journal). **2.** any shaky, rattling object. **3.** *Slang.* a very talkative person; chatterbox.

rattletraps, odds and ends: *Rattletraps for the mantelpiece, gimcracks for the table . . .* (Mary C. Jackson).

—*adj.* rickety; rattling.

rat·tling (rat′ling), *adj.* **1.** that rattles: *a rattling tea kettle.* **2.** fast and lively; brisk: *a rattling speech, a rattling pace.* **3.** *Informal.* very fine; great: *He preached . . . a sermon . . . that gave him a rattling reputation* (Mark Twain).

—*adv. Informal.* remarkably; extremely: *rattling good stuff* (H.G. Wells); *a rattling big distance off* (Mark Twain). —**rat′tling·ly,** *adv.*

rat·tly (rat′lē), *adj.* that rattles: *From Mombasa, a rattly, narrow-gauge railway begins*

the steep climb to the inland plateau (Newsweek). [< *rattl*(e)¹ + *-y*¹]
rat·ton (rat′ən), *n. Dialect.* a rat. [< Old French *raton* < *rat* rat, probably < Vulgar Latin *rattus*]
rat·toon (ra tün′), *n., v.* ratoon.
rat·trap (rat′trap′), *n.* **1.** a trap for rats. **2.** a hopeless situation. —*adj.* of, having to do with, or like a rattrap.
rat·ty (rat′ē), *adj.,* **-ti·er, -ti·est. 1.** of rats; like rats: *ratty odors.* **2.** full of rats: *Your German dungeons are mortal shivering ratty places* (George Meredith). **3.** *Slang.* poor; shabby: *an old ratty deck of cards* (Mark Twain).
rau·ci·ty (rô′sə tē), *n.* hoarseness; harshness.
rau·cous (rô′kəs), *adj.* hoarse; harsh-sounding: *the raucous caw of a crow.* [< Latin *raucus* (with English *-ous*)] —**rau′cous·ly,** *adv.* —**rau′cous·ness,** *n.* —**Syn.** husky.
raunch·i·ness (rôn′chē nis, rän′-), *n. U.S. Slang.* raunchy quality or state.
raunch·y (rôn′chē, rän′-), *adj.* **raunch·i·er, raunch·i·est.** *U.S. Slang.* carelessly untidy; sloppy; shabby: ... *a bunch of raunchy, rebellious kids* (Harper's).
rau·po (rou′pō), *n.* a bulrush of New Zealand used for building native houses, thatching roofs, etc. [< Maori *raupo*]
rau·wol·fi·a (rô wol′fē ə), *n.* **1.** any of a group of tropical trees and shrubs of the dogbane family, especially a small, evergreen shrub of southern Asia: *Dr. Wilkins was the first Western physician to use the Indian snakeroot, rauwolfia, in the treatment of high blood pressure* (Science News Letter). **2.** an alkaloid drug derived from the root of this shrub, used for reducing high blood pressure and in the treatment of mental illness. It is the source of many similar drugs, such as reserpine. [< New Latin *Rauwolfia* the genus name < Leonard *Rauwolf,* a German botanist of the 1500's]
rav·age (rav′ij), *v.,* **-aged, -ag·ing,** *n.* —*v.t.* to lay waste; damage greatly; destroy: *The forest fire ravaged many miles of country.* —*v.i.* to work destruction. —*n.* violence; great damage; destruction; devastation: *War causes ravage.* [< French *ravager* < Middle French *ravage* destruction, especially by rain and snowfall < *ravir;* see RAVISH] —**rav′ag·er,** *n.*
rave¹ (rāv), *v.,* **raved, rav·ing,** *n., adj.* —*v.i.* **1.** to talk wildly: *An excited, angry person raves; so does a madman.* **2.** to talk with too much enthusiasm: *She raved about her food.* **3.** to howl; roar; rage: *The wind raved about the lighthouse.* —*v.t.* to express in a frenzied or wild manner.
—*n.* **1.** a raving; frenzy or great excitement: *after our little hour of strut and rave* (Lowell). **2.** *Slang.* **a.** unrestrained praise. **b.** an infatuation, especially such as occurs in adolescence.
—*adj. Informal.* unrestrainedly enthusiastic in praising: *The play got rave notices in the local press.*
[perhaps < Old French *raver,* variant of *rêver* to dream, wander, rave; origin uncertain]
—**Syn.** *v.i.* **1.** storm, rant.
rave² (rāv), *n.* one of the side pieces in the body of a wagon, sleigh, etc. [origin uncertain]
rav·el (rav′əl), *v.,* **-eled, -el·ing** or (*especially British*) **-elled, -el·ling,** *n.* —*v.t.* **1.** to separate the threads of; fray: *Ravel a bit of the leftover cloth to mend the tear in your dress.* **2.** to make plain or clear; unravel: *Must I ravel out My weaved-up folly* (Shakespeare). **3.** to tangle; involve; confuse. —*v.i.* **1.** to fray out; separate into threads: *The sweater has raveled at the elbow.* **2.** to become tangled, involved, or confused.
—*n.* **1.** an unraveled thread or fiber: *Since then the splits and ravels have shown up . . . so that it is now doubtful whether the fabric can ever be repaired* (Harper's). **2.** a tangle; complication; entanglement.
[probably < earlier Dutch *ravelen*] —**rav′el·er,** *especially British,* **rav′el·ler,** *n.*
—**Syn.** *v.t.* **2.** disentangle. **3.** enmesh.
rave·lin (rav′lin), *n.* a triangular outwork in a fortification, outside of the main ditch and having two embankments forming a projecting angle. [< Middle French *ravelin,* perhaps < Old French *revelin* kind of shoe < Italian *ravellino,* variant of *rivellino*]
rav·el·ing (rav′ə ling, rav′ling), *n.* something raveled out, as a thread drawn from a woven or knitted fabric.
rav·el·ling (rav′ə ling, rav′ling), *n. Especially British.* raveling.
rav·el·ment (rav′əl mənt), *n.* **1.** entanglement; confusion. **2.** a raveling.
ra·ven¹ (rā′vən), *n.* a large, black bird like a crow, but larger. Ravens inhabit Europe, Asia, and North America, and have long been regarded as a portent of evil or death. —*adj.* deep, glossy black: *raven locks.* [Old English *hræfn*]

Raven¹ (about 2 ft. long)

rav·en² (rav′ən), *v.t.* **1.** to devour voraciously: *a roaring lion ravening the prey* (Ezekiel 22:25). **2.** to plunder; prey on. —*v.i.* to be ravenous: *The more they fed, they ravened still for more* (John Dryden).
—*n.* rapine; plunder; robbery.
—*adj.* ravin; ravenous.
[< Old French *raviner* (originally) fall impetuously or precipitously < *ravine* violent action; see RAVINE]
Ra·ven (rā′vən), *n.* the southern constellation Corvus. [< *raven*]
rav·en·ing (rav′ə ning), *adj.* greedy and hungry: *a ravening wolf.* [< *raven*² + *-ing*²]
rav·en·ous (rav′ə nəs), *adj.* **1.** very hungry. **2.** greedy. **3.** rapacious. [< Old French *ravinos* (with English *-ous*) rapacious, violent < *ravine;* see RAVINE. Related to RAVEN².] —**rav′en·ous·ly,** *adv.* —**rav′en·ous·ness,** *n.* —**Syn. 1.** famished. **2.** gluttonous, voracious. **3.** plundering.
rav·er (rā′vər), *n.* a person who raves.
ra·vi·gote (rá vē gôt′), *n.* a sauce or dressing consisting of a mixture of spinach purée, tarragon, chervil, parsley, chives, and other herbs, used with vinegar as a seasoning. [< French *ravigote* < *ravigoter* revive]
rav·in (rav′ən), *n.* rapine: *Blood and ravin and robbery are their characteristics* (George Rawlinson).
—*v.t., v.i.* raven².
—*adj.* ravenous: *Better 'twere I met the ravin lion* (Shakespeare).
[< Old French *ravine* robbery. Doublet of RAPINE, RAVINE.]
ra·vine (rə vēn′), *n.* a long, deep, narrow gorge worn by running water: *The river had worn a ravine between the two hills.* [< French, Old French *ravine* violent rush, robbery < Latin *rapīna* < *rapere* to snatch. Doublet of RAPINE, RAVIN.]
ravine deer, an East Indian antelope, the male of which has a second pair of small horns on the forehead in front of the principal pair. [because it frequents ravines]
rav·ing (rā′ving), *adj.* **1.** that raves; delirious; frenzied; raging. **2.** *Informal.* remarkable; extraordinary: *a raving beauty.* —*n.* delirious, incoherent talk. —**rav′ing·ly,** *adv.*
rav·i·o·li (rav′ē ō′lē), *n.pl.* small, thin pieces of dough filled with chopped meat, cheese, etc., cooked in boiling water, and usually served with a highly seasoned tomato sauce. [< Italian *ravioli,* or *raviuoli,* plural < *rapa* beet < Vulgar Latin *rāpa,* feminine singular < Latin, plural of *rāpum* beet, turnip]
rav·ish (rav′ish), *v.t.* **1.** to fill with delight: *My friend was ravished with the beauty, innocence, and sweetness that appeared in all their faces* (Joseph Addison). **2.** to carry off by force. **3.** to rape. **4.** to plunder; despoil: *the ease with which the Spaniards had ravished the city* (John L. Motley). [< Old French *raviss-,* stem of *ravir* < Vulgar Latin *rapīre,* for Latin *rapere* to seize. Related to RAPE¹.] —**rav′ish·er,** *n.* —**Syn. 1.** enrapture, entrance, enchant, transport.
rav·ish·ing (rav′i shing), *adj.* very delightful; enchanting: *jewels of ravishing beauty.* —**rav′ish·ing·ly,** *adv.*
rav·ish·ment (rav′ish mənt), *n.* **1.** rapture; ecstasy. **2.** the act of carrying off by force. **3.** rape.
ra·vis·sant (rá vē säN′), *adj. French.* ravishing; enchanting. [< French *ravissant,* present participle of *ravir* < Old French; see RAVISH]
raw (rô), *adj.* **1.** not cooked: *raw meat, raw oysters. Many fruits are eaten raw.* **2.** in the natural state; not manufactured, treated, or prepared: *raw cotton, raw materials, raw hides. When raw umber is heated, it becomes burnt umber, which has a deep reddish color* (World Book Encyclopedia). **3.** not experienced; not trained: *a raw recruit.* **4.** damp and cold: *raw weather, a raw wind.* **5.** with the skin off; sore: *a raw wound, a raw spot.* **6.** uncivilized; brutal: *the raw frontier.* **7.** having a crude quality; not refined in taste: *a raw piece of work, a raw story.* **8.** *U.S. Slang.* harsh; unfair: *have a raw deal.* —*n.* **1.** the raw flesh. **2.** a raw or sore spot on the body.
in the raw, nude: *He swims in the raw when no one else is around.*
[Old English *hrēaw*] —**raw′ly,** *adv.* —**raw′ness,** *n.*
—**Syn.** *adj.* **2. Raw, crude** mean not processed or prepared for use. **Raw** applies to a material or natural product that has not yet been processed for use or shaped or made into something by treating, tanning, finishing, manufacturing, etc.: *Raw milk has not been pasteurized to make it safe to drink.* **Crude** applies to a product in a natural state, not freed from impurities or prepared for use or greater usefulness and value by refining, tempering, or treating with chemicals and heat: *Crude rubber is treated with sulfur and heat to make it more elastic and durable.* **3.** ignorant, inexperienced.
raw-boned (rô′bōnd′), *adj.* having little flesh on the bones; gaunt: *She was extremely tall and thin and walked with a camel's swaying, raw-boned gait* (New Yorker).
raw·head (rô′hed′), *n.* a goblin of ghastly appearance.
raw·hide (rô′hīd′), *n., v.,* **-hid·ed, -hid·ing.** —*n.* **1.** the untanned skin of cattle. **2.** a rope or whip made of this. —*v.t.* to whip with a rawhide.
ra·win (rā′win), *n.* **1.** the determination of wind speed and direction by the tracking of a balloon with radar or radiocompass. **2.** wind tracked in this manner. [< *ra*(dar) + *win*(d)]
ra·win·sonde (rā′win sond), *n.* **1.** the gathering of temperature, pressure, wind speed or other atmospheric information by means of a balloon-borne radiosonde tracked by radiocompass and sometimes radar. **2.** a radiosonde used for this purpose. [< *rawin* + (radio)*sonde*]
raw·ish (rô′ish), *adj.* somewhat raw.
raw material, a substance in its natural state; anything that can be manufactured, treated, or prepared to make it more useful or increase its value: *Young men are the raw material of an army. These imports are mainly raw materials that are duty-free, or have low tariff rates because the U.S. requires them* (Time). *You* [*the Press*] *deal with the raw material of opinion* (Woodrow Wilson).
raw milk, unpasteurized milk.
raw silk, silk reeled from the cocoons before being thrown or spun: *He had on a brown-and-black-striped raw silk jacket, gray flannel slacks, and a proper tie* (New Yorker).
rax (raks, räks), *Scottish.* —*v.i.* **1.** to stretch. **2.** to reach out. —*v.t.* **1.** to stretch out. **2.** to hand over. [Old English *raxan*]
ray¹ (rā), *n.* **1.** a line or beam of light. **2. a.** a line or stream of heat, electricity, or energy. **b.** any stream of particles moving in the same line. **3.** a thin line like a ray, coming out from a center. **4.** a slight trace; faint gleam: *Not a ray of hope pierced our gloom.* **5.** light; radiance: *lamps that shed at eve a cheerful ray* (Thomas Gray). **6.** a line of sight. **7.** a glance of the eye: *All eyes direct their rays On him* (Alexander Pope). **8.** a part like a ray: **a.** one of the arms or branches of a starfish. **b.** the marginal portion of the flower head of certain composite plants, composed of ray flowers or petals. **c.** one of these ray flowers. **d.** a branch of an umbel. **e.** one of the processes which support and extend the fin of a fish. **f.** one of the vertical bands of tissue between the pith and the bark of a tree or other plant. **9.** one of any system of lines, parts, or things radially arranged.
—*v.i.* **1.** to issue as rays. **2.** to shine. **3.** to extend in lines from the center. —*v.t.* **1.** to send forth in rays; radiate. **2.** to treat with rays, as with X rays. **3.** to throw rays upon. [< Old French *rai* < Latin *radius.* Doublet of RADIUS.]
—**Syn.** *n.* **1.** See **beam.**
ray² (rā), *n.* any of several varieties of fishes, related to the sharks, that have broad, flat bodies with very broad pectoral fins. The electric ray has organs with which it shocks or kills its prey. Various rays include the sting rays, the electric rays, etc. *In early Roman times*

Electric Ray² (to 5 ft. long)

the standard cure for gout was a shock from the torpedo or electric ray (Earl S. Herald). [< Old French *raie* < Latin *raia*]

ra·yah or **ra·ya** (rä′yə), *n.* a Turkish subject who is not a Moslem. [< French *raïa* < Turkish *râya* < Arabic *ra'āyā* subjects, peasants < *ra'ā* he pastured]

rayed (rād), *adj.* having rays.

ray flower or **floret,** one of the marginal flowers or florets of a daisy, aster, or other composite flower head, resembling a petal.

ray fungus, actinomycete.

ray gun, 1. a gun or other instrument that is supposed to shoot radioactive rays: *He may slog through mud or he may ride into battle at supersonic speeds firing some weird futuristic ray gun* (Newsweek). **2.** anything resembling such a gun, as a scientific instrument producing a form of radiation.

ray hair, one of the slender filaments in the fin fold of an embryo fish.

ray·ing (rā′ing), *n.* exposure to radioactivity.

Ray·leigh wave (rā′lē), a vertical, ripple-like wave on or just below the surface of the earth, caused by seismic disturbances: *Measurement of crustal thickness over the entire U.S. was made by noting dispersion in phase velocity of earthquake Rayleigh waves* (Science News Letter). [<J.W.S. *Rayleigh,* 1842-1919, a British physicist, who first described it in 1900]

ray·less (rā′lis), *adj.* **1.** without rays. **2.** sending out no rays. **3.** dark; gloomy: *rayless night.*

rayless goldenrod, any of various plants related to the goldenrod which contain the poisonous substance that causes trembles in cattle and sheep.

Ray·naud's disease (rā nōz′), a primary disorder of the vascular system, characterized by spasms and cyanosis of the extremities, especially in the fingers and toes, due to the obstruction of blood supply and local asphyxia. [< Maurice *Raynaud,* 1834-1881, a French physician]

ray·on (rā′on), *n.* **1.** a fiber or fabric made from cellulose treated with chemicals. Rayon is used instead of silk, wool, and cotton and can be made to look like any of these, especially silk. *Rayon, which has only recently come into extensive use, is a creation of the chemist* (Monroe M. Offner). **2.** cloth made of this fiber. —*adj.* made of rayon: *If a rayon fiber is dyed and then the dye is leached out, the skin remains darker* (New Scientist). [American English < *ray*[1] beam, light. Compare French *rayon* ray of light.]

ray·on·nant (rā′ə nənt), *adj.* **1.** sending out rays. **2.** having radiating lines, as some architectural or other decoration. [< French *rayonnant,* present participle of *rayonner* to send out rays < *rayon* ray of light, ultimately < Latin *radius*]

raze (rāz), *v.t.,* **razed, raz·ing. 1.** to tear down; destroy completely; demolish: *to raze a building.* **2.** *Obsolete.* to scrape off; erase. **3.** *Obsolete.* to scrape. Also, **rase.** [< French, Old French *raser* to scrape, shave < Vulgar Latin *rāsāre* < Latin *rādere* to scrape, shave] —**Syn. 1.** level.

ra·zee (rā zē′), *n., v.,* **-zeed, -zee·ing.** —*n.* *Obsolete.* a ship reduced in height by the removal of the upper deck. —*v.t.* **1.** to cut down (a ship) by removing the upper deck. **2.** to abridge. [< French (*vaisseau*) *rasé* (literally) scraped warship; *rasé,* past participle of *raser;* see RAZE]

ra·zon (rā′zon), *n.* a bomb with movable control surfaces in the tail that can be adjusted by radio signals from a plane to control the bomb in range and azimuth. [< *r*(ange) + *az*(imuth) *on*(ly)]

ra·zor (rā′zər), *n.* an implement with a sharp blade for shaving. —*v.t.* **1.** to shave with a razor: *The trapper razored his face clean of his beard.* **2.** to remove with a razor: *to razor a beard.* [< Old French *rasor,* and *rasour* < *raser* to scrape; see RAZE]

ra·zor·a·ble (rā′zər ə bəl), *adj.* fit to be shaved.

ra·zor·back (rā′zər bak′), *n.* **1.** a kind of thin, half-wild hog with a ridged back: *Razorbacks are common in the southern United States.* **2.** a finback (whale); rorqual. —*adj.* razor-backed: ... *razorback hills covered with jungles* (Newsweek).

ra·zor-backed (rā′zər bakt′), *adj.* having a very sharp back or ridge: *a razor-backed animal.*

ra·zor·bill (rā′zər bil′), *n.* the razor-billed auk: *The razorbills, ... which with puffins and guillemots, make the island's cliffs exciting and beautiful for the birdwatcher in May, June, and July* (Sunday Times).

ra·zor-billed auk (rā′zər bild′), an auk of the North Atlantic resembling the great auk but smaller.

razor clam or **fish,** any of various bivalve mollusks with a long, narrow shell: *On the salt shores there were razor clams and oysters, and mullet in the canals ...* (Harper's).

razor edge, 1. a keen, razorlike edge. **2.** a precarious situation close to the verge of destruction: *to stand on the razor edge of a cliff.*

ra·zor-edged (rā′zər ejd′), *adj.* **1.** having a razor edge: *In recent works, he divides the painting into razor-edged triangles rimmed with black* (Time). **2.** keen; incisive; trenchant: *razor-edged wit.*

ra·zor-sharp (rā′zər shärp′), *adj.* sharp as a razor; very sharp: *Bellboys tiptoed by the razor-sharp scimitars of the fitfully dozing guards* (Newsweek). *His poetic gift is delicate, razor-sharp, and very special* (Atlantic).

razor shell, 1. the shell of a razor clam. **2.** a razor clam.

ra·zor·strop (rā′zər strop′), *n.* a strap of leather for sharpening a razor; strop.

ra·zor-thin (rā′zər thin′), *adj.* thin as a razor's edge; extremely thin or slight: *He sported a razor-thin red moustache* (Newsweek). *His popular vote lead was razor-thin* (Wall Street Journal).

razz (raz), *U.S. Slang.* —*v.t.* to laugh at; make fun of. —*v.i.* to tease. —*n.* strong disapproval or criticism; derision: *The Red Swede got the grand razz handed to him* (Sinclair Lewis). [American English, back formation < *raspberry*]

raz·zi·a (raz′ē ə), *n.* a military raid: ... *responded with a tactic called the razzia — a swift, merciless strike at a native village, sparing nothing and nobody* (Time). [< French *razzia* < Arabic *ghāzia,* variant of *ghazāh* war; foray < *ghasw* to make war]

raz·zle (raz′əl), *n.* razzle-dazzle.

raz·zle-daz·zle (raz′əl daz′əl), *n., adj., v.,* **-zled, -zling.** —*n.* **1.** *U.S. Slang.* bewilderment: *The store sells anything from diapers to tombstones, and pulls customers in from six counties with a sales formula combining low prices and razzle-dazzle* (Wall Street Journal). **2.** a revolving platform on which people are moved about in amusingly irregular ways. **3.** (in sports, especially football), an intricate movement by the players of a team, intended to deceive or bewilder their opponents. **4.** *Slang.* intoxication.
—*adj. U.S. Slang.* bewildering; showy: *He specializes in the razzle-dazzle finish, in which the hero gallops on to the scene when all seems darkest and the curtain falls* (New York Times).
—*v.t. U.S. Slang.* to confuse; bewilder: *She beat boys at mumblety-peg, whizzed past them in foot races and razzle-dazzled them in basketball* (Time). [American English, varied reduplication of *dazzle*]

raz·zle-daz·zler (raz′əl daz′lər), *n.* *U.S. Slang.* **1.** a person or thing that razzle-dazzles. **2.** something that astonishes with its glaring incongruities.

razz·ma·tazz (raz′mə taz′), *n. U.S. Slang.* razzle-dazzle; fanfare: ... *a high-powered product, successfully designed for theatergoers with a taste of unabashed razzmatazz and schmaltz* (Christian Science Monitor).

Rb (no period), rubidium (chemical element).

r.b.i., rbi (no periods), or **RBI** (no periods), (in baseball) run or runs batted in.

R.C. or **RC** (no periods), **1.** Red Cross. **2.** Reserve Corps. **3.** Roman Catholic.

R.C.A., 1. Royal Canadian Academy of Arts. **2.** Royal Canadian Army.

R.C.A.F. or **RCAF** (no periods), Royal Canadian Air Force.

R.C.Ch., Roman Catholic Church.

R.C.M.P. or **RCMP** (no periods), Royal Canadian Mounted Police.

R.C.N. or **RCN** (no periods), Royal Canadian Navy.

r-col·or (är′kul′ər), *n. Phonetics.* an accompanying retroflex articulation of a vowel resulting in an *r*-like quality.

r-col·ored (är′kul′ərd), *adj. Phonetics.* pronounced with accompanying retroflex articulation resulting in an *r*-like quality: *an r-colored vowel.*

r-col·or·ing (är′kul′ər ing), *n. Phonetics.* r-color.

R.C.P., Royal College of Physicians (of England).

R.C.S., Royal College of Surgeons (of England).

rd., 1. rix-dollar. **2.** road. **3.** rod or rods. **4.** round.

Rd (no period), formerly, radium (chemical element). Now, **Ra** (no period).

Rd., 1. rix-dollar. **2.** Road.

R/D, *Banking.* refer to drawer.

R.D., Rural Delivery.

RDB (no periods), Research and Development Board.

R.D.C. or **RDC** (no periods), Rural District Council.

RDX (no periods), a powerful and highly sensitive crystalline explosive used in combination with other explosive substances in bombs, depth charges, etc.; cyclonite: *RDX is far more violent than TNT, having at least 50% more power* (Science News Letter). *Formula:* $C_3H_6N_6O_6$ [perhaps < *R*(esearch and) *D*(evelopment E)*x*(plosive)]

re[1] (rā), *n.* the second tone of the musical diatonic scale. [< Medieval Latin *re* < Latin *re*(*sonāre*) to resound. See GAMUT.]

re[2] (rē), *prep.* with reference to; in the matter or case of; about; concerning: *re your letter of the 7th instant.* [< Latin (*in*) *rē* (in) the matter of]

➤ **Re** is used in the heading of certain legal documents and to some extent in business writing. In ordinary prose, the equivalent English prepositions are preferable.

Re (rā), *n.* Ra (the great sun god of the ancient Egyptians). [< Egyptian *r'* the sun]

re-, *prefix.* **1.** again; anew; once more, as in *reappear, rebuild, reheat, reopen.*
2. back, as in *recall, repay, replace.* Also, sometimes **red-** before vowels.
[< Latin *re-,* or < French, Old French *re-* < Latin]

➤ **re-.** Usually words formed of the prefix *re-* and another word are not hyphened: *rearrange, refine, remit.* However, words formed with the prefix *re-,* meaning again are hyphened (1) when the form with hyphen can have a different meaning from the form without: *reform,* to make better —*re-form,* to shape again, and (2) (rarely) for emphasis, as in "now *re-seated* in fair comfort," or in informal or humorous compounds: *re-re-married.*

The meaning of each of the following words is found by adding *again* or *anew* to the main part. The pronunciation of the main part is not changed.

re′a·bridge′
re′ab·solve′
re′ac·cept′
re′ac·cept′ance
re′ac·com′plish
re′ac·com′plish·ment
re′ac·cost′
re′ac·count′
re′ac·cu′mu·late
re′ac·cu′mu·la′tion
re′ac·cu·sa′tion
re′ac·cus′tom
re′ac·knowl′edge
re′ac·knowl′edg·ment
re′ac·quaint′
re′ac·quaint′ance
re′ac·qui·si′tion
re′a·dapt′a·bil′i·ty
re′a·dapt′a·ble
re′ad·ap·ta′tion
re′a·dap′tive
re′ad·here′
re′ad·he′sion
re′ad·ju′di·cate
re′ad·ju′di·ca′tion
re′ad·min′is·ter
re′ad·mi·ra′tion
re′ad·mire′
re′a·dop′tion
re′ad·vance′ment
re·ad′ver·tise
re′ad·ver·tise′ment
re′ad·vise′
re′aer·a′tion
re′af·fil′i·ate
re′af·fil′i·a′tion
re·ag′i·tate
re′ag·i·ta′tion

re′a·line′
re′al·le·ga′tion
re′al·lege′
re′al·lot′
re′al·lot′ment
re′al·low′
re′al·low′ance
re·al′ter
re′al·ter·a′tion
re′a·mend′
re′a·mend′ment
re′-A·mer′i·can·ize
re·am′pli·fy
re′a·nal′y·sis
re·an′a·lyze
re·an′chor
re·an′no·tate
re′an·nounce′
re′an·nounce′ment
re′a·pol′o·gize
re′ap·plaud′
re·ap′pli·cant
re′ap·pli′er
re′ap·praise′ment
re′ap·prov′al
re′ap·prove′
re′a·rouse′
re′ar·range′a·ble
re′ar·rang′er
re′ar·ray′
re′ar·rest′
re′ar·riv′al
re′ar·rive′
re′as·cend′an·cy
re′as·cend′ant
re′as·cend′en·cy
re′as·cend′ent
re·ask′
re′as·pire′

re′as·sail′
re′as·sault′
re′as·say′
re′as·sig·na′tion
re′at·tack′
re′at·tend′
re′at·tend′ance
re′at·tract′
re·au′dit
re′au·then′ti·cate
re′au·then′ti·ca′tion
re′au·thor·i·za′tion
re·au′thor·ize
re′a·vail′
re′a·vail′a·ble
re′a·vow′
re′a·vow′al
re′a·wake′
re′a·wak′en·ment
re·bait′
re·bake′
re·bal′last
re·band′age
re·ban′ish
re·ban′ish·ment
re′bar·ba·ri·za′tion
re·bar′ba·rize
re·beau′ti·fy
re′be·gin′
re′be·gin′ning
re·bend′
re′be·stow′
re′be·stow′al
re·bite′
re·blast′
re·bless′
re·book′
re·bore′
re·bot′tle
re·bounce′
re·bound′a·ble
re·brace′
re·brew′
re·bring′
re·broad′cast
re·bub′ble
re·buck′le
re·bud′
re·budg′et
re·buf′fet
re·bunch′
re·bun′dle
re·bur′den
re·bur′i·al
re·but′ton
re·buy′
re·ca′ble
re·cal′cine
re·cal′cu·late
re′cal·cu·la′tion
re·cal′i·brate
re′cal·i·bra′tion
re·calk′
re·can′vas
re·cart′
re·cash′
re·catch′
re′ce·ment′
re·cen′tral·i·za′tion
re·chain′
re·cheer′
re·chew′
re-Chris′tian·ize
re·civ′i·lize
re′clas·si·fi·ca′tion
re·clas′si·fy
re·clean′
re·cleanse′
re·clear′
re·climb′
re·close′
re′co·ag′u·late
re′co·ag′u·la′tion
re·coast′
re·coat′
re·cock′
re·code′
re′cod·i·fi·ca′tion
re·cod′i·fy
re·coin′er
re′col·late′
re′col·la′tion
re′com·mu′ni·cate
re′com·pare′
re′com·par′i·son
re′com·pel′
re·com′pen·sate
re′com·pi·la′tion
re′com·pile′
re′com·pile′ment
re′com·plain′
re′com·plete′
re′com·ple′tion
re·com′pli·cate
re′com·pli·ca′tion
re′com·pound′
re′con·ceal′
re′con·ceal′ment
re′con·cede′
re′con·ceive′
re′con·cep′tion
re′con·ces′sion
re′con·fer′
re′con·fess′
re′con·fine′
re′con·fine′ment
re′con·geal′
re′con·nec′tion
re·con′quer·or
re′con·sole′
re′con·strue′
re′con·sult′
re′con·sul·ta′tion
re·con′tact
re·con′tem·plate
re′con·tem·pla′tion
re′con·tin′u·ance
re′con·tin′ue
re′con·tract′
re′con·trac′tion
re′con·trast′
re′con·va·lesce′
re′con·va·les′cence
re′con·va·les′cent
re′con·verge′
re′con·vert′er
re′con·voke′
re·cook′
re·cop′y·right′
re·cork′
re′cor·rect′
re′cor·rec′tion
re·cost′
re′cos·tume′
re·cou′ple
re·cred′it
re·cru′ci·fy
re′cul·ti·va′tion
re·curl′
re·cush′ion
re·date′
re′de·bate′
re·deb′it
re′de·cay′
re′de·ci′sion
re′de·clare′
re′de·cline′
re·ded′i·ca·to′ry
re′de·feat′
re′de·fend′
re′de·fer′
re′de·fi′ance
re′de·fy′
re′de·lib′er·ate
re′de·lib′er·a′tion
re′de·liv′er·ance
re′de·liv′er·y
re′dem·on·stra′tion
re′de·scrip′tion
re′des·ig·na′tion
re′de·sire′
re′de·sir′ous
re′de·tect′
re′de·vote′
re·dic′tate
re′dic·ta′tion
re′dif·fer·en′ti·ate
re′dif·fer·en′ti·a′tion
re′dif·fuse′
re·dig′
re′di·ges′tion
re·dip′
re′dis·charge′
re·dis′ci·pline
re′dis·cuss′
re′dis·cus′sion
re′dis·patch′
re′dis·perse′
re′dis·play′
re′dis·po·si′tion
re′dis·pute′
re′dis·sol′u·ble
re′dis·so·lu′tion
re′dis·solv′a·ble
re′dis·tend′
re′dis·til·la′tion
re′dis·trib′ut·er
re′dis·trib′u·tive
re′dis·trib′u·tor
re′dis·trib′u·to′ry
re·dive′
re′di·vi′sion
re·dock′
re·doom′
re·dredge′
re·drill′
re·dust′
re′ë·di′tion
re′ë·ject′
re′ë·jec′tion
re′ë·ject′ment
re′ël·e·va′tion
re′ëm·bat′tle
re′ëm·bel′lish
re′ëm·brace′ment
re′ëm·i·gra′tion
re′ë·mis′sion
re′ëm·pow′er
re′ën·a′ble
re′ën·a′ble·ment
re′ë·nam′el
re′ën·close′
re′ën·clo′sure
re′ën·dear′
re′ën·dear′ment
re′ën·dow′ment
re·ën′er·gize
re′ën·forc′er
re′ën·fran′chise
re′ën·fran′chise·ment
re′ën·gen′der
re′ën·join′
re′ën·kin′dle
re′ën·large′
re′ën·large′ment
re′ën·light′en
re′ën·light′en·ment
re′ën·list′er
re′ën·liv′en
re′ën·roll′
re′ën·roll′ment
re′ën·shrine′
re′ën·sphere′
re′ën·ter·tain′
re′ën·ter·tain′ment
re′ën·thrall′
re′ën·tice′
re′ën·ti′tle
re′ën·tomb′
re′ën·train′
re′ë·nun′ci·ate
re′ë·nun′ci·a′tion
re′ë·rec′tion
re′ës·cape′
re′ës·cort′
re′ës·pous′al
re′ës·pouse′
re′ës·tab′lish·er
re′ës·ti·ma′tion
re′ë·vap′o·rate
re′ëx·alt′
re·ëx′ca·vate
re′ëx·ca·va′tion
re′ëx·ci·ta′tion
re′ëx·cite′
re·ëx′er·cise
re′ëx·ert′
re′ëx·hale′
re′ëx·haust′
re′ëx·hi·bi′tion
re′ëx·ist′
re′ëx·ist′ence
re′ëx·ist′ent
re′ëx·pect′
re′ëx·pec·ta′tion
re′ëx·per′i·ment
re′ëx·pla·na′tion
re′ëx·pose′
re′ëx·po′sure
re′ëx·pound′
re′ëx·press′
re′ëx·pres′sion
re′ëx·pul′sion
re′ëx·tend′
re′ëx·ten′sion
re′ëx·tract′
re·fall′
re·fal′low
re·fan′
re′fer·ment′
re′fer·ti·li·za′tion
re·find′
re·fin′ger
re·flame′
re·flash′
re′float·a′tion
re·floor′
re·for′ward
re′foun·da′tion
re·frac′ture
re·fresh′en
re·fright′en
re·frus′trate
re·fry′
re·gar′nish
re·gar′ri·son
re·glo′ri·fied
re·gloss′
re·grasp′
re·grind′er
re·grip′
re·grow′
re′guar·an·tee′
re·guide′
re·hal′low
re·ham′mer
re·hard′en
re·har′ness
re·heap′
re·hoist′
re·hum′ble
re′hu·mil′i·ate
re·hung′
re·ice′
re′i·den′ti·fi·ca′tion
re′i·den′ti·fy
re′ig·ni′tion
re′il·lume′
re′il·lu′mi·nate
re′il·lu′mi·na′tion
re′il·lu′mine
re′im·merse′
re′im·mer′sion
re·im′pact
re′im·part′
re′im·plant′
re′im·press′
re′in·duce′ment
re′in·duc′tion
re′in·fer′
re′in·fest′
re′in·fes·ta′tion
re′in·fil′trate
re′in·flict′
re·in′flu·ence
re′in·fu′sion
re′in·hab′i·ta′tion
re′in·her′it
re′i·ni′ti·ate
re′i·ni′ti·a′tion
re·in′jure
re·ink′
re′in·oc′u·late
re′in·oc′u·la′tion
re′in·quire′
re′in·quir′y
re′in·stal·la′tion
re′in·still′
re′in·sti·tu′tion
re′in·struc′tion
re′in·sult′
re′in·ter′ro·ga′tion
re′in·trude′
re′in·tru′sion
re′in·va′sion
re′in·ven′tion
re′in·ven′tor
re′in·vert′
re′in·voke′
re′in·volve′ment
re·i′so·late
re·lace′
re·lance′
re·land′
re·latch′
re·lead′
re·li′cense
re·lick′
re·lift′
re·lim′it
re′lim·i·ta′tion
re·liq′ue·fy
re·list′
re·lit′i·gate
re·lock′
re·lodge′
re·look′
re′mag·net·i·za′tion
re·mag′net·ize
re·mail′
re·man′tle
re′man·u·fac′ture
re·map′
re·march′
re′mas·ti·ca′tion
re·match′
re′ma·te′ri·al·ize
re·meas′ure·ment
re·mem′o·rize
re·mend′
re′min·er·al·i·za′tion
re·min′er·al·ize
re·min′gle
re·mix′ture
re·mo′bi·lize
re·mort′gage
re′no·ti·fi·ca′tion
re·no′ti·fy
re′ob·ser·va′tion
re′ob·serve′
re′ob·tain′ment
re′oc·cur′
re′oc·cur′rence
re′op·po·si′tion
re·or′ches·trate
re·or′na·ment
re·out′fit
re′o·ver·flow′
re·own′
re′ox·i·da′tion
re·ox′i·dize
re·pack′er
re·page′
re·pan′el
re·par′a·graph
re·park′
re·pave′ment
re·pawn′
re·ped′dle
re·peg′
re·pen′
re·pe′nal·ize
re′per·form′
re′per·form′ance
re′pe·rus′al
re′pe·ruse′
re·pick′
re·pin′
re·pitch′
re·plane′
re·pleat′
re·plow′
re·plun′der
re·point′
re′pol·lute′
re·pop′u·late
re·pow′der
re′pre·cip′i·tate
re′pre·cip′i·ta′tion
re′pre·pare′
re·press′
re·pres′sure
re·pres′sur·ize
re·price′
re·prime′
re′pro·cur′a·ble
re′pro·cure′
re′pro·nounce′
re′pro·pos′al
re′pro·pose′
re·pros′e·cute
re′pros·e·cu′tion
re·prove′
re·pub′lish
re·pump′
re·pun′ish
re·pun′ish·ment
re′pu·ri·fi·ca′tion
re·pur′pose
re′pur·suit′
re′qual·i·fi·ca′tion
re·qual′i·fy
re·ques′tion
re′quo·ta′tion
re·quote′
re·raise′
re·rate′
re·read′er
re·reel′
re′re·fine′
re′re·flect′
re′re·flec′tion
re′re·form′
re·reg′is·ter
re′reg·is·tra′tion
re′re·it′er·ate
re′re·late′
re′re·lease′
re′re·mit′
re·rent′
re·rent′al
re′re·pair′
re′re·peat′
re′re·port′
re′rep·re·sent′
re′rep·re·sen·ta′tion
re′re·side′
re′re·solve′
re′re·veal′
re′rev·e·la′tion
re′re·vise′
re·ring′
re·riv′et
re-Ro′man·ize
re·rub′
re·salt′
re·scrub′
re′se·crete′
re′se·lect′
re·sen′tence
re·share′
re·shave′
re·sheathe′
re·shift′
re·shine′
re·shin′gle
re·shut′
re·shut′tle
re·sight′
re·sing′
re·sink′
re·slash′
re·slay′
re·slide′
re·smelt′
re·smile′
re·snub′
re·soak′
re·soil′
re′so·lid′i·fy
re·solve′
re·spar′kle
re·sphere′
re·spin′
re·splice′
re·split′
re·spot′
re·spring′
re·sprin′kle
re·sprout′
re·stack′
re·stain′
re·steal′
re·steel′
re·stem′
re·stitch′
re·stress′
re·stuff′
re·sub′ju·gate
re′sub·li·ma′tion
re′sub·lime′
re′sub·mis′sion
re′suc·ceed′
re·suf′fer
re′sug·gest′
re·suit′
re·sup′
re′sup·press′
re′sur·prise′
re′sur·ren′der
re′sus·pend′
re·swal′low
re·swell′
re·syn′the·size
re·tack′
re·tail′or
re·talk′
re·taste′
re·tax′
re′tax·a′tion
re·tel′e·graph
re·tel′e·phone
re·tes′ti·fy
re·thatch′
re·thread′
re·throne′
re·tie′
re·till′
re·tin′
re·tor′ture
re·toss′
re·track′
re′trans·plant′
re′trans·port′
re·trav′el
re′trav·erse′
re·trip′
re·turn′
re·twine′
re·twist′
re·un′du·late
re′un·fold′
re·urge′
re·ut′ter·ance
re·va′por·ize
re·ver′si·fy
re·vis′u·al·ize
re·vow′
re·voy′age
re·warm′
re·wax′
re·weave′
re·wet′
re·whirl′
re·whit′en
re·wid′en
re·wound′
re·yoke′

r.e., right end.
Re (no period), rhenium (chemical element).
Re., rupee or rupees.
R.E., an abbreviation for the following:
1. Reformed Episcopal.
2. Right Excellent.
3. Royal Engineers of Great Britain.
4. Royal Exchange of Great Britain.

REA (no periods) or **R.E.A.**, Rural Electrification Administration.

re·ab·sorb (rē′əb sôrb′, -zôrb′), *v.t.* to absorb again or anew.

re·ab·sorp·tion (rē′əb sôrp′shən, -zôrp′-), *n.* **1.** the act of reabsorbing. **2.** the state of being reabsorbed.

re·ac·com·mo·date (rē′ə kom′ə dāt), *v.t.*, **-dat·ed, -dat·ing.** to accommodate or adjust afresh or again: *The hotel refused to reaccommodate us in other rooms.*

re·ac·com·pa·ny (rē′ə kum′pə nē), *v.t.*, **-nied, -ny·ing.** to accompany again.

re·ac·cuse (rē′ə kūz′), *v.t.*, **-cused, -cus·ing.** to accuse again or afresh; make a renewed accusation against.

reach (rēch), *v.t.* **1.** to get to; come to; arrive at: *to reach the top of a hill, to reach the end of a book, to reach an agreement.* **2.** to stretch out; hold out: *A tree reaches out its branches.* **3. a.** to extend to: *The radio reaches millions.* **b.** to get in touch with (someone): *I could not reach him by telephone.* **4.** to touch; get in touch with by anything extended, cast, etc.: *The ladder just reaches the roof. The anchor reached bottom.* **5.** to move to touch or seize (something); try to get: *to reach a package on a high shelf.* **6.** to get at; influence: *Some men are reached by flattery. The speaker reached the hearts of his hearers.* **7.** to amount to; be equal to: *The cost of the war reached billions.*
—*v.i.* **1.** to stretch: *to reach toward a book.* **2.** to extend in space, operation, effect, influence, etc.: *a dress reaching to the floor. The power of Rome reached to the ends of the known world.* **3.** to get or come; function; carry: *farther than the eye can reach.* **4.** to make a stretch in a certain direction: *The man reached for his gun.* **5.** to make a stretch of certain length with the hand, etc.: *I cannot reach to the top of the wall.* **6.** to amount (to): *amounts reaching to a considerable sum.* **7.** to succeed in coming to a place, point, person, etc.: *They could not reach back to the boat before it was dark* (Daniel Defoe). **8.** to sail on a course with the wind forward of the beam.
—*n.* **1.** a stretching out; reaching: *By a long reach, the drowning man grasped the rope.* **2.** the extent or distance of reaching: *out of one's reach.* **3.** range; power; capacity: *the reach of the mind.* **4.** a continuous stretch or extent: *a reach of woodland.* **5.** the part of a river, channel, or lake between bends. **6.** the part of a canal between locks. **7.** the course or distance sailed on one tack. **8.** a pole from the rear axle of a wagon or carriage to the bar above the front axle.
[Old English *rǣcan*] —**reach′er,** *n.*
—**Syn.** *v.t.* **1.** attain, gain.

reach·a·ble (rē′chə bəl), *adj.* that can be reached; within reach: *New York has good evidence that the goal is reachable* (Time).
—**Syn.** accessible, attainable.

reach·less (rēch′lis), *adj.* beyond reach; unattainable; lofty: *the reachless height of an eagle's nest.*

reach-me-down (rēch′mē doun′), *n., adj. British Informal.* hand-me-down: ... *reach-me-downs from other men's wardrobes* (London Times).

re·ac·quire (rē′ə kwīr′), *v.t.*, **-quired, -quir·ing.** to acquire anew: *The United States routinely reacquires military equipment given to allies* (New York Times).

re·act (rē akt′), *v.i.* **1.** to act back; have an effect on the one that is acting: *Unkindness often reacts on the unkind person and makes him unhappy.* **2. a.** to act in response: *Dogs react to kindness by showing affection.* **b.** to respond in some manner; have an opinion to some proposal: *How did he react to the idea when you told him? Plants react to light.* **3.** to act chemically: *Acids react on metals.* **4.** to return to a previous state, level, etc.
react against, to act in opposition to (some force): *I know that some individuals react against the strongest impediments* (Matthew Arnold).
[< *re-* back + *act*, verb. Compare Medieval Latin *reactus*, past participle of *reagere.*]

re-act (rē akt′), *v.t.* to act over again: *to re-act a scene from a play.* [< *re-* again + *act*]

re·act·ance (rē ak′təns), *n. Electricity.* that part of the impedance of an alternating-current circuit which is due to self-induction and capacity: *amplifiers ... for microwave amplification by variable reactance* (Wall Street Journal). [< *react* + *-ance*]

re·act·ant (rē ak′tənt), *n. Chemistry.* a substance that enters into a chemical reaction: *The influence of the concentrations of the reactants on the rates of chemical reactions was discovered very early in the development of chemical kinetics ...* (K. D. Wadsworth).

re·ac·tion (rē ak′shən), *n.* **1.** an action in the opposite direction: *Fever is a common reaction from a chill.* **2.** a political tendency toward a previous state of affairs. **3. a.** an action in response to some influence or force: *Our reaction to a joke is to laugh. The doctor observed carefully his patient's reactions to certain tests.* **b.** *Informal.* a response to an idea, plan, etc.; attitude; feeling; opinion: *What was his reaction to the plan?* **4. a.** the chemical action of two substances on each other: *Putting an acid and a metal together causes a reaction.* **b.** the change resulting from such chemical action: ... *whether reaction occurs may depend on the timing of internal vibration of each of the molecules* (K. D. Wadsworth). **5.** the response of a nerve, muscle, or organ to a stimulus: *They were designed to elucidate the reaction of the human body to the various stresses ...* (E. F. Roots). **6.** the response of the body to a test for immunization or the like: *A more general distinction depends on the extent of reaction shown by antiserum prepared against one strain of the virus ...* (A. W. Haslett). **7.** an equal and opposite force which a body exerts against a force that acts upon it: ... *in no case is it of importance which of the equal and opposite forces is considered the action and which the reaction* (Shortley and Williams). **8.** a process in which the nucleus of an atom becomes transformed, as in the disintegration of radioactive substances; nuclear reaction: *Reactions of the general type in which one of the two deuteron particles enters the hit nucleus and the other continues on its way* (A.W. Haslett). **9.** a drop in prices following a rise in prices, as on a stock market.

re·ac·tion·al (rē ak′shən əl), *adj.* of or having to do with reaction.

re·ac·tion·ar·y (rē ak′shə ner′ē), *adj., n., pl.* **-ar·ies.** —*adj.* having to do with, marked by, or favoring reaction, especially in politics: *The economic recession brought about a reactionary feeling to low tariffs.* —*n.* a person who favors or tends toward reaction, especially in politics; an extreme conservative.

reaction engine, an engine which expels a stream of matter at high velocity, the reaction from which creates a forward accelerating force; jet engine.

re·ac·tion·ism (rē ak′shə niz əm), *n.* reactionary principles and ideas; inclination toward a previous state of affairs, especially in politics; conservatism.

re·ac·tion·ist (rē ak′shə nist), *adj., n.* reactionary.

reaction key, *Psychology.* an instrument to record movement of response in a reaction experiment.

re·ac·tion·less (rē ak′shən lis), *adj.* without reaction, as of certain machines in which the magnetic circuit is neither strengthened nor weakened.

reaction time, the interval of time between a stimulus or signal and the response to it: *The reaction time of a V-bomber, even under ideal conditions and with advance preparation, cannot be much under four minutes* (Manchester Guardian).

re·ac·ti·vate (rē ak′tə vāt), *v.t.*, **-vat·ed, -vat·ing.** to make active again; restore to active service: *The Army announced that the old 101st Airborne Division, famous for its stand at Bastogne in the second world war, will be reactivated at Fort Campbell, Kentucky* (Newsweek).

re·ac·ti·va·tion (rē′ak tə vā′shən), *n.* a reactivating or being reactivated: *The government has authorized this month the reactivation of thirteen more labor unions* (New York Times).

re·ac·tive (rē ak′tiv), *adj.* **1.** tending to react: *Moreover, all the steps, apart from the first, require little or no energy of activation, because they are all reactions of highly reactive atoms with molecules* (K. D. Wadsworth). **2.** having to do with or characterized by reaction, especially in politics.

reactive circuit, a circuit with impedance from inductance or capacity or to both.

reactive coil, a wire coil, often with an iron core, to produce reactance.

reactive drop, the fall of potential in a circuit from reactance.

re·ac·tiv·i·ty (rē′ak tiv′ə tē), *n.* the power or state of being reactive, as in a chemical combination: *The existence of such ... ions as intermediates in organic reactions is well established, and their reactivity can be readily measured by the rate at which they react with powerful acidic (negative) ions* (R. F. Homer).

re·ac·tor (rē ak′tər), *n.* **1.** a special assembly for the production of a limited release of atomic energy, consisting of layers of fissionable material, such as uranium, spaced with moderators, such as graphite and heavy water, which slow down the speed and number of the neutrons intended for splitting the uranium nuclei; pile; nuclear reactor; atomic reactor: *The goal is to find economical ways of chemically treating water from the Columbia River so that it can be used to cool Hanford reactors operating at higher power than at present* (Science). **2.** *Electricity.* a type of condenser characterized by slow resistance and high inductance. **3.** a person or animal that reacts positively to a medical test, as for allergy. **4.** a person or animal that reacts.

read[1] (rēd), *v.*, **read** (red), **read·ing,** *n.* —*v.t.* **1.** to get the meaning of (writing or printing): *to read a book. The blind girl reads special raised print by touching it. I know enough German to read German.* **2.** to find out from reading or writing: *to read the news.* **3.** to speak (printed or written words); say aloud: *Read this story to me.* **4.** to show by letters, figures, signs, etc.: *The thermometer reads 70 degrees. The ticket reads "From New York to Boston."* **5.** to give as the word or words in a particular passage: *For "fail," a misprint, read "fall."* **6.** to study (a subject): *to read law or medicine.* **7.** to get the meaning of; understand: *God reads men's hearts.* **8.** to give the meaning of; interpret: *A prophet reads the future.* **9.** to introduce (something not expressed or directly indicated) by one's manner of understanding or interpreting: *to read a hostile intent in a friendly letter.* **10.** to bring or put by reading: *He reads himself to sleep.* **11.** to give (a lecture or lesson) as a reprimand. **12.** (of an electronic device) to absorb information directly from (written or printed matter) by means of a photoelectric cell: *The ... Unit both punches and reads paper tape or unit cards that activate other equipment* (Wall Street Journal).
—*v.i.* **1.** to get the meaning of something written or printed: *to learn to read and write. The blind read with their fingers.* **2.** to learn from writing or printing: *We read of heroes of other days.* **3.** to say aloud the words one sees or touches: *to read to a child before bedtime.* **4.** to study by reading: *He ... was ... set to read with the best private tutors that could be found* (Samuel Butler). **5.** to produce a certain impression when read; mean; be in effect when read: *This does not read like a child's composition.* **6.** to convey a statement when read: *The telegram reads as follows.* **7.** to be worded in a certain way: *This line reads differently in the first edition.* **8.** to admit of being read or interpreted: *A rule that reads two different ways.*
read between the lines. See under **line**[1], *n.*
read in, to feed information into a computer: *All data has to be read in to computers, and there is great interest in machines which can do their own reading* (New Scientist).
read into, to interpret in a certain way, often attributing more than intended: *He reads something of himself into the composition he is reviewing* (Arthur C. Ainger).
read out, to transmit (data) by radio transmitter: *Three radio receiving stations, to read out telemetry data from the satellite, are being established in Brazil* (New York Times).
read out of, to expel from (a political party, etc.): *Chiang would be read out of the U.N. probably by the next General Assembly* (Newsweek).
read up on, to study by reading about: *to read up on the latest scientific advances.*
—*n. Informal.* an act or spell of reading: *Woe betide those who settle down with this book to a steady read through 550 pages from beginning to end* (Economist).
[Old English *rǣdan* to guess; read; counsel]
—**Syn.** *v.t.* **4.** indicate, register. **7.** comprehend. **8.** explain, decipher. **9.** infer.

read[2] (red), *adj.* having knowledge gained by reading; informed: *a well-read man. He was deeply read in the ancients* (Henry Fielding). —*v.* the past tense and past participle of **read:** *I read that book last year. Joe has read it too.* [(originally) past participle of *read*[1]]

read·a·bil·i·ty (rē′də bil′ə tē), *n.* readable quality.

read·a·ble (rē′də bəl), *adj.* **1.** easy or pleasant to read; interesting: *Treasure Island is a very readable story.* **2.** that can be read; legible. —**read′a·ble·ness,** *n.*

read·a·bly (rē′də blē), *adv.* in a readable manner; so as to be readable; legibly.

re·a·dapt (rē′ə dapt′), *v.t.* to adapt anew: *To readapt, in a purified state, the old eras* (Thomas Carlyle).

re·ad·dress (rē′ə dres′), *v.t.* **1.** to put a new address on. **2.** to speak to again. **3.** to apply (oneself) anew.

read·er (rē′dər), *n.* **1.** a person who reads: *a good reader, a light reader.* **2.** a book for learning and practicing reading. **3.** a person employed to read manuscripts and estimate their fitness for publication: *The ideal publisher's reader should have two perfections — perfect taste and perfect knowledge of what the various kinds of other people deem to be taste* (Arnold Bennett). **4.** a proofreader. **5. a.** *Especially British.* an instructor in certain universities: *He came under Dr. Martin Johnson, the present Reader in Astrophysics at Birmingham* (New Scientist). **b.** an assistant who grades and corrects examinations, reads papers, etc., for a professor. **6.** a person who reads or recites to entertain an audience. **7.** a person who reads aloud the lessons or other parts of the service in a church. **8.** an electronic device that absorbs information directly from written or printed matter through a photoelectric cell or scanner: *a "character recognition" type of reader in its controls instrument division which turns out punched cards rather than electrical impulses* (Wall Street Journal).

read·er·ship (rē′dər ship), *n.* **1.** the reading audience, especially of a particular author, publication, or type of reading matter: *The distribution of readership has not been determined, but undoubtedly a large number of these readers are young* (Atlantic). **2.** the office of a reader, as in a university.

read·i·ly (red′ə lē), *adv.* **1.** quickly; promptly; without delay: *A bright boy answers readily when called on.* **2.** easily; without difficulty: *I enjoy the feeling ... that everything around me is in its place, within easy reach, and readily accessible* (Harper's).

read-in (rēd′in′), *n.* **1.** the reading of appropriate literary passages at a meeting as a form of protest against war, racial segregation, etc.: *... a read-in for Peace in Vietnam, where several poets read from their work* (Stanley Kunitz). **2.** the feeding of information into a computer: *During read-in ... the source connected to any store can be changed by depressing the appropriate button* (New Scientist).

read·i·ness (red′ē nis), *n.* **1.** the condition of being ready; preparedness: *to be in readiness for any emergency.* **2.** quickness; promptness. **3.** ease; facility: *readiness of thought.* **4.** willingness.

read·ing (rē′ding), *n.* **1.** the act or process of getting the meaning of writing or printing: *The teaching of reading has not changed in a generation* (Time). **2.** the study of books, etc.: *Reading has objective values, such as giving facts and arousing interests* (Emory S. Bogardus). *Reading maketh a full man* (Francis Bacon). **3.** a speaking out loud of written or printed words; public recital: *Reading aloud requires stamina in the reader as well as the read to* (London Times). **4.** written or printed matter read or to be read: *It is in newspapers that we must look for main reading of this generation* (Thomas De Quincey). *Remembering his early love of poetry and fiction, she unlocked a bookcase, and took down several books that had been excellent reading in their day* (Hawthorne). **5.** a thing shown by letters, figures, or signs: *The reading of the thermometer was 96 degrees.* **6.** the form of a given word or passage in a particular copy or edition of a book: *No two editions have the same reading for that passage.* **7.** interpretation: *Each actor gave the lines a different reading.* **8.** the extent to which one has read; literary knowledge. **9.** the formal recital of a bill, or part of it, before a legislature.

—*adj.* **1.** that reads: *the reading public.* **2.** used in or for reading: *reading glasses.*

reading desk, a desk to hold a book while a person reads, especially when standing; lectern.

reading glass, a magnifying glass usually used to read fine print or details of maps.

reading room, a special room for reading in a library, club, etc.

re·ad·journ (rē′ə jėrn′), *v.t., v.i.* to adjourn again: *Parliament assembling again ... was then readjourned by the king's special command till Tuesday next* (Sir Henry Wotton).

re·ad·journ·ment (rē′ə jėrn′mənt), *n.* a succeeding adjournment; adjournment anew.

re·ad·just (rē′ə just′), *v.t., v.i.* to adjust again; arrange again: *the day hospital ... for patients who ... need help in readjusting to the world at large* (Time). —**re′ad·just′er,** *n.*

re·ad·just·ment (rē′ə just′mənt), *n.* **1.** the process of readjusting. **2.** the process of being readjusted. **3.** alterations in the policies or structure of a business to correct a harmful condition: *After every war, business must go through a period of readjustment, and that readjustment sometimes proves painful* (Newsweek).

re·ad·mis·sion (rē′əd mish′ən), *n.* admission again or anew: *In an exhausted receiver, animals that seem as they were dead revive upon the readmission of fresh air* (John Arbuthnot).

re·ad·mit (rē′əd mit′), *v.t.,* **-mit·ted, -mit·ting.** to admit again.

re·ad·mit·tance (rē′əd mit′əns), *n.* permission to enter again; readmission: *Humbly petitioning a readmittance into his college* (Thomas Warton).

re·a·dopt (rē′ə dopt′), *v.t.* to adopt again: *The boundary which had first passed was re-adopted by a large vote* (Bayard Taylor).

re·a·dorn (rē′ə dôrn′), *v.t.* to adorn anew: *With Scarlet Honours readorn'd* (Sir Richard Blackmore).

read·out (rēd′out), *n.* **1.** the display, usually in digits, of processed information by a computer. **2.** the transmission of quantitative data such as that taken by a telemeter.

re·ad·vance (rē′əd vans′, -väns′), *v.i., v.t.,* **-vanced, -vanc·ing.** to advance again or afresh: *Which if they miss, they yet should readvance to former height* (Ben Jonson).

read·y (red′ē), *adj.,* **read·i·er, read·i·est,** *v.,* **read·ied, read·y·ing,** *n.* —*adj.* **1.** prepared for action or use at once; prepared: *Dinner is ready. The soldiers are ready for battle. We were ready to start at nine. The cannons are pointed, and ready to roar* (Byron). **2.** willing: *The soldiers were ready to die for their country. She is ready to forgive.* **3.** quick; prompt: *a ready welcome.* **4.** quick in thought or action; dexterous: *a ready wit.* **5.** apt; likely; liable: *She is too ready to find fault.* **6.** immediately available: *ready money.*

make ready, to prepare: *His companions made ready to fight* (William Longman).

—*v.t.* to make ready; prepare: *The expedition readied itself during the summer* (Atlantic).

ready up, to make ready; prepare for a special purpose: *It was the women's job to ready up the house for the party; the men went out to buy the food and drinks.*

—*n.* **1.** the condition or position of being fit for action: *While soldiers walked along the shore with their guns at the ready, holiday-makers were following along behind them* (London Times). **2.** *Slang.* ready money; cash.

[Middle English *redi* < Old English *rǣde* mounted (ready to ride) + *-ig* -y[1]. Related to RIDE.]

—**Syn.** *adj.* **2.** disposed. **3, 4. Ready, prompt** mean quick to understand, observe, or act in response. **Ready** implies being both quick and apt: *With ready fingers the surgeon explored the wound.* **Prompt** emphasizes being quick to act when the occasion demands: *He is prompt to help students.* **5.** prone.

read·y-made (red′ē mād′), *adj.* **1.** ready for immediate use; made for anybody who will buy; not made to order: *Department stores sell ready-made clothes.* **2.** all the same, as if produced by mass production, and kept in readiness for any use or occasion: *ready-made opinions. They were ... spies and agents ready-made for either party* (Robert Louis Stevenson). —*n.* a ready-made object: *Some maternity shops, in addition to selling ready-mades, will custom-design clothes* (Maclean's).

read·y-mix (red′ē miks′), *adj.* that contains the proper inactive ingredients and is ready for use after mixing with water, milk, etc.: *ready-mix cement, ready-mix cake.* —*n.* a preparation that is ready for use after mixing with a liquid solution: *The American consumer ... insists on better cuts of beef, fancier grades of vegetables,* [*and*] *ready-mixes* (Newsweek).

ready reckoner, *British.* a table, or collection of tables, showing at a glance the results of such arithmetical calculations as are most frequently required in ordinary business, housekeeping, etc.: *Having a poor head for figures, I was not at ease with ready reckoners* (London Times).

Ready Reserve, *U.S.* reserve members of the armed forces who train at certain intervals in preparation for active duty in an emergency: *That service will consist of six months' training, at which time he will move into the Ready Reserve and have an obligation there for nine and one-half years* (New York Times).

Ready Reservist, a member of the Ready Reserve: *The President could also clear the way for calling up Ready Reservists* (New York Times).

ready room, a room where members of an aircrew meet to receive a briefing or a call to fly.

read·y-to-wear (red′ē tə wãr′), *adj.* ready-made: *Others prefer to make their own clothes because they feel that ready-to-wear garments have too little individuality* (World Book Encyclopedia). —*n.* ready-made clothing: *He would like some day to design ready-to-wear to be manufactured in America* (New York Times).

read·y·wit·ted (red′ē wit′id), *adj.* mentally alert.

re·af·firm (rē′ə fėrm′), *v.t.* to affirm again or anew: *The electors have since ... reaffirmed and strengthened that decision* (Spectator). —**re′af·firm′er,** *n.*

re·af·firm·ance (rē′ə fėr′məns), *n.* reaffirmation.

re·af·fir·ma·tion (rē′af ər mā′shən), *n.* renewed affirmation; a repeated affirmation.

re·af·for·est (rē′ə fôr′əst, -for′-), *v.t.* to cover again with forest; reforest.

re·af·for·est·a·tion (rē′ə fôr′ə stā′shən, -for′-), *n.* a second afforestation; promotion of renewed forest growth.

re·a·gent (rē ā′jənt), *n.* a substance used to detect the presence of other substances by the chemical reactions it causes: *The addition to the blood of small amounts of reagents such as citrates, which can bind chemically and inactivate calcium ions ... prevents coagulation quite effectively* (K. S. Spiegler).

re·a·gin (rē′ə jin), *n.* **1.** one of a group of antibodies that reacts with the allergens of hay fever, asthma, etc. **2.** a substance in serum and cerebrospinal fluid that behaves like an antibody in complement fixation and similar reactions. [< *reag*(ent) + *-in*]

re·al[1] (rē′əl, rēl), *adj.* **1.** existing as a fact; not imagined or made up; actual; true: *a real experience, the real reason.* **2.** genuine; not artificial: *the real thing, a real diamond, real money.* **3.** *Law.* of or having to do with immovable property. **4.** of or having to do with things. **5.** *Mathematics.* either rational or irrational, not imaginary. **6.** *Optics.* of or having to do with an image formed by actual convergence of rays: *A real image can be caught on a screen, a virtual image cannot* (Shortley and Williams). **7.** *Economics.* measured by reference to useful goods rather than money: *In a period of rising prices, real incomes fall if money incomes remain steady.* **8.** *Philosophy.* existing in or having to do with things, and not words or thought merely.

—*adv. U.S. Substandard.* very; extremely: *real soon. It was real kind of you to come.*

—*n.* something real or having a real existence.

for real, *Informal.* **a.** genuine; authentic: *"Here's Love"—something about a Macy Santa Claus who thinks he's for real* (New Yorker). **b.** in reality; really: *President Johnson ... told Katzenbach that next day he would name him Attorney General for real* (Time).

[< Late Latin *reālis* < Latin *rēs, reī* matter, thing]

—**Syn.** *adj.* **1. Real, actual, true** mean existing as a fact. **Real** means that what is described is in fact what it seems, is thought, or is said to be, not pretended, imaginary, or made up: *Give your real name.* **Actual** means that what it describes has already happened or come into existence, and is not merely capable of doing so: *Name an actual case of bravery.* **True** means in agreement with what is real or actual, not false: *Tell the true story.* **2.** authentic.

re·al[2] (rē′əl; *Spanish* rä äl′), *n., pl.* **re·als,** *Spanish.* **re·a·les** (rä ä′lās). a former small Spanish silver coin worth about 12½ cents. It was widely used in the American colonies at one time and was referred to as a *bit.* [< Spanish *real* < Latin *rēgālis* regal < *rēx, rēgis* king. Doublet of REGAL, ROYAL.]

Real[2] coined in Spanish Mexico about 1800

real estate, *U.S.* land together with the buildings, fences, trees, water, and minerals that belong with it. **—real′-es·tate′,** *adj.*

re·al·gar (rē al′gər), *n.* arsenic disulfide, used in fireworks. It is found in a native state as a lustrous orange-red mineral and is also prepared artificially. *Formula:* As_2S_2 [< Medieval Latin *realgar,* probably < Spanish *rejalgar* < Arabic *rahgh-al-gār,* variant of *rahghu-lgār* (literally) powder of the cave; form apparently from a textual error for *rahghu-lfār* rat powder]

re·al·i·a (rē ā′lē ə), *n. pl.* actual objects, such as types of woods or fabrics, used as tools in teaching. [< Late Latin *reālia,* neuter plural of *reālis* real; see REAL[1]]

re·a·lign (rē′ə līn′), *v.t., v.i.* to align again or anew: *to realign wheels of a car. Just behind the film the carbon atoms realign themselves and form diamonds* (Scientific American). *Some political scientists have urged that the two major parties realign . . . that all conservatives move into the Republican party and all liberals be driven into the Democratic party* (World Book Encyclopedia).

re·a·lign·ment (rē′ə līn′mənt), *n.* a realigning; new alignment: *. . . party realignment along clear-cut principles* (Time).

re·al·ise (rē′ə līz), *v.t., v.i.,* **-ised, -is·ing.** *Especially British.* realize: *The question is whether the dramatist can adequately express these eternal qualities in abstractions from the situations that realise them* (Observer).

re·al·ism (rē′ə liz əm), *n.* **1.** practical tendency: *His realism caused him to dislike fanciful schemes. With the inexorable realism of her sex she easily dismissed . . . theories, and accommodated herself to the fact* (Arnold Bennett). **2.** Also, **Realism.** (in art and literature) the picturing of life as it actually is: *When we think of Realism we think of Ibsen . . . because in his social plays he not only used the form but pressed it very close to its ultimate limits* (Arthur Miller). **3.** the doctrine that material objects have a real existence independent of our consciousness of them. **4.** the doctrine that general ideas have a real existence independent of the mind.

re·al·ist (rē′ə list), *n.* **1.** a person interested in what is real and practical rather than what is imaginary or theoretical: *They are all realists and consider it futile, on most issues, to try to buck Mr. Eisenhower* (Newsweek). **2.** a writer or artist who represents things as they are in real life. **3.** a person who believes in realism. *—adj.* realistic: *It can be seen as a dramatic and realist attempt to reveal ultimate degradation* (Punch).

re·al·is·tic (rē′ə lis′tik), *adj.* **1.** like the real thing; lifelike. **2.** representing life in literature or art as it actually is: *The realistic novel, which was created by Defoe under George I., was already foreshadowed in the admirable character sketches of Addison* (William E. H. Lecky). **3.** seeing things as they really are; practical. **4.** having to do with realists or realism.

re·al·is·ti·cal·ly (rē′ə lis′tə klē), *adv.* in a realistic manner; with realism.

re·al·i·ty (rē al′ə tē), *n., pl.* **-ties. 1.** actual existence; true state of affairs: *Ghosts have no place in reality.* **2.** a real thing; actual fact: *Slaughter and destruction are terrible realities of war.*

in reality, really; actually; in fact; truly: *We thought he was serious, but in reality he was joking.*

—Syn. 1. actuality. **2.** truth, verity.

re·al·iz·a·ble (rē′ə lī′zə bəl), *adj.* that can be realized: *a realizable goal, realizable capital.*

re·al·i·za·tion (rē′ə lə zā′shən), *n.* **1.** a clear understanding; full awareness; perception: *The explorers had a realization of the dangers they must face.* **2.** a realizing or being realized: *the realization of your hopes.* **3.** the exchange of property for its money value. **4.** the obtaining or acquiring (of money, a fortune, etc.). **—Syn. 1.** comprehension. **2.** consummation, fulfillment.

re·al·ize (rē′ə līz), *v.,* **-ized, -iz·ing.** *—v.t.* **1.** to understand clearly; be fully aware of: *Does he fully realize the risks he's taking? She realizes how hard you worked.* **2.** to make real; bring into actual existence: *Her uncle's present made it possible for her to realize her dream of going to college.* **3.** to cause to seem real. **4.** to change (property) into money: *Before going to England to live, he realized all his American property.* **5.** to obtain as a return or profit: *He realized $10,000 from his investment.* **6.** to bring as a return or profit: *The prices realized were disappointing to the sellers.* *—v.i.* **1.** to convert property into money: *He realized with great prudence while this mine was still at its full vogue* (Thackeray). **2.** to make a profit. **3.** to change an asset, right, etc., into money or other real property. **—re′al·iz′er,** *n.* **—Syn.** *v.t.* **1.** comprehend, conceive. **2.** achieve.

re·al·iz·ing (rē′ə lī′zing), *adj.* that realizes; clear and vivid: *a realizing sense of danger.* **—re′al·iz′ing·ly,** *adv.*

re·al-life (rē′əl līf′), *adj.* true to life; real: *a real-life story. There seems to be a growing desire for toys that are . . . closely related to real-life situations* (New Yorker).

re·al·lo·cate (rē al′ə kāt), *v.t.,* **-cat·ed, -cat·ing.** to allocate again or anew; assign or distribute again.

re·al·lo·ca·tion (rē′al ə kā′shən), *n.* a new or fresh assignment or distribution: *The result clearly indicated a reallocation reflecting $109,000 for land and $191,000 for depreciable assets, and this appraisal was accepted by the taxing authorities* (Wall Street Journal).

re·al·ly (rē′ə lē, rē′lē), *adv.* **1.** actually; truly; in fact: *things as they really are.* **2.** indeed: *Oh, really?*

re·al·ly (rē′ə lī′), *v.,* **-lied, -ly·ing.** *—v.t.* **1.** to form or arrange again; recompose: *The enemy did not pursue, which gave us time to stop and re-ally our men* (Sir Henry Slingsby). **2.** to connect; unite. *—v.i.* to rally: *They re-allied and assembled themselves together.*

realm (relm), *n.* **1.** a kingdom. **2.** a region or sphere in which something rules or prevails: *the realm of death. One realm we have never conquered—the pure present* (D.H. Lawrence). **3.** a particular field of something: *the realm of biology.* **4.** *Geography.* a prime division of the earth's surface, containing one or more regions; zoological region of the first order.

abjure the realm, (formerly, in England) to take an oath to leave the country and never return: *Even while abjurations were in force, such a criminal was not allowed to take sanctuary and abjure the realm* (William Blackstone).

[Middle English *realme* < Old French *realme,* alteration (influenced by *reial* royal) of *reiemme* < Gallo-Romance *regiminem,* accusative of Latin *regimen.* Doublet of REGIME, REGIMEN.]

—Syn. 3. province.

realm·less (relm′lis), *adj.* without a realm.

real·ness (rē′əl nis, rēl′-), *n.* the state or condition of being or appearing real; manifest genuineness; freedom from artifice or any deception: *There is such a realness to his narration that one is willing to overlook his many deficiencies in the art of expression* (Science).

real number, any rational or irrational number.

Re·al·po·li·tik (rā äl′pō′li tēk′), *n. German.* political realism; practical politics: *Together with the Russian unideological Realpolitik, which means the Russians want to keep what they have but are not out to conquer the world, there is another factor of accommodation, the spontaneous wishes of the Russian people* (Canadian Forum).

real property, real estate.

Re·al·schu·le (rā äl′shü′lə), *n., pl.* **-len** (-lən). a German secondary school that emphasizes science and modern languages. [< German *Realschule* < *real* real, practical + *Schule* school]

real-time (rē′əl tīm′), *n.* equivalence in time or speed between the output of an electronic computer and a particular physical process which needs this output for its effective operation. *—adj.* having to do with or operating in real-time.

Re·al·tor or **re·al·tor** (rē′əl tər, -tôr), *n. U.S. Trademark.* a person engaged in the real-estate business who is a member of the National Association of Real Estate Boards. [American English, apparently < *realt*(y) + *-or*]

re·al·ty[1] (rē′əl tē), *n. U.S.* real estate. [< *real*[1] (definition 3) + *-ty*]

re·al·ty[2] (rē′əl tē), *n. Obsolete.* sincerity; honesty. [< Old French *realte* < Medieval Latin *regalitas, -atis* < Latin *rēgālis;* see REGAL]

real wages, wages measured in actual purchasing power.

ream[1] (rēm), *n.* **1.** 480 or 500 sheets of paper of the same size and quality. **2.** 516 sheets of printing paper. **3.** a very large quantity: *ream upon ream of nonsense.* [< Old French *raime,* or *rayme* < Spanish *resma* < Arabic *rizmah* bundle]

ream[2] (rēm), *v.t.* **1.** to enlarge or shape (a hole). **2.** to remove with a reamer. [Middle English *reamen;* origin uncertain]

ream[3] (rēm, rām), *Scottish.* *—n.* **1.** cream. **2.** a froth or scum.

—v.i. to froth or foam. *—v.t.* to skim.

[Old English *rēam*]

ream·er (rē′mər), *n.* **1.** a tool for enlarging or shaping a hole. **2.** a utensil for squeezing the juice out of oranges, lemons, etc.

Reamer (def. 1)

re·am·pu·ta·tion (rē′am pyə tā′shən), *n.* amputation on a limb, a part of which has already been removed.

re·an·i·mate (rē an′ə māt), *v.t.,* **-mat·ed, -mat·ing.** to give fresh spirit, vigor, activity, etc., to.

re·an·i·ma·tion (rē′an ə mā′shən), *n.* **1.** the act or operation of reanimating: *Whatever method of heating was used, artificial respiration was essential for reanimation* (New Scientist). **2.** a reanimated state.

re·an·nex (rē′ə neks′), *v.t.* to annex again, as territory that has been disjoined: *Saint Quentin, which . . . had been a Flemish town, was to be reannexed* (John L. Motley).

re·an·nex·a·tion (rē′an ik sā′shən), *n.* **1.** the act of reannexing. **2.** a being reannexed.

re·a·noint (rē′ə noint′), *v.t.* to anoint again.

reap (rēp), *v.t.* **1.** to cut (grain). **2.** to gather (a crop). **3.** to cut grain or gather a crop from: *to reap fields.* **4.** to get as a return or reward: *Kind acts reap happy smiles.* *—v.i.* **1.** to reap a crop. **2.** to get a return. [Old English *repan,* variant of *rīpan*] **—Syn.** *v.t.* **4.** earn. *-v.i.* **2.** profit.

reap·a·ble (rē′pə bəl), *adj.* that can be reaped.

reap·er (rē′pər), *n.* a person or machine that cuts grain or gathers a crop.

reaper and binder, a machine that cuts and gathers grain, and ties the stalks into bundles.

reap·ing machine (rē′ping), a reaper.

re·ap·par·el (rē′ə par′əl), *v.t.,* **-eled, -el·ing** or (*especially British*) **-elled, -el·ling.** to clothe again.

re·ap·pa·ri·tion (rē′ap ə rish′ən), *n.* a reappearance.

re·ap·pear (rē′ə pir′), *v.i.* to appear again: *See! the dull stars roll round and reappear* (Alexander Pope).

re·ap·pear·ance (rē′ə pir′əns), *n.* a reappearing.

re·ap·pli·ca·tion (rē′ap lə kā′shən), *n.* **1.** an applying again. **2.** a being reapplied.

re·ap·ply (rē′ə plī′), *v.t., v.i.,* **-plied, -ply·ing.** to apply again.

re·ap·point (rē′ə point′), *v.t.* to appoint again.

re·ap·point·ment (rē′ə point′mənt), *n.* a renewed appointment: *Reappointment in April for another four-year term of U.S. Surgeon General Scheele* (Time).

re·ap·por·tion (rē′ə pôr′shən, -pōr′-), *v.t.* to apportion again.

re·ap·por·tion·ment (rē′ə pôr′shən mənt, -pōr′-), *n.* a new distribution or arrangement: *the reapportionment of members of Congress or of Congressional districts under a new census.*

re·ap·prais·al (rē′ə prā′zəl), *n.* a new and fresh appraisal; reconsideration: *The situation calls for a reappraisal of all U.S. policies and contacts abroad, particularly in Latin America* (Wall Street Journal).

re·ap·praise (rē′ə prāz′), *v.t.,* **-praised, -prais·ing.** to reconsider; make a fresh valuation of: *Samuel Eliot Morison's "Strategy and Compromise" reappraises all the major strategic problems and decisions which faced the Allies during the war* (Newsweek).

re·ap·proach (rē′ə prōch′), *v.i., v.t.* to approach again.

re·ap·pro·pri·ate (rē′ə prō′prē āt), *v.t.*, **-at·ed, -at·ing.** to appropriate again.

re·ap·pro·pri·a·tion (rē′ə prō′prē ā′shən), *n.* a new or different appropriation.

rear[1] (rir), *n.* **1.** the back part; back: *the rear of a car.* **2.** the space or position behind, or at the back of, anything: *The soldiers ... fired upon them from the rear* (George Bancroft). **3.** the part of an army, fleet, etc., farthest from the line of battle.

at or **in the rear of,** behind: *The houses were built in 1877; at the rear of them was a 9-inch sewer* (Law Times).

bring up the rear, to move onward as the rear part; come last in order: *Lauener was in front, ... while I brought up the rear* (John Tyndall).

—adj. at the back; in the back: *the rear door of a car.*

[(originally) short for *arrear*]

rear[2] (rir), *v.t.* **1.** to make grow; help to grow; bring up: *The mother was very careful in rearing her children.* **2.** to breed (livestock). **3.** to set up; build: *The men of old reared altars to the gods. The pioneers soon reared churches in their settlements.* **4.** to lift up; raise: *The snake reared its head.* **5.** *British Dialect.* to set upright: *Gently rear'd By the angel, on thy feet thou stood'st at last* (Milton). **6.** to exalt. *—v.i.* to rise on the hind legs; rise, as a horse, bear, or other animal: *The horse reared as the fire engine dashed past.*

rear oneself, to get up on one's feet; rise up: *The unruly beast presently reared himself* (Henry Fielding).

[Old English *rǣran* to raise, related to *rīsan* to rise] **—rear′er,** *n.*

—Syn. *v.t.* **3.** erect. **4.** elevate.

➤ See **raise** for usage note.

rear[3] (rir), *adj. British Dialect.* rare; underdone. [Old English *hrēr*]

Rear Adm., Rear Admiral.

rear admiral, a naval officer ranking next above a captain and next below a vice-admiral. *Abbr.:* Rear Adm.

rear-driv·en (rir′driv′ən), *adj.* driven by power on to the rear axle: *Most modern automobiles and trucks are rear-driven.*

rear-end (rir′end′), *adj.* at the rear end: *Reflecting sheeting outlining the rear of a motor vehicle, to lessen danger of rear-end collisions* (Science News Letter).

rear-en·gine (rir′en′jin), *adj.* having an engine in the rear, as in an automobile: *There are reports here that Chevrolet may bring out a rear-engine sports car* (New York Times).

rear-en·gined (rir′en′jind), *adj.* rear-engine: *Clark has raced and won in rear-engined cars* (Time).

rear·guard (rir′gärd′), *adj.* designed or carried out to prevent, delay, or evade; diverting or delaying as a defensive measure: *rearguard tactics. In seeking to keep races apart he is fighting a rearguard action against a world trend* (Manchester Guardian Weekly).

rear guard, the part of an army that protects the rear.

re·ar·gue (rē är′gyü), *v.t.*, **-gued, -gu·ing.** to argue over again: *Although defense counsel may still have weighty objections ... they are likely to reserve their complaints for appeal rather than reargue them* (Manchester Guardian).

re·ar·gu·ment (rē är′gyə mənt), *n.* the process of renewing an argument, as of a case in court; a new pleading upon the same matter: *The Court ... held the cases under advisement ... and then directed the reargument conducted last December* (Atlantic).

rear·horse (rir′hôrs′), *n.* a mantis (insect). [< *rear*[2] to rise up + *horse* (because of the customary stance of the mantis)]

rearing pond, a pond in which the young are reared, usually at a fish hatchery.

re·arm (rē ärm′), *v.t., v.i.* **1.** to arm again; arm oneself again. **2.** to supply with new or better weapons. **—re·arm′er,** *n.*

re·ar·ma·ment (rē är′mə mənt), *n.* a re-arming: *While the French generally are for the North Atlantic alliance they are not for German rearmament* (New York Times).

rear·most (rir′mōst), *adj.* farthest in the rear; last.

rear·mouse (rir′mous′), *n., pl.* **-mice.** reremouse.

re·ar·range (rē′ə rānj′), *v.t.*, **-ranged, -rang·ing.** **1.** to arrange in a new or different way. **2.** to arrange again.

re·ar·range·ment (rē′ə rānj′mənt), *n.* a new or different arrangement.

rear sight, the sight closer to the user's eye in a weapon that has a pair of sights.

rear-view mirror (rir′vyü′), a movable mirror attached to a motor car or truck that gives the driver a view of what is behind him: *In the rear-view mirror he'd seen a car's headlights coming up behind him* (New Yorker).

rear·ward (rir′wərd), *adv., adj.* toward or in the rear: *A rearward view discloses a fine grouping of the hills which have been passed* (Henry I. Jenkinson). *—n.* the rear, especially of an army or fleet. [< Anglo-French *rerewarde* < *rere* rear, back + *warde* ward, guard]

rear·wards (rir′wərdz), *adv.* rearward.

re·as·cend (rē′ə send′), *v.i., v.t.* to ascend again.

re·as·cend·an·cy (rē′ə sen′dən sē), *n.* a reascending; return to ascendancy: *What started under Stalin ... is the reascendancy of nationalism over Communism, of self-interest over ideology* (Time).

re·as·cen·sion (rē′ə sen′shən), *n.* the act of reascending.

re·as·cent (rē′ə sent′), *n.* **1.** the act of re-ascending. **2.** a rise, as of ground, following a descent.

rea·son (rē′zən), *n.* **1.** a cause; motive; ground: *I have my own reasons for doing this.* **2.** a justification; explanation: *What is your reason for doing such poor work?* **3.** the ability to think and draw conclusions: *It may be true, as Immanuel Kant remarks in the immortal introductory sentence to the "Critique of Pure Reason," that reason is presented with questions it can neither answer nor ignore* (Robert Bierstedt). **4.** a reasonable or sensible view of a matter; right thinking; good sense. **5.** sanity: *That poor old man has lost his reason.* **6.** *Obsolete.* justice; satisfaction: *to do one reason.*

bring to reason, to cause to be reasonable: *The stubborn child was at last brought to reason.*

by reason of, on account of; because of: *I cannot go so fast as I would, by reason of this burden that is on my back* (John Bunyan).

in reason, within reasonable and sensible limits: *I will do anything in reason.*

stand to reason, to be reasonable and sensible: *It stands to reason that the rich never have justice done them in plays and stories; for the people who write are poor* (William Black).

—v.i. **1.** to think; think logically: *Man can reason. An idiot cannot reason.* **2.** to draw conclusions or inferences from facts or premises. **3.** to consider; discuss; argue: *Reason with Helen and try to make her change her mind. They reasoned among themselves, saying, It is because we have taken no bread* (Matthew 16:7). *—v.t.* **1.** to persuade by reasoning: *Don't fancy that men reason themselves into convictions* (Charles Kingsley). **2.** to argue, conclude, or infer: *to reason a point.* **3.** to support with reasons. **4.** to reason about or discuss (what, why, etc.): *I will not reason what is meant hereby* (Shakespeare).

reason away, to get rid of by reasoning: *He is so blinded by his ideas that he finds no trouble in reasoning away their many contradictions and absurdities.*

reason out, to think through and come to a conclusion; think out: *By thus reasoning out the probable consequences of an action, motives ... may lose more or less of their force* (William B. Carpenter).

[< Old French *reson*, and *raisun* < Latin *ratiō, -ōnis.* Doublet of RATIO, RATION.] **—rea′son·er,** *n.*

—Syn. *n.* **1. Reason, cause, motive** mean the ground or occasion for an event, action, etc. **Reason** applies to a ground or occasion that explains something that has happened, or one given as an explanation, which may or may not be the true cause or motive: *The reason he went to Arizona was the climate.* **Cause** applies to a person, thing, incident, or condition that directly brings about an action or happening: *The cause was his doctor's warning.* **Motive** applies to the feeling or desire that makes a person do what he does: *His motive was to regain his health.*

rea·son·a·bil·i·ty (rē′zə nə bil′ə tē, rēz′-nə-), *n.* reasonable quality or state.

rea·son·a·ble (rē′zə nə bəl, rēz′nə-), *adj.* **1.** according to reason; sensible; not foolish. **2.** not asking too much; fair; just. **3.** not high in price; inexpensive: *a reasonable dress.* **4.** able to reason. **—rea′son·a·ble·ness,** *n.*

—Syn. 1. Reasonable, rational mean according to reason. **Reasonable** implies being governed by reason and hence showing good judgment: *He took a reasonable view of the dispute and offered a solution that was fair, sensible, and practical.* **Rational** implies having the power to think logically and hence doing or saying what is sensible: *His approach to the problem was rational.*

rea·son·a·bly (rē′zə nə blē, rēz′nə-), *adv.* in a reasonable manner; with reason.

rea·soned (rē′zənd), *adj.* based on reasoning or reasons; reasonable: *This editorial gave a very reasoned approach to the problem facing our nation* (Wall Street Journal).

rea·son·ing (rē′zə ning, rēz′ning), *n.* **1.** the process of drawing conclusions from facts: *Philosophers have constantly failed to provide validity for principles of reasoning employed in science by reference to reason itself* (A.E. Bell). **2.** reasons; arguments.

rea·son·less (rē′zən lis), *adj.* **1.** lacking the power to reason: *reasonless creatures.* **2.** lacking good judgment or sense. **3.** without reason; unreasonable. **—rea′son·less·ly,** *adv.* **—rea′son·less·ness,** *n.*

reason of state, a political motive for some action or measure on the part of a ruler, government, or public officer, especially one not expedient to set forth publicly.

re·as·sem·blage (rē′ə sem′blij), *n.* a second assemblage.

re·as·sem·ble (rē′ə sem′bəl), *v.t., v.i.*, **-bled, -bling.** to come or bring together again: *One by one, the 65 crystal chandeliers in the U.S. Capitol had been taken down, disassembled, washed prism by prism, reassembled and rehung* (Time).

re·as·sem·bly (rē′ə sem′blē), *n., pl.* **-blies.** a second assembly; reassemblage: *The reassembly of the atoms that compose the human body* (Samuel Johnson).

re·as·sert (rē′ə sėrt′), *v.t.* to assert again: *During the past two and a half years, more European central banks have been reasserting their authority as guardians of their nations' currencies* (Newsweek).

re·as·ser·tion (rē′ə sėr′shən), *n.* a repeated assertion of the same thing; the act of asserting again.

re·as·sess (rē′ə ses′), *v.t.* to assess again: *The rateable value of certain property having been reassessed at a much higher sum* (Law Times Report).

re·as·sess·ment (rē′ə ses′mənt), *n.* a renewed or repeated assessment.

re·as·sign (rē′ə sīn′), *v.t.* to assign again: *In December, 1955, the suit says, the royalty agreement was reassigned to Pressed Metals* (Wall Street Journal).

re·as·sign·ment (rē′ə sīn′mənt), *n.* a renewed or repeated assignment.

re·as·sim·i·late (rē′ə sim′ə lāt), *v.t.*, **-lat·ed, -lat·ing.** to assimilate again.

re·as·sim·i·la·tion (rē′ə sim′ə lā′shən), *n.* a reassimilating.

re·as·so·ci·ate (rē′ə sō′shē āt), *v.t., v.i.*, **-at·ed, -at·ing.** to come together again: *The Indian families ... separate in the winter season ... and reassociate in the spring and summer* (Alexander Henry).

re·as·so·ci·a·tion (rē′ə sō′sē ā′shən, -shē-), *n.* a coming together again; a joining or bringing into renewed association.

re·as·sort (rē′ə sôrt′), *v.t.* **1.** to assort again. **2.** to assort repeatedly.

re·as·sume (rē′ə süm′), *v.t.*, **-sumed, -sum·ing.** to assume or take again; resume: *He would, by letter, turn [his duties] over to the Vice-President until he recovered, at which time he could write another letter, reassuming his post* (Newsweek).

re·as·sump·tion (rē′ə sump′shən), *n.* a second assumption.

re·as·sur·ance (rē′ə shůr′əns), *n.* **1.** new or fresh assurance. **2.** the restoration of courage or confidence. **3.** *British.* reinsurance: *The total of sums assured under new policies in the year was over £56,700,000, after deduction of reassurances* (London Times).

re·as·sure (rē′ə shůr′), *v.t.*, **-sured, -sur·ing.** **1.** to restore to confidence: *The captain's confidence during the storm reassured the passengers.* **2.** to assure again. **3.** *Especially British.* to insure again.

re·as·sur·ing (rē′ə shůr′ing), *adj.* that reassures; comforting; encouraging: *The President's reassuring words can offer no guarantee against a relapse into foolishness* (Wall Street Journal). —**re′as·sur′ing·ly,** *adv.*

reast·y (rēs′tē), *adj.*, **reast·i·er, reast·i·est.** *Dialect.* rancid: *For six months the food ... was only some reasty bacon and Indian corn* (A. Welby). [< Old French *resté* left over, past participle of *rester* to remain; see REST²]

re·a·ta (rē ä′tə), *n.* a lariat: *Papa got on his horse and splashed out into the shallows, shaking a wide loop into his plaited Mexican horsehide reata* (New Yorker). [< Spanish *reata* rope]

re·at·tach (rē′ə tach′), *v.t.* to attach again.

re·at·tach·ment (rē′ə tach′mənt), *n.* a second or repeated attachment: *Some of them have yielded along a plane passing through them ... but the reattachment is very strong* (John Tyndall).

re·at·tain (rē′ə tān′), *v.t.* to attain again.

re·at·tain·ment (rē′ə tān′mənt), *n.* the act of reattaining.

re·at·tempt (rē′ə tempt′), *v.t.* to attempt again. —*n.* a new attempt.

re·auc·tion (rē ôk′shən), *v.t.* to auction again.

Réaum., Réaumur thermometer.

Ré·au·mur or **Re·au·mur** (rā′ə myůr; *French* rā ō mYr′), *adj.* of or in accordance with the thermometric scale introduced about 1730 by René Antoine Ferchault de Réaumur, a French physicist, in which the freezing point of water is 0 degrees and the boiling point 80 degrees. *Abbr.:* R.

reave¹ (rēv), *v.t.*, **reaved** or **reft, reav·ing.** *Archaic.* **1.** to take by force; take away. **2.** to deprive by force; strip; rob: *to reave the orphan of his patrimony* (Shakespeare). [Old English *rēafian.* Related to BEREAVE, ROB, ROVER².]

reave² (rēv), *v.t., v.i.*, **reaved** or **reft, reav·ing.** *Archaic.* to tear; split. [Middle English *reve;* apparently < *reave¹*; influenced by *rive*]

reav·er (rē′vər), *n.* a robber or plunderer; marauder; raider: *This paper is remarkable for the sagacity which tracks the footsteps of the literary reaver* (William Hamilton).

re·a·wak·en (rē′ə wā′kən), *v.t., v.i.* to awaken again: *The consciousness of the truth ... reawakens* (Popular Science Monthly).

re·a·ware (rē′ə wãr′), *adj.* aware again: *Their portentous advent made him reaware of the unimaginable shapes that lie ahead* (New Yorker).

reb or **Reb** (reb), *n. U.S. Historical.* a rebel in the American Civil War: *"Hello, Charley," he said, "Where you been?" ... "Out hearing the Rebs," he said* (Stephen Vincent Benét).

re·bab (rə bäb′), *n.* **1.** an ancient stringed instrument with a pear-shaped or a long, narrow body, a vaulted back, and no neck. It was played originally with the fingers and later with a bow. **2.** any of various stringed instruments played with a bow, in use among the Moslems of northern Africa. [< Persian and Arabic *rabāb.* Related to REBEC.]

re·bap·tism (rē bap′tiz əm), *n.* a second baptism.

re·bap·tize (rē′bap tīz′), *v.t.* **-tized, -tiz·ing.** **1.** to baptize a second time: *People called them Anabaptists, or "rebaptizers," because they rebaptized all who joined them* (World Book Encyclopedia). **2.** to baptize by a new name; rename. —**re′bap·tiz′er,** *n.*

re·bar·ba·tive (ri bär′bə tiv), *adj.* **1.** crabbed; cross: *a rebarbative old man.* **2.** unattractive: *a rebarbative hat.* [< French *rébarbatif* < Old French < *rebarber* oppose, confront (literally, beard to beard) < *re-* + *barbe* beard < Latin *barba*]

re·bate¹ (rē′bāt, ri bāt′), *n., v.*, **-bat·ed, -bat·ing.** —*n.* a return of part of money paid; partial refund; discount: *An interesting feature of German price lists for the outside world is the appearance of rebates to shipbuilders—rebates for indirect exports, which recall the cartel* (London Times). [< Old French *rabat* < *rabatre* beat down; see the verb]
—*v.t.* **1.** to give as a rebate: *to rebate one third of the price.* **2.** to make dull; blunt.
[< Old French *rebatre* beat down < *re-* back + *abattre* beat down < *a-* to (< Latin *ad-*) + *batre* to beat < Latin *battuere*] —**re′bat·er,** *n.*

re·bate² (rē′bāt, rab′it), *n., v.t., v.i.*, **-bat·ed, -bat·ing.** rabbet.

re·ba·to (rə bä′tō), *n., pl.* **-toes.** a stiff collar of lace worn by both men and women, especially in western Europe and England, from about 1590 to 1630. [alteration of French, Old French *rabat,* or < obsolete French *rabateau* < *rebatre;* see REBATE¹, verb]

re·bec or **re·beck** (rē′bek), *n.* a three-stringed musical instrument, somewhat like a violin, used in the Middle Ages: *And the jocund rebecks sound* (Milton). [< Middle French *rebec,* alteration (influenced by Old French *bec* beak, because of the shape of the instrument) of Old French *rebebe,* or *rubebe,* probably < Old Provençal *rebec,* and *rebeb* < Arabic *rabāb* rebab]

Rebec

Re·bec·ca or **Re·bek·ah** (ri bek′ə), *n.* (in the Bible) the wife of Isaac and the mother of Esau and Jacob. Genesis 24-25.

reb·el (*n., adj.* reb′əl; *v.* ri bel′), *n., adj., v.*, **re·belled, re·bel·ling.** —*n.* **1.** a person who resists or fights against authority instead of obeying: *The rebels armed themselves against the government.* **2.** Also, **Rebel.** *U.S. Historical.* a Confederate, especially a Confederate soldier: *The Rebels are reported to have ordered an entire fleet from French builders* (New Mexican Review). [< Old French *rebelle,* learned borrowing < Latin *rebellis* < *rebellāre;* see the verb]
—*adj.* **1.** defying law or authority: *a rebel army.* **2.** Also, **Rebel.** *U.S. Historical.* Confederate: *the Rebel flag.*
—*v.i.* **1.** to resist or fight against law or authority. **2.** to feel a great dislike or opposition: *We rebelled at having to stay in on so fine a day.*
[< Old French *rebeller* < Latin *rebellāre* < *re-* again + *bellāre* to wage war < *bellum* war. Doublet of REVEL.] —**re·bel′ler,** *n.*
—**Syn.** *n.* **1.** insurgent. —*v.i.* **1.** revolt, mutiny.

reb·el·dom (reb′əl dəm), *n.* **1.** a region controlled by rebels. **2.** rebels as a group. **3.** rebellion.

re·bel·lion (ri bel′yən), *n.* **1.** an armed resistance or fight against one's government: *The nobles rose in rebellion against the king.* **2.** resistance against any power or restriction: *sullen rebellion against fate* (Rudyard Kipling). [< Latin *rebelliō, -ōnis* < *rebellis* rebel < *rebellāre;* see REBEL, verb] —**Syn. 1.** insurrection, revolution, sedition. See **revolt.**

re·bel·lious (ri bel′yəs), *adj.* **1.** defying authority; acting like a rebel. **2.** hard to manage; hard to treat. —**re·bel′lious·ly,** *adv.* —**re·bel′lious·ness,** *n.* —**Syn. 1.** mutinous. **2.** disobedient. —**Ant. 2.** submissive.

rebel yell, a long, shrill yell given by Confederate soldiers while going into battle in the U.S. Civil War.

re·bid (*v.* rē bid′; *n.* rē′bid′), *v.*, **-bid, -bidding,** *n.* —*v.t.* to bid again: *Possibly he should have ... rebid one of his suits* (London Times). —*n.* a subsequent bid made by a player: *The two no-trump was a demand for a rebid.*

re·bill (rē bil′), *v.t.* to bill again.

re·bind (rē bīnd′), *v.t.*, **-bound, -bind·ing.** to bind (a book, etc.) again or anew: *The book with the broken back needs rebinding.*

re·birth (rē′bėrth′, rē bėrth′), *n.* **1.** a new birth; being born again. **2.** a reviving; coming back into existence or into a condition of strength, power, etc.: *a rebirth of confidence, a rebirth of national pride.*

re·block (rē blok′), *v.t.* **1.** to provide with new block or a new block. **2.** to remold: *to reblock a hat.*

re·bloom (rē blüm′), *v.i.* to bloom again: *They ... Gather'd the blossom that rebloom'd* (Tennyson).

re·blos·som (rē blos′əm), *v.i.* to blossom again: *Mere dandies are but cut flowers in a bouquet—once faded, they never can reblossom* (Edward G. Bulwer-Lytton).

reb·o·ant (reb′ō ənt), *adj.* resounding loudly: *The echoing dance Of reboant whirlwinds* (Tennyson). [< Latin *reboāns, -antis,* present participle of *reboāre* to resound, bellow back < *re-* again + *boāre* to bellow < Greek *boân*]

re·boil (rē boil′), *v.t.* to cause to boil again; subject again to boiling.

re·boise·ment (ri boiz′mənt), *n.* a conversion into woodland; reforestation. [< French *reboisement* < *reboiser* reforest < *re-* again (< Latin *re-*) + *boiser* to plant with trees < *bois* wood < Medieval Latin *boscus*]

re·bop (rē′bop′), *n. U.S. Slang.* bebop: *Ella [Fitzgerald] it was who ... popularized ... the word rebop* (Time).

re·born (rē bôrn′), *adj.* born again.

re·bo·so (rā bō′sō), *n., pl.* **-sos.** rebozo.

re·bound¹ (*v.* ri bound′; *n.* rē′bound′, ribound′), *v.i.* **1.** to spring back: *I never think I have hit hard unless it rebounds* (Samuel Johnson). **2.** to resound. **3.** to get back to a good condition; bounce back; recover: *Government securities rebounded yesterday after a week of steady declines* (Wall Street Journal). **4.** *Archaic.* to leap; spring. —*v.t.* **1.** to cause to spring back. **2.** to echo back. —*n.* **1.** a springing back; rebounding: *the rebound of a ball.* **2.** *Basketball.* a ball that bounds off the backboard when a scoring attempt has been missed.
on the rebound, in a state of shock caused by the abrupt ending of a love affair: *to become engaged on the rebound.*
[< Old French *rebondir* < *re-* back, re- + *bondir* to bound, spring, resound, perhaps < Gallo-Romance *bombītīre,* ultimately < Latin *bombus* a booming sound < Greek *bómbos*]
—**Syn.** *v.i.* **1.** recoil.

re·bound² (rē bound′), *v.* the past tense and past participle of **rebind.**

re·bound·er (rē′boun′dər), *n.* a basketball player skilled at catching and controlling a ball that rebounds from the backboard: *Brannum was the top rebounder of the contest with 13, one more than Gallatin* (New York Times).

re·bo·zo (rā bō′sō, -zō), *n., pl.* **-zos.** a shawl or long scarf worn by Spanish-American women over the head and shoulders: *Men and women crossed themselves; women pulled their rebozos over the faces of the babies they were carrying* (Atlantic). [American English < Spanish *rebozo* shawl; a muffling of oneself < *bozo* the area around the mouth]

re·breathe (rē brēᴛʜ′), *v.t.*, **-breathed, -breath·ing.** to breathe again.

re·broad·cast (rē brôd′kast′, -käst′), *v.*, **-cast** or **-cast·ed, -cast·ing,** *n.* —*v.t., v.i.* **1.** to broadcast again: *His radio messages to the U.S.S.R. are now translated and rebroadcast* (Newsweek). **2.** to relay by broadcast (messages, speeches, etc., received from a broadcasting station). —*n.* a program, etc., rebroadcast: *Rebroadcasts of earlier Playhouse 90 productions on tape and film were to follow* (New Yorker).

re·buff (ri buf′), *n.* a blunt or sudden check to a person who makes advances, offers help, makes a request, etc.; snub: *The child's offer to help her sister met with the rebuff, "Let me alone."* —*v.t.* to give a rebuff to. [< Middle French *rebuffe* < Italian *ribuffo,* and *rabuffo* < *rabuffare* disarrange, alteration of *baruffare* to scuffle < Germanic (compare Old High German *biroufan* to tussle, pluck out)] —**Syn.** *v.t.* check.

re·build (rē bild′), *v.t.*, **-built, -build·ing.** to build again or anew: *They [children] are building new bone while adults are simply rebuilding some of their skeleton* (Newsweek). —**re·build′er,** *n.*

re·built (rē bilt′), *v.* the past tense and past participle of **rebuild:** *The damaged section of the school was entirely rebuilt.*

re·buk·a·ble (ri byü′kə bəl), *adj.* deserving of rebuke.

re·buke (ri byük′), *v.*, **-buked, -buk·ing,** *n.* —*v.t.* **1.** to express disapproval of; reprove: *The teacher rebuked the child for throwing paper on the floor.* **2.** *Obsolete.* to repress; check: *Under him My genius is rebuk'd: as, it is said, Mark Antony's was by Caesar* (Shakespeare). —*n.* an expression of disapproval; scolding: *a sharp rebuke.* [< Anglo-French *rebuker,* Old French *rebuchier* < *re-* back + *buchier* to strike < *bûche,* and *busche* a log, wood < Vulgar Latin *būsca*] —**re·buk′er,** *n.* —**re·buk′ingly,** *adv.* —**Syn.** *v.t.* **1.** reprimand, censure. See **reprove.**

re·buke·ful (ri byük′fəl), *adj.* full of rebuke; of a rebuking character, as words.

re·bunk·er (rē bung′kər), *v.i., v.t.* to refill the bunkers with coal; coal again.

re·bur·y (rē ber′ē), *v.t.*, **-bur·ied, -bur·y·ing.** to bury again: *Reburied hastily at dead of night* (Thomas Carlyle).

re·bus (rē′bəs), *n., pl.* **-bus·es.** a representation of a word or phrase by pictures suggesting the syllables or words: *A picture of a cat on a log is a rebus for "catalog."* [< Latin *rēbus* by means of objects, ablative plural of *rēs* thing, object]

re•bus sic stan•ti•bus (rē′bəs sik stan′tə bəs), *Latin.* things remaining the same: *There is a legal principle which holds that even the most solemnly recorded agreements are to be valid only for as long as they were intended to be valid—rebus sic stantibus, or while circumstances remain the same* (New Yorker).

re•but (ri but′), *v.t.,* **-but•ted, -but•ting. 1.** to oppose by evidence on the other side or by argument; try to disprove: *to rebut the arguments of the other team in a debate.* **2.** *Obsolete.* to repel; repulse. [< Old French *reboter* < *re-* back + *boter* to butt, strike < Germanic (probably unrecorded Frankish *botan* to strike)] —**Syn. 1.** refute, contradict, dispute.

re•but•ta•ble (ri but′ə bəl), *adj.* that can be rebutted; subject to rebuttal.

re•but•tal (ri but′əl), *n.* a rebutting: *The State Department issued a 2,700-word rebuttal, complete with texts of proposals and counterproposals* (Newsweek).

re•but•ter[1] (ri but′ər), *n.* **1.** a person who rebuts. **2.** an argument that rebuts. [< *rebut* + *-er*[1]]

re•but•ter[2] (ri but′ər), *n. Law.* an answer such as a defendant makes to a plaintiff's surrejoinder. [< Old French *reboter,* noun use of infinitive; see REBUT]

rec., 1. receipt. **2.** recipe. **3. a.** record. **b.** recorded. **c.** recorder.

re•cal•ci•trance (ri kal′sə trəns), *n.* a refusal to submit, conform, or comply: *The years of delay in initiating a continental defense . . . arose from the cover that secrecy afforded to the recalcitrance of a few arrogant men* (Bulletin of Atomic Scientists).

re•cal•ci•tran•cy (ri kal′sə trən sē), *n.* recalcitrance.

re•cal•ci•trant (ri kal′sə trənt), *adj.* resisting authority or control; disobedient: *a recalcitrant child.* —*n.* a recalcitrant person or animal. [< Latin *recalcitrāns, -antis,* present participle of *recalcitrāre* kick back < *re-* back + *calx, calcis* heel]

re•cal•ci•trate (ri kal′sə trāt), *v.i.,* **-trat•ed, -trat•ing.** to show strong objections, opposition, or resistance.

re•cal•ci•tra•tion (ri kal′sə trā′shən), *n.* opposition; repugnance.

re•ca•lesce (rē′kə les′), *v.i.,* **-lesced, -lesc•ing.** to show recalescence.

re•ca•les•cence (rē′kə les′əns), *n.* the increased brilliancy and sudden emission of heat of a cooling metal, especially iron, at a certain temperature. [< Latin *recalēscēns, -entis,* present participle of *recalēscere* < *re-* again + *calēscere* grow warm. Compare CALESCENT.]

re•ca•les•cent (rē′kə les′ənt), *adj.* that shows recalescence.

re•call (*v.t.* ri kôl′; *n.* ri kôl′, rē′kôl′), *v.t.* **1.** to call back to mind; remember: *to recall a name. I can recall stories that my mother told me years ago.* **2.** to call back; order back: *The ambassador was recalled. The captain was recalled from the front line.* **3.** to bring back; restore; revive: *recalled to life.* **4.** to take back; withdraw: *The order has been given and cannot be recalled.*

—*n.* **1.** a recalling to mind: *A few people with remarkable memories are said to have "total recall."* **2.** a calling back; ordering back. **3.** a signal used in calling back men, ships, etc. **4.** a taking back; undoing; revocation; annulment. **5.** the removal of a public official from office by vote of the people. —**Syn.** *v.t.* **1.** recollect. See **remember. 4.** revoke, retract.

re•call•a•ble (ri kô′lə bəl), *adj.* that can be recalled.

re•call•ment (ri kôl′mənt), *n.* **1.** the act of calling back. **2.** an invitation or summons to return.

re•can•des•cence (rē′kan des′əns), *n.* a growing brighter; renewed candescence.

re•cant (ri kant′), *v.t.* **1.** to take back formally or publicly; withdraw or renounce (a statement, opinion, purpose, etc.): *Critics of the government were publicly recanting their "errors"* (Newsweek). **2.** to retract (a promise, oath, etc.). **3.** to give up (a purpose). —*v.i.* to renounce an opinion or allegiance: *Though he was tortured to make him change his religion, the prisoner would not recant. . . . a bill . . . which would make the threat of perjury more real and thus make it infinitely more dangerous to recant* (Saturday Review). [< Latin *recantāre* < *re-* back + *cantāre* (frequentative) < *canere* to sing] —**re•cant′er,** *n.*

re•can•ta•tion (rē′kan tā′shən), *n.* the act of recanting: *The drama of the Inquisition lies in Galileo's abject recantation of his life's work* (Time).

re•cap[1] (*v.* rē′kap′, rē kap′; *n.* rē′kap′), *v.,* **-capped, -cap•ping,** *n.* —*v.t.* to put a strip of rubber or similar material on the tread of (a worn surface of an automobile tire), by using heat and pressure to make a firm union. —*n.* a recapped tire: *Volume of retreading has been growing, with 32 million recaps sold last year* (Wall Street Journal). [< *re-* again + *cap,* verb]

re•cap[2] (*v.* ri kap′; *n.* rē′kap), *v.,* **-capped, -cap•ping,** *n. Informal.* —*v.t., v.i.* to recapitulate. —*n.* a recapitulation: *Here's a recap of Orange Bowlers' paths to Miami* (Birmingham News). [short for *recapitulate*]

re•cap•i•tal•i•za•tion (rē kap′ə tə lə zā′shən), *n.* the act of recapitalizing: *Recapitalization and a new incorporation . . . were approved by stockholders* (Wall Street Journal).

re•cap•i•tal•ize (rē kap′ə tə līz), *v.t., v.i.,* **-ized, -iz•ing.** to capitalize again; renew or alter the capitalization of.

re•ca•pit•u•late (rē′kə pich′ə lāt), *v.t., v.i.,* **-lat•ed, -lat•ing. 1.** to repeat or recite the main points of; tell briefly; sum up. **2.** *Biology.* to repeat or reënact successive steps in a process: *The theory that ontogeny recapitulates phylogeny is no longer accepted.* [< Latin *recapitulāre* (with English *-ate*[1]) < *re-* again + *capitulum* chapter, section (diminutive) < *caput, capitis* head]

re•ca•pit•u•la•tion (rē′kə pich′ə lā′shən), *n.* **1.** a brief statement of the main points; summary: *One gets the notion that his book is in a sense an unconscious recapitulation of the process of growth* (New Yorker). **2.** *Biology.* the repetition in a young animal of evolutionary stages in the evolution of the species. **3.** *Music.* the section of a movement repeating the theme of the exposition, after the development.

Recapitulation doctrine or **theory,** the theory that the development of an organism recapitulates the life history of the race to which it belongs.

re•ca•pit•u•la•tive (rē′kə pich′ə lā′tiv), *adj.* **1.** having to do with or characterized by recapitulation; giving a summary of the chief parts or points. **2.** of or having to do with the biological doctrine of recapitulation.

re•ca•pit•u•la•tor (rē kə pich′ə lā′tər), *n.* a person or thing that recapitulates.

re•ca•pit•u•la•to•ry (rē′kə pich′ə lə tôr′ē, -tōr′-), *adj.* recapitulative.

re•cap•ture (rē kap′chər), *v.,* **-tured, -tur•ing,** *n.* —*v.t.* **1.** to capture again; have again. **2.** to recall: *The picture album recaptured the days of the horse and buggy.* **3.** (of the government) to take (a company's excess profits). —*n.* **1.** a taking or being taken a second time. **2.** the thing that is taken. **3.** *U.S.* the act of taking a company's excess profits, especially the profits of a public utility by the government.

re•car•bon (rē′kär′bən), *v.t.* to supply (an arc lamp) with new carbons.

re•car•ry (rē kar′ē), *v.t.,* **-ried, -ry•ing. 1.** to carry back, as in returning. **2.** to carry again or in a reversed direction: *When the Turks besieged Malta or Rhodes . . . pigeons are then related to carry and recarry letters* (Izaak Walton).

re•cast (*v.* rē kast′, -käst′; *n.* rē′kast′, -käst′), *v.,* **-cast, -cast•ing,** *n.* —*v.t.* **1.** to cast again or anew: *to recast a bell.* **2.** to make over; remodel: *to recast a sentence.*
—*n.* **1.** a recasting. **2.** something formed by recasting.

recd. or **rec'd.,** received.

re•cede[1] (ri sēd′), *v.i.,* **-ced•ed, -ced•ing. 1.** to go backward; move backward: *Houses and trees seem to recede as you ride past in a train.* **2.** to slope backward: *He has a chin that recedes.* **3.** to withdraw: *He receded from the agreement.* **4.** to go or fall back; decline in character or value. [< Latin *recēdere* < *re-* back + *cēdere* to go] —**Syn. 1.** retreat, retire.

re•cede[2] (rē sēd′), *v.t.,* **-ced•ed, -ced•ing.** to cede again. [< *re-* back + *cede*]

re•ced•ence (ri sē′dəns), *n.* a receding.

re•ceipt (ri sēt′) *n.* **1.** a written statement that money, a package, a letter, etc., has been received. **2.** a receiving or being received: *the receipt of a letter.* **3.** *Dialect.* a recipe. **receipts,** money received; amount or quantity received: *Our expenses were less than our receipts.*
—*v.t.* to write on (a bill, etc.) that something has been received or paid for. —*v.i. U.S.* to give a receipt.
[alteration (influenced by Latin *recepta,* feminine past participle of *recipere*) of Middle English *receit* < Anglo-French *receite,* Old French *reçoite,* earlier *recete* < Latin *recipere;* see RECEIVE]
➜ **receipt, recipe.** Both words mean a formula, directions for preparing something to eat. Locally one or the other may be preferred by cooks, but they are interchangeable in meaning.

re•ceipt•or (ri sē′tər), *n.* **1.** a person who receipts. **2.** *U.S. Law.* a person to whom attached property is bailed.

re•ceiv•a•ble (ri sē′və bəl), *adj.* **1.** fit for acceptance: *Gold is receivable all over the world.* **2.** on which payment is to be received: *Bills receivable is the opposite of bills payable.* **3.** which is to be received.
—*n.* **receivables,** accounts already or soon due, or similar assets.

re•ceiv•al (ri sē′vəl), *n.* the act of receiving.

re•ceive (ri sēv′), *v.,* **-ceived, -ceiv•ing.** —*v.t.* **1.** to take (something offered or sent); take into one's hands or possession: *to receive gifts.* **2.** to have (something) bestowed, conferred, etc.: *to receive a name, to receive a degree.* **3.** to be given; get: *to receive a letter from home.* **4.** to take; support; bear; hold: *The boat received a heavy load.* **5.** to take or let into the mind: *to receive new ideas.* **6.** to accept as true or valid: *a theory widely received.* **7.** to agree to listen to: *to receive confession.* **8.** to experience; suffer; endure: *to receive a blow.* **9.** to let into one's house, society, etc.: *The people of the neighborhood were glad to receive the new family.* **10.** to admit to a place; give shelter to: *to receive strangers.* **11.** to admit to a state or condition: *to receive a person into the church.* **12.** to meet (guests, etc.); greet upon arrival: *Crowds gathered to receive the queen.*
—*v.i.* **1.** to take, accept admit, or get something: *Freely ye have received, freely give* (Matthew 10:8). *Everyone shall receive according to his deserts* (Joseph Butler). **2.** to be at home to friends and visitors: *She receives on Tuesdays.* **3.** *Radio, Television.* to change electrical waves into sound signals or image patterns. **4.** to take the sacrament of Holy Communion. **5.** to return a served ball, as in tennis.
[< Old North French *receivre,* Old French *reçoivre* < Latin *recipere* < *re-* back + *capere* to take]
—**Syn.** *v.t.* **1. Receive, accept** mean to take what is given, offered, or delivered. **Receive** carries no suggestion of positive action or of activity of mind or will on the part of the receiver, and means nothing more than to take to oneself or take in what is given or given out: *He received a prize.* **Accept** always suggests being willing to take what is offered, or giving one's consent: *She received a gift from him, but did not accept it.*

Re•ceived Standard (ri sēvd′), the English spoken by educated Englishmen everywhere.

re•ceiv•er (ri sē′vər), *n.* **1.** a person who receives. **2.** a thing that receives: **a.** the part of the telephone held to the ear; a telephone receiver: *Even before I picked up the receiver, I knew that something was wrong* (New Yorker). **b.** a receiving set for radio or television. **3.** *Law.* a person appointed by law to take charge of the property of others: *Mr. Jones will act as receiver for the firm that has failed in business.* **4.** a treasurer. **5.** a person who knowingly receives stolen goods or harbors offenders. **6.** *Chemistry.* **a.** a vessel for receiving and condensing the product of distillation. See **retort** for picture. **b.** a vessel for receiving and containing gases.

receiver general, (in Massachusetts) an elected state official who collects assessments.

re•ceiv•er•ship (ri sē′vər ship), *n.* **1.** the position of a receiver in charge of the property of others. **2.** the condition of being in the control of a receiver.

re•ceiv•ing blanket (ri sē′ving), a small, light blanket used to wrap an infant in, especially after a bath: *Her husband has used more diapers and receiving blankets than she has in three years with two children* (New York Times).

receiving line, a group of persons standing

in line to receive the guests as they arrive, as at a formal reception, etc.

receiving set, 1. an apparatus for receiving sound, or sound and picture images, sent by radio waves; a radio or television set. 2. an apparatus for receiving messages sent by telegraph or teletype.

re·cel·e·brate (rē sel′ə brāt), *v.t.*, **-brat·ed, -brat·ing.** to celebrate again.

re·cel·e·bra·tion (rē′sel ə brā′shən), *n.* 1. a celebrating a second time. 2. a being celebrated again.

re·cen·cy (rē′sən sē), *n.* a being recent.

re·cense (ri sens′), *v.t.*, **-censed, -cens·ing.** to review; revise.

re·cen·sion (ri sen′shən), *n.* 1. the revision of a text, especially when critical. 2. a revised version of a text. [< Latin *recēnsiō, -ōnis* < *recēnsēre* survey, count over < *re-* again + *cēnsēre* count. Related to CENSUS.]

re·cen·sion·ist (ri sen′shə nist), *n.* a person who reviews or revises, as an editor.

re·cent (rē′sənt), *adj.* 1. done or made not long ago: *recent events.* 2. not long past; modern: *a recent period in history.* 3. *Poetic.* lately or newly come. [< Latin *recēns, -entis* new, fresh] —**re′cent·ness,** *n.*

Re·cent (rē′sənt), *n.* 1. the present geological epoch, after the Pleistocene epoch of the Cenozoic era: . . . *the Holocene or Recent has lasted only 20,000 years* (Beals and Hoijer). 2. the series of rocks formed during this epoch. —*adj.* of or having to do with this epoch or its rocks. [< *recent*]

re·cent·ly (rē′sənt lē), *adv.* lately; not long ago.

re·cept (rē′sept), *n. Psychology.* an idea supposedly formed in animals' minds by the reception of similar percepts, such as successive percepts of the same object. [< Latin *receptum,* (originally) neuter past participle of *recipere;* see RECEIVE]

re·cep·ta·cle (ri sep′tə kəl), *n.* 1. any container or place used to put things in to keep them conveniently: *Bags, baskets, and vaults are all receptacles.* 2. the end of the stem that bears the sepals, petals, stamens, and pistils of a flower: *All these parts—calyx, corolla, stamens, and carpels—are attached to the receptacle, the somewhat specialized summit of the pedicel* (Fred W. Emerson). 3. a socket to insert a plug in, to make an electrical connection. [< Latin *receptāculum* (diminutive) < *recipere;* see RECEIVE]

re·cep·ti·ble (ri sep′tə bəl), *adj.* 1. that can be received; receivable. 2. that can receive.

re·cep·tion (ri sep′shən), *n.* 1. the act of receiving: *calm reception of bad news.* 2. the fact of being received. 3. the manner of receiving: *a warm reception.* 4. a gathering to receive and welcome people: *Our school gave a reception to welcome our new principal.* 5. *Radio, Television.* a. the quality of the sound or image reproduced in a receiving set. b. the act or process of receiving radio waves. [< Latin *receptiō, -ōnis* < *recipere;* see RECEIVE]

reception center, a place at which people are received and taken care of in some way.

re·cep·tion·ist (ri sep′shə nist), *n.* a person employed to receive callers: *She is a receptionist in a doctor's office.*

reception room, a room for the reception of visitors.

re·cep·tive (ri sep′tiv), *adj.* able, quick, or willing to receive ideas, suggestions, impressions, stimuli, etc.: *a receptive mind.* —**re·cep′tive·ly,** *adv.* —**re·cep′tive·ness,** *n.*

re·cep·tiv·i·ty (rē′sep tiv′ə tē), *n.* the ability or readiness to receive.

re·cep·tor (ri sep′tər), *n.* 1. a receiver. 2. a cell or group of cells sensitive to stimuli; sense organ: *The eye has two kinds of visual receptors, rods and cones* (Science News Letter). 3. a chemical radical in a cell, to which a virus or protein substance becomes attached. [< Latin *receptor* receiver]

re·cess (*n.* rē′ses *for 1,* ri ses′, rē′ses *for 2 and 3; v.* ri ses′), *n.* 1. the time during which work stops: *There will be a short recess before the next meeting. Our school has an hour's recess at noon.* 2. a part in a wall set back from the rest; alcove; niche: *This long seat will fit nicely in that recess.* 3. an inner place or part; quiet, secluded place: *the recesses of a cave, the recesses of one's secret thoughts.*
—*v.i.* to take a recess: *The convention recessed until afternoon.* —*v.t.* 1. to put in a recess; set back: *to recess a window.* 2. to make a recess in: *to recess a wall.*
[< Latin *recessus, -ūs* a retreat < *recēdere;* see RECEDE[1]]
—**Syn.** *n.* 1. intermission.

Recess (def. 2)

re·ces·sion[1] (ri sesh′ən), *n.* 1. a going backward; moving backward. 2. a sloping backward. 3. withdrawal, as of the minister and choir after the service in some churches. 4. a period of temporary business reduction, shorter and less extreme than a depression: *When the country entered the 1949 recession, many analysts again warned business to batten down the hatches* (Newsweek). [< Latin *recessiō, -ōnis* < *recēdere;* see RECEDE[1]]

re·ces·sion[2] (ri sesh′ən), *n.* a ceding back to a former owner. [< *re-* + *cession*]

re·ces·sion·al (ri sesh′ə nəl), *adj.* 1. sung or played while the clergy and the choir retire from the church at the end of a service: *a recessional hymn.* 2. of or having to do with recession. —*n.* a recessional hymn or piece of music: *The attendant minister pronounced the benediction, the organ played the recessional* (Atlantic). [< *recession*[1] + *-al*[1]]

recessional moraine, a terminal moraine formed when a receding glacier halts temporarily.

re·ces·sive (ri ses′iv), *adj.* 1. likely to go back; receding. 2. *Biology.* of or having to do with a recessive character: *Blue eyes are recessive in a person, brown eyes dominant. In peas tallness is dominant, dwarfness recessive* (Heber W. Youngken). 3. (of accent) tending to move from one syllable of a word to a syllable nearer the beginning of the word: *recessive stress is a tendency in current English* (Simeon Potter).
—*n. Biology.* 1. a recessive character or gene: *In a heterozygote the genes are of two kinds, dominants and recessives* (Heber W. Youngken). 2. an individual possessing or transmitting a recessive character. —**re·ces′sive·ly,** *adv.*

recessive character, the one of any pair of opposite characters that is latent in an animal or plant, when both are present in the germ plasm: *Recessive characters, even in the presence of dominant ones, are quite easily recognized* (G. Fulton Roberts).

Rech·a·bite (rek′ə bīt), *n.* a total abstainer from alcoholic drinks: *Yet snobs every bit as accomplished are to be found among both Rechabites and non-denominational water-drinkers* (Punch). [< Late Latin *Rechabīta,* plural, translation of Hebrew *Rēkābim* < *Rēkāb,* the father of the founder of a sect which refused to drink wine (Jeremiah 35:2-19); spelling influenced by English *-ite*[1]]

re·change (rē chānj′), *v.*, **-changed, -chang·ing,** *n.* —*v.t., v.i.* to change again or anew. —*n.* a second or further change.

re·chan·nel (rē chan′əl), *v.t.*, **-neled, -nel·ing** or (*especially British*) **-nelled, -nel·ling.** to channel in a new form or direction: *It is difficult to predict whether . . . we can measurably rechannel the buying demands of the public* (Wall Street Journal).

re·charge (rē chärj′), *v.*, **-charged, -charg·ing,** *n.* —*v.t., v.i.* to charge again or anew; reload: *The storage battery is recharged by passing a current through the unit in the reverse direction of the discharge* (Wall Street Journal). —*n.* a second or additional charge: *In recent years the artificial recharge of water-bearing strata has been carried out experimentally* (New Scientist).

re·charge·a·ble (rē chär′jə bəl), *adj.* chargeable again.

re·char·ter (rē chär′tər), *v.t.* to charter again or anew. —*n.* 1. a chartering again. 2. a second or additional charter.

re·chauf·fé (rā′shō fā′), *n., pl.* **-fés** (-fā′). 1. a warmed-up dish of food. 2. a rehash of literary material, etc. [< French *réchauffé* (literally) warmed over < *ré-* again + *échauffer* to warm up < *e-* out, ex-[1] + Old French *chaufer.* Compare CHAFE.]

re·cheat (ri chēt′), *n. Archaic, Hunting.* 1. the calling together of the hounds. 2. a call on the horn to gather the hounds at the beginning or end of a chase: *The chase was declared to be ended . . . when the recheat should be blown* (Scott). [< Old French *racheter,* and *rachater* reassemble, rally]

re·check (*v.* rē chek′; *n.* rē′chek′), *v.t., v.i.* to check again. —*n.* a checking again; double-check.

re·cher·ché (rə shãr′shā; *French* rə shershā′), *adj.* 1. sought after; in great demand; rare: *The exhibition consists of a recherché choice of the finest productions of their archaic arts ever discovered* (New Yorker). 2. too studied; far-fetched. [< French *recherché* sought after < Old French *rechercher* seek after carefully < *re-* again + *chercher.* Compare SEARCH.]

re·choose (rē chüz′), *v.t.*, **-chose, -cho·sen.** to choose again: *The old-time ceremony of rechoosing a representative* (North Star).

re·chris·ten (rē kris′ən), *v.t.* to christen a second time; rename.

re·cid·i·vate (ri sid′ə vāt), *v.i.*, **-vat·ed, -vat·ing.** 1. to fall back or relapse; return to a former state, way of acting, etc.: *Thus then to recidivate, and to go against her own act and promise . . .* (Lancelot Andrewes). 2. to relapse into crime: *No sooner did he leave prison, than he recidivated into petty felonies.* [< Medieval Latin *recidivatus,* past participle of *recidivare;* see RECIDIVIST]

re·cid·i·va·tion (ri sid′ə vā′shən), *n.* 1. a falling back into a former state, way of acting, etc.; relapse. 2. the relapse of a criminal into crime.

re·cid·i·vism (ri sid′ə viz əm), *n.* a repeated or habitual relapse, especially into crime: *There is considerable recidivism among some juvenile offenders due to alcoholic liquor* (Clyde B. Vedder). [< *recidiv*(ist) + *-ism*]

re·cid·i·vist (ri sid′ə vist), *n.* a person who relapses, especially a habitual criminal: *Major Lloyd-George . . . described the recidivist, or persistent offender, as "the central problem of any penal system"* (London Times). —*adj.* of recidivism: *Nobody can write off the condition of Quebec's jails and Quebec's appalling recidivist rate* (Maclean's). [< French *récidiviste* < Middle French *recidiver* to relapse, learned borrowing from Medieval Latin *recidivare* < Latin *recidīvus;* see RECIDIVOUS]

re·cid·i·vis·tic (ri sid′ə vis′tik), *adj.* recidivous.

rec·i·div·i·ty (res′ə div′ə tē), *n.* a tendency to relapse, especially into crime.

re·cid·i·vous (ri sid′ə vəs), *adj.* liable to relapse, especially into crime. [< Latin *recidīvus* (with English *-ous*) < *recidere* fall back < *re-* back + *cadere* to fall]

rec·i·pe (res′ə pē), *n.* 1. a set of directions for preparing something to eat: *Give me your recipe for cookies.* 2. a set of directions for preparing anything. 3. a means for reaching some state or condition: *a recipe for happiness.* 4. a medical prescription. 5. a receipt. [< Latin *recipe* take!, imperative of *recipere;* see RECEIVE]

re·ci·pher (rē sī′fər), *v.t.* to encipher an already coded message: *The purpose of such a table would be to convert plain language letters or punctuation into figures which could then be subsequently reciphered* (London Times).

re·cip·i·ence (ri sip′ē əns), *n.* reception; a receptiveness.

re·cip·i·en·cy (ri sip′ē ən sē), *n.* recipience.

re·cip·i·ent (ri sip′ē ənt), *n.* a person or thing that receives something: *The recipients of the prizes had their names printed in the paper.* —*adj.* receiving; willing to receive: *The price charged for surplus would have to be either nil or appreciably lower . . . than the commercial price prevailing in the recipient country* (Wall Street Journal). [< Latin *recipiēns, -entis,* present participle of *recipere;* see RECEIVE]

re·cip·ro·cal (ri sip′rə kəl), *adj.* 1. in return: *Although I gave him many presents, I had no reciprocal gifts from him.* 2. existing on both sides; mutual: *reciprocal liking, reciprocal distrust. Kindness is generally reciprocal* (Samuel Johnson). 3. inversely proportional; inverse. 4. *Grammar.* expressing mutual action or relation. In "The two children like each other," *each other* is a reciprocal pronoun.
—*n.* 1. a number so related to another that when multiplied together they give one: *3 is the reciprocal of 1/3, and 1/3 is the reciprocal of 3.* 2. a thing which is reciprocal to something else; counterpart.
[< Latin *reciprocus* returning]

re·cip·ro·cal·i·ty (ri sip′rə kal′ə tē), *n.* the quality or state of being reciprocal.

re·cip·ro·cal·ly (ri sip′rə klē), *adv.* in a reciprocal way; each to the other; mutually.

reciprocal ohm, *Electricity.* an ohm.

reciprocal trade, an arrangement between

countries to reduce or do away with tariffs, duties, quotas of commodities, etc., in trading with each other; a most-favored-nation trade agreement.

reciprocal translocation, *Genetics.* an interchange of parts between pairs of chromosomes.

re·cip·ro·cate (ri sip′rə kāt), *v.,* **-cat·ed, -cat·ing.** —*v.t.* **1.** to give, do, feel, or show in return: *She likes me, and I reciprocate her liking.* **2.** to cause to move with an alternating backward and forward motion. —*v.i.* **1.** to make return, as for something given; make interchange. **2.** (of mechanical parts) to move with an alternate backward and forward motion. [< Latin *reciprocāre* (with English *-ate*¹) < *reciprocus* returning, alternating]

re·cip·ro·cat·ing engine (ri sip′rə kā′ting), an engine in which the piston and piston rod move back and forth in a straight line.

re·cip·ro·ca·tion (ri sip′rə kā′shən), *n.* **1.** the act of reciprocating: *the reciprocation of a favor received. With a sincere reciprocation of all your kindly feeling* (Dickens). **2.** the state of being in a reciprocal or harmonious relation. **3.** the backward and forward motion of mechanical parts.

re·cip·ro·ca·tive (ri sip′rə kā′tiv), *adj.* having to do with or characterized by reciprocation.

re·cip·ro·ca·tor (ri sip′rə kā′tər), *n.* a person or thing that reciprocates.

re·cip·ro·ca·to·ry (ri sip′rə kə tôr′ē, -tōr′-), *adj.* reciprocative.

rec·i·proc·i·tar·i·an (res′ə pros ə târ′ē ən), *adj.* of or having to do with reciprocity especially of commercial privileges between two governments. —*n.* a person who favors reciprocity, especially in trade agreements.

rec·i·proc·i·ty (res′ə pros′ə tē), *n., pl.* **-ties.** **1.** reciprocal state; mutual action: *We in the Central, at least, are not too proud to welcome a little reciprocity* (Wall Street Journal). **2.** a mutual exchange, especially of special privileges in regard to trade between two countries, as by the mutual lowering of tariffs.

re·cir·cle (rē sėr′kəl), *v.t., v.i.,* **-cled. -cling.** to circle again: *The airplane recircled the field.*

re·cir·cu·late (rē sėr′kyə lāt), *v.t., v.i.,* **-lat·ed, -lat·ing.** to circulate anew: *As the amount of impurities picked up from the system is small, the water can be recirculated instead of running to waste* (New Scientist).

re·cir·cu·la·tion (rē′sėr kyə lā′shən), *n.* a renewed circulation.

re·ci·sion (ri sizh′ən), *n.* a cutting back or away. [< Latin *recīsiō, -ōnis* < *recīdere* cut out < *re-* back + *caedere* to cut]

ré·cit (rā sē′), *n.* a short narrative: *He has given us a pleasant series of récits from the flow of his thinking and doing* (Saturday Review). [< French *récit* narrative < *réciter* to narrate < Latin *recitāre;* see RECITE]

recit., *Music.* recitative¹.

re·cit·al (ri sī′təl), *n.* **1.** the act of reciting; telling facts in detail: *Her recital of her experiences in the hospital bored her hearers.* **2.** a story; account. **3.** a musical entertainment, usually given by a single performer. **4.** a public performance given by a group of dancers (often dance pupils). **5.** (formerly) a concert consisting of selections from one composer. —**Syn. 2.** narration.

re·cit·al·ist (ri sī′tə list), *n.* a musician, singer, or actor who gives recitals: *Until last summer, Pianist de Groot was a two-handed recitalist of solid international reputation* (Time).

re·ci·tan·do (rā′chē tän′dō), *adj. Music.* reciting; half spoken or declaimed, after the manner of a recitative. [< Italian *recitando,* present participle of *recitare* recite]

rec·i·ta·tion (res′ə tā′shən), *n.* **1.** a reciting. **2.** a reciting of a prepared lesson by pupils before a teacher. **3.** a repeating of something from memory. **4.** a piece repeated from memory. [< Latin *recitātiō, -ōnis* < *recitāre;* see RECITE]

rec·i·ta·tion·ist (res′ə tā′shə nist), *n.* a person who recites poetry or prose before an audience.

rec·i·ta·tive¹ (res′ə tə tēv′), *n.* **1.** a style of music halfway between speaking and singing: *Operas often contain long passages of recitative. There's a lot of that recitative that is in the character of the songs and fits the opera perfectly* (Atlantic). **2.** a passage, part, or piece in this style: *Lerner's nimble recitatives and patter songs . . . provide as agreeable a pattern as anyone could wish for* (Saturday Review). —*adj.* resembling recitation or declamation: *Kabuki actors must attain not only great control of the voice, for their parts are spoken in a "high" recitative style* (Atlantic). [< Italian *recitativo* < Latin *recitāre;* see RECITE]

rec·i·ta·tive² (res′ə tā′tiv, ri sī′tə-), *adj.* **1.** that recites. **2.** having to do with a recital. [< *recit*(e) + *-ative;* perhaps influenced by *recitative*¹]

rec·i·ta·ti·vo (res′ə tə tē′vō), *n., pl.* **-vos,** *adj.,* recitative¹. [< Italian *recitativo*]

re·cite (ri sīt′), *v.,* **-cit·ed, -cit·ing.** —*v.t.* **1.** to say over; repeat: *to recite a lesson. He can recite that poem from memory.* **2.** to give an account of in detail: *Will you recite the names of the pupils who have not been absent this term?* **3.** to repeat (a poem, speech, etc.) to entertain an audience. —*v.i.* **1.** to repeat something; say part of a lesson: *The teacher called on me to recite.* **2.** *Obsolete.* to relate, rehearse, etc. [< Latin *recitāre* < *re-* back, again + *citāre* call, summon (frequentative) < *ciēre* to rouse, call] —**re·cit′er,** *n.*

—**Syn.** *v.t.* **1.** rehearse. **2.** relate, narrate.

re·cit·ing note or **tone** (ri sī′ting), a note in Gregorian music on which several syllables are recited in monotone.

reck (rek), *Archaic.* —*v.i.* **1.** to care; heed: *The brave soldier recked little of danger.* **2.** to be important or interesting; matter. —*v.t.* **1.** to have regard for: *May ye better reck the rede than ever did th' adviser!* (Robert Burns). **2.** to matter to; concern: *Of night, or loneliness, it recks me not* (Milton). [Old English *reccan*]

reck·less (rek′lis), *adj.* rash; heedless; careless: *Reckless of danger, the boy played with a loaded gun. Reckless driving causes many automobile accidents.* [Old English *recceleās,* related to *reccan* reck] —**reck′less·ly,** *adv.* —**reck′less·ness,** *n.* —**Syn.** See **rash.**

reck·ling (rek′ling), *n. British Dialect.* the smallest and weakest one in a litter of animals or a family of children: *There lay the reckling, one But one hour old!* (Tennyson). [origin unknown]

reck·on (rek′ən), *v.t.* **1.** to find the number or value of; count up: *Reckon the cost before you decide.* **2.** to consider; judge; account: *He is reckoned the best speller in the class.* **3.** *Informal and Dialect.* to think; suppose: *I reckon this always, that a man is never undone till he be hanged* (Shakespeare). —*v.i.* **1.** to count; make a calculation. **2.** to depend; rely: *You can reckon on our help.* **3.** to settle; settle accounts.

reckon up, to count up: *There were 786 small red roses . . . at the first count and . . . there will still be all those forget-me-nots to reckon up* (Punch).

reckon with, to take into consideration; deal with something or someone: *But in general what is in a politician's head is actual places and people, contingencies immediately to be reckoned with* (Edmund Wilson).

[Middle English *recken,* Old English *gerecenian*]

—**Syn.** *v.t.* **1,** *v.i.* **1.** compute, calculate. —*v.t.* **2.** regard, deem, esteem.

reck·on·a·ble (rek′ə nə bəl), *adj.* capable of being reckoned: *They [statements] will be used to determine reckonable earnings quickly* (London Times).

reck·on·er (rek′ə nər), *n.* **1.** a person who reckons. **2.** a help in reckoning, such as a book of tables.

reck·on·ing (rek′ə ning, rek′ning), *n.* **1.** a method of computing; count; calculation: *By my reckoning we are miles from home.* **2.** the settlement of an account. **3.** a bill, especially at an inn or tavern: *The company having now pretty well satisfied their thirst, nothing remained but to pay the reckoning* (Henry Fielding). **4. a.** the calculation of the position of a ship. **b.** the position calculated.

re·claim (ri klām′), *v.t.* **1.** to bring back to a useful, good condition: *The farmer reclaimed the swamp by draining it. Henrietta reclaimed him from a life of vice* (Macaulay). **2.** to demand the return of. **3.** to make tame; subdue. —*v.i.* **1.** to exclaim; protest. **2.** *Obsolete.* to call out; cry loudly. [< Old French *reclaimer,* and *reclamer* to protest; invoke, appeal, learned borrowings from Latin *reclāmāre* cry out loudly (against) < *re-* back + *clāmāre* cry out] —**re·claim′er,** *n.* —**Syn.** *v.t.* **1.** See **recover.**

re-claim (rē klām′), *n.* a new or renewed claim.

re·claim·a·ble (ri klā′mə bəl), *adj.* that can be reclaimed.

re·claim·ant (ri klā′mənt), *n.* a person who reclaims.

rec·la·ma·tion (rek′lə mā′shən), *n.* **1.** a reclaiming or being reclaimed; restoration to a useful, good condition: *the reclamation of deserts by irrigation.* **2.** the act of protesting; protest: *My reclamation was not well received* (Richard A. Proctor). [< Latin *reclāmātiō, -ōnis* < *reclāmāre;* see RECLAIM¹]

ré·clame (rā klàm′), *n. French.* **1.** advertisement; notoriety: *The vessel . . . had achieved a certain dubious réclame shortly before* (New Yorker). **2.** desire for publicity.

re·clasp (rē klasp′, -kläsp′), *v.t., v.i.* to clasp anew: *When two laminae, which have been separated by accident or force, are brought together again, they immediately reclasp* (William Paley).

re·clean·er (rē klē′nər), *n.* the screening attachment of a bean thresher or pea huller that cleans beans or peas before they are put into bags.

re·clin·a·ble (ri klī′nə bəl), *adj.* capable of reclining or being reclined: *Both front seats are fully reclinable* (London Times).

rec·li·nate (rek′lə nāt), *adj. Botany.* bent or curved downward, as a leaf in a bud. [< Latin *reclīnātus,* past participle of *reclīnāre;* see RECLINE]

re·cline (ri klīn′), *v.,* **-clined, -clin·ing.** —*v.i.* to lean back; lie down: *The tired girl reclined on the couch.* —*v.t.* to lay down. [< Latin *reclīnāre* < *re-* back + *clīnāre* to lean] —**re·clin′er,** *n.*

re·clothe (rē klōᴛʜ′), *v.t.,* **-clothed, -cloth·ing.** to clothe again.

rec·luse (*n.* rek′lüs, ri klüs′; *adj.* ri klüs′), *n.* a person who lives shut up or withdrawn from the world: *a bachelor and something of a recluse in his private house, where he lived alone* (W. H. Hudson). —*adj.* shut up or apart from the world: *a recluse life.* [< Old French *reclus,* or *recluse,* feminine, past participle of *reclure* < Latin *reclūdere* to shut up, enclose < *re-* back + *claudere* to shut] —**re·cluse′ly,** *adv.* —**re·cluse′ness,** *n.*

re·clu·sion (ri klü′zhən), *n.* **1.** a shutting up or being shut up in seclusion. **2.** solitary confinement. **3.** the condition or life of a recluse: *She is one of the few nuns in the world with ecclesiastical permission to attempt the hermitlike life known as reclusion* (Time).

re·clu·sive (ri klü′siv), *adj.* characterized by seclusion; recluse.

re·coal (rē kōl′), *v.t.* to supply again with coal: *to recoal a steamship.* —*v.i.* to take on a fresh supply of coal.

rec·og·nise (rek′əg nīz), *v.t., v.i.,* **-nised, -nis·ing.** *Especially British.* recognize: *No two people speak with exactly the same accent, yet we rarely have difficulty in recognising what they say* (New Scientist).

rec·og·ni·tion (rek′əg nish′ən), *n.* **1.** a knowing again; recognizing. **2.** a being recognized: *By a good disguise he escaped recognition.* **3.** acknowledgment: *We insisted on complete recognition of our rights.* **4.** notice: *The new club member sought recognition by the chair.* **5.** favorable notice; acceptance: *The actor soon won recognition from the public.* **6.** a formal acknowledgment conveying approval or sanction: *the recognition of a new country by the United Nations.* [< Latin *recognitiō, -ōnis* < *recognōscere;* see RECOGNIZE]

—**Syn. 3.** admission. **5.** appreciation.

rec·og·ni·tion·al (rek′əg nish′ən əl), *adj.* of or having to do with recognition.

recognition color, a color on an animal supposed to be of use to others of its species as a means of recognition.

recognition mark, 1. a mark of recognition or identification. **2.** recognition color.

recognition service, a church service held to introduce a new pastor to his congregation.

recognition signal, a coded signal by which a military unit, vessel, or aircraft can identify itself to friendly forces.

re·cog·ni·tive (ri kog′nə tiv), *adj.* having to do with recognition.

re·cog·ni·to·ry (ri kog′nə tôr′ē, -tōr′-), *adj.* recognitive.

rec·og·niz·a·bil·i·ty (rek′əg nī′zə bil′ə tē), *n.* recognizable quality.

rec·og·niz·a·ble (rek′əg nī′zə bəl), *adj.* that can be recognized. —**Syn.** identifiable.

rec·og·niz·a·bly (rek′əg nī′zə blē), *adv.* in a recognizable manner; so as to be recognized.

re·cog·ni·zance (ri kog′nə zəns, -kon′ə-), *n.* **1.** *Law.* **a.** a bond binding a person to do some particular act. **b.** the sum of money to be forfeited if the act is not performed. **2.** recognition. **3.** *Archaic.* a badge; token: *That recognizance and pledge of love which I first gave her* (Shakespeare). [alteration (influenced by Latin *recognōscere*) of Middle English *reconysaunce* < Old French *reconnaissance*, and *recognoissance* < *reconoistre;* see RECOGNIZE. Doublet of RECONNAISSANCE.]

rec·og·nize (rek′əg nīz), *v.*, **-nized, -nizing.** —*v.t.* **1.** to know again: *You have grown so that I scarcely recognized you.* **2.** to identify: *to recognize a person from a description.* **3.** to acknowledge acquaintance with; greet: *to recognize a person on the street.* **4.** to acknowledge; accept; admit: *to recognize a claim. A patriot recognizes his duty to defend his country. I recognize your right to ask that question.* **5.** to take notice of: *Anyone who wishes to speak in a public meeting should stand up and wait till the chairman recognizes him.* **6.** to show appreciation of: *Honesty and perseverance in students are quickly recognized by teachers.* **7.** to acknowledge and agree to deal with: *For some years other nations did not recognize the new government of Russia.* —*v.i. Law.* to bind a person by bond to do some particular act. [alteration of Old French *reconuiss-*, stem of *reconoistre* < Latin *recognōscere* < *re-* again + *com-* (intensive) + *gnōscere* to learn. Doublet of RECONNOITER.] —**Syn.** *v.t.* **4.** concede, grant.

rec·og·nized (rek′əg nīzd), *adj.* acknowledged; admitted; approved; received: *a recognized method of procedure. Every newspaper and periodical of recognized standing . . .* (Edward Bok).

re·cog·ni·zee (ri kog′nə zē′, -kon′ə-), *n. Law.* the person to whom a recognizance is made.

rec·og·niz·er (rek′əg nī′zər), *n.* a person who recognizes.

re·cog·ni·zor (ri kog′nə zôr′, -kon′ə-), *n. Law.* a person who enters into a recognizance.

re·coil (*v.* ri koil′; *n.* ri koil′, rē′koil), *v.i.* **1.** to draw back; shrink back: *Most people would recoil at seeing a snake in the path. The . . . British had recoiled five and twenty miles* (H. G. Wells). **2.** to spring back: *The gun recoiled after I fired.* **3.** to react: *The good or evil we confer on others, very often . . . recoils on ourselves* (Henry Fielding).

—*n.* **1.** a recoiling: *This is the expulsion of a jet of gas or other substance in one direction causing a recoil or thrust in the opposite direction* (New York Times). **2.** a state of having recoiled: *in recoil from danger.* **3.** the distance or force with which a gun, spring, etc., springs back.

[< Old French *reculer* < *re-* back + *cule* rump < Latin *cūlus*] —**re·coil′er,** *n.*

—**Syn.** *v.i.* **1.** flinch. **2.** kick.

recoil cylinder, a cylinder with a piston and piston rod that are forced through the length of the cylinder when a gun recoils.

re·coil·less (ri koil′lis), *adj.* (of a firearm) having no appreciable recoil: *a recoilless rifle.*

recoil spring, a spring to check a piece which recoils.

re·coin (rē koin′), *v.t.* to coin again or anew.

re·coin·age (rē koi′nij), *n.* **1.** coinage anew. **2.** a new coinage.

rec·ol·lect (rek′ə lekt′), *v.t.* **1.** to call back to mind; remember: *I know why I began the Memoir. It was an experiment to see how much I could really recollect if I once began to try* (William De Morgan). **2.** to recall (oneself) to something temporarily forgotten. —*v.i.* to have a recollection; remember. [< Latin *recollectus*, past participle of *recolligere;* see RE-COLLECT] —**Syn.** *v.t.* **1.** See **remember.**

re-col·lect (rē′kə lekt′), *v.t.* **1.** to collect again. **2.** to recover control of (oneself). [partly < Latin *recollectus*, past participle of *recolligere* < *re-* again + *colligere* (compare COLLECT[1]), later partly < English *re-* + *collect*[1]]

Rec·ol·lect (rek′ə lekt), *n.* (in the Roman Catholic Church) a member of a division of the Observant Franciscans following an especially strict rule. [< Latin *recollectus;* see RECOLLECT (because the members sought comfort in the recollection of God)]

rec·ol·lect·ed (rek′ə lek′tid), *adj.* remembered. [< *recollect* + *-ed*[2]] —**rec′ol·lect′ed·ness,** *n.*

re-col·lect·ed (rē′kə lek′tid), *adj.* composed; sure of oneself. [< *re-collect* + *-ed*[2]] —**re′-col·lect′ed·ness,** *n.*

rec·ol·lec·tion (rek′ə lek′shən), *n.* **1.** the act or power of recalling to mind: *Recollection of the distant events is difficult.* **2.** memory; remembrance: *This has been the hottest summer within my recollection.* **3.** a thing remembered: *a vivid recollection of a dream.* —**Syn. 2.** See **memory.**

rec·ol·lec·tive (rek′ə lek′tiv), *adj.* having recollection; characterized by recollection. —**rec′ol·lec′tive·ly,** *adv.*

Rec·ol·let (rek′ə let; *French* rā kô le′), *n.* a Recollect: *It was the Recollets who first brought Christianity to Canada* (George Buxton). [< Middle French *récollet*]

re·col·o·ni·za·tion (rē′kol ə nə zā′shən), *n.* **1.** the act of recolonizing: *There were many projects afloat for the recolonization of different parts of Hellas* (J. T. Bent). **2.** the state or condition of being recolonized.

re·col·o·nize (rē kol′ə nīz), *v.t.*, **-nized, -niz·ing.** to colonize (a place) anew: *After this devastation, the Persian court . . . were desirous of recolonizing the town* (William Taylor).

re·col·or (rē kul′ər), *v.t.* to color or dye again. —*v.i.* to flush again: *The swarthy blush recolors in his cheeks* (Byron).

re·comb (rē kōm′), *v.t.* to comb again: *Recombing a maze of tunnels in Boi Loi forest, army patrols suddenly found themselves under . . . machine-gun fire* (Time).

re·com·bi·nant (ri kom′bə nənt), *n.* **1.** something that combines again. **2.** *Biology.* a crossover: *The recombinants always inherit a larger fraction of their genetic characteristics from their mother than from their father* (Scientific American).

re·com·bi·na·tion (rē′kom bə nā′shən), *n.* **1.** a recombining. **2.** *Biology.* a crossover.

re·com·bine (rē′kəm bīn′), *v.t., v.i.*, **-bined, -bin·ing.** to combine again or anew.

re·com·fort (rē kum′fərt), *v.t. Archaic.* to comfort again; cheer; console.

re·com·mence (rē′kə mens′), *v.*, **-menced, -menc·ing.** —*v.i.* to begin again to be; begin again. —*v.t.* to cause to begin again to be; begin again. [< Old French *recommencer* < *re-* re- + *commencer.* Compare COMMENCE.]

re·com·mence·ment (rē′kə mens′mənt), *n.* the act or fact of beginning anew; commencement again.

rec·om·mend (rek′ə mend′), *v.t.* **1.** to speak in favor of; suggest favorably: *to recommend a person for the job. The waiter recommended fried chicken as the best dish on the menu. Can you recommend a good adventure story?* **2.** to advise; counsel: *The doctor recommended that she stay in bed.* **3.** to make pleasing or attractive: *The location of the camp recommends it as a summer home.* **4.** to hand over for safekeeping; commit; entrust: *I . . . devoutly recommended my spirit to its Maker* (Robert Louis Stevenson). —*n. Informal.* a recommendation. [< Medieval Latin *recommendare* < Latin *re-* again + *commendāre.* Compare COMMEND.]

rec·om·mend·a·ble (rek′ə men′də bəl), *adj.* worthy of being recommended.

rec·om·men·da·tion (rek′ə men dā′shən), *n.* **1.** a recommending. **2.** anything that recommends a person or thing. **3.** words of advice or praise. **4.** a thing recommended.

rec·om·men·da·to·ry (rek′ə men′də tôr′ē, -tōr′-), *adj.* serving to recommend; recommending: *I was to take with me letters recommendatory to a number of his friends* (Benjamin Franklin).

rec·om·mend·er (rek′ə men′dər), *n.* a person or thing that recommends.

re·com·mis·sion (rē′kə mish′ən), *v.t.* to commission anew: *The Royal Navy's oldest aircraft carrier, Victorious . . . was recommissioned at Portsmouth yesterday* (London Times). *They will be recommissioned with the grades which they held in the Russian army* (London Times).

re·com·mit (rē′kə mit′), *v.t.*, **-mit·ted, -mit·ting. 1.** to commit again. **2.** to refer again to a committee.

re·com·mit·ment (rē′kə mit′mənt), *n.* **1.** a recommitting. **2.** a being recommitted.

re·com·mit·tal (rē′kə mit′əl), *n.* recommitment.

rec·om·pense (rek′əm pens), *v.*, **-pensed, -pens·ing,** *n.* —*v.t.* **1.** to pay (a person); pay back; reward: *The travelers recompensed the man who so carefully directed them.* **2. a.** to make a fair return for (an action, anything lost, damage done, hurt received, etc.): *Liberally recompensing their services . . . he took leave of his faithful followers* (William H. Prescott). **b.** *Archaic.* to atone for: *. . . the future must recompense the past* (Robert Browning). **3.** *Obsolete.* to give in return: *Recompense no man evil for evil* (Romans 12:17).

—*n.* **1.** a payment; reward; return: *The money was in recompense for the damage to his car.* **2.** amends: *Some recompense To comfort those that mourn* (Robert Burns).

[< Late Latin *recompēnsāre* < Latin *re-* back + *compēnsāre.* Compare COMPENSATE.]

—**Syn.** *v.t.* **1.** repay, compensate, remunerate, requite.

re·com·pose (rē′kəm pōz′), *v.t.*, **-posed, -pos·ing. 1.** to compose again: *Whatever is decomposed may be recomposed by the being who first composed it* (Joseph Priestley). **2.** to rearrange. **3.** to restore to composure: *Our spirits, when disordered, are not to be recomposed in a moment* (Henry Fielding).

re·com·po·si·tion (rē′kom pə zish′ən), *n.* **1.** a recomposing: *I have taken great pains with the recomposition of this scene* (Charles Lamb). **2.** a being recomposed.

re·com·press (rē′kəm pres′), *v.t.* to compress again.

re·com·pres·sion (rē′kəm presh′ən), *n.* **1.** the act of recompressing. **2.** the state of being recompressed.

re·com·pu·ta·tion (rē′kom pyə tā′shən), *n.* **1.** the act of recomputing. **2.** the state of being recomputed: *The recomputation of all numerical quantities involving the Sun's distance as a unit* (George F. Chambers).

re·com·pute (rē′kəm pyüt′), *v.t.*, **-put·ed, -put·ing.** to compute again; recalculate.

re·con (rē′kon), *n. Biology.* the smallest molecular unit of genetic material out of which the larger units, the muton and cistron, are built: *The ultimate unit of molecular structure, the "recon," was found equal to one base pair of nucleic acid. The muton was approximately ten base pairs long* (Science News Letter). [< *rec*(ombination) + *-on*, as in *muton*]

re·con·cen·trate (rē kon′sən trāt), *v.t.*, **-trat·ed, -trat·ing. 1.** to concentrate again. **2.** to bring (forces) together at some point: *to reconcentrate troops before an offensive.*

re·con·cen·tra·tion (rē′kon sən trā′shən), *n.* a concentrating again.

re·con·cep·tu·al·i·za·tion (rē′kən sep′chü ə lə zā′shən), *n.* **1.** the process of conceptualizing again or anew: *The work involved a reconceptualization of an organization's problems and a redefining of assumptions and expectations* (Emory S. Bogardus). **2.** a new conceptualization.

rec·on·cil·a·bil·i·ty (rek′ən sī′lə bil′ə tē), *n.* the fact or quality of being reconcilable.

rec·on·cil·a·ble (rek′ən sī′lə bəl), *adj.* that can be reconciled. —**rec′on·cil′a·ble·ness,** *n.*

rec·on·cil·a·bly (rek′ən sī′lə blē), *adv.* in a reconcilable manner.

rec·on·cile (rek′ən sīl), *v.t.*, **-ciled, -cil·ing. 1. a.** to make friends again: *The children had quarreled but were soon reconciled. Being all now good friends, for common danger . . . had effectually reconciled them* (Daniel Defoe). **b.** to win over: *to reconcile a hostile person.* **2.** to settle (a quarrel, disagreement, etc.): *The teacher had to reconcile disputes among her pupils.* **3.** to make agree; bring into harmony: *It is impossible to reconcile his story with the facts.* **4.** to make satisfied; make no longer opposed: *It is hard to reconcile oneself to being sick a long time. Custom reconciles us to everything* (Edmund Burke). **5.** to purify by special ceremonies: *The places of assembly . . . were cleansed, or repaired, refitted and reconciled, and opened to . . . public . . . worship* (Nicholas P. S. Wiseman). [< Latin *reconciliāre* < *re-* back + *conciliāre.* Compare CONCILIATE.] —**rec′on·cil′er,** *n.*

rec·on·cile·ment (rek′ən sīl′mənt), *n.* reconciliation.

rec·on·cil·i·a·tion (rek′ən sil′ē ā′shən), *n.* **1.** a reconciling; bringing together again in friendship or harmony: *the absence of any appearance of reconciliation between the theory and practice of life* (Emerson). **2.** a being reconciled; settlement or adjustment of disagreements, differences, etc. —**Syn. 2.** agreement.

rec·on·cil·i·a·to·ry (rek′ən sil′ē ə tôr′ē, -tōr′-), *adj.* tending to reconcile.

re·con·den·sa·tion (rē′kon den sā′shən), *n.* the act of recondensing.

re·con·dense (rē′kən dens′), *v.t., v.i.,* **-densed, -dens·ing.** to condense again: *Vapour, which rises in the air and is recondensed on mountain heights* (John Tyndall).

rec·on·dite (rek′ən dīt, ri kon′-), *adj.* **1.** hard to understand; profound: *The recondite principles of philosophy* (Henry Mackenzie). **2.** little known; obscure: *a recondite writer, recondite writings.* **3.** hidden from view; concealed. [< Latin *reconditus,* past participle of *recondere* store away < *re-* back + *condere* to store < *com-* up + *dare* to put, lay] —**rec′on·dite′ly,** *adv.* —**Syn. 1.** abstruse.

rec·on·dite·ness (rek′ən dīt′nis), *n.* profound or hidden meaning.

re·con·di·tion (rē′kən dish′ən), *v.t.* to restore to a good or satisfactory condition; put in good condition by repairing, making over, etc.: *to recondition an old house.* —**Syn.** renovate.

re·con·di·tion·er (rē′kən dish′ə nər), *n.* a person or thing that reconditions.

re·con·duct (rē′kən dukt′), *v.t.* to conduct back or again: *Amidst this new creation want'st a guide To reconduct thy steps?* (John Dryden).

re·con·firm (rē′kən fėrm′), *v.t.* to confirm anew.

re·con·fir·ma·tion (rē′kon fər mā′shən), *n.* **1.** the act of reconfirming. **2.** the state or condition of being reconfirmed: *a reconfirmation of the alliance.*

re·con·nais·sance (ri kon′ə səns), *n.* an examination or survey, especially for military purposes. [< French *reconnaissance* < Old French *recognoissance.* Doublet of RECOGNIZANCE.]

reconnaissance in force, *Military.* an attack to discover the position and strength of an enemy.

reconnaissance satellite, an artificial satellite used to gather strategic information through photography, television, etc.: *It would be cheaper for Russia to spy on the U.S. through normal channels than by putting a reconnaissance satellite into orbit* (Science News Letter).

re·con·nect (rē′kə nekt′), *v.t.* to connect again: *The alliance . . . would be a link reconnecting England with the Empire* (James A. Froude).

re·con·nois·sance (ri kon′ə səns), *n.* reconnaissance.

rec·on·noi·ter (rek′ə noi′tər, rē′kə-), *v.,* **-tered, -ter·ing.** —*v.t.* **1.** to approach and examine or observe in order to learn something; make a survey of (the enemy, the enemy's strength or position, a region, etc.) in order to gain information for military purposes: *Our scouts will reconnoiter the enemy's position before we attack.* **2.** to survey (a tract or region) for engineering or geological purposes. —*v.i.* to approach a place and make a first survey of it: *It seemed wise to reconnoiter before entering the town.* [< obsolete French *reconnoître* < Old French *reconoistre.* Doublet of RECOGNIZE.]

rec·on·noi·ter·er (rek′ə noi′tər ər, rē′kə-), *n.* a person who reconnoiters or makes a preliminary survey.

rec·on·noi·tre (rek′ə noi′tər, rē′kə-), *v.t., v.i.,* **-tred, -tring.** *Especially British.* reconnoiter.

rec·on·noi·trer (rek′ə noi′trər, rē′kə-), *n. Especially British.* reconnoiterer.

re·con·quer (rē kong′kər), *v.t.* to conquer again; recover by conquest.

re·con·quest (rē kon′kwest, -kong′-), *n.* a reconquering.

re·con·se·crate (rē kon′sə krāt), *v.t.,* **-crat·ed, -crat·ing.** to consecrate anew: *This scheme . . . would reconsecrate our wells To good Saint Fillan and to fair Saint Anne* (Wordsworth).

re·con·se·cra·tion (rē′kon sə krā′shən), *n.* a renewed consecration: *There were some difficulties in deciding whether, if the altar was destroyed or removed, a reconsecration of the church would be required* (William Maskell).

re·con·sid·er (rē′kən sid′ər), *v.t.* to consider again: *The judge reconsidered his decision.* —*v.i.* to take up a matter again.

re·con·sid·er·a·tion (rē′kən sid′ə rā′shən), *n.* **1.** the act of reconsidering: *Her newest book is a reconsideration of some of the greatest Western writers* (Newsweek). **2.** a being reconsidered.

re·con·sign (rē′kən sīn′), *v.t.* to consign again: *Officials said 4,000 tons will be sold in the open market and the remainder will be reconsigned to the original suppliers* (Wall Street Journal).

re·con·sign·ment (rē′kən sīn′mənt), *n.* **1.** a consigning again. **2.** a change of destination during transportation.

re·con·sol·i·date (rē′kən sol′ə dāt), *v.t.,* **-dat·ed, -dat·ing.** to consolidate anew: *A petrifying fluid, with which a broken stone will be reconsolidated like a broken limb* (Richard J. Sullivan).

re·con·sol·i·da·tion (rē′kən sol′ə dā′shən), *n.* the act of reconsolidating, or the state of being reconsolidated; a second or renewed consolidation: *the reconsolidation of a scattered conscience* (John Donne).

re·con·stit·u·ent (rē′kən stich′ü ənt), *adj.* **1.** building up. **2.** causing the formation of new tissues. —*n.* a drug that reconstitutes what has been wasted by disease.

re·con·sti·tute (rē kon′stə tüt, -tyüt), *v.t.,* **-tut·ed, -tut·ing. 1.** to form again; bring back to its original form or consistency: *to reconstitute frozen orange juice by adding water.* **2.** to pulverize (coarse or damaged leaves of tobacco), press the dust into sheets, and use them as material for cigars.

re·con·sti·tut·ed (rē kon′stə tü′tid, -tyü′-), *adj.* that has been formed again or brought back to its original consistency: *reconstituted milk, reconstituted lemon juice.*

re·con·sti·tu·tion (rē′kon stə tü′shən, -tyü′-), *n.* the act or process of forming anew, or of bringing together again the parts or constituents of anything that has been broken or destroyed.

re·con·struct (rē′kən strukt′), *v.t.* to construct again; make over; rebuild; restore. —**Syn.** renew, remodel.

re·con·struct·ed (rē′kən struk′tid), *adj.* **1.** made again. **2.** artificially made from bits of real gems: *a reconstructed ruby.*

re·con·struct·i·ble (rē′kən struk′tə bəl), *adj.* that can be reconstructed: *Some of the statues were fragmentary but reconstructible* (William A. Ritchie).

re·con·struc·tion (rē′kən struk′shən), *n.* **1.** the act of constructing again. **2.** the state of being constructed again. **3.** something reconstructed.

Re·con·struc·tion (rē′kən struk′shən), *n. U.S.* **1.** the process by which the Southern states after the Civil War were reorganized and their relations with the national government were reëstablished. **2.** the period when this was done, from 1865 to 1877.

Re·con·struc·tion·ism (rē′kən struk′shən iz əm), *n.* a movement in American Judaism considering Judaism as a religious civilization and favoring those institutions, customs, etc., that are meaningful to Jews of all backgrounds and denominations.

Re·con·struc·tion·ist (rē′kən struk′shən ist), *adj.* of or having to do with Reconstructionism. —*n.* a supporter of Reconstructionism.

re·con·struc·tive (rē′kən struk′tiv), *adj.* tending to reconstruct.

reconstructive surgery, a branch of surgery dealing with the repair of congenital or acquired defects or malformations of body tissues: *Reconstructive and plastic surgery would be done by Dr. Arthur T. Barsky and his staff* (Norman Cousins).

re·con·struc·tor (rē′kən struk′tər), *n.* a person who constructs or restores again.

re·con·tam·i·nate (re′kən tam′ə nāt), *v.t.,* **-nat·ed, -nat·ing.** to contaminate again.

re·con·tam·i·na·tion (rē′kən tam′ə nā′shən), *n.* **1.** the act of recontaminating. **2.** the state or condition of being recontaminated.

re·con·trol (rē′kən trōl′), *v.,* **-trolled, -trol·ling,** *n.* —*v.t.* to put new controls upon; place again under price or rent control: *Four owners of the 29 establishments that had been recontrolled had filed plans with the Buildings Department to convert the building back to apartment house use* (New York Times). —*n.* a recontrolling; renewal of controls.

re·con·vene (rē′kən vēn′), *v.i., v.t.,* **-vened, -ven·ing.** to convene again.

re·con·ver·sion (rē′kən vėr′zhən, -shən), *n.* **1.** conversion again or anew. **2.** conversion back to a previous state or belief.

re·con·vert (rē′kən vėrt′), *v.t., v.i.* **1.** to convert back to a previous state or belief. **2.** to convert again: *After the war the factories that produced tanks were reconverted to produce tractors.*

re·con·vey (rē′kən vā′), *v.t.* **1.** to convey again or back to a previous place or position. **2.** *Law.* to make over again or restore to a former owner.

re·con·vey·ance (rē′kən vā′əns), *n.* conveyance again; conveyance back.

re·con·vict (rē′kən vikt′), *v.t.* to convict again.

re·con·vic·tion (rē′kən vik′shən), *n.* the act of reconvicting: *Were it the rule . . . that a longer sentence was to be expected at each reconviction, crime would at once largely diminish* (Daily News).

re·coop·er (rē kü′pər, -kůp′ər), *v.t.* to repair (barrels, casks, or the like).

re·cop·y (rē kop′ē), *v.t.,* **-cop·ied, -cop·y·ing.** to copy again.

re·cord (*v.* ri kôrd′; *n., adj.* rek′ərd), *v.t.* **1.** to set down in writing so as to keep for future use: *Listen to the speaker and record what he says. A long inscription . . . records how Amenhotep . . . slew seven kings with his own hand* (Amelia B. Edwards). **2.** to put in some permanent form; keep for remembrance: *We record history in books. The widespread destruction recorded the effectiveness of the atomic bomb.* **3.** to put on a phonograph disk, or on magnetic tape or wire: *Both will be recorded, and both brought their composers $1,200 each* (Newsweek).

—*n.* **1.** anything written and kept: *Her diary was a record of her childhood.* **2. a.** an official written account: *The secretary kept a record of what was done at the meeting. 43 out of 100 firms that lose their accounts receivable and other business records in a fire never reopen* (New Yorker). **b.** an official copy of a document: *The county clerk has a record of the deed to this house. The record of his case is in the court clerk's file.* **3.** a disk or cylinder used on a phonograph. **4.** the known facts about what a person, animal, ship, etc., has done: *He has a fine record at school. Burton's record looked all right* (Newsweek). **5.** *U.S.* a criminal record. **6.** the best, greatest, or least yet done; best or greatest amount, rate, speed, etc., yet attained: *to hold the record for the high jump, to break the record for the broad jump.* **7.** a recording or being recorded: *What happened is a matter of record.*

go on record, to state publicly for the record: *The candidate went on record as an opponent of nuclear tests.*

off the record, not to be recorded or quoted: *Politicians often say things off the record that it would be impolitic to say directly.*

of record, according to official record: *He says he and his wife and two adult children together own beneficially and of record 30,800 Libby shares* (Wall Street Journal).

on record, recorded; set down; registered: *The date of her birth is on record in Dade County, Florida.*

—*adj.* making or affording a record: *a record wheat crop.*

[< Old French *recorder* < Latin *recordārī* remember, call to mind < *re-* back + *cor, cordis* heart, mind]

re·cord·a·ble (ri kôr′də bəl), *adj.* **1.** that can be recorded: *. . . the smallest recordable activity is a few millionths of a volt* (Floyd and Silver). **2.** worth recording.

rec·or·da·tion (rek′ər dā′shən), *n.* **1.** the act of recording. **2.** a record. **3.** *Obsolete.* remembrance. [< Latin *recordātiō, -ōnis* < *recordārī;* see RECORD]

re·cor·da·tive (ri kôr′də tiv), *adj.* that records or keeps in memory; commemorative.

re·cor·da·to·ry (ri kôr′də tôr′ē, -tōr′-), *adj.* having to do with the keeping of records.

record breaker, a person, thing, or event that is faster, bigger, or in any way better than any other of the same class: *In his long term at New Haven, Kiphuth produced dozens of topflight swimmers, and many were record breakers* (Time).

re·cord-break·ing (rek′ərd brā′king), *adj.* surpassing any recorded performance or production of its kind.

record changer, a turntable for a phonograph with a device that holds several records above the turntable, letting each record down automatically after the previous one has been played: *If your setup includes a record changer, you may need to replace that, too* (Atlantic).

re·cord·er (ri kôr′dər), *n.* **1.** a person whose business is to make and keep records. **2.** a machine that records: *a tape recorder. A microfilm recorder takes small pictures of documents.* **3.** a title given to certain judges in some cities. **4.** a wooden musical wind

Recorder (def. 4)

instrument with a flutelike tone: *flutes and soft recorders* (Milton). *More recorders are being tootled nowadays than at any time since the development of the modern orchestra* (Newsweek). **5.** a person who records sounds or sound effects for motion pictures or phonograph records: *There is no specialization among technical workers, except in the case of sound mixers and recorders* (New York Times). —**Syn. 1.** registrar.

re·cord·er·ship (ri kôr′dər ship), *n.* the position or term of a recorder.

re·cord·hold·er (rek′ərd hōl′dər), *n.* a person who holds the record for some achievement: *He defeated the world recordholder . . . and won the 5000 meter race* (New York Times).

re·cord·ing (ri kôr′ding), *n.* **1.** a phonograph record: *Virtually all major-label recordings and most on small-company labels are now released in both stereo and mono (standard) form* (Harper's). **2.** the original transcription of any sound or combination of sounds: *A recording of the Liverpool performance is to be broadcast on April 7* (Sunday Times).

recording head, magnetic head: *The television program is recorded by . . . a recording head, a small horseshoe electromagnet* (New York Times).

re·cord·ist (ri kôr′dist), *n.* a person who cuts phonograph records or makes tape recordings, especially as a hobby: *Like the photographer with his various darkroom techniques, the recordist has a number of methods at his disposal for the creation of compositions in sound* (Glen Southworth).

record library, a collection of phonograph records.

re·cord·mak·er (rek′ərd mā′kər), *n.* a person or company that makes phonograph records: *Now the endless search for operatic treasure has driven the recordmakers back to Gluck* (Time).

record player, a phonograph: *Of course teenagers collect records and nearly all have a record player* (Punch). See **phonograph** for picture.

re·cor·o·na·tion (rē′kôr ə nā′shən, -kor-), *n.* a recrowning or being recrowned.

re·count (ri kount′), *v.t.* **1.** to tell in detail; give an account of: *They used to recount . . . the exploits of their youth* (Gilbert White). **2.** to tell one by one; enumerate: *to recount the items in a list.* [< Anglo-French, Old French *reconter* < *re-* again + *conter* to relate. Compare COUNT[1].] —**Syn. 1.** describe.

re-count (*v.* rē kount′; *n.* rē′kount′, rē-kount′), *v.t.* to count again. —*n.* a second count: *A re-count of the votes was made.* [< *re-* + *count*[1]]

re·count·al (ri koun′təl), *n.* a narration.

re·coup (ri küp′), *v.t.* **1.** to make up for: *He recouped his losses.* **2.** to repay: *It was necessary for parliament to intervene to compel the landlord to recoup the tenant for his outlay on the land* (W. S. Gregg). **3.** *Law.* to deduct: *The defendant may recoup damages before paying his lawyer's fee.*

—*n.* the act of recouping; deduction.

[< Old French *recouper* < *re-* back + *couper* to cut, divide with a stroke < *coup.* Compare COUP.]

—**Syn.** *v.t.* **2.** reimburse, recompense.

re·coup·a·ble (ri kü′pə bəl), *adj.* that can be recouped.

re·coup·er (ri kü′pər), *n.* a person who recoups or keeps back.

re·coup·ment (ri küp′mənt), *n.* **1.** the act of recouping. **2.** the state of being recouped.

re·course (rē′kôrs, -kōrs; ri kôrs′, -kōrs′), *n.* **1.** a turning for help or protection; an appealing: *Our recourse in illness is to a doctor.* **2.** a person or thing appealed to or turned to for help or protection: *A child's great recourse in trouble is its mother.* **3.** the right to demand compensation from someone, especially the right which the holder of a bill of exchange has to come back upon the drawer and endorsers if the acceptor fails to meet it. **4.** *Obsolete.* access; admission.

have recourse to, to turn to for help; appeal to: *If threats and persuasions proved ineffectual, he had often recourse to violence* (Edward Gibbon).

[< Old French *recours* < Latin *recursus, -ūs* a return, retreat < *recurrere;* see RECUR]

re·cov·er (ri kuv′ər), *v.t.* **1.** to get back (something lost, taken away, or stolen); regain: *to recover a lost ring, to recover one's health and strength after a long illness.* **2.** to make up for (something lost or damaged): *to recover lost time.* **3.** to bring back to life, health, one's senses, or normal condition: *Our men . . . took up three men; one of which was just drowning, and it was a good while before we could recover him* (Daniel Defoe). **4.** to get back to the proper position or condition: *He started to fall but recovered himself.* **5.** to obtain by judgment in a law court: *to recover damages.* **6.** to rescue; deliver. **7.** to regain in usable form; reclaim: *Many useful substances are now recovered from materials that used to be thrown away.* **8.** to return (a bayonet, sword, etc.) to a certain position, as after use. **9.** *Archaic.* to get to; reach. —*v.i.* **1.** to get well; get back to a normal condition: *She is recovering from a cold. The man recovered of the bite—The dog it was that died* (Oliver Goldsmith). **2.** to obtain judgment in one's favor in a law court. **3.** *Sports.* to make a recovery.

—*n. Sports.* a recovery, especially a getting back to the proper position in fencing or boxing.

[< Anglo-French *recoverer,* Old French *recovrer* < Latin *recuperāre.* Doublet of RECUPERATE.]

—**Syn.** *v.t.* **1. Recover, reclaim, retrieve** mean to get something back. **Recover** means to get something back again after losing it: *He recovered the stolen furs.* **Reclaim** means to get something back after temporarily giving it up: *At the end of the trip he reclaimed his luggage.* **Retrieve** means to get something back after letting it lapse or deteriorate: *It took him a long time to retrieve his reputation.*

re-cov·er (rē kuv′ər), *v.t.* to put a new cover on: *to re-cover a couch with new material.*

re·cov·er·a·bil·i·ty (ri kuv′ər ə bil′ə tē), *n.* the state, property, or possibility of being recovered: *. . . duration of flight, ability to take readings at constant altitudes, and recoverability of equipment are more important considerations* (J. Gordon Vaeth).

re·cov·er·a·ble (ri kuv′ər ə bəl), *adj.* **1.** that can be regained. **2.** that can be restored from sickness, faintness, or the like. **3.** that can be brought back to a former condition. **4.** that can be obtained from a debtor or possessor: *The debt is recoverable.*

re·cov·er·er (ri kuv′ər ər), *n.* **1.** a person who recovers. **2.** recoveror.

re·cov·er·or (ri kuv′ər ər), *n. Law.* a person who obtains a judgment in his favor in a law court.

re·cov·er·y (ri kuv′ər ē, -kuv′rē), *n., pl.* **-er·ies. 1.** a recovering. **2.** a coming back to health or normal condition: *recovery from fever.* **3.** a getting back something that was lost, taken away, or stolen: *The insurance company helped the police in the recovery of the stolen property. The recovery of Bagdad was impossible unless the British were driven back to the Sinai desert* (John Buchan). **4.** a getting back to a proper position or condition: *He started to fall, but made a quick recovery.* **5.** the return to a position of guard after a lunge in fencing, an attack in boxing, etc. **6.** the obtaining of some property or right by the judgment of a law court. **7.** the act of locating and repossessing a missile, nose cone, etc., after a flight in space, usually by snaring it during descent through the atmosphere or by finding it in the ocean.

recovery room, a room used in a hospital to treat patients recovering after an operation: *The child spent the next critical hours in the recovery room* (Harper's).

recpt., receipt.

rec·re·ance (rek′rē əns), *n.* recreancy.

rec·re·an·cy (rek′rē ən sē), *n.* **1.** cowardice. **2.** unfaithfulness; treason.

rec·re·ant (rek′rē ənt), *adj.* **1.** cowardly: *a recreant knight who would run in the face of battle.* **2.** unfaithful; disloyal; traitorous: *The recreant nobles forced King John to sign the Magna Charta.*

—*n.* **1.** a coward: *Hold! Recreants! Cowards! What, fear ye death and fear not shame?* (Richard Brinsley Sheridan). **2.** a traitor.

[< Old French *recreant* (one) confessing himself beaten, present participle of *recreire* to surrender allegiance, yield < Latin *re-* back + *crēdere* entrust (to), believe] —**rec′re·ant·ly,** *adv.*

—**Syn.** *adj.* **1.** pusillanimous. **2.** faithless, false. -*n.* **2.** betrayer.

rec·re·ate (rek′rē āt), *v.,* **-at·ed, -at·ing.** —*v.t.* to refresh with games, pastimes, exercises, etc. —*v.i.* to take recreation. [< Latin *recreāre* (with English *-ate*[1]) to restore < *re-* again + *creāre* to create]

re-cre·ate (rē′krē āt′), *v.t.,* **-at·ed, -at·ing.** to create anew: *One thing that . . . aided me in renewing and re-creating the stalwart soldier . . . was the recollection of those . . . words of his "I'll try, Sir"* (Hawthorne). [< *re-* + *create*]

rec·re·a·tion (rek′rē ā′shən), *n.* play; amusement: *Walking, gardening, and reading are quiet forms of recreation.* —**Syn.** diversion, relaxation.

re-cre·a·tion (rē′krē ā′shən), *n.* **1.** a creating anew: *His re-creation of the experiences of the Polonskys . . .* (Saturday Review). **2.** a new creation.

rec·re·a·tion·al (rek′rē ā′shə nəl), *adj.* of or having to do with recreation: *the recreational facilities of the playground.*

recreational therapist, a person who treats disabled persons, guiding them in specific types of recreational activity to promote their rehabilitation.

rec·re·a·tion·ist (rek′rē ā′shə nist), *n.* a person who is interested or engaged in recreational activities: *There is some fear by recreationists that the oil industry's proposals would spoil beaches* (New York Times).

recreation room, a room used for recreational purposes, as games, dancing, etc.

rec·re·a·tive (rek′rē ā′tiv), *adj.* refreshing; restoring.

re·cre·a·tor (rē′krē ā′tər), *n.* a person who creates anew: *Though Mr. Solti was thus a little disappointing as a recreator of monumental form, I found his virtues as a meticulous craftsman quite arresting* (New Yorker).

rec·re·ment (rek′rə mənt), *n.* **1.** a substance which after having been separated from the blood is returned to it; a secretion from one part of the body that is absorbed by another, as gastric juice. **2.** the useless part of a substance; dross. [< French *récrément,* learned borrowing from Latin *recrēmentum* dross < *re-* back + *cernere* to separate, sift]

rec·re·men·tal (rek′rə men′təl), *adj.* of or having to do with recrement.

rec·re·men·ti·tious (rek′rə men tish′əs), *adj.* **1.** consisting of recrement. **2.** useless.

re·cres·cence (ri kres′əns), *n.* regrowth, especially of lost parts of an organism.

re·crim·i·nate (ri krim′ə nāt), *v.i., v.t.,* **-nat·ed, -nat·ing.** to accuse (someone) in return: *Tom said Harry had lied, and Harry recriminated by saying Tom had lied too. To criminate and recriminate never yet was the road to reconciliation in difference among men* (Edmund Burke). [< Medieval Latin *recriminare* (with English *-ate*[1]) < Latin *re-* again + *crīminārī* accuse < *crīmen, -inis* a charge] —**Syn.** countercharge.

re·crim·i·na·tion (ri krim′ə nā′shən), *n.* accusing in return; counter accusation: *The quarreling children were full of recrimination.*

re·crim·i·na·tive (ri krim′ə nā′tiv, -nə-), *adj.* recriminatory.

re·crim·i·na·to·ry (ri krim′ə nə tôr′ē, -tōr′-), *adj.* of or involving recrimination: *a recriminatory remark.*

rec room (rek), *Informal.* recreation room: *We were playing ping-pong in the rec room* (Atlantic).

re·cross (rē krôs′, -kros′), *v.t., v.i.* **1.** to cross again in returning: *He knew that time, weather, and scarcity of supplies must wear Cromwell out and compel him to recross the border* (Henry Morley). **2.** to cross a second time or anew.

re·crown (rē kroun′), *v.t.* to crown again: *To recrown the soul and make it master of the flesh* (F. D. Huntington).

re·cru·desce (rē′krü des′), *v.i.,* **-desced, -desc·ing.** to break out again; become active again. [< Latin *recrūdēscere* become raw, grow worse < *re-* again + *crūdēscere* become raw < *crūdus* raw]

re·cru·des·cence (rē′krü des′əns), *n.* a breaking out afresh; renewed activity: *the recrudescence of an influenza epidemic.* [< Latin *recrūdēscēns, -entis,* present participle of *recrūdēscere;* see RECRUDESCE] —**Syn.** return, recurrence.

re·cru·des·cen·cy (rē′krü des′ən sē), *n.* recrudescence.

re·cru·des·cent (rē′krü des′ənt), *adj.* breaking out again.

re·cruit (ri krüt′), *n.* **1.** a newly enlisted soldier or sailor: *To have a wholly Regular Army we should need about 100,000 regular recruits, of whom there is no sign* (London

Times). **2.** a new member of any group or class: *The Nature Club needs recruits. Mr. E. H. Machin ("that most enterprising and enlightened recruit to the ranks of theatrical managers")* (Arnold Bennett). **3.** *Archaic.* a fresh supply of something. [< obsolete French *recrute* < *recruter;* see the verb]

—*v.t.* **1.** to get (men) to join an army, navy, etc. **2.** to strengthen or supply (an army, navy, etc.) with new men. **3.** to get (new members). **4.** to increase or maintain the number of: *to recruit a colonial population with new settlers.* **5.** to furnish with a fresh supply or stock; renew; replenish: *Before sailing, we recruited our provisions.* **6.** to renew the health, strength, or spirits of; refresh: *The rest and the refreshment of the fruit . . . recruited him, and he moved on languidly* (Cardinal Newman). —*v.i.* **1.** to get new men for the army, navy, etc.: *The country's first act would be to recruit for the navy* (Edward Bok). **2.** to renew health, strength, or spirits; recuperate: *After that Mr. Scott found it necessary to recruit for two months at Scarborough "with a course of quinine"* (Lytton Strachey). **3.** *Archaic.* to gain new supplies of anything lost or wasted. [< French *recruter* < *recrue* recruit; (literally) new growth < Old French *recroître* < *re-* again + *croître* to grow < Latin *crēscere.* Compare CRESCENT.]

—**Syn.** *n.* **2.** novice, tyro.

re·cruit·er (ri krü′tər), *n.* a person who recruits.

re·cruit·ment (ri krüt′mənt), *n.* **1.** the act or business of recruiting: *The recruitment and retention of individuals of outstanding ability became an element of national security* (Bulletin of Atomic Scientists). **2.** a being recruited.

re·crys·tal·li·za·tion (rē′kris tə lə zā′shən), *n.* repeated crystallization of the same substance: *Recrystallization has been found to take place mainly at temperatures near the freezing point . . . as is broadly the case with most temperate glaciers* (E.F.Roots).

re·crys·tal·lize (rē kris′tə līz), *v.t., v.i.,* **-lized, -liz·ing.** to crystallize again.

rec. sec., recording secretary.

rect., **1.** receipt. **2.** rectified. **3.** rector. **4.** rectory.

rec·tal (rek′təl), *adj.* **1.** of or having to do with the rectum. **2.** for use in the rectum: *a rectal thermometer.*

rec·tal·ly (rek′tə lē), *adv.* in or through the rectum.

rec·tan·gle (rek′tang′gəl), *n.* a four-sided figure with four right angles. [alteration of Medieval Latin *rectiangulum* < Late Latin, neuter of *rectiangulus* having a right angle < Latin *rēctus* right (< *regere* straighten, rule) + *angulus* angle, corner]

Rectangles

rec·tan·gled (rek′tang′gəld), *adj.* **1.** right-angled. **2.** *Heraldry.* formed with right angles or a right angle.

rec·tan·gu·lar (rek tang′gyə lər), *adj.* **1.** shaped like a rectangle. **2.** having one or more right angles. **3.** placed at right angles.

rec·tan·gu·lar·i·ty (rek′tang gyə lar′ə tē), *n.* rectangular quality or state.

rec·tan·gu·lar·ly (rek tang′gyə lər lē), *adv.* with or at right angles.

rec·tan·gu·lar·ness (rek tang′gyə lər nis), *n.* rectangularity.

rec·te et re·tro (rek′tē et rē′trō), *Music, Latin.* **1.** to be repeated backward. **2.** (literally) right and backward.

rec·ti·fi·a·ble (rek′tə fī′ə bəl), *adj.* that can be rectified.

rec·ti·fi·ca·tion (rek′tə fə kā′shən), *n.* the act of rectifying: *A nationwide campaign on the "rectification of food sales" is going on throughout Red China* (New York Times).

rec·ti·fi·ca·tive (rek′tə fə kā′tiv), *adj.* rectifying; corrective.

rec·ti·fi·ca·to·ry (rek′tə fə kə tôr′ē, -tōr′-), *adj.* rectificative.

rec·ti·fi·er (rek′tə fī′ər), *n.* **1.** a person or thing that makes right, corrects, adjusts, etc. **2.** a device for changing alternating current into direct current: *Biggest market for the rare metal is in rectifiers, devices used in radio* (Wall Street Journal).

rec·ti·fy (rek′tə fī), *v.t.,* **-fied, -fy·ing.** **1.** to make right; put right; adjust; remedy: *The storekeeper admitted his mistake and was willing to rectify it. It is ecology again which helps to analyze the situation and rectify it* (F. S. Bodenheimer). **2.** to change (an alternating current) into a direct current. **3.** to purify; refine: *to rectify a liquor by distilling it several times.* **4.** *Geometry.* to determine the length of (a curve, arc, etc.). [< Medieval Latin *rectificare* < Latin *rēctus* right, correct (< *regere* straighten, rule) + *facere* to make]

—**Syn.** **1.** correct, amend.

rec·ti·lin·e·al (rek′tə lin′ē əl), *adj.* rectilinear.

rec·ti·lin·e·ar (rek′tə lin′ē ər), *adj.* **1.** forming a straight line. **2.** bounded or formed by straight lines: *. . . flat and fertile fields, intensely green, and rectilinear roads edged with poplars, reminiscent of the large, geometric beauty of the Ile de France* (Harper's). **3.** characterized by straight lines. **4.** in a straight line; moving in a straight line: *The simplest kind of displacement of a particle occurs in rectilinear motion, which is motion along a straight line* (Shortley and Williams). [< Late Latin *rectilīneus* (< *rēctus* straight + *līnea* line) + English *-ar*] —**rec′ti·lin′e·ar·ly,** *adv.*

rec·ti·tude (rek′tə tüd, -tyüd), *n.* **1.** upright conduct or character; honesty; righteousness: *The name of Brutus would be a guaranty to the people of rectitude of intention* (James A. Froude). **2.** correctness: *rectitude of judgment.* **3.** straightness; direction in a straight line. [< Late Latin *rēctitūdō* < Latin *rēctus* straight, correct] —**Syn.** **1.** integrity, virtue.

rec·to (rek′tō), *n., pl.* **-tos.** the right-hand page of an open book: *The title page is always on the right side or the recto, of the leaf; the left side is known as the verso* (Van Allen Bradley). [< Latin (*foliō*) *rēctō* facing (leaf of a book); *rēctō*, ablative of *rēctus* right (hand)]

rec·to·cele (rek′tə sēl), *n.* a rectal hernia extending into the vagina. [< *rectum* + Greek *kēlē* tumor, rupture]

rec·tor (rek′tər), *n.* **1.** a clergyman in the Protestant Episcopal Church or the Church of England who has charge of a parish. **2.** a priest in the Roman Catholic Church who has charge of a congregation or religious house. **3.** the head of a school, college, or university, especially in Scotland: *After Jefferson's death in 1826,* [*Madison*] *became rector, or president, of the University of Virginia* (Ralph L. Ketcham). **4.** the person in control; director. [< Latin *rēctor, -ōris* ruler < *regere* to rule; straighten]

rec·tor·ate (rek′tər it), *n.* the position, rank, or term of a rector. [< *rector* + *-ate*[3]]

rec·to·ri·al (rek tôr′ē əl, -tōr′-), *adj.* of a rector or a rectory: *rectorial tithes.*

rec·tor·ship (rek′tər ship), *n.* a rectorate.

rec·to·ry (rek′tər ē, -trē), *n., pl.* **-ries.** **1.** a rector's house; parsonage. **2.** *British.* a rector's benefice with all its rights, tithes, and lands.

rec·tri·ces (rek trī′sēz), *n.* the plural of **rectrix.**

rec·trix (rek′triks), *n., pl.* **-tri·ces.** one of the strong feathers in the tail of a bird. The rectrices serve as a rudder in flight. [< Latin *rēctrix, -īcis* < *regere* to straighten (because of their use in directing the flight)]

rec·tum (rek′təm), *n., pl.* **-ta** (-tə). the lowest part of the large intestine. See **liver**[1] for diagram. [< New Latin *rectum,* for Latin (*intestīnum*) *rēctum* straight (intestine); *rēctum,* (literally) neuter past participle of *regere* to straighten, rule]

rec·tus (rek′təs), *n., pl.* **-ti** (-tī). any of several very straight muscles (in the abdomen, thigh, eye, etc.). [< New Latin (*musculus*) *rectus* straight (muscle); *rectus,* (literally) past participle of Latin *regere* to straighten, rule]

re·cu·ler pour mieux sau·ter (rə kʏ lā′ pür myœ sō tā′), *French.* to draw back in order to leap better.

re·cul·ti·vate (rē kul′tə vāt), *v.t.,* **-vat·ed, -vat·ing.** to cultivate anew: *to recultivate land, to recultivate a friendship.*

re·cum·ben·cy (ri kum′bən sē), *n.* a recumbent position or condition.

re·cum·bent (ri kum′bənt), *adj.* **1.** lying down; reclining; leaning. **2.** inactive; idle; listless. **3.** *Biology.* leaning or resting on anything: *a recumbent plant.* [< Latin *recumbēns, -entis,* present participle of *recumbere* to recline < *re-* back + *-cumbere* to lie down] —**re·cum′bent·ly,** *adv.*

re·cu·per·ate (ri kyü′pə rāt, -kü′-), *v.,* **-at·ed, -at·ing.** —*v.i.* to recover from sickness, exhaustion, loss, etc. —*v.t.* **1.** to restore to health, strength, etc. **2.** to recover; regain: *Some of its heat will be recuperated to produce electric current* (New York Times). [< Latin *recuperāre* (with English *-ate*[1]), apparently < *re-* back + *capere* to receive, take. Doublet of RECOVER.]

re·cu·per·a·tion (ri kyü′pə rā′shən, -kü′-), *n.* recovery from sickness, loss, etc.

re·cu·per·a·tive (ri kyü′pə rā′tiv, -kü′-), *adj.* **1.** of recuperation: *the recuperative powers of youth.* **2.** aiding recuperation: *a recuperative rest.* —**re·cu′per·a′tive·ness,** *n.*

re·cu·per·a·tor (ri kyü′pə rā′tər, -kü′-), *n.* **1.** a person who recovers. **2.** a device that utilizes normally waste heat from a furnace to heat incoming air.

re·cu·per·a·to·ry (ri kyü′pər ə tôr′ē, -kü′-; -tōr′-), *adj.* recuperative.

re·cur (ri kėr′), *v.i.,* **-curred, -cur·ring.** **1.** to come up again; occur again; be repeated: *Leap year recurs every four years. My holiday visits . . . seemed to them to recur too often, though I found them few enough* (Charles Lamb). **2.** to return in thought or speech: *The builder recurred to the matter of the cost of remodeling our house.* **3.** to have recourse; resort: *to recur to an expedient.* [< Latin *recurrere* < *re-* back + *currere* to run] —**Syn.** **2.** revert.

re·cur·rence (ri kėr′əns), *n.* an occurrence again; repetition; return: *More care in the future will prevent recurrence of the mistake.*

re·cur·rent (ri kėr′ənt), *adj.* **1.** recurring; occurring again; repeated: *recurrent attacks of asthma.* **2.** turned back so as to run in the opposite direction. [< Latin *recurrēns, -entis,* present participle of *recurrere;* see RECUR] —**re·cur′rent·ly,** *adv.*

re·cur·ring decimal (ri kėr′ing), a circulating decimal.

re·cur·sive (ri kėr′sive), *adj. Mathematics.* recurring; repeated: *recursive functions. The set 2, 4, 6, 8, . . . is recursive because all its integers can be described as divisible by two* (Time). [< Latin *recursus* (past participle of *recurrere* to recur) + English *-ive*] —**re·cur′sive·ly,** *adv.*

re·cur·vate (ri kėr′vit, -vāt), *adj.* recurved. [< Latin *recurvātus,* past participle of *recurvāre* < *re-* back + *curvus* curve]

re·cur·va·ture (ri kėr′və chůr), *n.* a turning back upon a previous direction, usually from a westward path to an eastward one: *the recurvature of the path of a hurricane.*

re·curve (ri kėrv′), *v.t., v.i.,* **-curved, -curv·ing.** to curve back; bend back.

rec·u·san·cy (rek′yə zən sē, ri kyü′-), *n.* a being recusant. —**Syn.** recalcitrance.

rec·u·sant (rek′yə zənt, ri kyü′-), *adj.* **1.** refusing to submit. **2.** (formerly) refusing to attend the services of the Church of England or to acknowledge the ecclesiastical supremacy of the Crown.

—*n.* **1.** a person who refuses to submit. **2.** (formerly) a Roman Catholic who refused to attend the services of the Church of England.

[< Latin *recūsāns, -antis,* present participle of *recūsāre* refuse; see RECUSE]

re·cuse (ri kyüz′), *v.t.,* **-cused, -cus·ing.** **1.** to reject. **2.** *Law.* to reject or challenge (a judge or juror) as disqualified to act. [< Old French *recuser,* learned borrowing from Latin *recūsāre* to refuse, object < *re-* back + *causāre* plead a cause < *causa* cause]

re·cut (rē kut′), *v.t.,* **-cut, -cut·ting.** to cut again.

re·cy·cle (rē sī′kəl), *v.,* **-cled, -cling,** *n.* —*v.t.* to put through a cycle again or through a new cycle; return for further treatment or use: *There is nothing in untouched nature to compare with our extravagant use of energy and our failure to recycle essential materials* (Bulletin of Atomic Scientists). —*n.* the act or process of recycling: *Because internal recycle builds up the chemicals, layer upon layer, the granules are spherical in shape* (Scotsman).

red[1] (red), *n., adj.,* **red·der, red·dest.** —*n.* **1.** the color of blood; the color in a rainbow having the longest light wave, opposite violet. **2.** any shade of that color: *Red is obliged to include many of the browns, which are deep shades of red and hues closely akin to it* (Matthew Luckiesh). **3.** a red pigment or dye. **4.** red cloth or clothing: *to wear red.* **5.** a red or reddish person, animal, or thing. **6.** a Red; radical; revolutionary: *But he can hardly be called a pink, much less a red* (Time).

in the red, *Informal.* in debt; losing money: *Promoter Frank J. Bruen declined to make any further estimates as to what the show would draw or whether there was a chance to save it from going heavily "in the red"* (Baltimore Sun).
out of the red, *Informal.* showing a profit: *About 966 copies more and the title will be out of the red* (Publishers' Weekly).
see red, to become very angry: *It maddened me, I think, and I saw red—and before I knew what I was doing I stabbed him* (London Daily Mail).
—*adj.* **1.** having the color of blood, being like it, or suggesting it: *red hair.* **2.** sore; inflamed: *red eyes.* **3.** blushing; flushed: *He might be sticking his neck out in predicting that the venture would get anywhere at all, and that his face would indeed be red if it didn't* (New Yorker). **4.** red-hot; glowing. **5.** of or having to do with the north pole of a magnet. **6.** Red; radical; revolutionary.
[Old English *rēad*]

red[2] (red), *v.t.*, **red, red·ding.** redd[1].

Red (red), *adj.* **1.** extremely radical; revolutionary. **2.** having to do with the Soviet Union or any communist country: *Red guns from the Chinese mainland lobbed 66 shells on the offshore Quemoy islands* (Wall Street Journal).
—*n.* **1.** a radical; revolutionary: *Communists, extreme socialists, and anarchists are often called Reds.* **2.** an inhabitant of the Soviet Union or any communist country.
[< *red*[1] (the color of the flag of the International Communist Movement)]

red-, *prefix.* a form of **re-** in some cases before vowels, as in *redeem.*

re·dact (ri dakt′), *v.t.* **1.** to draw up or frame (a statement, announcement, etc.): *The House of Commons was busy redacting a "Protestation"* (Thomas Carlyle). **2.** to prepare (material) for publication; put into proper literary form; revise; edit. [< Latin *redactus,* past participle of *redigere;* see REDACTION]

re·dac·tion (ri dak′shən), *n.* **1.** the preparation of another person's writings for publication; revising; editing. **2.** the form or version of a work as prepared by revision or editing. [< Latin *redactiō, -ōnis* < *redigere* reduce < *re-* back + *agere* bring]

re·dac·tor (ri dak′tər), *n.* a person who redacts; editor.

red adder, the copperhead (snake): *Copperhead is a poisonous American snake, one of the pit vipers; it is also known as the pilot snake, red adder, and redeye* (Clifford H. Pope).

red admiral, a butterfly having blue-black wings with white spots and red bands.

red alert, an alert to warn that an attack by enemy aircraft is imminent, as when hostile aircraft appear in an air defense sector.

red algae, a large group of characteristically red or purplish, mostly marine, algae, such as carrageen. The color depends on the combination of chlorophyll, red pigment, and in some, blue pigment: *Red algae supply agar-agar, an important substance used in bacteriology laboratories* (Lewis H. Tiffany).

re·dan (ri dan′), *n.* a fortification with two walls forming an angle that points outward. [< French *redan,* variant of *redent* a double notching < Latin *re-* again + *dēns, dentis* tooth]

red ant, any of various small, reddish ants, such as the Pharaoh's ant.

red·ar·gue (red är′gyü), *v.t.*, **-gued, -gu·ing.** *Scottish.* **1.** to prove (a person) to be wrong by argument. **2.** to prove (a statement, argument, etc.) to be false or incorrect: *I may . . . redargue your claim and statements, as the result of a mistake* (William Hamilton). [< Latin *redarguere* disprove < *re-* back + *arguere* to argue]

red·ar·gu·tion (red′är gyü′shən), *n. Rare.* disproof of a statement, etc.; refutation. [< Latin *redargūtiō, -ōnis* < *redarguere* redargue]

red arsenic, realgar.

red astrachan, an early variety of apple having a yellowish skin spotted and streaked with red, and a crisp, juicy pulp of rich, acid flavor.

red-backed mouse (red′bakt′), redback vole: *Red-backed mice . . . began invading the cabin in such numbers that it looked as if I would soon be starving* (Maclean's).

red-backed sandpiper, a dunlin.

red-backed shrike, a small European shrike, with a chestnut brown back and a gray crown.

red-backed spider, a poisonous spider related to the black widow, found in Australia, New Zealand, and the East Indies.

red·back vole (red′bak′), any of a group of small rodents (voles) with reddish fur on the back, found especially in northern regions.

red-bait (red′bāt′), *v.i., v.t.* to accuse or harass (a person or persons) with being Communist, usually without sufficient evidence: *In this buffeting from all sides, Kennedy is pictured as both "red-baiting" and "soft on Communism"* (Time).

red-bait·er (red′bā′tər), *n.* a person who is given to red-baiting.

red bat, a North American migratory tree bat having reddish fur tipped with white.

red beds, *Geology.* a series of deep-red, sandy, sedimentary strata of the Permian or Triassic periods, often containing gypsum or salt deposits. It is a conspicuous formation in the Rocky Mountains.

red beet, the common beet, eaten as a vegetable.

red-bel·lied terrapin (red′bel′ēd), a large turtle with a reddish shell and abdomen, found along the Atlantic Coast of the United States.

red-bellied woodpecker, a woodpecker of the eastern United States having black-and-white bars across the back of the head. The male also has red on the crown and the abdomen.

red birch, river birch.

red·bird (red′bėrd′), *n.* **1.** the cardinal (bird). **2.** the scarlet tanager. **3.** the summer tanager. **4.** the European bullfinch.

red-blind (red′blīnd′), *adj.* unable to distinguish the color red.

red-blind·ness (red′blīnd′nis), *n.* the state of being red-blind, unable to distinguish the color red.

red blood cell or **corpuscle,** red corpuscle.

red-blood·ed (red′blud′id), *adj.* full of life and spirit; virile; vigorous: *It is a fight which should fire the hearts of all red-blooded Americans and stir their wills to action* (Newsweek).

red brass, an alloy of copper and zinc, with more copper than in the normal composition of brass; tombac.

red·breast (red′brest′), *n.* **1.** the robin: *Keats' redbreast yet whistles in the spring-time garden-croft* (New York Times). **2.** the knot, a wading bird.

red-breast·ed bream (red′bres′tid), a sunfish of the eastern United States with a reddish belly.

red-breasted merganser, a variety of merganser with a long crest and, in the male, white collar and reddish-brown breast, most common in marine waters of the Northern Hemisphere.

red-breasted nuthatch, a small nuthatch with reddish underparts, found in forested areas of northern North America.

red·brick (red′brik′), *British.* —*adj.* of or having to do with a university other than Oxford or Cambridge: *Thus the prospects are not very bright for an ordinary man holding a B.Sc. gained at a redbrick university, however good he is* (New Scientist). —*n.* Also, **Redbrick. 1.** a university other than Oxford or Cambridge. **2.** a student or graduate of such a university: *Of the 175 University men, some 100, or 57 per cent, are Redbricks* (London Times).

red·bud (red′bud′), *n.* any of various North American and Asian trees or shrubs of the pea family, bearing many small, pink, bud-like flowers early in the spring, as the Judas tree.

red·bug (red′bug′), *n.* **1.** a chigger: *Chiggers, called redbugs down South, cause the most exquisite itching* (Science News Letter). **2.** the cotton stainer.

red cabbage, a variety of cabbage with deep-purple leaves which become reddish when cooked.

red·cap (red′kap′), *n.* **1.** *U.S.* a porter at a railroad station, bus station, etc. He usually wears a red cap as part of his uniform. *No redcaps were in sight and Sam had two bags* (Harper's). **2.** *British Slang.* a military policeman. He wears a hat with a red band as part of his uniform. **3.** the European goldfinch.

Red·cap (red′kap′), *n.* any of an English breed of chickens with a rose comb and black, brown, and deep-red plumage.

red carpet, a carpet laid down for royalty or other notable persons to walk on when being received formally or given preferential treatment.
roll out the red carpet, to receive or treat royally or preferentially by or as if by laying down a red carpet: *The hotel rolled out the red carpet for the President.*

red-car·pet (red′kär′pit), *adj.* royal; preferential; favored: *The visiting premier received red-carpet treatment.*

red-car·pet·ed (red′kar′pə tid), *adj.* laid with a red carpet: *Workmen rushed to load the . . . red-carpeted room with palms* (Time).

red caviar, salmon roe eaten as a delicacy.

red cedar, 1. any of several varieties of North American juniper. **2.** their wood, used in making pencils, for interior finishing, etc. **3.** a giant arbor vitae of western North America. **4.** its wood.

red cell, red corpuscle.

red cent, *U.S. Informal.* a copper cent. It is no longer current.
not worth a red cent, worthless: *His advice about gardening wasn't worth a red cent.*

Red Chamber, the Senate of the Canadian Parliament: *At present, in the 102-member Red Chamber, there are 21 vacancies* (Ottawa Citizen).

Red Chinese, 1. the natives or inhabitants of Red China (the People's Republic of China, a Communist state). **2.** of or having to do with Red China or its people: *the Red Chinese regime.*

red clay, *Geology.* a reddish-brown mud that covers the ocean bottoms at depths below 12,000 feet. It consists of very fine particles of volcanic ash, mica, quartz, pumice, and meteoritic material.

red clover, a variety of clover that has ball-shaped heads of reddish-purple flowers, cultivated as food for horses, cattle, etc., and as a cover crop. It is the state flower of Vermont.

Red Clover

red·coat (red′kōt′), *n.* a British soldier. In former times, the red coat was worn by most infantry and certain other regiments. *The red-coats are abroad . . . these English must be looked to* (James Fenimore Cooper).

red-coat·ed (red′kō′tid), *adj.* wearing a red coat or coats.

red-cock·ad·ed woodpecker (red′ko kā′did), a woodpecker of the southern United States having black-and-white bars across the back and white cheeks.

red corpuscle, one of the tiny, red-colored cells in the blood, formed in bone marrow and containing hemoglobin; red blood cell; erythrocyte.

Red Crescent, the Moslem counterpart of the Red Cross.

red cross, a red Greek cross on a white ground, the emblem of the Red Cross.

Red Cross, 1. an international organization to care for the sick and wounded in war and to relieve suffering caused by floods, fire, diseases, and other calamities. **2.** a national society that is a branch of this organization. **3.** the cross of Saint George, England's national emblem.

red crossbill, a variety of crossbill of northern North America and the Appalachians, the male of which has dull-red plumage.

redd[1] (red), *v.t.*, **redd, redd·ing.** *British Dialect.* to clear; clean; tidy. Also, **red.** [apparently Old English *rǣdan* arrange, put in order]

redd[2] (red), *n.* **1.** the spawn of fish and frogs. **2.** a nest made by a fish in which to spawn. [origin uncertain]

red deer, 1. a reddish-brown deer about 4 feet high, native to the forests of Europe and Asia, and formerly very abundant in England. **2.** the common Virginia or white-tailed deer in its summer coat.

red·den (red′ən), *v.t.* to make red. —*v.i.* **1.** to become red. **2.** to blush. —**Syn.** *v.t.* ruddy.

red·den·dum (re den′dəm), *n., pl.* **-da** (-də). *Law.* a reservation in a deed giving the grantor a new share of a previous grant. [< Latin *reddendum,* neuter gerundive of *reddere;* see RENDER]

red·dish (red′ish), *adj.* somewhat red. —**red′dish·ness,** *n.*

reddish egret, a grayish heron of the West Indies, Mexico, and the Gulf States with a cinnamon head and neck. There is also a pure white color phase.

red·dle (red′əl), *n., v.t.,* **-dled, -dling.** raddle[2].

red·dled (red′əld), *adj.* raddled.

red·dle·man (red′əl man), *n., pl.* **-men.** raddleman.

red dog[1], **1.** the lowest grade of flour produced in milling. **2.** a mixture of slate, ash, and waste from a coal mine, used sometimes in surfacing temporary roads.

red dog[2], a card game in which each player bets on his ability to show a card from his hand of the same suit but higher than the one turned up from the remaining cards in the deck.

red-dog (red′dôg′, -dog′), *v.t., v.i.* **-dogged, -dog·ging.** *Football.* to pursue and harass (the ball carrier or passer).

red drum or **drumfish,** a large drumfish of the Atlantic Coast of North America.

Red Duster, Red Ensign (def. 1): *The Red Duster was uniquely honoured on the occasion of the Japanese capitulation in Rangoon at the end of the last war* (London Times).

red dwarf, one of a group of faint stars of the main-sequence group having a cooler temperature and lower luminosity than the others.

rede (rēd), *v.,* **red·ed, red·ing,** *n. Archaic.* —*v.t.* **1.** to advise. **2.** to interpret; explain. **3.** to tell.
—*n.* **1.** advice. **2.** a story. **3.** an interpretation. **4.** a plan. [Middle English *reden* Old English *rǣdan.* Compare READ[1].]

re·deal (rē dēl′), *v.,* **-dealt, -deal·ing,** *n.* —*v.i., v.t.* to deal again. —*n.* a dealing again; new deal.

red-ear sunfish (red′ir′), a small fresh-water sunfish of the southeastern United States, having a reddish gill covering.

re·de·ceive (rē′di sēv′), *v.t.,* **-ceived, -ceiv·ing.** to deceive again.

re·de·cide (rē′di sīd′), *v.t.,* **-cid·ed, -cid·ing.** to decide again: *Cases which if not obsolete have been in principle redecided in more modern decisions* (Law Times).

re·dec·o·rate (rē dek′ə rāt), *v.t., v.i.,* **-rat·ed, -rat·ing.** to decorate again or anew, especially by putting new paint, paper, etc., on the walls, ceiling, and floor of a room.

re·dec·o·ra·tion (rē′dek ə rā′shən), *n.* **1.** a redecorating. **2.** a being redecorated.

re·ded·i·cate (rē ded′ə kāt), *v.t.,* **-cat·ed, -cat·ing.** to dedicate anew: *Those who ... have rededicated themselves unto the Lord* (Charles Haddon Spurgeon).

re·ded·i·ca·tion (rē′ded ə kā′shən), *n.* the act of rededicating: *There was a rededication service at the church* (London Daily News).

re·deem (ri dēm′), *v.t.* **1.** to buy back: *The property on which the money was lent was redeemed when the loan was paid back.* **2.** to pay off: *We redeemed the mortgage.* **3.** to carry out; make good; fulfill: *We redeem a promise by doing what we said we would.* **4.** to set free; rescue; save: *to be redeemed from sin. Like some merchant who, in storm, Throws the freight over to redeem the ship* (Robert Browning). **5.** to make up for; balance: *A very good feature will sometimes redeem several bad ones.* **6.** to reclaim (land): *a tract redeemed from the sea* (Thomas Hardy). [< Latin *redimere* < *re-* back + *emere* to buy] —**Syn. 1.** regain. **4.** liberate, deliver, release.

re·deem·a·bil·i·ty (ri dē′mə bil′ə tē), *n.* redeemable quality or state: *He said his group opposed the [trading] stamps because there was "consistently inadequate protection on redeemability"* (Wall Street Journal).

re·deem·a·ble (ri dē′mə bəl), *adj.* **1.** that can be redeemed. **2.** that will be redeemed or paid: *These bonds are redeemable in 1978.* —**re·deem′a·ble·ness,** *n.*

re·deem·a·bly (ri dē′mə blē), *adv.* so as to be redeemable.

re·deem·er (ri dē′mər), *n.* a person who redeems.

Re·deem·er (ri dē′mər), *n.* Jesus Christ, the Saviour of the world.

re·deem·ing (ri dē′ming), *adj.* that redeems; saving: *a redeeming feature.*

re·de·fect (rē′di fekt′), *v.t.* to forsake again; defect afresh.

re·de·fec·tion (rē′di fek′shən), *n.* the act of defecting or deserting again. The desertion by a political refugee of the country in which he found asylum and his return to his original country is redefection. *The young Russians had no words to explain their redefection* (Time).

re·de·fec·tor (rē′di fek′tər), *n.* a person who commits a redefection.

re·de·fine (rē′di fīn′), *v.t.,* **-fined, -fin·ing.** to define again: *One of the ancient terms it might be well to revive and redefine* (William Minto).

re·def·i·ni·tion (rē′def ə nish′ən), *n.* a redefining: *The whole tenor of his labors was towards an assertion, purification, and redefinition of Transcendentalism* (David Masson).

re·de·liv·er (rē′di liv′ər), *v.t.* **1.** to deliver back; return. **2.** to deliver again.

re·de·mand (rē′di mand′, -mänd′), *v.t.* **1.** to demand back. **2.** to demand again. —*n.* a redemanding.

re·de·mand·a·ble (rē′di man′də bəl, -män′-), *adj.* that can be redemanded.

re·dem·on·strate (rē dem′ən strāt), *v.t.,* **-strat·ed, -strat·ing.** to demonstrate again.

re·demp·tion (ri demp′shən), *n.* **1.** a redeeming. **2.** a being redeemed. **3.** deliverance; rescue. **4.** deliverance from sin; salvation. [< Latin *redēmptiō, -ōnis* < *redimere;* see REDEEM. Doublet of RANSOM.]

re·demp·tion·al (ri demp′shə nəl), *adj.* of or having to do with redemption.

re·demp·tion·er (ri demp′shə nər), *n.* one of the early emigrants to America, who gave the right to his services for a certain time in payment for his passage.

Re·demp·tion·ist (ri demp′shə nist), *n.* a member of the Roman Catholic Order of the Holy Trinity; Trinitarian.

re·demp·tive (ri demp′tiv), *adj.* serving to redeem.

re·demp·tor (ri demp′tər), *n.* a redeemer.

Re·demp·tor·ist (ri demp′tər ist), *n.* a member of the Congregation of the Most Holy Redeemer, a Roman Catholic order founded in Italy in 1732 and devoted to work among the poor. [< French *rédemptoriste* < Latin *redēmptor, -ōris* (< *redimere;* see REDEEM) + French *-iste* -ist]

re·demp·to·ry (ri demp′tər ē), *adj.* redemptive.

re·demp·tress (ri demp′tris), *n.* a woman redeemer.

re·demp·trix (ri demp′triks), *n., pl.* **-demp·trix·es, -demp·tri·ces** (-demp tri′ sēz). redemptress.

Red Ensign or **red ensign, 1.** the form of the national flag of Great Britain used as an ensign by merchant ships, consisting of a red flag with the Union Jack in the upper corner close to the flagstaff. **2.** (until 1965) the flag of Canada, consisting of a red flag containing the national arms of Canada, with the Union Jack in the upper corner close to the flagstaff. It has been replaced by a flag with a red maple leaf centered on a white background.

re·de·ny (rē′di nī′), *v.t., v.i.,* **-nied, -ny·ing.** to deny again.

re·de·ploy (rē′di ploi′), *v.t.* to change the position of (troops) from one theater of war to another: *At the same time, he will redeploy French forces for even more effective action against the rebel guerrillas* (Newsweek).

re·de·ploy·ment (rē′di ploi′mənt), *n.* **1.** a redeploying. **2.** a being redeployed.

re·de·pos·it (rē′di poz′it), *v.t.* to deposit again. —*n.* a new deposit.

re·dep·o·si·tion (rē′dep ə zish′ən, -dē pə-), *n.* **1.** the act of redepositing. **2.** the state or condition of being redeposited: *Changes ... brought about by the deposition, removal, and redeposition of gravel, sand, and fine sediment* (Charles Lyell).

re·de·scend (rē′di send′), *v.i., v.t.* to descend again: *That fatal child ... Who waits ... To redescend and trample out the spark* (Shelley). *Having reached the pinnacle of generalization, we may redescend the ladder* (William Hamilton).

re·de·scent (rē′di sent′), *n.* a descending or falling again.

re·de·scribe (rē′di skrīb′), *v.t.,* **-scribed, -scrib·ing.** to describe a second time; describe again.

re·de·sign (rē′di zīn′), *v.t.* to design again: *The t does not look well: I shall have to redesign it* (William Morris). —*n.* **1.** the act or process of redesigning: *There is still considerable scope for increasing the Caravelle's payload, but no prospect for improving its speed without a complete redesign of wing* (New Scientist). **2.** a new design: *It's just a coincidence that large-scale redesigns ... are coming up at a time when the industry woefully needs some help* (Wall Street Journal).

re·des·ig·nate (rē dez′ig nāt), *v.t.,* **-nat·ed, -nat·ing.** to designate again.

re·de·ter·mi·na·tion (rē′di tėr′mə nā′shən), *n.* a fresh determination: *The importance of a redetermination was thus rendered more obvious* (George F. Chambers).

re·de·ter·mine (rē′di tėr′mən), *v.t.,* **-mined, -min·ing.** to determine again: *To redetermine their boundaries after the subsidence of the flood* (John W. Draper).

re·de·vel·op (rē′di vel′əp), *v.t.* **1.** to develop again. **2.** *Photography.* to put into a second developer after bleaching to tone the image. **3.** to improve (land or buildings), especially by rebuilding: *Eight downtown blocks now have been cleared and 7 million dollars are being spent to redevelop them for a parkway* (Newsweek).
—*v.i.* to develop again.

re·de·vel·op·er (rē′di vel′ə pər), *n.* a person, thing, or company that redevelops land or buildings: *The federal government will then lend the locality the money it needs to acquire and clear blighted land for subsequent sale to private redevelopers* (Harper's).

re·de·vel·op·ment (rē′di vel′əp mənt), *n.* **1.** the act or process of redeveloping. **2.** a being redeveloped.

red·eye (red′ī′), *n.* **1. a.** a cyprinoid fish with a red iris; rudd. **b.** a blue-spotted fresh-water sunfish of the eastern United States. **c.** a rock bass. **2.** the red-eyed vireo. **3.** the copperhead, a poisonous North American snake. **4.** *U.S. Slang.* strong, cheap whiskey: *He drank enough redeye before he was 20 to make Lost Weekend seem like a short beer* (Time).

red-eyed (red′īd′), *adj.* **1.** having a red iris: *At his feet sat a white-coated, red-eyed dog* (Dickens). **2.** having eyes surrounded by a red ring, as some birds: *The red-eyed flycatcher is an inhabitant of the whole of our forests* (James Audubon). **3.** having the eyes reddened by tears, lack of sleep, excessive fatigue, etc.: *Before it's all over, negotiators and labor reporters will be weary and red-eyed* (Newsweek).

red-eyed towhee, the common towhee of eastern North America.

red-eyed vireo, a large vireo of temperate North America with white under parts and a white stripe over the eye. See **vireo** for picture.

red-faced (red′fāst), *adj.* **1.** having a red face: *The stout, red-faced Dutch plantation owner, immaculate in white linens, pours a bottle of Heineken's beer into a glass on the veranda table* (Wall Street Journal). **2.** flushed with embarrassment, anger, etc.: *[He] retorted with a blistering lecture about the ethics of business and government, and sent them away red-faced with shock* (Newsweek).

red fescue, a grass with small, reddish spikelets grown for pasture and used in lawns: *A good lawn mixture should also include red fescues* (Science News Letter).

red·field·i·a (red fēl′dē ə), *n.* a tall grass, with a loose, diversely spreading flower cluster, found in sandy parts of the western United States. [< New Latin *Redfieldia* the genus name < John H. *Redfield,* 1815-1895, an American botanist]

Red·field's grass (red′fēldz), redfieldia.

red·fin (red′fin′), *n.* any of various small, fresh-water, cyprinoid fishes with reddish fins, as the shiner.

red fir, 1. any of various firs of the western United States, especially a variety of Oregon, California, and Nevada growing to a height of 200 feet. **2.** their reddish wood. **3.** the Douglas fir.

red fire, a chemical preparation that burns with a red light, used in fireworks, signals, etc.

red·fish (red′fish′), *n., pl.* **-fish·es** or (*collectively*) **-fish. 1.** the red or sockeye salmon. **2.** the rosefish. **3.** the red drum.

red flag, 1. a symbol of rebellion, revolution, etc. **2.** a sign of danger. **3.** a thing that stirs up anger.

red-foot·ed booby (red′fu̇t′id), a gull-like sea bird about the size of a small goose, which lives on tropical islands.

red fox, 1. the common reddish fox of North America. **2.** a related fox of Europe. **3.** the reddish fur of a fox. See **fox** for picture.

red fuming nitric acid, a highly corrosive and unstable form of nitric acid used in combination with aniline in rocket fuels.

red giant, *Astronomy.* a star of great size and brightness which has a comparatively cool surface temperature.
red grouse, a variety of grouse of Great Britain and Ireland that does not turn white in winter.
Red Guard, a member of a mass movement of young Chinese communists proclaiming rigid adherence to Maoist doctrines. The Red Guard were at the forefront of the Chinese cultural revolution of 1966-67.
red gum[1], **1.** any of several Australian eucalyptus trees which yield a reddish gum, used as an astringent, for coughs, etc. **2.** the sweet gum. [< *red*[1] + *gum*[1]]
red gum[2], strophulus, a reddish eruption of the skin affecting infants. [alteration of earlier *red-gownd,* or *red-gowm,* apparently < *red*[1] + obsolete *gound* foul matter, Old English *gund* matter, pus; spelling influenced by *gum*[1]]
red-haired (red′hãrd′), *adj.* having red hair.
red-hand (red′hand′), *adj. Scottish.* red-handed.
red-hand·ed (red′han′did), *adj.* **1.** having hands red with blood. **2.** in the very act of crime, mischief, etc.: *a man caught red-handed in robbery.* —**red′-hand′ed·ly,** *adv.* —**red′-hand′ed·ness,** *n.*
red hat, 1. a cardinal's hat. **2.** the position or rank of a cardinal. **3.** a cardinal.
red·head (red′hed′), *n.* **1.** a person having red hair. **2.** a kind of North American duck related to and resembling the canvasback but with a grayer body. The adult male has a reddish-brown head. **3.** the redheaded woodpecker.
red·head·ed (red′hed′id), *adj.* **1.** having red hair. **2.** having a red head.
redheaded woodpecker, a black-and-white North American woodpecker with a bright-red head and neck. See **woodpecker** for picture.
red heat, 1. the condition of being red-hot. **2.** the accompanying temperature.
red herring, 1. the common smoked herring. **2.** something used to draw attention away from the real issue.
red hind, a kind of olive-colored grouper with red spots. It is an important food fish of the Carribbean.
red-hot (red′hot′), *adj.* **1.** red with heat; very hot: *a red-hot iron.* **2.** enthusiastic; excited; violent: *a red-hot radical.* **3.** fresh from the source: *red-hot rumors.*
—*n.* Also, **red hot.** *U.S. Slang.* a frankfurter.
red-hot poker, 1. any of a group of African plants of the lily family with tall, slender spikes of red and yellow flowers. **2.** the flower of any of these plants.
re·did (rē did′), *v.* the past tense of **redo:** *We redid it as a collection of short stories* (Newsweek).
re·dif·fu·sion (rē′di fyü′zhən), *n.* **1.** the act of rediffusing. **2.** the state or condition of being rediffused.
re·di·gest (rē′də jest′, -dī-), *v.t.* to digest again: *Kant ate up all Hume and redigested him* (David Masson).
red Indian, a North American Indian: *I have always understood that the pipe originated among the red Indians of North America* (Sunday Times).
➔ See **American Indian** for usage note.
red·in·gote (red′ing gōt), *n.* **1.** (formerly) a man's outer coat with long skirts overlapping in front. **2.** a somewhat similar coat now worn by women, sometimes forming part of a dress: *Veneziani's redingote, to be worn over a dress or as a dress, is reproduced in black cotton faille* (New Yorker). [< French *redingote* < English *riding coat*]

Redingote (def. 1)

red ink, 1. ink having a red color, used in bookkeeping for recording debit items and balances. **2.** *U.S.* financial loss; deficit: *Colleges battle red ink with a scattering of tuition fee hikes* (Wall Street Journal). —**red′-ink′,** *adj.*
red·in·te·grate (red in′tə grāt), *v.* **-grat·ed, -grat·ing.** —*v.t.* to make whole again; restore to a perfect state; renew; reëstablish. —*v.i.* to become whole again; be renewed. [< Latin *redintegrāre* (with English *-ate*[1] < *re-* again + *integrāre* make whole, renew < *integer* whole. Compare INTEGER.]
red·in·te·gra·tion (red′in tə grā′shən), *n.* **1.** restoration; renewal; reëstablishment: *A redintegration of love began to take place between the Colonel and his relatives in Park Lane* (Thackeray). **2.** *Psychology.* the tendency of elements once combined as parts of a single mental state to recall or suggest one another at a later time.
red·in·te·gra·tive (red in′tə grā′tiv), *adj.* of or having to do with redintegration.
red·in·te·gra·tor (red in′tə grā′tər), *n.* a person or thing that redintegrates.
re·di·rect (rē′də rekt′, -dī-), *v.t.* to direct again or anew. —*adj. Law.* of or having to do with a second examination of a witness by the party calling him, after cross-examination.
re·di·rec·tion (rē′də rek′shən, -dī-), *n.* a redirecting.
re·dis·count (rē dis′kount), *v.t.* to discount again; discount (a bill of exchange) for another, who has already discounted it. —*n.* **1.** a rediscounting. **2.** *Informal.* a commercial paper that has been rediscounted.
rediscount rate, the rate of discount charged by a Federal Reserve Bank on loans to commercial member banks.
re·dis·cov·er (rē′dis kuv′ər), *v.t.* to discover again. —**re′dis·cov′er·er,** *n.*
re·dis·cov·er·y (rē′dis kuv′ər ē, -kuv′rē), *n., pl.* **-er·ies.** a discovering again.
re·dis·lo·ca·tion (rē′dis lō kā′shən), *n.* **1.** repeated dislocation. **2.** *Medicine.* dislocation recurring after reduction.
re·dis·pose (rē′dis pōz′), *v.t.,* **-posed, -pos·ing.** to dispose or adjust again.
re·dis·po·si·tion (rē′dis pə zish′ən), *n.* **1.** the act or process of redisposing. **2.** rearrangement: *Redisposition of the Minister's functions, Mr. Wilson said, would be announced later* (London Times).
re·dis·solve (rē′di zolv′), *v.t., v.i.,* **-solved, -solv·ing.** to dissolve again: *As the light wreaths of cloud passed over the ridge ... they were immediately redissolved* (Charles R. Darwin).
re·dis·till (rē′dis til′), *v.t.* to distill again.
re·dis·til·late (rē′dis′tə lāt), *n.* something that is produced by a second or repeated distillation.
re·dis·trib·ute (rē′dis trib′yüt), *v.t.* **-ut·ed, -ut·ing.** to distribute again or anew.
re·dis·tri·bu·tion (rē′dis trə byü′shən), *n.* a distribution made again or anew: *The first and most popular measure in an agrarian society usually calls for the expropriation and redistribution of land* (Preston E. James).
re·dis·tri·bu·tion·al (rē′dis trə byü′shənəl), *adj.* of, having to do with, or characterized by redistribution: *To guarantee continuous economic growth, he thinks we need "large-scale redistributional reforms" that would lighten the tax load on the poor* (New Yorker).
re·dis·trib·u·tive (rē′dis trib′yə tiv), *adj.* redistributional: *Some of the large sum of money which will now be spent by the government will be raised by new redistributive taxation* (Canadian Saturday Night).
re·dis·trict (rē dis′trikt), *v.t. U.S.* to divide into districts again, often for voting purposes. [American English < *re-* again + *district,* verb]
re·di·vide (rē′də vīd′), *v.t., v.i.,* **-vid·ed, -vid·ing.** to divide again: *The Empire was redivided, and territorially reorganized* (Cornelius C. Felton).
red·i·vi·vous (red′ə vī′vəs), *adj. Obsolete.* liable to revive; reappearing. [< Latin *redivīvus* (with English *-ous*) < *re-* again + *vīvus* living, alive]
red·i·vi·vus (red′ə vī′vəs), *adj.* alive again; restored; renewed: *the Napoleonic empire redivivus* (George W. Curtis). [< Latin *redivīvus* < *re-* again + *vīvus* living, alive]
red jasmine, the frangipani.
red kangaroo, a large, reddish kangaroo of Australia. It is the largest marsupial in existence, standing nearly seven feet tall.
red lane, *Informal.* the throat.
red lattice, *Obsolete.* **1.** a lattice painted red, formerly the sign of an alehouse. **2.** an alehouse.
red lead, a red oxide of lead, used in paint, in making cement for pipes, and in making glass: *A variety of red lead, "orange mineral," is used in making red paint, printing ink and dipping paint* (W. R. Jones). *Formula:* Pb_3O_4
red lead ore, crocoite.
red·leg (red′leg′), *n.* an infectious disease of frogs, usually prevalent in the fall, characterized by hemorrhagic congestion of the legs and abdomen.
red-let·ter (red′let′ər), *adj.* **1.** marked by red letters. **2.** memorable; especially happy: *Graduation is a red-letter day in one's life.* —**Syn. 2.** notable.
red light, 1. a traffic signal or other warning to stop. **2.** a children's game of tag. One player turns his back and counts to ten while the others try to advance and tag him before he reaches ten and calls "red light."
red-light (red′līt′), *adj.* **1.** having a red light or lights. **2.** characterized by many brothels, disorderly places, etc.: *a red-light district, red-light conditions.*
Red Lion and Sun, the Iranian Red Cross.
red·ly (red′lē), *adv.* with a red color or glow: *The blaze was redly reflected in the waters of the strait* (George Borrow).
red man, an American Indian.
red maple, 1. any of several varieties of maple tree with reddish-brown wood and bright-red flowers that appear in the spring before the leaves, especially a large maple of eastern North America. **2.** the wood of any of these trees, used in cabinetwork.
Red Mass, (in the Roman Catholic Church) a Mass celebrated in honor of the Holy Ghost. The officiating priests wear red vestments.
red meat, a meat that is red when raw: *Red meat includes beef, veal, pork, mutton, and lamb.*
red mud, 1. red clay. **2.** residue of impurities, as silicon oxide, iron oxide, etc., resulting from the processing of alumina.
red mullet, any of a group of reddish fishes valued as food.
red·neck (red′nek′), *n. U.S. Slang.* a poor, white, Southern farmer; sharecropper.
red-necked (red′nekt′), *adj. U.S. Slang.* excitable; ill-tempered; angry.
red·ness (red′nis), *n.* red quality; red color.
red nose, a disease of the upper respiratory tract of cattle; mucosal disease.
re·do (rē dü′), *v.t.,* **-did, -done, -do·ing.** to do again; do over: *He ... ends by redoing the work of all of them* (Atlantic).
red oak, 1. any of various North American oaks with hard, reddish-brown, coarse-grained wood: *The red oak is one of the most favored American ornamental trees* (T. Ewald Maki). **2.** the wood of any of these trees.
red ocher, an earthy, reddish hematite; raddle.
red·o·lence (red′ə ləns), *n.* a being redolent.
red·o·len·cy (red′ə lən sē), *n.* redolence.
red·o·lent (red′ə lənt), *adj.* **1.** having a pleasant smell; fragrant. **2.** smelling strongly; giving off an odor: *a house redolent of fresh paint.* **3.** suggesting thoughts or feelings: *"Ivanhoe" is a name redolent of romance. Oxford is redolent of age and authority* (Emerson). [< Latin *redolēns, -entis,* present participle of *redolēre* emit scent < *re-* back + *olēre* to smell] —**red′o·lent·ly,** *adv.* —**Syn. 1.** aromatic. **3.** reminiscent.
re·done (rē dun′), *v.* the past participle of **redo.**
red osier, 1. any of various willows with reddish bark. **2.** *U.S.* a dogwood having reddish branches and shoots resembling those of the osier.
re·dou·ble (rē dub′əl), *v.,* **-bled, -bling,** *n.* —*v.t.* **1.** to double again. **2.** to increase greatly; double: *When he saw land ahead, the swimmer redoubled his speed.* **3.** to repeat; echo. **4.** (in games) to double (an opponent's double). —*v.i.* **1.** to double back: *The fox redoubled on his trail to escape the hunters.* **2.** to be doubled; become twice as great: *The clamour redoubled when it was known that the convert ... had accepted the Deanery of Saint Paul's* (Macaulay). **3.** to resound: *A stunning clang of massive bolts redoubling beneath the deep* (Shelley).
—*n.* the act of redoubling; a double of a double.
[< Middle French *redoubler* < *re-* re- + *doubler* to double]
re·dou·ble·ment (rē dub′əl mənt), *n.* a redoubling: *a redoublement of agitation.*
re·doubt[1] (ri dout′), *n.* **1.** a small fort standing alone: *They will meet American power in the air and sea lanes between the mainland and the Nationalist redoubt* (New Yorker). **2.** a fortified enclosure in front or

on the flanks of a permanent fortification: *Conservatism, entrenched in its immense redoubts* (Emerson). [< French *redoute* < earlier Italian *ridotta* < Vulgar Latin *reductus, -ūs* a retreat < Latin *redūcere;* see REDUCE; spelling influenced by *redoubt*[2]]

re·doubt[2] (ri dout′), *v.t., v.i.* to fear. [< Old French *redouter,* and *redoubter* < *re-* again + *doubter.* Compare DOUBT.]

re·doubt·a·ble (ri dou′tə bəl), *adj.* **1.** that should be feared or dreaded: *a redoubtable warrior.* **2.** commanding respect: *that you marry this redoubtable couple together—Righteousness and Peace* (Oliver Cromwell). *Michael I. Pupin . . . had become professor of electromechanics and a redoubtable inventor* (Harper's). [< Old French *redoutable* < *redouter* to dread < *re-* again + *douter.* Compare DOUBT.] —**re·doubt′a·ble·ness,** *n.* —**Syn. 1.** formidable.

re·doubt·a·bly (ri dou′tə blē), *adv.* in a redoubtable manner; formidably.

re·doubt·ed (ri dou′tid), *adj.* **1.** dreaded; formidable. **2.** respected; renowned.

re·dound (ri dound′), *v.i.* **1.** to come back as a result; contribute: *The noble deeds of women redound to the glory of womanhood.* **2.** to come back; recoil: *Disgrace redounds upon a person who lies or cheats.* **3.** to proceed; arise; issue: *the anxiety of spirit which redoundeth from knowledge* (Francis Bacon). —*n.* the fact of redounding or resulting: *Not without redound Of use and glory to yourselves ye come* (Tennyson).
[< Old French *redonder,* learned borrowing from Latin *redundāre* overflow < *re-* back + *undāre* to surge, rise in waves < *unda* wave]

red·out (red′out′), *n.* a sudden rush of blood to the head producing a red blur before the eyes: *At 3 or 4 G's in certain spins and loops the pilot experiences a redout* (World Book Encyclopedia). [< *red*[1]*;* patterned on *blackout*]

red·o·wa (red′ə wə, -və), *n.* **1.** a Bohemian dance popular in the 1800's. One form in triple time resembles the waltz or mazurka; another in duple time resembles the polka. **2.** music for these dances. [< German *Redowa* < Czech *rejdovák* < *rejdovati* steer about, drive < *rejd* turn, circular dance]

red·ox (red′oks), *adj. Chemistry.* producing or containing the processes of reduction and oxidation: *In the redox cell . . . the fuel and oxygen do not react directly with each other* (Scientific American). [< *red*(uction) + *ox*(idation)]

red-pen·cil (red′pen′səl), *v.t.,* **-ciled, -cil·ing** or (*especially British*) **-cilled, -cil·ling.** to correct or edit with or as if with a red lead pencil; blue-pencil: *I have been redpencilling student papers for a good many years and I ought by now to have become resigned or cynical* (Wall Street Journal).

red pepper, 1. a plant of the nightshade family that has a podlike fruit that turns red when ripe. There are many varieties of red pepper, including the sweet pepper and chili. **2.** the ground, dried seeds or fruits of any of these plants, used as a seasoning; cayenne pepper.

red phalarope, a phalarope with reddish under parts which breeds in arctic regions and winters at sea in southern waters.

red phosphorus, an allotropic form of phosphorus: *Red phosphorus is far less reactive than white phosphorus* (New Scientist).

red pine, 1. a pine of the northern United States and Canada, often over 100 feet tall, with smooth, reddish, hard wood of low resin content: *Red pine, also called Norway Pine, is a large, straight tree much prized for its lumber* (Richard J. Preston). **2.** the wood, much used for lumber in construction.

red·poll (red′pōl′), *n.* **1.** any of several varieties of small, brownish finches of arctic regions, having a pink or red cap on the head. During the winter they appear in the northern United States. **2.** Red Polled.

red·polled (red′pōld′), *adj.* having red on the top of the head.

Red Polled or **Poll,** any of a breed of reddish, hornless, short-haired cattle raised in England.

red porgy, a porgy that is crimson with blue spots.

red quebracho, a tree of the cashew family, growing in Argentina, whose wood and bright-red bark are used in tanning and dyeing.

re·draft (*v.* rē draft′, -dräft′; *n.* rē′draft′, -dräft′), *v.t.* to draft again or anew. —*n.* **1.** a second draft. **2.** a draft on the drawers or endorsers of a protested bill of exchange for the amount of the bill plus costs and charges.

red rag, 1. a source of extreme provocation or annoyance; something which excites violent anger (from the belief that a red rag will incite a bull): *The phrase "secret diplomacy" has long been a red rag to American public opinion* (Wall Street Journal). **2.** a variety of rust in grain. **3.** *Slang.* the tongue: *Stop that . . . red rag of yours, will you* (William S. Gilbert).

re·drape (rē drāp′), *v.t.,* **-draped, -drap·ing.** to drape again.

red raspberry, the common European or American variety of raspberry.

re·draw (rē drô′), *v.t.,* **-drew, -drawn, -draw·ing.** to make a redraft of. —**re·draw′er,** *n.*

re·dress (*v.* ri dres′; *n.* rē′dres, ri dres′), *v.t.* **1.** to set right; repair; remedy. **2.** to adjust evenly again: *I called the New World into existence to redress the balance of the Old* (George Canning).
—*n.* **1.** a setting right; reparation; relief: *Any man deserves redress if he has been injured unfairly. My griefs . . . finding no redress, ferment and rage* (Milton). **2.** the means of a remedy: *There was no redress against the lawless violence to which they were perpetually exposed* (John L. Motley).
[< Middle French *redresser* < *re-* again + Old French *dresser* to straighten, arrange. Compare DRESS, verb.]
—**Syn.** *n.* **1.** restitution.

re-dress (rē dres′), *v.t.* to dress again.

re·dress·a·ble (ri dres′ə bəl), *adj.* that can be redressed.

re·dress·al (ri dres′əl), *n.* a redressing or being redressed: *In spite of a redressal of the situation . . . they lost five wickets for 116* (London Times).

re·dress·er (ri dres′ər), *n.* a person that redresses: *Don Quixote . . . the redresser of injuries* (Thomas Shelton).

re·dres·sor (rē dres′ər), *n.* a person or thing that redresses.

re·dress·ment (ri dres′mənt), *n.* a redressal.

re·drew (rē drü′), *v.* the past tense of **redraw.**

re·drive (rē drīv′), *v.t.,* **-drove** or (*Archaic*) **-drave, -driv·en, -driv·ing.** to drive back; drive again: *As to and fro the doubtful Galliot rides, Here driven by Winds, and there redriven by Tides* (John Dryden).

red·root (red′rüt′, -rút′), *n.* **1.** a North American plant of the bloodwort family with sword-shaped leaves, woolly, yellow flowers, and a red root used in dyeing. **2.** any of various other plants with red roots, such as the bloodroot, the alkanet, and a pigweed.

re·drop (rē drop′), *v.i., v.t.,* **-dropped** or **-dropt, -drop·ping.** to drop again.

red rose, the emblem of the house of Lancaster.

red rot, a fungous disease which attacks sugar cane and sorghum, discoloring the pith and rotting the seeds and stalks.

re·dry (rē drī′), *v.t., v.i.,* **-dried, -dry·ing.** to dry again.

red sage, a tropical American plant of the verbena family, with yellow flowers that change to bright orange or red.

red salmon, the sockeye salmon.

red sandalwood, 1. an East Indian tree of the pea family, with dark-red wood. **2.** its wood, used for construction and as the source of a red dye.

red sanders or **red sanderswood,** red sandalwood.

red scale, a scale insect that attacks orange, grapefruit, and other citrus trees: *An almost microscopic wasp is being toughened with radiation in preparation for an attack on California's red scale, a major pest of citrus orchards* (Scientific American).

red-shaft·ed flicker (red′shaf′tid), a variety of flicker of western North America, with red feathers under the wings and tail.

red·shank (red′shangk′), *n.* an Old World bird related to the snipe, having red legs: *Some plovers and redshanks coming to winter in Britain, also unseasonally adorned, proved to be radioactive* (New Scientist).

red shift, *Astronomy.* a shift of the light of stars, nebulae, and other luminous bodies toward the red end of the spectrum, indicating movement outward at increasing speed, and leading to the belief that the universe is constantly expanding at ever greater rates of speed.

red shirt, a member of an organization who wore red shirts, especially a follower of Giuseppe Garibaldi in the struggle for Italian unity in the 1800's.

red-short (red′shôrt′), *adj.* brittle when at a red heat: *Iron and steel with too much sulfur are red-short.* —**red′-short′ness,** *n.*

red-shoul·dered hawk (red′shōl′dərd), a common hawk of eastern North America with broad wings and tail, that feeds largely on rodents and insects.

Red Sindhi, a red Brahman variety of cattle that originated in the province of Sind in Pakistan.

red·skin (red′skin′), *n., adj.* North American Indian: *We have had more difficulty with white desperadoes than with redskins* (Theodore Roosevelt). [American English < *red*[1] + *skin*]

red spider, a mite that damages fruit trees and evergreens by sucking the juice from leaves: *The red spider (which is neither red nor a spider, but yellowish-green and a mite) is fighting for its place in the Top Ten orchard pests* (Punch).

red squill, a squill having a reddish bulb, used as a rat poison.

red squirrel, a common North American squirrel having reddish fur.

red·start (red′stärt′), *n.* **1.** an American fly-catching warbler with orange-red or yellow markings on the tail and wings. **2.** the painted redstart. **3.** a small, common European songbird with a reddish tail. [American English < *red*[1] + *start*[2] a tail]

Redstart (def. 1)
(about 5½ in. long)

red stele, a disease of strawberries caused by a fungus that attacks the roots, causing the plants either to become stunted or to die: *Red stele attacks the roots, turning the steles or central part of the plant roots red* (Science News Letter).

red tab, *British Slang.* a high-ranking military officer: *A carload of red tabs and brass hats arrives* . . . (J.B. Priestley). [because of the red tabs on officers' collars]

red·tail (red′tāl′), *n.* red-tailed hawk: *One of his special interests is the redtail—the big, handsome, and once common bird of prey that frontier tradition calls the chicken hawk* (New Yorker).

red-tailed hawk (red′tāld′), a common North American, broad-winged hawk with a reddish-brown tail. See **hawk** for picture.

red tape, 1. tape having a red color, used for tying up official papers. **2.** too much attention to details and forms; bureaucracy: *A House Banking subcommittee assailed what it called the red tape and delays in the program to eliminate slums* (Wall Street Journal). —**red′-tape′,** *adj.*

red-tap·ism (red′tā′piz əm), *n.* too much attention to details and form.

red-throat·ed diver (red′thrō′tid), any of a species of small loons distinguished by an elongated patch of dark bay color on the throat: *The red-throated diver is the smallest species of the genus, as well as the most common* (William Yarrel).

red tide, a reddish discoloration on the surface of sea water produced at times by the sudden clustering together of billions of one-celled organisms that are toxic to fish. The red tide appears chiefly in the waters around Florida and in the Gulf of Mexico: *Unusually sultry weather plus an abundant rainfall appears to be the reason for Florida's latest red tide* (Science News Letter).

red·top (red′top′), *n.* a kind of grass grown for forage and pasture. One variety has large, reddish, spreading flower clusters.

re·duce (ri düs′, -dyüs′), *v.,* **-duced, -duc·ing.** —*v.t.* **1.** to make less; make smaller; decrease: *to reduce expenses, to reduce one's weight.* **2.** to make lower in degree, intensity, etc.; weaken; dilute. **3.** to bring down; lower: *Misfortune reduced that poor woman to begging.* **4.** to bring to a certain state, form, or condition; change: *The teacher soon reduced the noisy class to order. I was reduced to tears by the cruel words.* **5.** to change to another form: *to reduce a statement to writing. If you reduce 3 lbs. 7 oz. to ounces, you have*

55 ounces. **6.** to bring under control; conquer; subdue: *The army reduced the fort by a sudden attack.* **7.** to restore to its proper place or normal condition: *A doctor can reduce a fracture or dislocation.* **8.** *Chemistry.* **a.** to combine with hydrogen. **b.** to remove oxygen from. **c.** to change (a compound) so that the valence of the positive element is lower. **9.** *Mathematics.* to simplify (an expression, formula, etc.). **10.** to smelt: *to reduce the ores of silver or copper.* **11.** *Biology.* to bring about meiosis in (a cell). **12.** to thin (paint) with oil or turpentine. **13.** to treat (a photographic negative) to make less dense. **14.** *Astronomy.* to correct (observations) by making allowances.
—*v.i.* to become less; be made less; become less in weight. [< Latin *redūcere* < *re-* back + *dūcere* bring, lead]
—**Syn.** *v.t.* **1.** lessen, diminish. **3.** humble, debase, degrade.

re·duced (ri düst′, -dyüst′), *adj.* **1.** diminished in number, quantity, amount, or size: *I . . . reproduced some of his plates on a reduced scale* (Clements R. Markham). **2.** weakened; impaired: *The English leaders appear to have had no conception of the extremely reduced state of the French* (James Mill). **3.** impoverished: . . . *retired to the rural districts in reduced circumstances* (John Ruskin).

re·duc·er (ri dü′sər, -dyü′-), *n.* **1.** a person or thing that reduces. **2.** a threaded cylindrical piece for connecting pipes of different sizes. **3.** a solution for reducing the density of photographic negatives.

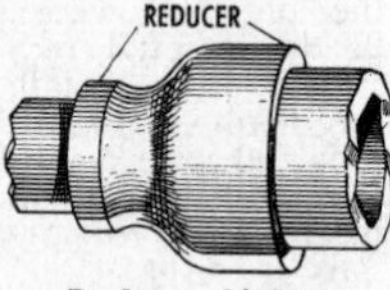

Reducer (def. 2)

re·duc·i·bil·i·ty (ri dü′sə bil′ə tē, -dyü′-), *n.* the quality or state of being reducible.

re·duc·i·ble (ri dü′sə bəl, -dyü′-), *adj.* that can be reduced: *4/8 is reducible to 1/2.* —**re·duc′i·ble·ness,** *n.*

re·duc·i·bly (ri dü′sə blē, -dyü′-), *adv.* in a reducible manner.

re·duc·ing agent (ri dü′sing, -dyü′-), any chemical substance that reduces or removes the oxygen in a compound.

reducing furnace, a furnace for reducing ores from oxides or separating metal from other substances by a nonoxidizing heat or flame.

reducing sugar, a saccharide, as glucose or fructose, that causes the reduction of copper or silver salts in alkaline solutions.

reducing valve, a valve for automatically reducing the pressure of steam or air in a closed heating system, boiler, etc.

re·duc·tant (ri duk′tənt), *n.* a reducing agent: *Chlorophyll is thus a very peculiar substance: it can act both as an oxidant and as a reductant* (Scientific American).

re·duc·tase (ri duk′tās, -tāz), *n.* any enzyme that promotes reduction of an organic compound. [< *reduct*(ion) + *-ase*]

re·duc·ti·o ad ab·sur·dum (ri duk′shē ō ad ab sėr′dəm), *Latin.* reduction to absurdity; method of proving something false by showing that conclusions to which it leads are absurd.

re·duc·tion (ri duk′shən), *n.* **1.** a reducing or being reduced: *a reduction in weight.* **2.** the amount by which a thing is reduced: *The reduction in cost was $5.* **3.** the form of something produced by reducing; copy of something on a smaller scale. **4.** *Biology.* meiosis. **5.** *Chemistry.* a reaction in which each of the atoms or groups of atoms affected gains one or more electrons. The atom or group of atoms that lose electrons becomes oxidized. [< Latin *reductiō, -ōnis* < *redūcere;* see REDUCE]

re·duc·tion·al (ri duk′shə nəl), *adj.* of or having to do with reduction.

reduction division, meiosis.

reduction gear, a gear that reduces the speed of rotation of a motor, turbine, etc., to a lower speed in transmitting the driving force to a machine or device.

re·duc·tion·ism (ri duk′shə niz əm), *n.* the tendency to reduce different ideas, theories, etc., to a single unifying principle, especially in science.

re·duc·tion·ist (ri duk′shə nist), *n.* a person who favors reduction or reductionism. —*adj.* favoring reduction or reductionism.

re·duc·tion·is·tic (ri duk′shə nis′tik), *adj.* reductionist.

re·duc·tive (ri duk′tiv), *adj.* reducing; tending to reduce. —*n.* a thing that reduces. —**re·duc′tive·ly,** *adv.*

re·duc·tor (ri duk′tər), *n.* a device reducing ferric to ferrous sulphate by zinc: *A reductor is used in the analysis of iron and steel.*

re·dun·dance (ri dun′dəns), *n.* redundancy.

re·dun·dan·cy (ri dun′dən sē), *n., pl.* **-cies.** **1.** more than is needed. **2.** a redundant thing, part, or amount. **3.** the use of too many words for the same idea; wordiness: *She is afflicted with a passion for redundancy* (Atlantic). **4.** the part of a communication that can be omitted without loss of essential information. **5.** *British.* an excess or surplus of workers in a factory, industry, etc., especially as a result of modernization or automation: *Workers at the Acton factory, where about a thousand people are employed, became worried last month about redundancy and the introduction for some of them of a four-day week* (Manchester Guardian Weekly).

re·dun·dant (ri dun′dənt), *adj.* **1.** extra; not needed. **2.** that says the same thing again; using too many words for the same idea; wordy: "*We two both had an apple each*" *is a redundant sentence.* **3.** having some unneeded or unusual part, as a verb that has more than one form for a tense. **4.** *British.* (of a worker or workers) dismissed or facing dismissal from work because unneeded or superfluous: *redundant railwaymen.* [< Latin *redundāns, -antis,* present participle of *redundāre;* see REDOUND] —**re·dun′dant·ly,** *adv.* —**Syn.** **1.** superfluous.

re·du·pli·cate (*v.* ri dü′plə kāt, -dyü′-; *adj.* ri dü′plə kit, -dyü′-; -kāt), *v.,* **-cat·ed, -cat·ing,** *adj.* —*v.t.* **1.** to double; repeat. **2. a.** to repeat (a letter or syllable) in forming a word. **b.** to form by such repetition. —*v.i.* to become doubled.
—*adj.* **1.** doubled; repeated. **2.** *Botany.* valvate, with the edges folded back so as to project outward.
[< Latin *reduplicāre* (with English *-ate*[1]) < *re-* again + *duplicāre.* Compare DUPLICATE.]

re·du·pli·ca·tion (ri dü′plə kā′shən, -dyü′-), *n.* **1.** a reduplicating or being reduplicated; doubling; repetition. **2.** something resulting from repeating; duplicate; copy: *To the prisoner each day seemed a reduplication of the preceding day.* **3. a.** repetition, as of a syllable or the initial part of a syllable: *Years might pass without my thinking of reduplication, but then suddenly a fresh double word, "tsetse fly" or "Berber", would come along* (Guy Endore). **b.** a syllable so formed. **c.** a word containing such a syllable: *Razzle-dazzle and bonbon are reduplications.*

re·du·pli·ca·tive (ri dü′plə kā′tiv, -dyü′-), *adj.* tending to reduplicate; having to do with or marked by reduplication: *Memory, as has well been said, is reconstructive, rather than reduplicative* (Scientific American).

re·du·pli·ca·to·ry (ri dü′plə kə tôr′ē, -tōr′-; -dyü′-), *adj.* reduplicative; repetitious.

re·dux (rē′duks), *adj.* brought back or returned, as from a distance or from exile. [< Latin *redux* leading back < *redūcere;* see REDUCE]

red·ward (red′wərd), *adv.* toward the red end of the spectrum.

red·ware[1] (red′wãr′), *n.* a large brown seaweed found off northern Atlantic coasts.

red·ware[2] (red′wãr′), *n.* a coarse, unglazed pottery made of clay containing iron oxide.

red-wat (red′wot′), *adj. Scottish.* soaked with blood.

red·wa·ter (red′wôt′ər, -wot′-), *n.,* or **red water, 1.** a usually fatal, bacterial disease of cattle characterized by internal hemorrhages and red urine. **2.** a malarial fever in cattle caused by a sporozoan parasite which is transmitted by ticks: *Blood parasites akin to the protozoa . . . cause red water in cattle and malaria in man* (New Scientist).

red·wing (red′wing′), *n.* **1.** an American blackbird, the male of which has a scarlet patch on each wing. See **blackbird** for picture. **2.** a common European song thrush that has reddish color on the under side of the wings.

red-winged blackbird (red′wingd′), the redwing of America: *Bobwhites raise their young in the blackberry thicket and red-winged blackbirds nest in the buttonbushes* (Harper's). See **blackbird** for picture.

red wolf, a grayish, reddish, or blackish wolf of areas of the southern United States, smaller than the gray or timber wolf.

red·wood (red′wůd′), *n.* **1. a.** an evergreen tree of the taxodium family found along areas of the California and southern Oregon coasts. It is among the world's largest trees, reaching a height of 359 feet and an age of several thousand years. *The coast redwoods—Sequoia sempervirens—are not the oldest trees in California, although decidedly the tallest* (Newsweek). **b.** its brownish-red wood. **2. a.** any of various trees with a reddish wood, chiefly of tropical regions. **b.** any red-colored wood.

Redwood Branch (def. 1a)

red-wood (red′wüd′, -wōd′, -wůd′), *adj. Scottish.* stark mad.

red-wud (red′wud′), *adj. Scottish.* red-wood.

re·dye (rē dī′), *v.t.,* **-dyed, -dye·ing.** to dye again.

red-yel·low (red′yel′ō), *n.* a color between red and yellow. —*adj.* of such hue.

re·ëch·o (rē ek′ō), *v.,* **-ëch·oed, -ëch·o·ing,** *n., pl.* **-ëch·oes.** —*v.i., v.t.* to echo back; *The thunder reëchoed far behind.* —*n.* an echo of an echo. —**Syn.** *v.i., v.t.* resound, reverberate.

re-ech·o (rē ek′ō), *v.,* **-ech·oed, -ech·o·ing,** *n., pl.* **-ech·oes.** reëcho.

reech·y (rē′chē), *adj. Obsolete.* **1.** smoky; dirty. **2.** rancid.

reed (rēd), *n.* **1.** a kind of tall grass with a jointed stalk that grows in wet places. **2.** such stalks. **3.** anything made from the stalk of a reed or anything like it: *A musical instrument played by blowing through it and an arrow are both reeds.* **4.** a thin piece of wood or metal in a musical instrument that produces sound when a current of air moves it. **5.** a small convex molding; reeding. **6.** (in the Bible) a Hebrew unit of length; 6 cubits.
—*adj.* producing tones by means of reeds: *a reed organ.*
—*v.t.* **1.** to thatch with reeds. **2.** to decorate with reeding.
[Old English *hrēod*] —**reed′like′,** *adj.*

reed-bed (rēd′bed′), *n.* a bed or growth of reeds: *At the far end of the lake are islands of swampy ground where willows and alders flourish amid reed-beds* (Manchester Guardian).

reed·bird (rēd′bėrd′), *n.* the bobolink.

reed·buck (rēd′buk′), *n., pl.* **-bucks** or (*collectively*) **-buck.** any of several tan African antelopes that live in marshy regions. Only the males have horns. [translation of Afrikaans and Dutch *rietbok*]

reed bunting, a European bunting that lives in marshes.

reed canary grass, a common species of canary grass, grown in the Northern Hemisphere for use as fodder. A variegated form of it is the ribbon grass of gardens.

re·ëd·i·fy or **re-ed·i·fy** (rē ed′ə fī), *v.t.,* **-fied, -fy·ing.** to rebuild; restore.

reed·i·ness (rē′dē nis), *n.* reedy quality or condition.

reed·ing (rē′ding), *n.* **1.** a small convex molding. **2.** these moldings on the surface of a column. **3.** ornamentation consisting of such moldings.

reed instrument, a musical instrument the tone of which is produced by the vibrations of a thin piece of wood or metal: *Oboes, clarinets, and saxophones are reed instruments.*

re·ëd·it or **re-ed·it** (rē ed′it), *v.t.* to edit again.

reed·ling (rēd′ling), *n.* a small European bird that lives in reedy places. The male has a tuft of black feathers on each side of the head.

reed mace, *British.* the cattail plant.

reed organ, a musical instrument producing tones by means of small metal reeds. Two common forms are the harmonium, in which the air is forced outward through the reeds, and the American organ, in which the air is sucked inward.

reed pipe, an organ pipe with a reed.

reed stop, a set of reed pipes in an organ, controlled by one stop knob.

re·ëd·u·cate or **re-ed·u·cate** (rē ej′ů kāt), *v.t.,* **-cat·ed, -cat·ing.** to educate again, especially to new ideas, methods, etc., to reform or rehabilitate: *The author's ideal prison would be . . . a walled city, where the* *prisoner would . . . reëducate himself in preparation for the time he is released* (Saturday Review).

re·ëd·u·ca·tion or **re-ed·u·ca·tion** (rē′ej ů kā′shən), *n.* **1.** a reëducating. **2.** a being reëducated.

re·ëd·u·ca·tion·al or **re-ed·u·ca·tion·al** (rē′ej ů kā′shə nəl), *adj.* of, having to do with, or for reëducation.

reed warbler, a common European warbler found in wet, reedy places.

reed wire, a flattened wire used in musical instruments, as in the fastening of the mouthpieces of reeds.

reed·y (rē′dē), *adj.*, **reed·i·er, reed·i·est. 1.** full of reeds: *the broad, reedy fen* (Robert Louis Stevenson). **2.** made of a reed or reeds. **3.** like a reed or reeds. **4.** sounding like a reed instrument: *a thin, reedy voice.*

reef[1] (rēf), *n.* **1.** a narrow ridge of rocks or sand at or near the surface of the water: *The ship was wrecked on a hidden reef.* **2.** a vein or lode in mining. [probably < earlier Dutch *riffe,* or *rif.* Compare RIFFLE[1].] —**Syn. 1.** shoal.

reef[2] (rēf), *n.* **1.** a part of a sail that can be rolled or folded up to reduce the sail's size. **2.** the size a sail is reduced to by reefing. **3. a.** the act of reefing. **b.** a method of reefing. —*v.t.* **1.** to reduce the size of (a sail) by the rolling or folding up of it. **2.** to reduce the length of (a topmast, bowsprit, etc.) by lowering, etc. [ultimately < Scandinavian (compare Old Icelandic *rif* rib, reef, ridge)]

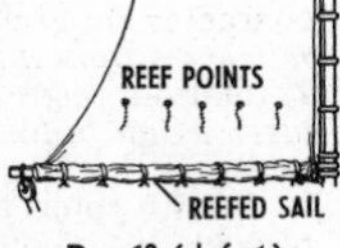

Reef[2] **(def. 1)**

reef·a·ble (rē′fə bəl), *adj.* that can be reefed.

reef band, a band of canvas sewed across a sail to strengthen it for the strain of the reef points.

reef·er[1] (rē′fər), *n.* **1.** a person who reefs. **2.** a short coat of thick cloth, worn especially by sailors and fishermen. **3.** *Informal.* a midshipman. **4.** a long scarf or muffler.

reef·er[2] (rē′fər), *n. U.S. Slang.* a cigarette containing marijuana. [American English; origin uncertain, perhaps < *reef*[2] (because both the sail and cigarette are rolled)]

reef·er[3] (rē′fər), *n. U.S. Slang.* a refrigerator railroad car or truck trailer: *This new car with its sub-freezing temperatures makes the old-style, ice-packed reefer as obsolete as the steam locomotive* (Wall Street Journal).

reef·ing (rē′fing), *n.* the process of taking out ore rock.

reef knot, a square knot.

reef-knot (rēf′not′), *v.t.*, **-knot·ted, -knot·ting.** to tie in a reef knot: *to reef-knot a line.*

reef point, one of the cords to reef a sail.

reef·y (rē′fē), *adj.* **1.** marked by reefs or rocks: *the reefy entrance to a harbor.* **2.** characterized by reefs: *a reefy coast.*

reek (rēk), *n.* **1.** a strong, unpleasant smell; vapor: *the pungent reek of camels* (Rudyard Kipling). **2.** the condition of reeking: *in a reek of a sweat.* **3.** *Dialect.* smoke. [Old English *rēc*]
—*v.i.* **1.** to send out vapor or a strong, unpleasant smell: *a reeking pond of stagnant water, to reek with the smell of cooking.* **2.** to be wet with sweat or blood: *their horses reeking with the speed at which they had ridden* (Scott). **3.** to be filled with something unpleasant or offensive: *a manner reeking with arrogance.* —*v.t.* **1.** to dry or coat by smoking, as meat, or molds for steel. **2.** to give out strongly or unmistakably: *His manner reeks arrogance.*
[Middle English *reken,* Old English *rēocan.* Related to REEK, noun.] —**reek′er,** *n.*

reek·y (rē′kē), *adj.*, **reek·i·er, reek·i·est.** reeking.

reel[1] (rēl), *n.* **1.** a frame turning on an axis, for winding thread, yarn, a fish line, rope, wire, etc. **2.** a spool; roller. **3.** something wound on a reel: *two reels of motion-picture film.* **4.** a length of motion - picture film on a reel.

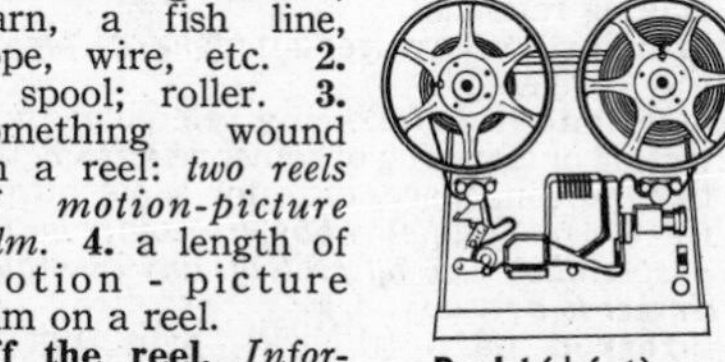
Reels[1] **(def. 1) on movie projector**

off the reel, *Informal.* quickly and easily: [*The story*] *seems to me to be so constituted as to require to be read off the reel* (Dickens). *He won five races off the reel* (St. James' Gazette).
—*v.t.* **1.** to wind on a reel. **2.** to draw with a reel or by winding: *to reel in a fish.*

reel off, to say, write, or make in a quick, easy way: *to reel off facts and figures from memory.*
[Old English *hrēol*]

reel[2] (rēl), *v.i.* **1.** to sway, swing, or rock under a blow, shock, etc.: *The ship shook and reeled in the storm.* **2.** to sway in standing or walking. **3.** to be in a whirl; be dizzy. **4.** to go with swaying or staggering movements. **5.** to sway; stagger; waver: *The ship shook and reeled in the storm.* —*v.t.* to cause to reel or reel along.
—*n.* a reeling or staggering movement.
[Middle English *relen,* probably < *reel*[1], verb]
—**Syn.** *v.i.* **2. Reel, stagger** mean to stand or move unsteadily. **Reel** suggests dizziness and a lurching movement: *Sick and faint, he reeled when he tried to cross the room.* **Stagger** suggests moving with halting steps and without much sense of balance: *The boy staggered in with the wood.*

reel[3] (rēl), *n.* **1.** a lively dance. Two kinds are the Highland reel and the Virginia reel. **2.** the music for it. [apparently < *reel*[2]]

reel·a·ble (rē′lə bəl), *adj.* that can be wound on a reel.

reel-and-bead molding (rēl′ən bēd′), a molding alternating disklike parts with long beads.

re·ë·lect or **re-e·lect** (rē′i lekt′), *v.t.* to elect again.

re·ë·lec·tion or **re-e·lec·tion** (rē′i lek′shən), *n.* election again for the same office: *Another factor which hinders many officials in their work is the recurring and frequent need to stand for re-election* (Punch).

reel·er (rē′lər), *n.* **1.** a person who winds silk, cord, etc., on a reel. **2.** a person who makes reels. **3.** a motion picture in terms of the length of the film on a reel or reels. [< *reel*[1] + *-er*[1]]

re·ël·e·vate or **re-el·e·vate** (rē el′ə vāt), *v.t.*, **-vat·ed, -vat·ing.** to elevate again.

re·ël·i·gi·bil·i·ty or **re-el·i·gi·bil·i·ty** (rē′el ə jə bil′ə tē), *n.* **1.** the condition of being qualified to be elected again to the same office. **2.** a state of being again eligible.

re·ël·i·gi·ble or **re-el·i·gi·ble** (rē el′ə jə bəl), *adj.* **1.** qualified to be elected again to the same office. **2.** once again eligible, as for parole, athletic competition, etc.: *a bill to make the tribunes legally reëligible* (James A. Froude).

reel towel, a roller towel.

re·ëm·bark or **re-em·bark** (rē′em bärk′), *v.t., v.i.* to embark again.

re·ëm·bar·ka·tion or **re-em·bar·ka·tion** (rē′em bär kā′shən), *n.* a putting on board or a going on board a ship or plane again.

re·ëm·bod·y or **re-em·bod·y** (rē′em bod′ē), *v.t.*, **-bod·ied, -bod·y·ing.** to embody again: *I propose . . . now to reëmbody my views in a more popular form* (Balfour Stewart).

re·ëm·brace or **re-em·brace** (rē′em brās′), *v.t., v.i.*, **-braced, -brac·ing.** to embrace again: *His Majesty, who wept like a paternal bear, on reëmbracing Wilhelmina* (Thomas Carlyle).

re·ëm·broi·dered or **re-em·broi·dered** (rē′em broi′dərd), *adj.* overlaid with an embroidered design: *Another dance dress . . . is of moonstone gray satin covered with re-ëmbroidered gray lace* (New Yorker).

re·ë·merge or **re-e·merge** (rē′i mėrj′), *v.i.*, **-merged, -merg·ing.** to emerge again: *to reëmerge from obscurity.*

re·ë·mer·gence or **re-e·mer·gence** (rē′i mėr′jəns), *n.* the act of emerging after having been submerged or covered: *This sudden reëmergence of Flaubert comes in answer to a need* (New Yorker).

re·ë·mer·gent or **re-e·mer·gent** (rē′i mėr′jənt), *adj.* reëmerging: *His tall, awkward angularity was a symbol of his own and his country's pride . . . the reëmergent spirit of France* (Time).

re·ëm·i·grate or **re-em·i·grate** (rē em′ə grāt), *v.i.*, **-grat·ed, -grat·ing.** to emigrate again.

re·ë·mit or **re-e·mit** (rē′i mit′), *v.t.*, **-mit·ted, -mit·ting. 1.** to emit again. **2.** *Especially U.S.* to reissue (bills, banknotes, etc.)

re·ëm·pha·sis or **re-em·pha·sis** (rē em′fə sis), *n., pl.* **-ses** (-sēz). the act of reëmphasizing: *Today there is a re-emphasis on healthy, hard-hitting selling* (Time).

re·ëm·pha·size or **re-em·pha·size** (rē em′fə sīz), *v.t., v.i.*, **-sized, -siz·ing.** to emphasize again.

re·ëm·ploy or **re-em·ploy** (rē′em ploi′), *v.t.* to take back into employment.

re·ëm·ploy·ment or **re-em·ploy·ment** (rē′em ploi′mənt), *n.* a reëmploying or being reëmployed.

re·ën·act or **re-en·act** (rē′en akt′), *v.t.* to enact again, as a law: *The Construction of Ships was forbidden to Senators, by a Law made by Claudius, the Tribune . . . and reënacted by the Julian Law of Concessions* (John Arbuthnot).

re·ën·ac·tion or **re-en·ac·tion** (rē′en ak′shən), *n.* the act of reënacting; reënactment.

re·ën·act·ment or **re-en·act·ment** (rē′en akt′mənt), *n.* the enactment a second time of a law, an event, etc.: *Dore Schary . . . has agreed to produce on the Capitol Steps a re-enactment of Lincoln's second inauguration* (New York Times).

re·ën·coun·ter or **re-en·coun·ter** (rē′en koun′tər), *v.t., v.i.* to meet again: *We do not reëncounter the past* (Scientific American). —*n.* a meeting again, as after separation or absence: *She had said it on that occasion of their first reëncounter* (A.S.M. Hutchinson).

re·ën·cour·age or **re-en·cour·age** (rē′en kėr′ij), *v.t.*, **-aged, -ag·ing.** to encourage again.

re·ën·cour·age·ment or **re-en·cour·age·ment** (rē′en kėr′ij mənt), *n.* the act of reëncouraging.

re·ën·dow or **re-en·dow** (rē′en dou′), *v.t.* to endow again.

re·ën·force or **re-en·force** (rē′en fôrs′, -fōrs′), *v.t.*, **-forced, -forc·ing.** reinforce.

re·ën·force·ment or **re-en·force·ment** (rē′en fôrs′mənt, -fōrs′-), *n.* reinforcement.

re·ën·gage or **re-en·gage** (rē′en gāj′), *v.t., v.i.*, **-gaged, -gag·ing.** to engage again.

re·ën·gage·ment or **re-en·gage·ment** (rē′en gāj′mənt), *n.* engagement again.

re·ën·gine or **re-en·gine** (rē en′jən), *v.t.*, **-gined, -gin·ing.** to provide with other engines: *Certain ships required to be reëngined* (Standard).

re·ën·gi·neer or **re-en·gi·neer** (rē′en jə nir′), *v.t.* to engineer again: *The intent is to reëngineer an entire industry—operations, equipment, corporate structures and all* (Wall Street Journal).

re·ën·grave or **re-en·grave** (rē′en grāv′), *v.t.*, **-graved, -grav·ing.** to engrave again.

re·ën·joy or **re-en·joy** (rē′en joi′), *v.t.* to enjoy a second time.

re·ën·joy·ment or **re-en·joy·ment** (rē′en joi′mənt), *n.* **1.** the act of reënjoying. **2.** a renewed enjoyment, as after a lapse.

re·ën·list or **re-en·list** (rē′en list′), *v.t., v.i.* to enlist again or for an additional term: *The Roman general was eager . . . to reënlist so brave a soldier in the service of the empire* (John L. Motley).

re·ën·list·ment or **re-en·list·ment** (rē′en list′mənt), *n.* the act or fact of reënlisting.

re·ën·slave or **re-en·slave** (rē′en slāv′), *v.t.*, **-slaved, -slav·ing.** to enslave again; cast again into bondage.

re·ën·slave·ment or **re-en·slave·ment** (rē′en slāv′mənt), *n.* **1.** the act of reënslaving or subjecting anew to slavery. **2.** the condition of being reënslaved.

re·ën·ter or **re-en·ter** (rē en′tər), *v.i., v.t.* to enter again; come or go in again: *to reënter a room, to reënter public life.*

re·ën·ter·ing angle (rē en′tər ing), an angle that turns inward, being greater than 180 degrees. See **salient** for diagram.

reëntering polygon, a polygon having at least one reëntering angle.

re·ën·throne or **re-en·throne** (rē′en thrōn′), *v.t.*, **-throned, -thron·ing.** to enthrone again; restore to the throne.

re·ën·throne·ment or **re-en·throne·ment** (rē′en thrōn′mənt), *n.* the act of enthroning again; restoration to the throne.

re·ën·trance or **re-en·trance** (rē en′trəns), *n.* **1.** a second entering. **2.** a coming back in after going out.

re·ën·trant or **re-en·trant** (rē en′trənt), *adj.* that reenters. —*n.* an angle, bend, etc., that turns inward.

re·ën·try or **re-en·try** (rē en′trē), *n., pl.* **-tries. 1.** a new or fresh entry; second entry:

They will be barred from reëntry into Singapore (New York Times). **2.** *Law.* the act or fact of taking possession again. **3.** a playing card that will take a trick and thus let the player get the lead. **4.** the return of a missile, rocket, etc., into the earth's atmosphere after flight into outer space: *The "heat barrier" . . . puts a limit on the speed of airplanes and creates a reëntry problem for rockets and satellites returning to earth* (Scientific American).

re·ë·quip or **re-e·quip** (rē′i kwip′), *v.t.*, **-quipped, -quip·ping.** to equip again.

re·ë·quip·ment or **re-e·quip·ment** (rē′i kwip′mənt), *n.* **1.** the act of reëquipping. **2.** the state or condition of being reëquipped: *The process of reëquipment being thus obvious* (Joshua Larwood).

re·ë·rect or **re-e·rect** (rē′i rekt′), *v.t.* to erect again.

reest[1] (rēst), *v.t., v.i., Scottish.* to cure or become cured by smoking. [origin uncertain. Compare obsolete *reese* to char, smoke, and Danish *riste* to grill or broil.]

reest[2] (rēst), *v.i. Scottish* (of horses) to balk. [probably variant of *rest*[1], verb. Compare Scottish *arreest* to arrest.]

re·ës·tab·lish or **re-es·tab·lish** (rē′es tab′lish), *v.t.* to establish again; restore. —**Syn.** reinstate.

re·ës·tab·lish·ment or **re-es·tab·lish·ment** (rē′es tab′lish mənt), *n.* an establishing or a being established again; restoration.

re·ës·ti·mate or **re-es·ti·mate** (*v.* rē′es′tə māt; *n.* rē′es′tə mit, -māt), *v.*, **-mat·ed, -mat·ing,** *n.* —*v.t., v.i.* to estimate again. —*n.* the act or process of reëstimating: *The Mayor promised that the reëstimate of borrowing would not interfere with the . . . budget* (New York Times).

re·ë·val·u·ate or **re-e·val·u·ate** (rē′i val′yu̇ āt), *v.t., v.i.*, **-at·ed, -at·ing.** to evaluate again.

re·ë·val·u·a·tion or **re-e·val·u·a·tion** (rē′i val′yu̇ ā′shən), *n.* **1.** the act of reevaluating. **2.** the state or condition of being reëvaluated.

reeve[1] (rēv), *n.* **1.** the chief official of a town or district in England: *A lord "who has so many men that he cannot personally have all in his own keeping" was bound to set over each dependent township a reeve, not only to exact his lord's dues, but to enforce his justice within its bounds* (John R. Green). **2.** a bailiff; steward; overseer. **3.** a local official of a town or village in Canada: *There are several mayors, aldermen and reeves besides those I have already mentioned whose chances are fair* (Toronto Telegram). [Old English *gerēfa.* Compare SHERIFF.]

reeve[2] (rēv), *v.t.*, **reeved** or **rove, reev·ing. 1.** to pass (a rope) through a hole, ring, etc. **2.** to fasten by placing through or around something. **3.** to pass a rope through (a block, ring, etc.). [origin uncertain. Compare Dutch *reven* to reef a sail.]

reeve[3] (rēv), *n.* a female ruff (sandpiper). [perhaps related to RUFF[1]]

reeve·ship (rēv′ship), *n.* the position or term of office of a reeve: *It was the first election for the reeveship fought by Mr. Shepard* (Kingston, Ontario Whig-Standard).

re·ëx·am·i·na·tion or **re-ex·am·in·a·tion** (rē′eg zam′ə nā′shən), *n.* **1.** a second or renewed examination: *Medical experts suggest that a reëxamination of disabled veterans take place every year* (Harper's). **2.** *Law.* the examination of a witness after cross-examination.

re·ëx·am·ine or **re-ex·am·ine** (rē′eg zam′ən), *v.t.*, **-ined, -in·ing. 1.** to examine again. **2.** *Law.* to examine (a witness) again after cross-examination.

re·ëx·change or **re-ex·change** (rē′eks chānj′), *v.*, **-changed, -chang·ing,** *n.* —*v.t.* to exchange again or anew. —*n.* **1.** a second exchange. **2.** *Commerce.* **a.** the recovery of the amount plus expenses of inconvenience for a dishonored foreign bill of exchange. **b.** the draft recovering the amount. **c.** the expense of inconvenience.

re·ëx·hib·it or **re-ex·hib·it** (rē′eg zib′it), *v.t.* to exhibit again or anew. —*n.* a second or renewed exhibit.

re·ëx·pand or **re-ex·pand** (rē′ek spand′), *v.t., v.i.* to expand again after contraction: *One was taken out and placed in cold water, and it reëxpanded* (Charles Darwin).

re·ëx·pan·sion or **re-ex·pan·sion** (rē′ek span′shən), *n.* the act of reëxpanding.

re·ëx·pel or **re-ex·pel** (rē′ek spel′), *v.t.*, **-pelled, -pel·ling.** to expel again: *On the expiration of the sentence he will be reëxpelled* (Daily News).

re·ëx·pe·ri·ence or **re-ex·pe·ri·ence** (rē′ek spir′ē əns), *n., v.*, **-enced, -enc·ing.** —*n.* a renewed or repeated experience. —*v.t.* to experience again.

re·ëx·plain or **re-ex·plain** (rē′ek splān′), *v.t., v.i.* to explain again or anew.

re·ëx·plore or **re-ex·plore** (rē′ek splôr′, -splōr′), *v.t., v.i.*, **-plored, -plor·ing.** to explore again.

re·ëx·port or **re-ex·port** (*v.* rē′ek spôrt′, -spōrt′; *n.* rē eks′pôrt, -pōrt), *v.t.* to export (imported goods). —*n.* **1.** something that is reëxported: *Reëxports over the same period have been 14 per cent up on the year* (Manchester Guardian). **2.** a reëxporting or being reëxported: *Foreign sugars have not been taken to Hawaii for reëxport to the Pacific Coast* (American).

re·ëx·por·ta·tion or **re-ex·por·ta·tion** (rē′eks pôr tā′shən, -pōr-), *n.* the act of exporting imported goods.

ref., 1. referee. **2.** reference. **3.** referred. **4.** reformation. **5.** reformed. **6.** reformer.

re·fab·ri·cate (rē fab′rə kāt), *v.t.*, **-cat·ed, -cat·ing.** to fabricate afresh.

re·face (rē fās′), *v.t.*, **-faced, -fac·ing. 1.** to repair the face or surface of (a building, wall, stone, etc.). **2.** to put a new facing in (a garment, etc.).

re·fash·ion (rē fash′ən), *v.t.* to reshape: *The nineteenth century historian, who refashions the past on the lines of his own mind* (Mrs. Humphry Ward).

re·fash·ion·er (rē fash′ə nər), *n.* a person who fashions or shapes anew.

re·fash·ion·ment (rē fash′ən ment), *n.* the act of fashioning or forming again or anew.

re·fas·ten (rē fas′ən, -fäs′-), *v.t.* to fasten again: *It was so negligently refastened* (Scott).

Ref. Ch., Reformed Church.

re·fect (ri fekt′), *v.t. Archaic.* to refresh with food or drink. [< Latin *refectus,* past participle of *reficere;* see REFECTORY]

re·fec·tion (ri fek′shən), *n.* **1.** refreshment by food or drink. **2.** a meal; repast: *They sat on Meredith's big porch . . . and ate a substantial refection* (Booth Tarkington). [< Latin *refectiō, -ōnis* < *reficere;* see REFECTORY]

re·fec·tion·er (ri fek′shə nər), *n.* a person in a monastery, abbey, or the like, in charge of the refectory and of supplies of food: *two most important officers of the convent, the kitchener and the refectioner* (Scott).

re·fec·to·ri·al (rē′fek tôr′ē əl, -tōr′-), *adj.* **1.** having to do with refection. **2.** used for refection.

re·fec·to·ri·an (rē′fek tôr′ē ən, -tōr′-), *n.* refectioner.

re·fec·to·ry (ri fek′tər ē), *n., pl.* **-ries.** a room for meals, especially in a monastery, convent, or school: *School was dismissed, and all were gone into the refectory to tea* (Charlotte Brontë). See **abbey** for diagram. [< Late Latin *refectōrium* < Latin *reficere* to refresh < *re-* again + *facere* make]

refectory table, a long, narrow, heavy table, especially one having simple lines and sturdy construction: *A beautiful oak refectory table . . . used at meal times four hundred years ago by Italian monks* (Maclean's).

re·fer (ri fėr′), *v.*, **-ferred, -fer·ring.** —*v.i.* **1.** to direct attention: *The minister often refers to the Bible.* **2.** to relate; apply: *The rule refers only to special cases.* **3.** to turn for information or help: *Writers often refer to a dictionary.* —*v.t.* **1. a.** to send or direct for information, help, or action: *We referred him to the boss.* **b.** to direct the attention of: *The asterisk refers the reader to a footnote. These weird sisters . . . referred me to the coming on of time, with "Hail, King that shalt be!"* (Shakespeare). **2.** to hand over; submit: *Let's refer the dispute to the umpire. She treated me with a certain consideration, and often referred questions to me* (Francis M. Crawford). **3.** to consider as belonging or due; assign: *Many people refer their failures to bad luck instead of to poor work.* **4.** *Archaic.* to defer. [< Latin *referre* < *re-* back + *ferre* take, bring]

—**Syn.** *v.i.* **1. Refer, allude** mean to speak of something in a way to turn attention to it. **Refer** means to make direct or specific mention. **Allude** means to mention indirectly: *She never referred to the incident but often alluded to it by hinting.*

➔ **refer back.** Though *refer back* is not uncommon, it is regarded as nonstandard because *back* is clearly redundant: *The relative pronoun refers (back) to its antecedent.*

ref·er·a·ble (ref′ər ə bəl), *adj.* that can be referred.

ref·er·ee (ref′ə rē′), *n., v.*, **-eed, -ee·ing.** —*n.* **1.** a judge of play in games and sports. **2.** a person to whom something is referred for decision or settlement. —*v.t., v.i.* to act as referee; act as referee in: *He had never refereed Saddler before, but he had heard about his propensity for bringing out the worst in other fighters' natures* (New Yorker).

ref·er·ence (ref′ər əns, ref′rəns), *n., adj., v.*, **-enced, -enc·ing.** —*n.* **1.** a referring or being referred. **2.** direction of the attention, as by a footnote: *This history contains many references to larger histories.* **3.** a statement, book, etc., to which the attention is directed: *You will find that reference on page 16.* **4.** something used for information or help: *A dictionary is a book of reference.* **5.** a person who can give information about another person's character or ability: *He gave his bank as a reference for credit.* **6.** a statement about someone's character or ability: *The boy had excellent references from men for whom he had worked.* **7.** relation; respect; regard: *This test is to be taken by all pupils without reference to age or grade.*

in or **with reference to,** in relation to; with respect to; about; concerning: *The same notation . . . was used to express the properties of the ellipse in reference to its axes* (Dionysius Lardner). *All existing lives must, with reference to their environment, be the best possible lives* (Henry Drummond).

make reference to, to mention: *Do not make any reference to his lameness.*

—*adj.* used for information or help.

—*v.t.* **1.** to provide with references or a point of reference: . . . *such control [is] not difficult when referenced to positions of fixed stars, or points on earth . . .* (Bulletin of Atomic Scientists). **2.** to assign as a reference: *This is a private communication and should be referenced as such* (Science).

reference book, 1. a book referred to for information on a special or general subject, often having the subject headings in alphabetical order, as a dictionary, encyclopedia, or almanac. **2.** (in libraries) a book held for consultation, but not available for loan.

reference library, a library consisting largely of reference books which are consulted only in the library.

reference mark, a number, letter, star (*), dagger (†), etc., used to refer a reader from the text to a footnote, an appendix, etc.

ref·er·end (ref′ər ənd), *n.* a person or thing referred to; referent.

ref·er·en·da·ry[1] (ref′ə ren′dər ē), *n., pl.* **-da·ries. 1.** any of various medieval court or state officials to whom petitions or other matters were referred. **2.** a referee. [< Medieval Latin *referendarius* < Latin *referendus* one to whom a matter must be referred; (literally) gerundive of *referre;* see REFER]

ref·er·en·da·ry[2] (ref′ə ren′dər ē), *adj.* of or like a referendum. [< *referend*(um) + *-ary*]

ref·er·en·dum (ref′ə ren′dəm), *n., pl.* **-dums, -da** (-də). **1.** the process of submitting a law already passed by the lawmaking body to a direct vote of the citizens for approval or rejection. **2.** the submitting of any matter to a direct vote. [< Latin *referendum* that which must be referred; (literally) neuter gerundive of *referre;* see REFER]

ref·er·ent (ref′ər ənt), *n.* **1.** a person who is consulted. **2.** a person or object referred to: *Individuals may differ widely in the referents they have for the same word* (Ogburn and Nimkoff). —*adj.* referring; containing a reference. [< Latin *referēns, -entis,* present participle of *referre;* see REFER]

ref·er·en·tial (ref′ə ren′shəl), *adj.* of or making reference.

ref·er·en·tial·ly (ref′ə ren′shə lē), *adv.* by way of reference.

re·fer·ral (ri fėr′əl), *n.* a referring; the directing or assigning of someone or something to a person, place, etc., for some purpose: *the referral of a patient by his family doctor to a specialist, the referral of an unemployed worker to a factory.*

re·ferred pain (ri fėrd′), pain that proceeds from a part or organ other than the part or organ actually affected or irritated: *Pain from the heart may be felt in the left arm. . . . This referred pain may be accounted for by the fact that nerves from the involved structures enter the spinal cord at the same level* (Martin E. Spencer).

re·fer·rer (ri fėr′ər), *n.* a person who refers.

re·fer·ri·ble (ri fėr′ə bəl), *adj.* referable.

re·fer·ti·lize (rē fėr′tə līz), *v.t.*, **-lized, -liz·ing.** to fertilize again.

ref·fo (ref′ō), *n. Australian Slang.* a European refugee.

re·fight (rē fīt′), *v.t.*, **-fought, -fight·ing.** to fight again: *If we could each of us refight our battles, doubtless our tactics would be different* (Margaret Goodman).

re·fig·ure (rē fig′yər), *v.t., v.i.*, **-ured, -ur·ing. 1.** to go over again; figure anew: represent anew: *When the fog is vanishing away, Little by little doth the sight refigure Whate'er the mist that crowds the air conceals* (Longfellow). **2.** *Astronomy.* to correct or restore the parabolic figure of (a lens or mirror), usually of a telescope. **3.** to make a renewed arithmetical calculation: *The results were compared and found to be all different, which meant . . . the refiguring of the whole thing again* (Westminster Gazette).

re·fill (*v.* rē fil′; *n.* rē′fil′), *v.t., v.i.* to fill again. —*n.* something to refill a thing.

re·fill·a·ble (rē fil′ə bəl), *adj.* that can be refilled.

re·fi·nance (rē fī′nans; rē′fī nans′, -fə-), *v.t.*, **-nanced, -nanc·ing.** to finance again or anew, as by arranging new terms, or borrowing to settle notes.

re·fine (ri fīn′), *v.*, **-fined, -fin·ing.** —*v.t.* **1.** to free from impurities: *Sugar, oil, and metals are refined before being used. Over the past 100 years, the sugar industry has steadily improved its techniques for extracting . . . and refining the crystallized grains* (Newsweek). **2.** to make fine, polished, or cultivated: *Love refines the thoughts* (Milton). **3.** to change or remove by polishing, purifying, etc. **4.** to make very fine, subtle, or exact. —*v.i.* **1.** to become free from impurities. **2.** to become fine, polished, or cultivated. **3.** to use nicety or subtlety of thought or language; make fine distinctions.

refine on or **upon, a.** to improve: *Our laws have considerably refined . . . upon the invention* (William Blackstone). **b.** to excel: *Chaucer has refined on Boccace, and has mended the stories which he has borrowed* (John Dryden).

[< *re-* + *fine*[1] make fine; probably patterned on Middle French *raffiner* < *re-* + Old French *affiner.* Compare AFFINED.]

re·fined (ri fīnd′), *adj.* **1.** freed from impurities: *refined sugar, refined gold. They claimed that the refined products of the crude oil were also theirs* (London Times). **2.** freed or free from grossness, coarseness, crudeness, vulgarity, or the like. **3.** having or showing nice feeling, taste, manners, etc.; well-bred. **4.** fine; subtle: *refined distinctions.* **5.** minutely precise: *refined measurements.* —**Syn. 2.** polished, cultured.

re·fin·ed·ly (ri fī′nid lē), *adv.* in a refined manner; with nicety or elegance.

re·fine·ment (ri fīn′mənt), *n.* **1.** fineness of feeling, taste, manners, or language: *little refinements of conversation.* **2.** the act or result of refining. **3.** improvement; advance: *refinements in the design of a new engine.* **4.** a fine point; subtle distinction. **5.** an improved, higher, or extreme form of something: *Such refinements of cruelty as were practiced by Caligula* (Winston Churchill). —**Syn. 1.** culture, polish.

re·fin·er (ri fī′nər), *n.* a person or thing that refines: *Oil refiners on the Gulf Coast trimmed bulk gasoline prices a quarter cent a gallon* (Wall Street Journal).

re·fin·er·y (ri fī′nər ē, -fīn′rē), *n., pl.* **-er·ies.** a building and machinery for purifying metal or sugar, distilling petroleum, or other such processes: *The Bureau of Mines has sold its shale-oil refinery at Rifle, Colo.* (Newsweek).

re·fin·ish (rē fin′ish), *v.t.* to finish again.

re·fire (rē fīr′), *v.t.*, **-fired, -fir·ing.** to fire again: *to refire a furnace. Red China . . . clearly feared that the Dalai Lama's escape would refire his people's will to resist* (Time).

re·fit (rē fit′), *v.*, **-fit·ted, -fit·ting,** *n.* —*v.t.* to fit, prepare, or equip for use again: *to refit an old ship.* —*v.i.* to get fresh supplies: *His ship put into Portsmouth to refit* (Lytton Strachey). —*n.* a refitting: *An explosion occurred last night in the diesel room of H.M.S. Daring under refit in Devonport dockyard* (London Times).

re·fit·ment (rē fit′mənt), *n.* the act of refitting; refit: *Later this year the Queen Elizabeth is due for a major refitment at a Clydeside shipyard* (London Times).

re·fix (rē fiks′), *v.t.* to set up again; attach again in the same or another place.

re·fix·a·tion (rē′fik sā′shən), *n.* a renewed fixing.

refl., an abbreviation for the following:
1. reflection.
2. a. reflective. **b.** reflectively.
3. reflex.
4. a. reflexive. **b.** reflexively.

re·flate (ri flāt′), *v.t., v.i.*, **-flat·ed, -flat·ing.** reinflate.

re·fla·tion (ri flā′shən), *n.* inflation stimulated to restore business conditions to their level before the recession: *You regard deflation as the danger and a little reflation as desirable?* (Punch). [< *re-* + (in)*flation*]

re·fla·tion·ar·y (ri flā′shə ner′ē), *adj.* of or inducing reflation: *Of more immediate . . . importance are the two very mildly reflationary steps which the Chancellor has taken* (Economist).

re·flect (ri flekt′), *v.t.* **1.** to turn back or throw back (light, heat, sound, etc.): *The sidewalks reflect heat on a hot day.* **2.** to give back a likeness or image of: *A mirror reflects your face and body.* **3.** to reproduce or show like a mirror: *The newspapers reflected the owner's opinions.* **4.** to serve to cast or bring: *A brave act reflects credit on the person who does it.* —*v.i.* **1.** to cast back light, heat, sound, etc.: *The sun's rays reflected on the ocean.* **2.** to give back an image: *A mirror reflects.* **3.** to think; think carefully: *Take time to reflect before doing important things.* **4.** to cast blame, reproach, or discredit: *Bad behavior reflects on home training.* [< Latin *reflectere* < *re-* back + *flectere* to bend] —**Syn.** *v.i.* **3.** meditate, ponder, deliberate. See **think.**

re·flect·ance (ri flek′təns), *n.* the amount of light reflected by a surface in proportion to the amount of light falling on the surface: *It is evident that reflectance is related in a general way to the lightness of the color perceived* (Deane B. Judd).

re·flect·er (ri flek′tər), *n.* reflector.

re·flect·i·ble (ri flek′tə bəl), *adj.* that can be reflected.

re·flect·ing microscope (ri flek′ting), a microscope that uses mirrors rather than lenses to magnify.

reflecting telescope, a telescope in which the image is produced by a concave mirror or speculum and magnified.

LIGHT RAYS
SMALL MIRROR
EYEPIECE
IMAGE
MIRROR (OBJECTIVE)

Reflecting Telescope has large, concave mirror (objective) in which light rays are focused and then reflected to small mirror; from this, rays are reflected to eyepiece.

re·flec·tion (ri flek′shən), *n.* **1.** a reflecting or being reflected. **2.** something reflected. **3.** likeness; image: *You can see your reflection in a mirror.* **4.** thinking; careful thinking: *On reflection, the plan seemed too dangerous.* **5.** an idea or remark resulting from careful thinking; idea; remark: *He made very wise reflections and observations upon all I said* (Jonathan Swift). **6.** a remark, action, etc., that casts blame or discredit. **7.** blame; discredit. **8.** *Anatomy.* **a.** the bending of a part back upon itself. **b.** the part bent back.

re·flec·tion·al (ri flek′shə nəl), *adj.* **1.** of reflection. **2.** caused by reflection.

reflection plotter, a radar device by which ships and aircraft can determine and keep track of the position of other craft in the area: *By watching the ship progress across the radar screen, and by comparing its position to the marked spot on the reflection plotter, the navigator can see at a glance the direction which the ship is taking* (Science News Letter).

re·flec·tive (ri flek′tiv), *adj.* **1.** reflecting: *the reflective surface of polished metal.* **2.** reflected: *reflective light or glory.* **3.** thoughtful: *a reflective look.* —**re·flec′tive·ly,** *adv.* —**re·flec′tive·ness,** *n.* —**Syn. 3.** contemplative, meditative.

re·flec·tiv·i·ty (rē′flek tiv′ə tē), *n.* the quality or state of being reflective.

re·flec·tom·e·ter (rē′flek tom′ə tər), *n.* an instrument for measuring the reflecting power of surfaces.

re·flec·tom·e·try (rē′flek tom′ə trē), *n.* the measurement of the reflecting power of surfaces, as with a reflectometer: *The use of a reference standard is avoided in the so-called absolute methods of reflectometry* (Hardy and Perrin).

re·flec·tor (ri flek′tər), *n.* **1.** any thing, surface, or device that reflects light, heat, sound, etc., especially a piece of glass or metal, usually concave, for reflecting light in a required direction: *It is no coincidence that polished silver is the best light reflector known as well as being the best electrical conductor* (J. Crowther). **2.** a telescope with a concave mirror; reflecting telescope.

Reflector (def. 1) for flash bulb on camera

re·flec·tor·ize (ri flek′tə rīz), *v.t.*, **-ized, -iz·ing.** to treat with a substance that reflects light at night: *to reflectorize road signs, reflectorized cloth.*

re·flec·to·scope (ri flek′tə skōp), *n.* an electronic device for examining metallic objects or parts by passing ultrasonic waves through them. The slightest flaw breaks the pattern of the waves: *Among these is a now standard instrument, called the reflectoscope, for detecting hidden cracks, bubbles, or other flaws in a metal* (Scientific American). [< *reflecto*(r) + *-scope*]

re·flet (rə fle′), *n.* **1.** the reflection of light or color. **2.** luster; iridescence. [< French *reflet* reflection < Italian *riflesso,* learned borrowing from Latin *reflexus, -ūs* a bending back < *reflectere* reflect]

re·flex (*adj., n.* rē′fleks; *v.* ri fleks′), *adj.* **1.** not voluntary; not controlled by the will; coming as a direct response to a stimulation of some sensory nerve cells: *Sneezing is a reflex act. Sometimes he binds his limbs with rope so that reflex movements will not jar his hand* (Newsweek). **2.** bent back; turned back: *reflex light.* **3.** *Radio.* having amplifier tubes that function as both radio-frequency and audio-frequency amplifiers simultaneously. **4.** (of an angle) more than 180 degrees and less than 360 degrees.

—*n.* **1.** an involuntary action in direct response to a stimulation of some nerve cells: *Sneezing, vomiting, and shivering are reflexes. Simple reflexes are considered to be independent of any learning process* (S.A. Barnett). **2.** something reflected; image; reflection: *A law should be a reflex of the will of the people.* **3.** a copy. **4.** a reflex receiving set.

—*v.t.* to bend back; turn back.

[< Latin *reflexus, -ūs* < *reflectere;* see REFLECT]

reflex arc, the nerve path in the body leading from stimulus to reflex action. The impulse travels inward to a nerve center and the response outward to the organ or part where the action takes place. *If one of the large motor nerves of a salamander or a fish is cut, the animals reëstablish normal reflex arcs and recover coördination* (Scientific American).

reflex camera, a camera in which the image received through the lens is reflected by a mirror onto a horizontal piece of ground glass, for viewing and focusing.

re·flexed (ri flekst′), *adj.* turned, bent, or folded back: *. . . reflexed bracts that conceal the flowers* (Joseph Hooker).

re·flex·i·ble (ri flek′sə bəl), *adj.* that can be reflected.

re·flex·i·bil·i·ty (ri flek′sə bil′ə tē), *n.* ability to be reflected.

re·flex·ion (ri flek′shən), *n.* reflection.

re·flex·ion·al (ri flek′shə nəl), *adj.* reflectional.

re·flex·ive (ri flek′siv), *adj.* **1.** *Grammar.* expressing an action that turns back on the subject. **2.** occurring in reaction. **3.** *Obsolete.* reflective.

—*n. Grammar.* a reflexive verb or pronoun. In "The boy hurt himself," *hurt* and *himself* are reflexives. —**re·flex′ive·ly,** *adv.* —**re·flex′ive·ness,** *n.*

➔ **reflexive pronouns.** The pronouns *myself, yourself, himself,* etc., are called *reflex-*

ive when they refer to the subject and are used as direct objects, indirect objects, or objects of prepositions: *He shaves himself. She bought herself two hats.* When used as modifiers, they are called intensifying pronouns or adjectives: *He himself is going. He is going himself.*

re·flex·iv·i·ty (rē′flek siv′ə tē), *n.* the quality or condition of being reflexive.

re·flex·ly (rē′fleks lē, ri fleks′-), *adv.* in a reflex manner: *The cat continued to survive for many hours, an unconscious automaton, yet reacting reflexly to many stimuli* (New Scientist).

re·flex·ness (ri fleks′nis), *n.* the state or condition of being reflex.

re·flex·o·log·i·cal (ri flek′sə loj′ə kəl), *adj.* of or having to do with reflexology: *To rework these disciplines in terms of Pavlov's reflexological conceptions, invited for these disciplines the same fate that befell genetics* (Bulletin of Atomic Scientists).

re·flex·ol·o·gy (rē′flek sol′ə jē), *n.* the belief that all behavior is a series of reflexes: *In reflexology and its offspring we have the beginnings ... of a rational account of behavior in terms of its bodily mechanisms, especially the central nervous system* (S.A. Barnett).

re·float (rē flōt′), *v.t.* to float, or set afloat, again: *The company undertook to refloat, at their own expense, any vessel that went ashore in the canal* (Manchester Guardian).

re·flo·res·cence (rē′flô res′əns, -flō-), *n.* a blossoming again.

re·flo·res·cent (rē′flô res′ənt, -flō-), *adj.* coming into bloom again; reflowering.

re·flour·ish (rē flėr′ish), *v.i.* to revive, flourish, or bloom anew.

re·flow (rē flō′) *v.i.* to flow back; ebb.

re·flow·er (rē flou′ər), *v.i.* to flower again. —*v.t.* to cause to flower or bloom again.

ref·lu·ence (ref′lu̇ əns), *n.* an ebb or backward movement.

ref·lu·ent (ref′lu̇ ənt), *adj.* flowing back; ebbing. [< Latin *refluēns, -entis,* present participle of *refluere* flow back < *re-* back + *fluere* to flow]

re·flux (rē′fluks), *n.* a flowing back; the ebb of a tide. [< *re-* + *flux*]

re·foc·il·late (ri fos′ə lāt), *v.t.*, **-lat·ed, -lat·ing.** to revive, refresh, reanimate, comfort, etc. (a person, the spirits, senses, etc.): *About every three hours his man was to bring him a roll and a pot of ale to refocillate his wasted spirits* (John Aubrey). [< Late Latin *refocillātus,* past participle of *refocillāre* to warm into life again, revive < Latin *re-* back + *focillāre* to warm into life < *focus* hearth]

re·foc·il·la·tion (ri fos′ə lā′shən), *n.* **1.** the act of refocillating; refreshment; reanimation: *He ... kindly performed all offices of ease and refocillation to these wayfaring strangers* (John Donne). **2.** that which causes or brings such refreshment, reanimation, etc.: ... *some precious cordial, some costly refocillation* (Thomas Middleton).

re·fo·cus (rē fō′kəs), *v.t., v.i.*, **-cused, -cus·ing** or (*especially British*) **-cussed, -cus·sing.** to focus again: *A pulpit ... capable of refocusing religion* (North American Review).

re·fold (rē fōld′), *v.t.* to fold again: *to refold and rearrange the clothing and bedding in a store room* (System of Medicine).

re·for·est (rē fôr′ist, -for′-), *v.t., v.i.* to replant with trees.

re·for·est·a·tion (rē′fôr ə stā′shən, -for-), *n.* a replanting with trees: *In Spain, reforestation will ultimately improve the quality of the soil, increase crops, and provide lumber for housing* (Atlantic).

re·forge (rē fôrj′, -fōrj′), *v.t.*, **-forged, -forg·ing.** to forge or form again; to fabricate or fashion anew; make over.

re·forg·er (rē fôr′jər, -fōr′-), *n.* a person or thing that reforges; one who makes over.

re·form (ri fôrm′), *v.t.* **1.** to make better: *Prisons should try to reform criminals instead of just punishing them.* **2.** to improve by removing faults or abuses: *to reform a city administration.* **3.** to crack and refine (petroleum, gas, etc.): *The use of a platinum-containing catalyst for the reforming of straight-run gasoline has undergone rapid acceptance by the petroleum industry* (Vladimir Haensel). —*v.i.* to become better: *The boy promised to reform if given another chance.* —*n.* a changing for the better; improvement, especially one made by removing faults or abuses: *The new government put through many needed reforms. The most fundamental reform, then, is a reform in fundamental point of view* (Bulletin of Atomic Scientists). —*adj.* of reform; favoring reform: *a reform movement within a party, a reform mayor.* [< Latin *reformāre* < *re-* again + *formāre* to form < *forma* form]

Re·form (ri fôrm′), *adj.* of or having to do with the liberal branch of Judaism, as contrasted with the Orthodox and Conservative branches: *The Reform Branch ... members seek to interpret Jewish religious law in accordance with the needs of contemporary life* (New York Times). [< *reform*]

re-form (rē fôrm′), *v.t.* to form again. —*v.i.* to take a new shape: *The effect ... is comparable to ... watching clouds form and reform in the changing light of a hot afternoon* (Atlantic).

re·form·a·bil·i·ty (ri fôr′mə bil′ə tē), *n.* the quality or condition of being reformable: *Though appalled at the conditions that obtained in the thirteenth century, a particularly dark time for ... Japan, he believed in the reformability of man and society* (New Yorker).

re·form·a·ble (ri fôr′mə bəl), *adj.* that can be reformed.

ref·or·ma·tion (ref′ər mā′shən), *n.* a reforming or being reformed; change for the better; improvement.

Ref·or·ma·tion (ref′ər mā′shən), *n.* the great religious, social, and political movement in Europe in the 1500's that aimed at reform within the Roman Catholic Church but led to the establishment of Protestant churches.

re-for·ma·tion (rē′fôr mā′shən), *n.* a formation over again.

ref·or·ma·tion·al (ref′ər mā′shə nəl), *adj.* of or having to do with reformation.

Ref·or·ma·tion·al (ref′ər mā′shə nəl), *adj.* of or having to do with the Reformation.

re·for·ma·tive (ri fôr′mə tiv), *adj.* that reforms; tending toward or inducing reform: *We are advised by the Prison Commissioners that periods of that kind are of very little value for reformative training* (Economist).

re-for·ma·tive (rē fôr′mə tiv), *adj.* having the power of forming over again.

re·for·ma·tive·ly (ri fôr′mə tiv lē), *adv.* in a reformative manner.

re·for·ma·tive·ness (ri fôr′mə tiv nis), *n.* a reformed quality or state.

re·form·a·to·ry (ri fôr′mə tôr′ē, -tōr′-), *adj., n., pl.* **-ries.** —*adj.* serving to reform; intended to reform: *reformatory laws.* —*n.* an institution for reforming young offenders against the laws; prison for young criminals: *[The prison farm] can be combined with any advantages in occupational training that reformatories may afford* (Emory S. Bogardus).

re·formed (ri fôrmd′), *adj.* improved; amended.

Re·formed (ri fôrmd′), *adj.* of or having to do with the Protestant churches, especially the Calvinistic as distinguished from the Lutheran.

re·form·er (ri fôr′mər), *n.* **1.** a person who reforms, or tries to reform, some state of affairs, custom, etc.; supporter of reforms. **2.** a device used to reform petroleum, natural gas, etc.

re·form·ism (ri fôr′miz əm), *n.* social or political reform.

re·form·ist (ri fôr′mist), *n.* a reformer. —*adj.* of reformists or reformism: *The move is part of the Government's stiffening resistance to the liberal and reformist influence of modern education and communications media* (New York Times).

reform school, a reformatory: *The word "rehabilitation" was practically unheard of in those days, and reform schools were raw institutions* (New Yorker).

re·for·mu·late (rē fôr′myə lāt), *v.t.*, **-lat·ed, -lat·ing.** to formulate anew: *Luther's doctrine of justification by faith reformulated Gospel truth for the Reformation era* (Academy).

re·for·mu·la·tion (rē′fôr myə lā′shən), *n.* the act of reformulating: *a reformulation of the indictments.*

re·for·ti·fi·ca·tion (rē′fôr tə fə kā′shən), *n.* **1.** the action of fortifying again. **2.** a new fortification: *The reduction of the size of the city by Venetians, and its refortification on a more contracted circumference* (Daily News).

re·for·ti·fy (rē fôr′tə fī), *v.t.*, **-fied, -fy·ing.** to fortify again: *I am repeating a judgment formed long ago, and often refortified* (John H. Skrine).

re·fought (rē fôt′), *v.* the past tense and past participle of **refight.**

re·found[1] (rē found′), *v.t.* to set up or found anew; reëstablish: *Abingdon School, one of the oldest in the country, was founded or, as some aver, refounded in 1563* (London Times). [< *re-* + *found*[2]]

re·found[2] (rē found′), *v.t.* to cast or found anew; recast: *All our cannon ... needed to be refounded* (Thomas Carlyle). [< *re-* + *found*[3]]

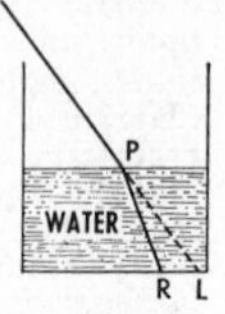

Refract (def. 1)

re·fract (ri frakt′), *v.t.* to bend (a ray) from a straight course: *Water refracts light.* In the diagram, the ray of light SP in passing into the water is refracted from its original direction SPL to SPR. [< Latin *refractus,* past participle of *refringere* < *re-* back + *frangere* to break]

re·frac·tile (ri frak′təl), *adj.* exhibiting refraction; refractive.

re·frac·til·i·ty (rē′frak til′ə tē), *n.* the character of being refractile.

re·fract·ing telescope (ri frak′ting), a telescope in which the image is produced by a lens (the objective) and magnified by the eyepiece: *In combination, two double convex lenses can form a refracting telescope* (Robert H. Baker).

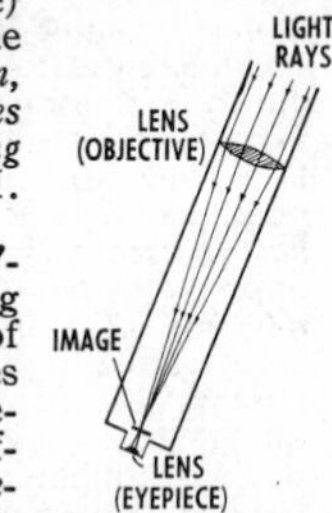

Refracting Telescope has large lens (objective) in which light rays are gathered and an image is formed; this is magnified for observer in smaller lens (eyepiece).

re·frac·tion (ri frak′shən), *n.* **1. a.** the turning or bending of a ray of light when it passes obliquely from one medium into another of different density: *The refraction of light that gives a diamond its fire is based on certain mathematical laws* (New Yorker). **b.** the turning or bending of sound waves, a stream of electrons, etc., when passing from one medium to another of different density: *When a tracking radar is used for guidance of an ICBM or IRBM ... an error in apparent direction of the missile can be produced by refraction of the microwaves in clouds* (Kenneth F. Gantz). **2.** the measuring of the refraction of the eye, a lens, etc.

re·frac·tion·al (ri frak′shə nəl), *adj.* of or having to do with refraction.

re·frac·tion·ate (ri frak′shə nāt), *v.t.* **-at·ed, -at·ing.** to fractionate again.

refraction circle, an instrument with a graduated circle for determining indexes of refraction.

re·frac·tion·ist (ri frak′shə nist), *n.* **1.** a person skilled in determining the amount of refraction in a lens. **2.** an optometrist.

re·frac·tive (ri frak′tiv), *adj.* **1.** refracting; having power to refract. **2.** having to do with or caused by refraction. —**re·frac′tive·ly** *adv.* —**re·frac′tive·ness,** *n.*

refractive index, index of refraction: *A lens made of strontium titanate has a very high refractive index, as compared with flint glass and crown glass lenses* (Science News Letter).

re·frac·tiv·i·ty (rē′frak tiv′ə tē), *n.* the quality or condition of being refractive.

re·frac·tom·e·ter (rē′frak tom′ə tər), *n.* **1.** an instrument for measuring refraction: *Typical of automatic control of the quality of products is the recent commercial introduction of refractometers for monitoring processes involving liquids* (David M. Kiefer). **2.** an instrument for determining the refractive condition of the eye.

re·frac·to·met·ric (ri frak′tə met′rik), *adj.* having to do with the measurement of refractive indexes.

re·frac·tom·e·try (rē′frak tom′ə trē), *n.* the use of refractometers.

re·frac·tor (ri frak′tər), *n.* **1.** anything that refracts. **2.** a refracting telescope.

re·frac·to·ri·ly (ri frak′tər ə lē), *adv.* stubbornly; obstinately.

re·frac·to·ri·ness (ri frak′tər ē nis), *n.* a refractory quality or condition: *During the refractory state this patient developed the anti-clotting substance that Dr. Rosenthal believes causes the trouble in plasma refractoriness* (Science News Letter).

re·frac·to·ry (ri frak′tər ē), *adj., n., pl.* **-ries.** —*adj.* **1.** hard to manage; stubborn; obstinate: *Mules are refractory.* **2.** not yielding readily to treatment: *a refractory cough.* **3.** hard to melt, reduce, or work: *Some ores are more refractory than others. The shock wave . . . has a temperature . . . several times the melting temperature of tungsten, the most refractory of metals* (Atlantic). **4. a.** (of a muscle, nerve, etc.) that responds less readily to stimulation after a response. **b.** of the period in which this occurs.
—*n.* **1. a.** an ore, cement, ceramic material, or similar substance that is hard to melt, reduce, or work. **b.** a brick made of refractory material, used for lining furnaces, etc. **2.** *Obsolete.* a refractory person.

ref·ra·ga·ble (ref′rə gə bəl), *adj. Obsolete.* that can be disproved. [apparently back formation < *irrefragable*]

re·frain[1] (ri frān′), *v.i.* to hold oneself back: *Refrain from wrongdoing. I have hitherto refrained from appealing to you* (George Bernard Shaw). —*v.t.* **1.** *Archaic.* to hold back; restrain: *I have refrained my feet from every evil way* (Psalms 119:101). **2.** *Obsolete.* to keep from; abstain. [< Old French *refrener,* learned borrowing from Latin *refrēnāre* < *re-* back + *frēnāre* to restrain, furnish with a bridle < *frēnum* a bridle] —**re·frain′er,** *n.*
—**Syn.** *v.i.* **Refrain, abstain** mean to keep oneself from (doing) something. **Refrain** implies checking an impulse or urge to do it: *He politely refrained from saying what he thought of her hat.* **Abstain** implies holding back from it by force of will, deliberately doing without something one really wants but believes harmful: *He is abstaining from pie.*

re·frain[2] (ri frān′), *n.* **1.** a phrase or verse repeated regularly in a song or poem: *In "The Star-Spangled Banner" the refrain is "O'er the land of the free and the home of the brave.* **2.** the music for it. [< Old French *refrain,* alteration of *refrait* (originally) past participle of *refraindre* break off, modulate < Vulgar Latin *refrangere* break off (in Late Latin, lessen), for Latin *refringere;* see REFRACT]

re·frame (rē frām′), *v.t.,* **-framed, -fram·ing.** to frame anew.

re·fran·gi·bil·i·ty (ri fran′jə bil′ə tē), *n.* **1.** the property of being refrangible. **2.** the amount of refraction (of light rays, etc.) that is possible.

re·fran·gi·ble (ri fran′jə bəl), *adj.* that can be refracted: *Rays of light are refrangible.* [< *re-* + Latin *frangere* to break + English *-ible*] —**re·fran′gi·ble·ness,** *n.*

re·freeze (rē frēz′), *v.t.,* **-froze, -fro·zen, -freez·ing.** to freeze a second time.

re·fresh (ri fresh′), *v.t.* to make fresh again; renew: *He refreshed his memory by a glance at the book. She refreshed herself with a cup of tea.* —*v.i.* to become fresh again. [< Old French *refrescher* < *re-* again + *fresche* fresh < Germanic (compare Old High German *frisc,* Middle High German *fresch*)]
—**Syn.** *v.t.* freshen, renovate, revive, enliven.

re·fresh·ant (ri fresh′ənt), *n.* that which refreshes or invigorates.

re·fresh·er (ri fresh′ər), *adj.* helping to renew knowledge or abilities, or to bring a person new needed knowledge: *to take a refresher course in typing.* —*n.* **1.** a person or thing that refreshes: *Lemonade on a hot day is a good refresher.* **2.** *Especially British.* an extra fee paid to a lawyer in a prolonged case.

re·fresh·ing (ri fresh′ing), *adj.* **1.** that refreshes: *refreshing sleep.* **2.** welcome as a pleasing change. —**re·fresh′ing·ly,** *adv.* —**re·fresh′ing·ness,** *n.*

re·fresh·ment (ri fresh′mənt), *n.* **1.** a refreshing or being refreshed. **2.** a thing that refreshes.
refreshments, food or drink: *to serve refreshments at a party.*

re·frig·er·ant (ri frij′ər ənt), *adj.* **1.** refrigerating; cooling. **2.** reducing bodily heat or fever.
—*n.* **1.** something that cools: *Ice is a refrigerant.* **2.** a liquid or gas such as ammonia, used in mechanical refrigerators, freezers, etc., to produce a low temperature. **3.** a medicine for reducing fever: *Aspirin and quinine are refrigerants.*

re·frig·er·ate (ri frij′ə rāt), *v.t.,* **-at·ed, -at·ing.** to make or keep cold or cool: *Milk, meat, and ice cream must be refrigerated to prevent spoiling.* [< Latin *refrīgerāre* (with English *-ate*[1]) < *re-* against + *frīgere* to freeze, related to *frīgidus* cold, frigid]

re·frig·er·a·tion (ri frij′ə rā′shən), *n.* the act or process of cooling or keeping cold.

re·frig·er·a·tive (ri frij′ə rā′tiv), *adj.* that refrigerates. —*n.* something that refrigerates.

re·frig·er·a·tor (ri frij′ə rā′tər), *n.* **1.** a box, room, etc., for keeping foods, etc., cool, by means of a mechanism, formerly by ice: *The name refrigerator implies an apparatus whose purpose is to cool; but the same apparatus can be used as a heater—when so used it is called a heat pump* (Shortley and Williams). **2.** something that cools. [< obsolete French *refrigerateur,* ultimately < Latin *refrīgerāre;* see REFRIGERATE]

re·frig·er·a·to·ry (ri frij′ər ə tôr′ē, -tōr′-), *adj., n., pl.* **-ries.** —*adj.* that refrigerates. —*n.* a refrigerant or refrigerator.

re·frin·gen·cy (ri frin′jən sē), *n.* refringent or refractive power.

re·frin·gent (ri frin′jənt), *adj.* refracting; refractive: *a refringent prism.* [< Latin *refringēns, -entis,* present participle of *refringere;* see REFRACT]

Ref. Sp., Reformed Spelling (a method of simplifying English spelling, as by writing *tho* and *nok* instead of *though* and *knock*).

reft[1] (reft), *v. Archaic.* reaved; a past tense and a past participle of **reave**[1]; deprived by force: *The barons reft King John of his power.*

reft[2] (reft), *v. Archaic.* reaved; a past tense and past participle of **reave**[2].

re·fu·el (rē fyü′əl), *v.,* **-eled, -el·ing** or (*especially British*) **-elled, -el·ling.** —*v.t.* to supply with fuel again. —*v.i.* to take on a fresh supply of fuel: *A Boeing KC-97 tanker . . . feeds a Boeing B-47 jet medium bomber by the "flying boom" method, one of two principal ways to refuel in midair* (New York Times).

re·fu·el·er (rē fyü′ə lər), *n.* a person or thing that refuels.

re·fu·el·ler (rē fyü′ə lər), *n. Especially British.* refueler.

ref·uge (ref′yüj), *n., v.,* **-uged, -ug·ing.** —*n.* **1.** shelter or protection from danger, trouble, etc.: *The cat took refuge from the dogs in a tree.* **2.** a resort, shift, or expedient in any emergency: *I consider proverbs as the refuge of weak minds* (Henry Kingsley).
—*v.t. Archaic.* to give refuge to. —*v.i. Archaic.* to give refuge; take refuge. [< Old French *refuge,* learned borrowing from Latin *refugium* < *re-* back + *fugere* to flee + *-ium* place for] —**Syn.** *n.* **1.** safety, security.

ref·u·gee (ref′yə jē′, ref′yə jē), *n., v.,* **-geed, -gee·ing.** —*n.* a person who flees for refuge or safety in time of persecution, war, disaster, etc.: *the great drive of the Germans towards Antwerp . . . which swept before it multitudes of Flemish refugees* (H.G. Wells). —*v.i.* **1.** to become a refugee. **2.** to take refuge in another country. [< French *réfugié* (literally) past participle of Middle French *réfugier,* learned borrowing from Latin *refugere* to flee; see REFUGE]

ref·u·gee·ism (ref′yə jē′iz əm), *n.* the state or condition of a refugee.

re·ful·gence (ri ful′jəns), *n.* radiance; brightness; splendor.

re·ful·gen·cy (ri ful′jən sē), *n.* refulgence.

re·ful·gent (ri ful′jənt), *adj.* shining brightly; radiant; splendid: *a refulgent sunrise.* [< Latin *refulgēns, -entis,* present participle of *refulgēre* < *re-* back + *fulgēre* to shine] —**re·ful′gent·ly,** *adv.*

re·fund[1] (*v.* ri fund′; *n.* rē′fund), *v.t.* **1.** to pay back; repay: *If the shoes do not wear well, the shop will refund your money.* **2.** *Obsolete.* to pour in or out again. —*v.i.* to make repayment. —*n.* a return of money paid. [< Latin *refundere* < *re-* back + *fundere* pour] —**re·fund′er,** *n.*

re·fund[2] (rē fund′), *v.t.* to change (a debt, loan, etc.) into a new form: *These maturing obligations will either be redeemed . . . or will be refunded into other obligations* (Andrew W. Mellon). [< *re-* + *fund*]

re·fund·a·bil·i·ty (ri fun′də bil′ə tē), *n.* the quality or condition of being refundable: *on-the-spot refundability.*

re·fund·a·ble (ri fun′də bəl), *adj.* capable of being refunded: *In Michigan the three-cent tax on gasoline for marine use is not refundable when used in boats longer than sixteen feet* (New York Times).

re·fund·ment (ri fund′mənt), *n.* **1.** the act or process of refunding; repayment. **2.** a thing or amount refunded.

re·fur·bish (rē fėr′bish), *v.t.* to polish up again; do up anew; brighten; renovate: *to refurbish an old house.*

re·fur·bish·ment (rē fėr′bish mənt), *n.* a renovation.

re·fur·nish (rē fėr′nish), *v.t.* to furnish over again.

re·fur·nish·ment (rē fėr′nish mənt), *n.* **1.** a refurnishing. **2.** a being refurnished.

re·fus·a·ble (ri fyü′zə bəl), *adj.* that can be refused.

re·fus·al (ri fyü′zəl), *n.* **1.** the act of refusing: *His refusal to play the game provoked the other boys.* **2.** the right to refuse or take a thing before it is offered to others: *Give me the refusal of the car till tomorrow.* —**Syn. 1.** denial, dissent.

re·fuse[1] (ri fyüz′), *v.,* **-fused, -fus·ing.** —*v.t.* **1.** to say no to; decline to accept; reject: *to refuse an offer.* **2.** to deny (a request, demand, or invitation); decline to give or grant: *to refuse admittance.* **3.** to decline (to do something): *The commander . . . refused to discuss questions of right* (George Bancroft). **4.** (of a horse) to decline to jump over. **5.** to hold or move (troops) back from the regular alignment, when about to meet the enemy. **6.** *Obsolete.* to give up; abandon; renounce: *Deny thy father and refuse thy name* (Shakespeare). —*v.i.* to say no; decline to accept or consent: *She is free to refuse.* [< Old French *refuser* < Latin *refundere;* see REFUND[1]] —**re·fus′er,** *n.*
—**Syn.** *v.t.* **1. Refuse, decline, reject** mean not to accept something offered. **Refuse** is the blunt term, implying a direct and sometimes an ungracious denial: *He refused to go with me.* **Decline** is more polite, implying a reluctant rather than direct denial: *He declined my invitation.* **Reject** is more emphatic than *refuse,* implying a very positive and brusque denial: *He rejected my friendly advice.*

ref·use[2] (ref′yüs), *n.* useless stuff; waste; rubbish: *The garbage men took away all the refuse from the streets.* —*adj.* rejected as worthless or of little value; discarded; useless: *Every thing that was vile and refuse, that they destroyed utterly* (I Samuel 15:9). [probably < Old French *refus* refusal; also, what is refused; (literally) past participle of *refuser;* see REFUSE[1]] —**Syn.** *n.* trash.

ref·u·ta·bil·i·ty (ref′yə tə bil′ə tē, ri fyü′-), *n.* the quality of being refutable.

ref·u·ta·ble (ref′yə tə bəl, ri fyü′-), *adj.* that can be refuted: *Their pretensions lead to refutable illusions* (Bulletin of Atomic Scientists).

ref·u·ta·bly (ref′yə tə blē, ri fyü′-), *adv.* in a refutable manner.

re·fu·tal (ri fyü′təl), *n.* refutation.

ref·u·ta·tion (ref′yə tā′shən), *n.* the disproof of a claim, opinion, or argument: *There is, however, more to life, and especially intellectual life, than the detection and refutation of error* (Bulletin of Atomic Scientists).

re·fu·ta·tive (ri fyü′tə tiv), *adj.* serving to refute.

re·fu·ta·to·ry (ri fyü′tə tôr′ē, -tōr′-), *adj.* refutative.

re·fute (ri fyüt′), *v.t.,* **-fut·ed, -fut·ing. 1.** to prove (a claim, opinion, or argument) to be false or incorrect; disprove: *How would you refute the statement that the cow jumped over the moon or that truth will prevail?* **2.** to prove (a person) to be in error; confute. [< Latin *refūtāre* < *re-* back + *-fūtāre* beat, drive]

re·fut·er (ri fyü′tər), *n.* a person or thing that refutes.

reg., an abbreviation for the following:
1. regent.
2. regiment.
3. region.
4. register.
5. registered.
6. registrar.
7. registry.
8. a. regular. **b.** regularly.
9. regulation.
10. regulator.

Reg., 1. Queen (Latin *regina*). **2.** Regent.

re·gain (*v.* ri gān′; *n.* rē′gān′), *v.t.* **1.** to get again; recover: *to regain health. I began by degrees to regain confidence* (Benjamin Jowett). **2.** to get back to; reach again: *They had now regained the shores of the lake* (Thomas L. Peacock).
—*n.* **1.** the act or process of regaining; recovery: *Pakistan's strongest foreign policy has been a negative one: fear of India, revenge on India, and regain of Kashmir* (Atlantic). **2.** an amount regained or recovered.

re·gain·a·ble (ri gā′nə bəl), *adj.* that can be regained.

re·gain·ment (ri gān′mənt), *n.* the act of regaining.

re·gal[1] (rē′gəl), *adj.* **1.** belonging to a king; royal. **2.** fit for a king; kinglike; stately; splendid; magnificent. [< Latin *rēgālis* <

rēx, rēgis king. Doublet of REAL², ROYAL.]
—**Syn. 1.** See **royal.**

re·gal² (rē′gəl), *n.* a small, portable organ used in the 1500's and 1600's, having one, or sometimes two, sets of reed pipes played with keys by the right hand, while a small bellows was worked by the left hand. [< Middle French *régale,* perhaps < *régal* regal < Latin *rēgālis;* see REGAL¹]

re·gale (ri gāl′), *v.,* **-galed, -gal·ing,** *n.* —*v.t.* **1.** to entertain agreeably; delight with something pleasing: *The old sailor regaled the boys with sea stories.* **2.** to entertain or refresh with a choice meal: *The rabbits regaled themselves with the young lettuce.* —*v.i.* to feast: *to regale on raspberries and cream.*
—*n.* **1.** a feast: *They indulged in a regale, relishing their buffalo beef with inspiring alcohol* (Washington Irving). **2.** choice food or drink. **3.** refreshment.
[< French *régaler* < Old French *regale,* noun < *gale* joy < *galer* make merry]

re·gale·ment (ri gāl′mənt), *n.* refreshment; entertainment; gratification.

re·gal·er (ri gā′lər), *n.* a person or thing that regales.

re·ga·li·a (ri gā′lē ə, -gāl′yə), *n.pl.* **1.** the emblems of royalty: *Crowns, scepters, etc., are regalia.* **2.** the emblems or decorations of any society, order, etc.: *Tom joined the new order of Cadets of Temperance, being attracted by the showy character of their "regalia"* (Mark Twain). **3.** clothes, especially fine clothes: *in party regalia.* **4.** the rights and privileges of a king. [< Latin *rēgālia* royal things, neuter plural of *rēgālis;* see REGAL]

re·gal·ist (rē′gə list), *n.* a royalist.

re·gal·i·ty (ri gal′ə tē), *n., pl.* **-ties. 1.** royalty; sovereignty; kingship. **2.** a right or privilege having to do with a king. **3.** a kingdom. **4.** in Scotland: **a.** a territory under the rule of a duke, baron, or other person appointed by the king: *The cultivators of each barony or regality . . . are obliged to bring their corn to be grinded at the mill of the territory* (Scott). **b.** such a grant by the king.

re·gal·ly (rē′gə lē), *adv.* royally.

regal moth, a large, hairy moth with olive forewings and orange-red hind wings, both spotted with yellow. Its wingspread is about five inches.

Regal Moth
(wingspread, 5 in.)

re·ga·lo (rä gä′lo, ri gā′-), *n. Archaic.* an elegant entertainment; choice food and drink. [< Italian *regalo* a gift]

re·gal·va·nize (rē gal′və nīz), *v.t.,* **-nized, -niz·ing.** to galvanize anew.

re·gard (ri gärd′), *v.t.* **1.** to think of; consider: *He is regarded as the best doctor in town.* **2.** to show thought or consideration for; care for; respect: *She always regards her parents' wishes.* **3.** to take notice of; pay attention to; heed: *None regarded her screams.* **4.** to look at; look closely at; watch: *He regarded me sternly. The cat regarded me anxiously when I picked up her kittens.* **5.** to concern; relate to: *As regards money, I have enough.* —*v.i.* **1.** to look closely. **2.** to pay attention.
as regards, so far as it concerns; as for; as to: *He was in a thoroughly sound condition as regards intellect* (Law Times).
—*n.* **1.** consideration; thought; care: *Have regard for the feelings of others.* **2.** a look; steady look; gaze: *Claude turned and met the stranger's regard with a faint smile* (George W. Cable). **3.** esteem; favor; good opinion: *I once thought you had a kind of regard for her* (George Borrow). **4.** a particular matter; point: *You are wrong in this regard.* **5.** *Obsolete.* importance to others: *I am a bard of no regard Wi' gentlefolks, and a' that* (Robert Burns).
in or **with regard to,** about; concerning; relating to: *The teacher wishes to speak to you with regard to being late. And in regard to remarkable persons in general, Michelet always shows them in relation to the social group which has molded them* (Edmund Wilson).
regards, good wishes; an expression of esteem: *He sends his regards.*
without regard to, not considering: *without regard to public opinion.*
[< Old French *regarder* < *re-* back + *garder,* earlier *guarder* guard. Doublet of REWARD, verb.]
—**Syn.** *v.t.* **1.** deem, hold. **2.** esteem. *-n.* **1.** See **respect.**

re·gard·a·ble (ri gär′də bəl), *adj.* that can be or should be regarded.

re·gard·ant (ri gär′dənt), *adj. Heraldry.* looking backward: *a lion regardant.* [< Old French *regardant* (originally) present participle of *regarder* regard]

re·gard·ful (ri gärd′fəl), *adj.* **1.** heedful; observant; mindful. **2.** considerate; respectful. —**re·gard′ful·ly,** *adv.* —**re·gard′ful·ness,** *n.*

re·gard·ing (ri gär′ding), *prep.* with regard to; concerning; about: *a prophecy regarding the future of life on this planet.*

re·gard·less (ri gärd′lis), *adj., adv.* with no heed; careless: *regardless of expense.* —**re·gard′less·ness,** *n.*

re·gard·less·ly (ri gärd′lis lē), *adv.* heedlessly; carelessly.

re·gards (ri gärdz′), *n.pl.* See under **regard,** *n.*

re·gath·er (rē gaтн′ər), *v.t., v.i.* to gather again or anew.

re·gat·ta (ri gat′ə), *n., pl.* **-tas. 1.** a boat race. **2.** a series of boat races: *the annual regatta of the yacht club.* **3.** a gondola race originally held in Venice. [< Italian *regata,* or dialectal (Venetian) Italian *regatta*]

Regatta Day, a former legal holiday in Hawaii, observed on the third Saturday in September.

re·gauge (rē gāj′), *v.t.,* **-gauged, -gaug·ing.** to gauge anew.

regd., registered.

re·gear (rē gir′), *v.t.* to gear again: *Specifically, it [a country] needs to regear and speed its missile program, and to reshape its alliances* (Time).

re·ge·late (rē′jə lāt, rē′jə lāt′), *v.i.,* **-lat·ed, -lat·ing.** to freeze together again.

re·ge·la·tion (rē′jə lā′shən), *n.* a freezing together again of two pieces of ice having moist surfaces, at a temperature above the freezing point. [< *re-* again + Latin *gelātiō, -ōnis.* Compare GELATION.]

Ré·gence (rē′jəns; *French* rā zhäɴs′), *adj.* of, having to do with, or characteristic of the French Regency, or the style of furniture of that period: *There are 10 pieces of furniture available, from a Régence armchair to a stool with upholstered legs* (New York Times). [< French *Régence* < *régence* regency]

re·gen·cy (rē′jən sē), *n., pl.* **-cies. 1.** the position, office, or function of a regent or body of regents: *The Queen Mother held the regency till the young king became of age.* **2.** a body of regents. **3.** government by a regent or body of regents. **4.** the period during which there is a regency.

Re·gen·cy (rē′jən sē), *n.* **1.** the period from 1811 to 1820 in English history, during which George, Prince of Wales, acted as regent. **2.** the period from 1715 to 1723 in French history, during which Philip, Duke of Orleans, acted as regent. —*adj.* of or having to do with the English or French Regency or the style of furniture of these periods.

French Regency Mirror

re·gen·er·a·cy (ri jen′ər ə sē), *n.* regenerate state.

re·gen·er·ate (*v.* ri jen′ə rāt; *adj.* ri jen′ər it), *v.,* **-at·ed, -at·ing,** *adj.* —*v.t.* **1.** to give a new and better spiritual life to: *Being converted regenerated the man. The doctrine of the Church is, that children are regenerated in holy baptism* (Charles Kingsley). **2.** to improve the moral condition of; put new life and spirit into: *a band of Christian reformers, coming to purify and regenerate the land* (Washington Irving). **3.** to grow again; form (new tissue, a new part, etc.) to replace what is lost: *If a young crab loses a claw, it can regenerate a new one.* **4.** *Physics.* to cause (a substance) to return intermittently to its original state or condition. **5.** *Electronics.* to increase the amplification of, by transferring a portion of the power from the output circuit to the input circuit. **6.** *Machinery.* to make use of (pressure, heat, energy, etc.) that would normally be unused.
—*v.i.* to reform; be regenerated: *Blood vessels regenerate very quickly* (Bernard Donovan).
—*adj.* **1.** born again spiritually. **2.** made over in better form; formed anew morally.
[< Latin *regenerāre* (with English *-ate*¹) make over < *re-* again + *generāre* to produce. Compare GENERATE.]

re·gen·er·a·tion (ri jen′ə rā′shən), *n.* **1.** a regenerating or being regenerated; the rebirth of the spirit: *Spiritual regeneration begins naturally among the poor and humble* (James A. Froude). **2. a.** the formation of new animal tissue to repair the waste of the body or to replace worn-out tissue. **b.** the reproduction of lost parts or organs. **3.** *Electronics.* the amplification of the strength of a radio signal by transferring a portion of the power from the output circuit to the input circuit.

re·gen·er·a·tive (ri jen′ə rā′tiv, -ər ə-), *adj.* regenerating; tending to regenerate.
—**re·gen′er·a·tive·ly,** *adv.*

re·gen·er·a·tor (ri jen′ə rā′tər), *n.* **1.** a person or thing that regenerates. **2.** a device in a furnace, engine, etc., for heating incoming air.

re·gen·er·a·tress (ri jen′ə rā′tris), *n.* a woman regenerator.

re·gent (rē′jənt), *n.* **1.** a person who rules when the regular ruler is absent, unfit, or temporarily disqualified: *The Queen will be the regent till her son grows up.* **2.** a member of a governing board: *Many universities have boards of regents. An individual alumnus, industrialist, regent or philanthropist can aid this effort by discussing the problem at the institutional level* (Newsweek). **3.** *Obsolete.* a ruler; governor.
—*adj.* **1.** acting as a regent. **2.** *Obsolete.* ruling; governing.
[< Latin *regēns, -entis,* present participle of *regere* to rule, direct, straighten]

regent bird, an Australian bowerbird, the male of which has velvety, black-and-yellow feathers. [< the Prince *Regent* of England, afterward George IV, 1762-1830]

re·gent·ship (rē′jənt ship), *n.* the position of a regent; regency: *If York have ill demean'd himself in France, Then let him be denied the regentship* (Shakespeare).

re·ger·mi·nate (rē jėr′mə nāt), *v.i.,* **-nat·ed, -nat·ing.** to germinate again: *This tree regerminates perpetually* (Thomas Taylor).

re·ger·mi·na·tion (rē′jėr mə nā′shən), *n.* a sprouting or germination anew: *He expresses an assured hope, that the time of his renovation or regermination would come* (G. S. Faber).

re·ges or **Re·ges** (rē′jēz), *n.* the plural of **rex** or **Rex.**

reg·i·cid·al (rej′ə sī′dəl), *adj.* of or having to do with regicide or a regicide.

reg·i·cide¹ (rej′ə sīd), *n.* the crime of killing a king: *The shadow of the coming regicide had held Fairfax's conscience on tenterhooks* (Newsweek). [< Latin *rēx, rēgis* + English *-cide*²]

reg·i·cide² (rej′ə sīd), *n.* **1.** a person who kills a king. **2.** Often, **Regicide.** one of the judges who sentenced Charles I to death. [< Latin *rēx, rēgis* + English *-cide*¹]

re·gi·dor (rā′hē dôr′), *n., pl.* **-do·res** (-dô′rās). *Spanish.* an alderman: *I was the regidor, and now you expect me to move down to the position of police chief* (Oscar Lewis).

ré·gie (rā zhē′, rā′zhē), *n.* **1.** an excise or revenue service or department, as in France. **2.** a government monopoly, as of tobacco, used as a means of taxation. [< French *régie* < *régir* govern, learned borrowing from Latin *regere* to rule, straighten]

re·gild (rē gild′), *v.t.* to gild anew.

re·gime or **ré·gime** (ri zhēm′, rā-), *n.* **1.** the system of government or rule; prevailing system: *Under the old regime women could not vote. The Russians may mean what they say when they describe their present régime as a transitory stage* (Bulletin of Atomic Scientists). **2.** *Informal.* a system of living; regimen: *The baby's regime includes two naps a day.* [< French *régime,* learned borrowing from Latin *regimen.* Doublet of REGIMEN.]

reg·i·men (rej′ə men, -mən), *n.* **1.** a set of rules or habits of diet, exercise, or manner of living intended to improve health, reduce weight, etc. **2.** the act of governing; government; rule. **3.** *Grammar.* the influence of one word in determining the case or mood of another; government. [< Latin *regimen, -inis* < *regere* to rule, straighten. Doublet of REGIME.]

reg·i·ment (*n.* rej′ə mənt; *v.* rej′ə ment), *n.* **1.** an army unit consisting of several com-

panies of soldiers, usually commanded by a colonel. In the United States it formerly consisted of three battalions, but no longer exists as a tactical unit. *Each division will comprise five battle groups (instead of the traditional three regiments)* (Newsweek). **2.** a large number: *He was living in that magnificent house all alone, with a whole regiment of servants* (Arnold Bennett). **3.** *Archaic.* rule or authority.
—*v.t.* **1.** to form into a regiment or organized group. **2.** to assign to a regiment or group. **3.** to treat in a strict or uniform manner: *A totalitarian state regiments its citizens.* **4.** to put in order or organize into some system.
[< Late Latin *regimentum* rule, direction < Latin *regere* to rule, straighten]

reg·i·men·tal (rej′ə men′təl), *adj.* of a regiment; having to do with a regiment: *He led the regimental band ashore at Normandy, on D Day* (Newsweek).
—*n.* **regimentals,** a military uniform: *Colonel Forster . . . in his regimentals* (Jane Austen). —**reg′i·men′tal·ly,** *adv.*

reg·i·men·ta·tion (rej′ə men tā′shən), *n.* **1.** formation into organized or uniform groups. **2.** a making uniform. **3.** subjection to control: *In time of war there may be regimentation of our work, play, food, and clothing. The whole plan would lead to complete regimentation of farming, with each farmer told exactly how many pounds or bushels of every crop he could sell* (Newsweek).

re·gim·i·nal (ri jim′ə nəl), *adj.* having to do with a regimen.

re·gi·na (ri jī′nə, -jē′-), *n.* a queen. [< Latin *rēgīna*]

re·gi·nal (ri jī′nəl), *adj.* queenly. [< Medieval Latin *reginalis* < Latin *rēgīna* queen]

re·gion (rē′jən), *n.* **1.** any large part of the earth's surface: *the region of the equator.* **2.** a place; space; area: *an unhealthful region. No other region offers so much of everything industry needs . . . as the Gulf South* (Newsweek). *He [Constantine] divided Constantinople into fourteen regions or quarters* (Edward Gibbon). **3.** a part of the body: *the region of the heart.* **4.** sphere; domain: *the region of art, the region of imagination.* **5.** a division of the sea according to depth. **6.** a division of the atmosphere according to height. **7.** a division of the earth according to plant or animal life. [< Anglo-French *regiun,* Old French *region,* and *reion,* learned borrowings from Latin *regiō, -ōnis* direction (in space); country < *regere* to direct, rule, straighten]

re·gion·al (rē′jə nəl), *adj.* of, in, or having to do with a particular region: *a regional storm, a regional disorder of the body.* —**re′gion·al·ly,** *adv.*

re·gion·al·ism (rē′jə nə liz′əm), *n.* **1.** narrow or steadfast attachment to a certain region: *The regionalism of American writing falls into place beside that of Scotland or Ireland* (London Times). **2.** an expression, dialect, custom, etc., peculiar to a region.

re·gion·al·ist (rē′jə nə list), *n.* a person who practices regionalism: *Their main platform, at first sight surprisingly, is a United Europe—"we are regionalists not nationalists nowadays," their spokesman insists* (Economist). —*adj.* of or inclined to regionalism: *a regionalist writer or artist.*

re·gion·al·is·tic (rē′jə nə lis′tik), *adj.* of, having to do with, or characterized by regionalism: *Our leaders . . . are at the same time oblivious, or at least insensitive, to the phenomenon of a new nationalistic and regionalistic mood* (New York Times).

re·gion·al·i·za·tion (rē′jə nə lə zā′shən), *n.* **1.** the act of regionalizing. **2.** the state of being regionalized.

re·gion·al·ize (rē′jə nə līz), *v.t.,* **-ized, -iz·ing.** to organize or divide by regions; decentralize: *to regionalize trade.*

re·gird (rē gėrd′), *v.t.,* **-girt** or **-gird·ed, -gird·ing.** to gird again.

ré·gis·seur (rā zhē sœr′), *n. French.* a stage manager or director of a theatrical production: *Among the things lost in the fire we can't replace . . . were our régisseur's notes on the staging of nearly all our ballets* (New Yorker).

reg·is·ter (rej′ə stər), *n.* **1.** a list; record: *A register of attendance is kept at our school.* **2.** the book in which a list or record is kept: *a hotel register.* **3.** a thing that records: *A cash register shows the amount of money taken in.* **4.** registration or registry. **5.** a registrar. **6. a.** an opening in a wall or floor with an arrangement to regulate the amount of air or heat that passes through: *Did you ever come into the house on a cold winter day and stand over the register of a hot-air heating system?* (Beauchamp, Mayfield, and West). **b.** the plate for regulating the draft in a furnace. **7.** the range of a voice or an instrument: *The last verse . . . goes as low as my register will reach* (Rudyard Kipling). **8.** the set of pipes of an organ stop. **9.** the exact fit or correspondence of lines, columns, colors, etc., in printing. **10.** the exact adjustment of the focus in a camera. **11.** a customs document declaring the nationality of a ship. **12.** a storage device in which the arithmetic unit of a computer stores data temporarily.
—*v.t.* **1.** to write in a list or record: *Register the names of the new members.* **2.** to indicate; record: *The thermometer registers 90 degrees.* **3.** to show (surprise, joy, anger, etc.) by the expression on one's face or by actions. **4.** to have (a letter, parcel, etc.) recorded in a post office, paying extra postage for special care in delivery: *Please register this letter.* **5.** to cause (lines, columns, colors, etc.) to fit or correspond exactly in printing. —*v.i.* **1.** to write or have one's name written in a list or record: *Twenty-six million French men and women had registered to vote* (Newsweek). **2.** to show surprise, joy, anger, etc., by one's expression or actions. **3.** (of lines, columns, colors, etc.) to fit or correspond exactly in printing.
[< Medieval Latin *registrum,* alteration of Late Latin *regesta, -ōrum* list, (originally) things transcribed < Latin *regerere* to record < *re-* back + *gerere* carry, bear] —**reg′is·ter·er,** *n.*

reg·is·tered (rej′ə stərd), *adj.* **1.** recorded: *A registered bond is listed by name, number, etc., and interest is mailed to the owner.* **2.** recognized by law; certified: *a registered accountant.* **3.** purebred; pedigreed: *a registered cow.*

registered letter, a letter for which a special fee has been paid, the delivery of which is recorded by the post office.

registered nurse, a graduate nurse licensed by the State authority to practice nursing. *Abbr.:* R.N.

register of wills, a clerk of the probate court who records wills, reports from executors, etc.

reg·is·tra·bil·i·ty (rej′ə strə bil′ə tē), *n.* the quality or condition of being able to register or be registered.

reg·is·tra·ble (rej′ə strə bəl), *adj.* that can be registered.

reg·is·tral (rej′ə strəl), *adj.* preserved in, copied from, and authenticated by a register.

reg·is·trant (rej′ə strənt), *n.* a person who registers: *the registrant of a patent.*

reg·is·trar (rej′ə strär, rej′ə strär′), *n.* an official who keeps a register; official recorder: *the registrar of a college. I married her before the registrar at Letchbury* (Samuel Butler). [variant of Middle English *registrer,* or earlier *registrary,* perhaps < *register,* verb, or < Medieval Latin *registrarius* < *registrum*]

reg·is·trate (rej′ə strāt), *v.i.,* **-trat·ed, -trat·ing.** to use various organ stops while playing a piece of music. [apparently back formation < *registration*]

reg·is·tra·tion (rej′ə strā′shən), *n.* **1.** a registering. **2.** an entry in a register. **3.** the number of people registered: *Public interest was so high that registration was 1,200,000 above past records* (Time). **4.** the combination of organ stops for a piece of music. **5.** the adjustment of lines, etc., in printing; register.

reg·is·tra·tion·al (rej′ə strā′shə nəl), *adj.* of or having to do with registration: *registrational procedures.*

registration area, that section of a country in which births, deaths, etc., officially registered by the local government serve as a basis for calculating the vital statistics of the country's population.

registration statement, *U.S.* a statement of information about a proposed issue of stock filed with the Securities and Exchange Commission before the issue is marketed: *When a registration statement is filed with the S.E.C. setting out information about a new offering, it is usually granted clearance by the agency in 20 days* (Wall Street Journal).

reg·is·trer (rej′ə strər), *n. Obsolete.* a registrar. [Middle English *registrer;* see REGISTRAR]

reg·is·try (rej′ə strē), *n., pl.* **-tries. 1.** a registering; registration. **2.** a place where a register is kept; office of registration. **3.** a book in which a list or record is kept.

re·gi·us (rē′jē əs, -jəs), *adj.* royal. [< Latin *rēgius* < *rēx, rēgis* king]

regius professor, a professor in a British university holding a position founded by a royal grant: *When he was made regius professor of modern history at Cambridge . . . he found his proper niche* (Time).

ré·glage (rā gläzh′), *n.* **1.** regulation; adjustment. **2.** *Military.* the regulation and spotting of artillery fire, especially by aircraft observation. [< French *réglage* < *régler* regulate < Late Latin *rēgulāre;* see REGULATE]

re·glaze (rē glāz′), *v.t.,* **-glazed, -glaz·ing.** to glaze again.

reg·let (reg′lit), *n.* **1.** *Architecture.* a narrow, flat molding. **2.** *Printing.* **a.** a thin strip of wood used in place of leading to space lines of type. **b.** the wood for making these strips. [earlier, column in a book < Middle French *réglet* (diminutive) < Old French *regle* < Latin *rēgula;* see RULE]

re·glo·ri·fy (rē glôr′ə fī, -glōr′-), *v.t.,* **-fied, -fy·ing.** to glorify again.

re·glow (rē glō′), *v.i.* to glow again. —*n.* a glowing again.

re·glue (rē glü′), *v.t.,* **-glued, -glu·ing.** to glue again.

reg·ma (reg′mə), *n., pl.* **-ma·ta** (-mə tə). a dry fruit of three or more carpels that separate from the axis at maturity, as in various geraniums. [< New Latin *regma* < Greek *rhēgma, -atos* a break < *rhēgnýnai* to break]

reg·nal (reg′nəl), *adj.* of or having to do with a reigning sovereignty, or a reign: *the third regnal year of a king.* [< Medieval Latin *regnalis* < Latin *rēgnum* reign < *rēx, rēgis* king]

reg·nan·cy (reg′nən sē), *n., pl.* **-cies.** a reign.

reg·nant (reg′nənt), *adj.* **1.** ruling; reigning: *Queen regnant. The members of virtually every royal house, regnant or deposed, in Europe are related to Europe's most prospering crown, Britain's* (Time). **2.** exercising sway or influence; predominant. **3.** prevalent; widespread: *The belief in witchcraft and diabolical contracts which was regnant in his day . . .* (Matthew Arnold). [< Latin *rēgnāns, -antis,* present participle of *rēgnāre* to rule < *rēgnum* kingdom < *rēx, rēgis* king]

reg·nat po·pu·lus (reg′nat pop′yə ləs), *Latin.* the people rule (the motto of Arkansas).

reg·num (reg′nəm), *n. Latin* **1.** dominion; rule. **2.** a period of power or rule.

reg·o·lith (reg′ə lith), *n.* the mantle of weathered debris that covers solid rock. [< Greek *rhēgos* blanket (< *rhēgein* to dye) + *lithos* stone]

re·gorge (rē gôrj′), *v.,* **-gorged, -gorg·ing.** —*v.t.* **1.** to disgorge; vomit. **2.** to swallow again. —*v.i.* to flow back.

Reg. Prof., Regius Professor.

re·gra·da·tion (rē′grā dā′shən), *n.* regression; retrogradation.

re·grade (*v.i. and v.t. 2* ri grād′; *v.t. 1* rē grād′), *v.,* **-grad·ed, -grad·ing.** —*v.i.* to retire; go back; retrograde: *They saw the darkness commence at the eastern limb of the sun, and proceed to the western, till the whole was eclipsed; and then regrade backwards, from the western to the eastern, till his light was fully restored* (Hales). —*v.t.* **1.** to grade again: *The city was torn up from one end to the other, and regraded* (Century Magazine). **2.** *Obsolete.* to degrade: *Elutherius . . . ordained that none should be regraded before he were condemned* (George Saltern). [< *re-* back + Latin *gradī* go]

re·graft (rē graft′, -gräft′), *v.t.* to graft again: *When a large tree has been deprived of its branches, to be regrafted, it often becomes unhealthy.*

re·grant (rē grant′, -gränt′), *v.t.* to grant again. —*n.* the renewal of a grant.

re·grass (rē gras′, -gräs′), *v.t.* **1.** to cause to produce grass again. **2.** to bring back to the condition of good pasture land.

re·grate (ri grāt′), *v.t.,* **-grat·ed, -grat·ing. 1.** to buy up (grain, provisions, etc.) to sell again at a profit in or near the same market. It was formerly forbidden by law. **2.** to sell again (commodities so bought); retail. [< Old French *regrater;* origin uncertain]

re·grat·er or **re·gra·tor** (ri grā′tər), *n.* a person who regrates; retailer.

re·greet (rē grēt′), *Obsolete.* —*v.t.* **1.** to greet again. **2.** to greet in return. **3.** to salute. —*n.* a greeting.

re·gress (*v.* ri gres′; *n.* rē′gres), *v.i.* **1.** to go back; return. **2.** to move in a backward direction: *They indicate a retreating area of sedimentation, as when a sea regresses from the land* (Raymond C. Moore). **3.** to return to an earlier or less advanced state. —*v.t. Psychology.* to cause regression in (a person).
—*n.* **1.** a going back; return. **2.** a backward movement or course.
[< Latin *regressus,* past participle of *regredī* < *re-* back + *gradī* to go, step]

re·gres·sion (ri gresh′ən), *n.* **1.** the act of going back; backward movement. **2.** *Psychology.* the reversion of a person to an earlier stage or mode of thinking, feeling, acting, etc., as a way of trying to escape difficult problems by assuming the characteristics of childhood or in response to hypnotic suggestion: *It is a short step to assume that fixation and regression are not independent of each other . . . the stronger the fixations . . . the more easily will the function yield . . . by regressing on to those fixations . . .* (Sigmund Freud). **3.** *Biology.* the reversion of offspring toward a more average condition, as the tendency of children of tall parents to be shorter than their parents. **4.** *Statistics.* the tendency of one variable that is correlated with another to revert to the general type and not to equal the amount of deviation of the second variable.

regression coefficient, *Statistics.* the numerical value best expressing the regression of a variable.

re·gres·sive (ri gres′iv), *adj.* **1.** going back; backward: *I'm regressive, yes, but very tired, too* (Newsweek). **2.** *Phonetics.* changing its sound by assimilation under the influence of the sound that follows. —**re·gres′sive·ly,** *adv.* —**re·gres′sive·ness,** *n.*

re·gres·siv·i·ty (rē′gre siv′ə tē), *n.* the quality of being regressive; retrograde tendency or policy.

re·gres·sor (ri gres′ər), *n.* a person or thing that regresses.

re·gret (ri gret′), *n., v.,* **-gret·ted, -gret·ting.** —*n.* the feeling of being sorry; sorrow; sense of loss: *It was a matter of regret that I could not see my mother before leaving.*
regrets, a polite reply declining an invitation: *She could not come but sent regrets.*
[< Middle French *regret* < Old French *regretter;* see the verb]
—*v.t.* to feel regret about: *We regretted his absence from the party.* —*v.i.* to feel regret: *Those who had umbrellas were putting them up; those who had not were regretting and wondering how long it would last* (Elizabeth Gaskell).
[< Old French *regretter* to regret, (originally) bewail (a death); origin uncertain; perhaps < Scandinavian (compare Old Icelandic *grāta* cry). Compare GREET².]
—**Syn.** *n.* **Regret, remorse** mean a feeling of sorrow for a fault or wrongdoing. **Regret** suggests sorrow or dissatisfaction about something one has done or failed to do, sometimes something one could not help: *With regret he remembered his forgotton promise.* **Remorse** suggests the mental suffering of a gnawing or guilty conscience: *The boy was filled with remorse for the worry he had caused his mother.*

re·gret·ful (ri gret′fəl), *adj.* feeling or expressing regret. —**re·gret′ful·ly,** *adv.* —**re·gret′ful·ness,** *n.*

re·gret·ta·ble (ri gret′ə bəl), *adj.* that should be or is regretted: *It is regrettable that many students cannot spell accurately.*

re·gret·ta·bly (ri gret′ə blē), *adv.* with regret; regretfully: *My mother and sisters, who have so long been regrettably prevented from making your acquaintance* (Henry James).

re·gret·ter (ri gret′ər), *n.* a person who regrets.

re·grind (rē grīnd′), *v.t.,* **-ground, -grinding.** to grind again.

re·group (rē grüp′), *v.t., v.i.* to group anew: *Children refine new ideas, regroup facts, and project their minds and their emotions outside of themselves* (Saturday Review). *As his army paused to regroup, the Premier broadcast "a solemn appeal to the rebels to lay down their arms"* (Time).

re·group·ment (rē grüp′mənt), *n.* a rearrangement in groups: *The talks yesterday reportedly concerned technical questions relating to regroupment of forces* (Wall Street Journal).

re·growth (rē grōth′), *n.* **1.** a growing again. **2.** new or second growth: *Amid the ruins . . . he towered up, gigantic, glowering, indispensable, the sole agency by which time could be gained for healing and regrowth* (Wall Street Journal).

regt., regiment.

Regt., **1.** regent. **2.** regiment.

reg·u·la (reg′yə lə), *n., pl.* **-lae** (-lē). *Architecture.* a band or fillet at the base of the Doric entablature, bearing droplike ornaments on the lower side. [< Latin *rēgula;* see RULE]

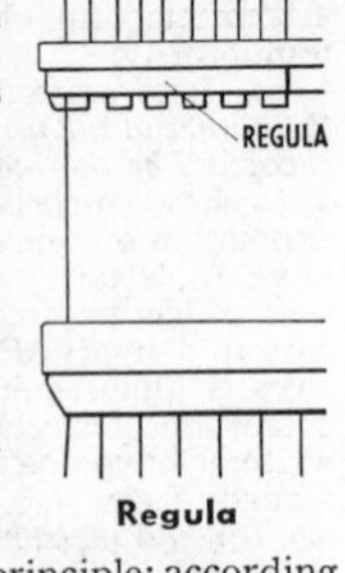

Regula

reg·u·la·ble (reg′yə lə bəl), *adj.* regulatable.

reg·u·lar (reg′yə lər), *adj.* **1.** fixed by custom or rule; usual; normal: *regular gasoline, regular grind coffee. Six o'clock was his regular hour of rising. Our regular sleeping place is in a bedroom.* **2.** following some rule or principle; according to rule: *A period is the regular ending for a sentence. S or es is the regular ending for a plural.* **3.** coming, acting, or done again and again at the same time: *regular attendance at church. Sunday is a regular holiday.* **4.** steady; habitual: *A regular customer trades often at the same store.* **5.** even in size, spacing, or speed; well-balanced; *regular features, regular teeth.* **6.** symmetrical. **7.** having all its angles equal and all its sides equal: *a regular polygon.* **8.** having all the same parts of a flower alike in shape and size. **9.** orderly; methodical: *to lead a regular life.* **10.** properly fitted or trained: *The regular cook in our cafeteria is sick.* **11.** *Grammar.* having the usual changes of form to show tense, number, person, etc.: *"Ask" is a regular verb.* **12.** *Informal.* **a.** thorough; complete: *a regular bore.* **b.** fine; agreeable; all-right: *He's a regular fellow.* **13.** permanently organized: *If we had a wholly regular army we could meet our present commitments with at least 100,000 fewer men because of the saving in overheads, avoidance of waste in movements, and so forth* (London Times). **14.** of or belonging to the permanent army of a country: *Police and military forces . . . had been under the unified command of a regular army general* (Newsweek). **15.** having to do with or conforming to the requirements of a political party or other organization: *the regular candidate, a regular ticket.* **16.** belonging to a religious order bound by certain rules: *The regular clergy live in religious communities.* **17.** *Sports.* first; varsity; best: *He was on the regular team for three seasons.*
—*n.* **1.** a member of a regularly paid group of any kind: *The army was made up of regulars and volunteers.* **2.** *U.S.* a party member who faithfully stands by his party. **3.** a person belonging to a religious order bound by certain rules. **4.** a regular customer, contributor, etc. **5.** *Sports.* a player on the regular team: *Holmes, who replaced Jim Looney, injured regular, in the third quarter, took advantage of an erratic . . . pass defense to score* (New York Times). **6.** a size of garment for men of average height and weight: *Men's: shorts, regulars, longs in standard sizes* (New Yorker).
[< Latin *rēgulāris* < *rēgula;* see RULE]
—**Syn.** *adj.* **1.** typical, standard **4.** constant. See **steady.**

Regular Army, the part of the Army of the United States that is made up of professionals and provides a permanent standing army.

reg·u·lar·ise (reg′yə lə rīz), *v.t.,* **-ised, -ising.** *Especially British.* regularize.

reg·u·lar·i·ty (reg′yə lar′ə tē), *n.* a being regular; order; system; steadiness: *The seasons come and go with regularity.*

reg·u·lar·i·za·tion (reg′yə lər ə zā′shən), *n.* **1.** the act or process of making regular: *[He] said that the Waterfront Commission had been facing up to the staggering problems of regularization of port conditions* (New York Times). **2.** the state of being made regular.

reg·u·lar·ize (reg′yə lə rīz), *v.t.,* **-ized, -izing.** to make regular: *Having regularized the procedure, we went on to the bars* (New Yorker).

reg·u·lar·ly (reg′yə lər lē), *adv.* **1.** in a regular manner. **2.** at regular times.

reg·u·lat·a·ble (reg′yə lā′tə bəl), *adj.* that can be regulated.

reg·u·late (reg′yə lāt), *v.t.,* **-lat·ed, -lat·ing.** **1.** to control by rule, principle, or system: *Private schools regulate the behavior of students.* **2.** to keep at some standard: *This instrument regulates the temperature of the room.* **3.** to adjust to ensure correct working: *to regulate a watch.* **4.** to put in good condition: *to regulate digestion.* **5.** to systematize; regularize: *to regulate one's habits of work or leisure.* [< Late Latin *rēgulāre* < Latin *rēgula;* see RULE]

reg·u·la·tion (reg′yə lā′shən), *n.* **1.** control by rule, principle, or system. **2.** a rule; law: *traffic regulations. Government regulations controlled the prices of rooms* (Newsweek).
—*adj.* **1.** according to or required by a regulation; standard: *a regulation tennis court. Soldiers wear a regulation uniform.* **2.** usual; ordinary.

reg·u·la·tion·ist (reg′yə lā′shə nist), *n.* a person who favors regulations in a particular matter.

reg·u·la·tive (reg′yə lā′tiv), *adj.* regulating: *Patents are being used as . . . regulative instruments in antitrust decrees* (Wall Street Journal).

reg·u·la·tor (reg′yə lā′tər), *n.* **1.** a person or thing that regulates. **2.** a device in a clock or watch to make it go faster or slower. **3.** a very accurate clock used as a standard of time. **4.** a valve to regulate the passage of air, gas, steam, water, etc. **5.** *Electricity.* a device to control the current, speed, voltage, or the like, of a machine, transformer, etc.

reg·u·la·to·ry (reg′yə lə tôr′ē, -tōr′-), *adj.* regulating: *The conferees will find out what regulatory moves are afoot in the various state legislatures* (Wall Street Journal).

reg·u·line (reg′yə lin, -līn), *adj.* of or having to do with a regulus. [< *regul*(us) + *-ine*¹]

reg·u·lus (reg′yə ləs), *n., pl.* **-lus·es, -li** (-lī). a product of the smelting of various ores, as copper, lead, and silver, consisting of an impure metallic mass: *Antimony metal is sometimes still referred to by the ancient name regulus* (W. Norton Jones). [< Medieval Latin *regulus* (diminutive) < Latin *rēx, rēgis* king (because it combined readily with the king's metal, gold)]

Reg·u·lus (reg′yə ləs), *n.* a white star of the first magnitude in the constellation Leo: *Another first-magnitude star now visible is Regulus, in Leo, the Lion, near which Jupiter stands in the east* (Science News Letter). [< Latin *rēgulus* (diminutive) < *rēx, rēgis* king (because of its magnitude)]

re·gur·gi·tate (rē gėr′jə tāt), *v.,* **-tat·ed, -tat·ing.** —*v.i.* (of liquids, gases, undigested foods, etc.) to rush, surge, or flow back. —*v.t.* to throw up; vomit: *Ants feed their young on regurgitated food. Many of the sea birds swallow fish and later regurgitate the partially digested fish to feed their young* (A.M. Winchester). [< Medieval Latin *regurgitare* to overflow < Latin *re-* back + *gurges, -itis* whirlpool]

re·gur·gi·ta·tion (rē gėr′jə tā′shən), *n.* **1.** a regurgitating. **2.** the flow of blood back into the heart through a defective heart valve.

re·ha·bil·i·tant (rē′hə bil′ə tənt), *n.* a person who has been rehabilitated: *Nearly 85 per cent of rehabilitants return to work* (Time).

re·ha·bil·i·tate (rē′hə bil′ə tāt), *v.t.,* **-tated, -tat·ing.** **1.** to restore to a good condition; make over in a new form: *The old house is to be rehabilitated.* **2.** to restore to a former standing, rank, rights, privileges, reputation, etc.: *The former criminal completely rehabilitated himself and was trusted and respected by all.* [< Medieval Latin *rehabilitare* (with English *-ate*¹) < Latin *re-* again + *habilitāre* < *habilis* fit, suited < *habēre* to hold, have]

re·ha·bil·i·ta·tion (rē′hə bil′ə tā′shən), *n.* the act or process of rehabilitating something or someone: *the rehabilitation of an injured person. Vocational rehabilitation services could be available to . . . newly disabled each year who could benefit from rehabilitation* (New York Times).

re·ha·bil·i·ta·tive (rē′hə bil′ə tā′tiv), *adj.* of or for rehabilitation: *. . . such rehabilitative techniques as prisons without bars* (Atlantic).

re·han·dle (rē han′dəl), *v.t.,* **-dled, -dling.** to handle or have to do with again; remodel.

re·hang (rē hang′), *v.t.,* **-hung** or (*especially for execution or suicide*) **-hanged, -hang·ing.** to hang again: *He hung and rehung the pictures* (Thackeray).

re·har·mo·nize (rē här′mə nīz), *v.t.*, **-nized, -niz·ing. 1.** *Music.* to provide (a melody or theme) with a new harmony; rearrange harmonically. **2.** to bring back into harmony or agreement.

re·hash (*v.* rē hash′; *n.* rē′hash), *v.t.* to deal with again; work up (old material) in a new form: *The question had been rehashed again and again.* —*n.* **1.** a rehashing. **2.** something old put into a different form: *That composition is simply a rehash of an article in the encyclopedia.*

re·hear (rē hir′), *v.t.*, **-heard, -hear·ing.** to hear over again: *At the request of the New Jersey Bar Association the case was reheard last week* (New York Times).

re·hear·ing (rē hir′ing), *n.* **1.** a second hearing; reconsideration. **2.** *Law.* a second hearing or trial; a new trial in chancery, or a second argument of a motion or an appeal: *If by this decree either party thinks himself aggrieved, he may petition the chancellor for a rehearing* (Sir William Blackstone).

re·hears·al (ri hėr′səl), *n.* **1.** a rehearsing. **2.** a performance beforehand for practice or drill: *More rehearsals might have helped the cast* (Newsweek).

re·hearse (ri hėrs′), *v.*, **-hearsed, -hears·ing.** —*v.t.* **1.** to practice (a play, part, etc.) for a public performance: *We rehearsed our parts for the school play.* **2.** to drill or train (a person, etc.) by repetition. **3.** to tell in detail; repeat: *She rehearsed all the happenings of the day from beginning to end.* **4.** to tell one by one; enumerate: *An act of the English parliament rehearsed the dangers to be apprehended* (George Bancroft). —*v.i.* to recite; rehearse a play, part, etc.: *You look as if you were rehearsing for a villain in a play* (Booth Tarkington). [< Anglo-French *rehearser,* Old French *rehercier,* and *reherser* to rake over < *re-* again + *hercier* to rake, harrow < *herce,* or *herse* a harrow, rake < Latin *hirpex, -icis*] —**re·hears′er,** *n.* —**Syn.** *v.t.* **4.** relate, recount.

re·heat (rē hēt′), *v.t., v.i.* to heat over again: *Part of last night's dinner was reheated for lunch today.* —*n.* an afterburner in a jet motor.

re·heat·er (rē hē′tər), *n.* something that reheats.

re·heel (rē hēl′), *v.t.* to supply a heel to, especially in knitting or mending.

re·hire (rē hīr′), *v.*, **-hired, -hir·ing,** *n.* —*v.t.* to hire again. —*n.* a renewed hiring.

Re·ho·bo·am (rē′ə bō′əm), *n.* **1.** (in the Bible) a son of Solomon and the first king of Judah, who refused to lower taxes, thus causing the revolt and secession of the northern tribes of Israel: *Rehoboam . . . was the son of Solomon and Naamah, a woman who belonged to the tribe of Ammon* (Hendrik van Loon). I Kings 11:43, 12:1-24. **2.** Also, **rehoboam.** a bottle that holds 156 ounces.

re·hos·pi·tal·i·za·tion (rē hos′pə tə lə zā′shən), *n.* the act of rehospitalizing.

re·hos·pi·tal·ize (rē hos′pə tə līz), *v.t.*, **-ized, -iz·ing.** to hospitalize again.

re·house (rē houz′), *v.t.*, **-housed, -hous·ing.** to house (a person, etc.) again; provide with other houses: *There's enough quick-growing pulpwood in the Amazon Valley alone to let us rehouse the whole world every ten years* (New Yorker).

re·hu·mid·i·fy (rē′hyü mid′ə fī), *v.t.*, **-fied, -fy·ing.** to make moist again; redampen.

re·hy·drate (rē hī′drāt), *v.t.*, **-drat·ed, -drat·ing.** to cause to become a hydrate again.

re·hy·dra·tion (rē′hī drā′shən), *n.* the state or condition of becoming a hydrate again.

rei (rā), *n.* a form sometimes used as the singular of **reis.**

Reich (rīH), *n.* Germany; the German state. [< German *Reich* empire < Middle High German *rīch* < Old High German *rīhhi,* ultimately < a Celtic word]

Reichs·bank (rīHs′bangk′; *German* rīHs′bängk′), *n.* the state bank of Germany. [< German *Reichsbank* < *Reich* Reich + *Bank* bank]

Reichs·füh·rer (rīHs′fY′rər), *n. German.* the leader of the Reich.

reichs·mark (rīHs′märk′), *n., pl.* **-marks** or **-mark.** the former unit of money of Germany, established in 1924. It was originally worth about 40 cents, and was replaced by the Deutsche mark in West Germany in 1948. *Abbr.:* Rm. [< German *Reichsmark* < *Reich* Reich + *Mark* mark, unit of currency]

reichs·pfen·nig (rīHs′pfen′ig), *n., pl.* **-pfen·nigs, -pfen·ni·ge** (-pfen′i gə). a small German coin that was worth about 1/100 of a reichsmark. [< German *Reichspfennig* < *Reich* Reich + *Pfennig.* Compare PFENNIG.]

Reichs·rat or **Reichs·rath** (rīHs′rät′), *n.* **1.** (formerly) the parliament in the Austrian part of the Austro-Hungarian Empire. **2.** the former national council of Germany under Hitler, now called the Bundesrat. [< German *Reichsrat* < *Reich* Reich + *Rat* council]

Reichs·tag (rīHs′täk′), *n.* the former elective legislative assembly of Germany. The West German equivalent is now called the Bundestag. [< German *Reichstag* < *Reich* Reich + *tagen* to deliberate]

Reichs·wehr (rīHs′vār′), *n.* the police force that Germany was permitted to have instead of an army after the end of World War I: *It looked dangerously like the Reichswehr, which Hitler had built into the Wehrmacht* (Time). [< German *Reichswehr* < *Reich* Reich + *Wehr* defense]

reif (rēf), *n. Obsolete.* plunder. [Old English *rēaf.* Related to REAVE[1].]

re·i·fi·ca·tion (rē′ə fə kā′shən), *n.* the regarding or treating of an idea as a thing; materialization.

re·i·fy (rē′ə fī), *v.t.*, **-fied, -fy·ing.** to make (an abstraction) material or concrete: *to reify an abstract concept.* [< Latin *rēs, reī* thing + English *-fy;* perhaps patterned on *deify*]

reign (rān), *n.* **1.** the period of power of a ruler: *Queen Victoria's reign lasted sixty-four years.* **2.** royal power; rule: *The reign of a wise ruler benefits his country.* **3.** existence everywhere; prevalence: *Our city must dedicate itself to a reign of law and order* (New York Times). **4.** *Obsolete.* a kingdom; realm; domain: *Then stretch thy sight o'er all her rising reign* (Alexander Pope).
—*v.i.* **1.** to be a ruler: *A king reigns over his kingdom. The laws reigned, and not men* (George Bancroft). **2.** to exist everywhere; prevail: *On a still night silence reigns.*
[< Old French *reigne* reign, realm < Latin *rēgnum* < *rēx, rēgis* king]

re·ig·nite (rē′ig nīt′), *v.t.*, **-nit·ed, -nit·ing.** to ignite again: *Matters are straightened out by the gods, who reignite the flame with a bolt of lightning* (New Yorker).

Reign of Terror, a period of the French Revolution from about March, 1793, to July, 1794, during which many persons considered undesirable by the ruling group were ruthlessly executed.

reign of terror, a period or situation in which a community lives in fear of death or violence because of the extremist methods used by a political group to win or keep power: *Northern Rhodesia is in the grip of a "reign of terror" reminiscent of Nazi Germany* (New York Times).

re·im·burs·a·ble (rē′im bėr′sə bəl), *adj.* that can be reimbursed; that must be reimbursed.

re·im·burse (rē′im bėrs′), *v.t.*, **-bursed, -burs·ing.** to pay back; refund: *satisfied that the expenses already incurred were likely to be reimbursed* (John Galt). *You reimburse a person for expenses made for you.* [< *re-* + obsolete *imburse* put into a purse < Medieval Latin *imbursare* < *in-* into + *bursa* purse (in Late Latin, hide, skin); patterned on French, Middle French *rembourser* < *embourser*]

re·im·burse·ment (rē′im bėrs′mənt), *n.* a paying back; repayment.

re·im·burs·er (rē′im bėr′sər), *n.* a person who reimburses.

re·im·plant (rē′im plant′, -plänt′), *v.t.* to implant again.

re·im·plan·ta·tion (rē′im plan tā′shən), *n.* the replacing or resetting of a part of the body that has been severed or removed.

re·im·port (*v.* rē′im pôrt′, -pōrt′; *n.* rē im′pôrt, -pōrt), *v.t.* to import (something previously exported): *We used to grow cotton in America, export it to England, and then reimport it as finished cloth.* —*n.* reimportation.

re·im·por·ta·tion (rē′im pôr tā′shən, -pōr-), *n.* **1.** an importing of something previously exported. **2.** goods reimported.

re·im·pose (rē′im pōz′), *v.t.*, **-posed, -pos·ing.** to impose again or anew: *Soviet overlordship could be reimposed only by force* (Newsweek).

re·im·po·si·tion (rē′im pə zish′ən), *n.* **1.** a reimposing. **2.** a tax levied once more or in a new form: *Such reimpositions are always over and above the taille of the particular year in which they are laid on* (Adam Smith).

re·im·preg·nate (rē′im preg′nāt), *v.t.*, **-nat·ed, -nat·ing.** to impregnate again.

re·im·pres·sion (rē′im presh′ən), *n.* **1.** a second impression. **2.** a reprinting. **3.** a reprint.

re·im·print (rē′im print′), *v.t.* to imprint anew; reprint.

re·im·pris·on (rē′im priz′ən), *v.t.* to imprison again: *Till . . . the Uncontrollable be got, if not reimprisoned, yet harnessed* (Thomas Carlyle).

re·im·pris·on·ment (rē′im priz′ən mənt), *n.* the act of confining in prison a second time for the same cause, or after a release from prison.

rein (rān), *n.* **1.** a long, narrow strap or line fastened to a bridle or bit, by which to guide and control an animal: *A driver or rider of a horse holds the reins in his hands.* **2.** a means of control and direction: *Few kings now hold the reins of government.*

draw rein, a. to tighten the reins: *He drew rein to check the fleeing horse.* **b.** to slow down; stop: *The marchers drew rein in the square.*

give rein to, to let move or act freely, without guidance or control: *The Romantic poets gave rein to their imaginations.*

keep a tight rein on, to check or restrain; control closely: *The past two governors may have submitted spendthrift budgets, but they weren't approved by the legislature, which has been keeping a tight rein on the purse* (Wall Street Journal).

take the reins, assume control: *Part of the Vice-President's job is to take the reins if the President falls ill.*

—*v.t.* **1.** to check or pull with reins: *The coachman reins his smoking bays Beneath the elm-tree's shade* (Oliver Wendell Holmes). **2.** to guide and control: *Rein your tongue.* **3.** to equip with reins. —*v.i.* **1.** to bring, turn, draw, or pull something by means of reins. **2.** to rein a horse.

rein in or **up,** to cause to stop or go slower: *another rider, meeting him and reining in* (George W. Cable).

[< Old French *rene* < Vulgar Latin *retina* a bond, check < Latin *retinēre* to hold back; see RETAIN]

re·in·au·gu·rate (rē′in ô′gyə rāt), *v.t.*, **-rat·ed, -rat·ing.** to inaugurate afresh.

re·in·car·nate (rē′in kär′nāt), *v.t.*, **-nat·ed, -nat·ing.** to give a new body to (a soul).

re·in·car·na·tion (rē′in kär nā′shən), *n.* **1.** the rebirth of the soul in a new body. **2.** a new incarnation or embodiment.

re·in·car·na·tion·ist (rē′in kär nā′shə nist), *n.* a person who believes in reincarnation.

re·in·cite (re′in sīt′), *v.t.*, **-cit·ed, -cit·ing.** to incite again; reanimate; reëncourage: *The hurricane seemed to have been reincited instead of exhausted* (Charlotte Smith).

re·in·cor·po·rate (rē′in kôr′pə rāt), *v.t., v.i.*, **-rat·ed, -rat·ing.** to incorporate again.

re·in·cor·po·ra·tion (rē′in kôr′pə rā′shən), *n.* a reincorporating or being reincorporated: *Potomac said it will seek stockholder approval of its reincorporation under the new District of Columbia Business Incorporation Act* (Wall Street Journal).

re·in·crease (rē′in krēs′), *v.t.*, **-creased, -creas·ing.** to increase again; augment; reinforce.

re·in·cur (rē′in kėr′), *v.t.*, **-curred, -cur·ring.** to incur a second time.

rein·deer (rān′dir′), *n., pl.* **-deer** or **-deers.** a large arctic deer with branching antlers, a semidomesticated strain of an Old World caribou which was introduced into Alaska in the 1890's. It is used to pull sleighs and also for meat, milk, and hides. *Santa Claus' sleigh is drawn by reindeer.* [< Scandinavian (compare Old Icelandic *hreindȳri* < *hreinn* reindeer + *dȳr* animal)]

Reindeer (about 3½ ft. high at the shoulder)

reindeer moss, a gray, branched lichen, the chief winter food of reindeer: *Green woodland mosses and a yielding sponge of reindeer moss carpet the ground* (New Yorker).

re·in·dict (rē′in dīt′), *v.t.* to indict again: *The prosecution said it planned to reindict the remaining defendants on simpler charges* (Newsweek).

re·in·doc·tri·nate (rē′in dok′trə nāt), *v.t.*, **-nat·ed, -nat·ing.** to indoctrinate again.

re·in·doc·tri·na·tion (rē′in dok′trə nā′shən), *n.* **1.** the act of reindoctrinating. **2.** the state of being reindoctrinated.

re·in·duce (rē′in düs′, -dyüs′), *v.t.*, **-duced, -duc·ing. 1.** to induce anew or again. **2.** *Obsolete.* to bring back; reintroduce: *There was a design . . . to reinduce Secular Priests into Monks' places* (Thomas Fuller).

re·in·fect (rē′in fekt′), *v.t.* to infect again.

re in·fec·ta (rē in fek′tə), *Latin.* the matter being unfinished.

re·in·fec·tion (rē′in fek′shən), *n.* infection a second time or subsequently.

re·in·flame (rē′in flām′), *v.t.*, **-flamed, -flam·ing.** to inflame anew; rekindle; warm again.

re·in·flate (rē′in flāt′), *v.t., v.i.*, **-flat·ed, -flat·ing** to inflate again.

re·in·fla·tion (rē′in flā′shən), *n.* inflation again or anew.

re·in·force (rē′in fôrs′, -fōrs′), *v.*, **-forced, -forc·ing,** *n.* —*v.t.* **1.** to strengthen with new force or materials: *to reinforce an army or a fleet, to reinforce a garment with an extra thickness of cloth, to reinforce a wall or a bridge.* **2. a.** to strengthen; make stronger or more effective: *to reinforce an argument, a plea, or an effect.* **b.** to add to; increase; supplement: *to reinforce a stock or a supply.* —*n.* **1.** something that reinforces or strengthens. **2.** the thicker metal at the rear part of a cannon to strengthen the barrel where the charge is exploded. Also, **reënforce.**

[earlier *re-enforce* < *re-* + *enforce;* perhaps patterned on Middle French *renforcer*] —**re′in·forc′er,** *n.*

re·in·forced concrete (rē′in fôrst′,-fōrst′), concrete with metal embedded in it to make the structure stronger: *Reinforced concrete, or concrete in which steel rods are embedded, must be used for concrete structures like floors, arches, and tanks* (Monroe M. Offner).

reinforced plastic, plastic for construction strengthened with glass fibers and polyester resins, used in foundations, walls, roofs, boats, tanks, etc.: *Limited quantities of complete sports-car bodies have been made of reinforced plastics and many automobile components are now made of this material* (F. H. Carmen).

re·in·force·ment (rē′in fôrs′mənt, -fōrs′-), *n.* **1.** the act of reinforcing. **2.** a being reinforced. **3.** something that reinforces.

reinforcements, extra soldiers, warships, planes, etc.: *Reinforcements were sent to the battle front.* Also, **reënforcement.**

re·in·form (rē′in fôrm′), *v.t.* to inform again or in a new way.

re·in·fuse (rē′in fyüz′), *v.t.*, **-fused, -fus·ing.** to infuse again or in a new way.

re·in·gest (rē′in jest′), *v.t.* to ingest again.

re·in·hab·it (rē′in hab′it), *v.t.* to inhabit again.

re·in·ject (rē′in jekt′), *v.t.* to inject again.

reins (rānz), *n.pl. Archaic.* **1.** the kidneys. **2.** the lower part of the back. **3.** the feelings: *The righteous God trieth the hearts and reins* (Psalms 7:9). [partly Old English *renys* < Latin *rēnēs*, plural of *rēn, rēnis* kidney, partly < Old French *reins,* or *rens* < Latin]

re·in·scribe (rē′in skrīb′), *v.t.*, **-scribed, -scrib·ing.** (in French law) to record or register a second time: *In Louisiana, originally a French colony, the old French law requires a mortgage to be periodically reinscribed in order to preserve its priority.*

re·in·sert (rē′in sėrt′), *v.t.* to insert again or in a new way: *All these deletions must be reinserted* (Atlantic).

re·in·ser·tion (rē′in sėr′shən), *n.* **1.** the act of reinserting. **2.** a second insertion.

reins·man (rānz′mən), *n., pl.* **-men.** a person who holds the reins; driver: *a skillful reinsman. The colts are members of the Del Miller stable, but the Pennsylvania reinsman will not drive either in the Delaware classic* (New York Times).

re·in·spect (rē′in spekt′), *v.t.* to inspect again: *We went to the Uffizi gallery, and reinspected the greater part of it* (Hawthorne).

re·in·spec·tion (rē′in spek′shən), *n.* the act of inspecting a second time.

re·in·spire (rē′in spīr′), *v.t.*, **-spired, -spir·ing.** to inspire again or in a new way.

re·in·stall (rē′in stôl′), *v.t.* to install over again.

re·in·stall·ment (rē′in stôl′mənt), *n.* **1.** a reinstalling. **2.** an additional installment.

re·in·state (rē′in stāt′), *v.t.*, **-stat·ed, -stat·ing.** to restore to a former position or condition; establish again: *to reinstate a member of the club. . . . The broken glass hacked out and reinstated* (Samuel Butler).

re·in·state·ment (rē′in stāt′mənt), *n.* **1.** restoration to a former position or condition: *The reinstatement and restoration of corruptible things is the noblest work of natural philosophy* (Francis Bacon). **2.** *Psychoanalysis.* alleviation of anxiety by infantile ritualistic acts to please a supposed father or mother.

re·in·sti·tute (rē in′stə tüt, -tyüt), *v.t.*, **-tut·ed, -tut·ing.** to institute again.

re·in·sti·tu·tion (rē′in stə tü′shən, -tyü′-), *n.* the act of reinstituting or state of being reinstituted: *There will never again be any reinstitution of slavery* (Horace Bushnell).

re·in·struct (rē′in strukt′), *v.t.* to instruct again or in turn.

re·in·struc·tion (re′in struk′shən), *n.* a reinstructing: *A course of reinstruction in the dry rudiments of knowledge* (Pall Mall Gazette).

re·in·sur·ance (rē′in shůr′əns), *n.* **1.** a reinsuring. **2.** the amount covered by it.

re·in·sure (rē′in shůr′), *v.t.*, **-sured, -sur·ing.** to insure again; insure under a contract by which a first insurer relieves himself from the risk and transfers it to another insurer. —**re′in·sur′er,** *n.*

re·in·te·grate (rē in′tə grāt), *v.t.*, **-grat·ed, -grat·ing.** to integrate over again or in a new way.

re·in·te·gra·tion (rē′in tə grā′shən), *n.* a reintegrating; a making whole again.

re·in·ter (rē′in tėr′), *v.t.*, **-terred, -ter·ring.** to inter again.

re·in·ter·ment (rē′in tėr′mənt), *n.* **1.** a reinterring. **2.** a being reinterred.

re·in·ter·pret (rē′in tėr′prit), *v.t.* to interpret afresh: *It needs a scientific telescope, it needs to be reinterpreted and artificially brought near us* (John Martineau).

re·in·ter·pre·ta·tion (rē′in tėr′prə tā′shən), *n.* the act of reinterpreting.

re·in·ter·ro·gate (rē′in ter′ə gāt), *v.t.*, **-gat·ed, -gat·ing.** to interrogate again; question repeatedly: *For interrogated, say reinterrogated: for . . . he must always have been interrogated in the first instance* (Jeremy Bentham).

re·in·trench (rē′in trench′), *v.t.* to intrench again or in a new way.

re·in·tro·duce (rē′in trə düs′ -dyüs′), *v.t.*, **-duced, -duc·ing.** to introduce again or in a new way.

re·in·tro·duc·tion (rē′in trə duk′shən), *n.* a reintroducing.

re·in·vade (rē′in vād′), *v.t.*, **-vad·ed, vad·ing.** to invade again or in turn.

re·in·vent (rē′in vent′), *v.t.* to devise or create anew, independently, and without knowledge of a previous invention: *After Spenser . . . had reinvented the art of writing well* (James Russell Lowell).

re·in·vest (rē′in vest′), *v.t., v.i.* to invest again or in a new way.

re·in·ves·ti·gate (rē′in ves′tə gāt), *v.t.*, **-gat·ed, -gat·ing.** to investigate again: *When I acquainted my friend with these facts he reinvestigated the specimen* (Jonathan Hutchinson).

re·in·ves·ti·ga·tion (rē′in ves′tə gā′shən), *n.* the act of reinvestigating: *Inconclusive results often demand reinvestigation.*

re·in·vest·ment (rē′in vest′mənt), *n.* **1.** a reinvesting. **2.** a second investment.

re·in·vig·or·ate (rē′in vig′ə rāt), *v.t.*, **-at·ed, -at·ing.** to invigorate again; give fresh vigor to: *Spain . . . was in some degree reinvigorated by the infusion of a foreign element into her government* (William E. H. Lecky).

re·in·vig·or·a·tion (rē′in vig′ə rā′shən), *n.* a reinforcement.

re·in·vi·ta·tion (rē′in və tā′shən), *n.* the act of inviting again; reinviting.

re·in·vite (rē′in vīt′), *v.t.*, **-vit·ed, -vit·ing.** to invite again.

re·in·volve (rē′in volv′), *v.t.*, **-volved, -volv·ing.** to involve anew.

re·ir·ra·di·ate (rē′i rā′dē āt), *v.t.*, **-at·ed, -at·ing.** to irradiate again.

reis (rās), *n.pl.* a former Portuguese and Brazilian unit of money. Nine Portuguese reis or eighteen Brazilian reis were worth one United States cent. [< Portuguese *reis,* plural of *real* real, unit of currency. Compare REAL².]

re·is·su·ance (rē ish′ů əns), *n.* an issuing again, or being issued again: *American Columbia pulls the Weingartner Beethoven symphonies out of circulation just as a French company announces their reissuance* (Atlantic).

re·is·sue (rē ish′ü, -yü), *v.*, **-sued, -su·ing,** *n.* —*v.t., v.i.* to issue again or in a new way: *The rifles are being reissued this week* (Newsweek). —*n.* a second or repeated issue: *the reissue of a best seller at a lower price. Its reissue is a lively event in a dull publishing season* (Time).

rei·ter (rī′tər), *n.* a German mounted soldier, especially in the wars of the 1500's and 1600's. [< German *Reiter* (literally) rider < *reiten* to ride. Relate to RIDER.]

re·it·er·ate (rē it′ə rāt), *v.t.*, **-at·ed, -at·ing.** to say or do several times; repeat (an action, demand, etc.) again and again: *The boy reiterated his assurances that he would be very careful with my bicycle.* [< Latin *reiterāre* < *re-* again + *iterāre* to repeat < *iterum,* adverb, again] —**Syn.** See **repeat.**

re·it·er·a·tion (rē it′ə rā′shən), *n.* **1.** a saying again. **2.** something repeated.

re·it·er·a·tive (rē it′ə rā′tiv), *adj.* repetitious. —**re·it′er·a·tive·ly,** *adv.*

reiv·er (rē′vər), *n. Scottish.* reaver; robber; raider. [ultimately < Old English *rēafian* to take by force. Related to BEREAVE, ROB.]

re·ja (rā′hä), *n. Spanish.* a decorative screen or grating protecting a window or before an altar, chapel, or choir of a church.

re·ject (*v.* ri jekt′; *n.* rē′jekt), *v.t.* **1.** to refuse to take, use, believe, consider, grant, etc.: *He rejected our help. He tried to join the army but was rejected.* **2.** to throw away as useless or unsatisfactory: *Reject all apples with soft spots.* **3.** to vomit. **4.** to repulse or rebuff (a person or appeal). **5.** *Biology.* to resist the introduction of (foreign tissue or other matter) in an organism by the mechanism of immunity: *Trouble is, the human body has a habit of trying to reject any tissue or organism that is foreign to its own chemistry* (Time).

—*n.* a rejected person or thing: [*His*] *wardrobe must have been made up of Salvation Army rejects* (New Yorker).

[< Latin *rejectus,* past participle of *rejicere* < *re-* back + *jacere* throw] —**re·ject′er,** *n.*

—**Syn.** *v.t.* **1.** decline, rebuff, repulse. See **refuse.**

re·ject·a·ble (ri jek′tə bəl), *adj.* capable of being rejected; worthy or suitable to be rejected.

re·jec·ta·men·ta (ri jek′tə men′tə), *n.pl.* **1.** things or matter rejected as useless or worthless; refuse; waste. **2.** excrement. [< New Latin *rejectamenta* < Latin *rejectus;* see REJECT]

re·ject·ee (ri jek′tē′, -jek′tē), *n.* a reject.

re·jec·tion (ri jek′shən), *n.* **1.** a rejecting. **2.** a being rejected: *A child who feels unloved, unwanted, or unworthy of his parents' interest is said to be suffering from rejection* (Sidonie M. Gruenberg). **3.** a thing rejected. **4.** *Biology.* immunological resistance of an organism to the introduction of foreign tissue or other matter: *It is well known that immunity problems, including rejection of transplants and infection resulting because drugs have destroyed the body's ability to resist disease, have been unsolved* (Science News Letter).

rejection slip, a note from a publisher rejecting the accompanying returned manuscript: *For the first time out of twenty tries I got a check instead of a rejection slip* (James Thurber).

re·jig (*n.* rē′jig′; *v.* ri jig′), *n., v.*, **-jigged, -jig·ging.** *British Slang.* —*n.* an overhauling or streamlining. —*v.t.* to rejigger: *The Treasury rejigged an old wartime poster to read in effect "Spend to Defend the Right to be Free"* (Punch).

re·jig·ger (ri jig′ər), *v.t. U.S. Slang.* to change or rearrange, especially by clever handling or juggling; work over in a new form: *Sir Arthur . . . had rejiggered his assistant's records* (Time).

re·joice (ri jois′), *v.*, **-joiced, -joic·ing.** —*v.i.* to be glad; be filled with joy: *Mother rejoiced at our success. I should rejoice to see you married to a good man* (John Galsworthy). —*v.t.* **1.** to make glad; fill with joy: *Good news rejoices the heart.* **2.** *Obsolete.* to be joyful at: *Ne'er mother Rejoiced deliverance more* (Shakespeare). [< Old French *rejoïss-,* stem of *rejoïr* < *re-* again + *esjoïr* < *es-* (Latin *ex-*) out (of) + *joïr* be glad < Vulgar

 PRONUNCIATION KEY: hat, āge, cãre, fär; let ēqual, tėrm; it, īce; hot, ōpen, ôrder; oil, out; cup, pu̇t, rüle;

Latin *gaudīre*, for Latin *gaudēre* be glad] —**re·joic′er,** *n.* —**Syn.** *v.t.* **1.** cheer, delight.

re·joice·ful (ri jois′fəl), *adj.* joyful; joyous: *In the meanwhile, the King makes a rejoiceful entrance into Excester* (John Speed).

re·joic·ing (ri joi′sing), *n.* **1.** the feeling or expression of joy: *There were great festivities—illuminations, state concerts, immense crowds, and general rejoicings* (Lytton Strachey). **2.** an occasion for joy. **3.** *Obsolete.* a cause of joy: *Thy word was unto me the joy and rejoicing of mine heart* (Jeremiah 15:16). —**re·joic′ing·ly,** *adv.*

re·join[1] (rē join′), *v.t.* **1.** to join again; unite again. **2.** to join the company of again. —*v.i.* to come together again; be reunited.

re·join[2] (ri join′), *v.t.* to answer; reply. —*v.i.* **1.** to make answer to a reply or remark. **2.** *Law.* to answer the plaintiff's reply to the defendant's plea. [< Old French *rejoindre* < *re-* back + *joindre.* Compare JOIN.]

re·join·der (ri join′dər), *n.* **1.** an answer to a reply; response: *a debater's rejoinder.* **2.** *Law.* a defendant's answer to the plaintiff's reply to the defendant's plea. [< Middle French, Old French *rejoindre,* noun use of infinitive < *re-* back + *joindre.* Compare JOIN.] —**Syn. 1.** retort.

re·judge (rē juj′), *v.t.,* **-judged, -judg·ing.** to judge over again or in a new way.

re·jug·gle (rē jug′əl), *v.t.,* **-gled, -gling.** to juggle again: *The U.S. High Commissioner in Okinawa rejuggled the city assembly quorum rules of Naha, the capital, and forced out a Communist mayor* (Wall Street Journal).

re·jus·ti·fi·ca·tion (rē′jus tə fə kā′shən), *n.* the act of rejustifying.

re·jus·ti·fy (rē jus′tə fī), *v.t.,* **-fied, -fy·ing.** to justify again.

re·ju·ve·nate (ri jü′və nāt), *v.t.,* **-nat·ed, -nat·ing. 1.** to make young or vigorous again; give youthful qualities to. **2.** *Geology.* **a.** to cause (a stream) to flow faster and erode land quicker by increasing the declivity of the land it flows over. **b.** to begin a new cycle of erosion in (a region) by upheaval of the land surrounding a stream. [< *re-* + Latin *juvenis* young]

re·ju·ve·nat·ing·ly (ri jü′və nā′ting lē), *adv.* in a manner that rejuvenates: *The imagination can only boggle fitfully at what exotic preparation soaks rejuvenatingly into her lilylike complexion* (Punch).

re·ju·ve·na·tion (ri jü′və nā′shən), *n.* **1.** a rejuvenating. **2.** a being rejuvenated.

re·ju·ve·na·tor (ri jü′və nā′tər), *n.* a person or thing that rejuvenates.

re·ju·ve·nesce (ri jü′və nes′), *v.t., v.i.,* **-nesced, -nesc·ing. 1.** to make or become young again. **2.** *Biology.* to undergo or produce rejuvenescence.

re·ju·ve·nes·cence (ri jü′və nes′əns), *n.* **1.** the renewal of youth or youthful vigor. **2.** *Biology.* **a.** the process by which the contents of a cell break the cell wall and form a new cell with a new wall. **b.** the renewal of vitality by the exchange of material between two distinct cells, as during conjugation. [< *re-* again + Latin *juvenēscēns, -entis,* present participle of *juvenēscere* grow young < *juvenis* young]

re·ju·ve·nes·cent (ri jü′və nes′ənt), *adj.* **1.** becoming young again. **2.** making young again.

re·ju·ve·nize (ri jü′və nīz), *v.t.,* **-nized, -niz·ing.** to rejuvenate.

re·kin·dle (rē kin′ dəl), *v.t., v.i.,* **-dled, -dling.** to kindle again or anew.

re·kin·dle·ment (rē kin′dəl mənt), *n.* **1.** a rekindling. **2.** a being rekindled.

re·knit (rē nit′), *v.t.,* **-knit·ted** or **-knit, -knit·ting.** to knit (up) again; refasten: *The renewal of the parental reknits the fraternal tie* (W.R. Williams).

rel., an abbreviation for the following:
1. relating.
2. a. relative. **b.** relatively.
3. religion.

re·la·bel (rē lā′bəl), *v.t.,* **-beled, -bel·ing.** to label again.

re·laid (rē lād′), *v.* the past tense and past participle of **re-lay.**

re·lapse (ri laps′; *also for n.* rē′laps), *v.,* **-lapsed, -laps·ing,** *n.* —*v.i.* to fall or slip back into a former state, way of acting, etc.: *After one cry of surprise she relapsed into silence. The next day the doctors were back; Tom had relapsed* (Mark Twain). —*n.* a falling or slipping back into a former state, way of acting, etc.: *his relapse into silence* (Edith Wharton). *He seemed to be getting over his illness but had a relapse.* [< Latin *relāpsus,* past participle of *relābī* < *re-* back + *lābī* to slip] —**re·laps′er,** *n.*

re·laps·ing fever (ri lap′sing), any of several infectious diseases characterized by recurrent episodes of chills, fever, and neuromuscular pain, and caused by spirochetes transmitted by lice or ticks.

re·late (ri lāt′), *v.,* **-lat·ed, -lat·ing.** —*v.t.* **1.** to give an account of; tell: *The traveler related his adventures* **2.** to connect in thought or meaning: *"Better" and "best" are related to "good."* —*v.i.* **1.** to be connected in any way: *We are interested in what relates to ourselves. The critic eye ... examines bit by bit: How parts relate to parts, or they to whole* (Alexander Pope). **2.** to have a feeling of association or mutual relationship with another or others: *Some teen-agers relate better to their friends than to their family.* **3.** *Obsolete.* to give an account of something. [< Latin *relātus,* past participle of *referre;* see REFER] —**re·lat′er,** *n.* —**Syn.** *v.t.* **1.** recount, recite, narrate. *-v.i.* **1.** pertain.

re·lat·ed (ri lā′tid), *adj.* **1.** connected: *Montesquieu had shown how human institutions were related to racial habit and climate* (Edmund Wilson). **2.** belonging to the same family; connected by a common origin: *French and Spanish are related languages.* **3.** *Music.* relative. **4.** narrated. —**re·lat′ed·ness,** *n.* —**Syn. 2.** allied, cognate, akin.

re·la·tion (ri lā′shən), *n.* **1.** a connection in thought or meaning: *Your answer has no relation to the question.* **2.** connection between persons, groups, countries, etc.: *The relation of mother and child is the closest in the world.* **3.** a person who belongs to the same family as another, such as a father, brother, aunt, or relative. **4.** reference; regard. **5. a.** the act of telling; account: *We were amused by his relation of his adventures.* **b.** a narrative: *We must be content in our ignorance with a brief and summary relation* (Lytton Strachey). **6.** *Law.* **a.** a reference to an earlier date. **b.** the charge of the person who brings a lawsuit.
in or **with relation to,** having to do with; about; concerning: *We must plan with relation to the future.*
[< Latin *relātiō, -ōnis* < *referre;* see REFER] —**Syn. 2.** alliance, relationship, affiliation.

re·la·tion·al (ri lā′shə nəl), *adj.* **1.** that relates. **2.** having to do with relations. **3.** showing relation between elements in grammar.

re·la·tion·ship (ri lā′shən ship), *n.* **1.** a connection. **2.** the condition of belonging to the same family.

rel·a·tive (rel′ə tiv), *n.* **1.** a person who belongs to the same family as another, such as a father, brother, or aunt: *Moody put nearly all of his estate in a tax-exempt foundation, passing out only about $1.5 million to relatives and associates* (Newsweek). **2.** a relative pronoun.
—*adj.* **1.** related or compared to each other: *Before ordering our dinner, we considered the relative merits of chicken and roast beef.* **2.** depending for meaning on a relation to something else: *East is a relative term; for example, Chicago is east of California but west of New York.* **3.** *Grammar.* introducing a subordinate clause; referring to another person or thing. In "The man who wanted it is gone," *who* is a relative pronoun, and *who wanted it* is a relative clause. **4.** *Music.* having a close harmonic relation; having the same signature: *a relative minor.*
relative to, a. about; concerning: *some inquiries relative to the character and usages of the remote Indian nations* (Francis Parkman). **b.** in proportion to: *Price is relative to demand.*
[< Late Latin *relātīvus* < Latin *referre;* see REFER] —**rel′a·tive·ness,** *n.*

➔ **relative clauses.** A relative clause is an adjective clause introduced by a relative pronoun (*that, which, who, whose,* etc.), or a relative adverb (*where, when, why*), or by neither (an asyndetic clause): The ball *that had been lost* was found by the caddy. The man *whose ball was lost* was angry. Mike's plane, *which was lost in the storm,* landed safely in a field. This is the place *where they met.* The ring *he bought* was expensive (asyndetic).

➔ **relative pronouns.** There are two classes: (1) Those such as *that, which, of which, who, whose, what,* and *whom,* which introduce adjective clauses and refer to an antecedent in the main clause: A man *who* was there gave us the details. Our team, *which* scored first, had the advantage. We didn't take the same trail *that* they did. He did *what* he thought best. *Who* refers to persons; *which,* to animals or objects; *that,* to persons, animals, or objects; *what* to objects. (2) Those such as *whoever, whichever,* and *who,* which introduce noun clauses and have no definite antecedent: You may have *whichever* you like. I know *who* did it.

relative frequency, *Statistics.* the ratio of the number of actual occurrences to the possible occurrences.

relative humidity, the ratio between the water vapor in the air and the amount of water vapor the air could contain at a given temperature: *Relative humidity is most accurately measured by determining the dew point* (Shortley and Williams).

rel·a·tive·ly (rel′ə tiv lē), *adv.* **1.** in a relative manner; in relation to something else; comparatively: *a relatively small difference.* **2.** in relation or with reference (to): *the value of one thing relatively to other things.* **3.** in proportion (to): *a subject little understood relatively to its importance.*

relative maximum, *Mathematics.* a value of a variable greater than any values close to it.

rel·a·tiv·ism (rel′ə tə viz′əm), *n.* the philosophical doctrine of the relativity of knowledge, truth, or certainty.

rel·a·tiv·ist (rel′ə tə vist), *n.* **1.** a person who believes in relativism. **2.** a person who believes in the theory of relativity: *The now dormant relativists may awaken to brave new concepts that will reorient us in the universe of matter and ideas* (Harlow Shapley). —*adj.* relativistic: *In Dewey's relativist world consequences were the definite test of all thinking, and experience the only ultimate authority* (Newsweek).

rel·a·tiv·is·tic (rel′ə tə vis′tik), *adj.* **1.** of or having to do with relativism or relativists. **2.** of or having to do with relativity: *Relativistic phenomena generally cause a lot of intellectual difficulties for the non-scientist* (Atlantic).

rel·a·tiv·is·ti·cal·ly (rel′ə tə vis′tə klē), *adv.* in a relativistic manner: *Although the name of a particle, or its electric charge, is a relativistically invariant concept, its ... angular momentum is not* (David Park).

rel·a·tiv·i·ty (rel′ə tiv′ə tē), *n.* **1.** a being relative. **2.** *Philosophy.* existence only in relation to the human mind. **3.** *Physics.* the character of being relative rather than absolute, as ascribed to motion or velocity. **4.** a theory expressed in certain equations by Albert Einstein. According to it, the only velocity we can measure is velocity relative to some body; observers on any celestial body may regard that body as motionless except for its rotation and acceleration and obtain the same observations as they would on any other celestial body, and will then obtain always the same value for the velocity of light; the mass of a moving body increases in relation to its velocity; in a certain sense space is curved. *One of the fundamental postulates of relativity is that the velocity of light is the same in all circumstances, even when the source and the observer are in relative motion* (W.H. Marshall).

relativity of knowledge, 1. *Philosophy.* the doctrine that all human knowledge is relative to the human mind. The mind can know only the effects which things produce upon it and not what the things themselves are. **2.** *Psychology.* the theory that the consciousness of objects comes only from their relations to one another.

rel·a·tiv·ize (rel′ə tə vīz), *v.t.,* **-ized, -iz·ing.** to make relative· *Recognition of the reality of evil necessarily relativizes the good* (Carl G. Jung).

re·la·tor (ri lā′tər), *n.* **1.** a person who relates or narrates. **2.** *Law.* an individual who brings a charge that causes the State to initiate legal action. [< Latin *relātor* < *referre;* see REFER]

re·launch (rē lônch′, -länch′), *v.t., v.i.* to launch again.

re·laun·der (rē lôn′dər, -län′-), *v.t., v.i.* to launder anew.

re·lax (ri laks′), *v.t.* **1.** to make less stiff or firm; loosen: *Relax your muscles to rest them.* **2.** to make less strict or severe; lessen in force: *Discipline was relaxed on the last day of school. Gloria ... slowly relaxes her threaten-*

ing attitude (George Bernard Shaw). **3.** to relieve from work or effort; give recreation or amusement: *Relax your mind.* **4.** to weaken; slacken: *to relax precautions against attack. Don't relax your efforts because the examinations are over.* —*v.i.* **1.** to become less tense or firm; loosen up: *Her compressed lips relaxed as she became less angry.* **2.** to become less strict or severe; grow milder: *Alick . . . never relaxed into the frivolity of unnecessary speech* (George Eliot). **3.** to reduce strain and worry; be lazy and carefree: *They come for rest, for fun, for the pure luxury of relaxing in Nassau sunshine* (New Yorker). *Take a vacation and relax.* **4.** to lessen force or intensity; diminish: *The waves relaxed in their force until they did little more than play upon the side of the wreck* (Frederick Marryat). [< Latin *relaxāre* < *re-* back + *laxāre* to undo < *laxus* loose. Doublet of RELEASE.] —**re·lax′er,** *n.*

re·lax·ant (ri lak′sənt), *n.* a practice or drug serving to produce relaxation: *Anesthesia proper begins with injections of thiopental and a muscle relaxant of the curare family* (Time).

re·lax·a·tion (rē′lak sā′shən), *n.* **1.** a loosening: *the relaxation of the muscles.* **2.** a lessening of strictness, severity, force, etc.: *the relaxation of discipline.* **3.** relief from work or effort; recreation; amusement: *Walking and reading were the only relaxations permitted on Sunday.* **4.** pardon; remission. **5.** the state or condition of being relaxed: *Mr. Lunt's always extraordinary relaxation on the stage has reached the point where practically everything he does gives the impression of being an immediate and happy improvisation* (New Yorker).

relaxation time, the time required, in many physical phenomena involving change or disturbance, for the elements of the process to recover equilibrium, or to effect some desired or expected result.

re·lax·a·tive (ri lak′sə tiv), *adj.* tending to relax; of the nature of relaxation.

re·laxed (ri lakst′), *adj.* **1.** free from restraint or restrictions; not strict or precise: *Shakespeare . . . is relaxed and careless in critical places* (William Hazlitt). **2.** slackened, mitigated, or modified with respect to strictness: *When the law has become relaxed, public opinion takes its place* (James A. Froude).

re·lax·ed·ly (ri lak′sid lē), *adv.* in a relaxed manner.

re·lax·in (ri lak′sin), *n.* a hormone produced by the corpus luteum during pregnancy which relaxes the pelvic ligaments. It is used in medicine to control premature labor and ease normal labor. [< *relax* + *-in*]

re·lay (rē′lā, ri lā′), *n., v.,* **-layed, -lay·ing.** —*n.* **1.** a fresh supply: *New relays of men were sent to the battle front. The distances at which we got relays of horses varied greatly* (Alexander W. Kinglake). **2. a.** a relay race. **b.** one part of a relay race. **3.** an electromagnetic device in which a weak current controls a strong current. A relay is used in transmitting telegraph or telephone messages over long distances. **4.** a device that extends or reinforces the action or effect of an apparatus, as a servomotor. **5.** a group of persons taking turns in any work or activity; shift. **6.** the act of passing on a ball, puck, etc., from one player to another.

—*v.t.* **1.** to take and carry or send farther: *Messengers will relay your message. He relays to Marx the stories that are reaching him from friends in Germany* (Edmund Wilson). **2.** to transmit by an electrical relay. **3.** to provide or replace with a fresh supply. —*v.i.* to relay signals, a message, etc.

[< Old French *relai* a reserve pack of hounds or other animals < *relaier* exchange tired animals for fresh < *re-* back + *laier* to leave, perhaps < Germanic (compare Low German *lâtan*)]

re-lay (rē lā′), *v.t.,* **-laid, -lay·ing.** to lay again: *At the same time that more and more people were trying to drive, more and more highways were being torn up and re-laid* (Harper's). [< *re-* + *lay*[1]]

relay race, a race in which each member of a team runs, swims, etc., only a certain part of the distance.

relay station, an instrument or object that transmits or reflects electrical signals from one place to another: *The moon, long a symbol linked to lovers, may soon be used as a relay station for their intercontinental telephone calls* (Newsweek).

relay switch, a switch operating an electric relay.

re·leap (rē lēp′), *v.t., v.i.,* **-leaped** or **-leapt, -leap·ing.** to leap back or over again: *I resolved to pluck up courage and releap the dangerous abyss* (Edward G. Bulwer-Lytton).

re·learn (rē lėrn′), *v.t.,* **-learned** or **-learnt, -learn·ing.** to learn again: *We must relearn the lesson that St. Augustine is forever insisting upon* (Charles Gore).

re·leas·a·ble (ri lē′sə bəl), *adj.* that can be released: *One pound of uranium carries more releasable energy than 1500 tons of coal.*

re·lease (ri lēs′), *v.,* **-leased, -leas·ing,** *n.* —*v.t.* **1.** to let go; let loose. **2.** to set free; relieve: *The nurse will be released from duty at seven o'clock. Release me from this life, From this intolerable agony!* (Robert Southey). **3. a.** to give up (a legal right, claim, etc.). **b.** to make over to another (property, etc.). **4.** to permit to be published, shown, sold, etc.: *to release a news dispatch, to release a motion picture.* **5.** *Obsolete.* to pardon.

—*n.* **1.** a letting go; setting free: *the release of strain from an engine.* **2.** freedom; relief: *This medicine will give you a release from pain.* **3.** a part that releases other parts of a machine, etc.: *Press the release and the box will open.* **4. a.** the legal surrender of a right, estate, etc., to another. **b.** the document that does this. **5.** permission for publication, exhibition, sale, etc.: *Now in the final stages of editing, the two-hour picture is scheduled for midsummer release* (Newsweek). **6. a.** an article, statement, etc., distributed for publication: *a news release.* **b.** a phonograph record, motion picture, etc., similarly released: *One of the most satisfying of the recent releases in his "Blues in Orbit"* (Punch). **7.** *Phonetics.* the breaking of the closure in the articulation of a stop, as *b, t,* and *k* sounds. **8.** *Obsolete.* a pardon.

[< Old French *relaissier* < Latin *relaxāre.* Doublet of RELAX.] —**re·leas′er,** *n.*

—**Syn.** *v.t.* **1. Release, free** mean to set loose from something that holds back or keeps confined. **Release** suggests relaxing the hold on the person or thing and letting him or it go again: *He released the brakes of the truck.* **Free,** more general in meaning and application, suggests removing or unfastening whatever is holding him or it back: *He freed the bird from the cage.* **2.** See **dismiss.**

re-lease (rē lēs′), *v.t.,* **-leased, -leas·ing.** to lease again.

re·leased time (ri lēst′), *U.S.* time given up by public schools for religious education or other legally appointed instruction outside of school: *On Thursdays, the children at the elementary schools nearby are let out an hour early for released time* (New Yorker).

re·leas·ee (ri lē′sē), *n.* a person to whom a release is given: *The University of Illinois concluded a study of the . . . careers of prisoners released from federal institutions, finding among other things that the most significant factor in the success of releasees was their ability to obtain a job* (Charles V. Bennett).

re·lease·ment (ri lēs′mənt), *n.* the act of releasing; release.

rel·e·ga·ble (rel′ə gə bəl), *adj.* that can be relegated.

rel·e·gate (rel′ə gāt), *v.t.,* **-gat·ed, -gat·ing.** **1.** to send away, usually to a lower position or condition: *to relegate a dress to the rag bag. We have not relegated religion (like something we were ashamed to show) to obscure municipalities or rustic villages* (Edmund Burke). **2.** to send into exile; banish. **3.** to hand over (a matter, task, etc.). **4.** to refer (a person), as for information. [< Latin *relēgāre* (with English *-ate*[1]) < *re-* back + *lēgāre* to despatch < *lēgātus* having a commission or contract < *lēx, lēgis* law, contract]

rel·e·ga·tion (rel′ə gā′shən), *n.* a relegating or being relegated: *Grimsby, struggling to avoid relegation, only briefly threatened to make a match of it with the Division leaders* (Sunday Times).

re·lend (rē lend′), *v.t.,* **-lent, -lend·ing.** to lend again.

re·lent (ri lent′), *v.i.* **1.** to become less harsh or cruel; be more tender and merciful: *The captain at last relented, and told him that he might make himself at home* (Herman Melville). **2.** *Obsolete.* to melt. —*v.t. Obsolete.* **1.** to slacken. **2.** to soften in feeling. **3.** to make dissolve. [perhaps < Latin *re-* again + *lentus* slow, viscous]

re·lent·less (ri lent′lis), *adj.* without pity; unyielding; harsh: *relentless determination. The storm raged with relentless fury.* —**re·lent′less·ly,** *adv.* —**re·lent′less·ness,** *n.* —**Syn.** ruthless, implacable.

re·let (rē let′), *v.t.,* **-let, -let·ting.** to let anew, as a house.

rel·e·vance (rel′ə vəns), *n.* relevancy: *Today, however, reserve forces have lost much of their relevance, and the need is for men on the ground in peacetime* (London Times).

rel·e·van·cy (rel′ə vən sē), *n.* a being relevant.

rel·e·vant (rel′ə vənt), *adj.* bearing upon or connected with the matter in hand; to the point: *The witness' testimony is not relevant to the case.* [< Latin *relevāns, -antis* relieving, present participle of *relevāre;* see RELIEVE] —**rel′e·vant·ly,** *adv.* —**Syn.** applicable, appropriate. See **pertinent.**

re·le·vé (rə lə vā′), *n. French.* (in ballet) the raising of the body on the fully or partly pointed toe.

re·li·a·bil·i·ty (ri lī′ə bil′ə tē), *n.* the quality or state of being reliable; trustworthiness; dependability.

re·li·a·ble (ri lī′ə bəl), *adj.* worthy of trust; that can be depended on: *reliable sources of news.* —**re·li′a·ble·ness,** *n.*

—**Syn. Reliable, trustworthy** mean worthy of being depended on or trusted. **Reliable** implies that a person or thing can safely be believed and counted on to do or be what is expected, wanted, or needed: *I have always found this to be a reliable brand of canned goods.* **Trustworthy** implies that a person is fully deserving of complete confidence in his truthfulness, honesty, good judgment, etc.: *He is a trustworthy news commentator.*

re·li·a·bly (ri lī′ə blē), *adv.* in a reliable manner; to a reliable extent or degree.

re·li·ance (ri lī′əns), *n.* **1.** trust; dependence: *A child has reliance on his mother.* **2.** confidence. **3.** a thing on which one depends.

re·li·ant (ri lī′ənt), *adj.* **1.** relying; depending. **2.** confident. **3.** relying on oneself.

rel·ic (rel′ik), *n.* **1.** a thing, custom, etc., that remains from the past: *This ruined bridge is a relic of the Civil War. Another relic of colonialism in Macassar is the Grand Hotel* (New York Times). **2.** something belonging to a holy person, kept as a sacred memorial. **3.** an object having interest because of its age or its associations with the past; keepsake; souvenir.

relics, a. remains; ruins: *It is only in this last period . . . that we find the relics of the war chariot among the contents of the tomb* (Daniel Wilson). **b.** *Archaic.* the remains of a person; corpse: *How long he lived after that year, I cannot tell, nor where his relics were lodg'd* (Anthony Wood).

[< Old French *relique* < Latin *reliquiae,* feminine plural, remains (in Late Latin, relics) < *re-* back + *linquere* leave]

rel·ict (rel′ikt), *n.* **1.** a widow. **2.** a plant or animal surviving from an earlier period. [< Late Latin *relicta* widow; (originally) feminine past participle of Latin *relinquere* leave < *re-* back + *linquere* leave]

re·lief (ri lēf′), *n.* **1.** the lessening of, or freeing from, a pain, burden, difficulty, etc. **2.** something that lessens or frees from pain, burden, difficulty, etc.; aid; help. **3.** help given to poor people. **4.** something that makes a pleasing change or lessens strain. **5.** release from a post of duty, often by the coming of a substitute: *This nurse is on duty from seven in the morning until seven at night, with only two hours' relief.* **6.** a change of persons on duty. **7.** persons who relieve others from duty, or a person who does this. **8.** the projection of figures and designs from a surface in sculpture, drawing, painting, etc. **9.** a figure or design standing out from the surface from which it is cut, shaped, or stamped: *Twenty-one paintings and reliefs make up the Nicholson collection at the Durlacher* (New Yorker). **10.** the appearance of standing out given to a drawing or painting by the use of shadow, shading, color, or line. **11.** different heights of the earth's surface. **12.** (in feudal law) money which the heir of a deceased tenant paid to the lord on taking possession of the estate.

Relief (def. 8)
Left, bas relief; right, high relief

in relief, a. standing out from a surface: *a church with its dark spire in strong relief against the clear, cold sky* (Washington Irving). **b.** in a strong, clear manner; with distinctness: *His noble nature stood out in relief from the evil of his surroundings.*
on relief, receiving money to live on from public funds: *His family has been on relief ever since he died.*
[< Old French *relief* < *relever;* see RELIEVE; (definition 8) < Old French *relief* < Italian *rilievo;* see RELIEVO]

re·lief·er (ri lē′fər), *n.* **1.** *Baseball.* a relief pitcher: *Jim Konstanty, the reliefer responsible for the 1950 pennant, is now rated a starter* (Time). **2.** *U.S. Informal.* a person who is on relief: *. . . putting able-bodied reliefers to work for the city* (Wall Street Journal).

relief map, a map that shows the different heights of a surface by using shading, colors, solid materials, etc.

relief pitcher, *Baseball.* a pitcher who enters a game to relieve another pitcher, usually a pitcher who specializes in this and seldom starts a game.

relief printing, letterpress; printing from type.

relief valve, a valve set to open at a given pressure of steam, air, or water; safety valve.

re·li·er (ri lī′ər), *n.* a person who relies.

re·liev·a·ble (ri lē′və bəl), *adj.* that can be relieved.

re·lieve (ri lēv′), *v.t.*, **-lieved, -liev·ing. 1.** to make less; make easier; reduce the pain or trouble of: *Aspirin will usually relieve a headache.* **2.** to set free: *Your coming relieves me of the bother of writing a long letter. This relieved Ernest of a good deal of trouble* (Samuel Butler). **3.** to bring aid to; help: *Soldiers were sent to relieve the fort.* **4.** to give variety or a pleasing change to: *The black dress was relieved by red trimming.* **5.** to free (a person on duty) by taking his place. **6.** *Sports.* to substitute for (another player, as a pitcher in a baseball game). **7.** to make stand out more clearly. [< Old French *relever* < Latin *relevāre* to lighten < *re-* back + *levāre* to raise < *levis* light (in weight)] —**Syn. 1.** alleviate, mitigate.

re·liev·er (ri lē′vər), *n.* **1.** a person or thing that relieves. **2.** *Baseball.* a relief pitcher: *Collins worked the reliever for a pass, filling the bases* (New York Times).

re·lie·vo (ri lē′vō), *n., pl.* **-vos.** (in painting, sculpture, etc.) relief. [alteration of Italian *rilievo* < *rilevare* to raise < Latin *relevāre;* see RELIEVE]

re·light (rē līt′), *v.t., v.i.*, **-lighted** or **-lit, -light·ing.** to light again or anew: *The furnace relighted yesterday has a 250-ton capacity* (Wall Street Journal). [< *re-* + *light*[1]]

re·li·gieuse (rə lē zhyœz′), *n., pl.* **-gieuses** (-zhyœz′). *French.* a nun: *I was the last one they expected to become a religieuse, and I couldn't explain it to them* (Maclean's).

re·li·gieux (rə lē zhyœ′), *n., pl.* **-gieux** (-zhyœ′). *French.* a man belonging to a religious order, community, etc.

re·lig·i·o-eth·i·cal (ri lij′ē ō eth′ə kəl), *adj.* having to do with or based upon both religion and ethics: *Islam arose as a movement of socioeconomic justice and reform backed by certain religio-ethical ideas about God, man, and the universe* (London Times).

re·lig·i·o la·i·ci (ri lij′ē ō lā′ə sī), *Latin.* the religion of the layman.

re·lig·i·o lo·ci (ri lij′ē ō lō′sī), *Latin.* the sacred character of a place.

re·li·gion (ri lij′ən), *n.* **1.** belief in God or gods. **2.** worship of God or gods. **3.** a particular system of religious belief and worship: *the Christian religion, the Moslem religion.* **4.** a matter of conscience: *She makes a religion of keeping her house neat.*
experience religion, to become converted: *Some went so far as to doubt if she had ever experienced religion* (Oliver Wendell Holmes).
[< Latin *religiō, -ōnis* respect for what is sacred; probably (originally) care for (worship and traditions) < *relegere* go through, or read again < *re-* again + *legere* to read; *religiō* was apparently strongly influenced, in popular thought, by the verb *religāre* to bind, in the sense "place an obligation on"]

re·li·gion·ar·y (ri lij′ə ner′ē), *adj.* having to do with religion: *religionary intolerance.*

re·li·gion·ism (ri lij′ə niz əm), *n.* **1.** an excessive inclination toward religion. **2.** an exaggerated zeal in religion.

re·li·gion·ist (ri lij′ə nist), *n.* **1.** a person devoted to religion. **2.** a religious zealot or bigot: *He plunged from the ark into the canal . . . unsuccessfully pursued by a small band of whooping religionists* (New Yorker).

re·li·gion·less (ri lij′ən lis), *adj.* without religion; irreligious.

re·lig·i·o-po·lit·i·cal (ri lij′ē ō pə lit′ə kəl), *adj.* having to do with or based upon both religion and politics: *These are to draw into closer amity the two religio-political communities in the province* (London Times).

re·li·gi·os·i·ty (ri lij′ē os′ə tē), *n.* affectation of religious feeling: *There is too much noisy religiosity on the public level in the U.S.* (Time). [< Latin *religiōsitās* < *religiōsus* religious < *religiō;* see RELIGION]

re·lig·i·o·so (ri lij′ē ō′sō), *adj., adv. Music.* expressing religious sentiment; devotional: *What appeals to me as impressive and rewarding is Poulenc's willingness to follow his expressive urge where it leads him, whether the mode is . . . secular, religioso, whatever* (Saturday Review). [< Italian *religioso* < Latin *religiōsus* religious]

re·li·gious (ri lij′əs), *adj.* **1.** of religion; connected with religion: *religious freedom, religious differences. Technically speaking a religious book is produced by a religious writer* (Harper's). **2.** much interested in religion; devoted to the worship of God or gods: *to be very religious.* **3.** belonging to an order of monks, nuns, friars, etc. **4.** of or connected with such an order: *a shaven head, and a religious habit* (Joseph Addison). **5.** strict; done with care: *Mother gave religious attention to the doctor's orders.*
—*n.* **1.** a monk, nun, friar, etc.; member of a religious order. **2.** such persons as a group: *One of Sister Benedicta's fellow religious at Echt soon received a brief message* (Time).
[perhaps < Anglo-French *religius,* Old French *religious,* learned borrowing from Latin *religiōsus* < *religiō;* see RELIGION]
—**re·li′gious·ly,** *adv.* —**re·li′gious·ness,** *n.*
—**Syn.** *adj.* **2.** pious, devout. **5.** exact, scrupulous.

religious education, instruction in the beliefs of a religion, as in Sunday school: *Religious houses were closed . . . and religious education in the schools was all but ended by harassment* (Time).

re·line (rē līn′), *v.t.*, **-lined, -lin·ing. 1.** to mark with new lines; renew the lines of. **2.** to put a new lining in.

re·lin·quish (ri ling′kwish), *v.t.* **1.** to give up; let go: *The small dog relinquished his bone to the big dog. She has relinquished all hope of going to Europe this year.* **2.** *Obsolete.* to withdraw from; leave: *Most of them relinquished Spain, as a country where they could no longer live in security* (Washington Irving). [< Middle French, Old French *relinquiss-,* stem of *relinquir* < Latin *relinquere* < *re-* back + *linquere* leave] —**re·lin′quish·er,** *n.* —**Syn. 1.** abandon, renounce.

re·lin·quish·ment (ri ling′kwish mənt), *n.* a giving up; abandonment; surrender: *The most important change is relinquishment of day-to-day Allied control over West Berlin legislation* (New York Times).

rel·i·quar·y (rel′ə kwer′ē), *n., pl.* **-quar·ies,** *adj.* —*n.* a small box or other receptacle for a relic or relics: *We stopt at St. Denis,* [*and*] *saw . . . crucifixes, . . . crowns, and reliquaries of inestimable value* (Thomas Gray).
—*adj.* of or having to do with a relic or relics: *. . . two most curious specimens of reliquary superstition* (George S. Faber). *There could be no doubt that here was an Italian 15th century reliquary bust* (Time).
[< French *réliquaire* < Old French *reliquaire* < *relique;* see RELIC]

rel·ique (rel′ik; *French* rə lēk′), *n. Archaic.* a relic. [< Middle French, Old French *relique;* see RELIC]

re·liq·ui·ae (ri lik′wē ē), *n.pl.* remains, as those of fossil animals or plants. [< Latin *reliquiae;* see RELIC]

re·liq·ui·date (rē lik′wə dāt), *v.t.*, **-dat·ed, -dat·ing.** to liquidate anew; adjust a second time.

re·liq·ui·da·tion (rē′lik wə dā′shən), *n.* a second or renewed liquidation; a renewed adjustment.

rel·ish (rel′ish), *n.* **1.** a pleasant taste; good flavor: *Hunger gives a relish to simple food.* **2. a.** something to add flavor to food, such as olives, pickles, peppers, etc. **b.** chopped pickles, peppers, etc., with slightly sweet seasoning. **3.** a slight dash (of something). **4.** liking; appetite; enjoyment: *The hungry boy ate with great relish. The teacher . . . has no relish for John's jokes. The cheerfulness of the children added a relish to his existence* (Jane Austen).
—*v.t.* **1.** to like; enjoy: *A cat relishes cream. He did not relish the prospect of staying after school. This doctrine . . . was not much relished by a great part of the audience* (Robert Graves). **2.** to give flavor to; make pleasing.
—*v.i.* to have a taste: *It will make everything relish of religion* (Jeremy Taylor).
[earlier *reles* < Old French, remainder < *relesser,* or *relaissier;* see RELEASE] —**rel′ish·er,** *n.* —**rel′ish·ing·ly,** *adv.*

rel·ish·a·ble (rel′i shə bəl), *adj.* that can be relished.

re·lis·ten (rē lis′ən), *v.i.* to listen again or anew: *The brook . . . seems, as I relisten to it, Prattling the primrose fancies of the boy* (Tennyson).

re·live (rē liv′), *v.*, **-lived, -liv·ing.** —*v.i.* to live again or anew. —*v.t.* to live over or through again: *She relived the scene of their good-bye* (Lionel Merrick).

re·load (rē lōd′), *v.t., v.i.* to load again.

re·load·er (rē lō′dər), *n.* a self-loading conveyer to collect and transport coal from a storage yard to railroad cars, vessels, or nearby storage places.

re·loan (rē lōn′), *v.t.* to loan again.

re·lo·cate (rē lō′kāt), *v.*, **-cat·ed, -cat·ing.** —*v.i. U.S.* to resettle. —*v.t.* to locate again or anew: *Programs must be worked out to ease the impact of technological changes by retraining and relocating workers* (Wall Street Journal).

re·lo·ca·tion (rē′lō kā′shən), *n.* a relocating or being relocated.

re·lo·ca·tor (rē lō′kā tər), *n.* **1.** one that relocates. **2.** a device to find the range and direction of a target to aim shore batteries.

rel. pron., relative pronoun.

re·lu·cent (ri lü′sənt), *adj.* **1.** casting back light. **2.** shining; bright. [< Latin *relūcēns, -entis* < *relūcēre* to shine out, glow < *re-* back + *lūcere* to shine, related to *lūx, lūcis* light[1]] —**Syn. 2.** refulgent.

re·luct (ri lukt′), *v.i.* **1.** to offer resistance or opposition: *I . . . reluct at the inevitable course of destiny* (Charles Lamb). **2.** to be relucent. [< Latin *reluctārī;* see RELUCTANT]

re·luc·tance (ri luk′təns), *n.* **1.** a reluctant feeling or action; unwillingness: *There is nothing we receive with so much reluctance as Advice* (Joseph Addison). **2.** slowness in action because of unwillingness: *Facts were never pleasing to him. He acquired them with reluctance and got rid of them with relief* (James M. Barrie). **3.** *Physics.* the resistance offered to the passage of magnetic lines of force. It is equivalent to the ratio of the magnetomotive force to the magnetic flux. —**Syn. 1.** disinclination.

re·luc·tan·cy (ri luk′tən sē), *n., pl.* **-cies.** reluctance: *One immediate effect . . . has been a reluctancy of scrap copper holders to make offers of their supplies to custom smelters* (Wall Street Journal).

re·luc·tant (ri luk′tənt), *adj.* **1.** showing unwillingness; unwilling: *He put the flimsy paper down with a slow, reluctant movement* (H. G. Wells). **2.** slow to act because unwilling: *He was very reluctant to give his money away.* **3.** *Archaic.* resisting; opposing. [< Latin *reluctāns, -antis* struggling against, present participle of *reluctārī* < *re-* back + *luctārī* to struggle] —**re·luc′tant·ly,** *adv.*
—**Syn. 1. Reluctant, loath** mean unwilling to do something. **Reluctant** implies mere lack of willingness, due to distaste for what is to be done, to irresolution, or simply to laziness: *He was reluctant to leave his cozy chair by the fire.* **Loath** implies strong unwillingness because one feels the thing to be done is extremely disagreeable or hateful; *His parents were loath to believe their son would steal.*

rel·uc·tiv·i·ty (rel′ək tiv′ə tē), *n. Physics.* the ratio of the intensity of the magnetic field to the magnetic induction of a substance; the reciprocal of permeability.

re·lume (ri lüm′), *v.t.*, **-lumed, -lum·ing.** to relight or rekindle: *I know not where is that Promethean heat That can thy light relume* (Shakespeare). [apparently < Latin *relūmināre* < *re-* again + *lūmināre* light up < *lūmen, -inis* light[1]]

re·lu·mine (ri lü′mən), *v.t.*, **-mined, -min·ing.** to relume.

re·ly (ri lī′), *v.i.*, **-lied, -ly·ing.** to depend; trust: *Rely on your own efforts. I rely upon your word absolutely. The Assembly, which could not rely on the Armed Forces . . . was*

too weak to defy Algiers (Observer). [< Old French *relier* < Latin *religāre* bind fast < *re-* back + *ligāre* to bind]
—**Syn. Rely, depend** mean to have confidence in someone or something. **Rely** suggests counting on, or putting one's trust in, someone or something one has reason to believe will never fail to do what is expected or wanted: *He relies on his parents' advice.* **Depend** suggests confidently taking it for granted, with or without reason, that a person or thing will give the help or support expected or needed, and often suggests leaning on others: *She depends on her friends to make her decisions.*

rem (rem), *n., pl.* **rem** or **rems.** a unit for measuring absorbed doses of radiation, equivalent to one roentgen of gamma rays. [< *r*(oentgen) *e*(quivalent) *m*(an)]

REM (no periods), rapid eye movement (a phenomenon occurring during sleep, thought to be a manifestation of dreaming).

rem., remark or remarks.

re·made (rē mād′), *v.* the past tense and past participle of **remake.**

re·main (ri mān′), *v.i.* **1.** to continue in a place; stay: *We shall remain at the seashore till October.* **2.** to continue; keep on; last: *The town remains the same year after year.* **3.** to be left: *A few apples remain on the trees. If you take 2 from 5, 3 remains.*
—*n.* **remains, a.** what is left: *Feed the remains of the meal to the dog. She cleared away the remains of lunch* (William De Morgan). **b.** a dead body: *Washington's remains are buried at Mount Vernon.* **c.** a writer's works not yet published at the time of his death: *He left behind him many valuable remains, which Bion Proconnesius is said to have translated* (Jacob Bryant). **d.** things left from the past, such as a building, a monument, or parts of an animal or plant: *the remains of an ancient civilization.*
[< Old French *remaindre* < Latin *remanēre* < *re-* back + *manēre* to stay]
—**Syn.** *v.i.* **1.** See **stay.**

re·main·der (ri mān′dər), *n.* **1.** the part left over; the rest: *After studying an hour, she spent the remainder of the afternoon in play. If you take 2 from 9, the remainder is 7.* **2.** one of the copies of a book left in the publisher's hands after the sale has practically ceased. **3.** *Law.* a future estate so created as to take effect after another estate, such as a life interest, has come to an end. **remainders,** stamps voided for postal use: *to collect remainders.*
—*adj.* remaining; left over: *Their memories are dimm'd and torn, Like the remainder tatters of a dream* (Thomas Hood).
—*v.t.* to sell as a remainder: *to remainder books.*
[< Anglo-French *remainder,* Old French *remaindre,* noun use of infinitive; see REMAIN]
—**Syn.** *n.* **1.** residue, remnant, balance, surplus.

re·main·der·man (ri mān′dər man′), *n., pl.* **-men.** *Law.* a person to whom a remainder is devised.

re·mains (ri mānz′), *n.pl.* See under **remain,** *n.*

re·make (*v.* rē māk′; *n.* rē′māk′), *v.,* **-made, -mak·ing,** *n.* —*v.t.* to make anew; make over: *They have united under God to remake the world* (Newsweek). —*n.* a remade version of a motion picture, recording, etc.: *This is a remake of Alfred Hitchcock's fondly remembered 1935 mystery . . . based on the John Buchan novel* (Maclean's). —**re·mak′er,** *n.*

re·man (rē man′), *v.t.,* **-manned, -man·ning. 1.** to furnish with a fresh supply of men: *to reman a fleet.* **2.** to restore the manliness or courage of.

re·man·ci·pa·tion (rē′man sə pā′shən), *n.* (in Roman law) the act of retransferring.

re·mand (ri mand′, -mänd′), *v.t.* **1.** to send back. **2. a.** to send back (a prisoner or an accused person) to prison: *He is charged with treason and remanded for interrogation* (Time). **b.** to send (a case) back to the court it came from for further action there. **3.** to recall; revoke: *I will remand the order I despatched to my banker* (Charlotte Brontë).
—*n.* a remanding.
[< Late Latin *remandāre* < Latin *re-* back + *mandāre* to consign, order]

remand home, *British.* detention home: *Can detention in a remand home be regarded as educational?* (Manchester Guardian).

re·mand·ment (ri mand′mənt), *n.* a remanding.

rem·a·nence (rem′ə nəns), *n.* **1.** the state or quality of being remanent. **2.** *Physics.* the flux density remaining in a substance after the magnetizing force has ceased.

rem·a·nent (rem′ə nənt), *adj.* **1.** remaining. **2.** additional. [< Latin *remanēns, -entis,* present participle of *remanēre;* see REMAIN]

re·ma·nié (rə man yā′), *adj.* **1.** (of fossils) derived from an older bed or layer. **2.** recemented, as a glacier formed by the falling of fragments of ice.
—*n.* **1.** a characteristic portion of one formation occurring in another younger one. **2.** a fossil found in a bed of more recent origin than that in which it was first buried.
[< French *remanié,* past participle of *remanier* to handle again, change < *re-* + *manier* to handle < *main* hand < Latin *manus*]

re·mark (ri märk′), *v.t.* **1.** to say; speak; comment: *He remarked that my hands would be better for a wash.* **2.** to notice; observe: *Did you remark that queer cloud?* **3.** *Obsolete.* to distinguish: *His manner remarks him; there he sits* (Milton). —*v.i.* to make a remark; comment.
—*n.* **1.** something said in a few words; short statement; comment: *The president made a few remarks.* **2.** the act of noticing; observation. **3.** remarque.
[< French *remarquer* < *re-* again + Middle French *marquer,* variant of Old North French *merquier,* Old French *merchier* to mark, notice < Germanic (probably unrecorded Frankish *merkjan*)]
—**Syn.** *v.t.* **2.** note.

re·mark·a·ble (ri mär′kə bəl), *adj.* worthy of notice; unusual: *a remarkable memory. This story of Mongolian conquests is surely the most remarkable in all history* (H. G. Wells). —**re·mark′a·ble·ness,** *n.* —**Syn.** notable, noteworthy, extraordinary, singular. —**Ant.** commonplace.

re·mark·a·bly (ri mär′kə blē), *adv.* notably; unusually.

re·marque (ri märk′), *n.* in the graphic arts: **1.** a distinguishing mark indicating a particular stage of a plate, as a small sketch engraved on the margin of a plate, and usually removed after a fixed number of early proofs have been taken. **2.** a proof, print, or plate having such a distinguishing mark. [< French *remarque* < *remarquer;* see REMARK]

re·mar·riage (rē mar′ij), *n.* a second or subsequent marriage: *A special commission of the United Lutheran Church of America . . . has just called for a relaxation of the church's strict laws on divorce, remarriage, and birth control* (Newsweek).

re·mar·ry (rē mar′ē), *v.t., v.i.,* **-mar·ried, -mar·ry·ing.** to marry again: *Widows might remarry if they liked* (Frederic W. Farrar). *His property was confiscated and his wife remarried to another* (George Grote).

re·mas·ti·cate (rē mas′tə kāt), *v.t.,* **-cat·ed, -cat·ing.** to chew again, as the cud; ruminate.

Rem·brandt·esque (rem′bran tesk′), *adj.* in the manner or style of Rembrandt: *One goes through a vast Rembrandtesque shed opening upon a great sunny field* (H. G. Wells). [< *Rembrandt* van Rijn, 1606–1669, the Dutch painter + *-esque*]

re·meas·ure (rē mezh′ər, -mā′zhər), *v.t.,* **-ured, -ur·ing.** to measure again: *Measuring and remeasuring, with . . . tremendous strides, the length of the terrace* (Scott).

re·me·di·a·ble (ri mē′dē ə bəl), *adj.* that can be remedied or cured.

re·me·di·a·bly (ri mē′dē ə blē), *adv.* in a remediable manner or condition.

re·me·di·al (ri mē′dē əl), *adj.* **1.** remedying; curing; helping; relieving. **2.** intended to improve related study habits and skills: *Students who read poorly will have to take a course in remedial reading.* [< Late Latin *remediālis* < Latin *remedium;* see REMEDY]

re·me·di·al·ly (ri mē′dē ə lē), *adv.* so as to remedy.

re·me·di·a·tion (ri mē′dē ā′shən), *n.* the act or process of remedying: *Only one instructor attempted to familiarize the student with the symptoms, causes and remediation of severe reading disabilities* (New Yorker).

rem·e·di·less (rem′ə dē lis), *adj.* without remedy; incurable; irreparable.

rem·e·dy (rem′ə dē), *n., pl.* **-dies,** *v.,* **-died, -dy·ing.** —*n.* **1.** a means of removing or relieving diseases or any bad condition; cure: *Aspirin and a mustard plaster are two old cold remedies. Religion, and not atheism, is the true remedy for superstition* (Edmund Burke). **2.** a legal redress; legal means of enforcing a right or redressing a wrong. **3.** (in coinage) an allowance at the mint for deviation from standard weight and fineness.
—*v.t.* to put right; make right; cure: *A thorough cleaning remedied the trouble.*
[probably < Anglo-French *remedie,* Old French *remede,* learned borrowing from Latin *remedium* < *re-* again + *medērī* to heal]
—**Syn.** *n.* **1.** restorative, corrective. *-v.t.* See **cure.**

re·melt (rē melt′), *v.t., v.i.* to melt again.

re·mem·ber (ri mem′bər), *v.t.* **1.** to have (something) come into the mind again; call to mind; recall: *to remember a name. He suddenly remembered that he had left the windows open.* **2.** to keep in mind; take care not to forget: *Remember me when I'm gone.* **3.** to make a gift to; reward; tip: *Grandfather remembered us all in his will.* **4.** to mention (a person) as sending friendly greetings; recall to the mind of another: *He asked to be remembered to you.* **5.** *Archaic.* to remind.
—*v.i.* **1.** to have memory: *Dogs remember.* **2.** to recall something. **3.** *Archaic.* to have recollection: *I remember Of such a time* (Shakespeare). [< Old French *remembrer* < Latin *rememorārī* < *re-* again + *memor, -oris* mindful of] —**re·mem′ber·er,** *n.*
—**Syn.** *v.t.* **1. Remember, recall, recollect** mean to think of something again by an act of memory. **Remember** applies whether the act requires conscious effort or not: *I remember many stray incidents from my childhood.* **Recall** (as well as *recollect*) applies particularly when the act requires conscious effort: *It took me a long time to recall one curious incident.* **Recollect** suggests that the thing remembered is somewhat hazy: *As I recollect the incident occurred when I was about four.*

re·mem·ber·a·ble (ri mem′bər ə bəl), *adj.* that can be or is worthy of being remembered.

re·mem·brance (ri mem′brəns), *n.* **1.** the power to remember; act of remembering; memory. **2.** the state of being remembered: *America holds its heroes in grateful remembrance.* **3.** any thing or action that makes one remember a person; keepsake; souvenir. **remembrances,** greetings: *Give my remembrances to your sister when you write to her.*

Remembrance Day, November 11, the anniversary in Great Britain and Canada of cessation of fighting (1918) in World War I.

re·mem·branc·er (ri mem′brən sər), *n.* a person or thing that reminds one; reminder.

Re·mem·branc·er (ri mem′brən sər), *n.* *British.* **1.** any of certain officials of the Court of the Exchequer. The King's (or Queen's) Remembrancer, who collects the sovereign's debts, is the only one still in existence and serves as an officer of the Supreme Court. **2.** an officer of the corporation of the City of London.

re·merge (rē mėrj′), *v i.,* **-merged, -merg·ing.** to merge again: *A remoter realm, out of which we emerged, and into which we again remerge* (Spectator).

re·mex (rē′meks), *n.* singular of **remiges.**

rem·i·cle (rem′ə kəl), *n.* **1.** the outermost predigital of a bird's wing. **2.** the outermost feather attached to the second phalanx of the middle finger of a bird's wing.

rem·i·ges (rem′ə jēz) *n., plural of* **re·mex** (rē′meks). the feathers of a bird's wing that enable it to fly; flight feathers. [< Latin *rēmiges,* plural of *rēmex, -igis* oarsman < *rēmus* oar, rudder]

REMIGES

Remiges

re·mig·i·al (ri mij′ē əl), *adj.* of or having to do with the remiges. [< Latin *rēmex, -igis* oarsman (< *rēmus* oar, rudder) + English *-al*[1]]

rem·i·grant (rem′ə grənt), *n.* a person or animal that remigrates. Certain insects leave one plant and migrate to a different plant to breed, but a later generation returns to the original plant.

re·mi·grate (rē mī′grāt), *v.i.,* **-grat·ed, -grat·ing.** to migrate again or back.

re·mi·gra·tion (rē′mī grā′shən), *n.* a remigrating.

re·mil·i·ta·ri·za·tion (rē′mil ə tər ə zā′shən), *n.* **1.** the act of remilitarizing: *The German Federal Republic entered upon the* *path of remilitarization and was included in the military grouping of the western powers* (London Times). **2.** the state or condition of being remilitarized.

re·mil·i·ta·rize (rē mil′ə tə rīz), *v.t.,* **-rized, -riz·ing.** to militarize anew.

re·mind (ri mīnd′), *v.t.* to make (one) think (of something); cause to remember: *This picture reminds me of a story. The time of year reminds me how the months have gone* (Dickens). —*v.i.* to bring something to mind. [< *re-* again + *mind*[1], verb]

re·mind·er (ri mīn′dər), *n.* something to help one remember.

re·mind·ful (ri mīnd′fəl), *adj.* **1.** reminiscent: *keepsakes remindful of one's friends.* **2.** mindful: *to be remindful of one's duties.*

rem·i·nisce (rem′ə nis′), *v.i.,* **-nisced, -nisc·ing.** to talk or think about past experiences or events: *He reminisces of years gone by . . .* (Commentary). [back formation < *reminiscence*] —**rem′i·nis′cer,** *n.*

rem·i·nis·cence (rem′ə nis′əns), *n.* **1.** a remembering; recalling past happenings, etc. **2.** a thing that makes one remember or think of something else.

reminiscences, an account of something remembered; recollection: *reminiscences of college, reminiscences of an old man.*

[< Latin *reminīscentia* < *reminīscēns, -entis,* present participle of *reminīscī* remember < *re-* again + *min-,* root of *meminī* to remember, related to *mēns* mind]

rem·i·nis·cent (rem′ə nis′ənt), *adj.* **1.** recalling past events, etc.: *reminiscent talk.* **2.** awakening memories of something else; suggestive: *A manner reminiscent of a statelier age.* —**rem′i nis′cent·ly,** *adv.*

rem·i·nis·cen·tial (rem′ə nə sen′shəl), *adj.* of or having to do with reminiscence. —**rem′i·nis·cen′tial·ly,** *adv.*

re·mise[1] (ri mīz′), *v.t.,* **-mised, -mis·ing.** *Law.* to give up a claim to; surrender by deed: *to remise a right or property.* [< Middle French *remise* restoration, noun use of feminine past participle of Old French *remettre,* learned borrowing from Latin *remittere;* see REMIT]

re·mise[2] (ri mēz′), *n.* **1.** a house for a carriage. **2.** a carriage hired from a livery stable. [< French *remise* < Old French *remettre;* see REMISE[1]]

re·miss (ri mis′), *adj.* **1.** careless; slack; neglectful; negligent: *A policeman who lets a thief escape is remiss in his duty.* **2.** lacking force or energy. [< Latin *remissus,* past participle of *remittere* < *re-* back + *mittere* let go, send] —**re·miss′ly,** *adv.* —**re·miss′ness,** *n.* —**Syn. 1.** derelict, thoughtless. **2.** mild.

re·mis·si·bil·i·ty (ri mis′ə bil′ə tē), *n.* remissible quality or state.

re·mis·si·ble (ri mis′ə bəl), *adj.* that can be remitted.

re·mis·sion (ri mish′ən), *n.* **1.** a letting off (from debt, punishment, etc.): *The bankrupt sought remission of his debts.* **2.** pardon; forgiveness: *Remission of sins is promised to those who repent.* **3.** a lessening (of pain, force, labor, etc.): *The storm continued without remission.* **4.** *Obsolete.* relaxation.

re·mis·sive (ri mis′iv), *adj.* **1.** inclined to remission. **2.** characterized by remission.

re·mit (ri mit′), *v.,* **-mit·ted, -mit·ting,** *n.* —*v.i.* **1.** to send money to a person or place: *Enclosed is our bill: please remit.* **2.** to become less. —*v.t.* **1.** to send (money due). **2.** to refrain from carrying out; refrain from exacting; cancel: *The governor remitted the prisoner's punishment.* **3.** to pardon; forgive: *the power to remit sins.* **4.** to make less; decrease: *After we had rowed the boat into calm water we remitted our efforts. In return the Government remits income tax on my subscriptions* (London Times). **5.** to send back (a case) to a lower court for further action. **6.** to put back. **7.** to postpone. **8.** *Obsolete.* to send back, especially to prison. —*n.* **1.** the transfer of a case from one court or judge to another. **2.** *Obsolete.* remission; pardon.

[< Latin *remittere* send back, let go < *re-* back + *mittere* let go, send]

—**Syn.** *v.i.* **2,** *v.t.* **4.** abate, slacken, diminish.

re·mit·ment (ri mit′mənt), *n.* remittance.

re·mit·ta·ble (ri mit′ə bəl), *adj.* that can be remitted: *Cash dividends could be paid in whatever currency might be remittable from Brazil* (Wall Street Journal).

re·mit·tal (ri mit′əl), *n.* remission. [< *remit* + *-al*[2]]

re·mit·tance (ri mit′əns), *n.* **1.** a sending money to someone at a distance. **2.** the money that is sent: *Thus he was able to send his friend regular remittances; and in the August of 1851 a new source of income opened for Marx* (Edmund Wilson).

remittance man, an emigrant who is supported or assisted by remittances from home: *I was a combination Sorbonne student and remittance man* (New Yorker).

re·mit·tence (ri mit′əns), *n.* a remitting.

re·mit·ten·cy (ri mit′ən sē), *n.* a remitting.

re·mit·tent (ri mit′ənt), *adj.* lessening for a time; lessening at intervals: *a remittent type of fever.* —**re·mit′tent·ly,** *adv.*

remittent fever, a fever in which the symptoms lessen and then return, without ever disappearing entirely.

re·mit·ter[1] (ri mit′ər), *n.* **1.** *Law.* the principle or operation by which a person having two titles to an estate and receiving it by the later or more defective one is adjudged to hold it by the earlier and more valid one. **2.** *Law.* the remitting of a case to another court for decision. **3.** restoration, as to a former right or condition.

re·mit·ter[2] (ri mit′ər), *n.* a person or thing that remits.

re·mit·tor (ri mit′ər), *n. Law.* a person who makes a remittance.

re·mix (rē miks′), *v.t.,* **-mixed** or **-mixt, -mix·ing.** to mix again: *It may then be overhauled and remixed with more earth* (L. F. Allen).

rem·nant (rem′nənt), *n.* **1.** a small part left: *Since the factory moved, this town has only a remnant of its former population. Though terribly offended, he retained some remnant of dignity.* **2.** a piece of cloth, ribbon, lace, etc., left after the rest has been used or sold: *She bought a remnant of silk at a bargain.* —*adj. Archaic.* remaining. [< Old French *remenant,* present participle of *remenoir,* also *remanoir,* and *remaindre;* see REMAIN] —**Syn.** *n.* **1.** rest, fragment.

rem·nan·tal (rem nan′təl), *adj.* of or having to do with a remnant.

re·mod·el (rē mod′əl), *v.t.,* **-eled, -el·ing** or (*especially British*) **-elled, -el·ling. 1.** to model again. **2.** to make over: *The old barn was remodeled into a house.*

re·mod·el·er (rē mod′ə lər), *n.* a person who remodels: *In this historic neighborhood, remodelers were busy restoring to their original elegance dozens of 18th century row houses* (Time).

re·mod·el·ler (rē mod′ə lər), *n. Especially British.* remodeler: *I will pass to Bacon, the great remodeller of science* (William R. Grove).

re·mod·el·ment (ri mod′əl mənt), *n.* **1.** a remodeling. **2.** a being remodeled.

re·mod·i·fi·ca·tion (rē′mod ə fə kā′shən), *n.* the act of modifying again; a repeated modification or change.

re·mod·i·fy (rē mod′ə fī), *v.t.,* **-fied, -fy·ing.** to modify again; shape anew; re-form: *Before America was remodified by the arts of Europe* (Thomas Hope).

re·mo·lade (rā′mə läd′), *n.* remoulade.

re·mold (rē mōld′), *v.t.* to mold or shape over again or in a new way.

re·mon·e·ti·za·tion (rē mon′ə tə zā′shən, -mun′-), *n.* **1.** a remonetizing. **2.** a being remonetized.

re·mon·e·tize (rē mon′ə tīz, -mun′-), *v.t.,* **-tized, -tiz·ing.** to restore to use as legal tender: *to remonetize silver.* [American English < *re-* again + *monetize;* probably patterned on *demonetize*]

re·mon·strance (ri mon′strəns), *n.* **1.** a protest; complaint: *Almost every word . . . is . . . in the nature of remonstrance for some breach of decorum* (George Bernard Shaw). **2.** *Historical.* a formal statement in protest to a ruler, government, etc. **3.** *Obsolete.* demonstration; manifestation: *remonstrance of my hidden power* (Shakespeare). [< Medieval Latin *remonstrantia* < *remonstrare;* see REMONSTRATE]

Re·mon·strant (ri mon′strənt), *n.* a member of the Arminian party in the Dutch Reformed Church. [< Medieval Latin *remonstrans, -antis,* present participle of *remonstrare;* see REMONSTRATE]

re·mon·strant (ri mon′strənt), *adj.* remonstrating; protesting. —*n.* a person who remonstrates. [< *Remonstrant*] —**re·mon′strant·ly,** *adv.*

re·mon·strate (ri mon′strāt), *v.,* **-strat·ed, -strat·ing.** —*v.i.* to object; protest: *The teacher remonstrated with the boy about his low grades. The people of Connecticut . . . remonstrated against the bill* (George Bancroft). —*v.t.* **1.** to reason or plead in protest. **2.** *Obsolete.* to point out; show. [< Medieval Latin *remonstrare* point out, show < Latin *re-* back + *mōnstrāre* point out < *mōnstrum* a sign. Compare MONSTER.]

re·mon·stra·tion (rē′mon strā′shən, rem′-ən-), *n.* a remonstrating: *He went many times over the case of his wife, the judgement of the doctor, his own repeated remonstration* (Harper's).

re·mon·stra·tive (ri mon′strə tiv), *adj.* remonstrating.

re·mon·stra·tor (ri mon′strā tər), *n.* a remonstrant.

re·mon·tant (ri mon′tənt), *adj.* (of roses) blooming more than once in a season. —*n.* a remontant rose. [< French *remontant,* present participle of *remonter* < Old French; see REMOUNT]

rem·on·toir (rem′ən twär′), *n.* a device in a clock or watch that keeps action of a pendulum or balance uniform. [< French *remontoir* < *remonter;* see REMOUNT]

rem·o·ra (rem′ər ə), *n.* **1.** any of certain fishes, found especially in tropical waters, with a sucker on the top of the head by which it can attach itself to ships, other fishes, etc., for transportation: *This is the remora, hitchhiker of the oceans, known to seafaring men the world over as the "pilot fish" or "shark sucker"* (Science News Letter). **2.** *Obsolete.* an obstacle; obstruction. [< Latin *remora* delay, hindrance < *re-* back + *mora* a wait, pause (because it was believed that if it attached itself to a ship, the ship's course would be hindered)]

Remoras (def. 1—2 to 3 ft. long) attached to sand shark

re·morse (ri môrs′), *n.* **1.** deep, painful regret for having done wrong: *The thief felt remorse for his crime and confessed. The critic else proceeds without remorse, Seizes your fame* (Alexander Pope). **2.** *Obsolete.* sorrow; pity; compassion: *the tears of soft remorse* (Shakespeare). [< Old French *remors* < Latin *remordēre* to disturb < *re-* again + *mordēre* to bite] —**Syn. 1.** compunction, contrition. See **regret.**

re·morse·ful (ri môrs′fəl), *adj.* feeling or expressing remorse: *So groan'd Sir Lancelot in remorseful pain* (Tennyson). —**re·morse′ful·ly,** *adv.* —**re·morse′ful·ness,** *n.*

re·morse·less (ri môrs′lis), *adj.* without remorse; pitiless; cruel. —**re·morse′less·ly,** *adv.* —**re·morse′less·ness,** *n.*

re·mote (ri mōt′), *adj.,* **-mot·er, -mot·est,** *n.* —*adj.* **1.** far away; far off: *a remote country. The North Pole is a remote part of the world.* **2.** out of the way; secluded: *This remote village is so out of the way that mail comes only once a week.* **3.** distant: *a remote relative, the remote past.* **4.** slight; faint: *I haven't the remotest idea what you mean.* **5.** *Obsolete.* foreign or alien (to). —*n.* a radio or television program originating outside of the studio: *In John A. Schneider's dream of 1975, there was . . . Ed Sullivan bringing in a remote from one of the big craters of the moon* (New York Times). [< Latin *remōtus,* past participle of *removēre;* see REMOVE] —**re·mote′ness,** *n.* —**Syn.** *adj.* **1.** See **distant.**

remote control, the operation or control from a distance of a machine, action, etc., by electrical impulses, radio, etc.: *a calculator or television set operated by remote control, an airplane flying by remote control. As air battle commanders watch the picture, they can direct interception by remote control* (Time).

re·mote-con·trol (ri mōt′kən trōl′), *adj.* by remote control: *remote-control steering or flying, remote-control television.*

re·mote-con·trolled (ri mōt′kən trōld′), *adj.* remote-control.

re·mote·ly (ri mōt′lē), *adv.* in a remote manner; distantly; slightly: *These points are not even remotely connected.*

re·mo·tion (ri mō′shən), *n.* **1.** removal. **2.** remoteness. **3.** *Obsolete.* departure.

re·mou·lade or **ré·mou·lade** (rā′mə läd′; *French* rā mü läd′), *n.* a sauce, usually containing hard-boiled egg yolks, eggs, capers, oil, vinegar, etc., used as a salad dressing. Also, **remolade.** [< French *rémoulade,* earlier *ramolade;* origin unknown; form influenced by French *remoulade* farrier's unguent < Italian *remolata* < Late Latin *remolum*]

re·mould (rē mōld′), *v.t. Especially British.* remold.

re·mount (*v.* rē mount′; *n., adj.* rē′mount′, rē mount′), *v.t.* **1.** to mount again: *to remount a picture.* **2.** to furnish with fresh horses. —*v.i.* **1.** to mount a horse or other animal again. **2.** to move upward again.
—*n.* a fresh horse, or a supply of fresh horses, for use: *Some of the cavalry had received remounts* (Sir Arthur Conan Doyle).
—*adj.* of or having to do with remounts.
[< Old French *remonter* < *re-* again + *monter.* Compare MOUNT[1].]

re·mov·a·bil·i·ty (ri mü′və bil′ə tē), *n.* the quality or state of being removable.

re·mov·a·ble (ri mü′və bəl), *adj.* that can be removed. —**re·mov′a·ble·ness,** *n.*

re·mov·a·bly (ri mü′və blē), *adv.* so as to be removable.

re·mov·al (ri mü′vəl), *n.* **1.** a removing; taking away: *After the removal of the soup, fish was served.* **2.** change of place: *The store announces its removal to larger quarters.* **3.** dismissal from an office or position.

re·move (ri müv′), *v.,* **-moved, -mov·ing,** *n.* —*v.t.* **1.** to move from a place or position; take off; take away: *People remove their hats in a theater.* **2.** to get rid of; put an end to: *An experiment removed all our doubt about the fact that water is made up of two gases.* **3.** to kill. **4.** to dismiss from an office or position: *to remove an official for taking bribes.* —*v.i.* to go away; move away: *till Birnam wood remove to Dunsinane* (Shakespeare).
—*n.* **1.** a moving away: *It is an English proverb that three removes are as bad as a fire* (Cardinal Newman). **2.** a step or degree of distance: *His cruelty was only one remove from crime. At every remove the mountain seemed smaller. It's a far remove from Paradise Is Spanish port* (John Masefield). **3.** *British.* one course of a meal.
[< Old French *remouvoir* < Latin *removēre* < *re-* back + *movēre* to move]
—**Syn.** *v.t.* **1.** dislodge, shift, displace.

re·moved (ri müvd′), *adj.* **1.** distant; remote: *a house far removed from the city.* **2.** separated by one or more steps or degrees of relationship: *a cousin once removed.*

re·mov·ed·ness (ri mü′vid nis), *n.* the quality or state of being removed.

re·mov·er (ri mü′vər), *n.* a person or thing that removes: *a bottle of ink remover.*

rem·pli (räN plē′), *adj. Heraldry.* covered with a different tincture, except for a bordering space: *a rempli chief.* [< French *rempli,* past participle of *remplir* to fill up < *re-* again + *emplir* to fill < Latin *implēre.* Compare IMPLEMENT.]

re·mu·da (*Spanish* rā mü′ᴛʜä; *Anglicized* ri myü′də), *n.* the saddle horses of a ranch, from which the cowboys choose their mounts for the day: *At night, it would make the wearer invisible, so he could steal horses from the best guarded remuda* (Harper's). [American English < American Spanish *remuda* spare horse < *re-* again + *mudar* to change < Latin *mūtāre*]

re·mu·ner·ate (ri myü′nə rāt), *v.t.,* **-at·ed, -at·ing.** to pay for work, services, trouble, etc.; reward: *The boy who returned the lost jewels was remunerated. The harvest will remunerate the laborers for their toil.* [< Latin *remūnerāre* (with English *-ate*[1]) < *re-* back + *mūnerāre* to give < *mūnus, -eris* gift]
—**Syn.** recompense. See **pay.**

re·mu·ner·a·tion (ri myü′nə rā′shən), *n.* reward; pay; payment: *Remuneration to employes for the quarter was down $3 million* (Wall Street Journal).

re·mu·ner·a·tive (ri myü′nə rā′tiv, -nər ə-), *adj.* paying; profitable: *remunerative work.* —**re·mu′ner·a′tive·ly,** *adv.* —**re·mu′ner·a′tive·ness,** *n.*

re·mu·ner·a·tor (ri myü′nə rā′tər), *n.* a person who remunerates.

re·mur·mur (rē mėr′mər), *Poetic.* —*v.i.* to respond or resound with murmurs. —*v.t.* to repeat in murmurs: *The trembling trees . . . Her fate remurmur to the silver flood* (Alexander Pope).

Re·mus (rē′məs), *n. Roman Mythology.* the twin brother of Romulus. As children they were nursed by a wolf; later Romulus founded Rome and slew Remus for leaping contemptuously over the wall of his new city.

Ren·ais·sance (ren′ə säns; ren′ə säns′, -zäns′; ri nā′səns), *n.* **1.** the great revival of art and learning in Europe during the 1300's, 1400's, and 1500's. **2.** the period of time when this revival occurred. **3.** the style of art, architecture, etc., of this period. —*adj.* of or having to do with the Renaissance: *Renaissance sculpture.*
[< French, Old French *renaissance* < *re-* again + *naissance* birth < Latin *nāscentia* birth, origin < *nāscī* be born. Compare NATIVE.]

ren·ais·sance (ren′ə säns; ren′ə säns′, -zäns′; ri nā′səns), *n.* a revival; new birth: *a renaissance of free men* (Newsweek).

Renaissance architecture, the style of architecture imitating the classical Roman. It originated in Italy in the first half of the 1400's, afterward spreading over Europe.

Early Renaissance Architecture
Cappella Pazzi, Florence

Re·nais·sant (ri nā′sənt), *adj.* of or having to do with the Renaissance. [< French *renaissant*]

re·nal (rē′nəl), *adj.* of the kidneys; having to do with the kidneys: *a renal artery. The veins which carry blood to the kidneys constitute the renal portal system* (Hegner and Stiles). [< Latin *rēnālis* < *rēn, rēnis* kidney]

renal corpuscle, one of the filtering structures in the cortex of the kidney, composed of a glomerulus and Bowman's capsule; Malpighian body: *The renal corpuscles with the uriniferous tubules are the essential excretory units in the vertebrate animals generally* (A. Franklin Shull).

renal gland or **capsule,** the adrenal gland; suprarenal gland.

re·name (rē nām′), *v.t.,* **-named, -nam·ing.** to give a new name to; name again.

Ren·ard (ren′ərd), *n.* Reynard, the nickname for a fox.

Re·nas·cence (ri nas′əns, -nā′səns), *n.* the Renaissance.

re·nas·cence (ri nas′əns, -nā′səns), *n.* **1.** a revival; new birth; renewal: *a renascence of religion. She wanted to lie . . . and wait, as a patient animal waits, for her renascence* (New Yorker). **2.** a being renascent: *a period of moral renascence* (H.G. Wells).

re·nas·cent (ri nas′ənt, -nā′sənt), *adj.* being born again; reviving; springing again into being or vigor. [< Latin *renāscēns, -entis,* present participle of *renāscī* < *re-* again + *nāscī* be born. Compare NATIVE.]

re·na·tion·al·ise (rē nash′ə nə līz, -nash′nə-), *v.t.,* **-ised, -is·ing.** *Especially British.* renationalize.

re·na·tion·al·i·za·tion (rē nash′ə nə lə zā′shən, -nash′nə-), *n.* a renationalizing or being renationalized: *With the return of the Conservative Government measures of renationalization . . . are no longer risks to be discounted* (London Times).

re·na·tion·al·ize (rē nash′ə nə līz, -nash′nə-), *v.t.,* **-ized, -iz·ing.** to nationalize again; restore to government control: *Socialists have repeatedly threatened to renationalize steel as soon as possible if the conservatives denationalize it* (Newsweek).

re·nav·i·gate (rē nav′ə gāt), *v.i., v.t.,* **-gat·ed, -gat·ing.** to navigate again.

re·nav·i·ga·tion (rē′nav ə gā′shən), *n.* the act of renavigating.

ren·con·tre (ren kon′tər; *French* räN kôN′trə), *n.* a rencounter. [< French, Middle French *rencontre;* see RENCOUNTER]

ren·coun·ter (ren koun′tər), *n.* **1.** a hostile meeting; conflict; battle; duel. **2.** a chance meeting: *All my acquaintance with him was confined to an occasional rencounter in the hall* (Charlotte Brontë).
—*v.t.* to come upon: *I had the good fortune to rencounter you at Durrisdeer* (Robert Louis Stevenson). —*v.i.* to meet in conflict.
[< Middle French, Old French *rencontre* < *rencontrer* to meet < *re-* again + *encontrer.* Compare ENCOUNTER.]

rend (rend), *v.,* **rent, rend·ing.** —*v.t.* **1.** to pull apart violently; tear: *Wolves will rend a lamb.* **2.** to split: *Lightning rent the tree.* **3.** to disturb violently: *John was rent by a wish to keep the money he found and the knowledge that he ought to return it.* **4.** to remove with force or violence: *I will surely rend the kingdom from thee* (I Kings 11:11). —*v.i.* to rip. [Old English *rendan*] —**rend′er,** *n.*

ren·der (ren′dər), *v.t.* **1.** to cause to become; make: *An accident has rendered him helpless.* **2.** to give; do: *She rendered us a great service by her help.* **3.** to offer for consideration, approval, payment, etc.; hand in; report: *The treasurer rendered an account of all the money spent.* **4.** to give in return: *Render thanks for your blessings.* **5.** to pay as due: *The conquered rendered tribute to the conqueror.* **6.** to bring out the meaning of; represent: *The actor rendered the part of Hamlet well.* **7.** to play or sing (music): *to render an old English ballad.* **8.** to change from one language to another; translate: *to render "Peer Gynt" into English.* **9.** to give up; surrender. **10.** to melt (fat, etc.); clarify or extract by melting: *Fat from hogs is rendered for lard.* **11.** to cover (bricks, stone, etc.) with a first coat of plaster. —*v.i. Obsolete.* to make return or recompense.
—*n.* **1.** a first coat of plaster. **2.** *Law.* a return; payment in money, kind, or service made by a tenant to his superior.
[< Old French *rendre* < Vulgar Latin *rendere,* alteration of Latin *reddere* give as due; to pay < *re-* back, again + *dare* give] —**ren′der·er,** *n.*

ren·der·a·ble (ren′dər ə bəl), *adj.* that can be rendered.

ren·der·ing (ren′də ring), *n.* **1. a.** the act of yielding, giving, offering, etc.: *Love itself is, in its highest state, the rendering of an exquisite praise to body and soul* (John Ruskin). **b.** that which is rendered or given: *Alas! our renderings are nothing . . .; we are like the barren field* (Philip Henry). **2.** translation; interpretation: *Correct rendering is very often conspicuously absent from our authorized version of the Old Testament* (Matthew Arnold). **3. a.** reproduction; representation: *The painter has shown himself extremely skilful in his rendering of curious effects of light* (London Times). **b.** performance: *The Opera Society had given an excellent rendering of "Patience" in the Founders' Hall* (Graham Greene).

ren·dez·vous (rän′də vü), *n., pl.* **-vous** (-vüz), *v.,* **-voused** (-vüd), **-vous·ing** (-vü′ing). —*n.* **1.** an appointment or engagement to meet at a fixed place or time; meeting by agreement: *Each tribe had usually some fixed place of rendezvous* (Scott). *This country has a rendezvous with destiny* (Franklin D. Roosevelt). **2.** a meeting place; gathering place: *The family had two favorite rendezvous, the library and the garden.* **3.** a place agreed on for a meeting at a certain time, especially of troops, ships, etc. **4.** the meeting of two or more persons or objects at a prearranged time and place: *Gemini's primary purpose is to practice rendezvous in earth orbit* (Time).
—*v.i.* to meet at a rendezvous. —*v.t. U.S.* to bring together (troops, ships, space capsules, etc.) at a fixed place.
[< Middle French *rendezvous* < *rendez-vous* betake (literally, present) yourself < Old French *rendre* (see RENDER), *vous* < Latin *vōs* you, plural]

ren·di·tion (ren dish′ən), *n.* **1.** a rendering: *Not the newspaper articles which were a sensationalized rendition of his tour . . .* (Saturday Review). **2.** the rendering of a dramatic part, music, etc. **3.** a translation. [< Middle French *rendition* < Old French *rendre;* see RENDER]

rend·rock (rend′rok′), *n.* an explosive mixture used chiefly in blasting, containing nitroglycerine, kieselguhr, wood pulp, etc.

ren·e·gade (ren′ə gād), *n., adj., v.,* **-gad·ed, -gad·ing.** —*n.* a deserter from a religious faith, a political party, etc.; traitor; one who abandons his principles or his people. —*adj.* deserting; apostate; disloyal: *But he is not, like Joyce, a bitterly renegade Catholic* (The Reporter). —*v.i.* to turn renegade. [< Spanish *renegado* renegado < Medieval Latin *renegare* to deny; see RENEGE] —**Syn.** *n.* recreant, backslider. *-adj.* traitorous.

ren·e·ga·do (ren′ə gā′dō), *n., pl.* **-does,** *adj., v.i. Archaic.* renegade. [< Spanish *renegado* < Medieval Latin *renegare;* see RENEGE]

re·nege (ri nig′, -nēg′), *v.,* **-neged, -neg·ing,** *n.* —*v.i.* **1.** to fail to follow suit when able to do so; revoke: *It is against the rules of cards to renege.* **2.** *Informal.* to back out; fail to keep a promise: *Most of the 57 members who had backed an amendment to admit women reneged* (Newsweek). —*v.t. Archaic.* to deny; renounce.

—*n.* a failure to follow suit in cardplaying when able to do so; revoke.
[< Medieval Latin *renegare* < Latin *re-* back + *negāre* deny] —**re·neg′er,** *n.*

re·ne·go·ti·a·ble (rē′ni gō′shē ə bəl, -shə-bəl), *adj.* that can be renegotiated: *Average profits on the much larger renegotiable defense business have plummeted* (Wall Street Journal).

re·ne·go·ti·ate (rē′ni gō′shē āt), *v.t., v.i.,* **-at·ed, -at·ing.** to negotiate again or anew, especially a contract, to eliminate excessive profits.

re·ne·go·ti·a·tion (rē′ni gō′shē ā′shən), *n.* a renegotiating or being renegotiated: *Far from encouraging is the threat of renegotiation of profits on Government contracts* (Wall Street Journal).

re·nerve (rē nėrv′), *v.t.,* **-nerved, -nerv·ing.** to restore vigor or courage to.

re·new (ri nü′, -nyü′), *v.t.* **1.** to make new again; make like new; restore: *Rain renews the greenness of the fields.* **2.** to make spiritually new: *Grant that we . . . may daily be renewed by thy holy spirit* (Book of Common Prayer). **3.** to begin again; get again; say, do, or give again: *to renew an attack, one's youth, one's vows, or one's efforts.* **4.** to replace by new material or a new thing of the same sort; fill again: *The well renews itself no matter how much water is taken away.* **5.** to give or get for a new period: *We renewed our lease for another year.* —*v.i.* **1.** to renew a lease, note, etc. **2.** to begin again. **3.** to become new again. —**re·new′er,** *n.*
—**Syn.** *v.t.* **1,** *v.i.* **3. Renew, restore, renovate** mean to put back in a new or former condition. **Renew** means to put back in a condition like new something that has lost its freshness, force, or vigor: *He renewed the finish of the table.* **Restore** means to put back in its original, former, or normal condition something that has been damaged, worn out, partly ruined, etc.: *That old Spanish mission has been restored.* **Renovate** means to put in good condition or make like new by cleaning, repairing, redecorating, etc.: *The store was renovated.*

re·new·a·bil·i·ty (ri nü′ə bil′ə tē, -nyü′-), *n.* the quality or condition of being renewable: *The original complaint . . . charged the company had misrepresented in advertising the renewability of its policies* (Wall Street Journal).

re·new·a·ble (ri nü′ə bəl, -nyü′-), *adj.* that can be renewed: *a renewable contract.*

re·new·al (ri nü′əl, -nyü′-), *n.* a renewing or being renewed: *When hot weather comes there will be a renewal of interest in swimming.*

re·new·ed·ly (ri nü′id lē, -nyü′-), *adv.* anew.

R. Eng., Royal Engineers.

ren·i·form (ren′ə fôrm, rē′nə-), *adj.* kidney-shaped: *a reniform leaf, a reniform shell.* [< Latin *rēn, rēnis* kidney + English *-form*]

Reniform Leaf

re·nin (rē′nin), *n.* a protein enzyme in the kidney that raises blood pressure when injected into the blood stream: *Page made important discoveries on the workings of renin, an enzyme secreted by the kidney when it is starved of blood* (Time). [< Latin *rēn, rēnis* kidney + English *-in*]

ren·i·punc·ture (ren′ə pungk′chər, rē′nə-), *n.* surgical puncture of the capsule of the kidney, for relief of pain. [< Latin *rēn, rēnis* kidney + English *puncture*]

re·ni·ten·cy (ri nī′tən sē, ren′ə-), *n.* resistance; recalcitrance.

re·ni·tent (ri nī′tənt, ren′ə-), *adj.* **1.** resisting pressure; resistant. **2.** recalcitrant. [< French *rénitent,* learned borrowing from Latin *renītēns, -entis,* present participle of *renītī* to resist < *re-* back + *nītī* to struggle, fight]

ren·net (ren′it), *n.* **1.** a mass of curdled milk found in the fourth stomach of a calf or other ruminant. **2.** an extract of this stomach, containing rennin, used for curdling milk in making cheese, rennet pudding (as junket), etc.: *The milk proteins are clotted, either by the action of lactic acid produced by bacteria growing in the milk, or by the addition of rennet* (Science News). [Middle English *rennet* < *rennen* to run, Old English *rinnan,* or < Scandinavian (compare Old Icelandic *renna*)]

rennet pepsin, pepsin from the stomach of the calf.

rennet stomach, the abomasum of a ruminant.

ren·nin (ren′in), *n.* a gastric enzyme that coagulates or curdles milk. It occurs in young infants, in calves, and also in certain lower animals and plants.

re·nog·ra·phy (rə nog′rə fē), *n.* the study of the kidneys by means of radiography: *To assist in the appraisal of kidney function, the new technique of renography is invaluable* (Frank P. Mathews). [< Latin *rēn, rēnis* kidney + English *-graphy*]

re·nom·i·nate (rē nom′ə nāt), *v.t.,* **-nat·ed, -nat·ing.** to nominate again.

re·nom·i·na·tion (rē′nom ə nā′shən), *n.* a nominating or being nominated again.

re·nom·i·nee (rē nom′ə nē′), *n.* a person who is renominated.

re·nounce (ri nouns′), *v.,* **-nounced, -nounc·ing.** —*v.t.* **1.** to declare that one gives up; give up entirely; give up: *He renounces his claim to the money. The shipwrecked sailor renounced all hope of rescue.* **2.** to cast off; refuse to recognize as one's own: *He renounced his disobedient son.* **3.** to give up, surrender, or resign by a greater or lesser sacrifice of one's own wishes or feelings: *The mind which renounces, once and for all, a futile hope, has its compensations in evergrowing calm* (George Gissing). **4.** (in card games) to play (a suit) different from that led, having no card of the suit led. —*v.i.* **1.** to make formal surrender. **2.** to play a card of a different suit from that led.
[< Old French *renoncer,* learned borrowing from Latin *renūntiāre* < *re-* back + *nūntiāre* to announce < *nūntius* messenger]
—**Syn.** *v.t.* **1.** forego, forsake, relinquish. **2.** repudiate.

re·nounce·a·ble (ri noun′sə bəl), *adj.* that can be renounced.

re·nounce·ment (ri nouns′mənt), *n.* the act of renouncing; renunciation.

re·nounc·er (ri noun′sər), *n.* a person who renounces; person who disowns or disclaims.

ren·o·vate (ren′ə vāt), *v.,* **-vat·ed, -vat·ing,** *adj.* —*v.t.* **1.** to make new again; make over; restore to good condition: *to renovate a garment. He had cleaned and renovated the dark little hole of a cabin* (Joseph Conrad). **2.** to restore to vigor; invigorate; refresh. **3.** make over in a new or better form; regenerate: *We want men and women who shall renovate life and our social state* (Emerson).
—*adj. Archaic,* renovated.
[< Latin *renovāre* (with English *-ate*[1]) < *re-* again + *novāre* make new < *novus* new]
—**Syn.** *v.t.* **1.** See **renew.**

ren·o·vat·er (ren′ə vā′tər), *n.* renovator.

ren·o·va·tion (ren′ə vā′shən), *n.* a restoration to good condition; renewal.

ren·o·va·tor (ren′ə vā′tər), *n.* a person or thing that renews or restores.

re·nown (ri noun′), *n.* **1.** fame: *A hero in war often wins renown.* **2.** *Obsolete.* **a.** report; rumor. **b.** reputation: *a young gentlewoman of a most chaste renown* (Shakespeare).
—*v.t.* to make famous: *The things of fame that do renown this city* (Shakespeare). —*v.i.* to brag; swagger.
[< Anglo-French *renoun,* Old French *renon,* or *renom* < *renommer* make famous < *re-* again, re- + *nommer* to name < Latin *nōmināre* < *nōmen, -inis* name]
—**Syn.** *n.* **1.** celebrity, distinction.

re·nowned (ri nound′), *adj.* famed; famous: *Peace hath her victories No less renowned than war* (Milton). —**Syn.** See **famous.**

rens·se·laer·ite (ren′sə lə rīt, ren′sə lãr′-īt), *n.* a variety of talc with a fine, compact texture that can be worked on a lathe. [American English < Stephen Van *Rensselaer,* 1764-1839, an American statesman]

rent[1] (rent), *n.* **1.** a regular payment for the use of property. **2.** *Economics.* what is paid for the use of natural resources. **3.** a house or other property for which rent is received. **4.** *Obsolete.* a revenue; income: *What are thy rents? What are thy comings-in?* (Shakespeare).
for rent, to be given in return for rent paid: *The apartment is for rent.*
—*v.t.* **1.** to pay for the use of (property): *We rent a house from Mr. Smith.* **2.** to receive pay for the use of (property): *He rents several other houses.*
—*v.i.* to be leased or let for rent: *This farm rents for $1,500 a year.*
[< Old French *rente* < Vulgar Latin *rendita* < *rendere;* see RENDER]

rent[2] (rent), *n.* **1.** a torn place; tear; split: *a rent in a shirt. See what a rent the envious Casca made* (Shakespeare). **2.** a break of relations; separation; schism; rupture. [< obsolete *rent* tear, variant of *rend*]
—*adj.* torn; split.
—*v.* the past tense and past participle of **rend:** *The tree was rent by the wind.*
[past participle of *rend*] —**Syn.** *n.* **1.** breach.

rent·a·bil·i·ty (ren′tə bil′ə tē), *n.* **1.** the quality of being rentable. **2.** the capacity of a property to produce income above cost of up-keep.

rent·a·ble (ren′tə bəl), *adj.* that can be rented.

rent-a-car (rent′ə kär′), *n. U.S.* a car rented for a day, week, etc., for a fixed sum or according to mileage: *Hotel reservations, sightseeing arrangements, rent-a-cars, etc., are all taken care of* (New Yorker).

rent·al (ren′təl), *n.* **1.** *U.S.* an amount received or paid as rent: *The yearly rental of her house is $4,000.* **2.** a list of tenants and of rents received or due. **3.** an apartment or house offered for rent: *There are not many rentals available in Fairfield County.*
—*adj.* of or in rent: *a rental agent.*
[< Anglo-French or Medieval Latin (England) *rentale,* both < Old French *rente* < Vulgar Latin *rendita* < *rendere;* see RENDER]

rental library, a circulating library that makes a charge for lending books.

rent control, the regulation of rent by a government.

rente (räNt), *n. French.* income; revenue.

ren·ten·mark (ren′tən märk′), *n.* a temporary German mark used in 1923 and 1924, representing a mortgage of all German property: *All Reichsmarks were called in and rentenmarks issued in exchange—one trillion Reichsmarks for one rentenmark* (Wall Street Journal). [< German *Rentenmark* < *Rente* revenue (< French *rente*) + *Mark* mark, unit of currency]

rent·er (ren′tər), *n.* a person who pays rent for using another's property. —**Syn.** lessee.

rentes (räNt), *n.pl.* **1.** the interest paid on French government bonds. **2.** such bonds. [< French *rentes,* plural of *rente* rent, income, revenue < Old French *rente;* see RENT[1]]

ren·tier (räN tyā′), *n. French.* a person who has a fixed income, as from lands, stocks, etc.: *Any observer . . . would have taken them for good rentiers, given to sport, literature, art, and especially to music* (New Yorker).

ren·tière (räN tyer′), *n. French.* a woman rentier.

rent party, a party to which admission is charged for the purpose of paying the rent of the host: *Monk was playing jazz at . . . rent parties up in Harlem* (Time).

rent roll, *Especially British.* a list of rents received or due.

rent-seck (rent′sek′), *n.* (formerly) a rent established with the agreement that if the tenant fell behind in payments the owner could not seize the tenant's goods. [< Anglo-French *rente secque* (literally) dry rent; *rente* < Vulgar Latin *rendita* < *rendere* (see RENDER), *secque* < Latin *siccus* dry, sec]

re·nu·mer·ate (rē nü′mə rāt, -nyü′-), *v.t.,* **-at·ed, -at·ing.** to count or number again.

re·nun·ci·ant (ri nun′sē ənt), *n.* one who renounces, especially one who renounces the world.

re·nun·ci·ate (ri nun′sē āt), *v.t.,* **-at·ed, -at·ing.** to renounce.

re·nun·ci·a·tion (ri nun′sē ā′shən), *n.* the act of renouncing; giving up of a right, title, possession, etc.: *The bonzes preach only patience, humility and the renunciation of the world* (Edward Gibbon). [< Latin *renūntiātiō, -ōnis* < *renūntiāre;* see RENOUNCE]
—**Syn.** rejection.

re·nun·ci·a·tive (ri nun′sē ā′tiv), *adj.* that renounces.

re·nun·ci·a·to·ry (ri nun′sē ə tôr′ē, -tōr′-), *adj.* that renounces; renunciative.

ren·ver·sé (rän′ver sā′), *n. Ballet.* a bending or swaying movement of the body, as to simulate loss of balance, usually executed while turning: *Like a jet of force he darts forward in deep plié, in renversé, bent sideways, bent double* (Saturday Review). [< French *renversé,* past participle of *renverser* to turn back]

re·oc·cu·pa·tion (rē′ok yə pā′shən), *n.* the act of occupying again; renewed occupation.

re·oc·cu·py (rē ok′yə pī), *v.t.,* **-pied, -py·ing.** to occupy (a place or position) again: *After a lapse of years a new people with new fashions of pottery and implements reoccupied the site* (Scientific American).

re·o·pen (rē ō′pən), *v.t.* **1.** to open again: *He reopened the window when it grew warmer.* **2.** to discuss again: *The matter is* *settled and cannot be reopened.* —*v.i.* **1.** to open again. **2.** to resume: *School will reopen in September.*

re·o·pen·er (rē ō′pə nər), *n. U.S.* a reopener clause.

reopener clause, *U.S.* a clause in a contract between a labor union and a company allowing either party to call for a resumption of negotiations before the contract expires: *The industry traditionally has negotiated wage increases every year, alternately under the reopener clause and in the negotiation of two-year master contract* (Wall Street Journal).

re·op·pose (rē′ə pōz′), *v.t.*, **-posed, -pos·ing.** to oppose again.

re·or·dain (rē′ôr dān′), *v.t.* **1.** to ordain, appoint, or establish again. **2.** *Ecclesiastical.* to ordain (a person) again; invest afresh with holy orders: *It is proposed that bishops should form part of the structure of the Methodist Church . . . but not that existing ministers should necessarily be reordained by Anglican bishops ordained by Anglicans* (Manchester Guardian Weekly).

re·or·der (rē ôr′dər), *v.t., v.i.* **1.** to put in order again; rearrange. **2.** to give a second or repeated order for goods; order again. —*n.* a second or repeated order for goods.

re·or·di·nate (rē ôr′də nāt), *v.t.*, **-nat·ed, -nat·ing.** to institute or establish again.

re·or·di·na·tion (rē′ôr də nā′shən), *n.* a second or repeated ordination.

re·or·gan·ise (rē ôr′gə nīz), *v.t., v.i.*, **-ised, -is·ing.** *Especially British.* reorganize.

re·or·gan·i·za·tion (rē′ôr gə nə zā′shən), *n.* **1.** the act or process of organizing again or anew: *I have already commenced a reorganization of the cavalry* (Duke of Wellington). **2.** the reconstruction or rehabilitation of a business that is in the hands of a receiver. **3.** the condition of being reorganized.

re·or·gan·ize (rē ôr′gə nīz), *v.t., v.i.*, **-ized, -iz·ing.** **1.** to organize anew; form again; arrange in a new way: *Classes will be reorganized after the first four weeks.* **2.** to form a new company to operate (a business in the hands of a receiver). —**Syn.** *v.t.* **1.** rearrange, readjust.

re·or·gan·iz·er (rē ôr′gə nī′zər), *n.* a person who organizes anew or again.

re·o·ri·ent (*v.* rē ôr′ē ent, -ōr′-; *adj.* rē ôr′ē ənt, -ōr′-), *v.t., v.i.* to orient again or in a new way: *Those reoriented to the white man's ways and his eating habits, soon start picking up his citified diseases* (Maclean's). —*adj. Archaic.* rising again: *the life reorient out of dust* (Tennyson).

re·o·ri·en·tate (rē ôr′ē en tāt, -ōr′-), *v.t., v.i.*, **-tat·ed, -tat·ing.** to reorient: *It would have given the Government sufficient time to reorientate British agricultural policy* (Manchester Guardian Weekly).

re·o·ri·en·ta·tion (rē ôr′ē en tā′shən, -ōr′-), *n.* **1.** the act or process of reorienting: *Reorientation of the developed countries' current aid programmes would involve an annual total of $450,000* (London Times). **2.** the condition of being reoriented.

re·o·vi·rus (rē′ō vī′rəs), *n.* any of a group of ECHO viruses associated with upper respiratory and gastrointestinal disorders, especially in man. [< *r*(espiratory) *e*(uteric) *o*(rphan) *virus*]

rep[1] (rep), *n.* a ribbed fabric of wool, silk, rayon, or cotton. Woolen rep is used especially for upholstery. Also, **repp, reps.** [probably < French *reps;* origin uncertain]

rep[2] (rep), *n. Slang.* reputation: *We can't afford to have our reps ruined by being seen with you* (Sinclair Lewis).

rep[3] (rep), *n.* (formerly) a unit of radiation; rad.

rep., **1.** repeat. **2. a.** report. **b.** reported. **3.** reporter. **4.** representative. **5.** republic.

Rep (no period), *Slang.* Repertory Company or Theater.

Rep., **1.** Representative. **2.** Republic. **3.** Republican.

re·pac·i·fy (rē pas′ə fī), *v.t.*, **-fied, -fy·ing.** to pacify again.

re·pack (rē pak′), *v.t., v.i.* to pack again: *to repack a suitcase.*

re·pack·age (rē pak′ij), *v.t.*, **-aged, -ag·ing.** to package again, especially in a more attractive container: *It plans to repackage the company's products with the aim of achieving greater eye-appeal and of preserving the product's freshness for a longer period* (Wall Street Journal).

re·paid (ri pād′), *v.* the past tense and past participle of **repay:** *He repaid the money he had borrowed.*

re·paint (rē pānt′), *v.t., v.i.* to paint again. —*n.* a part of a picture that has been repainted.

re·pair[1] (ri pãr′), *v.t.* **1.** to put in good condition again; mend: *He repairs shoes.* **2.** to make up for; remedy: *How can I repair the harm done? The loss of such a man could not easily be repaired* (Macaulay).

—*n.* **1.** the act or work of repairing. **2.** an instance or piece of repairing: *Repairs on the school building are made during the summer.* **3.** condition fit to be used: *The State keeps the roads in repair.* **4.** condition with respect to repairing: *The house was in bad repair.*

[Middle English *reparen* < Latin *reparāre* < *re-* again + *parāre* prepare]

—**Syn.** *v.t.* **1.** restore, renovate. See **mend.**

re·pair[2] (ri pãr′), *v.i.* **1.** to go (to a place): *It was to Malvern he repaired after his London triumph in the spring of 1924* (Atlantic). **2.** *Obsolete.* to return. —*n. Archaic.* a place repaired to; resort. [< Old French *repairier* < Late Latin *repatriāre* return to one's own country. Doublet of REPATRIATE.]

re·pair·a·ble (ri pãr′ə bəl), *adj.* that can be repaired.

re·pair·er (ri pãr′ər), *n.* a person or thing that repairs.

repair link, a specially made link for replacing a broken link in a chain.

re·pair·man (ri pãr′man′, -mən), *n., pl.* **-men.** a man whose work is repairing machines, etc.: *a television repairman.*

repair shop, a shop, store, or department for making repairs: *a shoe repair shop.*

re·pand (ri pand′), *adj. Botany.* having the margin slightly uneven or wavy: *a repand leaf.* [< Latin *repandus* < *re-* back + *pandus* bent]

rep·a·ra·ble (rep′ər ə bəl, ri pãr′-), *adj.* that can be repaired or remedied. [< Latin *reparābilis* < *reparāre;* see REPAIR[1]]

rep·a·ra·bly (rep′ər ə blē), *adv.* so as to be reparable.

rep·a·ra·tion (rep′ə rā′shən), *n.* **1.** a giving of satisfaction or compensation for wrong or injury done. **2.** compensation for wrong or injury: *to make reparation.* **3.** a repairing or being repaired; restoration to good condition: *The building stood from century to century . . . without need of reparation* (Samuel Johnson).

reparations, compensation for the devastation of territory during war: *After World War I England and France demanded reparations from Germany.*

[< Old French *reparacion,* learned borrowing from Latin *reparātiō, -ōnis* < *reparāre;* see REPAIR[1]]

re·par·a·tive (ri par′ə tiv), *adj.* **1.** tending to repair: *reparative power, a reparative process.* **2.** having to do with or involving reparation.

re·par·a·to·ry (ri par′ə tôr′ē, -tōr′-), *adj.* reparative.

rep·ar·tee (rep′ər tē′), *n.* **1.** a witty reply or replies: *Droll allusions, good stories, and smart repartees . . . fell thick as hail* (Charles J. Lever). **2.** talk characterized by clever and witty replies: *accomplished in repartee.* **3.** cleverness and wit in making replies: *framing comments . . . that would be sure to sting and yet leave no opening for repartee* (H. G. Wells). [< French *repartie* < *repartir* to reply, set out again, ultimately < Latin *re-* back, again + *pars, partis* a part, portion, share] —**Syn. 1.** sally, retort.

re·par·ti·mien·to (rā pär′ti myen′tō), *n., pl.* **-tos** (-tōs). **1.** a partition. **2.** an allotment. **3.** (in Spanish America) a territory granted by the early conquerors to their comrades and followers. It included the right to the labor of the native inhabitants. [< Spanish *repartimiento* < *repartir* < *re-* back (< Latin) + *partire* leave < Latin *partīrī* part]

re·par·ti·tion (rē′pär tish′ən, -pər-), *n.* **1.** partition; distribution; allotment. **2.** a redistribution. —*v.t.* to partition again or in a new way.

re·pass (rē pas′, -päs′), *v.t., v.i.* **1.** to pass back: *to repass the gravy.* **2.** to pass again: *to repass a car.*

re·pas·sage (rē pas′ij), *n.* **1.** a passage back. **2.** a passing again.

re·past (ri past′, -päst′), *n.* **1.** a meal; attractive meal; food: *to serve a delicious repast.* **2.** a taking of food; eating: *a brief repast.* **3.** *Archaic.* mealtime.

—*v.t., v.i. Archaic.* to provide a feast for; feed. [< Old French *repast* < Late Latin *repāscere* feed again < Latin *re-* again + *pāscere* to feed]

re·pa·tri·ate (rē pā′trē āt), *v.*, **-at·ed, -at·ing,** *n.* —*v.t.* **1.** to send back to one's own country: *After peace was declared, refugees and prisoners of war were repatriated.* **2.** to restore to citizenship. —*v.i.* to go back to one's own country. —*n.* a repatriated person: *To provide the means of transportation necessary for the transfer of repatriates to the frontier of their countries* (New York Times). [< Late Latin *repatriāre* (with English *-ate*[1]) < Latin *re-* back + *patria* native land < *pater, patris* father. Doublet of REPAIR[2].]

re·pa·tri·a·tion (rē pā′trē ā′shən), *n.* a returning or being returned to one's own country: *They hid the two convicted men, who were to have been brought ashore for repatriation to Britain* (London Times).

re·pave (rē pāv′), *v.t.*, **-paved, -pav·ing.** to pave again or anew.

re·pay (ri pā′), *v.*, **-paid, -pay·ing.** —*v.t.* **1.** to pay back; give back: *He repaid the money he had borrowed.* **2.** to make return for: *No thanks can repay such kindness.* **3.** to make return to: *The boy's success repaid the teacher for her efforts.* —*v.i.* to make repayment or return: *Vengeance is mine; I will repay, saith the Lord* (Romans 12:19). [< Old French *repaier* < *re-* back, re- + *paier* to pay] —**re·pay′er,** *n.* —**Syn.** *v.t.* **1.** refund.

re·pay·a·ble (ri pā′ə bəl), *adj.* that can be repaid; that must be repaid: *These would be repayable in local currency, which later might be used for further development programs* (New York Times).

re·pay·ment (ri pā′mənt), *n.* payment in return for something.

re·peal (ri pēl′), *v.t.* **1.** to take back; do away with; withdraw: *Prohibition was repealed in the 1930's.* **2.** *Obsolete.* to call back. —*n.* the act of repealing; abolition: *He voted for the repeal of that law.* [< Anglo-French *repeler,* Old French *rapeler* < *re-* back + *apeler* to call, appeal < Latin *appelāre* accost, related to *appellere* < *ad-* to + *pellere* strike, hit]

—**Syn.** *v.t.* **1.** revoke, rescind, annul, abrogate. *-n.* abrogation, revocation, withdrawal.

re·peal·a·ble (ri pē′lə bəl), *adj.* that can be repealed.

re·peal·er (ri pē′lər), *n.* **1.** a person or thing that repeals. **2.** *U.S.* a bill, or a clause of a bill, to repeal some legislative measure: *The repealer is retroactive to Jan. 1, 1954, when the provisions took effect* (New York Times). **3.** a person who believes in or works for the repeal of something.

re·peat (ri pēt′), *v.t.* **1.** to do or make again: *to repeat an error.* **2.** to say again: *to repeat a word for emphasis. I do but repeat what has been said a thousand times* (Sir Richard Steele). **3.** to say over; recite: *Jean can repeat many poems from memory.* **4.** to say after another says: *Repeat the pledge to the flag after me.* **5.** to tell to another or others: *Promise not to repeat the secret.* —*v.i.* **1.** to do or say something again. **2.** *U.S.* to vote more than once in an election. **3.** (of food) to rise in the gullet, so as to be tasted again.

repeat itself, to happen over again at a later time: *History repeats itself.*

repeat oneself, to say what one has already said: *A man must necessarily repeat himself who writes eighty-five stories . . . in less than twenty years* (Leslie Stephen).

—*n.* **1.** a repeating. **2.** a thing repeated. **3.** *Music.* **a.** a passage to be repeated. **b.** a sign indicating this, usually a row of dots. **4.** *Commerce.* a reorder for goods.

Repeat (noun def. 3b)
Left, begin repeat; right, end repeat

—*adj.* done again; repeated: *a repeat performance, repeat sales.* [< Old French *repeter,* learned borrowing from Latin *repetere* do or say again, attack again < *re-* again + *petere* aim at, seek]

—**Syn.** *v.t.* **1, 2,** *v.i.* **1. Repeat, reiterate** mean to do or say again. **Repeat,** the more general word, means to say, do, make, or perform something over again, once or many times: *The Glee Club will repeat the program next week.* **Reiterate** implies repeating again and again, and applies especially to something said: *We reiterated our requests for better bus service.*

re·peat·a·bil·i·ty (ri pē′tə bil′ə tē), *n.* the fact or quality of being repeatable: *The* *accuracy and repeatability of evaporation measurements* . . . (New Scientist).

re·peat·a·ble (ri pē′tə bəl), *adj.* **1.** that can be repeated: *We found that the test was repeatable as often as we cared to apply it* (Scientific American). **2.** that is fit to repeat: *His joke is not repeatable.*

re·peat·a·bly (ri pē′tə blē), *adv.* in a repeatable manner; so as to be repeatable: *It consists of a glass channel 115 ft. long which reproduces the sort of highly simplified cross-section through the ocean that can be studied exactly, in detail, and repeatably* (New Scientist).

re·peat·ed (ri pē′tid), *adj.* said, done, or made more than once: *Her repeated efforts at last won success.*

re·peat·ed·ly (ri pē′tid lē), *adv.* again and again; more than once: *He pointed out repeatedly that there are four cuisines in France, not just one, each with rewards to the epicure* (Atlantic). —**Syn.** frequently, often.

re·peat·er (ri pē′tər), *n.* **1.** a type of gun that can be fired several times without reloading. A lever, bolt, etc., must be moved after each shot. **2.** a watch or clock that, if a spring is pressed, indicates the correct time by striking the last hour, plus the number of quarter hours, five-minute periods, or minutes which have passed since then. **3.** *U.S.* a person who votes more than once in an election. **4.** *U.S.* a student who takes a course again or fails to pass on to the next grade. **5.** *Informal.* a person who is repeatedly sent to prison or a reformatory; habitual criminal: *It sometimes has become the rule to place on probation adolescents who have become "repeaters"* . . . (Emory S. Bogardus). **6. a.** a device that amplifies voice sounds in telephonic communication. Repeaters are built into underwater cables at certain intervals and relay the amplified sounds over long distances. **b.** a similar device for amplifying and relaying radio, telegraph, and radar signals. **7.** a repeating decimal. **8.** any person or thing that repeats.

re·peat·ing decimal (ri pē′ting), a decimal in which the same figure or series of figures is repeated infinitely. *Examples:* .3333+, .2323+.

repeating rifle, a rifle that fires several shots without reloading; repeater.

re·pe·chage (rep′ə shäzh; *French* rə pe-shäzh′), *n. Sports.* a trial race in which runners-up in early heats receive a second chance to qualify for the final race. [< French *repêchage* (literally) fishing up again]

re·pel (ri pel′), *v.,* **-pelled, -pel·ling.** —*v.t.* **1.** to force back; drive back; drive away: *They repelled the enemy.* **2.** to keep off or out; fail to mix with: *Oil and water repel each other. This tent repels moisture.* **3.** to force apart or away by some inherent force: *The positive poles of two magnets repel each other.* **4.** to be displeasing to; cause disgust in: *Spiders and worms repel me.* **5.** to reject: *to repel a proposition, to repel a charge. Katy . . . repelled this opinion with indignation* (James Fenimore Cooper). —*v.i.* **1.** to cause dislike; displease: *Evil odors invariably repel.* **2.** to act with a force that drives or keeps away something. [< Latin *repellere* < *re-* back + *pellere* to drive, strike]

re·pel·lence (ri pel′əns), *n.* repulsion.

re·pel·len·cy (ri pel′ən sē), *n.* repulsion.

re·pel·lent (ri pel′ənt), *adj.* **1.** disagreeable; distasteful: *Mr. Stern has a cold, repellent manner. Cheating is repellent to an honest boy.* **2.** repelling; driving back. —*n.* **1.** something that repels: *a mosquito repellent, a water repellent. It is neither an attractant nor a repellent to unconditioned salmon* (Scientific American). **2.** a medicine or application that reduces tumors, swellings, or eruptions. —**re·pel′lent·ly,** *adv.* —**Syn.** *adj.* **1.** repugnant.

re·pel·ler (ri pel′ər), *n.* a person or thing that repels.

re·pel·ling (ri pel′ing), *adj.* that repels; repulsive; displeasing: *a repelling sense of humor, a repelling insect.* —**re·pel′ling·ly,** *adv.* —**re·pel′ling·ness,** *n.*

re·pent[1] (ri pent′), *v.i.* **1.** to feel sorry for sin and seek forgiveness: *He had done wrong, but repented.* **2.** to feel sorry; regret something done in the past: *Married in haste, we may repent at leisure* (William Congreve). —*v.t.* **1.** to feel sorrow for (one's sins) and ask forgiveness. **2.** to feel sorry for; regret: *She bought the red hat and has repented her choice. I had soon reason to repent those foolish words* (Jonathan Swift). [< Old French *repentir* < *re-* again, re- + Vulgar Latin *pēnitire* < Latin *paenitēre* cause to regret or repent] —**re·pent′er,** *n.*

re·pent[2] (rē′pənt), *adj.* **1.** (of a plant) growing along the ground, or horizontally beneath the surface, and taking root as it grows. **2.** (of an animal) creeping; crawling. [< Latin *rēpēns, -entis,* present participle of *rēpere* to creep, crawl. Compare REPTILE.]

re·pent·ance (ri pen′təns), *n.* **1.** sorrow for doing wrong. **2.** sorrow; regret. —**Syn. 1.** contrition.

re·pent·ant (ri pen′tənt), *adj.* repenting; feeling repentance or regret; sorry for wrongdoing: *a repentant criminal, repentant tears.* [< Old French *repentant,* present participle of *repentir* repent] —**re·pent′ant·ly,** *adv.*

re·peo·ple (rē pē′pəl), *v.t.,* **-pled, -pling. 1.** to people anew. **2.** to restock with animals. [< Old French *repeupler* < *re-* again, re- + *peupler* to populate < *peuple* people]

re·per·cus·sion (rē′pər kush′ən), *n.* **1.** an indirect influence or reaction from an event: *repercussions of war. The repercussions of this victory went round the country* (Time). **2.** a sound flung back; echo: *Like the echo which is a repercussion of the original voice* (Cardinal Newman). **3.** a springing back; rebound; recoil: *the repercussion of a cannon.* **4.** a driving back. **5.** *Music.* **a.** the repetition of a tone or chord. **b.** the repetition of the theme in a fugue, especially the theme and answer in all voices. **6.** *Medicine.* **a.** a method of diagnosing pregnancy; ballottement. **b.** a driving in or away, as of a tumor or eruption. [< Latin *repercussiō, -ōnis* < *repercutere* < *re-* back, again + *percutere* strike, beat. Compare PERCUSSION.] —**Syn. 2.** reverberation.

re·per·cus·sive (rē′pər kus′iv), *adj.* **1.** causing repercussion. **2.** reverberated. —**re′per·cus′sive·ly,** *adv.*

re·per·fo·rate (ri pėr′fə rāt), *v.t.,* **-rat·ed, -rat·ing.** to perforate again: *Paper tape has first to be prepared at the sending end and then reperforated at the receiving end for feeding into the computer* (Manchester Guardian).

re·per·fo·ra·tor (ri pėr′fə rā′tər), *n.* a machine that receives information on punched tape and duplicates it on a similar tape for retransmission.

rep·er·toire (rep′ər twär, -twôr), *n.* the list of plays, operas, parts, pieces, etc., that a company, an actor, a musician, or a singer is prepared to perform. [< French *répertoire,* learned borrowing from Late Latin *repertōrium.* Doublet of REPERTORY.]

ré·per·toire (rā per twär′), *n. French.* repertoire.

rep·er·to·ri·al (rep′ər tôr′ē əl, -tōr′-), *adj.* of or having to do with a repertory or repertories: *As for his repertorial policy and directorial style, these are explained in two ways* (London Times).

rep·er·to·ry (rep′ər tôr′ē, -tōr′-), *n., pl.* **-ries. 1.** a catalogue or list of things; repertoire: *One of the best . . . was the revival in the repertory of the Comédie-Française . . . of Racine's Old Testament tragedy "Athalie"* (New Yorker). **2.** any store or stock of things ready for use. **3.** a storehouse. **4.** a repertory company or theater. [< Late Latin *repertōrium* inventory < Latin *reperīre* to find, get < *re-* again + *parere* beget, produce. Doublet of REPERTOIRE.] —**Syn. 3.** depository, depot.

repertory company or **theater,** a permanent organization of actors presenting a repertoire of plays, usually producing them alternately: *Dallas supports a symphony orchestra, a civic opera company, and a repertory theater* (H. B. Carroll).

rep·e·tend (rep′ə tend, rep′ə tend′), *n.* that part of a repeating decimal that is repeated indefinitely. [< Latin *repetendus,* gerundive of *repetere;* see REPEAT]

ré·pé·ti·teur (rā pā tē tœr′), *n. French.* **1.** a person who coaches the singers of an opera company. **2.** a person who oversees the rehearsals and performances of a ballet company. **3.** an assistant teacher at a lycée. **4.** a private tutor.

rep·e·ti·tion (rep′ə tish′ən), *n.* **1.** a repeating; doing again; saying again: *Repetition helps learning. Nature is an endless combination and repetition of a very few laws* (Emerson). **2.** a thing repeated. [< Latin *repetītiō, -ōnis* < *repetere;* see REPEAT]

rep·e·ti·tion·ar·y (rep′ə tish′ə ner′ē), *adj.* like or characterized by repetition.

rep·e·ti·tious (rep′ə tish′əs), *adj.* full of repetitions; repeating in a tiresome way. —**rep′e·ti′tious·ly,** *adv.* —**rep′e·ti′tious·ness,** *n.* —**Syn.** reiterative.

re·pet·i·tive (ri pet′ə tiv), *adj.* of or characterized by repetition: *The text itself is loaded with clichés, grossly repetitive, and stylistically dull* (Scientific American). —**re·pet′i·tive·ly,** *adv.* —**re·pet′i·tive·ness,** *n.*

re·pho·to·graph (rē fō′tə graf, -gräf), *v.t.* to photograph again: *He then had these new versions rephotographed and sent them to various friends in England* (W.H. Auden).

re·phrase (rē frāz′), *v.t.,* **-phrased, -phras·ing.** to phrase again; phrase in a new or different way: *to rephrase a question.*

re·pine (ri pīn′), *v.i.,* **-pined, -pin·ing.** to be discontented; fret; complain: *Through the long and weary day he repined at his unhappy lot* (Washington Irving).

re·pin·er (ri pī′nər), *n.* a person who repines or murmurs complainingly.

re·pin·ing·ly (ri pī′ning lē), *adv.* with murmuring complaint.

re·place (ri plās′), *v.t.,* **-placed, -plac·ing. 1.** to fill or take the place of: *Tom replaced Dick as captain. Most telephone operators have been replaced by dial telephones.* **2.** to get another in place of: *I will replace the cup I broke.* **3.** to put back; put in place again: *Please replace the books on the shelf.*
—**Syn. 1. Replace, supersede, supplant** mean to take the place of another. **Replace** means to take or fill as substitute or successor the place formerly held by another: *When one of the players on the team was hurt, another replaced him.* **Supersede,** used chiefly of things, suggests causing what is replaced to be put aside as out-of-date, no longer useful, etc.: *Buses have superseded streetcars.* **Supplant,** when used of a person, suggests forcing him out and taking over his place by scheming or treachery: *The dictator supplanted the president.*

re·place·a·bil·i·ty (ri plā′sə bil′ə tē), *n.* the fact or quality of being replaceable: *There was also need for interchangeability, standardization, and replaceability of building components* (London Times).

re·place·a·ble (ri plā′sə bəl), *adj.* that can be replaced: *The concurring individuals . . . appear but as insignificant and replaceable instruments* (W. Taylor).

re·place·ment (ri plās′mənt), *n.* **1.** the act of replacing: *the replacement of wooden cars by steel cars.* **2.** the state of being replaced. **3.** something or someone that replaces, as a man in military service who replaces another of similar training or skill. **4. a.** *Geology.* the process by which one mineral replaces another in a crystalline form. **b.** the process by which an edge or angle of a crystal is worn off and replaced by one or more faces. —**Syn. 3.** substitute.

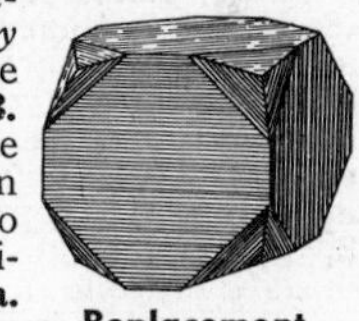
Replacement (def. 4b) of angles of a cube by faces of a trapezohedron

re·plac·er (ri plā′sər), *n.* **1.** a person or thing that replaces, or restores to the former or proper place. **2.** a person or thing that takes the place of another; substitute.

re·plan (rē plan′), *v.t., v.i.,* **-planned, -plan·ning.** to plan again: *Next time we cannot replan, train, produce weapons, or make mistakes* (Bulletin of Atomic Scientists). *Our cities are being replanned for cars* (New Yorker).

re·plant (rē plant′, -plänt′), *v.t.* **1.** to plant again: *I'm going to have to replant all the bushes around the house* (Look). **2.** to reinstate. —*v.i.* to provide and set fresh plants. —*n.* something that is replanted.

re·plant·a·ble (rē plan′tə bəl, -plän′-), *adj.* that can be planted again.

re·plan·ta·tion (rē′plan tā′shən), *n.* the act of planting again.

re·play (rē plā′), *v.t.* to play (a match, etc.) again. —*n.* a replayed match.

re·plead (rē plēd′), *v.i., v.t.,* **-plead·ed** or **-pled, -plead·ing.** to plead again.

re·plead·er (rē plē′dər), *n. Law.* **1.** a second pleading. **2.** the right of pleading again. [< *replead* + *-er*[5]]

re·pled (rē pled′), *v.* repleaded; a past tense and a past participle of **replead.**

re·plen·ish (ri plen′ish), *v.t.* to fill again; provide a new supply for: *Her supply of towels needs replenishing. One cannot take from a water supply at a greater rate than it is replenished* (R. N. Elston). [< Old French *repleniss-*, stem of *replenir* < Latin *re-* again + *plēnus* full, related to *plēre* fill. Compare REPLETE.] —**re·plen′ish·er,** *n.* —**Syn.** refill, renew.

re·plen·ish·ment (ri plen′ish mənt), *n.* **1.** a replenishing or being replenished. **2.** a fresh supply.

re·plete (ri plēt′), *adj.* abundantly supplied; filled: *The Disneyland tour was replete with unexpected thrills. The old men would sit at their tables, replete and sleepy* (H. G. Wells). [< Middle French *replète* < Latin *replētus*, past participle of *replēre* < *re-* again + *plēre* to fill, related to *plēnus* full] —**Syn.** full, abounding.

re·ple·tion (ri plē′shən), *n.* **1.** fullness. **2.** excessive fullness. **3.** *Medicine.* plethora; a disease caused by excess of red corpuscles in the blood or an increase in the quantity of blood in the body.

re·plev·i·a·ble (rē plev′ē ə bəl), *adj. Law.* that can be replevied.

re·plev·in (ri plev′ən), *n.* **1.** the recovery of goods taken from a person upon his giving security that the case shall be tried in court and the goods returned if he is defeated. **2.** the writ by which the goods are thus recovered. —*v.t.* to recover (goods) by replevin. [< Anglo-French *replevine* < *replever*, Old French *replevir;* see REPLEVY]

re·plev·i·sa·ble (ri plev′ə sə bəl), *adj.* repleviable.

re·plev·y (ri plev′ē), *v.*, **-plev·ied, -plev·y·ing,** *n., pl.* **-plev·ies.** —*v.t., v.i.* to recover by replevin. —*n.* replevin. [< Old French *replevir* < *re-* again + *plevir* to pledge]

rep·li·ca (rep′lə kə), *n.* **1.** a copy of a work of art executed by the original artist: *The artist made a replica of his picture.* **2.** a copy; reproduction: *Michael is a replica of his father in looks and voice.* [< Italian *replica* < *replicare* to reproduce < Latin *replicāre* unroll; see REPLY] —**Syn. 2.** facsimile.

rep·li·case (rep′lə kās), *n.* an enzyme used in the replication of RNA.

rep·li·cate (*adj.* rep′lə kit; *v.* rep′lə kāt), *adj., v.,* **-cat·ed, -cat·ing.** —*adj.* folded back on itself: *a replicate leaf.*
—*v.t.* **1.** to fold or bend back. **2.** to copy; reproduce: *What then distinguishes virus DNA, which replicates itself at the expense of other pathways of cellular anabolism?* (Science). **3.** to say in reply. —*v.i.* to fold or bend back.
[< Latin *replicātus*, past participle of *replicāre* fold back; see REPLY]

rep·li·cat·ed (rep′lə kā′tid), *adj.* replicate.

rep·li·ca·tion (rep′lə kā′shən), *n.* **1.** a fold. **2.** a reproducing: *Sometimes, because of a mistake in some step of the replication process, a daughter cell gets a gene carrying a garbled message* (Scientific American). **3.** a copy. **4.** a reply; rejoinder. **5.** reverberation; echo. **6.** a plaintiff's reply to the defendant's plea.

re·pli·er (ri plī′ər), *n.* a person who replies.

re·plume (rē plüm′), *v.t.*, **-plumed, -plum·ing.** to rearrange; put in proper order again; preen, as a bird its feathers.

re·ply (ri plī′), *v.*, **-plied, -ply·ing,** *n., pl.* **-plies.** —*v.i.* **1.** to answer by words or action; answer; respond: *She replied to the question with emphasis. The enemy replied to the offer with heavy gunfire.* **2.** *Law.* (of a plaintiff) to answer a defendant's plea.
—*v.t.* to give as an answer: *He replied that he had caught cold and could not come.*
—*n.* **1.** the act of replying. **2.** an answer.
[< Old French *replier* < Latin *replicāre* unroll, fold back < *re-* back + *-plicāre* to fold]

re·po·lar·ize (rē pō′lər īz), *v.t., v.i.*, **-ized, -iz·ing.** to polarize again.

re·pol·ish (rē pol′ish), *v.t.* to polish again: *His silver . . . requires to be purified and repolished throughout* (William Taylor).

ré·pon·dez s'il vous plaît (rā pôN dā′ sēl vü ple′), *French.* please reply (placed on formal invitations). *Abbr.:* R.S.V.P.

re·port (ri pôrt′, -pōrt′), *n.* **1.** an account of something seen, heard, read, done, or considered: *The reports of my death are greatly exaggerated* (Mark Twain). **2.** an account officially expressed, generally in writing: *a school report, a committee report to the President, a court report of the judicial opinion.* **3.** the sound of a shot or an explosion: *the report of a gun.* **4.** common talk; rumor: *Report has it that the Smiths are leaving town.* **5.** reputation: *a just man of good report.*
—*v.t.* **1.** to make a report of; announce. **2.** to give a formal account of; state officially: *Our treasurer reports that all dues are paid up.* **3.** to take down in writing; write an account of. **4.** to repeat (what one has heard, seen, etc.); bring back an account of; describe: *The radio reported many homes destroyed by the tornado.* **5.** to announce as a wrongdoer; denounce: *to report a prowler to the police.* **6.** to present (oneself): *We . . . went on shore with the lieutenant to report ourselves to the admiral* (Frederick Marryat). —*v.i.* **1.** to make a report: *The rules committee will report after lunch.* **2.** to act as a reporter. **3.** to relate; tell. **4.** to present oneself: *Report for duty at 9 A.M.*
report out, to return (a bill) from committee to a lawmaking body with a formal report: *The Senate subcommittee . . . has already reported out four civil-rights bills* (Newsweek).
[< Old French *report* < *reporter*, learned borrowing from Latin *reportāre* < *re-* back + *portāre* to carry]
—**Syn.** *n.* **1.** narrative, description. **4.** gossip, hearsay. *-v.t.* **1.** narrate.

re·port·a·ble (ri pôr′tə bəl, -pōr′-), *adj.* that can be reported; worth reporting.

re·port·age (ri pôr′tij, -pōr′-), *n.* a reporting, especially in the style of newspaper reporters: *Some novelists occasionally write reportage, and with interesting results; it outclasses their fiction* (New Yorker).

report card, a report sent by a school to parents or guardians, indicating the quality of a student's work.

re·port·ed·ly (ri pôr′tid lē, -pōr′-), *adv.* according to reports: *Hayakawa is reportedly seventy years old, jovially admits to only forty-five* (New Yorker).

re·port·er (ri pôr′tər, -pōr′-), *n.* **1.** a person who reports. **2.** a person who gathers news for a newspaper, radio or television station, etc.: *In a very real sense, a newspaper can be only as good as its reporters* (New Yorker). **3.** a person who takes down reports of law cases: *a court reporter.*

rep·or·to·ri·al (rep′ər tôr′ē əl, -tōr′-), *adj.* of or having to do with reporters: *a reportorial style of writing.* —**rep′or·to′ri·al·ly,** *adv.*

re·pos·al (ri pō′zəl), *n.* the act of reposing.

re·pose[1] (ri pōz′), *n., v.*, **-posed, -pos·ing.** —*n.* **1.** rest; sleep: *Do not disturb her repose.* **2.** quietness; ease: *She has repose of manner.* **3.** peace; calmness: *the repose of the country.* **4.** a restful quality.
—*v.i.* **1.** to lie at rest: *The cat reposed upon the cushion.* **2.** to lie in a grave: *In quiet she reposes* (Matthew Arnold). **3.** to rest from work or toil; take a rest: *Many people from the North repose in Florida during the winter season.* **4.** to be supported. **5.** to depend; rely (on): *The explorers reposed on the judgment of their Indian scout.* —*v.t.* **1.** to lay to rest: *Repose yourself in the hammock.* **2.** to refresh by rest: *We stopped at a little public-house where we reposed ourselves* (Richard Graves).
[< Old French *repos* < *reposer* < Late Latin *repausāre* cause to rest < *re-* again + *pausāre* to pause. Compare POSE[1].]
—**Syn.** *n.* **2.** composure. **3.** tranquillity.

re·pose[2] (ri pōz′), *v.t.*, **-posed, -pos·ing.** to put; place: *We repose complete confidence in his honesty.* [< Latin *repositus*, past participle of *repōnere* < *re-* back + *pōnere* to place]

re·pose·ful (ri pōz′ fəl), *adj.* calm; quiet: *Mr. Abramovitz and his interior decorator . . . have created a beautiful and reposeful interior* (Reporter). —**re·pose′ful·ly,** *adv.* —**re·pose′ful·ness,** *n.* —**Syn.** peaceful, restful.

re·pos·er (ri pō′zər), *n.* a person who reposes.

re·pos·ing room (ri pō′zing), a room in which the deceased is laid out at a funeral.

re·pos·it (ri poz′it), *v.t.* **1.** to deposit. **2.** to lay up; store. **3.** to put back. [< Latin *repositus*, past participle of *repōnere;* see REPOSE[2]]

re·po·si·tion (rē′pə zish′ən, rep′ə-), *n.* **1.** the act of depositing. **2.** replacement. **3.** *Archaic.* restoration to office or possession. —*v.t.* **1.** to restore (a bone, organ of the body, etc.) to its normal position. **2.** to place in a new position.

re·pos·i·to·ry (ri poz′ə tôr′ē, -tōr′-), *n., pl.* **-ries.** **1.** a place or container where things are stored or kept: *The box was the repository for old magazines. A library is a repository of information.* **2.** a person to whom something is confided or entrusted: *Pepper alone had been the repository of my secret* (Thomas B. Aldrich). [< Latin *repositōrium* < *repōnere;* see REPOSE[2]]

re·pos·sess (rē′pə zes′), *v.t.* **1.** to possess again; get possession of again. **2.** to put in possession again. —**Syn. 1.** recover.

re·pos·ses·sion (rē′pə zesh′ən), *n.* the act or process of repossessing.

re·post (ri pōst′), *n., v.* riposte.

re·pot (rē pot′), *v.t.*, **-pot·ted, -pot·ting.** **1.** to replace in pots. **2.** to shift (plants) from one pot to another, usually of a larger size, or to remove from the pot and replace more or less of the old earth with fresh earth.

re·pous·sé (rə pü sā′), *adj.* **1.** raised in relief by hammering on the reverse side: *A repoussé design can be made on thin metal.* **2.** ornamented or made in this manner. —*n.* repoussé work. [< French *repoussé* < Middle French *repousser* < *re-* back + *pousser* to push]

Repoussé Work on Louis XV étui

repp (rep), *n.* rep, a heavy ribbed fabric.

repped (rept), *adj.* transversely corded, like rep.

repr., **1. a.** represented. **b.** representing. **2. a.** reprint. **b.** reprinted.

rep·re·hend (rep′ri hend′), *v.t.* to reprove; rebuke; blame. [< Latin *reprehendere* (originally) pull back < *re-* back + *prehendere* to grasp] —**Syn.** reproach, censure, reprimand, upbraid.
➔ This word is often confused with *apprehend,* to take into custody, arrest.

rep·re·hen·si·bil·i·ty (rep′ri hen′sə bil′ə tē), *n.* the character of being reprehensible.

rep·re·hen·si·ble (rep′ri hen′sə bəl), *adj.* deserving reproof, rebuke, or blame: *Cheating is a reprehensible act.* —**Syn.** blameworthy, culpable.

rep·re·hen·si·bly (rep′ri hen′sə blē), *adv.* in a reprehensible manner.

rep·re·hen·sion (rep′ri hen′shən), *n.* reproof; rebuke; blame. [< Latin *reprehēnsiō, -ōnis* < *reprehendere* reprehend]

rep·re·hen·sive (rep′ri hen′siv), *adj.* reprehensible. —**rep′re·hen′sive·ly,** *adv.*

rep·re·sent (rep′ri zent′), *v.t.* **1.** to stand for; be a sign or symbol of: *Letters represent sounds. The fifty stars in our flag represent the fifty States. A policeman represents the power of the law.* **2.** to express by signs or symbols: *to represent ideas by words.* **3.** to act in place of; speak and act for: *We chose a committee to represent us. The Colonies . . . complain that they are taxed in a Parliament in which they are not represented* (Edmund Burke). **4.** to act the part of: *Each child will represent an animal at the party.* **5.** to show in a picture, statue, carving, etc.; give a likeness of; portray: *This picture represents the end of the world.* **6.** to be a type of; be an example of: *A log represents a very simple type of boat.* **7.** to be the equivalent of; correspond to. **8.** to describe; set forth: *He represented the plan as safe, but it was not.* **9.** to bring before the mind; make one think of: *His fears represented the undertaking as impossible.* [< Latin *repraesentāre* < *re-* back + *praesēns, -entis* present[1]] —**rep′re·sent′er,** *n.*

re-pre·sent (rē′pri zent′), *v.t.* to present over again or in a new way.

rep·re·sent·a·ble (rep′ri zen′tə bəl), *adj.* that can be represented.

rep·re·sen·ta·tion (rep′ri zen tā′shən), *n.* **1.** the act of representing. **2.** the condition or fact of being represented: *Taxation without representation is tyranny. The United States Congress is elected on the basis of proportional representation.* **3.** representatives considered as a group. **4.** a likeness; picture; model. **5.** the performance of a play; presentation: *a representation of the story of Rip Van Winkle.* **6.** the process or faculty of forming mental images or ideas. **7.** a protest; complaint: *to make representations to the police about a nuisance.* **8.** an account; statement: *They deceived us by false representations.* **9.** *Law.* a statement of fact, implied or expressed, made by a party to a transaction and tending to facilitate conclusion of the transaction. —**Syn. 3.** delegation. **4.** image. **5.** production. **7.** remonstrance.

rep·re·sen·ta·tion·al (rep′ri zen tā′shə-nəl), *adj.* **1.** of or having to do with a form of art that emphasizes realistic and conventional representation of subjects and the use of traditional materials: *We have run through the satisfactions of representational art to the puzzling outlines of abstract art* (Atlantic). **2.** of or having to do with representation: *representational government.* —**rep′re·sen·ta′tion·al·ly,** *adv.*

rep·re·sen·ta·tion·al·ism (rep′ri zen tā′-shə nə liz′əm), *n.* **1.** the theory or principles of representational art. **2.** the style or practice of representational art: *The mere fact of the show certainly means that abstraction is going to have to move over and make room for a new kind of U.S. representationalism* (Time).

rep·re·sen·ta·tion·al·ist (rep′ri zen tā′-shə nə list), *n.* a person who produces or favors representational art.

rep·re·sent·a·tive (rep′ri zen′tə tiv), *n.* **1.** a person appointed to act or speak for others: *He is the club's representative at the convention. The Philippines also declined to send a representative, but are expected to send an observer* (New York Times). **2.** a member of a legislative body. **3.** an example; type: *The tiger is a representative of the cat family.* —*adj.* **1.** having its citizens represented by chosen persons: *a representative government.* **2.** representing: *Images representative of animals were made by the children.* **3.** enough like all those of its kind to stand for all the rest: *Oak, birch, and maple are representative American hardwoods.* —**rep′re·sent′a·tive·ly,** *adv.* —**rep′re·sent′a·tive·ness,** *n.*

—**Syn.** *n.* **1.** agent, deputy. *-adj.* **3.** typical.

Rep·re·sent·a·tive (rep′ri zen′tə tiv), *n.* *U.S.* a member of the lower house of Congress (the House of Representatives) or of a corresponding body of any of certain state legislatures. *Abbr.:* Rep.

re·press (ri pres′), *v.t.* **1.** to prevent from acting; check: *She repressed an impulse to cough. To save his life he could not repress a chuckle* (Booth Tarkington). **2.** to keep down; put down: *The dictator repressed the revolt.* **3.** *Psychoanalysis.* to make the object of repression; force (a painful or undesirable memory or impulse) from the conscious mind into the unconscious mind. [< Latin *repressus,* past participle of *reprimere* < *re-* back + *premere* to press] —**re·press′er,** *n.* —**Syn. 1.** curb, restrain. **2.** suppress.

re·press·i·ble (ri pres′ə bəl), *adj.* that can be repressed.

re·pres·sion (ri presh′ən), *n.* **1.** the act of repressing: *The repression of a laugh made Jim choke. Fourteen months of military repression . . . plainly had failed* (Newsweek). **2.** the state of being repressed: *Repression only made her behave worse.* **3.** *Psychoanalysis.* a defense mechanism by which unacceptable or painful impulses, emotions, or memories are put out of the conscious mind, their energy or effect remaining (according to Freudian theory) in the unconscious, where it influences personality and behavior. —**Syn. 2.** constraint.

re·pres·sive (ri pres′iv), *adj.* tending to repress; having power to repress: *The people of Cyprus "will carry on their sacred struggle without fear of any repressive measures or prison cells"* (London Times). —**re·pres′sive·ly,** *adv.* —**re·pres′sive·ness,** *n.* —**Syn.** inhibitory.

re·pres·sor (ri pres′ər), *n.* **1.** a person or thing that represses. **2.** a substance that represses chemical or organic activity: *The activity of many enzymes . . . is regulated by feedback mechanisms, repressors, and inhibitors* (New Scientist).

re·priev·al (ri prē′vəl), *n.* a reprieve.

re·prieve (ri prēv′), *v.,* **-prieved, -priev·ing,** *n.* —*v.t.* **1.** to delay the execution of (a person condemned to death): *The governor reprieved the condemned man just the day before the scheduled execution.* **2.** to give relief from any evil or trouble.

—*n.* **1.** a delay in carrying out a punishment, especially of the death penalty. **2.** temporary relief from any evil or trouble.

[< obsolete *repry* to remand, detain < Old French *repris,* past participle of *reprendre* take back < Latin *reprehendere* (see REPREHEND); form perhaps influenced by Middle English *repreve* reprove]

—**Syn.** *v.t.* **2.** relieve.

rep·ri·mand (*n.* rep′rə mand, -mänd; *v.* rep′rə mand′, -mänd′), *n.* a severe or formal reproof: *the sharp reprimands that were sure to follow every act of negligence* (John F. Kirk). —*v.t.* to reprove severely or formally; censure: *Captain Wilson sent for the master, and reprimanded him for his oppression* (Frederick Marryat). [< French *réprimande,* earlier *réprimende,* learned borrowing from Latin *reprimenda* a thing to be repressed, feminine gerundive of *reprimere* repress] —**rep′ri·mand′er,** *n.* —**Syn.** *v.t.* reprehend.

re·print (*v.* rē print′; *n.* rē′print′), *v.t.* to print again; print a new impression of. —*n.* **1.** a reprinting; a new impression of a printed work. **2.** *Philately.* a stamp printed from the original plate after the issue has been discontinued. —**re·print′er,** *n.*

re·pris·al (ri prī′zəl), *n.* **1.** injury done in return for injury, especially by one nation or group to another: *The policy of reprisals is the fruit of cold, unemotional . . . reasoning* (Harper's). **2.** a compensation. [< Old French *reprisaille* < Italian *ripresaglia,* or < Medieval Latin *represalia,* ultimately < Latin *reprēnsus,* past participle of *reprēndere, reprehendere;* see REPREHEND] —**Syn. 1.** retaliation.

re·prise (rə prēz′), *n.* **1.** a renewal or resumption of an action; repetition: *Most of Van Fleet's testimony was a reprise of things he had said before* (Time). **2.** *Music.* a repetition or return to the first theme or subject. [< Old French *reprise,* feminine of *repris,* past participle of *reprendre* (literally) take back; see REPRIEVE]

re·pris·es (ri prī′ziz), *n.pl. Law.* an annual deduction, duty, or payment out of a manor or an estate.

re·pris·ti·nate (rē pris′tə nāt), *v.t.,* **-nat·ed, -nat·ing.** to restore to the original state.

re·pris·ti·na·tion (rē pris′tə nā′shən), *n.* a restoration to the original state.

re·pro (rē′prō), *n., pl.* **-pros.** *Informal.* a reproduction: *The cost is too high for most, but if you don't jib at repros you can buy a copy* (London Times).

re·proach (ri prōch′), *n.* **1.** blame: *conduct above reproach.* **2.** disgrace: *to bring reproach on one's family.* **3.** an object of blame, censure, or disapproval. **4.** an expression of blame, censure, or disapproval: *Mr. Travers . . . overwhelmed him with reproaches* (Joseph Conrad).

—*v.t.* **1.** to blame: *Father reproached me for being late.* **2.** to disgrace; shame: *to reproach one's life.*

[< Old French *reproche* < *reprocher* < Vulgar Latin *repropiāre* lay at the door of < Latin *re-* again + *prope* near] —**re-proach′er,** *n.*

—**Syn.** *n.* **1.** censure. **2.** discredit. *-v.t.* **1.** upbraid, reprove, rebuke. See **blame.**

re·proach·a·ble (ri prō′chə bəl), *adj.* deserving of reproach. —**re·proach′a·ble·ness,** *n.*

re·proach·a·bly (ri prō′chə blē), *adv.* in a reproachable manner.

re·proach·ful (ri prōch′fəl), *adj.* **1.** full of reproach; expressing reproach: *a reproachful expression.* **2.** *Obsolete.* disgraceful; blameworthy. —**re·proach′ful·ly,** *adv.* —**re·proach′ful·ness,** *n.*

re·proach·ing·ly (ri prō′ching lē), *adv.* reproachfully.

re·proach·less (ri prōch′lis), *adj.* without reproach; irreproachable.

rep·ro·ba·cy (rep′rə bə sē), *n.* reprobate state.

rep·ro·bate (rep′rə bāt), *n., adj., v.,* **-bat·ed, -bat·ing.** —*n.* an unprincipled scoundrel: *a penniless, drunken reprobate* (Theodore Watts-Dunton).

—*adj.* **1.** morally abandoned; unprincipled. **2.** condemned as worthless or inferior. **3.** *Theology.* beyond salvation.

—*v.t.* **1.** to disapprove; condemn; censure. **2.** to reject; refuse. **3.** *Theology.* to exclude from the number of elect or from salvation. [< Late Latin *reprobātus,* past participle of *reprobāre* reprove, reject < Latin *re-* against, dis- + *probāre* approve < *probus* good] —**Syn.** *adj.* **1.** depraved, corrupt, dissolute, profligate.

rep·ro·ba·tion (rep′rə bā′shən), *n.* **1.** disapproval; condemnation; censure: *dispensing reprobation for misconduct* (George Meredith). **2.** exclusion from salvation by God.

rep·ro·ba·tive (rep′rə bā′tiv), *adj.* reprobating; expressing reprobation. —**rep′ro·ba′tive·ly,** *adv.*

re·proc·ess (rē pros′es; *especially British* rē prō′ses), *v.t.* to process again.

re·proc·essed (rē pros′est; *especially British* rē prō′sest), *adj.* salvaged and made over again into the same material, as wool that has been made into clothes, etc., then unraveled, and remade into yarn: *A fabric manufacturer who has just returned from Europe contends that foreign textile mills are shipping fabrics containing used and reprocessed material into the United States labeled as all-wool products* (New York Times).

re·pro·duce (rē′prə düs′, -dyüs′), *v.,* **-duced, -duc·ing.** —*v.t.* **1.** to produce again: *A radio reproduces sounds.* **2.** to produce (offspring): *One function of all animals is to reproduce their own kind.* **3.** to make a copy of: *A camera will reproduce a picture.* —*v.i.* to produce offspring: *Most plants reproduce by seeds.* —**re′pro·duc′er,** *n.* —**Syn.** *v.i.* propagate, generate.

re·pro·duc·i·bil·i·ty (rē′prə dü′sə bil′ə-tē, -dyü′-), *n.* a being reproducible.

re·pro·duc·i·ble (rē′prə dü′sə bəl, -dyü′-), *adj.* that can be reproduced: *For such a method to work it is necessary for several conditions to be met; . . . the film formed must be optically active; . . . the film must be reproducible* (Science News Letter).

re·pro·duc·i·bly (rē′prə dü′sə blē, -dyü′-), *adv.* in a reproducible manner; so as to be reproducible: *It soon became apparent that although individual cryotrons are relatively simple to make, trying to make them reproducibly is quite another matter* (New Scientist).

re·pro·duc·tion (rē′prə duk′shən), *n.* **1.** a reproducing or being reproduced. **2.** a copy. **3.** the process by which animals and plants produce individuals like themselves: *Reproduction is one of the two essential features of life* (Scientific American).

re·pro·duc·tive (rē′prə duk′tiv), *adj.* **1.** that reproduces. **2.** for or concerned with reproduction. —**re′pro·duc′tive·ly,** *adv.* —**re′pro·duc′tive·ness,** *n.*

re·pro·duc·tiv·i·ty (rē′prə duk tiv′ə tē), *n.* the quality or power of being reproductive: *Insects' tremendous reproductivity is one reason for the havoc they can cause* (Wall Street Journal).

re·pro·gram (rē prō′gram, -grəm), *v.t.,* **-gramed, -gram·ing** or **-grammed, -gram·ming.** to program again: *NASA is obligated to tell the Congress how it will reprogram the money the Congress has appropriated for the agency* (San Francisco Chronicle).

re·proof (ri prüf′), *n.* words of blame or disapproval; blame: *Reproofs from authority ought to be grave, not taunting* (Francis Bacon). [< Middle French *reprove,* and *reprouve* < *reprover;* see REPROVE; form influenced by *proof*]

re·prov·a·ble (ri prü′və bəl), *adj.* deserving reproof.

re·prov·al (ri prü′vəl), *n.* a reproving; reproof.

re·prove (ri prüv′), *v.t.,* **-proved, -prov·ing.** to find fault with; blame: *She reproved the boy for teasing the cat.* [< Old French *reprover,* learned borrowing from Late Latin *reprobāre* reprove; (originally) reject; see REPROBATE] —**re·prov′ing·ly,** *adv.*

—**Syn. Reprove, rebuke** mean to criticize or blame someone for a fault. **Reprove** suggests expressing disapproval or blame directly to the person at fault, usually without scolding and with the purpose or hope of correcting the fault: *The principal reproved the students who had been smoking in the locker room.* **Rebuke** means to reprove sharply and sternly, with authority and often in public: *The Commissioner rebuked the patrolmen who had been neglecting duty.*

re·prov·er (ri prü′vər), *n.* a person or thing that reproves.

reps (reps), *n.* rep, a heavy ribbed fabric.

rep·tant (rep′tənt), *adj.* **1.** creeping; crawling. **2.** growing along the ground or horizontally beneath the surface. [< Latin *rēptāns, -antis,* present participle of *rēptāre* to creep (frequentative) < *rēpere* to crawl]

rep·tile (rep′təl, -tīl), *n.* **1. a.** any of a class of cold-blooded animals with dry, scaly skin and a backbone, as snakes, turtles, lizards, alligators, and crocodiles. Reptiles were the dominant form of life during the Mesozoic. **b.** *Informal.* any creeping or crawling animal. **c.** *Informal.* an amphibian. **2.** a low, mean, despicable person.

—*adj.* **1.** of or like a reptile; crawling; creeping. **2.** low; mean; venal: *a reptile press.* —**rep′tile·like′,** *adj.*

[< Late Latin *rēptile*, (originally) neuter of *rēptilis* crawling < Latin *rēpere* to crawl]

rep·til·i·an (rep til′ē ən), *adj.* **1.** of reptiles; having to do with reptiles. **2.** like a reptile; base; mean: *a reptilian nature.* —*n.* a reptile.

rep·til·i·form (rep′tə lə fôrm), *adj.* having the form of a reptile; reptilelike.

rep·ti·liv·o·rous (rep′tə liv′ər əs), *adj.* feeding on reptiles. [< *reptile* + Latin *vorāre* devour + English *-ous*]

Repub., **1.** Republic. **2.** Republican.

re·pub·lic (ri pub′lik), *n.* **1.** a nation or state in which the citizens elect representatives to manage the government. **2.** the form of government existing in such a state. **3.** any body of persons or things: *the republic of authors and scholars.* [< Middle French *république*, learned borrowing from Latin *rēs pūblica* public interest; the state; *rēs* affair, matter(s); things; *pūblica*, feminine adjective, public] —**Syn. 1.** commonwealth.

re·pub·li·can (ri pub′lə kən), *adj.* **1.** of a republic; like that of a republic: *republican institutions. Many countries have a republican government.* **2.** favoring a republic. **3.** (of birds) living in communities, as the cliff swallow.
—*n.* a person who favors a republic: *The republicans fought with the royalists.*

Re·pub·li·can (ri pub′lə kən), *U.S.* —*adj.* of or having to do with the Republican Party.
—*n.* a member of the Republican Party. *Abbr.:* Rep.

republican grosbeak, a weaverbird of South Africa, many pairs of which build in common an enormous umbrellalike nest.

Republican Grosbeak (5 in. long)

re·pub·li·can·ism (ri pub′lə kə niz′əm), *n.* **1.** a republican government. **2.** republican principles; adherence to republican principles: *Republicanism was in the air. Radical opinion in England ... suddenly grew more extreme than it had ever been since 1848* (Lytton Strachey).

Re·pub·li·can·ism (ri pub′lə kə niz′əm), *n. U.S.* the principles or policies of the Republican Party.

re·pub·li·can·i·za·tion (ri pub′lə kə nə zā′shən), *n.* the act or process of republicanizing.

re·pub·li·can·ize (ri pub′lə kə nīz), *v.*, **-ized, -iz·ing.** —*v.t.* to make republican. —*v.i.* to show republican tendencies.

Republican Party, **1.** one of the two main political parties now existing in the United States. **2.** (originally) the Antifederal Party which later became the Democratic-Republican Party.

re·pub·li·ca·tion (rē′pub lə kā′shən), *n.* **1.** publication anew. **2.** a book or the like published again.

republic of letters, **1.** all people engaged in literary or learned work. **2.** the field of literature.

re·pu·di·ate (ri pyü′dē āt), *v.t.*, **-at·ed, -at·ing.** **1.** to refuse to accept; reject: *The old man shook his head, gently repudiating the imputation* (Dickens). **2.** to refuse to acknowledge or pay: *to repudiate a debt, to repudiate a claim.* **3.** to cast off; disown: *to repudiate a son.* **4.** to put away by divorce. [< Latin *repudiāre* (with English *-ate*[1]) < *repudium* divorce, rejection, perhaps < *re-* back, away + unrecorded *podium* a kicking, related to *pēs, pedis* foot] —**Syn. 1.** disclaim.

re·pu·di·a·tion (ri pyü′dē ā′shən), *n.* the act of repudiating, or fact or condition of being repudiated: *repudiation of a doctrine or public debt.*

re·pu·di·a·tion·ist (ri pyü′dē ā′shə nist), *n.* a person who favors repudiation, especially of a public debt.

re·pu·di·a·tive (ri pyü′dē ā′tiv), *adj.* characterized by repudiation.

re·pu·di·a·tor (ri pyü′dē ā′tər), *n.* a person who repudiates or favors repudiation.

re·pugn (ri pyün′), *v.t.* **1.** to oppose; object to. **2.** to cause repugnance in. —*v.i. Obsolete.* to be opposed. [< Old French *repugner*, learned borrowing from Latin *repūgnāre;* see REPUGNANT]

re·pug·nance (ri pug′nəns), *n.* **1.** a strong dislike, distaste, or aversion: *Some people feel a repugnance for snakes.* **2.** a contradiction; inconsistency: *repugnance between statements.* —**Syn. 1.** antipathy.

re·pug·nan·cy (ri pug′nən sē), *n., pl.* **-cies.** repugnance.

re·pug·nant (ri pug′nənt), *adj.* **1.** distasteful; disagreeable; offensive: *Work is repugnant to lazy people.* **2.** objecting; averse; opposed: *We are repugnant to every sort of dishonesty.* **3.** inconsistent; contrary (to): *a clause repugnant to the body of the act.* [< Latin *repūgnāns, -antis*, present participle of *repūgnāre* to resist < *re-* back + *pūgnāre* to fight < *pūgna* a fight, battle] —**re·pug′nant·ly,** *adv.* —**Syn. 1.** objectionable.

re·pulse (ri puls′), *v.*, **-pulsed, -puls·ing,** *n.* —*v.t.* **1.** to drive back; repel: *Our soldiers repulsed the enemy. Thy faithful dogs ... who ... will ... Repulse the prowling wolf* (John Dryden). **2.** to refuse to accept; reject: *She coldly repulsed him.*
—*n.* **1.** a driving back, or being driven back: *After the second repulse, the enemy surrendered.* **2.** refusal; rejection.
[< Latin *repulsus*, past participle of *repellere* repel] —**re·puls′er,** *n.*

re·pul·sion (ri pul′shən), *n.* **1.** strong dislike or aversion: *a look of repulsion.* **2.** a repelling or being repelled; repulse. **3.** *Physics.* the tendency of particles or forces to increase their distance from one another: *Protons exert forces of repulsion on other protons, electrons exert forces of repulsion on other electrons ...* (Sears and Zemansky). —**Syn. 1.** repugnance.

re·pul·sive (ri pul′siv), *adj.* **1.** causing strong dislike or aversion: *Snakes are repulsive to some people.* **2.** tending to drive back or repel. **3.** *Physics.* of the nature of or characterized by repulsion. —**re·pul′sive·ly,** *adv.* —**re·pul′sive·ness,** *n.* —**Syn. 1.** revolting.

re·pur·chase (rē pėr′chəs), *v.*, **-chased, -chas·ing,** *n.* —*v.t.* to buy again; buy back. —*n.* the act of buying back. —**re·pur′chas·er,** *n.*

rep·u·ta·bil·i·ty (rep′yə tə bil′ə tē), *n.* reputable quality.

rep·u·ta·ble (rep′yə tə bəl), *adj.* **1.** having a good reputation; well thought of; in good repute: **2.** *a reputable man, a reputable newspaper.* **2.** (of words) having acceptable usage. —**rep′u·ta·ble·ness,** *n.* —**Syn. 1.** respectable, estimable.

rep·u·ta·bly (rep′yə tə blē), *adv.* in a reputable manner; without disgrace or discredit: *He conducts his business reputably.*

rep·u·ta·tion (rep′yə tā′shən), *n.* **1.** what people think and say the character of a person or thing is; character in the opinion of others: *He had the reputation of being very bright. This store has an excellent reputation for fair dealing.* **2.** a good name; good reputation: *to ruin one's reputation.* **3.** fame: *a man of some local reputation.* —**Syn. 1.** name, repute.

re·pute (ri pyüt′), *n., v.*, **-put·ed, -put·ing.** —*n.* **1.** reputation: *a weekly paper of fair repute* (George Gissing). *This is a district of bad repute on account of so many robberies.* **2.** good reputation; credit. [< verb] —*v.t.* to suppose to be; consider; suppose: *He is reputed the richest man in the State.* [< Latin *reputāre* < *re-* back, again + *putāre* to think; cleanse, prune (a tree)]

re·put·ed (ri pyü′tid), *adj.* accounted or supposed to be such: *the reputed author of a book.*

re·put·ed·ly (ri pyü′tid lē), *adv.* by repute; supposedly.

req., **1.** required. **2.** requisition.

re·quest (ri kwest′), *v.t.* **1.** to ask for; ask as a favor: *He requested a loan from the bank.* **2.** to ask: *He requested her to go with him.*
—*n.* **1.** the act of asking: *She did it at our request. Your request for a ticket was made too late.* **2.** what is asked for: *He granted my request.* **3.** the state of being asked for or sought after: *She is such a good singer that she is in great request.*
by request, in response to a request: *Records are played by request on some radio programs.*
[< Old French *requester* < *requeste* < Vulgar Latin *requaesita*, for Late Latin *requaesīta*, past participle of *requaerere* < Latin *re-* again, back + *quaerere* to ask, seek] —**re·quest′er,** *n.*
—**Syn.** *v.t.* **1.** See **ask.** **2.** beg, beseech, entreat.

Req·ui·em or **req·ui·em** (rek′wē əm, rē′kwē-), *n.* **1. a.** a Mass for the dead; musical church service for the dead. **b.** the music for it. **2.** any musical service or hymn for the dead. **3.** anything that suggests a service or hymn for the dead: *Every bird thy requiem sings* (Robert Burns). [< Latin *requiem*, accusative of *requiēs* rest < *re-* (intensive) + *quiēs, -ētis* quiet (*requiem* is the first word of the Mass for the dead)]

re·qui·es·cat (rek′wē es′kat), *n. Latin.* "May he (or she) rest (in peace)," a wish or prayer for the dead.

re·qui·es·cat in pa·ce (rek′wē es′kat in pā′sē), *Latin.* "May he (or she) rest in peace," a wish or prayer for the repose of the dead: *They will get a much more sympathetic treatment from a Christian friend who will mumble a requiescat in pace over their bones* (Time). *Abbr.:* R.I.P.

re·quir·a·ble (ri kwīr′ə bəl), *adj.* that can be required.

re·quire (ri kwīr′), *v.*, **-quired, -quir·ing.** —*v.t.* **1.** to have need for; need; want: *We shall require more spoons at our party.* **2.** to command; order; demand: *That condition requires immediate attention.* **3.** to put under an obligation or necessity: *Circumstances may require us to submit.* **4.** *Archaic.* to ask for; seek. —*v.i.* to make necessary: *to do as the law requires, ready to act if circumstances require.* [< Latin *requīrere* < *re-* back, again + *quaerere* to ask, seek. Related to REQUEST.] —**Syn.** *v.t.* **2.** See **demand.**

re·quired course (ri kwīrd′), a course of study that all students of a school or department must take, usually to fulfill the requirements for a major or for graduation.

required reading, a book or books that all students of a class or school must read: *Stalin's Short History of the Communist Party, which was required reading for university students [in the USSR], was withdrawn* (London Times).

re·quire·ment (ri kwīr′mənt), *n.* **1.** a need; thing needed: *Food is a requirement of life. Patience is a requirement in teaching.* **2.** a demand; thing demanded: *He has fulfilled all requirements for graduation.* —**Syn. 1.** essential.

req·ui·site (rek′wə zit), *adj.* required by circumstances; needed; necessary: *the qualities requisite for a leader, the number of votes requisite for election.* —*n.* a thing needed: *Food and air are requisites for life.* [< Latin *requīsītus*, past participle of *requīrere;* see REQUIRE] —**req′ui·site·ly,** *adv.* —**req′ui·site·ness,** *n.* —**Syn.** *adj.* essential, indispensable.

req·ui·si·tion (rek′wə zish′ən), *n.* **1.** the act of requiring. **2.** a demand made, especially a formal written demand: *the requisition of supplies for troops.* **3.** the state of being required for use or called into service: *The car was in constant requisition for errands.* **4.** an essential condition; requirement.
—*v.t.* **1.** to demand or take by authority: *to requisition supplies, horses, or labor.* **2.** to make demands upon: *The army requisitioned the village for food.*
—**Syn.** *v.t.* **1.** commandeer.

re·quit·a·ble (ri kwī′tə bəl), *adj.* that can be requited: *God's favours ..., how little they are requitable, for we can give Him nothing but His own* (Robert Boyle).

re·quit·al (ri kwī′təl), *n.* repayment; payment; return: *What requital can we make for all his kindness to us?* —**Syn.** recompense.

re·quite (ri kwīt′), *v.t.*, **-quit·ed, -quit·ing.** **1.** to pay back; make return for: *The Bible says to requite evil with good.* **2.** to make return to; reward: *My father will be glad to requite you for this night's hospitality* (Bret Harte). **3.** to make retaliation for; avenge. [< *re-* back + *quite*, variant of *quit*] —**re·quit′er,** *n.* —**Syn. 1.** repay, reward.

re·quite·ment (ri kwīt′mənt), *n.* requital.

re·ra·di·ate (rē rā′dē āt), *v.t., v.i.*, **-at·ed, -at·ing.** to send out (radio signals, etc.) again into the surrounding area by reflection or transmission.

re·ra·di·a·tion (rē′rā dē ā′shən), *n.* a radiating again; radiation received and given off again: *Reradiation may cause distorted reception by radios.*

re·ran (rē ran′), *v.* the past tense of **rerun.**

re·read (rē rēd′), *v.t., v.i.*, **-read** (-red′), **-read·ing.** to read again or anew.

re·read·a·ble (rē rē′də bəl), *adj.* that can be reread; worth rereading: *She tells retellable and rereadable stories* (Punch).

rere·brace (rir′brās′), *n.* a piece of armor for the upper arm, from the shoulder to the elbow. [< unrecorded Anglo-French *rerebras* < *rere-* back, rear + *bras* arm. Compare French *arrièrebras* (literally) rear arm.]

rere·dos (rir′dos), *n.* **1.** a screen or a decorated part of the wall behind an altar: *From the nave, the flat wall appears to be an apse behind the reredos, with the figures of Moses and Aaron standing out as clear as statues* (Manchester Guardian). **2.** *Archaic.* the back of a fireplace. [< Anglo-French *reredos,* short for *areredos* < Old French *a-* to + *rere* rear¹ (< Latin *retrum*) + *dos* back¹ < Latin *dossus,* variant of *dorsum.* Compare ARREARS.]

Reredos (def. 1)
Lichfield Cathedral, England

rere·mouse (rir′mous′), *n., pl.* **-mice.** *Archaic.* a bat. [Old English *hreremūs* < *hrere* (uncertain meaning and origin) + *mūs* mouse]

re·roll (rē rōl′), *v.t.* to roll again: *100,000 tons of aluminum ... stock ... will be purchased by the four stockholders and re-rolled into light gauge aluminum* (Wall Street Journal).

re·roll·er (rē rōl′ər), *n.* a person or thing that rerolls: *The cold-rolling firms take steel from the rerollers and pickle it to clean off scale* (London Times).

re·route (rē rüt′, -rout′), *v.t.,* **-rout·ed, -rout·ing.** to send by a new or different route.

re·run (*v.* rē run′; *n.* rē′run′), *v.,* **-ran, -run, -run·ning,** *n.* —*v.t., v.i.* to run again. —*n.* **1.** a running again: *the rerun of a race.* **2.** a television program or motion-picture film that is shown again: *We even saw one TV program that was a rerun of a Summit review —which was taped to begin with—and the next day, ... there was a re-review of the review* (Saturday Review).

res (rēz), *n., pl.* **res** (rēz). *Latin.* **1.** a matter. **2.** a case in law.

res., **1.** reserve. **2.** residence. **3.** resides. **4.** resigned. **5.** resistance.

res ad·ju·di·ca·ta (rēz ə jü′də kā′tə), *Latin.* **1.** a case in which a final decision has been reached by a court of highest authority. **2.** (literally) a case decided.

re·said (rē sed′), *v.* the past tense and past participle of **resay.**

re·sail (rē sāl′), *v.t., v.i.* **1.** to sail again. **2.** to sail back.

re·sal·a·ble (rē sā′lə bəl), *adj.* that can be resold; fit to be resold; easily resold: *Cigarettes, radios, and cameras ... are resalable on the black market for several times their original cost* (Time).

re·sale (rē′sāl′, rē sāl′), *n.* **1.** a selling again: *the resale of a house.* **2.** a selling at retail: *This store has a 20 per cent markup over the wholesale price for resale.*

resale price maintenance, *Especially British.* fair trade: *Resale price maintenance ... has been a controversial point with British Governments for the past 12 years* (London Times).

re·sa·lute (rē′sə lüt′), *v.t.,* **-lut·ed, -lut·ing.** **1.** to salute or greet anew. **2.** to salute in return.

re·say (rē sā′), *v.t.,* **-said, -say·ing.** to say again; repeat: *Am I resaying the moldy theory that women have no need, some say no capacity, to create art, because they can create babies?* (Harper's).

re·scind (ri sind′), *v.t.* to deprive of force; repeal; cancel: *to rescind a law.* [< Latin *rēscindere* < *re-* back + *scindere* to cut, related to Greek *schízein.* Compare SCHISM.] —**re·scind′er,** *n.* —**Syn.** revoke.

re·scind·a·ble (ri sin′də bəl), *adj.* that can be rescinded.

re·scind·ment (ri sind′mənt), *n.* rescission.

res·cin·na·mine (ri sin′ə mēn), *n.* a gray or whitish alkaloid obtained from rauwolfia, used as a sedative and tranquilizer. *Formula:* $C_{35}H_{42}N_2O_9$

re·scis·sion (ri sizh′ən), *n.* a rescinding. [< Latin *rēscissiō, -ōnis* < *rēscindere;* see RESCIND] —**Syn.** annulment.

re·scis·so·ry (ri sis′ər ē, -siz′-), *adj.* serving to rescind.

re·score (rē skôr′, -skōr′), *v.t.,* **-scored, -scor·ing.** to score again or in a new way.

re·screen (rē skrēn′), *v.t.* to screen again.

re·script (rē′skript), *n.* **1.** a written answer to a question or petition. **2.** an official announcement; edict; decree. **3.** a rewriting: *I wrote it three times—chastening and subduing the phrases at every rescript* (Charlotte Brontë). **4.** an official answer from the Pope or a Roman emperor on some question referred to them. [< Latin *rēscriptum,* (originally) neuter past participle of *rēscrībere* to write in reply < *re-* back + *scrībere* to write]

res·cue (res′kyü), *v.,* **-cued, -cu·ing,** *n.* —*v.t.* **1.** to save from danger, capture, harm, etc.; free; deliver: *The firemen rescued the children from the burning house.* **2.** *Law.* **a.** to take (a person) forcibly or unlawfully from a jail, policeman, etc. **b.** to take (property) from legal custody.
—*n.* **1.** a saving or freeing from danger, capture, harm, etc.: *A dog was chasing our cat when Mary came to the rescue.* **2.** *Law.* the forcible or unlawful taking of a person or thing from the care of the law. [< Old French *rescou-,* stem of *rescourre* < *re-* again + *escourre* to shake, stir < Latin *excutere* < *ex-* out + *quatere* to shake] —**res′cu·er,** *n.*
—**Syn.** *v.t.* **1. Rescue, deliver** mean to save or free from danger, harm, or restraint. **Rescue** means to save, by quick and forceful action, a person from immediate or threatened danger or harm, such as death, injury, attack, capture, or confinement: *Searchers rescued the boys lost in the mountains.* **Deliver** means to set someone free from something holding him in captivity or under its power or control, such as prison, slavery, oppression, suffering, temptation, or evil: *Advancing troops delivered the prisoners.*

rescue grass, a variety of brome grass native to South America, grown for forage.

re·search (ri sėrch′, rē′sėrch), *n.* a careful hunting for facts or truth about a subject, inquiry; investigation: *The researches of men of science have done much to lessen disease.* —*v.i.* to make researches: *On these three subjects he is directed to read and research—corn laws, finance, tithes* (Robert Southey). —*v.t.* to search into; investigate carefully: *He had employed himself ... in researching history* (Mrs. A.M. Bennett). [< Middle French *recerche* < Old French *recercher* < *re-* again + *cercher,* later, *chercher* to seek for, search] —**Syn.** *n.* study.

re-search (rē sėrch′), *v.t., v.i.* to search again or repeatedly: *The lads searched and re-searched this place, but in vain* (Mark Twain).

re·searched (ri sėrcht′, rē′sėrcht), *adj.* based upon research: *Although the work is heavily researched, it does not get entangled with historical theories and countertheories* (Wall Street Journal).

re·search·er (ri sėr′chər, rē′sėr′-), *n.* a person who makes researches; investigator.

re·search·ful (ri sėrch′fəl), *adj.* characterized by research; inquisitive: *Pity that the researchful notary has not ... told us in what century ... he was a writer* (Samuel Taylor Coleridge).

research reactor, an atomic reactor for the study of fission, nuclear energy, etc., or for research in radioactivity, medicine, biology, etc.

re·seat (rē sēt′), *v.t.* **1.** to seat again. **2.** to put a new seat on. **3.** to put in place again: *to reseat a valve.* **4.** to restore parliamentary rights and privileges to.

ré·seau (rā zō′), *n.* **1.** *Astronomy.* a crisscross of squares photographed on the same plate as a star for the purpose of measurement. **2.** a sensitive filter screen used in making color films. **3.** a network. **4.** the mesh in lace. [< French *réseau,* probably < Old French *roisel* (diminutive) < *roiz* < Latin *rētēs,* plural of *rēte* net]

re·sect (ri sekt′), *v.t. Surgery.* to cut away; pare off; remove a part of. [< Latin *resectus,* past participle of *resecāre* to cut off < *re-* back + *secāre* to cut]

re·sec·tion (ri sek′shən), *n.* the surgical removal of a portion of some structure, especially bone. [< Latin *resectiō, -ōnis* < *resecāre;* see RESECT]

re·sec·tion·al (ri sek′shə nəl), *adj.* of or having to do with a resection: *In some places lung collapse procedures such as artificial pneumothorax were abandoned in favour of resectional surgery* (J.A. Myers).

re·sec·to·scope (ri sek′tə skōp), *n.* a thin, tubular, cutting instrument with a sliding knife, which allows a resection to be performed without any opening other than that made by the instrument itself.

re·se·da (ri sē′də), *n.* **1.** any mignonette. **2.** grayish green. —*adj.* grayish-green. [< Latin *resēda*]

res·e·da·ceous (res′ə dā′shəs), *adj.* belonging to a family of dicotyledonous, largely Mediterranean plants typified by the mignonette. [< New Latin *Resedaceae* the reseda family (< Latin *resēda*) + English *-ous*]

re·see (rē sē′), *v.t.,* **-saw, -seen, -see·ing.** to see again: *If I could see and resee a hundred times this Captain's shifty slow fox trot, ... I feel sure I should not tire of it* (Manchester Guardian Weekly).

re·seed (rē sēd′), *v.t., v.i.* to seed again: *A large part of the increase occurred in Europe, where a considerable acreage of damaged wheat was reseeded to barley* (Wayne Dexter).

re·seg·men·ta·tion (rē′seg mən tā′shən), *n.* **1.** a dividing into segments. **2.** a dividing of segments into smaller segments.

re·seg·re·gate (rē seg′rə gāt), *v.t.,* **-gat·ed, -gat·ing.** **1.** to segregate (a racial group) again or in a new way. **2.** to renew segregation in: *In effect the schools have been resegregated on an overwhelmingly Negro basis* (Wall Street Journal).

re·seg·re·ga·tion (rē seg′rə gā′shən), *n.* a resegregating; renewed segregation: *Shifts in residential patterns since then have resulted in large-scale resegregation* (New York Times).

re·seize (rē sēz′), *v.t.,* **-seized, -seiz·ing.** **1.** to seize again; seize a second time. **2.** to put into possession of; reinstate. **3.** *Law.* to take possession of, as of lands and tenements which have been disseized.

re·sei·zure (rē sē′zhər), *n.* a second seizure; the act of seizing again.

re·sell (rē sel′), *v.t.,* **-sold, -sell·ing.** to sell again.

re·sem·blance (ri zem′bləns), *n.* **1.** likeness; similar appearance: *Twins often show great resemblance. There are certain resemblances between the two cases.* **2.** appearance: *under the resemblance of a mist.* **3.** a copy; image. [< Anglo-French *resemblance* < Old French *resembler* to resemble]
—**Syn. 1. Resemblance, similarity** mean a likeness between two persons or things. **Resemblance** emphasizes looking alike or having some of the same external features or superficial qualities: *There is some resemblance between the accounts of the fire, but all the important details are different.* **Similarity** suggests being of the same kind or nature, or having some of the same essential qualities: *The similarity between the two reports suggests that one person wrote both.*

re·sem·blant (ri zem′blənt), *adj.* resembling; similar: *The yearling was surely the mare's son, because two homelier but more resemblant animals never lived* (New Yorker).

re·sem·ble (ri zem′bəl), *v.t.,* **-bled, -bling.** **1.** to be like; be similar to; have likeness to in form, figure, or qualities: *An orange resembles a grapefruit.* **2.** *Archaic.* to liken; compare: *Unto what is the kingdom of God like? and whereunto shall I resemble it?* (Luke 13:18). [< Old French *resembler* < *re-* again + *sembler* to appear < Latin *simulāre* (originally) to copy < *similis* similar]

re·sem·bler (ri zem′blər), *n.* a person or thing that resembles some other person or thing.

re·send (rē send′), *v.t.,* **-sent, -send·ing.** **1.** to send again or in a new way. **2.** to send back.

re·sent (ri zent′), *v.t.* **1.** to feel injured and angry at; feel indignation at: *She resented being called a baby. He naturally resented the promotion of his younger colleague to a rank above his own.* **2.** to show such feeling by action or speech: *Putting his hand upon his sword, the knight threatened to resent this insult.* [< French *ressentir* < *re-* back + *sentir* < Latin *sentīre* to feel] —**re·sent′er,** *n.*

re·sent·ful (ri zent′fəl), *adj.* feeling resentment; injured and angry; showing resentment: *a resentful child, a resentful remark.* —**re·sent′ful·ly,** *adv.* —**re·sent′ful·ness,** *n.*

re·sent·ment (ri zent′mənt), *n.* **1.** the feeling that one has at being injured or insulted; indignation: *Everyone feels resent-*

ment at being treated unfairly. Resentment is never an asset (Atlantic). **2.** a showing of this feeling by action or speech. —**Syn. 1.** pique, umbrage.

res·er·pine (res′ər pin, -pēn; rə sėr′-), *n.* a powerful alkaloid obtained from the juices of the rauwolfia plant, used as a tranquilizer and sedative, in reducing high blood pressure, and in the treatment of mental illness. *Formula:* $C_{33}H_{40}N_2O_9$ [apparently < New Latin *R(auwolfia) serp(entina)* the rauwolfia plant + English *-ine*²]

res·er·va·tion (rez′ər vā′shən), *n.* **1.** a keeping back; hiding in part; something not expressed: *She outwardly approved of the plan but with the mental reservation that she would change it to suit herself.* **2.** a limiting condition: *We accepted the plan with two reservations. The United States accepted the World Court with reservations plainly stated.* **3.** *U.S.* land set aside for a special purpose: *The government has set apart Indian reservations.* **4.** an arrangement to keep a thing for a person; securing of accommodations, etc.: *We made reservations for rooms at the hotel.* **5.** something reserved.

off the reservation, away from the norm or from the expected way of acting, thinking, etc.: *Though some of them strayed off the reservation . . ., most of New York's influential labor leaders are firmly in the Wagner-Screvane camp* (Harper's).

—**Syn. 2.** limitation. **3.** reserve.

re·serve (ri zėrv′), *v.*, **-served, -serv·ing,** *n., adj.* —*v.t.* **1.** to keep back; hold back: *Mother reserved her complaint about my messy room until my friend left. Take each man's censure, but reserve thy judgment* (Shakespeare). **2.** to set apart: *time reserved for recreation. He reserves his evenings for reading to his son.* **3.** to save for use later: *Reserve enough money for your fare home.* **4.** to set aside for the use of a particular person or persons: *to reserve a table at a restaurant.*

—*n.* **1.** the actual cash in a bank or assets that can be turned into cash quickly: *Reserves are a specified portion of deposits banks are required to keep in cash at Federal Reserve Banks, plus a part of the cash in their own vaults* (Wall Street Journal). **2.** a body of soldiers, ships, aircraft, etc., kept ready to help the main force in battle: *A facet of the proposed program which is of interest to science and industry would be a continuous "screening" of men in the reserve* (Newsweek). **3.** public land set apart for a special purpose: *a forest reserve.* **4.** anything kept back for future use: *a reserve of food or energy.* **5.** the act of keeping back or holding back: *You may speak before her without reserve.* **6.** the fact or condition of being kept, set apart, or saved for use later: *to keep money in reserve.* **7.** a keeping one's thoughts, feelings, and affairs to oneself; self-restraint; lack of friendliness: *to maintain a polite reserve when talking about politics.* **8.** an exception or qualification to the acceptance of some idea, belief, etc.: *The scientists accepted the new theory with some reserves.* **9.** a silent manner that keeps people from making friends easily: *The deaf man's reserve was mistaken for haughtiness.* **10.** an avoidance of excess, fads, or the like, in literary or artistic work.

reserves, soldiers or sailors not in active service but ready to serve if needed: *The reserves were quickly mobilized during the war.*

—*adj.* kept in reserve; forming a reserve: *a reserve stock, a reserve force. A way to measure the banks' relative reserve position . . . is the amount they need to borrow from the Federal Reserve Bank to meet their reserve requirements* (Wall Street Journal).

[< Latin *reservāre* < *re-* back + *servāre* to keep] —**re·serv′er,** *n.*

—**Syn.** *v.t.* **1.** retain.

reserve bank, one of the twelve Federal Reserve Banks.

reserve book, a book held in reserve, usually one which cannot be taken from the library.

re·served (ri zėrvd′), *adj.* **1.** kept in reserve; kept by special arrangement: *a reserved seat.* **2.** set apart: *a reserved section at the stadium.* **3.** self-restrained in action or speech: *reserved comment. As a statesman he was reserved, seldom showing his own thoughts* (James A. Froude). **4.** disposed to keep to oneself: *A reserved boy does not make friends easily.* —**Syn. 1.** withheld, retained. **3.** restrained, reticent.

re·serv·ed·ly (ri zėr′vid lē), *adv.* in a reserved manner.

re·serv·ed·ness (ri zėr′vid nis), *n.* the character of being reserved.

reserved powers, *U.S.* the powers not granted by the Constitution to the Federal government but reserved for the states or the people.

reserve officer, an officer in the reserves.

re·serves (ri zėrvz′), *n.pl.* See under **reserve,** *n.*

re·serv·ist (ri zėr′vist), *n.* a soldier or sailor not in active service but available if needed: *50,000 reservists were recalled to the colors* (Time).

res·er·voir (rez′ər vwär, -vwôr, -vôr), *n.* **1.** a place where water is collected and stored for use, especially an artificial basin created by the damming of a river: *This reservoir supplies the entire city.* **2.** anything to hold a liquid: *the ink reservoir of a fountain pen, an oil reservoir for an engine.* **3.** a place where anything is collected and stored: *His mind was a reservoir of facts.* **4.** a great supply: *a reservoir of manpower. There exists in the world today a gigantic reservoir of good will toward us, the American people* (Wendell Willkie). **5.** a part of an animal or plant in which some fluid or secretion is collected or retained. [< French *réservoir* < Old French *reserver* to reserve]

re·set (*v.* rē set′; *n.* rē′set′), *v.*, **-set, -set·ting,** *n.* —*v.t.* **1.** to set again: *The diamond was reset in platinum. John's broken arm had to be reset.* **2.** to set (type) again.

—*n.* **1.** the act of resetting. **2.** a thing reset. **3.** matter set in type again.

re·set·ta·ble (rē set′ə bəl), *adj.* that can be reset.

re·set·tle (rē set′əl), *v.t., v.i.*, **-tled, -tling.** to settle again; reëstablish; relocate.

re·set·tle·ment (rē set′əl mənt), *n.* a settling again.

res ges·tae (rēz jes′tē), *Latin.* **1.** deeds; achievements. **2.** *Law.* facts; accompanying facts.

resh (rāsh), *n.* the twentieth letter of the Hebrew alphabet. [< Hebrew *resh*]

re·shape (rē shāp′), *v.t.*, **-shaped, -shap·ing.** to shape anew; form into a new or different shape.

re·ship (rē ship′), *v.*, **-shipped, -ship·ping.** —*v.t.* **1.** to ship again: *to reship merchandise to Chicago.* **2. a.** to put on board of a ship again. **b.** to transfer to a different ship. —*v.i.* (of men) to take ship again.

re·ship·ment (rē ship′mənt), *n.* **1.** a shipping again. **2.** that which is shipped again.

re·shoot (rē shüt′), *v.t., v.i.*, **-shot, -shoot·ing.** to shoot again or in a new way: *And then the scene was shot and reshot from the new angle* (New Yorker).

re·shuf·fle (rē shuf′əl), *v.*, **-fled, -fling,** *n.* —*v.t.* **1.** to arrange again: *It is like forever shuffling and reshuffling a pack of cards* (Maclean's). **2.** to arrange in a new or different way: *The Premier, who delights in political intricacy, has appointed or reshuffled no fewer than 104 Cabinet ministers* (Time). —*n.* a new or different arrangement; shakeup.

re·shuf·fle·ment (rē shuf′əl mənt), *n.* a reshuffling; reshuffle: *In the course of a simultaneous reshufflement of the government, Lajos Fehér . . . was appointed one of the four vice-premiers* (Stephen Borsody).

re·side (ri zīd′), *v.i.*, **-sid·ed, -sid·ing. 1.** to live (in or at) for a long time; dwell: *This family has resided in Richmond for 100 years.* **2.** to be (in); exist (in): *Her charm resides in her happy smile.* [< Latin *residēre* < *re-* back + *sedēre* to sit, settle] —**Syn. 2.** inhere.

res·i·dence (rez′ə dəns), *n.* **1.** a house; home; abode: *a fine residence. Many of these residences, which are among the most magnificent country homes on the face of the earth, are now going to solitary ruin* (Newsweek). **2.** a residing; living; dwelling: *Long residence in France made him very fond of the French.* **3.** the period of residing in a place. **4.** the fact of living or staying regularly at or in some place for the discharge of special duties, or to comply with some regulation: *the residence of a rector in his benefice, a two-year requirement of residence for students.* **5.** the seat of some power, principle, activity, or the like.

in residence, living in a place while on duty or doing active work: *a doctor in residence.*

—**Syn. 1.** dwelling, habitation.

res·i·den·cy (rez′ə dən sē), *n., pl.* **-cies. 1.** residence. **2.** the position of a doctor who continues practicing in a hospital after completing his internship. **3. a.** (formerly) the official residence of a representative of the British governor general of India at a native court. **b.** the official residence of a diplomatic officer or governor general. **4.** (formerly) an administrative division of the Dutch East Indies.

res·i·dent (rez′ə dənt), *n.* **1.** a person living in a place, not a visitor: *The residents of the town are proud of its new library.* **2.** a resident physician, especially one who has completed internship. **3.** an official sent to live in a foreign land to represent his country. **4.** (formerly) a representative of the British governor general of India at a native court. **5.** (formerly) the governor of an administrative division of the Dutch East Indies.

—*adj.* **1.** dwelling in a place; staying: *A resident owner lives on his property. Grandmother wants a resident companion.* **2.** living in a place while on duty or doing active work: *Doctor Jones is a resident physician at the hospital.* **3.** not migratory: *English sparrows are resident birds.*

[< Latin *residēns, -entis,* present participle of *residēre* reside]

res·i·dent·er (rez′ə den′tər), *n. Scottish and U.S.* a resident; an inhabitant.

res·i·den·tial (rez′ə den′shəl), *adj.* **1.** of, having to do with, or fitted for homes or residences: *They live in a good residential district.* **2.** having to do with residence: *a residential qualification for schoolteachers.*

res·i·den·ti·ar·y (rez′ə den′shē er′ē, -shər-), *adj., n., pl.* **-ar·ies.** —*adj.* **1.** residing in a place; resident. **2.** involving official residence: *a residentiary canonry.*

—*n.* **1.** a resident. **2.** a clergyman who is bound to official residence.

res·i·dent·ship (rez′ə dənt ship), *n.* the condition or station of a resident.

re·sid·er (ri zī′dər), *n.* a resident.

re·sid·u·a (ri zij′ü ə), *n.* plural of **residuum.**

re·sid·u·al (ri zij′ü əl), *adj.* **1.** of or forming a residue; remaining; left over: *Residual fuel oil is the thick, heavy oil left over after refining crude oil.* **2.** left after subtraction. **3.** *Geology.* resulting from the weathering of rock: *residual clay soil, a residual deposit.*

—*n.* **1.** the amount left over; remainder. **2.** a residual quantity. **3.** a fee paid to a performer for each rerun of a television commercial, motion picture, etc.

residual oil, a heavy liquid hydrocarbon obtained as a residual by-product of petroleum distillation, used mainly as an industrial fuel: *Residual oil is used by schools and factories as both a fuel and a heating oil* (Wall Street Journal).

residual quantity, *Algebra.* a binomial having one of its terms negative, as 2a – b.

re·sid·u·ar·y (ri zij′ü er′ē), *adj.* **1.** receiving or entitled to the remainder of an estate: *a residuary legatee.* **2.** residual.

res·i·due (rez′ə dü, -dyü), *n.* **1.** what remains after a part is taken; remainder: *The syrup had dried up, leaving a sticky residue at the bottom of the jar. The solution of almost any problem in science leaves, as a residue, other unsolved questions* (Fred W. Emerson). **2.** *Law.* the part of a testator's estate that is left after all debts, charges, and particular devises and bequests have been satisfied: *Mr. Smith's will directed that after the payment of all debts and $10,000 to his brother, the residue of his property should go to his son.* **3.** *Chemistry.* an atom or group of atoms considered as a radical or part of a molecule.

[< Old French *residu,* learned borrowing from Latin *residuum* left over. Doublet of RESIDUUM.]

re·sid·u·um (ri zij′ü əm), *n., pl.* **-sid·u·a. 1.** what is left at the end of any process; residue; remainder. **2.** *Law.* the residue of an estate. [< Latin *residuum* < *re-* back + *sedēre* to sit. Doublet of RESIDUE.]

re·sign (ri zīn′), *v.i.* **1.** to give up a job, office, position, etc.: *The manager of the football team resigned.* **2.** to yield; submit: *resigned to one's fate.* —*v.t.* to give up (an office, position, right, etc.): *The manager of the local newspaper resigned his position.*

resign oneself, to submit quietly; adapt oneself without complaint: *John had to resign himself to a week in bed when he hurt his back.*

[< Old French *resigner* < Latin *resīgnāre* to unseal < *re-* back + *sīgnāre* to sign, seal < *sīgnum* a seal] —**re·sign′er,** *n.*

➤ **Resign** is often followed by *from,* though sometimes the object follows without the from: *Jim resigned from the editorship of the school paper.* Or: *Jim resigned the editorship of the school paper.*

re-sign (rē sīn′), *v.t.* to sign again.

res·ig·na·tion (rez′ig nā′shən), *n.* **1.** the act of resigning: *There have been so many resignations from the committee that a new one must be formed.* **2.** a written statement giving notice that one resigns. **3.** patient acceptance; quiet submission: *She bore the pain with resignation.* —**Syn. 3.** acquiescence, meekness.

re·signed (ri zīnd′), *adj.* **1.** accepting what comes without complaint: *resigned obedience.* **2.** characterized by or showing resignation: *a resigned smile* (Joseph Conrad). —**Syn. 1.** submissive, acquiescent.

re·sign·ed·ly (ri zī′nid lē), *adv.* in a resigned manner; with resignation: *Several Greek families have resignedly packed their pathetic belongings and left, to the accompaniment of Turkish jeers and gestures of throat-slitting* (Observer).

re·sign·ed·ness (ri zī′nid nis), *n.* resignation.

re·sile (ri zīl′), *v.i.,* **-siled, -sil·ing. 1.** to spring back, as an elastic body does. **2.** to draw back, as from an agreement or purpose. **3.** to shrink back, as in fear or disgust. [< Middle French *resiler,* learned borrowing from Latin *resilīre* to recoil; see RESILIENT]

re·sil·i·ence (ri zil′ē əns, -zil′yəns), *n.* **1.** the power of springing back; resilient quality or nature; elasticity: *Rubber has resilience.* **2.** buoyancy; cheerfulness: *a man of great resilience.*

re·sil·i·en·cy (ri zil′ē ən sē, -zil′yən-), *n.* resilience.

re·sil·i·ent (ri zil′ē ənt, -zil′yənt), *adj.* **1.** springing back; returning to the original form or position after being bent, compressed, or stretched: *resilient steel, resilient turf.* **2.** readily recovering; buoyant; cheerful: *a resilient nature that throws off trouble.* [< Latin *resiliēns, -entis,* present participle of *resilīre* to rebound, recoil < *re-* back + *salīre* to jump, leap] —**re·sil′i·ent·ly,** *adv.*

re·sil·i·om·e·ter (ri zil′ē om′ə tər), *n.* an instrument for measuring resilience.

res·in (rez′ən), *n.* **1.** a sticky, yellow or brown substance that flows from certain plants and trees, especially the pine and fir. It is used in medicine and varnish. Copal, rosin, and amber are types of resin. **2.** any of a large group of resinlike substances that are made artificially and are used especially in making plastics. —*v.t.* to treat, rub, or coat with resin. [< Latin *rēsina* < *rasis* raw pitch] —**res′in·like′,** *adj.*

res·in·ate (rez′ə nāt), *n., v.,* **-at·ed, -at·ing.** —*n.* a mixture of certain acids in resin, used in making soap, paints, etc.: *New uses already are being found for tung oil through the addition of zinc resinate* (E.G. Moore). —*v.t.* to flavor or impregnate with resin.

resin cyst, a cyst or sac, in wood, containing resin.

resin duct, a canal in the wood of trees, especially conifers, through which resin is secreted and conducted: *The remainder of the softwood structure is composed of narrow rays, usually only one cell wide, and in some cases a small amount of vertical parenchyma and resin ducts* (E.W.J. Phillips).

resin gnat, a small dipterous insect whose larvae live in exuding masses of resin on pine trees and feed on the abraded bark.

Resin Gnat (Line shows actual length.)

re·sin·ic (re zin′ik), *adj.* of or having to do with resin.

res·in·if·er·ous (rez′ə nif′ər əs), *adj.* yielding resin: *a resiniferous tree.*

res·in·i·fy (rez′ə nə fī), *v.,* **-fied, -fy·ing.** —*v.t.* to make resinous. —*v.i.* to become resinous.

res·in·oid (rez′ə noid), *adj.* resinlike. —*n.* a resinlike substance.

res·i·no·sis (rez′ə nō′sis), *n.* an abnormal outflow of resin from a coniferous tree.

res·in·ous (rez′ə nəs), *adj.* **1.** of resin: *Two British scientists ... succeeded in preparing resinous materials which contained ion-exchange groups* (K. S. Spiegler). **2.** like resin. **3.** containing resin; full of resin. [< Latin *rēsīnōsus* < *rēsina;* see RESIN] —**res′in·ous·ly,** *adv.*

resin passage, a resin duct.

res in·te·gra (rēz in′tə grə), *n. Latin.* a matter not yet acted on, or a point of law not yet adjudicated.

res in·ter a·li·os (rēz in′tər ā′li ōs), *Latin.* **1.** the acts of third parties, or strangers to a proceeding, not relevant to the case. **2.** (literally) transactions between others.

res·in·y (rez′ə nē), *adj.* resinous.

res·i·pis·cence (res′ə pis′əns), *n.* **1.** a change to a better frame of mind. **2.** repentance.

res·i·pis·cent (res′ə pis′ənt), *adj.* changing to a better frame of mind. [< Latin *resipiscens, -entis,* present participle of *resipiscere* recover one's senses < *re-* again + *sapere* be wise]

res ip·sa lo·qui·tur (rēz ip′sə lō′kwə tər), *Latin.* the thing itself speaks; the case speaks for itself.

re·sist (ri zist′), *v.t.* **1.** to act against; strive against; oppose: *to resist change. The window resisted his efforts to open it.* **2.** to strive successfully against; keep from: *I could not resist laughing.* **3.** to withstand the action or effect of (an acid, storm, etc.): *A healthy body resists disease.* —*v.i.* to act against something; oppose something.
—*n.* **1.** a coating put on a surface to make it withstand the action of weather, acid, etc. **2.** a coating on parts of a fabric that are not to be colored, when the fabric is dyed.
[< Latin *resistere* < *re-* back + *sistere* take a stand, stand < *stāre* stand] —**re·sist′ing·ly,** *adv.*
—**Syn.** *v.t.* **1.** withstand. See **oppose.**

re·sist·ance (ri zis′təns), *n.* **1.** the act of resisting: *The bank clerk made no resistance to the robbers.* **2.** the power to resist: *She has little resistance to germs and so is often ill. Get enough sleep and eat well-balanced meals to help keep up resistance built up during the cold months* (Time). **3.** a thing or act that resists; opposing force; opposition: *An airplane can overcome the resistance of the air and go in the desired direction, while a balloon simply drifts.* **4.** the property of a conductor that opposes the passage of an electric current and changes electric energy into heat: *Copper has a low resistance. Resistance is the electrical counterpart of friction, and can serve the same damping function* (Roy F. Allison). **5.** a conductor, coil, etc., that offers resistance. **6.** *Physics* an opposing force, especially one tending to prevent motion. [< Middle French *resistance,* alteration of earlier *résistence* < *résister* resist < Latin *resistere;* see RESIST]

Re·sist·ance (ri zis′təns), *n.* an underground movement in a country against foreign military control, as those of France, Holland, and Norway during World War II.

resistance coil, a coil or wire made of metal that has a high resistance, used especially for measuring resistance, reducing voltage or amperage, and producing heat.

resistance thermometer, an electric thermometer based on the variation in conductivity of metals as a result of changing temperature.

re·sist·ant (ri zis′tənt), *adj.* resisting. —*n.* **1.** a resister. **2.** *Dyeing.* a resist.

ré·sis·tant (rā zēs tän′), *n. French.* a member of the Resistance: *During the German occupation, he defended some of the French résistants in the special courts* (New Yorker).

resist dyeing, the process of dyeing in a pattern with a resist.

re·sist·ent (ri zis′tənt), *adj.* resistant.

re·sist·er (ri zis′tər), *n.* **1.** a person or thing that resists. **2.** resistor.

re·sist·i·bil·i·ty (ri zis′tə bil′ə tē), *n.* the quality of being resistible.

re·sist·i·ble (ri zis′tə bəl), *adj.* that can be resisted: *earthquakes ... the least resistible of natural violence* (Samuel Johnson).

re·sis·tive (ri zis′tiv), *adj.* resisting; capable of or inclined to resist.

re·sis·tiv·i·ty (rē′zis tiv′ə tē), *n., pl.* **-ties.** *Electricity.* the resistance of the equivalent of one cubic centimeter of a given substance.

re·sist·less (ri zist′lis), *adj.* **1.** that cannot be resisted: *A resistless impulse made him wander over the earth.* **2.** that cannot resist. —**re·sist′less·ly,** *adv.* —**re·sist′less·ness,** *n.* —**Syn. 1.** irresistible.

re·sis·tor (ri zis′tər), *n.* a conducting body or device to control voltage in an electric circuit, especially of a radio or television set, or other electronic equipment, because of its resistance: *... a resistor is simply a poor conductor of electricity* (John R. Pierce).

re-site (rē sīt′), *v.t.,* **-sit·ed, -sit·ing.** to place on a new site: *If ... it was necessary ultimately to re-site the statue, the islanders would accept that decision graciously* (London Times).

re-size (rē sīz′), *v.t.,* **-sized, -siz·ing.** to size again or anew: *Ads in other column widths can either be resized or they can be floated in the new width* (New York Times).

res ju·di·ca·ta (rēz jü′də kā′tə), *Latin.* res adjudicata.

re-slant (rē slant′, -slänt′), *v.t.* **1.** to slant again. **2.** to slant in a new direction: *Wholehearted notions, when expressed with force and conviction by exceptional men, may serve to reslant the views of whole generations* (Sunday Times).

res·na·tron (rez′nə tron), *n.* a vacuum tube for generating large amounts of high-frequency power, as for jamming radar in warfare. [< *res*(o)*na*(tor) + (elec)*tron*]

res nul·li·us (rēz nul′ē əs), *Latin.* a thing belonging to no one: *The moon, however, is almost certainly res nullius, and therefore capable of appropriation through effective occupation* (Bulletin of Atomic Scientists).

re-sod (rē sod′), *v.t.,* **-sod·ded, -sod·ding.** to sod again: *The only thing that can be done is to completely resod the lawn, after fumigating with methyl bromide* (Science News Letter).

re·sold (rē sōld′), *v.* the past tense and past participle of **resell.**

re·sole (*v.* rē sōl′; *n.* rē′sōl′), *v.,* **-soled, -sol·ing,** *n.* —*v.t.* to put a new sole on (a shoe, etc.). —*n.* a new sole on a shoe, boot, etc.

re·sol·u·bil·i·ty (ri zol′yə bil′ə tē, -sol′-), *n.* the quality of being resoluble.

re·sol·u·ble[1] (rə zol′yə bəl, rez′ə lə-), *adj.* that can be resolved; resolvable: *The distinctiveness of all that which we call brogue, accent, etc., is ultimately resoluble into a specialty of modulation* (John Earle). [< Late Latin *resolūbilis* < Latin *resolvere;* see RESOLVE] —**re·sol′u·ble·ness,** *n.*

re·sol·u·ble[2] (rē sol′yə bəl), *adj.* that can be dissolved again: *... a precipitate partly resoluble in carbonate of ammonia* (Andrew Ure). [< *re-* + *soluble* (def. 1)]

res·o·lute (rez′ə lüt), *adj.* **1.** having a fixed resolve; determined: *He was resolute in his attempt to climb to the top of the mountain.* **2.** constant in pursuing a purpose; bold: *The risks will be greater in a few years, if we* [*the U.S.A.*] *dare not be resolute now* (Elmer Davis). **3.** indicating or suggesting firmness and determination: *a resolute attitude, a resolute chin.* [< Latin *resolutus,* past participle of *resolvere;* see RESOLVE] —**res′o·lute′ly,** *adv.* —**res′o·lute′ness,** *n.*

res·o·lu·tion (rez′ə lü′shən), *n.* **1.** a thing decided on; thing determined: *He made a resolution to get up early.* **2.** the act of resolving or determining. **3.** the power of holding firmly to a purpose; determination: *Lincoln's resolution overcame the obstacles of poverty.* **4.** a formal expression of opinion: *The club passed a resolution thanking Mr. Kay for his help throughout the year. Strong resolutions were adapted* [*in Parliament*] *against the queen* (Macaulay). **5.** a breaking into parts. **6.** the act or result of solving; solution: *Of this question ... we must be content to live without the resolution* (Samuel Johnson). **7.** *Medicine.* the reduction or disappearance of inflammation without the formation of pus. **8.** *Music.* **a.** the progression of a voice part or of the harmony as a whole from a discord to a concord. **b.** the tone or chord by which this is effected. **9.** *Optics.* the ability of a lens to produce separate images of objects that are very close together: *Resolution is the capacity of a lens to show two close objects as two, rather than as a single fuzzy one* (Scientific American).

res·o·lu·tion·er (rez′ə lü′shə nər), *n.* a person making, accepting, or approving a resolution.

res·o·lu·tion·ist (rez′ə lü′shə nist), *n.* a resolutioner.

re·solv·a·bil·i·ty (ri zol′və bil′ə tē), *n.* the property of being resolvable; resolvableness.

re·solv·a·ble (ri zol′və bəl), *adj.* that can be resolved. —**re·solv′a·ble·ness,** *n.*

re·solve (ri zolv′), *v.,* **-solved, -solv·ing,** *n.* —*v.t.* **1.** to make up one's mind; determine; decide: *He resolved to do better work in the future. Richard resolved to reform* (Newsweek). **2.** to break up; distinguish parts within: *to resolve a compound into its parts.*

3. to answer and explain; solve: *His letter resolved all our doubts. The conviction ... neither solves the mystery of Rémon's death nor resolves Panama's political problems* (Newsweek). 4. to decide by vote: *It was resolved that our school have a lunchroom.* 5. to change: *The assembly resolved itself into a committee. Earth, that nourished thee, shall claim thy growth, to be resolved to earth again* (William Cullen Bryant). 6. to produce separate images of; make distinguishable by optical instruments, radar, etc.: *to resolve a cluster of stars with a high-powered telescope.* 7. *Music.* to cause (a voice part or harmony) to progress from a discord to a concord. 8. *Medicine.* to cause (inflammation) to disappear without the formation of pus. —*v.i.* 1. to come to a decision; decide (on): *consultations ... in which much was proposed, but nothing resolved on* (Scott). 2. to break into parts: *This chemical resolves when distilled at a high temperature.* 3. *Music.* to progress from a discord to a concord.

—*n.* 1. a thing determined on: *He kept his resolve to do better.* 2. firmness in carrying out a purpose; determination: *George Washington was a man of great resolve.*

[< Latin *resolvere* < *re-* back + *solvere* loosen] —**re·solv′er,** *n.*

—**Syn.** *v.t.* 1. See **decide.**

re·solved (ri zolvd′), *adj.* determined; resolute; firm.

re·solv·ed·ly (ri zol′vid lē), *adv.* in a determined manner; with resolution: *We ... do most heartily and resolvedly offer, and engage our lives and fortunes to Your service* (London Gazette).

re·solv·ed·ness (ri zol′vid nis), *n.* determination; resolution; firmness.

re·sol·vent (ri zol′vənt), *adj.* resolving; solvent. —*n.* 1. a remedy that reduces swellings or inflammation. 2. a solvent. [< Latin *resolvēns, -entis,* present participle of *resolvere;* see RESOLVE]

re·solv·ing power (ri zol′ving), 1. the ability of a lens to produce separate images of objects very close together: *The device has a resolving power of 600,000 which means it can separate one part in 600,000* (Science News Letter). 2. the ability of electronic equipment, as radar or a radio telescope, or of photographic equipment to produce distinguishable images: *The ability of a photographic material to record fine detail—its resolving power—is limited by its granular structure* (Hardy and Perrin).

res·o·nance (rez′ə nəns), *n.* 1. a resounding quality; being resonant: *the resonance of an organ.* 2. a reinforcing and prolonging of sound by reflection or by vibration of other objects: *The sounding board of a piano gives it resonance.* 3. the condition of an electrical circuit adjusted to allow the greatest flow of current at a certain frequency: *A radio set must be in resonance to receive music or speech from a radio station.* 4. *Chemistry.* the oscillation of molecules between two or more structures, each possessing indentical atoms but different arrangements of electrons. 5. *Nuclear Physics.* any of a group of energy states that behave like elementary particles but may be temporary associations of unstable particles such as mesons and hyperons.

res·o·nant (rez′ə nənt), *adj.* 1. continuing to sound; resounding; echoing. 2. tending to increase or prolong sounds. 3. of or in resonance. [< Latin *resonāns, -antis,* present participle of *resonāre* < *re-* back + *sonāre* to sound, related to *sonus* sound] —**res′o·nant·ly,** *adv.*

resonant jet, a pulsejet.

res·o·nate (rez′ə nāt), *v.i.,* **-nat·ed, -nat·ing.** 1. to exhibit resonance; resound. 2. to oscillate with the same frequency as the source: *The wavelength of the radio waves can be calculated from the measured size of the particular cavity in which they will "tune" or resonate* (Scientific American). [< Latin *resonāre* (with English *-ate*[1]); see RESONANT]

res·o·na·tor (rez′ə nā′tər), *n.* 1. something that produces resonance; appliance for increasing sound by resonance. 2. a device for detecting electromagnetic radiation, as radio broadcasting waves. [< New Latin *resonator* < Latin *resonāre* to resonate]

res·o·na·to·ry (rez′ə nə tôr′ē, -tōr′-), *adj.* producing resonance.

re·sorb (ri sôrb′), *v.t.* to absorb again. [< Latin *resorbēre* < *re-* again + *sorbēre* drink in]

re·sorb·ence (ri sôr′bəns, -sōr′-), *n.* reabsorption.

re·sorb·ent (ri sôr′bənt, -sōr′-), *adj.* absorbing again.

res·or·cin (rez ôr′sin), *n.* resorcinol.

res·or·ci·nal (rez ôr′sə nəl), *adj.* having to do with resorcinol.

res·or·cin·ol (rez ôr′sə nol, -nōl), *n.* a white, crystalline compound, used in medicine as an antiseptic, and in making dyes, adhesives, etc. *Formula:* $C_6H_6O_2$ [< *res*(in) + *orcinol*]

re·sorp·tion (ri sôrp′shən), *n.* 1. a resorbing. 2. a being resorbed. 3. the remelting and reabsorbing of a crystal by the molten magma in the formation of igneous rocks.

re·sorp·tive (ri sôrp′tiv), *adj.* having to do with or characterized by resorption.

re·sort (ri zôrt′), *v.i.* 1. to go; go often: *Many people resort to the beaches in hot weather.* 2. to turn for help: *The mother resorted to punishment to make the child obey.* —*n.* 1. an assembling; going to (a place, etc.) often: *A park is a place of popular resort in good weather.* 2. a place people go to: *There are many summer resorts in the mountains.* 3. the act of turning for help; recourse: *The resort to force is forbidden in this school.* 4. a person or thing turned to for help: *Good friends are the best resort in trouble.*

[< Old French *resortir* < *re-* back + *sortir* go out] —**re·sort′er,** *n.*

re·sound (ri zound′), *v.i.* 1. to give back sound; echo: *The hills resounded when we shouted.* 2. to sound loudly: *Radios resound from every house.* 3. to be filled with sound: *The room resounded with the children's shouts.* 4. to be much talked about: *The fame of the first flight across the Atlantic resounded all over the world.* —*v.t.* 1. to give back (sound); echo: *The buildings resounded the siren's warning.* 2. to repeat loudly; celebrate: *to resound a hero's praise.* [< Latin *resonāre;* see RESONATE] —**re·sound′er,** *n.*

re-sound (rē sound′), *v.t., v.i.* to sound again.

re·sound·ing (ri zoun′ding), *adj.* 1. that resounds; making an echoing sound; sounding loudly: *He struck his breast a resounding blow* (Joseph Conrad). 2. ringing; sonorous: *a speech ... in which ... plain talk and resounding eloquence were mingled together* (Lytton Strachey). —**re·sound′ing·ly,** *adv.*

re·source (ri sôrs′, -sōrs′; rē′sôrs, -sōrs), *n.* 1. any supply that will meet a need: *to have resources of money, of quick wit, or of strength.* 2. any means of getting success or getting out of trouble: *Climbing a tree is a cat's resource when chased by a dog.* 3. skill in meeting difficulties, getting out of trouble, etc.: *Many of the early explorers were men of great resource.*

resources, the actual and potential wealth of a country: *natural resources, human resources.*

[< French *resource,* earlier *resourse* < Old French *resourdre* to rally, to rise again < Latin *re-* again + *surgere* to rise]

re·source·ful (ri sôrs′fəl, -sōrs′-), *adj.* 1. good at thinking of ways to do things; quick-witted. 2. abounding in resources; rich: *The United States is a resourceful country.* —**re·source′ful·ly,** *adv.* —**re·source′ful·ness,** *n.*

re·source·less (ri sôrs′lis, -sōrs′; rē′sôrs-, -sōrs-), *adj.* without resource; lacking resources: *The creation of an artificial, resourceless, hapless, meaningless State—inexorably correcting itself* (Manchester Guardian). —**re·source′less·ly,** *adv.* —**re·source′less·ness,** *n.*

re·sourc·es (ri sôr′siz, -sōr′-; rē′sôr-, -sōr-), *n.pl.* See under **resource,** *n.*

re·sow (rē sō′), *v.t., v.i.,* **-sowed, -sown** or **-sowed, -sow·ing.** to sow again: *It'll cost 20% to 25% more to resow those bare spots this spring* (Wall Street Journal).

resp., 1. a. respective. b. respectively. 2. respiration. 3. respondent.

re·speak (rē spēk′), *v.,* **-spoke, -spo·ken, -speak·ing.** *v.i.* to speak again: *I listened to the Prime Minister speak and respeak on subjects of which I have some knowledge* (Sunday Times). —*v.t.* to reëcho; resound: *... the heavens shall bruit again, respeaking earthly thunder* (Shakespeare).

re·spect (ri spekt′), *n.* 1. honor; esteem: *Children should show respect to those who are older and wiser. We hold the flag of our country in respect.* 2. consideration; regard: *We should show respect for school buildings, parks, and other public property.* 3. a feature; point; matter; detail: *The plan is unwise in many respects.* 4. relation; reference. 5. unfair consideration; partiality: *It is not good to have respect of persons in judgment* (Proverbs 24:23).

in respect of, with reference or comparison to: *The interest income ... will now in fact be equally free from tax in respect of approved contracts* (London Times).

in respect that, because of the fact that; since: *To a bad clergyman this may be an advantage, in respect that it allows him to remain bad* (William E. Gladstone).

in respect to, in relation, reference, or regard to (something): *It is generally agreed in Cambridge that Harvard would certainly not care to be in M.I.T.'s shoes in respect to involvement in government projects* (Christopher Rand).

respects, expressions of respect; regards: *We must pay our respects to the governor.*

with respect to, with relation, reference, or regard to (something): *We must plan with respect to the future.*

—*v.t.* 1. to feel or show honor or esteem for: *We respect an honest person.* 2. to show consideration for: *Respect the ideas and feelings of others.* 3. to relate to; refer to; be connected with.

[< Latin *respectus, -ūs* regard, (literally) a looking back < *respicere* look back, have regard for < *re-* back + *specere* to look. Doublet of RESPITE.] —**re·spect′er,** *n.*

—**Syn.** *n.* 1. reverence, veneration. 2. **Respect, regard** mean consideration, felt or shown, for someone or something of recognized worth. **Respect** implies both recognizing and properly honoring the worth of someone or something: *A soldier may feel respect for an officer he dislikes.* **Regard** implies recognizing but not necessarily honoring or even admiring the worth of someone or something: *It is difficult to respect someone for whose abilities one has small regard.* 3. particular.

re·spect·a·bil·i·ty (ri spek′tə bil′ə tē), *n., pl.* **-ties.** 1. the quality or condition of being respectable: *By maintaining a modicum of respectability ... they steer clear of harsher reprisals* (Newsweek). 2. respectable social standing. 3. respectable people, as a group: *Nearly the whole respectability of the town was either fussily marshalling processions or gazing down at them* (Arnold Bennett).

re·spect·a·bil·ize (ri spek′tə bə līz), *v.t.,* **-ized, -iz·ing.** to make respectable; consider or treat as respectable: *By forgetting the discreditable or by slowly transforming the discreditable into the creditable, as one tends to do in thinking about the dead, I had, so to speak, respectabilized him* (New Yorker).

re·spect·a·ble (ri spek′tə bəl), *adj.* 1. worthy of respect; having a good reputation: *Respectable citizens obey the laws.* 2. having fair social standing; honest and decent: *His parents were poor but respectable people.* 3. fairly good; moderate in size or quality: *John's record in school was always respectable but not brilliant.* 4. good enough to use; fit to be seen: *Though respectable, her clothes were certainly not stylish.*

—*n.* a respectable person: *Pleasance plays the husband as the abject dog beneath the good grey skin of a middle-aged respectable who has made his pile and lost his nerve* (Time).

re·spect·a·bly (ri spek′tə blē), *adv.* 1. in a manner to merit respect: *What a mother she was! ... Through what troubles she struggled to bring up her children respectably* (Mrs. J. H. Riddell). 2. moderately; pretty well.

re·spect·ful (ri spekt′fəl), *adj.* showing respect; polite: *He was always respectful to older people.* —**re·spect′ful·ly,** *adv.* —**re·spect′ful·ness,** *n.*

re·spect·ing (ri spek′ting), *prep.* regarding; about; concerning: *A discussion arose respecting the merits of different automobiles.*

re·spec·tive (ri spek′tiv), *adj.* belonging to each; particular; individual: *The classes went to their respective rooms.*

re·spec·tive·ly (ri spek′tiv lē), *adv.* as regards each one in his turn or in the order mentioned: *Bob, Dick, and Tom are 16, 18, and 20 years old respectively.*

re·spects (ri spekts′), *n.pl.* See under **respect,** *n.*

re·spect·wor·thy (ri spekt′wėr′ᴛʜē), *adj.,* **-thi·er, -thi·est.** worthy of respect; deserving respect: *And it is just these children who, almost by definition, have seldom experienced adequate respectworthy authority at home or at school* (Manchester Guardian Weekly).

re·spell (rē spel′), *v.t.* to spell over again, especially in another language or in the symbols of some phonetic transcription.

re·spi·ce fi·nem (res′pə sē fī′nem), *Latin.* consider the end; look to the end.

re·spir·a·bil·i·ty (rə spīr′ə bil′ə tē, res′-pər-), *n.* the quality of being respirable.

re·spir·a·ble (ri spīr′ə bəl, res′pər-), *adj.* **1.** that can be breathed. **2.** able to breathe.

res·pi·ra·tion (res′pə rā′shən), *n.* **1.** the act of inhaling and exhaling; breathing: *A bad cold hinders respiration. Of course, it is your breathing, or respiration, that gets the used air out of the air sacs in your lungs and takes in fresh air* (Beauchamp, Mayfield, and West). **2.** *Biology.* the energy-producing process by which an animal, plant, or living cell secures oxygen from the air or water, distributes it, utilizes it for oxidation of food materials, and gives off carbon dioxide: *The remarkable thing about respiration is that it releases energy from food in living cells* (Heber W. Youngken).

res·pi·ra·tor (res′pə rā′tər), *n.* **1.** a device used to help a person breathe: *Respirators are used by underwater swimmers and in giving artificial respiration.* **2.** a device, usually of gauze, worn over the nose and mouth to prevent inhaling harmful substances.

res·pi·ra·to·ry (res′pər ə tôr′ē, -tōr′-; ri-spīr′ə-), *adj.* having to do with, or used for, breathing: *The lungs are respiratory organs.*

respiratory pigment, any substance that carries oxygen in the blood, such as hemoglobin and hemocyanin: *It was further discovered that . . . the respiratory pigment of blood is not identical with the haemoglobin in muscle cells that makes meat red* (H. Munro Fox).

re·spire (ri spīr′), *v.,* **-spired, -spir·ing.** —*v.i.* **1.** to breathe; inhale and exhale. **2.** to breathe freely again, after anxiety, trouble, etc.: *The Imperial City stands released From bondage threatened by the embattled East, and Christendom respires* (Wordsworth). —*v.t.* to breathe in and out; inhale and exhale (air, gas, etc.): *I seemed to respire hope and comfort with the free air* (Washington Irving). [< Latin *respīrāre* < *re-* back, again + *spīrāre* to breathe]

res·pi·rom·e·ter (res′pə rom′ə tər), *n.* a device for measuring the degree and nature of respiration.

res·pite (res′pit), *n., v.,* **-pit·ed, -pit·ing.** —*n.* **1.** a time of relief and rest; lull: *a respite from toil, a slight respite from the storm. The cold war goes on without respite.* **2.** a putting off; delay, especially in carrying out a sentence of death; reprieve. —*v.t.* to give a respite to. [< Old French *respit* < Vulgar Latin *respectus* delay < Late Latin *respectus, -ūs* recourse, refuge < Latin, regard; (literally), a looking back. Doublet of RESPECT.]

re·splend (ri splend′), *v.i. Archaic.* to shine brilliantly. [< Latin *resplendēre;* see RESPLENDENT]

re·splend·ence (ri splen′dəns), *n.* great brightness; gorgeous appearance; splendor.

re·splend·en·cy (ri splen′dən sē), *n.* resplendence.

re·splend·ent (ri splen′dənt), *adj.* very bright; shining; splendid: *The queen was resplendent with jewels.* [< Latin *resplendēns, -entis,* present participle of *resplendēre* to glitter < *re-* back + *splendēre* to shine] —**re·splend′ent·ly,** *adv.*

re·spoke (rē spōk′), *v.* the past tense of **respeak.**

re·spo·ken (rē spō′kən), *v.* the past participle of **respeak.**

re·spond (ri spond′), *v.i.* **1.** to answer; reply: *He responded briefly to the question.* **2.** to act in answer; react: *A dog responds to kind treatment by loving its master. She responded quickly to the medicine.*
—*n.* **1.** a response made in church. **2.** a half pillar or the like engaged in a wall to support an arch. [< Old French *respondre* < Latin *respondēre* < *re-* back + *spondēre* to promise] —**Syn.** *v.i.* **1.** See **answer.**

re·spon·de·at su·pe·ri·or (ri spon′dē at sů pir′ē ôr), *Latin.* **1.** a phrase used to express the doctrine that the principal is responsible for the acts of his agents when done within the scope of their employment. **2.** (literally) let the principal answer.

re·spond·ence (ri spon′dəns), *n.* **1.** a response. **2.** *Obsolete.* an agreement.

re·spond·en·cy (ri spon′dən sē), *n., pl.* **-cies.** respondence.

re·spond·ent (ri spon′dənt), *n.* **1.** a person who responds. **2.** a defendant, especially in a divorce case: *All five men are respondents in a kickback investigation by the Waterfront Commission* (New York Times).
—*adj.* **1.** answering; responding: *to hear the king's speech and the respondent address read* (Horace Walpole). **2.** *Obsolete.* agreeing.

res·pon·den·ti·a (res′pon den′shē ə), *n.* a loan on the cargo of a vessel, to be repaid only if the goods arrive safely at their destination. [< New Latin *respondentia* < Latin *respondēre;* see RESPOND]

re·spond·er (ri spon′dər), *n.* **1.** a respondent. **2.** a device that reacts to stimuli, as a transmitter that returns signals in a radar system: *Each responder can be set by the pilot to give out such code signal as he has been ordered to use* (New Scientist).

re·sponse (ri spons′), *n.* **1.** an answer by word or act: *Her response to my letter was prompt. She laughed in response to his jokes. Free men cannot be frightened by threats and . . . aggression would meet its own response* (John F. Kennedy). **2.** the words said or sung by the congregation or choir in answer to the minister. **3.** the reaction of body or mind to a stimulus. [< Latin *respōnsum,* (originally) neuter past participle of *respondēre;* see RESPOND] —**Syn. 1.** rejoinder, reply.

re·spon·si·bil·i·ty (ri spon′sə bil′ə tē), *n., pl.* **-ties. 1.** a being responsible; obligation: *A little child does not feel much responsibility. No one gave them responsibility because it was felt they did not want it* (Time). **2.** a person or thing for which one is responsible: *A debt and little children to care for are her responsibilities.*

re·spon·si·ble (ri spon′sə bəl), *adj.* **1.** obliged or expected to account (for, to): *Each pupil is responsible for the care of the books given him. The people had given him his command, and to the people alone he was responsible* (James A. Froude). **2.** deserving credit or blame: *The bad weather is responsible for the small attendance. Who is responsible for all these changes?* **3.** trustworthy; reliable: *A responsible person should take care of the money.* **4.** involving obligation or duties: *The presidency is a very responsible position.* **5.** able to discharge obligations or pay debts: *responsible tenants.* **6.** able to tell right from wrong; able to think and act reasonably: *Insane people are not responsible.*
—*n.* **1.** a person of responsibility. **2.** an actor who undertakes to play any part which may be temporarily required: *Hearing that one of their 'responsibles' had just left, I went straight to the manager . . . and was accepted* (Jerome K. Jerome). —**re·spon′si·ble·ness,** *n.*
—**Syn.** *adj.* **1.** accountable, answerable. —**Ant.** *adj.* **3.** negligent, careless.

Responsible Government, the system of government established in Canada in 1849, by which the governor general's cabinet of ministers had to have the confidence of the Canadian legislature and not merely that of the governor general.

re·spon·si·bly (ri spon′sə blē), *adv.* in a responsible manner.

re·spon·sion (ri spon′shən), *n.* response.
responsions, (at Oxford University) the first examination that candidates for the degree of B.A. are required to pass; smalls. [< Latin *respōnsiō, -ōnis* < *respondēre;* see RESPOND]

re·spon·sive (ri spon′siv), *adj.* **1.** making answer; responding: *a responsive glance.* **2.** easily moved; responding readily: *a very friendly person with a responsive nature, to be responsive to kindness.* **3.** using or containing responses: *responsive reading in church in which minister and congregation read in turn.* **4.** corresponding. —**re·spon′sive·ly,** *adv.*

re·spon·sive·ness (ri spon′siv nis), *n.* **1.** the quality of being responsive. **2.** the speed with which a part of a machine returns to stability after a shift.

re·spon·siv·i·ty (rē′spon siv′i tē), *n.* the character of being responsive; mental responsiveness.

re·spon·so·ry (ri spon′sər ē), *n., pl.* **-ries.** (in church music) a response, especially an anthem sung by a soloist and choir, following a reading from the Bible. [< Late Latin *respōnsōria* < Latin *respondēre;* see RESPOND]

re·spray (rē sprā′), *v.t.* to spray again, as with paint: *A motorist seldom gets his car resprayed just for the sake of changing the colour* (Sunday Telegraph). —*n.* a respraying: *A motor car may need both a new camshaft and a respray* (New Scientist).

res pu·bli·ca (rēz pub′lə kə), *Latin.* the republic; the State.

rest[1] (rest), *n.* **1.** sleep: *The children had a good night's rest.* **2.** ease after work or effort: *The seventh day is the sabbath of rest . . . ye shall do no work therein* (Leviticus 23:3). **3.** freedom from anything that tires, troubles, disturbs, or pains; quiet: *The medicine gave the sick man a short rest from pain.* **4. a.** an absence of motion: *The driver brought the car to a rest.* **b.** inactivity of growth or development; dormant state or condition. **5.** a support; something to lean on: *a head rest, a rest for a billiard cue.* **6.** a place for resting: *a rest for sailors.* **7.** *Music.* **a.** a pause. **b.** a mark to show a pause. **8.**

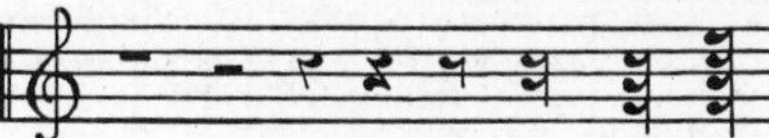

Rests[1] (def. 7b)
From left to right: whole, half, quarter, quarter, eighth, sixteenth, thirty-second, sixty-fourth

a short pause in reading; caesura. **9.** death; the grave.
at rest, a. asleep: *What Sir, not yet at rest? the king's abed* (Shakespeare). **b.** not moving: *The lake was at rest.* **c.** free from pain, trouble, etc.: *The injured man is now at rest.* **d.** dead: *Welcome the hour, my aged limbs Are laid with thee at rest!* (Robert Burns).
lay to rest, to bury: *Lay his bones to rest.*
[Old English *reste, ræste*]
—*v.i.* **1.** to be still or quiet; sleep: *Lie down and rest. My mother rests for an hour every afternoon.* **2.** to be free from work, effort, care, trouble, etc.: *Schoolteachers can rest in the summer. On the seventh day God ended his work . . . and he rested on the seventh day from all his work* (Genesis 2:2). **3.** to stop moving; come to rest; stop: *The ball rested at the bottom of the hill.* **4.** to lie, recline, sit, lean, etc., for rest or ease: *He spent the whole day resting in a chair. The younger ones . . . think that now the country is free, it can rest on its oars* (New Yorker). **5.** to be supported; lean: *The ladder rests against the wall. The roof rests on columns.* **6.** to look; be fixed: *Our eyes rested on the open book.* **7.** to be at ease: *Don't let Mrs. Smith rest until she promises to visit us.* **8.** to be or become inactive: *Let the matter rest.* **9.** to rely (on); trust (in); be based: *Our hope rests on you.* **10.** to lie; be found; be present: *In a democracy, government rests with the people. A smile rested on her lips.* **11.** to be dead; lie in the grave: *The old man rests at last with his forefathers.* **12.** *Law.* to end voluntarily the introduction of evidence in a case: *The state rests.* **13.** (of agricultural land) to be unused for crops, especially in order to restore fertility.
rest up, to get a thorough rest: *New Yorkers are all home or out of town today resting up for another week of the greatest city in the world* (New York Times).
—*v.t.* **1.** to give rest to; refresh by rest: *Stop and rest your horse. It rests one's feet to take off one's shoes. Is my boy, God rest his soul, alive or dead?* (Shakespeare). **2.** to cause to stop moving. **3.** to let remain inactive: *Rest the matter there.* **4.** to place for support; lay; lean: *to rest one's head in one's hands. Straight he took his bow of ash-tree, On the sand one end he rested* (Longfellow). **5.** to cause to rely or depend; base: *We rest our hope on you.* **6.** to fix (the eyes, etc.): *She rested her eyes on him steadily* (Henry James). **7.** *Law.* to end voluntarily the introduction of evidence in (a case at law): *The lawyer rested his case.*
[Old English *restan*]

rest[2] (rest), *n.* **1.** what is left; those that are left: *The sun was out in the morning but it clouded over at noon and rained for the rest of the day. One horse was running ahead of the rest.* **2.** *British.* the reserve or surplus funds of a bank, especially of the Bank of England. —*v.i.* to continue to be; remain: *You may rest assured that I will keep my promise. The final decision rests with* *father.* [< Middle French *reste* < *rester* to remain < Latin *restāre* be left < *re-* back + *stāre* to stand]

rest[3] (rest), *n.* (in medieval armor) a support for the butt of a lance attached to the breastplate or cuirass. A knight set his lance in rest as he prepared to charge the enemy: *Each ready lance is in the rest* (Scott). [short for Middle English *arest* arrest, noun; perhaps influenced by *rest*[1]]

re·staff (rē staf′, -stäf′), *v.t.* to staff again with new personnel: [*The hospital*] *will be confiscated and restaffed with Soviet doctors arriving late this month from Moscow* (Time).

re·stage (rē stāj′), *v.t.*, **-staged, -stag·ing.** **1.** to stage again or in a new way: *Antony Tudor has consented to restage four of his most famous ballets for the Ballet Theatre* (New York Times). **2.** to reënact (an event): *Refused immediate reinstatement of his citizenship, he drifted into semiobscurity until 1953, when he tried to restage his old camping act in front of Buckingham Palace* (Newsweek).

re·start (rē stärt′), *v.t., v.i.* to start again; recommence: *The trial restarts on January 19* (Manchester Guardian Weekly). —*n.* a fresh start; recommencement.

re·state (rē stāt′), *v.t.*, **-stat·ed, -stat·ing.** **1.** to state again or anew. **2.** to state in a new way.

re·state·ment (rē stāt′mənt), *n.* **1.** a statement made again: *But once in a while there is a need for a summing up, or a restatement of belief* (Time). **2.** a new statement.

res·tau·rant (res′tər ənt, -tə ränt), *n.* a place to buy and eat a meal. [American English < French *restaurant*, (originally) present participle of Old French *restaurer* to restore < Latin *restaurāre*]

res·tau·ra·teur (res′tə rə tėr′), *n.* the keeper of a restaurant. [< French *restaurateur* < Old French *restaurer;* see RESTAURANT]

rest cure, a treatment for nervous disorders consisting of a complete rest, usually combined with systematic feeding, massage, etc.: *He fainted not long ago in the midst of a speech, and was known to be considering a rest cure* (Wall Street Journal).

re·ster·i·lize (rē ster′ə līz), *v.t.*, **-lized, -liz·ing.** to sterilize again.

res·tes (res′tēz), *n.* plural of **restis.**

rest·ful (rest′fəl), *adj.* **1.** full of rest; giving rest: *a restful nap.* **2.** quiet; peaceful. —**rest′ful·ly,** *adv.* —**rest′ful·ness,** *n.*

rest·har·row (rest′har′ō), *n.* any of a group of low European herbs or shrubs of the pea family, with pink, white, or yellow flowers and tough roots. [< *rest*[3] + *harrow*]

Restharrow

rest home, **1.** a place where old people are cared for; old-age home: *Amos Alonzo Stagg, the grand old man of football, died at a rest home in California at the age of 102* (New York Times). **2.** a convalescent or nursing home.

rest·house (rest′hous′), *n.* **1.** a boarding house or inn for persons requiring rest and recreation. **2.** (in India) a building in which travelers can obtain rest and shelter: *Even leaving the resthouse after breakfast, we had ample time on arrival to set up easels, get our paints, and do some work before the elephants returned* (Atlantic).

res·tif (res′tif), *adj. Archaic.* restive.

res·ti·form (res′tə fôrm), *adj.* cordlike. [< New Latin *restiformis* < Latin *restis* a cord + *forma* form]

restiform body, one of a pair of large, cordlike bundles of nerve fibers lying one on each side of the medulla oblongata and connecting it with the cerebellum.

re·stim·u·late (rē stim′yə lāt), *v.t.*, **-lat·ed, -lat·ing.** to stimulate anew: *Even his obviously dwindling affection was restimulated by her quite visible need of help* (Theodore Dreiser).

re·stim·u·la·tion (rē stim′yə lā′shən), *n.* the act of restimulating or the state of being restimulated: *a restimulation of the economy.*

rest·ing (res′ting), *adj. Botany.* dormant, as spores, especially of algae and fungi, that can germinate only after a period of dormancy: *When a cell is not dividing or preparing to divide it is said to be in the resting stage* (A.M. Winchester).

res·tis (res′tis), *n., pl.* **res·tes.** restiform body.

res·ti·tute (res′tə tüt, -tyüt), *v.t.*, **-tut·ed, -tut·ing.** **1.** to give back (something lost or taken). **2.** to make good (loss, damage, or injury). [< Latin *restituere;* see RESTITUTION]

res·ti·tu·ti·o in in·te·grum (res tə tü′shē ō in in′ti grəm), *Latin.* restoration in its entirety to the previous condition (used in law when a court annuls a transaction or contract and orders the restoration of what has been received or given under it).

res·ti·tu·tion (res′tə tü′shən, -tyü′-), *n.* **1.** the giving back of what has been lost or taken away: *Charlemagne tried to enforce the restitution of the Roman lands.* **2.** the act of making good any loss, damage, or injury: *It is only fair that those who do the damage should make restitution.* **3.** *Physics.* the return of an elastic body to its original form or position when released from strain. [< Latin *restitūtiō, -ōnis* < *restituere* restore, rebuild, replace < *re-* again + *statuere* to set up < *stāre* to stand] —**Syn. 1.** return, restoration. **2.** reparation, amends.

res·ti·tu·tive (res′tə tü′tiv, -tyü′-), *adj.* having to do with restitution.

re·stit·u·to·ry (ri stit′yə tôr′ē, -tōr′-), *adj.* restitutive.

res·tive (res′tiv), *adj.* **1.** restless; uneasy: *a restive audience. A restive, resurgent Germany, ten years after the abyss of total defeat, holds the answers* (Newsweek). **2.** hard to manage: *a restive child.* **3.** refusing to go ahead; balky: *a restive mule.* [< Old French *restif, restive* motionless < *rester* rest[2] < Latin *restāre*] —**res′tive·ly,** *adv.* —**res′tive·ness,** *n.* —**Syn. 2.** intractable, refractory.

rest·less (rest′lis), *adj.* **1.** unable to rest; uneasy: *The dog seemed restless, as if he sensed some danger.* **2.** without rest or sleep; not restful: *The sick child passed a restless night.* **3.** rarely still; never quiet; always moving: *That nervous boy is very restless.* **4.** preventing rest: *Ease to the body some, none to the mind From restless thoughts* (Milton). —**rest′less·ly,** *adv.* —**rest′less·ness,** *n.*

restless cavy, the wild guinea pig.

rest mass, *Physics.* the mass of an atom, electron, etc., when it is at a low velocity or when regarded as not being in motion.

re·stock (rē stok′), *v.t., v.i.* to supply with a new stock; replenish.

re·stor·a·ble (ri stôr′ə bəl, -stōr′-), *adj.* that can be restored.

res·to·ra·tion (res′tə rā′shən), *n.* **1.** a restoring; bringing back to a former or normal condition: *the restoration of a man to his office, the restoration of peace after war.* **2.** a being restored; recovery: *a restoration from sickness.* **3.** something restored.

Res·to·ra·tion (res′tə rā′shən), *n.* **1. a.** the reëstablishment of the monarchy in 1660 under Charles II of England. **b.** the period from 1660 to 1688 in England, during which Charles II and James II reigned. **2.** the return of the Bourbons to power in France in 1813, and again in 1815. **3.** the return of the Jews to Palestine about 537 B.C.

Restoration comedy, the comedy of manners, marked by wit and social satire, that arose and flourished in England during the Restoration period.

res·to·ra·tion·ism (res′tə rā′shə niz əm), *n.* doctrines or belief of the restorationists.

res·to·ra·tion·ist (res′tə rā′shə nist), *n.* **1.** a person who believes in the doctrine of the final restoration of all men to a state of happiness and the favor of God. **2.** a person who restores old or dilapidated buildings.

re·stor·a·tive (ri stôr′ə tiv, -stōr′-), *adj.* capable of restoring; tending to restore health or strength: *a restorative medicine. The government has promised two million restorative dollars* (New Yorker). —*n.* something that restores health and strength: *Ammonia is used as a restorative when a person has fainted.* —**re·stor′a·tive·ly,** *adv.*

re·store (ri stôr′, -stōr′), *v.t.*, **-stored, -stor·ing.** **1.** to bring back; establish again: *to restore order.* **2.** to bring back to a former condition or to a normal condition: *to restore an old house, to restore a painting, to restore a person to consciousness. The Bishops were restored to their seats in the Upper House* (Macaulay). **3.** to give back; put back: *The thief was forced to restore the money to its owner.* **4.** *Obsolete.* to compensate for: *But if the while I think on thee, dear friend, all losses are restored and sorrows end* (Shakespeare). [< Old French *restorer* < Latin *restaurāre*] —**Syn. 2.** See **renew.**

re·stor·er (ri stôr′ər, -stōr′-), *n.* a person or thing that restores.

re·stow (rē stō′), *v.t.* to stow again; repack: *The two astronauts . . . were busy restowing all of the gear in their cabin* (New York Times).

rest period, **1.** a short period during working hours for rest, relaxation, or amusement, as in a factory, school, or military base. **2.** *Botany.* a period in which a plant is inactive or does not grow.

restr., restaurant.

re·strain (ri strān′), *v.t.* **1.** to hold back; keep down; keep in check; keep within limits: *She could not restrain her curiosity to see what was in the box. History shows that very few rulers restrained their powers of their own accord. We no longer have "disturbed wards" and it's a rare case when we have to restrain anyone* (Wall Street Journal). **2.** to keep in prison; confine. [< Old French *restreindre, restraindre* < Latin *restringere;* see RESTRICT] —**Syn. 1.** detain, repress, curb. See **check.**

re·strain·a·ble (ri strā′nə bəl), *adj.* that can be restrained.

re·strain·ed·ly (ri strā′nid lē, -strānd′-), *adv.* in a restrained manner; with restraint: *These and the other like precepts of our Saviour, are not to be taken strictly, but restrainedly* (William Burkitt).

re·strain·er (ri strā′nər), *n.* **1.** a person or thing that restrains. **2.** a chemical, such as potassium bromide, added to a photographic developer to slow down its action.

re·strain·ing order (ri strā′ning), *U.S.* an order issued by a law court enjoining a person or group to stop all action or proceedings until an injunction applied for is granted or denied: *The Government's application for a temporary restraining order to prevent the merger was denied by the court* (Wall Street Journal).

re·straint (ri strānt′), *n.* **1.** the act of restraining; holding back or hindering from action or motion: *Noisy children sometimes need restraint.* **2.** the condition of being restrained; confinement: *Restraint is for the savage, the rapacious, the violent: not for the just, the gentle, the benevolent* (Herbert Spencer). **3.** a means of restraining: *They threw off all restraints, conventions, pretences* (Arnold Bennett). **4.** a tendency to restrain natural feeling; reserve. [< Old French *restrainte* < *restraindre;* see RESTRAIN] —**Syn. 1.** restriction, check, curb.

restraint of trade, any limitation or prevention of free competition in business, as by creating a monopoly, fixing prices, or limiting markets.

re·strict (ri strikt′), *v.t.* **1.** to keep within limits; confine: *Our club membership is restricted to twelve. His activities were restricted by old age.* **2.** to put limitations on: *to restrict the meaning of a word.* [< Latin *restrictus*, past participle of *restringere* < *re-* back + *stringere* draw tight]

re·strict·ed (ri strik′tid), *adj.* **1.** kept within limits; limited: *She is on a very restricted diet, and can have no sweets.* **2.** having restrictions or limiting rules: *Factories may not be built in this restricted residential section. The restricted shares would be convertible into unrestricted parent company common* (Wall Street Journal). **3.** limited to certain groups (a euphemism for a policy of racial or religious discrimination). —**re·strict′ed·ly,** *adv.*

re·strict·ee (ri strik′tē′, -strik′tē), *n.* a person who is restricted to a particular area, such as a ghetto.

re·stric·tion (ri strik′shən), *n.* **1.** something that restricts; limiting condition or rule: *The restrictions on the use of the playground are: no fighting; no damaging property.* **2.** a restricting or being restricted: *This park is open to the public without restriction.*

re·stric·tion·ism (ri strik′shə niz əm), *n.* the practice or policy of setting up restrictions, especially on import trade.

re·stric·tion·ist (ri strik′shə nist), *n.* a person in favor of restrictions, especially one who advocates the limitation of imports. —*adj.* having to do with restrictionism.

re·stric·tive (ri strik′tiv), *adj.* restricting; limiting: *Some laws are prohibitive; some are only restrictive.* —**re·stric′tive·ly,** *adv.*

restrictive clause, an adjective clause that qualifies its noun so definitely that it cannot be left out without changing the sense. *Example:* All employees *who have been with this firm for five years* will receive bonuses.
➔ Notice that the restrictive clause in the sentence above is not set off by commas; a nonrestrictive clause is: *John Jones, who has been with the firm for five years, will receive a bonus.*
restrictive covenant, *U.S.* an agreement among property owners in a given area to restrict the use of land or the kind of residents, especially as to race or religion.
re·strike (*v.* rē strīk′; *n.* rē′strīk′), *v.*, **-struck, -strik·ing,** *n.* —*v.t.* **1.** to strike again. **2.** to stamp (a coin) again, especially with a different impression. —*n.* an impression, as of a coin, medal, woodcut, etching, etc., made from a plate, die, or similar source that has already been used; a second or subsequent impression: *When Giacometti returned to the atelier after about ten minutes, I was studying the framed Cézanne etching, in an effort to determine, beneath its dusty glass, the vintage and source of the restrike* (Atlantic).
re·string (rē string′), *v.t.*, **-strung, -string·ing.** to put a new string or new strings on: *to restring beads on a necklace.*
rest room, *U.S.* a room in a public building, business establishment, theater, etc., that provides toilet facilities: *Many department stores have lunchrooms and rest rooms for the convenience of their customers* (Fred M. Jones).
re·struc·ture (rē struk′chər), *v.t.*, **-tured, -tur·ing.** to structure anew: *Thinking is a guided process of restructuring a problem situation until it takes on the configuration of a solution* (Scientific American).
re·stud·y (rē stud′ē), *n.*, *pl.* **-stud·ies,** *v.t.*, **-stud·ied, -stud·y·ing.** —*n.* a new study: *Another part of the new program, he said, includes a restudy of merchandising techniques* (Wall Street Journal). —*v.t.* to study anew: *Bernstein knew that Walter was not well, and sat up restudying the scores, just in case* (Time).
re·style (rē stīl′), *v.t.*, **-styled, -styl·ing.** to change the style of; redesign: *The industry spent some $750,000,000 to restyle its 1959 models* (Glenn Fowler).
re·sub·ject (rē′səb jekt′), *v.t.* to subdue again.
re·sub·jec·tion (rē′səb jek′shən), *n.* a fresh subjection; a renewed subjugation.
re·sub·mit (rē′səb mit′), *v.t.*, **-mit·ted, -mit·ting.** to submit again, as for consideration or judgment: *The President planned to resubmit other important proposals that the last Democratic Congress failed to adopt* (Newsweek).
re·sult (ri zult′), *n.* **1.** that which happens because of something; what is caused: *The result of the fall was a broken leg.* **2.** a good or useful result: *We want results, not talk.* **3.** a quantity, value, etc., obtained by calculation. [< verb]
—*v.i.* **1.** to be a result; follow as a consequence: *Sickness often results from eating too much.* **2.** to have as a result; end: *Eating too much results often in sickness.*
[< Latin *resultāre* to rebound (frequentative) < *resilīre* rebound; see RESILIENT]
—**Syn.** *n.* **1.** consequence, outcome. See **effect.**
re·sult·ant (ri zul′tənt), *adj.* resulting. —*n.* **1.** a result. **2.** *Physics.* any force that has the same effect as two or more forces acting together.
re·sult·ful (ri zult′fəl), *adj.* fruitful; effective.
re·sult·less (ri zult′lis), *adj.* without results; fruitless; ineffective.
re·sum·a·ble (ri zü′mə bəl), *adj.* that can be resumed.
re·sume (ri züm′), *v.*, **-sumed, -sum·ing.** —*v.t.* **1.** to begin again; go on: *Resume reading where we left off.* **2.** to get or take again: *Those standing may resume their seats.* **3.** to take back: *concessions which the sovereign had freely made and might at his pleasure resume* (Macaulay). —*v.i.* to begin again; continue. [< Latin *resūmere* < *re-* again + *sūmere* take up] —**re·sum′er,** *n.*
ré·su·mé or **res·u·me** (rez′ü mā′, rez′ə-mā), *n.* **1.** a summary. **2.** *U.S.* a biographical summary, especially of a person's education and business career. [< French *résumé,* noun use of past participle of Middle French *résumer* to resume, learned borrowing from Latin *resūmere*]
re·sump·tion (ri zump′shən), *n.* **1.** a resuming: *the resumption of duties after absence.* **2.** *U.S. History.* the return to specie payments by the government: *The Resumption Act of 1875 provided for resumption on January 1, 1879.* [< Late Latin *resumptiō, -ōnis* < Latin *resūmere;* see RESUME]
re·sump·tive (ri zump′tiv), *adj.* **1.** tending to resume. **2.** that summarizes. —**re·sump′tive·ly,** *adv.*
res u·ni·ver·si·ta·tis (rēz yü′nə vėr′sə-tā′tis), *Latin.* **1.** places of common access, as the churches and parks of a city. **2.** (literally) things of the community.
re·su·pi·nate (ri sü′pə nāt), *adj. Botany.* bent backward; inverted; appearing as if upside down. [< Latin *resupīnātus,* past participle of *resupīnāre* < *resupīnus;* see RESUPINE]
re·su·pi·na·tion (ri sü′pə nā′shən), *n. Botany.* a resupinate condition; inversion of parts.
re·su·pine (rē′sü pīn′), *adj.* lying on the back; supine. [< Latin *resupīnus* < *re-* back + *supīnus* supine, lying on the back]
re·sup·ply (rē′sə plī′), *v.*, **-plied, -ply·ing,** *n.*, *pl.* **-plies.** —*v.t.* to supply again or anew; provide with a fresh supply. —*n.* a fresh supply.
re·sur·face (rē sėr′fis), *v.t.*, **-faced, -fac·ing.** to provide with a new or different surface.
re·sur·gam (ri sėr′gam), *Latin.* I shall rise again.
re·surge (ri sėrj′), *v.i.*, **-surged, -surg·ing.** to rise again: *The reason Explorer I's apparently dead radio resurged to life . . . was reported* (Science News Letter). [< Latin *resurgere* < *re-* again + *surgere* to rise]
re·sur·gence (ri sėr′jəns), *n.* a rising again: *a resurgence of unfriendly feeling.*
re·sur·gent (ri sėr′jənt), *adj.* rising or tending to rise again: *A restive, resurgent Germany, ten years after the abyss of total defeat, holds the answers—the answers which might well decide the cold war and with it the fate of generations to come* (Newsweek). —*n.* a person who has risen again.
res·ur·rect (rez′ə rekt′), *v.t.* **1.** to raise from the dead; bring back to life. **2.** to bring back to sight, use, etc.: *to resurrect an old law.* **3.** to take out of a grave. [back formation < *resurrection*]
res·ur·rec·tion (rez′ə rek′shən), *n.* **1.** a coming to life again; rising from the dead. **2.** a being alive again after death. **3.** a restoration from decay, disuse, etc. [< Latin *resurrēctiō, -ōnis* < *resurgere* < *re-* again + *surgere* to rise]
Res·ur·rec·tion (rez′ə rek′shən), *n.* the rising again of Christ after His death and burial.
res·ur·rec·tion·al (rez′ə rek′shə nəl), *adj.* of or having to do with resurrection.
res·ur·rec·tion·ar·y (rez′ə rek′shə ner′ē), *adj.* **1.** having to do with or of the nature of resurrection. **2.** having to do with resurrectionism.
res·ur·rec·tion·ism (rez′ə rek′shə niz-əm), *n.* the practice of exhuming and stealing dead bodies, especially for dissection.
res·ur·rec·tion·ist (rez′ə rek′shə nist), *n.* **1.** a person who brings something to life or view again. **2.** a person who exhumes and steals dead bodies, especially for dissection. **3.** a person who believes in resurrection.
resurrection man, a body snatcher.
resurrection plant, **1.** any of several mosslike plants which form a nestlike ball when dry and expand when moistened. It is a variety of selaginello. **2.** any of various other plants having the same property, as the rose of Jericho or one of the fig marigolds.
res·ur·rec·tive (rez′ə rek′tiv), *adj.* causing resurrection; bringing the dead to life.
re·sur·vey (*v.* rē′sər vā′; *n.* rē sėr′vā), *v.t.* **1.** to examine over again: *to resurvey a problem.* **2.** to survey (land, etc.) again. —*n.* a new survey.
re·sus·ci·ta·ble (ri sus′ə tə bəl), *adj.* that can be resuscitated.
re·sus·ci·tate (ri sus′ə tāt), *v.*, **-tat·ed, -tat·ing.** —*v.t.* **1.** to bring back to life or consciousness; revive: *The doctor resuscitated the man who was overcome by gas.* **2.** to renew or restore (a thing).
—*v.i.* to come to life or consciousness again. [< Latin *resuscitāre* (with English *-ate*[1]) < *re-* again + *sub-* (from) under + *citāre* to rouse (frequentative) < *ciēre* stir up]
re·sus·ci·ta·tion (ri sus′ə tā′shən), *n.* **1.** restoration to life or consciousness. **2.** restoration.
re·sus·ci·ta·tive (ri sus′ə tā′tiv), *adj.* helping to resuscitate.
re·sus·ci·ta·tor (ri sus′ə tā′tər), *n.* **1.** a respirator: *It consists of a resuscitator which weighs only 28 lbs. and so can be taken to the scene of emergency* (New Scientist). **2.** a person who resuscitates.
ret (ret), *v.t.*, **ret·ted, ret·ting.** to expose (flax, hemp, etc.) to moisture or soak in water, in order to soften by partial rotting. [probably < Middle Dutch *reten*]
ret., **1.** retard. **2.** retired. **3.** returned.
re·ta·ble (ri tā′bəl), *n.* a shelf for lights, flowers, etc., or the frame for a picture, or the like, above and behind an altar. [< French *rétable* < Spanish *retablo,* adaptation of Catalan *retaule,* earlier *reataula* < *rea-* behind (< Latin *retrō-*) + *taula* table < Latin *tabula* tablet]
re·tail (*n., adj., v.t. 1, v.i.* rē′tāl; *v.t. 2* ri tāl′), *n.* the sale of goods in small quantities at a time: *Our grocer buys at wholesale and sells at retail.*
—*adj.* **1.** in small lots or quantities: *The wholesale price of this coat is $20; the retail price is $30.* **2.** selling in small quantities: *the retail trade, a retail merchant.*
—*v.t.* **1.** to sell in small quantities: *to retail a dress at ten dollars.* **2.** to tell over again: *She retails everything she hears about her acquaintances.* —*v.i.* to be sold in small quantities or at retail: *This radio retails for $14.95.*
[< Old French *retaille* scrap < *retaillier* cut up < *re-* back + *taillier* to cut < Late Latin *tāliāre* < Latin *tālea* rod]
re·tail·er (rē′tā lər), *n.* a retail merchant or dealer: *The task of holding thousands of retailers to the agreement that they will observe minimum list prices is well nigh impossible* (Newsweek).
re·tail·ing (rē′tā ling), *n.* the selling of goods at retail: *The problem of productivity is being made more difficult by the attempt to include retailing under the National Labor Standards Act* (John W. Wingate).
retail store, *U.S.* a store selling items in small quantities directly to the consumer: *. . . in direct competition with private retail stores where members of the armed services get goods at a price which imposes a considerable part of the cost on the taxpayer* (Newsweek).
re·tain (ri tān′), *v.t.* **1.** to continue to have or hold; keep: *China dishes retain heat longer than metal pans do.* **2.** to keep in mind; remember: *She retained the tune but not the words of the song.* **3.** to employ by payment of a fee: *He retained the best lawyer in the State.* [< Old French *retenir* < Vulgar Latin *retenīre,* for Latin *retinēre* < *re-* back + *tenēre* to hold] —**Syn. 1.** See **keep.**
re·tain·a·ble (ri tā′nə bəl), *adj.* that can be retained.
retained earnings (ri tānd′), earned surplus: *Mr. Johnson said the program will be financed by funds generated internally and retained earnings* (Wall Street Journal).
retained object, an object in a passive construction corresponding to the direct or indirect object in an active construction. *Example:* The boy was given a *nickel.* A nickel was given to the *boy.*
re·tain·er[1] (ri tā′nər), *n.* **1.** a person who serves someone of rank; vassal; attendant; follower. **2.** a person kept in service; attendant: *that old retainer, Bridget the cook* (Winston Churchill). [< *retain* + *-er*[1]]
re·tain·er[2] (ri tā′nər), *n.* **1.** a fee paid to secure services: *This lawyer receives a retainer before he begins work on a case.* **2.** a retaining of a person's service. [< noun use of Old French *retenir;* see RETAIN]
re·tain·ing wall (ri tā′ning), a wall built to hold back a mass of earth, water, etc.
re·tain·ment (ri tān′mənt), *n.* the act of retaining; retention.
re·take (*v.* rē tāk′; *n.* rē′tāk′), *v.*, **-took, -tak·en, -tak·ing,** *n.* —*v.t.* **1.** to take again. **2.** to take back. —*n.* a retaking: *a retake of a scene in a motion picture.*
re·tak·er (rē tā′kər), *n.* one who takes again what has been taken; a recaptor.
re·tal·i·ate (ri tal′ē āt), *v.*, **-at·ed, -at·ing.** —*v.i.* to pay back wrong, injury, etc.; return like for like, usually to return evil for evil: *If we insult people, they will retaliate.* —*v.t.* to return in kind: *He retaliated on the . . . Huns of Pannonia the same calamities which they had inflicted on the nations* (Edward Gibbon). [< Latin *retāliāre* (with English

-ate[1]) < *re-* back + unrecorded *tāl-* payment; perhaps influenced by *tālis* such (a)]

re·tal·i·a·tion (ri tal′ē ā′shən), *n.* **1.** a paying back of a wrong, injury, etc.; return of evil for evil. **2.** an act of reprisal.

re·tal·i·a·tive (ri tal′ē ā′tiv), *adj.* disposed to retaliate; retaliatory: *My retaliative spirit ... told me that it was beneath my dignity* (Metropolis).

re·tal·i·a·tor (ri tal′ē ā tər), *n.* a person who retaliates: *It is often difficult to tell offenders from retaliators* (London Times).

re·tal·i·a·to·ry (ri tal′ē ə tôr′ē, -tōr′-), *adj.* returning like for like, especially evil for evil: *a retaliatory raid, retaliatory weapons.*

re·tard (ri tärd′), *v.t.* **1.** to make slow; delay the progress of; keep back; hinder: *Bad roads retarded the car.* **2.** to defer; postpone: *to advance or retard the hour of refection beyond the time* (Scott). **3.** to adjust (the ignition system of a gasoline engine) so that the spark occurs at a later point in the cycle of movement of the piston. —*v.i.* to be delayed or hindered.
—*n.* delay; retardation.
in retard, retarded; delayed: *I was far in retard ... in real knowledge* (John Ruskin).
[< Latin *retardāre* < *re-* back + *tardāre* to slow < *tardus* slow] —**re·tard′er,** *n.*

re·tard·an·cy (ri tär′dən sē), *n.* the quality or state of being retardant.

re·tard·ant (ri tär′dənt), *n.* something that delays an action, process, or effect, usually a chemical. —*adj.* retarding; tending to hinder: *We know the retardant effect of society upon artists of exalted sensibility* (Edmund C. Stedman).

re·tard·ate (ri tär′dāt), *n.* a person who is retarded: *"Criminal" covers a broad span of lawbreakers from the psychopath to the mental retardate* (Science News Letter).

re·tar·da·tion (rē′tär dā′shən), *n.* **1.** the act of retarding: *causing a retardation of reading ... and some ... relaxation of memory* (Francis Bacon). **2.** the state of being retarded. **3.** that which retards; hindrance. **4.** a decrease in velocity; negative acceleration. **5.** *Music.* a discord similar to suspension, resolving upward instead of downward.

re·tard·a·tive (ri tär′də tiv), *adj.* tending to retard.

re·tard·a·to·ry (ri tär′də tôr′ē, -tōr′-), *adj.* tending to retard; of a retarding effect.

re·tard·ed (ri tär′did), *adj.* slow in development; backward: *Retarded children—I.Q. between 65 and 90—have the capacity to learn if properly taught* (Scientific American).

re·tard·ment (ri tärd′mənt), *n.* retardation.

retch (rech), *v.i.* to make efforts to vomit; make straining movements like those of vomiting. [Old English *hrǣcan* clear the throat]

retd., **1.** retained. **2.** retired. **3.** returned.

ret′d., returned.

re·te (rē′tē), *n., pl.* **-ti·a** (-shē ə, -tē-). a network, as of fibers, nerves, or blood vessels. [< Latin *rēte, -is* net, related to *rārus* thin, of loose texture]

re·tell (rē tel′), *v.t.,* **-told, -tell·ing.** to tell again.

re·tell·a·ble (rē tel′ə bəl), *adj.* that can be retold; worth retelling.

re·tem (rē′tem), *n.* a desert shrub of the Near East with small, white flowers and rushlike branches. It is the juniper mentioned in the Old Testament. [< Arabic *ratam*]

re·te mi·ra·bi·le (rē′tē mi rab′ə lē), *pl.* **re·ti·a mi·ra·bi·li·a** (rē′shē ə mir′ə bil′ē ə, rē′tē ə). an elaborate network or plexus of small arteries and veins forming one unified system between two parts of a larger artery or vein, and usually found near the junction of an extremity and the main body. [< Latin *rēte, -is* net, *mīrābile* wonderful]

re·tene (rē′tēn, ret′ēn), *n.* a white, crystalline hydrocarbon obtained from the tar of resinous woods, certain fossil resins, etc. *Formula:* $C_{18}H_{18}$ [< Greek *rhētínē* (pine) resin + English *-ene*]

re·ten·tion (ri ten′shən), *n.* **1.** a retaining. **2.** a being retained. **3.** the power to retain. **4.** the ability to remember. [< Latin *retentiō, -ōnis* < *retinēre* retain]

re·ten·tion·ist (ri ten′shə nist), *adj.* favoring the retention of a law, policy, etc. —*n.* a retentionist person or group.

re·ten·tive (ri ten′tiv), *adj.* **1.** able to hold or keep: *a retentive substance.* **2.** able to remember: *a retentive memory.* —**re·ten′tive·ly,** *adv.* —**re·ten′tive·ness,** *n.*

re·ten·tiv·i·ty (rē′ten tiv′ə tē), *n.* **1.** the power to retain; retentiveness. **2.** the capacity of a substance to retain induced magnetic force after the source of the magnetization has been removed. **3.** the power of resisting magnetization.

re·te·nue (rə tə NY′), *n. French.* reserve; discretion; prudence.

re·te·pore (rē′tə pôr, -pōr), *n.* any of a group of bryozoans that form corallike colonies. [< New Latin *Retepora* the genus name < Latin *rēte, -is* net + *porus* pore[2]]

Retepore (diameter, 2 in.)

re·test (*v.* rē test′; *n.* rē′test′), *v.t.* to test again: *As for pilots, the airlines select only one applicant out of 20, spend $1,000 an hour to train him,* [*and*] *retest him every six months* (Time). —*n.* a retesting; repeated test: *We encourage members to take retests* (London Times).

re·think (rē thingk′), *v.t.* **-thought, -think·ing.** to think out, or think over, again; consider afresh: *Rahner believes that each generation must rethink the problems of theology* (London Times).

re·ti·ar·i·us (rē′shē ãr′ē əs), *n., pl.* **-ar·i·i** (-ãr′ē ī). a gladiator equipped with a net and a trident. [< Latin *rētiārius* < *rēte, -is* net]

re·ti·ar·y (rē′shē er′ē), *adj.* **1.** using a net or any entangling device. **2.** making a web: *a retiary spider.* **3.** netlike.

ret·i·cence (ret′ə səns), *n.* the tendency to be silent or say little; reserve in speech.

ret·i·cent (ret′ə sənt), *adj.* disposed to keep silent or say little; not speaking freely; reserved in speech: *She had been shy and reticent with me, and now ... she was telling me aloud the secrets of her inmost heart* (W.H. Hudson). [< Latin *reticēns, -entis,* present participle of *reticēre* keep silent < *re-* back + *tacēre* be silent] —**ret′i·cent·ly,** *adv.*
—**Syn.** reserved, taciturn. See **silent.**

ret·i·cle (ret′ə kəl), *n.* a line, or a network of fine lines, wires, or the like, placed in the focus of the objective of a telescope or other optical instrument to make accurate observation easier. [< Latin *rēticulum.* Doublet of RETICULE, RETICULUM.]

re·tic·u·lar (ri tik′yə lər), *adj.* **1.** having the form of a net; netlike. **2.** intricate; entangled. [< New Latin *reticularis* < Latin *rēticulum;* see RETICULUM] —**re·tic′u·lar·ly,** *adv.*

reticular formation, a network of small nerve cells extending from the diencephalon downward through the spinal cord, with distinct formations in the medulla oblongata and mesencephalon. It exerts control over the body's motor activities. *The reticular formation is now often referred to as the "working centre" of the brain* (New Scientist).

re·tic·u·late (*adj.* ri tik′yə lit, -lāt; *v.* ri-tik′yə lāt), *adj., v.,* **-lat·ed, -lat·ing.** —*adj.* netlike; covered with a network: *Reticulate leaves have the veins arranged like the threads of a net.* —*v.t.* to cover or mark with a network. —*v.i.* to form a network. [< Latin *rēticulātus* < *rēticulum;* see RETICULUM] —**re·tic′u·late·ly,** *adv.*

re·tic·u·lat·ed (ri tik′yə lā′tid), *adj.* reticulate: *the reticulated rivers in the central valley* (David Livingstone).

re·tic·u·la·tion (ri tik′yə lā′shən), *n.* **1.** a reticulated formation, arrangement, or appearance; network. **2.** one of the meshes of a network.

Reticulation (def. 1) Roman Masonry

ret·i·cule (ret′ə-kyül), *n.* **1.** a woman's small handbag: *women in cloaks, bearing reticules and bundles* (Henry James). **2.** a reticle. [< French *reticule,* learned borrowing from Latin *rēticulum* net. Doublet of RETICLE, RETICULUM.]

Re·tic·u·li (ri tik′yə lī), *n.* genitive of **Reticulum.**

re·tic·u·lo·cyte (ri tik′yə lə sīt), *n.* a red blood cell that is not fully developed. Reticulocytes comprise from 0.1 to 1 per cent of the red blood cells. [< Latin *rēticulum* net + English *-cyte*]

re·tic·u·lo·cy·to·sis (ri tik′yə lə sī tō′sis), *n.* the presence of an unusually large number of reticulocytes in the blood.

re·tic·u·lo·en·do·the·li·al system (ri-tik′yə lō en′dō thē′lē əl), a system of cells in the body, especially in the spleen, lymph nodes, bone marrow, and liver, that function in freeing the body of foreign matter and disease germs, in the formation of certain blood cells, and in the storing of fatty substances: *They found that cortisone depressed the activity of the blood cell forming reticuloendothelial system, particularly the spleen* (Science News Letter). [< Latin *rēticulum* net + English *endothelial*]

re·tic·u·lo·sis (ri tik′yə lō′sis), *n.* reticulocytosis.

re·tic·u·lum (ri tik′yə ləm), *n., pl.* **-la** (-lə). **1.** any reticulated system or structure; network. **2.** the second stomach of animals that chew the cud: *When first eaten the food passes into the rumen, later balls of this food, called the cud, are passed into the reticulum and up to the esophagus back into the mouth for thorough chewing* (A.M. Winchester). See **abomasum** for picture. [< Latin *rēticulum* (diminutive) < *rēte, -is* net. Doublet of RETICLE, RETICULE.]

Re·tic·u·lum (ri tik′yə ləm), *n., genitive* **Re·tic·u·li.** a southern constellation near Argo.

re·ti·form (rē′tə fôrm, ret′ə-), *adj.* netlike; reticulate. [< New Latin *retiformis* < Latin *rēte, -is* net + *forma* form]

ret·i·na (ret′ə nə), *n., pl.* **-nas, -nae** (-nē). a membrane at the back of the eyeball composed of layers of nervous tissue, with light-sensitive rods and cones near its outer surface, and continuous on its inner surface with the optic nerve. It receives the images of things looked at. *Towards the periphery of the retina the proportion of rods increases. That is why a very faint star can often be seen only when one looks slightly to one side of it* (Science News). See **accommodation** for picture. [< Medieval Latin *retina,* probably < Latin *rēte, -is* net]

ret·i·nac·u·lar (ret′ə nak′yə lər), *adj.* of or having to do with a retinaculum.

ret·i·nac·u·lum (ret′ə nak′yə ləm), *n., pl.* **-u·la** (-yə lə). **1.** *Botany.* a viscid gland on the stigma of orchids and plants of the milkweed family for holding the pollen masses together. **2.** *Anatomy.* a bridle or frenum; a fibrous structure binding down the tendons of muscles. **3.** *Zoology.* **a.** a small scale or plate which in some insects checks too much protrusion of the sting. **b.** an arrangement of hooks, or of hooks and bristles, whereby the fore and hind wings of insects are interlocked when in flight. [< Latin *retinaculum* a band, halter < *retinēre* to hold back; see RETAIN]

ret·i·nal (ret′ə nəl), *adj.* of or on the retina: *retinal images.*

re·tin·a·lite (ri tin′ə līt), *n.* a waxy, resinous variety of serpentine.

re·tine (ri tēn′), *n.* a chemical substance which retards the growth of cells: *Theoreticians suggested that a cancerous condition may result if retine is not in balance with promine, a similar chemical which stimulates cancer growth* (Milton Golin). [< *ret*(ard) + *-ine*]

ret·i·nene (ret′ə nēn), *n.* a yellow pigment in the retina of the eye that decomposes to form vitamin A: *The retinene, in the presence of the enzymes ... is changed to vitamin A* (Science News Letter). *Formula:* $C_{20}H_{28}O$ [< *retin*(a) + *-ene*]

ret·i·nite (ret′ə nīt), *n.* any of various fossil resins, especially one of those derived from brown coal. [< French *rétinite* < Greek *rhētínē* resin + French *-ite* -ite[1]]

ret·i·ni·tis (ret′ə nī′tis), *n.* inflammation of the retina. [< *retin*(a) + *-itis*]

ret·i·no·blas·to·ma (ret′ə nō blas tō′mə), *n.* cancer of the eye. It is very rare and can be inherited.

ret·i·no·cer·e·bral (ret′ə nō ser′ə brəl, -sə-rē′brəl), *adj.* having to do with both the retina and the brain.

ret·i·nol[1] (ret′ə nōl, -nol), *n.* a yellowish oil obtained by the distillation of rosin, used in printing inks, lubricants, etc. [< Greek *rhētínē* resin + English *-ol*[2]]

ret·i·nol[2] (ret′ə nōl, -nol), *n.* vitamin A.

ret·i·nop·a·thy (ret′ə nop′ə thē), *n.* a noninflammatory disorder of the retina. [< *retina* + *-pathy*]
ret·i·no·scope (ret′ə nə skōp), *n.* an ophthalmoscope.
ret·i·no·scop·ic (ret′ə nə skop′ik), *adj.* of or having to do with retinoscopy.
ret·i·nos·co·pist (ret′ə nos′kə pist), *n.* an optometrist or ophthalmologist who practices retinoscopy.
ret·i·nos·co·py (ret′ə nos′kə pē, ret′ə nə skō′-), *n.* examination of the retina with the aid of an ophthalmoscope to measure the amount of refraction of the eye.
ret·i·nue (ret′ə nü, -nyü), *n.* a group of attendants or retainers: *The King's retinue accompanied him on the journey.* [< Old French *retinue,* (originally) feminine past participle of *retenir* to retain < Latin *retinēre*]
ret·i·nued (ret′ə nüd, -nyüd), *adj.* accompanied by a retinue: *Rickey arrived, heavily retinued, and began rumbling forebodings* (New Yorker).
re·tir·a·cy (ri tīr′ə sē), *n.* retirement.
re·tir·al (ri tīr′əl), *n.* retirement: *employees of retiral age or with short service* (Sunday Times).
re·tire (ri tīr′), *v.*, **-tired, -tir·ing.** —*v.i.* **1.** to give up an office, occupation, etc.: *Our teachers retire at 65. You and your wife talk about ways of safeguarding the family life values you enjoy and look forward to the day when you can retire* (Newsweek). **2.** to go away, especially to be quiet: *She retired to a convent. The Roman senators still retired in the winter season to the warm sun, and the salubrious springs, of Baiæ* (Edward Gibbon). **3.** to go back; retreat: *The enemy retired before the advance of our troops.* **4.** to go to bed: *We retire early.* **5.** to recede or appear to recede: *Gradually the shore retired from view.* —*v.t.* **1.** to remove from an office, occupation, etc. **2.** to withdraw; draw back; send back: *The government retires worn or torn dollar bills from use.* **3.** to take up and pay off (bonds, loans, etc.). **4.** to put out (a batter, side, etc.) in baseball and cricket. [< Middle French *retirer* < *re-* back + *tirer* draw < Vulgar Latin *tirāre,* perhaps < a Germanic word] —**Syn.** *v.i.* **2.** See **depart.**
re·tired (ri tīrd′), *adj.* **1.** withdrawn from one's occupation: *a retired sea captain, a retired teacher. Retired Heavyweight Champion Gene Tunney seconded Rose's sentiment* (Time). **2.** retiring; reserved: *She has a shy, retired nature.* **3.** secluded; shut off; hidden: *a retired spot.*
—*n.* a retired person.
retired list, a list of persons who have been retired from active service in the armed services.
re·tir·ee (ri tī′rē), *n.* a person who retires from his occupation.
re·tire·ment (ri tīr′mənt), *n.* **1.** a retiring or being retired; withdrawal: *The teacher's retirement from service was regretted by the school. He thus had a choice of prison in the U.S. or retirement in Italy* (Newsweek). **2.** a quiet way or place of living: *She lives in retirement, neither making nor receiving visits.*
re·tir·er (ri tīr′ər), *n.* a person who retires or withdraws.
re·tir·ing (ri tīr′ing), *adj.* shrinking from society or publicity; reserved; shy; bashful. —**re·tir′ing·ly,** *adv.* —**re·tir′ing·ness,** *n.*
re·ti·trate (rē tī′trāt, -tit′rāt), *v.t.*, **-trat·ed, -trat·ing.** to titrate (a solution) again after some change, as that caused by exposure to the air.
re·told (rē tōld′), *v.* the past tense and past participle of **retell.**
ret·o·na·tion wave (ret′ə nā′shən, rē′tə-), a backward wave of compression, as when gases explode within a glass tube.
re·took (rē tu̇k′), *v.* the past tense of **retake.**
re·tool (rē tül′), *v.i.* to change the tools, machinery, designs, etc., in a plant to make new models or products. —*v.t.* to make over for this purpose.
re·tor·sion (ri tôr′shən), *n.* retortion.
re·tort[1] (ri tôrt′), *v.i.* to reply quickly or sharply. —*v.t.* **1.** to say in sharp reply: *"It's none of your business," he retorted.* **2.** to return in kind; turn back on: *to retort insult for insult or blow for blow.*
—*n.* **1.** the act of retorting. **2.** a sharp or witty reply: *"Why are your teeth so sharp?" asked Red Ridinghood. "The better to eat you with" was the wolf's retort.*
[< Latin *retortus,* past participle of *retorquēre* turn back < *re-* back + *torquēre* to twist]
re·tort[2] (ri tôrt′, rē′tôrt), *n.* **1.** a container used for distilling or decomposing substances by heat. **2.** a container for heating an ore to separate the metal by distillation. —*v.t.* to distill by heating in a retort: *Retorting of this mass of broken shale in place might release an additional 25 million barrels of petroleum products* (Scientific American). [< Vulgar Latin *retorta,* (originally) feminine past participle of Latin *retorquēre;* see RETORT[1]]

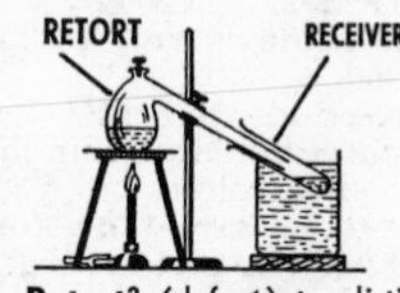

Retort[2] (def. 1) to distill water. Steam from boiling water in retort condenses in receiver immersed in cold water. Impurities are left in retort.

re·tort·er (ri tôr′tər), *n.* a person who retorts metals.
re·tor·tion (ri tôr′shən), *n.* **1.** the act of turning or bending back. **2.** *International Law.* a retaliation in kind by one state upon the citizens of another by imposing equivalent restrictions to those originally imposed on the citizens of the other state. [< Vulgar Latin *retortiō, -ōnis* < Latin *retorquēre;* see RETORT[1]]
re·touch (rē tuch′, rē′tuch′), *v.t.* to improve (a photographic negative, painting, composition, etc.) by new touches, or slight changes: *Retouched and smoothed and prettified to please* (Berton Braley). —*n.* a second or further touch given to a picture, composition, etc., to improve it. —**re·touch′er,** *n.*
re·tour (re tür′), *v.i.* **1.** to revert (to a person). **2.** to return (to a place).
re·trace (ri trās′), *v.t.*, **-traced, -trac·ing.** **1.** to go back over: *We retraced our steps to where we started. Slowly, hesitatingly, he retraced the route the doctor had taken, down the steps onto the tough rocky ground* (Graham Greene). **2.** to trace again in memory; recall: *Shall one retrace his life?* (Ernest Dowson). **3.** to go over again with the sight or attention. [< Middle French *retracer* < *re-* back + Old French *tracier* to trace[1]]
re-trace (rē trās′), *v.t.*, **-traced, -trac·ing.** to trace over again: *re-traced lines in a drawing.* [< *re-* + *trace*[1]]
re·trace·a·ble (ri trā′sə bəl), *adj.* that can be retraced.
re·tract (ri trakt′), *v.t.* **1.** to draw back or in: *to retract a plane's landing gear. The dog snarled and retracted his lips.* **2.** to withdraw; take back: *to retract an offer or an opinion.* —*v.i.* **1.** to be able to draw back or in: *claws that retract.* **2.** to make a withdrawal; be taken back. [< Latin *retractus,* past participle of *retrahere* < *re-* back + *trahere* to draw] —**Syn.** *v.t.* **2.** revoke, rescind, recall.
re·tract·a·bil·i·ty (ri trak′tə bil′ə tē), *n.* the property of being retractable.
re·tract·a·ble (ri trak′tə bəl), *adj.* that can be retracted or drawn back: *In 1957 the Ford Division of the Ford Motor Company introduced the first all-steel retractable hardtop to be produced in mass quantities* (Charles F. Kettering).
re·trac·ta·tion (rē′trak tā′shən), *n.* a retracting of a promise, statement, etc.
re·tract·ed (ri trak′tid), *adj. Phonetics.* pronounced with the tongue drawn farther back than normal for a particular vowel.
re·trac·tile (ri trak′təl), *adj.* that can be drawn back or in.
re·trac·til·i·ty (rē′trak til′ə tē), *n.* the quality of being retractile.
re·trac·tion (ri trak′shən), *n.* **1.** a drawing or being drawn back or in. **2.** a taking back; withdrawal of a promise, statement, etc.: *The newspaper published a retraction of the erroneous report.* **3.** retractile power.
re·trac·tive (ri trak′tiv), *adj.* tending or serving to retract.
re·trac·tor (ri trak′tər), *n.* **1.** a person or thing that draws back something. **2.** a muscle that retracts an organ, protruded part, etc. **3.** a surgical instrument or appliance for drawing back an organ or part.
re·train (rē trān′), *v.t.* to train again in order to teach a new skill, reinforce something already learned, etc.: *Every dancer in the company either has been trained by Balanchine from an early stage, or has been retrained according to Balanchine's principles of dance technique* (New Yorker). —*v.i.* to undergo retraining.
re·tral (rē′trəl), *adj.* at the back; posterior: *Beneath the retral ethmoidal spike is seen the olfactory groove* (Journal of Microscopic Sciences). [< Latin *retrō* back(wards) + English *-al*[1]]
re·tral·ly (rē′trə lē), *adv.* in a retral manner; posteriorly.
re·trans·fer (*v.* rē′trans fėr′, -trans′fėr; *n.* rē trans′fėr), *v.*, **-ferred, -fer·ring,** *n.* —*v.t.* **1.** to transfer back to a former place or condition. **2.** to transfer a second time.
—*n.* **1.** a transfer back to a previous place or condition. **2.** a second transfer.
re·trans·form (rē′trans fôrm′), *v.t.* to transform again or to a previous state.
re·trans·for·ma·tion (rē′trans fər mā′shən), *n.* a retransforming.
re·trans·late (rē′trans lāt′, -tranz-; rē trans′lāt, -tranz′-), *v.t.*, **-lat·ed, -lat·ing.** to translate back into the original form or language: *Of Cicero . . . he had translated and retranslated every extant oration* (James Pycroft).
re·trans·la·tion (rē′trans lā′shən, -tranz-), *n.* **1.** the act or process of retranslating. **2.** what is retranslated.
re·trans·mis·sion (rē′trans mish′ən, -tranz-), *n.* transmission back to a source or to a new destination: *Six long panels of solar batteries . . . supply electrical power to the satellite for retransmission of signals received from earth* (New York Times).
re·trans·mit (rē′trans mit′, -tranz-), *v.t.*, **-mit·ted, -mit·ting.** to transmit back again or further on: *The response is received by the satellite and again retransmitted at high power* (New Scientist).
re·tread (*v.* rē tred′; *n.* rē′tred′), *v.*, **-tread·ed, -tread·ing,** *n.* —*v.t.* to put a new tread on. —*n.* **1.** a tire that has been retreaded: *The exemption from the camelback tax would affect retreads for small and medium cars* (Wall Street Journal). **2.** *Informal.* **a.** a restoration or renewal of an old or worn thing, event, idea, etc.: *[He] regards the issue of "bossism" as a retread of the successful Wagner campaign theme of four years ago* (New York Times). **b.** the thing, event, idea, etc., itself. [< *re-* + *tread,* noun]
re-tread (rē tred′), *v.t., v.i.*, **-trod, -trod·den** or **-trod, -tread·ing.** to tread back over. [< *re-* + *tread,* verb]
re·treat (ri trēt′), *v.i.* **1.** to go back; move back; withdraw: *Seeing the big dog, the tramp retreated rapidly.* **2.** to incline backward, as an airfoil or other part of an aircraft. —*v.t.* **1.** to draw back; take away; remove. **2.** *Chess.* to move (a piece) back. [probably < noun]
—*n.* **1.** the act of going back or withdrawing: *The army's retreat was orderly.* **2.** a signal for retreat: *The drums sounded a retreat.* **3.** the ceremony at sunset during the lowering of the flag. **4.** a safe, quiet place; place of rest or refuge: *a country retreat.* **5.** a retirement, or period of retirement, by a group of people for religious exercises and meditation: *The monks conducted a retreat.* **6.** an asylum for insane people and for habitual drunkards. **7.** the amount of curve or backward slope, as of an airfoil or other part of an aircraft.
beat a retreat, to run away; retreat: *The cat beat a hasty retreat toward the barn in the face of the oncoming pack of yelping hounds.*
[< Old French *retraite,* (originally) past participle of *retraire* < Latin *retrahere* retract < *re-* back + *trahere* to draw, pull. Related to RETRACT.] —**re·treat′er,** *n.*
—**Syn.** *n.* **1.** withdrawal.
re-treat (rē trēt′), *v.t.* to treat again: *The tissue residue is then re-treated with alcohol at 99°* (A.M. Brown).
re·treat·al (ri trē′təl), *adj.* **1.** of or relating to retreat. **2.** *Geology.* relating to something that has retreated; recessional.
re·treat·ant (ri trē′tənt), *n.* a person who takes part in a religious retreat: *A nun read spiritual writings to the retreatants at the lunch period* (Seattle Times Pictorial).
re-treat·ment (rē trēt′mənt), *n.* further or renewed treatment: *The quick re-treatment of the relapsing patient is one of the most satisfying aspects of current psychiatric treatment in England* (Atlantic).
re·tree (ri trē′), *n.* broken, wrinkled, or imperfect paper. [perhaps < French *retrait* < Middle French *retirer;* see RETIRE]

re·trench (ri trench′), *v.t.* **1.** to cut down; reduce (expenses, etc.). **2.** *Military.* to protect by a retrenchment. —*v.i.* to reduce expenses: *In hard times, we must retrench to keep out of debt.* [< Old French *retrencher* < *re-* back + *trencher* to cut] —**re·trench′er,** *n.* —**Syn.** *v.i.* economize.

re·trench·ment (ri trench′mənt), *n.* **1.** a reduction of expenses: *Plant closing and retrenchment were the order of the day* (Wall Street Journal). **2.** a cutting down; cutting off. **3.** a second defense within an outer line of fortification.

re·tri·al (rē trī′əl, rē′trī-), *n.* a second trial.

ret·ri·bu·tion (ret′rə byü′shən), *n.* a deserved punishment; return for evil done, or sometimes for good done: *Accusation was preferred and retribution most singular was looked for* (Charles Lamb). [< Latin *retribūtiō, -ōnis* < *retribuere* < *re-* back + *tribuere* to assign, related to *tribus, -ūs* tribe]

re·trib·u·tive (ri trib′yə tiv), *adj.* paying back; bringing or inflicting punishment in return for some evil, wrong, etc.: *In death he suffered, with a kind of retributive justice* (Wall Street Journal). —**re·trib′u·tive·ly,** *adv.*

re·trib·u·tor (ri trib′yə tər), *n.* a person who makes retribution.

re·trib·u·to·ry (ri trib′yə tôr′ē, -tōr′-), *adj.* retributive.

re·triev·a·ble (ri trē′və bəl), *adj.* that can be retrieved.

re·triev·a·bly (ri trē′və blē), *adv.* with a possibility of retrieval or recovery.

re·triev·al (ri trē′vəl), *n.* the act of retrieving; recovery.

re·trieve (ri trēv′), *v.,* **-trieved, -triev·ing,** *n.* —*v.t.* **1.** to get again; recover: *to retrieve a lost pocketbook.* **2.** to bring back to a former or better condition; restore: *to retrieve one's fortunes.* **3. a.** to make good; make amends for; repair: *to retrieve a mistake, to retrieve a loss or defeat.* **b.** to rescue; save: *to retrieve the nations sitting in darkness from eternal perdition* (William H. Prescott). **4.** to find and bring to a person. —*v.i.* to find and bring back killed or wounded game.
—*n.* the act of retrieving; recovery, or possibility of recovery.
[< Old French *retruev-,* stem of *retrouver* < *re-* again + *trouver* to find]
—**Syn.** *v.t.* **1.** See **recover.**

re·trieve·ment (ri trēv′mənt), *n.* **1.** a retrieving. **2.** a being retrieved.

re·triev·er (ri trē′vər), *n.* **1.** a dog belonging to one of several powerfully built breeds trained to find killed or wounded game and bring it to a hunter: *A good retriever can be a big help to the hunter and wildlife* (Science News Letter). **2.** any dog trained to retrieve game. **3.** a person or thing that retrieves.

Curly-coated Retriever (def. 1) (23 in. high at the shoulder)

retro-, *prefix.* backward; back; behind, as in *retroactive, retrorocket, retrospection.* [< Latin *retrō* back, backward]

ret·ro·act (ret′rō akt′), *v.i.* **1.** to operate in a backward direction; affect what is past. **2.** to react.

ret·ro·ac·tion (ret′rō ak′shən), *n.* **1.** a retroactive force. **2.** an action in return; reaction.

ret·ro·ac·tive (ret′rō ak′tiv), *adj.* acting back; having an effect on what is past. —**ret′ro·ac′tive·ly,** *adv.*

ret·ro·ac·tiv·i·ty (ret′rō ak tiv′ə tē), *n.* a being retroactive or retrospective.

ret·ro·bron·chi·al (ret′rə brong′kē əl), *adj.* situated or occurring behind the bronchi.

ret·ro·car·di·ac (ret′rə kär′dē ak), *adj.* situated behind the heart.

ret·ro·cede[1] (ret′rə sēd′), *v.i.,* **-ced·ed, -ced·ing.** to go back; recede. [< Latin *retrōcēdere* < *retrō-* backward + *cēdere* go]

ret·ro·cede[2] (ret′rə sēd′), *v.t.,* **-ced·ed, -ced·ing.** to cede back (territory, etc.).

ret·ro·ced·ent (ret′rə sē′dənt), *adj.* going back.

re·tro·ces·sion[1] (ret′rə sesh′ən), *n.* a going back.

ret·ro·ces·sion[2] (ret′rə sesh′ən), *n.* a ceding back.

re·tro·ces·sion·al (ret′rə sesh′ə nəl), *adj.* having to do with or involving retrocession.

ret·ro·ces·sive[1] (ret′rə ses′iv), *adj.* going back.

ret·ro·ces·sive[2] (ret′rə ses′iv), *adj.* ceding back.

ret·ro·choir (ret′rə kwīr, rē′trə-), *n.* the space in a large church behind the choir or the main altar.

ret·ro·cog·ni·tion (ret′rə kog nish′ən), *n.* a supernatural familiarity with happenings in the past.

ret·ro·cog·ni·tive (ret′rə kog′nə tiv), *adj.* having to do with retrocognition.

re·trod (rē trod′), *v.* the past tense and a past participle of **re-tread.**

ret·ro·dis·placed (ret′rə dis plāst′), *adj.* displaced backward.

ret·ro·dis·place·ment (ret′rə dis plās′mənt), *n.* displacement backward: *retrodisplacement of the uterus.*

ret·ro·fire (ret′rō fīr), *n., v.,* **-fired, -fir·ing.** —*n.* the firing of a retrorocket: *When a Gemini capsule is about to re-enter the atmosphere, it will be positioned for retrofire by computers on the ground* (Time). —*v.i.* to fire a retrorocket.

ret·ro·fit (ret′rə fit′), *v.,* **-fit·ted, -fit·ting,** *n.* —*v.t.* to modify (a piece of equipment), especially in an aircraft, to include changes made in later production of the same type. —*n.* a retrofitting of an aircraft or piece of equipment.

ret·ro·flec·tion (ret′rə flek′shən), *n.* retroflexion.

ret·ro·flex (ret′rə fleks), *adj.* **1.** bent backward. **2.** having the tip raised and bent backward. **3.** made by raising the tip of the tongue and bending it backward: *Most Americans have a retroflex vowel in "hurt."* —*v.t., v.i.* **1.** to raise and bend backward the tip of (the tongue). **2.** to pronounce with the tip of the tongue raised and bent backward.
[< Latin *retrōflexus,* past participle of *retrōflectere* < *retrō-* back + *flectere* to bend]

ret·ro·flexed (ret′rə flekst), *adj.* retroflex.

ret·ro·flex·ion (ret′rə flek′shən), *n.* **1.** a bending backward, especially of the uterus. **2.** pronunciation with a bending backward and raising of the tip of the tongue.

ret·ro·gra·da·tion (ret′rə grā dā′shən), *n.* **1.** a backward movement; retreat; decline; deterioration. **2.** *Astronomy.* an apparent backward motion of a planet or asteroid from east to west.

ret·ro·grade (ret′rə grād), *adj., v.,* **-grad·ed, -grad·ing.** —*adj.* **1.** moving backward; retreating. **2.** becoming worse; declining; deteriorating. **3.** inverse or reversed, as order: *After the brilliant quantitative work of W.D. Wright, . . . it seems somewhat retrograde to examine one's sensations with little pieces of coloured paper* (Tansley and Weale). **4.** *Astronomy.* characterized by retrogradation. **5.** *Obsolete.* opposed; contrary: *It is most retrograde to our desire* (Shakespeare). —*v.i.* **1.** to move or go backward. **2.** to fall back toward a worse condition; grow worse; decline; deteriorate: *All that is human must retrograde if it do not advance* (Edward Gibbon). **3.** *Astronomy.* (of a planet or asteroid) to appear to move backward from east to west: *Once during each synodic period the planet turns and moves westward, or retrogrades, for a time before resuming the eastward motion* (Robert H. Baker). —*v.t.* to cause to go backward; turn back: *We see, now, events forced on, which seem to retard or retrograde the civility of ages* (Emerson).
[< Latin *retrōgradus* < *retrōgradī* to go back < *retrō-* backward + *gradī* to go, step]
—**ret′ro·grade′ly,** *adv.*

ret·ro·gress (ret′rə gres, ret′rə gres′), *v.i.* **1.** to move backward; go back. **2.** to become worse; decline; deteriorate. [< Latin *retrōgressus,* past participle of *retrōgradī;* see RETROGRADE]

ret·ro·gres·sion (ret′rə gresh′ən), *n.* **1.** a backward movement. **2.** a becoming worse; falling off; decline; deterioration; degeneration. **3.** *Astronomy.* retrogradation.

ret·ro·gres·sive (ret′rə gres′iv), *adj.* **1.** moving backward. **2.** becoming worse; declining; deteriorating. —**ret′ro·gres′sive·ly,** *adv.*

ret·ro·ject (ret′rə jekt), *v.t.* to cast or throw back.

ret·ro·jec·tion (ret′rə jek′shən), *n.* **1.** a putting back to an earlier date. **2.** *Medicine.* the washing out of a cavity or canal outward from within.

ret·ro·lent·al fi·bro·pla·sia (ret′rə len′təl fī′brə plā′zhə), a growth of fibrous tissue behind the lens of the eye, occurring in premature infants and resulting in blindness. It is caused chiefly by administering too much oxygen to the premature child. [< *retro-* + Latin *lēns* (compare LENS) + English *-al*[1]]

ret·ro·rock·et (ret′rō rok′it), *n.* a small rocket at the front of a rocket or spacecraft. It is set off to reduce speed for landing or for reëntry. *The way to bring a satellite, manned or unmanned, down to the atmosphere is to fire a forward-pointing retrorocket to reduce its speed* (Time).

re·trorse (ri trôrs′), *adj.* turned backward; turned in a direction opposite to the usual one. [< Latin *retrōrsus,* contraction of *retrōversus;* see RETROVERSION] —**re·trorse′ly,** *adv.*

ret·ro·se·quence (ret′rō sē′kwəns), *n.* the sequence of events before, during, and after a retrofiring: *John Glenn, aboard a command ship off the Japanese coast, provided the countdown for the retrosequence* (Hugh Odishaw).

ret·ro·spect (ret′rə spekt), *n.* **1.** a survey of past time, events, etc.; thinking about the past: *My retrospect of life recalls to my view many opportunities of good neglected* (Samuel Johnson). *We may be presenting, not simply retrospects of bygone episodes of this campaign year, but the two stories that will make the politics of 1952 memorable* (Harper's). **2.** a looking back; reference: *He deprecated any invidious retrospect as to what had happened in former debates* (William E.H. Lecky).
in retrospect, when looking back: *He saw, in retrospect, that another course of action should have been taken.*
—*v.t.* to think of (something past). —*v.i.* **1.** to look back in thought. **2.** to refer (to).
[< Latin *retrōspectus* < *retrōspicere* to look back < *retrō-* back + *specere* to look]

ret·ro·spec·tion (ret′rə spek′shən), *n.* **1.** the act or fact of looking back on things past; survey of past events or experiences: *Old people often enjoy retrospection.* **2.** a reference to something.

ret·ro·spec·tive (ret′rə spek′tiv), *adj.* **1.** looking back on things past; surveying past events or experiences. **2.** looking or directed backward: *Frequent retrospective glances . . . served to assure me that our retreat was not cut off* (Herman Melville). **3.** applying to the past; retroactive.
—*n.* a retrospective show: *Twenty-three paintings, 1930-54 make up the Ben Shahn retrospective at the Downtown Gallery* (New York Times). —**re′tro·spec′tive·ly,** *adv.*

retrospective show, an exhibition of paintings reviewing the work of an artist or group of artists over a number of years: *the Picasso retrospective show at the Museum of Modern Art.*

ret·rous·sage (ret′rü säzh′; *French* rə trüsȧzh′), *n.* a method used in the printing of etchings to produce effective tone, as in foregrounds or shadows, by skillfully bringing out the ink from the filled lines with a soft cloth. [< French *retroussage*]

ret·rous·sé (ret′rü sā′; *French* rə trü sā′), *adj.* turned up: *a retroussé nose.* [< French *retroussé,* past participle of Middle French *retrousser* < *re-* back + Old French *trousser* truss (up), load. Compare TROUSSEAU.]

ret·ro·ver·sion (ret′rə vėr′zhən, -shən), *n.* a turning or being turned backward; displacement backwards: *a retroversion of the uterus.* [< Latin *retrōversus* (< *retrō-* back + *vertere* to turn) + English *-ion*]

ret·ro·vert (ret′rə vėrt), *v.t.* to turn backward; displace as by tipping backward, as the uterus.

re·try (rē trī′), *v.t.,* **-tried, -try·ing.** to try again.

ret·si·na (ret′sə nə), *n.* a Greek wine flavored with resin.

ret·ting (ret′ing), *n.* the process of wetting flax, hemp, etc., and allowing it to decay until the fibers can be easily separated from the woody parts of the stalks.

re·tube (rē tüb′, -tyüb′), *v.t.,* **-tubed, -tub·ing.** to provide with a new tube or tubes: *to retube a boiler, a gun, etc.*

re·tune (rē tün′, -tyün′), *v.t.,* **-tuned, -tun·ing.** to tune (a musical instrument) again.

re·turf (rē tėrf′), *v.t.* to lay with new turf.

re·turn (ri tėrn′), *v.i.* **1.** to go back; come back: *to return this summer. We will return to this hard example after doing the easy ones. And the spirit shall return unto God who gave it* (Ecclesiastes 12:7). **2.** to make an answer or reply: *A plain-spoken . . . critic might here perhaps return upon me with my own expressions* (Robert Louis Stevenson).

—*v.t.* **1.** to bring, give, send, hit, put, or pay back: *Return that book to the library. You took this cap; return it at once. Return good for evil. She admired my dress, and I returned the compliment.* **2.** to yield: *The concert returned about $50 over expenses.* **3.** to report or announce officially: *The jury returned a verdict of guilty.* **4.** to reply; answer: *"No!" he returned crossly.* **5.** to elect to a lawmaking body: *Many Presidents have been returned to office for a second term.* **6.** (in card games) to lead (the suit led by one's partner). **7.** to continue (a wall, molding, etc.); turn at an angle. **8.** to reflect (light, sound, etc.).
—*n.* **1.** a going or coming back; a happening again: *We look forward all winter to our return to the country. We wish you many happy returns of your birthday.* **2.** a thing returned. **3.** a bringing back; giving back; sending back; hitting back; putting back; paying back: *The boy's bad behavior was a poor return for his uncle's kindness.* **4. a.** Often, **returns.** profit; amount received: *The returns from the sale were more than $100. Return on investment is the product of two ratios: the margin of profit on sales, and the rate of turnover of capital* (Wall Street Journal). **b.** a report; account: *to make out an income-tax return. The election returns are all in.* **5.** a reply; answer. **6.** (in card games) a lead responding to the suit led by one's partner. **7.** a bend or turn in a river, part of a machine, part of a building, etc.

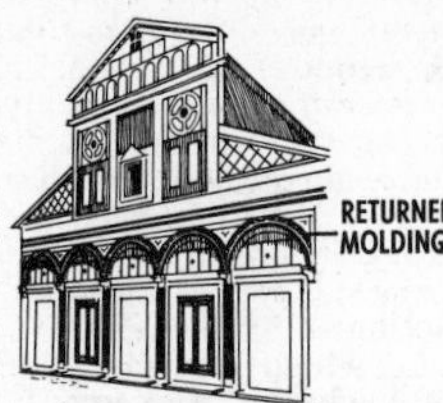

Returned Molding (def. 7)

in return, as a return; to return something: *thanks in return for aid.*
—*adj.* **1.** of or having to do with a return: *a return ticket.* **2.** sent, given, done, etc., in return: *a return game, a return cargo.* **3.** repeated: *a return engagement.* **4.** that bends or turns, often turning back on itself: *the return angle of the nave.* **5.** causing or allowing the return of some part of a device to its normal or starting position: *a return spring, a return valve.*
[< Old French *retourner* < *re-* back + *tourner* to turn]
—**Syn.** *v.t.* **4.** respond. *-n.* **1.** recurrence.

re·turn·a·ble (ri tėr′nə bəl), *adj.* **1.** that can be returned: *returnable merchandise.* **2.** meant or required to be returned: *They hinted that returnable missiles from either of these planets could introduce something on the earth* (Science News Letter).

return address, the address of the sender on a letter, package, etc.

re·turn·ee (ri tėr′nē′, -tėr′nē), *n.* **1.** a person who comes back: *The total number of returnees rose at the appliance division plant* (Wall Street Journal). **2.** a person who sends something back.

re·turn·er (ri tėr′nər), *n.* a person or thing that returns.

re·turn·ing board (ri tėr′ning), *U.S.* a board appointed in some States to determine the results of elections.

returning officer, *Especially British.* **1.** the officer at an election who reports the returns to the proper authority. **2.** the officer who returns writs or other documents to the issuing court.

re·turn·less (ri tėrn′lis), *adj.* **1.** without return; not returning: *Gone to the mould now, whither all that be vanish returnless* (Lowell). **2.** not allowing or being capable of return: *The boat had put a returnless distance between them* (Harriet Beecher Stowe).

re·tuse (ri tüs′, -tyüs′), *adj. Botany.* having an obtuse or rounded apex with a shallow notch in the center, as a leaf. [< Latin *retūsus,* past participle of *retundere* to blunt; beat back < *re-* back + *tundere* to beat]

Retuse Leaf

re·type (rē tīp′), *v.,* **-typed, -typ·ing.** —*v.t.* **1.** to typify anew. **2.** to recopy with a typewriter. —*v.i.* to acquire a stock of new type.

Reu·ben (rü′bən), *n.* in the Bible: **1.** the oldest son of Jacob. Genesis 29:32. **2.** the tribe of Israel that was made up of his descendants. Numbers 32.

re·u·ni·fi·ca·tion (rē′yü nə fə kā′shən, rē-yü′-), *n.* **1.** the action or process of reunifying: *reunification of the two sections of Germany.* **2.** the state of being reunified.

re·u·ni·fy (rē yü′nə fī), *v.t.,* **-fied, -fy·ing.** to bring back together again: *This includes preserving Berlin from eventual incorporation into the East German Regime, and ... reunifying her under a democratic process* (Sunday Times).

re·un·ion (rē yün′yən), *n.* **1.** a coming together again: *the reunion of parted friends.* **2.** a being reunited. **3.** a social gathering of persons who have been separated or who have interests in common: *a college reunion.*

re·un·ion·ism (rē yün′yə niz əm), *n.* the principles of reunionists; the belief in reunion.

re·un·ion·ist (rē yün′yə nist), *n.* a person who believes in or works for reunion, especially reunion of the Anglican Church with the Roman Catholic Church.

re·un·ion·is·tic (rē yün′yə nis′tik), *adj.* of or having to do with reunionism or reunionists.

re·u·nite (rē′yü nīt′), *v.,* **-nit·ed, -nit·ing.** —*v.t.* to bring together again: *Mother and child were reunited after years of separation.* —*v.i.* to come together again. [< Medieval Latin *reunitus,* past participle of *reunire* < Latin *re-* again + *unīre* to unite] —**re′u·nit′er,** *n.*

re·u·nit·ed·ly (rē′yü nī′tid lē), *adv.* in a reunited manner.

re-up (rē up′), *v.i.,* **-upped, -up·ping.** *U.S. Slang.* to rejoin the army, navy, etc.; reënlist: *More cooks, truck drivers, and other practitioners of "soft skills" actually "re-up" ... than the services need* (Newsweek).

re·up·hol·ster (rē′up hōl′stər), *v.t.* to put new upholstery on.

re·us·a·ble (rē yü′zə bəl), *adj.* that can be used again.

re·use (*v.* rē yüz′; *n.* rē yüs′), *v.,* **-used, -us·ing,** *n.* —*v.t.* to use again: *Almost all swimming pools built today are filtered, reusing the same water* (Newsweek). —*n.* a using again.

rev (rev), *n., v.,* **revved, rev·ving.** *Informal.* —*n.* a revolution (of an engine or motor). —*v.t.* to increase the speed of (an engine or motor). —*v.i.* to be revved.

rev., an abbreviation for the following:
1. revenue.
2. reverse.
3. review.
4. a. revise. **b.** revised. **c.** revision.
5. revolution.
6. revolving.

Rev., **1.** Revelation (book of the Bible). **2.** Reverend.

re·vac·ci·nate (rē vak′sə nāt), *v.t.,* **-nat·ed, -nat·ing.** to vaccinate again.

re·vac·ci·na·tion (rē′vak sə nā′shən), *n.* a vaccinating again, especially after the lapse of a number of years.

re·val·i·date (rē val′ə dāt), *v.t.,* **-dat·ed, -dat·ing.** to validate or confirm anew: *From July 1 to December 1, all citizens and aliens were required to revalidate their identity cards* (William S. Stokes).

re·val·i·da·tion (rē val′ə dā′shən), *n.* a revalidating or being revalidated: *Mr. Dirsmith advocates the revalidation of ideas established by Frank Lloyd Wright* (New York Times).

re·val·or·i·za·tion (ri val′ər ə zā′shən), *n.* the act or process of revalorizing: *Increasingly French Canadians are unwilling to let any traditional institution or constitutional limitation interfere with [monetary] revalorization* (William Kenneth Gibb).

re·val·or·ize (ri val′ə rīz), *v.t.,* **-ized, -iz·ing.** to assign a new value to (a currency, price, etc.); valorize anew.

re·val·u·a·tion (rē′val yu̇ ā′shən), *n.* **1.** a second or revised valuation: *The dollar suffered from rumors of Continental currency revaluations* (Wall Street Journal). **2.** a reëvaluation.

re·val·ue (rē val′yü), *v.t.,* **-ued, -u·ing.** **1.** to value anew: *to revalue a property.* **2.** to reëvaluate: *to revalue a classic.*

re·valve (rē valv′), *v.t.,* **-valved, -valv·ing.** to put new valves in.

re·vamp (rē vamp′), *v.t.* to patch up; repair: *to revamp an old car, to revamp plans.* —*n.* something revamped. [American English]

re·vanche (rə väNsh′), *n.* revenge: *Peace was not to return that easily. At week's end the revanche went on* (Time). [< French *revanche,* Old French *revenge;* see REVENGE]

re·vanch·ism (rə väN′shiz əm), *n.* the beliefs or practices of the revanchists.

re·vanch·ist (rə väN′shist), *n.* a person who advocates taking up arms against a country, government, etc., solely for revenge. —*adj.* of or having to do with revanchists or revanchism: *a revanchist party.*

re·veal (ri vēl′), *v.t.* **1.** to make known: *Promise never to reveal my secret. The wrath of God is revealed from heaven against all ungodliness and unrighteousness of men* (Romans 1:18). **2.** to display; show: *to reveal a room by opening a door. Her laugh revealed her even teeth.*
—*n.* **1.** a jamb. **2.** that part of a jamb between the face of a wall and that of the frame containing the door or window. **3.** the border of an automobile window.
[< Latin *revēlāre* < *re-* back + *vēlāre* to cover, veil < *vēlum* veil]
—**re·veal′er,** *n.*
—**Syn.** *v.t.* **1. Reveal, disclose** mean to make known something hidden or secret. **Reveal** applies especially when the thing has been unknown or undisplayed before: *At the new school he revealed an aptitude for science.* **Disclose** applies especially when the thing has been kept secret: *She disclosed that she had been married for a month.*

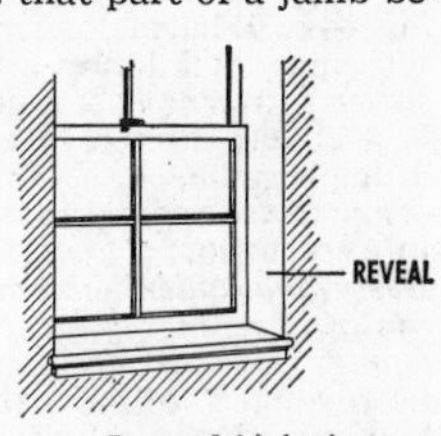

Reveal (def. 2)

re·veal·a·ble (ri vē′lə bəl), *adj.* that can be revealed.

revealed theology, the study of theology from the standpoint of supernatural revelation, without the aid of natural reason.

re·veal·ing (ri vē′ling), *adj.* disclosing something not known before or not shown: *a revealing novel, speech, or dress.*

re·veal·ing·ly (ri vē′ling lē), *adv.* in a revealing manner: *The characters are no longer so fully and revealingly lived with, hence so expressive or large* (Time).

re·veal·ment (ri vēl′mənt), *n.* a revelation.

re·veg·e·tate (rē vej′ə tāt), *v.i.,* **-tat·ed, -tat·ing.** **1.** to grow again. **2.** to grow plants again; become green with plants again.

re·veg·e·ta·tion (rē′vej ə tā′shən), *n.* a revegetating or being revegetated: *Revegetation of the eroded slopes is a related activity* (Science News Letter).

rev·eil·le (rev′ə lē; *British* ri val′ē), *n. Military.* **1.** a signal on a bugle, whistle, or drum to waken soldiers or sailors in the morning: *The bugler blew reveille.* **2.** the first military formation of the day, at which the roll is usually taken. [< French *réveillez* awaken, imperative of *réveiller* < Old French < *re-* again + *eveiller* < Latin *ex-* out + *vigilāre* be awake < *vigil, -ilis* awake]

rev·el (rev′əl), *v.,* **-eled, -el·ing** or (*especially British*) **-elled, -el·ling,** *n.* —*v.i.* **1.** to take very great pleasure (in): *The children revel in country life. Young boys who liked Enright's "Kinty" ... should revel in the excitement, color, and action of this little story* (Saturday Review). **2.** to make merry. —*n.* a merrymaking; noisy good time: *Christmas revels with feasting and dancing were common in England.* [< Old French *reveler* be disorderly, make merry < Latin *rebellāre.* Doublet of REBEL, verb.]

rev·e·la·tion (rev′ə lā′shən), *n.* **1.** the act of making known: *The revelation of the thieves' hiding place by one of their own number caused their capture. Revelation of serious unrest in the army has an added significance* (London Times). **2.** the thing made known: *Her true nature was a revelation to me.* **3.** God's disclosure of Himself and of His will to His creatures. [< Latin *revēlātiō, -ōnis* < *revēlāre* to reveal]

Rev·e·la·tion (rev′ə lā′shən), *n.* Also, **Revelations.** the last book of the New Testament, supposed to have been written by the Apostle John. Its full title in the Authorized Version (1611) is *The Revelation of Saint John the Divine. Abbr.:* Rev.

rev·e·la·tion·ist (rev′ə lā′shə nist), *n.* **1.** a person who believes in divine revelation. **2.** a person who makes a revelation.

rev·e·la·tor (rev′ə lā′tər), *n.* a revealer.

rev·e·la·to·ry (rev′ə lə tôr′ē, -tōr′-), *adj.* **1.** that makes known; revealing: *The novel is the most sincere, honest, and revelatory fictional treatment of the Soviet epoch to come out of Russia* (Atlantic). **2.** of religious revelation.

rev·el·er (rev′ə lər), *n.* a person who revels or takes part in a revel.

rev·el·ler (rev′ə lər), *n. Especially British.* reveler.

rev·el·ry (rev′əl rē), *n., pl.* **-ries.** boisterous reveling or festivity; wild merrymaking.

rev·e·nant (rev′ə nənt), *n.* a person who returns, especially as a spirit after death; ghost. [< French *revenant,* present participle of Old French *revenir* to come back; see REVENUE]

re·venge (ri venj′), *n., v.,* **-venged, -veng·ing.** —*n.* **1.** harm done in return for a wrong; returning evil for evil; vengeance: *a blow struck in revenge.* **2.** a desire for vengeance. **3.** a chance to win in a return game after losing a game.
—*v.i.* to take vengeance. —*v.t.* to do harm in return for: *I will revenge that insult. Every malcontent embraced the fair opportunity of revenging his private or imaginary wrongs* (Edward Gibbon).
be revenged, to have the person that hurt you get hurt in return: *She has . . . a most decided desire to be revenged of him* (Scott).
revenge oneself, to pay back to a person the injury he did to one: *The cat revenged itself on the teasing boy by scratching him.*
[< Old French *revenge,* variant of *revenche* < *revenger* avenge < Latin *re-* back + *vindicāre* to avenge] —**re·veng′ing·ly,** *adv.*
—**Syn.** *v.t.* **Revenge, avenge** mean to punish someone in return for a wrong. **Revenge** applies when it is indulged in to get even: *Gangsters revenge the murder of one of their gang.* **Avenge** applies when the punishment seems just: *We avenged the insult to our flag.*

re·venge·ful (ri venj′fəl), *adj.* feeling or showing a strong desire for revenge: *I had a keen, revengeful sense of the insult* (Hawthorne). —**re·venge′ful·ly,** *adv.* —**re·venge′ful·ness,** *n.*

re·venge·ment (ri venj′mənt), *n.* a revenging.

re·veng·er (ri ven′jər), *n.* a person who revenges; avenger.

re·ve·nons à nos mou·tons (rəv nôɴ′ à nō mü tôɴ′), *French.* **1.** let us return to our business. **2.** (literally) let us return to our sheep.

rev·e·noo·er (rev′ə nü′ər), *n. U.S. Dialect.* revenuer: *Tax extraction is getting less painful for taxpayers, revenooers claim* (Wall Street Journal).

rev·e·nue (rev′ə nü, -nyü), *n.* **1.** money coming in; income: *The government gets revenue from taxes.* **2.** a particular item of income. **3.** a source of income. **4.** the government department that collects taxes: *the Internal Revenue Service.* [< Middle French *revenue* < Old French, a return, feminine past participle of *revenir* come back < Latin *revenīre* < *re-* back + *venīre* come]

revenue agent, a government employee who collects or enforces the collection of taxes, duties, etc.

revenue bond, *U.S.* a bond issued by a city, state, etc., payable out of its future income.

revenue cutter, a small, armed coastguard ship used to prevent smuggling, etc.

rev·e·nu·er (rev′ə nü′ər, -nyü′-), *n. U.S. Informal.* **1.** a revenue agent, especially one enforcing the laws against the illegal distilling or smuggling of alcoholic liquor: *Last year revenuers cooled 22,913 stills in the U.S.* (Time). **2.** an employee of the Internal Revenue Service: *Revenuers again urge taxpayers to pay closer heed to their arithmetic in filling out returns* (Wall Street Journal).

revenue stamp, a stamp to show that money has been paid to the government as a tax on something.

re·verb (ri vėrb′), *v.t., v.i. Archaic.* to reverberate. [short for *reverberate*]

re·ver·ber·ant (ri vėr′bər ənt), *adj.* reverberating: *So reverberant* [*was*] *the air, they could hear the man's footsteps on the stony hillside* (Caine Hall).

re·ver·ber·ate (ri vėr′bə rāt), *v.,* **-at·ed, -at·ing.** —*v.i.* **1.** to echo back: *His voice reverberates from the high ceiling.* **2.** to be cast back; be reflected a number of times, as light or heat. **3.** to be deflected, as flame in a reverberatory furnace. —*v.t.* **1.** to reëcho (a sound or noise). **2.** to cast back; reflect (light or heat). **3.** to deflect (flame or heat) on something, as in a reverberatory furnace. [< Latin *reverberāre* (with English *-ate*[1]) beat back < *re-* back + *verberāre* to beat < *verber, -eris* (originally) whip, lash]

re·ver·ber·a·tion (ri vėr′bə rā′shən), *n.* **1.** an echoing back of sound; echo: *Reverberations of the split were felt all over the country* (New Yorker). **2.** the reflection of light or heat. **3.** a being reflected. **4.** that which is reverberated; reëchoed sound: *Shoutings and pistol-shots sent their hollow reverberations to the ear* (Mark Twain).

reverberation time, the time it takes for a sound made in a room, once its source is stopped, to decrease to one millionth of its initial value: *The changes will bring the hall's reverberation time, the acoustician's measure of echo, from 1.6 seconds to 2.1 seconds* (New York Times).

re·ver·ber·a·tive (ri vėr′bə rā′tiv), *adj.* reverberating.

re·ver·ber·a·tor (ri vėr′bə rā′tər), *n.* **1.** a person or thing that reverberates. **2.** a reflecting lamp.

re·ver·ber·a·to·ry (ri vėr′bər ə tôr′ē, -tōr′-), *adj., n., pl.* **-ries.** —*adj.* **1.** characterized by or produced by reverberations; deflected. **2.** built with a vaulted roof so that heat and flame are deflected onto the ore or metal but the fuel remains in a separate compartment: *a reverberatory furnace or kiln.* —*n.* a reverberatory furnace or kiln.

re·vere[1] (ri vir′), *v.t.,* **-vered, -ver·ing.** to love and respect deeply; honor greatly; show reverence for: *We revere sacred things.* [< Latin *reverērī* < *re-* back + *verērī* to stand in awe of, to fear]
—**Syn. Revere, reverence** mean to feel deep respect for someone or something. **Revere** implies deep respect mixed with love, and applies especially to persons: *The Army of Virginia revered General Robert E. Lee.* **Reverence** implies, in addition, wonder or awe, and applies especially to things: *We reverence the tomb of the Unknown Soldier.*

re·vere[2] (ri vir′), *n.* revers.

re·vere·a·ble (ri vir′ə bəl), *adj.* worthy of being revered.

rev·er·ence (rev′ər əns, rev′rəns), *n., v.,* **-enced, -enc·ing.** —*n.* **1.** a feeling of deep respect, mixed with wonder, awe, and love: *He had . . . a sincere reverence for the laws of his country* (Macaulay). **2.** a deep bow: *He made a profound reverence to the ladies* (Fanny Burney). **3.** *Obsolete.* deference.
—*v.t.* to regard with reverence; revere: *We reverence the battlefield at Gettysburg. Ye shall keep my sabbaths and reverence my sanctuary* (Leviticus 19:30).
[< Latin *reverentia* < *reverēns;* see REVERENT] —**Syn.** *n.* **1.** veneration, adoration. *-v.t.* See **revere**[1].

Rev·er·ence (rev′ər əns, rev′rəns), *n.* a title used in speaking of or to a clergyman: *Your Reverence, His Reverence.*

rev·er·enc·er (rev′ər ən sər, rev′rən-), *n.* a person who feels or shows reverence.

rev·er·end (rev′ər ənd, rev′rənd), *adj.* **1.** worthy of great respect. **2.** having to do with or characteristic of clergymen. —*n. Informal.* a clergyman. [< Latin *reverendus* (he who is) to be respected, gerundive of *reverērī* to revere]

Rev·er·end (rev′ər ənd, rev′rənd), *n.* a title for clergymen. *Abbr.:* Rev.
➔ **Reverend,** in formal usage, is preceded by *the,* is not applied to the last name alone, and is usually not abbreviated: *the Reverend James Shaw, the Reverend J.T. Shaw, the Reverend Mr. Shaw.* The abbreviation (*Rev.*) is used in newspapers and in more or less informal writing: *Reverend James Shaw, Reverend J.T. Shaw, Rev. James Shaw, Rev. J.T. Shaw.* It is also used in addressing an envelope: *"The Rev. Allen Price."*

rev·er·ent (rev′ər ənt, rev′rənt), *adj.* feeling reverence; showing reverence: *He gave reverent attention to the sermon.* [< Latin *reverēns, -entis,* present participle of *reverērī* to revere] —**rev′er·ent·ly,** *adv.*

rev·er·en·tial (rev′ə ren′shəl), *adj.* reverent: *reverential awe.* —**rev′er·en′tial·ly,** *adv.*

rev·er·ie (rev′ər ē), *n.* **1.** dreamy thoughts; dreamy thinking of pleasant things: *She was so lost in reverie that she did not hear the doorbell ring. He loved to indulge in reveries about the future.* **2.** the condition of being lost in dreamy thoughts. **3.** a fantastic idea; ridiculous fancy. **4.** *Music.* a composition suggesting a dreamy or musing mood. Also, **revery.** [< Old French *reverie* (originally) raving, delirium < *rever* to dream]

re·vers (rə vir′, -vãr′), *n., pl.* **-vers** (-virz′, -vãrz′). **1.** a part of a garment turned back to show the lining or facing. **2.** an imitation of such a part. **3.** the material covering either of these. Also, **revere.** [< French *revers* < Old French, adjective *reverse* < Latin *reversus;* see REVERSE]

re·ver·sal (ri vėr′səl), *n.* a change to the opposite; reversing or being reversed: *a reversal of attitude, a reversal in the weather. The high court's opinion was a reversal of the lower court's decision.*

re·verse (ri vėrs′), *n., adj., v.,* **-versed, -vers·ing.** —*n.* **1.** the opposite or contrary: *She did the reverse of what I ordered.* **2. a.** the gear or gears that reverse the movement of machinery. **b.** the arrangement of such a gear or gears. **c.** the position of the control that moves such a gear or gears. **3.** a change to bad fortune; check; defeat: *He used to be rich, but he met with reverses. Caesar was never more calm than under a reverse* (James A. Froude). **4.** the back: *His name is on the reverse of the medal.* **5.** an opposite direction; a contrary motion: *a reverse in dancing, a locomotive moving in reverse.*
—*adj.* **1.** turned backward; opposite or contrary in position or direction: *Play the reverse side of that record on the phonograph.* **2.** acting in a manner contrary or opposite to that which is usual. **3.** causing an opposite or backward movement: *the reverse gear of an automobile.*
—*v.t.* **1.** to turn the other way; turn inside out; turn upside down: *Reverse your sweater or you will put it on wrong side out. If you reverse those two pieces, the puzzle will fit together.* **2.** to work or revolve in the opposite direction. **3.** to change to the opposite; repeal: *The court reversed its decree of imprisonment, and the man went free.* **4.** to use or do in a way opposite to the usual method: *to reverse the usual order of conducting business.* —*v.i.* **1.** to put or work an engine, etc., in the opposite direction: *Alternating current reverses from negative to positive about 60 times a second.* **2.** to turn in a direction opposite to the usual one while dancing.
[< Latin *reversus,* past participle of *revertere* turn around; see REVERT] —**re·vers′er,** *n.*
—**Syn.** *n.* **3.** setback, failure. *-v.t.* **1. Reverse, invert** mean to turn something the other way. **Reverse** is the more general in application, meaning to turn to the other side or in an opposite position, direction, order, etc.: *In this climate one needs a coat that can be reversed when it begins to rain.* **Invert** means to turn upside down: *Invert the glasses to drain.*

reverse or **reversed fault,** *Geology.* a fault in which one side has moved above and over the other side, as in a thrust fault.

re·verse·ly (ri vėrs′lē), *adv.* **1.** in a reverse position, direction, or order: *Stated reversely, the law of rent is necessarily the law of wages and interest taken together* (Henry George). **2.** on the other hand; on the contrary.

re·verse·ment (ri vėrs′mənt), *n.* reversal.

reverse osmosis, a process for desalting or purifying water, using a semipermeable membrane of cellulose acetate through which the water is forced by high pressure.

reverse shell, a spiral shell, as of a gastropod, in which the whorl rises from right to left, in the reverse of the usual direction; sinistral shell.

Reverse Shell

re·ver·si (ri vėr′sē), *n.* a game for two played on a board, using counters that are differently colored on the opposite sides. The object is to surround the opponent's counters, giving one the right to reverse them to one's own color and thus capture them. *Last month we asked if it was possible for a player, in less than 10 moves, to win a game of reversi by eliminating all enemy pieces* (Scientific American). [< French *reversi*]

re·vers·i·bil·i·ty (ri vėr′sə bil′ə tē), *n.* the fact or quality of being reversible.

re·vers·i·ble (ri vėr′sə bəl), *adj.* **1.** that can be reversed; that can reverse: *reversible seats on a train.* **2.** (of a fabric, etc.) finished on both sides so that either can be used as the right side: *Men to whom life had appeared as a reversible coat —seamy on both sides* (O. Henry). —*n.* a garment, as a raincoat, made so that either side may be worn exposed.

re·vers·i·ble-pitch propeller (ri vėr′sə bəl pich′), a propeller that can reverse its pitch for reverse thrust to slow down an aircraft, especially while landing.

reversible reaction, a chemical reaction the progress of which may be halted and reversed or, after change has taken place, be caused to occur again in reverse, so as to leave the substances involved once again in their original state: *A reaction in which the products can interact to form the starting materials is known as a reversible reaction* (Parks and Steinbach).

re·vers·i·bly (ri vėr′sə blē), *adv.* in a reversible manner; so as to be reversible.

re·vers·ing layer (ri vėr′sing), the thin innermost layer of the atmosphere of the sun and other stars: *The reversing layer is a mass of vapors, entirely of the earthly elements, that stretches some 1200 miles above the photosphere* (Bernhard, Bennett, and Rice).

re·ver·sion (ri vėr′zhən, -shən), *n.* **1.** a return to a former condition, practice, belief, etc.; return: *It had become, by one of those periodic reversions to the ways of the eighteenth century . . . a question of dominating importance* (Lytton Strachey). **2.** the return of property to the grantor or his heirs. **3.** an estate returning to the person who granted it or his heirs. **4.** the right to possess a certain property under certain conditions. **5.** *Biology.* a return to an earlier type. **6.** *Obsolete.* a remainder. [< Latin *reversiō, -ōnis* < *revertere* turn around; see REVERT]

re·ver·sion·al (ri vėr′zhə nəl, -shə-), *adj.* of, having to do with, or involving a reversion.

re·ver·sion·ar·y (ri vėr′zhə ner′ē, -shə-), *adj.* reversional.

re·ver·sion·er (ri vėr′zhə nər, -shə-), *n. Law.* a person who possesses the reversion to an estate, office, or the like.

re·vert (ri vėrt′), *v.i.* **1.** to go back; return: *My thoughts reverted to the last time I had seen her.* **2.** to go back to any former possessor: *If a man dies without heirs, his property may revert to the State.* **3.** *Biology.* to go back to an earlier stage of development.
—*n.* a person who returns to his original, or a previous, faith.
[< Old French *revertir* < Latin *revertere* < *re-* back + *vertere* to turn]

re·vert·er[1] (ri vėr′tər), *n.* a person or thing that reverts. [< *revert* + *-er*[1]]

re·vert·er[2] (ri vėr′tər), *n. Law.* reversion, as of an estate. [< noun use of Anglo-French *reverter* to revert]

re·vert·i·ble (ri vėr′tə bəl), *adj.* that can revert.

rev·er·y (rev′ər ē), *n., pl.* **-er·ies.** reverie.

re·vest (rē vest′), *v.t.* **1.** to vest (a person, etc.) again with ownership, office, etc. **2.** to vest (power, etc.) again (in a person). —*v.i.* to become vested again; revert to a former owner. [< Old French *revestir,* learned borrowing from Latin *revestīre* < *re-* again + *vestīre* to clothe < *vestis* garment]

re·vet (ri vet′), *v.t.,* **-vet·ted, -vet·ting.** to face (a wall, embankment, etc.) with masonry or other material. [< French *revêtir* < Old French *revestir;* see REVEST]

re·vet·ment (ri vet′mənt), *n.* a retaining wall; facing of stone, brick, cement, etc. [< French *revêtement* < Old French *revestir;* see REVEST]

re·vi·brate (rē vī′brāt), *v.,* **-brat·ed, -brat·ing.** —*v.i.* to vibrate again: *The chord once touched, every note revibrated* (Jane Porter). —*v.t.* to cause to vibrate again.

re·vi·bra·tion (rē′vī brā′shən), *n.* the act of vibrating back.

re·vict·ual (rē vit′əl), *v.,* **-ualed, -ual·ing** or (*especially British*) **-ualled, -ual·ling.** —*v.t.* to victual again; furnish again with provisions: *The Roman fleet after it had been revictualled and repaired, stood right across the Mediterranean* (Bosworth Smith). —*v.i.* to renew one's stock of provisions: *An invading army . . . is therefore greatly harassed and cannot easily revictual* (Daily News).

re·vict·ual·ment (rē vit′əl mənt), *n.* the state or condition of being revictualed.

re·view (ri vyü′), *v.t.* **1.** to study again; look at again: *Review today's lesson for tomorrow. He reviewed the scene of the crime.* **2.** to look back on: *Before falling asleep, she reviewed the day's happenings. Now let's review the situation* (W. H. Hudson). **3.** to examine again; look at with care; examine: *A superior court may review decisions of a lower court.* **4.** to inspect formally: *The President reviewed the fleet.* **5.** to examine to give an account of: *Mr. Brown reviews books for a living.*
—*v.i.* to review books, plays, etc. [partly < noun, partly earlier *re-view* < *re-* + *view,* verb]
—*n.* **1.** a studying again: *Before the examinations we have a review of the term's work.* **2.** a looking back on; survey: *A review of the trip was pleasant. I have lived a life of which I do not like the review* (Samuel Johnson). **3.** a reëxamination. **4.** an examination; inspection: *A review of the troops will be held during the general's visit to the camp.* **5.** an account of a book, play, etc., giving its merits and faults: *Her book is clever . . . If it is put into capable hands for review! that's all it requires* (George Meredith). **6.** a magazine containing articles on subjects of current interest, including accounts of books, etc.: *a law review, a financial review, a motion-picture review.* **7.** revue.
[< Middle French *reveüe,* feminine past participle of *revoir* < Old French *reveoir, reveeir* see again < Latin *revidēre* < *re-* again + *vidēre* to see]
—**Syn.** *n.* **5. Review, criticism** mean an account discussing and evaluating a book, play, art exhibit, etc. **Review** applies particularly to an account giving some idea of what the book or play, etc., is about, its good and bad points, and the reviewer's critical or personal opinion: *That magazine contains good reviews of current books.* **Criticism** applies particularly to an account giving a critical judgment based on deep and thorough study and applying sound critical standards of what is good and bad in books, music, pictures, etc.: *I read a good criticism of Faulkner's works.*

re·view·a·ble (ri vyü′ə bəl), *adj.* that can be reviewed.

re·view·al (ri vyü′əl), *n.* **1.** a reviewing. **2.** a review.

re·view·er (ri vyü′ər), *n.* **1.** a person who reviews. **2.** a person who writes articles discussing books, plays, etc.: *After a fortnight of low ratings and blows from the reviewers, an emergency meeting of network bigwigs was held to try to pep up the show* (Newsweek).

re·view·ing authority (ri vyü′ing), one having authority to review decisions, as a military commander reviewing a court-martial record.

reviewing stand, a grandstand from which a parade is reviewed.

re·vile (ri vīl′), *v.,* **-viled, -vil·ing.** —*v.t.* to call bad names; abuse with words: *The tramp reviled the man who drove him off.* —*v.i.* to speak abusively. [< Old French *reviler* despise < *re-* again + *vil* vile] —**re·vil′ing·ly,** *adv.*

re·vile·ment (ri vīl′mənt), *n.* **1.** the act of reviling. **2.** contemptuous or insulting language.

re·vil·er (ri vī′lər), *n.* a person who acts or speaks abusively: *Nor thieves, nor covetous, nor drunkards, nor revilers, nor extortioners, shall inherit the kingdom of God* (I Corinthians 6:10).

re·vis·a·ble (ri vī′zə bəl), *adj.* that can be revised.

re·vis·al (ri vī′zəl), *n.* **1.** a revising. **2.** a revision.

re·vise (ri vīz′), *v.,* **-vised, -vis·ing,** *n.* —*v.t.* **1.** to read carefully in order to correct or make improvements; look over and change; examine and improve: *to revise a manuscript, to revise a textbook, to revise a local ordinance.* **2.** to change; alter: *to revise one's opinion.*
—*n.* **1.** the process of revising. **2.** a revised form or version. **3.** a proof sheet printed after corrections have been made.
[< Old French *reviser,* learned borrowing from Latin *revīsere,* probably < *re-* again + *vidēre* to see]

Re·vised Standard Version (ri vīzd′), an American Protestant revision of the New Testament, published in 1946; of the whole Bible, in 1952. *Abbr.:* R.S.V.

Revised Version, the revised form of the Authorized (King James) Version of the Bible. The New Testament was published in 1881 and the Old Testament in 1885. *Abbr.:* R.V.

re·vis·er (ri vīz′ər), *n.* **1.** a person who revises, reviews, or makes corrections or desirable changes, especially in a literary work. **2.** *Printing.* a person who revises proofs.

re·vi·sion (ri vizh′ən), *n.* **1.** the act or work of revising: *a very great work, the revision of my dictionary* (Samuel Johnson). *We'd rather wait for orderly, treaty-type revisions* (Newsweek). **2.** a revised form: *A revision of that book will be published in June.* **3.** *British.* a careful scrutiny or review of work: *The month before the final examination is given to careful revision of the subjects.*

re·vi·sion·al (ri vizh′ə nəl), *adj.* of or having to do with revision.

re·vi·sion·ar·y (ri vizh′ə ner′ē), *adj.* revisional.

re·vi·sion·ism (ri vizh′ə niz əm), *n.* the beliefs or practices of the Communist revisionists: *The attack on . . . revisionism (Tito) will be coupled with a final assault against the "anti-party group" of Malenkov . . . Molotov "and others"* (Sunday Times).

re·vi·sion·ist (ri vizh′ə nist), *n.* **1.** a person who favors or supports revision: *Martin Luther, a sixteenth century revisionist* (New Yorker). **2.** a reviser, especially one of those who made the Revised Version of the Bible. **3.** a Communist who tends to a somewhat flexible or nationalistic interpretation of Marxism, believing in the revision of doctrines according to changing national needs.
—*adj.* favoring revision or revisionism.

re·vis·it (rē viz′it), *v.t.* to visit again; return to: *He revisited his birthplace and he traveled over again to places where he had been as a boy actor* (Atlantic).

re·vi·sor (ri vī′zər), *n.* reviser.

re·vi·so·ry (ri vī′zər ē), *adj.* of or having to do with revision: *a revisory committee.*

re·vi·tal·ize (rē vī′tə līz), *v.t.,* **-ized, -iz·ing.** to restore to vitality; put new life into: *. . . to revitalize the Federal business-regulating agencies* (Wall Street Journal).

re·viv·a·ble (ri vī′və bəl), *adj.* that can be revived.

re·viv·al (ri vī′vəl), *n.* **1.** a bringing or coming back to life or consciousness: *On his revival from the swoon . . ., he recovered his speech and sight* (Edward Gibbon). **2.** a restoration to vigor or health: *He had an amazing revival after his operation.* **3.** a bringing or coming back to style, use, activity, etc.: *the revival of a play of years ago.* **4.** an awakening or increase of interest in religion. **5.** special services or efforts made to awaken or increase interest in religion.
—**Syn. 1.** reanimation, resuscitation. **2.** reinvigoration.

re·viv·al·ism (ri vī′və liz əm), *n.* **1.** a form of religious activity that is apparent in revivals: *Revivalism, the archbishop admits, accomplishes some things for which God should be praised* (Newsweek). **2.** a tendency to revive what belongs to the past.

re·viv·al·ist (ri vī′və list), *n.* a person who holds special services to awaken interest in religion, especially an evangelistic preacher: *The 36-year-old revivalist [Billy Graham] has shied away from Manhattan ever since he began his mass evangelism campaigns in Los Angeles in 1949* (Newsweek). —*adj.* revivalistic: *The tone of his argument is now without revivalist fervor* (George Gaylord Simpson).

re·viv·al·is·tic (ri vī′və lis′tik), *adj.* of revivalism or revivalists: *Cocky, voluble Democrat Maynard E. ("Jack") Sensenbrenner, 57, campaigned for his fourth term in the typical give-'em-hell, revivalistic style* (Time).

Revival of Learning, Letters, or **Literature,** the Renaissance in its relation to learning.

re·viv·a·to·ry (ri viv′ə tôr′ē, -tōr′-), *adj.* that revives; reviving.

re·vive (ri vīv′), *v.,* **-vived, -viv·ing.** —*v.t.* **1.** to bring back to life or consciousness: *to revive a half-drowned person.* **2.** to bring back to a fresh, lively condition. **3.** to make fresh; restore: *Hot coffee revived the cold, tired man.* **4.** to bring back to notice, use, fashion, memory, activity, etc.: *to revive an old song. . . . Petrarch . . . indulged his fancy by deliberately reviving Latin words and constructions* (Simeon Potter). **5.** *Chemistry.* to restore to its natural form; reduce to its uncombined state. —*v.i.* **1.** to come back to life or consciousness: *The half-drowned swimmer revived. Henry is dead and never shall revive* (Shakespeare). **2.** to come back to a fresh, lively condition: *Flowers revive in water.* **3.** to become fresh. **4.** to come back to notice, use, fashion, memory, activity, etc.: *The fine arts revived during the Renaissance.* **5.** *Chemistry.* to recover its natural or uncombined state. [< Latin *revīvere* < *re-* again + *vīvere* to live] —**Syn.** *v.t.* **3.** refresh.

re·viv·er (ri vī′vər), *n.* **1.** a person who revives or restores anything to use or prominence. **2.** a person who recovers anything from inactivity, neglect, or disuse. **3.** that which invigorates or revives. **4.** a compound used for renovating clothes: *'Tis a deceitful* *liquid, that black and blue reviver* (Dickens). **5.** *Law.* revivor.

re·viv·i·fi·ca·tion (rē viv′ə fə kā′shən), *n.* **1.** restoration to life. **2.** *Chemistry.* the reduction of a metal in combination to its metallic state.

re·viv·i·fi·er (rē viv′ə fī′ər), *n.* a person or thing that revivifies.

re·viv·i·fy (rē viv′ə fī), *v.t., v.i.,* **-fied, -fy·ing.** to restore to life; give new life to.

rev·i·vis·cence (rev′ə vis′əns), *n.* a return to life or vigor.

rev·i·vis·cen·cy (rev′ə vis′ən sē), *n.* reviviscence.

rev·i·vis·cent (rev′ə vis′ənt), *adj.* returning to life or vigor. [< Latin *revīviscens, -entis,* present participle of *reviviscere* revive < *re-* again + *vīvere* to live]

re·vi·vor (ri vī′vər), *n.* an action to revive a lawsuit, etc., interrupted by the death of one of the parties, or by some other circumstance.

rev/min, revolutions per minute: *a speed of 15,500 rev/min.*

rev·o·ca·bil·i·ty (rev′ə kə bil′ə tē, ri vō′-), *n.* the quality of being revocable.

rev·o·ca·ble (rev′ə kə bəl, ri vō′-), *adj.* that can be repealed, canceled, or withdrawn. —**rev′o·ca·ble·ness,** *n.*

rev·o·ca·bly (rev′ə kə blē, ri vō′-), *adv.* in a revocable manner; so as to be revocable.

rev·o·ca·tion (rev′ə kā′shən), *n.* a repeal; canceling; withdrawal: *the revocation of a law.* [< Latin *revocātiō, -ōnis* < *revocāre;* see REVOKE] —**Syn.** revoking, rescinding, annulment.

rev·o·ca·to·ry (rev′ə kə tôr′ē, -tōr′-), *adj.* revoking; recalling; repealing.

re·voice (rē vois′), *v.t.,* **-voiced, -voic·ing. 1.** to voice again; echo. **2.** to readjust the tone of: *to revoice an organ pipe.*

re·vok·a·ble (rev′ə kə bəl, ri vō′-), *adj.* revocable.

re·voke (ri vōk′), *v.,* **-voked, -vok·ing,** *n.* —*v.t.* **1.** to take back; repeal; cancel; withdraw: *The king revoked his decree.* **2.** *Obsolete.* to call back. —*v.i.* to fail to follow suit in playing cards when one can and should; renege.
—*n.* **1.** (in cards) a failure to follow suit when one can and should; renege. **2.** revocation.
[< Latin *revocāre* < *re-* back + *vocāre* call, related to *vōx, vocis* voice] —**re·vok′er,** *n.*

re·volt (ri vōlt′), *n.* the act or state of rebelling: *The town is in revolt. It was not possible to think of such things without a revolt of his whole being* (Edith Wharton).
—*v.i.* **1.** to turn away from and fight against a leader; rise against the government's authority: *The people revolted against the dictator.* **2.** to turn away with disgust: *Our whole hearts revolt against the way women have hitherto been treated* (William H. Mallock). —*v.t.* to cause to feel disgust: *There were several . . . whom this brutality revolted* (Robert Louis Stevenson).
[< Middle French *révolte* < Italian *rivolta,* ultimately < Latin *revolvere;* see REVOLVE] —**re·volt′er,** *n.*
—**Syn.** *n.* **Revolt, insurrection, rebellion** mean a rising up in active resistance against authority. **Revolt** emphasizes casting off allegiance and refusing to accept existing conditions or control: *The revolt of the American colonists developed into revolution.* **Insurrection** applies to an armed uprising of a group, often small, poorly organized, and selfishly motivated: *The insurrection was started by a few malcontents.* **Rebellion** applies to open armed resistance organized to force the government to do something or to overthrow it: *A rebellion may become civil war.* -*v.t.* repel, sicken.

re·volt·ing (ri vōl′ting), *adj.* disgusting; repulsive: *a revolting odor.* —**re·volt′ing·ly,** *adv.*

rev·o·lute[1] (rev′ə lüt), *adj. Botany.* rolled or curled backward or downward, as the tips or margins of some leaves, fronds, etc. [< Latin *revolūtus,* past participle of *revolvere;* see REVOLVE]

rev·o·lute[2] (rev′ə lüt′), *v.i.,* **-lut·ed, -lut·ing.** *Informal.* to engage in a political revolution. [back formation < *revolution*]

rev·o·lu·tion (rev′ə lü′shən), *n.* **1.** a complete overthrow of an established government or political system: *The American Revolution from 1763 to 1783 gave independence to the colonies. Geria, after the Revolution, got free primary and secondary schooling* (Harper's). **2.** a complete change: *The automobile caused a revolution in ways of traveling.* **3.** movement in a circle or curve around some point: *One revolution of the earth around the sun takes a year.* **4. a.** the act or fact of turning round a center or axis; rotation: *The revolution of the earth causes day and night.* **b.** the time or distance of one revolution. **5.** a complete cycle or series of events: *The revolution of the four seasons fills a year.* [< Latin *revolūtiō, -ōnis* < *revolvere;* see REVOLVE]

rev·o·lu·tion·ar·y (rev′ə lü′shə ner′ē), *adj., n., pl.* **-ar·ies.** —*adj.* **1.** of a revolution; connected with a revolution: *In considering the policy to be adopted for suppressing the insurrection, I have been anxious and careful that the inevitable conflict for this purpose shall not degenerate into a violent and remorseless revolutionary struggle* (Abraham Lincoln). **2.** bringing or causing great changes: *The antibiotics were a revolutionary advance in medical treatment.*
—*n.* a revolutionist: *the heated and headlong revolutionary* (Christopher Morley). *A group of revolutionaries go to the most extravagant lengths in order to blow up a politician's funeral* (Newsweek).

Revolutionary calendar, a calendar introduced in France October 5, 1793, which gave new names to the months. It began counting time from September 22, 1792.

Revolutionary War, the war from 1775 to 1783 by which the thirteen American colonies won independence from England.

rev·o·lu·tion·ise (rev′ə lü′shə nīz), *v.t.,* **-ised, -is·ing.** *Especially British.* revolutionize.

rev·o·lu·tion·ist (rev′ə lü′shə nist), *n.* a person who advocates, or takes part in, a revolution: *There is nothing of the rebel or the revolutionist about him* (Harper's).

rev·o·lu·tion·ize (rev′ə lü′shə nīz), *v.t.,* **-ized, -iz·ing. 1.** to change completely; produce a very great change in: *The automobile and radio have revolutionized country life. Charles S. Thomas said today that atomic energy was "certainly going to revolutionize the Navy"* (New York Times). **2.** to cause a revolution in the government of.

re·volv·a·ble (ri vol′və bəl), *adj.* that can be revolved.

re·volve (ri volv′), *v.,* **-volved, -volv·ing,** *n.* —*v.i.* **1.** to move in a circle; move in a curve round a point: *The moon revolves round the earth.* **2.** to turn round a center or axis; rotate: *The wheels of a moving car revolve.* **3.** to move in a complete cycle or series of events: *The seasons revolve.* **4.** to be turned over in the mind. —*v.t.* **1.** to cause to move round. **2.** to cause to move about a central point. **3.** to turn over in the mind; consider from many points of view: *Long stood Sir Belevedere, revolving many memories* (Tennyson).
—*n. Especially British.* a revolving stage: *Sliding walls and revolves . . . realign themselves as street scenes and interiors, and accelerate like a merry-go-round for the police chase in the last act* (London Times).
[< Latin *revolvere* < *re-* back, again + *volvere* to roll]
—**Syn.** *v.i.* **1.** See **turn.**

re·volv·er (ri vol′vər), *n.* **1.** a pistol with a revolving cylinder in which the cartridges are contained, that can be fired several times without reloading: *Revolvers with cylinders that have six chambers are called six-shooters.* **2.** a person or thing that revolves.

re·volv·ing (ri vol′ving), *adj.* **1.** that revolves: *The royal view would include a section of the tower's electric ad board and all of the revolving crane* (New Yorker). **2.** of or having to do with an internal-combustion airplane engine whose cylinders revolve about a stationary crankshaft.

revolving credit, credit that is automatically renewed on payment of debts, bills, etc.: *American Standard in January arranged with a group of banks a revolving credit of up to $50 million* (Wall Street Journal).

revolving door, a door set in a cylinder having an opening on two sides and four sections at right angles that revolve on a central axis: *Downstairs some German schoolgirls are happily crowding two at a time through the revolving door, each leaf of which bears the sign "Push one at a time, please"* (Manchester Guardian Weekly).

revolving fund, 1. a fund used for loans. **2.** a fund established by the U.S. government from which money can be lent to organizations important to the general welfare, as utilities.

revolving stage, a stage with a circular platform that revolves to allow for quick scene changes: *The use of the revolving stage to provide swift vignettes of a carousing . . . London has merit* (Howard Taubman).

re·vote (rē vōt′), *v.,* **-vot·ed, -vot·ing,** *n.* —*v.t.* to grant, settle, or decree again by a new vote. —*n.* a second or repeated vote; a renewed grant.

Revs., Reverends.

Rev. Stat., Revised Statutes.

re·vue (ri vyü′), *n.* a theatrical entertainment with singing, dancing, parodies of recent movies and plays, humorous treatments of current happenings and fads, etc.: *One of those dismal . . . revues, that are neither comedies nor farces, nor anything but shambling, hugger-mugger contraptions into which you fling anything that comes handy* (Alfred G. Gardiner). [< French *revue* < Middle French *reveüe;* see REVIEW, noun]

re·vul·sion (ri vul′shən), *n.* **1.** a sudden, violent change or reaction: *My feeling for my new friend underwent a revulsion when I discovered his cruelty and dishonesty.* **2.** the drawing of blood from one part of the body to another part, as by counterirritation. **3.** a drawing or being drawn back or away, especially suddenly or violently: *The revulsion of capital from the woolen industry.* **4.** the fact of being withdrawn. **5.** a sudden reverse tendency, as in business: *to sustain the credit of the merchants under the revulsion consequent on peace* (George Bancroft). [< Latin *revulsiō, -ōnis* < *revellere* < *re-* back + *vellere* tear away]

re·vul·sive (ri vul′siv), *adj.* tending to produce revulsion.

Rev. Ver., Revised Version.

re·ward (ri wôrd′), *n.* **1.** a return made for something done: *to give a reward for good behavior. Hanging was the reward of treason and desertion* (William Stubbs). **2.** money given or offered for the capture of criminals, the return of lost property, etc.: *Rewards totaling $150,000 attracted 5,000 letters with tips* (Newsweek).
—*v.t.* **1.** to give a reward to: *Excellent results rewarded him for his efforts.* **2.** to give a reward for: *She rewarded his past services with liberality* (Lytton Strachey).
[< Old North French *reward* < *rewarder,* variant of Old French *regarder,* earlier *reguarder* < *re-* back + *guarder* to guard, care for. Doublet of REGARD.] —**re·ward′er,** *n.*
—**Syn.** *v.t.* **1.** recompense, repay.

re·ward·a·ble (ri wôr′də bəl), *adj.* that can be rewarded; worthy of reward.

re·ward·ful (ri wôrd′fəl), *adj.* yielding a reward: *He was happy, because his labor of love was also rewardful.*

re·ward·ing (ri wôr′ding), *adj.* that rewards; useful; beneficial: *a rewarding experience. You will find this book very rewarding.*

re·ward·ing·ly (ri wôr′ding lē), *adv.* in a rewarding manner; profitably; usefully: *It is Mr. Curtis's method . . . to quote a line from one of the giants of Western culture . . ., stroll inquisitively around it, and set down the thoughts it inspires in his rewardingly unconventional mind* (New Yorker).

re·ward·less (ri wôrd′lis), *adj.* without reward.

re·wa·ter (rē wôt′ər, -wot′-), *v.t., v.i.* **1.** to water again. **2.** to place in water again.

re·win (rē win′), *v.t., v.i.,* **-won, -win·ning.** to win back or again; regain; recover: *. . . desert your comrades in their great battle to rewin the lands of their fathers* (Pall Mall Gazette).

re·wire (rē wīr′), *v.t., v.i.,* **-wired, -wir·ing. 1.** to put new wires on or in. **2.** to telegraph again.

re·word (rē wėrd′), *v.t.* **1.** to repeat in other words; rephrase. **2.** to repeat exactly.

re·work (rē wėrk′), *v.t.* to work over again; reprocess; revise: *He had done most of the writing and rewriting himself, reworking key passages again and again* (Time).

re·write (*v.* rē rīt′; *n.* rē′rīt′), *v.,* **-wrote, -writ·ten, -writ·ing,** *n.* —*v.t., v.i.* **1.** to write again; write in a different form; revise. **2.** *U.S.* to write (a news story) from material supplied over the telephone or in a form that cannot be used as copy.
—*n.* **1.** a rewriting. **2.** *U.S.* a news story that has to be rewritten. —**re·writ′er,** *n.*

rewrite man, *U.S.* a newspaper reporter or editor skilled in rewriting.

rex or **Rex** (reks), *n., pl.* **re·ges** or **Re·ges.** *Latin.* king.

Rex cat, any of a breed of short-haired cats with soft, closely curled coats and curly whiskers.

Rex·ine (rek′sēn), *n. Trademark.* an artificial leather used in upholstery, bindings for books, etc.

Reyn·ard (ren′ərd, rā′närd), *n.* the name for the fox in stories and poems, especially in the medieval beast epic, *Reynard the Fox.* [earlier *Renard* < Old French *Renart,* or *Renard,* probably < Middle Flemish *Reinaert*]

reyn·ard (ren′ərd, rā′närd), *n.* a fox.

Rey·nolds' number (ren′əldz), a mathematical factor used to express the relation between the velocity, viscosity, density, and dimensions of a fluid in any system of flow. It is used in aerodynamics to correct the results of tests of scale-model airplanes in wind tunnels. [< Osborne *Reynolds,* 1842-1912, a British scientist, who determined it]

rez-de-chaus·sée (rā′də shō sā′), *n. French.* the ground floor; first story.

re·zone (rē zōn′), *v.t.,* **-zoned, -zon·ing.** to zone again; change the present zoning of: *to rezone an area.*

rf., *Baseball.* **1.** right field. **2.** right fielder.

r.f., **1.** radio frequency. **2.** rapid-fire.

RF (no periods), radio frequency.

R.F., **1.** radio frequency. **2.** rapid-fire. **3.** French Republic (French, *République française*).

R.F.A., Royal Field Artillery.

RFC (no periods), Reconstruction Finance Corporation.

R.F.C., (formerly) Royal Flying Corps.

R.F.D., Rural Free Delivery.

r.g., right guard.

R.G.A., Royal Garrison Artillery.

R.G.G., Royal Grenadier Guards.

R.G.S., Royal Geographical Society.

r.h., **1.** relative humidity. **2.** *Music.* right hand.

Rh (no period), **1.** Rhesus factor. **2.** rhodium (chemical element).

R.H., **1.** Royal Highlanders. **2.** Royal Highness.

R.H.A., Royal Horse Artillery.

Rhab·di·tis form (rab dī′tis), a free-swimming sexual stage in the development of certain parasitic nematodes. [< New Latin *rhabditis* < Greek *rhábdos* rod]

rhab·do·man·cy (rab′də man′sē), *n.* **1.** divination by means of a rod or wand. **2.** the art of discovering water, ores, etc., by means of a divining rod; dowsing. [< Greek *rhabdomanteíā* < *rhábdos* rod + *manteíā* divination]

rhab·do·man·tist (rab′də man′tist), *n.* a person who divines by means of a rod or wand; dowser.

rhab·do·my·o·ma (rab′dō mī ō′mə), *n., pl.* **-mas, -ma·ta** (-mə tə). a tumor that is usually benign and composed chiefly of striated muscle fiber. [< New Latin *rhabdomyoma* < Greek *rhábdos* rod + *mŷs, myós* muscle + *-ōma* a growth]

rhab·do·some (rab′də sōm), *n.* a graptolite produced by gemmation from a sicula. [< Greek *rhábdos* rod + *sôma* body]

rha·chis (rā′kis), *n., pl.* **rha·chis·es, rhach·i·des** (rak′ə dēz, rā′kə-). rachis.

Rhad·a·man·thine (rad′ə man′thin), *adj.* **1.** of or having to do with Rhadamanthus. **2.** very strict.

Rhad·a·man·thus (rad′ə man′thəs), *n. Greek Mythology.* a son of Zeus and Europa, and brother of King Minos of Crete. Because he showed the spirit of justice in all his life, he was made a judge in Hades after he died.

Rhae·tian (rē′shən), *adj.* **1.** of or having to do with Rhaetia, the ancient name for a district comprising southeastern Switzerland, part of Tyrol, and adjoining regions. **2.** Rhaeto-Romanic.

Rhae·tic (rē′tik), *adj. Geology.* of or having to do with certain strata, extensively developed in the Rhaetian Alps, having features of both the Triassic and the Jurassic periods.

Rhae·to-Ro·man·ic (rē′tō rō man′ik), *adj.* of or having to do with a group of Romance dialects spoken in the Rhaetian Alps. —*n.* the Rhaeto-Romanic dialects.

rham·na·ceous (ram nā′shəs), *adj. Botany.* belonging to the buckthorn family. [< New Latin *Rhamnaceae* the family name (< *Rhamnus* the typical genus < Late Latin *rhamnus* the buckthorn < Greek *rhámnos*) + English *-ous*]

rhap·sode (rap′sōd), *n.* an ancient Greek rhapsodist. [< Greek *rhapsōdós* < *rháptein* sew + *ōidḗ* song, ode]

rhap·sod·ic (rap sod′ik), *adj.* rhapsodical: *In Florence he sat at the feet of Poet Theodor Daubler, whose rhapsodic verse, mystically urging man to free his spirit from the pull of Earth, appealed to Barlach's own yearnings* (Time).

rhap·sod·i·cal (rap sod′ə kəl), *adj.* of, having to do with, or characteristic of rhapsody; extravagantly enthusiastic; ecstatic: *It is a powerful piece of work, long, elaborate, rhapsodical, and digressive* (Atlantic). —**rhap·sod′i·cal·ly,** *adv.*

rhap·so·dist (rap′sə dist), *n.* **1.** a person who talks or writes with extravagant enthusiasm. **2.** a professional reciter of epic poetry in ancient Greece. **3.** any professional reciter or singer of poems.

rhap·so·dis·tic (rap′sə dis′tik), *adj.* rhapsodical.

rhap·so·dize (rap′sə dīz), *v.,* **-dized, -diz·ing.** —*v.i.* to talk or write with extravagant enthusiasm: *rhapsodising on this and that—poetry, politics, life, and death* (Maurice H. Hewlett). —*v.t.* to recite as a rhapsody.

rhap·so·dy (rap′sə dē), *n., pl.* **-dies. 1.** an utterance or writing marked by extravagant enthusiasm: *She went into rhapsodies over her garden.* **2.** *Music.* an instrumental composition, irregular in form, resembling an improvisation: *Liszt's Hungarian Rhapsodies.* **3.** an epic poem, or a part of such a poem, suitable for recitation at one time. [< Latin *rhapsōdia* < Greek *rhapsōidiā* verse composition < *rháptein* to stitch + *ōidḗ* song, ode]

rhat·a·ny (rat′ə nē), *n., pl.* **-nies. 1.** a trailing South American shrub of the pea family whose dried root is used in tanning, in medicine as an astringent, and to color port wine. **2.** a closely related plant, whose root is similarly used. **3.** the root of either of these plants. [< Spanish *ratania* or *rataña* < Quechua (Peru) *rataña*]

Rhatany (def. 1)

Rhe·a (rē′ə), *n. Greek Mythology.* a daughter of Uranus and Gaea, the wife of Cronus, and mother of Zeus, Hera, Poseidon, Hades, Hestia, and Demeter. She was called the "Mother of the Gods."

rhe·a (rē′ə), *n.* any of several large, flightless birds of South America that are much like the ostrich, but are smaller and have three toes instead of two. [< New Latin *Rhea* the genus name < Latin *Rhea* Rhea]

Rhea (about 3 ft. high)

rhe·bok (rē′bok; *Afrikaans* rā′bok), *n.* one of several varieties of comparatively small South African antelopes with slender, sharp horns: *The vaal rhebok is not among the fastest of antelopes* (C.S. Stokes). [< Dutch and Afrikaans *reebok* roe buck]

rhe·in (rē′in), *n.* a yellow, crystalline acid found in the leaves of the rhubarb and senna. *Formula:* $C_{15}H_8O_6$ [< Greek *rhéon* rhubarb + English *-in*]

Rhein·gold (rīn′gōld′), *n. German and Norse Mythology.* a magic hoard of gold owned by the Nibelungs and later by Siegfried. Also, **Rhinegold.** [< German *Rheingold* (literally) Rhine gold]

rhe·mat·ic (ri mat′ik), *adj.* **1.** having to do with the formation of words. **2.** having to do with or derived from a verb. [< Greek *rhēmatikós* < *rhêma, -atos* verb, word < *eírein* say, speak. Related to RHETOR.]

rhe·nic (rē′nik), *adj.* having to do with or containing rhenium. [< *rhen*(ium) + *-ic*]

Rhen·ish (ren′ish), *adj.* of the river Rhine or the regions near it. —*n.* Rhine wine. [< Latin *Rhēnus* the Rhine + English *-ish*[1]]

rhe·ni·um (rē′nē əm), *n.* a rare, hard, grayish metallic element with chemical properties similar to those of manganese and a very high melting point (above 3,000 degrees centigrade): *Aircraft metallurgists are excited about the rare element rhenium, which is found occasionally in copper ores* (Newsweek). *Symbol:* Re; *at.wt.:* (C^{12}) 186.2 or (O^{16}) 186.22; *at.no.:* 75; *valence:* 3, 4, 6, 7. [< New Latin *rhenium* < Latin *Rhēnus* Rhine + New Latin *-ium,* a suffix meaning "element"]

rheo-, *combining form.* stream; electric current: *Rheostat = an instrument that regulates the strength of an electric current.* [< Greek *rhéos* a flowing, stream < *rheîn* to flow]

rheo., rheostat or rheostats.

rhe·o·log·i·cal (rē′ə loj′ə kəl), *adj.* of or having to do with rheology: *The rheological properties of clay dispersions are of particular importance in the ceramic and petroleum industries* (Science News). —**rhe′o·log′i·cal·ly,** *adv.*

rhe·ol·o·gist (rē ol′ə jist), *n.* an expert in rheology: *The fundamental task of the experimental rheologist is to measure viscosity and other flow problems* (New Scientist).

rhe·ol·o·gy (rē ol′ə jē), *n.* the science that deals with flow and alteration of form of matter.

rhe·om·e·ter (rē om′ə tər), *n.* **1.** an instrument for measuring the flow of blood. **2.** an instrument for measuring electric currents.

rhe·o·scope (rē′ə skōp), *n.* an instrument that indicates the presence of an electric current.

rhe·o·scop·ic (rē′ə skop′ik), *adj.* electroscopic.

rhe·o·stat (rē′ə stat), *n.* an instrument for regulating the strength of an electric current by introducing a variable resistance into the circuit.

rhe·o·stat·ic (rē′ə stat′ik), *adj.* having to do with a rheostat.

rhe·o·tac·tic (rē ə tak′tik), *adj.* of or having to do with the movements of organisms in currents of liquid.

rhe·o·tax·is (rē′ə tak′sis), *n.* the movement of a cell or organism in response to the stimulus of a current of water or air. [< *rheo-* + Greek *táxis* arrangement]

rhe·o·trope (rē′ə trōp), *n.* a device for reversing the direction of an electric current.

rhe·ot·ro·pism (rē ot′rə piz əm), *n. Biology.* the orientation in growth of plants or sessile animals in response to a current of water or air.

rhe·sis (rē′sis), *n.* **1.** a saying; a speech; a passage in a play, poem, or book. **2.** a set speech or discourse. [< Greek *rhêsis*]

rhe·sus (rē′səs), *n.* a small, yellowish-brown monkey with a short tail, found in India, and often used in medical research. See **monkey** for picture. [< New Latin *rhesus* the species name, arbitrary use of Latin *Rhēsus* Rhesus]

Rhe·sus (rē′səs), *n. Greek Legend.* a Thracian ally of the Trojans, slain by Odysseus and Diomedes, because they knew that an oracle had said that Troy would not fall if Rhesus's horses drank from the Xanthus River.

Rhesus factor, Rh factor.

rhet., **1.** rhetoric. **2.** rhetorical.

Rhe·tic (rē′tik), *adj.* Rhaetic.

rhe·tor (rē′tər), *n.* **1.** a master or teacher of rhetoric. **2.** an orator, especially a professional one. [< Latin *rhētor* < Greek *rhḗtōr, -oros* < *eírein* to say]

rhet·o·ric (ret′ər ik), *n.* **1.** the art of using words in speaking or writing so as to persuade or influence others: *The communication of those thoughts to others falls under the consideration of rhetoric* (John Stuart Mill). **2.** the language used: *Blifil suffered himself to be overpowered by the forcible rhetoric of the squire* (Henry Fielding). **3.** a book on rhetoric: *Aristotle himself has given it a place in his Rhetoric among the beauties of that art* (Joseph Addison). **4.** mere display in language: *the exaggerated rhetoric of presidential campaigns ...* (New York Times); *the limp loquacity of long-winded rhetoric, so natural to men and soldiers in an hour of emergency* (Algernon Charles Swinburne). [< Latin *rhētorica* < Greek *rhētorikḗ* (*téchnē*) (art) of an orator < *rhḗtōr;* see RHETOR]

rhe·tor·i·cal (ri tôr′ə kəl, -tor′-), *adj.* **1.** of or having to do with rhetoric. **2.** using rhetoric. **3.** intended especially for display; artificial: *a rhetorical style, rhetorical language.* **4.** oratorical: *But easier it was for him, with a rhetorical flourish ... to dash his opinion out of countenance* (Samuel Purchas).

rhe·tor·i·cal·ly (ri tôr′ə klē, -tor′-), *adv.* in a rhetorical manner; according to the rules of rhetoric: *to treat a subject rhetorically, a discourse rhetorically delivered.*

rhetorical question, a question asked only for effect, not for information: *"Who can tell whether or not life exists in other worlds?" is a rhetorical question.*

rhet·o·ri·cian (ret′ə rish′ən), *n.* **1.** a person skilled in rhetoric: *Her poetry is the diary or autobiography . . . of an acute psychologist, a wonderful rhetorician, and one of the most wonderful writers who ever lived* (Harper's). **2.** a person given to display in language.

rheum[1] (rüm), *n. Archaic.* **1.** a watery discharge, such as mucus, tears, or saliva: *A few drops of women's rheum, which are As cheap as lies* (Shakespeare). **2.** a cold; catarrh: *But he was brooding even more than usual on the frailty of the human body in general and his own aches and rheums in particular* (Atlantic). [< Old French *reume,* learned borrowing from Latin *rheuma* < Greek *rheûma, -atos* a flowing < *rheîn* to flow]

rhe·um[2] (rē′əm), *n.* rhubarb. [< New Latin *Rheum* the genus name < Greek *rhêon*]

rheu·mat·ic (rü mat′ik), *adj.* **1.** of rheumatism: *rheumatic symptoms.* **2.** having rheumatism; liable to have rheumatism: *Silk mittens . . . covered her rheumatic hands* (Edith Wharton). **3.** causing rheumatism. **4.** caused by rheumatism.
—*n.* a person who has or is liable to have rheumatism.
rheumatics, *Informal.* rheumatism: *a new cure for the rheumatics* (Robert Louis Stevenson).
[< Latin *rheumaticus* < Greek *rheumatikós* < *rheûma;* see RHEUM[1]] —**rheu·mat′i·cal·ly,** *adv.*

rheumatic fever, an acute disease, usually attacking children, and characterized by fever, pains in the joints, and often inflammation in the heart, causing harmful aftereffects: *But iritis, a chronic eye ailment that was the residue of an earlier bout with rheumatic fever, ended his schooling* (Time).

rheu·ma·tism (rü′mə tiz əm), *n.* **1.** a disease with inflammation, swelling, and stiffness of the joints. **2.** rheumatic fever. [< Latin *rheumatismus* < Greek *rheumatismós* < *rheumatízein* < *rheûma;* see RHEUM[1]]

rheumatism weed, 1. Indian hemp. **2.** pipsissewa.

rheu·ma·toid (rü′mə toid), *adj.* **1.** resembling rheumatism: *The center would continue the Masons' research project in rheumatic fever and rheumatoid diseases, started in 1946* (New York Times). **2.** having rheumatism. —**rheu′ma·toi′dal·ly,** *adv.*

rheu·ma·toi·dal (rü′mə toi′dəl), *adj.* rheumatoid.

rheumatoid arthritis, inflammation and stiffness of the joints, often crippling in its effects: *Rheumatoid arthritis is a seasonal disease that is likely to begin or grow worse in the colder months* (Science News Letter).

rheu·ma·tol·o·gist (rü′mə tol′ə jist), *n.* an expert in rheumatology: *Once a major cause of arthritis, infections by common bacteria . . . no longer give the rheumatologists much concern* (Time).

rheu·ma·tol·o·gy (rü′mə tol′ə jē), *n.* the study and treatment of rheumatism and related diseases: *Medical science was a late starter in the field of rheumatology, which comprises the study of a group of diseases numbering 50 or more which kill infrequently but cripple greatly* (London Times).

rheum·y (rü′mē), *adj.,* **rheum·i·er, rheum·i·est. 1.** full of rheum: *Nobody recognized the aging white-haired man who walked about Moscow, staring with rheumy eyes at the broad streets and tall buildings* (Time). **2.** causing rheum; damp and cold.

rhex·is (rek′sis), *n.* rupture of a blood vessel or of any organ. [< Greek *rhêxis* < *rhegnýnai* break]

Rh factor, a substance often found in the blood of human beings and the higher mammals. Blood containing this substance is Rh positive and does not combine favorably with blood which is Rh negative and lacks this substance. Also, **Rhesus factor.** [< *rh*(esus); it was first discovered in the blood of the rhesus monkey]

R.H.G., Royal Horse Guards.

rhig·o·lene (rig′ə lēn), *n.* an extremely volatile liquid obtained from petroleum. It is used to produce local anesthesia by freezing. [< Greek *rhîgos* cold + English *-ol*[2] + *-ene*]

rhi·nal (rī′nəl), *adj.* of or having to do with the nose; nasal. [< Greek *rhîs, rhīnós* nose + English *-al*[1]]

rhi·nar·i·um (rī nãr′ē əm), *n., pl.* **-nar·i·a** (-nãr′ē ə). **1.** the front part of the clypeus of neuropteran insects, certain beetles, etc. **2.** the area of bare skin around the nostrils of ruminants; muffle. [< New Latin *rhinarium* < Greek *rhîs, rhīnós* nose]

Rhine·gold (rīn′gōld′), *n.* Rheingold.

Rhine·land·er (rīn′lan′dər), *n.* a native or inhabitant of the Rhineland region of West Germany.

rhi·nen·ce·phal·ic (rī′nen sə fal′ik), *adj.* having to do with the rhinencephalon.

rhi·nen·ceph·a·lon (rī′nen sef′ə lon), *n., pl.* **-la** (-lə). the part of the brain most closely connected with the olfactory nerves: *All the brain damage occurred in a region of the cerebrum known as the rhinencephalon* (Science News Letter). [< New Latin *rhinencephalon* < Greek *rhîs, rhīnós* nose + New Latin *encephalon* encephalon]

rhine·stone (rīn′stōn′), *n.* an imitation diamond, made of glass or paste. [translation of French *caillou du Rhin* Rhine pebble, originally made at Strasbourg]

Rhine wine (rīn), **1.** wine produced in the valley of the Rhine. Most Rhine wines are white wines. **2.** a similar wine made elsewhere.

rhi·ni·tis (rī nī′tis), *n.* inflammation of the nose or its mucous membrane. [< New Latin *rhinitis* < Greek *rhîs, rhīnós* nose + New Latin *-itis* -itis]

rhi·no[1] (rī′nō), *n., pl.* **-nos** or **-no.** *Informal.* a rhinoceros: *We saw two rhino come down to the river to drink* (J.H. Patterson).

rhi·no[2] (rī′nō), *n. Slang.* money; cash: *ready rhino.* [origin unknown]

rhi·noc·er·os (rī nos′ər əs), *n., pl.* **-os·es** or (*collectively*) **-os.** any of various large, thick-skinned mammals of Africa and Asia with one or two upright horns on the snout. There are five living species, all of which eat grass and other plants. [< Latin *rhīnoceros* < Greek *rhinókerōs* < *rhîs, rhīnós* nose + *kéras* horn]

Indian Rhinoceros
(about 8 ft. long)

rhinoceros beetle, any of several large scarabaeid beetles, mainly of the southern United States. The male has a large horn on the head.

rhinoceros iguana, a rare iguana lizard of the West Indies with three blunt horns on its snout.

rhi·nog·e·nous (rī noj′ə nəs), *adj.* of nasal origin.

rhi·no·lar·yn·gol·o·gy (rī′nō lar′ing gol′ə jē), *n.* the branch of medicine dealing with diseases of the nose and larynx. [< Greek *rhîs, rhīnós* nose + English *laryngology*]

rhi·no·lith (rī′nə lith), *n.* a calculus formed in the nasal cavities.

rhi·no·log·i·cal (rī′nə loj′ə kəl), *adj.* having to do with rhinology.

rhi·nol·o·gist (rī nol′ə jist), *n.* a specialist in diseases of the nose.

rhi·nol·o·gy (rī nol′ə jē), *n.* the branch of medicine dealing with the nose and its diseases. [< Greek *rhîs, rhīnós* nose]

rhi·no·pha·ryn·ge·al (rī′nō fə rin′jē əl, -far′in jē′-), *adj.* of or having to do with the nose and the pharynx.

rhi·no·phar·ynx (rī′nō far′ingks), *n.* nasopharynx.

rhi·no·plas·tic (rī′nə plas′tik), *adj.* of or having to do with rhinoplasty.

rhi·no·plas·ty (rī′nə plas′tē), *n.* plastic surgery of the nose. [< Greek *rhîs, rhīnós* nose + *plastós* something molded]

rhi·nor·rhe·a (rī′nə rē′ə), *n.* excessive secretion of mucus from the nose: *If the patient is allergic, the onset is frequently sudden, with profuse watery rhinorrhea, sneezing and nasal blockage* (Francis Loeffler Lederer). [< Greek *rhîs, rhīnós* nose + *rheîn* flow]

rhi·no·scope (rī′nə skōp), *n.* an instrument for examining the nasal passages. [< Greek *rhîs, rhīnós* nose + English *-scope*]

rhi·nos·co·py (rī nos′kə pē), *n.* use of the rhinoscope.

rhi·no·vi·rus (rī′nō vī′rəs), *n.* any of a group of viruses associated with the common cold and other respiratory diseases. [< Greek *rhîs, rhīnós* nose + English *virus*]

R. Hist. S., Royal Historical Society.

rhi·zo·bic (rī zō′bik), *adj.* of or having to do with the rhizobia.

rhi·zo·bi·um (rī zō′bē əm), *n., pl.* **-bi·a** (-bē ə). any of a group of rod-shaped, nitrogen-fixing bacteria that live symbiotically in nodules on the roots of leguminous plants. [< New Latin *rhizobium* < Greek *rhíza* root + *bíos* life]

rhi·zo·car·pic (rī′zə kär′pik), *adj.* rhizocarpous.

rhi·zo·car·pous (rī′zə kär′pəs), *adj.* having the stem annual but the root perennial. The perennial herbs are rhizocarpous. [< Greek *rhíza* root + *karpós* fruit + English *-ous*]

rhi·zo·caul (rī′zə kôl), *n. Zoology.* the rootlike part of a polyp, used for attachment to some support. [< Greek *rhíza* root + *kaulós* stalk]

rhi·zo·ceph·a·lous (rī′zə sef′ə ləs), *adj.* of or belonging to a group of crustaceans that are parasitic on crabs, living within the host as a mass of modified cells resembling rootlike processes. [< New Latin *Rhizocephala* the order name (< Greek *rhíza* root + *kephalḗ* head) + English *-ous*]

rhi·zo·gen·ic (rī′zə jen′ik), *adj.* producing roots: *rhizogenic cells or tissues.* [< Greek *rhíza* root + English *-gen* + *-ic*]

rhi·zog·e·nous (rī zoj′ə nəs), *adj.* rhizogenic.

rhi·zoid (rī′zoid), *adj.* rootlike. —*n.* one of the rootlike filaments by which a moss, fern, liverwort, or fungus is attached to the substratum. —**rhi′zoid·like′,** *adj.*

rhi·zoi·dal (rī zoi′dəl), *adj.* resembling a rhizoid.

rhi·zo·mat·ic (rī′zə mat′ik), *adj.* having to do with rhizomes; having the appearance of a rhizome.

rhi·zom·a·tous (rī zom′ə təs, -zō′mə-), *adj.* **1.** of or having to do with a rhizome. **2.** having rhizomes: *But if more plants of the rhizomatous type are wanted, a leaf is pulled off and inserted in regular soil* (New York Times).

rhi·zome (rī′zōm), *n.* a rootlike stem lying along or under the ground, which usually produces roots below and shoots from the upper surface; rootstock: *In some underground stems, that is rhizomes, many of these leaves develop very poorly, taking the form of scales* (Fred W. Emerson). [< Greek *rhízōma* < *rhizoûn* cause to strike root < *rhíza* root]

A
B
C
Rhizomes
A, Solomon's-seal; B, trillium; C, jack-in-the-pulpit

rhi·zo·mic (rī zō′mik, -zom′-), *adj.* belonging to or consisting of rhizomes.

rhi·zo·morph (rī′zə môrf), *n.* a rootlike filament of hypha in various fungi. [< Greek *rhíza* root + *morphḗ* form]

rhi·zo·mor·phous (rī′zə môr′fəs), *adj. Botany.* rootlike in form. [< Greek *rhíza* root + *morphḗ* form + English *-ous*]

rhi·zoph·a·gous (rī zof′ə gəs), *adj.* feeding on roots. [< Greek *rhíza* root + *phageîn* eat + English *-ous*]

rhi·zoph·i·lous (rī zof′ə ləs), *adj.* growing or parasitic upon roots.

rhi·zo·pho·ra·ceous (rī′zō fə rā′shəs), *adj.* belonging to a family of mostly tropical trees and shrubs typified by the mangrove. [< New Latin *Rhizophoraceae* the family name (< Greek *rhíza* root + *phérein* bear) + English *-ous*]

rhi·zo·pod (rī′zə pod), *n.* any of a group of one-celled animals that form temporary projections of protoplasm for moving about and taking in food: *Amoebas are rhizopods. Most of the animals caught in this way are rhizopods—sluggish amoebae encased in minute hard shells* (Scientific American). [< New Latin *Rhizopoda* the class name < Greek *rhíza* root + *poús, podós* foot]

rhi·zop·o·dan (rī zop′ə dən), *n.* a rhizopod. —*adj.* of or having to do with a rhizopod.

rhi·zop·o·dous (rī zop′ə dəs), *adj.* rhizopodan.

rhi·zo·pus (rī′zə pəs), *n.* any of a group of fungi that includes bread mold and potato rot. [< New Latin *Rhizopus* the genus name < Greek *rhíza* root + *poús, podós* foot]

rhi·zot·o·mist (rī zot′ə mist), *n.* a person who collects roots to use as medicine.

rhi·zot·o·my (rī zot′ə mē), *n., pl.* **-mies.**

the surgical operation of cutting a spinal nerve root. [< Greek *rhíza* root + *-tomiā* a cutting]

Rh negative, lacking the Rh factor (in the blood).

rho (rō), *n.* the 17th letter of the Greek alphabet (Ρ, ρ), corresponding to English *R, r.* [< Greek *rhô*]

rho·da·min (rō′də min), *n.* rhodamine.

rho·da·mine (rō′də mēn, -min), *n.* **1.** a red dye having brilliant fluorescent qualities, obtained by heating an amino derivative of phenol with phthalic anhydride and hydrochloric acid. *Formula:* $C_{28}H_{31}ClN_2O_3$ **2.** any of a group of related dyes. [< Greek *rhódon* rose + English *amine*]

Rhode Islander (rōd), a native or inhabitant of Rhode Island.

Rhode Island Red, any of an American breed of poultry of medium weight that have reddish feathers and a black tail.

Rhode Island White, any of an American breed of poultry similar to the Rhode Island Red but having white plumage.

Rhodes grass (rōdz), a perennial South African grass, grown in warm regions for forage.

Rho·de·sian (rō dē′zhən), *adj.* of or having to do with Rhodesia. —*n.* **1.** a native or inhabitant of Rhodesia. **2.** a student attending Oxford University on a Rhodes Scholarship.

Rhodesian man, a type of extinct man similar to the Neanderthal man, who lived in central and southern Africa in the early Stone Age, and whose remains were first discovered in northern Rhodesia.

Rhodesian ridgeback, any of a breed of fawn-colored hunting dogs native to South Africa, characterized by a ridge on its back which is formed by the hair growing forward instead of toward the back like the rest of his coat.

Rhodes scholar, a holder of a Rhodes scholarship.

Rhodes scholarship, a two- or three-year scholarship at Oxford University, founded by Cecil Rhodes. There are 96 of these scholarships open to candidates from the United States, and about 100 from the Commonwealth.

Rho·di·an (rō′dē ən), *adj.* of or having to do with the island of Rhodes. —*n.* a native or inhabitant of Rhodes.

rho·dic (rō′dik), *adj.* **1.** of or having to do with rhodium. **2.** containing rhodium, especially with a high valence.

rho·di·um (rō′dē əm), *n.* a rare, grayish-white metallic chemical element, forming salts that give rose-colored solutions. It is similar to aluminum, but harder, and occurs chiefly in platinum ores. *Symbol:* Rh; *at.wt.:* (C^{12}) 102.905 or (O^{16}) 102.91; *at.no.:* 45; *valence:* (usually) 3. [< Greek *rhódon* rose + New Latin *-ium,* a suffix meaning "element" (from the rosy color of its salts)]

rho·do·chro·site (rō′dō krō′sīt), *n.* a mineral consisting essentially of manganese carbonate and usually occurring in rose-red crystals; dialogite. *Formula:* $MnCO_3$ [< German *Rhodochrosit* < Greek *rhodóchrōs, -chrōtos* rose-colored (< *rhódon* rose + *chrōs, chrōtós* flesh-colored skin) + German *-it* -ite[1]]

rho·do·den·dron (rō′də den′drən), *n., pl.* **-drons, -dra** (-drə). any of a large group of shrubs or small trees of the heath family, cultivated chiefly for their leathery leaves and beautiful large, pink, purple, or white flowers: *The influence exerted by rhododendrons upon our gardens . . . has been . . . great* (London Times).

Branch of Rhododendron (great laurel)

[< New Latin *Rhododendron* the genus name < Greek *rhodódendron* < *rhódon* rose + *déndron* tree, related to *drŷs* tree]

➤ The terms **rhododendron** and **azalea** are often used interchangeably. They are not easily distinguishable on botanical characteristics, but popularly those that are evergreen are called *rhododendrons* and those that are deciduous *azaleas.*

rho·do·lite (rō′də līt), *n.* a rose-red variety of garnet, sometimes used as a gem. [< Greek *rhódon* rose + English *-lite*]

rhod·o·mon·tade (rod′ə mon tād′, -täd′), *n., adj., v.i.,* **-tad·ed, -tad·ing.** rodomontade.

rho·do·nite (rō′də nīt), *n.* a rose-red mineral, consisting essentially of manganese silicate. It is sometimes used as an ornamental stone. *Formula:* $MnSiO_3$ [< German *Rhodonit* < Greek *rhódon* rose + German *-it* -ite[1]]

rho·do·phy·ceous (rō′də fish′əs, -fī′shəs), *adj.* belonging to the red algae. [< New Latin *Rhodophyceae* the class name (< Greek *rhódon* rose + *phŷkos* seaweed) + English *-ous*]

rho·do·plast (rō′də plast), *n.* one of the chromatophores which bear the red coloring matter in the cells of the red algae. [< Greek *rhódon* rose + *plastós* something formed]

rho·dop·sin (rō dop′sin), *n.* a purplish-red protein pigment that is sensitive to light, found in the rods of the retina of the eye; visual purple: *Rhodopsin was found to be the visual pigment in all vertebrates from the primitive lamprey to man* (Science News Letter). [< Greek *rhódon* rose + *ópsis* sight + English *-in*]

rho·do·ra (rō dôr′ə, -dōr′-), *n.* a low variety of rhododendron of Canada and the northeast United States, with pink flowers that appear before the leaves do. [< New Latin *Rhodora* the genus name < Latin *rodarum* < a Gaulish word]

rho·do·sper·mous (rō′də spėr′məs), *adj.* of or belonging to the red algae.

rhomb (rom, romb), *n.* **1.** a rhombus. **2.** a rhombohedron. [< Middle French *rhombe,* learned borrowing from Latin *rhombus* < Greek *rhómbos;* see RHOMBUS]

rhombed (romd), *adj.* rhomboid.

rhom·ben·ceph·a·lon (rom′ben sef′ə lon), *n.* the hindbrain. [< New Latin *rhombencephalon* < Greek *rhómbos* (see RHOMBUS) + *en-* in + *kephalḗ* head]

rhom·bic (rom′bik), *adj.* **1.** having the form of a rhombus. **2.** having a rhombus as a base or cross section. **3.** bounded by rhombuses. **4.** *Chemistry.* having to do with a system of crystallization characterized by three unequal axes intersecting at right angles; orthorhombic.

rhom·bi·cal (rom′bə kəl), *adj.* rhombic.

rhom·bo·he·dral (rom′bə hē′drəl), *adj.* of, or in the form of, a rhombohedron.

rhom·bo·he·dron (rom′bə hē′drən), *n., pl.* **-dra** (-drə). a solid bounded by six rhombic planes. [< Greek *rhómbos* (see RHOMBUS) + *hédra* base]

rhom·boid (rom′boid), *n.* a parallelogram with equal opposite sides that is not a rectangle. —*adj.* shaped like a rhombus or rhomboid. [< Late Latin *rhomboīdes* < Greek *rhomboeidḗs* < *rhómbos* (see RHOMBUS) + *eîdos* form]

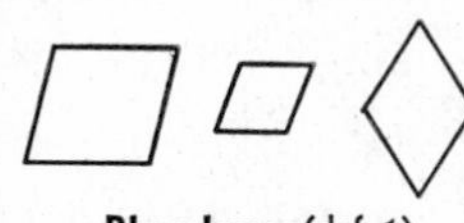

Rhomboids

rhom·boi·dal (rom boi′dəl), *adj.* rhomboid.

rhom·bus (rom′bəs), *n., pl.* **-bus·es, -bi** (-bī). **1.** a parallelogram with equal sides, having two obtuse angles and two acute angles; diamond. **2.** a rhombohedron. [< Latin *rhombus* < Greek *rhómbos* rhombus; spinning top < *rhémbein* to spin]

Rhombuses (def. 1)

rhon·chal or **rhon·cal** (rong′kəl), *adj.* of or having to do with a rhonchus.

rhon·chi·al (rong′kē əl), *adj.* rhonchal.

rhon·chus (rong′kəs), *n., pl.* **-chi** (-kī). a coarse sound resembling a snore, caused by obstruction of the bronchial tubes or trachea with secretions. [< Latin *rhoncus* a snoring, croaking, perhaps related to Greek *rhénchos* < *rénkein,* or *rhénchein* to snore]

rho·pal·ic (rō pal′ik), *adj.* of or having to do with a line of metrical verse in which each word contains one syllable or one letter more than the preceding word. *Example:* Spes Deus aeternae stationis conciliator (Ausonius). Also, **ropalic.** [< Late Latin *rhopalicus* < Greek *rhopalikós* < *rhópalon* a cudgel thicker at one end]

rho·ta·cism (rō′tə siz əm), *n.* **1.** an excessive use of the *r-* sound. **2.** a peculiar pronunciation of the *r*-sound, as with a burr. **3.** the conversion of another sound into the *r*-sound, especially the *s*-sound in Latin and Old Norse dialects. [< New Latin *rhotacismus* < Greek *rhōtakízein* overuse the letter *rhô* rho]

Rh positive, containing the Rh factor (in the blood): *When an individual's red cells contain this Rh factor, he is called "Rh positive"* . . . (Sidonie M. Gruenberg).

rhu·barb (rü′bärb), *n.* **1.** a garden plant of the buckwheat family, with very large leaves, whose thick and fleshy, sour stalks are used for making sauce, pies, etc. **2.** the leafstalks. **3.** the sauce made of them. **4.** a purgative medicine made from a kind of dried rhubarb. **5.** *U.S. Slang.* a heated dispute, usually marked by scornful comment: *The game was filled with rhubarbs. The Phils protested loudly that the run should have counted but lost the argument to Umpire Donatelli* (New York Times). [< Old French *rheubarbe,* learned borrowing from Medieval Latin *rheubarbarum* < Greek *rhéon bárbaron* foreign rhubarb]

rhumb (rum, rumb), *n.* **1.** any one of the 32 points of the compass. **2.** a rhumb line. [< Latin *rhombus* < Greek *rhómbos;* see RHOMBUS]

rhum·ba (rum′bə), *n., v.i.,* **-baed** (-bəd), **-ba·ing** (-bə ing). rumba.

rhum·ba·tron (rum′bə tron), *n. Electronics.* **1.** two hollow metal containers in a klystron for changing the flow of electrons into the ultra-high-frequency current. **2.** a klystron. [< *rhumba* + (elec)*tron* (because of the dancing motion of the electrons)]

rhumb line, a line on the surface of a sphere cutting all meridians at the same oblique angle.

rhumb sailing, sailing on a rhumb line.

rhyme (rīm), *v.,* **rhymed, rhym·ing,** *n.* —*v.i.* **1.** to sound alike, especially in the last part: *"Long" and "song" rhyme. "Go to bed" rhymes with "sleepy head."* **2.** to make rhymes. —*v.t.* **1.** to put or make into rhyme: *to rhyme a translation.* **2.** to use (a word) with another that rhymes with it: *to rhyme "love" and "dove."*
[Middle English *rimen* < Old French *rimer* < *rime;* see the noun]
—*n.* **1.** an agreement in the final sounds of words or lines. **2.** a word or line having the same last sound as another. **3.** verses or poetry with a regular return of similar sounds. Also, **rime.**
without rhyme or reason, having no system or sense: *On an irregular bare earth floor, machinery was strewn without apparent rhyme or reason* (New York Times).
[Middle English *rime* < Old French *rime,* probably < Latin *rhythmos* < Greek *rhythmós.* Doublet of RHYTHM.] —**rhym′er,** *n.*
➤ **rhyme, rime.** The simpler spelling seems to be gaining slowly on *rhyme.* It is not only simpler but was the original spelling in English.

rhyme royal, a seven-line stanza in iambic pentameter with the lines arranged *a b a b b c c.* Chaucer introduced it into English.

rhyme scheme, the pattern of rhymes used in a work in verse. *Example:* "*a a b b c c*" has a couplet rhyme scheme.

rhyme·ster (rīm′stər), *n.* a maker of rather poor rhymes or verse. Also, **rimester.**

rhym·ist (rī′mist), *n.* a person who uses rhymes.

rhyn·cho·ce·pha·li·an (ring′kō sə fā′lē ən, -fāl′yən), *adj.* belonging to an order of nearly extinct, small, lizardlike reptiles. —*n.* a rhynchocephalian reptile: *The tuatara of New Zealand is the only extant rhynchocephalian.* [< New Latin *Rhynchocephala* the order name (< Greek *rhýnchos* snout + *kephalḗ* head) + English *-ian*]

rhyn·choph·o·rous (ring kof′ər əs), *adj.* having a snout or rostrum, as a snout beetle or weevil. [< New Latin *rhynchophorus* (with English *-ous*) < *rhýnchos* snout + *phórein* to bear]

rhy·o·lite (rī′ə līt), *n.* a volcanic rock containing quartz with texture often showing the lines of flow. [< German *Rhyolit* < Greek *rhýāx, -ākos* lava flow; torrent (< *rhéin* to flow) + German *-it* -ite[1]]

rhy·o·lit·ic (rī′ə lit′ik), *adj.* of or resembling rhyolite: *The rhyolitic type of fissure eruption . . . is exemplified by one that took place in 1912 in the Valley of Ten Thousand Smokes in Alaska* (Scientific American).

rhyp·a·rog·ra·pher (rip′ə rog′rə fər), *n.* a person who paints or writes about mean or sordid subjects.

rhyp·a·ro·graph·ic (rip′ər ə graf′ik), *adj.* having to do with rhyparography.

rhyp·a·rog·ra·phist (rip′ə rog′rə fist), *n.* a rhyparographer.

rhyp·a·rog·ra·phy (rip′ə rog′rə fē), *n.* the painting or description of mean or sordid subjects. [< Greek *rhyparográphos* < *rhyparós* sordid + *gráphein* write, draw]

rhythm (riᴛʜ′əm), *n.* **1.** movement with a regular repetition of a beat, accent, rise and fall, or the like: *the rhythm of dancing, skating, swimming, the rhythm of the tides, the rhythm of one's heartbeats.* **2.** a repetition of an accent; arrangement of beats in a line of poetry: *The rhythms of "The Night Before Christmas" and "The Star-Spangled Banner" are different.* **3.** a grouping by accents or beats: *triple rhythm, rumba rhythm.* **4.** *Biology.* a pattern of involuntary behavior, action, etc., occurring regularly and periodically: *Furthermore, ants, which may be non-rhythmic, have been trained to feed at several time intervals, whereas bees, which have a marked rhythm and are active only in the daytime, cannot be trained on other than a 24-hour basis* (J.L. Cloudsley-Thompson). **5.** rhythm method. **6.** *Fine Arts.* the proper relation of parts producing a harmonious whole, especially by repeating certain forms, colors, etc. [< Latin *rhythmos* < Greek *rhythmós*, perhaps related to *rheîn* to flow. Doublet of RHYME.]

rhythm and blues, *U.S.* rock'n'roll with blues as its melodic element: *He began singing and playing his wailing mixture of rhythm and blues, jazz, and shoutin' gospel music* (Time).

rhythmed (riᴛʜ′əmd), *adj.* rhythmic.

rhyth·mic (riᴛʜ′mik), *adj.* rhythmical: *Berto Lardera . . . gets an almost musical sense of rhythmic movement in his pieces* (New Yorker). —*n.* rhythmics.

rhyth·mi·cal (riᴛʜ′mə kəl), *adj.* **1.** having rhythm: *rhythmical speech.* **2.** of or having to do with rhythm: *rhythmical structure in music.* —**rhyth′mi·cal·ly,** *adv.*

rhyth·mic·i·ty (riᴛʜ mis′ə tē), *n.* rhythmic character: *The rhythmicity of the heart is as much a built-in feature as the anatomical structure of its cells* (Scientific American).

rhyth·mics (riᴛʜ′miks), *n.* the science of rhythm and rhythmical structures.

rhyth·mist (riᴛʜ′mist), *n.* a person who is expert in, or has a fine sense of, rhythm.

rhyth·mi·za·ble (riᴛʜ′mī zə bəl), *adj.* capable of being rhythmically treated.

rhyth·mi·za·tion (riᴛʜ′mə zā′shən), *n.* **1.** the bringing of successive impressions into rhythmical form. **2.** the assuming of rhythmical form by such a succession.

rhythm method, a form of birth control involving a period of continence coordinated with the estimated period of ovulation.

rhy·ton (rī′ton), *n., pl.* **-ta** (-tə). a kind of drinking vessel used in ancient Greece, shaped like a horn and having the form of an animal's head at the lower end. [< Greek *rhytón* < *rheîn* to flow]

Antique State Rhyton
Vatican Museum, Rome

RI (no periods), respiratory infection (virus).

R.I., an abbreviation for the following: **1. a.** King and Emperor (Latin, *Rex et Imperator*). **b.** Queen and Empress (Latin, *Regina et Imperatrix*). **2.** Rhode Island. **3.** Royal Institute.

ri·a (rē′ä), *n.* an arm of the sea formed by a submerged valley with no indications of glacial action. [< Spanish *ría* mouth of a river. Compare *río* river.]

R.I.A., Royal Irish Academy.

ria coast, a coast with bays and headlands resulting from the partial submerging of the normal land surface.

ri·al (rē ôl′, -äl′), *n.* **1.** an Iranian silver coin and unit of money, worth about 1.3 cents: *The course costs six hundred rials, or about eight dollars, and lasts twelve weeks* (New Yorker). **2.** riyal. [< Persian, Arabic *riyāl* < Spanish *real.* Compare REAL², REGAL, ROYAL.]

Ri·al·to (rē al′tō), *n.* **1.** a former business district of Venice, Italy. **2.** a famous bridge in Venice, Italy, that crosses the Grand Canal. **3.** the theater district along Broadway in New York City or in other cities.

ri·al·to (rē al′tō), *n., pl.* **-tos.** an exchange; market place.

ri·an·cy (rī′ən sē), *n.* gaiety.

ri·ant (rī′ənt; *French* rē äɴ′), *adj.* laughing; smiling; gay. [< Middle French *riant,* present participle of Old French *rire* < Vulgar Latin *rīdere,* for Latin *rīdēre* to laugh] —**ri′ant·ly,** *adv.*

ri·ante (rē äɴt′), *adj.* riant. [< French *riante,* feminine of *riant* < Middle French *riant*]

RIAS (no periods), the American radio station in West Berlin. [< *R*(adio) *I*(n) *A*(merican) *S*(ector)]

ri·a·ta (rē ä′tə), *n.* a lariat. [< Spanish *reata*]

rib (rib), *n., v.,* **ribbed, rib·bing.** —*n.* **1.** one of the curved bones extending from the backbone and enclosing the upper part of the body: *Furthermore, certain parts of the skeleton, such as the skull and ribs, protect the delicate parts of your body from injury* (Beauchamp, Mayfield, and West). **2. a.** a piece that forms a frame: *the ribs of an umbrella.* **b.** *Aeronautics.* a structural member within a wing, running from the front to the back edge. **c.** any riblike part. **3.** a thick vein of a leaf. **4.** a ridge in a woven or knitted fabric. **5.** a cut of meat containing a rib: *a rib of beef.* **6.** one of the curved members of a ship's frame which go out from the keel. **7.** one of the arches forming the supports for a vault. **8.** a wife (in humorous allusion to the creation of Eve). **9.** *Informal.* **a.** a joke. **b.** a teasing or mocking; a satire on or parody of something: *All the stories are . . . acted with a tongue-in-cheek seriousness that adds up to a rib of Hollywood costume pictures* (Time).

tickle the ribs, to cause laughter: *a good joke to tickle the ribs.*

—*v.t.* **1.** to furnish or strengthen with ribs. **2.** to mark with riblike ridges. **3.** *Informal.* to tease: *to rib a person about a mistake.*

[Old English *ribb*] —**rib′like′,** *adj.*

R.I.B.A., Royal Institute of British Architects.

rib·ald (rib′əld), *adj.* offensive in speech; coarsely mocking; irreverent; indecent; obscene: *a ribald story, a ribald party.* —*n.* a person who is ribald or given to ribaldry. [< Old French *ribauld,* perhaps < Germanic (compare Old High German *hrībā, hrīpā* prostitute)] —**Syn.** *adj.* indelicate, gross.

rib·ald·ly (rib′əld lē), *adv.* in a ribald manner; irreverently; brazenly.

rib·ald·ry (rib′əl drē), *n., pl.* **-ries.** ribald language: *He ducked and dodged as he exchanged ribaldries with anyone who attempted to hit him* (Sunday Times). —**Syn.** obscenity.

rib·and¹ (rib′ənd, -ən), *n.* ribband.

rib·and² (rib′ənd), *n. Archaic.* ribbon.

rib·band (rib′band′, -ənd, -ən), *n.* a lengthwise timber or the like used to secure a ship's ribs in position while the outside planking or plating is being put on. [perhaps special use of a Middle English variant of *ribbon*]

ribbed (ribd), *adj.* having ribs or ridges: *a ribbed fabric.*

rib·bing (rib′ing), *n.* **1.** ribs collectively; a group or arrangement of ribs: *the delicate ribbing of a leaf, the ribbing of corduroy.* **2.** *Informal.* an act of mocking or teasing.

rib·ble-rab·ble (rib′əl rab′əl), *n.* **1.** confused, meaningless jabber or sounds. **2.** rabble.

rib·bon (rib′ən), *n.* **1.** a strip or band of silk, satin, velvet, etc.: *a yard of ribbon, a bow of ribbon.* **2.** anything like such a strip: *a typewriter ribbon, a ribbon of steel. I'll tell you how the sun rose—a ribbon at a time* (Emily Dickinson). **3.** a small badge of cloth worn in place of a decoration for bravery, etc.: *the red ribbon of the French Legion of Honor.* **4.** a ribband; lengthwise timber to hold a ship's ribs in position.

cut or **tear to ribbons, a.** to rip into small pieces; shred: *Her dress was torn to ribbons by the thorns and briers she had come through.* **b.** to insult or disparage thoroughly: *How disconcerting then to find that William Barkley had been allowed to cut Lord Beaverbrook to ribbons* (Punch).

ribbons, reins: *If he had ever held the coachman's ribbons in his hands, as I have in my younger days, he would know that stopping is not always easy* (George Eliot).

—*v.t.* **1.** to adorn with or as if with ribbons: *I could see all the inland valleys ribboned with broad waters* (Richard Blackmore). **2.** to separate into ribbons. —*v.i.* to take the shape of, or move in the winding manner of, a ribbon or ribbonlike strip: *Annecy boasts of a fourteenth-century castle and canals that ribbon through the old town* (Harper's).

[Middle English *ryban,* earlier *reban* < Old French *riban,* variant of *ruban,* perhaps < Germanic (compare Dutch *ringband*)] —**rib′bon·like′,** *adj.*

ribbon back, a back of a piece of furniture decorated with a ribbon design carved in wood.

ribbon building, *British.* the building of a ribbon development.

rib·bon·bush (rib′ən bu̇sh′), *n.* a tall shrub of the buckwheat family of tropical Pacific islands, with flat, ribbonlike branches and red or purplish fruit.

ribbon development, *British.* **1.** a row of houses, stores, etc., along a main road, extending outward from a town into the countryside: *Look at the ribbon development of cafes, hotels, villas, and beach huts that stretch out of Athens along the coast to Sounion* (Manchester Guardian Weekly). **2.** the building of such a row of houses, stores, etc.; ribbon building.

rib·boned (rib′ənd), *adj.* decorated with ribbons; marked with something suggesting ribbons; tied with a ribbon: *Their girl friends in ribboned pony tails and candy-striped pants play . . . on the jukebox* (Time).

rib·bon·fish (rib′ən fish′), *n., pl.* **-fish·es** or (*collectively*) **-fish.** any of several deep-sea fishes with a long, very slender, ribbonlike body, such as the dealfish and oarfish.

ribbon grass, a tall, white or yellowish striped grass of North America and Europe, sometimes grown for ornament: *She has been dreaming . . . about an old sidewalk with ribbon grass growing in the cracks* (New Yorker).

Rib·bon·man (rib′ən mən), *n., pl.* **-men.** a member of a secret society, the Ribbon Society, formed in the north of Ireland early in the 1800's in opposition to the Orangemen, and named from the green ribbon worn as a badge.

ribbon movement, the device on a typewriter that moves the ribbon.

ribbon rock, *Mining.* rock which occurs in veins.

rib·bons (rib′ənz), *n.pl.* See under **ribbon,** *n.*

ribbon seal, a brown seal of the northern Pacific, the male of which has a band of yellowish white about the neck, rump, and each front flipper.

Male Ribbon Seal
(about 6 ft. long)

ribbon snake, a small, striped garter snake common in central and eastern United States.

ribbon work, a decorative design of ribbons, often used in the Italian Renaissance.

ribbon worm, 1. any of a group of soft, thin, contractile worms varying in length from less than an inch to over 80 feet and living chiefly in the sea; nemertean: *Around the clam, the mud is alive with ribbon worms—scarlet, thin as threads* (New Yorker). **2.** a tapeworm.

rib·by (rib′ē), *adj.,* **-bi·er, -bi·est.** full of ribs; having prominent ribs: *All sorts of ribby ridges and intercostal hollows . . .* (C.E. Montague).

rib·cage (rib′kāj′), *n.* the barrel-shaped enclosure formed by the ribs of the chest; the framework of the ribs.

rib·let (rib′lit), *n.* a little rib: *a veal riblet.*

ri·bo·fla·vin (rī′bō flā′vin), *n.* a constituent of the vitamin B complex, present in liver, eggs, milk, spinach, etc.; lactoflavin. It is sometimes called vitamin G or B_2. Persons who lack riboflavin are retarded in growth. *Riboflavin is an important vitamin and one that the average person is likely to be short on* (Science News Letter). *Formula:* $C_{17}H_{20}N_4O_6$ [< *ribo*(se) + *flavin,* its earlier name in England]

ri·bo·nu·cle·ase (rī′bō nü′klē ās, -nyü′-), *n.* an enzyme that promotes the hydrolysis of ribonucleic acid: *The enzyme ribonuclease loses little of its activity when its molecule is partially degraded* (Scientific American).

ri·bo·nu·cle·ic acid (rī′bō nü klē′ik, -nyü-), a nucleic acid found in the cytoplasm and sometimes in the nucleus of the living cell, which consists of long chains of repeating units of ribose combined with phosphate and several chemical bases; ribose nucleic acid: *A second type of large molecule, ribonucleic*

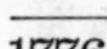

acid (RNA), carries the instructions from the genes to the building sites, where it directs the assembly of proteins (Scientific American). *Abbr.:* RNA (no periods).

ri·bo·nu·cle·o·pro·tein (rī′bō nü′klē ō-prō′tēn, -nyü′-), *n.* a combination of nucleic acids and proteins in the living cell, believed to be essential in the synthesis of protein. *Abbr.:* RNP (no periods).

ri·bose (rī′bōs), *n.* a pentose sugar, obtained in the dextrorotatory form chiefly from nucleic acids contained in plants: *Ribose is a sugar formed of five carbon atoms to the molecule, instead of the six that make up the more familiar glucose* (Science News Letter). *Formula:* $C_5H_{10}O_5$ [< a German alteration of English *arabinose*]

ribose nucleic acid, ribonucleic acid.

ri·bo·so·mal (rī′bə sō′məl), *adj.* of or having to do with a ribosome or ribosomes.

ri·bo·some (rī′bə sōm), *n.* a small structure in the cytoplasm of cells that carries on protein synthesis.

rib roast, a cut of beef including a part of one or more ribs, suitable for roasting.

rib·roast (rib′rōst′), *v.t. Archaic.* to belabor with blows; beat; drub; thrash.

rib-tick·ler (rib′tik′lər), *n. Informal.* a funny story or joke: *This collection of stories . . . happily intermingles the best humor of recent years with a few rib-ticklers from the past* (New Yorker).

rib-tick·ling (rib′tik′ling), *adj. Informal.* funny; jocular.

rib twist, a twist formed in glassware, by cutting a stem and twisting it to form spiral grooves.

rib-twist·ed (rib′twis′tid), *adj.* formed with a rib twist.

rib·wort (rib′wėrt′), *n.,* or **ribwort plantain,** **1.** a plantain having long, narrow leaves with prominent ribs. **2.** any of certain similar plantains.

Ri·car·di·an (ri kär′dē ən), *adj.* of or having to do with the theories of the English political economist David Ricardo, 1772-1823, or his followers. —*n.* a follower of Ricardo.

Ri·car·di·an·ism (ri kär′dē ə niz əm), *n.* the economic doctrines or methods of David Ricardo, 1772-1823, British economist.

rice (rīs), *n., v.,* **riced, ric·ing.** —*n.* **1.** the starchy seeds or grain of an annual cereal grass grown in warm climates. Rice is an important food in India, China, and Japan. **2.** the plant itself. —*v.t.* to reduce to a form like rice: *to rice potatoes.* [< Old French *ris* < Italian *riso* < Latin *oryza* < Greek *óryza*]

Panicle of Rice (def. 1)

rice·bird (rīs′bėrd′), *n.* **1.** a name for the bobolink in the southern United States. **2.** the Java sparrow.

rice bowl, an area where rice is grown extensively: *French Indo-China was once known as the rice bowl of the world* (New Yorker).

rice bran, the separated cuticle of the rice grain.

rice Christian, **1.** an Asian or African native who converts to Christianity solely to receive food provided by missionaries. **2.** a weak, vacillating Christian.

rice flour, **1.** ground rice, used in making puddings, face powder, etc. **2.** the layer of the rice kernel next to the cuticle, rubbed off as a powder in the processes of hulling and polishing.

rice grub, the larva of a scarabaeid beetle that damages the roots of upland rice in the southern United States.

rice paper, **1.** a thin paper made from the straw of rice. **2.** a paper made from the pith of a small tree of the ginseng family.

rice pounder, a person or machine that removes rice from its hull.

ric·er (rī′sər), *n.* a utensil for ricing cooked potatoes, etc., by pressing them through small holes.

rice rat, a gray or brownish rat of the southern United States and Mexico, found especially in wet, grassy areas.

ri·cer·ca·re (rē′cher kä′rā), *n., pl.* **-ri** (-rē). *Music.* **1.** a fugue using contrapuntal devices: *He had arranged the movements in an order which started with the three part ricercare on the royal theme* (London Times). **2.** an early form of the fugue, somewhat similar to a motet, but instrumental. [< Italian *ricercare* (literally) seek out < Latin *re-* again + *cicāre* go about]

rice stitch, a stitch in embroidery or crocheting resembling a grain of rice.

rice weevil, a beetle which feeds on rice and other stored grains. It is found in all parts of the world.

rice wine, sake, an alcoholic beverage made from fermented rice, popular in Japan.

rich (rich), *adj.* **1.** having much money or property: *Henry Ford and John D. Rockefeller were rich men.* **2.** well supplied; abounding: *The United States is rich in oil and coal. All this part of the river is rich in Indian history and traditions* (Mark Twain). **3.** abundant: *a rich supply.* **4.** producing or yielding abundantly; fertile: *rich soil, a rich mine.* **5.** having great worth; valuable: *a rich harvest, a rich suggestion.* **6.** costly; elegant: *rich dress, rich furnishings.* **7. a.** having many desirable elements or qualities. **b.** containing plenty of butter, eggs, flavoring, etc.: *a rich cake, rich milk.* **8.** (of colors, sounds, smells, etc.) deep; full; vivid: *a rich red, a rich tone.* **9.** (of wine, etc.) strong and finely flavored: *a rich, mellow sherry.* **10.** (of a fuel mixture) containing more fuel and less air than is normally required. **11.** *Informal.* **a.** very amusing. **b.** ridiculous; absurd. **12.** great, thorough, or fine: *A couple of boys left to themselves will furnish richer fun than any troop of trained comedians* (George Meredith).

strike it rich, *U.S. Informal.* **a.** to find rich ore, oil, etc.: *After three months of drilling in the desert, the prospectors struck it rich.* **b.** to have a sudden or unexpected great success: *The gaffer happens to be the head stableman on the opulent country estate of a former longshoreman who has struck it rich* (New Yorker).

—*n.* **the rich,** rich people: *The rich . . . do not, in general, require to be so much stimulated to benevolence* (Scott).

[probably fusion of Middle English *riche* (< Old French < Germanic), and Old English *rīce*]

—**Syn.** *adj.* **1. Rich, wealthy** mean having much money or property. **Rich** implies having more than enough money, possessions, or resources for all normal needs and desires: *With a five-dollar bill in his pocket, Tom felt rich.* **Wealthy** suggests greater and more permanent resources: *Some of our greatest universities, libraries, and museums were established by wealthy people.* **4.** productive, fruitful, fecund. **6.** expensive, sumptuous, luxurious.

Rich., Richard.

Rich·ard Roe (rich′ərd rō′), a fictitious name used in legal forms or proceedings for the name of an unknown person.

Rich·ard·so·ni·an (rich′ərd sō′nē ən), *adj.* of, having to do with, or characteristic of the English novelist Samuel Richardson, 1689-1761, or his writings: *When my Richardsonian epistles are published, there must be dull as well as amusing letters among them* (Macaulay). —*n.* an admirer or imitator of Richardson: *My own investigation . . . has led me to set a high value on the Richardsonians* (Robert Louis Stevenson).

Rich·ard·son's goose (rich′ərd sənz), Hutchins' goose. [< Sir John *Richardson,* 1787-1865, a Scottish naturalist]

Richardson's owl, a small, brown and white owl resembling the saw-whet owl, occurring in Canada and occasionally during the winter in northern United States.

rich·en (rich′ən), *v.t., v.i.* to make or become rich or richer.

rich·es (rich′iz), *n.pl.* wealth; abundance of property; much money, land, goods, etc.: *to rise from rags to riches.* [< Old French *richesse,* singular < *riche* rich] —**Syn.** affluence, opulence.

rich·ling (rich′ling), *n.* a rich person: *Kennedy was indeed born a richling . . . and could have had a patrician's life* (Conrad Jameson).

rich·ly (rich′lē), *adv.* **1.** in a rich manner: *storied windows richly light* (Milton). **2.** fully: *a richly deserved punishment.*

rich·ness (rich′nis), *n.* rich condition or quality.

rich rhyme, perfect rhyme.

Rich·ter scale (rik′tər), a scale for indicating the magnitude of earthquakes, ranging from 0 to 10. [< Charles Francis *Richter,* born 1900, an American seismologist]

rich·weed (rich′wēd′), *n.* **1.** a common urticaceous herb of North America and Japan. **2.** a plant of the mint family of eastern North America, used medicinally as a diuretic, tonic, etc. **3.** any of several ragweeds.

ri·cin (rī′sin, ris′in), *n.* a poisonous albumin found in castor-oil seeds. [< New Latin *Ricinus* the genus name of the plant < Latin *ricinus* the castor-bean plant, the croton; (originally) a tick (from its tick-shaped seeds)]

ric·in·o·le·ate (ris′ə nō′lē āt), *n.* a salt or ester of ricinoleic acid.

ric·in·o·le·ic acid (ris′ə nə lē′ik, -nō′lē-), an unsaturated, fatty hydroxy acid obtained from castor oil, used in soaps, finishing of textiles, etc. *Formula:* $C_{18}H_{34}O_3$ [< New Latin *Ricinus* the castor-bean genus (see RICIN) + English *oleic acid*]

ric·in·o·le·in (ris′ə nō′lē in), *n.* the glycerol ester of ricinoleic acid. It makes up about 80 per cent of castor oil. *Formula:* $C_{57}H_{104}O_9$ [< *ricinole*(ic acid) + *-in*]

rick[1] (rik), *n.* a stack of hay, straw, etc., especially one made so that the rain will run off it. —*v.t.* to form into a rick or ricks. [Old English *hrēac*] —**rick′er,** *n.*

rick[2] (rik), *v., n.* wrick.

rick·ard·ite (rik′ər dīt), *n.* a copper telluride occurring in small masses of metallic luster and bright purple color. *Formula:* Cu_4Te_3 [< Thomas A. *Rickard,* 1864-1953, an American mining engineer + *-ite*[1]]

rick·et·i·ness (rik′ə tē nis), *n.* shakiness; unsteadiness.

rick·ets (rik′its), *n.* a disease of childhood, caused by lack of vitamin D, and the resultant inability of the body to utilize calcium; rachitis. Rickets causes softening, and sometimes bending, of the bones, and can be prevented by providing the child plenty of sunlight and food rich in vitamin D and calcium. [apparently alteration of *rachitis*]

rick·ett·si·a (ri ket′sē ə), *n., pl.* **-si·ae** (-sē ē). any of a group of microorganisms intermediate between the bacteria and viruses, living in the tissue of arthropods, where they are transmitted to humans, causing such diseases as Rocky Mountain spotted fever, typhus, and Q fever: *Rickettsiae are of interest not only as a major cause of human disease but also as a new kind of organism for biologists to study* (Scientific American). [American English < New Latin *Rickettsia* < Howard T. *Ricketts,* 1871-1910, an American pathologist, who investigated the microorganisms]

rick·ett·si·al (ri ket′sē əl), *adj.* of or having to do with the rickettsiae.

rick·ett·si·al·pox (ri ket′sē əl poks′), *n.* a disease caused by a rickettsia, transmitted by a mite, with symptoms resembling those of chicken pox.

rick·et·y (rik′ə tē), *adj.* **1.** liable to fall or break down; shaky: *a rickety old chair.* **2.** having rickets; suffering from rickets. **3.** feeble in the joints. —**Syn. 1.** tottering.

rick·ey (rik′ē), *n.* **1.** a drink made with limes, sugar, carbonated water, and gin or other alcoholic liquor. **2.** a nonalcoholic carbonated drink made with lime juice. [American English, reputedly < a Colonel *Rickey*]

rick·le (rik′əl), *n. Scottish.* **1.** a heap. **2.** a small rick of hay or grain. [< *rick*[1] + *-le,* a diminutive suffix]

rick·rack (rik′rak′), *n.* a narrow, zigzag braid used as trimming. [American English, perhaps reduplication of *rack*[1], verb]

rick·shaw or **rick·sha** (rik′shô), *n.* a jinrikisha: *The trishaw, because of its speed, has almost completely replaced the rickshaw all over Southeast Asia* (Atlantic). See **jinrikisha** for picture.

rick·yard (rik′yärd′), *n.* a farmyard containing ricks of hay or corn; stackyard: *He swung himself over a gate into a rickyard, where blown chaff streamed across his vision like a sallow snowstorm* (New Yorker).

ric·o·chet (rik′ə shā′; *especially British* rik′ə shet′), *n., v.,* **-cheted** (-shād′), **-chet·ing** (-shā′ing) or (*especially British*) **-chet·ted** (-shet′id), **-chet·ting** (-shet′ing). —*n.* the skipping or jumping motion of an object as it goes along a flat surface: *the ricochet of a stone thrown along the surface of water.* —*v.i.* to move with a skipping or jumping motion: *The cannon balls struck the ground and ricochetted through the tall grass* (Ulysses S. Grant). *Ricocheting along the street, like a witch who had lost her broom, I streaked for home* (Tallulah Bankhead). [< French *ricochet;* origin uncertain] —**Syn.** *n.* carom. *-v.i.* bounce.

ri·cot·ta (ri kot′ə), *n.* a soft Italian cottage cheese. [< Italian *ricotta* < Latin *recocta,* feminine of *recoctus,* past participle of *recoquere* to cook again < *re-* again + *coquere* to cook]

ric·tal (rik′təl), *adj.* of or having to do with the rictus.

ric·tus (rik′təs), *n.* **1.** the cleft of the open mouth; the gape. **2.** an open position of the mouth: *the teeth disclosed in a perpetual rictus* (Robert Louis Stevenson). [< Latin *rictus, -ūs* a mouth opened wide, for laughter or food < *ringī* to gape]

rid[1] (rid), *v.t.,* **rid** or **rid·ded, rid·ding. 1.** to make free (of): *What will rid a house of rats?* **2.** *Obsolete.* to expel: *I will rid evil beasts out of the land* (Leviticus 26:6). **3.** *Obsolete.* to rescue.

be rid of, to be freed from: *Queen Victoria had called Gladstone a dreadful old man and longed to be rid of him* (Manchester Guardian Weekly).

get rid of, a. to get free from: *I can't get rid of this cold.* **b.** to do away with: *Poison will get rid of the rats in the barn.*

[probably fusion of Old English *āryddan,* or *geryddan* to strip, plunder and Middle English *rydan* < Scandinavian (compare Old Icelandic *rythja* to clear)]

rid[2] (rid), *v. Archaic.* a past tense and a past participle of **ride.**

rid·a·ble (rī′də bəl), *adj.* **1.** that can be ridden. **2.** that can be ridden over. Also, **rideable.**

rid·dance (rid′əns), *n.* **1.** a clearing away or out; removal: *He shall make even a speedy riddance of all them that dwell in the land* (Zephaniah 1:18). **2.** deliverance or rescue (from something): *a riddance from sin.*

good riddance, an exclamation expressing relief that something or somebody has been removed: *Good riddance to bad rubbish.*

—**Syn. 2.** liberation.

rid·den (rid′ən), *v.* a past participle of **ride:** *The horseman had ridden all day.*

rid·der (rid′ər), *n.* **1.** a person or thing that rids. **2.** *Obsolete.* a sieve.

rid·dle[1] (rid′əl), *n., v.,* **-dled, -dling.** —*n.* **1.** a puzzling question, statement, problem, etc., usually presented as a game or pastime. *Example:* When is a door not a door? *Answer:* When it is ajar. **2.** a person or thing that is hard to understand, explain, etc.: *All that Silver said was a riddle to him* (Robert Louis Stevenson). *Russia . . . is a riddle wrapped in a mystery inside an enigma* (Sir Winston Churchill).

—*v.i.* **1.** to speak in riddles. **2.** to ask riddles. —*v.t.* to solve (a riddle or question): *Riddle me this, and guess him if you can, who bears a nation in a single man?* (John Dryden).

[Middle English *redel* < earlier *redels,* taken as plural, Old English *rǣdels* < *rǣdan* to guess, explain] —**rid′dler,** *n.*

—**Syn.** *n.* **1.** enigma, puzzle, conundrum.

rid·dle[2] (rid′əl), *v.,* **-dled, -dling,** *n.* —*v.t.* **1.** to make many holes in: *The door of the fort was riddled with bullets.* **2.** to sift: *to riddle gravel.* [< noun] —*n.* a coarse sieve. [Old English *hriddel* sieve] —**Syn.** *v.t.* **1.** perforate.

rid·dle·me·ree (rid′əl mə rē′), *n.* rigmarole; nonsense: *On the basis of some such riddlemeree, Frisch has concocted a story about a man who loses himself in a fantasy* (New Yorker). [alteration of *riddle me a riddle, riddle my riddle*]

rid·dling·ly (rid′ling lē), *adv.* mysteriously.

ride (rīd), *v.,* **rode** or (*Archaic*) **rid, rid·den** or (*Archaic*) **rid, rid·ing,** *n.* —*v.i.* **1.** to sit on a horse and make it go. **2.** to sit on a camel, bicycle, etc., and make it go. **3.** to be carried along as if on horseback; be carried along by anything: *to ride on a train, to ride in a car.* **4.** to be capable of being ridden: *a horse that rides easily.* **5.** to be carried along in any way: *Disdain and scorn ride sparkling in her eyes* (Shakespeare). **6.** to float or move: *The ship rode into port. The moon rode clear and high in heaven* (Scott). **7.** to lie at anchor: *a windy, tossing anchorage where yawls and ketches ride* (John Masefield). **8.** to rest or turn on something, such as a pivot, axle, etc.: *Strong as the axletree on which heaven rides* (Shakespeare). **9.** to extend or project; overlap.

—*v.t.* **1.** to sit on and manage: *to ride a camel, to ride a bicycle. Sukarno and the ministers he has backed believe they can ride the Communist tiger* (Atlantic). **2.** to ride over, along, or through: *to ride a hundred miles.* **3.** to do or perform: *to ride a race.* **4.** to be mounted on; be carried on: *The gull rides the winds.* **5.** to move on; float along: *The ship rode the waves.* **6.** to extend or project over; overlap (something). **7.** to cause to ride or be carried: *The villagers had a strong desire to . . . ride him on a rail for body-snatching* (Mark Twain). **8.** to control, dominate, or tyrannize over: *to be ridden by foolish fears. The tradesman . . . is ridden by the routine of his craft* (Emerson). **9** *Informal.* to make fun of; tease; harass; nag: *Don't ride him for the blunder this time.* **10.** to keep (a ship) moored.

let ride, to leave undisturbed or inactive: *Let the matter ride until the next meeting.*

ride down, a. to knock down: *He rode down anyone who got in his way.* **b.** to overcome: *The support of the Commons . . . enabled Harley to ride down all resistance* (John R. Green). **c.** to overtake by riding: *He . . . was on the point of riding down a large old roomy family carriage* (Thackeray). **d.** to exhaust by riding: *The Czar was very active . . ., and rode down four horses* (London Gazette).

ride high, to enjoy success; do very well: *The conservatives, from looking like a beaten party earlier this year, are beginning to feel as if they were riding high* (Manchester Guardian).

ride out, a. to withstand (a gale or storm) without great damage: *The ship Lagoda . . . rode out the gale in safety* (Richard Henry Dana). **b.** to endure successfully: *Such weapons could ride out an enemy attack and still hit back effectively* (Wall Street Journal).

ride up, to slide up out of place: *That coat rides up at the back.*

—*n.* **1.** a trip on the back of a horse, in a carriage, car, train, boat, etc. **2.** a path, road, etc., made for riding.

hitch a ride, *U.S. Informal.* to get a free ride: *I had asked the Ambassador if I could hitch a ride back to Bad Godesberg with him* (New Yorker).

take for a ride, *Slang.* **a.** to murder: *Winford . . . was taken for a ride . . . and dumped out dead near Controni's Laurentian estate* (Maclean's). **b.** to cheat: *The taxpayer is being taken for a ride* (New York Times).

[Old English *rīdan*]

—**Syn.** *n.* **1. Ride, drive** mean a trip by some means of transportation. **Ride** suggests being carried along in or by something, as on horseback, in a boat, train, bus, etc., or in a car if one is going nowhere in particular or is strictly a passenger: *Let's go for a ride in my new car.* **Drive** suggests going in a particular direction, and applies particularly to a trip in a horse-drawn or motor vehicle one controls or operates himself or helps to direct: *Let's take a drive into the country.*

ride·a·ble (rī′də bəl), *adj.* ridable.

ri·deau (rē dō′), *n. Military.* a ridge of earth thrown up as a protection against the enemy. [< French *rideau* curtain]

rid·er (rī′dər), *n.* **1.** a person who rides: *The West is famous for its riders. Riders objected to jammed Friday night trains* (Newsweek). **2.** anything added to a record, document, legislative bill, or statement after it was supposed to be completed: *Now all the Council had to do was tack the rider on again and send the bill back to the Assembly* (Newsweek). **3.** an object resting on another, usually with one part hanging down on each side, as a strand of wire that can be moved back and forth on the beam of a balance as a minute weight. —**Syn. 2.** addendum.

ri·dered (rī′dərd), *adj. Mining.* of or having to do with rock containing ore or other minerals of a vein in strings or narrow strata.

rid·er·less (rī′dər lis), *adj.* without a rider.

ridge (rij), *n., v.* **ridged, ridg·ing.** —*n.* **1.** the long and narrow upper part of something: *the ridge of an animal's back, the ridge of a hill.* **2.** a line where two sloping surfaces meet: *the ridge of a roof.* **3.** a long, narrow chain of hills or mountains: *the Blue Ridge of the Appalachian Mountains.* **4.** any raised narrow strip: *the ridges on corduroy cloth, the ridges in plowed ground.* **5.** *Meteorology.* a trough of high barometric pressure: *A rather weak ridge of high pressure will extend from this high over the northern Mississippi Valley and the Northern Plains States* (New York Times).

—*v.t.* **1.** to form or make into ridges. **2.** to cover with ridges; mark with ridges. —*v.i.* to form ridges.

[Old English *hrycg*]

ridge·back (rij′bak′), *n.* the Rhodesian ridgeback.

ridge·board (rij′bôrd′, -bōrd′), *n.* a ridgepole.

ridge·piece (rij′pēs′), *n.* a ridgepole.

ridge·plate (rij′plāt′), *n.* a ridgepole.

ridge·pole (rij′pōl′), *n.* the horizontal timber along the top of a roof or tent.

ridg·er (ri′jər), *n.* a cultivator for heaping loose soil against young plants planted in rows. Its two hinged moldboards are side by side on a wheel at the rear.

ridge roof, a raised or peaked roof.

ridge·top (rij′top′), *n.* the top of a ridge: *I remember how . . . he picked his way up to the ridgetop* (Bud Boyd).

ridge·way (rij′wā′), *n.* a road along or following a ridge, especially the ridge of downs or low hills.

ridg·y (rij′ē), *adj.,* **ridg·i·er, ridg·i·est.** rising in a ridge or ridges: *ridgy ground, ridgy cloth. The ridgy summits of the eastern mountains of Clydesdale* (Jane Porter).

rid·i·cule (rid′ə kyül), *v.,* **-culed, -cul·ing,** *n.* —*v.t.* to laugh at; make fun of; mock: *My father discouraged me by ridiculing my performances* (Benjamin Franklin). [< noun]

—*n.* **1.** laughter in mockery; words or actions that make fun of somebody or something: *Silly mistakes and odd clothes often arouse ridicule.* **2.** *Archaic.* ridiculous quality or character: *to see the ridicule of this monstrous practice* (Joseph Addison). **3.** *Archaic.* something ridiculous.

[< French *ridicule* < Middle French, adjective < Latin *rīdiculum,* neuter of *rīdiculus;* see RIDICULOUS] —**rid′i·cul′er,** *n.*

—**Syn.** *v.t.* **Ridicule, deride, mock** mean to make fun of someone or something and cause him or it to be laughed at. **Ridicule** emphasizes making fun of a person or thing, in either a good-natured or an unkind way, with the intention of making him or it seem little and unimportant: *Boys ridicule their sisters' friends.* **Deride** emphasizes laughing in contempt and holding up to scorn: *Some people deride patriotic rallies and parades.* **Mock** means to ridicule or deride in a scornful way: *The impudent boys mocked the teacher. -n.* **1.** derision.

ri·dic·u·lous (ri dik′yə ləs), *adj.* deserving ridicule; absurd; laughable: *It would be ridiculous to walk backward all the time.* [< Latin *rīdiculōsus* < *rīdiculus* < *rīdēre* to laugh] —**ri·dic′u·lous·ly,** *adv.* —**ri·dic′u·lous·ness,** *n.*

—**Syn. Ridiculous, absurd, preposterous** mean not sensible or reasonable. **Ridiculous** emphasizes the laughable effect produced by something out of keeping with good sense: *His obvious attempts to be the life of the party were ridiculous.* **Absurd** emphasizes the contrast with what is true or sensible: *His belief that he was too clever to be caught in his wrongdoing was absurd.* **Preposterous** adds to *absurd* the idea of being contrary to nature: *The bandit made the preposterous suggestion that he would drop his gun if the policeman first dropped his.*

rid·ing[1] (rī′ding), *n.* **1.** the act of a person or thing that rides. **2.** a road for persons riding a bicycle or on horseback.

—*adj.* **1.** that rides; traveling. **2.** used for riding or when riding: *An average riding horse eats about 4 to 6 tons of hay a year* (Sunset).

rid·ing[2] (rī′ding), *n.* **1.** one of the three administrative divisions of Yorkshire, England. **2.** a similar division elsewhere: *He flew back to his own riding in Toronto just in time to watch the voters give him the greatest majority ever won by a candidate in the constituency's history* (Maclean's). [Middle English *thriding* < Scandinavian (compare Old Icelandic *thridjungr* one third); the *th-* was assimilated to a previous *-t* or *-th,* as in *East Thriding, North Thriding*]

riding boot, a high boot worn by horseback riders.

riding crop, a short whip with a loop on one end instead of a lash.

riding habit, a dress or suit worn by horseback riders. See **habit** for picture.

riding hood, a kind of hood or hooded cloak.

riding light, *Nautical.* a light hung on a ship riding at anchor.

ri·dot·to (ri dot′ō), *n., pl.* **-tos.** a public ball, often in masquerade. [< Italian *ridotto,* earlier *ridotta* a resort, retreat. Doublet of REDOUBT.]

ri·el (rē el′), *n.* a monetary unit of Cambodia, worth about 3 cents.

Rie·mann·i·an (rē′män′ē ən), *adj.* of or having to do with Georg Riemann, 1826-1866, German mathematician, or his mathematical theories and equations.

Ries·ling (rēs′ling, rēz′-), *n.* **1.** a dry, white wine. **2.** the grape from which this wine is made, grown in the upper Rhine and in California: *The best dry whites are made from the Riesling* (London Times). [< German *Riesling*]

riet·bok (rēt′bok), *n.* any of various medium-sized African antelopes, especially a reddish antelope inhabiting the marshy regions of central and southern Africa, of which only the males have horns; reedbuck. [< Afrikaans *rietbok* reed buck]

RIF (no periods) or **R.I.F.,** *U.S.* Reduction In Force (a notice of dismissal of government employees).

ri·fa·ci·men·to (rē fä′chē men′tō), *n., pl.* **-ti** (-tē). a recast or adaptation, especially of a literary or musical work. [< Italian *rifacimento* refashioning < *rifac-,* stem of *rifare* to remake < *ri-* re- + *fare* make < Latin *facere*]

rife (rīf), *adj.* **1.** happening often; common; numerous; widespread: *all those noises so rife in a Portuguese inn* (George Borrow). **2.** full; abounding: *The whole city was rife with rumors of political corruption.* [probably Old English *rīfe*] —**Syn. 1.** prevalent. **2.** replete.

riff (rif), *n.* a melodic phrase in jazz, especially as a recurring statement of the theme: *A welter of riffs, based on "St. Louis Blues," closed the program* (New Yorker). —*v.i.* to perform riffs. [origin uncertain]

Riff (rif), *n.* a native or inhabitant of the Rif in northern Africa.

Riff·i·an (rif′ē ən), *adj.* of or having to do with the Rif, in northern Africa, or its people. —*n.* a native or inhabitant of the Rif.

rif·fle¹ (rif′əl), *n., v.,* **-fled, -fling.** —*n.* **1.** *U.S.* a rapid. **2.** *U.S.* a ripple. **3.** the act of shuffling cards by bending the edges slightly.
—*v.t., v.i.* **1.** to shuffle (cards) by bending the edges slightly, so that the two divisions of the deck slide into each other. **2.** to bend the edges slightly and slip the pages of (a book, magazine, etc.) quickly out from under the thumb: *At home on East Street, he riffled through a 2-ft.-high stack of telegrams* (Time). **3.** *U.S.* to make (water) flow in riffles.
[American English, variant of *ripple¹,* or *ruffle¹*]

rif·fle² (rif′əl), *n.* **1.** an arrangement at the bottom of a sluice or the like, to catch and hold particles of gold. **2.** a slot or groove in such an arrangement. [perhaps < *riffle¹*]

rif·fler (rif′lər), *n.* a file with a curved end, for smoothing or shaping a depression. [< French *rifloir* < Old French *rifler;* see RIFLE¹]

riff·raff (rif′raf′), *n.* **1.** worthless people: *Bourgeois . . . is an epithet which the riffraff apply to what is respectable* (Anthony Hope). **2.** *Dialect.* trash. —*adj.* worthless. [Middle English *riffe and raff* < Old French *rif et raf,* and *rifle et rafle* every scrap < *rifler* to spoil, rifle² + *raffler* carry off] —**Syn.** *n.* **1.** rabble.

ri·fle¹ (rī′fəl), *n., v.,* **-fled, -fling.** —*n.* **1.** a gun with spiral grooves in its barrel to spin the bullet as it is fired. **2.** such a gun that is fired from the shoulder. **3.** one of the spiral grooves in the bore of a rifle. **4.** a soldier armed with a rifle; rifleman. **5.** a wooden block covered with emery to sharpen tools. [< verb]
—*v.t.* to cut spiral grooves in (a gun).
[probably < Old French *rifler* to scratch, groove, strip. Compare RIFLE².]

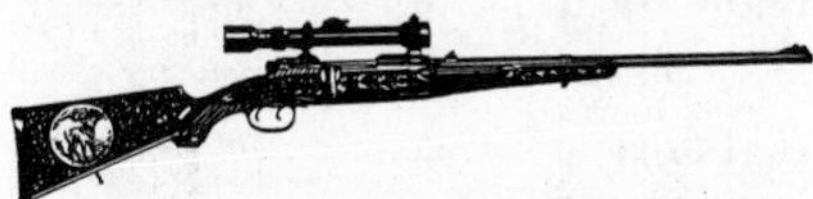
High-powered Rifle¹ (def. 1) with telescopic sight for big-game hunting

ri·fle² (rī′fəl), *v.t.,* **-fled, -fling. 1.** to search and rob; ransack and rob: *The thieves rifled all the drawers in the house.* **2.** to steal; take away. **3.** to strip bare: *The intruders rifled the whole orchard.* [< Old French *rifler* to scratch, groove, strip, perhaps < Germanic (compare Middle High German *riffeln* to comb, hackle thoroughly, Old High German *riffilōn* to comb flax)] —**Syn. 1.** pillage, plunder.

ri·fle·bird (rī′fəl bėrd′), *n.* **1.** an Australian bird. The male has a velvety-black plumage splendidly iridescent with purple, blue, green, etc. **2.** any of various related birds of Australia.

rifle grenade, a grenade fired from the muzzle of a rifle.

ri·fle·man (rī′fəl mən), *n., pl.* **-men. 1.** a soldier armed with a rifle. **2.** a man who uses a rifle: *The supply of fresh meat depends mainly on the skill of the riflemen* (Theodore Roosevelt).

rifle pit, a pit or short trench which shelters riflemen firing at an enemy.

ri·fler (rī′flər), *n.* **1.** a person who rifles; robber. **2.** *Falconry.* a hawk that does not return to the lure.

rifle range, 1. a place for practice in shooting with a rifle. **2.** the distance that a rifle will shoot a bullet.

ri·fle·ry (rī′fəl rē), *n., pl.* **-ries. 1.** shooting with a rifle, especially in target practice: *Montana's Lones Wigger, Jr. won two medals in riflery at Tokyo* (Time). **2.** firing from rifles: *Once before Shakespeare's cliff reverberated with the roar of riflery* (Punch).

ri·fling (rī′fling), *n.* **1.** the act or process of cutting spiral grooves in a gun barrel. **2.** the system of spiral grooves in a rifle.

rift (rift), *n.* a cleft; break; crack: *a rift in the earth. A rift in the clouds on a day threw a shaft of light upon her coffin . . .* (William Allen White). —*v.t., v.i.* to split; cleave. [< Scandinavian (compare Old Icelandic *ript* breach < *rīfa* to tear, rive)] —**Syn.** *n.* fissure.

rift saw, a saw for making boards, laths, etc.

rift-sawed (rift′sôd′), *adj.* sawed lengthwise into quarters before being sawed into boards.

rift valley, a valley formed by the lowering of an area of land between two nearly parallel faults; graben.

Rift Valley fever, a virus disease common in parts of Africa, affecting sheep, cattle, and sometimes man. [< *Rift Valley,* in Kenya, Africa]

rift·y (rif′tē), *adj.,* **rift·i·er, rift·i·est.** having rifts; rent; cracked; split.

rig¹ (rig), *v.,* **rigged, rig·ging,** *n.* —*v.t.* **1.** to equip (a ship) with masts, sails, ropes, etc.: *to rig a toy boat.* **2.** to move (a shroud, boom, stay, etc.) to its proper place: *to rig the mainmast and move forward rapidly.* **3.** to equip; fit out. **4.** *Informal.* to dress: *On Halloween the children rig themselves up in queer clothes.* **5.** to get ready for use: *Forward there! rig the head-pump!* (Richard Henry Dana). **6.** to put together in a hurry or by using odds and ends: *The boys rigged up a hut on the clothesline with a blanket.*
rig out, to fit out: *The free trappers, being newly rigged out and supplied, were in high spirits* (Washington Irving).
—*n.* **1.** the arrangement of masts, sails, ropes, etc., on a ship: *A schooner has a fore-and-aft rig; that is, the sails are set lengthwise on the ship.* **2.** *Informal.* clothes: *John's rig consisted of a silk hat and overalls.* **3. a.** outfit; equipment: *a camper's rig.* **b.** heavy machinery, or elaborate tools, such as those required to drill a well: *an oil rig.* **4.** *U.S. Informal.* **a.** an automobile or truck: *A terrified truck driver rode his runaway five-ton rig through Winsted at eighty miles an hour this morning with no brakes* (New York Times). **b.** a carriage, with its horse or horses.
[< Scandinavian (compare Danish *rigge,* perhaps < Low German *riggen,* variant of *rīgen* join together)]
—**Syn.** *n.* **3. a.** accouterment, tackle.

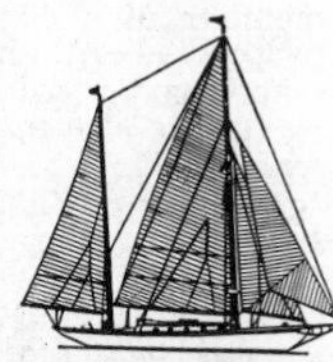
Rig¹ (def. 1) on a ketch

rig² (rig), *n. Scottish.* a ridge. [variant of *ridge*]

rig³ (rig), *n., v.,* **rigged, rig·ging.** —*n.* **1.** a prank; trick. **2.** a fraudulent scheme; swindle.
—*v.t.* **1.** to arrange dishonestly for one's own advantage: *to rig a race. Other costs and prices are rigged and falsified* (London Times). **2.** to arrange unfavorably: *The mathematical odds are rigged against the divorcee* (Life). [origin unknown]

rig·a·doon (rig′ə dün′), *n.* **1.** a lively dance for one couple. **2.** the quick, duple rhythm for this dance. **3.** a piece of music in such time. [< French *rigodon, rigaudon;* origin uncertain; probably < *Rigaud,* a Marseilles dancing master, who invented it]

rig·a·ma·role (rig′ə mə rōl), *n.* rigmarole.

Ri·gel (rī′jəl, -gəl), *n.* a star of the first magnitude in the foot of Orion. [< Arabic *rijl* foot]

rigged (rigd), *adj.* designed to deceive or defraud: *a rigged market.*

-rigged, *combining form.* having a —— rig: *Full-rigged = having a full rig.*

rig·ger (rig′ər), *n.* **1.** a person who rigs. **2.** a person who rigs ships, or works with hoisting tackle, etc. **3.** a person who assembles airplanes or adjusts their controls. **4.** a person who manipulates something fraudulently.

rig·ging¹ (rig′ing), *n.* **1.** the ropes, chains, etc., used to support and work the masts, yards, sails, etc., on a ship. **2.** tackle; equipment: *Do you need all that rigging for a trip of only two days?*

rig·ging² (rig′ing), *n. Scottish.* **1.** the roof of a house. **2.** the ridge of a roof. [< *rig²*]

Riggs' disease (rigz), pyorrhea of the gums. [American English < John M. *Riggs,* 1810-1885, an American dentist]

right (rīt), *adj.* **1.** good; just; lawful: *Jack did the right thing when he told the truth.* **2.** correct; true: *the right answer. A fool must now and then be right, by chance* (William Cowper). **3.** proper; fitting: *The right thing at the right time.* **4.** favorable: *If the weather is right, we'll go.* **5.** healthy; normal: *to be in one's right mind. He was thin and pale but he looks all right now.* **6.** meant to be seen; most important: *the right side of cloth.* **7.** the opposite of left; belonging to or having to do with the side of anything that is toward the east when the main side is turned north. **8.** straight: *a right line.* **9.** formed by a line drawn to another line or surface by the shortest course: *a right angle, a right cone.* **10.** *Archaic.* rightful; real: *the right owner.*
—*adv.* **1.** in a way that is good, just, or lawful: *He acted right when he told the truth.* **2.** correctly; truly: *She guessed right.* **3.** properly; well: *It serves you right to lose if you cheat.* **4.** favorably: *Such schemes don't always turn out right.* **5.** in a good or suitable condition: *Put things right. Don't mix up my papers; I shall never get them right again.* **6.** to the right hand: *to turn right.* **7.** exactly; just; precisely: *Your cap is right where you left it.* **8.** at once; immediately: *Stop playing right now.* **9.** very (used in some titles): *the right honorable, the right reverend. It is with stinging memories . . . that many people in the country who are not labourers come to the reading of the talk of right honourable gentlemen* (J. W. R. Scott). **10.** *Dialect.* extremely: *I am right glad to see you. He commands a right good crew* (W. S. Gilbert). **11.** in a straight line; directly: *Look me right in the eye.* **12.** completely: *His hat was knocked right off.*
right along, without stopping: *The traffic moved right along.*
right and left, a. to the right and the left; on every side: *He would lay about him right and left, what havoc he would make!* (London Examiner). **b.** continually; in great numbers; from all sides: *He is being robbed right and left* (Frank F. Moore). *The archaeologists . . . left the actual labor to the "experts" who committed archaeological atrocities right and left* (Atlantic).
right away or **right off,** at once; immediately: *He . . . had a kind of fit this noon and died right off* (Harper's).
—*n.* **1.** that which is right: *Do right, not wrong.* **2.** a just claim, title, or privilege: *the right to vote. The claimants submitted that the Japanese, . . . acquired no belligerent rights under international law and could acquire no right to the property* (London Times). **3.** fair treatment; justice: *payment*

as a matter of simple right. **4.** a blow struck with the right hand: *a hard right to the jaw.* **5.** the right side or what is on the right side: *to drive on the right, to turn to the right.* **6. a.** Often, **Right.** the part of a lawmaking body, made up of conservative or reactionary political groups, that sits to the right of the presiding officer. **b.** a conservative position or view. **7. a.** a privilege of subscribing for a stock or bond. **b.** a certificate granting such a privilege.
by right or **rights,** justly; properly: *Any little matters which ought to be ours by rights* (Dickens).
in one's own right, by inherent or personal right; independent of other conditions or qualifications: *The two-year college is an important educational institution in its own right, with its own special function and, hopefully, with its own distinguished future* (Harper's). *A novelist in her own right with a dozen books to her name . . .* (Manchester Guardian Weekly).
in the right, right: *Which party is in the right?*
rights, a. *U.S. Informal.* civil rights: *a rights group, the rights movement, Commission on Rights.* **b.** a share or interest in property: *With the rights to "Charley's Aunt" in hand, the fledgling producers could hardly be regarded as nonentities* (New Yorker).
to rights, *Informal.* in or into proper condition, order, etc.: *In my chamber, setting things and papers to rights* (Samuel Pepys).
—*v.t.* **1.** to make correct; put in order: *to right errors, to right one's accounts.* **2.** to do justice to: *to right the oppressed.* **3.** to put in the proper position: *to right an overturned car.* **4.** to inform (a person) correctly: *He was in error but I righted him.* —*v.i.* to get into proper position: *The ship righted as the wave passed.*
right about! turn in the opposite direction: *The command was given—right about!—and the troops marched back to the barracks.*
[Old English *riht*] —**right'er,** *n.*
—**Syn.** *adj.* **1.** equitable, ethical. **2.** accurate. **3.** fit, seemly, due, appropriate. **4.** suitable, propitious. **6.** principal, front, upper. *-adv.* **1.** justly. **3.** aptly. **4.** advantageously. **12.** altogether, quite. *-n.* **1.** morality, virtue. **2.** prerogative. *-v.t.* **1.** rectify, amend, adjust. **2.** vindicate.
➔ **Right** in the sense of "very" or "extremely" (*He's a right friendly man*) is now a localism.

Right (rīt), *adv.* very (used in titles): *The Right Honorable Thomas Jones, Lord Mayor of London.*

right·a·ble (rī'tə bəl), *adj.* that can be righted.

right·a·bout (rīt'ə bout'), *n.* **1.** the direction opposite to that which one is facing. **2.** a complete turn.
—*adj.* that is in the opposite direction: *a rightabout turn.*
—*adv.* in the opposite direction: *to turn rightabout.*

right about-face, 1. a turning in the opposite direction. **2.** a turn in the opposite direction; reversal: *a right about-face in policy.*

right-and-left (rīt'ənd left'), *adj.* **1.** made in pairs for the right and left side, as shoes or gloves. **2.** symmetrical to a central plane: *right-and-left engines.* **3.** having both a right-hand and a left-hand thread.

right angle, an angle of 90 degrees.

right-an·gled (rīt'ang'gəld), *adj.* **1.** containing a right angle or right angles. **2.** rectangular.

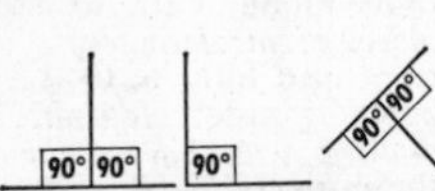

Right Angles

right ascen·sion, the arc of the celestial equator intercepted between the vernal equinox and the great circle of the celestial sphere passing through the celestial poles of a heavenly body whose position is being considered, reckoned toward the east and expressed in degrees or hours.

right bower, (in certain card games) the jack of trumps.

right-cen·ter (rīt'sen'tər), *adj.* of or belonging to the conservative or reactionary segment of a political party or group of the center. —*n.* a right-center party, group, or position.

right·down (rīt'doun'), *adj.* thorough; complete; out-and-out: *Such pretended favours and kindnesses as these are the most rightdown discourtesies in the world* (John Eachard). —*adv.* thoroughly; completely: *They . . . were rightdown honest, well-meaning people* (White Kennett).

right·en (rī'tən), *v.t. Archaic.* to set right.

right·eous (rī'chəs), *adj.* **1.** doing right; virtuous; behaving justly: *a righteous man.* **2.** morally right or justifiable: *a righteous cause. He was stirred by righteous wrath* (John Galsworthy). [Old English *rihtwīs* < *riht* right + *wīs* way, manner; altered by analogy with adjectives ending with *-eous*] —**right'eous·ly,** *adv.* —**Syn. 1.** upright, just.

right·eous·ness (rī'chəs nis), *n.* **1.** upright conduct; virtue: *Righteousness exalteth a nation* (Proverbs 14:34). *He [C. P. Scott] made righteousness readable* (James Bone). **2.** a being right and just: *the righteousness of a claim.* —**Syn. 1.** rectitude.

right face, a turn to the right.

right field, *Baseball.* the part of the outfield from the first-base foul line to center field. *Abbr.:* rf.

right fielder, *Baseball.* a player stationed in right field.

right·ful (rīt'fəl), *adj.* **1.** according to law; by rights; legal: *the rightful owner of this dog.* **2.** just and right; fair; proper. —**right'ful·ness,** *n.* —**Syn. 1.** lawful, legitimate. **2.** due.

right·ful·ly (rīt'fə lē), *adv.* **1.** in a rightful manner; according to right, law, or justice; legitimately: *a title rightfully vested.* **2.** properly; fittingly.

right hand, 1. the hand on the right side of the body, normally the stronger and more used of the two. **2.** a person of great usefulness to someone; very efficient or indispensable helper. **3.** the right side.

right-hand (rīt'hand'), *adj.* **1.** on or to the right: *a right-hand turn.* **2.** of, for, or with the right hand: *a right-hand drive.* **3.** most helpful or useful: *to be someone's right-hand man.*

right-hand·ed (rīt'han'did), *adj.* **1.** using the right hand more easily and readily than the left: *So Uncle Bob started early to convert a naturally right-handed boy into a southpaw* (Time). **2.** done with the right hand. **3.** made to be used with the right hand. **4.** turning from left to right: *a right-handed screw.* **5.** having a spiral that winds from left to right: *a right-handed thread.*

right-hand·ed·ness (rīt'han'did nis), *n.* **1.** the condition of being right-handed: *An example of right-handedness in this connection is the ordinary corkscrew that, when turned clockwise advances into a cork* (Science News Letter). **2.** dextrorotatory character.

right-hand·er (rīt'han'dər), *n.* **1.** a right-handed person, especially a baseball pitcher: *The towering right-hander also struck out nine Reds . . .* (New York Times). **2.** a blow given by the right hand.

right-hand rope, a rope laid up and twisted from left to right, such as common rope with three strands.

right·ism or **Right·ism** (rī'tiz əm), *n.* adherence or tendency to adhere to conservative or reactionary views in politics.

right·ist or **Right·ist** (rī'tist), *n.* **1.** a person who has conservative or reactionary ideas in politics: *Angrily the extreme rightists strode from the Chamber* (Time). **2.** a member of a conservative or reactionary party. —*adj.* having conservative or reactionary ideas in politics: *[He is] backed by rightist elements of the Liberal and Conservative Parties* (Wall Street Journal).

right·less (rīt'lis), *adj.* without rights.

right line, a straight line.

right·ly (rīt'lē), *adv.* **1.** justly; fairly. **2.** correctly; exactly; accurately: *He rightly guessed that I disapproved.* **3.** properly; suitably. [Old English *rihtlīce*] —**Syn. 3.** appropriately.

right-mind·ed (rīt'mīn'did), *adj.* having right opinions or principles. —**right'-mind'ed·ness,** *n.* —**Syn.** honest, upright.

right·ness (rīt'nis), *n.* **1.** goodness; uprightness. **2.** correctness. **3.** straightness. **4.** fitness.

right·o (rī'tō), *interj. Informal.* all right; O.K.

right of asylum, 1. the right of a state to shelter foreign political refugees in its embassies or other diplomatic establishments. **2.** the right of such a refugee to this protection.

right-of-cen·ter (rīt'əv sen'tər), *adj.* occupying a position on the right side of those in the center; holding a rightist view in politics; right-wing: *a right-of-center party or regime.*

right of search, the searching of a vessel or the examining of its papers, cargo, etc., by officers of a belligerent state to learn its nationality, whether it carries contraband, etc.

right of visit or **right of visit and search,** *Especially British.* right of search.

right of way, *pl.* **rights of way** or **right of ways. 1.** the right to go first; precedence over all others. **2.** the right to pass over property belonging to someone else. **3.** a strip of land on which a public highway, power line, railroad, etc., is built.

rights (rīts), *n.pl.* See under **right,** *n.*

Rights (rīts), *n.pl.* **Bill of.** See **Bill of Rights.**

right-to-work law (rīt'tə wėrk'), *U.S. Informal.* any of certain state laws that require an employer to disregard a worker's membership or nonmembership in a union as a condition of his employment, and forbid any agreement between an employer and a union to maintain a union shop: *Right-to-work laws ban the union shop, which requires a worker to join the union at a plant to continue working at the plant* (Wall Street Journal).

right triangle, a triangle one of whose angles is a right angle.

right·ward (rīt'wərd), *adv., adj.* on or toward the right: *When you throw a ball to your other assistant . . . it will again seem to drift rightward* (Scientific American).

right·wards (rīt'wərdz), *adv., adj.* rightward.

right whale, any of several whales with large heads from which whalebone and oil are obtained. Right whales have about 350 long, toothlike whalebones on each side of the mouth to sieve food from the water which they gulp. *Bowheads and right whales were depleted almost to extinction by the old open-boat whalers* (Scientific American).

right whale dolphin, a small black dolphin of Pacific waters, with a white belly and without a dorsal fin.

right wing, 1. Often, **Right Wing.** the conservative or reactionary members, especially of a political party: *There is no sign that the right wing of the party will call off its crusade to drive him from the party* (New York Times). **2.** persons or parties holding conservative or reactionary views.

right-wing (rīt'wing'), *adj.* belonging to or like the right wing.

right-wing·er (rīt'wing'ər), *n.* **1.** a right-wing member of a political group: *Scarcely had the Assembly reconvened when right-wingers launched an all-out attack* (Time). **2.** a person who has conservative or reactionary ideas in politics: *Right-wingers have waged a continuous war against teaching about the United Nations or using any UNESCO material* (Time).

right-wing·ism (rīt'wing'iz əm), *n.* the doctrines or practices of right-wingers: *There has been a lot of talk lately about right-wingism on college campuses* (Drew Pearson).

rig·id (rij'id), *adj.* **1.** stiff; firm; not bending: *a rigid support. Hold your arm rigid.* **2.** strict; not changing: *rigid discipline. In our home, it is a rigid rule to wash one's hands before eating. The young man is under the dictates of a rigid schoolmaster or instructor* (Sir Richard Steele). **3.** severely exact; rigorous: *a rigid examination.* **4.** (of an airship) having a framework within the envelope to maintain its shape. [< Latin *rigidus* < *rigēre* be stiff, perhaps related to *frīgidus* frigid] —**rig'id·ly,** *adv.* —**rig'id·ness,** *n.* —**Syn. 1.** unyielding, unbending. See **stiff. 3.** See **strict.**

ri·gid·i·fi·ca·tion (rə jid'ə fə kā'shen), *n.* **1.** the act or process of rigidifying: *Confinement obviously makes for rigidification of behavior* (New Scientist). **2.** the result of rigidifying; being rigidified: *personality rigidification.*

ri·gid·i·fy (rə jid'ə fī), *v.t., v.i.,* **-fied, -fy·ing.** to make or become rigid: *The proliferation of controls rigidifies the industry* (Wall Street Journal).

ri·gid·i·ty (rə jid'ə tē), *n., pl.* **-ties. 1.** stiffness; firmness. **2.** strictness; severity: *Here, as a singular exception, the rigidities which always accompany extreme discipline can be tolerated* (Wall Street Journal). —**Syn. 2.** stringency.

ri·gid·ize (ri'jə dīz), *v.t., v.i.,* **-ized, -iz·ing.** to rigidify: *Once inflated, the balloon is* *rigidized mechanically by stretching the skin beyond its elastic limit* (Science News Letter).

rig·ma·role (rig′mə rōl), *n.* foolish talk or activity; words or action without meaning; nonsense: *But was it not in order to cope with the situation ... that the Government set up in recent years ... the whole rigmarole of scheduling, listing, and building preservation orders?* (London Times). Also, **rigamarole.** [Middle English *ragman's roll* < *rageman* a list, catalogue + *roll*]

rig·ol (rig′əl), *n. Obsolete.* a ring, circle, or diadem. [< Middle French *rigole* < Old French *regol*, perhaps < Germanic (compare Old High German *rīga* circle, spiral)]

rig·o·lette (rig′ə let′), *n.* a kind of knitted wool scarf, worn as a headcovering by women. [< French *rigolette*]

rig·or (rig′ər), *n.* **1.** strictness; severity; harshness: *the rigor of a long, cold winter. Let him have all the rigor of the law* (Shakespeare). **2.** stiffness; rigidity. **3.** a chill caused by illness. [< Latin *rigor, -ōris* < *rigēre;* see RIGID] —**Syn. 1.** inclemency. **2.** inflexibility.

rig·or·ism (rig′ə riz əm), *n.* extreme strictness.

rig·or·ist (rig′ər ist), *n.* a person who believes in or supports extreme strictness, especially in matters of spiritual or moral conduct: *Even the moral rigorists who espouse suppression and try to enforce it are strong proponents of publicity* (Bulletin of Atomic Scientists). —*adj.* **1.** rigid; strict; exacting. **2.** having to do with rigorism.

rig·or·is·tic (rig′ə ris′tik), *adj.* rigorist.

rig·or mor·tis (rig′ər môr′tis; *especially British* rī′gôr môr′tis; *see note below*), the stiffening of the muscles after death, caused by the accumulation of metabolic products, especially lactic acid, in the muscles. [probably < Medieval Latin *rigor mortis* (literally) stiffness of death < Latin *rigor* rigor; *mortis,* genitive of *mors* death]

➤ The pronunciation (rī′gôr), conforming to the older fashion of pronouncing Latin words in English, has lost currency in the United States, but survives in Great Britain.

rig·o·ro·so (rig ə rō′sō), *adj. Music.* in strict time; in exact rhythm. [< Italian *rigoroso* rigorous]

rig·or·ous (rig′ər əs), *adj.* **1.** very severe; harsh; strict: *the rigorous discipline in a prison, a rigorous winter. The strike put the Administration's labor policy to a rigorous test* (New York Times). **2.** thoroughly logical and scientific; exact: *the rigorous methods of science.* —**rig′or·ous·ly,** *adv.* —**rig′or·ous·ness,** *n.* —**Syn. 1.** stern. See **strict.**

rig·our (rig′ər), *n. Especially British.* rigor.

rig-out (rig′out′), *n. Informal.* an outfit; costume: *This toggery of yours will never fit—you must have a new rig-out* (William T. Moncrieff).

Rigs·dag (rigz′däg′), *n.* the former parliament of Denmark. [< Danish *Rigsdag*]

rigs·da·ler (rigz′dä′lər), *n.* a former Danish silver coin, worth about 90 cents. [< Danish *rigsdaler* (literally) dollar of the realm. Compare REICH, DOLLAR.]

Rig-Ve·da (rig vä′də, -vē′-), *n.* the oldest and most important of the sacred books of the Hindus. [< Sanskrit *ṛigveda* < *ṛic-* praise + *veda* knowledge]

rig·wid·die (rig′wid ē), *n., adj. Scottish.* rigwoodie.

rig·wood·ie (rig′wu̇d ē), *Scottish.* —*n.* the rope or chain that goes over a horse's back. —*adj.* scrawny: *Rigwoodie hags* (Robert Burns). [< *rig*[2], variant of *ridge* spine + *withy* flexible]

R.I.I.A., Royal Institute of International Affairs.

rijks·daal·der (rīks′däl′dər; *informal* rīks′-dä′lər), *n.* rix-dollar. [< Dutch *rijksdaalder* (literally) dollar of the realm. Compare REICH, DOLLAR.]

rijst·ta·fel (rīst′tä′fəl), *n.* an elaborate meal consisting of rice with numerous side dishes of meats and vegetables, of Indonesian origin and popular in the Netherlands: *Rijsttafel is sort of an Indonesian "smorgasbord" dinner consisting of many different types of meat, vegetables, and rice dishes* (Newsweek). [< Dutch *rijst* rice + *tafel* table]

Riks·dag (riks′däg′), *n.* the Swedish legislature. [< Swedish *Riksdag*]

riks·da·ler (riks′dä′lər), *n.* a former Swedish silver coin. [< Swedish *riksdaler* (literally) dollar of the realm. Compare REICH, DOLLAR.]

rik·sha (rik′shô), *n. Informal.* a jinrikisha.

Riks·mål (riks′môl′), *n.* the older of the two varieties of standard, literary Norwegian (contrasted with *Landsmål*). It is a Norwegian form of Danish spoken in cities. [< Norwegian *Riksmål* < *riks,* genitive of *rik* realm + *mål* language, speech]

rile (rīl), *v.t.,* **riled, ril·ing.** *Especially U.S. Informal.* **1.** to disturb; irritate; vex: *There ain't no sense In getting riled* (Bret Harte). **2.** to roil (water, etc.). [American English, variant of *roil*]

rile·y (rī′lē), *adj. Especially U.S. Informal.* **1.** angry; irritable; vexed. **2.** roiled; turbid.

ri·lie·vo (rē lye′vō), *n., pl.* **-vi** (-vē). (in sculpture or painting) relief. [< Italian *rilievo*]

rill[1] (ril), *n.* a tiny stream; little brook: *I love thy rocks and rills, Thy woods and templed hills* (Samuel F. Smith). —*v.i.* to flow in a small stream. [compare Dutch *ril* groove, furrow] —**Syn.** *n.* rivulet, runnel.

rill[2] or **rille** (ril), *n.* a long, narrow valley on the surface of the moon: *There are many rills, or clefts—cracks of the order of half a mile wide and of unknown depth* (Robert H. Baker). [< German *Rille* a furrow]

rill·et (ril′it), *n.* a little rill.

ril·letts or **ril·lettes** (ri lets′, rē yet′), *n.pl.* a potted delicacy made of minced chicken, pork, truffles, etc., used in sandwiches or with salad. [< French *rillette* (diminutive) < *rille* piece of pork]

rim (rim), *n., v.,* **rimmed, rim·ming.** —*n.* an edge, border, or margin on or around anything: *the rim of a wheel, the rim of a cup, the south rim of the Grand Canyon. The basketball hit the rim of the basket and bounced off.* —*v.t.* **1.** to form a rim around; put a rim around: *Wild flowers and grasses rimmed the little pool.* **2.** to roll around the rim of: *The golf ball rimmed the cup and fell into the hole.*
[Old English *rima*]

ri·ma (rī′mə), *n., pl.* **-mae** (-mē). *Biology.* a long, narrow opening; fissure; cleft. [< Latin *rīma* cleft]

ri·mal (rī′məl), *adj.* of or having to do with a rima.

ri·ma·tion (rī mā′shən), *n.* a narrow opening or cleft; rima.

rim clutch, a clutch with a wheel fitted with a ring or cylindrical surface to grip the solid ring on the other wheel.

rime[1] (rīm), *v.i., v.t.,* **rimed, rim·ing,** *n.* rhyme: *Coleridge's "Rime of the Ancient Mariner."*

➤ See **rhyme** for usage note.

rime[2] (rīm), *n., v.,* **rimed, rim·ing.** —*n.* white frost; hoarfrost, especially from the freezing of vapor in drifting fog: *Evening cloud and whitening sunrise rime told of the coming of the wintertime* (John Greenleaf Whittier). —*v.t.* to cover with rime or something like rime: *The years had rimed his once black hair.* [Old English *hrīm*]

rim·er (rī′mər), *n.* a person who makes rhymes or verses, especially a maker of verses wherein rhyme or metrical form predominates over poetic thought or creation; an inferior poet; a minstrel.

rime·ster (rīm′stər), *n.* rhymester.

rim-fire (rim′fīr′), *adj.* **1.** (of a cartridge) having its primer at the rim of its base. **2.** (of a firearm) designed to fire rim-fire cartridges.

rim·land (rim′land′), *n.* the area or areas on or around the outer edges of a heartland: *Our strategic frontiers lie not along our own coastlines, but in the rimlands of Eurasia* (Wall Street Journal).

rim·less (rim′lis), *adj.* having no rim or rims: *rimless glasses.*

rimmed (rimd), *adj.* having a rim or rims.

ri·mose (rī′mōs, rī mōs′), *adj.* full of chinks or cracks. [< Latin *rīmōsus* < *rīma* chink, cleft]

rim·ous (rī′məs), *adj.* rimose.

rim·ple (rim′pəl), *n., v.i., v.t.,* **-pled, -pling.** *Dialect.* wrinkle; ripple. [Middle English *rymple.* Compare Middle Low German *rimpel.*]

rim·rock (rim′rok′), *n.* rock rising like a rim from the bedrock of an elevated piece of land, as above a basin.

rim saw, a saw with a ringlike, toothed cutting part mounted on the rim of a disk.

rim·shot (rim′shot′), *n. Jazz.* the sound made by simultaneously striking the rim and head of a snare drum: *The drummers experimented with jolting rimshots and heavy afterbeats, and for the first time the bass drum became a fixture in recording studios* (New Yorker).

rim·u·la (rim′yə lə), *n.* a small rima, especially of the spinal cord or brain.

rim·y (rī′mē), *adj.,* **rim·i·er, rim·i·est.** covered with rime or hoarfrost; frosty.

rin (rin), *n., pl.* **rin.** a Japanese money of account, worth 1/10 sen. [< Japanese *rin*]

rin·ceau (raN sō′), *n.pl.* **-ceaux** (-sō′). *French.* an ornamental scroll elaborated with acanthus leaves.

rind[1] (rīnd), *n.* the firm outer covering of oranges, melons, cheeses, etc.: *The bark of a tree or plant may be called the rind.* [Old English *rinde*] —**Syn.** peel, skin.

rind[2] (rīnd, rind), *n.* rynd.

rin·der·pest (rin′dər pest′), *n.* an acute and usually fatal, infectious virus disease of cattle, sheep, etc. It is marked by fever, dysentery, and inflammation of the mucous membranes. *Rinderpest is the world's deadliest cattle disease, killing 90% to 100% of the cattle it infects* (Science News Letter). [< German *Rinderpest* cattle plague < *Rinder,* plural of *Rind* ox + *Pest* pestilence, plague]

rind·less (rīnd′lis), *adj.* having no rind.

rin·for·zan·do (rin′fôr tsän′dō), *adj. Music.* with sudden increased force, as a single phrase or voice part to be made prominent. [< Italian *rinforzando,* gerund of *rinforzare* strengthen, reinforce]

ring[1] (ring), *n., v.,* **ringed, ring·ing.** —*n.* **1.** a circle: *The couples danced in a ring.* **2.** a thin circle of metal or other material: *a napkin ring, rings on her fingers, a wedding ring.* **3.** persons or things arranged in a circle: *A cottage ... close environ'd with a ring of branching elms* (William Cowper). **4.** the space between two circles having the same center. **5.** the outer edge or border of a coin, plate, wheel, or anything round. **6.** an enclosed space for races, games, circus performances, etc.: *The ring for a prize fight is square.* **7.** prize fighting. **8.** a space at a race track where bets are made. **9.** competition; rivalry; contest: *in the ring for election to the Senate.* **10.** a group of people combined for a selfish or bad purpose: *The police broke up a ring of smugglers operating in various ports. I had always understood that the theatrical "ring" was impenetrable to an outsider* (Arnold Bennett). **11.** a circular layer of wood produced yearly in a tree trunk; annual ring: *You can tell the age of a tree by counting the rings in its wood; one ring grows every year.* **12.** *Chemistry.* a closed chain of atoms linked by bonds that may be represented graphically in circular form. See **molecule** for picture.

run rings around, to surpass with great ease; beat easily: *It seems to be generally accepted that Mr. Wilson is running rings around the Opposition* (London Times).

—*v.t.* **1.** to put a ring around; enclose; form a circle around: *The cowboys ringed the herd before driving them into the pens. The circling sea that rings the earth* (William Morris). **2.** to toss a horseshoe, ring, etc., around (a certain mark or post): *Tom ringed the post.* **3.** to provide with a ring. **4.** to put a ring in the nose of (an animal). **5.** to cut away the bark in a ring around (a tree or branch). —*v.i.* **1.** to move in a ring. **2.** (of a hawk, etc.) to rise in circular flight. **3.** to form a ring or rings.
[Old English *hring*] —**ring′like′,** *adj.*
—**Syn.** *n.* **6.** arena. -*v.t.* **1.** encircle.

ring[2] (ring), *v.,* **rang** or (*now Dialect*) **rung, rung, ring·ing,** *n.* —*v.i.* **1.** to give forth a clear sound, as a bell does: *Did the telephone ring?* **2.** to cause a bell to sound: *Did you ring?* **3.** to call to church, prayers, etc., by ringing bells. **4.** to resound; sound loudly: *The room rang with shouts of laughter.* **5.** to echo; give back sound: *The camp rang with the bugle's call for reveille.* **6.** to be filled with report or talk: *The whole town is ringing with the good news.* **7.** to sound: *Your promises ring true. The sound of his voice rang in her ears for a long time.* **8.** to have a sensation as of sounds of bells; hear inner ringing: *My ears are ringing.*
—*v.t.* **1.** to cause to give forth a clear ringing sound: *Ring the bell. He rang his silver money upon the counter* (Owen Wister). **2.** to make (a sound) by ringing: *The bells rang a joyous peal.* **3.** to announce or proclaim by ringing; usher; conduct: *to ring a fire alarm. Big Ben rang out the hour. Ring out the old year; ring in the new.* **4.** to proclaim or repeat loudly everywhere: *to ring a person's praises.* **5.** to call on the telephone.

ring for, to summon by a bell: *to ring for a porter.*
ring in, a. *Informal.* to bring in dishonestly or trickily: *She can't be kept out of the case entirely, after all. We'll have to ring her in* (Theodore Dreiser). **b.** to record one's arrival at work on a time clock: *The foreman rings in five minutes before the workers ring in.*
ring off, to end a telephone call: *She heard him ring off, hang up the receiver, and go out into the hall* (Munsey's Magazine).
ring out, to record one's leaving from work on a time clock: *The day shift at the mill rings out at 5 P.M.*
ring up, a. to record (a specific amount) on a cash register: *The continued increase in the amount of consumer debt rang up more sales for the merchant* (Harry M. Kelly). **b.** to call on the telephone: *We did not look forward to the reproaches of Mrs. Slocum, who had already rung up the local policeman* (London Times).
—*n.* **1.** an act of ringing. **2.** a sound of a bell: *Did you hear a ring?* **3.** a sound like that of a bell: *the ring of skates on ice, the ring of voices in the halls. Tap the rim with your fingernail and the clear ring reveals the exquisite perfection of this crystal glassware* (Newsweek). **4.** a characteristic sound or quality: *a ring of sincerity, a ring of scorn in her voice.* **5.** a call on the telephone: *If Mr. Hogarth were to give me a ring in half an hour's time he could have the inquiry* (London Times). **6.** a set or peal of bells.
[Old English *hringan*]
➔ **Rung** as a past-tense form (*He rung the bell*), once standard and still widespread in nonstandard use, is now uncommon in cultivated English.

ring-a-le·vi·o (ring′ə lē′vē ō), *n.* a game in which one team must find hidden members of the opposing team, capture and imprison them, and prevent their being freed by their teammates. [origin uncertain]

ring armor, 1. armor made of chain mail. **2.** armor made of metal rings fastened on leather or cloth. See **mail**[2] for picture.

ring-a·round-the-ros·y (ring′ə round′-ᴛʜe rō′zē), *n.* a children's game in which the singing players skip around in a circle and drop to the floor on the song's last line.

ring-bark (ring′bärk′), *v.t.* to girdle (a tree, branch, etc.).

ring·bill (ring′bil′), *n.* ring-necked duck.

ring-billed gull (ring′bild′), a North American gull almost identical to the herring gull but smaller, and with a black ring around the bill.

ring binder, a loose-leaf notebook with hinged metal rings for holding the sheets of paper in place: *New editions of existing text books could be printed on single sheets of paper held together in a ring binder* (New Scientist).

ring·bolt (ring′bōlt′), *n.* a bolt with an eye in its head in which a ring is fitted.

ring·bone (ring′bōn′), *n.* an abnormal growth of bone on the pastern or coronet of a horse.

ring buoy, a ring-shaped life buoy: *Provide rescue equipment, such as a bamboo pole or ring buoy* (Good Housekeeping).

ring compound, a compound of several atoms united to form a ring; cyclic compound; closed-chain compound.

ring·craft (ring′kraft′, -kräft′), *n.* knowledge of or special skill in boxing in the ring: *The blame lies with a brutalized public, which values brawn before brain, which looks for knockouts but not for ringcraft* (John Reeves).

ring·dove (ring′duv′), *n.* **1.** a wood pigeon of Europe, with a whitish patch on either side of the neck; cushat. **2.** a pigeon of Europe and Asia, with a black half ring around its neck. It is related to the turtledove.

Ringdove (def. 1) (about 17 in. long)

ringed (ringd), *adj.* **1.** having or wearing a ring or rings. **2.** marked or decorated with a ring or rings. **3.** surrounded by a ring or rings. **4.** formed of or with rings; ringlike. **5.** *Zoology.* composed of ringlike segments; annulated. —**Syn. 3.** circled.

ringed plover, a plover of the Old World and eastern parts of arctic America, very similar to the semipalmated plover.

ringed seal, a common seal of arctic regions, brownish above and yellowish below with ringlike markings on the sides; floe rat.

rin·gent (rin′jənt), *adj.* gaping: *the ringent corollas of some flowers.* [< Latin *ringēns, -entis,* present participle of *ringī* to gape; show the teeth]

ring·er[1] (ring′ər), *n.* **1.** a person or thing that encircles, surrounds with a ring, etc. **2.** a horseshoe, quoit, etc., thrown so as to fall over a peg. **3.** the toss which does this. **4.** (in Australia) **a.** a very fast or expert sheepshearer. **b.** a cattle drover.

ring·er[2] (ring′ər), *n.* **1.** a person or thing that rings. **2.** a device for ringing a bell. **3.** *Slang.* a person or thing very much like another. **4.** *Slang.* **a.** a player who is not a regular member of the team that he is playing on. **b.** a horse, athlete, etc., competing or entering for competition under a false name or some other device to mask his identity, skill, or the like: *West appeared as a "ringer" for Nat (Killer) Jackson . . . and was knocked out by Brown in the third round* (New York Times).
be a (dead) ringer for, to be the image of: *He was a ringer for a ship's carpenter named Andersen* (New Yorker).

Ring·er's solution (ring′ərz), an aqueous solution of the chlorides of sodium, potassium, and calcium in the approximate proportion in which they are found in blood and tissue fluid. It is used to preserve mammalian tissue in experiments and as a synthetic body fluid to combat dehydration, acidosis, etc. [< Sydney *Ringer,* 1835-1910, an English physician]

ring fence, a fence completely enclosing some property.

ring finger, the finger next to the little finger, especially on the left hand.

ring gear, 1. the large circular gear in the differential of an automobile that engages the pinion gear. See picture under **differential gear. 2.** the circular gear with teeth on the inside within which the sun and planetary gears move in a planetary gear system.

ring·hals (ring′hals′), *n., pl.* **-hals·es.** a South African species of cobra with a narrow hood and a ring of color around its neck. It spits its venom into the face and eyes of its victims, causing burning pain and sometimes blindness: *I then saw a ringhals four feet away from me, which was reared up at the ready* (Cape Times). [< Afrikaans *ringhals* < *ring* ring + *hals* neck]

ring·ing[1] (ring′ing), *adj.* circling; running in circles.

ring·ing[2] (ring′ing), *adj.* having the sound of a bell; resounding.

ring·ing·ly (ring′ing lē), *adv.* with a ringing sound; resonantly; resoundingly: *He added ringingly that "there is no alternative to us but to defend our borders and our integrity"* (Time).

ring·lead (ring′lēd′), *v.t.,* **-led, -lead·ing.** to conduct or manage as ringleader. [back formation < *ringleader*]

ring·lead·er (ring′lē′dər), *n.* a person who leads others in opposition to authority or law: *the ringleaders of the mutiny.* [< *to lead the ring,* that is, to be the first]

ring·less (ring′lis), *adj.* without rings: *her ringless hand.*

ring·let (ring′lit), *n.* **1.** a little ring: *Drops of rain made ringlets in the pond.* **2.** a curl: *She wears her hair in ringlets.*

ring·let·ed (ring′lə tid), *adj.* having ringlets; curled.

ring·man (ring′mən), *n., pl.* **-men.** a person having to do with the prize ring or boxing.

ring·mas·ter (ring′mas′tər, -mäs′-), *n.* **1.** a man in charge of the performances in the ring of a circus. **2.** a person who takes complete charge or control of an undertaking: *The directors miss a firm but genial ringmaster whose flexibility of body and mind puts many younger men to shame* (London Times).
—*v.t.* **1.** to direct or manage as a circus ringmaster: *I saw the circus in action, ringmastered by Calder himself, back in the nineteen-forties* (New Yorker). **2.** to be in complete charge or control of (any undertaking): . . . *a convention so thoroughly ringmastered by the President that all the non-surprises came out of his pouch or hat* (Time).

ring nebula, 1. a kind of planetary nebula that looks like a ring when viewed through a telescope or on a photographic plate: *A survey of spectrograms . . . shows that some ring nebulae are indeed empty shells . . . . Other ring nebulae, however, show faint radiations of inert gases from within—radiations that indicate material does exist there* (Scientific American). **2. Ring Nebula,** the ring nebula in the constellation Lyra.

ring·neck (ring′nek′), *n.* any of various birds having the neck ringed with a band or bands of color, as certain ducks, plovers, and pheasants.

ring-necked duck (ring′nekt′), a North American duck, the male of which has a black head, back, and breast, and a faint chestnut ring about the neck.

ring-necked pheasant, a pheasant native to China, the male of which has bright-colored plumage, a long, pointed tail, and a white ring around the neck. It has become established in the central and northern United States and southern Canada. See **pheasant** for picture.

ringneck snake, any of several dark-colored North American snakes with yellow, orange or red bellies, and a yellow or orange ring about their necks.

Ring of the Nibelung, 1. *German Legend.* a magic ring made from the Rheingold by Alberich, a dwarf. **2.** a cycle of four operas by Richard Wagner.

ring ouzel, a European thrush which is black with a white marking on the breast.

ring plain, one of the nearly level circular areas on the moon's surface which are surrounded by high ridges and which have no central crater.

ring plover, 1. the semipalmated plover. **2.** the ringed plover.

ring post, one of the four posts of a boxing or wrestling ring.

ring road, *British.* a bypass.

ring shake, a crack in timber, usually caused by frost, in which the extremes of contraction and expansion tear apart the annular rings.

ring·side (ring′sīd′), *n.* **1.** the place just outside the ring at a circus, prize fight, etc. **2.** any place affording a close view.

ring·sid·er (ring′sī′dər), *n.* a person who sits or observes at the ringside: *Startled ringsiders heard that the official loser . . . had been robbed* (New Yorker).

ring snake, ringneck snake.

ring·spot (ring′spot′), *n.* **1.** a yellowish, necrotic discoloration in the form of spots or circles, symptomatic of a disease in plants. **2.** any of various plant diseases characterized by such discoloration: *tobacco ringspot.*

ring·ster (ring′stər), *n. U.S. Informal.* a member of a ring, especially a political ring.

ring-straked (ring′strākt′), *adj. Archaic.* ring-streaked.

ring-streaked (ring′strēkt′), *adj.* having streaks or bands of color around the body.

ring·tail (ring′tāl′), *n.* a small, squirrellike mammal with a pointed face and a long tail with black rings, found in southwest United States and Mexico; cacomistle. It is sometimes kept as a pet for catching rats and mice.

ring-tailed (ring′tāld′), *adj.* **1.** having the tail or the tail feathers marked with a ring or rings of a different color from the rest of the animal. **2.** having the end of the tail curled into a ring.

ring-tailed cat, the ringtail.

ring-tailed eagle, the golden eagle.

ring·toss (ring′tôs′, -tos′), *n.* quoits played with a ring of rope, plastic, etc., especially on shipboard: *One . . . little old woman was playing ringtoss in a fashion all her own* (New Yorker).

ring·worm (ring′wėrm′), *n.* a contagious skin disease, caused by fungi and characterized by ring-shaped patches.

rink (ringk), *n.* **1.** a sheet of ice for skating: *Jaffee developed muscles and endurance delivering newspapers on roller skates, then at 14 got a job sweeping ice at a New York rink* (Newsweek). **2.** a smooth floor for roller skating. **3.** a building for ice skating or roller skating. **4.** ice marked off for curling. **5.** a bowling green. **6.** a team of players in bowls,

 PRONUNCIATION KEY: hat, āge, cãre, fär; let, ēqual, tėrm; it, īce; hot, ōpen, ôrder; oil, out; cup, pu̇t, rüle;

curling, etc. [originally Scottish, perhaps < Old French *renc, reng* course, rank[1]]

rink·side (ringk′sīd′), *n.* the area beside a skating rink.

rink·y-dink (ring′kē dingk′), *U.S. Slang.* —*n.* that which is out-of-date and often trite or sentimental: *Eighteen-nineties rinky-dink, complete with fire engine, but the banjo band is above average* (New Yorker). —*adj.* out-of-date or trite; old and worn.

rins·a·ble (rin′sə bəl), *adj.* that can be rinsed: *Use a water rinsable paint remover* (New York Times).

rinse (rins), *v.,* **rinsed, rins·ing,** *n.* —*v.t.* **1.** to wash with clean water: *Rinse the soap out of your hair after you wash it.* **2.** to wash lightly: *Rinse your mouth with warm water.* **3.** to give a quick washing to, as by holding under a tap, without use of soap or other cleanser: *to rinse a glass before drinking.*
—*n.* **1.** a rinsing: *Give your hair a last rinse in cold water.* **2.** a preparation used in water to add color or luster to the hair.
[< Old French *reïncier,* ultimately < Latin *recēns, -entis* fresh]

rins·er (rin′sər), *n.* a person who rinses.

rins·ing (rin′sing), *n.* the act of one who rinses.
rinsings, a. the liquid or liquor with which anything has been rinsed out: *The beadle . . . washed down the greasy morsel with the last rinsings of the pot of ale* (Scott). **b.** dregs: *. . . being drenched with the rinsings of an unclean imagination* (James Russell Lowell).

ri·om·e·ter (rī om′ə tər), *n.* an instrument for recording the strength of radio noise and the level of its absorption by the ionosphere. [< *r*(elative)*i*(onospheric)*o*(pacity) *meter*]

ri·ot (rī′ət), *n.* **1.** a disturbance; confusion; disorder; wild, violent public disturbance. **2.** a loud outburst: *to break out in a riot of laughter.* **3.** loose living; wild reveling. **4.** a bright display: *The garden was a riot of color.* **5.** *Informal.* a very amusing person or performance: *He was a riot at the party.*
run riot, a. to act, speak, etc., without restraint; run wild: *Sometimes also . . . he runs riot, like Ovid, and knows not when he has said enough* (John Dryden). **b.** to grow wildly or luxuriantly: *The colors of the cliffs . . . run riot on a bright day* (William O. Douglas).
—*v.i.* **1.** to behave in a wild, disorderly way: *In protest, the Marathas rioted* (Newsweek). **2.** to revel. **3.** to live in a loose way. —*v.t.* to waste (money, time, etc.) in loose living: *He . . . Had rioted his life out, and made an end* (Tennyson).
[< Old French *riote* dispute < *rioter* to quarrel, ultimately < Latin *rūgīre* to roar]
—**ri′ot·er,** *n.* —**Syn.** *n.* **1.** outbreak, tumult.

Riot Act, an English statute of 1715 providing that if twelve or more persons assemble unlawfully and riotously, to the disturbance of the public peace, and refuse to disperse within an hour upon proclamation of the statute by a competent authority they shall be considered guilty of felony.
read the riot act, a. to give orders for disturbance to cease: *They find it necessary to enforce order, to read the riot act, [and] to issue an injunction to ensure respect for property* (Canadian Saturday Night). **b.** to reprimand, reprove, or admonish strongly: *Mr. Daly . . . read the riot act . . . and vanished into his den, leaving the naughty girls overwhelmed* (Dora Knowlton Ranous).

riot gun, a gun, especially a small shotgun, used in quelling riots: *The officers of the law, armed with tear gas and riot guns, cordoned off the area* (New Yorker).

ri·ot·ous (rī′ə təs), *adj.* **1.** taking part in a riot. **2.** boisterous; disorderly: *He was expelled from college for riotous conduct. Sounds of riotous glee came from the playhouse.* —**ri′ot·ous·ly,** *adv.* —**ri′ot·ous·ness,** *n.* —**Syn. 2.** turbulent, tumultuous.

riot squad, a body of police trained and equipped to deal with riots: *Riot squads and mounted police stood by in case of violence* (Wall Street Journal).

rip[1] (rip), *v.,* **ripped, rip·ping,** *n.* —*v.t.* **1.** to cut roughly; tear apart; tear off: *Rip the cover off this box.* **2.** to cut or pull out (the threads in the seams of a garment); take apart (a garment) by opening the seams. **3.** to saw (wood) along the grain, not across the grain. **4.** *Informal.* to speak or say with violence: *He ripped out an angry oath.* —*v.i.* **1.** to become torn apart. **2.** to come apart or be taken apart at a seam. **3.** *Informal.* to move fast or violently. **4.** *Informal.* to burst out angrily or violently: *Captain Peleg ripped and swore astern in the most frightful manner* (Herman Melville).
let her rip, *U.S. Slang.* to let a thing run its course, or do its best or worst: *In "Medea," I just open my big mouth and let her rip* (Time).
rip into, *Informal.* to attack violently: *Mr. Baird . . . rips into toadyism* (Orville Prescott).
—*n.* **1.** a torn place: *Please sew up this rip in my sleeve.* **2.** a seam burst in a garment.
[Middle English *rippen*]
—**Syn.** *v.t.* **1.** rend. See **tear.**

rip[2] (rip), *n.* **1.** a stretch of rough water made by cross currents meeting. **2.** a swift current made by the tide: *On some beaches the lifeguards mark rip currents . . . often moving the warning signs several times a day to keep up with the migration of the currents along the beach* (Scientific American). [American English, perhaps special use of *rip*[1]]

rip[3] (rip), *n. Informal.* **1.** a worthless or dissolute person: *the old rip, bewigged and gouty, ornate and enormous, with his jewelled mistress at his side* (Lytton Strachey). **2.** a worthless, worn-out horse. [origin uncertain]
—**Syn. 1.** rake, roué.

rip[4] (rip), *n. Scottish.* a handful of grain in the stalk. [variant of *reap* handful of grain, Old English *reopa* handful or sheaf of grain, related to *rīpan* reap]

R.I.P., may he or she (they) rest in peace (Latin, *Requiescat* (*requiescant*) *in pace*).

ri·par·i·al (ri pãr′ē əl, rī-), *adj.* riparian.

ri·par·i·an (ri pãr′ē ən, rī-), *adj.* of or on the bank of a river, a lake, etc.: *riparian rights, riparian property.* —*n.* a person who lives or owns property on the banks of a river, lake, etc. [< Latin *rīpārius* (< *rīpa* riverbank) + English *-an*]

rip cord, 1. a cord that opens a parachute when pulled. **2.** a cord on a balloon or airship which allows gas to escape when pulled, causing a rapid descent.

ripe[1] (rīp), *adj.,* **rip·er, rip·est. 1.** full-grown and ready to be gathered and eaten: *ripe fruit, ripe grain, ripe vegetables.* **2.** resembling ripe fruit in ruddiness and fullness: *ripe lips.* **3.** fully developed and fit to use: *ripe knowledge, a ripe cheese. I . . . saw, beneath his jaunty air, true mettle, and ripe bravery* (Richard Blackmore). **4.** ready to break or be lanced: *a ripe boil.* **5.** ready: *ripe for mischief. The country is ripe for revolt.* **6.** far enough along: *The hour is ripe to strike.* **7.** advanced in years: *a ripe old age.* [Old English *rīpe*]
—**ripe′ly,** *adv.* —**ripe′ness,** *n.* —**Syn. 1.** mellow, mature, matured, full-grown.

ripe[2] (rīp), *v.,* **riped, rip·ing.** *Obsolete.* —*v.t.* **1.** to search; rifle. **2.** to plunder. **3.** to poke. **4.** to wipe clean. —*v.i.* to make a search. [Old English *rȳpan*]

rip·en (rī′pən), *v.i.* to become ripe. —*v.t.* to make ripe.

rip·en·er (rī′pə nər), *n.* **1.** a person or thing that comes to ripeness. **2.** a person or thing that causes ripening.

ri·pid·o·lite (ri pid′ə līt, rī-), *n.* a mineral, a variety of chlorite; clinochlore. [< German *Ripidolith* (with English *-lite*) < Greek *rhipis, -idis* fan + *líthos* stone]

ri·pie·no (rē pyā′nō), *adj., n., pl.* **-ni** (-nē), **-nos.** —*adj.* supplementary or reinforcing. —*n.* a supplementary instrument or performer. [< Italian *ripieno* < Latin *re-* again + *plēnus* full]

ri·poste or **ri·post** (ri pōst′), *n., v.,* **-post·ed, -post·ing.** —*n.* **1.** *Fencing.* a quick thrust given after parrying a lunge. **2.** a quick, sharp reply or return. —*v.i.* to make a riposte; reply; retaliate. [< French *riposte* < Italian *risposta* a reply < *rispondere* respond < Latin *respondēre*] —**Syn.** *n.* **2.** retort.

rip-pan·el (rip′pan′əl), *n.* a part in the bag of a balloon or airship that can be ripped to let gas escape for a quick descent.

rip·per (rip′ər), *n.* **1.** a person who rips. **2.** a tool for ripping. **3.** Also, **ripper law, bill,** or **act.** *U.S.* a law taking away the power of appointment to office from its usual holders and conferring it on a chief executive, as the President, a governor, etc.

rip·ping (rip′ing), *adj. Especially British Slang.* fine; splendid: *a ripping good business* (H. G. Wells). —**rip′ping·ly,** *adv.*

rip·ple[1] (rip′əl), *n., v.,* **-pled, -pling.** —*n.* **1.** a very little wave: *Throw a stone into still water and watch the ripples spread in rings.* **2.** anything that seems like a tiny wave: *ripples in hair.* **3.** a sound that reminds one of little waves: *a ripple of laughter in the crowd.*
—*v.i.* **1.** to make a sound like rippling water. **2.** to form or have ripples. **3.** to flow with ripples on the surface. —*v.t.* to make little ripples on: *A breeze rippled the quiet waters.*
[origin uncertain]
—**Syn.** *n.* **1.** See **wave.**

rip·ple[2] (rip′əl), *n., v.,* **-pled, -pling.** —*n.* a tool with teeth for removing the seeds from flax, hemp, etc. —*v.t.* to remove the seeds from (flax, hemp, etc.) with a ripple. [compare Middle English *ripplen* comb seeds from flax]

ripple mark, one of the wavy lines made on sand, etc., by waves, wind, etc.: *Ripple marks are ridges and troughs that look like waves in rock* (Fenton and Fenton).

rip·pler (rip′lər), *n.* **1.** a person who ripples. **2.** a ripple.

rip·plet (rip′lit), *n.* a little ripple.

rip·pling (rip′ling), *adj.* that ripples; flowing in ripples: *rippling hair.* —**rip′pling·ly,** *adv.*

rip·ply (rip′lē), *adj.* characterized by ripples; rippling.

rip·rap (rip′rap′), *n., v.,* **-rapped, -rap·ping.** —*n.* **1.** a wall or foundation of broken stones thrown together irregularly. **2.** broken stones so used. —*v.t.* to build or strengthen with loose, broken stones. [American English, reduplication of *rap*[1], or related to *ripple*[1]]

rip·roar·ing (rip′rôr′ing, -rōr′-), *adj. Informal.* hilarious; uproarious; lively: *a rip-roaring good time.* [American English]

rip·roar·i·ous (rip′rôr′ē əs, -rōr′-), *adj. Slang.* riproaring. [American English < *rip*[1], patterned on *uproarious*]

rip·saw (rip′sô′), *n.* a saw for cutting wood along the grain, not across the grain.

rip·saw·yer (rip′sô′yər), *n.* a person who uses a ripsaw.

rip·snort·er (rip′snôr′tər), *n. U.S. Slang.* **1.** a thing that is unusually violent: *The new quake has an intensity of five, which is termed as "destructive, but not a ripsnorter"* (Wall Street Journal). **2.** a person who becomes violent or unusually angry. [American English, perhaps < *rip*[1] + *snort,* verb + *-er*[1]]

rip·snort·ing (rip′snôr′ting), *adj. U.S. Slang.* boisterous: *The outlook . . . was not for the kind of ripsnorting boom that Americans have recently become accustomed to* (Newsweek). *In the downtown saloons of the city a faint echo of Boise's ripsnorting frontier days can still be heard* (Time).

rip·tide (rip′tīd′), *n. U.S.* a tide that flows against another, causing a violent disturbance.

rip track, a railroad siding used for minor repairs.

Rip·u·ar·i·an (rip′yu̇ ãr′ē ən), *adj.* **1.** of or having to do with the ancient Franks who lived along the Rhine in the area around Cologne. **2.** of or having to do with the code of laws observed by them. —*n.* a Ripuarian Frank. [< Medieval Latin *Ripuarius* (origin uncertain) + English *-an*]

Rip Van Win·kle (rip′ van wing′kəl), **1.** a story by Washington Irving. **2.** its hero, who sleeps and wakes 20 years later to find everything changed. **3.** someone who is unaware of current events and conditions.

rise (rīz), *v.,* **rose, ris·en, ris·ing,** *n.* —*v.i.* **1.** to get up from a lying, sitting, or kneeling position: *to rise from a chair.* **2.** to get up from sleep or rest: *to rise at dawn.* **3.** to go up; come up; move up; ascend: *Mercury rises in a thermometer on a hot day. The curtain rose on the first act of the play. The fog is rising from the river.* **4.** to extend upward: *The tower rises to a height of 60 feet.* **5.** to slope upward: *The road rises up and over the hill.* **6.** to go higher; increase: *Butter rose five cents in price. The temperature is rising. During the spring thaw the river rises and often floods the valley.* **7. a.** to advance in importance, rank, etc.: *He rose from office boy to president.* **b.** to advance to a higher level of action, thought, feeling, expression, etc.: *His books never rise above mediocrity.* **8.** to become louder or of higher pitch: *His voice rose in anger.* **9. a.** to come to the surface of the water or ground: *The submarine rose near shore. The fish rose and seized the bait.* **b.** to come to

the surface of the skin; develop on the skin: *A blister rose on his heel.* **10.** to come above the horizon: *The sun rises in the morning.* **11.** to come into view: *Off in the distance the town rose before the travelers. A specter rose before his fevered mind.* **12.** to start; begin: *The river rises from a spring. Quarrels often rise from trifles.* **13.** to come into being or action: *The wind rose rapidly.* **14.** to be built up, erected, or constructed: *New houses are rising on the edge of town.* **15.** to become more animated or more cheerful: *Our spirits rose at the good news.* **16.** to revolt; rebel: *The slaves rose against their masters. At our heels all hell should rise With blackest insurrection* (Milton). **17.** to grow larger and lighter: *Yeast makes dough rise.* **18.** to come to life again: . . . *that Christ died for our sins . . . that he was buried, and that he rose again the third day* (I Corinthians 15:3-4). **19.** to end a meeting or session: *The senate rose for summer recess.*
—*v.t.* **1. a.** to cause to rise: *The dogs ran ahead to rise the birds. At almost every cast he rose a fish. He walked so far he rose a blister on his heel.* **b.** to cause to rise above the horizon by approaching nearer to it. **2.** to ascend; mount: *The Americans had to descend into a little hollow and rise a hill on its opposite side* (James Fenimore Cooper). **3.** *Dialect.* to increase; make higher: *to rise the price of provisions* (Lord Nelson).
rise to, to be equal to; be able to deal with: *They rose to the occasion.*
—*n.* **1.** an upward movement; ascent: *We watched the rise of the balloon.* **2.** an upward slope: *a rise in a road. The rise of that hill is gradual.* **3.** a piece of rising or high ground; a hill: *The house is situated on a rise. Slatter's hill . . . was a rise of ground covering perhaps, an acre and a quarter* (Thomas B. Aldrich). **4.** the vertical height of a slope, step, arch, etc. **5. a.** an increase: *The rise of the tide was four feet. There has been a great rise in prices since the war.* **b.** *British.* an increase in wages or salary: *It is a shame his firm won't give him a rise, but money isn't everything* (Punch). **6.** an advance in rank, power, position, etc.: *His rise in the army was swift.* **7.** an increase in loudness or to a higher pitch. **8.** a coming above the horizon. **9.** origin; beginning; start: *the rise of industrialism, the rise of a river, the rise of a storm, the rise of a new problem.* **10.** *U.S. Slang.* a response: *to get a rise out of a person by teasing him.* **11.** the coming of fish to the surface of the water to seize bait, etc.: *Mr. 'Ayward . . . he has plenty of rises but he don't hook them salmon* (Atlantic).
give rise to, to start; begin; bring about; cause: *His queer behavior gave rise to the fear that he was becoming insane.*
[Old English *rīsan*]
—**Syn.** *v.i.* **1.** arise, stand. **10, 11.** appear, emerge. **17.** swell, increase.
➔ In referring to people, **get up** is informal, **rise** is rather formal; **arise** is formal and poetic.

ris·en (riz′ən), *v.* the past participle of **rise:** *He had risen before dawn.*

ris·er (rī′zər), *n.* **1.** a person or thing that rises: *an early riser.* **2.** the vertical part of a step.

ris·i·bil·i·ty (riz′ə bil′ə tē), *n., pl.* **-ties.** the ability or inclination to laugh.
risibilities, the desire to laugh; sense of humor: *The articles are concerned . . . with the writers' lives, sensibilities and risibilities* (Harper's).
[< Late Latin *rīsibilitās* < Latin *rīdēre* to laugh]

ris·i·ble (riz′ə bəl), *adj.* **1.** able or inclined to laugh. **2.** of laughter; used in laughter: *By and by something would be said to touch his risible faculties* (W.H. Hudson). **3.** causing laughter; amusing; funny; comical: *a few wild blunders and risible absurdities* (Samuel Johnson). [< Late Latin *rīsibilis* < Latin *rīdēre* to laugh]

ris·ing (rī′zing), *n.* **1.** the act of a person or thing that rises: *the rising of the sun. Seven o'clock is my hour for rising.* **2.** a fight against the government; rebellion; revolt: *There was a rising now in Kent, my Lord of Norwich being at the head of them* (John Evelyn). **3.** *U.S.* **a.** a quantity of dough set to rise. **b.** the time dough is let rise before baking: *a short rising.* **4.** *Dialect.* an abnormal swelling, such as a boil, tumor, or abscess.
—*adj.* **1.** that rises: **a.** having an upward slope: *rising ground.* **b.** mounting: *a rising temperature, rising anger.* **c.** appearing above the horizon: *the rising sun.* **d.** increasing: *a rising wind.* **e.** advancing in power, influence, etc.: *a rising young lawyer.* **f.** growing: *the rising generation.* **2.** *Prosody.* (of a foot, rhythm, etc.) increasing in stress; having the ictus at the end.
—*prep.* **1.** approaching; about: *a horse rising five years old. Now, rising sixty-seven, he gets to Yankee Stadium daily before the first eager rookie* (Saturday Review). **2.** *U.S. Informal.* somewhat more than: *The enclosure contains something rising forty acres* (Outing Magazine).
—**Syn.** *n.* **2.** insurrection.

rising diphthong, a diphthong having more stress on the second element than on the first, as the element *i* of the diphthong *wi* in the word *win.*

risk (risk), *n.* **1.** a chance of harm or loss; danger: *He rescued the dog at the risk of his own life. If you drive carefully, there is no risk of being fined.* **2.** a person or thing with reference to the chance of loss from insuring him or it: *Very fat men and drunkards are not good risks.* **3.** the amount of possible loss. **4.** an insurance obligation: *Our company has no risks in that city.*
run or **take a risk,** to expose oneself to the chance of harm or loss: *She [Israel] now runs a great risk of bringing Egypt into the fray* (Manchester Guardian Weekly).
—*v.t.* **1.** to expose to the chance of harm or loss: *You risk your neck in trying to climb that tree. A soldier risks his life. To risk the certainty of little for the chance of much* (Samuel Johnson). **2.** to take the risk of: *They risked getting wet.* **3.** to bet; hazard: *to risk $85 on a horse race.*
[< French *risque* < earlier Italian *risco* < *risicare* to dare; (originally) skirt cliffs in sailing < Vulgar Latin *resecum* sharp cliff < Latin *resecāre* shorten, cut off < *re-* back + *secāre* cut]
—**Syn.** *n.* **1.** hazard, peril, jeopardy. —*v.t.* **1.** hazard, endanger, imperil, jeopardize.

risk capital, capital not covered by collateral and invested at the risk of a loss in the hope of profit: *It was risk capital from the United States which sparked many of Canada's major raw material development programs* (Wall Street Journal).

risk·i·ly (ris′kə lē), *adv.* in a risky or venturesome manner.

risk·i·ness (ris′kē nis), *n.* the quality of being risky or hazardous: *Small town banks have to assess the relative riskiness of their loans* (Wall Street Journal).

risk·less (risk′lis), *adj.* without risk: *He characterized these commitments as riskless investments since they are usually guaranteed by a bank* (Wall Street Journal).

risk·y (ris′kē), *adj.,* **risk·i·er, risk·i·est. 1.** full of risk; dangerous: *It's a risky thing getting mixed in any matters with the like of you* (John M. Synge). **2.** somewhat improper; risqué. —**Syn. 1.** hazardous, perilous, precarious, unsafe.

Ri·sor·gi·men·to (rē sôr′jē men′tō), *n., pl.* **-ti** (-tē). the revival of the political movement for the unification of Italy about 1815. [< Italian *risorgimento* < *risorgere* < Latin *resurgere* < *re-* back + *surgere* surge]

ri·sot·to (rē sôt′tō), *n.* a dish consisting of rice cooked in olive oil, then chicken broth, and served with the meat of the chicken, grated cheese, and a tomato sauce. [< Italian *risotto* < *riso* rice, learned borrowing from Late Latin *oryza;* see RICE]

ris·qué (ris kā′), *adj.* suggestive of indecency; somewhat improper: *a risqué joke.* [< French *risqué,* past participle of *risquer* to risk < *risque;* see RISK]

Riss (ris), *n.* the third glaciation of the Pleistocene period in Europe. [< *Riss* River, in southwestern Germany, Alpine locality of the glaciation]

ris·sole (ris′ōl; *French* rē sôl′), *n. French.* a fried ball or cake of meat or fish mixed with bread crumbs, egg, etc.

ris·so·lé (rē sô lā′), *adj. French.* browned in hot fat (in the oven or on top of the stove).

ris·to·ce·tin (ris′tō sē′tin), *n.* an antibiotic drug derived from a species of actinomycete, used in the treatment of pneumonia, meningitis, and other bacterial infections.

rit. or **ritard.,** ritardando.

Ri·ta·lin (ri tā′lin), *n. Trademark.* a drug used as a stimulant in the treatment of mental illness and certain depressive states. *Formula:* $C_{14}H_{13}NO_2$

ri·tard (rē tärd′, rē′tärd), *n. Music.* a gradual slowing down of tempo: *Purists today tend to frown on any kind of slowing up within a composition, unless the composer specifically indicates a ritard* (New York Times). [< *ritardando*]

ri·tar·dan·do (rē′tär dän′dō), *Music.* —*adj.* becoming gradually slower. —*n.* a piece or section of music in this style. [< Italian *ritardando,* gerund of *ritardare* to retard < Latin *retardāre*]

rite[1] (rīt), *n.* **1.** a solemn ceremony: *The church has rites for baptism, marriage, and burial. Secret societies have their special rites.* **2.** a particular form or system of ceremonies: *The Roman Catholic Church uses the Latin rite.* **3.** any customary ceremony or observance: *He omitted such empty rites as saying "Yes" or "Please"* (Arnold Bennett). [< Latin *rītus, -ūs*] —**Syn. 2.** See **ceremony.**

ri·te[2] (rī′tē), *adv.* (of an academic degree, as granted or obtained) in the proper or prescribed manner; not as an honorary distinction. [< Latin *rīte* < *rītus* rite]

rite·less (rīt′lis), *adj.* without rites or ceremonies: *riteless burial.*

rites de pas·sage (rēt′ də pä säzh′), *French.* **1.** the rites and ceremonies that mark such occasions as birth, naming, puberty, and marriage, especially in primitive societies. **2.** (literally) rites of passage.

ri·tor·nel·lo (rē′tôr nel′lō), *n., pl.* **-li** (-lē), **-los, -loes.** *Music.* **1.** an instrumental part in a piece of music written for solo or choral voice. **2.** one of the orchestral parts in a concerto for a particular instrument. [< Italian *ritornello* (diminutive) < *ritorno* a return]

ri·tour·nelle (rē tür nel′), *n. French.* ritornello.

Rit·ter (rit′ər), *n., pl.* **Rit·ter.** *German.* **1.** a knight. **2.** a member of a low order of the nobility in Germany and Austria.

rit·u·al (rich′ů əl), *n.* **1.** a form or system of rites: *The rites of baptism, marriage, and burial are parts of the ritual of the church. Secret societies have a ritual for initiating new members.* **2.** a book containing rites or ceremonies. **3.** the carrying out of rites: . . . *hear the ritual of the dead* (Tennyson). *17 teenagers gravely went through a ritual familiar to Boy Scouts the world over* (Time).
—*adj.* of or having to do with rites; done as a rite: *a ritual dance, ritual laws. As through a zodiac, moves the ritual year of England's Church* (Wordsworth).
[< Latin *rituālis* (adjective) < *rītus, -ūs* rite]

rit·u·al·ism (rich′ů ə liz′əm), *n.* **1.** fondness for ritual; insistence upon ritual: *Perhaps her touch of ritualism came from mere love of any form she could make sure of* (William Dean Howells). **2.** the study of ritual practices or religious rites.

rit·u·al·ist (rich′ů ə list), *n.* **1.** a person who practices or advocates observance of ritual. **2.** a person who studies or knows much about ritual practices or religious rites.

rit·u·al·is·tic (rich′ů ə lis′tik), *adj.* **1.** having to do with ritual or ritualism: *He might be struck by the ritualistic character that the interchange between the two sides came to assume* (Bulletin of Atomic Scientists). **2.** fond of ritual.

rit·u·al·is·ti·cal·ly (rich′ů ə lis′tə klē), *adv.* in a ritualistic manner; according to ritual.

rit·u·al·i·za·tion (rich′ů ə lə zā′shən), *n.* **1.** the act or process of ritualizing: *The first essential for ritualization of combat was to recognize one's enemy as being the same kind of creature playing according to the same rules as oneself* (Ivison Macadam). **2.** the result of ritualizing; being ritualized: *A widespread form of communication among animals and man called ritualization of behavior was discussed at a symposium in London* (New Scientist).

rit·u·al·ize (rich′ů ə līz), *v.t., v.i.,* **-ized, -iz·ing.** to make into or be a ritual: *the ritualized gift-giving of the Kwakiutl, Haida, and other tribes of the Northwest Coast of North America* (Melville J. Herskovits).

rit·u·al·ly (rich′ů ə lē), *adv.* with or according to a ritual.

ritual murder, the killing of a human being as a sacrifice to a deity.

ritz·y (rits′ē), *adj.,* **ritz·i·er, ritz·i·est.** *U.S. Slang.* smart; stylish; gaudy; classy: *Baia, a few miles north of Naples, was Rome's ritziest seaside resort* (Time). [< *Ritz,* name of the palatial hotels in London, Paris, New York, etc., founded by César Ritz, 1850-1918, a Swiss hotelier + English *-y*[1]]

riv., river.

riv•age (riv′ij), *n. Archaic.* a bank; coast; shore. [< Old French *rivage* < *rive* a bank, seashore < Latin *rīpa.* Compare RIVER[1], RIPARIAN.]

ri•val (rī′vəl), *n., adj., v.,* **-valed, -val•ing** or (*especially British*) **-valled, -val•ling.** —*n.* **1.** a person who wants and tries to get the same thing as another; one who tries to equal or do better than another: *The two baseball teams were rivals for the championship. There were no rivals: I had no competitor, none to dispute sovereignty or command with me* (Daniel Defoe). **2.** a thing that will bear comparison with something else; equal; match. **3.** *Obsolete.* a colleague; associate.
—*adj.* wanting the same thing as another; being a rival: *The rival store tried to get the other's trade.*
—*v.t.* **1.** to try to equal or outdo: *The stores rival each other in beautiful window displays.* **2.** to equal; match: *The sunset rivaled the sunrise in beauty. He soon rivaled the others in skill.* —*v.i.* to engage in rivalry; compete. [< Latin *rīvālis* one who uses the same stream < *rīvus* stream]
—**Syn.** *n.* **1.** competitor, contestant, antagonist.

ri•val•i•ty (rī val′ə tē), *n., pl.* **-ties.** rivalry.

ri•val•less (rī′vəl lis), *adj.* without a rival.

ri•val•rous (rī′vəl rəs), *adj.* causing rivalry; accompanied by rivalry; competitive: *Countries become threatened by disintegration and the rivalrous interventions of other powers* (Manfred Halpern).

ri•val•ry (rī′vəl rē), *n., pl.* **-ries.** an effort to obtain something another person wants; action, position, or relation of a rival or rivals; competition: *There is rivalry among business firms for trade.* —**Syn.** contest.

ri•val•ship (rī′vəl ship), *n.* the state or character of a rival; rivalry.

rive (rīv), *v.t., v.i.,* **rived, rived** or **riv•en, riv•ing.** to tear apart; split; cleave: *the anguish and despair that are . . . riving thousands of hearts* (Harriet Beecher Stowe). [< Scandinavian (compare Old Icelandic *rīfa*)]

riv•el (riv′əl), *v.t., v.i.,* **-eled, -el•ing** or (*especially British*) **-elled, -el•ling.** *Archaic.* to wrinkle; shrivel. [< unrecorded Old English *rifel* wrinkle, implied in *rifelede* wrinkled]

riv•en (riv′ən), *adj.* torn apart; split: *It* [*a tree*] *stood up, black and riven: the trunk, split down the centre, gaped ghastly* (Charlotte Brontë). —*v.* rived; a past participle of **rive.**

riv•er[1] (riv′ər), *n.* **1.** a large natural stream of water: *The Amazon River in South America, the largest river in the world, flows into the Atlantic Ocean.* **2.** any abundant stream or flow: *The full-flowing river of speech* (Tennyson).
sell down the river, a. *U.S.* (formerly) to punish (a slave) by selling him to a plantation owner on the lower Mississippi where conditions for slaves were severe: *Huck Finn helped Jim escape before Miss Watson could sell him down the river.* **b.** *Informal.* to hand over to an enemy; abandon in a cruel manner; betray: *Those African leaders . . . have now fallen victims of neocolonialism and sold their fellow Africans down the river* (Manchester Guardian).
[< Old French *rivere* < Vulgar Latin *rīpāria,* noun use of feminine of Latin *rīpārius* of a riverbank < *rīpa* bank, shore]
—**riv′er•like′,** *adj.*

riv•er[2] (rī′vər), *n.* a person or thing that rives.

riv•er•ain (riv′ə rān), *adj.* riverine; riparian. [< French *riverain* < *rivière* river]

riv•er•bank (riv′ər bangk′), *n.* the ground bordering a river.

river basin, the land that is drained by a river and its branches.

riv•er•bed (riv′ər bed′), *n.* the channel or bed in which a river flows.

river birch, a birch tree of the southeastern United States with shiny, reddish-brown bark, that grows along riverbanks and in swamps; red birch.

river blindness, onchocerciasis.

riv•er•boat (riv′ər bōt′), *n.* a boat for use on a river, usually having a flat bottom or very shallow draught: *He ran off . . . to complete his education as a deck hand and pilot on the riverboats of the Southwest* (Atlantic).

riv•er•boat•man (riv′ər bōt′mən), *n., pl.* **-men.** a man who works on a riverboat.

river cow, the manatee.

river crab, any of various fresh-water crabs living in the rivers and lakes of southern Europe.

riv•ered (riv′ərd), *adj.* having a river or rivers. [< *river*[1] + *-ed*[2]]

riv•er•front (riv′ər frunt′), *n.* **1.** the part of a town or city on or near a river or a harbor area: *Most of the town's business houses moved from the riverfront years ago* (Maclean's). **2.** the land in this part: *Out of work in St. Louis,* [*W.C.*] *Handy slept on the riverfront and knew the winter cold* (Newsweek).

riv•er•head (riv′ər hed′), *n.* the source of a river.

river hog, 1. any of various African wild hogs. **2.** the capybara.

river horse, a hippopotamus.

riv•er•ine (riv′ə rīn, -ər in), *adj.* **1.** of or having to do with a river. **2.** situated or living on the banks of a river. [< *river*[1] + *-ine*[1]]

riv•er•less (riv′ər lis), *adj.* without rivers.

riv•er•man (riv′ər man′), *n., pl.* **-men.** a man working or living on or near a river: *Of course the problem of water was as crucial to a rancher as it was to a riverman* (Atlantic).

river otter, 1. any of various otters inhabiting rivers and lakes or the nearby land, having webbed feet and a thick, tapered tail; land otter. **2.** its fur, used to make coats.

riv•er•scape (riv′ər skāp), *n.* **1.** a scene on a river. **2.** a picture representing such a scene.

riv•er•side (riv′ər sīd′), *n.* the bank of a river: *She had . . . come up to a little flat on the riverside not far from Westminster* (John Galsworthy). —*adj.* beside a river; on the bank of a river.

river trout, a brown trout of Europe, introduced into the United States.

river valley, a valley eroded or followed by a river.

riv•er•weed (riv′ər wēd′), *n.* any of various small, submerged, fresh-water plants.

riv•er•y (riv′ər ē), *adj.,* **-er•i•er, -er•i•est. 1.** abounding in streams or rivers: [*He*] *let his camera rove and dawdle among the streets and shops and pubs and quays of rainy, rivery Dublin* (Brendan Gill). **2.** resembling a river; riverlike.

riv•et (riv′it), *n.* a metal bolt with each end hammered into a head: *Rivets fasten heavy steel beams together.*
—*v.t.* **1.** to fasten with a rivet or rivets. **2.** to flatten (the end of a bolt) so as to form a head. **3.** to fasten firmly; fix firmly: *Equally unable to fly or to advance, he stood riveted to the spot* (James Fenimore Cooper).
[< Middle French, Old French *rivet* < *river* to fix, fasten < Vulgar Latin *rīpāre* come to shore < Latin *rīpa* bank] —**riv′et•er,** *n.*

BEAM HEAD RIVET BEAM HEAD
Rivet

ri•vi•er•a (riv′ē ãr′ə), *n.* a pleasant shore or coastline used for recreation. [< the *Riviera,* a section of the Mediterranean coast, famous as a resort]

ri•vière (rē vyer′), *n. French.* a necklace of gems, especially in more than one string: *A sale of jewels from various caskets . . . included an eighteenth-century diamond rivière of 47 stones, graduating to a large centre and with a cluster snap* (London Times).

Riv•o•li's hummingbird (riv′ə lēz), a large hummingbird with green, bronze, and purple plumage, brilliantly iridescent in the male, found from Arizona and New Mexico south to Nicaragua.

riv•u•let (riv′yə lit), *n.* a very small stream: *A fine stream, fed by rivulets and mountain springs, pours through the valley* (Washington Irving). [< Italian *rivoletto* (diminutive) < *rivolo* (diminutive) < *rivo* stream < Latin *rīvus* stream]

rix-dol•lar (riks′dol′ər), *n.* any of various silver coins of the Netherlands, Denmark, Germany, etc., now mostly out of use, which were worth about a dollar. [< earlier Dutch *rijcksdaler* (in Dutch, *rijksdaalder*), (literally) dollar of the realm. Compare RIGSDALER.]

ri•yal (ri yôl′, -yäl′), *n.* the unit of money of Saudi Arabia and Yemen; rial. [< Arabic *riyāl*]

Ri•zal Day (rē säl′), December 30, a legal holiday in the Philippine Islands, the anniversary of the death of José Rizal at the hands of the Spanish.

riz•zar (riz′ər), *v.t. Scottish.* to dry in the sun: *rizzared fish.* [< earlier Scottish *rissered* parched, perhaps < Middle French *ressoré* parched, dried < *re-* again (< Latin *re-*) + *serrer* to stretch (fish in order to dry them)]

RJ (no periods), road junction.

rm., 1. ream (of paper). **2.** room.

r.m., reichsmark or reichsmarks.

Rm., reichsmark or reichsmarks.

RM. or **RM** (no periods), reichsmark or reichsmarks.

R.M.A., Royal Military Academy (at Woolwich, England).

R.M.C., Royal Military College (at Sandhurst, England).

R meter, a roentgenometer: *Most X-ray technicians have R meters, however, and can measure the energy of the beam in terms of roentgens* (Scientific American).

R month, any of the months (September to April) in the name of which an *r* occurs and during which oysters are in season: *In this area clams may be had for the asking almost any day of the year, whereas oysters are relegated to the R months* (New York Times).

rms., 1. reams (of paper). **2.** rooms.

r.m.s., *Statistics.* root-mean-square.

R.M.S., 1. Royal Mail Service (of Great Britain). **2.** Royal Mail Steamship (of Great Britain).

Rn (no period), radon (chemical element).

R.N., 1. registered nurse. **2.** Royal Navy.

RNA (no periods), ribonucleic acid.

R.N.A.ase (är′en′ā′ās′), *n.* ribonuclease.

RNAS (no periods) or **R.N.A.S.,** Royal Naval Air Service (of Great Britain).

R.N.ase (är′en′ās′), *n.* ribonuclease.

R.N.C., Royal Naval College.

RNP (no periods), ribonucleoprotein.

R.N.R., Royal Naval Reserve.

R.N.V.R., Royal Naval Volunteer Reserve.

RNWMP (no periods) or **R.N.W.M.P.,** Royal Northwest Mounted Police (of Canada).

R.N.Z.A.F. or **RNZAF** (no periods), Royal New Zealand Air Force.

Ro (rō), *n.* an artificial language for international use, devised by Rev. Edward P. Foster, of Marietta, Ohio, and later of Waverly, West Virginia, first put forth in 1906. [a coined name]

ro., 1. recto. **2.** roan. **3.** rood.

R.O., 1. radio operator. **2.** recruiting officer.

roach[1] (rōch), *n.* a cockroach. [American English; short for *cockroach*]

roach[2] (rōch), *n., pl.* **roach•es** or (*collectively*) **roach. 1.** a European fresh-water fish with a greenish back, related to the carp. **2.** any of various similar fishes, such as the American sunfish. [< Old French *roche;* origin uncertain]

Roach[2] **(def. 1)**
(to 12 in. long)

roach[3] (rōch), *n.* **1.** an upward curve along the bottom of a square sail to improve the foot of the sail. **2.** the water thrown up behind a seaplane that is taking off or landing. [origin unknown]

roach[4] (rōch), *n. U.S. Slang.* the butt of a marijuana cigarette. [probably < *roach*[1]]

roach•back (rōch′bak′), *n.* the grizzly bear.

road (rōd), *n.* **1.** a highway between places; way made for automobiles or teams to travel on: *the road from Jonesville to New Plymouth. Our road went through the woods. You have to know every bump in the road* (Newsweek). *Abbr.:* Rd. **2.** a way or course: *the road to ruin, a road to peace. Man . . . shows formidable signs of taking the road of the dinosaurs, though by quite another track* (Loren Eiseley). **3.** *U.S.* a railroad: *The road stated that further considerations will be given at the September meeting* (Wall Street Journal). **4.** Also, **roads.** a place near the shore where ships can ride at anchor; roadstead: *The ship continued a fortnight in the roads, repairing some damage which had been done her in the late storm* (Daniel Defoe).
hold the road, to drive or travel on a road easily, smoothly, and safely: *The larger and heavier cars usually hold the road better than the small cars.*
on the road, a. traveling, especially as a salesman: *. . . his star salesman in from a good week on the road* (New York Times). **b.** *Theater, etc.* on tour, as in a theater company: *I was Blanche Wilmot, on the road for ten years, — never got a show in London* (Arnold Bennett).
take to the road, a. to go on the road; begin to travel: *To miss the holiday traffic, they took to the road before dawn.* **b.** to become a

highwayman: *So, I took to the road, and . . . the first man I robbed was a parson* (Jonathan Swift).

the road, the tour of a theater company, etc.: *Since the death, or at least near-death, of "the road," local theatres have multiplied prodigiously* (New York Times).

[Old English *rād* a riding; journey < *rīdan* to ride]

—**Syn. 1.** roadway, turnpike, thoroughfare. **2.** channel, route.

road·a·bil·i·ty (rō′də bil′ə tē), *n.* the ability of a vehicle to travel over roads of all kinds easily, smoothly, and safely: *Safety is built into a car with . . . precise steering, solid roadability and ruggedness* (Newsweek).

road agent, *U.S. History.* a highwayman in the days of stagecoach travel in the West.

road·bed (rōd′bed′), *n.* **1.** the foundation of a road or railroad. **2.** crushed stone and other materials to form such a foundation.

road·block (rōd′blok′), *n.* **1.** a barrier placed across a road to stop vehicles: *The police put up a roadblock to inspect all cars for the escaped convict. The soldiers threw up a roadblock to halt the enemy's advance.* **2.** any obstacle to the progress of something: *Legal roadblocks had been thrown in the way and finally sessions were deferred until next Monday* (Wall Street Journal). —*v.t.* to place a roadblock before; obstruct; block: *The police roadblocked all exits. Her refusal to sign the papers roadblocked the proceedings.*

road·build·er (rōd′bil′dər), *n.* a person who designs or builds roads: *The heedless roadbuilders were defeated and a Fire Island National Seashore was created* (New York Times).

road·build·ing (rōd′bil′ding), *n.* the designing or building of roads: *The Federal Government itself has provided the greatest incentive to reckless roadbuilding by supplying 90 per cent of funds* (New York Times). —*adj.* of or used in roadbuilding; having to do with roadbuilding: *roadbuilding equipment, roadbuilding costs.*

road camp, *U.S.* a camp housing a road gang.

road cart, a light, two-wheeled cart drawn by one horse.

road company, *U.S.* a traveling theatrical group: *The audition routine is the same for a road company as for a Broadway show* (Bruce Savan).

road·e·o (rō′dē ō), *n., pl.* **-e·os.** *U.S.* a contest or exhibition of skill in driving automobiles, trucks, etc.: *Alabama's annual truck roadeo will get under way at 9 a.m. Saturday . . . at Municipal Airport* (Birmingham News). [American English; blend of *road* and *rodeo*]

road gang, *U.S.* a group of prisoners assigned to work on roads.

road hog, *Informal.* a person who uses more of the road than is necessary, especially by driving in the center of the road: *Memorial Day road hogs trying to beat their neighbors to the beach* (Time).

road·hold·ing (rōd′hōl′ding), *n.* the ability of a vehicle to hold the road and be maneuvered at high speeds, especially when cornering: *The roadholding, steering and brakes could not be faulted* (Sunday Times).

road horse, a roadster (def. 2).

road·house (rōd′hous′), *n.* a restaurant on a highway outside of a city, where people can stop for refreshments and sometimes entertainment.

road·less (rōd′lis), *adj.* without roads.

road·mak·er (rōd′mā′kər), *n.* a roadbuilder.

road·mak·ing (rōd′mā′king), *n., adj.* roadbuilding.

road·man (rōd′man′, -mən), *n., pl.* **-men. 1.** a person who builds or repairs roads: *Extra roadmen were put on to renovate the wood paving* (Westminster Gazette). **2.** a person who travels the roads for any purpose, such as an itinerant salesman, truck driver, etc.: *Another method of direct selling is found in the system of canvassers and roadmen sent out by factories* (S. E. Sparling).

road map, a map for automobile travel that shows the roads in a region and indicates distances between cities and towns.

road·mend·er (rōd′men′dər), *n.* a person who mends roads: *Roadmenders on the night shift . . . hammered away with pneumatic drills, bawled "One, two, three, heave," and tossed paving stones about* (Punch).

road metal, broken stone, cinders, etc., used for roads and roadbeds.

road pen, a steel pen with two parallel points to draw roads in mapmaking.

road roller, a steam roller.

road runner, a long-tailed bird related to the cuckoo, living in the dry regions of the southwest United States; chaparral cock. Instead of flying, it usually runs, and can run at great speed.

road show, *U.S.* a traveling theatrical show: *He reached the movies by way of theatrical stock companies and road shows* (Newsweek).

road·side (rōd′sīd′), *n.* the side of a road: *Flowers grew along the roadside.* —*adj.* beside a road: *a roadside inn. Expect to be seeing a rash of roadside billboards soon* (Newsweek).

road sign, a sign along a road indicating speed limits, approaching curves, direction, distances, etc.: [*He*] *kept one eye on his rearview mirror and the other flashing between his speedometer and the road signs* (Maclean's).

road·stead (rōd′sted), *n.* a protected area near the shore where ships can ride at anchor; road: *the inner roadstead of the Port of Toulon* (Joseph Conrad). [Middle English *radestede* < *rade* road + *stede* place]

road·ster (rōd′stər), *n.* **1.** an automobile, common in the 1920's and 1930's, having either no top or a collapsible fabric top, a single wide seat, and, often, a rumble seat. **2.** a horse for riding or driving on the roads. **3.** (formerly) a bicycle for road use. **4.** the driver of a coach. **5.** a person accustomed to traveling on the roads.

Roadster (def. 1) (1924 model)

road·stone (rōd′stōn′), *n.* stone used for roadbuilding.

road test, a test of roadworthiness given to a vehicle: *The car's acceleration is only one of its many attractions, as I found out in a road test* (London Times).

road-test (rōd′test′), *v.t.* to subject to a road test: *The vehicle has been road-tested at maximum speed and has presented no problems* (Science News Letter).

road train, (in Australia) a group of trailers pulled by a truck, used to transport cattle and merchandise in parts of the country where there are no railroads.

road·way (rōd′wā′), *n.* **1.** a road. **2.** the part of a road used by wheeled vehicles.

road·work (rōd′wėrk′), *n.* running along a road, path, etc., as a form of physical training: *At five the next morning he is in Central Park, doing his roadwork — five miles in about forty-five minutes every day before breakfast* (New Yorker).

road·wor·thi·ness (rōd′wėr′ᴛʜē nis), *n.* the ability of a vehicle to perform well on the road: *The Government was given power to secure the testing of vehicles for roadworthiness by the Road Traffic Act of 1956* (Manchester Guardian).

road·wor·thy (rōd′wėr′ᴛʜē), *adj.* (of vehicles) in a suitable condition for use on the road: *Car owners who find that their cars have deteriorated to such an extent that they are no longer roadworthy dispose of them for what they can get* (London Times).

roam (rōm), *v.i.* to go about with no special plan or aim; wander: *to roam through the fields. Herds of horses and cattle roamed at will over the plain* (George W. Cable). *Her eyes were roaming about the room* (Hawthorne). —*v.t.* to wander over: *to roam the earth, to roam a city. Thunder clouds roamed the skies at Taunton yesterday* (London Times). —*n.* a walk or trip with no special aim; wandering: *a roam through the house.* [Middle English *romen;* origin uncertain] —**roam′er,** *n.*

—**Syn.** *v.t., v.i.* **Roam, rove, ramble** mean to wander. **Roam** suggests going about as one pleases over a wide area, with no special plan or aim: *The photographer roamed about the world.* **Rove** usually adds the suggestion of a definite purpose, though not of a settled destination: *Submarines roved the ocean.* **Ramble** suggests straying from a regular path or plan and wandering about aimlessly for one's own pleasure: *We rambled through the shopping district.*

roan (rōn), *adj.* **1.** yellowish- or reddish-brown sprinkled with gray or white. **2.** made of roan leather.
—*n.* **1.** a roan horse: *Beaufort's . . . brougham, drawn by a big roan* (Edith Wharton). **2.** a soft, flexible leather made from sheepskin, used in bookbinding. **3.** a roan color.

[< Middle French *roan* < Spanish *roano,* probably < Germanic (compare Gothic *raudan,* accusative, red)]

roar (rôr, rōr), *v.i.* **1.** to make a loud, deep sound; make a loud noise: *The lion roared. The bull roared with pain. The wind roared at the windows.* **2.** to laugh loudly or without restraint: *The whole audience roared with laughter at the clown.* **3.** to move with a roar: *The train roared past us.* **4.** (of a horse) to make a loud sound in breathing. —*v.t.* **1.** to utter loudly: *to roar out an order. The audience . . . roared its amusement* (Arnold Bennett). **2.** to make or put by roaring: *The crowd roared itself hoarse.*
—*n.* a loud, deep sound; loud noise: *a roar of laughter, the roar of a lion, the roar of a jet engine. The roar of the surf breaking upon the beach* (Herman Melville).

[Old English *rārian*] —**roar′er,** *n.*

—**Syn.** *v.t.* **1.** bellow, bawl, howl, yell.

roar·ing (rôr′ing, rōr′-), *adj.* **1.** that roars; extremely loud: *a roaring lion, a roaring wind.* **2.** characterized by noise or revelry; riotous: *a roaring party. He kept . . . a roaring table at which were collected the loose livers of the country round* (Washington Irving). **3.** *Informal.* brisk; successful: *a roaring trade.*
—*n.* **1.** the act of a person or thing that roars. **2.** a loud cry or sound. **3.** a disease of horses that causes them to breathe loudly. —**roar′ing·ly,** *adv.*

roaring forties, 1. a rough part of the northern Atlantic Ocean, between 40 degrees and 50 degrees north latitude. **2.** the region between 40 degrees and 50 degrees in the south latitude.

Roaring Twenties, the Jazz Age, 1920-1930.

roast (rōst), *v.t.* **1.** to cook by dry heat; cook before a fire; bake: *We roasted meat and potatoes.* **2.** to prepare by heating: *to roast coffee, roast a metal ore.* **3.** to make very hot: *Making a roaring fire, I roasted myself for half an hour, turning like a duck on a spit* (Weir Mitchell). **4.** *Informal.* **a.** to make fun of; ridicule. **b.** to reprove; criticize severely: *The Administration's high-level Business Advisory Council will be roasted by the House anti-monopoly subcommittee for refusing to produce its files for inspection* (Newsweek). —*v.i.* **1.** to be cooked by dry heat; be baked: *Put the meat in the oven to roast.* **2.** to be prepared by heating. **3.** to become very hot.
—*n.* **1.** a piece of roasted meat, or a piece of meat to be roasted: *to buy a roast for Sunday dinner.* **2.** the act or process of roasting. **3.** *U.S.* an informal outdoor meal, at which some food is cooked over an open fire: *a wienie roast.*

rule the roast, to be master, especially master of affairs in the home: *He had it all his own way, and ruled the roast . . . right royally* (Charles Kingsley).

—*adj.* roasted: *roast beef.*

[< Old French *rostir* < Germanic (compare Old High Germanic *rōstan*)]

roast·er (rōs′tər), *n.* **1.** a pan used in roasting. **2.** a chicken, a young pig, etc., fit to be roasted. **3.** a person or thing that roasts.

roast·ing (rōs′ting), *adj.* **1.** that roasts. **2.** exceedingly hot; scorching.

rob (rob), *v.,* **robbed, rob·bing.** —*v.t.* **1.** to take away from by force or threats; steal from: *Thieves robbed the bank of thousands of dollars. The tramps robbed the orchard.* **2.** to take away some characteristic; keep from having or doing: *The disease had robbed him of his strength. The shock of the explosion had robbed him of speech and movement* (Joseph Conrad). —*v.i.* to steal: *He said he would not rob again.*

rob one blind, *Slang.* to steal from someone who is unaware and, usually, trusting: *She* [*owned*] *the bar concession and the bartender was robbing her blind* (Atlantic).

rob Peter to pay Paul. See under **Peter.**

[< Old French *rober* < Germanic (compare Old High German *roubôn*). Related to REAVE[1].]

—**Syn.** *v.t.* **1.** plunder, pillage, loot.

rob·a·lo (rob′ə lō, rō′bə-), *n., pl.* **-los** or (*collectively*) **-lo.** any of a family of carnivorous fishes. Some varieties, as the snook, are esteemed as food. [< Spanish *róbalo,* or Portuguese *robalo* < Catalan, alteration of *llobarro,* ultimately < Latin *lupus* wolf]

rob·and (rob′ənd), *n.* a short piece of spun yarn or other material used to secure a sail to a yard, gaff, or the like. Also, **robbin.** [earlier Scottish *raband,* perhaps < Scandinavian (compare Old Icelandic *rābenda* bend a sail)]

rob·ber (rob′ər), *n.* a person who robs. —**Syn.** See **thief.**

robber baron, 1. a noble of former times who took property unfairly, especially from travelers through his lands. **2.** an American capitalist, in the late 1800's, who acquired wealth through ruthless business methods.

robber crab, coconut crab.

robber fly, any of a family of large, swift flies which prey upon other insects; bee killer.

robber frog, a large frog of Texas found among the rocks on river banks. It has a cry like the bark of a dog.

rob·ber·y (rob′ər ē, rob′rē), *n., pl.* **-ber·ies. 1.** the act of robbing; theft. **2.** *Law.* the felonious taking of property of another from his person or from his immediate presence, against his will, by violence or threats. [< Old French *roberie* < *rober;* see ROB]

rob·bin (rob′ən), *n.* a roband.

robe (rōb), *n., v.,* **robed, rob·ing.** —*n.* **1.** a long, loose outer garment: *Most Arabs wear robes.* **2.** a garment that shows a rank, office, etc.: *a judge's robe, the king's robes of state.* **3.** a covering or wrap: *Put a robe over you when you go for a ride on a cold day.* **4.** *U.S. and Canada.* (formerly) the dressed skin of a buffalo or other animal, used especially for protection against moisture and cold. **5.** a bathrobe or dressing gown.

the long robe, a. the legal profession: *The Houses . . . have likewise appointed a committee of the long robe to declare how the King ought . . . by the law to pass those ordinances* (Richard Montagu). **b.** the clerical profession: . . . *the long-lived gentlemen of the surplice and the long robe* (Punch).

the robe, *Especially British.* the legal profession: *rich advocates and other gentlemen of the robe* (John L. Motley).

the short robe, the military profession: *The king's council was made up of both men of the short robe and of the long robe, representing the army and the law.*

—*v.t., v.i.* to put a robe on; dress.

[< Old French *robe* (originally) plunder, booty < Germanic (compare Old High German) *rouba* spoils, booty, vestments. Compare ROB.]

robe de cham·bre (rôb′ də shäɴ′brə), *French.* a dressing gown.

robe de nuit (rôb′də nwē′), *French.* a nightgown.

robe de style (rôb′də stēl′), *French.* a formal gown with tight-fitting bodice and a full skirt.

rob·in (rob′ən), *n.* **1.** a large thrush of North America, brownish-gray with a reddish breast and white on the lower abdomen and throat. **2.** a small, brownish European thrush with a yellowish-red breast. [< *Robin,* proper name < Old French, (diminutive) < *Robert*]

American Robin (def. 1) (about 10 in. long)

Robin Good·fel·low (gu̇d′fel′ō), Puck, a mischievous fairy of English folklore: *That shrewd and knavish sprite call'd Robin Goodfellow* (Shakespeare).

rob·ing room (rō′bing), *British.* a room where ceremonial robes are put on.

Robin Hood, 1. the legendary leader of a band of outlaws in Sherwood Forest who robbed the rich and helped the poor. **2.** any similar champion of the common people: *Mexicans have argued whether Villa was the Robin Hood he claimed to be or just an ordinary hood* (Time).

ro·bin·i·a (rō bin′ē ə), *n.* any of a group of leguminous trees and shrubs of the central and southern United States, including the locust. [< New Latin *Robinia,* the genus name < Jean *Robin,* 1550-1629, a French botanist and royal gardener at Paris, whose son introduced the genus into Europe in 1635]

robin redbreast, the robin.

rob·in's-egg blue (rob′ənz eg′), greenish blue.

Rob·in·son Cru·soe (rob′ən sən krü′sō), **1.** the shipwrecked hero and narrator of Daniel Defoe's novel *Robinson Crusoe* (1719). **2.** any solitary castaway who survives through his own efforts.

ro·ble (rō′blā), *n.* any of several white oaks, especially a variety of California. [American English < American Spanish *roble* < Spanish, oak tree < Latin *rōbur, -oris* oak tree, heartwood]

ro·bomb (rō′bom′), *n.* a robot bomb. [< *ro*(bot) *bomb*]

rob·o·rant (rob′ər ənt), *adj.* strengthening. —*n.* a roborant medicine; tonic. [< Latin *rōborāns, -antis,* present participle of *rōborāre* to strengthen < *rōbur, -oris* strength; (originally) oak tree]

ro·bot (rō′bət, rob′ət), *n.* **1.** a machine made in imitation of a human being; a mechanical device that does some of the work of human beings: *robot explorers for neighboring planets* (Saturday Review). **2.** a person who acts or works without feeling, in a dull, mechanical way. [< Czech *robot* (coined by Karel Čapek for his play, *R.U.R.*); suggested by Czech *robota* work, *robotnik* serf] —**ro′bot·like′,** *adj.*

robot bomb, a jet-propelled airplane, steered by a mechanical device, without a pilot, which carries a heavy charge of explosives; buzz bomb.

ro·bot·ism (rō′bə tiz əm, rob′ə-), *n.* **1.** the condition of being a robot. **2.** mechanical behavior or character: *It shows how we can avoid robotism and build a society in which the emphasis is on man and not upon things* (Saturday Review).

ro·bot·is·tic (rō′bə tis′tik, rob′ə-), *adj.* of, having to do with, or like a robot; mechanical in behavior.

ro·bot·ize (rō′bə tīz, rob′ə-), *v.t.,* **-ized, -iz·ing. 1.** to make into a robot. **2.** to make mechanical; cause to function like a robot.

ro·bot·ry (rō′bə trē, rob′ə-), *n.* **1.** the condition of being a robot. **2.** robots as a group.

ro·bur (rō′bər), *n.* a species of oak common in England and much of Europe. Its hard, straight-grained wood, used for woodwork is pale when first cut, but on exposure gradually turns very dark. [<Latin *rōbur* oak]

ro·bur·ite (rō′bə rīt), *n.* a powerful, flameless explosive of very high power, consisting mostly of ammonium nitrate, used especially for blasting in mining. [< Latin *rōbur, -oris* strength; (originally) oak tree + English *-ite*[1]]

ro·bust (rō bust′, rō′bust), *adj.* **1.** strong and healthy; sturdy: *a robust person, a robust mind.* **2.** suited to or requiring bodily strength: *robust exercises. Crowds in this country . . . prefer a more robust game* (London Times). **3.** rough; rude: *the robuster sorts of evangelism* (John Galsworthy). [< Latin *rōbustus* (originally) oaken < *rōbur, -oris* oak tree, strength] —**ro·bust′ly,** *adv.* —**ro·bust′ness,** *n.* —**Syn. 1.** hardy, stalwart, stout, sound. See **strong.**

ro·bus·tious (rō bus′chəs), *adj.* **1.** rough; rude; boisterous: *Oh, it offends me to the soul to hear a robustious periwig-pated fellow tear a passion to tatters . . .* (Shakespeare). *A character who warms Marjorie's heart, and the reader's, is her uncle, Samson-Aaron, a robustious clown* (Time). **2.** robust; strong; stout. —**ro·bus′tious·ly,** *adv.* —**ro·bus′tious·ness,** *n.*

roc (rok), *n.* a legendary bird having enormous size and strength, and able to carry off huge animals, famous in such Arabian tales as *Sinbad.* [< Arabic *rukhkh*]

ro·caille (rō kī′; *French* rô kä′yə), *n.* **1.** a style of decoration of the 1700's, based on the forms of water-worn rocks and shells. **2.** rockwork in a garden that combines pebbles and shells in figures of sea gods, dolphins, etc., used as decoration. [< French *rocaille* rockwork, shellwork; see ROCOCO]

roc·am·bole (rok′əm bōl), *n.* a European plant closely related to the leek, used for flavoring in foods. [< French *rocambole* garlic; spice; origin uncertain]

Roch·dale principles or **system** (roch′-dāl), a cooperative system in which profits are divided among the members in proportion to their purchases. [< *Rochdale,* England, the site of the first cooperative store in England]

Roche limit (rôsh, rōsh), a distance of 2.44 times a planet's radius, measured from the planet's center, within which any satellite or heavenly body would be in danger of disruption due to the gravitational force of the planet: *There is no known case of a satellite existing within the Roche limit of a planet, though Saturn's rings lie well inside, and may be the debris of a former satellite which was pulled to pieces* (Listener). [< Edouard *Roche,* a French mathematician of the 1800's]

Ro·chelle powder (rō shel′), Seidlitz powder.

Rochelle salt, a colorless or white, crystalline compound, potassium sodium tartrate, used as a mild saline laxative, in the manufacture of cheese, and in silvering mirrors. The crystals are also used in electronic systems. *Formula:* $KNaC_4H_4O_6 \cdot 4H_2O$ [< *La Rochelle,* France (probably because it was exported from there)]

roche mou·ton·née (rôsh′ mü tô nā′), *French.* a moundlike piece of rock rounded and smoothed by glacial action; sheepback.

roch·et (roch′it), *n.* a vestment of linen or lawn, resembling a surplice, worn by bishops and abbots. [< Old French *rochet* < *roc* cloak < Germanic (compare Old High German *roc, rokkes* coat)]

rock[1] (rok), *n.* **1.** a large mass of stone: *The ship was wrecked on the rocks.* **2.** any piece of stone; a stone. **3.** *Geology.* **a.** the mass of mineral matter of which the earth's crust is made up. **b.** a particular layer or kind of such matter. **4.** something firm like a rock; support; defense: *Christ is called the Rock of Ages. The Lord is my rock* (II Samuel 22:2). **5.** something dangerous, as rocks are to ships. **6.** anything that suggests a rock: *The division of the profits was the rock on which the partners split.* **7.** something hard and uneven. **8.** rock candy: . . . *and fresh supplies of rock being carried into the sweetshops* (London Times). **9.** *Slang.* a precious stone, especially a diamond. **10.** a striped bass. **11.** a rock pigeon.

on the rocks, a. in or into a condition of ruin or failure: *Her marriage . . . went on the rocks in 1929* (Harper's). **b.** *Informal.* bankrupt: *After a year of high costs and poor sales the business found itself on the rocks.* **c.** *Informal.* (of alcoholic drinks) with ice but without soda water, etc.: *Here's where I discovered rum on the rocks* (New Yorker).

rocks, *Slang.* money: *Old man's piling up the rocks* (Rudyard Kipling).

—*adj.* made of rock: *a rock cavern.*

[< Old French *roque* < Vulgar Latin *rocca;* origin uncertain. Compare Old English *stānrocc.*] —**rock′like′,** *adj.*

rock[2] (rok), *v.i.* **1.** to move backward or forward, or from side to side; sway: *My chair rocks.* **2.** to be moved or swayed violently with emotion. **3.** *Mining.* to use a cradle or rocker in gold digging. —*v.t.* **1.** to move back and forth; sway from side to side; tip up and down: *The waves rocked the boat. The earthquake rocked the house.* **2.** to put (to sleep, rest, etc.) with swaying movements: *Mother rocked the baby to sleep.* **3.** to move or sway powerfully with emotion. **4.** *Engraving.* to prepare the surface of (a plate) for a mezzotint. **5.** *Mining.* to wash in a cradle or rocker: *to rock gold-bearing gravel.*

—*n.* **1.** a rocking movement. **2.** rock'n'roll. [Old English *roccian*]

—**Syn.** *v.i., v.t.* **1.** roll. See **swing.**

rock[3] (rok), *n. Archaic.* a distaff. [Middle English *rokke,* or *rooke.* Compare Middle Dutch *rocke.*]

rock-and-roll (rok′ən rōl′), *n., adj.* rock'n'roll: *These songs, with their driving beat and strong, jazzy rhythms, their "rock-and-roll" . . .* (New York Times).

rock·a·way (rok′ə wā), *n.* a light four-wheeled carriage. [American English < *Rockaway,* New Jersey, where many were made]

rock barnacle, any barnacle that attaches itself to rocks by its base rather than a stalk. See **barnacle** for picture.

rock bass, 1. an olive-green fish of eastern North America, about 9 inches long with a dark red iris; redeye. **2.** the striped bass. **3.** the cabrilla.

rock bottom, the very bottom; lowest.

rock-bot·tom (rok′bot′əm), *adj.* down to the very bottom; very lowest: *the rock-bottom price.* [American English < *rock,* probably for *bedrock* + *bottom*]

rock-bound (rok′bound′), *adj.* surrounded by rocks; rocky: *a rock-bound harbor.*

rock brake, any of a group of low ferns of cool areas of the Northern Hemisphere.

rock burst, a sudden, violent bursting of masses of rock from a weakened wall in a quarry, mine, etc.: *The rock burst [may] . . . occur in any man-made excavation if the rock is sufficiently highly stressed before stress relief, in the form of tunnelling, can take place* (New Scientist).

rock candy, sugar in the form of large, hard crystals.

rock cod, 1. a rockfish (def. 2). **2.** a small cod found on rocky sea bottoms or ledges.

Rock Cornish hen, a small hybrid fowl bred by crossing a Cornish chicken with a white Plymouth Rock, eaten as a delicacy.

rock crab, any of several different kinds of crab found on rocky sea bottoms.

rock·craft (rok′kraft′, -kräft′), *n.* skill in climbing rocks and cliffs.

rock crusher, 1. a person or machine that crushes rocks and stones. **2.** *Slang.* an overwhelmingly strong hand in cards: *Her bidding was cautious to a degree requiring a positive rock crusher for anything above the level of one* (London Times).

rock-cut (rok′kut′), *adj.* excavated in solid rock, as many of the cave tombs in Egypt, Asia Minor, and India.

rock crystal, a colorless, transparent variety of quartz that is often used for jewelry, ornaments, etc.

rock dove, a wild pigeon native to Europe and Asia, an ancestor of most common domestic breeds; rock pigeon.

rock drill, a machine for boring into rocks.

rock eel, gunnel.

rock·er (rok′ər), *n.* **1.** one of the curved pieces on which a cradle, rocking chair, etc., rocks. **2. a.** a rocking chair. **b.** a rocking horse. **3.** a person who rocks a cradle. **4.** a tool with a toothed edge, used to roughen the surface of a plate for an engraving. **5.** *Mining.* a cradle. **6.** an ice skate with a curved blade. **7.** an armlike piece attached to a rockshaft. **8.** Also, **Rocker.** *British Slang.* one of a group of teen-agers wearing leather jackets and jeans and traveling in gangs on motorcycles: *A rocker, sun winking on his belt studs, slouched in* (Punch).

off one's rocker, *U.S. Slang.* crazy; mad: *"I felt uncertain about going ahead with such an unusual thing," he told me. "People might think I was off my rocker if it ever got out"* (New Yorker).

rocker arm, an armlike piece attached to a rockshaft in machinery.

rock·er·y (rok′ər ē), *n., pl.* **-er·ies.** a pile of rough stones and soil on which to grow ferns and other plants; rock garden.

rock·et[1] (rok′it), *n.* a self-propelling

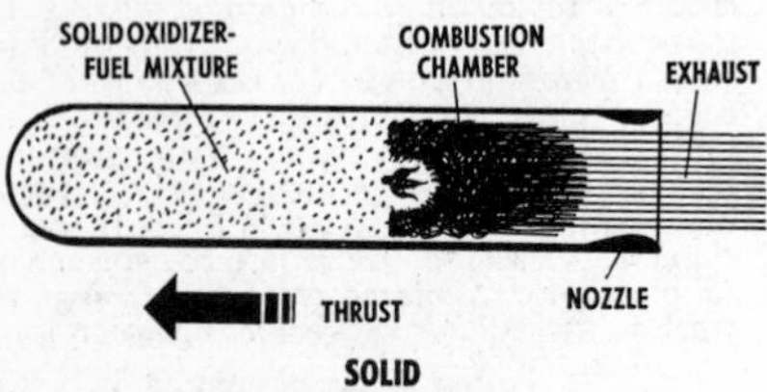

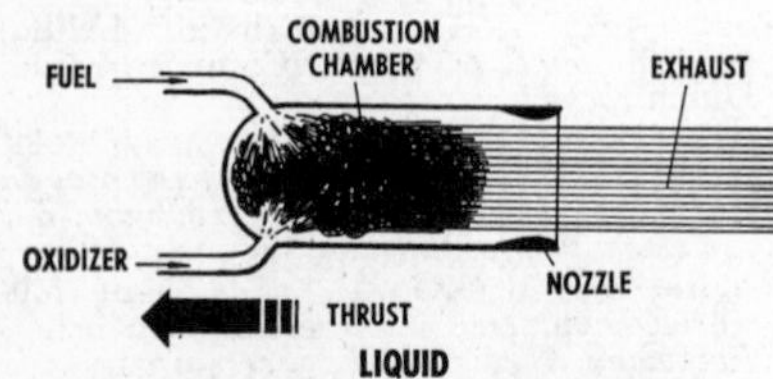

Solid and Liquid Fuel Rockets[1]
In a solid fuel rocket, the solid oxidizer-fuel mixture is already in the combustion chamber. In a liquid fuel rocket, the liquid oxidizer and fuel are fed into the combustion chamber separately. The propellants of both rockets are ignited, and the resultant expanding gases exhaust through the nozzle, producing thrust.

device operating by means of gases escaping from a nozzle or jet at the rear of a combustion chamber. The rocket principle is used in fireworks, signals of distress from ships, aerial targets, some types of projectiles, guided missiles, and as at least part of the driving power in some aircraft. *It should be noted that a rocket does not depend on the atmosphere for its propulsion, but actually would perform better in the absence of an atmosphere because of lessened air resistance* (Sears and Zemansky).
—*v.i.* **1.** to go like a rocket: *The racing car rocketed across the finish line to victory. Overnight the young singer rocketed to fame.* **2.** to fly straight up rapidly: *Pheasants often rocket when disturbed.* **3.** to be put into orbit with a rocket. —*v.t.* **1.** to put into orbit with a rocket: *Russia rocketed a second satellite into space carrying a small dog* (Wall Street Journal). **2.** to attack with rockets: *Rail and supply installations on both coasts were bombed and rocketed by naval ships and planes* (New York Times).
[< Italian *rocchetta,* probably (diminutive) < *rocca* distaff (from the similarity in shape) < a Germanic word]

rock·et[2] (rok′it), *n.* **1.** a garden plant of the mustard family with fragrant white or purplish flowers. **2.** a European plant of the mustard family used as a salad; rocket salad. [< earlier Italian *rochetta,* variant of *rucchetta* < *ruca* < Latin *ērūca* colewort]

rocket belt, a portable, rocket-powered device equipped with controls, used experimentally to propel a person through the air.

rocket bomb, a bomb propelled by a rocket.

rocket booster, a rocket engine used as a booster: *Ballistic missiles, once separated from their rocket boosters, can't be shifted to alternate targets or called back* (Wall Street Journal).

rock·et·eer (rok′ə tir′), *n.* a person who works with rockets, especially an expert in rocketry: *The sphere sent up Wednesday was the largest object sent into space by American rocketeers* (Chicago Tribune).

rock·et·eer·ing (rok′ə tir′ing), *n.* rocketry.

rocket engine, rocket[1].

rock·et·er (rok′ə tər), *n.* a bird that rockets.

rocket gun, a rocket launcher.

rocket launcher, any of various devices from which rockets are launched: *Wardell was attracted to Canada when our troops were first to use his rocket launcher* (Maclean's).

rock·et-pro·pelled (rok′it prə peld′), *adj.* propelled by one or more rockets or rocket engines: *Launching rocket-propelled missiles from a submerged submarine is not a new idea* (Time).

rocket propulsion, propulsion by means of rockets or rocket engines: *Development of new methods of rocket propulsion . . . will make interstellar travel more practical* (Science News Letter).

rock·et·ry (rok′ə trē), *n.* **1.** the science of building, using, and firing rockets. **2.** rockets collectively: *Small satellite spheres would be launched as test vehicles . . . to check the rocketry, instrumentation, and ground stations* (Wall Street Journal).

rocket salad, rocket[2].

rocket ship, a space vehicle using rocket propulsion for its chief or only source of power: *In a rocket ship accelerating toward the moon, a man's weight might be one-tenth of his normal weight, scientists calculate* (Wall Street Journal).

rocket sled, a sled with a rocket engine that operates on a rail and can be quickly accelerated to very high speeds, used in testing human tolerance, seat ejection, parachute opening, etc., under simulated flight conditions: *To toughen up for the physical trials and psychological terrors of space, they will spend hours in low pressure chambers, wind tunnels . . . they will be jolted on supersonic rocket sleds* (Time).

Rocket Sled

rock·et·sonde (rok′it sond), *n.* a rocket used to gather information on that portion of the lower atmosphere which is inaccessible to balloons. [< *rocket* + (radio)*sonde*]

rocket thrust, the thrust of a rocket engine or motor, usually expressed in pounds.

rocket vehicle, a vehicle propelled by a rocket motor or engine, used to carry a missile, satellite, etc.

rock·face (rok′fās′), *n.* the face of a rock or cliff: *Among these sea birds, the homely jackdaws . . . had their nests in crannies of the rockface* (Manchester Guardian Weekly).

rock·fall (rok′fôl′), *n.* **1.** a falling of rock down a slope, in a mine, etc.: *It was a rockfall in a cave in Iraq, probably caused by an earthquake, that killed the primitive man* (Science News Letter). **2.** the fallen rock.

Rock fever, undulant fever; brucellosis. [< the *Rock* of Gibraltar, where it is found]

rock-fill dam (rok′fil′), a dam built of coarse, heavy rocks and stones, graded in size to fit together compactly.

rock·fish (rok′fish′), *n., pl.* **-fish·es** or (*collectively*) **-fish. 1.** any of various fishes found among rocks, especially the striped bass. **2.** any of various groupers of the Atlantic Coast of the United States, such as the bonaci. **3.** a killifish of the Atlantic Coast of the United States. **4.** any of various edible fishes of the Pacific Coast of the United States, as the priestfish.

rock flour, rock meal: *At the beginning of the postglacial period, much of the country was covered with rock flour . . . carried by the moving ice and left* (W. H. Pearsall).

rock flower, any of a group of early-flowering shrubs found in arid parts of the southwestern United States.

rock garden, a garden on rocky ground or among rocks for the growing of flowers, ornamental plants, etc.

rock hind, a grouper found in tropical seas.

rock hound, *Slang.* a person who collects and studies rocks as a hobby.

rock·i·ly (rok′ə lē), *adv.* shakily; weakly.

rock·i·ness[1] (rok′ē nis), *n.* the state of being rocky; being full of rocks. [< *rocky*[1] + *-ness*]

rock·i·ness[2] (rok′ē nis), *n.* shakiness; unsteadiness; weakness. [< *rocky*[2] + *-ness*]

rock·ing chair (rok′ing), a chair mounted on rockers, or on springs, so that it can rock back and forth.

rocking horse, a toy horse on rockers for children to ride.

rocking stone, logan stone.

rocking valve, a cylindrical valve that opens and closes by rotating or oscillating.

rock·let (rok′lit), *n.* a small rock.

Boston Rocking Chair

rock lobster, any of a group of crayfish or lobsters common on the coast of Europe and South Africa; spiny lobster: *Some people complain that all our rock lobster is being exported* (Cape Times).

rock·man (rok′mən), *n., pl.* **-men. 1.** a man who splits slate in a quarry. **2.** a man who operates a jackhammer. **3.** a miner.

rock maple, the sugar maple.

rock meal, Bergmehl; a fine, mealy geological deposit that has been eaten in times of great scarcity.

rock milk, a powdery variety of calcium carbonate; agaric mineral.

rock'n'roll (rok′ən rōl′), *n.* a kind of folk music with a lively, rolling two-beat rhythm that accents every second beat, usually played with guitars, banjos, etc., for singing or dancing: *There is no denying that rock'n'roll evokes a physical response from even its most reluctant listeners, for that giant pulse matches the rhythmical operations of the human body* (Time). —*adj.* of or having to do with rock'n'roll: *rock'n'roll music, a rock'n'roll band.* —*v.i.* to dance to rock'n'roll: *Young Germans rock'n'roll because they like dancing* (Manchester Guardian Weekly).

rock'n'roll·er (rok′ən rō′lər), *n.* a person who plays, sings, or dances rock'n'roll.

rock oil, petroleum.

rock·oon (ro kün′), *n.* a solid-fuel rocket carried by a balloon into the upper atmosphere where it is released. The rockoon makes it possible for small rockets to reach high altitudes. [< *rock*(et) + (ball)*oon*]

rock pigeon, 1. the rock dove. **2.** a sand grouse.

rock pool, a pool of water remaining in a rocky or coral shore when the tide goes out: *There was in this small rock pool a limpet . . . clinging to the rock with all the strength of its single, sucking foot* (Punch).

rock ptarmigan, a brown and white ptarmigan or grouse of arctic America which changes in winter to pure white with a black tail and a black stripe on each cheek. See **ptarmigan** for picture.

rock rabbit, cony.
rock-ribbed (rok′ribd′), *adj.* **1.** having ridges of rock: *The hills rock-ribbed and ancient as the sun* (William Cullen Bryant). **2.** unyielding; rigid; inflexible: *rock-ribbed determination. Jake is a rock-ribbed old die-hard* (Sinclair Lewis). **3.** not likely to fail; sound: *a rock-ribbed bank.*
rock·rose (rok′rōz′), *n.* **1.** any of a group of low shrubs of the Mediterranean region, grown in rock gardens for their showy flowers. **2.** the flower.
rocks (roks), *n.pl.* See under **rock**[1], *n.*
rock salt, common salt got from mines; salt in large crystals.
rock·shaft (rok′shaft′, -shäft′), *n.* a shaft that rocks or oscillates on its journals instead of revolving, such as the shaft of a bell or a pendulum, or the shaft operating the valves of an engine.
rock·slide (rok′slīd′), *n.* **1.** a sliding down of a mass of rock on a steep slope: *Huge rockslides at times bury bulldozers and other machines* (Wall Street Journal). **2.** the mass that slides down.
rock squirrel, a large gray or blackish ground squirrel of the southwestern United States and Mexico.
rock temple, a temple cut out of solid rock, as in India.
rock waste, debris left by disintegration and decomposition of rock.
rock·weed (rok′wēd′), *n.* any of various seaweeds common on the rocks exposed at low tide: *a wagon-load of live lobsters, packed in rockweed* (Hawthorne).
rock wool, woollike fibers made from rock or slag and used for insulation and soundproofing.
rock·work (rok′wėrk′), *n.* **1.** a natural mass of rocks. **2.** masonry made to imitate natural rock. **3.** a rockery.
rock wren, a large, grayish-brown wren common in arid, rocky regions of western North America.
rock·y[1] (rok′ē), *adj.,* **rock·i·er, rock·i·est. 1.** full of rocks: *a rocky field.* **2.** made of rock. **3.** like rock; hard; firm; unyielding: *rocky determination, a rocky heart.*
rock·y[2] (rok′ē), *adj.,* **rock·i·er, rock·i·est. 1.** likely to rock; shaky: *That table is a bit rocky; put a piece of wood under the short leg.* **2.** unpleasantly uncertain. **3.** *Informal.* sickish; weak; dizzy.
Rocky Mountain goat, a goatlike animal of the northern Rockies; mountain goat.
Rocky Mountain sheep, the bighorn.
Rocky Mountain spotted fever, an infectious disease characterized by fever, pain, and a rash, caused by a rickettsia and transmitted by the bite of infected ticks. It was formerly believed to be prevalent chiefly in the Rocky Mountain area but is now known to occur throughout the Western Hemisphere. *Rocky Mountain spotted fever is no longer quite the worry that it was a few years ago* (Science News Letter).
ro·co·co (rō kō′kō, rō′kə kō′), *n.* a style of architecture and decoration with elaborate ornamentation, often combining shellwork, scrolls, foliage, etc., originated in France and much used in the early 1700's. —*adj.* **1.** of or having to do with this style. **2.** tasteless and florid: *... her unsophisticated intelligence gulped down his rococo allurements with peculiar zest* (Lytton Strachey). **3.** antiquated. [< French *rococo,* apparently < *rocaille* shellwork < Middle French *roc* rock[1]]

Rococo Interior (def. 1) in Schloss Bruchsal, Baden, Germany

rod (rod), *n.* **1.** a thin, straight bar of metal or wood. **2.** a thin, straight stick, either growing or cut off: *Jacob took him rods of green poplar, and of the hazel and chestnut tree* (Genesis 30:37). **3.** anything like a rod in shape. **4.** a stick used to beat or punish. **5.** punishment. **6.** a long, light pole; fishing rod. **7.** a measure of length; 5½ yards or 16½ feet. A square rod is 30¼ square yards or 272¼ square feet. **8.** a stick used to measure with. **9.** *U.S. Slang.* a pistol: *He was a show-off when he first got his rod* (Saturday Review). **10.** a branch of a family or tribe: *the rod of Jesse.* **11.** a staff or wand carried as a symbol of one's position: *hands that the rod of empire might have sway'd* (Thomas Gray). **12.** power; authority; tyranny. **13.** a divining rod. **14.** one of the microscopic sense organs in the retina of the eye that are sensitive to dim light: *The eye has two kinds of visual receptors, rods and cones* (Science News Letter). **15.** a cylindrical or rod-shaped bacterium; bacillus.
spare the rod, to fail to punish: "*Spare the rod and spoil the child" is an old saying.*
[Old English *rodd*] —**rod′like′,** *adj.*
rod·der (rod′ər), *n. U.S. Slang.* a hot-rodder: *Any rodder worth his salt knows as much ... about his car as the Detroit professionals* (Wall Street Journal).
rode (rōd), *v.* a past tense of **ride:** *We rode ten miles yesterday.*
ro·dent (rō′dənt), *n.* any of an order of mammals having two incisor teeth in each jaw especially adapted for gnawing wood and similar material: *Rats, mice, squirrels, porcupines, and beavers are rodents.* —*adj.* **1.** gnawing. **2.** of or like a rodent. [< Latin *rōdēns, -entis,* present participle of *rōdere* to gnaw] —**ro′dent·like′,** *adj.*
ro·den·tial (rō den′shəl), *adj.* of or having to do with rodents. [< New Latin *Rodentia* the order name (< Latin *rōdēns, -entis*) + English *-al*[1]] —**ro·den′tial·ly,** *adv.*
ro·den·ti·cide (rō den′tə sīd), *n.* a poison for rats and mice, or other rodents.
rodent ulcer, a malignant ulcer, usually of the face, which slowly works inward, destroying the deeper tissues and bone; noli-me-tangere.
ro·de·o (rō′dē ō, rō dā′-), *n., pl.* **-de·os,** *v.,* **-de·oed, -de·o·ing.** *U.S.* —*n.* **1.** a contest or exhibition of skill in roping cattle, riding horses, etc. **2.** *Western U.S.* the driving together of cattle. —*v.i.* to take part in a rodeo. [American English < Spanish *rodeo* < *rodear* to go around < Latin *rotāre* < *rota* wheel] —**Syn.** *n.* **2.** roundup.
Ro·din·esque (rō′də nesk′), *adj.* having to do with or characteristic of the French sculptor Auguste Rodin, 1840-1917, or his work: *As the artist moves steadily farther from his original Rodinesque realism towards figures of a more symbolic and ambiguous kind, his style retains considerable plastic strength* (London Times).
rod·let (rod′lit), *n.* a tiny rod.
rod·man (rod′mən), *n., pl.* **-men.** the man who carries the leveling rod in surveying.
rod mill, 1. a machine containing metal rollers for forming steel rods. **2.** the part of a plant containing such machines.
rod·ney (rod′nē), *n. British Dialect.* a vagrant; bum.
rod·o·mon·tade (rod′ə mon tād′, -täd′), *n., adj., v.,* **-tad·ed, -tad·ing.** —*n.* vain boasting; bragging; blustering talk: *A day it was of boast, swagger, and rodomontade* (Washington Irving). —*adj.* bragging; boastful; ranting. —*v.i.* to boast; brag. Also, **rhodomontade.** [< French *rodomontade* < Italian *rodomontata* < *Rodomonte,* a braggart king in Ariosto's work < dialectal *rodare* roll away (< Latin *rotāre* rotate < *rota* wheel) + *monte* mountain < Latin *mōns, montis*]
rod·ster (rod′stər), *n.* a person who fishes with a rod. [< *rod* + *-ster*]
roe[1] (rō), *n.* **1.** fish eggs. **2.** the spawn of various crustaceans. **3.** milt. [Middle English *rowe,* perhaps < *rown* (taken as a plural form) < Scandinavian (compare Old Icelandic *hrogn*)]
roe[2] (rō), *n., pl.* **roes** or (*collectively*) **roe. 1.** a small deer of Europe and Asia, with forked antlers. **2.** a hind. [< Old English *rā*]
roe·buck (rō′buk′), *n., pl.* **-bucks** or (*collectively*) **-buck.** a male roe deer.
roe deer, the roe of Europe and Asia. [Old English *rādēor* < *rā* roe + *dēor* deer]
roent·gen (rent′gən), *n.* the international unit of the intensity of X rays or gamma rays. It is the quantity of radiation that would produce, in air, ions carrying a positive or negative charge equal to one electrostatic unit in 0.001293 grams of air. *All nonhibernating gophers exposed to doses of 800 roentgens of X-rays died within fifteen days* (Newsweek). *Symbol:* r (no period). —*adj.* having to do with X rays or gamma rays. Also, **röntgen.** [< Wilhelm K. *Roentgen,* 1845-1923, a German physicist, who discovered X rays]

Roebuck

roent·gen·ize (rent′gə nīz), *v.t.,* **-ized, -iz·ing.** to expose to the action of X rays or gamma rays. Also, **röntgenize.**
roentgeno-, *combining form.* roentgen rays; X rays: *Roentgenogram = an X-ray photograph. Roentgenotherapy = therapy in which X rays are used.* [< *roentgen rays*]
roent·gen·o·gram (rent′gə nə gram), *n.* an X-ray photograph: *It is a roentgenogram of a woman of about fifty* (Harper's).
roent·gen·o·graph (rent′gə nə graf, -gräf), *n.* a roentgenogram.
roent·gen·o·graph·ic (rent′gə nə graf′ik), *adj.* of or having to do with roentgenography; radiographic.
roent·gen·og·ra·phy (rent′gə nog′rə fē), *n.* X-ray photography; radiography.
roent·gen·o·log·ic (rent′gə nə loj′ik), *adj.* of or having to do with roentgenology.
roent·gen·o·log·i·cal (rent′gə nə loj′ə kəl), *adj.* roentgenologic.
roent·gen·ol·o·gist (rent′gə nol′ə jist), *n.* a person skilled in roentgenology: *Several roentgenologists also said chest X-rays should be restricted to areas of high tuberculosis incidence* (Science News Letter).
roent·gen·ol·o·gy (rent′gə nol′ə jē), *n.* the branch of radiology having to do with X rays, especially as used in medical diagnosis and treatment.
roent·gen·o·lu·cent (rent′gə nə lü′sənt), *adj.* permitting X rays to pass through; radiolucent.
roent·gen·om·e·ter (rent′gə nom′ə tər), *n.* a device for measuring the intensity of X rays or gamma rays; R meter.
roent·gen·o·paque (rent′gə nō pāk′), *adj.* that cannot be penetrated by X rays.
roent·gen·o·par·ent (rent′gə nə pãr′ənt), *adj.* that can be seen with X rays. [< *roentgeno-* + (ap)*parent*]
roent·gen·o·scope (rent′gə nə skōp), *n.* a fluoroscope.
roent·gen·o·scop·ic (rent′gə nə skop′ik), *adj.* of or having to do with roentgenoscopy.
roent·gen·os·co·py (rent′gə nos′kə pē), *n.* direct examination with X rays.
roent·gen·o·ther·a·pist (rent′gə nə ther′ə pist), *n.* a person skilled in roentgenotherapy.
roent·gen·o·ther·a·py (rent′gə nə ther′ə pē), *n.* treatment of disease by means of X rays.
roentgen rays, X rays.
ro·ga·tion (rō gā′shən), *n.* **1.** a solemn prayer or supplication, especially as chanted on the three days before Ascension Day. **2.** in ancient Rome: **a.** the proposal of a law by consuls or tribunes to be approved by the people. **b.** a law so proposed. [< Latin *rogātiō, -ōnis* < *rogāre* to ask]
Rogation Days, the Monday, Tuesday, and Wednesday before Ascension Day, observed by solemn supplication.
rog·a·to·ry (rog′ə tôr′ē, -tōr′-), *adj.* that asks: *A judge in one country may issue a rogatory commission to a judge in another asking and authorizing him to collect evidence, question witnesses, etc.* [< Latin *rogātus,* past participle of *rogāre* to ask + English *-ory*[1]]
rog·er (roj′ər), *interj. U.S. Slang.* O.K.; message received and understood. [< *roger,* signaler's word for the letter *r,* used as abbreviation for "received"]
Rog·er (roj′ər), *n.* Jolly Roger; the black flag used by pirates. [special use of proper name]
rogue (rōg), *n., v.,* **rogued, ro·guing.** —*n.* **1.** a tricky, dishonest, or worthless person; rascal: *a rogue and cheat, hardened in crime.* **2.** a mischievous person: *The little rogue has his grandpa's glasses on.* **3.** an animal with a savage nature that lives apart from the herd: *The rogue ... is found among hippopotami, elk, deer, and other granivores as well as among ... the larger carnivores* (Richard F. Burton). **4.** *Biology.* an individual, usually a plant, that varies from the standard. **5.** *Archaic.* a vagrant; vagabond: *To hovel thee with swine, and rogues forlorn, in short and musty straw* (Shakespeare). —*v.t.* **1.** to eliminate defective plants from.

2. to cheat. —*v.i.* to be a rogue; act like a rogue.
[perhaps short for earlier *roger* beggar]
—**Syn.** *n.* **1.** knave, scoundrel. **2.** scamp.
rogue elephant, 1. a savage or destructive elephant driven away or living apart from a herd: *Forest officials and shikaris are searching the countryside ... for a rogue elephant which ... has already killed seven persons* (London Times). **2.** any hostile or dangerous social outcast.
ro·guer·y (rō′gər ē), *n., pl.* **-guer·ies. 1.** the conduct of rogues; dishonest trickery. **2.** playful mischief. —**Syn. 1.** knavery, rascality, fraud. **2.** mischievousness, waggery.
rogues' gallery, a collection of photographs of known criminals.
rogue's march, derisive music accompanying the expulsion of a person from a regiment, community, etc.
ro·guish (rō′gish), *adj.* **1.** playfully mischievous: *with a roguish twinkle in his eyes.* **2.** of, having to do with, or like rogues; dishonest; rascally: *These are the ideas of a roguish merchant rather than a statesman* (H.G. Wells). —**ro′guish·ly,** *adv.* —**ro′guish·ness,** *n.* —**Syn. 1.** waggish, sportive. **2.** knavish, tricky, fraudulent.
roi fai·né·ant (rwä′ fe nā äN′), *pl.* **rois fai·né·ants** (rwä′ fe nā äN′). *French.* **1.** a king whose governing powers have passed into the hands of subordinates (applied especially to the later Merovingian kings). **2.** (literally) idle king.
roil (roil), *v.t.* **1.** to make (water, etc.) muddy by stirring up sediment: *I had ... made a well of clear gray water, where I could dip up a pailful without roiling it* (Thoreau). **2.** to rile: *Some people get roiled up over petty things.* [< Old French *rouiller* to rust, make muddy < *rouil,* and *rouille* mud, rust, ultimately < Latin *rōbīgō, -inis* rust]
roil·y (roi′lē), *adj.,* **roil·i·er, roil·i·est.** *U.S.* **1.** muddy; turbid. **2.** riled; vexed.
rois·ter (rois′tər), *v.i.* to be boisterous; revel noisily; swagger: *these genial, roistering dare-devils [soldiers], who ... are supposed to carry their lives in their hands* (George Du Maurier). —*n. Archaic.* a boisterous fellow; noisy reveler: *an honest, social race of jolly roisters, who had no objection to a drinking bout, and were very merry in their cups* (Washington Irving). [< Old French *ruistre, ruiste* rude < Latin *rūsticus* rustic < *rūs, rūris* the country] —**rois′ter·er,** *n.* —**rois′ter·ing·ly,** *adv.*
rois·ter·ous (rois′tər əs, -trəs), *adj.* noisy; blustery; boisterous. —**rois′ter·ous·ly,** *adv.*
ROK (rok), *n.* **1.** Republic of Korea. **2.** a soldier in the South Korean army.
Ro·land (rō′lənd), *n.* one of Charlemagne's legendary chiefs, famous for his prowess. He and another hero, Oliver, once fought for five days without either's gaining the advantage.
a Roland for an Oliver, one thing thought to be a full match for another: [*He was*] *comforted ... by the thought that he had given Mrs. Carr a Roland for her Oliver* (H. Rider Haggard).
role or **rôle** (rōl), *n.* **1.** an actor's part in a play: *the leading role.* **2.** a part played in real life: *A mother's role is to comfort and console.* [< French *rôle* the roll (of paper, etc.) on which a part was written]
role-play·ing (rōl′plā′ing), *n.* a method of instruction or rehabilitation in which the students or subjects act out real-life situations and discuss and study them. It is used especially in training people to handle problems or in rehabilitating mental patients. *A.M.A.'s instruction in role-playing is provided in special three-day communications "clinics" and also during its three-week executive action sessions* (Wall Street Journal).
role-tak·ing (rōl′tā′king), *n. Sociology, Psychology.* acceptance and performance of rôles set by the culture.
roll (rōl), *v.i.* **1.** to move along by turning over and over: *The ball rolled away.* **2.** to become wrapped around itself or some other thing: *The string rolled into a ball. This wire rolls easily.* **3.** to move or be moved on wheels: *The car rolled along. He rolled onstage in a wheel chair* (Newsweek). **4.** to move smoothly: *Waves roll in on the beach. The years roll on.* **5.** to turn around; revolve: *His eyes rolled with fear.* **6.** (of a heavenly body, etc.) to perform a periodical revolution in an orbit: *The moon rolls about the earth.* **7.** to move from side to side: *The ship rolled in the waves.* **8.** to turn over, or over and over: *The horse rolled in the dust.* **9.** to walk with a swaying gait; swagger. **10.** to rise and fall again and again: *rolling country. Around me the prairie was rolling in steep swells and pitches* (Francis Parkman). **11.** to spread (out); spread (out) with a rolling pin, etc.: *to roll out dough to make a pie crust, to roll out a bolt of cloth.* **12.** to make deep, loud sounds: *Thunder rolls.* **13.** *Informal.* to abound (in); wallow: *to be rolling in money. The authors roll in luxury on the devastation of mankind* (Benjamin H. Malkin). **14.** (of a bird) to warble or trill in song. **15.** (of an airplane) to sway or turn on an axis parallel to the direction of flight: *The rate at which the wing rises, causing the aircraft to roll, depends on several things ...* (G.N. Lance). **16.** *Archaic.* to travel; wander; roam.
—*v.t.* **1.** to cause to move along by turning over and over: *to roll a hoop, to roll a barrel.* **2.** to wrap around on itself or on some other thing: *Roll the string into a ball. The boy rolled himself up in a blanket.* **3.** to move along on wheels or rollers: *to roll a bicycle.* **4.** to sweep along: *The tide was coming in, rolling quite big waves on to the rocks* (W.H. Hudson). **5.** to cause to turn around; rotate: *to roll one's eyes. To roll something between one's hands.* **6.** to cause to sway from side to side: *The huge waves rolled the ocean liner.* **7.** to cause to lie, turn over, etc., as on the back: *The dog rolled himself on the rug to scratch his back.* **8.** to make flat or smooth with a roller; spread out with a rolling pin, etc.: *Rolling the grass helps to make a smooth lawn. Roll the dough thin for these cookies.* **9.** *Printing.* to put ink on (type, etc.) with a roller. **10.** to beat (a drum) with rapid, continuous strokes. **11.** to utter with full, flowing sound. **12.** to utter with a trill: *to roll one's r's.* **13. a.** to cast (dice). **b.** to turn up (a number) on dice: *to roll a seven.* **14.** *U.S. Slang.* to rob (a person who is drunk or helpless), especially by turning him over to search through his pockets.
roll back, a. to cause (prices, wages, etc.) to return to a lower level: *The government ordered the farmers to roll back the prices of crops.* **b.** *Informal.* to set back; cause to fall behind: *Their overrash campaign promises to ... "roll back" the Soviet conquests* (Saturday Review).
roll up, to pile up or become piled up; increase: *Debts roll up fast. The deeper his inquiries went, the stronger the evidence rolled up* (Edward Bok).
[< Old French *roller* < Vulgar Latin *rotulāre* < Latin *rotula;* see the noun]
—*n.* **1. a.** something rolled up; cylinder formed by rolling (often forming a definite measure): *rolls of paper, a roll of carpet or film. A large, wrinkled roll of yellowish sea charts* (Herman Melville). *He pulled out a roll of bills as if to count them* (Rudyard Kipling). **b.** a scroll. **2.** a more or less rounded, cylindrical, or rolled-up mass: *a roll of butter. Her tiny hands, with ... rolls of aged fat encircling the wrist like ivory bracelets* (Edith Wharton). **3.** continued motion up and down, or from side to side: *The ship's roll made people sick.* **4.** a rapid, continuous beating on a drum. **5.** a deep, loud sound: *the roll of thunder.* **6.** the act of rolling. **7.** motion like that of waves; undulation: *the roll of a meadow.* **8.** a roller; revolving wheellike tool used by bookbinders. **9.** a record; list; list of names: *to call the roll. Employment rolls in mid-October stood at 65.2 million* (Newsweek). *Happy king, whose name The brightest shines in all the rolls of fame!* (Alexander Pope). **10. a.** a small piece of dough which is cut, shaped, and often doubled or rolled over and then baked: *a dinner roll.* **b.** a cake rolled up after being spread with something: *jelly roll.* **c.** any food prepared by being rolled up, such as meat. **11.** *Informal.* paper money rolled up. **12.** a part which is rolled or turned over: *the roll in a hem.* **13.** a cylindrical piece of wood or metal used to help move something. **14.** a rich or rhythmical flow of words: *the roll of a verse.* **15.** a rolling gait; swagger: *to walk with a roll.* **16.** a trill or warbling sound, especially of certain birds. **17.** a complete turn made by an airplane about its longitudinal axis without changing the direction of flight.
strike off the rolls, to expel from membership: *If I had ... thrown over a client of mine by such carelessness as that, I'd—I'd strike my own name off the rolls* (Anthony Trollope).
[< Old French *rolle* and *roule,* learned borrowings from Latin *rotula* (diminutive) < *rota* a wheel]
—**Syn.** *v.i., v.t.* **2.** curl, coil. **3.** wheel. *-v.i.* **7,** *v.t.* **6.** rock, sway. *-n.* **9.** roster, register. See **list.**
roll·a·ble (rō′lə bəl), *adj.* that can be rolled.
roll·a·way (rō′lə wā′), *n.* a bed that folds together and can be rolled away when not in use.
roll·back (rōl′bak′), *n.* a rolling back, especially of prices, wages, etc., to a lower level: *An extreme case is the 8½ cent wage rollback recently imposed on Southern Massachusetts textile employes* (Newsweek).
roll bar, a curved steel bar behind the seat of an open sports car that reaches above the heads of the passengers to protect them if the car turns over.
roll book, a book in which a record of attendance or roll calls is kept: *When [a new member] is introduced to the Society, he signs his name in a roll book with a quill pen* (W. M. Parker).
roll call, 1. the calling of a list of names, as of soldiers or pupils, to find out who is present: *Seventeen Congressmen were absent at the Congressional roll call.* **2.** the time of day of such a calling. **3.** a signal for such a calling, as by ringing a bell or sounding a bugle.
roll-call vote (rōl′kôl′), a voting or vote by a roll call, of the members of an assembled body, as in a legislature, society, union, etc.: *In 36 roll-call votes on domestic matters the majorities of both parties in the Senate agreed 18 times.*
roll·er (rō′lər), *n.* **1.** a thing that rolls; cylinder on which something is rolled along or rolled up: *The roller for this window shade is broken. The men used heavy logs as rollers to slide the heavy packing cases onto the truck. Many women use rollers to curl their hair. In the spring, our house was placed on rollers and moved over a block to a new site.* **2.** a cylinder of metal, stone, wood, etc., used for smoothing, pressing, crushing, etc.: *A heavy roller was used to smooth the tennis court. Wet clothes are put between the rollers of a clothes wringer to squeeze out the water in them.* **3.** a long rolled bandage. **4.** a long, swelling wave: *Huge rollers broke on the sandy beach.* **5.** a person who rolls something. **6. a.** a kind of canary that has a trilling voice. **b.** a kind of tumbler pigeon. **c.** any of various crowlike Old World birds that roll about while flying, especially during courtship. **7.** *Baseball.* a batted ball that rolls along the ground in fair or foul territory; grounder: *The relief pitcher caused the first batter to hit a weak roller permitting an out at the plate* (Atlantic). —**Syn. 4.** billow.
roller bearing, a bearing in which the shaft turns on rollers to lessen friction.
roller coaster, a railway for amusement, consisting of inclined tracks along which small cars roll, abruptly dip, turn, etc.
roll·ered (rō′lərd), *adj.* having rollers; mounted on rollers.
roller gate, a cylindrical gate at the top of a dam that regulates water level by rolling up or down an inclined track.
roller mill, a mill that crushes or grinds wheat or other grain by pulling or pushing it between horizontal rolls of steel.
roller skate, a skate with small wheels instead of a runner, for use on a floor or sidewalk.
roll·er-skate (rō′lər skāt′), *v.i.,* **-skat·ed, -skat·ing.** to move on roller skates.
roller towel, a long towel sewed together at the ends and hung on a roller.
roll film, photographic film rolled on a spool.
rol·lick (rol′ik), *v.i.* to enjoy oneself in a free, hearty way; be merry; frolic. [origin uncertain. Perhaps related to FROLIC.] —**rol′lick·er,** *n.*
rol·lick·ing (rol′ə king), *adj.* frolicking; jolly; lively: *A giddy and rollicking company were gathered at Judge Thatcher's* (Mark Twain). —**rol′lick·ing·ly,** *adv.* —**Syn.** sportive.
rol·lick·some (rol′ik səm), *adj.* rollicking.
roll·ing (rō′ling), *n.* the action, motion, or sound of anything that rolls or is being

rolled: *the rolling of a ball, the rolling of thunder.*
—*adj.* **1.** moving forward by continuous rolls: *a rolling ball.* **2.** that moves or runs on wheels: *a rolling cargo.* **3.** rising and falling in gentle slopes: *rolling land, rolling hills.* **4.** swaying from side to side: *a sailor's rolling gait.* **5.** making deep, loud, or swelling sounds; resounding: *rolling thunder.* **6.** continuously sounded; trilled. **7.** heaving; surging: *a rolling wave, a rolling billow of smoke.* **8.** recurring: *the rolling seasons.* **9.** turning or folding over: *a rolling collar.*

rolling chair, a wheeled chair, especially for outdoor use.

rolling hitch, a kind of hitch made round a spar, or the like, with the end of a rope, and which jams when the rope is pulled.

rolling mill, **1.** a factory where metal is rolled into sheets and bars. **2.** a machine for doing this: *The culprit was a "hot merchant mill"—a continuous rolling mill that forms angle iron, I-beams, round stock, sheets and various other shapes from hot steel billets* (Newsweek).

rolling pin, a cylinder of wood, plastic, or glass with a handle at each end, for rolling out dough.

rolling stock, the locomotives and cars of a railroad; wheeled vehicles generally.

roll-on-roll-off (rōl′on′rōl′ôf′; -ôn′-; -of′), *adj.* carrying loaded trucks, railroad cars, etc., that enter and leave under their own power for quick loading and unloading: *a roll-on-roll-off cargo ship. The advantage of roll-on-roll-off service . . . is that a truck's cargo need not be unloaded on one side of a bay or sound, ferried across, then reloaded on another truck on the opposite shore* (Wall Street Journal).

roll-out (rōl′out′), *n. Informal.* the first public showing of something new, as an aircraft, space vehicle, etc.

roll-top (rōl′top′), *adj.* having a top that rolls back: *a roll-top desk.*

roll-up (rōl′up′), *n. Australian Slang.* a meeting; a gathering of people.

roll·way (rōl′wā′), *n.* **1.** a way or place where things are rolled or moved on rollers, especially a place where logs are rolled into a stream. **2.** a pile of logs at the side of a stream ready to be moved.

ro·ly-po·ly (rō′lē pō′lē), *adj., n., pl.* **-lies.** —*adj.* short and plump: *a roly-poly child.* —*n.* **1.** a short, plump person or animal. **2.** a pudding made of jam or fruit spread on a rich dough, rolled up and cooked. [< reduplication of *roll*] —**Syn.** *adj.* pudgy.

Rom or **rom** (rom), *n.* a Gypsy man or boy. [< Romany *Rom*]

rom., roman (type).

Rom., an abbreviation for the following:
1. Roman.
2. Romance.
3. a. Romania. **b.** Romanian.
4. Romanic.
5. Romans (a book of the New Testament).

Ro·ma·ic (rō mā′ik), *n.* the everyday speech of modern Greece. —*adj.* of or having to do with this speech. [< Greek *Rhōmaïkós* (originally) of Rome, of the Roman Empire (in Late Greek, of the Eastern Empire)]

ro·ma·i·ka (rō mā′ə kə), *n.* a popular dance of modern Greece. [< New Greek *rhōmaïkē*]

ro·maine (rō mān′), *n.* a variety of lettuce having long, green leaves with crinkly edges, loosely joined at the base. [< French *romaine* < Old French, feminine adjective, Roman, learned borrowing from Latin *Rōmānus* (probably first introduced at Avignon in the days of the Avignon papacy)]

romaine salad, romaine lettuce served as a salad.

Ro·man (rō′mən), *adj.* **1.** of or having to do with Rome or its people. **2.** of or having to do with the Roman Catholic Church. **3.** roman.
—*n.* **1.** a native, inhabitant, or citizen of Rome. **2.** roman type. **3.** *Informal.* a Roman Catholic (used in an unfriendly way). **4. a.** the Italian dialect of modern Rome. **b.** Latin.
[< Latin *Rōmānus* < *Rōma* Rome < Etruscan (compare *Rūmōn*, Etruscan name for the Tiber)]

ro·man¹ (rō′mən), *n.* the style of type most used in printing and typewriting: *Most of this dictionary is in roman.* —*adj.* of or in roman. *Abbr.:* rom. [< *Roman* (because the style resembles that of Roman inscriptions)]

ro·man² (rô mäɴ′), *n. French.* **1.** a novel. **2.** a romantic tale in verse in old French literature.

ro·man à clef (rô mäɴ′ à klā′), *French.* a novel in which the characters and events represent real persons and events, but the story is told as if it were fictional: *He hints at parallels . . . and, by introducing well-known persons, gives the impression that he is writing a roman à clef* (New York Times).

Roman alphabet, the alphabet originally used by the Romans to write Latin. We use the Roman alphabet, with minor modifications, in writing English. *The early Roman alphabet had about 20 letters, and gradually gained 3 more* (World Book Encyclopedia).

Roman arch, a semicircular arch.

Roman architecture, the architecture of the ancient Romans, characterized by the development of the semicircular arch and vault, the dome, and the use of brick and concrete.

Roman calendar, the calendar of the ancient Romans that had 12 months of irregular numbers of days. The modern calendar is a modification of it.

Roman candle, a kind of firework consisting of a tube that shoots out balls of fire, etc.: *But when carbon 14 is mentioned, he lights up like a Roman candle* (Time).

Roman Catholic, **1.** of, having to do with, or belonging to the Christian church that recognizes the Pope as the supreme head. **2.** a member of this church.

Roman Catholic Church, the Christian church of which the Pope, or Bishop of Rome, is the supreme head.

Roman Catholicism, the doctrines, faith, practices, and system of government of the Roman Catholic Church.

ro·mance¹ (*n.* rō mans′, rō′mans; *v.* rō-mans′), *n., v.,* **-manced, -manc·ing.** —*n.* **1.** a love story. **2.** a story of adventure: *"The Arabian Nights" and "Treasure Island" are romances.* **3.** a medieval story or poem about heroic persons or exploits: *Have you read the romances about King Arthur and his Knights of the Round Table?* **4. a.** real events or conditions that are like such stories, full of love, excitement, or noble deeds: *Mamie beat her head against the bars of a little Indiana town and dreamed of romance and big things off somewhere the way the railroad trains all ran* (Carl Sandburg). **b.** the character or quality of such events or conditions: *Huge cloudy symbols of a high romance* (Keats). *This thing [lighting of the river] has knocked the romance out of piloting* (Mark Twain). **5.** interest in adventure and love: *You have no romance in you* (George Bernard Shaw). **6.** a love affair: *Miss Ailie had her romance* (James M. Barrie). **7.** a made-up story: *Nobody believes her romances about the wonderful things that have happened to her.* **8.** adventure stories, poems and stories of heroes, noble deeds, etc., as a class of literature; romantic literature: *I soon found . . . that the world in reality was very different from what it appeared in poetry and romance* (Richard Graves).
—*v.i.* **1.** to make up romances: *Some children romance because of their lively imaginations.* **2.** to think or talk in a romantic way: *Stop romancing and get down to work.* **3.** to exaggerate; lie: *Now when, for the first time, they told the truth, they were supposed to be romancing* (Macaulay).
[< Old French *romanz* verse narrative; vernacular, as in *romanz escrire* to write in the vernacular, "Roman" language < Vulgar Latin *rōmānicē scrībere* to write in Latin, instead of Frankish < Latin *Rōmānus* Roman < *Rōma* Rome]
—**Syn.** *n.* **1,2.** See **novel.**

ro·mance² (rō mans′), *n.* **1.** *Music.* **a.** a short, simple, sweet melody. **b.** a short melodic piece for a solo instrument or group of instruments, usually in a slow or moderate tempo. **2.** in Spanish literature: **a.** a short narrative poem. **b.** a short lyric. [< French *romance* < Spanish, a poem in stanzas < Old Provençal *romans.* Compare ROMANCE¹.]

Ro·mance (rō mans′, rō′mans), *n.* the group of Romance languages. —*adj.* of or having to do with the Romance languages. *Abbr.:* Rom. [< obsolete French (*langue*) *romance* < Old French *romanz;* see ROMANCE¹]

Romance languages, French, Italian, Spanish, Portuguese, Romanian, Provençal, and other languages that came from Latin, the language of the Romans.

ro·manc·er (rō man′sər), *n.* **1.** a writer of romance. **2.** a person who makes up false or extravagant stories.

Roman Circus, an entertainment of the ancient Romans, involving horse and chariot races, and later, wrestling and games.

Roman collar, a stiff, white band worn around the neck by clergymen, especially of the Roman Catholic faith.

Roman Curia, **1.** the group of judicial and executive departments that make up the governmental organization of the Roman Catholic Church, under the authority of the Pope. **2.** the papal court.

Roman Empire, the empire of ancient Rome that lasted from 27 B.C., when it was established by Augustus, to 395 A.D., when it was divided into the Eastern Roman Empire and the Western Roman Empire.

Ro·man·esque (rō′mə nesk′), *n.* **1.** a style of architecture using round arches and vaults, popular in Europe during the early Middle Ages, between the periods of Roman and Gothic architecture. **2.** a Romance language, especially Provençal.
—*adj.* **1.** of, in, or having to do with the Romanesque style of architecture. **2.** of or having to do with a Romance language, especially Provençal.
[< French *romanesque* < *roman* a roman² (< *romanz* romance¹) + *-esque* -esque]

Romanesque (def. 1)

ro·man-fleuve (rô mäɴ′ flœv′), *n. French.* a saga novel.

Roman holiday, **1.** a savage or barbaric spectacle suggesting the gladiatorial sports of the ancient Romans. **2.** any public event, entertainment, etc., providing enjoyment to some at the expense or through the sufferings of others: *[The] overture . . . was so fierce in its brilliance that one momentarily wondered if Berlioz was being butchered to make a Roman holiday* (London Times).

Ro·ma·ni·an (rō mā′nē ən, -mān′yən), *adj.* of or having to do with Romania, a country in southern Europe, its inhabitants, or their language. —*n.* **1.** a native or inhabitant of Romania. **2.** the Romance language of Romania. Also, **Roumanian, Rumanian.**

Ro·man·ic (rō man′ik), *adj.* **1.** derived from Latin: *French, Italian, and Spanish are Romanic languages.* **2.** derived from the Romans. [< Latin *Rōmānicus* < *Rōmānus* Roman < *Rōma;* see ROMAN]

Ro·man·ism (rō′mə niz əm), *n.* **1.** the spirit or institutions of ancient Rome. **2.** Roman Catholicism (used in an unfriendly way).

Ro·man·ist (rō′mə nist), *n.* **1.** a student of Roman law, institutions, etc. **2.** a member of the Roman Catholic church (used in an unfriendly way). —*adj.* belonging to the Church of Rome (used in an unfriendly way).

Ro·man·is·tic (rō′mə nis′tik), *adj.* **1.** Roman Catholic. **2.** having to do with Roman law. **3.** Romance.

Ro·man·i·za·tion (rō′mə nə zā′shən), *n.* a Romanizing.

Ro·man·ize (rō′mə nīz), *v.t., v.i.,* **-ized, -iz·ing.** **1.** to make or become Roman in character. **2.** to make or become Roman Catholic. **3.** to change or be changed into Roman characters.

Roman law, the system of laws of the ancient Romans. Roman law is the basis of civil law in many countries.

Roman nose, a nose having a prominent bridge: *. . . he had a Roman nose, and his cheek was like the rose in the snow* (Oliver Wendell Holmes).

Roman Nose
Male Portrait Head in Museo Mussolini

Roman numerals, the system of numerals like XXIII, LVI, and MDCCLX, used by the ancient Romans in numbering. In this system I = 1, V = 5, X = 10, L = 50, C = 100, D = 500, and M = 1,000.

Ro·ma·no (rō mä′nō), *n.* a hard Italian cheese with a dry, sharp, salty taste and a black, waxed rind, used grated for flavoring certain dishes. [< Italian *romano*]

Roman punch, lemon ice flavored with rum.

Roman Revival, a style of architecture and furnishings widespread during the first half of the 1800's, imitating classical Roman style and motifs.

Roman rite, the form of Roman Catholic ceremony used in celebrating Mass and in administering sacraments in the diocese of Rome.

Ro·mans (rō′mənz), *n.pl., singular in use.* a book of the New Testament written by Saint Paul: *The book of Romans is addressed to the Christian believers in Rome. Abbr.:* Rom.

Roman sandal, a low-heeled or heelless sandal with the front consisting entirely of equally spaced straps.

Ro·mansh or **Ro·mansch** (rō mansh′, -mänsh′), *n.* a Rhaeto-Romanic dialect of Switzerland: *Rhaeto-Romanic comes directly from ancient Latin and has two distinct dialects,* Ladin *and* Romansh (World Book Encyclopedia). [< Rhaeto-Romanic *rumantsch* < Vulgar Latin *Rōmānicē;* see ROMANCE[1]]

Roman snail, a European snail used for food. Once it was believed to have been introduced into Britain by the Romans.

ro·mant (rō mänt′), *n. Archaic.* romaunt.

ro·man·tic (rō man′tik), *adj.* **1.** characteristic of romances or romance; appealing to fancy and the imagination: *romantic tales of love and war. May thought it would be romantic to be an actress.* **2.** having ideas or feelings suited to romance: *The romantic schoolgirl's mind was full of handsome heroes, jewels, balls, and fine clothes.* **3.** suited to a romance: *soft, romantic music.* **4.** fond of making up fanciful stories. **5.** representing life in literature or art as one pleases; not realistic and not classical: *Romantic writing usually tells about the unusual and adventurous aspects of life, with particular freedom of form and expression.* **6. a.** not based on fact; fanciful; imaginary; unreal. **b.** not customary or practical; fantastic; extravagant; quixotic: *romantic illusions.* **7.** Also, **Romantic. a.** of or having to do with the Romantic Movement. **b.** of or having to do with a group of English poets of the late 1700's and early 1800's whose verse is characterized by a great freedom of form, with special emphasis on the imaginative power of the mind. The Romantic poets include William Wordsworth, Samuel Taylor Coleridge, Percy Bysshe Shelley, Lord Byron, and John Keats.

—*n.* **1.** a romanticist: *His "The Midnight Meditation" is as fine an expression as I know of the romantic's irremediable disconsolation* (Poetry). **2.** a romantic person.

romantics, a. romantic ideas, ways, etc.: *There you are with your romantics again* (William Black). **b.** Usually, *Romantics.* the Romantic poets of England: *The Romantics flourished in the late 1700's and early 1800's.*

[< French *romantique* (originally) romanesque < earlier *romant* a romance, variant of Old French *romanz;* see ROMANCE[1]]

—**Syn.** *adj.* **1.** imaginative, fanciful. **2.** sentimental.

ro·man·ti·cal (rō man′tə kəl), *adj. Archaic.* romantic.

ro·man·ti·cal·ly (rō man′tə klē), *adv.* in a romantic manner.

ro·man·ti·cise (rō man′tə sīz), *v.,* **-cised, -cis·ing.** *Especially British.* romanticize.

ro·man·ti·cism (rō man′tə siz əm), *n.* **1.** romantic spirit or tendency: *You hope she has remained the same, that you may renew that piece of romanticism that has got into your head* (W. Black). **2.** the romantic tendency in literature and art: *Romanticism represents life in its more unusual and exciting aspects and allows complete freedom of form.*

ro·man·ti·cist (rō man′tə sist), *n.* a follower of romanticism in literature or art: *Scott and Wordsworth were romanticists.*

ro·man·ti·ci·za·tion (rō man′tə sə zā′shən), *n.* **1.** the act or process of romanticizing: . . . *made insubstantial by a befuddlement of romanticization* (Edmund Wilson). **2.** the result of romanticizing; a being romanticized: *Some novels are romanticizations of historical truth.*

ro·man·ti·cize (rō man′tə sīz), *v.,* **-cized, -ciz·ing.** —*v.t.* to make romantic; give a romantic character to: *He romanticized his own asceticism* (Atlantic). *This is played in the original scoring . . . and also is broadly romanticized* (Atlantic). —*v.i.* to act, talk, or write in a romantic manner; be romantic.

Romantic Movement, the tendency toward romanticism in Western literature and art of the late 1700's and early 1800's.

ro·man·tics (rō man′tiks), *n.pl.* See under **romantic,** *n.*

Rom·a·ny (rom′ə nē), *n., pl.* **-nies,** *adj.* —*n.* **1.** a Gypsy. **2.** the Gypsies as a group. **3.** the language of the Gypsies: *to . . . speak Romany* (George Borrow).

—*adj.* belonging or having to do with the Gypsies, their customs, or their language: *the wildest Romany beliefs and superstitions* (Walter T. Watts-Dunton). Also, **Rommany.**

[< Romany *Romani* plural of *Romano,* adjective < *Rom* a Gypsy; man, husband]

Romany rye, a person who associates closely with Gypsies. [< *Romany, rye*[2]]

ro·man·za (rō man′zə), *n. Music.* a romance[2]. [< Italian *romanza*]

ro·maunt (rō mônt′, -mänt′), *n. Archaic.* a romantic poem or tale; romance. Also, **romant.** [< Old French *romaunt,* variant of *romant,* variant of *romanz;* see ROMANCE[1]]

Rom. Cath., Roman Catholic.

Rom. Cath. Ch., Roman Catholic Church.

Rome (rōm), *n.* the Roman Catholic Church.

Ro·me·o (rō′mē ō), *n., pl.* **-os. 1.** the hero of Shakespeare's play *Romeo and Juliet,* who died for love. **2.** a passionate lover. **3.** a lovesick young man. **4.** *U.S.* a code name for the letter *r,* used in transmitting radio messages.

Rome·ward (rōm′wėrd), *adj.* directed to, or tending toward, the Roman Catholic Church: *Romeward sympathies, Romeward tendencies.* —*adv.* **1.** in the direction of or toward Rome: *The campers left Naples heading Romeward.* **2.** toward the Roman Catholic Church or Roman Catholicism.

Rom·ish (rō′mish), *adj.* Roman Catholic (used in an unfriendly way). —**Rom′ish·ly,** *adv.* —**Rom′ish·ness,** *n.*

Rom·ma·ny (rom′ə nē), *n., pl.* **-nies,** *adj.* Romany.

romp (romp), *v.i.* **1.** to play in a rough, boisterous way; rush, tumble, and punch in play: *boys and girls romping together and running after one another* (Samuel Butler). **2. a.** to run or go rapidly and with little effort, as in racing. **b.** to win easily: *The favorite horse romped in by four lengths.*

—*n.* **1.** rough, lively play or frolic: *A pillow fight is a romp.* **2.** a girl or boy who likes to romp: *a brisk young creature of seventeen, who was of the order of romps or tomboys* (Thackeray). **3.** a swift but effortless victory in which all others are left behind, as in racing: *to win in a romp.*

[perhaps ultimately a variant of *ramp*[2], verb] —**romp′er,** *n.*

romp·ers (rom′pərz), *n.pl.* a loose outer garment, usually consisting of short bloomers and top, worn by young children at play.

romp·ing (rom′ping), *adj.* that romps; rompish: *The air she gave herself was that of a romping girl* (Sir Richard Steele). —**romp′ing·ly,** *adv.*

romp·ish (rom′pish), *adj.* given to romping. —**romp′ish·ly,** *adv.* —**romp′ish·ness,** *n.*

Rom·u·lus (rom′yə ləs), *n. Roman Mythology.* the founder and first king of Rome, who, together with his twin brother, Remus, was nourished by a wolf. The Romans later identified him with the god Quirinus.

ron·ca·dor (rong′kə dôr′), *n., pl.* **-dors** or (*collectively*) **-dor.** any of various carnivorous fishes of the Pacific Coast of North America. [< Spanish *roncador* < *roncar* snore < Late Latin *rhoncāre*]

ron·da·vel (ron′də vəl), *n.* (in South Africa) a round native hut, usually with a single room. Modernized rondavels with two or more rooms are frequently annexes of hotels. *You might be living in a motel if it were not that your cabin is a thatch-roofed circular hut called a rondavel* (Alan Moorehead). [< Afrikaans *rondawel*]

rond de jambe (rôN də zhäNb′), *pl.* **ronds de jambe** (rôN də zhäNb′), *French.* a circular movement of the leg in ballet, with the moving foot on the floor or in the air.

ron·deau (ron′dō, ron dō′), *n., pl.* **ron·deaux** (ron′dōz, ron dōz′). **1.** a short poem with thirteen (or ten) lines. The opening words are used in two places as a refrain. *The poem "In Flanders Fields" is a rondeau.* **2.** *Music.* a rondo. [< Middle French *rondeau,* variant of *rondel* < Old French. Doublet of RONDEL.]

ron·del (ron′dəl), *n.* a short poem, usually with fourteen lines and two rhymes. The initial couplet is repeated in the middle and at the end. [< Old French *rondel* (diminutive) < *ronde* round[1]. Doublet of RONDEAU.]

ron·de·let (ron′də let), *n.* a short poem similar to the rondel. It has a stanza of five or seven lines on two rhymes, with the opening words or word used as an unrhymed refrain. [< Old French *rondelet* (diminutive) < *rondel* rondel]

ron·di·no (ron dē′nō), *n. Music.* a short, simple form of rondo. [< Italian *rondino* (diminutive) < *rondo;* see RONDO]

ron·do (ron′dō, ron dō′), *n., pl.* **-dos. 1.** *Music.* a work or movement having one principal theme to which return is made after the introduction of each subordinate theme: *One of the remarkable compositions of Mozart's last years, this rondo spaces out a pretty, parlor-music theme with unusual interludes of poignance and even tragedy* (Time). **2.** rondeau. [< Italian *rondo* < French *rondeau, rondel* < Old French; see RONDEL]

ron·do·let·to (ron′də let′ō), *n.* a rondino.

ron·dure (ron′jər), *n. Archaic.* **1.** a circle; round space: *All things rare That heaven's air in this huge rondure hems* (Shakespeare). **2.** roundness. [< Middle French *rondeur* roundness < *ronde* round[1]]

ron·geur (rôN zhėr′), *n.* a surgical forceps for cutting and removing bone. [< French *rongeur* < Old French *ronger* to gnaw < *rougier* (< Vulgar Latin *rōdicāre* < Latin *rōdere*), blended with Old French *rungier* to ruminate < Latin *rūmigāre*]

ron·quil (rong′kəl), *n.* **1.** a food fish of the northern Pacific Ocean. **2.** any fish of the same group. [< Spanish *ronquillo* slightly hoarse (diminutive) < *ronco* hoarse]

rönt·gen (rent′gən), *n., adj.* roentgen.

rönt·gen·ize (rent′gə nīz), *v.t.,* **-ized, -iz·ing.** roentgenize.

röntgen rays, X rays; roentgen rays.

ron·yon (run′yən), *n. Archaic.* a scab (used in an unfriendly way of a woman). [< French *rogne* scab, mange]

'roo (rü), *n.* (in Australia) a kangaroo.

rood (rüd), *n.* **1. a.** 40 square rods; 1/4 of an acre. **b.** 1 square rod. **c.** a measure of length; 6 to 8 yards. **2.** *Archaic.* the cross on which Christ suffered and died: *Socrates drinking the hemlock, and Jesus on the rood* (W. H. Carruth). **3.** a representation of it; crucifix, as a large crucifix at the entrance to the chancel of a medieval church. [Old English *rōd* (apparently originally) pole]

rood beam, a beam across the entrance to the choir or chancel of a church to support the rood, and usually forming the head of a rood screen.

rood loft, a gallery in a church over a rood screen.

rood screen, a screen, often of elaborate design and properly surmounted by a rood, separating the nave from the choir or chancel of a church.

rood stair, a stairway leading to the top of the rood screen or rood loft.

rood steeple, a steeple built over the rood or over the intersection of the nave and transepts.

rood tower, a tower in the position of a rood steeple.

roof (rüf, rủf), *n., pl.* **roofs. 1.** the top covering of a building: *Structural alterations are being made, and the gutters could not take the water from the temporary roof* (London Times). **2.** something which in form or position resembles the roof of a building: *the roof of a car, the roof of a cave, the roof of the mouth.* **3.** a house; home.

raise the roof, *Informal.* to make a disturbance; create an uproar or confusion: *She [would] raise the roof when people didn't do what she wanted them to do* (New York Times).

—*v.t.* to cover with a roof; form a roof over: *rude log cabins, roofed with bark* (George Bancroft). *The trees roofed the glade where we camped.*

[Old English *hrōf*]

roof·age (rü′fij, rủf′ij), *n.* material for a roof; roofing.

roof deck, a flat roof or portion of a roof used for lounging, dining, etc.

roof·er (rü′fər, rúf′ər), *n.* a person who makes or repairs roofs.

roof garden, 1. a garden on the flat roof of a building: *She stayed at a "grand hotel" where there was a roof garden with an excellent view of the city* (New Yorker). **2.** the roof or top story of a building, ornamented with plants, etc., and used for a restaurant, theater, etc.

roof·ing (rü′fing, rúf′ing), *n.* material used for roofs: *Shingles are a common roofing for houses.*
—*adj.* used for roofs: *roofing tile, roofing nails.*

roof·less (rüf′lis, rúf′-), *adj.* **1.** having no roof. **2.** having no home or shelter: *a roofless orphan.*

roof·line (rüf′līn′, rúf′-), *n.* shape or outline of a roof, as of a car: *The new hardtop has a thin roofline that overhangs wrap-around rear-windows* (Wall Street Journal).

roof rat, a long-tailed black rat found about buildings in Europe, southern North America, and South America; black rat: *Later films in the series will show the habits and characteristics of the two most common rats found in the United States, roof rats and Norway rats* (Science News Letter).

roof·top (rüf′top′, rúf′-), *n.* the top of a roof: *The streets, balconies, and rooftops were packed with a clapping, shouting crowd* (Time).

roof·tree (rüf′trē′, rúf′-), *n.* **1.** the main horizontal timber along the top of a roof; ridgepole. **2.** a roof; home: . . . *to seek shelter under a strange rooftree* (Anthony Trollope).

roof truss, a truss in the framework of a roof, as the triangular one formed by two principal rafters and a tiebeam.

roo·i·nek (rō′i nek′, rü′-), *n.* (in South Africa) an Englishman (used in an unfriendly way). [< Afrikaans *rooinek* (literally) redneck < *rooi* red + *nek* neck]

rook[1] (rúk), *n.* **1.** a European crow that often nests in trees near buildings: *The rooks cawed peacefully in the old elms* (John Galsworthy). **2.** a person who cheats at cards, dice, etc. —*v.t.* to cheat. [Old English *hrōc*]

Rook[1] (def. 1) (about 19 in. long)

rook[2] (rúk), *n.* one of the pieces with which the game of chess is played; castle. It is placed at the corners of the board to begin the game, and moves any number of unoccupied squares along a rank or file.
[< Old French *roc* < Arabic *rukhkh.* Compare ROC.]

rook·er·y (rúk′ər ē), *n., pl.* **-er·ies. 1.** a breeding place of rooks; colony of rooks. **2.** a breeding place or colony where other birds or animals are crowded together: *a rookery of seals. Dr. Oliver L. Austin, Jr. . . . promptly led a small troop across 4 miles of unsettled ice to a huge penguin rookery* (Newsweek). **3.** a crowded, dirty tenement house or group of such houses.

rook·ie or **rook·y**[1] (rúk′ē), *n., pl.* **rook·ies.** *Slang.* **1.** an inexperienced recruit: *a police rookie, a rookie in the army.* **2.** a beginner; novice. **3.** *U.S.* a new candidate for an athletic team, especially a professional baseball player in his first season: *Last season he won twenty and was named rookie of the year in the American League* (New York Times). [perhaps alteration of *recruit,* influenced by *rook*[1], in earlier sense "simpleton"]

rook·y[2] (rúk′ē), *adj.,* full of rooks; visited often by rooks: *Light thickens and the crow Makes wing to the rooky wood* (Shakespeare).

room (rüm, rúm), *n.* **1.** a part of a house, or other building, with walls separating it from the rest of the building of which it is a part: *a dining room, a room in a school.* **2.** the people in a room: *The whole room laughed. The room applauded vociferously* (Thackeray). **3.** space occupied by, or available for, something: *The street was so crowded that the cars did not have room to move. There is little room to move in a crowd. I am pent up in frouzy lodgings, where there is not room enough to swing a cat* (Tobias Smollett). **4.** opportunity: *There is room for improvement in Bill's work.* **5.** *Archaic.* place; stead: *The inland counties had not been required to furnish ships, or money in the room of ships* (Macaulay). **6.** *Obsolete.* a position; post; office.
rooms, lodgings: *He travelled . . . to Islington, the locality of Mrs. Harper's latest "rooms"* (Leonard Merrick).
—*v.i.* to occupy a room; lodge: *Three girls from our town roomed together at college.*
—*v.t.* to provide with a room: *The door's open, and if they couldn't room any more guests they'd pretty soon close up, I guess* (Daily Telegraph).
[Old English *rūm*]

room·age (rü′mij, rúm′ij), *n.* room or space afforded.

room clerk, *U.S.* an employee in a hotel, motel, resort, etc., who assigns rooms to guests.

room divider, a panel, screen, set of shelves, etc., used as a partial partition: . . . *the room divider . . . has lately been debased into more or less trivial reproductions of the panels used in Japanese houses* (New Yorker).

room·er (rü′mər, rúm′ər), *n. U.S.* a person who lives in a rented room or rooms in another's house; lodger. [American English < *room* + *-er*[1]]

room·ette (rü met′, rú-), *n. U.S.* a small private bedroom on some railroad sleeping cars, often furnished with toilet and washing facilities.

room·ful (rüm′fúl, rúm′-), *n., pl.* **-fuls. 1.** enough to fill a room: *a roomful of books.* **2.** the people or things in a well-filled room.

room·i·ly (rü′mə lē, rúm′ə-), *adv.* in a roomy manner.

room·i·ness (rü′mē nis, rúm′ē-), *n.* spaciousness.

room·ing house (rü′ming, rúm′ing), *U.S.* a house with rooms to rent.

room·ing-in (rü′ming in′, rúm′ing-), *n.* **1.** living-in; the practice of living in a house in which one is employed as a domestic servant. **2.** lying-in; an arrangement in some hospitals whereby the mother of a newborn baby may keep it in her own room instead of in the nursery: *In both Britain and the U.S., hospitals that allow rooming-in by mothers can be counted on the fingers* (Time).

room·mate (rüm′māt′, rúm′-), *n.* a person who shares a room with another or others: *With a Frenchman and a Greek for my roommates* (J. L. Stephens).

rooms (rümz, rúmz), *n.pl.* See under **room,** *n.*

room service, a special service of a hotel, etc., whereby food, drinks, etc., may be ordered for delivery to one's room: *Entombed as he is, the playwright . . . can count on room service to sustain the slender thread of life* (Harper's).

room·y (rü′mē, rúm′ē), *adj.,* **room·i·er, room·i·est.** having plenty of room; large; spacious: *He lived . . . in a great roomy loghouse* (Theodore Roosevelt).

roor·back or **roor·bach** (rúr′bak), *n.* a false story or slander about a candidate for office, circulated for political effect. [American English; from a damaging statement about the character of James K. Polk, allegedly contained in *Roorback's Tour through the Western and Southern States, 1836,* a nonexistent travel book]

roose (rüz), *v.,* **roosed, roos·ing.** *Scottish.* —*v.t* to praise; extol; flatter. —*v.i.* to boast; be proud.
[< Scandinavian (compare Old Icelandic *hrōsa*)]

Roo·se·velt·i·an (rō′zə vel′tē ən), *adj.* of, having to do with, or characteristic of Franklin D. Roosevelt, 1882–1945, or Theodore Roosevelt, 1858–1919, or their policies as presidents of the United States: *a Rooseveltian New Deal.*

roost (rüst), *n.* **1.** a bar, pole, or perch on which birds rest or sleep: *the sudden rustling in the thicket of birds frightened from their roost* (Washington Irving). **2.** a place for birds to roost in. **3.** a place to rest or stay: *a hermit's roost in the mountains. Sam Lawson . . . continued to occupy his usual roost in the chimney-corner* (Harriet Beecher Stowe).
rule the roost, *Informal.* to be master: *CERN [European Council for Nuclear Research] will rule the roost in high-energy physics until the 30-Bev machine at Brookhaven National Laboratory goes into operation next year* (Time).
—*v.i.* **1.** to sit as birds do on a roost: *Curses are like young chickens, and still come home to roost* (Edward G. Bulwer-Lytton). **2.** to settle for the night.
—*v.t.* to afford a resting place to; accommodate; harbor.
[Old English *hrōst*]

roost·er (rüs′tər), *n.* **1.** *U.S.* a male domestic fowl; cock. **2.** a cocky man or boy. [apparently < *roost* + *-er*[1]] —**Syn. 1.** chanticleer.

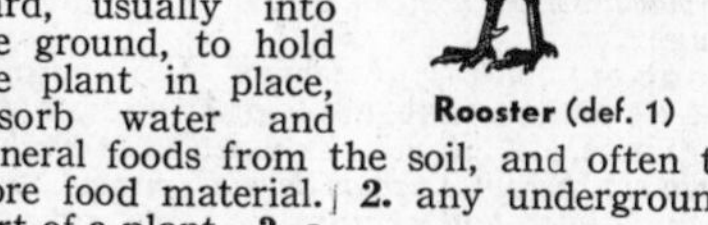
Rooster (def. 1)

root[1] (rüt, rút), *n.* **1.** the part of a plant, that grows downward, usually into the ground, to hold the plant in place, absorb water and mineral foods from the soil, and often to store food material. **2.** any underground part of a plant. **3. a.** something like a root in shape, position, use, etc.: *the root of a tooth, the roots of the hair.* **b.** the bottom of anything: *A burst of water driven as from the roots of the sea* (Shelley). **4.** the thing from which other things grow and develop; cause; source: *There are a thousand hacking at the branches of evil to one who is striking at the root* (Thoreau). **5.** the essential part; base: *to get to the root of a problem.* **6. a.** an ancestor: *myself should be the root and father Of many kings* (Shakespeare). **b.** an offspring: *It was said . . . that In that day there shall be a root of Jesse, which shall stand for an ensign of the people* (Isaiah 11:10). **7.** *Mathematics.* **a.** a quantity that produces another quantity when multiplied by itself a certain number of times: *2 is the square root of 4 and the cube root of 8* $(2 \times 2 = 4, 2 \times 2 \times 2 = 8)$. **b.** a quantity that satisfies an equation when substituted for an unknown quantity: *In the equation* $x^2+2x-3=0$, *1 and —3 are the roots.* **8. a.** a word from which others are derived. *Example: Room* is the root of *roominess, roomer, roommate,* and *roomy.* **b.** the supposed ultimate element of language. **9.** *Music.* the fundamental tone of a chord.

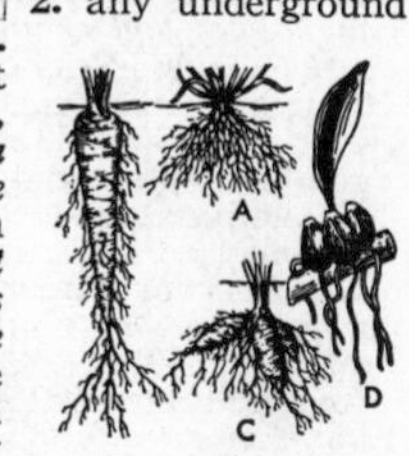

Roots[1]
A, grass; B, carrot; C, sweet potato; D, orchid

take root, a. to send out roots and begin to grow: *Thou . . . didst cause it [a vine] to take deep root, and it filled the land* (Psalms 80:9). **b.** to become firmly fixed: *One of the other secret organizations . . . took root on the coast* (Graham Greene).
—*v.i.* **1.** to send out roots and begin to grow; become fixed in the ground: *Some plants root more quickly than others.* **2.** to become firmly fixed. —*v.t.* **1.** to fix by the root. **2.** to fix firmly: *rooted to the spot. The principle . . . was firmly rooted in the public mind* (Macaulay). **3.** to pull, tear, or dig (up, out, etc.) by the roots; get completely rid of: *to root out common errors and superstitions.* [< Scandinavian (compare Old Icelandic *rōt*)]
—**Syn.** *v.t.* **3.** extirpate, exterminate.

root[2] (rüt, rút), *v.i.* **1.** to dig with the snout. **2.** to poke; pry; search: *to root for an answer.* —*v.t.* **1.** to turn over or dig up with the snout: *The pigs rooted up the garden.* **2.** to search (out); hunt (up): *to root the truth out of the prisoner.* [Old English *wrōtan*]

root[3] (rüt, rút), *v.i. U.S.* to cheer or support a contestant, etc., enthusiastically: *Who you rootin' for, for Republican candidate, Mr. Babbitt?* (Sinclair Lewis). [American English, probably < earlier sense "work hard" < *root*[2]]

root·age (rü′tij, rút′ij), *n.* **1.** the act of rooting. **2.** a being firmly fixed by means of roots.

root and branch, *Especially British.* **1.** radical; drastic; extreme: *Our . . . service is obsolete, requiring root and branch reform* (London Times). **2.** completely; utterly: *Political circumstances have forced him to oppose the Marples programme root and branch* (Manchester Guardian Weekly).

root beer, *U.S.* a carbonated soft drink flavored with the juice of the roots of certain plants, such as sarsaparilla, sassafras, etc.

root canal, a passage in the root of a tooth through which nerves and vessels pass to the pulp.

root cap, a mass of cells at the tip of growing roots that protects the active growing point immediately behind it: *The root cap grows from the inside and its old collapsing outer cells wear off as it is pushed through the soil* (Fred W. Emerson).

root collar, that place at the base of a tree where the swelling and spreading of the roots begin.

root·ed (rü′tid, rut′id), *adj.* **1.** having roots. **2.** having taken root; firmly fixed: *a deeply rooted belief.* —**root′ed·ly,** *adv.* —**root′ed·ness,** *n.*

root·er[1] (rü′tər, rut′ər), *n.* **1.** an uprooter. **2.** a machine that roots out or uproots trees, stumps, etc.: *Ranchmen now rely on mechanical equipment, such as dozers, pushers, rooters and cables and chains . . . to get rid of the pesky shrubs* (Science News Letter). **3.** a thing or person that takes root. [< *root*[1] + *-er*[1]]

root·er[2] (rü′tər, rut′ər), *n.* an animal that digs with its snout. [< *root*[2] + *-er*[1]]

root·er[3] (rü′tər, rut′ər), *n. U.S.* a person who cheers or supports enthusiastically: *The amateur baseball-team . . . made a schedule of games . . . The citizens accompanied it as "rooters"* (Sinclair Lewis). [< *root*[3] + *-er*[1]]

root fungus, fungus growing in symbiotic association with the roots of plants.

root graft, 1. the process of grafting scions directly onto a small part of a root. **2.** a natural joining of the roots of nearby plants.

root hair, a hairlike outgrowth from a root that absorbs water and dissolved minerals from the soil.

root·i·ness (rü′tē nis, rut′ē-), *n.* the quality of being rooty.

root·less (rüt′lis, rut′-), *adj.* having no roots; not firmly fixed or established.

root·less·ness (rüt′lis nis, rut′-), *n.* the state of having no roots; lack of ties to society, traditional values, etc.: *In the confused and precarious rootlessness of the modern world, a growing public seems to have turned to the past, to find . . . consolation* (Newsweek).

root·let (rüt′lit, rut′-), *n.* a little root; small branch of a root.

root maggot, one of several species of dipterous larvae which affect the roots of vegetables and other plants.

root mass, the lump of earth dug up when transplanting a plant, containing and protecting enough of the root system so that the plant can survive the shock of transplantation.

root-mean-square deviation (rüt′mēn′-skwãr′), standard deviation.

root neck, the line of union of the root and stem of a plant.

root rot, a disease which affects the roots of plants, causing decay and death. Fungi or bacteria are either the primary or the secondary cause of the disease. Unfavorable conditions of soil make plants more susceptible to it.

root·stalk (rüt′stôk′, rut′-), *n.* rootstock.

root·stock (rüt′stok′, rut′-), *n.* **1.** a rhizome. **2.** a root that serves as a stock for propagating plants. **3.** an earlier or original form; source.

root symbiosis, a symbiotic relation between certain bacteria and fungi and the roots of the higher plants.

root tubercle, *Botany.* one of the small rootlike growths or nodules produced on the roots of leguminous plants by nitrogen-fixing bacteria.

root·worm (rüt′wėrm′, rut′-), *n.* any of various worms or insect larvae that feed on the roots of plants.

root·y (rü′tē, rut′ē), *adj.,* **root·i·er, root·i·est. 1.** having many roots. **2.** like roots.

R.O.P., run-of-paper.

rop·a·ble (rō′pə bəl), *adj.* ropeable.

ro·pal·ic (rō pal′ik), *adj.* rhopalic.

rope (rōp), *n., v.,* **roped, rop·ing.** —*n.* **1.** a strong, thick line or cord, made by twisting smaller cords together. **2.** *U.S.* a lasso. **3.** a number of things twisted or strung together: *a rope of pearls.* **4.** a cord or noose for hanging a person. **5.** death by being hanged. **6.** a sticky, stringy, mass: *Molasses candy forms a rope.*

give one rope, to let one act freely: *Give this man rope—he's doing our work splendidly* (Thomas A. Guthrie). *Evidently, the best way . . . was to give him plenty of rope wherewith to hang himself* (Julian Hawthorne).

know or **learn the ropes, a.** to know or learn the various ropes of a ship: *The captain, who . . . knew the ropes, took the steering oar* (Richard Henry Dana). **b.** *Informal.* to know or learn about a business or activity: *After spending five years at that state-supported institution, she thought she knew the ropes about teaching* (New York Times).

on the ropes, a. driven against the ropes that enclose a boxing ring: *Clay had the contender on the ropes for most of the third round.* **b.** *Informal.* in trouble: *The Tories are on the ropes. . . . Diefenbaker has destroyed the . . . party as an effective instrument of government* (John T. McLeod).

ropes, the cords used to enclose a boxing ring or other space: *As he entered the ring, the champion leaped over the ropes.*

the end of one's rope, the end of one's resources, activities, etc.: *They have come to the end of their rope: their time is up* (Walter Besant).

—*v.t.* **1.** to tie, bind, or fasten with a rope. **2.** to enclose or mark off with a rope. **3.** *U.S.* to catch (a horse, calf, etc.) with a lasso; lasso: *He dexterously roped a horse* (Owen Wister). **4.** (in mountaineering) to attach (persons) to each other by a rope. —*v.i.* to form a sticky, stringy, mass: *Cook the syrup until it ropes when you lift it with a spoon.*

rope in, *Informal.* to get or take in by tricking: *I knew the first house would keep mum and let the rest of the town get roped in* (Mark Twain).

[Old English *rāp*]

rope·a·ble (rō′pə bəl), *adj.* **1.** *Australian.* uncontrollable; wild; untamable. **2.** *Australian Slang.* (of a person) intractable; obstinate; violently angry. Also, **ropable.**

rope·danc·er (rōp′dan′sər, -dän′-), *n.* a person who dances, walks, etc., on a rope stretched high above the floor or ground.

rope·danc·ing (rōp′dan′sing, -dän′-), *n.* the performance of a ropedancer.

rope of sand, something that cannot hold together; something that only looks like a bond, tie, or means of union: *the only man who could have used aright such a rope of sand as was the Creek confederacy* (Theodore Roosevelt).

rope race, the groove that a rope runs in, in a pulley block or similar device.

rop·er (rō′pər), *n.* **1.** a person who makes ropes. **2.** a person who uses a lasso: *A good roper will hurl out the coil with marvelous accuracy and force* (Theodore Roosevelt).

rop·er·y (rō′pər ē), *n., pl.* **-er·ies. 1.** a place where ropes are made; ropewalk. **2.** *Archaic.* trickery; knavery; roguery.

ropes (rōps), *n.pl.* See under **rope,** *n.*

rope tow, an endless, moving belt of rope driven by a motor for towing skiers up a hill: *Highmount has five rope tows, five slopes, five trails that include runs for the expert, and a ski school* (New York Times).

rope·walk (rōp′wôk′), *n.* a place where ropes are made. A ropewalk is usually a long, low shed.

rope·walk·er (rōp′wô′kər), *n.* **1.** a person who walks on a rope stretched high above the floor or ground. **2.** a ropedancer.

rope·way (rōp′wā′), *n.* an overhead stretch of rope or cable along which heavy objects are carried: *A 27-mile ropeway high in the Himalayas is being built to speed trade between Tibet and northern India* (Science News Letter).

rope yarn, the loosely twisted thread of hemp, or the like, which rope is made of.

rop·i·ly (rō′pə lē), *adv.* in a ropy or viscous manner.

rop·i·ness (rō′pē nis), *n.* the state of being ropy; stringiness.

rop·ing (rō′ping), *n.* **1.** the act of one who ropes. **2.** ropes collectively: *We had on board pretty good store of roping made of mats and flags* (Daniel Defoe). **3.** a ropelike formation.

rop·y (rō′pē), *adj.,* **rop·i·er, rop·i·est. 1.** forming sticky threads; stringy: *ropy syrup.* **2.** like a rope or ropes.

roque (rōk), *n.* a form of croquet played on a hard-rolled court and modified so as to demand greater skill: *Hustling for votes in Long Beach last month, he tried his hand at roque* (Time). [abstracted from *croquet*]

Roque·fort (rōk′fərt), *n.* **1.** a strongly flavored French cheese made of sheep's milk, veined with mold: *Roquefort, a French blue veined cheese, is perhaps the best example of a cheese that is till today definitely "regional"* (London Times). **2.** a cheese of similar flavor, made from cows' milk. [< *Roquefort,* a town in France, where originally made]

roq·ue·laure (rok′ə lôr, -lōr; *French* rôk-lōr′), *n.* a man's cloak reaching to the knee, worn during the 1700's and early 1800's: *a closely buttoned . . . roquelaure which enveloped him* (Edgar Allan Poe). [< French *roquelaure* < the Duc de *Roquelaure,* 1656-1738, who popularized it]

ro·quet (rō kā′), *v.,* **-queted** (-kād′), **-quet·ing** (-kā′ing), *n.* in croquet and roque: —*v.t.* **1.** to strike (another player's ball) with the ball being played. **2.** (of a ball) to make contact with (another ball). —*v.i.* to strike another ball with one's own ball in play. —*n.* the act of roqueting. [alteration of *croquet.* Compare ROQUE.]

ro·quette (rō ket′), *n.* rocket salad, a plant of the mustard family; rocket.

ro·ric (rôr′ik, rōr′-), *adj.* dewlike. [< Latin *rōs, rōris* dew + English *-ic*]

ror·qual (rôr′kwəl), *n.* any of the whalebone whales having a dorsal fin, especially a species of the Atlantic, Pacific, and Antarctic which grows 40 to 60 feet long; finback; razorback: *The blue whale belongs to the rorqual, or finback, group* (Scientific American). [< French *rorqual* < Norwegian *røyrkval,* perhaps < Old Icelandic *reytharhvalr* < *reythr* rorqual + *hvalr* whale]

Rorqual
(40 to 60 ft. long)

Ror·schach test (rôr′shäk), a psychological test for determining personality traits, based on the subject's response to ten different standardized inkblot designs. [< Hermann *Rorschach,* 1884-1922, a Swiss psychiatrist]

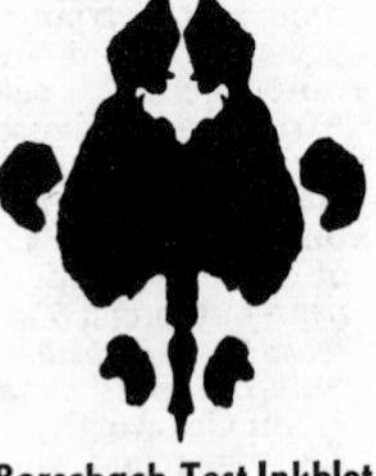

Rorschach Test Inkblot

ro·sace (rō′zās), *n.* a highly decorative circular ornament on a building, as a rondel filled with sculpture. [< Middle French *rosace* < *rose* rose]

ro·sa·ceous (rō zā′shəs), *adj.* **1.** belonging to the rose family. **2.** like a rose in form. **3.** rose-colored. [< Latin *rosāceus* (with English *-ous*) < *rosa* rose[1]] —**Syn. 3.** roseate.

ro·sa·lia (rō zāl′yə), *n. Music.* a form of melody in which a phrase or figure is repeated two or three times, each time a step or a half-step higher. [< Italian *rosalia* < *Rosalia, mia cara,* an old Italian popular song]

Ros·a·lind (roz′ə lind, -līnd), *n.* the heroine of Shakespeare's comedy *As You Like It.*

ros·an·i·lin (rō zan′ə lin), *n.* rosaniline.

ros·an·i·line (rō zan′ə lēn, -lin, -līn), *n.* **1.** a crystalline base derived from aniline, forming salts which yield red and other dyes. *Formula:* $C_{20}H_{21}N_3O$ **2.** any of the dyes obtained from this compound. [< *ros*(e) + *aniline*]

ro·sar·i·an (rō zãr′ē ən), *n.* a person who cultivates roses: *I am going to try a method of planting recommended to me by a consulting rosarian of the American Rose Society* (New York Times). [< Latin *rosārium* rose garden + English *-an*]

ro·sar·i·um (rō zãr′ē əm), *n., pl.* **-i·ums, -i·a** (-ē ə). a rose garden. [< Latin *rosārium* < *rosa* rose[1]]

ro·sa·ry (rō′zər ē), *n., pl.* **-ries. 1.** a string of beads for keeping count in saying a series of prayers: *The lama . . . fingered his rosary awhile* (Rudyard Kipling). **2. a.** a series of prayers consisting of a specified number of Aves (salutations to the Virgin Mary), of paternosters (repetitions of the Lord's Prayer), and Glorias (or doxologies). **b.** a string of beads of various sizes representing the same number of aves, paternosters, and glorias respectively, used for marking off these prayers. **3.** a rose garden; rose bed: *The rosary today displays a marvelous collection of 1,200 different roses* (New York Times). [< Medieval Latin *rosarium* < Latin *rosārium* rose garden < *rosa* rose[1]]

rosary pea, a tropical climbing shrub of the pea family whose seeds are used for beads and in rosaries; Indian licorice.

rose[1] (rōz), *n., adj., v.,* **rosed, ros·ing.** —*n.* **1.** a flower that grows on a bush with thorny stems. Roses are red, pink, white, or yellow and usually smell very sweet. Wild roses have one circle of petals; cultivated roses usually have more than one circle and are sometimes even cabbage-shaped in body. The rose is the state flower of Iowa, New York, and North Dakota. *Red as a rose is she* (Samuel Taylor Coleridge). *That which we call a rose by any other name would smell as sweet* (Shakespeare). **2.** the bush itself. **3.** any of various related or similar plants or flowers. **4.** a pinkish-red color: *shows in her cheek the roses of eighteen* (Alexander Pope). **5.** a perfume made from roses. **6.** something shaped like a rose or suggesting a rose: **a.** a rosette. **b.** the sprinkling nozzle of a water pot. **c.** a gem cut out with faceted top and flat base. **7.** a woman of great beauty, loveliness, or excellence. **8. a.** the compass card or the thirty-two-pointed figure on it showing the points of the compass. **b.** a thirty-two- or three-hundred-and-sixty-pointed figure printed on a map and showing compass directions.

under the rose, in secret; privately; sub rosa: *There was even a story told, with great mystery, and under the rose, of his having shot the devil with a silver bullet* (Washington Irving).

—*adj.* pinkish-red.

—*v.t.* **1.** to make rosy: *Till all the sails were darken'd in the west, And rosed in the east* (Tennyson). **2.** to scent or perfume with rose.

[Old English *rose, rōse* < Latin *rosa*] —**rose′like′,** *adj.*

rose[2] (rōz), *v.* the past tense of **rise.**

ro·sé or **Ro·sé** (rō zā′), *n.* a pink table wine: *Any normally white wine can be converted into a rosé simply by leaving the new wine in contact with the grapeskins for a bit longer than is usual* (New Yorker). [< French *rosé* (originally) pink < Old French *rose* rose[1], learned borrowing from Latin *rosa*]

rose acacia, a shrub of the pea family, a variety of locust, with large, rose-colored flowers, growing in the mountains from Virginia to Georgia.

ro·se·al (rō′zē əl), *adj.* rosy: *a roseal warmth of color* (Eden Phillpotts).

ro·se·ate (rō′zē it, -āt), *adj.* **1.** rose-colored; rosy: *the roseate glow of dawn.* **2.** cheerful: *the roseate face of a happy child.* **3.** optimistic: *roseate dreams of the future.* [< Latin *roseus* rosy (< *rosa* rose[1]) + English *-ate*[1]] —**ro′se·ate·ly,** *adv.*

roseate spoonbill, a spoonbill of warm or tropical parts of America, with plumage chiefly pink deepening in parts to red.

roseate tern, a black-capped tern of the coasts of temperate and tropical regions, with a blackish bill and slightly pinkish under parts.

rose·bay (rōz′bā′), *n.* **1.** the oleander. **2.** the rhododendron. **3.** the willow herb.

rose beetle, the rose bug.

rose-breast·ed grosbeak (rōz′bres′tid), a grosbeak of eastern North America, the male of which has a black head and back, white under parts, and a large triangle of rose on its breast. See **grosbeak** for picture.

rose·bud (rōz′bud′), *n.* the bud of a rose.

rose bug, a tan-colored bug destructive to roses, peonies, and certain other garden plants, especially by eating the blossoms.

rose·bush (rōz′bu̇sh′), *n.* a shrub or vine bearing roses.

rose campion, 1. a kind of pink with crimson flowers. **2.** the red corn cockle.

rose chafer, the rose beetle or bug.

rose cold, hay fever caused by pollen from roses and other plants.

rose color, a pinkish red.

rose-col·ored (rōz′kul′ərd), *adj.* **1.** pinkish-red. **2.** bright; cheerful; optimistic: *The colonel was . . . full of his rose-colored plans for the future* (Francis H. Smith).

rose comb, a type of low comb on certain breeds of chickens, as the Dominque, Wyandotte, and Hamburg, that is covered with rounded points and has a spike extending to the rear.

rose disease, erysipelas (of swine), in which reddish patches appear on the skin.

rose engine, a lathe for making decorative combinations of curved lines, as on watch-cases and on plates for printing banknotes, bonds, etc.

rose family, a large group of dicotyledonous trees, shrubs, and herbs, including the apple, pear, blackberry, spirea, hawthorn, and rose. Typical members of the rose family have alternate leaves, five-petaled flowers, and fruits with many seeds, and are dicots.

rose fever, rose cold: *A good many who are sneezing and sniffling in the spring, however, are victims of early hay fever, or rose fever as it used to be called, from pollens that are blown on spring breezes* (Science News Letter).

rose·fish (rōz′fish′), *n., pl.* **-fish·es** or (*collectively*) **-fish.** a food fish, mostly red in color, of the North Atlantic, now frozen and sold widely throughout the United States (under various names): *European and U.S. fishermen are taking cod, halibut, and rosefish ("ocean perch") further and further north in the Atlantic* (Newsweek).

rose geranium, any of a group of geraniums with fragrant, narrowly divided leaves, and small, pinkish flowers.

rose head, 1. a sprinkler nozzle with many small openings for making a spray. **2. a.** the head on a nail or spike with corrugations or facets. **b.** a nail having such a head.

rose hip, the fruit of the rose.

rose leaf, the petal of a rose.

ro·se·lite (rō′zə līt), *n.* a rose-colored mineral, an arsenate of calcium, cobalt, and magnesium.

ro·selle (rō zel′), *n.* a hibiscus native to tropical regions of the Old World, grown for its edible red calyx and involucre, and for a fiber made from its stem. [origin unknown]

rose mallow, any of a group of plants of the mallow family; hibiscus; mallow rose. The musk mallow and okra are rose mallows.

rose·mar·y (rōz′mãr′ē), *n., pl.* **-mar·ies.** an evergreen shrub of the mint family, native to southern Europe, whose leaves yield a fragrant oil used in making perfume, and are also much used in cooking. Rosemary is a symbol of remembrance. [earlier *rosmarine* < Latin *rōsmarīnus* (literally) dew of the sea < *rōs, rōris* dew + *marīnus* marine; influenced by *rose*[1] and *Mary*]

Sprig of Rosemary

rose moss, the garden plant portulaca.

rose noble, an English gold coin bearing an imprint of a rose on its face, first issued by Edward IV and then worth ten shillings: *Do away with the coin and you kill the phrase; no one cites saws about groats or rose nobles* (Punch).

rose of Jericho, a small plant of the mustard family, native to the arid deserts of southwestern Asia and northeastern Africa; resurrection plant. It rolls up as it dries but will open again when kept wet.

rose of Sharon, 1. a shrub of the mallow family with bright flowers; althea. **2.** a plant mentioned in the Bible, a kind of St.-John's-wort. **3.** a flower, identified as the autumn crocus, in the Revised Version of the Bible. Canticles (Psalms) 2:1.

ro·se·o·la (rō zē′ə lə), *n.* **1.** any rosy rash that occurs with various fevers: *Scientists finally have determined the cause of roseola or "baby measles," a common disease of infants* (Science News Letter). **2.** German measles. [< New Latin *roseola* (diminutive) < Latin *roseus* rosy < *rosa* rose[1]]

ro·se·o·lar (rō zē′ə lər), *adj.* **1.** of or having to do with roseola. **2.** showing a roseola.

rose pink, a soft, light pink color; rose color. —**rose′-pink′,** *adj.*

rose·point (rōz′point′), *n.* a fine lace first made in Venice, with raised flowers in large patterns: *She wore a gown of ivory satin, trimmed at the bodice with heirloom rosepoint lace worn by her mother and grandmother at their weddings* (New York Times).

rose quartz, a translucent or transparent quartz, varying in color from light rose-red to dark-pink: *Rose quartz . . . is colored by compounds of titanium or manganese* (Fenton and Fenton).

rose rash, roseola.

rose red, red with a tinge of purple.

rose-red (rōz′red′), *adj.* rose red in color.

rose scale, a scale insect occurring on the canes of the rose and raspberry and found also on the strawberry, pear, mango, and other plants.

ros·et (roz′it), *n. Scottish.* resin.

Ro·set·ta stone (rō zet′ə), a slab of black basalt found in 1799 near the mouth of the Nile. A decree carved on it in two kinds of ancient Egyptian writing and in Greek provided the most important key to the understanding of Egyptian hieroglyphics. [< *Rosetta* (< Arabic *Rashid*), a town near one of the mouths of the Nile]

ro·sette (rō zet′), *n.* an ornament, object, or arrangement shaped like a rose: *Rosettes are often made of ribbon. Carved or molded rosettes are used in architecture. Before a rosette of microphones, the President ignored the raindrops streaming down his face* (Time). [< French *rosette* (diminutive) < Old French *rose,* learned borrowing from Latin *rosa* rose[1]]

Architectural Rosettes
From left to right: Antique, Romanesque, Italian, Modern French

ro·set·ted (rō zet′id), *adj.* **1.** ornamented with rosettes. **2.** formed into rosettes.

rosette plant, a plant with clusters of leaves at the surface of the ground or at the summit of a caudex.

rose water, water made fragrant with oil of roses, used as a perfume and in some Oriental cooking.

rose-wa·ter (rōz′wôt′ər, -wot′-), *adj.* **1.** having the odor of rose water. **2.** affectedly delicate, nice, or fine.

rose window, an ornamental circular window, especially one with a pattern of small sections that radiate from a center (usually to be found in churches).

Gothic Rose Window

rose·wood (rōz′wu̇d′), *n.* **1.** a beautiful reddish wood used in fine furniture. **2.** any of various trees that it comes from, especially a group of tropical trees of the pea family.

Rosh Ha·sha·na or **Ha·sha·nah** (rosh hə shä′nə, rōsh), the Jewish New Year: *Jewish housewives already are planning family menus for the New Year holidays that begin a week from tomorrow with the feast of Rosh Hashanah* (New York Times). [< Hebrew *rōsh* head + *ha-shānāh* the year]

Rosh Ha·sho·na (hə shô′nə), Rosh Hashana.

Rosh Ho·desh (hō′desh), the first day (and, sometimes, the second day) of the new month in the Hebrew calendar beginning with the new moon, celebrated with special prayers. [< Hebrew *rōsh* head + *ḥodhesh* new moon]

Ro·si·cru·cian (rō′zə krü′shən), *n.* **1.** a member of a secret society prominent in the 1600's and 1700's which claimed to have a special and secret knowledge of nature and religion. **2.** a member of any of various similar societies founded later: *Today, headquarters of the Rosicrucians send over seven million pieces of mail annually to all parts of the world* (Maclean's). —*adj.* of or having to do with the Rosicrucians. [< a Latinized form (< Latin *rosa* rose[1] + *crux, crucis* cross) of *Rosenkreuz,* the supposed founder in 1484 of the order + *-ian*]

Ro·si·cru·cian·ism (rō′zə krü′shə niz əm), *n.* the theories and practices of Rosicrucians.

ros·i·ly (rō′zə lē), *adv.* **1.** with a rozy tinge or color. **2.** brightly; cheerfully.

ros·in (roz′ən), *n.* a hard, yellow, brown, or black substance that remains when turpentine is evaporated from pine resin: *Rosin is rubbed on violin bows, and on the shoes of acrobats to keep them from slipping. Rosin is made mainly from the gum of pine trees* (Wall Street Journal). —*v.t.* to cover or rub with rosin: *He takes good care . . . by rosining his bow* (Scientific American). [< Old French *rosine,* variant of *resine;* see RESIN]

Ros·i·nan·te (roz′ə nan′tē), *n.* **1.** Don Quixote's thin, worn-out horse. **2.** any poor horse. [< Spanish *Rocinante* < *rocín* a hack horse, jade]

rosin bag, *Baseball.* a small bag containing rosin used for drying the hands.

ros·i·ness (rō′zē nis), *n.* **1.** a rosy state. **2.** a rosy hue.

rosin oil, a yellowish, oily liquid; retinol.

ros·in·weed (roz′ən wēd′), *n.* any of various coarse North American plants of the composite family with resinous juice, especially the compass plant.

ros·in·y (roz′ə nē), *adj.* full of rosin; resinous.

ros·ma·rine (roz′mə rēn, -rīn), *n. Obsolete.* the walrus, formerly imagined as a sea monster which climbed cliffs to feed on dew: *greedy Rosmarines with visages deforme* (Edmund Spenser). [< Danish *rosmar* + English *-ine*[1]; influenced by obsolete *rosmarine* sea dew]

ro·so·lio (rō zōl′yō), *n.* a cordial made from raisins, etc., popular in southern Europe. [< Italian *rosolio* < Medieval Latin *ros solis* sundew, a plant; also, a liqueur < Latin *rōs, rōris* dew, *sōl, sōlis* sun]

ro·so·lite (rō′zə lit), *n.* a rose-colored garnet containing calcium and aluminum.

rosse (rôs), *adj. French.* characterized by a brutal or cynical disregard of convention.

ross·er (rôs′ər, ros′-), *n.* a lumberjack who barks and smooths the side of a log to make it slide easier. [origin unknown]

ros·se·rie (rôs rē′), *n. French.* cynical disregard of convention.

Ross seal (rôs, ros), a small, rather rare hair seal of antarctic regions.

Ross's goose, a white goose of arctic America with black primary feathers, similar to the snow goose, but smaller.

ros·tel·late (ros′tə lit, -lāt), *adj.* having a rostellum. [< New Latin *rostellatus* < Latin *rōstellum* (diminutive) < *rōstrum* beak; see ROSTRUM]

ros·tel·lum (ros tel′əm), *n., pl.* **-tel·la** (-tel′ə). **1.** any small part shaped like a beak, as the stigma of many violets. **2.** a modified stigma in many orchids that bears the glands to which the masses of pollen are attached. [< Latin *rōstellum* (diminutive) < *rōstrum;* see ROSTRUM]

ros·ter (ros′tər), *n.* **1.** a list giving each person's name and duties: *Many "servants" are mentioned in the roster of the Mayflower* (H.G. Wells). **2.** any list of persons or things: *In spite of the unique requirements for membership, the Club roster grows* (Newsweek). [< Dutch *rooster* list; (originally) gridiron < *roosten* to roast; the shift of meaning is because the parallel lines on a list resemble a gridiron]

ros·tral (ros′trəl), *adj.* **1.** of or having to do with a rostrum. **2.** adorned with beaks of warships. [< Late Latin *rōstrālis* < *rōstrum;* see ROSTRUM]

ros·trate (ros′trāt), *adj. Biology.* having a beaklike part.

ros·trum (ros′trəm), *n., pl.* **-trums, -tra** (-trə). **1.** a platform for public speaking: *Mr. Tappertit mounted on an empty cask which stood by way of a rostrum in the room* (Dickens). *A brief discussion of colonial affairs brought a few left-wing delegates to the rostrum to criticize the Government's policy* (London Times). **2.** the beak of an ancient war galley. **3.** a beaklike part, as a snout. [< Latin *rōstrum* beak, prow of a ship, related to *rōdere* gnaw (referring to the speakers' platform in the Roman forum, which was decorated with the beaks of captured galleys)] —**Syn. 1.** stage, dais.

ros·u·late (roz′yə lit, -lāt), *adj. Botany.* arranged in a rosette: *rosulate leaves.* [< Late Latin *rosula* (diminutive) < *rosa* rose[1] + English *-ate*[1]]

ros·y (rō′zē), *adj.,* **ros·i·er, ros·i·est. 1. a.** like a rose; rose-red; pinkish-red: *a rosy cloud, the rosy tints of sunset.* **b.** blushing. **2. a.** decorated with roses. **b.** made of roses. **3.** bright; cheerful: *a rosy future. Two Labor Department reports pictured a generally rosy employment picture across the nation* (Wall Street Journal).

rosy finch, any of several brownish finches with pinkish wings and rump and a gray patch on the back of the head, found in the mountains of western North America.

rot (rot), *v.,* **rot·ted, rot·ting,** *n., interj.* —*v.i.* **1.** to decay; spoil. **2.** to lose vigor; degenerate. —*v.t.* **1.** to cause to decay: *So much rain will rot the fruit.* **2.** to moisten or soak (flax, etc.) in order to soften; ret.
—*n.* **1.** the process of rotting; decay. **2.** rotten matter. **3.** a liver disease of animals, especially of sheep, caused by a liver fluke and marked by anemia, weakness, and swollen jaws. **4.** any of various diseases of plants marked by decay and caused by bacteria or fungi, as crown rot. **5.** any wasting disease. **6.** *Especially British Slang.* nonsense; rubbish: *I wish you wouldn't talk such infernal rot* (Arnold Bennett).
—*interj.* nonsense! rubbish! *There were exclamations of "Rot" and "Rubbish"* (London Times).
[Old English *rotian*]
—**Syn.** *v.i.* **1.** decompose, putrefy. See **decay.**

rot., 1. rotating. **2.** rotation.

ro·ta (rō′tə), *n., pl.* **-tas. 1.** a roster. **2.** a round; routine; rotation: *They have organized rotas and there are always three in the cottage, cooking, cleaning and mending* (Punch). **3.** (in the Roman Catholic Church) an ecclesiastical tribunal forming a court of final appeal. [< Latin *rota* a wheel]

ro·tam·e·ter (rō tam′ə tər), *n.* an instrument for measuring the distance covered by a wheel, for measuring curved lines, etc. [< Latin *rota* wheel + English *-meter*]

Ro·tar·i·an (rō tãr′ē ən), *n.* a member of a Rotary Club. —*adj.* belonging to or having to do with Rotary Clubs.

Ro·tar·i·an·ism (rō tãr′ē ə niz′əm), *n.* the theories and practices of Rotarians.

ro·ta·ry (rō′tər ē), *adj., n., pl.* **-ries.** —*adj.* **1.** turning like a top or a wheel; rotating. **2.** (of motion) circular: *In the windmills that operate pumps the rotary motion must be changed into reciprocating (back-and-forth) motion* (Beauchamp, Mayfield, and West). **3.** having parts that rotate. **4.** of or having to do with a rotary aircraft engine.
—*n.* **1.** a rotary engine or machine. **2.** *Especially U.S. and Canada.* a traffic circle: *At eight the next morning we came to the first traffic rotary outside New York, in New Jersey.* **3.** *Electricity.* a synchronous converter. [< Medieval Latin *rotarius* < Latin *rota* wheel]

Rotary Club, an association of business and professional men formed with the purpose of serving their community. All Rotary Clubs are united in an international organization.

rotary engine, 1. a turbine engine, electric motor, etc., in which the pistons, blades, armature, or similar parts rotate instead of moving in a straight line, or in which a cylinder rotates upon a piston. **2.** an internal-combustion engine in aircraft, having radially arranged cylinders that revolve around a common fixed crankshaft.

rotary hoe, any of various tools that cultivate soil with rotating prongs, blades, etc.

rotary plow or **tiller,** a tool with blades on a revolving horizontal shaft. The revolving blades rip up and break up the soil.

rotary press, a printing press using revolving cylinders for both the printing part and the surface to be printed.

rotary wing, the lifting surface of a helicopter or autogiro.

ro·tat·a·ble (rō′tā tə bəl, rō tā′-), *adj.* that can be rotated.

ro·tat·a·bly (rō′tā tə blē, rō tā′-), *adv.* in a rotatable manner; so as to be rotated.

ro·tate[1] (rō′tāt), *v.,* **-tat·ed, -tat·ing.** —*v.i.* **1.** to move around a center or axis; turn in a circle; revolve: *Wheels, tops, and the earth rotate.* **2.** to change in a regular order; take turns; alternate: *The officials will rotate in office.* —*v.t.* **1.** to cause to turn around. **2.** to cause to take turns: *to rotate men in office. Farmers rotate crops.* [< Latin *rotāre* (with English *-ate*[1]) < *rota* a wheel] —**Syn.** *v.i.* **1.** See **turn.**

ro·tate[2] (rō′tāt), *adj. Botany.* spreading out nearly flat like a wheel; wheel-shaped, as a corolla with a short tube and spreading limb. [< Latin *rota* wheel + English *-ate*[1]]

ro·ta·tion (rō tā′shən), *n.* **1. a.** the act or process of moving around a center or axis; turning in a circle; revolving: *the rotation of a top. The earth's rotation causes night and day.* **b.** the time required for one such movement. **c.** one such movement. **2.** change in a regular order. **3.** *Military.* the exchange of individuals or units in hazardous or uncomfortable areas with those more favorably located.
in rotation, in turn; in regular succession: *All being summoned in rotation, my own turn came at last* (Herman Melville).

ro·ta·tion·al (rō tā′shə nəl), *adj.* of or with rotation. —**ro·ta′tion·al·ly,** *adv.*

rotation of crops, the varying from year to year of the crops grown in the same field to keep the soil from losing its fertility.

ro·ta·tive (rō′tə tiv), *adj.* **1.** rotating. **2.** having to do with rotation.

ro·ta·tor (rō′tā tər), *n., pl.* **ro·ta·tors,** *also* **ro·ta·to·res** (rō′tə tôr′ēz, -tōr′-) *for 2.* **1.** a person or thing that rotates. **2.** a muscle that turns a part of the body: *Muscles that rotate a body part are called rotators, some of which move the structure clockwise and others move it counterclockwise* (A. M. Winchester). [< Latin *rotātor* < *rotāre;* see ROTATE[1]]

ro·ta·to·ry (rō′tə tôr′ē, -tōr′-), *adj.* **1.** rotating; rotary: *rotatory motion.* **2.** causing rotation: *a rotatory muscle.* **3.** passing or following from one to another in a regular order: *a rotatory office in a club.*

rotatory power, the property possessed by certain substances, solutions, etc., of rotating the plane of polarization.

ROTC (no periods) or **R.O.T.C.,** Reserve Officers' Training Corps.

rotche or **rotch** (roch), *n.* a small bird related to the auks; dovekie. [earlier *rotge;* origin uncertain]

rote[1] (rōt), *n.* a set, mechanical way of doing things.
by rote, by memory without thought of the meaning: *Most people learn their alphabet by rote. The hearers of such literature . . . had to get it by rote* (Maurice Hewlett).
[Middle English *rote;* origin uncertain]

rote[2] (rōt), *n.* a kind of medieval stringed musical instrument resembling a lyre. [< Old French *rote* < Medieval Latin *rotta,* or < a Germanic word < Celtic (compare Welsh *crwth* crowd[2])]

rote[3] (rōt), *n.* the sound of the sea or surf: *The rote of the sea from its sandy coast . . . Seemed the murmurous sound of the judgment host* (John Greenleaf Whittier). [origin uncertain. Compare Old Icelandic *rjōta,* Norwegian *rut.*]

ro·te·none (rō′tə nōn), *n.* a white, crystalline compound obtained from the roots of various plants, used as an insecticide and fish poison. It is harmless to birds and mammals. *Formula:* $C_{23}H_{22}O_6$ [origin unknown]

rot·gut (rot′gut′), *n. U.S. Slang.* cheap whiskey; bad or adulterated liquor.

ro·ti·fer (rō′tə fər), *n.* any of a group of complex, microscopic water animals that have one or more rings of cilia on a disk at one end of the body: *Small ponds appear choked with gelatinous algae and microscopic animals such as rotifers* (Gabriele Rabel). [< New Latin *Rotifera* the class name < Latin *rota* wheel + *ferre* to carry]

ro·tif·er·al (rō tif′ər əl), *adj.* **1.** of or having to do with the rotifers. **2.** having a wheel or wheellike organ.

ro·tif·er·ous (rō tif′ər əs), *adj.* rotiferal.

ro·tis·se·rie (rō tis′ər ē), *n.* **1.** a spit for roasting food, often enclosed in a hood and turned by an electric motor. **2.** a restaurant or shop that sells meats and poultry cooked on a spit. [< French *rotisserie* < *rôtir* roast]

rot·l (rot′əl), *n., pl.* **ar·tal. 1.** a unit of weight used in North Africa and nearby parts of Europe and Asia. It corresponds roughly to the pound but varies according to place. **2.** a dry measure, used in the same areas and also varying greatly. [< Arabic *raṭl* < Greek *lītra,* or Latin *lībra* a pound[1]]

ro·to·chute (rō′tə shüt), *n.* a parachute with freely turning blades, like the rotor of an autogiro, instead of a canopy to slow descent. [< *roto*(r) + (para)*chute*]

Ro·to·dyne (rō′tə dīn), *n. Trademark.* a jet-propelled helicopter that also has front propellers and small wings for forward movement: *The Rotodyne recently transported a whole casualty clearing station—doctors and nurses* (Sunday Times).

ro·to·graph (rō′tə graf, -gräf), *n.* a photograph printed by running a strip of sensitized paper under a negative, producing a succession of copies. [< Latin *rota* wheel + English *-graph*]

ro·to·gra·vure (rō′tə grə vyůr′, -grā′vyər), *n.* **1.** a process of printing from an engraved copper cylinder on which the pictures, letters, etc., have been depressed instead of raised. **2.** *U.S.* a print or section of a newspaper made by this process. **3.** a kind of paper on which rotogravure and many picture sections and picture magazines are usually printed: *[They] changed the weekly from rough newsprint to slick rotogravure* (Newsweek). [American English < *roto*-(graph) + *gravure*]

ro·tor (rō′tər), *n.* **1.** the rotating part of a machine or apparatus: *the rotor of a centrifugal pump. The blades of the rotors are carefully curved and streamlined to make the turbine as efficient as possible* (Beauchamp, Mayfield, and West). See the picture of **helicopter. 2.** the armature or other rotating part of an electric motor or dynamo. [short for *rotator*]

ro·tor·craft (rō′tər kraft′, -kräft′), *n., pl.* **-craft.** a helicopter or other aircraft driven by a rotor: *Despite his enthusiasm for rotorcraft, he makes it clear that they will not be used by private fliers for commuting* (New York Times).

rotor mast, (formerly) a rotating cylinder rising above the deck to propel a rotor ship.

rotor ship, (formerly) a ship equipped with a rotor mast in place of sails.

ro·to section (rō′tō), the section of a newspaper printed by rotogravure.

ro·to·till (rō′tə til′), *v.t.* to break up the soil with a rotary tiller: *In a mulched area, I never plow or rototill but simply open up a seed furrow with a hoe each spring* (New York Times).

ro·to·till·er (rō′tə til′ər), *n.* a rotary tiller: *A power cultivator of the rototiller type is the most efficient tool for the job* (New York Times).

rot·ten (rot′ən), *adj.* **1.** decayed; spoiled; decomposed: *a rotten egg, rotten wood. Beneath this is a zone of partly decayed stone or rotten rock* (Fenton and Fenton). **2.** bad-smelling; foul: *rotten air.* **3.** not in good condition; unsound; weak: *steep banks of rotten ice, which were breaking off and falling in all the time* (Theodore Roosevelt). *It is a reasoning weak, rotten, and sophistical* (Edmund Burke). **4.** corrupt; dishonest: *Something is rotten in the state of Denmark* (Shakespeare). **5.** *Slang.* bad; nasty: *to feel rotten, a rotten joke, to have a rotten time. He said furiously, "You loved Scobie," and added quickly, "Sorry. Rotten thing to say"* (Graham Greene). [< Scandinavian (compare Old Icelandic *rotinn*)] **—rot′ten·ly,** *adv.* **—Syn.** **2.** putrid, fetid.

rotten borough, 1. a borough in England before 1832 that had only a few voters, but kept the privilege of sending a member to Parliament. **2.** any election district with very few legal voters.

rot·ten·ness (rot′ən nis), *n.* **1.** rotten condition; decay: *The rottenness of the lumber made it useless.* **2.** a very bad condition; corruption.

rot·ten·stone (rot′ən stōn′), *n.* a decomposed limestone that resembles silica, used as a powder for polishing metals.

rot·ter (rot′ər), *n. British Slang.* a worthless or objectionable person; scoundrel: *a thorough rotter. One does not feel a rotter For one is doing good* (Punch). [< *rot,* verb + *-er*[1]]

rott·wei·ler (rot′wī′lər), *n.* any of a breed of short-haired, black and tan working dogs developed from cattle dogs used by the Romans. Today they are trained for police work. [< German *Rottweiler* < *Rottweil,* a city in West Germany]

ro·tund (rō tund′), *adj.* **1.** round; plump: *a rotund face.* **2.** sounding rich and full; full-toned: *a rotund voice.* [< Latin *rotundus,* related to *rota* wheel. Doublet of ROUND[1].] **—ro·tund′ly,** *adv.* **—ro·tund′ness,** *n.* **—Syn.** **2.** sonorous.

ro·tun·da (rō tun′də), *n.* **1.** a circular building or part of a building, especially one with a dome. **2.** a large, high, circular room: *The Capitol at Washington has a large rotunda. The band played in the rotunda in honor of the minister of Militia as he was dining* (Calgary [Alberta, Canada] Eye Opener). [< Italian *rotonda,* feminine of *rotundus,* learned borrowing from Latin *rotundus;* see ROTUND]

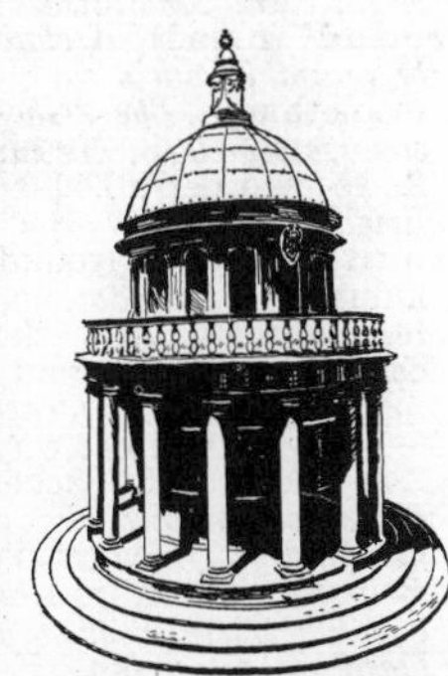

Renaissance Rotunda (def. 1), in Rome

ro·tun·di·ty (rō tun′də tē), *n., pl.* **-ties.** **1.** roundness; plumpness. **2.** something round. **3.** rounded fullness of tone: *[His] language was unequaled, said Churchill, "in point, in rotundity, in antithesis or in comprehension"* (Time). **—Syn.** **1.** chubbiness. **2.** sphere. **3.** sonority.

ro·ture (rô tʏr′), *n.* **1.** a low rank. **2.** *French-Canadian Law.* rented possession without any privileges. [< French *roture* < Middle French, newly cleared field < Latin *ruptūra* a breaking; see RUPTURE]

ro·tu·rier (rô tʏ ryā′), *n., pl.* **-riers** (-ryā′). a person of low rank. [< French *roturier* < *roture;* see ROTURE]

rou·ble (rü′bəl), *n.* ruble.

rouche (rüsh), *n.* ruche.

rou·é (rü ā′, rü′ā), *n.* a dissipated man; rake: *I knew him for a young roué of a vicomte—a brainless and vicious youth* (Charlotte Brontë). [< French *roué,* (originally) past participle of Old French *rouer* break on the wheel < *roue* wheel < Latin *rota* (first applied around 1720 to a group of profligates, companions of the Duc d'Orléans)] **—Syn.** profligate.

rouge (rüzh), *n., v.,* **rouged, roug·ing.** *—n.* **1.** a red powder, paste, or liquid for coloring the cheeks or lips. **2.** a red powder, chiefly ferric oxide, used for polishing metal, jewels, etc.

—v.t. to color with rouge: *She was admirably rouged and powdered* (Arnold Bennett).

—v.i. to use rouge on the face: *Fanny Minafer, who rouged a little* (Booth Tarkington).

[< French *rouge* < Old French *roge* red < Latin *rubeus* < *ruber* red]

rouge et noir (rüzh′ ā nwär′), a gambling game at cards, played on a table marked with two red and two black diamond-shaped spots that the players place their bets on. [< French *rouge et noir* red and black; see ROUGE; *noir* < Latin *niger*]

rouge flam·bé (rüzh′ flän bā′), *French.* **1.** an iridescent glaze of a red color. **2.** (literally) fired red.

rou·geot (rü zhō′), *n.* a disease of grape leaves, causing them to turn red and die. [< French *rougeot* < *rouge* red]

rough (ruf), *adj.* **1.** not smooth; not level; not even: *rough boards, rough bark, rough hilly country covered with rocks.* **2.** without polish or fine finish: *rough diamonds.* **3. a.** without luxury and ease: *rough life in camp.* **b.** without culture or refinement: *a rough soldier with little education.* **4.** not completed or perfected; done as a first try; without details: *a rough sketch, a rough idea. It is impossible to make any but the roughest guess at the numbers of these Northwestern Indians* (Theodore Roosevelt). **5.** coarse and tangled: *rough fur, a dog with a rough coat of hair.* **6.** likely to hurt others; not gentle; harsh; rude: *rough manners. My temper is rough, and will not be controlled* (William Godwin). **7.** disorderly; riotous: *a rough crowd.* **8.** *Informal.* unpleasant; hard; severe: *He was in for a rough time. Being out of work is rough on a man with a wife and children. It was early to prophesy and conditions were still "pretty rough," yet a courageous start had been made* (London Times). **9.** requiring merely strength rather than intelligence or skill: *rough work.* **10.** stormy: *rough weather.* **11.** violently disturbed or agitated: *a rough sea.* **12. a.** harsh, sharp, or dry to the taste: *rough wines.* **b.** harsh to the ear; grating; jarring: *rough sounds, a rough voice.* **13.** uneven in pulse or sound and operating improperly, as an internal-combustion engine that is misfiring: *The plane's Number 3 engine had backfired and had been rough* (New York Times). **14.** *Phonetics.* pronounced with an aspirate; having the sound of *h.*

—n. **1.** a coarse, violent person: *Without an army Pompey could do little against the roughs in the streets* (James A. Froude). **2.** rough ground. **3.** a rough thing or condition; hard or unpleasant side or part: *to take the rough with the smooth.* **4.** ground where there is long grass, etc., on a golf course: *He hooked his drive off the high tee into thick, impossible rough* (Time).

in the rough, a. not polished or refined; coarse; crude: *We must never forget that the truths of political economy are truths only in the rough* (John Stuart Mill). **b.** in an untidy or informal state; in an everyday condition: *I wish you'd come with me, and take her in the rough, and judge her for yourself* (Dickens). **c.** in an imperfect state; in a preliminary sketch or design: *Every kind of surface is first formed in the rough, and then finished by means of tools* (P. Nicholson).

—v.t. **1.** to make rough; roughen: *to rough the soles of new shoes to keep from slipping.* **2.** to treat roughly: *To back up the order it sent a squad of its Blue Shirt toughs to rough up the dean and the leaders of the anti-Falangist insurrection* (Atlantic). **3.** to shape or sketch roughly: *to rough out a plan, to rough in the outlines of a face.* *—v.i.* **1.** to become rough. **2.** to behave roughly.

rough it, to live without comforts and conveniences: *He looked old . . . as if he had roughed it all his life, and had found living a desperate long, hard grind* (George Du Maurier).

—adv. roughly.

[Middle English *rough,* Old English *rūh*]

—Syn. *adj.* **1.** uneven, irregular, broken, jagged. **3. a.** uncultivated, unpolished. **4.** approximate, imperfect, incomplete, preliminary. **5.** shaggy, bristly. **6.** discourteous, impolite, uncivil. **7.** boisterous, tumultuous. **8.** drastic, rigorous. **10.** inclement.

rough·age (ruf′ij), *n.* **1.** rough or coarse material. **2.** the coarser parts or kinds of food, such as bran, fruit skins, or straw.

rough-and-read·y (ruf′ən red′ē), *adj.* **1.** rough and crude, but good enough for the purpose; roughly effective: *Nor did he [Lincoln] make himself an exact lawyer; a rough-and-ready familiarity with practice . . . contented him* (Baron Charnwood). **2.** showing rough vigor rather than refinement: *He had a bluff, rough-and-ready face* (Robert Louis Stevenson).

rough-and-tum·ble (ruf′ən tum′bəl), *adj.* showing confusion and violence; with little regard for rules; roughly vigorous; boisterous: *a rough-and-tumble football game. In a rough-and-tumble campaign debate with Communist Party leader Jacques Duclos . . . Mendès-France vigorously flayed both the Reds and the right wing* (Newsweek). *—n.* a rough-and-tumble fight or struggle: *the rough-and-tumble of popular debate* (Baron Charnwood). **—Syn.** *adj.* riotous.

rough breathing, *Greek Grammar.* **1.** the mark (ʽ) placed over an initial vowel or rho (ρ) to indicate aspiration. **2.** having the sound of *h;* aspirated. [translation of Latin *spīritus asper*]

rough·cast (ruf′kast′, -käst′), *n., v.,* **-cast, -cast·ing.** *—n.* **1.** a coarse plaster for outside surfaces. **2.** a rough form.

—v.t. **1.** to cover or coat with coarse plaster. **2.** to make, shape, or prepare in a rough form: *to roughcast a story.* **—rough′cast′er,** *n.*

rough collie, a collie with a long, thick, coat.

rough cut, a type of tobacco chopped into irregular, small pieces.

rough-dry (ruf′drī′), *v.,* **-dried, -dry·ing,** *adj.* *—v.t.* to dry (clothes) after washing without ironing them. *—adj.* dried after washing but not ironed.

rough·en (ruf′ən), *v.t.* to make rough. *—v.i.* to become rough: *The broken landscape, by degrees Ascending, roughens into rigid hills* (James Thomson).

rough·er (ruf′ər), *n.* a workman who makes something in the rough; one who carries out the less finished operations of a work.

rough-hew (ruf′hyü′), *v.t.,* **-hewed, -hewed** or **-hewn, -hew·ing.** **1.** to hew (timber, stone, etc.) roughly or without smoothing or finishing. **2.** to shape roughly; give crude form to: *There's a divinity that shapes our ends, Rough-hew them how we will* (Shakespeare). **—rough′-hew′er,** *n.*

rough-hewn (ruf′hyün′), *adj.* **1.** roughly shaped: *His figures are rough-hewn, still bear the sculptor's chisel marks* (Time). **2.** without refinement; crude: . . . *[a] rough-hewn, painfully serious . . . Illinois stock and grain farmer* (Time).

rough·house (ruf′hous′), *n., v.,* **-housed, -hous·ing.** *Informal.* *—n.* rough play; rowdy conduct; disorderly behavior. *—v.i.* to act in a rough or disorderly way: *One driver on Second Avenue put off a group of pupils for roughhousing* (New York Times). *—v.t.* to disturb by such conduct: *to roughhouse a meeting or a speaker.*

rough·ish (ruf′ish), *adj.* rather rough.

rough-leg·ged hawk (ruf′leg′id), a North American, broad-winged hawk with plumage which varies from brown and white to a melanistic phase.

rough·ly (ruf′lē), *adv.* **1.** in a rough manner. **2.** approximately: *From New York to Los Angeles is roughly three thousand miles.* **—Syn.** **2.** about.

rough·neck (ruf′nek′), *n. Informal.* a rough, coarse fellow.

rough·ness (ruf′nis), *n.* **1.** the quality of being rough. **2.** rough condition. **3.** a rough part or place: *There were other breaks and roughnesses on that flat green expanse* (W. H. Hudson).

rough·ride (ruf′rīd′), *v.i., v.t.,* **-rode, -rid·den, -rid·ing.** **1.** to break in and ride (a rough, wild horse or horses). **2.** to ride over or overcome by rough tactics: *Tough as* *they were, they were supposed to have a rough time with Army's roughriding halfbacks* (Time).

rough·rid·er (ruf′rī′dər), *n.* **1.** a man used to rough, hard riding: *the roughrider of the plains, the hero of rope and revolver* (Theodore Roosevelt). **2.** a person who breaks in and rides rough, wild horses.

Rough·rid·ers (ruf′rī′dərz), *n.pl.* members of a volunteer cavalry regiment organized by Theodore Roosevelt and Leonard Wood during the Spanish-American War.

rough·shod (ruf′shod′), *adj.* having horseshoes with sharp calks to prevent slipping. **ride roughshod over,** to domineer over; show no consideration for; treat roughly.

rough sledding, *Informal.* unfavorable conditions; difficult going: *Many of these proposals could encounter rough sledding* (Wall Street Journal).

rough-winged swallow (ruf′wingd′), a grayish North American swallow with a brownish back, that nests in a hole which it digs in a bank.

roul., *Philately.* roulette.

rou·lade (rü läd′), *n., v.,* **-lad·ed, -lad·ing.** —*n.* **1.** a rapid succession of tones sung to a single syllable: *Singers stepped out of character at will, indulging in barbarous cadenzas or improvised roulades* (Time). **2.** a slice of meat rolled about a filling of chopped meat, carrot, parsley, seasonings, etc., and cooked. —*v.i. Music.* to sing roulades or divisions. [< French *roulade* < *rouler* to roll]

rou·leau (rü lō′), *n., pl.* **-leaux** or **-leaus** (-lōz′). **1.** a roll of coins wrapped in paper: *... a little leather case that was full of neat stacks of notes, with rubber bands around them, and rouleaux of coins* (New Yorker). **2.** a roll; coil. [< French *rouleau* < Middle French *rolel* < Old French *role* or *roule;* see ROLL]

rou·lette (rü let′), *n., v.,* **-let·ted, -let·ting.** —*n.* **1.** a gambling game in which the players bet on the turn of a wheel. **2.** a small wheel with sharp teeth for making lines of marks, dots, or perforations. **3.** *Philately.* one of the separations cut in a sheet of postage stamps. —*v.t.* to cut, mark, or pierce with a roulette. [< French *roulette* < Old French (diminutive) < *rouel* wheel (diminutive) < *roue* < Latin *rota* wheel. Compare ROWEL.]

roul·roul (rül′rül), *n.* a partridgelike bird of Java, Sumatra, Borneo, etc. The male has a rich-green body and a long, red crest.

Roum., 1. Roumania. **2.** Roumanian.

Rou·ma·ni·an (rü mā′nē ən, -mān′yən), *adj., n.* Romanian.

rounce (rouns), *n. Printing.* a pulley on a hand printing press with bands turned by a handle to run the type bed in and out under the platen. [< Dutch *rondse, ronse.* Compare *rond* round.]

round[1] (round), *adj.* **1.** shaped like a ball, a ring, a cylinder, or the like; having a circular or curved outline or surface: *a round hoop, a round bowl, a round hat box.* **2.** plump: *Her figure was short and round.* **3.** by, with, or involving a circular movement: *The waltz is a round dance.* **4. a.** full; complete; entire: *a round dozen; ... a round score of muskets* (Robert Louis Stevenson). **b.** large; considerable: *a good, round sum of money.* **5.** plainly expressed; plain-spoken; frank: *The boy's father scolded him in good round terms. I will a round unvarnish'd tale deliver* (Shakespeare). **6. a.** with a full tone: *a mellow, round voice.* **b.** full-bodied: *Fine beer, the experts say, should taste "round" ... no rough edges, a smooth harmony of flavors* (New Yorker). **7.** vigorous; brisk: *I passed at a round trot over the plains* (Francis Parkman). **8.** *Phonetics.* spoken with the lips rounded: *"O" is a round vowel.* **9.** that is in round numbers: *He returned me immediately an order on the paymaster for the round sum of one thousand pounds, leaving the remainder to the next account* (Benjamin Franklin). **10.** rough; approximate: *a round estimate. I may form a round guess ... what I might have to fear* (Scott).
—*n.* **1.** anything shaped like a ball, circle, cylinder, or the like: *The rungs of a ladder are sometimes called rounds.* **2.** a fixed course ending where it begins: *The watchman makes his round of the building every hour.* **3. a.** movement in a circle or about an axis: *the earth's yearly round.* **b.** a roundabout way or course: *You took them in a round, while they supposed themselves going forward* (Oliver Goldsmith). **4.** a series (of duties, events, drinks, etc.); routine: *a round of pleasures, a round of duties. Serve out a round of brandy to all hands* (Robert Louis Stevenson). **5.** the distance between any limits; range; circuit: *the round of human knowledge.* **6.** a section of a game or sport: *a round in a boxing match, a round of cards, the semifinal round in a tournament.* **7. a.** a discharge of firearms, artillery, bows and arrows, etc., especially by a group of soldiers at the same time. **b.** bullets, powder, shells, arrows, etc., for such a shot: *Only three rounds of ammunition were left.* **8.** an act that a number of people do together: *a round of applause, a round of cheers.* **9.** a dance in which the dancers move in a circle. **10.** a short song, sung by several persons or groups beginning one after the other: *"Three Blind Mice" is a round.* **11.** a cut of beef just above the hind leg and below the rump.

go the round, to be passed, told, shown, etc., by many people from one to another: *This celebrated epistle ... created quite a sensation ... as it went the round after tea* (Thomas Hughes).

in the round, a. in a form of sculpture in which the figures are apart from any background: *The cow's right horn must have been carried in the round, only the tip being attached to the background of the relief* (Alexander S. Murray). **b.** in the open; showing all sides or aspects: *The whole pavilion, in fact, is a huge museum of modern art in the round* (Manchester Guardian). *The new material ... does not alter our conception of Byron in any essential way, but it does help us to see him more in the round, both as a physical and as a social being* (New Yorker).

make or **go the rounds,** to go about from place to place in a certain course or through a certain area: *The watchman made the rounds of the factory twice each night. The candidate went the rounds of the neighborhood campaigning for votes.*

rounds, the ringing of a set of bells from the highest tone through the major scale to the lowest tone: *A man well practiced in all that pertained to bells, whether rounds [or] changes* (Frederic T. Jane).
—*v.t.* **1.** to make round: *The carpenter rounded the corners of the table. We round our lips when we say "oo." The healthy air rounded her cheeks.* **2.** to go wholly or partly around: *They rounded the island. The ship rounded Cape Horn.* **3.** to take a circular course about; make a complete or partial circuit of: *The car rounded the corner at high speed.* **4.** to fill; complete: *to round out a paragraph after much thought. We are such stuff as dreams are made on; and our little life is rounded with a sleep* (Shakespeare). **5.** to surround; encircle: *The hollow crown That rounds the mortal temples of a king* (Shakespeare). **6.** to cause to turn round or move in a circle: *She rounded her face toward him.* **7.** *Phonetics.* to utter (a vowel) with a small circular opening of the lips. —*v.i.* **1.** to become round: *The little boy's lips rounded when he tried to whistle.* **2.** to take a circular or winding course; make a complete or partial circuit: *The road rounded about the mountain. The night watchman rounds every half hour. I see ... The rounding seasons come and go* (John Greenleaf Whittier). **3.** to become finished or complete. **4.** to turn around; wheel about: *The men who met him rounded on their heels And wonder'd after him* (Tennyson).

round in, *Nautical.* to haul in: *Ease off the lee brace and round the yard in* (Richard Henry Dana).

round off, a. to make or become round: *The lower [stone] ... is shorter and rounded off, instead of being square at the corners* (Scott). **b.** to finish; complete: *A referendum held last month rounded off this period of anxiety* (Manchester Guardian Weekly). **c.** to express (a quantity) in round numbers, as in even tens, hundreds, thousands, etc.: *.364 rounded off to the nearest hundredth is .36; to the nearest tenth, .4.*

round on or **upon, a.** to attack or assail, especially in words: *Now everyone rounds on them and tells them that they are a selfish, grasping lot* (Punch). **b.** to turn informer against; betray: *The self-alienated man gives way to impulses to round upon his associates and accuse them* (Edmund Wilson).

round out, a. to make or become round: *Working at the wheel, the ceramist rounded out the corners, and the plate appeared finished.* **b.** to finish; complete: *to round out a paragraph, to round out a career.*

round to, *Nautical.* to come head up to the wind: *We rounded to and let go our anchor* (Richard Henry Dana).

round up, to draw or drive together: *to round up cattle.*
—*adv.* **1.** in a circle; with a whirling motion: *Wheels go round. The bird flew round and round.* **2.** on all sides; in every direction: *The travelers were compassed round by dangers. So twice five miles of fertile ground With walls and towers were girdled round* (Samuel Taylor Coleridge). **3.** in circumference: *The pumpkin measures 50 inches round.* **4.** by a longer road or way: *We went round by the candy store on our way home.* **5.** from one to another: *A report is going round that the schools will close.* **6.** through a round of time: *Summer will soon come round again. It fetched us a dollar a day apiece all the year round* (Mark Twain). **7.** about; around: *He doesn't look fit to be round.* **8.** here and there: *I am just looking round.* **9.** for all: *There is just enough cake to go round.* **10.** in the opposite direction or course; to the opposite opinion: *She continued to sit very still, without looking round* (John Galsworthy). *He brought me round to his opinion* (Samuel Butler).
—*prep.* **1.** on all sides of: *Bullets fell round him, but he was not hit.* **2.** so as to encircle or surround: *They built a fence round the yard. He ... saw ghosts dancing round him* (Thomas Love Peacock). *The Government yesterday put a smoke screen round the preparations for a show of force in the eastern Mediterranean* (London Times). **3.** so as to make a turn to the other side of: *He walked round the corner.* **4.** in a circuit or course through; to all or various parts of: *We took our cousins round the town.* **5.** about; around: *to stand still and look round one.* **6.** here and there in: *There are boxes for mail all round the city.* **7.** throughout (a period of time): *Verdant olives flourish round the year* (Alexander Pope). **8.** so as to revolve or rotate about: *a wheel's motion round its axis.*

get or **come round.** See under **get** and **come.**
[< Old French *rond, roont* < Latin *rotundus,* related to *rota* wheel. Doublet of ROTUND.]
—**round′ness,** *n.*
—**Syn.** *adj.* **1.** cylindrical, spherical, globular. **2.** stout.

➔ **round, around.** In informal usage *round* and *around* are used interchangeably, with a definite tendency to use *round* (or to clip the *a* of *around* so short that it would be taken for *round*). In formal English there is some tendency to keep *around* to mean "here and there" or "in every direction" and *round* for "in a circular motion" or "in a reverse motion": *I have looked all around. There aren't any around here. He is going round the world. Everyone turned round.*

round[2] (round), *Archaic.* —*v.i.* to whisper: *to round in one's ear.* —*v.t.* **1.** to whisper (something): *The "Ghosts of Life" rounded strange secrets in his ear* (Thomas Carlyle). **2.** to whisper to. [< obsolete *roun,* Old English *rūnian*]

round·a·bout (round′ə bout′), *adj.* **1.** indirect: *a roundabout route, to hear in a roundabout way.* **2.** that surrounds or encircles. **3.** cut round at the bottom: *a roundabout coat or jacket.*
—*n.* **1.** an indirect way, course, or speech. **2.** a short, tight jacket for men or boys: *His close-buttoned blue cloth roundabout was new and natty* (Mark Twain). **3.** *Especially British.* a merry-go-round: *a steam "roundabout," where wooden horses revolved to the blare of an organ* (Eden Phillpotts). **4.** *British.* a traffic circle: *Already a roundabout has been built at the capital's one road junction* (London Times). —**round′a·bout′ness,** *n.*
—**Syn.** *adj.* **1.** circuitous.

round angle, a complete circle; an angle of 360 degrees.

round arch, a semicircular arch.

round·arm (round′ärm′), *adj.* performed or executed with an outward, circular movement of the arm: *Taylor was frequently off the target with roundarm blows to the head* (London Times).

round clam, an almost circular, edible American clam; quahog.

round dance, **1.** a dance performed by couples and characterized by circular or revolving movements. **2.** a dance with dancers in a circle.

round·ed (roun′did), *adj.* **1.** round: *rounded edges.* **2.** *Phonetics.* spoken by rounding the lips: *a rounded vowel. The word "joke" has a rounded sound "o." One can learn to produce the rounded front vowels by practising lip-positions before a mirror* (Leonard Bloomfield). **3.** expressed in round numbers, as in even tens, hundreds, thousands, etc.: *The Federal Reserve places heaviest emphasis on its rounded index numbers in tracing the broad trend of production* (Wall Street Journal).

roun·del (roun′dəl), *n.* **1.** a small round ornament, window, panel, tablet, etc.: *... with freshly painted RAF roundels on its flanks and the red flaring tail of its rocket motor protruding from the back* (New Scientist). **2.** (in Heraldry) a circular figure used as a bearing, distinguished by its tincture: *a roundel sable.* **3.** a rondeau. **4.** roundelay, a dance. [< Old French *rondel* (diminutive) < *rond;* see ROUND[1]]

roun·de·lay (roun′də lā), *n.* **1.** a song or poem in which a phrase or a line is repeated again and again. **2.** a dance in which the dancers move in a circle; roundel. [< Old French *rondelet* (diminutive) < *rondel* rondel; influenced by *lay*[4]]

round·er (roun′dər), *n.* **1.** *U.S. Slang.* a person who makes the rounds of places of amusement, especially disreputable places. **2.** *Slang.* a habitual drunkard or criminal: *A "square John" is a man who does honest work for a living; a "rounder" is one who doesn't* (Maclean's). **3.** a person or thing that rounds something.

Round·er (roun′dər), *n. British.* a Methodist circuit preacher. [< *rounder*]

round·ers (roun′dərz), *n. pl.* a game, somewhat like baseball, played with a bat, ball, and bases.

round-eyed (round′īd′), *adj.* having the eyes rounded or wide open, as with wakefulness, astonishment, etc.; wide-eyed: *Strangely, I, who frequently grow round-eyed and alert as an owl at the stroke of midnight, find it pleasant to nap in daylight among friends* (Loren Eiseley).

round game, a game for four or more players during which each player plays for himself and does not have a partner.

round hand, a style of handwriting in which the letters are round and full.

Round·head (round′hed′), *n.* a Puritan in England during the English civil wars from 1642 to 1651. The Roundheads wore their hair cut short in contrast to the long curls of their opponents, the Cavaliers. *When, in October, 1641, the Parliament reassembled ... two hostile parties ... appeared confronting each other. During some years they were designated as Cavaliers and Roundheads. They were subsequently called Tories and Whigs* (Macaulay).

round·head·ed (round′hed′id), *adj.* **1.** having a round head or top: *a roundheaded screw.* **2.** with the hair on the head cut short. **3.** *Architecture.* topped with a semicircular arch.

Round·head·ed (round′hed′id), *adj.* of or having to do with the Roundheads; Puritan.

round·heel (round′hēl′), *n. U.S. Slang.* **1.** a person who is easily swayed or unable to resist a particular appeal. **2.** a promiscuous woman.

round·house (round′hous′), *n.* **1.** a circular building for storing or repairing locomotives, that is built about a turntable. **2.** a cabin on the after part of a ship's deck. **3.** *Obsolete.* a jail.
—*adj. Slang.* having or done with a sweeping or exaggerated curve, as a hook in boxing or a pitch in baseball: *Rocky crossed with a roundhouse right to the jaw* (Time).

round·ing (roun′ding), *adj.* that rounds; used in making something round: *a rounding tool, a rounding motion.*

round·ish (roun′dish), *adj.* somewhat round. —**round′ish·ness,** *n.*

round·let (round′lit), *n.* **1.** a small circle. **2.** a small circular object. [< Old French *roundelet, rondelet;* see RONDELET]

round lot, securities for trade, especially 100 shares of stock or $1,000 worth of bonds as a unit of exchange: *To encourage the small investor, which is the Stock Exchange's main current aim, commissions on many round lot transactions involving less than $1,000 would be lowered* (Wall Street Journal).

round·ly (round′lē), *adv.* **1.** in a round manner; in a circle, curve, globe, etc. **2.** plainly; bluntly; severely: *to refuse roundly; ... roundly proclaimed himself at the end no theist but a thoroughgoing agnostic* (Scientific American). **3.** fully; completely.

round number, **1.** a whole number without a fraction. **2.** a number in even tens, hundreds, thousands, etc.: *3874 in round numbers would be 3900 or 4000.*

round of beef, a cut of the thigh of beef through and across the bone.

round robin, **1. a.** a petition, protest, etc., with the signatures written in a circle, so that it is impossible to tell who signed first. **b.** any statement signed by a number of individuals. **2.** a contest in which every player or team plays every other player or team.

rounds (roundz), *n.pl.* See under **round**[1], *n.*

round-shoul·dered (round′shōl′dərd), *adj.* having the shoulders bent forward.

rounds·man (roundz′mən), *n., pl.* **-men.** **1.** a person who makes rounds of inspection, etc., especially a police inspector. **2.** *British.* a delivery man: *Between leaving school and going to the war, I was a milk roundsman* (Sunday Times).

round steak, a cut of beef just above the hind leg.

Round Table, **1.** the table around which King Arthur and his knights sat. **2.** King Arthur and his knights.

round table, a group of persons assembled for an informal discussion, etc.

round-ta·ble (round′tā′bəl), *adj.* of or at a round table; informal: *a round-table discussion.*

round-the-clock (round′ᴛʜə klok′), *adj.* continual; unceasing: *round-the-clock protection. Knowland told the Senate he hoped for a vote on his motion by the end of the week, even if he had to force round-the-clock sessions* (Wall Street Journal). —*adv.* throughout the day and night; without stopping: *to work round-the-clock.*

round·tree (round′trē′), *n.* the American mountain ash.

round trip, *U.S.* a trip to a place and back again. —**round′-trip′,** *adj.*

round-trip·per (round′trip′ər), *n. Slang.* a home run: *Mantle slammed his third round-tripper of the day and his twenty-first of the campaign* (New York Times).

round·up (round′up′), *n.* **1.** *U.S.* **a.** the act of driving or bringing cattle together from long distances: *The missing ones [cattle] are generally recovered in the annual roundups, when the calves are branded* (Theodore Roosevelt). **b.** the men and horses that do this. **2.** any similar gathering: *a roundup of old friends. The answer from a roundup of scholars and business leaders is an enthusiastic affirmative* (Wall Street Journal).

roun·dure (roun′jər, -dyůr), *n.* roundness; rounded form or space: *It is a city of dramatic hills ... that, in Marin County, across the Golden Gate, present even more striking bosses and roundures* (Lewis Mumford).

round window, an opening in the middle ear located below the oval window. It is covered with a membrane that serves as a secondary eardrum.

round·wood (round′wůd′), *n.* roundtree.

round·worm (round′wėrm′), *n.* any of a group of usually small, unsegmented worms that have slender, round bodies; nematode. Roundworms live in soil or water or are parasitic in animals and plants. *The hookworm, trichina, and filaria are roundworms. There is hardly a spot on the earth that does not contain roundworms* (A. M. Winchester).

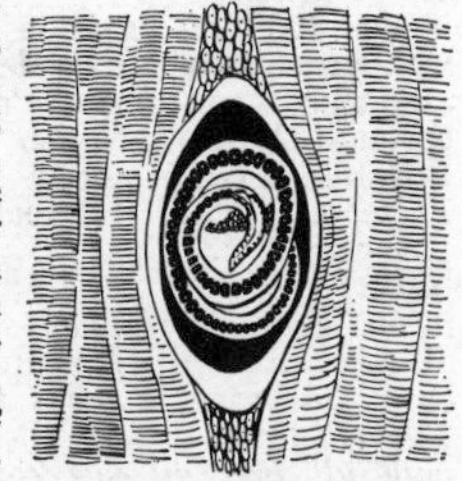
Roundworm
Trichina encysted in muscle tissue

round writing, handwriting with strong curves and exaggerated shading, used in lettering, ornamental engraving, etc.

roup[1] (rüp), *n.* **1.** either of two diseases of poultry and pigeons characterized by hoarseness and a discharge of catarrh from the eyes, nostrils, and throat. One form of roup, caused by a protozoan, is contagious and is often fatal; the other is caused by a lack of vitamin A in the diet. **2.** hoarseness or huskiness. [origin uncertain]

roup[2] (roup, rüp), *Scottish.* —*n.* an auction. —*v.i.* to cry or shout. —*v.t.* to auction: *An auctioneer ... rouped the kirk seats ... beginning by asking for a bid* (James M. Barrie). [< Scandinavian (compare Old Icelandic *raupa* boast)]

roup·et (rü′pit), *adj. Scottish.* roupy.

roup·y (rü′pē), *adj.* **1.** affected with the disease roup. **2.** hoarse or husky.

rous·ant (rou′zənt), *adj. Heraldry.* (of a bird) starting up as if about to fly.

rouse[1] (rouz), *v.,* **roused, rous·ing,** *n.* —*v.t.* **1.** to arouse; wake up; stir up: *I was roused by the telephone. The dogs roused a deer from the bushes. He was roused to anger by the insult. Ethan, with a touch of his whip, roused the sorrel to a languid trot* (Edith Wharton). *The Franks forgot their first panic, roused themselves, rallied, resisted, overcame* (G. P. R. James). *The ocean-going steamers ... roused in him wild and painful longings* (Arnold Bennett). **2.** *Nautical.* to haul with great force: *You and the boy, rouse the cable up ...* (Frederick Marryat). —*v.i.* to rise; wake; become active: *Morpheus rouses from his bed* (Alexander Pope).
—*n.* **1.** a rousing. **2.** a signal for rousing or action.
[(originally, of a hawk) to shake the feathers; origin uncertain]
—**Syn.** *v.t.* **1.** awaken, excite, provoke, stimulate, incite, inflame.

rouse[2] (rouz), *n. Archaic.* **1.** a drinking party; carouse: *Fill the cup and fill the can. Have a rouse before the morn* (Tennyson). **2.** a full draft of liquor; bumper. [perhaps short for *carouse*]

rouse·a·bout (rouz′ə bout′), *n. Australian.* a handyman, especially one on a sheep ranch.

rous·er (rou′zər), *n.* **1.** a person or thing that rouses to action. **2.** *Informal.* something interesting or astonishing: *The candidate's speech was a rouser.*

rous·ing (rou′zing), *adj.* **1.** that rouses; stirring; vigorous; brisk: *a rousing speech, to do a rousing business.* **2.** *Informal.* outrageous; extraordinary: *a rousing lie.*

rous·ing·ly (rou′zing lē), *adv.* in a rousing manner; briskly: *The alarming news ... has been promptly squashed by a local patriot who rousingly rebuts such defeatism* (Punch).

Rous sarcoma (rous), a contagious cancer of the connective tissue of poultry, believed to be caused by a virus. [< Francis P. *Rous,* born 1879, an American pathologist]

Rous·seau·an (rü sō′ən), *adj.* of, having to do with, or characteristic of the French author Jean Jacques Rousseau, 1712-1778, or his views on religion, politics, education, etc.: *The description of village conditions after the Revolution hardly encourages a Rousseauan view of peasant life* (Oscar Lewis).

Rous·seau·ism (rü sō′iz əm), *n.* the principles or doctrines of Jean Jacques Rousseau, especially in regard to social order and relations, or the social contract.

Rous·seau·ist (rü sō′ist), *n.* a follower of Rousseau or of his ideas. —*adj.* Rousseauan: *We still hold to a Rousseauist dread of the power of government* (Harper's).

Rous·seau·is·tic (rü′sō is′tik), *adj.* Rousseauan: *The existential hero of nothingness encounters the Rousseauistic myth of the innocent child of nature* (Time).

roust (roust), *v.t. Informal.* to rout; get; fetch: *to roust men out of their rooms.* [perhaps alteration of *rouse*[1]]

roust·a·bout (roust′ə bout′), *n. U.S.* an unskilled laborer on wharves, ships, ranches, etc.: *Roustabouts from the Clyde Beatty circus appeared to offer any manual labor needed* (Los Angeles Times). [American English < *roust* + *about*]

rout[1] (rout), *n.* **1.** the flight of a defeated army in disorder: *The enemy was in full rout. A retreat is painful enough; a rout borders on the unbearable* (New Yorker). **2.** a complete defeat accompanied by disorderly retreat: *All military skill of Frederick was required to prevent the defeat becoming a complete rout* (William E. H. Lecky). **3.** a group of followers; train; retinue. **4.** a noisy, disorderly crowd; mob; rabble. **5.** a riot; disturbance. **6.** *Archaic.* a crowd; band: *a*

rout of roisterers (Tennyson). **7.** *Archaic.* a large evening party.
—*v.t.* **1.** to put to flight: *Our soldiers routed the enemy.* **2.** to defeat completely.
[< Old French *route* detachment, ultimately < Latin *rumpere* to break. Doublet of ROUTE.]
—**Syn.** *n.* **4.** riffraff. *–v.t.* **2.** vanquish.

rout[2] (rout), *v.t.* **1.** to dig (out); get by searching: *Foraging about . . . I routed out some biscuit . . . and a piece of cheese* (Daniel Defoe). **2.** to put (out); force (out, up): *The farmer routed his sons out of bed at five o'clock. From even this stronghold the unlucky Rip was at length routed by his termagant wife* (Washington Irving). **3.** to root with the snout as pigs do. **4.** to hollow out; scoop out; gouge. —*v.i.* **1.** to dig with the snout: *The pigs were routing for nuts under the trees.* **2.** to poke; search; rummage: *He had been routing among the piled newspapers under the kitchen dresser* (H.G. Wells). [variant of *root*[2]]

rout[3] (rout), *v.i. Dialect.* to snore. [Old English *hrūtan*]

rout[4] (rout, rüt), *Dialect.* —*v.i.* to roar; bellow. —*n.* a roar; loud noise; uproar. Also, **rowt, rowte.** [< Scandinavian (compare Old Icelandic *rauta*)]

rout cake (rout), *British.* a kind of rich, sweet cake originally made for routs or evening parties. [< *rout*[1] (*n.* definition 7)]

route (rüt, rout), *n., v.,* **rout·ed, rout·ing.**
—*n.* **1. a.** a way to go; road: *to take the shortest route. They . . . arrived at the next inn upon the route of the stage-coach* (Henry Mackenzie). **b.** a fixed, regular course or area assigned to a person making deliveries, sales, etc.: *a newspaper route, a milk route. His route includes the south side of town.* **2.** an order for soldiers to move from one place to another. **3.** the course a kind of medicine takes through the body.
go the route, *Baseball.* to pitch a complete nine innings: *Paul Minner, a southpaw, went the route for the Cubs and gained his sixth victory* (New York Times).
—*v.t.* **1.** to arrange the route for: *The automobile club routed us on our vacation to Canada.* **2.** to send by a certain route: *The signs routed us around the construction work and over a side road. Route this memo through the sales department.*
[< French *route* < Old French < Latin *rupta* (*via*) (a way) opened up, (a passage) forced, feminine past participle of *rumpere* to break. Doublet of ROUT[1].]
—**Syn.** *n.* **1. a.** path.
➔ **route.** The pronunciation *rüt* is general, but *rout* is in common use, especially in the Army and informally, as of newspaper and delivery routes.

route march, a march of troops from one station to another, as to relieve a garrison, conducted in open order and without requiring keeping step or silence.

rout·er[1] (rou′tər), *n.* **1.** any of various tools or machines for hollowing out or furrowing. **2.** a person who routs. —*v.t.* to hollow out with a router. [< *rout*[2] + *-er*[1]]

rout·er[2] (rü′tər, rou′-), *n.* **1.** a person who arranges a route for someone or something. **2.** a thing that sends by a certain route. [< *rout*(e) + *-er*[1]]

routh (rüth, routh), *n. Scottish.* plenty. [origin unknown]

rou·tine (rü tēn′), *n.* **1.** a fixed, regular method of doing things; habitual doing of the same things in the same way: *Getting up and going to bed are parts of your daily routine. All this sort of thing was fresh and exciting at first, and then it began to fall into a routine and became habitual* (H.G. Wells). **2.** an act or skit that is part of some entertainment: *George Burns and Gracie Allen were famous for their vaudeville routines.* **3. a.** a set of coded instructions arranged in proper sequence to direct a computer to perform a sequence of operations. **b.** the sequence of operations performed by a computer.
—*adj.* using routine: *routine methods, routine workers.*
[< French *routine* < *route* route] —**rou·tine′ness,** *n.*

rou·tined (rü tēnd′), *adj.* **1.** subjected to or regulated by routine: *There we led a routined, rigorous existence in a residential community of over five hundred females* (Alison Adburgham). **2.** disciplined in routine; practiced: *Windgassen is a thoroughly experienced and routined Heldentenor* (Atlantic).

rou·ti·neer (rü′tə nir′), *n.* a person who acts by, or adheres to a routine: *My poem "Flying Crooked" was written as a satire on the ingenious routineers of poetry, as also on the ingenious routineers of science . . . who fail to understand that . . . erratic flight provides a metaphor for all original and constructive thought* (Robert Graves).

rou·tine·ly (rü tēn′lē), *adv.* **1.** as a matter of routine; regularly: *Routinely the youth squad checks bars for underage patrons* (Time). **2.** in a routine manner; without varying: *The reactor has since been rebuilt and has operated routinely since 1957* (Scientific American).

rout·ing plane (rou′ting), a router used to plane molding or to plane the edge of a board into a particular shape.

rou·tin·ism (rü tē′niz əm), *n.* adherence to routine.

rou·tin·ist (rü tē′nist), *n.* a person who believes in following or is dominated by routine.

rou·tin·i·za·tion (rü tē′nə zā′shən), *n.* **1.** the act or process of routinizing: *Professor Brown is evidently horrified by the routinization of the imaginative which occurs in the contemporary academy* (Harper's). **2.** the fact or state of being routinized: *Such routinization leaves little room for chance, luck, imagination, or excitement* (Science News Letter).

rou·tin·ize (rü tē′nīz), *v.t.,* **-ized, -iz·ing.** to cause to become a routine; make habitual: *to routinize a process or operation,* to routinize religion.

rout seat (rout), *British.* a light bench or chair rented for use at evening parties: *The waltz was over. He could see her now, on a rout seat against the wall* (John Galsworthy).

roux (rü), *n.* butter and flour cooked together to a stiff, brown paste, used to thicken and color sauces, soups, etc. [< French (*beurre*) *roux* reddish-brown (butter) < Latin *russus* red]

rove[1] (rōv), *v.,* **roved, rov·ing,** *n.* —*v.i.* to wander; wander about; roam: *He loved to rove over the fields and woods. For ten long years I roved about, living first in one capital, then another* (Charlotte Brontë). —*v.t.* to wander over; cross: *Their young men . . . roved the spurs of the Alleghenies, in quest of marketable skins* (George Bancroft). —*n.* a roving; ramble. [Middle English *roven* to shoot (arrows) at random targets while moving; origin uncertain] —**Syn.** *v.i.* ramble, range. See **roam.**

rove[2] (rōv), *v.* a past tense and a past participle of **reeve**[2].

rove[3] (rōv), *n., v.,* **roved, rov·ing.** —*n.* a sliver of wool, cotton, etc., drawn out and very slightly twisted in preparation for spinning. —*v.t.* to form (slivers of wool, cotton, etc.) into roves. [origin uncertain]

rove[4] (rōv), *n.* a small ring of metal in which the point of a nail is flattened in building boats. [< Scandinavian (compare Old Icelandic *rō*)]

rove beetle, any of a large group of long, thin beetles that run very fast and prey on other insects. Certain varieties live in decaying matter and in association with ants.

rove-o·ver (rōv′ō′vər), *adj.* of or having to do with a kind of poetic meter with a foot forming the end of one line and the first part of the next.

rov·er[1] (rō′vər), *n.* **1.** a person who roves; wanderer. **2.** a mark selected at random in archery. **3.** in croquet: **a.** a ball that goes through all the arches. **b.** the person playing this ball. **4.** *British.* a senior Boy Scout, 18 years or older. [< *rov*(e)[1] + *-er*[1]] —**Syn.** **1.** rambler.

rov·er[2] (rō′vər), *n.* **1.** a pirate: *the rovers whom Scandinavia had sent forth to ravage Western Europe* (Macaulay). **2.** a pirate ship: *Our ship . . . was surprised . . . by a Turkish rover of Sallee, who gave chase to us with all the sail she could make* (Daniel Defoe). [< Middle Dutch *roover opt zee* pirate, thief of the sea < *roven* to rob]

rov·er[3] (rō′vər), *n.* **1.** a machine or frame for roving cotton, wool, etc. **2.** a person who operates a roving frame or machine. [< *rov*(e)[3] + *-er*[1]]

row[1] (rō), *n.* **1.** a line of people or things: *rows of seats in a classroom or a theater, a row of houses. Corn is planted in rows.* **2.** a street with a line of buildings on either side.
hard row to hoe, a difficult thing to do: *The lecturer then set himself a hard row to hoe: the scholarly correction of everything his audience may have been taught at school about King John* (London Times).
in a row, a. in line; in alignment: *three houses in a row.* **b.** in succession; successively: *for the second day in a row.*
—*v.t.* to arrange in a row; place in rows.
[Old English *rāw*]
—**Syn.** *n.* **1.** file, series.

row[2] (rō), *v.i.* **1.** to use oars to move a boat: *Row to the island.* **2.** (of a boat) to be moved by the use of oars. —*v.t.* **1.** to move (a boat, etc.) by the use of oars. **2.** to convey in a rowboat: *We were rowed to the shore.* **3.** to perform (a race, etc.) by rowing. **4.** to row against in a race. **5.** to use (oars) for rowing. **6.** to have (oars): *a boat rowing 8 oars.*
—*n.* **1.** the act of using oars. **2.** a trip in a rowboat: *It's only a short row.*
[Old English *rōwan*] —**row′er,** *n.*

row[3] (rou), *n.* **1.** a noisy quarrel; disturbance; clamor: *It wasn't any ordinary difference of opinion; it was a "row"* (H.G. Wells). **2.** *Informal.* a squabble: *The children had a row over the bicycle.*
—*v.i. Informal.* to quarrel noisily; make noise. —*v.t. Informal.* to scold.
[origin uncertain]
—**Syn.** *n.* **1.** fracas, rumpus.

row·an (rō′ən, rou′-), *n.* **1.** the mountain ash. **2.** its red, berrylike fruit. [< Scandinavian (compare Norwegian dialectal *raun*)]

row·an·ber·ry (rō′ən ber′ē, rou′-), *n., pl.* **-ries.** the berry of the rowan.

rowan tree, the mountain ash; rowan.

row·boat (rō′bōt′), *n.* a boat moved by oars.

row crop (rō), a crop planted in rows, such as corn or cotton.

row·de·dow (rou′dē dou′), *n. Informal.* noise; uproar; disturbance. [probably < *row*[3]]

row·di·ly (rou′də lē), *adv.* in a rowdy way; disorderly.

row·di·ness (rou′dē nis), *n.* a being rowdy; disorderliness.

row·dy (rou′dē), *n., pl.* **-dies,** *adj.,* **-di·er, -di·est.** —*n.* a rough, disorderly, quarrelsome person. —*adj.* rough; disorderly; quarrelsome. [American English, probably < *row*[3]] —**Syn.** *n.* brawler.

row·dy·dow (rou′dē dou′), *n.* rowdedow.

row·dy·dow·dy (rou′dē dou′dē), *adj. Informal.* characterized by noisy roughness. [probably < *rowdedow,* influenced by *rowdy*]

row·dy·ish (rou′dē ish), *adj.* like a rowdy; rough and disorderly; quarrelsome. —**row′dy·ish·ness,** *n.*

row·dy·ism (rou′dē iz əm), *n.* disorderly, quarrelsome conduct; rough, noisy behavior: *rowdyism at Halloween.*

-rowed, *combining form.* having ___ rows: *Six-rowed = having six rows.*

row·el (rou′əl), *n., v.,* **-eled, -el·ing** or (*especially British*) **-elled, -el·ling.** —*n.* **1.** a small wheel with sharp points, attached to the end of a spur: *Striking his rowels into his horse, he was out of sight in an instant* (Jane Porter). **2.** a piece of silk, etc., inserted under the skin of an animal to cause a discharge of pus or fluid.
—*v.t.* **1.** to use a rowel on. **2.** to insert a rowel in (an animal).
[< Old French *roel, rouelle* (diminutive) < *roue* wheel < Latin *rota.* Compare ROULETTE.]

row·en (rou′ən), *n.* the second crop of grass or hay in a season; aftermath. [Middle English *rewayn,* apparently < unrecorded Old North French *rewain,* probably < Old French *re-* re- + *gaïn* gain[1]]

row house (rō), one of a row of attached houses of the same design, usually two floors high and occupied by one family.

row·ing boat (rō′ing), *British.* a rowboat.

row·lock (rō′lok′), *n.* a notch, metal support, etc., in which the oar rests in rowing; oarlock. [< *row*[2]; patterned on *oarlock*]

Rowlock
Top, detail; bottom, with oars on dinghy

rowt or **rowte** (rout), *v.,* **rowt·ed, rowt·ing,** *n. Scottish.* roar; bellow; rout. [variant of *rout*[4]]

rox·burghe (roks′bėr′ō), *n.* a bookbinding of plain leather with cloth or paper boards and gilt leaves. [< the third Duke of *Roxburghe,* 1740-1804, a British collector of books]

Roy., Royal.

roy·al (roi′əl), *adj.* **1. a.** of kings and queens: *the royal family.* **b.** belonging to the family of a king or queen: *a royal prince.* **2.** belonging to a king or queen: *royal power.* **3. a.** serving a king or queen: *the royal household.* **b.** founded, favored, or encouraged by a king or queen: *the Royal Academy.* **4.** from or by a king or queen: *a royal command.* **5.** of a kingdom: *a royal army or navy.* **6.** appropriate for a king; splendid: *a royal welcome, a royal feast.* **7.** like a king; noble; majestic: *The lion is a royal beast.* **8.** fine; excellent. **9.** rich and bright: *royal blue.* **10.** chemically inert; noble: *royal metals.*
—*n.* **1.** a small mast, sail, or yard, set above the topgallant. See picture under **sail. 2.** a size of writing paper (19 x 24 inches). **3.** a size of printing paper (20 x 25 inches).
[< Old French *roial, real* < Latin *rēgālis* < *rēx, rēgis* king. Doublet of REAL², REGAL.]
—**Syn.** *adj.* **1, 2. Royal, regal, kingly** mean of or belonging to a king or kings. **Royal** is the most general in application, describing people or things associated with or belonging to a king: *Sherwood Forest is a royal forest.* **Regal** emphasizes the majesty, pomp, and magnificence of the office, and is now used chiefly of people or things showing these qualities: *The general has a regal bearing.* **Kingly** emphasizes the personal character, actions, purposes, or feelings of or worthy of a king: *Tempering justice with mercy is a kingly virtue.* **6.** magnificent. **7.** august.

Royal Academy, a society founded in 1768 by George III of England to promote and encourage painting, sculpture, and architecture. *Abbr.:* R.A.

Royal Air Force, the air force of Great Britain. *Abbr.:* R.A.F.

royal antler, the third branch of an antler.

Royal Assent, (in England) the formal approbation given by the sovereign in Parliament to a bill that has been passed by the House of Lords and the House of Commons, after which it becomes law. The assent is usually given by a commission representing the sovereign and is read by the clerk of Parliament in Anglo-French.

royal coachman, a fishing fly with white wings, a greenish and red body, and a golden tail.

royal commission, in Canada: **a.** a group of people commissioned by the Crown to conduct an inquiry into any matter that concerns the federal or provincial governments. **b.** the inquiry conducted by such a group.

royal demesne, crown lands; the private property of the Crown.

royal fern, a fern with tall, upright fronds, growing in clumps.

royal flush, (in poker) a straight flush in which the highest card is an ace.

roy·al·ism (roi′ə liz-əm), *n.* adherence to a king or to a monarchy.

roy·al·ist (roi′ə list), *n.* a supporter of a king or of a royal government. —*adj.* of or having to do with royalism or royalists: *Judging by the newspaper space and fuss in our nation that is devoted to the Queen of England . . . a royalist party here ought to sweep the country* (Newsweek).

American Royal Fern (2 to 10 ft. high)

Roy·al·ist (roi′ə list), *n.* **1.** a supporter of Charles I in England in his struggle with Parliament; Cavalier. **2.** a supporter of the British in the American Revolution; Tory; Loyalist. **3.** a supporter of the Bourbons in France since 1793.

roy·al·is·tic (roi′ə lis′tik), *adj.* royalist.

roy·al·ize (roi′ə līz), *v.t.,* **-ized, -iz·ing.** to make royal.

royal jelly, a creamy, jellylike substance rich in vitamins and proteins, fed to the young larvae of bees and throughout the larval stage to queen bees to give the queen a longer life and greater fertility. A preparation containing royal jelly is used by women as a cosmetic. *The U.S. Government is inquiring whether the advertising and sale of royal jelly, the queen bee food, is a "racket"* (Science News Letter).

roy·al·ly (roi′ə lē), *adv.* in a royal manner; grandly; richly.

royal mast, the mast next above the topgallant mast.

royal moth, any of a group of large, hairy moths, including the regal moth and imperial moth.

royal palm, a tall palm tree that has a whitish trunk and is often planted for ornament. See the picture of **palm².**

Royal Peculiar, (in England) a particular parish or church which is exempted from any jurisdiction but that of the sovereign; sovereign's free chapel: *This Royal Peculiar became a centre of worship, teaching, social work, and reconciliation* (London Times).

royal poinciana, a tropical tree of the pea family often cultivated for its large spikes of scarlet and orange flowers; flamboyant.

Royal Society, an association, incorporated under Charles II of England in 1662, to advance science and encourage scientific research.

royal tennis, court tennis: *Royalty then adopted the game, and it was moved to indoor courtyards. This game, called . . . royal tennis, is still played today* (Helen I. Driver).

royal tern, a large tern, white with a grayish mantle. The royal tern is found along the coast in the warmer parts of North and South America.

roy·al·ty (roi′əl tē), *n., pl.* **-ties. 1.** a royal person; royal persons: *Kings, queens, princes, and princesses are royalty.* **2.** the rank or dignity of a king or queen; royal power: *The crown is a symbol of royalty.* **3.** royal quality; kingliness; nobility. **4.** a royal right or privilege. **5.** a royal domain; realm. **6. a.** a share of the receipts or profits paid to an owner of a patent or copyright: *He prevailed upon the management to pay a small royalty for the use of the fourth movement of Shostakovich's Fifth Symphony* (New Yorker). **b.** a payment for the use of any of various rights: *The joint enterprise will pay a royalty to the government, as the owner of the underground oil* (Time). [< Old French *roialte* < *roial;* see ROYAL]

royal water, aqua regia, a mixture of nitric acid and hydrochloric acid: *It is termed royal water because of [its] action upon the noble, or royal, metals* (W.N. Jones).

roz·zer (roz′ər), *n. British Slang.* policeman; detective. [origin unknown]

Rp., rupiah.

R.P., 1. Reformed Presbyterian. **2.** Regius Professor.

R.P.E., Reformed Protestant Episcopal.

r.p.m. or **rpm** (no periods), revolutions per minute.

RPM (no periods) or **R.P.M.,** resale price maintenance.

R.P.O., Railway Post Office.

r.p.s. or **rps** (no periods), revolutions per second.

rpt., report.

R.Q. or **r.q.,** respiratory quotient.

R.R., 1. railroad. **2.** Right Reverend. **3.** rural route.

RRB (no periods), Railroad Retirement Board.

RR Lyrae star, any of a class of variable stars with very short periods between fluctuations of brightness. Such fluctuations are usually less than a day.

rs., rupees.

Rs (no period), rupees.

Rs., 1. reis. **2.** rupees.

R.S., 1. recording secretary. **2.** Revised Statutes. **3.** Royal Society.

R.S.A., 1. Royal Scottish Academician. **2.** Royal Scottish Academy.

R.S.F.S.R. or **RSFSR** (no periods), Russian Soviet Federated Socialist Republic.

RSG (no periods) or **R.S.G.,** regional seat of government.

R.S.L., Royal Society of Literature.

R.S.M., regimental sergeant major.

R.S.P.C.A. or **RSPCA** (no periods), *British.* The Royal Society for the Prevention of Cruelty to Animals.

R.S.S., Fellow of the Royal Society (Latin, *Regiae Societatis Socius*).

R.S.V. or **RSV** (no periods), Revised Standard Version (of the Bible): *The work under consideration here, the Revised Standard Version (R.S.V.), issued with such fanfare last fall, is the latest great effort* (New Yorker).

R.S.V.P. or **r.s.v.p.,** please answer (French, *répondez s'il vous plaît*).

rt., right.

r.t., reverberation time.

RT (no periods), radiotelephone.

rte., route.

Rt. Hon., Right Honorable.

Rt. Rev., Right Reverend.

Rts., *Finance.* rights.

Ru, ruthenium (chemical element).

Ru. 1. Rumanian. **2.** runic.

ru·at coe·lum (rü′at sē′ləm), *Latin.* though the heavens fall.

rub (rub), *v.,* **rubbed, rub·bing,** *n.* —*v.t.* **1.** to move (one thing) back and forth (against another); move (two things) together: *Rub your hands to keep them warm. Solomon Gill rubbed his hands with an air of stealthy enjoyment* (Dickens). **2.** to move one's hand or an object over the surface of; push and press along the surface of: *The nurse rubbed my lame back.* **3.** to make or bring (to some condition) by sliding the hand or some object: *to rub silver bright, to rub the skin off one's back.* **4.** to clean, smooth, or polish by moving one thing firmly against another: *to rub a table with steel wool.* **5.** to irritate or make sore by rubbing. **6.** to annoy; make angry. —*v.i.* **1.** to press as it moves: *That door rubs on the floor. Stray, homeless cats rubbed against his legs* (Winston Churchill). **2.** to be capable of being rubbed; admit of rubbing. **3.** to keep going with difficulty: *Money is scarce, but we shall rub along.*
rub down, a. to clean (a horse) from dust and sweat by rubbing: *After the horses are rubbed down, the men proceed to the straw barn* (H. Stephens). **b.** to rub (the body); massage: *He went to the Turkish bath to have his aching back rubbed down.*
rub it in, *Informal.* to keep on mentioning something unpleasant: *Ye needn't rub it in any more* (Rudyard Kipling).
rub off, a. to remove by rubbing: *There's some dust on your sleeve; rub it off.* **b.** to be removed by rubbing: *Ink rubs off easily with this eraser.*
rub off on, to cling to; become a part of; take hold of: *Possibly some of Wilson's devotion to style has rubbed off on him* (Saturday Review).
rub out, a. to erase: *Rub that out and do it over again.* **b.** *U.S. Slang.* to murder: *Shoveling the money back into the house, the frantic badmen realize that the little old lady must be rubbed out* (Time).
—*n.* **1.** the act of rubbing: *Give the silver a rub with the polish.* **2.** something that rubs or hurts the feelings: *He didn't like her mean rub at his slowness.* **3.** a rough spot due to rubbing. **4.** a difficulty: *The rub came when both boys wanted to sit with the driver. To sleep: perchance to dream: ay, there's the rub* (Shakespeare).
[Middle English *rubben.* Compare Low German *rubben,* Danish *rubbe.*]
—**Syn.** *v.t.* **5.** chafe.

rub·a·boo or **rub·ba·boo** (rub′ə bü′), *n. Canadian.* a soup made by boiling pemmican in water with flour and other ingredients. [< Canadian French *rababou* < Algonkian]

rub-a-dub (rub′ə dub′), *n., v.,* **-dubbed, -dub·bing.** —*n.* **1.** the sound of a drum being beaten. **2.** a similar sound. —*v.i.* to make such a sound. [probably imitative]

ru·ba·'i (rü bä′ē), *n., pl.* **ru·bái·yát** (rü′bī-yät, -bē-) a quatrain. [< Arabic *rubā'i* having four]

Ru·bái·yát (rü′bī yät, -bē-), *n.pl.* a collection of poems by Omar Khayyám or its translation by Edward FitzGerald. [< Arabic *rubā'iyāt,* feminine plural of *rubā'īya* quatrain < *rubā'i* ruba'i]

ru·basse (rü bas′, -bäs′), *n.* quartz crystals containing particles of hematite which reflect a bright-red color, used as a gem. [< earlier French *rubace* < stem of *rubis* ruby]

ru·ba·to (rü bä′tō), *adj., n., pl.* **-tos.** *Music.* —*adj.* having certain notes of a measure arbitrarily lengthened while others are correspondingly shortened. —*n.* a rubato tempo or passage. [< Italian *(tempo) rubato* (literally) robbed (time), past participle of *rubare* to rob]

rub·ber¹ (rub′ər), *n.* **1.** an elastic substance obtained from the milky juice of various tropical plants, or made synthetically by various chemical processes. Rubber will

not let air or water through. Pure rubber is a whitish hydrocarbon that becomes black and more easily worked when vulcanized for commercial use. *Natural rubber is made up of long molecules consisting of simple hydrocarbons strung together end to end like beads in a necklace* (Edith Goldman). **2.** something made from this substance: *We wear rubbers on our feet when it rains. Pencils often have rubbers for erasing pencil marks.* **3.** a person or thing that rubs. **4.** *Baseball.* **a.** the rectangular piece of rubber on the pitcher's mound. **b.** home plate.
—*adj.* made of rubber: *Since the 1930's when rubber foam first bounded into the auto industry, its use as a padding for seats has climbed* (Wall Street Journal).
—*v.i. Slang.* to stretch the neck or turn the head to look at something.
[(definition 1) for *India rubber* (from its use originally as an eraser)] —**rub′ber-like′,** *adj.*
rub·ber[2] (rub′ər), *n.* in bridge or certain other card games: **1.** a series of two games out of three or three games out of five won by the same side. **2.** the deciding game in such a series: *If each side has won two games, the fifth game will be the rubber.*
rubber band, a circular strip of rubber, used to hold things together: *I keep a rubber band around the small cardboard tickets that I get with every purchase at the bakery* (Atlantic). —**Syn.** elastic.
rubber cement, an adhesive consisting of natural or synthetic rubber in a solvent, used to bond leather, paper, rubber, etc.
rubber check, *Slang.* a check refused by the bank on which it is drawn because of insufficient money on deposit to cover the amount; check that bounces.
rubber game, the deciding game or match in an odd-numbered series in baseball, boxing, etc.
rub·ber·ise (rub′ə rīz), *v.t.,* **-ised, -is·ing.** *Especially British.* rubberize.
rub·ber·ize (rub′ə rīz), *v.t.,* **-ized, -iz·ing.** to cover or treat with rubber: *rubberized cloth.*
rub·ber·neck (rub′ər nek′), *U.S. Slang.* —*n.* a sightseer, especially an unsophisticated one: *A good-sized crowd of rubbernecks quickly gathered, anxious to see who had been bold enough to jaywalk when the heat was on* (New Yorker).
—*v.i.* **1.** to stare: *Everyone has gone ashore to buy, to drink, to rubberneck* (New Yorker). **2.** to go sightseeing: *He rubbernecked through Cairo last week* (Time).
—*adj.* of or for sightseeing: *a rubberneck tour. She had flown through the Middle East with rubberneck stops at Beirut, Damascus, Amman, Jerusalem, and Tel Aviv* (Time).
—**rub′ber·neck′er,** *n.*
rubber plant, 1. any plant yielding rubber. **2.** an ornamental house plant of the mulberry family with oblong, shining, leathery leaves.
rubber stamp, 1. a stamp made of rubber, used with ink for printing dates, signatures, etc. **2.** *Informal.* a person or group that approves or endorses something without thought or as a formality: *Russia charged that the General Assembly was merely a rubber stamp* (Newsweek).
rub·ber-stamp (*v.* rub′ər stamp′; *adj.* rub′ər stamp′), *v.t.* **1.** to print or sign with a rubber stamp: *He read through my sheaf of papers and rubber-stamped each of them three or four times* (New Yorker). **2.** *Informal.* to approve or endorse (a policy, bill, etc.) without thought or as a formality.
—*adj.* **1.** using a rubber stamp. **2.** *Informal.* that approves or endorses without thought or as a formality.
rubber tree, a tree from which rubber is produced, as the hevea.
rub·ber·y (rub′ər ē), *adj.* like rubber; elastic; tough.
rub·bing (rub′ing), *n.* a representation of a design in relief obtained by pressing a thin tough paper, as parchment, onto the surface and rubbing it with a heelball, charcoal, etc.: *These rubbings from medieval English brass plates commemorate the contemporary nobility* (New York Times).
rubbing alcohol, denatured alcohol, usually slightly scented.
rubbing table, a table to massage a person on.
rub·bish (rub′ish), *n.* **1.** waste stuff of no use; trash: *Pick up the rubbish and burn it.* **2.** silly words and thoughts; nonsense: *The jumbled rubbish of a dream* (Tennyson). *All this modern newspaper rubbish about a New York aristocracy* (Edith Wharton). [Middle English *robys, robbous;* origin uncertain] —**Syn. 1.** litter, debris, refuse.
rub·bish·ing (rub′i shing), *adj.* rubbishy; trashy: *The chief problem here is how such a rubbishing melodrama could possibly have been co-authored, directed and produced by the eminent French director* (Newsweek).
rub·bish·y (rub′i shē), *adj.* **1.** full of or covered with rubbish. **2.** of or like rubbish; trashy; paltry: *The doggerel expresses the rubbishy lives of the modern London sophisticates* (Time).
rub·ble (rub′əl), *n.* **1.** rough broken stones, bricks, etc.: *the rubble left by an explosion or earthquake.* **2.** masonry made of this: *The house was built of rubble and plaster.* —*adj.* made of or like rubble: *rubble masonry, rubble ballast.* [Middle English *robel;* origin uncertain]
rub·ble·work (rub′əl wėrk′), *n.* masonry built of rubble or roughly dressed stones.
rub·bly (rub′lē), *adj.* full of, consisting of, or like rubble: *These combined with the rubbly, half-demolished buildings in the older sections to give the whole city an air of impermanence* (New Yorker).
rub·down (rub′doun′), *n.* a rubbing of the body; massage.
rube (rüb), *Slang.* —*n.* an unsophisticated countryman: *Generations of comedians have vulgarized Peoria as the symbol of the rube and the boob* (Saturday Evening Post).
—*adj.* of a rube; like rubes: *a rube town. One of your rube detectives should come over to my cottage* (Charles Dutton). [American English, earlier *reub,* abbreviation of *Reuben,* a proper name]
ru·be·an·ic acid (rü′bē an′ik), a reddish powder made from hydrogen sulfide and cyanogen, used as a reagent. *Formula:* $C_2H_4N_2S_2$
ru·be·fa·cient (rü′bə fā′shənt), *adj.* causing redness, especially of the skin: *a rubefacient liniment.* —*n.* a rubefacient application, such as a mustard plaster. [< Latin *rubefaciēns, -entis,* present participle of *rubĕfacere* < *rubeus* red + *facere* make]
ru·be·fac·tion (rü′bə fak′shən), *n.* **1.** a making red. **2.** redness of the skin, especially as caused by a rubefacient.
Rube Gold·berg (rüb′ gōld′bėrg), (of an invention, device, scheme, etc.) ridiculously complicated: *He called the three-gun color tube used by present manufacturers, "a Rube Goldberg contraption if there ever was one"* (Wall Street Journal). [< *Rube Goldberg,* an American cartoonist noted for a cartoon series depicting fantastically complicated mechanical inventions for performing the simplest tasks]
ru·bel·la (rü bel′ə), *n.* German measles: *Rubella (German measles) in pregnant women caused severe damage to the fetus* (Bulletin of Atomic Scientists). [< New Latin *rubella,* neuter plural of Latin *rubellus* reddish (diminutive) < *rubeus* red]
ru·bel·lite (rü bel′īt), *n.* a pink or red variety of tourmaline, used as a gem. [< Latin *rubellus* (see RUBELLA) + English *-ite*[1]]
Ru·ben (rü′bən), *n.* (in the Douay Bible) Reuben.
Ru·ben·esque (rü′bə nesk′), *adj.* suggestive or characteristic of the paintings or style of Rubens: *The models of his choice are of rather Rubenesque fullness* (Observer). [< Peter Paul *Rubens,* 1577-1640, the Flemish painter + *-esque*]
Ru·ben·si·an (rü ben′sē ən), *adj.* Rubenesque: *He drew soothing pictures of Rubensian nudes, quiet beaches, bustling cities* (Time).
ru·be·o·la (rü bē′ə lə, rü′bē ō′-), *n.* **1.** measles. **2.** German measles. [< New Latin *rubeola* < a diminutive form of Latin *rubeus* red]
ru·be·o·lar (rü bē′ə lər, rü′bē ō′-), *adj.* of, having to do with, or like rubeola.
ru·bes·cence (rü bes′əns), *n.* a growing or being red.
ru·bes·cent (rü bes′ənt), *adj.* becoming red; blushing. [< Latin *rubēscēns, -entis,* present participle of *rubēscere* become red < *rubēre* be red, related to *ruber* red]
ru·bi·a·ceous (rü′bē ā′shəs), *adj.* belonging to the madder family: *The coffee plant, gardenia, and bluet are rubiaceous plants.* [< New Latin *Rubiaceae* the order name (< *Rubia* the madder genus < Latin *rubia* madder < *rubeus* red) + English *-ous*]
ru·bi·celle (rü′bə sel), *n.* a yellow or orange-red spinel. [< French *rubicelle,* (apparently diminutive) < earlier *rubace;* see RUBASSE]
Ru·bi·con (rü′bə kon), *n.* a limit to a course of action from which one cannot turn back. **cross** or **pass the Rubicon,** to make an important decision from which one cannot turn back: [*Napoleon*] *would . . . have crossed the Rubicon at the head of the popular party* (Scott). *A pause—in which I began to steady the palsy of my nerves, and to feel that the Rubicon was passed* (Charlotte Brontë). [< *Rubicon,* a small river in eastern Italy that was part of the boundary between the Roman republic and its provinces. By crossing the Rubicon into Italy in 49 B.C., Julius Caesar started the civil war that made him master of Rome.]
ru·bi·cund (rü′bə kund), *adj.* reddish; ruddy: *the cheery, rubicund faces of children* (Harriet Beecher Stowe). [< Latin *rubicundus* < *rubeus* red] —**Syn.** florid.
ru·bi·cun·di·ty (rü′bə kun′də tē), *n.* rubicund quality or state.
ru·bid·i·um (rü bid′ē əm), *n.* a soft, silver-white metallic chemical element resembling potassium. It decomposes water and ignites spontaneously when exposed to air. *Rubidium and cesium, like the other alkali metals, never occur free in nature* (W. N. Jones). *Symbol:* Rb; *at.wt.:* (C^{12}) 85.47 or (O^{16}) 85.48; *at.no.:* 37; *valence:* 1. [< New Latin *rubidium* < Latin *rubidus* red < *rubēre* be red (from the two red lines in its spectrum)]
ru·bied (rü′bēd), *adj.* colored like the ruby.
ru·big·i·nose (rü bij′ə nōs), *adj.* rubiginous.
ru·big·i·nous (rü bij′ə nəs), *adj.* **1.** rusty; rust-colored. **2.** (of plants) affected with rust or blight. [< Latin *rūbīginōsus* < *rūbīgō, -inis* rust, mold, related to *ruber* red]
ru·bi·go (rü bī′gō), *n.* a reddish ferric oxide, used as a pigment and in polishing compounds; rouge. [< Latin *rūbīgō*]
ru·bi·ous (rü′bē əs), *adj.* red; rubied.
ru·ble (rü′bəl), *n.* a Russian monetary unit and silver coin or piece of paper money, worth $1.11. 100 kopecks = 1 ruble. *Abbr.:* r. Also, **rouble.** [< Russian *rubl′*]
ru·bor (rü′bər), *n.* redness of the skin. [< Latin *rubor* < *rubēre* be red]
rub·out (rub′out′), *n. U.S. Slang.* a murder; gangland killing: *Frankie was the picture of innocence, said he ran because "I thought it was a rubout"* (Time).
rub rail, 1. a protective guard on the gunwale of a boat: *Then it came to me: . . . get a leg hooked over the rub rail and onto the deck, and then pull up* (Harper's). **2.** a metal projection on cars and trucks, as a bumper, to guard against scraping. **3.** any raillike protection.
ru·bric (rü′brik), *n.* **1.** the title or heading of a chapter, a law, etc., written or printed in red or in special lettering. **2.** a direction for the conducting of religious services, inserted in a prayer book, ritual, etc. **3.** any heading, rule, or guide: *I think that the rubrics of the materialist dialectic are useful aids to thought* (Scientific American). *I talked to him till I was black in the face, and all I got out of him was the law and the rubrics* (Frank O'Connor). **4.** *Archaic.* **a.** red ocher. **b.** a red color.
—*adj.* rubrical.
[< Old French *rubrique,* learned borrowing from Late Latin *rubrīca* rubric < Latin, red color, red coloring matter < *ruber* red]
ru·bri·cal (rü′brə kəl), *adj.* **1.** red. **2.** printed or written in red or in special lettering. **3.** of, having to do with, or according to religious rubrics. —**ru′bri·cal·ly,** *adv.*
ru·bri·cate (rü′brə kāt), *v.t.,* **-cat·ed, -cat·ing. 1.** to mark or color with red. **2.** to furnish with rubrics. **3.** to regulate by rubrics. [< Latin *rubrīcāre* (with English *-ate*[1]) to color red < *rubrīca* red coloring matter; see RUBRIC]
ru·bri·ca·tion (rü′brə kā′shən), *n.* **1.** the act of rubricating. **2.** that colored red.
ru·bri·ca·tor (rü′brə kā′tər), *n.* a person who inserts rubrics in a manuscript.
ru·bri·cian (rü brish′ən), *n.* a person who studies or is an expert in religious rubrics.
ru·bric·i·ty (rü bris′ə tē), *n.* **1.** the assumption of a red color: *the periodical . . . rubricity of the Nile* (Auckland C. Geddes). **2.** adherence to liturgical rubrics.
ru·by (rü′bē), *n., pl.* **-bies,** *adj.* —*n.* **1.** a clear, hard, red precious stone. It is a variety of corundum. *Formula:* Al_2O_3 **2.** its color, a deep, glowing red: *the natural*

ruby of your cheek (Shakespeare). **3.** something made of ruby, especially a bearing in a watch. **4.** red wine: *Still the Vine her ancient Ruby yields* (Edward FitzGerald). **5.** *British.* (in printing) a size of type; approximately 5½ points. In the United States it is called *agate.* **6.** *British Slang.* blood.

—*adj.* deep, glowing red: *ruby lips.*

[< Old French *rubis,* plural of *rubi,* ultimately < Latin *rubeus* red] —**ru′by·like′,** *adj.*

ru·by-crowned kinglet (rü′bē kround′), a tiny, grayish, North American bird with a bright ruby patch on the crown that is exposed during excitement, courtship, etc.

ruby silver, 1. pyrargyrite. **2.** proustite.

ruby spaniel, a chestnut red variety of the English toy spaniel.

ru·by·tail (rü′bē tāl′), *n.* any of various small, solitary, stinging insects that are brilliantly colored and lay their eggs in the nests of other insects. One variety has a ruby-colored abdomen.

ru·by-throat·ed hummingbird (rü′bē-thrō′tid), a hummingbird of eastern North America with bright-green plumage above. The male also has a brilliant-red throat.

ru·cer·vine (rü sėr′vīn, -vin), *adj.* of or having to do with a group of large East Indian deer that have branching antlers and long tines extending forward over the brow. [< New Latin *Rucervus* the genus name (< Malay *rūsa* deer + Latin *cervus* deer) + English *-ine*[1]]

ruche (rüsh), *n.* a full pleating or frill of lace, ribbon, net, etc., used as trimming, especially on the collars and cuffs of women's dresses. Also, **rouche.** [< French *ruche* (originally) beehive (from its shape)]

ruched (rüsht), *adj.* **1.** made into a ruche or ruches: *The top and hem are ruched nylon and lace* (Sunday Times). **2.** having a ruche or ruches: *a ruched collar, a ruched dress.*

ruch·ing (rü′shing), *n.* **1.** trimming made of ruches. **2.** material used to make ruches.

ruck[1] (ruk), *n.* **1.** a crowd. **2.** the great mass of common or inferior people or things. **3.** the horses left behind in a race: *a brilliant young charioteer in the ruck of the race* (George Meredith). [< Scandinavian (compare Norwegian *ruka* little heap)]

ruck[2] (ruk), *n.* **1.** a crease; wrinkle. **2.** a ridge. —*v.i.* to become creased or wrinkled. —*v.t.* **1.** to crease; wrinkle. **2.** to gather in folds. [apparently < Scandinavian (compare Norwegian *rukka,* Old Icelandic *hrukka*)]

ruck·sack (ruk′sak′, růk′-), *n.* a kind of knapsack, usually of canvas with two shoulder straps. [< German *Rucksack* < dialectal *Ruck,* variant of *Rücken* back + *Sack* sack]

Rück·um·laut (rʏk′ům′lout), *n. German.* the absence of umlaut.

ruck·us (ruk′əs), *n. U.S. Slang.* a noisy disturbance or uproar; row: *Like most old campaigners, Harry Truman often likes to stir up a ruckus* (Newsweek). [American English, perhaps blend of *ruction* and *rumpus*]

ruc·tion (ruk′shən), *n. Informal.* a disturbance; quarrel; row: *when the racial ructions rise* (Rudyard Kipling). [perhaps alteration of *insurrection*]

ruc·us (ruk′əs), *n. U.S. Slang.* ruckus.

rud (rud), *n.* **1.** *Archaic.* red or ruddy color. **2.** *Dialect.* ruddle. **3.** *Obsolete.* complexion. [Old English *rudu,* related to *rēad* red]

rud·beck·i·a (rud bek′ē ə), *n.* any of various herbs of the composite family with showy flowers consisting of petals around a conical dark center; coneflower: *The yellow daisy or the black-eyed Susan is a common rudbeckia.* [< New Latin *Rudbeckia* the genus name < Olaus *Rudbeck,* 1630-1702, a Swedish botanist]

rudd (rud), *n.* a red-finned, European fresh-water fish related to the carp. [earlier *rowde,* apparently a use of *rud* redness, Old English *rudu;* see RUD]

rud·der (rud′ər), *n.* **1.** a hinged flat piece of wood or metal at the rear end of a boat or ship, by which it is steered. **2.** a similar piece in an airplane, dirigible, etc., hinged vertically (for right-and-left steering). **3.** a person or thing that guides, directs, or controls. [Middle English *roder* < Old English *rōthor*]

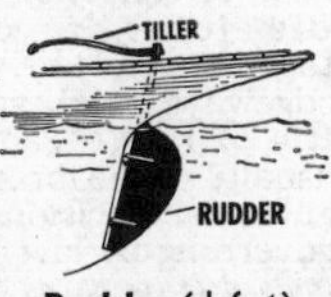

Rudder (def. 1)

rudder bar, a foot-operated bar in the cockpit of certain light airplanes, to which the control cables leading to the rudder are attached.

rud·dered (rud′ərd), *adj.* having a rudder.

rud·der·head (rud′ər hed′), *n.* the upper end of the rudder, into which the tiller is fitted.

rud·der·less (rud′ər lis), *adj.* without a rudder; without controls; drifting; aimless: *a rudderless boat. Left rudderless, Pakistan drifted on the currents of opportunism, intrigue and corruption* (Atlantic).

rud·der·post (rud′ər pōst′), *n.* **1.** an extension of the sternpost on which the rudder is hung. **2.** a rudderstock.

rud·der·stock (rud′ər stok′), *n.* the part of a rudder by which it is connected to the ship.

rud·di·ly (rud′ə lē), *adv.* **1.** in a ruddy manner. **2.** with a ruddy hue.

rud·di·ness (rud′ē nis), *n.* the quality or state of being ruddy; redness; rosiness.

rud·dle (rud′əl), *n., v.,* **-dled, -dling.** —*n.* red ocher. —*v.t.* to mark or color with ruddle. [apparently < *rud*]

rud·dle·man (rud′əl mən), *n., pl.* **-men.** a dealer in ruddle.

rud·dock (rud′ək), *n., pl.* **-docks** or (*collectively*) **-dock.** the European robin: *The sweet And shrilly ruddock, with its bleeding breast* (Thomas Hood). [Old English *rudduc,* related to *rudu* red; see RUD]

rud·dy (rud′ē), *adj.,* **-di·er, -di·est,** *adv., v.,* **-died, -dy·ing.** —*adj.* **1.** red; reddish: *the ruddy glow of a fire. As dear to me as are the ruddy drops That visit my sad heart* (Shakespeare). **2. a.** healthy red: *ruddy cheeks.* **b.** having such a color in the cheeks: *a short, stout, ruddy young fellow* (Herman Melville). **3.** *British Slang.* bloody; blinking: *But one thinks the bad words—one says them back of one's teeth while one is nodding and smiling at the ruddy idiot* (Smith's London Journal).

—*adv. British Slang.* very; surely; extremely: *He was ruddy near right! We'll ruddy well see the admiral* (Maclean's).

—*v.t.* to make ruddy; redden: *A wondrous blaze was seen to gleam . . . It ruddied all the copsewood glen* (Scott).

[Old English *rudig,* related to *rudu;* see RUD]

—**Syn.** *adj.* **1.** rubicund, florid. **2. a.** rosy.

ruddy duck, a small North American fresh-water duck with a long, broad bill, a stiff tail, and white cheeks; fool duck. The male is reddish-brown in the spring and summer.

ruddy turnstone, an American shore bird related to the plover, black, white, and chestnut above, black and white below in breeding plumage. It uses its wedge-shaped bill to turn over stones in search of food.

rude (rüd), *adj.,* **rud·er, rud·est. 1.** not courteous; impolite: *It is rude to stare at people.* **2.** roughly made or done; without finish or polish; coarse: *rude tools, a rude cabin, a rude sketch; . . . a rude bed upon the floor* (Dickens). **3.** rough in manner or behavior; violent; harsh: *the rude winds of winter. Rude hands seized the dog and threw him into the car. In far less polished days, A time when rough rude men had naughty ways* (Robert Burns). **4.** harsh to the ear; unmusical. **5.** not having learned much; rather wild; barbarous: *Life is rude in tribes that have few tools. . . . the rude forefathers of the hamlet* (Thomas Gray). **6.** belonging to the poor or to uncultured people; without luxury or elegance; simple: *a rude, primitive culture. The temple . . . is of rude design and indifferent execution* (Amelia B. Edwards). **7.** not fully or properly developed. **8.** robust; sturdy; vigorous: *rude health, rude strength.* **9.** *Archaic.* inexpert; unskilled. [< Latin *rudis*] —**Syn. 1.** uncivil, discourteous, impertinent, impudent. **2.** unwrought, raw, crude. **5.** primitive.

rude·ly (rüd′lē), *adv.* in a rude manner.

rude·ness (rüd′nis), *n.* roughness; coarseness; bad manners; violence: *His rudeness is inexcusable.*

rudes·by (rüdz′bē), *n., pl.* **-bies.** *Archaic.* a rude or unmannerly fellow: *Rudesby, be gone!* (Shakespeare).

Rü·des·heim·er (rʏ′dəs hī′mər), *n.* a fine white Rhine wine. [< German *Rüdesheimer* < *Rüdesheim,* a town on the Rhine]

ru·di·ment (rü′də mənt), *n.* **1.** a part to be learned first; beginning: *the rudiments of grammar. Mr. Geoffry Wildgoose received the first rudiments of his education at a little free-school* (Richard Graves). **2.** something in an early stage; undeveloped or imperfect form: *a youth . . . who apparently had not in him even the rudiments of worldly successfulness* (Arnold Bennett). **3.** an organ or part incompletely developed in size or structure: *the rudiments of wings on a baby chick.* [< Latin *rudīmentum* < *rudis* rude, ignorant]

ru·di·men·tal (rü′də men′təl), *adj.* rudimentary.

ru·di·men·ta·ri·ly (rü′də men′tər ə lē, -trə-), *adv.* in a rudimentary manner or state; elementarily.

ru·di·men·ta·ri·ness (rü′də men′tər ē nis, -trē-), *n.* rudimentary quality or state.

ru·di·men·ta·ry (rü′də men′tər ē, -trē), *adj.* **1.** that is to be learned or studied first; elementary. **2.** in an early stage of development; undeveloped. —**Syn. 1.** See **elementary. 2.** embryonic.

rue[1] (rü), *v.,* **rued, ru·ing,** *n.* —*v.t.* to be sorry for; regret: *She will rue the day she insulted your mother. Thou shalt rue this treason* (Shakespeare). *Was ever son so rued a father's death?* (Shakespeare). —*v.i. Archaic.* to feel sorrow; lament. —*n. Archaic.* sorrow; repentance; regret: *With rue my heart is laden For golden friends I had* (A. E. Housman). [Middle English *rewen,* Old English *hrēowan;* compare *ruth*] —**Syn.** *v.t.* deplore.

rue[2] (rü), *n.* a plant of the Mediterranean region with leaves that have a strong smell and a bitter taste. [< Old French *rue* < Latin *rūta,* perhaps < Greek *rhȳtē*]

rue[3] (rʏ), *n. French.* street.

rue anemone (rü), a small North American perennial plant of the crowfoot family with white or pinkish flowers that bloom in the spring; windflower.

rue family (rü), a group of chiefly tropical or subtropical herbs, shrubs, and trees, many of which yield an aromatic oil. The family is dicotyledonous and includes the rue, citrus fruits, dittany, and hop tree.

rue·ful (rü′fəl), *adj.* **1.** sorrowful; unhappy; mournful: *a rueful expression.* **2.** causing sorrow or pity: *a rueful sight.* —**rue′ful·ly,** *adv.* —**rue′ful·ness,** *n.* —**Syn. 1.** doleful, woeful, lugubrious, melancholy.

ru·er (rü′ər), *n.* a person who rues.

ru·fes·cence (rü fes′əns), *n.* reddishness.

ru·fes·cent (rü fes′ənt), *adj.* reddish. [< Latin *rūfēscēns, -entis,* present participle of *rūfēscere* become reddish < *rūfus* reddish, red-haired, related to *ruber* red]

ruff[1] (ruf), *n.* **1.** a deep frill stiff enough to stand out, worn around the neck by men and women in the 1500's. **2.** a collar of specially marked feathers or hairs on the neck of a bird or other animal. **3.** a sandpiper of Europe and Asia the male of which has ear tufts and a ruff on the neck during the breeding season. The female ruff is called a reeve. [perhaps related to RUFFLE[1], perhaps < *rough*]

Ruff[1] (def. 1)

ruff[2] (ruf), *v.t., v.i.* to trump in a card game: *West had to ruff with a good trump and the prospective penalty was down to 100* (Observer). —*n.* **1.** the act of trumping. **2.** *Obsolete.* a card game resembling whist. [< Middle French *roffle* < Old French *ronfle, romfle*]

ruff[3] or **ruffe** (ruf), *n.* a small European fresh-water fish similar to the perch. [perhaps < Middle English *roughe* rough (probably from its prickles)]

ruffed (ruft), *adj.* having a ruff.

ruffed grouse, a North American grouse with a tuft of feathers on each side of the neck and a fan-shaped tail. It is called a partridge in New England and a pheasant in the southern United States. See the picture of **grouse**[1].

ruffed lemur, a black and white lemur with a woolly ruff of hair on the sides of its face.

ruf·fi·an (ruf′ē ən), *n.* a rough, brutal, or cruel person: . . . *an abominable lot of lawless ruffians* (Joseph Conrad). —*adj.* rough; brutal; cruel: *He heard a ruffian voice in the alley and hurried along.* [< Middle French *rufian* < Italian *ruffiano* a pander; meaning perhaps influenced by *rough*] —**Syn.** *n.* bully, rowdy, rough, hoodlum.

ruf·fi·an·ism (ruf′ē ə niz′əm), *n.* brutal conduct; ruffianly conduct or character.

ruf·fi·an·ly (ruf′ē ən lē), *adj.* like a ruffian; rough, lawless, and brutal.

ruf·fle[1] (ruf′əl), *v.*, **-fled, -fling,** *n.* —*v.t.* **1. a.** to make rough or uneven; wrinkle; rumple: *A breeze ruffled the lake. He ruffled up his gray moustache with thumb and forefinger* (Booth Tarkington). **b.** to cause to rise in anger or fear: *The hen ruffled her feathers at the sight of the dog.* **2. a.** to gather into a ruffle. **b.** to trim with ruffles. **3.** to disturb; annoy: *Nothing can ruffle her calm temper. He was not ruffled by the immense disappointment* (Arnold Bennett). **4.** to shuffle (playing cards). **5.** to turn over (the pages of a book) rapidly. —*v.i.* to become ruffled: *The flag ruffled in the breeze. "Of course you consider it would have been so," sighed the lady, ruffling* (George Meredith). —*n.* **1.** roughness or unevenness in some surface; wrinkling. **2. a.** a strip of cloth, ribbon, or lace gathered along one edge and used for trimming. Ruffles used to be much worn; even men had shirts with ruffles. **b.** something resembling this, such as the ruff on a bird. **3.** disturbance; annoyance: *the ordinary rubs and ruffles which disturb even the most uniform life* (Scott). **4.** disorder; confusion. [Middle English *ruffelen.* Compare Low German *ruffelen* to rumple, Old Icelandic *hrufla* to stretch.] —**Syn.** *v.t.* **1. a.** roughen. **3.** disquiet, discompose.

Ruffles[1] **(def. 2a) (19th century)**

ruf·fle[2] (ruf′əl), *n.*, *v.*, **-fled, -fling.** —*n.* a low, steady beating of a drum. —*v.t.* to beat (a drum) in this way. [perhaps imitative]

ruf·fle[3] (ruf′əl), *v.*, **-fled, -fling,** *n.* —*v.i.* **1.** to be violent or rough, as wind or waves. **2.** to make a display; swagger: *Here he was, a provincial man of business, ruffling it with the best of them!* (Arnold Bennett). **3.** *Archaic.* to struggle; contend.
—*n. Archaic.* a struggle; fight; brawl: *the ruffle betwixt the Scottish Archers and the provost-marshal's guard* (Scott). [Middle English *ruffelyn;* origin uncertain]

ruf·fler[1] (ruf′lər), *n.* **1.** a person or thing that ruffles or annoys: *that enemy of all repose and ruffler of even tempers—the mosquito* (Herman Melville). **2.** an attachment for a sewing machine to gather cloth into ruffles. [< *ruffl*(e)[1] + *-er*[1]]

ruf·fler[2] (ruf′lər), *n.* **1.** *Archaic.* a bully; ruffian. **2.** *Obsolete.* one of a group of roving bullies in the 1500's. [< *ruffl*(e)[3] + *-er*[1]]

ruf·fly (ruf′lē), *adj.* having ruffles.

ru·fous (rü′fəs), *adj.* **1.** reddish or reddish-brown: *rufous hair, rufous granite.* **2.** red-faced; ruddy: *The rufous, foxy little dentist would give another turn of the screw to the instruments of torture I wore in my mouth* (New Yorker). [< Latin *rūfus* (with English *-ous*)]

rufous hummingbird, a hummingbird of western North America, the male of which has bright rufous upper parts and a bright scarlet throat.

rug[1] (rug), *n.* **1.** a heavy floor covering: *a rag rug, a grass rug.* **2.** a thick, warm cloth used as covering: *He wrapped his woolen rug around him.*
cut a rug, *U.S. Slang.* to dance in a lively manner: *Shirley, who is an expert dancer, cut many a rug at the Stage Door Canteen* (Time).
pull the rug (out) from under, to upset the plans of: *Until the afternoon, there seemed some hope of a settlement. Then the Supreme Court pulled the rug out from under the President* (Newsweek).
sweep under the rug, *Informal.* to conceal (a problem, difficulty, etc.), especially from the public: *For years this national scandal has been swept under the rug* (Harper's).
[< Scandinavian (compare Norwegian dialectal *rugga* coarse coverlet)]

rug[2] (rug), *v.*, **rugged, rug·ging,** *n. Scottish.* —*v.t., v.i.* to pull roughly; tug. —*n.* a rough pull; jerk. [< Scandinavian (compare Old Icelandic *rugga*)]

ru·ga (rü′gə), *n., pl.* **-gae** (-jē). a wrinkle; fold; ridge. [< Latin *rūga* a crease, wrinkle]

ru·gate (rü′gāt), *adj.* wrinkled; rugose.

Rug·bei·an (rug bē′ən), *adj.* **1.** of or having to do with Rugby, England, or its inhabitants. **2.** of or having to do with the school for boys there. —*n.* a man who has been educated at Rugby.

Rug·by (rug′bē), *n.*, or **Rugby football,** an English form of football, in which the forward pass is not allowed and play is stopped only for penalties. [< *Rugby,* a famous school for boys in Rugby, England]

rug·ged (rug′id), *adj.* **1.** rough; wrinkled; uneven: *rugged ground. So onward, o'er the rugged way That runs through rocks and sand* (Oliver Wendell Holmes). **2.** strong; vigorous; sturdy: *a rugged figure in rawhide boots and coonskin cap* (Winston Churchill). *Pioneers were rugged people.* **3.** strong and irregular: *rugged features.* **4.** harsh; stern; severe: *rugged times.* **5.** rude; unpolished; unrefined: *rugged manners; . . . rugged maxims hewn from life* (Tennyson). **6.** stormy: *rugged weather.* **7.** harsh to the ear: *rugged sounds.* **8.** *Obsolete.* rough; shaggy: . . . *the rugged Russian bear* (Shakespeare). [< Scandinavian (compare Swedish *rugga* to roughen)] —**rug′ged·ly,** *adv.* —**rug′ged·ness,** *n.* —**Syn. 1.** craggy, scraggy, furrowed. **7.** discordant.

Rug·ger or **rug·ger** (rug′ər), *n. British Informal.* Rugby: *I was subjected to so much compulsory chapel, rugger, battle training . . . that I was too exhausted to absorb much of the excellent tuition* (Manchester Guardian).

ru·gose (rü′gōs, rü gōs′), *adj.* having rugae or wrinkles; wrinkled; ridged: *a rugose leaf.* [< Latin *rūgōsus* < *rūga* wrinkle] —**ru′gose·ly,** *adv.*

ru·gos·i·ty (rü gos′ə tē), *n., pl.* **-ties. 1.** wrinkled condition. **2.** a wrinkle.

Ruhm·korff coil (rüm′kôrf), an induction coil. [< H.D. *Ruhmkorff,* 1803-1877, a German inventor]

ru·in (rü′ən), *n.* **1.** something left after destruction, decay, or downfall, especially a building, wall, etc., that has fallen to pieces: *That ruin was once an ancient castle. A paralysis had ravaged his stately form, and left it a shaking ruin* (Washington Irving). **2.** very great damage; destruction; overthrow; decay: *His enemies planned the duke's ruin.* **3.** a condition of destruction, decay, or downfall: *The house had gone to ruin and neglect.* **4.** the cause of destruction, decay, or downfall: *Drink was his ruin.* **5.** bankruptcy. **6.** a falling or tumbling down, as of a building. **7.** the dishonor of a woman.
ruins, a. that which is left after destruction, decay, or downfall, as a building, wall, etc., that has fallen to pieces: *the ruins of an ancient city.* **b.** injuries or damage done or received: *Till thy father hath made good The ruins done to Malta and to us* (Christopher Marlowe).
—*v.t.* **1.** to bring to ruin; destroy; spoil: *The rain has ruined my new dress. Too much smoking and drinking will ruin your health.* **2.** to make bankrupt: *His father, a printer, had been ruined by Napoleon's suppression of the press* (Edmund Wilson). —*v.i.* **1.** to be destroyed; come to ruin. **2.** *Archaic.* to fall with a crash: *Hell saw Heaven ruining from heaven* (Milton).
[< Old French *ruin,* learned borrowing from Latin *ruīna* a collapse < *ruere* to collapse] —**ru′in·er,** *n.*
—**Syn.** *n.* **2. Ruin, destruction** mean great damage. **Ruin** implies total or extensive damage caused by external force or especially by natural processes, such as decay: *Proper care protects property from ruin.* **Destruction** implies damage, extensive or not, caused by external forces, such as wind, explosion, etc.: *The storm caused widespread destruction.* -*v.t.* **1.** demolish, wreck. See **spoil. 2.** impoverish.

ru·in·a·ble (rü′ə nə bəl), *adj.* that can be ruined.

ru·in·ate (rü′ə nāt), *v.*, **-at·ed, -at·ing,** *adj. Archaic.* —*v.t., v.i.* to ruin. —*adj.* ruined: *a famous city now ruinate* (Milton).

ru·in·a·tion (rü′ə nā′shən), *n.* ruin; destruction; downfall: *Pride is the ruination of many a successful man.*

ru·ined (rü′ənd), *adj.* reduced to ruins; damaged beyond repair; destroyed.

ru·in·ous (rü′ə nəs), *adj.* **1.** bringing ruin; causing destruction: *ruinous expense; . . . a ruinous war . . .* (Edward Gibbon). *Of all those expensive and uncertain projects . . . there is none perhaps more perfectly ruinous than the search after new silver and gold mines* (Adam Smith). **2.** fallen into ruins; in ruins: *. . . a ruinous wooden fence . . .* (Hawthorne). **3.** of ruins; made of ruins: *Damascus . . . shall be a ruinous heap* (Isaiah 17:1). —**ru′in·ous·ly,** *adv.* —**ru′in·ous·ness,** *n.* —**Syn. 1.** calamitous, disastrous. **2.** dilapidated.

ru·ins (rü′ənz), *n.pl.* See under **ruin,** *n.*

rul·a·ble (rü′lə bəl), *adj.* that can be ruled; governable.

rule (rül), *n.*, *v.*, **ruled, rul·ing.** —*n.* **1.** a statement of what to do and not to do; principle governing conduct, action, arrangement, etc.; law: *the rules of a club, to obey the rules of the game, the rules of the road, the rules of grammar and spelling.* **2.** an order by a law court, based upon a principle of law. A special rule is limited to a particular case; a general rule regulates the procedure or decisions of a court. **3.** a set of rules; code. A religious order lives under a certain rule: *the rule of St. Benedict.* **4.** control; government: *In a democracy the people have the rule. A wife's rule should only be over her husband's house, not over his mind* (John Ruskin). **5.** a regular method; a thing that usually happens or is done; what is usually true: *Fair weather is the rule in Arizona.* **6.** a straight strip used to measure or as a guide to drawing; ruler. **7.** a thin, type-high strip of metal, for printing a line or lines. **8.** *Obsolete.* conduct; behavior.
as a rule, normally; generally: *As a rule, hail falls in summer* (Thomas H. Huxley). *As a rule it should not take more than an hour to reach areas of natural terrain from the center of a city* (Saturday Review).
out of rule, contrary to practice or custom: *Miss Portman . . . blushes for you . . . when you propose that she, who is not yet a married woman, should chaperon a young lady. It is quite out of rule* (Maria Edgeworth).
rules, *British, Obsolete.* **a.** an area near a prison, where certain prisoners were permitted to live: *He was permitted to live in the rules—consequently his punishment was merely nominal* (The Examiner). **b.** the freedom of such an area: *Any prisoner for debt may . . . enjoy the rules, or liberty to walk abroad* (John Entick).
—*v.i.* **1.** to make a rule; decide. **2.** to make a formal decision: *The judge ruled against them.* **3.** to exercise highest authority; govern; direct: *this love of life, which in our nature rules* (George Crabbe). *Let them obey that know not how to rule* (Shakespeare). **4.** to prevail; be current: *Prices of wheat and corn ruled high all the year.* —*v.t.* **1.** to declare (a rule); decide (something): *The umpire ruled that the ball was foul.* **2.** to decide formally: *The judge ruled a mistrial.* **3.** to exercise highest authority over; control: *the evil influence that rules your fortunes* (Hawthorne). *To rule men, we must be men* (Benjamin Disraeli). **4.** to prevail in; dominate: *Wit rules all his poems.* **5.** to mark with lines: *He used a ruler to rule the paper.* **6.** to mark off.
rule out, to decide against; exclude: *Mr. Shepilov yesterday did not rule out possible aid for the Aswan project* (London Times).
[< Old French *riule, reule* < Latin *rēgula* straight stick, related to *regere* to rule, straighten, and to *rēx, rēgis* king. Doublet of RAIL[1].]
—**Syn.** *n.* **1.** regulation, order, precept. **4.** direction, authority, dominion, sway. -*v.i., v.t.* **3. Rule, govern** mean to control by the exercise of authority or power. **Rule** implies control over others through absolute power both to make laws and to force obedience: *He tries to rule his family as a dictator rules a nation.* **Govern** implies sensible control by the wise use of authority or power, usually for the good of the thing, person, or nation governed: *Parents govern a child until he develops the power to govern himself.*

rule·book (rül′bu̇k′), *n.*, or **rule book,** a book or collection of rules.

rule joint, a joint hinging two strips together end to end, each strip turning edgeways, used especially in folding rules.

rule of law, 1. a recognized legal principle, usually in the form of a maxim, applied as a guide for decisions in doubtful cases. **2.** a governing by law or laws: *As human society evolved from clans to nations, we have learned that rule of force is war, and rule of law is peace—the only peace possible* (Bulletin of Atomic Scientists).

rule of the road, 1. any of the regulations of a country, state, etc., with regard to the passing of vehicles on a highway. **2.** any of the regulations embodied in a code of rules for the safe handling of ships meeting or passing each other: *If [a naval manoeuvre] requires ships to pass starboard side to starboard side, the rule of the road is waived* (Listener).

rule of three, a method of finding the fourth term in a mathematical proportion when three are given. The product of the means equals the product of the extremes.

rule of thumb or **rule o' thumb, 1.** a rule based on experience or practice rather than on scientific knowledge: *The practical men believed that the idol whom they worship —rule of thumb—has been the source of the past prosperity, and will suffice for the future* (Thomas H. Huxley). **2.** a rough practical method of procedure: *People were not so introspective then . . . they lived more according to a rule of thumb* (Samuel Butler). *A rule of thumb for reviewing is that one must first discern the author's intention and then judge how well he carried it off* (Wall Street Journal). —**rule′-of-thumb′,** *adj.*

rul·er (rü′lər), *n.* **1.** a person who rules. **2.** a straight strip of wood, metal, etc., used in drawing lines or in measuring. **3.** a person or machine that makes lines on paper. —**Syn. 1.** sovereign. **2.** rule.

rul·er·ship (rü′lər ship), *n.* the position or power of a ruler: *In the Kremlin, the rulership by committee will bring more jockeying for power* (Newsweek).

rules (rülz), *n.pl.* See under **rule,** *n.*

Rules Committee, a standing committee in the U.S. House of Representatives concerned with the general rules governing the House, all proposals for amendments, and the introduction of bills for consideration on the floor: *All major and controversial legislation must be approved by the Rules Committee before it can reach the floor for action* (Wall Street Journal).

rul·ing (rü′ling), *n.* **1.** a decision of a judge or court: *a ruling on a point of law.* **2.** a ruled line or lines. **3.** the act of making lines on paper, fabric, etc. **4.** government. —*adj.* **1.** that rules; governing; controlling: *The tiny principality would become French territory if the ruling prince had no male issue* (Newsweek). **2.** predominating; prevalent; chief: *Samuel Johnson was the ruling authority on English in the 1700's.* —**rul′ingly,** *adv.*

ru·ly (rü′lē), *adj.* orderly.

rum[1] (rum), *n.* **1.** an alcoholic liquor made from sugar cane, molasses, etc. **2.** alcoholic liquor. [apparently short for obsolete *rumbullion* rum; origin unknown]

rum[2] (rum), *adj. Especially British Slang.* odd; strange: *Deuced rum sensation!* (John Galsworthy). [perhaps < Romany *rom* male, husband]

Rum., 1. Rumania. **2.** Rumanian.

Ru·man (rü′mən, rü män′), *adj., n., pl.* **-mans.** Rumanian.

Ru·ma·ni·an (rü mā′nē ən, -mān′yən), *adj., n.* Romanian.

Ru·mansh (rü mansh′, -mänsh′), *adj., n.* Rhaeto-Romanic.

rum·ba (rum′bə), *n., v.,* **-baed** (-bəd), **-ba·ing** (-bə ing). —*n.* **1.** a dance in quadruple time that originated among the Cuban Negroes: *For years he has been taking dancing lessons "for exercise," and his creditable rumba, flavored with Victorian courtliness, has won him several competitive awards* (New York Times). **2.** music for such a dance. —*v.i.* to dance the rumba. Also, **rhumba.** [< Cuban Spanish *rumba* (literally) spree]

rum·ba·ba (rum′bä′bə), *n.* baba au rhum.

rum·ble (rum′bəl), *v.,* **-bled, -bling,** *n.* —*v.i.* **1.** to make a deep, heavy, continuous sound: *The thunder rumbled overhead.* **2.** to move with such a sound: *The train rumbled on through a landscape* (Arnold Bennett). —*v.t.* **1.** to utter with a rumbling sound. **2.** to cause to move with a rumbling sound. **3.** to polish, mix, etc., in a tumbling box. —*n.* **1.** a deep, heavy, continuous sound: *We heard the far-off rumble of thunder. "Wouldn't you have thought," . . . she ventured in her throaty military rumble . . .* (Mary McCarthy). **2.** *U.S. Slang.* a teen-age gang fight: *The Minotaurs, like many of the longer-established gangs, avoid "rumbles" (mass fights) if a sneak raid on an enemy will avenge an insult or settle a score* (New York Times). **3.** the rear part of a carriage or old automobile containing an extra seat or a place for baggage. **4.** a tumbling box. [Middle English *romblen.* Compare Middle Dutch *rommelen.*] —**rum′bling·ly,** *adv.*

rum·bler (rum′blər), *n.* **1.** a person or thing that rumbles. **2.** a resounding line of poetry.

rumble seat, an extra, open seat in the back of some older automobiles.

Rumble Seat on 1926 coupe

rum·bly (rum′blē), *adj.* **1.** that rumbles. **2.** causing rumbling. **3.** accompanied by rumbling.

rum·bus·tious (rum bus′chəs), *adj. Informal.* boisterous; unruly: *. . . a fortnightly newspaper, a rumbustious and gossipy affair . . .* (Punch). *The sperm whales are such . . . rumbustious fellows* (Charles Kingsley). [variant of *robustious*] —**rum·bus′tious·ly,** *adv.*

ru·men (rü′mən), *n., pl.* **-mi·na** (-mə nə). **1.** the first stomach of an animal that chews the cud: *Sheep, as cattle and goats do, have an "extra stomach," the rumen, where rough feed is predigested with the help of bacteria* (Science News Letter). See the picture of **abomasum. 2.** the cud of such an animal. [< Latin *rūmen, -inis* gullet]

ru·me·not·o·my (rü′mə not′ə mē), *n.* the cutting into the rumen of a cud-chewing animal to permit the evacuation of gases, impacted food, etc.

ru·mi·nant (rü′mə nənt), *n.* a herbivorous animal that chews the cud: *Cows, sheep, and camels are ruminants.* —*adj.* **1.** belonging to the group of ruminants. **2.** meditative; reflective. [< Latin *rūminans, -antis,* present participle of *rūmināre* to chew a cud < *rūmen, -inis* gullet] —**Syn.** *adj.* **2.** contemplative, musing.

ru·mi·nate (rü′mə nāt), *v.,* **-nat·ed, -nat·ing.** —*v.i.* **1.** to chew the cud. **2.** to ponder; meditate: *He ruminated on the strange events of the past week. Mr. Wendover . . . stood gloomily ruminating in front of the fire* (Mrs. Humphry Ward). —*v.t.* **1.** to chew again: *A cow ruminates its food.* **2.** to turn over in the mind; meditate on: *to ruminate strange plots of dire revenge* (Shakespeare). [< Latin *rūmināre* (with English *-ate*[1]); see RUMINANT] —**ru′mi·nat′ing·ly,** *adv.* —**Syn.** *v.i.* **2.** cogitate, reflect.

ru·mi·na·tion (rü′mə nā′shən), *n.* **1.** a chewing of the cud. **2.** meditation; reflection.

ru·mi·na·tive (rü′mə nā′tiv), *adj.* inclined to ruminate; meditative.

ru·mi·na·tor (rü′mə nā′tər), *n.* a person who ruminates.

rum·mage (rum′ij), *v.,* **-maged, -mag·ing,** *n.* —*v.t.* **1.** to search thoroughly by moving things about: *I rummaged three drawers before I found my gloves. He rummaged his pockets* (Mark Twain). **2.** to pull from among other things; bring to light: *She rummaged change from the bottom of her purse. Theobald had rummaged up a conclusion from some odd corner of his soul* (Samuel Butler). —*v.i.* to search in a disorderly way: *He rummaged in the drawer for a sheet of paper* (Edith Wharton). [< noun] —*n.* **1.** a rummaging search. **2.** a rummage sale. **3.** odds and ends. **4.** *Obsolete.* a disturbance. **5.** *Obsolete.* **a.** the stowing or removing of cargo on a ship. **b.** a ship's hold. [earlier *romage* < Middle French *arrumage* < *arrumer* stow cargo < unrecorded *rum,* variant of *run* hold of a ship < Germanic (compare Dutch *ruim*)] —**Syn.** *v.t.* **1.** See **search.**

rum·mag·er (rum′ə jər), *n.* **1.** a person who searches. **2.** *Obsolete.* a person who arranges cargo in a ship.

rummage sale, a sale of odds and ends, old clothing, etc., usually held to raise money for charity.

rum·mer (rum′ər), *n.* **1.** a large drinking glass, especially with a tall, stemless, cylindrical form. **2.** a cupful of wine or other liquor. [probably < Dutch *romer, roemer* a fancy, show-off glass, (literally) boaster]

Bavarian Rummer (def. 1)

rum·my[1] (rum′ē), *adj.,* **-mi·er, -mi·est.** *Slang.* odd; strange: *There seemed to be some rummy mystery about his absence* (A. S. M. Hutchinson). [< *rum*[2] + *-y*[1]]

rum·my[2] (rum′ē), *n., v.,* **-mied, -my·ing.** —*n.* a card game in which points are scored by melding sets of three or four cards of the same rank or sequences of three or more cards of the same suit. —*v.i.* to end the game by using or discarding the last card in one's hand. [American English; origin uncertain]

rum·my[3] (rum′ē), *n., pl.* **-mies,** *adj.* —*n. U.S. Slang.* a drunkard. —*adj.* of or like rum: *a rummy flavor.* [American English < *rum*[1] + *-y*[1]]

ru·mor (rü′mər), *n.* **1.** a story or statement talked of as news without any proof that it is true: *The rumor spread that a new school would be built here. The rumor of what had happened . . . had spread about the premises* (Arnold Bennett). **2.** vague, general talk: *Rumor has it that the new girl went to school in France. According to the rumor of the times, she may have been a daughter of Lord Byron* (Time). **3.** *Archaic.* reputation; fame: *Great is the rumour of this dreadful knight* (Shakespeare). **4.** *Obsolete.* confused noise; din.
—*v.t.* to tell or spread by rumor: *It was rumored that the government was going to lower taxes.*
[< Old French *rumor* great uproar < Latin *rūmor, -ōris* rumor, noise] —**ru′mor·er,** *n.*
—**Syn.** *n.* **1.** report.

ru·mor·mon·ger (rü′mər mung′gər, -mong′-), *n.* a person who spreads rumors.

ru·mor·ous (rü′mər əs), *adj.* **1.** of or like rumor. **2.** *Archaic.* murmurous.

ru·mour (rü′mər), *n., v.t. British.* rumor.

rump (rump), *n.* **1.** the hind part of the body of an animal, where the legs join the back. **2.** a cut of beef from this part. **3.** an unimportant or inferior part; remnant.
—*adj.* small; unimportant; inferior, as of a splinter group: *Both were named by acclamation at a rump convention of southern Democrats* (Milwaukee Journal).
[< Scandinavian (compare Swedish *rumpa* rump)]

Rump (rump), *n.* the Long Parliament in England after the exclusion, in December, 1648, of about 100 members who favored compromise with King Charles I: *The Rump alone was left to stand for the old tradition of Parliament* (Henry Morley).

rump·bone (rump′bōn′), *n.* the bone of the rump; sacrum.

Rump Congress, the Congress of the United States without the representatives from the southern states during the Civil War and Reconstruction period.

Rum·pel·stilt·skin (rum′pəl stilt′skin), *n.* a dwarf of German folklore who helps a miller's daughter by spinning straw into gold on condition that she give him her first-born child. He later agrees to relent if she can guess his name, and when she does so, he destroys himself in a rage.

rum·ple (rum′pəl), *v.,* **-pled, -pling,** *n.* —*v.t.* to crumple; crush; wrinkle; disorder: *a rumpled sheet of paper, to rumple up hair. Don't play in your best dress; you'll rumple it.* —*v.i.* to become wrinkled, crumpled, or disordered. [apparently < noun] —*n.* a wrinkle; crease. [< earlier Dutch *rompel*] —**Syn.** *v.t., v.i.* pucker, crease.

rum·ply (rum′plē), *adj.,* **-pli·er, -pli·est.** rumpled; disorderly; wrinkled: *The men among them followed Sinatra's style; they had rumply hair, wistful smiles, and casual charm* (Maclean's).

rum·pot (rum′pot′), *n. Slang.* a drunkard: *I had hysterical thoughts of Henry Fielding's wonderful rumpot, Squire Western, roaring in on the scene* (Maclean's).

Rump Parliament, the Rump.

rum·pus (rum′pəs), *n. Informal.* **1.** a noisy quarrel; disturbance: *He . . . knocked down so many students and easels and drawing-boards . . . and made such a terrific rumpus* (George Du Maurier). **2.** noise; uproar: *The affair caused considerable rumpus.* [origin uncertain]

rumpus room, *U.S.* a room in a house set apart for parties, games, etc.: *. . . a gaudy rumpus room, the ceilings decorated with Venetian carnival masks* (Saturday Review).

rum·run·ner (rum′run′ər), *n. U.S.* a person or ship that smuggles alcoholic liquor. [American English < *rum* + *runner*]

rum·run·ning (rum′run′ing), *n.* the act of smuggling alcoholic liquor. —*adj.* that smuggles alcoholic liquor.

run (run), *v.,* **ran, run, run·ning,** *n., adj.* —*v.i.* **1.** to move the legs quickly; go faster than walking: *A horse can run faster than a man.* **2. a.** to go hurriedly; hasten:

Run for help. What need a man ... run to meet what he would most avoid? (Milton). **b.** to make a quick trip: *Let's run over to the lake for the weekend.* **3.** to flee: *Run for your life.* **4. a.** to go; move; keep going: *This train runs between Chicago and Los Angeles.* **b.** to sail or be driven: *The ship ran aground on the rocks.* **c.** to turn; revolve: *A wheel runs on an axle.* **5.** to go on; proceed: *Prices of hats run as high as $50.00.* **6.** to creep; trail; climb: *Vines run up the side of the chimney.* **7.** to pass quickly: *Time runs on. The thought ran through his mind that he might forget his speech.* **8.** to stretch; extend: *Shelves run along the walls. A fence runs around the house. The road runs south from New York to Atlanta.* **9.** to flow: *Blood runs from a cut. But if ye will not hear it, my soul shall weep in secret places for your pride; and mine eye shall weep sore, and run down with tears, because the Lord's flock is carried away captive* (Jeremiah 13:17). **10.** to discharge fluid, mucus, or pus: *My nose runs whenever I have a cold.* **11.** to get; become: *Never run into debt. The well ran dry.* **12.** to have a specified character, quality, form, size, etc.: *These potatoes run large. Her hair runs to curls.* **13.** to spread: *The color ran when the dress was washed. Ink runs on a blotter.* **14.** to continue; last: *a lease to run two years. The play ran for a whole season.* **15.** to have currency or be current; occur: *The story runs that school will close early today. In haste I snatch up my pen ... to give you news as it runs* (Alexander Hamilton). **16.** to have legal force. **17. a.** to take part in a race or contest. **b.** to finish a race, contest, etc., in a certain way: *The horse ran last.* **18.** to be a candidate for election: *to run for president.* **19.** to move easily, freely, or smoothly; keep operating: *A rope runs in a pulley. The engine ran all day without overheating.* **20.** to be worded or expressed: *How does the first verse run?* **21.** to go about without restraint: *children allowed to run about the streets.* **22.** to drop stitches; ravel: *Nylon stockings often run.* **23.** to soften; become liquid; melt: *The wax ran when the candles were lit.* **24.** to pass to or from the sea; migrate, as for spawning: *The salmon are running.* **25.** to return often to the mind: *That tune has been running in my head ever since I first heard it.* **26. a.** to make many and urgent demands for money or payment: *to run on a bank.* **b.** to collect, accumulate, or become payable in due course, as interest on a loan.

—*v.t.* **1.** to cause to run; cause to move: *to run a horse up and down a track.* **2. a.** to perform by, or as if by, running: *to run a race, to run an errand.* **b.** to cover by running: *to run ten miles.* **3.** to go along (a way, path, etc.): *to run the course until the end.* **4.** to pursue; chase (game, etc.): *to run a fox. The chief difficulty in running buffalo ... is that of loading the gun ... at full gallop* (Francis Parkman). **5.** to cause to pass quickly: *He ran his hand over the pipe to see if it was hot before grabbing it. She ran her eyes over the old notes before discarding them.* **6.** to trace: *Run that report back to its source.* **7.** to put; spread; lead: *to run a shelf along a wall.* **8.** to drive; force; thrust: *He ran a splinter into his hand. I ... chanced to run my nose directly against a post* (Sir Richard Steele). **9. a.** to flow with: *The streets ran blood.* **b.** to cause to flow. **10. a.** to bring into a certain state by running: *to run oneself out of breath.* **b.** to lead or force into some state, action, etc.: *... to run myself into trouble ...* (Scott). *He runs his father in debt* (Thoreau). **11.** to expose oneself to: *to run a risk.* **12.** to cause to move easily, freely, or smoothly; cause to keep operating: *to run a machine.* **13.** to conduct; manage: *to run a business. Was it not obvious ... that this was how the whole of society should be run?* (Edmund Wilson). **14.** to sew temporarily and quickly by pushing a needle in and out with even stitches in a line; baste: *to run a hem.* **15.** to get past or through: *Enemy ships tried to run the blockade.* **16.** to smuggle: *to run rum. The plan was to bargain with the slave to run him to Canada for a stipulated sum* (St. Louis Reveille). **17.** to publish (an advertisement, story, etc) in a newspaper: *He ran an ad in the evening paper.* **18.** to shape by melting: *to run bullets through a mold.* **19. a.** to carry; take; transport: *Can you run this book over to the library for me?* **b.** to discharge; be able to carry: *a drain that runs 10 gallons of water every hour.* **20.** to put up as a candidate: *The Democrats ran Mr. Stevenson for the Presidency twice.* **21.** to enter (a horse, etc.) in a race. **22.** *Football.* to run off (a play). **23.** to contend with in a race: *I will run you a mile.* **24.** to make an unbroken sequence of (shots, strokes, etc.) in billiards, pool, etc. **25.** to draw or trace (a line, etc.) on a surface.

run across, to meet by chance; find: *Until two years ago I had never run across this deviation in my patients* (Maclean's).

run away, to escape by running; flee in a hurry: *When he saw the policeman, the thief ran away.*

run away with, a. to overcome: *Don't let your passion run away with your senses* (John Gay). **b.** to win easily over others: *He ran away with every prize in the tournament.* **c.** to elope with: *Dutton ... leaving Win in the lurch, ran away with another man's wife* (Tobias Smollett).

run down, a. to cease to go; stop working: *The toys that had been set in motion for the baby had all stopped and run down long ago* (Dickens). **b.** to pursue till caught or killed; hunt down: *A weasel will occasionally run down the strongest hare* (Cornhill Magazine). **c.** to knock down by running against: *We stand a good chance of being run down by a tram* (Titan Magazine). **d.** to speak unfavorably about; disparage: *He found himself run down as a superficial prating quack* (Joseph Addison). **e.** to decline or reduce in vigor or health: *She had run down ... both mentally and physically, and was in a generally unstrung condition* (Lady Duffus Hardy). **f.** to fall off, diminish, or decrease; deteriorate: *[She] had let everything run down; she had, in truth, no money for repairs* (Harper's).

run for it, to run for safety: *As soon as they heard the siren, they ran for it.*

run in, a. *Slang.* to arrest and put in jail: *Yusef is a very bad man. Why don't the authorities run him in?* (Graham Greene). **b.** to pay a short visit: *It might be a relief to her to run in to me whenever she pleased* (Margaret O.W. Oliphant). **c.** to set (type or copy) without a break in the running text: *to run in indented lines.*

run into, a. to meet by chance: *If you run into him after not seeing him for a year or so he grabs you by the arm as if he's overjoyed* (Maclean's). **b.** to crash into; collide with: *A large steamer ... ran into her, doing considerable damage* (Law Reports).

run off, a. to cause to be run or played: *On the theory that the more plays a team runs off the greater its chances of scoring, Wilkinson had Oklahoma running as many as three plays in 38 seconds* (Newsweek). **b.** to print: *to run off 1000 copies for a first edition.* **c.** to run away; flee: *They cast their arms to the ground, and ran off ... as fast as they could* (Henry Brooke).

run on, a. to continue in operation, effect, etc.: *This abuse has been allowed to run on unchecked for too long.* **b.** to elapse: *... as months ran on and rumour of battle grew* (Tennyson). **c.** to continue speaking: *"I'm a fool—I always was," he ran on, hurriedly* (F.W. Robinson). **d.** to expand; develop: *The proposed six lessons ran on into perhaps eight or nine* (John Ruskin). **e.** to set (type or copy) without a break in the running text: *to run on paragraphs.*

run out, to come to an end; become exhausted: *Time was running out and no solution was in sight* (Maclean's).

run out of, to use up; have no more: *When we had run out of money, we had no living soul to befriend us* (Manchester Guardian).

run out on, *Informal.* **a.** to fail to help; desert: *Only a coward would run out on his best friend at a difficult time.* **b.** to back out of; renege on: *The club's board of directors ran out on their long-standing promise to support him* (New York Times). **c.** to run away from; escape: *He ran out on me without paying his rent.*

run over, a. to ride or drive over: *The car ran over some glass.* **b.** to overflow: *Now was my heart full of joy, ... and mine affections running over with love* (John Bunyan). **c.** to go through quickly: *The particulars of his life have been often written, and therefore I shall run them over briefly* (Horace Walpole).

run through, a. to use up, spend, or consume rapidly or recklessly: *Working women run through an average of 36 pairs of nylons a year* (Wall Street Journal). **b.** to pierce: *I ran one of the assassins through the body* (Henry Brooke). **c.** to review; rehearse: *The teacher ran through the homework assignment a second time. The players ran through the new football plays before the game.*

run up, *Informal.* **a.** to make quickly: *to run up a good lead.* **b.** to collect; accumulate: *Don't run up a big bill.*

—*n.* **1.** the act of running: *to set out at a run.* **2. a.** a spell or period of causing a machine, etc., to operate: *a factory with a run of 8 hours a day.* **b.** the amount of anything produced in such a period: *Refinery runs averaged 975,874 barrels daily* (Wall Street Journal). **3.** a spell of causing something liquid to run or flow, or the amount that runs: *the run of sap from maple trees.* **4. a.** a trip: *Through freight trains make the run from Chicago to New York in as little as 22 hours* (Newsweek). **b.** a quick trip: *to take a run up to the country for the day.* **5. a.** a unit of score in baseball or cricket. **b.** an unbroken sequence of scoring plays in billiards, pool, etc. **6.** a continuous spell or course; continuous extent: *a run of bad luck, a run of fine weather.* **7. a.** a succession of performances, showings, etc.: *This play has had a two-year run.* **b.** a continuous series or succession of something; succession of demands: *There was a run on the bank to draw out money.* **c.** a spell of being in demand or favor: *A history of the Bloody Assizes ... was expected to have as great a run as the Pilgrim's Progress* (Macaulay). **8.** onward movement; progress; course; trend: *the run of events.* **9.** *Music.* a rapid succession of tones. **10.** kind or class: *the common run of mankind. As for the usual run of concerts, he hated them* (Samuel Butler). **11.** freedom to go over or through, or to use: *The guests were given the run of the house.* **12.** a flow or rush of water; small stream: *There is no ... Flat rich Land to be found—till one gets far enough from the River to head the little runs and drains* (George Washington). **13. a.** a number of fish moving together: *a run of salmon.* **b.** (of fish) a moving up a river from the sea to spawn. **14.** a way; track; trough; pipe. **15. a.** a stretch or enclosed space for animals: *a dog run, a chicken run.* **15. b.** (in Australia) a large area for grazing sheep. **16.** a place where stitches have slipped out or become undone: *a run in a stocking.* **17.** a landing of smuggled goods. **18.** the extreme after part of a ship's bottom. **19.** a track or support on which something can move. **20.** the direction, line, or lie of anything: *the run of the grain of wood.*

a run for one's money, a. strong competition: *Determined to give the large chain a run for its money, he opened a discount store.* **b.** satisfaction for one's expenditures, efforts, etc.: *The travel agent promised to give the tourists a run for their money.*

in the long run, on the whole; in the end: *A full investigation would, in the long run, do less harm than continued official silence* (David McReynolds).

in the short run, in the immediate present; for the moment: *In the short run, the mood of the investors is what counts* (New Yorker).

on the (or **a**) **dead run,** moving at full speed: *Mr. Nixon is on the dead run from the time he wakes up at 7:30 a.m. ... until 1:30 next morning* (Wall Street Journal).

on the run, a. hurrying: *You could see the people tearing down on the run* (Mark Twain). **b.** in retreat or rout; fleeing: *Since then Lahorie had been on the run for six years, hidden for part of that time by Hugo's mother* (New Yorker). **c.** while running: *He caught the ball on the run.*

—*adj.* **1.** melted: *run butter.* **2.** melted and run into a mold; cast: *run steel.* **3.** (of a fish) having ascended a stream from the sea. **4.** smuggled: *The pirates brought in run goods at night.*

[Old English *rinnan;* the vowel may be from the Old English past participle *runnon*]

—**Syn.** *v.i.* **1.** sprint, gallop. **2. a.** hurry, rush, race, speed. –*v.t.* **12, 13.** operate.

run·a·bout (run′ə bout′), *n.* **1.** a light automobile or carriage with a single seat. **2.** a small motorboat. **3.** a person who runs about from place to place, as a vagabond or peddler.

run·a·gate (run′ə gāt′), *n. Archaic.* **1.** a runaway; fugitive. **2.** a vagabond; wanderer. [alteration of Middle English *renegat* renegade; influenced by *run* + earlier *agate* away]

run·a·round (run′ə round′), *n.* **1.** *Informal.*

evasion or indefinite postponement of action, especially in regard to a request; avoidance: *Even those who would probably get visas hate to take the risk of getting a consular runaround* (Time). **2.** type set less than the full measure to permit the insertion of an illustration or the like.

run·a·way (run′ə wā′), *n.* **1.** a person, horse, etc., that runs away. **2.** a running away; eloping.
—*adj.* **1.** running with nobody to guide or stop it; out of control: *a runaway horse. Her knees bounced up and down like runaway jackhammers* (Time). **2.** done by runaways: *a runaway marriage.* **3.** easily won; one-sided: *a runaway victory. The book turned out to be a runaway best seller* (Time). **4.** escaped; fugitive: *runaway slaves.*

runaway shop, a plant moved to another site by the employer to escape local union demands.

run·back (run′bak′), *n.* **1.** *Football.* the run made by a player who has received the ball as a result of an opponent's kick or an intercepted pass: *His 86-yard run was a record for a Rose Bowl punt runback to a touchdown* (New York Times). **2.** the area between the base line and the backstop on a tennis court, etc.

run·ci·ble spoon (run′sə bəl), a fork with three short, wide prongs, used as a spoon in eating ice cream, etc. [apparently < *run-c*(inate) + *-ible*]

run·ci·nate (run′sə nit, -nāt), *adj.* having coarse, toothlike notches or lobes pointing backward: *Dandelion leaves are runcinate.* [< Latin *runcina* plane (but taken as "saw") < Greek *rhykánē;* influenced by Latin *runcāre* to clear (of thorns)]

Runcinate Leaves of dandelion

run·dle (run′dəl), *n.* **1.** a rung of a ladder. **2.** a bar of a kind of pinion. **3.** a wheel; rotating part. [Middle English *rundel,* variant of *roundel*]

rund·let (rund′lit), *n. Archaic.* **1.** an old measure of liquid equal to about 18 gallons. **2.** a cask; small barrel: *... twelve small rundlets of fine powder for our small-arms ...* (Daniel Defoe). Also, **runlet.** [Middle English *rowndelet, rondelet* < Old French (diminutive) < *rondelle* small tun < *rond* round]

run·down (run′doun′), *n. Informal.* an account; summary: *Mr. Myerberg gave us a brief rundown on his career* (New Yorker). [< *run* + *down*]

run-down (*adj.* run′doun′; *n.* run′doun′), *adj.* **1.** tired; sick: *If you are generally "run-down," ask your doctor about preventive measures against respiratory infections* (Time). **2.** falling to pieces; partly ruined. **3.** that has stopped going or working.
—*n.* **1.** *Baseball.* the attempt to tag out a base runner caught off base between two players. **2.** decrease; decline: *... a run-down in the labor force due to rapid mechanization* (Wall Street Journal). [< *run down,* idiom]

rune[1] (rün), *n.* **1.** any letter of an ancient Germanic alphabet. **2.** a mark that looks like a rune and has some mysterious, magic meaning: *Wise he was, and many curious arts, Postures of runes, and healing herbs he knew* (Matthew Arnold). **3.** a verse or sentence that has a magic meaning. [Old English *rūn* < Scandinavian (compare Old Icelandic *rūn* secret, rune)]

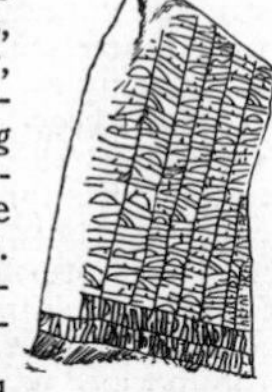
Runes[1] (def. 1) on tablet

rune[2] (rün), *n.* **1.** an old Scandinavian poem or song: *Of the Troll of the Church they sing the rune By the Northern Sea in the harvest moon* (John Greenleaf Whittier). **2.** *Poetic.* a poem; song; verse. [< Finnish *runo* < Scandinavian (compare Old Icelandic *rūn*)]

runed (ründ), *adj.* inscribed with runes.

rune-stone (rün′stōn′), *n.* a stone having runic inscriptions: *Professor Hagen, philologist, made an intensive study of the Kensington rune-stone* (New York Times).

rung[1] (rung), *v.* a past tense and the past participle of **ring**[2]: *The bell has rung.*

rung[2] (rung), *n.* **1.** a round rod or bar used as a step of a ladder. **2.** a crosspiece set between the legs of a chair or as part of the back or arm of a chair. **3.** a spoke of a wheel. **4.** a bar of wood having a similar shape and use. **5.** *Scottish.* a stout staff; cudgel. [Old English *hrung*]

ru·nic[1] (rü′nik), *adj.* consisting of runes; written in runes; marked with runes. [< *run*(e)[1] + *-ic*]

ru·nic[2] (rü′nik), *adj.* like a rune. [< *run*(e)[2] + *-ic*]

run·i·form (rün′ə fôrm), *adj.* having the appearance of runes.

run-in (run′in′), *n.* **1.** *Informal.* a quarrel; sharp disagreement; row. **2.** *Printing.* copy to be set starting on the same line and right after what comes before it. —*adj. Printing.* that is a run-in.

run·kle (rung′kəl), *n., v.,* **-kled, -kling.** *Scottish.* wrinkle; crease.

run·let[1] (run′lit), *n.* a small stream. [< *run,* noun + *-let*] —**Syn.** rivulet, runnel.

run·let[2] (run′lit), *n.* rundlet.

run·na·ble (run′ə bəl), *adj.* suitable for the chase, as deer; warrantable: *His coat was in perfect condition, ... and he was a runnable deer, that is, of age and size sufficient for the chase* (Richard Jefferies).

run·nel (run′əl), *n.* **1.** a small stream or brook: *... hearing no sound except ... the various gurgling noises of innumerable runnels* (W. H. Hudson). **2.** a small channel for water; gutter. [Old English *rynel,* related to *rinnan* run; probably influenced by Middle English *runnen* run]

run·ner (run′ər), *n.* **1.** a person, animal, or thing that runs; racer: *Most of our relay runners will be competing in individual events during the afternoon* (London Times). **2. a.** *Baseball.* a base runner: *The game was close with two out and runners at first and third.* **b.** *Football.* the ball carrier. **c.** a messenger: *a runner for a bank or brokerage house.* **3.** a person who runs or works a machine, etc. **4.** either of the long narrow pieces on which a sleigh or sled slides. **5.** the blade of a skate. **6.** a long, narrow strip: *We have a runner of carpet in our hall, and runners of linen and lace on our dressers.* **7.** a smuggler; person or ship that tries to evade somebody. **8. a.** a slender stem that takes root along the ground, thus producing new plants: *Strawberry plants spread by runners. Many plants produce runners and rhizomes that effectively extend the area they occupy* (Fred W. Emerson). **b.** a plant that spreads by such stems. **9.** any of various climbing bean plants: *the scarlet runner.* **10.** a raveled place: *There was a runner in her stocking, an affecting thinness to her ankles* (New Yorker). **11.** the rotating part of a turbine. **12.** a jurel of the Atlantic Coast of America. **13.** a person who tries to get business for a hotel, tradesman, etc. **14.** a collector, agent, or the like, for a bank, brokerage house, etc. **15.** a channel along which molten metal runs from the furnace to the mold. **16.** the millstone which turns against a fixed stone in a grinding mill. —**Syn. 2. c.** courier.

Runner (def. 8a) of a strawberry plant

runner bean, a climbing bean plant; runner.

run·ner-up (run′ər up′), *n.* a player or team that takes second place in a contest.

run·ning (run′ing), *n.* **1.** the act of a person or thing that runs: *running a race, running a store.* **2.** that which runs.
in the running, a. in the race or competition; having a chance to win: *Although he is no longer the leading candidate, he is still in the running.* **b.** among the leading competitors in a race or contest: *Experts place that horse in the running.*
out of the running, a. out of the race or competition: *The new British champion crashed and put himself out of the running* (London Times). **b.** not among the leading competitors in a race or contest: *Out of the running for the second season, he is considered a poor bet.*
—*adj.* **1.** cursive: *Running handwriting joins all letters of a word together.* **2.** discharging matter: *a running sore.* **3.** flowing: *running water.* **4.** liquid; fluid: *molten running iron.* **5.** going or carried on continuously: *a running commentary.* **6.** current: *the running month.* **7.** repeated continuously: *a running pattern.* **8.** following in succession: *for three nights running.* **9.** prevalent: *Stores were advised to ... watch selling carefully to guide reorders on running styles* (New York Times). **10.** moving or proceeding easily or smoothly. **11.** moving when pulled or hauled: *a running rope.* **12.** slipping or sliding easily: *a running knot or noose.* **13.** (of plants) creeping or climbing; sending out runners. **14.** that is measured in a straight line. **15.** of the run of a train, bus, etc.: *the running time between towns.* **16.** performed with or during a run: *a running leap.* **17.** operating, as a machine; going; working. **18.** of a horse: **a.** traveling with speed at a run. **b.** trained to travel at a run.

running bale, a finished bale of cotton as it comes from the gin and is ready for market: *Running bales ... usually vary somewhat in weight from the Agriculture Department's statistical 500-pound bale* (Wall Street Journal).

running board, a metal or wood piece along the side of a truck, and of older automobiles, near the ground.

running bowline, a bowline knot made round a part of the same rope to form a noose.

running gear, 1. the wheels and axles of an automobile, locomotive, or other vehicle. **2.** ropes used to adjust a vessel's sails.

running hand, handwriting in which each word is formed without lifting the pen or pencil from the paper.

running head, a heading printed at the top of each page of a book, etc.

running knot, a knot so made as to slide along the rope.

running light, a light required on a ship or aircraft while navigating at night.

running mate, 1. a. a candidate running on the same ticket with another, but for a less important office, such as a candidate for vice-president. **b.** any companion or associate. **2.** a horse that paces another in a race.

running noose, a noose with a running knot.

running part, part of a tackle that is free to slide, as between sheaves or pulleys.

running shed, *British.* a roundhouse for locomotives.

running shoe, track shoe: *How fast you move depends on how good you are, and if running shoes fit you'll be encouraged to wear them* (London Times).

running start, 1. a flying start. **2.** an advantage gained by beginning early: *He designed the machines that later gave Renault a running start in the postwar period* (Wall Street Journal).

running stitch, several short, even stitches taken with the needle at one time.

running title, a title of a book or article printed at the top of the left-hand pages, or of all the pages.

run·ny (run′ē), *adj.,* **-ni·er, -ni·est.** that runs: *a runny nose. A runny faucet leaks.*

run-off (run′ôf′, -of′), *n.* **1.** something that runs off, as rain that flows off the land in streams: *... lead to compacting of the surface soil and to greatly increased surface run-off of rainwater* (W. H. Pearsall). **2.** a final, deciding race or contest.

run-off primary, *U.S.* a second primary held between the two candidates polling the greatest number of votes in the first primary.

run-of-pa·per (run′əv pā′pər), *adj.* (of an advertisement) not requiring special or preferred placement in a newspaper; that may be placed on any page or in any section. *Abbr.:* R.O.P.

run-of-riv·er (run′əv riv′ər), *adj.* run-of-the-river.

run-of-the-mill (run′əv ᴛʜə mil′), *adj.* average or commonplace; ordinary; unselected: *a run-of-the-mill play.* [earlier *run of the mill* coarsely finished or unrefined mill products]

run-of-the-mine (run′uv ᴛʜə mīn′), *adj.* run-of-the-mill: *Though the third act is not, like the first, a fiasco, it is run-of-the-mine entertainment* (Time). [earlier *run of the mine* crude, unsorted coal, or ores]

run-of-the-riv·er (run′əv ᴛʜə riv′ər), *adj.* (of a hydroelectric power plant) using the flow of a stream as it occurs; having no reservoir for storing power: *Kariba ... has ample long-term storage and can provide continuous firm power; Kafne, being virtually run-of-the-river, could not* (London Times).

run-on (run′on′, -ôn′), *adj.* **1.** *Printing.* **a.** continued or added without a break at the end: *Run-on chapters may begin anywhere on a page.* **b.** run-in. **2.** *Prosody.* continuing without pause from one line of verse to another.
—*n.* **1.** *Printing.* matter to be run-on. **2.** run-on entry.

run-on entry, (in a dictionary) a derived word that is not defined but is shown at the end of the entry for the word from which it is formed. *Rurally* may be found as a run-on entry under *rural.*

run·out (run′out′), *n. U.S. Slang.* a running out on someone; escape.
take a runout powder, to run away; take a powder: *They* [*tenants in arrears*] *readily take a runout powder, and they do not even shrink from suicide* (New Yorker).

run-o·ver (run′ō′vər), *adj.* worn-out: *Even the shoes I wear are, despite run-over heels . . . the same* (Harper's).

run·rig (run′rig′), *British.* —*n.* **1.** land divided into parallel strips or rigs, with alternate rigs belonging to different owners. **2.** a ridge of turf separating two parallel strips. —*adv.* in separate strips farmed by different holders.

run sheep run, a children's game similar to hide-and-seek but played with two sides. As one side hunts for the other side, the leader of the group in hiding remains at the base and warns his teammates with signals.

runt (runt), *n.* **1. a.** a stunted animal, person, or plant. **b.** the smallest animal of a litter. **2.** an ox or cow of a small breed. **3.** *British Dialect.* an old or decayed stump of a tree. **4.** *Scottish.* the stalk or stem of a plant. [perhaps unrecorded Old English *hrunta* (compare *Hrunting,* Beowulf's sword) < *hrung* rung[2]] —**Syn. 1. a.** dwarf.

run-through (run′thrü′), *n. Informal.* **1.** a brief review; summary: *He began with a run-through of Freud's . . . speculations on telepathy as a . . . means of human communication* (New Yorker). **2.** a rehearsal of a play or other prepared entertainment: *a final run-through of a play before opening night.*

runt·i·ness (run′tē nis), *n.* runty quality or condition.

runt·ish (run′tish), *adj.* runty.

runt·y (run′tē), *adj.,* **runt·i·er, runt·i·est.** stunted; dwarfish.

run-up (run′up′), *n.* **1.** an increase: *a run-up in prices.* **2.** *British.* the act of sending a ball up to the goal or into a position for final play: *. . . to restrict a bowler's run-up to 20 yards* (London Times). **3.** the running or speeding up of an engine in order to test, check, or warm it.

run·way (run′wā′), *n.* **1.** a way, track, groove, trough, or the like, along which something moves, slides, etc. **2.** the beaten track of deer or other animals. **3.** an enclosed place for animals to run in: *When I got home with her, I unbridled her in the runway of the barn which was about twelve feet wide and fifty feet long* (Harper's). **4.** a strip having a hard surface on which planes take off and land. **5.** a stream bed. **6.** a groove to return bowling balls to the head of the alley. —**Syn. 2.** spoor.

ru·pee (rü pē′), *n.* **1.** the monetary unit of either India or Pakistan, worth about 21 cents. *Abbr.:* R. **2.** a unit of money of Nepal worth about 13 cents. **3.** a silver or nickel coin or piece of paper money worth one rupee. [< Hindi *rūpiyah* < Sanskrit *rūpya* wrought silver or gold]

ru·pes·tri·an (rü pes′trē ən), *adj.* found on rocks: *rupestrian inscriptions. This rupestrian art, which is of mysterious origin and said to be very beautiful, was an important find* (New Yorker). [< New Latin *rupestris* (< Latin *rūpes* rock) + English *-ian*]

ru·pes·trine (rü pes′trin), *adj. Biology.* living or growing among rocks.

ru·pi·ah (rü pē′ə), *n.* the unit of money of Indonesia, worth about 2¼ cents. [< Indonesian *rupiah* < Hindi *rūpiyah* rupee]

rup·tur·a·ble (rup′chər ə bəl), *adj.* that can be ruptured.

rup·ture (rup′chər), *n., v.,* **-tured, -tur·ing.** —*n.* **1.** a break; breaking: *the rupture of a blood vessel. During the war it was found that in zones of secondary damage rupture of welding was rare* (London Times). **2.** a breaking off of friendly relations that threatens to become actual war: *The smothered dissensions among the emigrants suddenly broke into open rupture* (Francis Parkman). **3.** the sticking out of some tissue or organ of the body through the wall of the cavity that should hold it in; hernia.
—*v.t.* **1.** to break; burst; break off. **2.** to affect with hernia. —*v.i.* **1.** to suffer a break. **2.** to suffer a hernia.
[< Latin *ruptūra* < *rumpere* to burst]

ru·ral (rúr′əl), *adj.* **1.** in the country; belonging to the country; like that of the country: *As cities grow, they spread farther and farther into what were once rural areas. The smell of grain, or tedded grass, or kine, Or dairy, each rural sight, each rural sound* (Milton). **2.** of or having to do with agriculture: *rural economy.* [< Late Latin *rūrālis* < *rūs, rūris* country] —**ru′ral·ly,** *adv.* —**ru′ral·ness,** *n.*
—**Syn. 1. Rural, rustic, pastoral** mean of, relating to, or characteristic of the country as opposed to the city. **Rural** is the most objective term, implying neither favor nor disfavor (*rural roads*) or mild, general favor (*healthful rural life*). **Rustic** implies simplicity and roughness, regarded favorably (*rustic charm*) or unfavorably (*rustic speech*). **Pastoral** implies idyllic simplicity, suggesting shepherds, grazing flocks, green pastures, and serene peace: *He paints pastoral pictures.*

rural dean, a priest holding the first rank among the clergy of a district outside the cathedral city.

ru·ra·les (rü rä′lās), *n.pl.* mounted police in Mexico, originally made up largely of revolutionaries of President Diaz: *The rurales, I was told, prefer not to take prisoners* (New Yorker). [< Spanish (*guardias*) *rurales* rural (guards)]

rural free delivery, the delivery of mail in country districts by regular carriers. *Abbr.:* R.F.D.

ru·ral·ism (rúr′ə liz əm), *n.* **1.** rural character; rural life. **2.** an expression, idiom, or custom peculiar to the country.

ru·ral·ist (rúr′ə list), *n.* **1.** a person who leads or advocates a rural life. **2.** a person skilled in the management of rural affairs, the cultivation or development of country regions, etc. **3.** a person who lives or works in the country: *Then they drive the country roads, visiting ruralists in tobacco fields or strawberry patches* (Wall Street Journal).

ru·ral·i·ty (rú ral′ə tē), *n., pl.* **-ties. 1.** rural character. **2.** a rural characteristic, matter, or scene.

ru·ral·i·za·tion (rúr′ə lə zā′shən), *n.* a ruralizing.

ru·ral·ize (rúr′ə līz), *v.,* **-ized, -iz·ing.** —*v.t.* to cause to become rural. —*v.i.* to spend time in the country.

rural route, a mail-delivery circuit in the country; route for rural free delivery: *Entrants will be accepted from Thamesville and surrounding rural routes* (Chatham, Ontario, Daily News). *Abbr.:* R.R.

rur·ban (rur′bən, rúr′-), *adj. U.S.* of or having to do with a group or an area marked by both rural and urban features. [< *rur*(al) + (ur)*ban*]

ru·ri·dec·a·nal (rúr′ə dek′ə nəl, -di kā′-), *adj.* of or having to do with a rural dean or deans: *As the basic unit of church synodal government, these ruridecanal synods will elect representatives to the diocesan synods and General Synod of the church* (Time).

Ru·ri·ta·ni·an (rúr′ə tā′nē ən, -tān′yən), *adj.* **1.** characteristic of an imaginary kingdom or land. **2.** of or having to do with a romanticized, glamorous concept of royalty. [< *Ruritania,* the fictional kingdom in *The Prisoner of Zenda,* a novel by Anthony Hope, 1863-1933, a British novelist + *-an*]

Rus., **1.** Russia. **2.** Russian.

ru·sa (rü′sə), *n.* any of a group of large East Indian deer with a mane; sambar. [< New Latin *Rusa* the genus < Malay *rūsa* deer]

ru·sal·ka (rü säl′kə), *n. Russian Legend.* a water nymph. [< Russian *rusalka*]

ruse (rüz, rüs), *n.* a trick; stratagem: *It was a ruse on the part of the governing authorities . . . to get the rioters out of the city* (Cardinal Newman). [< Old French *ruse* < *ruser* to dodge, get out of the way < Late Latin *refusāre* < Latin *recusāre* push back, deny] —**Syn.** artifice, dodge, wile. See **stratagem.**

ru·sé (rü zā′), *adj.* artful; cunning; sly. [< French *rusé,* past participle of *ruser;* see RUSE]

rush[1] (rush), *v.i.* **1.** to move with speed or force: *to rush from the room, to rush to the station. The river rushed past. Our sail was now set, and, with the still rising wind, we rushed along* (Herman Melville). **2.** to run forward to make an attack: *The crazed man rushed at the doctor who was trying to help him. All his creditors would have come rushing on him in a body* (Thackeray). **3.** to come, go, pass, act, etc., with speed or haste: *color rushing to the face, thoughts rushing through the mind. He rushes into things without knowing anything about them.*
—*v.t.* **1.** to attack, overcome, or take with much speed and force: *They rushed the enemy.* **2.** to send, push, force, carry, etc., with speed or haste: *Rush this order, please. We rushed him home before the rain began. The sick child was rushed to the hospital.* **3.** to urge to hurry: *Don't rush me.* **4.** *U.S. Informal.* to give much attention to, especially to persuade to join a fraternity or sorority: *There were a lot of students who weren't rushed or pledged who found solace in the Y . . . or musical clubs* (Eva Thompson). **5.** to advance (a football) by running.
—*n.* **1.** the act of rushing: *The rush of the flood swept everything before it. The little girl told her sad story in a rush of tears. There was a general rush of the men towards the beach* (Herman Melville). **2.** busy haste; hurry: *the rush of city life. So sorry to have kept you waiting, but we're rather in a rush to-day* (G. K. Chesterton). **3.** the effort of many people to go somewhere or get something: *the Christmas rush, the gold rush.* **4.** eager demand; pressure: *a rush for tickets to a play, a rush on steel stocks. A sudden rush of business kept everyone working hard.* **5.** an attempt to carry the ball through the opposing line in football. **6.** *U.S.* a scrimmage held as a form of sport between groups or classes of students. **7.** an attack: *The infantry rush which followed captured them* (John Buchan). **8.** *U.S. Informal.* a rushing, as for a fraternity or sorority.
rushes, the first filmed scenes of a part of a motion picture: *Sometimes . . . I'm not satisfied with the rushes and they let me dub in new lines* (Maclean's).
with a rush, suddenly; quickly: *The Confederate States perceive that they cannot carry all before them with a rush* (London Times).
—*adj.* **1.** requiring haste: *A rush order must be filled at once.* **2.** *U.S. Informal.* of or having to do with rushing: *Formal rush week for all sororities on the campus will be Oct. 1 to Oct. 6* (Denver Tribune).
[Middle English *ruschen* force out of place by violent impact, probably < Old French *russher,* variant of *ruser;* see RUSE] —**rush′er,** *n.* —**Syn.** *v.i.* **1.** dash, hurry, speed.

rush[2] (rush), *n.* **1.** any of a group of grasslike plants with smooth, pithy or hollow stems, that grow in wet ground. **2.** a stem of such a plant, used for making chair seats, baskets, floor mats, etc.: *a heap of dried leaves and rushes . . . for rest at night* (Cardinal Newman). **3.** something of little or no value. [Old English *rysc*]

rush·bear·ing (rush′bãr′ing), *n.* an annual ceremony in northern districts of England, consisting of carrying rushes and garlands to the church and strewing the floor or decorating the walls with them, usually made the occasion of a general holiday.

rush candle, a rushlight.

rush·ee (rush ē′), *n. U.S. Informal.* a student undergoing rushing in a college.

rush hour, *U.S.* the time of day when traffic is heaviest or when trains, buses, etc., are most crowded.

rush·ing (rush′ing), *n. U.S. Informal.* **1.** the act of paying special attention to someone, especially to persuade to join a fraternity or sorority: *Howard has a normally lively interest in extracurricular activities like . . . fraternity and sorority rushing* (Life). **2.** the period when fraternity rushing takes place. —*adj.* **1.** moving or going with speed; dashing. **2.** proceeding with great activity: *a rushing business.* —**rush′ing·ly,** *adv.*

rush·light (rush′līt′), *n.* a candle with a wick made from a rush.

rush·like (rush′līk′), *adj.* like a rush or reed.

rush line, the forward line in football; line.

rush·y (rush′ē), *adj.,* **rush·i·er, rush·i·est. 1.** abounding with rushes; covered with rushes: *Artemis haunted streams and rushy pools* (Maurice Hewlett). **2.** made of rushes: *my rushy couch* (Oliver Goldsmith). **3.** like rushes: *rushy herbs.*

ru·sine antler (rü′sīn, -sin), an antler with a single brow tine and a simple fork at the end of the main stem. [< New Latin *Rusa* (see RUSA) + English *-ine*[1]]

rus in ur·be (rus′ in ėr′bē), *Latin.* the country in the city.

rusk (rusk), *n.* **1.** a piece of bread or cake toasted in the oven. **2.** a kind of light, sweet biscuit. [< Spanish, Portuguese *rosca* roll, twist of bread; (literally) spiral; origin uncertain]

Russ (rus), *n., pl.* **Russ,** *adj.* —*n.* **1.** a Russian (used in an unfriendly way). **2.** the Russian language. —*adj.* Russian. [< Russian *Rus'* the Russians, Russia, ultimately < *Ros*(lagen), in Sweden, where the founders of Russia came from]

Russ., 1. Russia. 2. Russian.

Rus·sell diagram (rus′əl), *Astronomy.* a diagram of the relation between the brightness and temperature of stars. [< Henry N. *Russell,* 1877-1957, an American astronomer, who devised it]

Rus·sell·ite (rus′ə līt), *n.* a member of Jehovah's Witnesses. [< Charles T. *Russell,* 1852-1916, an American religious leader, founder of Jehovah's Witnesses + *-ite*[1]]

Russell's viper, a large, very poisonous snake with bright reddish-brown spots, common to southeastern Asia.

rus·set (rus′it), *adj.* **1.** yellowish-brown or reddish-brown. **2.** rustic; homely; simple. **3.** made of russet (cloth). **4.** made of leather that has not been blackened: *russet shoes.* —*n.* **1.** a yellowish brown or reddish brown. **2.** a coarse, russet-colored cloth: *The English peasants used to make and wear russet.* **3.** a kind of winter apple with a rough, brownish skin. **4.** leather that is finished but not polished.
[< Old French *rousset* (diminutive) < *rous* < Latin *russus* red, related to *ruber* red]

rus·set-backed thrush (rus′it bakt′), the olive-backed thrush, especially the variety of the Pacific Coast of North America.

rus·set·y (rus′ə tē), *adj.* having a color like russet.

rus·sia (rush′ə), *n.* Russia leather.

Russia leather, a fine, smooth leather, often dark-red, originally produced in Russia by careful tanning and dyeing and then rubbing with birch oil.

Rus·sian (rush′ən), *adj.* of or having to do with Russia (the Soviet Union), its people, or their language: *The Western world was treated to the first publication of general Soviet economic statistics, including the Russian census . . . since 1939* (Newsweek). —*n.* **1.** a native or inhabitant of Russia, especially a member of the dominant Slavic people of the Soviet Union. **2.** the East Slavic language of Russia, the most widely used of the Slavic languages.

Russian Blue cat, any of a breed of short-haired cats with thick, bluish-gray fur.

Russian Church, a self-governing branch of the Eastern or Orthodox Church, with its see at Moscow; Russian Orthodox Church. It was the national church of Russia before 1918.

Russian dressing, mayonnaise with chili sauce, usually used as a salad dressing.

Rus·sian·ism (rush′ə niz′əm), *n.* **1.** a tendency to favor Russia. **2.** prevalence of Russian ideas or spirit: *Stravinsky . . . abandoned his so-called Russianism and began to compose in a style that had sharp classical references* (John Brodbin Kennedy). **3.** a word, phrase, or meaning typically Russian: *He accuses Mr. Nabokov of using Russianisms* (London Times).

Rus·sian·i·za·tion (rush′ə nə zā′shən), *n.* **1.** the act of Russianizing. **2.** the condition of being Russianized.

Rus·sian·ize (rush′ə nīz), *v.t., v.i.,* **-ized, -iz·ing.** to make or become Russian in customs, language, etc.

Russian olive, oleaster (def. 1).

Russian Orthodox Church, Russian Church: *The Soviet Communist party is in the process of reappraising its campaign against the Russian Orthodox Church* (New York Times).

Russian Revolution, the revolution in which the Russian people, especially the workers, soldiers, and sailors, overthrew the government of the Czar in 1917, and established the Soviet Union.
➔ **Russian Revolution.** The Russian Revolution has two parts: "the February Revolution," of March, 1917 (February, Old Style), establishing the Kerensky government, and "the October Revolution," of November, 1917 (October, Old Style), establishing the Lenin or Bolshevik government.

Russian roulette or **Roulette,** a game of chance played with a revolver loaded with one bullet. After spinning the chamber a player points the gun at his head and pulls the trigger. *A Frenchman was shooting up the German air force with a forward-firing machine gun that worked much on the principle of "Russian roulette"—you just fired and took a chance that the propeller would not be hit* (Wall Street Journal).

Russian tea, *Especially British.* tea flavored with lemon but not milk.

Russian thistle, a large weed of the goosefoot family with spiny branches, that develops into a troublesome tumbleweed.

Russian wolfhound, any of a breed of tall, slender, swift dogs that have silky hair; borzoi.

Rus·si·fi·ca·tion (rus′ə fə kā′shən), *n.* Russianization: *The Russification of the nationalists in the Tsarist tradition . . .* (Observer).

Rus·si·fy (rus′ə fī), *v.t., v.i.,* **-fied, -fy·ing.** Russianize.

Russo-, *combining form.* Russian: *Russophilia = great admiration for the Russians.* [< *Russia,* or *Russ*]

Rus·so-Byz·an·tine (rus′ō biz′ən tēn, -tīn; -bi zan′tin), *adj.* both Russian and Byzantine; Russian, as developed from the Byzantine style: *Russo-Byzantine architecture.*

Russo-Byzantine Architecture (Cathedral of Assumption, Moscow)

Rus·so-Jap·a·nese (rus′ō-jap′ə nēz′, -nēs′), *adj.* having to do with or between Russia and Japan: *the Russo-Japanese War of 1904-1905.*

Rus·so·phile (rus′ə fīl, -fil), *n.* a person who greatly admires or favors Russia, Russian methods, etc.

Rus·so·phil·i·a (rus′ə fil′ē ə), *n.* great admiration of Russia, Russian methods, Russian policies, etc.

Rus·soph·i·lism (rə sof′ə liz əm), *n.* the beliefs and theories of a Russophile.

Rus·so·phobe (rus′ə fōb), *n.* a person with an excessive fear or hatred of Russia, Russian methods, etc.

Rus·so·pho·bi·a (rus′ə fō′bē ə), *n.* an excessive fear or hatred of Russia, Russian methods, etc.

rust (rust), *n.* **1.** the reddish-brown or orange coating that forms on iron or steel when exposed to air or moisture. **2.** any film or coating on any other metal due to oxidation or corrosion: *Aluminum has built-in protection against rust* (Newsweek). **3.** a harmful growth, habit, influence, or agency. **4.** Also, **rust fungus. a.** a plant disease that spots leaves and stems. **b.** any of various fungi that produce this disease: *wheat rust.* **5.** a reddish brown or orange.
—*v.i.* **1.** to become covered with rust: *Don't let your tools or machines rust. From the practical standpoint, the most undesirable property of iron is its tendency to rust* (W. N. Jones). **2.** to become spoiled by not being used: *Don't let your mind rust during the vacation. Neglected talents rust into decay* (William Cowper). **3.** to have the disease rust. **4.** to become rust-colored. —*v.t.* **1.** to coat with rust. **2.** to spoil by not using. **3.** to cause to have the disease rust.
—*adj.* reddish-brown or orange.
[Old English *rūst*]

rust·a·ble (rus′tə bəl), *adj.* that can become rusted or rusty.

rust-col·ored (rust′kul′ərd), *adj.* reddish brown or orange.

rus·tic (rus′tik), *adj.* **1.** belonging to the country; suitable for the country; rural: *a rustic lane in the quiet countryside. Some rustic phrases which I had learned at the farmer's house* (Jonathan Swift). **2.** simple; plain: *His rustic speech and ways made him uncomfortable in the city school.* **3.** rough; awkward. **4.** made of branches with the bark still on them: *rustic furniture, a rustic fence.* **5.** having the surface rough or the joints deeply sunk or chamfered: *rustic masonry.*
—*n.* **1.** a country person: *The rustics gathered at the country fair.* **2.** a crude or boorish person considered as coming from the country.
[< Latin *rūsticus* < *rūs, rūris* country]
—**Syn.** *adj.* **1.** See **rural.**

rus·ti·cal (rus′tə kəl), *adj., n. Archaic.* rustic.

rus·ti·cal·ly (rus′tə klē), *adv.* in a rustic manner; plainly; crudely.

rus·ti·cate (rus′tə kāt), *v.,* **-cat·ed -cat·ing.** —*v.i.* to go to the country; stay in the country: *Month after month, he rusticated in solitary grandeur in Pasadena* (New Yorker). —*v.t.* **1.** to send to the country. **2.** *British.* to send (a student) away from a university or college as a punishment. **3.** to make (masonry) with a rough surface or sunken joints. [< Latin *rūsticārī* (with English *-ate*[1]) < *rūsticus;* see RUSTIC]

rus·ti·ca·tion (rus′tə kā′shən), *n.* **1. a.** a rusticating. **b.** a being rusticated. **2.** residence in the country. **3.** *British.* the temporary dismissal of a student from a college or university as a punishment.

rus·ti·ca·tor (rus′tə kā′tər), *n.* a person who rusticates.

rus·tic·i·ty (rus tis′ə tē), *n., pl.* **-ties. 1.** a rustic quality, characteristic, or peculiarity: *a rusticity of manner.* **2.** rural life. **3.** awkwardness; ignorance.

rust·i·ly (rus′tə lē), *adv.* in a rusty state; in such a manner as to suggest rustiness.

rust·i·ness (rus′tē nis), *n.* the quality or condition of being rusty.

rus·tle (rus′əl), *n., v.,* **-tled, -tling.** —*n.* **1.** the sound that leaves make when moved by the wind, or a sound like this. **2.** *U.S. Informal.* hustle: *to get a rustle on.* [< verb]
—*v.i.* **1.** to make a light, soft sound of things gently rubbing together: *Leaves rustled in the breeze.* **2.** to move or stir, making such a sound: *the wind rustling through the woods.* **3.** *U.S. Informal.* to move, work, or act with energy. **4.** *U.S. Informal.* to steal cattle; be a rustler. —*v.t.* **1.** to move or stir (something) so that it makes a rustle: *to rustle the papers. Memory was turning over the leaves of her volume, rustling them to and fro* (Hawthorne). **2.** *U.S. Slang.* to do or get with energy: *I'll sure buy Pedro back . . . just as soon as ever I rustle some cash* (Owen Wister). **3.** *U.S. Informal.* to steal (cattle).
[Middle English *rustelen,* perhaps Old English *hrūxlian* make noise]

rus·tler (rus′lər), *n.* **1.** *U.S. Informal.* a cattle thief: *The cattle thieves—the rustlers—were gaining in numbers and audacity* (Owen Wister). **2.** *U.S. Informal.* an active, energetic person. **3.** a person or thing that rustles; rustling leaf, bird, etc. [American English < *rustl*(e) to steal cattle + *-er*[1]]

rust·less (rust′lis), *adj.* free from rust; resisting rust.

rus·tling·ly (rus′ling lē), *adv.* with a rustle.

rust·proof (rust′prüf′), *adj.* resisting rust.

rus·tre (rus′tər), *n. Heraldry.* a bearing in the form of a lozenge with a hole in the middle. [< French *rustre*]

rust·y[1] (rus′tē), *adj.,* **rust·i·er, rust·i·est. 1.** covered with rust; rusted: *a rusty knife.* **2.** made by rust: *a rusty stain, a rusty spot.* **3.** colored like rust. **4.** faded; shabby: *a rusty black; . . . a little rusty, musty old fellow, always groping among ruins* (Washington Irving). **5.** damaged by lack of use: *Mother's grammar is rusty, she says. Editorial contacts were getting rusty* (Newsweek). **6.** out of practice: *Hector . . . Who in this dull and continued truce Is rusty grown* (Shakespeare). **7.** affected with the disease rust: *rusty wheat.*

rust·y[2] (rus′tē), *adj.,* **rust·i·er, rust·i·est.** stubborn; contrary; cross: *The people got rusty about it, and would not deal* (Scott).
ride or **run rusty,** to act in a stubborn, contrary, or disagreeable way: *How the devil am I to get the crew to obey me? Why, even Dick Fletcher rides rusty on me now and then* (Scott).
[perhaps alteration of *resty,* variant of *restive;* perhaps influenced by *rusty*[1] in sense "surly"]

rusty blackbird, a blackbird of northern and eastern North America, solid black in the spring and rusty in the fall.

rut[1] (rut), *n., v.,* **rut·ted, rut·ting.** —*n.* **1.** a track made in the ground, as by wheels; furrow; groove: *A sleepy land, where under the same wheel The same old rut would deepen year by year* (Tennyson). **2.** a fixed or established way of acting: *It's time to pull out of the rut of earthbound traffic* (Newsweek). —*v.t.* to make ruts in: *The road was beaten into paste and rutted two feet deep by the artillery* (Sir Arthur Conan Doyle). [perhaps variant of *route*] —**Syn.** *n.* **2.** routine.

rut[2] (rut), *n., v.,* **rut·ted, rut·ting.** —*n.* **1.** sexual excitement of deer, goats, sheep, etc., occurring at regular intervals. **2.** the period during which it lasts. —*v.i.* to be in rut. [< Old French *rut,* and *ruit* < Latin *rugītus, -ūs* a bellowing < *rūgīre* to bellow]

ru·ta·ba·ga (rü′tə bā′gə, -beg′ə), *n.* a kind of large, yellow or white turnip. [< Swedish dialectal *rotabagge*]

ru·ta·ceous (rü tā′shəs), *adj.* **1.** belonging to the rue family: *Orange and lemon trees are rutaceous plants.* **2.** of or like rue. [< New Latin *Rutaceae* the rue family < Late Latin *rūtāceus* having to do with rue < Latin *rūta* a bitter herb < Greek *rhytē* rue]

ruth (rüth), *n. Archaic.* **1.** pity; compassion: *I came back to her now with no other emotion than a sort of ruth for her great sufferings* (Charlotte Brontë). **2.** sorrow. [Middle English *rewthe* < *rewen* to rue[1], Old English *hrēowan*]

Ruth (rüth), *n.* in the Bible: **1.** the wife of Boaz. She is famous for her devotion to her mother-in-law, Naomi. **2.** the book of the Old Testament that tells about her.

Ru·the·ni·an (rü thē′nē ən), *adj.* of or having to do with Ruthenia, a part of the Soviet Union, or with its people, or their language. —*n.* **1.** a native or inhabitant of Ruthenia. **2.** the language of Ruthenia, a form of Ukrainian.

ru·then·ic (rü then′ik, -thē′nik), *adj.* of or having to do with ruthenium, especially with a high valence.

ru·the·ni·ous (rü thē′nē əs), *adj.* of or having to so with ruthenium, especially with a low valence.

ru·the·ni·um (rü thē′nē əm), *n.* a brittle, gray metallic chemical element similar to platinum. It is a rare metal found in platinum ores. *Symbol:* Ru; *at.wt.:* (C^{12}) 101.07 or (O^{16}) 101.1; *at.no.:* 44; *valence:* 2, 3, 4, 6, 7, 8. [< New Latin *ruthenium* < Medieval Latin *Ruthenia* Russia (because it was discovered in platinum ores from the Urals)]

ruth·ful (rüth′fəl), *adj. Archaic.* **1.** compassionate. **2.** sorrowful.

ruth·less (rüth′lis), *adj.* having no pity; showing no mercy; cruel: *What a ruthless thing is this . . . to take away the life of a man?* (Shakespeare). —**Syn.** hard-hearted, relentless, merciless, pitiless.

ruth·less·ly (rüth′lis lē), *adv.* cruelly.

ruth·less·ness (rüth′lis nis), *n.* ruthless action or behavior: *He harassed them and embarrassed them with absolute ruthlessness* (Atlantic).

ru·ti·lant (rü′tə lənt), *adj.* shining; glowing; gleaming. [< Latin *rutilāns, -antis,* present participle of *rutilāre* glow with red-gold light < *rutilus;* see RUTILE]

ru·ti·lat·ed (rü′tə lā′tid), *adj.* containing needles of rutile: *rutilated quartz.*

ru·tile (rü′tēl, -tīl), *n.* a mineral consisting of titanium oxide, often with a little iron. It has a metallic or diamondlike luster, and is usually reddish-brown or black. *Formula:* TiO_2 [< French *rutile* < German *Rutil* < Latin *rutilus* red-gold, related to *ruber* red]

ru·tin (rü′tin), *n.* a substance found in the leaves of the buckwheat, pansy, tobacco, and other plants, that relaxes and expands blood vessels. It is effective in preventing small hemorrhages. *Formula:* $C_{27}H_{30}O_{16}$ [< Latin *rūta* rue + English *-in*]

rut·ti·ness (rut′ē nis), *n.* rutty quality or state.

rut·tish (rut′ish), *adj.* lustful; lascivious.

rut·ty (rut′ē), *adj.,* **-ti·er, -ti·est. 1.** full of ruts: *a rutty country road.* **2.** ruttish.

R.V. or **RV** (no periods), Revised Version of the Bible.

RW., railway.

R.W., 1. Right Worshipful. **2.** Right Worthy.

Rwan·dese (rů än′dēz′, -dēs′), *adj., n., pl.* **-dese.** —*adj.* of or having to do with the republic of Rwanda (formerly part of Ruanda-Urundi) in central Africa. —*n.* a native or inhabitant of Rwanda.

Rx (är′eks′), *n., pl.* **Rx's. 1.** a medical prescription: *More and more physicians are specifying by brand or manufacturers' names the products to be used in filling their "Rx's"* (New York Times). **2.** any remedy; course; solution: *Rx for a healthy summer* (Consumer Report). [< *Rx,* symbol (short for Latin *recipe* take)]

Rx (no periods) or **rx** (no periods), **1.** (in medical prescriptions) take (Latin, *recipe*). **2.** tens of rupees.

-ry, *suffix.* **1.** occupation or work of a ——: *Dentistry = the occupation or work of a dentist. Chemistry = the occupation or work of a chemist.*
2. act of a——: *Mimicry = act of a mimic.*
3. quality, state, or condition of a——: *Rivalry = the condition of a rival.*
4. group of——s, considered collectively, as in *jewelry, peasantry.*
[short for *-ery*]

Ry., railway.

ry·al (rī′əl), *n.* **1.** an old English gold coin; rose noble. **2.** an old gold or silver coin of Scotland. [Middle English *ryal,* variant of *royal*]

ry·a·ni·a (rī ā′nē ə), *n.* the ground wood of a tropical American tree, used as an insecticide. [< New Latin *Ryania* genus name of the tree]

rye[1] (rī), *n.* **1.** a hardy, annual cereal grass grown in cold regions as a cover and forage crop and for its grain. **2.** its seeds or grain, used to make flour and whiskey. **3.** flour made from them: *Peasants in Germany and Russia ate a great deal of almost black rye bread.* **4.** *U.S.* whiskey made from rye: *After a long day's work they often shared a bottle of rye and sang songs* (Maclean's). [Old English *ryge*]

Rye[1] (def. 1)

rye[2] (rī), *n.* (among Gypsies) a gentleman. [< Gypsy *rei, rai* lord]

rye·grass (rī′gras′, -gräs′), *n.* any of several grasses having spicules growing in a zigzag pattern along the stem, used for pastures and lawns.

ryke (rīk), *v.i.,* **ryked, ryk·ing.** *Scottish.* to reach.

rynd (rīnd, rind), *n.* a piece of iron fastened across the hole of an upper millstone, and serving to support the stone. Also, **rind.** [early variant of *rind*[2]]

ry·ot (rī′ət), *n.* (in India) a small farmer; peasant. [earlier *riat* < Hindustani *raiyat,* ultimately < Arabic *ra'āyyah* non-Moslem subjects of Moslem rulers]

Ryu·kyu·an (rē yü′kyü ən), *n.* a native or inhabitant of the Ryukyu Islands, southwest of Japan. —*adj.* of or having to do with the Ryukyu Islands.

S Roman 100's A.D. — Greek 600's B.C. — Phoenician 1000's B.C. — Semitic 1500's B.C. — Egyptian 3000's B.C.

Ss Ss *Ss* *Ss*

S or **s** (es), *n., pl.* **S's** or **Ss, s's** or **ss. 1.** the 19th letter of the English alphabet. **2.** any sound represented by this letter. **3.** (as a symbol) the 19th (or more usually 18th, either *I* or *J* being omitted) of an actual or possible series. **4. a.** the shape of the letter: *The road curved in a big S.* **b.** anything shaped like an S.

's, *Informal.* a spelling representing the informal pronunciation of:
a. is. *Examples:* There's nothing there. That's it.
b. has. *Examples:* She's done it. That's been done.
c. us. *Example:* Let's do it.

-s[1], a suffix used to form the plural of most nouns whose singular does not end in an *s* or *z* sound, as in *boys, dogs, hats, houses.* It also forms the plural of noun substitutes, such as symbols. [Middle English *-es,* or *-s,* Old English *-as,* suffix denoting the nominative or accusative plural of certain masculine nouns]

-s[2], a suffix used to form the third person singular of verbs in the present indicative active, as in *lies, runs, rides, sees, asks, bites, bluffs.* [Middle English *-es,* or *-s,* Old English, (originally) suffix denoting the second person singular]

-s[3], a suffix used to form some adverbs, as in *needs, unawares.* [Middle English, Old English *-es,* (originally) suffix denoting the genitive singular of masculine and neuter nouns and adjectives]

-'s, a suffix used to form the possessive case of nouns in the singular, as in *fellow's, man's, child's, book's, elf's,* and also of plural nouns not ending in *s,* as in *men's, children's, alumni's.* (When the singular ends with an *s* sound, the possessive is sometimes indicated by the apostrophe above, as *Jesus', goodness' sake,* etc.) [Middle English, Old English *-es,* or *-s;* see -S[3]]

s., an abbreviation for the following:
1. half (Latin, *semi*).
2. *Anatomy.* sacral.
3. saint.
4. school.
5. scribe.
6. second or seconds.
7. section.
8. see.
9. series.
10. set or sets.
11. shilling or shillings.
12. a. sign. **b.** signed.
13. silver.
14. singular.
15. sire (in animal pedigrees).
16. society.
17. solo.
18. son or sons.
19. soprano.
20. a. south. **b.** southern.
21. steamer.
22. steel.
23. stem.
24. stratus (cloud).
25. substantive.
26. succeeded.
27. sun.

S (no period), an abbreviation or symbol for the following:
1. Saxon.
2. a. South. **b.** Southern.
3. specific heat.
4. sulfur (chemical element).

S., an abbreviation for the following:
1. fellow (of a society, etc.; Latin, *socius*).
2. page or pages (German, *Seite*).
3. Sabbath.
4. saint.
5. Saturday.
6. Saxon.
7. school.
8. sea.
9. Senate (bill; used with a number).
10. September.
11. signor.
12. socialist.
13. society.
14. soprano.
15. a. south. **b.** southern.
16. Sunday.
17. surplus.

s.a., an abbreviation for the following:
1. semiannual.
2. subject to approval.
3. undated (Latin, *sine anno,* without a year).
4. under the year (Latin, *sub anno*).

Sa (no period), samarium (chemical element).

SA (no periods), **1.** storm troops (German, *Sturmabteilung*). **2.** surface-to-air.

S.A., an abbreviation for the following:
1. corporation (for French *Société Anonyme,* Spanish *Sociedad Anónima,* Italian *Società Anonima,* etc.).
2. Salvation Army.
3. *Slang.* sex appeal.
4. a. South Africa. **b.** South African.
5. a. South America. **b.** South American.
6. a. South Australia. **b.** South Australian.
7. storm troops (German, *Sturmabteilung*).

Saar·land·er (sär′lan′dər), *n.* a native or inhabitant of the Saar (territory in West Germany).

Sab., Sabbath.

sab·a·dil·la (sab′ə dil′ə), *n.* **1.** a Mexican and Central American plant of the lily family with long, grasslike leaves and bitter seeds. **2.** the seeds, used in medicine as a source of veratrine, and in making an insecticide. [< New Latin *Sabadilla* the genus name < Spanish *cebadilla* (diminutive) < *cebada* barley; ultimately < Latin *cibus* food nourishment]

Sa·bae·an (sə bē′ən), *adj., n.* Sabean.

Sa·ba·ism (sā′bē iz əm), *n.* star worship. [< Hebrew *ṣābā* host (of heaven) + English *-ism.* Compare SABAOTH.]

Sa·ba·ist (sā′bē ist), *n.* a worshiper of stars.

Sab·a·oth (sab′ē oth, -ōth; sə bā′ōth), *n.pl.* armies; hosts: *The Lord of Sabaoth* (Romans 9:29). [< Latin *Sabaōth* < Greek *Sabaṓth* of hosts < Hebrew *ṣəbā'oth* armies]

sab·a·ton (sab′ə ton), *n.* **1.** a shoe or half boot made of satin, cloth of gold, etc., worn by persons of wealth in the 1400's. **2.** an armed foot covering, broad and blunted at the toes, worn by warriors in armor in the 1500's: *At the commencement of the 16th century, the pointed sollerets were succeeded by broad sabatons, cut off square or rounded at the toes* (Charles Bontell). [< Old Provençal *sabaton* < *sabata* shoe. Related to SABOT.]

Sab·bat (sab′ət), *n.* a midnight meeting of demons, sorcerers, and witches, presided over by the Devil, supposed in medieval times to have been held annually as an orgy or festival; witches' Sabbath. [< French *Sabbat* (literally) Sabbath < Latin *sabbatum;* see SABBATH]

Sab·ba·tar·i·an (sab′ə târ′ē ən), *n.* **1.** a person who observes Saturday, the seventh day of the week, as the Sabbath, as many Jews do. **2.** a Christian who favors a very strict observance of Sunday. *—adj.* of or having to do with the Sabbath, Sabbatarians, or Sabbath observance: *He was sharply criticized by strict Sabbatarian elements when he first began playing golf on Sundays* (Newsweek).
[< Late Latin *Sabbatārius* of the Sabbath (in Latin, plural, keepers of the Sabbath < *sabbatum* sabbath) + English *-an*]

Sab·ba·tar·i·an·ism (sab′ə târ′ē ə niz′əm), *n.* the beliefs or practices of the Sabbatarians.

Sab·bath (sab′əth), *n.* a day of the week used for rest and worship: *Sunday is the Christian Sabbath; Saturday is the Jewish Sabbath. . . . Severe and sunless remembrances of the Sabbaths of childhood* (Hawthorne).
—adj. of, belonging to, or suitable for the Sabbath.
[< Latin *sabbatum* < Greek *sábbaton* < Hebrew *shabbāth* < *shābath* he rested] **—Syn.** *n.* See **Sunday.**

sab·bath (sab′əth), *n.* a time or period of rest, quiet, etc. [< *Sabbath*]

Sab·bath-day's journey (sab′əth dāz′), the distance in ancient times that a Jew might lawfully travel on the Sabbath: *Then returned they . . . from the mount called Olivet, which is from Jerusalem a Sabbath-day's journey* (Acts 1:12).

Sab·bath·less (sab′əth lis), *adj.* having or observing no Sabbath, or day of rest: *Sabbathless Satan! he who his unglad task ever plies* (Charles Lamb).

Sabbath School, 1. Sunday School. **2.** a school for religious instruction held on Saturday by Seventh-Day Adventists.

sab·bat·ic (sə bat′ik), *adj., n.* sabbatical. [< Greek *sabbatikós* < *sábbaton;* see SABBATH]

sab·bat·i·cal (sə bat′ə kəl), *adj.* **1.** of or suitable for the Sabbath. **2.** of or for a rest from work.
—n. **1.** a sabbatical leave: *I can't imagine being an ambassador for life, so this is only a sort of unique sabbatical* (New Yorker). **2.** a sabbatical year.

sabbatical leave, a leave of absence for a year or half year given to college and university teachers, commonly once in seven years, for study, travel, or rest: *John Wheeler from Princeton interrupted a well-deserved sabbatical leave in Europe* (Science).

sab·bat·i·cal·ly (sə bat′ə klē), *adv.* in a sabbatical manner.

sabbatical year, 1. (among the ancient Jews) every seventh year, during which fields were left untilled, debtors released, etc. **2.** sabbatical leave.

Sab·ba·tism (sab′ə tiz əm), *n.* observance of the Sabbath or of a sabbath. [< Late Latin *sabbatismus* < Greek *sabbatismós* < *sábbaton* Sabbath + *-ismos* -ism]

Sa·be·an (sə bē′ən), *adj.* **1.** of or having to do with Sheba, an ancient kingdom of Arabia, noted for its trade in spices and gems. **2.** fragrant; rich: *Sabaean odours from the spicy shore of Araby the bless'd* (Milton).
—n. an inhabitant of Sheba. Also, **Sabaean.**
[< Latin *Sabaeus* (< Greek *Sabaîos* < *Sába* an ancient name of Sheba, a city in Yemen) + English *-an*]

Sa·bel·li·an (sə bel′ē ən), *n.* **1.** a member of a group of related peoples who inhabited parts of ancient Italy, comprising the Sabines, Samnites, and others. **2.** a group of early Italic dialects spoken by these people. **3.** a follower of Sabellius, about 220 A.D., a philosopher of northern Africa, who believed that the Father, Son, and Holy Spirit are merely different aspects or modes of one Divine person.
—adj. **1.** of or having to do with the Sabellians or their language. **2.** having to do with the Sabellians or their doctrine.
[< Latin *Sabellī,* for *Sabīnī* Sabines + English *-an*]

Sa·bel·li·an·ism (sə bel′ē ə niz′əm), *n.* the doctrinal view of the Trinity maintained by Sabellius and his followers.

sa·ber (sā′bər), *n.* **1.** a heavy sword, usually slightly curved, having a single cutting edge. **2.** a soldier armed with a saber. **3. a.** a sword used in fencing, similar to the foil but with two cutting edges. **b.** the sport or skill of fencing with such a sword. *—v.t.* to strike, cut, wound, or kill with a saber. Also, *especially British,* **sabre.** [< French *sabre,* alteration of *sable* < earlier German *Sabel* (now *Säbel*) < Hungarian *szablya* < Slavic (compare Russian *sáblja*), perhaps < Semitic (compare Arabic *sajf,* Aramaic *sajpā*)]

Saber (def. 1)

sa·bered (sā′bərd), *adj.* armed or equipped with a saber: *sabered cavalry charging on horseback.* Also, *especially British,* **sabred.**

sa·ber-legged (sā′bər legd′, -leg′id), *adj.* (of a horse) having a congenital malformation of the hind leg that extends the foot forward in a curve like that of a saber.

sa·ber·like (sā′bər līk′), *adj.* shaped like a saber; curved; crescentic: *There is one extinct land family, the sabertooths, which had saber-like upper canine teeth* (William C. Beaver).

saber rattling, a bold or reckless exhibition of military power; threat of violent action in behalf of a cause: *Under present military conditions it is senseless for the Federal government to use a policy of saber rattling to force the Russians to the conference table* (Newsweek).

saber saw, a kind of electric jigsaw: *A portable saber saw is needed to cut out the animals* (New York Times).

sa·ber·tooth (sā′bər tüth′), *n.* the saber-toothed tiger.

sa·ber-toothed (sā′bər tütht′), *adj.* having very long, curved, upper canine teeth.

saber-toothed tiger, a large, extinct, tigerlike carnivorous mammal whose upper canine teeth were long and curved.

Saber-toothed Tiger (6 ft. long)

Sa·bi·an (sā′bē ən), *n.* **1.** a member of a religious sect in Babylonia classed in the Koran with the Moslems, Jews, and Christians, as believers in the true God. **2.** a member of a sect of star worshipers in Mesopotamia in the 800's. [< Arabic *Ṣābi'* Sabian + English *-an*]

Sa·bi·an·ism (sā′bē ə niz′əm), *n.* star worship.

sa·bin (sā′bin), *n.* a unit to measure the sound absorption qualities of a surface. It is equivalent to one square foot of a completely absorptive surface. [< Wallace C. *Sabine,* 1868-1919, an American physicist]

Sa·bine (sā′bīn), *n.* **1.** a member of an ancient tribe in central Italy which was conquered by the Romans in the 200's B.C. **2.** their Italic language. —*adj.* of or belonging to the Sabines or their language. [< Latin *Sabīnus*]

Sabine's gull, a small gull of arctic regions with a forked tail and black and white wings. [< Sir Edward *Sabine,* 1788-1883, a British scientist and arctic explorer]

Sabin vaccine, a vaccine for preventing the development of paralytic polio. It consists of living but attenuated polioviruses, and it is taken orally in a single dose. [< Albert B. *Sabin,* born 1906, an American virologist, who developed it]

sa·ble (sā′bəl), *n.* **1.** a small carnivorous mammal of northern Europe and Asia, valued for its dark-brown, glossy fur. It is related to the marten. **2.** its fur, one of the most costly furs. **3.** the marten of North America; American sable. **4. a.** the color black: *clothes of sable.* **b.** black clothing, especially as a symbol of mourning. **5.** *Heraldry.* black, as one of the heraldic colors, in engraving represented by crossing horizontal and vertical lines.

Sable (def. 1) (including tail, about 27 in. long)

sables, *Poetic.* mourning garments: *Nay then let the Devil wear black, for I'll have a suit of sables* (Shakespeare).

—*adj. Archaic.* black; dark: . . . *did a sable cloud Turn forth her silver lining on the night?* (Milton).

[< Old French *sable,* probably < Medieval Latin *sabellum* < Slavic (compare Russian *sobol',* Polish *soból*)] —**sa′ble·ness,** *n.*

sable antelope, a large South and East African, antelope with large, sickle-shaped horns. The male is black, the female red-dish-brown.

sa·ble·fish (sā′bəl fish′), *n., pl.* **-fish·es** or (*collectively*) **-fish.** the beshow, a fish of the west coast of North America.

sa·bles (sā′bəlz), *n.pl.* See under **sable,** *n.*

sab·ot (sab′ō; *French* sȧ bō′), *n.* **1.** a shoe hollowed out of a single piece of wood, worn by peasants in France, Belgium, etc. **2.** a coarse leather shoe with a thick wooden sole. **3.** a cuplike cap fitted to the base of a shell or other projectile to position it correctly in the barrel, prevent the escape of gases, and make contact with the rifling. [< French *sabot* < Old French *çabot,* alteration of unrecorded *çavate* old shoe (influenced by *bot,* or *botte* boot), perhaps < Arabic *ṣabbāṭ* sandal, shoe]

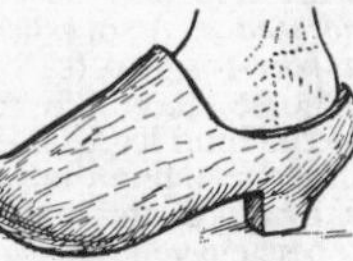
Sabot (def. 1)

sab·o·tage (sab′ə täzh), *n., v.,* **-taged, -tag·ing.** —*n.* **1.** damage done to work, tools, machinery, etc., by workmen as an attack or threat against an employer: *A part of the syndicalist's method is sabotage, which originally referred to throwing a shoe into a machine so as to stop production and to further revolution* (Emory S. Bogardus). **2.** such damage done by civilians of a conquered nation to injure the conquering forces: *The jailed cardinal furnished a rallying cause for anti-Communist agitation and sabotage in Hungary* (Time). **3.** damage done by enemy agents or sympathizers in an attempt to slow down a nation's war effort. **4.** malicious attacking of or secret working against any cause to which cooperation is due.

—*v.t.* to damage or destroy by sabotage: *to sabotage a defense plant. Conservatives sabotaged the heavy spending program.* [< French *sabotage* < *saboter* to bungle, walk noisily < *sabot* wooden shoe (possibly because wooden shoes were thrown into machinery to damage it); see SABOT]

sab·o·teur (sab′ə tėr′), *n.* a person who engages in sabotage. [< French *saboteur,* ultimately < *sabot;* see SABOT]

sa·bra (sä′brə), *n., pl.* **-bras.** a person born in Israel: *Only three of the authors are sabras, born in Palestine and accustomed to the language from infancy* (Time). [< Hebrew *ṣābrāh* cactus (because the person is thought of as tough on the outside and soft on the inside)]

sa·bre (sā′bər), *n., v.t.* **-bred, -bring.** *Especially British.* saber.

sa·bred (sā′bərd), *adj. Especially British.* sabered.

sa·bre·tache (sā′bər tash, sab′ər-), *n.* a leather case hanging from the left side of a cavalryman's sword belt. [< French *sabretache,* alteration of German *Säbeltasche* < *Säbel* (see SABER) + *Tasche* a case, pouch]

sa·breur (sȧ brœr′), *n. French.* a person, especially a cavalryman, who fights with a saber.

Sa·bri·na (sə brī′nə), *n.* the legendary daughter of Lócrine and Estrildis. She was drowned in the river Severn and became its nymph.

sab·u·los·i·ty (sab′yə los′ə tē), *n.* sandiness; grittiness.

sab·u·lous (sab′yə ləs), *adj.* consisting of sand; full of sand; sandy; gritty. [< Latin *sabulōsus* < *sabulum* sand]

sac (sak), *n.* a baglike part in an animal or plant, often containing a liquid: *the sac of a honeybee, the ink sac of an octopus.* [< French, Old French *sac* < Latin *saccus;* see SACK[1]] —**sac′like′,** *adj.* —**Syn.** cyst, vesicle.

Sac (sak, sôk), *n., adj.* Sauk.

SAC (no periods) or **S.A.C.,** Strategic Air Command.

sac·a·ton (sak′ə tōn′), *n.* any of several coarse grasses of the dry regions of southwestern United States, grown for pasture or hay; zacatón. [American English < Spanish *zacatón* zacatón]

sac·cad·ic (sə kä′dik), *adj.* jerky: *The eyeball does not follow a continuous path but jumps discontinuously, in so-called saccadic movement* (New Scientist). [< French *saccade* (< Old French *saquer, sacher* to pull, draw) + English *-ic*]

sac·cate (sak′āt), *adj.* **1.** having the form of a sac or pouch. **2.** having a sac or pouch. [< Latin *saccus* a bag, sack + English *-ate*[1]]

sac·cat·ed (sak′ā tid), *adj.* saccate.

sac·cha·rate (sak′ə rāt), *n.* **1.** a salt of any saccharic acid. **2.** a compound of a metallic oxide with a sugar: *calcium saccharate.* **3.** a sucrate. [< *sacchar*(ic acid) + *-ate*[2]]

sac·char·ic (sə kar′ik), *adj.* having to do with or obtained from a sugar. [< Greek *sákcharis* (see SACCHARIN) + English *-ic*]

saccharic acid, a dibasic acid, occurring in three optically different forms, produced by oxidizing glucose and various other hexose sugars. *Formula:* $C_6H_{10}O_8$

sac·cha·ride (sak′ə rīd, -ər id), *n.* **1.** a saccharate; compound of a metallic oxide with a sugar. **2.** a carbohydrate which contains sugar. **3.** a compound of sugar with a base.

sac·cha·rif·er·ous (sak′ə rif′ər əs), *adj.* yielding or containing sugar. [< Greek *sákcharis* (see SACCHARIN) + English *-ferous*]

sac·char·i·fi·ca·tion (sə kar′ə fə kā′shən, sak′ər ə-), *n.* transformation into sugar.

sac·char·i·fy (sə kar′ə fī, sak′ər ə-), *v.t.,* **-fied, -fy·ing.** to change (starch, etc.) into sugar; saccharize.

sac·cha·rim·e·ter (sak′ə rim′ə tər), *n.* a device for determining the amount of sugar in a solution, especially a kind of polarimeter. [< French *saccharimètre* < Greek *sákcharis* (see SACCHARIN) + French *-mètre* -meter]

sac·cha·rin (sak′ər in), *n.* a white, crystalline substance, obtained from coal tar, used as a substitute for sugar. A pellet of it has as much sweetening power as several hundred times its weight of cane sugar. *Calory counters and diabetics can eat products containing either of the two chemical sweeteners, saccharin or the newer cyclamate* (Wall Street Journal). *Formula:* $C_7H_5NO_3S$ [< Medieval Latin *saccharum* sugar (< Greek *sákcharon,* for *sákcharis* < Pali *sakkharā* < Sanskrit *śarkarā* candied sugar; originally, gravel, grit) + English *-in*[1]]

sac·cha·rine (sak′ər in, -ə rīn), *adj.* **1.** very sweet; sugary: *a saccharine smile. He knew how to handle youngsters without being saccharine or patronizing* (Newsweek). **2.** of or having to do with sugar. —*n.* saccharin. —**sac′cha·rine·ly,** *adv.* —**Syn.** *adj.* **1.** honeyed.

saccharine sorghum, sweet sorghum, used for making molasses or syrup and as a food for livestock.

sac·cha·rin·i·ty (sak′ə rin′ə tē), *n.* the quality of being saccharine.

saccharin sodium, a white, crystalline powder used as a substitute for sugar. It is a sodium salt of saccharin, up to 500 times as sweet as sugar; Crystallose. *Formula:* $C_7H_4NNaO_3S.2H_2O$

sac·cha·rize (sak′ə rīz), *v.t.,* **-rized, -riz·ing.** to change into sugar; saccharify.

sac·cha·roid (sak′ə roid), *adj. Geology.* having a granular texture like that of loaf sugar.

sac·cha·roi·dal (sak′ə roi′dəl), *adj.* saccharoid.

sac·cha·ro·lyt·ic (sak′ə rə lit′ik), *adj.* having the power of chemically splitting sugar.

sac·cha·rom·e·ter (sak′ə rom′ə tər), *n.* a device for measuring the amount of sugar in a solution, as a form of hydrometer.

sac·cha·rose (sak′ə rōs), *n.* cane or beet sugar; sucrose. *Formula:* $C_{12}H_{22}O_{11}$ [< Greek *sákcharis* (see SACCHARIN)]

sac·ci·form (sak′sə fôrm), *adj.* sac-shaped; saclike. [< Latin *saccus* sac + English *-form*]

sac·cos (sak′os), *n.* a short vestment corresponding to the Western dalmatic, worn in the Eastern Church by metropolitans. Also, **sakkos.** [< New Greek *sakkos* < Greek *sákkos* sack[1]]

sac·cu·lar (sak′yə lər), *adj.* having to do with or having the form of a saccule or sac.

sac·cu·late (sak′yə lāt), *adj.* formed of little sacs; divided into saclike dilations.

sac·cu·lat·ed (sak′yə lā′tid), *adj.* sacculate.

sac·cu·la·tion (sak′yə lā′shən), *n.* **1.** the formation of a saccule or saccules. **2.** a sacculate part.

sac·cule (sak′ūl), *n.* **1.** a little sac. **2.** the smaller of the two membranous sacs in the labyrinth of the internal ear: . . . *there are two other organs in the inner ear which are believed to register gravity. These are the tiny cavities known as the "utricle" and "saccule" which contain microscopic solid particles called "otoliths" or, literally, "ear stones"* (Arthur C. Clarke). [< Latin *sacculus* (diminutive) < *saccus;* see SACK[1]]

sac·cu·lus (sak′yə ləs), *n., pl.* **-li** (-lī). a saccule.

sa·cer·do·cy (sas′ər dō′sē), *n., pl.* **-cies. 1.** sacerdotal or priestly character or dignity. **2.** a priestly office or system.

sa·cer·do·tal (sas′ər dō′təl), *adj.* **1.** of priests or the priesthood; priestly: *Régine took on the job of tending the church altar and the sacerdotal robes* (Time). **2.** of, based on, or having to do with the doctrine that the priesthood is invested by ordination with supernatural powers. [< Latin *sacerdōtālis* < *sacerdōs, -ōtis* priest < *sacra* rites + a stem *dōt-* to put, set]

sa·cer·do·tal·ism (sas′ər dō′tə liz əm), *n.* **1. a.** the sacerdotal system; spirit or methods of the priesthood. **b.** (in an unfavorable sense) priestcraft. **2.** the theory that the priesthood is invested by ordination with supernatural powers.

sa·cer·do·tal·ly (sas′ər dō′tə lē), *adv.* in a sacerdotal manner.

SACEUR (no periods), Supreme Allied Commander, Europe.

sac fungus, an ascomycete.

sa·chem (sā′chəm), *n.* **1.** (among some North American Indians) the chief of a tribe or a confederation: *Tammany was sachem of the Delaware Indians in the 1600's.* **2.** *U.S.* one of a body of twelve high officials in the Tammany Society of New York: *the sachem of Tammany Hall.* [American English < Algonkian (Narragansett) *sâchimau* chief. Related to SAGAMORE.]

sa·chem·ship (sā′chəm ship), *n.* the office or position of a sachem.

Sa·cher·tor·te (zä′Hər tôr′tə), *n., pl.* **-tor·ten** (-tôr′tən), a rich layer cake filled with apricot jam and covered with chocolate frosting: *The miniature Sachertorten . . . will be flown in from Vienna* (New York Times). [< *Sacher*, a hotel in Austria specializing in this cake + German *Torte* torte]

sa·chet (sa shā′; *especially British* sash′ā), *n.* **1.** a small bag or pad containing perfumed powder, usually placed among articles of clothing. **2.** perfumed powder. [< French, Old French *sachet* (diminutive) < *sac* sack, bag]

sachet powder, strongly perfumed powder used in sachets.

sack[1] (sak), *n.* **1.** a large bag, usually made of coarse cloth: *Sacks are used for storing and carrying grain, flour, potatoes, coal, etc.* **2.** such a bag with what is in it: *He bought two sacks of corn.* **3.** the amount that a sack will hold: *We burned two sacks of coal.* **4.** *U.S.* any bag or what is in it: *a sack of candy.* **5.** *U.S. Slang.* (in baseball) a base. **6.** *Slang.* a bed. **7.** dismissal from employment or office: *to get the sack, give a person the sack.*

hit the sack, *Slang.* to go to bed: *The exhausted campers hit the sack and fell asleep at once.*

hold the sack, *Informal.* to be left emptyhanded; be left to suffer the consequences: *We will be holding the sack for an additional . . . deficit of nearly $1000* (University of Kansas Graduate Magazine).

—*v.t.* **1.** to put into a sack or sacks. **2.** to dismiss from employment or office; fire.

sack out, *Slang.* to go to bed: *It's still too early to sack out.*

[Middle English *sacke*, or *secke*, Old English *sacc* < Latin *saccus* < Greek *sákkos* < Semitic (compare Hebrew *shaq*)] —**sack′like′**, *adj.* —**Syn.** *n.* **1.** See **bag.**

sack[2] (sak), *v.t.* to plunder (a captured city, town, etc.); loot and despoil; pillage. [< noun]

—*n.* the act of sacking; plundering of a captured city: *The city was sure to be delivered over to fire, sack, and outrage* (John L. Motley).

[< Middle French *sac* < Italian *sacco* < Vulgar Latin *saccāre* take by force; origin uncertain] —**Syn.** *v.t.* devastate.

sack[3] (sak), *n.* **1.** a loose jacket worn by women and children: *a knitted sack for a baby.* **2.** a kind of loose gown formerly worn by women or a long back piece fastened to the gown at the shoulders and forming a train. Also, **sacque.** [apparently < *sack*[1]. Compare Dutch *zak*, German (*französischer*) *Sack*.]

sack[4] (sak), *n.* **1.** sherry. **2.** any of certain other strong, light-colored wines formerly exported from Spain and certain other parts of southern Europe. [< French (*vin*) *sec* dry (wine) < Latin *siccus*]

sack bearer, the larva of a North American moth, which feeds on oak leaves and protects itself with a case made of leaves.

sack·but (sak′but), *n.* **1.** a musical wind instrument of the Middle Ages, somewhat like the trombone: *Three unusual early French hunting madrigals then swirl through abstruse modes with double-reeds . . . xylophone . . . and sackbut . . .* (New Yorker). **2.** an ancient stringed instrument mentioned in the Bible. Daniel 3. [< Middle French, Old French *saquebute*, Old North French *saqueboute* hooked lance for unhorsing an enemy; (literally) pull-push < *saquer* to pull (probably < *sac* < Latin *saccus*; see SACK[1]) + *bouter* to push. Compare BUTT[3].]

Nuremberg Sackbut (def. 1) (1557)

sack·cloth (sak′klôth′, -kloth′), *n.* **1.** a coarse cloth for making sacks; sacking. **2.** a coarse fabric worn as a sign of mourning or penitence: *The sackcloth of the Bible was a dark fabric of goats' or camels' hair.*

in sackcloth and ashes, with grief, humiliation, or abject penitence: *The culprit's only proper course would seem to be repentance in sackcloth and ashes* (Arthur Krock).

sack cloud, a form of mammatocumulus in which the pocket hanging from the cloud becomes so deep as to resemble a sack or bag, sometimes seeming to reach to the ground.

sack coat, a man's short, loose-fitting coat for ordinary wear.

sack dress, a loose-fitting dress with straight lines: *Fashions changed again briefly in the late 1950's to . . . chemises and sack dresses and high-waisted empire lines similar to those of the early 1800's* (Betsy Talbot Blackwell).

sack·er[1] (sak′ər), *n.* a person who sacks or plunders. [< *sack*[2] + *-er*[1]]

sack·er[2] (sak′ər), *n. Baseball Slang.* a baseman: *But Thompson, in his haste to make the throw, didn't wait for Davey Williams, Giant second sacker, to reach the bag* (New York Times). [< *sack*[1] + *-er*[2]]

sack·ful (sak′fu̇l), *n., pl.* **-fuls. 1.** enough to fill a sack. **2.** *Informal.* a great quantity; large amount.

sack·ing (sak′ing), *n.* a coarse cloth closely woven of hemp, cotton, flax, jute, etc., used for making sacks, bags, etc.

sack·less (sak′lis), *adj.* **1.** *Scottish.* **a.** harmless. **b.** lacking energy, spirit, or sense. **c.** feeble-minded. **2.** *Obsolete.* **a.** guiltless. **b.** secure. [Old English *saclēas*, perhaps < *sacu* sake, behalf + *-lēas* -less or, perhaps < Scandinavian (compare Old Icelandic *saklauss*)]

sack race, a race in which each competitor is enveloped in a sack, the mouth of which is secured around his neck or waist.

SACLANT (no periods), Supreme Allied Commander, Atlantic.

sacque (sak), *n.* sack[3]. [Gallicized variant of *sack*[3]]

sa·cral[1] (sā′krəl), *adj.* of or having to do with sacred rites or observances. [< Latin *sacer, sacris* sacred + English *-al*[1]]

sa·cral[2] (sā′krəl), *adj.* of, having to do with, or in the region of the sacrum. [< New Latin *sacralis* < Latin (*os*) *sacrum* sacrum; (literally) sacred (bone), neuter of *sacer*, adjective, sacred]

sac·ra·ment (sak′rə mənt), *n.* **1.** any of certain solemn ceremonies or religious acts of the Christian church. Roman Catholic and Eastern Church use recognizes seven sacraments: Baptism, Confirmation, Eucharist, Penance, Extreme Unction, Holy Orders, and Matrimony. From the 1500's, Protestants generally have recognized two sacraments only—Baptism and Communion. **2.** Often, **Sacrament. a.** Communion (the Eucharist or Lord's Supper). **b.** the consecrated bread and wine. **c.** the bread alone (the Host). **3.** something especially sacred: *To the true mystic, life itself is a sacrament* (W. R. Inge). **4.** a sign; token; symbol. **5.** a solemn promise; oath. [< Old French *sacrement*, learned borrowing from Latin *sacrāmentum* a consecrating (usually an oath or surety) < *sacrāre* to consecrate < *sacer* holy, sacred] —**Syn. 1.** rite. **5.** vow.

sac·ra·men·tal (sak′rə men′təl), *adj.* **1.** of or having to do with a sacrament; used in a sacrament: *sacramental wine.* **2.** especially sacred: *The fulfillment of her father's lifelong ambition about this library was a sacramental obligation for Romola* (George Eliot). —*n.* (in the Roman Catholic Church) a rite or ceremony similar to but not included among the sacraments. The use of holy water or oil or the sign of the cross is a sacramental. —**Syn.** *adj.* **2.** consecrated, hallowed, holy.

sac·ra·men·tal·ism (sak′rə men′tə liz əm), *n.* the doctrine that there is in the sacraments themselves by Christ's institution a direct spiritual power to confer grace upon the recipient: *She goes in for a kind of sacramentalism, holding that there is a difference between the medieval belief and the later view* (Manchester Guardian).

sac·ra·men·tal·ist (sak′rə men′tə list), *n.* a person who holds the doctrine of sacramentalism.

sac·ra·men·tal·ly (sak′rə men′tə lē), *adv.* after the manner of a sacrament.

sac·ra·men·tar·i·an (sak′rə men târ′ē ən), *adj.* of or having to do with the sacraments. [< *sacramentary*, adjective + *-an*]

Sac·ra·men·tar·i·an (sak′rə men târ′ē-ən), *n.* **1.** a person who believes that the bread and wine of Communion are the symbol of Christ's sacrifice, but not actually His flesh and blood. **2.** a person who believes that the sacraments in themselves confer spiritual grace upon the recipient; a sacramentalist. —*adj.* of or having to do with the Sacramentarians. [< German *Sakramentarian* (coined by Martin Luther) < Medieval Latin *sacramentarius*, adjective, sacramentary]

sac·ra·men·ta·ry (sak′rə men′tər ē), *adj., n., pl.* **-ries.** —*adj.* sacramental; sacramentarian. —*n.* a book containing religious offices or services formerly in use in the Western Church, containing the rites and prayers connected with the sacraments and other ceremonies. [< Medieval Latin *sacramentarium* < Latin *sacrāmentum;* see SACRAMENT]

Sac·ra·men·ta·ry (sak′rə men′tər ē), *n., pl.* **-ries.** Sacramentarian. [variant of *Sacramentarian*]

sacrament cloth, the veil or cloth which covers the pyx or vessel containing the reserved Eucharist.

sacrament house, the tabernacle for the reserved Eucharist.

sa·crar·i·um (sə krãr′ē əm), *n., pl.* **-i·a** (-ē ə). **1.** the sanctuary of a church. **2.** (in Roman Catholic use) a piscina; basin used to dispose of water after certain ablutions. **3.** (in ancient Rome) a shrine or sanctuary. [< Latin *sacrārium* < *sacrāre* to consecrate < *sacer* sacred]

Sa·cra Ro·ma·na Ro·ta (sā′krə rō mā′nə rō′tə), rota; an ecclesiastical tribunal forming a court of final appeal. [< New Latin *Sacra Romana Rota* (literally) sacred Roman wheel]

sa·cre (sā′kər), *v.t.,* **-cred, -cring.** to consecrate; hallow (now only as in *sacred* and *sacring*). [< Old French *sacrer*, learned borrowing from Latin *sacrāre;* see SACRARIUM]

sa·cré (sȧ krā′), *adj.* **1.** sacred. **2.** damned; cursed; confounded. [< French *sacré*, past participle of *sacrer* to consecrate, learned borrowing from Latin *sacrāre;* see SACRARIUM]

Sa·cré-Coeur (sȧ′krā kœr′), *n.* Sacred Heart (of Jesus). [< French *Sacré-Cœur* (literally) sacred heart]

sa·cred (sā′krid), *adj.* **1.** belonging to or dedicated to God or a god; holy: *the sacred altar. A church is a sacred building. This statement says that the people of Cyprus "will carry on their sacred struggle without fear of any repressive measures or prison cells"* (London Times). **2.** connected with religion; religious: *sacred writings, sacred music. What is called sacred may be any object. Thus the thunderbird or the coyote may be sacred in one group but not in another . . . the objects chosen to be sacred are those which are related to the unknown forces of mana, or other powers* (Ogburn and Nimkoff). **3.** worthy of reverence: *the sacred memory of a dead hero. To a feather-brained schoolgirl nothing is sacred* (Charlotte Brontë). **4.** set apart for or dedicated to some person, object, or purpose: *This monument is sacred to the memory of the Unknown Soldier.* **5.** secured by reverence, sense of justice, or the like, against violation, infringement, or encroachment: *sacred oaths. Their property would be held sacred* (Macaulay). **6.** properly immune from violence, interference, etc.; sacrosanct; inviolable: *The persons of Saturninus and Glaucia were doubly sacred, for one was tribune and the other praetor* (James A. Froude). **7.** *Rare.* accursed: *For sacred hunger of my Gold I die* (John Dryden). [(originally) past participle of *sacre*] —**Syn. 1.** consecrated. See **holy.**

sacred baboon, the hamadryad, revered in ancient Egypt.

Sacred College, the cardinals of the Roman Catholic Church collectively; College of Cardinals. The Sacred College elects and advises the Pope.

sacred cow, 1. a cow believed to be sacred in certain religions, as among the Hindus: *On the balcony of a dingy little flat in Old Delhi, looking down on a street that swarmed with sacred cows, bullock carts, peddlers and beggars . . .* (Maclean's). **2.** any person or thing regarded as being so sacred or privileged as to be above opposition or criticism: *The need for widespread secrecy has become a sacred cow, a belief hedged by the deepest emotions and accepted without question by many Americans* (Bulletin of Atomic Scientists). *Is foreign policy a "sacred cow," an inscrutable object of worship to be accepted without question?* (Wall Street Journal).

sacred ibis, an Egyptian wading bird with white and black feathers and a downward-curving bill.

sacred lotus, a variety of nelumbo or lotus of southern Asia and Australia, with large white, pink, or red flowers and leaves up to three feet wide.

sa•cred•ly (sā′krid lē), *adv.* **1.** in a sacred manner; with due reverence; religiously: *to observe the Sabbath sacredly.* **2.** with strict care; inviolably: *a secret to be sacredly kept.*

sa•cred•ness (sā′krid nis), *n.* the quality or state of being sacred.

sacred orders, holy orders.

Sacred Way, 1. the ancient road from Athens to Eleusis, starting at the Dipylon Gate and traversing the Pass of Daphne. **2.** the first street of ancient Rome to be established on the low ground beneath the hills.

sac•ri•fice (sak′rə fīs), *n., v.,* **-ficed, -fic•ing.** —*n.* **1. a.** the act of offering to a god, especially for the purpose of propitiation or homage: *Sacrifices were invaluable features of early religions. By this method the relationships with the gods were renewed and strengthened* (Emory S. Bogardus). **b.** the animal or other thing offered: *The ancient Hebrews killed animals on the altars as sacrifices to God.* **2. a.** a giving up of one thing for another; destruction or surrender of something valued or desired for the sake of a higher object or more pressing claim: *Our teacher does not approve of any sacrifice of studies to sports. Wisdom and sacrifices are demanded from all sides* (Science News Letter). **b.** the thing so given up or destroyed. **3. a.** a loss brought about in selling something below its value: *He will sell his house at a sacrifice because he needs money.* **b.** something that is sold below its value. **4.** *Baseball.* a sacrifice hit: *The Phillies caused consternation by . . . advancing a man to third on a sacrifice and an error* (Christopher "Christy" Mathewson).

make the supreme sacrifice, to give one's life; die: *On Memorial Day we honor the men in our armed forces who made the supreme sacrifice for their country.*

—*v.t.* **1.** to make an offering of; offer as a sacrifice: *They sacrificed oxen, sheep, and doves.* **2. a.** to give up (something) for some higher advantage or dearer object: *A mother will sacrifice her life for her children.* **b.** to permit injury or disadvantage to, for the sake of something else: *to sacrifice business for pleasure.* **3.** to sell or get rid of at a loss. **4.** *Baseball.* to help (a runner) to advance by a sacrifice: *He sacrificed Mantle to second base.* —*v.i.* **1.** to offer up a sacrifice. **2.** *Baseball.* to make a sacrifice hit.

[< Old French *sacrifice,* learned borrowing from Latin *sacrificum* < *sacrificāre* < *sacra* rites, neuter plural of *sacer* holy + *facere* to perform, do] —**Syn.** *n.* **1.a.** immolation. *-v.t.* **1.** immolate.

sacrifice fly, *Baseball.* a sacrifice hit in the form of a fly to the outfield.

sacrifice hit, *Baseball.* a bunt or fly that enables a base runner to advance a base although the batter is put out. It does not count as an official time at bat.

sac•ri•fic•er (sak′rə fī′sər), *n.* a person who sacrifices, especially a priest.

sac•ri•fi•cial (sak′rə fish′əl), *adj.* **1.** having to do with, connected with, or used in sacrifice: *sacrificial rites.* **2.** involving sacrifice or loss to the seller: *a sacrificial sale of summer dresses.*

sacrificial lamb, a person or thing sacrificed for some gain or advantage: *The firemen may have to be the "sacrificial lamb" in obtaining concessions from the carriers* (Wall Street Journal).

sac•ri•fi•cial•ly (sak′rə fish′ə lē), *adv.* as regards sacrifices; after the manner of a sacrifice.

sac•ri•lege (sak′rə lij), *n.* the intentional injury of anything sacred or held sacred; disrespectful treatment of anyone or anything sacred: *Robbing the church was a sacrilege.* [< Old French *sacrilege,* learned borrowing from Latin *sacrilegium* temple robbery < *sacrum* sacred object; (originally) neuter of *sacer* sacred + *legere* to take; select] —**Syn.** profanation.

sac•ri•le•gious (sak′rə lij′əs, -lē′jəs), *adj.* **1.** committing sacrilege; guilty of sacrilege. **2.** involving sacrilege: *sacrilegious acts.* —**Syn. 1.** impious, irreverent.

➔ The more common pronunciation (sak′rə-lij′əs) has arisen on the analogy of *sacrilege* (sak′rə lij) and of *religious.* It is a frequent cause of misspelling.

sac•ri•le•gious•ly (sak′rə lij′əs lē, -lē′jəs-), *adv.* in a sacrilegious manner; with sacrilege.

sac•ri•le•gious•ness (sak′rə lij′əs nis, -lē′-jəs-), *n.* the character of being sacrilegious.

sac•ri•le•gist (sak′rə lē′jist), *n.* a person guilty of sacrilege.

sa•cring (sā′kring), *n.* a consecrating, especially that of the bread and wine in the Mass. [< *sacr*(e) + *-ing*[1]]

sacring bell, in the Roman Catholic Church: **1.** a small bell rung at the elevation of the Host. **2.** the ringing of the bell at the elevation of the Host.

sa•crist (sā′krist), *n.* a sacristan. [< Old French *sacriste,* learned borrowing from Latin *sacrista.* Doublet of SACRISTAN, SEXTON.]

sac•ris•tan (sak′rə stən), *n.* **1.** a person in charge of the sacred vessels, robes, etc., of a church or monastery. **2.** *Obsolete.* a sexton. [< Medieval Latin *sacristanus* < Latin *sacrista* a sacristan < *sacer* holy. Doublet of SACRIST, SEXTON.]

sac•ris•ty (sak′rə stē), *n., pl.* **-ties.** the place where the sacred vessels, robes, etc., of a church or monastery are kept. [< Medieval Latin *sacristia* < Latin *sacrista;* see SACRISTAN] —**Syn.** vestry.

sa•cro•coc•cyx (sā′krō kok′siks), *n.* the sacrum and coccyx regarded as one bone.

sa•cro•il•i•ac (sā′krō il′ē ak, sak′rō-), *adj.* **1.** of or having to do with the sacrum and the ilium: *sacroiliac articulation.* **2.** designating the joint between the sacrum and the ilium. —*n.* the sacroiliac joint: *Strictly speaking, the sacroiliac is an area at the base of the spine; everybody has one* (Atlantic). [< New Latin *sacrum* sacrum + English *iliac*]

sacroiliac disease, inflammation of the sacroiliac.

sac•ro•sanct (sak′rō sangkt), *adj.* very holy; most sacred; inviolable: *He reluctantly accepts the sacrosanct character of FBI files* (Scientific American). *Nowadays modernism is sacrosanct under the name of experimentation* (Harper's). [< Latin *sacrōsānctus* < *sacrō,* ablative of *sacer* sacred + *sānctus,* past participle of *sancīre* ordain, establish] —**sac′ro•sanct′ness,** *n.*

sac•ro•sanc•ti•ty (sak′rō sangk′tə tē), *n.* being sacrosanct; especial sacredness; inviolability: *Posadovsky asked whether the basic, minimum civil liberties—"the sacrosanctity of the person"—could be infringed and even violated if the party leader so decided* (Atlantic).

sa•cro•sci•at•ic (sā′krō sī at′ik, sak′rō-), *adj.* of or having to do with the sacrum and the ischium: *the sacrosciatic notch.* [< New Latin *sacrum* sacrum + English *sciatic*]

sa•crum (sā′krəm), *n., pl.* **-cra** (-krə), **-crums.** a compound, triangular bone at the lower end of the spine, made by the joining of several vertebrae, and forming the back of the pelvis: *In the sacral region the vertebrae in some animals are considerably thickened without great change while in others they are much flattened and more or less fused into a platelike structure, the sacrum* (A. Franklin Shull). [< Late Latin (*ōs*) *sacrum* sacred (bone), translation of Greek *hieròn ostéon* (probably because it was offered as a dainty in sacrifices)]

sad (sad), *adj.,* **sad•der, sad•dest. 1.** not happy; full of sorrow; grieving; in low spirits: *You feel sad if your best friend goes away. Mary was sad because she lost her money. I was very sad, I think sadder than at any one time in my life* (John Bunyan). **2.** characterized by sorrow; sorrowful: *a sad life, a sad occasion. The death of a pet is a sad loss.* **3.** causing sorrow; distressing: *a sad accident.* **4.** expressing sorrow; gloomy; downcast: *sad looks, a sad countenance. Of all sad words of tongue or pen, the saddest are these: "It might have been!"* (John Greenleaf Whittier). **5.** dull in color; not cheerful-looking; dark: *The general colouring was uniform and sad* (Robert Louis Stevenson). **6.** extremely bad; shocking: *a sad mess. In the present sad state of international distrust, there is only a faint hope of achieving such a step in political evolution* (Bulletin of Atomic Scientists). **7.** *Dialect.* (of bread, pastry, etc.) that has not risen properly; heavy. [Old English *sæd* sated; later, weary] —**Syn. 1. Sad, dejected, depressed** mean unhappy or in a state of low spirits. **Sad** is the general term, and implies nothing as to the degree, duration, or cause of the state: *Moonlight makes her sad.* **Dejected** implies a very low but usually temporary state of unhappiness due to some specific cause: *She is dejected over his leaving.* **Depressed** implies a temporary and usually not very low state of unhappiness due to some vague or general cause: *He is depressed by the state of the world.* **3.** deplorable, lamentable, calamitous, disastrous. —**Ant. 1.** glad, cheerful.

sad•den (sad′ən), *v.t.* to make sad or sorrowful; depress in spirits: *Her gloomy presence saddens all the scene* (Alexander Pope). —*v.i.* to become sad or gloomy: *Better be merry with the fruitful grape than sadden after none, or bitter, fruit* (Edward Fitzgerald).

sad•den•ing•ly (sad′ə ning lē), *adv.* in a way that saddens: *The horde of entries from fictitious MPs' wives were so saddeningly authentic that one wondered whether the ladies weren't actual political spouses* (Punch).

sad•dhu (sä′dü), *n.* sadhu.

sad•dle (sad′əl), *n., v.,* **-dled, -dling.** —*n.* **1.** a seat for a rider on a horse's back, on a bicycle, etc. **2.** the part of a harness that holds the shafts, or to which a checkrein is attached. **3.** something resembling a saddle in shape, position, or use. **4.** a ridge between two hills or mountain peaks: *The colors of the cliffs that rim this saddle run riot on a bright day* (William O. Douglas). **5.** a cut of mutton, venison, etc., consisting of the upper back portion and both loins, used as food. **6.** the rear part of the back of a male fowl, extending to the tail. **7.** the bearing on the axle of a railroad car. **8.** the part of certain gun carriages which supports the trunnions. **9.** *Bookbinding.* the center portion of the back of the binding; outer part of the spine.

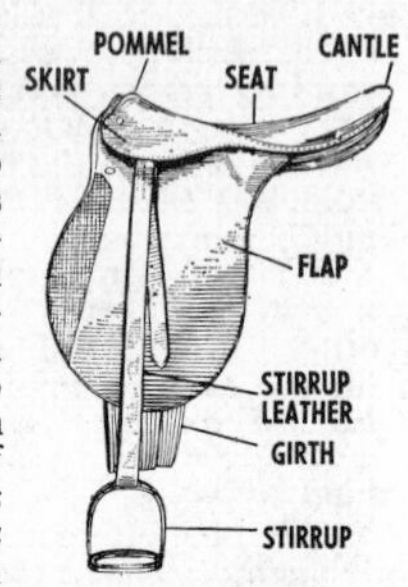

English Saddle (def. 1)

in the saddle, in a position of control or command: [*He*] *resigned in the belief that things would soon break down without him and he would be back in the saddle more firmly seated than before* (Observer). *But key men opposing the civil rights legislation were in the saddle at the moment the bill arrived* (New York Times).

—*v.t.* **1.** to put a saddle on: *to saddle up a horse.* **2.** to load with (something) as a burden; burden: *He is saddled with a big house which he neither needs nor wants.* **3.** to put as a burden on: *If you like not my company, you can saddle yourself on someone else* (Robert Louis Stevenson). **4.** to train (a race horse). —*v.i.* to get into the saddle.

[Old English *sadol*]

—**Syn.** *v.t.* **2.** encumber.

—**sad′dle•like′,** *adj.*

sad•dle•back (sad′əl bak′), *n.* **1.** a hill or summit shaped like a saddle. **2.** the great black-backed gull. **3.** the saddleback seal.

saddleback caterpillar, a green caterpillar having a brown mark shaped like a saddle on its back and stinging hairs which can cause severe irritation to the skin: *Other common stingers are the saddleback caterpillar* (Time).

sad•dle-backed (sad′əl bakt′), *adj.* **1.** having the back, upper surface, or edge curved like a saddle: *a saddle-backed hill, a saddle-backed horse.* **2.** (of birds, etc.) having saddlelike markings on the back.

saddleback seal, a gray or yellowish seal with a black face and a black or brown band along the back and sides, found in arctic regions south to the St. Lawrence River; harp seal.

sad•dle•bag (sad′əl bag′), *n.* one of a pair of bags laid across the back of a horse, mule, etc., behind the saddle.

sad•dle-billed stork (sad′əl bild′), a large white and blackish stork of tropical Africa, with scarlet on the knees, feet, and bill.

saddle blanket, a saddlecloth.

sad•dle•bow (sad′əl bō′), *n.* the arched front part of a saddle or saddletree.

sad•dle•cloth (sad′əl klôth′, -kloth′), *n.* a

 PRONUNCIATION KEY: hat, āge, cãre, fär; let, ēqual, tėrm; it, īce; hot, ōpen, ôrder; oil, out; cup, pu̇t, rüle;

cloth put between an animal's back and the saddle.

saddle gall, a raw area formed on a horse's back by uneven pressure of the saddle.

saddle horse, a horse used, trained, or suited by breeding for riding.

sad·dle·mak·er (sad′əl mā′kər), *n.* a saddler: *He was apprenticed to a Dublin saddlemaker* (New Yorker).

sad·dler (sad′lər), *n.* a person who makes, mends, or sells saddles and harness.

saddle nose, a nose considerably depressed at the bridge because of fracture or disease.

saddle roof, a ridged roof with two gables: *Stubbins' Berlin Congress Hall, with its jaunty saddle roof, clearly sought to express the concept of freedom in the speech which it was built to house* (Harper's).

sad·dler·y (sad′lər ē), *n., pl.* **-dler·ies. 1.** the work of a saddler. **2.** the shop of a saddler. **3.** saddles, harness, and other equipment for horses.

saddle shell, 1. a shell suggesting a saddle in shape, as that of a bivalve mollusk of East Indian seas. **2.** a mollusk with such a shell.

saddle shoe, an oxford shoe, usually white, with the instep crossed by a band of leather or synthetic fabric of a (usually) contrasting color, worn especially for sports and casual wear: *The saddle shoes and the dark Shaker-knit sweater . . . gave him the air of a college athlete home for vacation* (New Yorker).

saddle soap, a substance, now usually consisting chiefly of a mild soap and neat's-foot oil, used for cleaning and conditioning saddles, harnesses, boots, etc.

sad·dle·sore (sad′əl sôr′, -sōr′), *adj.* sore or stiff from riding horseback: *"Jorrocks," at the New Theatre, London, is an innocuous musical derived from the Surtees novels about the saddlesore grocer among the grandees of the hunting field* (Manchester Guardian Weekly).

sad·dle·tree (sad′əl trē′), *n.* **1.** the frame of a saddle. **2.** *U.S.* the tulip tree.

Sad·du·ce·an or **Sad·du·cae·an** (saj′ə-sē′ən, sad′yə-), *adj.* of or having to do with the Sadducees. *—n.* a Sadducee.

Sad·du·cee (saj′ə sē, sad′yə-), *n.* one of a Jewish sect, of the time of Christ, that rejected the oral law and denied the resurrection of the dead and the existence of angels. The sect stood for hereditary priestly authority. *Next to the Pharisees in power, but not quite so numerous, were the Sadducees* (Hendrik van Loon). [Old English *sadducēas,* plural < Latin *Saddūcaeus* of the *Saddūcaeī,* the Sadducees < Late Greek < *Saddoukaîoi* the Sadducees < Hebrew *ṣaddūqī* < *ṣaddūq* Zadok, apparently the Hebrew high priest in the time of David (II Samuel 8:17, Ezekiel 40:46)]

Sad·du·cee·ism (saj′ə sē iz′əm, sad′yə-), *n.* **1.** the beliefs and practices of the Sadducees. **2.** skepticism.

sa·dha·na (sä′də nə), *n. Hinduism.* the spiritual training leading to the state of samadhi: *Ganja was there considered a beginning of sadhana* (Allen Ginsberg). [< Sanskrit *sādhana* < *sādhu* straight, virtuous]

sa·dhe (sä dā′, tsä′dē), *n.* the eighteenth letter of the Hebrew alphabet. Also, **tsadi.** [< Hebrew *ṣadhe*]

sa·dhu (sä′dü), *n.* a Hindu holy man: *Sadhu is the Sanskrit word for "straight," and the straight-living, ascetic sadhus of India were once the bearers of Hindu holiness* (Time). Also, **saddhu, sadu.** [< Sanskrit *sādhu* straight, virtuous]

sad·i·ron (sad′ī′ərn), *n.* a heavy flatiron for pressing clothes. [< *sad* in obsolete sense of "firm" + *iron*]

sa·dism (sā′diz əm, sad′iz-), *n.* **1.** a form of sexual perversion marked by a love of cruelty: *By his own principles he would stand convicted of various abnormalities, including masochism, sadism . . .* (Harper's). **2.** an unnatural love of cruelty. [< French *sadisme* < the Count or Marquis Donatien de *Sade,* 1740–1814, who wrote of it]

sa·dist (sā′dist, sad′ist), *n.* a person who practices or is affected with sadism.

sa·dis·tic (sə dis′tik, sā-), *adj.* of or relating to sadism or to sadists: *Those who torture others in mind or body in order to gain ego satisfaction are sadistic* (George Simpson). —**sa·dis′ti·cal·ly,** *adv.*

sad·ly (sad′lē), *adv.* **1.** sorrowfully; mournfully. **2.** in a manner to cause sadness; lamentably; deplorably: *Authors . . . are sadly prone to quarrel* (William Cowper).

sad·ness (sad′nis), *n.* sorrow; grief. —**Syn.** melancholy, dejection.

sa·do·mas·och·ism (sā′dō mas′ə kiz əm, -maz′-), *n.* a form of perversion marked by a love for both receiving and inflicting pain; masochism and sadism combined.

sa·do·mas·och·ist (sā′dō mas′ə kist, -maz′-), *n.* a person who exhibits sadomasochism.

sa·do·mas·och·is·tic (sā′dō mas′ə kis′tic, -maz′-), *adj.* of or having to do with sadomasochism; exhibiting both sadism and masochism.

sad sack, *Informal.* **1.** a poor, bewildered soldier who blunders his way through the mazes of army life, constantly making mistakes and getting into trouble: *The Hemingway-type hero is no Jake, no Lieut. Henry, but the saddest of fictional sad sacks, called, of all things, Tyree Shelby* (Time). **2.** any bewildered, blundering person: *Ian Carmichael is a sort of egghead's sad sack* (Newsweek). [< *sad* + slang *sack* a sleepy, lazy, slovenly soldier; popularized in the comic strip drawn by Sergeant George Baker]

sa·du (sä′dü), *n.* sadhu: *Disguised as sadus (holy men), they duped pious Hindus into parting with their hoarded valuables* (Time).

sae (sā), *adv., conj., interj., pron. Scottish.* so.

s.a.e., self-addressed envelope: *The book of etiquette surely would award a black mark to those advertisers who invite their correspondents to "send s.a.e." and then neglect to answer* (London Times).

S.A.E. or **SAE** (no periods), Society of Automotive Engineers.

SAE number, a number established by the Society of Automotive Engineers to designate the viscosity of a lubricant. SAE 10 is light oil; SAE 40 is heavy oil.

sa·e·ta (sä ā′tä), *n.* a Spanish song of mourning or penitence sung during the processions of Holy Week: *Seville is the sound of the saetas* (Frances Parkinson Keyes). [< Spanish *saeta* (literally) arrow, dart < Latin *sagitta* arrow]

sae·ter (sē′tər), *n., pl.* **-ters** or **-ter.** in Norway: **1.** a mountain pasture. **2.** a mountain dairy farm. [< Norwegian *saeter*]

sa·fa·ri (sə fär′ē), *n., pl.* **-ris. 1.** a journey or hunting expedition in eastern Africa. **2.** the people and animals employed on such an expedition. **3.** any long journey or expedition: *Erhard ended his two-day safari in Texas this afternoon with a clutch of double handshakes* (Manchester Guardian Weekly). [< Swahili *safari* < Arabic *safar* journey, voyage]

safe (sāf), *adj.,* **saf·er, saf·est,** *n. —adj.* **1.** free from harm, danger, or loss: *safe from disease or enemies. Keep money in a safe place.* **2.** having been kept from or escaped injury, damage, or danger; not harmed; uninjured: *to bring goods safe to land. He returned from war safe and sound.* **3.** not likely to cause harm or injury; not dangerous: *a safe bridge. The old building was pronounced safe.* **4.** out of danger; secure: *We felt safe with the dog in the house.* **5.** put beyond the power of doing harm; no longer dangerous: *a criminal safe in prison.* **6.** not taking risks; cautious; careful: *a safe guess, a safe move, a safe driver.* **7.** that can be depended on; reliable; trustworthy: *a safe guide. A Manchester cloth firm got out a range of nearly forty colours—and the stores took less than a dozen of them, all in "safe" colours* (Observer). **8.** *Baseball.* (of a batter or base runner) reaching a base or home plate without being out. **9.** (of a state, county, etc.) not likely to be lost to an opposing party in an election.

—n. **1.** a steel or iron box for money, jewels, papers, etc., often built into a wall. **2.** a place made to keep things safe: *a meat safe.*

[< Old French *sauf,* earlier *salf* < Latin *salvus.* Compare SAVE[1].]

Floor Safe (def. 1)

—**Syn.** *adj.* **1. Safe, secure** mean free from danger, harm, or risk. **Safe** emphasizes being not exposed to danger, harm, or risk: *The children are safe in their own yard.* **Secure** emphasizes being protected or guarded against loss, attack, injury, or other anticipated or feared danger or harm and having no worry or fear: *A child feels secure with his mother.*

safe·blow·er (sāf′blō′ər), *n.* a safecracker who blows open safes by means of explosives.

safe·blow·ing (sāf′blō′ing), *n.* an opening of safes by explosives. *—adj.* that opens safes by explosives: *One of Harry Steed's most famous safeblowing jobs never brought him a nickel* (Newsweek).

safe·break·er (sāf′brā′kər), *n.* a safecracker.

safe·break·ing (sāf′brā′king), *n.* a safecracking.

safe-con·duct (sāf′kon′dukt), *n.* **1.** the privilege of passing safely through a region, especially in time of war: *The nurse was given safe-conduct through the enemy's camp.* **2.** a paper granting this privilege. **3.** the act of conducting or convoying in safety. —**Syn. 2.** passport.

safe·crack·er (sāf′krak′ər), *n.* a person who opens or is skilled at opening safes for purposes of robbery, by manipulation of the tumblers of the lock, removal of the door, or blowing it open with explosives: *A smash-and-grab epidemic cleaned out jewelers' windows in several Paris suburbs, and safecrackers were busy all over the country* (Maclean's).

safe·crack·ing (sāf′krak′ing), *n.* the work or skill of a safecracker: *To maintain that schools for safecracking or pocket-picking . . . should be allowed to operate without limitations . . . would be absurd* (New York Times).

safe deposit, a place in which valuables may be stored in safety: *The rest languish in safe deposits* (Manchester Guardian).

safe-de·pos·it box (sāf′di poz′it), a box for storing valuables, especially in the vault of a bank.

safe·guard (sāf′gärd′), *v.t.* **1.** to keep safe; guard against hurt, danger, or attack; protect: *to safeguard the country from surprise attack. Pure food laws safeguard our health.* **2.** to guard; convoy. [< noun]

—n. **1.** a protection; defense: *Keeping clean is a safeguard against disease. Personnel security programs can and should incorporate more of our traditional legal safeguards* (Bulletin of Atomic Scientists). **2.** a guard; convoy.

[< Old French *sauvegarde* < *sauve,* feminine of *sauf* safe + *garde* guard]

—**Syn.** *n.* **1.** security, shield. **2.** escort.

safe hit, *Baseball.* a base hit; safety.

safe·keep·ing (sāf′kē′ping), *n.* the act of keeping safe; protection; preservation; custody; care: *He gave a fascinating eyewitness account of the stickup and said he gave his share to Jazz Maffie for safekeeping* (Newsweek).

safe·light (sāf′līt′), *n.* a lamp or bulb used in a darkroom to provide light of a color or intensity which will not affect a photographic paper, emulsion, etc.: *Films are better processed in the dark. Theoretically, red or deep orange safelights are permissible for some, but no light at all is the really safe thing* (New York Times).

safe·ly (sāf′lē), *adv.* **1.** without hurt or injury: *to return home safely.* **2.** without risk; securely: *He could not safely venture to outrage all his Protestant subjects at once* (Macaulay). **3.** without risk of error: *I can safely say.* **4.** *Obsolete.* in close custody: *Till then I'll keep him dark and safely lock'd* (Shakespeare).

safe·ness (sāf′nis), *n.* the state or character of being safe or of conferring safety.

safe period, the period in the female menstrual cycle when conception is least likely to take place.

safe·ty (sāf′tē), *n., pl.* **-ties,** *adj. —n.* **1.** the quality or state of being safe; freedom from harm or danger: *A bank affords safety for your money. You can cross the road in safety when the policeman holds up his hand.* **2.** freedom from risk or possible damage or hurt; safeness: *I am very well satisfied of the safety of the experiment* (Lady Mary Wortley Montagu). **3.** a device to prevent injury or accident. **4.** a device that controls part of the firing mechanism and prevents a gun from being fired: *The hunters clicked off their safeties* (Harper's). **5.** *Football.* **a.** act of putting a football down behind one's own goal line when the impetus of the ball has come from one's own team. It counts two points for the other team: *Iowa's Hawkeyes edged into a 2-to-0 lead with a safety in the second quarter* (New York

Times). **b.** the two points so scored. **c.** a safety man. **6.** *Baseball.* a base hit; hit. —*adj.* giving safety; making harm unlikely: *One large market visualized for the process is steel-toed safety shoes for industry* (Wall Street Journal).
—**Syn.** *n.* **1.** security. —*adj.* protective.

safety belt, **1.** a belt attached to the seat of an airplane, used to hold the passenger or pilot in the seat and so protect him from bumps, etc.: *Just then the plane . . . lurched and plunged at the same time, . . . and I thought it better to get back to the reassurance of my safety belt* (Patricia Collinge). **2.** a similar belt attached to the seat of an automobile or other vehicle: . . . *a campaign to get drivers to fit and use safety belts in their cars* (New Scientist). **3.** a strap, or pair of short straps, used by window washers, linemen, tree workers, etc., to prevent falling. **4.** a life belt.

Safety Belts (def. 2)

safety bicycle, the early name for a bicycle with two low wheels, as distinguished from the older type with one high and one small wheel and no gears or clutch.

safety catch, a catch or stop attached to a mechanical contrivance, used as a safeguard, as in firearms, hoisting apparatus, etc.

safety chain, a chain used for additional security, as on a door latch, a pocket watch, the coupling of railway cars, etc.: *A falling drill joint snapped its safety chain and struck a workman* (London Times).

safety factor, **1.** the proportion of the ultimate strength of a material to the maximum strains that can be brought upon it. **2.** an element, condition, quality, etc., that helps to bring about safety: *The unions claim the jobs not only are needed but are a vital safety factor* (Wall Street Journal).

safety fuse, **1.** a fuse filled or saturated with a slow-burning composition. **2.** *Electricity.* a fuse.

safety glass, window glass that is hard to break, made of two or more panes of glass joined together by a transparent adhesive.

safety harness, a combination of straps and belt attached to the seat of an automobile, etc., used to hold a person in the seat while traveling. A safety harness is considered safer than a safety belt.

safety island, safety zone.

safety lamp, **1.** a miner's lamp in which the flame is kept from setting fire to explosive gases by a piece of wire gauze. **2.** an electric lamp similarly protected.

safety man, *Football.* a defensive player stationed behind the line in order to receive a punt or tackle a runner who has broken through the backfield: *There was no one between him and a touchdown except the safety man* (New Yorker).

safety match, a match that will ignite only when rubbed on a specially prepared surface.

safety pin, **1.** a pin bent back on itself to form a spring and having a guard that covers the point and prevents accidental unfastening. **2.** a pin on a grenade or mine that ignites the fuse when pulled; pin.

safety razor, a razor having the blade protected to prevent cutting the skin deeply.

safety valve, **1.** a valve in a steam boiler or the like that opens and lets steam or fluid escape when the pressure becomes too great. **2.** something that helps a person get rid of anger, nervousness, etc., in a harmless way. —**Syn.** **2.** outlet.

safety zone, a part of a road set off by painted strips, a fence, or a curb, to protect people from traffic while they are waiting for a bus, or to cross a street, etc.

saf·fi·an (saf′ē ən), *n.* a kind of leather made from goatskin or sheepskin tanned with sumac and dyed in various colors without a previous treating with fats. [< Russian *saf'jan* < Rumanian *saftian* < Persian *sakhtijān*]

saf·flow·er (saf′lou′ər), *n.* **1.** a thistlelike Old World composite herb with large, white to brilliant red flower heads: *Safflower seed has found outlets . . . in vegetable oil, meal for turkey feed . . . plastics and chemicals* (Wall Street Journal). **2.** its dried petals used in making certain red dyestuffs, and in medicine as a substitute for saffron. **3.** the red dyestuff. [earlier *safflore* (spelling influenced by *flower*), probably < Dutch *saflor* < earlier Italian *saffiore*, alteration of *zaffrole;* origin uncertain]

safflower oil, an oil derived from the seeds of the safflower, used for cooking and lighting, and in medicine to reduce the level of cholesterol in the blood: *More and more safflower oil is going into cooking oil, margarine, and other edible products where emphasis is on low fat diets* (Wall Street Journal).

saf·fron (saf′rən), *n.* **1.** an autumn crocus with purple flowers having orange-yellow stigmas. **2.** an orange-yellow coloring matter consisting of the dried stigmas of this crocus. Saffron is used to color and flavor candy, drinks, etc. **3.** an orange yellow.
—*adj.* orange-yellow.
[Middle English *safran, safroun* < Old French *safran*, learned borrowing from Medieval Latin *safranum* < Arabic *za'farān;* influenced by Italian *zafferano*]

saffron yellow, orange yellow.

S. Afr., **1.** South Africa. **2.** South African.

saf·ra·nin (saf′rə nin), *n.* safranine.

saf·ra·nine (saf′rə nēn, -nin), *n.* any of a class of organic synthetic dyes, chiefly red, derivatives of azonium compounds, used for dyeing wool, silk, etc., and as a microscopic stain. *Formula:* $C_{18}H_{14}N_4$ [< German *Safranin* < Middle High German *safran* (< Old French *safran;* see SAFFRON) + *-in* -ine[2]]

S. Afr. D., South African Dutch.

saf·rol (saf′rōl, -rol), *n.* safrole.

saf·role (saf′rōl), *n.* a colorless or faintly yellow, poisonous, oily liquid, obtained from oil of sassafras, used in making perfumes, soaps, and insecticides. *Formula:* $C_{10}H_{10}O_2$ [< German *Safrol*, short for *Sassafrol* < *Sassafras* sassafras (< Spanish *sasafras*) + *-ol* -ole]

saft (saft, säft), *adj., adv., n., interj. Scottish.* soft.

sag (sag), *v.,* **sagged, sag·ging,** *n.* —*v.i.* **1.** to sink under weight or pressure; bend or curve down in the middle, as a rope, beam, cable, plank, etc. **2.** to hang down unevenly: *Your dress sags in the back.* **3.** to become less firm or elastic; yield through weakness, weariness, or lack of effort; droop; sink: *The mind I sway by and the heart I bear, Shall never sag with doubt, nor shake with fear* (Shakespeare). **4.** to decline in price or value: *sagging cash incomes. Industrials sagged as a wave of selling began.* **5.** (of a ship) to drift from her course: *We're sagging South on the Long Trail* (Rudyard Kipling). —*v.t.* to cause to sag.
—*n.* **1.** the act, state, or degree of sagging: *Her voice is further let down by the sag of a large string orchestra* (New Yorker). **2.** a place where anything sags. **3.** a decline in price. **4.** the drift of a ship from her course.
[Middle English *saggen*, perhaps ultimately < Scandinavian (compare Old Icelandic *sekkva* to drift)]

SAG (no periods) or **S.A.G.,** Screen Actors Guild.

sa·ga (sä′gə), *n.* **1.** any of the prose narratives written in Iceland or Norway during the Middle Ages, especially those embodying the traditional history of Icelandic families or of the kings of Norway. **2.** a narrative having the characteristics of such sagas; any story of heroic deeds: *The story of this American's business career in the Philippines is a . . . saga that seems almost too overblown to be believed* (New Yorker). [< Scandinavian (compare Old Icelandic *saga*). Related to SAW[3], SAY[1].] —**Syn.** **2.** epic.

sa·ga·cious (sə gā′shəs), *adj.* **1.** wise in a keen, practical way; shrewd. **2.** resulting from or showing wisdom or sagacity: *He was observant and thoughtful, and given to asking sagacious questions* (John Galt). **3.** (of animals) intelligent. [< Latin *sagāx, -ācis* (with English *-ous*), related to *sāgus* prophetic] —**Syn.** **1.** astute, perspicacious. See **shrewd.**

sa·ga·cious·ly (sə gā′shəs lē), *adv.* in a sagacious manner; wisely; sagely: *Sagaciously, under their spectacles, did they peep into the holds of vessels* (Hawthorne).

sa·ga·cious·ness (sə gā′shəs nis), *n.* the quality of being sagacious; sagacity.

sa·gac·i·ty (sə gas′ə tē), *n., pl.* **-ties.** keen, sound judgment; mental acuteness; shrewdness: . . . *a mariner of infinite resource and sagacity* (Rudyard Kipling). —**Syn.** acumen, perspicacity.

sag·a·more (sag′ə môr, -mōr), *n.* (among the Algonkian Indian tribes of New England) a chief or great man, sometimes inferior to a sachem. [American English, earlier *sagamo* < Algonkian (Abnaki) *sa^{n}gma^n* chief, ruler. Related to SACHEM.]

saga novel, a long, rambling novel dealing in some detail with the lives of the members of a large family, or group of families, over several generations.

sage[1] (sāj), *adj.,* **sag·er, sag·est,** *n.* —*adj.* **1.** wise; able to give good advice: *a sage adviser. Cousin of Buckingham, and you sage, grave men* (Shakespeare). **2.** showing wisdom or good judgment: *a sage reply. The sage counsels of Lord Salisbury seemed to bring with them not only wealth and power, but security* (Lytton Strachey). **3.** wise-looking; grave; solemn: *Owls have the reputation of being sage birds.*
—*n.* a very wise man: . . . *a sage like Einstein* (Newsweek).
[< Old French *sage* < Vulgar Latin *sapius*, for Latin *sapiēns -entis*, present participle of *sapere* be wise. Compare SAPIENT.]
—**Syn.** *adj.* **1,2.** judicious, prudent. See **wise.**

sage[2] (sāj), *n.* **1. a.** a shrub of the mint family, whose grayish-green leaves are used as seasoning for sausages, stuffing, etc., and in medicine. See **bilabiate** for picture. **b.** its dried leaves. **2.** any of various other shrubs or herbs of the same genus; salvia. **3.** *U.S.* sagebrush. [< Old French *sauge* < Latin *salvia*. Doublet of SALVIA.]

SAGE (no periods) or **S.A.G.E.,** Semi-Automatic Ground Environment (a ground-operated system of the United States Air Force to detect and intercept enemy aircraft and missiles).

sage·brush (sāj′brush′), *n.* any of various aromatic, grayish-green shrubs of the composite family common on the dry plains and mountains of the western United States. The sagebrush is the state flower of Nevada: *Some ranchers are reported as utilizing sagebrush to keep stock alive* (British Columbia Mining Journal).

Sagebrush
(2 to 12 ft. high)

sage cock, a male sage grouse.

sage green, a dull grayish green: *The odd colors, like rusty orange and sage green, make them distinctive* (New Yorker).

sage grouse, the largest American grouse, living on the sagebrush plains of western North America.

sage hen, the sage grouse, especially the female.

sage·ly (sāj′lē), *adv.* in a sage manner; wisely.

sage·ness (sāj′nis) *n.* the quality of being sage; wisdom; sagacity.

sage sparrow. a grayish-brown sparrow of the arid regions of southwestern United States and nearby Mexico.

sage tea, an infusion of sage leaves, used as a mild tonic or stimulant.

sage thrasher, a grayish-brown and white thrasher of arid regions of western United States, similar to the mockingbird.

sag·ger or **sag·gar** (sag′ər), *n.* **1.** a case of fired clay in which porcelain and other delicate wares are enclosed while firing. **2.** the clay of which saggers are made. —*v.t.* to place or fire in a sagger. Also, **seggar.** [perhaps variant of dialectal *saggard*, perhaps contraction of *safeguard*]

sag·gy (sag′ē), *adj.,* **-gi·er, -gi·est.** sagging: *saggy trousers, saggy rubber.*

Sa·git·ta (sə jit′ə), *n., genitive* **Sa·git·tae.** a northern constellation south of Cygnus; the Arrow. [< Latin *Sagitta* < *sagitta* arrow]

Sa·git·tae (sə jit′ē), *n.* genitive of **Sagitta.**

sag·it·tal (saj′ə təl), *adj.* **1.** naming or having to do with a suture between the parietal bones of the skull: . . . *a sagittal crest running along the top of the skull* (New Scientist). **2.** naming or situated in the vertical plane dividing an animal into equal halves, or a plane parallel to it. **3.** of, like, or having to do with an arrow or arrowhead. [< New Latin *sagittalis* < Latin *sagitta* arrow (because of the suture's long and narrow shape)] —**sag′it·tal·ly,** *adv.*

Sag·it·tar·i·i (saj′ə tãr′ē ī), *n.* genitive of **Sagittarius** (the constellation).

Sag·it·tar·i·us (saj′ə tãr′ē əs), *n., genitive* (def. 1) **Sag·it·tar·i·i.** **1.** a southern constellation between Scorpio and Capricorn, originally thought of as arranged in the shape of a centaur drawing a bow; the Archer: *The center of our galaxy lies in the direction of Sagittarius.* **2.** the ninth sign of the zodiac: *The sun enters Sagittarius about November 22. Symbol:* ♐. **3.** *Heraldry.* a representation of an archer or centaur on a coat of arms. [< Latin *Sagittārius* (literally) the Archer < *sagitta* arrow]

Sag·it·tar·y (saj′ə ter′ē), *n.* **1.** a centaur fabled in medieval romance to have fought in the Trojan army against the Greeks. **2.** Sagittarius. [< Latin *Sagittārius*]

sag·it·tar·y (saj′ə tər′ē), *n., pl.* **-tar·ies.** **1.** an archer. **2.** a centaur. [variant of *Sagittarius*, in the heraldic sense]

sag·it·tate (saj′ə tāt), *adj.* shaped like an arrowhead: *Calla lilies have sagittate leaves.* [< New Latin *sagittatus* < Latin *sagitta* arrow]

Sagittate Leaf of calla lily

sa·git·ti·form (sə jit′ə fôrm, saj′ə tə-), *adj.* sagittate.

sa·go (sā′gō), *n., pl.* **-gos.** **1.** a starchy food used in making puddings, etc., obtained from the sago palm. **2.** the sago palm. [< Malay *sagu*]

sago palm, any of several East Indian palm trees from whose pith a starchy food is made.

sa·gua·ro (sə gwä′rō, -wä′-), *n., pl.* **-ros.** a very tall, columnar cactus of Arizona and neighboring regions, from 25 to 50 feet high. Its white blossom is the floral emblem of Arizona. *The watchtower of the hawk . . . was a giant saguaro cactus* (Atlantic). Also, **sahuaro.** See **giant cactus** for picture. [American English < Mexican Spanish *saguaro*]

sa·hua·ro (sə wä′rō), *n., pl.* **-ros.** the saguaro cactus.

sa·ic (sä ēk′), *n.* a kind of ketch very common in the Levant. [< French *saïque* < Turkish *şayka*]

saice (sīs), *n.* syce.

said (sed), *v.* past tense and past participle of **say**[1]: *He said he would come. She has said "No" every time.* —*adj.* named or mentioned before: *the said witness.* —**Syn.** *adj.* aforesaid, aforementioned.

➔ **said.** As an adjective *said* is largely confined to legal language, and is regarded as inappropriate elsewhere.

sai·ga (sī′gə), *n.* an antelopelike animal of western Asia and eastern Russia with a peculiarly expanded nose which serves to filter dust and warm the air breathed in. [< Russian *sajga* < a Turkic word]

Sai·gon·ese (sī′gə nēz′, -nēs′), *adj., n., pl.* **-nese.** —*adj.* of Saigon, the capital of South Vietnam, or its people. —*n.* a native of Saigon: *The Saigonese . . . have always been more concerned about their personal comfort than the prosecution of the war against the Communists* (New York Times).

sail (sāl), *n.* **1.** a piece of cloth spread to the wind to make a ship move through the water. **2.** sails: *with all sail set.* **3.** something like a sail, such as the part of an arm of a windmill that catches the wind: *Many recent submarines have a tall streamlined sail instead of a conning tower.* **4. a.** a ship having sails. **b.** such ships as a group: *To them the sinking only proved that the days of sail were done* (London Times). **5. a.** a trip or outing on a boat with sails. **b.** a trip or outing on any other vessel. **6.** *Poetic.* a bird's wing: *The mountain eagle . . . spread her dark sails on the wind* (Scott).

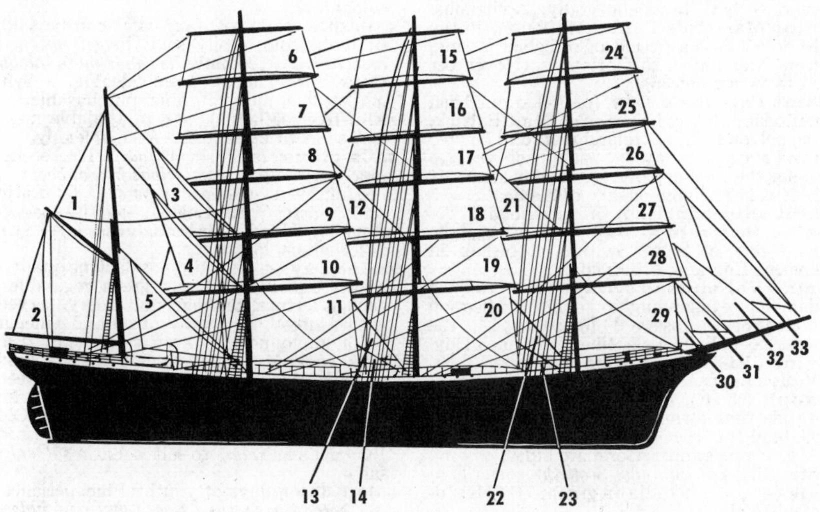

Sails (def. 1) on a full-rigged ship (four-masted bark)

1) Jigger topsail
2) Spanker
3) Jigger topgallant staysail
4) Jigger topmast staysail
5) Jigger staysail
6) Mizzen-royal
7) Mizzen upper topgallant
8) Mizzen lower topgallant
9) Mizzen upper topsail
10) Mizzen lower topsail
11) Crossjack
12) Mizzen-topgallant staysail
13) Mizzen-topmast staysail
14) Mizzenstaysail
15) Mainroyal
16) Main upper topgallant
17) Main lower topgallant
18) Main upper topsail
19) Main lower topsail
20) Mainsail
21) Maintopgallant staysail
22) Maintopmast staysail
23) Main staysail
24) Foreroyal
25) Fore upper topgallant
26) Fore lower topgallant
27) Fore upper topsail
28) Fore lower topsail
29) Foresail
30) Fore-topmast staysail
31) Inner jib
32) Upper jib
33) Flying jib

crowd sail, to hoist an unusual number of sails on a ship; carry a press of sail for the purpose of speed: *They crowded all the sail they could* (London Gazette).

make sail, a. to spread the sails of a ship: *The men . . . were making sail upon the yacht nimbly* (Clark Russell). **b.** to begin a trip by water: *We will make sail on Friday.*

set sail, to begin a trip by water: *We will set sail for Europe next week.*

take in sail, a. to lower or lessen the sails of a ship: *The men took in sail when the storm approached.* **b.** to lessen one's hopes, ambitions, etc.: *It is time to be old, to take in sail* (Emerson).

under sail, having the sails set: *Suppose . . . you see a ship . . . under sail, making towards the Land* (William Leybourn).

—*v.i.* **1. a.** to travel or go on water in a boat propelled by the action of wind on sails. **b.** to travel or go in a boat propelled by any means, as a steamship. **c.** to travel through the air in an airplane, balloon, glider, etc. **2.** to move on or through the water: *a schooner sailing for the Azores, two submarines sailing from New London to the Caribbean.* **3.** to move smoothly like a ship with sails: *The sea gull sailed by. Then all the great people sailed in state from the room* (Charlotte Brontë). **4.** to manage a ship or boat: *The boys are learning to sail this summer.* **5.** to begin a trip by water; set sail: *We sail at 2 p.m.* —*v.t.* **1.** to sail upon, over, or through: *It was the schooner Hesperus that sailed the wintry sea* (Longfellow). **2.** to manage or navigate (a ship or boat).

sail into, *Informal.* **a.** to attack; beat: *He sailed into me for no reason and gave me a black eye.* **b.** to criticize; scold: *The drama critics sailed into the new play.* **c.** to rush into; go into boldly or spiritedly: *Though paralysed by fright . . . I gritted my teeth and sailed into it* (Tallulah Bankhead).

[Old English *segl*]

—**Syn.** *v.i.* **1.** navigate, cruise.

➔ **Sail** is used collectively when it means sails for a sailing vessel (def. 2): *Our ship had all sail spread.* **Sail** may also mean a ship or ships (def. 4a and 4b). When it means ships it is used collectively and often with a numeral: *a fleet of thirty sail.*

sail·boat (sāl′bōt′), *n.* any boat that is moved by a sail or sails.

sail·boat·ing (sāl′bō′ting), *n.* the sport of navigating or riding in a sailboat: [*It*] *makes one think of summer sailboating with one's best girl* (New Yorker).

sail·cloth (sāl′klôth′, -kloth′), *n.* **1.** canvas or other sturdy material used for making sails. **2.** tarpaulin.

-sailed, *combining form.* having ___ sail or sails: *White-sailed = having white sails.*

sail·er (sā′lər), *n.* **1.** a ship with reference to its sailing power: *the best sailer in the fleet, a fast sailer.* **2.** a sailing vessel.

sail·fish (sāl′fish′), *n., pl.* **-fish·es** or (*collectively*) **-fish.** **1.** any of several large salt-water fish related to the marlin and spearfish and having a long, high fin on its back. **2.** the basking shark: *The habit of swimming slowly at the surface has given rise to the common name of the animal* (*basking shark*) *. . . and to the alternative local name of sailfish* (New Scientist).

sail hook, a small hook used to hold sailcloth while it is being sewed.

sail·ing (sā′ling), *n.* **1.** the act of a person or thing that sails. **2.** the art of managing and maneuvering a ship; navigation; seamanship. **3. a.** the departure of a ship from port. **b.** its occupancy or load: *Transatlantic steamship lines report capacity sailings for April* (Newsweek).

sailing boat, *British.* a sailboat.

sailing vessel, any vessel, ranging in size from a boat to a ship (but usually the latter), that is moved by a sail or sails.

sail·less (sāl′lis), *adj.* without sails.

sail lizard, a large lizard of the Molucca Islands, with a crested tail.

sail·mak·er (sāl′mā′kər), *n.* **1.** a person who makes or repairs sails. **2.** *U.S. Navy.* a warrant officer in charge of maintaining sails, awnings, etc.

sail needle, a large, three-sided needle used to sew canvas.

sail·or (sā′lər), *n.* **1.** a person whose work is handling a sailboat or other vessel. In these days most sailors are on steamships. **2.** a member of a ship's crew, usually not an officer. **3.** a flat-brimmed hat modeled after the kind of hat sailors used to wear years ago; sailor hat.

good sailor, a person who does not get seasick: *Many of the passengers proved to be good sailors during the stormy voyage.*

poor or **bad sailor,** a person who readily becomes seasick: *He wished people who were bad sailors would not travel* (Mary Bridgman).

talk sailor, to use nautical language: *I . . . could talk sailor like an "old salt"* (Century Magazine).

—*adj.* like that of a sailor: *The little boy wore a sailor suit.* —**sail′or·ly,** *adj.*

sailor collar, a large collar, broad and square across the back, with ends tapering to a point to meet on the breast.

sailor hat, a flat-brimmed straw hat, worn by women and children and modeled after a hat formerly worn by sailors.

sa·gum (sā′gəm), *n., pl.* **-ga** (-gə). a kind of cloak worn by Roman soldiers and inferior officers. [< Latin *sagum*, or *sagus*, perhaps < a Celtic word]

Sa·hap·tan (sä hap′tən), *adj., n.* Shahaptian.

Sa·har·a (sə hãr′ə, -här′-), *n.* an arid place; desert. [< *Sahara*, the great desert in northern Africa]

Sa·har·an (sə hãr′ən, -här′-), *adj.* of or having to do with the Sahara, the largest desert in the world, in northern Africa, or the people living there: *A young Scots surgeon, Mungo Park, rode through Saharan sand and thorn* (Atlantic). —*n.* a native or inhabitant of the Sahara.

sa·hib (sä′ib), *n.* sir; master: *Natives in British India commonly call a European "sahib" when speaking to or of him. The sahibs have not all this world's wisdom* (Rudyard Kipling). [< Hindi *sāhib* < Arabic *ṣāḥib*]

sail·or·ing (sā′lər ing), *n.* the work or life of a sailor.
sail·or·like (sāl′ər līk′), *adj.* like or resembling a sailor.
sail·or·man (sā′lər man′), *n., pl.* **-men.** *Archaic.* a sailor; seaman.
sail·or's-choice (sā′lərz chois′), *n., pl.* **sail·or's-choic·es** or (*collectively*) **sail·or's-choice.** a local name of various American fishes: **a.** a grunt. **b.** a porgy. **c.** a pigfish. **d.** a pinfish.
sailor suit, a suit or outfit worn by children and women, with a sailor collar, middy blouse, etc., modeled after the uniform worn by sailors: . . . *the little figure in trim sailor suit and knickerbockers* (Punch).
sail·o·ver (sāl′ō′vər), *n.* a repeating of a yacht run previously interrupted or inconclusive: *They were going to see a series of yacht races, not the sort of sailovers they had seen in 1958* (Harper's).
sail·plane (sāl′plān′), *n., v.,* **-planed, -planing.** —*n.* a light glider capable of being maneuvered to take advantage of rising air currents so as to remain aloft, as distinguished from a heavy glider, designed to be towed by a powered aircraft: *Sailplanes are of course designed to meet rough weather, but it is quickly established that they need much too large a propulsive power to make them suitable as man-powered vehicles* (New Scientist).
—*v.i.* to fly in a sailplane.
sain (sān), *v.t. Archaic.* **1. a.** to make the sign of the cross on. **b.** to cross (oneself). **2.** to protect by prayer, etc., from evil influence. **3.** to bless. [Old English *segnian,* ultimately < Latin *signāre* to mark, especially with the sign of the cross < *sīgnum* sign (in Late Latin, sign of the cross)]
sain·foin (sān′foin), *n.* a low, pink-flowered, Old World perennial herb of the pea family, grown for forage. [< French *sainfoin* < *sain* wholesome, healthy (< Latin *sānus*) + *foin* < Old French *fein* hay < Latin *fēnum*]
saint (sānt; *see note below*), *n.* **1. a.** a very holy person; one who is pure in heart and upright in life: *a Buddhist saint.* **b.** a person thought of as like a saint. **2.** a person who has gone to heaven; one of the blessed dead in heaven (distinguished from the angels, who are superhuman beings): *We therefore pray thee, help thy servants . . . Make them to be numbered with thy Saints in glory everlasting* (Book of Common Prayer). **3.** a person declared to be a saint by the Roman Catholic Church. *Abbr.:* St. **4.** an angel: *The Lord came from Sinai . . .; he shined forth from mount Paran, and he came with ten thousands of saints* (Deuteronomy 33:2). **5.** Also, **Saint. a.** (in the New Testament) a member of the Christian church. **b.** a person belonging to any religious body whose members are called Saints. The Church of the Latter-Day Saints is a name for the Mormon Church.
—*v.t.* **1.** to make a saint of; canonize. **2.** to give the name of saint to; call or consider a saint. —*v.i.* to live or act as a saint.
—*adj.* holy; sacred (now only before proper names): *Saint John, Saint Paul.*
[< Old French *saint* < Latin *sānctus* holy, consecrated < *sancīre* consecrate, related to *sacer* holy, sacred]
➔ When it precedes a name, **Saint (St.)** is unstressed in British English and pronounced (sənt) or (sint); in present American use the word is ordinarily (sānt) in all contexts.
Saint. Names more commonly written in the abbreviated form, as *St. Anthony's fire, St.-John's-wort,* will be found in their alphabetical places following **St.**
Saint Ag·nes's Eve (ag′nə siz), the night of January 20, when a girl was supposed to see a vision of her future husband if she performed certain ceremonies.
Saint Andrew's cross, a cross shaped like the letter X.
Saint An·tho·ny's cross (an′thə niz), a cross in which the transverse bar lies on the top of the upright, like the letter T; tau cross.
Saint Bar·thol·o·mew's Day (bär thol′ə myüz), August 24, especially this day in the year 1572, on which a great massacre of Huguenots was begun in Paris by order of King Charles IX at the instigation of Catherine de Medici.
Saint Ber·nard (bər närd′), any of a breed of very large, red-and-white dogs with large heads. These intelligent dogs were first bred at the hospice of St. Bernard in the Swiss Alps to rescue travelers lost in the snow. Also, **St. Bernard.**

Saint Bernard (25½ to 29 in. high at the shoulder)

Saint David's Day, a holiday in honor of the patron saint of Wales (Saint David), observed March 1.
saint de bois (saɴ′ də bwä′), *French.* **1.** a hypocrite. **2.** (literally) a saint of wood.
Sainte (sānt, saɴt), *n.* the French feminine form of **Saint.** *Abbr.:* Ste.
saint·ed (sān′tid), *adj.* **1.** declared to be a saint; canonized. **2.** thought of as a saint; gone to heaven; dead (an occasional euphemism). **3.** very holy; sacred. **4.** saintly. —**Syn. 3.** consecrated, hallowed.
Saint George's cross (jôrj′iz), the Greek cross, red on a white ground, as used on the English flag.
saint·hood (sānt′hu̇d), *n.* **1.** the condition, status, or dignity of a saint. **2.** saints collectively.
saint·like (sānt′līk′), *adj.* like or befitting a saint; saintly.
saint·li·ness (sānt′lē nis), *n.* the quality or state of being saintly.
saint·ly (sānt′lē), *adj.,* **-li·er, -li·est. 1.** like, proper to, or befitting a saint; very holy: *I mention still Him whom thy wrongs, with saintly patience borne* (Milton). **2.** very good. —**Syn. 1.** angelic, godly. **2.** virtuous.
Saint Mar·tin's Lent (mär′tənz), (in the Middle Ages) a period of religious fasting, from Martinmas to Christmas (November 11 to December 25).
Saint Pat·rick's Day (pat′riks), an Irish national holiday, in honor of Saint Patrick, the patron saint of Ireland (March 17).
saint's day, a day set aside each year to honor the memory of a particular saint. It is usually the anniversary of his death.
saint·ship (sānt′ship), *n.* sainthood.
Saint Swith·in's Day (swiᴛʜ′inz), the feast day of Saint Swithin, a bishop in ancient England, observed July 15.
Saint Val·en·tine's Day (val′ən tīnz), a day for exchanging tokens of affection (valentines), observed February 14, the feast day of Saint Valentine; Valentine's Day.
Saint Vi·tus's dance (vī′tə siz), St. Vitus's dance, a nervous disorder.
Sa·iph (sä ēf′), *n.* a star of the second magnitude that forms part of the great quadrilateral of the constellation Orion. [< Arabic *saif* sword. Compare SEIF.]
sair (sãr), *adj., n., adv. Scottish.* sore.
sais (sīs), *n.* (in India) a groom. [< Hindustani *sāis*]
saith (seth), *v. Archaic.* says.
saithe (sāth), *n., pl.* **saithe.** the pollack, a salt-water food fish, especially when mature: *Those who think the epitome of the meal is smoked salmon may like to try smoked saithe* (London Times). [< Old Icelandic *seithr*]
Sa·kai (sä′kī), *n., pl.* **-kai. 1.** an aboriginal Malayan people or tribe. **2.** a member of this people or tribe.
sake[1] (sāk), *n.* **1.** cause; account; interest: *Put yourself to no trouble for our sakes.* **2.** purpose; end.
for old sake's sake, for the sake of old times or old friendship: *I continue to take an interest in him for old sake's sake as they say* (Robert Louis Stevenson).
for the sake of, a. because of; on account of: *He does not differ from that opinion for the sake of difference, but for the sake of the values embodied in perception* (Manchester Guardian Weekly). **b.** in order to help or please: *It became necessary for him to exert himself for the sake of his family* (James Payn).
for one's own sake, on one's own account; in order to help oneself: *For my own sake as well as for yours, I will do my very best* (Benjamin Jowett).
[Old English *sacu* a cause at law]
—**Syn. 2.** reason.
sa·ke[2] (sä′kē), *n.* an alcoholic beverage made from a fermented mash of rice, very popular in Japan. It somewhat resembles a still white wine, and is drunk by the Japanese in slightly warmed porcelain cups. [< Japanese *sake*]
sa·ker (sā′kər), *n.* a large Old World falcon used in falconry. [< Old French *sacre* < Arabic *ṣaqr*]
sa·ki (sak′ē, sä′kē), *n., pl.* **-kis.** a South American monkey with a bushy, nonprehensile tail and a long, thick coat of hair. There are several species. [< French *saki* < Tupi *sagui*]
sak·i·eh (sak′ē ä), *n.* a kind of waterwheel, powered by oxen or other draft animals, used for raising water in the Near East. [< Arabic *sāqiyah*]
sak·kos (sak′os), *n.* saccos.
Sak·ta (sak′tə), *n.* Shakta.
Sak·ti (sak′tē; *Sanskrit* shuk′tē), *n.* Shakti.
Sak·tism (sak′tiz əm), *n.* Shaktism.
sal (sal), *n.* salt (used especially in druggists' terms such as *sal ammoniac*). [< Latin *sāl, salis*]
sa·la (sä′lə), *n.* a large hall. [< Spanish *sala* hall, parlor < a Germanic word]
sa·laam (sə läm′), *n.* **1.** a greeting that means "Peace," used especially in Islamic countries or regions. **2.** a very low bow, with the palm of the right hand placed on the forehead. —*v.t.* to greet with a salaam. —*v.i.* to make a salaam. [< Arabic *salām* peace]
sa·laam a·lei·kum (sə läm′ ä lā′ku̇m), *Arabic.* peace be upon you (a greeting): *Clad in dignity and finery, the imam ascends the pulpit, murmurs "salaam aleikum," recites a text from the Koran, and begins a sermon* (Time).
sal·a·bil·i·ty (sā′lə bil′ə tē), *n.* salable quality or condition: *Each hi-fi store . . . will soon have an experienced repair staff to restore . . . items to salability* (Harper's). Also, **saleability.**
sal·a·ble (sā′lə bəl), *adj.* that can be sold; fit to be sold; easily sold: *Permit the new association . . . to make its bonds more salable* (New York Times). Also, **saleable.** —**Syn.** marketable, merchantable, purchasable.
sal·a·bly (sā′lə blē), *adv.* in a salable manner; so as to be salable. Also, **saleably.**
sa·la·cious (sə lā′shəs), *adj.* **1.** obscene; indecent; smutty: *a salacious joke or book.* **2.** lustful; lewd: *a salacious person.* [< Latin *salāx, -ācis* (with English *-ous*)] —**sa·la′cious·ly,** *adv.* —**sa·la′cious·ness,** *n.* —**Syn. 2.** lecherous, lascivious.
sa·lac·i·ty (sə las′ə tē), *n.* salacious quality.
sal·ad (sal′əd), *n.* **1.** raw green vegetables, such as lettuce, cabbage, and celery, served with a dressing, usually of oil and vinegar or of mayonnaise. Often cold meat, fish, eggs, cooked vegetables, or fruits are used along with, or instead of, the raw green vegetables. **2.** any green vegetable that can be eaten raw. **3.** *Dialect.* lettuce. [< Old French *salade* < Old Provençal *salada* < Vulgar Latin *salāre* to salt < Latin *sāl, salis* salt]
salad days, days of youthful inexperience: *My salad days, when I was green in judgement* (Shakespeare).
salad dressing, a sauce used in or on a salad, as oil and vinegar mixed with seasonings, or mayonnaise.
salad oil, 1. olive oil, usually of superior quality, used in dressing salads and for other culinary purposes. **2.** any oil used in salad dressing.
sal·a·man·der (sal′ə man′dər), *n.* **1.** a cold-blooded animal shaped like a lizard but belonging to the same group as frogs and toads, as the mud puppy of North America. Salamanders have moist, scaleless skin. The larvae, as well as some adults, are aquatic and breathe by gills. **2.** a legendary lizardlike animal supposed to live in or be able to endure fire. **3.** a person who likes or can stand a great deal of heat. **4.** a spirit or imaginary being supposed to live in fire (originally hypothesized by Paracelsus as inhabiting fire, one of the four elements). **5.** any of various articles formerly used in connection with fire or capable of withstanding great heat, as an iron or poker formerly used for lighting a pipe or igniting gunpowder or a plate used for browning puddings: *Press them tight into shells or a dish, and brown them with a*

American Spotted Salamander (def. 1) (6 to 8 in. long)

salamander (Sunday Times). [< Old French *salamandre* < Latin *salamandra* < Greek *salamándra*]

sal·a·man·drine (sal′ə man′drin), *adj.* **1.** resembling the legendary salamander in being able to live in or endure fire. **2.** *Zoology.* of, having to do with, resembling, or related to the salamanders. —*n. Zoology.* a salamander.

sa·la·mi (sə lä′mē), *n.* a kind of thick sausage, usually sliced and eaten cold, flavored with garlic or otherwise highly spiced. [< Italian *salami*, plural of *salame* < Vulgar Latin *salāmen* < Latin *sāl, salis* salt]

sal ammoniac, ammonium chloride.

sa·lar·i·at (sə lãr′ē at), *n.* the salaried class; the class of workers receiving a salary. [< French *salariat.* Compare PROLETARIAT.]

sal·a·ried (sal′ər id, sal′rid), *adj.* **1.** receiving a salary: *a salaried employee.* **2.** having a salary attached to it: *a salaried position.*

sal·a·ry (sal′ər ē, sal′rē), *n., pl.* **-ries.** a fixed payment made periodically to a person, especially by the week or month, for regular work: *Teachers, government officials, and clerks receive salaries. The fees annually paid to lawyers . . . amount in every court, to a much greater sum than the salaries of the judges* (Adam Smith). [< Anglo-French *salarie*, learned borrowing from Latin *salārium* soldier's allowance for salt; pay < *sāl, salis* salt] —**Syn.** stipend.

➤ **salary, wages.** Though these words are synonyms, *salary* generally refers to a fixed compensation for regular work (usually mental or professional) paid at longer intervals than *wages* (usually for manual or mechanical work).

sal·a·ry·less (sal′ər ē lis, sal′rē-), *adj.* without a salary.

sal At·ti·cum (sal at′ə kəm), *Latin.* sal Atticus.

sal At·ti·cus (sal at′ə kəs), *Latin.* pungent wit; Attic salt.

sal·chow (sal′kov), *n.* a jump in figure skating in which the skater leaps from the inside back edge of one skate, rotates in the air, and lands on the outside back edge of the other skate: *With all the confidence of a champion, long-legged Tenley glided out to begin her free skating—the difficult double loops and axels and double salchows of her own devising* (Time). [< Ulrich *Salchow*, a skater after whom the jump was named]

sale (sāl), *n.* **1.** the exchange of goods or property for money or some other valuable consideration; act of selling: *no sale yet this morning. The sale of his old home made him sad.* **2.** an amount sold: *Today's sales were larger than yesterday's.* **3.** a chance to sell; demand; market: *There is almost no sale for washboards in these days.* **4.** a selling at lower prices than usual: *This store is having a sale on suits.* **5.** a putting up of goods to be sold at auction, especially a public auction; auction.

for sale, to be sold: *My car is for sale.*

on sale, a. to be sold: *There are many houses on sale but few for rent.* **b.** available at a reduced price: *This ten-dollar hat is now on sale for five.* **c.** at a reduced price: *I bought this dress on sale.*

on sale or return, *Especially British.* **a.** on condition that the customer can decide after examining the item whether to buy it or return it; on approval: *The coat . . . had been delivered to the defendants on sale or return* (London Times). **b.** on condition that the retailer may return to the wholesaler any part of the goods that he fails to sell: *to buy a quantity of merchandise on sale or return.*

[Old English *sala*, perhaps < Scandinavian (compare Old Icelandic *sala*)]

—**Syn. 5.** vendue.

sale·a·bil·i·ty (sā′lə bil′ə tē), *n.* salability.

sale·a·ble (sā′lə bəl), *adj.* salable.

sale·a·bly (sā′lə blē), *adv.* salably.

sale and leaseback, an arrangement whereby a company sells all or part of its property to another organization and takes out a long-term lease on the property at the same time; leaseback. The original seller pays rent, which is considered a tax-deductible business expense.

sale and return, an arrangement whereby a retailer accepts goods from a wholesaler on condition that he may return any part of the goods that he fails to sell.

sal·ep (sal′ep), *n.* a starchy foodstuff consisting of the dried tubers of certain orchids, formerly also used as a drug. Also, **saloop.** [< French *salep*, or Spanish *salép* < Turkish *salep*, perhaps a contraction of Arabic *khaṣyu-ṭhtha'lab* testicles of a fox. Compare ORCHID.]

sal·e·ra·tus (sal′ə rā′təs), *n. U.S., Archaic.* **1.** sodium bicarbonate; baking soda. **2.** potassium bicarbonate, a compound similar to sodium bicarbonate, used in cookery. [American English < New Latin *sal aeratus* aerated salt]

sales (sālz), *n.pl.* the total volume of selling; selling activity: *How are sales today?* —*adj.* of or having to do with sales: *a sales engineer or manager, a sales plan.*

sales·clerk (sālz′klėrk′), *n.* a person whose work is selling in a store.

sales engineer, a salesman of mechanical, electrical, and other equipment who has had technical training and is familiar with the details of installation, operation, etc., of the equipment: *1,200 sales engineers . . . sell the domestic warm air furnaces and accessories* (Wall Street Journal).

sales·girl (sālz′gėrl′), *n.* a girl whose work is selling in a store: *The salesgirl showed her nearly all the hats in the shop.* —**Syn.** shopgirl.

Sa·le·sian (sə lē′zhən), *n.* a member of the Society of St. Francis of Sales, a Roman Catholic congregation of priests, clerics, and lay brothers, founded in 1846 mainly for education of the young. —*adj.* **1.** of or having to do with St. Francis of Sales or his writings on spiritual matters. **2.** of or having to do with the Society of St. Francis of Sales: *One word of sorrow, on the part of the Salesian Father, is enough to stop a boy who is about to do wrong* (The Month).

sales·la·dy (sālz′lā′dē), *n., pl.* **-dies.** a saleswoman.

sales·man (sālz′mən), *n., pl.* **-men.** a man whose work is selling: *Four salesmen were showing people suits and sweaters.*

sales·man·ship (sālz′mən ship), *n.* **1.** the work of a salesman. **2.** ability at selling.

sales·peo·ple (sālz′pē′pəl), *n.pl.* salespersons.

sales·per·son (sālz′pėr′sən), *n.* a person whose work is selling in a store: *[The] great advantage over most door-to-door selling, he thinks, is that the salesperson will be backed by the familiar name of a big local department store* (Wall Street Journal). —**Syn.** clerk.

sales promotion, the methods and activities involved in producing or increasing the sales of a product or service in addition to direct selling and advertising. Sales promotion includes getting publicity through various media, distributing samples, providing displays in stores, giving free demonstrations, etc.: *To increase exports one must spend freely on sales promotion of every kind* (London Times).

sales resistance, a customer's unwillingness to buy, due to price, class, nature, and appearance of goods, or other causes: *to overcome sales resistance.*

sales·room (sālz′rüm′, -rům′), *n.* a room where things are sold or shown for sale.

sales talk, 1. a talk by a salesman designed to sell something. **2.** any talk to convince or persuade.

sales tax, a tax based on the amount received for articles sold: *Her coat cost 25 dollars plus 75 cents sales tax.*

sales·wom·an (sālz′wům′ən), *n., pl.* **-women.** a woman whose work is selling in a store.

sale·work (sāl′wėrk′), *n.* **1.** work that is made for sale rather than for home use. **2.** work or things made in a perfunctory manner, and usually of inferior quality: *I see no more in you than in the ordinary of nature's salework* (Shakespeare).

sale·yard (sāl′yärd′), *n.* (in Australia) a yard where livestock is sold; stockyard.

Sa·li·an (sā′lē ən), *adj.* of or belonging to the Salii, a tribe of Franks who lived in the regions of the Rhine near the North Sea. —*n.* a member of this tribe of Franks.

Sal·ic (sal′ik, sā′lik), *adj.* based on or contained in the code of the Salian Franks. Also, **Salique.** [< Medieval Latin *Salicus* < Late Latin *Saliī, -orum* the Salian Franks]

sal·i·ca·ceous (sal′ə kā′shəs), *adj.* belonging to the family of trees and shrubs containing the willows and poplars. [< New Latin *Salicaceae* the willow family (< Latin *salix, -icis* willow) + English *-ous*]

sal·i·cin (sal′ə sin), *n.* a bitter, colorless, crystalline compound of glucose, obtained especially from the leaves and female flowers of various willows. It was formerly used in medicine as a tonic and to reduce fever. *Formula:* $C_{13}H_{18}O_7$ [< French *salicine* < Latin *salix, -icis* willow + French *-ine* -ine²]

sal·i·cine (sal′ə sin, -sēn), *n.* salicin.

Salic law, 1. the code of laws of the Franks. **2.** a law excluding women from succession to the crown.

sal·i·cyl·al·de·hyde (sal′ə sə lal′də hīd), *n.* a fragrant, colorless oil used in the manufacture of dyestuffs, odor bases, and petroleum additives, produced from phenol and chloroform. It is the aldehyde of salicylic acid. *Formula:* $C_7H_6O_2$ [< *salicyl*(ic) + *aldehyde*]

sal·i·cyl·am·ide (sal′ə sə lam′īd, -id), *n.* a yellowish, crystalline compound made by treating oil of wintergreen with concentrated ammonia. *Formula:* $C_7H_7NO_2$ [< *salicyl*(ic) + *amide*]

sal·i·cyl·ate (sal′ə sil′āt, sal′ə sil′-; sə lis′-ə lāt), *n.* any salt or ester of salicylic acid.

sal·i·cyl·ic (sal′ə sil′ik), *adj.* of or having to do with salicin.

salicylic acid, a white, crystalline or powdery acid, prepared by treating sodium phenolate with carbon dioxide, used as a mild antiseptic and preservative, and (in the form of salts) as a medicine for rheumatism, gout, etc. *Formula:* $C_7H_6O_3$ [< *salic*(in), from which it was first obtained + *-yl* + *-ic*]

sa·li·ence (sā′lē əns, sāl′yəns), *n.* **1.** the fact or condition of being salient. **2.** a salient or projecting object, part, or feature.

sa·li·en·cy (sā′lē ən sē, sāl′yən-), *n., pl.* **-cies.** salience.

sa·li·ent (sā′lē ənt, sāl′yənt), *adj.* **1.** standing out; easily seen or noticed; prominent; striking: *the salient features in a landscape, the salient points in a speech.* **2.** pointing outward; projecting: *a salient angle.* **3.** *Heraldry.* (of an animal in coats of arms) standing with forepaws raised, as if jumping. **4.** *Archaic.* **a.** leaping; jumping. **b.** (of animals) saltatorial.

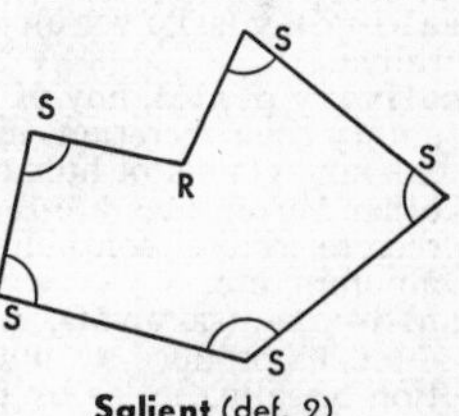

Salient (def. 2)
S, salient angles;
R, reentering angle

—*n.* **1.** a salient angle or part; projection: *The Soviet Union has thrust a huge salient into the heart of Europe* (Wall Street Journal). **2.** a part of a fort or line of trenches that projects toward the enemy.

[< Latin *saliēns, -entis*, present participle of *salīre* to leap] —**sa′li·ent·ly,** *adv.*

—**Syn.** *adj.* **1.** noticeable, conspicuous.

sa·li·en·ti·an (sā′lē en′shē ən, -shən), *adj.* of or belonging to a group of amphibians that includes the frogs and toads; anuran. —*n.* a salientian animal. [< New Latin *Salientia* the order name (< Latin *saliēns, -entis* leaping; see SALIENT) + English *-an*]

sa·lif·er·ous (sə lif′ər əs), *adj.* containing salt; producing salt. [< Latin *sāl, salis* salt + English *-ferous*]

sal·i·fi·a·ble (sal′ə fī′ə bəl), *adj.* that can be salified.

sal·i·fi·ca·tion (sal′ə fə kā′shən), *n.* **1.** the act of salifying. **2.** the state of being salified.

sal·i·fy (sal′ə fī), *v.t.,* **-fied, -fy·ing. 1.** to form into a salt, as by combination with an acid. **2.** to combine with a salt or add a salt to. [< French *salifier* < Latin *sāl, salis* salt]

sal·im·e·ter (sə lim′ə tər), *n.* salinometer.

sa·li·na (sə lī′nə), *n.* **1.** a salt marsh or spring. **2.** a saltworks. [< Spanish *salina* < Latin *salīnae, -ārum*, plural, saltworks < *sāl, salis* salt]

sal·i·na·tion (sal′ə nā′shən), *n. Especially British.* salinization: *. . . the salination of the soil which makes it barren* (Listener).

sa·line (sā′līn), *adj.* **1. a.** consisting of or constituting common salt: *saline particles, saline substances.* **b.** of salt; characteristic of salt; salty: *a saline taste.* **2.** containing common salt or any other salts: *saline waters.* **3. a.** of or having to do with chemical salts. **b.** (of medicines) consisting of or based on salts of the alkaline metals or magnesium; *a saline laxative.*

—*n.* **1.** a salt spring, well, or marsh; salina.

2. a salt of an alkali or magnesium, used as a cathartic. 3. a saline solution, especially one with a concentration similar to that of the blood, used in physiological investigations.
[< Latin *sāl, salis* salt + English *-ine*[1]]
sal·i·nelle (sal ə nel′), *n.* a mud volcano which pours out a saline product. [< French *salinelle* (diminutive) < *saline* saltworks < Latin *salīnae;* see SALINA]
sa·lin·i·ty (sə lin′ə tē), *n.* saline quality; saltiness: *Additional samples were drawn for later measurement ashore of salinity* (Science).
sa·lin·i·za·tion (sā′lən ə zā′shən, -līn-), *n.* the accumulation of salt, especially in the soil.
sal·i·nom·e·ter (sal′ə nom′ə tər), *n.* a hydrometer for measuring the percentage of salt present in a given solution. [< *salin-*(ity) + *-meter*]
Sa·lique (sȧ lēk′, sal′ik, sā′lik), *adj.* Salic.
Salis·bur·y steak (sôlz′ber′ē, -bər-; salz′-), chopped beef shaped before cooking into a patty about twice the size of a hamburger, usually served with a gravy.
Sa·lish (sā′lish), *n.* a Salishan Indian; Flathead. [American English < Salishan *sälst* people]
Sa·lish·an (sā′li shən, sal′i-), *adj.* of or having to do with an American Indian linguistic stock of the northwestern United States and British Columbia, including Flathead and Coeur-d'Alêne. —*n.* this linguistic stock.
sa·li·va (sə lī′və), *n.* the liquid that the salivary glands secrete into the mouth, serving to keep it moist, soften food, and start digestion of starch; spittle. [< Latin *salīva*] —**Syn.** spit.
sal·i·var·y (sal′ə ver′ē), *adj.* of or producing saliva.
salivary gland, any of various glands that empty their secretions into the mouth. The salivary glands of human beings and most other vertebrates are digestive glands that secrete saliva containing enzymes, salts, albumin, etc.
sal·i·vate (sal′ə vāt), *v.,* **-vat·ed, -vat·ing.** —*v.t.* to produce an unusually large secretion of saliva in, as by the use of mercury. —*v.i.* to secrete saliva: *[Pavlov] found that ... dogs ... would quite quickly associate the sound of the bell with food and soon the bell alone would cause them to salivate* (J. A. V. Butler). [< Latin *salīvāre* (with English *-ate*[1]) < *salīva* saliva]
sal·i·va·tion (sal′ə vā′shən), *n.* 1. the act or process of salivating: *It is supposed that in ... salivation the presence of food in the mouth activates a particular clump of nerve cells* (S. A. Barnett). 2. an abnormally large secretion of saliva, as caused by mercury, nervous disorders, etc.; ptyalism.
Salk vaccine (sôk, sôlk), a vaccine that prevents the development of paralytic polio. It is given as a series of injections and contains dead polioviruses that cause the body to react by producing antibodies. These antibodies protect the central nervous system from infection by live viruses. [< Jonas E. *Salk,* born 1914, an American bacteriologist, who developed it]
salle (sal), *n.* a hall: *The ballroom ... is a large room straining every nook to resemble a salle in the Palace of Versailles* (New Yorker). [< French *salle.* Related to SALA.]
salle à man·ger (sȧl′ ȧ mäɴ zhā′), *French.* dining room.
sal·len·ders (sal′ən dərz), *n.pl.* a dry, scabby condition of the hock of a horse, resembling psoriasis in humans. [< Middle French *solandres;* origin unknown]
sal·let (sal′it), *n.* (in medieval armor) a light rounded helmet, with or without a visor. [< Middle French *salade* < Italian *celata* < Latin *caelāre* to chisel < *caelum* chisel, related to *caedere* to cut]
sal·low[1] (sal′ō), *adj.* having a sickly, yellowish, or brownish-yellow color: *a sallow skin, a sallow complexion, a sallow person.* —*v.t.* to make yellowish or sallow. [Old English *sealwes*] —**sal′low·ness,** *n.*
sal·low[2] (sal′ō), *n.* 1. any willow. 2. a willow twig. [Old English *sealh*]
sal·low·ish (sal′ō ish), *adj.* somewhat sallow.
sal·low·y (sal′ō ē), *adj.* full of sallows (willows).
sal·ly (sal′ē), *n., pl.* **-lies,** *v.,* **-lied, -ly·ing.** —*n.* 1. a sudden attack on an enemy made from a defensive position; sortie: *The men in the fort made a brave sally and returned with many prisoners.* 2. any sudden rushing forth: *I come from haunts of coot and hern, I make a sudden sally, And sparkle out among the fern, To bicker down a valley* (Tennyson). 3. a sudden start into activity: *Nature goes by rule, not by sallies and saltations* (Emerson). 4. a going forth; trip; excursion: *I made my second sally into the world* (Daniel Defoe). 5. an outburst of anger, delight, wit, etc.: *Sudden sallies and impetuosities of temper* (Cardinal Manning). 6. a witty remark; witticism; quip: *She continued her story undisturbed by the merry sallies of her hearers.*
—*v.i.* 1. (of troops) to go suddenly from a defensive position to attack an enemy. 2. to rush forth suddenly; go out: *We sallied forth at dawn.* 3. to set out briskly or boldly: *I cannot praise a fugitive and cloistered virtue ... that never sallies out and sees her adversary* (Milton). 4. to go on an excursion or trip. 5. (of things) to issue forth, especially suddenly.
[< Old French *saillie* a rushing forth, outrush, noun use of feminine past participle of *saillir* leap < Latin *salīre*]
Sally Lunn or **sally lunn** (lun′), a slightly sweetened tea cake, served hot with butter. [< *Sally Lunn,* supposedly a woman who sold such cakes in Bath, England, in the late 1700's]
sally port, a protected gate or underground passage in a fort through which troops may pass when making a sally: *In the outwork was a sally port corresponding to the postern of the castle* (Scott).
sal·ma·gun·di (sal′mə gun′dē), *n.* 1. a dish of chopped meat, anchovies, eggs, onions, oil, seasonings, etc. 2. any mixture, medley, or miscellany. [< French *salmigondis* < Italian *salami conditi* pickled sausages; see SALAMI; *conditi,* past participle of *condere* to flavor < Latin *condīre* to preserve] —**Syn.** 2. jumble, hodgepodge.
sal·mi or **sal·mis** (sal′mē; *French* sȧl mē′), *n.* a highly seasoned stew, especially of game seared by roasting and then simmered in wine. [< French *salmi,* short for *salmigondis;* see SALMAGUNDI]
salm·on (sam′ən), *n., pl.* **-ons** or (*collectively*) **-on,** *adj.* —*n.* 1. a large marine and fresh-water fish with silvery scales and yellowish-pink flesh, common in the North Atlantic near the mouths of large rivers which it swims up in order to spawn. 2. a fish of this species that lives in lakes; landlocked salmon. 3. any of various other fishes of the same family common in the North Pacific, as the chinook salmon and sockeye salmon. 4. a yellowish pink like that of the flesh of the salmon; salmon pink: *More pastels, including pink and salmon, are crowding red as the traditional color for the humble building brick* (Wall Street Journal).

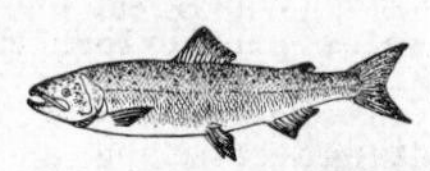
Atlantic Salmon (def. 1) (about 40 in. long)

—*adj.* yellowish-pink.
[< Old French *salmun* < Latin *salmō, -ōnis*]
salm·on·ber·ry (sam′ən ber′ē), *n., pl.* **-ries.** 1. the salmon-colored, edible fruit of a raspberry of the Pacific Coast of North America. 2. the plant itself, bearing red flowers: *The watercourse was a thicket of ... huckleberry, salmonberry, of alder and willow* (Maclean's).
salmon cloud, a band of parallel cirrostratus clouds stretching almost entirely across the sky and appearing, by perspective, to taper at the ends, so that it resembles the outline of a salmon.
salm·on-col·ored (sam′ən kul′ərd), *adj.* salmon.
sal·mo·nel·la (sal′mə nel′ə), *n., pl.* **-nel·las, -nel·lae** (-nel′ē). any of a group of bacteria that cause food poisoning, typhoid and paratyphoid fever, and other infectious diseases. [< New Latin *Salmonella* the genus name < Daniel E. *Salmon,* 1850-1914, an American pathologist]
sal·mo·nel·lo·sis (sal′mə nə lō′sis), *n.* any infectious disease caused by salmonella, such as cholera in fowls, typhoid fever, etc.
Sal·mo·ne·us (sal mō′nē əs, -nyüs), *n. Greek Mythology.* a king and one of the sons of Aeolus who proclaimed he was Zeus and scattered firebrands about pretending that they were thunderbolts. Zeus promptly hurled a real thunderbolt and killed him.
salm·on·id (sam′ə nid), *adj., n.* salmonoid.
sal·mo·noid (sal′mə noid), *adj.* 1. of or belonging to a family of fishes including the salmon and trout. 2. resembling a fish of this family. —*n.* a salmonoid fish.
salmon pink, a yellowish pink; salmon. —**salm′on-pink′,** *adj.*
salmon trout, 1. the sea trout of Europe. 2. the lake trout. 3. the steelhead. 4. any other large trout.
salmon wheel, a tall wheel, set in a rapid and turned by the current, which catches ascending salmon in scoop nets and throws them into a pen; fish wheel.
sal·ol (sal′ōl, -ol), *n.* a white, crystalline, aromatic powder, a salicylate of phenyl, prepared from phenol and salicylic acid. It is used as an antiseptic and to reduce fever. *Formula:* $C_{13}H_{10}O_3$ [< *sal*(icylic) + *-ol*[1]]
Sa·lo·me (sə lō′mē), *n.* (in the Bible) the daughter of Herodias, whose dancing so pleased Herod that he granted her anything she would ask. Instructed by her mother, she demanded the head of John the Baptist, which she then presented to Herodias on a platter. Her name is not given in the Bible. Matthew 14:3-11.
sa·lon (sə lon′; *French* sȧ lôɴ′), *n., pl.* **-lons** (-lonz′; *French* -lôɴ′). 1. a large room for receiving or entertaining guests: *The social and political elite of Paris ... filed into a cavernous salon in the Ministry of the Interior* (Newsweek). 2. the assembly of guests in such a room. 3. a. a place used to exhibit works of art. b. an exhibition of works of art. 4. a fashionable or stylish shop: *a fashion salon, a beauty salon.* [< French *salon* < Italian *salone* < *sala* hall < Germanic (compare Old High German *sal*). Related to SALOON.] —**Syn.** 3. a. gallery.
Sa·lon (sə lon′; *French* sȧ lôɴ′), *n.* the annual exhibition, in Paris, of the works of living artists. [< French *Salon* (originally held in one of the *salons* of the Louvre)]
sa·loon (sə lün′), *n.* 1. *U.S. and Canada.* a place where alcoholic drinks are sold and drunk: *The majority of the citizens of this village are tired of the saloon and want it to go* (Cowansville [Quebec] Observer). 2. a large room for general or public use: *The ship's passengers ate in the dining saloon.* 3. Also, **saloon car.** *British.* a. a sedan: *A black saloon whistled smoothly past us ...* (Geoffrey Household). b. a saloon carriage. 4. a salon (drawing room): *Her saloons were always attended, and by "nice people"* (Benjamin Disraeli). [American English < French *salon.* Related to SALON.] —**Syn.** 1. tavern, bar.
saloon car, saloon, def. 3.
saloon carriage, *British.* a railroad parlor car.
sa·loon·keep·er (sə lün′kē′pər), *n. U.S.* a man who keeps a saloon where alcoholic drinks are sold and drunk: *He excused himself and went about his business, as a good saloonkeeper should* (New Yorker).
sa·loop (sə lüp′), *n.* 1. a hot beverage made from salep or (later) sassafras, milk, and sugar, popular in England, especially in London, during the late 1700's and early 1800's: *This is saloop ... the delight, and ... too often the envy of the unpennied sweep* (Charles Lamb). 2. salep. [< earlier *salop,* variant of *salep*]
Sa·lo·pi·an (sə lō′pē ən), *adj.* of Shropshire, a county in western England. —*n.* a native of Shropshire. [< *Salop,* another name for Shropshire + *-ian*]
sal·pa (sal′pə), *n.* any of a group of transparent, spindle-shaped, free-swimming tunicates, reproducing asexually in one generation, sexually in the next. [< New Latin *Salpa* the genus name < Latin *salpa* a stockfish < Greek *salpē*]
sal·pi·con (sal′pə kon), *n.* cooked meat, mushrooms, truffles, etc., cut into small pieces and mixed with a rich sauce, used as a filling for patés, etc., or served separately. [< French *salpicon* < Spanish *salpicón* < *salpicar* sprinkle < *sal* salt + *picar* to pick]
sal·pi·form (sal′pə fôrm), *adj.* of or having the form or structure of a salpa; fusiform. [< New Latin *Salpa* salpa + English *-form*]
sal·pi·glos·sis (sal′pə glos′is), *n.* 1. any of a group of Chilean herbs of the nightshade family, having funnel-shaped flowers in rich colors, often variegated. 2. the flower of any of these plants. [< New Latin *Salpiglossis* the genus name < Greek *sálpinx, -pingos* trumpet + *glôssa* tongue (because of the shape of the stigma)]
sal·pin·gec·to·my (sal′pin jek′tə mē), *n.* salpingotomy.

sal·pin·gi·tis (sal′pin jī′tis), *n.* inflammation of the Fallopian or the Eustachian tubes. [< New Latin *salpinx, -pingos* Fallopian or Eustachian tube + English *-itis*]

sal·pin·got·o·my (sal′ping got′ə mē), *n., pl.* **-mies.** *Surgery.* **1.** the operation of cutting into a Fallopian tube. **2.** excision of a Fallopian tube. [< New Latin *salpinx, -pingos* Fallopian tube + Greek *-tomiā* a cutting]

sal·pinx (sal′pingks), *n., pl.* **sal·pin·ges** (sal pin′jēz). *Anatomy.* **1.** a Eustachian tube. **2.** a Fallopian tube. [< New Latin *salpinx, -pingos* < Greek *sálpinx, -pingos* trumpet]

sal·si·fy (sal′sə fī), *n.* **1.** a purple-flowered biennial composite plant native to Europe, having a long root somewhat resembling a parsnip and a flavor thought by some to resemble that of the oyster; oyster plant; vegetable oyster; oysterroot; goatsbeard. **2.** its root, eaten as a vegetable. [< French *salsifis* < Italian *sassefrica* < Latin *saxifraga.* Doublet of SAXIFRAGE.]

ROOTS

Salsify

sal·sil·la (sal sil′ə), *n.* any of a group of usually twining herbs of the amaryllis family of tropical America, that yield edible tubers. [< Spanish *salsilla* (diminutive) < *salsa* sauce < Latin; see SAUCE]

sal soda, sodium carbonate; washing soda. [< Latin *sal* salt]

sal·su·gi·nous (sal sü′jə nəs), *adj.* (of plants) growing in salty soil. [< Latin *salsūgō, -inis* saltness (< *salīre* to salt < *sāl, salis* salt) + English *-ous*]

salt (sôlt), *n.* **1.** a white substance, sodium chloride, very abundant in nature both in solution (in sea water) and in crystalline form (in beds in the earth), and extensively prepared for use as a seasoning, a preservative for food, and in many industrial processes. *Formula:* NaCl **2.** anything that gives liveliness, freshness, piquancy, or pungency to anything: *His character has the salt of honesty about it* (William Hazlitt). *Though we are justices and doctors and churchmen, Master Page, we have some salt of our youth in us* (Shakespeare). **3.** any of a group of compounds derived from acids by replacing the hydrogen wholly or partly with a metal or an electropositive radical: *Baking soda is a salt.* See the usage note below. **4.** a saltcellar. **5.** *Informal.* a sailor, especially an experienced one: *Nor, though I am something of a salt, do I ever go to sea as a Commodore, or a Captain or a Cook* (Herman Melville).

eat one's salt, to be one's guest: *He who abuses my hospitality shall never again eat my salt.*

rub salt in or **into the wound,** to aggravate a person, situation, etc., further: *As if to rub salt in the wound, a special report to Parliament by the Iron and Steel Board . . . takes a gloomy view of the industry's chances in export markets* (London Times).

salts, a. a medicine that causes movement of the bowels: *Epsom salts, Rochelle salts.* **b.** smelling salts: *Virginia had run for the salts as soon as she perceived that her mother was unwell* (Frederick Marryat).

with a grain or **pinch of salt,** with some reservation or allowance: *The author takes these statements with a grain of salt* (Wall Street Journal). *Many dockers are taking Mr. Gleason with a pinch of salt* (London Times).

worth one's salt, worth supporting, employing, etc.; capable or efficient: *It was plain from every line of his body that our new hand was worth his salt* (Robert Louis Stevenson).

—*adj.* **1.** containing salt: *salt water.* **2.** tasting like salt; saline; salty: *food that is too salt.* **3.** overflowed with or growing in salt water: *salt marshes, salt grasses.* **4.** cured or preserved with salt: *salt pork.* **5.** sharp; pungent; to the point; lively: *salt speech.*

—*v.t.* **1.** to mix or sprinkle with salt: *These [curds] are salted, adding about an ounce of salt to every three pounds of curd* (J.A. Barnett). **2.** to cure or preserve with salt, either in solid form or as brine. **3.** to provide with salt: *to salt cattle.* **4.** to make pungent; season: *conversation salted with wit.* **5.** *Chemistry.* **a.** to treat or impregnate with any salt. **b.** to add a salt to (a solution) in order to precipitate a dissolved substance. **c.** to precipitate (a dissolved substance) in this manner. **6.** *Slang.* to make appear more prosperous or productive, as a mine, an account, etc., by fraudulent or illegal means: *At the gold diggings of Australia, miners sometimes salt an unproductive hole by sprinkling a few grains of gold dust over it* (John C. Hotten).

salt away or **down, a.** to pack with salt to preserve: *fish salted down in a barrel.* **b.** *Slang.* to store away (money, stock, etc.); put by: *I can't help thinking he must be salting a lot of money away* (Booth Tarkington).

[Old English *sealt*] —**salt′like′,** *adj.*

—**Syn.** *n.* **2.** flavor. **5.** tar. —*adj.* **5.** piquant.

➔ **salt.** The nomenclature of chemical salts has reference to the acids from which they are derived. For example, sulfates, nitrates, carbonates, etc., imply salts of sulfuric, nitric, and carbonic acids. The suffix *-ate* implies the maximum of oxygen in the acids; the suffix *-ite* implies the minimum.

SALT (sôlt), *n.* Strategic Arms Limitation Talks (a series of conferences between the United States and the Soviet Union to limit nuclear armament).

sal·ta (sal′tə), *n.* a game similar to halma, and somewhat like Chinese checkers. [ultimately < Latin *saltāre* leap]

salt-and-pep·per (sôlt′ən pep′ər), *adj.* pepper-and-salt: *A blackish, salt-and-pepper carpeting covers the corridors* (Atlantic).

sal·tant (sal′tənt), *adj.* leaping, jumping, or dancing. [< Latin *saltāns, -antis,* present participle of *saltāre;* see SALTATE]

sal·ta·rel·lo (sal′tə rel′ō), *n., pl.* **-los. 1.** an animated Italian and Spanish dance in triple time, sometimes classed as a galliard or a jig and containing numerous skips or jumps. **2.** the music for it. [< Italian *saltarello* (diminutive) < *salto* a leap, jump < Latin *saltāre;* see SALTATE]

sal·tate (sal′tāt), *v.i.,* **-tat·ed, -tat·ing.** to leap; jump; dance. [< Latin *saltāre* (with English *-ate*[1]) (frequentative) < *salīre*]

sal·ta·tion (sal tā′shən), *n.* **1. a.** a leaping, bounding, or jumping: *Locusts . . . being ordained for saltation, their hinder legs do far exceed the other* (Thomas Browne). **b.** a leap. **2.** an abrupt movement, change, or transition. **3.** *Biology.* a mutation. **4.** the process by which material too heavy to remain in suspension is moved along by a current of water or air in a series of jumping movements. [< Latin *saltātiō, -ōnis* < *saltāre;* see SALTATE]

sal·ta·to (säl tä′tō), *n., pl.* **-tos.** *Music.* a technique of bowing a stringed instrument in which the bow is allowed to spring back from the string by its own elasticity. [< Italian *saltato* < *saltare* to spring < Latin *saltāre;* see SALTATE]

sal·ta·to·ri·al (sal′tə tôr′ē əl, -tōr′-), *adj.* **1.** of, having to do with, or characterized by leaping, jumping, or dancing. **2.** fitted or adapted for leaping.

sal·ta·to·ry (sal′tə tôr′ē, -tōr′-), *adj.* **1.** characterized by or adapted for leaping: *Nature hates calculators; her methods are saltatory and impulsive* (Emerson). **2.** having to do with or adapted for dancing. **3.** proceeding by abrupt movements.

salt·box (sôlt′boks′), *n. U.S.* an old-style, square-shaped, two-story house with a lean-to kitchen in the rear, originally built in Connecticut in the 1700's.

salt·bush (sôlt′bu̇sh′), *n.* any of a widely distributed group of grayish herbs or shrubs of the goosefoot family, especially common in poor soils of Australia and North America: *As cattle can live upon the saltbush, this country is thus suitable for pastoral pursuits* (William Westgarth).

salt cake, crude sodium sulfate that occurs as a by-product in the manufacture of hydrochloric acid from sodium chloride.

salt cedar, a variety of tamarisk native to southeastern Europe and western Asia, now naturalized in parts of the United States: *They are to see "forests" of salt cedar, a tree that . . . uses enormous quantities of water* (New York Times).

salt·cel·lar (sôlt′sel′ər), *n.* a shaker or small dish for holding salt, intended to be used at the table during meals. [< *salt*[1] + obsolete *saler* saltcellar < Old French *salier* < Latin *salārius* of salt < *sāl, salis* salt; influenced by *cellar*]

salt dome, *Geology.* a circular structure of sedimentary rocks resulting from the upward movement of a subterranean mass of salt: *In the northeastern area of the Caspian Sea, salt domes and subsalt formations have been discovered* (New Scientist).

salt·ed (sôl′tid), *adj.* **1.** seasoned, cured, or preserved with salt: *salted peanuts.* **2.** experienced; hardened: *An expert and thoroughly "salted" journalist* (Westminster Gazette). **3.** (of a mine) having the ore, gold dust, etc., placed fraudulently to deceive purchasers or investors. **4.** (of a nuclear weapon) treated so as to produce a large amount of radioactive fallout: *The technical feasibility of "salted" weapons . . . had been studied . . . but the Defense Department had never been asked by the AEC to produce these weapons* (Bulletin of Atomic Scientists). **5.** *Archaic or Dialect.* (of animals) immune to a disease from having had it.

salt·er (sôl′tər), *n.* **1.** a person who makes or sells salt. **2.** a person who salts meat, fish, hides, etc.

salt·ern (sôl′tərn), *n.* a saltworks. [Old English *sealtern, sealtærn* < *sealt* salt + *ærn* building]

salt·er·y (sôl′tər ē), *n., pl.* **-er·ies.** a factory that prepares salted fish for market.

salt flat, 1. a large, level area of flat land containing salt deposits: *It had come a very long way . . . across salt flats abandoned ten million years ago by the shingling off of waters* (Ray Bradbury). **2.** the basin of a playa.

salt·glaze (sôlt′glāz′), *n.* a glaze produced on ceramic ware by putting salt in the kilns during firing. —*adj.* having a saltglaze: *. . . a pair of saltglaze plates painted with two scenes of a gallant and a young woman in a garden* (London Times).

salt grass, any of various grasses that grow in land having large salt or alkali deposits. Some kinds are used for fodder and hay.

salt hay, hay consisting of salt grass, used for food and bedding, and as a mulch: *In the nineteenth century, salt hay from the meadows was of value as bedding for horses, packing for ice, and thatching for the roofs of barns, and was therefore cut annually, right down to the high-tide line* (New Yorker).

salt horse, *Nautical Slang.* salted beef: *There is nothing left us but salt horse and sea-biscuit* (Herman Melville).

sal·tier (sal′tir), *n.* saltire.

sal·ti·grade (sal′tə grād), *adj.* having limbs modified for leaping, as certain insects and spiders. [< New Latin *Saltigradae* the group name < Latin *saltus, -ūs* a leap (< *salīre* to leap) + *gradī* to go]

salt·i·ly (sôl′tə lē), *adv.* in a salty manner.

sal·tim·ban·co (sal′tim bang′kō), *n.* a mountebank; quack. [< Italian *saltimbanco* < *saltare* to leap + *in* on + *banco* bench. Compare MOUNTEBANK.]

sal·tim·banque (sal′tim bangk), *n.* a saltimbanco: *Circus is a simple, romantic ballet . . . dressed in costumes that suggest the saltimbanques of Picasso* (Time). [< French *saltimbanque*]

salt·ine (sôl tēn′), *n.* a thin, crisp, salted cracker. [apparently < *salt* + *-ine*[1]]

salt·i·ness (sôl′tē nis), *n.* the quality or state of being salty.

salt·ing (sôl′ting), *n.* **1.** the act of a person or thing that salts. **2.** *British.* a tract of land overflowed at times by the sea: *At the bridge of the lower saltings the cattle gather and blare* (Rudyard Kipling).

sal·tire (sal′tir), *n. Heraldry.* an ordinary in the form of a Saint Andrew's cross, formed by the crossing of a bend and a bend sinister: *The present British Union Jack dates only from 1801, when the saltire of St. Patrick was added* (Time). [< Old French *sautoir,* earlier *saltoir,* learned borrowing from Medieval Latin *saltatorium* a kind of stirrup; saltatory < Latin *saltāre* to leap; see SALTATE]

salt·ish (sôl′tish), *adj.* somewhat salty.

salt junk, *Nautical Slang.* hard salt meat.

salt lake, a salt-water lake. Salt lakes are found in areas of large salt deposits and are often saltier than oceans.

salt lick, 1. a place where natural salt is found on the surface of the ground and where animals go to lick it up; lick: *[Moose] also like to roll in mud holes and eat the salty earth or salt licks* (Victor H. Cahalane). **2.** a block of manufactured salt placed in a pasture for cattle and sheep to lick, in order to provide necessary salt in the diet.

salt·ly (sôlt′lē), *adv.* with a salt taste or smell.

salt marsh, a marsh regularly overflowed or flooded by salt water, as by the action of winds or tides: *Most types of environment are to be found . . . an exposed cliff-beach, salt marsh and tidal mud, and a shingle spit* (Science News).

salt mine, 1. a mine from which salt is extracted. **2.** a place or situation of drudgery or enslavement: *This is not a prep school for the industry salt mine* (Harper's).

salt·mouth (sôlt′mouth′), *n.* a wide-mouthed bottle suitable for holding solid chemicals.

salt·ness (sôlt′nis), *n.* saltiness: *Boyle wrote a remarkable essay on the saltness of the sea* (New Scientist).

salt of the earth, the best people: *He has been driven to imagining that his sole solidarity lies with a small number of superior persons who have been appointed as the salt of the earth . . .* (Edmund Wilson).

salt pan, 1. a large, shallow vessel in which salt water is evaporated to yield salt. **2.** a shallow depression in the ground in which salt water is evaporated in salt making. **3.** any dried-up salt lake or marsh, especially in Africa: *The water-holes of the salt pans are almost permanently ringed by zebra and wildebeest* (New Scientist).

salt·pans (sôlt′panz′), *n.pl.* saltworks.

salt·pe·ter or **salt·pe·tre** (sôlt′pē′tər), *n.* **1.** a salty, white mineral, used in making gunpowder, in preserving meat, and in medicine; potassium nitrate; niter. *Formula:* KNO_3 **2.** sodium nitrate, used as a source of nitrogen in fertilizing soil; Chile saltpeter. *Formula:* $NaNO_3$ [< Old French *salpetre*, learned borrowing from Medieval Latin *sal petrae* salt of rock < Latin *sāl, salis* salt, *petrae*, genitive of *petra* rock < Greek *pétrā*]

salt pit, a pit where salt is mined.

salt rheum, *Informal.* a skin eruption, as eczema: *Salt rheum . . . has long baffled the art of the most experienced physicians* (Canadian Courant).

salts (sôlts), *n.pl.* See under **salt,** *n.*

salt sage, shadscale: *Salt sage . . . the mainstay of domestic sheep and of the antelope, especially in the winter* (William O. Douglas).

salt·shak·er (sôlt′shā′kər), *n.* a container for salt, having a perforated top through which the salt is sprinkled.

salt spoon, a small spoon, usually having a round, deep bowl, used in taking salt at the table.

salt tree, 1. a leguminous tree with white, pinnate leaves, growing in central Asia. **2.** (in India) a species of tamarisk, the twigs of which are frequently covered with a slight efflorescence of salt.

sal·tus (sal′təs), *n., pl.* **-tus.** a breach of continuity, as in a process of reasoning; leap from premises to conclusion. [< Latin *saltus, -ūs* a leap < *salīre* to leap]

salt-wa·ter (sôlt′wôt′ər, -wot′-), *adj.* **1.** consisting of or containing salt water: *a salt-water bath.* **2.** living in the sea or in water like sea water: *a salt-water fish.* **3.** taking place or active in or about salt water: *a salt-water sport, a salt-water fisherman.*

salt-water taffy, *U.S.* a kind of taffy sold at seaside resorts, originally containing a very small amount of salt water as an ingredient: *The box of salt-water taffy from Atlantic City, mailed to the folks back home, was America's staple packaged delicacy for years* (Newsweek).

salt well, a well sunk, usually by boring, in order to procure brine.

salt·works (sôlt′wėrks′), *n.pl. or sing.* an establishment for the obtaining of salt in commercial quantities by evaporation of naturally salty water, as that in the sea.

salt·wort (sôlt′wėrt′), *n.* any of several plants that grow on beaches, in salt marshes, or in regions of alkaline soil: **1.** any of various plants of the goosefoot family, especially a prickly plant used in making soda ash (barilla). **2.** any of several glassworts.

salt·y (sôl′tē), *adj.,* **salt·i·er, salt·i·est. 1.** containing or impregnated with salt; tasting of salt: *What there is [of underground water] proves mostly too salty for human use continuously* (R. N. Elston). **2.** terse, witty, and (often) a bit improper: *a salty remark.* **3.** that manifests itself in salty language: *a salty sense of humor.* —**Syn. 1.** saline, briny. **2.** racy.

sa·lu·bri·ous (sə lü′brē əs), *adj.* favorable or conducive to health; healthful: *Their salubrious effects, which include the relief of pain . . . are seldom more than palliative and almost never permanent* (New Yorker). [< Latin *salūbris* (with English *-ous*), related to *salūs, -ūtis* good health] —**sa·lu′bri·ous·ly,** *adv.* —**sa·lu′bri·ous·ness,** *n.* —**Syn.** wholesome, salutary.

sa·lu·bri·ty (sə lü′brə tē), *n.* salubrious quality or condition; healthfulness: *The salubrity of their walk is sadly tinctured by carbon monoxide* (New Yorker).

sa·lu·ki (sə lü′kē), *n.* any sporting dog of what is probably the oldest known breed of dogs, familiar to the ancient Egyptians and Arabs and the "dog" of the Bible. It resembles the greyhound in build and has short, silky hair and fringed ears and tail. *Excavation of the Sumerian Empire of 7,000 to 6,000 B.C. has found evidence of . . . the saluki* (Cape Times). [< Arabic *salūqi* of *Salūq*, an ancient city of Arabia]

Sa·lus (sā′ləs), *n. Roman Mythology.* the goddess of health and prosperity, identified with the Greek Hygeia. [< Latin *Salūs, -ūtis* (originally) health]

sa·lus po·pu·li su·pre·ma lex es·to (sā′ləs pop′yə lī sə prē′mə leks es′tō), *Latin.* let the people's welfare be the supreme law (the motto of Missouri).

sal·u·tar·i·ly (sal′yə ter′ə lē), *adv.* in a salutary manner.

sal·u·tar·i·ness (sal′yə ter′ē nis), *n.* the state or quality of being salutary.

sal·u·tar·y (sal′yə ter′ē), *adj.* **1.** promoting or contributing to a more satisfactory condition; beneficial: *The professor gave the discouraged student salutary advice. Through a wise and salutory neglect [of the colonies], a generous nature has been suffered to take her own way to perfection* (Edmund Burke). **2.** good for the health; wholesome: *Walking is a salutary exercise.* [< Latin *salūtāris* < *salūs, -ūtis* good health] —**Syn. 1.** profitable, useful.

sal·u·ta·tion (sal′yə tā′shən), *n.* **1.** the act of greeting; saluting: *The man raised his hat in salutation. Out into the yard sallied mine host himself also, to do fitting salutation to his new guests* (Scott). **2. a.** something uttered, written, or done to salute. **b.** any of the various conventional forms of address with which a letter is begun, as "Dear Sir" or "My Dear Mrs. Jones."

sa·lu·ta·to·ri·an (sə lü′tə tôr′ē ən, -tōr′-), *n.* (in American colleges and schools) the student, usually the second highest in the class in scholarship, who delivers the address of welcome at the graduation exercises. [American English < *salutator*(y) + *-ian*]

sa·lu·ta·to·ry (sə lü′tə tôr′ē, -tōr′-), *adj., n., pl.* **-ries.** —*adj.* **1.** expressing greeting; welcoming. **2.** *U.S.* designating the address by the salutatorian at graduation exercises in a college or school.
—*n.* **1.** an address of greeting. **2.** *U.S.* an opening address welcoming guests at the graduation of a class.
[American English < Latin *salūtātōrius* < *salūtāre;* see SALUTE]

sa·lute (sə lüt′), *v.,* **-lut·ed, -lut·ing,** *n.* —*v.t.* **1.** to honor in a formal manner by raising the hand to the head, by firing guns, or by dipping flags, etc.: *We salute the flag every day at school.* **2.** to meet with kind words, a bow, clasp of the hand, kiss, etc.; greet: *The old gentleman walked along the avenue saluting his friends and receiving their salutes.* **3.** to come to (the eye or ear); strike; meet: *Shouts of welcome saluted their ears.*
—*v.i.* **1.** to perform a salutation. **2.** to make a salute.
—*n.* **1.** an act of saluting; expression of welcome, farewell, or honor. **2. a.** the act or gesture by which a superior officer, national flag, etc., is honored or shown respect. **b.** the position of the hand, rifle, etc., assumed in saluting.
[< Latin *salūtāre* to greet (wish health to) < *salūs, -ūtis* good health]
—**Syn.** *v.t.* **1.** welcome, hail.

Salute (def. 2) by a soldier

sa·lut·er (sə lü′tər), *n.* a person who salutes.

sal·u·tif·er·ous (sal′yü tif′ər əs), *adj.* **1.** healthful; salubrious. **2.** conducive to well-being, safety, or salvation. [< Latin *salūtifer* (< *salūs, -ūtis* good health + *ferre* to bear) + English *-ous*]

Salv., Salvador.

sal·va·ble (sal′və bəl), *adj.* **1.** (of a ship, cargo, etc.) salvageable. **2.** *Theology.* admitting of salvation. [< Late Latin *salvāre* to save (< Latin *salvus* safe) + English *-able*]

Sal·va·do·ran (sal′və dôr′ən, -dōr′-), *adj.* of or having to do with El Salvador, a country in western Central America, or its people. —*n.* a native or inhabitant of El Salvador.

Sal·va·do·re·an or **Sal·va·do·ri·an** (sal′və dôr′ē ən, -dōr′-), *adj., n.* Salvadoran: *Salvadoreans say United States corn is too hard for proper grinding* (New York Times).

sal·vage (sal′vij), *n., v.,* **-vaged, -vag·ing.** —*n.* **1.** the act of saving a ship or its cargo from wreck, capture, etc. **2.** a payment for saving it. **3.** the rescue of property from fire or other danger. **4. a.** the property salvaged or saved: *the salvage from a shipwreck or fire.* **b.** the value of this property, or the proceeds from its sale. **5. a.** any saving from ruin: *the salvage of one's dignity.* **b.** anything saved thus.
—*v.t.* **1.** to save from shipwreck, capture, fire, etc.: *The passengers and crew . . . were evacuated . . . except for the captain and six of his men, who are remaining, trusting that the ship . . . may be salvaged* (London Times). **2.** to save from damage or ruin: *to salvage a company.*
[< Middle French *salvage* < Medieval Latin *salvagium* < Late Latin *salvāre* < Latin *salvus* safe]

sal·vage·a·ble (sal′və jə bəl), *adj.* that can be salvaged: *Submarines preyed particularly on tankers during the war, but there is little hope that oil cargoes are salvageable* (Wall Street Journal).

sal·vag·er (sal′və jər), *n.* a person who salvages.

Sal·var·san (sal′vər san), *n. Trademark.* arsphenamine, a compound of arsenic formerly used in the treatment of syphilis, trench mouth, etc. [< German *Salvarsan* < Latin *salvus* safe + German *Arsenik* arsenic]

sal·va·tion (sal vā′shən), *n.* **1.** a saving or being saved; preservation from destruction, ruin, loss, or calamity: *Many a Burgoyne has capitulated because the means of salvation were not . . . put into his hands* (Archibald Alison). **2.** a saving of the soul; deliverance from sin and from punishment for sin. **3.** a person or thing that saves: *Christians believe that Christ is the salvation of the world. Sleep is the salvation of the nervous system* (M. L. Holbrook). [< Late Latin *salvātiō, -ōnis* < *salvāre* save < Latin *salvus* safe]
—**Syn. 2.** redemption.

Salvation Army, an international organization to spread Christianity and help the poor, founded in England in 1865 by William Booth: *A religious and charitable organization, the Salvation Army maintains its operations in 85 countries and colonies scattered over the world* (Donald McMillan).

sal·va·tion·ism (sal vā′shə niz əm), *n.* religious teaching which lays prime stress on the saving of the soul. [< *salvation* + *-ism*]

Sal·va·tion·ism (sal vā′shə niz əm), *n.* the principles or methods of the Salvation Army. [< *salvationism*]

sal·va·tion·ist (sal vā′shə nist), *n.* a teacher or disciple of salvationism: *They were rich . . . and were both internationally famous as applied salvationists* (New Yorker).

Sal·va·tion·ist (sal vā′shə nist), *n.* a member of the Salvation Army: *She was the daughter of Salvationists.* —*adj.* having to do with Salvationists or Salvationism: *Salvationist leaders from many countries met in London* (Norman S. Marshall).

salve[1] (sav, säv), *n., v.,* **salved, salv·ing.** —*n.* **1.** a soft, greasy substance put on wounds and sores; healing ointment: *a salve that is good for burns.* **2.** something soothing: *The kind words were a salve to his hurt feelings. Ronald had this salve for his conscience* (Charles Kingsley). **3.** *Slang.* praise; flattery.
—*v.t.* **1.** to put salve on. **2.** to soothe; smooth over: *He salved his conscience by the thought that his lie harmed no one.*
[Old English *sealf*]
—**Syn.** *n.* **1.** unguent.

salve[2] (salv), *v.t.,* **salved, salv·ing.** to save from loss or destruction; salvage. [back formation < *salvage*]

 PRONUNCIATION KEY: hat, āge, cãre, fär; let, ēqual, tėrm; it, īce; hot, ōpen, ôrder; oil, out; cup, pu̇t, rüle;

sal·ve[3] (sal′vē), *interj.* hail! "*Salve Regina, mater misericordiae,*" *he prayed* (Edgar Maass). [< Latin *salvē!* be in good health! probably imperative of *salvēre* < *salvus* safe, well]

sal·ver (sal′vər), *n.* a tray: *The first footman brought in a letter on a silver salver* (John Galsworthy). [< French *salve* < Spanish *salva* (literally) a foretasting < *salvar* in the sense of "safeguard (a superior) by pretasting food" < Late Latin *salvāre* save < Latin *salvus* safe]

sal·ver·form (sal′vər fôrm), *adj. Botany.* (of a corolla) shaped like a tube, with the limb spreading out flat.

sal·ver-shaped (sal′vər shāpt′), *adj.* salverform.

sal·vi·a (sal′vē ə), *n.* any of a group of herbs and shrubs of the mint family, especially the scarlet sage and the common garden sage; sage. *Salvia* is commonly used to refer to the ornamental varieties of sage. [< Latin *salvia,* probably < *salvus* healthy, safe (because of its supposed healing properties). Doublet of SAGE[2].]

sal·vif·ic (sal vif′ik), *adj.* tending to save; providing or causing salvation: *A number of liberal Catholic thinkers have suggested that unbaptized children may get to heaven after all because of God's "salvific will"—his desire that all mankind be saved* (Time). [< Late Latin *salvificus* < Latin *salvus* safe + *facere* to make]

sal·vo[1] (sal′vō), *n., pl.* **-vos** or **-voes. 1. a.** the discharge of several guns at the same time as a broadside or as a salute. **b.** the dropping by an aircraft of a complete rack of bombs at the same time over a target. **c.** the launching at the same time of every rocket in a group of rockets: *It could briefly match the firepower of a modern cruiser with its close-in salvos of rockets* (Time). **d.** the projectiles, bombs, etc., thus discharged, dropped, or fired. **2.** a round of cheers or applause. **3.** a barrage: *a salvo of rocks, a salvo of insults. Britain's electioneering war will begin with a salvo of statistics tomorrow* (Wall Street Journal). [< Italian *salva* < Latin *salvē* hail!; see SALVE[3]]

sal·vo[2] (sal′vō), *n., pl.* **-vos. 1.** a reservation (of a right, etc.); saving clause; proviso. **2.** a quibbling evasion. **3.** an expedient for saving a person's reputation or soothing offended pride or conscience. [< Medieval Latin *salvo jure* (literally) with a right being saved or reserved; ablative forms of Latin *salvus* safe, saved, and *jūs, jūris* law, a right]

sal vo·la·ti·le (vō lat′ə lē), **1.** ammonium carbonate; volatile salt. **2.** an aromatic solution of this, used to relieve faintness, headache, etc. [< New Latin *sal volatile* < Latin *sāl, salis* salt, and *volātile* volatile]

sal·vor (sal′vər), *n.* **1.** a person who salvages or attempts to salvage vessels, cargo, etc. **2.** a ship used in salvage.

Sam., Samuel (two books of the Old Testament, usually distinguished as I Sam. or 1 Sam.; II Sam. or 2 Sam.).

SAM (no periods), surface-to-air missile or missiles.

S. Am., 1. South America. **2.** South American.

sam (sam), *v.t.,* **sammed, sam·ming.** to sammy.

sa·madh (sə mäd′), *n.* a place of immolation or burial, especially the tomb of a Hindu yogi supposed to be lying in a state of trance. [< Hindustani *samādh* < Sanskrit *samādhi* (literally) deep meditation]

sa·ma·dhi (sə mä′dē), *n. Hinduism.* a state of mystical contemplation in which distinctions between the self and the outer world disappear: *Of samadhi it is said, "If a man goes into it a fool he comes out a sage"* (Manchester Guardian Weekly). [< Sanskrit *samādhi* deep meditation]

sam·a·ra (sam′ər ə, sə mãr′-), *n.* any dry fruit that has a winglike extension and does not split open when ripe; a key or key fruit: *The fruit of the maple tree is a double samara with one seed in each half.* [< Latin *samara* elm seed]

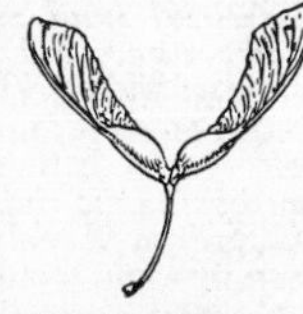
Double Samara of maple

Sa·mar·i·tan (sə mar′ə tən), *n.* **1.** a native or inhabitant of Samaria, a region and ancient kingdom of northern Palestine: *A rebellion under Justinian . . . brought down on the Samaritans total suppression* (New Yorker). **2.** a good Samaritan.
—*adj.* of or having to do with Samaria or its people.

sa·mar·i·tan·ism (sə mar′ə tə niz′əm), *n.* **1.** the religious doctrine of the Samaritans, a modification of Sadduceeism. **2.** a word, phrase, or expression peculiar to the Hebrew dialect of the Samaritans. **3.** charitableness or benevolence like that of the good Samaritan: *Samaritanism today means courage* (Maclean's).

sa·mar·i·um (sə mãr′ē əm), *n.* a grayish-white, rare-earth, metallic chemical element of the cerium group, discovered in 1879 in samarskite. *Symbol:* Sm; *at.wt.:* (C^{12}) 150.35 or (O^{16}) 150.35; *at.no.:* 62; *valence:* 2, 3. [< *samar*(skite) + New Latin *-ium,* a suffix meaning "element"]

sa·mar·skite (sə mär′skīt), *n.* a black mineral, containing niobium, uranium, cerium, samarium, etc. [< German *Samarskit* < a Colonel *Samarski,* a Russian official in the 1800's + German *-it* -ite[1]]

sam·ba (sam′bə), *n., pl.* **-bas,** *v.,* **-baed, -ba·ing.** —*n.* an African dance adapted and modified in Brazil as a ballroom dance, in syncopated duple time.
—*v.i.* to dance the samba: *Tangos and slow foxtrots are his favorites, but he can samba* (Time).
[< Portuguese *samba,* probably < an African word]

sam·bal (säm′bäl), *n.* a condiment of Malaya and Indonesia, as chutney, made of peppers, fruits, herbs, fish foods, etc., usually eaten with curry and rice: *There were curry of shrimp and curry of chicken . . . and an assortment of nine sambals, including chutney* (Craig Claiborne). [< Malay]

sam·ba·qui (säm bä′kē), *n.* any of the piles of shell and refuse found along the Brazilian coast, containing items deposited by prehistoric man. [< Portuguese *sambaquí* < a Tupi word]

sam·bar (sam′bər, säm′-), *n., pl.* **-bars** or (*collectively*) **-bar.** any of certain large, maned deer of Asia, especially a kind with massive, rusine antlers, found in India. [< Hindi *sāmbar* < Sanskrit *śambara* kind of deer]

sam·bo (sam′bō), *n., pl.* **-bos.** the child of a Negro and an Indian, or of a Negro and a mulatto (used in an unfriendly way). Also, **zambo.** [< Spanish *zambo*]

Sam Browne belt (sam′ broun′), a military belt consisting of a waist strap supported by a light strap passing over the right shoulder, worn by British and American army officers, especially in World War I. [< Sir *Samuel Browne,* 1824-1901, a British general, who invented it]

sam·buk (sam′bůk), *n.* a kind of small ship, similar to a dhow, used off western India and the Arabian coast: *He is also part owner of a leaky sambuk in which he ventures out into deeper waters in search of shark, rock cod, and kingfish* (London Times). [< Arabic *sambūq*]

sam·bu·ka (sam byü′kə), *n.* sambuke.

sam·buke (sam′byük), *n.* an ancient, triangular, stringed musical instrument, akin to the harp. [< Latin *sambūca* < Greek *sambȳkē*]

sam·bur (sam′bər, säm′-), *n., pl.* **-burs** or (*collectively*) **-bur.** sambar.

same (sām), *adj.* **1.** not another; identical: *We came back the same way we went. All the planets travel round the sun in the same direction.* **2.** just alike; not different: *Her name and mine are the same.* **3.** just spoken of; aforesaid: *The boys were talking about a queer man. This same man wore his hair very long and always dressed in white.* **4.** unchanged: *He is the same kind old man.*
—*pron.* the same person or thing: *It is the same in our age that it was in our youth* (Robert Southey).
all the same, a. notwithstanding; nevertheless: *All the same, I'm glad to be at home again* (John Ruskin). **b.** of little importance: *Whether or not it rains is all the same to me.*
just the same, a. in the same manner: *The stairs creaked just the same as ever.* **b.** nevertheless: *My mother was a lady . . . but just the same she ate boiled cabbage with a knife except when company came* (Hugh McHugh).
the same, in the same way or manner: *"Sea" and "see" are pronounced the same.*
[probably < Scandinavian (compare Old Icelandic *samr*)]
—**Syn.** *adj.* **1, 2. Same, identical** mean not different from something else or each other. When referring to something or someone already mentioned, either word applies: *That is the same* (or *identical*) *man I saw yesterday.* When describing two or more people or things, **same** implies likeness of some kind or degree; **identical** implies absolute likeness: *He always has the same lunch. Their cars are identical.* —**Ant.** *adj.* **2.** unlike.
➤ **Same,** the adjective, is always preceded by the definite article (*the*) or by a demonstrative pronoun (*this, that,* etc.).
➤ **Same** as a substitute for *it* or other pronouns is largely confined to legal usage and is regarded as nonstandard: *The committee has completed its report and will present same* (standard: *it*) *at the next meeting.*

Sa·mekh or **sa·mech** (sä′meн, -mek), *n.* the fifteenth letter of the Hebrew alphabet. [< Hebrew *sāmeḵ*]

same·ness (sām′nis), *n.* **1.** the state or quality of being the same; exact likeness. **2.** lack of variety; tiresomeness: *It seems that giants in industry are taking refuge in sameness* (Atlantic). —**Syn. 2.** uniformity, monotony.

S. Amer., 1. South America. **2.** South American.

Sa·mi·an (sā′mē ən), *adj.* of or having to do with the island of Samos, an island in the Aegean Sea, west of Asia Minor. —*n.* a native or inhabitant of Samos.

sam·iel (sam′yel), *n.* a hot, dry, sand-laden desert wind of Arabia and northern Africa; simoom: *the samiel or mortifying wind of the desert near Bagdad* (James Smith). [< Turkish *samyel* < *sam* poisonous (< Arabic *samm* poison) + *yel* wind]

sam·i·sen (sam′ə sen), *n.* a Japanese guitarlike instrument with three strings, played with a plectrum: *After dinner we listened to the strange music of the samisen* (New York Times). [< Japanese *samisen* < Chinese roots *som* three + *sien* string]

sam·ite (sam′īt, sā′mīt), *n.* a heavy, rich silk fabric, sometimes interwoven with gold, worn in the Middle Ages: *Clothed in white samite, mystic, wonderful* (Tennyson). [< Old French *samit,* short for Medieval Greek *hexamiton* (literally) six-threaded < Greek *héx* six + *mítos* thread]

Saml., Samuel (two books of the Old Testament, usually distinguished as I Saml. or 1 Saml.; II Saml. or 2 Saml.).

sam·let (sam′lit), *n.* a young or small salmon. [< *sa*(l)*m*(on) + *-let*]

sam·lor (sam′lər), *n.* a pedicab. [< Thai *samlor*]

sam·my (sam′ē), *v.t.,* **-mied, -my·ing. 1.** to dampen (skins) with cold water in dressing leather. **2.** to season (skins) to a uniform temper. [origin unknown]

Sam·nite (sam′nīt), *n.* one of a people of ancient Italy, believed to be an offshoot of the Sabines.
—*adj.* of or having to do with the Samnites or Samnium, an ancient country of central Italy.

Sa·mo·an (sə mō′ən), *adj.* of or having to do with Samoa, a group of islands in the South Pacific, or its people. —*n.* **1.** a native or inhabitant of Samoa. **2.** the Polynesian language of the Samoans.

sa·mo·gon (sä′mə gon), *n.* a Russian vodka illegally distilled from various elements, as sugar beets, potatoes, grain, etc.: *Too many people here know how to brew samogon, the Russian equivalent of moonshine* (Edmund Stevens). [< Russian *samogon*]

Sam·o·thra·cian (sam′ə thrā′shən), *adj.* of or having to do with the island of Samothrace, in the northern Aegean Sea. —*n.* a native or inhabitant of Samothrace.

sam·o·var (sam′ə vär, sam′ə vär′), *n.* a metal urn used for heating water for tea: *Tea was brewing in a big Kashmiri samovar nearby* (New Yorker). [< Russian *samovar* (literally) self-boiler < *sam* self + *varit′* boil]

Samovar

Sam·o·yed or **Sam·o·yede** (sam′ə yed′), *n.* **1.** one of a people living in Siberia and northeastern Russia. **2.** a group of Ural-Altaic languages spoken by these people. **3.** any of a Siberian breed of large working dogs having a long-haired, white or cream-colored coat, used in arctic regions to guard reindeer herds and pull sleds. —*adj.* of or having to do with the Samoyeds or their languages. [< Russian *samoyed*]

Samoyed (def. 3) (19 to 23½ in. high at the shoulder)

Sam·o·yed·ic (sam′ə yed′ik), *adj.* of or having to do with the Samoyeds or their languages. —*n.* their languages.

samp (samp), *n. U.S.* coarsely ground corn, boiled and eaten, usually with milk and sugar. [American English < Algonkian (Narragansett) *nasaump* porridge of meal]

sam·pa·gui·ta (sam′pə gē′tə), *n.* the fragrant white flower of an East Indian jasmine. It is the national flower of the Philippines. [< Tagalog *sampaga* + Spanish *-ita* (diminutive suffix)]

sam·pan (sam′pan), *n.* a type of small boat sculled by one or more oars at the stern and usually having a single sail and a roofing made of mats, used in China and nearby regions. [< Chinese *san pan* (literally) three boards, planks < Portuguese *champão;* origin uncertain]

Sampan

sam·phire (sam′fīr), *n.* **1.** a European plant of the parsley family, growing in clefts of rocks by the sea. Its aromatic, saline, fleshy leaves are used in pickles. **2.** glasswort. [earlier *sampere* < French (*herbe de*) *Saint Pierre* St. Peter's (herb)]

sam·ple (sam′pəl, säm′-), *n., adj., v.,* **-pled, -pling.** —*n.* a part to show what the rest is like; one thing to show what the others are like: *Get samples of blue silk for a dress. Pushing people aside to get in a car is a sample of his bad manners.* —*adj.* serving as a sample: *a sample copy, sample ores.* —*v.t.* to take a part of; test a part of: *We sampled the cake and found it very good. Each of us . . . seems to have sampled all the different varieties of human experience* (Mark Twain). [short for *essample,* variant of *example* < Old French *essample*] —**Syn.** *n.* specimen. See **example.**

sam·pler (sam′plər, säm′-), *n.* **1.** a person who samples. **2.** a piece of cloth embroidered to show skill in needlework. **3.** a mechanism for collecting samplings. **4.** something containing typical samples: *a sampler of Poe's work.* [short for Old French *essamplaire* < Latin *exemplārium* model pattern, original < Latin *exemplum* example]

sample room, *U.S.* **1.** a room where samples, especially of merchandise, are kept or shown. **2.** *Informal.* a barroom; saloon.

sam·pling (sam′pling, säm′-), *n.* **1.** a testing or trying of anything by means of samples, especially in order to determine its quality or nature: *A second requirement in prospecting in any area is to find the constitution of the surface layers of the sea bed by direct sampling* (Gaskell and Hill). **2.** an item or portion used as a sample: *Samplings were . . . tested out by a physician on eight military patients* (Newsweek).

sam·shu (sam′shü), *n.* **1.** a Chinese alcoholic beverage made from fermented rice or millet. **2.** alcoholic or intoxicating liquor generally. [< Cantonese *sam-shiu* (literally) three times distilled]

sam·sa·ra (səm sä′rə), *n. Hinduism.* the endless repetition of births, deaths, and rebirths to which man is subject. [< Sanskrit *samsāra*]

Sam·son (sam′sən), *n.* **1.** (in the Bible) one of the judges of Israel, a man of very great strength. Judges 13-16. **2.** any very strong man.

Sam·so·ni·an (sam sō′nē ən), *adj.* of, having to do with, or resembling Samson; showing great strength: [*He*] *gave a faintly Samsonian performance, for one had the odd impression that some of his prodigious strength left him after a capital loss* (London Times).

Sam·u·el (sam′yu̇ əl), *n.* **1.** (in the Bible) a Hebrew leader, judge, and prophet. He anointed Saul, the first king of Israel, and later, David. **2.** either of two of the historical books of the Old Testament, I Samuel and II Samuel, coming after Judges. In the Douay Bible, these books are called I Kings and II Kings. *Abbr.:* Sam.

sam·u·rai (sam′u̇ rī), *n., pl.* **-rai.** **1.** the military class in feudal Japan, consisting of the retainers of the great nobles: *The samurai generally thought print-making and even print-buying beneath their dignity* (Time). **2.** a member of this class. [< Japanese *samurai* warrior, knight]

san (san), *n. Informal.* a sanitorium: *One in five active cases doesn't go in the san* (Maclean's).

San (sän), *adj. Spanish and Italian.* Saint.

san·a·tive (san′ə tiv), *adj.* having the power to cure or heal; healing; curative. [< Late Latin *sānātīvus* < Latin *sānāre* to heal < *sānus* healthy] —**Syn.** therapeutic, sanatory, remedial.

san·a·to·ri·um (san′ə tôr′ē əm, -tōr′-), *n., pl.* **-to·ri·ums, -to·ri·a** (-tôr′ē ə, -tōr′-). **1.** sanitarium. **2.** a health resort, especially one in the hills or mountains of hot countries, as India, for summer use. [< New Latin *sanatorium,* neuter of Late Latin *sānātōrius* health-giving < Latin *sānāre* to heal < *sānus* healthy]

san·a·to·ry (san′ə tôr′ē, -tōr′-), *adj.* **1.** favorable to health; healing; curing. **2.** of or having to do with healing. [< Late Latin *sānātōrius;* see SANATORIUM]

san·be·ni·to (san′bə nē′tō), *n., pl.* **-tos.** **1.** a yellow penitential garment with a red Saint Andrew's cross before and behind, worn by a confessed heretic under trial by the Inquisition. **2.** a black garment ornamented with flames, devils, etc., worn by a condemned heretic at an auto-da-fé. [< Spanish *sanbenito* < *San Benito* Saint Benedict (because he introduced the scapular)]

sanc·ti·fi·ca·tion (sangk′tə fə kā′shən), *n.* **1.** the act of sanctifying or making holy: *God hath from the beginning chosen you to salvation through sanctification of the Spirit and belief of the truth* (II Thessalonians 2:13). **2.** the state of being sanctified; purification from sin; consecration.

sanc·ti·fied (sangk′tə fīd), *adj.* **1.** made holy; set apart for sacred services; consecrated; sacred. **2.** sanctimonious: *a sanctified whine.*

sanc·ti·fi·er (sangk′tə fī′ər), *n.* a person who sanctifies or makes holy.

sanc·ti·fy (sangk′tə fī), *v.t.,* **-fied, -fy·ing.** **1.** to make (a thing, quality, action, etc.) holy: *We will our youth lead on to higher fields, And draw no swords, but what are sanctify'd* (Shakespeare). **2.** to set apart as sacred; observe as holy; consecrate: *And God blessed the seventh day, and sanctified it* (Genesis 2:3). **3.** to make (a person) free from sin. **4.** to make right; justify: *Does the end sanctify the means?* (W. H. Hudson). [< Latin *sānctificāre* < *sānctus* holy (see SAINT) + *facere* make] —**Syn. 3.** redeem.

sanc·ti·fy·ing·ly (sangk′tə fī′ing lē), *adv.* in a manner or degree tending to sanctify or make holy.

sanc·ti·mo·ni·ous (sangk′tə mō′nē əs), *adj.* **1.** making a show of holiness; putting on airs of sanctity: *a sanctimonious hypocrite. The sanctimonious pirate, that went to sea with the ten Commandments, but scraped one out of the Table* (Shakespeare). **2.** *Obsolete.* consecrated; sacred; holy. —**sanc′ti·mo′ni·ous·ly,** *adv.* —**sanc′ti·mo′ni·ous·ness,** *n.* —**Syn. 1.** pharisaic.

sanc·ti·mo·ny (sangk′tə mō′nē), *n.* **1.** a show of holiness; affected or hypocritical devoutness; airs of sanctity. **2.** *Obsolete.* holiness; sanctity. [< Old French *sainctimonie,* learned borrowing from Latin *sānctimōnia* < *sānctus* holy; see SAINT]

sanc·tion (sangk′shən), *n.* **1. a.** permission with authority; approval: *Plans are also being prepared for the building of nine others, for which all necessary sanctions from various interested authorities have been obtained* (London Times). **b.** encouragement given to an opinion or practice by an influential person or by custom, public opinion, etc.: *Religion gave her sanction to that intense and unquenchable animosity* (Macaulay). **2.** a making legally authoritative or binding; solemn ratification or confirmation: *The day on which the royal sanction was . . . solemnly given to this great Act* (Macaulay). **3. a.** a provision of a law stating a penalty for disobedience to it or a reward for obedience. **b.** the penalty or reward. **4.** an action by several nations toward another nation, such as a blockade, restrictions on trade, or withholding loans, intended to force it to obey international law: *to apply economic sanctions, rather than to threaten with military ones.* **5.** a consideration that leads one to obey a rule of conduct. **6.** binding force: *This word* [*honor*] *is often made the sanction of an oath* (Jonathan Swift).
—*v.t.* **1.** to approve; allow: *Her conscience does not sanction repeating scandal.* **2.** to authorize: *The use of a site in Hyde Park, selected by the Prince, was sanctioned by the Government* (Lytton Strachey). **3.** to make valid or binding; confirm.
[< Latin *sānctiō, -ōnis* < *sānctus* holy; see SAINT] —**sanc′tion·er,** *n.*
—**Syn.** *n.* **1. a.** approbation. *-v.t.* **1.** See **approve.**

sanc·ti·tude (sangk′tə tüd), *n.* sanctity; holiness. [< Latin *sānctitūdō* < *sānctus* holy; see SAINT]

sanc·ti·ty (sangk′tə tē), *n., pl.* **-ties.** **1.** holiness of life; saintliness; godliness: *the sanctity of a saint.* **2.** holy character; sacredness: *the sanctity of a church, the sanctity of the home. His affirmations have the sanctity of an oath* (Charles Lamb).
sanctities, a. sacred obligations, feelings, etc.: *the sanctities of obedience and faith* (Emerson). **b.** objects possessing sanctity: *. . . the flower of olden sanctities* (Coventry Patmore).
[< Latin *sānctitās* < *sānctus* holy; see SAINT] —**Syn. 2.** inviolability.

sanc·tu·a·rize (sangk′chu̇ ə rīz), *v.t.,* **-rized, -riz·ing.** to shelter by means of a sanctuary or sacred privileges.

sanc·tu·ar·y (sangk′chu̇ er′ē), *n., pl.* **-aries.** **1.** a sacred place; holy spot; place where sacred things are kept: *A church is a sanctuary; so was the ancient Hebrew temple at Jerusalem.* **2. a.** the part of a church around the altar. **b.** the most sacred part of any temple. **c.** the sacred place where the Ark of the Covenant was kept in the temple at Jerusalem. **3.** a place of refuge or protection. **4.** immunity from the law; refuge; protection: *The escaped prisoner found sanctuary in the temple.* **5.** a refuge for wild life: *a bird sanctuary.* [< Latin *sānctuārium* < *sānctus* holy; see SAINT]

sanc·tum (sangk′təm), *n., pl.* **-tums,** (*Rare*) **-ta** (-tə). **1.** a sacred place. **2.** a private room or office where a person can be undisturbed. **3.** anything set apart as sacred. [< Latin *sānctum* originally adjective, neuter of *sānctus* holy; see SAINT] —**Syn. 2.** study.

sanc·tum sanc·to·rum (sangk′təm sangk tôr′əm, -tōr′-), **1.** the holy of holies. **2.** an especially private place; inner sanctum (often humorous in use): *. . . When she expressed an interest in be-bop he had unearthed the inner sanctum sanctorum of that art in Harlem and taken her there* (William Ard). [< Latin *sānctum sānctōrum* < Greek translation of Hebrew *qodhesh haqqodhāshīm*]

Sanc·tus (sangk′təs, sängk′tu̇s), *n.* **1.** a hymn beginning "Sanctus, Sanctus, Sanctus" in Latin and "Holy, holy, holy, Lord God of hosts" in English, ending the preface of the Mass or Eucharistic service. **2.** the musical setting of this. [< Latin *sānctus* holy; see SAINT (because it is the first word of the hymn)]

Sanctus bell, (in the Roman Catholic Church) the bell rung to signal the more solemn portions of the Mass, first rung at the Sanctus.

sand (sand), *n.* **1.** a material consisting of fine water-worn or disintegrated particles of rocks, mainly siliceous, finer than gravel: *the sand of the seashore.* **2. a.** the sand in an hourglass. **b.** a grain of this. **3.** *U.S. Informal.* courage; pluck; grit: *She had more sand in her than any girl I ever see* (Mark Twain). **4.** a yellowish red.
build on sand, to have a weak foundation or basis; have little support: *Their . . . material well-being is built on sand* (Manchester Guardian Weekly).
run into the sands, to become bogged down or reach a dead end: *The short novels of this middle period are much better than most of his longer ones, which are likely to start off invitingly but in the second volume to run into the sands* (New Yorker).
sands, a. a tract or region composed mainly of sand, as along a shore: *. . . the principal*

sands in the estuary of the Thames (Thomas H. Huxley). **b.** moments, minutes, or small portions of time (in allusion to the sand in the hourglass for measuring time); lifetime: *Now there were voices in France, too, which called for compromise and reform before the sands ran out* (Newsweek).
—*v.t.* **1.** to sprinkle with or as if with sand: *The highway department sanded the icy road.* **2.** to rub with sand, sandpaper, etc., in order to clean, polish, smooth, etc. **3.** to fill up (a harbor) with sand. **4.** to add sand to. **5.** to cover with sand; bury under sand.
—*adj.* yellowish-red.
[Old English *sand*]

san·dal[1] (san′dəl), *n., v.,* **-daled, -dal·ing** or (*especially British*) **-dalled, -dal·ling.**
—*n.* **1.** a kind of shoe made of a sole fastened to the foot by straps: *Our hero proudly strutting along the promenade, shod in sandals, wearing a short sleeved multi-coloured shirt . . .* (London Times). **2.** any of various kinds of low-cut shoes, slippers, etc. **3.** a light, low, rubber overshoe that has no heel.
—*v.t.* to furnish with sandals.
[< Old French *sandale,* learned borrowing < Latin *sandalium* < Greek *sandálion* (diminutive) < *sándalon*]

Sandals[1] (def. 1) Left and center, Greek; right, Roman

san·dal[2] (san′dəl), *n.* sandalwood. [< Medieval Latin *sandalum* < Greek *sántalon* < Arabic *ṣandal* < Persian *chandal,* ultimately < Sanskrit *candana*]

san·daled (san′dəld), *adj.* wearing sandals.

san·dalled (san′dəld), *adj. Especially British.* sandaled.

sandal tree, 1. the white sandalwood tree. **2.** an East Indian evergreen tree of the mahogany family, having edible fruit and a red, close-grained heartwood that takes a fine polish.

san·dal·wood (san′dəl wu̇d′), *n.* **1.** the hard, fragrant, close-grained, yellowish heartwood of any of a group of Asiatic trees, especially the white sandalwood. It is used for carving, making ornamental boxes, fans, etc., and is also burned as incense. **2.** the tree that it comes from. **3.** any of several other trees or their similar wood, especially the red sandalwood, an East Indian tree of the pea family. [< *sandal*[2] + *wood*[1]]

sandalwood oil, a fragrant oil extracted from the heartwood and roots of the sandalwood tree, used in incense and perfumes.

san·da·rac (san′də rak), *n.* **1.** a brittle, pale-yellow, translucent, slightly aromatic resin yielded by the bark of the sandarac tree, used as incense and in making varnish. **2.** the sandarac tree. **3.** red arsenic sulfide; realgar. [< Latin *sandaraca* < Greek *sandarákē*]

sandarac tree, a tree of northwest Africa of the cypress family, whose fragrant, hard wood is much used in building. It is the source of the resin sandarac.

sand·bag (sand′bag′), *n., v.,* **-bagged, -bag·ging.** —*n.* **1.** a bag filled with sand: *Sandbags are used to protect trenches and as ballast on a balloon.* **2.** a small bag of sand used as a club.
—*v.t.* **1.** to furnish with sandbags: *There was no flood here; nothing had been damaged; no one was sandbagging streets or houses* (Harper's). **2.** to hit or stun with or as if with a sandbag: *to be sandbagged by creditors, sandbagging tactics.*

sand·bag·ger (sand′bag′ər), *n.* **1.** a person who uses a sandbag, especially a robber who uses a sandbag to stun his victims. **2.** a sailboat that uses sandbags as ballast.

sand·bank (sand′bangk′), *n.* a ridge of sand in a sea or a river: *But many ships have foundered and lives have been lost on what must be one of the best known sandbanks in the world* (New Scientist).

sand bar, a ridge of sand formed at the mouth of a river or harbor, or along beaches, by the action of tides or currents: *Many heavily-laden streams deposit sand bars in their channels thus making their courses shallower and rendering them more likely to flood their valleys* (White and Renner).

sand bath, 1. a receptacle containing hot sand, in which a chemical retort or the like is heated. **2.** a therapeutic treatment in which the body is covered with warm sand. **3.** the shaking of the body and feathers in sand or dry dirt, a method by which birds clean and rid themselves of lice, etc.

sand belt, 1. a belt coated with sand or other abrasives, used in wood-polishing, surfacing, and finishing machines. **2.** an arid ridge of sand, often extending many miles.

sand binder, any plant which serves to bind or fix shifting sands.

sand·blast (sand′blast′, -bläst′), *n.* **1.** a blast of air or steam containing sand, used to clean, grind, cut, or decorate hard surfaces, such as glass, stone, or metal. **2.** the apparatus used to apply such a blast: *A sandblast is often used in cleaning the outside of buildings faced with stone.* —*v.t., v.i.* to use a sandblast on; clean, grind, cut, or decorate by a sandblast: *The accumulated grime was removed by sandblasting* (New York Times).

sand·blast·er (sand′blas′tər), *n.* **1.** a person who sandblasts. **2.** an apparatus that sandblasts: *. . . the hiss of the sandblaster, and the deep chorus of horns coming up from the streets in early morning* (Theodore Roethke).

sand-blind (sand′blīnd′), *adj. Archaic.* half-blind; dim-sighted; purblind. [perhaps alteration of unrecorded Old English *sam-blind* < *sām-* part, half + *blind* blind] —**sand′-blind′ness,** *n.*

sand·box (sand′boks′), *n.* **1.** a box for holding sand, especially for children to play in. **2.** a place in a locomotive to hold sand for use when the wheels slip. **3.** the sandbox tree.

sandbox tree, a tropical American tree of the spurge family, whose fruit (a woody capsule) bursts with a sharp report when ripe and dry, scattering the seeds: *The author . . . enlivens her general information with such specific details as how . . . the South American sandbox tree is supposed to call monkeys to dinner* (New Yorker).

sand·boy (sand′boi′), *n. British Informal.* **as happy (jolly, merry,** etc.) **as a sandboy,** completely happy; very glad or cheerful: "*Happy as a sandboy" about my deposit account* (London Times).

sand·bur or **sand·burr** (sand′bėr′), *n.* any of various weeds growing in sandy or waste places and bearing a small, burlike fruit.

sand-cast (sand′kast′, -käst′), *v.t., v.i.* to cast (metal) by pouring it in a sand mold.

sand-cast·ing (sand′kas′ting, -käs′-), *n.* the process of making a casting by pouring metal in a sand mold.

sand cherry, a shrub bearing small, bitter, black cherries, that grows on the sand dunes of the Great Lakes and in sandy areas elsewhere in the Middle West and Canada.

sand clock, a sandglass: *One child turned over the sand clock, another struck the ship's bell* (New Scientist).

sand cone, a low, conical projection of glacial ice the rapid melting of which is prevented by a covering of sand.

sand crab, any of a group of terrestrial American crabs living in burrows high up on sandy beaches; beach crab: *They are so common on some beaches that a sunbather stretching out on the sand must be careful or he might receive a pinch which informs him of the sand crab beneath him* (A.M. Winchester).

sand crack, a disease that causes cracks in the wall of a horse's hoof, often resulting in lameness.

sand·cul·ture (sand′kul′chər), *n.* a method of growing plants in wet sand, nutrients and moisture being supplied by means of regular feeding with a weak solution of the necessary chemicals.

sand dab, a flatfish.

san·dek (sän′dek), *n.* the person who holds a Jewish infant during the ceremony of circumcision and acts the part of a godfather. [< Yiddish *sandik* < Hebrew *sandiqōs*]

sand dollar, any of certain small, flat, round echinoderms related to the sea urchins, found on sandy bottoms of the Atlantic Ocean along the eastern coast of North America: *Heart urchins and sand dollars, lying in saturated sand, keep on sorting out bits of food* (New Yorker). [because its shape resembles that of a silver dollar]

sand dune, a dune: *sand dunes of the Great Lakes.*

sand·ed (san′did), *adj.* **1.** covered or sprinkled with sand: *a sanded floor.* **2.** adulterated with sand: *sanded sugar.* **3.** *Obsolete.* of a sandy color.

sand eel, sand launce: *Launce, or sand eels, dart through the shallow water seeking copepods* (New Yorker).

sand·er (san′dər), *n.* **1.** a person or apparatus that sands: *a road sander.* **2.** a person or apparatus that sandpapers: *a floor sander.*

sand·er·ling (san′dər ling), *n.* a small, gray and white shore bird of worldwide distribution, which follows the retreating waves along beaches in search of food.

sand·fish (sand′fish′), *n., pl.* **-fish·es** or (*collectively*) **-fish. 1.** any of a small family of scaleless fish of the northern Pacific with oddly fringed lips. They commonly bury themselves in the ocean bottom with only their head exposed. **2.** a small edible sea bass of Atlantic waters with a striped gray or tan body.

sand flea, 1. any flea found in sandy places. **2.** the chigoe. **3.** a beach flea or sand hopper: *The sand flea is really a shellfish, ⅛-inch long, and resembles a tiny lobster* (World Book Annual).

sand fly, 1. any of certain small, blood-sucking, dipteran flies that transmit certain diseases, such as kala-azar. **2.** any of certain similar flies.

sand·glass (sand′glas′, -gläs′), *n.* a device for measuring time by the flow of sand from one glass enclosure to another, especially an hourglass.

sand grass, any grass that grows on sandy soil, as by the seashore.

sand-grop·er (sand′grō′pər), *n. Australian Slang.* a native of Western Australia. [< *sand* + *groper* (because the original settlers were gold prospectors)]

sand grouse, any of a family of birds, similar to a pigeon, found in sandy regions of southern Europe, western Asia, and northern Africa.

san·dhi (san′dē, sän′-), *n.* the changes or differences in speech sounds, stress, or juncture that may occur when a word or phrase is used as part of a construction rather than spoken independently. The assimilation of sounds in the constructions *I'm ready, He's got it,* and *That'll do* are examples of sandhi. [< Sanskrit *saṁdhi* a placing together]

sandhi form, *Phonetics.* the form of a word or phrase used within a construction when it differs from the form used independently. The sentence *It's raining* has the sandhi form *'s* rather than the absolute form *is.*

sand hill, a hill or bank of sand; dune.

sand·hill crane (sand′hil′), a crane of North America with gray plumage and a bare, red forehead, that stands about four feet tall.

sand·hog (sand′hog′, -hôg′), *n. U.S.* a man who works under air pressure much higher than that of the atmosphere either underground, as in a boring for a tunnel, or underwater, as in a caisson: *Sandhogs working near the site of the leak had knocked off for lunch minutes earlier, so nobody was hurt* (Wall Street Journal).

sand hopper, a small crustacean found along beaches; beach flea: *The sand hopper, or beach flea, also appears to be passing through one of those dramatic moments of evolution in which a creature abandons an old way of life for a new* (New Yorker).

sand·i·ness (san′dē nis), *n.* sandy character: *the sandiness of the soil.*

san·di·ver (san′də vər), *n.* a scum that rises upon melted glass in the furnace. [Middle English *sandyver* < Old French *suin de verre; suin* suint, *de* of, *verre* glass]

S & L, Savings and Loan (Association): *Gibraltar S & L raises its savings rate to 5* (Wall Street Journal).

sand launce or **lance,** any of various small, elongate, marine fishes which burrow into the sand along beaches when the tide goes out; sand eel. [< *sand* + *launce,* variant of *lance* (because of its shape)]

sand leaf, one of the lowest, poor leaves on a tobacco plant, small and often sandy.

sand lily, a low, stemless, white-flowered plant of the lily family, found in the western United States.

sand·ling (sand′ling), *n.* a sanderling.

sand lizard, a common European lizard found in sandy areas: *A white mouse lost ten times as much water as a desert-dwelling sand lizard kept under the same conditions* (New Scientist).

sand·lot (sand′lot′), *adj. U.S.* of or having to do with games, especially baseball, played between informally organized teams of boys or men on undeveloped city lots, small fields, etc.: *Chicago's Mayor Richard J. Daley, a sandlot baseball second baseman during his spare time . . .* (Newsweek).

sand·lot·ter (sand′lot′ər), *n. U.S.* a boy who plays sandlot baseball, football, etc.: *Many major league ballplayers have grown up from sandlotters.*

sand·man (sand′man′), *n.* the fabled man who is supposed to make children sleepy by sprinkling sand on their eyes. [< *sand* + *man.* Compare German *Sandmann.*]

sand martin, the bank swallow.

sand mole, 1. a large South African mole rat that burrows in the sand. **2.** a smaller related species of South Africa, very troublesome in gardens.

sand painting, a design made by pouring various colored sands, powdered rock, charcoal, etc., on a flat, sandy surface. Sand paintings are used by some American Indian tribes in healing ceremonies and other rituals: *Taken together, the Navaho sand paintings are symbolic of an enormously complex myth cycle, recounting the creation of the universe, the preparation of the world for habitation by man, and the origins of most rituals and ceremonies* (Beals and Hoijer).

sand·pa·per (sand′pā′pər), *n.* a heavy paper having a gritty, abrasive substance such as silicon carbide or aluminum oxide glued on one side, used for smoothing, cleaning, or polishing, especially wood: *Today the word "sandpaper" is a misnomer; no sand is involved* (Wall Street Journal). —*v.t.* to rub (wood, metal, etc.) with sandpaper in order to smooth, clean, or polish.

sand·pa·per·y (sand′pā′pər ē), *adj.* like sandpaper; rough; grating: *Mr. John Reed's sandpapery tones and aptitude on the stage made him a Ko-Ko in the true . . . tradition* (London Times).

sand pear, a variety of pear native to China, with rough, gritty fruit.

sand pine, a small pine growing in sandy areas of Florida west to Alabama.

sand·pip·er (sand′pī′pər), *n.* any of various small, long-billed shore birds related to the plovers, as the common sandpiper of Europe, and the spotted sandpiper of North America.

Spotted Sandpiper (about 7 in. long)

sand·pit (sand′pit′), *n.* **1.** a pit from which sand is excavated: *I stood on the rim of a great saucer-shaped sandpit the other day* (Manchester Guardian Weekly). **2.** *British.* a sandbox for children: *She said swings were no longer enough, and regretted that in Birmingham water and sandpits were not allowed* (London Times).

sand plain, a small sandy plain, usually a flat-topped hill originally formed as a delta by water running out of a glacier.

sand·plov·er (sand′pluv′ər, -plō′vər), *n., pl.* **-ers** or (*collectively*) **-er.** a ringed plover or ringneck that frequents sandy beaches: *Sandplovers were breeding 2,000 miles outside their known range* (London Times).

sand rat, 1. a pocket gopher found in sandy areas on the western coast of North America. **2.** any of several rodents found in sandy areas, as the gerbil.

sand reef, a strip of low, sandy land, or barrier beach, built by the action of waves on a shallow sea floor not far from the coast and often enclosing a narrow lagoon.

sand ripple, alternate ridge and hollow formed in sand through the influence of waves, wind, or currents.

sands (sandz), *n.pl.* See under **sand,** *n.*

S. and s.c., sized and supercalendered.

sand sea, a large stretch of desert consisting of barchans: *A sand sea, with small crescentic dunes* [*that*] *migrate as entities across the desert floor* (Robert M. Garrels).

sand shark, a variety of shark common along the Atlantic Coast, which attains a length of almost eleven feet but is not known to attack humans.

sand·spit (sand′spit′), *n.* a low, sandy area jutting out into a lake or sea: *Many Northerners maintain palatial winter homes on this sand-spit 70 miles north of Miami Beach* (Wall Street Journal).

sand·spout (sand′spout′), *n.* a pillar of sand similar to a waterspout, produced by a whirlwind, as on a desert.

sand star, 1. a starfish. **2.** an ophiuran.

sand·stone (sand′stōn′), *n.* a sedimentary rock formed by the consolidation of sand, the grains being held together by a cement of silica or the like: *They used stone that lent itself to fine workmanship—chert, quartzite and a fine-grained sandstone* (Scientific American).

sand·storm (sand′stôrm′), *n.* a storm of wind that bears along clouds of sand: *The latest explosion had come in Jordan with the suddenness of a desert sandstorm* (Newsweek).

sand sucker, 1. a pump that removes wet sand, silt, or mud from an area: *Both expeditions made feverish plans to go after the copper lode with sand suckers and . . . power shovels* (Newsweek). **2.** a flatfish; sand dab.

sand table, a table with a rim, on which sand is spread for children's play or for modeling terrain for military study, etc.: *At three or four, the children go to a preprimary school, where they learn to run, hop, skip, play at sand tables, and even fingerpaint* (Time).

sand trap, a shallow pit filled with sand on a golf course, usually near a green, and serving as a hazard: *Great Britain's Prime Minister Harold Macmillan* (*in the low 80s*) *. . . can be reduced to hopeless and despairing silence when three tries fail to get him out of a sand trap* (Newsweek). *The ninth hole, a par four right by the clubhouse, continued to be a psychological sand trap worse than the course's 130 real ones* (Time).

sand tube, a tube of fused or sintered sand which has been melted together along the path of a stroke of lightning.

sand verbena, any of a group of low herbs of the four-o'clock family with verbenalike flowers, found in the western United States.

sand·vine (sand′vīn′), *n.* a vine of the milkweed family growing in the southeastern United States, having deeply cordate, ovate leaves, small whitish flowers in axillary cymes, and large follicles.

sand viper, 1. a hognose (snake). **2.** a horned viper.

sand wasp, a solitary wasp that nests in the sand.

sand wedge, a special golf club used for hitting out of sand traps: *He pulled out his sand wedge, swung—and blasted the ball straight into the cup* (Time).

sand·wich (sand′wich), *n.* **1.** two or more slices of bread with meat, jelly, cheese, or some other filling between them. **2.** something formed by similar arrangement: *When used as the outer leaf of an insulating sandwich, it provides a membrane which gives fairly good control of light and heat* (Scientific American).
—*v.t.* **1.** to put in (between): *to be sandwiched between two parked cars.* [*He*] *also lived in Paris from around 1924 to 1927, but . . . this visit was sandwiched between visits to his native Japan* (New Yorker). **2.** to put in a sandwich.
[< John Montagu, the fourth Earl of *Sandwich,* 1718-1792, supposedly the inventor]

sandwich board, a board carried by a sandwich man: [*One caricature*] *showed Hall Caine, with frenzied eyes and hair, bearing a sandwich board on which his name was inscribed in lavish capitals* (New Yorker).

sandwich course, *British.* a course in an industrial school that combines classroom study with practical experience in factories: *"Sandwich" courses—alternate periods of industrial and academic study—are being run in co-operation with technical colleges* (Punch).

Sandwich glass, glassware manufactured by the Boston and Sandwich Glass Company at Sandwich, Massachusetts, from 1825 to 1888. Sandwich glass often has elaborate designs to give a complex, lacelike effect.

sandwich man, a man carrying two advertising boards hung from his shoulders, one before him and one behind: *Walking on rosy clouds, he passed a sandwich man who handed him an advertising circular* (Time).

sandwich panel, a panel used in construction, made by bonding together several layers of material, as aluminum, steel, or plastic, so that one layer is sandwiched between two other layers: *Built of aluminum sandwich panels, it would weigh about half as much as a comparable conventional car* (Wall Street Journal).

sand·worm (sand′wėrm′), *n.* a lugworm: *Two Puerto Rican boys . . . were baiting fishhooks with sandworms in the hope of catching eels* (New Yorker).

sand·wort (sand′wėrt′), *n.* any of a group of low, scrubby herbs of the pink family most common in sandy soil, and bearing very small, white flowers.

sand·y (san′dē), *adj.,* **sand·i·er, sand·i·est. 1.** containing sand; consisting of sand; covered with sand: *Most of the shore is rocky, but there is a sandy beach.* **2. a.** yellowish-red: *sandy hair.* **b.** having such hair: *The ladies Fitz-Warene were sandy girls* (Benjamin Disraeli). **3.** shifting like sand; not stable: *But mark how sandy is your own pretence* (John Dryden).

sane (sān), *adj.,* **san·er, san·est. 1. a.** having a healthy mind; not crazy: *Their doctrine could be held by no sane man* (Robert Browning). **b.** not diseased or disordered: *a sane mind. The activity of sane minds in healthful bodies . . .* (Samuel Taylor Coleridge). **2. a.** having or showing good sense or sound judgment; sensible: *sane and equitable historic verdicts* (John Morley). **b.** regulated by reason; rational: *It is the American woman who is primarily responsible for the safe and sane Fourth* [*of July*] (Edward Bok). [< Latin *sānus* healthy] —**sane′ly,** *adv.* —**sane′ness,** *n.* —**Syn. 1.** sound.

SANE (sān), *n.* National Committee for a Sane Nuclear Policy.

San·for·ize (san′fə rīz), *v.t.,* **-ized, -iz·ing.** *Trademark.* to shrink (cotton, linen, or rayon fabric) by a patented process before it is made into a garment, that is then guaranteed a maximum shrinkage of one per cent. [American English < *Sanfor*(d) L. Cluett, born 1874, the inventor + *-ize*]

San Fran·cis·can (san′ fran sis′kən), a native or inhabitant of San Francisco, California.

sang (sang), *v.* the past tense of **sing.**

san·gar (sung′gər), *n.* a breastwork of stone. Also, **sungar.** [< Hindustani *saṅgar*]

san·ga·ree (sang′gə rē′), *n.* a tropical drink consisting of wine (usually red), water, sugar, spice, and sometimes brandy. [< Spanish *sangría* (literally) bleeding (because of its color) < *sangre* blood < Latin *sanguīs*]

säng·er·bund (zeng′ər bůnt), *n.* a German male singing society. [< German *Sängerbund* < *Sänger* (literally) singers + *Bund* group, federation]

säng·er·fest (zeng′ər fest), *n.* a German song festival, especially a gathering of German singing societies for competition: *The town's newest, and just about its best, triad, are half in earnest, half in fun during their up-tempo sängerfest* (New Yorker). [< German *Sängerfest* < *Sänger* (literally) singers + *Fest* festival, festivities]

sang-froid (säNfrwä′), *n.* coolness of mind; calmness; composure: *The Canadian bush pilots, on the other hand, tended to call it "pretty much routine, so long as you look where you are going"—a view which may be an overemphasis of their professional sang-froid* (Harper's). [< French *sang froid* (literally) cold blood, ultimately < Latin *sanguīs* blood, *frīgidus* frigid] —**Syn.** equanimity, imperturbability.

san·gha (sang′gə), *n.* the Buddhist monastic community; Buddhist monks and nuns collectively: *. . . the hundred thousand monks who wear the saffron robe of the Buddhist sangha* (Atlantic). [< Sanskrit *saṅgha*]

San·graal (sang grāl′), *n.* the Holy Grail. [< Old French *Saint Graal; Saint* holy (see SAINT), *Graal* Grail]

San·gre·al (sang′grē əl), *n.* the Holy Grail.

san·gri·a (sang grē′ə), *n.* a Spanish drink made of red or white wine mixed with fruit juice and club soda: *Along with the flamenco comes sangria* (Atlantic). [< Spanish *sangría* < *sangre* blood]

san·guic·o·lous (sang gwik′ə ləs), *adj.* inhabiting the blood, as a parasite. [< Latin *sanguīs* blood + *colere* inhabit + English *-ous*]

san·guif·er·ous (sang gwif′ər əs), *adj.* bearing or conveying blood, as a vein. [< Latin *sanguis* blood + English *-ferous*]

san·gui·fi·ca·tion (sang′gwə fə kā′shən), *n.* the production of blood.

san·gui·mo·tor (sang′gwə mō′tər), *adj.* of or having to do with the circulation of the blood. [< Latin *sanguis* blood + *mōtor* mover]

san·gui·nar·i·a (sang′gwə nãr′ē ə), *n.* **1.** the bloodroot, a plant with a red root, red sap, and a white flower that blooms in the spring. **2.** its rhizome, used in medicine as a stimulant, expectorant, and emetic. [American English < New Latin *sanguinaria* (because of its color) < Latin (*herba*) *sanguināria,* (originally) a kind of plant, probably polygonum; (literally) (herb) for stanching blood < *sanguīs, -inis* blood]

san·gui·nar·i·ly (sang′gwə ner′ə lē), *adv.* in a sanguinary manner; bloodthirstily.

san·guin·a·rine (sang gwin′ə rēn), *n.* an alkaloid obtained from the roots of the sanguinaria. *Formula:* $C_{20}H_{15}NO_5$

san·gui·nar·i·ness (sang′gwə ner′ē nis), *n.* sanguinary quality; bloodthirsty disposition.

san·gui·nar·y (sang′gwə ner′ē), *adj.* **1.** with much blood or bloodshed; bloody: *a sanguinary battle. We may not propagate Religion by wars or by sanguinary persecutions to force consciences* (Francis Bacon). **2.** delighting in bloodshed; bloodthirsty: *The sanguinary and ferocious conversation of his captor — the list of slain that his arm had sent to their long account . . . made him tremble* (G. P. R. James). **3.** imposing the death penalty freely: *sanguinary laws.* **4.** of blood. [< Latin *sanguinārius* < *sanguīs, -inis* blood]

san·guine (sang′gwin), *adj.* **1.** naturally cheerful and hopeful: *a sanguine disposition. The invincible hopefulness of his sanguine temperament had now got Mr. Britling well out of the pessimistic pit again* (H. G. Wells). **2.** confident; hopeful: *sanguine of success. I was not too sanguine of seeing an epic when I took my seat in the Garden on the night of the fight* (New Yorker). **3.** having a healthy red color; ruddy: *a sanguine complexion.* **4.** (in ancient and medieval physiology) having blood as the predominant humor, indicated by a ruddy complexion and a cheerful and ardent disposition. **5.** sanguinary: *All gaunt and sanguine beasts her gentle looks made tame* (Shelley).
—*n.* **1.** *Heraldry.* the blood-red color in coats of arms, in engravings represented by intersecting diagonal lines; murrey. **2. a.** a crayon colored red with iron oxide. **b.** a drawing executed with red chalks.
[< Middle French *sanguin,* learned borrowing from *sanguineus* < *sanguīs, -inis* blood]
—**san′guine·ly,** *adv.* —**san′guine·ness,** *n.*
—**Syn.** *adj.* **1, 2.** optimistic.

san·guin·e·ous (sang gwin′ē əs), *adj.* **1.** of blood; containing blood; bloody. **2.** red like blood. **3.** abounding with blood; full-blooded. **4.** sanguine; hopeful. **5.** bloodthirsty; sanguinary: *His passion, cruel grown, took on a hue fierce and sanguineous* (Keats).

san·guin·i·ty (sang gwin′ə tē), *n.* **1.** the quality of being sanguine: *But I distrust your sanguinity* (Jonathan Swift). **2.** consanguinity: *In the determination of adoption orders, . . . such considerations may [be] . . . subordinated to a theory of sanguinity* (London Times).

san·guin·o·lent (sang gwin′ə lənt), *adj.* bloody. [< Middle French *sanguinolent,* learned borrowing from Latin *sanguinolentus* < *sanguīs, -inis* blood + *-olentus* full of]

san·guiv·o·rous (sang gwiv′ər əs), *adj.* feeding on blood. [< Latin *sanguīs* blood + Latin *vorāre* to devour + English *-ous*]

San·he·drim (san′hi drim), *n.* Sanhedrin.

San·he·drin (san′hi drin), *n.* **1.** Also, **Great Sanhedrin.** the supreme council and highest religious and legal authority of the ancient Jewish nation, consisting of 70 members. **2.** a lower court of justice, of 23 members, with lesser or local jurisdiction. [< Hebrew *sanhedrīn* < Greek *synédrion* council, (literally) a sitting together < *syn-* together + *hédra* a seat]

san·i·cle (san′ə kəl), *n.* any of a group of herbs of the parsley family, once credited with great medicinal value; selfheal. [< Old French *sanicle,* learned borrowing from Medieval Latin *sanicula,* perhaps < Latin *sānus* healthy]

san·i·dine (san′ə dēn), *n.* a glassy form of orthoclase occurring in volcanic rocks. [< Greek *sanís, -idos* plank + English *-in* (because of its flat crystals)]

sa·ni·es (sā′nē ēz), *n.* a thin, greenish fluid containing pus mixed with serum or blood, discharged from ulcers, wounds, etc. [< Latin *saniēs* diseased blood]

san·i·fi·ca·tion (san′ə fə kā′shən), *n.* the process of rendering sanitary; the putting and keeping (something) in a sanitary condition.

san·i·fy (san′ə fī), *v.t.,* **-fied, -fy·ing.** to make healthy; improve the sanitary conditions of (a city, etc.). [< Latin *sānus* healthy + English *-fy*]

sa·ni·ous (sā′nē əs), *adj.* of, consisting of, or discharging sanies. [< Latin *saniōsus* < *saniēs* sanies]

san·i·tar·i·an (san′ə tãr′ē ən), *n.* a person who studies sanitation or favors sanitary reform. —*adj.* sanitary.

san·i·tar·i·ly (san′ə ter′ə lē), *adv.* as regards health or its preservation.

san·i·tar·i·ness (san′ə ter′ē nis), *n.* the state or condition of being sanitary.

san·i·tar·i·um (san′ə tãr′ē əm), *n., pl.* **-i·ums, -i·a** (-ē ə). **1.** an establishment for treatment of the sick or convalescent, especially those suffering from a long, slow disease like tuberculosis: *Once these were the houses of the rich; today they are sanitaria for the proletariat* (John Gunther). **2.** a health resort. Also, **sanatorium.** [< Latin *sānitas* health (< *sānus* healthy) + *-ārium* place for]

san·i·tar·y (san′ə ter′ē), *adj., n., pl.* **-tar·ies.** —*adj.* **1. a.** of or having to do with the conditions affecting health: *sanitary regulations, to improve the sanitary conditions of slums.* **b.** favorable to health; preventing disease; healthful. **2.** free from dirt and filth: *Food should be kept in a sanitary place.* —*n.* a public toilet or urinal. [< French *sanitaire* < Latin *sānitās* (< *sānus* healthy) + French *-aire* -ary] —**Syn.** *adj.* **1.** hygienic.

sanitary cordon, cordon sanitaire.

sanitary napkin, a soft, absorbent pad used to absorb the uterine discharge during menstruation.

sanitary ware, coarse glazed earthenware used for drainage, sewer pipes, and lavatory fittings.

san·i·tate (san′ə tāt), *v.,* **-tat·ed, -tat·ing.** —*v.t.* to subject to sanitation; make sanitary: *It seems incomprehensible that man can progress very far in sanitating the lowlands against malaria because of the staggering cost* (White and Renner). —*v.i.* to introduce sanitation. [back formation < *sanitation*]

san·i·ta·tion (san′ə tā′shən), *n.* the working out and practical application of sanitary measures: *When people gathered together and built large cities, many problems were raised concerning a proper water supply, a safe food supply, disposal of garbage and human wastes, keeping the city clean, and preventing the spread of disease. Most of these problems are related to sanitation* (Beauchamp, Mayfield, and West). [< *sanit*(ary) + *-ation*]

san·i·tize (san′ə tīz), *v.t.,* **-tized, -tiz·ing.** to make sanitary; disinfect: *The unit is intended to keep the water well above 145 degrees, "the lowest temperature at which clothes still could be sanitized"* (Newsweek).

san·i·tiz·er (san′ə tī′zər), *n.* a sanitizing substance or product: *We are also concerned with the hygiene of the operators and machinery in the factory, and we test manufacturers' claims for sanitizers* (New Scientist).

san·i·ty (san′ə tē), *n.* **1.** soundness of mind; mental health. **2.** soundness of judgment; sensibleness; reasonableness. [< Latin *sānitās* < *sānus* healthy]

san·jak (san′jak), *n.* a former Turkish administrative district, a subdivision of a vilayet. [< Turkish *sancak* (literally) flag]

San Jo·se scale (san hō zā′), a scale insect very injurious to fruit trees, first discovered in the United States at San Jose, California.

sank (sangk), *v.* the past tense of **sink:** *The ship sank before help reached her.*

San·khya (säng′kyə), *n.* one of the six principal systems of Hindu philosophy, based on the dualism of spirit and matter, with the latter deriving from the former. [< Sanskrit *sāṁkhya*]

san·nup (san′up), *n.* (among North American Indians) a married man. [American English < Algonkian (Penobscot, Passamaquoddy) *sanaⁿba, seenaⁿbe* man]

sans (sanz; *French* säɴ), *prep.* without: . . . *sans teeth, sans eyes, sans taste, sans everything* (Shakespeare). [< Old French *sans* < Latin *absentiā,* ablative, in the absence (of) < *abesse* to be away; Old French influenced by Latin *sine* without]

Sans., Sanskrit.

san·sa (san′sə), *n.* an African musical instrument consisting of a wooden box having at the top tongues of bamboo or iron which the performer vibrates with his thumbs. [< Arabic *ṣinj* cymbals]

San·scrit (san′skrit), *n.* Sanskrit.

sans-cu·lotte (sanz′kyů lot′), *n.* **1.** (in the French Revolution) a contemptuous term for a republican of the poorer classes in Paris, adopted by the revolutionists as a designation of honor. **2.** any extreme republican or revolutionary: *The scientists of today . . . are the sans-culottes of a second scientific revolution in which the prime methods of the laboratory are being conquered by a new and more thoroughgoing empiricism* (Scientific American).
[< French *sansculotte* (literally) without knee breeches (because the republicans substituted pantaloons for knee breeches); *sans* without, *culotte* knee breeches. Compare CULOTTES.]

sans-cu·lot·te·rie (sanz′kyů lot′ə rē), *n.* sansculottism: *You will then be arrested on a charge of lèse-majesté with overtones of sansculotterie* (Punch).

sans-cu·lot·tic (sanz′kyů lot′ik), *adj.* of the sans-culottes or sans-culottism.

sans-cu·lot·tid (sanz′kyů lot′id), *n.* sans-culottide.

sans-cu·lot·tide (sanz′kyə lot′id; *French* säɴkü lô tēd′), *n.* (in the French Revolutionary calendar) one of the 5 (in leap year 6) complementary days resulting from the division of the year into 12 months of 30 days each. They were added as festival days at the end of the month Fructidor. [< French *sans-culottide* < *sans-culotte* sansculotte]

sans-cu·lot·tish (sanz′kyů lot′ish), *adj.* sans-culottic.

sans-cu·lot·tism (sanz′kyů lot′iz əm), *n.* the principles or practices of sans-culottes.

sans doute (säɴ düt′), *French.* without doubt; beyond question.

San·sei or **san·sei** (sän′sā′), *n., pl.* **-sei** or **-seis.** an American citizen whose grandparents were Japanese immigrants: *The Nisei and their Sansei children have rapidly adopted American ways of life* (World Book Encyclopedia). [< Japanese *san* third + *sei* generation]

san·se·vie·ri·a (san′sə vir′ē ə), *n.* any of a group of Asiatic and African herbs of the agave family, various species of which are grown for their mottled, sword-shaped leaves; bowstring hemp. [< New Latin *Sansevieria* the genus name < the Prince of *Sanseviero,* 1710-1771, an Italian patron of learning]

sans gêne (säɴ zhen′), *French.* without constraint or embarrassment; without ceremony; free and easy: . . . *a love affair with a beautiful waif who is also decidedly sans gêne* (Atlantic).

Sansk., Sanskrit.

San·skrit (san′skrit), *n.* **1.** the ancient sacred and literary language of India, of importance in the study of Indo-European: *Sanskrit is of great interest to linguists because of the . . . stimulus which the introduction of Sanskrit to Western scholarship gave to the development of modern linguistic science* (H. A. Gleason, Jr.). **2.** the classical literary form of this language, as distinguished from the earlier Vedic. Also, **Sanscrit.** [< Sanskrit *saṃskṛta* prepared, cultivated (applied to the literary language as contrasted with the vernacular language). Compare PRAKRIT.]

A B C D

अ ब च ड

Sanskrit Characters (def. 1) equivalent to the first 4 letters of our alphabet

San·skrit·ic (san skrit′ik), *adj.* relating to, or derived from, Sanskrit.

San·skrit·ist (san′skrit ist), *n.* an expert in Sanskrit language or literature.

San·skrit·i·za·tion (san′skrit ə zā′shən), *n.* **1. a.** the act or process of Sanskritizing. **b.** the fact or result of being Sanskritized. **2.** (in India) the adoption of the customs, attitudes, and status symbols of an upper caste by a caste below it: *There is still a hierarchy, but castes can make their way upward within it by . . . Sanskritization* (London Times).

San·skrit·ize (san′skrit īz), *v.t.,* **-ized, -iz·ing.** **1.** to translate into Sanskrit. **2.** to render similar to Sanskrit; modify by Sanskritic influences.

sans pa·reil (säɴ pá re′yə), *French.* **1.** unequaled. **2.** (literally) without equal.

sans peur et sans re·proche (säɴ pœr′ ā säɴ rə prôsh′), *French.* without fear and without reproach; fearless and blameless.

sans-ser·if (sanz′ser′if), *n. Printing.* any of various styles of type without serifs: *The type was a very readable sans-serif, all upper case* (Atlantic). [< French *sans* without (< Old French; see SANS) + English *serif*]

sans sou·ci (säN sü sē′), *French.* without care or worry.

San·ta[1] (san′tə), *n.* Santa Claus. [American English, short for *Santa Claus*]

San·ta[2] (san′tə, sän′tä), *adj.* a Spanish or an Italian word meaning *holy* or *saint,* used in combinations, as in *Santa Maria, Santa Lucia.* [< Spanish, or Italian *santa,* feminine of *santo* < Latin *sānctus* holy. Compare SAINT, adjective.]

San·ta An·a (san′tə an′ə), a strong, hot, dry wind occurring in southern California usually in the winter: *Santa Anas are not strangers to the Los Angeles area* (Time). [< *Santa Ana,* a city and mountain range in southern California]

San·ta Claus (san′tə klôz′), Saint Nicholas, the saint of Christmas giving, according to modern conception a jolly old man with a white beard, dressed in a fur-trimmed red suit. [American English < dialectal Dutch *Sante Klaas* Saint Nicholas]

San·ta Fe·an (san′tə fā′ən), a native or inhabitant of Santa Fe, New Mexico: *Santa Feans can still proudly point to the nearby 1610 Palace of the Governors, the oldest capitol in the U.S.* (Time).

San·ta Ger·tru·dis (san′tə gėr trü′dis), a breed of cattle developed in the United States, that is a cross between a shorthorn and a brahma. It is able to withstand the humid heat of the South and Southwest. *Santa Gertrudis cattle are a deep cherry red, a color that is supposed to discourage flies and other stinging insects* (New Yorker).

san·tal (san′təl), *n.* sandalwood. [< Middle French *santal* < Medieval Latin *santalum,* variant of *sandalum.* Related to SANDAL[2].]

san·ta·la·ceous (san′tə lā′shəs), *adj.* belonging to a family of dicotyledonous plants typified by the sandalwood. [< New Latin *Santalaceae* the family name (< Medieval Latin *santalum,* variant of *sandalum;* see SANDAL[2]) + English *-ous*]

San·ta·li (sun tä′lē), *n.* a Munda language of central India.

san·ta·lin (san′tə lin), *n. Chemistry.* the coloring matter of red sandalwood, that forms minute red crystals. *Formula:* $C_{15}H_{14}O_5$ [< French *santaline* < Middle French *santal* santal]

San·ta Ma·ri·a (san′tə mə rē′ə), the flagship of Columbus on his voyage of 1492.

san·tir (sän tir′, san-; sän′tir), *n.* a kind of dulcimer of the Arabs and Persians. [< Arabic *santīr,* Persian *sāntūr,* alteration of Greek *psaltērion*]

San·to·brite (san′tə brīt), *n. Trademark.* a sodium salt used for the eradication of algae, slime, etc. *Formula:* C_6Cl_5ONa

san·tol (sän tōl′), *n.* an evergreen tree of the mahogany family, having axillary panicles of small sweet-scented flowers, and bearing a fleshy, acid fruit eaten especially in preserves. [< Tagalog *santól*]

san·to·li·na (san′tō lē′nə), *n.* a fragrant shrub, related to the camomile, that grows in the Mediterranean region: *A thick hedge of green santolina is on each side of the planting* (New York Times). [< Italian *santolina* < Latin *sānctus* holy + *līnum* flax]

san·ton[1] (san′tən), *n.* a Moslem holy man or ascetic; marabout: *He was* (*say the Arabian historians*) *one of those . . . santons, who pass their lives in hermitages, in fasting, meditation, and prayer, until they attain to the purity of saints and the foresight of prophets* (Washington Irving). [< French *santon* < Spanish *santón* (augmentative) holy man < *santo* saint; see SANTA[2]]

san·ton[2] (säN tôN′), *n.* a clay figurine of a religious nature, usually associated with the nativity scene, made in southern France: *Pierre . . . longed to enter the contest for shaping clay into santons . . . but his uncle wouldn't hear of it* (Atlantic). [< French *santon* < Provençal *santoun* (diminutive) little saint < *sant* saint < Latin *sānctus* holy; see SAINT]

san·ton·i·ca (san ton′ə kə), *n.* **1.** a European wormwood. **2.** its dried unexpanded flower heads, used as a vermifuge. [< New Latin *santonica* < Latin (*herba*) *santonica* < *Santoni* a Gaulish people in Aquitaine]

san·to·nin or **san·to·nine** (san′tə nin), *n.* a bitter, colorless, crystalline compound, obtained from santonica and used to destroy or expel intestinal worms. *Formula:* $C_{15}H_{18}O_3$ [< *santon*(ica) + *-in.* Compare French *santonine.*]

Saor·stat Eir·eann (sãr′stôt ãr′ən), Irish Free State (so designated in Irish Gaelic). [< Irish *Saorstat Eireann* < *saor* free + *stát* state (< English *state*) + *Eireann* having to do with Erin (Ireland)]

sap[1] (sap), *n., v.,* **sapped, sap·ping.** —*n.* **1.** the vital juice or fluid that is distributed through a plant, consisting of water and dissolved substances which serve to maintain the life and growth of the plant. Rising sap carries dissolved salts from the roots; sap traveling downward carries sugar, gums, resins, etc.: *The trees of the Lord also are full of sap* (English Book of Common Prayer). **2.** any life-giving liquid: *The world's whole sap is sunk* (John Donne). **3.** sapwood. **4.** *Slang.* a silly, stupid person; fool: *He would talk all the way back from school about what a sap she was* (Atlantic).
—*v.t. Obsolete.* to remove the sap from (wood, a tree, etc.).
[Old English *sæp*]

sap[2] (sap), *v.,* **sapped, sap·ping,** *n.* —*v.t.* **1.** to dig under or wear away the foundation of; undermine: *The walls of the boathouse had been sapped by the waves.* **2.** to weaken or destroy insidiously: *The extreme heat sapped our strength. New York's public school system is being harassed and sapped by increasing problems of discipline and delinquency* (New York Times). *Sapping a solemn creed with solemn sneer . . .* (Byron). **3. a.** to approach or undermine (a fortification) by means of protected trenches. **b.** to dig through (ground, an area, etc.) in constructing trenches. —*v.i.* to dig or use covered or protected trenches.
—*n.* **1.** a long, deep trench, protected by the earth dug up; trench dug to approach the enemy position when a besieged place is within range of fire: *They were now pushing forward saps into No Man's Land, linking them across, and so continually creeping nearer to the enemy and a practicable jumping-off place for attack* (H.G. Wells). **2.** the making of trenches to approach a besieged place or an enemy's position.
[< Middle French *sapper* < *sappe* spade, or Italian *zappare* < *zappa* spade, hoe; goat (because of the resemblance of the handle to a goat's horns), perhaps < Late Latin *sappa*]

sap·a·jou (sap′ə jü; *French* sȧ pȧ zhü′), *n.* any of a group of South and Central American monkeys, as the capuchin monkey. [< French *sapajou,* probably < a Tupi word]

Sapajou (including tail, about 40 in. long)

sa·pan·wood (sə pan′wu̇d′), *n.* sappanwood.

sap chafer, any of various beetles that feed on the nectar of flowers or the exuding sap of trees.

sap·head (sap′hed′), *n. Slang.* a silly, stupid person: *You don't seem to know anything, somehow—perfect saphead* (Mark Twain).

sap·head·ed (sap′hed′id), *adj. Slang.* silly; stupid.

sa·phe·na (sə fē′nə), *n., pl.* **-nae** (-nē). either of two large superficial veins of the leg, one extending along the inner side of the leg from the foot to the groin, and the other extending along the outer and posterior side from the foot to the knee. [< Medieval Latin *saphena* < Arabic *aṣ-ṣāfin* the hidden one; perhaps influenced by Greek *saphēnēs* clear (intellectually)]

sa·phe·nous (sə fē′nəs), *adj.* of, designating, or having to do with a saphena.

sa·phir d'eau (sȧ fēr′ dō′), *French.* water sapphire.

sap·id (sap′id), *adj.* **1.** having taste or flavor. **2.** having a pleasant taste or flavor; savory; palatable. **3.** pleasing to the mind or mental taste; agreeable. [< Late Latin *sapidus* savory, tasty < Latin *sapere* (originally) to have a taste]

sa·pid·i·ty (sə pid′ə tē), *n.* sapid quality; tastefulness; savor; relish.

sa·pi·ence (sā′pē əns), *n.* wisdom: *She was timeless, with a beauty that comes with sapience, valiant, artistic, and incredibly vital* (Atlantic).

sa·pi·en·cy (sā′pē ən sē), *n.* sapience.

sa·pi·ens (sā′pē ənz), *adj.* of, resembling, or having to do with modern man or Homo sapiens: *Beginning with the sapiens races of the late Pleistocene, we find well-developed chins* (Beals and Hoijer). [< (Homo) *sapiens*]

sa·pi·ent (sā′pē ənt), *adj.* wise; sage: *Nor bring . . . some doctor . . . To shake his sapient head and give the ill he cannot cure a name . . .* (Matthew Arnold). [< Latin *sapiēns, -entis* present participle of *sapere* be wise; (originally) to have a taste] —**sa′pi·ent·ly,** *adv.*

sa·pi·en·tial (sā′pē en′shəl), *adj.* belonging to or characterized by wisdom. [< Latin *sapientiālis* < *sapiēns;* see SAPIENT]

sap·in·da·ceous (sap′in dā′shəs), *adj.* belonging to the soapberry family of plants. [< New Latin *Sapindaceae* the family name (< *Sapindus* the typical genus < Latin *sāpō, -ōnis* soap + *Indicus* Indian) + English *-ous*]

sap·less (sap′lis), *adj.* **1.** without sap; withered; dry. **2.** without vitality, energy, or the like; insipid; trivial: *Now sapless on the verge of death he stands* (John Dryden).

sap·ling (sap′ling), *n.* **1.** a young tree, especially a young forest tree with a trunk three or four inches in diameter. **2.** a young or inexperienced person.

sap·o·dil·la (sap′ə dil′ə), *n.* **1.** a large evergreen tree of tropical America that yields chicle and bears brownish, rough-skinned, edible berries that look and taste somewhat like pears; mammee; sapota; naseberry. **2.** its fruit. [< Mexican Spanish *zapotilla* (diminutive) < *zapote;* see SAPOTA]

sapodilla family, a group of (chiefly) tropical, dicotyledonous trees and shrubs, with a milky juice. The fruit of certain species, as the sapodilla, star apple, and marmalade tree, is edible; other species are valued for their hard timber; and others yield gutta-percha and gums.

sap·o·na·ceous (sap′ə nā′shəs), *adj.* of the nature of or like soap; soapy. [< Medieval Latin *saponaceus* (with English *-ous*) < Latin *sāpō, -ōnis* soap]

sa·pon·i·fi·a·ble (sə pon′ə fī′ə bəl), *adj.* that can be saponified.

sa·pon·i·fi·ca·tion (sə pon′ə fə kā′shən), *n.* **1.** the act or process of saponifying: *The process for making a Fortisan rayon yarn from an acetate base* (*called saponification by the chemists*) *was perfected by Celanese researchers back in 1937* (Wall Street Journal). **2.** *Chemistry.* **a.** alkaline hydrolysis of any ester to form an alcohol and a salt or acid. **b.** any hydrolysis.

sa·pon·i·fi·er (sə pon′ə fī′ər), *n.* **1.** an apparatus for the manufacture of glycerin and soap by the decomposition of fats and oils. **2.** a substance that produces saponification, as caustic soda or potash.

sa·pon·i·fy (sə pon′ə fī), *v.,* **-fied, -fy·ing.** —*v.t.* **1.** to change (a fat or an oil) into soap by treating with an alkali: *Considerable preliminary concentration can be effected by saponifying the oil, that is by turning the glycerides of fatty acids which constitute the bulk of the oil into soaps, which are sodium salts of the fatty acids* (Science News). **2.** to decompose (an ester of an acid) into an alcohol and a salt of the acid. —*v.i.* to become soap. [< New Latin *sāpōnificāre* < Latin *sāpō, -ōnis* soap + *facere* to make]

sap·o·nin (sap′ə nin), *n.* any of the glucosides obtained from the soapwort, soapbark, soapberry, and many other plants, and forming (in solution) a soapy lather when shaken. The commercial substance, a mixture of saponins, is used to produce foam in beverages, as a detergent, and in fire extinguishers. [< French *saponine* < Latin *sāpō, -ōnis* soap + French *-ine* -ine[2]]

sap·o·nine (sap′ə nin, -nēn), *n.* saponin.

sap·o·nite (sap′ə nīt), *n.* a mineral having a soapy feel, occurring in soft, amorphous masses, filling veins and cavities in serpentine, traprock, etc. It is a hydrous silicate of aluminum and magnesium. [< Swedish *saponit* (translation of German *Seifenstein*) < Latin *sāpō, -ōnis* soap + *-it* -ite[1]]

sa·por (sā′pôr, -pər), *n.* that quality in a substance which is perceived by the sense of taste, as sweetness, bitterness, or sourness; taste; savor. [< Latin *sapor, -ōris* flavor, savor, related to *sapere* to taste, be wise]

sap·o·rif·ic (sap′ə rif′ik), *adj.* producing or imparting taste or flavor.

sap·o·rous (sap′ər əs), *adj.* having flavor or taste.

sa·po·ta (sə pō′tə), *n.* **1.** the sapodilla. **2.** (in tropical America) a general term for any of various different sapotaceous fruits or the trees that these fruits grow on. [< New Latin *sapota* < Mexican Spanish, variant of *sapote,* or *zapote,* short for Nahuatl *cuauhtzapotl* zapote tree]

sap·o·ta·ceous (sap′ə tā′shəs), *adj.* belonging to the sapodilla family.

sa·po·te (sə pō′tā), *n.* a tropical American tree with edible fruit; marmalade tree. [< Mexican Spanish *sapote;* see SAPOTA]

sa·pour (sā′pôr, -pər), *n. Especially British.* sapor.

sap·pan·wood (sə pan′wůd′), *n.* **1.** a wood yielding a red dye, obtained from an East Indian tree of the pea family. **2.** the tree itself. Also, **sapanwood.** [half-translation of Dutch *sapanhout; sapan* < Malay *sapañ*]

sap·per (sap′ər), *n.* **1.** *British.* a soldier employed in the construction of trenches, fortifications, etc. **2.** a person employed to render mines, bombs, etc., harmless: *The sappers had not yet examined the rubble and blasted buildings for . . . booby traps* (New York Times). [< *sap*[2] + *-er*[1]; patterned on Middle French *sappeur*]

Sap·phic (saf′ik), *adj.* **1.** of or having to do with Sappho, a Greek lyric poetess who lived about 600 B.C. **2.** having to do with certain meters, or a four-line stanza form, used by or named after her: *We send our thanks to you . . . in scattered Sapphic lines* (Atlantic).
—*n.* a Sapphic stanza, strophe, or line of verse.

Sap·phi·ra (sə fī′rə), *n.* (in the Bible) a woman who, with her husband Ananias, was struck dead for lying. Acts 5:1-10.

sap·phire (saf′īr), *n.* **1.** a bright-blue precious stone that is hard and clear like a diamond. It is a variety of corundum. **2.** the color of the sapphire; bright blue. **3.** anything thought of as resembling a sapphire: *Orselli considered the stars, each shining with a separate glory: golden Dubhe, blue Denebola, Vega the pale sapphire* (Henry Morton Robinson). **4.** a gem-quality corundum of any other color except red (commonly prefixed by the color): *a pink sapphire.*
—*adj.* **1.** bright-blue: *a sapphire gown, a sapphire sea.* **2.** made or consisting of a sapphire or sapphires: *a sapphire brooch.* [< Old French *safir,* learned borrowing from Latin *saphīrus* < Greek *sáppheiros* < Semitic (compare Hebrew *sappīr*) < Sanskrit *śani-priya* sapphire; dear to the planet Saturn]

sap·phire·ber·ry (saf′īr ber′ē), *n., pl.* **-ries.** a small tree native to Japan and China with fragrant white flowers and bright blue fruit.

sapphire blue, 1. a bright blue, the color of the gem. **2.** *Poetic.* any clear or deep blue.

sapphire quartz, a dark-blue variety of quartz.

sap·phir·ine (saf′ər in, -ə rīn), *adj.* of or like sapphire: *a sapphirine sky.* —*n.* **1.** a pale-blue or greenish mineral consisting of a silicate of aluminum and magnesium. **2.** *Especially British.* a blue variety of spinel.

sap·pi·ness (sap′ē nis), *n.* the quality or state of being sappy.

sap·py (sap′ē), *adj.,* **-pi·er, -pi·est. 1.** full of sap. **2.** vigorous; energetic. **3.** *Slang.* silly; foolish: . . . *a committee of sappy women* (Mark Twain).

sa·pre·mi·a or **sa·prae·mi·a** (sə prē′mē-ə), *n.* a form of blood poisoning due to the absorption of toxins produced by bacteria. [< Greek *saprós* rotten + English *-emia*]

sap·ro·gen·ic (sap′rə jen′ik), *adj.* **1.** producing decay: *saprogenic bacteria.* **2.** formed by putrefaction. [< Greek *saprós* rotten + English *-gen* + *-ic*]

sa·prog·e·nous (sə proj′ə nəs), *adj.* saprogenic.

sap·ro·lite (sap′rə līt), *n.* soft, partly decomposed rock remaining in its original place. [< Greek *saprós* rotten + English *-lite*]

sap·ro·lit·ic (sap rə lit′ik), *adj.* of, having to do with, or like saprolite.

sa·proph·a·gous (sə prof′ə gəs), *adj.* living on decomposing matter; saprophytic. [< New Latin *saprophagus* (with English *-ous*) < Greek *saprós* rotten + *phageîn* devour]

sap·ro·phyte (sap′rə fīt), *n.* any vegetable organism that lives on decaying organic matter: *Fungi that use dead plant or animal bodies, or the excreta or other wastes from animals, are known as saprophytes* (Fred W. Emerson). [< Greek *saprós* rotten + English *-phyte*]

sap·ro·phyt·ic (sap′rə fit′ik), *adj.* of or like a saprophyte; living on dead organic matter.

sap·ro·phyt·i·cal·ly (sap′rə fit′ə klē), *adv.* as a saprophyte; in the manner of a saprophyte.

sap·sa·go (sap′sə gō), *n.* a hard, greenish cheese flavored with melilot, originally made in Switzerland. [< alteration of German *Schabzieger* < *schaben* to shave, grate + Swiss German *Zieger* whey cheese, whey]

sap·suck·er (sap′suk′ər), *n.* any of various American woodpeckers, that feed on the sap and sapwood of trees. The common or yellow-bellied sapsucker drills rows of small holes in trees and eats the inner bark, and later the sap and insects that gather in the holes. [American English < *sap*[1] + *sucker*]

Yellow-bellied Sapsucker (about 8 in. long)

sap·wood (sap′wůd′), *n.* the soft, new, living wood between the bark and the hard, inner wood of most trees; alburnum.

Sar., 1. Sardinia. **2.** Sardinian.

SAR (no periods) or **S.A.R.,** Sons of the American Revolution.

sar·a·band (sar′ə band), *n.* **1.** a slow and stately dance of Spanish origin, originally for a single dancer but later performed by couples. **2.** the music for it. [< French *sarabande* < Spanish *zarabanda,* perhaps < Persian *serbend* a kind of dance]

Sar·a·cen (sar′ə sən), *n.* **1.** an Arab. **2.** a Moslem at the time of the Crusades. **3.** (among the later Greeks and Romans) a member of the nomadic peoples of the Syrian and Arabian deserts.
—*adj.* of or having to do with the Saracens. [partly Old English *Saracene,* plural < Late Latin *Saracēnī,* partly < Old French *sarrazin,* learned borrowing from Late Latin < Greek *Sarakēnós*]

Sar·a·cen·ic (sar′ə sen′ik), *adj.* of, having to do with, or characteristic of the Saracens.

Sar·a·cen·i·cal (sar′ə sen′ə kəl), *adj.* Saracenic.

Sar·ah (sãr′ə), *n.* (in the Bible) the wife of Abraham and the mother of Isaac. Genesis 17:15.

SARAH (no periods) or **S.A.R.A.H.,** Search and Rescue and Homing (a radio and radar beam device used in locating people lost at sea): *SARAH . . . weighs only about 3 lb. and can be carried in a Mae West* (London Times).

sa·ran (sə ran′), *n.* a thermoplastic resin produced as a fiber, film, or molded form and highly resistant to damage and soiling. It is used to package food, in automobile seat covers, in clothing, and for other commercial purposes.

sa·ran·gi (sä′rang gē), *n.* a stringed musical instrument of India resembling a violin: . . . *the sarangi, a chunky instrument fitted with 29 strings* (Time). [< Sanskrit *sāraṅgī*]

sa·ra·pe (sə rä′pē), *n.* serape: *He was a thoroughly Mexican personality and loved to wear brightly striped Mexican sarapes* (London Times).

Sa·ras·va·ti (sə räs′və tē), *n.* the Hindu goddess of learning, and patroness of the arts and music.

Sar·a·to·ga trunk (sar′ə tō′gə), a kind of large trunk formerly much used by women. [American English < *Saratoga Springs,* New York]

sar·casm (sär′kaz əm), *n.* **1.** the act of making fun of a person to hurt his feelings; bitter irony: *"How unselfish you are!" said Ellen in sarcasm as Mary took the biggest piece of cake. Sarcasm, I now see to be, in general, the language of the Devil* (Thomas Carlyle). **2.** a sneering or cutting remark; ironical taunt: *Blows are sarcasms turned stupid* (George Eliot). **3.** the substance of such a remark or remarks. [< Late Latin *sarcasmus* < Greek *sarkasmós* < *sarkázein* to sneer; (literally) strip off flesh < *sárx, sarkós* flesh]
➤ See **irony** for usage note.

sar·cas·tic (sär kas′tik), *adj.* characterized by, involving, or using sarcasm; cutting; sneering; ironical; taunting; caustic: *"Don't hurry!" was his sarcastic comment as I began to dress at my usual slow rate.*
—**Syn. Sarcastic, sardonic, satirical** mean scornful or contemptuous. **Sarcastic** implies exhibiting scorn in such a way as to hurt someone's feelings: *The teacher's sarcastic comment about the girl's essay made her cry.* **Sardonic** implies exhibiting scorn in a cold, aloof manner but not directed at anything or anyone in particular: *Our efforts to cheer him up produced only a sardonic smile.* **Satirical** implies exhibiting something in a scornful light but not necessarily so as to hurt anyone: *We were all amused by the satirical comparison of life at college and in the army.*

sar·cas·ti·cal·ly (sär kas′tə klē), *adv.* in a sarcastic manner; with bitter taunt.

Sar·cee (sär′sē), *n., pl.* **-cee** or **-cees. 1.** an Athapascan people of Alberta, Canada. Most of the Sarcee are now living on a reservation near Calgary. **2.** a member of this people. **3.** the Athapascan dialect of this people. Also, **Sarsi.**

sarce·net (särs′net), *n.* a soft, thin silk fabric, either plain or twilled, used especially for linings. Also, **sarsenet.** [< Anglo-French *sarzinett,* probably (diminutive) < *Sarzin,* Old French *sarrazin* Saracen (because of its resemblance to the garb of the Saracens)]

sar·co·carp (sär′kō kärp), *n.* **1.** the fleshy mesocarp of certain fruits, as the peach and plum. It is the part usually eaten. **2.** any fruit that is fleshy. [< Greek *sárx, sarkós* flesh + *karpós* fruit]

sar·code (sär′kōd), *n.* the protoplasm of a one-celled animal: *Two years later, in 1835, Dujardin, a French protozoologist, described the semifluid substance in unicellular animals and coined the term sarcode* (Hegner and Stiles). [< French *sarcode* < Greek *sarkṓdēs* fleshy < *sárx, sarkós* flesh + *eîdos* form]

sar·co·gen·ic (sär′kō jen′ik), *adj.* producing muscle or flesh. [< Greek *sárx, sarkós* flesh + English *-gen* + *-ic*]

sar·cog·e·nous (sär koj′ə nəs), *adj.* sarcogenic.

sar·coid (sär′koid), *n.* sarcoidosis.

sar·coi·do·sis (sär′koi dō′sis), *n.* a chronic disease in which tumorlike lesions develop in many parts of the body. Its cause is undetermined. *This disease was sarcoidosis, a chronic infectious disease affecting the eyes and face* (Science News Letter). *A mysterious and sometimes fatal tuberculosislike disease, sarcoidosis is linked to the Eastern pine tree* (Science News Letter). [< Greek *sarkoeidḗs* fleshy (< *sárx, sarkós* flesh + *eîdos* form) + English *-osis*]

sar·co·lac·tic acid (sär′kō lak′tik), the dextrorotatory form of lactic acid found in the blood and muscles as a result of the metabolism of glucose: *Sarcolactic acid . . . has been called the "acid of fatigue" . . . because a greater amount of sarcolactic acid is present in the muscles when a person is tired* (George L. Bush). [< Greek *sárx, sárkos* flesh + English *lactic acid*]

sar·co·lem·ma (sär′kō lem′ə), *n.* an elastic transparent membrane enclosing each of the fibers of striated muscle tissue, excepting that of the heart. [< Greek *sárx, sarkós* flesh + *lémma* lemma[2]]

sar·co·lem·mal (sär′kō lem′əl), *adj.* of or having to do with a sarcolemma or sarcolemmas: *Each giant fiber is surrounded by a stout sarcolemmal complex with associated nuclei* (Graham Hoyle).

sar·col·o·gy [sär kol′ə jē), *n.* the branch of anatomy that has to do with the fleshy parts of the body. [< Greek *sárx, sarkós* flesh + English *-logy*]

sar·col·y·sin (sär kol′ə sin), *n.* a nitrogen mustard used in treating malignant tumors. *Formula:* $C_{13}H_{18}Cl_2N_2O_2$

sar·co·ma (sär kō′mə), *n., pl.* **-mas, -ma·ta** (-mə tə). any of a class of cancers originating in nonepithelial tissue, chiefly connective tissue: *It is possible to have tumors of the mesoderm, these being usually known as sarcomata* (Science News). [< New Latin *sarcoma* < Greek *sárkōma, -atos* < *sarkôn* to produce flesh; grow fleshy < *sárx, sarkós* flesh]

sar·co·ma·toid (sär kō′mə toid), *adj.* sarcomatous.

sar·co·ma·to·sis (sär kō′mə tō′sis), *n.* a condition characterized by the formation of sarcomas in many parts of the body. [< New Latin *sarcomatosis* < *sarcoma, -atos* sarcoma + *-osis* -osis]

sar·com·a·tous (sär kō′mə təs), *adj.* having to do with or of the nature of a sarcoma.

sar·co·mere (sär′kə mir), *n.* one of the segments or pieces of a sarcostyle. [< Greek *sárx, sarkós* flesh + *méros* part]

sar·coph·a·gus (sär kof′ə gəs), *n., pl.* **-gi** (-jī), **-gus·es. 1.** a stone coffin, especially one ornamented with sculptures or bearing inscriptions: *The early doges had themselves buried, in St. Mark's porch, in sarcophagi that did not belong to them, displacing the bones of old pagans and Paleo-Christians* (New Yorker). **2.** a kind of limestone that the ancient Greeks used for coffins because they supposed it quickly consumed the flesh of corpses placed in it. [< Latin *sarcophagus* < Greek *sarkophágos* (originally) flesh-eating (stone) < *sárx, sarkós* flesh + *phageîn* to eat]

Sarcophagus (def. 1)

sar·co·phile (sär′kə fīl), *n.* the Tasmanian devil.

sar·co·plasm (sär′kō plaz əm), *n.* the clear protoplasmic substance which separates the fibrillae, or sarcostyles, in a striated muscle fiber. [< Greek *sárx, sarkós* flesh]

sar·co·plas·mic (sär′kō plaz′mik), *adj.* having to do with or of the nature of sarcoplasm.

sar·cop·tic (sär kop′tik), *adj.* of, having to do with, or caused by itch mites. [< *Sarcoptes,* genus of parasites including the itch mite < Greek *sárx, sarkós* flesh + *kóptein* to cut]

sarcoptic mange, a mange caused by the burrowing of itch mites into the skin: *Sarcoptic mange in a puppy could infect the whole household* (London Times).

sar·co·some (sär′kō sōm), *n.* any of the very small cell inclusions found in muscle tissue, believed to be a principal factor in keeping the heart muscle strong and active. [< Greek *sárx, sarkós* flesh + *sôma* body]

sar·co·spo·ri·di·o·sis (sär′kō spô rid′ē ō′sis, -spō-), *n.* a disease of animals caused by a parasite, believed to be a protozoan or fungus, which invades the muscles, especially the striated muscles. It is encountered frequently in ducks, sheep, swine, horses, reptiles, and birds. [< New Latin *Sarcosporidia* the order name of the parasite (< Greek *sárx, sarkós* flesh + *sporá* spore) + *-osis* -osis]

sar·co·style (sär′kō stīl), *n.* one of the delicate fibrillae which make up the fiber of a striated muscle.

sar·cous (sär′kəs), *adj.* having to do with or consisting of flesh or muscle. [< Greek *sárx, sarkós* flesh + English *-ous*]

sard (särd), *n.* a mineral, a variety of chalcedony, varying in color from brown to deep red, used in jewelry. [< Latin *sarda.* Compare SARDIUS.]

sar·da·na (sär dä′nə), *n.* the national dance of Catalonia, danced in a large ring with much twirling and hand-clapping to the rhythm of a flute and drum. [< Catalan *sardana*]

Sar·da·na·pa·li·an (sär′də nə pā′lē ən), *adj.* inordinately luxurious and effeminate. [< *Sardanapalus,* an Assyrian king, proverbial for his wealth and splendor + *-ian*]

sar·dar (sär′där, sər där′), *n.* sirdar: *That [leadership] is largely exercised by the tribal sardars* (London Times).

Sar·di·an (sär′dē ən), *adj.* of or having to do with Sardis, the ancient capital of Lydia in Asia Minor: *His monument ... [was] erected near Sardis by the joint efforts of the whole Sardian population* (George Grote). —*n.* a native or inhabitant of Sardis: *You have condemned and noted Lucius Pella for taking bribes here of the Sardians* (Shakespeare).

sar·dine[1] (sär dēn′), *n., pl.* **-dines** or (*collectively*) **-dine. 1.** a kind of small European marine fish, a young pilchard, preserved in oil for food. **2.** any of certain similar small fishes prepared in a similar way: *The 40-odd canneries in Maine provide all the domestic supply of small snack-type sardines* (Wall Street Journal).

packed like sardines, very much crowded: *We rode on the subway at rush hour, packed like sardines.*

[< Old French *sardine* < Italian *sardina* < Latin *sardīna* < *sarda* sardine, probably (literally) Sardinian fish]

sar·dine[2] (sär′din, -dīn), *n.* sard. [< Late Latin *sardinus,* apparently < Latin *sarda* sard]

Sar·din·i·an (sär din′ē ən), *adj.* of or having to do with Sardinia, a large island near Italy, its people, or their dialect. —*n.* **1.** a native or inhabitant of Sardinia. **2.** the Romance dialect spoken in Sardinia: *Sardinian is quite distinct from Italian* (H.A. Gleason, Jr.).

sar·di·us (sär′dē əs), *n.* **1.** sard. **2.** (in the Bible) one of the precious stones in the breastplate of the Jewish high priest, thought to have been a ruby. [< Late Latin (*lapis*) *sardius,* for Greek (*líthos*) *sárdios* (stone) of *Sardis,* a city in Lydia]

sar·don·ic (sär don′ik), *adj.* bitterly contemptuous; coldly scornful; mocking: *a sardonic outlook. I well remember his sardonic amusement over the hoopla occasioned in this country by the first Kinsey report* (Atlantic). [< French *sardonique* < Latin *sardonius* (< Greek *sardónios* of bitter or scornful smiles or laughter < *sardónion* a supposed Sardinian plant that produced hysterical convulsions + French *-ique* -ic] —**Syn.** derisive. See **sarcastic.**

sar·don·i·cal·ly (sär don′ə klē), *adv.* in a sardonic manner: *He laughed sardonically, hastily took my hand, and as hastily threw it from him* (Charlotte Brontë).

sar·don·i·cism (sär don′ə siz əm), *n.* the quality of being sardonic.

sar·do·nyx (sär′də niks), *n.* a variety of quartz containing layers of sard: *The engraved carnelian and sardonyx rings that fashionable Greeks wore on their toes ... had swivel mountings, so that the center was reversible* (New Yorker). [< Latin *sardonyx* < Greek *sardónyx,* probably < *sárdios,* or *sárdion* sardius + *ónyx* onyx]

sar·gas·so (sär gas′ō), *n.,* or **sargasso weed,** any of a group of olive-brown seaweeds that have berrylike air bladders and float in large masses; sargassum. [< Portuguese *sargasso,* or *sargaço,* perhaps < *sarga* a type of grape (because of the berrylike air sacs on the seaweed) or, perhaps < Latin *sargus* a kind of sea fish]

sar·gas·sum (sär gas′əm), *n.* any of a group of olive-brown seaweeds that inhabit the warmer waters of the globe, especially an area of the Atlantic off southern North America; gulfweed: *It is commonly supposed that this area [the Sargasso Sea] of the Atlantic is so thick with seaweed that ships cannot penetrate it. Although it is indeed strewn with floating sargassum, it is actually a biological desert* (J. H. Ryther). [< New Latin *Sargassum* the genus name < Portuguese *sargasso;* see SARGASSO]

sargassum fish, any of the frogfishes often found among floating masses of sargassum, common in warm parts of the Atlantic: *If you have trouble seeing the sargassum fish ... hidden among the tropic and semi-tropic sargassum sea weed ... so do his natural enemies* (Science News Letter).

sarge (särj), *n. U.S. Informal.* sergeant.

sar·go (sär′gō), *n.* a small, edible, silvery fish with dark spots on the body and yellow fins, a variety of grunt found off the Pacific Coast of North America. [< Spanish *sargo* < Latin *sargus;* see SARGASSO]

sa·ri (sä′rē), *n., pl.* **-ris.** the principal outer garment of Hindu women, a long piece of cotton or silk, sometimes brightly colored, wrapped around the middle of the body, with one end falling nearly to the feet and the other end thrown over the head: *The sari, which has come a long way since it left Delhi, now makes its influence felt in two-piece dacron-and-cotton dresses* (New Yorker). [< Hindi *sārī* < Prakrit *sāḍī* < Sanskrit *śāṭī* garment, petticoat]

sar·in or **Sar·in** (sar′in), *n.* a highly lethal nerve gas that is a compound of phosphorus: *A protecting antidote for the nerve gas called sarin has been developed* (Science News Letter). *Formula:* $C_4H_{10}FPO_2$ [< German *Sarin*]

sa·rin·da (sə rin′də), *n.* a stringed musical instrument of India, played with a bow, of the class characterized by the rebab. [< Hindustani *sārindā*]

sark (särk), *n. Scottish.* shirt. [Old English *serc*]

sar·ky (sär′kē), *adj. British Slang.* sarcastic: *Some do get a bit sarky* (Sunday Times).

Sar·ma·tian (sär mā′shən), *adj.* of or having to do with Sarmatia, an ancient region in Europe extending from the Vistula to the Volga, sometimes poetically identified with Poland or with the inhabitants of this region. —*n.* a native or inhabitant of Sarmatia.

sar·ment (sär′mənt), *n. Obsolete.* **1.** sarmentum. **2.** a cutting. [< Latin *sarmentum* twig]

sar·men·to·gen·in (sär men′tō jen′in), *n.* a glycoside obtained from the seeds of a tropical African vine of the dogbane family, used in the production of cortisone. *Formula:* $C_{23}H_{34}O_5$

sar·men·tose (sär men′tōs), *adj. Botany.* **1.** having runners. **2.** of or like a runner. [< Latin *sarmentōsus* < *sarmentum* twig]

sar·men·tous (sär men′təs), *adj.* sarmentose.

sar·men·tum (sär men′təm), *n., pl.* **-ta** (-tə). *Botany.* a runner (stem), as that of the strawberry. [< Latin *sarmentum* twig, related to *sarpere* to prune, trim]

sa·rod (sə rōd′), *n.* an ancient stringed instrument of India. It has twenty-five strings, ten of which are plucked, the other fifteen providing resonance. *Mr. Khan is a performer on the sarod, a stringed instrument of beautiful design that is plucked according to a highly intricate technique* (New Yorker). [< Hindi *sarod* < Persian *si* three + *rōd* string]

sa·rong (sə rông′, -rong′), *n.* **1.** a rectangular piece of cloth, usually a brightly colored printed material, worn as a skirt by men and women in the Malay Archipelago, East Indies, etc.: *The shop has a selection of filmy and transparent saris from India and hand-painted Javanese sarongs* (New York Times). **2.** a fabric used to make this garment. [< Malay *sarong,* perhaps ultimately < Sanskrit *śāṭa* cloth, garment]

sa·ros (sãr′os), *n. Astronomy.* a cycle of 18 years and 11⅓ days, in which solar and lunar eclipses repeat themselves. If the interval contains five leap years instead of four, it is 18 years and 10⅓ days. It was discovered by the ancient Chaldeans. [< Greek *sáros* < Semitic (compare Assyrian *shāru*)]

Sar·pe·don (sär pē′dən), *n. Greek Legend.* **1.** a son of Zeus and Europa, king of the Lycians, to whom Zeus granted the privilege of living for three generations. **2.** (in another account) a son of Zeus and Laodamia, leader of the Lycians in the Trojan War and an ally of the Trojans, killed by Patroclus.

sar·ra·ce·ni·a (sar′ə sē′nē ə), *n.* a bog plant with pitcher-shaped leaves and a more or less arching hood at the top, usually partly filled with rain water and decomposing insects on which the plant subsists; pitcher plant. [< New Latin *Sarracenia* the genus name < Dr. D. *Sarrazin,* a Canadian botanist of the 1600's who sent the first samples to Europe]

sar·ra·ce·ni·a·ceous (sar′ə sē′nē ā′shəs), *adj.* belonging to a family of American dicotyledonous bog herbs typified by the sarracenia.

sar·sa·pa·ril·la (sas′pə ril′ə, sär′sə-), *n.* **1.** any of a group of tropical American climbing or trailing plants of the lily family. **2.** the dried roots of any of these plants, formerly used in medicine as an alterative and as a tonic. **3.** a nonalcoholic, usually carbonated, beverage made from an infusion of these roots. [< Spanish *zarzaparrilla* < *zarza* bramble (perhaps < Basque *sartzia*) + *parrilla* (diminutive) < *parra* vine (origin uncertain)]

➔ The second pronunciation, although it agrees with the spelling, is rare in the United States.

sar·sar (sär′sər), *n.* a killingly cold wind. [< Arabic *ṣarṣar*]

sar·sen (sär′sən), *n.* any of a number of large boulders or blocks of sandstone found as parts or remnants of prehistoric buildings. The sarsens of Stonehenge, in England, are the most famous stones of this kind. *Those that first catch the attention are the immense sarsens, great monoliths of sandstone* (Scientific American). [apparently variant of *Saracen* (because they were originally thought to have built the buildings)]

sarse·net (särs′net), *n.* sarcenet.

Sar·si (sär′sē), *n., pl.* **-si** or **-sis.** Sarcee.

sar·tor (sär′tər, -tôr), *n.* a tailor (in humorously pedantic use). [< Latin *sartor*]

sar·to·ri·al (sär tôr′ē əl, -tōr′-), *adj.* **1.** of tailors or their work: *His sartorial taste runs to loud candy-striped shirts* (Newsweek). **2.** *Anatomy.* of or having to do with the sartorius. [< Latin *sartōrius* of a tailor (< *sarcīre* to patch) + English *-al*[1]] —**sar·to′ri·al·ly,** *adv.*

sar·to·ri·us (sär tôr′ē əs, -tōr′-), *n., pl.* **-to·ri·i** (-tôr′ē ī, -tōr′-). a flat, narrow muscle, the longest in the human body, running from the ilium to the top of the tibia, and crossing the thigh obliquely in front. [< New Latin *sartorius* < Latin *sartor, -ōris* tailor, patcher < *sarcīre* to patch]

Sar·tri·an or **Sar·tre·an** (sär′trē ən), *adj.* of, having to do with, or characteristic of the French existentialist philosopher and writer Jean Paul Sartre, his writings, or his ideas: *Honesty, objectivity, compassion and acceptance of total personal responsibility is the Sartrian prescription* (Sunday Times).

Sar·um use (sãr′əm), the order of divine service and the liturgy used in the diocese of Salisbury, England, from the late Middle Ages to the Reformation. [< Medieval Latin *Sarum,* for *Sarisburia* Salisbury]

Sar·us crane (sãr′əs), a large crane of India and Malaya: . . . *the first Sarus crane ever to hatch in the United States* (Science News Letter). [< Hindi *sāras* < Sanskrit *sārasa* of a lake]

Sa·sa·ni·an (sa sā′nē ən), *n., adj.* Sassanid: *The origins, languages, arts, governments, and beliefs of the . . . Sasanians and the rest are meticulously described* (London Times). *R. Naumann . . . continued the large-scale clearance of the Sasanian fire temple* (Robert J. Braidwood).

sash[1] (sash), *n.* **1.** a long, broad strip of cloth or ribbon, worn as an ornament or belt around the waist by women and children: *She wore a white dress with a blue sash around her waist.* **2.** a similar ornamental strip, often fringed, worn over one shoulder or around the waist as part of a uniform or as an emblem of rank, etc.: *Acting President Nereu Ramos took off the green-and-gold sash of office and draped it across the incoming President's breast* (Time). [earlier *shash* < Arabic *shāsh* muslin cloth (worn in turbans)]

sash[2] (sash), *n.* **1.** the frame for the glass in a window or door. **2.** such frames collectively. **3.** the part or parts of a window that can be moved so as to open or close it. —*v.t.* to provide with a sash or sashes. [earlier *shashes,* taken as plural < French *châssis,* or *châsse* frame or sash. Compare CHASSIS.]

sa·shay (sa shā′), *v.i. U.S.* **1.** *Informal.* to glide, move, or go about, especially lightly or casually: *When they passed the Wade Hampton Inn, they less walked than sashayed* (New Yorker). **2.** to do a chassé (now only in folk dancing). [American English, alteration of *chassé* a gliding step]

sash cord, 1. a rope which runs over a pulley and connects a window sash with its counterbalancing weight. **2.** the rope made for this purpose.

sa·shi·mi (sa shē′mē), *n.pl.* thin slices of raw fish, eaten as an appetizer in Japan. [< Japanese *sashimi*]

sash weight, a slender, metal weight hung within the frame of a window by a sash cord, and used to counterbalance the weight of the sash.

sa·sin (sā′sin), *n.* the common Indian antelope; the black buck. It is brown or black on the upper parts with a white abdomen and breast, and straight corkscrew horns. [origin uncertain. Compare Sanskrit *śaśin* of or having to do with a hare or deer.]

Sask., Saskatchewan.

sas·ka·toon (sas′kə tün′), *n. Canadian.* **1.** any of various shadbushes, especially the serviceberry and a species with purple fruit. **2.** the berry of any of these plants. [American English, apparently < Algonkian (Cree) *misâskwatomin* fruit of the *misâskwat* tree of many branches]

sass (sas, säs), *n.* **1.** *U.S. Dialect.* vegetables, especially those used in making sauces; sauce. **2.** *Informal.* rudeness; back talk; impudence.
—*v.t. Informal.* to be saucy to; sauce: *He'd come to me and sass me sumthin' dreadful, naggin' me to let him play* (New York Times).
—*v.i. Informal.* to talk or act rudely or impudently.
[< a variant pronunciation of *sauce*]

sas·sa·by (sas′ə bē), *n., pl.* **-bies** or (*collectively*) **-by.** a large, dark-red, South African antelope. [< dialectal Bantu *tsessébe*]

sas·sa·fras (sas′ə fras), *n.* **1.** a slender American tree of the laurel family, that has fragrant, yellow flowers, bluish-black fruit, and light, soft, yellowish wood. **2.** the aromatic dried bark of its root, used in medicine and to flavor candy, soft drinks, tea, etc. It yields an aromatic volatile oil used in making perfume. [American English < Spanish *sasafrás,* perhaps < an American Indian language, and later influenced by Spanish *sassifragia,* earlier *saxifragia;* see SAXIFRAGE]

Sassafras Branch (def. 1)

Sas·sa·ni·an (sa sā′nē ən), *n., adj.* Sassanid.

Sas·sa·nid or **Sas·sa·nide** (sas′ə nid), *n.* one of the Sassanidae. —*adj.* of or having to do with the Sassanidae.

Sas·san·i·dae (sa san′ə dē), *n.pl.* the dynasty that ruled Persia from 226 to 651 A.D. [< Medieval Latin *Sassanidae,* ultimately < Persian *Sāsān,* grandfather of Ardashir, the first king of the dynasty]

Sas·se·nach (sas′ə naн), *n. Scottish and Irish.* **1.** an Englishman: *It had been hoped that a special commemorative stamp would be issued . . . but the Sassenachs in Parliament in London would not agree* (Cape Times). **2.** the English; Englishmen collectively. [< Irish *sasanach* (literally) Saxon < Medieval Latin *Saxonicus.* Related to SAXON.]

sas·si·ly (sas′ə lē), *adv. Informal.* saucily: *All that viewers saw or heard was Elsa Maxwell sassily telling Host Jack Paar that Walter Winchell had never voted* (Time).

sas·si·ness (sas′ē nis), *n. Informal.* sauciness.

sas·sy[1] (sas′ē), *adj.,* **-si·er, -si·est.** *U.S. Informal.* saucy: *Also on the bill are Bobbi Wright, a Harlem miss with a sassy voice and great ebullience . . .* (New Yorker). [< *sass* + *-y*[1]]

sas·sy[2] (sas′ē), *n.* **1.** sassy bark. **2.** a large African tree of the pea family, whose poisonous bark is used by the natives as a poison to test a person at an ordeal, and for capturing fish; sassywood. [origin uncertain; perhaps < a West African word, or perhaps < English *sassy*[1]]

sassy bark, 1. the bark of the sassy tree. **2.** the sassy tree.

sas·sy·wood (sas′ē wu̇d′), *n.* the sassy tree.

sas·tra (säs′trə), *n.* **1.** (in Hindu use) any of certain sacred books constituting the sources of Hindu law. **2.** any of various authoritative books for instruction in some science or art. Also, **shastra.** [< Hindi *śāstr* < Sanskrit *śāstra*]

sas·tru·ga (sas trü′gə), *n., pl.* **-gi** (-gē). zastruga; windblown ridge of snow and ice: *Angry clouds drift over seas of corrugated sastrugi and sparkling glacial spillways* (Time). [< Russian *zastruga*]

sat (sat), *v.* a past tense and a past participle of **sit:** *Yesterday I sat in the train all day. The cat has sat at that mouse's hole for many hours.*

S.A.T. or **SAT** (no periods), Scholastic Aptitude Test.

Sat., 1. Saturday. **2.** Saturn.

Sa·tan (sā′tən), *n.* (especially in Christian theology) the supreme evil spirit; the enemy of goodness and great adversary of God and mankind; the Devil: *Satan finds some mischief still for idle hands to do* (Isaac Watts). *And he laid hold on the dragon, that old serpent, which is the Devil, and Satan, and bound him a thousand years* (Revelation 20:2). [Old English *Satan* < Latin *Satān* < Greek *satanâs,* adapted from *satân* < Hebrew *shāṭān* adversary]

sa·tang (sä tang′), *n., pl.* **-tang.** a Thai bronze coin and money of account, worth 1/100 of a baht. [< Thai *satān* (literally) having one hundred < *sata* hundred < Sanskrit *śata*]

sa·tan·ic or **Sa·tan·ic** (sā tan′ik, sə-), *adj.* **1.** of Satan. **2.** like that of Satan; very wicked: *Though he is capable of satanic mockery . . . the mocker cannot jeer at such a doom without breaking . . . his own neck as well* (Edmund Wilson). —**Syn. 2.** diabolical, devilish, infernal.

sa·tan·i·cal (sā tan′ə kəl, sə-), *adj.* satanic.

sa·tan·i·cal·ly (sā tan′ə klē, sə-), *adv.* in a satanic manner; with the wicked and malicious spirit of Satan; devilishly.

Sa·tan·ism (sā′tə niz əm), *n.* **1.** the worship of Satan. Satanism had a vogue in France during the 1800's. It was mostly a form of decadence rather than actual belief in Satan. **2.** the principles of or rites used in this worship. **3.** devilishness; a satanic or diabolical disposition, doctrine, etc.: *With such a mixture of . . . loyalty, mysterious Satanism, and reputation for conquests over her sex . . . Bothwell must have fascinated the Queen* (Andrew Lang).

sa·tan·ist (sā′tə nist), *n.* a very wicked person.

Sa·tan·ist (sā′tə nist), *n.* a believer in Satanism.

sa·tan·oph·a·ny (sā′tə nof′ə nē), *n., pl.* **-nies. 1.** an appearance of Satan. **2.** the condition of being possessed by a devil. [< *Satan;* patterned on *theophany*]

Sa·tan·o·pho·bi·a (sā′tə nə fō′bē ə), *n. Rare.* fear of the Devil. [< Greek *Satanâs* (see SATAN) + English *-phobia*]

S.A.T.B., soprano, alto, tenor, bass: *Standard carol books still more or less automatically gear their arrangements to the S.A.T.B. church choir* (London Times).

satch·el (sach′əl), *n.* a small bag for carrying clothes, books, etc.; handbag: *The whining schoolboy, with his satchel and shining morning face* (Shakespeare). [< Old French *sachel* < Latin *saccellus* money bag, purse, (diminutive) < *sacculus* (diminutive) < *saccus;* see SACK[1]]

satchel charge, an explosive charge that can be carried and set off either by one person or a small group: *The satchel charges would replace the unwieldy TNT charges used heretofore by engineers . . . to demolish bridges* (New York Herald Tribune).

sate[1] (sāt), *v.t.,* **sat·ed, sat·ing. 1.** to satisfy fully (any appetite or desire): *A long drink sated his thirst.* **2.** to supply with more than enough, so as to disgust or weary; glut. [alteration of earlier *sade,* Old English *sadian* to glut (compare SAD); influenced by Latin *satiāre* satiate] —**Syn. 2.** See **satiate.**

sate[2] (sat, sāt), *v. Archaic.* sat; a past tense and a past participle of **sit.**

sa·teen (sa tēn′), *n.* a cotton cloth made to imitate satin, often used for lining sleeves. [variant of *satin;* probably influenced by *velveteen*]

sate·less (sāt′lis), *adj. Archaic.* that cannot be sated; insatiable.

sat·el·lite (sat′ə līt), *n.* **1. a.** a heavenly body that revolves around a planet, especially around one of the nine major planets of the solar system: *The moon is a satellite of the earth. The number of known satellites in the solar system, including the earth's moon, rose to 32* (Newsweek). **b.** a sphere or other object launched into an orbit around the earth; earth satellite: *The satellite was launched by one of the Army's four-stage Juno II rockets . . .* (World Book Encyclopedia). **2. a.** a follower or attendant upon a person of importance: *Three thousand armed satellites escorted his steps* (John L. Motley). **b.** a subservient follower: *Legree encouraged his two black satellites to a kind of coarse familiarity with him* (Harriet Beecher Stowe). **3.** a country that is nominally independent but is actually controlled by a more powerful country, especially such a country under Russian control: *South Africa produces . . . as much uranium as the U.S.S.R. and her satellites put together* (Economist).
—*adj.* **1.** secondary; minor: *a satellite navy, a satellite group, party, regime, etc.* **2.** allied; associated: *Percival maintains that Canada's supremacy in hockey is being lost because*

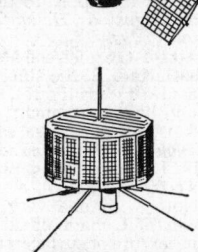

Satellites (def. 1b)
Top, Explorer IV, used to obtain radiation, temperature, and cosmic dust data in space; bottom, Tiros I, used to photograph storm centers

coaching and conditioning in the NHL and its satellite leagues hasn't advanced (Eric Hutton).
[< Middle French *satellite,* learned borrowing from Latin *satelles, -itis* attendant]

sat·el·lit·ic (sat′ə lit′ik), *adj.* of, having to do with, or of the nature of a satellite: *With a directed booster at the end, this rocket could have been fired into a satellitic orbit* (Scientific American).

sat·el·lit·ism (sat′ə lī tiz′əm), *n.* the policy or practice of seeking political satellites: *The nationalism learned from the West makes the new nations sensitive to Communist satellitism* (American Scholar).

sat·el·li·za·tion (sat′ə lə zā′shən), *n.* the act or process of seeking political satellites: *Understanding of a wider world would help Canadians resist American satellization* (Canadian Saturday Night).

sat·el·loid (sat′ə loid), *n.* **1.** a space vehicle that travels at less than the speed required for it to remain long in orbit: *The glider is now a satelloid ... travelling 1,000 mph less than the velocity needed to make it an orbiting space fixture* (Newsweek). **2.** a manned and rocket-powered space vehicle that is part airplane and part satellite, made to orbit the earth for a short time and return intact: *Pilots of experimental rocket aircraft ... are only a few years before pilots of "satelloids," a class of semi-space ships now being developed* (Newsweek).

sa·tem language (sä′tem, sā′-), one of the eastern division of the Indo-European languages, including Indo-Iranian, Armenian, Balto-Slavic, and Albanian. [< Avestan *satəm* hundred]

sa·ti·a·bil·i·ty (sā′shē ə bil′ə tē, -shə bil′-), *n.* capability of being satiated.

sa·ti·a·ble (sā′shē ə bəl, -shə bəl), *adj.* that can be satiated. —**sa′ti·a·ble·ness,** *n.*

sa·ti·a·bly (sā′shē ə blē, -shə-), *adv.* so as to satiate.

sa·ti·ate (*v.* sā′shē āt; *adj.* sā′shē it, -āt), *v.,* **-at·ed, -at·ing,** *adj.* —*v.t.* **1.** to feed fully; satisfy fully. **2.** to weary or disgust with too much; glut; cloy: *Alice was so satiated with bananas that she would not even look at one.* —*adj.* filled to satiety; satiated: *In life's cool evening, satiate of applause* (Alexander Pope). [< Latin *satiāre* (with English *-ate*[1]) < *satis* enough]
—**Syn.** *v.t.* **1. Satiate, sate, surfeit** mean to fill with more than enough to satisfy. **Satiate** means to feed, literally or figuratively, a person, mind, etc., to the point where something that did please or was wanted no longer gives pleasure: *Children who are given every toy they see become satiated.* **Sate** usually means to satisfy a desire or appetite so fully that it dies: *Will nothing sate his lust for power?* **Surfeit** means to eat or supply to the point of being sick or disgusted: *He surfeited them with candy and sodas.*

sa·ti·a·tion (sā′shē ā′shən), *n.* **1.** the act of satiating. **2.** the state of being satiated.

sa·ti·e·ty (sə tī′ə tē), *n.* the feeling of having had too much; disgust or weariness caused by excess; satiated condition: *Of knowledge there is no satiety* (Francis Bacon). [< Latin *satietās* < *satis* enough]

sat·in (sat′ən), *n.* a silk, rayon, or acetate cloth with one very smooth, glossy side. —*adj.* **1.** made of satin. **2.** of or like satin in texture or surface; smooth and glossy: *The color finish—of semi-gloss or satin appearance—is said to be permanent* (Wall Street Journal). [< Old French *satin,* also *zatanin,* perhaps < Spanish *aceituni* < Arabic *zaitūnī* having to do with or from *Zaitūn,* adaptation of Chinese *Tzu-t'ing* Chuanchow]

sat·i·net or **sat·i·nette** (sat′ə net′), *n.* **1.** an imitation satin cloth, especially of silk mixed with cotton. **2.** a cloth woven with a cotton warp and woolen woof and having a satinlike surface. **3.** *Obsolete.* a thin satin.

sat·in·flow·er (sat′ən flou′ər), *n.* honesty (the plant).

satin glass, white opaque glass flashed with a color and treated with hydrofluoric acid to produce a satiny finish: *In England, Thomas Webb and Sons of Stourbridge produced much coloured glass including satin glass* (London Times).

sat·in·pod (sat′ən pod′), *n.* honesty (the plant).

satin spar, a fibrous variety of calcite or gypsum.

satin stitch, an embroidery stitch made by filling in a design with straight or slanting, parallel stitches, close enough together to look satiny and to look nearly the same on the reverse side.

sat·in·wood (sat′ən wu̇d′), *n.* **1.** the beautiful, smooth, yellowish-brown wood of an East Indian tree of the mahogany family, used to ornament furniture: *This wardrobe is made of stinkwood with satinwood panels* (Cape Times). **2.** the tree itself. **3.** a small West Indian tree of the rue family, having hard, fine-grained, orange-colored wood, used especially for cabinetwork.

sat·in·y (sat′ə nē), *adj.* like satin in smoothness and gloss: *The wood is a satiny hand-rubbed and hand-waxed cypress, almost impervious to the elements* (New Yorker).

sat·ire (sat′īr), *n.* **1.** the use of sarcasm or irony to attack or ridicule a habit, idea, custom, etc., that is, or is considered to be, foolish, wrong, etc.: *Satire ... to tell men freely of their foulest faults, to laugh at their vain deeds and vainer thoughts* (John Dryden). *Satire should, like a polished razor keen, wound with a touch that's scarcely felt or seen* (Lady Mary Wortley Montagu). **2.** a poem, essay, story, etc., that attacks or ridicules in this way: *Some of Aesop's "Fables" are satires.* [< Middle French *satire,* learned borrowing from Latin *satira,* variant of (*lanx*) *satura* medley; (literally) mixed (dish) < *satis* enough]
➤ See **irony** for usage note.

sa·tir·ic (sə tir′ik), *adj.* **1.** of or containing satire: *a satiric novel or poem.* **2.** fond of using satire: *a satiric poet.*

sa·tir·i·cal (sə tir′ə kəl), *adj.* **1.** fond of using satire. **2.** satiric; of or containing satire. —**sa·tir′i·cal·ness,** *n.* —**Syn. 1.** sarcastic, ironical, cutting, caustic, sneering. See **sarcastic.**

sa·tir·i·cal·ly (sə tir′ə klē), *adv.* in a satirical manner; with sarcastic or witty treatment: *What has a pastoral tragedy to do with a paper of verses satirically written?* (John Dryden).

sat·i·rise (sat′ə rīz), *v.t.,* **-rised, -ris·ing.** *Especially British.* satirize.

sat·i·rist (sat′ər ist), *n.* **1.** a writer of satires: *The follies and vices of their own times are the chief subjects of satirists.* **2.** a person who uses satire.

sat·i·rize (sat′ə rīz), *v.t.,* **-rized, -riz·ing.** to attack with satire; criticize with mockery; seek to improve by ridicule.

sat·i·riz·er (sat′ə rī′zər), *n.* a person who satirizes.

sat·is·fac·tion (sat′is fak′shən), *n.* **1.** the act of satisfying; fully supplying or gratifying wants or wishes; fulfillment of conditions or desires: *The problem has been settled to the satisfaction of all concerned. The satisfaction of hunger requires food.* **2.** the condition of being satisfied; a pleased and contented feeling or state of mind: *Mary felt satisfaction at winning a prize. Jones expressed the utmost satisfaction at the account* (Henry Fielding). **3.** anything that makes a person feel pleased or contented: *It is a great satisfaction to have things turn out just the way you want. I cannot express what a satisfaction it was to me, to come into my old hutch* (Daniel Defoe). **4.** a response, information, etc., that fully meets doubts, objections, demands, etc. **5.** the payment of debt; the discharge of an obligation or claim; making up for a wrong or injury done. **6.** the performance by a penitent, especially as part of the sacrament of penance, of the expiatory act set forth by Church authority.
give satisfaction, a. to satisfy: *If this product does not give satisfaction, your money will be refunded.* **b.** to fight a duel because of an insult: *It is called "giving a man satisfaction" to urge your offence against him with your sword* (Sir Richard Steele).
[< Latin *satisfactiō, -ōnis* < *satisfacere;* see SATISFY]
—**Syn. 1.** gratification. **2.** contentment, complacency. **5.** reparation, atonement, expiation, amends. —**Ant. 2.** discontent, dissatisfaction.

sat·is·fac·to·ri·ly (sat′is fak′tər ə lē, -trə-), *adv.* in a satisfactory manner; so as to give satisfaction.

sat·is·fac·to·ri·ness (sat′is fak′tər ē nis, -trē-), *n.* satisfactory character or state; the power of satisfying or contenting.

sat·is·fac·to·ry (sat′is fak′tər ē, -trē), *adj.* **1.** good enough to satisfy; satisfying. **2.** *Theology.* expiatory; making reparation. —**Syn. 1.** gratifying, pleasing, adequate, sufficient.

sat·is·fi·er (sat′is fī′ər), *n.* a person or thing that satisfies.

sat·is·fy (sat′is fī), *v.,* **-fied, -fy·ing.** —*v.t.* **1.** to give enough to (a person); fulfill (desires, hopes, demands, etc.); put an end to (needs, wants, etc.): *to satisfy one's curiosity. He satisfied his hunger with a sandwich and milk. What do you suppose will satisfy the soul, except to walk free and own no superior?* (Walt Whitman). **2.** to meet fully (an objection, doubt, demand, etc.). **3.** to set free from doubt or uncertainty; convince: *The teacher is satisfied that his statement is true.* **4.** to pay (a debt or creditor). **5.** to make right (a wrong); make reparation to (a person): *After the accident he satisfied all claims for the damage he had caused.* **6.** to fulfill the conditions of: *to satisfy an algebraic equation.* —*v.i.* **1.** to make contented; give satisfaction; please. **2.** to make up for a wrong or injury. [< Middle French *satisfier,* learned borrowing from Latin *satisfacere* < *satis* enough + *facere* do]
—**Syn.** *v.t.* **1. Satisfy, content** mean to meet, wholly or partly, a person's desires and wants. **Satisfy** means to give enough to fulfill a person's desires, hopes, needs, etc.: *The little mongrel satisfied the boy's desire for a dog.* **Content** means to give enough to please a person and keep him from being unhappy because he does not have everything he wants: *A letter from her daughter once a week contented her.*

sat·is·fy·ing·ly (sat′is fī′ing lē), *adv.* so as to satisfy; satisfactorily.

sa·to·ri (sä tôr′ē, -tōr′-), *n.* spiritual enlightenment, the goal of Zen Buddhism: *His meditations may lead him to a mental crisis that produces a flash of intuitive insight known as satori* (New Yorker). [< Japanese *satori*]

sa·trap (sā′trap, sat′rap), *n.* **1.** a ruler, often a tyrant, who is subordinate to a higher ruler. **2.** a governor of a province under the ancient Persian monarchy. [< Latin *satrapes* < Greek *satrápēs* < Old Persian *xšathra-pāvan* guardian of the realm]

sa·trap·y (sā′trə pē, sat′rə-), *n., pl.* **-trap·ies.** the province, position, or authority of a satrap: *Eventually, the three sects ... developed huge financial and territorial satrapies in return for their subservience to colonialism* (Newsweek).

sat·u·ra·ble (sach′ər ə bəl), *adj.* that can be saturated; capable of saturation.

sat·u·rant (sach′ər ənt), *adj.* saturating. —*n.* any substance that charges, impregnates, or neutralizes completely.

sat·u·rate (sach′ə rāt), *v.,* **-rat·ed, -rat·ing,** *adj.* —*v.t.* **1.** to soak thoroughly; fill completely: *During the fog, the air was saturated with moisture. Saturate the moss with water before planting the bulbs in it. The whole spiritual atmosphere was saturated with cant* (James A. Froude). **2.** *Chemistry.* to cause (a substance) to combine with or dissolve the greatest possible amount of another substance: *This saturated solution of sugar cannot dissolve any more sugar.* **3.** *Physics.* to magnetize (a substance) so that the intensity of its magnetization reaches its maximum value. **4.** to cover with or concentrate bombs on (a target) so as to destroy completely.
—*adj.* **1.** (of colors) intense; deep. **2.** saturated.
[< Latin *saturāre* (with English *-ate*[1]) to glut, sate < *satur* full < *satis* enough]
—**Syn.** *v.t.* **1.** steep, drench, imbue.

sat·u·rat·ed (sach′ə rā′tid), *adj.* **1.** soaked thoroughly; wet. **2.** (of colors) containing no white. **3.** *Chemistry.* **a.** that has combined with or taken up in solution the largest possible proportion of some other substance: *When the relative humidity reaches 100 per cent the air is said to be saturated* (Finch and Trewartha). **b.** (of an organic compound) lacking double or triple bonds and having no free valence, as hydrocarbons of the methane series: *The members of the Methane Series do not form addition products and are therefore said to be saturated* (Parks and Steinbach). **4.** *Physics.* charged to the full extent of its capacity: *Further increase of plate potential does not increase the plate current, which is then said to become saturated* (Sears and Zemansky). **5.** (of minerals) containing the greatest proportion of silica possible.

saturated fat, solid or semisolid animal fat, such as butter and lard, that contains mainly saturated fatty acids. A diet high in such fat is believed to raise the cholesterol level in the blood, and is associated with certain heart diseases: *The degree of saturation depends on the number of hydrogen atoms on the fat molecule. Saturated fats can accommodate no more hydrogens* (Time).

sat·u·rat·er (sach′ə rā′tər), *n.* saturator.

sat·u·ra·tion (sach′ə rā′shən), *n.* **1.** the act or process of saturating: *The process of saturation is employed in changing liquid fats into solid fats . . .* (Harbaugh and Goodrich). **2.** the fact of being saturated; saturated condition: *The saturation of a color increases as the amount of white in it is decreased. The body is first magnetized to saturation . . . the field reduced to zero and it remains permanently magnetized* (Science News).

saturation bombing, a method of bombing in which the heaviest possible tonnage or largest possible number of bombs is concentrated on a target so as to destroy it completely: *They used a new strategy of saturation bombing, aimed at stopping the Communist rail supply to the front so that it stayed stopped* (New York Times).

saturation point, 1. the point at which a substance will combine with or take up in solution no more of another substance. **2.** the condition in which a person can endure no more: *The meeting was filled almost to the saturation point with upsets* (New Yorker).

sat·u·ra·tor (sach′ə rā′tər), *n.* a person or thing that saturates: *a saturator for supplying air saturated with water vapor.*

Sat·ur·day (sat′ər dē, -dā), *n.* the seventh and last day of the calendar week, following Friday. *Abbr.:* Sat.
[Old English *Sæterdæg,* also *Sæterndæg,* half-translation of Latin *Sāturnī diēs* day of Saturn (the planet)]

Sat·urn (sat′ərn), *n.* **1.** the ancient Roman god of agriculture and the harvest, identified with the Greek Cronus, believed to have ruled during a golden age and to have been deposed by his son Jupiter. **2.** the second largest planet in the solar system, and sixth in distance from the sun. Its orbit lies between those of Jupiter and Uranus and takes 29.46 years to complete, at a mean distance from the sun of 886,000,000 miles. It is surrounded by a system of three rings made up of small particles. *Saturn, the only planet easily visible on July evenings, shines toward the south* (Science News Letter). **3.** a space vehicle having several small rocket engines designed to furnish a thrust of 1.5 million pounds. **4.** (in alchemy and old chemistry) the metal lead. [< Latin *Sāturnus;* associated by the Romans with *satiō* sowing < *serere* to sow]

Sat·ur·na·le (sat′ər nā′lē), *n.* the singular of **Saturnalia.**

Sat·ur·na·li·a (sat′ər nā′lē ə, -nāl′yə), *n.pl.* the ancient Roman festival of Saturn, celebrated in December with much feasting and merrymaking. [< Latin *Sāturnālia* < *Sāturnus* Saturn]

sat·ur·na·li·a (sat′ər nā′lē ə, -nāl′yə), *n.pl.* any period of unrestrained revelry and license. [< *Saturnalia*]

Sat·ur·na·li·an (sat′ər nā′lē ən, -nāl′yən), *adj.* of or having to do with the Roman Saturnalia.

sat·ur·na·li·an (sat′ər nā′lē ən, -nāl′yən), *adj.* riotously merry; reveling without restraint. [< *Saturnalian*]

Sa·tur·ni·an (sə tėr′nē ən), *adj.* **1.** of or having to do with the god Saturn, whose reign is referred to as "the golden age." **2.** prosperous, happy, or peaceful. **3.** of or having to do with a form of verse used in early Roman poetry. **4.** of or having to do with the planet Saturn.

sa·tur·ni·id (sə tėr′nē id), *n.* any of a family of thick-bodied, giant silkworm moths, as the Cecropia moth, the luna moth, and the Polyphemus moth. *—adj.* of or belonging to this family of moths. [< New Latin *Saturniidae* the family name < *Saturnia* the typical genus < Latin *Sāturnius* having to do with Saturn (because of its titanic size)]

sat·ur·nine (sat′ər nīn), *adj.* **1.** gloomy; grave; taciturn: *The saturnine young man returned to France as the dashing hero of a cause célèbre* (Time). **2.** *Astrology.* born under or affected by the influence of the planet Saturn. **3.** suffering from or caused by lead poisoning. **4.** (in old chemistry) of, having to do with, or like lead. [< *Saturn,* the planet (because it was supposed to make those born under its sign morose) + *-ine*[1]] **—sat′ur·nine′ly,** *adv.* **—Syn. 1.** cheerless, glum.

sat·ur·nism (sat′ər niz əm), *n.* chronic lead poisoning.

Sat·ya·gra·ha (sut′yə gru′hə), *n.* (in India) a policy of passive resistance and withdrawal of cooperation with the state, begun by the followers of Gandhi in 1919 as a protest against certain abuses: *. . . as Gandhi conceived it—not only as a technique but as a soul force, Satyagraha* (Atlantic). [< Sanskrit *satyāgraha* justified obstinacy < *satya* truth + *ā-graha* a hanging on < *grah* to grasp]

Sat·ya·gra·hi (sut′yə gru′hē), *n.* one who favors the policy of Satyagraha.

sat·yr (sat′ər, sā′tər), *n.* **1.** an ancient Greek deity of the woods, who was part man and part beast. The satyrs were followers of Bacchus, the god of wine. **2.** a man who is beastly in thought and action: *From forty to fifty a man is at heart either a stoic or a satyr* (Arthur Wing Pinero). **3.** a man having satyriasis. **4.** any of a family of brown or grayish butterflies that have eyespots on the wings. [< Latin *satyrus* < Greek *sátyros*]

sat·y·ri·a·sis (sat′ə rī′ə sis), *n.* a morbid and uncontrollable sexual desire in a man. [< New Latin *satyriasis* < Greek *satyríāsis* < *sátyros* satyr]

sa·tyr·ic (sə tir′ik), *adj.* of or having to do with a satyr or satyrs.

sa·tyr·i·cal (sə tir′ə kəl), *adj.* of or like a satyr; satyric: *Boasting the most improbable plot since the satyrical heyday of Thorne Smith . . .* (Time).

satyr play, a ribald drama of ancient Greece, with a chorus of satyrs or satyr-like characters, written to be performed following a trilogy of tragedies at the spring-time Dionysian Festival: *The Athenians . . . would sit through three tragedies and a satyr play in one morning* (London Times).

sauce (sôs), *n., v.,* **sauced, sauc·ing.** *—n.* **1.** something, usually a liquid, served with food to make it taste better: *cranberry sauce with turkey, mint sauce with lamb, egg sauce with fish, and many different sauces with puddings.* **2.** *U.S.* stewed fruit: *applesauce.* **3.** something that adds interest or relish: *Fame is only one of the sauces of life* (A.C. Benson). **4.** *Informal.* sauciness; impertinence: *Jaunty girls gave sailors sauce* (Atlantic). **5.** *U.S.* garden sauce.
—v.t. **1.** to prepare with sauce; season: *to sauce meat with pepper. Now the shish kebab, sauced in Burgundy . . .* (New Yorker). **2.** to give interest or flavor to. **3.** *Informal.* to be saucy to. **4.** to reduce the harshness of: *to sauce criticism with flattery.*
[< Old French *sauce,* earlier *saulse* < Latin *salsa,* feminine adjective, salted, ultimately < *sāl, salis* salt]
—Syn. *n.* **4.** pertness, flippancy.

sauce Béarnaise, béarnaise sauce: *He lives a strangely vigorous life without butter, sauce Béarnaise, or dessert, and with mineral water instead of wine* (Newsweek).

sauce·boat (sôs′bōt′), *n.* a dish for serving sauce, usually with a lip.

sauce·box (sôs′boks′), *n. Informal.* a saucy person, especially a girl or young child.

sauce·pan (sôs′pan′), *n.* **1.** a metal dish with a handle and usually a lid, used for boiling, stewing, etc.: *Hotplates have special "glide-over" tops that remove the danger of tipping saucepans* (London Times). **2.** a small skillet with a long handle formerly used for boiling sauces and other small things.

sauce·pot (sôs′pot′), *n.* a saucepan.

sau·cer (sô′sər), *n.* **1.** a small, shallow dish to set a cup on. **2.** a small, round dish with its edge curved up: *to give a cat a saucer of cream.* **3.** anything round and shallow like a saucer.
[< Old French *saucier* sauce dish < *sauce;* see SAUCE] **—sau′cer·like′,** *adj.*

saucer eye, a large, round eye.

sau·cer-eyed (sô′sər īd′), *adj.* having very large, round eyes: *Saucer-eyed children sat watching the circus performers.*

sau·cer·ful (sô′sər fůl), *n., pl.* **-fuls.** enough to fill a saucer.

sauce suprême, a velouté made from chicken stock; suprême.

sau·cier (sō syā′), *n. French.* a cook who specializes in preparing sauces.

sau·ci·ly (sô′sə lē), *adv.* impudently; pertly: *She then smiled saucily in his face* (Charles Reade).

sau·ci·ness (sô′sē nis), *n.* impudence; pertness; rudeness: *Her sauciness was always charming because it was without emphasis* (George Eliot).

sau·cis·son (sō sē sôN′), *n. French.* a long pipe or bag made waterproof and filled with powder to serve as a fuse.

sau·cy (sô′sē), *adj.,* **-ci·er, -ci·est. 1.** showing lack of respect; impudent; rude: *saucy language or conduct.* **2.** pert; smart: *a saucy new hat.* **3.** *Obsolete.* scornful; disdainful: *In saucy state the griping broker sits* (John Gay). **—Syn. 1.** See **impertinent.**

Sa·u·di (sä ü′dē, sou′-), *adj.* Saudi Arabian. *—n.* **1.** a native or inhabitant of Saudi Arabia; Saudi Arabian. **2.** a member or supporter of the royal dynasty of Saudi Arabia.

Saudi Arabian, 1. of or having to do with the kingdom of Saudi Arabia, its people, or their language. **2.** a native or inhabitant of Saudi Arabia. Also, **Saudi.**

Sau·er·bra·ten (zou′ər brä′tən), *n. German.* a pot roast marinated in vinegar and herbs before cooking.

sauer·kraut (sour′krout′), *n.* cabbage cut fine, salted, and allowed to ferment. [< German *Sauerkraut* < *sauer* sour + *Kraut* vegetable, cabbage]

sau·ger (sô′gər), *n.* a North American pike perch smaller than a walleye. [American English; origin uncertain]

saugh (sôH, souH, säH), *n. Scottish.* a willow; sallow. [Old English *salh,* variant of *sealh* sallow[2]]

Sauk (sak, sôk), *n.* a member of a tribe of North American Indians of Algonkian stock who formerly lived west of Lake Michigan and now live in Oklahoma, Iowa, and Kansas. *—adj.* of or having to do with this tribe. Also, **Sac.**

Saul (sôl), *n.* in the Bible: **1.** the first king of Israel. I Samuel 9-31. **2.** the original name of the Apostle Paul. He was also known, prior to his conversion, as Saul of Tarsus. Acts 9:1-31.

sault (sü), *n.* a rapid in a river: *Sault Sainte Marie.* [< Canadian French *sault,* variant of Old French *saut* < Latin *saltus, -ūs* a leap < *salīre* leap. Compare ASSAULT.]

Saul·teaux (sôl tō′), *n., pl.* **-teaux** (-tō′, -tōz′), *adj. —n.* **1.** a member of a tribe of Ojibwa Indians inhabiting the woodlands of western Ontario, north of Lake Huron and Lake Superior. **2.** the language of this tribe.
—adj. of or having to do with this tribe or its language.
[< French *Saulteaux* < *sault* falls, rapids + *eaux,* plural of *eau* water; because the tribe annually met at the rapids of Sault Ste. Marie in Ontario]

sau·na (sou′nä), *n.* **1.** a steam bath that originated in Finland: *The sauna and Finland are so wedded that wherever the Finn goes, the sauna goes with him* (Harper's). **2.** a building used for such steam baths: *And a $20,000 sauna (steam) bath had to be constructed* (Wall Street Journal). [< Finnish *sauna*]

saun·ter (sôn′tər, sän′-), *v.i.* to walk along slowly and aimlessly; stroll: *to saunter through the park.*
—n. **1.** a leisurely or careless gait: *The other . . . walked slowly, with a sort of saunter, towards Adam* (George Eliot). **2.** a stroll: *a week-day saunter through the less busy parts of the metropolis* (Charles Lamb).
[origin uncertain] **—saun′ter·er,** *n.* **—saun′ter·ing·ly,** *adv.*

sau·rel (sôr′əl), *n., pl.* **-rels** or (*collectively*) **-rel.** any of various carangoid salt-water fishes common off the Atlantic coasts of Europe and America; scad; horse mackerel. Saurels are fusiform in shape with vertical plates arming the entire lateral line. [< French *saurel* < Old French *saur, sor* herring < a Germanic word]

sau·ri·an (sôr′ē ən), *adj.* **1.** belonging to or having to do with the lizards, or, formerly, with the lizards, the crocodiles, and certain extinct forms. **2.** of or like a lizard. *—n.* **1.** a lizard. **2.** any similar reptile, such as a crocodile or dinosaur.
[< New Latin *Sauria* an earlier order name (< Greek *saûros* lizard) + English *-an*]

saur·is·chi·an (sô ris′kē ən), *adj.* of or having to do with an order of carnivorous and herbivorous dinosaurs, having the lower pelvic elements directed downward, of the Mesozoic, including the sauropods, tyrannosaurus, etc. *—n.* a saurischian dinosaur. [< New Latin *Sauria* an earlier order name (< Greek *saûros* lizard) + Greek *ischíon* hip + English *-ian*]

sau·ro·pod (sôr′ə pod), *adj.* of or belonging to a group of herbivorous dinosaurs with a small head, long neck and tail, and limbs with five toes, comprising the largest-known land animals. —*n.* an animal of this group. [< New Latin *Sauropoda* the order name < Greek *saûros* lizard + *poús, podós* foot]

Sauropod (diplodocus) (over 80 ft. long)

sau·rop·o·dous (sô rop′ə dəs), *adj.* of or having to do with the sauropods.

sau·ry (sôr′ē), *n., pl.* **-ries** or (*collectively*) **-ry.** any of various small, slender, long-snouted fish related to the needlefishes and flying fishes. [apparently < New Latin *saurus* the species name < Greek *saûros* lizard]

sau·sage (sô′sij), *n.* chopped pork, beef, or other meats, seasoned and usually stuffed into a thin tube. [< Old North French *saussiche,* Old French *saucisse* < Vulgar Latin *salcīcia* < Latin *salere* to salt < *sāl, salis* salt. Compare SAUCE.]

sausage balloon, a long, cylindrical balloon used for observation in the late 1800's and as a barrage balloon in World War I.

sausage curl, a curl of hair resembling a sausage.

sausage tree, any of a group of African trees of the bignonia family with panicles of orange or reddish flowers, especially a variety grown for its long, edible fruit.

saus·su·rite (sôs′yə rīt, sô sûr′īt), *n.* a very compact mineral formed by the alteration of feldspar, composed chiefly of zoisite. [< Professor Horace B. de *Saussure,* 1740-1799, a Swiss naturalist, who described it first]

sau·té (sō tā′, sô-), *adj., n., v.,* **-téed, -té·ing.** —*adj.* cooked or browned in a little fat. —*n.* a dish of food cooked or browned in a little fat. —*v.t.* to fry quickly in a little fat: *crabmeat sautéed with butter.* [< French *sauté,* past participle of *sauter* to jump < Latin *saltāre* hop, dance (frequentative) < *salīre* to leap]

sau·terne or **Sau·terne** (sō tėrn′, sô-), *n.* **1.** a white wine made in the region south of Bordeaux, France: *In bad years the Sauternes are less sweet, but there's no such thing as "dry Sauternes"* (Atlantic). **2.** a similar wine made elsewhere. [< *Sauternes,* a town in France near where the grapes are grown]

sau·toir (sō twär′), *n.* **1.** a long ribbon, chain, or the like, worn about the neck, and drawn together some distance above the lower ends, often used to hold eyeglasses. **2.** *Heraldry.* saltire. [< French *sautoir;* see SALTIRE]

sauve qui peut (sōv′ kē pœ′), *French.* **1.** a general rout; hasty flight: *We did manage in our sauve qui peut to reach the top of that almost vertical wall where the path came out of the beechwoods* (New Yorker). **2.** (literally) let whoever can, save (himself).

sav·a·ble (sā′və bəl), *adj.* that can be saved. Also, **saveable.**

sav·age (sav′ij), *adj., n., v.,* **-aged, -ag·ing.** —*adj.* **1.** wild or rugged; uncultivated: . . . *a wild savage land of mountains, rivers, and forests* (W. H. Hudson). **2.** not civilized; barbarous: *savage customs; the barriers, which had so long separated the savage and the civilized nations of the earth* (Edward Gibbon). **3.** ready to fight; fierce; cruel; brutal: *a savage dog, a savage temper.* **4. a.** enraged; furiously angry: *Come, Jasper, you need not look so savage* (W. S. Hayward). **b.** rough or unsparing in speech: *He turned and gave a short savage order to one of his men* (Graham Greene). **5.** undomesticated; untamed. **6.** *Archaic.* (of a plant) uncultivated: *St. Foin . . . grows naturally savage without sowing or tillage* (Jethro Tull). **7.** *Archaic.* rude; unpolished: . . . *To savage music, wilder as it grows* (Shelley).
—*n.* **1.** a member of a people in the lowest stage of development or civilization; uncivilized person: *nations of savages . . . barbarous and brutish to the last degree* (Daniel Defoe). **2.** a fierce, brutal, or cruel person: *Witness the patient ox . . . Driv'n to the slaughter . . . while the savage at his heels Laughs at the frantic suff'rer's fury* (William Cowper). **3.** a person ignorant or neglectful of the rules of good behavior. **4.** *Obsolete.* a wild animal: *When the grim savage [the lion], to his rifled den Too late returning, snuffs the track of men* (Alexander Pope).
—*v.t.* **1.** (of an animal) to attack viciously, especially with the teeth. **2.** to assail in a ferocious manner; subject to savage attack: *The current vogue in satire . . . is to savage every father figure in sight* (Manchester Guardian)
[< Old French *sauvage* < Late Latin *salvāticus,* for Latin *silvāticus* < *silva* forest] —**Syn.** *adj.* **2.** primitive. **3.** ferocious. See **fierce.**

sav·age·ly (sav′ij lē), *adv.* in a savage manner; cruelly; fiercely: *The football player tackled the runner savagely. Your wife and babes savagely slaughter'd* (Shakespeare).

sav·age·ness (sav′ij nis), *n.* **1.** wildness: *the savageness of a jungle scene.* **2.** savage or uncivilized condition: *the savageness of some remote African tribes.* **3.** cruelty; fierceness: *In spite of the savageness of his satires . . . [Alexander Pope's] natural disposition seems to have been an amiable one* (Lowell).

sav·age·rous (sav′ij rəs), *adj. Dialect.* savage; fierce. [< *savage* + (dange)*rous*]

sav·age·ry (sav′ij rē), *n., pl.* **-ries. 1.** wildness: *The appearance of the rock-bound coast is one of unrelieved savagery* (George Augustus Sala). **2.** an uncivilized condition: *to live in savagery.* **3.** fierceness; cruelty; brutality: *What they could not get by borrowing or adapting, they went after with a savagery that bloodied history* (Time). **4.** savage persons or beasts as a group: *That the white settlers were not entirely overwhelmed in the first mad, blood-thirsting rush of relentless savagery is a matter for marvel* (Robert S. S. Baden-Powell). —**Syn. 3.** ferocity.

sav·ag·ism (sav′ə jiz əm), *n.* savagery: *There are various kinds of life: . . . that of youth and age, of ignorance and knowledge, of civilization and savagism* (William Sparrow).

sa·van·na or **sa·van·nah** (sə van′ə), *n.* **1.** a treeless, grassy plain, especially one in the southeastern United States or tropical America. **2.** a region of grassland with scattered trees lying between the equatorial forest and the hot deserts in either hemisphere. [< Spanish *sabana* < earlier *zavana* < Arawak (Haiti)]

savanna sparrow, a streaked, brownish, North American sparrow of the open fields and marshes.

sa·vant (sə vänt′, sav′ənt; *French* sȧväN′), *n., pl.* **-vants** (*French* -väN′). a man of learning: *This seemed to make him a savant on subjects political* (Atlantic). *Saint-Simon divided mankind into three classes: the savants, the propertied, and the unpropertied* (Edmund Wilson). [< Old French *savant,* present participle of *savoir* know < Vulgar Latin *sapēre,* for Latin *sapere* be wise] —**Syn.** sage, scholar.

sa·vate (sȧ vȧt′), *n.* a French style of boxing in which the feet and head are used as well as fists: *In the French savate, kicking is a legal form of attack* (New Yorker). [< French *savate* (literally) old shoe; origin uncertain. Compare SABOT.]

save¹ (sāv), *v.,* **saved, sav·ing,** *n.* —*v.t.* **1.** to make safe from harm, danger, loss, etc.; rescue: *to save a drowning man.* **2.** to keep safe from harm, danger, hurt, loss, etc.; protect: *to save one's honor. The loan saved my credit, and made my fortune* (Edward G. Bulwer-Lytton). **3.** to lay aside; store up: *to save pieces of string, to save money for his son's education.* **4.** to keep from spending or wasting: *Save your strength.* **5.** to prevent; make less: *to save work, to save trouble, to save expense. A stitch in time saves nine.* **6.** to treat carefully to lessen wear, weariness, etc.: *Large print saves one's eyes.* **7.** *Theology.* to set free from sin and its results: *Jesus came to save the people of the world.* **8.** *Especially British.* to avoid missing: *The note must go this instant to save the post* (Thackeray). —*v.i.* **1.** to keep a person or thing from harm, danger, loss, etc. **2.** to lay up money; add to one's property. **3.** to avoid expense or waste; be economical: *She saves in every way she can.*
—*n.* the act of saving, especially by keeping an opponent from scoring in a game: *The . . . goalie . . . had a comparatively easy time of it. He had to make only three saves in the first period* (New York Times).
[< Old French *sauver,* earlier *salver* < Late Latin *salvāre* < Latin *salvus* safe]
—**Syn.** *v.t.* **1, 7.** deliver, redeem. **2.** safeguard, shield, preserve. **3.** hoard, reserve.

save² (sāv), *prep.* except; but: *He works every day save Sundays. He heard no other sound save . . . his own breathing* (James M. Barrie). —*conj.* **1.** excepting. **2.** *Archaic.* unless. [variant of *safe,* in sense of "not being involved"; probably patterned on French *sauf* safe, used in an absolute construction]

save·a·ble (sā′və bəl), *adj.* that can be saved. Also, **savable.**

save-all (sāv′ôl′), *n.* **1.** a means for preventing loss or waste, especially a receptacle for collecting things that would otherwise be lost or not used. **2.** a penny bank. **3.** *Dialect.* a pinafore or overall.

sav·e·loy (sav′ə loi), *n. British.* a highly seasoned, dried pork sausage. [< French *cervelas,* earlier *cervelat.* Compare CERVELAT.]

sav·er (sā′vər), *n.* a person or thing that saves: *A washing machine is a saver of time and strength.*

sav·in or **sav·ine** (sav′in), *n.* **1.** a juniper shrub whose tops yield an oily drug used in medicine. **2.** this drug. **3.** the red cedar. [Old English *safine* < Vulgar Latin *savina* < Latin (*herba*) *sabīna* Sabine herb]

sav·ing (sā′ving), *adj.* **1.** that saves. **2.** tending to save up money; avoiding waste; economical: *Old-fashioned housewives were usually very saving.* **3.** making a reservation: *a saving clause.* **4.** *Theology.* delivering from sin: *Good works may exist without saving principles . . .; but saving principles . . . never can exist without good works* (Samuel Taylor Coleridge). **5.** compensating; redeeming: *Rich in saving common sense* (Tennyson).
—*n.* **1. a.** the act of saving money, time, labor, etc.; economy: *Saving, in short, enriches, and spending impoverishes* (John Stuart Mill). **b.** an instance of this; a reduction in the spending of money, time, etc.: *It will be a saving to take this short cut.* **2.** that which is saved, especially a sum of money: *The discount gave me a saving of $25.* **3.** *Law.* a reservation; exception.
savings, money saved: *With our policyholder dividends your total savings can be really surprising* (Newsweek).
—*prep.* **1.** save; except: *Saving a few crusts, we had eaten nothing all day.* **2.** with all due respect to or for: *saving your presence.*
—*conj.* with the exception of: *And what pleasure more has he that possesses them, saving that he may look upon them with his eyes?* (Miles Coverdale). —**sav′ing·ly,** *adv.* —**sav′ing·ness,** *n.* —**Syn.** *adj.* **1.** preserving. **2.** thrifty, provident, sparing, frugal.

saving grace, 1. a redeeming feature. **2.** *Theology.* God's grace that gives salvation.

sav·ings account (sā′vingz), an account in a savings bank.

savings and loan association, a bank that is owned by its members, who can borrow money to improve real estate: *Under Federal tax laws, savings banks and savings and loan associations may transfer all earnings to surplus, which is tax-free up to 12 per cent of deposits* (New York Times).

savings bank, a bank which pays interest on all deposits and accepts money only for savings and investment. It does not transfer money to other banks or persons on checks written by the depositors. *Commercial bankers say that because of a difference in tax treatment and authorized investment policies, savings banks are able to pay a higher interest rate on savings than are commercial banks* (New York Times).

savings bond, a bond issued by the U.S. Government to help pay its expenses and encourage personal saving. Bonds can be cashed with interest after a certain time and have been used in wartime to help curb inflation by absorbing excess private funds.

sav·ior (sāv′yər), *n.* a person who saves or rescues: *He was extolled as the savior of the country* (Washington Irving). [< Old French *sauveour,* adaptation of Late Latin *salvātor* < *salvāre* to save] —**Syn.** deliverer.

sav·iour (sāv′yər), *n. Especially British.* savior.

Sav·iour or **Sav·ior** (sāv′yər), *n.* Jesus Christ.

sa·voir-faire (sav′wär fãr′), *n.* knowledge of just what to do and how to do it; social grace; tact: *It was typical of the confusion — the absence of savoir-faire—that he had expected from Earline* (New Yorker). [< French *savoir-faire* (literally) knowing how to act]

sa·voir-vi·vre (sav′wär vē′vrə), *n.* knowledge of the world and of the usages of polite society; good breeding: *Our society is to have the utmost polish, ease, and grace of manner, and the completest savoir-vivre* (William H. Mallock). [< French *savoir-vivre* (literally) knowing how to live] —**Syn.** urbanity.

Sa·vonne·rie carpet (sä vun rē′), a carpet from Savonnerie, France, where the first carpet factory of modern times was established in 1627. The texture of such a carpet is rich and velvety, with a deep pile surface.

sa·vor (sā′vər), *n.* **1.** taste or smell; flavor: *This soup has a savor of onion.* **2.** a distinctive quality; noticeable trace: *There is a savor of conceit in everything he says. The savor of death from all things there that live . . .* (Milton). **3.** a pleasing flavor; interesting quality: *a dull life, quite without savor.* **4.** *Archaic.* repute; estimation.
—*v.i.* **1.** to taste or smell (of): *That sauce savors of lemon.* **2.** to have the quality or nature (of): *a request that savors of a command. The plot savored of treason.* —*v.t.* **1.** to perceive or appreciate by taste or smell; enjoy the savor of: *He savored the soup with pleasure. In his youth the cavalier had savored life to the full.* **2.** to give flavor to; season. **3.** to show traces of the presence or influence of: *Bad manners savor a bad education. Willful barrenness, that . . . savors only rancor and pride . . .* (Milton). **5.** *Obsolete.* to discern; note; perceive.
[< Old French *savour, savur* < Latin *sapor, -ōris,* related to *sapere* to taste, be wise] —**sa′vor·er,** *n.*
—**Syn.** *n.* **1,** *v.i.* **2.** smack¹.

sa·vor·i·ly (sā′vər ə lē), *adv.* in a savory manner; with a pleasing taste or smell.

sa·vor·i·ness (sā′vər ē nis), *n.* savory quality; pleasing taste or smell: *the savoriness of an orange or of meat.*

sa·vor·less (sā′vər lis), *adj.* without flavor; insipid.

sa·vor·ous (sā′vər əs), *adj.* savory.

sa·vor·y¹ (sā′vər ē), *adj.,* **-vor·i·er, -vor·i·est,** *n., pl.* **-vor·ies.** —*adj.* **1.** pleasing in taste or smell: *The savory smell of roasting turkey greeted us as we entered the house.* **2.** giving a relish; salty or piquant and not sweet. **3.** morally pleasing; agreeable.
—*n.* a small portion of highly seasoned food served at the beginning or end of a dinner to stimulate the appetite or digestion: *Later over soup, steak and savory, served by several maids, there were painful attempts at conversation* (New Yorker).
[< Old French *savoure,* past participle of *savourer* to taste < *savour;* see SAVOR]
—**Syn.** *adj.* **1.** appetizing, palatable, tasty, toothsome.

sa·vor·y² (sā′vər ē), *n., pl.* **-vor·ies.** any of several fragrant, often woody herbs of the mint family, used for seasoning food. [Middle English *saverey* < Old French *savoreie,* alteration of Latin *saturēia*]

sa·vour (sā′vər), *n., v.i., v.t. Especially British.* savor: . . . *a name of evil savour in the land* (Tennyson). *And now, with so little left, each moment must be savoured to the full* (London Times).

sa·vour·y¹ (sā′vər ē), *adj.,* **-vour·i·er, -vour·i·est,** *n., pl.* **-vour·ies.** *Especially British.* savory¹.

sa·vour·y² (sā′vər ē), *n., pl.* **-vour·ies.** *Especially British.* savory².

sa·voy (sə voi′), *n.* a variety of common cabbage with a compact head and wrinkled leaves. [< French *chou de Savoie* (Savoy cabbage) < *Savoie* Savoy, a region in France]

Sa·voy·ard (sə voi′ərd), *n.* **1.** a native or inhabitant of Savoy, a region in eastern France. **2.** an actor, producer, or warm admirer of Gilbert and Sullivan's operas, many of which were first produced at the Savoy Theater, London: *Making public for the first time such items as Gilbert's own plot-books, it is a "must" for all Savoyards and lovers of light opera* (Saturday Review). —*adj.* of Savoy or its people.

Savoy cake, a ladyfinger.

Savoy medlar, a European shrub or tree, related to the shadbush.

sav·vy (sav′ē), *v.,* **-vied, -vy·ing,** *n., adj. Slang.* —*v.t., v.i.* to know; understand: *You think you are wise, but there's a lot of things you don't savvy* (Owen Wister). —*n.* understanding; intelligence; sense: *I said he had savvy enough to find the index in "Gray's Anatomy"* (Sinclair Lewis). *Author Laing shows enough savvy about supermarkets to have been born and bred in one* (Time). —*adj.* intelligent; sensible; knowing: . . . *a savvy farm spokesman and Ike's campaign adviser on agriculture* (Time). [partly < French *savez(-vous)?* do you know? partly < Spanish *sabe (usted)* (or *sabes*) you know, both < Vulgar Latin *sapēre,* for Latin *sapere* be wise, be knowing; have taste]

saw¹ (sô), *n., v.,* **sawed, sawed** or **sawn, saw·ing.** —*n.* **1.** a tool for cutting, made of a thin blade with sharp teeth on the edge: *The saw . . . is made of a new . . . stainless steel* (Newsweek). **2.** a machine with such a tool for cutting. **3.** a tool without teeth that wears its way through stone, etc.

CIRCULAR
CROSSCUT HAND
TWO-HANDED CROSSCUT
Saws (def. 1)

—*v.t.* **1.** to cut with a saw. **2.** to make with a saw: *Boards are sawed from logs.* **3.** to cut as if with a saw; move through as if sawing: *Do not saw the air too much with your hand* (Shakespeare). **4.** to work (something) from side to side like a saw. —*v.i.* **1.** to use a saw: *Can you saw straight?* **2.** to be sawed: *Pine saws more easily than oak.* **3.** to cut as a saw does.
[Old English *sagu, saga*] —**saw′er,** *n.* —**saw′like′,** *adj.*

saw² (sô), *v.* the past tense of **see**¹: *I saw a robin yesterday.*

saw³ (sô), *n.* a wise saying; proverb: *"A stitch in time saves nine" is a familiar saw. It is an old Wall Street saw that "the market never discounts anything twice"* (Newsweek). [Old English *sagu,* related to *secgan* to say¹] —**Syn.** maxim, adage.

saw·back (sô′bak′), *n.* a regularly serrate ridge or mountain.

saw·bill (sô′bil′), *n.* any of various birds with a serrate bill, such as the motmot.

saw·bones (sô′bōnz′), *n. Slang.* a doctor; surgeon: *The kindly sawbones nodded* (Atlantic).

saw·buck (sô′buk′), *n. U.S.* **1.** a sawhorse. **2.** *Slang.* a ten-dollar bill. **3.** *Slang.* a twenty-dollar bill. [American English, probably < Dutch *zaagbok*]

saw·der (sô′dər), *n. Informal.* flattery; blarney: *My Lord Jermyn seems to have his insolence as ready as his soft sawder* (George Eliot). [variant of *solder*]

saw·dust (sô′dust′), *n.* small particles of wood made by sawing: *We prefer hardwood sawdust, like birch, maple, and oak* (New Yorker).
—*adj.* **1.** filled or covered with sawdust: *a sawdust doll, a sawdust floor.* **2.** of or having to do with a tent show or tent meeting at which the floor is covered with sawdust: *a sawdust star, a sawdust preacher.* **3.** unsubstantial; insignificant: *[Mussolini] knew himself to be a sawdust Caesar* (Punch).
—*v.t.* to cover, sprinkle, or strew with sawdust.

sawdust trail, *U.S.* **1.** the trail of revivalists; the round of revival meetings and activities: . . . *an insider looking disdainfully out the stained-glass window of the established church at . . . the sawdust trail* (Robert MacBain). **2.** the road of repentance or conversion: *to hit the sawdust trail.* [because repentant sinners at a tent meeting go down the sawdust-covered aisle to the altar]

sawed-off (sôd′ôf′, -of′), *adj.* **1.** cut or sawed short: *sawed-off matchsticks. He tried to hide a sawed-off shotgun . . . by shoving it down the side of his rubber boot* (Maclean's). **2.** *U.S. Slang.* small in size; short: *An amiable, sawed-off little man, with a manner as unobtrusive as his . . . crew haircut* (Newsweek).

saw·fish (sô′fish′), *n., pl.* **-fish·es** or (*collectively*) **-fish.** a fish like a shark, having a long, flat snout with a row of sharp teeth on each edge. The sawfish grows to about 20 feet long and bears live young.

saw·fly (sô′flī′), *n., pl.* **-flies.** any of a group of hymenopterous insects. The female sawfly has a sawlike organ for cutting slits in plants to hold her eggs.

saw grass, *U.S.* any of various plants of the sedge family having long, slender, saw-toothed leaves.

saw·horse (sô′hôrs′), *n.* a frame for holding wood that is being sawed.

saw log, a log fit for sawing into boards: *Crooked and diseased trees can be sold as pulpwood, while straight, healthy trees grow into valuable saw logs* (Science News Letter).

saw·man (sô′mən), *n., pl.* **-men.** a man who works with a saw: *The sawman in a steel mill . . . tries to calculate how to divide up billets hundreds of feet in length* (New Scientist).

saw·mill (sô′mil′), *n.* **1.** a building or place where machines saw timber into planks, boards, etc. **2.** a machine for such sawing.

saw·mill·er (sô′mil′ər), *n.* the proprietor or manager of a sawmill.

saw·mill·ing (sô′mil′ing), *n.* the business or work of sawing wood in a sawmill.

sawn (sôn), *v.* sawed; a past participle of **saw**¹.

Saw·ney (sô′nē), *n., pl.* **-neys.** *Informal.* **1.** a nickname for a Scotsman. **2.** a fool or simpleton: *He's a Sawney but you must not drive him to bay* (Cardinal Newman). [variant of *Sandy,* short for *Alexander*]

sawn·wood (sôn′wu̇d′), *n.* wood cut up for lumber.

Saw·ny (sô′nē), *n., pl.* **-nies.** Sawney.

saw palmetto, a shrublike palmetto with leafstalks with spiny teeth, found in the southern United States and the West Indies.

saw·pit (sô′pit′), *n.* a pit over which a log is sawed into planks by two men, the pit allowing room for the blade and for the bottom sawyer to work.

saw set, an instrument used to set the teeth of a saw.

saw·tim·ber (sô′tim′bər), *n.* trees large enough to be cut for lumber: *The growth of new sawtimber at last almost matches the amount cut down* (Time).

saw-tooth (sô′tüth′), *adj.* saw-toothed: *They found that during a dream the eyeballs move rapidly and brain waves take on a saw-tooth pattern quite different from the long, rolling waves of dreamless sleep* (Scientific American).

saw-toothed (sô′tütht′), *adj.* **1.** having teeth on the edge, like a saw. **2.** notched like teeth on a saw; serrate.

saw-whet owl (sô′hwet′), a small, brown and white owl of North America, which has an extremely harsh and rasping call: *But we almost missed the tiny saw-whet owl, motionless on a dead limb just out of arm's reach* (Atlantic). [because the owl's call sounds like the filing of a *saw*]

saw·yer (sô′yər), *n.* **1.** a man whose work is sawing timber into planks, boards, etc. **2.** any of various beetles whose larvae bore large holes in wood. **3.** *U.S.* a tree with one end caught in the bed of a stream and the other swaying with the current: . . . *abundance of water from shore to shore, and no bars, snags, sawyers, or wrecks in his road* (Mark Twain). [< *saw*¹ + *-yer,* as in *lawyer*]

sax¹ (saks), *n.* a tool for trimming slate roof tiles and for making nail holes in them. [Old English *seax* knife, dagger]

sax² (saks), *n., pl.* **sax·es.** *Informal.* **1.** a saxophone: *[He] turned down an offer to play his sax on a U.S. vaudeville circuit* (Maclean's). **2.** a saxophone player: *The five saxes play with savage bite or else hum in their eerie, split harmonies behind a pagan trumpet solo* (Time). [short for *saxophone*]

Sax., **1.** Saxon. **2.** Saxony.

sax·a·tile (sak′sə təl), *adj. Biology.* saxicoline. [< Latin *saxātilis* < *saxum* rock, stone]

Saxe blue (saks), **1.** a dye obtained from indigo dissolved in sulfuric acid, used for dyeing wool and silk. **2.** a deep blue, brighter than indigo blue. [< French *Saxe* Saxony]

sax·horn (saks′hôrn′), *n.* a brass musical instrument like a trumpet, having valves, a loud, full tone, and a wide range. A tuba is a large saxhorn with a bass tone. [< Adolphe *Sax,* 1814-1894, a Belgian inventor. Compare SAXOPHONE.]

sax·ic·a·vous (sak sik′ə vəs), *adj.* rock-boring, as certain mollusks. [< New Latin *saxicavus* (with English *-ous*) < Latin *saxum* rock + *cavāre* to hollow]

sax·ic·o·line (sak sik′ə lin, -lin), *adj. Biology.* living on or among rocks; saxatile. [< Latin *saxum* rock, stone + *colere* inhabit + English *-ine*¹]

sax·ic·o·lous (sak sik′ə ləs), *adj.* saxicoline.

sax·i·fra·ga·ceous (sak′sə frə gā′shəs), *adj.* belonging to the saxifrage family. [< New Latin *Saxifragaceae* the family name (< *Saxifraga* the typical genus, saxifrage) + English *-ous*]

sax·i·frage (sak′sə frij), *n.* any of a group of low, spreading plants, most of which have rosettes of thick leaves with silvery, toothed edges. Saxifrages are often grown in rock gardens for their clusters of white, yellow, or red flowers. *Saxifrage leaves resemble cacti in their adaptation to dry climate* (Scientific American). [< Old French *saxifrage, sassifrage* < Latin *saxifraga* < *saxum* rock + a root of *frangere* to break. Doublet of SALSIFY.]

saxifrage family, a group of dicotyledonous herbs, shrubs, and small trees found chiefly in temperate and frigid regions. The family includes the saxifrage, gooseberry, currant, hydrangea, syringa, and miterwort.

Sax·on (sak′sən), *n.* **1.** a member of a Germanic tribe living in northwestern Germany in ancient times. With the Angles and Jutes, the Saxons conquered England in the 400's and 500's A.D. **2.** the language of the Saxons. **3.** Anglo-Saxon; Old English. **4.** a native or inhabitant of Saxony, a former province in northwestern Germany, now a region in East Germany.
—*adj.* **1.** of or having to do with the early Saxons or their language. **2.** Anglo-Saxon: *His [Thoreau's] character ... in singular combination with a very strong Saxon genius* ... (Emerson). **3.** English. **4.** of or having to do with Saxony in modern Germany.
[probably < Old French *Saxon,* learned borrowing from Latin *Saxo, Saxonēs,* plural < Germanic (compare Old High German *Sahso*)]

Saxon architecture, a rough, unrefined variety of Romanesque architecture common in England before the Norman conquest.

Sax·o·ni·an (sak sō′nē ən), *adj.* **1.** of or having to do with Saxony in modern Germany; Saxon. **2.** of or having to do with a division of the Permian period at the end of the Paleozoic era.

Sax·on·ism (sak′sə niz əm), *n.* **1.** Saxon or Anglo-Saxon character. **2.** an attachment for what is Anglo-Saxon. **3.** an Anglo-Saxon idiom.

Sax·on·ist (sak′sə nist), *n.* a Saxon scholar; person learned in Anglo-Saxon.

Sax·on·ize (sak′sə nīz), *v.t.,* **-ized, -iz·ing.** to make Saxon or Anglo-Saxon: *Other invaders ... poured in ... till the island was Saxonized* (Charles H. Pearson).

Sax·o·ny or **sax·o·ny** (sak′sə nē), *n., pl.* **-nies. 1.** a woolen fabric of high quality with a glossy surface: ... *fine saxonies, cheviots, flannels and worsteds* (New Yorker). **2.** a fine knitting yarn with a close twist.

sax·o·phone (sak′sə fōn), *n.* a brass musical wind instrument with keys for the fingers and a reed mouthpiece like that of a clarinet. [< Adolphe *Sax,* 1814-1894, a Belgian inventor + *-phone*]

Saxophone

sax·o·phon·ic (sak′sə fon′ik), *adj.* of or for the saxophone.

sax·o·phon·ist (sak′sə fō′nist), *n.* a saxophone player: *A talented jazz saxophonist* ... (Newsweek).

sax·tu·ba (saks′tü′bə, -tyü′-), *n.* a large saxhorn having a deep tone. [< *sax-,* as in *saxhorn* + *tuba*]

say[1] (sā), *v.,* **said, say·ing,** *n.* —*v.t.* **1.** to speak: *What did you say? Learn to say "please" and "thank you." And Enid could not say one tender word* (Tennyson). **2.** to put into words; express; declare; state: *to say what you think. We hear it said that men go down before your spear* ... (Tennyson). **3.** to recite; repeat: *to say one's prayers, to say grace.* **4.** to take as an estimate; suppose: *a bookcase containing, say, 100 books. You can learn to dance in, say, ten lessons.* **5.** to express an opinion: *It is hard to say which dress is prettier. Can anyone really say he is wrong?*
—*v.i.* **1.** to say words; talk: *So he says.* **2.** to express an opinion.
not to say, to use a more moderate word or statement than: *His language was irreverent, not to say blasphemous.*
that is to say, that is; in other words: *She invited us to her birthday party on Labor Day; that is to say, next Monday.*
to say nothing of, without mentioning: *She is a beautiful young woman, to say nothing of her kindness and generosity.*
—*n.* **1.** what a person says or has to say: *He said his say and sat down.* **2.** *Informal.* a turn to say something, or to make a suggestion, decision, or reply: *It is now my say. To guard the security of its loan, the bank wants a say in any future Egyptian borrowings* (Newsweek).
have a say, to have the right to be consulted; have the power to make or help make a decision: *The landscape architect has a say not only in the development but in the planning and siting of these roads* (Observer).
have the say, *U.S.* to be in command: *Who has the say in the matter?*
[Middle English *seien,* Old English *secgan*] —**say′er,** *n.*
—**Syn.** *v.t.* **1.** utter, articulate, enunciate. **2.** tell, announce, assert, allege. **3.** recount. **4.** assume.
➔ **Say** is the general word for speaking: *Please say when you have had enough.* **Talk** implies a series of sayings, a conversation: *They talked all evening about old times.* **State** implies a formal saying or, as the word itself suggests, a statement: *Would you please state your frank opinion of the plan?*

say[2] (sā), *v.t., n. Obsolete.* assay; trial; taste; sample. [short for *assay*]

say[3] (sā), *n. Obsolete.* a cloth of silk or wool resembling serge, and from which serge was developed. [< French *saie* < Latin *saga,* plural of *sagum* military cloak]

sa·ya (sä′yä), *n., pl.* **-yas.** a skirt worn in the Philippines in the manner of a sarong. [< Tagalog *saya*]

say·a·ble (sā′ə bəl), *adj.* that can be said: *Browning has said all that was sayable concerning the celebrated cause* (F.M. Wilson).

say·est (sā′ist), *v. Archaic.* say. "Thou sayest" means "you say."

sa·yid (sī′id, sä′yid), *n.* (in Moslem countries) the title given to a person supposed to be descended from Mohammed through his daughter Fatima: *A young sayid, or holy man, presented himself for employment the first day* (Atlantic). Also, **sayyid.** [< Arabic *sayyid* lord]

say·ing (sā′ing), *n.* **1.** making a statement: *Saying and doing are two things, we say* (Thomas Heywood). **2.** something said; statement. **3.** a proverb: *"Haste makes waste" is a saying.*
go without saying, to be too obvious to need mention: *It goes without saying that you are always welcome at our house.*
—**Syn. 1.** utterance, declaration, assertion. **2.** adage, saw, maxim.

say·nète (se net′), *n.* **1.** (in Spain) a short, amusing dramatic piece with few characters. **2.** (in France) a somewhat similar short dramatic piece. [< French *saynète* < Spanish *sainete* (literally) a delicacy < *sain* fat. Compare SAINETE.]

sa·yo·na·ra (sä′yō nä′rä), *n. Japanese.* goodbye; farewell: *Michener's novel concludes with the lovers forlornly bidding each other sayonara* (New Yorker).

says (sez), *v.* the 3rd person singular, present indicative of **say**[1]: *He says "No" to everything.*

Say's law (sāz), *Economics.* the theory that in a system of free enterprise the goods produced represent demand as well as supply, so that total supply and total demand are equal, and overproduction is impossible. [< Jean Baptiste *Say,* 1767-1832, a French economist who formulated the theory]

say-so (sā′sō′), *n. Informal.* **1.** an unsupported statement; one's mere word: *They'd grab a bright idea right away, just on the say-so of somebody they trusted* (New Yorker). **2.** authority; power: *We would want the say-so on where the buildings are put up and what kind of buildings* (Wall Street Journal).

Say's phoebe (sāz), a small bird of western North America with a brownish-gray back and a rust-colored chest, a kind of phoebe. [< Thomas *Say,* 1787-1834, an American naturalist]

sayst (sāst), *v. Archaic.* sayest; say. "Thou sayst" means "You say."

say·yid (sī′id), *n.* sayid.

Saz·e·rac (saz′ə rak), *n.* a cocktail made with bourbon, absinthe, bitters, and sugar, and served with ice and a twist of lemon peel. [probably < a French proper name]

sb., substantive.

s.b. or **sb** (no periods), stolen base or stolen bases.

Sb (no period), antimony (chemical element; Latin, *stibium*).

S.B., an abbreviation for the following:
1. Bachelor of Science (Latin, *Scientiae Baccalaureus*).
2. simultaneous broadcast.
3. South Britain (England and Wales).

SBA (no periods) or **S.B.A.,** *U.S.* Small Business Administration: *SBA lends to small business, helps it get government contracts, provides information* ... (Newsweek).

SBIC (no periods) or **S.B.I.C.,** small business investment company.

sbir·ro (zbir′rō), *n., pl.* **-ri** (-rē). (in Italy) a policeman. [< Italian *sbirro,* variant of *birro* < Late Latin *birrus* a cloak (because they are worn by policemen)]

'sblood (zblud), *interj. Archaic.* "God's blood," used as an oath.

SBR (no periods), styrene-butadiene rubber.

sc (no periods), small capitals.

sc., an abbreviation for the following:
1. he or she engraved or carved it (Latin, *sculpsit*).
2. namely (Latin, *scilicet*).
3. scale.
4. scene.
5. a. science. **b.** scientific.
6. screw.
7. scruple or scruples (in apothecaries' weight).

s.c., an abbreviation for the following:
1. (of paper) sized and calendered.
2. small capitals.
3. (of paper) super-calendered.

Sc (no period), **1.** scandium (chemical element). **2.** strato-cumulus (cloud).

Sc., **1.** science. **2.** Scotch. **3.** Scots. **4.** Scottish.

S.C., an abbreviation for the following:
1. Sanitary Corps.
2. Signal Corps.
3. South Carolina.
4. Staff College.
5. Staff Corps.
6. Supreme Court.

scab (skab), *n., v.,* **scabbed, scab·bing.** —*n.* **1.** a crust that forms over a sore during healing: *A scab formed on the spot where he was vaccinated.* **2.** a skin disease in animals, especially sheep; mange. **3. a.** any of several fungous diseases of plants, usually producing dark, crustlike spots. **b.** one of these spots. **4.** *Slang.* a workman who will not join a labor union or who takes a striker's place: *Thousands of workers poured through picket lines amid shouts of "scabs," "blacklegs" and "traitors" and into auto making factories* (Wall Street Journal). **5.** *Slang.* a rascal; scoundrel.
—*v.i.* **1.** to become covered with a scab. **2.** *Slang.* to act or work as a scab.
[< Scandinavian (compare Danish *skab*)]

scab·bard (skab′ərd), *n.* a sheath or case for the blade of a sword, dagger, etc. —*v.t.* to put into a scabbard; sheathe. [alteration (perhaps influenced by *halberd*) of Middle English *scauberc* < Anglo-French *escaubers,* plural, Old French *escalberc,* perhaps < Germanic]

scabbard fish, any of various fishes with a long, thin, silvery body and a long dorsal fin, as a variety found in the Pacific off North America.

scabbed (skabd), *adj.* **1.** having scab or mange. **2.** covered with scabs. **3.** *Obsolete.* mean; contemptible.

scab·bi·ly (skab′ə lē), *adv.* in a scabby manner.

scab·bi·ness (skab′ē nis), *n.* scabby quality or condition.

scab·ble (skab′əl), *v.t.,* **-bled, -bling.** to shape or dress (stone) roughly: *The facings of the stones in Hadrian's Wall are sometimes roughly tooled or ... scabbled with the pick* (Thomas Wright). [variant of *scapple* < Old French *escapeler, eschapeler* to dress timber]

scab·bling (skab′ling), *n.* a chip of stone.

scab·by (skab′ē), *adj.,* **-bi·er, -bi·est. 1.** covered with scabs. **2.** consisting of scabs. **3.** having scab or mange. **4.** *Informal.* low; mean; contemptible.

sca·bies (skā′bēz, -bē ēz), *n.* a skin disease caused by mites that live as parasites under the skin and cause itching; the itch. [< Latin *scabiēs,* related to *scabere* to scratch]

sca·bi·et·ic (skā′bē et′ik), *adj.* of or having scabies or mange.

sca·bi·o·sa (skā′bē ō′sə), *n.* scabious, the group of plants. [< New Latin *Scabiosa* the genus name < Medieval Latin *scabiosa;* see SCABIOUS[2]]

sca·bi·ous[1] (skā′bē əs), *adj.* **1.** scabby. **2.** of or like scabies or mange. [< Latin *scabiōsus* mangy, rough < *scabiēs;* see SCABIES]

sca·bi·ous[2] (skā′bē əs), *n.* any of a group of herbs with long, tough stems and dense flower heads of various colors. [< Medieval Latin *scabiosa* (literally) having to do with the itch, noun use of feminine of Latin *scabiōsus* scabious[1]]

scab·land (skab′land′), *n.* an area stripped of topsoil by flood waters, leaving low hills of bare rock, as in the Pacific Northwest.

scab·rin (skab′rin), *n.* a potent insecticide obtained as an oily yellow liquid from the roots of various plants of the composite family. *Formula:* $C_{22}H_{35}NO$ [< New Latin *scabra* species name of a plant that yields it + English *-in*]

sca·brous (skā′brəs), *adj.* **1.** rough with very small points or projections: *scabrous skin.* **2.** full of difficulties; harsh; thorny. **3.** hard to treat with decency; indelicate; risqué: *With the rout at its height, fire breaks out, and the guests perish in a scabrous cartoon sequence* (Harper's). [< Late Latin *scabrōsus* < Latin *scaber* scaly, related to *scabere* to scratch, scrape] —**sca′brous·ly,** *adv.* —**sca′brous·ness,** *n.* —**Syn. 1.** scraggly.

scad (skad), *n.* a saurel: *What makes the scad sad is that its other name is horse mackerel, and nobody loves it* (Sunday Times). [origin uncertain; perhaps < Scandinavian (compare Norwegian dialectal *skad.* Compare SHAD.]

scads (skadz), *n.pl. Slang.* a large quantity or number: *scads of trouble, scads of people.* [American English; origin uncertain]

scaf·fold (skaf′əld), *n.* **1.** a temporary structure for holding workmen and materials during the construction, repair, or decoration of a building. **2.** a raised platform on which criminals are put to death, especially by hanging: *Truth forever on the scaffold, wrong forever on the throne* (Lowell). **3.** a platform, stage, or stand for exhibiting shows, seating spectators, or the like. **4.** any raised framework. **5.** scaffolding material.
—*v.t.* to furnish with a scaffold; support with a scaffold: *The walls were scaffolded for the use of firearms* (Scott).
[Middle English *scafald* < Old French *eschaffault,* also *escadafaut*]

Scaffold (def. 1)

scaf·fold·er (skaf′əl dər), *n. British.* a person who erects scaffolding.

scaf·fold·ing (skaf′əl ding), *n.* **1.** a scaffold or a system of scaffolds: *A fire which broke out in scaffolding that had been erected round it during repair work . . .* (London Times). **2.** materials for scaffolds.

scagl·ia (skal′yə), *n.* an Italian limestone, similar to the chalk of England. [< Italian *scaglia* < a Germanic word. Compare SHALE.]

scagl·io·la (skal yō′lə), *n.* plasterwork that imitates marble, granite, etc., used in decorating interior walls, etc. [< Italian *scagliuola* (diminutive) < *scaglia;* see SCAGLIA]

scal·a·ble (skā′lə bəl), *adj.* that can be scaled or climbed: *The cliff hereabouts was . . . scalable in a score of places* (Sir Arthur Quiller-Couch).

sca·lade (skə lād′), *n. Obsolete.* escalade.

scal·age (skā′lij), *n.* **1. a.** an amount deducted from the listed weight, price, etc., to allow for moisture, leakage, or the like. **b.** the act of making such an allowance or deduction. **2.** the estimated board feet of lumber obtainable from a log, tree, stand of timber, etc.

sca·lar (skā′lər), *adj.* **1.** *Mathematics.* real: *a scalar number.* **2.** capable of being represented by a point on a scale. **3.** of or resembling a musical or other scale: *. . . a dozen choruses full of double-stops, immense scalar leaps* (New Yorker). —*n.* a scalar number. [< Latin *scālāris* like a ladder < *scālae* ladder; see SCALE[3]]

sca·lar·e (skə lãr′ē, -lä′rē), *n.* a small South American fish that has a silvery body with black bars and large fins, commonly raised in aquariums; angelfish. [< New Latin *scalare,* noun use of neuter of Latin *scālāris* like a ladder; see SCALAR]

sca·lar·i·form (skə lar′ə fôrm), *adj.* ladderlike: *scalariform plant cells.* [< Latin *scālāris* like a ladder (see SCALAR)]

sca·la·tion (skā lā′shən), *n.* the nature and form of the scales in fishes, snakes, etc.

scal·a·wag (skal′ə wag), *n.* **1.** *Informal.* a good-for-nothing person; scamp; rascal: *They are mostly crooks and scalawags* (Time). **2.** a white Southerner who acted with the Republican Party after the Civil War (an unfriendly term used by Southern Democrats). Also, **scallawag, scallywag.** [American English; origin uncertain]

scald[1] (skôld), *v.t.* **1.** to burn with hot liquid or steam: *She scalded herself with hot grease.* **2.** to pour boiling liquid over; use boiling liquid on: *Scald the dishes before drying them. You scald a pig after you slaughter it* (New Yorker). **3.** to heat almost to the boiling point but not quite: *to scald milk.* **4.** to burn as if with boiling water: *The tears that scald the cheek . . .* (William Cullen Bryant). **5.** *Obsolete.* to inflame; irritate: *Would not a secret . . . scald you to keep it?* (Philip Massinger). —*v.i.* **1.** to be heated almost to boiling, but not quite. **2.** to become burned by hot liquid or steam.
—*n.* **1.** a burn caused by hot liquid or steam: *The scald on her hand came from carelessly lifting a pot cover.* **2.** a browning of foliage by very hot weather. **3.** any of several parasitic plant diseases, especially of cranberries.
[< Old North French *escalder* < Late Latin *excaldāre* bathe (off) in hot water < Latin *ex-* off + *calidus* hot]

scald[2] (skôld, skäld), *n.* skald: *Never was I so enthralled either by saga-man or scald* (Longfellow). [older spelling of *skald*]

scald[3] (skôld), *Obsolete.* —*adj.* **1.** scabby. **2.** mean; contemptible. —*n.* a scab; scruff. Also, **scalled.** [< *scalled,* adjective < *scall;* see SCALL]

scald·ed (skôl′did), *adj. Obsolete.* scald[3].

scald·ic (skôl′dik, skäl′-), *adj.* skaldic.

scald·ing (skôl′ding), *adj.* **1.** that scalds; hot enough to scald: *scalding water. He . . . drinks his tea scalding* (Scott). **2.** producing an effect or sensation like that of scalding: *scalding tears. Our venomous and scalding words . . . burn like coals* (John Jackson). —**scald′ing·ly,** *adv.*

scal·di·no (skäl dē′nō), *n., pl.* **-ni** (-nē). a small earthenware brazier used in Italy: *He took my poor plaything, and thrust it down among the coals of his scaldino* (William Dean Howells). [< Italian *scaldino* < *scaldare* to heat]

scale[1] (skāl), *n., v.,* **scaled, scal·ing.** —*n.* **1. a.** one of the thin, flat, hard plates forming the outer covering of many fishes, snakes, and lizards. **b.** a part like this in other animals, as one of the very small plates covering the wings of moths and butterflies or one of the plates covering the tails of certain mammals. **c.** such scales collectively: *And fishes which were isles of living scale . . .* (Shelley). **2.** a thin layer like a scale: *Scales of skin peeled off after she had scarlet fever.* **3.** a thin piece of metal or other material. **4. a.** a mineral coating formed on the inside of a boiler, kettle, etc., by water during heating. **b.** an oxide formed on metals when heated. **5. a.** one of the parts that unite to cover a bud in winter. Scales are modified rudimentary leaves found on the leaf buds of most perennial deciduous plants. **b.** a part like those of the leaf bud, as one of the layers of an onion bulb, or one of the scalelike leaves of a rhizome or pine cone. **6.** an insect that has a shieldlike covering under which it hides and feeds; scale insect.
—*v.t.* **1.** to remove scales from: *He scaled the fish with a sharp knife.* **2.** to remove in thin layers. **3.** to cover with scales. **4.** to throw (a thin flat object) so that it moves edgewise: *to scale a paper plate.* **5.** *Scottish.* to cause to separate; disperse; scatter: *to scale a crowd.* —*v.i.* **1.** to come off in scales: *The paint is scaling off the house.* **2.** to become coated with scale.
[< Old North French *escale* < Germanic (compare Old High German *scāla* shell, husk). Compare SCALE[2].] —**scale′like′,** *adj.*

scale[2] (skāl), *n., v.,* **scaled, scal·ing.** —*n.* the dish or pan of a balance.
scales, a balance; instrument for weighing: *bathroom scales. The butcher weighed the turkey on the scales.*
tip the scales, a. to have as one's weight: *Quarterback Joseph Weiss . . . stands 6 ft. 4 in. and tips the scales at an even 200 lbs.* (Time). **b.** to overbalance one for another: *He also believes that the scales have been unduly tipped in favor of ambitious, power-hungry labor bosses by . . . legislation of the New Deal period* (Wall Street Journal).
turn the scale or **scales, a.** to weigh slightly more than: *He had weighed it carefully . . . and it turned the scale at thirty-four pounds* (J.K. Jerome). **b.** to determine the success or superiority of one of two opposing actions or sides; preponderate; decide: *The scale was turned in favour of strong measures by the voice of the native troops* (William Stubbs).
—*v.t.* **1.** to weigh: *to scale 180 pounds. Thousands of trout fishermen have never seen a brook trout that scaled six pounds* (New York Times). **2.** to weigh in or as if in scales; measure; compare: *You have found, scaling his present bearing with his past, that he's your fixed enemy* (Shakespeare). —*v.i.* **1.** to be weighed. **2.** to have weight.
[< Scandinavian (compare Old Icelandic *skāl*). Compare SHALE, SHELL, SCALL.]

scale[3] (skāl), *n., v.,* **scaled, scal·ing.** —*n.* **1.** a series of steps or degrees; scheme of graded amounts, especially from the lowest to the highest: *The scale of wages in this factory ranges from ten dollars to twenty dollars a day. He was not at all certain that it did not sometimes happen lower down the scale* (London Times). **2. a.** a series of marks made along a line or curve at regular distances to use in measuring: *A thermometer has a scale.* **b.** an instrument marked in this way, used for measuring, etc. **3. a.** the size of a plan, map, drawing, or model compared with what it represents: *a map drawn to a scale of one inch for each 100 miles.* **b.** the equally divided line on a map, plan, chart, etc., that indicates this relationship. **4.** relative size or extent: *to entertain on a lavish scale.* **5.** a system of numbering: *The decimal scale counts by tens, as in cents, dimes, dollars.* **6.** *Music.* a series of tones ascending or descending in pitch: *She practiced scales on the piano. Abbr.:* sc. **7.** a graded series of tests or problems used to measure intelligence, learning, adjustment, etc. **8.** *Obsolete.* **a.** a ladder or staircase or other means of ascent: *A scale by which the soul ascends from mighty means to more important ends* (William Cowper). **b.** a rung of a ladder.
—*v.t.* **1.** to climb up or over: *They scaled the wall by ladders.* **2.** to reduce or increase by a certain proportion: *The 22 striking unions — which had scaled down their wage demands to an 18½-cent-an-hour boost . . .* (Newsweek). *Their figures must be scaled up to contemporary levels* (London Times). **3.** to make according to a scale. **4.** to measure by, or as if by, a scale. **5.** to estimate the number of board feet in (logs or trees). —*v.i.* **1.** to go upward; climb. **2.** to form a graduated series.
[< Latin *scālae,* ladder, steps < *scandere* to climb]
—**Syn.** *v.t., v.i.* **1.** ascend, mount.

scale·board (skāl′bôrd′, -bōrd′; skab′ərd), *n.* **1.** a very thin board used for the back of a picture, veneer, etc. **2.** a thin strip of wood used in aligning hand-set type. [< *scale*[1] + *board*]

scaled-down (skāld′doun′), *adj.* scale-down: *It might be difficult for the Soviets to achieve even the scaled-down goals of the new plan* (Wall Street Journal).

scale dove, any of various small doves or pigeons of tropical America having feathers that look like scales.

scale-down (skāl′doun′), *adj.* being reduced by a certain proportion: *Mill buying was scale-down in nature with the cotton textile market currently in a lull* (Wall Street Journal). —*n.* a proportional reduction: *They're buying a little on a scale-down in the stocks they like* (New York Times).

scaled-up (skāld′up′), *adj.* scale-up: *The Russian machine is mostly a scaled-up copy of the Berkeley Bevatron and the Cosmotron* (Time).

scale insect, any of various small sucking insects, the females of which are highly destructive of fruit trees and garden plants and have the body and eggs covered by a shield formed by a secretion from the body. Certain kinds are a source of lac or dye.

scale leaf, one of the parts that unite to cover a bud in winter; scale.

scale·less (skāl′lis), *adj.* without scales, as the catfish.

scale model, a model of something with all parts proportional: *a scale model of the new hospital.*

scale moss, any of various liverworts with small, overlapping, scalelike leaves.

sca·lene (skā lēn′, skā′lēn), *adj.* **1.** (of a triangle) having three unequal sides. See **triangle** for picture. **2.** (of a cone, etc.) having the axis inclined to the base. [< Late Latin *scalēnus* < Greek *skalēnós* uneven < *skélos* leg]

scalene muscle, any of several triangular muscles that connect the upper ribs with vertebrae.

sca·le·nus (skā lē′nəs), *n., pl.* **-ni** (-nī). a scalene muscle.

scal·er (skā′lər), *n.* **1.** a person or thing that scales: *We are soul-probers, starmappers, wood-walkers, scalers of Everests, pursuers of tomorrow and tomorrow and tomorrow* (Atlantic). **2.** an instrument for removing scales from fish. **3.** a device that records impulses electronically by selecting them in groups when the impulses run through a circuit too rapidly to be measured by the metering equipment: *A scaler unit counts the scatter or impulses for one or two minutes* (New Scientist). **4.** an instrument used by dentists to remove tartar from the teeth.

scales (skālz), *n.pl.* See under **scale²**, *n.*

Scales (skālz), *n.pl. Astronomy.* Libra; the Balance. [translation of Latin *Lībra*]

scale-up (skāl′up′), *adj.* increased by a certain proportion: *Trading was slow but mill and commission house buying met mostly scale-up hedging and liquidation* (Wall Street Journal). —*n.* a proportional increase: *The scale-up from pilot plant to full production was a billion to one, surely the greatest in technological history* (Scientific American).

scal·i·ness (skā′lē nis), *n.* scaly quality or condition.

scal·ing (skā′ling), *n.* **1.** scales. **2.** the arrangement of scales, as on a fish.

scaling ladder, a ladder for climbing walls.

scall (skôl), *n.* a scabby eruption, especially on the scalp. [probably < Scandinavian (compare Old Icelandic *skalle* a bald head)]

scal·la·wag (skal′ə wag), *n.* scalawag.

scalled (skôld), *adj. Obsolete.* scald³.

scal·lion (skal′yən), *n.* **1.** a kind of onion that does not form a large bulb. **2.** the shallot. **3.** the leek. [< Anglo-French *scaloun* < Latin (*caepa*) *Ascalōnia* (onion) from *Ascalon*, in Palestine]

Scaling Ladder

scal·lop (skol′əp, skal′-), *n.* **1. a.** a shellfish somewhat like a clam. In some species the large muscle that opens and closes the shell is edible. **b.** this muscle, used as food. **c.** one of the two rounded, fanlike, ribbed parts of the shell: *Pilgrims returning from Palestine formerly wore scallops as a sign of their pilgrimage.* **2.** a small dish or scallop shell, in which fish or other food is baked and served. **3.** one of a series of curves on an edge of a dress, etc. —*v.t.* **1.** to bake with sauce and bread crumbs in a dish; escallop: *scalloped oysters, scalloped potatoes.* **2.** to make with a series of curves on: *She scalloped the edges of the shelf paper.* Also, **scollop.** [earlier, short for *escallop*¹]

Scallop Shell (def. 1c)

scal·lop·er (skol′ə pər, skal′-), *n.* **1.** a person or thing that scallops. **2.** a boat used to gather scallops. Also, **scolloper.**

scal·lop·ing (skol′ə ping, skal′-), *n.* **1.** an ornamental edging. **2.** the embroidery stitch used in making a variety of such edging.

scal·lop·pi·ne (skal′ə pē′nē), *n.* thin slices of veal pounded flat and cooked in Marsala wine, sometimes with mushrooms, cheese, tomato paste, etc. [alteration of Italian *scaloppini*]

scal·ly·wag (skal′ē wag), *n.* scalawag: *a band of scallywags and self-seekers* (Manchester Guardian).

sca·lo·gram (skā′lə gram), *n.* a graded series of related questions or problems which become progressively more difficult to answer. Scalograms are used in psychological and other tests to measure the uniformity and consistency of responses. [< *scale*³ + *-gram*¹]

scalp (skalp), *n.* **1.** the skin and hair on the top and back of the head. **2. a.** a part of this skin and hair cut off as a token of victory. Some Indians of North America used to collect the scalps of their enemies. **b.** a part of this skin and hair thought of as cut off in revenge, defeat, etc., especially to advance one's own cause: *The angry Chancellor made no bones of the fact he was out to get Dehler's political scalp* (Newsweek). **3.** *Informal.* a small profit made by quickly buying and selling.
—*v.t.* **1.** to cut or tear the scalp from: *A party of St. Francis Indians . . . scalped one of his companions* (George Bancroft). **2.** *Informal.* to buy and sell to make small, quick profits. **3.** to trade in (theater tickets, stocks, etc.), especially buying at face value and selling at higher prices. —*v.i.* to buy and sell theater tickets, stocks, etc., to make small, quick profits: *A corporation like the Pennsylvania Railroad must protect itself against loss through scalping* (Nation).
[perhaps < Scandinavian (compare Old Icelandic *skālpr* sheath)]

scalp dance, a ceremonial dance of the American Indians in which the scalps of enemies were used in celebrating a victory.

scal·pel (skal′pəl), *n.* a small, straight knife used in surgery and in dissections. [< Latin *scalpellum* (diminutive) < *scalprum* knife, related to *scalpere* to carve]

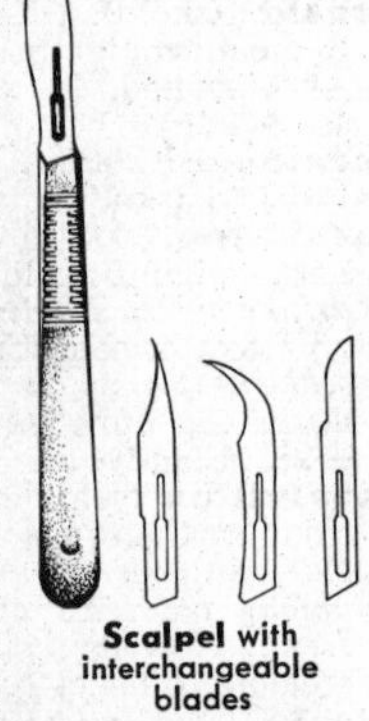

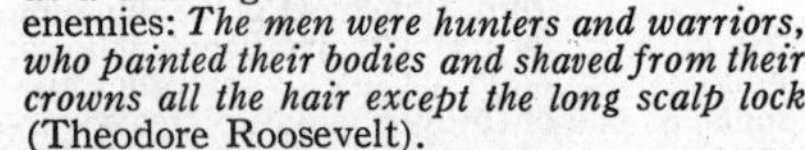

Scalpel with interchangeable blades

scalp·er (skal′pər), *n. Informal.* a person who scalps, especially tickets, stocks, etc.: *The fact that so many shows are sold out for months in advance to benefit theater parties makes it easier for the scalper to operate* (Time).

scalp lock, a long lock or tuft of hair left on the head by certain North American Indians to show their status as warriors and as a challenge to their enemies: *The men were hunters and warriors, who painted their bodies and shaved from their crowns all the hair except the long scalp lock* (Theodore Roosevelt).

scal·prum (skal′prəm), *n., pl.* **-pra** (-prə). the cutting edge of an incisor tooth. [< Latin *scalprum* knife]

scal·y (skā′lē), *adj.,* **scal·i·er, scal·i·est. 1.** covered with scales; having scales like a fish: *This iron pipe is scaly with rust.* **2.** suggesting scales. **3.** consisting of scales or scale. **4.** that comes off in scabs. **5.** having scale insects; infested with scale. **6.** *Slang.* mean; shabby; stingy. [< *scal*(e)¹ + *-y*¹]

scaly anteater or **lizard,** a pangolin, a toothless, scaly mammal of tropical Asia and Africa.

scam·ble (skam′bəl), *v.i., v.t.,* **-bled, -bling,** *n. Archaic.* scramble. [origin uncertain]

scam·mon·ic (skə mon′ik), *adj.* derived from scammony: *a scammonic medicine.*

scam·mo·ny (skam′ə nē), *n., pl.* **-nies. 1.** a twining Asiatic plant of the morning-glory family, a variety of convolvulus. **2.** a gum resin obtained from its root, used as a purgative. [Old English *scammonie* < Latin *scammōnia* < Greek *skammōniā*]

scamp (skamp), *n.* a worthless person; rascal; rogue: *Old Dodd had a scamp of a son who had run away from school* (Margaret Kennedy). —*v.t.* to do (work, etc.) in a hasty, careless manner: *I will undertake to say he never scamped a job in the whole course of his life* (Samuel Butler). *The motivations of the novel are scamped in the film* (Newsweek). —*v.i. U.S.* to be stingy; skimp. [perhaps < dialectal *scamp* to roam, probably < *scamper*] —**scamp′er,** *n.*

scam·per (skam′pər), *v.i.* **1.** to run quickly; go hastily: *The mice scampered when the cat came.* **2.** to run away or decamp: *The wagoners took each a horse out of his team and scampered* (Benjamin Franklin). —*n.* a quick run: *Let the dog out for a scamper.* [< Old French *escamper* to run away, ultimately < Latin *ex-* out of + *campus* field]

scam·pi (skäm′pē), *n.pl. Italian.* shrimp.

scamp·ish (skam′pish), *adj.* like a scamp; rascally.

scan (skan), *v.,* **scanned, scan·ning,** *n.* —*v.t.* **1.** to look at closely; examine with care: *His mother scanned his face to see if he was telling the truth.* **2.** to glance at; look over hastily. **3. a.** to mark off (lines of poetry) into feet. *Example:* Sing′ a/ song′ of/ six′ pence. **b.** to read or recite (poetry), marking off the lines into feet. **4.** (in television) to expose (bits of a surface) in rapid succession to beams of electrons in order to transmit a picture. The electron beam moves in successive horizontal lines from top to bottom analyzing the light values of the object. **5.** to search (an area) with radar. —*v.i.* **1. a.** to conform to metrical rules for marking off lines of poetry into feet: *The new poets scan* (Time). **b.** to scan verse. **2.** (in television) to scan a surface in transmitting a picture.
—*n.* **1.** the act or fact of scanning: *Radio astronomers began an intensive radio scan of the sun* (Scientific American). **2.** the area of vision in television or radar.
[< Latin *scandere* to scan; (originally) to climb, related to *scālae* ladder]
—**Syn.** *v.t.* **1.** scrutinize. **2.** skim.

Scan., **1.** Scandinavia. **2.** Scandinavian.

Scan-A-Grav·er (skan′ə grā′vər), *n. Trademark.* a device that makes engravings from photographs by the reaction of electrons to the varying density of black in the photograph.

Scand., **1.** Scandinavia. **2.** Scandinavian.

scan·dal (skan′dəl), *n., v.,* **-daled, -dal·ing** or (*especially British*) **-dalled, -dal·ling.** —*n.* **1.** a shameful action, condition, or event that brings disgrace or offends public opinion: *It was a scandal for the city treasurer to take tax money for his own use. The state-government scandals of 1939-1940 retired him to private life when he first was governor* (Newsweek). **2.** damage to reputation; disgrace: *to avoid scandal at all costs. O the disgrace of it! The scandal, the incredible come-down* (Max Beerbohm). **3.** public talk about a person that will hurt his reputation; malicious gossip: *You'll have no scandal while you dine, but honest talk and wholesome wine* (Tennyson). **4.** discredit to religion caused by irreligious conduct or moral lapse.
be the scandal of, to scandalize: *The visiting dignitaries who got into a public brawl were the scandal of the town.*
—*v.t.* **1.** *Archaic.* to spread scandal about (a person); defame. **2.** *Obsolete.* to disgrace.
[< Latin *scandalum* (cause for) offense, temptation < Greek *skándalon* scandal, offense; (originally) trap with a springing device. Doublet of SLANDER.]
—**Syn.** *n.* **2.** discredit, disrepute, dishonor. **3.** slander, calumny, defamation.

scan·dal·ise (skan′də līz), *v.t.,* **-ised, -is·ing.** *Especially British.* scandalize: *It was evidently at the piano that he hit upon those bold and abrupt harmonies which so scandalised Rimsky-Korsakov* (Sunday Times).

scan·dal·i·za·tion (skan′də lə zā′shən), *n.* **1.** the act of scandalizing. **2.** the condition or fact of being scandalized: *The Prince and his wife, to the amusement of some and the scandalization of others, indulged in a violent bout of fisticuffs in open court* (Daily Telegram).

scan·dal·ize (skan′də līz), *v.t.,* **-ized, -iz·ing.** to offend or horrify by doing something considered wrong or improper; shock: *She scandalized her grandmother by smoking cigarettes.*

scan·dal·iz·er (skan′də lī′zər), *n.* a person who slanders.

scan·dal·mon·ger (skan′dəl mung′gər, -mong′-), *n.* a person who spreads scandal and malicious gossip: *Political scandalmongers were even tossed a surprising and piquant new morsel* (Newsweek).

scan·dal·ous (skan′də ləs), *adj.* **1.** disgraceful; shameful; shocking: *a scandalous crime.* **2. a.** spreading scandal or slander; slandering. **b.** fond of scandal. —**scan′dal·ous·ly,** *adv.* —**scan′dal·ous·ness,** *n.* —**Syn. 1.** disreputable, infamous. **2. a.** slanderous, defamatory, libelous.

scandal sheet, a newspaper or magazine devoted primarily to items of a notorious, scandalous, or gossipy nature.

scan·da·roon (skan də rün′), *n.* a variety of homing pigeon, with a long head and body, long legs, wide shoulders, and a long curved bill. [< *Scanderoon,* variant of *İskenderon,* a seaport in southern Turkey]

scan·dent (skan′dənt), *adj.* climbing: *a scandent vine.* [< Latin *scandēns, -entis,* present participle of *scandere* to climb]

scan·di·a (skan′dē ə), *n.* a white, infusible powder, an oxide of scandium. *Formula:* Sc_2O_3 [< New Latin *scandia* < *scandium;* see SCANDIUM]

Scan·di·an (skan′dē ən), *adj., n.* Scandinavian. [< Latin *Scandia* Scandinavia + English *-an*]

scan·dic (skan′dik), *adj.* of or having to do with scandium.

Scan·di·na·vi·an (skan′də nā′vē ən, -nāv′yən), *adj.* of or having to do with Scandinavia, its people, or their languages. —*n.* **1.** a native or inhabitant of Scandinavia. **2.** the languages of Scandinavia and Iceland, both modern and historical; North Germanic.

scan·di·um (skan′dē əm), *n.* a rare, gray, metallic chemical element, found in euxenite and various other minerals: *Observations show that scandium is rather abundant in some of the stars* (Scientific American). *Symbol:* Sc; *at.wt.:* (C^{12}) 44.956 or (O^{16}) 44.96; *at.no.:* 21; *valence:* 3. [< New Latin *scandium* < Latin *Scandia* Scandinavia]

scan·na·ble (skan′ə bəl), *adj.* that can be scanned.

scan·ner (skan′ər), *n.* **1.** a person or thing that scans. **2.** (in television) a scanning disk. **3.** the rotating antenna that sends out and receives radar signals: *The scanner is mounted in the nose of the aircraft and must be capable of operating under all conditions of pressure and temperature encountered in flight* (New Scientist). **4.** a photoelectric cell that scans printed data and converts it into the electric impulses fed into a computer or data-processing machine.

scan·ning (skan′ing), *n.* **1.** close investigation or consideration; critical examination or judgment: *The private interpretation of the Scripture [is] exposed to every man's scanning in his mother tongue* (Thomas Hobbes). **2.** scansion: *This scanning was a liberal art that we learned at grammar school* (Andrew Marvell). **3.** (in television) the process in which an electron beam scans the picture area.
—*adj.* **1.** that scans or examines closely; critical; searching: *When his eyes fell again they glanced round with a scanning coolness* (George Eliot). **2.** spoken in a measured manner, with more or less regular pauses between syllables, characteristic of certain nervous diseases, as multiple sclerosis: *scanning speech.*

scanning disk, 1. a filter disk made up of sections of red, blue, and green, placed in front of the camera lens and the receiver in one type of color television. **2.** a mechanical device used for scanning in early television.

scan·sion (skan′shən), *n.* the marking off of lines of poetry into feet; scanning. The marks for scansion are - or ′ for a long or stressed syllable, ˘ for a short syllable, / for a foot division, and ^ for a pause. *Example:* And firéd / thĕ shót / heărd roúnd / thĕ wórld /. In the oral scansion of poetry, a reader stresses the long syllables heavily. [< Latin *scānsiō, -ōnis* < *scandere* to scan]

scan·sion·ist (skan′shə nist), *n.* a person skilled in scansion.

scan·so·ri·al (skan sôr′ē əl, -sōr′-), *adj.* **1.** having to do with or adapted for climbing: *Woodpeckers have scansorial feet.* **2.** habitually climbing: *a scansorial bird.* [< Latin *scānsōrius* used for climbing (< *scandere* to climb; scan) + English *-al*[1]]

scant (skant), *adj.* **1.** not enough in size or quantity; meager; poor: *a coat that is short and scant, scant consideration, scant help. When the canal was undertaken, he got scant recognition from de Lesseps* (Edmund Wilson). **2.** barely enough; barely full; bare: *Use a scant cup of butter in the cake. But there was scant time for resolutions and reflections* (Lytton Strachey).
scant of, having a limited supply: *He's fat, and scant of breath* (Shakespeare).
—*v.t.* **1.** to make scant or small; cut down in amount; limit: *Don't scant the butter if you want a rich cake. Any number of moments lacked their sovereign power to move—and not least from scanting Shakespeare's sovereign powers of language* (Time). **2.** to limit the supply of; withhold: *You have obedience scanted* (Shakespeare).
—*adv. Dialect.* scarcely; barely; hardly: *His manner was scant civil* (Robert Louis Stevenson). [< Scandinavian (compare Old Icelandic *skamt* short)] —**scant′ness,** *n.*
—**Syn.** *adj.* **1.** inadequate, insufficient.

scant·ies (skan′tēz), *n.pl.* very short, snug-fitting panties for women. [blend of *scanty* and *panties*]

scant·i·ly (skan′tə lē), *adv.* in a scanty manner; insufficiently; inadequately: *scantily attired. The living room was scantily and dingily furnished.*

scant·i·ness (skan′tē nis), *n.* the quality or fact of being scanty: *Miss Tox's dress ... had a certain character of angularity and scantiness* (Dickens).

scant·ling (skant′ling), *n.* **1. a.** a small beam or piece of timber, often used as an upright piece in the frame of a building. **b.** such beams or timbers collectively. **2.** the width and thickness of a board, beam, cut stone, or other building material, used as a measure of size. **3.** the dimensions of the various parts of a vessel in shipbuilding. **4.** a small quantity or amount; modicum. **5.** *Archaic.* a portion; share; allowance: *The muleteer ... thought not of tomorrow ... provided he got but his scantling o Burgundy* (Laurence Sterne). [variant of earlier *scantillon* < Old French *escantillon* splinter, ultimately < Vulgar Latin *cantus.* Compare CANT².]

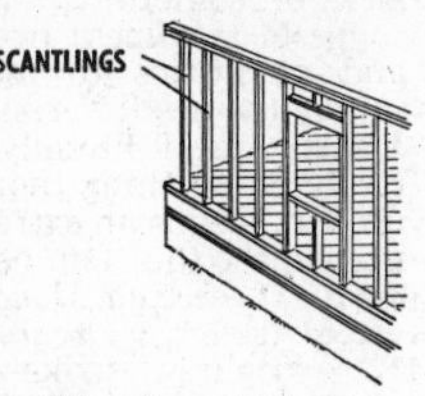

Scantlings (def. 1a)

scant·ly (skant′lē), *adv.* **1.** scantily; in a scant manner or degree; slightingly: *A grace but scantly thine* (Tennyson). **2.** *Archaic.* scarcely; hardly; barely: *Marmion, whose soul could scantly brook, Even from his king, a haughty look* (Scott).

scant·y (skan′tē), *adj.,* **scant·i·er, scant·i·est. 1.** existing or present in small or insufficient quantity; not enough; not abundant: *His scanty clothing did not keep out the cold. My paper is scanty and time more so* (William Penn). **2.** not ample or copious; barely enough; meager: *a scanty meal, a scanty harvest. Congregations were scanty* (Andrew Lang). **3.** deficient in extent, compass, or size: *Our minds are narrow and scanty in their capacities* (Isaac Watts). [perhaps back formation < *scantiness* < *scant*]
—**Syn. 1, 2. Scanty, sparse, meager** mean less than is needed or normal. **Scanty** implies falling short of the needed or standard amount: *The scanty rainfall is causing a water shortage.* **Sparse** implies a thin scattering of what there is, particularly of numbers or units: *He carefully combs his sparse hair.* **Meager** implies thinness, a lack of something necessary for fullness, completeness, richness, strength, etc.: *Meager soil produces meager crops.*

SCAP (no periods), Supreme Commander for the Allied Powers (in Japan): *In the truce tents at Panmunjom and at SCAP headquarters in Tokyo, dejection seized the U.N. team* (Time).

scape[1] (skāp), *n., v.,* **scaped, scap·ing.** *Archaic.* escape.

scape[2] (skāp), *n.* **1.** *Botany.* a leafless flower stalk rising from the ground, such as that of the narcissus, dandelion, or hyacinth. **2.** something like a stalk, such as the shaft of a feather or the shaft of a column. [< Latin *scāpus* stalk]

scape[3] (skāp), *n.* a view of scenery of any kind: *to sketch a scape in pencil.* [abstracted from *landscape*]

'scape (skāp), *n., v.t., v.i.,* **'scaped, 'scap·ing.** *Archaic.* escape: *hair-breadth 'scapes* (Shakespeare). [short for *escape*]

scape·goat (skāp′gōt′), *n.* **1.** a person or thing made to bear the blame for the mistakes of others: *He has been made the scapegoat for many of the sins ... of other individuals* (Edward A. Freeman). **2.** a goat on which the sins of the people were laid by the ancient Jewish high priests on the Day of Atonement. The goat was then driven into the wilderness. Leviticus 16:5-22.
—*v.t.* to make a scapegoat of: *This suggests that witches did not simply exist in nature in the form of demented women—but that the Inquisition created them by scapegoating innocent women* (New York Times). [< *scape*¹, variant of *escape* + *goat*]

scape·goat·ism (skāp′gō′tiz əm), *n.* the act or practice of seeking out a scapegoat to lay blame on: *Much of the anti-American feeling that does exist in Europe can be charged to scapegoatism* (Newsweek).

scape·grace (skāp′grās′), *n.* a reckless, good-for-nothing person; scamp: *He ... was the most charming young scapegrace in the army* (Thackeray). [short for (person who e)*scape*(s) *grace*]

scape·ment (skāp′mənt), *n.* an escapement in a clock or watch.

scape wheel, the toothed wheel in the escapement of a watch or clock that actuates the pendulum or balance. [< *scape*¹, variant of *escape* + *wheel*]

scaph·o·ce·phal·ic (skaf′ō sə fal′ik), *adj.* (of a skull) boat-shaped; very long and narrow. [< Greek *skáphē* boat + English *cephalic*]

scaph·oid (skaf′oid), *adj.* **1.** boat-shaped. **2.** navicular. —*n. Anatomy.* the navicular. [< Greek *skaphoeidḗs* < *skáphē* boat, tub, trough (< *skáptein* to dig, carve) + *eîdos* form]

scaph·o·pod (skaf′ə pod), *n.* any of a group of marine mollusks with a conical, tubular shell open at both ends. Scaphopod shells were used as money by Pacific coast Indians. [< New Latin *Scaphopoda* the class name < Greek *skáphē* boat, trough + *poús, podós* foot]

sca·pi·form (skā′pə fôrm), *adj.* having the form of a stalk or shaft. [< Latin *scāpus* stalk + English *-form*]

sca·pig·er·ous (skə pij′ər əs), *adj.* having a stalk without leaves. [< Latin *scāpus* stalk + *gerere* to bear + English *-ous*]

scap·o·lite (skap′ə līt), *n.* any of a group of minerals of variable composition, essentially silicates of aluminum, calcium, and sodium, occurring in tetragonal crystals and also massive, such as wernerite. [< German *Skapolith* < Greek *skâpos* shaft (with English *-lite*)]

sca·pose (skā′pōs), *adj. Botany.* **1.** having scapes. **2.** consisting of or like a scape. [< *scap*(e)² + *-ose*¹]

scap·ple (skap′əl), *v.t.,* **-pled, -pling.** scabble.

s.caps., small capitals.

scap·u·la (skap′yə lə), *n., pl.* **-lae** (-lē), **-las. 1.** a shoulder blade. **2.** one of the other bones of the pectoral arch of some vertebrates. [< New Latin *scapula* shoulder blade < Late Latin, shoulder < Latin *scapulae,* plural, shoulders]

scap·u·lal·gi·a (skap′yə lal′jē ə), *n.* pain in the scapular region. [< *scapul*(a) + *-algia* < Greek *álgos* pain]

scap·u·lar (skap′yə lər), *adj.* of the shoulder or shoulder blade.
—*n.* **1.** a loose, sleeveless garment hanging from the shoulders, worn by members of certain religious orders in the Roman Catholic Church: *She knelt once more before him to be formally clothed with the girdle, scapular, and white veil betokening Sister Laurentia's official reception into the thirteen-centuries-old Order of St. Benedict* (Atlantic). **2.** two small pieces of woolen cloth joined by string passing over the shoulders, worn under the ordinary clothing by Roman Catholics as a mark of religious devotion. **3.** a bird's feather growing in the shoulder region where the wing joins the body. **4.** a bandage that goes over the shoulder. **5.** a scapula.
[< New Latin *scapularis* < Late Latin *scapulāre* scapular, tippet < *scapula* shoulder, scapula]

scap·u·lar·y (skap′yə ler′ē), *adj., n., pl.* **-lar·ies.** scapular.

scap·u·li·man·cy (skap′yə lə man′sē), *n.* divination by means of the cracks in an animal's shoulder blade scorched in a fire. [< Latin *scapula* shoulder + Greek *manteíā* divination]

scap·u·lo·pex·y (skap′yə lə pek′sē), *n.* a condition in which the scapula cannot be moved away from the ribs, as when the scapular muscles are paralyzed. [< *scapula* + Greek *pêxis* a fixing < *pḗgnyai* to fix, place]

scar[1] (skär), *n., v.,* **scarred, scar·ring.** —*n.* **1.** the mark left by a healed cut, wound, burn, or sore: *a small vaccination scar. He jests at scars that never felt a wound* (Shakespeare). **2.** any mark like this: *See the scars your shoes have made on the chair. War leaves many deep scars on the minds of* *men.* **3. a.** *Botany.* a mark where a leaf has formerly joined the stem. **b.** *Zoology.* a cicatrix.

—*v.t.* to mark with a scar: *Yet I'll not shed her blood, Nor scar that whiter skin of hers than Snow* (Shakespeare). —*v.i.* to form a scar; heal: *His wound is scarring well.*

[< Old French *escarre* < Late Latin *eschara* scab < Greek *eschárā* scab; hearth. Doublet of ESCHAR.]

scar[2] (skär), *n.* **1.** a steep, rocky place on the side of a mountain; precipice; cliff. **2.** a low rock in the sea. Also, **scaur.** [< Scandinavian (compare Old Icelandic *sker* reef). Related to SKERRY.]

SCAR (no periods), Special Committee on Antarctic Research (an organization set up to continue the work of the International Geophysical Year).

scar·ab (skar′əb), *n.* **1. a.** a beetle, especially the sacred beetle of the ancient Egyptians; a variety of scarabaeid beetle. **b.** an image of this beetle. Scarabs were much used in ancient Egypt as charms or ornaments. **2.** a gem cut in the form of a beetle. **3.** any dung beetle. [< Middle French *scarabée,* learned borrowing from Latin *scarabaeus* < Greek *kárabos* beetle; crayfish]

Scarab (def. 1b)
A, top; B, bottom

scar·a·bae·an (skar′ə bē′ən), *adj., n.* scarabaeid.

scar·a·bae·id (skar′ə bē′id), *adj.* of or having to do with a large group of broad, thick-bodied beetles with antennae ending in flattened segments. Scarabaeid beetles include the chafers, June bugs, and Japanese beetles. —*n.* a scarabaeid beetle. [< New Latin *Scarabaeidae* the family name < Latin *scarabaeus;* see SCARAB]

scar·a·bae·oid (skar′ə bē′oid), *adj.* **1.** of, having to do with, or like a scarabaeid. **2.** resembling a scarab (image or gem). —*n.* a scarab, either much conventionalized or an imitation.

scar·a·bae·us (skar′ə bē′əs), *n., pl.* **-bae·us·es, -bae·i** (-bē′ī). a scarab. [< New Latin *scarabaeus* < Latin, beetle; see SCARAB]

scar·a·boid (skar′ə boid), *adj., n.* scarabaeoid.

Scar·a·mouch (skar′ə müsh), *n.* a cowardly braggart in traditional Italian comedy. [< French *Scaramouche* < Italian *Scaramuccia* (literally) skirmish. Compare SKIRMISH.]

scar·a·mouch (skar′ə mouch, -müsh), *n.* **1.** a cowardly braggart: *The habit of this greasy Don was very proper for a scaramouch . . . being a dirty calico, with all the tawdry and trapping of a fool's coat* (Daniel Defoe). **2.** a rascal; scamp: *He swore that no scaramouch of an Italian robber would dare to meddle with an Englishman* (Washington Irving). [< *Scaramouch*]

scarb tree (skärb), a wild or seedling apple tree.

scarce (skãrs), *adj.,* **scarc·er, scarc·est,** *adv.* —*adj.* hard to get; rare: *Good cooks are scarce. Very old stamps are scarce. Milk was scarce during the strike.*

make oneself scarce, *Informal.* **a.** to go away: *Please do make yourself scarce. You are in my way, and I'm very busy* (Arnold Bennett). **b.** to stay away: *My liberty was granted only on condition of making myself scarce in the two Castilles* (Benjamin Malkin).

scarce as hen's teeth, *Informal.* very scarce: *Now good comedians are as scarce as hen's teeth* (Newsweek).

—*adv.* scarcely: *I scarce kept myself from shedding tears* (George Gissing).

[< Old North French *escars* < Vulgar Latin *excarpsus,* for Latin *excerpsus* extracted, past participle of *excerpere* select, excerpt < Latin *ex-* out + *carpere* to pluck] —**scarce′ness,** *n.*

—**Syn.** *adj.* See **rare.**

scarce·ly (skãrs′lē), *adv.* **1.** barely; not quite: *I can scarcely hear your voice. We could scarcely see through the thick fog.* **2.** decidedly not: *He can scarcely have said that.* **3.** very probably not: *I will scarcely pay that much.* —**Syn. 1.** See **hardly.**

➔ **scarcely.** Since its negative force is weak, *scarcely* readily lends itself to use in a concealed double negative: *For a while we couldn't scarcely see a thing.* In standard English this would be: *For a while we could scarcely see a thing.*

scarce·ment (skãrs′mənt), *n.* in building: **1.** a setoff in the face of a wall or in a bank of earth. **2.** a footing or ledge formed by a setoff in a wall.

scar·ci·ty (skãr′sə tē), *n., pl.* **-ties.** too small a supply; lack; rarity: *There is still a scarcity of food in Istanbul, and restaurants are unable to supply their customers* (London Times).

—**Syn. Scarcity, dearth** mean a shortage or lack of something. **Scarcity** particularly suggests smallness or shortness of supply and quantities to meet the demand or satisfy the need: *There is a scarcity of nurses.* **Dearth,** used literally of food or figuratively of anything thought of as wanted or needed, means an extreme scarcity amounting almost to a famine: *There seems to be a dearth of news on Mondays.*

scare[1] (skãr), *v.,* **scared, scar·ing,** *n.* —*v.t.* **1.** to frighten; strike with sudden fear or terror: *Scaring a child is wrong. The play* [*is*] *a plausible melodrama that is likely to scare the living daylights out of you* (New York Times). "*Wasn't the rabbit scared, Uncle Remus?*" *asked the little boy* (Joel Chandler Harris). *The noise of thy crossbow Will scare the herd* (Shakespeare). **2.** to frighten (away); drive off: . . . *the poet must pull down the shade so that they may not scare off his fancies* (Edmund Wilson). *The watchdog scared away the robber by barking.* —*v.i.* to become frightened; be scared: *Courageous people don't scare easily.*

scare up, *Informal.* to get; raise, locate, or prepare: *to scare up a few extra blankets on a cold night.*

—*n.* **1.** a fright; sudden fright: *Peyrol actually laughed at this momentary scare* (Joseph Conrad). **2.** a frightened condition.

—*adj. U.S. Informal.* **1.** causing fear; frightening; alarming: *scare headlines, scare statistics.* **2.** designed to frighten or alarm: *scare tactics, scare propaganda.*

[alteration of Middle English *skerre* < Scandinavian (compare Old Icelandic *skirra* < *skjarr* timid)] —**scar′ing·ly,** *adv.*

—**Syn.** *v.t.* **1.** terrify, alarm. See **frighten.**

scare[2] (skãr), *n.* the part of a golf club where the head joins the shaft. [originally Scottish < Scandinavian (compare Old Icelandic *skör* joint)]

scare buying, buying more than one needs in fear of threatened or alleged shortage: *Not since the Korean war touched off scare buying in 1951 have the stores shown such improvement* (Wall Street Journal).

scare·crow (skãr′krō′), *n.* **1.** a figure of a man dressed in old clothes, set in a field to frighten birds away from crops: *The farmer decided to build a scarecrow so terrifying it would scare the hateful crows to death when they got a good look at it* (New Yorker). **2.** a person dressed in ragged clothes: *There ranged themselves in front of the schoolmaster's desk, half-a-dozen scarecrows, out at knees and elbows* (Dickens). **3.** anything that fools people into being frightened; bugbear; bugaboo.

scared (skãrd), *adj.* frightened; afraid; terrified: *Don't be scared, the dog won't bite you. We were scared and ran away.*

run scared, a. to run a political campaign as if in fear of losing: *Though confident, Republicans run scared* (Wall Street Journal). **b.** to run fast or hard, as if in fear: *I don't like to say that the Nashua stable, warming up here in Saratoga, will run scared* (Newsweek).

scared·y cat (skãr′dē), fraidy cat.

scare·head (skãr′hed′), *n.* a newspaper headline in very large type, and usually of a sensational nature.

scare·mon·ger (skãr′mung′gər, -mong′-), *n.* a person who spreads alarming reports, rumors, etc.; alarmist: *He declared "scaremongers" are at work attempting to frighten automobile workers with the "bogeyman of automation"* (Wall Street Journal).

scare·mon·ger·ing (skãr′mung′gər ing, -mong′-), *n.* the spreading of alarming reports: *No incidents were reported from the disturbed areas today, but . . . the atmosphere in the affected areas was still tense owing to "sporadic attempts at scaremongering"* (Times of India).

scar·er (skãr′ər), *n.* a person or thing that scares.

scarf[1] (skärf), *n., pl.* **scarfs** or (*especially British*) **scarves,** *v.* —*n.* **1. a.** a long, broad strip of silk, lace, etc., worn about the neck, shoulders, head, or waist. **b.** a muffler. **2.** a long strip of cloth, etc., used as a cover for a bureau, table, piano, etc. **3.** a necktie with hanging ends. **4.** a sash worn across the chest to indicate membership in some ceremonial order.

—*v.t.* **1.** to clothe, cover, or wrap with, or as if with, a scarf. **2.** to wrap about or around a person in the manner of a scarf. **3.** *Archaic.* to deck with flags: *The scarfed bark puts from her native bay* (Shakespeare).

[< Old North French *escarpe* < Germanic (compare Old High German *scharpe* bag, pocket)]

scarf[2] (skärf), *n., pl.* **scarfs,** *v.* —*n.* **1. a.** a joint in which the ends of beams are cut so that they lap over and join firmly. **b.** an end cut in this way. **2.** a cut made in the body of a whale.

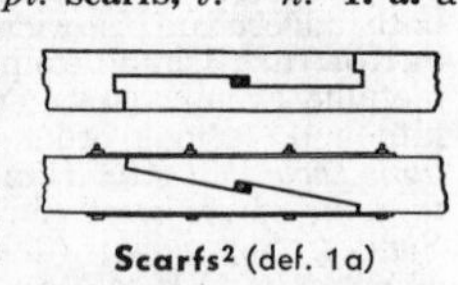

Scarfs[2] (def. 1a)

—*v.t.* **1.** to join by a scarf. **2.** to form a scarf on (a beam). **3.** to remove the skin and blubber from (a whale). **4.** *Metallurgy.* to remove surface blemishes from (steel ingots) by spraying with oxygen before rolling: *There is increasing demand for oxygen in the "scarfing" . . . of steel ingots or billets* (Wall Street Journal).

[perhaps < Scandinavian (compare Swedish *skarv*)] —**scarf′er,** *n.*

scar-faced (skär′fāst′), *adj.* having a scarred face; with scars on the face.

scarfed (skärft), *adj.* wearing a scarf or scarfs; decorated with or as if with a scarf: *The scarfed bark puts from her native bay* (Shakespeare). Also, **scarved.**

scarf joint, a scarf in a beam, etc.

scarf·pin (skärf′pin′), *n.* an ornamental pin worn in a scarf or necktie.

scarf·skin (skärf′skin′), *n.* the outer layer of skin; epidermis. [< *scarf*[1], in the sense of "light outer covering" + *skin*]

scar·i·fi·ca·tion (skar′ə fə kā′shən), *n.* **1.** a scarifying. **2.** a scratch or scratches: . . . *scarification in elaborate geometrical patterns . . .* (Atlantic).

scar·i·fi·ca·tor (skar′ə fə kā′tər), *n.* **1.** a person who scarifies. **2.** a surgical instrument for scarifying. [< New Latin *scarificator* < Late Latin *scarīficāre;* see SCARIFY]

scar·i·fi·er (skar′ə fī′ər), *n.* **1.** a person or thing that scarifies. **2.** *Agriculture.* a cultivator with prongs for loosening the soil without turning it over.

scar·i·fy (skar′ə fī), *v.t.,* **-fied, -fy·ing. 1. a.** to make scratches or cuts in the surface of (the skin, etc.). **b.** to cover with scratches: *These . . . could be stamped out of plastic or Fiberglas with a scarified top* (New Yorker). *Fixing her nails in his antagonist's face, she scarified all one side of his nose* (Tobias Smollett). **2.** to criticize severely; hurt the feelings of; wound; harrow: *He . . . cut up a rising genius or scarified some unhappy wretch* (Benjamin Disraeli). **3.** to loosen (soil) without turning it over. **4.** to slit the coats of (seeds) to hasten sprouting. **5.** to make cuts in the bark of (a tree) as a treatment or to tap the sap. [< Old French *scarifier,* learned borrowing from Late Latin *scarīficāre* < Latin *scarīfāre* < Greek *skarīphâsthai* to scratch < *skarîphos* stylus] —**scar′i·fy′ing·ly,** *adv.*

scar·i·ous (skãr′ē əs), *adj.* **1.** *Botany.* thin, dry, and membranous: *the scarious bracts of many composites.* **2.** *Zoology.* scabby; scurfy. [< New Latin *scariosus;* origin uncertain]

scar·la·ti·na (skär′lə tē′nə), *n.* **1.** scarlet fever. **2.** a mild form of scarlet fever. [< New Latin *scarlatina* < Italian *scarlattina,* feminine of *scarlattino* (diminutive) < *scarlatto* scarlet]

scar·la·ti·nal (skär′lə tē′nəl), *adj.* like or resulting from scarlatina.

scar·la·ti·noid (skär′lə tē′noid, skär lat′ə-), *adj.* resembling scarlatina or its eruption. [< *scarlatin*(a) + *-oid*]

scar·less (skär′lis), *adj.* **1.** having no scar; unscarred. **2.** leaving no scar.

scar·let (skär′lit), *n.* **1.** a very bright red, much lighter than crimson. **2.** cloth or clothing having this color: *Alas, alas, that great city, that was clothed in fine linen, and purple, and scarlet* (Revelation 18:16).

—*adj.* **1.** very bright red. **2.** red, as with shame: *Embarrassed, her face turned scarlet.* **3.** glaring; flagrant; notorious: *scarlet sins, a scarlet crime.*

[short for Old French *escarlate* < Medieval Latin *scarlatum*, perhaps ultimately < Persian *saqlāt* rich cloth]

scar·let·ber·ry (skär′lit ber′ē), *n., pl.* **-ries.** **1.** the bittersweet. **2.** its berry.

scarlet cross, the scarlet lychnis.

scarlet fever, a very contagious disease caused by a streptococcus and characterized by a scarlet rash, sore throat, and fever.

scarlet ibis, an ibis of tropical South America, about two feet long, with completely scarlet plumage except for black primary feathers.

scarlet letter, a scarlet letter "A" worn as punishment for adultery, as by Hester Prynne in Nathaniel Hawthorne's *The Scarlet Letter*.

scarlet lychnis, a common garden plant of the pink family with showy, red or white flowers; Maltese cross.

scarlet oak, a kind of oak of eastern North America whose leaves turn a brilliant scarlet in fall.

scarlet pimpernel, an herb of the primrose family with bright-scarlet flowers that close in cloudy or rainy weather.

scarlet plume, a shrubby variety of spurge native to Mexico, with scarlet appendages extending from between the lobes of the involucre.

scarlet runner, a tall, twining bean of tropical America having showy, scarlet flowers and long pods with large, black, edible seeds.

scarlet sage, a common garden plant of the mint family with clusters of bright-red flowers, a variety of salvia.

scarlet tanager, the common tanager of eastern North America; redbird. The male has black wings and tail and a scarlet body.

Scarlet Woman, the woman described in Revelation 17, variously interpreted as representing pagan Rome, papal Rome, or the spirit of worldliness and evil.

scarlet woman, a harlot; whore.

scarp (skärp), *n.* **1.** a steep slope: *sheer scarps of grey rock* (Henry Kingsley). **2.** the inner slope or side of a ditch surrounding a fortification; escarp. *—v.t.* to make into a steep slope; slope steeply: *The rock on which this fort stands was scarped towards the city* (Garnet J.W. Wolseley). [< Italian *scarpa* slope. Compare ESCARP.]

scarp·er (skär′pər), *v.i. British Slang.* to run away; go away; leave in a hurry: *A raft of people got the wind up and scarpered for foreign climes* (Punch). [apparently < Italian *scappare* escape]

scart (skärt), *Scottish. —n.* **1.** a scratch. **2.** a mark made by a pen. *—v.t., v.i.* to scratch or scrape. [alteration of *scrat;* see SCRATCH]

scar tissue, the new connective tissue that forms when a wound, sore, or ulcer heals. Scar tissue forms after granulation. *A grafting technique . . . could eliminate scar tissue in wounds that are healing* (Science News Letter).

scarved (skärvd), *adj.* scarfed: *high scarved necklines* (Daily Telegram).

scarves (skärvz), *n. Especially British.* scarfs; a plural of **scarf.**

scar·y (skãr′ē), *adj.,* **scar·i·er, scar·i·est.** *Informal.* **1.** causing fright or alarm: *a scary ghost story. Maxwell Anderson's scary melodrama dealing with a winsome little girl who is also homicidal* . . . (New Yorker). **2.** easily frightened: *A scary comrade in the woods is apt to make a short path long* (James Fenimore Cooper). **—Syn. 2.** timorous.

scat[1] (skat), *interj., v.,* **scat·ted, scat·ting.** *Informal. —interj.* an exclamation used to drive away an animal. *—v.i.* to go away, especially in a hurry. [perhaps < *hiss* + *cat*]

scat[2] (skat), *n.* a tax; tribute. Also, **scatt.** [originally Scottish < Scandinavian (compare Old Icelandic *skattr*). Related to SCOT, tax.]

scat[3] (skat), *n., v.,* **scat·ted, scat·ting,** *adj. Slang. —n.* nonsense chatter and sounds, usually sung or spoken rapidly to jazz music. *—v.i., v.t.* to sing or speak scat: *Miss Fitzgerald, in the space of four records, sings, scats, hums, and noodles her way through thirty-seven . . . tunes* (New Yorker). *—adj.* of or having to do with scat: *a scat session, a scat singer.*

scat·back (skat′bak′), *n. Football.* a swift, agile back, usually of relatively small stature: *If anyone wonders where the old-fashioned 165-lb. scatbacks went, he might take a look at all those 275-lb. defensive tackles playing football these days* (Time). [< *scat*[1] + *back*[1]]

scath (skath), *v.t., n. Dialect.* scathe.

scathe (skāᴛʜ), *v.,* **scathed, scath·ing,** *n. —v.t.* **1.** to blast or sear with invective; wither with satire: *His satire flashed about, . . . scathing especially his old enemies the monks* (James A. Froude). **2.** to injure or destroy by fire, lightning, etc.; sear; scorch: *. . . a place where the tree had been scathed by lightning* (Washington Irving). **3.** *Archaic.* to injure; damage.
—n. **1.** *Archaic.* a hurt; harm. **2.** *Archaic.* a matter for sorrow or regret. **3.** *Obsolete.* an injury.
[< Scandinavian (compare Old Icelandic *skathi,* noun; *skatha,* verb)]

scathe·ful (skāᴛʜ′fəl), *adj. Archaic.* hurtful; harmful; injurious.

scathe·less (skāᴛʜ′lis), *adj.* without harm; unhurt: *It is a game from which you will come out scatheless, but I have been scalded* (Anthony Trollope). **—Syn.** uninjured, unharmed.

scath·ing (skā′ᴛʜing), *adj.* bitterly severe; withering: *a scathing remark, scathing criticism.* **—scath′ing·ly,** *adv.* **—Syn.** stinging.

scat·o·log·ic (skat′ə loj′ik), *adj.* scatological.

scat·o·log·i·cal (skat′ə loj′ə kəl), *adj.* of or having to do with scatology.

sca·tol·o·gy (skə tol′ə jē), *n.* **1. a.** the study of fossil excrement to learn about animals. **b.** the branch of medicine that deals with diagnosis by means of the feces. **2. a.** the study of or an interest in obscenity, especially in literature. **b.** obscene literature: *. . . especially in the light of this year's Broadway scatology . . .* (Time). [< Greek *skôr, skatós* excrement + English *-logy*]

sca·toph·a·gous (skə tof′ə gəs), *adj.* feeding upon dung. [< Greek *skôr, skatós* excrement + *phageîn* eat + English *-ous*]

sca·tos·co·py (skə tos′kə pē), *n.* examination of the feces for the purpose of diagnosis or divination. [< Greek *skôr, skatós* excrement + English *-scopy*]

scatt (skat), *n.* scat[2].

scat·ter (skat′ər), *v.t.* **1.** to throw here and there; sprinkle: *The farmer scattered corn for the chickens. Scatter ashes on the icy sidewalk.* **2.** to distribute here and there: *So long as works of art are scattered through the nation, no universal destruction of them is possible* (John Ruskin). **3.** to separate and drive off in different directions: *The police scattered the mob.* **4.** *Physics.* to throw back or deflect (rays of light, radioactive particles, etc.) in all directions: *There would be no lens surfaces to scatter light, and the working distance could be quite large* (J. G. Thomas). *—v.i.* to separate and go in different directions: *The hens scattered when they saw the hawk.*
—n. **1.** the act or fact of scattering: *There was a general scatter of the party who had come to see the duel* (Samuel Lover). **2.** anything that is scattered: *significant rock formations on the scatter of islands west of Ellesmere* (New Scientist). **3.** *Slang.* an apartment; room: *The Grand Duke hurries straightway to Marian's scatter, where she tenderly awaits Orloff* (New Yorker).
[perhaps unrecorded Old English *sceaterian.* Compare SHATTER.] **—scat′ter·er,** *n.*
—Syn. *v.t.* **1.** strew, sow. **3. Scatter, dispel, disperse** mean to separate and drive away. **Scatter** applies to persons or objects, and means to separate and drive them off in different directions: *The wind scattered my papers.* **Dispel** applies only to things that cannot be touched, such as clouds and feelings, and means to drive them completely away: *The sun dispelled the fog.* **Disperse** applies to an organized or compact group, and means to scatter the individuals in every direction but not so that they cannot come together again: *Storms dispersed the convoy.*

scat·ter·a·tion (skat′ə rā′shən), *n.* **1.** the act of scattering. **2.** the fact of being scattered: *The scatteration of economic authority in Washington is notorious* (Harper's). **3.** the policy of spreading grants of money over many small projects instead of concentrating them on a few of greater value.

scat·ter·brain (skat′ər brān′), *n.* a thoughtless, heedless person: *The scatterbrains . . . are deeply involved in personal problems while behind the wheel of a car and are inclined to daydream* (New York Times).

scat·ter·brained (skat′ər brānd′), *adj.* not able to think steadily; thoughtless; heedless; flighty: *So here is the Government officially encouraging a scatterbrained attitude* (Wall Street Journal).

scat·ter·brains (skat′ər brānz′), *n.* a scatterbrain.

scatter communication, long distance communication using the troposphere or other areas of atmospheric ionization to deflect radio waves over a long distance.

scat·tered (skat′ərd), *adj.* **1.** disunited or dispersed; disorganized: *He . . . began to collect his scattered forces* (Thomas Macaulay). **2.** occurring at wide intervals; placed here and there; spread over a wide area: *scattered clouds. Ye scattered birds that faintly sing* (Robert Burns). **—scat′tered·ly,** *adv.* **—scat′tered·ness,** *n.*

scat·ter·good (skat′ər gu̇d′), *n.* a person who is very wasteful; a spendthrift.

scat·ter·gun (skat′ər gun′), *n. U.S. Informal.* a shotgun.

scat·ter·ing (skat′ər ing), *adj.* **1.** widely separated; occurring here and there: *scattering drops of rain.* **2.** divided in small numbers among several candidates: *scattering votes.* *—n.* a small amount or number scattered or interspersed: *There seldom were more than a half-dozen senators on the floor at one time and only a scattering of people in the Senate galleries* (Newsweek). **—scat′tering·ly,** *adv.* **—Syn.** *adj.* **1.** sporadic.

scattering layer, a layer of plankton or other organisms in the ocean that reflects and scatters sound waves.

scatter pins, small ornamental pins worn in groups on the clothing by women and girls: *Scatter pins . . . come in three graduated sizes, to twinkle on the lapel of your new spring suit* (New York Times).

scatter propagation, scatter communication: *Reception far beyond the horizon is usually impossible, except by the brute-force methods of scatter propagation* (New Scientist).

scatter rug, a small rug, covering part of a floor.

scatter shot, 1. buckshot. **2.** the spread of small shot from a shotgun.

scat·ter·shot (skat′ər shot′), *adj.* spreading widely like the burst of shot from a shotgun: *The old tendency to place politics in a sharply defined category ignores the scattershot impacts of political power* (Saturday Review).

scatter transmission, scatter communication.

scat·ty (skat′ē), *adj.,* **-ti·er, -ti·est.** *Especially British Informal.* scatterbrained: *. . . the same scatty, mixed-up international . . . literary conference* (Manchester Guardian).

sca·tu·ri·ent (skə tůr′ē ənt, -tyůr′-), *adj.* streaming or flowing out; gushing forth: *He wielded . . . a pen so scaturient and unretentive, that . . . he himself must have been often astonished . . . at the extent of his lucubrations* (Edinburgh Review). [< Latin *scatūriēns, -entis,* present participle of *scatūrīre* stream forth < *scatēre* gush]

scaup duck (skôp), any of several broad-billed wild ducks related to the canvasback; widgeon. The males have glossy black heads and necks. [perhaps variant of dialectal *scalp* bank that provides a bed for shellfish]

scaur[1] (skôr), *n.* a scar[2]. [variant of *scar*[2]]

scaur[2] (skôr), *v.t., v.i. Scottish.* scare[1].

scav·enge (skav′ənj), *v.,* **-enged, -eng·ing.** *—v t.* **1. a.** to clean (a street, surface of a river, etc.) by removing filth, rubbish, etc. **b.** to pick over (a dump, garbage, etc.) for things to use or sell. **2.** to expel burned gases from (the cylinder of an internal-combustion engine). **3.** to clean (molten metal) by chemically removing its impurities. *—v.i.* **1.** to act as a scavenger. **2.** to undergo scavenging. [back formation < *scavenger*]

scav·en·ger (skav′ən jər), *n.* **1.** an animal that feeds on decaying matter: *Vultures, jackals, and some snails and beetles are scavengers. Turkey buzzards . . . their services as scavengers are invaluable* (Frank M. Chapman). **2.** a person who cleans streets, etc., taking away the dirt and filth: *An army of scavengers . . . was cleansing the asphalt roadway* (George Du Maurier). [alteration of Middle English *skavager* inspector < Anglo-French *scawager* < *scawage* a toll < Old North French *escauwage* < *escauwer* to inspect < Flemish *scauwen.* Compare PASSENGER, MESSENGER.]

Sc. B., Bachelor of Science (Latin, *Scientiae Baccalaureus*).

Sc. D., Doctor of Science (Latin, *Scientiae Doctor*).

sceat (shat), *n.* a small Old English silver coin, about 15 grains in weight, used in the 600's and 700's A.D. Also, **sceatta.** [Old English *sceat, scætt*]

sceat·ta (shat′ə), *n.* sceat: *A silver sceatta of the early eighth century [is] the first such find at Winchester* (London Times).

sce·na (shā′nə), *n.* **1.** a scene in an opera: *The big scena of madness in the second act . . . brought out her most affecting and colorful tone* (Manchester Guardian Weekly). **2.** a composition consisting largely of recitative of a dramatic and impassioned character, for one or more voices and accompaniment, either forming part of an opera or composed separately for the concert room. [< Italian *scena* < Latin *scēna* scene]

sce·nar·i·o (si nãr′ē ō, -när′-), *n., pl.* **-i·os.** **1.** the outline of a motion picture, giving the main facts about the scenes, persons, and acting. **2.** an outline of any play, opera, etc.: *The two men met, and the scenario for "La Chambre" is the result* (New Yorker). [< Italian *scenario* < *scena* scene < Latin *scēna*]

sce·nar·ist (si nãr′ist, -när′-), *n.* a person who writes scenarios.

scend (send), *v.i.* (of a ship) to lurch upward on the swell of a wave: *to pitch and scend.*
—*n.* a sudden upward heave on the swell of a wave. Also, **send.**
[spelling variant of *send*]

scene (sēn), *n.* **1. a.** the time, place, circumstances etc., of a play or story: *The scene of the novel is laid in Virginia during the Civil War.* **b.** the place where anything is carried on or takes place: *the scene of an accident, the scene of my childhood.* **2.** the painted screens, hangings, etc., used on the stage to represent places: *The scene represents a city street.* **3.** a part of an act of a play: *The king first appears in Act I, Scene 2.* **4.** a particular incident of a play, story, etc.: *the balcony scene in "Romeo and Juliet."* **5.** an action, incident, situation, etc., occurring in reality or represented in literature or art: *He painted a series of pictures called "Scenes of My Boyhood."* **6.** a view; picture: *The white sailboats in the blue water made a pretty scene.* **7.** a show of strong feeling in front of others; exhibition; display: *The child kicked and screamed and made such a scene that his mother was ashamed of him.* **8.** *Slang.* any place or location: *Besides the hipster scene at the club, there were two other scenes where pot was common* (Maclean's). **9.** *Archaic.* the stage of a theater.
behind the scenes, a. out of sight of the audience: *Things happening in the action of the play, and supposed to be done behind the scenes* (John Dryden). **b.** privately; secretly; not publicly: *Important conferences were held behind the scenes.* **c.** privy to what is going on; in a capacity to be in on or to influence matters privately decided: *Miss Pratt . . . had obtained the entrée to a number of great houses, and was behind the scenes in many fashionable families* (Maria Edgeworth).
make the scene, *Slang.* **a.** to appear or be present, especially at a fashionable place or event: *A slim, elegantly dressed character . . . used to make the jazz scene at the club* (Maclean's). **b.** to be popular or successful: *These days the girl who can't perform a mean frug . . . will never make the scene* (Time).
[< Middle French *scene*, learned borrowing from Latin *scēna* < Greek *skēnḗ* (originally) tent, in the theater, where actors changed costumes]
—**Syn. 6.** See **view.**

scen·er·y (sē′nər ē, sēn′rē), *n., pl.* **-er·ies.** **1.** the general appearance of a place: *mountain scenery.* **2.** the painted hangings, fittings, etc., used in a theater to represent places: *The scenery pictures a garden in the moonlight.*
chew the scenery, to act in an exaggerated fashion; overact: *. . . a family unabashedly given to chewing the scenery* (New Yorker).
—**scen′er·y·less′,** *adj.*

scene·shift·er (sēn′shif′tər), *n.* a person who shifts and arranges the scenes in a theater: *Sceneshifters at Wood Green studios walked off the set* (Punch).

scene-steal·er (sēn′stē′lər), *n.* an actor who seizes all the attention of an audience with his performance: *The scene-stealer is often a butler or a maid seeking stardom.*

sce·nic (sē′nik, sen′ik), *adj.* **1. a.** of or having to do with natural scenery: *The scenic splendors of Yellowstone Park are famous.* **b.** having much fine scenery; picturesque: *a scenic highway.* **2.** belonging to the stage of a theater; of or having to do with stage effects: *The production of the musical comedy was a scenic triumph.* **3.** representing an action, incident, situation, etc., in art: *There is far less antagonism between what is decorative and what is scenic in painting than is sometimes supposed* (C.H. Moore).
—*n.* a moving picture of natural scenes.
—**sce′ni·cal·ly,** *adv.*

sce·ni·cal (sē′nə kəl, sen′ə-), *adj.* scenic.

scenic dome, a glass or plastic dome on top of a railway car through which passengers can view the passing scenery: *Canadian Pacific's sleek scenic dome streamliner speeds across Canada* (Maclean's).

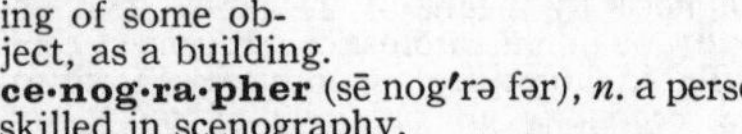

Scenic Dome

sce·no·graph (sē′nə graf, -gräf), *n.* a perspective drawing of some object, as a building.

sce·nog·ra·pher (sē nog′rə fər), *n.* a person skilled in scenography.

sce·no·graph·ic (sē′nə graf′ik, sen′ə-), *adj.* of or having to do with scenography.

sce·no·graph·i·cal (sē′nə graf′ə kəl, sen′ə-), *adj.* scenographic.

sce·nog·ra·phy (sē nog′rə fē), *n.* **1.** the representing of objects according to the rules of perspective. **2.** scene painting, especially for the ancient Greek stage. [< Latin *scēnographia* < Greek *skēnographíā* < *skēnḗ* scene, stage + *-graphíā* description of < *gráphein* to draw, write]

scent (sent), *n.* **1.** smell: *The scent of roses filled the air. Several drops of a strong flower scent . . . were added* (Scientific American). **2.** the sense of smell: *Bloodhounds have a keen scent.* **3. a.** the smell left in passing: *The dogs followed the fox by scent.* **b.** the trail of such a smell: *to lose or recover the scent.* **4.** perfume: *She uses too much scent.* **5.** a means by which a person or thing can be traced: *The police are on the scent of the thieves.* **6.** the paper scraps left as a trail in the game of hare and hounds. [< verb]
—*v.t.* **1. a.** to smell; recognize by smell: *The dog scented a rabbit and ran off after it.* **b.** to detect as if by smell; have a suspicion of: *I scent a trick in his offer. The Tory rank and file, scenting Labor blood, are convinced that they can sweep the country* (Time). **2.** to fill with odor. **3.** to perfume: *She scented the room to rid it of the fish smell.*
—*v.i.* to hunt by using the sense of smell: *The dog scented about till he found the trail of the rabbit.*
[< Old French *sentir* to smell, sense < Latin *sentīre* to sense, feel]

-scented, *combining form.* **1.** having scent, or the sense of smell: *Keen-scented = having a keen sense of smell.*
2. having a scent or odor: *Sweet-scented = having a sweet scent.*

scent gland, a gland which secretes an odoriferous substance: *the scent glands of . . . female moths* (New Scientist).

scent·less (sent′lis), *adj.* having no smell.
—**Syn.** odorless.

scep·sis (skep′sis), *n.* skepsis.

scep·ter (sep′tər), *n.* **1.** the rod or staff carried by a ruler as a symbol of royal power or authority. **2.** royal or imperial power or authority; sovereignty: *The Persian conqueror governed his new subjects with an iron scepter* (Edward Gibbon).
—*v.t.* **1.** to furnish with a scepter. **2.** to touch with a scepter as a sign of royal assent.
[< Old French *sceptre*, learned borrowing from Latin *scēptrum* < Greek *skē̂ptron* staff]

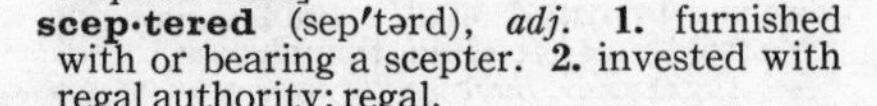

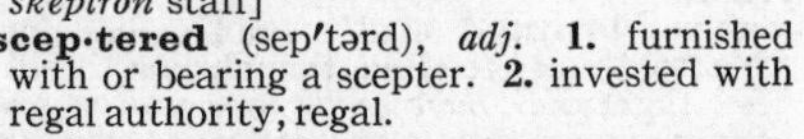

Scepter (def. 1)

scep·tered (sep′tərd), *adj.* **1.** furnished with or bearing a scepter. **2.** invested with regal authority; regal.

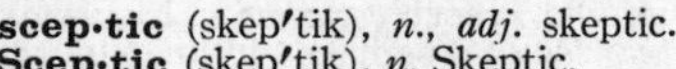

scep·tic (skep′tik), *n., adj.* skeptic.

Scep·tic (skep′tik), *n.* Skeptic.

scep·ti·cal (skep′tə kəl), *adj.* skeptical.

scep·ti·cism (skep′tə siz əm), *n.* skepticism: *A wise scepticism is the first attribute of a good critic* (Herman Melville).

scep·ti·cize (skep′tə sīz), *v.i.,* **-cized, -cizing.** skepticize.

scep·tre (sep′tər), *n., v.t.,* **-tred, -tring.** *Especially British.* scepter.

sch., **1.** school. **2.** schooner.

Schab·zie·ger (shäp′tsē gər), *n. German.* sapsago.

Scha·den·freu·de (shä′dən froi′də), *n. German.* malicious joy or pleasure: *The Germans may feel some of the emotion which they call Schadenfreude . . . at the spectacle of their wartime enemies falling out among themselves* (Wall Street Journal).

schanz (skäns), *n.* (in South Africa) a small fort or barricade of stones, earth, etc. [< Afrikaans *schanz* < Dutch *schans*]

Scha·per glass (shä′pər), a low, cylindrical drinking glass. [< Johann *Schaper*, a German glass-painter of the 1600's]

schat·chen (shät′Hən), *n. Yiddish.* a marriage broker.

sched·u·lar (skej′u̇ lər; *especially British or Canadian* shed′yu̇ lər), *adj.* of, by, or according to a schedule.

sched·ule (skej′u̇l; *especially British or Canadian* shed′yül), *n., v.,* **-uled, -ul·ing.**
—*n.* **1.** a written or printed statement of details; list: *A timetable is a schedule of the coming and going of airplanes, trains, or buses. The teacher posted the schedule of classes.* **2.** the time fixed for the doing of something, arrival at a place, etc.: *The plane was an hour behind schedule.* **3. a.** a blank form on which to fill out particulars under several headings: *List the expenditures under schedule B of this income-tax form.* **b.** an official statement arranged under prescribed headings, such as assets and liabilities, of particulars liable to income tax, or the like. **4.** an appendix to a legislative act or a legal document containing a statement of details not included in the body of the main document. **5.** *Obsolete.* a scroll of parchment or paper containing a writing; document.
—*v.t.* **1.** to make a schedule of; enter in a schedule. **2.** to plan or arrange (something) for a definite future date: *to schedule the convention for the fall.*
[< Old French *cedule*, learned borrowing from Late Latin *schedula* (diminutive) < Latin *scheda* < Greek *schédē* sheet of papyrus < *skízein* to split] —**sched′ul·er,** *n.*

Sched·uled Caste (skej′u̇ld; *especially British or Canadian* shed′yüld), a name for the untouchables of India.

schee·lite (shā′līt, shē′-), *n.* a mineral, calcium tungstate, an ore of tungsten, found chiefly in brilliant crystals of various colors: *But they had found crystals of pinkish scheelite indicating tungsten beds . . .* (Harper's). *Formula:* $CaWO_4$
[< Karl W. *Scheele*, 1742-1786, a Swedish chemist, who discovered tungstic acid in it + *-ite*[1]]

schef·fer·ite (shef′ə rīt), *n.* a mineral, a variety of pyroxene, usually of yellowish or reddish-brown color, containing manganese and often iron. [< H.T. *Scheffer*, 1710-1759, a Swedish chemist + *-ite*[1]]

Sche·her·a·za·de (shə her′ə zä′də, -hir′-), *n.* the young bride of the Sultan in the *Arabian Nights* who related tales nightly to him to save her life.

sche·ma (skē′mə), *n., pl.* **-ma·ta** (-mə tə). **1.** a diagram; plan; scheme. **2.** (in Kantian philosophy) any one of certain forms or rules of the "productive imagination" through which the understanding is able to apply its "categories" to the manifold of sense perception in the process of realizing knowledge or experience. **3.** a draft of decrees to be issued by an ecumenical council: *This schema consisted of . . . such topics as the principles of liturgical renewal, the eucharistic mystery, the sacraments and sacramentals* (New Yorker). [< Latin *schēma* < Greek *schēma, -atos* figure, appearance. Doublet of SCHEME.]

sche·mat·ic (skē mat′ik), *adj.* **1.** having to do with or like a diagram, plan, or scheme; diagrammatic: *My representations became even more schematic and abstract* (Time). **2.** suggested or modified by a preconceived system.

sche·mat·i·cal·ly (skē mat′ə klē), *adv.* **1.** by means of or using a schematic diagram.

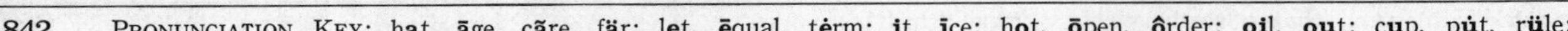

2. in a definite pattern; according to a symmetrical plan.

sche·ma·tise (skē′mə tīz), *v.t., v.i.*, **-tised, -tis·ing.** *Especially British.* schematize.

sche·ma·tism (skē′mə tiz əm), *n.* **1.** an arrangement by diagrams, outlines, etc. **2.** a schematic presentation. **3.** an arrangement; structure.

sche·ma·ti·za·tion (skē′mə tə zā′shən), *n.* reduction to a scheme or formula; arrangement according to a scheme or formula.

sche·ma·tize (skē′mə tīz), *v.t., v.i.*, **-tized, -tiz·ing.** to reduce to or arrange according to a scheme or formula: . . . *violin-and-drum harmonies that orchestrate the human spectacle instead of schematizing it into moral judgments* (Atlantic). [< Greek *schēmatízein* assume a form < *schêma, -atos* a form; see SCHEME]

scheme (skēm), *n., v.*, **schemed, schem·ing.** —*n.* **1.** a program of action; plan: *He has a scheme for doubling his income from the business. It forms no part of our scheme to tell what became of the remainder* (Thackeray). **2.** a self-seeking or underhanded project; plot: *a scheme to cheat the government.* **3.** a system of connected things, parts, thoughts, etc.: *a scheme of theology. The color scheme of the room is blue and gold.* **4.** a diagram; outline; table: *a scheme of postal rates.* **5.** a visionary plan; foolish project. **6.** *Obsolete.* an astrological diagram of the heavens.
—*v.i.* to devise plans, especially underhanded or evil ones; plot: *Those men were scheming to bring the jewels into the country without paying duty.* —*v.t.* to devise as a scheme; plan; plot.
[< Latin *schēma* < Greek *schêma, -atos* figure, appearance < *échein* to have. Doublet of SCHEMA.]
—**Syn.** *n.* **1.** design, project. *-v.i., v.t.* See **plot.**

schem·er (skē′mər), *n.* a person who plans or plots; plotter.

schem·ing (skē′ming), *adj.* making tricky schemes; crafty. —**schem′ing·ly,** *adv.* —**Syn.** plotting, intriguing, contriving, designing, wily.

sche·moz·zle (shə moz′əl), *n. Especially British Slang.* **1.** a mix-up; mess; confusion: *Nobody knows . . . how fearsome a schemozzle will develop at the Motorway's terminal points* (Punch). **2.** a fight; quarrel: [*He had*] *to leave the field with a cut forehead after a schemozzle* (Listener). Also, **shemozzle.** [probably alteration of Yiddish *shlemazl* an unlucky person or thing]

schenk beer (shengk), a mild German beer brewed for immediate use, and not stored like lager. [< German *Schenkbier* < *schenken* pour out; retail + *Bier* beer]

scher·zan·do (sker tsän′dō), *adj. Music.* playful; sportive (a direction). [< Italian *scherzando* < *scherzare* to play, sport < *scherzo;* see SCHERZO]

scher·zo (sker′tsō), *n., pl.* **-zos, -zi** (-tsē). *Music.* a light or playful part of a sonata or symphony. It developed from the minuet: *The symphony . . . is a joyous affair . . . containing a quite charming first movement, a vigorous and infectious scherzo for woodwinds and brass, and a finale full of very exuberant clanging and booming* (New Yorker). [< Italian *scherzo* < German *Scherz* a joke]

Schick test (shik), a test to determine susceptibility to or immunity from diphtheria, made by injecting a dilute diphtheria toxin under the skin. Reddening of the skin shows lack of immunity. [< Dr. Béla *Schick,* 1877–1967, an Austrian pediatrician, who developed it]

Schie·dam (skē dam′), *n.* Hollands (a type of gin). [< *Schiedam,* a town in Holland, where it is distilled]

schil·ler (shil′ər), *n.* a peculiar, almost metallic luster, sometimes with iridescence, occurring on certain minerals, such as hypersthene. [< German *Schiller* play of colors]

schil·ler·i·za·tion (shil′ər ə zā′shən), *n.* a process of change in crystals giving rise to a schiller, appearing when the crystal is turned in various directions.

schil·ler·ize (shil′ə rīz), *v.t.*, **-ized, -iz·ing.** to give a schiller to (a crystal) by rearranging tiny particles within the crystal along certain planes.

schil·ling (shil′ing), *n.* **1.** a copper and nickel coin and unit of money used in Austria since 1925, worth about 3.85 cents. **2.** a former German coin worth 12 pfennigs. [< German *Schilling*]

schip·per·ke (skip′ər kē), *n.* any of a breed of small, sturdy dogs with erect ears and a rather rough, black coat. [< Dutch dialectal *schipperke* (literally) little boatman < Dutch *schipper* skipper[1] (from its use as a watchdog on canal boats)]

Schipperke
(12 to 13 in. high at the shoulder)

schism (siz′əm), *n.* **1.** a division into opposing groups: . . . *the possibility of a serious schism in the ranks of one of the two big British parties* (Wall Street Journal). **2.** a discord or breach between persons or things. **3. a.** the division, either of the whole Church or of some portion of it, into separate and hostile organizations, on account of some difference of opinion over matters of faith or discipline. **b.** the offense of causing or trying to cause such a schism. **c.** a sect or group formed by such a schism. [< Latin *schisma* < Greek *schísma, -atos* < *schízein* to split]

Schism (siz′əm), *n.* **Great, 1.** the division between the Latin and Greek churches, which began in the 800's A.D. **2.** the division (1378-1417) between supporters of the two popes.

schis·mat·ic (siz mat′ik), *adj.* **1.** of, having to do with, or of the nature of a schism. **2.** causing or likely to cause schism. **3.** inclined toward, or guilty of, schism. —*n.* a person who tries to cause a schism or takes part in a schism.

schis·mat·i·cal (siz mat′ə kəl), *adj.* schismatic.

schis·mat·i·cal·ly (siz mat′ə klē), *adv.* in a schismatic manner; by schism.

schis·ma·tize (siz′mə tīz), *v.i.*, **-tized, -tiz·ing. 1.** to act as a schismatic. **2.** to belong to a schismatic body.

schist (shist), *n.* a kind of crystalline metamorphic rock composed mainly of mica that splits easily into layers: *In a few places the rocks are less coarsely crystalline, and are varieties of green slate and schist* (E.F. Roots). [< French *schiste,* learned borrowing from Latin *schistos* < Greek *schistós* cleft, separated < *schízein* to split]

schis·to·cyte (skis′tə sīt), *n.* a segmenting red blood cell. [< Greek *schistós* cleft + English *-cyte* hollow body < Greek *kytos*]

schis·to·cy·to·sis (skis′tə sī tō′sis), *n.* division of a red blood cell. [< New Latin *schistocytosis* < Greek *schistós* cleft + *kýtos* hollow body + English *-osis*]

schis·to·glos·si·a (skis′tə glos′ē ə), *n.* a congenitally cleft tongue.

schist·oid (shis′toid), *adj.* somewhat like schist.

schis·tor·rha·chis (skis tor′ə kis), *n.* spina bifida. [< New Latin *schistorrhachis* < Greek *schistós* cleft + *rhachis* spine]

schist·ose (shis′tōs), *adj.* of or like schist; having the structure of schist; laminated.

schis·to·some (shis′tə sōm), *n.* any of various trematode worms that infest the blood of mammals in tropical countries, causing schistosomiasis. [< New Latin *Schistosoma* the genus name < Greek *schistós* divided (see SCHIST) + *sôma, -atos* body]

schis·to·so·mi·a·sis (shis′tə sō mī′ə sis), *n.* a disease prevalent in Africa and other tropical areas, occurring in human beings and animals, and caused by schistosomes infesting the blood; bilharziasis: *Bilharziasis or schistosomiasis* (*due to parasitic worms in the veins of the intestine or bladder*), *which is spreading in some countries like Brazil, is not yet controlled by efficient therapeutic or prophylactic means* (New Scientist). [< *schistosom*(e) + *-iasis*]

schist·ous (shis′təs), *adj.* **1.** schistose. **2.** formed of schist.

schiz-, *combining form.* the form of **schizo-** before vowels, as in *schizoid.*

schi·zan·thus (ski zan′thəs), *n.* any of a group of variously colored annual and biennial herbs, native to Chile, that are often cultivated, especially in greenhouses, for their showy and abundant flowers. [< Greek *schízein* + *ánthos* flower]

schiz·o (skiz′ō, skit′sō), *n., pl.* **-os.** *Slang.* a schizophrenic: *Treatment turns out to be only palliative at best; the truth is they are schizos, whose psychic split is too wide ever to be healed* (Harper's).

schizo-, *combining form.* split; divided; a cleavage: *Schizocarp = a fruit that divides when ripe. Schizogenesis = reproduction by dividing.* Also, **schiz-** before vowels. [< Greek *schízein* to divide, split]

schiz·o·carp (skiz′ə kärp), *n. Botany.* any dry fruit that divides, when ripe, into two or more one-seeded seed vessels that do not split open, as in the carrot and celery. [< *schizo-* + Greek *karpós* fruit]

schiz·o·car·pous (skiz′ə kär′pəs), *adj. Botany.* of or like a schizocarp.

schi·zog·a·my (ski zog′ə mē), *n. Biology.* reproduction in which a sexual form is produced by fission or by budding from a sexless one, as in some worms.

schiz·o·gen·e·sis (skiz′ə jen′ə sis), *n. Biology.* reproduction by fission, as in the schizophytes. [< New Latin *schizogenesis* < Greek *schízein* divide + *génesis* reproduction]

schi·zog·e·nous (ski zoj′ə nəs), *adj.* reproducing by schizogenesis: *Internal glands and secretion reservoirs are termed schizogenous when the secreting cells split apart at the center of the group and draw away from the line of separation, as in the stems and leaves of the pines* (Heber W. Youngken).

schiz·o·go·ni·a (skiz′ə gō′nē ə), *n.* schizogony.

schiz·o·gon·ic (skiz′ə gon′ik), *adj.* having to do with or exhibiting schizogony.

schi·zog·o·nous (ski zog′ə nəs), *adj.* schizogonic.

schi·zog·o·ny (ski zog′ə nē), *n.* schizogenesis.

schiz·oid (skiz′oid, skit′soid), *adj.* **1.** having schizophrenia. **2.** like or tending toward schizophrenia: *A journalist writing of a visit to Reverón's thatched hut some time after his first schizoid crisis in 1945 describes the artist's bizarre method of painting* (Newsweek). —*n.* a person who has, or tends toward, schizophrenia; schizophrenic.

schiz·o·my·cete (skiz′ō mī sēt′), *n.* a bacterium. [< *schizo-* + Greek *mýkēs, -ētos* fungus]

schiz·o·my·ce·tous (skiz′ō mī sē′təs), *adj.* of or belonging to bacteria.

schiz·o·my·co·sis (skiz′ō mī kō′sis), *n.* any disease caused by bacteria.

schiz·ont (skiz′ont), *n.* (in sporozoans) a fully developed trophozoite that divides by fission into a number of new cells. [< *Schiz-* + Greek *ôn, óntos* being]

schiz·o·pel·mous (skiz′ə pel′məs), *adj.* (of birds) having two flexor tendons for the toes; nomopelmous. [< *schizo-* + Greek *pélma* sole of the foot + English *-ous*]

schiz·o·phrene (skiz′ə frēn, skit′sə-), *n.* a person suffering from schizophrenia.

schiz·o·phre·ni·a (skiz′ə frē′nē ə, -frēn′yə; skit′sə-), *n.* **1.** a mental disease in which the patient dissociates himself from his environment, and deteriorates in character and personality: *She was a victim of the most common form of mental illness, schizophrenia —a loss of touch with reality, a disintegration of personality* (Wall Street Journal). **2.** the condition of having or showing markedly inconsistent or contradictory qualities; split personality: *He finds America suffering from schizophrenia, pulled in opposite directions between an idealism . . . and a realism that is not consistently followed through* (Wall Street Journal). [< New Latin *schizophrenia* < Greek *schízein* to split + *phrēn, phrenós* mind]

schiz·o·phren·ic (skiz′ə fren′ik, skit′sə-), *adj.* of or having to do with schizophrenia; affected with schizophrenia: *It has long been known that schizophrenic patients show biological and chemical changes as well as mental changes* (Wall Street Journal). —*n.* a person affected with schizophrenia: *About half of all hospital beds are occupied by mental patients and about half of the latter are schizophrenics* (Wall Street Journal). —**schiz′o·phren′i·cal·ly,** *adv.*

schiz·o·phren·i·form (skiz′ə fren′ə fôrm, skit′sə-), *adj.* taking on the form of schizophrenia; like schizophrenia: *Schizophreniform confusion may occur in perhaps 20% of the cases* (Kalman Gyarfas).

schiz·o·phy·ceous (skiz′ə fī′shəs, -fish′əs), *adj.* of or belonging to a group of marine and fresh-water blue-green algae that often pollute reservoirs, etc. [< New Latin *Schizophyceae* the class name (< Greek *schízein* split + *phýkos* seaweed)]

schiz·o·phyte (skiz′ə fīt), *n.* any of the bacteria and blue-green algae, reproducing by simple fission or by spores, that are sometimes classified as a group. [< *schizo-* + Greek *phytón* plant]

schiz·o·phyt·ic (skiz′ə fit′ik), *adj.* of or belonging to the schizophytes.

schiz·o·pod (skiz′ə pod), *adj.* of or belonging to the soft-shelled, shrimplike crustaceans with branched limbs that were formerly classified as a group. —*n.* a schizopod crustacean. [< New Latin *Schizopoda* the order name < Greek *schizópous, -podos* with parted toes < *schízein* split + *poús, podós* foot]

schi·zop·o·dous (ski zop′ə dəs), *adj.* schizopod.

schiz·o·thy·mi·a (skiz′ə thī′mē ə, skit′sə-), *n.* a condition bordering on schizophrenia. [< New Latin *schizothymia* < Greek *schízein* split + *thȳmós* spirit]

schiz·o·thy·mic (skiz′ə thī′mik, skit′sə-), *adj.* of or having to do with schizothymia.

schiz·o·zo·ite (skiz′ə zō′īt), *n.* an organism reproduced by schizogamy. [< *schizo-* + Greek *zôion* animal + English *-ite*]

schlaf·rock (shläf′rôk), *n.* a dressing gown. [< German *Schlafrock* < *schlafen* to sleep + *Rock* coat, gown]

schle·miel or **schle·mihl** (shlə mēl′), *n. Slang.* a clumsy person; bungler; gullible fool. [American English < Yiddish *shlumiel* < the Hebrew name *Shelumiel* (compare Numbers 7:36)]

Schlemm's canal (shlemz), a venous canal or sinus near the junction of the sclera and cornea of the eye that serves to drain the aqueous humor. [< Friedrich S. *Schlemm,* 1795-1858, a German anatomist]

schlepp (shlep), *Slang. v.t., v.i.* to move slowly, with difficulty, or unwillingly; drag: *He slaved for years like a dog, schlepped through rain and snow to put bread in his children's mouths* (New Yorker). —*n.* a stupid, foolish, or dull person. [< Yiddish *shlepen* to drag]

schlie·ren (shlir′ən), *n.pl.* **1.** streaks of irregularly shaped igneous rock, that differ in texture or composition from the main mass. **2.** *Physics.* **a.** areas in a medium where refraction varies as a result of differences in density. **b.** the shadows cast on a screen when light is refracted by these areas so that it cannot hit the screen.

—*adj.* **1.** of or having to do with schlieren: *Focused shadowgraphs were taken through windows. They are known as schlieren photographs and show the shock waves about the model* (Science News Letter). **2.** using schlieren to study substances or their behavior in motion, to indicate irregularities in glass, heat convection, shock wave patterns, etc.: *This schlieren system is probably best known from its use in photographing the shock waves formed by air passing at great speeds over airplane models in wind tunnels* (Science News Letter).

[< German *Schlieren* < *Schlier* marl, or perhaps < *Schliere* slime]

schlie·ric (shlir′ik), *adj.* of or having to do with schlieren.

schlock (shlok), *Slang. n.* junk; trash: *What might have been at least an amusing trifle becomes merely another piece of schlock* (Russell Baker). —*adj.* junky; cheap. [< Yiddish *shlok* junk]

schlock·meis·ter (shlok′mīs′tər), *n. U.S. Slang.* a person who supplies giveaway shows, celebrities, etc., with various products in exchange for free advertisement of those products: *A schlockmeister [is] defined in the radio-TV lexicon as "somebody in the business of giving away somebody else's merchandise"* (Time). [apparently < Yiddish *shlok* junk + German *Meister* master]

schloss (shlôs), *n.* a castle: *The first Haydn [concert] was to have been given at the Schloss Esterhazy, in the reception hall* (Atlantic). [< German *Schloss*]

schmaltz or **schmalz** (shmälts), *n.* **1.** *Slang.* **a.** cloying sentimentalism in music, art, literature, etc.: *Here were no treacly saxophone sections, no "crooners"—none of the cloying, fake romanticism which made our dance halls misty with schmaltz* (Punch). **b.** anything characterized by such sentimentalism. **2.** chicken fat. [< German *Schmalz* (literally) fat]

schmaltz·y (shmält′sē), *adj.,* **schmaltz·i·er, schmaltz·i·est.** *Slang.* of or characterized by schmaltz; cloyingly sentimental: *Big, schmaltzy dance bands* (Wall Street Journal).

schmalz·y (shmält′sē), *adj.,* **schmalz·i·er, schmalz·i·est.** schmaltzy.

Schmidt camera (shmit), a camera with a concave spherical mirror to converge light rays to a focal point, together with a thin correcting plate or lens to overcome spherical aberration. [< Bernard *Schmidt,* died 1935, a German optics specialist]

Schmidt telescope, a telescope with an objective that uses an optical system like that of the Schmidt camera.

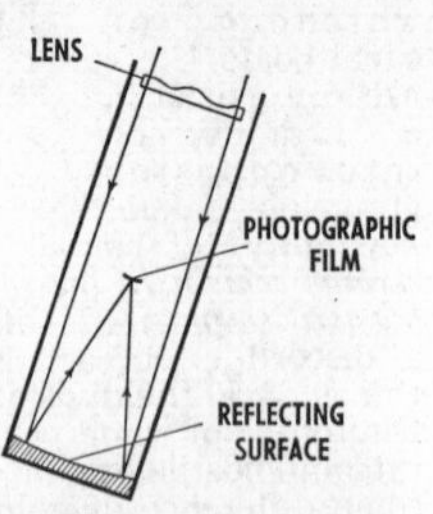

Schmidt Telescope has partly concave, partly convex lens through which light rays pass to be focused and reflected on curved photographic film.

schmier·kä·se (shmir′kā′zə), *n.* cottage cheese. [< German *Schmierkäse* (literally) smear cheese]

schmo or **schmoe** (shmō), *n. Slang.* a silly person; fool: *He's no schmo. He's a brilliant guy that needs editing* (Newsweek). Also, **shmo.** [< a Yiddish word]

schmoos or **schmoose** (shmüz), *n., v.,* **schmoosed, schmoos·ing.** *Slang.* —*n.* chatter; gossip; idle talk: *After a good deal of weighty schmoos, its membership announced that daydreams are a major crash factor on superhighways* (New Yorker). —*v.i.* to gossip; talk idly: *It was a quiet time in the delicatessen ... and the three of us started schmoosing for a few minutes* (New Yorker). [< Yiddish *shmues* < Hebrew *shamuot* news]

schna·bel (shnä′bəl), *n.* a whitefish of Europe. [< German *Schnabel* beak]

schna·bel·kan·ne (shnä′bəl kän′ə), *n.* a jug or vessel with a long spout. [< German *Schnabelkanne* (literally) beak can]

schnap·per (shnap′ər, snap′-), *n.* a reddish food fish of Australia and New Zealand. [perhaps < German *Schnapper* kind of fish]

schnapps or **schnaps** (shnäps), *n.* **1.** Hollands. **2.** any alcoholic liquor: *But the city did have a splendid period of song and schnapps, of beer gardens and opera and theater* (Newsweek). [< German *Schnapps* (originally) a mouthful, gulp < *schnappen* gulp, gasp]

schnau·zer (shnou′zər), *n.* any of a breed of wire-haired German terriers with a long head, small ears, and heavy eyebrows, mustache, and beard. There are three sizes, miniature, standard and giant. [< German *Schnauzer,* also *Schnauze* snout]

Standard Schnauzer (17 to 20 in. high at the shoulder)

schneck·en (shnek′ən), *n.pl.* snail-shaped rolls made from a sweet dough, with yeast, butter, cinnamon or other spices, and nuts. [< German *Schnecken* (literally) snails]

schnei·der (schnī′dər), *v.t.* (in various card games) to beat (an opponent) by a decisive margin, usually by taking all possible points: *I'm going to schneider you* (New Yorker). —*n.* a schneidering: *Australia frankly anticipates that the challenge round will be a rout, a schneider, a kick in the pants* (Newsweek). [< German *Schneider* tailor]

schnell (shnel), *adj., adv. Music.* fast; quick. [< German *schnell*]

schnit·zel (shnit′səl), *n.* a veal cutlet, usually seasoned with lemon juice, parsley, capers, and sardines. [American English < German *Schnitzel* cutlet < *schnitzen* carve (frequentative) < *schneiden* to cut]

schnook (shnůk), *n. Slang.* a simple or stupid person. [origin unknown]

schnor·kle or **schnor·kel** (shnôr′kəl), *n.* a snorkel: *In the spring of 1944 operational U-boats of the older types began to be equipped with the "Schnorkel," which enabled them both to recharge batteries while submerged and to draw fresh air into the boat* (Sunday Times).

schnor·rer (shnôr′ər, shnōr′-), *n. Slang.* a beggar; sponger: *I had lunch with him one day a couple of weeks ago. A real schnorrer, but sort of likable* (New Yorker). [< Yiddish *shnorer* < *shnoren* beg < Middle High German]

Schoen·berg·i·an (shœn bėr′gē ən), *adj.* of or having to do with the Austrian composer Arnold Schoenberg (1874-1951), his music, or his musical style. —*n.* an admirer of Schoenberg's musical style or theories.

schol., scholium.

scho·la can·to·rum (skō′lə kan tôr′əm, -tōr′-), **1.** a choir school or choir associated with a cathedral or monastery. **2.** the part of a church reserved for the use of the choir. [< Latin *schola cantōrum* school of singers]

schol·ar (skol′ər), *n.* **1.** a learned person; person having much knowledge: *a Latin scholar. To talk in public, to think in private, to read and to hear, to inquire and answer inquiries, is the business of a scholar* (Harper's). **2.** a pupil at school; student; learner: *a poor scholar, failing in every course.* **3.** a student who is given money by some institution to help him continue his studies. **4.** a person who is able to read and write (usually in illiterate use). [< Late Latin *scholāris* < Latin *schola;* see SCHOOL[1]] —**Syn. 1.** savant, sage. **2.** See **student.**

schol·arch (skol′ärk), *n.* the head of a school, especially of a school of philosophy in ancient Athens. [< Greek *scholárchēs* < *scholḗ* (see SCHOOL[1]) + *árchein* to lead]

schol·ar·li·ness (skol′ər lē nis), *n.* scholarly quality or character.

schol·ar·ly (skol′ər lē), *adj.* **1.** of a scholar; like that of a scholar: *scholarly habits; ... a slight scholarly stoop* (Robert Bridges). **2.** fit for a scholar. **3.** having much knowledge; learned; erudite. **4.** fond of learning; studious. **5.** thorough and orderly in methods of study.

—*adv.* in a scholarly manner: *Speak scholarly and wisely* (Shakespeare).

schol·ar·ship (skol′ər ship), *n.* **1. a.** the possession of knowledge gained by study; quality of learning and knowledge: *Scholarship, ... education, in a country like ours, is a branch of statesmanship* (Newsweek). **b.** the collective attainments of scholars; sphere of learning: *modern French scholarship.* **2. a.** a grant of money to help a student continue his studies. **b.** a fund to provide this money. **c.** the position or status of a student thus aided. —**Syn. 1. a.** erudition.

scho·las·tic (skə las′tik), *adj.* **1.** of schools, scholars, or education; academic: *scholastic achievements or methods.* **2.** of or like scholasticism.

—*n.* **1.** Also, **Scholastic.** a person who favors scholasticism. **2.** a theologian and philosopher of the Middle Ages. **3.** a man who is studying to become a Jesuit priest.

[< Latin *scholasticus* < Greek *scholastikós* < *scholágein* be a scholar, devote one's leisure to learning < *scholḗ;* see SCHOOL[1]]

scho·las·ti·cal (skə las′tə kəl), *adj.* scholastic.

scho·las·ti·cal·ly (skə las′tə klē), *adv.* in a scholastic way or manner; in scholastic respects: *A Federal judge ruled today that the University of Alabama must open its doors to all Negroes scholastically qualified to pursue courses there* (New York Times).

Scholastic Aptitude Test, *U.S.* a test prepared and supervised by the College Entrance Examination Board to test the general intelligence and academic aptitude of a prospective applicant to a college.

scho·las·ti·cate (skə las′tə kāt, -kit), *n.* a house of study for Jesuits before ordination. [< New Latin *scholasticatus* < Latin *scholasticus;* see SCHOLASTIC]

scho·las·ti·cism (skə las′tə siz əm), *n.* **1.** Also, **Scholasticism.** the system of theological and philosophical teaching in the Middle Ages, based chiefly on the authority of the church fathers and of Aristotle, and characterized by a formal method of discussion. **2.** adherence to the teachings of the schools or to traditional doctrines and methods.

scho·li·a (skō′lē ə), *n.* a plural of **scholium.**

scho·li·ast (skō′lē ast), *n.* **1.** a commentator upon the works of an author. **2.** a commentator upon the ancient classics: *From their seats ... arose the gentler and graver ghosts ...—of Grecian or of Roman lore—to crown ... the ... love labours of their unwearied scholiast* (Charles Lamb). [< Medieval Greek *scholiástēs* < *schólion;* see SCHOLIUM]

scho·li·as·tic (skō′lē as′tik), *adj.* of or having to do with a scholiast or his work.

scho·li·um (skō′lē əm), *n., pl.* **-li·a** or **-li·ums. 1.** an explanatory note or comment, especially upon a passage in the Greek or Latin classics. **2.** a note added by way of illustration or amplification. [< Medieval Latin *scholium* < Greek *schólion* (diminutive) < *scholē* discussion; see SCHOOL¹]

school¹ (skül), *n.* **1. a.** a place for teaching and learning: *an elementary or high school, public or private schools, a dancing school.* **b.** instruction in school; education received at school: *Most children start school when they are about 5 years old.* **c.** a regular course of meetings of teachers and pupils for instruction: *a summer school.* **d.** one session of such a course: *to stay after school.* **e.** those who are taught and their teachers: *The entire school was present.* **2.** any place, situation, experience, etc., as a source of instruction or training: *the school of adversity. The men of 1776 were trained in the strictest school of . . . discipline* (E. Everett). **3.** a place of training or discipline. **4. a.** a group of people holding the same beliefs or opinions: *a gentleman of the old school.* **b.** a group of people taught by the same person or following the methods of the same person or group of people: *the Dutch school of painting.* **5. a.** a particular department or group in a university, specializing in a particular branch of leaning: *a school of medicine, a school of music.* **b.** a room, rooms, building, or group of buildings in a university, set apart for the use of one department: *The art school is across the street from the main campus.* **6.** *Military, Naval.* **a.** special drill regulations or drill applying to the individual, squad, etc.: *the school of the squad.* **b.** the performance of a drill in accordance with such regulations. **7.** (in the Middle Ages) a place where lectures were given in logic, metaphysics, and theology.
—*v.t.* **1.** to teach; educate in a school. **2.** to train; discipline: *School yourself to control your temper.* **3.** to instruct (a person) how to act: *Herodias schooled Salome in the part she was to play* (H.R. Reynolds).
—*adj.* of or having to do with a school or schools.
[Old English *scōl* < Latin *schola* < Greek *scholē* discussion; (originally) leisure, related to *échein* to have]
—**Syn.** *n.* **1. a.** academy.

school² (skül), *n.* a large group of the same kind of fish or water animals swimming together: *a school of mackerel.* —*v.i.* to swim together in a school. [< Dutch *school.* Related to SHOAL².]

school age, 1. the age at which a child begins to go to school. **2.** the years during which going to school is compulsory or customary.

school·a·ger (skül′ā′jər), *n.* a young person of school age.

school·bag (skül′bag′), *n.* a bag or case to carry books, papers, etc., to and from school.

school board, a local board or committee managing the public schools: *Houston's KUHT has found that its telecasts of school board meetings draw audiences of 280,000, outrating commercial competition* (Newsweek).

school·book (skül′bu̇k′), *n.* a book for study in schools.

school·boy (skül′boi′), *n.* a boy attending school.

school·boy·ish (skül′boi′ish), *adj.* like or characteristic of a schoolboy: *His prose style, though lucid, is awkward and repetitious — it has a schoolboyish ring* (Atlantic).

school bus, a bus that carries children to and from school.

school·child (skül′chīld′), *n., pl.* **-children.** a schoolboy or schoolgirl.

school·craft (skül′kraft′, -kräft′), *n. Archaic.* knowledge taught in the schools.

school day, 1. a day on which school is in session. **2.** the time of such a session.

school district, an area of a town, county, etc., having its own school or schools. The school district usually serves as a unit of local taxation.

school edition, the form of a book published for use in the classroom: *Many novels are published in paperback school editions with notes and glossaries in the back.*

school·er (skü′lər), *n.* a schoolchild: *By winter's end, there will be enough vaccine for everyone under 20, and for third shots for the grade schoolers* (Newsweek).

school·fel·low (skül′fel′ō), *n.* a companion at school.

school figure, one of a required set of figures or movements in a skating competition: *School figures . . . include turns like threes, double threes, brackets, and loops, and combinations thereof* (New Yorker).

school·girl (skül′gėrl′), *n.* a girl attending school. —*adj.* of or like that of a young girl: *a schoolgirl figure.*

school·girl·ish (skül′gėr′lish), *adj.* like or characteristic of a schoolgirl: *She said to Johnny at lunch, in her schoolgirlish way, "Can you come to the office afterward?"* (New Yorker).

school·house (skül′hous′), *n.* a building used as a school.

school·ing (skü′ling), *n.* **1.** instruction in school; education received at school. **2.** training: *At a riding academy both horses and riders receive schooling.* **3.** the cost of instruction. **4.** *Archaic.* a reprimand; reproof.

school land, *U.S.* land set apart for the maintenance of a school.

school-leav·er (skül′lē′vər), *n. British.* a person who leaves or quits school before he completes his course of study: *The chief works of literature, in particular those of our century, are unknown to most school-leavers* (Manchester Guardian).

school-leav·ing (skül′lē′ving), *n. British.* a leaving or quitting of school before completion of the course of study: *The raising of the school-leaving age to 16 in the late 1960's is the principal proposal of the Crowther report* (Manchester Guardian).

school·less (skül′lis), *adj.* without a school; deprived of a school or schooling: *It thus appeared that Little Rock's high-school students might as well settle down to a long schoolless winter* (Time).

school·ma'am (skül′mam′), *n. Informal or Dialect.* a woman teacher.

school·maid (skül′mād′), *n. Archaic.* a schoolgirl.

school·man (skül′mən), *n., pl.* **-men. 1.** a man engaged in teaching or in managing a school. **2.** Also, **Schoolman.** a teacher in a university of the Middle Ages; medieval theologian. **3.** an expert in traditional learning, formal logic, etc.

school·marm (skül′märm′), *n. Informal or Dialect.* a woman teacher.

school·marm·ish (skül′mär′mish), *adj. Informal.* like or characteristic of a schoolmarm: *A frail, schoolmarmish Dublin spinster named Evie Hone . . . is considered one of the top stained-glass artists of her time* (Time).

school·mas·ter (skül′mas′tər, -mäs′-), *n.* **1.** a man who teaches in or manages a school. **2.** any person or thing that teaches or disciplines. **3.** a snapper of the West Indies and adjacent waters.
—*v.t.* to supervise or instruct as a schoolmaster. —*v.i.* to be a schoolmaster.

school·mas·ter·ing (skül′mas′tər ing, -mäs′-), *n.* the occupation or profession of a schoolmaster.

school·mas·ter·ish (skül′mas′tər ish, -mäs′-), *adj.* like or characteristic of a schoolmaster: *. . . a bookish fantasia about history, full of . . . bloodless schoolmasterish jokes* (Harper's).—**school′mas′ter·ish·ly,** *adv.*

school·mas·ter·ly (skül′mas′tər lē, -mäs′-), *adj.* like or characteristic of a schoolmaster: *Mr. Louw spoke in schoolmasterly tones to 150 newsmen gathered in South Africa House* (Times of India).

school·mate (skül′māt′), *n.* a companion at school.

school·mis·tress (skül′mis′tris), *n.* a woman who teaches in or manages a school.

school·room (skül′rüm′, -ru̇m′), *n.* a room in which pupils are taught.

school section, (in Canada) a section of government land given to a local government by the federal government for the support of public schools: *We brought the school section from a state of bankruptcy to a flourishing and healthy condition* (Elora, Ontario, Observer).

school·ship (skül′ship′), *n.* a seagoing vessel used as a school for practical instruction in seamanship.

school·teach·er (skül′tē′chər), *n.* a person who teaches in a school. —**Syn.** instructor.

school·teach·er·ish (skül′tē′chər ish), *adj.* like or characteristic of a schoolteacher: *Her hair is short, gray, curly, and parted in the middle, giving her a slightly schoolteacherish look, which is often intensified by a pair of rimless spectacles* (New Yorker).

school·teach·er·ly (skül′tē′chər lē), *adj.* like or characteristic of a schoolteacher: *He gave us . . . a thoughtful, schoolteacherly talk on how clean the election was going to be* (Christopher Rand).

school·teach·ing (skül′tē′ching), *n.* the occupation or profession of a schoolteacher: [*He*] *gave up schoolteaching to become executive secretary of the Massachusetts Audubon Society* (New Yorker).

school·time (skül′tīm′), *n.* **1.** the time at which school begins or during which school continues. **2.** the period of life which is passed at school.

school tuna, a tuna fish ranging from 20 to 100 pounds.

school·ward (skül′wərd), *adv., adj.* toward school: *They reluctantly trudged schoolward* (*adv.*). *They found many distractions on their schoolward journey* (*adj.*).

school·work (skül′wėrk′), *n.* a student's work in school.

school·yard (skül′yärd′), *n.* ground around a school, used for play, games, etc.

school year, the part of the year during which school is in session.

schoon·er (skü′nər), *n.* **1.** *U.S.* a ship with two or more masts and fore-and-aft sails. **2.** a prairie schooner. **3. a.** *U.S. Informal.* a large glass for beer: *He ordered a schooner of beer and knocked it off with unaffected enthusiasm* (New Yorker). **b.** *British.* a customary measure of beer. [American English, probably < dialectal *scoon* to skim]

Schooner (def. 1)

schooner rig, a fore-and-aft rig.

schoon·er-rigged (skü′nər rigd′), *adj.* having fore-and-aft sails.

Scho·pen·hau·er·i·an (shō′pən hou′ə rē ən), *adj.* of, having to do with, or characteristic of the German philosopher Arthur Schopenhauer (1788-1860) or his doctrines. —*n.* a believer in or supporter of the philosophical doctrines of Schopenhauer.

Scho·pen·hau·er·ism (shō′pən hou′ə riz əm), *n.* the philosophy of Arthur Schopenhauer, German philosopher; belief that life is evil, and cannot be made good.

schorl (shôrl), *n.* a mineral, tourmaline, especially black tourmaline. [< German *Schörl*]

schor·la·ceous (shôr lā′shəs), *adj.* of the nature of, resembling, or containing schorl.

schot·tische or **schot·tish** (shot′ish), *n.* **1.** a dance in 2/4 time, somewhat like the polka but slower, popular in the 1800's. **2.** the music for it. [< German *Schottische* (originally) Scottish]

schr. or **Schr.,** schooner: *The Schr. Rival.*

Schreck·lich·keit (shrek′liʜ kīt), *n. German.* **1.** frightfulness. **2.** terrifying measures used as a means of coercion, as in war.

schrei·ber·site (shrī′bər sīt, -zīt), *n.* a phosphide of iron and nickel occurring only in meteoric iron. *Formula:* $(Fe,Ni)_3P$ [< German *Schreibersit* < Carl von *Schreibers,* an Austrian museum director + *-it* -ite]

schrik (skrik), *n. Afrikaans.* sudden terror.

Schrö·ding·er wave equation (shrœ′ding ər), a general equation of wave mechanics describing the behavior of atomic particles passing through a field of force. [< Erwin *Schrödinger,* 1887-1961, an Austrian physicist, who formulated this equation in 1926]

schtik (shtik), *n. Slang.* a characteristic, routine, gimmick, trick, etc., especially used by an entertainer: *John Barber's schtik is to flay his native land* (Maclean's). [< Yiddish *shtik* piece, slice]

Schu·bert·i·an (shü bėr′tē ən), *adj.* of, having to do with, or characteristic of Franz Schubert, 1797-1828, Austrian musical composer: *Autumn, a setting of verses by Harmony Twitchell Ives, is a work of almost Schubertian beauty and expressiveness* (New York Times). —*n.* an admirer of Franz Schubert's style or theory of music.

schuh·platt·ler (shü′plät′lər), *n.* a Bavarian folk dance for couples, in which the woman turns slowly in place, while her partner dances around her slapping his thighs and the soles of his shoes. [< German *Schuhplattler* < *Schuh* shoe + dialectal *Plattler* one who strikes]

schuit (skoit), *n.* a short, somewhat bargelike ship used on the rivers and canals of the Netherlands. It has a sloop rigging but is now powered by motor. Also, **schuyt.** [< Dutch *schuit*]

Schu·man Plan (shü′mən), a plan providing for the pooling of the coal and steel resources of France, Italy, West Germany, Belgium, The Netherlands, and Luxemburg, with production supervised by a joint authority. [< Robert *Schuman,* 1886-1963, a French political figure, who devised it]

schuss (shůs), *v.,* **schussed, schuss·ing,** *n.* in skiing: *—v.i.* to make a run at top speed over a straight course: *He was schussing down Hahnenkamm at something like 50 miles an hour when he hit a bare spot* (Newsweek). *—n.* **1.** a fast run down a straight course. **2.** the course itself. [< German *Schuss*]

Schutz·staf·fel (shůts′shtä′fəl), *n.* the SS Troops, especially those of the German army during World War II. [< German *Schutzstaffel*]

schuyt (skoit), *n.* schuit.

schwa (shwä), *n.* **1.** an unstressed vowel sound such as *a* in *about* or *u* in *circus,* represented by the symbol ə. **2.** a neutral vowel. **3.** the symbol ə. [< German *Schwa* < Hebrew *shəwa*]

Schwann cell (shwän, shvän), any of the cells that form a myelin sheath around the nerve fibers or axons in the peripheral nervous system. [< Theodor *Schwann,* 1810-1882, a German anatomist]

Schwär·me·rei or **schwär·me·rei** (shver′mə rī′), *n. German.* enthusiasm; devotion: *We had a great schwärmerei for Frank which would come like measles and go as completely* (New Yorker).

Schweit·zer's reagent (shvīt′sərz), a reagent used to test for the presence of wool, consisting of an hydroxide of copper combined with ammonia. [< Matthias *Schweitzer,* 1818-1860, a German chemist]

Schwei·zer·kä·se or **schwei·zer·kä·se** (shvīt′sər kā′zə), *n. German.* Swiss cheese.

Schwer·punkt (shvār′půngkt′), *n. German.* **1.** a military maneuver using tanks supported by aircraft, mobile artillery, and motorized infantry in an attempt to overwhelm and break through an enemy's line on a narrow front. **2.** the portion of an enemy's line that is the objective of such an assault.

Schwyz·er·dütsch (shvēt′sər dych′), *n.* the German dialect of Switzerland. [< Schwyzerdütsch *Schwyzerdütsch* Swiss German < *Schwyz* Switzerland + *dütsch* German]

sci., **1.** science. **2.** scientific.

sci·ae·nid (sī ē′nid), *adj., n.* sciaenoid.

sci·ae·noid (sī ē′noid), *adj.* of or belonging to a large group of spiny-finned carnivorous fishes usually with air bladders that make a drumming sound. It includes the drumfishes and some kingfishes. *—n.* a sciaenoid fish. [< Latin *sciaena* kind of fish (< Greek *skíaina*) + English *-oid*]

sci·a·gram (sī′ə gram), *n.* a skiagram.

sci·a·graph (sī′ə graf, -gräf), *n., v.* skiagraph.

sci·a·graph·ic (sī′ə graf′ik), *adj.* skiagraphic.

sci·ag·ra·phy (sī ag′rə fē), *n.* skiagraphy.

sci·am·a·chy (sī am′ə kē), *n., pl.* **-chies.** **1.** fighting with a shadow; futile combat with an imaginary enemy. **2.** a sham combat. Also, **sciomachy.** [< Greek *skiāmachía* < *skiāmacheîn* fight against a shadow < *skiá, -âs* shadow + *máchē* battle < *máchesthai* to fight]

sci·at·ic (sī at′ik), *adj.* **1.** of the hip: *the sciatic artery.* **2.** affecting the sciatic nerves: *sciatic neuralgia.* [< Medieval Latin *sciaticus,* alteration of Latin *ischiadicus* < Greek *ischiadikós* < *ischíon* hip joint]

sci·at·i·ca (sī at′ə kə), *n.* **1.** pain in a sciatic nerve and its branches. **2.** a neuralgia of the hips, thighs, and legs. [< Medieval Latin *sciatica* (*passio*) sciatic (disease), feminine of *sciaticus;* see SCIATIC]

sci·at·i·cal (sī at′ə kəl), *adj.* of sciatica; affected with sciatica. **—sci·at′i·cal·ly,** *adv.*

sciatic nerve, a large nerve emerging from the pelvis and extending along the back part of the thigh and leg to the foot.

sci·ence (sī′əns), *n.* **1. a.** knowledge of facts and laws arranged in an orderly system: *Science is verified knowledge; that is, knowledge that can be validated and communicated to other people* (George Simpson). **b.** a branch of such knowledge: *Biology, chemistry, physics, and astronomy are natural sciences. Economics and sociology are social sciences. Agriculture and engineering are applied sciences.* **2.** the search for truth: *a martyr to science. Be love my youth's pursuit, and science crown my age* (Thomas Gray). **3.** skill; technique: *A good boxer must have science as well as strength and speed.* [< Old French *science,* learned borrowing from Latin *scientia* knowledge < *sciēns, -entis,* present participle of *scīre* to know] **—Syn. 3.** proficiency.

Sci·ence (sī′əns), *n.* Christian Science.

science fair, a group of exhibits, each demonstrating a scientific principle, process, development, etc.

science fiction, a novel, short story, play, or the like, based on some actual or fanciful elements of science: *Science fiction is as old as the myth of Icarus and Daedalus* (New York Times).

science fictioneer, a writer of science fiction: *Cartoonists and science fictioneers still picture a planet inhabited by little green men with floppy antennae sprouting out of little green heads* (Time).

sci·en·ter (sī en′tər), *n. Law.* **1.** a clause in a complaint or indictment charging that the defendant has knowledge which makes him responsible or guilty. **2.** the fact that the defendant has such knowledge. [< Latin *scienter* knowingly, with knowledge]

sci·en·tial (sī en′shəl), *adj.* **1.** of or having to do with science or knowledge. **2.** having knowledge.

sci·en·tian (sī en′shən), *adj.* of or characterized by scientism.

sci·en·tif·ic (sī′ən tif′ik), *adj.* **1. a.** based on, regulated by, or done according to the facts and laws of science: *a scientific arrangement of fossils, scientific farming.* **b.** using the facts and laws of science: *a scientific farmer.* **2.** of or having to do with science; used in science: *scientific books, scientific laws, scientific instruments.* **3. a.** systematic; accurate; exact: *a scientific survey.* **b.** trained in skill or technique: *a scientific boxer, a scientific engraver.* [< Late Latin *scientificus* < *scientia* knowledge (see SCIENCE) + *facere* to make]

sci·en·tif·i·cal·ly (sī′ən tif′ə klē), *adv.* **1.** in a scientific manner: *Einstein thought scientifically.* **2.** according to the facts and laws of science: *A perpetual motion machine is scientifically impossible. It is easier to believe than to be scientifically instructed* (John Locke).

scientific method, an orderly method used by scientists to solve problems, in which a recognized problem is subjected to thorough investigation, and the resulting facts and observations are analyzed, formulated in a hypothesis, and subjected to verification by means of experiments and further observations.

sci·en·tism (sī′ən tiz′əm), *n.* **1.** the habit of thought and manner of expression characteristic of scientists: *The lingo of scientism is still used by businessmen* (Wall Street Journal). **2.** the tendency to reduce all reality and experience to mathematical descriptions of physical and chemical phenomena: *Those of us who think that scientific method is applicable to political problems are apt to be told, rather sharply, that we are talking "Scientism"* (Saturday Review).

sci·en·tist (sī′ən tist), *n.* a person who is trained in, or is familiar with, science, usually physical or natural science.

Sci·en·tist (sī′ən tist), *n.* a Christian Scientist.

sci·en·tis·tic (sī′ən tis′tik), *adj.* of or like the methods of a scientist; scientific. **—sci′en·tis′ti·cal·ly,** *adv.*

sci·en·tize (sī′ən tīz), *v.,* **-tized, -tiz·ing.** *—v.t.* to treat in a scientific manner; organize scientifically: *to scientize raw data.* *—v.i.* to lay down scientific propositions; theorize: *That there are patterns in events is a conclusion of scientizing, not a postulate on which it is based* (Bulletin of Atomic Scientists).

sci·en·tol·o·gy (sī′ən tol′ə jē), *n.* a religion and system of healing founded by L. Ron Hubbard, emphasizing pastoral counseling to heal the spirit and thereby alleviate physical ailments.

sci-fi (sī′fī′), *n. Slang.* science fiction.

scil., scilicet; namely.

scil·i·cet (sil′ə set), *adv.* to wit; namely. [< Latin *scīlicet* < *scīre* to know + *licet* it is allowed] *Abbr.:* sc.

scil·la (sil′ə), *n.* any of a group of early-blooming, ornamental plants of the lily family with bluish or white flowers; squill. [< Latin *scilla* < Greek *skílla*]

Scil·la (sil′ə; *Italian* shēl′lä), *n.* Scylla.

Scil·lo·ni·an (si lō′nē ən), *n.* a native or inhabitant of the Scilly Isles, a small group of islands southwest of England: *Scillonians are as sturdily individual as the rocks* (London Times). *—adj.* of or having to do with the Scilly Isles or the Scillonians.

scim·i·tar or **scim·i·ter** (sim′ə tər), *n.* a short, curved sword used by Turks, Persians, and other Oriental peoples. Also, **simitar.** [< Italian *scimitarra,* perhaps < Persian *shimshīr*]

Scimitar

scin·coid (sing′koid), *adj.* **1.** belonging to the same group of reptiles as the skinks. **2.** resembling the skinks. *—n.* a skink. [< Latin *scincus* skink[1] + English *-oid*]

scin·coi·di·an (sing koi′dē ən), *adj., n.* scincoid.

scin·tig·ra·phy (sin tig′rə fē), *n.* a means of obtaining diagnostic pictures of internal organs by administering radioisotopes to the patient and subsequently recording their distribution with a device related to the scintillation counter. [< *scinti*(llation) + *-graphy*]

scin·til·la (sin til′ə), *n.* a spark; particle; trace: *not a scintilla of truth. There was approval in the lady's gaze. There was, however, not a scintilla of recognition in it* (Leonard Merrick). [< Latin *scintilla* spark. Doublet of STENCIL, TINSEL.] **—Syn.** jot, mite.

scin·til·lant (sin′tə lənt), *adj.* scintillating; sparkling.

scin·til·late (sin′tə lāt), *v.,* **-lat·ed, -lat·ing.** *—v.i.* to sparkle; flash; twinkle: *The snow scintillates in the sun like diamonds.* *—v.t.* to flash with; shower like sparks: *to scintillate wit.* [< Latin *scintillāre* < *scintilla* a spark] **—Syn.** *v.i.* glitter, glisten.

scin·til·lat·ing (sin′tə lā′ting), *adj.* that scintillates; sparkling: *The Berlin Philharmonic may not be the most scintillating orchestra in the world, but it is . . . magnificent* (New Yorker). **—scin′til·lat′ing·ly,** *adv.*

scin·til·la·tion (sin′tə lā′shən), *n.* **1.** a sparkling; a flashing. **2.** a spark; flash: *Let the scintillations of your wit be like . . . summer lightning, lambent but innocuous* (Edward M. Goulburn). **3.** the twinkling of the stars. **4.** *Physics.* a flash or spark produced by ions in a phosphor, as when an alpha particle impinges on certain solid materials, especially zinc sulfide.

scintillation counter, a device which detects and counts radioactive particles by counting the number of scintillations when radiation strikes a luminescent liquid, crystal, or gas. It is sensitive to gamma rays which the Geiger counter is not.

scintillation detector, a scintillation counter.

scin·til·la·tor (sin′tə lā′tər), *n.* **1.** a scintillating star. **2.** the liquid, crystal, or gas used as the source of scintillations in a scintillation counter.

scin·til·les·cent (sin′tə les′ənt), *adj.* scintillating.

scin·til·lom·e·ter (sin′tə lom′ə tər), *n.* **1.** a scintillation counter. **2.** an instrument for measuring the intensity of the scintillation of the stars.

sci·o·graph (sī′ə graf, -gräf), *n.,v.* skiagraph.

sci·o·graph·ic (sī′ə graf′ik), *adj.* skiagraphic.

sci·o·lism (sī′ə liz′əm), *n.* superficial knowledge: *The sciolism of literary or political adventurers* (George Eliot). [< Late Latin *sciolus* one who knows a little (< *scius* knowing < *scīre* to know) + English *-ism*]

sci·o·list (sī′ə list), *n.* a person who pretends to have more knowledge than he really has: *It is of great importance that those whom I love should not think me a precipitate, silly, shallow sciolist in politics* (Macaulay). **—Syn.** charlatan, quack.

sci·o·lis·tic (sī′ə lis′tik), *adj.* of, or like sciolism or sciolists.

sci·o·lous (sī′ə ləs), *adj.* having only superficial knowledge; shallow. [< Late Latin *sciolus* one who knows a little (diminutive) < Latin *scīre* to know; + English *-ous*]

sci·om·a·chy (sī om′ə kē), *n., pl.* **-chies.** sciamachy.

 PRONUNCIATION KEY: hat, āge, cãre, fär; let, ēqual, tėrm; it, īce; hot, ōpen, ôrder; oil, out; cup, půt, rüle;

sci·o·man·cy (sī′ə man′sē), *n.* divination by means of the shades of the dead. [< Greek *skiá* shadow, shade + *manteíā* divination]
sci·on (sī′ən), *n.* **1.** a descendant; heir: . . . *it became more obvious that Bertie [Prince Albert] was a true scion of the House of Brunswick* (Lytton Strachey). *The present Mr. Chadwick was a worthy scion of a worthy stock* (Anthony Trollope). **2.** a bud or branch cut for grafting or planting; cutting; slip. Also, **cion.** [< Old French *cion,* perhaps < Latin *sectiō, -ōnis* a cutting, section] —**Syn. 1.** offspring.
➔ See **cion** for usage note.
sci·oph·i·lous (sī of′ə ləs), *adj. Botany.* growing or living by preference in the shade; shade-loving. [< Greek *skiá* shadow + English *-phil* + *-ous*]
sci·o·phyte (sī′ə fīt), *n.* a sciophilous plant. [< Greek *skiá* shadow + English *-phyte*]
sci·re fa·ci·as (sī′rē fā′shē as), *Law.* **1.** a writ requiring the party against whom it is brought to show cause why a judgment, letters patent, etc., should not be executed, vacated, or annulled. **2.** a proceeding based on such a writ. [< Latin *scīre faciās* you must make known]
scir·rhoid (skir′oid, sir′-), *adj.* resembling a scirrhus.
scir·rho·ma (ski rō′mə, si-), *n., pl.* **-ma·ta** (-mə tə). scirrhus. [< New Latin *scirrhoma.*]
scir·rhos·i·ty (ski ros′ə tē, si-), *n., pl.* **-ties.** scirrhous condition; a morbid hardness.
scir·rhous (skir′əs, sir′-), *adj.* **1.** of, caused by, or like a scirrhus. **2.** hard.
scir·rhus (skir′əs, sir′-), *n., pl.* **scir·rhi** (skir′ī, sir′-), **scir·rhus·es. 1.** a hard, fibrous cancer. **2.** a hard tumor. [< New Latin *scirrhus* < Latin *scirros* < Greek *skirrhós* hard]
scis·sel (sis′əl), *n.* the metal scrap from some process, as that left after cutting blanks for coins. [< French *cisaille* < *cisailler* clip with shears]
scis·sile (sis′əl), *adj.* that can be easily cut, divided, or split: *Slate is a scissile rock.* [< Latin *scissilis* < *scindere* to cut]
scis·sion (sizh′ən, sish′-), *n.* the act of cutting, dividing, or splitting; division; separation. [< Late Latin *scissiō, -ōnis* < Latin *scindere* to split]
scis·sor (siz′ər), *v.t., v.i.* to cut with scissors: *The author does not scissor the story neatly out of whole cloth to a preconceived pattern* (Time). [< *scissors*] —**scis′sor·er,** *n.*
scis·sor·like (siz′ər līk′), *adj.* similar to scissors in shape, operation, etc.
scis·sors (siz′ərz), *n.pl. or sing.* **1.** a tool or instrument for cutting that has two sharp blades with handles so fastened that they will work toward each other. **2. a.** a wrestling hold with the legs clasped around an opponent. **b.** a movement of the legs while vaulting or high jumping that is like the movement of scissors blades. **c.** the scissors kick. [< Old French *cisoires,* plural < Late Latin *cīsōria,* plural of *cīsōrium* tool for cutting < Latin *caedere* to cut; confused with Latin *scissōr* a cutter < *scindere* to cleave, split] —**Syn. 1.** shears.
➔ **scissors.** In the sense of a cutting instrument, scissors is plural: *The scissors aren't sharp.* The word is singular in the sense of a movement of the legs: *The wrestler got a scissors about his opponent's body.*
scis·sors-and-paste (siz′ərz ən pāst′), *adj.* put together like a scrapbook; derivative; superficial: *His latest book is a scissors-and-paste affair, consisting mostly of anecdotes* (New Yorker).
scissors kick, a movement of the legs in swimming like the movement of scissors blades.
scis·sor·tail (siz′ər tāl′), *n.* a grayish flycatcher of the southern United States, Mexico, and Central America, with a very long, deeply forked tail that opens and closes as it flies.
scis·sor-tailed flycatcher (siz′ər-tāld′), a scissortail.
scis·sure (sizh′ər, sish′-), *n.* **1.** a longitudinal opening cut in a body. **2.** a division or schism; split. **3.** *Anatomy.* a natural opening in an organ or part. [< Latin *scissūra* < *scindere* cut]

Scissortail
(about 14 in. long)

sci·u·rine (sī′yů rīn, -yůr in), *adj.* of or belonging to a group that includes the squirrels, chipmunks, and certain related rodents. —*n.* a squirrel or other sciurine animal. [< Latin *sciūrus* squirrel (< Greek *skíouros* < *skiá* shadow + *ourá* tail) + English *-ine*[1]]
sci·u·roid (sī yůr′oid), *adj.* **1.** sciurine. **2.** like a squirrel's tail; curved and bushy: *the sciuroid spikes of certain grasses.* [< Latin *sciūrus* (see SCIURINE) + English *-oid*]
sclaff (sklaf, skläf), *v.t., v.i. Golf.* **1.** to scrape (the ground) with a golf club before hitting the ball. **2.** to hit (a golf ball) after scraping the ground with the club.
—*n.* **1.** *Golf.* a sclaffing stroke. **2.** *Scottish.* the noise made by a slight, glancing blow. [probably imitative] —**sclaff′er,** *n.*
Sclav (sklav, skläv), *n., adj. Obsolete.* Slav.
Sclav·ic (sklav′ik, sklä′vik), *adj., n. Obsolete.* Slavic.
Scla·vo·ni·an (sklə vō′nē ən), *adj., n. Obsolete.* Slavonian.
SCLC (no periods) or **S.C.L.C.,** Southern Christian Leadership Conference (an organization of Southern churches formed in 1956 to campaign for Negro civil rights).
scler-, *combining form.* the form of **sclero-** sometimes used before vowels, as in *sclereid.*
scle·ra (sklir′ə), *n.* the sclerotic coat of the eyeball. [< New Latin *sclera* < *Greek sklērós* hard < *skéllein* to dry up]
scler·al (sklir′əl), *adj.* of or having to do with the sclerotic coat of the eyeball.
scle·re·id (sklir′ē id), *n. Botany.* a thickened, sclerotic cell; stone cell.
scle·ren·chy·ma (skli reng′kə mə), *n. Botany.* tissue composed of thickened and hardened cells from which the protoplasm has disappeared. It is found chiefly as a strengthening and protecting tissue in the stem and in such hard parts of plants as nut shells. [< New Latin *sclerenchyma* < Greek *sklērós* hard (see SCLERA) + New Latin *enchyma* enchyma]
scle·ren·chym·a·tous (sklir′eng kim′ə-təs), *adj.* of or like sclerenchyma: *sclerenchymatous tissue, a sclerenchymatous polyp.*
scle·ri·a·sis (skli rī′ə sis), *n.* **1.** a hardening of body tissue. **2.** scleroderma. [< New Latin *scleriasis* < Greek *sklēríāsis* < *sklērós* hard; see SCLERA]
scle·rite (sklir′īt), *n. Zoology.* a chitinous or calcareous plate, spicule, etc., of an invertebrate animal, especially one of the plates of the exoskeleton of a grasshopper or similar arthropod. [< Greek *sklērós* hard + English *-ite*[1]]
scle·rit·ic (skli rit′ik), *adj.* **1.** of or like a sclerite; hardened or chitinized. **2.** of or having to do with scleritis.
scle·ri·tis (skli rī′tis), *n.* inflammation of the sclerotic coat of the eyeball.
sclero-, *combining form.* **1.** hard: *Sclerodermatous = having a hard body covering.* **2.** having to do with the sclerotic coat of the eyeball: *Scleroiritis = inflammation of the sclerotic coat and iris of the eye.* Also, **scler-** before vowels. [< Greek *sklērós*]
scle·ro·cau·ly (sklir′ə kô′lē), *n.* a condition of plant stems in which they become slender, hard, and dry. [< Greek *sklēros* hard + *kaulos* stem + English *-y*]
scle·ro·cor·ne·al (sklir′ə kôr′nē əl), *adj.* of or having to do with the sclerotica and cornea together.
scle·ro·dac·tyl·i·a (sklir′ə dak til′ē ə), *n.* atrophy and deformity of the fingers, with thickening and hardening of the skin covering them. [< New Latin *sclerodactylia* < *sclero-* + Greek *dáktylos* finger]
scle·ro·der·ma (sklir′ə dėr′mə), *n.* a disease in which the skin becomes hard and rigid. [< New Latin *scleroderma* < Greek *sklērós* hard + *dérma* skin]
scle·ro·der·ma·tous (sklir′ə dėr′mə təs), *adj. Zoology.* having a hard body covering, as of plates or scales.
scle·ro·der·mi·a (sklir′ō dėr′mē ə), *n.* scleroderma.
scle·roid (sklir′oid), *adj. Biology.* hard; indurated. [< *scler-* + *-oid*]
scle·ro·i·ri·tis (sklir′ō ī rī′tis), *n.* inflammation of the sclerotic coat and iris of the eye. [< *sclero-* + *ir*(is) + *-itis*]
scle·ro·ma (skli rō′mə), *n., pl.* **-ma·ta** (-mə tə). a hardening of body tissue. [< New Latin *scleroma* < Greek *sklērōma* < *sklērós* hard (see SCLERA) + *-ōma* a growth]
scle·rom·e·ter (skli rom′ə tər), *n.* an instrument for measuring the hardness of a substance, especially a mineral. [< *sclero-* + *-meter*]
scle·ro·phyll (sklir′ə fil), *n.* a plant with small, leathery leaves that reduce evaporation, making the plant adaptable to dry conditions. [< *sclero-* + Greek *phýllon* leaf]
scle·ro·phyl·lous (sklir′ə fil′əs), *adj. Botany.* **1.** having leathery leaves which resist easy loss of moisture. **2.** made up of sclerophylls.
scle·ro·phyl·ly (sklir′ə fil′ē), *n.* a thickened and hardened condition of foliage due to sclerenchyma.
scle·ro·pro·tein (sklir′ə prō′tēn, -tē in), *n.* an albuminoid.
scle·ro·sal (skli rō′səl), *adj.* having to do with sclerosis.
scle·ro·scope (sklir′ə skōp), *n.* an instrument for testing the hardness of metal. [< *sclero-* + *-scope*]
scle·rose (skli rōs′), *v.t., v.i.,* **-rosed, -ros·ing.** to harden; affect with sclerosis. [back formation < *sclerosed*]
scle·rosed (skli rōst′, sklir′ōst), *adj.* affected with sclerosis: *sclerosed tissue.* [< *scleros*(is) + *-ed*[2]]
scle·ro·sis (skli rō′sis), *n., pl.* **-ses** (-sēz). **1.** a hardening of a tissue or part of the body by an increase of connective tissue or the deposition of salts at the expense of more active tissue. **2.** a hardening of a tissue or cell wall of a plant by thickening or the formation of wood. [< New Latin *sclerosis* a hardness, hard tumor < Greek *sklērōsis* hardening < *sklērós* hard; see SCLERA]
scle·ro·tial (skli rō′shəl), *adj.* of or having to do with a sclerotium or sclerotia.
scle·rot·ic (skli rot′ik), *n.* the hard, white outer membrane of the eye, continuous with the cornea.
—*adj.* **1.** of or having to do with the sclerotic. **2.** of, with, or having sclerosis. **3.** *Botany.* hardened; stony in texture. [< New Latin *scleroticus* < Greek *sklērós* hard; see SCLERA]
scle·rot·i·ca (skli rot′ə kə), *n.* the sclerotic coat of the eyeball. [< New Latin *sclerotica*]
scle·ro·ti·oid (skli rō′shē oid), *adj.* having to do with or resembling a sclerotium.
scle·ro·tit·ic (sklir′ō tit′ik), *adj.* affected with sclerotitis or scleritis.
scle·ro·ti·tis (sklir′ō tī′tis), *n.* scleritis.
scle·ro·ti·um (skli rō′shē əm), *n., pl.* **-ti·a** (-shē ə). *Botany.* a tuberlike body of reserve food material that forms the mycelium of certain fungi. [< New Latin *sclerotium* < Greek *sklērótēs* hardness < *sklērós* hard]
scle·ro·ti·za·tion (sklir′ə tə zā′shən), *n.* sclerosis.
scle·ro·tize (sklir′ə tīz), *v.t., v.i.,* **-tized, -tiz·ing.** to sclerose.
scle·ro·toid (sklir′ə toid), *adj.* sclerotioid.
scle·rot·o·my (skli rot′ə mē), *n., pl.* **-mies.** a surgical incision into the sclerotic coat of the eyeball, as for the extraction of foreign bodies. [< *sclero-* + Greek *-tomíā* a cutting]
scle·rous (sklir′əs), *adj.* hardened; hard; bony. [< *scler-* + *-ous*]
Sc.M., Master of Science (Latin, *Scientiae Magister*).
sco·bic·u·lar (skō bik′yə lər), *adj.* scobiform.
sco·bic·u·late (skō bik′yə lāt), *adj.* scobiform.
sco·bi·form (skō′bə fôrm), *adj.* having the form of or resembling sawdust: *scobiform seeds.* [< Latin *scobis* (or *scobs*) sawdust, filings + English *-form*]
sco·del·la (skō del′ə), *n.* a majolica vessel in the form of a shallow bowl on a footed stem. Also, **scudella.** [< Italian *scodella* < Latin *scutella* platter; see SCUTTLE[1]]
scoff[1] (skôf, skof), *v.i.* to make fun to show one does not believe something; mock: *We scoffed at the idea of drowning in three inches of water. Fools, who came to scoff, remain'd to pray* (Oliver Goldsmith). —*v.t.* to jeer at; deride: *He . . . scoff'd their easy fears* (Robert Southey). [< noun]
—*n.* **1.** mocking words or acts: *With scoffs and scorns and contumelious taunts* (Shakespeare). **2.** something ridiculed or mocked: *The principles of liberty were the scoff of every grinning courtier* (Macaulay).
[< Scandinavian (compare Danish *skuffe* to deceive, earlier, to mock, ridicule, fool <

Middle Low German *schoven* deceive)] —**scoff′er,** *n.*

—**Syn.** *v.i., v.t.* **Scoff, jeer, sneer** mean to express scorn or contempt for someone or something. **Scoff** implies speaking mockingly about something others respect or believe in: *He scoffs at religion.* **Jeer** implies expressing mocking by loud, coarse laughter: *The mob jeered when the speaker got up to talk.* **Sneer** implies expressing mocking by look, tone, or manner of speech: *He sneers at everything sentimental.*

scoff[2] (skôf, skof), *Slang.* —*n.* food; a meal. —*v.t., v.i.* to eat heavily. [< Afrikaans *scoff* < Dutch *schoft* a meal]

scoff·ing·ly (skôf′ing lē, skof′-), *adv.* in a scoffing manner.

scoff·law (skôf′lô′, skof′-), *n. U.S. Informal.* a person with little regard for the law; person who regularly flouts the law: *One of the twins was named the city's champion scofflaw, with eighty-six traffic and parking violations dating from 1947* (New York Times).

scoke (skōk), *n.* the pokeweed.

scold (skōld), *v.t.* to find fault with; blame with angry words: *His mother scolded him for tracking in dirt on her clean floor.* —*v.i.* **1.** to find fault; talk angrily: *Don't scold so much.* **2.** *Obsolete.* to quarrel noisily; brawl. [< noun]

—*n.* a person who scolds, especially a noisy, scolding woman: *In older times, scolds were punished by being ducked in ponds.*

[probably < Scandinavian (compare Old Icelandic *skāld* poet, in sense of "lampooner")] —**scold′er,** *n.*

—**Syn.** *v.t., v.i.* **1. Scold, upbraid, chide** mean to find fault with someone. **Scold** particularly suggests cross and usually constant faultfinding, often without good reason: *That woman is always scolding the children in our neighborhood.* **Upbraid** suggests sharp and severe censure or blame for a definite fault: *He upbraided them for tormenting animals.* **Chide** usually suggests mild disapproval or blame, intended to correct: *He chided her for carelessness.*

scold·ing (skōl′ding), *adj.* that scolds: *I have seen tempests, when the scolding winds have riv'd the knotty oaks* (Shakespeare). —*n.* the act of a person who scolds: *Was not mamma often in an ill-humor; and were they not all used to her scoldings?* (Thackeray). —**scold′ing·ly,** *adv.*

scold's bit or **bridle,** branks.

scol·e·cite (skol′ə sīt, skō′lə-), *n.* a mineral, a hydrous silicate of calcium and aluminum, found in needle-shaped crystals and fibrous or radiated masses. *Formula:* $CaAl_2Si_3O_{10}.3H_2O$ [< German *Scolezit* < Greek *skōlēx, -ēkos* worm + German *-it* -ite[1]]

sco·lex (skō′leks), *n., pl.* **sco·le·ces** (skō lē′sēz), **scol·i·ces** (skol′ə sēz, skō′lə-). **1.** the larva of a tapeworm or similar parasitic worm. **2.** the head of the adult form. [< New Latin *scolex* < Greek *skōlēx, -ēkos* worm, grub]

sco·li·id (skō′lē id), *adj.* of or having to do with a family of hairy wasps whose larvae are parasitic on the larvae of certain beetles. —*n.* a scoliid wasp. [< New Latin *Scoliidae* the family name]

sco·li·on (skō′lē on), *n., pl.* **-li·a** (-lē ə). a short song sung in turn by the guests at an ancient Greek banquet. [< Greek *skólion* < *skoliós* curved]

sco·li·o·sis (skō′lē ō′sis, skol′ē-), *n.* a lateral curvature of the spine. [< New Latin *scoliosis* < Greek *skolíōsis* curvature, crookedness < *skoliós* crooked]

scol·lop (skol′əp), *n., v.t.* scallop. —**scol′lop·er,** *n.*

scol·o·pen·drid (skol′ə pen′drid), *n.* any of a group of chilopods including many large and poisonous centipedes. —*adj.* of or belonging to this group. [< New Latin *Scolopendridae* the centipede family < Latin *scolopendra* a kind of multipede < Greek *scolópendra*]

scol·o·pen·drine (skol′ə pen′drīn, -drin), *adj.* of or having to do with the scolopendrids.

sco·lyt·id (skə lit′id), *n.* any of a group of bark beetles, one variety of which carries the fungus of Dutch elm disease. [< New Latin *Scolytidae* the family name < *Scolytus* the typical genus < Greek *skolýptein* to peel, strip]

scom·bri·form (skom′brə fôrm), *adj.* scombroid.

scom·brin (skom′brin), *n.* a protamine found in the testicles of the mackerel. [< Greek *skómbros* mackerel]

scom·broid (skom′broid), *adj.* **1.** of or belonging to a group of fishes including the mackerels and tunas. **2.** resembling the mackerel. —*n.* a mackerel or mackerellike fish. [< New Latin *Scombroidea* the group name < Latin *scomber* mackerel < Greek *skómbros*]

sconce[1] (skons), *n.* a bracket projecting from a wall, used to hold a candle or other light, often with a reflector. [perhaps < Old French *esconse* lantern, hiding place < Medieval Latin *sconsa* < Latin *abscondere* to hide < *ab-* away + *condere* place, put]

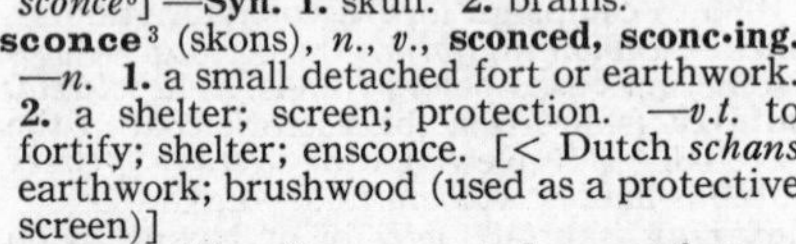
Sconce[1]

sconce[2] (skons), *n. Informal.* **1.** the head, especially, the top of the head: *Peter Stuyvesant dealt him a thwack over the sconce with his wooden leg* (Washington Irving). **2.** sense; wit. [perhaps special use of *sconce*[1]] —**Syn. 1.** skull. **2.** brains.

sconce[3] (skons), *n., v.,* **sconced, sconc·ing.** —*n.* **1.** a small detached fort or earthwork. **2.** a shelter; screen; protection. —*v.t.* to fortify; shelter; ensconce. [< Dutch *schans* earthwork; brushwood (used as a protective screen)]

sconce[4] (skons), *v.,* **sconced, sconc·ing,** *n.* —*v.t.* to mulct; fine for some breach of conventional usage. —*n.* the fine imposed.

scone (skōn, skon), *n.* **1. a.** a thick, flat cake cooked on a griddle. **b.** a similar cake baked in an oven. Some scones taste much like baking-powder biscuits; some are like buns. **2.** one of the four pieces into which such a cake is often cut. [originally Scottish, probably < Middle Dutch *schoon(brot)* fine (bread)]

Scone (skün, skon), *n.* **Stone of,** a stone underneath the coronation throne in Westminster Abbey. It was the traditional coronation seat of the kings of Scotland, and was brought to England by King Edward I in 1296.

S. Con. Res., Senate concurrent resolution (used with a number).

scoop (sküp), *n.* **1.** a tool like a shovel, but having a short handle and a deep hollow part for dipping out or shoveling up and carrying loose materials: **a.** a kitchen utensil to take out flour, sugar, etc. **b.** a large ladle. **2.** the part of a dredge, steam shovel, etc., that takes up the coal, sand, etc. **3.** the act of taking up with, or as if with, a scoop. **4. a.** the amount taken up at one time by a scoop: *She used two scoops of flour and one of sugar.* **b.** *Informal.* a big haul, as of money made in speculation, etc. **5.** a place scooped or hollowed out; hollow. **6.** *Slang.* **a.** the publishing of a piece of news before a rival newspaper does. **b.** the piece of news. **7.** a spoon-shaped surgical instrument used to extract matter from cavities.

—*v.t.* **1. a.** to take up or out with a scoop, or as a scoop does: *Scoop out a quart of grain. The children scooped up the snow with their hands to build a snow man.* **b.** *Informal.* to gather up or in as if with a scoop: *Werner was with us when father scooped us all up and took us to the concert at the Stadium* (Harper's). **2.** to hollow out; dig out; to make by scooping: *The children scooped holes in the sand.* **3.** to empty with a scoop. **4.** *Slang.* to publish a piece of news before (a rival newspaper). **5.** *Informal.* to sing (a note or phrase) by sliding to the correct pitch from a note below: *She is given to scooping her notes and is unable to produce convincing chest tones* (New Yorker).

[< Middle Dutch *schoepe* bucket, and *schoppe* shovel] —**scoop′er,** *n.*

—**Syn.** *n.* **4. a.** scoopful. **5.** cavity. —*v.t.* **2.** excavate.

scoop·ful (sküp′fu̇l), *n., pl.* **-fuls.** enough to fill a scoop.

scoop neck or **neckline,** a rounded, fairly low-cut neck on a dress, blouse, etc.

scoop-necked (sküp′nekt′), *adj.* having a scoop neck.

scoop net, a net to scoop something out of the water, as a person in a rescue operation: *The pilot ... was rescued within a few minutes by a scoop net attached to a helicopter* (London Times).

scoot (sküt), *Informal.* —*v.i.* to go quickly; dart. —*n.* the act of scooting. —*interj.* be off with you! scat! [(originally) Scottish, to squirt, gush, eject, perhaps < a Scandinavian word. Related to SHOOT.]

scoot·er[1] (skü′tər), *n.* **1.** a child's vehicle consisting of two wheels, one in front of the other, and a footboard between, steered by a handlebar and propelled by pushing against the ground with one foot. **2.** a similar vehicle run by a motor; motor scooter. See **motor scooter** for picture. **3.** *U.S.* a sailboat with runners, for use on either water or ice.

—*v.i.* to sail or go in or on a scooter.

[< *scoot,* verb]

scoot·er[2] (skü′tər), *n.* scoter.

scoot·er·ist (skü′tər ist), *n.* a person who rides a motor scooter: *In Manhattan traffic ... the race is to the scooterist* (New York Times).

scop (skop, skōp), *n.* an Anglo-Saxon poet or minstrel; bard. [Old English *scop*]

sco·pal·a·mine (skō pə lam′ēn, -in), *n.* scopolamine.

scope[1] (skōp), *n.* **1. a.** the distance the mind can reach; extent of view: *Very hard words are not within the scope of a child's understanding.* **b.** the area over which any activity operates or is effective; range of application: *within the scope of an investigation. Beyond the scope of all speculation* (Edmund Burke). **2.** room to range; space; opportunity: *Football gives scope for courage and quick thinking. I gave full scope to my imagination* (Laurence Sterne). **3.** the range or length of flight of an arrow or other missile. **4. a.** extent; length; sweep: *The yacht's gig was towing easily at the end of a long scope of line* (Joseph Conrad). **b.** the length of cable at which a ship rides when at anchor. **5.** *Archaic.* an aim; purpose; ultimate object. [< Italian *scopo,* learned borrowing from Late Latin *scopus* < Greek *skopós* aim, object < *skopeîn* behold, consider] —**Syn. 1.** compass. See **range.**

scope[2] (skōp), *n. Informal.* **1.** a radarscope. **2.** a telescopic sight for a rifle: *All were equipped with 20-power scopes* (New York Times). [back formation < *telescope, radarscope*]

-scope, *combining form.* an instrument for viewing, examining, or observing: *Stethoscope = an instrument for examining the chest. Telescope = an instrument for viewing distant objects.* [< New Latin *-scopium* < Greek *-skopion* < *skopeîn* look at, examine]

sco·po·la (skō′pə lə), *n.* the dried rhizome and larger roots of a plant of the nightshade family, used as a source of atropine and scopolamine.

sco·pol·a·mine (skō pol′ə mēn, -min; skō′pə lam′ēn, -in), *n.* a drug used to dilate the pupils of eyes, as a depressant, to produce a partial stupor known as "twilight sleep," and to induce confession in criminals. *Formula:* $C_{17}H_{21}NO_4$ [< New Latin *Scopola canicola* a plant of the nightshade family that yields this drug (< Giacomo *Scopoli,* 1723-1788, an Italian naturalist) + English *amine*]

sco·po·line (skō′pə lēn, -lin), *n.* a crystalline, narcotic compound obtained from scopolamine by decomposition. *Formula:* $C_8H_{13}NO_2$

scop·u·la (skop′yə lə), *n., pl.* **-las** or **-lae** (-lē). a small brushlike pad of stiff hairs on the tarsi of bees and spiders. [< New Latin *scopula* < Latin *scōpula;* see SCOPULATE]

scop·u·late (skop′yə lāt, -lit), *adj. Zoology.* shaped like a broom or brush; brushlike. [< New Latin *scopulatus* < Latin *scōpula* broom twig (diminutive) < *scōpa* twig]

-scopy, *combining form.* observation; examination: *Cranioscopy = examination of the cranium.* [< Greek *skopiā́* watchtower < *skopeîn* look at]

SCOR (no periods) or **S.C.O.R.,** Special Committee on Oceanic Research (an organization set up by the International Council of Scientific Unions to continue the activities begun during the International Geophysical Year).

scor·bu·tic (skôr byü′tik), *adj.* **1.** of, having to do with, or like scurvy. **2.** affected with scurvy. [< New Latin *scorbuticus* < *scorbutus* scurvy < French *scorbut* < a Germanic word]

scor·bu·ti·cal (skôr byü′tə kəl), *adj.* scorbutic.

scor·bu·tus (skôr byü′təs), *n.* scurvy. [< New Latin *scorbutus;* origin uncertain]

scorch[1] (skôrch), *v.t.* **1.** to burn slightly; burn on the outside of: *to scorch a shirt in ironing it.* **2.** to dry up; wither: *grass*

scorched by the sun. **3.** to criticize with burning words. —*v.i.* **1.** to be or become scorched. **2.** *Informal.* to drive or ride very fast.
—*n.* a slight burn.
[origin uncertain]
scorch² (skôrch), *v.t. Obsolete.* to slash with a knife. [alteration of *score*]
scorched earth (skôrcht), destruction by government orders of all things useful to an invading army.
scorched-earth (skôrcht′ėrth′), *adj.* of or having to do with destruction of all things useful to an invading enemy: *a scorched-earth policy.*
scorch·er (skôr′chər), *n.* **1.** a person or thing that scorches. **2.** *Informal.* a very hot day. **3.** *Informal.* a person who drives or rides very fast. **4.** *Informal.* a scathing rebuke; withering criticism.
scorch·ing (skôr′ching), *adj.* that scorches; burning; withering. —**scorch′ing·ly,** *adv.*
scor·da·to (skôr dä′tō), *adj. Music.* put out of tune; tuned in an unusual manner for the purpose of producing particular effects. [< Italian *scordato,* past participle of *scordare* put out of tune]
scor·da·tu·ra (skôr′dä tü′rä), *n., pl.* **-tu·re** (-tü′rā), **-tu·ras.** *Music.* an intentional deviation from the usual tuning of a stringed instrument for some particular effect. [< Italian *scordatura*]
score (skôr, skōr), *n., v.,* **scored, scor·ing.** —*n.* **1.** the record of points made in a game, contest, test, etc.: *to keep score. The score was 9 to 2 in our favor. The student made such a high score on his tests that he received a scholarship.* **2. a.** an amount owed; debt; account: *I agreed that he should pay the score at our next meeting* (Washington Irving). **b.** *Archaic.* a record kept by notches or marks. **c.** *Archaic.* a notch, cut, or mark made in keeping an account or a record. **3.** a group or set of twenty; twenty: *A score or more were present at the party.* **4.** a written or printed piece of music arranged for different instruments or voices: *the score of an opera.* **5.** a cut; scratch; stroke; mark; line: *scores made on a tree for its sap. The carpenter used a nail to make a score on the board.* **6.** *Sports.* a line to show the beginning or end of a course, range, etc., as the line at which a marksman stands to shoot. **7.** the act of making or winning a point; successful stroke, rejoinder, etc. **8.** an account; reason; ground: *Don't worry on that score. She was excused on the score of illness. The chemical industry is not alone in entertaining doubts on that score* (London Times).
pay off or **settle a score,** to get even for an injury or wrong: *many an old score to settle with one's enemies.*
scores, a large number: *Scores died in the epidemic.*
the score, *Informal.* the truth about anything or things in general; the facts: *The new man doesn't know what the score is yet.*
—*v.t.* **1. a.** to make as points in a game, contest, test, etc.: *to score two runs in the second inning. He scored 85 per cent on the entrance test.* **b.** to keep a record of (the number of points made in a game, contest, etc.). **c.** to be counted as in the score: *In American football, a touchdown scores six points.* **d.** to make as an addition to the score; gain; win: *He scored 35 points in the last basketball game. The new play scored a great success with the critics.* **2.** to keep a record of as an amount owed; set down; mark: *The innkeeper scored on a slate the number of meals each person had.* **3. a.** to arrange (a piece of music) for different instruments or voices: *to score a sonata for piano and strings.* **b.** to write out (music) in score. **4.** to cut; scratch; mark; line: *He scored the board with a pencil and ruler before sawing it. Mistakes are scored in red ink. Passages had been scored in his favourite books* (Thackeray). **5.** to blame or scold severely; berate: *The President scored the newspapers for their warmongering reporting.* **6.** to make long cuts in the surface of, before cooking: *to score a ham before baking.* —*v.i.* **1. a.** to make points in a game, contest, etc., or on a test: *to be in a position to score. In baseball, only the side at bat can score.* **b.** to keep a record of the number of points in a game, etc.: *The teacher will appoint some pupil to score for both sides.* **2.** to achieve a success; succeed. **3.** to make notches, cuts, lines, etc.: *Glass is hard to score and cut without the proper tools.* **4.** *Obsolete.* to run up a score (debt).
[Old English *scoru* < Scandinavian (compare Old Icelandic *skor* notch, tally stick; score)]
score·board (skôr′bôrd′, skōr′bōrd′), *n.* **1.** a board on which the running score or the results of sporting events are posted. **2.** a record of any contest, situation, etc.: *The earnings scoreboard for the first ... quarter is not yet complete* (Newsweek).
score·book (skôr′bu̇k′, skōr′-), *n.* a book for recording the scores of games and, sometimes, the performance of the players.
score·card (skôr′kärd′, skōr′-), *n.,* or **score card,** a card to keep the score of a game on, especially while it is being played: *He strolled through the final 36 holes with a steady 141; came home with an overall scorecard that showed 283 strokes* (Time).
score·keep·er (skôr′kē′pər, skōr′-), *n.* a person who scores a game or keeps a record of certain events: *Dun and Bradstreet, the master scorekeeper of business failures, has found that more than nine out of ten business failures were caused by lack of experience or incompetence* (Harper's).
score·keep·ing (skôr′kē′ping, skōr′-), *n.* the act or process of keeping score; scoring.
score·less (skôr′lis, skōr′-), *adj.* **1.** having no score: *The game ended in a scoreless tie.* **2.** making no score or mark.
scor·er (skôr′ər, skōr′-), *n.* **1.** a scorekeeper, or person who grades tests. **2.** a person who makes a score in a game, contest, or, sometimes, a test. **3.** a person or thing that scores or notches.
scores (skôrz, skōrz), *n.pl.* See under **score,** *n.*
score·sheet (skôr′shēt, skōr′-), *n.* a sheet of paper upon which a record of the tallies or runs in baseball, cricket, etc., may be written.
sco·ri·a (skôr′ē ə, skōr′-), *n., pl.* **sco·ri·ae** (skôr′ē ē, skōr′-). **1.** the slag or refuse left from ore after the metal has been melted out; dross. **2.** cinderlike fragments of lava. [< Latin *scōria* < Greek *skōriā* < *skôr, skatós* dung]
sco·ri·ac (skôr′ē ak, skōr′-), *adj.* scoriaceous.
sco·ri·a·ceous (skôr′ē ā′shəs, skōr′-), *adj.* **1.** like slag or clinkers. **2.** consisting of slag, clinkers, etc. [< Greek *skōriā* dross (see SCORIA) + English *-aceous*]
sco·ri·fi·ca·tion (skôr′ə fə kā′shən, skōr′-), *n.* **1.** the act of scorifying. **2.** (in assaying) a process by which gold or silver is separated from its ore by heating with lead, the impurities being removed as a slag.
sco·ri·fi·er (skôr′ə fī′ər, skōr′-), *n.* a thing that scorifies.
sco·ri·form (skôr′ə fôrm, skōr′-), *adj.* in the form of scoria; like scoria.
sco·ri·fy (skôr′rə fī, skō′-), *v.t.,* **-fied, -fy·ing.** to reduce to scoria. [< *scori*(a) + *-fy*]
scor·ing (skôr′ing, skōr′-), *n.* **1.** the act of making a score. **2.** a score made. **3. a.** the act or process of arranging a piece of music for different instruments, or voices. **b.** the result of this: *... little song-like snatches that rise to the surface of his complex and highly original scoring* (New Yorker).
—*adj.* resulting in a score: *Leggett threw a 21-yard scoring pass* (New York Times).
scorn (skôrn), *v.t.* **1.** to look down upon; think of as mean or low; despise: *Honest boys scorn sneaks and liars. Death had he seen ... knew all his shapes, and scorn'd them all* (Scott). **2.** to reject or refuse as low or wrong: *The judge scorned to take a bribe. I scorn the counterfeit sentiment you offer* (Charlotte Brontë). **3.** *Obsolete.* to mock; deride. —*v.i. Obsolete.* to mock; scoff.
—*n.* **1.** a feeling that a person, animal, or act is mean or low; contempt: *We feel scorn for a traitor. The red glow of scorn and proud disdain* (Shakespeare). **2.** a person, animal, or thing that is scorned or despised: *That bully is the scorn of the school. Oh! aren't you the scorn of women?* (J. M. Synge). **3.** mockery; derision. **4.** *Archaic.* an expression of contempt; taunt; insult.
[Middle English *schornen* < Old French *escarnir* < Germanic (compare Old High German *skernôn*)] —**scorn′er,** *n.*
—**Syn.** *v.t.* **1.** disdain, spurn. *-n.* **1. Scorn, contempt, disdain** mean disgust, or feeling that a person or thing is mean, low, or worthless. **Scorn** implies disgust mixed with anger and bitterness: *We feel scorn for a draft dodger.* **Contempt** implies disgust combined with strong disapproval: *We feel contempt for a coward.* **Disdain** implies feeling oneself above anything so mean or low: *We feel disdain for a person who cheats.*
scorn·ful (skôrn′fəl), *adj.* showing contempt; full of scorn; mocking: *He spoke of our old car in a scornful voice.* —**scorn′ful·ly,** *adv.* —**scorn′ful·ness,** *n.* —**Syn.** disdainful, derisive, contemptuous.
scor·o·dite (skôr′ə dīt, skor′-), *n.* a mineral, a hydrous ferric arsenate, occurring in orthorhombic crystals and in earthy form, and usually of a greenish or brown color. *Formula:* $FeAsO_4.2H_2O$ [< German *Skorodit* < Greek *skórodon* garlic (because of its smell when heated) + German *-it* -ite¹]
scor·pae·nid (skôr pē′nid), *n.* a scorpaenoid.
scor·pae·noid (skôr pē′noid), *adj.* of or belonging to a family of marine fishes that have spiny fins, including the scorpionfishes. —*n.* a scorpaenoid fish. [< Latin *scorpaena* a kind of fish (< Greek *skórpaina*) + English *-oid*]
scor·pene (skôr′pēn), *n.* a scorpaenoid fish of the southern coast of California. [< French *scorpène* < Latin *scorpaena;* see SCORPAENOID]
Scor·pi·i (skôr′pē ī), *n.* genitive of **Scorpius.**
Scor·pi·o (skôr′pē ō), *n., genitive* (def. 1) **Scor·pi·o·nis. 1.** Scorpius. **2.** the eighth sign of the zodiac. The sun enters Scorpio about October 24. [< Latin *Scorpiō, -ōnis* (literally) scorpion < Greek *skorpíōn, -ōnos* Scorpio; scorpion]
scor·pi·oid (skôr′pē oid), *adj.* **1. a.** of or belonging to a group of animals including the scorpions. **b.** like a scorpion. **2.** *Botany.* curved at the end like the tail of a scorpion: *In the borage family, certain plants are called scorpioid because the cyme unrolls as the flowers expand.* [< Greek *skorpioeidḗs* < *skórpios* scorpion + *eîdos* form]
scor·pi·on (skôr′pē ən), *n.* **1.** any of a group of small animals belonging to the same group as the spider and having a poisonous sting at the end of its tail. **2.** a kind of whip made of knotted cords or with lead or steel spikes. I Kings 12:11. [< Old French *scorpion,* learned borrowing from Latin *scorpiō, -ōnis* < Greek *skorpíōn, -ōnos*]

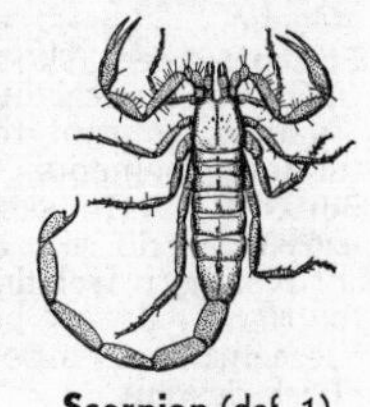
Scorpion (def. 1) (1½ to 8 in. long)

Scor·pi·on (skôr′pē-ən), *n.* Scorpio.
scor·pi·on·fish (skôr′pē ən fish′), *n., pl.* **-fish·es** or (*collectively*) **-fish.** any of a group of marine fishes having spines on the head and fins.
scorpion fly, any of a group of insects, the male of which has an extension of the abdomen resembling the stinger of a scorpion.
scor·pi·on·ic (skôr′pē on′ik), *adj.* of or having to do with the scorpion.
Scor·pi·o·nis (skôr pē ō′nis), *n.* genitive of **Scorpio.**
Scorpion's Heart, the bright-red star Antares, in the constellation Scorpio.
Scor·pi·us (skôr′pē əs), *n., genitive* **Scor·pi·i.** **1.** a southern constellation that was thought of as arranged in the shape of a scorpion. It is between Libra and Sagittarius. **2.** Scorpio in the zodiac.
scor·za·lite (skôr′zə līt), *n.* a blue mineral, a phosphate of iron and aluminum, occurring in crystalline or massive form.
scot (skot), *n.* one's share of a payment; payment; tax. [probably fusion of Old English *gesceot* with Scandinavian (compare Old Icelandic *skot*). Related to SHOT.] —**Syn.** assessment.
Scot (skot), *n.* **1.** a native or inhabitant of Scotland; Scotchman. **2.** one of an ancient Gaelic-speaking people living in Ireland, Scotland, etc. Scotland is named after them. [Old English *Scottas* the Irish, the Scotch < Late Latin *Scottus*]
➔ See **Scotchman** for a usage note.
Scot., 1. Scotch. **2.** Scotland. **3.** Scottish.
scot and lot, a municipal tax formerly assessed proportionately upon members of a community.
pay off scot and lot, to pay off completely; settle with: *I'll pay you off scot and lot by and by* (Dickens).
scotch (skoch), *v.t.* **1. a.** to make harmless: *We have scotched the snake, not killed it* (Shakespeare). **b.** to stamp on or stamp out;

crush: *He did so with sufficient force . . . to scotch once and for all any lingering doubts or rumours that the pound is to be devaluated* (London Times). **2.** to cut; score; gash. **3.** to block or wedge (a wheel, log, etc.) so as to prevent moving or slipping.
—*n.* **1.** a cut; score; gash. **2.** a line drawn on the ground, as in hopscotch. **3.** a block placed under a wheel, log, etc., to prevent moving or slipping.
[origin uncertain; perhaps < Anglo-French *escoche,* Old French *coche* notch, nick, ultimately < Latin *coccum* berry of scarlet oak (notchlike in appearance)]
—**Syn.** *v.t.* **1. a.** disable, cripple.

Scotch (skoch), *adj.* **1.** of or having to do with Scotland, its people, or their language. **2.** *Informal.* stingy; mean; parsimonious.
—*n.* **1.** the people of Scotland as a group. **2.** the dialect of English spoken by the people of Scotland. **3.** Scotch whisky. **4.** a dry snuff.
➔ **Scotch, Scots, Scottish** have the same literal meaning but are only in part interchangeable. *Scotch* is a familiar form before certain nouns (*Scotch whisky, Scotch broth*); in Scotland itself, this form does not have wide usage. *Scots* is used outside of Scotland in a few collocations (*Middle Scots, Scots law, Scots Guards*). *Scottish* is used widely in Scotland, and is elsewhere perhaps more literary (*Scottish history, the Scottish character*).

Scotch blessing, *Informal.* a stern rebuke.

Scotch broth, a soup containing pearl barley, meat, and small pieces of vegetables.

Scotch cap, any of various brimless caps worn in Scotland, as the glengarry or the balmoral.

Scotch elm, the wych-elm, a tall elm of Europe and Asia.

Scotch-Gael·ic (skoch′gā′lik), *n.* Scottish Gaelic.

Scotch·gard (skoch′gärd′), *n. Trademark.* a fluorochemical substance used for making textiles resistant to water, oils, and other staining elements.

Scotch-I·rish (skoch′ī′rish), *adj.* **1.** of or having to do with a part of the population of Northern Ireland descended from Scotch settlers. **2.** of both Scotch and Irish descent. —*n.* a person of both Scotch and Irish descent.

Scotch·lite (skoch′līt), *n. Trademark.* a luminous, adhesive tape that reflects light after dark.

Scotch·man (skoch′mən), *n., pl.* **-men.** a native or inhabitant of Scotland.
➔ **Scotchman, Scotsman, Scot.** In Scotland, *Scotsman* is the preferred and current form; *Scot* is an occasional, somewhat literary, and inoffensive variant, especially in the plural: *Scots! wha hae wi' Wallace bled* . . . (Robert Burns). *Scotchman,* overwhelmingly the most common term in most other parts of the English-speaking world, is virtually never used by natives of the country.

Scotch mist, **1.** a very dense, wet, penetrating mist like that common in the Highlands of Scotland. **2.** a steady, soaking rain.

Scotch pine, a European and Asian pine with reddish-tinged wood, used for lumber, as a source of tar, as a Christmas tree, etc. It has become naturalized in areas of eastern North America.

Scotch tape, **1.** a transparent, cellophane, adhesive tape for mending, patching, sealing, etc. **2.** *Trademark.* any of several kinds of transparent or opaque adhesive tapes.

scotch-tape (skoch′tāp′), *v.t.,* **-taped, -taping.** to mend, patch, seal, etc., with Scotch tape: *Scotch-taping the family's finger painting on the kitchen walls* . . . (New York Times).

Scotch terrier, a Scottish terrier.

Scotch verdict, an inconclusive verdict.

Scotch whisky, a whiskey distilled in Scotland from barley malt, having a slightly smoky flavor.

Scotch·wom·an (skoch′wu̇m′ən), *n., pl.* **-wom·en.** a woman who is a native or inhabitant of Scotland.
➔ See **Scotchman** for a usage note.

Scotch woodcock, cooked eggs served on toast with anchovy paste.

Scotch·y (skoch′ē), *adj.,* **Scotch·i·er, Scotch·i·est.** having the characteristics of what is Scotch; suggesting Scotch people or ways.

sco·ter (skō′tər), *n.* any of several large, black sea ducks, native to arctic regions and common in northern seas, usually called coot in the United States; surf duck. Also, **scooter.** [origin uncertain]

scot-free (skot′frē′), *adj.* **1.** free from injury, punishment, etc.; unharmed: *to go scot-free. Although an Englishman who indulged in similar escapades last year was fined $29, Thompson went scot-free* (Newsweek). **2.** *Obsolete.* free from payment of scot (tax), tavern score, fine, etc.

sco·tia (skō′shə), *n.* a concave molding, as at the base of a column. [< Latin *scotia* < Greek *skotíā* a shadowed (because sunken or hollowed) molding at the base of a pillar; (originally) darkness < *skótos* the dark]

Sco·tia (skō′shə), *n. Poetic.* Scotland. [< Medieval Latin *Scotia* < Late Latin *Scōtus,* variant of *Scottus* a Scot]

Scot·ic (skot′ik), *adj.* of or relating to the Scots.

Sco·tism (skō′tiz əm), *n.* the doctrines of the scholastic theologian John Duns Scotus, about 1265 to about 1308, or his followers. Its fundamental doctrine is that distinctions of the mind are real, although they exist only in their relation to mind.

Sco·tist (skō′tist), *n.* a follower of John Duns Scotus: *Scotists and Thomists now in peace remain* (Alexander Pope).

Scot·land Yard (skot′lənd), **1.** the headquarters of the London police. **2.** the London police, especially the department that does detective work. [< the name of the building in London where it was located]

scot·o·din·i·a (skot′ə din′ē ə), *n.* a dizziness combined with dimness of vision. [< New Latin *scotodinia* < Greek *skótos* darkness + *dînos* a whirling]

sco·to·ma (skə tō′mə), *n., pl.* **-ma·ta** (-mə tə). a loss of vision in a part of the visual field. [< Late Latin *scotōma* dimness of vision < Greek *skotōma, -atos* dizziness, vertigo < *skótos* darkness]

sco·tom·a·tous (skə tom′ə təs), *adj.* having to do with or affected with a scotoma.

sco·to·pho·bi·a (skō′tə fō′bē ə), *n.* an abnormal fear of the dark; nyctophobia. [< Greek *skótos* darkness + English *-phobia*]

sco·to·pi·a (skō tō′pē ə), *n.* **1.** adaptation to darkness. **2.** the ability to see in darkness. [< New Latin *scotopia* < Greek *skótos* darkness + *ōps, ōpós* eye]

sco·top·ic (skō top′ik, -tō′pik), *adj.* **1.** that can adapt to darkness. **2.** that can see in darkness.

Scots (skots), *adj.* **1.** Scottish. **2. a.** in the older Scottish currency: *two pounds Scots.* **b.** in the older Scottish weights and measures: *one Scots pint.*
—*n.* **1.** (*pl.*) the people of Scotland. **2.** (*sing.*) the dialect of English spoken in Scotland.
[Scottish short form of earlier *Scottis* (see SCOTCH) < Late Latin *Scottus* a SCOT]
➔ See **Scotch** for a usage note.

Scots·man (skots′mən), *n., pl.* **-men.** a Scotchman; Scot: *I think my father was a Scotsman* (James Barrie).
➔ See **Scotchman** for a usage note.

Scots pine, the Scotch pine.

Scots·wom·an (skots′wu̇m′ən), *n., pl.* **-wom·en.** a woman who is a native or inhabitant of Scotland.
➔ See **Scotchman** for a usage note.

Scot·ti·cism (skot′ə siz əm), *n.* an idiom or way of speaking peculiar to Scottish English.

Scot·tie (skot′ē), *n.* Scotty.

Scot·tish (skot′ish), *adj.* of or having to do with Scotland, its people, or their language. —*n.* **1.** the people of Scotland. **2.** the dialect of English spoken by the people of Scotland. *Abbr.:* Sc. —**Scot′tish·ness,** *n.*
➔ See **Scotch** for a usage note.

Scottish deerhound, any of a breed of dog similar to the greyhound but larger and with a rough coat. It was developed by the Scottish nobility for hunting deer.

Scottish Deerhound (28 to 32 in. high at the shoulder)

Scottish Gaelic, the Celtic language of the Scottish Highlanders; Erse.

Scottish Rite, one of the two advanced branches of membership in the Freemasons (the other being the York Rite).

Scottish terrier, any of a breed of short-legged terriers with rough, wiry hair and pointed, standing ears. Its short coat can range from black or gray to a sandy color; Scotch terrier.

Scottish Terrier (about 10 in. high at the shoulder)

Scott's oriole, an oriole of Mexico and southwestern United States, the male of which is light yellow with black head, throat, back, wings, and tail.

Scot·ty (skot′ē), *n., pl.* **-ties.** *Informal.* **1.** a Scottish terrier. **2.** a nickname for a Scotchman.

scoun·drel (skoun′drəl), *n.* a person without honor or good principles; villain; rascal: *The scoundrels who set fire to the barn have been caught.* —*adj.* scoundrelly; villainous; unprincipled; base: . . . *these scoundrel Doones* (Richard D. Blackmore). —**Syn.** *n.* blackguard, scamp.

scoun·drel·dom (skoun′drəl dəm), *n.* scoundrels, or their ways or habits.

scoun·drel·ism (skoun′drə liz əm), *n.* **1.** the character or conduct of a scoundrel. **2.** a scoundrelly action: *A dirty little boy! Capable no doubt of a thousand kindred scoundrelisms* (H. G. Wells).

scoun·drel·ly (skoun′drə lē), *adj.* **1.** having the character of a scoundrel. **2.** having to do with or characteristic of a scoundrel.

scour[1] (skour), *v.t.* **1.** to clean or polish by vigorous rubbing: *to scour the floor with a brush and soapsuds.* **2.** to remove dirt or grease from (anything) by rubbing: *to scour soiled clothing, scour woolens.* **3.** to make clear by flowing through or over: *The stream had scoured a channel.* **4.** to clean; cleanse; purge, as an animal. **5.** to rid or clear of what is undesirable: . . . *to scour the sea of the pirates* (Sir Philip Sidney). **6.** to beat; scourge; punish: *But I will pay the dog, I will scour him* (Henry Fielding). —*v.i.* **1.** to rub something vigorously to clean or polish it. **2.** to remove dirt or grease from clothing, etc.
—*n.* **1.** the act of scouring. **2.** the cleansing substance used in scouring woolens, etc. **3.** a place in a river where the bottom is scoured by the stream.
scours, *U.S.* diarrhea in cattle, especially calves: *His calves will very likely take the "scours"* (D.G. Mitchell).
[probably < Middle Dutch *schuren,* perhaps ultimately < Latin *ex-* completely + *cūra* care]

scour[2] (skour), *v.t.* **1.** to move quickly over: *Men scoured the country looking for the lost child.* **2.** to look into every part of; search: *to scour one's memory for a forgotten date. He cannibalized damaged machinery to get spare parts to get other machines running, repaired buildings, put order into production lines, scoured Germany for raw materials* (Wall Street Journal). —*v.i.* to go swiftly in search or pursuit: *The horsemen . . . gave reins to their steeds and scoured for the frontier* (Washington Irving). [perhaps < Scandinavian (compare Old Icelandic *skura* rush violently), or perhaps < Old French *escourre* run forth < Latin *excurrere.* Compare EXCURSION.] —**Syn.** *v.t.* **2.** comb.

scour·er[1] (skour′ər), *n.* **1.** a person who scours. **2.** a thing for scouring or scrubbing: *Brushes, sponges, etc., are household scourers.* **3.** a purgative agent; cathartic. [< *scour*[1] + *-er*[1]]

scour·er[2] (skour′ər), *n.* a rowdy person who ranged through the streets at night in England during the 1600's and 1700's, breaking windows, picking fights, etc. [< *scour*[2] + *-er*[1]]

scour·fish (skour′fish′), *n., pl.* **-fish·es** or (*collectively*) **-fish.** the escolar. [because of its rough skin]

scourge (skėrj), *n., v.,* **scourged, scourg·ing.** —*n.* **1.** a whip; lash. **2.** any means of punishment. **3.** some thing or person that causes great trouble or misfortune, as an outbreak of disease or a war: *Malaria, an old scourge, is now confined to the far jungles* (Time).
—*v.t.* **1.** to whip; flog; punish severely; chastise: *the waves . . . scourged with the*

 PRONUNCIATION KEY: hat, āge, cãre, fär; let, ēqual, tėrm; it, īce; hot, ōpen, ôrder; **oil**, **out**; cup, pu̇t, rüle;

wind's invisible tyranny (Shelley). **2.** to trouble very much; afflict; torment.
[< Anglo-French *escorge,* and *escurge,* Old French *escorgiee,* ultimately < Latin *ex-* + *corrigia* strap, latchet < *corium* a hide]

scourg·er (skėr′jər), *n.* a person who scourges or punishes; flagellant.

scour·ing cinder (skour′ing), a slag low in silica which wears out the lining of a furnace.

scouring pad, a soft mass of steel wool, plastic mesh, etc., used for cleansing and polishing

scouring rush, any of various horsetail plants formerly used to scour and polish.

scour·ings (skour′ingz), *n.pl.* **1.** dirt, refuse, material, etc., removed by, or as if by, scouring; dregs: *a gang built up from the scourings of the slums.* **2.** refuse removed from grain before milling.

scours (skourz), *n.pl.* See under **scour**[1], *n.*

scour·way (skour′wā′), *n.* a channel eroded by a stream, especially by a former glacial stream.

scour·wort (skour′wėrt′), *n.* the soapwort.

scouse (skous), *n.* a kind of sailors' stew made with sea biscuit, onions, cabbage or other vegetables, water, and salt; lobscouse. [short for *lobscouse*]

scouse kettle, *Nautical.* an iron kettle for cooking.

scout[1] (skout), *n.* **1. a.** a person sent to find out what the enemy is doing. A scout wears a uniform; a spy does not. **b.** a warship, airplane, etc., used to find out what the enemy is doing. **2.** a person who is sent out to get information. **3.** a person sent out to get information about athletes or athletic teams. **4.** the act of scouting: *on scout, to the scout.* **5.** a person belonging to the Boy Scouts or Girl Scouts. **6.** *Slang.* a fellow; person: *He's a good scout. George, old scout, you were sore-headed about something* (Sinclair Lewis). **7.** *British.* a college servant at Oxford University.
—*v.i.* to act as a scout; hunt around to find something: *Go and scout for firewood for the picnic.* —*v.t.* to observe or examine to get information; reconnoiter.
[< Old French *escoute* act of listening, listener < *escouter* listen, ultimately < Latin *auscultāre*] —**scout′er,** *n.* —**scout′ing·ly,** *adv.*

scout[2] (skout), *v.t.* to refuse to believe in; reject with scorn: *He scouted the idea of a dog with two tails. A large, looming man, Wenning is alleged to have been a significant athlete at college . . . although he scouts the idea* (Newsweek). —*v.i.* to scoff: *They might scout at Moby Dick as a monstrous fable* (Herman Melville). [< Scandinavian (compare Old Icelandic *skūta* to taunt)]

scout car, any of various fast, open-top vehicles designed for military reconnaissance.

scout·craft (skout′kraft′, -kräft′), *n.* knowledge and skill in activities required to be a good Boy or Girl Scout.

scouth (sküth), *n. Scottish.* **1.** opportunity; scope. **2.** abundance; plenty.

scout·ing (skou′ting), *n.* the activities of scouts.

scout·mas·ter (skout′mas′tər, -mäs′-), *n.* **1.** the man in charge of a troop of Boy Scouts. **2.** the leader of a band of scouts.

scow (skou), *n.* a large, flat-bottomed boat used to carry freight, coal, sand, etc. [American English < Dutch *schouw*]

Scows being towed by tugboat

scowl (skoul), *v.i.* **1.** to look angry or sullen by lowering the eyebrows: *She scowls dreadfully . . . out of pure ugliness of temper* (Hawthorne). **2.** to have a gloomy or threatening aspect. —*v.t.* **1.** to affect by scowling. **2.** to express with a scowl: *to scowl one's disapproval.*
—*n.* **1.** an angry, sullen look; frown. **2.** a gloomy or threatening aspect.
[Middle English *scoulen.* Compare Danish *skule* cast down the eyes.] —**scowl′er,** *n.* —**scowl′ing·ly,** *adv.* —**Syn.** *v.i.* **1, 2.** See **frown.**

scr., scruple or scruples.

scrab·ble (skrab′əl), *v.,* **-bled, -bling,** *n.* —*v.i.* **1.** to scratch or scrape about with hands, claws, etc.; scramble: *to scrabble up a sand bank. She scrabbled among the papers* (H.G. Wells). **2.** to struggle or scramble feverishly, desperately, etc.: *to scrabble for scraps of food, to scrabble for a living. Similar cars driven by other men scream and scrabble for a footing on the roadway* (Atlantic). **3.** to scrawl; scribble. —*v.t.* **1.** to scratch; scrape: *But Tubal got him a pointed rod, and scrabbled the earth for corn* (Rudyard Kipling). **2.** to scratch or rake hurriedly; obtain by scratching or raking about. **3.** to scrawl (something) or upon (something).
—*n.* **1.** a scrabbling; scramble. **2.** a scrawling character, writing, etc.
[< Dutch *schrabbelen* (frequentative) < *schrabben* to scratch]

Scrab·ble (skrab′əl), *n. Trademark.* a game played on a board with blocks having printed letters which the players try to fit together to spell words.

scrab·bly (skrab′lē), *adj.* minor; unimportant: *They are writing about . . . scrabbly little social problems* (Harper's).

scrag (skrag), *n., v.,* **scragged, scrag·ging.** —*n.* **1.** a lean, skinny person or animal: *An old bony horse is a scrag.* **2.** a lean, bony part: *A scrag of mutton is the neck.* **3.** *Slang.* the neck.
—*v.t. Slang.* **1.** to hang on the gallows. **2. a.** to wring the neck of. **b.** to strangle.
[< Scandinavian (compare Swedish dialectal *skragge* old and torn thing)]

scrag·gi·ness (skrag′ē nis), *n.* scraggy quality or condition.

scrag·gling (skrag′ling), *adj.* irregular in outline or distribution; straggling: *The remains [of Hastings Castle] being somewhat scanty and scraggling* (Hawthorne).

scrag·gly (skrag′lē), *adj.,* **-gli·er, -gli·est.** rough; irregular; ragged: *a scraggly growth of trees or hair.*

scrag·gy[1] (skrag′ē), *adj.,* **-gi·er, -gi·est. 1.** lean; thin; bony: . . . *his sinewy, scraggy neck* (Scott). **2.** meager; scanty. —**Syn. 1.** scrawny.

scrag·gy[2] (skrag′ē), *adj.,* **-gi·er, -gi·est.** rough in surface; broken in line; jagged; irregular; scraggly: *old scraggy bushes* (W. H. Hudson). *The note was written in Meshach's scraggy and irregular hand* (Arnold Bennett).

scraich or **scraigh** (skrāʜ), *v.i., v.t., n. Scottish.* screech.

scram (skram), *v.,* **scrammed, scram·ming,** *interj. U.S. Slang.* —*v.i.* to go at once; leave immediately. —*interj.* begone! scat! [American English; perhaps short for *scramble*]

scram·ble (skram′bəl), *v.,* **-bled, -bling,** *n.* —*v.i.* **1.** to make one's way by climbing, crawling, jumping, etc.: *The boys scrambled up the steep, rocky hill.* **2.** to struggle with others for something: *to scramble for a living, to scramble for office. The boys scrambled to get the football.* **3.** *U.S. Slang.* (in the Air Force) to get an airplane into the air hurriedly, usually to intercept unidentified planes: *You tumble out of bed . . . You are to scramble on a practice flight to intercept an "enemy" bomber* (World Book Encyclopedia). —*v.t.* **1.** to collect or gather up in a hurry or without method: *Juliet, scrambling up her hair, darted into the house* (Bulwer-Lytton). **2.** to toss or mix together in a confused way. **3.** to cook and stir (eggs) in a pan with the whites and yolks mixed together. **4.** *U.S. Slang.* (in the Air Force) to put (airplanes) into the air hurriedly, usually to intercept unidentified airplanes: *Reservists . . . stood ready to scramble fighters aloft to intercept any unidentified planes* (Time). **5.** to break up or mix (a message, radio or television signal, etc.) so that it cannot be received and understood without special equipment: *The broadcasting is done by coding or scrambling the pictures so that the general public can't receive them unless they pay for a special device to unscramble the broadcast on their sets* (Wall Street Journal).
—*n.* **1.** a climb or walk over rough ground: *It was a long scramble through bushes and over rocks to the top of the hill.* **2.** a struggle to possess: *the scramble for wealth and power.* **3.** any disorderly struggle or activity: *The pile of boys on the football seemed a wild scramble of arms and legs.* **4.** *U.S. Slang.* (in the Air Force) the act or process of scrambling: *If there's a scramble, you fly, regardless of weather* (New Yorker).
[perhaps variant of *scrabble*]

scram·bler (skram′blər), *n.* **1.** a person who scrambles. **2.** a device for breaking up a telephone, radio, or television signal, etc.

scram·bling·ly (skram′bling lē), *adv.* in a scrambling or haphazard manner.

scram·bly (skram′blē), *adj.,* **scram·bli·er, scram·bli·est.** scrambled; disorganized: *I find the lovers' climactic quarrel in Act II a scratchy, scrambly business* (Punch).

scram·jet (skram′jet′), *n.* a jet engine, similar to the ramjet, which obtains its thrust by burning fuel in a supersonic airstream: *Scramjets theoretically could extend flight speeds to at least Mach 14* (New Scientist). [< *s*(upersonic) *c*(ombustion) *ramjet*]

scran (skran), *n.* **1.** *Dialect.* scraps of food; provision; fare. **2.** *Irish Slang.* luck: *bad scran.* [origin uncertain]

scran·nel (skran′əl), *adj. Archaic.* **1.** thin; slight: *Their lean and flashy songs grate on their scrannel pipes of wretched straw* (Milton). **2.** squeaky and harsh. [< Scandinavian (compare Norwegian dialectal *skran* lean, shriveled)]

scrap[1] (skrap), *n., v.,* **scrapped, scrap·ping,** *adj.* —*n.* **1.** a small piece; little bit; small part left over: *a scrap of paper. The cook gave some scraps of meat to the dog. The girls haven't a scrap of imagination* (John Galsworthy). **2.** a bit of something written or printed; a short extract: *She read aloud scraps from the letter.* **3.** old or discarded metal fit only to be melted and made again: *About half of all our new steel is old steel, otherwise known as scrap* (New Yorker).
scraps, the remains of animal fat after the oil has been tried out: *He had codfish and pork scraps for dinner.*
—*v.t.* **1.** to make into scraps; break up. **2.** to throw aside as useless or worn out; discard: *Existing plans could be scrapped and fresh ones made* (London Times).
—*adj.* **1.** in the form of scraps: *scrap metal.* **2.** made of scraps or fragments; useful only as scrap.
[< Scandinavian (compare Old Icelandic *skrap* scraps, trifles)] —**Syn.** *n.* **1.** remnant.

scrap[2] (skrap), *n., v.i.,* **scrapped, scrap·ping.** *Slang.* fight; quarrel; struggle: *Well, let's not scrap about it* (Sinclair Lewis). [probably variant of *scrape,* noun, definition 4]

scrap·bas·ket (skrap′bas′kit, -bäs′-), *n.* a basket or other container for scraps, as of paper.

scrap·book (skrap′bu̇k′), *n.* a book in which pictures or clippings are pasted and kept.

scrape (skrāp), *v.,* **scraped, scrap·ing,** *n.* —*v.t.* **1.** to rub with something sharp or rough; make smooth or clean thus: *Scrape your muddy shoes with this knife.* **2. a.** to remove by rubbing with something sharp or rough: *The man scraped some paint off the table when he pushed it through the doorway.* **b.** to scratch or graze by rubbing against something rough: *She fell and scraped her knee on the sidewalk.* **3.** to rub with a harsh sound: *to scrape the floor with one's chair. Don't scrape your feet on the floor.* **4.** to dig: *The child scraped a hole in the sand.* **5.** to collect by scraping or with difficulty: *The hungry boy scraped up the last crumbs from his plate. He scraped together enough money for his first year at college.* **6.** to smooth the surface of (an unpaved road), as with a bulldozer. —*v.i.* **1.** to graze (against, on). **2.** to rub harshly: *The branch of the tree scraped against a window.* **3.** to give a harsh sound; grate. **4.** to gather together money, etc., with labor and difficulty; hoard up. **5.** to manage with difficulty: *That family can just scrape along but never asks for charity.* **6.** to bow with a drawing back of the foot: *Bowing and scraping and rubbing his hands together* (Anthony Trollope).
scrape through, to manage to just get by: *to scrape through a narrow opening.*
—*n.* **1.** the act of scraping. **2.** a scraped place. **3.** a harsh, grating sound: *the scrape of the bow of a violin.* **4.** a position hard to get out of; difficulty; predicament: *Boys often get into scrapes.* **5.** a bow with a drawing back of the foot.
[perhaps alteration of Old English *scrapian,* influenced by Scandinavian (compare Old Icelandic *skrapa*)]

scrap·er (skrā′pər), *n.* **1.** an instrument or tool for scraping: *a paint scraper, a shoe scraper.* See **solder** for picture. **2.** a person who scrapes: **a.** a person who scrapes together money meanly; miser. **b.** a fiddler, as a person who scrapes the strings (used in an unfriendly way). **c.** a barber, as a person who scrapes the skin in shaving.

scrap·heap (skrap′hēp′), *n.* **1.** a pile of scraps. **2.** a place for useless or worn-out things. —*v.t.* **1.** to consign to a scrapheap. **2.** to discard as useless or worthless.

scrap·ie (skrā′pē), *n.* a virus disease of sheep which attacks the nervous system, usually causing death: *Scrapie is . . . so named because bleating victims rub themselves against posts or wire to relieve the itching* (Time).

scrap·ing (skrā′ping), *n.* **1.** the act of a person or thing that scrapes. **2.** the sound produced by this.

scrapings, that which is scraped off, up, or together: *An apprentice . . . thinking of . . . the miseries of the milk and water, and thick bread and scrapings* (Dickens).

scrap iron, broken or waste pieces of old iron, for remelting or reworking.

scrap·man (skrap′man′), *n., pl.* **-men.** a junkman who deals in old or discarded metal: *The affluent society only wants new cars and the scrapman has lost interest in the old ones* (New Scientist).

scrap·page (skrap′ij), *n.* **1.** a scrapping, especially of old cars. **2.** what is scrapped; amount scrapped.

scrap·per (skrap′ər), *n. Slang.* **1.** a person who scraps or fights; boxer: *a good light-weight scrapper.* **2.** a person given to fighting: *He's a real scrapper for a little boy.*

scrap·pi·ly (skrap′ə lē), *adv.* in scraps or fragments; fragmentarily; desultorily.

scrap·pi·ness (skrap′ē nis), *n.* scrappy character or condition; fragmentariness; disconnectedness.

scrap·ple (skrap′əl), *n.* scraps of pork or other meat boiled with corn meal or flour, made into cakes, sliced, and fried. [American English; diminutive of *scrap*[1]]

scrap·py[1] (skrap′ē), *adj.,* **-pi·er, -pi·est. 1.** made up of odds and ends: *a scrappy meal of leftovers.* **2.** fragmentary; disconnected; disjointed: *a scrappy conversation.* [< *scrap*[1] + *-y*[1]]

scrap·py[2] (skrap′ē), *adj.,* **-pi·er, -pi·est.** *Slang.* fond of fighting; pugnacious. [< *scrap*[2] + *-y*[1]] —**Syn.** quarrelsome.

scraps (skraps), *n.pl.* See under **scrap**[1], *n.*

scrap·yard (skrap′yärd′), *n.* the place where a scrapman stores his items and carries on his business: *By 1967 most cars will reach the scrapyard by their tenth birthday* (London Times).

scratch (skrach), *v.t.* **1.** to break, mark, or cut slightly with something sharp or rough: *Your shoes have scratched the chair.* **2.** to tear or dig with the claws or nails: *The cat scratched him.* **3.** to rub or scrape to relieve itching, give pleasure, or from force of habit: *He scratched his head. Don't scratch your mosquito bites.* **4.** to rub with a harsh noise; rub: *He scratched a match on the wall.* **5.** to write or draw in a hurry or carelessly; scribble: *I also scratched down another ballad* (Scott). **6.** to scrape out; strike out; draw a line through: *I have often scratched out passages from papers and pamphlets* (Jonathan Swift). **7.** to withdraw (a horse, etc.) from a race or contest: *High Gun, a good horse in America who has been difficult to train this season, was officially scratched yesterday* (London Times). **8.** to gather by effort; scrape: *The oil wealth has yet to trickle down to many thousands of half-nomadic rural Venezuelans, who scratch subsistence diets out of jungle clearings* (Time). **9.** *U.S.* **a.** to split (one's ballot) but still support most of the members of one's party. **b.** to fail to support part of (a party ticket). **c.** to erase the name of (a candidate) on a party ticket. —*v.i.* **1.** to use the claws, nails, etc., for tearing a surface, digging, etc. **2.** to rub some part of one's body to relieve itching, give pleasure, or from force of habit. **3.** to rub with a slight grating noise: *This pen scratches.* **4.** to get along with difficulty. **5.** to withdraw from a race or contest. **6.** to make a miss or fluke in billiards or pool.

—*n.* **1.** a mark made by scratching: *There are deep scratches on this desk.* **2.** a very slight cut: *He escaped with only a scratch on his face.* **3.** a rough mark made by a pencil, pen, etc.; hasty scrawl; scribble. **4.** the sound of scratching: *the scratch of a pen or match.* **5.** any act of scratching. **6. a.** the line marking the starting place of a race or contest. **b.** the starting place, time, or status of a competitor who has neither allowance nor penalty. **c.** such a competitor. **7.** (formerly) a line at which boxers met and began to fight. **8.** in billiards or pool: **a.** a miss. **b.** a fluke. **9.** a scratch wig.

from scratch, from nothing; from the beginning: *Its [Yemen's] rulers are virtually starting from scratch, not only in industrialization but in administration* (Manchester Guardian Weekly).

up to scratch, up to standard; in good condition: *"The Lost Princess" is . . . a shepherd's daughter, who has also been taken in hand by the wise woman but who fails to come up to scratch* (New Yorker).

—*adj.* **1.** for quick notes, a first draft, etc.: *scratch paper.* **2.** collected or prepared hastily and often of poor quality: *a scratch football team, a scratch crew, a scratch meal.* **3.** done by chance; dependent on chance: *a scratch shot.* **4.** without a handicap in a race.

[perhaps alteration of earlier *scrat* scratch; influenced by obsolete *cratch* scratch; origin uncertain] —**scratch′er,** *n.*

Scratch (skrach), *n.* the Devil; Old Scratch.

scratch·board (skrach′bôrd′, -bōrd′), *n.* a kind of cardboard covered with chalk, used for drawings in pen and ink, crayon, etc. Its prepared surface can also be scratched out with a cutting tool to achieve certain effects of lighting.

scratch·es (skrach′iz), *n.pl.* (*usually sing. in use*) a disease of horses characterized by chapping and dry cracks near the fetlock.

scratch gage or **gauge,** a tool for marking on metal, having a hard steel point.

scratch hit, a poorly hit ball in baseball that results in a base hit because of some circumstance.

scratch·i·ly (skrach′ə lē), *adv.* in a scratchy manner; unevenly; raggedly.

scratch·i·ness (skrach′ē nis), *n.* scratchy quality or condition.

scratch pad, a pad of paper for hurried notes or first-draft writing.

scratch sheet, *U.S. Slang.* a publication that lists the horses scratched from a race and other racing information; form sheet.

scratch test, a test for allergy to a particular substance, made by scratching the skin with a dose of the substance.

scratch wig, a wig covering only part of the head.

scratch·y (skrach′ē), *adj.,* **scratch·i·er, scratch·i·est. 1.** that scratches, scrapes, or grates: *a scratchy pen.* **2.** consisting of mere scratches: *a scratchy drawing, scratchy writing.* **3.** scanty; straggling: *scratchy hair.*

scrawl (skrôl), *v.t., v.i.* to write or draw poorly or carelessly. —*n.* **1.** poor, careless handwriting. **2.** something scrawled, such as a hastily or badly written letter or note. [perhaps < obsolete *scrawl* spread out the limbs, sprawl; gesticulate; perhaps alteration of *crawl,* influenced by *sprawl*] —**scrawl′er,** *n.*

scrawl·y (skrô′lē), *adj.,* **scrawl·i·er, scrawl·i·est.** awkwardly written or drawn.

scraw·ni·ness (skrô′nē nis), *n.* scrawny quality or appearance.

scraw·ny (skrô′nē), *adj.,* **-ni·er, -ni·est.** *U.S. Informal.* lean; thin; skinny: *Turkeys have scrawny necks.* [American English, perhaps variant of dialectal *scranny.* Compare SCRANNEL.]

screak (skrēk), *v.i.* **1.** to screech; scream. **2.** to creak. —*n.* a shrill cry; screech. [apparently < Scandinavian (compare Swedish *skrika*)]

scream (skrēm), *v.i.* **1.** to make a loud, sharp, piercing cry, as in fright, anger, or sudden pain: . . . *the desperate screaming of a frightened woman* (Joseph Conrad). **2.** to give forth a characteristic shrill cry, as certain birds and animals, or a whistle: *I heard the owl scream and the crickets cry* (Shakespeare). **3.** to laugh loudly. **4. a.** to speak loudly: *Stop screaming! we can hear you.* **b.** to write excitedly. **5.** to produce a vivid impression or startling effect: *The colors of her pink sweater and orange blouse screamed at each other.* —*v.t.* **1.** to utter loudly: *It was so noisy in the room that I had to scream my name.* **2.** to bring about by screaming: *Bugles . . . to scream us out of bed* (Scott).

—*n.* **1.** a loud, sharp, piercing cry, as of fright, extreme pain, etc.: *loud screams of laughter* (W. H. Hudson). **2.** a shrill sound like a scream: *The screams of the engines announced that the day was done* (Leonard Merrick). **3.** something extremely funny: *Ted observed that her friends were "a scream of a bunch"* (Sinclair Lewis).

[perhaps unrecorded Old English *scrǣman*]

—**Syn.** *v.i.* **1. Scream, shriek** mean to make a loud, sharp, piercing sound. **Scream** suggests a loud, high-pitched, piercing cry expressing fear, pain, or almost hysterical anger or joy: *She screamed when she saw the child fall.* **Shriek** suggests a more high-pitched, wild, hair-raising and back-tingling cry, expressing extreme terror, horror, agony, or uncontrolled rage or laughter: *The prisoner shrieked when he was tortured.*

scream·er (skrē′mər), *n.* **1.** a person or thing that screams. **2.** any of a group of aquatic South American birds that are about the size of a swan and have a loud cry. Screamers have long unwebbed toes, sharp spurs on the wings and a layer of air-filled cells under the skin. **3. a.** a headline in very large type across the page. **b.** an exclamation point. **4.** *Slang.* **a.** an exceptional person, animal, or thing: *[Her] whirlwind tour of the dress racks was punctuated by such remarks as "That's a screamer" . . . while she discarded dresses of overbold and too-subtle patterns* (New York Times). **b.** a very thrilling or funny story. **5.** *Slang.* **a.** a very long shot in golf. **b.** a hard-hit ball in baseball: *to hit a screamer deep to the outfield.*

scream·ing (skrē′ming), *adj.* **1.** that screams; sounding shrilly: *High the screaming fife replies* (A.E. Housman). **2.** calling forth screams of laughter: *a screaming farce, a screaming joke.* **3.** startling: *screaming headlines, screaming colors.*

scream·ing·ly (skrē′ming lē), *adv.* **1.** in a screaming tone. **2.** so as to call forth screams.

screaming mee·mies (mē′mēz), *U.S. Slang.* extreme nervousness or hysteria, due to such causes as excessive drinking, acute anxiety, etc.; jitters: *So the hero promptly comes down with pneumonia, while the heroine gets the screaming meemies and tries to drown herself* (Time).

scream·y (skrē′mē), *adj.,* **scream·i·er, scream·i·est.** *Informal.* **1.** inclined to scream: *The crew . . . will have been selected with meticulous care to exclude screamy or jittery types* (Time). **2.** screaming: *screamy songs, screamy coloring.*

scree (skrē), *n.* a steep mass of loose rocky fragments lying at the base of a cliff or on the side of a mountain; talus. [< *screes,* plural, probably spelling for earlier *screthes* < Scandinavian (compare Old Icelandic *skrithna* landslide, related to *skrītha* to slide)]

screech (skrēch), *v.i., v.t., n.* scream; shriek: *"Help! help!" she screeched. The woman's screeches brought the police.* [apparently alteration of Middle English *scritchen;* perhaps imitative] —**screech′er,** *n.* —**screech′·ing·ly,** *adv.*

screech owl, 1. any of a group of small, gray or reddish-brown American owls with hornlike tufts of feathers and a long, quavering cry rather than a hoot. **2.** any owl that screeches, as distinguished from one that hoots. **3.** *British.* the barn owl. It has a very shrill, explosive cry.

Screech Owl (def. 1) (about 9 in. long)

screech·y (skrē′chē), *adj.,* **screech·i·er, screech·i·est. 1.** screeching: . . . *a shrill, screechy voice* (W. H. Hudson). **2.** given to screeching: *a screechy woman.*

screed (skrēd), *n.* **1. a.** a long speech or writing; harangue; tirade. **b.** a long roll or list. **2.** a strip of plaster (or wood) of the proper thickness, applied to the wall as a guide in plastering. **3.** *Dialect.* **a.** a fragment; shred. **b.** a torn piece of some cloth. **c.** a bordering strip; edging. **4.** *Scottish.* **a.** a sound as of the tearing of cloth. **b.** a rent; tear. **5.** *Obsolete.* a drinking bout.

—*v.t., v.i. Dialect.* to shred; tear; rip.

[< variant of Old English *scrēade* shred; influenced by Scandinavian words beginning with *sk-*]

screen (skrēn), *n.* **1. a.** a covered frame that hides, protects, or separates: *a fire screen, a folding screen.* **b.** wires woven together with small openings in between, used as a protection: *We have screens on our windows to keep out the flies.* **c.** an ornamental partition. **2.** anything like a screen: *A screen of trees hides our house from the road. An impenetrable screen of secrecy . . .* (William

De Morgan). **3.** a surface on which motion pictures, etc., are shown. **4.** motion pictures; motion-picture industry; films. **5.** a sieve for sifting sand, gravel, coal, seed, etc. **6.** a body of soldiers detached toward the enemy to protect an army. **7.** an escort of destroyers, etc., to protect battleships, aircraft carriers, merchant convoys, etc., as against submarine attack. **8.** *Physics.* a barrier against some special form of energy. **9.** (in photoengraving) a transparent plate with fine lines that cross at right angles, used to produce the minute dots in halftones.

—*v.t.* **1. a.** to shelter, protect, or hide with or as if with a screen: *She screened her face from the fire with a fan.* **b.** to save from danger, punishment, or exposure; shield: *The mother tried to screen her guilty son. Great exertions were made to screen him from justice, but in vain* (Washington Irving). **2. a.** to show (a motion picture) on a screen: *See the film of this adventurous journey, now being screened at main cinemas throughout South Africa* (Cape Times). **b.** to adapt (a story, etc.) for reproduction as a motion picture. **c.** to photograph with a motion-picture camera. **3. a.** to sift with a screen: *to screen sand.* **b.** to test to sort out the good from the bad: *He said that the Government should have screened vaccine batches more carefully* (New York Times). **c.** to test the fitness of (persons) for a job: *Many government agencies screen their employees for loyalty.* **4.** to print with a screen or in the silk-screen process: [*It*] *is perhaps the handsomest paper of the lot, and certainly the most meticulously screened* (New Yorker). —*v.i.* to be suitable for reproducing on a motion-picture screen.

[< Old French *escren;* origin uncertain] —**screen′er,** *n.* —**screen′like′,** *adj.*

—**Syn.** *n.* **1. a.** shield, protection, fender.

screen·a·ble (skrē′nə bəl), *adj.* that can be screened.

screen grid, an electrode placed between the control grid and the plate of certain vacuum tubes to reduce capacitance between the electrodes.

screen·ing (skrē′ning), *n.* a fine wire mesh for making screens, filters, etc.

screenings, matter separated out by sifting through a sieve or screen.

screen·land (skrēn′land′), *n.* filmland.

screen memory, *Psychoanalysis.* a minor or trivial memory of childhood which conceals and helps to keep repressed a more important and disturbing recollection.

screen·o (skrē′nō), *n.* a form of bingo originally played in movie houses.

screen pass, *Football.* a forward pass in which the offensive linemen form a protective screen in front of the receiver.

screen·play (skrēn′plā′), *n.* a motion-picture story in manuscript form, including the dialogue, descriptions of scenes, action, camera directions, etc.; a scenario with dialogue.

screen-print (skrēn′print′), *v.t.* to print with a screen or in the silk-screen process: *These designs . . . can also be screen-printed on . . . any of several fabrics* (New Yorker).

screen test, a test of how an actor performs or looks in a motion picture.

screen-test (skrēn′test′), *v.t.* to put (an actor) to a screen test: *The producer screen-tested her and gave her a small romantic role* (Newsweek).

screen·wip·er (skrēn′wī′pər), *n. British.* windshield wiper.

screen·writ·er (skrēn′rī′tər), *n.* a person who writes screenplays.

screw (skrü), *n.* **1.** a kind of nail, with a ridge twisted evenly around its length and often a groove across the head: *Turn the screw to the right to tighten it.* **2. a.** a cylinder with a ridge winding around it; external screw. **b.** the part into which this cylinder fits and advances; internal screw. **3.** anything that turns like a screw or looks like one, such as a corkscrew or the boring part of a gimlet. **4. a.** a turn of a screw; screwing motion. **b.** a twist or turn such as that applied to a screw: *Strained to the last screw he can bear . . .* (William Cowper). **5.** a contortion, as of the body or face: *The Englishman . . . listened to them all with a certain screw of the mouth, expressive of incredulity* (Washington Irving). **6.** a propeller that moves a boat. **7. a.** a very stingy person; miser. **b.** a person who drives a sharp bargain: *He's a terrible screw at a bargain* (Harriet Beecher Stowe). **8.** *Especially British.* a small amount of tobacco, snuff, salt, etc., wrapped up in a twist of paper. **9.** a broken-down horse. **10.** *Especially British Slang.* salary; wages: *I shall have something left out of this week's screw* (Leonard Merrick). **11.** *Slang.* a guard in a prison. **12.** a former instrument of torture for compressing the thumbs; thumbscrew.

Screws (def. 1) From left to right: oval, round, and flat heads

a screw loose, something out of order: *There's a screw loose in your affairs* (Dickens).

have a screw loose, *Slang.* to be crazy or eccentric: *When he came across a person who was "limited intellectually" he normally referred to him as "having a screw loose"* (London Times).

put the screws on, to use pressure or force to get something: *Love strains the heartstrings of the human race, and not unfrequently puts the screws on so hard as to snap them asunder* (E.G. Paige).

—*v.t.* **1.** to turn as one turns a screw; twist: *Screw the lid on the jar.* **2. a.** to fasten or tighten with a screw or screws: *to screw hinges to a door.* **b.** to work (a screw) by turning. **3.** to force, press, or stretch tight by using screws, pegs, etc.: *to screw the strings of a guitar.* **4. a.** to force to do something. **b.** to force (prices) down. **c.** to force (a seller) to lower his price. **d.** to force people to tell or give up (something): *to screw information or money out of a person.* **5.** to gather for an effort: *He finally screwed up enough courage to try to dive.* **6.** to wind; twist; contort: *His face was screwed up with fear.* —*v.i.* **1.** to turn like a screw. **2.** to be fitted for being put together or taken apart by a screw or screws. **3. a.** to turn with a twisting motion; wind. **b.** to become twisted or turned. **4.** to force a person to tell or give up something.

screw up, *Slang.* to make a mess of; do or get all wrong; foul up: *The film, like the play, is a heavyweight contest with a couple of bantamweights thrown into the ring to screw things up* (Manchester Guardian Weekly).

[< Old French *escroue* nut, screw, perhaps < Latin *scrōfa* sow[2] (in Medieval Latin, engine for undermining walls)] —**screw′er,** *n.*

screw auger, an auger with a spiral shank.

screw·ball (skrü′bôl′), *n.* **1.** *Slang.* an eccentric person. **2.** *Baseball.* a pitch thrown with a break or spin opposite to that of a curve. —*adj. Slang.* eccentric; erratic.

screw bean, 1. a tree of the pea family, growing in the southwestern United States and in Mexico, and having twisted pods that are used as fodder; tornillo. **2.** the pod.

screw cap, a threaded cap or cover for a jar, pipe, etc.

screw·drive (skrü′drīv′), *v.t.,* **-drove, -driv·en, -driv·ing.** to drive in with or as if with a screwdriver: *He stared at me for some moments fixedly as though he would screwdrive his gaze through my brain* (Clark Russell).

screw·driv·en (skrü′driv′ən), *adj.* driven by a screw propeller: *The "Great Britain" . . . was then the largest ship afloat, the first iron-built screwdriven ship to cross the Atlantic* (London Times).

screw·driv·er (skrü′drī′vər), *n.* **1.** a tool for putting in or taking out screws by turning them. **2.** a drink made of vodka and orange juice.

screwed (skrüd), *adj.* **1.** fastened or furnished with screws. **2.** having threads, like those of a screw. **3.** Also, **screwed up.** twisted round; contorted. **4.** *Especially British Slang.* drunk; intoxicated.

screw eye, a screw with a head shaped like a loop.

screw·head (skrü′hed′), *n.* the upper end of a screw, into which the screwdriver is fitted for turning.

screw hook, a screw with a head shaped like a hook.

screw jack, a jackscrew.

screw·loose (skrü′lüs′), *Slang.* —*adj.* very eccentric. —*n.* a screwloose person.

screw·man (skrü′man′), *n., pl.* **-men.** *U.S.* a stevedore who stows compressed cotton bales in the hold of a vessel.

screw pine, any of a group of tropical plants found chiefly in the Malay Archipelago and Pacific islands, having tufts or crowns of long, tough, prickly leaves, strong aerial roots, and a roundish, edible fruit; pandanus.

screw propeller, a revolving hub with radiating blades for propelling a steamship, aircraft, etc.: *Screw propellers . . . were first used on ocean-going ships in 1839* (Beauchamp, Mayfield, and West).

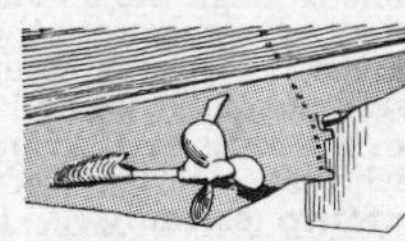

Screw Propeller on ocean liner

screw thread, 1. the spiral ridge of a screw. **2.** one complete turn of the thread of a screw, as a unit of length of a screw's axis.

screw·worm (skrü′wėrm′), *n.* the larva of the screwworm fly.

screwworm fly, a blowfly that deposits its eggs in the sores of animals, the eggs developing into tiny larvae which eat into the wound. The screwworm fly injures and kills cattle and other livestock in the southern and southwestern United States.

screw·y (skrü′ē), *adj.,* **screw·i·er, screw·i·est.** *Slang.* very odd or peculiar: *a screwy person, screwy weather.*

scrib·al (skrī′bəl), *adj.* **1.** of or having to do with a scribe. **2.** made by a scribe or copyist: *a scribal error.*

scrib·ble[1] (skrib′əl), *v.,* **-bled, -bling,** *n.* —*v.t.* **1.** to write or draw carelessly or hastily: *to scribble verses.* **2.** to write in an untidy or illegible hand: *to scribble a note.* **3.** to cover or fill with meaningless scrawls, sloppy writing, worthless matter, etc.: *walls scribbled over with names.* —*v.i.* **1.** to write or draw carelessly or hastily: *. . . some poor devil in Grub Street scribbling for his dinner* (Robert Louis Stevenson). *Another damned thick square book! Always scribble, scribble, scribble! Eh, Mr. Gibbon?* (William Henry, Duke of Gloucester). **2.** to make meaningless marks.

—*n.* **1.** something scribbled. **2.** hurried or irregular marks: *Did you ever behold such a vile scribble as I write?* (Hawthorne).

[< Medieval Latin *scribillare,* ultimately < Latin *scrībere* to write]

scrib·ble[2] (skrib′əl), *v.t.,* **-bled, -bling.** to comb or tease coarsely, as wool. [probably < Low German (compare German *schrubbeln*)]

scrib·bler (skrib′lər), *n.* **1.** a person who scribbles. **2.** an author of little or no importance.

scrib·bling (skrib′ling), *n.* **1.** the act of a person who scribbles: *. . . the insatiate itch of scribbling* (William Gifford). **2.** a scribble; scrawl.

scribe (skrīb), *n., v.,* **scribed, scrib·ing.** —*n.* **1.** a person whose occupation is writing: *Before the invention of printing there were many scribes.* **2.** a member of the class of professional interpreters of the Jewish law. **3.** any of various officials of ancient or former times who performed clerical or secretarial duties. **4.** a writer; author (often used humorously). **5.** a marking tool; scriber. **6.** *Archaic.* a person skilled in penmanship.

—*v.t.* **1.** to mark or cut with something sharp. **2.** *Archaic.* to write down; inscribe. —*v.i.* **1.** to use a scriber to mark lines. **2.** to write. [< Latin *scrība* < *scrībere* to write]

scrib·er (skrī′bər), *n.* **1.** a pointed tool for marking or cutting lines on wood, stone, metal, etc. **2.** a person who scribes.

scrieve (skrēv), *v.i.,* **scrieved, scriev·ing.** *Scottish.* to move or glide along swiftly. [apparently < Scandinavian (compare Old Icelandic *skrefa* to stride)]

scrim (skrim), *n.* a thin, loosely woven cotton or linen material, used for window curtains, etc. [origin unknown]

scrim·mage (skrim′ij), *n., v.* **-maged, -mag·ing.** —*n.* **1.** a rough fight or struggle: *. . . one of those chums that stand up for a fellow in a scrimmage and look after him should he be hurt* (Joseph Conrad). **2. a.** a play in football that takes place when the two teams are lined up and the ball is snapped back. **b.** playing football for practice: *an hour of scrimmage between the first and second teams.*

—*v.i.* **1.** to take part in a rough fight or struggle. **2.** to take part in a scrimmage in football. **3.** to bustle about, especially in search of something. —*v.t.* to oppose in football practice: *to scrimmage the second team.* Also, *especially British,* **scrummage.** [variant of *skirmish*]

scrimmage line, *Football.* an imaginary line through the forward end of the football and running across the field; line of scrimmage. A player cannot cross the line of scrimmage before a play starts.

scrim·mag·er (skrim′ə jər), *n.* a person who takes part in a scrimmage.

scrimp (skrimp), *v.t.* **1.** to be sparing of; use too little of. **2.** to treat stingily or very economically. —*v.i.* to be very economical; stint; skimp: *Many parents have to scrimp to keep their children in college. To scrimp on the Government's spending is to put a crimp in the economy* (Wall Street Journal).
—*adj.* scanty; meager; deficient.
—*n. Informal.* a miser. [origin uncertain]

scrimp·i·ly (skrim′pə lē), *adv.* in a scrimpy manner.

scrimp·i·ness (skrim′pē nis), *n.* scrimpy quality; meagerness.

scrimp·y (skrim′pē), *adj.,* **scrimp·i·er, scrimp·i·est.** too small; too little; scanty; meager.

scrim·shank (skrim′shangk′), *v.i. British Military Slang.* to shirk duty. [origin unknown] —**scrim′shank′er,** *n.*

scrim·shaw (skrim′shô′), *n.* **1.** the handicrafts practiced by sailors as a pastime during long whaling or other voyages: *In an art form known as scrimshaw, a nineteenth century whaler has carved his memories on a horn cup* (Maclean's). **2.** the products of these, as small manufactured articles, or carvings on bone, shells, etc.
—*v.t.* to decorate or produce as scrimshaw.
—*v.i.* to do scrimshaw work.
[American English; origin unknown]

scrip[1] (skrip), *n.* **1.** a receipt, certificate, or other document showing a right to something. **2. a.** a certificate entitling the holder to a fraction of a share of stock. **b.** Also, **scrip dividend.** a stock dividend in the form of a note payable at a later date. **3.** *U.S.* **a.** paper money in amounts of less than a dollar, formerly issued in the United States. **b.** any of various other paper currencies, as those issued by an occupying power during or after a war, by a government in time of emergency, etc.: . . . *the mine companies began paying the miners half in gold and half in scrip, or checks with no redemption date* (World Book Encyclopedia). **c.** a piece of such currency. **3.** *Obsolete.* a small scrap of writing; writing. [variant of *script*]

scrip[2] (skrip), *n. Archaic.* a small bag. [probably < Scandinavian (compare Old Icelandic *skreppa*)]

Scrip., Scripture.

script (skript), *n.* **1. a.** written letters, figures, signs, etc.; handwriting. **b.** a kind of writing; system of alphabetical or other written characters: *German script.* **2.** any of various styles of type that look like handwriting. **3. a.** the manuscript of a play or actor's part: . . . *to work over a script that some lonely playwright has put together* (New Yorker). **b.** manuscript used in making a motion picture; screenplay. **c.** manuscript used in broadcasting. **4.** *Law.* an original or principal document, as distinguished from a copy, duplicate, etc. **5.** *Archaic.* something written; a piece of writing.
—*v.t.* **1.** to write a script for. **2.** to turn into a script: *Famous and familiar stories are being scripted for some major TV shows* (Maclean's). —*v.i.* to write radio or television programs or screenplays.
[< Latin *scrīptum,* (originally) neuter past participle of *scrībere* write. Compare SHRIFT, SCREED.]

Script., Scripture.

script editor, an editor who corrects and prepares scripts for radio or television.

script·er (skrip′tər), *n. U.S. Informal.* a scriptwriter. [< *script* + *-er*[1]]

scrip·to·ri·al (skrip tôr′ē əl, -tōr′-), *adj.* of, having to do with, or using script.

scrip·to·ri·um (skrip tôr′ē əm, -tōr′-), *n., pl.* **-to·ri·ums, -to·ri·a** (-tôr′ē ə, -tōr′-). a writing room, especially a room in a monastery set apart for writing or copying manuscripts: . . . *the very scriptorium where the ink was set to the parchment* (Atlantic). [< Late Latin *scriptorium,* (originally) neuter adjective < Latin *scrībere* write]

scrip·tur·al (skrip′chər əl), *adj.* **1.** Also, **Scriptural. a.** of, in, or from the Scriptures. **b.** according to the Scriptures; based on the Scriptures. **2.** of or having to do with writing. —**scrip′tur·al·ness,** *n.*

scrip·tur·al·ism (skrip′chər ə liz′əm), *n.* literal adherence to the Scriptures.

scrip·tur·al·ist (skrip′chər ə list), *n.* **1.** a person who adheres literally to the Scriptures. **2.** a person well acquainted with the Scriptures.

scrip·tur·al·ly (skrip′chər ə lē), *adv.* in a scriptural manner; in accordance with the Scriptures.

Scrip·ture (skrip′chər), *n.* **1.** the Bible. **2.** a particular passage or text of the Bible. *Abbr.:* Script.
the Scriptures or **the Holy Scriptures,** the Bible: *I would teach the knowledge of the Scriptures only* (Joseph Priestley).
[< Late Latin *Scrīptūra* < Latin *scrīptūra* a writing < *scrībere* write]

scrip·ture (skrip′chər), *n.* **1.** any sacred writing: *Most men do not know that any nation but the Hebrews have had a scripture* (Thoreau). **2.** *Archaic.* an inscription or superscription. **3.** *Archaic.* a written record; writing. [< *Scripture*]

scrip·tured (skrip′chərd), *adj.* **1.** covered with writing. **2.** *Obsolete.* **a.** well acquainted with the Scriptures. **b.** decreed by the Scriptures.

scrip·tur·ist (skrip′chər ist), *n.* scripturalist.

script·writ·er (skript′rī′tər), *n.* a person who writes scripts.

scri·vel·lo (skri vel′ō), *n., pl.* **-vel·loes** or **-vel·los.** a small elephant's tusk, used for making billiard balls. [< Portuguese *escrevelho*]

scriv·en (skriv′ən), *v.t., v.i. Archaic.* to write or work as a scrivener. [back formation < *scrivener*]

scrive·ner (skriv′nər), *n.* **1.** *Archaic.* **a.** a public writer of letters or documents for others; clerk: . . . *a notched and cropt scrivener . . . that sucks his substance . . . through a quill* (Charles Lamb). **b.** a notary. **2.** any professional writer (used in an unfriendly way). [< obsolete *scrivein* scrivener < Old French *escrivein* < Vulgar Latin *scrībānus* < Latin *scrība* scribe < *scrībere* write]

scro·bic·u·late (skrō bik′yə lit, -lāt), *adj.* furrowed or pitted. [< New Latin *scrobicula* a small pit (< Latin *scrobiculus* (diminutive) < *scrobis, -is* ditch, trench) + English *-ate*[1]]

scrod (skrod), *n. U.S.* **1.** a young codfish, especially one that is cut up or filleted for cooking. **2.** a piece of such a cod: *to order broiled scrod.* [American English; origin unknown]

scrof·u·la (skrof′yə lə), *n.* a form of tuberculosis characterized by the enlargement of the lymphatic glands, especially those in the neck: . . . *sufferers applying to be touched by King Charles II for scrofula—"king's evil"* (London Times). [< Medieval Latin *scrofula* < Latin *scrōfulae,* plural < *scrōfa* a sow (reason for use is unknown)]

scrof·u·la·root (skrof′yə lə rüt′, -rủt′), *n.* the dogtooth violet.

scrof·u·la·weed (skrof′yə lə wēd′), *n.* the rattlesnake plantain.

scrof·u·lism (skrof′yə liz əm), *n.* the state of being scrofulous.

scrof·u·lo·sis (skrof′yə lō′sis), *n.* scrofulism.

scrof·u·lous (skrof′yə ləs), *adj.* **1.** of or having to do with scrofula: *He suffered from a scrofulous ear complaint* (Newsweek). **2.** like scrofula. **3.** having scrofula. **4.** (of literature, etc.) morally corrupt. —**scrof′u·lous·ly,** *adv.* —**scrof′u·lous·ness,** *n.*

scrog (skrog), *n. Scottish.* **1.** a stunted bush. **2.** a branch broken from a tree.
scrogs, thicket; underbrush: *I have gathered nuts from the scrogs of Tynron* (Blackwood's Magazine).
[compare dialectal *scrag* tree stump; origin uncertain]

scrog·gy (skrog′ē), *adj.,* **-gi·er, -gi·est.** *Scottish.* **1.** full of scrogs. **2.** stunted.

scroll (skrōl), *n.* **1. a.** a roll of parchment or paper, especially one with writing on it: *He slowly unrolled the scroll as he read from it.* **b.** a list of names, events, etc.; roll; schedule: *to be entered in the scrolls of history.* **2.** an ornament resembling a partly unrolled sheet of paper, or having a spiral or coiled form, as the spiral ornaments in the Ionic and Corinthian capitals or the curved head of a violin, cello, etc. **3.** *Obsolete.* **a.** a piece of writing, as a letter. **b.** a draft or copy of a letter, etc.
—*v.t.* **1.** to write down on a scroll; inscribe. **2.** to form into a scroll. **3.** to ornament with scrolls.
[alteration (influenced by *roll*) of Middle English *scrow* < Anglo-French *escrowe,* Old French *escroue* a scrap, perhaps < Germanic (compare Old High German *scrōt*)] —**scroll′-like′,** *adj.*

Scroll (def. 1a)

scroll·er·y (skrō′lər ē, skrōl′rē), *n.* scrollwork.

scroll painting, 1. the ancient Chinese and Japanese art of painting figures and scenes on scrolls, usually telling a story. **2.** a painting of this kind: *Japanese scroll paintings are done on long strips of paper, usually about 12 inches high, which are rolled from one spindle to another* (Atlantic).

scroll saw, a very narrow saw for cutting thin wood in curved or ornamental patterns.

scroll·work (skrōl′wėrk′), *n.* **1.** decorative work in which scrolls are much used. **2.** ornamental work cut with a scroll saw.

scrooch (skrüch), *v.i. Dialect.* to crouch; cower: *Scrooch down and see if you can't wriggle down underneath* (J.C. Lincoln).

scrooge (skrüj), *v.t., v.i.,* **scrooged, scroog·ing,** *n.* scrouge.

Scrooge (skrüj), *n.* **1.** the embittered old miser in Charles Dickens' story *"A Christmas Carol": Exhibits . . . showed . . . that ugly office furniture is as out of date as Scrooge* (New York Times). **2.** Usually, **scrooge.** any greedy and stingy person; miser: . . . *scrooges and sourpusses whose blood rarely flows and then at subnormal temperatures* (Wall Street Journal).

scroop (skrüp), *Dialect.* —*v.i.* to grate; creak; squeak. —*n.* a grating, creaking, or squeaking noise. [probably imitative]

scroph·u·lar·i·a·ceous (skrof′yə lãr′ē ā′shəs), *adj.* belonging to the figwort family: *Snapdragon and foxglove are scrophulariaceous plants.* [< New Latin *Scrophularia* the typical genus (< *scrophula* < Medieval Latin *scrofula;* see SCROFULA) + English *-aceous*]

scro·tal (skrō′təl), *adj.* of or having to do with the scrotum.

scro·tum (skrō′təm), *n., pl.* **-ta** (-tə), **-tums.** the pouch that contains the testicles. [< Latin *scrōtum*]

scrouge (skrüj, skrouj), *v.,* **scrouged, scroug·ing,** *n. Informal.* —*v.t., v.i.* to squeeze; press; crowd: . . . *oysters grew faster than they did all scrouged together on natural beds* (New Yorker). —*n.* a crowd. Also, **scrooge.** [apparently alteration of earlier *scruze* squeeze, press together; origin uncertain]

scroug·er (skrü′jər), *n. U.S. Slang.* **1.** a person who scrouges. **2.** anything exceptional in size, capacity, etc.; whopper.

scrounge (skrounj), *v.,* **scrounged, scroung·ing.** *Slang.* —*v.t.* **1.** to take dishonestly; pilfer. **2.** to beg; get by begging: *to scrounge a meal. I scrounged an umbrella and Margaret and I walked home together in the rain* (Al Schacht). —*v.i.* **1.** to search about for what one can find: *He scrounged around in junk shops and acquired . . . the French mantel clock* (Atlantic). **2.** to sponge (on). [apparently alteration of dialectal *scrunge* pilfer, steal]

scroung·er (skroun′jər), *n. Slang.* a person who begs or cadges; sponger.

scroyle (skroil), *n. Obsolete.* a rascal.

scrub[1] (skrub), *v.,* **scrubbed, scrub·bing,** *n.* —*v.t.* **1.** to rub hard; wash or clean by rubbing: *to scrub dirty clothes. It was the hour when cooks and doormen walk dogs, and when porters scrub the lobby floor mats with soap and water* (New Yorker). **2.** to remove impurities from (a gas). **3.** *U.S. Slang.* to cancel: *The design was scrubbed at the drawing-board stage as being impractical.* —*v.i.* to wash.
—*n.* a scrubbing: *Give your hands a good scrub before dinner.*
[perhaps < Middle Dutch *schrubben* or < Scandinavian (compare Norwegian dialectal *skrubba*)]

scrub[2] (skrub), *n.* **1. a.** low, stunted trees or shrubs: *Sometimes the Colonel and I would go wandering through the trenches, which are gradually disappearing under a tangle of scrub* (New Yorker). **b.** land overgrown with stunted trees or shrubs, as the Australian bush. **2. a.** anything small, or below the usual size: *He is a little scrub of a man.* **b.** a steer, horse, etc., of mixed stock, often inferior in size or disposition to the purebred. **c.** a mean, insignificant person. **3.** a person who has to work hard or do menial work to make a living; drudge. **4.** a player not on the regular team, etc.

scrubs, a team of inferior or substitute players: *His brother made the varsity, but he played with the scrubs.*

—*adj.* **1.** small; poor; inferior: *A scrub wagon team of four . . . unkempt, dejected, and vicious-looking broncos* (Theodore Roosevelt). **2.** *Sports.* **a.** made up of inferior, substitute, or untrained players: *a scrub ball team.* **b.** of, having to do with, or for such players: *a scrub game, scrub practice.*

[< Scandinavian (compare Middle Danish *skrubbe* brushwood)]

scrub·ba·ble (skrub′ə bəl), *adj.* that can be scrubbed or will not be injured by scrubbing: *A new flat wall paint that is odorless, scrubbable, and tough enough to resist chipping has been developed* (Wall Street Journal).

scrub·bed (skrub′id), *adj. Archaic.* stunted; scrubby.

scrub·ber (skrub′ər), *n.* **1.** a person who scrubs. **2.** a scrubbing brush: *a back scrubber.* **3.** an apparatus for washing gas.

scrub·bi·ness (skrub′ē nis), *n.* scrubby quality or condition.

scrub·bing brush (skrub′ing), a brush with hard bristles for scrubbing.

scrub·bird (skrub′bėrd′), *n.* either of two wrenlike perching birds that live in the dense scrub of Australia. One kind is nearly extinct.

scrub brush, a scrubbing brush: *Cleaning an industrial building used to mean an old lady with a scrub brush and soap* (Wall Street Journal).

scrub·by (skrub′ē), *adj.,* **-bi·er, -bi·est. 1.** below the usual size; low; stunted; small: *a scrubby tree.* **2.** covered with scrub: *scrubby land.* **3.** shabby; mean: . . . *a scrubby loft in the West Thirties full of noise and commotion* (New Yorker). —**Syn. 1.** undersized.

scrub fowl, scrub hen.

scrub hen, the Australian mound builder or megapode, which lives in the thick underbrush or scrub.

scrub jay, the Florida jay.

scrub·land (skrub′land′), *n.* land overgrown with scrub: *Tractors have been used to clear scrubland for cultivation* (London Times).

scrub nurse, a nurse in charge of the instruments in the operating room of a hospital: *The senior scrub nurse knew the senior surgeon's methods so well that he rarely had to ask for an instrument* (Time).

scrub oak, any of various small, scrubby oaks growing in sandy or barren soil, as the bur oak.

scrub pine, any of various low pines that commonly grow in poor or sandy soil, especially: **a.** a pine found from New York to Georgia, usually small and straggly but reaching a height of 100 feet in the western part of its range. **b.** the Pacific Coast variety of the lodgepole pine.

scrubs (skrubz), *n.pl.* See under **scrub**², *n.*

scrub typhus, a disease with fever, inflammation of the lymph glands, and neuritis. It is caused by a rickettsia that is transmitted by certain chiggers.

scrub·wom·an (skrub′wům′ən), *n., pl.* **-wom·en.** a cleaning woman.

scrub wren, a small, insect-eating passerine bird related to the thrush, common in parts of Australia.

scruff (skruf), *n.* the skin at the back of the neck; back of the neck: *to pick up a cat by the scruff of the neck.* Also, **scuff.** [perhaps alteration of *scuff;* origin uncertain]

➔ See **nape** for usage note.

scruf·fi·ness (skruf′ē nis), *n.* **1.** scruffy quality or condition; scaliness. **2.** meanness; shabbiness.

scruf·fle (skruf′əl), *v.i., v.t.,* **-fled, -fling,** *n. British Dialect.* scuffle.

scruf·fler (skruf′lər), *n. British Dialect.* scuffler.

scruf·fy (scruf′ē), *adj.,* **-fi·er, -fi·est. 1.** *Especially British.* covered with dandruff; scaly: *A scruffy, somewhat aggressively-inclined individual, aged sixteen . . .* (Punch). **2.** mean; shabby: *a scruffy lie. In all this ancient pomp, there was one concession to scruffy present reality* (Time).

scrum (skrum), *n. British.* a scrummage in Rugby football: *Sykes went over for a try from a scrum five yards from the Rhodesian line* (London Times). [short for *scrummage*]

scrum-half (skrum′haf′, -häf′), *n., pl.* **-halves.** *Rugby.* the halfback who rolls the ball into scrummage: *He had the figure of a scrum-half and the fluency of a Parliamentary candidate* (Sunday Times).

scrum·mage (skrum′ij), *n., v.,* **-maged, -mag·ing.** *British.* —*n.* a formation in Rugby used to begin play again after it has been stopped, in which the ball is rolled between two lines of no more than three players each, each of whom tries to kick the ball to other players lined up in back of him: *The early play was mainly a hard slog of scrummage, lineout, and maul* (London Times). —*v.i.* to take part in a scrummage. —*v.t.* to begin play by rolling (the ball) in a scrummage. [variant of *scrimmage*]

scrum·mag·er (skrum′ə jər), *n. British.* a person who takes part in a scrummage.

scrump·tious (skrump′shəs), *adj. Slang.* elegant; first-rate, splendid: *Probably the lumber-yard isn't as scrumptious as all these Greek temples* (Sinclair Lewis). [American English; origin uncertain]

scrunch (skrunch), *v.t., v.i.* to crunch; crush; crumple; squeeze: *Every part of it . . . may be profitably scrunched between molars* (New Yorker). *Don't scrunch up like that, Huckleberry—set up straight* (Mark Twain). —*n.* **1.** the noise made by scrunching. **2.** an act of scrunching. [perhaps < *crunch*]

scru·ple (skrü′pəl), *n., v.,* **-pled, -pling.** —*n.* **1. a.** a feeling of uneasiness that keeps a person from doing something; uneasiness affecting the conscience: *to have scruples about gambling.* **b.** a feeling of doubt about what one ought to do; hesitation to do something: *No scruple of caution ever holds him back from prompt action.* **2.** a weight of 20 grains. Three scruples make 1 dram. **3. a.** an ancient Roman weight equal to 1/24 ounce. **b.** an ancient Roman coin. Its weight in gold determined its value. **4.** a very small amount: . . . *the smallest scruple of her excellence* (Shakespeare).

make scruple, to hesitate or be reluctant, especially because of conscientiousness: *She made no scruple of oversetting all human institutions* (Hawthorne).

—*v.i.* to hesitate or be unwilling (to do something): *A dishonest man does not scruple to deceive others. As a Parliamentarian he has never scrupled to use any weapon which comes to hand* (Harper's). —*v.t.* to have or make scruples about.

[< Latin *scrūpulus* a feeling of uneasiness (diminutive) < *scrūpus* uneasiness, anxiety such as the pricking of conscience like the pricking of a sharp stone; (originally) sharp stone]

scru·pu·los·i·ty (skrü′pyə los′ə tē), *n., pl.* **-ties. 1.** a being scrupulous; strict regard for what is right; scrupulous care: *Albert, with characteristic scrupulosity, attempted to thread his way through the complicated labyrinth of European diplomacy . . .* (Lytton Strachey). **2.** an instance of this.

scru·pu·lous (skrü′pyə ləs), *adj.* **1.** having or showing a strict regard for what is right: *a scrupulous man, scrupulous honesty.* **2.** attending thoroughly to details; very careful: *A soldier must pay scrupulous attention to orders.* [< Latin *scrūpulus* (see SCRUPLE) + English *-ous*] —**scru′pu·lous·ly,** *adv.* —**scru′pu·lous·ness,** *n.*

—**Syn. 1.** conscientious. **2. Scrupulous, punctilious** mean very careful and exact. **Scrupulous** implies attending thoroughly to details and following strictly what one knows is right or true: *She takes scrupulous care of the children's health.* **Punctilious** emphasizes paying special and often excessive attention to fine points of laws, rules, and requirements for conduct, behavior, or performance of duties: *He is punctilious in returning borrowed books.*

scru·ta·ble (skrü′tə bəl), *adj.* that can be penetrated or understood by investigation. [< Latin *scrūtārī* examine + English *-able*]

scru·ta·tor (skrü tā′tər), *n. British.* a person who examines or investigates, especially a scrutineer. [< Latin *scrūtātor* < *scrūtārī* examine]

scru·ti·neer (skrü′tə nir′), *n. British.* a person who inspects and counts election ballots: *Our scrutineers who go home red-eyed every evening . . .* (Cape Times).

scru·ti·nise (skrü′tə nīz), *v.,* **-nised, -nis·ing.** *Especially British.* scrutinize.

scru·ti·nize (skrü′tə nīz), *v.t.,* **-nized, -niz·ing.** to examine closely; inspect carefully: *The jeweler scrutinized the diamond for flaws. But never before have so many citizens been scrutinized with suspicion* (Scientific American). —**scru′ti·niz′ing·ly,** *adv.*

scru·ti·niz·er (skrü′tə nī′zər), *n.* a person who scrutinizes or examines with critical care.

scru·ti·nous (skrü′tə nəs), *adj.* scrutinizing; searching; critical. —**scru′ti·nous·ly,** *adv.*

scru·ti·ny (skrü′tə nē), *n., pl.* **-nies. 1.** a close examination; careful inspection: *His work may look all right, but it will not bear scrutiny.* **2.** a looking searchingly at something; searching gaze: *I observed him throwing a glance of scrutiny over all the passengers* (Charlotte Brontë). **3.** an official examination of the votes cast at an election. [< Late Latin *scrūtinium* < Latin *scrūtārī* to examine, investigate]

scru·to (skrü′tō), *n. Theater.* a trap door or doorway which springs into place after being used for quick appearances and disappearances.

scru·toire (skrü twär′), *n.* escritoire (a desk).

scry (skrī), *v.,* **scried, scry·ing.** —*v.i.* to see images revealing remote future events by looking into a crystal or the like. —*v.t. British Dialect.* to descry; see; perceive. [short for *descry*] —**scry′er,** *n.*

SCS (no periods), Soil Conservation Service.

S. Cu., strato-cumulus.

SCUA (no periods), Suez Canal Users' Association.

scu·ba (skü′bə), *n.* the underwater breathing equipment used by skindivers: *Skindivers who use scuba favor contact [lenses] because spectacles . . . are cumbersome inside a watertight face mask* (Time). —*adj.* having to do with, comprising, or using underwater breathing equipment: *scuba diving, scuba gear, scuba diver.* [< *s*(elf)-*c*(ontained) *u*(nderwater) *b*(reathing) *a*(pparatus)]

Scuba

scud (skud), *v.,* **scud·ded, scud·ding,** *n.* —*v.i.* **1.** to run or move swiftly: *Clouds scudded across the sky driven by high winds. For months, Donald Campbell's 2½-ton turbojet speedboat, Bluebird, has scudded through a series of trial runs* (Newsweek). **2.** *Nautical.* to run before a storm with little or no sail set: *We were scudding before a heavy gale, under bare poles* (Frederick Marryat). —*n.* **1.** a scudding. **2.** clouds or spray driven by the wind, as in a storm at sea: *At 500 feet [altitude] you break out under the dark scud, into a rainy but fairly clear area* (Atlantic). **3.** *Dialect.* **a.** a brief, driving shower of rain or fall of snow. **b.** a sudden gust of wind. **4.** *Scottish.* a slap.

[perhaps variant of *scut,* or < Scandinavian (compare Danish *skyde* shoot, glide)]

scud·der (skud′ər), *n.* a person or thing that scuds.

scu·del·la (skü del′ə), *n.* scodella.

scu·do (skü′dō), *n., pl.* **-di** (-dē). **1.** a former Italian silver coin and money of account, worth about a dollar. **2.** a former gold coin of the same value. [< Italian *scudo* coin marked with a shield; (literally) a shield < Latin *scūtum* shield]

scuff¹ (skuf), *v.i.* to walk without lifting the feet; shuffle: *to scuff through sand, to scuff into a room.* —*v.t.* to wear or injure the surface of by hard use: *to scuff one's shoes.*

—*n.* **1. a.** the act of scuffing. **b.** the noise made by scuffing. **2.** a slipper with only a sole and toe piece: *Travel scuffs of the softest glove leather . . .* (New Yorker). **3.** *Scottish.* a glancing blow.

[perhaps variant of *scuffle,* or perhaps < Scandinavian (compare Swedish *skuffa* shove, push)]

scuff² (skuff), *n.* scruff.

scuf·fle (skuf′əl), *v.,* **-fled, -fling,** *n.* —*v.i.* **1.** to struggle or fight in a rough, confused manner: *Somewhere in the darkness two rats*

scuffled (Graham Greene). **2.** to go or move in hurried confusion: *Drive the populace headlong past it as fast as they can scuffle* (John Ruskin). **3.** to shuffle. *—v.t.* to stir the surface of (land), hoe (a crop), or cut up (weeds) by means of a scuffle hoe: *This land was ploughed deep and ... harrowed and scuffled till there was tilth enough for planting* (London Times).
—n. **1.** a confused, rough struggle or fight: *The mob followed ... a scuffle ensued ...* (Cardinal Newman). **2.** a shuffling: *They could hear a scuffle of feet* (George J. Whyte-Melville). **3.** a scuffle hoe.
[apparently a frequentative form of *scuff*]
—Syn. *n.* **1.** tussle, scrimmage.

scuffle hoe, a hoe which is pushed instead of pulled.

scuf·fler (skuf′lər), *n.* a person or thing that scuffles.

scuff·proof (skuf′prüf′), *adj.* resistant to scuffing: *scuffproof leather.*

scug (skug), *n. British Slang.* an ill-favored, untalented, and unpopular schoolboy.

scul·dud·der·y (skul dud′ər ē), *n. Archaic.* **1.** *U.S.* skulduggery. **2.** *Scottish.* obscenity.

sculk (skulk), *v.i., n.* skulk. **—sculk′er,** *n.*

scull[1] (skul), *n.* **1.** an oar worked with a side twist over the end of a boat to make it go. **2.** one of a pair of oars used, one on each side, by a single rower. **3.** the act of propelling by sculls. **4.** a light racing boat for one or more rowers. **5.** any boat propelled by a scull or sculls. *—v.t.* to propel (a boat) by a scull or sculls. *—v.i.* to scull a boat.
[origin unknown]

Scull[1] **(def. 1)**

scull[2] (skul), *n. Scottish.* a large, shallow basket. [< a Scandinavian word]

scull·er (skul′ər), *n.* **1.** a person who sculls. **2.** a boat propelled by sculling.

scul·ler·y (skul′ər ē, skul′rē), *n., pl.* **-ler·ies,** *adj. —n.* **1.** *Especially British.* a small room where the dirty, rough work of a kitchen is done. **2.** *Obsolete.* **a.** the department of a household that cares for the plates, dishes, and kitchen utensils. **b.** the room or rooms for this department.
—adj. Especially British. of or having to do with a scullery: *a scullery maid, scullery work.*
[< Old French *escuelerie* < *escuelle* dish < Vulgar Latin *scūtella,* for Latin *scutella* (diminutive) < *scutra* platter]

scul·lion (skul′yən), *n. Archaic.* **1.** a servant who does the dirty, rough work in a kitchen: *... to hear the clinking of the plates ... as the scullion rinsed them and put them by* (Samuel Butler). **2.** a low, contemptible person. [< Old French *escouillon, escouvillon* a swab, cloth < *escouve* broom < Latin *scōpa*]

sculp (skulp), *v.t., v.i. Informal.* to carve; engrave; sculpture: *There's some bohemians up that dirt road there. They all sculp or weave or something* (New Yorker). [< Latin *sculpere* carve]

sculp., **1.** sculpsit. **2.** sculptor. **3.** sculptural. **4.** sculpture.

scul·pin (skul′pin), *n.* **1.** any of a group of small fish with large pectoral fins and eyes near the top of a big head. Sculpins are found in salt and fresh water and are not considered edible by most people. **2.** a scorpionfish or rockfish of the southern Californian coast. [perhaps alteration of *scorpene*]

sculps. or **sculpt.,** sculpsit.

sculp·sit (skulp′sit), *Latin.* he or she carved it.

sculpt (skulpt), *Informal. —v.t.* to sculpture: *Michel Daum of France sculpted an abstract seagull in brilliantly clear crystal* (New York Times). *—v.i.* to make sculptures: *Parents .painted, drew and sculpted alongside their grade-school-age children* (Time). [< French *sculpter* < Latin *sculpere* carve]

sculpt., **1.** sculptor. **2.** sculptural. **3.** sculpture.

sculp·tor (skulp′tər), *n.* a person who carves or models figures; artist in sculpture. Sculptors usually make statues of stone, wood, or bronze. [< Latin *sculptor, -ōris,* variant of *scalptor* < *scalpere* to carve]

Sculp·tor (skulp′tər), *n., genitive* **Sculp·to·ris.** a southern constellation near Grus. [short for New Latin (*Apparatus*) *Sculptoris*]

Sculp·to·ris (skulp tôr′is, -tōr′-), *n.* genitive of **Sculptor.**

sculp·tress (skulp′tris), *n.* a woman sculptor.

sculp·tur·al (skulp′chər əl), *adj.* of or having to do with sculpture; like sculpture: *... one rolled-up sleeve baring a sculptural forearm* (Joseph Conrad). **—sculp′tur·al·ly,** *adv.*

sculp·ture (skulp′chər), *n., v.,* **-tured, -tur·ing.** *—n.* **1.** the art of carving or modeling figures. Sculpture includes the cutting of statues from blocks of marble or wood, casting in bronze, and modeling in clay or wax: *Sculpture gives expression to the most prized personality traits ...* (Emory S. Bogardus). **2.** sculptured work: *temples adorned with sculpture.* **3.** a piece of such work: *Most of Stankiewicz's sculptures are extremely funny* (Newsweek).
—v.t. **1.** to carve, model, or cast (a design or figure). **2.** to cover or ornament with sculpture. **3.** *Geology.* to alter the contour of by erosion.
[< Latin *sculptūra,* variant of *scalptūra* < *scalpere* to carve]

sculp·tured (skulp′chərd), *adj.* **1.** carved or molded in sculpture: *Hood and fenders of the highly-styled car are sculptured* (Wall Street Journal). **2.** covered or ornamented with sculpture.

sculp·tur·er (skulp′chər ər), *n. Obsolete.* a person who sculptures; sculptor.

sculp·tur·esque (skulp′chə resk′), *adj.* resembling or suggesting sculpture. **—sculp′tur·esque′ly,** *adv.* **—sculp′tur·esque′ness,** *n.*

scum (skum), *n., v.,* **scummed, scum·ming.** *—n.* **1. a.** a thin layer that rises to the top of a liquid: *Green scum floated on top of the pond. The idea is prevalent that algae, especially those which form a scum on the water, are loathsome or filthy. This is far from the truth* (Fred W. Emerson). **b.** the refuse that rises to the surface of metals in a molten state. **2.** low, worthless people; dregs: *The saloon was filled with the scum of the town. ... rascals, the scum of the earth* (William Godwin).
—v.i. to form scum; become covered with a scum. *—v.t.* **1.** to remove scum from; skim. **2.** to form scum on; cover with scum: *A thick mist scummed the windshields* (Time).
[perhaps < Middle Dutch *schuum,* or Danish *skum*]

scum·ble (skum′bəl), *v.,* **-bled, -bling,** *n. Painting and Drawing. —v.t.* **1.** to soften the effect of (colors or the harder lines), as by overlaying with a thin coat of opaque or semiopaque color, or by spreading the lines. **2.** to produce (an effect) by either or both of these processes. *—n.* **1.** the act or technique of overlaying paint or color. **2.** the effect produced. **3.** the paint or color used.
[perhaps a frequentative form of *scum,* verb]

scum·my (skum′ē), *adj.,* **-mi·er, -mi·est. 1.** consisting of or containing scum: *a scummy pond.* **2.** low; mean; worthless: *a scummy fellow, a scummy trick.*

scun·ner (skun′ər), *n.* **1.** a feeling of disgust or loathing: *Small wonder that I developed a subconscious scunner on philanthropists and all their works* (New Yorker). **2.** an object of disgust. *—v.i., v.t.* to sicken; disgust. [origin unknown]

scup (skup), *n., pl.* **scups** or (*collectively*) **scup.** a narrow, high-backed sea fish used for food, common on the eastern coast of the United States; a variety of porgy. [American English, short for earlier *scuppaug* < Algonkian (Narragansett) *mishcuppauog,* plural of *mishcup*]

scup·per (skup′ər), *n.* an opening in the side of a ship to let water run off the deck: *The fruit fell from his hand. Before it had rolled to the scupper, Able was rising from his chair* (Atlantic). *—v.t. Slang.* to catch by surprise and kill or destroy; overwhelm: *The greater part of our tank force has recently been scuppered* (Atlantic). [origin uncertain]

scup·per·nong (skup′ər nông, -nong), *n.* **1.** a large, yellowish-green grape, a variety of the muscadine or fox grape, grown in the southern United States. **2.** a wine made from these grapes. [American English < *Scuppernong* River, North Carolina, near which the grape was first cultivated]

scup·seat (skup′sēt′), *n.* a wooden seat on which a sailor sits while working aloft where he can obtain no foothold.

scupper shoots, tubes which carry overboard the water from the spar deck.

scur (skėr), *v.* skirr.

scurf (skėrf), *n.* **1.** small scales of dead skin; dandruff. **2.** any scaly matter on a surface. **3.** something no longer useful or essential, that can be sloughed off. [Old English *scurf* < Scandinavian (compare Old Swedish *skurf*)]

scurf·i·ness (skėr′fē nis), *n.* a being scurfy; scurfy condition.

scurf·y (skėr′fē), *adj.,* **scurf·i·er, scurf·i·est. 1.** covered with scurf. **2.** of or like scurf.

scur·rile or **scur·ril** (skėr′əl), *adj. Archaic.* scurrilous. [< Latin *scurrīlis;* see SCURRILOUS]

scur·ril·i·ty (skə ril′ə tē), *n., pl.* **-ties. 1.** coarse joking: *... based on the proposition that millions like to wallow in scurrility* (Time). **2.** indecent abuse. **3.** an indecent or coarse remark.

scur·ri·lous (skėr′ə ləs), *adj.* **1.** coarsely joking; using abusive or derisive language: *a scurrilous political writer.* **2.** abusive and indecent; foul: *scurrilous language. ... so indiscreet as to print scurrilous reflections on the government of neighbouring states* (Benjamin Franklin). [< Latin *scurrīlis* (with English *-ous*) < *scurra* buffoon] **—scur′ri·lous·ly,** *adv.* **—scur′ri·lous·ness,** *n.*

scur·ry (skėr′ē), *v.,* **-ried, -ry·ing,** *n., pl.* **-ries.** *—v.i.* to run quickly; hurry: *We could hear mice scurrying about in the walls. —n.* **1.** a hasty running; hurrying: *With much fuss and scurry, she at last got started.* **2.** a short, quick run or race on horseback. [short for *hurry-scurry*]

S-curve (es′kėrv′), *n.* a curve shaped like the capital letter S.

scur·vied (skėr′vēd), *adj.* affected with scurvy; scorbutic.

scur·vi·ly (skėr′və lē), *adv.* in a scurvy manner; meanly; shabbily.

scur·vi·ness (skėr′vē nis), *n.* meanness; baseness; shabbiness.

scur·vish (skėr′vish), *n.* the evening primrose. [alteration of *scabious*[2]]

scur·vy (skėr′vē), *n., adj.,* **-vi·er, -vi·est.** *—n.* a disease characterized by weakness, swollen and bleeding gums, livid spots on the skin, and prostration, caused by lack of vitamin C in the diet. Scurvy used to be common among sailors when they had little to eat except bread and salt meat. [< adjective] *—adj.* **1.** low; mean; contemptible: *a scurvy fellow, a scurvy trick. A wooden tenement known as the Old Brewery ... had the reputation of being the scurviest hovel in town* (New Yorker). **2.** *Obsolete.* scurfy; scabby. [variant of *scurfy*]

scurvy grass, a plant of the mustard family, found in the arctic and northern regions, formerly used as a remedy for scurvy.

scut (skut), *n.* **1.** an erect, short tail, especially that of a hare, rabbit, or deer. **2.** *Slang.* a mean fellow. [origin uncertain. Compare Old Icelandic *skutr* stern.]

scu·ta (skyü′tə), *n.* plural of **scutum.**

scu·tage (skyü′tij), *n.* (in the feudal system) a payment exacted in lieu of military service. [< Medieval Latin *scutagium* < Latin *scūtum* a shield]

scu·tate (skyü′tāt), *adj.* **1.** *Zoology.* having shieldlike plates or large scales of bone, shell, etc. **2.** *Botany.* round: *Nasturtiums have scutate leaves.* [< Latin *scūtātus* having a shield < *scūtum* shield]

scutch (skuch), *v.t.* **1.** to free (flax or hemp fiber) from woody parts by beating. **2.** to separate (cotton fibers) after loosening and cleansing.
—n. **1.** a scutcher. **2.** a tool with perpendicular double edges to trim brick.

scutch·eon (skuch′ən), *n.* **1.** an escutcheon. **2.** *Zoology.* a scutum.

scutch·eoned (skuch′ənd), *adj.* having scutcheons.

scutch·er (skuch′ər), *n.* **1.** a tool for scutching flax, cotton, etc. **2.** a person or thing that scutches.

scute (skyüt), *n.* a scutum; shieldlike plate of bone, shell, etc. [< Latin *scūtum* shield]

scu·tel·la (skyü tel′ə), *n.* plural of **scutellum.**

scu·tel·lar (skyü tel′ər), *adj.* of or having to do with a scutellum.

scu·tel·late (skyü′tə lāt, skyü tel′it), *adj. Biology.* **1.** having scutella. **2.** formed into a scutellum. **3.** hollow like a shield; platter-shaped. [< New Latin *scutellātus* < Latin *scutella* platter < *scutra* dish, but taken as < New Latin *scutellum;* see SCUTELLUM]

scu·tel·lat·ed (skyü′tə lā′tid), *adj.* scutellate.

scu·tel·la·tion (skyü'tə lā'shən), *n.* **1.** arrangement of scales. **2.** a scaly covering, as on a bird's leg.
scu·tel·lum (skyü tel'əm), *n., pl.* **-la.** *Biology.* a small plate, scale or other shieldlike part, as on the feet of certain birds, the bodies of insects, or a cotyledon of some grasses. [< New Latin *scutellum* (diminutive) < Latin *scūtum* shield]
Scu·ti (skyü'tī), *n.* genitive of **Scutum.**
scu·ti·form (skyü'tə fôrm), *adj.* shield-shaped. [< Latin *scūtum,* shield]
scu·to bo·nae vo·lun·ta·tis tu·ae co·ro·nas·ti nos (skyü'tō bō'nē vol'ən tā'tis tyü'ē kor'ə nas'tī nōs), *Latin.* with the shield of Thy favor Thou hast encompassed us (motto of Maryland). Psalms 5:12.
scut·ter (skut'ər), *Dialect.* —*v.i.* to scurry: *Two pedestrians . . . were sent scuttering on their way by a short burst of angry toots* (London Times). —*n.* a scuttering; scurrying.
scut·tle[1] (skut'əl), *n.* **1.** a kind of bucket for holding or carrying coal. See **coal scuttle** for picture. **2.** *Obsolete.* a broad, shallow basket for carrying grain, vegetables, etc. [Old English *scutel* < Latin *scutella* platter (diminutive) < *scutra* dish] —**Syn. 1.** hod.
scut·tle[2] (skut'əl), *v.,* **-tled, -tling,** *n.* —*v.i.* to run with quick, hurried steps; scamper; scurry: *The women had grasped the peril of their position and were scuttling away* (New Yorker). —*n.* a short, hurried run. [variant of earlier *scuddle,* frequentative of *scud*]
scut·tle[3] (skut'əl), *n., v.,* **-tled, -tling.** —*n.* **1.** an opening in the deck or side of a ship, with a lid or cover. **2.** an opening in a wall or roof, with a lid or cover. **3.** the lid or cover for any such opening.
—*v.t.* **1. a.** to make a hole or holes in the bottom or sides of (a ship) to sink it: *His Black Sea fleet had been scuttled* (London Times). **b.** to open the seacocks or valves of (a ship) to sink it. **2.** to cut a hole or holes in the deck of (a ship) to salvage the cargo. **3. a.** to give up; let go: *The West was willing to scuttle the present . . . government in favor of a truly neutralist one* (Time). **b.** to undermine; destroy: *His weakness for the rash remark eventually would scuttle him* (New Yorker).
[perhaps < Middle French *escoutille* < Spanish, or directly < Spanish *escotilla* hatchway, perhaps < a Germanic word]
scut·tle·butt (skut'əl but'), *n.* **1.** *U.S. Slang.* rumor and stories not based on fact; gossip: *Moscow scuttlebutt says Ekaterina is now a sports car buff* (Time). **2. a.** a water cask for drinking, with a hole in the top for a cup or dipper, kept on the deck of a ship. **b.** a drinking fountain. [< *scuttle*[3] + *butt*[4] (def. 1, because the scuttle was a place to gossip)]
scut·tler[1] (skut'lər), *n.* a person who hurries off, usually in an undignified manner.
scut·tler[2] (skut'lər), *n.* a person who scuttles a ship, especially with the design of "losing" her and claiming the insurance money: *The overinsured as well as the scuttler should be punished severely* (Daily News).
scu·tum (skyü'təm), *n., pl.* **-ta. 1.** *Zoology.* a shieldlike part of a bone, shell, etc., as on a turtle or armadillo; scute. **2.** a large, oblong Roman shield. [< Latin *scūtum* shield]
Scu·tum (skyü'təm), *n., genitive* **Scu·ti.** a southern constellation near Sagittarius. [< New Latin *Scutum* < Latin *scūtum* shield]
S.C.V., *U.S.* Sons of Confederate Veterans.
scye (sī), *n.* the armhole of a garment, into which the sleeve is set. [origin unknown]
Scyl·la (sil'ə), *n.* a mythical monster with six heads and twelve arms that lived opposite the whirlpool Charybdis and snatched sailors from ships. Also, **Scilla.**
between Scylla and Charybdis, between two dangers: *to guide the ship of state between the Scylla of provocation and the Charybdis of appeasement* (New York Herald Tribune).
[< *Scylla,* a rock opposite the whirlpool Charybdis at the extreme southwestern tip of Italy]
scy·phif·er·ous or **scy·phiph·o·rous** (sī fif'ər əs), *adj. Botany.* bearing a scyphus. [< New Latin *scyphus* (see SCYPHUS) + English *-ferous*]
scy·phi·form (sī'fə fôrm), *adj. Botany.* cup-shaped.
scy·phis·to·ma (sī fis'tə mə), *n., pl.* **-ma·ta** (-mə tə). a scyphozoan embryo that multiplies by budding, and gives rise to permanent colonies of scyphozoans. [< New Latin *scyphistoma* < *scyphus* + *stoma* < Greek *stóma* mouth]
scy·phis·tome (sī fis'tōm), *n.* scyphistoma.
scy·pho·zo·an (sī'fə zō'ən), *n.* any of a group of marine coelenterates including many of the large jellyfishes. —*adj.* of or belonging to the scyphozoans. [< New Latin *scyphus* (see SCYPHUS) + Greek *zôion* animal + English *-an*]
scyph·u·la (sif'yə lə), *n., pl.* **-lae** (-lē). scyphistoma. [< New Latin *scyphula,* diminutive of *scyphus*]
scy·phus (sī'fəs), *n., pl.* **-phi** (-fī). **1.** *Botany.* a cup-shaped part, such as the end of a lichen's fruit stalk or the corolla of a flower. **2.** an ancient Greek cup. [< New Latin *scyphus* < Latin, a large drinking cup < Greek *skýphos*]
scythe (sīᴛʜ), *n., v.,* **scythed, scyth·ing.** —*n.* a long, thin, slightly curved blade on a long handle, for cutting grass, etc. —*v.t.* to cut or mow with a scythe. —*v.i.* to use a scythe: *Far away . . . men were scything* (John Galsworthy). [Old English *sīthe;* spelling later influenced by Latin *scindere* to cut]

Scythe

scythed (sīᴛʜd), *adj.* having scythes or sharp blades attached to the wheels, as ancient war chariots did: *Let Destiny drive forth her scythed car through the . . . trembling mass of humanity!* (Scott).
scythe·man (sīᴛʜ'mən), *n., pl.* **-men. 1.** a man who uses a scythe: *It suggested the simple, ancient grace of a good scytheman or sower* (New Yorker). **2.** time and death personified.
Scyth·i·an (sith'ē ən), *adj.* of or having to do with ancient Scythia, its people, or their language. —*n.* **1.** a native or inhabitant of ancient Scythia. **2.** the Iranian language of these people.
Scythian lamb, 1. a mythical creature, half animal, half plant, formerly supposed to inhabit Scythia. **2. a.** the shaggy rhizome of an Asiatic fern which when inverted and trimmed somewhat resembles a small lamb. **b.** the fern itself.
s.d., 1. sight draft. **2.** sine die. **3.** standard deviation.
S.D., 1. Doctor of Science (Latin, *Scientiae Doctor*). **2.** South Dakota. **3.** standard deviation.
S. Dak., South Dakota.
'sdeath (zdeth), *interj. Archaic.* "God's death," used as an oath: *'Sdeath! sir, do you question my understanding?* (Thomas Love Peacock).
S. Doc., Senate document (used with a number).
SDS (no periods) or **S.D.S.,** Students for a Democratic Society.
S-dump (es'dump'), *n.* a chute curved or bent resembling the letter S.
s.e., 1. southeast. **2.** southeastern.
Se (no period), selenium (chemical element).
SE (no periods) or **S.E., 1.** southeast. **2.** southeastern.
sea (sē), *n.* **1.** the great body of salt water that covers almost three fourths of the earth's surface; the ocean. **2.** any large body of salt water, smaller than an ocean, partly or wholly enclosed by land: *the North Sea, the Mediterranean Sea, the Dead Sea.* **3.** a large lake of fresh water: *the Sea of Galilee.* **4. a.** the swell of the ocean: *a heavy sea. Some ship in distress, that cannot live in such an angry sea* (Longfellow). **b.** a large, heavy wave: *A high sea swept away the ship's masts.* **5.** an overwhelming amount or number: *To take arms against a sea of troubles . . .* (Shakespeare). **6.** a broad expanse: *a sea of upturned faces.* **7.** one of the dark, flat plains of the moon once thought to be seas; mare: *The dark markings which are called "seas," even though they are entirely dry, make up the surface of the "man in the moon"* (Science News Letter). See **mare** for picture.
at sea, a. out on the sea; on shipboard: *We were at sea out of sight of land for ten days.* **b.** puzzled; confused: *I can't understand this problem; I'm all at sea.*
follow the sea, to be a sailor: *As a boy, Columbus dreamed of following the sea.*
go to sea, a. to become a sailor: *The captain had gone to sea when he was barely seventeen.* **b.** to go on a sea voyage: *The family went to sea last month.*
put to sea, to begin a sea voyage: *The Ottoman fleet . . . putting to sea from Constantinople, landed in Candy* (Jean Chardin).
take to sea, (of a ship or person) to start a voyage; embark: *The ships of the Spanish Armada took to sea in 1588.*
[Old English *sǣ*]
sea anchor, 1. a drag used in a gale to prevent a ship from drifting and to keep its head to the wind. It usually consists of a floating framed cone of canvas with its large, open base toward the ship. **2.** any of various somewhat similar devices by which a seaplane or amphibious aircraft may be held more or less stationary with its hull pointed into the wind, used especially after a forced landing at sea.
sea anemone, any of numerous flowerlike polyps with a fleshy, cylindrical body and a mouth surrounded by many tentacles: *I have found myself in the world of the sea anemones —creatures that spread a creamy-hued crown of tentacles above the shining brown columns of their bodies* (New Yorker). See **anemone** for picture.
sea bag, a large canvas bag that seamen use to carry clothing and other articles to and from a ship: *The third mate emerged from the deckhouse and thumped down his sea bag* (Atlantic).
sea bass, 1. a common food and game fish of the Atlantic Coast of the northeastern United States with a peculiar tail fin. **2.** any of various similar fishes.
sea bean, 1. the large, hard, beanlike edible seed of a tropical, leguminous climbing plant often carried by ocean currents to distant shores. **2.** the plant producing this seed. **3.** any of various small univalve shells somewhat resembling coffee beans.
sea bear, 1. the polar bear. **2.** any of various fur seals, especially the northern fur seal.
sea·bed (sē'bed'), *n.* the bottom of the sea; ocean bed; sea-bottom: *A careful survey of the seabed is needed before laying an underwater pipeline* (New Scientist).
Sea·bee (sē'bē'), *n.* a member of the construction battalion of the United States Navy, composed of mechanics, carpenters, welders, etc., who normally take no part in combat. [< pronunciation of the initials *C.B.* of Construction Battalion]
sea beef, the flesh of the porpoise or the whale.
sea bird, any bird that lives on or near the sea, as the petrels, gannets, and jaegers. —**Syn.** seafowl.
sea biscuit, a hard biscuit prepared for long keeping; hardtack; ship biscuit.
sea bladder, a Portuguese man-of-war.
sea·board (sē'bôrd', -bōrd'), *n.* land near the sea; seacoast; seashore: *New York City is on the Atlantic seaboard.* —*adj.* bordering on the sea. [earlier *sea-bord,* adjective < *sea* + *bord, board* side, border < Old French *bord*]
sea boat, a vessel considered with reference to her behavior at sea: *What . . . makes one ship a better sea boat than another* (New Scientist).
sea boots, high, waterproof boots for use at sea: *Scarcely . . . had I rolled into my bunk than I found myself pulling on my sea boots and reaching for my cap* (Atlantic).
sea·born (sē'bôrn'), *adj.* **1.** born in or of the sea. **2.** produced in or by the sea.
sea·borne (sē'bôrn', -bōrn'), *adj.* **1.** conveyed by sea; carried on the sea: *Authorities reported today that tens of thousands of penguins were dying on islands off the Cape coast because their feathers were clogged with seaborne oil* (New York Times). **2.** (of a ship) carried or floating on the sea.
sea-bot·tom (sē'bot'əm), *n.* the bottom or lowest depth of the sea: *For a particular area of the sea-bottom . . . there were approximately a million tons of available molluscs, worms and crustacea* (New Scientist).
sea bread, hardtack; ship biscuit.
sea bream, 1. any of certain edible marine fishes belonging to the same family as the porgies, especially a common European species. **2.** any fish belonging to this family.
sea breeze, a breeze blowing from the sea toward the land: *Late every afternoon, practically the year round, a stiff sea breeze blows in from the Pacific, carrying with it on many days fog heavy enough to require windshield wipers and headlights* (Harper's).

SEAC (no periods), Standard Eastern Automatic Computer (a high-speed, electronic computing machine used by the National Bureau of Standards).

sea calf, the common hair seal of the North American coasts; harbor seal.

sea captain, the master (captain) of a seagoing vessel, especially a merchant vessel; man whose profession is to command at sea.

sea change, 1. a change wrought by the sea: *Nothing of him that doth fade but doth suffer a sea change into something rich and strange* (Shakespeare). **2.** any radical or complete change; transformation: *In its transition to the screen ... Shaw's novel ... has undergone quite a sea change* (New Yorker).

sea cliff, a cliff facing the sea, usually formed by the erosive action of waves at its base: *During the early 1930's I often visited the sea cliffs of the British Isles where sea birds breed in vast numbers* (Scientific American).

sea coal, *British Archaic.* coal dug from the earth and formerly carried to London by sea, as distinguished from charcoal.

sea·coast (sē′kōst′), *n.* the land along the sea: *the seacoast of North America.*

sea·cock (sē′kok′), *n.* **1.** (in a marine steam engine) a cock or valve in the injection water pipe which passes from the sea to the condenser. It is supplementary to the ordinary cock at the condenser and is intended to serve in case this should be damaged. **2.** any cock or valve forming a connecting passage from a ship's hull to the sea: *Tuckfield opened a seacock, and the forward escape hatch began to fill with water* (Time).

sea·cop·ter (sē′kop′tər), *n.* a helicopter with a floating hull, that can operate from land or water. [< *sea* + (heli)*copter*]

sea cow, 1. a manatee, dugong, or other plant-eating water mammal. **2.** a walrus. **3.** *Obsolete.* a hippopotamus.

sea·craft (sē′kraft′, -kräft′), *n., pl.* **-craft. 1.** a seagoing vessel: *The first ship was ... followed by almost every kind of seacraft imaginable—colliers, yachts, motor boats, fishing smacks, launches, and motor lifeboats* (Maclean's). **2.** seagoing vessels collectively: *Mr. Krause ... picked me out as a man likely to be interested in unconventional seacraft* (New Yorker). **3.** skill in navigation.

sea crayfish. the spiny lobster.

sea crow, 1. the coot. **2.** the oyster catcher.

sea cucumber, any of a group of small echinoderms, most of which have flexible bodies that look somewhat like cucumbers; holothurian.

Sea Cucumber (to 2 ft. long)

sea devil, 1. a large fish related to the shark; devilfish. **2.** a shark having large, winglike fins; angelfish.

sea dog, 1. a sailor, especially one who has had long experience: *an old fighting sea dog* (Joseph Conrad). **2.** a privateer or pirate. **3. a.** the common or harbor seal. **b.** the dogfish, a small shark. **4.** a fogdog.

sea·drome (sē′drōm′), *n.* a large floating structure providing a landing place at sea for aircraft (such as was projected during the 1920's for transoceanic flights). [< *sea* + (air)*drome*]

sea duck, any of a group of ducks including the scoters and eiders, members of which dive for their food, have a lobate hind toe and are found chiefly on salt water.

sea dust, *Geology.* dust of deserts, usually of brick-red color, borne away by the wind and descending at a long distance.

sea eagle, 1. any of several eagles that feed mainly on fish, especially a species of northern Europe, and the Steller's sea eagle, found on islands off the Alaskan and Siberian coasts. **2.** the osprey.

sea-ear (sē′ir′), *n.* an abalone.

sea elephant, a kind of very large seal, the male of which has a trunklike snout; elephant seal: *The sea elephant, like the mammoth kangaroo whose remains are preserved in fossils, is practically extinct, at least in Australian waters* (New Yorker).

sea fan, a fan-shaped coral, especially a species of the Caribbean and the Gulf of Mexico.

sea·far·er (sē′fãr′ər), *n.* **1.** a sailor. **2.** a traveler on the sea. —**Syn. 1.** mariner, seaman.

sea·far·ing (sē′fãr′ing), *adj.* going, traveling, or working on the sea: *Sailors are seafaring men.* —*n.* **1.** the business or calling of a sailor. **2.** the act or fact of traveling by sea: *His novel is salt-encrusted in the best tradition of literary seafaring* (Newsweek).

sea feather, a sea pen.

sea fight, a fight between ships at sea; naval battle.

sea floor, the floor or bottom of a sea or ocean; seabed: *Temperatures of the oceans at various times in Geologic past may be revealed by ... chemical studies of calcium carbonate on ancient sea floors* (Science News Letter).

sea·flow·er (sē′flou′ər), *n.* a sea anemone or related organism.

sea foam, 1. the foam of the sea. **2.** meerschaum.

sea·food (sē′füd′), *n. U.S.* edible salt-water fish and shellfish: *Seafood ... is more apt to be cooked with cornflakes than with a delicate wine sauce* (Harper's).

sea·fowl (sē′foul′), *n., pl.* **-fowls** or (*collectively*) **-fowl.** sea bird.

sea front, 1. land fronting the sea; water front. **2.** that portion or side of a building, etc., which faces the sea.

sea gate, an entrance from the sea into a bay, harbor, or the like.

sea-girt (sē′gėrt′), *adj.* surrounded by the sea: *Since the Arctic is almost a landlocked sea, while the Antarctic is a seagirt land, certain important climatic differences are to be expected between the two regions* (Finch and Trewartha).

sea god, a god of the sea, as Neptune or Nereus: *Proteus, that sea god who can change his shape at will ...* (Time).

sea goddess, a goddess of the sea, as Amphitrite, wife of Poseidon.

sea·go·ing (sē′gō′ing), *adj.* **1.** going by sea; seafaring. **2.** fit for going to sea: *a powerful seagoing tug.* **3.** (of fishes) catadromous. —*n.* a going or traveling by sea.

sea gooseberry, any of a group of radially symmetrical marine organisms resembling jellyfish, such as certain ctenophore.

sea grape, a tropical American shrub or small tree of the buckwheat family, having white flowers and attractive autumn foliage, and bearing bunches of grapelike fruit that are made into jelly and a beverage.

sea grass, any of various grasses or grasslike plants that grow by or in the sea, such as the glasswort, eelgrass, and sea pink.

sea green, a pale bluish-green color. —**sea′-green′,** *adj.* —**Syn.** aquamarine.

sea gull, a gull, a water bird with long wings and webbed feet.

sea heath, a heathlike shrub of European coasts.

sea hedgehog, sea urchin.

sea hog, a porpoise.

sea holly, a coarse European herb of the parsley family, a variety of eryngo, with toothed or spiny leaves whose root was formerly candied for use as a sweetmeat.

sea horizon, the circle which bounds the view of the observer at sea.

sea horse, 1. any of a group of small fish with a prehensile tail and a head suggesting that of a horse, living in warm waters; hippocampus. **2.** a walrus. **3.** a mythical sea animal with the foreparts of a horse and the hind parts of a fish. The Nereids are fabled to have used sea horses for riding, and Neptune to have used them for drawing his chariot. *Notice Neptune, though, taming a sea horse ... cast in bronze for me!* (Robert Browning). **4.** a large, white-crested wave.

Sea Horse (def. 1) (6 to 10 in. long)

sea ice, frozen seawater. Sea ice has many salt-water pockets. *Both the theory and tests disprove the long-held rule that sea ice is only one-third as strong as fresh-water ice* (Science News Letter).

sea-is·land cotton (sē′ī′lənd), **1.** a long-staple variety of cotton formerly grown on the islands off the coast of South Carolina and Georgia and now grown especially in the West Indies. **2.** the plant producing it.

sea kale, a broad-leaved plant of the mustard family, growing near the sea, cooked and eaten as a vegetable in certain countries of Europe.

sea·kind·ly (sē′kīnd′lē), *adj.* easy to handle at sea: *Her hull shape ... has proved staunch and seakindly* (Manchester Guardian Weekly).

sea king, a Scandinavian pirate chief of the Middle Ages. [translation of Old Icelandic *sǣkonungr*]

seal[1] (sēl), *n.* **1.** a design stamped on a piece of wax or other soft material, to show ownership or authenticity: *The seal of the United States is attached to important government papers.* **2.** a stamp for marking things with such a design: *Mabel has a seal with her initials M.B. on it, with which she stamps sealing wax to fasten her letters securely.* **3.** a piece of wax, paper, metal, etc., on which the design is stamped. **4.** a thing that fastens or closes something tightly. **5.** something that secures; pledge: *under seal of secrecy.* **6.** something that settles or determines: *the seal of authority.* **7.** a mark; sign: *Sea sands are made beautiful by their bearing the seal of the motion of the waters* (John Ruskin). *The haughty ... passions that set their seal upon her brow ...* (Dickens). **8.** a stamp: *Christmas seals, Easter seals.* **9.** a small quantity of water left in a trap to prevent the escape of foul air from a sewer or drain.

The Great Seal[1] of the United States (def. 1)

set one's seal to, a. to put one's seal on: *The king set his seal to the decree.* **b.** to approve: *To this truth Mr. Hobbs sets his seal with all willingness imaginable* (Henry More).

the seals, *British.* the symbols of public office: *The King sent him to the Earl of Jersey, with a peremptory order to return the seals* (Philip Henry Stanhope).

—*v.t.* **1.** to mark (a document) with a seal: *The deed was signed, sealed, and delivered.* **2.** to make binding by affixing seals; authenticate: *The treaty was signed and sealed by both governments.* **3.** to stamp as an evidence of standard measure or quality or legal size: *to seal weights and measures.* **4.** to close tightly; fasten; shut: *Seal the letter before mailing it. She sealed the jars of fruit. Her promise sealed her lips. His eyes were sealed with sleep. Every train passing through on the mainline ... had its windows sealed with steel shutters* (Newsweek). **5.** to close up the cracks of: *They sealed the log cabin with clay.* **6.** to fix firmly: *But ah, she gave me never a look for her eyes were seal'd to the holy book* (Matthew Arnold). **7.** to settle; determine: *The judge's words sealed the prisoner's fate.* **8.** to give a sign that (a thing) is true: *to seal a promise with a kiss. They sealed their bargain by shaking hands.* **9.** to set apart; decide beyond recall; destine: *the God ... who had watched over the growth of a family into a nation, who had sealed that family for Himself ...* (Sir John R. Seeley). **10.** (in Mormon use) to set apart and bind spiritually forever by a solemn ceremony, as in marriage. **11.** *Electricity.* to bring into position so that the circuit is complete, as a plug and jack.

seal off or **up,** to shut up within impenetrable barriers; make inaccessible: *a ship sealed up in ice. Zoo officials ... put the sad little ape in quarantine in a sealed-off room* (Time).

[< Old French *seel* < Vulgar Latin *sigellum* < Latin *sigillum* (diminutive), related to *sīgnum* a sign]

seal[2] (sēl), *n., pl.* **seals** or (*collectively for 1*) **seal,** *v.* —*n.* **1.** any of a suborder of carnivorous marine mammals with limbs developed into large flippers for swimming and an elongated body covered with thick fur or bristle. Some kinds are hunted for their valuable fur. Seals include the family of eared seals, as the northern fur seal of the Bering Sea, and the family of earless or hair seals, as the harbor seal of North American coasts. **2.** the fur of the fur seal;

Fur Seal[2] (def. 1) (about 6 ft. long)

sealskin. **3.** some other fur used as a substitute for sealskin: *Hudson seal is obtained from the muskrat.* **4.** leather made from the skin of a seal. **5.** seal brown.
—*v.i.* to hunt or take seals.
[Old English *sēolwes,* genitive of *seolh*]
—**seal′like′,** *adj.*

seal[3] (sēl), *v.t.* seel.

Sea·lab (sē′lab′), *n.* a submerged, stationary laboratory engaged in underwater oceanographic research: *The goal of the Sealabs is to develop techniques whereby men can operate on the ocean floor* (New York Times).

seal·a·ble (sē′lə bəl), *adj.* that can be sealed.

sea lamprey, a marine lamprey of the Atlantic coasts of Europe and North America which spawns in fresh water. It has become landlocked in the Great Lakes and certain other waters, where it is highly destructive of lake trout and other fish. See **lamprey** for picture.

sea lane, a particular course or route regularly used by most ships when crossing an ocean or large area of water: *Their navy dominated the strategic sea lanes to the Dardanelles* (Harper's).

seal·ant (sē′lənt), *n.* a compound for sealing: *a paint sealant. Research developed new synthetic rubber sealants that replaced putty and made possible today's glass-and-steel-wall skyscrapers* (World Book Encyclopedia).

sea lavender, any of a group of mostly perennial herbs with many tiny, lavender, yellow, or multicolored flowers that retain their color long after being cut and dried.

sea lawyer, *Slang.* a sailor inclined to find fault and to argue.

seal brown, a rich, dark-brown color.
—**seal′-brown′,** *adj.*

sea leather, the skin of sharks, porpoises, dogfishes, etc., prepared to be used for the same purposes as ordinary leather.

sealed (sēld), *adj.* **1.** authenticated or ratified by a seal. **2.** guaranteed as to exactness, measure, quality, etc., by a seal. **3.** fastened with a seal. **4.** closed to knowledge; unknown.

sealed-beam headlight (sēld′bēm′), an automobile headlight in which filament, lens, and reflector form a single unit, insuring the correct focus of the filament and the constant reflecting power of the lens.

sealed bid, a confidential bid, as for a contract, usually submitted in a sealed envelope: *Civil Service and the sealed bid, those dread enemies of patronage . . .* (Wall Street Journal).

sealed book, something unknown or undiscoverable: *The young generation was always something of a sealed book to him* (John Galsworthy).

sealed orders, sealed written orders to be opened after leaving port, instructing the commander of a ship where to proceed on a voyage.

sea legs, legs accustomed to walking steadily on a rolling or pitching ship: *Michel, who had good sea legs, kept his balance to the movements of the craft* (Joseph Conrad).

get one's sea legs, to become accustomed to the motion of a ship, especially after an initial period of seasickness: *In addition to all this, I had not got my sea legs* (Richard Henry Dana).

sea leopard, a large, spotted seal of the southern and antarctic seas, that attacks little seals and penguins: *The sea leopard . . . so far as is known, has never killed a man. But that is not for want of trying* (New York Times).

seal·er[1] (sē′lər), *n.* **1.** a person or thing that seals. **2.** a local or municipal official, appointed to examine and test weights and measures for accuracy.

seal·er[2] (sē′lər), *n.* **1.** a person who hunts seals. **2.** a ship used for hunting seals.

seal·er·y (sē′lər ē), *n., pl.* **-er·ies. 1.** the act or occupation of hunting seals; sealing. **2.** a place where seals are hunted.

sea letter, a document formerly issued by the civil authorities of a port in which a vessel was fitted out, certifying her nationality, and specifying the kind, quantity, ownership, and destination of her cargo.

sea lettuce, a green seaweed whose fronds look like strips of lettuce. They are sometimes eaten.

sea level, the surface of the sea, especially when halfway between mean high and low water. Heights of mountains are measured as so many feet above sea level: *In each hemisphere, sea level is low during the spring and high in the fall* (Jan Hahn).

sea·lift (sē′lift′), *n.* a system of using ships for transportation of military personnel and equipment to places where land approaches are closed or inadequate: *You have to be accurate about your tables of organization and order of battle and in your calculations of airlift and sealift* (Christopher Rand).

sea lily, a crinoid, a flowerlike invertebrate animal.

sea line, 1. the horizon at sea; line where sea and sky seem to meet. **2.** a long line for fishing in deep water.

seal·ing (sē′ling), *n.* the hunting and taking of seals, as an occupation or commercial undertaking.

sealing wax, a substance consisting of resin, shellac, and turpentine, and resembling hard, brittle wax when cool, but soft when heated, used for sealing letters, packages, etc.

sea lion, any of certain large, eared seals, growing about seven to twelve feet long, as the Steller's sea lion of the northern Pacific and the California sea lion of the Pacific Coast from California south.

Sea Lion (10 ft. long)

seal limb or **limbs,** phocomelia.

seal point, a variety of Siamese cat having a cream-colored body and dark-brown points (ears, face, feet, and tail). [< *seal* (brown) + *point* (def. 8)]

seal ring, a finger ring engraved with a seal design so that it can be used as a signet ring.

seals (sēlz), *n.pl.* See under **seal**[1], *n.*

seal·skin (sēl′skin′), *n.* **1.** the skin of a fur seal, prepared for use: *a coat of brown sealskin.* **2.** a garment or article made of this fur. —*adj.* made of sealskin.

sea lungwort, a fleshy herb of the borage family, growing along the northern coasts of North America, Europe, and Asia; oyster plant; oyster leaf.

Sea·ly·ham terrier, or **Sea·ly·ham** (sē′lē ham, -əm), *n.* any of a breed of small Welsh dogs with short legs, a square jaw, and a rough, shaggy, white coat, sometimes marked with lemon, tan, or brown on the head and ears. It resembles the Scottish terrier but regularly has the tail docked. [< *Sealyham,* an estate in Pembrokeshire, Wales, where the breed was originated]

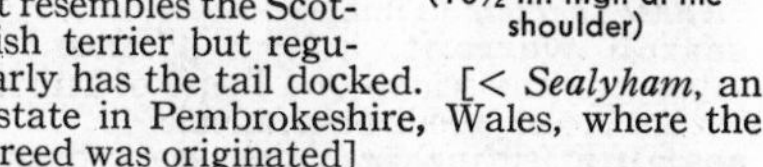
Sealyham Terrier (10½ in. high at the shoulder)

seam[1] (sēm), *n.* **1.** the line formed by sewing the edges of two pieces of cloth, canvas, leather, etc., together: *the seams of a coat, the seams of a sail.* **2.** any line where edges join: *The seams of the boat must be filled in if they leak.* **3.** any mark or line like a seam. **4.** *Geology.* a layer or stratum: *a seam of coal.* **5.** (in knitting) a line of purled stitches. **6.** *Dialect.* sewing; needlework.
—*v.t.* **1.** to sew the seam or seams of; join with a seam or seams. **2.** to mark (a surface, as the face) with lines or indentations; furrow, scar, or wrinkle: *Marshes, seamed and crossed with narrow creeks . . .* (John Greenleaf Whittier). **3.** (in knitting) to make a seam or apparent seam in; purl. —*v.i.* **1.** to crack open. **2.** (in knitting) to form a seam; purl. **3.** *Dialect.* to sew.
[Old English *sēam.* Related to SEW.]

seam[2] (sēm), *n. Dialect.* fat; grease; lard. [< Old French *saim* < Vulgar Latin *sagīmen* < Latin *sagīna*]

sea maid, 1. a mermaid. **2.** a goddess or nymph of the sea.

sea maiden, a sea maid.

sea·man (sē′mən), *n., pl.* **-men. 1.** a sailor; mariner: *a fine seaman.* **2. a.** a sailor below the rank of officer. **b.** *U.S. Navy.* a sailor of any of the three lowest enlisted grades, below a petty officer.

sea·man·like (sē′mən līk′), *adj.* of or like a seaman; like that of a good seaman: *seamanlike skill in tying knots. The charges . . . were that he failed to ensure that adequate seamanlike precautions were taken to safeguard the lives of the boarding party* (London Times).
—*adv.* in a seamanlike manner.

sea·man·ly (sē′mən lē), *adj., adv.* seamanlike.

sea·man·ship (sē′mən ship), *n.* **1.** skill in managing a ship at sea. **2.** the skill of a good seaman.

sea·mark (sē′märk′), *n.* **1.** a lighthouse, beacon, or other landmark that can be seen from the sea, used as a guide for a ship's course. **2.** a line on the shore that shows the upper limit of the tide.

sea mat, a bryozoan that forms flat, matted seaweed: *Certain groups, including fishes . . ., sea pens, brittle stars, and sea mats . . . do not appear to extend appreciably below 6,000 metres* (C.M. Yonge).

seamed (sēmd), *adj.* **1.** joined with a seam or seams, as by sewing. **2.** cleft, furrowed, or marked with seams: *a seamed face. A great ship, an East Indiaman, with rusty, seamed, blistered sides . . .* (George W. Curtis).

sea·men (sē′mən), *n.pl.* sailors.

seam·er (sē′mər), *n.* **1.** a person or thing that seams. **2.** a kind of sewing machine for seaming fabrics together. **3.** a machine for bending two pieces of sheet metal to unite them in a seam or joint.

sea mew, a sea gull, especially a common European species.

sea mile, a nautical mile (6,076.1033 feet).

sea milkwort, a plant of the primrose family, common on the seacoast; milkwort.

seam·i·ness (sē′mē nis), *n.* seamy state or quality.

seam·less (sēm′lis), *adj.* without a seam or seams: *seamless stockings, seamless shoes.*
—**seam′less·ly,** *adv.*

sea monster, 1. a huge fish, cetacean, or the like. **2.** a fabulous marine animal of terrifying proportions and shape.

sea moss, 1. a bryozoan. **2.** a seaweed, such as carrageen.

sea·mount (sē′mount′), *n.* a tall, cone-shaped hill or mountain with a flat top, arising from the sea bottom; guyot: *Explorers of the ocean depths have been turning up so many new peaks, ridges, basins, seamounts and other underwater landmarks that naming them all has become a major problem in the flourishing science of oceanography* (Science News Letter).

sea mouse, any of a group of large polychaete sea worms covered with long, fine, hairlike setae, that give it a mouselike appearance.

seam·ster (sēm′stər), *n.* a person whose occupation is sewing (originally applied to a woman, but now only to a man); tailor. Also, **sempster.** [Old English *sēamestre* (originally), feminine of *sēamere* tailor < *sēam* seam[1]]

seam·ster·ing (sēm′stər ing), *n.* the work of a seamstress: *She's been picking up a living at seamstering in Melchester for several months* (Thomas Hardy).

seam·stress (sēm′stris), *n.* **1.** a woman whose work is sewing. **2.** a girl or woman who sews; needlewoman: *an excellent seamstress, a born seamstress.* Also, **sempstress.**

seam·y (sē′mē), *adj.,* **seam·i·er, seam·i·est. 1.** having or showing a seam or seams: *the seamy side of a garment.* **2.** least pleasant; worst: *A policeman sees much of the seamy side of life.*

Sean·ad Eir·eann (shan′əᴛʜ ãr′ən), or **Sean·ad,** *n.* the upper house of the legislature (*Oireachtas*) of the Irish Republic. [< Irish *Seanad Eireann*]

sé·ance (sā′äns), *n.* **1.** a meeting of people trying to communicate with spirits of the dead by the help of a medium: *. . . attending spiritual lectures and séances, whenever a noted medium visited the place* (John Hay). **2.** a sitting or session, as of a learned society or other body of persons. [< French *séance* a sitting < *seoir* to sit < Latin *sedēre*]

sea nettle, a jellyfish, so called because of the stinging organs (nematocysts) in its tentacles.

sea nymph, a nymph supposed to inhabit the sea; Nereid.

sea onion, the squill, a plant of the lily family: *The sea onion grows around the Mediterranean Sea* (Harold N. Moldenke).

sea otter, a large, rare otter with webbed feet, found mainly along the shores of California and the Aleutian Islands. Its fur is considered the most valuable of all fur-bearing animals, but it is now protected by law in American waters.

Sea Otter (including tail, 4 to 6 ft. long)

sea pen, any of a group of anthozoan polyps that form featherlike colonies; sea feather.

sea·perch (sē′pėrch′), *n.* any of a family of small, mostly marine fish that bear live young; surf fish.

sea pie[1], a sailors' dish composed of meat, vegetables, etc., cooked between layers of dough.

sea pie[2], *Especially British.* the oyster catcher, so called from its pied coloration.

sea·piece (sē′pēs′), *n.* a picture representing a scene at sea: . . . *a piece representing Sir F. Drake's action in the year 1580, an excellent seapiece* (John Evelyn).

sea pigeon, a black guillemot having the size of a small duck and a plump, dovelike appearance.

sea pink, any of a group of low evergreen plants of temperate regions bearing usually pink flowers; thrift: *In May and June the island is carpeted with vivid stretches of sea pinks, bluebells . . .* (Sunday Times).

sea plain, a plain produced by the erosive action of waves, currents, tides, etc.

sea·plane (sē′plān′), *n.* **1.** an airplane that can rise from and alight on water; hydroplane. **2.** an airplane that can take off from or land on either land or water; amphibian.

sea porcupine, any of various globefishes with skin covered with spiny processes.

sea·port (sē′pôrt′, -pōrt′), *n.* **1.** a port or harbor on the seacoast: *Seaports, the termini of ocean trade routes, are both the creations and creators of such routes* (White and Renner). **2.** a city or town with a harbor that ships can reach from the sea: *San Francisco and New Orleans are seaports.*

sea post, the postal service conducted at sea, concerned with the sorting of mail on ocean steamers so as to be in readiness for prompt transmission to the various destinations on arrival in port.

sea power, **1.** a nation having a strong navy. **2.** naval strength.

sea purse, the horny case or pouch that a skate, ray, or shark secretes around its eggs to protect them and anchor them to rocks, weeds, etc.

sea·quake (sē′kwāk′), *n.* a sudden agitation of the sea caused by a volcanic eruption or earthquake at the bottom of the sea: *Destructive tidal waves are caused by . . . seaquakes* (Harry A. Marmer).

sear[1] (sir), *v.t.* **1.** to burn or char the surface of: *to sear a roast. The hot iron seared the cloth. The trees were seared by lightning.* **2.** to make hard and unfeeling: . . . *manifesting . . . a more seared and callous conscience than even Nero himself* (Henry Fielding). **3.** to cause to dry up; wither; blight: *When summer sears the plains . . .* (William Cowper).
—*v.i.* **1.** to become dry, burned, or hard. **2.** to become hardened or callous: *Her conscience sears* (William Morris). [Old English *sēarian,* verb < *sēar* dried up]
—*n.* a mark made by searing.
—*adj.* Also, **sere.** *Archaic.* dried up; withered.
[Old English *sēar*]
—**Syn.** *v.t.* **1.** See **burn.**

sear[2] (sir), *n.* the pivoted piece in a gunlock that holds the hammer at full cock or half cock until released by the trigger. [probably < Old French *serre* something that grasps; a lock < *serrer* to grasp, ultimately < Latin *sera* bar for fastening a door]

sea raven, a large fish with a long, spiny dorsal fin, a variety of sculpin common on the North Atlantic Coast of America.

search (sėrch), *v.i.* to try to find by looking; seek: *We searched all day for the lost cat.*
—*v.t.* **1.** to go over carefully in trying to find something. **2.** to examine, especially for something concealed: *to search one's baggage. The boys searched the entire cave for the hidden treasure.* **3.** to look through (writings, records, etc.) in order to discover if certain things are there: *Search the Scriptures* (John 5:39). **4.** to examine by probing: *The doctor searched the wound for the bullet.* **5.** (of wind, cold, firearms, etc.) to pierce; penetrate. **6.** *Archaic.* to look for; try to find: *My fancy ranging thro' and thro', to search a meaning for the song* (Tennyson).

search me, *U.S. Slang.* **a.** I don't have it: "*Where is my book?*" "*Search me.*" **b.** I don't know: "*Why does he act so strangely?*" "*Search me.*"

search out, a. to look for: *His primary object is to search out the truth* (Weekly Times). **b.** to find by searching: *He searched out all the facts of the case.*

—*n.* **1.** the act of searching: *to give up the search, the search after knowledge. John found his book after a long search.* **2.** the act of stopping and examining a neutral vessel on the high seas in time of war to discover if it is violating neutrality.

in search of, trying to find; looking for: *Aubrey Jones has been voyaging lately in search of fresh talent* (Manchester Guardian Weekly).

[< Old French *cerchier* < Late Latin *circāre* go about, wander < Latin *circus* circle] —**search′er,** *n.*

—**Syn.** *v.i., v.t.* **1, 2, 3. Search, explore, rummage** mean to look through a place for something. **Search** implies looking for something known or thought to be there: *Men searched the woods for the murderer.* **Explore** implies looking for whatever may be there: *Geologists explored the newly discovered mineral deposit.* **Rummage** suggests searching among the contents and moving them about: *He rummaged through the drawers looking for a map.*

search·a·ble (sėr′chə bəl), *adj.* that can be searched or explored.

search coil, a small coil of insulated wire used for measuring the strength of magnetic fields by means of the currents induced in the coil.

search ephemeris, an ephemeris calculated from an approximate orbit of a comet or planet to help to find it or its position.

search·ing (sėr′ching), *adj.* **1.** examining carefully; thorough: *a searching investigation.* **2.** keenly observant; penetrating: . . . *the searching eye of heaven . . .* (Shakespeare). *He felt quite calm under his searching glance* (Dickens). **3.** piercing; sharp; keen: *a searching wind.* —**search′ing·ly,** *adv.* —**search′·ing·ness,** *n.*

search·light (sėrch′līt′), *n.* **1.** a device that can throw a very bright beam of light in any direction desired. **2.** the beam of light so thrown: *The searchlights had begun their nightly wanderings* (John Galsworthy).

search party, a group of persons searching for someone or something lost, in hiding, etc.: *Search parties went out in all directions without success* (Time).

search warrant, a legal document authorizing the search of a house or building, as for stolen goods or criminals.

sear·ing (sir′ing), *adj.* that sears; burning; scorching.

searing iron, an iron which is heated for use in cauterizing, branding, etc.

sear·ing·ly (sir′ing′lē), *adv.* in a searing manner; scorchingly: *The life of the Black Muslim leader as he told it, searingly . . .* (New York Times).

sea risk, risk or hazard at sea; danger of injury or destruction by the sea.

sea robber, a pirate. —**Syn.** corsair, buccaneer.

sea robin, **1.** any of a group of marine gurnards (fish) with a large head, mailed cheeks, and separate pectoral rays, especially certain reddish or brownish American species. **2.** the red-breasted merganser.

sea room, space at sea free from obstruction, in which a ship can be maneuvered or navigated easily and safely: *The sloop . . . at length . . . recovered sea room enough to weather the Point of Warroch* (Scott).

sea route, **1.** a path or course followed by or mapped out for ships: *Whenever it is decided that a sea-route is "essential to the trade and economy of the nation," ships using the route are entitled to a subsidy* (Atlantic). **2.** markings on a chart giving point of departure, course, and destination for a ship's voyage.

sea rover, **1.** a pirate. **2.** a pirate ship.

sea salt, salt (sodium chloride) obtained by the evaporation of sea water.

sea·scape (sē′skāp′), *n.* **1.** a picture of a scene or scenery at sea: *The work in the current showing consists principally of landscapes, seascapes, and still lifes* (New Yorker). **2.** a view of scenery on the sea: *The landing . . . offers a large, beautiful seascape* (Atlantic). [< *sea* + *scape*[3]] —**Syn. 1.** marine.

sea scorpion, **1.** a eurypterid: *Sea scorpions . . . are among the rarest fossils found in the Cincinnati area* (Science News Letter). **2.** a sculpin. **3.** a scorpionfish.

sea scout, a boy trained in seamanship by the Boy Scout organization.

sea scouting, training in seamanship by the Boy Scout organization.

sea serpent, **1.** a huge, snakelike animal said to have been repeatedly seen at sea: *For all he knew at the time he set out, he'd find nothing but man-eating sea serpents before his ships toppled over the edge of the world* (New Yorker). **2.** a sea snake.

Sea Serpent, the southern constellation Hydra.

sea shell, the shell of any salt-water mollusk, such as an oyster, conch, or abalone.

sea·shore (sē′shôr′, -shōr′), *n.* **1.** the land along the sea; coast. **2.** the area between the lines of ordinary high tide and ordinary low tide. —*adj.* of or at the seashore: *a seashore resort.* —**Syn.** *n.* **1.** seacoast.

sea·sick (sē′sik′), *adj.* sick because of a ship's motion.

sea·sick·ness (sē′sik′nis), *n.* sickness caused by a ship's motion.

sea·side (sē′sīd′), *n.* the land along the sea; seacoast; seashore. —*adj.* of or at the seaside: *a seaside inn.*

seaside sparrow, a dingy, grayish sparrow with a yellow mark in front of the eye, found in saltwater marshes from Massachusetts to Florida and Texas.

Sea Sled, *Trademark.* a sledlike motorboat capable of great speed, having a square bow and stern, and an inverted V-shaped, longitudinal trough extending along the bottom of the hull.

sea slug, **1.** any of a group of marine gastropods lacking shells in the adult state, and somewhat resembling land slugs; nudibranch. **2.** a sea cucumber.

sea snail, a marine gastropod with a spiral shell resembling a helix, such as the periwinkle.

sea snake, **1.** any of a group of poisonous snakes with finlike tails that live in tropical seas: *The true sea snakes have a poison as deadly as that of the cobra* (Science News Letter). **2.** a sea serpent.

sea soldier, a marine.

sea·son (sē′zən), *n.* **1.** one of the four periods of the year, spring, summer, autumn, and winter, each beginning astronomically at an equinox or solstice, but popularly at various dates in different climates. **2.** a period of the year with reference to the particular conditions of weather, temperature, etc., that characterize it: . . . *a most extraordinary wet and cold season* (John Evelyn). **3.** any period of time marked by something special or characteristic: *the Christmas season, the harvest season, a season of peace.* **4.** the time when something is occurring, active, at its best, or in fashion: *the hunting, fishing, or baseball season, the theatrical season, the oyster season.* **5.** the period of the year when a place is most frequented or active: *the London or Florida season.* **6.** a period or time: . . . *at a certain season of our life . . .* (Thoreau). **7.** a suitable or fit time: *But that was no season for internal dissensions* (Macaulay).

for a season, for a time; for an indefinite period: *Thou shalt be blind, not seeing the sun for a season* (Acts 13:11).

in good season, early enough: *The two young men desired to get back again in good season* (Dickens).

in season, a. at the right or proper time: *Mr. March has to be home by a certain day; and we shall just get back in season* (William Dean Howells). **b.** in the time or condition for eating, hunting, etc.: *They [pinks] are not in season, your honour* (Samuel Foote). **c.** early enough: *News of this intention reached him in season to effect his escape* (W. Walker).

in season and out of season, at all times: *He will be repeating his folly in season and out of season, until at last it has a hearing* (Arthur Helps).

out of season, not in season: *So spake the fervent Angel, but his zeal none seconded, as out of season judg'd* (Milton).

—*v.t.* **1.** to add salt, pepper, spices, herbs, etc., to (food) to improve its flavor: *to season*

soup with salt. **2.** to give interest or character to: *to season conversation with wit.* **3.** to make fit for use by a period of keeping or treatment: *Wood is seasoned for building by drying and hardening it. Knowledge and timber shouldn't be much used till they are seasoned* (Oliver Wendell Holmes). **4.** to make fit physically: *... an extremely vigorous person ... tanned and seasoned by the life of his class, by the yachting, hunting, and shooting* (Mrs. Humphry Ward). **5.** to make used; accustom: *Soldiers are seasoned to battle by experience in war.* **6.** to make less severe; moderate; temper: *... when mercy seasons justice* (Shakespeare). *—v.i.* **1.** to become fit for use. **2.** to become hardened or inured.
[Middle English *sesun* < Old French *seison* < Latin *satiō, -ōnis* a sowing < *serere* to sow]
—**Syn.** *v.t.* **3.** age, mature, ripen. **4.** harden. **5.** inure, habituate, acclimate. **6.** soften, alleviate.

➔ **seasons.** *Winter, spring, summer, fall,* and *autumn* are not capitalized except for stylistic emphasis, as sometimes in poetry.

sea·son·a·ble (sē′zə nə bəl, sēz′nə-), *adj.* **1.** suitable to the season: *Hot weather is seasonable in July.* **2.** coming at the right or proper time: *The Red Cross brought seasonable aid to the flood victims.* **3.** in good season; early: *to leave at a seasonable hour.* —**sea′son·a·ble·ness,** *n.* —**Syn. 2.** opportune, timely.

sea·son·a·bly (sē′zə nə blē, sēz′nə-), *adv.* in due time or season; at the right moment; sufficiently early: *to sow or plant seasonably.*

sea·son·al (sē′zə nəl), *adj.* **1.** having to do with the seasons: *seasonal variations in the weather.* **2. a.** depending on a season: *a seasonal business.* **b.** employed only during a certain season: *a seasonal worker.* **3.** recurring at regular intervals; periodical.

sea·son·al·i·ty (sē′zə nal′ə tē), *n.* the quality or condition of being seasonal; periodicity: *This masterly analysis of the agricultural implications of seasonality deserves serious study* (New Scientist).

sea·son·al·ly (sē′zə nə lē), *adv.* according to season; periodically.

sea·soned (sē′zənd), *adj.* **1.** matured, hardened, or accustomed by some process of seasoning: *seasoned timber, seasoned troops.* **2.** tested and approved by time; experienced; trained: *This was the finding last week of the seasoned political observers* (Newsweek). **3.** flavored with seasoning.

sea·son·er (sē′zə nər), *n.* **1.** a person or thing that seasons. **2.** *U.S.* a fisherman who hires for the season. **3.** *U.S. Informal.* a loafer; beachcomber.

sea·son·ing (sē′zə ning, sēz′ning), *n.* **1.** something that gives a better flavor to food. Salt, pepper, spices, and herbs are seasonings. **2.** something that gives interest or character: *We like conversation with a seasoning of humor.* —**Syn. 1.** condiment.

season ticket, a ticket that gives its holder the right to attend a series of games or entertainments, to make a daily trip on a railroad for a stated period of time, etc.

sea spider, 1. any of a group of tiny spiderlike marine arthropods. **2.** a spider crab.

sea squirt, a small, soft-bodied marine animal that squirts water when it contracts; a simple ascidian: *The salient contradiction here is between the adult sea squirt, which is anchored to a rock, and its free-swimming and seemingly much more advanced and go-ahead larvae* (Observer).

sea stack, a sharp, isolated hill rising from the sea-bottom.

sea star, 1. starfish. **2.** any star which guides mariners at sea.

sea step, one of a set of narrow steps on the side of a ship, used in going on board from a boat when the side ladders are unshipped.

sea swallow, a tern: *The swifts have gone, but the terns — "sea swallows" — still linger near their nesting places* (London Times).

sea swell, a wave of symmetrical form which has outrun the wind which produced it.

seat[1] (sēt), *n.* **1.** something to sit on, as a chair, stool, bench, or sofa: *Take a seat, please.* **2.** a place to sit: *Can you find a seat on the train?* **3.** that part of a chair, stool, bench, etc., on which one sits: *This bench has a broken seat.* **4.** that part of the body on which one sits, or the clothing covering it: *The seat of his trousers was patched.* **5.** a place in which one has the right to sit: *Please reserve a seat on the next airplane for me. Our seats are in the fifth row of the first balcony.* **6.** a right to sit as a member, or the position of being a member, of a lawmaking or deliberative body, a stock exchange, or the like: *Ohio's five-term Governor Frank Lausche, fabled Democratic votegetter ... announced that day his candidacy for Bender's Senate seat* (Time). **7.** manner of sitting on horseback: *He ... had the graceful seat of an experienced horseman* (Dickens). **8.** that on which anything rests or appears to rest; base.
—*v.t.* **1.** to place on a seat or seats; cause to sit down: *to seat a person on a chair, to seat oneself at the piano.* **2.** to have seats for (a specified number): *a hall seating 300 people.* **3.** to provide with a seat or seats: *to seat a church for 1,000 people.* **4.** to put a seat on (a chair, trousers, etc.). **5.** to establish or give the right to sit in a lawmaking body, a stock exchange, or the like: *General Romulo ... declared he was still opposed to seating the Chinese Communists in the United Nations* (New York Times).
be seated, a. to sit down: *Please be seated.* **b.** to be sitting: *He was seated in A Chariot of an inestimable value* (Shakespeare).
[< Scandinavian (compare Old Icelandic *sǣti*)] —**seat′less,** *adj.*

seat[2] (sēt), *n.* **1.** an established place or center: *A university is a seat of learning.* **2.** a city or place in which a government, throne, or the like is established; capital: *Our county seat has a large high school. The seat of our government is in Washington, D. C.* **3. a.** the throne of a king, bishop, or the like. **b.** the authority or dignity of a king, bishop, or the like. **4.** a residence; home: *The family seat of the Howards is in Kent.* **5.** location; situation; site: *the seat of a disease. The seat of ethics is in our hearts, not in our minds* (Atlantic).
—*v.t.* to fix in a particular or proper place; locate.
be seated, to be situated in a certain position or place; be located: *London ... is seated on clay* (Thomas Henry Huxley).
[probably extended use of *seat*[1]; influenced by uses of Latin *sēdes*]
—**Syn.** *n.* **4.** abode.

sea tangle, any of various brown seaweeds.

seat belt, a safety device in an automobile or airplane consisting of straps fastened to the seat and buckled across the occupant's lap; safety belt: *To cut the mounting toll of deaths and injuries on the highway, the latest cars offer lifesaving seat belts ... so crucial in keeping driver and passengers from being hurled against windshields or car fixtures in case of collisions* (Time). See **safety belt** for picture.

-seated, *combining form.* having a ___ seat or seats: *Two-seated = having two seats.*

seat·er (sē′tər), *n.* **1.** a person who seats. **2.** *U.S. Historical.* a person who assigned seats at a meeting of settlers or citizens.

seat·ing (sē′ting), *n.* **1.** the act of providing with a seat or seats. **2. a.** the arrangement of seats in a building, for a party, etc. **b.** the seats themselves. **3.** material for the seats of chairs, etc. **4. a.** a support. **b.** a part resting on a support.

seat·mate (sēt′māt′), *n.* a person sitting next to one on a bus, train, aircraft, etc.: *Aboard the plane he had struck up a casual conversation with his seatmate, a man he had never met before* (Wall Street Journal).

seat-mile (sēt′mīl′), *n.* one mile multiplied by the number of seats in a plane, used as a unit in determining the costs, profits, etc., in air transportation: *A fifty-seat plane flying a 1,000 mile trip flies 50,000 seat-miles.*

SEATO (no periods) or **S.E.A.T.O.,** Southeast Asia Treaty Organization (group of eight nations, consisting of Australia, France, Great Britain, New Zealand, Pakistan, the Philippines, Thailand, and the United States, that signed a treaty in 1954 for common defense against military aggression in southeastern Asia).

seat-of-the-pants (sēt′əv ᴛʜə pants′), *adj. Slang.* **1.** experienced in navigating without instruments: *He applied the principles that he found most successful as a seat-of-the-pants bush flier, in outwitting the wind* (Atlantic). **2.** based upon accumulated experience: *The architect ... must still have the capacity for a fair measure of seat-of-the-pants design* (New Scientist).

sea train, a seagoing vessel with tracks on its deck for railroad cars, used especially in coastal traffic.

sea trout, 1. any of various species of trout which spend part of their life in salt water, as the brown trout of Europe. **2.** any of several weakfishes.

Se·at·tle·ite (sē at′ə līt), *n.* a native or inhabitant of Seattle, Washington: *Seattleites regard Canlis as their most elegant and expensive restaurant* (Harper's).

sea turn, a gale or breeze coming from the sea, generally accompanied by mists.

sea turtle, any of various large turtles or tortoises living in the sea; any marine chelonian, having the limbs formed as flippers, as the green turtle, leatherback, and loggerhead. See **turtle** for picture.

seat·work (sēt′wėrk′), *n.* work or assignments that a child does at his seat in the classroom.

seau (sō), *n., pl.* **seaux** (sōz; *French* sō). a pail-shaped vessel belonging to a dinner service, made by English potters in the 1700's. [< French *seau* bucket]

sea unicorn, the narwhal, so called from the single hornlike tusk of the male, sometimes 8 feet long.

sea urchin, 1. any of a class of echinoderms, consisting of marine animals having a rounded or disklike body and a hard shell formed of calcareous plates bearing many movable spines. **2.** a tall shrub of western Australia with globular clusters of crimson flowers whose yellow styles project beyond the perianth.

Sea Urchin (diameter, about 3 in.)

sea·view (sē′vyü′), *n.* **1.** a view or prospect of the sea, or at sea: *a room with a seaview.* **2.** a picture representing a scene at sea; seascape.

sea wall, a strong wall or embankment made to prevent the waves from wearing away the shore, to act as a breakwater, etc.: *Sea walls to protect the Netherlands against flooding from the sea were the unanimous recommendation of the Government's Delta Commission* (Warren E. Howland).

sea walnut, any of various ctenophores resembling a walnut in shape.

sea·wan (sē′wən), *n.* loose or unstrung beads made from shells, once used by certain tribes of North American Indians as money. Also, **sewan.** [earlier *sewan* < Algonkian (Narragansett) *siwan* scattered, (literally) unstrung < *siwen* he scatters]

sea·want (sē′wənt), *n.* seawan.

sea·ward (sē′wərd), *adv., adj.* toward the sea: *a seaward breeze. The river glided seaward* (Robert Louis Stevenson). —*n.* the direction toward the sea or away from land: *The island lies a mile to seaward.*

sea·wards (sē′wərdz), *adv.* seaward.

sea·ware (sē′wãr′), *n.* seaweed, especially coarse seaweed used as manure. [Old English *sǣwār* < *sǣ* sea + *wār* alga]

sea·wa·ter (sē′wôt′ər, -wot′-), *n.* the salt water of the sea or ocean: *Seawater can get as cold as 28 degrees without freezing because of the salt in solution* (Science News Letter).

sea·way (sē′wā′), *n.* **1.** a way over the sea, especially a regular shipping lane. **2.** the sea as a means of communication; the open sea. **3.** the progress of a ship through the waves; headway: *to lose seaway.* **4.** a rough sea: *... a very safe boat ... buoyant and clever in a seaway* (Robert Louis Stevenson). **5.** an inland waterway that connects with the open sea and is deep enough to permit ocean shipping: *The seaway, however, will provide the deep channel only from Lake Erie east through the St. Lawrence River* (New York Times).

sea·weed (sē′wēd′), *n.* any plant or plants growing in the sea, especially any of various algae growing in the sea.

sea whip, a gorgonian coral of slender, straight, or spiral shape that has small branches or is branchless: *... forests of sea whips, sea fans, and giant sponges* (Harper's).

sea wind, a wind blowing from the sea toward the land.

sea wolf, 1. a pirate. **2.** a privateering vessel.

sea worm, any free-moving worm living in salt water; marine annelid.

sea·wor·thi·ness (sē′wėr′ᴛʜē nis), *n.* the quality or condition of being seaworthy.

sea·wor·thy (sē′wėr′ᴛʜē), *adj.* fit for sailing on the sea; able to stand storms at sea: *a seaworthy ship or hull.*

sea wrack, seaweed, especially any of the large, coarse kinds cast upon the shore.

se·ba·ceous (si bā′shəs), *adj.* **1.** having to do with fat; fatty; greasy. **2.** secreting sebum. [< Latin *sēbum* tallow, grease, suet + English *-aceous*] —**Syn. 1.** oily, oleaginous.

sebaceous gland, any of the glands in the deeper layer of the skin that supply oil to the skin and hair.

se·bac·ic acid (si bas′ik, -bā′sik), a white crystalline acid obtained by the distillation of castor oil, used to make fruit flavors, perfumes, lubricants, etc. *Formula:* $C_{10}H_{18}O_4$ [< French *sébacique* < Latin *sēbum* tallow, grease]

se·bes·ten or **se·bes·tan** (si bes′tən), *n.* **1.** a plumlike fruit borne by an East Indian tree of the borage family, used in the East, and formerly in Europe, for medicinal purposes. **2.** the tree it grows on. **3.** the fruit of a related species or the tree it grows on. [< Arabic *sabastān* < Persian *sapistān*]

se·bif·er·ous (si bif′ər əs), *adj.* **1.** producing or secreting fat, as certain glands. **2.** *Botany.* producing vegetable wax or tallow. [< Latin *sēbum* tallow, grease + *ferre* to carry + English *-ous*]

se·bip·a·rous (si bip′ər əs), *adj.* producing fatty matter (sebum). [< Latin *sēbum* tallow, grease + *parere* to bear + English *-ous*]

seb·or·rhe·a or **seb·or·rhoe·a** (seb′ə-rē′ə), *n.* an abnormal discharge from the sebaceous glands, forming an oily coating on the skin. [< New Latin *sebum* tallow, grease + Greek *rhein* to flow]

seb·or·rhe·al or **seb·or·rhoe·al** (seb′ə-rē′əl), *adj.* having to do with or affected with seborrhea.

seb·or·rhe·ic or **seb·or·rhoe·ic** (seb′ə-rē′ik), *adj.* of or having to do with seborrhea.

se·bum (sē′bəm), *n.* the fatty secretion of the sebaceous glands. [< New Latin *sebum* < Latin *sēbum* tallow, grease]

sec (sek), *adj.* (of wines) dry; not sweet (applied originally and still especially to champagne). [< French *sec* (literally) dry < Latin *siccus*]

sec (no period), secant.

sec., an abbreviation for the following:
1. according to (*Latin,* secundum).
2. secant.
3. second or seconds.
4. secondary.
5. secretary.
6. section or sections.
7. sector.

SEC (no periods) or **S.E.C.,** Securities and Exchange Commission.

se·cant (sē′kənt, -kant), *n.* **1.** *Geometry.* a line that intersects a curve at two or more points. **2.** *Trigonometry.* **a.** the ratio of the length of a hypotenuse of a right-angled triangle to the length of the side adjacent to an acute angle. It is the reciprocal of the cosine. **b.** a straight line drawn from the center of a circle through one extremity of an arc to the tangent from the other extremity of the same arc. **c.** the ratio of the length of this line to the length of the radius of the circle. *Abbr.:* sec (no period). —*adj.* intersecting: *a secant plane.* [< Latin *secāns, -antis,* present participle of *secāre* to cut]

Secant (def. 2): The ratio of AB to AD is the secant of the angle A, and AB is the secant of the arc CD.

sec·a·teurs (sek′ə tėrz), *n.pl. Especially British.* pruning shears: *She snipped at the roses with her secateurs* (Punch). [< French *sécateur* (singular) < Latin *secāre* to cut]

sec·co (sek′ō), *adj. Music.* dry; unaccompanied; plain. —*n.* secco painting. [< Italian *secco* < Latin *siccus* dry]

secco painting, painting on dry plaster with water colors; tempera.

se·cede (si sēd′), *v.i.,* **-ced·ed, -ced·ing.** to withdraw formally from an organization: [*President*] *Buchanan reiterated that the South had no right to secede* (Herbert Agar). [< Latin *sēcēdere* < *sē-* apart + *cēdere* go]

se·ced·er (si sē′dər), *n.* one who withdraws formally from association with an organization.

se·cern (si sėrn′), *v.t., v.i.* **1.** to discriminate. **2.** *Physiology.* to secrete. [< Latin *sēcernere* < *sē-* aside, apart + *cernere* distinguish]

se·cern·ent (si sėr′nənt), *adj. Physiology.* that secretes.

se·cern·ment (si sėrn′mənt), *n. Physiology.* secretion.

se·ces·sion (si sesh′ən), *n.* **1.** the act of formally withdrawing from an organization; a seceding. **2.** Also, **Secession.** *U.S. History.* the seceding of the eleven Southern states from the Union in 1860-61, which culminated in the Civil War. [< Latin *sēcessiō, -ōnis* < *sēcēdere;* see SECEDE]

se·ces·sion·al (si sesh′ə nəl), *adj.* of or having to do with secession.

se·ces·sion·ism (si sesh′ə niz əm), *n.* the principles of those in favor of secession.

se·ces·sion·ist (si sesh′ə nist), *n.* **1.** a person or group that favors secession or joins in a secession. **2.** Also, **Secessionist.** *U.S. History.* a person who supported or participated in the secession of the Southern states from the Union in 1860-61. —*adj.* favoring secession; separatist: *... still another attempt to force the secessionist province of Katanga back under the authority of the central government* (Time). —**Syn.** *n.* **1.** seceder.

sec.-ft., second-foot.

sech (no periods), hyperbolic secant.

seck (sek), *adj.* (of rents) not returning a profit. [< Anglo-French (*rente*) *secque* dry (rent), ultimately < Latin *siccus* dry]

Seck·el or **seck·el** (sek′əl, sik′-), *n.* an American variety of small, sweet, reddish-brown pear. Also, **Sickle.** [American English < *Seckel,* a Philadelphian, who introduced the variety]

sec. leg., secundum legem.

Sec. Leg., Secretary of Legation.

se·clude (si klüd′), *v.t.,* **-clud·ed, -clud·ing. 1.** to keep apart from company; shut off from others: *He secludes himself and sees only his close friends.* **2.** *Obsolete.* to shut or keep out; exclude: *He has the doors and windows open in the hardest frosts, secluding only the snow* (John Evelyn). [< Latin *sēclūdere* < *sē-* apart + *claudere* shut] —**Syn. 1.** withdraw, isolate, sequester.

se·clud·ed (si klü′did), *adj.* shut off from others; undisturbed; remote: *a secluded village.* —**se·clud′ed·ly,** *adv.* —**se·clud′ed·ness,** *n.* —**Syn.** withdrawn, isolated.

se·clu·sion (si klü′zhən), *n.* **1.** the act of secluding. **2.** the state of being secluded; retirement: *Brought up ... in severe seclusion ...* (John Ruskin). **3.** a secluded place: *Sweet seclusions for holy thoughts and prayers* (Longfellow). [< Medieval Latin *seclusio, -onis* < Latin *sēclūdere;* see SECLUDE]

se·clu·sion·ist (si klü′zhə nist), *n.* a person who favors or advocates seclusion, such as a supporter of monasticism or one who opposes the admission of foreigners to his country.

se·clu·sive (si klü′siv), *adj.* **1.** fond of seclusion. **2.** tending to seclude. —**se·clu′sive·ly,** *adv.* —**se·clu′sive·ness,** *n.*

sec·o·bar·bi·tal (sē′kō bär′bə tôl, -tal), *n.* a white barbiturate used (usually in the form of secobarbital sodium) as a sedative for nervousness and sleeplessness. *Formula:* $C_{12}H_{18}N_2O_3$

secobarbital sodium, the form of secobarbital commonly used in medicine. *Formula:* $C_{12}H_{17}N_2O_3Na$

Sec·o·nal (sek′ə nəl, -nôl, -nol), *n. Trademark.* secobarbital.

sec·ond[1] (sek′ənd), *adj.* **1.** coming next after the first: *the second seat from the front, the second volume of a book, second prize.* **2.** below the first: *the second officer on a ship.* **3.** inferior to the first; next to the best: *second quality.* **4.** another: *to take a second sheet of paper. Napoleon has been called a second Caesar.* **5.** *Music.* **a.** lower in pitch. **b.** rendering a part lower in pitch: *second soprano.* —*adv.* in the second group, division, rank, etc.; secondly: *to speak second.*
—*n.* **1.** a person or thing that is second. **2. a.** a person who aids or supports another; backer. **b.** a person who attends a boxer or duelist: *Seated in his corner, Cockell was closely examined by his seconds, who did their best to close a deep cut between the eyes* (London Times). **3.** *Music.* **a.** a tone on the next degree from a given tone. **b.** the interval between two consecutive tones of the scale. **c.** the harmonic combination of such tones. **d.** the second part in a concerted piece. **e.** a voice or instrument rendering such a part. **f.** the second tone in any scale. **g.** the subordinate part in a duet; secondo. **4.** the forward gear or speed of an automobile, having a ratio to the engine speed between that of low and high. **seconds, a.** articles below first quality: *These stockings are seconds and have some slight defects.* **b.** an inferior, coarse flour: *Some millers sell only seconds.* **c.** the bread made from it: *to buy seconds at the baker's.*
—*v.t.* **1. a.** to support; back up; assist: *Deeds must second words when needful* (Thomas Arnold). **b.** to attend (a boxer or duelist). **2.** to express approval or support of (a motion, amendment, proposal, or the one who makes it). **3.** *British.* to transfer temporarily to another assignment, by secondment. **4.** *Obsolete.* to repeat, as an action. [< Old French *seconde,* learned borrowing from Latin *secundus* (literally) following, second (of a series), present participle of *sequī* follow. Doublet of SECUND.]

sec·ond[2] (sek′ənd), *n.* **1.** 1/60 of a minute; 1/3600 of an hour. **2.** a very short time; instant; moment. **3.** 1/3600 of a degree of an angle (often indicated by the symbol ″): *12°10′30″ means 12 degrees, 10 minutes, 30 seconds. Abbr.:* sec.
[< Old French *seconde* < Medieval Latin *secundum* second; division of time; also *secunda* (*minuta*) second (minute), that is, the result of the second division of the hour by sixty]

sec·ond-act (sek′ənd akt′), *v.t., v.i. Slang.* to steal into a theater during the intermission before the second act without paying admission. —**sec′ond act′er.**

Second Advent, the second coming of Christ at the millennium.

Second Adventist, a person who believes in the Second Advent; millenarian or premillenarian.

sec·ond·ar·i·ly (sek′ən der′ə lē), *adv.* **1.** indirectly. **2.** subordinately. **3.** *Obsolete.* secondly.

sec·ond·ar·i·ness (sek′ən der′ē nis), *n.* **1.** subordinate character or position. **2.** secondary quality.

sec·ond·ar·y (sek′ən der′ē), *adj., n., pl.* **-ar·ies.** —*adj.* **1.** next after the first in order, place, time, etc.: *a secondary layer of tissue. Other industries, especially the lighter ones, are called secondary because they employ the products of previous manufacture as their raw materials* (Finch and Trewartha). **2.** not main or chief; having less importance: *Reading fast is secondary to reading well.* **3.** not original; derived: *a secondary source of the report.* **4.** *Chemistry.* involving the substitution of two atoms or groups. **5.** *Electricity.* of or having to do with a coil or circuit in which a current is produced by induction. **6.** *Geology.* produced from another mineral by decay, alteration, or the like. **7.** (of suffixes, derivation, etc.) added to or based on a form which is itself a derivative.
—*n.* **1.** a person or thing that is secondary, second in importance, or subordinate. **2.** a secondary accent. **3.** a secondary coil. **4.** a secondary feather. **5.** a satellite of a planet. [< Latin *secundārius* of the second class or quality < *secundus;* see SECOND[1]]
—**Syn.** *adj.* **2.** subordinate, subsidiary, auxiliary, inferior, minor. **3.** derivative.

secondary accent, 1. a stress accent that is weaker than the strongest stress in a word (primary accent), but stronger than no stress, as on the second syllable of *ab·bre′vi·a′tion.* **2.** the mark (′) used to show a stress that is weaker than a primary accent.

secondary boycott, the practice of combining to prevent the handling of goods of one manufacturer, employer, union, etc., as a means of intimidating or coercing a second manufacturer, employer, group of workers, etc.: *Reps. Griffin ... and Landrum ... presented last-minute counterproposals in the troublesome areas of curbs on secondary boycotts and picketing* (Wall Street Journal).

secondary cell, a storage battery.

secondary coil, a coil in which an electric current is produced by induction, as in a transformer.

secondary distribution, secondary offering.

secondary electron, an electron given off by secondary emission. An anode struck by electrons flowing from a cathode will give off secondary electrons.

secondary emission, the freeing of electrons from the surface of a metal or other substance by bombardment with other electrons or ions.

secondary feather, one of the flight feathers on the forearm of a bird's wing.

secondary group, *Sociology.* a specialized, often formal, group whose members have less intimate contact with each other than those of a primary group: *In the setting of secondary groups, since only superficial and limited aspects of personality are controlled, there is more freedom for the individual but this freedom may lead to loneliness and confusion* (Ogburn and Nimkoff).

secondary metal, metal obtained from scrap or as a by-product in producing other metal.

secondary offering, the putting up for sale of a large block of stock that has been held by a stockholder or corporation, often to settle an estate, liquidate holdings, etc.: *As in the case of all secondary offerings, the proceeds accrue to selling stockholders and not to the company* (Wall Street Journal).

secondary rainbow, an outer and fainter rainbow parallel with the primary bow, formed by rays reflected twice within each raindrop.

secondary root, *Botany.* a branch of a primary root.

secondary school, a school for instruction above the elementary level but below the collegiate level; a high school or (in England) a public school.

secondary seventh chord, *Music.* a seventh chord constructed upon any tone other than the dominant.

secondary syphilis, syphilis in its second stage, characterized by anemia, skin disease, inflammation of mucous membranes, and swelling of lymph glands.

secondary wave, an earthquake wave in which rock particles vibrate at right angles to the direction of travel.

se·con·da vol·ta (sä kōn′dä vôl′tä), *Music.* the second time. [< Italian *seconda vòlta*]

second ballot, 1. an electoral method in which a second or supplementary election is held when no candidate has secured a majority of the votes cast. **2.** the second poll itself.

second banana, *Slang.* **1.** a comedian who supports the leading comic actor: *Art Carney has emerged as one of the best known second bananas in television, but he has no desire to be a top banana such as his boss* (New York Times). **2.** the person next below a leader in any field; second-in-command.

sec·ond-best (sek′ənd best′), *adj.* next in quality to the first: *In that case the second-best solution would be for Britain and France to put their nuclear forces under some form of joint control* (Manchester Guardian Weekly). —*n.* a person or thing inferior to the best.
—*adv.* **come off second-best,** to be defeated in a contest: *I am glad to hear of fighting, even though we come off second-best* (Abigail Adams).

second childhood, a foolish or childish condition caused by old age; dotage.

sec·ond-class (sek′ənd klas′, -kläs′), *adj.* **1.** of or belonging to the class next after the first: *second-class mail.* **2.** having to do with the second grade of conveyances or accommodations for travel: *a second-class car, a second-class ticket.* **3.** of inferior grade or quality; second-rate.
—*adv.* on a second-class ship, train, etc.: *to travel second-class.*

second-class matter, (in the postal system of the United States) newspapers and other periodicals, issued at stated intervals, and sent from the office of publication.

Second Coming, Second Advent.

sec·ond-de·gree burn (sek′ənd di grē′), a burn in which blisters are formed.

second-degree murder, *Law.* homicide committed unintentionally but without justification.

sec·ond-drawer (sek′ənd drôr′), *adj. Informal.* of lesser importance; secondary; second-rate: *The defendants in the trial were second-drawer leaders of the U.S. Communist Party* (Time).

se·conde (si kond′; *French* sə gôNd′), *n. Fencing.* the second in a series of eight defensive positions or parries. [< French *seconde,* feminine of *second* second¹]

Second Empire, of or having to do with a style of dress, furniture, etc., derived from the Empire style and in fashion during the second French Empire (1852-1870).

sec·ond·er (sek′ən dər), *n.* a person who seconds; person who approves and supports what another attempts, affirms, or proposes: *the seconder of a motion.*

second fiddle, a secondary part.
be or **play second fiddle (to),** to take a lesser part or position; play a secondary role: *In any case, the Navy is playing second fiddle to the Air Force* (New York Times).

sec·ond-foot (sek′ənd fu̇t′), *n., pl.* **-feet.** foot-second. *Abbr.:* sec.-ft.

second gear, an intermediate speed gear of an automobile; second.

sec·ond-gen·er·a·tion missile (sek′ənd-jen′ə rā′shən), a guided missile improved by experience gained from constructing earlier missiles.

sec·ond-guess (sek′ənd ges′), *v.t.* to say afterwards what someone ought to have said; to use hindsight to correct: *Armed with . . . their most involved charts and theories, the economists are out in force to second-guess the President and his own economic advisers* (Newsweek). —**sec′ond-guess′er,** *n.*

sec·ond-hand (sek′ənd hand′), *adj.* **1.** not original; obtained from another: *second-hand information.* **2.** not new; used or worn already by someone else: *a second-hand car, second-hand clothes, second-hand books.* **3.** dealing in used goods: *a second-hand bookshop. Uncle Gilbert advised my grandmother to get rid of everything—sell it to a second-hand dealer* (New Yorker).
—*adv.* from somewhere other than the original source; not directly: *Babylonian culture could continue to reach Canaan second-hand* (S. Cook).

second hand, 1. the hand on a clock or watch showing the passage of time in seconds. It moves around the dial once in a minute. **2.** *Obsolete.* an intermediary; middleman.

sec·ond-in-com·mand (sek′ənd in kə-mand′), *n., pl.* **sec·onds-in-com·mand.** a person ranking in authority next to the one in charge: *He is showing increased inclination to choose the current second-in-command as the successor to the departing agency chief* (Atlantic).

second intention, the healing of a wound by the formation of granulated tissue in the wound cavity.

Second International, an international socialistic society formed in Paris in 1889, and succeeded by the Socialist and Labor International in 1923.

second lieutenant, *U.S.* a commissioned officer of the air force, army, or marines having the lowest rank, next below a first lieutenant, often having command of a platoon.

sec·ond·ly (sek′ənd lē), *adv.* in the second place.

sec·ond·ment (sek′ənd mənt), *n. British.* temporary transfer to another position or staff, usually without loss of position or seniority in the organization from which the transfer takes place: *What is still lacking in most advanced countries, including Britain, is a regular system of secondment under which the expert and the teacher can work for a fixed period in an undeveloped country* (New Scientist).

second mortgage, a mortgage second in point of claim to a first mortgage.

second nature, a habit, quality, knowledge, etc., that a person has acquired and had for so long that it seems to be almost a part of his nature.

se·con·do (sä kōn′dō), *n., pl.* **-di** (-dē). *Music.* **1.** the subordinate part, as in a duet. **2.** the performer of this part. [< Italian *secondo* < Latin *secundus;* see SECOND¹]

second person, 1. the form of a pronoun which refers to the person spoken to, as *you, your,* etc. **2.** the form of a verb which has *you* as its subject.

second pilot, a copilot.

second quarter, 1. the period between the first half moon and full moon. **2.** the phase of the moon when it has revolved far enough to reveal its entire face; full moon.

sec·ond-rate (sek′ənd rāt′), *adj.* **1.** rated as second-class. **2.** inferior: *a very second-rate meal.* —**sec′ond-rate′ness,** *n.* —**Syn. 2.** middling.

sec·ond-rat·er (sek′ənd rā′tər), *n.* a second-rate person or thing.

Second Reich, the German Empire begun by Otto Von Bismarck in 1871 and terminated in 1919 by the defeat of the Germans in World War I.

Second Republic, the government of France from 1848 to 1852.

sec·ond-run (sek′ənd run′), *adj.* **1.** (of a new motion picture) not shown for the first time; shown after its general release; not first-run: *The movies were second-run and six a day* (Atlantic). **2.** (of a theater) featuring second-run motion pictures: *The number of cinemas has been reduced . . . by the closing of second-run houses* (Manchester Guardian Weekly).

sec·onds (sek′əndz), *n.pl.* See under **second¹,** *n.*

second sight, the supposed power of seeing distant objects or future events as if they were present. —**Syn.** clairvoyance.

sec·ond-sight·ed (sek′ənd sī′tid), *adj.* having second sight.

second sound, *Physics.* the rapid heat transfer of helium at very low temperatures by a motion like that of sound waves.

second speed, second gear; second.

sec·ond-sto·ry man (sek′ənd stôr′ē, -stōr′-), *U.S.* a cat burglar.

sec·ond-strike (sek′ənd strīk′), *adj.* **1.** (of a nuclear weapon or force) able to retaliate or strike back after a nuclear attack. **2.** of retaliation; retaliatory: *second-strike capability.*

sec·ond-string (sek′ənd string′), *adj.* **1.** second-rate; secondary; subordinate: *second-string executives, a second-string college.* **2.** *Sports.* not of the first or regular team: *a second-string quarterback.*

sec·ond-string·er (sek′ənd string′ər), *n. Informal.* a second-string person; subordinate.

second thought, a thought or idea occurring later.
on second thought, upon further consideration: *On second thought, how can we be sure?*

Second Triumvirate, the alliance in ancient Rome (43 B.C.) of Octavius, Mark Antony, and Lepidus.

second wind, 1. a renewal of regular breathing and energy while continuing the activity that brought about the original loss of breath or fatigue. **2.** any renewal of energy: *Packaging workers seem to go faster when they get their second wind after a cup of coffee* (Wall Street Journal).

Second World War, the world war, 1939-1945, that ended with the defeat of the Axis powers, Germany, Italy, Japan, and their allies; World War II.

sec·par (sek′pär′), *n.* parsec.

se·cre·cy (sē′krə sē), *n., pl.* **-cies. 1.** the condition of being secret: *to carry out a plan in secrecy.* **2.** the condition of being kept secret: *to observe the strictest secrecy.* **3.** the ability to keep things secret: *to give a promise of secrecy.* **4.** a tendency to conceal; lack of frankness: *to maintain secrecy as to one's plans.* [alteration of Middle English *secretie* < *secre* secret + *-tie* -ty]

se·cret (sē′krit), *adj.* **1.** kept from the knowledge of others: *a secret marriage, a secret errand.* **2.** keeping to oneself what one knows: *He is as secret as a mouse.* **3.** known only to a few: *a secret society.* **4.** kept from sight; hidden: *a secret drawer, a secret passage.* **5.** retired; secluded: *a secret place.* **6.** working or acting in secret: *a secret agent, secret police.* **7.** very hard to understand or discover.
—*n.* **1.** something secret or hidden; mystery: *Can you keep a secret?* **2.** a thing known only to a few: *The secret of the authorship was known to only one man* (Edward Bok). *Each cherished a secret, which she did not confide to the other* (Longfellow). **3.** a hidden cause or reason: *the secret of her charm.*
in secret, in private; not openly or publicly: *I spake openly to the world . . . in secret have I said nothing* (John 18:20).
[< Old French *secret,* learned borrowing from Latin *sēcrētus,* past participle of *sēcernere* set apart < *sē-* apart + *cernere* to separate. Doublet of SECRETE.] —**se′cret·ness,** *n.*
—**Syn.** *adj.* **1. Secret, covert, clandestine** mean done, made, or carried on without the knowledge of others. **Secret** is the general term, and applies to concealment of any kind and for any purpose: *They have secret plans.* **Covert** suggests partial concealment, and applies to anything kept under cover, disguised, or not openly revealed: *A hint is a covert suggestion.* **Clandestine** suggests concealment for an unlawful or wicked purpose: *He feared someone would learn of his clandestine trips.* **2.** uncommunicative, secretive. **4.** concealed, covered. **7.** obscure, recondite, esoteric.

Se·cret (sē′krit), *n.* a prayer or prayers following the Offertory and before the Preface of the Mass, recited inaudibly, except for the last phrase, by the celebrant.

se·cre·ta (si krē′tə), *n.pl.* the products of secretion. [< New Latin *secreta,* neuter plural of Latin *sēcrētus;* see SECRET]

se·cre·tage (sē′krə tij), *n.* a process in preparing furs, using mercury or some of its salts to impart the property of felting to the fur. [< French *secrétage*]

secret agent, an agent of the government secret service; a spy: . . . *Soviet technicians who were actually secret agents* (Newsweek).

se·cre·ta·gogue (si krē′tə gôg, -gog), *n.* a substance that promotes secretion: *These secretagogues are distinct from the irritant substances contained in many tear gases that induce reflex tearing* (Scientific American). [< New Latin *secreta* secreta + Greek *agōgós* leading < *ágein* to lead]

sec·re·taire (sek′rə tãr′), *n.* a high desk shaped like a cabinet, with drawers and pigeonholes. [< French *secrétaire*]

sec·re·tar·i·al (sek′rə tãr′ē əl), *adj.* of a secretary; having to do with a secretary: *She learned to do stenography, typewriting, and other secretarial work.*

sec·re·tar·i·at (sek′rə tãr′ē it, -at), *n.* **1. a.** the office or position of secretary, now especially of a secretary as the administrative head of a government department or similar organization. **b.** the department itself, including staff, buildings, etc.: *Coordinating the labors of these far-flung agencies and linking them to the U.N. proper is the job of the Secretariat* (Time). **2.** a group of secretaries within a government, department, etc. **3.** the place where a secretary transacts business. [< French *secrétariat* < Old French *secretaire* secretary, learned borrowing from Late Latin *sēcrētārius*]

sec·re·tar·i·ate (sek′rə tãr′ē it), *n.* secretariat.

sec·re·tar·y (sek′rə ter′ē), *n., pl.* **-tar·ies.** **1.** a person who writes letters, keeps records, etc., for a person, company, club, etc.: *a private secretary. Our club has a secretary who keeps the minutes of the meeting.* **2.** an official who administers a department of the government: *The Secretary of the Treasury is the head of the Treasury Department.* **3.** a diplomatic agent, usually of a lower rank in an embassy or legation, often designated as first secretary, second secretary, etc. *Abbr.:* sec. **4.** a writing desk with a set of drawers and often with shelves for books. [< Late Latin *sēcrētārius* confidential officer < Latin *sēcrētum* a secret, neuter of *sēcrētus;* see SECRET] —**Syn. 1.** clerk.

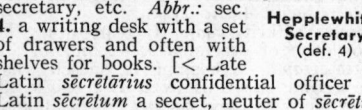

Hepplewhite Secretary (def. 4)

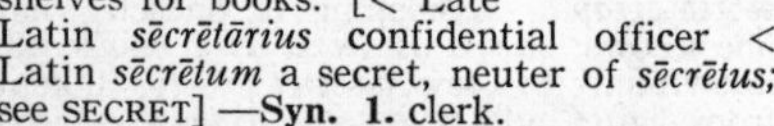

secretary bird, a large, long-legged African bird of prey that feeds on reptiles, so called because its crest suggests pens stuck behind the ear.

Secretary Bird (including tail, 4 ft. long)

sec·re·tar·y-gen·er·al (sek′rə ter′ē-jen′ər əl,-jen′rəl), *n., pl.* **sec·re·tar·ies-gen·er·al.** the chief secretary; administrative head of a secretariat, as in certain societies, the United Nations, etc.

Secretary of State, 1. *U.S.* **a.** the head of the State Department and principal advisor to the President on foreign affairs. **b.** an officer of a State government in charge of making and keeping records. **2.** *British.* the head of any of various government departments.

sec·re·tar·y·ship (sek′rə ter′ē ship), *n.* the position, duties, etc., of a secretary.

secret ballot, voting in secret, usually on printed or written ballots that are put in a ballot box.

se·crete[1] (si krēt′), *v.t.,* **-cret·ed, -cret·ing.** **1.** to hide; keep secret: *A certain French lady . . . had secreted herself on board the vessel* (John Leland). **2.** to remove secretly; appropriate in a secret manner: *He was delivering back to the Company money of their own, which he had secreted from them* (Edmund Burke). [< Latin *sēcrētus.* Doublet of SECRET.] —**Syn. 1.** conceal, ensconce.

se·crete[2] (si krēt′), *v.t.,* **-cret·ed, -cret·ing.** to make, prepare, or produce by the process of secretion: *Glands in the mouth secrete saliva. Most people secrete the appropriate blood group substances (antigens) in bodily secretions such as saliva and tears* (Science News). [back formation < *secretion*]

se·cre·tin (si krē′tin), *n.* an intestinal hormone that stimulates secretion of the pancreatic juice by the pancreas.

se·cre·tion (si krē′shən), *n.* **1.** a substance, as bile, saliva, milk, etc., separated from or formed out of the blood or sap of an animal or plant: *Bile is the secretion of the liver.* **2.** the act or process of secreting or producing such a substance. **3.** a concealing; hiding. [< Latin *sēcrētiō, -ōnis* < *sēcrētus;* see SECRET]

se·cre·tion·al (si krē′shə nəl), *adj.* of or having to do with secretion; secretory.

se·cre·tion·ar·y (si krē′shə ner′ē), *adj.* secretional.

se·cre·tive (si krē′tiv), *adj.* **1.** having the habit of secrecy; not frank and open: *There was certainly nothing secretive or hidden in the Poujadists' campaign, animated as it was by shouting hecklers . . . that echoed in every corner of France* (New Yorker). **2.** causing or aiding secretion. —**se·cre′tive·ly,** *adv.* —**se·cre′tive·ness,** *n.* —**Syn. 1.** reticent.

se·cret·ly (sē′krit lē), *adv.* without knowledge by others.

se·cre·to-in·hib·i·to·ry (si krē′tō in hib′ə tôr′ē, -tōr′-), *adj.* that diminishes secretion of the glands: *secreto-inhibitory nerves.*

se·cre·to·mo·tor (si krē′tō mō′tər), *adj.* that increases secretion of the glands.

se·cre·tor (si krē′tər), *n.* a person or thing that secretes: *the silk secretor of a spider. These latter subjects, called secretors, also pour out their specific water-soluble blood group substances in the digestive juices* (New Scientist).

se·cre·to·ry (si krē′tər ē), *adj., n., pl.* **-ries.** —*adj.* of or causing secretion; secreting. —*n.* an organ of the body that secretes.

secret police, a governmental police force working to control and spy on persons considered dangerous or subversive, as in certain dictatorial governments: *For another term he would continue to ignore the civil rights of citizens, muzzle press, radio, and T.V., and liquidate all opposition with the help of his efficient secret police and their legion of local spies* (Atlantic).

secret service, 1. a branch of a government that makes secret investigations. **2.** official service of a secret nature. **3.** Secret Service. —**se′cret-serv′ice,** *adj.*

Secret Service, the branch of the United States Treasury Department concerned with discovering and preventing counterfeiting, with protecting the President, and, in wartime, with espionage.

secret society, an organization to promote some cause by secret methods, its members being sworn to observe secrecy.

secs., 1. seconds. **2.** sections.

sect (sekt), *n.* **1.** a group of persons having the same principles, beliefs, or opinions: *a philosophical sect. Each religious sect in the town had its own church.* **2.** a religious group separated from an established church. **3.** *Obsolete.* a class or kind (of persons). [< Latin *secta* party, school, probably < *sectārī* keep following < *sequī* to follow] —**Syn. 1.** denomination.

sect., section.

sec·ta (sek′tə), *n.* in Old English law: **1.** a case in court; suit. **2.** the witnesses brought to court by a plaintiff to prove his arguments. [< Latin *secta* party, school]

sec·tar·i·al (sek tãr′ē əl), *adj.* sectarian.

sec·tar·i·an (sek tãr′ē ən), *adj.* **1.** of or having to do with a sect. **2.** characteristic of one sect only; strongly prejudiced in favor of a certain sect. —*n.* **1.** a devoted member of a sect, especially a narrow-minded or strongly prejudiced member of a sect. **2.** a member of a religious group separated from an established church; nonconformist. —**Syn.** *adj.* **1.** denominational. *-n.* **2.** dissenter.

sec·tar·i·an·ism (sek tãr′ē ə niz′əm), *n.* the spirit or tendencies of sectarians; adherence or too great devotion to a particular sect, especially a religious sect.

sec·tar·i·an·ize (sek tãr′ē ə nīz), *v.t.,* **-ized, -iz·ing.** to make sectarian.

sec·ta·ry (sek′tər ē), *n., pl.* **-ries,** *adj.* —*n.* a member of a particular sect, especially a member of a religious group separated from an established church: *It is not as religious sectaries they [school inspectors] have to discharge their duties, but as civil servants* (Matthew Arnold). —*adj.* sectarian. [< Medieval Latin *sectarius* < Latin *secta;* see SECT]

sec·tile (sek′təl), *adj.* (of a mineral or the like) that can be cut smoothly by a knife but cannot withstand pulverization: *If the specimen can be cut by a knife, like a piece of hard tar, and yet shatters under a sharp blow, it is sectile* (Scientific American). [< Latin *sectilis* < *secāre* to cut]

sec·til·i·ty (sek til′ə tē), *n.* the property of being easily cut; sectile character.

sec·tion (sek′shən), *n.* **1.** a part separated or cut off; part; division; slice: *Mother cut the pie into eight equal sections. His section of the family estate was larger than his brother's.* **2.** a division of a book, a law, or the like: *Chapter X has seven sections. Our arithmetic book has several sections on fractions.* **3.** a region; part of a country, city, etc.: *The city has a business section and a residential section.* **4.** a district one mile square; 640 acres: *A township usually contains 36 sections.* **5.** one of the parts of something that is built of a number of similar parts: *the sections of a bookcase.* **6.** the act of cutting or dividing. **7.** a representation of a thing as it would appear if cut straight through. **8.** a thin slice of a tissue, mineral, or the like, cut off for microscopic examination. **9.** the part of a railroad line maintained by one group of workmen: *The front coach was crowded with Galicians going down the line to work on the section* (Calgary, Canada, Eye Opener). **10.** *U.S.* a part of a sleeping car containing an upper and a lower berth. **11.** *U.S.* one of two or more trains operating on the same schedule: *The second section of the Twentieth Century Limited arrived five minutes after the first.* **12.** *Bookbinding.* a number of sheets folded together to form a unit. *Abbr.:* sec. —*v.t.* **1.** to cut into sections. **2.** to cut through so as to present a section. [< Latin *sectiō, -ōnis* < *secāre* to cut]

sec·tion·al (sek′shə nəl), *adj.* **1.** having to do with a particular section; local: *sectional interests, sectional prejudices, sectional legislation.* **2.** made of sections or parts: *a sectional bookcase.* —*n.* a sectional couch, bookcase, etc. —**sec′tion·al·ly,** *adv.* —**Syn.** *adj.* **1.** regional.

sec·tion·al·ism (sek′shə nə liz′əm), *n.* too great regard for sectional interests; sectional prejudice or hatred: *When the people of a region become self-centered and neglect their relation to the larger national unity, they suffer from sectionalism or provincialism* (Emory S. Bogardus). —**Syn.** parochialism.

sec·tion·al·ist (sek′shə nə list), *n.* a person who advocates sectional aims or interests: *Calhoun had discarded his nationalism and had become a sectionalist* (World Book Encyclopedia).

sec·tion·al·i·za·tion (sek′shə nə lə zā′shən), *n.* the act of making sectional in scope or spirit.

sec·tion·al·ize (sek′shə nə līz), *v.t.,* **-ized, -iz·ing.** **1.** to make sectional in scope or spirit: *The principal results of the struggle were to sectionalize parties.* **2.** to divide into sections; divide (land or an area) into plots or districts.

section boss, *U.S.* section foreman.

section foreman, *U.S.* the foreman of a section gang.

section gang or **crew,** *U.S.* a group of workmen who maintain a single railroad section.

section hand or **man,** *U.S.* a worker on a section gang.

sec·tor (sek′tər), *n.* **1.** *Geometry.* the part of a circle, ellipse, etc., between two radii and the included arc. **2.** a clearly defined military area which a given military unit protects or covers with fire; part of a front held by a unit. **3.** an instrument consisting of two rulers connected by a joint, used in measuring or drawing angles. —*v.t.* to divide into sectors; provide with sectors. [< Late Latin *sector, -ōris* (in Latin, a cutter) < *secāre* to cut]

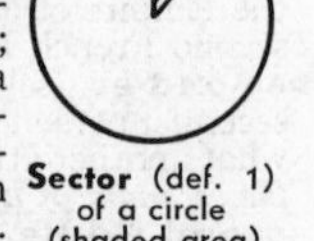

Sector (def. 1) of a circle (shaded area)

sec·tor·al (sek′tər əl), *adj.* of or having to do with a sector: *sectoral spaces.*
sec·to·ri·al (sek tôr′ē əl, -tōr′-), *adj.* **1.** of, having to do with, or resembling a sector. **2.** adapted for cutting, as certain teeth; carnassial.
sector scan, a radar scan through a limited angle to provide a continuous surveillance of a particular area or airspace.
sec·u·lar (sek′yə lər), *adj.* **1.** connected with the world and its affairs; of things not religious or sacred; worldly: *secular music, a secular education. Bishops now were great secular magistrates, and . . . were involved in secular occupations* (Cardinal Newman). **2.** living in the world; not belonging to a religious order: *a secular priest. Those northern nations easily embraced the religion of those they subdued, and by their devotion gave great authority and reverence, and thereby ease, to the clergy, both secular and regular* (Sir William Temple). **3.** occurring once in an age or century: *When Augustus celebrated the secular year, which was kept but once in a century . . .* (Joseph Addison). **4.** lasting through long ages; going on from age to age: *the secular cooling or refrigeration of the globe.*
—*n.* a secular priest; clergyman living among the laity and not in a monastery: *While the Danish wars had been fatal to the monks — the "regular clergy" as they were called — they had also dealt heavy blows at the seculars, or parish priests* (J.R. Green).
[< Latin *saeculāris* < *saeculum* age, span of time; later, the present age or world, the world]
sec·u·lar·ise (sek′yə lə rīz), *v.t.,* **-ised, -is·ing.** *Especially British.* secularize.
sec·u·lar·ism (sek′yə lə riz′əm), *n.* **1.** skepticism in regard to religion; the ignoring or exclusion of religious duties, instruction, or considerations: *Caught between secularism and militant Hindu fanaticism, the missionaries themselves are gloomy* (Newsweek). **2.** opposition to the introduction of religion into public schools and other public affairs. —**Syn. 1.** worldliness.
sec·u·lar·ist (sek′yə lər ist), *n.* a believer in secularism. —*adj.* secularistic.
sec·u·lar·is·tic (sek′yə lə ris′tik), *adj.* of or characterized by secularism.
sec·u·lar·i·ty (sek′yə lar′ə tē), *n., pl.* **-ties. 1.** secular spirit or quality; worldliness. **2.** a secular matter.
sec·u·lar·i·za·tion (sek′yə lər ə zā′shən), *n.* a secularizing or being secularized.
sec·u·lar·ize (sek′yə lə rīz), *v.t.,* **-ized, -iz·ing. 1.** to make secular or worldly; separate from religious connection or influence: *to secularize Sunday, to secularize education.* **2.** to transfer (property) from the possession of the church to that of the government. **3.** to transfer (clergy) from regular or monastic to secular: *to secularize a monk.*
sec·u·lar·iz·er (sek′yə lə rī′zər), *n.* a person or thing that secularizes.
sec·u·lar·ly (sek′yə lər lē), *adv.* in a secular or worldly manner.
se·cund (sē′kund, sek′und), *adj. Botany.* arranged on one side only; unilateral: *The flowers of the lily of the valley and the false wintergreen are secund.* [< Latin *secundus* following. Doublet of SECOND[1].]

Secund Flowers of lily of the valley

se·cun·dif·lo·rous (sek′ən dif′lə rəs), *adj.* having secund flowers or inflorescence.
sec·un·dine (sek′ən dīn, -din), *n. Botany.* the second or inner coat or integument of an ovule.
secundines, the afterbirth: *to deliver the baby and the secundines.* [< Late Latin *secundīnae,* plural < Latin *secundus;* see SECOND[1]]
se·cun·dum (si kun′dəm), *prep. Latin.* according to; in accordance with.
se·cun·dum le·gem (si kun′dəm lē′jəm), *Latin.* according to law.
se·cur·a·ble (si kyůr′ə bəl), *adj.* that can be secured.
se·cure (si kyůr′), *adj., v.,* **-cured, -cur·ing.** —*adj.* **1.** safe against danger, loss, attack, escape, etc.: *Keep the prisoner secure within the dungeon. This is a secure hiding place. Land in a growing city is a secure investment.* **2.** that can be counted on; sure; certain: *We know in advance that our victory is secure.* **3.** free from care, fear, or worry: *He hoped for a secure old age.* **4.** firmly fastened; not liable to give way: *The boards of this bridge do not look secure.*
—*v.t.* **1.** to make safe; protect: *You cannot secure yourself against all risks and dangers. Every loan was secured by bonds or mortgages.* **2.** to make (something) sure or certain: *Their manner of building secured a certain air of solidity and grandeur* (P.H. Hunter). **3.** to make firm or fast: *Secure the locks on the windows. Having secured my boat, I took my gun and went on shore* (Daniel Defoe). **4.** to get by effort; obtain: *to secure tickets for a play, to secure the attention of an audience, to secure a hearing at court.* **5.** to seize and confine: *They . . . formed a conspiracy to seize the ship and secure me* (Jonathan Swift). —*v.i.* to make oneself safe; be safe: *We must secure against the dangers of the coming storm.*
[< Latin *sēcūrus* < *sē-* free from + *cūra* care. Doublet of SURE, SICKER.] —**se·cure′ly,** *adv.* —**se·cure′ness,** *n.*
—**Syn.** *adj.* **1.** See **safe. 4.** fast, firm, stable, immovable. -*v.t.* **1.** guard, defend, shield. **2.** assure, insure. **3.** fasten, tie. **4.** gain.
se·cur·er (si kyůr′ər), *n.* a person or thing that secures.
se·cu·ri·ties (si kyůr′ə tēz), *n.pl.* See under **security,** *n.*
se·cu·ri·ty (si kyůr′ə tē), *n., pl.* **-ties,** *adj.* —*n.* **1.** freedom from danger, care, or fear; feeling or condition of being safe: *Insurance is the modern Aladdin's lamp from which flows the power to protect the possessions of man—give security and peace of mind* (Newsweek). **2.** freedom from doubt; certainty. **3.** overconfidence; carelessness. **4.** something that secures or makes safe: *My watchdog is a security against burglars. Rubber soles are a security against slipping.* **5.** something given as a pledge that a person will fulfill some duty, promise, etc.: *A life-insurance policy may serve as security for a loan.* **6.** a person who agrees to be responsible for another; surety: *Father was security for Mr. Johnson.*
securities, an evidence of debt or of property ownership; bond or stock certificates: *These public securities can be sold for $5,000.*
—*adj.* of or having to do with the security of a country, business, etc.: *a security agent, agreement, or procedure.*
—**Syn.** *n.* **1.** confidence. **4.** safety, protection, defense.
security analyst, a person who analyzes and evaluates stocks and bonds: *The job of a security analyst is not to report facts, but to evaluate them* (New York Times).
security clearance, 1. permission given to a person or group, after official investigation, to enter or work in classified areas, deal with confidential or secret material, meet with high government officials, etc. **2.** the investigation conducted before giving such clearance or permission: *Although not strictly Government employees, the contract experts have been required . . . to undergo security clearance* (New York Times).
Security Council, a body in the United Nations consisting of five permanent member nations and six rotating members, concerned primarily with preserving world peace. The Security Council can investigate any situation that might cause international friction, and may ask member nations to furnish troops and order them into areas of international conflict.
security police, secret police.
security risk, 1. an employee or prospective employee of the Federal government, who is regarded as unreliable or dangerous in positions involving national security because of weakness of character, criminal record, affiliation with subversive organizations, etc. **2.** any condition or development regarded as a risk to national security.
security system, any system for maintaining or safeguarding national or international security: *Under a general security system set up under the auspices of the United Nations, a control commission . . . would have the supervision of troubled areas and would provide the warning signal for any growing risk of aggression* (Atlantic).
se·cu·tor (si kyü′tər), *n.* a light-armed gladiator with a square shield and a sword who opposed the retiarius in the gladiatorial contests of ancient Rome. [< Latin *secūtor* (literally) pursuer < *sequī* to follow, pursue]
secy. or **sec'y.,** secretary.
SED (no periods), Socialist Unity Party (German, *Sozialistische Einheitspartei Deutschlands*), the Communist party in East Germany.
se·dan (si dan′), *n.* **1.** a type of closed automobile having a front and a rear seat and seating four or more persons. **2.** a sedan chair. [origin uncertain]
sedan chair, a covered chair for one person, carried on poles by two men, much used in London, Paris, etc., during the 1600's, 1700's, and early 1800's.

Sedan Chair

se·date[1] (si dāt′), *adj.* calm, quiet, and composed; undisturbed by passion or excitement: *She is very sedate for a child and would rather read and sew than play. One of those calm, quiet, sedate natures, to whom the temptations of turbulent nerves or vehement passions are things utterly incomprehensible* (Harriet Beecher Stowe). [< Latin *sēdātus,* past participle of *sēdāre* to calm; (originally) to seat, related to *sedēre* to sit] —**se·date′ly,** *adv.* —**se·date′ness,** *n.*
—**Syn.** placid, staid, sober, collected, unruffled.
se·date[2] (si dāt′), *v.t.,* **-dat·ed, -dat·ing.** to treat or calm with sedatives: *They tried . . . to sedate her, and take care of her—and she would not let them* (Theodore H. White). [back formation < *sedation*]
se·da·tion (si dā′shən), *n. Medicine.* **1.** the state of being calm, relaxed, or free from excitement. **2.** the act of producing such a state, especially through a diminishing of the rate of functional activity; treatment with sedatives.
sed·a·tive (sed′ə tiv), *n.* **1.** a medicine that lessens pain or excitement. **2.** anything soothing or calming.
—*adj.* **1.** *Medicine.* lessening pain or excitement; lowering functional activity; calmative: *a sedative drug.* **2.** soothing; calming: *. . . soothing the cares of Polynesian life in the sedative fumes of tobacco* (Herman Melville).
—**Syn.** *n.* **2.** salve.
se de·fen·den·do (sē def′en den′dō), *Law.* in self-defense (a plea offered to justify homicide). [< Latin *sē dēfendendō* (literally) in defending himself; *sē* oneself, *dēfendendō,* ablative of the gerund of *dēfendere* defend]
sed·en·tar·i·ly (sed′ən ter′ə lē), *adv.* in a sedentary manner.
sed·en·tar·i·ness (sed′ən ter′ē nis), *n.* the state or habit of being sedentary.
sed·en·tar·y (sed′ən ter′ē), *adj.* **1.** used to sitting still much of the time; inactive: *Sedentary people get little physical exercise.* **2.** that keeps one sitting still much of the time: *Bookkeeping is a sedentary occupation.* **3.** moving little and rarely. **4.** *Zoology.* **a.** living in one place, as English sparrows; not migratory or moving far: *Pigeons are sedentary birds.* **b.** attached to one spot; not moving: *a sedentary mollusk.* **c.** spinning a web and lying in wait: *I discovered that this was no web-spinning, sedentary spider, but a wandering hunter* (W.H. Hudson). [< Latin *sedentārius* ultimately < *sedēre* to sit]
sed·en·ta·tion (sed′ən tā′shən), *n.* the state of having become sedentary.
Se·der (sā′dər), *n., pl.* **Se·ders, Se·dar·im** (se där′im). the religious service and feast held in Jewish homes on the first two nights (or first night only) of Passover. [< Hebrew *sēder* (literally) order, arrangement]
sedge (sej), *n.* **1.** any of a large group of grasslike plants of the sedge family, growing chiefly in wet places. **2.** any of various coarse, grassy, rushlike or flaglike plants growing in wet places. [Old English *secg*]
sedged (sejd), *adj.* **1.** bordered with sedge: *sedged brooks.* **2.** *Obsolete.* made of sedge.
sedge family, a large group of monocotyledonous herbs resembling grasses but having solid, three-sided stems and small, inconspicuous flowers usually in spikes or heads. The family includes the sedge, papyrus, chufa, and bulrush.
sedge hen, the clapper rail.
sedge·land (sej′land′), *n.* land between high and low watermarks.
sedge warbler, any of a group of small, Old World birds commonly found in marshy areas.
sedg·y (sej′ē), *adj.* **1.** abounding in or covered with sedge; bordered with

Sedge (def. 1) (2 to 3 ft. high)

sedge: *a sedgy brook.* **2.** like sedge: *The water . . . stirred a sedgy growth of reeds bordering its margin* (Herman Melville).

se·dia ges·ta·to·ria (se′dyä jes′tä tô′ryä), *Italian.* the portable throne on which the Pope is borne on ceremonial occasions.

se·di·le (si dī′lē), *n., pl.* **-dil·i·a** (-dil′ē ə). one of the three seats in the chancel for the use of the clergy officiating in the Eucharist. [< Latin *sedīle* seat < *sedēre* to sit]

sed·i·ment (sed′ə mənt), *n.* **1.** any matter that settles to the bottom of a liquid; dregs. **2.** *Geology.* earthy or detrital matter suspended in or deposited by water, wind, or ice: *Each year the Nile overflows and deposits sediment on the surrounding fields.* —*v.t., v.i.* to deposit as or form sediment. [< Latin *sedimentum* < *sedēre* to settle; sit] —**Syn.** *n.* **1.** lees.

sed·i·men·tal (sed′ə men′təl), *adj.* sedimentary.

sed·i·men·ta·ri·ly (sed′ə men′tər ə lē), *adv.* in the form of a sedimentary deposit.

sed·i·men·ta·ry (sed′ə men′tər ē), *adj.* **1.** of sediment; having to do with sediment. **2.** *Geology.* formed by the depositing of sediment: *Shale is a sedimentary rock. . . . Sedimentary rocks—the hardened remnants of sediments laid down by ancient rivers and seas* (Scientific American).

sed·i·men·ta·tion (sed′ə men tā′shən), *n.* a depositing of sediment.

sed·i·men·to·log·i·cal (sed′ə men′tə loj′ə kəl), *adj.* of or having to do with sedimentology.

sed·i·men·tol·o·gist (sed′ə men tol′ə jist), *n.* a specialist in sedimentology: *Sedimentologists are trying to acquire a deeper physical, chemical and biological insight into modern sediments and apply this knowledge to interpreting sediments of the past* (New Scientist).

sed·i·men·tol·o·gy (sed′ə men tol′ə jē), *n.* the branch of geology that deals with the formation and structure of sediments.

se·di·tion (si dish′ən), *n.* **1.** speech or action causing discontent or rebellion against the government; incitement to discontent or rebellion: *Sedition against the Federal Government, the Court held, is a field in which Congress alone has jurisdiction to enact laws* (Wall Street Journal). **2.** *Archaic.* a revolt; rebellion. [< Old French *sedicion,* learned borrowing from Latin *sēditiō, -ōnis* < *sē-* apart + *īre* to go]

se·di·tion·ar·y (si dish′ə ner′ē), *adj., n., pl.* **-ar·ies.** —*adj.* having to do with or involving sedition; seditious. —*n.* a person who promotes or is guilty of sedition.

se·di·tious (si dish′əs), *adj.* **1.** stirring up discontent or rebellion: *a seditious speech.* **2.** taking part in or guilty of sedition: *a seditious person, a seditious faction.* **3.** having to do with or arising from sedition: *seditious strife.* —**se·di′tious·ly,** *adv.* —**se·di′tious·ness,** *n.*

Sed·litz powder (sed′lits), Seidlitz powder.

Se·dor·mid (si dôr′mid), *n. Trademark.* a synthetic drug used as a sedative and hypnotic. *Formula:* $C_9H_{16}N_2O_2$

sed·ra (sed′rə), *n., pl.* **-ras, -rath** (-rōth). *Judaism.* a weekly section of the Pentateuch which is read in the synagogue on the Sabbath. [< Aramaic *sedrah* order, arrangement. Compare Hebrew *sēder* Seder.]

se·duce (si düs′, -dyüs′), *v.t.,* **-duced, -duc·ing. 1.** to tempt to wrongdoing; persuade to do wrong: *Benedict Arnold, seduced by the offer of great wealth, tried to betray his country to the enemy.* **2.** to lead away from virtue; lead astray: *Caelius . . . tried to seduce Caesar's garrison and was put to death for his treachery* (James A. Froude). **3.** to win over; beguile; entice: *Pandora was seduced by curiosity. . . . Or if not drive, seduce them to our party* (Milton). **4.** to entice to a surrender of chastity.
[< Latin *sēdūcere* < *sē-* aside, away + *dūcere* to lead] —**se·duc′ing·ly,** *adv.*
—**Syn. 1.** corrupt. **2.** mislead. **4.** betray.

se·duc·ee (si dü′sē′, -dyü′-), *n.* a person who is seduced: *Huxley, Mann, Constant, and Stendhal convey the seducee as something more than the ever reluctant object* (Observer).

se·duce·ment (si düs′mənt, -dyüs′-), *n.* seduction.

se·duc·er (si dü′sər, -dyü′-), *n.* a person, especially a man, who seduces.

se·duc·i·ble (si dü′sə bəl, -dyü′-), *adj.* that can be seduced; corruptible.

se·duc·tion (si duk′shən), *n.* **1.** the act of seducing. **2.** the condition of being seduced. **3.** something that seduces; temptation; attraction. [< Latin *sēductiō, -ōnis* < *sēdūcere;* see SEDUCE]
—**Syn. 3.** enticement.

se·duc·tive (si duk′tiv), *adj.* **1.** that tempts or entices; alluring: *a very seductive offer.* **2.** captivating; charming: *a quick and extra-ordinarily seductive smile* (Arnold Bennett). **3.** arousing physical desire: *a woman with a very seductive figure.* —**se·duc′tive·ly,** *adv.* —**se·duc′tive·ness,** *n.*

se·duc·tress (si duk′tris), *n.* a woman who seduces.

sé·dui·sant (sā dwē zäN′), *adj. French.* seductive; enticing; alluring; captivating.

sé·dui·sante (sā dwē zäNt′), *adj. French.* (of a woman) alluring; captivating.

se·du·li·ty (si dü′lə tē, -dyü′-), *n.* sedulous quality; sedulous application or care.

sed·u·lous (sej′ů ləs), *adj.* hard-working; diligent; painstaking: *The most sedulous friend of union . . . was Benjamin Franklin* (George Bancroft). *The laziest will be sedulous and active where he is in pursuit of what he has much at heart* (Jonathan Swift). [< Latin *sēdulus* (with English *-ous*) < *sē dolō* diligently; (literally) without deception; *sē,* for *sine* without, *dolō,* ablative of *dolus* guilt, deceit] —**sed′u·lous·ness,** *n.*
—**Syn.** industrious, assiduous, persevering, untiring.

sed·u·lous·ly (sej′ů ləs lē), *adv.* in a sedulous manner; diligently; industriously: *Each of them had his own Bible, and sedulously looked up the texts cited by the preachers* (Newsweek).

se·dum (sē′dəm), *n.* any of a large group of fleshy plants of the orpine family, most of which have clusters of yellow, white, or pink flowers; stonecrop. [< Latin *sedum* houseleek]

see[1] (sē), *v.,* **saw, seen, see·ing.** —*v.t.* **1.** to look at; perceive with the eyes: *See that black cloud.* **2.** to use the eyes to see (things): *to see a tennis match or a play.* **3.** to perceive with the mind; understand: *I see what you mean. I did not immediately see the purpose of his lordship's question* (Scott). **4.** to find out; learn: *I will see what needs to be done. Please see who is at the door.* **5.** to take care; make sure: *See that you lock the back door. See that the records are brought up to date.* **6.** to think; consider: *You may go if you see fit to do so.* **7.** to have knowledge or experience of: *to see service in two wars. That coat has seen hard wear. The wisest men whom the world has seen* (Scott). **8.** to go with; attend; escort: *to see a girl to her door.* **9. a.** to have a talk with; meet: *He wishes to see you alone.* **b.** to call on: *I went to see a friend.* **c.** to receive a call from: *She is too ill to see anyone.* **d.** to visit; attend: *We plan to see the World's Fair.* **10.** (in card games) to meet (a bet) by staking an equal sum; call.
—*v.i.* **1.** to perceive objects with the eyes: *I write and read till I can't see, and then I walk* (Lady Mary Wortley Montagu). **2.** to have the power of sight: *The blind do not see.* **3.** to perceive with the mind; understand: *I have explained it very carefully. Do you see now?* **4.** to find out: *Ah, something terrible has happened! I must run and see!* (Hawthorne). **5.** to look; behold: *But, see, the evening star comes forth* (Tennyson).

see after, to take care of: *Here Tom, Tom, see after the luggage* (Henry Kingsley).

see into, to understand the real character or hidden purpose of: *Well hath your Highness seen into this Duke* (Shakespeare).

see off, to go with to the starting place of a journey: *Escorted by a multitude of relatives and friends, who all went down . . . to see them off* (Washington Irving).

see out, a. to go through with; finish: *He evidently meant to see this thing out* (J.K. Jerome). **b.** to survive: *Dev is in his eighties and may not see out his second Presidential term* (Manchester Guardian Weekly).

see through, a. to understand the real character or hidden purpose of: *She was quite indifferent whether Edwin saw through her dodge or not* (Arnold Bennett). **b.** to go through with (a matter) to the end; finish: *I'm responsible and I'll see it through the only way I can* (Graham Greene). *Mr. Brown . . . will remain at the Department of Economic Affairs to see the prices and incomes policy through* (Manchester Guardian Weekly). **c.** to watch over or help (a person) through a difficulty: *We will see him through if he were to burn the college down* (Henry Kingsley).

see to (it), to look after; take care of; to make sure: *Inflation has seen to it that the £20,000 . . . is no longer the "fortune" it used to be* (Manchester Guardian Weekly). *He would see to it that his sons took a livelier interest in politics* (H.G. Wells).
[Old English *sēon*]
—**Syn.** *v.t.* **1. See, perceive, observe** mean to become aware of something through sight. **See,** the general word, implies awareness but not necessarily conscious effort or recognition: *We saw someone standing in the doorway.* **Perceive** implies conscious notice or recognition of what is seen: *We perceived the figure to be your mother.* **Observe** implies conscious effort and attention: *We observed a change in her.* **2.** watch, witness, regard, view. **3.** apprehend, discern. **4.** ascertain. **6.** judge, deem.
➔ Nonstandard forms of the past tense are *see, seen,* and *seed: Jack seen him drive away,* etc. In the Eastern States, for which evidence is available, *see* is the predominant dialectal form in New England, most of New York State, and northern Pennsylvania, and also occurs in parts of the coastal South; *seen* predominates in central and southern Pennsylvania, New Jersey, Delaware, Maryland, West Virginia, and South Carolina, and occurs at least sporadically everywhere else; *seed* is restricted to the South.

see[2] (sē), *n.* **1.** the position or authority of a bishop. **2.** the district under a bishop's authority; diocese; bishopric. [< Old French *sie,* or *sied* < Latin *sēdēs* abode < *sedēre* to sit]

see·a·ble (sē′ə bəl), *adj.* that can be seen; visible.

See·beck effect (zā′bek, sē′-), the production of a current in a circuit composed of two different metals when the junctions between these metals are maintained at different temperatures. [< Thomas J. *Seebeck,* 1770-1831, a German physicist, who discovered it]

see·catch (sē′kach′), *n., pl.* **-catch·ie** (-kach′ē). the adult male of the fur seal. [< Russian *sekach*]

seed (sēd), *n., pl.* **seeds** or **seed,** *adj., v.* —*n.* **1. a.** *Botany.* the thing from which a flower, vegetable, or other plant grows; a fertilized and mature ovule of the flowering plants, found within the pericarp and containing an organized embryo. **b.** any seedlike part of certain plants, as the fruit of the strawberry. **2.** a bulb, sprout, or any part of a plant from which a new plant will sprout. **3.** the source or beginning of anything: *to sow the seeds of trouble. Every guilty deed holds in itself the seed of retribution and undying pain* (Longfellow). **4.** children; descendants: *The Jews are the seed of Abraham.* **5.** semen; sperm. **6.** very young oysters; seed oysters. **7.** a minute bubble arising in glass during fusion. **8.** *Sports.* a player whose name has been seeded in the draw of a tournament.

go or **run to seed,** to come to the end of vigor, usefulness, prosperity, etc.: *. . . whenever I think of Watts or Harlem or even the little cities going quietly to seed* (New York Times).
—*adj.* of or containing seeds; used for seeds.
—*v.t.* **1.** to sow with seed; scatter seeds over: *The farmer seeded his field with corn.* **2.** to sow (seeds): *Dandelions seed themselves.* **3.** to remove the seeds from: *to seed raisins.* **4.** *Sports.* to scatter or distribute (the names of players) so that the best players do not meet in the early part of a tournament. **5.** to scatter dry ice or other chemicals into (clouds) from an airplane in an effort to produce rain: *Rainfall can be increased by 9 to 17 per cent or more by seeding clouds with silver iodide smoke* (Newsweek). —*v.i.* **1.** to sow seed. **2.** to produce seed; shed seeds; grow to maturity: *Some plants will not seed in a cold climate.*
[Old English *sǣd*] —**seed′like′,** *adj.*

seed·age (sē′dij), *n.* the propagation of plants by means of seeds and spores.

seed·ball (sēd′bôl′), *n.* **1.** a capsule containing seeds. **2.** a mass of utricles or other one-seeded fruits.

seed·bed (sēd′bed′), *n.* **1.** a piece of ground prepared for planting seed: *For a good seedbed, topsoil is needed . . . about eight inches* *deep after it has settled* (New York Times). **2.** a place where something originates or develops; breeding ground: *The Middle East provides 80 per cent of the oil required by the European economy . . . and could be the seedbed of a war* (Atlantic).

seed bud, *Botany.* **1.** the part of a plant that develops into a seed; ovule. **2.** the bud of a plant still in the seed; plumule.

seed·cake (sēd′kāk′), *n.* **1.** a cake or cooky flavored with caraway or other spicy seeds. **2.** the cake left after the oil has been pressed from cotton seeds.

seed capsule, a seed vessel; pericarp.

seed·case (sēd′kās′), *n.* any pod, capsule, or other dry, hollow fruit that contains seeds; seed vessel; pericarp.

seed coat, the outer covering of a seed.

seed coral, coral in tiny pieces, used to make jewelry.

seed corn, corn grown or saved for use as seed.

seed-corn maggot (sēd′kôrn′), the small, yellowish larva of a fly native to Europe but now widespread in the United States. It is highly destructive to the seeds or seedlings of corn, peas, beans, potatoes, and many other plants.

seed·eat·er (sēd′ē′tər), *n.* **1.** the grassquit. **2.** any granivorous bird.

seed·ed (sē′did), *adj.* modified, placed, or fixed by seeding, as at tennis.

-seeded, *combining form.* having — seed or seeds: *One-seeded = having one seed.*

seed·er (sē′dər), *n.* **1.** a person who seeds. **2.** a machine or device for planting seeds. **3.** a machine or device for removing seeds.

seed·i·ly (sē′də lē), *adv.* shabbily: *The poor artist was seedily dressed.*

seed·i·ness (sē′dē nis), *n.* seedy condition.

seed·ing (sē′ding), *n.* **1.** a sowing of seed; sowing with seed. **2.** the production of seed. **3.** the distribution of players in a tournament. **4.** the dropping of dry ice or other chemicals into clouds.

seed-lac (sēd′lak′), *n.* an especially pure form of lac.

seed leaf, the embryo leaf in the seed of a plant; cotyledon.

seed·less (sēd′lis), *adj.* having no seeds: *seedless grapefruit.* —**seed′less·ness,** *n.*

seed·ling (sēd′ling), *n.* **1.** a young plant grown from a seed. **2.** a young tree less than three feet high.
—*adj.* **1.** developed or raised from seed. **2.** like a small seed; existing in a rudimentary state. **3.** (of oysters) hatched from seed.

seed·man (sēd′mən), *n., pl.* **-men.** seedsman.

seed money, *U.S.* money used by a foundation to support or finance various causes: *Mrs. Lasker is no mere giver-away of grants. . . . The concept underlying her gifts is that of "seed money" designed to "finance the financing" of unheralded but notably worthwhile projects* (Saturday Review).

seed·ness (sēd′nis), *n. Dialect.* seedtime.

seed oyster, a very young oyster ready for planting.

seed pearl, a very small pearl, often imperfect.

seed plant, any plant that bears seeds. Most seed plants have flowers and produce seeds enclosed in fruits; some, such as the pines, form naked seeds on cones.

seeds·man (sēdz′mən), *n., pl.* **-men.** **1.** a sower of seed. **2.** a dealer in seed.

seed snipe, any of a group of short-legged birds resembling the quail and plover, found on rocky and barren ground of South America.

seed·time (sēd′tīm′), *n.* the season for sowing seeds.

seed tree, **1.** any tree which bears seed. **2.** *Forestry.* a tree which provides the seed for natural reproduction.

seed vessel, any pod, capsule, or other hollow fruit that contains seeds; pericarp.

seed weevil, any of various small weevils that feed on the seeds of beans, peas, and similar plants.

seed·y (sē′dē), *adj.,* **seed·i·er, seed·i·est.** **1.** full of seed. **2.** having gone to seed. **3. a.** no longer fresh or new; shabby: *seedy clothes. . . . a seedy man who had evidently spent the night in a doorway* (Thomas Bailey Aldrich). **b.** *Informal.* somewhat ill: *He had felt seedy all day and had taken no food* (George Du Maurier). —**Syn. 3. a.** threadbare.

seed year, *Forestry.* a year in which a given species of tree bears seed, especially one in which it bears abundantly.

seedy toe, a condition in horses characterized by a separation of the hoof wall from the sensitive tissue below. [because the tissue appears to be granular]

see·ing (sē′ing), *conj.* in view of the fact; considering; since: *Seeing that it is 10 o'clock, we will wait no longer. Deep harm to disobey, seeing obedience is the bond of rule* (Tennyson).
—*n.* **1.** the act of a person or thing that sees: *a play worth seeing.* **2.** sight; vision. **3.** the degree to which the atmosphere remains still and steady with respect to observation of heavenly bodies through a telescope: *Seeing is the scientists' term for the same effect that causes stars to "twinkle"* (Science News Letter).
—*adj.* that sees. —**Syn.** *conj.* because.

seeing eye, a device that detects an object and often activates some mechanism to which it is connected: *The photoelectric cell has become familiar in the form of . . . the "seeing eye" for opening doors* (Scientific American).

Seeing Eye, an organization that breeds and trains dogs as guides for blind people.

seeing eye dog, a dog trained as a guide for the blind.

seek (sēk), *v.,* **sought, seek·ing.** —*v.t.* **1.** to try to find; look for: *The boys are seeking a good camping place.* **2.** to hunt; search for: *to seek something lost.* **3.** to try to get: *to seek relief from pain, to seek someone's friendship. Most men seek wealth; all men seek happiness. Friends sought his advice.* **4.** to try; attempt; endeavor: *to seek to right a wrong. We sought to make peace between Pat and Tom. The schools seek to be laboratories where moral action is encouraged and practiced* (Atlantic). **5.** to go to: *Being sleepy, he sought his bed.* —*v.i.* **1.** to search: *Seek, and ye shall find* (Matthew 7:7). **2.** *Archaic.* to go: *Wisdom's self oft seeks to sweet retired solitude* (Milton).
be sought after, to be desired or in demand: *His company is greatly sought after.*
to seek, a. to be sought; to be found: *The reason is not far to seek.* **b.** absent; lacking: *Intelligence is sadly to seek among them.* **c.** *Archaic.* at a loss; puzzled: *For the details of our itinerary, I am all to seek* (Stevenson).
[Old English *sēcan.* Compare BESEECH.] —**seek′er,** *n.*

seek·ing (sē′king), *n.* the act of trying to find something: *a seeking after riches.*
of one's (own) seeking, due to one's own fault: *The misfortune is entirely of my own seeking* (T. Hook).
—*adj.* that seeks; searching: *a seeking intellect.* —**seek′ing·ly,** *adv.*

seel (sēl), *v.t.* **1.** *Falconry.* **a.** to stitch together the eyelids of (a hawk while being trained). **b.** to stitch up (a bird's eyes). **2.** *Archaic.* to make blind: *She that, so young, could give out such a seeming, to seel her father's eyes up close as oak* (Shakespeare). Also, **seal.** [Middle English *silen* < Old French *ciller,* or *siller* < *cil* eyelash < Latin *cilium*]

see·ly (sē′lē), *adj. Dialect.* **1.** insignificant; trifling. **2.** mean; poor. **3.** feeble; frail. [earlier form of *silly*]

seem (sēm), *v.i.* **1.** to appear to be: *This apple seemed good but was rotten inside. Does this room seem hot to you? He seemed a very old man. He seemed very strong for his age.* **2.** to appear: *The dog seems to like that bone. This, it seems, is your idea of cleaning a room.* [< Scandinavian (compare Old Icelandic *sœma* conform to)] —**seem′er,** *n.*
—**Syn. 1. Seem, appear** mean to give the impression or have the outward look of being something that it may or may not be in fact or reality. **Seem** emphasizes the impression created; **appear** emphasizes the outward looks: *He appears pale but he seems not to be sick.*

seem·ing (sē′ming), *adj.* that appears to be; apparent: *a seeming advantage.* —*n.* appearance; likeness: *It was worse in its seeming than in reality.* —**Syn.** *adj.* ostensible. -*n.* semblance.

seem·ing·ly (sē′ming lē), *adv.* as far as appearances go; apparently: *This hill is, seemingly, the highest around here.*

seem·ing·ness (sē′ming nis), *n.* **1.** plausibility. **2.** semblance.

seem·li·ness (sēm′lē nis), *n.* **1.** fitness; propriety; decency; decorum: *England is the country, so we have always been taught to believe, for seemliness and moderation* (London Times). **2.** pleasing appearance; attractiveness.

seem·ly (sēm′lē), *adj.,* **-li·er, -li·est,** *adv.* —*adj.* **1.** fitting or becoming with respect to good taste; suitable; proper: *Some old people do not consider modern dances seemly. All loved Art in a seemly way With an earnest soul and a capital A* (James Jeffrey Roche). **2.** *Archaic.* having a pleasing appearance: *. . . a seemly Georgian residence* (Arnold Bennett). —*adv.* properly; becomingly; fittingly: *Nor is it seemly or piously attributed to the justice of God* (Milton). [< Scandinavian (compare Old Icelandic *sœmiligr*)] —**Syn.** *adj.* **1.** See **fitting.**

seen (sēn), *v.* the past participle of **see**[1]: *Have you seen William?* —*adj.* skilled; versed; experienced: *A schoolmaster well seen in music* (Shakespeare).

See of Rome, Holy See.

seep (sēp), *v.i.* to leak slowly; ooze; trickle: *Water seeps through sand. The independence seeped out of him* (Sinclair Lewis). —*n.* **1.** moisture that seeps out. **2.** a small spring. [apparently variant of *sipe* leak, Old English *sīpian* to sink low. Compare SIP.]

seep·age (sē′pij), *n.* **1.** a seeping; slow leakage; oozing. **2.** moisture or liquid that seeps.

seep·y (sē′pē), *adj.* **1.** full of moisture. **2.** poorly drained: *seepy land.*

seer[1] (sir *for 1;* sē′ər *for 2*), *n.* **1.** a person who foresees or foretells future events; prophet: *Seers . . . are . . . ever with us, whether they call themselves oracles, shamans, soothsayers, psychical mediums, or, in up-to-date parlance, "sensitives"* (New Yorker). **2.** a person who sees. —**Syn. 1.** augur, prognosticator.

seer[2] (sir), *n.* ser.

seer·ess (sir′is), *n.* a woman seer; prophetess.

seer·ship (sir′ship), *n.* the office or function of a seer.

seer·suck·er (sir′suk′ər), *n.* a thin rayon (originally, linen) or cotton cloth with alternate stripes of plain and crinkled material, used especially for clothing worn during hot weather. [earlier *sirsaka* < Hindustani < Persian *shīr o shakkar* (literally) milk and sugar (in allusion to the stripes)]

see·saw (sē′sô′), *n.* **1.** a plank resting on a support near its middle so the ends can move up and down. **2.** a children's game in which the children sit at opposite ends of such a plank and move alternately up and down or back and forth. **3.** a moving up and down or back and forth: *With uncanny skill he has managed to place himself at the exact dead center of the seesaw of French politics* (Atlantic). **4.** (in whist) a crossruff.
—*v.i., v.t.* **1.** to move up and down on a balanced plank. **2.** to move up and down or back and forth: *The ancient inn . . . whose flapping sign these fifty years has seesawed to and fro* (Oliver Wendell Holmes).
—*adj.* moving up and down or back and forth: *I don't remember ever being seesaw . . . when I'd made my mind up* (George Eliot). [apparently varied reduplication of *saw*[1]]

seethe (sēᴛʜ), *v.,* **seethed** or (*Obsolete*) **sod, seethed** or (*Obsolete*) **sod·den, seeth·ing,** *n.* —*v.i.* **1. a.** to bubble and foam: *Water seethed under the falls.* **b.** *Archaic.* to boil. **2.** to be excited; be disturbed; be agitated: *The crew was seething with discontent and ready for open rebellion.* —*v.t.* to soak; steep: *They drown their wits, seethe their brains in ale* (Robert Burton).
—*n. Rare.* a state of agitation.
[Old English *sēothan*] —**seeth′ing·ly,** *adv.* —**Syn.** *v.i.* **2.** See **boil.**

see-through (sē′thrü′), *adj.* having a transparent surface or very sheer body one can see through: *. . . see-through inflatable vinyl pillows decorated with boldly colored patterns silk-screened on the inside* (Time).

seg., segment.

se·gar (si gär′), *n.* cigar.

seg·gar (seg′ər), *n., v.t.* sagger.

seg·ment (seg′mənt), *n.* **1.** a part cut, marked, or broken off; division; section: *A tangerine is easily pulled apart into its segments. There is a solid segment of educated citizens in the Latin American countries as well as in the United States* (Newsweek). **2.** *Geometry.* **a.** a part of a circle, sphere, or other figure cut off by a line or plane, especially a part bounded by an

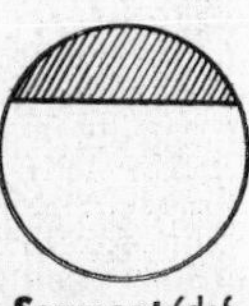

Segment (def. 2a) of a circle (shaded area)

arc and its chord, or by two parallel lines or planes. **b.** any of the finite sections of a divided line. **3.** *Biology.* one of a series of parts having a more or less similar structure: *a segment of a tapeworm.*
—*v.t., v.i.* to divide into segments.
[< Latin *segmentum* < *secāre* to cut]
—**Syn.** *n.* **1.** portion, piece.

seg·men·tal (seg men′təl), *adj.* **1.** composed of segments. **2.** of or having to do with segments. **3.** having the form of a segment of a circle: *a segmental arch.*

segmental apparatus, the brain exclusive of the cerebrum and the cerebellum; brain stem.

seg·men·tal·ly (seg men′tə lē), *adv.* in segments.

seg·men·tar·y (seg′mən ter′ē), *adj.* segmental.

seg·men·ta·tion (seg′mən tā′shən), *n.* **1.** division into segments. **2.** the growth and division of a cell into two, four, eight cells, and so on.

segmentation cavity, the cavity of the blastula.

se·gno (sā′nyō), *n., pl.* **-gni** (-nyē). *Music.* a sign, especially the sign (:𝄋:) used to indicate the beginning or (rarely) the end of repetitions. [< Italian *segno* (literally) sign < Latin *signum.* Doublet of SIGN.]

se·go (sē′gō), *n., pl.* **-gos.** sego lily. [American English < Shoshonean (Paiute) *sego*]

sego lily, 1. a plant of the lily family that has trumpet-shaped flowers, common in the western part of the United States. Its blossom is the floral emblem of Utah. **2.** its edible bulb.

seg·re·ga·ble (seg′rə gə bəl), *adj. Genetics.* able to undergo segregation.

seg·re·gate (*v.* seg′rə gāt; *adj.* seg′re git, -gāt), *v.,* **-gat·ed, -gat·ing,** *adj.* —*v.t.* **1.** to separate from others; set apart; isolate: *The doctor segregated the child sick with scarlet fever to protect the other patients.* **2.** to cause (a race, social group, etc.) to keep apart from other groups, as by maintaining separate schools, separate public facilities, etc. —*v.i.* **1.** to separate from the rest and collect in one place. **2.** *Genetics.* to undergo segregation.
—*adj.* segregated.
[< Latin *sēgregāre* (with English *-ate*[1]) < *sē-* apart (from) + *grex, gregis* herd]

seg·re·ga·tion (seg′rə gā′shən), *n.* **1.** a separation from others; setting apart; isolation: *the segregation of lepers.* **2.** the separation of a race, social group, etc., from other groups, especially in schools, theaters, restaurants, etc. **3.** a thing separated or set apart; isolated part, group, etc. **4.** *Genetics.* the separation of opposing (allelomorphic) pairs of genes or characters, occurring during meiosis, in the gametes formed by a biparental organism.

seg·re·ga·tion·ist (seg′rə gā′shə nist), *n.* a person who believes in the separation of a race, social group, etc., from other groups in schools, theaters, restaurants, etc. —*adj.* of or having to do with segregationists or segregation.

seg·re·ga·tive (seg′rə gā′tiv), *adj.* **1.** tending to segregate. **2.** keeping apart from others; unsociable.

seg·re·ga·tor (seg′rə gā′tər), *n.* a person or thing that segregates.

se·gue (sā′gwā), *n., v.,* **-gued, -gue·ing.** *Music.* —*n.* a direction at the end of a movement to proceed with the following movement immediately. —*v.i.* to proceed immediately with the following movement; attacca. [< Italian *segue,* third person singular of *seguire* follow < Latin *sequī*]

se·gui·dil·la (sā′gē ᴛʜēl′yä), *n.* **1.** a Spanish dance in triple rhythm for two persons. **2.** the music (instrumental or vocal) for such a dance. [< Spanish *seguidilla* < *seguida* sequence; (literally) a following < *seguir* to follow < Latin *sequī*]

sei (sā), *n.* sei whale.

sei·cen·tist (sā chen′tist), *n.* an Italian artist or man of letters of the 1600's.

sei·cen·to (sā chen′tō), *n.* the 1600's (used especially in Italian art and literature of that period). [< Italian *seicento,* short for *mille seicento* one thousand and six hundred (that is, after 1600)]

seiche (sāsh), *n.* an occasional rhythmical movement from side to side of the water of a lake, with fluctuation of water level, thought to be caused by sudden local variations in atmospheric pressure. [< Swiss French *seiche*]

sei·chom·e·ter (sā shom′ə tər), *n.* an instrument measuring the fluctuations of the level of the water in lakes.

sei·del (zī′dəl), *n.* a mug for beer. [< German *Seidel* < Latin *situla* bucket]

Seid·litz powder (sed′lits), a saline laxative consisting of two powders, one tartaric acid and the other a mixture of sodium bicarbonate and Rochelle salt (potassium sodium tartrate); Rochelle powder. These are dissolved separately, and the solutions are mixed and drunk while effervescing. Also, **Sedlitz powder.** [patterned on earlier *Seidlitz salt* (because of the similarity in use) < *Seidlitz,* a village in Czechoslovakia, the site of a mineral spring]

seif (sīf), *n.* a long dune found in sandy deserts in which the winds are variable. [< Arabic *saif* sword (because of its shape)]

sei·gneur (sēn yėr′; *French* se nyœr′), *n.* **1.** a feudal lord or landowner; seignior: *A grand seigneur was a person of high rank or one who behaved as a person of high rank should.* **2.** (formerly, in Canada) the holder of a landed estate the title to which had its origin in a feudal grant from the king of France. [< French *seigneur* < Old French *seignor* seignior < Latin *seniōrem,* accusative of *senior.* Doublet of SEIGNIOR, SIEUR.]
—**Syn. 1.** liege.

sei·gneur·i·al (sēn yůr′ē əl), *adj.* of or having to do with a seigneur or seigniory: *I have seized . . . seigneurial rights on five lands situated in the above mentioned disjointed part of the seigniory* (Quebec Gazette).

seign·ior (sēn′yər), *n.* **1. a.** a feudal lord; nobleman who held his lands by feudal grant. **b.** any lord (holder) of a manor; gentleman. **2.** a title of respect, formerly corresponding (especially in France) approximately to *Sir.* [< Old French *seignor,* or *seignior* < Latin *senior.* Doublet of SEIGNEUR, SIEUR.]

seign·ior·age (sēn′yər ij), *n.* **1.** something claimed by a sovereign or superior as a prerogative. **2.** a charge for coining gold or silver. **3.** the difference between the face value of a coin and the cost of the bullion and the minting of it.

seign·ior·al (sēn′yər əl), *adj.* seigniorial.

seign·ior·i·al (sēn yôr′ē əl, -yōr′-), *adj.* of or having to do with a seignior.

seign·ior·y (sēn′yər ē), *n., pl.* **-ior·ies. 1.** the authority, rights, or privileges of a seignior. **2.** a feudal lord's domain. **3.** a group of feudal lords. Also, **signory.** [< Old French *seignorie* < *seignor;* see SEIGNIOR]

seine (sān), *n., v.,* **seined, sein·ing.** —*n.* a fishing net with floats at the top and weights at the bottom, so that it hangs down in the water.
—*v.i.* to fish or catch fish with a seine. —*v.t.* **1.** to catch (fish, etc.) with a seine. **2.** to fish (a body of water) with a seine or seines.
[Old English *segne* < Latin *sagēna* < Greek *sagēnē*]

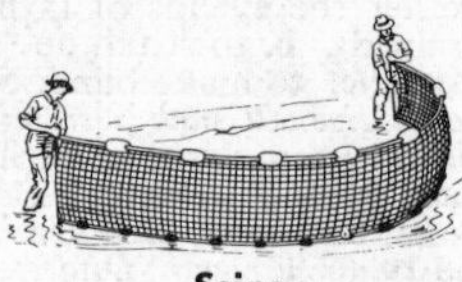

Seine

seine boat, a boat for carrying and paying out a seine.

sein·er (sā′nər), *n.* a boat used in fishing with a seine: *Only seamen of lifelong skill . . . could navigate . . . the seiners and trollers bobbing a hundred miles off the Pacific coast* (Maclean's).

seise (sēz), *v.t.,* **seised, seis·ing.** *Archaic or Law.* seize. [spelling variant of *seize*]

seised (sēzd), *adj. Law.* having ownership and right of possession, especially of a freehold estate.

sei·sin (sē′zin), *n.* seizin.

seism (sī′zəm, -səm), *n.* an earthquake.

seis·mal (sīz′məl, sīs′-), *adj.* seismic.

seis·met·ic (sīz met′ik, sīs-), *adj.* seismic.

seis·mic (sīz′mik, sīs′-), *adj.* **1.** of earthquakes; having to do with or characteristic of an earthquake. **2.** caused by an earthquake. [< Greek *seismós* earthquake (< *seíein* shake) + English *-ic*]

seis·mi·cal (sīz′mə kəl, sīs′-), *adj.* seismic.
—**seis′mi·cal·ly,** *adv.*

seis·mic·i·ty (sīz mis′ə tē, sīs-), *n.* **1.** liability to earthquakes. **2.** the relative frequency of earthquakes in a given area: *One involves finding the number of earthquakes of this size in two places of well-measured seismicity, Southern California and New Zealand* (Bulletin of Atomic Scientists).

seis·mism (sīz′miz əm, sīs′-), *n.* the phenomena of earthquakes, collectively.

seismo-, *combining form.* earthquake: *Seismology = the scientific study of earthquakes.* [< Greek *seismós* < *seíein* shake]

seis·mo·gram (sīz′mə gram, sīs′-), *n.* the record of an earthquake made by a seismograph.

seis·mo·graph (sīz′mə graf, -gräf; sīs′-), *n.* an instrument for recording automatically the direction, intensity, and duration of earthquakes: *At one stage, the West discovered to its dismay that underground* [*atomic*] *tests could be concealed from seismographs by exploding the bombs in caves* (Time).

seis·mog·ra·pher (sīz mog′rə fər, sīs-), *n.* a person skilled in seismography.

seis·mo·graph·ic (sīz′mə graf′ik, sīs′-), *adj.* **1.** of a seismograph. **2.** of seismography.

seis·mo·graph·i·cal (sīz′mə graf′ə kəl, sīs′-), *adj.* seismographic.

seis·mog·ra·phy (sīz mog′rə fē, sīs-), *n.* **1.** the art of using the seismograph in recording earthquakes. **2.** the branch of seismology dealing especially with the mapping and description of earthquakes.

seismol., 1. seismological. **2.** seismology.

seis·mo·log·i·cal (sīz′mə loj′ə kəl, sīs′-), *adj.* of or having to do with seismology.
—**seis′mo·log′i·cal·ly,** *adv.*

seis·mol·o·gist (sīz mol′ə jist, sīs-), *n.* a person skilled in seismology.

seis·mol·o·gy (sīz mol′ə jē, sīs-), *n.* the scientific study of earthquakes and other movements of the earth's crust: *Seismology has lifted our notions about the interior of our planet from the realm of wild speculation to the stage of scientific measurement and well-reasoned inferences* (Scientific American).

seis·mom·e·ter (sīz mom′ə tər, sīs-), *n.* a seismograph.

seis·mo·met·ric (sīz′mə met′rik, sīs′-), *adj.* of or having to do with seismometry.

seis·mo·met·ri·cal (sīz′mə met′rə kəl, sīs′-), *adj.* seismometric.

seis·mom·e·try (sīz mom′ə trē, sīs-), *n.* the scientific recording and study of earthquake phenomena, especially by means of the seismometer.

seis·mo·scope (sīz′mə skōp, sīs′-), *n.* a simple form of seismograph; instrument for indicating the occurrence of earthquake shocks.

seis·mo·scop·ic (sīz′mə skop′ik, sīs′-), *adj.* relating to or furnished by the seismoscope.

seis·mo·tec·ton·ic (sīz′mə tek ton′ik, sīs′-), *adj. Geology.* having to do with the structure of the earth's crust that is connected with earthquakes.

seis·mot·ic (sīz mot′ik, sīs-), *adj.* of or having to do with earthquakes; seismic.

sei whale, a very common rorqual of a bluish-black color; sei: *When the blue whale was reduced to the point of near extinction . . . the deep sea fleets promptly turned to the sei whale. From what can be learned of this form of overkill, the sei should be protected* (New Scientist). [partial translation of Norwegian *seihval* < *sei* coalfish + *val* whale]

seiz·a·ble (sē′zə bəl), *adj.* that can be seized: *rich foreign lands, full of seizable wealth* (H.G. Wells).

seize (sēz), *v.,* **seized, seiz·ing.** —*v.t.* **1.** to take hold of suddenly; clutch; grasp: *In fright she seized his arm.* **2.** to grasp with the mind; apprehend: *to seize an idea, to seize the point. He was confronted with what was really the more difficult task of seizing the trend of contemporary events* (Edmund Wilson). **3. a.** to take possession of by force; capture: *The soldiers seized the city.* **b.** to take prisoner; arrest; catch: *to seize a man wanted for murder.* **4.** to take possession of: *to be seized with terror. A fever seized him.* **5.** to take possession of (goods) by a judicial order or other legal authority: *to seize smuggled goods.* **6.** *Law.* to put in legal possession of (a feudal holding, property, etc.); establish in (an office, dignity, etc.). **7.** *Nautical.* to bind, lash, or join by winding around cord, wire, etc.: *to seize one rope to another.* —*v.i. Metallurgy.* to cohere.
seize on or **upon, a.** to take hold of suddenly; to take possession of: *Victoria seized upon the idea with avidity* (Lytton Strachey). *The machine seized on Gerard's bend and he was thrown to the track* (London Times). **b.** to take advantage of; make use of: *That group . . . seized upon the day of his burial to bring out . . . a fierce manifesto against him* (Edmund Wilson).

seize up, a. (of bearings, joints, etc.) to cohere; become jammed: *Human hip bones seize up due to arthritis or have to be removed because of tumours* (New Scientist). **b.** *British Informal.* to become deadlocked; break down: *There is at present a real risk that the negotiations . . . will seize up* (Listener).
[< Old French *seisir* < Late Latin *sacīre,* perhaps < Germanic (compare Old High German *satjan* put in possession)]
—Syn. *v.t.* **1, 2. Seize, grasp, clutch** mean to take hold of something, literally or figuratively. **Seize** suggests taking hold suddenly and with force, or (used figuratively of the mind) understanding something hard to get the meaning of: *The dog seized the sausages.* **Grasp** suggests seizing and holding firmly with the fingers, claws, talons, etc., closed around the object, or to understand fully: *The eagle grasped the snake.* **Clutch** suggests grasping eagerly, sometimes greedily, and tightly as in a clenched fist: *The child clutched his toy.*

seiz·er (sē′zər), *n.* a person or thing that seizes.

seize-up (sēz′up′), *n.* **1.** the state of bearings, etc., being seized up. **2.** *British Informal.* a jam-up; breakdown: *. . . the degree of road congestion which will mean a total seize-up* (London Times).

sei·zin (sē′zin), *n. Law.* the possession of a freehold estate; possession of land under rightful title. Also, **seisin.** [< Old French *saisine* < *saisir,* or *seisir;* see SEIZE]

seiz·ing (sē′zing), *n.* **1.** the act of binding, lashing, or fastening together with several turns of a small rope, cord, etc. **2.** a fastening made in this way. **3.** a small rope, cord, wire, etc., used for this.

Seizings (def. 2)

sei·zor (sē′zər, -zôr), *n. Law.* a person who seizes or is authorized to seize.

sei·zure (sē′zhər), *n.* **1.** the act of seizing. **2.** the condition of being seized. **3.** a sudden attack of disease: *The seizure was, I think, not apoplectical* (Samuel Johnson). **4.** a sudden attack, as of some emotion, or of panic.

se·jant or **se·jeant** (sē′jənt), *adj.* (of heraldic animals) sitting with the forelegs upright. [Middle English *seiaunte,* and *seand* < Old French *seiant,* and *seant,* present participles of *seier,* or *seoir* to sit < Latin *sedēre*]

Sejm (sām), *n.* **1.** the constituent assembly of the Polish Republic from 1918 to 1922. **2.** (later) the lower house of the Polish parliament. **3.** (currently) the Polish parliament. [< Polish *sejm* assembly]

sel (sel), *n. Scottish.* self.

sel., 1. selected. **2.** selection or selections.

se·la·chi·an (si lā′kē ən), *adj.* of or belonging to an order of fishes, including the sharks and rays.
—*n.* a shark, dogfish, or other selachian fish.
[< New Latin *Selachii* the order name < *Selache* the genus name < Greek *seláchē,* plural of *sélachos* shark, ray < *sélas* light, flame (because of their phosphorescence) + English *-an*]

sel·a·choid (sel′ə koid), *adj.* sharklike; of the group comprising the sharks.

se·la·dang (sə lä′däng), *n.* the gaur. [< Malay *seladang*]

sel·a·gi·nel·la (sel′ə jə nel′ə), *n.* any of a group of mosslike plants related to the ferns, having delicate, low stems. [< New Latin *selaginella* (diminutive) < Latin *selāgo, -inis* club moss]

se·lah (sē′lə), *n.* a Hebrew word occurring frequently in the Psalms, supposed to be a musical direction. It perhaps means "Pause here." [< Hebrew *selāh*]

se·lam·lik (se läm′lik), *n.* the part of a Turkish house reserved for men. [< Turkish *selâmlık* < Arabic *salām* peace + Turkish *-lik,* a noun suffix]

sel·dom (sel′dəm), *adv.* rarely; not often: *He is seldom ill. Seldom is advice given, seldomer still is the advice worth anything* (Harper's). —*adj.* rare; infrequent: *Blunting the fine point of seldom pleasure* (Shakespeare). [Old English *seldum,* alteration of *seldan,* on the analogy of adverbial dative plurals ending in *-um*]
➔ **Seldom ever** (*I seldom ever do that*) is regarded as nonstandard. *Seldom if ever* is the standard form: *In Bengal to move at all is seldom if ever done* (Noel Coward).

se·lect (si lekt′), *v.t.* to pick out from a number; choose: *John's uncle let him select his own Christmas present. The soul selects her own society, then shuts the door* (Emily Dickinson). —*v.i.* to make a selection: *to select on the basis of quality.*
—*adj.* **1.** picked as best; chosen specially: *The captain needs a select crew for this dangerous job.* **2.** choice; superior: *That store carries a very select line of merchandise.* **3.** careful in choosing; particular as to friends, company, etc.; exclusive: *a very select club.*
—*n.* **1.** a person or thing that is selected. **2.** something select or choice.
[< Latin *sēlectus,* past participle of *sēligere* < *sē-* apart + *legere* choose] **—se·lect′ly,** *adv.* **—se·lect′ness,** *n.*
—Syn. *v.t.* See **choose.** *-adj.* **2.** picked.

se·lect·a·ble (si lek′tə bəl), *adj.* that can be selected.

select committee, a small committee of a legislative body appointed to consider and report on a special matter: *The Select Committee of the House of Commons . . . has now reported on the affairs of the Coal Board* (Manchester Guardian Weekly).

select council, (in certain cities of the United States) the higher branch of the local legislative body.

se·lect·ee (si lek′tē′), *n.* **1.** a person selected for military service; draftee. **2.** a person who has been selected for any purpose: *There, spread out across the stage, were the selectees, . . . fat men, spinsters, and devout-looking young girls* (Harper's).

se·lec·tion (si lek′shən), *n.* **1.** choice: *Her selection of a hat took a long time. The shop offered a very good selection of hats.* **2.** a person, thing, or group chosen: *The plain blue hat was her selection.* **3.** a passage or piece, or a number of passages or pieces, selected from one or more books: *a volume of prose or poetical selections, a book containing a selection from an author's works.* **4.** any process by which certain animals or plants survive and reproduce their kind, while other less suitable ones die, or are prevented from breeding: *I have called this principle, by which each slight variation, if useful, is preserved, by the term Natural Selection* (Charles Darwin). **5.** (in Australia) **a.** the act of choosing a piece of land under the Australian land laws. **6.** the land so chosen.

se·lec·tion·ist (si lek′shə nist), *n.* a person who adheres to a theory of selection.

se·lec·tive (si lek′tiv), *adj.* **1.** having the power to select; selecting. **2.** having to do with selection. **3.** responding to oscillations of a certain frequency only: *When a selective radio is tuned to one station, those on other wave lengths are excluded.*

selective buying, *U.S.* a boycott: *Brazier . . . threatened today "a massive wave of sit-ins, picketing, and selective buying campaigns" if integration demands are not met* (New York Times).

se·lec·tive·ly (si lek′tiv lē), *adv.* in a selective manner; by selection.

Selective Service, the selection of persons from the total manpower of the United States for compulsory military service, as established by Federal law.

selective transmission, an automotive transmission system that permits shifting from neutral into any other gear, without the necessity of passing progressively through the different changes of gears as in some early automobiles.

se·lec·tiv·i·ty (si lek′tiv′ə tē), *n.* **1.** the quality of being selective: *Caution in the financial district . . . has made for great selectivity in buying of securities* (Wall Street Journal). **2.** the property of a circuit, instrument, or the like, by virtue of which it responds to electric oscillations of a particular frequency; especially, the ability of a radio receiving set to receive certain frequencies or waves to the exclusion of others.

se·lect·man (si lekt′mən), *n., pl.* **-men.** a member of a board of town officers in New England (exclusive of Rhode Island), chosen each year to administer the local government. [American English]

se·lec·tor (si lek′tər), *n.* **1.** a person who selects or chooses. **2.** a mechanical or electrical device that selects: *Cars with automatic transmissions have selectors for the driver to choose the gear he wishes.* **3.** (in Australia) a settler who acquires land cheaply from the government.

selector switch, 1. a switch used in telephone exchanges to connect subscribers' phones automatically. **2.** the switch for changing from one television channel to another.

sel·e·nate (sel′ə nāt), *n.* a salt of selenic acid. [< *selen*(ic acid) + *-ate*[2]]

Se·le·ne (si lē′nē), *n. Greek Mythology.* the goddess of the moon, daughter of Hyperion and Thea, and later identified with Artemis. [< Greek *Selēnē* (literally) moon < *sélas* light, flame]

se·le·nic (si lē′nik, -len′ik), *adj.* **1.** of selenium. **2.** containing selenium, especially with a valence of six.

selenic acid, a strong, corrosive dibasic acid resembling sulfuric acid. In a water solution, it can dissolve gold, copper, etc. *Formula:* H_2SeO_4

sel·e·nide (sel′ə nīd, -nid), *n. Chemistry.* a compound of selenium with a more electropositive element or radical.

sel·e·nif·er·ous (sel′ə nif′ər əs), *adj.* containing or yielding selenium, as ore.

se·le·ni·ous (si lē′nē əs), *adj.* **1.** of selenium. **2.** containing selenium, especially with a valence of four.

selenious acid, a dibasic acid formed from selenium and nitric acid, used as a chemical reagent. *Formula:* H_2SeO_3

sel·e·nite[1] (sel′ə nīt, si lē′-), *n.* a salt of selenious acid. [< *selen*(ious acid) + *-ite*[2]]

sel·e·nite[2] (sel′ə nīt, si lē′-), *n.* a variety of gypsum found in transparent crystals and foliated masses. [< Latin *selēnītēs* < Greek *selēnī́tēs* (*líthos*) moon (stone) < *selḗnē* moon < *sélas* light (because its brightness was supposed to wax and wane with the moon)]

se·le·ni·um (si lē′nē əm), *n.* a rare, nonmetallic chemical element resembling both sulfur and tellurium in chemical properties. Because its electrical resistance varies with the amount of light, it is used in photoelectric cells. *Symbol:* Se; *at.wt.:* (C^{12}) 78.96 or (O^{16}) 78.96; *at.no.:* 34; *valence:* 1, 2, 4, 6. [< New Latin *selenium* < Greek *selḗnē* moon (because its properties follow those of tellurium)]

selenium cell, a photoelectric cell consisting of selenium placed between electrodes, valued for certain optical experiments because of the property of selenium of varying in electrical resistance under the action of light: *The camera has a selenium cell that adjusts the lens while the camera is being aimed, closing the aperture if the light grows brighter and opening it if the light grows dim* (Newsweek).

se·le·no·cen·tric (si lē′nō sen′trik), *adj.* **1.** having to do with the center of the moon. **2.** with the moon as center: *. . . a system for placing a spacecraft into a selenocentric or near-lunar orbit* (London Times).

sel·e·nog·ra·pher (sel′ə nog′rə fər), *n.* a person skilled in selenography: *When a telescope user ceases to look at the moon in a merely desultory manner and begins to observe it, he has begun to be a selenographer* (Scientific American).

se·le·no·graph·ic (si lē′nə graf′ik), *adj.* of or having to do with selenography.

selenographic chart, a map of the moon.

sel·e·nog·ra·phist (sel′ə nog′rə fist), *n.* a selenographer.

sel·e·nog·ra·phy (sel′ə nog′rə fē), *n.* the science dealing with the moon, especially its physical features. [< New Latin *selenographia* < Greek *selḗnē* moon + *-graphíā* -graphy]

se·le·no·log·i·cal (si lē′nə loj′ə kəl), *adj.* of or having to do with selenology.

sel·e·nol·o·gist (sel′ə nol′ə jist), *n.* a person skilled in selenology.

sel·e·nol·o·gy (sel′ə nol′ə jē), *n.* the science dealing with the moon, especially its astronomical features.

se·le·no·trop·ic (si lē′nə trop′ik), *adj. Botany.* turning toward the moon; taking a particular direction under the influence of the moon's light. [< Greek *selḗnē* moon + *-tropos* a turning + English *-ic*]

sel·e·not·ro·pism (sel′ə not′rə piz əm), *n.* selenotropic tendency or movement.

se·le·nous (si lē′nəs), *adj.* selenious.

Se·leu·cid (sə lü′sid), *n.* one of the Seleucidae. —*adj.* of or having to do with the Seleucidae. [< Latin *Seleucidēs* < Greek *Seleukídēs* < *Séleukos* Seleucus I, founder of the Seleucidae]

Se·leu·ci·dae (sə lü′sə dē), *n.pl.* a dynasty that reigned in Syria, Persia, Bactria, and elsewhere in western Asia from 312 to about 64 B.C. It was founded by Seleucus I, one of the generals of Alexander the Great.

Se·leu·ci·dan (sə lü′sə dən), *adj.* Seleucid.

self (self), *n., pl.* **selves,** *adj., pron., pl.* **selves,** *v.* —*n.* **1.** one's own person: *his very self, her sweet self.* **2.** one's own welfare, interests, etc.: *It is a good thing to think more of others and less of self.* **3.** the nature, character, etc., of a person or thing: *She does not seem like her former self. It seemed . . . as if he had two distinct yet kindred selves* (H.G. Wells). **4.** *Philosophy.* the individual consciousness of a being in its relationship to its own self. **5.** a flower that is the same color throughout.
—*adj.* being the same throughout; all of one kind, quality, color, material, etc.
—*pron.* myself; himself; herself; yourself: *a check made payable to self.*
—*v.t., v.i.* to fertilize (a flower) with its own pollen: *Several inbred lines from a parent rose are being produced by "selfing." Each of these lines will be further selfed* (Science News Letter).
[Old English *self*]
—**Syn.** *adj.* uniform, unmixed.
➔ **Self** as a suffix forms the reflexive and intensive pronouns: *myself, yourself, himself, herself, itself, oneself, ourselves, yourselves, themselves.* These are used chiefly for emphasis (*I can do that myself*) or as reflexive objects (*I couldn't help myself*).
➔ The pronominal use of **self** (*payable to self, a room for self and wife*) is largely confined to commercial English, and is not regarded as standard.

self-, *prefix.* **1.** of or over oneself, as in *self-conscious, self-control, self-assured.*
2. by or in oneself or itself; without outside aid, as in *self-appointed, self-inflicted, self-evident, self-styled.*
3. to or for oneself, as in *self-addressed, self-respect.*
4. oneself (as object), as in *self-accusing, self-serving.*
5. automatic or automatically, as in *self-starter, self-closing, self-loading.*

self-a·ban·don·ment (self′ə ban′dən mənt), *n.* disregard of self or of self-interest.

self-a·base·ment (self′ə bās′mənt), *n.* abasement of self; humiliation of oneself.

self-ab·hor·rence (self′ab hôr′əns, -hor′-), *n.* abhorrence or detestation of oneself.

self-ab·ne·gat·ing (self′ab′nə gā′ting), *adj.* self-denying.

self-ab·ne·ga·tion (self′ab′nə gā′shən), *n.* self-denial: *There is even in the most selfish passion a large element of self-abnegation* (Harper's).

self-ab·sorbed (self′ab sôrbd′, -zôrbd′), *adj.* absorbed in oneself or one's own thoughts, affairs, etc.

self-ab·sorp·tion (self′ab sôrp′shən, -zôrp′-), *n.* absorption in oneself or one's own thoughts, affairs, etc.

self-a·buse (self′ə byüs′), *n.* **1.** abuse of oneself. **2.** masturbation.

self-ac·cu·sa·tion (self′ak′yů zā′shən), *n.* the act of accusing oneself: *Too liberal self-accusations are generally but so many traps for acquittal with applause* (Samuel Richardson).

self-ac·cus·ing (self′ə kyü′zing), *adj.* accusing oneself: *self-accusing guilt.*

self-ac·knowl·edged (self′ak nol′ijd), *adj.* acknowledged by oneself.

self-act·ing (self′ak′ting), *adj.* **1.** working of itself: *Man is a self-acting machine* (George Meredith). **2.** acting automatically without the manipulation or mechanism which would otherwise be required: *the self-acting feed of a boring mill.*

self-ac·tion (self′ak′shən), *n.* action that is independent of external impulse.

self-ac·tive (self′ak′tiv), *adj.* acting of or by itself; acting independently of external impulse.

self-ac·tiv·i·ty (self′ak tiv′ə tē), *n.* inherent or intrinsic power of acting or moving.

self-ac·tor (self′ak′tər), *n.* a self-acting machine or part of a machine.

self-ad·ap·ta·tion (self′ad ap tā′shən), *n.* the adaptation of an organism in response to new conditions.

self-ad·dressed (self′ə drest′), *adj.* addressed to oneself: *a self-addressed envelope.*

self-ad·just·ing (self′ə jus′ting), *adj.* adjusting itself; requiring no external adjustment: *The system is self-adjusting and finds a new balance when it is disturbed* (New Scientist).

self-ad·min·is·tered (self′ad min′ə stərd), *adj.* administered by oneself.

self-ad·mi·ra·tion (self′ad′mə rā′shən), *n.* admiration of oneself; self-conceit.

self-ad·mir·ing (self′ad mī′ring), *adj.* full of admiration for oneself. —**self′-ad·mir′ing·ly,** *adv.*

self-ad·mit·ted (self′ad mit′id), *adj.* admitted by oneself; self-confessed: *a self-admitted gambler, self-admitted doubts, self-admitted guilt.*

self-ad·van·tage (self′ad van′tij, -vän′-), *n.* one's own advantage.

self-ad·van·ta·geous (self′ad′vən tā′jəs), *adj.* advantageous to or for oneself.

self-ad·ver·tise·ment (self′ad′vər tīz′mənt; -ad vėr′tis-, -tiz-; self′ad′vər tiz′-), *n.* advertisement of oneself; showing off oneself in a deliberate manner.

self-ag·gran·dize·ment (self′ə gran′diz mənt), *n.* aggrandizement of oneself.

self-a·lign·ing or **self-a·lin·ing** (self′ə lī′ning), *adj.* aligning automatically.

self-a·nal·y·sis (self′ə nal′ə sis), *n., pl.* **-ses** (-sēz). **1.** self-examination. **2.** autoanalysis (def. 1).

self-an·ni·hi·la·tion (self′ə nī′ə lā′shən), *n.* destruction or obliteration of self: *To sink the soul into the lowest state of humility, what the schoolmen call self-annihilation* (Joseph Addison).

self-ap·par·ent (self′ə par′ənt), *adj.* apparent to oneself, or in itself.

self-ap·plause (self′ə plôz′), *n.* approval or commendation of oneself: *She . . . with self-applause her wild creation views* (Alexander Pope).

self-ap·pli·ca·tion (self′ap′lə kā′shən), *n.* application of oneself or itself.

self-ap·point·ed (self′ə poin′tid), *adj.* appointed or nominated by oneself: *Leigh Hunt himself was, as Mr. Colvin has observed, a kind of self-appointed poet laureate of Hampstead* (Athenaeum).

self-ap·prais·al (self′ə prā′zəl), *n.* appraisal of oneself.

self-ap·prov·al (self′ə prü′vəl), *n.* approval of oneself.

self-ap·prov·ing (self′ə prü′ving), *adj.* **1.** implying approval of one's own conduct or character. **2.** justifying such approval.

self-as·ser·tion (self′ə sėr′shən), *n.* insistence on one's own wishes, opinions, claims, etc.

self-as·ser·tive (self′ə sėr′tiv), *adj.* putting oneself forward; insisting on one's own wishes, opinions, etc. —**self′-as·ser′tive·ly,** *adv.* —**self′-as·ser′tive·ness,** *n.*

self-as·sumed (self′ə sümd′), *adj.* assumed by one's own act or authority: *a self-assumed title.*

self-as·sur·ance (self′ə shůr′əns), *n.* self-confidence.

self-as·sured (self′ə shůrd′), *adj.* self-confident; sure of oneself.

self-at·tach·ment (self′ə tach′mənt), *n.* attachment to oneself or itself.

self-au·thor·ized (self′ô′thə rīzd), *adj.* authorized by oneself.

self-a·ware (self′ə wãr′), *adj.* **1.** having self-awareness. **2.** self-conscious: *Although the eyes of the nation were not upon them, the demeanor of the event's main participants . . . was . . . unmistakably self-aware* (Truman Capote).

self-a·ware·ness (self′ə wãr′nis), *n.* awareness of oneself; self-realization: *There are a few glints of self-awareness, such as his realization that his diary had taken a political-literary rather than a personal form* (New Yorker).

self-bal·anc·ing (self′bal′ən sing), *adj.* automatically balancing oneself or itself.

self-belt (self′belt′), *n.* a belt attached to and made of the same material as a garment: *It would consist of a blouse of green-brown with a self-belt* (New York Times).

self-be·tray·al (self′bi trā′əl), *n.* betraying of oneself; self-deception.

self-bind·er (self′bīn′dər), *n.* **1.** a machine that gathers cut grain and ties it with wire into sheaves. **2.** a reaper or harvester with such an attachment.

self-bow (self′bō′), *n. Archery.* a bow made of a single piece of wood, or of two pieces spliced endwise at the handle.

self-care (self′kãr′), *n.* care of oneself.

self-cen·sor·ship (self′sen′sər ship), *n.* censorship of oneself or itself: *I foresee that self-censorship in television programs will be severe* (Lee De Forest).

self-cen·tered (self′sen′tərd), *adj.* **1.** occupied with one's own interests and affairs. **2.** selfish. **3.** being a fixed point around which other things move. —**self′-cen′tered·ly,** *adv.* —**self′-cen′tered·ness,** *n.*

self-cen·tred (self′sen′tərd), *adj. Especially British.* self-centered.

self-charg·ing (self′chär′jing), *adj.* automatically charging itself.

self-cho·sen (self′chō′zən), *adj.* chosen by oneself; not imposed; voluntary: *Freedom of religious practice can be observed in homes and churches under . . . self-chosen guidance* (New York Times).

self-cleans·ing (self′klen′zing), *adj.* automatically cleansing itself.

self-clos·ing (self′klō′zing), *adj.* closing of itself; closing or shutting automatically: *a self-closing bridge, a self-closing door.*

self-cock·ing (self′kok′ing), *adj.* (of a gun) cocking automatically; having the hammer cocked and released by simply pulling the trigger.

self-col·or (self′kul′ər), *n.* **1.** one uniform color, as of a dyed fabric. **2.** natural (undyed) color.

self-col·ored (self′kul′ərd), *adj.* **1.** of one uniform color. **2.** of the natural color.

self-com·mand (self′kə mand′, -mänd′), *n.* control of one's actions or feelings; self-control: *a combat between native ardour of temper and the habitual power of self-command* (Scott).

self-com·ment (self′kom′ent), *n.* comment of or over oneself.

self-com·mun·ion (self′kə myün′yən), *n.* communion with oneself.

self-com·pas·sion (self′kəm pash′ən), *n.* compassion for oneself; self-pity.

self-com·pla·cence (self′kəm plā′səns), *n.* self-complacency.

self-com·pla·cen·cy (self′kəm plā′sən sē), *n.* a being self-satisfied; complacence.

self-com·pla·cent (self′kəm plā′sənt), *adj.* pleased with oneself; self-satisfied; complacent. —**self′-com·pla′cent·ly,** *adv.*

self-com·plete (self′kəm plēt′), *adj.* complete in oneself or itself.

self-com·posed (self′kəm pōzd′), *adj.* calm; composed.

self-con·ceit (self′kən sēt′), *n.* too much pride in oneself or one's ability; conceit: *Conquest brings self-conceit and intolerance* (Havelock Ellis). —**Syn.** egotism.

self-con·ceit·ed (self′kən sē′tid), *adj.* having or showing self-conceit.

self-con·cen·trat·ed (self′kon′sən trā′tid), *adj.* concentrated on or over oneself.

self-con·cen·tra·tion (self′kon′sən trā′shən), *n.* concentration over oneself.

self-con·cep·tion (self′kən sep′shən), *n.* conception of oneself; view of oneself: *An individual's self-conception often differs from the conception others have of him.*

self-con·cern (self′kən sėrn′), *n.* self-interest.

self-con·dem·na·tion (self′kon′dem nā′shən), *n.* condemnation by oneself of one's own action.

self-con·demned (self′kən demd′), *adj.* condemned by one's own conscience or confession.

self-con·fessed (self′kən fest′), *adj.* confessed by oneself; self-admitted: *a self-confessed failure, a self-confessed sadist. Eddington's self-confessed addiction to thinking of the electron as a "hard, red, shiny ball"* (Science News Letter).

self-con·fi·dence (self′kon′fə dəns), *n.* belief in one's own ability, power, judgment, etc.; confidence in oneself.

self-con·fi·dent (self′kon′fə dənt), *adj.* believing in one's own ability, power, judgment, etc. —**self′-con′fi·dent·ly,** *adv.*

self-con·grat·u·la·tion (self′kən grach′ə lā′shən), *n.* congratulation of oneself: *Her [his wife's] practical capacity was for him a matter for continual self-congratulation* (H. G. Wells).

self-con·grat·u·la·to·ry (self′kən grach′ə lə tôr′ē, -tōr′-), *adj.* congratulating oneself: *a self-congratulatory mood.*

self-con·scious (self′kon′shəs), *adj.* **1.** made conscious of how one is appearing to others; embarrassed, especially by the presence or the thought of other people and their attitude toward one; shy: *self-conscious of a world looking on* (Thomas Carlyle). **2.**

 PRONUNCIATION KEY: hat, āge, cãre, fär; let, ēqual, tėrm; it, īce; hot, ōpen, ôrder; oil, out; cup, pů t, rüle;

Philosophy. having consciousness of oneself, one's actions, sensations, etc. —**self′-con′scious·ly,** *adv.* —**self′-con′scious·ness,** *n.*
self-con·se·quence (self′kon′sə kwens, -kwəns), *n.* a sense of one's own importance; self-importance.
self-con·sist·en·cy (self′kən sis′tən sē), *n., pl.* **-cies.** the quality or state of being self-consistent: *This Administration has achieved a self-consistency of foreign policy which its predecessor never acquired* (Wall Street Journal).
self-con·sist·ent (self′kən sis′tənt), *adj.* consistent with oneself or itself; having its parts or elements in agreement.
self-con·sti·tut·ed (self′kon′stə tü′tid, -tyü′-), *adj.* constituted by oneself or itself: *a self-constituted board of inquiry.*
self-con·tained (self′kən tānd′), *adj.* **1.** saying little; reserved: *They are rather silent, self-contained men when with strangers* (Theodore Roosevelt). **2.** containing in oneself or itself all that is necessary; independent of what is external: *When London was smaller, and the parts of London more self-contained and parochial* (G.K. Chesterton). **3.** having all its working parts contained in one case, cover, or framework: *A watch is self-contained.* **4.** *British.* (of a house) having approaches, entrances, and apartments restricted to the use of a single household. —**self′-con·tained′ness,** *n.*
self-con·tain·ment (self′kən tān′mənt), *n.* the condition of being self-contained.
self-con·tempt (self′kən tempt′), *n.* contempt for oneself: *Perish in thy self-contempt!* (Tennyson).
self-con·tent (self′kən tent′), *n.* self-satisfaction.
self-con·tent·ed (self′kən ten′tid), *adj.* self-satisfied.
self-con·tent·ment (self′kən tent′mənt), *n.* self-satisfaction.
self-con·tra·dic·tion (self′kon′trə dik′shən), *n.* **1.** contradiction of oneself or itself. **2.** a statement containing elements that are contradictory.
self-con·tra·dic·to·ry (self′kon′trə dik′tər ē), *adj.* contradicting oneself or itself.
self-con·trol (self′kən trōl′), *n.* control of one's actions, feelings, etc.: *His handsome face had all the tranquillity of Indian self-control; a self-control which prevents the exhibition of emotion* (Francis Parkman).
self-con·trolled (self′kən trōld′), *adj.* having or showing self-control.
self-con·vict·ed (self′kən vik′tid), *adj.* convicted by one's own consciousness, knowledge, or avowal: *Guilt stands self-convicted when arraign'd* (Richard Savage).
self-cor·rect·ing (self′kə rek′ting), *adj.* correcting automatically.
self-cor·rec·tion (self′kə rek′shən), *n.* automatic correction of oneself or itself.
self-cor·rupt·ed (self′kə rup′tid), *adj.* corrupted by oneself or itself.
self-cre·at·ed (self′krē ā′tid), *adj.* created, brought into existence, or constituted by oneself: *The particular, partly self-created, character of Gibbon's mind* ... (R.H. Hutton).
self-crit·i·cal (self′krit′ə kəl), *adj.* critical of oneself.
self-crit·i·cism (self′krit′ə siz əm), *n.* criticism of oneself.
self-de·ceit (self′di sēt′), *n.* self-deception.
self-de·ceit·ful (self′di sēt′fəl), *adj.* self-deceptive.
self-de·ceived (self′di sēvd′), *adj.* deceived by oneself.
self-de·ceiv·er (self′di sē′vər), *n.* a person who practices self-deception.
self-de·ceiv·ing (self′di sē′ving), *adj.* self-deceptive.
self-de·cep·tion (self′di sep′shən), *n.* the act or fact of deceiving oneself; self-delusion; self-deceit.
self-de·cep·tive (self′di sep′tiv), *adj.* deceiving oneself.
self-de·clared (self′di klãrd′), *adj.* declared by oneself; self-proclaimed: *a self-declared conservative, self-declared limitations.*
self-ded·i·ca·tion (self′ded′ə kā′shən), *n.* dedication of oneself to some person or purpose.
self-de·feat·ing (self′di fē′ting), *adj.* defeating oneself or itself; contrary to one's or its own purpose, interests, etc.: *U.S. taxation on foreign business activity is self-defeating* (Time). *In the long run, it is self-defeating to allocate aid only to known political allies* (Manchester Guardian).
self-de·fence (self′di fens′), *n. Especially British.* self-defense.
self-de·fense (self′di fens′), *n.* defense of one's own person, property, reputation, etc.: *Homicide in self-defense ... upon a sudden affray, is ... excusable, rather than justifiable, by the English law* (William Blackstone).
self-de·fen·sive (self′di fen′siv), *adj.* tending to defend oneself; of the nature of self-defense.
self-de·fined (self′di fīnd′), *adj.* defined by oneself or itself.
self-de·fin·ing (self′di fī′ning), *adj.* defining by oneself or itself; self-explanatory.
self-def·i·ni·tion (self′def′ə nish′ən), *n.* definition of one's own character, identity, etc.: *Africa's central problem is political self-definition* (New York Times).
self-de·lud·ed (self′di lü′did), *adj.* deluded by oneself: *He had warned the self-deluded members of the Conservative party* (Leeds Mercury).
self-de·lu·sion (self′di lü′zhən), *n.* the act or fact of deluding oneself; self-deception.
self-de·ni·al (self′di nī′əl), *n.* sacrifice of one's own desires and interests; going without things one wants. —**Syn.** self-sacrifice, abstemiousness, austerity.
self-de·ny·ing (self′di nī′ing), *adj.* sacrificing one's own wishes and interests; unselfish. —**self′-de·ny′ing·ly,** *adv.*
self-de·pend·ence (self′di pen′dəns), *n.* reliance on oneself with a feeling of independence of others; self-reliance.
self-de·pend·ent (self′di pen′dənt), *adj.* depending on oneself, or on one's own efforts, etc.; self-reliant: *Left early to his own guidance, he had begun to be self-dependent while yet a boy* (Hawthorne). —**self′-de·pend′ent·ly,** *adv.*
self-dep·re·cat·ing (self′dep′rə kā′ting), *adj.* deprecating of oneself.
self-dep·re·ca·tion (self′dep′rə kā′shən), *n.* deprecation of oneself.
self-de·rived (self′di rīvd′), *adj.* derived from oneself or from itself.
self-de·sir·a·ble (self′di zīr′ə bəl), *adj.* desirable in or of oneself or itself.
self-de·spair (self′di spãr′), *n.* despair of oneself; a despairing view of one's character, prospects, etc.
self-de·stroy·ing (self′di stroi′ing), *adj.* self-destructive: *He unfolded a six-point plan for dealing with ... self-destroying conflict* (London Times).
self-de·struc·tion (self′di struk′shən), *n.* the destruction of oneself or itself.
self-de·struc·tive (self′di struk′tiv), *adj.* **1.** tending to destroy oneself or itself: *Suicide is a self-destructive urge or act. The Nationalists, like many Americans, believe in the self-destructive attributes of Communism* (Manchester Guardian). **2.** causing its own destruction: *Each balloon has a self-destructive device to release the gas if anything goes wrong* (Newsweek). —**self′-de·struc′tive·ly,** *adv.* —**self′-de·struc′tive·ness,** *n.*
self-de·ter·mi·na·tion (self′di tėr′mə nā′shən), *n.* **1.** direction from within only, without influence or force from without. **2.** the deciding by the people of a nation what form of government they shall have, without reference to the wishes of any other nation, especially one to which it has been subject.
self-de·ter·mined (self′di tėr′mənd), *adj.* determined by oneself or itself; having the power of self-determination.
self-de·ter·min·ing (self′di tėr′mə ning), *adj.* determining one's own acts; having the power of self-determination.
self-de·vel·op·ment (self′di vel′əp mənt), *n.* **1.** development of oneself: *The secret of true happiness consists of self-discovery [and] self-development* (Atlantic). **2.** spontaneous development: *If the alleged cases of self-development be examined it will be found that the new truth affirms ... a relation between the original subject of conception and some new subject conceived later on* (William James).
self-de·vo·tion (self′di vō′shən), *n.* self-sacrifice.
self-de·vo·tion·al (self′di vō′shə nəl), *adj.* characterized by self-devotion.
self-dif·fer·en·ti·a·tion (self′dif′ə ren′shē ā′shən), *n. Biology.* the differentiation shown in organs, tissues, etc., that are relatively independent of neighboring structures in their development.
self-dif·fu·sion (self′di fyü′zhən), *n.* the diffusion of atoms within a metal that is composed of chemically identical atoms, especially at high temperature.
self-di·ges·tion (self′də jes′chən, -dī-), *n. Physiology.* digestion or breakdown of cells or tissue by enzymes produced by these cells; autolysis.
self-di·rect·ed (self′də rek′tid, -dī-), *adj.* directed by oneself.
self-di·rec·tion (self′də rek′shən, -dī-), *n.* control or management of oneself; self-guidance.
self-dis·ci·pline (self′dis′ə plin), *n.* careful control and training of oneself.
self-dis·clo·sure (self′dis klō′zhər), *n.* disclosure of oneself; self-revelation: *"The Young Tigers" is a candid self-disclosure of what makes a man tick* (London Times).
self-dis·con·tent·ed (self′dis′kən ten′tid), *adj.* discontented with or over oneself.
self-dis·cov·er·y (self′dis kuv′ər ē, -kuv′rē), *n.* discovery of one's identity, position in society, etc.
self-dis·par·age·ment (self′dis par′ij-mənt), *n.* disparagement of oneself.
self-dis·sat·is·fac·tion (self′dis sat′is-fak′shən), *n.* dissatisfaction with or over oneself.
self-dis·trust (self′dis trust′), *n.* distrust of oneself; lack of confidence in one's own abilities: *I ... urge, in trembling self-distrust, a prayer without a claim* (John Greenleaf Whittier).
self-dis·trust·ful (self′dis trust′fəl), *adj.* distrustful of oneself or one's own abilities.
self-doubt (self′dout′), *n.* doubt of oneself; doubt of one's own abilities, worth, decisions, motives, etc.
self-dram·a·ti·za·tion (self′dram′ə tə zā′shən, -drä′mə-), *n.* dramatization of oneself.
self-dram·a·tize (self′dram′ə tīz, -drä′mə-), *v.i.,* **-tized, -tiz·ing.** to dramatize oneself.
self-drive car (self′drīv′), *British.* a car for rent, driven by the renter: *Now, you can hire a ... self-drive car and leave it at your destination at no extra charge* (Sunday Times).
self-driv·en (self′driv′ən), *adj.* driven by itself; automatic.
self-ed·u·cat·ed (self′ej′ů kā′tid), *adj.* self-taught; educated by one's own efforts.
self-ed·u·ca·tion (self′ej′ů kā′shən), *n.* education by or through one's own efforts.
self-ef·face·ment (self′ə fās′mənt), *n.* the act or habit of keeping oneself in the background, as in modesty or humility: *Self-effacement in a generation of self-salesmanship* (Hugh R. Orr).
self-ef·fac·ing (self′ə fā′sing), *adj.* effacing oneself or keeping oneself in the background. —**self′-ef·fac′ing·ly,** *adv.*
self-e·lec·ted (self′i lek′tid), *adj.* **1.** elected by oneself; self-appointed. **2.** (of a body) elected by its members: *Self-elected Town Councils* (Macaulay).
self-em·ployed (self′em ploid′), *adj.* not employed by others; working for oneself: *The Senate Finance Committee decided to make social security voluntary for physicians, dentists, lawyers, farmers, and other self-employed persons* (Time).
self-en·am·ored (self′en am′ərd), *adj.* enamored of or over oneself.
self-en·forc·ing (self′en fôr′sing, -fōr′-), *adj.* enforcing by oneself or itself.
self-es·teem (self′es tēm′), *n.* **1.** the thinking well of oneself; self-respect. **2.** the thinking too well of oneself; conceit.
self-e·val·u·a·tion (self′i val′yů ā′shən), *n.* evaluation of oneself.
self-ev·i·dent (self′ev′ə dənt), *adj.* evident by itself; needing no proof; axiomatic: *We hold these truths to be self-evident* (Declaration of Independence). *The self-evident fact that growth is the result of eating and drinking* (Benjamin Jowett). —**self′-ev′i·dent·ly,** *adv.*
self-ex·am·i·na·tion (self′eg zam′ə nā′shən), *n.* an examination into one's own state, conduct, motives, etc.
self-ex·ci·ta·tion (self′ek′sī tā′shən), *n.* the excitation of the field of a generator by currents taken from its own armature.
self-ex·cit·ed (self′ek sī′tid), *adj.* (of a generator) excited by the current of its own armature.
self-ex·cit·ing (self′ek sī′ting), *adj.* capable of self-excitation: *a self-exciting dynamo.*
self-ex·cus·ing (self′ek skyü′zing), *adj.* excusing oneself.

self-ex·e·cut·ing (self′ek′sə kyü′ting), *adj.* becoming effective automatically under circumstances or at a time as specified, and needing no legislation to enforce it: *a self-executing clause in a treaty or contract.*

self-ex·ile (self′eg′zīl, -ek′sīl), *n.* **1.** voluntary exile: *to live in self-exile.* **2.** a self-exiled person.

self-ex·iled (self′eg′zīld, -ek′sīld), *adj.* voluntarily exiled; absent by choice from one's native land.

self-ex·ist·ence (self′eg zis′təns), *n.* the property or fact of being self-existent.

self-ex·ist·ent (self′eg zis′tənt), *adj.* **1.** existing independently of any other cause. **2.** having an independent existence.

self-ex·plain·ing (self′ek splā′ning), *adj.* self-explanatory.

self-ex·plan·a·to·ry (self′ek splan′ə tôr′ē, -tōr′-), *adj.* explaining itself; that needs no explanation; obvious.

self-ex·po·sure (self′ek spō′zhər), *n.* exposure of oneself.

self-ex·pres·sion (self′ek spresh′ən), *n.* the expression of one's personality.

self-ex·pres·sive (self′ek spres′iv), *adj.* expressive of one's personality: *In place of a self-expressive art created by the imagination, tastes, and desires of the artist, Cage purposes an art born of chance and indeterminacy in which every effort is made to extinguish the artist's own personality* (New Yorker).

self-feed·er (self′fē′dər), *n.* a machine that feeds itself automatically, as a printing press.

self-feed·ing (self′fē′ding), *adj.* that feeds itself automatically: *a self-feeding press.*

self-feel·ing (self′fē′ling), *n. Psychology.* selfish feeling or emotion.

self-fer·tile (self′fėr′təl), *adj. Botany.* **1.** (of a flower) having the property of fertilizing itself by the action of its pollen on its stigma. **2.** (of a plant) fertilized by the pollen of its own flowers alone.

self-fer·til·i·ty (self′fėr til′ə tē), *n. Botany.* the ability to fertilize itself.

self-fer·ti·li·za·tion (self′fėr′tə lə zā′shən), *n. Botany.* the fertilization of the ovules of a flower by pollen from the same flower; autogamy.

self-fer·ti·lized (self′fėr′tə līzd), *adj. Botany.* (of a flower) fertilized by its own pollen; autogamous.

self-fig·ured (self′fig′yərd), *adj.* woven with figures in its own color: *a self-figured fabric.*

self-fill·er (self′fil′ər), *n.* any of various types of fountain pen that can be filled by operating some mechanism while the lower part of the pen is dipped in ink.

self-fill·ing (self′fil′ing), *adj.* that can fill itself.

self-flag·el·la·tion (self′flaj′ə lā′shən), *n.* flagellation of oneself; punishment of oneself: *. . . a kind of solemnity and mental or moral self-examination and self-flagellation* (Theodore Dreiser).

self-for·get·ful (self′fər get′fəl), *adj.* forgetful of oneself or one's own individuality; showing no thought of one's own advantage or interest. —**self′-for·get′ful·ly,** *adv.* —**self′-for·get′ful·ness,** *n.*

self-for·get·ting (self′fər get′ing), *adj.* self-forgetful.

self-ful·fill·ment or **self-ful·fil·ment** (self′fu̇l fil′mənt), *n.* achievement of one's true needs, aspirations, etc., by one's own efforts or actions; self-realization.

self-gen·er·at·ed (self′jen′ə rā′tid), *adj.* generated by oneself or itself, independently of any external agency.

self-gen·er·at·ing (self′jen′ə rā′ting), *adj.* automatically generating.

self-giv·ing (self′giv′ing), *adj.* giving of oneself for others; self-sacrificing: *A flow of this divine self-giving charity* (Frederick W. Robertson).

self-glo·ri·fi·ca·tion (self′glôr′ə fə kā′shən, -glōr′-), *n.* glorification or exaltation of oneself: *The unconscious Captain walked out in a state of self-glorification* (Dickens).

self-glo·ri·fy·ing (self′glôr′ə fī′ing, -glōr′-), *adj.* glorifying or exalting oneself: *. . . occasionally desisting from his own self-glorifying diatribes* (Theodore Dreiser).

self-glo·ry (self′glôr′ē, -glōr′-), *n.* vainglory; boasting: *. . . narcissuslike in its self-glory* (Time).

self-gov·erned (self′guv′ərnd), *adj.* **1.** having self-government: *a self-governed state.* **2.** governing one's own actions or affairs; independent. **3.** marked by or exercising self-control.

self-gov·ern·ing (self′guv′ər ning), *adj.* that governs itself; having self-government; autonomous.

self-gov·ern·ment (self′guv′ərn mənt, -ər-), *n.* **1. a.** government of a state or group by its own citizens or members: *self-government through elected representatives.* **b.** the state of having such a government. **2.** government of one's actions, affairs, etc., by oneself or independently of others. **3.** self-control; self-command: *Virtuous self-government . . . improves the inward constitution or character* (Joseph Butler).

self-grat·i·fi·ca·tion (self′grat′ə fə kā′shən), *n.* the gratification of oneself or one's desires, vanity, etc.

self-grat·u·la·tion (self′grach′ə lā′shən), *n.* self-congratulation.

self-grat·u·la·to·ry (self′grach′ə lə tôr′ē, -tōr′-), *adj.* self-congratulatory.

self-guid·ance (self′gī′dəns), *n.* guidance of oneself in one's own course, action, etc.: *He may lose the powers of self-guidance, and in a wrong course his very vitalities hurry him to perdition* (George Meredith).

self-guid·ed (self′gī′dəd), *adj.* directed along a course by self-contained devices, such as a homing mechanism: *a self-guided missile.*

self-hard·en (self′här′dən), *v.i.* (of steel) to harden without the usual quenching process.

self-hard·en·ing (self′här′də ning), *adj.* hardening without the usual quenching process: *self-hardening steel.*

self-hate (self′hāt′), *n.* self-hatred.

self-ha·tred (self′hā′trid), *n.* a very strong dislike of oneself; hate of oneself.

self·heal (self′hēl′), *n.* **1.** a weed of the mint family, with blue or purple flowers, formerly supposed to heal wounds; allheal. **2.** any of various other plants formerly supposed to possess healing powers, as the sanicle.

Selfheal (def. 1)

self-heal·ing (self′hē′ling), *adj.* healing by itself without external application: *a self-healing wound.*

self-help (self′help′), *n.* **1.** a helping oneself; getting along without assistance from others: *The first lesson the backwoodsmen learned was the necessity of self-help* (Theodore Roosevelt). **2.** *Law.* the act or right of redressing or preventing wrongs by one's own actions, without recourse to legal process.

self-help·ful (self′help′fəl), *adj.* helping oneself. —**self′-help′ful·ness,** *n.*

self·hood (self′hu̇d), *n.* **1.** the quality by virtue of which one is oneself; personal individuality. **2.** devotion to self; self-centeredness. **3.** one's personal interests or character; one's personality: *In cultivating manhood we develop selfhood* (Century Magazine).

self-hyp·no·sis (self′hip nō′sis), *n.* self-induced hypnosis; autohypnosis.

self-i·den·ti·cal (self′ī den′tə kəl), *adj.* identical with itself.

self-i·den·ti·ty (self′ī den′tə tē), *n.* the identity of a thing with itself.

self-im·age (self′im′ij), *n.* self-conception: *The human inherently protects himself against threats to his self-image—that is, to his image of the world and the way he masters or copes with it* (Bulletin of Atomic Scientists).

self-im·mo·la·tion (self′im′ə lā′shən), *n.* self-sacrifice: *It was not mere sorrow that kept her so strangely sequestered; it was devotion, it was self-immolation; it was the laborious legacy of love* (Lytton Strachey).

self-im·por·tance (self′im pôr′təns), *n.* a having or showing too high an opinion of one's own importance; conceit; behavior showing conceit.

self-im·por·tant (self′im pôr′tənt), *adj.* having or showing too high an opinion of one's own importance. —**self′-im·por′tant·ly,** *adv.*

self-im·posed (self′im pōzd′), *adj.* imposed on oneself by oneself: *a self-imposed task.*

self-im·prove·ment (self′im prüv′mənt), *n.* improvement of one's character, mind, etc., by one's own efforts: *The first thing I discovered was that those who are most interested in self-improvement are those who need it least* (New Yorker).

self-im·prov·ing (self′im prü′ving), *adj.* improving oneself by one's own efforts.

self-in·clu·sive (self′in klü′siv), *adj.* inclusive of oneself or itself.

self-in·crim·i·nat·ing (self′in krim′ə nā′ting), *adj.* accusing of oneself.

self-in·crim·i·na·tion (self′in krim′ə nā′shən), *n.* the incriminating of oneself through one's own testimony: *He pleaded his privilege against self-incrimination under the fifth amendment of the Constitution* (Wall Street Journal).

self-in·curred (self′in kėrd′), *adj.* incurred by oneself.

self-in·duced (self′in düst′, -dyüst′), *adj.* **1.** induced by oneself or itself. **2.** *Electricity.* produced by self-induction.

self-in·duc·tion (self′in duk′shən), *n. Electricity.* the production of an electromotive force in a circuit by a varying current in that circuit.

self-in·dul·gence (self′in dul′jəns), *n.* the gratification of one's own desires, passions, etc., with too little regard for the welfare of others.

self-in·dul·gent (self′in dul′jənt), *adj.* characterized by self-indulgence: *a capricious and self-indulgent valetudinarian* (James Boswell). —**self′-in·dul′gent·ly,** *adv.*

self-in·fec·tion (self′in fek′shən), *n. Medicine.* auto-infection.

self-in·flict·ed (self′in flik′tid), *adj.* inflicted on oneself by oneself, as a wound.

self-i·ni·ti·at·ed (self′i nish′ē ā′tid), *adj.* begun by oneself or itself.

self-i·ni·ti·at·ing (self′i nish′ē ā′ting), *adj.* initiating by itself; occurring spontaneously or automatically.

self-in·ju·ri·ous (self′in ju̇r′ē əs), *adj.* injurious to or for oneself.

self-in·ju·ry (self′in′jər ē), *n., pl.* **-ries.** injury to or for oneself.

self-in·oc·u·la·tion (self′i nok′yə lā′shən), *n. Medicine.* auto-inoculation.

self-in·sur·ance (self′in shu̇r′əns), *n.* the insuring of oneself, one's own property, etc., through oneself rather than through an insurance company, as by setting aside a fund for the purpose.

self-in·sured (self′in shu̇rd′), *adj.* insured by oneself rather than through an insurance company.

self-in·sur·er (self′in shu̇r′ər), *n.* a person or company that is self-insured: *Self-insurers are companies . . . that can prove financial responsibility and so run their own insurance system* (Wall Street Journal).

self-in·tel·li·gi·ble (self′in tel′ə jə bəl), *adj.* intelligible of oneself or itself.

self-in·ter·est (self′in′tər ist, -trist), *n.* **1.** interest in one's own welfare or advantage with too little care for the welfare of others; selfishness: *. . . the self-interest of the calculating statesman* (Henry Morley). **2.** personal interest or advantage.

self-in·ter·est·ed (self′in′tər ə stid, -trəs-; -tə res′tid), *adj.* motivated solely by regard for one's own welfare or advantage; showing self-interest. —**self′-in′ter·est·ed·ness,** *n.*

self-in·vit·ed (self′in vī′tid), *adj.* **1.** not waiting for an invitation; invited by oneself. **2.** occasioned, encouraged, or incited by oneself.

self·ish (sel′fish), *adj.* **1.** caring too much for oneself and too little for others: *This selfish, well-fed and supremely indifferent old man . . .* (Edith Wharton). **2.** showing care solely or chiefly for oneself: *selfish motives. Want makes almost every man selfish* (Samuel Johnson). —**self′ish·ly,** *adv.* —**self′ish·ness,** *n.*

self-jus·ti·fi·ca·tion (self′jus′tə fə kā′shən), *n.* justification of oneself.

self-jus·ti·fy·ing (self′jus′tə fī′ing), *adj.* **1.** justifying oneself; excusing oneself. **2.** *Printing.* justifying lines of type automatically: *a self-justifying typesetter.*

self-knowl·edge (self′nol′ij), *n.* the knowledge of one's own character, ability, etc.

self-lac·er·a·tion (self′las′ə rā′shən), *n.* a laceration of oneself; self-inflicted injury: *We have become guilty of thinking that all American autobiographies will contain vicious self-lacerations* (Manchester Guardian Weekly).

self·less (self′lis), *adj.* having no regard or thought for self; unselfish. —**self′less·ly,** *adv.* —**self′less·ness,** *n.*

self-lim·it·ed (self′lim′ə tid), *adj.* (of a

disease) that runs a definite course, being little modified by treatment: *Influenza is self-limited, usually lasting three or four days* (Science News Letter).

self-lim·it·ing (self′lim′ə ting), *adj.* **1.** limiting or controlling oneself or itself; self-regulating. **2.** self-limited: *a self-limiting illness.*

self-liq·ui·dat·ing (self′lik′wə dā′ting), *adj.* that will convert goods into cash quickly.

self-load·ing (self′lō′ding), *adj.* that loads itself; automatic.

self-lock·ing (self′lok′ing), *adj.* locking automatically.

self-love (self′luv′), *n.* **1.** love of oneself; selfishness. **2.** conceit. **3.** *Philosophy.* the regard for one's own well-being or happiness, considered as a natural and proper relation of a man to himself. **4.** narcissism.

self-lov·ing (self′luv′ing), *adj.* loving oneself too much.

self-lu·bri·cat·ing (self′lü′brə kā′ting), *adj.* lubricating automatically.

self-lu·mi·nos·i·ty (self′lü′mə nos′ə tē), *n.* the property or condition of being self-luminous; luminosity caused by the spontaneous vibratory motions of the particles of the luminous body: *Bodies like radium that exhibit self-luminosity in the dark . . .* (Nature).

self-lu·mi·nous (self′lü′mə nəs), *adj.* having in itself the property of giving off light, as the sun, flames, etc.: *The necessity for an outward flow of energy explains why a star must be self-luminous* (Scientific American).

self-made (self′mād′), *adj.* **1.** made by oneself. **2.** successful through one's own efforts, especially without material aid from one's family.

self-mas·ter·y (self′mas′tər ē, -mäs′-), *n.* the mastery of oneself; self-control.

self-mate (self′māt′), *n.* a checkmate produced in chess by the side that is mated; suimate.

self-med·i·ca·tion (self′med′ə kā′shən), *n.* **1.** the taking of medicines without the advice of a doctor: *Many compounded the mischief by harmful self-medication, especially with laxatives* (Time). **2.** the proper medical treatment of oneself, in the absence of doctors: *Space men and women . . . should be trained in self-medication and, particularly, the use of antibiotics* (New Yorker).

self-mock·er·y (self′mok′ər ē), *n.* mockery of oneself; a scoffing at one's own talents, personality, appearance, etc.: *Self-mockery may sometimes mask great conceit.*

self-mor·ti·fi·ca·tion (self′môr′tə fə kā′shən), *n.* mortification of oneself, one's passions, etc.

self-mor·ti·fied (self′môr′tə fīd), *adj.* mortified of oneself.

self-moved (self′müvd′), *adj.* moved of itself, without external agency.

self-mov·ing (self′mü′ving), *adj.* that can move by itself; moving spontaneously or automatically.

self-mur·der (self′mėr′dər), *n.* the taking of one's own life; suicide.

self-mur·der·er (self′mėr′dər ər), *n.* a person who kills himself; suicide.

self-mu·ti·la·tion (self′myü′tə lā′shən), *n.* injury inflicted upon oneself.

self-ne·glect (self′ni glekt′), *n.* neglect of oneself.

self-ob·sessed (self′əb sest′), *adj.* obsessed of or over oneself; self-concentrated.

self-ob·ses·sion (self′əb sesh′ən), *n.* obsession of or over oneself; self-concentration.

self-oc·cu·pied (self′ok′yə pīd), *adj.* **1.** occupied with oneself; self-absorbed. **2.** self-employed.

self-o·pin·ion (self′ə pin′yən), *n.* **1.** opinion of oneself. **2.** conceit. **3.** obstinacy in one's own opinion.

self-o·pin·ion·at·ed (self′ə pin′yə nā′tid), *adj.* **1.** having an exaggerated opinion of oneself; conceited. **2.** stubborn.

self-o·pin·ioned (self′ə pin′yənd), *adj.* self-opinionated.

self-op·posed (self′ə pōzd′), *adj.* opposed to oneself or itself; having parts or elements that are opposed one to another.

self-or·dained (self′ôr dānd′), *adj.* ordained by oneself or itself.

self-or·gan·ized (self′ôr′gə nīzd), *adj.* organized of or by oneself.

self-out·lawed (self′out′lôd′), *adj.* outlawed by oneself.

self-par·o·dy (self′par′ə dē), *n.* a parody of oneself; a ridiculous exaggeration of one's own characteristics: *Lord Attlee was one of the most enigmatic Prime Ministers, a reticent Englishman to the point of self-parody* (Manchester Guardian Weekly).

self-per·cep·tion (self′pər sep′shən), *n.* perception of or by oneself.

self-per·fect (self′pėr′fikt), *adj.* perfect in oneself or itself.

self-per·pet·u·at·ing (self′pər pech′u̇ ā′ting), *adj.* perpetuating oneself or itself: *The largest single block of stock is owned by a charitable foundation whose trustees are self-perpetuating* (Wall Street Journal).

self-per·pet·u·a·tion (self′pər pech′u̇ ā′shən), *n.* perpetuation of oneself or itself: *Self-perpetuation of the organization is assured* (Harper's).

self-pit·y (self′pit′ē), *n.* pity for oneself, especially to excess: *Honesty rare as a man without self-pity* (Stephen Vincent Benét).

self-pit·y·ing (self′pit′ē ing), *adj.* characterized by self-pity: *sharply pathetic, but not self-pitying . . .* (Manchester Guardian). —**self′-pit′y·ing·ly,** *adv.*

self-pleased (self′plēzd′), *adj.* pleased with oneself; self-complacent.

self-poised (self′poizd′), *adj.* **1.** poised or balanced of itself or without external aid: *Thy form self-poised as if it floated on the air* (Longfellow). **2.** having or showing mental poise, steadiness, or self-possession, regardless of external circumstances: *Decorous and self-poised, he was only passionate before the enemy* (John L. Motley).

self-po·lic·ing (self′pə lē′sing), *adj.* policing of oneself or itself. —*n.* the act or process of policing oneself or itself: *He favored self-policing by the industry* (New York Times).

self-pol·li·nat·ed (self′pol′ə nā′tid), *adj.* (of a flower) pollinated by its own stamens.

self-pol·li·na·tion (self′pol′ə nā′shən), *n.* the transfer of pollen from a stamen to a stigma of the same flower.

self-pol·lu·tion (self′pə lü′shən), *n.* masturbation.

self-por·trait (self′pôr′trit, -trāt; -pōr′-), *n.* a portrait executed by a person of himself: *Inevitably, a good many strokes on the self-portrait he was so carefully painting revealed traits he would have liked to conceal* (Newsweek).

self-pos·sessed (self′pə zest′), *adj.* having or showing control of one's feelings and acts; not easily excited, embarrassed, or confused; calm: *. . . as impenitent and self-possessed a young lady as one would desire to see* (George Bernard Shaw). *In a moment he recovered his usual self-possessed manner* (W. H. Hudson). —**Syn.** composed, collected, poised, assured, unruffled.

self-pos·ses·sion (self′pə zesh′ən), *n.* control of one's feelings and actions; self-command; composure; calmness: *Their quiet self-possession and dignified ease impressed me pleasurably* (Samuel Butler). —**Syn.** equanimity, imperturbability.

self-pow·ered (self′pou′ərd), *adj.* powered automatically.

self-praise (self′prāz′), *n.* praise of oneself by oneself.

self-prep·a·ra·tion (self′prep′ə rā′shən), *n.* preparation of or by oneself.

self-pres·er·va·tion (self′prez′ər vā′shən), *n.* preservation of oneself from harm or destruction: *the instinct of self-preservation.*

self-pride (self′prīd′), *n.* pride in oneself, one's achievements, or one's position; personal pride: *But it is also true that most people have independence and self-pride enough to prefer work to unemployment* (Wall Street Journal).

self-prim·ing (self′prī′ming), *adj.* priming automatically.

self-pro·claimed (self′prə klāmd′), *adj.* made known by oneself about oneself; self-declared: *a self-proclaimed connoisseur of art.*

self-pro·duced (self′prə düst′, -dyüst′), *adj.* produced by or from within oneself or itself.

self-prof·it (self′prof′it), *n.* a person's own profit or advantage; self-interest: *. . . unbias'd by self-profit* (Tennyson).

self-pro·pelled (self′prə peld′), *adj.* propelled by an engine, motor, etc., within itself.

self-pro·pel·ling (self′prə pel′ing), *adj.* that moves under its own power, as an automobile: *Yonder self-propelling man-of-war with the armour-plated upper deck (and by this . . . he meant the crocodile) . . .* (Rudyard Kipling).

self-pro·pul·sion (self′prə pul′shən), *n.* movement forward or onward by one's own power: *The charter contains no instrument of self-propulsion* (New York Times).

self-pro·tec·tion (self′prə tek′shən), *n.* protection of oneself; self-defense.

self-pro·tec·tive (self′prə tek′tiv), *adj.* protecting of or over oneself or itself.

self-pu·ri·fi·ca·tion (self′pyůr′ə fə kā′shən), *n.* a purification of oneself.

self-ques·tion·ing (self′kwes′chə ning), *adj.* questioning of oneself.

self-rais·ing (self′rā′zing), *adj.* self-rising.

self-rat·ing scale (self′rā′ting), a rating scale on which a person evaluates himself in various areas, as personality, character, or ability.

self-re·al·i·za·tion (self′rē′ə lə zā′shən), *n.* the fulfillment by one's own efforts of the possibilities of development of the self.

self-re·cord·ing (self′ri kôr′ding), *adj.* that makes a record of its own operations; recording automatically; self-registering.

self-re·crim·i·na·tion (self′ri krim′ə nā′shən), *n.* self-accusation; self-reproach: *She mixed self-recrimination with self-justification until it was enough to make a man's head swim* (New Yorker).

self-re·gard (self′ri gärd′), *n.* **1.** regard of or consideration for oneself. **2.** self-respect.

self-re·gard·ing (self′ri gär′ding), *adj.* looking towards or centering upon oneself; self-serving: *The pleasures and pains of amity and enmity are of the self-regarding cast* (Jeremy Bentham).

self-reg·is·ter·ing (self′rej′ə stər ing), *adj.* registering automatically.

self-reg·u·lat·ing (self′reg′yə lā′ting), *adj.* regulating oneself or itself: *. . . a hearing aid with a self-regulating noise suppressor to dull sudden, loud sharp noises* (Science News Letter).

self-reg·u·la·tion (self′reg′yə lā′shən), *n.* regulation by or of oneself or itself.

self-reg·u·la·tive (self′reg′yə lā′tiv), *adj.* tending or serving to regulate oneself or itself.

self-re·la·tion (self′ri lā′shən), *n.* the identity of a thing with itself.

self-re·li·ance (self′ri lī′əns), *n.* reliance on oneself, one's own acts, abilities, etc.: *. . . A greater self-reliance must work a revolution in all the offices and relations of men* (Emerson).

self-re·li·ant (self′ri lī′ənt), *adj.* having or showing self-reliance. —**self′-re·li′ant·ly,** *adv.*

self-re·nun·ci·a·tion (self′ri nun′sē ā′shən), *n.* renunciation of one's own will, interests, etc.; self-sacrifice.

self-re·nun·ci·a·to·ry (self′ri nun′sē ə-tôr′ē, -tōr′-), *adj.* self-sacrificing.

self-re·pair (self′ri pãr′), *n.* repair by itself without external application: *. . . the faculties of self-repair of the humblest living tissues* (New Scientist).

self-rep·li·ca·tion (self′rep′lə kā′shən), *n.* self-reproduction: *. . . the more generalized activities of the cell, notably its self-replication* (Scientific American).

self-re·pressed (self′ri prest′), *adj.* repressed by oneself.

self-re·pres·sion (self′ri presh′ən), *n.* repression of oneself or one's own impulses, desires, etc.

self-re·proach (self′ri prōch′), *n.* blame by one's own conscience.

self-re·proach·ful (self′ri prōch′fəl), *adj.* reproaching oneself.

self-re·pro·duc·ing (self′rē′prə dü′sing, -dyü′-), *adj.* reproducing of oneself or itself.

self-re·pro·duc·tion (self′rē′prə duk′shən), *n.* reproduction or copy of oneself or itself.

self-re·proof (self′ri prüf′), *n.* reproof of oneself by oneself.

self-re·spect (self′ri spekt′), *n.* respect for oneself; proper regard for the dignity of one's character or position, with recognition of its obligations of worthy conduct; proper pride: *With shame and repentance . . . had come a strange new feeling—that of a dawning self-respect* (George Du Maurier).

self-re·spect·ing (self′ri spek′ting), *adj.* having self-respect; properly proud: *. . . the shame of boasting that shuts the mouths of self-respecting Scots* (Ian Maclaren).

self-re·spon·si·bil·i·ty (self′ri spon′sə-bil′ə tē), *n., pl.* **-ties.** responsibility to or for oneself.

self-re·strained (self′ri strānd′), *adj.* restrained by oneself or itself; showing self-restraint.

self-re·straint (self′ri strānt′), *n.* restraint imposed by oneself on one's actions, etc.; self-control.

self-rev·e·la·tion (self′rev′ə lā′shən), *n.* revelation of oneself; disclosure of one's real self.

self-right·eous (self′rī′chəs), *adj.* thinking that one is more moral than others; thinking that one is very good and pleasing to God: *She's narrow and self-righteous* (Eden Phillpotts). **—self′-right′eous·ly,** *adv.* **—self′-right′eous·ness,** *n.*

self-right·ing (self′rī′ting), *adj.* that can right itself after being upset: *a self-righting life raft.*

self-ris·ing (self′rī′zing), *adj.* that has a leavening agent mixed with it during its manufacture; self-raising: *self-rising flour.*

self-rule (self′rül′), *n.* self-government: *As urgent as the rumble of talking drums, the spirit of self-rule swept across Africa* (Time).

self-sac·ri·fice (self′sak′rə fīs), *n.* sacrifice of one's own interests and desires for the sake of one's duty or the welfare of others.

self-sac·ri·fic·ing (self′sak′rə fī′sing), *adj.* giving up things for someone else; unselfish: *self-sacrificing love.*

self-sales·man·ship (self′sālz′mən ship), *n.* ability at selling oneself to others.

self·same (self′sām′), *adj.* very same; identical: *A bird sings the selfsame song, with never a fault in its flow* (Thomas Hardy).

self-same·ness (self′sām′nis), *n.* the quality or state of being self-same; identicalness.

self-sat·is·fac·tion (self′sat′is fak′shən), *n.* satisfaction with oneself; complacency.

self-sat·is·fied (self′sat′is fīd), *adj.* pleased with oneself, one's achievements, etc.: ... *the self-satisfied smirk of flash Toby Crackit* (Dickens).

self-schooled (self′sküld′), *adj.* **1.** schooled by oneself; self-educated. **2.** disciplined by oneself.

self-school·ing (self′skü′ling), *n.* **1.** schooling of oneself. **2.** disciplining of or by oneself.

self-scru·ti·ny (self′skrü′tə nē), *n., pl.* **-nies.** scrutiny of oneself or itself.

self-seal·ing (self′sē′ling), *adj.* closing tightly or fastening by itself.

self-search·ing (self′sėr′ching), *adj.* examining one's actions, motives, etc., carefully. *—n.* careful examination of one's motives or actions: *The flurry ... of self-searching that succeeded the Nixons' encounter with spittle, stone, and slurs ...* (Harper's).

self-seek·er (self′sē′kər), *n.* a person who seeks his own interests, welfare, advancement, etc., without regard for that of others: *So the three self-seekers banded and beset the one unselfish* (Charlotte Brontë).

self-seek·ing (self′sē′king), *adj.* selfish. *—n.* selfishness.

self-se·lec·tion (self′si lek′shən), *n.* **1.** selection by oneself. **2.** the selection of merchandise in a retail store by customers without the help of salespeople.

self-serv·ice (self′sėr′vis), *n.* the act or process of serving oneself in a restaurant, store, etc. *—adj.* of or designating a restaurant, store, etc., in which one serves oneself.

self-serv·ing (self′sėr′ving), *adj.* serving one's own interests; seeking advantage for oneself: *Often he is a self-serving schemer, intent on discrediting those who stand between him and the presidency of the great corporation* (Atlantic). **—self′-serv′ing·ly,** *adv.*

self-slaugh·ter (self′slô′tər), *n.* the killing of oneself; suicide.

self-so·lic·i·tude (self′sə lis′ə tüd, -tyüd), *n.* anxiety for oneself.

self-sown (self′sōn′), *adj.* **1.** sown by itself: *flowers self-sown by last year's plants.* **2.** sown by any agency other than man, as by the wind or by birds.

self-sta·bi·liz·ing (self′stā′bə lī′zing), *adj.* automatically stabilizing of oneself or itself.

self-start·er (self′stär′tər), *n.* **1.** an electric motor or other device used to start an engine automatically. **2.** an automobile whose engine is equipped with such a device. **3.** *U.S. Informal.* a person who initiates work, projects, etc., by himself, not by the urging of others.

self-ster·ile (self′ster′əl), *adj.* unable to fertilize itself, as certain flowers or plants.

self-ste·ril·i·ty (self′stə ril′ə tē), *n.* the inability of a flower or plant to fertilize itself.

self-striped (self′strīpt′), *adj.* woven with stripes in its own color, as a self-colored fabric.

self-styled (self′stīld′), *adj.* so called by oneself or itself: *a self-styled leader whom no one follows, the self-styled party of progress.*

self-sub·sist·ence (self′səb sis′təns), *n.* subsistence by oneself without dependence on anything external.

self-sub·sist·ent (self′səb sis′tənt), *adj.* subsisting alone without dependence on or support of anything external.

self-suf·fi·cien·cy (self′sə fish′ən sē), *n.* **1.** the ability to supply one's own needs. **2.** conceit; self-assurance.

self-suf·fi·cient (self′sə fish′ənt), *adj.* **1.** asking no help; independent: *a grave and self-sufficient child.* **2.** having too much confidence in one's own resources, powers, etc.; conceited.

self-suf·fic·ing (self′sə fī′sing), *adj.* self-sufficient.

self-suf·fic·ing·ness (self′sə fī′sing nis), *n.* self-sufficiency.

self-sug·gest·ed (self′səg jes′tid), *adj.* suggested to or by oneself; caused by self-suggestion.

self-sug·ges·tion (self′səg jes′chən), *n.* **1.** suggestion to oneself; autosuggestion. **2.** a suggestion arising of itself.

self-sup·port (self′sə pôrt′, -pōrt′), *n.* unaided support of oneself or itself.

self-sup·port·ed (self′sə pôr′tid, -pōr′-), *adj.* supported by oneself or itself without outside aid.

self-sup·port·ing (self′sə pôr′ting, -pōr′-), *adj.* supporting oneself or itself without outside aid; earning one's expenses; getting along without help: *a self-supporting private college. The children would soon become self-supporting and independent* (Samuel Butler).

self-sur·ren·der (self′sə ren′dər), *n.* a complete yielding to another person, to emotion, to religion, etc.

self-sus·tained (self′sə stānd′), *adj.* sustained by oneself or itself without outside aid.

self-sus·tain·ing (self′sə stā′ning), *adj.* self-supporting.

self-tap·ping screw (self′tap′ing), a screw that cuts its own internal screw thread in metal: *The three-cornered screws are self-tapping* (New York Times).

self-taught (self′tôt′), *adj.* **1.** taught by oneself without aid from others; self-educated: *a self-taught cook. That egotism ... characteristic of self-taught men* (William Hazlitt). **2.** (of knowledge) acquired by one's own unaided efforts.

self-think·ing (self′thing′king), *adj.* thinking for oneself; forming one's own opinions and not borrowing them ready-made from others, or merely following prevalent fashions of thought.

self-thread·ing (self′thred′ing), *adj.* threading of itself; threading automatically.

self-tim·er (self′tī′mər), *n.* a device on a camera that opens and closes the shutter automatically after a certain lapse of time. A self-timer enables the photographer to take his own picture.

self-tor·ment (self′tôr′ment), *n.* a tormenting of oneself: ... *the stupid self-torments of an ascetic* (Scott).

self-tor·ture (self′tôr′chər), *n.* torture inflicted on one by oneself.

self-un·der·stand·ing (self′un′dər stand′ing), *n.* understanding of oneself; self-knowledge.

self-un·load·er (self′un lōd′ər), *n.* a cargo ship with self-contained handling machinery which can unload bulk cargo without help from shore conveniences: *The self-unloader ... [in which] a discharge arm carrying a conveyor belt extends from the ship, and the cargo pours off its end in a smooth stream* (New Scientist).

self-vin·di·ca·tion (self′vin′də kā′shən), *n.* vindication of oneself.

self-whole (self′hōl′), *adj.* complete in or of oneself or itself.

self-will (self′wil′), *n.* an insistence on having one's own way; obstinacy.

self-willed (self′wild′), *adj.* insisting on having one's own way; objecting to doing what others ask or command: *The children ... were young and self-willed and rude, and would not learn to do as they were bid* (George MacDonald). **—self′-willed′ness,** *n.*

self-wind·er (self′wīn′dər), *n.* a self-winding timepiece: *The new 15-jewel clock is a self-winder, deriving its power from the driver's turning of the wheel and from the vibration of the car* (Wall Street Journal).

self-wind·ing (self′wīn′ding), *adj.* **1.** that is wound automatically. **2.** that is wound by the movements of the person wearing it: *a self-winding watch.*

se·li·ha (sə lē′ḤÄ), *n., pl.* **-hes** (-Həs), **-hoth** (-Hōth). *Judaism.* pentitential prayers recited on fast days, on the week preceding Rosh Hashana, on the ten days between Rosh Hashana and Yom Kippur, etc. [< Hebrew *seliḥah* < *sā-laḥ,* forgive, pardon]

Sel·juk (sel jük′), *adj.* of or having to do with certain Turkish dynasties, or the tribes to which they belonged, that ruled over large parts of Asia from the 1000's to the 1200's. *—n.* a member of a Seljuk tribe or dynasty. [< Turkish *Selçuk,* the name of the legendary leader]

Sel·juk·i·an (sel jü′kē ən), *adj., n.* Seljuk.

sell[1] (sel), *v.,* **sold, sell·ing,** *n. —v.t.* **1.** to exchange for money or other payment: *to sell a house.* **2.** to keep regularly for sale; deal in: *A butcher sells meat.* **3.** to give up; betray: *The traitor sold his country for money. You would have sold your king to slaughter* (Shakespeare). **4.** to take money or a reward for, or make profit or gain of (something not a proper object for such action): *to sell one's vote. When perjury ... Sells oaths by tale, and at the lowest price ...* (William Cowper). **5.** to cause to be accepted, approved, or adopted by representations and methods characteristic of salesmanship: *to sell an idea to the public.* **6.** to promote the sale of: *Advertisements sold many new cars.* **7.** *Slang.* to cheat; trick; hoax. *—v.i.* **1.** to dispose of something for money or other payment; engage in selling. **2.** to be in demand as an article of sale; find purchasers; be on sale; be sold: *This article sells well. Strawberries sell at a high price in January.* **3.** *Informal.* to gain acceptance, approval, or adoption: *an idea that will sell.*

sell off, to dispose of by sale: *Reynolds Metals sold off ... a new stock* (Wall Street Journal).

sell on, *U.S.* **a.** to inspire with the desire to buy or possess something: *I was sold on the house the minute I saw it.* **b.** *Informal.* to show or convince of the value, truth, etc., of something: *They failed to sell the Supreme Court on this argument* (Wall Street Journal).

sell out, a. to sell all that one has of; get rid of by selling: *All the tickets have been sold out. A couple of years from now you'll kick yourself around the block for selling out cheap* (New York Times). **b.** *Slang.* to betray by a secret bargain: *The self-alienated man gives way to impulses to round upon his associates and accuse them of selling out the cause* (Edmund Wilson). **c.** (1) to sell at the market price (stock, commodities, etc., held on margin where the nominal owner fails to meet his margin requirements): *I wrote ... a power of attorney to him [the broker] to sell out the stock* (Frederick Marryat). (2) to sell thus the stocks, commodities, etc., of (an individual, etc.): *When margins went up, several of the investors were sold out at a loss.*

sell short, a. to sell stocks or commodities not in one's possession at the time of sale, hoping to buy them at a lower rate before the time of delivery and make a profit: *People sell short when they expect the market to decline. It is risky to sell short.* **b.** *U.S. Slang.* to have a low opinion of; belittle; downgrade: *Nobody but nobody was selling him short on this occasion* (New York Times).

sell up, *Especially British.* **a.** to dispose of the whole of (one's stock, property, etc.) by sale: *Soon afterwards he sold up his English home and settled abroad permanently* (London Times). **b.** to dispose of the whole or a portion of a bankrupt person's goods for the benefit of creditors: *He ... would ... drink his glass with a tenant and sell him up the next day* (Thackeray).

—n. **1.** *Slang.* a cheat; trick; hoax. **2.** *British Slang.* letdown; disappointment. **3.** *U.S. Informal.* **a.** sales quality; salability: *He has shrewdly applied his promotion sense to get "sell" out of it [the magazine]* (Harper's). **b.** selling activity.

[Old English *sellan* sell; give]

—Syn. *v.t.* **1.** barter, trade, vend.

sell[2] (sel), *n. Scottish.* self.

sell[3] (sel), *n. Archaic.* **1.** a seat. **2.** a saddle. [< Old French *selle* < Latin *sella* seat, related to *sēdes* seat]

sell·a·ble (sel′ə bəl), *adj.* that can be sold; salable.

sel·lan·ders (sel′ən dərz), *n.pl.* sallenders.

sell·er (sel′ər), *n.* **1.** a person who sells. **2.** a thing considered with reference to its sale: *This book is a best seller.*

seller's market, an economic condition in which the demand for goods exceeds the supply of them, and prices are usually high.

sell·ing (sel′ing), *adj.* **1. a.** that is sold: *a steadily selling item.* **b.** *Archaic.* easily salable. **2.** at which sale is or can be accomplished: *a low selling price.* **3.** that is engaged in selling.
—*n.* the act of one who sells.

selling plate, a selling race.

sell·ing-plat·er (sel′ing plā′tər), *n.* a horse that competes in a selling race.

selling price, the price at which an article is offered for sale.

selling race, a race for horses which are to be offered for sale after the race at prices stated when they are entered.

sell·off (sel′ôf′, -of′), *n.* a widespread selling of stocks, securities, etc.

sell·out (sel′out′), *n.* **1.** *U.S. Informal.* a selling out; betrayal. **2.** a performance of a play, sports event, etc., for which no unsold seats are left. **3.** a selling of all that one has: *a near sellout of their first issue.*

Sel·syn (sel′sin), *n. Trademark.* a synchro unit designed for various purposes, as for synchronizing gunfire with a radar scanner or the projectors of a three-dimensional motion picture with each other. [< *sel*(f) + *syn*(chronous)]

Selt·zer (selt′sər), *n.*, or **Seltzer water, 1.** a bubbling mineral water containing salt and calcium and magnesium carbonates. **2. a.** an artificial mineral water of similar composition. **b.** any carbonated water. [alteration of earlier *Selters* < German *Selterser* < *Selters,* a village in Germany, where it is found]

sel·va (sel′və), *n., pl.* **-vas.** a tract of densely wooded country, as that lying in the basin of the Amazon River in South America. [< Portuguese *selva* < Latin *silva* wood]

sel·vage or **sel·vedge** (sel′vij), *n.* **1.** the edge of a woven fabric finished off so as to prevent raveling. **2.** any similar strip or surplus section of material, especially wallpaper. **3.** the edge plate of a lock, through which the bolt shoots. **4.** a border; edge: *Ducks gobble at the selvage of the brook* (John Masefield). [probably < earlier Flemish *selfegghe* self-edge (because it serves as an edge for itself)]

selves (selvz), *n., pron.* plural of **self.**

sem., semicolon.

Sem., 1. seminary. **2.** Semitic.

se·mai·nier (sə men′yā), *n.* a tall, narrow chest, having seven drawers, one for each day of the week. [< French *semainier* < *semaine* week < Late Latin *septimāna,* feminine of Latin *septimānus* of seven < *septem* seven]

se·man·teme (sə man′tēm), *n. Linguistics.* a morpheme that has lexical rather than mere grammatical meaning. [< French *sémantème* < *sémantique* semantics + *-ème,* as in *phonème* phoneme]

se·man·tic (sə man′tik), *adj.* **1.** having to do with meaning, especially the meaning of linguistic forms and expressions: *There is a semantic difference between bear* (*animal*) *and bear* (*carry*), *though the two words are identical in sound and spelling.* **2.** having to do with semantics. —**se·man′ti·cal·ly,** *adv.*

se·man·ti·cist (sə man′tə sist), *n.* a person skilled in or who studies semantics.

se·man·tics (sə man′tiks), *n.* **1.** the branch of linguistics that involves the scientific study of word meanings, especially their development and alteration. **2.** the scientific study of symbols as denotative units, of their relationship to each other, and of their impact on society. [< Late Latin *sēmanticus* < Greek *sēmantikós* significant < *sēmaínein* signify, show < *sêma, -atos* sign]

sem·a·phore (sem′ə fôr, -fōr), *n., v.,* **-phored, -phor·ing.** —*n.* **1.** an upright post or structure with movable arms, or an arrangement of lights, lanterns, flags, etc., now used especially in railroad signaling. **2.** a signaling by means of a flag held in either hand, a letter of the alphabet being represented by each of certain positions of the flags with reference to the body of the signaler. —*v.t., v.i.* to signal by semaphore. [< Greek *sêma, -atos* signal + English *-phore*]

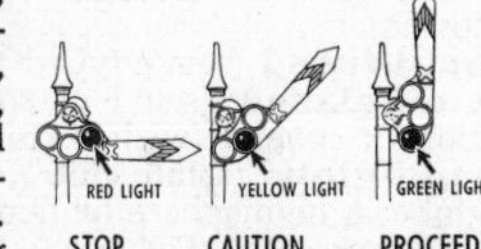

Semaphore

sem·a·phor·ic (sem′ə fôr′ik, -fōr′-), *adj.* of, having to do with, or by means of a semaphore: *They flash a semaphoric SOS* (Time).

se·ma·si·o·log·i·cal (sə mā′sē ə loj′ə kəl), *adj.* having to do with semasiology.

se·ma·si·ol·o·gist (sə mā′sē ol′ə jist), *n.* a semanticist.

se·ma·si·ol·o·gy (sə mā′sē ol′ə jē), *n.* semantics (def. 1). [< Greek *sēmasíā* meaning < *sēmaínein* (see SEMANTIC) + English *-logy*]

se·mat·ic (si mat′ik), *adj. Biology.* serving as a sign or warning of danger: *The conspicuous colors or markings of various poisonous animals may be sematic.* [< Greek *sêma, -atos* sign + English *-ic*]

sem·bla·ble (sem′blə bəl), *Archaic.* —*adj.* **1.** like; similar (to). **2.** suitable. **3.** seeming. —*n.* something similar; likeness. [< Old French *semblable* < *sembler;* see SEMBLANCE]

sem·bla·bly (sem′blə blē), *adv. Archaic.* similarly.

sem·blance (sem′bləns), *n.* **1. a.** outward appearance: *His story had the semblance of truth, but was really false.* **b.** an assumed or unreal appearance of something; mere show: *He was convicted without even the semblance of a trial.* **2. a.** a likeness; image or copy of something: *These clouds have the semblance of a huge head.* **b.** the fact or quality of being like something; resemblance: *I see there was some semblance betwixt this good Man and me* (John Bunyan). **3.** *Archaic.* the appearance or outward aspect of a person or thing: *Mine outward semblance doth deceive the truth* (Milton). [< Old French *semblance* < *sembler* to seem, resemble < Latin *similāre* < *similis* similar]

sem·blant (sem′blənt), *adj. Archaic.* **1.** like; similar. **2.** seeming

sem·ble (sem′bəl), *v.i.* "it seems," a legal term used impersonally in judicial utterances to precede an incidental statement of opinion on a point of law which it is not necessary to decide in the case. [< French *semble* it seems]

sem·bling (sem′bling), *n.* the attraction of male insects to a captive female. [obsolete *semble* to come together, assemble + *-ing*[1]]

se·mé or **se·mée** (sə mā′), *adj. Heraldry.* strewn with small stars, flowers, etc. [< Old French *semee,* feminine past participle of *semer* to sow < Latin *sēmināre* < *sēmen, -inis* seed]

se·mei·ol·o·gy (sē′mī ol′ə jē), *n.* **1.** the science of signs. **2.** sign language. **3.** the branch of medicine dealing with symptoms; symptomatology. Also, **semiology.** [< Greek *sēmeîon* sign + English *-logy*]

se·mei·ot·ic (sē′mī ot′ik), *adj.* **1.** of or having to do with the general theory of signs. **2.** relating to symptoms; symptomatic. Also, **semiotic.** [< Greek *sēmeiōtikós* significant < *sēmioûn* interpret as a sign < *sēmeîon* sign]

se·mei·ot·i·cal (sē′mī ot′ə kəl), *adj.* semeiotic.

se·mei·ot·ics (sē′mī ot′iks), *n.* semiotics.

Sem·e·le (sem′ə lē), *n. Greek Mythology.* the daughter of Cadmus and Harmonia, mother by Zeus of Dionysus. Insisting upon seeing Zeus as he appeared among the gods, Semele was consumed by lightning, but her unborn child was rescued by Zeus.

sem·el·in·ci·dent (sem′əl in′sə dənt), *adj.* (of a disease) occurring only once; providing immunity against future infection. [< Latin *semel* once + English *incident*]

se·men (sē′mən), *n., pl.* **sem·i·na** (sem′ə nə). the fluid produced in the male reproductive organs, containing the male reproductive cells (spermatozoa) that fertilize the ova. [< Latin *sēmen, -inis,* related to *serere* to sow. Compare SEASON.]

se·mes·ter (sə mes′tər), *n.* **1.** a division, often one half, of a school year; term of instruction lasting usually from 15 to 18 weeks. **2.** (in German universities) a period or term of six months, including the vacation periods. [American English < German *Semester* < Latin (*cursus*) *sēmēstris* (period) of six months < *sēmēstris* semiannual < *sex* six + *mēnsis* month]

se·mes·tral (sə mes′trəl), *adj.* relating to a semester; half-yearly; semiannual.

se·mes·tri·al (sə mes′trē əl), *adj.* semestral.

sem·i (sem′ē), *n. British Informal.* a semidetached house.

semi-, *prefix.* **1.** exactly half: *Semicircle = a half circle. Semirevolution = one half revolution. Semitone = one half tone.*
2. about half; partly; incompletely: *Semicivilized = partly civilized. Semibarbarian = partly barbarian. Semisecret = not completely secret.*
3. half a (period of time); twice. Semi——ly means in each half of a ——, or twice in a ——: *Semiannually = every half year or twice a year.* [< Latin *sēmi-*]
➔ **a. Semi-** is not usually hyphened except before proper names (*semi-Christian*) or words beginning with *i* (*semi-invalid*). In British use the hyphen tends to be retained in words formed in English by adding the prefix to an existing form (*semi-detached*), as distinguished from words derived from forms without the hyphen in Latin, French, etc. **b. Semi-** is usually pronounced (sem′ē-) before both vowels and consonants, sometimes (sem′ə-) before consonants, and occasionally (sem′ī-).

sem·i·ab·stract (sem′ē ab′strakt, -ab-strakt′), *adj.* partly abstract.

sem·i·ad·her·ent (sem′ē ad hir′ənt), *adj. Botany.* having the lower half adherent, as a seed or stamen.

sem·i·ag·ri·cul·tur·al (sem′ē ag′rə kul′chər əl), *adj.* not completely agricultural.

sem·i·air-cooled (sem′ē ãr′küld), *adj.* partially but not entirely air-cooled.

sem·i·an·gle (sem′ē ang′gəl), *n.* the half of a given or measuring angle.

sem·i·an·nu·al (sem′ē an′yủ əl), *adj.* **1.** occurring every half year. **2.** lasting a half year, as a plant.

sem·i·an·nu·al·ly (sem′ē an′yủ ə lē), *adv.* twice a year; once in every six months.

sem·i·an·nu·lar (sem′ē an′yə lər), *adj.* forming a half circle; semicircular.

sem·i·an·thra·cite (sem′ē an′thrə sīt), *n.* a coal intermediate between anthracite and bituminous coal. It is softer and more volatile than anthracite.

sem·i·a·quat·ic (sem′ē ə kwat′ik, -kwot′-), *adj.* partly aquatic; growing or living close to water, and sometimes found in water.

sem·i·arc (sem′ē ärk′), *n.* half an arc.

sem·i·arch (sem′ē ärch′), *n. Architecture.* half an arch: *to determine the center of gravity of a semiarch.*

sem·i·ar·id (sem′ē ar′id), *adj.* having very little rainfall.

sem·i·a·the·ist (sem′ē ā′thē ist), *n.* a partial adherent of the tenets or theories of atheism; part atheist.

sem·i·at·tached (sem′ē ə tacht′), *adj.* **1.** partially attached or united: *a semiattached house.* **2.** partially bound by affection, interest, or special preference of any kind: *We would have been semiattached, as it were. We would have locked up that room in either heart where the skeleton was, and said nothing about it* (Thackeray).

sem·i·au·to·bi·o·graph·i·cal (sem′ē ô′tə bī′ə graf′ə kəl), *adj.* partly autobiographic.

sem·i·au·to·mat·ic (sem′ē ô′tə mat′ik), *adj.* **1.** partly automatic; automatic in some aspect or aspects of its operation. **2.** (of a firearm) capable of or designed for ejecting the empty cartridge and loading the next cartridge by an automatic mechanism, but requiring a press of the trigger to fire each shot; self-loading. —*n.* a semiautomatic firearm.

sem·i·au·ton·o·mous (sem′ē ô ton′ə məs), *adj.* not completely self-governing.

sem·i·au·ton·o·my (sem′ē ô ton′ə mē), *n* partial self-government: *Sicily and Sardinia have gained regional semiautonomy* (Charles F. Delzell).

sem·i·ax·is (sem′ē ak′sis), *n.* half an axis, as of a hyperbola.

sem·i·bar·bar·ic (sem′ē bär bar′ik), *adj.* not completely barbaric; partly civilized: *a semibarbaric people.*

sem·i·bar·ba·rism (sem′ē bär′bə riz əm), *n.* the condition or state of being semibarbaric.

sem·i·bar·ba·rous (sem′ē bär′bər əs), *adj.* semibarbaric.

sem·i·bay (sem′ē bā′), *n. Architecture.* half a bay: *Not, as usual, embracing two bays, but two of these semibays* (G.Gilbert Scott).

sem·i·blind (sem′ē blīnd′), *adj.* partly blind: *Once it happ'd that, semiblind, he* [*love*] *met thee on a summer day* (Thomas Hood).

sem·i·breve (sem′ē brēv′), *n. Especially British.* the longest note in common use in music; whole note.

sem·i·cal·car·e·ous (sem′ē kal kãr′ē əs), *adj.* **1.** partly chalky. **2.** approaching chalk in substance or appearance.

sem·i·car·ba·zide hydrochloride (sem′ē kär′bə zīd), a white, crystalline compound used as a reagent for ketones and aldehydes. *Formula:* CH_6CN_3O

sem·i·car·ti·lag·i·nous (sem′ē kär′tə-laj′ə nəs), *adj.* gristly; imperfectly cartilaginous.

sem·i·cell (sem′ē sel′), *n.* (in a certain green algae) one of the halves of a desmid cell.

sem·i·cen·te·nar·y (sem′ē sen′tə ner′ē, -sen ten′ər-; *especially British* sem′ē sen-tē′nər ē), *n., pl.* **-nar·ies,** *adj.* —*n.* a fiftieth anniversary. —*adj.* having to do with a period of fifty years.

sem·i·cen·ten·ni·al (sem′ē sen ten′ē əl), *adj.* occurring at the end of fifty years; celebrating the completion of fifty years, or half a century: *a semicentennial celebration.*
—*n.* a fiftieth anniversary or the celebration of this.

sem·i·cen·tu·ry (sem′ē sen′chər ē), *n., pl.* **-ries.** half a century; fifty years.

se·mi·cha (sə mē′Hə), *n., pl.* **-chas** (-Həs), **-choth** (-Hōth). *Judaism.* **1.** ordination into the rabbinate. **2.** the certificate or diploma of an ordained rabbi.
[< Hebrew *semiḥāh,* literally, leaning upon someone < *sāmaḥ* to lean]

sem·i·chem·i·cal (sem′ē kem′ə kəl), *adj.* partly chemical.

sem·i·cho·ric (sem′ē kôr′ik, -kōr′-, -kor′-), *adj.* having to do with or of the nature of a semichorus.

sem·i·cho·rus (sem′ē kôr′əs, -kōr′-), *n. Music.* **1.** a half chorus; a number of voices chosen from a full chorus, whether from all or from some of the parts. **2.** a passage or piece to be sung by such a selection of voices.

sem·i-Chris·tian (sem′ē kris′chən), *adj.* half-Christian.

sem·i·cir·cle (sem′ē sėr′kəl), *n.* **1.** the half of a circle: **a.** either of the two identical figures formed by bisection of a circle. **b.** the arc formed by half the circumference of a circle. **2.** anything having, or arranged in, the form of half a circle: *We sat in a semicircle around the fire.*

Semicircle (def. 1)

sem·i·cir·cu·lar (sem′ē sėr′kyə lər), *adj.* having the form of half a circle. —**sem′i·cir′cu·lar·ly,** *adv.*

semicircular canal, any of three curved, tubelike canals in the internal ear that help to maintain balance.

sem·i·cir·cum·fer·ence (sem′ē sər kum′-fər əns), *n.* the half of a circumference.

sem·i·cirque (sem′ē sėrk′), *n. Poetic.* a semicircular formation or arrangement; semicircle: *Upon a semicirque of turf-clad ground* (Wordsworth).

sem·i·civ·i·li·za·tion (sem′ē siv′ə lə zā′-shən), *n.* the state of being partly civilized.

sem·i·civ·i·lized (sem′ē siv′ə līzd), *adj.* partly civilized.

sem·i·clas·sic (sem′ē klas′ik), *adj.* semiclassical. —*n.* an artistic work based on classical motives; a semiclassical book, musical composition, etc.

sem·i·clas·si·cal (sem′ē klas′ə kəl), *adj.* partly classical.

sem·i·clo·sure (sem′ē klō′zhər), *n.* half or partial closure.

sem·i·co·ag·u·lat·ed (sem′ē kō ag′yə lā′-tid), *adj.* incompletely coagulated; partly thickened.

sem·i·co·lon (sem′ē kō′lən), *n.* a mark of punctuation (;) that shows a separation not so distinct as that indicated by a period but more so than that indicated by a comma. A semicolon is used in ordinary prose, especially: **a.** between coordinate clauses not connected by a coordinating conjunction and for clarity: *A teacher affects eternity; he can never tell where his influence stops* (Henry Brooks Adams). **b.** between sentence elements that are rather long or are subdivided by commas: *A fundamental, and as many believe, the most essential part of Christianity, is its doctrine of reward and punishment in the world beyond; and a religion which had nothing at all to say about this great enigma we should hardly feel to be a religion at all* (G. Lowes Dickinson).

sem·i·co·lo·ni·al (sem′ē kə lō′nē əl), *adj.* partly colonial.

sem·i·col·umn (sem′ē kol′əm), *n.* the half of a column (taken lengthwise); an engaged column of which one half projects from the wall.

sem·i·co·lum·nar (sem′ē kə-lum′nər), *adj.* of or like a semicolumn; flat on one side and rounded on the other, as a stem, leaf, or petiole.

sem·i·co·ma (sem′ē kō′mə), *n., pl.* **-mas.** a partial coma.

sem·i·co·ma·tose (sem′ē kō′-mə tōs, -kom′ə-), *adj.* partly unconscious: *She complained of ... headache, became semicomatose* ... (A.M. Hamilton).

Roman Semicolumns
Maison Carée, France

sem·i·com·ic (sem′ē kom′ik), *adj.* partly comical: *He looked semitragic. semicomic, like a mask with two sides* (Lady Morgan).

sem·i·com·mer·cial (sem′ē kə mėr′shəl), *adj.* partly commercial.

sem·i·con·duct·ing (sem′ē kən duk′ting), *adj.* of, being, or designating a semiconductor: *Transistors and solar batteries are semiconducting devices.*

sem·i·con·duc·tion (sem′ē kən duk′shən), *n.* the transmission of electricity by a semiconductor.

sem·i·con·duc·tive (sem′ē kən duk′tiv), *adj.* semiconducting: ... *semiconductive materials for electric signal translation* (London Times).

sem·i·con·duc·tor (sem′ē kən duk′tər), *n. Electronics.* a mineral crystal, such as germanium or silicon, that conducts electricity with an efficiency between that of metals and insulators. Semiconductors convert alternating current into direct current and sunlight into electricity. They are also used as amplifiers replacing vacuum tubes in radios, and in certain electronic instruments.

sem·i·con·ic (sem′ē kon′ik), *adj.* semiconical.

sem·i·con·i·cal (sem′ē kon′ə kəl), *adj.* having the form of half a cone.

sem·i·con·scious (sem′ē kon′shəs), *adj.* half-conscious; not fully conscious. —**sem′i·con′scious·ly,** *adv.* —**sem′i·con′scious·ness,** *n.*

sem·i·con·so·nant (sem′ē kon′sə nənt), *n.* **1.** a sound having a partly consonantal character, as *y* in *you;* a semivowel viewed as a consonant. **2.** a letter or character representing such a sound.

sem·i·con·tin·u·ous (sem′ē kən tin′yu̇ əs), *adj.* partly continuous.

sem·i·con·tin·u·um (sem′ē kən tin′yu̇-əm), *n., pl.* **-tin·u·a** (-tin′yu̇ ə). a cohesive but not perfect mathematical series; continuum with its ends cut off.

sem·i·con·ver·sion (sem′ē kən vėr′zhən, -shən), *n.* an incomplete conversion.

sem·i·crys·tal·line (sem′ē kris′tə lin, -līn), *adj.* half- or imperfectly crystallized: *Primitive limestone of a ... semicrystalline grain* (Edinburgh Review).

sem·i·cyl·in·der (sem′ē sil′ən dər), *n.* the half of a cylinder (taken lengthwise).

sem·i·cy·lin·dric (sem′ē sə lin′drik), *adj.* shaped like or resembling a cylinder divided lengthwise.

sem·i·cy·lin·dri·cal (sem′ē sə lin′drə kəl), *adj.* semicylindric.

sem·i·dai·ly (sem′ē dā′lē), *adv., adj.* twice a day.

sem·i·dark·ness (sem′ē därk′nis), *n.* part darkness: *The vast apartment is in semi-darkness* (Charles J. Lever).

sem·i·deaf (sem′ē def′), *adj.* not entirely deaf; able to hear a little.

sem·i·de·pend·ent (sem′ē di pen′dənt), *adj.* half dependent or depending.

sem·i·des·ert (sem′ē dez′ərt), *adj.* half-desert; mostly barren, with a sparse vegetation. —*n.* a semidesert area or region.

sem·i·de·tached (sem′ē di tacht′), *adj.* **1.** partly detached. **2.** *Especially British.* designating either of two houses joined by a common wall but separated from other buildings.

sem·i·de·vel·oped (sem′ē di vel′əpt), *adj.* not fully developed.

sem·i·di·am·e·ter (sem′ē dī am′ə tər), *n.* the half of a diameter; radius.

sem·i·di·gest·ed (sem′ē də jes′tid, -dī-), *adj.* partly digested.

sem·i·di·lap·i·da·tion (sem′ē də lap′ə-dā′shən), *n.* the condition or state of being partly ruined; incomplete dilapidation: *Nightmare Abbey ... in a highly picturesque state of semidilapidation* ... (Thomas Love Peacock).

sem·i·di·ur·nal (sem′ē dī ėr′nəl), *adj.* **1.** occurring every twelve hours. **2.** accomplished in half a day; continuing half a day. **3.** *Astronomy.* of or having to do with the arc described by a heavenly body in half the time between its rising and setting. **4.** *Entomology.* partly diurnal; flying at twilight: *semidiurnal moths.*

sem·i·di·vine (sem′ē də vīn′), *adj.* partly divine.

sem·i·doc·u·men·ta·ry (sem′ē dok′yə-men′tər ē, -trē), *adj., n., pl.* **-ries.** —*adj.* partly documentary; presenting or dramatizing factual information but using fictional details, settings, characters, etc.: *a semidocumentary film.* —*n.* a semidocumentary book, motion picture, television program, etc.

sem·i·dome (sem′ē dōm′), *n.* half a dome, especially one formed by a vertical section: *There is an apse at each end of the building ... covered by a semidome* (G. H. Moore).

Semidome over apse of Suleimanie Mosque, Istanbul

sem·i·do·mes·tic (sem′ē də mes′tik), *adj.* partly domestic: *some semidomestic breeds* (Charles Darwin).

sem·i·do·mes·ti·cat·ed (sem′ē də mes′tə-kā′tid), *adj.* partly domesticated: *the semidomesticated buffalo* (W.C.L. Martin).

sem·i·dor·mant (sem′ē dôr′mənt), *adj.* half-asleep.

sem·i·dry·ing (sem′ē drī′ing), *adj.* partly drying.

sem·i·ed·u·cat·ed (sem′ē ej′u̇ kā′tid), *adj.* partly educated.

sem·i·el·lipse (sem′ē i lips′), *n.* the half of an ellipse bisected by one of its diameters, especially the transverse.

sem·i·el·lip·tic (sem′ē i lip′tik), *adj.* semielliptical.

sem·i·el·lip·ti·cal (sem′ē i lip′tə kəl), *adj.* shaped like half of an ellipse, especially one that is cut transversely.

sem·i·em·pir·i·cal (sem′ē em pir′ə kəl), *adj.* partly empirical.

sem·i·e·rect (sem′ē i rekt′), *adj.* partly erect.

sem·i·fas·cist (sem′ē fash′ist), *adj.* partly fascist.

sem·i·fer·al (sem′ē fir′əl), *adj.* partly wild; feral to some extent.

sem·i·feu·dal (sem′ē fyü′dəl), *adj.* partly feudal.

sem·i·fic·tion·al (sem′ē fik′shə nəl), *adj.* partly imaginative.

sem·i·fi·nal (sem′ē fī′nəl), *n.* one of the two matches, rounds, etc., that immediately precede the final one. —*adj.* having to do with or designating a round, match, etc., immediately before the final one.

sem·i·fi·nal·ist (sem′ē fī′nə list), *n.* a contestant in the semifinal round.

sem·i·fin·ished (sem′ē fin′isht), *adj.* partly finished.

sem·i·fit·ted (sem′ē fit′id), *adj.* partly fitted.

sem·i·fit·ting (sem′ē fit′ing), *adj.* partly or loosely fitting, as a garment.

sem·i·fixed (sem′ē fikst′), *adj.* partly fixed.

sem·i·flex·ion (sem′ē flek′shən), *n.* the posture of a limb or joint halfway between extension and complete flexion.

sem·i·fluc·tu·at·ing (sem′ē fluk′chu̇ ā′-ting), *adj. Medicine.* (of a tumor, etc.) giving a sensation of elasticity when tapped.

sem·i·flu·id (sem′ē flü′id), *adj.* imperfectly fluid; extremely viscous. —*n.* a substance that flows but is very thick; semifluid substance: *A soft-boiled egg is a semifluid.*

sem·i·flu·id·i·ty (sem′ē flu̇ id′ə tē), *n.* the state of being semifluid.

sem·i·for·mal (sem′ē fôr′məl), *adj.* partly formal.

sem·i·fused (sem′ē fyüzd′), *adj.* half-fused.

sem·i·glazed (sem′ē glāzd′), *adj.* slightly glazed; covered with a thin gloss.

sem·i·globe (sem′ē glōb′), *n.* the half of a globe; a hemisphere or hemispherical form, structure, etc.: *The hills ... swell in beautiful semiglobes* (A. Young).

sem·i·glob·u·lar (sem′ē glob′yə lər), *adj.* of the form of a semiglobe or hemisphere.

sem·i·gov·ern·men·tal (sem′ē guv′ərn-men′təl, -ər-), *adj.* partly governmental.

sem·i·har·dy (sem′ē här′dē), *adj.* partly hardy.

sem·i·hex·ag·o·nal (sem′ē hek sag′ə nəl), *adj.* having the form of half a hexagon.

sem·i·hol·i·day (sem′ē hol′ə dā), *n.* a partial holiday; half holiday: *Marriage and divorce were on the rise . . . and deaths took a semiholiday* (Robert A. Irwin).

sem·i·ho·ral (sem′ē hôr′əl, -hōr′-), *adj.* half-hourly.

sem·i·hu·man (sem′ē hyü′mən), *adj.* partly human.

sem·i·hy·a·line (sem′ē hī′ə lin, -līn), *adj.* partly hyaline or glassy; semitransparent.

sem·i·im·mersed (sem′ē i mėrst′), *adj.* partially immersed.

sem·i·in·de·pend·ence (sem′ē in′di pen′dəns), *n.* partial freedom from control, etc.; incomplete independence.

sem·i·in·de·pend·ent (sem′ē in′di pen′dənt), *adj.* not fully independent; half- or partly dependent.

sem·i·in·dus·tri·al·ized (sem′ē in dus′trē ə līzd), *adj.* not fully industrialized.

sem·i·in·tox·i·ca·tion (sem′ē in tok′sə kā′shən), *n.* partial intoxication.

sem·i·in·va·lid (sem′ē in′və lid), *adj.* not completely well; partly invalid. —*n.* a semi-invalid person.

sem·i·lan·ce·o·late (sem′ē lan′sē ə lāt, -lit), *adj.* lanceolate on one side only; partly lanceolate.

sem·i·leg·end·ar·y (sem′ē lej′ən der′ē), *adj.* partly legendary: *a semilegendary story.*

sem·i·le·thal (sem′ē lē′thəl), *adj.* partly lethal.

sem·i·liq·uid (sem′ē lik′wid), *adj., n.* semifluid.

sem·i·li·quid·i·ty (sem′ē li kwid′ə tē), *n.* semifluidity.

sem·i·lit·er·ate (sem′ē lit′ər it), *adj.* partly literate; semieducated.

sem·i·loy·al·ty (sem′ē loi′əl tē), *n., pl.* **-ties.** partial loyalty.

sem·i·lu·nar (sem′ē lü′nər), *adj.* shaped like a half moon; crescent-shaped. —*n.* something of semilunar shape.

semilunar bone, the second bone of the proximal row of the carpus, counting from the thumb side; lunate bone.

semilunar valve, 1. one of a set of three crescent-shaped flaps or valves at the opening of the aorta that prevent the blood from flowing back into the ventricle. **2.** one of a similar set of valves at the opening of the pulmonary artery.

sem·i·ma·jor axis (sem′ē mā′jər), **1.** *Mathematics.* one half of the length or major axis of an ellipse or ellipsoid. **2.** *Astronomy.* the mean distance of a planet from the sun.

sem·i·man·u·fac·ture (sem′ē man′yə fak′chər), *n.* a partly manufactured product, used in making end products. Steel and yarn are semimanufactures.

sem·i·man·u·fac·tured (sem′ē man′yə fak′chərd), *adj.* partly or incompletely manufactured: *semimanufactured materials.*

sem·i·me·chan·i·cal (sem′ē mə kan′ə kəl), *adj.* half-mechanical.

sem·i·mem·bra·no·sus (sem′ē mem′brə nō′səs), *n., pl.* **-si** (-sī). a long, membranous muscle of the back of the thigh, arising from the ischiadic tuberosity, and inserted chiefly into the upper end of the tibia. It flexes and rotates the leg and extends the thigh.

sem·i·mem·bra·nous (sem′ē mem′brə nəs, -mem brā′-), *adj. Anatomy.* partly membranous; intersected by several broad, flat tendinous intervals, as the semimembranosus.

sem·i·met·al (sem′ē met′əl), *n.* an element that is nonmalleable and only partly metallic, as arsenic or tellurium.

sem·i·me·tal·lic (sem′ē mə tal′ik), *adj.* partly metallic: *a compound of zinc and the semimetallic element germanium* (Harper's).

sem·i·mil·i·tar·y (sem′ē mil′ə ter′ē), *adj.* partly military: *a semimilitary costume.*

sem·i·mil·le·nar·y (sem′ē mil′ə ner′ē), *adj.* lasting 500 years.

sem·i·mi·nor axis (sem′ē mī′nər), *Mathematics.* one half of the minor axis of an ellipse or ellipsoid.

sem·i·mo·bile (sem′ē mō′bəl), *adj.* partly mobile: *A missile from one of these semimobile* [*launching*] *sites had shot down the American aircraft 40 miles from Hanoi* (London Times).

sem·i·month·ly (sem′ē munth′lē), *adj., adv., n., pl.* **-lies.** —*adj.* occurring or appearing twice a month. —*adv.* twice a month. —*n.* something that occurs or appears twice a month, especially a magazine or other periodical published twice a month.

sem·i·mute (sem′ē myüt′), *adj.* nearly mute; almost unable to speak.

sem·i·mys·ti·cal (sem′ē mis′tə kəl), *adj.* partly mystical.

sem·i·myth·i·cal (sem′ē mith′ə kəl), *adj.* half-imaginary; part myth.

sem·i·na (sem′ə nə), *n.* the plural of **semen.**

sem·i·nal (sem′ə nəl), *adj.* **1.** of, having to do with, or of the nature of the semen of men and animals. **2.** containing or conveying semen. **3.** having to do with reproduction. **4.** of or of the nature of seed. **5.** like seed; having the possibility of future development: *a seminal idea. There appeared other prophets who were trying to create by themselves small seminal new worlds inside the old* (Edmund Wilson). [< Middle French *séminal,* learned borrowing from Latin *sēminālis* < *sēmen, -inis* seed, related to *serere* to sow] —**sem′i·nal·ly,** *adv.*

sem·i·nar (sem′ə när), *n.* **1.** a group of college or university students engaged in advanced study and original research under the guidance of a professor. **2.** the course of study or work for such a group. **3.** the room or other place in which such a group meets. **4.** a course of study, discussion, or work undertaken by any group of people; workshop: *Some companies send their staffs to "secretaries' seminars"* (New York Times). [American English < German *Seminar* < Latin *sēminārium* plant nursery, hotbed < *sēmen, -inis* seed. Doublet of SEMINARY.]

sem·i·nar·i·an (sem′ə nãr′ē ən), *n.* a student at a seminary, now especially a religious seminary: . . . *nuns in white cotton habit, priests and Catholic seminarians in black . . .* (Time).

sem·i·nar·ist (sem′ə ner′ist), *n.* a seminarian.

sem·i·nar·y (sem′ə ner′ē), *n., pl.* **-nar·ies. 1.** a school, especially one beyond high school. **2.** an academy or boarding school, especially for young women. **3.** a school or college for training students to be priests, ministers, etc. **4.** a place for instruction, training, or development. **5.** a place of origin and early development: . . . *a nursery and seminary of blunder* (Lowell). **6.** *Obsolete.* a seminar. [earlier, a seedbed < Latin *sēminārium.* Doublet of SEMINAR.]

sem·i·nate (sem′ə nāt), *v.t.,* **-nat·ed, -nat·ing.** to sow; propagate; disseminate. [< Latin *sēmināre* (with English *-ate*[1]) to sow < *sēmen, -inis* seed]

sem·i·na·tion (sem′ə nā′shən), *n.* a sowing; propagation; dissemination.

sem·i·nat·u·ral (sem′ē nach′ər əl, -nach′rəl), *adj.* half-natural.

sem·i·nif·er·ous (sem′ə nif′ər əs), *adj.* **1.** bearing or producing seed. **2.** conveying, containing, or producing semen. [< Latin *sēmen, -inis* seed + English *-ferous*]

sem·i·niv·o·rous (sem′ə niv′ər əs), *adj.* eating or feeding on seeds: *seminivorous birds.* [< Latin *sēmen, -inis* seed + *vorāre* devour + English *-ous*]

sem·i·noc·tur·nal (sem′ē nok tėr′nəl), *adj. Astronomy.* having to do with or accomplished in half a night.

Sem·i·nole (sem′ə nōl), *n., pl.* **-nole** or **-noles,** *adj.* —*n.* a member of a confederation of tribes of American Indians that left the Creek Confederacy and settled in Florida. Most Seminoles now live in Oklahoma; the remainder are in Florida. —*adj.* of or having to do with this tribe. [American English < Muskhogean (Creek) *simanóle* one who has camped away from the regular towns, perhaps < Spanish *cimarrón* wild]

sem·i·no·ma (sem′ə nō′mə), *n., pl.* **-mas, -ma·ta** (-mə tə). a tumor in a seminal passage or organ. [< Latin *sēmen, -inis* semen + English *-oma*]

sem·i·no·mad·ic (sem′ē nō mad′ik), *adj.* partly nomadic.

sem·i·nude (sem′ē nüd′, -nyüd′), *adj.* partly naked.

sem·i·ob·scu·ri·ty (sem′ē əb skyůr′ə tē), *n., pl.* **-ties.** the condition of being half-concealed; partial obscurity.

sem·i·oc·ca·sion·al (sem′ē ə kā′zhə nəl), *adj.* occurring once in a while. —**sem′i·oc·ca′sion·al·ly,** *adv.*

sem·i·oc·tag·o·nal (sem′ē ok tag′ə nəl), *adj.* having the form of half an octagon.

sem·i·of·fi·cial (sem′ē ə fish′əl), *adj.* partly official; having some degree of official authority or knowledge. —**sem′i·of·fi′cial·ly,** *adv.*

se·mi·ol·o·gy (sē′mē ol′ə jē), *n.* semeiology.

sem·i·o·paque (sem′ē ō pāk′), *adj.* imperfectly opaque; only partially transparent.

sem·i·or·bic·u·lar (sem′ē ôr bik′yə lər), *adj.* having the form of half a sphere.

sem·i·os·se·ous (sem′ē os′ē əs), *adj.* half bony; partly osseous.

se·mi·ot·ic (sē′mē ot′ik), *adj.* having to do with signs or symptoms; semeiotic.

se·mi·ot·ics (sē′mē ot′iks), *n.* **1.** the branch of medicine concerned with the study of symptoms; symptomatology. **2.** the study or science of signs. Also, **semeiotics.** [< Greek *sēmeiōtikós* (see SEMEIOTIC) + English *-ics*]

sem·i·o·val (sem′ē ō′vəl), *adj.* having the form of half an oval; semielliptical.

sem·i·o·vate (sem′ē ō′vāt), *adj. Zoology.* having the form of half an ovate surface or plane.

sem·i·o·vip·a·rous (sem′ē ō vip′ər əs), *adj.* bearing living young so incompletely developed that they remain within the mother's pouch for a time: *Kangaroos are semioviparous.* [< *semi-* + *oviparous*]

sem·i·o·void (sem′ē ō′void), *adj.* having the form of half an ovoid solid.

sem·i·ox·y·gen·at·ed (sem′ē ok′sə jə nā′tid), *adj.* incompletely combined with oxygen.

sem·i·pal·mate (sem′ē pal′māt), *adj.* incompletely webbed; with the toes webbed only part way, as the feet of certain birds.

sem·i·pal·mat·ed (sem′ē pal′mā tid), *adj.* semipalmate.

semipalmated plover, a small brown and white plover with a single black ring about the neck, that breeds in arctic regions and winters in South America.

semipalmated sandpiper, a small, common, brown and white American sandpiper with partially webbed toes; oxeye.

sem·i·pal·ma·tion (sem′ē pal mā′shən), *n.* the state of being semipalmate.

sem·i·pa·ral·y·sis (sem′ē pə ral′ə sis), *n., pl.* **-ses** (-sēz). a partially crippled condition; incomplete paralysis.

sem·i·pa·ram·e·ter (sem′ē pə ram′ə tər), *n.* half a parameter.

sem·i·par·a·sit·ic (sem′ē par′ə sit′ik), *adj.* **1.** *Biology.* usually living on a host but able to live on decaying or dead organic matter. **2.** *Botany.* living on a host, but containing chlorophyll and therefore able to manufacture carbohydrates from the air, as mistletoe.

sem·i·par·a·sit·ism (sem′ē par′ə sī tiz′əm), *n.* incomplete or partial parasitism.

sem·i·ped (sem′ə ped), *n. Prosody.* a metrical unit consisting of half a foot. [< Latin *sēmipēs, -pedis* < *sēmi-* semi- + *pēs, pedis* foot]

sem·i·per·ma·nent (sem′ē pėr′mə nənt), *adj.* not made to last; temporary: *a semipermanent residence, semipermanent telegraph lines.*

sem·i·per·me·a·ble (sem′ē pėr′mē ə bəl), *adj.* partly permeable; permeable to some substances but not to others: *A semipermeable membrane allows the solvent, but not much of the dissolved substance, to pass through.*

sem·i·pet·ri·fied (sem′ē pet′rə fīd), *adj.* partly petrified.

sem·i·plas·tic (sem′ē plas′tik), *adj.* imperfectly plastic; in a state between plasticity and rigidity.

sem·i·po·lit·i·cal (sem′ē pə lit′ə kəl), *adj.* half-political: *a semipolitical, semisacerdotal fraternity* (Thomas Hughes).

sem·i·pop·u·lar (sem′ē pop′yə lər), *adj.* partly popular.

sem·i·por·ce·lain (sem′ē pôr′sə lin, -pōr′-; -pôrs′lən, -pōrs′-), *n.* **1.** an inferior grade of porcelain. **2.** earthenware made to resemble porcelain.

sem·i·po·rous (sem′ē pôr′əs, -pōr′-), *adj.* partly porous.

sem·i·post·al (sem′ē pōs′təl), *adj.* (of a postage stamp) valued at more than the face amount. —*n.* a semipostal stamp.

sem·i·pre·cious (sem′ē presh′əs), *adj.* having value, but not sufficient value to rank as gems: *Amethysts and garnets are semiprecious stones; diamonds and rubies are precious stones.*

sem·i·pri·vate (sem′ē prī′vit), *adj.* partly private: *a semiprivate thoroughfare, semiprivate conferences.*

sem·i·pro (sem′ē prō′), *n., pl.* **-pros,** *adj.* —*n.* a person who plays a sport for money, especially on a part-time basis. —*adj.* of or for semipros: *a semipro baseball team.*

sem·i·pro·fes·sion·al (sem′ē prə fesh′ə nəl, -fesh′nəl), *adj.* partly professional.

sem·i·prone (sem′ē prōn′), *adj.* partly prone.

sem·i·pub·lic (sem′ē pub′lik), *adj.* partly or to some degree public.

sem·i·py·ram·i·dal (sem′ē pə ram′ə dəl), *adj.* having the form of a pyramid of three, four, or more sides, vertically bisected.

sem·i·qua·ver (sem′ē kwā′vər), *n. Music.* a sixteenth note.

Se·mir·a·mis (sə mir′ə mis), *n.* an ancient Assyrian princess who lived about 800 B.C. In ancient legend she was famous for her beauty, wisdom, and sensuality, and was said to have founded Babylon.

sem·i·re·cum·bent (sem′ē ri kum′bənt), *adj.* semiprone; partly recumbent.

sem·i·reg·u·lar (sem′ē reg′yə lər), *adj.* having to do with or containing a quadrilateral which has four equal sides, but only pairs of equal angles.

sem·i·re·li·gious (sem′ē ri lij′əs), *adj.* partly religious: . . . *on subjects semireligious and semischolastic* (Cardinal Newman).

sem·i·re·tired (sem′ē ri tīrd′), *adj.* not completely retired.

sem·i·re·tire·ment (sem′ē ri tīr′mənt), *n.* the condition of being partly retired.

sem·i·re·trac·tile (sem′ē ri trak′təl), *adj.* partly retractile.

sem·i·rev·o·lu·tion (sem′ē rev′ə lü′shən), *n.* half a revolution.

sem·i·rig·id (sem′ē rij′id), *adj.* **1.** partly rigid. **2.** (of aircraft) having a balloon whose shape is maintained by a rigid keel-like structure which carries passengers, etc.: *A dirigible is semirigid.*

sem·i-Ro·man·ized (sem′ē rō′mə nīzd), *adj.* partly Romanized: *the semi-Romanized Britons* (Westminster Review).

sem·i·round (sem′ē round′), *adj.* having one curved and one flat side. —*n.* a thing that is semiround.

sem·i·ru·ral (sem′ē rür′əl), *adj.* partly rural: *a semirural suburb.*

sem·i·sac·er·do·tal (sem′ē sas′ər dō′təl), *adj.* half-priestly.

sem·i·sa·cred (sem′ē sā′krid), *adj.* partly sacred: *His eulogy of Latin as if it were a semisacred language* . . . (Manchester Guardian Weekly).

sem·i·sav·age (sem′ē sav′ij), *adj.* semibarbaric; half-civilized. —*n.* a half-civilized person.

sem·i·scho·las·tic (sem′ē skə las′tik), *adj.* partly scholastic.

sem·i·sci·en·tif·ic (sem′ē sī′ən tif′ik), *adj.* partly scientific: *semiscientific observations.*

sem·i·se·cre·cy (sem′ē sē′krə sē), *n., pl.* **-cies.** the condition of partial or incomplete secrecy: *working in semisecrecy.*

sem·i·se·cret (sem′ē sē′krit), *adj.* partly secret.

sem·i·sed·en·tar·y (sem′ē sed′ən ter′ē), *adj.* partly sedentary.

sem·i·seg·ment (sem′ē seg′mənt), *n.* the half of a segment.

sem·i·se·ri·ous (sem′ē sir′ē əs), *adj.* half-serious.

sem·i·skilled (sem′ē skild′), *adj.* partly skilled.

sem·i·smile (sem′ē smīl′), *n.* a faint smile; a suppressed or forced smile.

sem·i·so·cial·ist (sem′ē sō′shə list), *n.* a partly socialistic person. —*adj.* not completely socialistic.

sem·i·soft (sem′ē sôft′, -soft′), *adj.* of medium softness: . . . *an excellent semisoft cheese* (New Yorker).

sem·i·sol·id (sem′ē sol′id), *adj.* partly solid. —*n.* a partly solid substance.

sem·i·so·phis·ti·cat·ed (sem′ē sə fis′tə kā′tid), *adj.* not completely sophisticated.

sem·i·spher·i·cal (sem′ē sfer′ə kəl), *adj.* hemispherical.

sem·i·stag·na·tion (sem′ē stag nā′shən), *n.* the condition of being partly stagnated.

sem·i·star·va·tion (sem′ē stär vā′shən), *n.* the condition of being nearly starved: *Tolerably cheerful in the midst of his semistarvation* (Thackeray).

sem·i·starved (sem′ē stärvd′), *adj.* half-starved.

sem·i·sub·ter·ra·ne·an (sem′ē sub′tə rā′nē ən), *adj.* partly underground: *The semisubterranean house was in excellent state of preservation* (Science News Letter).

sem·i·su·per·nat·u·ral (sem′ē sü′pər nach′ər əl, -nach′rəl), *adj.* partly divine and partly human; demigodlike: *The Greeks . . . were surrounded with a world of semisupernatural beings* (R.S. Perrin).

sem·i·sweet (sem′ē swēt′), *adj.* not too sweet; partially or moderately sweetened: . . . *semisweet, white, rice wine* (Maclean's).

sem·i·syn·thet·ic (sem′ē sin thet′ik), *adj.* partly artificial or synthetic.

Sem·ite (sem′īt, sē′mīt), *n.* **1.** a member of the linguistic family that includes the Hebrews, Arabs, Syrians, Phoenicians, Assyrians, etc.; person who speaks a Semitic language as his native tongue. **2.** a descendant of Shem. [< New Latin *Semita* < Late Latin *Sēm* Shem < Greek *Sēm*]

sem·i·ter·res·tri·al (sem′ē tə res′trē əl), *adj.* partly terrestrial: *Gorillas, equally semiterrestrial* . . . (Atlantic).

Se·mit·ic (sə mit′ik), *adj.* of or having to do with the Semites or their languages: *a Semitic nation.* —*n.* the Semitic family of languages, including Hebrew, Arabic, Aramaic, Phoenician, and Assyrian.

Se·mit·ics (sə mit′iks), *n.* the study of the Semitic languages and literature.

Sem·i·tism (sem′ə tiz əm, sē′mə-), *n.* **1.** Semitic character, especially the ways, ideas, influence, etc., of the Jews. **2.** a Semitic word or idiom.

Sem·i·tist (sem′ə tist, sē′mə-), *n.* a person skilled in Semitic languages and literature.

Sem·i·tize (sem′ə tīz, sē′mə-), *v.t.,* **-tized, -tiz·ing.** to make Semitic in character, language, etc.

sem·i·ton·al (sem′ē tō′nəl), *adj.* semitonic.

sem·i·tone (sem′ē tōn′), *n. Music.* **1.** one of the smaller intervals of the modern scale; half tone; half step. **2.** a tone at such an interval from another tone.

sem·i·ton·ic (sem′ē ton′ik), *adj.* having to do with or consisting of a semitone or semitones.

sem·i·to·tal·i·tar·i·an (sem′ē tō tal′ə târ′ē ən), *adj.* partly totalitarian.

sem·i·trag·ic (sem′ē traj′ik), *adj.* partly tragic.

sem·i·trail·er (sem′ē trā′lər), *n.* a type of truck trailer that is supported at its forward end on the same wheels as the rear of the cab and engine (tractor) unit.

Semitrailer attached to tractor

sem·i·trans·lu·cent (sem′ē trans lü′sənt), *adj.* imperfectly translucent.

sem·i·trans·par·en·cy (sem′ē trans pãr′ən sē), *n., pl.* **-cies.** imperfect transparency; partial opaqueness.

sem·i·trans·par·ent (sem′ē trans pãr′ənt, -par′-), *adj.* imperfectly transparent.

sem·i·trop·i·cal (sem′ē trop′ə kəl), *adj.* halfway between tropical and temperate; partly tropical: *Florida is a semitropical state.*

sem·i·trop·ics (sem′ē trop′iks), *n.pl.* a semitropical region or regions; subtropics.

sem·i·tu·bu·lar (sem′ē tü′byə lər, -tyü′-), *adj.* like the half of a tube divided longitudinally; elongate, with parallel margins, one surface being strongly convex and the other strongly concave.

sem·i·ur·ban (sem′ē ėr′bən), *adj.* partly urban: *The swamping of the agricultural labourers by the semiurban population* . . . (Manchester Examiner).

sem·i·vault (sem′ē vôlt′), *n.* the half of a vault.

sem·i·vi·bra·tion (sem′ē vī brā′shən), *n.* a half vibration.

sem·i·vit·re·ous (sem′ē vit′rē əs), *adj.* partially vitreous, as mineral constituents of volcanic rocks.

sem·i·vit·ri·fi·ca·tion (sem′ē vit′rə fə kā′shən), *n.* **1.** the process of partly vitrifying anything. **2.** a substance or mass semivitrified or partially converted into glass.

sem·i·vit·ri·fied (sem′ē vit′rə fīd), *adj.* imperfectly vitrified; partially converted into glass.

sem·i·vol·a·tile (sem′ē vol′ə təl), *adj.* partly volatile.

sem·i·vol·can·ic (sem′ē vol kan′ik), *adj.* characterized by volcanic outbreaks without the emission of lava.

sem·i·vol·un·tar·y (sem′ē vol′ən ter′ē), *adj.* partly voluntary.

sem·i·vow·el (sem′ē vou′əl), *n.* **1.** a sound that is both a vowel and a consonant; a speech sound having vowellike articulatory and acoustic qualities, but functioning as a consonant, as the English sounds represented by *y* in *yes* and *w* in *well.* **2.** a letter or character representing such a sound. *W* and *y* are semivowels in *win* and *yet.*

sem·i·week·ly (sem′ē wēk′lē), *adj., adv., n., pl.* **-lies.** —*adj.* occurring or appearing twice a week. —*adv.* twice a week. —*n.* something that occurs or appears twice a week, especially a magazine or other periodical published twice a week.

sem·i·year·ly (sem′ē yir′lē), *adj., adv., n., pl.* **-lies.** —*adj.* occurring or appearing twice a year. —*adv.* twice a year. —*n.* something that occurs or appears twice a year.

sem·o·li·na (sem′ə lē′nə), *n.* the coarsely ground hard parts of wheat remaining after the fine flour has been sifted through, used in making puddings, macaroni, etc. [alteration of Italian *semolino* (diminutive) < *semola* bran < Latin *simila* the finest flour]

sem·per e·a·dem (sem′pər ē′ə dem), *Latin.* always the same (motto of Queen Elizabeth I of England, 1533-1603).

sem·per fi·de·lis (sem′pər fi dē′lis, -del′is), *Latin.* always faithful (motto of the U.S. Marine Corps).

sem·per i·dem (sem′pər ī′dem), *Latin.* always the same.

sem·per pa·ra·tus (sem′pər pə rā′təs), *Latin.* always prepared; always ready (motto of the U.S. Coast Guard).

sem·per·vi·rent (sem′pər vī′rənt), *adj.* evergreen, as plants. [< Latin *semper* always + *virēns, -entis,* present participle of *virēre* be green]

sem·per·vir·id (sem′pər vir′id), *adj.* sempervirent. [< Latin *semper* always + *viridis* green]

sem·per·vi·rine (sem′pər vī′rən, -rēn), *n.* an alkaloid made from the dried root of the yellow jasmine, used as a sedative.

sem·per·vi·vum (sem′pər vī′vəm), *n.* any of a genus of crassulaceous plants that includes the houseleek and many other species. [< Latin *semper* always + *vīvus* alive]

sem·pi·ter·nal (sem′pi tėr′nəl), *adj.* everlasting; eternal: *All truth is from the sempiternal source of light divine* (William Cowper). [< Late Latin *sempiternalis* < Latin *sempiternus* everlasting < *semper* forever] —**sem′pi·ter′nal·ly,** *adv.*

sem·pli·ce (sem′plē chā), *adj. Music.* unaffected; simple; to be played in an unadorned and unpretentious manner in both tempo and expression (a direction). [< Italian *semplice* < Latin *simplex, -icis* simple]

sem·pre (sem′prā), *adv. Music.* always; in the same (or the designated) style throughout. [< Italian *sempre* < Vulgar Latin < Latin *semper* always]

semp·ster (sem′stər, semp′-), *n.* seamster.

semp·stress (sem′stris, semp′-), *n.* seamstress.

sen (sen), *n., pl.* **sen. 1.** a Japanese copper or bronze coin worth 1/100 of a yen. **2.** a Cambodian coin worth 1/100 of a riel. **3.** an Indonesian coin worth 1/100 of a rupiah. [< Japanese *sen*]

Sen. or **sen., 1. a.** Senate. **b.** senator. **2.** senior.

sen·a·ry (sen′ər ē), *adj.* **1.** of or having to do with the number six. **2.** *Mathematics.* having six for the base: *the senary scale.* [earlier, six < Latin *sēnārius* of six each < *sēnī* six each, related to *sex* six]

sen·ate (sen′it), *n.* **1.** an assembly or council of citizens having the highest deliberative functions in the government of a state. **2.** the supreme council of state in ancient Rome, whose membership and functions varied at different periods. **3. a.** a legislative assembly of a state or nation. **b.** the upper and smaller branch of such an assembly. **4.** a governing or disciplinary body in certain universities. [< Old French *senat,* learned borrowing from Latin *senātus, -ūs* < *senex, senis* old man]

Sen·ate (sen′it), *n.* **1.** the upper house of Congress (of the United States of America) or of a State legislature. **2.** the upper house of the legislature of certain other countries, such as Canada and Australia.

sen·a·tor (sen′ə tər), *n.* a member of a senate. [< Latin *senātor, -ōris* < *senātus;* see SENATE]

sen·a·to·ri·al (sen′ə tôr′ē əl, -tōr′-), *adj.* **1.** of, characteristic of, or befitting a senator or senators: *a senatorial election.* **2.** consisting of senators: *a senatorial subcommittee.* **3.** *U.S.* entitled to elect a senator: *a senatorial district.* —**sen′a·to′ri·al·ly,** *adv.*

senatorial courtesy, *U.S.* the custom of the Senate of not confirming nominations for office made by the President without the approval of the senators from the State where the nominee lives.

sen·a·to·ri·an (sen′ə tôr′ē ən, -tōr′-), *adj.* senatorial (used chiefly with reference to the senators of ancient Rome).

sen·a·tor·ship (sen′ə tər ship), *n.* the position, duties, etc., of a senator.

sen·a·to·ry (sen′ə tôr′ē, -tōr′-), *n., pl.* **-ries.** (in French history) a landed estate granted to a senator under the consulate and the first empire.

se·na·tus con·sul·tum (sə nā′təs kən sul′təm), *pl.* **se·na·tus con·sul·ta** (sə nā′təs kən sul′tə). *Latin.* a decree of the senate of ancient Rome.

send (send), *v.,* **sent, send·ing,** *n.* —*v.t.* **1.** to cause to go or pass from one place to another: *to send a child on an errand.* **2.** to cause (a person) to live in a certain place, engage in certain employment, or the like, for a period of time: *to send a boy to college, to send a man to Congress.* **3.** to refer (a reader) to some author, authority, etc.: *to send a reader to the dictionary.* **4.** to cause to be carried: *to send good news, to send one's compliments. We sent the letter by air mail.* **5.** to cause to come, occur, be, etc.: *Send help at once. Ah, spring was sent for lass and lad* (A. E. Housman). **6.** to cause (something) to go (down, up, etc.): *The news sent the stock market up.* **7.** to compel or force to go: *The blow sent him staggering to a chair. The arrival of the police sent the rioters flying in all directions.* **8.** to throw, propel, discharge, or otherwise impel (a missile) in a particular direction: *to send a ball or an arrow.* **9.** to give forth, off, or out as light, heat, odor, smoke, or sound; emit: *The volcano sent clouds of smoke into the air.* **10. a.** to transmit (radio signals, etc.). **b.** to transmit (a current, electromagnetic wave, etc.) by means of pulsation. **11.** *Slang.* to excite greatly or inspire, especially by jazz: *Two pumas snarled savagely at an Irish Jig but Home Sweet Home and Annie Laurie sent them* (Cape Times). **12.** *Archaic.* to cause to be or become: *God send him well!* (Shakespeare).
—*v.i.* **1.** to send a message or messenger: *to send for a doctor, to send for a taxi. I have sent every half hour to know how she does* (Samuel Richardson). **2.** of a ship: **a.** to lurch forward into the trough of a wave. **b.** to scend; pitch.
send down, *British.* to expel from a university: *Another told us that he had been sent down from Oxford before coming to Exeter* (Listener).
send packing, to send away in a hurry; dismiss without delay or formality: *Sure as fate, we'll send you packing* (Robert Browning).
send up, *U.S. Informal.* to send to prison: *They sent that fellow Sparser up for a year* (Theodore Dreiser).
—*n.* **1.** the driving impulse or force of a wave or waves on a ship: *The Mayflower ... stood for the open Atlantic, borne on the send of the sea* (Longfellow). **2.** a sudden lurch forward of a ship into the trough of a wave. [Old English *sendan*]
—**Syn.** *v.t.* **1.** dispatch. **5.** bestow. **7.** drive, impel. **12.** grant.

sen·dal (sen′dəl), *n.* **1.** a thin, rich silk fabric used during the Middle Ages. **2.** a garment made of it. [< Old French *cendal,* perhaps ultimately < Greek *sindṓn, -ónos* fine cloth]

send·er (sen′dər), *n.* **1.** a person or thing that sends. **2.** a transmitter, as in telegraphy.

send-off (send′ôf′, -of′), *n. Informal.* **1.** a friendly demonstration in honor of a person setting out on a journey, course, career, etc. **2.** a start (favorable or unfavorable) given to a person or thing: *Each of these groups sent representatives today to a press conference ... to give the new bill a send-off* (New York Times).

send-up (send′up′), *n. British Informal.* a caricature; burlesque; take-off: *It [the book] is a splendidly detached send-up of the brainy female* (Punch).

Sen·e·ca (sen′ə kə), *n.* a member of the largest tribe of the Iroquois Confederacy of American Indians, living in western New York. —*adj.* of this tribe. [American English < Dutch *Sennacaas* the Five Nations < Algonkian (Mohegan) *A'sinnika* a place name < *ahsinni* stone, rock + *-ika* place of]

Sen·e·can (sen′ə kən), *adj.* of or having to do with Seneca, a Roman Stoic philosopher, and the tragedies written by him and his imitators.

Seneca snakeroot, the senega.

sen·e·ga (sen′ə gə), *n.* **1.** the dried root of a milkwort of eastern North America, used medicinally as an expectorant; rattlesnake root. **2.** the plant itself. [American English < New Latin *senega* the species name, alteration of *Seneca*]

Senega (def. 2) or Seneca snakeroot

Sen·e·gal·ese (sen′ə gô lēz′, -lēs′), *adj., n., pl.* **-ese.** —*adj.* of or having to do with Senegal, a republic in western Africa, its people, or their language. —*n.* **1.** a native or inhabitant of Senegal. **2.** their language.

Sen·e·gam·bi·an (sen′ə gam′bē ən), *adj.* **1.** of or having to do with both Senegal and Gambia. **2.** of or having to do with Senegambia, a region in western Africa between the Senegal and Gambia rivers.

se·nes·cence (sə nes′əns), *n.* the fact or condition of growing old: *Senescence begins, and middle age ends, the day your descendants outnumber your friends* (New Yorker).

se·nes·cent (sə nes′ənt), *adj.* growing old; beginning to show old age. [< Latin *senēscēns, -entis,* present participle of *senēscere* grow old, related to *senex, senis* old]

sen·es·chal (sen′ə shəl), *n.* a steward in charge of a royal palace, nobleman's estate, etc., in the Middle Ages. Seneschals often had the power of judges or generals. [< Old French *seneschal,* ultimately < Germanic (compare Gothic *sinista* oldest, *skalks* servant)]

sen·es·chal·ship (sen′ə shəl ship), *n.* the office of seneschal.

se·nhor (sā nyōr′), *n., pl.* **se·nho·res** (sā nyō′rās). *Portuguese.* **1.** Mr.; sir. **2.** a gentleman.

se·nho·ra (sā nyō′rə), *n. Portuguese.* **1.** Mrs.; Madam. **2.** a lady.

se·nho·ri·ta (sā′nyō rē′tə), *n. Portuguese.* **1.** Miss. **2.** a young lady.

se·nile (sē′nīl, -nəl), *adj.* **1.** of or belonging to old age. **2.** showing the weakness of old age; characterized by senility: *a senile condition.* **3.** caused by old age: *senile diseases.* **4.** *Geology.* having reached an advanced stage of erosion; made flat or level by the action of water, wind, etc.: *a senile valley.* —*n.* a senile person. [< Latin *senīlis* < *senex, senis* old] —**se′nile·ly,** *adv.*

senile psychosis or **dementia,** a mental disorder caused by atrophy of the brain due to old age, characterized by loss of memory, depression, confusion, delusions, and irrational behavior.

se·nil·i·ty (sə nil′ə tē), *n.* **1.** the mental and physical weakness due to old age; dotage. **2.** old age: *He is yet in green and vigorous senility* (Charles Lamb).

sen·ior (sēn′yər), *adj.* **1.** older: *a senior citizen, senior children.* **2.** elder, especially designating a father whose son has the same name: *John Parker, Senior. Abbr.:* Sr. **3.** higher in rank or longer in service: *Mr. Jones is the senior member of the firm of Jones and Brown. Thus, usually a more senior person such as a professor or reader finds it much easier to get assistance than does a young lecturer with a bright idea* (Listener). **4.** *U.S.* of or having to do with the graduating class: *the senior year.*
—*n.* **1.** a person who is older than another: *Paul is his brother's senior by two years.* **2.** a person of higher rank or longer service. **3.** *U.S.* a member of the graduating class of a high school or college. **4.** (in English universities) a graduate or faculty member who assists in the college government.
[< Latin *senior, -ōris,* comparative of *senex, senis* old. Doublet of SIRE.]

senior high school, *U.S.* a school attended after junior high school. It has grades 10, 11, and 12.

sen·ior·i·ty (sēn yôr′ə tē, -yor′-), *n., pl.* **-ties. 1.** the state or fact of being older: *Harry felt that two years' seniority gave him the right to advise his brother.* **2.** priority or precedence in office or service. **3.** *British.* the body of seniors of a college or public school.

senior optime, *British.* an optime placed in the second class.

senior school, (in Great Britain) a school for pupils from 14 to 17 years of age.

sen·na (sen′ə), *n.* **1.** a laxative extracted from the dried leaves or fruit of any of several cassia plants. **2.** the dried leaves of any of these plants. **3.** any of a group of plants of the pea family; cassia. [< New Latin *senna* < Arabic *sanā*]

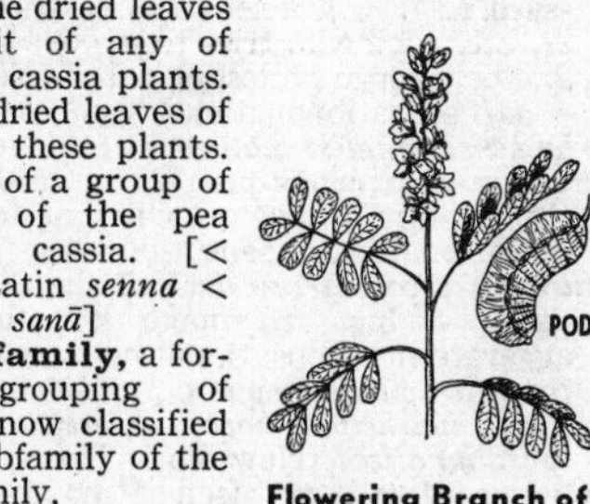

Flowering Branch of Senna (def. 3)

senna family, a former grouping of plants now classified as a subfamily of the pea family.

sen·net[1] (sen′it), *n.* a particular set of notes played on a trumpet or cornet as a signal for an important entrance or exit. The word occurs chiefly in the stage directions of Elizabethan plays. [variant of *signet*]

sen·net[2] (sen′it), *n.* any of several barracudas of Atlantic waters.

Sen·nett's white-tailed hawk (sen′its), a hawk with white underparts and a black band on the tail, found from Texas south to Patagonia. [< George B. *Sennett,* 1840-1900, an American ornithologist]

sen·night (sen′īt, -it), *n. Archaic.* seven nights and days; week: *She shall never have happy hour, unless she marry within this sennight* (Ben Jonson). [Old English *seofon nihta* seven nights]

sen·nit (sen′it), *n.* **1.** a kind of flat, braided cordage used on shipboard, formed by plaiting strands of rope yarn or other fiber. **2.** plaited straw or palm leaves for making hats.

se·no·pi·a (sə nō′pē ə), *n.* a condition of old people in which persons formerly having myopic vision acquire apparently normal sight. [< New Latin *senopia* < Latin *senex* old + Greek *ōps* eye]

se·ñor (sā nyōr′), *n., pl.* **-ño·res** (-nyō′res). *Spanish.* **1.** Mr.; sir. *Abbr.:* Sr. **2.** a gentleman.

se·ño·ra (sā nyō′rä), *n. Spanish.* **1.** Mrs.; Madam. **2.** a lady.

se·ño·ri·ta (sā′nyō rē′tä), *n. Spanish.* **1.** Miss. **2.** a young lady.

sen·sate[1] (sen′sāt), *adj. Obsolete.* **1.** endowed with sense or sensation. **2.** perceived by the senses. [< Late Latin *sensātus* < *sēnsus, -ūs;* see SENSE]

sen·sate[2] (sen′sāt), *v.t.,* **-sat·ed, -sat·ing.** to perceive by a sense or the senses; have a sensation of. [< Latin *sēnsus, -ūs* (see SENSE) + English *-ate*[1]]

sen·sa·tion (sen sā′shən), *n.* **1.** the action of any of the senses; power to see, hear, feel, taste, smell, etc.: *A dead body is without sensation. Blindness is loss of the sensation of sight.* **2.** a particular mental condition produced by the stimulation of a sense organ or nerves; feeling: *Ice gives a sensation of coldness; polished wood, of smoothness; sugar, of sweetness. Jim has a sensation of dizziness when he walks along cliffs.* **3.** a vague, generalized feeling: *a sensation of tiredness or of apprehension. The moviegoer is thus left with the highly unpleasant sensation ...* (Time). **4. a.** a state of strong or excited feeling: *The announcement of war caused a sensation throughout the nation.* **b.** a cause of such feeling: *The election of a President for a fourth term was a great sensation. Atomic developments are the greatest sensations of the present age.* **5.** *Psychology.* experience received directly through the sense organs. [< Late Latin *sēnsātiō, -ōnis* < *sensātus* having feelings, sense < Latin *sēnsus, -ūs;* see SENSE] —**Syn. 1.** See **sense.**

sen·sa·tion·al (sen sā′shə nəl, -sāsh′nəl), *adj.* **1.** arousing strong or excited feeling: *There were sensational developments in the murder case.* **2.** trying to arouse strong or excited feeling: *a sensational novel. Writing for the papers had made Miss Stackpole sensational* (Henry James). **3.** of the senses; having to do with sensation. **4.** of, based on, or adhering to sensationalism in philosophy. —**sen·sa′tion·al·ly,** *adv.* —**Syn. 1.** exciting, thrilling, dramatic, startling.

sen·sa·tion·al·ism (sen sā′shə nə liz′əm, -sāsh′nə-), *n.* **1.** sensational methods; writing, language, etc., aimed at arousing strong or excited feeling. **2.** the philosophical theory or doctrine that all ideas are derived solely through sensation. **3.** *Ethics.* sensualism. **4.** *Psychology.* sensationism.

sen·sa·tion·al·ist (sen sā′shə nə list, -sāsh′nə-), *n.* **1.** a sensational writer, speaker, etc.; one who tries to make a sensation. **2.** a believer in philosophical sensationalism. —*adj.* sensationalistic: *It could be exploited by sensationalist managers* (London Times).

sen·sa·tion·al·is·tic (sen sā′shə nə lis′tik, -sāsh′nə-), *adj.* of or having to do with sensationalism or sensationalists.

sen·sa·tion·al·ize (sen sā′shə nə līz), *v.t.,* **-ized, -iz·ing.** to make sensational; exaggerate in a sensational manner: *Certainly juvenile delinquency is a problem today. But it will not help to have it misrepresented and sensationalized* (New York Times).

sen·sa·tion·ism (sen sā′shə niz əm), *n. Psychology.* the doctrine that all states of consciousness are derived from sensations.

sen·sa·tion·ist (sen sā′shə nist), *n.* a psychologist who believes in sensationism.

sen·sa·to·ry (sen′sə tôr′ē, -tōr′-), *adj.* of or having to do with sensation; sensory.

sense (sens), *n., v.,* **sensed, sens·ing.** —*n.* **1. a.** the power of the mind to know what happens outside itself: *Sight, hearing, touch, taste, and smell are the five principal senses.* **b.** a receptor, or group of receptors, whereby an animal receives and responds to external or internal stimuli. **2.** a feeling: *a sense of warmth, a sense of incompleteness. The extra lock on the door gave him a sense of security. He seems to have no sense of shame. Duty well done brings a sense of pleasure.* **3.** a faculty, perception, or sensation not based on the five senses: *a sixth sense.* **4. a.** the five senses viewed collectively as a faculty. **b.** the exercise or function of this faculty; sensation. **5.** the faculties of the mind or soul, compared or contrasted with the bodily senses: *moral sense.* **6.** understanding; appreciation: *Everyone thinks he has a sense of humor. She has a poor sense of duty.* **7.** an instinctive or acquired faculty of perception or accurate estimation: *a sense of direction, a sense of beauty.* **8.** Often, **senses.** normal, sound condition of mind: *He must be out of his senses to act so.* **9.** good judgment; intelligence: *He had the good sense to keep out of foolish quarrels. Common sense would have prevented the accident.* **10.** the recognition (of a duty, virtue, etc.) as incumbent upon one or as fitting and proper: *a sense of justice. Will his words carry this sense of American responsibility for freedom attained through regard for the eternal rules of order?* (Time). **11.** meaning: *He was a gentleman in every sense of the word.* **12.** discourse that has a satisfactory or intelligible meaning: *to speak or write sense.* **13.** the general opinion: *The sense of the assembly was clear even before the vote.* **14.** *Mathematics.* either of two opposite directions in which motion takes place.

in a sense, in some respects; to some degree: *The consciousness of the body is of course, in a sense, its inner nature* (A. Barratt).

make sense, to be understandable; be reasonable: *The sentence James wrote on the board didn't make sense. The words "Cow cat bless Monday" do not make sense.*

sense of humor, the ability to see a joke, or to see and state the amusing side of things: *Nothing spoils a romance so much as a sense of humour in the woman* (Oscar Wilde).

—*v.t.* **1.** to be aware of; feel: *She sensed that he was tired.* **2.** to understand: *It's better sometimes for me to know what a show represents to the public than to know what it is on the stage, and I can sense that more clearly by not seeing it* (New Yorker).

[< Latin *sēnsus, -ūs* < *sentīre* perceive, know, feel]

—**Syn.** *n.* **1.a, 2. Sense, sensation, sensibility** mean the power or act of feeling or perceiving. **Sense** applies to the power of the mind to respond to stimulation from within or without and to accord it proper recognition: *He has a sense of well-being.* **Sensation** applies particularly to the response to stimulation of a bodily organ like the eyes or nerves: *He has no sensation in his feet.* **Sensibility** applies particularly to emotional or esthetic response: *He lacks the sensibility of a true poet. Nothing is little to him that feels it with great sensibility* (Samuel Johnson). **11.** See **meaning.**

sense datum, a fact of experience resulting directly from the stimulation of one of the senses.

sen·sei (sen sā′), *n. Japanese.* master; teacher: *It was most startling, also, to observe the respect for the sensei, or teacher, in Japan* (Atlantic).

sense·less (sens′lis), *adj.* **1.** unconscious: *A blow on the head knocked him senseless.* **2.** foolish; stupid: *a senseless fellow, a senseless strategy.* **3.** meaningless: *senseless words.* **4.** lacking mental perception or appreciation: *I am senseless of your wrath* (Shakespeare). —**sense′less·ly,** *adv.* —**sense′less·ness,** *n.*

sense organ, a specialized organ, as an eye, ear, or taste bud, by which a person or an animal receives sensations, as of heat, colors, sounds, or smells; receptor.

sense perception, perception by the senses.

sense stress, the stress pattern of a phrase or sentence; sentence stress.

sen·si·bil·i·ty (sen′sə bil′ə tē), *n., pl.* **-ties. 1.** the ability to feel or perceive: *Some drugs lessen a person's sensibilities.* **2.** the quality of being easily and strongly affected by emotional influences; sensitiveness: *a sensibility to the beauties of nature.* **3.** a fineness of feeling; delicate sensitiveness of taste: *... the admiration of every traveller of sensibility and taste* (William Prescott). **4.** a tendency to feel hurt or offended too easily; susceptibility. **5.** keen awareness; consciousness: *a person's sensibility of his own good fortune. ... Expressed great sensibility of your loss* (Samuel Johnson). **6.** the property, as in plants or certain instruments, of being readily affected by external influences.

sensibilities, sensitive feelings; emotional capacities: *Something intensely human, narrow, and definite pierces to the seat of our sensibilities more readily than huge occurrences and catastrophes* (Oliver Wendell Holmes).

—**Syn. 1.** See **sense. 2.** impressibility.

sen·si·bi·lize (sen′sə bə līz), *v.t.,* **-lized, -liz·ing.** to make sensitive; sensitize. —**sen′si·bi·liz′er,** *n.*

sen·si·ble (sen′sə bəl), *adj.* **1.** having or showing good judgment; wise: *Now do be sensible. One hears very sensible things said on opposite sides* (George Eliot). **2.** aware; conscious: *I am sensible of your kindness. Mr. Peter G. Roberts said how deeply sensible he was of the great honour done him by his appointment as chairman of the board* (London Times). **3.** that can be noticed: *There is a sensible difference between yellow and orange.* **4.** that can be perceived by the senses: *the sensible horizon.* **5.** large enough to be perceived or considered; considerable: *a sensible reduction in expenses.* **6.** capable of feeling or perceiving, as organs, tissues, or parts of the body. **7.** sensitive: *sensible of shame.* **8.** sensitive to external influences, as a balance or thermometer. [< Latin *sēnsibilis* < *sēnsus, -ūs*; see SENSE] —**sen′si·ble·ness,** *n.*

—**Syn. 1. Sensible, practical** mean having or showing good sense. **Sensible** applies particularly to the common sense shown in acting and speaking, and implies both natural intelligence and good judgment: *He is too sensible to do anything foolish.* **Practical** applies particularly to the common sense used in the performance of everyday tasks, and implies the ability to see what must or can be done and to use the best means at hand to accomplish it: *He is a practical man and does not understand dreamers and pure scientists.* **2.** sentient, cognizant. **3.** perceptible. **5.** appreciable.

sensible temperature, temperature as felt by a person and recorded by the wet-bulb thermometer.

sen·si·bly (sen′sə blē), *adv.* **1.** in a sensible manner; with good sense. **2.** so as to be felt. —**Syn. 1.** judiciously, reasonably. **2.** perceptibly.

sen·sil·lum (sen sil′əm), *n., pl.* **-la** (-lə). an elementary sense organ, as a single epithelial cell at the end of a sensory nerve fiber. [< New Latin *sensillum* (diminutive) < Latin *sēnsus* sense]

sens·ing device or **instrument** (sen′sing), *Aeronautics.* a device or instrument, such as an antenna, gyroscope, or photocell, that reacts in some way when acted upon by electronic or other waves coming from an object.

sen·si·tive (sen′sə tiv), *adj.* **1.** receiving impressions readily: *The eye is sensitive to light.* **2. a.** easily affected or influenced: *The mercury in the thermometer is sensitive to changes in temperature.* **b.** easily affected by certain agents: *paper sensitive to white light.* **c.** (of a radio receiving set) readily affected by incoming radio waves. **d.** fluctuating or tending to fluctuate rapidly, as prices, stock, etc. **3.** easily hurt or offended: *Alice is sensitive when scolded. He was keenly sensitive to personal slight or insult* (William H. Prescott). **4.** of, having to do with, or connected with the senses or sensation: *the sensitive perception of objects.* **5.** *Medicine.* unusually susceptible, as to a serum. **6.** *Biology.* able to respond to stimulation by various external agents, as light, gravity, etc. **7.** *Botany.* responding to external stimuli by moving, as the leaves of the sensitive plant. **8.** involving classified documents, etc.: *The second phase of the program involves the investigation of all employees occupying sensitive positions* (New York Times).

—*n.* **1.** a person who is sensitive to psychic, hypnotic, or spiritualistic influences; medium. **2.** a person having a highly developed sensitive faculty: *He was a sublime emotional Englishman, who lived by atmosphere. He was a great sensitive* (G. K. Chesterton).

[< Old French *sensitif, sensitive,* learned borrowing from Medieval Latin *sensitivus* < Latin *sēnsus, -ūs*; see SENSE] —**sen′si·tive·ly,** *adv.* —**sen′si·tive·ness,** *n.*

—**Syn.** *adj.* **2. a. Sensitive, susceptible** mean easily affected or influenced. **Sensitive** suggests having, by nature or because of a physical or emotional condition, a specially keen or delicate capacity for feeling (physical or mental) or responding to an influence: *Sensitive people are quickly touched by something beautiful or sad.* **Susceptible** suggests having a nature, character, or makeup that makes a person unable to resist some influence: *Susceptible people are easily tricked.*

sensitive fern, a North American fern in which the segments of the fronds tend to fold together after being detached.

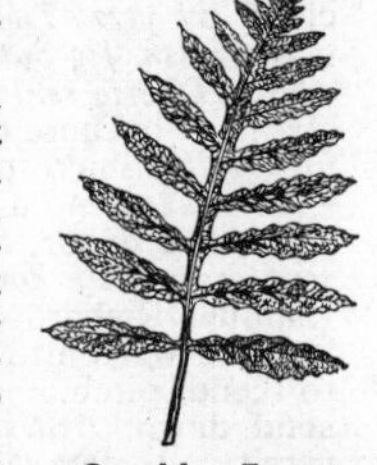

Sensitive Fern

sensitive plant, 1. a tropical American plant of the pea family often grown in greenhouses, whose leaflets fold together at the slightest touch. **2.** any of various other plants showing sensitiveness to touch.

sen·si·tiv·i·ty (sen′sə tiv′ə tē), *n., pl.* **-ties. 1.** the quality or state of being sensitive: *Sentimentality and sensitivity, not in the maudlin but in the highest sense, are perhaps the greatest and most important qualities in a good mother* (New York Times). **2. a.** the capacity of an organism or part to respond to stimuli; irritability. **b.** the degree of this. **3.** the degree of responsiveness of an electrical or electronic device, as to a signal.

sen·si·ti·za·tion (sen′sə tə zā′shən), *n.* the act, process, or result of sensitizing or making sensitive.

sen·si·tize (sen′sə tīz), *v.t.,* **-tized, -tiz·ing. 1.** to make sensitive. **2.** *Photography.* to make (a plate, film, etc.) sensitive to light. **3.** *Immunology.* to make unusually sensitive to a protein or other substance by repeated injections.

sen·si·tiz·er (sen′sə tī′zər), *n.* **1.** a person or thing that sensitizes. **2.** *Photography.* the chemical agent or bath by which films or substances are made sensitive to light.

sen·si·tom·e·ter (sen′sə tom′ə tər), *n.* a device or apparatus for determining degree of sensitiveness, especially to light, of the eye, or of photographic plates, films, etc. [< *sensit*(ivity) + *-meter*]

sen·si·to·met·ric (sen′sə tə met′rik), *adj.* of or having to do with sensitometry: *the sensitometric characteristics of a photographic emulsion.*

sen·si·tom·e·try (sen′sə tom′ə trē), *n.* the determination of the degree of sensitivity of photographic materials.

sen·sor (sen′sər, -sôr), *n.* the part of a control panel that detects and indicates changes in temperature, radiation, etc. [apparently back formation < *sensory*]

sen·so·ri·al (sen sôr′ē əl, -sōr′-), *adj.* sensory.

sen·so·ri·mo·tor (sen′sər ē mō′tər), *adj.* of or having to do with both sensory and motor activity in the body: *All ... was removed, except for the sensorimotor cortex* (Harper's).

sen·so·ri·um (sen sôr′ē əm, -sōr′-), *n., pl.* **-so·ri·ums, -so·ri·a** (-sôr′ē ə, -sōr′-). **1.** the supposed seat of sensation in the brain, usually taken as the cortex or gray matter. **2.** the whole sensory apparatus of the body. **3.** the brain or mind (an unscientific use of the word). [< Late Latin *sēnsōrium* < Latin *sēnsus, -ūs;* see SENSE]

sen·so·ry (sen′sər ē), *adj.* **1.** of or having to do with sensation: *The eyes and ears are sensory organs.* **2.** (of nerves, ganglia, etc.) conveying an impulse from the sense organs to a nerve center: *Thus we see that some of the nerves are sensory and pick up sensations from sense organs to carry them to the main cords and brain, while others are motor and carry impulses from the brain and main nerves to the muscles in order to produce the proper response to the stimulation* (A. M. Winchester).

sensory perception, perception by the senses; sense perception.

sen·su·al (sen′shü əl), *adj.* **1.** of, having to do with, or appealing to the bodily senses rather than the mind or soul: *sensual pleasures.* **2.** caring too much for the pleasures of the senses; indifferent to intellectual and moral interests: *a coarse and sensual glutton. ... The average sensual man ... whose ideal is the free, gay, pleasurable life of Paris* (Matthew Arnold). **3.** lustful; lewd; unchaste. **4.** indicative of a sensual disposition: *sensual lips.* **5.** of or having to do with the senses or sensation; sensory: *Of music Doctor Johnson used to say that it was the only sensual pleasure without vice* (William Seward). **6.** having to do with the doctrine of sensationalism. [< Latin *sēnsuālis* < *sēnsus, -ūs;* see SENSE] **—sen′su·al·ly,** *adv.*
—Syn. 1, 2. Sensual, sensuous mean of or concerned with the senses. **Sensual,** usually derogatory, describes things that give pleasurable satisfaction to the bodily appetites, and people who indulge their desires for gross physical pleasure: *A glutton derives sensual pleasure from eating.* **Sensuous,** always favorable, describes people highly sensitive to beauty and the pure pleasure of the senses, and things that give such pleasure through the senses: *She derives sensuous delight from traditional church music.* **3.** wanton, lecherous. **—Ant. 3.** continent, chaste.

sen·su·al·ism (sen′shü ə liz′əm), *n.* **1.** sensuality. **2.** the ethical doctrine that gratification of the senses is the main object of life.

sen·su·al·ist (sen′shü ə list), *n.* **1.** a person who indulges too much in the pleasures of the senses. **2.** a believer in the ethical doctrine of sensualism.

sen·su·al·is·tic (sen′shü ə lis′tik), *adj.* having to do with sensualism.

sen·su·al·i·ty (sen′shü al′ə tē), *n., pl.* **-ties. 1.** sensual nature: *Claude's agonizing longing for purity struggles against a sensuality that is wholly animal* (Saturday Review). **2.** excessive indulgence in the pleasures of the senses. **3.** lewdness; lasciviousness.

sen·su·al·i·za·tion (sen′shü ə lə zā′shən), *n.* **1.** the act of sensualizing. **2.** the state of being sensualized.

sen·su·al·ize (sen′shü ə līz), *v.t.,* **-ized, -iz·ing.** to make sensual.

sen·su·os·i·ty (sen′shü os′ə tē), *n.* sensuous quality; sensuousness.

sen·su·ous (sen′shü əs), *adj.* **1.** of or derived from the senses; having an effect on the senses; perceived by the senses: *the sensuous thrill of a warm bath, a sensuous love of color. The sensuous joy from all things fair his strenuous bent of soul repressed* (John Greenleaf Whittier). **2.** enjoying the pleasures of the senses. [< Latin *sēnsus, -ūs* (see SENSE) + English *-ous*] **—sen′su·ous·ly,** *adv.* **—sen′su·ous·ness,** *n.* **—Syn. 1, 2.** See **sensual.**

sent (sent), *v.* the past tense and past participle of **send:** *They sent the trunks last week. Nan was sent on an errand.*

sent., sentence.

sen·tence (sen′təns), *n., v.,* **-tenced, -tenc·ing.** **—***n.* **1.** a group of words (or sometimes a single word) that constitute a grammatically complete and independent utterance. A sentence normally contains a subject and predicate: *"Boys and girls" is not a sentence. "The boys are here" is a sentence. Examples: He is good* (declarative sentence); *Is he good?* (interrogative sentence); *Be good!* (imperative sentence); *Good boy!* (exclamatory sentence). **2.** an opinion pronounced on some particular question; decision: *My sentence is for open war* (Milton). **3.** *Law.* **a.** a decree or decision by a judge or court, especially of the punishment to be imposed on a lawbreaker. **b.** the punishment itself: *The remaining two months of his sentence slipped by ... rapidly* (Samuel Butler). **4.** *Music.* a phrase or (sometimes) a period. **5.** *Mathematics.* a group of symbols that expresses a complete idea or a requirement. *Examples:* $4+2=6$ is a closed sentence expressing a complete idea. $X+2=6$ is an open sentence expressing a requirement. **6.** *Archaic.* a short, wise saying; proverb: *Who fears a sentence or an old man's saw shall by a painted cloth be kept in awe* (Shakespeare).
—*v.t.* to pronounce punishment on: *The judge sentenced the thief to five years in prison.* [< Old French *sentence,* learned borrowing from Latin *sententia* (originally) opinion < *sentīre* to feel, perceive]

sen·tenc·er (sen′tən sər), *n.* a person who pronounces sentence; judge.

sentence stress or **accent,** the varying emphasis given to words that affects the meaning of a sentence. *Example:* "*He* killed the dog, not his brother," vs. "He killed the *dog,* not his *brother.*"

sen·ten·tial (sen ten′shəl), *adj.* **1.** having to do with or of the nature of a judicial sentence or decree. **2.** having to do with a grammatical sentence.

sen·ten·tious (sen ten′shəs), *adj.* **1.** full of meaning; saying much in few words: *grave reflections and sententious maxims.* **2.** speaking as if one were a judge settling a question. **3.** inclined to make wise sayings; abounding in proverbs: *... a long, sententious letter, full of Latin quotations* (Charles Kingsley). [< Latin *sententiōsus* < *sententia;* see SENTENCE] **—sen·ten′tious·ly,** *adv.* **—sen·ten′tious·ness,** *n.* **—Syn. 1.** pithy. **3.** epigrammatic.

sen·tience (sen′shəns), *n.* **1.** capacity for feeling: *Some people believe in the sentience of flowers.* **2.** mere responsiveness to sensory stimuli; sensory capacity, as of the skin to pain.

sen·tien·cy (sen′shən sē), *n.* sentience.

sen·tient (sen′shənt), *adj.* that can feel; having feeling: *Poets are very apt to credit inanimate objects with sentient feelings.* **—***n.* a person or thing that feels. [< Latin *sentiēns, -entis,* present participle of *sentīre* to feel] **—sen′tient·ly,** *adv.*

sen·ti·ment (sen′tə mənt), *n.* **1. a.** a mixture of thought and feeling: *Admiration, patriotism, and loyalty are sentiments.* **b.** Often, **sentiments.** a mental attitude; personal opinion: *What are his sentiments in the matter?* **2.** feeling, especially refined and tender feeling: *a sentiment of pity.* **3. a.** emotional regard to ideal considerations, as a principle of action or judgment: *a man completely without sentiment.* **b.** such regard carried to or possessed in an excessive degree, especially to the degree of maudlin sentimentality: *Ann thinks clearly but Kate is full of sentiment.* **4.** a thought or saying that expresses feeling: *a very charming sentiment. Now, here is a little girl who wants my autograph and a 'sentiment'* " (Longfellow). [< Medieval Latin *sentimentum* < Latin *sentīre* to feel]
—Syn. 1. b. view, thought. **2. Sentiment, sentimentality** mean refined or tender feeling, or a quality or characteristic showing or produced by feeling. **Sentiment** suggests genuine, sincere, refined, tender, or noble feeling: *Christmas and birthdays are times for sentiment.* **Sentimentality** suggests affected or false, excessive or exaggerated feeling: *Sentimentality toward criminals is as dangerous as it is disgusting.* **4.** maxim, epigram.

sen·ti·men·tal (sen′tə men′təl), *adj.* **1.** having or showing much tender feeling: *sentimental poetry, a touchingly sentimental letter.* **2.** likely to act from feelings rather than from logical thinking: *a sentimental schoolgirl.* **3.** of sentiment; dependent on sentiment: *She values her mother's gift for sentimental reasons.* **4.** having too much sentiment. **—sen′ti·men′tal·ly,** *adv.* **—Syn. 4.** emotional, gushing.

sen·ti·men·tal·ise (sen′tə men′tə līz), *v.i., v.t.,* **-ised, -is·ing.** *Especially British.* sentimentalize.

sen·ti·men·tal·ism (sen′tə men′tə lizəm), *n.* **1.** a tendency to be influenced by sentiment rather than reason; excessive indulgence in sentiment. **2.** a display of sentimentality.

sen·ti·men·tal·ist (sen′tə men′tə list), *n.* a sentimental person; a person who indulges in sentimentality.

sen·ti·men·tal·i·ty (sen′tə men tal′ə tē), *n., pl.* **-ties. 1.** a tendency to be influenced by sentiment rather than reason; sentimental quality, disposition, behavior, etc. **2.** a sentimental notion or the like. **—Syn. 1.** See **sentiment.**

sen·ti·men·tal·ize (sen′tə men′tə līz), *v.,* **-ized, -iz·ing.** **—***v.i.* to indulge in sentiment; affect sentiment: *He had left his father tearfully sentimentalizing about the Queen* (Arnold Bennett). **—***v.t.* **1.** to make sentimental: *Coming away from New England has sentimentalized us all* (Harriet Beecher Stowe). **2.** to be sentimental about: *to sentimentalize one's college days.*

sen·ti·nel (sen′tə nəl), *n., v.,* **-neled, -nel·ing** or (*especially British*) **-nelled, -nel·ling.** **—***n.* **1.** a person stationed to keep watch and guard against surprises; sentry: *The party now approached the sentinels on guard at the castle* (Scott). **2.** a person or thing that watches, or stands as if watching, like a sentinel: *The tree stood like a lonely sentinel against the sky.*
stand sentinel, to act as a sentinel; keep watch: *One of the campers stood sentinel while the others slept.*
—*v.t.* **1.** to stand guard over; watch as a sentinel: *... when the watches of the night were set, and the band on deck sentinelled the slumbers of the band below* (Herman Melville). **2.** to furnish with or as if with a sentinel or sentinels. **3.** to post as a sentinel.
[< Middle French *sentinelle* < Italian *sentinella* < Late Latin *sentīnāre* pump out the bilge water from a ship; to be in difficulty or danger < Latin *sentīna* bilge water]

sen·try (sen′trē), *n., pl.* **-tries,** *v.,* **-tried, -try·ing.** **—***n.* **1.** a soldier stationed at a post to watch, protect, and guard; guard; sentinel. **2.** a person or thing that keeps guard like a military sentry. **3.** the occupation, duty, or service of a sentry; watch kept by a sentry.
stand sentry, to keep watch; guard: *We stood sentry over the sleepers.*
—*v.t.* to guard as a sentry does.
[perhaps short for earlier *centrinel,* variant of *sentinel*]

Sentry Box

sentry box, a small building for sheltering a sentry on a post or watch.

sen·try-go (sen′trē gō′), *n.* *Especially British.* the patrol or duties of a sentry.

Se·nu·si or **Se·nus·si** (se nü′sē), *n., pl.* **-si.** a North African of a fanatical and warlike Moslem sect.

Se·nu·si·an (se nü′sē ən), *adj.* of or having to do with the Senusi.

sep., 1. sepal. **2.** separate.

Sep., 1. September. **2.** Septuagint.

se·pal (sē′pəl), *n.* one of the leaflike divisions of the calyx, or outer covering of a flower. In a carnation, the sepals make a green cup at the base of the flower. In a tulip, the sepals are bright, just like the petals. *... the calyx consists of sepals, distinct as in the tomato, or united as in the Easter lily* (Harbaugh and Goodrich). [< French *sépale* < New Latin *sepalum,* apparently coined from Greek *skepē* covering]

PETAL
SEPAL
Sepal

-sepaled, *combining form.* having —— sepals: *Four-sepaled = having four sepals.*

sep·al·ine (sep′ə lin, -līn), *adj.* of or belonging to the sepal of a flower.

sep·al·o·dy (sep′ə lō′dē), *n.* the change in form of petals or other flower organs into sepals or organs resembling sepals.

sep·al·oid (sep′ə loid), *adj.* of or like a sepal.

sep·al·ous (sep′ə ləs), *adj.* having sepals.

sep·a·ra·bil·i·ty (sep′ər ə bil′ə tē, sep′rə-), *n.* the quality of being separable.

sep·a·ra·ble (sep′ər ə bəl, sep′rə-), *adj.* that can be separated; divisible. **—sep′a·ra·ble·ness,** *n.*

sep·a·ra·bly (sep′ər ə blē, sep′rə-), *adv.* in a separable manner; so as to be separable.

sep·a·rate (*v.* sep′ə rāt; *adj., n.* sep′ər it, sep′rit), *v.,* **-rat·ed, -rat·ing,** *adj., n.* **—***v.t.* **1.** to be between; keep apart; divide: *The*

Atlantic Ocean separates America from Europe. **2.** to take apart; part; disjoin: *to separate church and state.* **3.** to cause to live apart: *Disagreement over how to spend their money separated the husband and wife.* **4.** to divide or part (a mass, compound, whole, etc.) into elements, sizes, etc.; divide into parts or groups: *to separate a tangle of string.* **5. a.** to put apart; take away: *Separate your books from mine.* **b.** to set apart for a special purpose; segregate. **6.** *U.S.* to discharge from an office, service, school, etc.; dismiss. —*v.i.* **1.** to draw, come, or go apart; become disconnected or disunited: *The rope separated under the strain.* **2.** to part company: *After school, the children separated in all directions.* **3.** to live apart: *A husband and wife may separate by agreement or by order of a court.* **4.** to become parted from a mass or compound, as crystals.

—*adj.* **1.** divided; not joined: *Our teeth are separate.* **2.** apart from others; without access; shut off from others: *He leads a separate life away from the community. He sought them both, but wish'd his hap might find Eve separate* (Milton). **3.** existing independently; distinct: *to keep private matters separate from official business.* **4.** belonging to one; not shared with others: *separate rooms. Those twins have separate problems in school—one cannot read well and the other is poor at arithmetic.* **5.** individual; single: *each separate part of a machine; . . . a hundred trifles too insignificant for separate notice* (Arnold Bennett).

—*n.* something separate, especially an article or document issued separately.

separates, women's blouses, skirts, sweaters, and other articles of two-piece, outer clothing, not usually part of a suit: *Among the cotton-knit separates from Italy are cardigans . . . teamed with pullovers that have wide square necks and no sleeves* (New Yorker).

[< Latin *sēparāre* (with English *-ate*[1]) < *sē-* apart + *parāre* make equal < *pār, paris* equal] —**sep′a·rate·ness,** *n.*

—**Syn.** *v.t.* **2. Separate, divide** mean to part or put apart two or more people, things, or elements. **Separate** applies when they have formerly been together, whether or not actually connected or united: *We have decided to separate the twins for the summer.* **Divide** applies when they have formerly constituted a mass, body, or whole: *The teacher divides the class for field trips.*

separate but equal, *U.S.* of or having to do with a policy of racial segregation between Negroes and whites in education, employment, transportation, etc., while providing equal facilities for all: *In the South, the "separate but equal" doctrine, which was struck down by the 1954 Supreme Court ruling, had led to the establishment of dual school systems* (New York Times).

sep·a·rate·ly (sep′ər it lē, sep′rit-), *adv.* in a separate manner; one by one; one at a time.

separate school, in Canada: **1.** a Roman Catholic parochial school. **2.** any school that is not part of the public-school system.

sep·a·ra·tion (sep′ə rā′shən), *n.* **1.** the act of separating; dividing; taking apart: *Three groups of unit operations exist, concerned respectively with size reduction, mixing, and physical separation of materials* (J. F. Pearson). **2.** the condition of being separated: *The friends were glad to meet after so long a separation. The apparent separation of two stars depends not only on the distance between them, but also on their distance from us* (W. H. Marshall). **3.** a place where two or more objects separate; line or point of separating: *We now come to the separation of the [two] branches of the river* (William Chambers). **4.** the living apart of husband and wife by agreement or by order of a court. **5.** *U.S.* discharge from an office, service, school, etc.; dismissal.

separation center, *U.S.* a military base where men in the armed forces are released from service.

separation pay, severance pay: *Three former managers seeking back wages and separation pay* (Canada Month).

sep·a·ra·tism (sep′ər ə tiz′əm, sep′rə-), *n.* the principle or policy of separation; opposition to ecclesiastical or political union.

sep·a·ra·tist (sep′ə rā′tist, -ər ə-; sep′rə-), *n.* **1.** a member of a group that withdraws or separates from a larger group. **2.** a person who favors separation from a church or state. —*adj.* of or characteristic of separatists or separatism: *The report accuses [him] of aiding the separatist tendency of the services* (Wall Street Journal).

sep·a·ra·tive (sep′ə rā′tiv), *adj.* tending to separate; causing separation.

sep·a·ra·tor (sep′ə rā′tər), *n.* **1.** a person or thing that separates, especially a machine for separating the cream from milk, wheat from chaff or dirt, etc.: *The pieces that sift through are then dumped into a separator — a large vat shaped like an inverted cone* (New Yorker). **2.** any of various devices used for dressing ore. [< Latin *sēparātor* < *sēparāre;* see SEPARATE]

sep·a·ra·to·ry (sep′ər ə tôr′ē, -tōr′-), *adj.* that separates; separative: *My reservoir is a separatory funnel and the water drips into a pair of collectors that formerly held frozen orange juice* (Scientific American).

sep·a·ra·tum (sep′ə rā′təm), *n., pl.* **-ta** (-tə). a copy of an article read at a meeting, or printed in the journal, of a learned society or the like; separate. [< New Latin *separatum* < Latin *sēparāre;* see SEPARATE]

Se·phar·dic (si fär′dik), *adj.* of or having to do with the Sephardim: *the daughter of a rich Sephardic family — educated by private tutors, a friend of Emerson* (New Yorker).

Se·phar·dim (si fär′dim), *n.pl.* Spanish-Portuguese Jews and their descendants, as contrasted with the Ashkenazim or German-Polish Jews and their descendants: *They have encountered in the less traveled quarters of Greater New York . . . the Hasidim and Sephardim* (New Yorker). [< Hebrew *səfardīm,* plural of *səfārāth,* a country mentioned in Obadiah 20, perhaps Spain]

se·pi·a (sē′pē ə), *n., pl.* **-pi·as, -pi·ae** (-pē ē), *adj.* —*n.* **1.** a brown paint or ink prepared from the inky fluid of cuttlefish. **2.** a dark brown. **3. a.** a drawing made with this color. **b.** a photograph tinted in this color. **4.** any of a group of cuttlefish having an internal shell. —*adj.* **1.** dark-brown. **2.** done in sepia: *a sepia print.*

[< Latin *sēpia* < Greek *sēpíā* cuttlefish < *sēpein* make foul; to rot, related to *sápros* rotten]

se·pi·o·lite (sē′pē ə līt), *n.* meerschaum, native hydrous silicate of magnesium. [< German *Sepiolith* (with English *-lite*) < Greek *sēpion* cuttlebone (< *sēpíā;* see SEPIA) + *lithos* stone]

se·poy (sē′poi), *n.* (formerly) a native of India who was a soldier in the British army or a member of the army of the British East India Company in the 1700's and early 1800's. [probably < Portuguese *sipae* < Hindustani *sipāhī* soldier, horseman < Persian < *sipāh* army. Compare SPAHI.]

sep·pu·ku (sep′pü′kü), *n. Japanese.* hara-kiri: *The Japanese hara-kiri or seppuku . . . was formerly confined to nobles and warriors* (A. L. Kroeber).

sep·sine (sep′sēn, -sin), *n.* any of certain poisonous ptomaines formed by decaying yeast, blood, etc. [< *seps*(is) + *-ine*[2]]

sep·sis (sep′sis), *n.* **1. a.** a poisoning of the system by disease-producing bacteria and their toxins absorbed into the blood stream from festering wounds, etc.; blood poisoning. **b.** the condition of being infected with such bacteria as streptococci or staphylococci. **2.** putrefaction. [< New Latin *sepsis* < Greek *sêpsis* putrefaction < *sēpein* to rot, related to *sápros* foul, rotten]

sept (sept), *n.* **1.** a clan, especially of descendants of a common ancestor. **2.** an ancient Irish clan. [probably early variant of *sect;* influenced by Latin *sēptum* enclosure; see SEPTUM]

sept-, *combining form.* seven: *Septangular = having seven angles.* Also, **septem-, septi-** before consonants. [< Latin *septem*]

Sept (no period), September.

Sept., **1.** September. **2.** Septuagint.

sep·ta (sep′tə), *n.* plural of **septum.**

sep·tal (sep′təl), *adj.* of or having to do with a septum: *a septal filament.*

sep·tan·gu·lar (sep tang′gyə lər), *adj.* having seven angles.

sep·tar·i·an (sep tãr′ē ən), *adj.* **1.** of or having to do with a septarium. **2.** containing a septarium.

sep·tar·i·um (sep tãr′ē əm), *n., pl.* **-i·a** (-ē ə). *Geology.* a rounded lump of minerals occurring in layers in sand, clay, etc. A septarium is usually of calcium carbonate or carbonate of iron, having a network of cracks filled with calcite and other minerals. [(originally) a septate object < New Latin *septarium* < Latin *sēptum* septum, a divider]

sep·tate (sep′tāt), *adj.* divided by a septum or septa: *. . . all other filamentous fungi are more or less completely septate (that is, the cells are separated from each other by cross walls) . . .* (Fred W. Emerson). [< New Latin *septatus* < Latin *sēptum* septum]

sep·tat·ed (sep′tā tid), *adj.* septate.

sep·ta·tion (sep tā′shən), *n.* septate condition.

sep·ta·va·lent (sep′tə vā′lənt, sep tav′ə-), *adj.* septivalent.

sep·tec·to·my (sep tek′tə mē), *n., pl.* **-mies.** surgical removal of part of the nasal septum. [< *sept*(um) + Greek *ektomḗ* a cutting out]

septem-, *combining form.* a form of **sept-,** as in *septemvirate.*

Sep·tem·ber (sep tem′bər), *n.* the ninth month. It has 30 days. *Abbr.:* Sept. [< Latin *September, -bris* < *septem* seven (because of its position in the early Roman calendar)]

Sep·tem·brism (sep tem′briz əm), *n.* the principles and actions of the Septembrists.

Sep·tem·brist (sep tem′brist), *n.* (in French history) a person who instigated or took part in the massacre of the royalists and political prisoners in Paris, September 2-6, 1792.

sep·te·mi·a (sep tē′mē ə), *n.* septicemia.

sep·tem·par·tite (sep′tem pär′tīt), *adj. Botany.* divided nearly to the base into seven parts.

sep·tem·vir (sep tem′vər), *n., pl.* **-vi·ri** (-və rī), **-virs.** one of seven men who hold some office or authority. [< Latin *septemviri,* plural < *septem* seven + *viri,* plural of *vir* man]

sep·tem·vi·rate (sep tem′və rāt), *n.* **1.** the office of a septemvir. **2.** government by septemviri. **3.** a group of seven men in office or authority. **4.** any group of seven.

sep·te·nar·y (sep′tə ner′ē), *adj., n., pl.* **-nar·ies.** —*adj.* **1.** of or having to do with the number seven. **2.** forming a group of seven. **3.** septennial.

—*n.* **1.** the number seven. **2.** a group or set of seven things. **3.** a period of seven years. **4.** *Prosody.* a line of seven feet or seven accented syllables.

[< Latin *septēnārius* < *septēnī* seven each < *septem* seven]

sep·ten·nate (sep ten′āt), *n.* a period of seven years. [< French *septennat* < Latin *septennis*]

sep·ten·ni·al (sep ten′ē əl), *adj.* **1.** lasting seven years. **2.** occurring every seven years. [< Latin *septennium* seven-year period (< *septem* seven + *annus* year) + English *-al*[1]] —**sep·ten′ni·al·ly,** *adv.*

sep·ten·ni·um (sep ten′ē əm), *n., pl.* **-ten·ni·ums, -ten·ni·a** (-ten′ē ə). a period of seven years. [< Latin *septennium;* see SEPTENNIAL]

sep·ten·tri·on (sep ten′trē ən), *n. Archaic.* **1.** the north: *Thou art as opposite to every good . . . as the south to the septentrion* (Shakespeare). **2.** a northerner. —*adj.* septentrional: *A ridge of hills, that screened the fruits of the earth, and seats of men from cold Septentrion blasts* (Milton). [< Latin *septentriō, -ōnis*]

sep·ten·tri·o·nal (sep ten′trē ə nəl), *adj.* **1.** northern. **2.** of or from the north: *For Paris, this has been the longest, coldest stretch of septentrional weather known since . . . 1940* (New Yorker).

Sep·ten·tri·ons (sep ten′trē ənz), *n.pl. Archaic.* the constellation of the Great Bear. [< Latin *septentriōnēs* (literally) the seven oxen that circle the polestar, singular of *septentriō, -ōnis* the north]

sep·tet or **sep·tette** (sep tet′), *n.* **1.** a musical composition for seven voices or instruments. **2.** seven singers or players. **3.** any group of seven. [< German *Septet* < Latin *septem* seven; patterned on German *Duett* duet]

sept·foil (sept′foil′), *n. Architecture.* an ornament with seven cusps or points. [< Late Latin *septifolium* < Latin *septem* seven + *folium* leaf]

septi-, *combining form.* a form of **sept-** before consonants, as in *septivalent.*

sep·tic (sep′tik), *adj.* **1.** causing infection or putrefaction: *We did, of course, practice* *rigid asepsis (avoidance of infection) but septic surgery could be a nightmare* (Harper's). **2.** caused by infection or putrefaction. —*n.* a substance that causes or promotes sepsis. [< Latin *sēpticus* < Greek *sēptikós* < *sēpein* to rot, related to *sápros* foul, rotten]

sep·ti·ce·mi·a or **sep·ti·cae·mi·a** (sep′tə sē′mē ə), *n.* blood poisoning, especially in which bacteria as well as their toxins enter the blood stream. [< New Latin *septicemia* < Greek *sēptikós* septic + *haîma* blood]

sep·ti·ce·mic or **sep·ti·cae·mic** (sep′tə sē′mik), *adj.* **1.** causing septicemia. **2.** caused by or having septicemia.

septicemic plague, a virulent form of plague that infects the blood stream directly, causing death before there is time for the formation of buboes.

sep·ti·cid·al (sep′tə sī′dəl), *adj. Botany.* (of dehiscent seed capsules) bursting along the septa: *There are three kinds of valvular dehiscence: septicidal, loculicidal, and septifragal* (Heber W. Youngken). [< *septum* + Latin *caedere* to cut -*cide*[1] + -*al*[1]] —**sep′ti·cid′al·ly,** *adv.*

sep·tic·i·ty (sep tis′ə tē), *n.* septic character or quality: *septicity in sewage* (New Scientist).

sep·ti·cize (sep′tə sīz), *v.t.*, **-cized, -ciz·ing.** to make septic.

sep·ti·co·py·e·mi·a or **sep·ti·co·py·ae·mi·a** (sep′tə kō pī ē′mē ə), *n.* septic pyemia.

septic sore throat, a throat condition caused by a streptococcic infection.

septic tank, a tank in which sewage is decomposed by anaerobic bacteria: *Septic tanks meant for open areas were installed among patches of homes because sewers could not be built fast enough* (Wall Street Journal).

sep·ti·form (sep′tə fôrm), *adj.* sevenfold.

sep·tif·ra·gal (sep tif′rə gəl), *adj. Botany.* characterized by the breaking away of the valves from the septa in dehiscence: *Septifragal dehiscence is that form in which there occurs a breaking away of the valves from the septa or partitions, as in Stramonium and Morning Glory fruits* (Heber W. Youngken). [< *septum* + Latin *frag-*, stem of *frangere* to break + English -*al*[1]]

sep·til·lion (sep til′yən), *n.* **1.** (in the United States and France) 1 followed by 24 zeros; 1,000 to the eighth power. **2.** (in Great Britain) 1 followed by 42 zeros; 1,000,000 to the seventh power. —*adj.* that is a septillion in number. [< French *septillion* < Latin *septem* seven; patterned on *million* million]

sep·til·lionth (sep til′yənth), *adj., n.* **1.** last in a series of a septillion. **2.** one (or being one) of a septillion equal parts.

sep·ti·mal (sep′tə məl), *adj.* having to do with or based on the number seven. [< Latin *septimus* seventh (< *septem* seven) + English -*al*[1]]

sep·time (sep′tēm), *n. Fencing.* the seventh in a series of eight defensive positions or parries. [< Latin *septimus* < *septem* seven]

sep·tin·su·lar (sep tin′sə lər, -syə-), *adj.* **1.** Also, **Septinsular.** having to do with seven islands, especially the Ionian Islands that made up the Septinsular Republic of 1800-1807. **2.** consisting of seven islands. [< *sept-* + Latin *insula* island + English -*ar*]

sep·ti·par·tite (sep′tə pär′tīt), *adj.* consisting of seven parts.

sep·ti·syl·la·ble (sep′tə sil′ə bəl), *n.* a word of seven syllables.

sep·ti·va·lent (sep′tə vā′lənt, sep tiv′ə-), *adj. Chemistry.* having a valence of 7. Also, **septavalent.**

sep·tu·a·ge·nar·i·an (sep′chü ə jə nãr′ē-ən, -tyü-), *adj.* of the age of 70 years, or between 70 and 80 years old. —*n.* a person who is 70, or between 70 and 80 years old. [< Latin *septuāgēnārius* septuagenary + English -*an*]

sep·tu·ag·e·nar·y (sep′chü aj′ə ner′ē, -tyü-), *n., pl.* **-nar·ies,** *adj.* —*n.* a septuagenarian. —*adj.* **1.** septuagenarian. **2.** consisting of 70. [< Latin *septuāgēnārius* < *septuāgēnī* seventy each < *septem* seven]

Sep·tu·a·ges·i·ma (sep′chü ə jes′ə mə, -tyü-), *n.*, or **Septuagesima Sunday,** the third Sunday before Lent. [< Late Latin *septuāgēsima* (literally) seventieth]

Sep·tu·a·gint (sep′chü ə jint, -tyü-), *n.* the Greek translation of the Old Testament that was made before the time of Christ. Ptolemy II of Egypt is supposed to have brought seventy scholars to Alexandria, and in seventy days they are supposed to have completed the translation from Hebrew to Greek. *Abbr.:* LXX (no periods). [earlier, the seventy translators < Late Latin *septuāgintā* (*interpretes*) seventy (interpreters) < Latin]

Sep·tu·a·gin·tal (sep′chü ə jin′təl, -tyü-), *adj.* of or having to do with the Septuagint.

sep·tum (sep′təm), *n., pl.* **-ta.** a dividing wall, as of membrane, bone, or cartilage; a partition, such as that between the nostrils or between the ventricles of the heart: *The inside of a green pepper is divided into chambers by septa. The pleasure areas in the monkey brain are the septum and putamen deep in the middle of the brain* (Science News Letter). [< Latin *sēptum*, variant of *saeptum* a fence < *saepīre* to hedge in < *saepēs, -is* a hedge, fence]

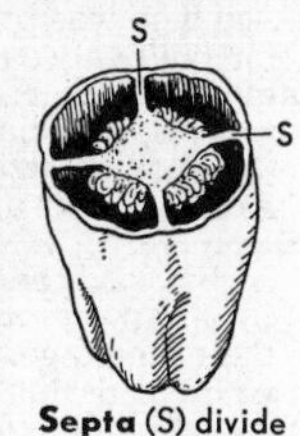

Septa (S) divide interior of green pepper

sep·tu·or (sep′chü ôr, -tyü-), *n.* a septet.

sep·tu·ple (sep′tü pəl, -tyü-; sep tü′-, -tyü′-), *adj., n., v.*, **-pled, -pling.** —*adj.* **1.** seven times as great; sevenfold. **2.** *Music.* characterized by seven beats to the measure. —*n.* a number or amount seven times as great as another.
—*v.t.* to make seven times as great. —*v.i.* to become seven times as great.
[< Late Latin *septuplus* < Latin *septem* seven + -*plus* -fold]

sep·tu·plet (sep′tü plit, -tyü-; sep tü′-, -tyü′-), *n.* **1.** one of seven offspring born to the same mother at the same time. **2.** a group of seven things.

sep·ul·cher (sep′əl kər), *n.* **1.** a place of burial; tomb; grave. **2.** (formerly) a structure in a church in which sacred objects were deposited on the Thursday or Friday before Easter to be taken out at Easter. —*v.t.* to bury (a dead body) in a sepulcher. [< Old French *sepulcre*, learned borrowing from Latin *sepulcrum* < *sepelīre* to bury]

se·pul·chral (sə pul′krəl), *adj.* **1.** of sepulchers or tombs: *They are more than sepulchral effigies: they exist in their own right as an embodiment of worldly power* (Atlantic). **2.** of burial: *sepulchral ceremonies.* **3.** deep and gloomy; dismal; suggesting a tomb: *sepulchral darkness. He heard his own name spoken in the hollow, sepulchral tones of death* (James Fenimore Cooper). —**se·pul′chral·ly,** *adv.* —**Syn. 2.** funeral. **3.** funereal.

sep·ul·chre (sep′əl kər), *n., v.t.*, **-chred, -chring.** *Especially British.* sepulcher.

sep·ul·ture (sep′əl chər), *n. Archaic.* **1.** burial: *Even the honours of sepulture were long withheld from his remains* (Macaulay). **2.** a place of burial; sepulcher. [< Old French *sepulture*, learned borrowing from Latin *sepultūra* < *sepelīre* to bury]

seq., **1.** sequel. **2.** the following (Latin, *sequens*).

seqq., the following (items) (Latin, *sequentia*).

se·qua·cious (si kwā′shəs), *adj.* **1.** proceeding smoothly and regularly: *a sequacious argument.* **2.** disposed to follow, especially in an unreasoning manner. **3.** following: *We find individuals . . . like the Sophists of old, leading after them . . . troops of sequacious hearers* (Bishop Hampden). [< Latin *sequāx, -ācis* a follower, one following (< *sequī* to follow) + English -*ous*] —**se·qua′cious·ly,** *adv.* —**se·qua′cious·ness,** *n.*

se·quac·i·ty (si kwas′ə tē), *n.* **1.** the quality or condition of being sequacious. **2.** *Obsolete.* ductility; pliability (of matter).

se·quel (sē′kwəl), *n.* **1.** that which follows; continuation: *She referred to the expected decease of her mother, and the gloomy sequel of funeral rites* (Charlotte Brontë). **2.** something that follows as a result of some earlier happening; result: *Among the sequels of the party were many stomach aches. Our dreams are the sequel of our waking knowledge* (Emerson). **3.** a complete story continuing an earlier one about the same people: *Robert Louis Stevenson's "David Balfour" is a sequel to his "Kidnapped."* **4.** *Obsolete.* an inference. [< Old French *sequelle*, learned borrowing from Latin *sequēla* < *sequī* to follow] —**Syn. 2.** consequence, outcome.

se·que·la (si kwē′lə), *n., pl.* **-lae** (-lē). **1.** a thing following or resulting: *I was just getting into the inevitable simmering sequelae of ripostes to the editor* (New Yorker). **2.** a disease or abnormal condition which is the result of a previous disease. [< Latin *sequēla* sequel]

se·quence (sē′kwəns), *n.* **1.** the coming of one thing after another; succession; order of succession: *Arrange the names in alphabetical sequence. By using the method of priority and sequence a good deal can be learned about how much mechanical invention influences social change* (Ogburn and Nimkoff). **2.** a connected series: *a sonnet sequence.* **3.** something that follows; result: *Crime has its sequence of misery.* **4.** (in card playing) a set of three or more cards of the same suit following one after another in order of value. **5. a.** part of a motion picture consisting of an episode without breaks. **b.** any group of scenes of a motion picture taken as a unit. **6.** *Music.* a series of melodic or harmonic phrases repeated three or more times at successive pitches upward or downward. **7.** (in the Roman Catholic Church) a hymn sung after the Gradual and before the Gospel. [< Late Latin *sequentia* < Latin *sequēns;* see SEQUENT] —**Syn. 1.** See **series.**

se·quenc·er (sē′kwən sər), *n.* a device that determines or regulates a sequence, as an electronic device on a space vehicle.

se·quent (sē′kwənt), *adj.* **1.** following; subsequent: *a sequent king.* **2.** following in order; consecutive: *The galleys have sent a dozen sequent messengers . . . at one another's heels* (Shakespeare). **3.** following as a result; consequent.
—*n.* that which follows; result; consequence.
[< Latin *sequēns, -entis*, present participle of *sequī* to follow]
—**Syn.** *adj.* **2.** successive. -*n.* sequel.

se·quen·tial (si kwen′shəl), *adj.* **1.** forming a sequence or connected series; characterized by a regular sequence of parts. **2.** sequent. —**se·quen′tial·ly,** *adv.*

se·ques·ter (si kwes′tər), *v.t.* **1. a.** to remove from public use or from public view; seclude: *The shy old lady sequestered herself from all strangers.* **b.** to keep (something or someone) apart from all others; isolate: *The virtue of art lies in detachment, in sequestering one object from the embarrassing variety* (Emerson). **2.** to take away (property) for a time from an owner until a debt is paid or some claim is satisfied. **3.** to seize by authority; take and keep: *The United States sequestered the land and homes of all Japanese citizens living in the United States during World War II.* **4.** *Chemistry.* to prevent precipitation of (metallic ions) in solution by the addition of a chemical compound. [< Latin *sequestrāre* place in safekeeping < *sequester, -trī* trustee, mediator; (originally) following, interposing, related to *sequī* to follow] —**Syn. 3.** confiscate.

se·ques·tered (si kwes′tərd), *adj.* **1.** withdrawn; secluded: *Along the cool sequester'd vale of life They kept the noiseless tenor of their ways* (Thomas Gray). **2.** living in retirement or seclusion.

se·ques·tra·ble (si kwes′trə bəl), *adj.* that can be sequestered; separable.

se·ques·trant (si kwes′trənt), *n.* a chemical compound that takes away or prevents the usual precipitation reactions of metallic ions in solution: *Many of the most common and most easily obtainable sequestrants are designed to soften water by pre-empting calcium and magnesium salts* (Newsweek).

se·ques·trate (si kwes′trāt), *v.t.*, **-trat·ed, -trat·ing. 1.** to confiscate. **2.** *Archaic.* to sequester.

se·ques·tra·tion (sē′kwes trā′shən, si-kwes′-), *n.* **1. a.** the seizing and holding of property until a debt is paid or legal claims are satisfied. **b.** a writ authorizing this. **2.** forcible or authorized seizure; confiscation: *His former delinquencies . . . were severely punished by fine and sequestration* (Scott). **3.** separation or withdrawal from others; seclusion.

se·ques·tra·tor (sē′kwes trā′tər, si kwes′-trā-), *n.* **1.** a person who holds property in trust when there are outstanding claims. **2.** a person authorized to collect and administer the income of a sequestrated estate: *The Puritan, a conqueror, a ruler, a persecutor, a sequestrator, had been detested* (Macaulay). **3.** a person who sets apart; separator.

se·ques·trec·to·my (sē′kwes trek′tə mē), *n., pl.* **-mies.** the surgical removal of a sequestrum.

se·ques·trum (si kwes′trəm), *n.*, *pl.* **-tra** (-trə). a dead part of bone separated from the living part, as in necrosis. [< New Latin *sequestrum* < Latin, a separation, neuter of *sequester;* see SEQUESTER]

se·quin (sē′kwin), *n.* **1.** a small spangle used to ornament dresses, scarfs, etc.: *An evening sheath of black marquisette, whose skirt is spangled with black sequins, is mated to a black sweater top* (New Yorker). **2.** a former Italian and Turkish gold coin, worth about $2.25. [< French *sequin* < Italian *zecchino* < *zecca* a mint < Arabic *sikka* a die used in minting]

se·quined (sē′kwind), *adj.* ornamented with sequins: *decorated with lightly sequined leaves.*

se·qui·tur (sek′wə tər), *n.* an inference or conclusion that follows from the premises: *Lee Goodman, a mad rhetorician of many words and few sequiturs* . . . (New Yorker). [abstracted from *non sequitur*]

se·quoi·a (si kwoi′ə), *n.* either of two kinds of very tall evergreen trees of the taxodium family growing in California: **a.** the redwood. **b.** the giant sequoia or big tree. [American English < New Latin *Sequoia* the genus name < *Sequoya* < Muskogean (Cherokee) *Sikwayi,* the Cherokee Indian who invented the Cherokee system of writing]

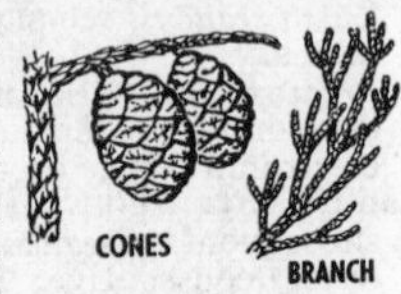

Giant Sequoia Branch and Cones

ser (sir), *n.* a weight of India, officially about 2 pounds but varying according to locality. Also, **seer.** [earlier *seer* < Hindi *ser* (in Prakrit, a kind of measure), probably ultimately < Sanskrit *kṣetra* field]

ser., **1.** series. **2.** sermon.

se·ra (sir′ə), *n.* serums; a plural of **serum:** *Future work . . . will also be directed towards the production of immune sera* (New Scientist).

se·rac (sā răk′), *n.* a large block or pinnaclelike mass of ice on a glacier, formed by the intersection of two or more crevasses: *We tried an obvious line, cut up and over a whaleback of a serac, and found a clear passage through* (London Times). [< Swiss French *sérac*]

se·ra·glio (sə ral′yō, -räl′-), *n.*, *pl.* **-glios.** **1.** the women's quarters of a Moslem house or palace; harem. **2.** a Turkish palace. [< Italian *serraglio* (influenced by *serrare* to close, lock up, ultimately < Latin *sera* bar, bolt) < Turkish *saray;* see SERAI] —**Syn.** **1.** zenana.

se·rai (sə rī′, -rä′ē), *n.* **1.** (in Eastern countries) a hotel for caravans or an inn for travelers. **2.** a seraglio. [< Turkish *saray* palace, lodging < Persian *serāī*]

se·rail (sə rāl′), *n.* a seraglio.

ser·al (sir′əl), *adj.* of or having to do with an ecological sere. [< *sere*² + *-al*¹]

se·rang (sə rang′), *n.* an Indian or Pakistani head of a lascar crew, about like a boatswain in status and duties or sometimes employed in an engine room. [Anglo-Indian < Persian *sarhang* commander]

se·ra·pe (sə rä′pē), *n.* a shawl or blanket, often having bright colors, worn by Spanish Americans: *The Mexican influence pops up in broad, "serape" stripes, named for the Mexican blanket* (Wall Street Journal). Also, **sarape.** [American English < Mexican Spanish *serape,* or *sarape*]

Mexican Serape

ser·aph (ser′əf), *n.*, *pl.* **-aphs** or **-a·phim.** **1.** one of the highest order of angels, of a warm, loving nature: *With a love that the winged seraphs of Heaven coveted her and me* . . . (Edgar Allan Poe). **2.** (in the Bible) one of the six-winged celestial beings seen hovering above the throne of God in Isaiah's vision. Isaiah 6:2.
[new singular < *seraphim,* plural, Old English *seraphim* < Late Latin *seraphīm* < Greek *serapheím* < Hebrew *śārāfīm*]

se·raph·ic (sə raf′ik), *adj.* **1.** of seraphs. **2.** like a seraph; angelic: *At the royal palace, his fingertips pressed together in the customary seraphic greeting, Sihanouk played benign host* (Time). —**se·raph′i·cal·ly,** *adv.*

se·raph·i·cal (sə raf′ə kəl), *adj.* seraphic.

ser·a·phim (ser′ə fim), *n.* seraphs; a plural of **seraph.**

Se·rap·ic (sə rap′ik), *adj.* of or having to do with Serapis.

Se·ra·pis (sə rā′pis), *n.* an Egyptian god of the lower world, whose worship was a combination of Egyptian and Greek cults, and who was promoted under the Ptolemies for political reasons.

ser·as·kier (ser′ə skir′), *n.* a Turkish general, especially the commander-in-chief. [< Turkish *seraskier* < Persian *ser* head + Arabic *'askar* army]

Serb (sėrb), *n.* **1.** a native or inhabitant of Serbia. **2.** the language of Serbia; Serbo-Croatian. —*adj.* of Serbia, its people, or their language. [< Serbian *srb*]

Serb., **1.** Serbia. **2.** Serbian.

Ser·bi·an (sėr′bē ən), *adj.* of Serbia, its people, or their language. —*n.* Serb.

Ser·bo-Cro·at (sėr′bō krō′at), *adj.*, *n.* Serbo-Croatian.

Ser·bo-Cro·a·tian (sėr′bō krō ā′shən), *adj.* **1.** both Serbian and Croatian. **2.** of or having to do with Serbo-Croatian or the Serbo-Croatians.
—*n.* **1.** the chief Southern Slavic language spoken in Yugoslavia. **2.** a person whose native language is Serbo-Croatian.

Ser·bo·ni·an bog (sər bō′nē ən), any difficult or embarrassing situation from which it is almost impossible to free oneself; distracting state of affairs: *In the "Serbonian bog" of this base oligarchy they are all absorbed, sunk and lost forever* (Edmund Burke). [< Greek *Serbōnís* (*límnē*) (lake) Serbonis, in Egypt, in which armies are said to have been swallowed up + English *-ian*]

ser·dab (sėr′dab, sėr dab′), *n.* **1.** (in western Asia) a cellar or underground chamber. **2.** (formerly in Egypt) a narrow chamber in a tomb, holding a statue of the dead person. [< Arabic *serdāb* < Persian]

sere¹ (sir), *adj. Archaic.* withered; sear. [variant of *sear*¹]

sere² (sir), *n.* the complete series of changes in a given plant area; the succession of plant communities from the initial to the final or climax stage. [< *series;* perhaps influenced by Latin *serere* join, connect]

se·reh (sē′re), *n.* a serious disease of sugar cane which attacks and destroys the entire grass. It is especially common in India and the Malay Archipelago. [from a native name]

se·rein (sə raN′), *n.* a fine rain falling from an apparently clear sky, especially after sunset. The clouds may be too thin to be seen, or may be to the windward side. [< French *serein,* ultimately < Latin *sērum* evening, neuter of *sērus* late]

ser·e·nade (ser′ə nād′), *n.*, *v.*, **-nad·ed, -nad·ing.** —*n.* **1.** music played or sung outdoors at night, especially by a lover under his lady's window. **2.** a piece of music suitable for such a performance. **3.** *Music.* a work of four to eight connected instrumental movements, usually written for a small orchestra
—*v.t.* to sing or play a serenade to. —*v.i.* to sing or play a serenade.
[< French *sérénade* < Italian *serenata* < Latin *serēnus* serene; influenced by Italian *sera* evening < Latin *sērus* late]

ser·e·nad·er (ser′ə nā′dər), *n.* a person who serenades.

ser·e·na·ta (ser′ə nä′tə), *n.*, *pl.* **-tas, -te** (-tā). **1.** a cantata, usually pastoral or dramatic. **2.** a serenade for a small orchestra. [< Italian *serenata;* see SERENADE]

ser·en·dip·i·tous (ser′ən dip′ə təs), *adj.* having to do with, resulting from, or characterized by serendipity: *As a serendipitous by-product of volcano research, scientists have found new fresh-water sources* (Time). —**ser′en·dip′i·tous·ly,** *adv.*

ser·en·dip·i·ty (ser′ən dip′ə tē), *n.* the ability to find, by accident, interesting items of information, unexpected proof of one's theories, etc., especially while looking for something else; discovery of things not sought: *And there was plenty of serendipity demonstrated on the two-week tour for science writers to cancer research centers* (New York Herald Tribune). [(coined by Horace Walpole) < "The Three Princes of *Serendip*" (old name of Ceylon), a fairy tale whose heroes made such discoveries]

ser·en·dip·per (ser′ən dip′ər), *n.* a person who has the gift of serendipity or who finds things unsought. [probably back formation < *serendipity*]

se·rene (sə rēn′), *adj.* **1.** peaceful; calm; tranquil: *serene happiness, a serene smile. He kept serene and calm, by . . . knowing nothing of the dangers which surrounded him* (Daniel Defoe). **2.** not cloudy; clear and pleasant: *a serene sky. One serene and moonlight night, when all the waves rolled by like scrolls of silver* . . . (Herman Melville). **3.** bright; clear and fine: . . . *many a gem of purest ray serene* . . . (Thomas Gray).
—*n.* an expanse of clear sky or calm sea: *The bark that plows the deep serene* . . . (William Cowper).
[< Latin *serēnus*] —**se·rene′ly,** *adv.* —**se·rene′ness,** *n.*
—**Syn.** *adj.* **1.** placid, untroubled. See **peaceful.**

Se·rene (sə rēn′), *adj.* of or having to do with a reigning prince, member of a royal house, etc. (used in a title).

se·ren·i·ty (sə ren′ə tē), *n.*, *pl.* **-ties.** **1.** quiet peace; peacefulness; calmness: *He was always a cool man; nothing could disturb his serenity* (Mark Twain). **2.** clearness; brightness of air and sky. —**Syn.** **1.** tranquillity, placidity.

Se·ren·i·ty (sə ren′ə tē), *n.*, *pl.* **-ties.** a title of honor given to reigning princes and other dignitaries: *His Serenity, the Pope.*

serf (sėrf), *n.* **1.** a slave who cannot be sold off the land, but passes from one owner to another with the land. **2.** a person treated almost like a slave; person who is mistreated, underpaid, etc., with little or no hope of advancement, change, or the like. **3.** *Obsolete.* a slave. [< Old French *serf* < Latin *servus* slave] —**serf′like′,** *adj.*

serf·age (sėr′fij), *n.* **1.** the condition of a serf. **2.** the serf system. **3.** the serf class.

serf·dom (sėrf′dəm), *n.* **1.** the condition of a serf: *Break up ere long The serfdom of this world!* (Elizabeth Barrett Browning). **2.** the custom of having serfs or people treated almost like slaves. Serfdom existed all over Europe in the Middle Ages and lasted in Russia until the middle 1800's: *The Soviet rulers are learning from experience that serfdom is not a profitable method of production* (Wall Street Journal).

serf·hood (sėrf′hu̇d), *n.* the condition of a serf.

serg. or **Serg.,** sergeant.

serge (sėrj), *n.* a kind of cloth having slanting lines or ridges on its surface. Worsted serge is used for coats and suits. Silk serge is used for linings. [< Old French *serge* < Vulgar Latin *sārica,* variant of Latin *sērica* (*vestis*) silken (garment), feminine of *sēricus* < Greek *sērikós* silken; Chinese < *Sēres* the Chinese (because they are thought to be the originators of silk)]

ser·gean·cy (sär′jən sē), *n.*, *pl.* **-cies.** the position, rank, or duties of a sergeant.

ser·geant (sär′jənt), *n.* **1.** a noncommissioned officer of a grade higher than corporal, especially: **a.** (in the U.S. Air Force, Marine Corps, and formerly the Army) a master sergeant, technical sergeant, or staff sergeant. **b.** (in the U.S. Army, since 1948) a master sergeant or a sergeant first class. **2.** a police officer ranking next above a patrolman, constable, trooper, etc., and next below a lieutenant or captain. *Abbr.:* Sgt. **3.** a sergeant at arms. **4.** a sergeant-at-law. **5.** *Obsolete.* an attendant; servant, as of a soldier. **6.** *Obsolete.* an officer of the court who arrested offenders, issued summonses, and enforced court orders: *This fell sergeant, death, Is strict in his arrest* (Shakespeare). **7.** *Especially British, Obsolete.* a person, below a knight, and holding land in return for military service. Also, especially British, **serjeant.** [Middle English *sergeaunte* < Old French *sergent, serjent* < Latin *serviēns, -entis* serving (in Late Latin, a public official), present participle of *servīre* to serve < *servus* slave]

sergeant at arms, or **ser·geant-at-arms** (sär′jənt ət ärmz′), *n.*, *pl.* **sergeants at arms, ser·geants-at-arms.** an officer who keeps order in a legislature, law court, etc.

ser·geant-at-law (sär′jənt ət lô′), *n.*, *pl.* **ser·geants-at-law.** (formerly) a barrister of superior rank in England.

sergeant first class, (in the United States Army, since 1948) a noncommissioned officer next below a master sergeant and next above a sergeant. *Abbr.:* Sfc.

sergeant fish, **1.** a large, semitropical marine fish with spiny fins and a black stripe along its side, similar to a mackerel; cobia. **2.** the robalo.

sergeant major, *pl.* **sergeants major.** **1.** a sergeant who assists an adjutant at an army headquarters. A sergeant major is the highest enlisted man in a battalion or larger unit. *A former commando sergeant major ... He looked too lawless for any policeman* (Geoffrey Household). **2.** a damselfish of tropical American waters; pintano.

ser·geant·ship (sär′jənt ship), *n.* the position, rank, or duties of a sergeant.

ser·geant·y (sär′jən tē), *n., pl.* **-geant·ies.** a form of feudal tenure in England for some personal service to the king. [< Old French *sergentie* < *sergent;* see SERGEANT]

sergt. or **Sergt.,** sergeant.

se·ri·al (sir′ē əl), *n.* **1.** a story published, broadcast, or televised one part at a time in a magazine or newspaper or on the radio or television: *The film is an extension of the popular television serial* (Sunday Times). **2.** a report published like a serial, especially at long intervals; periodical.
—*adj.* **1.** of serials; having to do with a serial: *the serial rights of a novel.* **2.** published, broadcast, or televised one part at a time: *a serial publication, a serial story.* **3.** of a series; arranged in a series; making a series: *Place volumes 1 to 5 on the shelf in serial order.* **4.** *Music.* twelve-tone: *Some of the serial composers replied that serialism provided them with a viable basis for writing music* (Listener).
[< New Latin *serialis* < Latin *seriēs* series]

se·ri·al·ise (sir′ē ə līz), *v.t.,* **-ised, -is·ing.** *Especially British.* serialize.

se·ri·al·ism (sir′ē əl iz əm), *n.* the twelve-tone system or technique of atonal music.

se·ri·al·ist (sir′ē ə list), *n.* **1.** a writer of serials. **2.** a composer or musician who uses the serial technique. —*adj.* of serialism; serial (def. 4).

se·ri·al·i·ty (sir′ē al′ə tē), *n.* serial character; occurrence or arrangement in a series.

se·ri·al·i·za·tion (sir′ē ə lə zā′shən), *n.* publication in serial form: *The answer to this riddle lies, of course, in the increased support of fiction by magazine and newspaper serialization and by book clubs and other reprinters* (Saturday Review).

se·ri·al·ize (sir′ē ə līz), *v.t.,* **-ized, -iz·ing. 1.** to publish in a series of installments: *Gordon's Monthly was serializing the novel in America* (Arnold Bennett). **2.** to arrange in a series.

se·ri·al·ly (sir′ē ə lē), *adv.* in a series; as a serial.

serial number, an individual number given to a person, article, etc.

se·ri·ar·y (sir′ē ər′ē), *adj.* of, having to do with, or belonging in a series.

se·ri·ate (sir′ē it, -āt), *adj.* arranged or occurring in one or more series or rows. —**se′ri·ate·ly,** *adv.*

se·ri·a·tim (sir′ē ā′tim, ser′-), *adv.* in a series; one after the other: *This question subdivides into several questions, which we will consider seriatim* (Herbert Spencer). —*adj.* following one after the other; arranged in a series: *There are places where force would be lost by dividing it into two or three successive and seriatim sentences* (John Earle). [< Medieval Latin *seriatim* < Latin *seriēs* series]

se·ri·a·tion (sir′ē ā′shən, ser′-), *n.* **1.** formation of or into a series. **2.** *Archaeology.* a method of arranging artifacts from a particular civilization in a sequence to show the changes in style that reflect the cultural change: *Behind the fragments is a seriation diagram, in which the relative abundance of each kind of pottery is plotted against time* (Scientific American).

se·ri·ceous (sə rish′əs), *adj.* **1. a.** made of silk. **b.** silky. **2.** covered with fine, silky hairs. [< Late Latin *sēriceus* (with English *-ous*) < Latin *sēricus* silken; see SERGE]

ser·i·ci·cul·tur·al (ser′ə si kul′chər əl), *adj.* sericultural.

ser·i·ci·cul·ture (ser′ə si kul′chər), *n.* sericulture.

ser·i·ci·cul·tur·ist (ser′ə si kul′chər ist), *n.* a sericulturist.

ser·i·cin (ser′ə sin), *n.* the gelatinous element of raw silk. [< Latin *sēricum* silk, neuter of *sēricus* (see SERGE) + English *-in*]

ser·i·cite (ser′ə sīt), *n.* a variety of muscovite with a silky luster, occurring in fine scales of greenish- or yellowish-white color. [< Latin *sēricum* silk + English *-ite*[1]]

ser·i·cit·i·za·tion (ser′ə sī′tə zā′shən), *n.* the alteration of a mineral or rock to sericite.

ser·ic·te·ri·um (ser′ik tir′ē əm), *n., pl.* **-te·ri·a** (-tir′ē ə). a glandular apparatus in insects, especially silkworms, for the secretion of silk. [< New Latin *sericterium* < Latin *sēricum* silk]

se·ric·ter·y (sə rik′tər ē), *n., pl.* **-ter·ies.** sericterium.

ser·i·cul·tur·al (ser′ə kul′chər əl), *adj.* **1.** having to do with sericulture. **2.** engaged in sericulture.

ser·i·cul·ture (ser′ə kul′chər), *n.* the breeding and care of silkworms for the production of raw silk. [short for French *sériciculture* < Latin *sēricum* silk (see SERGE) + *cultūra* culture]

ser·i·cul·tur·ist (ser′ə kul′chər ist), *n.* a person who raises silkworms or studies the breeding and care of silkworms: *Mr. Tomioka, who is a graduate sericulturist, or silk scientist, has devoted thirty years to the study and development of the industry in his homeland* (New York Times).

ser·i·e·ma (ser′ē ē′mə, -ā′-), *n.* **1.** a large, long-legged, crested screamer (bird), found especially in Brazil. **2.** a somewhat smaller related bird, found especially in Argentina. [earlier *çariama* < New Latin *Cariama* the genus name < Tupi (Brazil) *sarīa* the native name]

se·ries (sir′ēz), *n., pl.* **-ries. 1.** a number of similar things in a row: *A series of rooms opened off the long hall.* **2.** a number of things placed one after another. **3.** a number of things, events, etc., coming one after the other; succession: *a series of experiments. A series of rainy days spoiled their vacation.* **4.** coins, stamps, or the like, of a particular issue, ruler, country, etc. **5.** written or artistic works that are produced one after another, usually having a common subject or purpose, and often by a single author, artist, or composer: *The so-called "series books" are often helpful in breaking the ice for the reluctant reader* (Sidonie M. Gruenberg). **6.** an electrical arrangement in which a number of batteries, condensers, etc., are connected so that a current flows in turn through each one. **7.** *Mathematics.* a succession of terms related by some law, and consequently predictable. **8.** *Geology.* a division of rocks included in a system, and formed during a geological epoch. **9.** a group of elements of a sentence written one after another. *Abbr.:* ser. [< Latin *seriēs* < *serere* to join]
—**Syn. 1. Series, sequence, succession** mean a number of things, events, etc., arranged or coming one after another in some order. **Series** applies to a number of similar things with the same purpose or relation to each other: *He gave a series of lectures on Mexico.* **Sequence** implies a closer or unbroken connection, in thought, between cause and effect, in numerical or alphabetical order, etc.: *He reviewed the sequence of events leading to the discovery.* **Succession** emphasizes following in order of time, sometimes of place, usually without interruption: *He had a succession of illnesses.*

➔ **series.** Commas are used between the items of a series of three or more short items. Usage is divided over the insertion of a comma before *and* preceding the last item of the series: *pen, ink, and paper* or *pen, ink and paper.*

series dynamo, a series-wound dynamo.

series generator, series dynamo.

series motor, a series-wound motor.

series turn, any one of the ampere turns in a series winding.

series winding, *Electricity.* a winding of a motor or dynamo whereby the field magnet coils are connected in series with the armature and carry the same current.

se·ries-wound (sir′ēz wound′), *adj. Electricity.* that has series winding: *a series-wound motor.*

ser·if (ser′if), *n.* a thin or smaller line used to finish off a main stroke of a letter, as at the top and bottom of *l* and *M*, or ending the cross stroke in *T*. Also, **cerif, ceriph.** [origin uncertain]

se·rif·ic (sə rif′ik), *adj.* having to do with the making of silk threads: *the serific glands of a silkworm.* [< Latin *sēri*(cum) + English *-fic*]

ser·i·graph (ser′ə graf, -gräf), *n.* a color print made by serigraphy or the silkscreen process: *Georg Jensen has shown particularly shrewd judgment in exhibiting the shop's collection of fine serigraphs* (New Yorker).

se·rig·ra·pher (sə rig′rə fər), *n.* a person who makes serigraphs; one who uses serigraphy.

ser·i·graph·ic (ser ə graf′ik), *adj.* of or having to do with serigraphy.

se·rig·ra·phy (sə rig′rə fē), *n.* the art of producing handmade prints in several colors by pressing oil paint or similar pigment through a series of silk screens. [< Latin *sēricum* silk, neuter of *sēricus* (see SERGE) + English *-graphy*]

ser·in[1] (ser′in), *n.* a small finch of central and southern Europe, closely related to the canary. [< French *serin* canary; origin uncertain]

ser·in[2] (ser′in, sir′-), *n.* serine.

ser·ine (ser′ēn, -in; sir′-), *n.* a colorless, crystalline compound, an amino acid, present in many proteins or produced synthetically. *Formula:* $C_3H_7NO_3$ [< *ser*(um) + *-ine*[2]]

se·rin·ga (sə ring′gə), *n.* **1.** any of a group of Brazilian trees of the spurge family, which yield rubber. **2.** syringa. [< French *seringa* < New Latin *syringa* syringa]

se·ri·o·com·e·dy (sir′ē ō kom′ə dē), *n., pl.* **-dies.** a seriocomic play, incident, situation, etc.

se·ri·o·com·ic (sir′ē ō kom′ik), *adj.* partly serious and partly comic: *Irony ... assumes that man is a seriocomic animal* (James Harvey Robinson). [< *serio*(us) + *comic*] —**se′ri·o·com′i·cal·ly,** *adv.*

se·ri·o·com·i·cal (sir′ē ō kom′ə kəl), *adj.* seriocomic.

se·ri·ous (sir′ē əs), *adj.* **1. a.** thoughtful; grave: *a serious face.* **b.** thought-provoking; not superficial: *a serious style of writing. The symphonic upswing reflects to some extent a general increase in interest in serious music* (Wall Street Journal). **2.** in earnest; not joking; sincere: *He was serious about the subject.* **3. a.** needing thought; important: *Choice of one's lifework is a serious matter.* **b.** significant; large; considerable: *to take a serious part in the negotiations.* **4.** important because it may do much harm; dangerous: *The badly injured man was in serious condition. We live in serious times* (James Fenimore Cooper). [< Late Latin *sēriōsus* < Latin *sērius* earnest] —**se′ri·ous·ly,** *adv.* —**se′ri·ous·ness,** *n.* —**Syn. 1. a.** solemn, sober. See **grave. 3. a.** weighty, momentous. **4.** critical, alarming.

se·ri·ous-mind·ed (sir′ē əs mīn′did), *adj.* earnest; having serious intentions: *A serious-minded politician who ... has proved himself a master of detail on any political level* (Newsweek).

ser·jeant (sär′jənt), *n. British.* sergeant.

ser·mon (sėr′mən), *n.* **1.** a public talk on religion or something connected with religion: *Ministers preach sermons in church. A sermon requires meditation, leisure, and a certain loneliness* (J.W.R. Scott). **2.** a serious talk about morals, conduct, duty, etc.: *After the guests left, the boy got a sermon on table manners from his father.* **3.** a long, tiresome speech; harangue. [< Latin *sermō, -ōnis* a talk; (originally) a stringing together of words, perhaps < *serere* join]

ser·mon·esque (sėr′mə nesk′), *adj.* in the manner of a sermon.

ser·mon·ette or **ser·mon·et** (sėr′mə net′), *n.* a short sermon: *His conversations also ranged far and wide, including a sermonette on the hazards of jaywalking* (Time).

ser·mon·ic (sėr mon′ik), *adj.* of, having to do with, or like a sermon. —**ser·mon′i·cal·ly,** *adv.*

ser·mon·i·cal (sėr mon′ə kəl), *adj.* sermonic.

ser·mon·ise (sėr′mə nīz), *v.i., v.t.,* **-ised, -is·ing.** *Especially British.* sermonize.

ser·mon·ize (sėr′mə nīz), *v.,* **-ized, -iz·ing.** —*v.i.* to give a sermon; preach: *... recalling a time when preachers sermonized against jazz in the churches* (Harper's). —*v.t.* to preach or talk seriously to; lecture: *I see no right you have to sermonize me* (Charlotte Brontë).

ser·mon·iz·er (sėr′mə nī′zər), *n.* a preacher or writer of sermons.

ser·mon·ol·o·gy (sėr′mə nol′ə jē), *n.* the art of writing and preaching sermons; homiletics.

Sermon on the Mount, Christ's sermon to his disciples, as reported in Matthew 5-7 and Luke 6:20-49.

sero-, *combining form.* **1.** serum: *Serodiagnosis = diagnosis by means of serums.* **2.** serum and ___: *Seromucous = containing serum and mucus.*
[< Latin *serum* whey, liquid]

se·ro·di·ag·no·sis (sir′ō dī′əg nō′sis), *n., pl.* **-ses** (-sēz). a diagnosis by means of serums. [< *sero-* + *diagnosis*]

se·ro·log·ic (sir′ə loj′ik), *adj.* serological.

se·ro·log·i·cal (sir′ə loj′ə kəl), *adj.* of or having to do with serology: *Serological tests and examination by electron microscope have established that the two viruses are distinct* (New Scientist).

se·ro·log·i·cal·ly (sir′ə loj′ə klē), *adv.* **1.** in a serologic manner. **2.** from the point of view of serology: *one of approximately 80 serologically different coatings that surround the bacteria* (Science News Letter).

se·rol·o·gist (si rol′ə jist), *n.* a person skilled in serology.

se·rol·o·gy (si rol′ə jē), *n.* the scientific study of the use of serums in curing or preventing disease. [< *sero-* + *-logy*]

se·ro·mu·cous (sir′ō myü′kəs), *adj.* **1.** containing both serum and mucus. **2.** of the nature of both serum and mucus.

se·ro·mus·cu·lar (sir′ō mus′kyə lər), *adj.* having to do with both the serous and muscular coats of the intestine.

Se·ro·my·cin (sir′ō mī′sin), *n. Trademark.* an antibiotic effective against tuberculosis and certain other bacterial infections: *Seromycin may be able to cure tuberculosis by itself, though it may be given combined with streptomycin* (Science News Letter). *Formula:* $C_3H_6N_2O_2$

se·root (sə rüt′), *n.*, or **seroot fly,** a fly of the upper Nile region whose female sucks much blood and often transmits diseases. It is related to the horsefly. [< an African word]

se·ro·sa (si rō′sə), *n.* a serous membrane. [< New Latin *serosa* < Latin *serum* whey, liquid]

se·ro·si·tis (sir′ə sī′tis), *n.* inflammation of a serous membrane. [< New Latin *serositis* < *serōsus* serous + English *-itis*]

se·ros·i·ty (si ros′ə tē), *n., pl.* **-ties. 1.** a serous condition. **2.** serous fluid; serum. [< New Latin *serositas* < *serosus* serous < Latin *serum* whey, liquid]

se·ro·ther·a·pist (sir′ō ther′ə pist), *n.* a serum therapist.

se·ro·ther·a·py (sir′ō ther′ə pē), *n.* serumtherapy.

se·rot·i·nal (si rot′ə nəl), *adj.* serotine[1].

ser·o·tine[1] (ser′ə tin, -tīn), *adj.* late blooming, developing, or appearing: *a serotine plant.* [< Latin *sērōtinus* < *sērō*, adverb < *sērus* late]

ser·o·tine[2] (ser′ə tin, -tīn), *n.* a small European bat that flies late in the evening. [< French *sérotine* < feminine of Latin *sērōtinus;* see SEROTINE[1]]

se·rot·i·nous (si rot′ə nəs), *adj.* serotine[1].

se·ro·to·nin (sir′ō tō′nən), *n.* a hormonelike substance in the blood that causes blood vessels to constrict and aids in blood clotting. It is an indole, chemically related to adrenalin, that also occurs in the brain and in smooth muscles of the intestines. *Discovery that reserpine, the tranquilizing drug ... causes the body to unload serotonin ... found in many tissues, including the brain, suggested that some psychoses may result from abnormal serotonin metabolism* (Science News Letter). *Formula:* $C_{10}H_{12}N_2O$

se·ro·type (ser′ə tīp), *n.* a group of bacteria or other microorganisms that have the same combination of antigens.

se·rous (sir′əs), *adj.* **1.** of serum; having to do with serum. **2.** like serum; watery: *Tears are drops of a serous fluid.* **3.** secreting or carrying serum. [< Middle French *séreux* (with English *-ous*) < Latin *serum* whey, liquid]

serous fluid, any of various animal liquids resembling blood serum, such as the fluids of the serous membranes.

serous membrane, any of various thin membranes of connective tissue, as the peritoneum and pericardium, lining certain cavities of the body and moistened with a serous fluid.

ser·ow (ser′ō), *n.* any of a group of sturdy, dark-colored, goatlike antelopes of eastern Asia. [< the native name]

Ser·pa·sil (sėr′pə səl), *n. Trademark.* reserpine.

Ser·pens (sėr′penz), *n., genitive* **Ser·pen·tis.** a long, narrow constellation on the celestial equator near Scorpio: *The head of Serpens is represented by an X-shaped group of stars just to the south of the crown* (Science News Letter). [< Latin *Serpēns,* (originally) present participle of *serpere;* see SERPENT]

ser·pent (sėr′pənt), *n.* **1. a.** a snake; big snake. **b.** any of various animals in legend supposed to be like a snake in shape but usually of enormous size and often living in the sea or a lake. **2.** a sly, treacherous person. **3.** a bass wood-wind instrument with three U-shaped turns, used especially in the 1700's and 1800's: *The fiddles finished off with a screech, and the serpent emitted a last note that nearly lifted the roof* (Thomas Hardy). **4.** a firework that whizzes up with a snaky twist. **5.** *Archaic.* any of various animals thought of as creeping and dangerous, as crocodiles, spiders, etc. [< Latin *serpēns, -entis,* (originally) present participle of *serpere* to creep]

Ser·pent (sėr′pənt), *n.* (in the Bible) the Devil; Satan. Genesis 3:1-13.

ser·pen·tar·i·a (sėr′pən tãr′ē ə), *n.* **1.** the root of the Virginia snakeroot. **2.** the plant itself. [< Late Latin *serpentāria* < Latin *serpēns;* see SERPENT]

ser·pen·tar·i·um (sėr′pən tãr′ē əm), *n., pl.* **-i·ums, -i·a** (-ē ə). a place where serpents are kept for safety or for exhibition. [New Latin *serpentarium* < Latin *serpēns, -entis* serpent]

Serpent Bearer, Serpens.

ser·pen·ti·form (sər pen′tə fôrm), *adj.* having the form of a serpent; serpentlike.

ser·pen·tine (*adj., v.* sėr′pən tēn, -tīn; *n.* sėr′pən tēn), *adj., n., v.,* **-tined, -tin·ing.** —*adj.* **1.** of or like a serpent. **2.** twisting; winding. **3.** cunning; sly; treacherous: *a serpentine suggestion.* **4.** diabolical; Satanic: *serpentine cunning.*

—*n.* **1.** a soft, waxy mineral consisting chiefly of a hydrous silicate of magnesium, usually green, and sometimes spotted like a serpent's skin. *Formula:* $Mg_3Si_2O_5(OH)_4$ **2.** anything twisted or winding like a snake: *... entangled in a serpentine of military red tape* (Science). *The road winds up in serpentines through woods* (London Times).

—*v.i., v.t.* to wind like a snake: *the electronic safari that serpentined through French Equatorial Africa ... under the intrepid leadership of TV's Arthur Godfrey* (Time). [< Late Latin *serpentīnus* < Latin *serpēns;* see SERPENT]

ser·pen·tined (sėr′pən tēnd, -tīnd), *adj.* **1.** having serpents; infested with snakes: *... the disappearance of two other woodsmen in the alligatored and serpentined gloom* (Newsweek). **2.** twisted or winding like a snake: *serpentined mountain roads.*

ser·pen·tin·ite (sėr′pən tē′nīt), *n.* a rock made up chiefly of the mineral serpentine.

ser·pen·tin·ize (sėr′pən tē′nīz), *v.t.,* **-ized, -iz·ing.** to convert into serpentine: *They [the rocks] are made of so-called serpentinite and serpentinized peridotite* (New Scientist).

ser·pen·ti·nous (sėr′pən tī′nəs), *adj.* of, having to do with, or like the mineral serpentine.

Ser·pen·tis (sėr pen′tis), *n.* genitive of **Serpens.**

ser·pent·ry (sėr′pən trē), *n.* serpents as a group.

ser·pig·i·nous (sər pij′ə nəs), *adj.* of or having to do with serpigo. [< Medieval Latin *serpigo, -inis* serpigo + English *-ous*]

ser·pi·go (sər pī′gō), *n.* ringworm or a similar spreading skin disease. [< Medieval Latin *serpigo, -inis* < Latin *serpere* to creep]

ser·ra·del·la (ser′ə del′ə), *n.* serradilla.

ser·ra·dil·la (ser′ə dil′ə), *n.* a plant of the pea family, cultivated in Europe for forage, etc. [< Portuguese *serradilla* (diminutive) < *serrado* serrate < Latin *serrātus;* see SERRATE]

ser·ra·noid (ser′ə noid), *adj.* of or belonging to a group of fishes with spiny fins, including the sea basses, jewfishes, and groupers. —*n.* a serranoid fish. [< New Latin *Serranus* the typical genus (< Latin *serra* a saw, sawfish) + English *-oid*]

ser·rate (ser′āt, -it), *adj., v.,* **-rat·ed, -rat·ing.** —*adj.* notched like the edge of a saw; toothed. —*v.t.* to make serrate; notch like a saw. [< Latin *serrātus* < *serra* a saw]

Serrate Leaf

ser·rat·ed (ser′ā tid), *adj.* serrate: *The mountains to the northeast are serrated and lovely* (Atlantic).

ser·ra·tion (se rā′shən), *n.* **1.** a serrate edge or formation. **2.** one of its series of notches. **3.** a serrate condition.

ser·ra·ture (ser′ə chər), *n.* serration.

ser·re·file (ser′ə fīl), *n. Military.* any of the men forming a line behind the last regular rank at the rear of a body of troops. [< French *serre-fille* < *serrer* close up + *file* file[1]]

serre-fine (sãr′fēn′), *n.* a small forceps used for closing a blood vessel during an operation. [< French *serre-fine* < *serre* clamp (< *serrer* to close) + *fine* fine]

ser·ri·corn (ser′ə kôrn), *adj.* **1.** having serrate antennae. **2.** belonging to a group of beetles whose antennae are usually serrate, as the firefly. —*n.* a serricorn beetle. [< New Latin *serricornis* < Latin *serra* saw + *cornū* horn]

ser·ried (ser′ēd), *adj.* crowded closely together: *On every side rose up the serried ranks of pine trees* (Bret Harte). [adjectival use of past participle of *serry*] —**Syn.** compact, dense.

ser·ri·form (ser′ə fôrm), *adj.* toothed like a saw; serrate. [< Latin *serra* saw + English *-form*]

ser·ru·la (ser′yə lə, ser′ə-), *n., pl.* **-lae** (-lē). *Biology.* a comblike ridge found on the appendages of arachnids, such as spiders, scorpions, and mites. [< Latin *serrula* (diminutive) < *serra* saw]

ser·ru·late (ser′yə lit, -lāt; ser′ə-), *adj.* very finely notched: *a serrulate leaf.* [< New Latin *serrulatus* < Latin *serrula* (diminutive) < *serra* a saw]

ser·ru·lat·ed (ser′yə lā′tid, ser′ə-), *adj.* serrulate.

ser·ru·la·tion (ser′yə lā′shən, ser′ə-), *n.* **1.** serrulate condition or form. **2.** serration; one of a series of minute notches.

ser·ry (ser′ē), *v.,* **-ried, -ry·ing.** —*v.i.* to stand or press close: *High shoulders, low shoulders, broad shoulders, narrow ones, Round, square and angular serry and shove* (William E. Henley). —*v.t.* to close up, especially troops in ranks: *The little band of devoted cavaliers about the king serried their forces* (Washington Irving). [< French *serré*, past participle of *serrer* press close; fasten < Vulgar Latin *serrāre* to bar, fasten, for Latin *serāre* < *sera* a bar, bolt of a door]

ser·tu·lar·i·an (sėr′chu̇ lãr′ē ən), *n.* any of a group of very simple invertebrate water animals or coelenterates, growing in branching colonies: *On what, I wondered, were these sertularians — carnivorous, like all hydroids — feeding?* (New Yorker). —*adj.* of or having to do with a sertularian. [< New Latin *Sertularia* the genus name < Latin *sertula* (diminutive) < *serta* garland; + English *-an*]

ser·tu·lum (sėr′chə ləm), *n., pl.* **-la** (-lə). selection of plants scientifically studied or described. [< New Latin *sertulum,* diminutive of Latin *sertula,* see SERTULARIAN]

ser·tum (sėr′təm), *n., pl.* **-ta** (-tə). a report or dissertation upon a collection of plants. [< unrecorded Latin *sertum,* assumed singular of *serta* garland]

se·rum (sir′əm), *n., pl.* **-rums** or **-ra. 1.** the clear, pale-yellow, watery part of the blood that separates from the clot when blood coagulates. **2.** liquid used to prevent or cure a disease, usually obtained from the blood of an animal that has been made immune to the disease, as diphtheria antitoxin: *Such serums, containing substances that will fight the particular diseases, are used for immunization* (Sidonie M. Gruenberg). **3.** any watery animal fluid: *Lymph is a serum.* **4.** the watery substance of plants. **5.** *Obsolete.* whey. [< Latin *serum* whey, liquid]

se·rum·al (sir′ə məl) *adj.* of, having to do with, or like a serum.

serum albumin, the albumin found in blood serum. It is the largest component of blood plasma and is a substitute for plasma.

serum disease, serum sickness.

serum globulin, the globulin found in blood serum.

serum hepatitis, a noninfectious hepatitis caused by a virus that is carried by human blood, often accompanied by jaundice: *During World War II ... serum hepatitis was transmitted through plasma to many persons in the armed forces* (Scientific American).

serum sickness, illness from an abnormal sensitivity to an injection of animal serum: *The only side effects noticed were a few cases of "delayed serum sickness" reactions, none of them serious* (Wall Street Journal).

se·rum·ther·a·py (sir′əm ther′ə pē), *n.* the treatment of disease by the injection of the serum of immunized animals.

serv., 1. servant. **2.** service.

serv·a·ble (sėr′və bəl), *adj.* that can be served.

ser·val (sėr′vəl), *n.* an African wildcat that has a brownish-yellow coat with black spots. [< New Latin *serval* the species name < French < Portuguese (*lobo*) *cerval* lynx < Latin *cervārius* (*lupus*) lynx; wolf that attacks a stag < *cervus* stag]

Serval (including tail, 4 to 5 ft. long)

serv·ant (sėr′vənt), *n.* **1.** a person employed in a household. **2.** a person employed by another or others: *a loyal civil servant. Policemen and firemen are public servants.* **3.** a person devoted to any service: *. . . returning missionaries whose pitiable condition told the world how Communist China feels about servants of God* (Time). **4.** (formerly) a slave: *Why don't we teach our servants to read?* (Harriet Beecher Stowe). [< Old French *servant,* present participle of *servir* serve] —**Syn. 1.** domestic. **2.** employee.

serv·ant·less (sėr′vənt lis), *adj.* having no servant: *. . . with all the mechanised comfort of the servantless American way of life* (Manchester Guardian).

serv·ant·ship (sėr′vənt ship), *n.* the condition of being a servant.

serve (sėrv), *v.,* **served, serv·ing,** *n.* —*v.i.* **1.** to be a servant; give service; work; perform official duties: *He served as butler. He left work for three weeks to serve on a jury. He had served with distinction in the war against Napoleon* (Lytton Strachey). **2.** to wait at table; bring food or drink to guests. **3.** to be useful; be what is needed; be of use: *Boxes served as seats. Short greeting serves in time of strife* (Scott). **4.** to be favorable or suitable, as wind, weather, occasion, etc.: *The ship will sail when the time and tide serve. We must take the current when it serves, Or lose our ventures* (Shakespeare). **5.** to start play by hitting the ball in tennis and similar games. **6.** to act as server at Mass.
—*v.t.* **1.** to be a servant of; give service to; work for or in: *A slave serves his master. Over 10,000,000 served their country as soldiers in World War II. In the soul Are many lesser faculties that serve Reason as chief* (Milton). **2. a.** to wait on at table; bring food or drink to. **b.** to put (food or drink) on the table: *to serve pie for dessert. They did not expect to sleep in hammocks, clean their messes . . . or serve up their meals* (London Times). **3.** to supply; furnish; supply with something needed: *The dairy serves us with milk. The pump . . . that serves water to his garden* (John Evelyn). **4.** to help; aid: *Let me know if I can serve you in any way.* **5.** to be favorable or suitable to; satisfy; answer the requirements of: *If fortune serve me, I'll requite this kindness* (Shakespeare). **6.** to be useful to; fulfill: *This will serve my purpose. My stomach serves me instead of a clock* (Jonathan Swift). **7.** to treat; reward: *The punishment served him right. I could . . . deprive him of all his possessions and serve him as he served me* (W.H. Hudson). **8.** to pass; spend; go through: *He served a term as ambassador. Tokyo Rose will be released from the Federal Reformatory . . . her ten-year sentence served* (Newsweek). **9. a.** to deliver (an order from a court, a writ, etc.). **b.** to present (with an order from a court, etc.): *He was served with a notice to appear in court.* **10.** to put (the ball) in play by hitting it in tennis and similar games. **11.** to operate or be a member of the crew that operates (a cannon, machine gun, etc.). **12.** *Nautical.* to bind or wind (a rope, etc.) with small cord to strengthen or protect it.
—*n.* in tennis, etc.: **1.** the act or way of serving a tennis ball or the like: *And an innovation this year was a so-called tennis clinic to give the spectators a better idea of . . . different types of serves, volleys, lobs* (New Yorker). **2.** the ball, shuttlecock, etc., served: *The serve fell over the line and was out of play.*
[< Old French *servir* < Latin *servīre* (originally) be a slave < *servus* slave]

serv·er (sėr′vər), *n.* **1.** a person who serves. **2.** a tray for dishes, etc., as a salver. **3.** any of various pieces of tableware for serving food, usually a spatula: *a cake or pie server.* **4.** an attendant who serves the celebrant at low Mass: *The interview was like a ritual between priest and server* (Graham Greene). **5.** the player who puts the ball in play in certain games, as tennis.

serv·er·y (sėrv′ər ē), *n., pl.* **-er·ies.** a small room between the kitchen and dining room from which a butler, maid, etc., serves; butler's pantry.

Ser·vi·an (sėr′vē ən), *adj., n.* (formerly) Serbian.

serv·ice[1] (sėr′vis), *n., adj., v.,* **-iced, -ic·ing.** —*n.* **1.** a helpful act or acts; aid; conduct that is useful to others: *a neighborly service. George Washington performed many services for his country. Myriads of souls were born again to ideas of service and sacrifice in those tremendous days* (H.G. Wells). **2.** a supply; arrangements for supplying: *The train service was good. A big snowstorm interrupted telephone service in the town.* **3.** occupation or employment as a servant: *to go into service, domestic service.* **4.** work for others; performance of duties; work: *Mrs. Brown no longer needs the service of a doctor.* **5.** advantage, benefit; use: *This coat has given me great service. Every available vehicle was pressed into service.* **6. a.** a department of government or public employment: *the civil service.* **b.** the persons engaged in it: *The foreign service is having a banquet tonight.* **7.** the army, navy, air force, etc.: *We entered the service together. All the services use machines to reveal on paper the performance of guided missiles, rockets, and other new "hardware"* (Newsweek). **8.** duty in the army, navy, air force, etc.: *to be on active service.* **9. a.** a religious meeting, ritual, or ceremony, especially as worship in a prescribed form: *the marriage service. We attend church services twice a week.* **b.** the music for those parts of a liturgy that are sung: *When the English Church became completely separate from the Roman Catholic Church, composers wrote new services and anthems for English words* (World Book Encyclopedia). **10.** regard; respect; devotion: *Sir, my service to you* (Oliver Goldsmith). **11. a.** the manner of serving food: *Their world-famous cuisines are equalled by the . . . service to be found in these great hotels* (Time). **b.** the food served. **12.** a set of dishes, etc.: *a solid silver tea service.* **13.** *Law.* the serving of a process or writ upon a person. **14.** in tennis, etc.: **a.** the act or manner of putting the ball in play: *Knight won that game and settled the set and match on his service in the next* (London Times). **b.** the ball as put into play. **c.** a turn at starting the ball in play. **15.** *Nautical.* a small cord wound about a rope, etc., to strengthen or protect it. **16.** the loading and firing of a cannon, machine gun, etc., by a gun crew. **17.** *Archaic.* the devotion of a lover: *So well he wooed her . . . with humble service, and with daily suit* (Edmund Spenser).

at one's service, a. ready to do what one wants: *My name is Matthew Bramble, at your service* (Tobias Smollett). **b.** ready or available for one to use: *My means, which are certainly ample, are at your service* (Benjamin Jowett).

break service, *Tennis.* to win a game from the server: *He went on to win the match after he broke service.*

of service, helpful; useful: *The reader who wishes to work this out for himself will find the following references of service* (Thomas Mitchell).

services, work in the service of others; helpful labor: *goods and services. It is estimated that consumers will spend more than . . . $85 billions for services such as rent, education, laundering, repairs, utilities, and the like* (New York Times).

—*adj.* **1.** belonging to or assisting household servants, tradespeople, etc.: *a service pantry. They . . . went out through the kitchen, with its smell of gas leaks, to the service door* (New Yorker). **2.** belonging to a branch of the armed forces, especially on active duty: *a service cap.* **3.** used for ordinary occasions: *a service uniform.*
—*v.t.* **1.** to make fit for service; keep fit for service: *The mechanic serviced our automobile.* **2.** to provide with a service of any kind: *Two trains serviced the town.*
[< Old French *service, servise* < Latin *servitium* < *servus* slave; see SERF]

serv·ice[2] (sėr′vis), *n.* **1.** the service tree. **2.** *U.S.* the shadbush.
[earlier *serves,* plural of *serve,* Old English *syrfe* < Vulgar Latin *sorbea* < Latin *sorbus* sorb]

serv·ice·a·bil·i·ty (sėr′vi sə bil′ə tē), *n.* a being serviceable; usefulness: *One of the admirable things about . . . crystal is its serviceability* (New Yorker).

serv·ice·a·ble (sėr′vi sə bəl), *adj.* **1.** useful for a long time; able to stand much use: *a sturdy, serviceable coat. Most cars are very serviceable.* **2.** capable of giving good service; useful: *You are useful to Mrs. Gradgrind, and . . . you are serviceable in the family also* (Dickens). **3.** *Archaic.* willing to be useful: *The footmen might be aptly compared to the waiters of a tavern, if they were more serviceable* (Tobias Smollett).
—**serv′ice·a·ble·ness,** *n.* —**Syn. 1.** durable. **2.** helpful.

serv·ice·a·bly (sėr′vi sə blē), *adv.* in a serviceable manner; so as to be serviceable.

serv·ice·ber·ry (sėr′vis ber′ē), *n., pl.* **-ries.** **1.** the fruit of a service tree. **2.** the shadbush.

service board, *Nautical.* a small grooved, flat board with a handle, used in place of a serving mallet for winding a service on small rope; serving board.

service book, a book containing forms for divine service, as the Book of Common Prayer of the Anglican churches.

service box, (in handball, rackets, squash, etc.) the designated area in which the server must stand when putting the ball in play.

service ceiling, the height above sea level at which an airplane is unable to climb faster than 100 feet per minute.

service charge, a charge made for services given: *Revolving credit plans generally involve a service charge which is based on the monthly unpaid balance* (Wall Street Journal).

service club, 1. a club formed to promote the interests of its members and of the community, as Rotary or Kiwanis. **2.** *Especially U.S.* a recreation center for soldiers and sailors. **3.** *Especially British.* a men's club of members or retired members of the armed forces.

service command, an administrative and tactical division of the United States Army corresponding to an area of the world or a section of the United States in which troops are located.

service court, (in tennis, handball, etc.) the space of an opponent's court into which the ball must be served.

service flag, a flag with a star for each member of a family, school, organization, etc., in the U.S. Armed Forces during World War II.

service line, 1. a line drawn across a tennis court parallel to the net and 21 feet away from it to mark off the service court. **2.** a corresponding line in handball, jai alai, etc., drawn parallel to the wall or board.

serv·ice·man (sėr′vis man′, -mən), *n., pl.* **-men. 1.** a member of the armed forces. **2.** a person who maintains or repairs machinery or some kind of equipment: *The automobile serviceman has to work like a medical man* (Maclean's).

service mark, a mark or symbol used by a business or organization to distinguish its services from the services of others: *Service marks are to services what trademarks are to goods* (New York Times).

service medal, *U.S.* a medal for military service in a particular campaign or for a period of service.

service plate, a large dinner plate to hold other plates with food during the course of the meal: *A service plate is used at a formal dinner with a cocktail, soup, or fish course, or with a salad which is served as a separate course* (Helen Marley).

service road, 1. access road. **2.** a road, generally paralleling an expressway, to carry local traffic and to provide access to adjoining property.

serv·ic·es (sėr′vi siz), *n.pl.* See under **service**[1], *n.*

service side, (in court tennis) the side of the court from which service is made.

service station, 1. *U.S.* a place for supplying automobiles with gasoline, oil, water, etc. **2.** a place where repairs, parts, adjustments, etc., can be obtained for mechanical or electrical devices: *Towboats on the Mississippi can now pull into a "service station" here just about as easily as landlubbers pull into the corner garage* (Wall Street Journal).

service stripe, *U.S.* **1.** a diagonal stripe worn on the left sleeve of a uniform, to show three years of military service. **2.** a small stripe or bar worn on the sleeve of railroad conductors or other uniformed employees to show the number of years of service.

service tree, 1. a European, Asian, and African tree of the rose family, bearing a small, pear-shaped or round fruit called the serviceberry, sorb, or sorb apple, that is edible when overripe. 2. a closely related bush or small tree, the wild service tree, bearing harsh, bitter fruit; checker tree or sorb. 3. the shadbush; serviceberry.

serv·ice·wom·an (sėr′vis wu̇m′ən), *n., pl.* **-wom·en.** a female member of the armed forces.

Serv·i·dor (sėr′və dôr), *n. Trademark.* a cabinet, built in the door to a hotel room. It has a locked door on either side to permit clothes, etc., to be picked up or delivered without opening the main door to the room.

ser·vi·ent (sėr′vē ənt), *adj. Especially Law.* subordinate. [< Latin *serviēns, -entis,* present participle of *servīre* serve]

servient tenement, *Law.* a tenement which is subject to an easement in favor of a dominant tenement.

ser·vi·ette (sėr′vē et′), *n. Especially British.* a table napkin: *His serviette was tucked under his chin* (Arnold Bennett). [< Middle French *serviette* < Old French *servir* serve]

ser·vile (sėr′vəl), *adj.* 1. like that of slaves; mean; base: *servile flattery. I did not . . . aim at gaining his favor by paying any servile respect to him* (Benjamin Franklin). 2. of slaves; having to do with slaves: *a servile revolt, servile work.* 3. fit for a slave. 4. yielding through fear, lack of spirit, etc.: *An honest judge cannot be servile to public opinion.* 5. *Obsolete.* (of a people, state, etc.) politically enslaved. [< Latin *servīlis* < *servus* a slave] —**ser′vile·ly,** *adv.* —**ser′vile·ness,** *n.*
—**Syn.** 1. slavish, cringing, fawning, groveling. —**Ant.** 1. masterful, imperious, haughty.

ser·vil·i·ty (sėr vil′ə tē), *n., pl.* **-ties.** attitude or behavior fit for a slave; servile yielding: *Arrogance and servility, the common products of ignorance* (J.W.R. Scott).

serv·ing (sėr′ving), *n.* 1. the act of a person or thing that serves. 2. a portion of food or drink served to a person at one time; helping. 3. *Nautical.* a material used for serving a rope, etc.

serving board, *Nautical.* service board.

serving mallet, *Nautical.* a mallet-shaped piece of wood, used for serving ropes. It has a groove on one side to fit a rope.

serving man, a male servant.

Ser·vite (sėr′vīt), *n.* a mendicant friar or nun of a religious order founded in Italy in the 1200's, and following the rule of Saint Augustine. [< Medieval Latin *Servitae,* plural < Latin *servus* slave, servant]

ser·vi·tial (sėr vish′əl), *adj.* having to do with service, as that between servant and master or child and parent. [< Latin *servitium* service + English *-al*[1]]

ser·vi·tor (sėr′və tər), *n.* a servant; attendant: *My noble queen . . . henceforth I am thy true servitor* (Shakespeare). [< Old French *servitor,* learned borrowing from Late Latin *servitor* < Latin *servīre* serve]

ser·vi·to·ri·al (sėr′və tôr′ē əl, -tōr′-), *adj.* of or having to do with a servitor.

ser·vi·tor·ship (sėr′və tər ship), *n.* the position of a servitor.

ser·vi·tress (sėr′və tris), *n.* a woman servant or attendant.

ser·vi·tude (sėr′və tüd, -tyüd), *n.* 1. slavery; bondage: *A disturbed liberty is better than a quiet servitude* (Joseph Addison). 2. forced labor as a punishment: *The criminal was sentenced to five years' servitude.* 3. *Law.* a. the condition of property subject to a right of enjoyment possessed by some person other than its owner, or attaching to some other property. b. such a right of enjoyment. [< Old French *servitude,* learned borrowing from Latin *servitūdō, -inis* < *servus* a slave] —**Syn.** 1. enslavement, subjection.

ser·vo (sėr′vō), *n., pl.* **-vos,** *adj.* —*n.* 1. a servomechanism: *A knowledge of servos and environmental test gear would be an asset* (Observer). 2. servosystem. —*adj.* that uses a servomotor or is part of a servosystem: *a servo device.* [short for *servomechanism*]

servo brake, an automobile brake with shoes so connected that one shoe passes on the force exerted on it by the rotating drum to increase the action of the other.

ser·vo·con·trol (sėr′vō kən trōl′), *n.* any of various devices by which a supplementary source of power is activated to assist in the movement, manipulation, guidance, etc., of some equipment.

ser·vo·con·trolled (sėr′vō kən trōld′), *adj.* controlled or activated by a servocontrol or servosystem.

Ser·vo-Cro·a·tian (sėr′vō krō ā′shən), *adj., n.* Serbo-Croatian.

ser·vo·mech·a·nism (sėr′vō mek′ə niz-əm), *n.* 1. servocontrol. 2. servomotor: *I have said nothing about the servomechanisms and electronic "black boxes" which perform the various control functions* (New Scientist).

ser·vo·mo·tor (sėr′vō mō′tər), *n.* an auxiliary motor to supplement the primary source of power in the movement, guidance, etc., of a heavy or complex device: *The company's commercial items include various servomotors and other airborne components used in private and commercial aircraft* (Wall Street Journal). [< French *servo-moteur* < Latin *servus* slave + *mōtor* a mover]

ser·vo·sys·tem (sėr′vō sis′təm), *n.* a system of servocontrols or servomotors to move or guide a heavy or complex device.

Ser·vus ser·vo·rum De·i (sėr′vəs sėr vôr′-əm dē′ī, -vōr′-), *Latin.* servant of the servants of God (a title used by the Popes).

ses·a·me (ses′ə mē), *n.* 1. an Asian plant cultivated in tropical countries for its small seeds. 2. a. Also, **sesame seed.** its seeds, used to flavor bread, candy, and other foods. b. sesame oil. 3. a magic password; an open sesame: *No Tory, however wise, . . . could have obtained the sesame to those apartments* (Edward R. Bulwer-Lytton). [< Latin *sēsama, sēsamum* < Greek *sēsámon* < Semitic (compare Syriac *shushmâ*)]

SEEDS POD

Sesame (def. 1)

sesame oil, a bland, yellow oil extracted from sesame seeds, used in cooking, salads, medicine, and cosmetics.

ses·a·moid (ses′ə moid), *adj.* of or having to do with certain small, oval, nodular bones or cartilages, as in the kneecap. —*n.* a sesamoid bone or cartilage. [< Greek *sēsamoeidēs* < *sēsamon* (see SESAME) + *eîdos* form]

ses·a·mum (ses′ə məm), *n.* sesame. [< Latin *sēsamum;* see SESAME]

ses·qui·cen·ten·ni·al (ses′kwi sen ten′ē-əl), *n.* a 150th anniversary or its celebration: *The sesquicentennial of the Declaration of Independence was held in 1926.* —*adj.* having to do with, or marking the completion of, a period of a century and a half. [American English < Latin *sēsqui-* one and a half + English *centennial*]

ses·qui·ox·ide (ses′kwi ok′sīd), *n.* a compound of oxygen and another element in the proportion of three atoms of oxygen to two of the other. [< Latin *sēsqui-* one and a half + English *oxide*]

ses·quip·e·dal (ses kwip′ə dəl, ses′kwi-pē′-), *adj.* sesquipedalian.

ses·qui·pe·da·li·an (ses′kwi pə dā′lē ən), *adj.* 1. very long; containing many syllables. 2. using or given to using long words: *The words gathered size like snowballs, and towards the end of her letter Miss Jenkyns used to become quite sesquipedalian* (Elizabeth Gaskell). 3. measuring a foot and a half.
—*n.* a very long word.
[< Latin *sēsquipedālis* a foot and a half long (< *sēsqui-* one and a half + *pēs, pedis* foot) + English *-ian*]

ses·qui·pe·da·li·an·ism (ses′kwi pə dā′lē-ə niz′əm), *n.* the practice of using long words.

ses·qui·pe·dal·i·ty (ses′kwi pə dal′ə tē), *n.* sesquipedalianism.

sess , session.

ses·sile (ses′əl), *adj.* 1. a. *Botany.* attached by the base instead of by a stem, as a leaf having no petiole or a flower having no peduncle or pedicel: *If no style intervenes between the ovary and stigma, the stigma is said to be sessile, as in the poppy* (Heber W. Youngken). b. *Zoology.* attached by the base and having no connecting neck, as certain organs or animals: *Some barnacles are sessile.* 2. *Zoology.* sedentary; fixed to one spot; not able to move around, as barnacles and sponges: *A small group of about a dozen species of sessile, marine, wormlike animals . . . secrete a hard tube in which they dwell* (A.M. Winchester). [< Latin *sessilis* sitting < *sedēre* to sit]

Sessile Leaves (def. 1a)

ses·sil·i·ty (se sil′ə tē), *n.* the condition of being sessile.

ses·sion (sesh′ən), *n.* 1. a. a sitting or meeting of a court, council, legislature, etc.: *Congress is now in session.* b. a series of such sittings: *. . . the Administration's hopes and plans for the next session of Congress* (Time). c. the term or period of such sittings: *This year's session of Congress was unusually long.* 2. one of the periods of lessons and study into which a school day or year is divided: *the afternoon session, the summer session.* 3. any meeting: *a heated session with the head of the department. After 100 sessions, the entire group is better in health and better adjusted* (Newsweek). 4. *Archaic.* any sitting or being seated: *Vivien . . . Leapt from her session on his lap* (Tennyson).

in session, meeting: *The teachers were in session all Saturday morning.*

sessions, a. (in the United States) local courts dealing especially with lesser criminal offenses: *He was brought before the town court of sessions on a charge of petty larceny.* b. Also, **sessions of the peace.** (in Great Britain) periodic sittings held by justices of the peace: *A favourite at the Old Bailey, and eke at the sessions* (Dickens).
[< Latin *sessiō, -ōnis* < *sedēre* to sit]

ses·sion·al (sesh′ə nəl), *adj.* 1. of a session; having to do with sessions. 2. occurring every session.

ses·terce (ses′tėrs), *n.* an ancient Roman silver or brass coin of small value, worth 1/4 of a denarius. [< Latin *sēstertius* (originally) adjective, two and a half < *sēmis* half (< *sēmi-* half + *as* monetary unit) + *tertius* third]

ses·ter·ti·um (ses tėr′shē əm), *n., pl.* **-ti·a** (-shē ə). an ancient Roman unit of money equal to a thousand sesterces. [(erroneously formed as a neuter singular to Latin *sēstertia*) short for *mīlia sēstertium* thousands of sesterces]

ses·ter·ti·us (ses tėr′shē əs), *n., pl.* **-ti·i** (-shē ī). sesterce. [< Latin *sēstertius*]

ses·tet (ses tet′), *n.* 1. a musical sextet. 2. the last six lines of a sonnet, especially of an Italian or Petrarchan sonnet. [< Italian *sestetto* (diminutive) < *sesto* sixth < Latin *sextus* < *sex* six]

ses·ti·na (ses tē′nə), *n., pl.* **-nas, -ne** (-nā). a poem of six six-line stanzas and a concluding triplet. The last words of the first stanza are repeated in the other five stanzas in different order, and in the concluding triplet. *John Ashbery, in his first book, . . . comes up with a canzone, a pantoum, a sestina, and an eccentric sonnet* (New Yorker). [< Italian *sestina* < *sesto;* see SESTET]

Se·su·to (se sü′tō), *n.* the Bantu language of the Basuto people.

set (set), *v.,* **set, set·ting,** *adj., n.* —*v.t.* 1. to put in some place; put; place: *to set a box on its end, to set a lamp on the table.* 2. a. to put in the right place, position, or condition: *to set a broken bone. The hunters set traps. Set the table for dinner.* b. to arrange (the hair) when damp to make it take a certain position. c. to raise or adjust (sails) to catch the wind. 3. to adjust according to a standard: *to set a clock.* 4. to cause to be; put in some condition or relation: *to set someone at ease, to set a prisoner free. A spark set the woods on fire. . . . the subtle strings that set the wheels of the whole world in motion* (Lytton Strachey). 5. a. to put (a price, etc.); fix the value of at a certain amount or rate: *He set the value of the watch at $500.* b. to put (a sum) down as a stake; bet: *to set $5 on a horse to win.* 6. to put as the measure of esteem of a person or thing: *to set more by action than by talk.* 7. to post, appoint, or station for the purpose of performing some duty: *to set a detective on a person.* 8. a. to fix; arrange; appoint: *to set a time limit for taking an examination, to set the rules for the contest, to set the stage for the scene in a play, to set the scene for negotiations.* b. to allot or assign: *to set a difficult job for oneself.* 9. to provide for others to follow: *to set a good example, to set a pace, to set the fashion.* 10. to put in a fixed, rigid, or settled state; fix: *to set one's teeth, to set one's heart on something. If he sets his mind on it, he will do it.* 11. to make firm or hard: *to set mortar, to set the white of an egg by boiling it.* 12. to put in a frame or other thing that holds: *The windows were set in stone. The jeweler set a diamond in gold.* 13. to adorn; ornament: *to set a bracelet* *with diamonds.* **14. a.** to put (a hen) to sit on eggs to hatch them. **b.** to place (eggs) under a hen or in an incubator, to be hatched. **15.** to encourage to attack; cause to be hostile: *He set his dogs upon the prowler.* **16.** to cause to take a particular direction; direct: *to set one's feet homeward.* **17.** (of a dog) to mark the position of (game) by stopping and pointing the muzzle. **18.** *Music.* **a.** to adapt; fit: *to set words to music.* **b.** to arrange (music) for certain voices or instruments. **19.** *Printing.* to put (type) in the order required: *Walt Whitman set the type himself for his "Leaves of Grass."* **20.** to make (a color of fabrics, etc.) fast. **21.** to adjust (a machine, instrument, or one of the parts) to work properly or maintain a certain position: *to set the focus of a microscope, to set a wheel.* **22.** to give a sharp edge to (a blade): *to set a razor.* **23.** to change into curd; curdle, as milk. **24.** to mix (batter, dough, etc., containing yeast) and leave it to rise. **25.** to remove the wrinkles from (an animal hide or leather) by pressing: *The hides are set or put through a machine which presses out the wrinkles and in general smooths the leather to a uniform evenness* (August C. Orthmann). **26.** (in cards) to put down or defeat (a contract): *West was able to set the contract with his two aces and long trump.*

—*v.i.* **1.** to hang or fit in a particular manner: *That coat sets well.* **2.** to go down; sink; wane: *The sun sets in the west. His power has begun to set.* **3.** to begin to move: *He set across the river.* **4.** to make an attack: *The Indians set upon the wagon train just before nightfall.* **5.** to begin to apply; begin to apply oneself: *Have you set to work?* **6.** to become fixed; become firm or hard: *Jelly sets as it cools.* **7.** to be arranged; be fixed: *His face is set in stern lines.* **8.** (of the wind, a current, etc.) to have a direction; tend: *The current sets to the south.* **9.** (of a hen) to sit on eggs. **10.** (of color) to become fast and permanent. **11.** to form fruit in the blossom: *The blossoms were abundant, but they failed to set.* **12.** (of a dog) to indicate the position of game by standing stiffly and pointing with the nose.

set about, to start work upon; begin: *to set about one's business. Set about your washing.*

set against, a. to make unfriendly toward; cause to be hostile: *They set his friends against him.* **b.** to balance; compare: *Setting the probabilities of the story against the credit of the witnesses* (Henry Brougham).

set apart, to reserve: *to set some food apart for winter.*

set aside, a. to put to one side: *Set this aside, till I call for it* (Jehan Palsgrave). **b.** to put by for later use; reserve: *to set money aside for one's education.* **c.** to discard; dismiss or leave out; reject; annul: *Sometimes a higher court sets aside the decision in a lawsuit.*

set back, a. to stop; hinder; check: *All his efforts were set back.* **b.** *U.S. Informal.* to cost (a person) so much: *The new car set him back a lot of money.*

set down, a. to deposit or let alight; put down: *to set down a suitcase. The bus set him down near town.* **b.** to put down in writing or printing: *to set down a story.* **c.** to consider; ascribe: *to set someone's actions down to ignorance.*

set forth, a. to make known; express; declare: *to set forth one's opinions on a subject.* **b.** to start to go: *to set forth on a trip.*

set in, a. to begin: *Winter set in.* **b.** to blow or flow toward the shore: *The current of the flood set in close by the shore* (Daniel Defoe).

set loose, to release; let go; set free: *The horses were set loose from the stables to graze and roam in the fields.*

set off, a. to cause to go off; explode: *to set off a charge of dynamite.* **b.** to start to go: *Sir Robert set off on a week's tour of his new domain* (Manchester Guardian Weekly). **c.** to touch off; instigate: *The war against Red guerrilla units ... set off the heaviest fighting in many months* (Wall Street Journal). **d.** to counterbalance; compensate: *The loss feared in one branch ... would be set off by a gain in the other* (London Times). **e.** to show to advantage; enhance: *Dress helped to set off her many charms* (Temple Bar). **f.** to allot or assign, especially for some special purpose away from the rest: *A part of the hospital was set off for the care of contagious disease.*

set on, a. to attack: *The dog set on him.* **b.** to urge to attack: *Prospero and Ariel setting them on* (Shakespeare).

set out, a. to start to go: *They set out on the hike with plenty of water.* **b.** to spread out to show, sell, or use: *to set out a flag, to set out goods for sale.* **c.** to plant: *to set out tomato plants in the spring.* **d.** to plan; intend (to do something): *to set out to reform the courts. The Treasury did not set out consciously to reduce the debt* (New York Times). **e.** to put down: *The communiqué set out what it was thought right to set out as the result of the discussions* (London Times).

set right, a. to restore to the right condition: *It would set him right in their eyes* (H.G. Wells). **b.** to correct: *to set errors right. I ... found myself capable of setting him right as to many of his antiquated notions* (Washington Irving).

set to, a. to begin: *to set to work.* **b.** to begin fighting: *The two boys set to.*

set up, a. to build; erect: *to set up a monument.* **b.** to begin; start: *Scholarships should be set up by the local colleges to enable the Southern teachers to obtain ... additional credits* (New York Times). **c.** to assemble: *Flemish weavers set up their looms and taught the English to weave cloth* (M. J. Guest). **d.** to put up; raise in place, position, power, pride, etc.: *They set him up above his rivals.* **e.** to raise; utter: *to set up a cry.* **f.** to claim; pretend: *to set up to be honest.*

set upon, to fall upon a person or enemy without warning; attack: *The marines were set upon by snipers* (New York Times).

—*adj.* **1. a.** fixed or appointed beforehand; established: *a set time, set rules, a set speech.* **b.** prepared; ready: *A bipartisan group of Northern liberals is set to try again for Federal aid to school construction* (Newsweek). **2.** fixed; rigid: *a set smile.* **3.** firm; hard. **4.** resolved; determined: *He is set on going today.* **5.** *Informal.* stubbornly fixed; obstinate: *She's an old maid and kind o' set in her ways* (Harriet Beecher Stowe). **6.** (of a kind of weather) persistent: *set snows.* **7.** having a specified build, look, etc.: *deep-set eyes.*

all set, *Informal.* fully prepared; ready: *She was all set to leave for Europe when she took sick and had to cancel her trip.*

—*n.* **1. a.** a number of things belonging together; outfit: *a set of teeth, a set of furniture, a set of tools, a set of dishes.* **b.** a set of furniture: *a dining-room set.* **c.** books, usually by the same author, or covering the same subject, or of the same type: *a set of Dickens, a set of plays.* **2.** a number of people with similar habits, interests, the same occupation, etc.: *a golfing set, a fast set. And this, at least according to Spens's translation, is how the Socrates set talked at meals* (Atlantic). **3.** a device for receiving or sending by radio, telephone, telegraph, etc. **4. a.** the scenery of a play or scene; setting: *The set ... shows an impoverished attic room, with a mean bed and table, a telephone, and a huge curtained window* (New Yorker). **b.** the scenery for a motion picture: *With all its championship furnishings Cortina, a popular resort ... took on the freshly built look of a Hollywood set* (Newsweek). **5.** the way a thing or person is put or placed; form; shape: *a man of heavy set. His jaw had a stubborn set.* **6.** a direction; tendency; course; drift: *The set of opinion was toward building a new bridge.* **7.** the arrangement of the hair after it has been dampened. **8.** warp; bend; displacement: *a set to the right. The specimen does not return to its original length but retains a permanent strain or a set* (Sears and Zemansky). **9.** a slip or shoot for planting: *onion sets.* **10.** a young fruit just formed from a blossom. **11.** the act or manner of setting. **12.** a group of six or more games in tennis. One side must win six games and at least two more than the other side. *It was decided that the match would be for the best seven of thirteen sets* (New Yorker). **13.** the way in which anything fits: *the set of a coat.* **14.** the direction in which a current flows or a wind blows. **15.** a dog's pointing in the presence of game: *Brownie got her set. She held it and we hurried* (New Yorker). **16. a.** the number of couples required for a square dance. **b.** the figures of a square dance. **17.** a clutch of eggs. **18.** the lateral bending of the teeth of a saw. **19.** *Psychology.* a temporary condition of an organism making a certain type of response or activity easier. **20.** *Philately.* stamps of similar subject matter: *"I've brought you some stamps ... And here's a complete set of Liberians"* (Graham Greene). **21.** *Mathematics.* a group of numbers, points, or other elements having common properties: *The number 3 belongs to the set of prime numbers.* **22.** *Basketball.* a set shot.

[Old English *settan.* Related to SIT.]

—**Syn.** *v.t.* **1, 4.** See **put. 8. b.** prescribe. —*v.i.* **2.** decline. —*adj.* **1. a.** determined, prescribed. —*n.* **1. a.** collection, group.

➔ **set, sit.** People and things sit (past, *sat*) or they are *set* (past, *set*), meaning placed: *I like to sit in a hotel lobby. I have sat in this same seat for a long time. She set the soup down with a flourish. The post was set three feet in the ground.* A hen, however *sets* (on her eggs).

Set (set), *n.* the ancient Egyptian god of evil, who oppressed souls after death. He was represented as having an animal's head with a pointed snout.

SET (no periods) or **S.E.T.,** *British.* Selective Employment Tax.

se·ta (sē′tə), *n., pl.* **-tae** (-tē). *Biology.* any slender, stiff, bristlelike structure: *Earthworms have two pairs of setae on each segment.* [< Latin *sēta, saeta* bristle]

se·ta·ceous (si tā′shəs), *adj. Biology.* **1.** bristlelike; bristle-shaped. **2.** furnished with bristles; bristly. [< New Latin *setaceus* (with English *-ous*) < Latin *sēta* bristle]

SETAF (no periods), Southern European Task Force (a division of NATO).

se·tal (sē′təl), *adj.* of or having to do with setae.

set-a·side (set′ə sīd′), *n. U.S.* **1.** raw materials, food, etc., reserved by federal order, especially for the use of the armed forces: *The Office of Defense Mobilization ordered smaller set-asides of aluminum, copper, steel and nickel alloys for military production* (Wall Street Journal). **2.** anything put in reserve.

set·back (set′bak′), *n.* **1.** a check to progress; reverse: *a temporary setback in one's fortunes, an unexpected setback in a patient's recovery.* **2.** a setting back at different heights of the outside wall in a tall building to give better light and air in the street. **3.** a lessening in the thickness of a wall. **4.** a flat, plain projection of a wall. —**Syn. 1.** relapse, retardation.

Setbacks (def. 2) on office building

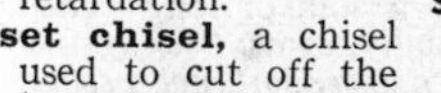

set chisel, a chisel used to cut off the heads of rivets and bolts.

set·down (set′doun′), *n.* a humiliating rebuke or rebuff: *I wish you had been there ... to have given him one of your setdowns* (Jane Austen).

Seth (seth), *n.* (in the Bible) the third son of Adam. Genesis 4:25.

se·tif·er·ous (si tif′ər əs), *adj.* having setae. [< Latin *sēta* bristle + English *-ferous*]

se·ti·form (sē′tə fôrm), *adj.* shaped like setae: *The antennae of a dragonfly are setiform.* [< Latin *sēta* bristle]

se·tig·er·ous (si tij′ər əs), *adj. Zoology.* setaceous: *the setigerous growth on the skin of pigs.* [< Latin *sētiger* (< *sēta* bristle + *gerere* to bear) + English *-ous*]

set-in (set′in′), *adj.* sewn into a garment as a separate piece.

se·tip·a·rous (si tip′ər əs), *adj.* producing setae. [< Latin *sēta* bristle + *parere* give birth + English *-ous*]

set·line (set′līn′), *n.* **1.** a long fish line having short lines and baited hooks attached, laid on the bottom, its ends anchored. **2.** a trotline.

set·off (set′ôf′, -of′), *n.* **1.** a setting off on a trip; start; departure. **2.** a thing used to set off or adorn; ornament; decoration. **3.** something that counterbalances or makes up for something else; compensation; offset. **4. a.** the settlement of a debt by means of a claim in the debtor's favor. **b.** a claim so used. **5.** a setback on a building. —**Syn. 2.** trimming.

se·ton (sē′tən), *n. Obsolete.* **1.** thread or horsehair inserted beneath the skin to keep open an artificial passage or issue. **2.** the passage or issue. [< Medieval Latin *seto, -onis* < *seta* silk < Latin *sēta* bristle]

se·tose (sē′tōs, si tōs′), *adj.* bristly; setaceous. [< Latin *sētōsus* < *sēta* bristle]

set·out (set′out′), *n.* **1.** a start; outset: *The parties were pretty equal at the setout* (Byron). **2. a.** a display, as of a set of china. **b.** a spread of food; buffet. **3.** an entertainment for a group of people; party: *This was a very different setout, a children-and-parents party with a puppet show* (New Yorker). **4.** a person's costume or get-up. **5.** a turnout, such as a carriage with its horses, harness, etc. **6.** outfit; equipment.

set piece, 1. a usually formal or stylized scene in a painting, story, play, motion picture, etc., often written or painted to tell a story of its own. **2.** a set scene.

set point, 1. the established point that determines a set of variables or frame of reference for the quantity being controlled: *The control engineer . . . would expect the body's temperature control system to have a "set point," but this cannot easily be established physiologically* (New Scientist). **2.** the concluding point that is needed to win a set in tennis.

set scene, *Theater.* a stage set not painted on a flat or drop.

set·screw (set′skrü′), *n.* a machine screw used to fasten gears, pulleys, etc., to a shaft: *Three setscrews permit accurate adjustment in level* (World Book Encyclopedia).

Setscrews
From top to bottom: square, headless slotted, and socket

set shot, *Basketball.* a long shot at the basket, usually from beyond the foul line or from a corner with the player standing still: *He will have to develop a variety of offensive skills: hooks and jump shots from close in, set shots from the outside, driving lay-ups . . .* (Time).

set square, a flat triangular instrument, with one right angle and the other angles of either 60° and 30° or both of 45°, used in mechanical or architectural drawing.

sett (set), *n. Archaic.* set (still used in certain technical senses): *These "fancy figures," . . . became popular as the last dance in a "sett"* (New Yorker).

set·ta·ble (set′ə bəl), *adj.* that can be set.

set·te·cen·to (set′tā chen′tō), *n.* the 1700's (used especially in connection with a period of Italian art and literature). [< Italian *settecento* seven hundred, short for *millesettecento* one thousand and seven hundred]

set·tee[1] (se tē′), *n.* a sofa or long bench with a back and, usually, arms: *Over against one wall was . . . not a davenport, not a settee, but simply a battered old leather couch* (Robert Traver). [perhaps a variant of *settle*[2]]

set·tee[2] (se tē′), *n.* a ship having a long, sharp bow and two or three masts with lateen sails, used on the Mediterranean. [alteration of Italian *saettia*]

set·ter (set′ər), *n.* **1.** a person or thing that sets: *a setter of type, a setter of jewels.* **2.** a long-haired hunting dog trained to stand motionless and point his nose toward the game that he scents, as the Irish setter and English setter.

set theory, a mathematical system or theory that deals with sets, their properties, and their relationships: *Set theory is widely used in teaching to demonstrate how things can be grouped and how groups are related to one another* (Scientific American).

set·ting (set′ing), *n.* **1.** a frame or other thing in which something is set: *The mounting of a jewel is its setting.* **2. a.** the scenery of a play, including the lighting and other things that contribute to the play. **b.** a single scene or set. **3.** the place, time, etc., of a play or story. **4.** surroundings; background: *a fashionable setting, against a lofty mountain setting.* **5. a.** music composed to go with certain words. **b.** music composed or arranged for particular instruments: *a symphonic setting.* **6.** the eggs that a hen sets on for hatching: *He had been given the hen while she was broody and had bought a setting of New Hampshire eggs to put under her* (George Johnston). **7.** the act of a person or thing that sets. —**Syn. 6.** clutch.

setting hammer, 1. a tinsmith's hammer, having a square head and a chisel-shaped peen. **2.** a specially shaped light hammer to swage the teeth of saws in setting them.

setting point, the place or point at which an adjustment or setting can be made in a mechanism.

setting screw, 1. a screw by which cams or timing devices may be adjusted to work as desired. **2.** a setscrew.

set·ting-up exercises (set′ing up′), exercises that require no equipment, as push-ups, sit-ups, etc.; calisthenics.

set·tle[1] (set′əl), *v.*, **-tled, -tling.** —*v.t.* **1. a.** to make a decision on; decide: *to settle an argument. The lama waved a hand to show that the matter was finally settled in his mind* (Rudyard Kipling). **b.** to agree upon (a time, place, plan, etc.); fix beforehand: *to settle a course of action, Thus, the preliminaries settled . . .* (William Cowper). **2.** to put in order; arrange: *I must settle all my affairs before going away for the winter.* **3.** to pay; arrange payment of: *to settle a bill.* **4.** to cause to take up residence in a place, especially a new country, town, etc.: *to settle one's family in the country.* **5.** to establish colonies in; colonize: *The English settled New England.* **6.** to set in a fairly permanent position, place, or way of life: *to settle one's son in business. We quickly settled ourselves in our new house.* **7.** to arrange in a desired or comfortable position; adjust: *to settle one's feet in the stirrups. The cat settled herself in the chair.* **8.** to make quiet: *A vacation will settle your nerves.* **9.** to cause to sink down: *The end of that wall has settled four inches.* **10.** to make (a liquid) clear: *A beaten egg or cold water will settle coffee.* **11.** to cause (dregs or other impurities) to sink to the bottom. **12.** to make firm and compact; cause to subside into a solid or more compact mass: *to settle the contents of a barrel, to settle soil by watering it.* **13.** *Law.* to decide (a case) by arrangement between the parties.

—*v.i.* **1. a.** to come to a conclusion; resolve: *Have you settled on a time for leaving?* **b.** to arrange matters in dispute; come to terms or agreement (with): *to settle with a union.* **2.** to be put in order, especially by closing an account (with). **3.** to take up residence (in a new country or place): *to settle in New York.* **4.** (of a bird or insect) to alight: *Flies everywhere settled in clouds, and the hospital was full of malaria patients* (Graham Greene). **5.** to be set in a fairly permanent position, place, or way of life: *He settled into his new position at the company very quickly.* **6. a.** to come to rest in a particular place; lodge: *A heavy fog settled over the airport.* **b.** to come to a definite condition: *His cold settled in his lungs. The elements of war are often gradually accumulating before they settle into an open rupture* (Benjamin Disraeli). **7.** to come to a desired or comfortable position. **8.** to become quiet or composed: *The children were too excited with their Christmas presents to settle at once.* **9.** to go down; sink gradually, especially by its own weight: *The house settled after a time and the walls began to crack.* **10.** (of a liquid) to become clear by depositing dregs or impurities. **11.** (of dregs) to sink to the bottom. **12.** to become firm and compact, as soil.

settle down, a. to live a more regular life: *Botanizing, music, writing the first chapters of his Confessions, Rousseau seemed to be settling down at Wootton* (Listener). **b.** to direct steady effort or attention: *When he finally settled down to his work he managed to complete it in two hours.* **c.** to calm down; become quiet: *The baby kept crying and refused to settle down.*

settle for, to be content with; agree upon; accept, often less than one wanted: *But neither the star nor the composer was willing to settle for that kind of routine triumph* (Henry Hewes).

settle on or **upon,** to give (property, a right, etc.) to by law: *The day that Miss Rayne becomes Lady Coombe, I will settle a thousand a year on her for her private use* (Florence Marryat).

[Old English *setlan* < *setl*; see SETTLE[2]]

—**Syn.** *v.t.* **1.b, 2.** set. See **fix.** -*v.i.*, *v.i.* **8.** compose, calm.

set·tle[2] (set′əl), *n.* a long bench: *The man on the settle waited a minute, and then got up and passed the length of the bar . . .* (Geoffrey Household). [Old English *setl* a sitting place; an abode]

Settle[2]

set·tled (set′əld), *adj.* **1.** fixed in place or position; having a fixed home: *Most Indians never were settled people until the government set up reservations.* **2.** populated: *a densely settled region.* **3.** fixed or established: *. . . the settled course of things* (Joseph Butler). **4.** placed on a permanent basis, as government. **5.** maintained or continuing without change: *settled fair weather.* **6.** fixed; firmly seated; unchanging: *. . . his old buoyancy and confidence gave way to something like settled gloom* (Edmund Wilson). **7. a.** steadfast, staid, or sober, as the character, mind, etc. **b.** indicating such a character, as the countenance. **8. a.** established in a regular way of life, or in fixed ways: *a settled married man, a settled old woman.* **b.** steady or orderly: *the settled life of an old man.* **9.** established in an office, charge, etc. **10.** secured to a person by a legal act or process, as an estate or property. **11. a.** appointed or fixed definitely, as a time, etc. **b.** decided definitely, as a question or a matter in doubt. **12.** adjusted or closed, as an account by payment. —**set′tled·ness,** *n.*

set·tle·ment (set′əl mənt), *n.* **1.** the act of settling. **2.** the state of being settled. **3.** the establishment of a person in life, in marriage, in employment, etc., or of oneself in a fixed place, a permanent residence, etc. **4.** a deciding or determining of a time, question, dispute, etc.: *the settlement of a date. Until a compromise settlement was achieved, that issue alone prolonged the strike for almost a month* (Newsweek). **5. a.** a putting in order; arrangement: *Dulles publicly "dissociated" the U.S. from the settlement* (Newsweek). **b.** the resulting condition of affairs; an established order of things. **6.** the payment of an account: *Settlement of all claims against the firm will be made shortly.* **7.** the settling of persons in a new country or area; colonization: *the settlement of the Dutch in New Amsterdam.* **8.** a colony: *England had many settlements along the Atlantic Coast.* **9.** a group of buildings and the people living in them: *Indians often attacked the little settlements of the colonists.* **10.** a place in a poor, neglected neighborhood where work for its improvement is carried on: *Hull House is a famous settlement on the west side of Chicago.* **11. a.** the settling of property upon someone: *She received $200,000 by a marriage settlement.* **b.** the amount so given: *As to his own settlement, the Duke observed that he would expect the Duke of York's marriage to be considered the precedent* (Lytton Strachey). **12.** legal residence. **13.** a gradual sinking or subsidence of a structure, etc.

settlements, breaks or other damage caused by the settlement of a building or structure: *They complained to the builder about the extent of the house's settlements.*

set·tle·ment-work·er (set′əl mənt wėr′kər), *n.* a person who gives his time to help in the work of a neighborhood settlement.

set·tler (set′lər), *n.* **1.** a person who settles in a new country, an undeveloped region, etc.: *the original settlers of America.* **2.** a person who settles: *a settler of disputes.* **3.** *Law.* a person who settles property on someone. —**Syn. 1.** colonist.

settler's twine, a grasslike plant of the arum family, used by pioneers in New South Wales and Queensland as cord or string.

set·tling (set′ling), *n.* **1. a.** the act of a thing that settles; sinking down: *As the new house begins to age, its parts begin to shrink, stretch, bend, shift, and crack. This natural process is called "settling"* (New York Times). **b.** the result of this. **2.** the act of a person who settles.

settlings, things in a liquid which settle to the bottom; sediment; dregs: *Yet 'tis but the lees and settlings of a melancholy blood* (Milton).

settling tank, a tank for holding a liquid until the suspended matter or sediment settles: *The Duke of a century ago was a believer in large reserves, for he installed settling tanks sufficient for 300 acres* (New Scientist).

set·tlor (set′lər), *n. Law.* a person who settles property on someone. Also, **settler.**

set-to (set′tü′), *n., pl.* **-tos.** *Informal.* **1.** a fight; dispute: *a sudden set-to between two children. As India watches our current set-to with China, her ideals tend to push her to the Chinese side* (New Yorker). **2.** a contest; match; bout: *Such bi-weekly set-tos are a "reformed" remnant of medieval tournaments* (Time). [< *set to*, idiom]

set·up (set′up′), *n.* **1. a.** an arrangement of apparatus, machinery, etc.: *But before*

Chicago can reap the benefits . . . of increased trade, it must practically rebuild its entire port setup (Newsweek). **b.** the arrangement of an organization: *an efficient setup, to learn the setup of a company.* **2.** *U.S. Informal.* **a.** a glass and ice cubes, often with carbonated water, ginger ale, etc., for a person to mix an alcoholic drink for himself. **b.** a place setting for a customer in a restaurant. **3.** *Slang.* **a.** a contest or match where the outcome is assured. **b.** anything that is very easy to do or whose outcome is readily predictable: *That job would be a setup for any good carpenter. This release from . . . obligatory reading has resulted in a euphoria that makes me a setup for a book* (Harper's). **4.** *U.S. Archaic.* the manner of holding the head and body; carriage.

sève (sev), *n. French.* the special flavor and aroma of a wine.

sev·en (sev′ən), *adj.* being one more than six. —*n.* **1.** one more than six; 7. **2.** a playing card, throw of the dice, etc., with seven spots. [Old English *seofon*]

Sev·en (sev′ən), *n.* the original seven members of the EFTA (European Free Trade Association); Outer Seven.

Seven against Thebes, *Greek Legend.* the seven heroes, Adrastus, Amphiaraus, Capaneus, Hippomedon, Parthenopaeus, Polynices, and Tydeus, who made an expedition against Thebes to put Polynices on the throne.

sev·en-a-side (sev′ən ə sīd′), *n.* (in Rugby) a game or match played with seven men on each side.

seven champions of Christendom, (in medieval tales) the national saints of England, Scotland, Wales, Ireland, France, Spain, and Italy (George, Andrew, David, Patrick, Denis, James, and Anthony).

seven deadly sins, pride, covetousness, lust, anger, gluttony, envy, sloth.

sev·en·fold (sev′ən fōld′), *adv.* **1.** seven times as much or as many. **2.** seven times as much or as often; in the proportion of seven to one.
—*adj.* **1.** seven times as much or as many: *Last year's total was . . . about a sevenfold increase* (Newsweek). **2.** having seven parts.

Seven Hills, the hills upon and about which ancient Rome was built (the Aventine, Caelian, Capitoline, Esquiline, Palatine, Quirinal, and Viminal).

sev·en-league boots (sev′ən lēg′), the magical boots in the fairy tale of Hop o'my Thumb, which enabled the wearer to cover seven leagues at each stride.

seven liberal arts, the seven studies which constituted the quadrivium and trivium of the Middle Ages.

seven seas or **Seven Seas,** all the oceans (the Arctic, Antarctic, North Atlantic, South Atlantic, North Pacific, South Pacific, and Indian oceans): *to sail the seven seas.*

sev·en·teen (sev′ən tēn′), *n., adj.* seven more than ten; 17. [Old English *seofontēne*]

sev·en·teenth (sev′ən tēnth′), *adj., n.* **1.** next after the 16th; last in a series of 17. **2.** one, or being one, of 17 equal parts.

sev·en·teen-year locust (sev′ən tēn′yir′), a cicada that requires about seventeen years to develop from egg to adult. The larva burrows underground and feeds on roots, emerging after seventeen years to live a short time as an adult. *Seventeen-year locusts . . . climb trees in the summer and produce a lonesome continuous singing* (A.M. Winchester).

Seventeen-year Locust (1¼ in. long)

sev·enth (sev′ənth), *adj.* **1.** next after the sixth; last in a series of 7: *Saturday is the seventh day of the week.* **2.** being one of 7 equal parts.
—*n.* **1.** next after the sixth; last in a series of 7. **2.** one of 7 equal parts: *A day is one seventh of a week.* **3.** *Music.* **a.** the interval between two tones that are seven degrees apart. **b.** the harmonic combination of two such tones. **c.** the seventh tone of a scale.

seventh chord, *Music.* a chord consisting of a fundamental tone together with its third, fifth, and seventh.

sev·enth-day or **Sev·enth-Day** (sev′ənth dā′), *adj.* **1.** of, having to do with, or belonging to any of several Christian denominations observing Saturday, the seventh day of the week, as the principal day of rest and religious observance: *Seventh-Day Adventists of New York and New England gave $10,556,633 in tithes and foreign-mission offerings in the last four years* (New York Times). **2.** of or having to do with the seventh day, especially as the Sabbath.

seventh heaven, 1. the highest place or condition of joy and happiness. **2.** the highest part of heaven.

sev·enth·ly (sev′ənth lē), *adv.* in the seventh place.

sev·en·ti·eth (sev′ən tē ith), *adj., n.* **1.** next after the 69th; last in a series of 70. **2.** one, or being one, of 70 equal parts.

sev·en·ty (sev′ən tē), *n., pl.* **-ties,** *adj.* —*n.* seven times ten; 70.
the Seventy, a. the scholars who translated the Septuagint into Greek: *The Seventy render it . . . "ta glyptà," by which they understand graven images* (Edward Stillingfleet). **b.** (in the Bible) the disciples appointed by Jesus to preach the gospel. Luke 10:1-20: *Matthias . . . was one of the Seventy that was chosen and ordained by the other Apostles to succeed Judas in the Apostolate* (John Scott). **c.** the Great Sanhedrin: *The thief was brought before the Seventy for trial.*
—*adj.* seven times ten; 70.
[Old English *seofontig,* short for *hundseofontig*]

sev·en·ty-five (sev′ən tē fīv′), *n.* a 75-millimeter gun, especially the standard artillery piece of the French in World War I.

sev·en·ty·fold (sev′ən tē fōld′), *adj., adv.* **1.** 70 times as many. **2.** 70 times as much.

sev·en-up (sev′ən up′), *n.* a card game for two or more players, to each of whom six cards are dealt, in which there are four special chances of scoring a point, seven points constituting a game.

Seven Wonders of the World, the seven most remarkable structures of ancient times (the Egyptian Pyramids, the Mausoleum at Halicarnassus, the Temple of Artemis at Ephesus, the walls and hanging gardens of Babylon, the Colossus of Rhodes, the statue of Zeus by Phidias at Olympia, and the Pharos (lighthouse) at Alexandria).

sev·er (sev′ər), *v.t.* **1.** to cut apart; cut off: *to sever a rope. The ax severed the branch from the trunk.* **2.** to break off: *The two countries severed friendly relations.* —*v.i.* to part; divide; separate: *The church severed into two factions. The frayed rope suddenly severed and the swing fell down. Ae fond kiss and then we sever* (Robert Burns). [< Anglo-French *severer,* Old French *sevrer* < Vulgar Latin *sēperāre,* for Latin *sēparāre* to separate]

sev·er·a·bil·i·ty (sev′ər ə bil′ə tē, sev′rə-), *n.* the quality or condition of being severable.

sev·er·a·ble (sev′ər ə bəl, sev′rə-), *adj.* **1.** that can be severed or separated. **2.** *Law.* that can be separated into distinct rights or obligations.

sev·er·al (sev′ər əl, sev′rəl), *adj.* **1.** being more than two or three but not many; some; a few: *to gain several pounds. Some of the men . . . remembered . . . to have seen several strangers on the road* (Robert Louis Stevenson). **2.** individual; respective; different: *The boys went their several ways.* **3.** considered separately as distinct or single: *The several steps in the process of making paper were shown in a movie.* **4.** *Law.* binding or bound separately or distinctly. **5.** *Archaic.* different: *. . . three several times astonished* (George Eliot). **6.** *Archaic.* single.
—*n.* more than two or three but not many; some; a few: *Several have given their consent.*
[< Anglo-French *several* < Medieval Latin *seperalis, separalis* < Latin *sēpar, -aris* distinct < *sēparāre* to separate]

sev·er·al·fold (sev′ər əl fōld′, sev′rəl-), *adv., adj.* several times as much or as many: *It is possible to reduce those effects several-fold* (Scientific American). *It has led to a several-fold increase in yields since 1910* (New Scientist).

sev·er·al·ly (sev′ər ə lē, sev′rə-), *adv.* **1.** separately; singly; individually: *Consider these points, first severally and then collectively. He turned severally to each for their opinion* (Oliver Goldsmith). **2.** respectively. **3.** *Archaic.* apart from others; independently.

sev·er·al·ty (sev′ər əl tē, sev′rəl-), *n., pl.* **-ties. 1.** the state of being separate or distinct. **2.** the condition of being held or owned by separate or individual rights. **3.** land so held.
in severalty, *Law.* in a person's own right without being joined in interest by another: *They hold their shares in severalty.*

sev·er·ance (sev′ər əns, sev′rəns), *n.* **1.** a severing. **2.** a being severed; separation; division. **3.** a breaking off: *the severance of diplomatic relations between two countries.* [< Anglo-French *severance,* Old French *sevrance* < *sevrer* to sever]

severance pay, additional pay granted to employees that are leaving a business, company, etc., based on length of service: *Some actors didn't fit their roles, and had to be dismissed with severance pay* (Newsweek).

severance tax, *U.S.* a tax on the amount of ore, oil, gas, timber, etc., processed during a certain period, levied on producers in certain states: *Not only is there no severance tax, but Wyoming has no personal or corporate income tax and no bonded indebtedness* (Time).

se·vere (sə vir′), *adj.,* **-ver·er, -ver·est. 1.** very strict; stern; harsh: *severe self-denial. The judge imposed a severe sentence on the criminal.* **2.** serious; grave: *a severe illness.* **3.** very plain or simple; without ornament: *She has a severe haircut like a boy's.* **4.** sharp; violent: *severe criticism, severe pain, a severe winter.* **5.** difficult; taxing: *The new gun had to pass a series of severe tests.* **6.** rigidly exact, accurate, or methodical: *severe reasoning.* [< Latin *sevērus*] —**se·vere′ly,** *adv.* —**se·vere′ness,** *n.*
—**Syn. 1. Severe, stern** mean strict or hard, especially in holding to rules or standards and in enforcing order and obedience. **Severe** applies to things as well as people, and implies unvarying strictness verging on harshness and totally lacking in sympathy: *His parents are severe.* **Stern** implies hardness of manner and appearance, sometimes assumed only for the occasion: *The coach is stern when boys break training.* **3.** chaste, unadorned. **5.** exacting. **6.** precise, rigid.

se·ver·i·ty (sə ver′ə tē), *n., pl.* **-ties. 1.** strictness; sternness; harshness: *The children feared their new neighbor because of his severity.* **2.** simplicity of style or taste; plainness: *The severity of a nun's dress is often becoming.* **3.** violence; sharpness: *the severity of storms, pain, disease, or grief, etc.* **4.** seriousness; gravity. **5.** accuracy; exactness. **6.** something severe.

se·vil·la·na (sä′vēl yä′nä), *n.* the form of seguidilla performed in Seville, Spain. [< Spanish *sevillana* (literally) of Seville]

Sè·vres (sev′rə), *n.* a choice and costly kind of porcelain made in Sèvres, France. —*adj.* of or designating this porcelain: *a Sèvres vase.* [< *Sèvres,* a town in France]

sew (sō), *v.,* **sewed, sewed** or **sewn, sew·ing.** —*v.i.* to work with needle and thread. —*v.t.* **1.** to fasten with stitches. **2.** to attach by stitches: *to sew on a button.* **3.** to use a needle and thread to make, mend, etc.
sew up, a. to close with stitches: *The doctor sewed up the wound.* **b.** *U.S. Informal.* to make certain: *Betsy Davison had a job sewed up at an uptown private nursery school* (Mary McCarthy).
[Old English *seowian*]

sew·age (sü′ij), *n.* the waste matter carried off in sewers and drains.

sewage farm, a farm which disposes of sewage by using it to irrigate and fertilize the fields.

se·wan (sē′wən), *n.* loose shell beads used as money by American Indians; seawan.

Sew·ard's Folly (sü′ərdz), Alaska, acquired by the United States from Russia in 1867 when William Henry Seward was Secretary of State: *The utmost political pressure and personal cajolery were necessary to get Congress to agree to the consummation of "Seward's Folly"* (Atlantic).

sew·er[1] (sü′ər), *n.* an underground pipe or channel for carrying off waste water and refuse. [< Old French *sewiere* sluice from a pond, ultimately < Latin *ex* out + *aquāria* (water) vessel < *aqua* water] —**Syn.** drain, conduit.

sew·er[2] (sō′ər), *n.* a person or thing that sews. [< *sew* + *-er*[1]]

sew·er[3] (sü′ər), *n.* (formerly) a head servant in charge of arranging the table and serving the meals: *The sewer with savoury meats Dish after dish served them* (William Cowper). [short for Anglo-French *assoeur* (literally) seater < Vulgar Latin *assedēre,* for Latin *assidēre* to sit by < *ad-* by + *sedēre* to sit]

sew·er·age (sü′ər ij), *n.* **1.** the removal of waste matter by sewers: *Candidates must have had previous . . . experience in sewerage, sewage disposal or plumbing* (London News Chronicle). **2.** a system of sewers. **3.** sewage.

sew·ing (sō′ing), *n.* **1.** work done with a needle and thread. **2.** something to be sewed. *—adj.* for sewing; used in sewing: *a sewing room.* —**Syn.** *n.* **1.** needlework.

sewing circle, a group of women who meet regularly to sew for their church, for charity, etc.: *Her sewing circle was to meet at her house . . . and most of the members were too decrepit to climb the stairs* (New Yorker).

sewing machine, a machine for sewing or stitching cloth.

sewing silk, silk thread.

sewn (sōn), *v.* sewed; a past participle of **sew.**

sex (seks), *n.* **1.** one of the two divisions of human beings, animals, etc.: *Men, bulls and roosters are of the male sex; women, cows and hens are of the female sex.* **2. a.** the character of being male or female: *People were admitted without regard to age or sex.* **b.** the physical quality in plants of having male or female functions. **3.** the differences in structure and function between male and female: *The young need . . . to be told . . . all we know of three fundamental things; the first of which is God . . . and the third Sex* (H.G. Wells). **4.** the attraction of one sex for the other: *the place of sex in literature.*
the sex, *Rare.* women: *The sex of Venice are undoubtedly of a distinguished beauty* (Arthur Young).
—adj. of sex; having to do with sex.
[< Latin *sexus, -ūs*]

sex-, *combining form.* six: *Sexangular* = *having six angles.* Also, **sexi-.** [< Latin *sex* six]

sex·a·ge·nar·i·an (sek′sə jə nãr′ē ən), *adj.* of the age of 60 years, or between 60 and 70 years old. *—n.* a person who is 60, or between 60 and 70, years old. [< Latin *sexāgēnārius* sexagenary + English *-an*]

sex·ag·e·nar·y (sek saj′ə ner′ē), *adj., n., pl.* **-nar·ies.** *—adj.* **1.** of or having to do with the number 60. **2.** composed of or going by sixties. **3.** sexagenarian.
—n. a sexagenarian.
[< Latin *sexāgēnārius* < *sexāgēnī* sixty each < *sexāgintā* sixty]

Sex·a·ges·i·ma (sek′sə jes′ə mə), *n.,* or **Sexagesima Sunday,** the second Sunday before Lent. [< Latin *sexāgēsima* (literally) sixtieth < *sexāgintā* sixty]

sex·a·ges·i·mal (sek′sə jes′ə məl), *adj.* having to do with or based upon the number 60: *A sexagesimal fraction is one whose denominator is 60 or a power of 60. Each table is transcribed in the now standard adaptation of Hindu-Arabic numerals to the sexagesimal notation of the Babylonians* (Science). *—n.* a sexagesimal fraction. [< Medieval Latin *sexagesimalis* < Latin *sexāgēsimus* sixtieth < *sexāgintā* sixty]

sex·an·gu·lar (seks ang′gyə lər), *adj.* hexagonal. [< *sex-* + *angular*]

sex appeal, attraction for the opposite sex: *She has a large endowment of the "plus" quality of femininity, the unexplainable but unmistakable flair called "sex appeal"* (Sunday Express).

sex·a·va·lent (sek′sə vā′lənt, sek sav′ə-), *adj.* sexivalent.

sex·cen·te·nar·y (seks sen′tə ner′ē, -senten′ər-), *adj., n., pl.* **-nar·ies.** *—adj.* having to do with the number 600. *—n.* **1.** a period of 600 years. **2.** a 600th anniversary. [< Latin *sexcentēnī* 600 each (< *sexcentī* 600 < *sex* six + *centum* 100) + English *-ary*]

sex chromosome, a chromosome carrying the genes which determine sex in certain animals and plants.

sexed (sekst), *adj.* having sex or the characteristics of sex.

sex·en·ni·al (seks en′ē əl), *adj.* **1.** of or for six years. **2.** occurring every six years. *—n.* a sexennial celebration or other event. [< Latin *sexennium* period of six years (< *sex* six + *annus* year) + English *-al*[1]] —**sex·en′ni·al·ly,** *adv.*

sex·en·ni·um (seks en′ē əm), *n., pl.* **-en·ni·ums, -en·ni·a** (-en′ē ə). a period of six years. [< Latin *sexennium;* see SEXENNIAL]

sex hormone, a hormone which influences the development or stimulates the function of reproductive organs and other sexual characteristics: *Scientists call the female sex hormones estrogens and the male hormones androgens* (Science News Letter).

sex hygiene, the hygiene of sex and sexual activity.

sexi-, *combining form.* a form of **sex-,** as in *sexivalent.*

sex·i·ly (sek′sə lē), *adv. Informal.* in a sexy manner

sex·i·ness (sek′sē nis), *n. Informal.* the quality of being sexy.

sex·i·po·lar (sek′si pō′lər), *adj.* having six poles.

sex·i·va·lent (sek′si vā′lənt), *adj.* having a valence of six.

sex kitten, *Slang.* sexpot.

sex·less (seks′lis), *adj.* without sex or the characteristics of sex; asexual. —**sex′less·ly,** *adv.* —**sex′less·ness,** *n.*

sex-link·age (seks′ling′kij), *n. Biology.* the state or condition of being sex-linked.

sex-linked (seks′lingkt′), *adj. Biology.* of or having to do with a characteristic, such as hemophilia, that is transmitted by genes located in the sex chromosomes: *Traits such as color blindness are said to be sex-linked* (Hegner and Stiles).

sex·o·log·i·cal (sek′sə loj′ə kəl), *adj.* of or having to do with sexology.

sex·ol·o·gist (sek sol′ə jist), *n.* a person who studies or is an expert in sexology: *Havelock Ellis, one of the great pioneer sexologists . . .* (Sunday Times).

sex·ol·o·gy (sek sol′ə jē), *n.* the science dealing with sex and sexual conduct.

sex·par·tite (seks pär′tīt), *adj.* divided into or consisting of six parts. [< New Latin *sexpartitus* < Latin *sex* six + *partītus* partite, past participle of *partīre* to divide]

sex·pot (seks′pot′), *n. Slang.* a very sexy or seductive woman.

sex ratio, the proportion of males born to females born: *The number of males per 100 females is the sex ratio* (Science News Letter).

sext or **Sext** (sekst), *n.* **1.** the fourth of the seven canonical hours set aside for prayer and meditation. **2.** the office or service for this hour, originally fixed for noon, the sixth hour after sunrise: *Throughout the day, Maryknollers recite all . . . the hours—Matins, Lauds, Prime, Terce, Sext, None, Vespers and Compline* (Time). [< Latin *sexta* (*hōra*) sixth (hour) < *sex* six. Doublet of SIESTA.]

sex·tain (seks′tān), *n.* a stanza of six lines. [perhaps alteration of obsolete French *sestine;* patterned on *quatrain*]

sex·tan (seks′tən), *n.* a fever or ague characterized by paroxysms that recur every sixth day, both days of consecutive occurrence being counted.
—adj. **1.** of such a fever or ague. **2.** recurring every sixth day. [< New Latin *sextana* (*febris*) sextan (fever) < Latin *sex* six]

Sex·tans (seks′tənz), *n., genitive* **Sex·tan·tis.** a constellation south of Leo; the Sextant. [< New Latin *Sextans;* see SEXTANT]

sex·tant (seks′tənt), *n.* **1.** an instrument used by navigators, surveyors, etc., for measuring the angular distance between two objects. Sextants are used at sea to measure the altitude of the sun, a star, etc., in order to determine latitude and longitude: *Scientific research has produced another device to make aircraft navigation easier and safer—an automatic celestial sextant* (New York World Telegram). **2.** one sixth of a circle. [< New Latin *sextans* (apparently coined by Tycho Brahe) sextant < Latin *sextāns, -antis* a sixth < *sex* six]

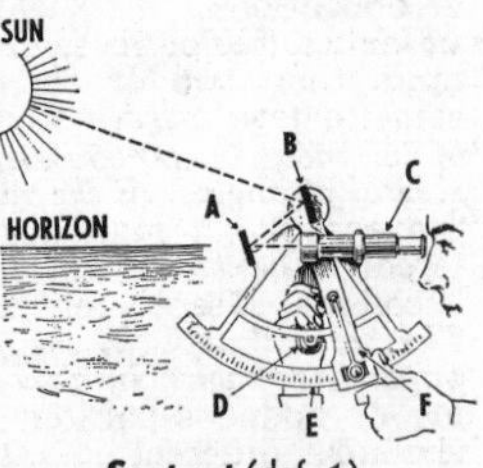

Sextant (def. 1)
A, mirror; B, mirror; C, telescope; D, handle; E, graduated arc; F, hand

Sex·tant (seks′tənt), *n.* the constellation Sextans. [< *sextant*]

Sex·tan·tis (sek stan′tis), *n.* genitive of **Sextans.**

sex·tet or **sex·tette** (seks tet′), *n.* **1. a.** a piece of music for six voices or instruments. **b.** six singers or players: *An attempt to recreate the smooth sound of the old John Kirby sextet by reassembling all the original members . . .* (New Yorker). **2.** any group of six. [partly < German *Sextett,* partly alteration of *sestet;* influenced by Latin *sex* six]

sex·tile (seks′təl), *Astrology. —adj.* of or having to do with the aspect of two heavenly bodies 60 degrees distant from each other. *—n.* a sextile aspect. [earlier, one sixth of the zodiac < Latin *sextīlis* (*mēnsis*) old name of August; (literally) pertaining to the sixth month < *sex* six]

sex·til·lion (seks til′yən), *n.* **1.** (in the United States and France) 1 followed by 21 zeros; 1,000 to the seventh power. **2.** (in Great Britain) 1 followed by 36 zeros; 1,000,000 to the sixth power. *—adj.* that is a sextillion in number. [< French *sextillion* < Latin *sextus* sixth; patterned on *million* million]

sex·til·lionth (seks til′yənth), *adj., n.* **1.** last in a series of a sextillion. **2.** one, or being one, of a sextillion equal parts.

sex·tip·a·ra (seks tip′ə rə), *n.* a woman who has passed through six pregnancies. [< Latin *sextus* sixth + *parere* to bring forth]

sex·to·dec·i·mo (seks′tō des′ə mō), *n., pl.* **-mos,** *adj. —n.* **1.** a size of a book, or of its pages, made by folding a sheet of paper into sixteen parts to form leaves about 4½ x 6¾ inches. **2.** a book with pages this size. *—adj.* of this size; having pages this size. [< Latin *sextō,* ablative of *sextus* sixth (< *sex* six) + *decimō,* ablative of *decimus* tenth < *decem* ten]

sex·tole (seks′tōl), *n.* sextolet.

sex·to·let (seks′tə let′), *n. Music.* a group of six notes to be played in the time of four: *It was apparent when it came to the rippling sextolets later on that his taste was amply supported by his technique* (London Times). [< Latin *sextus* sixth + English *-let*]

sex·ton (seks′tən), *n.* a man who takes care of a church. A sexton's duties, in addition to acting as janitor, sometimes include ringing the bell, digging graves, etc. [< Old French *segrestein* and *secrestein,* learned borrowing from Medieval Latin *sacristanus.* Doublet of SACRISTAN.]

sexton beetle, any of certain beetles that bury small dead animals in which they have deposited their eggs. Their larvae eat the decaying flesh.

sex·tu·ple (seks′tu̇ pəl, -tyu̇-; seks tü′-, -tyü′-), *adj., n., v.,* **-pled, -pling.** *—adj.* **1.** consisting of six parts; sixfold. **2.** six times as great. **3.** *Music.* characterized by six beats to the measure: *sextuple rhythm.*
—n. a number or amount six times as great as another.
—v.t., v.i. to make or become six times as great.
[< Latin *sextus* sixth; patterned on *quadruple*]

sex·tu·plet (seks′tu̇ plit, -tyu̇-; seks tü′-, -tyü′-), *n.* **1.** one of six children, animals, etc., born of the same mother at the same time. **2.** any group of six; six persons or things. [< *sextuple,* patterned on *quadruplet*]

sex·tu·plex (seks′tu̇ pleks, -tyu̇-), *adj.* **1.** sixfold. **2.** of or having to do with a system of telegraphy by which six messages may be transmitted simultaneously over one wire. [< Medieval Latin *sextuplex* sixfold < Latin *sex* six; patterned on *quadruplex*]

sex·tu·pli·cate (*adj., n.* seks tü′plə kit, -tyü′-; *v.* seks tü′plə kāt, -tyü′-), *adj., v.,* **-cat·ed, -cat·ing,** *n. —adj.* **1.** sixfold; sextuple. **2.** *Mathematics.* raised to the sixth power.
—v.t. to make sixfold; sextuple.
—n. one of six things, especially six copies of a document, exactly alike.
in sextuplicate, in six copies, exactly alike: [*She*] *took down the . . . testimony in sextuplicate* (Newsweek).
[< Medieval Latin *sextuplicatus,* past participle of *sextuplicāre* < *sextuplex;* see SEXTUPLEX]

sex·u·al (sek′shu̇ əl), *adj.* **1.** of or having to do with sex. **2.** of or between the sexes: *sexual love. Her very frankness suggested a perfect sexual equality* (Bret Harte). **3.** having to do with the relations between the sexes: *sexual morality, sexual excess.* **4.** having sex; separated into two sexes. [< Late Latin *sexuālis* < Latin *sexus, -ūs* sex]

sexual generation, the sexual phase in the alternation of generations.

sex·u·al·ism (sek′shu̇ ə liz′əm), *n.* **1.** sexuality as a principle of action or thought. **2.** sexuality: *He has a puritanical obsession about showing sexualism onstage* (Time).

sex·u·al·i·ty (sek′shu̇ al′ə tē), *n.* **1.** sexual character; possession of sex. **2.** the possession of sexual powers or capability of sexual feelings. **3.** attention to sexual matters.

sex·u·al·ly (sek′shu̇ ə lē), *adv.* **1.** by means of sex. **2.** in regard to sex.

sexual selection, *Biology.* natural selection perpetuating certain characteristics that attract one sex to the other, such as bright feathers in birds: *I conclude that of all the causes which have led to the differences in external appearance between the races of men . . . sexual selection has been by far the most efficient* (Charles Darwin).

sex·u·pa·ra (sek sü′pə rə), *n. pl.* parthenogenetic female organisms which give birth to males and to females that lay fertilized eggs. [< New Latin *sexupara* < Latin *sexus, -ūs* sex + *parere* to bring forth]

sex·u·pa·rous (sek sü′pə rəs), *adj.* having to do with sexupara.

sex·y (sek′sē), *adj.*, **sex·i·er, sex·i·est.** *Informal.* sexually appealing or stimulating; having sex appeal: *sexy photographs, sexy beauties. With words and music just simple, sad and sexy enough to make it sound like a hit* (Time).

Seym (sām), *n.* Sejm; the Polish Parliament: *This handful of Catholic deputies, permitted to sit in the Seym under the one-list system of election, represents more of the Polish people than the ruling United Workers Party* (Wall Street Journal).

sf., sforzando.

SF (no periods), science fiction: *Long ago the SF writer was deprived of his Bug-eyed Monsters and compelled to use jargon that bore at least a superficial patina of conviction to the student of physics* (Punch).

Sfc., sergeant, first class.

sfer·ics (sfer′iks), *n.* atmospherics: *Another possible means of identifying a tornado at a distance is the phenomenon known as "sferics"* (Scientific American).

sfor·zan·do (sfôr tsän′dō), *adj., n., pl.* **-dos, -di** (-dē). *Music.* —*adj.* with special emphasis (used as a direction). —*n.* a note or passage played with special emphasis or rendered louder than the rest: *In Beethoven his sforzandi were often hard and ugly* (London Times). [< Italian *sforzando,* present participle of *sforzare* to force]

➔ **Sforzando** is usually considered as calling for a stronger emphasis than either of the accent symbols > or ∧.

sfor·za·to (sfôr tsä′tō), *adj.* sforzando. [< Italian *sforzato,* past participle of *sforzare* to force]

sfz., sforzando.

s.g., specific gravity.

S.G., solicitor general.

S.-G., Secretary-General (of the United Nations).

Sga·na·relle (zgȧ nȧ rel′), *n.* the name given to a comic character in Molière comedies.

sgd., signed.

sgraf·fi·to (zgraf fē′tō), *n., pl.* **-ti** (-tē). a type of decoration scratched through a layer of paint, plaster, clay, etc.; graffito: . . . *embellished with sgraffito designs of foliage on a slightly ridged surface* (New Yorker). [< Italian *sgraffito.* Compare GRAFFITO.]

Sgt. or **sgt.,** sergeant.

sh or **'sh** (sh), *interj.* a shortened form of **hush,** used in urging silence: *"Sh!" she whispered. "Never mind what you make"* (Leonard Merrick).

sh., **1.** share. **2.** *Bookbinding.* sheep. **3.** sheet. **4.** shilling or shillings. **5.** shoal. **6.** short.

SH (no periods), sulfhydryl.

SHA (no periods), sidereal hour angle: *The star's SHA and declination are found in the star table* (Robert H. Baker).

shab (shab), *n.* **1.** *British Dialect.* scab, a disease of animals. **2.** *Obsolete.* a scab. [Old English *sceabb*]

Sha·ban (shə bän′), *n.* the eighth month of the Moslem calendar. [< Arabic *shaʿbān*]

Shab·bat (shə bät′), *n. Hebrew.* the Jewish Sabbath.

shab·bi·ly (shab′ə lē), *adv.* in a shabby manner: *Schumann's exacting Toccata was also rather shabbily treated* (London Times).

shab·bi·ness (shab′ē nis), *n.* the quality or state of being shabby.

shab·ble (shab′əl), *n. Archaic.* **1.** a saber. **2.** a curved sword. [< Italian *sciabola.* Ultimately related to SABER.]

Shab·bos (shä′bəs), *n. Yiddish.* the Jewish Sabbath.

shab·by (shab′ē), *adj.,* **-bi·er, -bi·est. 1.** much worn: *His old suit looks shabby. The other had his hand bound up with shabby strips of a tropical shirt* (Graham Greene). **2.** wearing old or much worn clothes; poorly dressed. **3.** not generous; mean; unfair: *It is shabby not to speak to an old friend because he is poor. On the floor of the House, Rep. Tumulty . . . denounced Dulles for "shabby treatment of Corsi"* (Wall Street Journal).

shab·by-gen·teel (shab′ē jen tēl′), *adj.* shabby but genteel; making or showing an effort to keep up appearances.

shab·by-gen·til·i·ty (shab′ē jen til′ə tē), *n.* the condition of being shabby-genteel.

shab·le (shab′əl), *n.* shabble.

shab·rack (shab′rak), *n.* a saddlecloth used in European armies: . . . *upon chestnut horses, with their leopard skin shabracks and their little red panaches* (Sir Arthur Conan Doyle). [< French *schabraque* < German *Schabracke,* perhaps < Turkish *chaprak*]

Sha·bu·oth or **Sha·bu·ot** (shä vü′ōth, -ōt), *n.* the Jewish holiday, seven weeks after Passover, called Pentecost or the Feast of Weeks. Also, **Shavuos.** [< Hebrew *shabuoth* (literally) weeks, plural of *shabuā*]

shack[1] (shak), *U.S. and Canada.* —*n.* **1.** a roughly built hut or cabin: *a shack in the woods. The Caney Creek Community Center was born in a one-room shack* (Newsweek). **2.** *Informal.* **a.** a house in bad condition. **b.** a house that is poorly built, designed, etc. —*v.i. Slang.* **1.** to live at a place; dwell: *He shacks in a boarding house.* **2.** Usually, **shack up.** to stay in a place: *I was going to shack up in a hotel for a couple of days* (J.D. Salinger).

[American English; origin uncertain; perhaps back formation < *ramshackle*]

—**Syn.** *n.* **1.** shanty.

shack[2] (shak), *v.t.* shag[2].

shack·le (shak′əl), *n., v.,* **-led, -ling.** —*n.* **1.** a metal band fastened around the ankle or wrist of a prisoner, slave, etc. Shackles are usually fastened to each other, the wall, floor, etc. **2.** the link fastening together the two rings for the ankles and wrists of a prisoner. **3.** anything that prevents freedom of action, thought, etc.: . . . *the bars and shackles of civilization* (Mark Twain). *He frequently writes of the shackles imposed by the Japanese family system* (Atlantic). **4.** a thing for fastening or coupling, leaving some freedom of movement: *The springs of a car are secured on each end by shackles.*

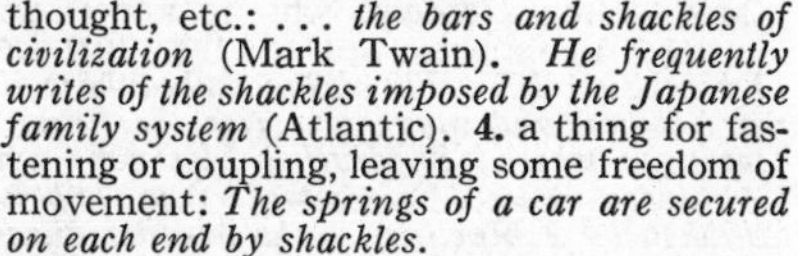

Shackles (def. 1)

—*v.t.* **1.** to put shackles on. **2.** to restrain; hamper. **3.** to fasten or couple with or as with a shackle: . . . *who were not shackled to the past in their thinking* (New York Times). [Old English *sceacel*]

—**Syn.** *n.* **3.** impediment, obstacle. *-v.t.* **2.** obstruct, restrict.

shack·ler (shak′lər), *n.* a person or thing that shackles.

shack·town (shak′toun′), *n. U.S. and Canada.* a group or settlement of makeshift shacks; shantytown: *To prevent the creation of a shacktown, the Kent Township Council hurriedly rammed through a building bylaw* (Maclean's).

shad (shad), *n., pl.* **shad** or (*for different kinds*) **shads. 1.** any of several salt-water fishes related to the herrings, that ascend rivers every spring to spawn. The shad common on the North Atlantic Coast is a valuable food fish. **2.** any of various other related salt-water fishes. [Old English *sceadd*]

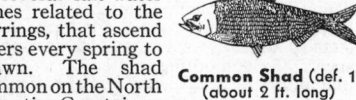

Common Shad (def. 1) (about 2 ft. long)

shad·ber·ry (shad′ber′ē), *n., pl.* **-ries. 1.** the fruit of the shadbush. **2.** shadbush.

shad·blos·som (shad′blos′əm), *n.* shadbush.

shad·blow (shad′blō′), *n.* shadbush.

shad·bush (shad′bu̇sh′), *n.* any of a group of North American shrubs or small trees of the rose family, with white flowers and berrylike fruit, which blossoms about the time when shad appear in the rivers; Juneberry; serviceberry.

shad·chan (shäd′ʜən), *n., pl.* **-cho·nim** (-ʜô′nim). *Yiddish.* a professional matchmaker or marriage broker.

Shadbush Branch

Shad·dai (shad′ī), *n.* one of the names of God in the Old Testament. [< Hebrew *shadday*]

shad·dock (shad′ək), *n.* **1.** the pear-shaped fruit of a tree of the rue family, like a coarse, dry, inferior grapefruit. **2.** the tree that it grows on. [< a Captain *Shaddock,* who introduced the fruit into the West Indies in the 1600's]

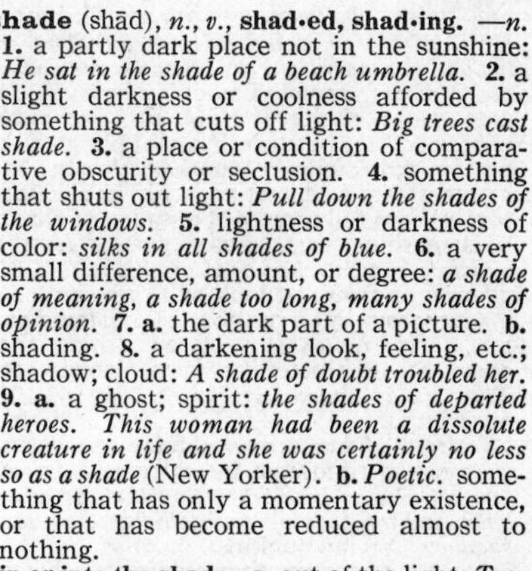

shade (shād), *n., v.,* **shad·ed, shad·ing.** —*n.* **1.** a partly dark place not in the sunshine: *He sat in the shade of a beach umbrella.* **2.** a slight darkness or coolness afforded by something that cuts off light: *Big trees cast shade.* **3.** a place or condition of comparative obscurity or seclusion. **4.** something that shuts out light: *Pull down the shades of the windows.* **5.** lightness or darkness of color: *silks in all shades of blue.* **6.** a very small difference, amount, or degree: *a shade of meaning, a shade too long, many shades of opinion.* **7. a.** the dark part of a picture. **b.** shading. **8.** a darkening look, feeling, etc.; shadow; cloud: *A shade of doubt troubled her.* **9. a.** a ghost; spirit: *the shades of departed heroes. This woman had been a dissolute creature in life and she was certainly no less so as a shade* (New Yorker). **b.** *Poetic.* something that has only a momentary existence, or that has become reduced almost to nothing.

in or **into the shade, a.** out of the light: *Two maximum thermometers are issued—one to observe the greatest heat in the sun, the other in the shade* (Edmund Parkes). **b.** in or into a condition of being unknown or unnoticed: *Bacon still remained in the shade* (Richard W. Church).

shades, sunglasses: *Your teen-age daughter asks what you think of her shades, which you are canny enough to know are her sunglasses* (New York Times).

(the) shades, a. the darkness of evening or night: *The shades . . . had by this time fallen upon the quiet city* (Thackeray). **b.** the inhabitants of hell, as a group: *A journey after death to reach the home of shades* (Charles Keary). **c.** hell: *See! on one Greek three Trojan ghosts attend, This, my third victim, to the shades I send* (Alexander Pope).

—*v.t.* **1.** to screen from light; darken. **2.** to make darker than the rest, as by using darker paint in a picture. **3.** to make dark or gloomy. **4.** to lessen slightly: *Some companies are offering allowances and dealers are shading prices* (Wall Street Journal). —*v.i.* to show small differences; change little by little: *This scarf shades from deep rose to pale pink.*

[Old English *sceadu.* Compare SHADOW.]

—**Syn.** *n.* **5.** See **color.**

shad·ed (shā′did), *adj.* **1. a.** protected from light or heat: *There are shaded walks for study and contemplation* (Margaret Calderwood). **b.** covered with a shade: *The shaded lamps were lighted* (Iza Duffus Hardy). **2.** covered with shadow: *O'er the shaded billows rushed the night* (Alexander Pope). **3.** having colors gradually passing into one another; marked with gradations of color. **4.** (in painting and drawing) furnished with colors or markings to indicate shade.

shade·less (shād′lis), *adj.* having or affording no shade: *A gap in the hills, an opening shadeless and shelterless* (Wordsworth).

shade tree, 1. any tree that gives shade. **2.** any of certain species of trees, as most maples, that provide good shade.

shad·fly (shad′flī′), *n., pl.* **-flies.** a May fly or similar insect that appears at or near the time when shad start up the river.

shad·i·ly (shā′də lē), *adv.* in a shady manner.

shad·i·ness (shā′dē nis), *n.* the quality or condition of being shady.

shad·ing (shā′ding), *n.* **1.** a covering from the light. **2.** the use of black or color to give the effect of shade in a picture. **3.** a slight variation or difference of color, character, etc.

sha·doof (shä düf′), *n.* a long rod with a bucket on one end and a weight on the other, used for raising water in the Near East. [< Arabic *shādūf*]

shad·ow (shad′ō), *n.* **1.** shade made by some person, animal, or thing: *Sometimes a person's shadow is much longer than he is, and sometimes much shorter.* **2.** shade, darkness, or partial shade. **3.** the dark part of a place or picture. **4.** a little bit; small degree; slight suggestion: *There's not a shadow of a doubt about his guilt.* **5.** a ghost; specter: *There sat the Shadow fear'd of man* (Tennyson). **6. a.** a faint image: *You look worn to a shadow.* **b.** anything that is unsubstantial or unreal, having the appearance of being real: *Titles are shadows, Crowns are empty things* (Daniel Defoe). *What shadows we are,* *and what shadows we pursue* (Edmund Burke). **7.** a reflected image: *And on the bay the moonlight lay, And the shadow of the Moon* (Samuel Taylor Coleridge). **8.** protection; shelter: *Hide me under the shadow of thy wings* (Psalms 17:8). **9.** a person who follows another closely and secretly, as a detective. **10.** a constant companion; follower. **11. a.** sadness; gloom. **b.** something that causes gloom: *Love is sunshine, hate is shadow* (Longfellow). **12.** a gloomy or troubled look or expression. **13.** a temporary interruption: *A shadow came over their friendship.* **14.** something that obscures the luster of fame, glory, etc.: *There is a shadow over his reputation.* **15.** obscurity.

be afraid of one's own shadow, to be unreasonably timorous; be extremely frightened: *One gets the impression that the whole back line [of people] are afraid of their own shadows* (Vivian Jenkins).

cast a long shadow, to wield great influence or power: [*She*] *is always driven by the need for self-assertion, whether it involves ... meddling with politics and art, or merely casting a long shadow over all the people she encounters* (Atlantic).

(the) shadows, the darkness after sunset: *Shadows of the evening Steal across the sky* (Sabine Baring-Gould).

under or **in the shadow of,** very near to: *The friends met in a little cafe under the shadow of St. Peter's.*

—*v.t.* **1.** to protect from light; shade: *The grass is shadowed by huge oaks.* **2.** to cast a shadow on. **3.** to represent faintly. **4.** to follow closely and secretly. **5.** to make sad or gloomy. **6.** to represent in a prophetic way.

shadow forth, to represent faintly: *By the same four* [*creatures*], *in the opinion of many of the Fathers, are shadowed forth the four Evangelists* (Thomas Godwin).

—*adj.* of or belonging to a shadow cabinet: *Labour's principal speaker was Mr. James Callaghan, the shadow Chancellor of the Exchequer* (Manchester Guardian Weekly).

[Old English *sceadwe*, oblique case of *sceadu* shade. Compare SHADE.] —**shad′ow·er,** *n.*

shadow band, one of a series of roughly parallel broken bands, alternately bright and dark, and moving with an irregular, flickering motion over every light-colored surface during a solar eclipse. It is seen just before and after the period of total eclipse. *The fact that shadow bands are not visible at all eclipses proves satisfactorily their atmospheric origin* (New Scientist).

shadow bird, the umbrette.

shad·ow·box (shad′ō boks′), *v.i.* to engage in shadowboxing.

shadow box, 1. a box or boxlike structure with artificial lighting to draw attention to and highlight certain features of an object or painting displayed in it: *There was a great framed shadow box containing a representation of the coronation of Czar Alexander II* (New Yorker). **2.** a device to shield a projection surface for viewing a film in daylight.

shad·ow·box·ing (shad′ō bok′sing), *n.* boxing with an imaginary opponent for exercise or training: *In the morning he did fifteen minutes' shadowboxing before going down to breakfast* (Atlantic).

shadow cabinet, 1. a group of influential advisers chosen by the head of a government; kitchen cabinet: *Some back-benchers are commenting bitterly on the judgment of the shadow cabinet* (Sunday Times). **2.** a similar group of advisers forming the governing body of a minority or opposition party: *Labor's shadow cabinet ... men who would be Cabinet ministers if their party returned to power* (Time).

shadow dance, a dance in which the shadows of the performers (who are invisible) are thrown on a screen.

shad·ow·graph (shad′ō graf, -gräf), *n.* **1.** a picture produced by throwing a shadow on a lighted screen. **2.** an X-ray picture. **3.** a shadow play.

shad·ow·graph·er (shad′ō graf′ər, -gräf′-), *n.* shadowgraphist.

shad·ow·graph·ic (shad′ō graf′ik), *adj.* having to do with or done by shadowgraphy.

shad·ow·graph·ist (shad′ō graf′ist, -gräf′-), *n.* a person who is skilled or trained in shadowgraphy.

shad·ow·graph·y (shad′ō graf′ē, -gräf′-), *n.* the producing of shadowgraphs.

shad·ow·i·ly (shad′ō ə lē), *adv.* in a shadowy manner: *The Infanta is only shadowily visible through the darkly luminous galleries* (Time).

shad·ow·i·ness (shad′ō ē nis), *n.* shadowy or unsubstantial character or quality.

shad·ow·land (shad′ō land′), *n.* a region of shadows, phantoms, unrealities, or uncertainties: *Congress ... has a responsibility to watch carefully over an agency it created to stand watch in that shadowland between peace and war* (Wall Street Journal).

shad·ow·less (shad′ō lis), *adj.* having or casting no shadow: *He was content to drink in the new, exciting talk of pure, shadowless colors* (Time). —**shad′ow·less·ly,** *adv.*

shadow of death, (in the Bible) the darkness or gloom of death, especially approaching or imminent death: *Before I go whence I shall not return, even to the land of darkness and the shadow of death* (Job 10:21).

shadow play, an entertainment in which the shadows of actors, puppets, or other forms are cast upon a screen placed between the stage and the auditorium: *In these shadow plays, the figures are made of cardboard with translucent paper for the eyes and mouth* (Atlantic).

shad·ow·y (shad′ō ē), *adj.* **1.** having much shadow or shade; shady: *We are glad to leave the hot sun and come into the cool shadowy room.* **2.** like a shadow; dim, faint, or slight: *a shadowy figure. He saw a shadowy outline on the window curtain. But as for who the shadowy seller of the forgeries was, no one had the slightest idea* (New Yorker). **3.** not real; ghostly; imaginary. **4.** *Obsolete.* symbolic. —**Syn. 1.** dark, obscure. **2.** fleeting, vague, indistinct.

Sha·drach (shā′drak, shad′rak), *n.* (in the Bible) a companion of Daniel, one of the three young Hebrews who remained unharmed in Nebuchadnezzar's fiery furnace. Daniel 2:49-3:30. *The oil that calked the walls of Babylon and may have fired the furnace through which Shadrach, Meshach and Abednego walked unscathed now bubbles through huge pipelines to the Mediterranean* (Time).

shad·scale (shad′skāl′), *n.* a low scaly shrub of the goosefoot family growing in dry, salty areas of the western United States: *Commonest of the uranium-indicating plants are rabbit brush, shadscale ...* (Science News Letter).

sha·duf (shä düf′), *n.* shadoof.

shad-wait·er (shad′wā′tər), *n.* a whitefish of lakes of Siberia and North America from New England to Alaska.

shad·y (shā′dē), *adj.*, **shad·i·er, shad·i·est. 1.** in the shade; shaded. **2.** giving shade. **3.** *Informal.* of doubtful honesty, character, etc.: *He has engaged in rather shady occupations.* —**Syn. 1.** shadowy. **3.** dubious, questionable.

SHAEF (no periods), Supreme Headquarters, Allied Expeditionary Forces.

shaft (shaft, shäft), *n.* **1.** the long, slender stem of an arrow, spear, etc. **2.** an arrow or spear. **3.** something aimed at a person like an arrow or spear: *shafts of ridicule. A shield against its shafts of doubt* (John Greenleaf Whittier). *The shaft of love ... had struck me* (Arnold Bennett). **4. a.** a ray or beam of light. **b.** anything like a shaft of light: *Mr. Campbell's observations are a refreshing and badly needed shaft of common sense* (Wall Street Journal). **5.** one of the two wooden poles between which a horse is harnessed to a carriage, etc. **6. a.** a column. **b.** a column or obelisk erected as a memorial. **c.** a flagpole. **d.** the part of a candlestick that supports the branches. **7.** the main part of a column. **8.** a bar to support parts of a machine that turn, or to help move parts, as gears or pulleys, and to transmit power by turning, as the drive shaft of an automobile. **9.** the handle of a hammer, ax, golf club, etc.: *In Oxford, a woman was killed by lightning when it struck the metal shaft of her umbrella* (London Times). **10.** a stem; stalk: *... the symmetrical shaft of the cocoanut tree* (Herman Melville). **11.** the rib of a feather. See **feather** for picture. **12.** a deep passage sunk in the earth: *The entrance to a mine is called a shaft. He had been caught by a landslide in a tiny shaft of the cave* (Newsweek). **13.** a well-like passage; long, narrow space: *an elevator shaft.* [Old English *sceaft*] —**shaft′like′,** *adj.*

shaft·ed (shaf′tid, shäf′-), *adj.* having a shaft or shafts.

shaft house, a heavy framework at the top of a mine shaft, to support the hoisting machinery, sometimes enclosed.

shaft·ing (shaf′ting, shäf′-), *n.* **1.** shafts. **2.** a system of shafts, especially for transmitting power to machinery. **3.** material for shafts.

shaft·man (shaft′man′, -mən; shäft′-), *n., pl.* **-men.** a man employed to sink shafts or to keep shafts in repair: *a colliery shaftman.*

shag[1] (shag), *n., v.,* **shagged, shag·ging.** —*n.* **1. a.** rough, matted hair, wool, etc. **b.** a mass of this: *the shag of a dog.* **2. a.** the long, rough nap of some kinds of cloth, especially a layer of woven loops, longer and coarser than pile: *a shag rug.* **b.** a cloth having such a nap, especially a fabric of worsted or silk. **3.** a tangled mass of shrubs, trees, foliage, etc. **4.** a strong tobacco cut into fine shreds. **5.** a cormorant, especially a European species which in the breeding season has a short, upright crest.

—*v.t.* **1.** to make rough or shaggy (with a growth of trees or the like). **2.** *Obsolete.* to make a long or rough nap or pile on (a fabric).

[perhaps Old English *sceacga* matted hair, wool]

➤ See **pile**[3] for usage note.

shag[2] (shag), *v.,* **shagged, shag·ging.** —*v.t. Informal.* to catch or retrieve and throw back (a ball): *At ten, he was shagging flies at the Toronto Maple Leaf baseball practices* (Maclean's). —*v.i. U.S. Slang.* to go away; leave at once; get out.

shag[3] (shag), *n., v.,* **shagged, shag·ging.** —*n.* a hopping dance popular in the 1930's: *As they swoop and leap to the remembered acrobatics of the Lindy, the Shag ... time is, in a sense, expunged* (New Yorker). —*v.i.* to dance the shag. [< earlier *shag* to shake. Related to SHAKE.]

shag·a·nap·pi or **Shag·a·nap·pi** (shag′ə nap′ē), *n., pl.* **-pis,** *adj.* —*n. U.S.* **1. a.** a thread, cord, or thong made from rawhide. **b.** rawhide cut into strips. **2.** a rough pony. —*adj.* rough; tough. [American English < Algonkian (compare Cree *pisaganâbiy*)]

shag·bark (shag′bärk′), *n.* **1.** a hickory tree of eastern North America whose rough bark peels off in long strips. **2.** the nut of this tree. Shagbarks have fairly thin shells and are considered the best hickory nuts. **3.** its wood. **4.** a cotton fabric of rough texture somewhat like shagbark: *Sun dresses of pink or orchid shagbark, a cotton into which raised pin dots and stripes are woven ...* (New Yorker). Also, **shellbark.** [American English < *shag*[1] + *bark*]

shag-eared (shag′ird′), *adj.* having hairy ears: *a shag-eared pony.*

shag·ged (shag′id), *adj.* **1. a.** covered with shaggy hair. **b.** like shaggy hair. **2.** covered with a rough growth of vegetation: *a deep mountain glen, wild, lonely, and shagged* (Washington Irving). **3.** having a jagged or broken surface.

shag·gi·ly (shag′ə lē), *adv.* roughly.

shag·gi·ness (shag′ē nis), *n.* the quality of being shaggy.

shag·gy (shag′ē), *adj.,* **-gi·er, -gi·est. 1.** covered with a thick, rough mass of hair, wool, etc.: *a shaggy dog.* **2.** long, thick, and rough: *shaggy eyebrows, a shaggy mustache.* **3.** unkempt in appearance, especially needing a haircut or shave. **4.** covered with a rough, tangled growth of plants. **5.** having a long, rough nap; of coarse texture: *... wearing a heavy overcoat and shaggy felt hat* (New Yorker).

shaggy dog story, a story which relates, usually at great length, a number of unimportant incidents in building up to an unexpected or ridiculous climax. [< an original story of this type in which a *shaggy dog* appeared]

shag·gy-mane (shag′ē mān′), *n.* a fungus having a white top that is good to eat.

sha·green (shə grēn′), *n.* **1.** a kind of untanned leather with a granular surface made from the skin of the horse, ass, shark, seal, and other animals. **2.** the rough skin of some sharks. [< French *chagrin* < Turkish *sağri* rump of a horse. Compare CHAGRIN.]

Shah or **shah** (shä), *n.* **1.** the title of the ruler of Iran. **2.** a title of local chiefs in various Asian countries, especially India. [< Persian *shāh*]

Sha·hap·ti·an (shä hap′tē ən), *adj.* of or

having to do with an American Indian linguistic family that includes the language of the Nez Percés. —*n.* **1.** an Indian of this linguistic family. Shahaptians lived in the northern part of the valley of the Columbia River. **2.** this linguistic family. Also, **Sahaptan.** [American English < Salishan *Sahāptini*, plural of *Sáptini* a Salishan name for the Nez Percé Indians]

Shah·dom or **shah·dom** (shä′dəm), *n.* the territory under the rule of a Shah.

Shah·in·shah (shä′in shä′), *n.* King of Kings, a title of the ruler of Iran: *Iran . . . where dynasties of tremendous warrior Shahinshahs march back to the seventh century B.C. . . .* (New Yorker). [< Persian *shāhinshāh*]

Shah·na·mah (shä nä′mə), *n.* a great Persian epic, completed about 1010 A.D. It is the oldest known work written in modern Persian.

shah·rith (shäн′ris, -rith), *n. Judaism.* the daily morning prayer or service. [< Hebrew *shaḥarith* < *shaḥar morning*]

shaikh (shēk; *especially British* shāk), *n. Especially British.* sheik.

shaikh·dom (shēk′dəm; *especially British* shāk′-), *n. Especially British.* sheikdom.

shai·tan (shī tän′), *n.* **1.** in Moslem usage: **a.** Often, **Shaitan.** Satan; the Devil. **b.** an evil spirit, especially one of an order of the jinn. **2.** a vicious person or animal. Also, **sheitan.** [< Arabic *shaiṭān* < Hebrew *sāṭān* adversary]

Shak., Shakespeare.

shak·a·ble (shā′kə bəl), *adj.* that can be shaken.

shake (shāk), *v.,* **shook, shak·en, shak·ing,** *n.* —*v.t.* **1.** to cause to move quickly backward and forward, up and down, or from side to side: *to shake a rug, to shake one's head in sorrow or dissent.* **2.** to bring, throw, force, rouse, scatter, etc., by or as if by movement: *to shake snow off one's clothes.* **3.** to clasp (hands) in greeting, congratulating, etc., another: *Marshal Bulganin paused on the way to his seat . . . and then walked towards Dr. Adenauer to shake hands* (London Times). **4.** to make tremble: *The explosion shook the building.* **5.** to cause to totter or waver: *to shake the very foundations of society.* **6.** to disturb; make less firm or sure; upset: *His lie shook my faith in his honesty. I'd jump up abruptly, in the middle of a word, but I still couldn't shake them* (New Yorker). **7.** *Informal.* to get rid of (a person); give up (a habit): *Can't you shake him?* **8.** *Music.* to execute with a trill; trill. **9.** to mix (dice) before throwing.
—*v.i.* **1.** to move quickly backwards and forwards, up and down, or from side to side: *branches shaking in the wind.* **2.** to be shaken: *Sand shakes off easily.* **3.** to tremble: *He is shaking with cold. The house shook in the storm. The boy shook with fear at the sound of the howling dog.* **4.** to become weakened or unsteady; totter; waver: *His courage began to shake.* **5.** *Music.* to trill.

shake down, a. to bring or throw down by shaking: *Parts of two monasteries had been shaken down by earthquakes* (Henry F. Tozer). **b.** to cause to settle down: *It now appears that Korea, communism and foreign policy in particular have been fairly well shaken down as issues* (New York Times). **c.** to bring into working order: *He finally managed to shake down the troublesome motor and get on his way.* **d.** *Slang.* to get money from dishonestly; extort: *. . . a fantastic story of how two men had tried to shake him down for $500,000* (Time).

shake off, to get rid of: *I am glad I have wholly shaken off that family* (Jonathan Swift).

shake up, a. to shake hard: *We shake up a mixture of liquids of different densities* (Thomas Henry Huxley). **b.** to stir up: *Bob . . . hollers to his horses, and shakes 'em up, and away we goes* (Thomas Hughes). **c.** to jar in body or nerves: *The bad news shook her up considerably.*
—*n.* **1.** the act or fact of shaking: *a shake of the head.* **2.** *Informal.* an earthquake. **3.** a drink made by shaking ingredients together: *a milk shake.* **4.** *Slang.* a moment: *I'll be there in two shakes.* **5.** *Music.* a rapid alternation of a note with the note above it or below it; trill. **6. a.** a crack in a growing tree; fissure. **b.** such cracks as a group. **7.** a fissure in rock, mineral strata, etc.

no great shakes, *Informal.* not unusual, extraordinary, or important: *Her early novels were no great shakes, as she herself fully realized* (New York Times).

the shakes, *Informal.* **a.** any disease characterized by a trembling of the muscles and limbs: *Anxiety symptoms were relieved, he revealed, and the "shakes" lessened* (Newsweek). **b.** nervousness caused by fear or horror: *The Administration is not planning any action now toward a blockade of Red China, a possibility British and French leaders have had the shakes over* (Wall Street Journal).
[Old English *sceacan* to vibrate, make vibrate; move (away)]
—**Syn.** *v.i.* **3. Shake, tremble, quiver** mean to move with irregular, rapid and repeated movements from side to side or up and down. **Shake,** the general word, suggests a rapid, irregular, more or less violent or abrupt motion: *He shook with laughter.* **Tremble,** used chiefly of people or animals, suggests uncontrollable, continued shaking with quick, short movements, caused by fear, strong feeling, cold, etc.: *In his excitement his hands trembled.* **Quiver** suggests a slight trembling motion: *The dog's nostrils quivered at the scent.*

shake·a·ble (shā′kə bəl), *adj.* shakable.

shake-down[1] or **shake·down**[1] (shāk′doun′), *n.* **1.** *Informal.* a bringing into proper condition or working order by use, practice, etc.: *The new ocean liner was given a shakedown by a trial voyage.* **2.** a makeshift bed: *We made a shakedown of straw and blankets on the floor.* **3.** the process of shaking down: *Now give the bed a shake-down* (Thomas Hardy).
—*adj. Informal.* having to do with a trial and adjustment of new equipment, sometimes to permit a crew to become familiar with it: *a shakedown cruise.*

shake-down[2] or **shake·down**[2] (shāk′doun′), *n. Slang.* an exaction of money, etc., by compulsion, especially as in various forms of graft: *. . . letters alleging pay-offs, graft and shake-downs in military clothing contracts* (New York Times). [< *shakedown* (Slang), translation of Italian *riscuotere* to collect, shake down (e.g., fruit from a tree)]

shake·fork (shāk′fôrk′), *n.* **1.** a large wooden fork, used especially for lifting and shaking threshed straw to separate the grain. **2.** a bearing having the shape of a Y with blunted ends that do not reach the edge of the shield on a coat of arms.

shak·en (shā′kən), *v.* the past participle of **shake.**

shake·out (shāk′out′), *n. Informal.* **1. a.** a recession in a particular type of business, industry, trade, or other area of the economy, especially when accompanied by a disappearance of small competitors, marginal enterprises, and the like: *A shakeout already is under way that will end with six or eight producers dominating the field* (Wall Street Journal). *So far, unemployment hasn't approached the level of the last business shakeout in the 1949-50 winter* (Wall Street Journal). **b.** a similar decline in the stock market, resulting in widespread sellout of securities: *The stock market last week saw its sharpest shakeout since May* (Time). **2.** a drastic reorganization of policy, personnel, etc., usually resulting in the dismissal of some employees; shake-up: *. . . a possible shakeout of leading personalities associated with the succession* (Birmingham Post-Herald).

shak·er (shā′kər), *n.* **1.** a person who shakes something. **2.** a machine or utensil used in shaking. **3.** a container for pepper, salt, etc., having a perforated top.

Shak·er (shā′kər), *n.* a member of an American religious sect, so called from movements of the body that formed part of their worship. Shakers owned all property in common.
—*adj.* designating, or in the style of, furniture made by the Shakers.

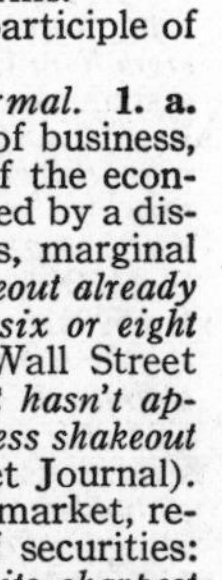

Shaker Chair

Shak·er·ess (shā′kər is), *n.* a woman Shaker.

Shak·er·ism (shā′kə riz əm), *n.* the principles and practices of the Shakers.

Shak·er·knit (shā′kər nit′), *adj.* (of a sweater, scarf, etc.) knitted in a plain stitch with coarse yarn, as some of the garments worn by the Shakers.

shakes (shāks), *n.pl.* See under **shake,** *n.*

Shake·spear·e·an (shāk spir′ē ən), *adj., n.* Shakespearian.

Shake·spear·e·a·na (shāk′spir ē ä′nə, -an′ə, -ā′nə), *n.pl.* Shakespeariana.

Shake·speare-Ba·con Controversy (shāk′spir bā′kən), an argument over the claim that Sir Francis Bacon wrote the plays usually attributed to Shakespeare.

Shake·spear·i·an (shāk spir′ē ən), *adj.* of, having to do with, or suggestive of Shakespeare or his works. —*n.* a specialist in the study of the works of Shakespeare.

Shake·spear·i·a·na (shāk′spir ē ä′nə, -an′ə, -ā′nə), *n.pl.* items, details, publications, etc., relating to Shakespeare.

Shake·spear·i·an·ism (shāk spir′ē ə niz′əm), *n.* **1.** the form of expression peculiar to Shakespeare. **2.** devotion to Shakespeare. **3.** the influence of Shakespeare.

Shakespearian sonnet, the Elizabethan sonnet.

Shake·sper·i·an (shāk spir′ē ən), *adj., n.* Shakespearian.

shake·up (shāk′up′), *n. Informal.* a sudden and complete change; drastic rearrangement of policy, personnel, etc.: *a shakeup in the government. Shakeups are under way in Russia's Far Eastern embassies* (Newsweek).

shak·i·ly (shā′kə lē), *adv.* in a shaky manner.

shak·i·ness (shā′kē nis), *n.* the condition of being shaky.

shak·ing (shā′king), *n.* **1.** the act of a person or thing that shakes. **2.** that which is shaken down. **3.** the ague.
shakings, bits of cordage, canvas, etc., used in making oakum: *The sailors swept up the shakings from the deck.*
—*adj.* that shakes. —**shak′ing·ly,** *adv.*

shaking palsy, Parkinson's disease: *Parkinsonism, or shaking palsy, is no longer a hopeless, progressive, incurable disease* (Science News Letter).

shak·o (shak′ō), *n., pl.* **shak·os.** a high, stiff military hat with a plume or other ornament: *His hat was a giant, moth-eaten bearskin shako* (New Yorker). [< French *schako* < Hungarian *csákó* peaked cap; (originally) point of a cow's horn]

Shako

Shak·sper·i·an or **Shak·sper·e·an** (shāk spir′ē ən), *adj., n.* Shakespearian.

Shak·ta (shuk′tə), *n.* a worshiper of Shakti. Also, **Sakta.**

shak·ti (shuk′tē), *n.* (in Hinduism) creative energy; vital force. [< Sanskrit *śakti* power, force]

Shak·ti (shuk′tē), *n.* in Hinduism: **1.** the female principle: *As Shakti, or Female Energy, she symbolizes the whole universe* (New York Times). **2.** a goddess, Devi, the consort of Shiva. Also, **Sakti.** [< Sanskrit *śakti* power, force]

Shak·tism (shuk′tiz əm), *n.* the worship of Shakti. Also, **Saktism.**

sha·ku (shä′kü), *n.* a Japanese measure of length, equal to about 11¾ inches. [< Japanese *shaku* foot]

sha·ku·do (shä′kü dō′), *n.* a Japanese alloy of copper with from one to ten per cent of gold, much used for ornamental metalwork. It is often subjected to a chemical process which produces a blue patina and exposes a thin film of gold. [< Japanese *shakudō* red copper]

sha·ku·ha·chi (shä′kü hä′chē), *n.* a Japanese bamboo flute with five holes: *One black-and-gray-robed soloist warbled the mournful, breathy tones of the shakuhachi* (Time). [< Japanese *shakuhachi*]

shak·y (shā′kē), *adj.,* **shak·i·er, shak·i·est. 1.** shaking: *a shaky voice, shaky writing.* **2.** liable to break down or give way; not firm or solid; weak: *a shaky porch, a shaky ladder. The movement made a start, if a somewhat shaky one, on the tasks of reshaping its organization and attitudes to meet the needs of the times* (London Times). **3.** not to be depended on; not reliable: *a shaky bank, a shaky knowledge of history.*

shale (shāl), *n.* a fine-grained rock, formed from clay or mud, that splits easily into thin layers: *In the United States and elsewhere, large supplies of oil-yielding organic matter are contained in compact shales* (Gilluly, Waters, and Woodford). [Old English *scealu*]

shale oil, petroleum obtained by the destructive distillation of shale.

shall (shal; *unstressed* shəl), *v., pres.* **shall,** *2nd sing. also* (*Poetic*) **shalt;** *past* **should,** *2nd sing. also* (*Archaic*) **should•est** or **shouldst.** *Shall* is an auxiliary expressing future time, determination or obligation, or uncertainty. **1.** In general, *shall* in the first person expresses simple futurity, in the second and third, determination or obligation: *I shall miss you. You shall hear from us. He shall not do it.* **2.** In questions, *shall* is used in the first person to express simple futurity and in the second if *shall* is expected in the answer: *Shall I go? Shall you come?* **3.** In an indirect quotation, *shall* is used in the first person to express simple futurity and in the second and third to express determination or obligation: *He says I shall go. He says you shall wait.* **4.** In subordinate clauses introduced by *if, when,* etc., *shall* is used in the first person to express simple futurity and in the second and third to express uncertainty: *When I shall see her, I shall give her your message. If he shall come, we shall be saved.* [Old English *sceal* (infinitive *sculan*)]
➔ See **will**[1] for usage note.

shal•loon (sha lün′), *n.* a twilled woolen cloth used chiefly for linings. [Middle English *chaloun* (material used as) a coverlet < Old French *chalon* < *Châlons-sur-Marne,* a city in France]

shal•lop (shal′əp), *n. Archaic.* **1.** any of various small, light, open boats with sail or oars, or both, often like a dinghy: . . . *a shallop flitteth, silken sailed* (Tennyson). **2.** any of various small, sloop-rigged vessels used as vessels of war. [< Middle French *chaloupe* < Dutch *sloep,* perhaps < *sloepen* to guide. Doublet of SLOOP.]

shal•lot (shə lot′, shal′ət), *n.* **1.** a small plant of the amaryllis family, much like an onion, but with a bulb composed of sections or cloves; eschalot. **2.** a bulb or clove of this plant. [short for *eschalot* < Middle French *eschalotte,* alteration of Old French *eschaloigne* scallion]

shal•low (shal′ō), *adj.* **1.** not deep: *shallow water, a shallow dish. Scobie dropped asleep—into one of those shallow sleeps that last a few seconds* (Graham Greene). **2.** lacking depth of thought, knowledge, feeling, etc.; superficial: *a shallow mind, a shallow person.*
—*n.* a shallow place: *The boys splashed in the shallows of the pond. Here was something beyond the shallows of ladies'-school literature* (George Eliot).
—*v.i.* to become less deep. —*v.t.* to make less deep.
[Middle English *shalowe,* perhaps related to Old English *scealdn* shallow. Compare SHOAL[1].] —**shal′low•ly,** *adv.* —**shal′low•ness,** *n.*

shal•lu (shal′ü, sha lü′), *n.* a variety of grain sorghum introduced into the United States from India about 1890.

shal•ly (shal′ē), *v.i.,* **-lied, -ly•ing.** shilly-shally: *Hem and Haw were the sons of sin Created to shally and shirk* (Bliss Carman).

shalm (shôm), *n.* shawm.

sha•lom (shä lōm′, shô-), *n., interj. Hebrew.* **1.** peace. **2. a.** hello. **b.** good-by.

shalt (shalt), *v. Poetic.* 2nd person singular present of **shall.** "Thou shalt" means "You shall": *Thou shalt not kill.*

shal•y (shā′lē), *adj.* **1.** of or containing shale: *shaly sandstone.* **2.** like shale.

sham (sham), *n., adj., v.,* **shammed, shamming.** —*n.* **1.** pretense; fraud: *If peace is sought to be defended or preserved for the safety of the luxurious and the timid, it is a sham* (Emerson). *But when it came to sham—either academic or political—he could be merciless* (Time). **2.** counterfeit; imitation. **3.** a cover or the like to give a thing a different outward appearance: *a pillow sham.* **4.** *Obsolete.* a hoax.
—*adj.* **1.** pretended; feigned: *We fight our sham battles, and go through the drill we learned when we thought the causes mattered* (Harper's). **2.** counterfeit; imitation: *sham diamonds.*
—*v.t.* **1.** to assume the appearance of; feign: *to sham illness, to sham sleep.* **2.** to create a false imitation of: . . . *tawdry frescoes shamming stonework* (J.A. Symonds). **3.** *Obsolete.* to trick. —*v.i.* to make false pretenses; pretend: *The boy is not really angry but only shamming.*
[(originally) dialectal variant of *shame*]
—**Syn.** *n.* **1.** hypocrisy. **2.** forgery.

sha•mal (shə mäl′), *n.* a cold northwest wind that periodically blows across parts of central Asia and the Persian Gulf: *The shamal howled down from central Russia, chilling desert lands* (Newsweek). [< Arabic *shamāl* left hand; north; north wind]

sha•man (shä′mən, sham′ən), *n.* **1.** a priest or medicine man of certain Ural-Altaic tribes of northern Asia: *The province of the shaman is the world of ideas, especially about the unknown* (Ogburn and Nimkoff). **2.** a medicine man, as among certain American Indians: *Some tribes believe that shamans, or medicine men, can communicate directly with spirits* (World Book Encyclopedia). [< Russian *shamán* < Tungus *šaman* < Pali *samana* < Sanskrit *śramaṇa* Buddhist monk; (literally) self-tormentor < *śramati* he tires, fatigues]

sha•man•ic (shə man′ik), *adj.* having to do with or proper to shamans or shamanism.

sha•man•ism (shä′mə niz əm, sham′ə-), *n.* **1.** the primitive religion of the Ural-Altaic peoples of northern Asia, embracing a belief in controlling spirits who can be influenced only by shamans. **2.** any similar religion, as that of certain American Indians: *Though these practitioners are paid for their services, there are none who devote full time to shamanism* (Beals and Hoijer).

sha•man•ist (shä′mə nist, sham′ə-), *n.* a believer in shamanism.

sha•man•is•tic (shä′mə nis′tik, sham′ə-), *adj.* of shamanists; having to do with shamanism: *According to traditional beliefs, the spirits of the departed can be called back to this world—usually by shamanistic rites* (Atlantic).

Sha•mash (shä′mäsh), *n.* the sun god of Babylonian and Assyrian mythology. He makes crops grow and protects against illness.

sham•a•teur (sham′ə chu̇r, -chər, -tu̇r, -tər), *n. Slang.* a player classed as an amateur even though he is paid like a professional: *The amateur-professional status of boxing behind the Iron Curtain is confused because of different conceptions of amateur, professional, "shamateurs" and state amateurs* (New York Times). [blend of *sham* and *amateur*]

sham•a•teur•ism (sham′ə chə riz′əm, -tə-), *n. Slang.* **1.** the use of shamateurs in sports: *Miller is unhappy about the state of cricket . . . finding it corrupted by shamateurism, red tape, conservatism and closed-shop professionalism* (Punch). **2.** the condition of being a shamateur.

sham•ba (sham′bə), *n.* (in East Africa) a piece of cultivated land: *At dawn, parties form up to draw water, to drive cattle, and to work on the shambas* (London Times). [< Swahili *shamba*]

sham•ble (sham′bəl), *v.,* **-bled, -bling,** *n.* —*v.i.* to walk awkwardly or unsteadily: *He shambled around the floor like a lost kid* (Time). —*n.* a shambling walk. [probably special use of *shamble,* singular of obsolete *shambles* tables, benches (from the straddling legs of a bench)] —**sham′bling•ly,** *adv.*

sham•bles (sham′bəlz), *n.pl. or sing.* **1. a.** a place of butchery or of great bloodshed: *the gloomy bigot . . . who . . . converted all these gay cities into shambles* (John L. Motley). **b.** a confusion; mess; general disorder: *to make a shambles of a clean room. He left his affairs in a complete shambles when he died. The voice radio was a shambles of several different operators speaking at once* (New Yorker). **c.** a slaughter house; abattoir: . . . *he was felled like an ox in the butcher's shambles* (Dickens). **2.** *British.* **a.** tables or stalls for the sale of meat, especially in a public market. **b.** a butcher's shop. **c.** *Obsolete.* tables or counters for displaying goods, etc. [Old English *sceamel* counter in a market, bench, ultimately < Latin *scamellum* (diminutive) < *scamnum* bench, stool]

sham•bly (sham′blē), *adj.,* **-bli•er, -bli•est.** characterized by an awkward, irregular gait or motion; ungainly: *Leacock was a shaggy, shambly sort of man* (Canadian Saturday Night).

shame (shām), *n., v.,* **shamed, sham•ing.** —*n.* **1.** a painful feeling of having done something wrong, improper, or silly: *to blush with shame.* **2.** a loss of reputation; disgrace; dishonor: *Free from these slanders, and this open shame* (Shakespeare). **3.** a fact to be sorry about; circumstance that brings disgrace, dishonor, or regret: *It is a shame to be so wasteful.* **4.** a person or thing to be ashamed of; cause of disgrace. **5.** a sense of what is decent or proper.
for shame! shame on you!: *At which remark . . . Miss Caroline very properly said, "For shame, Becky!"* (Thackeray).
put to shame, a. to disgrace; make ashamed: *The drunkard put to shame his wife and children.* **b.** to surpass; make dim by comparison: *Every ship from the New World came freighted with marvels which put the fictions of chivalry to shame* (Francis Parkman).
—*v.t.* **1.** to cause to feel shame; make ashamed. **2.** to drive or force by shame or fear of shame: *Bill was shamed into combing his hair.* **3.** to bring disgrace upon: *He has shamed his parents.* **4.** to surpass; make dim by comparison; outshine: *She'll shame 'em with her good looks, yet* (Dickens).
[Old English *sceamu*]
—**Syn.** *n.* **1.** humiliation, mortification. *-v.t.* **1.** humiliate, mortify.

sha•me•a•nah (shä′mē ä′nə), *n.* shamiana.

shame•faced (shām′fāst′), *adj.* **1.** showing shame and embarrassment: *It was pitiful to see his confusion and hear his awkward and shamefaced apologies* (Mark Twain). **2.** bashful; shy. [earlier, *shamefast;* later taken as if from *shame* + *face*] —**Syn. 1.** abashed. **2.** diffident.

shame•fac•ed•ly (shām′fā′sid lē, shām′-fāst′-), *adv.* in a shamefaced manner; modestly; bashfully.

shame•fac•ed•ness (shām′fā′sid nis, shām′fāst′-), *n.* **1.** modesty; bashfulness; shyness. **2.** the state of being ashamed; ashamedness.

shame•fast (shām′fast, -fäst), *adj. Obsolete.* shamefaced. [Old English *sceamfæst* firm in modesty, shame] —**shame′fast•ly,** *adv.* —**shame′fast•ness,** *n.*

shame•ful (shām′fəl), *adj.* causing shame; bringing disgrace. —**shame′ful•ly,** *adv.* —**shame′ful•ness,** *n.* —**Syn.** dishonorable.

shame•less (shām′lis), *adj.* **1.** without shame; improper: *a shameless woman.* **2.** not modest: *shameless boldness;* . . . *this shameless falsehood* (Edmund Burke). —**shame′less•ly,** *adv.* —**shame′less•ness,** *n.* —**Syn. 2.** impudent, brazen.

sha•mes (shä′məs), *n., pl.* **sha•mos•im** (shä-mos′im), a person who takes care of a synagogue; synagogue sexton or caretaker. [< Yiddish *shames* < Hebrew *shammash*]

sha•mi•a•na (shä′mē ä′nə), *n.* (in India) an awning set on poles, often with open sides: *The Chief Minister of Maharashtra, Mr. Y. B. Chavan, being sworn in by the Governor . . . at a colorful ceremony held in a shamiana . . .* (Times of India). [< Hindustani *shamiyāna* < Persian]

sham•mer (sham′ər), *n.* a person who shams.

sham•my (sham′ē), *n., pl.* **-mies,** or **shammy leather,** chamois.

sham•ois or **sham•oy** (sham′oi), *n.* chamois.

sham•poo (sham pü′), *v.,* **-pooed, -poo•ing,** *n.* —*v.t.* **1.** to wash (the hair or scalp). **2.** to wash the hair or scalp of (a person). **3.** to massage.
—*n.* **1.** a washing of the hair or scalp. **2.** a preparation used for shampooing: *a liquid shampoo.* **3.** a massage.
[Anglo-Indian < Hindustani *chāmpō,* imperative (literally) press, knead < Sanskrit *cap* knead] —**sham•poo′er,** *n.*

sham•rock (sham′rok), *n.* **1.** a bright-green leaf composed of three parts. The shamrock is the national emblem of Ireland: *A son of the Ould Sod who still sports a blackthorn stick, shamrock tie pin, shamrock cuff links, and heavy brogue* (Newsweek). **2.** any of various plants that have leaves like this, such as white clover, the wood sorrel, etc. The name is now most commonly applied to a yellow-flowered clover. [< Irish *seamrōg* (diminutive) < *seamar* clover]

Shamrock (def. 1)

sha•mus (shā′məs), *n. U.S. Slang.* a detective: *Nick Marshall, London shamus, in pickle when client he never saw turns up dead in shabby hotel . . .* (Saturday Review). [< Yiddish *shames* sexton, caretaker; see SHAMES]

Shan (shän, shan), *n.* **1.** a member of certain tribes of southeastern Asia, especially in the Shan state of Upper Burma. **2.** the Thai language of these people.

shan•a•chy or **shan•a•chie** (shan′ə kē), *n., pl.* **-chies.** (in Ireland) a traveling minstrel or storyteller who tells of ancient times and traditions: *Fortunately for the readers of this handsome volume, artist-shanachie Reynolds sidestepped in time* (Saturday Review).

shan·dry·dan (shan′drē dan), *n.* **1.** a light two-wheeled cart or gig. **2.** any old-fashioned, rickety conveyance. [compare dialectal *shandry* a light cart on springs; origin unknown]
shan·dy (shan′dē), *n.* shandygaff.
shan·dy·gaff (shan′dē gaf), *n.* beer and ginger ale mixed. [perhaps < dialectal *shandy* wild, half crazy + *gaff*[2] in the sense "vociferous joking"]
Shang (shäng), *n.* the ruling Chinese dynasty from 1523-1028 B.C., known for weapons and other instruments of bronze.
Shan·gaan (shän gän′), *n.* a member of a Bantu people in the northern Transvaal in South Africa. [< Bantu *Shangana*]
shang·hai (shang′hī, shang hī′), *v.t.*, **-haied, -hai·ing. 1.** to make unconscious by drugs, liquor, etc., and put on a ship to serve as a sailor. **2.** *Informal.* to bring or get by trickery or force: *Thirteen bewildered strollers in Foley Square were legally "shanghaied" . . . to complete a trial jury* (New York Times).
[American English (from the practice of securing sailors by illicit means for long voyages, often to *Shanghai,* China)]
Shang·hai (shang′hī, shang hī′), *n.* one of a longlegged breed of domestic fowl. [< *Shanghai,* a seaport in China]
Shan·gri·la or **Shan·gri-La** (shang′grí lä′), *n.* an idyllic earthly paradise: *The austere serenity of Shangri-La. Its . . . pale pavilions shimmered in repose from which all the fret of existence had ebbed away* (James Hilton). [< the name of an inaccessible land in the remote Himalayas in *Lost Horizon,* 1933, a novel by James Hilton]
shank (shangk), *n.* **1.** the part of the leg between the knee and the ankle. **2. a.** the corresponding part in animals. **b.** a cut of meat from the upper part of the leg of an animal. **3.** the whole leg: *to stir one's shanks.* **4.** any part like a leg, stem, or shaft: *The shank of a fishhook is the straight part between the hook and the loop.* **5.** the body of a printing type. **6. a.** the narrow part of a shoe connecting the broad part of the sole with the heel. **b.** the piece of metal, fiber, etc., used to shape this part. **7.** the latter end or part of anything: *the shank of the day.* **8.** *Music.* a crook.
by shank's mare, on foot; by walking: *Pilgrims had converged from all over India—by train, by cart and by shank's mare* (Scientific American).
go or **ride on shank's mare,** to go on foot; walk: *I'd rather . . . ride on shank's mare* (S. Bishop).
—*v.t.* to strike (a golf ball) with the heel of an iron club: *He had a quick snatch at the ball, shanked it and took five* (London Times).
shank it, to walk: *Let him shank it! We're in no hurry to have him home* (George Douglas).
shank off, to rot at the stem: *Entire beds [of pansies] have been known to shank off during a very hot summer* (J. Turner).
[Old English *sceanca*]
shank·bone (shangk′bōn′), *n.* the shinbone of an animal: *Someone discovered that bluefish would strike at the shankbone of an alley cat* (Time).
shan·ny (shan′ē), *n., pl.* **-nies** or (*collectively*) **-ny.** the smooth blenny of Europe. [origin uncertain]
shan't (shant, shänt), shall not.
shant·ey (shan′tē), *n., pl.* **-eys.** chantey.
shan·tung or **Shan·tung** (shan′tung, shan tung′), *n.* **1.** a heavy pongee, a kind of soft silk. **2.** a similar cloth made of rayon or cotton. [< *Shantung,* a province in China]
shan·ty[1] (shan′tē), *n., pl.* **-ties.** a roughly built hut or cabin; shack: *Her childhood was spent in a succession of Florida and Georgia cracker shanties, in dreary sawmill towns* (Time). [American English, perhaps < Canadian French *chantier* lumberjack's headquarters, in French, timber yard, dock < Latin *canthērius* framework, rafter; beast of burden]
shan·ty[2] (shan′tē), *n., pl.* **-ties.** chantey. [variant of *chantey*]
shanty boat, a rude houseboat used especially on the Mississippi River and in logging areas.
shan·ty·man (shan′tē man′, -mən), *n., pl.* **-men. 1.** a lumberman. **2.** a backwoodsman.
shan·ty·town (shan′tē toun′), *n.,* or **shanty town,** *U.S.* **1.** a poor, run-down section of a city or a town: *Rural workers flock to oilfields and cities, only to sit idle in shantytowns* (Time). **2.** a settlement of makeshift shacks, tents, etc., usually near a new military installation, factory, etc.: *Shantytowns spring up overnight on the outskirts of Lima and other cities* (Atlantic).
shap·a·ble (shā′pə bəl), *adj.* that can be shaped.
shape (shāp), *n., v.,* **shaped, shap·ing.** —*n.* **1.** outward contour or outline; form; figure: *All circles have the same shape; rectangles have different shapes. A white shape stood at his bedside.* **2.** an assumed appearance; guise; disguise: *A witch was supposed to take the shape of a cat or bat.* **3.** condition: *The athlete exercised to keep himself in good shape.* **4.** a definite form; arrangement; order: *Take time to get your thoughts into shape. He collected his cut of the surplus value in the shape of the rent which was paid him* (Edmund Wilson). **5.** a kind; sort: *Dangers of ev'ry shape and name . . .* (William Cowper). **6.** a mold or pattern for giving shape to something. **7.** something shaped, as jelly, pudding, etc., shaped in a mold or metal of any of various shapes: *But the English firmly entrenched behind impenetrable ramparts of . . . cold shape and suet pudding, have gone right on boiling their Brussels sprouts* (Time).
in shape, *Informal.* in good condition or health: *In 1955, at Key West, Ernest [Hemingway] looks old, fat, lined, flat-footed. But in 1958, in Ketchum, he is back in shape* (New Yorker).
lick into shape, *Informal.* to make presentable or usable: *to lick a story into shape. They . . . promised their cooperation in licking it into shape* (London Times).
take shape, to have or take on a definite form: *The general outlines of "Where's Charley?" began to take shape* (New Yorker).
[Old English *gesceap*]
—*v.t.* **1.** to form; make into a form: *The child shapes clay into balls.* **2.** to adapt in form: *That hat is shaped to your head.* **3.** to give definite form or character to: *events which shape people's lives.* **4.** to direct; plan; devise; aim: *to shape one's course in life.* **5.** to express in words: *to shape a question or a reply. She had a way of idiomatically shaping a musical phrase that cannot be taught* (New York Times). **6.** mold; pattern. **7.** *Obsolete.* to appoint; decree; determine. —*v.i.* **1.** to take shape; assume form: *clay shapes easily. His plan is shaping well.* **2.** to turn out; happen.
shape up, a. to take on a certain form or appearance; develop: *The plans for the new building are shaping up nicely.* **b.** to show a certain tendency: *What had shaped up as a Democratic cat-and-dog fight became . . . a "high-level" debate* (Newsweek).
[Middle English *shapen,* Old English *sceapen,* past participle of *scieppan* to create]
—**Syn.** *n.* **1.** cast, build. See **form.**
SHAPE (no periods), Supreme Headquarters, Allied Powers in Europe: *We at SHAPE are basing all our operational planning on using atomic and thermonuclear weapons in our defense* (Time).
shaped (shāpt), *adj.* formed by shaping; made into a particular shape: *a shaped mirror.*
-shaped, *combining form.* having a ——— shape or shapes: *Cone-shaped = having a cone shape. Many-shaped = having many shapes.*
shaped charge, a cone-shaped explosive charge used especially in armor-piercing shells, such as those of a bazooka: *AEC's scientists hope to develop an atomic explosive that exerts much of its force in one direction, as a "shaped charge" does* (Time).
shape·less (shāp′lis), *adj.* **1.** without definite shape: *a shapeless old hat.* **2.** having an unattractive shape: *a fat, shapeless woman.* —**shape′less·ly,** *adv.* —**shape′less·ness,** *n.* —**Syn. 1.** formless. **2.** unshapely.
shape·li·ness (shāp′lē nis), *n.* the state of being shapely.
shape·ly (shāp′lē), *adj.,* **-li·er, -li·est.** having a pleasing shape; well-formed: *. . . a delicate shapely little hand* (W.H. Hudson).
shap·er (shā′pər), *n.* **1.** a person who makes, forms, or shapes. **2.** (in metalwork) a combined lathe and planer, which can be used, with attachments, for doing a great variety of work. **3.** a stamp or press for cutting and molding sheet metal or certain plastics. **4.** (in woodworking) a planer for cutting moldings, panels, etc., having irregular forms.
shape-up (shāp′up′), *n. U.S.* a system of hiring longshoremen whereby the men line up each workday to be selected for work by the foreman: *The dock workers remained in groups on the outside, refusing to heed the shape-up or work call* (New York Times).
sha·poo (shä′pü), *n.* a mountain sheep of central Asia which resembles the bighorn of North America. [< Tibetan *sha-pho*]
shar·a·ble (shãr′ə bəl), *adj.* shareable.
shard[1] (shärd), *n.* **1.** a broken piece; fragment. **2.** a piece of broken earthenware or pottery. **3.** the hard case that covers a beetle's wing; elytron. Also, **sherd.** [Old English *sceard* fragment]
shard[2] (shärd), *n. British Dialect.* excrement; a mass of cow dung. [origin uncertain]
shard beetle, any of various dung beetles.
shard-born (shärd′bôrn′), *adj.* **1.** born or generated in shards or dung: *. . . The shard-born beetle . . .* (Shakespeare). **2.** borne on shards or elytra (due to a misinterpretation of Shakespeare).
shard·ed (shär′did), *adj.* having shards or elytra, as a beetle; coleopterous: *Sharded insects . . . vastly outnumber all the other forms of active life we see* (New York Times).
share[1] (shãr), *n., v.,* **shared, shar·ing.** —*n.* **1.** the part belonging to one individual; portion; part: *to have more than one's share of work, to take little share in a conversation.* **2.** a part of anything owned in common with others: *One of the boys offered to sell his share in the boat.* **3.** each of the parts into which the ownership of a company or corporation is divided. Shares are usually in the form of transferable certificates of stock. *The ownership of this railroad is divided into several million shares. With borrowed money, they bought 59,100 shares . . . then agreed to resell the block* (Newsweek). *Abbr.:* sh.
go shares, to share in something: *If you find the treasure we will go shares* (H. Rider Haggard).
on shares, sharing in the risks and profits. *Men can always be had to go on shares, which is by far the most profitable method, both to the employers and the fishermen* (Jeremy Belknap).
—*v.t.* **1.** to use together; enjoy together; have in common: *The sisters share the same room.* **2.** to divide into parts, each taking a part: *to share one's food with others.* **3.** to divide: *. . . a thin oaten cake, shared into fragments* (Charlotte Brontë). —*v.i.* to have a share; take part: *to share in the expenses. All shared in making the picnic a success.*
share and share alike, a. to share alike in; have equal shares in a will, insurance policy, etc.: *I bequeath to my nephews and nieces . . . the whole of my . . . personal effects, share and share alike* (Frederick Marryat). **b.** to share everything with others: *Children should not fight about who is to have a toy, but should share and share alike.*
[Old English *scearu* a cutting, shaving, division, related to *scieran* to cut, shear]
—**Syn.** *n.* **1.** allotment, quota. *-v.t.* **1. Share, participate, partake** mean to use, enjoy, or have something in common with another. **Share,** meaning either to give or to take a part, emphasizes the idea of common possession, enjoyment, use, etc.: *He shares a room with his brother.* **Participate,** more formal, followed by *in,* means to take part together with others in an idea, feeling, or action: *He participated in the discussion.* **Partake,** now formal, and usually followed by *of,* means to take one's (own) share of food, pleasure, qualities, etc.: *He partook of our meal.*
share[2] (shãr), *n.* the part of a plow that cuts through the soil; plowshare: *Until fairly recent times . . . the share was simply a heavy piece of pointed wood . . .* (Beals and Hoijer). [Old English *scear,* related to *scieran* to cut, divide]
share·a·ble (shãr′ə bəl), *adj.* that can be shared: *The basis of federal payments would amount to about half the shareable costs of hospital services* (Wall Street Journal). Also, **sharable.**
share·crop (shãr′krop′), *v.i., v.t.,* **-cropped, -crop·ping.** to farm as a sharecropper: *Later they sharecropped, saved money, bought their own land, grew cotton, corn and rice* (Time).
share·crop·per (shãr′krop′ər), *n.* a person who farms land for the owner in return for part of the crops: *Sharecroppers and tenant farmers left the farm and turned to the rapidly growing opportunities in industry* (Time). [American English < earlier *share-crop,* adjective]
share·hold·er (shãr′hōl′dər), *n.* a person owning shares of stock; stockholder: *This*

railroad has many thousands of shareholders. At the meeting shareholders approved a three-for-one split of the common stock (Wall Street Journal).

share·hold·ing (shãr′hōl′ding), *n.* stockholding; shareownership: *Chase Manhattan plans to acquire . . . an important shareholding in an overseas banking corporation* (New York Times).

share·out (shãr′out′), *n.* distribution (of prizes, shares, commodities, etc.) in shares: *In the shareout of decorations which had accompanied victory his name had been noticeably absent* (Sunday Times).

share·own·er (shãr′ō′nər), *n.* shareholder.

share·own·er·ship (shãr′ō′nər ship), *n.* ownership of shares of stock: *Without stock markets this free exchange of shareownership obviously would be extremely difficult, if not totally impossible* (Alfred L. Malabre, Jr.).

shar·er (shãr′ər), *n.* a person or thing that shares.

Sha·ri·a or **Sha·ri·ah** (shə rē′ə), *n.* the religious law of the Moslems, consisting of the Koran and the traditional sayings of Mohammed: *They urge the enforcement of a modified Sharia law and propagate the principle of a theocratic state* (Atlantic). Also, **Sheria.** [< Arabic *sharī'a* road to the watering place, law]

shark[1] (shärk), *n.* any of a group of fishes, mostly marine, certain kinds of which are large and ferocious, and destructive to other fishes and sometimes dangerous to man.

Blue Shark[1] (7½ to 12 ft. long)

Sharks have streamlined, spindlelike bodies, with gill slits on the sides and thick, dull-colored skin, and swim by movements of the tail: *A world's record brown shark . . . has been caught in Florida waters* (New York Times). [origin uncertain] —**shark′like′,** *adj.*

shark[2] (shärk), *n.* **1.** a dishonest person who preys on others. **2.** *Slang.* a person unusually good at something; expert: *a shark at bridge.*
—*v.i.* **1.** to act or live by preying on others; live by trickery. **2.** to be a card sharper.
—*v.t.* **1.** to obtain by trickery, fraud, or theft. **2.** *Archaic.* to collect quickly.
[probably < *shark*[1]]

shark-liv·er oil (shärk′liv′ər), oil extracted from the liver of sharks, used as a source of vitamin A and as a preservative: *Shark-liver oil contains a far higher concentration of vitamin A than cod-liver oil, but cod are infinitely less troublesome to catch* (Wall Street Journal).

shark·proof (shärk′prüf′), *adj.* able to withstand an attack by a shark; protected against sharks: *The sharkproof cage, made of chicken wire and supported by empty gasoline drums . . .* (New Yorker).

shark·skin (shärk′skin′), *n.* **1.** a cloth made from fine threads of wool, rayon, or cotton, used in suits: . . . *dapper, aromatic men in sharkskin and effulgent neckties* (New Yorker). **2. a.** the skin of a shark. **b.** leather made from the skin of a shark.

shark sucker, a fish, widely distributed over warm seas, that attaches itself by means of a sucker to large fish without regard to their species; remora.

sharp (shärp), *adj.* **1.** having a thin cutting edge or a fine point: *a sharp knife, a sharp pin, a pencil with a sharp point.* **2.** having a point; not rounded: *a sharp nose, a sharp corner on a box.* **3.** with a sudden change of direction; abrupt: *a sharp turn in the road.* **4.** very cold; nippy: *sharp weather, a sharp morning.* **5.** severe; biting: *sharp words, a sharp note of reproof. The coal industry urged Congress to place sharp curbs on imports of residual fuel oil* (Wall Street Journal). **6.** feeling somewhat like a cut or prick; affecting the senses keenly: *a sharp taste, a sharp noise, a sharp pain.* **7.** clear; distinct: *the sharp contrast between black and white.* **8.** quick in movement; brisk: *a sharp walk or run.* **9.** fierce; violent: *a sharp attack or struggle.* **10.** keen; eager: *a sharp desire, a sharp appetite.* **11.** being aware of things quickly: *sharp ears. Their lack of immediate concern . . . doesn't mean bankers and economists aren't following it with a sharp eye* (Wall Street Journal). **12.** wide-awake; watchful; vigilant: *to keep a sharp watch.* **13.** quick in mind; shrewd; clever: *a sharp critic, sharp at a bargain. With their own sharp and realistic minds, they had lopped off the sentimentality and fantasy* (Edmund Wilson). **14.** high in pitch; shrill: *a sharp cry of fear.* **15.** *Music.* **a.** above the true pitch. **b.** raised a half step in pitch: *G sharp.* **c.** having sharps in the signature. **16.** *Phonetics.* (of a consonant) pronounced with breath and not with voice; voiceless. **17.** *U.S. Slang.* attractive; handsome.
—*adv.* **1.** promptly; exactly: *Come at one o'clock sharp.* **2.** in a sharp manner; in an alert manner; keenly: *Look sharp!* **3.** suddenly; abruptly: *to pull a horse up sharp.* **4.** *Music.* above the true pitch: *to sing sharp.*
—*n.* **1.** *Music.* **a.** a tone one half step above a given tone. **b.** the sign (♯) for this. **2.** a swindler; sharper: . . . *chiseling tactics on the part of back-alley sharps* (Wall Street Journal). **3.** *Informal.* an expert: *What the sales manager was about to say would seem painfully old-hat to a personnel sharp* (Atlantic).
sharps, a. the hard part of wheat, requiring a second grinding: *These sharps were ground a second time, . . . and the produce was 46 lb. of . . . barley* (Farmer's Magazine). **b.** long needles with very sharp points: *The sharps are those usually called "sewing needles"* (Michael Morrall).
—*v.t. Music.* to raise (a note) in pitch, especially by one half step. —*v.i. Music.* to sound a note above the true pitch.
[Old English *scearp*] —**sharp′ly,** *adv.* —**sharp′ness,** *n.*
—**Syn.** *adj.* **2.** angular, pointed. **5.** sarcastic, tart, caustic. **6.** piercing, intense, painful. **11.** quick, discerning, perspicacious. **13. Sharp, keen, acute,** used figuratively to describe a person or the mind, mean quickly aware or penetrating. **Sharp** suggests being well suited to cutting or piercing through things, and implies cleverness, shrewdness, quickness to see and take advantage, sometimes dishonestly: *He is a sharp lawyer.* **Keen** suggests being shaped to slash through things, and implies clearness and quickness of perception and thinking: *He has a keen mind.* **Acute,** literally meaning coming to a sharp point, implies penetrating perception, insight, or understanding: *He is an acute interpreter of current events.*

sharp-cut (shärp′kut′), *adj.* **1.** cut sharply to give a clear outline. **2.** sharply defined; distinct; clear.

sharp-edged (shärp′ejd′), *adj.* **1.** having a sharp edge or edges. **2.** caustic; sarcastic: *Harold Talburt is a veteran political cartoonist, known for his sharp-edged lampoons* (Newsweek). **3.** trenchant; incisive: *Instead of the . . . sharp-edged direction that Herman Shumlin brought to the play, there is in the film a sluggish, confused manipulation of ideas and players* (Time).

sharp·en (shär′pən), *v.t.* to make sharp or sharper: *to sharpen a pencil, sharpen your wits.* —*v.i.* to become sharp or sharper.

sharp·en·er (shär′pə nər), *n.* a person or thing that sharpens: *a pencil sharpener.*

sharp·er (shär′pər), *n.* **1.** a swindler; cheat. **2.** a gambler who makes a living by cheating at cards, etc.: *a card sharper.*

sharp-eyed (shärp′īd′), *adj.* **1.** having keen sight: *a sharp-eyed person, sharp-eyed mice.* **2.** watchful; vigilant: *The top candidates were counting the early returns, like sharp-eyed pineapple sorters in a canning factory* (Time).

sharp-fanged (shärp′fangd′), *adj.* **1.** having sharp teeth. **2.** biting; caustic; sarcastic.

sharp·ie (shär′pē), *n.* **1.** a long, flat-bottomed boat with a centerboard and one or two masts, each rigged with a triangular sail. **2.** *U.S. Slang.* a sharper; cheat: *We hear of a girl who was loaded with furs and automobiles by a sharpie using absconded funds* (Alistair Cooke).

Sharpie (def. 1)

sharp·ish (shär′pish), *adj.* somewhat sharp: *Second-half profits . . . were only fractionally down whereas there was a sharpish setback in the first six months* (London Times).

sharp-nosed (shärp′nōzd′), *adj.* **1.** having a pointed nose or end: *sharp-nosed pliers.* **2.** having a keen scent: *sharp-nosed dogs.*

sharps (shärps), *n.pl.* See under **sharp,** *n.*

sharp-set (shärp′set′), *adj.* **1.** keen; eager. **2.** very hungry: *Being sharp-set, we told him to get breakfast* (Herman Melville).

sharp-shinned (shärp′shind′), *adj.* having slender shanks.

sharp-shinned hawk, a small North American hawk with short wings, long tail, and a white breast barred with reddish-brown.

sharp·shoot·er (shärp′shü′tər), *n.* **1.** a person who shoots very well. **2.** a soldier chosen to do accurate shooting: *The absence of a sharpshooter . . . blunted the sharp edge of their attack and minimised their chances of victory* (Times of India).

sharp·shoot·ing (shärp′shü′ting), *n.* the act of a sharpshooter. —*adj.* that acts as a sharpshooter.

sharp-sight·ed (shärp′sī′tid), *adj.* **1.** having sharp sight: *He is as sharp-sighted as a hawk* (Scott). **2.** sharp-witted: *a sharp-sighted move.* —**sharp′-sight′ed·ness,** *n.*

sharp-tailed (shärp′tāld′), *adj.* having a sharp-pointed tail or tailfeathers.

sharp-tailed grouse, a grouse of the northwestern United States and Canada with a short, pointed tail; pintail.

sharp-tailed sandpiper, a sandpiper of Asia that is seen along the Pacific coast of North America during migration.

sharp-tailed sparrow, a sparrow found in marshes of the eastern United States and Canada.

sharp-tongued (shärp′tungd′), *adj.* sharp or bitter of speech; severely critical; cutting; biting: *They were oblivious of the scornful comments of their sharp-tongued neighbors* (New Yorker).

sharp-wit·ted (shärp′wit′id), *adj.* having or showing a quick, keen mind. —**Syn.** bright, clever.

sharp·y (shär′pē), *n., pl.* **sharp·ies.** *U.S. Slang.* sharpie (def. 2): *Peddling useless drugs, fake remedies and gadgets in the United States mails is a lucrative source of income for some of the meanest sharpies in the world* (Science News Letter).

shash·lik (shäs lik′), *n.* shish kebab.

Shas·ta daisy (shas′tə), **1.** a cultivated variety of daisy having large flowers with white rays. **2.** its flower. [American English < Mount *Shasta,* a mountain in California]

Shas·tan (shas′tən), *adj., n. Geology.* Comanchean.

shas·tra (shäs′trə), *n.* sastra.

shat·ter (shat′ər), *v.t.* **1.** to break into pieces: *A stone shattered the window.* **2.** to disturb greatly; destroy: *The great mental strain and overwork shattered his mind. Her hopes were shattered. A great postwar illusion . . . was shattered decisively last week by the people of France themselves* (Newsweek). **3.** *Obsolete.* to scatter; disperse. —*v.i.* to be shattered.
—*n.* **1.** a shattering: *The stone hit the window and a shatter of glass fell on their heads.* **2.** a shattering quality or condition: *Only superior audio equipment can begin to play back a brilliantly recorded piano disc without shatter or distortion* (Harper's).
shatters, fragments: *If ever the heart come to be sensible of its blows, it will break all to shatters* (William Fenner).
[Middle English *schater(en)* cause (leaves, etc.) to fall; to disperse. Perhaps related to SCATTER.]
—**Syn.** *v.t.* **1.** *v.i.* smash, splinter. See **break.**

shat·ter·er (shat′ər ər), *n.* a person or thing that shatters or makes a shatter.

shat·ter·ing (shat′ər ing), *adj.* **1.** that shatters; destructive: *We felt the shattering impact as the ship hit the rocks.* **2.** startling; emotionally overpowering: *To see this play is to undergo a shattering experience. Her answer . . . was as shattering as it was rapid* (Thomas DeQuincey). **3.** (of sound) ear-splitting; very loud: *The shattering trumpet shrilleth high* (Tennyson).
—*n.* **1.** a breaking into pieces. **2.** the broken pieces; shatters. —**shat′ter·ing·ly,** *adv.*

shat·ters (shat′ərz), *n.pl.* See under **shatter,** *n.*

shat·ter·proof (shat′ər prüf′), *adj.* that will not shatter: *The door . . . is said to be weather-resistant, shatterproof, and warp-proof* (Science News Letter).

shat·ter·y (shat′ər ē), *adj.* **1.** liable to be shattered. **2.** easily crumbled, as rock or soil.

Sha·van·te (shə van′tē), *n., pl.* **-tes** or **-te.** **1.** a member of a Brazilian tribe of the Ge linguistic family living along the Tocantins

River in Brazil. **2.** the language of this tribe.

shave (shāv), *v.*, **shaved, shaved** or **shav·en, shav·ing,** *n.* —*v.t.* **1.** to cut hair from (the face, chin, etc.) with a razor. **2.** to cut off (hair) with a razor. **3.** to cut off in thin slices; cut in thin slices: *She shaved the chocolate.* **4.** to cut very close. **5.** to come very close to; graze: *The car shaved the corner.* **6.** *U.S. Informal.* to discount (a promissory note) at a very high rate of interest. **7.** *Informal.* to reduce: *Mondolini, sentenced in absentia . . . had his term shaved to two years* (Maclean's). —*v.i.* **1.** to remove hair with a razor **2.** to be hard or extortionate in bargains.
—*n.* **1.** the cutting off of hair with a razor. **2.** any of various tools for shaving, scraping, removing very thin slices, etc. **3.** a shaving; thin slice. **4.** *Informal.* a narrow miss or escape: *The racing cars passed each other by a shave.*
[Old English *sceafan* to shave]

shave·ling (shāv′ling), *n.* **1.** a tonsured monk, friar, or priest (an unfriendly use). **2.** a youth.

shav·en (shā′vən), *adj.* **1.** shaved. **2.** closely cut. **3.** tonsured. —*v.* shaved; a past participle of **shave.**

shav·er (shā′vər), *n.* **1.** a person who shaves. **2.** an instrument for shaving. **3.** *Informal.* a youngster; small boy: *Young shavers like you don't have pipes* (William De Morgan).

shave·tail (shāv′tāl′), *n. U.S. Slang.* a new second lieutenant: *Every military type is represented—the good soldier, the coward, the goldbrick, the rank-happy shavetail* (Time). [American English; earlier, an army mule (because of the appearance of their tails)]

Sha·vi·an (shā′vē ən), *adj.* **1.** of or having to do with George Bernard Shaw. **2.** characteristic of George Bernard Shaw: *Shavian wit. He is a dapper and well-to-do gentleman who sports a Shavian beard* (Time). —*n.* a devoted admirer of George Bernard Shaw, his works, or his theories.

shav·ing (shā′ving), *n.* **1.** the act or process of cutting hair from the face, chin, etc., with a razor. **2.** the act of scraping or cutting a thin slice off a surface. **3.** Often, **shavings.** a very thin slice or piece taken off a surface: *shavings of cheese. Shavings of wood are cut off by a plane.*

shaving brush, a brush used to put on the lather before shaving: *You'll find an old-fashioned silver-handled shaving brush, with excellent badger bristles* (New Yorker).

shaving cream, a creamy preparation put on the face for shaving.

shaving lotion, a fragrant lotion usually containing alcohol, applied to the face before or after shaving to soothe the skin.

shaving mug, a mug used to hold soap or lather for shaving.

Sha·vu·os (shä vü′ōth, shə vü′əs), *n.* Shabuoth.

shaw (shô), *n.* **1.** *Archaic.* a thicket; small wood: *He can turn it into a thing of natural beauty all on its own, if he takes many hints from neighboring lanes and shaws* (Observer). **2.** *Scottish.* the stalks and leaves of potatoes, turnips, etc. [Old English *sceaga.* Related to SHAG[1].]

shawl (shôl), *n.* a square or oblong piece of cloth to be worn about the shoulders or head. [< Persian *shāl*] —**Syn.** scarf.

shawl collar, a yokelike collar and lapel reaching from the neck to the chest or waistline: . . . *a wrapped cocoon coat with a wide shawl collar* (New Yorker).

shawled (shôld), *adj.* wearing or covered with a shawl.

shawl pattern, a pattern on cloth, resembling patterns on Oriental shawls.

shawm (shôm), *n.* any of certain wood-wind musical instruments like the oboe or clarinet, used especially in the Middle Ages: *The instrument had a sweet, thin, flutelike tone, comparable to that of a shepherd's shawm* (New Yorker). [apparently new singular < Middle English *shalmys* (taken as plural) < Old French *chalemie,* variant of *chalemel.* Doublet of CHALUMEAU.]

Shaw·nee (shô nē′), *n., pl.* **-nee** or **-nees,** *adj.* —*n.* **1.** a member of a tribe of American Indians formerly centered in the Tennessee Valley, but widespread, now living in Oklahoma. **2.** the Algonkian language of this tribe. —*adj.* of or belonging to this tribe. [American English < Algonkian (Shawnee) *Shawunogi* southerners]

Shaw·nee·wood (shô nē′wu̇d′), *n.* the western catalpa.

Shaw·wal (shô wäl′), *n.* the tenth month of the Moslem calendar. [< Arabic *shawwāl*]

shay (shā), *n. Informal.* a light carriage with two wheels and one seat; chaise. [< *chaise* (taken as plural). Doublet of CHAISE, CHAIR, CATHEDRA.]

she (shē), *pron., sing. nom.* **she,** *poss.* **her** or **hers,** *obj.* **her;** *pl. nom.* **they,** *poss.* **their** or **theirs,** *obj.* **them;** *n., pl.* **shes.** —*pron.* **1.** the girl, woman, or female animal spoken about or mentioned before. **2.** anything thought of as female and spoken about or mentioned before: *She was a fine old ship.* —*n.* a girl; woman; female animal: *Is it a he or a she?* [probably Old English *sēo,* or *sīe,* demonstrative pronoun]

she-, *combining form.* a female ——: *She-goat = a female goat.*

shea (shē), *n.* an African tree of the sapodilla family, whose seeds yield shea butter; butter tree. [< Mandingo *si, sye*]

shea butter, a fat obtained from the seeds of the shea, used as food and in Europe for the manufacture of soap, etc.

shead·ing (shē′ding), *n.* a civil division on the Isle of Man. [variant of earlier *shedding,* verbal noun < *shed,* in early meaning "to divide"]

sheaf (shēf), *n., pl.* **sheaves,** *v.* —*n.* a bundle of things of the same sort bound together or so arranged that they can be bound together: *a sheaf of wheat, a sheaf of arrows.* —*v.t.* to bind into a sheaf or sheaves: *Anyone with a patch of land worth talking about was out cutting hay or sheafing corn* (New Yorker). [Old English *scēaf*]

sheal (shēl), *v.t. British Dialect.* to shell (peas, etc.).

sheal·ing (shē′ling), *n. Scottish.* shieling.

shear (shir), *v.,* **sheared** or (*Archaic*) **shore, sheared** or **shorn, shear·ing,** *n.* —*v.t.* **1.** to cut with shears or scissors. **2.** to remove (wool or fleece) by cutting or clipping: *to shear wool from sheep.* **3.** to cut the wool or fleece from: *The farmer sheared his sheep.* **4.** to cut close; cut off; cut. **5.** to break by a force causing two parts or pieces to slide on each other in opposite directions: *Too much pressure on the handles of the scissors sheared off the rivet holding the blades together.* **6.** to strip or deprive as if by cutting: *The assembly of the people had been shorn of its legislative powers* (James A. Froude). **7.** *Dialect.* to reap with a sickle. —*v.i.* **1.** *Dialect.* to use a sickle on crops. **2.** *Archaic.* to cut through something with the aid of a weapon.
—*n.* **1.** the act or process of shearing. **2.** that which is taken off by shearing. **3.** one blade of a pair of shears. **4.** a pair of shears. **5.** any of various machines for cutting metal, especially sheet metal. **6. a.** a force causing two parts or pieces to slide on each other in opposite directions. **b.** the strain or deformation resulting from this; shearing stress.
[Old English *sceran.* Compare SHARE[1], SHARE[2].] —**shear′er,** *n.*

shear boom, (in lumbering) a boom fixed to guide floating logs in the desired direction.

shear flocks, the part of the nap which is cut from cloth while it is being sheared.

shear·ing (shir′ing), *n.* **1.** the act of a person or thing that shears. **2.** an instance of shearing.

shearings, something cut off with shears or some other sharp instrument: *Put the shearings of scarlet cloth upon the coals* (G. Smith).

shearing plane, *Geology.* the plane along which rupture from shearing stress takes place in rocks.

shearing stress, the stress in a body caused by shear.

shear legs, a hoist for heavy weights; shears.

shear·ling (shir′ling), *n.* **1.** a sheep that has been shorn once. **2.** the fleece of such a sheep: . . . *western canvas jacket with shearling type lining* (New Yorker).

shear·man (shir′mən), *n., pl.* **-men.** a person who shears cloth.

shear plane, *Geology.* shearing plane.

shears (shirz), *n.pl.* **1.** large scissors: *barber's shears, tin shears.* **2.** any cutting instrument resembling scissors. **3.** an apparatus for hoisting heavy weights, consisting of two or more poles fastened together at the top to support a block and tackle. [Old English *scēara,* plural of *scēar.* Compare SHARE[2].]

shear·wa·ter (shir′wôt′ər, -wot′-), *n.* any of several sea birds related to the petrel, with long bills and long wings which appear to shear or cleave the water.

shear wave, a wave in an elastic medium which causes movement of the medium but no change in its volume. A secondary wave is a shear wave.

shear zone, *Geology.* a belt of rock crushed and metamorphosed by compression: *Along shear zones massive rocks become schists.*

sheat·fish (shēt′fish′), *n., pl.* **-fish·es** or (*collectively*) **-fish.** a very large European catfish sometimes weighing as much as 400 pounds. [alteration of earlier *sheath-fish;* influenced by German *Scheide* sheath]

sheath (shēth), *n., pl.* **sheaths** (shēᴛʜz), *v.* —*n.* **1.** a case or covering for the blade of a sword, knife, etc. See **bowie knife** for picture. **2.** any similar covering, especially on an animal or plant: **a.** *Botany.* the part of an organ rolled around a stem or other body to form a tube: *In the grasses, the blade arises, not from a petiole, but from a sheath* (Fred W. Emerson). **b.** *Zoology.* the elytron of a beetle. **3.** a narrow, tight-fitting dress with straight lines: *In the past few years fashion has tricked herself out in the sack, the chemise, the trapeze, the baby doll, the sheath* (Punch). —*v.t.* to sheathe.
[Old English *scēath*]

sheath·bill (shēth′bil′), *n.* either of two white, pigeonlike sea birds related to the plovers, with a horny case partly covering the bill. It lives in cold regions of the Southern Hemisphere.

sheathe (shēᴛʜ), *v.t.,* **sheathed, sheath·ing. 1.** to put (a sword, etc.) into a sheath or scabbard. **2.** to enclose in a case or covering: *a mummy sheathed in linen, doors sheathed in metal. He is a motorboat fancier, and his latest vessel . . . is sheathed in teak* (New Yorker). **3.** to retract (claws). **4.** to plunge or bury (a sword, tusk, etc.) in the body of an opponent, victim, etc.: *Not I, till I have sheathed my rapier in his bosom . . .* (Shakespeare). —**Syn. 2.** incase.

sheath·er (shē′ᴛʜər), *n.* a person who sheathes.

sheath·ing (shē′ᴛʜing), *n.* **1.** a casing; covering, as the first covering of boards on a house, nailed to the rafters, or the thin protective covering of copper, etc., on the hull of a vessel. **2.** the material used for either of these, especially boards, plywood, etc. **3.** the act of putting on or into a sheath.

sheath knife, a knife carried in a sheath.

sheath-winged (shēth′wingd′), *adj.* having the wings sheathed in elytra, as a beetle.

shea tree, the shea.

sheave[1] (shēv), *v.t.,* **sheaved, sheav·ing.** to gather and tie into a sheaf or sheaves: *to sheave wheat.* [< *sheaf,* by analogy to plural *sheaves*]

sheave[2] (shēv, shiv), *n.* a wheel with a grooved rim, as the wheel of a pulley. [Middle English *sheeve,* variant of *schive*]

sheaves (shēvz; *for 2 also* shivz), *n.* **1.** the plural of **sheaf. 2.** the plural of **sheave**[2].

She·ba (shē′bə), *n.* **Queen of,** (in the Bible) a queen who visited Solomon to learn of his great wisdom. I Kings 10:1-13.

she·bang (shə bang′), *n. U.S. Slang.* **1.** an outfit; concern: *A single skilled button pusher can run the whole shebang* (New Yorker). **2.** an affair; event: *They went to a big shebang last night and slept late this morning.* [American English; earlier, dilapidated shelter, conveyance, etc.; perhaps alteration of French *char à bancs* car with benches]

She·bat (shə bät′), *n.* (in the Jewish calendar) the fifth month of the civil year and the eleventh month of the ecclesiastical year, beginning in January. [< Hebrew *shəbāṭ*]

she·been (shi bēn′), in Ireland and Scotland: —*n.* a place where alcoholic liquor is sold without a license: *But after winning a big fight he goes to a shebeen . . . to celebrate* (Cape Times). —*v.i.* to operate a shebeen. [apparently < Irish *séibín* alehouse]

she·chi·ta or **she·chi·tah** (shə ʜē′tə), *n.* the Jewish method of slaughtering animals according to rabbinical law. [< Hebrew *shəḥīṭāh*] Also, **shehita, shehitah.**

shed[1] (shed), *n.* **1.** a building used for shelter, storage, etc., usually having only one story: *a wagon shed, a tool shed, a train shed.* **2.** a hut; cottage: *To shame the meanness of his humble shed* (Oliver Goldsmith). **3.** any covering, as the lair of an animal. [Middle English *shadde* apparently variant of *shade,* Old English *scead* shelter] —**shed′like′,** *adj.*

shed[2] (shed), *v.,* **shed, shed·ding,** *n.* —*v.t.* **1.** to pour out; let fall: *The girl shed tears. A man who is good enough to shed his blood for his country is good enough to be given a square deal afterward* (Theodore Roosevelt). **2.** to throw off: *The umbrella sheds water. The snake sheds his skin. The duke shed his coat* (Mark Twain). **3.** to cause to flow: *Ulysses here the blood of victims shed* (Joseph Addison). **4.** to scatter abroad; give forth: *The sun sheds light. Flowers shed perfume. They [the reports] were aimed at shedding light on the need for additional power* (New York Times). —*v.i.* **1.** to throw off a covering, hair, etc.: *That snake has just shed.* **2.** to drop or fall, as leaves or grain from the ear.
—*n.* **1.** something that is or has been shed. **2.** a watershed or ridge of high ground.
[Old English *scēadan*] —**Syn.** *v.t.* **2.** molt, discard. **4.** emit, diffuse.

shed[3] (shād), *n., pl.* **she·dim.** (in Jewish folklore) an evil spirit or demon. [< Hebrew *shēdh* < Assyrian *shēdu*]

she'd (shēd; *unstressed* shid), **1.** she had. **2.** she would.

shed·der (shed′ər), *n.* **1.** a person or thing that sheds. **2. a.** a crab or lobster beginning to shed its shell. **b.** a lobster that has just grown its new shell. **c.** a soft-shell crab.

she-dev·il (shē′dev′əl), *n.* a woman or girl who is like a devil in character or actions.

she·dim[1] (shā′dim), *n.* plural of **shed**[3].

she·dim[2] (shā′dim), *n.* plural of **shedu.**

shed roof, a pent roof.

she·du (shā′dü), *n., pl.* **-dim.** an Assyrian protective spirit or demigod: *Passages and doorways [of an excavated Nimrod palace] were often flanked by winged monsters, part human, sometimes leonine, sometimes bovine, known as the good shedu* (New Yorker). [< Assyrian *shēdu*]

sheen (shēn), *n.* **1.** gleaming brightness; luster: *the sheen of satin or polished silver.* **2.** gorgeous attire: *In costly sheen . . . arrayed* (Byron).
—*v.i. Poetic.* to glisten.
—*adj. Poetic.* bright; shining; resplendent.
[Old English *scēne, sciene* bright]
—**Syn.** *n.* **1.** See **polish.**

sheen·y (shē′nē), *adj.* bright; lustrous: *The silken sheeny woof* (Tennyson).

sheep (shēp), *n., pl.* **sheep. 1.** any of a group of cud-chewing mammals raised for wool and mutton. Sheep are closely related to the goats and sometimes have horns. **2.** a weak, timid, or stupid person. **3.** leather made from the skin of sheep; sheepskin.

Hampshire Sheep (def. 1)

make sheep's eyes at, to give a loving, longing look at: *The horrid old Colonel . . . was making sheep's eyes at a half-caste girl* (Thackeray).
separate the sheep from the goats, *Especially British.* to separate what is good from what is bad (originally in allusion to the division into "sheep" and "goats", those saved or lost at the Last Judgment): *One sad consequence of the massive output of television and radio is that it is virtually impossible to separate the sheep from the goats* (London Times).
[Old English *scēap*]

sheep·back (shēp′bak′), *n.* roche moutonnée, a rock subjected to glacial action. [because it is rounded like a sheep's back]

sheep·ber·ry (shēp′ber′ē), *n., pl.* **-ries. 1.** a tall North American shrub of the honeysuckle family, bearing clusters of small white flowers and edible, black, berrylike fruit. **2.** the fruit itself. **3.** the black haw or its fruit.

sheep·bine (shēp′bīn′), *n.* a small species of bindweed that grows as a weed in fields of Europe and North America.

sheep bug, the sheep ked.

sheep·bur (shēp′bėr′), *n.* the cocklebur.

sheep·cot (shēp′kot′), *n.* sheepcote.

sheep·cote (shēp′kōt′), *n.* shelter for sheep. —**Syn.** fold.

sheep·dip (shēp′dip′), *n.* a disinfecting mixture used for dipping sheep.

sheep dog, a collie or other dog trained to help a shepherd watch and tend sheep.

sheep fescue, a low, tufted fescue grass with fine leaves and culms, native in many mountain regions, and forming the bulk of the sheep pasturage in the Scottish Highlands. Also, **sheep's fescue.**

sheep fly, a European fly related to the screwworm fly of the United States. Its larvae infest the bodies of live sheep, especially in Great Britain and Ireland.

sheep·fold (shēp′fōld′), *n.* a pen for sheep.

sheep·herd·er (shēp′hėr′dər), *n.* a person who watches and tends large numbers of sheep while they are grazing on unfenced land: *The majority of Alberta sheep are out on range in care of a "sheepherder"* (Canadian Geographical Journal).

sheep·herd·ing (shēp′hėr′ding), *n.* the herding of sheep in large numbers on unfenced land. —*adj.* of or having to do with sheepherding.

sheep·hook (shēp′hu̇k′), *n.* a shepherd's staff. Its upper end is usually curved or bent into a hook.

sheep·ish (shē′pish), *adj.* **1.** awkwardly bashful or embarrassed: *a sheepish smile.* **2.** like a sheep; timid; weak; stupid: *. . . saying the downright things that the sheepish society around her is afraid to utter* (Alexander Kinglake). —**sheep′ish·ly,** *adv.* —**sheep′ish·ness,** *n.* —**Syn. 1.** diffident. **2.** timorous.

sheep ked, a small bloodsucking fly that is a harmful parasite on sheep; sheep tick.

sheep laurel, a low North American shrub of the heath family, similar to the mountain laurel but lower and with purple or red flowers; lambkill. It is said to be poisonous to sheep.

sheep·like (shēp′līk′), *adj.* meek; submissive; sheepish: *sheeplike conformity. In sheeplike acquiescence we trail into our overall game of follow-the-foolish* (Wall Street Journal). —*adv.* meekly; submissively: *. . . stoops your pride And leads your glories sheeplike to the sword* (Christopher Marlowe).

sheep·man (shēp′man′), *n., pl.* **-men. 1.** a person who owns and raises sheep: *Veritable dynasties were built up by cattlemen and sheepmen* (Harper's). **2.** a sheepherder.

sheep range, a tract of land on which sheep are pastured.

sheep scab, a contagious disease of sheep due to mites which live on the skin and cause the formation of scabs with the fall of the wool; acariasis of sheep.

sheep's fescue, sheep fescue.

sheep·shank (shēp′shangk′), *n.* **1.** a leg of a sheep. **2.** something lank, slender, or weak. **3.** a kind of knot, hitch, or bend made on a rope to shorten it temporarily.

Sheepshank (def. 3)

sheeps·head (shēps′hed′), *n., pl.* **-heads** or (*collectively for 1 and 2*) **-head. 1.** a large salt-water food fish related to the porgies, common on the Atlantic Coast of the United States. **2.** the fresh-water drumfish of the Mississippi River and the Great Lakes. **3.** the head of a sheep, especially as food. **4.** a fool; simpleton.

sheep·shear·er (shēp′shir′ər), *n.* **1.** a person who shears sheep: *. . . Judah was comforted, and went up unto his sheepshearers to Timnath* (Genesis 38:12). **2.** a machine for shearing sheep.

sheep·shear·ing (shēp′shir′ing), *n.* **1.** the act of shearing sheep. **2.** the time of year for shearing sheep. **3.** the feast held at that time.

sheep-sick (shēp′sik′), *adj.* (of pasture land) exhausted or diseased by excessive sheep-pasturing and no longer fit for this use.

sheep·skin (shēp′skin′), *n.* **1.** the skin of a sheep, especially with the wool on it. **2.** leather or parchment made from it. **3. a.** *U.S. Informal.* a diploma. **b.** a person holding a diploma: *The accumulation of sheepskins has helped give the city good government, good schools . . .* (Wall Street Journal).

sheep sorrel, a kind of sorrel with reddish flowers, common as a weed on poor soil.

sheep tick, the sheep ked: *Sheep ticks are properly not ticks at all, but wingless flies* (Science News Letter).

sheep·walk (shēp′wôk′), *n.* sheep range.

sheep·weed (shēp′wēd′), *n.* **1.** the soapwort. **2.** the butterwort. **3.** a velvetleaf.

sheep·y (shē′pē), *adj.,* **sheep·i·er, sheep·i·est.** characteristic of or resembling sheep; sheeplike; sheepish: *He called the social English the most sheepy of sheep* (George Meredith).

sheer[1] (shir), *adj.* **1.** very thin; almost transparent: *a sheer white dress.* **2.** unmixed with anything else; complete: *sheer nonsense, sheer weariness.* **3.** straight up and down; very steep: *From the top of the wall there was a sheer drop of 100 feet to the water below.* **4.** *Obsolete.* bright; shining; shiny.
—*adv.* **1.** completely; quite. **2.** very steeply.
—*n.* **1.** a thin, fine, almost transparent cloth. **2.** a dress made of this: *She wore a billowing pink sheer to the Junior Prom.*
[Middle English *scere* clear, free, partly Old English *scīr* bright; vowel influenced by Old Icelandic *skǣrr* bright] —**sheer′ness,** *n.* —**Syn.** *adj.* **2.** unadulterated, pure, absolute, utter.

sheer[2] (shir), *v.i.* to turn from a course; turn aside; swerve: *Birds perching on the surrounding roofs took to flight immediately, while those passing over on the wing sheered off* (New Scientist). —*v.t.* to cause to sheer.
—*n.* **1.** a turning of a ship from its course. **2.** the upward curve of a ship's deck or lines from the middle toward each end. **3.** the position in which a vessel at anchor is placed to keep her clear of the anchor.
[probably < Dutch *scheren.* Compare SHEAR, verb in the sense of "to form two parts or pieces by cutting or breaking."]
—**Syn.** *n.* **1.** deviation.

sheer·hulk (shir′hulk′), *n.* an old ship with hoists mounted on it, used for loading, etc.

sheer legs, a hoist for heavy weights; shears.

sheer·ly (shir′lē), *adv.* absolutely; thoroughly; quite: *Some of the audience may have come sheerly out of curiosity* (Newsweek).

sheet[1] (shēt), *n.* **1.** a large piece of cotton, linen, nylon, or other cloth used to sleep on or under. **2.** a broad, thin piece of anything: *a sheet of glass, a sheet of iron.* **3. a.** a single piece of paper. **b.** a piece of paper printed and folded to page size; unbound page of a book: *He checks the paper itself for finish . . . examines sheets for cleanliness* (Newsweek). **c.** a piece of paper printed with rows of postage stamps. **4.** a newspaper. **5.** a broad, flat surface: *a sheet of ice, a sheet of flame. The rain came down in sheets.* **6.** a nearly horizontal, thin layer of rock or gravel.
—*adj.* rolled out in a sheet during the manufacturing process: *sheet steel.*
—*v.t.* to furnish or cover with a sheet or layer: *. . . a sheeted ghost* (Longfellow). *The river was sheeted with ice* (Washington Irving). —*v.i.* to spread or flow in a sheet or layer: *The water sheeted down* (Observer).
[Old English *scēte, sciete* a cloth, covering]
—**sheet′less,** *adj.* —**sheet′like′,** *adj.*

sheet[2] (shēt), *Nautical.* —*n.* a rope attached to a lower or after corner of a sail, to control the angle at which a sail is set: *Better change to heavy jib sheets* (Newsweek).
a sheet in the wind or **wind's eye,** *Informal.* tipsy: *Maybe you think we were all a sheet in the wind's eye. But . . . I was sober* (Robert Louis Stevenson).
sheets, the space at the bow or stern of an open boat: *The sheets are usually called either foresheets or sternsheets.*
three sheets in the wind, *Informal.* very drunk: *He . . . seldom went up to the town without coming down three sheets in the wind* (Richard Henry Dana).
—*v.t.* **sheet home,** to stretch (a square sail) as flat as possible by pulling hard on the sheets fastened to it: *The topsails were let fall and sheeted home* (Michael Scott).
[Old English *scēata* lower part of sail, piece of cloth. Related to SHEET[1].]

sheet anchor, 1. a large anchor used only in emergencies. **2.** a final reliance or resource: *The United States Supreme Court . . . has been called the sheet anchor of our governmental system* (Harper's). [earlier *sheat-,* variant of Middle English *shutte* (*anker*); origin uncertain]

sheet bend, a kind of knot used to fasten two ropes together; becket bend; hawser bend.

sheet erosion, the washing away of soil in layers from barren, sloping land by rainfall.

sheet-fed (shēt′fed′), *adj.* (of a printing press) having the paper fed in single sheets instead of from a continuous roll.

sheet glass, glass made into large, flat sheets before cooling.

sheet ice, ice formed on the surface of a body of water.

sheet·ing (shē′ting), *n.* **1.** a cotton or linen cloth for bed sheets, etc.: ... *heavy industrial cloth, such as "sheetings" used in cloth bags, auto upholstery and other industrial products* ... (Wall Street Journal). **2.** a lining or covering of timber or metal, used to protect a surface: *a plywood sheeting.* **3.** the act or process of making into or covering with sheets.

sheet iron, iron in sheets or thin plates.

sheet lightning, lightning in broad flashes: *sheet lightning often occurs without a thunderstorm in the summer.*

sheet metal, metal in thin pieces or plates. —**sheet′-met′al,** *adj.*

sheet music, music printed on unbound sheets of paper: *Sheet music doesn't sell the way it did in the old days* (Atlantic).

sheet·pile (shēt′pīl′), *n.* a piling formed of thick planks driven between the main piles of a cofferdam or other hydraulic work to retain or to exclude water: *The cofferdams are basically a series of interlocking cells filled with sand and walled by steel sheetpile* (William W. Jacobus).

sheet·pil·ing (shēt′pī′ling), *n.* sheetpile.

sheets (shēts), *n.pl.* See under **sheet**², *n.*

sheet·y (shē′tē), *adj.* **1.** consisting of or resembling sheets. **2.** (of rocks) showing a tendency to break up into thin tabular masses.

Shef·field plate (shef′ēld), an especially durable silver plate made by rolling out sheets of copper and silver fused together. [< *Sheffield,* a city in England, where the process was perfected]

she·hi·ta or **she·hi·tah** (shə ʜē′tə), *n.* shechita.

sheik or **sheikh** (shēk; *especially British* shāk), *n.* **1.** an Arab chief or head of a family, village, or tribe: *One by one, the tribal sheiks who had strayed to the Saudi side ... led their camel-riding followers into the Sultan's camp to beg forgiveness* (Newsweek). **2.** a Moslem religious leader. **3.** a title of respect used by Moslems. **4.** *Slang.* a man supposed to be irresistibly fascinating to women; great lover. [< Arabic *shaikh* (originally) old man < *shākha* he grew (or was) old] Also, *especially British,* **shaikh.**

sheik·dom or **sheikh·dom** (shēk′dəm; *especially British* shāk′dəm), *n.* the territory ruled by a sheik: *Now Arabs from up and down the Persian Gulf have been attracted by the sheikdom's high wages* (Newsweek).

sheik·ly or **sheikh·ly** (shēk′lē; *especially British* shāk′lē), *adj.* of, having to do with, or characteristic of a sheik: *The imposition of sheikhly authority on those who do not want it* ... (Manchester Guardian).

shei·la (shē′lə), *n. Australian Slang.* a young woman: *The men love their work, their wives, and the odd sheila down at Melbourne for the races* (Manchester Guardian Weekly). [< *Sheila,* a proper name]

sheil·ing (shē′ling), *n.* **Scottish.** shieling.

shei·tan (shī tän′), *n.* shaitan.

shek·el (shek′əl), *n., pl.* **shek·els, she·ka·lim** (shə kä′lim). **1.** an ancient silver coin of the Hebrews that weighed about half an ounce. **2.** an ancient unit of weight originating in Babylonia, equal to about 1/2 of an ounce.

Hebrew Shekel (def. 1)

shekels, *Slang.* coins; money: *Ordinary degrees in technology were bringing in the shekels* (Economist). [< Hebrew *sheqel* < *shāqal* he weighed (it)]

She·ki·nah (shi kē′nə, -ʜē′nə, -kī′nə), *n.* (in Jewish theology) the divine presence, or a visible symbol of it, as the glory of light or the cloud resting over the mercy seat. [< Hebrew *shəkīnāh* < *shākan* he rested, dwelt]

shel·drake (shel′drāk′), *n., pl.* **-drakes** or (*collectively*) **-drake. 1.** any of a group of large ducks, many of which resemble geese and have variegated plumage. **2.** any merganser. [< obsolete *sheld* variegated + *drake*]

Sheldrake (def. 1) (body, about 1 ft. long)

shel·duck (shel′duk′), *n.* the sheldrake (def. 1).

shelf (shelf), *n., pl.* **shelves. 1. a.** a thin, flat piece of wood, metal, stone, etc., fastened to a wall or frame to hold things, such as books, dishes, etc. **b.** the contents of a shelf: *to read a whole shelf in a week.* **2.** anything like a shelf, as a ledge of land or rock, especially a submerged ledge or bedrock: *to hit a shelf of coral. In the Gulf the shelf—the offshore sea bottom—is muddy* (Scientific American). **3.** *Archery.* the part of the hand that the arrow rests on as the bow is drawn.

off the shelf, directly from stock on hand; without requiring special preparation or modification: [*When*] *aircraft themselves could almost be purchased off the shelf, it was not difficult for a company to obtain new aircraft to meet unexpected needs* (London Times).

(put) on the shelf, put aside as no longer useful or desirable: *The trouble is that the Americans obsessed with their purity of purpose, stubbornly cling to an idea that should either be dropped or at least put on the shelf* (Canadian Forum).

[perhaps < Middle Low German *schelf*] —**shelf′like′,** *adj.*

shelf·ful (shelf′fu̇l′), *n., pl.* **-fuls.** the amount a shelf can hold; a full shelf.

shelf fungus, bracket fungus.

shelf ice, a ledge of ice sticking out into the sea from an ice sheet: *Some species of marine plants even manage to thrive in the lightless waters beneath the shelf ice* (Scientific American).

shelf ladder, a ladder used in libraries and stores for reaching high shelves and drawers. It is fitted with wheels at the top and bottom on which it can be moved.

shelf life, the length of time a product may be shelved or stored without becoming spoiled or useless: *the shelf life of a drug.*

shelf list, a list of the books in a library in the order of their location.

shelf sea, the part of the sea that covers a continental shelf.

shell (shel), *n.* **1.** a hard outer covering of an animal, as of oysters and other mollusks, beetles and some other insects, turtles, etc. **2.** the hard outside covering of an egg. **3.** the hard outside covering of a nut, seed, fruit, etc. **4.** something like a shell; outer part or appearance: *Going to church is only the mere shell of religion. The shell of party polemics, that convention which is in itself an abrogation of peacetime relations and an obstacle to serious discussions* ... (Edmund Wilson). **5. a.** a metal case filled with explosives, and sometimes chemicals, gas, etc., designed to be fired by artillery and to burst in or over the target. **b.** a paper cartridge filled with small shot and gunpowder to use in a shotgun. **c.** a cartridge-like firework that explodes in the air. **6.** any framework or outside covering of a structure: *Only the shell of the old building remained after the fire had burned out the inside.* **7.** a long, narrow racing boat of light wood, rowed by a crew using long oars. **8.** a hollow case of pastry or the lower crust of a pie. **9.** any orbit with electrons revolving about the nucleus of an atom: *When a shell is complete, the electron system is very stable, and the element is chemically inert* (J. Little). **10.** a mollusk, especially a shellfish.

come out of one's shell, to stop being shy or reserved; join in conversation, etc., with others: *Under the soothing influence of coffee and tobacco, he came out of his shell* (C.F.M. Bell).

go or **retire into one's shell,** to become shy and reserved; refuse to join in conversation, etc., with others: [*He*] *rarely spoke unless personally appealed to, and speedily retired into his shell again* (Henry Vizetelly).

shells, burnt limestone before it is slaked: *He brings his lime from the kiln, lays it in small heaps, about a firlot of shells in each heap* (John Sinclair).

—*v.t.* **1.** to take out of a shell: *to shell peas.* **2.** to separate (grains of corn) from the cob. **3.** to bombard by cannon or mortar fire: *Communist artillery today shelled two Chinese Nationalist islets in Amoy Bay* (New York Times). —*v.i.* **1.** to fall or come out of the shell. **2.** to come away or fall off as an outer covering does. **3.** to fire cannon or mortar shells.

shell out, *Informal.* to hand over (money); pay up: *The U.S. will keep shelling out aid abroad as long as the menace of Communism persists* (Wall Street Journal).

—*adj.* **1.** having a shell, as an animal, fruit, etc. **2.** consisting or formed of a shell or shells; ornamented with shells. **3.** having the shape of a shell or a shell pattern.

[Old English *scell, sciell.* Perhaps related to SHALE.] —**shell′-like′,** *adj.*

—**Syn.** *n.* **1.** carapace.

she'll (shēl; *unstressed* shil), **1.** she shall. **2.** she will.

shel·lac (shə lak′), *n., v.,* **-lacked, -lack·ing.** —*n.* **1.** a liquid that gives a smooth, shiny appearance to wood, metal, etc. Shellac is made from refined lac dissolved in alcohol. **2.** refined lac, used in sealing wax, phonograph records, etc.

—*v.t.* **1.** to put shellac on; cover or fasten with shellac. **2.** *Slang.* to defeat completely: *The cool-headed squad that shellacked Italy last week operated with precision and brutal efficiency* (Time).

[< *shell* + *lac*¹; translation of French *laque en écailles* lac in thin plates] —**shel·lack′er,** *n.*

shel·lack (shə lak′), *n., v.t.,* shellac.

shell·back (shel′bak′), *n.* **1.** an experienced sailor. **2.** a person who has crossed the equator on shipboard.

shell·bark (shel′bärk′), *n.* shagbark.

shell bean, 1. any of various beans that are shelled before cooking only the seeds being eaten; field bean. **2.** the plant bearing such beans.

shell·burst (shel′bėrst′), *n.* the explosion of a shell.

shell concrete, reinforced concrete in the form of very thin, curved slabs resembling the shape of sea shells, used especially to build domelike roofs or buildings spanning large spaces: *Exhibition halls, warehouses, and factories in shell concrete can become objects of surprising geometric beauty* (Time).

-shelled, *combining form.* having a —— shell: *A hard-shelled crab = a crab having a hard shell.*

shell·er (shel′ər), *n.* **1.** a person who shells something, as peas or clams. **2.** a tool or machine used in shelling.

Shel·ley·an (shel′ē ən), *adj.* of or having to do with the English poet Percy Bysshe Shelley (1792-1822) or his works.

shell eye, a primitive organ of sight found on the shells of various univalve and bivalve mollusks.

Shel·ley·esque (shel′ē esk′), *adj.* Shelleyan.

shell·fire (shel′fīr′), *n.* the firing of explosive shells; artillery fire.

shell·fish (shel′fish′), *n., pl.* **-fish·es** or (*collectively*) **-fish.** a water animal (not a fish in the ordinary sense) having a shell, especially a mollusk or a crustacean: *Clams, oysters, crabs, and lobsters are shellfish.* [Old English *scielfisc*]

shell·fish·er·y (shel′fish′ər ē), *n.* the business or industry of gathering oysters, clams, and other shellfish.

shell game, 1. a gambling game in which a pea or other object is placed under one of several walnut shells that are rapidly rearranged, after which bets are made on the shell concealing the pea. **2.** a swindling form of this, in which the person arranging the shells conceals the pea in his hand. **3.** anything regarded as a game of chance and especially as a swindle or fraud.

shell·heap (shel′hēp′), *n.* kitchen midden.

shell hole, a hole in the ground formed by the explosion of a mine or shell: *He ... enlisted when the time came, refused a commission, and died in a shell hole* (Manchester Guardian Weekly).

shell house or **home,** a house that is unfinished on the inside, the remaining work being done by the purchaser.

shell jacket, a mess jacket, especially one worn in place of a tuxedo jacket.

shell-lac (shə lak′), *n., v.t.,* **-lacked, -lack·ing.** shellac.

shell·less (shel′lis), *adj.* having no shell, as some mollusks.

shell number, the number of shells of a given atom.

shell pink, a soft, delicate pink with a tinge of yellow.

shell·proof (shel′prüf′), *adj.* able to withstand the impact and explosive force of shells, bombs, etc.

shell road, a road surface composed of sea shells.

shells (shelz), *n.pl.* See under **shell,** *n.*

shell shock, any of the many types of nervous or mental disorder resulting from the strain of combat in war; combat fatigue; combat neurosis.

shell-shocked (shel′shokt′), *adj.* suffering from shell shock.

shell·work (shel′wėrk′), *n.* decorative work made of or made to look like sea shells.

shell·y (shel′ē), *adj.*, **shell·i·er, shell·i·est.** **1.** abounding in shells. **2.** consisting of a shell or shells. **3.** shell-like.

shel·ter (shel′tər), *n.* **1.** something that covers or protects from weather, danger, or attack: *Trees are a shelter from the sun. Only people who were secure in strong blast-proof shelters would have any chance of survival* (Bulletin of Atomic Scientists). *They pull some of the flotsam from the sea and make a pathetic shelter* (Time). **2.** protection; refuge: *We took shelter from the storm in a barn. The tribunals ought to be sacred places of refuge, where . . . the innocent of all parties may find shelter* (Macaulay). **3.** a place of temporary lodging for the homeless poor.
—*v.t.* to protect; shield; hide: *It is a serious crime to shelter a known criminal from the police.* —*v.i.* to find or take shelter: *This is a night when polecats and rabbits would shelter together in peace* (Henry Kingsley).
[origin uncertain] —**shel′ter·er,** *n.*
—**Syn.** *n.* **1.** safeguard, defense, shield. *-v.t.* screen, harbor.

shelter belt, trees planted in a row to prevent soil erosion from water or wind.

shelter half, *pl.* **shelter halves.** a rectangular piece of canvas that is half of a shelter tent.

shel·ter·ing·ly (shel′tər ing lē), *adv.* in a sheltering position or manner; so as to shelter.

shel·ter·less (shel′tər lis), *adj.* **1.** giving no shelter: *The wind blew across the shelterless beach.* **2.** having no shelter: *a shelterless roadstead.*

shelter tent, a small tent, usually made of pieces of waterproof cloth that fasten together.

shelter trench, a trench hastily excavated to obtain shelter from enemy fire.

shelter wood, shelter belt.

shel·ter·y (shel′tər ē), *adj.* giving shelter: *. . . the warm and sheltery shores of Gibraltar and Barbary* (Gilbert White).

shel·ty or **shel·tie** (shel′tē), *n.*, *pl.* **-ties.** **1.** a Shetland pony. **2.** a Shetland sheep dog. [probably < the Orkney-Shetland pronunciation of Old Icelandic *Hjalti* Shetlander]

shelve[1] (shelv), *v.t.*, **shelved, shelv·ing.** **1.** to put on a shelf. **2.** to lay aside by removing (a person) from active service or failing to consider (a question or request): *Let us shelve that argument.* **3.** to furnish with shelves. [apparently < *shelf; -v-*, as in *sheave*, verb]

shelve[2] (shelv), *v.i.*, **shelved, shelv·ing.** to slope gradually: *. . . a shelving part of the shore* (Thomas Love Peacock). [origin uncertain; perhaps a figurative use of *shelf* in sense of "ledge"] —**Syn.** incline, slant.

shelves (shelvz), *n.* plural of **shelf.**

shelv·ing (shel′ving), *n.* **1.** wood, metal, etc., for shelves: *The carpenter ordered 40 feet of pine shelving.* **2.** shelves collectively. **3.** the act of laying aside.

shelv·y (shel′vē), *adj.* sloping gradually: *I had been drowned but that the shore was shelvy and shallow* (Shakespeare).

Shem (shem), *n.* (in the Bible) the oldest of the three sons of Noah, regarded as the ancestor of the Semitic peoples. Genesis 10:21-31.

She·ma (shə mä′, shmä), *n.* the name given to the verse "Hear, O Israel: the Lord our God is one Lord," recited by Jews as a confession or reiteration of faith. Deuteronomy 6:4. [< Hebrew *shəma'* hear, imperative]

Shem·ite (shem′īt), *n.* a Semite.

She·mit·ic (she mit′ik), *adj.* Semitic.

she·mit·ta or **she·mit·tah** (shə mē′tə), *n.* the Jewish sabbatical year: *A year of shemitta, when the land must lie fallow and all loans must be canceled* (J.B. Agus). [< Hebrew *shəmittāh*]

she·moz·zle (shə moz′əl), *n.* schemozzle.

she·nan·i·gan (shə nan′ə gən), *n. Informal.* **shenanigans,** mischief or trickery; nonsense: *Their predecessors could be bluffed by students marking all answers to a multiple-choice question; not these: they reject an exam paper at the first sign of shenanigans* (Maclean's). [American English; origin uncertain]

shend (shend), *v.t.*, **shent, shend·ing.** *Archaic.* **1** to put to shame or confusion. **2.** to blame; reproach. **3.** to defeat; destroy. **4.** to damage. [Middle English *shenden* revile, Old English *scendan*]

sheng (sheng), *n.* a small hand organ first used in China around 1250, the forerunner of the modern accordion, harmonica, and concertina: *Sir Thomas Beecham, an irascible 77, soothed himself by trying to make music on a sheng* (Time). [< Chinese *shêng*]

shent (shent), *Archaic.* —*adj.* **1.** shamed. **2.** blamed; scolded. **3.** defeated. **4.** ruined. **5.** damaged.
—*v.* the past tense and past participle of **shend.**

shen·ti (shen′tē), *n.* a loincloth of white cotton or linen worn by men in ancient Egypt.

she oak, **1.** any of the casuarina trees of Australia. **2.** *Australian Slang.* beer.

She·ol (shē′ōl), *n.* a Hebrew name for the abode of the dead. [< Hebrew *shə'ol*]

she·ol (shē′ōl), *n. Informal.* hell.

shep·herd (shep′ərd), *n.* **1.** a man who takes care of sheep. **2.** a person who cares for and protects. **3.** a spiritual guide; pastor.
the Shepherd, Jesus Christ; Good Shepherd. John 10:11-16.
—*v.t.* **1.** to take care of. **2.** to guide; direct: *The teacher shepherded the children safely out of the burning building.*
[Old English *scēaphierde* < *scēap* sheep + *hierde* herder < *heord* a herd]
—**Syn.** *n.* **3.** clergyman. *-v.t.* **1.** tend.

shepherd dog, sheep dog.

shep·herd·ess (shep′ər dis), *n.* a woman who takes care of sheep.

shepherd god, a god worshiped especially by shepherds.

Shepherd Kings, the Hyksos, a succession or dynasty of kings of Egypt. [translation of Greek *basileîs poiménes*]

shepherd's check, **1.** a black-and-white pattern of small checks. **2.** a fabric, usually woolen, with this pattern.

shepherd's pie, a meat pie covered with mashed potatoes rather than pastry.

shep·herd's-purse (shep′ərdz pėrs′), *n.* a weed of the mustard family that has small, white flowers and purselike pods. [< the resemblance of its pods to shepherds' purses or pouches]

Shep·pard's adjustment (shep′ərdz), an adjustment to correct certain statistical errors caused by assuming that all cases in one class interval have the same value exactly, whereas they actually may have any value within the class interval. [< William F. *Sheppard*, a British statistician of the 1900's]

sher·ard·ize (sher′ər dīz), *v.t.*, **-ized, -iz·ing.** to coat (iron articles) with zinc. [< *Sherard* Cowper-Coles, a British scientist, died 1936, who invented the process + *-ize*]

Sher·a·ton (sher′ə tən), *adj.* in or having to do with the style of furniture designed by Thomas Sheraton. It is marked especially by straightness of line, simplicity of form, and little use of ornament. [< Thomas *Sheraton*, 1751-1806, an English cabinetmaker and furniture designer]

Sheraton Table

sher·bet (shėr′bət), *n.* **1.** a frozen dessert made of fruit juice, sugar, and water, milk, or whites of eggs. **2.** a cooling drink made of fruit juice, sugar, and water, popular in the Orient. **3.** a dish, usually with a long stem, to hold frozen sherbet. [< Turkish *şerbet* < Arabic *sharbat* a drink]

sherd (shėrd), *n.* shard[1]: *In the street between the little palace and the shops we came upon a few fragmentary sherds of Aegean painted pottery* (Scientific American).

She·ri·a (shə rē′ə), *n.* Sharia.

she·rif or **she·reef** (shə rēf′), *n.* **1.** a descendant of Mohammed through his daughter Fatima. **2.** an Arab prince or ruler, especially the chief magistrate of Mecca or (formerly) the sovereign of Morocco. **3.** *Archaic.* a Moslem priest. [< Arabic *sharīf* exalted < *sharafa* he was exalted]

sher·iff (sher′if), *n.* the most important law-enforcing officer of a county, in the United States elected by popular vote: *A sheriff appoints deputies to help him keep order in the county.*
[Old English *scīrgerēfa* < *scīr* shire + *gerēfa* reeve[1]]

sher·iff·al·ty (sher′ə fəl tē), *n.*, *pl.* **-ties.** shrievalty.

sher·iff·dom (sher′if dəm), *n.* **1.** the district or territory under a sheriff's jurisdiction. **2.** the office of sheriff.

sher·iff·ship (sher′if ship), *n.* sheriffdom.

she·ris·ta·dar (she ris′tə där′), *n.*, *pl.* **-dars.** (in India) an officer or clerk, as of a court, who keeps records.

sher·lock (shėr′lok), *n. Informal.* a private detective. [< *Sherlock* Holmes, a fictional detective created by Sir Arthur Conan Doyle, 1859-1930]

Sher·lock·i·an (shėr lok′ē ən), *adj.* of or having to do with Sherlock Holmes; Holmesian. —*n.* an admirer or devotee of Sherlock Holmes: *The excisions . . . will nevertheless be annoying to many a good Sherlockian* (Atlantic).

Sher·pa (shėr′pə), *n.* a member of a Mongoloid ethnic group of Nepal. Sherpas have served as guides and porters for most of the expeditions to climb Mount Everest. *Foot over foot for five weeks, the 13 Britons and the 35 Sherpas . . . drive up a jagged icefall of 3,000 feet* (Time).

sher·ris (sher′is), *n. Archaic.* sherry.

sher·ry (sher′ē), *n.*, *pl.* **-ries.** **1.** a strong wine made in southern Spain. It varies in color from pale yellow to brown. **2.** any similar wine: *This week we can offer our Golden Cyprus Sherry in a medium sweet or medium dry* (London Times).
[new singular < *sherris* (taken as plural) wine from (earlier name) *Sherries* < earlier Spanish (*vino de*) *Xeres*, a Spanish town (modern *Jerez*)]

sherry cobbler, a drink of sherry, sugar, lemon, and water.

sher·wa·ni (shər wä′nē), *n.* a long, tight, buttoned coat with a high collar, worn in India as a man's formal dress. [< Hindi *shĕrwānī*]

she's (shēz; *unstressed* shiz), **1.** she is: *She's going home tomorrow.* **2.** she has: *She's already gone home.*

shet (shet), *v.t.*, *v.i.*, *adj.*, *n. Dialect.* shut.

sheth (sheth), *n.* **1.** one of the ribs of the framework for the bottom or sides of a wagon. **2.** the part of a plow to which the moldboard, share, etc., are attached. [Middle English *schethe.* Related to SHED[1].]

Shet·land (shet′lənd), *n.* **1.** a Shetland pony. **2.** Also, **shetland.** Shetland wool: *He'll want this bulky brushed shetland pullover* (Wall Street Journal). [< *Shetland* Islands, near Scotland and the Orkneys, where the breed originated, and the wool was spun]

Shetland pony, a small, sturdy, rough-coated pony, originally from the Shetland Islands.

Shetland Pony (2 to 4 ft. high at the shoulder)

Shetland sheep, one of a breed of sheep native to the Shetland Islands.

Shetland sheep dog, a small, long-haired working dog of a breed originated in the Shetland Islands. It has a black or brown coat with white or tan markings.

Shetland Sheep Dog (14 to 16 in. high at the shoulder)

Shetland wool, a fine, hairy, strong worsted spun from the wool of Shetland sheep, widely used in knitting fine shawls, garments, etc.

sheugh or **sheuch** (shyüн), *n. Scottish.* a furrow; ditch; gully. [Middle English *sough*]

shew (shō), *v.t.*, *v.i.*, **shewed, shewn, shew·ing,** *n.*, *adj. Especially British.* show.

shew·bread (shō′bred′), *n.* the unleavened bread placed near the altar every Sabbath by the ancient Jewish priests as an offering to God. Leviticus 24:5-9. Also, **showbread.** [< *shew* + *bread*; influenced by German *Schaubrot* (coined by Luther), translation of Hebrew *lechem pānī'm* (literally) face bread (because it was shown, not eaten)]

SHF (no periods), superhigh frequency.

Shi·ah or **Shi·a** (shē′ə), *n.* **1.** one of the two great Moslem sects, centered in Iran, which regards Ali, the son-in-law of Mohammed, as the true successor of Mohammed and rejects the first three caliphs and the Sunnite book of tradition handed down under their protection. **2.** a Shiite. [< Arabic *shīʻah* sect]

shib·bo·leth (shib′ə lith), *n.* any test word, watchword, or pet phrase of a political party, a class, a sect, etc. [< Hebrew *shibbōleth* stream; used as a password by the Gileadites to distinguish the fleeing Ephraimites, because the Ephraimites could not pronounce *sh.* Judges 12:4-6.]

shi·bu·i·chi (shē′bü ē′chē), *n.* an alloy widely used in Japanese decorative art. It is made of three parts copper to one part silver. [< Japanese *shibuichi* < *shi* four + *bu* part + *ichi* one]

shick·er (shik′ər), *Australian Slang. adj.* drunk. —*n.* drunkard. [< Yiddish *shiker* < Hebrew *shikkūr*]

shied (shīd), *v.* a past tense and past participle of **shy:** *The horse shied and threw the rider.*

shiel (shēl), *n. Scottish.* **1.** a hut; shanty. **2.** a shepherd's summer hut. [Middle English *shale, schele;* origin uncertain]

shield (shēld), *n.* **1.** a piece of armor carried on the arm or in the hand to protect the body in battle, used in ancient and

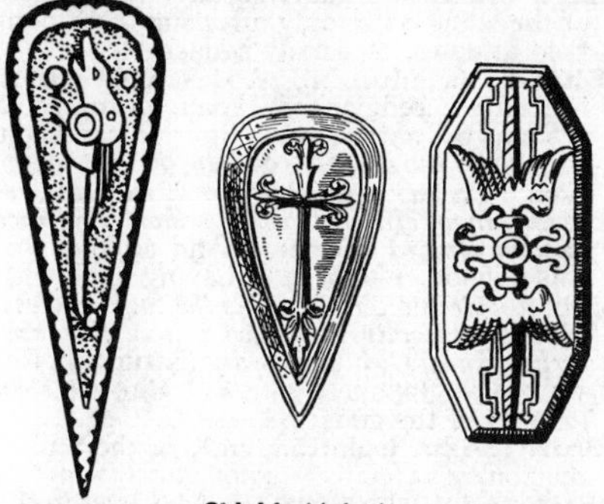

Shields (def. 1)
Left, Romanesque; center, Medieval; right, Roman

medieval warfare. **2.** anything used to protect: *A heavy face shield protects a welder's face and eyes from being burned. Active French forces in the Allied "shield" in Europe now stand officially at four divisions* (New York Times). **3.** something shaped like a shield. **4.** a covering for moving parts of machinery. **5. a.** any substance to protect against exposure to radiation, especially in nuclear reactors, as lead or water. **b.** a barrier built out of one of these substances. **6. a.** a framework pushed ahead in a tunnel to prevent the earth from caving in while the tunnel is being lined. **b.** a movable framework protecting a miner at his work. **7.** a steel screen or plate attached to a cannon, howitzer, etc., to protect the crew, mechanism, etc. **8. a.** a policeman's badge. **b.** an escutcheon. **9.** a piece of fabric, often rubberized, worn inside a dress at the armpit. **10.** *Zoology.* a protective plate covering a part, as a scute, carapace, or plastron.
—*v.t.* **1.** to be a shield to; protect; defend; shelter: *to shield one from attack, to shield one from the sun, to shield a criminal.* **2.** *Obsolete.* to avert; prevent. —*v.i.* to act or serve as a shield.
[Old English *sceld, scield*] —**shield′er,** *n.* —**shield′like′,** *adj.*

shield-back (shēld′bak′), *n.* a chair with a back whose center resembles a shield, a design much used by George Hepplewhite in England in the 1700's.

shield-bear·er (shēld′bãr′ər), *n.* (formerly) a soldier who carried his chief's shield.

shield·ing (shēl′ding), *n.* a substance that shields against radiation; shield.

shield·less (shēld′lis), *adj.* without a shield; unprotected.

Shield of So·bies·ki (sō byes′kē, sô-), *Astronomy.* a constellation over the bow of Sagittarius, represented as a shield having a cross. [< John *Sobieski*, 1624-1696, a king of Poland]

shield pigeon, one of a breed of domesticated pigeons of small size, having a white head and body, parti-colored wings, and no crest.

shield-shaped (shēld′shāpt′), *adj.* like a shield in shape.

shield volcano, a low, flat, dome-shaped volcano, built up of coalescing and overlapping lava streams with almost no explosive activity and with relatively little pyroclastic material: *Most shield volcanoes are composed of basalt, though a few are andesite* (Gilluly, Waters, and Woodford).

shiel·ing (shē′ling), *n. Scottish.* **1.** a shiel. **2.** a piece of pasture: *... song ... she and her colleagues may have chanted on the lone shieling* (Punch). Also, **shealing, sheiling.**

shi·er[1] (shī′ər), *n.* a horse that shies. Also, **shyer.**

shi·er[2] (shī′ər), *n.* a person who shies (throws). Also, **shyer.**

shi·er[3] (shī′ər), *adj.* a comparative of **shy**[1].

shi·est (shī′ist), *adj.* a superlative of **shy**[1].

shift (shift), *v.t.* **1.** to move or change (something) from one place, position, person, sound, etc., to another: *to shift the responsibility to someone else, to shift a heavy bag from one hand to the other. The Administration is only shifting its stance a little to meet the old challenger in the continuation of the old bout* (Observer). **2.** to remove and replace with another or others; change: *to shift the scenes on a stage. But nothing would shift the General Staff's blind belief in the Maginot Line and static warfare* (Observer). **3.** to change from one set of (gears) to another in an automobile. **4.** *Archaic.* to change the clothes of. **5.** to get rid of. **6.** *Obsolete.* to divide; distribute.
—*v.i.* **1.** to move from one place, position, person, sound, etc., to another: *The wind shifted to the southeast. Scobie shifted uncomfortably in his chair* (Graham Greene). **2.** to manage to get along; contrive: *When his parents died, Tom had to shift for himself.* **3.** to be rather dishonest; scheme. **4.** *Archaic.* to change one's clothing. **5.** to connect the motor to a different set of gears in an automobile: *He had to shift as he drove around the corner and up the hill.* **6.** *Obsolete.* to make a distribution.
—*n.* **1.** a change of position, direction, or attitude; a substituting in the place of another person or thing; change: *a shift of the wind, a shift in policy. There are two shifts of work at the factory.* **2.** a group of workmen; group: *This man is on the night shift.* **3.** the time during which such a group works: *He works a day shift.* **4.** a way of getting on; scheme; trick; artifice: *The lazy man tried every shift to avoid doing his work.* **5.** a change in the arrangement of players before a football is put into play. **6.** *Geology.* a slight fault or dislocation in a seam or stratum. **7.** *Linguistics.* sound change that affects the phonetic and phonemic system of a language or language group. **8. a.** a woman's chemise. **b.** a loosely fitting dress like a chemise, but with straighter lines: *The shift is nothing more than an easy-fitting sheath, ... street-length or to the floor* (Time). **9.** *Music.* **a.** a change of the hand's position on the fingerboard of a string instrument. **b.** one of the positions thus reached. **c.** a moving of the trombone slide to vary the pitch. **10.** *Archaic or Dialect.* a change of clothing.
make shift, a. to manage to get along: *He made shift pretty well till he got to low land, and then had to drop upon his hands and knees and crawl* (Arthur Quiller-Couch). **b.** to manage with effort or difficulty: *When she first came here she could speak no English; now she can make shift to talk it a little* (Charlotte Brontë). **c.** to do as well as one can: *Act then as persons ... who accordingly make shift and put up with anything that comes to hand* (Cardinal Newman).
[Old English *sciftan* arrange] —**shift′er,** *n.*
—**Syn.** *v.t., v.i.* **1.** transfer. -*n.* **2.** crew, gang. **4.** expedient.

shif·ta or **Shif·ta** (shif′tə), *n., pl.* **-ta** or **-tas.** a member of a nomadic band of Somalis engaged in terrorist and guerrilla activities in Somalia, Kenya, and Ethiopia: *Kenya's Shifta "war" began more than a year ago [in 1964] when the Shifta urged that part of the Northern Frontier should secede to neighbouring Somalia* (London Times). [< Amharic *shifta* (literally) bandit]

shift·i·ly (shif′tə lē), *adv.* in a shifty manner; cowardly; underhandedly.

shift·i·ness (shif′tē nis), *n.* the character of being shifty; sneakiness.

shift joint, in masonry: **1.** the placing of a stone or brick so that the vertical joints will come over the solid members of the course below. **2.** the stone or brick so placed.

shift key, a typewriter key that shifts the type to print upper-case letters.

shift·less (shift′lis), *adj.* lazy; inefficient: *Going to hunt up her shiftless husband at the inn* (Thomas Hardy). —**shift′less·ly,** *adv.* —**shift′less·ness,** *n.*

shift·work (shift′wėrk′), *n.* work done by those working in shifts: *In nursing, for example, shiftwork and weekend work may cause difficulty* (London Times).

shift·y (shif′tē), *adj.,* **shift·i·er, shift·i·est.** **1.** not straightforward; tricky: *shifty eyes, a very shifty fellow.* **2.** full of shifts; well able to look out for oneself.

shift·y-eyed (shif′tē īd′), *adj.* having shifty eyes: *a shifty-eyed gambler.*

shig·el·lo·sis (shig′ə lō′sis), *n., pl.* **-ses** (-sēz). bacillary dysentery. [< New Latin *Shigella,* genus name of the bacillus]

Shi·ism (shē′iz əm), *n.* the principles or doctrines of the Shiites.

Shi·ite (shē′īt), *n.* a member of the Shiah sect of the Moslem religion. [< *Shi*(ah) (see SHIAH) + English *-ite*[1]]

Shi·it·ic (shē it′ik), *adj.* of or having to do with the Shiites.

shi·kar (shi kär′), in India: —*n.* hunting; sport: *His service in the Indian Army and his periods of leave ... were almost invariably spent on shikar* (London Times). —*v.t.* to hunt. [< Hindi *shikār* < Persian]

shi·ka·ra (shē′kər ə), *n.* a long, narrow boat with a peak at each end, used in Kashmir: *Shikaras ... are used for quick trips around the city or for romantic outings on moonlit nights* (New Yorker). [< Kashmiri *shikhara*]

shi·ka·ri or **shi·ka·ree** (shi kä′rē), *n.* in India: **1.** a hunter, especially a native hunter: *These became a professional group, the European shikaris, the White Hunters of song and story* (Harper's). **2.** a native guide or assistant to a European sportsman. [< Hindi *shikārī* < Persian < *shikār* shikar]

shik·sa or **shik·se** (shik′sə), *n. Yiddish.* **1.** a non-Jewish girl. **2.** an unobservant or irreligious Jewish girl.

shill[1] (shil), *U.S. Slang.* —*n.* a person hired by a gambler, auctioneer, etc., to pose as a bystander and decoy others to bet, buy, bid, etc.: *An almost universal characteristic of booms is the sprouting of fast operators, shills and suckers* (Wall Street Journal). —*v.t.* to be a shill for: *I certainly could use a character like you just to sit alongside me on the show and shill my pitch* (Harper's). —*v.i.* to work as a shill; act as a lure: *to shill for a gambler. This is ... the fish that shills for a poisonous anemone, luring other fish to their destruction* (Time). [< earlier *shillaber;* origin uncertain]

shill[2] (shil), *adj. Obsolete.* shrill. [Middle English *schille,* Old English *scyl*]

shil·la·la or **shil·la·lah** (shə lā′lē, -lə), *n.* shillelagh.

shil·le·lagh or **shil·le·lah** (shə lā′lē, -lə), *n. Irish.* a stick to hit with; cudgel: *Meanwhile, Teddy Roosevelt was taking after the big trusts, wielding the shillelagh of the Sherman Act* (Harper's). [< *Shillelagh,* a town and barony in Ireland]

shil·ling (shil′ing), *n.* **1.** a British money of account and silver coin worth about 12 cents. Twenty shillings make a pound. *Abbr.:* s. **2.** a corresponding piece of money of one of the thirteen American colonies. **3.** a former Scottish coin and money of account, worth one English penny in the 1600's.
to take the King's or **Queen's shilling,** (formerly) to enlist as a soldier in the British Army by accepting a shilling from a recruiting officer.
[Old English *scilling*]

shilling mark, 1. the mark (/) used to divide shillings and pence. *Example:* The hat was cheap at 16/4d. **2.** this mark used for other purposes in writing and printing; virgule; slash.

shilling shocker, *British.* a short, sensational novel, originally sold for a shilling: *She wanted to prove that she could write rather better than the fair young ladies of London society whose shilling shockers littered the shelves of circulating libraries up and down the country* (Listener).

shil·lings·worth (shil′ingz wėrth′), *n. British.* as much as can be bought for a shilling: *A good shillingsworth of dry fino was jerked out of the glass* (Punch).

shil·ly-shal·ly (shil′ē shal′ē), *adj., v.,* **-lied, -ly·ing,** *n.* —*adj.* vacillating; wavering; hesitating; undecided. —*v.i.* to be undecided; vacillate; hesitate. —*n.* inability to decide; hesitation. [< earlier *shill I, shall I,* varied reduplication of *shall I?*] —**Syn.** *adj.* irresolute.
shilp·it (shil′pit), *adj. Scottish.* **1.** sickly; feeble; puny. **2.** (of drink) weak; insipid. [origin unknown]
shi·ly (shī′lē), *adv.* shyly.
shim (shim), *n., v.,* **shimmed, shim·ming.** —*n.* a thin strip of metal or wood, etc., used to raise a part, make it fill some other part, or fill up a space. —*v.t.* to put a shim or shims in. [American English; origin uncertain]
shim·mer (shim′ər), *v.i.* to gleam faintly: *The satin shimmers.* —*n.* a faint gleam or shine: *The pearls have a beautiful shimmer.* [Old English *scimerian*]
shim·mer·ing (shim′ər ing), *adj.* softly bright or gleaming; lambent: *He directed without quite the verve needed to give Richard Strauss' shimmering music its best display* (Wall Street Journal). —**shim′mer·ing·ly,** *adv.*
shim·mer·y (shim′ər ē), *adj.* shimmering; gleaming softly: *The moon, full last night, will be up soon, casting a shimmery reflection in the pond* (New York Times).
shim·mey (shim′ē), *n., v.i.* shimmy.
shim·my[1] (shim′ē), *n., pl.* **-mies,** *v.,* **-mied, -my·ing.** —*n.* **1.** an unusual shaking or vibration: *a sudden shimmy of a ladder. The basic causes of dangerous nosewheel shimmy in aircraft have been uncovered* (Science News Letter). **2.** a jazz dance popular in the early 1920's, a fox trot with much shaking of the body.
—*v.i.* **1.** to shake; vibrate. **2.** to dance the shimmy.
[American English; origin uncertain]
shim·my[2] (shim′ē), *n., pl.* **-mies.** *Informal.* chemise. [variant of *chemise*]
shi·mo·se (shi mō′se), *n.* a Japanese explosive consisting largely of picric acid. [short for earlier *shimonose* < M. *Shimonose* Kogakubachi, a Japanese inventor of the 1800's]
shin[1] (shin), *n., v.,* **shinned, shin·ning.** —*n.* **1.** the front part of the leg from the knee to the ankle. **2.** the lower part of the leg in beef cattle. **3.** the shinbone.
—*v.i., v.t.* to climb by clasping or holding fast with the hands or arms and legs and drawing oneself up: *to shin up a tree.*
[Old English *scinu*]
shin[2] (shēn), *n.* the twenty-first letter of the Hebrew alphabet. Also, **sin.** [< Hebrew *shin*]
shin·bone (shin′bōn′), *n.* the front bone of the leg below the knee; tibia.
shin·dig (shin′dig), *n. U.S. Slang.* a merry or noisy dance, party, etc.: *... rented an airport hangar to toss a shindig at which an estimated ton of food was served* (New York Times). [American English, perhaps < *shindy;* influenced by *shin*[1] + earlier *dig* a blow]
shin·dy (shin′dē), *n., pl.* **-dies.** *Slang.* **1.** a disturbance; rumpus: *to kick up a shindy. The tension is increased by the fact that the marshal in a recent shindy ... has lost the use of his trigger finger* (Newsweek). **2.** a shindig. [origin uncertain]
shine (shīn), *v.,* **shone** or (*especially for v.t. 2*) **shined, shin·ing,** *n.* —*v.i.* **1.** to send out light; be bright with light; reflect light; glow: *The sun shines by day, the moon by night. Wax makes the floors shine. What fun shone in his eyes ...* (Charlotte Brontë). **2.** to do very well; be brilliant; excel: *to shine in school, to shine in conversation.* —*v.t.* **1.** to cause to shine: *to shine a light in someone's face.* **2.** to make bright; polish: *to shine shoes. After roughing up one side of the ball, pitchers used to shine ... the other side on a part of their uniform heavily dosed with paraffin* (Time).
shine up to, *Slang.* to try to please and get the friendship of: *Mother was always hectorin' me about getting married, and wantin' I should shine up to this likely girl and that* (Congregationalist).
—*n.* **1.** light; brightness. **2.** luster; polish; gloss; sheen, as of silk or metal. **3.** fair weather; sunshine: *rain or shine.* **4. a.** a polish put on shoes. **b.** the act of putting on such a polish. **5.** *Slang.* a fancy; liking. **shines,** *Slang.* a trick; prank: *He's up to his old shines again.*
take a shine to, *Slang.* to become fond of; like: *He took a shine to you that night you saw him* (Winston Churchill).
take the shine out of, off, or **off of,** *Informal.* **a.** to take the brightness or cheer from: *... enough to take more of the shine out of things than church-going on Sundays could put in again* (George MacDonald). **b.** to outshine: *I am only sorry I didn't bring Seth Sprague along with me, with his pitch pipe, just to take the shine off of them there singers* (Seba Smith).
[Old English *scīnan*] —**Syn.** *v.i.* **1.** beam, gleam. -*n.* **1.** radiance, gleam.
shin·er (shī′nər), *n.* **1.** a person or thing that shines. **2.** any of a group of small American freshwater fish with glistening scales, related to the carp and dace. **3.** *Slang.* a black eye. **4.** *British Slang.* a guinea or a sovereign.
shin·gle[1] (shing′gəl), *n., v.,* **-gled, -gling.** —*n.* **1.** a thin piece of wood, etc., used to cover roofs, walls, or the like. Shingles are laid in overlapping rows with the thicker ends exposed. **2.** *U.S. Informal.* a small signboard, especially for a doctor's or lawyer's office. **3.** a short haircut.
hang out one's shingle, *Informal.* to open an office (used only of professional men): *He studied law ... and hung out his shingle* (Albion W. Tourgee).

Shingles[1] (def. 1) on a roof

—*v.t.* **1.** to cover with shingles: *to shingle a roof.* **2.** to cut (the hair) short.
[variant of earlier *shindle* < Latin *scindula*]
shin·gle[2] (shing′gəl), *n. Especially British.* **1.** loose stones or pebbles such as lie on the seashore; coarse gravel. **2.** a beach or other place covered with this. [earlier *chingle;* origin uncertain. Compare Norwegian *singling* small round pebble.]
shin·gle[3] (shing′gəl), *v.t.,* **-gled, -gling.** to hammer or squeeze (a mass of iron taken from a puddling furnace) to press out the slag and impurities. [< French *cingler* < German *zängeln* < *Zange* tongs]
shingle bolt, a block of wood ready to be cut into shingles.
shin·gled (shing′gəld), *adj.* covered with loose pebbles: *I was content to rove the shingled beach* (Walter de la Mare).
shin·gler[1] (shing′glər), *n.* **1.** a person who shingles houses. **2.** a person or a machine that cuts and prepares shingles.
shin·gler[2] (shing′glər), *n.* a person or thing that shingles iron.
shin·gles (shing′gəlz), *n. sing. or pl.* a virus disease that causes painful irritation of a group of cutaneous nerves and an outbreak of itching spots or blisters. The commonest location is on the chest or lower part of the back. *[Senator] Tydings was laid low by a serious attack of shingles, and had to withdraw from the race* (Time). [< Medieval Latin *cingulus,* variant of Latin *cingulum* (translation of Greek *zōstēr* girdle, shingles; see ZOSTER) girdle < *cingere* to gird]
shin·gling (shing′gling), *n. Geology.* the arrangement of flat pebbles or boulders by streams in such a manner that they overlap like shingles.
shin·gly (shing′glē), *adj.* consisting of or covered with small, loose stones or pebbles: *a shingly beach. ... a shingly spit on the Hampshire shore* (John Morley).
Shin·gon (shin′gon), *n.* a mystical Buddhist sect in Japan, teaching that truth is inherent in all living beings and may be developed by special rituals: *Japan's 1,139 year old Buddhist Shingon ... sect became the first in the country to form a labor union with priests as members* (Time).
shin guard, or **shin·guard** (shin′gärd′), *n.* a pad, worn by baseball catchers, ice hockey players, etc., to protect the leg.
shin·i·ly (shī′nə lē), *adv.* in a shiny manner; glossily.
shin·i·ness (shī′nē nis), *n.* shiny or glossy character or condition; glossiness; sheen.
shin·ing (shī′ning), *adj.* **1.** that shines; bright. **2.** brilliant; outstanding: *... a man of shining talents* (Benjamin Disraeli). —**shin′ing·ly,** *adv.* —**shin′ing·ness,** *n.*
—**Syn. 1.** glowing, radiant, glistening. **2.** distinguished, eminent.
shining light, a person conspicuous for some excellence (after John 5:35): *Pavlov, ... however brilliant his methodological innovations and experimental contributions, was no shining light as a theorist* (Bulletin of Atomic Scientists).
shin·leaf (shin′lēf′), *n.* any of a group of low perennial herbs of the Northern Hemisphere, related to the pipsissewa and pinedrops, with creeping underground stems, evergreen leaves, and racemes of white, greenish, or purplish flowers; wintergreen. [< the use of this plant as a shinplaster]
shin·ner·y (shin′ər ē), *n., pl.* **-ner·ies.** cheniere.
shin·ney (shin′ē), *n., v.i.* shinny[1].
shin·ny[1] (shin′ē), *n., pl.* **-nies,** *v.,* **-nied, -ny·ing.** —*n.* **1.** a simple kind of field hockey, played with a ball or the like and sticks curved at one end. **2.** the stick used in this game.
—*v.i.* **1.** to play shinny. **2.** to drive the ball in shinny. Also, **shinty.**
[origin uncertain]
shin·ny[2] (shin′ē), *v.i., v.t.,* **-nied, -ny·ing.** *Informal.* to shin; climb. [< *shin*]
shin·plas·ter (shin′plas′tər, -pläs′-), *n.* **1.** *Informal.* a five-dollar bill or less of United States paper money that has depreciated greatly in value. **2.** a plaster for a sore leg, often paper wet with vinegar.
shin splints, inflammation and soreness of the shins commonly affecting track-and-field athletes, especially runners.
Shin·to (shin′tō), *n., pl.* **-tos,** *adj.* —*n.* **1.** the native religion of Japan, primarily a system of nature worship and ancestor worship: *The result was Shinto, the Way of the Gods — a lock step of temporal rule and religion, more efficient perhaps than any since ancient Sparta* (Time). **2.** an adherent of this religion. —*adj.* of or having to do with Shinto: *Shinto girls worship the Sun Goddess, but ecumenically they also believe that sincerity binds God and man* (Saturday Review). [< Japanese *shintō* < Chinese *shên tao* way of the gods]
Shin·to·ism (shin′tō iz əm), *n.* the Shinto religion.
Shin·to·ist (shin′tō ist), *n.* a believer in the Shinto religion.
Shin·to·is·tic (shin′tō is′tik), *adj.* of or having to do with Shinto or Shintoism.
shin·ty (shin′tē), *n., pl.* **-ties.** shinny[1].
shin·y (shī′nē), *adj.,* **shin·i·er, shin·i·est.** **1.** shining; bright: *a shiny new penny.* **2.** worn to a glossy smoothness: *a coat shiny from hard wear.*
ship (ship), *n., v.,* **shipped, ship·ping.** —*n.* **1.** a large seagoing vessel with masts and sails. **2.** any large vessel for use on water or in air, such as a steamship, a battleship, an airship, etc. **3.** a large, square-rigged sailing vessel typically with three masts, but rarely with more, and a bowsprit. **4.** the officers and crew of a vessel.
about ship! a command to turn a ship so it will be on the other tack: *The cry of "about ship!" rang out, and the men scrambled to reset the sails.*
dress ship, a. to run flags on a line across the mastheads the full length of the ship as a decoration: *The crew dressed ship on docking and on sailing.* **b.** *U.S. Navy.* to hoist and fly ensigns on each masthead and on the flagstaff: *The captain gave the order to dress ship as soon as they came in sight of the fleet.*
jump ship, a. to desert a ship: *The convicts who had been impressed as sailors jumped ship at the first opportunity.* **b.** to leave any place or cause suddenly and without notice: *In a crisis, he will jump ship rather than face danger.*
when one's ship comes home or **in,** when one's fortune is made; when one has money: *I will take a long vacation when my ship comes in.*
—*v.t.* **1.** to put, take, or receive (persons or goods) on board a ship. **2.** to send or carry from one place to another by a ship, train, truck, etc.: *Did he ship it by express or by freight?* **3.** *Informal.* to send off; get rid of: *When I start using that sextant in the nose I have to unstrap myself, ship my parachute ... take off my helmet* (Harper's). **4.** (of a ship) to take in (water) over the side as a vessel does when the waves break over it: *We shipped a sea that drenched us all to the skin* (Tobias Smollett). **5.** to engage for service on a ship: *to ship a new crew.* **6.** to fix in a ship or boat in its proper place for use: *to ship a rudder.* —*v.i.* **1.** to go on board a ship. **2.** to travel on a ship; sail. **3.** to take a job on a ship: *He shipped as cook.*
ship oars. See under **oar,** *n.*
ship out, a. to leave; depart: *My father never*

shipped out . . . (Harry Brown). **b.** to send away: *State troopers, brought in to help curb protests, were shipped out* (Time).
[Old English *scip*]
—**Syn.** *v.t.* **2.** convey, transport. *-v.i.* **1.** embark.
➔ The distinction between **ship** and **boat** is primarily one of size, the former designating larger and the latter smaller vessels. *Boat* is applied, however, to some vessels of large size, such as ferryboats, that operate in harbors and narrow waters, and (loosely, chiefly in landsmen's use) to what are technically and officially ships, for example river steamships and even ocean liners.
-ship, *suffix.* **1.** office, status, or rank of ——, as in *clerkship, dictatorship, governorship, kingship, professorship.*
2. the quality, state, or condition of ——, as in *authorship, hardship, kinship, partnership.*
3. the act, acts, or qualities, or the power or skill in action, characteristic of ——, as in *comradeship, gamesmanship, horsemanship, dictatorship, kingship, scholarship.*
4. relation between ——s, as in *cousinship.*
5. the number of ——s, as a group, as in *readership.*
[Middle English *-ship,* Old English *-scipe.* Related to SHAPE.]
ship biscuit, a kind of hard biscuit used on shipboard; hardtack.
ship·board (ship′bôrd′, -bōrd′), *n.* **1.** a ship. **2.** *Obsolete.* the side of a ship.
on shipboard, on or inside a ship; aboard ship: *Being then on shipboard, bound for Bengal* (Dickens).
—adj. aboard ship; at sea: *shipboard life, a shipboard wedding.*
ship·borne (ship′bôrn′, -bōrn′), *adj.* carried in a ship: *A shipborne wave recorder from the National Institute of Oceanography* . . . (New Scientist).
ship bread, ship biscuit; hardtack.
ship·break·er (ship′brā′kər), *n.* **1.** a person who deals in old, unfit ships that are broken up for sale: *Unless a larger volume of merchant tonnage is sold for scrap soon, shipbreakers generally expect again to face a rather lean time* (Economist). **2.** a person whose work is breaking up such ships.
ship·break·ing (ship′brā′king), *n.* the work or occupation of a shipbreaker: *The possibilities of shipbreaking as an alternative employment at Scapa Flow, where naval establishments are to be closed* . . . (London Times).
ship·build·er (ship′bil′dər), *n.* a person who designs or constructs ships.
ship·build·ing (ship′bil′ding), *n.* **1.** the designing or building of ships. **2.** the art of building ships. *—adj.* of or used in shipbuilding; having to do with shipbuilding: *Engineering and shipbuilding employers at Nantes late last night decided on a general lock-out* (London Times).
ship canal, a canal wide and deep enough for ships.
ship chandler, a dealer who supplies ships with necessary stores.
ship chandlery, the business of, or goods dealt in by, a ship chandler.
ship·en·tine (ship′ən tēn), *n.* a four-masted vessel having the first three masts square-rigged and the last one fore-and-aft-rigged. [< *ship;* patterned on *barkentine*]
ship fever, typhus as occurring on overcrowded ships.
ship·fit·ter (ship′fit′ər), *n.* a person who fits together parts of ships: *When one starts paying welders, shipfitters, electricians, etc., for unnecessary work* . . . *millions are easily added to the cost of shipbuilding* (Wall Street Journal).
ship·ful (ship′fu̇l), *n., pl.* **-fuls.** a quantity or number sufficient to fill a ship.
ship·lap (ship′lap′), *n.* **1.** a flush, overlapping joint between boards, formed by cutting corresponding rabbets in the adjoining edges and lapping the boards to the depth of the rabbets. **2.** boards so rabbeted. *—adj.* **1.** having such rabbets: *shiplap siding.* **2.** utilizing lumber so milled: *shiplap construction.*
ship·less (ship′lis), *adj.* **1.** unoccupied by ships. **2.** possessing no ships; deprived of one's ship or ships.
ship·load (ship′lōd′), *n.* a full load for a ship: *Between 65 and 75 shiploads of Soviet military equipment and personnel have unloaded at Cuban ports* (Time). —**Syn.** cargo.
ship·man (ship′mən), *n., pl.* **-men. 1.** the master of a ship; shipmaster. **2.** *Archaic.* a sailor.
ship·mas·ter (ship′mas′tər, -mäs′-), *n.* the master, commander, or captain of a ship.
ship·mate (ship′māt′), *n.* **1.** a fellow sailor on a ship: *Members of the catering staff walked off the ship in protest against the threatened dismissal of two of their shipmates* (London Times). **2.** a person who sails on the same ship; fellow passenger: *He also told of catching 75-pound groupers* . . . *from the crash boat he and a shipmate were [on]* (Newsweek).
ship·ment (ship′mənt), *n.* **1.** the act of shipping goods: *A thousand boxes of oranges are ready for shipment.* **2.** the goods sent at one time to a person, firm, etc.: *a shipment to Europe, a large shipment of nails. We received two shipments from Chicago.* —**Syn. 2.** consignment.
ship money, an old English tax to provide money to build ships in time of war. It was abolished by an act of Parliament in 1640.
ship of state, the government: . . . *sail on, O Ship of State! Sail on, O Union strong and great!* (Longfellow).
ship of the desert, a camel.
ship of the line, a sailing warship of the largest class, carrying 74 or more guns, big enough to be part of the line of battle of a fleet.

Ship of the Line (1700's)

ship-of-war (ship′əv wôr′), *n.* a warship.
ship·own·er (ship′ō′nər), *n.* a person who owns a ship or ships.
ship·own·ing (ship′ō′ning), *n.* ownership in a ship or ships. *—adj.* that owns a ship, etc.
ship·pa·ble (ship′ə bəl), *adj.* that can be shipped.
ship·pen (ship′ən), *n. Scottish.* shippon.
ship·per (ship′ər), *n.* a person, company, etc., that ships goods: *shippers of bulk cargo.*
shipper fork, a two-pronged device for guiding a belt from one pulley to another on a machine.
ship·ping (ship′ing), *n.* **1.** the act or business of sending goods by water, rail, etc.: *Mr. Hecht brought his own kind of jet propulsion into shipping long before the airplane people even dreamed of it* (New York Times). **2. a.** ships collectively: *the seagoing shipping of the world.* **b.** the ships of a nation, city, or business: *British merchant shipping.* **c.** their total tonnage: *an increase of 250,000 deadweight tons in merchant shipping.* **3.** *Obsolete.* a voyage: *God send 'em good shipping* (Shakespeare).
shipping clerk, 1. a person whose work is to see to the packing and shipment of goods. **2.** any person who works in a shipping room.
shipping fever, a disease similar to influenza, attacking cattle, horses, etc., that are being shipped. The exhaustion of travel and changes in climate, water, and feed cause them to lose appetite, and to develop fever and a cough and red, watery eyes.
shipping lane, a regular route for ships, usually provided with aids to navigation; lane: *It is really impossible to predict how many icebergs will float south of the 48th parallel and into the world's busiest shipping lanes each year* (Science News Letter).
shipping line, a company that has ships for transporting goods or passengers.
shipping room, a room in a business house, factory, warehouse, etc., where consignments of goods are made up and packed, and from which they are sent.
shipping ton, a unit of measure of the carrying capacity of a ship, equal to 40 cubic feet.
ship·pon (ship′ən), *n. Scottish.* a cattle barn: *Nearly an hour later, the cows turned out, the shippon swept, an irate figure* . . . *came striding into the yard* (London Times). [Old English *scypen.* Related to SHOP.]
ship-rigged (ship′rigd′), *adj.* **1.** rigged with square sails on all three masts. **2.** carrying square sails; square-rigged: *a ship-rigged mast.*
ship's bell, the bell on a ship that is struck every half hour to tell time, indicate the time of the watch, etc.
ship's boat, a rowboat, launch, or the like, carried on or towed by a ship for use in landing passengers, as a lifeboat, and for other purposes.
ship·shape (ship′shāp′), *adj.* in good order; trim: *We finally got the rocket shipshape just before the admiral in charge of aviation policy arrived* (Atlantic). *—adv.* in a trim, neat manner. —**Syn.** *adj.* tidy.
ship's husband, a man who has the care of a ship while in port; a person who oversees the general interests of a ship, as berthing, provisioning, repairing, and entering and clearing.
ship·side (ship′sīd′), *n.* the area alongside which a ship is docked: *Cargo has to be moved to shipside* (Harper's).
ship's papers, the documents giving information as to the ship's nationality, owner, etc., which every ship must carry.
ship-to-shore (ship′tu̇ shôr′, -shōr′), *adj.* passing from a ship to the shore; working between a ship and shore: *In a ship-to-shore call she urged her husband not to waste his time meeting her at the pier* (Harper's). *—adv.* from a ship to the shore: *to radio ship-to-shore.*
ship·way (ship′wā′), *n.* **1.** the structure on which a ship is built; ways: *The entire assembly is hoisted into the spider-web of girders that make up the shipway, for quick insertion* (Wall Street Journal). **2.** a ship canal.
ship·worm (ship′wėrm′), *n.* any of various clams, having small valves and wormlike bodies, which burrow into the wood of ships, docks, etc.; teredo; copperworm: *Old spars cast up on the beach are full of the workings of the mollusk known as the shipworm* (New Yorker).
ship·wreck (ship′rek′), *n.* **1.** the destruction or loss of a ship by foundering, by striking a rock or shoal, etc.: *Only two people were saved from the shipwreck.* **2.** a wrecked ship or what remains of it; wreckage. **3.** a total loss or ruin; destruction: *the shipwreck of one's plans.*
—v.t. **1.** to wreck; ruin; destroy: *a career shipwrecked by war.* **2. a.** to cause (a person) to suffer shipwreck: *shipwrecked by a hurricane.* **b.** to cause the loss of (goods) by shipwreck. *—v.i.* to suffer shipwreck.
ship·wright (ship′rīt′), *n.* a man who builds or repairs ships: *Since the sections obviously were to be attached to the ship* . . . *the shipwrights said they were the ones to drill the holes* (Wall Street Journal).
ship·yard (ship′yärd′), *n.* a place near the water where ships are built or repaired.
shir·a·lee (shir′ə lē), *n. Australian Slang.* a bundle of personal belongings; swag.
Shi·ra·zi (shi rä′zē), *n.* a Zanzibari of mixed African and Persian descent. [< *Shiraz,* a city in southwestern Iran]
shire (shīr), *n.* **1.** one of the counties into which Great Britain is divided: *They mean to live to themselves more than ever in the shires* (J. W. R. Scott). **2.** (in Australia) one of the larger divisions of a state local administration. **3.** *Obsolete.* a province; district; region. [Old English *scīr*]
➔ **Shire** (def. 1) is now restricted chiefly to literary use and applied mainly to counties with names ending in *-shire;* **county** is the usual official term.
Shire (shīr), *n.* a shire horse: *The Shire descended from the great war horses ridden by heavily armored knights of the Middle Ages* (Margaret Cabell Self). [< *the Shires,* a section of England, where they are raised]
shire horse, any of a breed of large, strong draft horses with long hair on the back of the legs from the knees and hocks down, bred for a time in the midland counties of England.
shire town, the town where the business of a shire is transacted: *As Richibucto is the shire town of Kent, there are good accommodations for travellers* (Gun and Rod).
shirk (shėrk), *v.t., v.i.* to avoid or get out of doing (work, a duty, etc.): *Dev lost his job because he shirked his work. Common men cannot shirk world politics and at the same time enjoy private freedom* (H. G. Wells). *—n.* a person who does not do his share; a person who avoids work, duty, obligations, etc.: *You think we're all a lot of shirks* (Edith Wharton). [origin uncertain. Compare SHARK[2].] —**shirk′er,** *n.* —**Syn.** *v.t.* evade, shun, neglect.
shirr (shėr), *v.t.* **1.** to draw up or gather (cloth) on parallel threads, especially to trim (a garment) with shirring. **2.** to bake (eggs) in a shallow dish, or in individual dishes, with butter, and (sometimes) cream,

bread crumbs, etc. —*n.* a shirred arrangement of cloth. [American English; origin unknown]

shirr·ing (shėr′ing), *n.* a gathering of cloth by sewing with parallel threads and pulling on the threads: *If above-the-waistline pleating, shirring, or tucking requires fullness over Body Basic measurements, the following restrictions apply* . . . (Bernice G. Chambers).

shirt (shėrt), *n.* **1.** a man's or boy's garment, usually of cotton, linen, or other washable fabric, for the upper part of the body, commonly buttoning down the front, with long or short sleeves, worn as an outer garment or under a vest or jacket: *a formal white shirt, a sport shirt.* **2. a.** any of various women's or girls' garments patterned on this. **b.** a shirtwaist. **3.** an undergarment for the upper part of the body; undershirt. **4.** a nightshirt.

keep one's shirt on, *U.S. Slang.* to stay calm; keep one's temper: *It don't make any difference . . . so you can just keep your shirt on* (R.D. Saunders).

lose one's shirt, *U.S. Slang.* to lose everything one owns: *The same people who hopefully predicted that my father would lose his shirt now say that he had the Midas touch* (New Yorker).

—*v.t.* to clothe with or as if with a shirt.

[Old English *scyrte.* Related to SKIRT.]

shirt·band (shėrt′band′), *n.* the neckband, collar, or other band of a shirt.

shirt dress, a shirtwaist dress; shirtwaister: *. . . pale blue Osmaline shirt dress, the bib front hand-embroidered in silk, the collar, cuffs, and sleeves silk-stitched* (Sunday Times).

shirt front, the part of a shirt covering the chest.

shirt·ing (shėr′ting), *n.* cloth for making shirts: *He is also one of the most brilliant designers of shirting alive today* (New Yorker).

shirt·less (shėrt′lis), *adj.* without a shirt or shirts: *Hundreds of barefooted and shirtless Chinese youths crowded into the chamber* (Atlantic).

shirt·mak·er (shėrt′mā′kər), *n.* a person whose work is making or altering shirts, etc.: *They owed the hotel, the doctor, and all the dressmakers and shirtmakers of France* (Harper's).

shirt·sleeve (shėrt′slēv′), *n.* a sleeve of a shirt.

in (one's) shirtsleeves, with one's jacket or coat off; wearing one's shirt: *Lincoln thought it friendly to open the door himself in his shirtsleeves when two most elegant ladies came to call* (Baron Charnwood). *Working in shirtsleeves, Jake and Roy eschewed the usual trappings of executive life* (Time).

—*adj.* **1.** informal; direct: *a shirtsleeve conference, shirtsleeve diplomacy.* **2.** plain-spoken; homespun; folksy: *He was the local shirtsleeve philosopher* (New Yorker).

[American English < *shirt sleeve*]

shirt·sleeved (shėrt′slēvd′), *adj.* in shirtsleeves; wearing a shirt or shirts without a coat: *shirt-sleeved men watering their lawns in the gentle half-light* (Time).

shirt·tail (shėrt′tāl′), *n.* the divided lower part of a shirt, especially the back part: *His dress, however, has improved . . . and although he occasionally wears his shirttails out they are more often neatly tucked in* (New Yorker).

hang onto one's shirttails, to depend completely upon one: *The Tunisian newspaper L'Action . . . said "the hard reality teaches us every day that hanging onto the shirttails of the West brings us only insults and humiliation"* (Wall Street Journal).

—*adj.* casual; informal: *a shirttail conference.*

shirt·waist (shėrt′wāst′), *n.* a woman's or girl's tailored blouse, usually with a collar and cuffs, worn with a separate skirt. —*adj.* having a bodice that resembles a shirt: *Bright yellow silk shantung covered with white Dalmatian dots makes a trim shirtwaist dress with a small tie at the neckline* (New York Times). [American English < *shirt* + *waist*]

shirt·waist·er (shėrt′wās′tər), *n.* a one-piece dress with a shirtwaist top: *Of these charming shirtwaisters, some printed, others in woven cotton, the best are high waisted, slim* (Observer).

shirt·y (shėr′tē), *adj.*, **shirt·i·er, shirt·i·est.** *British Slang.* ill-tempered; ill-natured.

shish·ka·bob (shish′kə bob′), *n.* shish kebab.

shish ke·bab (shish′ kə bob′), square pieces of lamb or beef roasted or broiled on a spit with tomatoes, peppers, onion slices, etc. [< Armenian *shish kabab*]

shit·tah (shit′ə), *n.*, or **shittah tree,** (in the Bible) a tree from which shittim was obtained, probably a species of acacia with a hard, durable wood. Isaiah 41:19. [< Hebrew *shiṭṭāh*]

shit·tim (shit′im), *n.*, or **shittim wood,** (in the Bible) the tough, durable wood of the shittah tree, from which the Ark of the Covenant and various parts of the Jewish tabernacle were built. Exodus 25:10-27:6. [< Hebrew *shiṭṭim*, plural of *shiṭṭāh* shittah]

shiv (shiv), *n. U.S. Slang.* a knife or razor. [perhaps earlier *chiv, chive* knife, file < a Romany word]

shiv·a (shiv′ə), *n.*, *pl.* **shiv·as.** *Judaism.* the period of mourning for a parent, brother, sister, husband, or wife, consisting of seven days. [< Hebrew *shib'ah* seven]

Shi·va (shē′və), *n.* Siva.

shiv·a·ree (shiv′ə rē′), *n.*, *v.*, **-reed, -ree·ing.** *U.S.* —*n.* a mock serenade made by beating on kettles, pans, etc., especially one performed by neighbors and friends outside the bedroom of a newly married couple; charivari. —*v.t.* to greet or serenade with a shivaree: *A crowd . . . started out to 'shivaree' (mob and din to madness) the old man* (Guide). [American English; spelling of a pronunciation of *charivari*]

shive[1] (shiv), *n.* **1.** a thin, flat cork for stopping a wide-mouthed bottle. **2.** *British Dialect.* a slice, especially of bread. [origin uncertain. Compare Middle Dutch *scheve.*]

shive[2] (shīv), *n.* **1.** a particle of husk. **2.** a piece of thread or fluff on the surface of cloth, etc.

shives, the refuse of hemp or flax: *Chipboard can also be made from peanut shells, flax shives and bagasse* (Wall Street Journal).

[Middle English *schive.* Compare Middle Low German *schīve.*]

shiv·er[1] (shiv′ər), *v.i.* **1.** to shake with or as if with cold, fear, excitement, etc.; tremble; quiver: *The leaves shivered in the breeze. He shivered as with an ague* (Hawthorne). *As a dog withheld a moment . . . shivers ere he springs* (Tennyson). **2.** to sound or resound vibrantly: *a cry that shiver'd to the tingling stars* (Tennyson). —*v.t.* to cause (a sail or sails) to flutter through the action of the wind on the edge or edges, as by luffing the helm.

—*n.* a shaking from or as if from cold, fear, etc.: *Cold shivers went down Trilby's back as she listened* (George Du Maurier).

the shivers, a fit of shivering; ague; chills: *It gives me the cold shivers when I think what might have become of me* (Century Magazine).

[Middle English *schiveren;* origin uncertain]

—**shiv′er·er,** *n.* —**shiv′er·ing·ly,** *adv.*

—**Syn.** *v.i.* **1. Shiver, shudder, quake** mean to shake or tremble. **Shiver,** used chiefly of people and animals, suggests a quivering of the flesh: *He crept shivering into bed.* **Shudder** suggests sudden, sharp shivering of the whole body in horror or extreme disgust: *He shuddered at the ghastly sight.* **Quake** suggests violent trembling with fear or cold, or shaking and rocking from a violent disturbance: *The house quaked to its foundations.*

shiv·er[2] (shiv′ər), *v.t.* to break into small pieces; shatter or split into fragments or pieces: *a tree shivered by lightning. He shivered the mirror with a hammer.* —*v.i.* to be shattered or split; fly into small pieces: *His statue fell, and shivered on the stones* (James A. Froude).

—*n.* a small piece; splinter: *thorns of the crown and shivers of the cross* (Tennyson).

shiv·ers (shiv′ərz), *n.pl.* See under **shiver**[1], *n.*

shiv·er·some (shiv′ər səm), *adj.* **1.** causing shivers: *. . . the wintry river in which dear Mr. Crisparkle enjoyed his shiversome but innocent immersions* (London Times). **2.** shuddersome.

shiv·er·y[1] (shiv′ər ē, shiv′rē), *adj.* **1.** quivering from or as if from cold, fear, etc., shivering: *Shivery, we had another drink; climbed into the car, and moved on* (Atlantic). **2.** inclined to shiver, especially from cold: *. . . the frail, shivery . . . little being, enveloped in a tangle of black silk wraps* (Harriet Beecher Stowe). **3.** chilly: *shivery weather.* **4.** causing shivers, especially from fear: *a shivery experience.* [< *shiver*[1] + *-y*[1]]

shiv·er·y[2] (shiv′ər ē, shiv′rē), *adj.* apt to shatter or split; brittle. [< *shiver*[2] + *-y*[1]]

shives (shīvz), *n.pl.* See under **shive**[2], *n.*

shi·voo (shi vü′), *n. Australian Slang.* a noisy party or celebration.

shi·vy or **shi·vey** (shī′vē), *adj.* containing shives, as of wool, hair, etc.

shmo (shmō), *n.*, *pl.* **shmos, shmoes.** *Slang.* schmo: *A couple of shmos like you and me, we can't even get up our rent* (New Yorker).

shnook (shnu̇k), *n.* schnook.

shoal[1] (shōl), *n.* **1.** a place where the water of a sea, lake, or stream is shallow. **2.** a sandbank, sand bar, or ledge of rock, coral, etc., that makes the water shallow, especially one showing at low water: *The ship was wrecked on the shoals.* **3.** *Nautical.* a bank, mound, etc., of sand, muck, etc., that is never more than 36 feet beneath the surface of the sea.

—*adj.* (of water, a channel, etc.) not deep; shallow.

—*v.i.* (of water, a channel, etc.) to become shallow or more shallow: *He anchored them fast where the Texel shoaled* (Henry Newbolt). —*v.t.* **1.** to cause (a piece of water) to become shallow. **2.** to obstruct by shoals. **3.** to proceed from a greater to a lesser depth of (water): *There was no apparent change in colour to indicate that they shoaled their water* (Frederick Marryat).

[Old English *sceald* shallow, adjective]

shoal[2] (shōl), *n.* a large number; crowd: *a shoal of mackerel, a shoal of tourists, a shoal of troubles, etc. The letters which followed her in shoals from Berlin flattered her to the skies* (Mrs. Humphry Ward). —*v.i.* to form into a shoal or shoals; crowd together. [perhaps Old English *scolu* host (of people), school of fish, or perhaps < Middle Dutch *schole* a host, flock, shoal. Related to SCHOOL[2].]

shoal·i·ness (shō′lē nis), *n.* shoaly condition.

shoal·ness (shōl′nis), *n.* shoaliness.

shoal·y (shō′lē), *adj.* full of shoals or shallow places: *a shoaly channel.*

shoat (shōt), *n.* a young weaned pig able to feed itself: *The hood was thin and narrow, like a shoat's nose—you remember the way all Model-T Fords were built* (Marjorie Kinnan Rawlings). Also, **shote.** [origin uncertain]

sho·chet (shō′Hət), *n.*, *pl.* **sho·chets, sho·che·tim** (shō′Hə tim). shohet.

shock[1] (shok), *n.* **1. a.** a sudden and violent shake, blow, or crash; collision: *Earthquake shocks are often felt in Japan. The two cars crashed head on with a terrible shock.* **b.** the effect of such a shake, blow, etc.: *The shock broke the windows.* **2.** a sudden, violent, or upsetting disturbance: *His death was a great shock to his family. A shock, chill and painful, deprived me of speech* (Owen Wister). **3.** a sudden collapsing or weakening of the body or mind caused by some violent impression on the nerves: *The operation was successfully performed, but the patient suffered from shock.* **4.** *Informal.* a sudden attack of illness that makes a person senseless or takes away the power to move or speak; paralysis. **5.** the disturbance produced by the passage of an electric current through the body.

—*v.t.* **1. a.** to strike together violently. **b.** to shake or weaken by sudden collision. **2.** to cause to feel surprise, horror, or disgust: *That child's bad language shocks everyone. Ernest was terribly shocked when he heard of the loss of his money* (Samuel Butler). **3.** to cause (a person or part of the body) to suffer a physical, especially a nervous, shock. **4.** to give (a person or part of the body) an electric shock. —*v.i.* to collide with a shock: *All at fiery speed the two shock'd on the central bridge* (Tennyson).

[probably < French *choc*, noun, and *choquer*, verb, perhaps < a Germanic word]

—**Syn.** *n.* **1.** concussion, jolt, impact. —*v.t.* **1. a.** jar, jolt, collide. **2.** horrify, startle.

shock[2] (shok), *n.* **1.** a group of cornstalks or bundles of grain set up on end together in the field in order to dry or to await harvesting; shook. **2.** a large collection of various things; heap: *Lilacs, wind-beaten, staggering under a lopsided shock of bloom* (Amy Lowell).

—*v.t.* to make into a shock or shocks: *to shock corn.* —*v.i.* to make shocks: *If you will shock, I will tie.*

[origin uncertain]

shock[3] (shok), *n.* **1.** a thick, bushy mass: *He has a shock of red hair.* **2.** a dog having long, shaggy hair, especially a poodle. —*adj.* (of hair) rough and thick; shaggy. [origin uncertain]

shock·a·bil·i·ty (shok′ə bil′ə tē), *n.* the state or quality of being shockable.

shock·a·ble (shok′ə bəl), *adj.* that can be shocked; easily shocked: *Shock treatment is a waste of effort and electricity without an abundant presence of shockable people* (London Times).

shock absorber, 1. anything that absorbs or lessens a shock or shocks. **2.** a mechanical or hydraulic device on automobiles to absorb or lessen the shocks caused by rough roads. See **suspension system** for picture. **3.** a hydraulic device in the landing gear of airplanes, by which the shock of the wheels striking the ground in landing is absorbed.

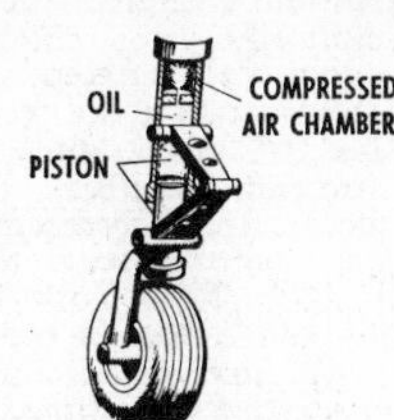

Shock Absorber (def. 3) Shock of the wheel hitting ground moves the piston upward, forcing oil into compressed air chamber, thus cushioning landing.

shock action, a mass attack; attack by an overwhelming force on a limited front, such as by an armored unit or units given close tactical support by artillery or aircraft, or both.

shock cord, a cord consisting of a bundle of rubber strands that permit stretching, used as a shock absorber: *an airplane shock cord.*

shock dog, a dog with long, shaggy hair.

shock·er[1] (shok′ər), *n.* **1.** *Informal.* a highly sensational written work, especially a story: *That young man loves to read shockers.* **2.** *Slang.* a person or thing that shocks: *You never know what he'll do next—a real shocker, isn't he?*

shock·er[2] (shok′ər), *n.* a person or device that shocks cornstalks and grain.

shock-head (shok′hed′), *n.* **1.** a head covered with a thick, bushy mass of hair. **2.** a shock-headed person. —*adj.* shock-headed. [< *shock*[3] + *head*]

shock-head·ed (shok′hed′id), *adj.* having a thick, bushy mass of hair.

shock·ing (shok′ing), *adj.* **1.** that shocks: *Mice soon learn to avoid the shocking current, which occurs at about 5-minute intervals* (Science). **2.** causing intense and painful surprise. **3.** offensive; disgusting; revolting: *it was a shocking sight . . . For many thousand bodies . . . lay rotting in the sun* (Robert Southey). **4.** *Informal.* very bad: *shocking manners.* —**shock′ing·ly,** *adv.* —**shock′ing·ness,** *n.* —**Syn. 2.** appalling. **3.** outrageous, scandalous.

shocking pink, 1. a very strong, bright pink color: . . . *dresses of shocking pink, blue, and cerise* (Manchester Guardian Weekly). **2.** of such a color; intensely pink: . . . *shocking pink and lavender flowers* (New Yorker).

shock·proof (shok′prüf′), *adj.* **1.** capable of withstanding or resisting shock: *a shockproof watch.* **2.** safe from electric shock: *The heating pad is waterproof, shockproof . . . and will not overheat* (Newsweek).

shock-re·sist·ant (shok′ri zis′tənt), *adj.* capable of resisting shock; shockproof: *Plastic mirrors, unlike those of glass, do not shatter, are shock-resistant, and do not steam or cloud* (Science News Letter).

shock stall, the stall of an aircraft traveling near the speed of sound, in which the separation of the airflow to the rear of the shock wave causes an increase in drag and a decrease in lift: *The use of swept-back wings raises the critical Mach number for the aircraft and allows the higher speeds to be reached without the danger of shock stall* (O. G. Sutton).

shock tactics, the use of masses of troops, heavy artillery, armored units, etc., to break through an enemy line.

shock therapy, the treatment of mental disorder through shock induced by chemical or electric means.

shock treatment, 1. shock therapy: *The aim of shock treatment is to break up the patient's pattern of recent mental associations* (New York Times). **2.** any act that is deliberately intended to shock: *In 1861 he* [*William Henry Seward*] *had been willing to provoke war with England and Spain in the rash hope that the shock treatment of trouble abroad would draw the seceded states back into the Union* (Atlantic).

shock troops, troops chosen and specially trained for making attack.

shock tube, a long, gas-filled tube for testing the effects of shock waves upon scale models of airplanes, missiles, satellites, etc. The tube is usually divided into two compartments, separated by a diaphragm; one, containing the model to be tested has low pressure, and the other, high. An explosion in the high-pressure compartment breaks the diaphragm and creates a shock wave of very high speed and temperature in the other.

shock wave, 1. a disturbance of the atmosphere produced by the movement of an aircraft, rocket, etc., at velocities greater than that of sound: *The shock wave created in the atmosphere by a reentering 5000-mile missile has a temperature in the tens of thousands of degrees Centigrade* (Atlantic). **2.** a similar effect caused by the expansion of gases away from an explosion: *There was an enormous explosion ashore, and the small boat, gathering way, rocked as the hot shock wave reached them* (Nicholas Monsarrat).

shod (shod), *v.* the past tense and past participle of **shoe:** *The blacksmith shod the horses. Her feet were shod in silver slippers.*

shod·di·ly (shod′ə lē), *adv.* in a shoddy manner: *Mayapan had been known as a collection of ruins of shoddily built temples and colonnaded halls* (Scientific American).

shod·di·ness (shod′ē nis), *n.* the quality or state of being shoddy.

shod·dy (shod′ē), *adj.,* **-di·er, -di·est,** *n., pl.* **-dies.** —*adj.* **1.** seeming to be better than it is; poorly made, designed, etc.: *a shoddy necklace, shoddy merchandise. It* [*painting*] *was all false, insincere, shoddy* (W. Somerset Maugham). **2.** mean; shabby: *shoddy treatment, a shoddy trick.* **3.** made of woolen waste.

—*n.* **1. a.** an inexpensive kind of wool made of woolen waste, old rags, yarn, etc. **b.** a coarse fabric made of this wool and some new wool. **2.** anything inferior made to look like what is better; pretense, sham: *a person with no taste for the shoddy in art or life.*

[origin uncertain]

shoe (shü), *n., pl.* **shoes** or (*Archaic*) **shoon,** *v.,* **shod, shoe·ing.** —*n.* **1.** an outer covering for a person's foot: *From his high-laced shoes . . . to the paper holders into which he jams his . . . cigar, Ludwig Erhard has remained true to his staid . . . upbringing* (Time). **2.** something like a shoe in shape, position, or use. **3.** a horseshoe. **4.** a metal rim, ferrule, band, casing, etc., to protect the end of a staff, pole, cane, spear, etc. **5.** the part of a brake that presses on a wheel or brake drum to slow down or stop a vehicle: *In bonding brake lining . . . a cement is used between the shoes and lining* (Automotive Encyclopedia). See **brake drum** for picture. **6.** the outer casing of an automobile tire, enclosing the inner tube or air chamber. **7.** a metal strip on the bottom of a runner of a sleigh or sled. **8.** a metal plate upon which a moving part of a mechanism bears. **9.** a sliding plate or contact by which a locomotive or an electric car takes current from the third rail. See **third rail** for picture.

fill one's shoes, take a person's place; fill another's position: *Mr. Macmillan has now put an end to the buzz of speculation about who was going to fill his shoes* (Mollie Panter-Downes).

in another's shoes, in another's place, situation, or circumstances: *I judge I should put more to risk if I were in his shoes* (John Adams).

the shoe is on the other foot, the situation is reversed: *All of us have a chance to help, as we would want to be helped if the shoe were on the other foot* (New York Times).

where the shoe pinches, where the real trouble or difficulty lies: *Oh, is that where the shoe pinches?* (Charles Reade).

—*v.t.* **1.** to put shoes on; furnish with a shoe or shoes: *A blacksmith shoes horses.* **2.** to protect or arm at the point; edge or face with metal: *a stick shod with steel.*

[Old English *scōh*]

➤ **shoe.** In the United States, *shoe* normally applies to footwear ending below, at, or just above the ankle, as distinguished from *boot,* which applies to footwear reaching at least to the middle of the calf. In British use, *shoe* is commonly applied to oxfords, opera pumps, and other low-cut footwear, while *boot* applies to footgear covering the whole foot including the ankle.

shoe·bill (shü′bil′), *n.* a large, grayish wading bird of central Africa, especially along the White Nile, that has a broad bill shaped somewhat like a shoe, and is related to the herons and storks.

shoe·black (shü′blak′), *n.* a person who cleans and polishes shoes to earn money; bootblack.

shoe boil, a flabby growth over the elbow of a horse, due to lying on hard floors or with the front feet doubled under the body.

shoe·box (shü′boks′), *n.* **1.** a thin cardboard box, usually of a standard size, used for holding shoes: *The instrument weighs less than 20 pounds and is only slightly larger than a shoebox* (Science News Letter). **2.** *Informal.* something that resembles a shoebox, especially a building: *He has been nurturing his company in a glorified Manhattan shoebox called City Center* (Time).

shoe·brush (shü′brush′), *n.* a brush for cleaning and polishing shoes.

shoe·horn (shü′hôrn′), *n.* a curved piece of metal, wood, plastic, etc., for inserting in a shoe at the heel to assist in slipping it on easily. —*v.t.* to put or force (into) as if with a shoehorn: *The new buildings will shoehorn another 125,000 to 150,000 office workers into one of the world's most congested areas* (New York Times).

shoe·lace (shü′lās′), *n.* a cord, braid, or leather strip for fastening a shoe: *Thirteen warnings in quick succession that his shoelaces were undone would have worn down even Lord Chesterfield* (Punch).

shoe·less (shü′lis), *adj.* without a shoe or shoes: *a shoeless horse. Why do you roam about shoeless and in rags?* (Wall Street Journal).

shoe·mak·er (shü′mā′kər), *n.* a person who makes or mends shoes. —**Syn.** cobbler.

shoe·mak·ing (shü′mā′king), *n.* a making or mending of shoes: *A person untrained to shoemaking does not offer his services as a shoemaker to the foreman of a shop* (Mark Twain).

sho·er (shü′ər), *n.* a person who shoes horses, mules, etc.

shoe·shine (shü′shīn′), *n.* **1.** the act of shining or polishing the shoes: *Sometimes Mr. Bruce and I . . . would stop . . . for a cup of coffee at the snack bar or a shoeshine in the barbershop* (New Yorker). **2.** the condition or appearance of shoes after being shined: *He's* [*a salesman's*] *a man way out there in the blue, riding on a smile and a shoeshine* (Arthur Miller). **3.** a shoeshine boy.

shoeshine boy, *U.S.* a boy who shines shoes to earn money; shoeblack: *The other day a high-ranking, nattily-dressed official . . . stopped to bawl out a ragged group of shoeshine boys on a busy street corner* (Wall Street Journal).

shoe·shop (shü′shop′), *n.* a shoe store: *In the shoeshops, boxes are scattered over the floors . . . at Bank Holiday* (Manchester Guardian).

shoe store, an establishment that sells shoes at retail.

shoe·string (shü′string′), *n.* **1.** a shoelace. **2.** *Informal.* a very small amount of money used to start or carry on a business, investment, etc.: *They don't amount to a shoestring* (Punch).

on a shoestring, *Informal.* with very little capital; on a small margin: *In general, an off-Broadway theater is financed on a shoestring* (Newsweek).

—*adj. Informal.* having or based on very little capital: *a shoestring budget. The agency was a shoestring operation at first* (Harper's).

shoestring catch, *Baseball.* a catch made close to the ground while running: *Don Mueller missed an attempt for a shoestring catch and the ball rolled to the bullpen* (New York Times).

shoestring gambler, *U.S.* a petty or tinhorn gambler.

shoestring potatoes, *U.S.* potatoes cut in long, stringlike pieces; julienne potatoes: *The food was simple but superior—hot consommé, mixed grill, shoestring potatoes . . . and coffee* (New Yorker).

shoe tree, a shaped block inserted into a shoe to keep it in shape or for stretching it.

sho·far (shō′fär, -fər), *n.* shophar, a musical instrument made of a curved ram's horn: *The ancient Hebrews decreed that a warning* *blast should be sounded on the shofar to mark the third case of an infectious disease in the community* (Time).

shog (shog), *v.*, **shogged, shog·ging,** *n. Dialect.* —*v.t.* to shake (something) from side to side; jolt; jog. —*v.i.* to shake to and fro; rock.
—*n.* **1.** a shake, jerk, or jog. **2.** a shogging gait.
[Middle English *shogge;* origin uncertain]

sho·gi (shō′gē), *n.* the game of chess as played in Japan: *Shogi . . . where the captured piece becomes the property of the capturing side to be used for that side's offensive* (Science News Letter). [< Japanese *shōgi* chess]

sho·gun (shō′gun, -gün), *n.* the former hereditary commander in chief of the Japanese army. The shoguns were the real rulers of Japan for hundreds of years until 1867. [< Japanese *shōgun* < Chinese *chiang chün* army leader]

sho·gun·ate (shō′gun it, -āt; -gün-), *n.* **1.** the position, rank, or rule of a shogun. **2.** government by shoguns: . . . *the arrival of Commodore Matthew C. Perry in 1853 with both the shogunate and feudalism ending shortly thereafter* (Atlantic).

sho·het (shō′hət), *n., pl.* **sho·hets, sho·he·tim** (shō′hə tim). a Jewish slaughterer who is learned in the rabbinical laws of slaughtering animals. Also, **shochet.** [< Hebrew *shōḥet*]

sho·ji (shō′jē), *n.*, or **shoji screen,** a sliding screen of semitransparent paper used to make up the partitions or walls of a Japanese house: *Shoji screens slide in front of a glass bedroom wall* (Sunset). [< Japanese *shōji*]

shone (shōn), *v.* a past tense and past participle of **shine:** *The sun shone all last week. It has not shone since.*

shoo (shü), *interj., v.,* **shooed, shoo·ing.** —*interj.* **1.** an exclamation used to scare away cats, hens, birds, etc. **2.** scat! go away!
—*v.t.* to scare or drive away by or as if by calling "Shoo!": *Shoo those flies away from the sugar. If a cow came into this farmyard everybody in the place would be shooing it out again* (H. G. Wells). —*v.i.* **1.** to call "Shoo!" **2.** to hurry away in obedience to a call of "Shoo."
[probably imitative. Compare Low German *schu,* French *shou.*]

shoo·fly (shü′flī′), *n., pl.* **-flies.** the wild indigo. [from the belief that attaching the plant to a harness will keep away horseflies]

shoo-fly pie, a pie or cake made of flour, crumbs, brown sugar, and molasses: *Shoo-fly pie . . . is a breakfast cake, he insists, and it's perfectly permissible to dunk it* (Wall Street Journal). [from the sweetness of the pie, which attracts flies that have to be shooed away]

shoo-in (shü′in′), *n. U.S. Informal.* **1.** an easy or sure winner: *He had been considered a shoo-in, but now the strategists are not so sure* (Newsweek). **2.** an easy race, contest, etc., to win; sure thing: *The election will be no shoo-in for the Republicans* (New York Daily News). [< *shoo* + *in*]

shook[1] (shu̇k), *n.* **1.** a set of staves and pieces for top and bottom sufficient for a single barrel, keg, etc. **2.** a set of the parts of a box or article of furniture, ready to be put together. [American English, apparently special use of *shook,* old past participle of *shake*]

shook[2] (shu̇k), *v.* the past tense of **shake:** *They shook with laughter. The solitary monk [Martin Luther] who shook the world* (Robert Montgomery).

shook[3] (shu̇k), *n.* a shock of corn or bundles of grain.

S-hook (es′hu̇k′), *n.* a double-pointed hook with the points turned in opposite directions.

shook-up (shu̇k′up′), *adj. Slang.* shaken; disturbed; upset: *I can't get particularly shook-up about a couple of days' delay* (The Nation).

shool (shül), *n., v.t., v.i. Dialect.* shovel.

shoon (shün), *n. Archaic.* shoes; a plural of **shoe.**

shoot (shüt), *v.,* **shot, shoot·ing,** *n.* —*v.t.* **1.** to hit, wound, or kill with a bullet, arrow, etc.: *to shoot a rabbit.* **2.** to send forth or let fly (a bullet, arrow, etc.) from a firearm, bow, or the like. **3.** to send forth like a shot or an arrow; send swiftly: *He shot question after question at us.* **4.** to fire or use (a gun or other firearm); discharge (a bow, catapult, etc.). **5.** to kill game in or on (an area): *He shot the east side of the mountain.* **6.** to move suddenly and swiftly: *He shot back the bolt.* **7.** to pass quickly along, through, under, or over: *to shoot a rapid or a bridge, to shoot Niagara Falls in a barrel.* **8.** to send out (rays, flames, etc.) swiftly and forcibly; dart: *The sun obliquely shoots his burning ray* (Alexander Pope). **9.** to put forth (buds, leaves, branches, etc.). **10. a.** to send (a ball, etc.) toward the goal, pocket, etc., in attempting to score. **b.** to score (a goal, points, etc.) by doing this: *He shot two goals.* **11.** to propel (a marble), as from the thumb and forefinger: *He taught them to fly kites and shoot marbles* (Washington Irving). **12.** to cast or toss (the dice) in playing craps. **13.** to take a picture with a camera; photograph; film: *A television outfit went there to shoot the story of George Voskovec, a Czech actor* (New Yorker). **14.** to measure the altitude of: *to shoot the sun.* **15.** to vary with some different color, etc.: *Her dress was shot with threads of gold. The river lay in pools of the most enchanting sea green shot with watery browns* (Robert Louis Stevenson). **16.** to dump; empty out. **17.** to straighten or fit the boards of (a joint) by planing. **18.** to open, loosen, remove, etc., by setting off a charge of an explosive: *to shoot an oil well.* **19.** to pull (one's cuffs) out so that they project beyond the sleeves of one's coat.
—*v.i.* **1.** to send forth a bullet, arrow, or other missile from a firearm, bow, or the like: *The boys shot at the mark. Who's there? . . . speak quickly, or I shoot* (Shakespeare). **2.** (of a gun, etc.) to send a bullet; go off: *This gun shoots straight.* **3.** to move suddenly and swiftly; go: *A car shot by us. Flames shot up from the burning house.* **4.** to hurt sharply from time to time: *Pain shot up his arm.* **5.** to come forth from the ground; grow rapidly: *Buds shoot forth in the spring. To rear the tender thought, To teach the young idea how to shoot* (James Thomson). **6.** to put forth buds or shoots, as a plant; germinate: *Always cut close, not leaving any stump to shoot again* (James Abercrombie). **7.** to project sharply; jut out: *a cape that shoots out into the sea.* **8. a.** to take a snapshot or film a motion picture. **b.** to begin photographing a scene. **c.** to film part of a motion picture. **9.** to follow or practice the sport of hunting or killing game with a gun: *He went into the mountains to fish and shoot.* **10.** to propel a ball, marble, etc. (in a certain manner or direction), especially in an effort to score. **11.** to produce or form crystals, as a solution, or a salt.

shoot at or **for,** *Informal.* to aim at; aspire to: *I shoot at no advantage to myself* (Robert Louis Stevenson). *The Air Force will "shoot" for the moon in August* (Christian Science Monitor).

shoot down, a. to kill by a shot: *The corporal was shot down by a sniper.* **b.** to cause (an airplane, etc.) to fall down by shooting: *The ace was credited with having shot down more than twenty enemy aircraft.*

shoot it out, *U.S.* to shoot until one side wins; fight it out with guns: *He shot it out with the gunman . . . [who] was wounded in the head* (New York Times).

shoot off, to discharge; fire: *A bonfire was lighted, the pipes were played, and guns were shot off* (Lytton Strachey).

shoot up, a. to grow tall or large quickly, as a plant, building, young person, etc.: *The corn is shooting up in the warm weather. Take that son of yours, shootin' up like a weed* (Charles Sale). **b.** *U.S.* to shoot at in a reckless way: *The rival hoodlums shot each other up.* **c.** *U.S. Informal.* to rush through (a place) shooting wildly in all directions: *The angry cowboys went on a rampage and shot up the town.*

—*n.* **1. a.** a shooting practice. **b.** a trip, party, or contest for shooting; shooting match or contest. **c.** a game-shooting expedition: *What a grand shoot it was in those far-off days . . . there were pheasants, partridges, grouse, and blackgame* (London Times). **2. a.** the act of sprouting or growing. **b.** the amount of growth in a certain period. **c.** any new part growing out, as a young bud or stem; offshoot: *The rosebush is putting out new shoots. These changes in volume and consequent pressures may in part serve the germinating seed by eventually permitting the emergence of the delicate root and shoot from the seed coat without damage* (A. M. Mayer). **3.** a short, sharp twinge of pain. **4.** a sloping trough for conveying coal, grain, water, etc., to a lower level; chute. **5.** a swift or sudden movement of something as though shooting or being shot in a particular direction. **6.** the time between strokes in rowing. **7.** the launching of a missile or rocket: *Since its first shoot early in 1957, it has had more than forty successful launchings* (Wall Street Journal). **8.** one movement of the shuttle between the threads of the warp in weaving, or a thread so placed; cast or throw.
[Middle English *schoten,* Old English *scēotan*]
—**Syn.** *v.i.* **7.** extend.

shoot·a·ble (shü′tə bəl), *adj.* that can be shot; fit for shooting.

shoot·er (shü′tər), *n.* **1.** a person who shoots: *Most shooters interested in the future of their sport refrain from hunting until the end of May* (New York Times). **2.** something that shoots or is used for shooting: *Each player uses a larger marble, the shooter, to knock, or "shoot," the small marbles out of the ring* (World Book Encyclopedia). *Then Jack drew his shooter out and shot Billy Bill through the head* (William Black). **3.** (in the petroleum industry) a person who shoots oil wells with nitroglycerin.

shoot·ing (shü′ting), *n.* **1.** the act of a person or thing that shoots. **2.** a shoot or sprout. **3.** the exclusive right to kill game on a particular tract: *Gentlemen . . . combine and lease the shooting over wide areas* (Richard Jefferie). **4.** the tract itself.

shooting box, *Especially British.* a small house used by hunters during the shooting season; hunting lodge.

shooting gallery, a long room or a deep booth fitted with targets for practice in shooting.

shooting iron, *Informal.* a gun, especially a rifle or pistol; firearm: *What he called "shooting irons" were his weapons* (Joseph Conrad).

shooting lodge, *British.* a shooting box; hunting lodge.

shooting star, 1. a meteor resembling a star seen falling or darting through the sky: *A knowledge of the constellations is a great help in reporting these shooting stars* (Bernhard, Bennett, and Rice). **2.** any of a group of North American plants of the primrose family with clusters of nodding, rose, purple, or white flowers whose petals and sepals turn backward.

shooting stick, 1. an implement used by printers to tighten or loosen the quoins in a chase by striking with a mallet. **2.** a walking stick with a small, hinged seat: *The Oklahoma oil broker rested on a shooting stick between each stroke* (Time).

shooting war, a war in which military weapons are used: *If a shooting war does come, then whatever technological advantages we hold at that critical moment may be of transcending importance* (Bulletin of Atomic Scientists).

shoot-off (shüt′ôf′, -of′), *n.* a supplementary contest to decide a tie in a shooting match: *The twenty-third annual Great Eastern skeet shoot was completed . . . with shoot-offs in nearly every event* (New York Times).

shoot-out (shüt′out′), *n. U.S. Informal.* a duel with guns; gunfight: *He was always in the middle of the big cops-and-robbers shoot-outs* (Time).

shop (shop), *n., v.,* **shopped, shop·ping.** —*n.* **1.** a place where things are sold; store, especially one dealing in a single type or limited range of commodities. **2.** a place where things are made or repaired; workshop: *He works in a carpenter's shop.* **3.** a place where a certain kind of work is done: *a barber shop.* **4.** *Informal.* a person's place of business or occupation. **5.** *British Slang.* an engagement or job in the theatrical business: *You'll be able to get me a shop! If Ross takes the piece . . .* (Leonard Merrick).

set up shop, a. to start work or business: *Every morning the fruit and vegetable man sets up shop at the corner.* **b.** to start a business: *He set up shop in the fur trade.*

shut up shop, a. to end work or business: *The grocer shuts up shop at six.* **b.** to close a business: *With another loss as large as this one, we will have to shut up shop.*

talk shop, to talk about one's work: *There is a coffee break in the afternoon, or tea in the library, when the associates gather with the partners and talk shop* (Harper's).

—*v.t.* **1.** to visit (a store or stores) to examine merchandise, compare prices, etc., especially as a shopper. **2.** to do one's shopping in: *In older times most people shopped*

the general store. **3.** *U.S. Slang.* to dismiss from a job or position. **4.** *British Slang.* **a.** to give a job to, especially in the theatrical business: *I can't shop everybody; there aren't enough parts to go around* (Leonard Merrick). **b.** to shut up or cause to be shut up in prison. —*v.i.* to visit stores to look at or to buy things: *We shopped all morning for a coat. I thought Joan was going with you, and that you would be shopping* (Benjamin Disraeli).
shop around, *U.S.* to look around intensively for something, as for a bargain, better position, etc.: *People aren't shopping around for jobs the way they used to* (Wall Street Journal).
[Old English *sceoppa* a (lean-to) booth. Related to SHIPPON.]

shop assistant, *British.* a salesclerk; salesman or saleswoman.

shop·break·ing (shop′brā′king), *n.* the act of breaking into and entering a store to steal or commit some other crime: *The two brothers were convicted of shopbreaking and received prison sentences* (London Times).

shop·front (shop′frunt′), *n.* the front or front room of a store.

shop·girl (shop′gėrl′), *n.* a girl who works in a shop or store.

sho·phar (shō′fär, -fər), *n.* an ancient Hebrew musical instrument of the trumpet kind, usually made of a curved ram's horn, still used in certain religious services, as on Yom Kippur. Also, **shofar.** [< Hebrew *shōfār*]

shop·keep·er (shop′kē′pər), *n.* the owner or manager of a shop or store. —**Syn.** tradesman.

shop·keep·ing (shop′kē′ping), *n.* the keeping of a shop; business of a shopkeeper.

shop·lift (shop′lift′), *v.t., v.i.* to steal goods from a store while pretending to be a customer. [back formation < *shoplifting*]

shop·lift·er (shop′lif′tər), *n.* a person who steals goods from a shop or store while pretending to be a customer. [< *shop* + *lifter* thief < *lift* to steal, take away]

shop·lift·ing (shop′lif′ting), *n.* the stealing of goods from a store while pretending to be a customer: *From shoplifting and petty thievery, the addict quickly graduates to major crimes* (New York Times).

shop·man (shop′mən), *n., pl.* **-men. 1.** a shopkeeper. **2.** *Especially British.* a salesman in a shop.

shoppe (shop), *n.* shop.
➔ This archaic spelling is used sometimes for a quaint, old-world effect, especially in names of small specialty shops and similar establishments: *His ferryboat was beached . . . and turned into a gift shoppe* (Time).

shop·per (shop′ər), *n.* **1.** a person who visits stores to look at or buy things: *bargain basement shoppers* ... (Newsweek). **2.** a person hired to buy goods at retail for another, especially one hired by a retail store to buy items of merchandise from competitive stores in order to determine how similar items offered by it compare in price and quality; comparison shopper.

shop·ping (shop′ing), *n.* the buying of groceries, clothes, etc.: *Mother does her shopping on Wednesdays and Saturdays.*
go shopping, to go to a store or stores in order to buy groceries, clothes, etc.: *We go shopping every Thursday at the shopping center.*

shopping cart, a small, four-wheeled cart, used by customers in a supermarket or other self-service store to carry goods from the shelves to the clerk at the cash register or checkout counter.

shopping center, a cluster of retail stores and shops, with parking facilities, planned and built as a unit on or near a main road in a suburban or new community: *"The average housewife prefers a one-stop shopping center" and she also desires the "self-service method" of selling* (Wall Street Journal).

shop·py (shop′ē), *adj.* **1.** having to do with or characteristic of shops. **2.** consisting of many shops. **3.** having to do with a person's interest in his occupation, hobby, trade, etc.; talking shop.

shop steward, a union worker in a factory or company elected to act as spokesman for his fellow workers in dealing with management, maintaining union regulations, etc.

shop·talk (shop′tôk′), *n.* **1.** the informal language of an occupation: *the shoptalk of lawyers, the shoptalk of actors.* **2.** the discussion of business or professional matters, especially outside of office hours; talking shop: *Mere shoptalk, while of course it is heard, is not encouraged or admired for its own sake* (New York Times).
➔ **shoptalk.** For the most part shoptalk consists of the necessary names for materials, processes, tools, etc.—for everything that is commonly referred to in the line of work. While many of these words are in good standing, they are not often needed outside of the vocation.

shop·walk·er (shop′wô′kər), *n. Especially British.* a floorwalker.

shop·win·dow (shop′win′dō), *n.* a window of a shop or store in which goods are displayed for sale; show window.

shop·wom·an (shop′wu̇m′ən), *n., pl.* **-wom·en.** a woman who works in a shop or store; shopgirl.

shop·work·er (shop′wėr′kər), *n.* a person who works in a shop or workshop.

shop·worn (shop′wôrn′, -wōrn′), *adj.* soiled, frayed, etc., by being displayed and handled in a shop or store; old and worn; threadbare: *After all these years and books, another factual account of the crucial European battles of World War II may sound like pretty shopworn fare* (Wall Street Journal).

sho·ran (shôr′an, shōr′-), *n.* a method of navigating an airplane or ship. The time between sending signals to two fixed stations and receiving signals from the stations determines the sender's position: *Surveys over water generally depend on radio navigation aids such as shoran* (Scientific American). [< *sho*(rt) *ra*(nge) *n*(avigation)]

shore[1] (shôr, shōr), *n., v.,* **shored, shor·ing.** —*n.* **1.** land at the edge of a sea, lake, river, etc.: *The [Mississippi] River cuts at the shores to give itself man-size room; past Memphis and Vicksburg and New Orleans* (Newsweek). **2.** land near a sea; coast: . . . *I have seen the kingly ocean gain advantage on the kingdom of the shore* (Shakespeare). **3.** the land (as contrasted with the sea): *Our marines serve both on sea and on shore.* **4.** *Law.* the ground lying between the ordinary high-water and low-water marks; foreshore. **5.** *U.S.* the seashore as a place of vacation resort: *to go to the shore for the summer.*
in shore, in or on the water, but near to the shore or nearer to the shore: *Steer in shore of them* (Frederick Marryat).
off shore, in or on the water, but not far from the shore: *The yacht was anchored off shore opposite Sandy Point.*
shores, land: *As one who long detain'd on foreign shores pants to return* (William Cowper).
—*v.t.* to put or set ashore: *to shore goods or passengers. The boat was temporarily shored on the beach* (J. Spence).
[Middle English *schore,* perhaps < Low German, or Middle Dutch]
—**Syn.** *n.* **1.** strand. **2.** seaboard.

shore[2] (shôr, shōr), *n., v.,* **shored, shor·ing.** —*n.* a prop placed against or beneath something to hold it in place or support it; strut. —*v.t.* to prop or support with, or as if with, shores: *We laid the ship aground . . . and shored her up on each side* (Daniel Defoe). *The hydraulic mechanism also has been shored up by inserting metal filters in place of paper ones* (Wall Street Journal). [Middle English *schore,* perhaps < Middle Dutch, a prop]

Shores[2] supporting ship frame

shore[3] (shôr, shōr), *v. Archaic.* a past tense of **shear.**

shore[4] (shôr, shōr), *v.t.,* **shored, shor·ing.** *Scottish.* **1.** to threaten. **2.** to scold. **3.** to offer. [origin unknown]

shore-based (shôr′bāst′, shōr′-), *adj.* having its base of operations on or near the shore; land-based: *shore-based radar, shore-based aircraft.*

shore bird, any bird that frequents the shores of seas, inlets, lakes, etc.: *Plovers, snipes, and sandpipers are shore birds.*

shore crab, the green crab of Europe and the Atlantic coast of America.

shore dinner, *U.S.* a dinner featuring various seafoods: . . . *memories of Chesapeake Bay, Cape Cod, and innumerable shore dinners* (New Yorker).

shore fast, the length of cable which secures a ship to the dock; hawser.

shore-go·ing (shôr′gō′ing, shōr′-), *n.* a going, staying, or living on shore. —*adj.* going or living on shore; having to do with life on shore.

shore leave, leave for a member or members of a ship's crew to go ashore: *Though we made two ports in Australia, no shore leave was granted* (Harper's).

shore·less (shôr′lis, shōr′-), *adj.* **1.** having no shore; having no low land adjacent to the water: *a rocky, shoreless island.* **2.** boundless: *He was adrift on the shoreless tides of delirium* (Rudyard Kipling).

shore·line (shôr′līn′, shōr′-), *n.* the line where shore and water meet: *The National House and Farms Association, Inc., will transfer title to the lake with its several miles of shoreline* (New York Times).

shore patrol, a detail or detachment of two or more enlisted men of the United States Navy or Coast Guard assigned to maintain order among personnel of their own branch of the service while ashore in a particular city, district, etc.

Shore Patrol, the policing branch of the United States Navy and Coast Guard, as a distinct division of the service. *Abbr.:* SP (no periods), S.P.

shor·er (shôr′ər, shōr′-), *n.* **1.** a person whose work it is to prop up structures, etc., as during construction operations. **2.** something that shores; a prop.

shores (shôrz, shōrz), *n.pl.* See under **shore**[1], *n.*

shore·scape (shôr′skāp′, shōr′-), *n.* **1.** a view of scenery on a shore: *Morning showed shorescapes of a most inviting aspect; fields . . . thick forests . . . with ash trees at the riverbanks* (Wall Street Journal). **2.** a picture or painting showing a scene on a shore: *Thirty recent, pretty, and repetitious shorescapes . . .* (Time). [< *shore* + *scape*[3]]

shore·side (shôr′sīd′, shōr′-), *adj.* of, on, or toward the shore; along the shore. —*n.* the land along the shore.

shore wall, an accumulation of sand and gravel pushed up into mounds by the expansion and contraction of ice formed on rivers or lakes.

shore·ward (shôr′wərd, shōr′-), *adv., adj.* toward the shore: *Now the great winds shoreward blow* (Matthew Arnold). (*adv.*). *The shoreward portion . . . was found to lie on a nearly exposed rock bottom . . . due to the vigorous wave and current action* (Science News Letter). (*adj.*).

shore·wards (shôr′wərdz, shōr′-), *adv.* shoreward.

shor·ing (shôr′ing, shōr′-), *n.* **1.** a system of shores or props, as for supporting a building, ship, or dock. **2.** the act of building or providing with shores.

shorn (shôrn, shōrn), *v.* a past participle of **shear:** *The sheep was shorn of its wool.* —*adj.* **1.** sheared: *Early in the period choice 102-pound shorn lambs sold for $21.50* (Wall Street Journal). **2.** deprived: *a man newly shorn of his wealth.*

short (shôrt), *adj.* **1.** not long; having small extent from end to end: *a short distance, a short time, a short street. The life so short, the craft so long to learn* (Geoffrey Chaucer). **2.** not tall; having little height: *a short man, short grass.* **3.** extending or reaching but a little way: *a short memory.* **4. a.** not coming up to the right amount, measure, standard, etc.: *short weight. The cashier is short in his accounts.* **b.** not having enough; scanty: *a short supply of money. The explorers managed on a short allowance of food. He was short with his rent for the approaching quarter day* (H.G. Wells). **5.** so brief as to be rude: *He was so short with me that I felt hurt.* **6.** not long-winded; concise: *Let me pray you to be short and explicit in what you have to say* (Scott). **7.** *Phonetics.* (of vowels or sounds) occupying a relatively short time in utterance. The vowels are short in *fat, net, not, up.* **8.** breaking or crumbling easily: *Pastry is made short with lard and butter.* **9.** not owning at the time of sale the stocks, securities, commodities, that one sells: *A trader is short when he sells something he does not have, usually in the expectation that the price will go down before he must deliver* (New York Times). **10.** of, noting, or having to do with sales of stocks, securities, or commodities that the seller does not possess; having to do with a short sale or short selling. **11.** depending for profit on a decline in prices. **12.** (of a bill, note, etc.) that is to be paid within a short time, as within ten days.
run short, a. not have enough: *Let me know if you run short of money before then.* **b.** not

be enough: *There was a great dearth of arms . . . and the supply in the Tower soon ran short* (Garnet J.W. Wolseley).
short for, an abbreviated term for: *The word 'phone' is short for 'telephone.'*
short of, a. not up to; less than: *Nothing short of your best work will satisfy me. Fine seasoned regiments were short of half their strength* (Baron Charnwood). **b.** in want of; lacking: *He is short of funds right now. Allow me to take your hat—we are rather short of pegs* (Dickens). **c.** on the near side of: *He halted . . . at Malmesbury, twenty miles short of Bath* (John F. Kirk).
short on, poorly furnished with; having little of; lacking: *U.S. housewives, long on gadgets and short on help, often look enviously to the Old World as a place where . . . willing hands are plentiful* (Time).
—*adv.* **1.** so as to be or make short: *to throw short.* **2.** abruptly; suddenly: *The horse pulled up short.* **3.** briefly. **4.** on the near side of an intended or particular point: *to stop short of actual crime.* **5.** *Commerce.* without possessing at the time the stocks, securities, or commodities sold.
be caught short. See under **caught.**
sell short. See under **sell**[1], *v.*
—*n.* **1. a.** something short. **b.** what is deficient or lacking. **2.** a short circuit. **3.** *Commerce.* **a.** a person who has sold or is selling short: *This not only put the company in effective competition with the shorts as bidders for the stock . . .* (Wall Street Journal). **b.** a short sale: *to cover one's shorts.* **c.** stock, etc., sold short: *The biggest gains were made in shorts where the 4½ per cent . . . stock . . . gained ¾* (Economist). **4.** any short motion picture as a cartoon, newsreel, etc., especially one shown on the same program with a full-length picture (feature). **5.** *Baseball.* the position of shortstop: *to play short.* **6. a.** a fish too small to be worth keeping, or to keep legally. **b.** *Especially Northeastern U.S.* a lobster with a body measurement below that required for keeping legally. **7.** a short sound or syllable. **8.** a shot that strikes in front of the target, as while firing to adjust the range. **9.** a size of garment for men who are shorter than average.
for short, by way of abbreviation; as a nickname: *Robert is often called Rob for short.*
in short, briefly: *The twins no longer derive their sustenance from Nature's founts—in short, they are weaned* (Dickens).
shorts, a. short, loose trousers often worn in sports: *I . . . stood outside in football shorts, nailed boots, and sweater* (Blackwood's Magazine). **b.** similar short trousers, worn as an undergarment by men: *a set of undershirt and shorts.* **c.** a baby's short clothes: *Six months passed . . . and then he [the baby] was put into shorts* (Frederick Marryat). **d.** knee breeches; smallclothes: *The little old gentleman . . . follows him, in black shorts and white silk stockings* (Walter Besant). **e.** a mixture of bran and coarse meal: *The farmers ate middlings, shorts, or corn meal at least once a day.*
squeeze the shorts, to demand and get higher prices (for securities, etc.) from short sellers at the time they must make delivery: *Firms that squeeze the shorts compel short sellers to buy back the stocks at a heavy loss to themselves.*
—*v.t., v.i.* to short-circuit: *On the top floor the electrician shorted five pairs of wires . . . leaving one free wire* (Scientific American).
[Old English *sceort*] —**short′ness,** *n.*
—**Syn.** *adj.* **1. Short, brief** mean of small extent. **Short** may refer to either space or time, and often suggests being curtailed or unfinished: *Because he was late he could take only a short walk today.* **Brief** usually refers to time and means coming to an end quickly. When applied to speeches or writings, it is more likely to suggest leaving out unnecessary details than cutting off the end: *A brief essay is short but to the point.* **5.** abrupt, curt, sharp.
short account, 1. the account of a person who sells stocks or commodities short. **2.** all short sales of one stock or commodity, or of an entire market at a given time.
short·age (shôr′tij), *n.* **1.** too small an amount; lack: *a shortage of rain. There is a shortage of grain because of poor crops. There is still an acute shortage of housing facilities in the large cities of this country* (Andrew W. Mellon). **2.** the amount by which something is deficient: *The total shortage was $500.*
—**Syn. 1.** deficiency.
short and, the sign &; ampersand.
short-arm (shôrt′ärm′), *adj.* short-armed.
short-armed (shôrt′ärmd′), *adj.* **1.** that has short arms; not long of arm or reach. **2.** that travels a short distance and is delivered with the arm not fully straight: *a short-armed jab to the chin.*
short ballot, *U.S.* a simplified ballot having only the principal offices filled through election.
short-billed marsh wren (shôrt′bild′), a wren of eastern North America with white streaks on the crown that nests in wet, grassy marshes and meadows.
short bit, *U.S. Dialect.* 10 cents; a dime.
short·bread (shôrt′bred′), *n.* a rich cake or cookie that crumbles easily.
short-breathed (shôrt′bretht′), *adj.* **1.** short of breath; short-winded: *Being short-breathed and unable to go up even a gentle hill without panting and puffing . . .* (Blackwood's Magazine). **2.** lacking prolonged effort; fleeting; short-lived: *Chávez's invention is too short-breathed to sustain the big romantic proportions [of the music] that he has elected to fill* (London Times).
short·cake (shôrt′kāk′), *n.* **1. a.** a cake made of rich biscuit dough and shortening, usually slightly sweetened, covered or filled with berries or other fruit. **b.** a sweet cake filled with fruit. **2.** any of various rich cookies or small cakes resembling shortbread, but unsweetened. **3.** *Archaic.* shortbread.
short-change (shôrt′chānj′), *v.t.*, **-changed, -chang·ing. 1.** to give less than the right change to (a person), especially intentionally. **2.** to give less than is considered a proper return, full share, etc.; cheat: *to short-change the public, to be short-changed in getting an education.*
short-chang·er (shôrt′chān′jər), *n.* a person who short-changes.
short circuit, a side circuit of electricity that is formed when insulation wears off a wire or wires that touch each other or some connecting conductor, so that the main circuit is by-passed: *A short circuit usually blows a fuse and may cause a fire by heating wires.*
short-cir·cuit (shôrt′sėr′kit), *v.t.* **1.** to make a short circuit in (an electric system). **2.** (of a conductor) to carry (a current) by acting as a short circuit. **3.** to cut off the current from (part of an apparatus) by making a short circuit. **4.** *Surgery.* to make a direct passage from (an organ) into some other part when the normal passage is obstructed. **5.** *Informal.* to get around; avoid; by-pass: *It was he who . . . contrived to short-circuit the . . . defense order* (Harper's). —*v.i.* to make a short circuit.
short·com·ing (shôrt′kum′ing), *n.* a fault; defect: *a person with many shortcomings.*
—**Syn.** failing.
short commons, little to eat: *In a word, the Army is on short commons and the lack of funds is apparent everywhere* (London Times).
short covering, the buying of securities, commodities, etc., to cover a short sale.
short cut, 1. a less distant or quicker way between two places. **2.** a quick or quicker way: *There are no short cuts to wisdom and learning.*
short-cut (shôrt′kut′), *v.*, **-cut, -cut·ting.** —*v.i.* to use a short cut. —*v.t.* to avoid by using a short cut: *to short-cut a city. One reason for short-cutting the legal order . . . is the unwillingness some judges are showing now to sign such orders* (New York Times).
short-dat·ed (shôrt′dā′tid), *adj.* **1.** falling due at an early date: *short-dated bills, bonds, or notes.* **2.** having little time to run: *a short-dated life or career.*
short-day plant (shôrt′dā′), a plant that blooms only when its daily exposure to light is relatively short, as in the spring or late fall when the days are short and the nights are long: *Sugar cane, wild strawberries, violets, and poinsettias are some short-day plants.*
short division, a method of dividing numbers in which the various steps of the division are worked out mentally. It is used to divide small numbers.
short-eared owl (shôrt′ird′), an owl about 15½ inches long that frequents open, marshy areas and often hunts during the day; hawk owl.
short·en (shôr′tən), *v.t.* **1.** to make shorter; cut off: *to shorten the working day. She has had all her dresses shortened. Envy and wrath shorten the life* (Ecclesiasticus 30:24). **2.** to make seem shorter: *Thus were the hours of labour shortened . . . by shrewd remarks and bits of local gossip* (Joseph Conrad). **3.** to make rich with butter, lard, etc.; add shortening to: *She used butter to shorten her cake.* **4.** to lessen the area of (a vessel's sails) by reefing or furling; take in (sail). **5.** (in the Bible) to reduce the reach or power of: *Behold, the Lord's hand is not shortened, that it cannot save* (Isaiah 59:1). **6.** to treat or pronounce (a vowel or syllable) as short.
—*v.i.* **1.** to become shorter; dwindle in size: *The days shorten in November in the United States.* **2.** (of odds or prices) to decrease.
—**short′en·er,** *n.*
—**Syn.** *v.t.* **1. Shorten, curtail, abbreviate** mean to make shorter. **Shorten** is the general word meaning to reduce the length or extent of something: *The new highway shortens the trip.* **Curtail,** more formal, means to cut something short by taking away or cutting off a part, and suggests causing loss or incompleteness: *Bad news made him curtail his trip.* **Abbreviate,** used chiefly of words and phrases, means to shorten by leaving out syllables, letters, or sounds, by sometimes using initial letters or substitutions: *Abbreviate "pound" to "lb." after numerals.*
short-end·er (shôrt′en′dər), *n. U.S. Informal.* a contestant who is not favored to win; underdog: *Truman is the patron saint of short-enders; favorites never invoke him* (New Yorker).
short·en·ing (shôr′tə ning, shôrt′ning), *n.* **1.** butter, lard, or other fat, used to make pastry, cake, etc., rich or crumbly: *Shortening, like salad oil, starts out as roughly refined "summer oil"* (Wall Street Journal). **2.** the act of a person or thing that shortens.
Short·er Catechism (shôr′tər), the shorter of two catechisms used by the Presbyterian Church.
short·fall (shôrt′fôl′), *n.* a falling short; failure to reach an expected amount; decrease: *a shortfall in purchasing.*
short-fired (shôrt′fird′), *adj.* (of china and pottery) not sufficiently baked.
short·hair cat, or **short·hair** (shôrt′här′), *n.* any of a breed of medium-sized, domestic cats having long, slender bodies and short hair: *Shorthair of the Year was . . . a black Manx male* (Theodore M. O'Leary).
short·hand (shôrt′hand′), *n.* **1.** a method of rapid writing that uses symbols capable of rapid transcription in place of letters, syllables, words, and phrases; stenography: *Sometimes it is possible to make actual notes in shorthand or longhand, and occasionally a simultaneous electrical recording may be made of the interview* (Anthony H. Richmond). **2.** writing that contains these symbols. **3.** any shortened form or system of communicating: *Sociologists all have their own shorthand or jargon* (Listener).
—*adj.* **1.** using shorthand: *a shorthand clerk.* **2.** written in shorthand: *shorthand notes.*

Gregg Shorthand (def. 2) for: "The booklet will also tell you about the many services that are available to customers of our bank."

short-hand·ed (shôrt′han′did), *adj.* not having enough workmen or helpers; undermanned; understaffed: *The Giants . . . are so short-handed in the backfield that . . . Steve [the coach] no longer has a choice* (New York Times). —**short′-hand′ed·ness,** *n.*
short-hand-typ·ist (shôrt′hand′tī′pist), *n. British.* a stenographer: *Shorthand-typist, knowledge of bookkeeping essential, required for small City office* (London Times).
short-hand-writ·er (shôrt′hand′rī′tər), *n. British.* a shorthand-typist.
short-haul (shôrt′hôl′), *adj.* of or having to do with transportation over relatively short distances: *a short-haul airline.*
short-head·ed (shôrt′hed′id), *adj.* having a short head; brachycephalic. —**short′-head′ed·ness,** *n.*

 PRONUNCIATION KEY: hat, āge, cãre, fär; let, ēqual, tėrm; it, īce; hot, ōpen, ôrder; oil, out; cup, pu̇t, rüle;

short·horn (shôrt′hôrn′), *n.* any of a breed of cattle with short horns, raised chiefly for beef: *The Shorthorn is generally considered a dual-purpose breed, though different strains have been selected primarily for meat or for milk production* (Ralph W. Phillips).

Shorthorn Cow (48 to 52 in. high at the shoulder)

short-horned (shôrt′hôrnd′), *adj.* having short horns: *a short-horned cow or bull.*

short-horned grasshopper, any of a family of grasshoppers having short antennae and commonly migrating in great swarms; locust.

short hundred-weight, the American hundred-weight, equal to 100 pounds.

shor·ti·a (shôr′tē ə), *n.* any of a group of perennial plants, of the mountains of North and South Carolina and of Japan, with evergreen leaves and nodding white or rose flowers. Shortia, prized in cultivation, was long thought the rarest of North American plants. [American English < New Latin *Shortia* the genus name < Charles W. *Short*, 1794-1863, an American botanist]

short·ie (shôr′tē), *n.* **1.** a garment of short length: *Trousers . . . tapering elegantly from under my new camel shortie with Avenger type breast-pocket flap* (Basil Boothroyd). **2.** *Informal.* a short person. —*adj.* (of a garment) of short length: *The third was wearing an old trilby hat and a blue shortie raincoat* (London Times). Also, **shorty.**

short interest, a quantity of borrowed stock sold in a short sale; number of shares sold short.

short iron, a golf club with an iron or steel head inclined at a relatively large angle to its short shaft, suitable for shots close to the green.

short·ish (shôr′tish), *adj.* rather short: *a shortish run, visit, speech, etc.*

short-joint·ed (shôrt′join′tid), *adj.* **1.** (of plants) having short gaps between the joints. **2.** (of a horse) having a short pastern.

short·leaf pine (shôrt′lēf′), a pine tree of the southern and eastern United States having short needles and small cones.

short-leg·ged (shôrt′leg′id, -legd′), *adj.* having short legs.

short-list (shôrt′list′), *v.t. British.* to include in a list of chosen applicants or candidates, from which a final selection will be made: *Candidates short-listed will be interviewed on 27th July* (London Times).

short-lived (shôrt′livd′, -livd′), *adj.* **1.** living only a short time; having a short life: *a short-lived plant.* **2.** lasting only a short time; fleeting; brief: *a short-lived improvement, short-lived hope.*

➔ The first and more common pronunciation also accords better with the etymology, since the underlying form is the noun *life*, not the verb *live*. The second pronunciation is nevertheless an established variant, and the prevailing one in British English. An exactly parallel situation exists with regard to *long-lived*.

short·ly (shôrt′lē), *adv.* **1.** in a short time; before long; soon: *I will be with you shortly.* **2.** a short time (after or before): *He went shortly before they came.* **3.** in a few words; briefly; concisely: *"The business of America is business," said Calvin Coolidge shortly.* **4.** briefly and rudely; abruptly; curtly: *"I think very differently," answered Elizabeth shortly* (Jane Austen). —**Syn. 1.** presently. **3.** tersely.

short·nose gar (shôrt′nōz′), a North American gar ranging from the Great Lakes to the Gulf Coast, that grows up to 3 feet in length.

short-or·der (shôrt′ôr′dər), *adj. U.S.* preparing or selling meals, sandwiches, etc., that can be quickly cooked or made on order: *a short-order cook, a short-order diner.*

short-pe·ri·od variable (shôrt′pir′ē əd), a variable star whose period from one peak of brightness to the next is less than 100 days.

short position, short interest: *They said dealers in New York and Paris are believed to hold substantial short positions in sterling* (Wall Street Journal).

short-range (shôrt′rānj′), *adj.* not reaching far; having a limited use or application: *a short-range view, a short-range forecast, a short-range objective, a short-range missile.*

short-run (shôrt′run′), *adj.* for or lasting a brief time: *Four steps—one a short-run corrective measure and three for the long pull —should be promptly taken* (Harper's).

shorts (shôrts), *n.pl.* See under **short,** *n.*

short sale, the sale of what a person does not have but hopes to buy at a lower price before the time of delivery.

short seller, a person who sells stocks or commodities short.

short selling, the act of selling stocks or commodities short.

short shrift, 1. little mercy, consideration, or delay: *Flagrant violators will get short shrift, the chief said* (New York Times). *Mr. Guyot, the only Communist speaker, was given short shrift by the Assembly* (London Times). **2.** a short time for confession and absolution. **make short shrift of,** to give little consideration to: *The unification of Germany . . . led to making short shrift of the claims of non-German neighbors in regions where Germans, too, were involved* (Edmund Wilson).

short-sight·ed (shôrt′sī′tid), *adj.* **1.** not able to see far; nearsighted; myopic: *He was very short-sighted, and this early encouraged his preference for reading rather than sport* (Manchester Guardian). **2. a.** lacking in foresight; not prudent: *It is short-sighted and self-deluding to ascribe more than a small part of Russian success to efficient espionage* (Bulletin of Atomic Scientists). **b.** characterized by or proceeding from lack of foresight: *a short-sighted strategy. Heaven mocks the short-sighted views of man* (Horace Walpole). —**short′-sight′ed·ly,** *adv.* —**short′-sight′ed·ness,** *n.*

short snort·er (snôr′tər), *Slang, especially in the 1930's and 1940's.* **1.** a dollar bill or other piece of paper currency autographed by some or all of those who have shared in a transoceanic flight with its owner. **2.** a person who shared in such a flight and had to buy drinks for others who made the flight if he could not produce his autographed bill on demand.

short-spo·ken (shôrt′spō′kən), *adj.* **1.** speaking in a short or brief manner; concise: *The short-spoken Air Force veteran with . . . a limp in his leg was asked by a friend how it happened* (Wall Street Journal). **2.** curt.

short-staple (shôrt′stā′pəl), *adj.* (of cotton, etc.) having the fiber short.

short·stop (shôrt′stop′), *n.* **1.** (in baseball) an infielder stationed between second base and third base. **2.** an acid solution used to halt the developing process in photography; stop bath.

short story, a prose story with a full plot, but much shorter than a novel: *Mr. [Gore] Vidal is a novelist, and in short stories he tends to take an episode and fine it down* (Punch). —**short′-sto′ry,** *adj.*

short subject, a short motion picture running from 7 to 20 minutes between feature films: *Cartoons, newsreels, and travelogues are short subjects.*

short sweetening, *U.S. Dialect.* sugar.

short-swing (shôrt′swing′), *adj. U.S. Finance.* based on or covering a six-month or shorter period in which a transaction is concluded: *short-swing trading.*

short-tailed hawk (shôrt′tāld′), a small broad-winged hawk of light and dark color phases, found from Florida and Mexico south to Argentina.

short-tailed shrew, a large, very common shrew found throughout the eastern half of the United States and into southern Canada; blarina.

short-tailed weasel, a brown weasel of North America with white feet, throat, and belly. In winter it turns all white except for a black tip on the tail.

short-tem·pered (shôrt′tem′pərd), *adj.* easily made angry; quick-tempered.

short-term (shôrt′tėrm′), *adj.* **1.** for a short period: *a short-term investment, short-term training.* **2.** falling due in a short time: *short-term notes, short-term interest.*

short-time (shôrt′tīm′), *adj.* of or for a short time; temporary: *short-time housing. No overtime work until laid-off and short-time workers are fully employed* (Wall Street Journal).

short-tim·er (shôrt′tī′mər), *n.* a person who serves or works for a short time: *Soldiers near the end of their enlistment or draft period describe themselves as short-timers, an old prison term* (David Boroff).

short ton, 2,000 pounds avoirdupois; net ton.

short-waist·ed (shôrt′wās′tid), *adj.* having a short waist; short from neck to waistline.

short wave, a radio wave having a wave length of 100 meters or less.

short-wave (shôrt′wāv′), *v.,* **-waved, -waving,** *adj.* —*v.t., v.i.* to transmit by short waves: *The President's speech was short-waved overseas.* —*adj.* of or by means of short waves: *When using short-wave diathermy, short-length radio waves are passed through the tissues from one rubber covered electrode to the other* (Howard A. Carter).

short·weight or **short-weight** (shôrt′-wāt′), *n.* a weight that is short of the weight charged for by the seller: *. . . the evil perpetrated by some stores of defrauding the public by shortweights in items they prepackage for sale* (New York Times). —*v.t., v.i.* to defraud by giving shortweight: *Ship's pursers . . . short-weighted . . . rancid salt pork* (Maclean's). *Arden and . . . O'Leary were also accused of short-weighting* (Wall Street Journal).

short-wind·ed (shôrt′win′did), *adj.* getting out of breath too quickly; having difficulty in breathing. —**short′-wind′ed·ness,** *n.*

short·y (shôr′tē), *n., pl.* **-ties,** *adj.* shortie: *Another shorty, this one a costume, involves a double-breasted coat . . . and a sheath* (Lois Long).

Sho·sho·ne (shō shō′nē), *n., pl.* **-nes** or **-ne,** *adj.* —*n.* **1.** a member of a tribe of North American Indians of Wyoming, Idaho, Utah, Colorado, and Nevada. **2.** the language of this tribe. —*adj.* of or having to do with this tribe or language. Also, **Shoshoni, Shoshonee.**

Sho·sho·ne·an (shō shō′nē ən), *adj.* belonging to or constituting a widely extended linguistic stock of North American Indians of the western United States including the Shoshone, Comanche, Ute, Hopi, and other tribes.

Sho·sho·nee (shō shō′nē), *n., pl.* **-nees** or **-nee,** *adj.* Shoshone.

Sho·sho·ni (shō shō′nē), *n., pl.* **-nis** or **-ni,** *adj.* Shoshone.

shot[1] (shot), *n., pl.* **shots** or (*for 3*) **shot** or **shots,** *v.,* **shot·ted, shot·ting,** *adj.* —*n.* **1. a.** the discharge of a gun, cannon, bow, etc.: *to fire a shot. He heard two shots.* **b.** the act of shooting: *. . . taken without shot or slaughter* (Charles Kingsley). **2. a.** the distance a weapon can shoot, or to which a missile will go: *We were within rifle shot of the fort.* **b.** the range or reach of anything like a shot: *Beyond the shot of tyranny* (Shelley). *Out of the shot and danger of desire* (Shakespeare). **3.** what is discharged in shooting: **a.** bullets, balls, or other projectiles designed to be discharged from a firearm or cannon by the force of an explosive: *Storm'd at with shot and shell* (Tennyson). **b.** a single ball of lead for a gun or cannon. **c.** tiny balls or pellets of lead, of which a number are combined in one charge, used chiefly in shotguns. **d.** one such ball or pellet. **4.** a heavy metal ball, usually weighing 16 pounds, used in the shot-put. **5.** a person who shoots, especially with a firearm: *He is a good shot.* **6. a.** an attempt to hit by shooting: *That was a good shot.* **b.** a remark aimed at some person or thing: *The speaker . . . presently delivered a shot which went home, and silence and attention resulted* (Mark Twain). **7. a.** an attempt or try: *to take a shot at the job.* **b.** a random guess. **c.** a bet; chance: *A 34-1 shot named Sky Clipper beat Bally Ache in a photo finish* (New Yorker). **8.** an aimed stroke or throw, or a scoring attempt in billiards, hockey, or various other games. **9.** anything like a shot; something emitted, cast, launched or set off, as a nuclear bomb, etc.: *After the fourteenth shot, no more Nevada tests are contemplated* (New York Times). **10.** *Informal.* an injection, as of a drug: *a typhoid shot.* **11.** *Informal.* one drink, usually a jigger, of alcoholic liquor: *a shot of whiskey.* **12.** an amount due or to be paid, especially at a tavern, or one's share in such payment. **13.** *Photography.* **a.** the taking of a picture. **b.** a picture taken with a camera; snapshot: *Last week, a visitor . . . took a shot of a squirrel, a close-up with a tiny Japanese camera* (New Yorker). **c.** the motion-picture record

of a scene: *For the final shot* [*John*] *Huston said: "I want you with your eyes staring open as . . . your dead hand beckons the man"* (Newsweek). **14.** in mining: **a.** a blast. **b.** the charge of powder sufficient for a blast.
a long shot. See under **long shot.**
call the shots or **one's shot,** *U.S. Informal.* **a.** to control the proceedings or outcome; direct; manage: *He let the Republicans call the shots, but when the hearings opened . . . he put the responsiblity on their shoulders* (Atlantic). **b.** to state what will happen or is happening: *Babe Ruth called his shot by pointing to the bleachers. Southern editors who . . . call their shots as they see them* (Time).
like a shot, at once; with great rapidity: *If anybody can suggest to me anything else that I can do—I'll do it like a shot* (Arnold Bennett).
not by a long shot. See under **long shot.**
put the shot, to send a heavy metal ball as far as one can with one push: *to put the shot in an athletic contest.*
shot in the arm, *Informal.* something that stimulates or revives; incentive; spur: *As a shot in the arm for industry, there could be generous investment allowances* (Sunday Times).
shot in the dark, *Informal.* a guess based upon little or no evidence; wild guess: *Nielsen really had no facts of any substance. . . . His innuendos about "covering up" were mere shots in the dark* (Blair Fraser).
stand shot, to meet the expense; pay the bill: *Are you going to stand shot to all this good liquor?* (Scott).
—*v.t.* **1.** to load with shot; furnish with shot: *Her* [*a ship's*] *shotted guns were discharging* (Scott). **2.** to weigh by attaching a shot or shots. **3.** to attempt; try.
—*adj.* **shot through with,** full of: *speeches shot through with wit.*
[Old English *sceot* < *scēotan* shoot]
—**Syn.** *n.* **5.** marksman. **7. b.** conjecture.

shot² (shot), *v.* the past tense and past participle of **shoot:** *Many years ago he shot a rival and was himself shot in revenge.*
—*adj.* **1. a.** woven or dyed so as to show a play of colors: *blue silk shot with gold.* **b.** variable, as a color; changeable. **2.** that has grown or sprouted, as a stalk, blade, etc. **3.** *Slang.* that has been used up, worn out, or ruined: *The game was shot for the Brooks in the third* [*inning*] (New York Times).

shot borer, a small beetle which bores many minute holes in trees; pin borer.

shot cartridge, a cartridge containing shot instead of a bullet.

shote (shōt), *n.* **1.** a young weaned pig; shoat. **2.** *Dialect.* a thriftless, worthless person.

shot·fire (shot'fīr'), *v.i.*, **-fired, -fir·ing.** *Mining.* to fire a blasting charge: *As detonator and high-explosive are embedded in the borehole, shotfiring can be done entirely by electrical means* (New Scientist).

shot·fir·er (shot'fīr'ər), *n.* a miner who fires blasting charges.

shot glass, a jigger: *Karl turned away from the beer pump . . . and lifted a shot glass from the end of the shelf along the wall* (Harper's).

shot·gun (shot'gun'), *n.*, *v.*, **-gunned, -gun·ning.** —*n.* any of various smoothbore guns for firing cartridges filled with very small shot, used for killing birds and small mammals. —*v.t.* **1.** to shoot with or as if with a shotgun: *The destroyer hunted back and forth, shotgunning depth charges left and right* (Time). **2.** *U.S. Informal.* to force, as into a shotgun marriage: *We distinguish between grooms who marry brides of their own choice and those who are shotgunned into marriage* (Scientific American). [American English]

Shotgun
Above, double-barreled shotgun; below, detail of gun opened showing both barrels

shotgun marriage or **wedding,** *U.S. Informal.* a forced marriage or wedding, as to save honor or reputation.

shotgun microphone, a microphone that can pick up and amplify very faint sounds.

shotgun prescription, *Informal.* a medical prescription that combines a great number of drugs of different properties.

shot hole, 1. a hole made by a gunshot. **2.** *Mining.* a hole drilled in rock to insert an explosive charge.

shot metal, an impure form of lead containing two percent of arsenic, used for making shot for cartridges.

shot-proof (shot'prüf'), *adj.* proof against shot: *An enormous vessel, with shot-proof bulwarks* (John L. Motley).

shot-put (shot'pu̇t'), *n.* a contest in which a person sends a heavy metal ball through the air as far as he can with one push.

shot-put·ter (shot'pu̇t'ər), *n.* a person who puts the shot in athletic contests.

shott (shot), *n.* a shallow, saline lake or marsh in Northern Africa, usually dry in the summer and filled with deposits of salt, gypsum, and sand. [< Arabic *shaṭṭ*]

shot·ten (shot'ən), *adj.* **1.** that has recently spawned: *a shotten herring.* **2.** exhausted; worthless. [apparently Old English *sceoten,* past participle of *scēotan* shoot]

shot tower, a high tower for making small shot by dropping molten lead from the top into water at the bottom.

shot·ty (shot'ē), *adj.* like small balls of lead.

should (shu̇d; *unstressed* shəd), *v., past tense of* **shall. 1.** See **shall** for ordinary uses. **2. Should** has special uses as an auxiliary: **a.** to express duty, obligation, or propriety: *You should try to make fewer mistakes. Conquest, lady, should soften the heart* (Scott). **b.** to make statements, requests, etc., less direct or blunt: *I should not call her beautiful.* **c.** to express uncertainty: *If John should win the prize, how happy he would be.* **d.** to make statements about something that might have happened but did not: *I should have gone if you had asked me.* **e.** to express a condition or reason for something: *He was pardoned on the condition that he should leave the country.* **f.** to imply that something is unreasonable, unbelievable, unjustifiable, etc. (in questions introduced by *why*): *Why should you think that I did not like the book?* [Old English *sceolde*]
➔ The frequent misspelling **should of** for *should have* arises out of the fact that *have* and *of,* when completely unstressed, are pronounced identically.

shoul·der (shōl'dər), *n.* **1.** the part of the body to which an arm or foreleg or wing is attached. **2.** the joint by which the arm or the foreleg is connected to the trunk. **3.** the part of a garment covering this. **4.** the foreleg and adjoining parts of a slaughtered animal, used for food. **5.** a shoulderlike part or projection: *Don't drive on the shoulder of the road.* **6.** *Printing.* the flat surface on a type extending beyond the base of the letter. **7.** (in fortification) the angle of a bastion included between the face and a flank.
put one's shoulder to the wheel, to set to work vigorously; make a great effort: *Instead of putting their shoulders to the wheel, the lazy workers stood idling in the shop.*
rub shoulders with, to mingle with; rub elbows with: *Never have we rubbed shoulders with as many ranking celebrities* (Vladimir Nabokov).
shoulders, a. the two shoulders and the upper part of the back, where burdens are sometimes carried: *The man carried a trunk on his shoulders.* **b.** the strength to support burdens; sustaining power: *to take the work or blame on one's own shoulders.*
shoulder to shoulder, a. side by side; together: *. . . that band of heroes who died shoulder to shoulder* (Michael Donovan). **b.** with united effort: *We are . . . strongest when we are labouring shoulder to shoulder for some common object* (Augustus Jessopp).
square one's shoulders, to bring the shoulders smartly back, so as to be at right angles with the vertical axis of the body: *The troops squared their shoulders and stood at attention while the general reviewed them.*
straight from the shoulder, a. with the fist brought to the shoulder and then swiftly sent forward: *No! Give me a chap that hits straight from the shoulder* (Charles Reade). **b.** frankly; directly: *The first speaker was evasive, but the second spoke straight from the shoulder about the college's financial difficulties.*
turn or **give a cold shoulder to.** See under **cold shoulder.**
—*v.t.* **1.** to take upon or support with the shoulder or shoulders: *Caleb . . . shouldered the round box and took a hurried leave* (Dickens). **2.** to bear (a burden, blame, etc.); assume (responsibility, expense, etc.): *People behave differently at home from at work, or when they have to shoulder responsibility from when they are acting as subordinates* (Anthony H. Richmond). **3.** to push or thrust with or as with the shoulder, especially energetically or with violence: *to shoulder someone aside, shoulder one's way through a crowd. Custom and prejudice . . . shouldering aside the meek and modest truth* (William Cowper). **4.** to furnish with one or more shoulderlike parts or projections. —*v.i.* to push with the shoulders: *to shoulder through a crowd.*
shoulder arms. See under **arms,** *n.pl.*
[Old English *sculdor*] —**shoul'der-like',** *adj.*

shoulder belt, *Military.* a belt worn over the shoulder and across the breast.

shoulder blade, the flat bone of the shoulder; scapula.

shoulder block, *Nautical.* a block with a projection on the shell to prevent the rope that is rove through it from becoming jammed.

shoulder bone, 1. the humerus. **2.** shoulder blade.

shoulder brace, an appliance for correcting or preventing round shoulders.

-shouldered, *combining form.* having ____ shoulders: *Round-shouldered = having round shoulders.*

shoulder galls, an irritation of the shoulder in horses due to poorly fitting collars.

shoul·der-high (shōl'dər hī'), *adj., adv.* so high as to reach the shoulders: *. . . a crowd of several hundreds who carried him shoulder-high* (London Times).

shoul·der-hit·ter (shōl'dər hit'ər), *n. U.S. Informal.* a person who hits from the shoulder; bully; rough.

shoulder knot, a knot of ribbon or lace worn on the shoulder, especially by fashionable men in the 1600's and 1700's.

shoulder loop, a narrow strap of cloth extending on each shoulder of a uniform coat from the sleeve to the collar, used for wearing insignia of rank.

shoulder pad, 1. a padded piece sewn inside the shoulder of a jacket or coat to give it form. **2.** a piece of equipment worn under the jersey to protect the shoulders and collarbone in football and certain other sports.

shoulder patch, a cloth insigne worn on the upper sleeve of a uniform, just below the seam of the coat or shirt.

shoulder piece, shoulder strap.

shoul·ders (shōl'dərz), *n.pl.* See under **shoulder,** *n.*

shoulder screw, an external screw having a shoulder which limits the distance to which it can be screwed in.

shoulder steak, a steak of beef cut from the fore quarter through the shoulder.

shoulder strap, 1. a strap (usually one of a pair) worn over the shoulder to hold a garment up. **2. a.** an ornamental strip fastened on the shoulder of an officer's uniform to show his rank. **b.** any of various strips of fabric sewn on the shoulders of a shirt, coat, etc., to which may be attached insignia of rank.

should·na (shu̇d'nə), *Scottish.* should not.

should·n't (shu̇d'ənt), should not.

shouldst (shu̇dst), *v. Archaic.* second person singular of **should.** "Thou shouldst" means "you should."

shout (shout), *v.i.* **1.** to call or cry loudly and vigorously: *The drowning boy shouted for help.* **2.** to talk or laugh very loudly: *The crowd shouted with laughter.* **3.** (in Australia) to treat, especially to a drink. —*v.t.* **1.** to express by a shout or shouts; utter (something) by shouting: *The Senate shouted its approval today of legislation to authorize the United States to join Canada in a survey of possible tidal power projects* (New York Times). **2.** (in Australia) to treat to (a drink or other refreshment).
shout down, to silence by very loud talk, shouts of disapproval, etc.: *When he got up to speak at the meeting, his opponents shouted him down.*
—*n.* **1.** a loud, vigorous call or cry: *Shouts of joy rang through the halls.* **2.** a loud outburst of laughter. **3.** in Australia: **a.** a free drink for everyone present. **b.** a turn in buying free drinks for everyone present.

[Middle English *shout;* origin uncertain. Perhaps ultimately related to SCOUT[2].] **—shout′er,** *n.* **—Syn.** *v.i.* **1.** See **cry.**

shout·ing (shou′ting), *n.* uproar; clamor: *Dobbin . . . kept up a great shouting* (Thackeray).

all over but the shouting, nearly completed, finished, or decided, with the result appearing certain: *Canadians who hoped that the various Medicare battles were all over but the shouting had better reach for their tranquilizers* (Jeff Holmes).

—adj. that shouts; clamorous; vociferous: *shouting spectators. The shouting seas drive by* (Rudyard Kipling). **—shout′ing·ly,** *adv.*

shove (shuv), *v.,* **shoved, shov·ing,** *n.* *—v.t.* **1.** to move (something) forward or along by the application of force from behind; push: *He shoved the bookcase into place.* **2.** to push roughly or rudely against; jostle (a person): *He . . . just shoved me out of the room* (Arnold Bennett). **3. a.** to put or thrust (carelessly or hastily) into a place or receptacle. **b.** to thrust (aside or away).

—v.i. **1.** to push; apply force against something in order to move it. **2.** to push or jostle in a crowd; make one's way by jostling or elbowing.

shove off, a. to push a boat away from the shore; row away: *Into the boat he sprang, and in haste shoved off to his vessel* (Longfellow). **b.** *Informal.* to leave a place; start on one's way: *The older boys told him to shove off and find some friends his own age.*

—n. **1.** an act of shoving; push: *Fred gave the boat a shove which sent it far out into the water. A minor shove by the government from time to time . . .* (Edmond Taylor). **2.** a rough or careless push or thrust: *Someone in the crowd gave him a shove that sent him flying.*

[Old English *scūfan*]

—Syn. *v.t.* **1.** thrust. See **push.**

shove-half·pen·ny or **shove-ha′pen·ny** (shuv′hā′pə nē, -hāp′nē), *n. British.* **1.** shuffleboard. **2.** a gambling game similar to shuffleboard.

shov·el (shuv′əl), *n., v.,* **-eled, -el·ing** or (*especially British*) **-elled, -el·ling.** *—n.* **1.** a tool with a broad blade or scoop attached to a handle, used to lift and throw loose matter: *a coal shovel, a snow shovel.* **2.** a shovelful. **3.** a shovel hat.

—v.t. **1.** to lift and throw with a shovel: *to shovel snow from the sidewalk. The men shoveled the sand into a cart.* **2.** to make with a shovel: *to shovel a path through the snow.* **3.** to lift and throw or place with a vigorous motion and in large quantities: *The hungry man greedily shoveled the food into his mouth.* *—v.i.* to work with a shovel; use a shovel.

Shovel (def. 1)

[Old English *scofl.* Related to SHUFFLE, SCUFFLE.] **—shov′el·like′,** *adj.*

shov·el·bill (shuv′əl bil′), *n.* shoveler; a duck with a broad, flat bill.

shov·el·board (shuv′əl bôrd′, -bōrd′), *n.* shuffleboard.

shov·el·er (shuv′ə lər, shuv′lər), *n.* **1.** a person or thing that shovels. **2.** any of a group of fresh-water ducks having broad, flat bills, especially a species found widely in the Northern Hemisphere: *Teal, shovelers . . . fluttered up from the roadside ditches . . .* (Atlantic).

shov·el·fish (shuv′əl fish′), *n., pl.* **-fish·es** or (*collectively*) **-fish.** shovelhead.

shov·el·ful (shuv′əl fu̇l), *n., pl.* **-fuls.** as much as a shovel can hold: *They were tossing small shovelfuls of sand, by turns* (New Yorker).

shovel hat, a hat with a broad brim turned up at the sides and projecting with shovel-like curves in front and behind. Some clergymen of the Church of England formerly wore shovel hats.

shov·el·head (shuv′əl hed′), *n.* **1.** a shark with a flattish head, similar and related to the hammerhead. **2.** the shovel-nosed sturgeon.

shov·el-head·ed (shuv′əl hed′id), *adj.* having a broad, flat snout, like a shovel.

shov·el·ler (shuv′ə lər, shuv′lər), *n. Especially British.* shoveler.

shov·el·nose (shuv′əl nōz′), *n.* **1.** any animal with the head or part of the head shaped like a shovel. **2.** the hammerhead shark. **3.** the shovel-nosed sturgeon.

shov·el-nosed (shuv′əl nōzd′), *adj.* having a wide, flat snout or beak.

shovel-nosed sturgeon, a small sturgeon of the Mississippi valley, that has a wide, blunt snout.

shovel plow, a plow with a simple triangular blade, used for cultivating the ground between growing crops.

shov·el·weed (shuv′əl wēd′), *n.* the shepherd's purse. [from its shovel-shaped pods]

shov·er (shuv′ər), *n.* a person or thing that shoves.

show (shō), *v.,* **showed, shown** or **showed, show·ing,** *n., adj.* *—v.t.* **1. a.** to let be seen; put in sight: *She showed her new hat. The dog showed his teeth.* **b.** to exhibit (animals, flowers, etc.) publicly: *to show one's dog.* **c.** to display (goods, wares, etc.), as for sale or exhibition: *to show the newest fashions.* **2.** to reveal; manifest; disclose: *to show great energy, to show one's good manners, to show signs of fear. The tendency was one which showed itself in various . . . directions* (James Bryce). **3.** to grant; give: *to show gratitude to a friend.* **4.** to point out: *to show someone the way to town or the sights of a town.* **5.** to guide or conduct; usher: *to show someone to his room, to show a person out.* **6. a.** to make known, evident, or clear; explain: *Only time will show the results of the experiment.* **b.** to make clear to; explain to: *Show us how to do the problem.* **7. a.** to prove or demonstrate (a fact, statement, etc.) by reasoning, experiment, etc. (used especially with *that* and a clause): *Many arguments are used to show that motion is the source of life* (Benjamin Jowett). **b.** (of a thing) to be a proof, evidence, sign, or indication of: *All of it goes to show how little we know of each other* (Sir Arthur Helps). **8.** to have visibly or in an exposed position: *a house showing signs of neglect, a dress showing coffee stains.* **9.** (of a list, record, recording instrument) to indicate: *a watch showing twelve o'clock.* **10.** *Especially Law.* **a.** to state, allege, or plead (a cause, reason, etc.). **b.** to produce (a document, etc.) for inspection.

—v.i. **1.** to be or become visible; make one's or its appearance: *Anger showed in his face.* **2.** to present an appearance; make a display: *Her imperfect and unequal gait, which showed to peculiar disadvantage . . .* (Scott). **3.** to be evident or noticeable: *a stain that shows.* **4.** *Informal.* to appear in or present a theatrical performance: *We are showing at the Orpheum.* **5.** *Sports.* **a.** to finish among the first three in a race. **b.** to finish third in a race (contrasted with *win* and *place*).

show off, to act or talk for show; make a deliberate or ostentatious display of one's abilities or accomplishments: *It is true that many of these boys try to show off and are irresponsible* (New York Times).

show up, a. to hold up for ridicule or contempt; expose: *The pompous student was shown up by the professor.* **b.** to stand out; be or become prominent: *[His face] showed up in the illumination of the dashboard, wide, pasty, untrustworthy* (Graham Greene). **c.** to put in an appearance; turn up (at an appointed time or place): *The golfer showed up one hour late for his match.*

—n. **1.** a sight; spectacle: *The jewels made a fine show.* **2.** any kind of public exhibition or display, especially a temporary one: *an art, flower, or horse show.* **3.** a play, motion picture, etc., or a performance of one of these: *The new show is a western. The late show starts at 11:00.* **4.** an object of scorn; something odd; queer sight: *Don't make a show of yourself.* **5.** a showing: *to vote by a show of hands.* **6.** a demonstration or display of military strength or of intention to take severe measures. **7.** ostentatious display; parade; pomp: *. . . Marx and others have said that it had more bulk and show of learning than content* (Edmund Wilson). **8.** an appearance: *a bed which made a poor show of comfort. There is some show of truth in his excuse.* **9.** an indication of the presence of metal in a mine, oil in a well, etc. **10.** a false or misleading appearance: *to hide treachery by a show of friendship.* **11.** *Informal.* a chance; opportunity: *He hasn't a ghost of a show.* **12.** *Sports.* third place, as in a horse race: *win, place, and show.*

for show, for effect; to attract attention: *A fine pair of organs, which I could not find they made use of in divine service, . . . but only for show* (John Evelyn).

run the show, *Informal.* to take complete charge of an operation or situation; assume control over something: *In Jackson . . . the mayor is running the show. The normally outspoken Gov. Barnett is remaining strangely quiet* (Wall Street Journal).

stand a show, *Informal.* to stand a chance; have a favorable prospect: *He stood no show of securing the nomination for the legislature* (Lisbon, North Dakota, Star).

steal the show, a. to attract the most attention, applause, or favor: *The Stravinsky [piece] stole the show, as it always has* (Howard Klein). **b.** to take away credit, applause, etc. (from someone): *Two relatively unknown American designers have stolen the show from older and better-established names* (Barbara Plumb).

—adj. **1.** fitted or used for show or display: *a show dog.* **2.** of or having to do with a theatrical show or shows. Also, *especially British,* **shew.**

[Old English *scēawian* look at]

—Syn. *n.* **2. Show, display** mean a public exhibiting. **Show** applies to anything on public view, and sometimes has unfavorable connotations, suggesting sham, shabbiness, etc.: *The show at the planetarium is well worth seeing.* **Display** applies particularly to something carefully arranged so as to call attention to its fineness, beauty, strength, or other admirable qualities: *That florist has the most beautiful displays in the city.* **10.** pretext, pretense.

show·a·ble (shō′ə bəl), *adj.* that can be shown.

show bill, a poster, placard, or the like, advertising a show.

show biz, *Slang.* show business: *. . . has brought the flair of show biz to the often-dull realm of televised talks and public affairs* (Maclean's).

show·boat (shō′bōt′), *n.* a steamboat with a theater for plays, especially one traveling on a river, carrying its own actors, and making frequent stops to give performances: *The showboat had a band of sixteen pieces, the majority of them trombones* (New Yorker).

—v.i. U.S. Informal. to show off; make a display: *They denounced him because he didn't showboat when Junior Stephens hit a home run* (Birmingham News). [American English < *show* + *boat*]

show box, a box in which objects of interest or curiosity are exhibited; a box containing a peep show.

show·bread (shō′bred′), *n.* shewbread.

show business, the business or world of entertainment or of professional entertainers: *There's no business like show business* (Irving Berlin). **—show′-busi′ness,** *adj.*

show·case (shō′kās′), *n., v.,* **-cased, -cas·ing.** *—n.* **1.** a glass case in which to display and protect articles in stores, museums, etc. **2.** any display or exhibit: *America is a showcase of civil liberty. An editorial page column has been developed as a showcase for good writing on any subject* (Harper's). *—v.t. Informal.* to display or present as if in a showcase: *This week's [program] . . . showcased the first of five plays on Lincoln* (Newsweek).

show cause order, an order of court requiring a person to present a reason why a judgment should not be executed or confirmed.

show·down (shō′doun′), *n.* **1.** a forced disclosure of facts, purposes, methods, etc., bringing a conflict, dispute, or the like to a decisive outcome: *to have a showdown with one's employer, to force a showdown with one's allies.* **2.** (in card games) the displaying of the hands of the players at the end of a round, especially in poker, by which the winner of the round is revealed. [American English < *show* + *down*]

show·er[1] (shou′ər), *n.* **1.** a short fall of rain: *a hard shower, a gentle shower.* **2.** anything like such a fall of rain: *a shower of tears, a shower of sparks from an engine.* **3.** *U.S.* a party for giving presents to a woman about to be married, have a baby, etc., especially presents of a similar kind: *a kitchen shower, a linen shower.* **4. a.** a bath in which water pours down on the body from above in small jets: *to take a shower.* **b.** an apparatus for producing such a bath: *to install a shower.* **c.** an enclosure containing such an apparatus: *a tiled shower.*

—v.i. **1.** to rain for a short time. **2.** to come in a shower: *The withered leaves came showering down* (Dickens). **3.** to cleanse or refresh

oneself by means of a shower bath. *—v.t.* **1.** to wet with or as with a shower; spray; sprinkle. **2. a.** to send in a shower or showers; pour down: *to shower bombs on a city. The women, from the roofs and windows, showered stones on the heads of the soldiers* (Edward Gibbon). **b.** to heap lavishly upon: *They showered gifts upon her.* **c.** *U.S.* to hold a shower for: *to shower a bride.* [Old English *scūr*]

show·er[2] (shō′ər), *n.* **1.** a person who shows, points out, or exhibits. **2.** an animal that shows well or makes a (good or bad) display of its qualities: *He is a smart shower and a well-made dog* (Kennel Gazette). [< *show* + *-er*[1]]

shower bath, 1. a bath in which water pours down on the body from above in small jets. **2.** apparatus for such a bath.

shower cap, a rubber or plastic cap worn to keep the hair dry when taking a shower.

shower curtain, a curtain around or at the side of a shower, to prevent splashing and for privacy.

show·er·i·ness (shou′ər ē nis), *n.* the state of being showery.

show·er-proof (shou′ər prüf′), *adj. British.* water repellent, as a garment or fabric.

shower stall, a stall shower.

show·er·y (shou′ər ē), *adj.* **1.** raining or falling in showers: *a showery summer afternoon* (Henry Morley). **2.** having many showers. **3.** like a shower.

show·folk (shō′fōk′), *n.pl.* people in show business; entertainers as a group: *For showfolk, the shape of success may be a name in lights, a signature on a contract, a kind review* (Time).

show·girl (shō′gėrl′), *n.* a chorus girl: *The showgirls minced their way across the huge stage, arms resplendently aloft, in costumes of stunning opulence* (Harper's).

show·ground (shō′ground′), *n.* an area set aside for exhibitions: *The showground, extending over 166 acres, is the largest that the Royal Agricultural Society has ever laid out* (London Times).

show·i·ly (shō′ə lē), *adv.* in a showy manner; with display.

show·i·ness (shō′ē nis), *n.* the state of being showy; pompousness.

show·ing (shō′ing), *n.* **1.** the act of displaying, exhibiting, or manifesting: *Out they [the programs] go to 150 television stations for immediate showing* (Newsweek). **2.** the fact of being displayed, etc.: *The work in the current showing consists principally of landscapes, seascapes, and still-lifes* (New Yorker). **3.** *Especially U.S.* **a.** a statement or presentation of figures, accounts, or the like: *He is wrong by his own showing.* **b.** *U.S.* an appearance or display of a specified kind: *to make a good showing.*

show jumper, a horse trained for and used in show jumping: *Concern is mounting among those who love horses . . . at the . . . abuse of show jumpers at horse shows* (Andrew Horsbrough Porter).

show jumping, an exhibition of skill in riding a horse over or between various hurdles: *Show jumping, as opposed to steeplechasing, is entirely artificial* (London Times).

show·man (shō′mən), *n., pl.* **-men. 1.** a man who manages a show. **2.** a person skilled in showmanship or publicity.

show·man·ly (shō′mən lē), *adj.,* **-li·er, -li·est.** like that of a showman; suitable for a showman: *The famous blues are played and sung in showmanly style* (Time).

show·man·ship (shō′mən ship), *n.* **1.** the management of shows. **2.** skill in managing shows or in publicity.

show-me (shō′mē′), *adj. U.S. Informal.* demanding demonstration; believing only on clear evidence: *a show-me attitude. The full house was in a show-me mood* (Time).

Show Me State, a nickname for Missouri.

shown (shōn), *v.* a past participle of **show:** *The clerk has shown the lady many hats.*

show-off (shō′ôf′, -of′), *n.* **1.** a showing off. **2.** *Informal.* a person who shows off: . . . *under the leader's or the group's influence the show-off or aggressive youngster often learns to channel his tendencies toward the common goal* (Sidonie M. Gruenberg).

show·piece (shō′pēs′), *n.* anything which provides a dazzling or ostentatious display.

show·place (shō′plās′), *n.* any place that attracts visitors for its beauty, interest, etc.

show·room (shō′rüm′, -rům′), *n.* a room used for the display of goods or merchandise, often of items that are samples of what may be bought, but not offered for sale themselves.

show·stop·per (shō′stop′ər), *n.* an act or performer so outstanding that the audience's spontaneous response or applause delays the continuation of the show.

show·time (shō′tīm′), *n.* the time at which a show is scheduled to begin: *An hour before showtime everything seems chaotic* (Harper's).

show trial, a public trial conducted solely for purposes of propaganda, especially in a totalitarian state: . . . *a show trial that featured abject confessions in old Stalinist tradition* (Time).

show window, a window in the front of a store, where things are shown for sale; shopwindow.

show·y (shō′ē), *adj.,* **show·i·er, show·i·est. 1.** making a display; striking; conspicuous: *A peony is a showy flower. She's showier and better-looking than they are* (Booth Tarkington). **2.** too bright and gay to be in good taste: *a showy red dress.* **3.** ostentatious: *They want to do vulgar, showy things* (H.G. Wells) **—Syn. 1.** See **gaudy. 2.** garish.

showy orchis, a common North American species of orchid bearing a spike of pink-purple flowers with a white lip.

sho·yu (shō′yü), *n.* soy sauce: . . . *a tray of steamed meat-filled Chinese dumplings surrounding a bowl of shoyu to dip them in* (Craig Claiborne). [< Japanese *shōyu* < Chinese (Peking) *chiang-yu*]

s. hp., shaft horsepower.

shpt., shipment.

shr., share or shares.

shrad·dha (shrä′də), *n.* sradha.

shrank (shrangk), *v.* a past tense of **shrink.**

shrap·nel (shrap′nəl), *n.* **1.** an artillery shell filled with pellets and powder, arranged to explode in the air and scatter pellets over a wide area. **2.** such shells collectively: *to fire a barrage of shrapnel.* **3.** one or more of the pellets or fragments scattered by the explosion of such a shell: *to be wounded by shrapnel.* [< Henry *Shrapnel,* 1761-1842, a British army officer, who invented it]

METAL CASE · SHRAPNEL PELLETS · DETONATOR · POWDER CHARGE

Shrapnel (def. 1)

shred (shred), *n., v.,* **shred·ded** or **shred, shred·ding.** *—n.* **1.** a very small piece torn off or cut off; very narrow strip; scrap: *The wind tore the sail to shreds.* **2.** a fragment; particle; bit: *There's not a shred of evidence that he took the money.*
—v.t. to make shreds of; reduce to shreds.
—v.i. to be reduced to shreds.
[Old English *scrēade.* Apparently related to SHROUD.]
—Syn. *n.* **2.** iota, whit.

shred·cock (shred′kok′), *n. British Dialect.* the fieldfare, a thrush.

shred·der (shred′ər), *n.* an instrument for shredding: *a cabbage shredder.*

shred·dy (shred′ē), *adj.,* **-di·er, -di·est.** torn into shreds; ragged.

shrew (shrü), *n.* **1.** a bad-tempered, quarrelsome woman: *Once the marriage contract is signed, the sweet little bride turns into an extravagant shrew* (Time). **2.** any of a family of small, mouselike mammals with a long snout and tiny eyes and ears that eat insects and worms: *A shrew has to eat about one and one-half times its body weight per day in order to live* (A.M. Winchester). [Middle English *schrewe* a rascal, villain; later, a scold, Old English *scrēawa* the animal] **—shrew′like′,** *adj.* **—Syn. 1.** vixen, termagant.

Common Short-tailed Shrew (def. 2)
(about 5 in. long)

shrewd (shrüd), *adj.* **1.** having a sharp mind; showing a keen wit; clever: *a shrewd argument. He was too shrewd to go along with them upon a road which could lead only to their overthrow* (James Froude). **2. a.** effective; sharp; hard: *a shrewd thrust, a shrewd blow.* **b.** *Archaic.* (of a weapon, the air, etc.) keen; piercing: *The night was shrewd and windy* (Irving). **3.** *Archaic or Dialect.* malicious; mischievous: *That shrewd and knavish sprite Call'd Robin Goodfellow* (Shakespeare). **4.** *Obsolete.* **a.** cunning; artful. **b.** dangerous; injurious: *That is a shrewd loss* (Scott). **c.** shrewish: *Thou wilt never get thee a husband if thou be so shrewd of thy tongue* (Shakespeare). [earlier *shrewed* malignant, ill-disposed, past participle of *shrew,* verb, in sense of "to scold, curse"] **—shrewd′ly,** *adv.* **—shrewd′ness,** *n.*
—Syn. 1. Shrewd, sagacious, astute mean having a sharp or keen mind and good judgment, especially in practical affairs. **Shrewd** implies the ability to see below the surface of things, and suggests natural cleverness in practical affairs or, sometimes, craftiness: *a shrewd businessman, a shrewd move.* **Sagacious** implies a wise and far-seeing understanding of practical affairs: *Lincoln was a sagacious man.* **Astute** implies shrewdness and sagacity plus the ability of being hard to fool: *He is an astute diplomat.*

shrewd·ie (shrü′dē), *n. Informal.* a shrewd person: . . . *under Manager Paul Richards, the old shrewdie, the Orioles flew all the way up to second place* (Time).

shrew·ish (shrü′ish), *adj.* that is, resembles, or is characteristic of a shrew; scolding; bad-tempered: *a shrewish remark. My wife is shrewish when I keep not hours* (Shakespeare). **—shrew′ish·ly,** *adv.* **—shrew′ish·ness,** *n.*

shrew mole, a small mole of the humid Pacific coast of the United States and British Columbia.

shrew·mouse (shrü′mous′), *n., pl.* **-mice.** shrew.

shriek (shrēk), *n.* **1.** a loud, sharp, shrill sound: *a shriek of terror, the shriek of an engine's whistle.* **2.** a loud, shrill laugh.
—v.i. to utter a shriek or shrieks: *Ghosts did shriek and squeal about the streets* (Shakespeare). *—v.t.* to utter (words) with a shriek or shrieks: *In . . . the confusion and uproar . . . Cicero could only shriek that he had saved his country* (James A. Froude).
[perhaps related to SCREAK] **—shriek′er,** *n.*
—Syn. *v.i.* See **scream.**

shriev·al (shrē′vəl), *adj.* of or having to do with a sheriff.

shriev·al·ty (shrē′vəl tē), *n., pl.* **-ties.** the office, term or jurisdiction of a sheriff.

shrieve[1] (shrēv), *n. Obsolete.* sheriff. [variant of *sheriff*]

shrieve[2] (shrēv), *v.t., v.i.,* **shrieved, shriev·ing.** *Archaic.* shrive.

shrift (shrift), *n. Archaic.* **1.** confession to a priest, followed by the imposing of penance and the granting of absolution. **2.** the act of shriving. [Old English *scrift* < Latin *scrīptus* written, past participle of *scrībere* write. Compare SHRIVE.]

shrike (shrīk), *n.* **1.** any of a group of songbirds with a strong, hooked and toothed beak that feeds on large insects, frogs, mice, and small birds; butcher bird: *The . . . shrike has an innate tendency to impale its food on sharp thorns* (J.A.V. Butler). **2.** a woman who attempts to destroy the man she loves. [Old English *scrīc* a thrush]

Loggerhead Shrike
(def. 1)
(9 in. long)

shrill (shril), *adj.* **1.** having a high pitch; high and sharp in sound; piercing: *a shrill cry or voice. Crickets, locusts, and katydids make shrill noises.* **2. a.** full of shrill sounds: *a gym shrill with young fans.* **b.** characterized or accompanied by sharp, high-pitched sounds: *the shrill merriment of children.* **3.** *Archaic.* **a.** keen; sharp: *The northern summer air is shrill and cold* (William E. Henley). **b.** pungent. **c.** poignant.
—v.i. **1.** to speak, cry, or sing with a shrill voice; make a shrill noise: *A wind that shrills All night in a waste land* (Tennyson). **2.** to sound sharply. *—v.t.* to utter or give forth (a sound, cry, words, etc.) in shrill tones; exclaim or proclaim with a shrill voice: *The locust shrills his song of heat* (John Greenleaf Whittier).
—n. a shrill sound, cry, etc.: *You may . . . almost fancy you hear the shrill of the midsummer cricket* (Henry James).
—adv. Rare. shrilly: *The hounds and horn Through the high wood echoing shrill* (Milton).
[Middle English *shrille*] **—shrill′ness,** *n.*
—Syn. *adj.* **1.** strident.

 PRONUNCIATION KEY: hat, āge, cãre, fär; let, ēqual, tėrm; it, īce; hot, ōpen, ôrder; oil, out; cup, pu̇t, rüle;

shrill·ish (shril′ish), *adj.* somewhat shrill.

shril·ly[1] (shril′lē), *adv.* in shrill tones; with a shrill voice.

shril·ly[2] (shril′ē), *adj.* somewhat shrill: *Some kept up a shrilly mellow sound* (Keats). [< *shrill* + *-y*[1]]

shrimp (shrimp), *n., pl.* **shrimps** or (*for 1, especially collectively*) **shrimp,** *v.* —*n.* **1.** any of certain small, long-bodied shellfish, several kinds of which are used for food: *Many shrimps, prawns, and other Crustacea show exogenous, light-stimulated diurnal rhythms of colour-change* (J.L. Cloudsley-Thompson). **2.** a small or insignificant person or thing: *Could she possibly care for a shrimp like himself* (George Du Maurier). —*v.i.* to fish for or catch shrimp: *Captain Davey . . . has been shrimping for 50 years* (Newsweek). [Middle English *shrimpe.* Compare Middle High German *schrimpen* shrink up.] —**shrimp′like′,** *adj.*

Common Shrimp of Great Britain (def. 1) (about 2 in. long)

shrimp boat, a fishing boat used in catching shrimp.

shrimp·er (shrim′pər), *n.* **1.** a person whose business or work is catching or selling shrimp: *Shrimping . . . paid shrimpers "somewhat less" than the $70 million they brought in 1954* (Wall Street Journal). **2.** a shrimp boat.

shrimp·ing (shrim′ping), *n.* the catching of shrimp for a living or for pleasure.

shrimp·y (shrim′pē), *adj.* **1.** of or like shrimp: *a shrimpy smell.* **2.** filled with shrimp; full of shrimp: *shrimpy waters, a shrimpy gulf.* **3.** small or insignificant; puny: *a shrimpy young man.*

shrine (shrīn), *n., v.,* **shrined, shrin·ing.** —*n.* **1.** a casket or box holding a holy object; reliquary. **2. a.** the tomb of a saint. **b.** a place where sacred relics are kept. **3.** an altar, small chapel, or other object or place of worship: *A very old priest in charge of the shrine tottered out to have a chat with the traveller* (London Times). **4.** a place or object considered as sacred because of its memories, history, etc.: *Shakespeare's birthplace is visited as a shrine. Shrines are now built for national heroes as they once were for saints* (Ogburn and Nimkoff).
—*v.t.* to enclose in a shrine or something like a shrine; enshrine.
[Old English *scrīn* < Latin *scrīnium* case or box for keeping papers. Compare SCREEN.]
—**Syn.** *n.* **3.** temple.

Shrin·er (shrī′nər), *n.* a member of the Order of the Mystic Shrine, an organization of high-ranking Masons.

shrink (shringk), *v.,* **shrank** or **shrunk, shrunk** or **shrunk·en, shrink·ing,** *n.* —*v.i.* **1.** to draw back; recoil: *The dog shrank from the whip. A shy person shrinks from meeting strangers.* **2. a.** to become smaller: *His wool sweater shrank when it was washed.* **b.** to become less: *a fortune shrinking to nothing, shrinking influence.* —*v.t.* to make smaller or less; cause to shrink: *Hot water shrinks wool. Are all thy conquests, glories, triumphs, spoils, Shrunk to this little measure?* (Shakespeare).
—*n.* a shrinking.
[Old English *scrincan*] —**shrink′er,** *n.* —**shrink′ing·ly,** *adv.*
—**Syn.** *v.i.* **1. Shrink, flinch** mean to draw back from something painful, unpleasant, or the like. **Shrink** suggests instinctive drawing back physically or mentally, by or as if by contracting or drawing away some part of the body in fear, horror, or sensitiveness, from something painful or disagreeable: *He shrank from admitting his guilt.* **Flinch** suggests drawing back or turning away in spite of one's desire or determination not to, from danger, an unpleasant or difficult task or duty, or, especially, pain: *Indians could bear torture without flinching.*
➤ **Shrunken** is still sometimes used as a past participle (*It had shrunken*), but is chiefly used as an adjective (*a shrunken face*).

shrink·a·ble (shring′kə bəl), *adj.* that can be shrunk; liable to shrink.

shrink·age (shring′kij), *n.* **1.** the fact or process of shrinking. **2. a.** the amount or degree of shrinking: *a shrinkage of two inches in the length of a sleeve.* **b.** a depreciation or decrease, as in value, power, etc.: *the shrinkage of a fortune or a nation's influence. This divine . . . was vindictively economical because of some shrinkage of his tithes* (H.G. Wells). **3.** the part of the total weight of a steer, hog, etc., lost in its shipment, butchering, and the subsequent curing of the meat: *You get away from that shrinkage . . . that you have when the cattle are hauled around first by the trader* (Wall Street Journal).

shrink·ing violet (shring′king), a person who is shy, timid, or self-effacing: *We expect our rulers to be reasonably ambitious; shrinking violets are unfit for the harsh experience of power* (John Grigg).

shrink·proof (shringk′prüf′), *adj.* that will not shrink; resistant to shrinking: *Orlon, Dacron and nylon also are more easily washable, more shrinkproof, and more spot-resistant than the others* (Wall Street Journal). —*v.t.* to make shrinkproof: *. . . experiments to find a way to shrinkproof and permanently crease wool* (Time).

shrive (shrīv), *v.,* **shrove** or **shrived, shriv·en** or **shrived, shriv·ing.** *Archaic.* —*v.t.* to hear the confession of, impose penance on, and grant absolution to. —*v.i.* **1.** to hear confession, impose penance, and grant absolution. **2.** to confess; go to confession: *And who art thou, thou Gray Brother, That I should shrive to thee?* (Scott).
shrive oneself, to confess to a priest and receive absolution: *Let me shrive me clean, and die* (Tennyson).
Also, *Archaic,* **shrieve.**
[Old English *scrīfan* < Latin *scrībere* write. Compare SHRIFT, SCREED.]

shriv·el (shriv′əl), *v.,* **-eled, -el·ing** or (*especially British*) **-elled, -el·ling.** —*v.t.* **1. a.** to dry up; wither: *The hot sunshine shriveled the grass.* **b.** to shrink and wrinkle: *skin shriveled by age.* **2.** to make helpless or useless. —*v.i.* **1.** to become contracted and wrinkled or curled (up), as from heat, cold, age, etc.; wither: *The fruit shriveled up. The men shriveled under the fierce blast of the captain's angry words.* **2.** to waste away; become useless. [origin uncertain] —**Syn.** *v.i.* **2.** atrophy.

shriv·en (shriv′ən), *v.* a past participle of **shrive:** *The penitent was shriven by the priest.*

shroff (shrof), *n.* **1.** (in India, etc.) a banker or moneychanger. **2.** (in China and other countries of the Far East) a native expert employed to test coins. —*v.t., v.i.* to test (coins) to separate the genuine from the false. [earlier *sheroff* < Arabic *sharrāf* < *sharafa* he exchanged]

shrof·fage (shrof′ij), *n.* **1.** the act or practice of shroffing coins. **2.** the charge for shroffing coins.

Shrop·shire (shrop′shir, -shər), *n.* any of an English breed of black-faced, hornless sheep, raised especially for meat. [< *Shropshire,* a county in England, where they were developed]

shroud (shroud), *n.* **1.** a cloth or garment in which a dead person is wrapped for burial; winding sheet. **2.** something that covers, conceals, or veils: *The fog was a shroud over the city.* **3.** one of the lines attached to the canopy of a parachute.
shrouds, a series of ropes, from a masthead to the side of a ship or a lower masthead, that help support the mast: *In an instant everyone sprung into the rigging, up the shrouds and out on the yards* (Richard H. Dana).
—*v.t.* **1.** to wrap for burial. **2.** to bury. **3.** to cover; conceal; veil: *The earth is shrouded in darkness.* **4.** *Archaic.* to shelter. —*v.i. Archaic.* to seek or find shelter; take refuge: *I will here shroud till the dregs of the storm be past* (Shakespeare).
[Old English *scrūd* a garment, clothing. Related to SHRED.]

SHROUDS

Shrouds

shroud knot, *Nautical.* a knot joining the two parts of a broken or severed shroud.

shroud-laid (shroud′lād′), *adj.* (of a rope) made with four strands woven from left to right or clockwise, usually around a central core.

shroud·less (shroud′lis), *adj.* **1.** without a shroud or winding sheet: *Shroudless and tombless they sunk to their rest* (Oliver Wendell Holmes). **2.** unshrouded; unobscured.

shrove (shrōv), *v.* a past tense of **shrive.**

Shrove Monday, the Monday before Ash Wednesday.

Shrove Sunday, the Sunday before Ash Wednesday; Quinquagesima Sunday.

Shrove·tide (shrōv′tīd′), *n.* the three days before Ash Wednesday, the first day of Lent. Shrovetide is a time for confession and absolution in preparation for the solemn Lenten period, and of rejoicing and feasting.

Shrove Tuesday, the day before Ash Wednesday; the last day before Lent.

shrub[1] (shrub), *n.* a perennial, woody plant smaller than a tree, usually with many separate stems starting from or near the ground; bush: *Rhododendrons, viburnums, and the box are shrubs. Shrubs are much like trees, but are smaller, more profusely branched and often have several main small stems* (Fred W. Emerson). [Old English *scrybb* brush-(wood), shrubbery] —**shrub′like′,** *adj.*

shrub[2] (shrub), *n.* a beverage made from fruit juice (especially lemon or orange juice), sugar, and usually, rum or brandy. [< Arabic *shurb* a drink. Compare SHERBET.]

shrub·ber·ied (shrub′ər ēd, shrub′rēd), *adj.* abounding in shrubbery.

shrub·ber·y (shrub′ər ē, shrub′rē), *n., pl.* **-ber·ies. 1.** shrubs collectively or in a mass. **2.** a place planted with shrubs.

shrub·bi·ness (shrub′ē nis), *n.* the state of being like a shrub or planted with shrubs.

shrub·by (shrub′ē), *adj.,* **-bi·er, -bi·est. 1.** like shrubs. **2.** covered with shrubs. **3.** consisting of shrubs.

shrug (shrug), *v.,* **shrugged, shrug·ging,** *n.* —*v.t., v.i.* to raise (the shoulders) as an expression of dislike, doubt, indifference, impatience, etc.: *He merely shrugged his shoulders in answer to our request for help.* (*v.t.*) *He shrugged and walked away.* (*v.i.*)
shrug off, to dismiss with indifference or contempt: *The foreman shrugged off his injury and went about his business.*
—*n.* **1.** a raising of the shoulders in this way: *He is a lively man, full of chat, and foreign shrugs and gestures* (Fanny Burney). **2.** a woman's short sweater or jacket.
[Middle English *schruggen;* origin uncertain]

shrunk (shrungk), *v.* a past tense and past participle of **shrink:** *His wool socks have shrunk so that he can't get them on.*

shrunk·en (shrung′kən), *adj.* grown smaller; shriveled: *a shrunken face, a shrunken fortune.* —*v.* shrunk; a past participle of **shrink.**
➤ See **shrink** for usage note.

shtetl (shtet′əl), *n.* a small Jewish community in any of the towns or villages of Eastern Europe, especially before World War II: *In the shtetl of Eastern Europe, . . . the wise scholar was a particularly important figure* (Saturday Review). [< Yiddish *shtetl* (literally) small town < Middle High German *stetel* (diminutive) < *stat* town]

shtg., shortage.

shu·ba (shü′bə), *n. Russian.* a long fur coat or outer garment.

shuck (shuk), *n.* **1.** a husk, pod, or shell, especially the outer covering or strippings of corn (maize), chestnuts, hickory nuts, etc.: *Every morsel, including potato peel and pea shucks, was carried to the compost heap* (Punch). **2.** the shell of an oyster or clam.
—*v.t.* **1.** to remove the husk, pod, or shell from (corn, etc.): *to shuck out . . . eight or ten ears of corn* (Edward Eggleston). **2.** to open the shells of (oysters or clams). **3.** *Informal.* Also, **shuck off, a.** to take off; remove: *Patrons shuck their shoes* (New York Times). **b.** to get rid of: *We must shuck off the habits of the past* (Harper's).
[origin uncertain] —**shuck′er,** *n.*

shuck-bot·tom (shuk′bot′əm), *adj. U.S.* (of a chair) having a seat made of the shucks or husks of corn. —*n.* a shuck-bottom chair.

shuck-bot·tomed (shuk′bot′əmd), *adj.* shuck-bottom.

shucks (shuks), *Informal.* —*interj.* an exclamation of impatience, irritation, etc. —*n.* a type of something valueless (used especially in negative phrases): *not worth shucks.* [American English, perhaps < *shuck*]

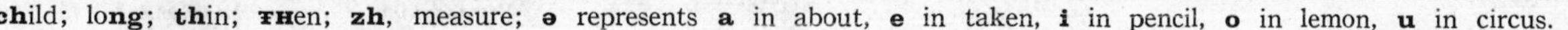

shud·der (shud′ər), *v.i.* to tremble with horror, fear, cold, etc.: *She starts, like one that spies an adder . . . the fear whereof doth make him shake and shudder* (Shakespeare).
shudder at, to feel dismay, horror, etc., at.
—*n.* a trembling; quivering.
the shudders, *Informal.* nervousness caused by fear or horror: *Such a prospect is giving Mr. Benson . . . and many wheat growers alike the shudders* (Wall Street Journal).
[Middle English *shodderen.* Compare Middle Low German *schöderen.*] —**shud′der·ing·ly,** *adv.* —**Syn.** *v.i.* See **shiver.**

shud·der·some (shud′ər səm), *n.* causing a shudder; fearsome.

shud·der·y (shud′ər ē), *adj.* characterized by or causing shudders: *I had the shuddery intuition that the moment his "good" eye had closed, the other one had started to see* (Frederic Morton).

shuf·fle (shuf′əl), *v.,* **-fled, -fling,** *n.* —*v.i.* **1.** to walk without lifting the feet: *The old man shuffles feebly along. The bear . . . comes . . . shuffling along at a strange rate* (Daniel Defoe). **2.** to dance with scraping motions of the feet. **3.** to act or answer in a tricky way: *He said and unsaid, sighed, sobbed, beat his breast, shuffled, implored, threatened* (James A. Froude). **4.** to get (through) somehow; do hurriedly or perfunctorily: *to shuffle through one's lessons.* **5.** to get (into clothing) in a clumsy or fumbling manner. **6.** to divide a deck of cards and, by distributing one half into the other, to mix them into random order: *They draw, they sit, they shuffle, cut and deal* (George Crabbe). —*v.t.* **1.** to scrape or drag (the feet). **2.** to perform (a dance or dance step) with such motions. **3.** to mix (a deck of cards) so as to change the order. **4.** to put or throw (together) in a mass indiscriminately, incongruously, or without order; huddle or jumble together: *Good days, bad days so shuffled together* (Charles Lamb). **5.** to push about; thrust or throw with clumsy haste: *He shuffled on his clothes and ran out of the house.* **6.** to move about this way and that; shift about: *to shuffle the papers on one's desk.*
shuffle off, a. to get rid of: *When we have shuffled off this mortal coil . . .* (Shakespeare). *[They] are obliged for propriety's sake to shuffle off the anxious inquiries of the public* (Thackeray). **b.** to proceed to go to: *to shuffle off to the seashore.* **c.** to die: *I mean in plain English that I am likely to shuffle off long before you kick the bucket* (Atlantic).
—*n.* **1.** a scraping or dragging movement of the feet: *When the hobble had a second life from 1908 to 1914 skirts appeared to clip the ankles, walking became a kind of shuffle or glide* (London Times). **2.** a dance or dance step with a shuffle: *. . . a powerhouse rhythm section which divides itself between a two-beat calypso and a hot-blooded shuffle* (Time). **3. a.** a shuffling of a deck of cards. **b.** the right or turn to shuffle (cards). **4.** a movement this way and that: *After a hasty shuffle through his papers the speaker began to talk.* **5.** an unfair act; trick; evasion: *Through some legal shuffle he secured a new trial.*
[perhaps < Low German *schuffeln.* Related to SHOVEL.]
—**Syn.** *v.i.* **3.** dodge, equivocate, quibble. -*n.* **5.** subterfuge.

shuf·fle·board (shuf′əl bôrd′, -bōrd′), *n.* **1. a.** a game played by pushing large wooden or iron disks, by means of a cue fitted with a shovellike head, into any of various numbered spaces marked out on a large flat surface, as the deck of a ship: *Shuffleboard, an interesting game for old and young alike, requires a concrete surface* (New York Times). **b.** the surface on which it is played. **2. a.** a former game in which pieces of money or counters were driven by the hand toward certain compartments or lines marked on a table; shovehalfpenny. **b.** the board or table used in this game. Also, **shovelboard.**

shuf·fler (shuf′lər), *n.* **1.** a person or thing that shuffles. **2.** an evasive person. **3.** a scaup duck.

shuf·fling (shuf′ling), *adj.* **1.** shifty or evasive, as persons or their actions: *her shuffling excuses* (Jane Austen); *a mean-spirited shuffling rascal in the very agonies of detection* (Scott). **2.** moving the feet over the ground or floor without lifting them, or characterized by such movement: *Sounds like the shuffling steps of those that bear Some heavy thing* (William Morris). —**shuf′fling·ly,** *adv.*

shul (shül), *n. Yiddish.* a synagogue: "*You mean church, Sergeant.*" "*I mean shul, Grossbart!*" (Philip Roth).

Shu·lam·ite or **Shu·lam·mite** (shü′lə mīt), *n.* the epithet of the woman beloved in the Song of Solomon 6:13.

shun (shun), *v.t.,* **shunned, shun·ning.** to keep away from; avoid: *to shun a person. She was lazy and shunned work. He shunned uttering a direct falsehood, but did not scruple to equivocate* (George Bancroft). [Old English *scunian*] —**shun′ner,** *n.* —**Syn.** See **avoid.**

Shu·nam·mite (shü′nə mīt), *n.* (in the Bible) an inhabitant of the town of Shunem in ancient Palestine. I Kings 1:3.

shun·less (shun′lis), *adj.* that cannot be shunned; inevitable: *shunless destiny* (Shakespeare).

shun·pike (shun′pīk′), *n. U.S. Slang* a road taken by travelers to avoid paying toll.

shunt (shunt), *v.t* **1. a.** to switch (a train) from one track to another: *The car was uncoupled from the rest of the train and shunted into a siding* (London Times). **b.** to switch (anything) to another route or place: *After the mixture . . . is ground, a small blower shunts the feed to the top of the crib* (Wall Street Journal). **2. a.** to push aside or out of the way; sidetrack: *My mind has been shunted off upon the track of other duties* (Lowell). **b.** to get rid of. **3.** *Electricity.* to carry (a part of a current) by means of a shunt. —*v.i.* **1.** (of a train) to move from one line of rails to another. **2.** to move out of the way; turn aside: *Trucks shunt . . . unceasingly . . . the drivers . . . displaying something like wizardry in maneuvering them through perennial traffic jams* (Bulletin of Atomic Scientists).
—*n.* **1.** a turning aside; shift. **2.** a railroad switch. **3.** a wire or other conductor, usually of relatively low resistance, joining two points in an electric circuit and forming an auxiliary circuit through which a part of the current will pass, used to regulate the quantity of current going through the main circuit; by-pass: *However, by inserting a low resistance shunt in parallel with the pivoted coil . . . any galvanometer may be modified to serve as an ammeter or voltmeter* (Sears and Zemansky). **4.** *Medicine.* a leakage within the heart: *Shunts . . . had previously been detected by having the patient breathe a mixture of the gas nitrous oxide and tracing its course through the circulatory system* (Science News Letter).
[origin uncertain] —**shunt′er,** *n.*
—**Syn.** *n.* **1.** deflection.

shunt dynamo, *Electricity.* a shunt-wound dynamo.

shunt motor, *Electricity.* a shunt-wound motor: *If the armature and the field windings are connected in series we have a series motor; if they are connected in parallel, a shunt motor* (Sears and Zemansky).

shunt winding, *Electricity.* a winding of a motor or generator whereby the field magnet coils are connected in parallel with the armature.

shunt-wound (shunt′wound′), *adj. Electricity.* that has shunt winding: *a shunt-wound motor.*

shure (shyr), *v. Scottish.* sheared; a past tense of **shear.**

shush (shush, shùsh), *v.t., v.i., n., interj.* hush: *My husband grumbled about the damage to the lawn but I shushed him* (Jean Winchester).

shut (shut), *v.,* **shut, shut·ting,** *adj., n.* —*v.t.* **1.** to close (a receptacle or opening) by pushing or pulling a lid, door, some part, etc., into place: *to shut a box, window, or gate.* **2.** to close (eyes, a knife, a book, etc.) by bringing parts together or by folding up. **3.** to close tightly; close securely; close doors or other openings of: *to shut a house for the summer.* **4.** to enclose; confine: *Shut the kitten in the basket. The criminal was shut in prison.* —*v.i.* to become shut; be closed: *The great gates slowly shut.*
shut down, a. to close by lowering: *We shut down all the windows when the storm began.* **b.** to close (a factory, mine, etc.) for a time; stop work: *We've got to shut down till the home demand begins again* (William Dean Howells). **c.** to settle down so as to cover or envelop: *Night shut down on the settlement* (Bret Harte). **d.** to put a stop or check (on); suppress: *The military junta shut down the radio and the press.*
shut in, a. to keep from going out, as by closing a door or receptacle: *The recluse shut himself in and refused to leave the house.* **b.** to enclose with a barrier; hem in: *Wooded hills . . . shut in the view on every side* (Edward A. Freeman).
shut off, a. to prevent the passage of (steam, etc.), as by closing a valve or tap: *The motion of the piston was equalized by shutting off the steam sooner or later from the cylinder* (Robert Stuart). **b.** to cut off; separate (from): *a lake shut off from the sea by a dike,*
shut out, a. to keep from coming in; deny right of entry to a place, etc.; exclude: *The curtains shut out the light. Shut the dog out of this room.* **b.** to prevent (an opponent, team, etc.) from scoring: *The pitcher shut out the other team, limiting them to three hits.*
shut up, a. to close the doors and windows of: *Noah, you shut up the shop* (Dickens). **b.** to keep from going out; enclose; confine: *She shuts her cats up during the day, but lets them roam the neighborhood at night.* **c.** *Informal.* to stop, or stop from, talking: *. . . the boy would be torn between anger and a desire to shut the man up . . .* (Edmund Wilson).
—*adj.* **1.** closed; fastened up; enclosed. **2.** *Phonetics.* **a.** formed by completely checking the outgoing breath. **b.** having sound stopped by a consonant at the end of a syllable.
—*n.* **1.** the act or time of shutting or closing. **2.** the line of junction of two pieces of welded metal.
[Old English *scyttan* to bolt up]
—**Syn.** *v.t.* **1.** *v.i.* See **close**[1].

shut-down (shut′doun′), *n.* a shutting down; a closing of a factory, mine, or the like, for a time: *The permanent shut-down was caused by an increase in use of oil and other domestic fuels* (Wall Street Journal).

shut-eye (shut′ī′), *n. Slang.* sleep: *All he wanted now was a little shut-eye, but an agent of the city editor turned up* (New Yorker).

shut-in (shut′in′), *adj.* **1. a.** not allowed or able to go out because of illness, weakness, etc. **b.** confined: *How can you stand the shut-in feeling those mountains give? They scare me* (New York Times). **2.** *Psychiatry.* reluctant to associate or communicate with others; solitary. —*n.* a person who is kept from going out by sickness or weakness: *You can take it from Colonel Martingale, who has been a shut-in lately, that the Gotham Stakes was as good a show as you could ask for* (New Yorker). [American English < *shut in,* idiom]

shut-off or **shut·off** (shut′ôf′, -of′), *n.* **1.** something that shuts off, as a valve or switch: *an automatic shut-off.* **2.** a being shut off: *a temporary shut-off of electricity.*

shut-out or **shut·out** (shut′out′), *n.* **1.** *U.S.* **a.** a game in which one side is kept from scoring: *to pitch a shut-out.* **b.** a preventing of the opposite side from scoring: *The home team won by a shut-out.* **2.** a lockout.

shut·ter (shut′ər), *n.* **1.** a movable cover, usually one of a pair, for the outside of a window; blind: *When we shut up our cottage for the winter, we put shutters on all the windows.* **2. a.** a movable cover, slide, etc., for closing any opening: *Every train . . . had its windows sealed with steel shutters* (Newsweek). **b.** a device that opens and closes in front of the lens of a camera in order to regulate the length of an exposure. **3.** a person or thing that shuts.
—*v.t.* to put a shutter or shutters on or over; close up; shut down: *We shuttered our windows before the storm. Shop owners shuttered their stores* (Wall Street Journal).

shut·ter·bug (shut′ər bug′), *n. U.S. Slang.* a devotee of photography; camera bug: *Its American distributor has sold 75,000 cameras to U.S. shutterbugs* (Newsweek).

shut·ter·less (shut′ər lis), *adj.* having no shutters.

shut·tle (shut′əl), *n., v.,* **-tled, -tling,** *adj.* —*n.* **1. a.** the device by which the woof thread is passed between the warp threads from one side of the web to the other in weaving: *My days are swifter than a weaver's shuttle* (Job 7:6). **b.** a similar device on which thread is wound, used for knitting, tatting, and embroidery. **c.** the holder for the lower thread in a sewing machine, that moves back and forth once for each stitch. **2.** any of various things, not connected with weaving or sewing, characterized by a back-and-forth motion. **3.** *U.S.* a shuttle train.
—*v.i., v.t.* **1.** to move quickly to and fro: *Frey shuttles between Lucerne and the Bürgenstock in a speedboat, making the run*

in seven minutes (New Yorker). *A face of . . . extreme mobility, which he shuttles about . . . in a very singular manner while speaking* (Thomas Carlyle). **2.** to transport or be transported by or as if by shuttle.
—*adj.* **1.** that shuttles; shuttling: *a shuttle bus, a shuttle flight, a shuttle service.* **2.** that is traversed by a shuttle: *a shuttle route.*
[Old English *scytel* a dart < *scēotan* to shoot]

shuttle box, a box attached to a loom to receive the shuttle at the end of its movement across the web.

shut·tle·cock (shut′əl kok′), *n.* **1. a.** a cork with feathers stuck in one end, that is hit back and forth by a small racket, called a battledore, in the old game of battledore and shuttlecock. **b.** battledore and shuttlecock. **2.** a feathered or plastic cork used in the game of badminton; bird.

Shuttlecock (def. 1a)

—*v.t.* to throw or send backward and forward; toss to and fro. —*v.i.* to move to and fro; shuttle: *The hot, tired, apologetic traveler shuttlecocks between one uniformed official . . . and another, getting more hot, more tired, more apologetic* (Mary Goldring).

shuttle shell, 1. the elongated fusiform shell of a marine gastropod, so called from the resemblance to a weaver's shuttle. **2.** the gastropod itself.

shuttle train, a train that runs back and forth over a short distance: . . . *shuttle trains which permit a skier several days of skiing without repeating a run* (Newsweek).

shy[1] (shī), *adj.*, **shy·er, shy·est** or **shi·er, shi·est,** *v.*, **shied, shy·ing,** *n., pl.* **shies.** —*adj.* **1. a.** uncomfortable in company; bashful; retiring: *John is shy and dislikes parties.* **b.** showing or resulting from bashfulness: *shy looks.* **2.** easily frightened away; timid: *A deer is a shy animal.* **3.** cautious; wary: *shy of an interview, shy of using a new tool.* **4.** not bearing well; unprolific, as plants, trees, etc. **5.** not having enough; short; scant: *He's shy on accessories* (Wall Street Journal). **6.** *Informal.* owing, as one's ante in poker; in arrears.
shy of, having little; lacking: *shy of funds, two months shy of being of voting age.*
—*v.i.* **1.** to start back or aside suddenly: *The horse shied at the newspaper blowing along the ground.* **2.** to shrink: *He would shy in pretended fright at every shadow* (New Yorker).
shy away from, to avoid out of shyness or fear; shrink from: *Some parents who shy away from a discussion group will feel more free to chat in a sewing class or furniture repair project* (New York Times).
—*n.* a sudden start to one side.
[Old English *scēoh.* Compare ESCHEW, SKEW.] —**shy′ness,** *n.*
—**Syn.** *adj.* **1. Shy, bashful** mean uncomfortable in the presence or company of others. **Shy** suggests a lack of self-confidence that makes a person unable to be easy and friendly in company and shrink from making friends or going up to others, and is shown by a reserved or timid manner: *People who appear snobbish are often really shy.* **Bashful** suggests shrinking by nature from being noticed, and is shown by awkward and embarrassed behavior in the presence of strangers: *The boy was too bashful to ask her to dance.* **3.** suspicious, distrustful.

shy[2] (shī), *v.*, **shied, shy·ing,** *n., pl.* **shies.** —*v.t., v.i.* to throw; fling: *The boy shied a stone at a tree.*
—*n.* **1.** a throw; fling: *Jack-in-the-box—three shies a penny* (Dickens). **2.** *Informal.* a verbal attack; sarcastic or taunting remark: *He wasn't above taking a few shies at his fellow school-board members.* **3.** *Informal.* a try; fling.
[origin uncertain]

shy·er[1] (shī′ər), *n.* a horse that shies. Also, **shier.**

shy·er[2] (shī′ər), *n.* a person who shies (throws). Also, **shier.**

Shy·lock (shī′lok), *n.* **1.** a greedy moneylender. **2.** any moneylender. [after *Shylock,* the relentless and vengeful moneylender in Shakespeare's *The Merchant of Venice*]

shy·ly (shī′lē), *adv.* in a shy manner. Also, **shily.**

shy·ster (shīs′tər), *n. U.S.* a lawyer or other person who uses improper or questionable methods in his business or profession: *They all set up some crazy foundation under the control of . . . the little shyster who drew the will* (New Yorker). [American English; origin uncertain]

si (sē), *n. Music.* (in solmization) the seventh tone of the scale; B; ti. [see GAMUT]

Si (no period), silicon (chemical element).

S.I., 1. Sandwich Islands. **2.** Staten Island (in New York).

si·al (sī′al), *n.* a granitelike rock rich in silica and aluminum. Sial is the chief rock underlying the land masses, as distinct from the ocean basins. [< *si*(lica) + *al*(uminum)]

si·al·a·gog·ic (sī al′ə goj′ik), *adj., n.* sialogogic.

si·al·a·gogue (sī al′ə gog, -gôg), *adj., n.* sialogogue.

si·al·ic (sī al′ik), *adj.* **1.** composed largely or chiefly of silica and aluminum: *Sial and granite are sialic rocks.* **2.** consisting largely of sial: *a sialic land basin.*

si·a·lid (sī′ə lid), *adj.* of or belonging to a family of insects that includes the hellgrammite. —*n.* a sialid insect. [< New Latin *Sialidae* the family name < *Sialis* the typical genus < Greek *sialís* a type of bird]

si·al·i·dan (sī al′ə dən), *adj., n.* sialid.

si·al·o·gog·ic (sī al′ə goj′ik), *adj.* stimulating or provoking an increased flow of saliva. —*n.* a sialogogue.

si·al·o·gogue (sī al′ə gog, -gôg), *adj.* producing a flow of saliva. —*n.* a drug that produces a flow of saliva. [< New Latin *sialagogus* < Greek *síalon* saliva + *agōgós* leading < *ágein* to lead]

si·a·loid (sī′ə loid), *adj.* resembling saliva. [< Greek *síalon* saliva + English *-oid*]

si·al·o·lith (sī al′ə lith), *n.* a salivary calculus. [< Greek *síalon* saliva + *líthos* stone]

si·al·o·li·thi·a·sis (sī al′ə li thī′ə sis), *n.* the production of salivary calculi. [< Greek *síalon* saliva + English *lithiasis*]

si·al·or·rhe·a or **si·al·or·rhoe·a** (sī al′ə-rē′ə), *n.* excessive flow of saliva. [< New Latin *sialorrhea, sialorrhoea* < Greek *síalon* saliva + *rhoia* flow < *rheîn* to flow]

si·a·mang (sē′ə mang, syä′mang), *n.* the largest of the gibbons, black, and having the second and third digits united to some extent. It inhabits Sumatra and the Malay Peninsula. [< Malay *siāmang* < *āmang* black]

Si·a·mese[1] (sī′ə mēz′, -mēs′), *adj., n., pl.* **-mese.** —*adj.* of or having to do with Siam (Thailand), a country in southeastern Asia, its people, or their language. —*n.* **1.** a native or inhabitant of Siam (Thailand), especially a member of its dominant Thai-speaking people. **2.** the official language of Siam (Thailand), belonging to the Thai linguistic family.

si·a·mese or **Si·a·mese**[2] (sī′ə mēz′, -mēs′), *v.t.*, **-mesed, -mes·ing.** to join; unite; couple: *The other pipes are siamesed together in pairs* (Science News Letter). *We are Siamesed to France* (Blackwood's Magazine). [< *Siamese* twins]

Siamese cat, any of a breed of short-haired cats with either light tan bodies and dark face, ears, feet, and tail, or with bluish-white bodies and bluish face, ears, feet, and tail, originally from Siam (Thailand): *Siamese cats seem less independent than other breeds . . . and utter loud, mournful "meows" until they receive attention* (Raymond D. Smith).

Blue Point Siamese Cat (including tail, 26 to 32 in. long)

Siamese connection, coupling, or **joint,** (in fire apparatus) a Y-shaped device by which two or more pipes or hoses discharge into one hose.

Siamese fighting fish, the betta or fighting fish: *The Siamese fighting fish* [*is*] *ordinarily a peaceable creature until another male of the same species appears* (Science News Letter).

Siamese twins, twins joined together at birth. [< twin boys, Eng and Chang, 1811-1874, born in Siam, who were so joined from birth]

sib[1] (sib), *adj.* related by blood; closely related; akin.
—*n.* **1.** a kinsman or kinswoman; relative: *The disease can be detected earlier if the children or sibs of patients are examined* (J.B.S. Haldane). **2.** one's kin; kinsfolk; relatives. **3.** a brother or sister.
[Old English *sibb*]
—**Syn.** *adj.* consanguineous.

sib[2] (sib), *n. U.S. Anthropology.* a group or clan whose members trace their descent from a common ancestor through one line only. [perhaps a special use of *sib*[1], or perhaps short for *sibling*]

Sib., 1. Siberia. **2.** Siberian.

Si·be·li·an (sə bā′lē ən), *adj.* of, having to do with, or characteristic of the Finnish composer Jean Sibelius (1865-1957) or his music: *The first two movements are intensely Sibelian* (Harold C. Schonberg). —*n.* a student or admirer of Sibelius or his works: *Collins was a really great Sibelian, and . . . his version of these two works was just about his finest achievement on record* (London Times).

Si·be·ri·a (sī bir′ē ə), *n.* a place of exile or imprisonment; remote assignment (used in a humorous way). [< *Siberia,* in Asia (traditional place of exile for Russian criminals)]

Si·be·ri·an (sī bir′ē ən), *adj.* of or having to do with Siberia, a large part of the Soviet Union extending across northern Asia. —*n.* a native or inhabitant of Siberia.

Siberian husky, a medium-sized working dog of a breed originating in Siberia. It has a thick coat of medium length and a brush tail, and is black, tan, or gray with white markings.

Siberian Husky (20 to 23½ in. high at the shoulder)

sib·i·lance (sib′ə ləns), *n.* **1.** a being sibilant. **2.** a hissing sound.

sib·i·lan·cy (sib′ə lən sē), *n., pl.* **-cies.** sibilance.

sib·i·lant (sib′ə lənt), *adj.* **1.** hissing: *When he spoke, his voice was usually low and sibilant* (New Yorker). **2.** *Phonetics.* articulated by forcing the breath stream through a very narrow passage, so that it makes a hissing sound, as English *s* in *so*, *z* in *zero*, *sh* in *show*, and *z* in *azure.* —*n.* a hissing or sibilant sound: *The voices are picked up at close range . . . without the unpleasant exaggerations of sibilants* (Harper's). [< Latin *sībilāns, -antis,* present participle of *sībilāre* to hiss] —**sib′i·lant·ly,** *adv.*

sib·i·late (sib′ə lāt), *v.*, **-lat·ed, -lat·ing.** —*v.i.* to hiss; utter a hissing sound. —*v.t.* **1.** to make sibilant. **2.** to pronounce with a hissing sound. [< Latin *sībilāre* (with English *-ate*[1]) to hiss]

sib·i·la·tion (sib′ə lā′shən), *n.* **1.** the act of sibilating or hissing. **2.** a hissing sound: *All metals quenched in water give a sibilation . . .* (Francis Bacon).

sib·i·la·to·ry (sib′ə lə tôr′ē, -tōr′-), *adj.* producing a hissing or sibilant effect.

Si·bir·ic (sī bir′ik), *adj.* of or having to do with the Asiatic peoples of Siberia, such as the Tungusic, Mongolic, Tartarian, Finnic, and Japanese groups. [< Russian *Sibirĭ* of Siberia + English *-ic*]

sib·ling (sib′ling), *n.* **1. a.** each or any one of two or more individuals born to the same parents but not at the same birth: *Siblings in a family group have special social relationships, not possessed by an only child . . .* (Emory S. Bogardus). **b.** each or any one of two or more individuals born to the same parents, including twins, triplets, etc. **2.** each or any one of two or more individuals having one parent in common. [< *sib*[1] + *-ling*]

sib·ship (sib′ship), *n.* the condition of being a sibling.

sib·yl (sib′əl), *n.* **1.** any of several prophetesses that the ancient Greeks and Romans consulted about the future: *Even the prophets and sibyls . . . show little or no connection with the traditional aspects they are expected to express* (Atlantic). **2. a.** a prophetess; fortuneteller. **b.** a witch, especially one with prophetic powers. [< Old French *sibile,* learned borrowing from Latin *Sibylla* < Greek *Síbylla*]

si·byl·ic or **si·byl·lic** (sə bil′ik), *adj.* sibylline.

sib·yl·line (sib′ə lēn, -līn, -lin), *adj.* **1.** of or like a sibyl; prophetic; mysterious: . . . *a* *numerical code . . . [that] seemed to be a row of sibylline figures* (New Yorker). **2.** said or written by a sibyl.

Sibylline Books, a collection of religious prophecies and oracular advice (in the realm especially of statecraft) in Greek hexameters, cherished and consulted by the ancient Romans and alleged to have been obtained from the Cumaean sibyl and brought to Rome by Tarquin the Proud, the seventh and last king of Rome.

Sibylline Oracles, a collection of apocalyptic writings, consisting partly of Jewish and partly of Christian material, composed in imitation of the Sibylline Books.

sib·yl·list (sib′ə list), *n.* a believer in sibylline prophecies or in the oracles of the Sibylline Books.

sic[1] (sik), *adv. Latin.* so; thus.

➔ **Sic** is used to show or emphasize the fact that something has been copied just as it is in the original. *Sic,* italicized and set in brackets, is used to mark an error in quoted matter: *The letter was headed "Danbury, Conneticut [sic], Jan. 2."*

sic[2] (sik), *v.t.,* **sicked, sick·ing. 1.** to set upon or attack. **2.** to incite to set upon or attack: *to sic a dog on a stranger.* [American English, spelling variant of *sick*[2], verb]

sic[3] (sik), *adj., pron. Dialect.* such. [Scottish variant of *such*]

Sic., 1. Sicilian. **2.** Sicily.

Si·ca·ni·an (si kā′nē ən), *adj., n.* Sicilian.

Si·car·i·us (si kãr′ē əs), *n., pl.* **-i·i** (-ē ī). one of a group of zealots in Palestine in the later years of Nero's reign who used murder and other forms of violence against the Romans. [< Latin *Sicārius* (literally) assassin < *sīca* dagger]

sic·ca (sik′ə), *n., pl.* **-cas.** a newly coined rupee. [< Hindi *sikkā* < Arabic *sikkah* a die for coining]

sic·ca·tive (sik′ə tiv), *adj.* drying. —*n.* a substance that hastens drying, especially one used in paint, such as linseed oil. [< Late Latin *siccātīvus* < Latin *siccāre* make dry < *siccus* dry]

sice[1] (sīs), *n.* the number six at dice. [< Old French *sis* < Latin *sex* six]

sice[2] (sīs), *n.* syce.

Si·cel·i·ot (si sel′ē ot), *n.* an ancient Greek settler in Sicily; Sicilian Greek. [< Greek *Sikeliṓtēs*]

Si·cil·ian (si sil′yən), *adj.* of or having to do with Sicily, the largest island in the Mediterranean, near the southwestern tip of Italy, its people, or their dialect. —*n.* **1.** a native or inhabitant of Sicily. **2.** the dialect of Italian spoken in Sicily.

si·cil·i·a·na (si sil′ē ä′nə), *n.* siciliano. [< Italian *siciliana,* feminine of *siciliano* Sicilian]

si·cil·i·a·no (si sil′ē ä′nō), *n.* **1.** a slow, pastoral dance of the peasants of Sicily, accompanied with singing. **2.** the music for this dance, in sextuple and moderately slow time, resembling the pastoral. [< Italian *siciliano* Sicilian]

si·cil·i·enne (si sil′ē en′), *n.* a heavy variety of mohair (fabric). [< French *sicilienne,* feminine of *sicilien* Sicilian]

sick[1] (sik), *adj.* **1.** in poor health; having some disease; ill. **2. a.** of, showing, or characterized by sickness: *a sick look.* **b.** of, for, or connected with a sick person: *sick leave, sick pay.* **3.** *Especially British.* vomiting or inclined to vomit; feeling nausea: *O lend me a basin, I am sick, I am sick* (Ben Jonson). **4.** affected with sorrow, longing, or some other strong feeling: *sick at heart, to be sick for old friends at home. Hope deferred maketh the heart sick* (Proverbs 13:12). **5.** thoroughly tired; weary: *to be sick of drudgery. He is sick of school.* **6.** *Informal.* disgusted; mortified; chagrined: *I am sick and tired of his complaints.* **7.** not in the proper condition; impaired; unsound: *The enterprise is sick* (Shakespeare). **8.** pale; wan. **9.** mentally ill: *People tend to believe that it is wrong and "sick" to feel anxious or guilty* (Time). **10.** grisly; sadistic; cruel: *a sick joke, sick humor. I've produced every type of picture except sick ones* (Walt Disney). **11.** *Agriculture.* **a.** (of soil) not producing a sufficient yield of a crop: *cotton-sick.* **b.** infested with destructive microorganisms.

—*n.* **the sick,** sick people collectively: *The sick were so numerous that it became necessary to call in . . . a nurse* (Medical and Physical Journal).

—*v.i.* to vomit: *Gertrude [was] sicking up the contents of the poisoned cup on to the floor* (Jeremy Kingston).

[Old English *sēoc*]

—**Syn.** *adj.* **1.** unwell, ailing, indisposed. **5.** satiated.

➔ In England, **sick** meaning "unwell" survives chiefly in attributive use: *a sick man.* As a predicate adjective (*to be* or *feel sick*), it has been narrowed to mean "nauseated, about to vomit" or "vomiting" and in the general sense has been replaced by *ill.* In America, *sick* may have this restricted meaning, but it is also regularly used in the older general sense: *He was violently sick behind the hedge. He was sick all last year.*

sick[2] (sik), *v.t.* to set upon or incite to attack; sic[2]: *Sick him, Towser.* [American English, perhaps < dialectal variant of *seek*]

sick bay, the part of or place on a ship in which drugs are kept, medical treatment given, etc.; ship's hospital, infirmary, or dispensary.

sick·bed (sik′bed′), *n.* the bed of a sick person: *She would get up from a sickbed to go shopping* (New Yorker).

sick benefit, money given to employees who cannot work because of illness, as arranged in a labor or insurance contract: *It said it will press for the following fringe-benefit improvements: . . . weekly sick benefits, life insurance, severance pay and pensions* (Wall Street Journal).

sick berth, sick bay.

sick call, 1. a summons to a doctor, clergyman, etc., to visit a sick person. **2.** *Military.* **a.** a call sounded by a bugle, trumpet, etc., as a signal to those who are sick to report to the hospital or medical officer. **b.** the assembling of those who are sick in answer to this call.

sick·en (sik′ən), *v.i.* **1.** to become sick: *to sicken with typhus. The bird sickened when kept in the cage.* **2. a.** to feel horror or nausea; experience revulsion (at something). **b.** to grow weary or tired (of a thing). **c.** to long eagerly. —*v.t.* **1.** to make sick: *The sight of blood sickened him.* **2.** to make weary or tired of something: *He was sickened by too much luxury.*

sick·en·er (sik′ə nər), *n.* something that sickens, especially something that nauseates or disgusts.

sick·en·ing (sik′ə ning, sik′ning), *adj.* **1.** making sick; causing nausea or faintness, disgust, or loathing: *a sickening sight; with monstrous head and sickening cry [the donkey]* (G.K. Chesterton). **2.** becoming sick; falling ill. —**sick′en·ing·ly,** *adv.* —**Syn. 1.** repulsive, offensive.

sick·er (sik′ər), *adj. Scottish.* **1.** that may be depended on; certain; sure. **2.** free from danger or harm; secure; safe. Also, **siker.** [Old English *sicor* < Latin *sēcūrus.* Doublet of SECURE, SURE.]

sick flag, a yellow flag indicating the presence of disease, displayed at a quarantined building, ship, etc., to prevent unauthorized communication.

sick headache, 1. a headache accompanied by nausea and stomach disorders. **2.** a migraine.

sick·ish (sik′ish), *adj.* **1.** somewhat ill or sick; indisposed. **2.** somewhat sickening: *The jam avenged itself by arousing a slightly sickish feeling* (Atlantic). —**sick′ish·ly,** *adv.* —**sick′ish·ness,** *n.*

sick·le (sik′əl), *n., v.,* **-led, -ling.** —*n.* a tool consisting of a short, curved blade on a short handle, used for cutting grass, reaping grain, etc. —*v.i.* to take on the shape of a sickle: *The tendency of red blood cells from such people to sickle can be readily demonstrated* (New Scientist). [Old English *sicol, sicel* < Latin *secula,* related to *secāre* to cut]

Sickles
Left, sickle; right, sickle emblem in flag of U.S.S.R.

Sick·le[1] (sik′əl), *n.* a group of stars shaped like a sickle in the northern constellation Leo. [< *sickle*]

Sick·le[2] (sik′əl) *n.* Seckel (pear).

sick leave, a leave of absence given to a worker because of illness, usually a certain number of days and with pay.

sick·le·bill (sik′əl bil′), *n.* **1.** a curlew, or any of various other birds with a curved bill. **2.** any of several kinds of birds of paradise of New Guinea.

sick·le-billed (sik′əl bild′), *adj.* having a falcate or sickle-shaped bill, as a bird.

sickle cell anemia, a hereditary form of anemia in which the normally round red blood cells become sickle-shaped, are ineffective in carrying oxygen, and are easily destroyed: *The hemoglobin molecule in the cell . . . and not the cell itself is the diseased factor in sickle cell anemia* (Science News Letter).

sick·led (sik′əld), *adj.* furnished with a sickle.

sickle feather, one of the long, curved feathers of a rooster's tail.

sick·le·man (sik′əl man′), *n., pl.* **-men.** a man who uses a sickle; reaper: *You sunburnt sicklemen, of August weary, Come hither from the furrow and be merry* (Shakespeare).

sick·le·mi·a (sik lē′mē ə), *n.* sickle cell anemia.

sick·le·pod (sik′əl pod′), *n.* a North American rock cress with long, curved pods.

sick·ler (sik′lər), *n.* a reaper; sickleman.

sick·le-shaped (sik′əl shāpt′), *adj.* shaped like a sickle; having a curved, hooklike form; falcate.

sick·li·ly (sik′lə lē), *adv.* in a sickly manner; sickly.

sick·li·ness (sik′lē nis), *n.* the state or fact of being sickly; ill health.

sick·ling (sik′ling), *n.* a changing in the shape of red blood cells from round to convex, as in sickle cell anemia: *Sickling is not dangerous unless it affects most of the hemoglobin, in which case it can cause fatal anemia* (Scientific American).

sick list, a list of workers, military personnel, students, etc., who are sick.

sick-list·ed (sik′lis′tid), *adj.* entered on the sick list; reported sick.

sick·ly (sik′lē), *adj.,* **-li·er, -li·est,** *adv., v.,* **-lied, -ly·ing.** —*adj.* **1.** often sick; not strong and healthy. **2.** of, having to do with, caused by, or suggesting sickness: *Her skin is a sickly yellow.* **3. a.** causing sickness: *That place has a sickly climate.* **b.** marked by the presence of sickness. **4.** faint; weak; pale: *a sickly glow.* **5.** weak; mawkish: *sickly sentimentality.*

—*adv.* in a sick manner. *to smile sickly.*

—*v.t.* **1.** to cover with a sickly hue: *Thus the native hue of resolution Is sicklied o'er with the pale cast of thought* (Shakespeare). **2.** to make sickly or pale.

—**Syn.** *adj.* **1.** ailing, indisposed. —**Ant.** *adj.* **1.** healthy, strong.

Sick Man of Europe, the Turkish or Ottoman Empire, or the Sultan of Turkey, used from the middle of the 1800's in allusion to the dying condition of the Turkish Empire (that ceased to exist in 1923).

sick·ness (sik′nis), *n.* **1. a.** the condition of being sick; illness; disease. **b.** a particular disease, as the cause of this; ailment; malady. **2.** nausea; vomiting. —**Syn. 2.** queasiness, squeamishness.

sick nurse, a nurse for sick persons.

sick parade, an inspection of those who are sick, as in the armed forces.

sick pay, sick benefit.

sick·room (sik′rüm′, -rům′), *n.* a room in which a sick person is cared for.

sic pas·sim (sik pas′im), *Latin.* so in various places.

sic sem·per ty·ran·nis (sik sem′pər tə-ran′is), *Latin.* thus always to tyrants (the motto of Virginia; known also as the utterance of John Wilkes Booth to the audience at Ford's Theatre just after his shooting of Lincoln).

sic tran·sit glo·ri·a mun·di (sik tran′-sit glôr′ē ə mun′dī, glōr′-), *Latin.* so passes away the glory of this world.

Si·cu·li·an (si kyü′lē ən), *adj.* of or having to do with the Siculi, an ancient people of central and southern Italy, who at a very early date colonized and gave name to the island of Sicily. —*n.* a member of the Siculi; an ancient Sicilian.

sic·ut pa·tri·bus, sit De·us no·bis (sik′-ət pā′trə bəs sit dē′əs nō′bis), *Latin.* May God be with us, as with our fathers (motto of Boston).

Sic·y·o·ni·an (sis′ē ō′nē ən), *adj.* of or having to do with Sicyon, an ancient city of northern Peloponnesus in Greece, or its territory Sicyonia, noted as an early center of art development. —*n.* a native or an inhabitant of Sicyon or Sicyonia.

SID (no periods), sudden ionospheric disturbance (usually caused by the sun).

si·da (sī′də), *n.* any of a group of herbs and

shrubs of the mallow family, found mostly in warm climates and usually having small yellow or white flowers, as Queensland hemp. [< New Latin *Sida* the typical genus < Greek *sidē* a water plant]

sid·dur (sid′ůr), *n.* the Jewish prayer book, with prayers for daily, Sabbath, and festival services. [< Hebrew *siddur* order]

side[1] (sīd), *n., adj., v.,* **sid·ed, sid·ing.** —*n.* **1.** a surface or line bounding a thing: *the sides of a square.* **2.** one of the two surfaces of an object that are not the front, back, top, or bottom: *a door at the side of a house, the sides of a bed, a table, a box, or a wagon.* **3.** one of the two surfaces of paper, cloth, a phonograph record, etc.: *Write on one side of the paper only. Play both sides of the record.* **4. a.** a particular surface: *the outer and inner sides of a hollow ball, the side of the moon turned toward the earth.* **b.** an aspect or view of something immaterial: *the better side of one's nature, the bright side of a difficulty, to hear all sides of an argument.* **5.** the slope of a hill or bank, especially one extending for a considerable distance. **6.** the bank or shore of a river or water, or the land bordering a river or water. **7.** either the right or the left part of the body of a person or animal: *a pain in one's side.* **8.** a position, place, area, etc., considered either as lying to the right or left of a central or a specified line, place, point, etc., or as extending in any direction from a certain place, point, etc.: *a region on both sides of a river, the west side of town, our side of the street, to turn to one side.* **9.** the position, course, attitude or part of one person or party against another: *faults on both sides, the winning side of a dispute.* **10. a.** a group of persons opposed to another group: *Both sides are ready for the contest.* **b.** a sports team: *The present Australian side is, on good pitches, a very powerful one* (Sunday Times). **11.** the line of descent; part of a family: *He is English on his mother's side.* **12.** *British Slang.* pretentious airs; arrogance: *remarkable for his want of anything like "side"* (Samuel Butler). **13.** either part of a ship's hull extending from stem to stern, above the water line. **14.** *British.* a spinning motion given a billiard ball by striking it at a point not directly in the middle; english. **15.** one page of an actor's lines.

by one's side, near one: *His mother was by his side all through his illness.*

off side, not in a position, according to the rules of the game, to participate in a play: *One of the ends was off side, having started to go out for the pass a second before the ball was put into play.*

on side, in position, according to the rules of the game, to participate in a play: *All players were on side for the kickoff.*

on the shady side of, older than; beyond the age of: *From looking at his face one would not think he was on the shady side of fifty.*

on the side, in addition to one's regular or ordinary duties: *Many producers of long-run shows are lenient about letting members of their casts earn money on the side* (New Yorker).

shiver my sides, a mock oath attributed to sailors: *If fairer can be said by mortal seaman, shiver my sides!* (Robert Louis Stevenson).

side by side, a. beside one another: *They walked side by side like a couple of policemen on duty* (Graham Greene). **b.** equally: *In the hourly earning of its employees . . . it ranked side by side with petroleum refining, an industry with a much higher profit margin* (New York Times).

split one's sides, to laugh or cause one to laugh very hard: *Unlike Mr. Milligan, who is forever trying to split our sides, he is content with inducing the wry chuckle, and this he does supremely well* (Manchester Guardian Weekly).

take sides, to place oneself with one person or group against another, as in an argument: *The bystander refused to take sides in the quarrel.*

this side of, short of; not spilling over into: *Its lean harmonies and themes keep the work this side of sentimentality* (Raymond Ericson).

—*adj.* **1.** situated or lying toward, at, or on the side: *side streets, the side aisles of a theater.* **2.** directed, tending, or coming from or toward one side; indirect: *a side view.* **3.** less important; subsidiary: *a side issue.*

—*v.t.* **1.** to provide with sides, as a building. **2.** to put aside: *Mrs. Wilson was "siding" the dinner things* (Elizabeth Gaskell).

—*v.i.* **side against,** to oppose: *Most of the smaller boys sided against the bully and gave him a licking.*

side with, to take the part of; favor (one among opposing or differing groups or persons): *The sisters always side with each other when the children quarrel. Scotchmen who sided alternately with the French and English interests* (Theodore Roosevelt).

[Old English *sīde*]

side[2] (sīd), *adj. Scottish.* reaching or hanging far down on the person; long. [Old English *sīd*]

side·arm (sīd′ärm′), *adj. Sports.* throwing or thrown from the side with the arm at waist height; not overhand or underhand: *a sidearm pitcher, a sidearm pitch.*

side arms, weapons worn at the side, such as a sword, dagger, revolver, or bayonet, typically belted on at the waist in a scabbard or holster.

side-ax (sīd′aks′), *n.* an ax with the handle slightly bent to one side to guard the hand.

side·band (sīd′band′), *n.* one of the bands comprising the frequencies on either side of the carrier frequency of a modulated wave when the carrier frequency is higher than the modulating frequency: *From this point of view existing plans in the United States for a Medical Radio System utilizing unused sidebands of existing FM broadcasting stations are of special interest* (New Scientist).

side·bar (sīd′bär′), *n.* **1.** a latitudinal bar or longitudinal sidepiece as in a carriage, saddle, etc. **2.** a news report or feature which supplements a major news story: *Brinkley produced some intriguing sidebars on candidates* (Time).

side bet, an additional bet, secondary to the main bet or betting.

side·board (sīd′bōrd′, -bōrd′), *n.* **1.** a piece of dining-room furniture with drawers and shelves for holding silver, linen, etc., and usually a flat top for dishes. **2.** an additional and removable board placed on the side of a truck, wagon, etc., as in slotted uprights, so as to increase the height of, or form, a side: *The general effect was that of a Sicilian market cart with painted and carved sideboards* (Lawrence Durrell).

Renaissance Sideboard (def. 1)

sideboards, *Slang.* side whiskers; sideburns: *to shave off one's sideboards.*

—**Syn. 1.** buffet.

side bones, the ossification of the lateral cartilages of a horse's foot.

side-box (sīd′boks′), *n.* a box or enclosed seat on the side in a theater.

side-boy (sīd′boi′), *n.* a boy assigned to the gangway of a ship to wait on an officer who is coming aboard or leaving.

side·burned (sīd′bėrnd′), *adj. U.S.* wearing sideburns: *A sideburned youth beats out an insolent rhythm on a resonant fantail deck* (New Yorker).

side·burns (sīd′bėrnz′), *n.pl. U.S.* short whiskers just below the hairline on both cheeks. [American English, alteration of *burnsides* < Ambrose E. *Burnside*, 1824-81, a Union general]

➔ **Sideburns—burnsides** are related etymologically but have rarely, if ever, been exactly synonymous. *Burnsides,* now chiefly historical in use, designates relatively long, heavy whiskers, patterned on those worn by General Burnside, 1824-1881. *Sideburns,* especially in current use, designates any hairy growth extending downward from a point just in front of the upper base of the ear, with length and closeness of cut being a matter of individual taste.

side·car (sīd′kär′), *n.* **1.** a car for a passenger, baggage, etc., attached to the side of a motorcycle: *Mercury . . . bought an aged and decrepit motorcycle, with a sidecar* (New Yorker). **2.** *U.S.* a cocktail made with cointreau, brandy, and lemon juice in approximately equal parts.

side chain, 1. a chain of atoms attached to the principal chain in the structure of a molecule: *One possible line of research . . . would be the production . . . of a basic penicillin nucleus and the attachment to it of different side chains* (London Times). **2.** a chain at the side of a vehicle, especially either of two chains that transmit motion from the engine to the driving wheels in some motor vehicles.

side chair, 1. an armless chair. **2.** one of a set of chairs, with or without arms, placed at the side of a table or room: *A matching side chair, low-armed and inviting, is $55* (New Yorker).

side chapel, a chapel in an aisle or at the side of a church.

side comb, a comb used in a woman's hair to retain a curl or lock on the side of the head.

-sided, *combining form.* having —— sides: *Slab-sided = having slab sides. Three-sided = having three sides.*

side dish, 1. an item of food served in addition to the main dish of a course or meal: *to have peas as a side dish.* **2.** a dish, especially a small dish, for a serving of such an item of food.

side door, a door at the side of a house or building, used as a secondary entrance: *He reached the building, and, entering through the side door on the sun porch, went straight to his rooms* (New Yorker).

side-dress (sīd′dres′), *v.t.* to fertilize (a plant or plants) with something as a side dressing: *to side-dress corn with nitrates.*

side dressing, a fertilizer scattered on or worked shallowly into the soil near the base of a plant, especially as a supplement to that placed in the soil at planting or to overcome some nutritional deficiency: *Side dressings of liquid fertilizer are applied as the plants need the nutrients* (Consumer Reports, 1952).

side drum, a snare drum, especially for a marching band: *So we got a battered old saxophone, a second-hand side drum, a stringbass . . .* (Harper's).

side effect, a secondary effect or reaction, usually undesirable or unpleasant: *The doctor cites the dangers of tranquilizers, among which were their side effects, drug dependency, habituation and addiction* (Science News Letter).

side entrance, a subsidiary entrance on the side into a building, vehicle, etc.

side-glance (sīd′glans′, -gläns′), *n.* a glance directed sideways; sidelong glance: *We got the drift, and our side-glances to each other said simply, "He stinks"* (Edward Weeks).

side·head (sīd′hed′), *n.* a subhead in the margin, as in the left-hand margin of a left-hand page, aligned with the first line of the paragraph or context to which it applies.

side·hill (sīd′hil′), *n. Canadian and U.S.* a hillside: *Horseherds ranged the valleys and sidehills* (Canadian Geographic Journal).

side horse, a gymnasium apparatus for jumping or vaulting exercises: *The men's Olympic events demand all-round agility on 1) a single horizontal bar, 2) two parallel bars, 3) a side horse, 4) a long horse, 5) a pair of suspended rings* (Time).

side issue, a matter not connected with the subject under discussion.

side-kick (sīd′kik′), *n. Informal.* a partner or close friend; crony: *Henry Fonda . . . and Anthony Quinn as his devoted but sinister side-kick are the most interesting characters in this solid "adult western"* (Maclean's).

side·lamp (sīd′lamp′), *n. Especially British.* the lamp on either side of a motor vehicle: *. . . the many heavy lorries which, even though they may use their headlamps in the country, only have one pinhead-size nearside sidelamp in the town* (R.J. Swan).

side·less (sīd′lis), *adj.* without sides; open at the sides: *[The car] had a sideless, makeshift hood of old sheet metal* (New Yorker).

side·light (sīd′līt′), *n.* **1.** light coming from the side. **2.** incidental information about a subject: *He adds illuminating and amusing sidelights* (Scientific American). *Such information may throw sidelight upon my story* (Herman Melville). **3.** either of two lights required to be carried by a moving ship at night, a red one on the port side and a green one on the starboard. **4.** a window or other opening for light in the side of a building, ship, etc. **5.** a window at the side of a door or (sometimes) a larger window, used especially with a solid door to permit daylight to enter a hall that would otherwise be dark.

side·line (sīd′līn′), *n., v.,* **-lined, -lin·ing.** —*n.* **1.** a line at the side of something. **2.** *Sports.* one of the lines, extending from one goal or end line to the other, on either side of a playing field, marking the limits of the ac-

tive playing area. **3. a.** a line of goods, trade, etc., that is additional, auxiliary, and secondary to the basic one or ones. **b.** any enterprise, business, etc., carried on apart from that in which one is chiefly or officially employed. **4.** a branch line (of a railroad).
sidelines, *Sports.* **a.** the area just outside the lines marking the limits of the active playing area of a playing field: *The spectators watched the game from the sidelines.* **b.** the position or status of those not actively taking part in a game: *In spite of Morgan's professed intention of retiring from competition after the Olympics, it was hardly to be expected that anyone so tireless and ambitious could remain on the sidelines for long* (London Times).
—*v.t.* to put on the sidelines; make inactive: *One was a right wing . . . who was sidelined for two weeks with an ankle injury* (New York Times).

side·ling (sīd′ling), *adv.* **1.** with a sideward movement; sideways; obliquely. **2.** sloping; steep.

side·long (sīd′lông′, -long′), *adj., adv.* to one side; toward the side: *a sidelong glance (adj.); a plow lying sidelong beside the fence (adv.).*

side·man (sīd′man′), *n., pl.* **-men.** *U.S.* a musician in a jazz ensemble other than the leader: *He began at $1,250 a week for himself and his three sidemen, or $750 for a one-night concert date* (New Yorker).

side meat, *U.S. Dialect.* **1.** salt pork. **2.** bacon.

side·note (sīd′nōt′), *n.* a note at the side of a written or printed page; a marginal note, as distinguished from a footnote.

side oats, a grama grass ranging from New Jersey to the Rocky Mountains and southward, bearing many short spikes along one side of the stem, used for forage.

side partner, a person who works alongside or alternately with another person.

side·piece (sīd′pēs′), *n.* a piece forming a side or part of a side, or fixed by the side, of something.

side play, motion which is not in the direction of the desired motion but at an angle to it, as in the parts of an automobile or other vehicle.

sid·er (sī′dər), *n.* a person who sides with a person, party, or cause; partisan; adherent.

sid·er·al (sid′ər əl), *adj.* **1.** sidereal. **2.** due to the stars.

si·de·re·al (sī dir′ē əl), *adj.* **1.** of or having to do with the stars or constellations: *our sidereal system.* **2.** *Astronomy.* measured by the apparent daily motion of the stars: *The sidereal month measures the moon's revolution in relation to a fixed star* (World Book Encyclopedia). [< Latin *sīdereus* astral (< *sīdus, -eris* star) + English *-al*[1]] —**Syn. 1.** astral, stellar.

sidereal time, time measured by the stars, or the hour angle of the vernal equinox. A sidereal day is the period between the departure and arrival of a star or of the vernal equinox at the meridian and is about 4 minutes shorter than a mean solar day. Sidereal hours, months, and years bear the same relation to the sidereal day that calendar hours, months, and years bear to the calendar day. *The minutes and seconds of solar time are each a little longer than the corresponding units of sidereal time* (Bernhard, Bennett, and Rice).

sid·er·ite (sid′ə rīt), *n.* **1.** a brownish or yellowish mineral consisting of iron carbonate, an iron ore, and crystallizing with perfect rhombohedral cleavage; chalybite: *Ores containing the carbonate of iron, siderite, are of many varieties* (W.R. Jones). *Formula:* $FeCO_3$ **2.** a meteorite consisting mainly of iron: *Meteorites are classified in three general divisions. Siderites are composed almost entirely of nickel-iron* (Science News Letter). **3.** *Obsolete.* loadstone. [< Latin *sidērītes* loadstone < Greek *sidērī́tēs* < *sídēros* iron]

sid·er·it·ic (sid′ə rit′ik), *adj.* of the nature of siderite.

side road, a secondary road alongside or turning off a main road: *New signs were posted along a side road leading westward from the Edmonton-Calgary highway* (Edmonton (Canada) Journal).

sid·er·o·graph·ic (sid′ər ə graf′ik), having to do with or produced by siderography: *siderographic art or impressions.*

sid·er·og·ra·phy (sid′ə rog′rə fē), *n.* the art of engraving on steel, especially a process in which the design is subsequently transferred by pressure to other steel surfaces. [< Greek *sídēros* iron + English *-graphy*]

sid·er·o·lite (sid′ər ə līt), *n.* a meteorite composed of a mixed mass of iron and stone: *Siderolites consist of nickel-iron and silicate minerals in roughly equal proportions* (Science News Letter). [< Greek *sídēros* iron + English *-lite*]

sid·er·o·na·trite (sid′ər ə nā′trīt), *n.* a hydrated sulfate of iron and sodium occurring in crystalline masses of a dark-yellow color.

sid·er·o·phile (sid′ər ə fīl), *adj. Geology.* having an affinity for metallic iron: *Chondrites contain, mingled together, lithophile, chalcophile, and siderophile elements* (Scientific American). [< Greek *sídēros* iron + English *-phile*]

sid·er·o·sis (sid′ə rō′sis), *n.* a chronic inflammatory disease of the lungs caused by inhalation of iron particles. [< New Latin *siderosis* < Greek *sídēros* iron + *-ōsis* condition]

sid·er·o·stat (sid′ər ə stat), *n. Astronomy.* a device for keeping the direction of the reflected light of a star constant, usually consisting of a plane mirror carried on an axis parallel to the earth's axis and rotating once every 48 hours. [< Latin *sīdus, -eris* star + English *-stat*]

sid·er·o·stat·ic (sid′ə rə stat′ik), *adj.* of or having to do with a siderostat.

sid·er·ur·gi·cal (sid′ər ėr′jə kəl), *adj.* having to do with siderurgy.

sid·er·ur·gy (sid′ər ėr′jē), *n.* the art of working in iron and steel. [< Greek *sidērourgíā* < *sidērourgós* ironworker < *sídēros* iron + *érgon* work]

side·sad·dle (sīd′sad′əl), *n.* a woman's saddle so made that both of the rider's legs are on the same side of a horse, now especially one with knoblike protuberances to support the knees of the rider, who sits facing forward with the right knee slightly raised above the left. —*adv.* with both legs on the same side of the horse: *to ride sidesaddle.*

side show, **1.** a small show in connection with a principal one: *the side shows of a circus.* **2.** any minor proceeding or affair connected with a more important one.

side·slip (sīd′slip′), *n., v.,* **-slipped, -slipping.** —*n.* **1.** the slipping to one side and downward of an airplane in flight; loss of altitude by a sliding sideward and downward, as along the plane of a bank. **2.** a slip to one side, as in skiing; skid. —*v.i.* to do or undergo a sideslip.

sides·man (sīdz′mən), *n., pl.* **-men.** *British.* **1.** an assistant to the churchwarden of a parish: *There has been a great deal of activity in Anglican parishes this past week with . . . annual parochial church meetings to elect parochial councillors and sidesmen* (Manchester Guardian). **2.** *Obsolete.* a person who takes sides; partisan.

side·split·ting (sīd′split′ing), *adj.* extremely funny: *a sidesplitting joke.*

side step, **1.** a step or stepping to one side. **2.** a step at the side of a ship, vehicle, etc.

side-step (sīd′step′), *v.t., v.i.,* **-stepped, -step·ping. 1.** to step aside: *to side-step in order to avoid a blow.* **2.** to avoid by or as if by stepping aside; evade: *to side-step a responsibility.* —**side′-step′per,** *n.*

side stroke, a swimming stroke in which the swimmer lies on his side in the water, pulling alternately with his arms while performing a scissors kick: *The side stroke is a restful stroke and is not used for racing* (World Book Encyclopedia).

side·swipe (sīd′swīp′), *v.,* **-swiped, -swiping,** *n. U.S.* —*v.t., v.i.* to hit with a sweeping blow along the side: *A chartered German plane en route to New York sideswiped a building and crashed in flames* (Wall Street Journal). —*n.* a sweeping blow along the side or indirectly: *The author takes some well-aimed sideswipes at our foreign policy* (New Yorker).

side table, **1.** a table placed near the wall of a room, especially a dining room. **2.** a table smaller than a dining table, placed to one side of it, and used in serving.

side tool, a tool with a cutting edge at the side.

side·track (sīd′trak′), *n.* **1.** a railroad siding. **2.** a being diverted or turned aside: *to stick to the business at hand and avoid sidetracks.*
—*v.t.* **1.** to switch (a train, car, etc.) to a siding; move off the main track. **2.** to put aside; turn aside: *The teacher refused to be sidetracked by the pupils' questions on other subjects.*

side trip, a short trip away from the main or direct route of a journey: *You can go straight up Highway 8A, making side trips to the ghost towns* (Sunset).

side·walk (sīd′wôk′), *n.* a place to walk at the side of the street, usually paved: *. . . the first chance most of our soldiers or airmen have ever had to know any French people except the samples on the sidewalks or in the bars* (New Yorker). —**Syn.** footway, footpath.

sidewalk superintendent, *Informal.* a person who stops on the street to observe the work of a construction or repair project: *Sidewalk superintendents can be a terrible nuisance, getting in the way of trucks, gear, and workmen* (New Yorker).

side wall, **1.** either of the two side portions of an automobile tire, extending from the tread toward the center of the circle described by the tire: *One of them is located in its normal rim position and the other in the side wall* (Wall Street Journal). **2.** the outer surface of one of these: *to buy tires with white side walls.*

side·wall (sīd′wôl′), *n.* a wall forming the side of a structure, room, or enclosure.

side·ward (sīd′wərd), *adj., adv.* toward one side.

side·wards (sīd′wərdz), *adv.* sideward: *to slip sidewards.*

side·way (sīd′wā′), *adv., adj.* sideways. —*n.* **1.** a side street, as distinguished from a main road; byway. **2.** a sidewalk.

side·ways (sīd′wāz′), *adv., adj.* **1.** toward one side: *to walk sideways. Backwards and forwards and sideways did she pass* (Rudyard Kipling). **2.** from one side: *a sideways glimpse.* **3.** with one side toward the front; with a side other than the usual side facing upward, outward, etc.: *to stand sideways, to place a book sideways on a shelf.* **4.** at one side of a place.

side-wheel (sīd′hwēl′), *adj.* (of a steamboat) having a paddle wheel on each side: *A leisurely trip up the Volga in a side-wheel steamer left over from Czarist days* (Time).

side-wheel·er (sīd′hwē′lər), *n.* a side-wheel steamer: *in 1839, twenty years after the "side-wheeler" Savannah made the first steamship crossing of the Atlantic Ocean* (Beauchamp, Mayfield, and West).

side whisker, a hair growing long on the side of the face.

side whiskers, the whiskers that grow on the cheek or side of the face: *Pale young men with larded hair and Valentino-black side whiskers* (Atlantic).

side-whisk·ered (sīd′hwis′kərd), *adj.* having side whiskers: *the sainted but side-whiskered Nathaniel Mugford* (Sinclair Lewis).

Side Whiskers

side wind, a wind blowing from or on a side of an aircraft, ship, etc.: *The airplane is usually drifting sideways under the influence of side winds but the 67 determines the drift and allows for it* (Time).

side·wind·er (sīd′wīn′dər), *n.* **1.** a small rattlesnake of the southwestern United States that travels in a sideways direction by looping its body: *Rattlesnakes in the desert areas include the western diamondback rattler and the . . . sidewinder* (Lucius M. Beebe). **2.** a heavy blow delivered from the side, in which the fist is swung at or near the level of the shoulder through an arc of approximately 45 degrees.

side·wipe (sīd′wīp′), *n., v.,* **-wiped, -wip·ing.** sideswipe.

side·wise (sīd′wīz′), *adv., adj.* sideways: *The market is moving sidewise and there's no real big piece of good news* (Wall Street Journal).

sid·ing (sī′ding), *n.* **1.** a short railroad track to which cars may be switched from a main track. **2.** *U.S.* the boards or other material used for the outside wall of certain types of frame buildings, nailed to a house over the sheathing or directly to the studs of a barn: *The personnel building now under construction is using aluminum siding and roofing.* —**Syn. 1.** sidetrack.

si·dle (sī′dəl), *v.,* **-dled, -dling,** *n.* —*v.i.* **1.** to move sideways: *"I can't bear those things," Wilson said, sidling through the door* (Graham Greene). **2.** to move sideways slowly so as not to attract attention: *The little boy shyly sidled up to the visitor.* —*n.* a movement sideways. [probably back formation < *sideling*]

Si·do·ni·an (sī dō′nē ən), *adj.* of or having to do with Sidon, a famous seaport of ancient Phoenicia. —*n.* a native or inhabitant of Sidon.

siè·cle (sye′klə), *n. French.* century; age; epoch (especially in English contexts in certain phrases, as *fin de siècle*).

siege (sēj), *n., v.,* **sieged, sieg·ing.** —*n.* **1.** the act, process, or operation of surrounding a fortified place by an army trying to capture it; besieging or being besieged: *The siege of Troy lasted for ten years. The country was in a state of siege, and tanks were lined up in front of the Presidential palace* (Newsweek). **2.** any long or persistent effort to overcome resistance; any long-continued attack: *a siege of illness.* **3.** *Obsolete.* a seat, especially one used by a person of rank or distinction. **4.** *Obsolete.* a place in which one has his seat or residence; a seat of rule, empire, etc.

lay siege to, a. to besiege: *The Greeks laid siege to Troy for ten years.* **b.** to attempt to win or get by long and persistent effort: *His great ambition made him lay siege to all those who could help him achieve it.*

—*v.t.* to besiege.

[Middle English *sege* seat < Old French *siege* < Vulgar Latin *sedium* < Latin *sedēre* to sit]

—**Syn.** *n.* **1. Siege, blockade** mean a military operation to cut off normal communications and supplies of a place. **Siege,** chiefly applied to a land operation, means surrounding a city or fortified place, cutting off all movement to and from it, and usually assaulting it: *The Japanese laid siege to Corregidor.* **Blockade** applies to an operation, chiefly but not always naval, to close a harbor, coast, or city and cut off its supplies, but does not suggest attacking it: *In the struggle against Napoleon the British proclaimed a blockade of the northern coast of Europe. In 1948-1949, the airlift defeated the Russian blockade of Berlin.*

Siege Perilous, the vacant seat at King Arthur's Round Table, that could be occupied only by the knight who was destined to find the Holy Grail. [< Middle French *siege perilous;* see SIEGE (definition 3)]

siege piece, a coin, commonly of unusual shape and rude workmanship, struck and issued in a place during a siege, when the operations of the ordinary mints are suspended or their issues are not available.

Newark Siege Piece (obverse)

siege train, the equipment of guns, carriages, ammunition, etc., carried with an army for the purpose of besieging.

Sieg·fried (sēg′frēd), *n. German Legend.* a hero who killed a dragon, won the Rheingold, the treasure of the Nibelungs, acquired Balmung, a magic sword, and rescued the Valkyrie Brünhilde from an enchanted sleep. [< German *Siegfried* (literally) peace of victory]

Siegfried Line, an elaborate network of German fortifications facing the French Maginot Line, built shortly before World War II.

Si·en·ese (sē′ə nēz′, -nēs′), *adj., n., pl.* **-ese.** —*adj.* of or having to do with Siena, a city and province of central Italy. —*n.* a native or inhabitant of Siena.

si·e·nite (sī′ə nīt), *n.* syenite, a crystalline rock.

si·en·na (sē en′ə), *n.* **1.** an earth containing oxides of iron and, commonly, of manganese, used as a yellowish-brown coloring matter (raw sienna) or as a reddish-brown coloring matter (burnt sienna) after having been roasted. **2.** a yellowish brown or reddish brown. [< Italian *sienna* short for *terra di Sienna* earth from Siena, a city in Italy]

sie·ro·zem (syer′ə zem), *n.* a grayish soil found in temperate or cool arid regions, supporting sparse, shrubby vegetation. It is low in humus and its lime is near or on the surface. [< Russian *serozëm* < *seryj* gray + *zemlja* land, soil]

si·er·ra (sē er′ə), *n.* **1.** a chain of hills or mountains with jagged peaks: *The road wound up the bold sierra which separates the great plateaus of Mexico and Puebla* (William H. Prescott). **2.** any of certain Spanish mackerels, as the cero. [American English < Spanish *sierra* (literally) a saw < Latin *serra*]

Si·er·ra (sē er′ə), *n. U.S.* a code name for the letter *s*, used in transmitting radio messages.

si·es·ta (sē es′tə), *n., v.,* **-taed, -ta·ing.** —*n.* a nap or rest taken at noon or in the afternoon, especially one commonly taken during the hottest hours of the day in Spanish-speaking countries of the tropics or subtropics. —*v.i.* to rest or take a nap; indulge in a siesta.

[< Spanish *siesta* < Latin *sexta* (*hōra*) sixth (hour) of the Roman day (that is midday). Doublet of SEXT.]

sieur (syœr), *n.* a former French title of respect for a man; Sir. [< Old French *sieur* < Vulgar Latin *seiōrem* < Latin *seniōrem,* accusative of *senior* senior. Doublet of SEIGNEUR, SEIGNIOR.]

Sie·va bean (sē′və), a twining species of bean related to the Lima bean, with broad and curved pods containing flat seeds.

sieve (siv), *n., v.,* **sieved, siev·ing.** —*n.* a utensil consisting typically of a circular frame and a bottom having holes that let liquids and smaller pieces pass through, but not the larger pieces: *Shaking flour through a sieve removes lumps. We use a sieve to strain soup.* —*v.t., v.i.* to put or pass through a sieve. [Old English *sife*] —**sieve′like′,** *adj.*

—**Syn.** *n.* strainer, colander.

sieve cell, *Botany.* an elongated cell whose thin walls have perforations, usually at each end, which allow communication between adjacent cells of a similar nature. Sieve cells form an essential element of the phloem of vascular plants.

sieve plate, *Botany.* one of the thin walls of a sieve cell.

sieve tissue, *Botany.* tissue composed of sieve cells or sieve tubes.

sieve tube, *Botany.* **1.** a tubelike structure composed of sieve cells placed end to end: *The thin-walled sieve tubes are often filled with colloidal material and have the appearance of containing live protoplasm* (Fred W. Emerson). **2.** one of the cells that make up this structure; sieve cell.

Sif (sif), *n. Norse Mythology.* the blond-haired wife of Thor.

sif·fle (sif′əl), *n. Medicine.* a sibilant râle. [earlier, verb, blow, whistle < Old French *siffler* < Latin *sīfilāre,* variant of *sībilāre* whistle]

sif·flöt (sē flœt′), *n.* **1.** a whistle flute. **2.** a flute stop in an organ having a whistling tone. [< German *Sifflöt* < French *siffloter* whistle < Old French *siffler;* see SIFFLE]

sift (sift), *v.t.* **1.** to separate large pieces from small by shaking in a sieve: *to sift the ashes.* **2.** to put through a sieve: *to sift sugar on the top of a cake.* **3.** to examine very carefully: *The jury sifted the evidence to decide if the man was guilty.* **4.** to subject (a person) to close questioning. —*v.i.* **1.** to use a sieve. **2.** to fall through, or as if through, a sieve: *The snow sifted softly down.* [Old English *siftan,* related to *sife* sieve] —**Syn.** *v.t.* **3.** scrutinize.

sift·er (sif′tər), *n.* a utensil or device for sifting: *a flour sifter.*

sift·ing (sif′ting), *n.* the act of a person or thing that sifts.

siftings, the parts of matter sifted out: *I would recommend to add to it . . . either sand, lime rubbish, or lime siftings* (Beck's Florist Journal).

sig., **1.** mark (Latin, *signa*). **2.** signal. **3.** signature.

Sig., **1.** (in pharmacy) signature. **2.** Signor. **3.** Signore. **4.** Signori.

Sig·a·to·ka (sig′ə tō′kə), *n.* a destructive, tropical American leaf-spot disease of bananas, caused by a fungus.

sigh (sī), *v.i.* **1.** to let out a very long, deep breath because one is sad, tired, relieved, etc. **2.** to make a sound like a sigh: *The wind sighed in the treetops. Nought but a lovely sighing of the wind* (Keats). **3.** to wish very much; long: *She sighed for home and friends.* **4.** to lament with sighing: *to sigh over one's unhappy fate.* —*v.t.* **1.** to say or express with a sigh. **2.** to lament (an event, circumstance, etc.) with sighing.

—*n.* the act or sound of sighing.

[Middle English *sighen,* probably back formation < *sighte,* preterit of Old English *sīcan*] —**sigh′er,** *n.* —**sigh′ing·ly,** *adv.*

—**Syn.** *v.i.* **3.** yearn.

sight (sīt), *n.* **1. a.** the power of seeing; eyesight; vision: *Birds have better sight than dogs.* **b.** mental or spiritual vision. **2.** the limit or range of one's vision: *to lose sight of a plane. Land was in sight.* **3. a.** the act or fact of seeing; look: *love at first sight.* **b.** examination; inspection; scrutiny: *a bill of sight.* **4.** a thing seen; view; glimpse (of something): *I caught a sight of him.* **5. a.** something worth seeing: *Niagara Falls is one of the sights of the world.* **b.** *Informal.* something that looks bad or odd: *Jane is a sight in that ugly dress.* **6.** a way of looking or thinking; regard; estimation; judgment; opinion: *Dolls are very precious in a little girl's sight.* **7.** *Informal.* a great number or quantity: *a sight of people; . . . an awful sight of money* (Mark Twain). **8.** an observation taken with a telescope or other instrument. **9.** an aim with a gun or other weapon. **10.** a device, or one of a pair of devices, on a gun, surveying instrument, etc., through which the line of direction to an object is set for aiming or observing.

a sight for sore eyes, a welcome or pleasing sight: *Elizabeth in the saddle must have been a sight for sore eyes* (London Times).

at sight, a. as soon as seen: *She reads music at sight.* **b.** as soon as presented; on demand: *Some banks will cash a check at sight.*

catch sight of, to see: *. . . when . . . we catch sight above our heads of the squinting oblique eye watching us pass* (Edmund Wilson).

heave in sight, to come into view as though rising above the horizon: *The great Spanish ships heave in sight, and a furious struggle begins* (John R. Green).

in sight of, where one can see: *After the long voyage, we were at last in sight of land. We are not yet in possession of . . . peace, but for the first time we are fairly in sight of it* (Spectator).

know by sight, to know sufficiently to recognize when seen: *I know her by sight, but we have never spoken to each other.*

on sight, as soon as seen; at sight: *The fugitive lived in fear of being shot on sight.*

out of sight, out of this world: *Bibi thinks he's out of sight* (F.P. Tullius).

out of sight of, where one cannot see or be seen by: *out of sight of land, out of sight of the neighbors.*

sights, goals; objectives: *to raise or lower one's sights. The countries of these regions have set their sights on full schooling by 1980* (New Scientist).

sight unseen, without seeing or examining (a person or thing) in advance: *She ordered the dress over the phone, sight unseen.*

—*v.t.* **1.** to see: *At last Columbus sighted land.* **2.** to aim at or observe (an object) by means of sights: *to sight a star.* **3.** to adjust the sight or align the sights of (a gun, instrument, etc.). **4.** to provide with a sight or sights. —*v.i.* to take aim or observation by means of a sight or sights: *The hunter sighted carefully before firing his gun.*

[Old English *gesiht.* Related to SEE[1].]

—**Syn.** *n.* **3. a.** glance, gaze.

sight bill, a bill payable at sight or on presentation.

sight·board (sīt′bôrd′, -bōrd′), *n.* a white screen at the end of a cricket field for making the ball more easily visible to the batsman.

sight draft, a draft payable at sight or on presentation. *Abbr.:* s.d.

sight·ed (sī′tid), *adj.* **1.** having sight or vision. **2.** having a sight or sights, as a firearm. —*n.* a person who has sight or vision.

-sighted, *combining form.* having —— sight: *Dim-sighted = having dim sight.*

sight gag, *U.S. Informal.* a wordless joke or prank that must be seen to be understood.

sight·hole (sīt′hōl′), *n.* a hole to see through in a surveying or other instrument.

sight·ing (sī′ting), *n.* **1.** an act or instance of seeing: *Sea-serpent sightings have diminished of late* (Time). **2.** the act of adjusting the sight or aligning the sights of a gun, instrument, etc.: *The rotation of the earth moves objects out of the field of vision before a sighting can be made and the camera put in place on a telescope* (Science News Letter).

sight·less (sīt′lis), *adj.* **1.** unable to see; blind. **2.** unable to be seen; invisible. —**sight′less·ly,** *adv.* —**sight′less·ness,** *n.*

sight·line (sīt′līn′), *n.* a straight line from the eye to the object looked at; line of sight: *The arrangement of seats will . . . make possible clear sightlines to the stage for every member of the audience* (New York Times).

sight·li·ness (sīt′lē nis), *n.* the state of being sightly; pleasing appearance; comeliness.

sight·ly (sīt′lē), *adj.,* **-li·er, -li·est. 1.** pleasing to the sight. **2.** *U.S.* **a.** that can be seen from a distance. **b.** affording a fine view. —**Syn. 1.** fair, handsome.

sight-read (sīt′rēd′), *v.t., v.i.* to read at first sight; engage or be skilled in sight reading: *Candidates must sight-read in addition to playing . . . orchestral passages* (Newsweek). [back formation < *sight reading*]

sight reader, a person who is skilled in or capable of sight reading.

sight reading, a reading of a piece of music or passage in a foreign language at first sight.

sight·screen (sīt′skrēn′), *n. Cricket.* a structure of canvas or wood behind the bowler, serving as a white background that enables the batsman to have a clear sight of the ball.

sight·see (sīt′sē′), *v.i.* to go sightseeing. [back formation < *sightseeing*]

sight·see·ing (sīt′sē′ing), *n.* a going around to see objects or places of interest: *a week-end of sightseeing.* —*adj.* that goes around to see objects or places of interest: *a sightseeing bus.*

sight·se·er (sīt′sē′ər), *n.* a person who goes around to see objects or places of interest: *For sightseers, Katmandu offered an unmatched piquancy* (Newsweek).

sight·wor·thy (sīt′wėr′ᴛʜē), *adj.,* **-thi·er, -thi·est.** worthy of being seen, or of being visited as a sight.

sig·il (sij′il), *n.* **1.** an occult mark or sign as in astrology or magic: *Sign and sigil, word of power, From the earth raised keep and tower* (Scott). **2.** a seal or signet. [< Late Latin *sigillum* < Latin *sigilla,* plural < *sīgnum* mark, sign. Doublet of SEAL[1].]

sigill., seal (Latin, *sigillum*).

sig·il·lar·y (sij′ə ler′ē), *adj.* having to do with seals or signets.

sig·il·late (sij′ə lāt), *v.t.,* **-lat·ed, -lat·ing. 1.** to mark with or as with impressions of a seal. **2.** to close by or as by sealing. [< Late Latin *sigillāre* (with English *-ate*[1]) to seal < *sigillum;* see SIGIL]

sig·il·lat·ed earth (sij′ə lā′tid), Lemnian earth, so called because it is made into cakes stamped with a seal.

sig·il·la·tion (sij′ə lā′shən), *n.* **1.** the act of marking or the state of being marked with or as with a seal. **2.** a mark or marking so made.

sig·il·log·ra·pher (sij′ə log′rə fər), *n.* a person who is skilled in sigillography.

sig·il·log·ra·phy (sij′ə log′rə fē), *n.* the science or study of seals or signets. [< Late Latin *sigillum* (see SIGIL) + English *-graphy*]

sig·ma (sig′mə), *n.* **1.** the 18th letter of the Greek alphabet (Σ, σ, s), corresponding to the English *S, s.* **2.** something shaped like the letter S. **3.** something shaped like the letter C (from the shape of the Greek letter in its uncial form). [< Greek *sígma*]

sig·mate (sig′mit, -māt), *adj., v.,* **-mat·ed, -mat·ing.** —*adj.* **1.** S-shaped; having the form of a sigma. **2.** shaped like a C. —*v.t.* to add a sigma or *s* to; change by the addition of an *s* at the end, as *upward* into *upwards.*

sig·ma·tion (sig mā′shən), *n.* the adding of a sigma or *s* at the end of a word or a syllable.

sig·ma·tism (sig′mə tiz əm), *n.* **1.** the use or presence of sigma or *s;* repetition or recurrence of *s* or of the *s*-sound. **2.** difficult or defective pronunciation of the sound *s.*

sig·moid (sig′moid), *adj.* **1.** shaped like the letter S: *P. F. Verhulst showed in 1838 that the growth of human population followed an S-shaped or sigmoid curve* (F. S. Bodenheimer). **2.** *Anatomy.* having to do with the sigmoid flexure of the colon. **3.** shaped like the letter C. [< Greek *sigmoeidḗs* < *sígma* sigma + *eîdos* form]

sig·moi·dal (sig moi′dəl), *adj.* sigmoid.

sigmoid flexure, 1. *Zoology.* an S-shaped curve. **2.** *Anatomy.* the S-shaped bend of the colon just before descending to the rectum.

sig·moid·o·scope (sig moi′də skōp), *n.* a tube about 10 inches long which is inserted through the anus for the purpose of examining the colon: *. . . the use of the sigmoidoscope in routine physical examination to spot cancer of the colon* (Frank P. Matthews).

sign (sīn), *n.* **1. a.** any mark used to mean, represent, or point out something: *to use a delete sign. Three balls are the sign of a pawnbroker. We lunched at the sign of the Red Lion.* **b.** *Mathematics.* a mark or symbol used to indicate an operation to be performed on a quantity or number, a relation of quantities or numbers, etc.: *The four signs of the arithmetic operations are addition* (+), *subtraction* (−), *multiplication* (×), *division* (÷). *The sign* (=) *means "equals." The signs* (+) *and* (−) *in algebra and higher mathematics define positive and negative numbers.* **c.** *Music.* a flat, sharp, or other symbol used in notation to give directions, indicate tonality, etc. **2.** a motion or gesture used to mean, represent, or point out something: *to talk to a deaf person by signs. The priest made the sign of the cross. A nod is a sign of agreement.* **3.** an inscribed board, plate, or space serving for advertisement, guidance, or information: *The sign reads, "Keep off the grass." The names of streets are on signs at the corners.* **4. a.** an indication: *The ruin is a sign of past grandeur. There are no signs of life about the house.* **b.** an indication of a disease: *Fever is often a sign of infection.* **5.** a trace: *The hunter found signs of deer.* **6.** an indication of a coming event: *The robin is a sign of spring. The star in the east was a sign of Christ's coming.* **7.** *Astrology, Astronomy.* any of the twelve divisions of the zodiac, each named for a constellation and each denoted by a special symbol. **8.** a miraculous occurrence.

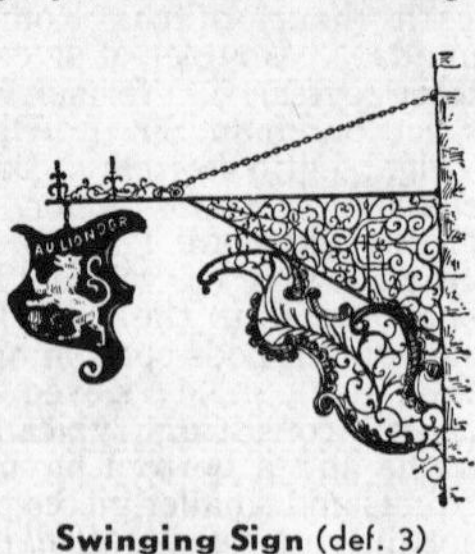

Swinging Sign (def. 3) (18th century)

—*v.t.* **1.** to attach one's name to: *Sign this letter. He signed the check.* **2.** to write: *Sign your initials here.* **3.** to designate (oneself) in a signature or signatures: *He signed himself "a constant reader."* **4.** to hire by a written agreement: *to sign a new ballplayer, to sign on a new crew.* **5.** to indicate; signify; betoken. **6.** to give a signal to; communicate by gesture: *to sign someone to enter, to sign assent.* **7.** to mark, protect, consecrate, etc., with the sign of the cross. **8.** to mark with a sign.

—*v.i.* **1.** to attach one's name to show authority, agreement, obligation, etc.; write one's name: *to sign on the dotted line.* **2.** to accept employment: *to sign for three years.* **3.** to make a sign or signal.

sign away, to give away by signing one's name: *. . . signing away vague and enormous sums of money. "I promise," he said, with a sense of despair, as though he were signing away the whole future* (Graham Greene).

sign off, to stop broadcasting after announcing the end of a program, etc.: *The show signs off at midnight.*

sign on, a. to join, enlist, etc., by written agreement; sign up: *He signed on as first mate.* **b.** to begin broadcasting: *The station signs on with the playing of the National Anthem.*

sign over, to hand over by signing one's name: *He has signed over one of his houses to his brother.*

sign up, to enlist, join, etc., by written agreement: *to sign up as a new member.*

[< Old French *signe,* learned borrowing from Latin *sīgnum*]

—**Syn.** *n.* **4. a.** See **mark. 6. Sign, omen** mean an indication of a coming event. **Sign** applies to something which provides objective evidence that the event can reasonably be expected: *Those big, black clouds are signs of a storm.* **Omen** applies to something which, particularly from a religious or superstitious point of view, is regarded as extraordinary and as a promise of something good or bad to come: *He believed his dream was an omen of death.*

sign·a·ble (sī′nə bəl), *adj.* **1.** that can be signed; requiring a signature. **2.** that can sign.

sig·nal (sig′nəl), *n., v.,* **-naled, -nal·ing** or (*especially British*) **-nalled, -nal·ling,** *adj.*—*n.* **1.** a sign, object, light, sound, or the like, giving notice of something: *A red light is a stop signal. A bell is often used as a signal that a train is approaching a crossing. A siren is used as a fire signal.* **2. a.** a sign agreed upon or understood as the occasion of concerted action: *to give the signal to advance.* **b.** an exciting cause; occasion: *This tyrannous act was the signal for insurrection.* **3.** a token; indication: *His wave was a signal of recognition.* **4.** (in card games) a bid or play that gives certain information to one's partner. **5.** *Electronics.* **a.** the waves, impulses, picture components, etc., serving to convey the communication, effect, etc.: *Signals describing the condition of the air are transmitted to the ground station by the radio sonde* (Herz and Tennent). **b.** the communication, effect, etc., thus conveyed. **c.** the wave serving to modulate the carrier wave.

signals, (in football) the numbers called by an offensive back, usually the quarterback, designating a particular play, or by a member of the defensive team to direct the positions of the players: *to call the signals.*

—*v.t.* **1.** to make signals to (a person, ship, etc.); summon, direct, or invite by signal: *He signaled the car to stop by raising his hand.* **2.** to make known by a signal or signals: *A bell signals the end of a school period.* —*v.i.* to give notice, warning, information, etc., by signal.

—*adj.* **1. a.** used as a signal or in signaling: *a signal light, a signal flag.* **b.** designating a place or thing from which signals are given or worked: *a signal box, signal tower.* **c.** of or having to do with signaling: *a signal officer.* **2.** remarkable; striking; notable: *a signal success. The aircraft was a signal invention.*

[alteration of Old French *seignal* < Medieval Latin *signale,* noun < Late Latin *sīgnalis,* adjective < Latin *sīgnum* sign] —**sig′nal·er,** *especially British,* **sig′nal·ler,** *n.*

—**Syn.** *adj.* **2.** conspicuous.

signal box, 1. a small house or tower in which railway signals are worked. **2.** the alarm box of a police or fire-alarm system.

Signal Corps, the branch of the United States Army in charge of communications and communication equipment, members of which are usually attached to units of other branches in tactical operations.

signal fire, a fire used in giving a signal: *Often fire-blackened on top, they may have served for signal fires . . . for the fierce, feuding warrior clans* (Time).

signal flag, a flag used in giving a signal.

sig·nal·ing (sig′nə ling), *n.* the act of using, controlling, or transmitting signals.

sig·nal·ize (sig′nə līz), *v.t.,* **-ized, -iz·ing. 1.** to make stand out; make notable: *The year 1961 was signalized by man's first voyage into space.* **2.** to point out; mention specially; draw attention to: *Need we have waited for Sweden to signalize the discovery?* (New York Times). **3. a.** to make signals to; communicate with by signal. **b.** to announce by a signal or signals.

sig·nal·ling (sig′nə ling), *n. Especially British.* signaling.

sig·nal·ly (sig′nə lē), *adv.* remarkably; strikingly; notably: *a signally imprudent policy.*

sig·nal·man (sig′nəl mən), *n., pl.* **-men. 1.** a man in charge of the signals on a railroad, especially one who sets the signals controlling the flow of traffic over a specified part of the line. **2.** a man who sends or receives messages by signaling in the army or navy.

sig·nal·ment (sig′nəl mənt), *n.* **1.** a description of a person wanted by the police. **2.** a distinguishing mark.

sig·nals (sig′nəlz), *n.pl.* See under **signal,** *n.*

signal service, 1. an organized system of service concerned with communicating by means of signals, especially in the military service. **2.** the organization or body having charge of such a system.

signal tower, a tower from which signals are sent or displayed, as by a semaphore.

sig·na·ry (sig′nər ē), *n., pl.* **-ries.** a list of the characters or signs of an ancient language, such as the hieroglyphic signs of ancient Egypt.

sig·na·tar·y (sig′nə ter′ē), *n., pl.* **-tar·ies,** *adj.* signatory.

sig·nate (sig′nāt), *adj.* **1.** distinguished in some way. **2.** *Zoology.* having spots or marks resembling letters.

sig·na·to·ry (sig′nə tôr′ē, -tōr′-), *n., pl.* **-ries,** *adj.* —*n.* **1.** any one of the signers of a document signed by two or more persons, whether on their own behalf or as authorized agents of a country, company, etc.: *Most of the signatories of the Declaration of Independence were intellectuals* (Harper's). **2.** a country, company, etc., on whose behalf such a person signs. —*adj.* signing: *signatory delegates, signatory nations.*

sig·na·ture (sig′nə chər, -chůr), *n.* **1. a.** a person's name written by himself. **b.** a writing of one's name, especially authenticating a document by doing so. **2.** *Music.*

a set of signs, usually placed at the beginning of a piece immediately after the clef, to show the pitch, key, and time; key signature or time signature. **3.** a signature mark. **4.** *Radio, Television.* a tune, song, or sound effect used to identify a particular program; theme. **5.** *Pharmacy.* the part of a prescription that is to be copied on the label, giving directions for taking the medicine. *Abbr.:* S (no period), Sig. **6.** *Nuclear Physics.* a characteristic track of bubbles or sparks made by a subatomic particle in a bubble or spark chamber, by means of which it may be identified. [< Late Latin *signātūra* marking (of sheep) < Latin *sīgnum* sign] —**Syn. 1. a.** autograph.

signature mark, in printing: **1.** a letter or number placed by the printer at the bottom of the first page of every sheet in a book, to show how it is to be folded and arranged in pages. **2.** a sheet with such a mark, especially when folded.

signature tune, theme song: *But they won't really have made a breakthrough until television programmes use hymns as signature tunes* (Punch).

sign·board (sīn′bôrd′ -bōrd′), *n.* a board having a sign, notice, advertisement, inscription, etc., on it; billboard.

sign·er (sī′nər), *n.* **1.** a person who signs. **2.** a person who writes his name in token of agreement, obligation, etc.: *the signers of the Declaration of Independence.*

sig·net (sig′nit), *n.* **1. a.** a small seal, usually one fixed in a finger ring. **b.** a small seal of this kind in formal or official use, especially as employed to give authentication or authority to a document: *The order was sealed with the king's signet.* **2. a.** an impressed seal or stamp, especially the stamp or impression of a signet. **b.** a mark, sign, or stamp.
—*v.t.* to stamp with a signet.
[< Old French *signet* (diminutive) < *signe* sign < Latin *sīgnum* seal]

signet ring, a ring for the finger set with a signet or seal.

sig·ni·fi·a·ble (sig′nə fī′ə bəl), *adj.* that can be signified.

sig·nif·i·cance (sig nif′ə kəns), *n.* **1.** importance; consequence: *The President wanted to see him on a matter of great significance.* **2.** the meaning of something; what is meant: *Do you understand the significance of H_2SO_4? She did not understand the significance of my nod.* **3.** significant quality; expressiveness: *the significance of her smile.* —**Syn. 1.** moment, weight, gravity. **2.** import, sense.

sig·nif·i·can·cy (sig nif′ə kən sē), *n.* significance.

sig·nif·i·cant (sig nif′ə kənt), *adj.* **1.** full of meaning; important; of consequence: *July 4, 1776, is a significant day for Americans.* **2.** having a meaning; expressive: *Smiles are significant of pleasure.* **3.** having or expressing a hidden meaning: *A significant nod from his friend warned him to stop talking.*
—*n.* something that expresses or conveys a meaning.
[< Latin *sīgnificāns, -antis,* present participle of *sīgnificāre;* see SIGNIFY] —**sig·nif′i·cant·ly,** *adv.*
—**Syn.** *adj.* **1.** momentous. **2.** See **expressive.**

sig·ni·fi·ca·tion (sig′nə fə kā′shən), *n.* **1.** meaning; sense; import: *The signification of a proposition is the sum total of the contextual senses of its parts* (Simeon Potter). **2.** the act or process of signifying: *Signification relies largely upon words and gestures.* —**Syn. 1.** significance.

sig·nif·i·ca·tive (sig nif′ə kā′tiv), *adj.* **1.** serving to signify; having a meaning. **2.** significant or suggestive. —**sig·nif′i·ca′tive·ly,** *adv.* —**sig·nif′i·ca′tive·ness,** *n.*

sig·nif·i·ca·tor (sig nif′ə kā′tər), *n.* **1.** a person or thing that signifies or indicates something. **2.** *Astrology.* the planet that rules a house.

sig·nif·i·ca·to·ry (sig nif′ə kə tôr′ē, -tōr′-), *adj.* serving to signify; significative.

sig·nif·ics (sig nif′iks), *n.* the science or the systematic study of the exact significance of terms in any department of education or learning: *Modern semantics originated in the early 1900's in what an English philosopher . . . called significs* (S. I. Hayakawa). [< *signif*(icance) + *-ics*]

sig·ni·fi·er (sig′nə fī′ər), *n.* a person or thing that signifies.

sig·ni·fy (sig′nə fī), *v.,* **-fied, -fy·ing.** —*v.t.* **1.** to be a sign of; mean: *"Oh!" signifies surprise.* **2.** to make known by signs, words, or actions: *He signified his consent with a nod.*
—*v.i.* to have importance; be of consequence; have significance; matter: *What a fool says does not signify. What does it signify how we dress here . . . where everybody knows us?* (Elizabeth Gaskell).
[< Latin *sīgnificāre* < *sīgnum* sign + *facere* to make] —**Syn.** *v.t.* **1.** represent, denote, imply, suggest. **2.** indicate, intimate.

si·gnior (sēn′yôr), *n.* signor.

sign language, 1. a system of communication in which motions stand for letters, words, ideas, etc. **2.** a system of gestures used by some Indians for communicating between tribes.

sign·less (sīn′ləs), *adj.* **1.** making no sign or manifestation; quiet; passive. **2.** having no algebraical sign, or being essentially positive, like the modulus of an imaginary, a tensor, etc.

sign manual, 1. a person's signature, especially that of a sovereign or magistrate, that authenticates an official document: *Ancient precedent had made the validity of an enormous number of official transactions dependent upon the application of the royal sign manual* (Lytton Strachey). **2.** a distinctively individual sign, stamp, or quality.

sign-off (sīn′ôf′, -of′), *n.* **1.** an act or instance of signing off; a going off the air: *From the moment the carrier went on the air to the sign-off at night, WJZ was on a sustaining basis* (Carl Dreher). **2.** a word or phrase used in signing off: *Miss Reed's television sign-off is "Have a Happy"* (New York Times).

sign of the zodiac, any one of the 12 zodiacal divisions: *The signs of the zodiac no longer agree with the constellations of the same name* (Robert H. Baker).

si·gnor (sē nyôr′), *n. Italian.* **1.** Mr.; sir. **2.** a gentleman.

si·gno·ra (sē nyō′rä), *n., pl.* **-re** (-rā). *Italian.* **1.** Mrs.; Madam. **2.** a lady.

si·gno·re (sē nyō′rā), *n., pl.* **-ri** (-rē). *Italian.* **1.** a gentleman. **2.** Mr.; sir.
➔ **Signore** becomes **signor** when it is used before a person's name.

si·gno·ri·a (sē′nyô rē′ä), *n., pl.* **-ri·as.** a governing body in old Italian republics, especially Venice. [< Italian *signoria*]

si·gno·ri·na (sē′nyô rē′nä), *n., pl.* **-ne** (-nā). *Italian.* **1.** Miss. **2.** a young lady.

si·gno·ri·no (sē′nyô rē′nō), *n., pl.* **-ni** (-nē). *Italian.* **1.** Master (as used to a boy or youth). **2.** a young gentleman.

si·gno·ry (sēn′yər ē), *n., pl.* **-ries. 1.** lordship; domination; rule. **2.** domain. **3.** a governing body, especially that by which Venice was ruled as a republic. [< Old French *signorie,* variant of *seignorie;* see SEIGNIORY; influenced by Italian *signoria*]

sign painter, a person who paints signs for tradesmen, etc.

sign·post (sīn′pōst′), *n.* **1.** a post having a sign, notice, or direction on it; guidepost. **2.** anything that marks, points, guides, or from which bearings may be taken, conclusions drawn, etc. —*v.t. British.* to equip or provide with signposts: *The police and the motoring organizations can be relied on to signpost alternative routes for motorists* (Punch).

sign-up (sīn′up′), *n.* an act or instance of signing up: *The budget calls for an even higher appropriation to keep up the momentum of future Job Corps sign-ups* (Arlen J. Large).

Sig·urd (sig′ėrd), *n.* a hero in the *Volsunga Saga,* identified with the German Siegfried.

si jeu·nesse sa·vait, si vieil·lesse pou·vait (sē zhœ nes′ sȧ ve′ sē vye yes′ pü ve′), *French.* if youth but knew, if age but could.

si·ka (sē′kə), *n.* a small deer native to Japan and China, having a brown coat that is spotted with white in the summer. [< Japanese *shika* deer]

sike (sīk), *n. Scottish.* **1.** a small stream of water; rill; streamlet. **2.** a ditch or channel through which such a stream flows. [Old English *sīc*]

sik·er (sik′ər), *adj. Scottish.* safe; sure; dependable; sicker. [Old English *sicor*]

Sikh (sēk), *n.* a member of a religious sect of northern India, founded in the early 1500's as an offshoot of Hinduism, from which it differs sharply, especially in being monotheistic and in denying caste: *As everyone knows, the Sikhs were some of the finest fighting men of the Indian armies* (Atlantic).
—*adj.* of or having to do with the Sikhs. [< Hindi *sikh* disciple]

Sikh·ism (sē′kiz əm), *n.* the religious system and practices of the Sikhs: *Sikhism is a monotheistic religion incorporating elements of Hinduism, Islam and other religions* (New York Times).

Sik·kim·ese (sik′ə mēz′, -mēs′), *adj., n., pl.* **-ese.** —*adj.* of or having to do with Sikkim, a small state in the Himalayas, or its people.
—*n.* a native or inhabitant of Sikkim: *The Sikkimese wistfully pine for more autonomy under India, which handles their defense and foreign affairs* (Time).

si·lage (sī′lij), *n.* green fodder, now usually chopped stalks of slightly immature corn, for winter feeding of livestock, especially cattle, stored in a silo or other airtight chamber and preserved by the partial fermentation of its carbohydrate components; ensilage. [alteration of *ensilage,* probably influenced by *silo*]

sil·ane (sil′ān), *n.* a compound of silicon and hydrogen. It is a colorless gas that burns spontaneously with a brilliant white flame when exposed to air. *Formula:* SiH_4

Si·las·tic (sə las′tik), *n. Trademark.* a silicone plastic much used in making artificial parts for damaged organs of the body: *Silastic was the material from which Dr. DeBakey made the artificial ventricle* (London Times).

si·le·na·ceous (sī′lə nā′shəs), *adj.* belonging to the pink family of plants; caryophyllaceous. [< New Latin *Silene* (< Latin *Sīlēnus* Silenus) + English *-aceous*]

si·lence (sī′ləns), *n., v.,* **-lenced, -lenc·ing,** *interj.* —*n.* **1.** an absence of all sound or noise; stillness; noiselessness: *The teacher asked for silence. And silence, like a poultice, comes to heal the blows of sound* (Oliver Wendell Holmes). **2.** the state of being or keeping silent; not talking: *to keep or break silence, to listen in silence. Mother passed over our foolish remarks in silence. Silence gives consent* (Oliver Goldsmith). **3. a.** an omission of mention or notice in a narrative. **b.** the omission or neglect to write, communicate, or reply (about something); secrecy: *Silence in matters of public interest is intolerable in a free society.*
—*v.t.* **1.** to stop the speech or noise of; make silent; quiet: *The nurse silenced the baby's crying. To silence envious tongues* (Shakespeare). **2.** to reduce to silence, as by restraint or prohibition; repress. **3.** to put at rest; stop the activity of: *to silence doubts, one's conscience, or scruples.* **4.** to stop (enemy guns, etc.) from firing by destroying or disabling with return fire: *Fighter-bombers ripped rails, knocked out rolling stock and silenced gun positions in attacks deep in North Korea* (New York Times).
—*interj.* be silent!
[< Old French *silence* < Latin *silentium* < *silēre* be silent]
—**Syn.** *n.* **1.** hush, quiet. **2.** reticence, reserve.

silence cloth, a sheet of thick cotton cloth or the like placed under the linen cloth on a dining table.

si·lenc·er (sī′lən sər), *n.* **1.** a device for deadening the sound of a gun, typically one that fits over and extends slightly forward of the barrel. **2.** *British.* a muffler on an internal-combustion engine. **3.** a person or thing that silences.

si·lent (sī′lənt), *adj.* **1.** quiet; still; noiseless: *a silent house, the silent hills.* **2.** not speaking; saying little or nothing: *Pupils must be silent in the study hour. Ulysses . . . was the most eloquent and the most silent of men* (William Broome). **3.** performed, made, suffered, etc., in silence or without speaking; unspoken; unsounded: *a silent prayer, silent agony, silent opposition, a silent movie.* **4.** omitting mention of something, as in a narrative: *An event has happened, upon which it is difficult to speak, and impossible to be silent* (Edmund Burke). **5.** not active or operative; quiescent: *a silent volcano.* **6.** (of a letter in spelling) not representing a sound: *The "b" in "dumb" is silent.*
—*n.* **silents,** motion pictures without recorded and synchronized sounds: *He confined his moviegoing to Charlie Chaplin silents* (Atlantic).
[< Latin *silēns, -entis,* present participle of *silēre* be silent] —**si′lent·ly,** *adv.* —**si′lent·ness,** *n.*

—**Syn. 1.** hushed. **2. Silent, taciturn, reticent** mean saying little or nothing. **Silent** especially means not talkative, characteristically speaking only when necessary or saying very little, but also means saying nothing on some particular occasion for some special reason: *He is a silent, thoughtful boy.* **Taciturn** means not fond of talking, being by nature inclined to be silent and avoid conversation: *He is a taciturn man who dislikes parties.* **Reticent** means not saying all one knows, disposed to keep silent, especially about private affairs: *He is reticent about his early life.*

silent butler, any of various boxlike or bowllike containers with handles and hinged tops, into which crumbs may be brushed, ashtrays emptied, etc.

si·len·ti·ar·y (sī len′shē er′ē), *n., pl.* **-ar·ies. 1.** a person who practices or advocates silence, especially from religious motives. **2.** an official appointed to enforce silence, as in a public assembly. **3.** an officer of the Byzantine court charged with maintaining silence within the imperial palace, and often acting as confidential adviser or agent. [< Late Latin *silentiārius* < Latin *silentium* silence]

si·lent le·ges in·ter ar·ma (sī′lənt lē′jēz in′tər är′mə), *Latin.* the laws are silent in the midst of war.

silent partner, a partner taking no open or active part in the firm's affairs.

silent service, *U.S.* submarines and their crews, as a part of the U.S. Navy or sometimes any navy. [because of their characteristic mode of operation]

silent system, a system of prison discipline that imposes complete silence on the prisoners.

silent vote, 1. the collective vote of those who take no avowed part in a campaign. **2.** the vote represented by the number of persons qualified to vote, but who do not vote.

Si·le·nus (sī lē′nəs), *n. Greek Mythology.* a minor woodland deity, the foster father and companion of Dionysus and leader of the satyrs. He is represented as a short, stout, bald old man.

si·le·nus (sī lē′nəs), *n., pl.* **-ni** (-nī). *Greek Mythology.* **1.** any of various minor deities of the forests, resembling the satyrs. **2.** a satyr. [< Latin *Sīlēnus* < Greek *Seilēnós* Silenus]

si·le·sia (sə lē′shə, -zhə; sī-), *n.* a fine, light, smooth cotton or linen cloth used for lining. [< *Silesia,* where it was first made]

Si·le·sian (sə lē′shən, -zhən; sī-), *adj.* of or having to do with Silesia, a region of central Europe, now included in eastern Germany, Czechoslovakia, and Poland. —*n.* a native or inhabitant of Silesia.

si·lex (sī′leks), *n.* **1.** flint; silica. **2.** a type of heat-resistant glass. [< Latin *silex, -icis* flint]

Si·lex (sī′leks), *n. Trademark.* a coffee maker made of silex glass.

sil·hou·ette (sil′ü et′), *n., v.,* **-et·ted, -et·ting.** —*n.* **1.** an outline portrait, especially in profile, cut out of a black paper or drawn and filled in with some single color. **2.** a dark image, as a shadow in profile, outlined against a lighter background: *the cat's dark silhouette on the wall* (John Greenleaf Whittier). **3.** the contour of a garment: *The slim silhouette gained over the full-skirted silhouette in women's daytime clothes* (World Book Annual).

in silhouette, in outline or profile, especially in black against a white background: *This framing of the trees, which stand out in silhouette against a bright blue sky* (Harper's).

—*v.t.* to show in outline: *The mountain was silhouetted against the sky.*

[< French *silhouette* < Étienne de *Silhouette,* 1709-67, French minister of finance in 1759]

Silhouette (def. 1)

sil·hou·et·tist (sil′ü et′ist), *n.* a maker of silhouettes.

sil·i·ca (sil′ə kə), *n.* a common mineral, silicon dioxide, a hard, white or colorless substance, that in the form of quartz enters into the composition of many rocks, and is contained in sponges and certain plants. Flint, sand, opal, and chalcedony are common silicas. It also occurs as opal. *Formula:* SiO_2 [< New Latin *silica* < Latin *silex, -icis* flint]

silica gel, a type of colloidal silica, resembling coarse sand, used as an adsorbent in air conditioners, petroleum refining, etc.

silica glass, a kind of glass made of pure silica which can withstand large and rapid temperature changes and is highly transparent to ultraviolet and infrared rays as well as to light: *Silica glass . . . is especially valuable for use in sanatoria windows and as lenses for ultraviolet lamps* (W. Norton Jones).

sil·i·cate (sil′ə kit, -kāt), *n.* a compound containing silicon with oxygen and a metal; a salt of silicic acid. Silicates constitute the greater number of the minerals that compose the crust of the earth. Mica, garnet, talc, asbestos, and feldspar are silicates.

sil·i·cat·ed (sil′ə kā′təd), *adj.* coated, mixed, combined, or impregnated with silica: *silicated soap.*

sil·i·ca·ti·za·tion (sil′ə kə tə zā′shən), *n.* the process of combining with silica so as to change to a silicate.

si·li·ceous or **si·li·cious** (sə lish′əs), *adj.* **1.** containing or consisting of silica; resembling silica: *Paleolithic stone tools were made by chipping or flaking hard siliceous (glasslike) materials like flint, quartzite, and obsidian* (Beals and Hoijer). **2.** growing best or solely in soil containing much silica. [< Latin *siliceus* (with English *-ous*) of flint < *silex, -icis* flint]

si·lic·ic (sə lis′ik), *adj.* **1.** containing silicon or silica: *The more volatile or acidic or silicic constituents of the fluid rock beneath the surface may have concentrated in the original uplifts* (Scientific American). **2.** of or obtained from silicon or silica.

silicic acid, any of various weak acids obtained from silicon. The formula of a common kind is H_4SiO_4

sil·i·cide (sil′ə sīd, -sid), *n.* a compound of silicon and another element or radical.

sil·i·cif·er·ous (sil′ə sif′ər əs), *adj.* yielding or containing silica; united with silica. [< Latin *silex, -icis* flint + English *-ferous*]

si·lic·i·fi·ca·tion (sə lis′ə fə kā′shən), *n.* conversion into silica.

si·lic·i·fied wood (sə lis′ə fīd), wood so impregnated or replaced by silica that it has become quartz or opal.

si·lic·i·fy (sə lis′ə fī), *v.,* **-fied, -fy·ing.** —*v.t.* to convert into or impregnate with silica: *The walnut kernels are . . . a golden brown in color and perfectly silicified* (Scientific American). —*v.i.* to become siliceous.

si·li·ci·um (sə lish′ē əm, -lis′-), *n.* silicon. [< New Latin *silicium* < Latin *silex, -icis* flint]

sil·i·cle (sil′ə kəl), *n. Botany.* a short, broad silique, as in shepherd's-purse. [probably < French *silicule,* learned borrowing from Latin *silicula* (diminutive) < *siliqua* seed pod]

sil·i·con (sil′ə kən), *n.* a nonmetallic chemical element found only in combination, chiefly with oxygen in silica. Next to oxygen, it is the most abundant element in nature and occurs in amorphous and crystalline forms. The crystalline form is much used in the manufacture of steel as a deoxidizing and hardening agent. *Silicon is present in the earth's crust to the extent of about 25.8 per cent, but, because of its activity, it is never found in the free state* (W.N. Jones). *Symbol:* Si; *at.wt.:* (C^{12}) 28.086 or (O^{16}) 28.09; *at.no.:* 14; *valence:* 4. [< *silica*]

silicon carbide, a substance that is almost as hard as diamond, used in grinding metals, beveling glass, in polishing powders and other abrasives, and as a semiconductor in transistors: *Better electronic tubes that glow blue when working, instead of red, may result from the discovery that silicon carbide is a good source of electrons* (Science News Letter). *Formula:* SiC

silicon dioxide, silica.

sil·i·cone (sil′ə kōn), *n.* any of a large group of organic compounds formed by the replacement of carbon with silicon, and obtained as oils, greases, plastics, and resins. Noted for their stability and their ability to resist extremes of heat and cold, they are used for lubricants, varnishes, and insulators. *Silicones are fluids and resins that keep clothes and shoes and brick walls dry in the rain* (Scientific American). [< *silic*(on) + *-one*]

sil·i·con·ize (sil′ə kə nīz), *v.t., v.i.,* **-ized, -iz·ing.** to combine, or cause to combine, with silicon.

sil·i·co·sis (sil′ə kō′sis), *n.* a disease of the lungs caused by continually breathing air filled with dust from quartz or silicates, formerly common among certain types of workers, as stonecutters. [< *silic*(on) + *-osis*]

sil·i·cot·ic (sil′ə kot′ik), *adj.* having to do with, causing, or suffering from silicosis. —*n.* a person having silicosis.

si·lic·u·la (sə lik′yə lə), *n., pl.* **-lae** (-lē). silicle. [< Latin *silicula,* a little husk or pod; see SILICLE]

si·lic·u·lar (sə lik′yə lər), *adj. Botany.* having the shape or appearance of a silicula or silicle.

sil·i·cule (sil′ə kyül), *n. Botany.* silicle.

si·lic·u·lose (sə lik′yə lōs), *adj. Botany.* **1.** bearing silicles. **2.** having the shape or appearance of a silicle.

si·lic·u·lous (sə lik′yə ləs), *adj. Botany.* siliculose.

sil·i·qua (sil′ə kwə), *n., pl.* **-quae** (-kwē). *Botany.* silique.

si·lique (sə lēk′, sil′ik), *n. Botany.* the characteristic podlike fruit of plants of the mustard family, a long, narrow, two-valved capsule which splits open from the bottom upward, exposing the seeds attached to two placentae. [< Latin *siliqua* seed pod]

si·liq·ui·form (sə lēk′wə fôrm), *adj.* having the form of a silique. [< Latin *siliqua* a husk, pod + *forma* form]

sil·i·quose (sil′ə kwōs), *adj. Botany.* **1.** bearing siliques. **2.** having the form of a silique.

sil·i·quous (sil′ə kwəs), *adj. Botany.* siliquose.

silk (silk), *n.* **1.** the lustrous, fine, strong fiber produced by the larvae of certain moths, spiders, etc., especially that obtained from the cocoon spun by the silkworm: *Raw silk that comes from Hong Kong . . . is much heavier* (New Yorker). **2.** a thread made of this. **3.** a cloth made of silk fiber: *Japanese silks, imported silks.* **4.** a garment of such material: *The little lady . . . had on . . . rather an old black silk* (Elizabeth Gaskell). **5.** any artificial thread or cloth resembling silk. **6.** *British.* the gown of silk which a king's or queen's counsel is entitled to wear. **7.** anything like silk: *corn silk.*

hit the silk, *Slang.* to parachute from a plane: *The rookie pilots soon learned how to hit the silk.*

silks, the blouses and caps worn by jockeys and harness race drivers and the coverings sometimes draped over their horses which, by their coloring, identify the owner of these horses; colors: *Citation raced under the silks of Calumet Farm.*

take silk, *British.* to become a king's or queen's counsel: *After he . . . had taken silk . . . he became at least as redoubtable a leader as his father had been* (London Times).

—*adj.* **1.** of, made of, or having to do with silk; silken: *May sewed the silk dress with silk thread. Conventional balloons of light rubberised silk fabric can take payloads of half a ton or more* (New Scientist). **2.** silky.

—*v.i. U.S.* (of corn) to produce silk.

[Old English *sioloc,* or *seolc* < Latin *sēricus* < *Sēres* the Chinese < Greek *Sêres*] —**silk′like′,** *adj.*

silk·a·line or **silk·a·lene** (sil′kə lēn′), *n.* a soft, thin, cotton fabric resembling silk. [American English < *silk*]

silk cotton, the silky, elastic down or fiber covering the seeds of certain tropical trees of the bombax family, used for packing, and for stuffing pillows and cushions.

silk-cot·ton family (silk′kot′ən), bombax family, a group of dicotyledonous tropical trees.

silk-cotton tree, any tree yielding silk cotton, especially the ceiba or kapok tree, of tropical America, the East Indies, and Africa, that bears large pods from which kapok or silk cotton is obtained.

silk·en (sil′kən), *adj.* **1. a.** made of silk: *a silken dress. The king wore silken robes.* **b.** of or having to do with silk stuffs or goods. **2.** like silk; soft, smooth, and glossy: *silken hair.* **3. a.** resembling silk in being soft and smooth; silky: *a silken manner or voice.* **b.** balmy; gentle: *a silken climate.* **4.** wearing silk clothes. **5.** elegant; luxurious.

—*v.t.* to make smooth and glossy like silk; give a silky luster to: [*A cream*] *to soften and silken your skin while you sleep* (New Yorker). —**silk′en·ly,** *adv.*

silk·er (sil′kər), *n.* **1.** a person or thing that

embroiders (the back of a glove, etc.) in silk. **2.** a person or thing that extracts silk from the cut kernels of corn.
silk fowl, a variety of white, domestic hen slightly larger than the bantam, having a silky plumage, dark, heavily feathered legs, a crested head, and purple face, comb, and wattles. Also, **silky.**
silk gland, any gland which secretes the substance of silk, as in the silkworm or silk spider; sericterium.
silk grower, a person who produces silk cocoons by raising silkworms, and the mulberries or other plants on which they feed.
silk hat, 1. a top hat. **2.** an opera hat.
silk·i·ly (sil′kə lē), *adv.* in a silky manner: *Each garment whispered silkily to the floor* (Harper's).
silk·i·ness (sil′kē nis), *n.* the state or quality of being silky.
silk·man (silk′man′), *n., pl.* **-men. 1.** a dealer in silk fabrics. **2.** a person employed in the manufacture of silks. **3.** the manufacturer or director of a silk mill.
silk moth, a bombycid moth whose larva is a silkworm.
silk·o·line (sil′kə lēn′), *n.* silkaline.
Silk Road, an ancient trade route between the Middle East and China. [because *silk* was a chief trade item]
silks (silks), *n.pl.* See under **silk,** *n.*
silk-screen (silk′skrēn′), *adj.* of or having to do with the process of printing colors on a variety of surfaces, especially cloth, paper, and linoleum, by means of a stencil put on silk or other fine cloth stretched over a frame: *The studio also contains equipment for making silk-screen or serigraphic prints* (Wall Street Journal).
—*n.* this process.
—*v.t.* to print, apply, etc., by the silk-screen process: *This Japanese-American [Norio Azuma] painstakingly silk-screens oil on canvas* (Time).
silk spider, any spider which spins a kind of silk, especially an orb weaver of the southern United States, which spins copiously, and is also notable for the unusual disparity of the sexes in size.
silk-stock·ing (silk′stok′ing), *adj.* **1.** made up of or populated by people of considerable means and social standing (who alone, in an earlier day, could afford to wear silk stockings): *a silk-stocking clientele, a silk-stocking district.* **2.** elegant; aristocratic: *a silk-stocking manner.*
—*n.* **1.** a well-to-do, elegant man or woman. **2.** *U.S.* a member of the Federalist or (later) Whig parties (to which, in the early 1800's, most well-to-do people belonged).
silk thrower, a person who produces or manufactures thrown silk, or organzine.
silk·weed (silk′wēd′), *n. U.S.* milkweed.
silk·worm (silk′wėrm′), *n.* any caterpillar that spins a cocoon made of silk, especially the larva of a domesticated moth, originally of China, that feeds on mulberry leaves: *Every silkworm that is to become a moth must first spin itself a cocoon* (Scientific American). [Old English *seolcwyrm*]

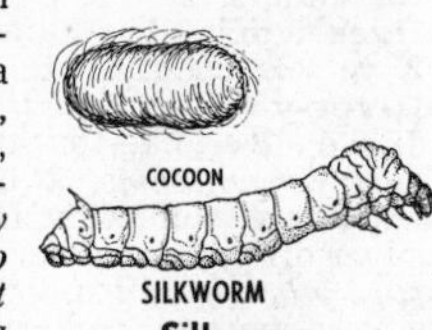

Silkworm (about 2 in. long)

silkworm moth, any of a family of large moths whose larvae spin cocoons of silk, as the luna moth and Polyphemus moth; saturniid.
silk·y (sil′kē), *adj.,* **silk·i·er, silk·i·est,** *n., pl.* **silk·ies.** —*adj.* **1.** like silk; smooth, soft, and glossy; silken: *A kitten has silky fur. At this stage the curd feels rather like rubber, though cheese makers say that when ready for milling . . . it should be silky in texture* (J.A. Barnett). **2.** made or consisting of silk. **3.** *Botany.* covered with fine, soft, closely set hairs having a silklike gloss, as a leaf.
—*n.* any of a breed of crested chickens with white, webless feathers of a peculiarly fluffy, silky texture; silk fowl. The silky weighs two to three pounds and has a purplish face and comb, small wings, and short tail.
silky oak, any of several Australian trees whose wood is used for ornament.
silky terrier, any of a breed of small terrier with long, silky, blue and tan hair, erect ears, and docked tail, weighing from 8 to 10 pounds.
sill (sil), *n.* **1.** a piece of wood, stone, metal, etc., across the bottom of a door, window, or house frame: *a cat sunning itself on a window sill.* See **lintel** for picture. **2.** a large beam of wood, metal, etc., or an equivalent structure of masonry, at or near the level of the ground, on which an outside wall of a building rests. **3.** any of various beams, blocks, or combinations of these serving a purpose similar to this, as at the base of an arch of a bridge. **4.** *Geology.* an intrusive sheet of igneous rock of approximately horizontal attitude. [Old English *syll*]
sil·la·bub (sil′ə bub), *n.* **1.** a dessert made of a mixture of whole milk or cream with wine or cider, usually slightly sweetened, and often including eggs, nutmeg, cinnamon, etc.: *Sillabub—at the Gore, anyway—consists of raspberries cooked in canary wine, whipped into cream and whites of eggs, and flavored with lemon peel, rosemary, honey, and nutmeg* (New Yorker). **2.** something unsubstantial and frothy, especially floridly vapid discourse or writing. Also, **syllabub.** [origin unknown]
sill cock, a faucet or valve for use at the sill of a house or building to allow a hose connection.
sill course, *Architecture.* a continual horizontal course closely connected with the sills of a row of windows, either immediately below the sills, or more properly with its lower bed on a line with the lower beds of the sills so that the sills form part of it.
sil·ler (sil′ər), *n., adj., v. Scottish.* silver.
sil·li·ly (sil′ə lē), *adv.* in a silly manner; foolishly.
sil·li·man·ite (sil′ə mə nit), *n.* a mineral consisting of a silicate of aluminum, and occurring in long, slender, crystalline needles or compact, fibrous masses; fibrolite. It is valuable commercially as a refractory or fire-resisting material. *Formula:* Al_2SiO_5 [< Benjamin *Silliman,* 1779-1864, an American scientist + *-ite*[1]]
sil·li·ness (sil′ē nis), *n.* **1.** the quality of being silly; senselessness. **2.** any instance of this; silly act, thing, etc.
sil·ly (sil′ē), *adj.,* **-li·er, -li·est,** *n., pl.* **-lies.** —*adj.* **1.** without sense or reason: *Mamma says that she [Jane Austen] was then the prettiest, silliest, most affected . . . butterfly she ever remembers* (Mary R. Mitford). **2.** of or characteristic of a silly person: *silly behavior, a silly remark.* **3.** *Scottish.* **a.** harmless; simple; innocent: *His silly sheep, what wonder if they stray?* (William Cowper). **b.** feeble-minded; imbecile: *William IV of England was called Silly Billy.* **c.** weak, feeble, or frail; sickly; ailing: *She was but of a silly constitution* (John Galt). **4.** *Informal.* stunned; dazed: *I was knocked silly by the news. He was knocked silly by the collision.* **5.** *Obsolete.* unsophisticated; rustic.
—*n.* a silly or foolish person.
[Middle English *syly* defenseless, weak, pitiable; variant of earlier *sely* seely, Old English *sǣlig* happy < *sǣl* happiness]
—**Syn.** *adj.* **1.** senseless, nonsensical, ridiculous. See **foolish.**
silly billy, *Informal.* a foolish person: *. . . pitifully unenlightened silly billies* (Punch).
silly season, *Informal.* a season when there is little news and the editors of newspapers are supposed to be obliged to use any material, however foolish, that comes to hand.
si·lo (sī′lō), *n., pl.* **-los,** *v.,* **-loed, -lo·ing.** —*n.* **1.** an airtight structure, usually a cylindrical tower of wood, metal, etc., but sometimes a pit, in which green fodder for livestock is stored. **2.** a shelter built underground with facilities for holding or launching a guided missile. —*v.t.* to put into or store in a silo; turn into silage; ensile. [< Spanish *silo* < Latin *sīrus* < Greek *sirós* grain cellar]

Silo (def. 1)

sil·ox·ane (sil ok′sān), *n.* any hydride of silicon in which silicon atoms alternate with atoms of oxygen. Siloxanes are very water-repellent and cannot be dissolved except by strong acids and alkalis. *Feeding a suspension in water of several kinds of siloxanes, put a tough coating over eroded areas of the stomach and duodenal tract* (Science News Letter). [< *sil*(icon) + *ox*(ygen) + *-ane*]
sil·phid (sil′fid), *n.* any of a family of clavicorn beetles that live mainly on carrion, as the sexton beetle. —*adj.* belonging to or having to do with this family. [< New Latin *Silphidae* the family name < Greek *sílphē* cockroach]
silt (silt), *n.* **1. a.** very fine particles of earth, sand, clay, etc., carried by moving water: *a river brown with silt. Silt is made up of tiny particles which are anywhere from .01 to .1 mm. (.0004 to .004 inches) in diameter.* **b.** such particles deposited as sediment: *The harbor is being choked with silt.* **2.** a deposit of sediment occurring as a stratum in soil.
—*v.t., v.i.* to fill or choke up with or as with silt: *At the same time, the harbor of Palaeopolis was silting up, so that its merchant ships could no longer bring in grain* (Harper's).
[probably < earlier Flemish *sulte* salt marsh, perhaps < a Scandinavian word. Related to SALT.]
sil·ta·tion (sil tā′shən), *n.* the formation or deposition of silt.
silt·stone (silt′stōn′), *n.* a fine-grained rock formed of consolidated silt: *The whole trench is conveniently capped by a layer of impermeable siltstone a few hundred feet below the present surface* (Time).
silt·y (sil′tē), *adj.* of, like, or full of silt: *A sediment composed dominantly of sand-sized particles but with a considerable amount of silt can be referred to as . . silty sand* (Robert M. Garrels).
si·lun·dum (si lun′dəm), *n.* a very hard, insoluble substance consisting partly or entirely of silicon carbide, used as an abrasive, for electrical resistors, etc. [< *sil*(icon) + (carbor)*undum*]
Sil·u·res (sil′yə rēz), *n.pl.* an ancient British tribe in southeastern Wales at the time of the Roman conquest. [< Latin *Silures*]
Si·lu·ri·an (sə lůr′ē ən, sī-), *n.* **1.** the third geological period of the Paleozoic era, after the Ordovician and before the Devonian, characterized by the development of early land invertebrate animals and land plants. The Silurian formerly included what is now Ordovician and what is now Silurian. *In Europe . . . the close of the Silurian witnessed the rise of the majestic Caledonian Mountains, which ranged northeastward across the British Isles and Scandinavia* (Carl O. Dunbar). **2.** the rock strata formed in this period.
—*adj.* **1.** of or having to do with this period or its rocks: *The total vegetation of the earth by the end of the Silurian period . . . appears to have been mostly algae floating in water and growing on wet soil* (Fred W. Emerson). **2.** of or belonging to the ancient Silures, or to the district inhabited by them.
[< *Silures* + *-ian* (because such rock deposits were found on the site where the Silures formerly lived)]
si·lu·rid (sə lůr′id, sī-), *adj.* of or belonging to a family of fresh-water catfish with long anal fins, found in Europe, Africa, and parts of Asia. —*n.* a silurid fish. [< New Latin *Siluridae* the family name < *Silurus* the typical genus < Latin *silūrus* < Greek *sílouros* a kind of river fish]
si·lu·roid (sə lůr′oid), *adj.* of the silurid fishes; catfishlike. —*n.* a siluroid fish.
sil·va (sil′və), *n.* **1.** the trees of a particular region or period collectively. **2.** a treatise on forest trees, or a descriptive list or catalogue of trees. Also, **sylva.** [< Latin *silva,* or *sylva* forest]
sil·van (sil′vən), *adj., n.* sylvan.
Sil·va·nus (sil vā′nəs), *n.* an ancient Italian god of woods, fields, and herds. [< Latin *Sylvānus* (originally) sylvan]
sil·ver (sil′vər), *n.* **1.** a precious, metallic, chemical element occurring both native and in combination, characterized in a pure state by its lustrous white color, great malleability and ductility, and liability to tarnish when exposed to sulfur. Silver is superior to any other substance in its ability to conduct heat and electricity. It is used for coins, jewelry, and spoons and other table utensils. *Symbol:* Ag; *at.wt.:* (C^{12}) 107.870 or (O^{16}) 107.873; *at.no.:* 47; *valence:* 1. **2.** this metal considered as a valuable possession or commodity. **3.** coins made from this or any other metal of a similar color, as cupronickel; money: *a pocket full of silver.* **4.** silverware; utensils or dishes made of silver or plated with it: *table silver.* **5.** something like

silver, as in luster or color. **6.** the color of silver; a shining whitish gray. **7.** *Photography.* a salt of silver, especially silver nitrate. —*adj.* **1.** made, consisting of, or plated with silver: *a silver spoon.* **2.** of, having to do with, connected with, or characteristic of silver: *silver ore.* **3.** producing, yielding, or selling silver: *a silver mine.* **4.** resembling silver, as in luster or color; silvery: *silver hair, a silver slipper. There's a silver lining to every cloud* (William S. Gilbert). **5.** having a clear, ringing sound like that of silver dropped on a hard surface; melodious: *But, there, the silver answer rang* (Elizabeth Barrett Browning). **6.** eloquent; persuasive: *a silver tongue.* **7.** of or advocating the use of silver as a standard of money: *the silver cabal.* **8.** having to do with the 25th anniversary of an event: *The children gave a party to celebrate their parents' silver wedding anniversary.*
—*v.t.* **1.** to cover or plate with silver: *A completely enclosed evacuated cylinder which was silvered on its inner surfaces to give the highest possible conductivity* (W. C. Vaughn). **2.** to coat at the back with a silvery amalgam: *to silver glass to make a mirror.* **3.** to give a silvery color to: *A waxing moon silvered the green hillside fields and sand dunes* (Time). —*v.i.* to take on a silvery hue or luster: *The old lady's hair had silvered.*
[Old English *siolfor*] —**sil′ver·er,** *n.* —**sil′ver·like′,** *adj.*

Silver Age, 1. *Greek and Roman Mythology.* the second age of the world, in which the state of mankind was inferior to that of the earlier Golden Age of noble grandeur and ideal innocence, but superior to that of any age that followed. **2.** the period in the literature of ancient Rome from the death of Augustus in 14 A.D. to about 180 A.D., in which writing is traditionally considered to have slipped from the peak of grandeur and grace of the immediately preceding Augustan age; age of Martial, Pliny, Juvenal, and Tacitus. [translation of Latin *argentea prōlēs* (used by Ovid), (literally) silver offspring]

silver age, any period following and inferior to that considered to have been the greatest or most brilliant in achievement.

silver bath, 1. *Photography.* a solution of silver nitrate, used especially for sensitizing collodion plates or paper for printing. **2.** a dish or tray for the use of such a solution.

silver beater, a person who prepares silver foil by beating.

silver bell, or **sil·ver-bell tree** (sil′vər-bel′), a small North American tree, related to the storax, often grown for its white, bell-shaped flowers.

sil·ver·ber·ry (sil′vər ber′ē), *n., pl.* **-ries.** a North American shrub related to the oleaster, having silvery leaves, flowers, and berries.

silver birch, 1. paper birch. **2.** yellow birch: *Silver birch has yellowish or dark-gray bark when fully grown* (T. Ewald Maki). **3.** a birch of northern Europe and of Asia having white bark and often used for ornamental purposes: . . . *a silver birch . . . distinguished by its long, pendulous branchlets* (Sunday Times).

silver bromide, a compound noted for its sensitivity to light, formed by the action of a bromide on an aqueous solution of silver nitrate. It is much used in photography. *Formula:* AgBr

silver certificate, paper money issued by the United States Government, bearing a promise to pay for its face value in silver coin on demand: *The silver dollars . . . were inconvenient to carry, and so the government began issuing paper money called silver certificates* (World Book Encyclopedia).

silver chloride, a compound noted for its sensitivity to light, used especially in photography for sensitizing paper: *The plate was prepared by the all but impossible process of precipitating silver chloride from solution . . . and syphoning off the liquid* (Science News Letter). *Formula:* AgCl

silver crescent, an American nymphalid butterfly, dark brown in color, with a band of orange across both wings, the undersides being marked with silvery lunules. It is of wide distribution, and its larvae feed on the foliage of a variety of composite plants.

silver doctor, an artificial fly with brown, green, blue, red, and yellow wings, a body of silver-colored tinsel, a yellow, red, blue, and green tail, and blue hackle, used especially in trout and salmon fishing.

silver dollar, a silver coin of the United States and Canada worth one dollar.

sil·ver·eye (sil′vər ī′), *n.* a bird whose leading common color mark is a white eye ring; white-eye.

silver fern, one of numerous ferns in which the under surface of the frond is covered with a white or silvery powder.

sil·ver·fish (sil′vər fish′), *n., pl.* **-fish·es** or (*collectively*) **-fish. 1. a.** a silvery or white variety of goldfish. **b.** any of certain other silvery fishes, as the tarpon and silversides. **2.** any of a group of small, wingless insects with silvery scales on the body and three bristles extending from the tip of the abdomen. It is injurious to books, wallpaper, certain fabrics, etc. *Silverfish are among the most primitive insects, according to the classification schemes of naturalists* (Science News Letter).

silver foil, silver leaf.

silver fox, 1. any red fox in the color phase during which its fur is composed of black hairs with white bands near the tips. **2.** this fur.

sil·ver-gilt (sil′vər gilt′), *n.* **1.** silver covered with gilding. **2.** gilded articles of silver.

silver glance, a variety of silver ore; argentite.

sil·ver-haired (sil′vər hãrd′), *adj.* having white or lustrous gray hair: *A tall, handsome, silver-haired man of sixty-five* (New Yorker).

silver hake, an edible, gray and silver hake common off the coast of New England.

sil·ver·i·ness (sil′vər ē nis), *n.* the state or character of being silvery.

sil·ver·ing (sil′vər ing), *n.* **1.** the act of a person or thing that silvers. **2.** silver plating.

silver iodide, a yellow compound of silver and iodine used in treating venereal diseases, in making photographic film, and in cloud seeding: *The scientists will heavily seed supercooled clouds, composed of water droplets below freezing temperature, with silver iodide to cause the droplets to change to ice* (Science News Letter). *Formula:* AgI

sil·ver·ite (sil′və rīt), *n.* **1.** a person who favors the free use of silver as money equally with gold; bimetallist. **2.** *U.S.* a person who advocates the free coinage of silver, particularly one who desires free coinage at the existing ratio with gold.

sil·ver·ize (sil′və rīz), *v.t.,* **-ized, -iz·ing.** to silver.

silver lace, a silver braid used for trimming uniforms, and the like.

silver leaf, silver beaten into very thin sheets.

sil·ver·ling (sil′vər ling), *n.* **1.** an old standard of value in silver. **2.** a piece of silver money: *There were a thousand vines at a thousand silverlings* (Isaiah 7:23).

silver lining, the brighter side of a sad or unfortunate situation: . . . *Dr. Francis E. Townsend whose old-age pension "Plan" once promised a silver lining beyond the Depression's storm clouds* (Time).

sil·ver·ly (sil′vər lē), *adv. Poetic.* with a silvery appearance or sound: *the dinn'd air vibrating silverly* (Keats).

sil·vern (sil′vərn), *adj. Archaic.* made of, consisting of, or resembling silver.

silver nitrate, a colorless, crystalline, poisonous salt that becomes gray or black in the presence of light and organic matter, obtained by treating silver with nitric acid. It is used as a reagent in photography, in dyeing, to silver mirrors, as an antiseptic, etc. *In contact with organic matter silver nitrate is reduced to metallic silver* (Monroe M. Offner). *Formula:* $AgNO_3$

silver owl, the barn owl.

silver paper, 1. a fine, white tissue paper. **2.** silver foil. **3.** *Especially British.* tin foil for wrapping candy, etc.

sil·ver-plat·ed (sil′vər plā′tid), *adj.* covered with a thin layer of silver or similar material: *On top of the closet sat a silver-plated sailing ship under full silver-plated sail and in its round side was an electric clock* (Harper's).

sil·ver·point (sil′vər point′), *n.* **1.** the process of making a drawing with a point or pencil of silver on specially prepared paper: *Fifty drawings in silverpoint, ink, tempera, and wax encaustic by a facile, delicate draftsman* (Time). **2.** a drawing made in this way.

silver print, a photographic positive made on paper sensitized by a silver salt.

silver screen, 1. a screen with a silver-like coating on which motion pictures are shown. **2.** motion pictures: *Yet if he orated on the silver screen he would be faintly ridiculous* (Maclean's).

sil·ver·side (sil′vər sīd′), *n.* **1.** silversides. **2.** *British.* the upper and choicer part of a round of beef: *I had kippers, finnan haddock, roast beef and boiled silverside* (Manchester Guardian).

sil·ver·sides (sil′vər sīdz′), *n., pl.* **-sides. 1.** any of a family of small, chiefly marine fishes having a silvery stripe along the body, as the grunion. **2.** any of certain fresh-water minnows related to the carps.

sil·ver·smith (sil′vər smith′), *n.* a person who makes articles of silver.

sil·ver·smith·ing (sil′vər smith′ing), *n.* the practice or business of a silversmith.

silver standard, a monetary system having a specific quantity of silver as the unit of money value, and in which all types of currency are redeemable with silver coin or bullion.

Silver Star, a decoration awarded by the United States for gallantry in action against an armed enemy, consisting of a five-pointed bronze star set at the center with a silver star, conferring a greater degree of honor than the Bronze Star but less than the Distinguished Service Cross: *[Vandenberg] won the DFC and Silver Star for combat missions over the Mediterranean* (Time).

Silver State, a nickname for Nevada.

silver stick, *British.* an officer of the royal palace, so called from the silvered wand which is his badge.

silver thaw, the phenomenon of rain freezing as it falls and forming a glassy coating on the ground, trees, etc.

sil·ver-tongued (sil′vər tungd′), *adj.* eloquent.

sil·ver·tree (sil′vər trē′), *n.* a small, evergreen tree with silvery, lance-shaped leaves, native to South Africa.

sil·ver·ware (sil′vər wãr′), *n.* **1. a.** eating utensils, serving dishes, etc., made of or plated with silver; silver tableware. **b.** metal eating utensils as distinguished from plates, glasses, etc. **2.** articles made of silver; ware of a silversmith.

silver wedding, the 25th anniversary of a wedding.

sil·ver·weed (sil′vər wēd′), *n.* **1.** an herb of the rose family, a variety of cinquefoil whose pinnate leaves are silvery on the underside. **2.** a closely related short-stemmed plant, naturalized in North America from Europe, whose palmate leaves are silvery on the underside.

silver work, 1. ornamental work in silver **2.** vessels, utensils, etc., made of silver.

sil·ver·y (sil′vər ē), *adj.,* **-ver·i·er, -ver·i·est. 1.** like silver; like that of silver: *silvery hair, silvery moonbeams.* **2.** having a clear, gentle resonance, somewhat like that of pieces of silver dropped on a hard surface; melodious: *silvery laughter, a silvery voice.* **3.** producing silver; containing silver.

sil·vics (sil′viks), *n.* **1.** the science dealing with the life of trees in a forest. **2.** the characteristics of a forest tree. Also, **sylvics.** [< Latin *silva* forest + English *-ics*]

sil·vi·cul·tur·al (sil′və kul′chər əl), *adj.* of or having to do with silviculture: *It seems more appropriate to consider silvicultural practices as preventive rather than control measures* (J.J. DeGryse). Also, **sylvicultural.**

sil·vi·cul·ture (sil′və kul′chər), *n.* the cultivation of woods or forests; the growing and tending of trees as a branch of forestry: *Silviculture is . . . the systematic growing of timber on a crop basis* (White and Renner). Also, **sylviculture.** [< Latin *silva* forest + *cultūra* culture]

sil·vi·cul·tur·ist (sil′və kul′chər ist), *n.* a person skilled in silviculture. Also, **sylviculturist.**

s'il vous plaît (sēl vü ple′), *French.* if you please.

si·ma (sī′mə), *n.* a basaltic rock rich in silica and magnesium. Sima is the chief constituent of the ocean floors. [< *si*(lica) + *ma*(gnesium)]

si·mar (si mär′), *n.* a loose, light robe with

a train formerly worn by women. Also, **cymar.** [< French *simarre* < Italian *zimarra,* variant of *cimarra.* Doublet of CHIMERE, CYMAR.]

sim·a·rou·ba (sim′ə rü′bə), *n.* **1.** any of a group of tropical American trees, having pinnate leaves and a plumlike fruit. **2.** the bark of the root, used as a tonic or astringent. [< French *simarouba* < Carib *simaruba*]

sim·a·rou·ba·ceous (sim′ə rü bā′shəs), *adj.* belonging to the quassia family of trees and shrubs, typified by the simarouba.

si·mat·ic (sī′mat′ik), *adj.* **1.** composed largely of silica and magnesium. **2.** consisting of sima: *a simatic ocean basin.*

sim·bil (sim′bəl), *n.* an African stork having a greenish and brownish-purple plumage with white under parts. [< a native name]

Sim·chas Torah (sim ʜäth′, sim′ʜäs), Simhath Torah.

Sim·e·on (sim′ē ən), *n.* **1.** in the Old Testament: **a.** the second son of Jacob and Leah. Genesis 29:33. **b.** one of the twelve tribes of Israel, that claimed him as ancestor. Numbers 26:12-14. **2.** (in the New Testament) a pious old man who saw the child Jesus in the temple at Jerusalem and recognized him as the promised Messiah. Luke 2:25-35.

Sim·hath To·rah (sim ʜäth′ tō rä′; sim′ʜäs tō′rä), a Jewish holiday (the Rejoicing in the Law) on the ninth and last day of the festival of Sukkoth, celebrating the end of the complete annual reading of the Pentateuch and the start of a new cycle with the beginning of Genesis.

sim·i·an (sim′ē ən), *adj.* **1.** like or characteristic of an ape or monkey; apelike: *The teeth were not forward-jutting . . . and had no simian gap* (Time). **2.** having to do with an ape or monkey. —*n.* an ape or monkey (often applied to an anthropoid ape). [< Latin *sīmia, sīmius* ape (< *sīmus* snubnosed < Greek *sīmós*) + English *-an*]

simian shelf, a bony shelf along the inside of the lower jawbone of anthropoid apes: *The reduction of the jaw, especially the elimination of the "simian shelf," gave the tongue freer movement and thus helped create the potentiality for speech* (Julian H. Steward).

sim·i·lar (sim′ə lər), *adj.* **1.** much the same; alike; like: *A creek and a brook are similar.* **2.** *Geometry.* (of figures) having the same shape but varying in size or position or both; having corresponding angles equal and corresponding sides proportional: *similar triangles.* [< French *similaire* < Latin *similis* like] —**sim′i·lar·ly,** *adv.*

sim·i·lar·i·ty (sim′ə lar′ə tē), *n., pl.* **-ties.** a being similar; likeness; resemblance: *The parallel does not end there, for both pieces had points of similarity* (New York Times). **similarities,** points of resemblance: *There are many curious similarities between the inhabitants of Europe and North America* (Saturday Review).
—**Syn.** See **resemblance.**

similar motion, *Music.* two parts or voices sounded together and moving in the same direction, both either ascending or descending in pitch, but not in the same intervals.

Similar Motion from score of music

sim·i·la·tive (sim′ə lā tiv), *adj.* **1.** expressing similarity. **2.** *Grammar.* denoting the case which expresses similarity. —*n.* a similative word or expression.

sim·i·le (sim′ə lē), *n.* an expressed comparison of two different things or ideas, especially as a figure of speech for rhetorical effect. *Examples:* a face like marble, as hard as nails, as brave as a lion. [< Latin *simile,* neuter adjective, like]

simile mark, *Music.* an abbreviation mark signifying that the contents of the last measure that was written out are to be repeated.

si·mi·li·a si·mi·li·bus cu·ran·tur (sə-mil′ē ə sə mil′ə bus kyů ran′tər), *Latin.* like things are cured by like things; like cures like (the basic formula of homeopathy).

si·mil·i·ter (sə mil′ə tər), *adv. Law.* in like manner; the technical designation of the common-law form by which, when the pleading of one party, tendering an issue, demands trial, the other accepts the issue by saying, "and the (defendant) doeth the like." [< Latin *similiter* < *similis* like, resembling]

si·mil·i·tude (sə mil′ə tüd, -tyüd), *n.* **1.** similarity; likeness; resemblance: *A striking similitude between the brother and sister now first arrested my attention* (Edgar Allan Poe). **2.** a comparison drawn between two things or facts: *She could think of no similitude to describe the sunset.* **3.** a parable or allegory (chiefly in Biblical use). **4.** a copy; image. [< Latin *similitūdō, -inis* < *similis* like] —**Syn. 2.** simile. **4.** counterpart.

sim·i·lize (sim′ə līz), *v.t.,* **-lized, -liz·ing.** to liken; compare. [< Latin *similis* like + English *-ize*]

sim·i·ous (sim′ē əs), *adj.* simian.

sim·i·tar (sim′ə tər), *n.* scimitar.

sim·mer (sim′ər), *v.i.* **1. a.** to make a murmuring or whispering sound while boiling gently: *The kettle simmered on the stove.* **b.** to be at or just below the boiling point; boil gently: *soup simmering on the stove.* **2.** to be on the point of breaking out: *He simmered with indignation, but said nothing.* —*v.t.* to keep at or just below the boiling point.
simmer down, a. to calm down from an angry or excited state; cool off: *The owner of the house was enraged, but he simmered down when the boys promised to pay for the broken window.* **b.** (of a liquid) to be reduced in quantity through continued simmering: *He left the brew on the fire for so long that it simmered down completely.*
—*n.* the process of cooking or being cooked at or just below the boiling point.
[earlier *simper;* probably imitative]
—**Syn.** *v.i.* **2.** See **boil.**

sim·nel (sim′nəl), *n.* **1.** a rich currant cake eaten on the Sunday in the middle of Lent in some parts of England. **2.** any of various breads or buns eaten in England until the late 1700's, made of fine flour and cooked partially or completely by boiling. [< Old French *simenel*]

si·mo·le·on (sə mō′lē ən), *n. Slang.* a dollar: *Fielding will be found . . . with a placid smile on his face and a hundred and twenty thousand simoleons in his jeans* (Calgary (Canada) Eye Opener). [American English, apparently < earlier *simon* a dollar; perhaps on analogy of French *napoleon,* a former gold coin]

Si·mon (sī′mən), *n.* in the Bible: **1.** the Apostle Peter's original name. Mark 3:16. **2.** one of the disciples chosen by Jesus as His Apostles; Simon Zelotes. Luke 6:15. **3.** a brother or relative of Jesus. Matthew 13:55. **4.** a Samaritan sorcerer. He was converted to Christianity by Philip and incurred the Apostle Peter's anger by trying to buy the power of imparting the Holy Ghost; Simon Magus. Acts 8:9-24. **5.** a tanner with whom the Apostle Peter stayed at Joppa. Acts 9:43.

si·mo·ni·ac (si mō′nē ak), *n.* a person who practices simony.

si·mo·ni·a·cal (sī′mə nī′ə kəl, sim′ə-), *adj.* **1.** guilty of simony. **2.** of or having to do with simony. —**si′mo·ni′a·cal·ly,** *adv.*

si·mo·nism (sī′mə niz əm, sim′ə-), *n.* the practice or advocacy of simony.

si·mo·nist (sī′mə nist, sim′ə-), *n.* a person who practices or advocates simony.

si·mo·nize (sī′mə nīz), *v.t.,* **-nized, -niz·ing.** to polish, especially with wax: *to simonize a car.* [< *Simoniz,* a trademark]

Simon Le·gree (li grē′), a harsh, cruel, or demanding employer, officer, etc. [< *Simon Legree,* a brutal slave overseer in Harriet Beecher Stowe's *Uncle Tom's Cabin*]

Simon Magus, Simon, the Samaritan sorcerer who was converted to Christianity.

Simon Peter, the Apostle Peter.

si·mon-pure (sī′mən pyůr′), *adj. Informal.* **1.** real; genuine; authentic; true: *simon-pure maple sugar.* **2.** that is morally pure: *He's not as simon-pure as he pretends.* [American English < *Simon Pure,* the name of a Quaker in Mrs. Centlivre's comedy *A Bold Stroke for a Wife* (1717), whose identity is questioned but proved genuine]

Simon Says, a children's game of calisthenics in which the players obey only those commands which the leader prefaces with the words "Simon says." Players who miss such a command or obey a command not prefaced by "Simon says" must drop out of the game.

si mo·nu·men·tum re·qui·ris, cir·cum·spi·ce (sī mon′yů men′təm ri kwī′ris sər kum′spə sē), *Latin.* if you would see his monument, look around (Sir Christopher Wren's epitaph in St. Paul's Cathedral, London).

si·mo·ny (sī′mə nē, sim′ə-), *n., pl.* **-nies. 1.** the making of money out of sacred things. **2.** the sin of buying or selling of positions, promotions, etc., in the church. [< Old French *simonie,* learned borrowing from Latin *simōnia* < *Simōn Magus,* who tried to buy the power of conferring the Holy Spirit. See Acts 8:9-24.]

Simon Ze·lo·tes (zə lō′tēz), Simon, one of the disciples chosen by Jesus as an Apostle.

si·moom (sə müm′), *n.* a hot, dry, suffocating, sand-laden wind that sweeps across the deserts of Arabia, Syria, and northern Africa at intervals during the spring and summer; samiel. [< Arabic *simūm* < *samma* he poisoned]

si·moon (sə mün′), *n.* simoom.

simp (simp), *n. U.S. Slang.* a simpleton; fool: *I guess it's a joke on me, I was such a simp* (Sinclair Lewis). [American English, short for *simpleton*]

sim·pai (sim′pī), *n.* the black-crested monkey of Sumatra, having a long, slender body, tail, and limbs, and highly variegated coloration. [< Malay *simpai*]

sim·pa·ti·ca (sim pä′ti kə), *adj.* feminine of **simpatico:** *To hear her say anyone was not simpatica gave me a turn* (Atlantic). [< Spanish *simpática*]

sim·pa·ti·co (sim pä′ti kō), *adj.* **1.** arousing a sympathetic response; agreeable: *It is important to find the simpatico agent who will give the traveler what he wants and not what the agent thinks he ought to want* (Atlantic). **2.** in agreement; in harmony; compatible: *If he goes, it won't be because the two are simpatico, . . . but because his business interests are at stake.* (Wall Street Journal). [< Spanish *simpático* < *simpatía* sympathy < Latin *sympathīa*]

sim·per (sim′pər), *v.i.* to smile in a silly, self-conscious, or affected way; smirk: *She stood before the mirror . . . simpering to her own image* (Hawthorne). —*v.t.* to express by a simper; say with a simper. —*n.* a silly, affected smile. [perhaps < Scandinavian (compare Norwegian *semper* smart)] —**sim′per·er,** *n.* —**sim′per·ing·ly,** *adv.*

sim·ple (sim′pəl), *adj.,* **-pler, -plest,** *n.* —*adj.* **1.** easy to do, understand, use, solve, or the like: *a simple problem, simple language, a simple explanation, a simple task.* **2.** not complex or complicated with respect to parts or structure; having few parts; not involved: *a simple pattern or design, a simple one-celled animal. A simple curve does not cross itself.* **3.** not divided into parts; uncompounded or unmixed (or nearly so); elementary; single: *a simple substance, a simple concept.* **4.** considered or taken by itself; with nothing added; mere; bare: *a simple majority. My answer is the simple truth.* **5.** unaffected; plain: *a simple tale, to write in a simple style.* **6.** free from duplicity or guile; undesigning; honest; sincere: *a simple heart. The short and simple annals of the poor* (Thomas Gray). **7.** not subtle; not sophisticated; innocent; artless: *He was a simple innocent boy* (Shelley). **8.** free from pride, ostentation, or display; not showing off; natural: *a simple life. She has a pleasant, simple manner. Arthur . . . neither wore on helm or shield the golden symbol of his kinglihood, But rode a simple knight among his knights* (Tennyson). **9.** without ornament; not rich or showy: *He eats simple food and wears simple clothes.* **10.** of humble birth or position; lowly; undistinguished: *His place of birth a solemn angel tells to simple shepherds* (Milton). **11.** common; ordinary: *a simple citizen, a simple private.* **12.** of little value or importance; insignificant; trifling; slight: *Great floods have flown from simple sources* (Shakespeare). **13.** dull; stupid; weak in mind: *Simple Simon met a pieman. Thou art as simple, I see, in this world's knowledge as ever* (Scott). **14.** *Chemistry.* **a.** composed of only one element; elementary. **b.** unmixed. **15.** *Botany.* not formed by a union of similar parts or groups of parts, as a stem which is not divided at the base.
—*n.* **1.** a foolish, stupid person. **2.** something unmixed or uncompounded. **3.** a medicine, etc., composed of only one constituent. **4. a.** a plant or herb used in

medicine: *Saphira read his medical library, added herbs and simples she knew from her childhood, plus other remedies* (Harper's). **b.** medicine made from it. **5.** *Archaic.* a person of poor or humble birth or position. [< Old French *simple* < Latin *simplex, -icis.* Doublet of SIMPLEX.] —**sim′ple·ness,** *n.*
—**Syn.** *adj.* **1.** See **easy. 4.** pure, absolute. **6.** open, straightforward. **7.** naïve, ingenuous. **8.** unassuming, unpretentious.

simple contract, *Law.* a contract or agreement not under seal.

sim·ple-faced (sim′pəl fāst′), *adj.* (of bats) having no foliaceous appendages on the snout.

simple fraction, a fraction in which both the numerator and the denominator are whole numbers. *Examples:* 1/3, 3/4, 219/125.

simple fracture, a fracture in which a broken bone does not penetrate the skin; closed fracture.

simple fruit, a fruit developed from a single matured ovary, as the tomato, apple, and acorn. Simple fruits are classified as either fleshy or dry.

sim·ple-heart·ed (sim′pəl här′tid), *adj.* **1.** having or showing a simple, unaffected nature: *The average simple-hearted lover of Westerns will be quite happy to see some of the familiar situations without bothering to understand exactly how they came about* (Punch). **2.** guileless; sincere.

simple honors, (in auction bridge) a bare majority of honors; three trump honors or three aces at no trump, held by one side.

simple interest, interest that is paid only on the principal of a loan, etc., and not on accrued interest.

simple leaf, a leaf consisting of a single blade: *The lamina of a simple leaf is never completely broken up into definite bladelike parts* (Heber W. Youngken).

simple machine, any of the elementary devices or mechanical powers on which other machines are based. The lever, wedge, pulley, wheel and axle, inclined plane, and screw are the six simple machines.

sim·ple-mind·ed (sim′pəl mīn′did), *adj.* **1.** artless; inexperienced. **2.** ignorant; foolish; stupid. **3.** feeble-minded. —**sim′ple-mind′ed·ly,** *adv.* —**sim′ple-mind′ed·ness,** *n.*
—**Syn. 1.** unsophisticated.

simple past, the past tense without reference to the duration of action; past absolute.

sim·pler (sim′plər), *n. Archaic.* a person who gathers simples or medicinal herbs, or is skilled in their uses; herbalist.

simple sentence, a sentence consisting of one main clause. *Example:* The whistle blows.

Simple Simon, a simpleton: *In looking for life on Mars we could establish for ourselves the reputation of being the greatest Simple Simons of all time* (New York Times).

simple time or **measure,** *Music.* a rhythm or time having two or three beats to a measure.

sim·ple·ton (sim′pəl tən), *n.* a silly person; fool. [< *simple*]

sim·plex (sim′pleks), *adj.* **1.** consisting of or characterized by a single part, structure, etc.; not compound. **2.** (in telegraphy) of or having to do with a system for sending messages in only one direction at a time. —*n.* a simple, uncompounded word. [< Latin *simplex* single < *sem-* one- (for *semel* once) + *-plex* -fold. Doublet of SIMPLE]

sim·pli·ci·den·tate (sim′plə sə den′tāt), *adj.* of or belonging to a former suborder containing all those animals now classified as rodents, and characterized by only one pair of upper incisor teeth. —*n.* a simplicidentate animal. [< Latin *simplex, -icis* single + English *dentate*]

sim·pli·cis·tic (sim′plə sis′tik), *adj.* simplistic: *But this is not science, only assumption; and art, meanwhile, forever subtle, eludes this simplicistic theory and continues to demonstrate that meaning is more than the sum of its parts* (Howard Mumford Jones).

sim·plic·i·ty (sim plis′ə tē), *n., pl.* **-ties. 1.** the state or quality of being simple. **2.** freedom from difficulty; clearness: *The simplicity of the book makes it suitable for children. Simplicity is become a very rare quality in a writer* (William Cowper). **3.** an absence of ornament or freedom from useless accessories; plainness: *A room in a hospital should be furnished with simplicity.* **4.** an absence of or freedom from luxury; plainness, especially rustic plainness, of life: *The simplicities of cottage life* (Wordsworth). **5.** an absence of show or pretense; sincerity; straightforwardness. **6.** a lack of shrewdness; dullness: *His simplicity made him easily fooled.* [< Latin *simplicitās* < *simplex, -icis* simple]

sim·pli·fi·ca·tion (sim′plə fə kā′shən), *n.* **1.** the act of simplifying: *The simplification . . . is aimed . . . at lightening unnecessary and unintended burdens on trade* (Wall Street Journal). **2.** the state of being simplified. **3.** a change to a simpler state or form: *Mounted above it was a large, multicolored simplification of the atom* (New Yorker).

sim·pli·fi·ca·tive (sim′plə fə kā′tiv), *adj.* tending to simplify.

sim·pli·fi·ca·tor (sim′plə fə kā′tər), *n.* a simplifier.

sim·pli·fi·er (sim′plə fī′ər), *n.* a person or thing that simplifies: *Lawyer Dulles, a great popularizer and simplifier, then told the U.S. what happened at Geneva* (Time).

sim·pli·fy (sim′plə fī), *v.t.,* **-fied, -fy·ing.** to make simple or simpler; make plainer or easier: *"Tho" is a simplified spelling of "though." The program has been modified, but not simplified, for their benefit* (Time). [< French, Old French *simplifier,* adaptation of Medieval Latin *simplificari* < Late Latin *simplus,* variant of Latin *simplex, -icis* simple + *facere* to make]

sim·plism (sim′pliz əm), *n.* **1.** the advocacy or cultivation of simplicity. **2.** an affected or labored simplicity.

sim·plis·tic (sim plis′tik), *adj.* endeavoring to explain everything, or too much, by a single principle: *The facts of nature and of life are more apt to be complex than simple. Simplistic theories are generally one-sided and partial* (James Freeman Clarke). —**sim·plis′ti·cal·ly,** *adv.*

sim·ply (sim′plē), *adv.* **1.** in a simple manner. **2.** without much ornament; without pretense or affectation; plainly: *Mary was simply dressed.* **3.** in simple language; clearly. **4.** merely; only: *The baby did not simply cry, he yelled.* **5.** foolishly: *He acted as simply as an idiot.* **6.** absolutely: *simply perfect, simply hopeless.*

sim·u·la·cra (sim′yə lā′krə), *n.* a plural of **simulacrum:** *We see why the greater part of the work done on the mechanical simulacra of the brain has been on machines which are more or less on a digital basis* (Norbert Wiener).

sim·u·la·cre (sim′yə lā′kər), *n. Archaic.* a material or mental representation; image of a person or thing. [< Old French *simulacre,* learned borrowing from Latin *simulācrum.* Doublet of SIMULACRUM.]

sim·u·la·crum (sim′yə lā′krəm), *n., pl.* **-cra** or **-crums. 1.** a faint, shadowy, or unreal likeness; mere semblance: *The dictator permitted only a simulacrum of democracy.* **2.** an image: *It exists on a little island in time as a simulacrum of Moslem culture in its purity* (New Yorker). [< Latin *simulācrum* < *simulāre* to simulate. Doublet of SIMULACRE.]

sim·u·lant (sim′yə lənt), *adj.* presenting the appearance of something else; simulating: *stamens simulant of petals.* [< Latin *simulāns, -antis,* present participle of *simulāre* to simulate]

sim·u·lar (sim′yə lər), *n.* a person or thing that simulates; simulator. —*adj.* **1.** simulated; pretended. **2.** simulative of something. [< Latin *simulāre;* perhaps influenced by *similar*]

sim·u·late (sim′yə lāt), *v.,* **-lat·ed, -lat·ing,** *adj.* —*v.t.* **1.** to pretend; feign: *Ann simulated interest to please her friend. A government . . . in word and action simulating reform* (Matthew Arnold). **2.** to act like; look like; imitate: *Certain insects simulate leaves.* —*adj.* simulated. [< Latin *simulāre* (with English *-ate*[1]) < *similis* like] —**Syn.** *v.t.* **1.** sham.

sim·u·la·tion (sim′yə lā′shən), *n.* **1.** the act or practice of simulating; pretense; feigning: *Simulation is a pretence of what is not, and Dissimulation a concealment of what is* (Sir Richard Steele). **2.** an acting or looking like; imitation: *a harmless insect's simulation of a poisonous one.*

sim·u·la·tive (sim′yə lā′tiv), *adj.* characterized by simulation. —**sim′u·la′tive·ly,** *adv.*

sim·u·la·tor (sim′yə lā′tər), *n.* **1.** a person who simulates or pretends. **2.** a thing that simulates, as an apparatus that duplicates airplane or missile flight conditions: *Eastern Air Lines has installed half a dozen new simulators within the past year to train pilots to land when visibility is bad* (Wall Street Journal).

si·mul·cast (sī′məl kast′, -käst′), *v.,* **-cast** or **-cast·ed, -cast·ing,** *n.* —*v.t., v.i.* to transmit (a program) over radio and television simultaneously: *The Firestone Hour . . . is "simulcast" at 8:30* (New York Times). —*n.* **1.** the act of so transmitting or fact of being so transmitted. **2.** a program so transmitted: *The audience will get the usual feature and, in addition, the simulcast* (Newsweek). [< *simul*(taneous) + (broad)*cast*]

si·mu·li·um fly (sə myü′lē əm), any of a group of small flies or gnats found near rivers and streams throughout the world, as the black fly. Several varieties are the carriers of onchocerciasis. *The simulium fly . . . [carries] microscopic worms that multiply under the skin of bitten persons, working their way toward the eyes* (Science News Letter). [< New Latin *Simulium* the genus name < Latin *simulāre* to simulate]

si·mul·ta·ne·i·ty (sī′məl tə nē′ə tē, sim′-əl-), *n.* the quality or fact of being simultaneous; occurrence at the same time: *It is this simultaneity of the end of history as we knew it in the Western world, and the beginning of history in Asia and Africa, which makes the present world situation so confused and unpredictable* (Bulletin of Atomic Scientists).

si·mul·ta·ne·ous (sī′məl tā′nē əs, sim′əl-), *adj.* existing, done, operating, or happening at the same time: *The two simultaneous shots sounded like one. Everyone in the audience burst into simultaneous applause.* [< Medieval Latin *simultaneus* (with English *-ous*) simulated < Latin *similis* like; confused in sense with Latin *simul* at the same time] —**si′mul·ta′ne·ous·ly,** *adv.* —**si′mul·ta′ne·ous·ness,** *n.* —**Syn.** coincident, contemporaneous.

simultaneous equations, two or more equations that have to be satisfied by the same set of values of the unknowns.

si·murgh (sē múrg′), *n.* a monstrous bird of Persian mythology, corresponding to the Arabian roc. [< Persian *sīmurgh* < Pahlavi *sīn* eagle + *murgh* bird]

sin[1] (sin), *n., v.,* **sinned, sin·ning.** —*n.* **1. a.** a breaking of the law of God deliberately: *human sin. Men have dulled their eyes with sin* (Henry Van Dyke). **b.** the state or condition resulting from this: *born and raised in sin.* **2.** an immoral act; wrongdoing: *Lying, stealing, dishonesty, and cruelty are all sins.* **3.** a violation of any rule or standard, as of taste, propriety, etc.
—*v.i.* **1.** to break the law of God; be a sinner: *The tempter, or the tempted, who sins most?* (Shakespeare). **2.** to offend (against some principle, standard, etc.); do or be wrong: *more sinned against than sinning* (Shakespeare). *Faces sinning against all proportion* (Byron). —*v.t.* **1.** to do, perform, or perpetrate sinfully; commit (a sin): *A man . . . who had sinned all the sins* (H. G. Wells). **2. a.** to bring (oneself into a state, or beyond something) by sinning. **b.** to drive (away) by sinning: *Souls which have sinned away the grace of God and are beyond its reach* (Edward B. Pusey).
[Old English *synn* wrongdoing, injury, hostility]

sin[2] or **sin'** (sin), *prep., conj., adv. Scottish.* since.

sin[3] (sēn), *n.* shin, the twenty-first letter of the Hebrew alphabet. [< Hebrew *sin*]

sin (no period), the mathematical notation for sine, used in formulas and equations.

Si·nae·an (si nē′ən, sī-), *adj.* Chinese. [< Latin *Sīnae* the Chinese (< Greek *Sīnai*) + English *-an*]

Si·nai (sī′nī), *n.* **Mount,** (in the Bible) the mountain, often identified with one on the Sinai Peninsula, but by some thought to have been in Arabia, on which Moses received the Law and the Ten Commandments. Exodus 19, 20, 34.

Si·na·ic (sī nā′ik), *adj.* Sinaitic.

Si·na·it·ic (sī′nā it′ik), *adj.* having to do with Mount Sinai.

sin·al·bin (sin al′bin), *n.* a crystalline glucoside present in the seeds of the white mustard. *Formula:* $C_{30}H_{42}N_2O_{15}S_2$ [< Latin *sināpis* mustard + *alba* white + English *-in*]

Si·nan·thro·pus pe·ki·nen·sis (sin′an-thrō′pəs pē′kə nen′sis, si nan′thrə-), Peking man: *Sinanthropus pekinensis, first found in 1929, by W.C. Pei, reopened the whole problem of early man in the Far East* (Melville J. Herskovits). [< New Latin *Sinanthropus* *pekinensis* < Greek *Sînai* the Chinese + *ánthrōpos* man; *pekinensis* of Peking]

sin·a·pin (sin′ə pin), *n.* sinapine.

sin·a·pine (sin′ə pēn, -pin), *n.* an alkaloid present in the seeds of the black mustard. *Formula:* $C_{16}H_{25}NO_6$ [< Latin *sināpis* + English *-ine*[2]]

sin·a·pism (sin′ə piz əm), *n.* a mustard plaster. [< Latin *sināpismus* < Greek *sināpismós* (use of) a mustard plaster < *sínāpi* mustard < *nâpy*]

Sin·bad (sin′bad), *n.* **1.** a sailor in *The Arabian Nights* who had seven extraordinary voyages. **2.** any sailor. Also, **Sindbad.**

since (sins), *prep.* **1.** from a past time continuously till now: *The package has been ready since noon. We have been up since five.* **2.** at any time between some past time or event and the present: *We have not seen him since Saturday.*
—*conj.* **1.** from the time that; in the course of the period following the time when: *He has written home but once since he left us.* **2.** continuously or counting from the time when: *Charles has worked hard since he left school.* **3.** because; seeing that; inasmuch as: *Since you feel tired, you should rest.*
—*adv.* **1.** from that time till now; continually afterward: *John caught cold on Saturday and has been in bed ever since.* **2.** at some time between a particular past time and the present; subsequently; later: *At first he refused but since has accepted.* **3.** before now; ago: *I heard that old joke long since.*
[Middle English *sinnes*, Old English *siththan* then later < *sīth*, preposition, late]
➤ See **because** for usage note.

sin·cere (sin sir′), *adj.*, **-cer·er, -cer·est. 1.** free from pretense or deceit; genuine; real; honest: *sincere affection, a sincere person, to be sincere in one's apologies.* **2.** *Obsolete.* free from adulterants; pure; unadulterated: *As newborn babes, desire the sincere milk of the word, that ye may grow thereby* (I Peter 2:2). **3.** *Obsolete.* free from hurt; uninjured. [< Latin *sincērus*] **—sin·cere′ly,** *adv.* **—sin·cere′ness,** *n.* **—Syn. 1.** true, heartfelt, straightforward.

sin·cer·i·ty (sin ser′ə tē), *n.*, *pl.* **-ties.** the character, quality, or state of being sincere; freedom from pretense or deceit; honesty; straightforwardness: *No one doubts the sincerity of Abraham Lincoln.*
sincerities, *Archaic.* sincere feelings or actions.

sin·cip·i·tal (sin sip′ə təl), *adj.* of or having to do with the sinciput.

sin·ci·put (sin′sə put, -pət), *n.* **1.** the front part of the head. **2.** the upper part of the skull. [< Latin *sinciput* < *sēmi* half + *caput, -itis* head]

Sind·bad (sin′bad), *n.* Sinbad.

Sin·dhi (sin′dē), *n.* an Indic language spoken in Sind, a province in West Pakistan.
—*adj.* of or having to do with Sind, its people, or their language: *The Sindhi politicians claimed that the peasants of Sind would oppose the immigration of landless farmers from the adjacent Punjab region* (Atlantic).

sine[1] (sīn), *n.* **1.** (in a right triangle) the ratio of the length of the side opposite an acute angle to the length of the hypotenuse. The sine, secant, and tangent are the three fundamental trigonometric functions. *Abbr.:* sin (no period). **2.** (originally) a perpendicular drawn from one extremity of an arc of a circle to the diameter which intersects its other extremity [< Latin *sinus, -ūs* bend; fold in a garment, bosom (in Medieval Latin, a translation of Arabic *jaib* sine; (originally) bosom of a garment)]

B b A a C

Sine[1] (def. 1) In the diagram, the sine of angle a is BC/AB; the sine of angle b is AC/AB

si·ne[2] (sī′nē), *prep. Latin.* without.

si·ne·cure (sī′nə kyůr, sin′ə-), *n.* **1.** an extremely easy job; position requiring little or no work and usually paying well: *His job has become a profession instead of a drowsy sinecure, as it was in the eighteenth century* (New Yorker). **2.** an ecclesiastical benefice without cure of souls. [< Medieval Latin (*beneficium*) *sine cura* (benefice) without cure (of souls) < Latin *sine*, preposition; *cūrā*, ablative singular of *cūra* care]

si·ne·cur·ism (sī′nə kyů riz′əm, sin′ə-), *n.* the practice of holding or permitting sinecures.

si·ne·cur·ist (sī′nəkyůr′ist, sin′ə-), *n.* a person who holds or seeks to obtain a sinecure.

sine curve, a curve showing the relationship between the size of an angle and its sine, plotted by using the successive values as coordinates.

si·ne di·e (sī′nē dī′ē, sī′nə), without a day specified for another meeting, trial, etc.; indefinitely: *The committee adjourned sine die. Abbr.:* s.d. [< Medieval Latin *sine die* without a day (being set)]

si·ne qua non (sī′nē kwā non′, sī′nə), something essential; indispensable condition: *Prior settlement of the Saar problem was bound to be the sine qua non for any such eventuality* (Atlantic). [< Late Latin *sine quā non* (literally) without which not]

sin·ew (sin′yü), *n.* **1.** a tough, strong band or cord that joins muscle to bone; tendon: *You can see the sinews in a cooked chicken leg.* **2.** a means of strength; source of power: *Men and money are sinews of war.* **3.** *Obsolete.* a nerve.
sinews, strength; energy; force: *He is well liked, but as a leader he lacks sinews.*
—*v.t.* to furnish or strengthen with or as if with sinews: *Ourselves well sinewed to our defence* (Shakespeare).
[Old English *sionu*]

sine wave, a simple wave, as an electromagnetic or sound wave, that can be graphically represented as a sine curve: *Strictly speaking, a sine wave can be a sine wave only if it has a constant amplitude* (John R. Pierce).

sin·ew·i·ness (sin′yü ē nis), *n.* the state or character of being sinewy: *They are a deplorable lot, having . . . the predatory sinewiness of hunting leopards* (Manchester Guardian).

sin·ew·less (sin′yü lis), *adj.* **1.** lacking sinews. **2.** lacking vigor; feeble; weak; powerless.

sin·ew·y (sin′yü ē), *adj.* **1.** having strong or well-developed sinews; strong; powerful: *A blacksmith has sinewy arms.* **2.** vigorous; forcible: *a sinewy mind.* **3. a.** like sinews; tough; stringy. **b.** furnished with or full of sinews.

sin·fo·ni·a (sin′fə nē′ə; *Italian* sēn′fô nē′ä), *n.*, *pl.* **-ni·e** (-nē′ā). *Music.* **1.** a symphony. **2.** (originally) any of various instrumental pieces, as a sonata, or an overture or interlude in an opera or oratorio: *Haydn and Mozart wrote classic symphonies developed from the earlier sinfonia* (World Book Encyclopedia). [< Italian *sinfonia* symphony]
➤ The Italian **sinfonia** in the 1600's and 1700's was an instrumental piece in an opera or oratorio, later usually the overture, especially the Italian allegro overture from which the symphony developed. In Italian the word *sinfonia* still means both "overture" and "symphony."

sin·fo·niet·ta (sin′fən yet′ə), *n.* **1.** any of various short instrumental pieces patterned on the symphony: *The stirring sinfoniettas from the double pianos . . . begin at eight-thirty* (New Yorker). **2.** a small orchestra, especially one consisting entirely or chiefly of strings: *Max Goberman . . . led the New York Sinfonietta in all-Vivaldi programs* (New Yorker). [< Italian *sinfonietta* (diminutive) < *sinfonia* symphony]

sin·ful (sin′fəl), *adj.* full of sin or sins; wicked; wrong: *a sinful man, a sinful act.* **—sin′ful·ly,** *adv.* **—sin′ful·ness,** *n.* **—Syn.** depraved, immoral, evil.

sing (sing), *v.*, **sang** or (sometimes) **sung, sung, sing·ing,** *n.* —*v.i.* **1.** to make music with the voice: *to sing in a choir, to sing while working. He sings on the radio.* **2.** to make pleasant musical sounds: *Birds sing.* **3.** to tell in song or poetry: *Homer sang of Troy. Thus have I sung of fields, and flocks, and trees . . .* (John Dryden). **4.** to admit of being sung: *This arrangement of the song sings more easily than that one.* **5. a.** to make a ringing, murmuring, whistling, humming, or buzzing sound: *The teakettle sang.* **b.** to move with such a sound: *The stone sang past my head* (Sir Arthur Conan Doyle). **6.** to have a sensation of a ringing, buzzing, or humming sound; tingle: *A bad cold made his ears sing.* **7.** *Slang.* to reveal; inform; tell all: *[He] hopes to get consideration on his twelve-year jail sentence in return for singing in public* (Newsweek). —*v.t.* **1.** to utter musically: *He almost seemed to sing his lines from the play.* **2.** to chant; intone: *the priest sings Mass.* **3.** to tell of in song or poetry: *The poet sang the deeds of heroes.* **4.** to proclaim: *to sing a person's praises.* **5. a.** to bring, send, put, etc., by or with singing: *Sing the baby to sleep.* **b.** to escort or wait upon with singing: *to sing the old year out and the new year in.*
sing out, to call loudly; shout: *Suddenly a scout sang out that a party was in sight* (Benjamin Disraeli).
sing small, to change to a humble tone or manner: *Sir R. Peel endorsed the remonstrance and I had to sing small* (William E. Gladstone).
—*n.* **1.** a singing, ringing, or whistling sound: *the sing of a bullet in flight.* **2.** a singing, especially in a group.
[Old English *singan*]
—Syn. *v.i.* **1.** carol, warble, croon.
➤ **Sung** as the past tense form was once common but is now rare in standard English.

sing., singular.

sing·a·ble (sing′ə bəl), *adj.* that can be sung; that is easily sung: *[It] contains some passages of gripping theatre and lush, singable music* (New Yorker).

sing-a·long (sing′ə lông′, -long′), *n. U.S.* **1.** a musical act in which the audience joins in the singing of familiar songs: *. . . a singalong with a trio of Texas folk singers* (Time). **2.** a phonograph recording of such an act or of songs used in such an act.

singe (sinj), *v.*, **singed, singe·ing,** *n.* —*v.t.* **1.** to burn a little: *The cook singed the chicken to remove the fine hairs.* **2.** to burn the ends or edges of: *The barber singed my hair after he cut it.* **3.** to remove by slight burning: *to singe off the bristles.* **4.** to injure slightly; harm: *A scandal singed the mayor's reputation.*
—*n.* a slight burn; scorch.
[Old English *sengan*]

sing·er (sing′ər), *n.* **1.** a person who sings: *You can hear famous singers on the radio.* **2.** a bird that sings; songbird: *Our canary is a fine singer.* **—Syn. 1.** chorister, vocalist, songster.

Sin·gha·lese (sing′gə lēz′, -lēs′), *n.*, *pl.* **-lese,** *adj.* —*n.* **1.** the principal native people of Ceylon, an island in the Indian Ocean. **2.** a member of this people. **3.** the Indic language of this people.
—*adj.* having to do with Ceylon, its principal native people, or their language. Also, **Sinhalese.**
[< Sanskrit *Siṅhala* Ceylon + English *-ese*]

sing·ing (sing′ing), *n.* **1.** the sound made by one that sings: *Her singing was wildly applauded.* **2.** a ringing in the ears.
—*adj.* **1.** that sings. **2.** of or like singing; musical.

singing bird, a songbird; oscine bird.

singing flame, a flame, as a gas jet, which, when burned in a tube of proper length, produces a clear, musical note.

singing school, a school in which singing and the simple fundamentals of music are taught.

singing voice, the voice as used in singing: *Her singing voice was small, but true and clear* (Harper's).

sin·gle (sing′gəl), *adj.*, *n.*, *v.*, **-gled, -gling.** —*adj.* **1.** one and no more; only one: *Please give me a single piece of paper. The spider hung by a single thread.* **2.** of or for only one; individual: *a single bed, a single room in a hotel.* **3.** without others; alone: *Behold her, single in the field* (Wordsworth). **4. a.** not married: *They rent rooms to single men.* **b.** of or in the unmarried state: *single life.* **5.** between two persons; having only one on each side: *The knights engaged in single combat.* **6.** (of a flower) having only one set of petals: *Most cultivated roses have double flowers with many petals; wild roses have single flowers with five petals.* **7.** consisting of one part, element, or member; not double; not multiple: *single houses.* **8.** sincere; honest; genuine: *She showed single devotion to her religion. To those whose views are single and direct, it is a great comfort to have to do business with frank and honorable minds* (Thomas Jefferson). **9.** unique; singular; unmatched; unusual: *Favor your country with your counsels on such an important and single occasion* (John Jay). **10.** (of the eye) seeing rightly or justly; without defect: *If . . . thine eye be single, thy whole body shall be full of light* (Matthew 6:22).
—*n.* **1. a.** a single person or thing; individual. **b.** *Informal.* a single performer; soloist: *Patty Andrews . . . is dickering with one of the networks for a TV show next fall as a result of*

her successful stand as a "single" in Las Vegas (Newsweek). **2.** a hit in baseball that allows the batter to reach first base only: *The Red Sox filled the bases on a double by Sam White, a walk to Harry Agganis and a single by Jensen* (New York Times). **3.** a hit in cricket for which one run is scored. **4.** a game for two people only. **5.** a phonograph record having only one song or tune on a side: *Victor . . . has let these two ladies share a new long-playing record made up of old singles* (New Yorker). **6.** a form of change in bell ringing.
singles, a match or game, especially in tennis, played with only one player on each side: *He likes to play singles rather than doubles.*
—*v.t.* to pick from among others: *The teacher singled Harry out for praise. Romance had singled Jim for its own* (Joseph Conrad).
—*v.i.* **1.** to make a hit in baseball that allows the batter to reach first base safely. **2.** (of a horse) to move at a single-foot.
[< Old French *sengle, single* < Latin *singulus*]
—**Syn.** *adj.* **1. Single, sole, only** mean one as distinguished from more than one. **Single** implies one and no more: *She buys a single new dress each year.* **Sole** implies being by itself, the only one there is or that there is to be considered: *My sole purpose is to help you.* **Only** implies being one of a class (actual or conceivable) of which it is the best or the single representative: *She is the only girl in the world for me. She is his only daughter.* **3.** solitary. **4. a.** unmarried. **b.** celibate.

sin·gle-act·ing (sing′gəl ak′ting), *adj.* **1.** that acts in one direction only: *A single-acting engine exerts force on the piston or pistons only on one end.* **2.** that operates simply.

sin·gle-ac·tion (sing′gəl ak′shən), *adj.* **1.** single-acting. **2.** (of a revolver) cocked and fired in separate motions: *In a single-action revolver, the user pulls back the hammer by hand; he then pulls the trigger to fire.*

single blessedness, the condition of being unmarried; celibacy: *She was left unplucked on the stalk of single blessedness* (John Galt).

single bowknot, a type of knot forming only one loop.

sin·gle-breast·ed (sing′gəl bres′tid), *adj.* (of a coat or jacket) overlapping across the breast just enough to fasten with only one row of buttons.

sin·gle-chan·nel (sing′gəl chan′əl), *adj.* monaural; monophonic: *Single-channel . . . sound can never achieve auditory perspective, no matter how carefully the sound equipment is designed* (New York Times).

single combat, combat with one on each side.

single cross, the hybrid produced by a single crossing of two inbred lines; single-cross hybrid.

sin·gle-cross (sing′gəl krôs′, -kros′), *adj. Genetics.* that is of the first generation produced by crossing two inbred lines: *a single-cross hybrid.*

sin·gle-deck·er (sing′gəl dek′ər), *adj.* having only one deck or level: *a single-decker bus, a single-decker grandstand.*

single entry, a simple system of bookkeeping in which there is one account to which all items are debited or credited. —**sin′gle-en′try,** *adj.*

sin·gle-eyed (sing′gəl īd′), *adj.* **1.** having but one eye. **2.** seeing rightly; just; honest; straightforward: *He was single-eyed in all his dealings.*

single file, a line of persons or things arranged one behind another: *to march in single file.*

sin·gle-foot (sing′gəl fu̇t′), *n.* a gait of a horse in which one foot is put down at a time; rack. First there is one foot on the ground, then two, then one, then two, and so on. —*v.i.* (of a horse) to go or move at a single-foot: *Two mounted cops led the procession, to clear traffic, and the easy-gaited little cutting horses single-footing in their wake made the police geldings look like draft stock* (New Yorker).

sin·gle-hand·ed (sing′gəl han′did), *adj.* **1.** without help from others; working alone; unassisted; unaided: *Single-handed . . . she performed all the labors of Mr. Jonathan Rossiter's little establishment* (Harriet Beecher Stowe). **2.** using, requiring, or managed by only one hand or only one person: *a single-handed catch, a single-handed saw.* —**sin′gle-hand′ed·ly,** *adv.*

sin·gle-heart·ed (sing′gəl här′tid), *adj.* **1.** free from deceit; sincere; straightforward. **2.** having only one purpose: *He was single-hearted in his aim* (W. Somerset Maugham). —**sin′gle-heart′ed·ly,** *adv.* —**sin′gle-heart′ed·ness,** *n.* —**Syn. 1.** ingenuous.

single knot, a knot similar to a half hitch.

sin·gle-leaf (sing′gəl lēf′), *n.* a piñon or pine of western North America, with leaves growing singly or in clusters of two; nut pine.

sin·gle-mind·ed (sing′gəl mīn′did), *adj.* **1.** having only one purpose in mind. **2.** sincere; straightforward; single-hearted: *An unpretending, single-minded, artless girl — infinitely to be preferred by any man of sense and taste* (Jane Austen). —**sin′gle-mind′ed·ly,** *adv.* —**sin′gle-mind′ed·ness,** *n.* —**Syn. 2.** guileless.

sin·gle-name paper (sing′gəl nām′), *Banking.* a promissory note endorsed only by the maker.

sin·gle·ness (sing′gəl nis), *n.* **1.** oneness; state or quality of being single. **2.** the unmarried state; celibacy. **3.** freedom from deceit; sincerity; honesty; integrity: *That we may do the work which Thou givest us to do . . . with singleness of heart* (Book of Common Prayer). —**Syn. 3.** uprightness.

sin·gle-phase (sing′gəl fāz′), *adj.* of or having to do with an alternating current having one phase: *a single-phase circuit.*

single phaser, *Electricity.* a single-phase alternating-current generator.

sin·gles (sing′gəlz), *n.pl.* See under **single,** *n.*

sin·gle-seat·er (sing′gəl sē′tər), *n.* an aircraft or other vehicle that seats only one person: *The top speed of the little Handley Page single-seater will be below 300 mph* (New Scientist).

single sideband, *Radio.* a transmitter or system that uses only one of the two sidebands of a frequency, eliminating the carrier signal completely. A single sideband permits more frequencies to exist and requires less space between them: *Seamon lives in Port Washington, L.I.,* [*and*] *talks from his den to people all over the world through his single sideband amateur radio station* (Time).

sin·gle-stage (sing′gəl stāj′), *adj.* having a propulsive force of only one charge and thus capable of reaching only one level of ascent: *a single-stage rocket or missile.*

single standard, 1. a monetary standard or system based upon a single metal only as the circulating medium, usually gold; monometallism. **2.** a standard of moral behavior that is the same for both men and women.

single stem, a skiing maneuver involving stemming with one ski.

sin·gle·stick (sing′gəl stik′), *n.* **1.** a stick held in one hand, used in fencing, striking, etc. **2.** fencing with such a stick: *. . . an exciseman, whom he challenged to a bout of singlesticks* (Tobias Smollett). **3.** any short stick for striking; cudgel.

sin·gle·stick·er (sing′gəl stik′ər), *n. Informal.* a one-masted vessel, especially a sloop.

sin·glet (sing′glit), *n.* **1.** a man's short-sleeved undershirt or jersey: *They were dressed in tattered singlets and equally tattered trousers* (New Yorker). **2.** any undershirt for men. **3.** *Nuclear Physics.* a resonance with a spin of zero.

single tax, 1. a tax on one kind of property only, especially a tax on land only. **2.** a system of public revenue based on such a tax, such as one urged by Henry George, American political economist, 1839-1897, and his followers. —**sin′gle-tax′,** *adj.*

sin·gle-tax·er (sing′gəl tak′sər), *n.* an advocate of a single tax: *He was an anarchist, a single-taxer, a vegetarian, a disciple of Gandhi* (New Yorker).

single ticket, *British.* a one-way ticket.

sin·gle·ton (sing′gəl tən), *n.* **1.** something occurring singly or apart from others. **2.** a playing card that is the only one of a suit in a player's hand.

sin·gle-track (sing′gəl trak′), *adj.* **1.** having only a single track: *a single-track railroad.* **2.** able to go or act in only one way; one-track: *a single-track mind.*

sin·gle·tree (sing′gəl trē′), *n.* whiffletree. [American English, variant of *swingletree*]

single wing back formation, *Football.* an offensive formation with one back behind and outside an end.

sin·glings (sing′glingz), *n.* (in distilling) the crude spirit which is the first to come over.

sin·glo (sing′glō), *n.* a kind of fine tea, consisting of large, flat leaves, not much rolled. [< *Sung-lo,* a range of hills in China]

sin·gly (sing′glē), *adv.* **1.** by itself; individually; separately: *Let us consider each point singly.* **2.** one by one; one at a time: *Misfortunes never seem to come singly.* **3.** by one's own efforts; without help; unaided; unassisted; single-handed.

sing-sing (sing′sing′), *n.* a West African kob antelope. [< a native word]

sing·song (sing′sông′, -song′), *n.* **1.** a monotonous, up-and-down rhythm: *In childhood singsong is not a defect; it is simply the first form of rhythmical sensibility* (C. S. Lewis). **2.** a monotonous tone or sound in speaking: *. . . the rapt singsong of the wayside fortuneteller* (Rudyard Kipling). **3.** a monotonous or jingling verse. **4.** *British.* an informal gathering where each person is expected to contribute a song; gathering for community singing: *Jack's wife had cooked us a banquet, after which there was a singsong, and many stories* (New Yorker).
—*adj.* monotonous in tone or rhythm: *a singsong recitation of the multiplication table. She spoke quietly, in a singsong voice* (Atlantic).
—*v.t., v.i.* to recite or speak in a singsong way.

Sing·spiel (zing′shpēl), *n. German.* **1.** a semidramatic work or performance presenting a story in song, and subordinating instrumental accompaniment to the vocal parts. **2.** (literally) a song play.

sin·gu·lar (sing′gyə lər), *adj.* **1.** extraordinary; unusual: *Einstein and Da Vinci were men of singular ability. "Treasure Island" is a story of singular interest to boys.* **2.** strange; odd; peculiar: *Detectives were greatly puzzled by the singular nature of the crime. He was called strange and singular long before he was acknowledged to be great* (Walter S. Landor). **3.** being the only one of the kind: *an event singular in history.* **4.** *Grammar.* **a.** signifying or implying only one person or thing: *the singular number, a singular verb form.* **b.** one in number: *"Boy" is singular; "boys" is plural.* **5.** separate; individual; private: *a singular matter.* **6.** *Logic.* of or having to do with some single thing, person, or instance; not general.
—*n.* **1.** *Grammar.* **a.** the number commonly used when referring to one person or thing. **b.** a form or class of forms used thus: *Book* is a singular; *books* is a plural. *Abbr.:* sing. **2.** *Logic.* a thing, person, or instance considered by itself; that which is not general.
[< Latin *singulāris* < *singulus* single] —**sin′gu·lar·ness,** *n.*
—**Syn.** *adj.* **1.** exceptional, uncommon, remarkable. **2.** queer, curious, eccentric. **3.** unique.

sin·gu·lar·i·ty (sing′gyə lar′ə tē), *n., pl.* **-ties. 1.** peculiarity; oddness; strangeness; unusualness: *The singularity of the dwarf's appearance attracted much attention. Singularity is almost invariably a clue* (Sir Arthur Conan Doyle). **2.** something singular; peculiarity; oddity: *The giraffe's chief singularity is the length of its neck.* **3.** individual character or property; individuality; distinctiveness.

sin·gu·lar·i·za·tion (sing′gyə lər ə zā′shən), *n.* **1.** a singularizing. **2.** a transformation from the plural to the singular number.

sin·gu·lar·ize (sing′gyə lə rīz), *v.t.,* **-ized, -iz·ing. 1.** to distinguish; signalize: *It also includes another sister from her order, who resents Sister Luke's excelling her and reports to the Mother Superior that she fears Sister Luke is showing off—singularizing herself* (New Yorker). **2.** to make singular or single; individualize.

sin·gu·lar·ly (sing′gyə lər lē), *adv.* in a singular manner; unusually; extraordinarily; peculiarly: *a man of singularly clear judgment and singularly lofty spirit* (Macaulay).

sinh (no periods), hyperbolic sine.

Sin·ha·la (sin′hə lə), *n.* the Indic language of Ceylon; Singhalese: *Mrs. Bandaranaike ordered that all official business must be con-*

 PRONUNCIATION KEY: hat, āge, cãre, fär; let, ēqual, tėrm; it, īce; hot, ōpen, ôrder; oil, out; cup, pu̇t, rüle;

ducted in Sinhala (Time). [< Sanskrit *Sinhala* Ceylon]

Sin·ha·lese (sin'hə lēz', -lēs'), *n., pl.* **-lese,** *adj.* Singhalese.

Sin·ic (sin'ik), *adj.* Chinese. [< Late Latin *Sīnae* the Chinese + English *-ic*]

Sin·i·cism (sin'ə siz əm), *n.* **1.** a Chinese mannerism, method, or custom; Chinese usage. **2.** affectation or adoption of what is Chinese.

Sin·i·cize or **sin·i·cize** (sin'ə sīz), *v.t.,* **-cized, -ciz·ing.** to make Chinese in character: *Emigration from the north China plain had, however, begun long before that, so that it is today completely sinicized* (London Times).

Sin·i·fy (sin'ə fī), *v.t.,* **-fied, -fy·ing.** Sinicize.

sin·i·grin (sin'ə grin), *n.* a colorless, crystalline glucoside present in the seeds of the black mustard. *Formula:* $C_{10}H_{16}KNO_9S_2 \cdot H_2O$ [< New Latin *Si(napis) nigr(a)* black mustard (< Latin *sināpis* mustard, *niger, -gra* black) + English *-in*]

sin·is·ter (sin'ə stər), *adj.* **1.** showing ill will; threatening: *a sinister rumor, a sinister look.* **2.** bad; evil; dishonest: *I hope . . . that you'll . . . not impute to me any impertinence or sinister design* (Oliver Goldsmith). **3.** bringing evil; disastrous; unfortunate: *Such a life was sinister to the intellect, and sinister to the heart* (Hawthorne). **4.** on the left; left: *My mother's blood runs in my dexter cheek and this sinister bounds in my father's* (Shakespeare). **5.** *Heraldry.* situated to the right of the one looking at the escutcheon: *sinister base, sinister chief.* [< Latin *sinister* left (from the belief that omens seen on the left side were unlucky)] —**sin'is·ter·ly,** *adv.* —**sin'is·ter·ness,** *n.* —**Syn. 1.** ominous, inauspicious. **2.** base. **3.** unlucky.

sin·is·ter·wise (sin'ə stər wīz'), *adv.* in a sinister manner.

si·ni·stra (sē nēs'trä), *adv. Music. Italian.* with the left hand (used in marking a note or passage that is to be performed with the left hand in preference to the right).

sin·is·trad (sin'ə strad), *adv.* to the left. [< Latin *sinistra* the left hand + *ad* to]

sin·is·tral (sin'ə strəl), *adj.* **1.** of or having to do with the left side; left; left-handed. **2.** (of a spiral shell) having the whorl rising from right to left as viewed from the outside: *In most species the shell is right-handed (dextral), being coiled clockwise as seen from the spire, but some are left-handed (sinistral)* (Tracy I. Storer). **3.** (of flatfishes) having what is properly the left side converted into the upper one. —**sin'is·tral·ly,** *adv.*

sin·is·tral·i·ty (sin'ə stral'ə tē), *n.* the condition or quality of being sinistral.

sin·is·troc·u·lar (sin'ə strok'yə lər), *adj.* using the left eye more than the right. [< Latin *sinister* left hand + English *ocular*]

sin·is·tro·dex·tral (sin'ə strō deks'trəl), *adj.* **1.** left-handed. **2.** moving from left to right: *sinistrodextral calligraphy.* [< Latin *sinister* left hand + *dexter* right hand + English *-al*]

sin·is·tror·sal (sin'ə strôr'səl), *adj.* sinistrorse. —**sin'is·tror'sal·ly,** *adv.*

sin·is·trorse (sin'ə strôrs, sin'ə strôrs'), *adj.* **1.** rising spirally from right to left: *the sinistrorse stem of a vine.* **2.** sinistral. [< Latin *sinistrōrsus* < *sinister* left (see SINISTER) + *versus,* past participle of *vertere* to turn] —**sin'is·trorse'ly,** *adv.*

sin·is·trous (sin'ə strəs), *adj.* **1.** sinister; disastrous; unlucky. **2.** (of flatfishes) sinistral.

sin·is·trous·ly (sin'ə strəs lē), *adv.* in a sinistrous manner.

Si·nit·ic (si nit'ik), *adj.* of or having to do with China or the various Chinese dialects; Sinic: *The Sinitic languages are used in eastern and parts of southeastern Asia* (World Book Encyclopedia). [< Late Latin *Sīnae* the Chinese + English *-ite*[1] + *-ic*]

sink (singk), *v.,* **sank** or (sometimes) **sunk, sunk** or (now chiefly used as an adjective) **sunk·en, sink·ing,** *n.* —*v.i.* **1.** to go down; fall slowly; go lower and lower: *She sank to the floor in a faint. The sun is sinking in the west.* **2.** to go under: *The ship is sinking.* **3.** to become lower or weaker: *The wind has sunk down.* **4.** to pass gradually (to or into a state of sleep, silence, oblivion, etc.): *to sink to rest.* **5.** to go deeply: *The ink sank into the blotting paper.* **6.** to become worse in health, morals, reputation, or social status: *His spirits sank. It is indeed possible for men to sink into machines* (John Ruskin). *He had sunk by this time to the very worst reputation* (Thackeray). **7.** to fall in; become hollow: *The sick man's cheeks have sunk.* —*v.t.* **1.** to make go down; make fall: *Lack of rain sank the reservoirs.* **2.** to make go under: *The submarine sank two ships.* **3.** to make lower; reduce: *Sink your voice to a whisper.* **4.** to make go deep; dig (a well, shaft, etc.): *The men are sinking a well.* **5.** to insert or fasten into a concavity, hollow space, etc.: *a stone sunk into the wall.* **6.** to keep quiet about; conceal: *to sink evidence. By merely . . . bestowing a rich aunt, and sinking half the children he was able to represent the whole family . . . in a most respectable light* (Jane Austen). **7.** to invest (money) unprofitably: *We sank twenty dollars in a machine that we never used.* **8. a.** (in basketball) to score: *[He] sank three baskets and eight of his ten foul attempts* (New York Times). **b.** (in golf) to hit (the ball) into a hole; score thus with (a stroke): *He sank a 20-foot putt for a birdie.*

sink in, to be understood or grasped: *The warning failed to sink in, and he got into trouble as a consequence.*

sink into, to be understood or grasped by: *Let the lesson sink into your mind.*

sink or swim, to succeed or fail depending on one's own efforts: *Father wouldn't help him; he was a man and left to sink or swim.*

—*n.* **1.** a shallow basin or tub with a drainpipe: *The dishes are in the kitchen sink.* **2.** a drain; sewer. **3.** a place where dirty water or any filth collects. **4.** a place of vice or corruption: *That roadhouse is a sink of iniquity.* **5.** a low-lying inland area where waters collect or where they disappear by sinking downward or by evaporation: *Some sinks are many feet deep, are steep-sided, and have obvious openings through which the surface drainage runs underground* (Finch and Trewartha). **6.** *Printing.* **a.** the extra space left at the top of a page for the beginning of a chapter or the like. **b.** the amount of this space.

[Old English *sincan*]

—**Syn.** *v.i.* **1.** subside, descend, fall, settle, decline. **2.** submerge. *-v.t.* **3.** diminish.

sink·a·ble (sing'kə bəl), *adj.* that can be sunk.

sink·age (sing'kij), *n.* **1. a.** the act of sinking; subsidence. **b.** an instance of this. **2.** something that sinks or has sunk. **3.** *Printing.* sink.

sink·er (sing'kər), *n.* **1.** a person or thing that sinks. **2.** a weight of lead, stone, etc., for sinking a fishing line or net in the water. **3.** *U.S. Slang.* a doughnut: *Sinkers and coffee, folks, get your doughnuts here* (Los Angeles Times). **4.** a pitch in baseball that drops suddenly as it approaches the batter.

sink·hole (singk'hōl'), *n.* **1.** the hole in a sink; hole for waste to pass through. **2.** a hole that drains surface water. **3. a.** a hole where water collects. **b.** *U.S.* a funnel-shaped cavity formed in limestone regions by the removal of the rock through action of rain or running water, or both: *As the caverns enlarge, their roofs become incapable of supporting themselves and collapse, forming sinkholes at the surface* (Robert M. Garrels). **4.** a place of vice and corruption: *Company towns and company stores were a polite expression for economic serfdom. We eliminated these sinkholes* (Atlantic).

sink·ing fund (sing'king), a fund formed by a government, corporation, or the like, usually by periodically setting aside certain amounts of money to accumulate at interest, for the paying off of a debt: *The new shares will have a sinking fund of $15,000 a year* (Wall Street Journal).

sinking spell, 1. a period when an ill person takes a turn for the worse; decline; relapse. **2.** any period of decline: *With higher rates ahead, U.S. bonds had another sinking spell last week* (Time).

sin·less (sin'lis), *adj.* without sin. —**sin'less·ly,** *adv.* —**sin'less·ness,** *n.*

sin·ner (sin'ər), *n.* **1.** a person who sins; person who disobeys divine law: *God be merciful to me a sinner* (Luke 18:13). **2.** a person who does wrong, fails in any duty, or violates some rule or custom. —**Syn. 1.** evildoer.

Sinn Fein (shin' fān'), a political organization in Ireland, founded about 1905, demanding complete political separation of all Ireland from Great Britain. [< Irish *Sinn Fein* (literally) we ourselves]

Sinn Fein·er (fā'nər), a member or supporter of the Sinn Fein.

Sinn Fein·ism (fā'niz əm), adherence to Sinn Fein.

Sino-, *combining form.* **1.** of China; Chinese ——: *Sinology = the study of Chinese customs, language, art, etc.* **2.** China (Chinese) and ——: *Sino-Japanese War = the war between China and Japan.* [< Late Latin *Sīnae* the Chinese]

si·no·a·tri·al node (sī'nō ā'trē əl), the sinus node.

sin offering, a sacrifice or other offering made to atone for sin. Exodus 29:14.

Si·no-Jap·a·nese (sī'nō jap'ə nēz', -nēs'; sin'ō-), *adj.* of both China and Japan: *Sino-Japanese design is almost exclusively an art of contours* (Bernard Berenson).

Si·no·log·i·cal (sī'nə loj'ə kəl, sin'ə-), *adj.* of or having to do with Sinology.

Si·nol·o·gist (sī nol'ə jist, si-), *n.* a student of Chinese language, customs, etc.; person skilled in Sinology.

Si·no·logue (sī'nə lôg, -log; sin'ə-), *n.* a Sinologist: *Indeed, most Sinologues to-day see the uniqueness of Chinese character as a cornerstone sustaining Chinese civilization* (London Times).

Si·nol·o·gy (sī nol'ə jē, si-), *n.* the study of Chinese history, customs, institutions, language, and literature.

Si·non (sī'nən), *n.* a treacherous or perfidious betrayer. [< *Sinon,* a Greek character in Homer's *Iliad,* who induced the Trojans to bring the wooden horse into Troy]

Si·no·phil (sī'nə fil, sin'ə-), *adj., n.* Sinophile.

Si·no·phile (sī'nə fīl, -fil; sin'ə-), *adj.* friendly to the Chinese; fond of Chinese ways, customs, etc. —*n.* a friend or admirer of the Chinese.

si·no·pi·a (si nō'pē ə), *n.* sinopis.

si·no·pis (si nō'pəs), *n.* a pigment of a fine red color, prepared from the earth sinople. [< Latin *Sinōpis;* see SINOPLE]

sin·o·pite (sin'ə pīt), *n.* sinople.

sin·o·ple (sin'ə pəl), *n.* **1.** a ferruginous clay, sometimes used as a pigment. Also, **sinopite. 2.** a kind of ferruginous quartz found in Hungary. [< Old French *Sinople* < Latin *Sinōpis* < Greek *Sinōpís* < *Sinṓpē,* a colony]

Si·no-So·vi·et (sī'nō sō'vē et, sin'ō-; -it; -sov'ē-), *adj.* of or between China and the Soviet Union: *The Sino-Soviet ideological dispute centers around Peking's demand for a much stronger stand against the West* (Wall Street Journal).

Si·no-Ti·bet·an (sī'nō ti bet'ən, sin'ō-), *n.* a linguistic grouping including the Chinese, Tibeto-Burman, and Thai language families. —*adj.* of or having to do with the people or the languages of this linguistic grouping: *In eastern and southern Asia we find the great Sino-Tibetan family, of which Chinese, in its many different languages, is the most important subgroup* (Beals and Hoijer).

SINS (no periods), Ship's Inertial Navigation System (used in nuclear-powered submarines).

sin·syne (sin'sīn), *adv. Scottish.* since then.

sin·ter (sin'tər), *n.* **1.** a hard incrustation or deposit formed on rocks, etc., by evaporation of mineral waters. **2.** *Metallurgy.* something produced by sintering. —*v.t. Metallurgy.* to fuse (various constituents) to form larger particles, masses, etc.: *In order to obtain a material of fairly high density, the beryllium compacts may be heat-treated, or sintered, in a high vacuum or in a protective atmosphere such as argon* (Science News Letter). [< German *Sinter* dross, slag; origin uncertain]

sin·u·ate (sin'yů āt, -it), *adj.* **1.** *Botany.* having the margin strongly or distinctly wavy: *a sinuate leaf.* **2.** bent in and out; winding; sinuous. [< Latin *sinuātus,* past participle of *sinuāre* bend, wind < *sinus, -ūs* a curve] —**sin'u·ate·ly,** *adv.* —**Syn. 2.** tortuous.

Sinuate Leaf (def. 1) of chestnut oak

sin·u·at·ed (sin'yů ā'tid), *adj.* sinuate.

sin·u·a·tion (sin'yů ā'shən), *n.* a winding; sinuosity.

sin·u·os·i·ty (sin'yů os'ə tē), *n., pl.* **-ties. 1.**

sinuous form or character; winding: *A snake has sinuosity. Meander is a river . . . famous for the sinuosity and often returning thereof* (Michael Drayton). **2.** a curve; bend; turn: *the endless sinuosities of the mountain road.*

sin·u·ous (sin′yu̇ əs), *adj.* **1.** having many curves or turns; winding: *The motion of a snake is sinuous. I have sinuous shells of pearly hue* (Walter S. Landor). **2.** indirect; devious; roundabout. **3.** morally crooked. **4.** *Botany.* sinuate.
[< Latin *sinuōsus* < *sinus, -ūs* a curve]
—**sin′u·ous·ly,** *adv.* —**sin′u·ous·ness,** *n.*
—**Syn. 1.** serpentine.

si·nus (sī′nəs), *n.* **1.** a cavity in a bone, especially one of the air cavities lined with mucous membrane in the bones of the skull that connect with the nasal cavity: *In some places this spongy bone is absorbed and air spaces termed sinuses develop* (Harbaugh and Goodrich). **2.** a long, narrow abscess with a small opening. **3.** a reservoir or channel for venous blood. **4.** a curved hollow; cavity. **5.** a curve; bend, as a curve between two projecting lobes of a leaf. [< Latin *sinus, -ūs* any bend or curve]

Si·nus Ir·i·dum (sī′nəs ir′ə dəm), a bay or irregularity along the shoreline of one of the great sealike areas on the moon: *Along the northeastern "shore" of Mare Imbrium is a beautifully curved "bay" known as the Sinus Iridum* (Bernhard, Bennett, and Rice). [< New Latin *Sinus Iridum* < Latin *sinus* bay, *iridum* of rainbows]

si·nus·i·tis (sī′nə sī′tis), *n.* inflammation of one of the sinuses of the head, especially a nasal sinus: *Some common symptoms of sinusitis are: headache (usually in the front, sometimes in the back of the head), pain around the eyes, fever, continuous post-nasal drip (discharge from the back of the nose into the throat)* (Sidonie M. Gruenberg).

sinus node, *Anatomy.* a mass of tissue in the right auricle of the heart near the point where the major veins enter, that originates the heartbeat; pacemaker: *An increase of temperature, acting through the sinus node, also leads to faster beating* (A. Franklin Shull).

si·nus·oid (sī′nə soid), *n. Mathematics.* sine curve: *When unrolled, each half of the paper will have a cut edge in the form of a sine curve, or sinusoid, one of the fundamental wave forms of physics* (Scientific American).

si·nus·oi·dal (sī′nə soi′dəl), *adj.* of or having to do with a sinusoid: *The eastward rotation of the earth will cause its path to describe a sinusoidal curve around the Equator* (James A. Van Allen).

si·nus·oi·dal·ly (sī′nə soi′də lē), *adv.* in the manner of a sinusoid: *The steady state current, like the terminal voltage, is seen to vary sinusoidally with the time* (Sears and Zemansky).

sinusoidal projection, a type of map projection in which the central meridian and the equator are shown as straight lines, but the other meridians are shown as curved lines: *In Mollweide's homalographic projection and the sinusoidal projection the meridians are equally spaced, as they are on a globe, and the parallels are truly parallel, as they also are on a globe* (Finch and Trewartha).

sinus ve·no·sus (vi nō′səs), **1.** the chamber in the heart of lower vertebrates to which the blood is returned by the veins: *The heart [of the alligator] lies in the anteroventral part of the thorax; it comprises a small sinus venosus, two auricles, and two ventricles* (Tracy I. Storer). **2.** the cavity in the embryonic auricle of mammals in which the various venous systems are joined. [< New Latin *sinus venosus* < Latin *sinus, -ūs* (see SINUS), *vēnōsus* venose]

Si·on (sī′ən), *n.* Zion.

Siou·an (sü′ən), *adj.* of or forming the group of North American Indian tribes, or the family of languages, including the Sioux (Dakota), Osage, Crow, etc. —*n.* this group or family.

Sioux (sü), *n., pl.* **Sioux** (sü, süz), *adj.* —*n.* a member of a tribe of American Indians of the Middle Western United States. —*adj.* of or having to do with the Sioux. [American English, apparently < earlier French *Nadowes(sioux)*, alteration of Algonkian (Ojibwa) *nadoweisiw* (diminutive) < *nadowe* snake; enemy]

Sioux State, a nickname of North Dakota.

sip (sip), *v.,* **sipped, sip·ping,** *n.* —*v.t., v.i.* **1.** to drink little by little: *She sipped her tea.* **2.** to take a mere taste of (something).
—*n.* **1.** a very small drink: *It [beer] can't be tasted in a sip* (Dickens). **2.** a mere taste: *His first sip brought an exclamation of disgust. A sip is all that the public . . . ever care to take from reservoirs of abstract philosophy* (Thomas De Quincey).
[Middle English *sippen;* origin uncertain]
—**Syn.** *v.t., v.i.* **1.** See **drink.**

sipe (sīp), *v.i.,* **siped, sip·ing.** *Scottish.* to trickle slowly; ooze. [Old English *sypian.* Related to SEEP.]

si·phon (sī′fən), *n.* **1.** a bent tube through which liquid can be drawn, by air pressure, over the edge of one container into another at a lower level. **2.** a bottle for soda water with a tube through which the liquid is forced out by the pressure of the gas in the bottle. **3.** a tube-shaped organ of a clam, oyster, or certain other shellfishes for drawing in and expelling water.

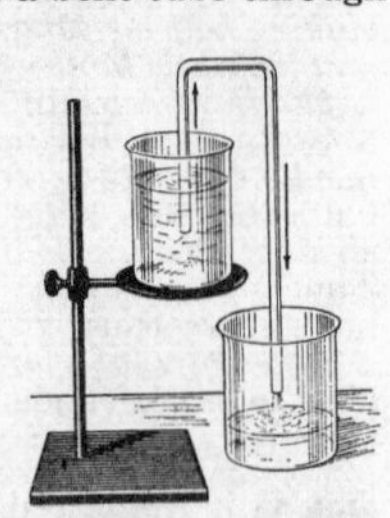

Siphon (def. 1)

—*v.t.* **1.** to draw off by means of a siphon: *The farmer siphoned water from the cellar into the ditch.* **2.** to draw off as if with a siphon: *The voters will decide whether to permit the state to siphon off surplus . . . Turnpike revenues to help solve the state's transportation problem* (Wall Street Journal). —*v.i.* to pass through a siphon. Also, **syphon.**
[< Latin *siphō, -ōnis* < Greek *sī́phōn, -ōnos* pipe]

si·phon·age (sī′fə nij), *n.* the action of a siphon.

si·phon·al (sī′fə nəl), *adj.* of or having to do with a siphon.

si·phon·ate (sī′fə nāt), *adj.* (of a mollusk, etc.) having a siphon or siphons.

siphon barometer, a barometer with the lower end of the tube bent in the form of a siphon.

siphon bottle, a bottle for aerated water, fitted with a siphon. The pressure of accumulating gas forces the water out when the valve is opened.

si·phon·ic (sī fon′ik), *adj.* **1.** siphonal. **2.** working by means of or on the principle of a siphon.

si·pho·no·phore (sī′fə nə fôr, -fōr; sī-fon′ə-), *n.* any of a group of pelagic, free-swimming hydrozoans that form colonies made up of different types of polyps, as the Portuguese man-of-war: *A siphonophore is not a single animal but a composite, or colony, of inseparably associated individuals —the multiple offspring of a single fertilized egg* (New Yorker). [< Greek *sī́phōn, -ōnos* siphon + English *-phore*]

si·pho·no·stele (sī′fə nə stēl, -stē′lē), *n. Botany.* vascular tissue in the form of a hollow tube with the pith in the center: *A siphonostele resembles the protostele except that a pith occurs in its center* (Heber W. Youngken). [< Greek *sī́phōn, -ōnos* siphon + English *stele*]

si·phun·cle (sī′fung kəl), *n.* **1.** *Zoology.* a small tube passing through the partitions in the shell of certain cephalopods: *The siphuncle, a coiled fleshy tube enclosed in a limy covering, extends through all the chambers, connecting them with the body of the nautilus* (World Book Encyclopedia). **2.** *Entomology.* either of two small tubular organs on the abdomen of an aphid, through which a waxy secretion is exuded. [< Latin *sīphunculus* (diminutive) < *siphō;* see SIPHON]

si·phun·cu·lar (sī fung′kyə lər), *adj.* of, having to do with, or like a siphuncle.

si·phun·cu·late (sī fung′kyə lāt, -lit), *adj.* having a siphuncle.

si·phun·cu·lat·ed (sī fung′kyə lā′tid), *adj.* siphunculate.

sip·id (sip′id), *adj.* **1.** having a pleasing taste or flavor. **2.** of agreeably distinctive character. [back formation < *insipid*]

sip·per (sip′ər), *n.* **1.** a person who sips or drinks: *Key factor in the surge toward drinks for fat-wary sippers is the development of cyclamate calcium to replace sugar* (Wall Street Journal). **2.** a straw for sipping liquid from a glass or bottle.

sip·pet (sip′it), *n.* **1.** a bit of toast or fried bread, such as is served in soup, as a garnish, etc. **2.** a bit; fragment. [< *sip* + *-et*]

sip·pi·o (sip′ē ō), *n.* a game like bagatelle, played with eight balls, driven into numbered holes or pockets by means of a cue ball struck with an ordinary cue.

Sip·py diet (sip′ē), a diet for the treatment of peptic ulcer by frequent feedings of small amounts of milk, cream, alkaline powders, cereal, eggs, and some other bland foods: *The Sippy diet [is] prescribed for approximately 90 per cent of the 2,440,000 ulcer patients in the United States* (Science News Letter). [< Bertram W. *Sippy,* 1886-1924, an American physician]

si·pun·cu·lid (sī pung′kyə lid), *n.* any of a group of elongated, tentacled marine worms that live in sand or mud, either within snail shells or free. [< New Latin *Sipunculus* the genus name < Latin *sīpunculus,* variant of *sīphunculus;* see SIPHUNCLE]

si quae·ris pen·in·su·lam a·moe·nam, cir·cum·spi·ce (sē kwī′ris pə nin′sü läm ä mē′näm sėr′kəm spē′sā), *Latin.* if you seek a pleasant peninsula, look about you (the motto of Michigan).

sir (sėr; *unstressed* sər), *n., v.,* **sirred, sir·ring.** —*n.* **1.** a respectful or formal term of address used to a man: *It's very kind of you, sir.* **2.** a title of respect formerly used before a man's name or a noun designating his profession: *I am one that would rather go with sir Priest than sir Knight* (Shakespeare). **3.** Mr. or Master (often used in scorn, contempt, indignation, etc.): *You, sir, have no business here; get out.* **4.** a lord or gentleman. In olden times, *sir* was equivalent to *sire.*
—*v.t., v.i.* to address as sir: *You mustn't sir me* (Graham Greene).
[probably unstressed variant of *sire*]

Sir (sėr; *unstressed* sər), *n.* **1.** a title of a knight or baronet: *Sir Walter Scott. Abbr.:* Sr. **2.** a title of respect or honor, used to a man.

➔ **Sir** is usually used with one given name plus the surname or with the given name alone, but not with the surname only. Thus *Sir William Craigie* might be addressed or referred to as *Sir William,* but not as *Sir Craigie.*

SIR (no periods), Submarine Intermediate Reactor, a nuclear reactor used in nuclear-powered submarines, utilizing liquid sodium metal as the heat exchanger.

sir·car (sėr′kär, sər kär′), *n.* sirkar.

sir·dar (sėr′där, sər där′), *n.* **1.** a military chief or leader in India. **2.** a chief or headman in India. **3.** the British commander of the Egyptian army in former times. **4.** an Indian valet or body servant. [< Anglo-Indian < Hindustani *sardār* chief < Persian *sar* head + *dār* having]

sir·dar·ship (sėr′där ship, sər där′-), *n.* the position or authority of a sirdar.

sire (sīr), *n., v.,* **sired, sir·ing.** —*n.* **1. a.** a male parent; father: *No children run to lisp their sire's return* (Thomas Gray). **b.** a male ancestor; forefather: *Strike—for the green graves of your sires!* (Fitz-Greene Halleck). **2.** the male parent: *Lightning was the sire of the race horse Danger.* **3.** a title of respect used formerly to a great noble and now to a king *"I'm killed, Sire," said the messenger to Napoleon.* **4.** *Obsolete.* a lord; master.
—*v.t.* to be the father of; beget: *Lightning sired the race horse Danger.*
[< Old French *sire* < Vulgar Latin *seior* < Latin *senior* older. Doublet of SENIOR.]

si·re·don (sī rē′dən), *n.* a salamander in its larval state, especially an axolotl. [< New Latin *Siredon* the genus name < Greek *seirēdṓn,* earlier *seirḗn* siren]

sir·ee (sə rē′), *n. Informal.* sirree.

sire·less (sīr′lis), *adj. Archaic.* without a sire; fatherless.

si·ren (sī′rən), *n.* **1.** *Greek and Roman Mythology.* a nymph who, by her sweet singing, lured sailors to their destruction upon the rocks. **2.** any woman who lures, tempts, or entices: . . . *that pretty little girl who used to live just around the corner, has returned to town . . . a full-fledged siren* (New Yorker). **3.** a kind of whistle that makes a loud, piercing sound. It consists of a disk pierced with holes and rotating over a stream of compressed air, steam, or the like: *a police siren, an air-raid siren. We heard the sirens of the fire engines.* **4.** any of a group of aquatic, eellike salamanders, having small forelimbs, no hindlimbs, and three pairs of external gills that remain even after the lungs are formed.
—*adj.* of or like a siren; tempting; charming: *siren words, siren charms. The siren call of alleged panaceas* (New York Times).
[< Latin *sīrēn* < Greek *seirḗn, -ênos*] —**si′ren·like′,** *adj.*
—**Syn.** *adj.* bewitching, alluring.

si·re·ni·an (sī rē′nē ən), *n.* any of a small group of aquatic, herbivorous mammals, distinguished from whales by their rounded, unnotched tails: *Manatees and dugongs are sirenians.* [< New Latin *Sirenia* the order name (< *Siren* the typical genus < Latin *sīrēn;* see SIREN) + English *-an*]

si·ren·ic (sī ren′ik), *adj.* **1.** seductive; alluring; sirenlike. **2.** melodious.

siren song, a call or song of enticement; something which attracts a person irresistibly: *Africa's siren song to aluminum manufacturers isn't emanating from the Belgian Congo alone, by any means* (Wall Street Journal).

siren suit, *British.* coveralls: *The siren suit became a favourite of Sir Winston's during the war* (London Times).

sir·gang (sėr′gang), *n.* a crested, crowlike bird of southern Asia, with light-green to blue feathers. [< a native word]

Sir·i·an (sir′ē ən), *adj.* of or having to do with Sirius.

si·ri·a·sis (si rī′ə sis), *n.* **1.** sunstroke; coup de soleil. **2.** exposure to the sun for medical purposes; sun bath; insolation. [< New Latin *siriasis* < Greek *seiriásis* < *seiriān* to be scorching]

Sir·i·us (sir′ē əs), *n.* the brightest (fixed) star in the sky, in the constellation Canis Major; the Dog Star. [< Latin *Sīrius* < Greek *Seírios*]

sir·kar (sėr′kär, sėr kär′), *n.* (in India) the government; the state. Also, **sircar.** [Anglo-Indian < Hindustani *sarkār* < Persian, < *sar* head + *-kār*, an agential suffix]

sir·loin (sėr′loin), *n.* **1.** *U.S.* **a.** a cut of beef from the back part of the loin, in front of the rump and round. **b.** a beefsteak cut from the portion of the loin immediately in front of this, beginning at the hip joint. **2.** *British.* porterhouse (steak): *Our "porterhouse" steak is their "sirloin"* (Holiday). [< variant of Old French *surlonge* < *sur* over + *longe* loin]

si·roc (sə rok′, sī′rok), *n. Archaic.* sirocco.

si·roc·co (sə rok′ō), *n., pl.* **-cos. 1.** a very hot, dry, and dust-laden wind blowing from the northern coast of Africa across the Mediterranean and parts of southern Europe: *Rain is followed usually by the sirocco—the hot wind from Africa—and the ground is quickly parched and cracked* (Atlantic). **2.** a moist, warm, south or southeast wind in these same regions: *Sometimes the sirocco extends to the northern shore of the Mediterranean where it becomes a warm and moist wind* (Thomas A. Blair). **3.** any hot, unpleasant wind: *The slow self-service elevator was an asphyxiating chamber with a fan that blew a withering sirocco* (New Yorker). [< Italian *scirocco* < Arabic *sharqī* east wind]

sir·rah (sir′ə), *n. Archaic.* fellow, used as a term of address to men and boys when speaking impatiently, contemptuously, angrily, etc.: *"Silence, sirrah," said the prince to the stableboy.* [apparently < *sir* + *ha*]

sir·ree (sə rē′), *n. Informal.* sir (emphasized). Also, **siree.**

sir-rev·er·ence (sėr′rev′ər əns), *n. Obsolete.* saving your reverence, an apology: *A very reverent body; ay, such a one as a man may not speak of, without he says sir-reverence* (Shakespeare). [alteration of *s'r reverence*, shortened pronunciation of *save your reverence*, translation of Latin *salva reverentia*]

Sir Rog·er de Cov·er·ley (sėr roj′ər dē kuv′ər lē), an old-fashioned English country-dance, something like the Virginia reel.

sir·up (sir′əp, sėr′-), *n.* syrup.

sir·up·y (sir′ə pē, sėr′-), *adj.* syrupy.

sir·vente (sir väNt′), *n.* a kind of satirical song of the medieval troubadours, usually about the faults and vices of society. [< French *sirvente* < Old Provençal *sirventes*, or *serventes*, perhaps < *servir* serve]

sis (sis), *n. U.S. Informal.* sister. [American English; short for *sister*]

sis·al (sis′əl, sī′səl), *n.,* or **sisal hemp. 1.** a strong, white fiber obtained from the leaves of either of two species of agave, used for making rope, twine, etc. **2.** either of the plants that it comes from: *Careful where you sit, bub; those blasted sisal plants are needle-sharp* (New Yorker). [< *Sisal*, a port in Yucatán, from which it was exported]

sis·co·wet (sis′kə wet), *n.* a very fat, thick-skinned variety of lake trout found in Lake Superior. [< Canadian French *siscowet*, alteration of Chippewa *pemitewiskawet* that which has oily flesh]

Sis·er·a (sis′ər ə), *n.* (in the Bible) a commander of the Canaanites against the Israelites, slain by Jael after his defeat in battle. Judges 4 and 5.

si sic om·ni·a (sī sik om′nē ə), *Latin.* if all had been thus.

sis·kin (sis′kin), *n.* any of a group of small finches, as a green-and-yellow European finch related to the goldfinch, and the pine siskin of North America. [probably < Middle Dutch *sijsken* < Slavic (compare Czech *čížek*)]

sis·mo·gram (sis′mə gram), *n.* seismogram.

sis·mo·graph (sis′mə graf, -gräf), *n.* seismograph.

sis·mo·graph·ic (sis′mə graf′ik), *adj.* seismographic.

siss (sis), *v.i.* to hiss. —*n.* a hiss. [imitative]

sis·si·fied (sis′ə fīd), *adj. Informal.* effeminate: *Wealthy oil men from Texas ... sometimes are prone to class blue-white diamonds as sissified* (Wall Street Journal).

sis·soo (sis′ü), *n.* **1.** a large, deciduous tree of the pea family, common in India, having durable, dark-brown wood used extensively for boats and furniture. **2.** its wood. [< Hindi *sīsū*]

sis·sy (sis′ē), *n., pl.* **-sies,** *adj.,* **-si·er, -si·est.** *Informal.* —*n.* **1.** a boy or man who behaves too much like a girl: *I could not for a moment tolerate the idea of being thought of as a "kid" or a sissy* (John Masters). **2.** sister. —*adj.* of or like a sissy; effeminate: *The feeling that it is sissy for a boy to take an interest in the arts has probably always existed among the middle class and is yet not extinct* (New Yorker). [probably diminutive form of *sis*]

sissy britches, *U.S. Slang.* **1.** a sissy. **2.** a coward.

sis·sy·ish (sis′ē ish), *adj. Informal.* of, like, or characteristic of a sissy: *In cities, suburbs, and small towns there is little—if any—outdoor work to be done, and many boys consider housework "sissyish"* (Sidonie M. Gruenberg).

sis·ter (sis′tər), *n.* **1. a.** a daughter of the same parents or parent. A girl is a sister to the other children of her parents or parent. **b.** a half sister; a stepsister. **2.** a person or thing resembling or closely connected with another: *Its smaller sister, the IRBM (intermediate range ballistic missile), could, at ranges of 600 to 1,500 miles, bombard many of the cities and airfields of Western Europe* (Hanson W. Baldwin). *Happiness and Intelligence are seldom sisters* (Thomas Love Peacock). **3.** a female fellow member of a society, church, etc.: *a sorority sister.* **4.** a member of a religious sisterhood or order of women; a nun. **5.** *British.* **a.** a nurse. **b.** a head nurse.
—*adj.* being a sister; related as if by sisterhood: *a sister ship.*
[< Scandinavian (compare Old Icelandic *systir*)]
➤ **Sister** is sometimes used alone as a word of address in very informal or nonstandard English as a substitute for "Miss" or "Madam": *Look, sister, I've told you the price three times now; it won't be less next time you ask.*

sister block, *Nautical.* a block with two sheaves in it, one above the other, used for various purposes.

sis·ter·hood (sis′tər hůd), *n.* **1.** the feeling of sister for sister; bond between sisters: *the bonds of sisterhood.* **2.** persons joined as sisters; association of women with some common aim or characteristic: *the great sisterhood of mothers. I'll dispose of thee, Among a sisterhood of holy nuns* (Shakespeare).

sister hook, *Nautical.* one of a pair of hooks working on the same axis and fitting closely together, much used about a ship's rigging.

sis·ter-in-law (sis′tər in lô′), *n., pl.* **sisters-in-law. 1.** the sister of one's husband or wife. **2.** the wife of one's brother. **3.** the wife of one's brother-in-law.

sis·ter·less (sis′tər lis), *adj.* having no sister.

sis·ter·li·ness (sis′tər lē nis), *n.* sisterly quality or state.

sis·ter·ly (sis′tər lē), *adj.* **1.** suitable for a sister; like a sister; very kindly: *sisterly interest, sisterly love.* **2.** of or having to do with a (religious) sisterhood: *a sisterly life.*

sis·tern (sis′tərn), *n.pl. Dialect.* sisters.

Sister of Charity, a member of a sisterhood, especially a Roman Catholic sisterhood, devoted to work among the poor and to nursing the sick.

Sister of Mercy, a member of a Roman Catholic sisterhood devoted to nursing the sick and to the education and care of the poor.

sis·te vi·a·tor (sis′tē vī ā′tər), *Latin.* stop, traveler.

Sis·tine (sis′tēn, -tīn, -tin), *adj.* of or having to do with any one of the five popes named Sixtus. Also, **Sixtine.** [< Italian *sistino* < *Sisto* (Pope Sixtus IV) < Latin *sextus* sixth]

Sistine Chapel, the chapel of the Pope in the Vatican at Rome, built for Pope Sixtus IV in 1473, decorated with frescoes by Michelangelo and other great artists.

Sistine Madonna, one of the best known of the many Madonnas painted by Raphael, done for the Church of Saint Sixtus at Piacenza, Italy.

sis·troid (sis′troid), *adj. Geometry.* contained between the convex sides of two curves that intersect each other.

sis·trum (sis′trəm), *n., pl.* **-trums, -tra** (-trə). an ancient metal instrument or rattle, having an oval frame with loosely fitting transverse rods, used especially in Egypt in the worship of Isis. [< Latin *sīstrum* < Greek *seîstron* < *seíein* to shake]

Sistrum

Sis·y·phe·an (sis′ə fē′ən), *adj.* of or having to do with Sisyphus.

Sis·y·phus (sis′ə fəs), *n. Greek Mythology.* a king of Corinth condemned forever to roll a heavy stone up a steep hill in Hades, only to have it always roll down again when he neared the top.

sit (sit), *v.,* **sat** or (*Archaic*) **sate, sat** or (*Obsolete*) **sit·ten, sit·ting,** *n.* —*v.i.* **1. a.** to rest on the lower part of the body, with the weight off the feet: *She sat in a chair.* **b.** to do this in a certain way: *to sit cross-legged, to sit close to a fire.* **2.** to have place or position: *The clock has sat on that shelf for years. We came upon a little village sitting in the hills.* **3.** to have a seat in an assembly, etc.; be a member of a council: *to sit in Congress.* **4.** to hold a session: *The court sits next month.* **5.** to place oneself in a position for having one's picture made; pose: *to sit for a portrait.* **6.** to be in a state of rest; remain inactive: *Shall your brethren go to war, and shall ye sit here?* (Numbers 32:6). **7.** to press or weigh: *Care sat heavily on his brow.* **8.** to fit: *The coat sits well.* **9.** to perch; roost: *The birds were sitting on the fence rail.* **10.** to cover eggs so that they will hatch; brood. **11.** to baby-sit.
—*v.t.* **1.** to cause to sit; seat: *The woman sat the little boy down hard.* **2.** to seat (oneself): *He boldly sat himself down at my fireside.* **3.** to sit on: *He sat his horse well.*

sit down, to take a seat; put oneself in a sitting position: *He sat down by the roadside to partake of his bread and cheese* (Arthur Conan Doyle).

sit in, a. to be present as a spectator or observer: *He was invited to sit in at the lecture.* **b.** to take part in an activity: *to sit in with a musical group, sit in at a game.* **c.** *U.S.* to take part in a sit-in: ... *Negro pupils sitting in at the nearly all-white school* (New York Times).

sit in on, to be present at, as a spectator or observer: *The Senate Finance and Assembly Ways and Means Committees now have a legal right to sit in on the budget-making process* (New York Times).

sit on or **upon, a.** to sit in judgment or council on; deliberate on: *A committee of ... friends ... sat upon our affairs* (Harper's). **b.** to have a seat on (a jury, commission, etc.): *He sat on the Royal Commission on Hospitals* (London Times). **c.** *Informal.* to check, rebuke, or snub: *My lady felt rebuked, and, as she afterward expressed it, sat upon* (Lynn Linton).

sit out, a. to remain seated during (a dance): [*She*] *only refused him once when she wanted to sit out with Cornelia* (Edna Lyell). **b.** to stay through (a performance, etc.): *This is the only meeting ... which it has been my privilege to sit out* (J. Johnston). **c.** to stay later than (another): *I thought I would sit the other visitors out* (W.E. Norris). **d.** *Informal.* to do nothing about; stay out of: *He's prudently sitting out the scandal* (Maclean's).

sit through, to remain seated during; be present or in attendance at: *to sit through a dull concert, to sit through a lecture.*

sit tight, *Informal.* **a.** to keep the same position, opinion, etc.: *When a company's business is down, it's far more inclined to sit tight and take a strike than when things are*

booming (Wall Street Journal). **b.** to let matters take their own course; refrain from action: *Be calm and sit tight and everything will turn out well.*
sit under, to attend the preaching, etc., of; listen to, as a customary hearer: *Members of Parliament, even Cabinet Ministers, sit under him [a clergyman]* (Thackeray).
sit up, a. to raise the body to a sitting position: *She heard, she moved, . . . and up she sat* (Tennyson). **b.** to keep such a position: . . . *the pale wasted form in the easy chair (for he sat up to the last)* (George Eliot). **c.** to stay up instead of going to bed: *They sat up talking till far into the night* (Edward Peacock). **d.** *Informal.* to start up in surprise: *He sat up and took notice in a hurry.*
—*n.* a stopping at a place for a short while; sojourn; stay: *The day before it was a trip round the Island and a sit in the arboretum* (Punch).
[Old English *sittan*]
➤ See **set** for usage note.

Si·ta (sē′tä), *n. Hindu Mythology.* the wife of the god Rama, and heroine of the Ramayana: *Sita, . . . who was kidnapped by the wicked king Ravana, withstood his attempts to seduce her, returned to her husband only to be banished by him for sixteen years because people of his kingdom couldn't believe that she could have remained chaste* (Santha Rama Rau).

si·tar (si tär′), *n.* a three-stringed guitar used in India: *[He] begins to play on his sitar, deliberately plucking a succession of ten or twelve notes, and then stops* (Newsweek). [< Hindi *sitār*]

si·tar·ist (si tär′ist), *n.* a player of the sitar: *Ravi Shankar—sitarist, with Kanai Dutta, tabla, and N.C. Mullick, tamboura* (New Yorker).

sit·a·tun·ga (sit′ə tu̇ng′gə), *n.* an antelope of central and eastern Africa which inhabits swampy, forested regions.

sit-down[1] (sit′doun′), *adj.* served to persons seated at a table: *Later, they were treated to a sit-down lunch consisting of fruit cup, roast beef, vegetables, and apple pie* (Wall Street Journal).

sit-down strike, or **sit-down**[2] (sit′doun′), *n.* **1.** a strike in which the workers stay in the factory, store, etc., without working until their demands are met or an agreement is reached: *Three thousand workers staged a sit-down strike today at the Bremen Goliath Automobile works* (New York Times). **2.** a demonstration in which participants sit down in a public place and refuse to move as a form of protest against discrimination, the use of nuclear weapons, etc.: *He was ready to call a sit-down strike in Congress against funds for the Congo* (Manchester Guardian Weekly).

site (sīt), *n., v.,* **sit·ed, sit·ing.** —*n.* **1.** the position or place (of a building, town, etc.): *This house has one of the best sites in town.* **2.** ground or area upon which something has been, is being, may be, or will be built, done, etc.: *the site of a pioneer settlement, of a steel mill, or of a battle. The chapel . . . stands on the site of the ancient church burnt not long ago* (William Dean Howells). —*v.t.* to place in a site; locate; situate: *There is also much to be said for siting industry so that the minimum fetching and carrying is required* (Sunday Times). [< Latin *situs, -ūs*] —**Syn.** *n.* **1.** location.

sit·fast (sit′fast′, -fäst′), *n.* saddle gall.

sith (sith), *prep., conj., adv. Archaic.* since. [Old English *sīth* after (in time)]

sith·en (sith′ən), *prep., conj., adv. Archaic.* sith; since.

sit-in (sit′in′), *n. U.S.* a taking of seats in a restaurant, etc., by a group as a form of protest against racial segregation.

Sit·ka spruce (sit′kə), a tall spruce tree of the Pacific Coast region from Alaska to California, valued for its lumber: *The arches are made from thinnings of Sitka spruce* (New Science). [< *Sitka,* a town in Alaska]

si·tol·o·gy (sī tol′ə jē), *n.* the science of food or diet; dietetics. [< Greek *sîtos* food, grain + English *-logy*]

si·to·ma·ni·a (sī′tō mā′nē ə), *n.* an abnormal craving for food. [< Greek *sîtos* food, grain + English *mania*]

si·to·pho·bi·a (sī′tō fō′bē ə), *n.* an abnormal dislike for food. [< Greek *sîtos* food, grain + English *-phobia*]

si·tos·ter·in (sī tos′tər in), *n.* sitosterol.

si·tos·ter·ol (sī tos′tə rōl, -rol), *n.* any of several crystalline alcohols or sterols, similar to cholesterol, present in wheat, corn, bran, Calabar beans, and other plants. [< Greek *sîtos* grain, food + English (chole)*sterol*]

si·to·tox·in (sī′tō tok′sin), *n.* a toxin or poison generated by a microorganism in vegetable food.

sit·rep (sit′rep′), *n.* a report on military activities and operations: . . . *the morning sitreps—situation reports on . . . U-boat attack and counterattack, British and German air raids, all the details of the day-to-day progress of the war* (John H. Peck). [< *sit*(uation) *rep*(ort)]

sit spin, (in figure skating) a spin on one leg with a gradual sinking into a sitting position in which the other leg is extended.

sit·ter (sit′ər), *n.* **1.** a person who sits: *The number of sitters in the pine pews of the chapels and the oak pews of the churches falls ever lower* (J.E.R. Scott). **2.** a person who is usually hired to take care of a child or children; baby sitter: *The self-contained little family is only made possible by the sitter—an outsider paid to come into the house and maintain it as a going concern, watching over sleeping children, giving the baby his supper, answering the telephone, and so forth* (Sidonie M. Gruenberg). **3.** a bird sitting on its eggs. **4.** anything easy or certain of performance: *In the last chukka, Hanut missed three shots running that normally would have been sitters for him* (London Times).

sit·ter-in (sit′ər in′), *n.* **1.** *British.* a baby sitter. **2.** a person who sits in or participates: *He's an amateur drummer and the inveterate sitter-in with any musical group that will invite him* (Maclean's).

sit·ting (sit′ing), *n.* **1.** the act of one that sits. **2. a.** a meeting or session of a legislature, court, etc.: *His [Babeuf's] defense, which lasted for six sittings of the court and fills more than three hundred pages, is an impressive and moving document* (Edmund Wilson). **b.** the period of time occupied by this. **3. a.** the time of remaining seated: *He read five chapters at one sitting.* **b.** a period of posing: *to do a portrait in three sittings.* **4. a.** the act of a bird, especially a hen, in setting; brooding. **b.** the number of eggs on which the bird sits; clutch. **5.** a seat for one person in a church or other place of worship: *The church is enlarged by at least five hundred sittings* (George Eliot).
—*adj.* **1.** that sits; seated: *a sitting dog, person, etc.* **2.** that sets; setting: *a sitting hen.* **3.** that has a seat in a legislative body, on a committee, etc.: *a sitting magistrate.* **4. a.** of or having to do with sitting: *a sitting posture.* **b.** used for sitting; in which one sits or may sit: *the sitting area of an auditorium, to find sitting space.* **c.** used in sitting: *the sitting muscles.*

sitting duck, *Informal.* an easy target or mark: . . . *a master detection system which can pinpoint every . . . submarine . . . at sea and makes the subs . . . sitting ducks* (Newsweek).

sitting room, a room to sit in, entertain guests in, etc.; living room or parlor, as distinguished from a bedroom, kitchen, etc.: *With each sleeping room was connected a sitting room, where fires were kept* (E. Banks).

sit·u·ate (sich′u̇ āt), *v.,* **-at·ed, -at·ing,** *adj.* —*v.t.* to place; locate: *They situated themselves in three separate chambers* (Thomas Paine).
—*adj. Archaic except Law.* having its location; placed; situated. [< Medieval Latin *situare* (with English *-ate*[1]) < Latin *situs, -ūs* location]

sit·u·at·ed (sich′u̇ ā′tid), *adj.* **1.** placed; located: *New York is a favorably situated city.* **2.** being in certain circumstances: *The doctor is well situated.*
➤ **Situated,** when followed by a preposition, is often an unnecessary sentence element: *He traveled to a small town in Canada called Picton, [situated] in Ontario.*

sit·u·a·tion (sich′u̇ ā′shən), *n.* **1.** a position; location; place: *Our house has an attractive situation on a hill.* **2. a.** combination of circumstances; case; condition: *Act reasonably in all situations.* **b.** position with regard to circumstances: *It is an awkward situation to be alone and without money in a strange city.* **3.** a place to work; job: *She is trying to find a situation.* **4.** a state of affairs, series of events, etc., in a play, novel, etc.: *a good opening situation. The play turned upon a typical French situation* (Mrs. Humphry Ward).
—**Syn. 1.** site, station, spot. **3.** post. See **position.**

sit·u·a·tion·al (sich′u̇ ā′shə nəl), *adj.* of or having to do with situations: *We must recognize that people are not just driven by situational pressures; they are also pulled by the ideals and goals of their cultures* (Scientific American).

situation comedy, comedy which depends for its humor upon one or more contrived situations: *A number of able comedians have been forced to rely on the artificial support of quiz-show routines, or of so-called situation comedy, which is far from being the same thing as pure, or "straight," comedy* (John Lardner).

situation ethics, a theory of ethics that rejects moral absolutes and maintains that ethical decisions must arise spontaneously from the demands of specific situations and contexts: *In 1956 the Holy Office condemned situation ethics for Roman Catholics as an illicit brand of subjectivism* (Time).

sit·u·a·tion·ism (sich′u̇ ā′shə niz′əm), *n.* **1.** a psychological theory which emphasizes the influence of a person's present situation in determining his behavior. **2.** situation ethics: *Situationism fails to consider that man is always acting within a community that cannot exist without law* (Time).

sit·u·a·tion·ist (sich′u̇ ā′shə nist), *n.* a person who favors or advocates situationism.

sit·u·la (sich′u̇ lə), *n., pl.* **-lae** (-lē). a deep, bucketlike vessel, vase, or urn used by the ancient Greeks and Romans. [< Latin *situla* bucket, urn]

sit-up (sit′up′), *n.* an exercise in which a person lies on his back with hands under his head, legs extended, and then sits up without raising the feet: *I've run to the point of exhaustion, and I've done push-ups and pull-ups and sit-ups until my muscles twitched like a thoroughbred's flanks* (Maclean's).

sit-up·on (sit′ə pon′, -pôn′), *n. Slang.* the rump: *The advertisements . . . would make Mrs. Grundy fall flat on her sit-upon* (London Times).

si·tus (sī′təs), *n.* position, situation, or location, especially the proper or original position, as of a part or organ. [< Latin *situs, -ūs*]

si·tus in·ver·sus (sī′təs in vėr′səs), a congenital defect of the human anatomy in which the organs of the right and left side are reversed. [< New Latin *situs inversus* < Latin *situs, -ūs* situs and *inversus* inverse]

sit·u·tun·ga (sit′ə tu̇ng′gə), *n.* sitatunga.

sit ve·ni·a ver·bo (sit vē′nē ə vėr′bō), *Latin.* pardon the expression.

sitz bath (sits), **1.** a tub to bathe in, in which the user sits so that only the hips and the lower part of the body are submerged. **2.** the bath so taken, especially a hot bath for easing muscular pain. [half-translation of German *Sitzbad* < *Sitz* seat, sitting position (< *sitzen* to sit) + *Bad* bath]

sitz·krieg (sits′krēg′; *German* zits′krēk′), *n.* warfare without movement; static warfare. [< German *Sitzkrieg* (literally) sitting war. Compare BLITZKRIEG.]

sitz·mark (sits′märk′; *German* zits′märk′), *n.* a hole in the snow made by a skier who falls backward and comes to rest approximately in a sitting position: *Thousands left their sitzmarks on the deep powder slopes of California's Sierras and Washington's Cascade range* (Time). [half-translation of German *Sitzmarke* < *Sitz* a sitting, seat + *Marke* sign]

SIU (no periods) or **S.I.U.,** Seafarers' International Union.

Si·va (sē′və, shē′-), *n.* one of the three chief Hindu divinities, known as "the Destroyer." Those who worship him as the primary Hindu divinity consider him to be the creative and reproductive force. Also, **Shiva.** [< Hindustani *Shiva* < Sanskrit *śiva* (literally) auspicious]

Si·va·ism (sē′və iz əm, shē′-), *n.* the worship of Siva.

Si·va·ist (sē′və ist, shē′-), *n.* a worshiper of Siva.

Si·va·is·tic (sē′və is′tik, shē′-), *adj.* of or having to do with Sivaism or Sivaists.

Si·va·ite (sē′və īt, shē′-), *n.* a person who worships Siva; an adherent of the worship of Siva.

Si·van (sē vän′, siv′ən), *n.* the third month of the Hebrew ecclesiastical year or the

ninth of the civil year, corresponding to May and sometimes part of June. [< Hebrew *siwān*]
si·va snake (sē′və), the king cobra.
siv·a·there (siv′ə thir), *n.* sivatherium.
siv·a·the·ri·um or **Siv·a·the·ri·um** (siv′ə thir′ē əm), *n.* a large, extinct mammal, a forebear of the modern giraffe but having a shorter neck and legs, a skull as large as an elephant's, and two pairs of horns, the posterior pair attaining a six-foot spread. Its fossil remains were found in the Tertiary strata of India. [< New Latin *Sivatherium* the genus name < *Siva* + Greek *theríon* beast]
si·ver (sī′vər), *n. Scottish.* a gutter, drain, or sewer. [perhaps < Old French *sewiere* sewer]
Si·wan (sē vän′, siv′ən), *n.* Sivan.
Si·wash (sī′wosh), *n.* a North American Indian of the northern Pacific Coast. —*adj.* of, having to do with, or like a Siwash. [< Chinook jargon < French *sauvage* savage]
six (siks), *n.* **1.** one more than five; 6. **2.** the number six. **3.** a playing card or die with six spots. **4.** anything identified as being or having six units, especially a six-cylinder automobile.
at sixes and sevens, a. in confusion: *As usual, things were also at sixes and sevens in the stake races for fillies* (New Yorker). **b.** in disagreement: *With the Democratic party at sixes and sevens since the Minnesota primary there will be a whole stable of dark horses in the background this year* (Wall Street Journal).
knock (or **hit**) **for six,** *British Slang.* to beat soundly; defeat; destroy: *Declaring that the Bill is a "serious infringement on the rights of women," they proceed to knock it for six* (London Times).
—*adj.* being one more than five.
[Old English *siex, six*]
Six (siks), *n.* the six original members of the European Common Market, Belgium, France, Italy, Luxemburg, the Netherlands, and West Germany; Inner Six.
six-by-six (siks′bī siks′), *n.* a motor truck with six wheels: *Engineers banging down the road in six-by-sixes, raising red dust* (New Yorker).
six·fold (siks′fōld′), *adj.* **1.** six times as much or as many; sextuple. **2.** having six parts. —*adv.* six times as much or as many.
six-foot (siks′fút′), *adj.* six feet long or tall.
six-foot·er (siks′fút′ər), *n.* a person who is six feet tall.
six-gun (siks′gun′), *n. U.S.* a six-shooter.
Six Nations, a federation of Iroquois Indian tribes. The Tuscarora tribe of Iroquois in 1722 joined the original federation of Iroquois tribes called the Five Nations.
606, the original name of arsphenamine: *Paul Ehrlich ... discovered Salvarsan or "606", the drug that attacked syphilis* (New Scientist).
six-pack (siks′pak′), *n.* a container holding six bottles, cans, or other items sold as a unit: *a six-pack of beer.*
six·pence (siks′pəns), *n.* **1.** a sum of six British pennies; six pence. Sixpence is worth about 7 cents of United States money. **2.** a British coin having this value, worth six pence or ½ of a shilling.
six·pen·ny (siks′pen′ē, -pə nē), *adj.* **1.** worth, costing, or amounting to sixpence. **2.** *British.* of little worth; cheap. **3.** two inches long; two-inch: *sixpenny nails.*
six·score (siks′skôr′, -skōr′), *adj. Archaic.* six times twenty; 120.
six-shoot·er (siks′shü′tər), *n.* **1.** a revolver of relatively large caliber (.44 or .45; never less than .38) having a cylinder with six chambers. **2.** any revolver.
six·some (sik′səm), *n.* **1.** a group of six people. **2.** a game played by six people. **3.** the players.
sixte (sikst), *n. Fencing.* the sixth in a series of eight defensive positions or parries. [< Old French *sixte,* variant of *siste* < *sis* six < Latin *sex*]
six·teen (siks′tēn′), *n., adj.* six more than ten; 16. [Old English *sixtēne*]
six·teen·mo (siks′tēn′mō), *n., pl.* **-mos,** *adj.* sextodecimo, an English reading of the abbreviation *16mo.*
six·teenth (siks′tēnth′), *adj.* **1.** next after the 15th; last in a series of 16. **2.** being one of 16 equal parts.
—*n.* **1.** the next after the 15th; last in a series of 16. **2.** one of 16 equal parts: *An ounce is one sixteenth of a pound.* **3.** *Music.* a sixteenth note.
sixteenth note, *Music.* a note having one sixteenth of the time value of a whole note; semiquaver. See **note** for picture.
sixth (siksth), *adj.* **1.** next after the fifth; last in a series of 6. **2.** being one of 6 equal parts.
—*n.* **1.** the next after the fifth; last in a series of 6. **2.** one of 6 equal parts. **3.** *Music.* **a.** a tone or note six steps apart in the diatonic scale, or the sixth step of a diatonic scale, from a given tone or note. **b.** the interval between such tones or notes. **c.** the harmonic combination of such tones. **d.** the sixth note or tone of a scale, six diatonic degrees above the tonic.
sixth chord, *Music.* a chord consisting of a note or tone, its third, and its sixth (symbol $^6_3$ or simply 6); the first inversion of a triad, with its original third in the bass; chord of the sixth.
sixth·ly (siksth′lē), *adv.* in the sixth place.
sixth sense, an unusual power of perception; intuition: *It was not a do-nothing Congress, but its political sixth sense may have helped to keep it from doing many things the country can well do without* (Wall Street Journal).
six·ti·eth (siks′tē ith), *adj.* **1.** next after the 59th; last in a series of 60. **2.** being one of 60 equal parts.
—*n.* **1.** the next after the 59th; last in a series of 60. **2.** one of 60 equal parts.
Six·tine (siks′tin), *adj.* Sistine.
six·ty (siks′tē), *n., pl.* **-ties,** *adj.* six times ten; 60.
like sixty, *Informal.* very fast: *to go like sixty.*
[Old English *siextig, sixtig*]
six·ty-fold (siks′tē fōld′), *adj., adv.* sixty times as much or as many.
$64 question, *U.S.* the key question; the final and most important question: *The answer to the $64 question has thus far been given by the politicians, with woefully inadequate consideration of the scientist's point of view* (Science News Letter). [< the name of a radio quiz program of the 1940's, which offered a prize of $64]
six·ty-fourth note (siks′tē fôrth′, -fōrth′), *Music.* a note having the time value of one sixty-fourth of a whole note; hemidemisemiquaver. See **note** for picture.
siz·a·ble (sī′zə bəl), *adj.* **1.** fairly large: *a sizable sum.* **2.** *Archaic.* of suitable or convenient size. Also, **sizeable.** —**siz′a·ble·ness,** *n.*
siz·a·bly (sī′zə blē), *adv.* to a sizable extent or degree. Also, **sizeably.**
siz·ar (sī′zər), *n.* a student who pays reduced rates in the colleges of Cambridge University in Cambridge, England, and of Trinity College in Dublin, Ireland. Also, **sizer.** [< *siz*(e)[1] + *-ar,* variant of *-er*[2]]
siz·ar·ship (sī′zər ship), *n.* the position, rank, or privileges of a sizar.
size[1] (sīz), *n., v.,* **sized, siz·ing,** *adj.* —*n.* **1.** the amount of surface or space a thing takes up: *The two boys are of the same size. The library has books of all sizes.* **2.** extent; amount; magnitude: *the size of an industry, the size of an undertaking.* **3.** one of a series of measures: *His shoes are size ten. The size of card I want is 3 by 5 inches.* **4.** *Informal.* the actual condition; true description: *That's about the size of it.* **5.** *Obsolete.* a ration, allowance, or standard of food or drink: *'Tis not in thee To grudge my pleasures ... to scant my sizes* (Shakespeare).
cut down to size, a. to reduce to (a specified size or number) by or as if by cutting: *to cut a plant down to size. Sportswriters had named his team the best in the country, and he was determined to cut his players down to fighting size* (Time). **b.** to diminish the sense of importance or ego of: *to cut a politician down to size.*
of a size, of the same size: *There are large and small pears, but the apples are all of a size.*
try for size, to try out or test for fit or appropriateness: *A British Railways liner train was tried for size at the first special depot* (London Times).
—*v.t.* **1.** to arrange or classify according to size or in sizes: *Will you size these nails? Why should a man's shirt be sized by his neck but his pyjamas by his chest?* (Observer). **2.** to make of a certain size. **3.** *Obsolete.* to regulate or control according to a fixed standard: ... *to size weights and measures* (Francis Bacon).
size up, *Informal.* **a.** to form an opinion of; estimate: *A fellow ought to ... look 'em [candidates] all over and size 'em up, and then decide carefully* (Sinclair Lewis). **b.** to come up to some size or grade: *It was a letter ... which sized up very well with the letters written in my part of the United States* (Owen Wister).
—*adj.* having size.
[Middle English *syse* an ordinance setting a fixed amount; also, assizes of justice; (perhaps originally) short for *assize*]
—**Syn.** *n.* **1, 2. Size, volume, bulk** mean the measure of something. **Size** applies particularly to the dimensions (length, width, and height or depth) of something, but also to the extent of surface occupied or number of individuals included: *What is the size of your herd?* **Volume** is used of something measured by the cubic inches, feet, etc., it occupies, especially something that rolls or flows: *The volume of water confined by Hoover Dam is tremendous.* **Bulk** means size or quantity measured in three dimensions, and often suggests largeness: *Let the dough double in bulk.*
size[2] (sīz), *n., v.,* **sized, siz·ing.** —*n.* a preparation made from glue, starch, or other sticky material; sizing. It is used for covering paper, plaster, etc., before paint is put on, for stiffening cloth, for glazing paper, etc. —*v.t.* to coat, treat, fill, or glaze with size. [< Old French *assise* a sitting, fixing, layer]
-size, *combining form.* a variant of **-sized,** as in *life-size.*
size·a·ble (sī′zə bəl), *adj.* sizable. —**size′a·ble·ness,** *n.*
size·a·bly (sī′zə blē), *adv.* sizably.
size copy, *British, Printing.* a dummy.
sized (sīzd), *adj.* having size, especially as specified: *variously sized garments.*
-sized, *combining form.* having or of ____ size: *Fair-sized = having fair size. Large-sized = of large size.* Also, **-size.**
siz·er[1] (sī′zər), *n.* a device for testing the size of articles, or for separating them according to size: *The raindrop sizer ... relays its information to a counter unit* (Science News Letter).
siz·er[2] (sī′zər), *n.* sizar.
size-up (sīz′up′), *n. Informal.* an estimate; opinion; consideration: *The United States is evolving a new defense policy, based on a new size-up of the world situation and a new concept of warfare* (Newsweek).
siz·ing (sī′zing), *n.* **1.** size; a preparation made from glue, starch, etc. **2.** the act or process of coating or treating with size.
siz·y (sī′zē), *adj.* of or like size; thick; viscous; glutinous. [< *siz*(e)[2] + *-y*[1]]
sizz (siz), *v.i.* to hiss; sizzle; make a hiss somewhat resembling a buzz. [imitative]
siz·zle (siz′əl), *v.,* **-zled, -zling,** *n.* —*v.i.* **1.** to make a hissing sound, as fat does when it is frying or burning. **2.** to be very hot: *to sizzle in a heat wave, to sizzle with anger.*
—*v.t.* **1.** to burn or scorch so as to produce a hissing sound. **2.** to burn up with intense heat: *A gas ... ionizes into a hot, high-speed jet that sizzles the surface of the two metals and joins them* (Science).
—*n.* a hissing sound; sizzling.
[imitative]
siz·zler (siz′lər), *n.* **1.** *Slang.* something outstanding, exciting, or dangerous: *But his Curnonsky folder was a sizzler: "Dangerous anarchist, without a fixed domicile since 1912"* (Atlantic). **2.** *Informal.* a very hot day: *Tuesday was really a sizzler.*
siz·zling (siz′ling), *adj.* **1.** that sizzles: *a sizzling steak, sizzling anger.* **2.** very hot: *sizzling weather.* —**siz′zling·ly,** *adv.*
S.J., Society of Jesus (the official name of the Jesuit order).
sjam·bok (sham′bok), *n.* a strong, heavy whip made from thick, tough hide, such as that of the rhinoceros or hippopotamus, used in South Africa for driving cattle, etc.: *Indignant citizens ... claimed to have witnessed assaults on Africans all over Capetown by police carrying batons and sjamboks* (Manchester Guardian). —*v.t.* to strike or drive with a sjambok: *Then I will sjambok them first, and hang them after* (G.H. Russell). [< earlier Afrikaans *sjambok* < Malay *sambok* < Persian *chābuk.* Compare CHABOUK.]
S.J.D., Doctor of Juridical Science (Latin, *Scientiae Juridicae Doctor*).
S.J. Res., *U.S.* Senate Joint Resolution (used with a number).

sk., sack.

skald (skôld, skäld), *n.* a Scandinavian poet and singer of ancient times: . . . *the lives of two Icelanders, Viking and his skald Thorgeir* (Observer). Also, **scald.** [< Scandinavian (compare Old Icelandic *skāld*)]

skald·ic (skôl′dik, skäl′-), *adj.* of or having to do with the skalds or their poetry and songs: *He* [*Odin*] *imperiled his life again to take away from the Giants the skaldic mead, which made anyone who tasted it a poet* (Edith Hamilton). Also, **scaldic.**

skat (skät), *n.* **1.** a card game for three players. Cards won in tricks are counted for points. **2.** the widow dealt in this game. [< German *Skat* (originally) two cards for discard < Italian *scarto* a discard < *scartare* discard < Latin *ex-* out of + *charta* chart. Compare CARD¹.]

skate¹ (skāt), *n., v.,* **skat·ed, skat·ing.** —*n.* **1.** a frame with a blade fixed to a shoe so that a person can glide over ice; ice skate. **2.** a similar frame or shoe with small wheels for use on any smooth, hard surface; roller skate.

—*v.i.* **1.** to glide or move along on skates. **2.** to slide or glide along: *Insects skated on the water* (Longfellow). *Many other savings institutions are skating close to their break-even points* (Wall Street Journal).

[< Dutch *schaats* (taken as plural) < Old French *escache* stilt < a Germanic word]

skate² (skāt), *n., pl.* **skates** or (*collectively*) **skate.** any of a group of broad, flat fishes related to the rays, usually having a pointed snout. The barn-door skate and the thornback are two kinds. [< Scandinavian (compare Old Icelandic *skata*)]

Barn-door Skate² (45 in. long)

skate³ (skāt), *n. U.S. Slang.* **1.** a term of contempt for an old, worn-out horse. **2.** a fellow: *He's a good skate. Dave's a cheap skate, all right* (Sinclair Lewis). [origin uncertain]

skate·bar·row (skāt′bar′ō), *n.* the egg case of a skate, ray, or other elasmobranch fish, often called a mermaid's purse. Its shape suggests a handbarrow.

skate·board (skāt′bôrd′, -bōrd′), *n.* a narrow board resembling a surfboard, with roller-skate wheels attached to each end, used for skating. —**skate′board′er,** *n.*

skat·er (skā′tər), *n.* **1.** a person who skates. **2.** any of various long-legged insects that glide over water.

skat·ing rink (skā′ting), **1.** a smooth sheet of ice for skating: *The first snowfall, usually shy, announced the prompt metamorphosis of our tennis court into a skating rink* (New Yorker). **2.** a smooth floor for roller skating.

skat·ol (skat′ōl, -ol), *n.* skatole.

skat·ole (skat′ōl), *n.* a bad-smelling substance produced by the decomposition of albuminous matter in the intestinal canal, and present in feces. *Formula:* C_9H_9N [< Greek *skôr, skatós* excrement + English *-ole*]

skean (shkēn, skēn), *n.* a type of dagger formerly used by foot soldiers in Ireland and Scotland. Also, **skene.** [< Irish Gaelic, Scottish Gaelic *sgian*]

skean dhu (ᴛʜü), a small dagger carried by Scottish Highlanders as an ornament, usually in a stocking: *He is armed with a claymore* (*broadsword*), *a dirk* (*dagger*), *and a skean dhu* (*a knife tucked in his sock*) (New York). [< *skean* + Scottish Gaelic *dubh* black]

sked (sked), *n. Informal.* schedule.

ske·dad·dle (ski dad′əl), *v.,* **-dled, -dling,** *n. Informal.* —*v.i.* to run away; leave suddenly and quickly; scatter in flight: *Meant to tame him* [*a gopher*] *but he got out of his box and skedaddled* (Atlantic). —*n.* a hasty flight or scattering. [origin uncertain]

skee (skē), *n., pl.* **skees** or **skee,** *v.i.,* **skeed, skee·ing.** ski.

skeet (skēt), *n.* a kind of trapshooting in which the clay pigeons are flung into the air at angles similar to those taken by a bird in flight: *The riding trails, skeet fields and trout streams are waiting* (New Yorker). [compare Old Icelandic *skjōta* shoot]

skeet·er (skē′tər), *n.* **1.** *U.S. Informal.* a mosquito. **2.** a small sailboat for riding on ice; iceboat.

skee·zicks or **skee·sicks** (skē′ziks), *n. U.S. Slang.* **1.** a worthless fellow; chap: *Suddenly, the man she wants . . . comes home from medical school, a fast-driving, wild-boozing, hard-gambling skeesicks* (Time). **2.** a mischievous child (usually applied playfully). [American English; origin unknown]

skeg (skeg), *n.* **1.** the part of a ship's keel nearest the stern. **2.** a projection of the after part of a ship's keel for the support of a rudder. [< Dutch *schegge,* perhaps < Scandinavian (compare Old Icelandic *skegg* a beak, beard)]

skeg·ger (skeg′ər), *n.* a salmon of the first year; a smolt.

skeigh (skēʜ), *adj. Scottish.* **1.** (of horses) skittish; mettlesome; spirited. **2.** (of persons) not easily approached or mastered; disdainful or proud. [compare Old English *scēoh* shy]

skein (skān), *n.* **1.** a small, coiled bundle of yarn, thread, etc. There are 120 yards in a skein of cotton yarn. **2.** a confused tangle: *Freights entering the yard are pushed up an artificial "hump," uncoupled, then allowed to roll into a skein of classification tracks* (Newsweek). **3.** a small cluster or arrangement like a skein. **4.** a flight or group of wild geese or ducks. **5.** an unbroken string or series: *Constance's unbeaten skein in this country was stopped at six* (New York Times). [< Old French *escaigne*]

Skein (def. 1)

skein·er (skā′nər), *n.* a person or machine that winds yarn into skeins.

skel·e·tal (skel′ə təl), *adj.* **1.** of or like a skeleton. **2.** attached to, forming, or formed by a skeleton: *The movement of your body is made possible by the skeletal muscles; that is, the muscles that are attached to the bones* (Beauchamp, Mayfield, and West).

skel·e·tal·ly (skel′ə tə lē), *adv.* with reference to skeletal structure.

skel·e·tog·e·nous (skel ə toj′ə nəs), *adj.* producing a skeleton: giving rise to a skeleton; osteogenetic: *skeletogenous tissue.*

skel·e·ton (skel′ə tən), *n.* **1. a.** the bones of a human being, or other vertebrate, fitted together in their natural places. The skeleton is a frame that supports the muscles, organs, etc., and protects the viscera. *By looking at a human skeleton . . . you quickly see that there is a central column of bones to which the ribs and the bones of our arms and legs are attached* (Beauchamp, Mayfield, and West). **b.** the hard supporting or covering part of an invertebrate animal, as the shell of a mollusk or crustacean. **2.** a very thin person or animal: *A long illness made a skeleton out of him.* **3.** a frame: *the steel skeleton of a building.* **4.** the basic features or elements; outline: *In a few days' time I sketched out the skeleton of my poem* (Washington Irving).

skeleton at the feast, a reminder of gloomy or depressing things in the midst of pleasure (because the Egyptians used to have a skeleton or mummy at feasts as a reminder of death): *With her constant complaints, she was always the skeleton at the feast.*

skeleton in the closet, cupboard, or **house,** a secret source of embarrassment, grief, or shame, especially to a family; hidden domestic trouble: *Some particulars regarding the Newcome family, which will show us that they have a skeleton or two in their closets, as well as their neighbours . . .* (Thackeray).

—*adj.* **1.** of, like, or consisting of a skeleton. **2.** greatly reduced in numbers; fractional: *Only a skeleton crew was needed while the ship was tied up in dock.*

[< New Latin *sceleton* < Greek *skeletón* (*sôma*) dried up (body) < *skéllein* dry out (up)]

—**Syn.** *n.* **3.** framework. **4.** sketch, draft.

skeleton clock, a clock that has no case, so that the interior wheelwork is visible.

skel·e·ton·ic (skel′ə ton′ik), *adj.* **1.** of a skeleton; like that of a skeleton. **2.** skeletonlike; meager: *A young Italian painter whose skeletonic works . . . are currently having a big success in the U.S.* (Life).

skel·e·ton·ize (skel′ə tə nīz), *v.,* **-ized, -iz·ing.** —*v.t.* **1.** to make a skeleton of; reduce to a skeleton: *The codes should be updated, the group said, to permit the construction of modern low-cost buildings such as ramp, "open-deck" and other skeletonized multi-story units* (New York Times). **2.** to draw up in outline; sketch out; outline: *a skeletonized report.* **3.** to greatly reduce the numbers of: *Lack of money forced the country to maintain only a skeletonized air force.* —*v.i.* to become a skeleton.

skel·e·ton·iz·er (skel′ə tə nī′zər), *n.* an insect which reduces leaves to skeletons.

skeleton key, a key made to open many locks, especially a thin, light key with most of the bit filed away.

skel·e·ton·less (skel′ə tən lis), *adj.* having no skeleton.

skel·e·ton·like (skel′ə tən līk′), *adj.* like a skeleton; bony; drawn; emaciated; gaunt: *I often thought of the skeletonlike patients we'd seen in the hospital, famine victims from outlying villages* (New Yorker).

skel·lum (skel′əm), *n. Archaic.* a rascal; scamp. [< Dutch *schelm* < German *Schelm*]

skelp¹ (skelp), *Scottish.* —*n.* a slapping blow or noise; smack. —*v.t.* to slap; smack: *In the year you refer to . . . I was getting skelped in the parish school* (Robert Louis Stevenson). —*v.i.* to hurry: *Skelping about here, destroying the few deer that are left* (Scott). [probably imitative]

skelp² (skelp), *n.* a strip of steel or iron used to make a pipe or tube.

skel·ter (skel′tər), *v.i.* to dash along; rush; hurry. [< short for *helter-skelter*]

Skel·ton·ic (skel ton′ik), *adj.* of, having to do with, or characteristic of John Skelton, the English poet, 1460?-1529, or his writings: *Skeltonic verse.*

Skel·ton·ics (skel ton′iks), *n.pl.* short, irregular lines of verse with frequent recurrence of the same rhyme.

ske·ne¹ (skē′nē), *n., pl.* **-nai** (-nī). the stage of an ancient Greek theater. [< Greek *skēnḗ* stage; scene]

skene² (shkēn, skēn), *n.* skean.

skep (skep), *n.* **1.** a beehive. **2.** a large, deep basket; hamper. **3.** the quantity of coal, grain, etc., held by a container of a certain size. [Middle English *sceppe* < Scandinavian (compare Old Icelandic *skeppa* basket)]

skep·sis (skep′sis), *n.* philosophic doubt; skeptical philosophy. Also, **scepsis.** [< Greek *sképsis* < *sképtesthai* reflect]

Skep·tic (skep′tik), *n.* a member or adherent of an ancient Greek school of philosophy that maintained that real knowledge of things is impossible. Also, **Sceptic.** [< Latin *Sceptici,* plural < Greek *sképtikoi* < *skeptikós* reflective < *sképtesthai* reflect]

skep·tic (skep′tik), *n.* **1.** a person who questions the truth of theories or apparent facts; doubter: *The skeptic doth neither affirm, neither deny, any position; but doubteth of it . . .* (Sir Walter Raleigh). **2.** a person who doubts or questions the possibility or certainty of our knowledge of anything. **3.** a person who doubts the truth of religious doctrines, or of religion in general: *The smugness has gone out of cynicism and the skeptics are asking the questions which will lead at length to affirmation of some kind* (Atlantic).

—*adj.* doubting; skeptical. Also, **sceptic.**

[< *Skeptic*]

—**Syn.** *n.* **3.** unbeliever, disbeliever, agnostic.

skep·ti·cal (skep′tə kəl), *adj.* **1.** of or like a skeptic; inclined to doubt; not believing easily: *a skeptical person.* **2.** questioning the truth of theories or apparent facts: *a skeptical remark, a skeptical approach.* Also, **sceptical.** —**skep′ti·cal·ly,** *adv.* —**skep′ti·cal·ness,** *n.* —**Syn. 1.** doubting, incredulous, disbelieving, distrustful.

skep·ti·cism (skep′tə siz əm), *n.* **1.** skeptical attitude; doubt; unbelief: *A wise skepticism is the first attribute of a good critic* (Lowell). *His skepticism made him distrustful of dreamy meddlers* (Atlantic). **2.** doubt or disbelief with regard to religion: *Since skepticism was current, even during the Middle Ages, there were those who scoffed* (Newsweek). **3.** the philosophical doctrine that nothing can be proved absolutely, and thus real knowledge of any kind is impossible. Also, **scepticism.** —**Syn. 1.** incredulity, mistrust, distrust.

skep·ti·cize (skep′tə sīz), *v.i.,* **-cized, -ciz·ing.** to act the skeptic; doubt; profess to doubt of everything. Also, **scepticize.**

sker·rick (sker′ik), *n. Australian.* the least possible amount; smallest piece: *There isn't a skerrick of meat in the pot.*

sker·ry (sker′ē), *n., pl.* **-ries.** *Scottish.* an isolated rock, rocky island, or reef. [< Old Icelandic *sker* reef]

sketch (skech), *n.* **1.** a rough, quickly done drawing, painting, clay model, or design: *The artist made many sketches in pencil before painting the portrait.* **2.** an outline; plan: *Give me a sketch of his career.* **3.** a brief description, story, play, etc.

—*v.t.* **1.** to make a sketch of; draw roughly.

2. to describe briefly, generally, or in outline: *Montesquieu sketched a government which should make liberty its end* (George Bancroft).
—*v.i.* to make a sketch; draw, paint, or model sketches.
[< Dutch *schets* < Italian *schizzo* < Latin *schedium* extemporaneous poem < Greek *schédios* impromptu] —**sketch′er,** *n.*
—**Syn.** *n.* **2.** draft, brief. —*v.t.* **1.** outline, delineate.

sketch·a·ble (skech′ə bəl), *adj.* suitable for being sketched.

sketch·block (skech′blok′), *n.* a pad of paper for sketching on.

sketch·book (skech′bu̇k′), *n.*, or **sketch book, 1.** a book to draw or paint sketches in: *In the sketchbook were 35 exquisite drawings no bigger than his hand* (Time). **2.** a book of descriptions, stories, plays, etc.: *Washington Irving's "Sketch Book."*

sketch·i·ly (skech′ə lē), *adv.* in a sketchy manner; incompletely; slightly; imperfectly: *a sketchily planned trip.*

sketch·i·ness (skech′ē nis), *n.* the state or quality of being sketchy.

sketch map, a map prepared without accurate measurement.

sketch plan, the first plan of a building, design; etc., suggesting matter to be developed in later detailed drawings.

sketch·y (skech′ē), *adj.*, **sketch·i·er, sketch·i·est. 1.** like a sketch; having or giving only outlines or main features. **2.** incomplete; slight; imperfect: *a sketchy recollection of an event, a sketchy costume, a sketchy meal.*
—**Syn. 2.** unfinished, crude.

skete (skēt), *n.* a community of monks or hermits of the Greek Church. [< New Greek *skētos* < Greek *askētēs* monk, ascetic]

skew (skyü), *adj.* **1.** twisted to one side; slanting. **2.** having a part that deviates from a straight line, right angle, etc.: *a skew chisel, a skew facet.* **3.** unsymmetrical. [< verb]
—*n.* **1.** a slant; twist: *As alignment is lost, flutter and skew set in* (Scientific American). **2.** a sideward movement.
on the or **a skew,** on the slant; slantwise: *Over the Lune, which is crossed on the skew, the span is 350 ft.* (London Times).
[< verb or adjective]
—*v.i.* **1.** to slant; twist. **2.** to turn aside; swerve. **3.** to look suspiciously or slightingly. —*v.t.* **1.** to give a slanting form, position, direction, etc., to. **2.** to represent unfairly; distort.
[< Old North French *eskiuer* shy away from, eschew < Germanic (compare Old High German *sciuhen*)]
—**Syn.** *adj.* **1.** askew, awry. **2.** crooked, bent.

skew arch, an arch whose axis is not perpendicular to the face of the wall or member against which it abuts.

skew·back (skyü′bak′), *n.* **1.** a sloping surface against which the end of an arch rests: *This skewback bearing is intended to support the end reactions of a road bridge ...* (New Science). **2.** a stone, course of masonry, iron plate, or the like, with such a surface.

skew·bald (skyü′bôld′), *adj.* (of horses) irregularly marked with patches of white, brown, or red. —*n.* a skewbald horse: *Crompton, on his skewbald, was the only scorer* (London Times). [Middle English *skewed.* Compare PIEBALD.]

skew curve, a curve in three dimensions.

skew·er (skyü′ər), *n.* **1.** a long pin of wood or metal stuck through meat to hold it together while it is cooking. **2.** something shaped or used like a long pin.
—*v.t.* **1.** to fasten with or as if with a skewer or skewers: *I ... jammed the hat on my head and skewered it savagely with the pins* (Arnold Bennett). **2.** to pierce with or as if with a skewer: *Whole new fields are opening up for free divers, who, like Cousteau, soon tire of skewering fish as too easy* (Time).
[earlier *skiver;* origin uncertain]

skew·er·wood (skyü′ər wu̇d′), *n.* the spindle tree, whose stems were used to make skewers.

skew-gee (skyü′jē′), *Informal.* —*adv.* crookedly; askew. —*adj.* crooked; skew; squint.

skew·ness (skyü′nis), *n.* **1.** the quality of being skew; onesidedness; distortion. **2.** *Statistics.* asymmetry, especially of a frequency distribution: *Skewness is the degree that a group of items varies from a normal frequency curve* (Emory S. Bogardus).

skew·whiff (skyü′hwif′), *adj., adv. British Dialect.* askew; awry: *It is falling into a skewwhiff perspective* (Atlantic).

ski (skē; *Norwegian* shē), *n., pl.* **skis** or **ski,** *v.,* **skied, ski·ing.** —*n.* **1.** one of a pair of long, flat, slender pieces of hard wood or light metal curved upward at the front, that can be fastened to a person's shoes to enable him to glide over snow: *With a pair of skis, a skilled traveler may keep up with a herd of reindeer and travel as many as seventy miles a day with a heavy pack* (Beals and Hoijer). See **herringbone** for picture. **2.** a skilike device fastened to the undercarriage of an airplane and used in place of wheels for landings on snow, mud, sand, etc.: *A Navy R4D (a modified DC-3) ... [made] a tricky ski landing—the first landing ever made at the South Pole* (Time).
—*v.i.* to glide over snow on skis: *to learn to ski. They tramped, they skated, they skied* (Sinclair Lewis). Also, **skee.**
[< Norwegian *ski.* Compare Old Icelandic *skīth* snowshoe]

ski·a·ble (skē′ə bəl), *adj.* that can be skied on: ... *a skiable mountain* (London Times).

ski·a·gram (skī′ə gram), *n.* **1.** a skiagraph; radiograph; X-ray picture. **2.** an outline of the shadow of an object filled in with black.

ski·a·gram·mat·ic (skī′ə grə mat′ik), *adj.* radiographic. —**ski′a·gram·mat′i·cal·ly,** *adv.*

ski·a·graph (skī′ə graf, -gräf), *n.* a radiograph; X-ray picture. —*v.t.* to take an X-ray photograph of. Also, **skiograph.** [< Greek *skiā́* shadow + English *-graph*]

ski·ag·ra·pher (skī ag′rə fər), *n.* **1.** a radiographer. **2.** anyone concerned with skiagraphy. Also, **skiographer.**

ski·a·graph·ic (skī′ə graf′ik), *adj.* having to do with skiagraphy. Also, **skiographic.**

ski·ag·ra·phy (skī ag′rə fē), *n.* **1.** radiography. **2.** the drawing of shadows or skiagrams.

ski·a·scope (skī′ə skōp), *n.* an instrument used in testing the refractive condition of the eye; retinoscope. [< Greek *skiā́* shadow + English *-scope*]

ski·as·co·py (skī as′kə pē), *n.* a method of testing the refractive condition of the eye; retinoscopy.

ski bob, a frame on two skis for gliding over snow: *The ski bob is rather like a converted bicycle, and the rider uses small skis on each foot for steering and stopping* (London Times).

ski boot, a boot of sturdy leather, specially made for protecting the foot while skiing.

ski bum *U.S. Slang.* a skiing enthusiast, especially one who drifts from job to job so that he may travel around to be near ski slopes, skiers, etc.

skice (skīs), *v.i.,* **skiced, skic·ing.** *British Dialect.* to run fast; move quickly; scurry. [origin unknown]

skid[1] (skid), *n., v.,* **skid·ded, skid·ding.** —*n.* **1.** a slip or slide sideways while moving. **2.** a piece of wood or metal to prevent a wheel from going round, as when going down a hill. **3.** a timber, frame, etc., on which something rests, or on which something heavy may slide. **4.** a runner on the bottom of an airplane to enable the airplane to slide along the ground when landing. **5.** a slightly raised wooden platform for carrying loads: *I was working for a florist back in the shambling thirties when iced skids of 250 roses sold for $2 at Faneuil Hall* (Atlantic).
on the skids, *Informal.* **a.** headed for dismissal, failure, or other disaster; failing; slipping: *Diem is said to suspect that pro-French Americans are trying to withhold further U.S. aid and thus put him on the skids* (Newsweek). **b.** on the way down; on the downgrade: *The aging boxer was plainly on the skids.*
put the skids under, *Informal.* to cause (someone or something) to head for failure or disaster; cause the ruin or downfall of: *This has really put the skids under Pearson. This is the knockout blow* (Time).
—*v.i.* **1.** to slip or slide sideways while moving: *The car skidded on the slippery road.* **2.** to slide along without going around, as a wheel does when held by a skid or brake. **3.** (of an airplane) to slide or be carried sideways, as when not banked enough while turning. —*v.t.* **1.** to slide along on a skid or skids. **2.** to prevent (a wheel) from going round by means of a skid. **3.** to cause (a vehicle or its wheels) to slide sideways while moving.
[origin uncertain. Compare Old Frisian *skīd* stick of wood. Related to SKI.]

skid[2] (skid), *v.i.,* **skid·ded, skid·ding.** to run or go quickly; scud. [variant of *scud*]

skid·der (skid′ər), *n.* **1.** a person or thing that skids. **2.** a person who uses a skid.

skid·doo (ski dü′), *v.i. Slang.* to be off; depart; vamoose. [American English, perhaps < *skedaddle,* or < *skid*[2]]

skid·dy (skid′ē), *adj.* liable to cause skidding.

skid fin, a finlike vertical plane set across the upper wing of some early aircraft to increase lateral stability.

skid·pan (skid′pan′), *n.* a device for slowing down the rotation of the wheels of a vehicle; drag.

skid·proof (skid′prüf′), *adj.* that prevents skidding or slipping: *skidproof soles on shoes, a skidproof surface on a bridge.*

skid road, (in lumbering) **1.** a road over which logs are dragged, usually with heavy skids partly sunk in the ground. **2.** Often, **Skid Road.** skid row: *It [Skid Road] originated in Seattle some seventy years ago, when logs were hauled through the town over an actual skid road made of logs laid crossways* (Saturday Review).

skid row, a slum street or section full of cheap saloons, rooming houses, etc., frequented by derelict men: *Many management men still stereotype an alcoholic as a red-nosed skid row bum* (Wall Street Journal).

skid·way (skid′wā′), *n.* **1. a.** two logs or timbers laid parallel at right angles to a road, on which to pile a tier of logs for loading. **b.** a way or path down which logs can slide as on a skid. **2.** a wide, sloping tunnel in the rear of a whaling factory ship, leading from water level up to the work deck, used to drag the whale out of the water.

skied[1] (skēd), *v.* the past tense and past participle of **ski.**

skied[2] (skīd), *v.* a past tense and past participle of **sky.**

ski·er (skē′ər), *n.* a person who uses or travels on skis: *an expert skier.*

skies (skīz), *n.* the plural of **sky:** *cloudy skies.*

skiff (skif), *n.* **1.** a small, light rowboat with a rounded bottom and flat stern. **2.** a small, light boat with a mast for a single triangular sail. [< French *esquif* < Italian *schifo* < Germanic (compare Old High German *schif*). Related to SHIP.]

skif·fle (skif′əl), *n., v.,* **-fled, -fling.** *Especially British Slang.* —*n.* a type of Dixieland jazz in which folk or popular songs are rendered to a rapid beat by small groups playing guitars and improvised instruments such as washboards, bottles, jugs, etc.: *U.S. rock 'n' roll, commercial hillbilly and folk music, warmed over and juiced up in a mishmash called skiffle* (Time). —*v.i.* to play skiffle.

skif·fler (skif′lər), *n. Especially British Slang.* a person who plays skiffle.

ski·ing (skē′ing), *n.* the act or sport of gliding over snow on skis: *to be skillful at skiing.*

ski·jor·ing (skē jôr′ing, -jōr′-), *n.* a sport in which a person is towed on skis over snow or ice by a horse or vehicle. [American English < Norwegian *skijøring* < *ski* ski + *kjøring* driving]

ski jump, 1. a jump made by a person on skis off the end of an elevated runway. **2.** an elevated runway for making such a jump: *To tourists, the new ski jump, a 40-minute walk from town, was Cortina's most spectacular new attraction* (Newsweek).

skil·ful (skil′fəl), *adj.* skillful. —**skil′ful·ly,** *adv.* —**skil′ful·ness,** *n.*

ski lift, any of various mechanisms for transporting skiers to the top of a slope, usually by means of a chair running on a suspended cable: *Liechtenstein has no ski lifts; the husky young Olympians must hike up the steep Alpine slopes on foot* (Time). See **chair lift** for picture.

skill[1] (skil), *n.* **1.** ability gained by practice, knowledge, etc.; expertness: *to drive a car with skill. The trained teacher covered the assigned lesson with skill. He had conducted an important negotiation with skill and tact* (Lytton Strachey). **2.** ability to do things well with one's body or with tools: *to have great inborn skill. Not everyone has the skill to become a watchmaker.* **3.** work that requires expert ability; craft: *to master the carpenter's skill, a lawyer's skill.* **4.** *Obsolete.* cause; reason: *I think you have as little skill to fear as I have purpose to put you to't* (Shakespeare). [< Scandinavian (compare Old Icelandic *skil* discernment < *skilja* distinguish, separate, part)]
—**Syn. 1.** facility, proficiency. **2.** dexterity, deftness, adroitness.

skill[2] (skil), *v.i. Archaic.* **1.** to make a difference; matter: *Whate'er he be, it skills not much, we'll fit him to our turn* (Shakespeare). **2.** to avail; help: *Whatever we say skills but little.*
[Middle English *skilen* cause a distinction; earlier, to separate < Scandinavian (compare Old Icelandic *skilja*)]

skilled (skild), *adj.* **1.** having skill; trained; experienced: *a skilled workman.* **2.** requiring skill; showing skill: *a skilled piece of work. Bricklaying is skilled labor.* —**Syn. 1.** See **expert.**

skil·less (skil′lis), *adj.* lacking skill; unskilled; unskillful: *Let me see the wound; I am not quite skilless* (Byron).

skil·let (skil′it), *n.* **1.** *U.S.* a shallow pan with a long handle, used for frying. **2.** a long-handled saucepan. [origin uncertain]

skill·ful (skil′fəl), *adj.* **1.** having skill; expert: *a skillful surgeon.* **2.** showing skill: *a skillful piece of bricklaying.* Also, **skilful.** —**skill′ful·ness,** *n.* —**Syn. 1, 2.** dexterous, deft, adroit, proficient.

skill·ful·ly (skil′fə lē), *adv.* with skill; expertly.

skil·ling (skil′ing), *n.* a copper coin and money of account formerly used in Scandinavian countries, having a value of less than one cent. [< Danish *skilling.* Compare SHILLING.]

skil·lion (skil′yən), *n. Australian.* a lean-to or shed.

skil·ly (skil′ē), *n. British.* **1.** a thin, watery soup or gruel formerly fed to prisoners and paupers: *The best thing . . . for the writer is to give him a bed in a doss house and a bowl of skilly and leave him alone* (Manchester Guardian). **2.** a drink made of oatmeal, sugar, and water formerly served to sailors in the British navy.

skim (skim), *v.,* **skimmed, skim·ming,** *n., adj.* —*v.t.* **1.** to remove from the top: *The cook skims the cream from the milk.* **2.** to take from the top of: *She skims the milk to get cream.* **3.** to move lightly over: *gulls skimming the waves. The pebble I threw skimmed the little waves. The skaters skimmed the ice.* **4.** to cause to fly lightly; send skimming: *You can skim a flat stone over the water.* **5.** to read or glance through very rapidly or carelessly; read with omissions: *It took me an hour to skim the book.* **6.** to cover with a thin layer of ice, scum, etc.
—*v.i.* **1.** to move lightly (over or through): *skaters skimming over the ice, to skim through the newspaper headlines.* **2.** to glide along: *swallows were skimming by.* **3.** to become covered with a thin layer of ice, scum, etc.: *The pond skimmed over with ice during the night.*
—*n.* **1.** something which is skimmed off. **2.** skim milk: *The upsweep in skim sales is documented in Federal figures of milk sales in a number of major metropolitan areas across the country* (Wall Street Journal). **3.** a skimming or moving lightly.
—*adj.* skimmed.
[perhaps variant of *scum,* or < Old French *escumer* < *escume* scum < Germanic (compare Old High German *scûm*)]

skim·ble-skam·ble or **skim·ble-scam·ble** (skim′bəl skam′bəl, skim′əl skam′əl), *Archaic.* —*adj.* rambling; confused; silly: *Such a deal of skimble-scamble stuff, as puts me from my faith* (Shakespeare). —*n.* nonsense; gabble. [varied reduplication of earlier *scamble* to struggle in an undignified manner, scramble for; origin uncertain]

ski·meis·ter (skē′mīs′tər), *n. German.* an expert or master skier.

skim·mer (skim′ər), *n.* **1.** a person or thing that skims. **2.** a long-handled, shallow ladle, full of holes, used in skimming liquids. **3.** any of three species of sea birds related to the gulls, that skims the surface of the water with the long, lower part of its bill to get food. **4.** a man's or woman's straw hat with a flat crown and wide brim: *Not since the heyday of the Homburg and the skimmer have hat makers had so much to be happy about* (Wall Street Journal). **5.** any of various clams or scallops: *We . . . watched Olaf* [*the walrus*] *munch some skimmer clams and herring out of a pail* (New Yorker).

Black Skimmer (def. 3) (16 in. long)

skim milk, milk from which the cream has been removed: *Skim milk masquerades as cream* (W. S. Gilbert).

skim·ming (skim′ing), *n.* **1.** the act of one that skims. **2.** that which is skimmed off: *greasy skimmings from soup.*

skimmings, *Metallurgy.* dross.

skimming dish, 1. a shallow dish used in skimming liquids; skimmer. **2.** something comparable to a skimming dish: *The adherents of the inexplicable . . . hinted that their antagonists were mere skimming dishes in point of depth* (George Eliot). **3.** a kind of shallow sailboat or speedboat.

skim·ming·ton (skim′ing tən), *n.* **1.** a burlesque procession or serenade formerly held in ridicule of a henpecked husband, common in villages and country districts of England; skimmity ride. **2.** *U.S. Dialect.* a mock serenade for newly married persons; charivari.

skim·mi·ty ride (skim′ə tē), skimmington.

Ski·mo (skē′mō), *n. Canadian Slang.* an Eskimo (used in an unfriendly way).

ski·mo·bile (skē′mə bēl), *n.* a small automobile running on tracks, for carrying skiers to the top of a slope.

skimp (skimp), *v.t.* **1.** to supply in too small an amount: *Don't skimp the butter in making a cake.* **2.** to do imperfectly: *The lazy boy skimped his job.* —*v.i.* **1.** to be very saving or economical: *She had to skimp to send her son to college.* **2.** to do something imperfectly: *He was always skimping on his assignments.*
—*adj.* scanty; skimpy.
[origin uncertain. Compare SCRIMP.]
—**skimp′ing·ly,** *adv.*

skimp·i·ly (skim′pə lē), *adv.* in a skimpy manner.

skimp·i·ness (skim′pē nis), *n.* skimpy quality or condition.

skimp·y (skim′pē), *adj.,* **skimp·i·er, skimp·i·est. 1.** not enough; scanty: *a skimpy portion of food, a skimpy bathing suit.* **2.** too saving or economical. —**Syn. 1.** meager. **2.** parsimonious.

skin (skin), *n., v.,* **skinned, skin·ning.** —*n.* **1.** the covering of the body in persons or animals, fruits, etc., especially when soft and flexible: *He slipped on a banana skin. The skin is the largest organ of the body and, next to the brain, the most complicated* (Science News Letter). **2. a.** the covering of an animal when stripped from the body to be dressed or tanned; hide; pelt: *The numbers of rabbits also fluctuate with the seasons, as can be seen from figures for exports of carcasses and skins* (Fenner and Day). **b.** a container for holding liquids, made of the hide of an animal: *a water skin, a wine skin.* **3. a.** the planking or iron plating covering the ribs or frame of a ship. **b.** the outside covering or casing of an aircraft, rocket, spacecraft, etc.: *. . . heat-resistant alloys for use in the skins of missiles* (Time). **4.** *Slang.* a cheat; swindler. **5.** *Slang.* a skinflint. **6.** *Slang.* a dollar: *We get only the 75 skins a month . . . And we can prove it* (Time). **7.** *Slang.* a drum: *He beats the skins with a fine, off-beat flavor* (New York Times). **8.** *Architecture.* a curtain wall, especially of lightweight metal or glass: *The outer skin of the building . . . is composed of two-story aluminum frames* (Wall Street Journal).

by (or **with**) **the skin of one's teeth,** with nothing to spare; very narrowly; barely: *About half way through I began to fear that the joke could not be sustained, but it was—by the skin of its teeth* (Listener). *His eldest son was implicated in the robbery . . ., and came off by the skin of his teeth* (Nation).

get under one's skin, a. to make one overly sensitive; irritate or annoy: *Don't let your opponents and what they say about you get under your skin* (Hubert H. Humphrey). **b.** to affect emotionally; stimulate or excite: *Venice gets under your skin, all right, and it stays there. Once you've been a part of it, . . . Venice will always be a part of you* (New Yorker).

in or **with a whole skin,** safe and sound: *He was besides in a very great fright, For a whole skin he liked to be in* (Robert Southey).

jump out of one's skin, to jump with extreme delight, excitement, high spirits, or surprise: *Scipio . . . was ready to jump out of his skin for joy at the sight of me* (Benjamin H. Malkin).

no skin off one's nose, back, teeth, etc., *Slang.* not one's concern; of no consequence or interest to one: *If Mr. Horvitz doesn't come into the service, it's no skin off my nose* (Jon C. Suggs).

save one's skin, to escape without harm: *He was taken prisoner . . . and had to turn Dervish to save his skin* (Sir Arthur Conan Doyle).

—*v.t.* **1.** to strip, rub, or scrape the skin off: *Jack skinned his knees when he fell. The hunter skinned the deer.* **2.** to cover with or as if with skin: *It will but skin and film the ulcerous place* (Shakespeare). **3.** *Slang.* to swindle of money, etc.; cheat; defraud. —*v.i.* **1.** to become covered with skin; form a new skin: *The wound gradually skinned over.* **2.** to shed skin. **3.** to pass barely; slip by narrowly: *We skinned past a seething snag* (New Yorker).

skin alive, *Informal.* **a.** to torture; flay: *They may skin me alive, if they please* (Benjamin Jowett). **b.** to beat up or punish: *His father will skin him alive if he comes home late.* **c.** to defeat completely: *Any amateur would be skinned alive when competing against the world champion.*

skin out, *Slang.* to slip away, especially hastily; make off; escape: *I used to skin out of the old Sunday School . . . every chance I got* (Sinclair Lewis).

[< Scandinavian (compare Old Icelandic *skinn*)]

—**Syn.** *n.* **2. a. Skin, hide, pelt** mean the outer covering of the body of an animal. **Skin** is the general word, applying to the covering of a person or animal: *The skin of a calf makes soft leather.* **Hide** applies particularly to the tough skin of a large animal, commercially raw or tanned: *The hide of a cow is tough.* **Pelt** applies particularly to the skin of a fur- or wool-bearing animal before dressing or tanning: *Trappers sell pelts of foxes; stores sell dressed skins.*

skin and bones, 1. extreme thinness or emaciation: *She languished and pined away to skin and bones* (Edward Herbert). **2.** a very thin person: *"I like to eat," said Otto. "Not like . . . skin and bones here"* (New Yorker).

skin boat, a boat made from animal skins extended over a frame: *Seals, walruses, and whales are used for the making of skin boats* (John C. Reed).

skin-bound (skin′bound′), *adj.* having the skin drawn tightly over the flesh.

skin-deep (skin′dēp′), *adj.* no deeper than the skin; shallow; slight: *a skin-deep wound, beauty that is only skin-deep.* —*adv.* in a superficial manner; slightly: *Stings that have penetrated more than skin-deep into my mind* (Edmund Burke).

skin disease, a disease affecting the skin: *Acne and eczema are skin diseases.*

skin-dive (skin′dīv′), *v.i.,* **-dived, -diving.** to engage in skin diving: *Fish, skin-dive, or water-ski at . . . Boca Chica lagoon* (New Yorker).

skin diver, a person engaged in skin diving as his work or as a sport: *Sunlight filters down through the crystal-clear waters so that skin divers 25 or 30 feet below the surface move in an enchanting world of liquid sunshine* (New Yorker).

skin diving, swimming under water, sometimes at considerable depth, without special diving equipment other than goggles, rubber flippers for the feet, and a portable breathing device: *As an ultimate in sports gear, an underwater camera has now been developed for the benefit of skin diving enthusiasts* (Newsweek).

skin effect, *Electricity.* a concentration of current density at the surface of a conductor, increasing with frequency and producing an increase in resistance.

skin·flint (skin′flint′), *n.* a mean, stingy person; miser: *And let him question such a thing as an appropriation for foreign aid to education; he is a skinflint without regard for the welfare of the world or even our own children* (Wall Street Journal).

skin friction, the friction developed between a solid and a fluid, especially the friction that occurs in the thin layer of air (boundary layer) over the surface of an aircraft moving at very high speeds, causing a sharp rise in temperature.

skin·ful (skin′fu̇l), *n., pl.* **-fuls. 1. a.** *In-*

formal. as much as a person or animal can hold or drink. **b.** *Slang.* as much as, or more than, one should drink at one time of alcoholic liquor. **2.** as much as a skin for liquids can hold.

skin game, *Informal.* a game or proceeding in which one is fleeced, cheated, or swindled: *The satellites fell victims to an incredible Soviet skin game. Poland was forced to buy Russian wheat at prices higher than Argentina's* (Newsweek).

skin grafting, the transferring of skin to another part of the body or to another person, to improve appearance, aid healing, etc.

skink[1] (skingk), *n.* any of a family of small, smooth-scaled lizards: *Many lizards that live on the ground can get along without any legs. Many kinds of skinks, for example, have no legs* (World Book Encyclopedia). [< Latin *scincus* < Greek *skínkos*]

Five-lined Skink[1] (to 8 in. long)

skink[2] (skingk), *v.t. Archaic.* to pour out or draw (liquor). [probably < Middle Dutch *schenken*]

skink·er (sking′kər), *n. Dialect.* a bartender; tapster: *If the skinker can't make your Dry Martini dry enough . . .* (New Yorker).

skin·less (skin′lis), *adj.* having no skin; having a very thin skin: *skinless franks.*

skinned (skind), *adj.* **1.** stripped of the skin: *a skinned rabbit.* **2.** *British.* peeled; alert: *"Her boy brought me a letter. You see I asked him to keep his eyes — skinned — is that the right word?"* (Graham Greene).

-skinned, *combining form.* having a ______ skin: *Dark-skinned = having a dark skin.*

skin·ner (skin′ər), *n.* **1.** a person who skins (animals). **2.** a person who prepares or deals in skins, furs, etc.: *When the skinners got through with the forests, fireweed, scrub jackpine, blueberries, and aspen took over the ravaged land* (Harper's). **3.** a fleecer. **4.** a teamster.

Skinner box, a box or cage, used in experiments with animal conditioning, in which an animal must learn to operate correctly a lever or other mechanism in order to escape punishment or obtain a reward. [< B.F. *Skinner,* an American psychologist]

skin·ner·y (skin′ər ē), *n., pl.* **-ner·ies. 1.** a place where skins are prepared, as for market. **2.** *Obsolete.* skins or furs.

skin·ni·ness (skin′ē nis), *n.* skinny quality or condition.

skin·ny (skin′ē), *adj.,* **-ni·er, -ni·est. 1.** very thin; very lean: *a tall skinny boy.* **2.** like skin. —**Syn. 1.** gaunt, lank.

skint (skint), *adj. British Slang.* without money; penniless: *The bloke's a ruddy tycoon and he's always skint by the end of the week* (Punch). [variant of *skinned*]

skin test, any test made on the skin, such as the Schick test or patch test, to determine susceptibility to a disease or allergic reaction to a substance.

skin-tight (skin′tīt′), *adj.* fitting tightly to the skin; close-fitting: *a skin-tight bathing suit or dress.*

ski·o·gram (skī′ə gram), *n.* skiagram.

ski·o·graph (skī′ə graf, -gräf), *n., v.t.* skiagraph.

ski·og·ra·pher (skī og′rə fər), *n.* skiagrapher.

ski·o·graph·ic (skī′ə graf′ik), *adj.* skiagraphic.

skip[1] (skip), *v.,* **skipped, skip·ping,** *n.* —*v.i.* **1. a.** to leap lightly; spring; jump: *lambs skipping in the fields.* **b.** to go along with light, springing movements: *The little girl skipped down the street.* **2.** to go bounding along a surface. **3.** to omit parts; pass from one thing to another, disregarding what intervenes: *Answer the questions in order without skipping. The art of reading is to skip judiciously* (Philip G. Hamerton). **4.** to change quickly from one task, pleasure, subject, etc., to another. **5.** *Informal.* to leave in a hurry: *The revolutionary Polish officers, whom Bakúnin had been to pains to procure, gave the situation up and skipped out* (Edmund Wilson). **6.** *U.S.* to be promoted past the next regular grade in school. —*v.t.* **1.** to spring or leap lightly over: *The girls skipped rope.* **2.** to send bounding along a surface: *Boys like to skip stones on the lake.* **3. a.** to pass over; fail to notice; omit: *She skips the hard words when she reads.* **b.** *U.S.* to advance past in being promoted in school: *Jean skipped a grade last year.* **4.** *Informal.* to dodge, avoid, or stay away from: *to skip school, to skip rehearsals.* **5.** *Informal.* to leave (a place) hurriedly; flee: *The swindler has skipped town.*

—*n.* **1.** a light leap, spring, or jump: *The child gave a skip of joy.* **2.** a gait, especially of children, in which hops and steps are alternated. **3.** a passing over. **4.** that which is or may be skipped: *In his books there are scarcely any of those passages which, in our school days, we used to call skip* (Macaulay). **5.** *Music.* a passing from one note to another more than one step away.

[compare Middle Swedish *skuppa,* Old Icelandic *skipa* undergo a change]

—**Syn.** *v.t.* **3. a.** disregard. -*n.* **3.** omission.

skip[2] (skip), *n., v.,* **skipped, skip·ping.** —*n.* the captain of a team at curling or bowling. —*v.t.* to command or direct (a team) as skip. [probably short for *skipper*[1]]

skip[3] (skip), *n.* (in mining or quarrying) a bucket, box, basket, cage, or wagon in which materials or men are drawn up or let down: *. . . and then spewed out as a kind of gravel into immense containers, or skips, that hold twelve tons of the stuff each* (New Yorker). [variant of *skep*]

ski pants, lightweight, close-fitting pants with tapering trouser legs, worn by skiers.

ski patrol, a rescue and first-aid unit that patrols skiing areas.

skip-bomb (skip′bom′), *v.t., v.i.* to attack by or as if by skip bombing: *When the promotions of eight . . . colonels came up for approval . . . Senator Smith quickly zoomed in to skip-bomb the biggest target in sight: lanky [actor] James Stewart* (Time).

skip bombing, a method of precision bombing in which an airplane flies just above the water toward a ship, dam, etc., releasing its bombs so that they strike the target at or just below the level of the water, somewhat like a torpedo.

Skip·e·tar (skip′ə tär), *n.* **1.** an Albanian. **2.** the language of the Albanians. [< Albanian *Shqiptarë* (literally) mountaineer < *shqip* mountain]

skip·jack (skip′jak), *n., pl.* **-jacks** or (*collectively for 1*) **-jack. 1.** any of various fishes that sometimes leap out of the water, as a variety of tuna: *Today, yellowfin and skipjack—the hearty, light meat tuna—constitute about 80 per cent of the total pack put up by the industry* (Time). **2.** a click beetle. **3.** *Archaic.* a pert, lively, conceited fellow.

ski·plane (skē′plān′), *n.* an airplane equipped with skis for landing and taking off on snow.

skip·pa·ble (skip′ə bəl), *adj.* that may be skipped or passed over: *The second half of the book makes skippable reading* (New Scientist).

skip·per[1] (skip′ər), *n.* **1.** the captain of a ship, especially of a yacht or a small trading or fishing boat: *A new skipper had been piped aboard* (Newsweek). **2.** *Informal.* any captain or manager: *the skipper of a baseball team.* —*v.t.* to be the skipper of; captain; command: *He skippered one of the first paddle-wheel steamers on the upper Mississippi* (Atlantic). [< Middle Dutch *schipper* < *schip* ship]

skip·per[2] (skip′ər), *n.* **1.** a person or thing that skips. **2.** any of certain insects that make skipping movements. **3.** any of a group of small, mothlike butterflies that fly with a darting, hopping motion. **4.** a maggot that lives in cheese, etc. **5.** the saury (fish). [< *skip*[1] + *-er*[1]]

skipper's daughters, tall white-crested waves; whitecaps: *The swell ran pretty high, and out in the open there were skipper's daughters* (Robert Louis Stevenson).

skip·pet (skip′it), *n.* a small, round wooden box, enclosing and protecting a seal attached by a ribbon, etc., to a document. [origin uncertain]

skip·ping rope (skip′ing), a length of rope, often with a handle at each end, for jumping or skipping over.

skip rope, skipping rope.

skip tracer, *Informal.* an investigator whose job it is to locate persons who run off without paying their bills, debts, etc.

skip-trac·ing (skip′trā′sing), *n. Informal.* the work of a skip tracer: *Practically every store, financial institution and doctor's office does a certain amount of its own skip-tracing* (Wall Street Journal).

skip vehicle, a space vehicle that is propelled into outer space at such trajectory and speed that, on its return to the upper atmosphere, it bounces back one or more times in the manner of a stone skipping across the surface of water.

skirl (skėrl), *v.t., v.i.* **1. a.** (of bagpipes) to sound loudly and shrilly **b.** to play a bagpipe: *An imposing 6-footer, the chief of Clan Fraser, he charged into battle in a green bonnet, carrying a submachine gun and flanked by two skirling pipers* (Newsweek). **2.** to cry out shrilly; scream: *The womenfolk fair skirled wi' fear* (James M. Barrie). **3.** to sing or play in loud, shrill tones: *The grunting horns and syncopated strings, the skirling clarinets . . . make a classical tour de force* (Harper's).

—*n.* the sound made by or as if by a bagpipe: *the skirl of the grey sea-birds* (Elizabeth C. Gaskell).

[Middle English *skrillen* < Scandinavian (compare Norwegian dialectal *skrylla*)]

skir·mish (skėr′mish), *n.* **1.** a brief fight between small groups of soldiers: *A skirmish . . . between Indian Army personnel and the Pakistani police* (New York Times). **2.** a slight conflict, argument, contest, etc. —*v.i.* to take part in a skirmish. [< Old French *eskirmiss-,* stem of *eskirmir* (originally) ward off < Germanic (compare Old High German *scirman* fight under cover). Compare SCRIMMAGE, SCARAMOUCHE.]

skir·mish·er (skėr′mi shər), *n.* **1.** a person who skirmishes: *Round its front played a crowd of skirmishers . . . flying, reforming, shrieking insults* (Rudyard Kipling). **2.** one of the soldiers sent out in advance of an army to clear the way for the main attack, to prevent a surprise attack by the enemy, etc.: *Despite his vigilance, small details of skirmishers now and then infiltrate his prepared position successfully* (New Yorker).

skirmish line, a line of skirmishers, thrown out to feel the enemy, protect the main body from unexpected attack, etc.

skirr (skėr), *Dialect.* —*v.i.* to go rapidly; rush; fly; scurry: *And make them skirr away as swift as stones enforced from the old Assyrian slings* (Shakespeare). —*v.t.* **1.** to go rapidly over; scour: *Mount ye, spur ye, skirr the plain, That the fugitive may flee in vain* (Byron). **2.** to throw with a rapid skimming motion.

—*n.* a grating, rasping, or whirring sound. [origin uncertain. Compare SCURRY.]

skir·ret (skir′it), *n.* a plant of the parsley family, formerly much cultivated in Europe for its edible tubers that taste somewhat like turnips.

[Middle English *skirwhit,* alteration by folk etymology (< obsolete *skire* pure + *white*) of Old French *eschervis,* variant of *carvi* caraway]

skirt (skėrt), *n.* **1.** the part of a dress that hangs down from the waist. **2.** a woman's or girl's outer garment that hangs from the waist: *The triangle flare skirt is fully lined . . . to give it a majestic sweep from a tiny waist to the billowed hem* (New Yorker). **3.** a petticoat. **4.** something like a skirt: *the skirts of a man's long coat.* **5.** *Slang.* a woman or girl: *She's as nice a looking skirt as there is in town* (Sinclair Lewis). **6.** the border; edge: *. . . a few heavy drops from the skirt of the passing cloud . . .* (Francis Parkman). **7.** the outer part of a place, group of people, etc.: *The school is . . . built right on the summer colony's skirts* (Wall Street Journal). **8.** one of the flaps hanging from the sides of a saddle. See **saddle** for picture. **9.** *British.* a cut of beef from the flank.

—*v.t.* **1.** to border; edge: *Those vast and trackless forests that skirted the settlements . . .* (Washington Irving). **2.** to pass along the border, edge, or side of: *to skirt a swamp. The boys skirted the forest because they did not want to go through it at night.* **3.** to be, lie, live, etc., along the border of: *So is man's narrow path By strength and terror skirted* (Emerson). —*v.i.* **1.** to be, lie, live, etc., along the border of a place, etc.: *A sandy desert . . . skirts along the doubtful confine of Syria* (Edward Gibbon). **2.** to pass along the border or edge: *Then I set off up the val-*

ley, skirting along one side of it (Richard D. Blackmore).
[< Scandinavian (compare Old Icelandic *skyrta* shirt, skirt, kirtle). Compare SHIRT.]
skirt dancer, a woman who does skirt dancing.
skirt dancing, a form of ballet dancing in which the effect is produced by graceful movements of a long, full skirt, often manipulated by the hands of the dancer.
-skirted, *combining form.* having a ——— skirt: *Short-skirted = having a short skirt.*
skirt·ing (skėr′ting), *n.* **1.** cloth for making skirts. **2.** *British.* a strip of masonry, wood, etc., placed along the base of a wall; baseboard.
skirtings, the trimmings or inferior parts of a fleece: *to separate skirtings.*
skirting board, *British.* baseboard; skirting.
skirt·less (skėrt′lis), *adj.* **1.** having no skirt: *a skirtless coat.* **2.** wearing no skirt: *Trousers, such as skirtless feminine bicyclists adopt* (London Daily News).
skirt·like (skėrt′līk′), *adj.* resembling a skirt or the act of skirting: *The rain moves as a curtain in an unfolding skirtlike movement* (Maclean's).
ski run, a snow-covered slope or steep runway used by skiers: *Several ski runs cut through the forest* (Atlantic).
skish (skish), *n.* a fisherman's game or sport in which bait-casting or fly-casting equipment is used to cast a plug or weight at a ring or other target from various distances: *In the skish distance bait, ⅝ oz., event, C.J. Lane won with a long cast of 273 ft.* (A.J. McClane). [a coined word; perhaps a blend of *skip*[1] and *fish*]
skit[1] (skit), *n.* a short sketch that contains humor or satire: *a television skit. When we graduated the school paper had skits about each one of us.* [perhaps < *skit*[2]] —**Syn.** squib.
skit[2] (skit), *v.i.*, **skit·ted, skit·ting.** *Scottish.* to dart; skip; leap. [perhaps back formation < *skittish*]
skite[1] (skīt), *n. Scottish.* **1.** a sudden, slapping blow at an angle. **2.** a slight shower; sprinkle. [perhaps < Scandinavian (compare Old Icelandic *skȳt;* see SKITTISH)]
skite[2] (skīt), *v.*, **skit·ed, skit·ing,** *n. Australian.* —*v.i.* to boast. —*n.* a boaster. [probably special use of *skite*[1]]
ski tow, a continuous rope on pulleys, kept moving by a motor, for pulling skiers to the top of a slope: *The city maintains two rinks, a toboggan run and a two-for-a-nickel ski tow* (Maclean's).
ski train, a special train for skiers traveling to skiing resorts.
ski troops, soldiers specially trained to fight and maneuver on skis, especially in northern or arctic areas: *The entire region surrounding the plant was patrolled by a regiment of ski troops* (Maclean's).
skit·ter (skit′ər), *v.i.* **1.** to move lightly or quickly; hurry about: *Motorscooters, ridden by sport-shirted youths, skittered among primitive horsemen in burnooses* (Time). **2.** *U.S.* to skim or skip along a surface: *... the Concepcion was skittering downstream at about fifteen knots* (Atlantic). **3.** *U.S.* (in fishing) to draw a spoon or baited hook over the surface of the water with a skipping motion. —*v.t.* **1.** to cause to skitter. **2.** *U.S.* (in fishing) to draw in (a spoon or baited hook) over the surface of the water with a skipping motion.
—*n.* a light skipping movement or the sound caused by this: *The slim shell trailed with dying headway to the skitter of the resting oars* (Scribner's Magazine).
[related to SKITTISH]
skit·ter·ish (skit′ər ish), *adj.* moving lightly and quickly; skimming; skipping.
skit·ter·y (skit′ər ē), *adj.* **1.** sliding; skidding; slippery: *The skittery [putting] greens proved too much for the U.S. Open Champion* (Time). **2.** frightened; nervous; skittish: *He had an exercise boy take Hill Gail out to the track so that his admittedly skittery horse could get accustomed to all the noise* (Newsweek).
skit·tish (skit′ish), *adj.* **1.** apt to start, jump, or run; easily frightened: *a skittish horse.* **2.** fickle; changeable: *a skittish wind.* **3.** difficult to manage; tricky: *a light, skittish boat.* **4.** shy and timid; coy: *a skittish young girl.* [perhaps < Scandinavian (compare Old Icelandic *skȳt-*, stem of *skjōta* shoot) + English *-ish*] —**skit′tish·ly,** *adv.* —**skit′tish·ness,** *n.*
—**Syn. 1.** excitable. **2.** capricious, volatile. **4.** bashful, demure.
skit·tle (skit′əl), *n., v.*, **-tled, -tling.** —*n.* one of the pins used in the game of skittles.
skittles, a game in which each player tries to knock down nine wooden pins by rolling balls or throwing wooden disks or balls at them: *Skittles resembles bowling.*
—*v.t. Cricket.* to get (batsmen) out rapidly in succession: *Jim Laker of England set a significant mark among bowlers when he skittled out nineteen Australians in two innings* (Newsweek).
[probably < Scandinavian (compare Danish *skyttel* shuttle)]
skittle alley, an alley used in the game of skittles.
skittle ball, a heavy disk, usually of hard wood, for throwing or sliding at the pins in the game of skittles.
skive[1] (skīv), *v.t.*, **skived, skiv·ing. 1.** to slice or split (leather, etc.) into layers. **2.** to shave (hides, etc.). **3.** to pare off. [perhaps < Scandinavian (compare Old Icelandic *skīfa*)]
skive[2] (skīv), *v.i.*, **skived, skiv·ing.** *Dialect.* **1.** to move lightly and quickly; dart. **2.** to go; depart: *He ... skived off to church* (Observer).
skiv·er (skī′vər), *n.* **1. a.** a person who skives. **b.** a tool that skives; knife for skiving: *In the early days of fine shoemaking, French craftsmen proudly used as their symbol the razor-sharp bench knife or skiver* (Wall Street Journal). **2.** a thin, soft leather sliced from the grain side of sheepskin, used for bookbinding and sweatbands in hats.
skiv·ey (skiv′ē), *n., pl.* **-eys.** *British Slang.* skivvy.
skiv·vies (skiv′ēz), *n.pl. U.S. Nautical Slang.* underwear: *Officers were in shirt sleeves; some of the crew lounged in their skivvies* (Newsweek).
skiv·vie shirt (skiv′ē), *U.S. Nautical Slang.* an undershirt.
skiv·vy (skiv′ē), *n., pl.* **-vies.** *British Slang.* a woman servant of low status, as a scullery maid.
ski·wear (skē′wãr′), *n.* clothes worn for skiing.
sklent (sklent), *Scottish.* —*v.i.* **1.** to slant. **2.** to deviate from the truth.
—*n.* **1.** a slant. **2.** a lie; fib.
—*adj.* slanting.
[variant of earlier *slent* < Scandinavian (compare Norwegian *slenta*)]
skoal (skōl), *n., interj.* a Scandinavian word used in drinking a health. It means "Hail" or "May you prosper." —*v.i.* to drink healths.
[< Danish *skaal,* Norwegian *skål* < Old Icelandic *skāl* bowl, shell]
sko·ki·aan (skō′kē än), *n.* (in South Africa) illegally distilled whiskey; moonshine. [< Afrikaans *skokiaan*]
skol·ly (skol′ē), *n., pl.* **-lies.** (in South Africa) a young native rascal or hoodlum: *There has always been an element of skolly crime in the Peninsula* (Cape Argus). [< Afrikaans *skollie*]
skoo·kum (skü′kəm), *adj. Dialect.* strong; fine; excellent; good. [American English < Chinook jargon *skookum*]
Skr., Sanskrit.
Skt., Sanskrit.
sku·a (skyü′ə), *n.*, or **skua gull,** any of several large brown sea birds that are related to the gulls and jaegers: *The skua gull though rarely abundant, is ubiquitous; it appears to be the only scavenger in inland Antarctica* (E. F. Roots). [alteration of Faroese *skūgvur*]

Skua (to 2 ft. long)

skul·dug·ger·y (skul dug′ər ē, -dug′rē), *n. U.S. Informal.* trickery; dishonesty: *That was the season when the Cobb-Lajoie duel for the batting championship brought angry charges of skulduggery and complicity* (New York Times). [American English; origin uncertain]
skulk (skulk), *v.i.* **1.** to keep out of sight to avoid danger, work, duty, etc.; hide or lurk in a cowardly way. **2.** to move in a stealthy, sneaking way: *The wolf was skulking in the woods near the sheep. It is a poor thing for a fellow to get drunk at night and skulk to bed* (Samuel Johnson).
—*n.* **1.** a person who skulks: *You are certainly no skulk when duty is to be done* (James Fenimore Cooper). **2.** *Archaic.* **a.** a group or collection of animals which skulk: *We say a flight of doves ... a skulk of foxes* (Washington Irving). **b.** a group of other animals or persons: *a skulk of thieves.*
[< Scandinavian (compare Danish *skulke*)]
—**skulk′er,** *n.* —**skulk′ing·ly,** *adv.*
—**Syn.** *v.i.* **1.** See **lurk.**
skull (skul), *n.* **1.** the bones of the head; the group of bones around the brain; cranium: *The human skull may conveniently be divided into three principal portions: the cranium or cranial vault, the face, and the lower jaw or mandible* (Beals and Hoijer). **2.** the head; brain: *Skulls that cannot teach and will not learn* (William Cowper). **3.** a crust which is formed by the cooling of molten metal on the sides of a ladle or other vessel.
—*v.t. Slang.* to hit on the skull: *I've seen more guys skulled by warm-up throwers on the sidelines than I've ever seen hit in a ball game* (New York Times).
[< Scandinavian (compare Norwegian dialectal *skul* shell)]
skull and crossbones, a picture of a human skull above two crossed bones. It was often used on pirates' flags as a symbol of death, and is now often used on the labels of poisonous drugs, etc.
skull·cap (skul′kap′), *n.* **1.** a close-fitting cap without a brim: *... a Presbyterian clergyman wearing a black silk skullcap, covering his short hair* (Scott). **2.** any of various plants of the mint family in which the calyx looks like a bowl-shaped helmet. **3.** the upper, caplike part of the skull; top or roof of the head: *The extinct Solo man was inferred from eleven skullcaps found in Java.*
skulled (skuld), *adj.* having a skull.
-skulled, *combining form.* having a ——— skull: *Thick-skulled = having a thick skull.*
skull·fish (skul′fish′), *n., pl.* **-fish·es** or (*collectively*) **-fish.** an old whale, or one more than two years of age.
skull practice, *U.S. Sports Slang.* a lesson or drill in which diagrams are used to explain the tactics of a game: *Skull practice ... held by a football coach and his players* (New Yorker).
skunk (skungk), *n., pl.* **skunks** or (*collectively for 1*) **skunk,** *v.* —*n.* **1.** any of several black, bushy-tailed, burrowing mammals of North and South America, usually with white markings on the back and tail. It is about the size of a cat and gives off a very strong, unpleasant smell when frightened or attacked. **2.** the fur of this animal, used in making coats, etc. **3.** *Informal.* a mean, contemptible person: *He must think me the most awful skunk* (John Galsworthy).

Striped Skunk (def. 1) (not including tail, 1½ ft. long)

—*v.t. U.S. Slang.* to defeat utterly, as in an unequal contest where one side is held scoreless: *He had got 292 votes in New Orleans, and had been skunked in only two parishes out of sixty-three* (New Yorker).
[American English < Algonkian (probably Abnaki) *seganku*]
skunk bear, the wolverine, whose appearance and markings are somewhat suggestive of a large skunk.
skunk blackbird, the male bobolink in full plumage. [because of the resemblance of the black and white coloration to that of the skunk]
skunk cabbage, 1. a low, broadleaved, ill-smelling North American plant of the arum family, growing commonly in moist ground. **2.** a similar and related plant of the Pacific Coast.
skunk·er·y (skung′kər ē), *n., pl.* **-er·ies.** a place where skunks are kept and raised for fur, etc.
skunk·weed (skungk′wēd′), *n.* skunk cabbage.
skunk·y (skungk′ē), *adj.*, **skunk·i·er, skunk·i·est. 1.** of a skunk; like that of a skunk: *People describe the odor as skunky* (New Yorker). **2.** befitting a skunk; nasty: *You try to shove him into any skunk corner ... and he lets you know* (Richard D. Blackmore).

Skup·shti·na (skúp′shti nä), *n.* **1.** the national assembly of Yugoslavia, consisting of a single chamber. **2.** the former national assembly of Serbia or of Montenegro, likewise consisting in each case of a single chamber. [< Serbian (*Narodna*) *Skupshtina* (National) Assembly]

skurf (skėrf), *v.i. Slang.* to ride on a skateboard: *Hundreds of vacationing teen-agers chanting "we want to skurf" wheeled to City Hall yesterday on their skateboards* (Toronto Globe and Mail). [blend of *skate* and *surf*] —**skurf′er,** *n.*

sky (skī), *n., pl.* **skies,** *v.,* **skied** or **skyed, sky·ing.** —*n.* **1.** Often, **skies.** the covering over the world; the region of the clouds or the upper air; the heavens: *a clear sky, to open the sky to aircraft of all nations.* **2. a.** the place where many people believe God and His angels live; heaven. **b.** the heavenly power; the Deity. **3.** climate: *I seek a warmer sky* (Tennyson). **4.** *Obsolete.* a cloud.

out of a clear (blue) sky, suddenly; unexpectedly: *He dropped upon me . . . out of a clear sky and began asking questions which I had to answer* (W.E. Norris).

the sky is the limit, there is no limit; everything is possible or achievable: *For a girl of real talent the sky is the limit* (London Times).

to the skies or **sky,** to the highest possible degree; very highly: *to praise to the skies.*

—*v.t.* **1.** to hit, throw, or raise high into the air, as in golf or cricket: *At 32 Lawrence snicked a "kicker" to McIntyre, and Jordoff, driving at Bedser, skied the ball to extra cover* (London Times). **2.** to hang (a picture, etc.) high up on the wall or near the ceiling, as at an exhibition.

[Middle English *skei* a cloud; the upper air < Scandinavian (compare Old Icelandic *skȳ* cloud)]

—**Syn.** *n.* **1.** firmament.

sky blue, a clear, soft blue; azure. —**sky′-blue′,** *adj.* —**Syn.** cerulean.

sky·borne (skī′bôrn′, -bōrn′), *adj.* airborne: *The first plane . . . was skyborne* (Time).

sky·cap (skī′kap′), *n. U.S.* a porter at an airport.
[< *sky* + *-cap,* as in *redcap*]

sky diver, a person who engages in sky diving: *Canada's sky divers are steadily gaining new converts to their sport—free-falling thousands of feet from an aircraft* (Maclean's).

sky diving, the sport, or military tactic, of diving from an airplane and dropping in a free fall for a great distance, controlling one's course by changing body positions, before releasing the parachute: *Sky diving is a relatively new sport that has quite a following in this small Southern California airstrip. Divers soar free like birds, sometimes for thousands of feet, before opening their parachutes* (Tuscaloosa News).

sky·er (skī′ər), *n.* a lofty hit at cricket: *He fell to a well-judged, running catch off a skyer* (London Times).

Skye terrier, or **Skye** (skī), *n.* any of an old Scottish breed of terriers having a long, low body with short, strong legs and long, shaggy hair. [< the Isle of *Skye,* near Scotland]

Skye Terrier (8½ to 9 in. high at the shoulder)

sky·ey (skī′ē), *adj.* **1.** of or from the sky: *A breath thou art, servile to all the skyey influences* (Shakespeare). **2.** very high; lofty. **3.** like the sky in color; sky-blue; azure.

sky·glow (skī′glō′), *n.* a shaft of light on the night sky, reflecting the lighting patterns of a city: *. . . to reduce skyglow, which could give navigational aid to enemy aircraft in an attack on principal U.S. target cities* (Bulletin of Atomic Scientists).

sky-high (skī′hī′), *adv., adj.* very high: *One firm in the advertising game that is not doing sky-high business is a skywriter here* (Wall Street Journal).

sky·hook (skī′hůk′), *n.* a flattish device that spirals slowly to earth when dropped from a plane, used to drop supplies of medicine, etc.

skyhook balloon, a large, open-necked plastic balloon used to carry scientific instruments for making meteorological studies or observing cosmic rays, the sun's spectrum, etc.: *A different method of taking a hurricane's picture is also a Navy project: a giant skyhook balloon carrying a camera gondola* (Science News Letter).

sky·ish (skī′ish), *adj. Poetic.* skyey; lofty.

sky·jack (skī′jak′), *v.t.* to take over (an aircraft) by force causing it to fly to a place other than its destination. —**sky′-jack′er,** *n.*

sky·lark (skī′lärk′), *n.* the common European lark, a small bird that sings very sweetly as it flies skyward: *A more inexhaustible singer than the skylark does not exist* (W.H. Hudson). —*v.i.* to play pranks; frolic: *The children were skylarking in the orchard.* —**sky′lark′er,** *n.*

English Skylark (about 7 in. long)

sky·less (skī′lis), *adj.* without visible sky; cloudy; dark; thick: *a skyless day.*

sky·light (skī′līt′), *n., v.,* **-light·ed** or **-lit, -light·ing.** —*n.* a window in a roof or ceiling. —*v.t.* to furnish with or light by a skylight or skylights: *All the inside rooms were skylighted.*

sky·line (skī′līn′), *n.* **1.** the line at which earth and sky seem to meet; horizon: *Often I had to crawl on all-fours to avoid appearing against the skyline on the ridge* (Theodore Roosevelt). **2.** the outline of buildings, mountains, trees, etc., as seen against the sky: *The tall buildings and towers of Manhattan make a remarkable skyline.*

sky·lin·er (skī′lī′nər), *n.* a large, usually luxurious, commercial passenger airplane: *You'll be delighted with the feeling of solid security you get from flight aboard this swift new skyliner* (New Yorker).

sky·lit (skī′lit′), *adj.* skylighted: *The long skylit corridor . . . leads to the ten consulting rooms* (Time). —*v.* skylighted; a past tense and a past participle of **skylight.**

sky·man (skī′man′), *n., pl.* **-men.** *Informal.* an aviator.

sky map, star map: *The frustrated stargazer can always find consolation in studying his sky map* (Atlantic).

sky·mo·tel (skī′mō tel′), *n.* a motel for air travelers, usually at or near an airport.

sky parlor, *Slang.* a garret or attic.

sky·phos (skī′fos′), *n., pl.* **-phoi** (-foi). an ancient Greek cup; scyphus: *. . . the pendant semicircle skyphos, which are found throughout the Aegean* (London Times). [< Greek *skýphos*]

sky pilot, 1. *Slang.* a clergyman; chaplain. **2.** *Informal.* an aviator: *The present bishop . . . flies his own plane, . . . to visit his far-flung missions, literally as well as figuratively a "sky pilot"* (Ernest Gruening).

sky·port (skī′pôrt′, -pōrt′), *n.* an airport for helicopters, built on top of a building.

sky·rock·et (skī′rok′it), *n.* a firework that goes up high into the air and (usually) bursts into a shower of stars, sparks, etc.; rocket.
—*v.i.* **1.** to move like a skyrocket; rise suddenly, make a brilliant show, and disappear. **2.** to rise to a great height quickly: *Prices were skyrocketing.*

sky·sail (skī′sāl′; *Nautical* skī′səl), *n.* a light sail set at the top of a mast above the royal on a square-rigged ship.

sky·scape (skī′skāp′), *n.* **1.** a view of the sky: *It was the unbroken horizon which impressed me . . . and the skyscapes which it afforded* (Robert Southey). **2.** a picture or representation of part of the sky: *The landscape and skyscape in the background are an oil painting stretched on canvas over a built-in frame* (New Yorker).

sky·scrap·er (skī′skrā′pər), *n.* a very tall building: *Where did the skyscraper get its name? From the topmost sail of the clipper ships, according to Lewis Mumford* (New York Times).

sky·scrap·ing (skī′skrā′ping), *adj.* very high; lofty: *The monumental form seems to combine Babel and Troy with intimations of modern Manhattan—its skyscraping towers connected at the top by railroad bridges* (Time).

sky sign, *British.* an advertisement, announcement, or direction, set up so as to be visible against the sky, as on the top of a building: *If you drive round London at night you keep coming across illuminated sky signs suspended eerily in places where memory tells you there aren't any buildings* (Punch).

Sky·sweep·er (skī′swē′pər), *n. Trademark.* an automatic anti-aircraft gun with radar and computer that tracks the target and aims the gun on the same carriage.

sky·ward (skī′wərd), *adv., adj.* toward the sky: *to move skyward* (*adv.*), *a skyward movement* (*adj.*).

sky·wards (skī′wərdz), *adv.* skyward.

sky wave, a radio wave sent from a transmitter into the atmosphere and sometimes reflected back to earth by the ionosphere: *This zone of intense auroral activity, floating above the Iceland-Greenland-Labrador axis, can so disorganize the ionosphere that sky waves are not bent back to the earth* (Newsweek).

sky·way (skī′wā′), *n.* **1.** a route for small private airplanes that lack the equipment to follow the federal airway system: *The 24 skyways are 40-mile wide routes picked for good emergency landing spaces between airports* (World Book Encyclopedia). **2.** an elevated highway for motor vehicles: *Motorists will be charged tolls to cross these arches, as well as the new skyway planned to eliminate the traffic bottleneck caused by the Welland Canal* (Maclean's).

sky·write (skī′rīt′), *v.t., v.i.,* **-wrote, -writ·ten, -writ·ing.** to advertise by skywriting.

sky·writ·er (skī′rī′tər), *n.* a person or thing that skywrites.

sky·writ·ing (skī′rī′ting), *n.* **1.** the tracing of letters, words, etc., against the sky by smoke or similar substance from an airplane. **2.** the letters, words, etc., so traced.

s.l., without place (Latin, *sine loco*).

S.L., 1. sergeant at law. **2.** solicitor at law. **3.** south latitude.

SLA (no periods), Special Libraries Association.

S.L.A. or **SLA** (no periods), State Liquor Authority.

slab[1] (slab), *n., v.,* **slabbed, slab·bing.** —*n.* **1.** a broad, flat, relatively thick piece (of stone, wood, meat, etc.): *This sidewalk is made of slabs of stone. The hungry boy ate a slab of cheese as big as his hand.* **2.** a rough, outside piece cut lengthwise from a log, used with or without the bark as siding, for stove wood, etc.: *Slabs are beams whose width is greater than their depth* (World Book Encyclopedia). **3.** *Slang.* the pitcher's plate on a baseball diamond; rubber.
—*v.t.* **1.** to make into slabs. **2.** to cut the outside pieces from (a log). **3.** to lay with slabs; cover with slabs.
[Middle English *slabbe;* origin uncertain]

slab[2] (slab), *adj. Archaic.* semisolid; viscid: *Make the gruel thick and slab* (Shakespeare). [< Scandinavian (compare Danish *slab* slippery; mire)]

slab·ber (slab′ər), *v.i., v.t., n.* slobber.

slab·ber·er (slab′ər ər), *n.* a person or animal that slabbers; driveler.

slab·ber·y (slab′ər ē), *adj.* covered with slobber; wet; sloppy.

slab·bing mill (slab′ing), a mill that rolls steel ingots into slabs for further processing.

slab·by (slab′ē), *adj.,* **-bi·er, -bi·est. 1.** thick; viscous: *The writing is largely slabby and indigestible* (Punch). **2.** *Archaic.* muddy; slimy; sloppy: *Bad slabby weather today* (Jonathan Swift).

slab·like (slab′līk′), *adj.* like a slab; broad, flat, and thick: *. . . the bare slablike surfaces that are transforming Park Avenue* (New Yorker).

slab-sid·ed (slab′sī′did), *adj.* **1.** having long, flat sides: *. . . a slab-sided, fourteen-storey block still at the skeletal stage* (Manchester Guardian). **2.** *Informal.* tall and lank: *. . . long-legged, slab-sided, lean, sunburnt . . . lads* (Henry Kingsley).

slab·stone (slab′stōn′), *n.* rock which splits readily into slabs or flags; flagstone.

slack[1] (slak), *adj.* **1.** not tight or firm; loose: *slack rigging, a slack bandage. The rope hung slack.* **2.** careless: *She is a slack housekeeper. He was slack in fulfilling his promises and responsibilities.* **3.** slow; sluggish: *The horse was moving at a slack pace. Then he took advantage of the change from ebb to slack tide to bring her alongside the bulkhead* (New York Times). **4.** not active; not brisk; dull: *a slack three weeks before harvest. Business is slack at this season.*
—*n.* **1.** the part that hangs loose: *Pull in the slack of the rope.* **2.** a dull season; quiet period; lull. **3.** a stopping of a strong flow of the tide or a current of water.
—*v.t.* **1.** to make less tight or firm; let up on; loosen; slacken. **2.** to make less active; moderate; abate: *He . . . without slacking his pace for an instant, stalked on* (Robert Louis Stevenson). **3.** to leave undone;

neglect; shirk. **4.** to slake (lime). *—v.i.* **1.** to become less tight or firm. **2.** to be or become slack; let up: *Still she went . . . slacking not, pausing not* (Harriet Beecher Stowe). **3.** (of lime) to become slaked.

slack off, a. to loosen: *Slack off the halyards a little so the sails will billow.* **b.** to lessen one's efforts: *The American artillery slacked off in its firing . . . and this tactical error undoubtedly allowed a lot of fleeing troops to make their way through Chambois* (Harper's).

slack up, to slow down; go more slowly: *One expected to see the locomotive pause, or slack up a little* (Mark Twain).

—adv. in a slack manner.

[Old English *slæc*] **—slack′ly,** *adv.* **—slack′ness,** *n.*

—Syn. *adj.* **2.** lax, indolent, negligent, remiss.

slack² (slak), *n.* dirt, dust, and small pieces left after coal is screened; small coal. [probably < Middle Dutch *slacke*]

slack³ (slak, släk), *n. Scottish.* **1.** a hollow between hills. **2.** a soft or boggy hollow. [< Scandinavian (compare Old Icelandic *slakki*)]

slack·age (slak′ij), *n.* the amount allowed for the droop or sag of a rope or cable when not fully strained; slack.

slack-baked (slak′bākt′), *adj.* **1.** not baked enough. **2.** poorly designed, made, etc.: *. . . down to the slack-baked buckles in his shoes* (Dickens). [< *slack*¹, adverb + *baked*]

slack·en (slak′ən), *v.t.* **1.** to make slower: *Don't slacken your efforts till the job is done.* **2.** to make looser: *to slacken a rope. Slackening the reins, I let my horse take his own course* (Francis Parkman). *—v.i.* **1.** to become slower; become less active, vigorous, brisk, etc.: *Work slackens on a hot day. His business always slackens in the winter.* **2.** to become loose: *The rope slackened as the wave sent the boat toward the pier.* **—slack′en·er,** *n.* **—Syn.** *v.t.* **1.** retard.

slack·en·ing (slak′ə ning), *n.* the action of making or becoming slack; diminution; lessening: *Zinc demand continues strong, with no indications of immediate slackening* (Wall Street Journal).

slack·er (slak′ər), *n.* a person who shirks work or evades his duty, especially an able-bodied man who evades military service in time of war: *Every shirker, every coward and slacker . . . decided at once to be a conscientious objector* (H.G. Wells).

slack·er·ism (slak′ə riz əm), *n.* the conduct of a slacker; attitude of shirkers: *Rear Admiral Emory S. Land, chairman of the Government shipbuilding agency, called "illegitimate absenteeism a first cousin to slackerism"* (Baltimore Sun).

slack-fill (slak′fil′), *v.t.* to fill loosely so that there is room for more: *When a manufacturer slack-fills his cereal box, he makes a few extra pennies on each sale* (Harper's).

slack-jawed (slak′jôd′), *adj.* with the jaw or mouth partly open and loose: *Bobby is credited . . . with "the Game of the Century" —one that chess buffs retrace in slack-jawed admiration* (Time).

slack-mouthed (slak′mouᴛʜd′, -moutht′), *adj.* slack-jawed: *Her slack-mouthed gibbering performance . . .* (Punch).

slack-off (slak′ôf′, -of′), *n. Informal.* a slowing down; a lessening; letup: *He explained that orders have been filled and an industry-wide slack-off exists* (Wall Street Journal).

slacks (slaks), *n.pl.* trousers worn by men and women as sportswear, for lounging, etc.

slack suit, a two-piece, informal suit consisting of a jacket or shirt and slacks, worn by both men and women.

slack tide, slack water: *The American Manufacturer, of the United States Lines, sailed early yesterday morning at slack tide from Pier 61, North River* (New York Times).

slack water, the time between tides when the water does not move either way: *These four dams when finished will provide slack water navigation from Astoria to Pasco, a distance of 328 miles* (Newsweek).

slack wire, a loosely stretched wire on which an acrobat performs: *A man twirling hoops while balancing on a slack wire* (New York Times).

slade (slād), *n. British Dialect.* **1.** a little valley; dell. **2.** an open space of green grass in a wood or between two woods. [Old English *slæd*]

slag (slag), *n., v.,* **slagged, slag·ging.** *—n.* **1.** the rough, hard waste left after metal is separated from ore by melting: *Some 357 million tons of stone, sand, gravel, and slag now go into building roads each year* (Newsweek). **2.** a light, spongy lava; the scoria from a volcano.

—v.t. **1.** to change into slag. **2.** to free from slag. *—v.i.* to form slag; become a slaglike mass.

[probably < Scandinavian (compare Swedish *slagg,* Norwegian *slagga* dross < Middle Low German *slagge*)]

—Syn. *n.* **1.** dross.

slag furnace, a furnace for the extraction of lead from slags, and from ores which contain little lead.

slag·gy (slag′ē), *adj.,* **-gi·er, -gi·est.** of, like, or having to do with slag.

slag·less·ness (slag′lis nis), *n.* the fact of having no slag or cinder.

slag wool, mineral wool.

slain (slān), *v.* the past participle of **slay:** *The sheep were slain by the wolves.*

slake (slāk; *also* slak, *especially for v.t. 3, v.i. 1*), *v.,* **slaked, slak·ing.** *—v.t.* **1.** to make (thirst, revenge, wrath, etc.) less active, vigorous, or intense by satisfying: *We slaked our thirst at the spring.* **2.** to put out (a fire). **3.** to change (lime) from calcium oxide to calcium hydroxide by leaving it in the moist air or putting water on it. **4.** *Archaic.* to make less painful: *Wake thou . . . and slake . . . A wound more fierce than his . . .* (Shelley). *—v.i.* **1.** (of lime) to become calcium hydroxide. **2.** to become less active, vigorous, intense, etc. [Middle English *slaken,* Old English *slacian* slacken < *slæc* slack] **—Syn.** *v.t.* **1.** assuage. **2.** extinguish.

slaked lime (slākt, slakt), calcium hydroxide: *Plaster contains slaked lime and sand.*

slake·less (slāk′lis), *adj.* that cannot be satisfied; insatiable: *a slakeless thirst.*

sla·lom (slä′ləm, -lōm; slal′əm), *n.* (in skiing) a zigzag race downhill. The skiers complete the run in turns, the winner being the one who does it fastest without error.

—v.i. to move as a skier doing the slalom; zigzag skillfully between objects: *I slalomed around cloverleafs trying to get turned the right way* (Maclean's). [< Norwegian *slalom*]

slam¹ (slam), *v.,* **slammed, slam·ming,** *n.* *—v.t.* **1.** to shut with force and noise; close with a bang: *He slammed the window down.* **2.** to throw, push, hit, or move hard with force: *Joe slammed himself down on his bed. Why, he'd have slammed you through the window* (Mark Twain). **3.** *U.S. Informal.* to criticize harshly: *His habit of slamming his friends made him unpopular.* *—v.i.* **1.** to shut with force and noise; close with a bang: *The door slammed.* **2.** to move hard with force: *My car slammed into the truck.*

—n. **1.** a violent and noisy closing, striking, etc.; bang: *John threw his books down with a slam.* **2.** *U.S. Informal.* harsh criticism.

slam² (slam), *n.* **1.** (in bridge) the winning of 12 (little, or small, slam) or all 13 (grand slam) tricks in a hand. **2.** a hand of whist in which one side wins all the tricks. **3.** a game of cards something like ruff, played in the 1600's. [origin uncertain]

slam·bang (slam′bang′), *Informal.* *—adv.* with a slam and a bang; with noisy or headlong violence: *The car went slambang into a fence.* *—adj.* violent and noisy; unrestrained: *. . . the slambang, profane hit play, "The Front Page"* (Newsweek). *—v.i.* to go with a slam and a bang; go noisily: *Zooey's razor, new blade and all slambanged down into the metal wastebasket* (J. D. Salinger).

slan·der (slan′dər, slän′-), *n.* **1. a.** a false report meant to do harm to the good name and reputation of another: *To speak no slander, no, nor listen to it* (Tennyson). **b.** *Law.* a spoken statement tending to damage a person's reputation. **2.** the spreading of false reports: *The worthiest people are the most injured by slander* (Jonathan Swift).

—v.t. to talk falsely about. *—v.i.* to speak or spread slander.

[< Anglo-French *esclandre* scandal, adapted from Latin *scandalum.* Doublet of SCANDAL.] **—slan′der·er,** *n.*

—Syn. *n.* **1. a.** defamation, calumny. *-v.t.* defame, calumniate.

➤ **Slander** and **libel** are sharply distinguished from each other in modern United States law. *Slander* applies only to what is spoken; *Libel* applies only to what is written or printed.

slander of title, *Law.* defamatory and false statements injuring one's property, real or personal, or one's title thereto.

slan·der·ous (slan′dər əs, -drəs; slän′-), *adj.* **1.** of, containing, or involving slander or a slander: *slanderous words.* **2.** speaking or spreading slanders: *Done to death by slanderous tongues* (Shakespeare). **—slan′der·ous·ly,** *adv.* **—slan′der·ous·ness,** *n.* **—Syn. 1.** calumnious, defamatory.

slang (slang), *n.* **1.** new, flashy, and popular words or phrases characterized by freshness and vividness, or ordinary words or phrases used in special and arbitrary senses: *The central characteristic of slang comes from the motive for its use: a desire for novelty, for vivid emphasis, for being in the know, up with the times or a little ahead . . . Many slang words have short lives — skiddoo, twenty-three, vamoose, beat it, scram, hit the trail, take a powder, drag out, shag out — have succeeded each other almost within a generation . . . The chief objections to slang, aside from its possible conspicuousness, are to its overuse, and to its use in place of more exact expressions* (Porter G. Perrin). *All slang is metaphor, and all metaphor is poetry* (G. K. Chesterton). **2.** the special talk or language of a particular class of people: *"Crib" means "cheat" in students' slang.* **3.** the special language of tramps, thieves, etc.; cant: *"Slang" in the sense of the cant language of thieves appears in print certainly as early as the middle of the last century [1700's]* (The Nation).

—v.t. **1.** to attack with abusive language; rail at; scold. **2.** to address in slang. *—v.i.* **1.** to rail at a person or persons: *They slanged away at each other* (Atlantic). **2.** to utter slang. [origin unknown]

slang·i·ly (slang′ə lē), *adv.* in a slangy manner.

slang·i·ness (slang′ē nis), *n.* slangy quality: *[The play] drew many a brickbat from critics . . . for its slanginess* (Newsweek).

slan·guage (slang′gwij), *n.* slangy language: *It is also best to avoid attempts to talk teen slanguage* (Time).

slang·y (slang′ē), *adj.,* **slang·i·er, slang·i·est. 1.** containing slang; full of slang: *Trilby's French was . . . droll, slangy, piquant . . .* (George Du Maurier). *You'd always thought of them before as being jazzy—you know, hep cats, slangy* (New York Times). **2.** using much slang: *She's slangy, and she'd shock your sort of woman out of her wits* (Leonard Merrick).

slank (slangk), *v. Archaic.* a past tense of **slink**¹.

slant (slant, slänt), *v.i.* to slope: *Most handwriting slants to the right.* *—v.t.* **1.** to cause to slant; slope: *to slant a roof.* **2.** *U.S.* to make (a story, news account, etc.) favorable, or unfavorable, to a particular person, group, cause, etc., by choosing or emphasizing certain facts: *Almost a third of them think that newspaper stories on their activities are "slanted"* (Time). [variant of Middle English *slenten* to slant, slip sideways < Scandinavian (compare Norwegian *slenta*)]

—n. **1.** slanting or oblique direction or position; slope: *a roof with a sharp slant.* **2.** a way of regarding something; mental attitude; point of view: *Then the matter was given an entirely new slant by discoveries from another quarter* (Scientific American). **3.** *U.S. Informal.* favorable or unfavorable bias (in a story, news account, etc.): *I have yet to see a piece of writing, political or nonpolitical, that doesn't have a slant* (New Yorker). **4.** *U.S.* a glance; look.

—adj. **1.** sloping. **2.** (of direction) oblique.

[short for Middle English *aslante,* probably < *a-* on + *slant,* or *slent* a slope]

—**Syn.** *v.i.* See **slope.** *-n.* **1.** incline.

slant drilling, slant-hole drilling: *Slant drilling involved the intentional slanting of oil wells to tap reserves under leases belonging to others* (Wall Street Journal).

slan·ten·dic·u·lar (slan′tən dik′yə lər, slän′-), *adj.* slantindicular. **—slan′ten·dic′u·lar·ly,** *adv.*

slant-eyed (slant′īd′, slänt′-), *adj.* having eyes that slant, as certain Oriental people.

slant-hole drilling (slant′hōl′, slänt′-), the drilling of oil wells in a slanting instead of a vertical direction, especially with the unlawful purpose of tapping oil belonging to adjacent properties.

slan·tin·dic·u·lar (slan′tən dik′yə lər, slän′-), *adj. Humorous.* slanting; oblique. [< *slantin*(g) + (perpen)*dicular*] —**slan′tin·dic′u·lar·ly,** *adv.*

slant·ing (slan′ting, slän′-), *adj.* that slants; oblique: *a slanting roof; slanting sunlight* (Winston Churchill). —**slant′ing·ly,** *adv.*

slant·ly (slant′lē, slänt′-), *adv.* in a slant or slanting direction.

slant·ways (slant′wāz′, slänt′-), *adv.* slantwise.

slant·wise (slant′wīz′, slänt′-), *adv.* in a slanting manner; obliquely: *A crab scuttles slantwise.* —*adj.* slanting; oblique: *The slantwise rain Of light through the leaves* (John Greenleaf Whittier).

slap[1] (slap), *n., v.,* **slapped, slap·ping,** *adv.* —*n.* **1.** a blow with the open hand or with something flat; smack. **2.** sharp words of blame; direct insult or rebuff.

slap in the face, *Informal.* a humiliating insult or rebuff: *His decision to recognize Red China was a slap in the face because he had given contrary assurances* (Atlantic).

slap on the wrist, *Informal.* a light scolding: *NASA received a slap on the wrist for the way it has handled project Surveyor* (New Scientist).

—*v.t.* **1.** to strike with the open hand; hit with something more or less flat; smack: *to slap a child for disobedience.* **2.** to put, dash, or cast with force: *She slapped the book down on the table.* —*v.i.* **1.** to strike with the open hand or with something flat: *He slapped at the fly with a folded newspaper.* **2.** to beat or hit with a slapping sound: *waves slapping against the dock. The piston was slapping in the cylinder.*

slap together, to put together in a slapdash manner: *Ira Levin has slapped together a busy lampoon of a yarn* (New York Times).

—*adv.* **1.** straight; directly: *He'll run slap into the sentries* (Rudyard Kipling). **2.** quickly; suddenly.

[< Low German *slappe*]

—**Syn.** *n.* **2.** rebuke, reproval. -*adv.* **2.** abruptly.

slap[2] (slap, släp), *n. Scottish.* an opening in a wall, hedge, etc.; narrow pass between hills. [< Flemish *slop* opening, passage]

slap·bang (slap′bang′), *adv.* **1.** without delay; immediately. **2.** without due consideration or regard to the consequences: *He was bent on getting the Army slapbang into the Air Force's business of long-range strategic attack* (Time). —*adj.* slapdash.

slap·dash (slap′dash′), *adv.* without much thought or care; hastily and carelessly: *I talked . . . and said a thousand silly things, slapdash* (Washington Irving).

—*adj.* hasty and careless: *Slapdash buildings were going up everywhere* (Time).

—*n.* **1.** hasty, careless action, methods, or work: *The rest is swashbuckle and slapdash, jousting and broadsword, banqueting and jesting, and a fine siege of a beleaguered castle* (Newsweek). **2.** rough plastering.

—**Syn.** *adv.* precipitately. -*n.* **1.** scramble.

slap-hap·py (slap′hap′ē), *adj. Slang.* dizzy and uncoordinated because of too many blows to the head; giddy; befuddled; senseless: *Two years has been long enough to inure the President against all slap-happy impulses* (Manchester Guardian Weekly).

slap·jack (slap′jak′), *n.* **1.** *U.S. Dialect.* a flapjack; griddlecake or pancake. **2.** a children's card game. [American English]

slap·per (slap′ər), *n.* a person or thing that slaps.

slap·py (slap′ē), *adj.,* **-pi·er, -pi·est.** smacking; spanking: *a slappy breeze, a slappy blow.*

slap·stick (slap′stik′), *n.* **1.** a device consisting of two long, narrow sticks fastened so as to slap together loudly when a clown, actor, etc., hits somebody with it. **2.** comedy full of rough play, pranks, etc.: *Behind all this slapstick there is a serious question waiting in the wings* (Wall Street Journal).

—*adj.* full of rough play, pranks, etc. In slapstick comedy, the actors knock each other around to make people laugh.

[American English < *slap*[1] + *stick*[1]]

slap-up (slap′up′), *adj. British Slang.* of superior quality; first-rate: *a slap-up hotel. Another in Pennsylvania will do this and add a slap-up dinner for two* (Manchester Guardian Weekly).

slash[1] (slash), *v.t.* **1.** to cut with a sweeping stroke of a sword, knife, ax, etc.; gash: *to slash a tree, to slash a person's face, etc. He slashed the bark off the tree with his knife.* **2.** to cut or slit (a garment) to let a different cloth or color show through. **3.** to whip severely; lash. **4.** to criticize sharply, severely, or unkindly: *The critics slashed the new play in the next morning's press.* **5.** to cut down severely; reduce a great deal: *His salary was slashed when business became bad.* **6.** to cut out parts of (a book, etc.); change greatly (a book, etc.). —*v.i.* **1.** to make a sweeping stroke or strokes: *We . . . came slashing down with the mad current into the narrow passage between the dykes* (Mark Twain). **2.** to criticize sharply, severely, or unkindly: *The writer slashed out against his critics.*

—*n.* **1.** a sweeping, slashing stroke: *the slash of the rain* (Hamlin Garland); *rough slashes of sarcasm* (Thomas Carlyle). **2.** a cut or wound made by such a stroke; gash. **3.** an ornamental slit in a garment that lets a different cloth or color show through. **4. a.** a clearing in a forest full of felled trees, branches, etc., allowed to lie as they fell, as a result of storm, fire, logging, etc. **b.** the tangle of fallen trees, branches, etc.: *Another change equally important, results from a more careful scientific disposal of slash and forest leftovers* (Atlantic). **5.** a severe cutting down; a great reduction: *Cotton has come down despite a drastic slash in plantings* (Wall Street Journal). **6.** *U.S.* the slanting line (/) used in writing and printing.

[Middle English *slaschen,* perhaps < Old French *esclachier* to break, variant of *esclater.* Compare ECLAT.]

slash[2] (slash), *n.* wet or swampy ground overgrown with bushes or trees. [American English; origin uncertain. Compare dialectal English *slashy* wet, miry.]

slash-and-burn (slash′ən bėrn′), *n.* a method of agriculture used by primitive peoples, in which trees were felled, and the land burned over just before planting season. This method was wasteful because it used up the nutrients of the soil very quickly. *Indians of the South American tropics used slash-and-burn agriculture* (Clifford Evans).

slash·er (slash′ər), *n.* **1.** a person who slashes; fighter; bully. **2.** (in textile manufacturing) a machine that sizes warp yarns before weaving.

slash·ing (slash′ing), *adj.* **1.** dashing; reckless. **2.** that slashes; cutting: *slashing criticism.*

—*n.* **1.** the act of a person or thing that slashes. **2.** a slash. —**slash′ing·ly,** *adv.*

slash pine, 1. a pine common in swamps of the southeastern United States: *The greatest proportion of forest and shelterbelt tree planting during the year was devoted to slash pine in the South* (Science News Letter). **2.** its hard, durable wood. **3.** the loblolly.

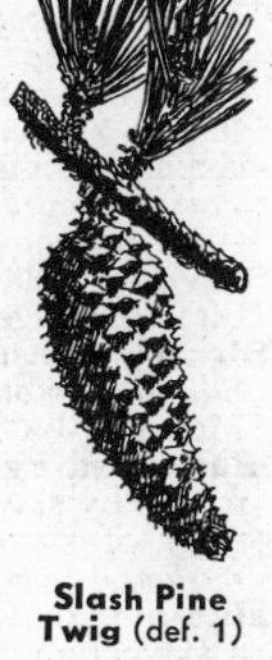

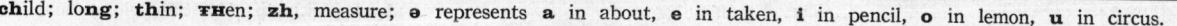

Slash Pine Twig (def. 1)

slash pocket, a diagonal pocket in an outer garment, with no flap on the outside: *It has a lining of Tattersall checks, an inside pocket, and the usual outside slash pockets* (New Yorker).

slat[1] (slat), *n., v.,* **slat·ted, slat·ting.** —*n.* a long, thin, narrow strip of wood or metal: *All the houses of the village were covered with slats or tiles* (J. Davies).

slats, *Slang.* the ribs.

—*v.t.* to provide or build with slats: *to slat a porch or roof.*

[ultimately < Old French *esclat* split piece < *esclater* to splinter, burst. Compare ÉCLAT.]

slat[2] (slat), *v.,* **slat·ted, slat·ting,** *n. Archaic.* —*v.t.* **1.** to flap, cast, or dash. **2.** to strike or beat; knock. —*v.i.* to flap violently: *The mainsail was blowing and slatting with a noise like thunder* (Richard Henry Dana).

—*n.* a slap.

[origin uncertain. Compare Old Icelandic *sletta* to slap, splash, etc.]

S. Lat. or **S. lat.,** south latitude.

slate[1] (slāt), *n., v.,* **slat·ed, slat·ing,** *adj.* —*n.* **1.** a fine-grained, bluish-gray rock that splits easily into thin, smooth layers. Slate is used to cover roofs and for blackboards. **2.** a thin piece of this rock: *Children used to write on slates, but now they use paper.* **3.** a dark, bluish-gray color. **4.** *U.S.* a list of candidates, officers, etc., to be considered for appointment, nomination, etc.: *Apprehensions of Administration leaders that the Republican right wing will try to put up a rival slate are declining* (Newsweek).

clean slate, a record unmarred by discreditable acts or failures to act: *to start life again with a clean slate.*

on the slate, on credit: *Old-age pensioners would not be able to pop into the corner shop for a quarter pound on the slate* (Punch).

—*v.t.* **1.** to cover with slate. **2.** to list on or as if on a slate: *He is slated for the office of club president.*

—*adj.* dark bluish-gray. [Middle English *sclate* < Old French *esclate,* variant of *esclat;* see SLAT[1]] —**slate′like′,** *adj.*

slate[2] (slāt), *v.t.,* **slat·ed, slat·ing. 1.** to thrash severely. **2.** to scold or criticize severely: *The reviewers slated his book.* [perhaps variant of *slat*[2]]

slate black, a slate color having less than one tenth the luminosity of white.

slate blue, a dull blue with a grayish tinge.

slate-col·ored junco (slāt′kul′ərd), a grayish North American junco with white belly and outer tail feathers.

slate gray, a relatively luminous slate color.

slate pencil, a pencil of soft slate or similar material, used for writing on a slate.

slat·er[1] (slā′tər), *n.* **1.** a person who covers roofs, etc., with slates. **2.** *Scottish.* a wood louse.

slat·er[2] (slā′tər), *n.* a violent critic.

slate writer, a person who practices slate writing.

slate writing, a sleight-of-hand trick in which a slate is written on apparently while tied or sealed face to face with another.

slath·er (slaтн′ər), *U.S. Slang.* —*n.* **slathers,** a large amount: *They get slathers of money—most a dollar a day, Ben Rogers says* (Mark Twain).

—*v.t.* to spread or pour lavishly: *to slather butter on toast, to slather cream in his coffee. He even smells stylish, slathering on . . . cologne so liberally that it lingers on long after he leaves the room* (Time).

[American English; origin unknown]

slat·ing (slā′ting), *n.* **1.** slates: *to buy slating for a barn.* **2.** the work or business of a slater.

slat·ted (slat′id), *adj.* furnished with, made of, or covered with slats: *a slatted frame.*

slat·ter (slat′ər), *v.t. British.* to spill; slop; scatter carelessly; waste. [origin uncertain]

slat·tern (slat′ərn), *n.* a woman or girl who is dirty, careless, or untidy in her dress, her ways, her housekeeping, etc. [related to SLATTER; origin uncertain. Compare Low German *slattje* slatternly woman.] —**Syn.** sloven.

slat·tern·li·ness (slat′ərn lē nis), *n.* slatternly quality or condition.

slat·tern·ly (slat′ərn lē), *adj.* slovenly; untidy: *. . . a slatternly girl, in shoes down at heel* (Dickens). *A slatternly calico wrapper hung from her shoulders* (Edith Wharton).

slat·y (slā′tē), *adj.,* **slat·i·er, slat·i·est. 1.** of, like, or having to do with slate. **2.** slate-colored: *The sun had disappeared under a cloud, and the sea had turned a little slaty* (G. Macdonald).

slaugh·ter (slô′tər), *n.* **1.** the killing of an animal or animals for food; butchering: *the slaughter of a steer, to fatten hogs for slaughter. They* [*passenger pigeons*] *were wiped out by one of the most relentless and perverse slaughters in history, exceeding in ruthlessness the better-known butchery of the buffalo* (Newsweek). **2.** brutal killing; much or needless killing: *the slaughter of the Innocents by Herod, the frightful slaughter on the highways.*

—*v.t., v.i.* **1.** to butcher: *Millions of cattle are slaughtered in Chicago every year.* **2.** to kill brutally; massacre.

[Middle English *slahter* < Scandinavian (compare Old Icelandic *slātr* butcher meat)] —**slaugh′ter·er,** *n.*

—**Syn.** *n.* **2.** murder, massacre.

slaugh·ter·house (slô′tər hous′), *n.* a place where animals are butchered and dressed for food and other products: *As a schoolboy, he had once spent one and sixpence for a horse on its way to the slaughterhouse* (Time). —**Syn.** abattoir.

slaugh·ter·man (slô′tər mən), *n., pl.* **-men. 1.** a man whose work is to slaughter animals for food. **2.** an executioner.

slaugh·ter·ous (slô′tər əs), *adj.* murderous; destructive: *Direness, familiar to my* *slaughterous thoughts, cannot once start me* (Shakespeare).

slaugh·ter·ous·ly (slô′tər əs lē), *adv.* murderously; so as to slay.

Slav (släv, slav), *n.* a member of a group of peoples in eastern Europe speaking related languages: *Russians, Ukrainians, Poles, Czechs, Slovaks, Moravians, Serbs, and Bulgarians are Slavs.* —*adj.* of, having to do with, or characteristic of Slavs; Slavic. [< Medieval Latin *Slavus* Slav; slave, ultimately < Slavic (compare Russian *slovo* word); original meaning was member of a single speech community]

Slav., **1.** Slavic. **2.** Slavonian. **3.** Slavonic.

Slav·dom (släv′dəm, slav′-), *n.* the group or race of people called Slavs; Slavs collectively: *the civilization of Slavdom.*

slave (slāv), *n., v.,* **slaved, slav·ing,** *adj.* —*n.* **1.** a person who is the property of another: *Slaves were bought and sold like horses. We'll visit Caliban, my slave* (Shakespeare). **2. a.** a person who submits to or follows another: *The head of a party and, consequently . . . the slave of a party . . .* (Macaulay). **b.** a person who is controlled or ruled by some desire, habit, or influence: *A drunkard is a slave of drink. Give me that man That is not passion's slave* (Shakespeare). **3.** a person who works like a slave. **4.** a slave ant. **5. a.** an electronic device that receives and relays radio signals transmitted by a master control, as in loran navigation. **b.** a mechanical or electric device, usually a kind of servomechanism, for manipulating objects by remote control, as in handling dangerous radioactive materials from outside a closed system.
—*v.i.* to work like a slave; work hard and long: *Many mothers slave for their children.* —*v.t.* to make a slave of; enslave.
—*adj.* **1.** of slaves; for slaves; done by slaves: *a slave dealer, a slave hunt, slave labor.* **2.** of or having to do with an apparatus or device which duplicates an action or transmits back a signal in the same form as sent: *The signal from the master goes directly to the navigator and also to the slave station, which, after synchronizing properly, retransmits the pulse* (James P. Baxter).
[< Old French *esclave* < Medieval Latin *Sclavus,* later *Slavus* Slav; slave < Late Greek *Sklábos* (first applied to enslaved Slavs)] —**slave′like′,** *adj.*

slave ant, an ant that is captured and forced to work for other ants in a way that suggests slavery.

slave bracelet, an identification bracelet worn around the ankle.

slave driver, **1.** a person who makes others work very hard; exacting taskmaster. **2.** an overseer of slaves.

slave fork, a long, heavy piece of wood with a forked end formerly used in Africa for securing a slave, as when on the march, the forked end being made fast about the neck of the slave.

slave·hold·er (slāv′hōl′dər), *n.* an owner of slaves: *The central character is . . . the daughter of a New Orleans slaveholder* (New Yorker).

slave·hold·ing (slāv′hōl′ding), *adj.* owning slaves. —*n.* the owning of slaves: *Secession was rebellion and revolution; but rebellion and revolution might be right, if only slaveholding was right* (New Yorker).

slave·less (slāv′lis), *adj.* without slaves: *a slaveless land* (John Greenleaf Whittier).

slave·ling (slāv′ling), *n.* a submissive or servile person or thing: *De Gaulle's government, describing American companies as monsters trying to turn France into an economic slaveling . . .* (Time).

slave maker, an ant that captures and forces other ants to work for it.

slave-mak·ing ant (slāv′mā′king), a slave maker.

slave market, **1.** a market where slaves are sold. **2.** a place or condition similar to or suggesting a slave market: *. . . in the slave markets where teachers are hired* (Time).

slave·own·er (slāv′ō′nər), *n.* an owner of slaves: *Archaeologists believe that it was a tomb of a slaveowner* (Science News Letter).

slav·er[1] (slā′vər), *n.* **1.** a dealer in slaves. **2.** a ship used in the slave trade. **3.** a white slaver.

slav·er[2] (slav′ər), *v.i.* to let saliva run from the mouth; drool: *Beneath [Tammany's] shaky perch slavered a whole litter of lesser tigers* (Time). —*v.t.* to wet with saliva; slobber.
—*n.* **1.** saliva running from the mouth. **2.** drivel; nonsense. **3.** gross flattery.
[< Scandinavian (compare Old Icelandic *slafra*). Compare SLOBBER.]

slav·er·y (slā′vər ē, slāv′rē), *n.* **1.** the condition or fact of being a slave: *Many African Negroes were captured and sold into slavery.* **2.** the custom of owning slaves: *Where slavery is permitted, certain men own others. Slavery is but half-abolished, emancipation is but half completed, while millions of freemen with votes in their hands are left without education* (Robert C. Winthrop). **3.** a condition like that of a slave: *The extreme slavery and subjection that courtiers live in . . .* (John Evelyn). **4.** hard work like that of a slave; drudgery. —**Syn. 1.** bondage, serfdom, thralldom, servitude.

slave state, **1.** one of the Slave States. **2.** a country ruled by absolute authority; dictatorship: *The difference between a free country and a slave state . . . is . . . individual incentive . . . freedom of individual choice . . . opportunity . . .* (Time).

Slave States, the 15 states of the United States in which slavery was legal before and during the Civil War: Virginia, North Carolina, South Carolina, Georgia, Florida, Alabama, Mississippi, Louisiana, Texas, Arkansas, and Tennessee; Missouri, Kentucky, Maryland, and Delaware. The last four states did not join the Confederacy.

slave trade, the business of procuring, transporting, and selling slaves, especially Negro slaves: *For 250 years, Bristol and Liverpool merchants grew fat on the profits of the Nigerian slave trade, shipping tens of thousands of blacks yearly to the U.S.* (Newsweek).

slave trader, a person who buys and sells slaves as a business; slaver.

slav·ey (slā′vē), *n., pl.* **-eys.** *Especially British Informal.* a maid of all work.

Slav·ic (slä′vik, slav′-), *adj.* of or having to do with the Slavs or their languages; Slavonic: *Slavic origin, Slavic heritage, Slavic music.* —*n.* a language or the group of languages spoken by the Slavs, including West Slavic (Polish, Czech, Slovak, Serbian, and the extinct Polabian), East Slavic (Russian, Ruthenian), and South Slavic (Bulgarian, Serbo-Croatian, and Slovene).

Slav·i·cism (slä′və siz əm, slav′ə-), *n.* Slavism.

slav·ish (slā′vish), *adj.* **1.** of or having to do with a slave or slaves. **2.** like a slave; mean; base: *slavish fears.* **3.** weakly submitting: *the thoughtless, slavish victim of inclination.* **4.** like that of slaves; fit for slaves: *a slavish race* (Alexander Pope). **5.** lacking originality and independence: *a slavish reproduction.* —**slav′ish·ly,** *adv.* —**slav′ish·ness,** *n.* —**Syn. 3.** servile.

Slav·ism (slä′viz əm, slav′iz-), *n.* the culture, languages, and spirit of the Slavs.

Slavo-, *combining form.* Slav or Slavs: *Slavophile = one who admires the Slavs.* [< Medieval Latin *Slavus;* see SLAV]

slav·oc·ra·cy (slāv ok′rə sē), *n.* **1.** domination by slaveholders. **2.** the dominating body of slaveholders. [American English < *slave* + *-ocracy,* as in *democracy*]

slav·o·crat (slāv′ə krat), *n.* a member of a slavocracy.

slav·o·crat·ic (slāv′ə krat′ik), *adj.* of or having to do with slavocracy or slavocrats.

Sla·vo·ni·an (slə vō′nē ən), *adj.* **1.** of or having to do with Slavonia, a region in northern Yugoslavia, or its people. **2.** Slavic.
—*n.* **1.** a native of Slavonia. **2.** a Slav. **3.** the Slavic language or languages; Slavic.

Sla·von·ic (slə von′ik), *adj.* **1.** Slavic. **2.** Slavonian.
—*n.* **1.** a Slav. **2.** the Slavic language or languages.

Slav·o·ni·za·tion (slä′və nə zā′shən, slav′ə-), *n.* **1.** a Slavonizing. **2.** a being Slavonized.

Slav·o·nize (slä′və nīz, slav′ə-), *v.t.,* **-nized, -niz·ing.** to make Slavonian or Slavic in character, sentiment, language, etc.

Slav·o·phil (slä′və fil, slav′ə-), *n.* Slavophile.

Slav·o·phile (slä′və fīl, -fil; slav′ə-), *n.* an admirer or friend of the Slavs or their culture.

Slav·o·phil·ic (slä′və fil′ik, slav′ə-), *adj.* admiring the Slavs; favoring Slavic interests.

Sla·voph·i·lism (slə vof′ə liz əm; slä′və-fə liz′-, slav′ə-), *n.* admiration for the Slavs or their culture.

Slav·o·phobe (slä′və fōb, slav′ə-), *n.* a person who fears or hates the Slavs or their policies.

slaw (slô), *n. U.S.* **1.** finely sliced or chopped cabbage, raw or cooked, served with dressing; coleslaw. **2.** a salad like coleslaw, made of cooked cabbage and served with a hot dressing. [American English, apparently short for *coleslaw*]

slay (slā), *v.t.,* **slew, slain, slay·ing.** **1.** to kill with violence: *A hunter slays wild animals. Jack slew the giant. Saul hath slain his thousands and David his ten thousands* (I Samuel 18:7). **2.** *U.S. Slang.* to amuse greatly: *That comedian just slays me.* **3.** *Obsolete.* to smite; strike. [fusion of Old English *slēan* to strike, and Middle English *slayen* to kill, Old English *slægen*] —**slay′er,** *n.* —**Syn. 1.** See **kill.**

➔ **Slay** now regularly has as its principal parts *slay, slew, slain.* In its slang sense, however, *slayed* (instead of *slew* or *slain*) is usual: *Our act simply slayed them in Las Vegas.*

sld., **1.** sailed. **2.** sealed.

SLD (no periods), Specific Language Disability (inability to decode and reproduce the written symbols of language due to physical or neurological causes).

sleave (slēv), *v.,* **sleaved, sleav·ing,** *n.* —*v.t.* to divide or separate (silk, etc.) into smaller threads.
—*n.* **1. a.** a small silk thread made by separating a thicker thread. **b.** silk in the form of such threads; floss. **2.** *Archaic.* anything confused and troublesome: *Sleep that knits up the ravel'd sleave of care* (Shakespeare).
[Old English *-slǣfan,* as in *tōslǣfan* to divide]

slea·zi·ly (slē′zə lē), *adv.* in a sleazy manner.

slea·zi·ness (slē′zē nis), *n.* sleazy quality.

slea·zy (slē′zē), *adj.,* **-zi·er, -zi·est.** flimsy and poor: *sleazy cloth, a sleazy dress. Wise pulled down the sleazy window shades* (Sinclair Lewis). *It is a stammered, sleazy chronicle, told by fits and starts in bits and pieces, and constantly interrupted by the director and actors* (Time). [origin uncertain]

sled (sled), *n., v.,* **sled·ded, sled·ding.** —*n.* **1. a.** a wooden framework mounted on runners for use on snow or ice. **b.** *British.* a toboggan. **2.** a sleigh. **3.** a framework that moves on rails at controlled speeds, for testing the effects of acceleration, deceleration, heat, shock, etc., produced on a vehicle or person.
—*v.i.* to ride in or on a sled. —*v.t.* to carry (something) on a sled: *to sled logs out of the forest.*
[< Middle Dutch *sledde*] —**sled′like′,** *adj.*

sled·der (sled′ər), *n.* **1.** a person who drives, rides on, or guides a sled. **2.** a horse, dog, etc., that pulls a sled.

sled·ding (sled′ing), *n.* **1.** the use of a sled. **2.** the condition of the snow for the use of sleds: *two months of good sledding.*

sled dog, a dog used to draw a sled in arctic regions. See **dog sled** for picture.

sledge[1] (slej), *n., v.,* **sledged, sledg·ing.** —*n.* **1.** a sled for carrying loads over snow, ice, rough ground, etc.: *. . . travelling is impossible by sledge because the ice is unsafe . . .* (Gabriele Rabel). **2.** *British.* a sleigh.
—*v.t.* to carry (something) on a sledge.
—*v.i.* to ride on a sledge: *On the shelf ice of this sound one can sledge without great difficulty . . .* (Gabriele Rabel).
[< Middle Dutch *sleedse;* influenced by *sled*]

sledge[2] (slej), *n.* a sledge hammer: *The building of the Great Pyramid . . . was pushed through with only the most rudimentary technical aids—the inclined plane, ropes, and sledges—before even the wagon wheel had been invented* (New Yorker). [Old English *slecg*]

sledge dog, sled dog.

sledge hammer, **1.** a large, heavy hammer. **2.** anything powerful and crushing: *Sarcasm can become a sledge hammer in a debate.*

Sledge Hammer (def. 1)

sledge-ham·mer (slej′ham′ər), *v.t.* to hit with, or as if with, a sledge hammer. —*adj.* powerful; crushing: *a sledge-hammer attack. In the past, the Russians have always used sledge-hammer tactics in trying to take over Iran* (Newsweek).

sleek (slēk), *adj.* **1.** soft and glossy; smooth:

sleek hair. **2.** having smooth, soft skin, hair, fur, etc.: *a sleek cat.* **3.** smooth of speech, manners, etc.: *a sleek salesman. He had a look of sleek intelligence* (Graham Greene). **4.** having clean lines; trim; smooth: *Pictures ... of sleek new-type jets and twin-engined helicopters prove the Russians are not lagging* (Newsweek).
—*v.t.* **1.** to smooth; remove roughness from. **2.** to make (the skin, hair, etc.) smooth and glossy. **3.** to make tidy: *to sleek up a room.* [Middle English *slike;* see SLICK, adjective] —**sleek'ly,** *adv.* —**sleek'ness,** *n.*

sleek·en (slē'kən), *v.t.* to make sleek; smooth.

sleek·er (slē'kər), *n.* a person or a tool that sleeks leather, etc.

sleek·it (slē'kit), *adj. Scottish.* **1.** sleek: *Wee, sleekit, cow'rin', timrous beastie ...* (Robert Burns). **2.** plausible; deceitful; sly. [variant of *sleeked,* past participle of *sleek*]

sleek·y (slē'kē), *adj.,* **sleek·i·er, sleek·i·est. 1.** sleek; smooth. **2.** plausible; artful; sly.

sleep (slēp), *v.,* **slept, sleep·ing,** *n.* —*v.i.* **1.** to rest body and mind; to be without ordinary consciousness: *We sleep at night.* **2.** to be in a condition like sleep: *The seeds sleep in the ground all winter. How sweet the moonlight sleeps upon this bank!* (Shakespeare). **3.** to rest, as in the grave; lie buried: *So David slept with his fathers and was buried in the city of David* (I Kings 2:10). **4.** *Botany.* to close petals or leaves, especially at night.
—*v.t.* **1.** to take rest in (sleep): *He slept the sleep of exhaustion.* **2.** to provide with or offer sleeping accommodation for: *a hotel that sleeps 500 people.*
sleep away, to pass or spend in sleeping: *She slept away the whole morning.*
sleep in, a. to sleep in the house where one works: *Some servants sleep in.* **b.** *British.* to sleep late; oversleep: *Saturday morning the boys and I let Merna and Willa sleep in* (Maclean's).
sleep off, to get rid of by sleeping: *to sleep off a headache.*
sleep on, to consider (something) overnight: *The attendant slept on the offer and then decided* (New York Times).
sleep out, a. to pass or spend in sleeping: *to sleep out the night.* **b.** to sleep outside one's home or the house where one works: *Our maid sleeps out.*
—*n.* **1.** a condition in which body and mind are very inactive, occurring naturally and regularly in animals: *Most people need eight hours of sleep a day. Tired nature's sweet restorer, balmy sleep!* (Edward Young). *The biological object of sleep seems to be recuperation, its psychological characteristic the suspension of interest in the outer world* (Sigmund Freud). **2.** a period of sleep: *a short sleep. Have a good sleep.* **3.** a state or condition like sleep: *to put one's doubts to sleep.* **4.** *Botany.* a movement of plants in which they assume at nightfall positions unlike those which they have maintained during the day; nyctitropism.
last sleep, death: *She was by his side until the last sleep closed his eyes.*
lose sleep over, to worry so as to be unable to sleep: *But can we convert back before the conference season, is what I lose sleep over* (Punch).
[Old English *slǣpan*]
—**Syn.** *v.i.* **1.** slumber, doze, drowse, nap, snooze. *-n.* **1.** slumber, doze, drowse, snooze, nap.

sleep·er (slē'pər), *n.* **1.** a person or thing that sleeps: *The noise woke the sleepers.* **2.** a railroad car with berths for passengers to sleep in. **3. a.** a horizontal beam. **b.** one of the substantial strips of wood laid over concrete to enable wood floors, etc., to be nailed to it. **4.** *British.* a tie to support a railroad track: *The steel rail, prised from the sleepers, had tilted over to one side* (Maclean's). **5.** *Informal.* something with little advance notice that makes an unexpected success: *I was in the peculiar spot of negotiating for a book that I hadn't read—but the deal went through in fine shape, and I think we've got a real sleeper* (Saturday Review).
sleepers, one-piece pajamas for little children, extending from the neck and covering the feet: *winter sleepers.*

sleep·er·ette (slē'pə ret'), *n. Especially British.* a sleeping compartment on a train or boat.

sleeper plane, an airplane with sleeping accommodations for passengers.

sleep·ful (slēp'fəl), *adj.* marked by sleep; restful through sleep: *sleepful nights.*

sleep·ful·ness (slēp'fəl nis), *n.* sleepiness.

sleep·i·ly (slē'pə lē), *adv.* in a sleepy manner.

sleep-in (slēp'in'), *adj.* sleeping in the place where one works: *Her mother was a sleep-in domestic servant who worked in another suburb of Cape Town* (New Yorker).

sleep·i·ness (slē'pē nis), *n.* sleepy condition; drowsiness.

sleep·ing (slē'ping), *n.* sleep. —*adj.* **1.** that sleeps: *a sleeping child.* **2.** used for sleeping on or in: *a sleeping porch, sleeping quarters.*

sleeping bag, a canvas or waterproof bag, usually warmly lined, to sleep in out-of-doors.

Sleeping Beauty, 1. a fairy-tale princess shut up in a castle and put to sleep by enchantment for a hundred years. The kiss of a young prince awakens her. **2.** a person who resembles or suggests this princess: *A modern Sleeping Beauty held in ... imprisonment by order of her husband* (Atlantic).

sleeping car, a railroad car with berths for passengers to sleep in.

sleeping partner, a partner who takes no active part in managing the business.

sleeping pill, a drug that causes sleep, prepared in pellet form: *Breakfast found the American group comparing sleeping pills and seasickness remedies* (Harper's).

sleeping powder, a drug that causes sleep.

sleeping sickness, 1. a protozoan disease of Africa carried by the tsetse fly, causing fever, inflammation of the brain, sleepiness and increasing weakness, and usually death; African sleeping sickness. **2.** a kind of epidemic encephalitis characterized by extreme drowsiness and muscular weakness, caused by a virus; lethargic encephalitis: *Sleeping sickness, the dread encephalitis, is not a strange disease afflicting only peoples in distant Africa or Asia* (Science News Letter).

sleep·less (slēp'lis), *adj.* **1.** without sleep; not sleeping; restless: *a sleepless night.* **2.** watchful; wide-awake: *sleepless vigilance.* **3.** always moving or acting: *the sleepless tides. Winds are rude in Biscay's sleepless bay* (Byron). —**sleep'less·ly,** *adv.* —**sleep'less·ness,** *n.*

sleep·walk (slēp'wôk'), *v.i.* to walk about while asleep. —*n.* a walk during sleep: *[a] sleepwalk that brought her near to the roof-edge and death ...* (Punch).

sleep·walk·er (slēp'wô'kər), *n.* a person who walks about while asleep. —**Syn.** somnambulist.

sleep·walk·ing (slēp'wô'king), *n.* the act of walking while asleep. —*adj.* **1.** that walks about while asleep. **2.** having to do with someone who walks while asleep: ... *who was superb in the sleepwalking scene* (Time).

sleep·wear (slēp'wãr'), *n.* pajamas, nightgowns, or other garments to be worn for sleeping: ... *children's sleepwear made with Acrilan acrylic fiber* (New Yorker).

sleep·y (slē'pē), *adj.,* **sleep·i·er, sleep·i·est. 1.** ready to go to sleep; inclined to sleep. **2.** not active; quiet: *a sleepy little town.* **3.** inducing sleep; soporific: *a warm, sleepy day. The sleepy sound of the chanting and the sleepier sound of the bells made her feel still more pressed* (Atlantic).
—**Syn. 1. Sleepy, drowsy** mean ready or inclined to sleep. **Sleepy** suggests being ready to fall asleep or having a tendency to sleep: *He never gets enough rest and is always sleepy.* **Drowsy** suggests being heavy or dull with sleepiness: *After lying in the sun, he became drowsy.*

sleep·y-eyed (slē'pē īd'), *adj.* looking as if ready to fall asleep: *A sleepy-eyed girl opened the door for us.*

sleepy grass, a stout bunch grass of the Rocky Mountains which, when eaten, has a narcotic effect on livestock lasting several days.

sleep·y·head (slē'pē hed'), *n.* a sleepy, drowsy, or lazy person: ... *small travelling alarm clocks, packed in miniature leather suitcases and designed to wake the sleepyhead in time* (New Yorker).

sleet (slēt), *n.* **1.** half-frozen rain; snow or hail mixed with rain: *In Texas, snow and sleet in near freezing temperatures iced over highways and closed schools* (Newsweek). **2.** a thin coating of ice formed when rain falls on a very cold surface; glaze.
—*v.i.* to come down in sleet: *It sleeted; then it snowed; then it rained.* —*v.t.* **1.** to send down like sleet. **2.** to beat or cover with sleet. [Middle English *slete*]

sleet·i·ness (slē'tē nis), *n.* sleety quality or condition.

sleet·y (slē'tē), *adj.,* **sleet·i·er, sleet·i·est. 1.** of or like sleet: *sleety showers.* **2.** characterized by sleet: *The weather was cold, wet, and sleety.*

sleeve (slēv), *n., v.,* **sleeved, sleev·ing.** —*n.* **1.** the part of a garment that covers the arm: *The scooped neckline blouse has a soft bow and short sleeves* (New Yorker). **2.** a tube into which a rod or another tube fits: *a cylinder sleeve.* **3.** the cover or jacket enclosing a phonograph record.
laugh in or **up one's sleeve,** to be amused but not show it; laugh inwardly: *His shrewd nephew was laughing at him in his sleeve* (Henry Kingsley).
up one's sleeve, in reserve; ready for use when needed: *Barrett had considerably more up his sleeve than the three lengths with which he finished* (London Daily News).
—*v.t.* **1.** to fix, fasten, or couple by means of a sleeve or tube. **2.** (of a garment) to provide with sleeves; fashion: *the drifting peignoir sleeved with puffs, steeped in lace* (New Yorker).
[Old English *slēfe, slīefe*]

sleeve board, a shaped board on which sleeves are ironed or pressed.

sleeved (slēvd), *adj.* having sleeves.

-sleeved, *combining form.* having ____ sleeves: *Long-sleeved = having long sleeves.*

sleeve dog, a dog small enough to be carried in the sleeve, as among the Chinese, Japanese, etc.

sleeve·less (slēv'lis), *adj.* **1.** without sleeves: *a sleeveless dress.* **2.** *Archaic.* futile; fruitless; useless: ... *a sleeveless errand* (Shakespeare). —**sleeve'less·ness,** *n.*

sleeve nut, a double nut which has right-hand and left-hand threads for joining the ends of rods or tubes; union.

sleeve valve, a sliding, cylindrical sleeve within an automobile's cylinder, having holes which its motion brings over ports in the cylinder for intake and exhaust.

sleigh (slā), *n.* **1.** a carriage or cart mounted on runners for use on snow or ice, pulled by one or more horses: *To grandfather's house we'll go; The horse knows the way To carry the sleigh Through the white and drifted snow* (Lydia Maria Child). **2.** sled: *A following of younger brothers on sleighs ...* (Maclean's).
—*v.i.* to travel or ride in a sleigh. [American English, earlier *slee* < Dutch, variant of *slede* sled]

sleigh bell, a small bell, usually a hollow ball of metal pierced by a slit and containing a loose pellet of metal, several of which are often attached to the harness of a horse drawing a sleigh: *But now the sleigh bells are jingling on the carriage outside, so heigh-ho, let's be away to the toy stores!* (New Yorker).

sleigh·ing (slā'ing), *n.* **1.** riding in a sleigh. **2.** the condition of the roads, a region, etc., for using a sleigh: *a week of good sleighing. Hard-packed snow makes good sleighing.*

sleight (slīt), *n.* **1.** skill; dexterity. **2.** a clever trick: *Unpractised in the sleights and artifices of controversy* (Benjamin Franklin). **3.** craft or cunning, used to deceive: *Every interest did, by right, or might, or sleight, get represented* (Emerson). [alteration of Middle English *slethe* < Scandinavian (compare Old Icelandic *slǣgth* < *slǣgr* sly)]

sleight of hand, 1. skill and quickness in moving the hands. **2.** the tricks or skill of a modern magician; juggling: ... *music that is free of self-conscious formulas and tricks of stylistic sleight of hand* (New Yorker). —**Syn. 2.** legerdemain.

slen·der (slen'dər), *adj.* **1.** long and thin; not big around: *A boy 6 feet tall and weighing 130 pounds is very slender. A pencil is a slender piece of wood.* **2.** slight; small: *a slender meal, a slender hope of success.* **3.** *Phonetics.* (of vowels) high. [Middle English *slendre,* and *sclendre,* origin uncertain] —**slen'der·ly,** *adv.* —**slen'der·ness,** *n.*
—**Syn. 1. Slender, slim** mean thin, not big around. **Slender** suggests pleasing, graceful thinness: *Most girls want to be slender. The legs of those chairs are slender.* **Slim** suggests lack of flesh or weakness of frame or build: *He is a slim boy, but he may fill out as he becomes older.*

slen·der·i·za·tion (slen'dər ə zā'shən), *n.* **1.** a slenderizing. **2.** a being slenderized.

slen·der·ize (slen'də rīz), *v.,* **-ized, -iz·ing.**

—*v.t.* **1.** to make slender or more slender; cause to lose weight: . . . *ideal for men and women who want to keep fit and aid their slenderizing campaign easily* (Wall Street Journal). **2.** to make appear less stout: *a slenderizing dress. Vertical lines in dress design tend to slenderize the matronly figure.* —*v.i.* to lose weight; reduce.

slender loris, a tailless, nocturnal lemur of India and Ceylon, about 5 inches long with very large eyes.

slen·tan·do (slen tän′dō), *adj. Music.* lentando; slackening; becoming slower. [< Italian *slentando,* present participle of *slentare* slacken]

slept (slept), *v.* the past tense and past participle of **sleep:** *The baby has slept soundly for several nights.*

sleugh (slü), *n.* slough; soft, muddy ground.

sleuth (slüth), *n.* **1.** *U.S.* a detective: *He remains the most reluctant of sleuths throughout the book* (Newsweek). **2.** a bloodhound. —*v.i.* to be or act like a detective. [< Scandinavian (compare Old Icelandic *slōth*) a trail] —**sleuth′er,** *n.*

sleuth·hound (slüth′hound′), *n.* **1.** a bloodhound. **2.** *U.S. Informal.* a detective.

slew[1] (slü), *v.* the past tense of **slay:** *Jack slew the giant.*

slew[2] (slü), *v.t., v.i., n.* turn; swing; twist: *The jeep slewed half round and lurched on one front wheel* (Harper's). Also, **slue.** [origin unknown]

slew[3] (slü), *n.* a swampy place; marshy inlet: *A slew is often covered with reeds and marsh grass.* Also, **slough, slue.** [American English, spelling for pronunciation of *slough*[1]]

slew[4] (slü), *n. Informal.* a large number or amount; lot: *Mulligan has been on the payroll of a slew of big-name companies himself* (Newsweek). Also, **slue.** [American English, perhaps through Anglo-Irish < Irish *sluagh* host, crowd]

slg., sailing.

slice (slīs), *n., v.,* **sliced, slic·ing.** —*n.* **1.** a thin, flat, broad piece cut from something: *a slice of bread, meat, or cake.* **2.** a part; share: *Each partner receives his slice of the profits.* **3.** a knife or spatula with a thin, broad blade, for serving food, turning meat while frying, etc.: *a fish slice.* **4.** a small spade-shaped tool used for taking up printing ink. **5.** *Sports.* **a.** a hit or stroke made in such a way that the ball curves in flight or after falling on the ground, as in golf, tennis, and baseball: [*She*] *employs heavy slice on the forehand side and considerable underspin on her backhand drive* (Sunday Observer). **b.** the course of the ball so hit: *The ball spun away in a wicked slice.*
—*v.t.* **1.** to cut into slices: *Slice the bread. We ate sliced peaches.* **2.** to cut through or across; divide: *The boat sliced the waves.* **3.** to cut off as a slice or slices. **4.** to divide into parts or shares: *The estate was sliced up into very small bequests.* **5.** to remove, take up, etc., with a slice or slice bar. **6.** *Sports.* to hit (a ball) so that it curves or spins: [*He*] *cannot be fooled consistently by even the smartest pitchers, is as likely to slice the ball as pull it* (New York Times). *He sliced his forehand unmercifully* (New Yorker). —*v.i.* **1.** *Sports.* to slice a ball, as in golf, tennis, etc. **2.** to admit of being sliced: *Firm tomatoes slice well.*
[probably short for Old French *esclice* thin chip < a Germanic word]

slice·a·ble (slī′sə bəl), *adj.* that can be sliced; easily sliced: *Hot bread is often not sliceable.*

slice bar, a long iron bar with a broad, flat end, used in a coal furnace to break up or clear away clinkers, ashes, etc.

slice-of-life (slīs′əv līf′), *adj.* describing or presenting an actual segment of life without modification by selection or arrangement of material: *The Czechs blend the understated documentary techniques with a slice-of-life narrative style* (Time).

slic·er (slī′sər), *n.* **1.** a person who slices. **2.** a tool or machine that slices: *a bread slicer, a meat slicer.*

slick (slik), *adj.* **1.** sleek; smooth: *slick hair.* **2.** slippery; greasy: *a road slick with ice or mud, etc.* **3.** clever; ingenious; skillful; deft: *a slick barber, a slick shortstop.* **4.** *Informal.* smooth of speech, manners, etc., but superficial; glib: *They were suspicious of Mr. Graham's advertising, which they thought "slick" and American* (New York Times). **5.** *Informal.* sly; tricky: *a slick operator.* **6.** *Informal.* of or like that of a smooth, tricky person; cunningly made up: *a slick excuse.*
—*v.t.* to make sleek or smooth: *Rain slicked the winding mountain roads* (Time). —*v.i.* to move in a smooth manner; glide; sweep: *Slowly, slowly, he slicked out* (Maclean's).
—*n.* **1.** a smooth place or spot: *a slick of mud on the road. Search planes found a life preserver and an oil slick where the fishing boat would have gone down* (Wall Street Journal). **2.** *U.S. Informal.* a magazine printed on heavy, glossy paper: *He had spent nearly twenty years writing mostly wilderness-adventure serials, first for the pulps and then for the "slicks"* (Newsweek). **3. a.** a tool used for scraping and smoothing leather. **b.** a trowel for smoothing the top of a mold in founding.
—*adv.* **1.** *Informal.* smoothly; slyly; cleverly. **2.** directly.
[Middle English *slike,* related to Old English *-slician* make smooth] —**slick′ly,** *adv.* —**slick′ness,** *n.*

slick chick, *U.S. Slang.* a good-looking, well-groomed girl.

slicked-up (slikt′up′), *adj. Slang.* **1.** made tidy; cleaned up: *a slicked-up living room. The result is an artificial slicked-up version of real life* (Observer). **2.** sleek; attractive: *slicked-up utilitarian gadgets.*

slick·en (slik′ən), *adj. British Dialect.* smooth; polished.

slick·ens (slik′ənz), *n.pl.* fine or powdered ore, debris, or the like, as from a stamping mill. [perhaps < German *Schlich*]

slick·en·side (slick′ən sīd′), *n. Geology.* a rock surface that has become more or less polished and striated from the sliding or grinding motion of an adjacent mass of rock.

slick·en·sid·ed (slik′ən sī′did), *adj.* of or like slickenside; having slickensides.

slick·er (slik′ər), *n.* **1.** *U.S.* a long, loose waterproof coat, made of oilskin or the like: *Fishermen used to wear slickers.* **2.** *Informal.* a sly, tricky person: *One of those city slickers sold him worthless shares.*
—*v.t. Slang.* to fool; trick.

slick-pa·per (slik′pā′pər), *adj.* printed on heavy, glossy paper: *A slick-paper magazine, entirely for sportscar buffs, will make its debut this summer* (Maclean's).

slick·ster (slik′stər), *n.* a sly, tricky person; slick or smooth operator: . . . *to negotiate such political shoals without giving the appearance of being a political slickster* (Wall Street Journal).

slid (slid), *v.* the past tense and a past participle of **slide:** *Minutes slid rapidly by.*

slid·a·ble (slī′də bəl), *adj.* that can slide.

slid·den (slid′ən), *v.* a past participle of **slide:** *He has slidden back into his old habits.*

slide (slīd), *v.,* **slid, slid** or **slid·den, slid·ing,** *n.* —*v.i.* **1.** to move smoothly along on a surface or in a groove: *The bureau drawers slide in and out.* **2.** to glide over the surface of ice or snow on the feet, or on a sled, toboggan, or the like: *When the snowstorm stops, let's go sliding down the hill.* **3.** to move or go easily, quietly, or secretly: *The burglar slid behind the curtains.* **4.** to pass by degrees; slip: *He has slid into bad habits. The car slid by us.* **5.** to pass without heeding or being heeded; go unregarded. *Alack, how good men, and the good turns they do us, slide out of memory* (Charles Lamb). **6.** to slip as one losing one's foothold: *The car slid into the ditch.* **7.** *Music.* to pass or progress from tone to tone without perceptible step or break. **8.** (in baseball) to launch a slide for a base or home plate. —*v.t.* **1.** to cause to move smoothly along on a surface or in a groove: *Slide the door back into the wall.* **2.** to put quietly or secretly: *He slid a gun into his pocket.*
let slide, to not bother about; neglect: *He let his studies slide. He let his business slide until he was bankrupt.*
—*n.* **1.** the act of sliding: *The children each take a slide in turn.* **2.** a smooth surface for sliding on: *The frozen brook makes a good slide.* **3.** a track, rail, groove, etc., on or in which something slides. **4.** something that works by sliding. **5.** the U-shaped tube of a trumpet or trombone that is pushed in or out to change the pitch of the tones. **6. a.** a mass of earth, snow, etc., sliding down; landslide; avalanche. **b.** the sliding down of such a mass. **c.** the place where this has occurred. **7.** a small thin sheet of glass, plastic, or the like. Objects are put on slides for microscopic examination. Slides with pictures on them are projected on a screen. **8.** *Music.* **a.** a rapid ascending or descending series of three or more notes, composed of grace notes which ornament the last or principal note. **b.** a passing from tone to tone without perceptible step or break; portamento. **9.** (in baseball) a throwing of the body, usually feet first, along the ground in running to a base, so as to avoid being tagged, to break up a double play, etc. **10.** a framed opening in a wall between two rooms for passing things through: *The cook put the dishes through the slide, and the maid, waiting in the china closet, received them and took them into the diningroom* (Harper's).
[Old English *slīdan*]
—**Syn.** *v.i.* **1. Slide, slip, glide** mean to move along smoothly, over a surface. **Slide** emphasizes continuous contact with a smooth or slippery surface: *The boat slid down the bank into the water.* **Slip** emphasizes a sudden, involuntary movement caused by a very smooth or slippery surface: *One of the climbers slipped on the rocks.* **Glide** emphasizes a continuous, easy, graceful movement, without reference to the surface: *The swans glide gracefully on the lake. The stream glides through the forest.*

slide bar, 1. a sliding bar in a machine, etc., as for opening or closing an aperture. **2.** a bar that serves as a guide, track, etc., for a sliding or reciprocating part.

slide fastener, a zipper.

slide knot, a slipknot tied with two half hitches.

slide projector, an instrument for projecting onto a screen the images on photographic slides.

slid·er (slī′dər), *n.* **1. a.** a person who slides. **b.** a sliding thing or part. **2.** (in baseball) a fast pitch that curves somewhat but without a pronounced break: *You throw the slider like you throw a football* (Newsweek). **3.** the toothed portion of a zipper: . . . *manufacturers of zipper hardware, including sliders, chain pulls and stops* (Wall Street Journal). **4.** the red-bellied terrapin.

slide rest, an appliance for holding tools in turning, enabling them to be held in different ways in relation to the material worked on: *Control of the cutting tool was taken from the skilled hands of the turner and put into a . . . slide rest* (Scientific American).

slide rule, a rule with a sliding section in the center, both marked with logarithmic scales, used by engineers, physicists, etc., for making rapid calculations: *Armed with their sharpest pencils, their longest slide rules, their most involved charts and theories, the economists are out in force to second-guess the President and his own economic advisers* (Newsweek).

Slide Rule

slide trombone, a trombone with a U-shaped bend near the cup mouthpiece, in which double telescoping tubes slide one upon the other to vary the length of the sounding tube and thus produce different tones.

slide valve, (in engines) a valve that slides (without lifting) to open or close an aperture.

slide·way (slīd′wā′), *n.* a guideway on which some part of a machine moves.

slid·ing (slī′ding), *adj.* having a part that slides; adjustable; changing.

sliding door, a door, usually in two leaves, that slides in grooves or along a track: *As Elizabeth pulled back one of the sliding doors to the room, she felt a flash of soft hair against her legs* (New Yorker).

sliding scale, 1. a scale of wages, prices, taxes, customs duties, etc., that can be adjusted according to certain conditions: *The sliding scale tax formula for lead and zinc imports was proposed by the Administration as part of its long-range program for the mineral industry* (Wall Street Journal). **2.** a slide rule.

sliding seat, 1. a seat, as in an outrigger, which moves backwards and forwards with the action of the rower. **2.** a seat which can be slid out beyond the gunwale of a yacht.

sli·er (slī′ər), *adj.* a comparative of **sly.**

sli·est (slī′ist), *adj.* a superlative of **sly.**

slight (slīt), *adj.* **1.** small; not much; not

important: *I have a slight headache. One slice of bread is a slight lunch. I hardly felt that slight scratch. Therefore I am glad to take this slight occasion—this trifling occasion* . . . (Dickens). **2.** not big around; slender; slim: *She is a slight girl.* **3.** flimsy; frail: *a slight structure, slight clothing, a slight excuse.*
—*v.t.* to pay too little attention to; treat as of little value or importance; neglect: *This maid slights her work. She felt slighted because she was not asked to the party.*
—*n.* an act of intentional neglect; slighting treatment shown to one who expects courtesy and friendliness: . . . *thwarted or stung by a fancied slight* . . . (Bret Harte). *Cinderella suffered many slights from her sisters.*
[Middle English *slight,* perhaps Old English *-sliht* level, as in *eorthslihtes* level with the ground] —**slight′ness,** *n.*
—**Syn.** *adj.* **1.** inconsiderable, trivial, trifling. **2.** thin. *-v.t.* **Slight, overlook, neglect** mean to pay too little attention to someone or something needing or deserving it. **Slight** emphasizes intentionally doing so: *Johnny slights his homework.* **Overlook** emphasizes unintentionally doing so: *He overlooked the telephone bill.* **Neglect** emphasizes doing so because of indifference, distaste, or laziness: *He neglects his teeth.*

slight breeze, *Meteorology.* a breeze having a velocity of 4-7 miles per hour.

slight·ing (slī′ting), *adj.* that slights; contemptuous; disdainful: *a slighting remark.* —**slight′ing·ly,** *adv.* —**Syn.** disparaging.

slight·ly (slīt′lē), *adv.* **1.** in a slight manner. **2.** to a slight degree; a little; somewhat: *I know him slightly.* **3.** in a slighting manner; disdainfully.

sli·ly (slī′lē), *adv.* slyly.

slim (slim), *adj.,* **slim·mer, slim·mest,** *v.,* **slimmed, slim·ming.** —*adj.* **1.** thin; slender: *a slim girl.* **2.** small or slight; weak: *a slim victory, a slim meal. The invalid's chances for getting well were very slim.* **3.** meager; scanty: *We had a slim attendance at the football game because of the rain.*
—*v.t., v.i.* to make or become slim or slender: *You'll love your new, lively, lissom self when you've slimmed with Formula 21* (Sunday Times).
slim down, to reduce in size or number: . . . *the Marine Corps began slimming down under budget restrictions* (World Book Annual).
[< Dutch *slim* bad] —**slim′ly,** *adv.* —**slim′ness,** *n.* —**Syn.** *adj.* **1.** See **slender.**

slime (slīm), *n., v.,* **slimed, slim·ing.** —*n.* **1.** soft, sticky mud or something like it: *His shoes were covered with slime from the swamp. At present, the most important commercial source of selenium is the anode mud or slime produced in the electrolytic refining of blister copper* (Wall Street Journal). **2.** a sticky, slippery, substance given off by snails, slugs, fish, etc. **3.** disgusting filth: *An honest man he is, and hates the slime That sticks on filthy deeds* (Shakespeare).
—*v.t.* **1.** to cover or smear with, or as with, slime. **2.** to clear (skins, fish, etc.) of slimy matter by scraping.
[Old English *slīm*]

slime mold or **fungus,** any of a group of primitive organisms consisting of a thin mass of naked protoplasm and occurring in slimy masses on damp soil and decaying logs, etc.

slime pit, 1. a tank or reservoir in which slimes are settled or stored. **2.** *Archaic.* a pit yielding liquid bitumen.

slim·i·ly (slī′mə lē), *adv.* in a slimy manner.

slim·i·ness (slī′mē nis), *n.* slimy quality or condition.

slim-jim (slim′jim′), *adj. Slang.* very slim: . . . *a coal shed full of slim-jim bottles* (Punch).

slim·line (slim′līn′), *adj.* having slim lines; long and slender: *New slimline model does more jobs in less space than any other copying machine* (Wall Street Journal).

slim·ming (slim′ing), *adj.* making one slim or slimmer: *Slimming diets, other than a sensible limitation of sweets and starches, are frowned upon for teenagers* (Sunday Times). —*n.* a making or becoming slim or slimmer; reducing: *Whenever women get together, sooner or later, the question of slimming arises* (Cape Times).

slim·mish (slim′ish), *adj.* somewhat slim.

slimp·sy (slimp′sē), *adj.,* **-si·er, -si·est.** *U.S. Informal.* slimsy.

slim·sy (slim′zē), *adj.,* **-si·er, -si·est.** *U.S. Informal.* flimsy; frail. [American English, apparently < *slim;* patterned on *flimsy*]

slim·y (slī′mē), *adj.,* **slim·i·er, slim·i·est. 1.** covered with slime: *Yea, slimy things did crawl with legs upon the slimy sea* (Samuel Taylor Coleridge). **2.** of or like slime: *the slimy sediment in a drain.* **3.** disgusting; filthy.

sling[1] (sling), *n., v.,* **slung, sling·ing.** —*n.* **1.** a strip of leather with a string fastened to each end, for throwing stones. **2.** a throw; hurling or casting. **3.** a hanging loop of cloth, usually fastened around the neck, to support an injured arm, hand, etc.: *First of the walking cases to come on shore was an elderly man with an arm in a sling* (Graham Greene). **4.** a loop of rope, band, chain, etc., by which heavy objects are lifted, carried, or held: *Rifles have slings to carry them over the shoulder. The men lowered the boxes into the cellar by a sling.*
slings, *Nautical.* **a.** a rope or chain at the center of a yard connecting it to a mast. **b.** a rope at the bow or stern for attaching a barrel, bale, etc., to be hoisted or lowered.
[Middle English *slynge.* Compare Swedish *slinga.*]
—*v.t.* **1.** to throw with a sling. **2.** to throw; cast; hurl; fling: *to sling stones.* **3.** to raise, lower, move, etc., with a sling or slings. **4.** to hang in a sling; hang so as to swing loosely: *The soldier's gun was slung over his shoulder.* **5.** to hang up or suspend (a hammock, etc.), from one part to another. **6.** *Slang.* to mix; serve.
[< Scandinavian (compare Old Icelandic *slyngva*)]

Sling[1] (def. 4)

sling[2] (sling), *n. U.S.* a drink consisting of an alcoholic liquor, usually gin, lemon or lime juice, sugar, and water. [compare earlier British *sling* a drink, "pull" from a bottle, and German *schlingen* to swallow]

sling·back (sling′bak′), *n.* a woman's shoe with an upper that tapers off to become a strap instead of a closed back around the heel of the wearer.

sling cart, a two-wheeled cart used for transporting cannon or other heavy objects, by slinging them by a chain from the axletree.

sling·er (sling′ər), *n.* **1.** a fighter armed with a sling. **2.** a worker in charge of slings used in hoisting, etc. **3.** a person who slings.

slinger ring, a tubular ring around the hub of the propeller of an airplane, through which deicing fluid is sprayed over the propeller blades.

sling·man (sling′mən), *n., pl.* **-men.** a soldier armed with a sling; slinger.

sling psychrometer, a pair of thermometers, one wet-bulb and the other dry-bulb, suspended by a chain and whirled about to bring the wet-bulb to a standard temperature for measuring the relative humidity.

sling pump, a slingback.

sling·shot (sling′shot′), *n. U.S.* a Y-shaped stick with a rubber band fastened to its prongs, used to shoot pebbles, etc.

sling·stone (sling′stōn′), *n.* a stone used as a missile to be hurled by a sling.

slink[1] (slingk), *v.i.,* **slunk** or (*Archaic*) **slank, slunk, slink·ing.** to move in a sneaking, guilty manner; sneak: *The dog slunk away with the stolen meat.* [Old English *slincan*] —**slink′ing·ly,** *adv.*

slink[2] (slingk), *v.,* **slinked** or **slunk, slink·ing,** *n., adj.* —*v.t.* (of domestic animals) to bring forth (young) prematurely. —*n.* a calf, etc., born prematurely. —*adj.* born prematurely. [< *slink*[1]]

slink·i·ly (sling′kə lē), *adv.* in a slinky manner: . . . *slinkily attired* . . . *actresses* (Punch).

slink·i·ness (sling′kē nis), *n.* **1.** sneakiness; furtiveness; stealthiness. **2.** the allure given by slinky clothes.

slink·skin (slingk′skin′), *n.* the skin of a slink, or leather made from such skin.

slink·weed (slingk′wēd′), *n.* the swamp loosestrife.

slink·y (sling′kē), *adj.,* **slink·i·er, slink·i·est. 1.** sneaky; furtive; stealthy. **2. a.** close-fitting, as if molded to the figure: *a slinky dress, a slinky negligee.* **b.** wearing, or as if wearing such clothes; sexy: *Her parody of the slinky and tarnished redhead whom the American colonel seeks to save* . . . *is a particularly engaging bit* (Wall Street Journal).

slip[1] (slip), *v.,* **slipped** or (*Archaic*) **slipt, slipped, slip·ping,** *n.* —*v.i.* **1.** to go or move smoothly, quietly, easily, or quickly: *She slipped out of the room. Time slips by. The ship slips through the waves. The drawer slips into place. He slipped into a clean shirt.* **2.** to move out of place; slide: *The knife slipped and cut him. My axe slipped out of my hand.* **3.** to slide suddenly without wanting to: *He slipped and fell on the icy sidewalk.* **4.** to make a mistake or error. **5.** to pass without notice; pass through neglect: *Don't let this opportunity slip.* **6.** to get away, escape, or be lost: *The point seems to have slipped from the old man's mind. Wealth or power slips from one.* **7.** to fall off; decline; deteriorate: *The market for cotton continues to slip. New car sales have slipped.*
—*v.t.* **1.** to cause to slip; put, push, or draw with a smooth or sliding motion: *to slip a shell into a rifle. He slipped the bolt of the lock. She slipped the ring from her finger.* **2.** to put (on) or take (off) quickly and easily: *Slip on your coat. Slip off your shoes.* **3.** to get loose from; get away from; escape from: *The dog has slipped his collar. Your name has slipped my mind.* **4.** to let go from a leash or slip; release: *He slipped the hound.* **5. a.** to allow (an anchor cable, etc.) to run out entirely, frequently with a buoy attached, often leaving an anchorage hastily. **b.** to drop or disengage (an anchor) in this way: *The ship has slipped anchor and is off.* **6.** to untie (a knot); undo: *The bonds of heaven are slipt, dissolved and loosed* (Shakespeare). **7.** (of animals) to bear (young) prematurely; slink. **8.** *Archaic.* to let pass; neglect.
let slip, to tell without meaning to: *I will not let his name slip* . . . *if I can help it* (Tennyson). *Lest* . . . *he should let anything slip that might give a clue to the place or people* (G. Macdonald).
slip one over on, *Informal.* to get the advantage of, especially by trickery; outwit: *The fox slipped one over on the hounds and got away.*
slip out, to become known; leak out: *When one side or the other had written any particularly spicy dispatch, news of it was sure to slip out* (Thackeray).
slip up, *Informal.* to make a mistake or error: *Slip up in my vernacular! How could I? I talked it when I was a boy* (Century Magazine).
—*n.* **1.** the act or fact of slipping: *His broken leg was caused by a slip on the ice.* **2. a.** a thing that covers and can be slipped on or off; covering: *Pillows are covered by slips. Slips are often put on furniture for the summer.* **b.** a sleeveless garment worn under a dress, gown, etc.: *Grace wore a pink slip under her party dress.* **c.** a child's pinafore or frock. **3.** a mistake; error; blunder: *to make slips in grammar. That remark was a slip of the tongue. There has been a bad slip somewhere* (New York Times). **4.** *U.S.* a space for ships between two wharves or in a dock. **5. a.** an inclined platform alongside of the water, on which ships are built or repaired. **b.** a similar platform, used as a landing place for ferries, small craft, amphibious aircraft, etc.: *They sent a boat up to tow us down here to the slip* (Atlantic). **6.** a leash for one or two dogs, designed for quick release. **7.** *Cricket.* **a.** a position behind and to the side of the wicketkeeper: *Nor is his a one-stroke mind, for he varied his lustier blows with deft glances through the slips and clean cover drives* (London Times). **b.** a player in this position. **8.** the difference between the actual speed of a ship or boat in water and the speed it would attain if the propeller, paddle wheel, etc., were working in a solid or less mobile substance **9.** *Geology.* **a.** a fault in rock due to the sinking of one section. **b.** a movement producing such a fault. **c.** the amount of such movement, measured by the amount of displacement along the fault plane.
give one the slip, *Informal.* to escape or get away from one; evade or elude one: *One of the principal officers of finance* . . . *had given the slip to his guards* (James Mill).
[perhaps < Middle Low German *slippen.* Compare Old English *slip-,* as in *slipor* (see SLIPPERY), *slipig* slimy.]
—**Syn.** *v.i.* **1.** See **slide.**

slip[2] (slip), *v.*, **slipped** or (*Archaic*) **slipt, slipped, slip·ping,** *n.* —*v.t.* to cut branches from (a plant) to grow new plants; take (a part) from a plant.
—*n.* **1. a.** a small, narrow piece of paper on which a record is made: *a laundry slip.* **b.** a narrow strip of wood, land, etc. **2.** a young, slender person: *She is just a slip of a girl.* **3.** a twig or small branch cut from a plant, used to grow a new plant: *Ruth has promised us slips from her rosebushes.* **4.** *British.* a galley proof. **5.** *U.S.* an ordinary church pew that is long, narrow, and open on the aisle. [probably < Middle Dutch, Middle Low German *slippen* to cut, slit]

slip[3] (slip), *n.* potter's clay made semifluid with water. It is used for coating or decorating pottery, cementing handles, etc.; barbotine. [apparently Middle English *slyppe* mud, Old English *slypa* a semiliquid mass]

slip·board (slip′bôrd′, -bōrd′), *n.* a board sliding in grooves.

slip·case (slip′kās′), *n.* a box or covering designed to protect one or more books, records, etc., so that only their backs or edges are exposed: *Four miniature books, in a decorated slipcase to match . . . are sheer delight to view and read* (Atlantic).

slip casting, a method of making pottery by pouring semifluid clay into plaster casts, used especially in the manufacture of whiteware with intricate shapes.

slip·cov·er (slip′kuv′ər), *n.* **1.** a removable cloth cover for a chair, sofa, etc.: *He found Marshall seated not behind a desk but in an armchair adorned with a gay print slipcover* (New Yorker). **2.** a dust jacket for a book.
—*v.t.* to cover with a slipcover: . . . *books to be bound, rebound or slipcovered* (New York Times).

slipe (slīp), *v.t.*, **sliped, slip·ing.** *Archaic.* to strip (off); peel.

slip glaze, a liquid glaze of clay mixed with ground minerals.

slip·horn (slip′hôrn′), *n.* *Informal.* trombone: *The boys played sliphorn and piano* (Time).

slip·knot (slip′not′), *n.* **1.** a knot made to slip along the rope or cord around which it is made. See **knot**[1] for picture. **2.** a knot that can be undone by pulling the end.

slip noose, a noose with a slip knot. It is made larger or smaller by sliding the knot on the cord, as on a lasso.

slip-on (slip′on′, -ôn′), *adj.* **1.** that can be put on or taken off easily or quickly: . . . *slip-on gloves with corduroy palms and plastic-leather backs* (New Yorker). **2.** that must be put on or taken off over the head.
—*n.* a slip-on glove, blouse, sweater, etc.

slip·o·ver (slip′ō′vər), *adj.* designed to be slipped on over the head: *a slipover sweater.*
—*n.* a slip-on.

slip·page (slip′ij), *n.* **1.** the act of slipping: *There were indications the profit margin slippage . . . could well bring total fourth-quarter profits below year-ago levels* (Wall Street Journal). **2.** the amount or extent of slipping, as in loss of working power in machinery.

slipped disk or **disc** (slipt), the loosening of an intervertebral disk, causing painful pressure on the spinal nerves: *Slipped disc . . . is the most common of all types of rheumatism* (Science News Letter).

slip·per (slip′ər), *n.* **1.** a kind of light, low shoe that is slipped on easily: *dancing slippers, bedroom slippers.* **2.** a person or thing that slips: *Most fats and oils have come down in price—lard, the fastest slipper, now wholesales in Chicago for less than 12 cents a pound.* (Wall Street Journal). —*v.t.* to hit or beat with a slipper. [< *slip*[1], verb + *-er*[1]]

slipper animalcule, a paramecium.

slip·pered (slip′ərd), *adj.* **1.** wearing slippers. **2.** associated with the wearing of slippers, especially their relaxing aspect: *His benign presence, slippered airs, and general good humour . . .* (London Times).

slip·per·i·ly (slip′ər ə lē, slip′rə-), *adv.* in a slippery manner.

slip·per·i·ness (slip′ər ē nis, slip′rē-), *n.* slippery quality or condition: *A graphite crystal consists of carbon atoms arranged in flat sheets which are only loosely bound together—hence the slipperiness of graphite and its use in "lead" pencils* (New Scientist).

slip·per·ing (slip′ər ing), *n.* a beating with a slipper: . . . *to give me a good slippering for my misbehavior* (Herman Melville).

slip·per·less (slip′ər lis), *adj.* without slippers: *His feet were slipperless, Eastern fashion* (F. Marion Crawford).

slipper limpet, a gastropod with a convex oval shell, containing a shelflike partition: *Starfish are destroyers of one oyster pest, the slipper limpet* (New Scientist).

slipper sock, a wool sock with a leather sole, usually worn for lounging indoors; muckluck: *The girls appeared . . . with scarfs bound around their pin curls, and wearing quilted robes and slipper socks* (Harper's).

slip·per·wort (slip′ər wėrt′), *n.* calceolaria, a tropical American plant of the figwort family.

slip·per·y (slip′ər ē, slip′rē), *adj.*, **-per·i·er, -per·i·est.** **1.** causing or likely to cause slipping: *A wet street is slippery. The steps are slippery with ice.* **2.** slipping away easily; difficult to catch or hold: *Wet soap is slippery.* **3.** not to be depended on; shifty; tricky: *The traditional con man was a slippery customer.* **4.** *Archaic.* licentious; wanton; unchaste: *Ha' not you seen Camillo? . . . or heard? . . . or thought? . . . My wife is slippery?* (Shakespeare). [< obsolete *slipper* slippery, Old English *slipor* + *-y*[1]]

slippery elm, **1.** an elm tree of eastern North America having a hard wood and a fragrant inner bark that becomes slimy or slippery when moistened, or in early spring. **2.** the inner bark.

slip·pi·ness (slip′ē nis), *n.* slipperiness.

slip proof, *British.* a galley proof.

slip·py (slip′ē), *adj.*, **-pi·er, -pi·est.** **1.** *Informal.* slippery: *steep, slippy-feeling rocks* (John M. Synge). **2.** *British Informal.* nimble, quick, or sharp: *Bring us two liqueur brandies, miss . . . And look slippy, if ye please* (Arnold Bennett).

slip·rail (slip′rāl′), *n.* (in Australia) a fence rail or section that can be removed to serve as a gate.

slip ring, one of two or more rings with which the brushes make connection in a dynamo or motor: *The alternating current dynamo is a device by which mechanical energy is converted into electrical energy. Slip rings help the electrons surge back and forth* (Louis T. Masson).

slip road, *British.* a road leading into an express highway: *Signs should also be erected . . . in positions where they can be seen by drivers before entering the motorway on the slip roads* (London Times).

slip rope, a rope so arranged that it may be readily let go.

slip seat, an upholstered seat which can be easily removed from a chair, stool, or bench.

slip·sheet (slip′shēt′), *v.t., v.i.* to place blank sheets of paper between (printed sheets) to prevent the offset of wet ink.
—*n.* a blank sheet used for this.

slip·shod (slip′shod′), *adj.* **1.** careless in dress, habits, speech, etc.; untidy; slovenly: *a slipshod performance. Slipshod handling once the packages reach the grocery can reduce even the finest brand to a sorry and sometimes dangerous mess* (Wall Street Journal). **2.** shuffling: *a slipshod gait.* **3.** wearing slippers or shoes worn down at the heel. —**slip′shod′ness,** *n.*

slip·slop (slip′slop′), *n.* **1.** sloppy food or drink. **2.** sloppy talk or writing. **3.** a blunder in the use of words.
—*adj.* sloppy; trifling.
[varied reduplication of *slop*[1]]

slip·stick (slip′stik′), *n.* *Slang.* a slide rule: *Mr. Crane has done his homework, including much hot labor with his slipstick* (Saturday Review).

slip stream, or **slip·stream** (slip′strēm′), *n.* a current of air produced by the propeller of an aircraft.

slipt (slipt), *v.* *Archaic.* a past tense of **slip**[1] and **slip**[2].

slip-up (slip′up′), *n.* *Informal.* a mistake; error; failure: *I want this job done right, with no slip-ups.*

slip·ware (slip′wãr′), *n.* earthenware which is coated with slip, or thinly diluted clay.

slip·way (slip′wā′), *n.* a platform sloping from a dock into the water, on which ships are built or repaired; slip: *On the slipway beside the basin there towered a tanker* (Punch).

slit (slit), *v.*, **slit, slit·ting,** *n.* —*v.t.* **1. a.** to cut or tear in a straight line: *to slit cloth into strips.* **b.** to make a long, straight cut or tear in: *to slit a shirt down the sides.* **2.** *Archaic.* to cut off; sever: *Comes the blind Fury with the abhorred shears And slits the thin-spun life* (Milton). —*n.* a straight, narrow cut, tear, or opening: *a slit in a bag, the slit in the letter box.* [Middle English *slitten*, related to Old English *slītan* to slit]

slit-eyed (slit′īd′), *adj.* having long and narrow eyes: . . . *scars on his simple, slit-eyed face* (New Yorker).

slith·er (sli*th*′ər), *v.i.* **1.** to slide down or along a surface, especially unsteadily or with noise: *Rocks slithered down the side of the cliff.* **2.** to go with a sliding motion; manner: *to slither into a room. Soon the cars would start slithering across the square like a funeral cortege* (New Yorker). —*v.t.* to cause to slither or slide.
—*n.* a slithering movement; slide.
[variant of dialectal *slidder*, Old English *slidrian*]

slith·er·y (sli*th*′ər ē), *adj.* slippery; crawly. [variant of dialectal *slidder* (see SLITHER) + *-y*[1]]

slit lamp, a lamp that projects a thin beam of light through a narrow slit, used in eye examinations: *Such cases should be referred to an ophthalmologist for an adequate slit lamp examination* (Science News Letter).

slit·ter (slit′ər), *n.* one that slits.

slit·tered (slit′ərd), *adj.* cut into strips with square ends, as the edge of a sleeve or garment.

slit trench, **1.** a narrow trench for one person or a small group, used as a shelter against shelling or bombing: *I was lucky, the going was good, and I rolled over into a shallow slit trench* (Cape Times). **2.** a similar trench in front or on the flank of a military position, as for an observation post, often in the shape of an L or V, so as to protect against enfilading fire.

sliv·er (sliv′ər), *n.* **1.** a long, thin piece that has been split off, broken off, or cut off; splinter. **2.** a loose fiber of wool, cotton, flax, etc.: *In the carding process, the wool passes through rows of teeth, which straighten and interblend the fibers into a flat band called a sliver* (World Book Encyclopedia). —*v.t., v.i.* to split or break into slivers. [Middle English *slivere*, related to Old English *-slīfan* to split, cleave]

sliv·o·vitz (sliv′ə vits), *n.* a strong brandy made from plums: *The Yugoslavs were cheerful and hospitable. They gave us fiery slivovitz with our dinner* (New Yorker). [< Serbo-Croatian *sljivovica* < *sljiva* plum]

slob (slob), *n.* **1.** *Slang.* a stupid, untidy, or clumsy person: . . . *and instead of asking, like some slobs, "Where do you want to go?" I say, "What is your pleasure, Madame?"* (New Yorker). **2.** *Irish.* **a.** mud or ooze. **b.** a stretch of it, especially along a seashore. **3.** in Newfoundland: **a.** slushy ice and snow. **b.** disintegrating pack ice. [probably < Irish *slab* mud]

slob·ber (slob′ər), *v.i.* **1.** to let saliva or other liquid run out from the mouth; slaver; drivel; drool. **2.** to speak in a silly, sentimental way: *Why is it that most Americans are always ready to slobber ecstatically over anything French?* (Time). —*v.t.* to wet or smear with saliva, etc.
—*n.* **1.** saliva or other liquid running out from the mouth; slaver. **2.** silly, sentimental talk or emotion. Also, **slabber.**
[probably ultimately < Middle Flemish *slobberen*] —**slob′ber·er,** *n.*

slob·ber·han·nes (slob′ər hon′əs), *n.* a game of cards for four persons, the object of every player being not to take the first trick, the last trick, or the queen of clubs.

slob·ber·i·ness (slob′ər ē nis), *n.* slobbering quality; sloppiness.

slob·ber·y (slob′ər ē), *adj.* **1.** slobbering. **2.** disagreeably wet; somewhat slimy; sloppy.

slob ice, disintegrating pack ice.

slock·en (slok′ən), *v.t.* *Scottish.* to quench. Also, **sloken.** [< Scandinavian (compare Old Icelandic *slokna* < *slökkva* go out, be slack)]

sloe (slō), *n.* **1.** a small, black or dark-purple, plumlike fruit with a sharp, sour taste. **2.** the thorny shrub that it grows on; blackthorn. **3.** any of several related shrubs or trees that bear dark purple fruit. [Old English *slāh*]

FRUIT
BRANCH
Sloe

sloe-eyed (slō′īd′), *adj.* black-eyed: *a sloe-eyed maiden.*

sloe gin, an alcoholic liquor like ordinary gin, but flavored with sloes instead of juniper berries: *Sloe gin is not a true gin, but a liqueur* (World Book Encyclopedia).

sloe plum, the fruit of the sloe.

slog (slog), *v.*, **slogged, slog·ging,** *n. Informal.* —*v.t.* to hit hard; slug. —*v.i.* **1.** to plod heavily. **2.** to work hard (at something).
—*n.* **1.** a hard blow. **2.** a spell of difficult, steady work: *The early play was mainly a hard slog of scrummage, lineout, and maul* (London Times).
[variant of *slug*[2]]

slo·gan (slō′gən), *n.* **1.** a word or phrase used by a business, club, political party, etc., to advertise its purpose; motto: *"Safety first" is our slogan.* **2.** a war cry; battle cry: *Sound the fife and cry the slogan—Let pibroch shake the air* (William E. Aytoun). *The bloody slogans of church-state and King-Commons still echoed in English ears . . .* (Time).
[< Scottish Gaelic *sluagh-ghairm* < *sluagh* army, host + *gairm* a cry]

slo·gan·eer (slō′gə nir′), *n.* a person who makes up or uses slogans: *. . . a sloganeer, a master of rhetoric and exhortation* (New York Times).

slo·gan·eer·ing (slō′gə nir′ing), *n.* the making up or use of slogans, as in advertising or political propaganda: *Some people seem to have accepted that epitome of simplified sloganeering—that foreign aid is like "pouring money down a rathole"* (Christian Science Monitor).

slo·gan·ize (slō′gə nīz), *v.t.*, **-ized, -iz·ing.** **1.** to reduce to a slogan: *We must have the courage to experiment with ideas among ourselves and within each of us—ideas which cannot be immediately sloganized or sold* (Bulletin of Atomic Scientists). **2.** to influence or persuade by slogans: *He . . . found the American people "sloganized" and the students "stereotyped"* (Newsweek).

slog·ger (slog′ər), *n. Informal.* a person who slogs.

sloid or **slojd** (sloid), *n.* sloyd.

slok·en (slok′ən), *v.t. Scottish.* slocken.

sloop (slüp), *n.* a fore-and aft rigged sailboat having one mast, a mainsail, a jib, and sometimes other sails. [< Dutch *sloep*, earlier *sloepe*. Doublet of SHALLOP.]

Sloop

sloop of war, (formerly) a small warship having guns on the upper deck only.

sloosh (slüsh), *n. Dialect.* **1.** a wash. **2.** the sound, as of washing. **3.** corn meal dough fried in bacon fat. [variant of *slosh*]

slop[1] (slop), *v.*, **slopped, slop·ping,** *n.* —*v.t.* **1.** to spill (liquid); splash: *He slopped water on me.* **2.** to spill liquid upon: *a table slopped with milk.* **3.** to give slop or slops to: *The farmer slopped the pigs.* —*v.i.* **1.** to run over in spilling: *I poured the milk from the bottle so fast that it slopped over the sides of the cup.* **2.** to splash through mud, slush, or water: *Then he slopped right along* (Mark Twain). *Beside the docks were the lees of the population, evidently much as they are today, slopping about among the pigs and the dogs* (Edmund Wilson).
slop over, *Slang.* to show too much feeling, enthusiasm, etc.; gush: *The "Herald" has slopped over this time, but it will steady itself as soon as it gets the facts* (New York Daily News).
—*n.* **1.** liquid carelessly spilled or splashed about. **2.** a thin, liquid mud or slush.
slops, a. dirty water; liquid garbage; dregs; swill: *kitchen slops.* **b.** liquid or semiliquid food, such as gruel, that is weak or not appetizing: *. . . please consider that you are steeping your poor original tea leaves in their fifth wash of hot water, and are drinking slops* (Atlantic). **c.** what is left of grain, etc., after distilling out the alcohol, used to make food for animals: *Farmers use slops to make food for their stock.*
[Middle English *sloppe* a mud hole; origin uncertain]

slop[2] (slop), *n.* a loose outer garment, such as a jacket, gown, or smock.
slops, a. cheap, ready-made clothing: *I bought an oilskin hat and a second-hand suit of slops* (W.S. Gilbert). **b.** clothes, bedding, etc., supplied to sailors on a ship: *A young sailor, with a face innocent of everything but a pride in his slops* (Leigh Hunt). **c.** loose trousers; wide, baggy breeches: *. . . two pair black silk slops, with hanging garters of carnation silk* (Scott).
[Middle English *sloppe* loose outer garment, later, loose trousers, apparently < Middle Dutch *slop*]

slop basin, bowl, or **bucket,** a container for holding slops, swill, etc.

slop book, (in the British navy) a register of clothing and small stores issued.

slop chest, *Nautical Slang.* a ship's store that sells clothing, tobacco, etc., to the crew during a voyage: *At sea, even the clothes the members wear come from S.I.U. operated "slop chests," or shipboard supply stores* (Wall Street Journal).

slope (slōp), *v.*, **sloped, slop·ing,** *n.* —*v.i.* to go up or down at an angle: *The land slopes toward the sea.* —*v.t.* to cause to go up or down at an angle: *As the enemy climbed the opposite cliff, we sloped our firing to follow them.*
—*n.* **1. a.** any line, surface, etc., that goes up or down at an angle: *the slope of a person's forehead.* **b.** a stretch of rising or falling ground: *to climb a steep slope.* **2.** the amount of slope: *The floor of the theater has a slope of four feet from back to front.*
[perhaps misdivision of *aslope*, adverb < Old English *āslopen*, past participle, slipped away]
—**Syn.** *v.i.* **Slope, slant** mean to go off at an angle from a straight line or level surface. **Slope** usually means to go up or down from a level, at a gradual degree unless otherwise specified: *The fields slope up to the foothills. One field slopes steeply.* **Slant** means to go or turn up or down, or to the side, at any degree: *That picture slants to the left.*

Slope (def. 1b)

slop·ing (slō′ping), *adj.* that slopes. —**slop′ing·ly,** *adv.* —**slop′ing·ness,** *n.*

slop·pi·ly (slop′ə lē), *adv.* in a sloppy or slovenly manner.

slop·pi·ness (slop′ē nis), *n.* sloppy quality or state.

slop·py (slop′ē), *adj.*, **-pi·er, -pi·est.** **1.** very wet; slushy: *sloppy ground, sloppy weather.* **2.** splashed or soiled with liquid: *a sloppy table, a floor sloppy with suds.* **3.** careless; slovenly: *to do sloppy work, to use sloppy English. By returning to Freud's original work, Trilling suggests, we can clear up some of our own sloppy thinking on the subject* (Newsweek). **4.** weak; silly; weakly sentimental: *sloppy sentiment.* **5.** loose or baggy; ill-fitting: *sloppy trousers.* **6.** watery; unappetizing: *a sloppy pudding.* [< *slop*[1] + *-y*[1]]

sloppy Joe, *U.S. Slang.* a large, loose or baggy sweater.

slops (slops), *n.pl.* See under **slop**[1] and **slop**[2], *n.*

slop·sell·er (slop′sel′ər), *n.* a person who sells ready-made, cheap, or inferior clothes.

slop·shop (slop′shop′), *n.* a store where cheap, ready-made clothing is sold.

slop·work (slop′wėrk′), *n.* **1.** the manufacture of cheap clothing. **2.** cheap clothing. **3.** any work done cheaply or poorly.

slop·work·er (slop′wėr′kər), *n.* a person who does slopwork.

slop·y (slō′pē), *adj.*, **slop·i·er, slop·i·est.** sloping; inclined; oblique.

slosh (slosh), *n.* **1.** slush. **2.** *Informal.* a watery or weak drink.
—*v.i.* **1.** to splash in or through slush, mud, or water. **2.** to go about idly; move aimlessly: *Devils don't slosh around much of a Sunday, I don't reckon* (Mark Twain). —*v.t.* **1.** to cause (a liquid) to splash around in a container by shaking or stirring: *He nervously sloshed the liquor around in his glass.* **2.** to pour or dash liquid upon: *He bangs his thumb, sloshes paint in his hair . . .* (New York Times). **3.** to beat; thrash.
[perhaps blend of *slop*[1] and *slush*]

slosh·y (slosh′ē), *adj.*, **slosh·i·er, slosh·i·est.** slushy.

slot[1] (slot), *n.*, *v.*, **slot·ted, slot·ting.** —*n.* **1.** a narrow opening or depression, such as a groove or notch, in a piece of metal, wood, etc., into which something can be pushed or fitted: *Put a penny in the slot to get a stick of gum from this machine.* **2.** a narrow opening on the leading edge of an airplane wing, formed by the wing and a movable auxiliary airfoil, designed to create a smooth flow over the wing and thus increase the lift, especially at relatively low speeds. **3.** *Informal.* a place or position in a schedule, list, series, etc.: *The program premiers next week in the 9:30-to-10:30 slot on Saturday evening* (Wall Street Journal).
—*v.t.* **1.** to make a slot or slots in. **2.** *U.S. Informal.* to put into a slot; schedule; slate: *The network slotted the new program for Sunday afternoon.*
[< Old French *esclot* the hollow between the breasts]

slot[2] (slot), *n.*, *v.*, **slot·ted, slot·ting.** —*n.* a track; trail: *They followed the slot made by the deer's footprints in the mud.* —*v.t.* to track by the slot: *They slotted the deer into the forest.* [< Old French *esclot*, probably < Scandinavian (compare Old Icelandic *slōth* track). Compare SLEUTH.]

sloth (slōth, slôth), *n.* **1.** unwillingness to work or exert oneself; laziness; idleness: *His sloth keeps him from engaging in sports.* **2.** a very slow-moving mammal of South and Central America that lives in trees. Sloths hang upside down from tree branches. One kind has three toes on the forefeet and another has two. **3.** *Archaic.* slowness. [Old English *slǣwth* < *slāw* slow] —**Syn. 1.** sluggishness, indolence.

Two-toed Sloth (def. 2—2 ft. long)

sloth bear, a long-haired bear that lives in India and Ceylon.

Sloth Bear (about 3 ft. high at the shoulder)

sloth·ful (slōth′fəl, slôth′-), *adj.* **1.** unwilling to work or exert oneself; lazy; idle: *He is the true slothful man that does no good* (Thomas Dekker). **2.** characterized by sloth: *slothful habits.* —**sloth′ful·ly,** *adv.* —**sloth′ful·ness,** *n.* —**Syn. 1, 2.** sluggish.

slot·hound (slot′hound′), *n.* a sleuthhound; bloodhound.

sloth monkey, the slow lemur; loris.

slot machine, a machine that is worked by dropping a coin into a slot. Some slot machines sell peanuts, sticks of gum, etc., others are used for gambling: *I see the latest slot machine will not only take pound notes but, through some complicated mechanism, also test if they are genuine* (Punch).

slot man, *U.S.* the news editor of a newspaper in charge of the copy desk: *When he walked into the newsroom, the whole copy desk except the slot man ducked for the washroom* (Time).

slot·ter (slot′ər), *n.* a person or a machine that makes slots: *In a slotter, or vertical shaper, the cutting tool moves up and down instead of back and forth* (World Book Encyclopedia).

slouch (slouch), *v.i.* **1.** to stand, sit, walk, or move in an awkward, drooping manner: *The weary man slouched along. Don't slouch, sit up straight.* **2.** to droop or bend downward: *The old hat slouched backward on his head.* —*v.t.* to cause to droop or bend down.
—*n.* **1.** a stooping or bending forward of the head and shoulders; awkward, drooping way of standing, sitting, or walking. **2.** a drooping or bending downward of a hat brim, etc. **3.** *U.S. Informal.* **a.** an awkward or inefficient person: *He's no slouch when it comes to square dancing.* **b.** a lazy, idle, or slovenly person.
[origin uncertain. Compare Old Icelandic *slōkr* a slouch, *slōka* to droop.]

slouch·er (slou′chər), *n.* a person who slouches, or walks with a slouching gait.

slouch hat, a soft hat, usually with a broad brim that bends down easily.

slouch·i·ly (slou′chə lē), *adv.* in a slouchy manner.

slouch·i·ness (slou′chē nis), *n.* slouchy quality or state.

slouch·ing (slou′ching), *adj.* **1.** that slouches; carrying oneself with a slouch: *. . . a tall, slouching fellow* (Francis Parkman). **2.** characterized by a slouch: *I adopted, along with my beggar's attire, a* *peculiar slouching and clownish gait* (William Godwin). —**slouch′ing·ly,** *adv.*

slouch·y (slou′chē), *adj.,* **slouch·i·er, slouch·i·est.** slouching awkwardly; carelessly untidy; slovenly.

slough[1] (slou *for 1 and 3;* slü *for 2*), *n.* **1.** a soft, deep, muddy place; mud hole: *We visited sloughs that always have water, no matter the severity of the drought* (William O. Douglas). **2.** *U.S. and Canada.* a swampy place; marshy inlet; slew. **3.** hopeless discouragement; degradation; decline: *Otto Kahn, the suave, music-loving-man-about-town, was . . . the man who rescued the Metropolitan Opera from a financial and artistic slough* (Newsweek). [Old English *slōh*]

slough[2] (sluf), *n.* **1.** the old dead skin shed or cast off by a snake. **2.** a layer of dead skin or tissue that drops or falls off as a wound, sore, etc., heals. **3.** anything that has been shed or cast off: *As savages become civilized, they cast off the slough of primitive ways and beliefs.* **4.** (in card games) a discard that might otherwise be a losing card.
—*v.t.* **1.** to drop off; throw off; shed: *Through the processes of excision and sloughing of certain structures which contain wastes, plants get rid of wastes* (Harbaugh and Goodrich). *She could slough off a sadness and replace it by a hope* (Thomas Hardy). **2.** (in card games) to discard (a losing card) on a trick.
—*v.i.* to be shed or cast; drop or fall: *A scab sloughs off when new skin takes its place.*
[Middle English *slouh;* origin uncertain]

slough of despond (slou), hopeless dejection; deep despondency. [< the *Slough of Despond,* in *Pilgrim's Progress,* by John Bunyan, 1628-1688, an English minister and religious writer]

slough·y[1] (slou′ē), *adj.,* **slough·i·er, slough·i·est.** soft and muddy; full of soft, deep mud; miry: *Secaucus, at the heart of a vast trash-filled marsh . . . is bounded by the ever dirty Hackensack River and two sloughy creeks* (Time).

slough·y[2] (sluf′ē), *adj.* of dead skin; covered with dead skin or tissue.

Slo·vak (slō′väk, -vak), *n.* **1.** a member of the Slavic people native to Slovakia: *The Slovaks are closely related to the Bohemians and the Moravians.* **2.** their Western Slavic language, closely related to Czech and Moravian. —*adj.* of or having to do with Slovakia, a province in eastern Czechoslovakia, its people, or their language. [< Czech, and Slovak *Slovák*]

Slo·va·ki·an (slō vä′kē ən, -vak′ē-), *n., adj.* Slovak.

slov·en (sluv′ən), *n.* a person who is untidy, dirty, or careless in dress, appearance, habits, work, etc.: *Since he had never taken any care of his personal appearance, he became every known variety of sloven* (Rudyard Kipling). —*adj.* untidy; dirty; careless; slovenly. [perhaps ultimately < Flemish *sloef* dirty, or Dutch *slof* careless]

Slo·vene (slō′vēn), *n.* **1.** a member of a Slavic group of people native to Slovenia, a region in northwestern Yugoslavia. The Slovenes are closely related to the Croats, Serbians, and other southern Slavs. **2.** their Southern Slavic language, closely related to Serbo-Croatian. —*adj.* of or having to do with Slovenia, its people, or their language. [< German *Slovene* < Slovenian *slovenec*]

Slo·ve·ni·an (slō vē′nē ən, -vēn′yən), *adj., n.* Slovene.

slov·en·li·ness (sluv′ən lē nis), *n.* lack of neatness; dirtiness; carelessness in appearance, dress, habits, work, etc.: *Slovenliness is no part of religion* (John Wesley).

slov·en·ly (sluv′ən lē), *adj.,* **-li·er, -li·est,** *adv.* —*adj.* untidy, dirty, or careless in dress, appearance, habits, work, etc.: *A thin elderly man, rather threadbare and slovenly* (Washington Irving). —*adv.* in a slovenly manner. —**Syn.** *adj.* unkempt, slatternly, slipshod, negligent.

slov·en·ry (sluv′ən rē), *n. Archaic.* slovenly character, condition, or procedure.

slow (slō), *adj.* **1.** taking a long time; taking longer than usual; not fast or quick: *a slow journey, a slow train, a slow messenger.* **2.** running behind time; at less than proper speed: *a slow runner. Seldom readers are slow readers* (Charles Lamb). **3.** indicating a time earlier than the correct time: *The clock was slow and I was late for school.* **4.** causing a low or lower rate of speed: *slow ground, a slow track.* **5.** burning or heating slowly or gently: *a slow flame.* **6. a.** naturally inactive; sluggish: *a slow fellow.* **b.** not quick to understand; dull: *a slow learner.* **7.** not interesting; not lively; boring: *a slow party.* **8.** not fast or hurried; leisurely: *music in a slow tempo; to proceed by slow marches and frequent halts* (Scott). **9. a.** not ready or willing: *slow to answer, slow in or of speech.* **b.** not readily stirred or moved; not hasty: *slow to anger, slow to take offense.* **10.** not brisk; slack: *Business is slow.* **11.** behind the times; not smart or up-to-date: *a slow town.* **12.** (of time) passing slowly or heavily: *As slow years pass . . .* (Shelley).
—*adv.* in a slow manner or way; slowly: *Drive slow. In front the sun climbs slow, how slowly!* (Arthur Hugh Clough).
—*v.t.* to make slow or slower; reduce the speed of: *to slow down a car.* —*v.i.* to become slow; go slower: *Slow up when you drive through a town. Slow down, you're walking too fast for me.*
[Old English *slāw*] —**slow′ly,** *adv.* —**slow′ness,** *n.*
—**Syn.** *adj.* **1. Slow, leisurely, deliberate** mean taking a long time to do something or to happen. **Slow,** the general term, suggests taking longer than usual or necessary: *We took the slow train.* **Leisurely** suggests slowness because of having plenty of time: *I like leisurely meals.* **Deliberate,** describing people or their acts, suggests slowness due to care, thought, or self-control: *His speech is deliberate.* **6. a.** phlegmatic. **7.** wearisome, tiresome. —**Ant.** *adj.* **1.** fast, swift, fleet, rapid.

➤ **Slow, slowly.** In standard English *slowly* is now the usual form of the adverb except in set phrases (*go slow, drive slow*) and in the comparative or superlative (where *slower* or *slowest* are often used instead of *more* or *most slowly*).

slow burn, a gradually increasing exasperation turning by degrees into intense, but still controlled, anger, used as a comic device by actors: *Jack Carson* [*was*] *master of the double-take and the slow burn* (Time).

slow coach, *Informal.* **1.** a slowpoke. **2.** an idle, inactive person. **3.** an old-fashioned person; fogy.

slow·down (slō′doun′), *n.* a slowing in rate of production, pace of work, etc.: *Most concerns* [*are*] *expecting the traditional midsummer month slowdown* (Wall Street Journal).

slow-foot·ed (slō′fu̇t′id), *adj.* advancing slowly; slow-moving; slow-paced: *. . . get slow-footed members of Congress off and running early* (Harper's).

slow·go·ing (slō′gō′ing), *adj.* slow in moving, proceeding, or acting; leisurely: *a calm, slowgoing Arkansan . . .* (Time).

slow·hound (slō′hound′), *n.* a sleuthhound.

slow·ish (slō′ish), *adj.* somewhat slow or dull: *An Allegretto that begins like a Siciliano but turns into a slowish waltz* (Manchester Guardian).

slow loris, a small nocturnal lemur of India and the East Indies, noted for the extreme slowness of its movements.

slow match, a fuse that burns very slowly, used to set fire to gunpowder, dynamite, etc.

slow-mo·tion (slō′mō′shən), *adj.* **1.** moving at less than normal speed: *Lewisohn is at his narrative best as he puts a slow-motion technique to work* (New York Times). **2.** showing action at much less than its actual speed: *a slow-motion movie.*

slow-mov·ing (slō′mü′ving), *adj.* **1.** that moves or goes slowly; slowgoing: *Large droves of patient, slow-moving cattle arrived* (Rolf Boldrewood). **2.** making slow progress; advancing or acting slowly: *. . . overloads himself with slow-moving stock* (Harper's).

slow·paced (slō′pāst′), *adj.* moving or advancing slowly: *He has written a slowpaced, leisurely, rambling and discursive novel about several of the most important issues of our time* (New York Times).

slow·poke (slō′pōk′), *n. U.S. Informal.* a very slow person or thing: *The meters' chief purposes are to turn over curb space . . . and cut down on double parking and the cruising of slowpokes looking for an empty space* (New Yorker).

slow-spo·ken (slō′spō′kən), *adj.* speaking at a slow pace: *. . . a slow-spoken man with a brooding look* (New Yorker).

slow·up (slō′up′), *n.* slowdown: *There has also been a moderate slowup in the rate of growth of mutual savings banks' deposits* (Wall Street Journal).

slow-wit·ted (slō′wit′id), *adj.* slow at thinking; dull; stupid.

slow·worm (slō′wėrm′), *n.* the blindworm, a small, snakelike lizard: *The pretty little slowworms that are not only harmless, but seem to respond to gentle and kindly treatment* (A. Jessop).

sloyd (sloid), *n.* a system of manual training for children in work with the hands and simple tools, as for woodworking and other crafts, originally developed and taught in Sweden. Also **sloid, slojd.** [< Swedish *slöjd* skill, dexterity]

slub (slub), *v.,* **slubbed, slub·bing,** *n.* —*v.t.* to twist (wool, yarn, etc.) slightly after carding, so as to prepare for spinning: *Stripes, checks and other fancy patterns, are formed in prominent looped or slubbed yarns against a flat ground* (London Times). —*n.* **1.** a partially twisted silk, wool, or cotton fiber or cloth made from such a fiber: *a bright pink chiffon dress has a matching silk slub jacket* (New York Times). **2.** a lump on a fiber that becomes attached to the yarn in spinning. [origin uncertain. Compare earlier *slub* a lump on a thread.]

slub·ber (slub′ər), *v.t. Dialect.* **1.** to stain; smear; daub; soil. **2.** to do, make, etc., in a hurried and careless manner. [probably < Low German *slubbern;* perhaps variant of *slobber*]

sludge (sluj), *n., v.,* **sludged, sludg·ing.** —*n.* **1.** soft mud; mire; ooze; slush. **2.** a soft, thick, muddy mixture, deposit, sediment, etc. **3.** small, broken, floating pieces of ice: *In winter there is sludge on the sea near the shore.*
—*v.t.* **1.** to convert into sludge. **2.** to stop up with liquid mud. **3.** to clear from sludge or mud. —*v.i.* to form sludge: *Unanswered is the question of what causes the blood to be over-viscous or to sludge* (Science News Letter).
[earlier *slutch;* origin uncertain]

sludg·er (sluj′ər), *n.* a pump or other apparatus for removing sludge from a bore.

sludg·y (sluj′ē), *adj.* consisting of sludge; miry; slushy.

slue[1] (slü), *v.t., v.i.,* **slued, slu·ing,** *n.* slew; turn; swing; twist. [earlier variant of *slew*[2]]

slue[2] (slü), *n.* slew; a swampy place; marshy inlet.

slue[3] (slü), *n.* slew; a large number or amount.

sluff (sluf), *n.* slough[2].

slug[1] (slug), *n., v.,* **slugged, slug·ging.** —*n.* **1.** a slow-moving, slimy animal like a snail, without a shell or with only a very small shell: *A study of the embryonic development of the slug reveals that a shell is formed in the embryo just as it is in the snail, but fails to continue its development to a functional size* (A.M. Winchester). **2.** a caterpillar or other insect larva that looks like a slug. **3.** any slow-moving animal, person, wagon, etc. **4.** a piece of lead or other metal for firing from a gun: *a slug from a .45-caliber revolver.* **5.** a lump of metal, usually rounded. **6.** *Printing.* **a.** a strip of metal used to space lines of type. A slug is more than 1/16 of an inch in thickness. Slugs are also used to fill out missing lines in page proofs, for printing temporary marks of identification, etc. **b.** a line of type cast in one piece by a linotype machine. **7.** *Physics.* (in the British system of units) a unit of mass, equal to about 32.17 pounds, which has an acceleration of one foot per second per second when acted upon by a force of one pound. **8.** *U.S. Slang.* a drink; shot: *a slug of whiskey.*
—*v.t.* **1.** *Printing.* to insert slugs between lines of (type). **2.** to load (a gun) with slugs.
—*v.i. Archaic.* **1.** to be inactive or slothful. **2.** to move slowly.
[Middle English *slugge* a slow person, perhaps < Scandinavian (compare Swedish dialectal *slogga* be sluggish)]
—**slug′like′,** *adj.*

Common Slug[1] (def. 1—to 2 in. long)

slug[2] (slug), *v.,* **slugged, slug·ging,** *n. Informal.* —*v.t., v.i.* **1.** to hit hard with the fist: *to slug a person on the chin.* **2.** to hit hard: *to slug a ball. He slugged two home runs in the deciding game of the series.*

slug it out, *U.S. Informal.* to fight or compete until one side wins; fight it out: *Retail casualties mount as St. Louis merchants slug it out with discount houses* (Wall Street Journal).
—*n.* a hard blow with the fist.

slug·a·bed (slug′ə bed′), *n.* a lazy, idle person who likes to lie in bed: *Occasionally lolling in bed until 6, Joe Moore would have been considered a slugabed by his great-grandfather, who, out of the necessity of his era, turned out at an invariable 4 a.m.* (Time).

slug·fest (slug′fest′), *n. U.S. Slang.* **1.** an occasion of much vigorous battling, contesting, etc.; fight; free-for-all: *The back-slapping camaraderie soon degenerated into a verbal slugfest* (Newsweek). **2.** a baseball game dominated by heavy hitting: *Last night's anticipated pitching duel . . . turned into a slugfest* (New York Times).

slug·gard (slug′ərd), *n.* a lazy, idle person: *Go to the ant, thou sluggard; consider her ways, and be wise* (Proverbs 6:6). —*adj.* lazy; idle. [< *slug*[1], verb + Old French *-ard,* a suffix meaning "one who does"] —**Syn.** *adj.* sluggish, slothful.

slug·gard·ly (slug′ərd lē), *adj.* lazy; indolent; slothful: *It failed . . . to rouse me from a sluggardly half-sleep* (London Times).

slug·ger (slug′ər), *n. Informal.* **1.** a person who slugs or hits hard, especially with the fists. **2.** a boxer; pugilist.

slug·ging (slug′ing), *n. Informal.* the act of a person who slugs or hits hard; hard hitting; beating.

slugging match, 1. a boxing match or fistfight involving hard hits. **2.** *Informal.* a sharp or forceful dispute: *The Pentagon vs. Congress slugging match over the choice . . .* (Wall Street Journal).

slug·gish (slug′ish), *adj.* **1.** not active; lacking energy or vigor: *a sluggish mind.* **2.** lazy; idle. **3.** moving very slowly; having little motion: *A sluggish river has very little current.* **4.** slow; tardy: *a sluggish digestion. Climbing again into his car, pushing at the sluggish starter* (Graham Greene). [< *slug*[1] + *-ish*] —**slug′gish·ly,** *adv.* —**slug′gish·ness,** *n.* —**Syn. 1.** dull, inert.

slug·horn (slug′hôrn′), *n.* a kind of trumpet: *His letters to Pauline Viardot have the sound of a journey to the Dark Tower on the part of a reluctant Childe Roland who is equipped with no resonant slughorn to challenge the evil spirits* (New Yorker). [variant of *slogan* battle cry]

slug·worm (slug′wėrm′), *n.* the slimy sluglike larva of any of various sawflies.

sluice (slüs), *n., v.,* **sluiced, sluic·ing.** —*n.* **1.** a structure with a gate or gates for holding back or controlling the water of a canal, river, or lake: *A big sluice has been constructed on the Austrian bank of the Danube and shipping can proceed through locks on the Bavarian side* (Wall Street Journal). **2.** a gate that holds back or controls the flow of water. When the water behind a dam gets too high, the sluices are opened. **3.** the water held back or controlled by such a gate. **4.** a valve, pipe, or other device that regulates the flow of water into or out of some receptacle. **5.** a means of controlling the flow or passage of anything: *War opens the sluices of hatred and bloodshed.* **6.** *Mining.* a long, sloping trough through which water flows, used to wash gold from sand, dirt, or gravel: *The sluice consists of an inclined channel through which runs a stream of water and into which the gold-bearing earth is shoveled* (White and Renner). **7.** a channel for carrying off overflow or surplus water.

Sluice (def. 6)

—*v.t.* **1.** to let out or draw off (water, etc.) by opening a sluice. **2.** to flush or cleanse with a rush of water; pour or throw water over; slush. **3.** to wash (gold) from sand, dirt, or gravel in a sluice. **4.** to carry or send (logs, etc.) along a channel of water. —*v.i.* to flow or pour in a stream; rush: *Water sluiced down the channel.*
[< Old French *escluse* < Late Latin *exclūsa* a barrier to shut out water < Latin *exclūdere* shut out < *ex-* out + *claudere* close, shut]

sluice gate, a gate to control the flow of water in a sluice.

sluice·way (slüs′wā′), *n.* **1.** a channel controlled or fed by a sluice. **2.** any small, artificial channel for running water.

sluic·y (slü′sē), *adj. Archaic.* **1.** pouring abundantly: *And oft whole sheets descend of sluicy rain* (John Dryden). **2.** wet: *the cool and sluicy sands* (Keats).

sluit (slüt), *n.* (in South Africa) a gully made by heavy rains. [< Afrikaans *sloot*]

slum (slum), *n., v.,* **slummed, slum·ming.** —*n.* a street, alley, etc., in a crowded, dirty part of a city or town: *We hear stories now and then of some boy from a slum who makes good and winds up with a fortune.*
the slums, a. a crowded, dirty part of a city or town, where the poorest people live: *If Judge Holtzoff's philosophy prevails, we shall have taken a long step backward toward the sweatshop and the slums* (Time). **b.** extreme poverty, low social class, etc., as in the slums: *to rise from the slums to power and wealth.*
—*v.i.* **1.** to go into or visit a slum or the slums, etc. **2.** to go into or visit any place thought of as greatly inferior to one's own.
[earlier, a room; origin uncertain]

slum·ber (slum′bər), *v.i.* **1.** to sleep; sleep lightly; doze. **2. a.** to be inactive: *a slumbering volcano, slumbering anger.* **b.** to be negligently inactive: *to slumber while one's enemies arm themselves.* —*v.t.* to pass in slumber: *The baby slumbers away the hours.*
—*n.* **1.** a sleep; light sleep: *He awoke from his slumber.* **2.** an inactive state or condition.
[Middle English *slumberen, slumeren* (frequentative) < Old English *slūma* sleep, noun] —**slum′ber·er,** *n.*

slum·ber·land (slum′bər land′), *n.* the imaginary country of slumber.

slum·ber·less (slum′bər lis), *adj.* without slumber; sleepless.

slum·ber·ous (slum′bər əs, -brəs), *adj.* **1.** sleepy; heavy with drowsiness: *slumberous eyelids.* **2.** causing or inducing sleep. **3.** having to do with, characterized by, or suggestive of sleep. **4.** inactive; sluggish. **5.** calm; quiet. —**slum′ber·ous·ly,** *adv.*

slumber party, *U.S.* a gathering of young girls in a home to spend the night together; pajama party: *They had been to a slumber party . . . and had not slept at all* (New Yorker).

slum·ber·y (slum′bər ē), *adj.* **1.** slumberous; sleepy. **2.** of or like slumber.

slum·brous (slum′brəs), *adj.* slumberous. —**slum′brous·ly,** *adv.*

slum clearance, the clearing away of slums in connection with a program of housing and redevelopment: *The largest efforts will be directed at slum clearance and improvement of blighted homes* (New York Times).

slum·dom (slum′dəm), *n.* **1.** the condition of being a slum: *Neglected, this property will slip by degrees into slumdom* (London Times). **2.** the people living in a slum.

slum·gul·lion (slum gul′yən), *n.* **1.** a stew of meat and vegetables, usually potatoes and onions. **2.** *Mining.* the thick and sticky refuse of the sluice boxes, generally of red, iron-bearing clay and water. **3.** *Slang.* a low, worthless fellow.

slum·gum (slum′gum), *n.* the impurities that remain as a residue after the wax is extracted from honeycombs.

slum·lord (slum′lôrd′), *n. U.S.* the owner of a run-down tenement house, usually in the slums: *The number of housing violations we have found* [*shows*] *how strongly we are attacking the slumlords* (Robert F. Wagner).

slum·mer (slum′ər), *n.* a person who visits slums for charitable purposes, curiosity, etc.

slum·mi·ness (slum′ē nis), *n.* the quality or condition of being slummy.

slum·ming (slum′ing), *n.* the visiting of slums, as for charitable purposes or from curiosity.

slum·my (slum′ē), *adj.,* **-mi·er, -mi·est. 1.** characteristic of a slum or of people living there: *a slummy street, accent, or manner.* **2.** full of slums.

slump (slump), *v.i.* **1.** to drop heavily: *The wagon, under a load . . . had slumped into a hole* (G.W. Cable). *She slumped into a chair and gasped with the heat* (Sinclair Lewis). **2.** to fall heavily or suddenly: *New England . . . put its brains to work and found new research and electronics industries after textiles slumped* (Time). **3.** to move, walk, sit, etc., heavily or with difficulty; slouch: *The bored students slumped in their seats.*
—*n.* **1.** a heavy drop or sudden fall; collapse. **2.** a great or sudden decline in prices, business or financial activity, etc.: *In 1929, in the great slump, disaster fell* (Atlantic). **3.** a drooping posture or stance.
[perhaps imitative]

slung (slung), *v.* the past tense and past participle of **sling**[1]: *They slung some stones and ran away. The boy had slung his books over his shoulder.*

slung shot, a piece of metal, stone, etc., fastened to a short strap, chain, etc., used as a weapon.

slunk[1] (slungk), *v.* a past tense and past participle of **slink**[1]: *The dog slunk away ashamed.*

slunk[2] (slungk), *v.* a past tense and a past participle of **slink**[2].

slur (slėr), *v.,* **slurred, slur·ring,** *n.* —*v.t.* **1.** to pass lightly over; go through hurriedly or carelessly. **2.** to pronounce indistinctly: *Many persons slur "ing" and "How do you do."* **3.** *Music.* **a.** to sing or play (two or more tones of different pitch) without a break; run together in a smooth, connected manner. **b.** to mark with a slur. **4.** to harm the reputation of; insult; slight. **5.** *Printing.* to smudge or blur; mackle. **6.** *Dialect.* to smear; stain; sully. —*v.i.* to speak or write sounds, letters, etc., so indistinctly that they run into each other.
—*n.* **1.** a slurred pronunciation, sound, word, etc. **2.** *Music.* **a.** a slurring of tones. **b.** a curved mark (⌢) (⌣) indicating this. **3.** an insulting or slighting remark; a blot or stain (upon reputation): *a slur on a person's good name. Then came the inevitable slur, or imagined slur, for Swift had the thinnest of skins* (Time). **4.** a mark; stain; blot. **5.** *Printing.* a smudged or blurred place; mackle.
[origin uncertain]

Slur (def. 2b)

slurp (slėrp), *U.S. Slang.* —*v.i.* to eat or drink something with a noisy gurgling sound: *I never slurp, nor gobble as if I'm starving* (Wall Street Journal).
—*v.t.* to eat or drink in this manner: *From the fishermen we learned how to pry them loose from the rocks, shuck them open with a knife, and slurp the soft pink pulp inside* (Atlantic).
—*n.* a slurping or gurgling sound: *. . . the last whirling slurp of water down a drain* (Harper's). [perhaps imitative]

slur·ry (slėr′ē), *n., pl.* **-ries,** *v.,* **-ried, -ry·ing.** —*n.* a semifluid substance, such as thin mud, slush, cement, or mortar prepared with a high percentage of water, etc.: *In the wet process, water is added during the grinding, until a soupy mixture called a slurry forms* (World Book Encyclopedia). —*v.t.* to make or convert into a slurry: *to slurry uranium ore, radioactive waste, etc.* [related to SLUR]

slush (slush), *n.* **1.** partly melted snow; snow and water mixed: *There was no traffic to turn the snow to slush* (James Barrie). **2.** soft mud; mire. **3.** silly, sentimental talk, writing, etc.; drivel. **4. a.** a mixture of grease and other materials for lubricating. **b.** a mixture of white lead and lime, used for painting parts of machinery to prevent them from rusting. **5.** used or spoiled fat from a ship's galley.
—*v.t.* **1.** to splash or soak with slush or mud. **2.** to grease, polish, or cover with slush: *The officer . . . ordered me to slush the mainmast . . . So I took my bucket of grease and climbed up* (Richard Henry Dana). **3.** to fill up or cover with mortar or cement. **4.** to wash with much water.
[origin uncertain. Perhaps related to SLUDGE.]

slush fund, 1. a fund of money for use, usually corrupt, in political campaigning or the like: *Enrico Mattei, the young oil czar, has rapidly sized up the situation and is using his slush funds for an all-out financing of the leftist groups inside the party* (Harper's). **2.** a fund of money obtained from the sale of waste fat on ship or in camp.

slush·i·ness (slush′ē nis), *n.* **1.** slushy quality or condition. **2.** sickening sentimentality: *Aside from their slushiness, the romantic epistles are historically interesting in graphically demonstrating the young prince's fickle ways* (Time).

slush lamp, a crude lamp that burns slush

or refuse fat, often made from an old tin can with a rag as a wick.

slush·y (slush′ē), *adj.*, **slush·i·er, slush·i·est.** **1.** full of or covered with slush: *slushy grass.* **2.** of or like slush. —*n.* **1.** *Slang.* a ship's cook. **2.** (in Australia) a cook's assistant on a sheep station during shearing time.

slut (slut), *n.* **1.** a dirty, untidy woman or girl; slattern. **2.** a woman or girl of loose morals. **3.** a female dog; bitch. [Middle English *slutte* a slovenly person]

slut·ter·y (slut′ər ē), *n.* the character or practices of a slut; sluttishness.

slut·tish (slut′ish), *adj.* **1.** dirty; untidy. **2.** loose in morals. —**slut′tish·ly,** *adv.* —**slut′tish·ness,** *n.*

sly (slī), *adj.*, **sly·er** or **sli·er, sly·est** or **sli·est,** *n.* —*adj.* **1.** able to do things without letting others know; acting secretly: *That girl is as sly as a fox. The sly cat stole the meat while the cook's back was turned.* **2.** cunning; crafty; tricky; wily: *He was, indeed, a little inquisitive; but I was sly, sir; devilish sly* (Richard Brinsley Sheridan). *Finney, the attorney, has been among them, asking sly questions* (Anthony Trollope). **3.** playfully mischievous or knowing; roguish: *a sly wink, a sly look.* **4.** *Obsolete.* skilled; wise.

—*n.* **on the sly,** in a sly way; secretly; stealthily: *Prominent politicians came to seek favors from him on the sly* (James Bryce).

[< Scandinavian (compare Old Icelandic *slægr*)] —**sly′ness,** *n.*

—**Syn.** *adj.* **1.** surreptitious, stealthy, furtive. **2. Sly, cunning** mean having or showing ability to get what one wants by secret or indirect means. **Sly** emphasizes lack of frankness and straightforwardness, and suggests stealthy actions or secrecy and deceit in dealing with others: *That sly girl managed to get her best friend's job.* **Cunning** emphasizes cleverness in getting the best of others by tricks or schemes, unfair dealing, or cheating: *A fox is cunning enough to cross a stream so that dogs cannot follow its scent. He showed a kind of low cunning in dealing with his customers.*

sly·boots (slī′büts′), *n.* a sly, cunning, or crafty person: *Sure enough, in a few weeks Mr. Jones gives his boys each a new top, but — what a slyboots he is! — there are no strings* (New Yorker).

sly·ly (slī′lē), *adv.* in a sly manner; secretly. Also, **slily.**

slype (slīp), *n.* a covered passage, especially from the transept of a cathedral to the chapter house. [origin uncertain]

sm., small.

Sm (no period), samarium (chemical element).

S.M., an abbreviation for the following:
1. Master of Science (Latin, *Scientiae Magister*).
2. Saint Mary.
3. Sergeant Major.
4. Soldier's Medal.
5. State Militia.

smack[1] (smak), *n.* **1.** a slight taste or flavor: *This sauce has a smack of nutmeg.* **2.** a trace; suggestion: *The old sailor still had a smack of the sea about him.* **3.** a small quantity; taste; mouthful.

—*v.i.* to have a taste, trace, or touch: *The Irishman's speech smacked of the old country.* [Old English *smæcc*]

—**Syn.** *n.* **2.** touch, dash, tinge.

smack[2] (smak), *v.t.* **1.** to open (the lips) quickly so as to make a sharp sound: *Tom . . . smacked his lips over the long-necked glass* (Thomas Hughes). **2.** to kiss loudly. **3.** to slap: *to smack someone in the face.* **4.** to bring, put, throw, or send with a sharp blow or smack: *to smack a ball, to smack a home run.* **5.** to crack (a whip, etc.). —*v.i.* to make or give out a smacking sound.

—*n.* **1.** a smacking movement of the lips: *Tasting the wine with a judicious smack* (Sir Richard Steele). **2.** the sharp sound made in this way. **3.** a loud kiss. **4.** a slap: *a smack in the nose.* **5.** a crack (of a whip, etc.): *The loud, resounding smack of its [beaver's] tail on the water was at first as startling as gunfire* (William O. Douglas).

—*adv. Informal.* **1.** suddenly and sharply; with or as with a smack: *He ran smack into the very man he was trying to avoid.* **2.** directly; squarely; completely: *He fell smack on his face.*

[ultimately imitative. Compare Dutch *smacken.*]

smack[3] (smak), *n.* **1.** a small sailboat with one mast rigged like a sloop or cutter, generally used as a coaster or for fishing. **2.** *U.S.* a similar fishing boat with a well for keeping fish alive. [probably < Dutch *smak*]

Smack[3] (def. 1)

smack-dab (smak′dab′), *adv. U.S. Informal.* directly; squarely; smack: *Then he zagged to his right and ran smack-dab through a fence* (New York Times). *If there was ever an Irishman body and soul, Mr. O'Casey is one. His heart is smack-dab in the middle of Ireland* (New York Times).

smack·er (smak′ər), *n.* **1.** a person or thing that smacks. **2.** *Informal.* a loud kiss; smack. **3.** a resounding blow. **4.** *U.S. Slang.* a dollar: *The price will be somewhere around ten thousand smackers* (Harper's).

smack·ing (smak′ing), *adj.* **1.** lively, brisk, or strong; spanking: *a smacking breeze.* **2.** given with a smack or the sound of a smack: *a smacking blow, a smacking kiss.*

smacks·man (smaks′mən), *n., pl.* **-men.** a person who owns or works on a smack.

small (smôl), *adj.* **1.** not large or great; little in size; not large as compared with other things of the same kind: *a small house, a small country or city.* **2.** not fully grown or developed; young: *small boys, small plants.* **3.** not great in amount, degree, extent, duration, value, strength, etc.: *a small dose, small hope of success. The cent is our smallest coin.* **4.** having low value or rank; low: *to play a small trump.* **5.** not important; of little interest: *Don't bother Mother with that small matter.* **6. a.** of low social position; poor: *Both great and small people mourned Lincoln's death.* **b.** of poor or minor ability, reputation, etc.; ordinary: *to make a small start. A small author, and smaller wit* (Benjamin Disraeli). **7.** having little land, capital, etc.; dealing, doing business, etc., on a limited scale: *a small farmer. A man who keeps a little shop is a small dealer.* **8.** having or showing littleness of mind or character; mean: *A boy with a small nature is not generous. A small-minded person attacks people for petty reasons.* **9.** gentle; soft; low: *the still, small voice of conscience.* **10.** diluted; weak. **11.** (of letters) not capital; lower-case.

feel small, to be ashamed or humiliated: *Mrs. Smith's kindness to Jack after he had broken her window made him feel small.*

no small, great; considerable: *a man of no small curiosity.*

—*adv.* **1.** into small pieces. **2.** in low tones. **3.** in a small manner.

sing small. See under **sing,** *v.*

—*n.* **1.** a small person, animal, or thing. **2.** the small, slender, or narrow part: *the small of the back.*

smalls, a. parcels, commodities, consignments, etc., of little size or weight: *Hitherto in Birmingham "smalls" had been defined to be quantities less than 2 cwt.* (London Times). **b.** knee breeches; smallclothes: *He whisked away our smalls and washed them with loving care* (Punch). **c.** *British Informal.* the first of three examinations which candidates for the degree of B.A. at Oxford University are required to pass; responsions: *I ought to be going up for smalls myself next term* (Thomas Hughes).

[Old English *smæl* slender, narrow] —**small′ness,** *n.* —**Syn.** *adj.* **1.** diminutive, undersized, tiny, minute. See **little. 3.** slight, inconsiderable. **5.** trifling, insignificant, trivial. **8.** selfish, illiberal, stingy.

small·age (smô′lij), *n.* celery, especially in its wild state, growing in marshy places, with the leafstalks little developed and having a sharp scent and bitter taste. [earlier *smalege,* Middle English *smale ache* < *smal* small + *ache* smallage; any celery or parsley < Old French *ache* < Latin *apium* parsley, or a related plant]

small ale, ale of low alcoholic strength, often made without hops; weak or light ale.

small arms, firearms that can be easily carried and used by a single person, such as rifles, pistols, submachine guns, etc.

small beer, 1. weak beer. **2.** matters or persons of little or no importance; trifles: *The economic problems that the east German State is now having to face are small beer compared with the problems it has already overcome* (Listener).

think small beer of, *Informal.* to have a poor or low opinion of: *She thinks small beer of painters, . . .—well, we don't think small beer of ourselves* (Thackeray).

small-bore (smôl′bôr′, -bōr′), *adj.* **1.** having a relatively narrow diameter or bore: *a small-bore pipe.* **2.** (of a rifle) firing a bullet of .22 caliber.

small calorie, the quantity of heat necessary to raise the temperature of a gram of water 1 degree centigrade; gram calorie.

small capital, a capital letter that is slightly smaller than the regular capital letter. This sentence shows 7½-point REGULAR CAPITALS and SMALL CAPITALS. *Abbr.:* s.c.

small change, 1. coins of small value, such as nickels, dimes, etc. **2.** anything small and unimportant: *We must teach our students to manipulate the small change of language, the common coinage of everyday talk* (Donald J. Lloyd).

small circle, a circle on the surface of a sphere whose plane does not pass through the center of the sphere.

small·clothes (smôl′klōz′, -klōᴛʜz′), *n.pl.* knee breeches, especially close-fitting ones, worn by men in the 1700's.

Small Cloud, the smaller of the two Magellanic Clouds, located in the constellation Tucana: *It has been possible to determine that the Small Cloud has basically the same spiral pattern as the Large Cloud* (Scientific American).

small coal, 1. slack; coal of small size. **2.** *Obsolete.* charcoal.

small cranberry, a small cranberry of Europe, Asia, and North America; European cranberry.

small fry, 1. babies or children; small or young creatures: *Small fry and their mothers may share similar creative art experiences at the People's Art Center* (New York Times). **2.** small fish. **3.** unimportant people or things: *The forest giants among the trees do not kill the small fry under them* (Scientific American).

small·hold·er (smôl′hōl′dər), *n.* a farmer who works a smallholding: *An aristocracy of planters . . . and a multitude of smallholders, grew cotton for the world by slave-labour* (Sir Winston Churchill).

small·hold·ing (smôl′hōl′ding), *n.* **1.** a piece of land smaller than an ordinary farm: *The workers each had their own smallholding of about an acre and had their own live stock — chickens, pigs, and cows* (Manchester Guardian). **2.** the practice or occupation of working such a piece of land.

small hours, the early hours of the morning, just after midnight: *Parliament adjourned in the small hours yesterday after both Chambers had sat late to deal with outstanding bills* (London Times).

small intestine, the slender part of the bowels, extending from the stomach to the large intestine, about twenty feet long in grown people: *The lower end of the small intestine opens into the side of the large intestine* (Beauchamp and West). See **intestine** for picture.

small·ish (smô′lish), *adj.* somewhat small; rather small: *Laura was smallish and dark, and disliked games* (Harper's).

small letter, an ordinary letter, not a capital; a lower-case letter.

small-mind·ed (smôl′mīn′did), *adj.* narrow-minded; petty; mean. —**small′-mind′ed·ness,** *n.*

small·mouth (smôl′mouth′), *n.* the smallmouth bass.

smallmouth bass, a North American fresh-water game fish similar to the largemouth bass, but with a shorter upper jaw and a weight of up to about 11 pounds; black bass.

small-mouthed black bass (smôl′mouᴛʜd′, -moutht′), the smallmouth bass.

small of the back, the narrowest part of the back.

small pastern bone, the lower of two pastern bones between the fetlock and the hoof of a horse, donkey, mule, etc.

small pica, 11-point type.

small potatoes, *U.S. Informal.* an unimportant person or thing; unimportant persons or things: *Against these increases, the cuts in spending looked like very small potatoes indeed* (Newsweek).

small·pox (smôl′poks′), *n.* a highly contagious disease, characterized by fever and blisterlike eruptions on the skin that often leave permanent scars shaped like little pits: *Smallpox is a viral disease that has been* *brought under control by the use of vaccine ...* (Sidonie M. Gruenberg). [< *small* + *pox,* for *pocks,* plural of *pock*]

smalls (smôlz), *n.pl.* See under **small,** *n.*

small saphenous vein, a large vein of the leg extending along the outer and posterior side.

small-scale (smôl′skāl′), *adj.* **1.** involving few persons or things; limited: *a small-scale offensive, operation, or business. Syria's own resources are adequate for only small-scale projects* (Wall Street Journal). **2.** made or drawn to a small scale: *a small-scale model. A small-scale map leaves out many details and covers a much larger area, such as the world* (World Book Encyclopedia).

small slam, *Bridge.* a little slam: *Secondly, the optimum contract might be a small slam in spades, bid and played by me* (Manchester Guardian).

small stores, (in the U.S. Navy) articles for personal use such as tobacco, soap, needles and thread, etc., for which the men pay.

small stuff, (on a ship) spun yarn, marline, houseline, and other small ropes.

small·sword (smôl′sôrd′, -sōrd′), *n.* (in fencing) a light sword tapering from the hilt to the point and designed for thrusting.

small talk, conversation about unimportant matters; chit-chat: *He mingled freely with other delegates, trying to make small talk and little jokes* (New York Times).

small-time (smôl′tīm′), *adj. Slang.* not first-rate; of lesser importance or consequence; mediocre: *It's a private-eye novel but you've not met (in fiction) an eye like small-time operative Barney Harris, who never had a criminal case before* (New York Times).

small-tim·er (smôl′tī′mər), *n. Slang.* a person who is small-time, especially a small-time hoodlum.

small-town (smôl′toun′), *adj. Especially U.S.* **1.** of or from a small town: *The father of the present editor was a wonderful small-town newspaperman* (New Yorker). **2.** as a small town is supposed to be; narrow; provincial: *Cosmopolitans, they do not sink into the ruts of a small-town life* (Harper's).

small-town·er (smôl′tou′nər), *n. Especially U.S.* a small-town person: *... the small-towners wearing their set, starched faces, all fever and suspicion, and proud to be there* (Atlantic).

smalt (smôlt), *n.* **1.** common glass colored a deep-blue by an oxide of cobalt and, after cooling, finely pulverized for use as a pigment: *Cobalt compounds, such as cobalt blue, ceruleum, new blue, smalt ... are used as pigments by artists and interior decorators, and in ceramics* (World Book Encyclopedia). **2.** the pigment prepared from this glass. [< Middle French *smalt,* or Italian *smalto* < Medieval Latin *smaltum,* apparently < a Germanic word]

smalt·ine (smôl′tin, -tēn), *n.* smaltite.

smalt·ite (smôl′tīt), *n.* a tin-white to steel-gray mineral consisting essentially of an arsenide of cobalt, but usually containing also nickel, and occurring in crystals or in compact or granular masses.

smal·to (zmäl′tō), *n., pl.* **-ti** (-tē). *Italian.* **1.** a colored glass or enamel used in mosaics. **2.** a piece of it.

smar·agd (smar′agd), *n.* emerald. [< Old French *smaragde* < Latin *smaragdus* < Greek *smáragdos*]

sma·rag·dine (smə rag′din), *adj.* of an emerald color. —*n.* an emerald.

sma·rag·dite (smə rag′dīt), *n.* a brilliant grass-green or emerald-green variety of amphibole. [< French *smaragdite* < Greek *smáragdos* smaragd + French *-ite* -ite[1]]

smarm (smärm), *Informal.* —*v.i.* to behave in an offensively flattering or toadying manner: *Her way of smarming up to the rich was disgusting.* —*n.* gushiness; slobber: *... a public conditioned by the melodic froth and smarm of the Viennese school* (Punch). [variant of dialectal *smalm;* origin unknown]

smarm·y (smär′mē), *adj.,* **smarm·i·er, smarm·i·est.** *Informal.* offensively flattering or ingratiating: *a smarmy smugness.*

smart (smärt), *adj.* **1.** sharp and severe; stinging: *He gave the horse a smart blow.* **2.** keen; active; lively: *They walked at a smart pace.* **3. a.** quick at learning; clever and bright: *a smart student.* **b.** sharp and shrewd in dealing with others: *a smart businessman.* **c.** witty, superficial, and often somewhat impertinent: *a smart reply.* **4. a.** fresh and neat in appearance: *smart in his uniform.* **b.** stylish; fashionable: *a smart hat, a smart hotel. Beth has a smart new dress.* **5.** *Informal or Dialect.* fairly large; considerable: *to walk a right smart distance. Madame ... left a smart legacy to the ... children* (Thackeray). **6.** *Archaic.* causing sharp pain. [Old English *smeart*]

—*adv.* in a smart manner. [< adjective]

—*v.i.* **1.** to feel sharp pain: *His eyes smarted from the smoke.* **2.** to cause sharp pain: *The cut smarts.* **3.** to feel distress or irritation: *He smarted from the scolding.* **4.** to suffer severely: *He shall smart for this.* —*v.t.* to cause sharp pain to or in.

[Old English *smeortan*]

—*n.* **1.** a sharp pain. **2.** keen mental suffering; grief; sorrow; remorse.

[< verb] —**smart′ly,** *adv.* —**smart′ness,** *n.*

smart al·eck (al′ik), *U.S. Informal.* a conceited, obnoxious person.

smart-al·eck·ism (smärt′al′ə kiz əm), *n. U.S. Informal.* behavior or language characteristic of a smart aleck: *The critic who depends on smart-aleckism to gain readership can damage reputations and spread false imputations* (Thomas H. Creighton).

smart-al·eck·y (smärt′al′ə kē), *adj. U.S. Informal.* like that of a smart aleck; cocky; pretentious; conceited: *The writing verges on the smart-alecky, but it is certainly entertaining* (Harper's).

smart·en (smär′tən), *v.t., v.i.* **1.** to improve in appearance; brighten: *The Council of Industrial Design felt sufficiently encouraged to open a souvenir section of its Design Index, with the object of smartening up tourist souvenirs* (Punch). **2.** to make or become brisker: *He choreographed three new ballets for the company and smartened up its dancing in general* (New Yorker).

smart money, 1. *U.S. Informal.* **a.** money for betting or investing by persons with special knowledge or experience, as on sporting events, the stock market, etc.: *The first game, at Yankee Stadium, made the smart money seem safe* (Time). **b.** the informed speculators or betters. **2.** *British.* **a.** money allowed to soldiers and sailors for injuries received while on service. **b.** money paid to obtain the discharge of a recruit. **c.** any compensation for injury. **3.** legal damages in excess of the injury done, as for gross misconduct on the part of the defendant. **4.** money paid to escape some unpleasant engagement or situation.

smart set, the extremely fashionable section of society.

smart·weed (smärt′wēd′), *n.* any of various weeds of the buckwheat family growing in low or wet places, as the water pepper.

smart·y (smär′tē), *n., pl.* **smart·ies,** *adj.,* **smart·i·er, smart·i·est.** *Informal.* —*n.* a would-be smart, clever, or witty person. —*adj.* cocky; pretentious: *Not a bad line, either, he conceded, except there were no smarty lawyers around to bring in a writ of habeas corpus* (Margery Allingham).

smart·y-pants (smär′tē pants′), *n. U.S. Slang.* a person who acts as if he knows everything; an intellectual snob; wiseacre.

smash (smash), *v.t.* **1. a.** to break into pieces with violence and noise: *to smash a window. The boat was smashed on the rocks.* **b.** to flatten by a crushing force: *to smash a hat.* **c.** to break, beat, or dash (in, off, down, etc.) with violence: *to smash a cup against a wall, to smash a door in, to smash a lock off.* **2.** to destroy; ruin: *to smash a person's hopes, to smash an argument.* **3.** to crush; defeat: *to smash an attack.* **4.** *Informal.* to cause to fail financially; bankrupt. **5.** to hit (a tennis ball) with a hard, fast overhand stroke; kill. **6.** to hit (a person or thing) with a hard blow. —*v.i.* **1.** to be broken to pieces: *The dishes smashed on the floor as the tray upset.* **2.** to rush violently; crash: *The car smashed into a tree.* **3.** to become ruined; fail financially; become bankrupt.

—*n.* **1. a.** a violent breaking; shattering; crash: *the smash of two automobiles.* **b.** the sound of a smash or crash: *the smash of broken glass. We heard a smash in the kitchen.* **2.** a crushing defeat; disaster; overthrow. **3.** a business failure; bankruptcy. **4.** a hard blow. **5.** a hard, fast overhand stroke in tennis. **6.** a drink made of water, mint, sugar, and brandy or other alcoholic liquor, served with ice: *I had a couple of smashes and marched in* (Maclean's). **7.** *U.S. Informal.* a smash hit: *"Guys and Dolls" — Broadway's musical smash ...* (Newsweek).

to smash, a. into broken pieces; into bits: *to break, fly, or go to smash.* **b.** to ruin: *The ... arrangements all went to smash* (Thomas Henry Huxley).

—*adj. U.S. Informal.* highly successful; very profitable: *a smash Broadway musical.* [origin uncertain. Compare Norwegian *smaske* smash to bits.] —**smash′er,** *n.*

—**Syn.** *v.t.* **1. a.** shatter. See **break. 1. b.** crush. **1. c.** batter. **2.** overcome, overwhelm, wreck.

smash·a·ble (smash′ə bəl), *adj.* that can be smashed.

smash-and-grab (smash′and grab′, -ən-), *adj. Especially British.* of or having to do with a robbery committed by smashing a shop window and snatching the goods displayed inside: *Thieves made five smash-and-grab raids during dense fog in Nottingham last night* (London Times).

smash·er·oo (smash′ə rü′), *n. Slang.* a smash hit: *Even the best-laid plans tend to bend before a runaway box office smasheroo* (Punch).

smash hit, *Especially U.S.* a highly successful performance or production, as of a play, motion picture, etc.: *It is a truism that Broadway critics are dangerously omnipotent, able to create a smash hit overnight or to kill a play stone dead* (Manchester Guardian Weekly).

smash·ing (smash′ing), *adj.* **1.** that smashes; shattering; crushing: *a smashing blow.* **2.** *Especially British Slang.* fine; excellent; splendid: *"Smashing" and "wizard" ... seem to have replaced the "ripping" of earlier days* (Holiday). —**smash′ing·ly,** *adv.*

smash-up (smash′up′), *n.* **1.** a bad collision; wreck: *But few people know the Air Force loses more personnel in auto smash-ups than in air accidents (83 killed in cars in two years; 72 in airplanes)* (Maclean's). **2.** a business failure; bankruptcy. **3.** a great misfortune; disaster. **4.** a failure in health; crack-up.

smatch (smach), *n. Archaic.* **1.** a smack, taste, or flavor. **2.** a trace or touch: *Thy life hath had some smatch of honour in it* (Shakespeare). **3.** a smattering: *... some Latin, and a smatch of Greek* (William Cowper). [Middle English *smach,* alteration of Old English *smæc* smack[1]]

smat·ter (smat′ər), *n.* slight knowledge; a smattering.

—*v.t.* **1.** to speak (a language) with only slight knowledge of it: *She could read, and write, and dance, and sing ... and smatter French* (Tobias Smollett). **2.** to study or learn superficially. —*v.i.* to have a slight or superficial knowledge.

smat·ter·er (smat′ər ər), *n.* a person who smatters; dabbler.

smat·ter·ing (smat′ər ing), *n.* **1.** slight or superficial knowledge: *a smattering of French.* **2.** a small amount or number: *Today some 15 firms offer on tape over 200 selections, most of them classical or semi-classical, compared with only a smattering two years ago* (Wall Street Journal). —*adj.* slight; superficial; imperfect: *a smattering knowledge of Russian.* —**smat′ter·ing·ly,** *adv.*

smaze (smāz), *n.* a combination of smoke and haze in the air.

sm. c. or **sm. caps.,** small capitals.

smear (smir), *v.t.* **1.** to cover or stain with anything sticky, greasy, or dirty: *She smeared her fingers with jam.* **2.** to rub or spread (oil, grease, paint, etc.): *to smear paint on one's hands.* **3.** to rub or wipe (a brush, hand, cloth, etc.) so as to make a mark or stain: *... smearing his sleeve across his mouth* (Dickens). **4.** to harm; soil; spoil: *to smear a person's good reputation.* **5.** *U.S. Slang.* to defeat; overwhelm. —*v.i.* to receive a mark or stain; be smeared: *Wet paint smears easily.* [Old English *smerian* rub with oil]

—*n.* **1.** a mark or stain left by smearing: *She put her lips to the bandage and left a little smear of orange lipstick* (Graham Greene). **2.** a small amount of something spread on a slide for microscopic examination, or on the surface of a culture medium. **3.** a mixture for glazing pottery by evaporating salt or other substances. **4.** the act of smearing a person's reputation; slander: *Criticism, as an instrument not of inquiry and reform, but of power, quickly degenerates into the techniques of deceit and smear* (Harper's). [Old English *smeoru* grease]

smear·case (smir′kās′), *n. U.S. Dialect.* cottage cheese. [< German *Schmierkäse* < *schmieren* to smear + *Käse* cheese]

smear·i·ness (smir′ē nis), *n.* the quality or condition of being smeared or smeary.

smear·y (smir′ē), *adj.*, **smear·i·er, smear·i·est.** **1.** smeared. **2.** tending to smear.

smec·tic (smek′tik), *adj.* **1.** cleansing; abstersive; detergent. **2.** (of crystals) consisting of a series of layers in which the molecules are arranged either in rows or at random. [< Latin *smēcticus* < Greek *smēktikós* < *smḗchein* to wipe; cleanse]

smed·dum (smed′əm), *n. Scottish.* **1.** mettle; spirit. **2.** powder. **3.** the finest part of ground malt. [Old English *smedma* fine powder, especially flour]

smeek (smēk), *n., v. Scottish.* smoke.

smeg·ma (smeg′mə), *n.* a sebaceous secretion, especially that found under the prepuce: *So far little is known about the cancer-producing properties, if any, of smegma* (Observer). [< Latin *smēgma* < Greek *smêgma* a detergent, soap or unguent < *smḗchein* to wipe; cleanse]

smell (smel), *v.*, **smelled** or **smelt, smell·ing,** *n.* —*v.t.* **1.** to perceive with the nose: *to smell smoke in the air.* **2.** to use the sense of smell on (something): *The dog smelled the tramp's legs.* **3.** to find a trace or suggestion of: *to smell danger. We smelled trouble.* —*v.i.* **1.** to use the sense of smelling. **2.** to give out a smell; have a scent: *The rose smells sweet.* **3.** to give out a bad smell; have a bad smell; stink: *Garbage smells.* **4.** to have the smell (of); have the trace (of): *The plan smells of trickery.*

smell out, to hunt or find by smelling or as if by smelling: *to smell out a secret. A dog will smell out a thief.*

smell up, *Informal.* to cause to have a bad smell: *to smell up the house cooking onions.*

—*n.* **1.** the sense of smelling: *Smell is keener in dogs than in men.* **2.** the quality in a thing that affects the sense of smell; odor: *the smell of burning cloth.* **3.** a trace; suggestion: *the smell of injustice.* **4.** an act of smelling; sniff: *to take a smell of something.*

[Middle English *smellen*]

—**Syn.** *n.* **2. Smell, odor** mean the property or quality of a thing that affects the sense organs of the nose. **Smell** is the general word, used especially when the effect on the sense organs is emphasized: *I like the smells in the country after a rain.* **Odor** is often interchanged with *smell,* but emphasizes and applies particularly to the actual property or quality itself, as belonging to and coming from what is smelled: *I find the odor of hay especially pleasing.*

smell·a·ble (smel′ə bəl), *adj.* that can be smelled: *To be smellable, a substance must be soluble in fat or water—preferably both* (Scientific American).

smell·er (smel′ər), *n.* **1.** a person or thing that smells. **2.** a person who tests by smelling. **3.** *Slang.* the nose or sense of smell. **4.** a sensitive hair or process such as one of a cat's whiskers; feeler.

smell-feast (smel′fēst′), *n. Archaic.* a person on the lookout for food at someone else's expense.

smell·ie (smel′ē), *n. Informal.* a motion picture in which odors are adapted to appropriate scenes.

smell·ing salts (smel′ing), a form of ammonia inhaled to relieve faintness, headaches, etc.

smell-less (smel′lis), *adj.* **1.** having no sense of smell. **2.** having no smell; odorless.

smell·y (smel′ē), *adj.*, **smell·i·er, smell·i·est.** having or giving out a strong or unpleasant smell: *I wonder what makes the sea so smelly. I don't like it* (Rudyard Kipling). —**Syn.** noisome, rank.

smelt[1] (smelt), *v.t.* **1.** to melt (ore) in order to get the metal out of it. **2.** to obtain (metal) from ore by melting: *It also smelts some high grade tin from ores* (Wall Street Journal). **3.** to refine (impure metal) by melting.

—*v.i.* **1.** to melt ore to extract metal, or melt metal to refine it. **2.** to be subjected to smelting.

[probably < Middle Low German *smelten* (originally) to melt]

smelt[2] (smelt), *n., pl.* **smelts** or (*collectively*) **smelt.** any of a family of small, edible fish with silvery scales, related to the salmon. Smelts live in cool oceans of the Northern Hemisphere, though some species swim up rivers to spawn and stay permanently in fresh water. [Old English *smelt*]

Smelt[2] (8 to 10 in. long)

smelt[3] (smelt) *v.* a past tense and a past participle of **smell.**

smelt·er (smel′tər), *n.* **1.** a person whose work or business is smelting ores or metals. **2.** a place where ores or metals are smelted. **3.** a furnace for smelting ores.

smelt·er·y (smel′tər ē), *n., pl.* **-er·ies.** a place where ores are smelted.

smew (smyü), *n.* a small, crested, mostly white merganser of northern Europe and Asia. [origin uncertain]

smice (smīs), *n.* a combination of fog and ice crystals in the air; ice-fog: *Smice rears its misty head during the night, sharply reducing visibility but is otherwise unharmful* (New York Times). [blend of *smoke* and *ice*]

smidge (smij), *n. Informal.* a smidgen: *In every case the veal, or the beef, is of good quality, without a smidge of fat or gristle* (New Yorker).

smidg·en or **smidg·eon** (smij′ən), *n. Informal.* a small piece or quantity: *He didn't have a smidgen of proof* (New Yorker). [origin uncertain]

smi·la·ca·ceous (smī′lə kā′shəs), *adj.* belonging to a group of plants of the lily family, as the smilax. [< New Latin *Smilaceae* the lily family (< Latin *smīlax;* see SMILAX) + English *-ous*]

smi·lax (smī′laks), *n.* **1.** a twining, trailing, African plant or vine of the lily family, much used by florists in decoration. **2.** any of a large group of tropical and temperate woody vines of the lily family, with prickly stems, umbrella-shaped clusters of flowers, and small blackish or red berries, as the sarsaparilla plant; greenbrier. [< Latin *smīlax, -acis* < Greek *smîlax, -akos* bindweed]

Branch of Smilax (def.2 —greenbrier)

smile (smīl), *v.*, **smiled, smil·ing,** *n.* —*v.i.* **1.** to look pleased or amused; show pleasure, favor, amusement, kindness, etc., by an upward curve of the mouth: *to smile at a friend. Why do you smile at what I say? One may smile, and smile, and be a villain* (Shakespeare). **2.** to look pleasant; be agreeable; look with favor: *From his early childhood good fortune smiled upon him. A sea that could not cease to smile* (Wordsworth). *The music does not really smile, and, indeed, is of the reserved kind that demands very many hearings* (London Times). **3.** to show scorn, disdain, etc., by a curve of the mouth: *She smiled bitterly.* —*v.t.* **1.** to give (a smile): *She smiled a sunny smile.* **2.** to express by a smile: *She smiled consent.* **3.** to bring, put, drive, etc., by smiling: *Smile your tears away.*

—*n.* **1.** an act of smiling: *a smile of pity. She met his eye with her sweet hospitable smile* (Henry James). **2.** a favoring look or regard; pleasant look or aspect: . . . *the smile of fortune* (Joseph Conrad).

[Middle English *smilen*]

smile·ful (smīl′fəl), *adj.* full of smiles; smiling.

smile·less (smīl′lis), *adj.* without a smile; serious; gloomy; cheerless.

smil·er (smī′lər), *n.* **1.** one who smiles. **2.** one who looks smilingly, as from pleasure, derision, or real or affected agreeableness.

smil·ey (smī′lē), *adj.* smiling; cheerful: *A smiley novel full of dry situation humour . . .* (Punch).

smil·ing (smī′ling), *adj.* that smiles; bright; cheerful; pleasant: *The April countryside is fresh and smiling* (Atlantic). —**smil′ing·ness,** *n.*

smil·ing·ly (smī′ling lē), *adv.* in a smiling manner; with a smile: *President Eisenhower and Premier Bulganin smilingly shook hands at the summit parley* (Time).

smi·lo·don (smī′lə don), *n.* any of a group of the largest saber-toothed tigers, that became extinct in the ice age. [< New Latin *Smilodon* the genus name < Greek *smīlē* knife + *odoús, odóntos* tooth]

smil·y (smī′lē), *adj.* smiley.

smirch (smėrch), *v.t.* to make dirty; soil with soot, dirt, dust, dishonor, disgrace, etc.: *This is an attempt by the Attorney General to smirch the union* (James Hoffa). —*n.* a dirty mark; blot; stain. [Middle English *smorchen* to discolor] —**smirch′er,** *n.* —**Syn.** *v.t.* sully.

smirk (smėrk), *v.i.* to smile in an affected, silly, self-satisfied way. —*n.* an affected, silly, self-satisfied smile. [compare Old English *smearcian* to smile]

smirk·y (smėr′kē), *adj.*, **smirk·i·er, smirk·i·est.** of the nature of a smirk; simpering: *a smirky smile.*

smit (smit), *v.* a past participle of **smite.**

smitch (smich), *n. Informal.* a particle; bit: *They didn't increase the visibility a smitch* (New Yorker). [origin uncertain. Compare SMIDGEN.]

smite (smīt), *v.*, **smote, smit·ten** or **smit, smit·ing.** —*v.t.* **1.** to strike; strike hard; hit hard: *The hero smote the giant with his sword. . . . those strange-looking instruments [golf clubs] which are used for smiting the little white ball* (Wall Street Journal). **2.** to affect with a sudden pain, disease, etc.: *The thief's conscience smote him. A grief that smites my very heart at root* (Shakespeare). **3.** to strike down; punish severely; destroy: *The Lord shall smite the proud* (John Greenleaf Whittier). —*v.i.* **1.** to come with force (upon): *The sound of a blacksmith's hammer smote upon their ears.* **2.** to come (together) forcibly or in conflict; strike or dash (on or against something): *His heart turned within him and his knees smote together* (Washington Irving).

[Old English *smītan*]

smit·er (smī′tər), *n.* **1.** a person or thing that smites or strikes. **2.** *Obsolete.* a sword; scimitar: *Put thy smiter up, and hear; I dare not tell the truth to a drawn sword* (Ben Jonson).

smith (smith), *n.* **1.** a man who makes or shapes things out of metal. **2.** a blacksmith. [Old English *smith*] —**Syn. 1.** metalworker.

smith·er·eens (smiᴛʜ′ə rēnz′), *n.pl. Informal.* small pieces; bits: *to smash a chair into smithereens.* [apparently < Irish *smidirin*]

smith·ers (smiᴛʜ′ərz), *n.pl. Informal.* smithereens.

smith·er·y (smith′ər ē), *n., pl.* **-er·ies. 1.** the work or craft of a smith. **2.** a smithy.

Smith·i·an (smith′ē ən), *adj.* of or having to do with Adam Smith, 1723-1790, a Scottish economist, or his economic doctrines: *Who can dispute the . . . Smithian righteousness of your position as a sound conservative, forever pointing with alarm* (Wall Street Journal).

Smith·so·ni·an Institution (smith sō′nē ən), an institution in Washington, D.C., founded to increase and spread knowledge by providing money for scientific research and publication, and exhibits of discoveries and inventions. [< James *Smithson,* 1765-1829, English chemist and mineralogist, who founded it]

smith·son·ite (smith′sə nīt), *n.* **1.** native carbonate of zinc. *Formula:* $ZnCO_3$ **2.** *British.* hemimorphite, a native hydrous silicate of zinc. *Formula:* $(ZnOH)_2SiO_3$ [< James *Smithson* (see SMITHSONIAN INSTITUTION) + *-ite*[1]]

smith·work (smith′wėrk′), *n.* the work of a smith; work in metals.

smith·y (smith′ē, smiᴛʜ′-), *n., pl.* **smith·ies,** *v.*, **smith·ied, smith·y·ing.** —*n.* the workshop of a smith, especially a blacksmith; forge: *Under a spreading chestnut tree The village smithy stands* (Longfellow). —*v.t.* to forge as a blacksmith.

smit·ten (smit′ən), *adj.* **1.** hard hit; struck. **2.** suddenly and strongly affected: *Sammy was smitten with show business about as soon as he could take a few dance steps* (Time). **3.** very much in love.

—*v.* a past participle of **smite:** *The giant was smitten by the sword of the knight.*

—**Syn.** *adj.* **3.** enamored.

smock (smok), *n.* **1.** a loose outer garment worn to protect clothing. **2.** *Archaic.* a chemise.

—*v.t.* **1.** to ornament (a dress, smock, etc.) with a honeycomb pattern made of lines of stitches crossing each other diagonally: *Friede, that beloved niece for whom her aunt had smocked frocks and embellished the collars with forget-me-nots . . .* (New Yorker). **2.** to clothe in a smock.

[Old English *smoc*]

smock frock, a smock reaching to the middle of the leg, worn especially by laborers in Europe.

smock·ing (smok′ing), *n.* a honeycomb pattern made of lines of stitches crossing each other diagonally and gathering the material, used to ornament smocks, dresses, etc.: *I wore brown holland smocks for everyday . . . blue serge with scarlet smocking for winter* (New Yorker).

smock mill, a type of windmill in which the mill house is fixed and only the top revolves with the wind: *The smock mill—the name taken from a fancied resemblance to the countryman's dress—was introduced from Holland* (London Times).

smog (smog), *n.* a combination of smoke and fog in the air: *Automobile exhaust fumes were blamed as one of the major causes of smog* (New York Times). [blend of *smoke* and *fog*]

smog·gy (smog′ē), *adj.* full of smog: *There was a virus in the . . . smoky, smoggy air* (Newsweek).

smok·a·ble (smō′kə bəl), *adj.* fit to be smoked: *The cigarette was bent in a couple of places, but it was smokable* (John O'Hara). —*n.* **smokables,** tobacco, especially in the form of cigars or cigarettes: *A fiendish consumer of cigars, the man had smokables bulging in his every jacket pocket.*

smoke (smōk), *n., v.,* **smoked, smok·ing.** —*n.* **1. a.** a mixture that can be seen of gases and particles of carbon that rise when anything burns; cloud from anything burning. **b.** a mass, cloud, or column caused by anything burning. **2.** something resembling this. **3. a.** something unsubstantial, quickly passing, or without value or result: *The affair ended in smoke.* **b.** something that clouds or is meant to confuse or hide an issue, etc. **4.** that which is smoked; cigar, cigarette, pipe, etc.: *A woman is only a woman, but a good Cigar is a Smoke* (Rudyard Kipling). **5.** an act or period of smoking tobacco. **6.** *Chemistry.* a colloidal system consisting of solid particles dispersed in a gas.

go up in smoke, to come to nothing; be unrealized; be without results: *Cardiff City's brave achievement, which won its full hour of praise, has gone up in smoke* (London Times).

watch one's smoke, *U.S. Slang.* to observe one's actions: *Out come the brandy, the long johns, the parka, and the racing goggles —and Lordy, watch his smoke* (Time).

—*v.i.* **1.** to give off smoke or steam, or something like it: *The fireplace smokes.* **2.** to move with great speed. **3.** to draw in and puff out the smoke of burning tobacco.

—*v.t.* **1.** to draw the smoke from (a pipe, cigar, or cigarette) into the mouth and puff it out again. **2.** to expose to the action of smoke. **3.** to cure (meat, fish, etc.) by exposing to smoke: *People smoke fish to preserve them.* **4.** to drive (out) by smoke, or as if by smoke: *to smoke bees out of a nest in an old tree.* **5.** to color, darken, or stain with smoke. **6.** to make, bring, pass, etc., by smoking. **7.** *Archaic.* to find out; suspect; notice. **8.** *Archaic.* to make fun of; ridicule.

smoke out, a. to drive out with smoke, as an animal from its hole: *We tried to smoke the woodchuck out of its hole.* **b.** to find out and make known: *. . . a set of traitors, who . . . will be smoked out like a nest of wasps* (Cardinal Newman).

[Old English *smoca*]

—**Syn.** *n.* **2.** fume, reek.

smoke ball, a spherical case filled with a composition which, while burning, emits a great quantity of smoke, used for concealment or for annoying an enemy's workmen in siege operations.

smoke-blue (smōk′blü′), *n., adj.* bluish gray: *A smoke-blue haze hangs over the mountains* (Atlantic).

smoke bomb, a bomb that gives off a dense cloud of smoke, used especially to conceal military movements.

smoke bush, smoke tree.

smoke-col·ored (smōk′kul′ərd), *adj.* of a dull-gray or brownish-gray color: *Smoke-colored cats have hair that is white at the base and black at the tips* (World Book Encyclopedia).

smoked (smōkt), *adj.* **1.** treated or cured with smoke: *Evenings Erhard dined heavily on Franconian smoked meat and dumplings* (Time). **2.** darkened by smoke: *smoked glass.* **3.** gray: *smoked pearl.*

smoke-dry (smōk′drī′), *v.t.,* **-dried, -dry·ing.** to dry or cure by exposing to smoke: *He cut up and smoke-dried the flesh* (W.H. Hudson).

smoke-eat·er (smōk′ē′tər), *n. U.S. Slang.* a fireman, especially of the U.S. Forest Service: *Smoke-eaters slash forest fire losses with the aid of World War II torpedo bombers* (Wall Street Journal).

smoke-filled room (smōk′fild′), *U.S.* a room in which influential politicians meet in private, especially at a political convention, to plan strategy or make deals: *The campaign for the Democratic nomination may well be decided in a smoke-filled room* (Newsweek). [in allusion to a hotel room in Chicago at which the decision to nominate Warren G. Harding as the Republican presidential candidate in 1920 was supposed to have been reached]

smoke·house (smōk′hous′), *n.* a building or place in which meat, fish, etc., are treated with smoke to keep them from spoiling. [American English < *smoke* + *house*]

smoke·jack (smōk′jak′), *n.* an apparatus for turning a roasting spit, set in motion by the current of rising gases in a chimney.

smoke jumper, a member of a unit of the U.S. Forest Service trained to parachute into remote areas to fight forest fires.

smoke·less (smōk′lis), *adj.* **1.** making or giving off little or no smoke: *smokeless fuel.* **2.** having little or no smoke. —**smoke′less·ly,** *adv.*

smokeless powder, a substitute for ordinary gunpowder that gives off little or no smoke when it explodes.

smoke pipe, the pipe that connects a furnace to the chimney.

smoke·pot (smōk′pot′), *n.* a pot for burning a mixture of fuels in order to produce a smoke screen.

smok·er (smō′kər), *n.* **1.** a person who smokes tobacco. **2.** a railroad car or a part of it where smoking is allowed. **3.** an informal gathering of men for smoking and entertainment. **4.** a person who smokes meat, fish, etc. **5.** something which throws out much smoke, as a smoky locomotive, or a device for smoking out bees: *After a piece of burlap has been ignited and stuffed into the tin, the bellows of the smoker is pumped (not too hard lest flames come out and scorch the bees' wings)* (New York Times).

smoke ring, smoke forced out between the lips of a smoker in the shape of a ring: *A gay blade of the 90's blew smoke rings in the eyes of his lady friend* (Newsweek).

smoke room, a smoking room.

smok·er·y (smō′kə rē), *n., pl.* **-er·ies.** a place in which to smoke; a smoking room.

smoke screen, 1. a mass of thick smoke used to hide a ship, airplane, etc., from the enemy. **2.** anything that serves some such purpose: *Seasoned observers of the Irish scene believe that the Partition provides an ideological smoke screen for a policy embarrassing to most Irishmen* (Newsweek).

smoke signal, 1. a signal made with smoke, usually by covering and uncovering a fire, used especially by American Indians. **2.** an indication; sign; trend: *The nation's purchasing agents are a tough-minded down-to-earth group of businessmen who keep their eyes peeled for every economic smoke signal* (Newsweek).

smoke·stack (smōk′stak′), *n.* **1.** a tall chimney: *. . . the broad expanse of roofs, the long, slanting conveyor belts, and the dark smokestacks characteristic of mines all over the world* (New Yorker). **2.** a pipe that discharges smoke, etc., as the funnel of a steamship or locomotive.

smoke tree, a small tree or shrub of the cashew family, with flower clusters that look somewhat like tiny puffs of smoke; feather tree.

smok·i·ly (smō′kə lē), *adv.* in a smoky manner; with much smoke; like smoke.

smok·i·ness (smō′kē nis), *n.* the state of being smoky.

smok·ing (smō′king), *n.* **1.** the act of a person or thing that smokes. **2.** the act or practice of smoking tobacco: *Captain Nutter gradually gave up smoking, which is an untidy, injurious . . . and highly pleasant habit* (Thomas B. Aldrich).

smoking car, a smoker on a train.

smoking jacket, a lounging jacket to be worn while smoking, originally to protect the clothing.

smoking room, a room set apart for smoking, as in a hotel, clubhouse, etc.: *. . . a prearranged rendezvous in a theater smoking room* (Time).

smo·ko (smō′kō), *n. Australian Slang.* a short period of rest, especially for workers.

smok·y (smō′kē), *adj.,* **smok·i·er, smok·i·est. 1. a.** giving off much smoke: *a smoky fire.* **b.** tending to send smoke out into the room: *a smoky fireplace.* **2.** full of smoke: *a smoky room.* **3.** darkened or stained with smoke: *the smoky buildings of a great industrial city.* **4.** like smoke; suggesting smoke: *a smoky gray, a smoky taste.* —**Syn. 3.** sooty.

smoky quartz, a brownish-yellow quartz; cairngorm.

smol·der (smōl′dər), *v.i.* **1.** to burn and smoke without flame: *The campfire smoldered for hours after the blaze died down.* **2.** to exist inwardly with little or no outward sign: *The people's discontent smoldered for years before it broke out into open rebellion.* **3.** to show suppressed feeling: *His eyes smoldered with anger.* [< noun]

—*n.* **1.** a slow, smoky burning without flame; smoldering fire. **2.** a feeling of heated emotion: *a smolder of indignation.* Also, **smoulder.**

[Middle English *smolder;* origin uncertain]

smolt (smōlt), *n.* a young salmon with silvery scales, that is no longer a parr, and is ready to descend, or has descended, to the sea for the first time. [Middle English *smolt.* Probably related to SMELT[2].]

smooch[1] (smüch), *v.t., n. U.S.* smudge.

smooch[2] (smüch), *v.i., v.t., n. U.S. Slang.* kiss. [alteration of *smouch*]

smoodge (smüj), *v.i. Australian.* **1.** to curry favor. **2.** to kiss.

smooth (smüᴛʜ), *adj.* **1.** having an even surface, like glass, silk, or still water; flat; level: *smooth stones, a smooth tire, a smooth road or path.* **2.** free from unevenness or roughness; proceeding evenly, calmly, or gently: *smooth sailing, a smooth voyage, a smooth landing, the smooth operation of a well-oiled machine.* **3.** without lumps: *smooth sauce.* **4.** without hair: *a smooth face, smooth leaves.* **5.** without trouble or difficulty; easy: *a smooth course of affairs.* **6.** calm; serene: *a smooth temper.* **7. a.** polished; pleasant; polite: *That salesman is a smooth talker.* **b.** too polished, pleasant, or polite to be sincere. **8.** not harsh in sound or taste: *smooth verses, a smooth wine.* **9.** (in Greek grammar) unaspirated.

—*adv.* in a smooth manner: *The course of true love never did run smooth* (Shakespeare).

—*v.t.* **1.** to make smooth or smoother; give an even, level, or glossy surface to: *Smooth the board with sandpaper before you paint it. He smoothed out the ball of crushed paper and read it.* **2.** to make easy; free from difficulty: *His tact smoothed the way to an agreement.* **3.** to make less harsh or crude; polish or refine (writing, manners, etc.). **4.** to soothe.

smooth away, to get rid of; iron out: *His problems were minor and were soon smoothed away.*

smooth down, a. to make smooth by pressing down: *She had an infant in one arm, and with the other she smoothed down her apron* (Scott). **b.** to calm; soothe: *She smoothed down her father's temper.*

smooth over, to make (something) seem less wrong, unpleasant, or conspicuous: *The OAS has for some time needed a broker in its ranks to smooth over the differences which last year's Dominican adventure not surprisingly created* (Manchester Guardian Weekly).

—*n.* **1.** an act of smoothing: *She . . . gave one smooth to her hair, and . . . let in her visitor* (Thackeray). **2.** something smooth; a smooth part or place.

[Old English *smōth*] —**smooth′er,** *n.* —**smooth′ly,** *adv.* —**smooth′ness,** *n.*

—**Syn.** *adj.* **1.** plain, sleek, glossy. See **level. 6.** placid, unruffled.

smooth blenny, a European blenny with a smooth skin and no filaments or appendages on the head, found chiefly under stones and in seaweed along the coast; shanny.

smooth·bore (smüᴛʜ′bôr′, -bōr′), *adj.* not rifled: *A smoothbore gun has no grooves in its barrel.* —*n.* a smoothbore gun. [American English < *smooth* + *bore*]

smooth breathing, *Greek Grammar.* **1.** the absence of aspiration of an initial vowel. **2.** the mark (’) placed over a vowel or diphthong to indicate this. [translation of Latin *spiritus lēnis,* a translation of Greek *pneûma psilón*]

smooth collie, a kind of collie with a short, smooth coat.

smooth dogfish, a small shark of the Atlantic Ocean.

smooth·en (smüᴛʜ′ən), *v.t.* to make smooth or smoother. —*v.i.* to become smooth or smoother.

smooth-faced (smüᴛʜ′fāst′), *adj.* **1.** having a smooth face; beardless; clean-shaven. **2.** having a smooth surface. **3.** agreeable in speech and manner; blandly ingratiating: *a smooth-faced hypocrite.*

smooth·ie or **smooth·y** (smü′ᴛʜē), *n., pl.* **smooth·ies.** *U.S. Slang.* a man who speaks, behaves, etc., in a polished manner, often insincerely, especially in trying to impress or court a woman: *The attentions paid to his wife ... by an amorous Hungarian smoothie at last roused him to lash out in the time-honoured manner* (Punch).

smooth muscle, involuntary muscle with fibers in smooth layers or sheets. The muscles of the stomach, intestine, and other viscera (except the heart) are smooth muscles.

smooth skate, a variety of skate of the Atlantic ocean.

smooth-spo·ken (smüᴛʜ′spō′kən), *adj.* speaking easily and plausibly; polished in speech: *a smooth-spoken young lady.*

smooth-talk·ing (smüᴛʜ′tô′king), *adj.* speaking smoothly and persuasively; trying to convince or persuade: *a smooth-talking salesman.*

smooth-tongued (smüᴛʜ′tungd′), *adj.* speaking smoothly; agreeable; plausible: *Poor Miss Canaris, the ingrown spinster, ... has her sad fling with a smooth-tongued crook* (Punch).

smor·gas·bord or **smör·gås·bord** (smôr′gəs bôrd, -bōrd; *Swedish* smœr′gōs bürd), *n.* **1. a.** an elaborate Scandinavian meal, with a large variety of meats, salads, fish, hors d'oeuvres, etc., served from a buffet. **b.** any buffet supper with an elaborate variety of food. **2.** any elaborate variety of things: *But to combat the accompanying inflation it has served up a regular smorgasbord of economic schemes* (Wall Street Journal). [American English < Swedish *smörgåsbord* < *smörgås* open-face sandwich + *bord* table]

smør·re·brød (smœr′ə brœᴛʜ′), *n.* an open-face sandwich served as an hors d'oeuvre. [< Danish *smørrebrød* < *smør* butter + *brød* bread]

smote (smōt), *v.* past tense of **smite.**

smoth·er (smuᴛʜ′ər), *v.t.* **1.** to make unable to get air; kill by depriving of air: *The gas almost smothered the coal miners but they got out in time.* **2.** to cover thickly: *In the fall the grass is smothered with leaves.* **3.** to deaden or put out by covering thickly: *to smother a fire with ashes.* **4. a.** to keep back; check; suppress: *to smother one's fears, to smother a committee's report. He smothered a sharp reply.* **b.** to cover up; conceal: *He smothered a yawn behind his hand.* **5.** to cook in a covered pot or baking dish: *smothered chicken.* —*v.i.* **1.** to be unable to breathe freely; suffocate: *We are smothering in this stuffy room.* **2.** to be suppressed, concealed, or stifled. **3.** *Dialect.* to smolder; burn slowly.
[Middle English *smortheren* suffocate with smoke < *smorther* smother, noun]
—*n.* **1.** a cloud of dust, smoke, spray, etc. **2.** anything that smothers or appears to smother. **3.** an excess of disorder; confusion: *a perfect smother of letters and papers.* **4.** the condition of being smothered. **5.** a smoking or smoldering state or condition.
[Middle English *smorther,* noun < Old English *smorian* to suffocate] —**smoth′er·er,** *n.*

smoth·er·a·tion (smuᴛʜ′ə rā′shən), *n.* the act of smothering, or the state of being smothered; suffocation.

smoth·er·ing·ly (smuᴛʜ′ər ing lē), *adv.* **1.** suffocatingly. **2.** so as to suppress.

smoth·er·y (smuᴛʜ′ər ē), *adj.* tending to smother; full of dust, smoke, spray, etc.; stifling: *a smothery atmosphere.*

smouch (smouch, smüch), *v.i., v.t., n. Archaic.* kiss. [compare German *Schmatz*]

smoul·der (smōl′dər), *v.i., n.* smolder.

s.m.p., without male offspring (Latin, *sine mascula prole*).

smudge (smuj), *n., v.,* **smudged, smudg·ing.** —*n.* **1.** a dirty mark; smear. **2. a.** a smoky fire made to drive away insects or to protect fruit from frost. **b.** any suffocating smoke. **3.** a dirty or smeared condition.
—*v.t.* **1.** to mark with dirty streaks; smear: *The child's drawing was smudged.* **2.** to smoke (an orchard) with a smudge or smudges to fumigate or prevent frostbite. —*v.i.* **1.** to make or leave a stain. **2.** to be smudged.
[origin uncertain. Probably related to SMUTCH.]
—**Syn.** *v.t., v.i.* **1.** stain, blacken, smirch.

smudge pot, a pot for burning oil or other smoke-producing fuels to protect plants and early blooming trees from frost: *Florida's citrus growing belt reported 30 degrees, but smudge pots and burning piles of wood saved most of the crop* (Wall Street Journal).

smudg·i·ly (smuj′ə lē), *adv.* in a smudgy manner.

smudg·i·ness (smuj′ē nis), *n.* the quality or state of being smudgy.

smudg·y (smuj′ē), *adj.,* **smudg·i·er, smudg·i·est.** **1.** smudged; marked with smudges. **2.** smoky. **3.** *British Dialect.* close or sultry: *smudgy air.*

smug (smug), *adj.,* **smug·ger, smug·gest.** **1.** too pleased with one's own goodness, cleverness, respectability, etc.; self-satisfied; complacent: *Nothing disturbs the smug beliefs of some narrow-minded people.* **2.** sleek; neat; trim. [earlier, trim, neat, perhaps < Dutch, Low German *smuk* trim, neat] —**smug′ly,** *adv.* —**smug′ness,** *n.* —**Syn. 2.** spruce.

smug·gle (smug′əl), *v.,* **-gled, -gling.** —*v.t.* **1.** to bring into or take out of a country secretly and against the law: *It is a crime to smuggle opium into the United States.* **2.** to bring, take, put, etc., secretly: *to smuggle presents into the attic.* —*v.i.* to practice smuggling. [earlier *smuckle,* apparently < Low German *smuggeln, smukkeln*]

smug·gler (smug′lər), *n.* **1.** a person who smuggles: *On Libya's unguarded coast near the age-old smugglers' notch of Zuara ...* (Newsweek). **2.** a ship used in smuggling.

smut (smut), *n., v.,* **smut·ted, smut·ting.** —*n.* **1. a.** soot, dirt, etc. **b.** a bit of this: *The controversial aft-placed funnel has been an unqualified success; not a smut, it is claimed, has yet besmirched her virgin decks* (London Times). **2.** a place soiled with smut. **3.** indecent, obscene talk or writing: *Smut Held Cause of Delinquency* (New York Times). **4. a.** a plant disease, especially of cereals, in which the ears of grain are changed to a black dust. **b.** any fungus producing such a disease.
—*v.t.* **1.** to mark or stain with smut; smudge; blacken; soil: *to smut one's hands with coal.* **2.** to affect a (plant) with the disease smut. —*v.i.* **1.** to be soiled with smut. **2.** (of grain) to become affected by smut.
[perhaps variant of Middle English *smotten,* related to Middle High German *smotzen.* Compare Old English *smitte.*]
—**Syn.** *n.* **3.** obscenity, ribaldry.

smut ball, **1.** the ball of black powder into which an ear of grain is changed by the smut fungus. **2.** a puffball.

smutch (smuch), *v.t.* to blacken with soot or dirt; smudge: *Let light forbear those lids; I have forbidden the feathery ash to smutch them* (Elinor Wylie). —*n.* a dirty mark; smudge. [origin uncertain. Probably related to SMUDGE.]

smutch·y (smuch′ē), *adj.,* **smutch·i·er, smutch·i·est.** marked with smutches; dirty.

smut grass, a rushy grass growing in warm regions, with spikes usually blackened by a smut; carpet grass.

smut·ti·ly (smut′ə lē), *adv.* in a smutty manner.

smut·ti·ness (smut′ē nis), *n.* the state or property of being smutty.

smut·ty (smut′ē), *adj.,* **-ti·er, -ti·est.** **1.** soiled with smut, soot, etc.; dirty. **2.** indecent; nasty; obscene: *"Let us not be smutty," appeals Lady Fidget, in the line Dame Edith Evans made famous* (London Times). **3.** having the plant disease smut. **4.** of the color of smut; dusky; dark. —**Syn. 1.** grimy. **2.** pornographic, salacious.

Smyr·ne·an (smėr′nē ən), *adj.* of or having to do with Smyrna, a seaport in western Turkey, on the Aegean Sea, or its people. —*n.* a native or inhabitant of Smyrna.

Smyr·ni·ot (smėr′nē ot) or **Smyr·ni·ote** (smėr′nē ōt), *adj., n.* Smyrnean.

smy·trie (smī′trē, smit′rē), *n. Scottish.* a group; litter. [compare Frisian *smite*]

s.n., without name (Latin, *sine nomine*).

Sn (no period), tin (chemical element).

Sn., Sanitary.

snack (snak), *n.* **1.** a light meal: *to eat a snack before going to bed. We bought a snack at a roadside stand.* **2.** a share; portion. **go snacks,** to have a share (in something): *The Princesses ... were mean enough to go snacks in the profits* (Temple Bar).
[< verb]
—*v.i.* to have a little bit to eat between meals: *He's forever snacking and will always be overweight.*
[Middle English *snaken* to snap (as a dog), perhaps < Middle Low German *snacken.* Compare SNATCH.]
—**Syn.** *n.* **2.** allotment.

snack bar, a lunch counter: *Lunch is often a sandwich and a piece of pie at the cloakroom snack bar* (Time).

snack table, a tray or small top on folding legs upon which a helping of food or refreshments may be placed.

snaf·fle[1] (snaf′əl), *n., v.,* **-fled, -fling.** —*n.* a slender, jointed bit used on a bridle; snaffle bit. —*v.t.* **1.** to control or manage by a snaffle. **2.** to put a snaffle on. [compare Dutch *snavel,* Frisian *snaffel* beak, mouth]

Snaffle

snaf·fle[2] (snaf′əl), *v.t.,* **-fled, -fling.** *Especially British Dialect.* to steal: *He returned to find that some had snaffled a few groceries* (Manchester Guardian Weekly). [origin uncertain]

snaffle bit, a snaffle.

sna·fu (sna fü′), *adj., v.,* **-fued, -fu·ing,** *n. Slang.* —*adj.* being in great disorder; snarled; confused.
—*v.t.* **1.** to put in disorder or in a chaotic state: *Shipments of the same drugs to our most severely hurt allies are snafued in bureaucracy* (Birmingham News). **2.** to mishandle; botch.
—*n.* **1.** a condition of great disorder; chaotic state of affairs: *There were a few inevitable snafus (an unscheduled tornado raised hob at Richmond, Va., and communication lines went dead)* (Newsweek). **2.** anything hopelessly mishandled; botched piece of work: *The former Ambassador ... left in July and snafus over political clearance held up another appointment* (Newsweek).
[< the initial letters of "situation normal—all fouled up"]

snag (snag), *n., v.,* **snagged, snag·ging.** —*n.* **1.** a tree or branch held fast in a river or lake, often forming a hazard to boats: *It required all his attention and skill ... to pilot her clear of sand bars and snags, or sunken trees* (Washington Irving). **2.** any sharp or rough projecting point, such as the broken end of a branch, the point of a nail, etc. **3.** the stump of a tooth; projecting tooth. **4.** a hidden or unexpected obstacle: *His plans hit a snag. The treaty might be signed at the end of this week if no last-minute snags appeared* (New York Times). **5.** an imperfectly developed branch of an antler.
—*v.t.* **1.** to hinder; block as with a snag: *The refugee issue had snagged treaty discussions* (New York Times). **2.** to run or catch on a snag. **3.** to clear of snags. —*v.i.* to run into a snag or obstacle: *Talks snagged on fringe issues* (Wall Street Journal).
[perhaps < Scandinavian (compare Norwegian dialectal *snage* point of land, *snag* stump, spike)]
—**Syn.** *n.* **4.** obstruction, impediment. -*v.t.* **1.** clog, obstruct.

snag boat, a vessel equipped to remove snags, etc., from rivers.

snagged (snagd), *adj.* having snags; jagged.

snag·gle·tooth (snag′əl tüth′), *n., pl.* **-teeth.** a tooth that grows apart from or beyond the others. [perhaps < a diminutive form of *snag* + *tooth*]

snag·gle-toothed (snag′əl tütht′), *adj.* having uneven, broken, or projecting teeth: *a snaggle-toothed grin.*

snag·gy (snag′ē), *adj.,* **-gi·er, -gi·est.** **1.** having snags: *a snaggy tree, a snaggy river.* **2.** projecting sharply or roughly.

snail (snāl), *n.* **1.** any of certain small, soft-bodied mollusks that crawl very slowly. Most snails have spirally coiled shells on their backs into which they can withdraw for protection. There are land snails, fresh water snails, and marine snails. **2.** a lazy, slow-moving person. [Old English *snægel*] —**Syn. 2.** sluggard.

Land Snail (def. 1) (about 1 in. long)

snail bore, a gastropod, as a whelk, etc., which bores and injures oysters.

snail·er·y (snā′lər ē), *n., pl.* **-er·ies.** a place for growing snails for food.

snail fever, a disease of man caused by any

of certain parasitic flatworms whose intermediate host is the mollusk; schistosomiasis.
snail·flower (snāl′flou′ər), *n.* a twining bean, often cultivated in tropical gardens and in greenhouses for its showy white and purple fragrant flowers.
snail·like (snāl′lik′), *adj.* like a snail in moving slowly; snail-paced.
snail-paced (snāl′pāst′), *adj.* very slow in pace or progress; sluggish: ... *the nation's snail-paced arms build-up* (Time).
snail-slow (snāl′slō′), *adj.* as slow as a snail; extremely slow.
snail's pace, a very slow pace: ... *to accelerate our lunar research from a mere snail's pace to a speed which should reveal many new discoveries* ... (Gilbert Fielder).
snake (snāk), *n., v.,* **snaked, snak·ing.** —*n.* **1.** any of a group of long, slender, crawling reptiles without limbs. Some snakes are poisonous. *Snakes have tails, which is not to say they are all tail* (Scientific American). **2.** a sly, treacherous person: *I am not ... a snake, to bite when I have learned to love* (Rudyard Kipling). **3.** anything resembling a snake, as a long, flexible, metal tool used by plumbers to clean out a drain.
—*v.i.* **1.** to move, wind, or curve like a snake: ... *new roads snaking into the mountainous interior* (Wall Street Journal). *Since the train was snaking along at a brisk clip, the diner swayed from side to side* (New Yorker). **2.** to creep along stealthily like a snake.
—*v.t.* **1.** *U.S. Informal.* to drag; haul, especially along the ground with chains or ropes: *Old Sam cut down most of the virgin timber on his farm, snaked it out by mules to his own sawmills* ... (Time). **2.** *U.S. Informal.* to yank; jerk: *to snake a car out of a ditch.* **3.** to clean out (a drain) with a plumber's snake.
[Old English *snaca*] —**snake′like′,** *adj.*
snake·bird (snāk′bėrd′), *n.* **1.** any of certain swimming birds with a long, snaky neck, as the water turkey of America. **2.** *British Dialect.* the wryneck, a bird that habitually twists its neck.

Snakebird
(about 3 ft. long)

snake·bite (snāk′bīt′), *n.* the bite of a snake, especially a poisonous snake: *Snakebite causes thousands of deaths in tropical regions every year* (Scientific American).
snake charmer, a person who is supposed to charm snakes, especially with music: ... *those who hold that it is the snake charmer's secret powers and not his flute that makes the cobra dance* ... (Manchester Guardian).
snake dance, 1. *U.S.* an informal parade of persons dancing in a zigzag line in celebration of a victory, event, etc.: *There were victory rallies and ... snake dances on the Missouri campus* (New Yorker). **2.** a ceremonial dance of the Hopi Indians, in which the dancers carry live snakes as an offering to the rain gods.
snake-dance (snāk′dans′, -däns′), *v.i.,* **-danced, -danc·ing.** to do a snake dance: *20,000 Togolese, shouting "ablode, ablode" (freedom), snake-danced through the palm-lined streets* (Time).
snake-danc·er (snāk′dan′sər, -dän′-), *n.* a person who does a snake dance.
snake doctor, 1. a doctor who treats snakebites. **2.** the hellgrammite. **3.** the dragonfly.
snake eater, 1. the secretary bird. **2.** the markhor.
snake eyes, *Slang.* two ones on a roll of dice: *A lot of the hotelmen-gamblers were rolling snake eyes* (Baltimore Sun).
snake feeder, 1. the dragonfly. **2.** the hellgrammite.
snake fence, a zigzag fence made of rails resting across one another at an angle.
snake·fish (snāk′fish′), *n., pl.* **-fish·es** or (*collectively*) **-fish.** any of various fishes more or less resembling a snake, as the lizard fish and the oarfish.
snake·head (snāk′hed′), *n.* the turtlehead, a plant of the figwort family.
snake·let (snāk′lit), *n.* a small snake: *Dozens of young snakelets have been seen crawling into the open jaws ... of certain pythons* (Popular Science Monthly).
snake moss, the common club moss.
snake·mouth (snāk′mouth′), *n.* a North American swamp orchid with a slender stem bearing a single, fragrant, rose-colored, nodding flower and a single leaf.
snake·neck (snāk′nek′), *n.* a snakebird.
snake oil, *U.S.* any of various preparations advertised as medicine supposed to cure certain ailments, such as rheumatism, colds, baldness, etc., formerly sold by peddlers posing as scientists, doctors, or the like.
snake pit, 1. a pit filled with snakes. **2.** *Informal.* a backward or overcrowded mental institution, prison, etc., especially one where outmoded theories and practices are perpetuated. **3.** any frightening or oppressive place or condition: *It's difficult to orient one's way in the snake pit we're living in* (Arthur Miller).
snake plant, the sansevieria.
snake·root (snāk′rüt′, -rủt′), *n.* **1.** any of various plants whose roots have been regarded as a remedy for snakebites, as the Virginia snakeroot, the Seneca snakeroot, the white snakeroot, the button snakeroot, or a kind of bugbane: *Rauwolfia, also known as the snakeroot plant, is the source of reserpine, [a] relaxing drug* (Science News Letter). See **senega** for picture **2.** the root of such plants.
snakes and ladders, a game played on a board, in which figures of ladders on the board permit progress while figures of snakes set the players back.
snake·skin (snāk′skin′), *n.* **1.** the skin of a snake. **2.** leather made from it.
snake·stone (snāk′stōn′), *n.* **1.** an ammonite. **2.** a porous substance supposed to extract the venom from snakebites.
snake·weed (snāk′wēd′), *n.* **1.** bistort. **2.** any of the weedy plants among which snakes are supposed to abound. **3.** any of a group of herbs of the composite family with small yellow flower heads.
snake·wood (snāk′wủd′), *n.* **1. a.** any of certain East Indian shrubs or trees whose wood is supposed to cure snakebites. **b.** the wood itself. **2. a.** a South American tree of the mulberry family with a mottled wood used for veneering, etc. **b.** the wood itself; letterwood: ... *such exotic varieties as ... dark red snakewood from British Guiana* (Time).
snak·i·ly (snā′kə lē), *adv.* in a snaky manner; windingly: *Usually it is shaped like a funnel, but sometimes it is tubular and gyrates snakily in the air* (New Yorker).
snak·i·ness (snā′kē nis), *n.* snaky character or appearance.
snak·y (snā′kē), *adj.,* **snak·i·er, snak·i·est. 1.** of a snake or snakes. **2.** like a snake; like the curving and turning of a snake; twisting; winding: ... *doing a snaky dance in front of a white statue* (New Yorker). **3.** having many snakes. **4.** sly; venomous; treacherous. **5.** formed with or composed of snakes, as the caduceus of Mercury.
snap (snap), *v.,* **snapped, snap·ping,** *n., adj., adv.* —*v.i.* **1.** to make a sudden, sharp sound: *Most pine snaps as it burns.* **2.** to move, shut, catch, etc., with a snap: *The door snapped shut behind him.* **3.** to break suddenly or sharply: *The violin string snapped.* **4.** to become suddenly unable to endure a strain: *His nerves snapped.* **5.** to make a sudden, quick bite or snatch: *The dog snapped at the child's hand.* **6.** to seize suddenly: *She snapped at the chance to go to Europe.* **7.** to speak quickly and sharply: *to snap impatiently at a person who is slow.* **8.** to move quickly and sharply: *The soldiers snapped to attention. Her eyes snapped with anger.* **9.** to take snapshots.
—*v.t.* **1. a.** to cause to make a sudden, sharp sound: *to snap one's fingers.* **b.** to crack (a whip). **2.** to cause to move, close, catch, etc., with a snap: *to snap a door shut, to snap the jaws together, to snap a bolt into place.* **3.** to break (something) suddenly or sharply: *to snap a stick in two; ... it seemed for a moment as if the tradition of generations might be snapped* ... (Lytton Strachey). **4.** to snatch quickly with the mouth; bite suddenly: *The dog snapped up the meat.* **5.** to seize suddenly: *to snap up a bargain.* **6.** to say quickly and sharply: *The sergeant snapped out an order.* **7.** to move quickly and sharply: *You better snap it up or you will never get the job done.* **8.** to take a snapshot of. **9.** *Football.* to pass (the ball) back from the center with a quick motion to start a play. **10.** *Baseball.* to throw (the ball) quickly: *to snap the ball to first base.*
snap back, *U.S. Informal.* to bounce back; recover suddenly: *Whitey Ford ... snapped back into his best pitching form* (New York Times).
snap into, to throw oneself into (an action): *Oh, snap into it! We want to get this done* (F.A. Pottle).
snap out of it, *Informal.* to change one's attitude, habit, etc., suddenly: *He was in a bad mood one minute, but then he snapped out of it and started to laugh.*
—*n.* **1.** a quick, sharp sound: *The box shut with a snap.* **2.** a sudden, sharp breaking or the sound of breaking. **3.** a quick, sudden bite or snatch: *The dog made a snap at the fly.* **4.** a quick, sharp speech: *When she was tired, she sometimes answered with a snap.* **5.** *Informal.* **a.** a quick, sharp way: *She moves with snap and energy.* **b.** liveliness or crispness in writing: *a delightful little tale, full of romance, snap, and brightness.* **6.** a short spell of cold weather. **7.** a fastener; clasp: *One of the snaps of your dress is unfastened.* **8.** a snapping of the fingers, especially as a sign of disregard, contempt, etc. **9.** a thin, crisp cooky: *a chocolate snap.* **10.** *Informal.* a snapshot. **11.** *Informal.* a snapdragon. **12.** *Slang.* an easy job, piece of work, etc.
not a snap, not at all: *I cared not a snap that he didn't write.*
—*adj.* **1.** made or done suddenly: *A snap judgment is likely to be wrong.* **2.** closing or fastening by action of a spring: *a snap bolt, a snap lock.* **3.** *Informal.* very easy: *a snap course at college.*
—*adv.* **1.** with a snap. **2.** without delay, hesitation, etc.
[earlier, to bite < earlier Dutch *snappen*]
SNAP (no periods), Systems for Nuclear Auxiliary Power (a series of nuclear devices to provide auxiliary power in satellites, space vehicles, etc.).
snap·back (snap′bak′), *n.* **1.** *U.S. Informal.* a snapping back to a former or normal condition; bounceback. **2.** in football: **a.** the passing back of the ball which puts it in play. **b.** the center.
snap bean, 1. any of several varieties of the common bean, whose unripe pods are used for food. **2.** the pod itself.
snap-brim (snap′brim′), *n.* a snap-brim hat.
snap-brim hat, a hat with a brim that can be turned down, especially in front.
snap·drag·on (snap′drag′ən), *n.* **1.** any of a group of herbs of the figwort family, especially a common garden plant with spikes of showy flowers of crimson, purple, white, yellow, etc. **2.** an old game in which people try to snatch raisins from burning brandy.
snap·hance (snap′hans), *n.* **1.** an early flintlock worked by a spring. **2.** a gun or pistol having such a lock: *The snaphance or flintlock was little used, at least in the early stages of the war* (John Morley).
[< Dutch *snaphaan* < *snappen* snap + *haan* hammer]
snap·haunce (snap′hôns), *n.* snaphance.
snap link, an open link closed by a spring, used to connect chains, parts of harness, etc.
snap-on (snap′on′, -ôn′), *adj.* that is or can be snapped into place: *Snap-on sunglasses that double as safety glasses come with adjustable parts* (Science News Letter).
snap·per (snap′ər), *n., pl.* **-pers** or (*collectively for 3*) **-per. 1.** a person or thing that snaps. **2.** a fastener; snap. **3.** a snapping turtle. **4. a.** any of a group of large, mostly red or yellowish fish of tropical seas used for food. **b.** any of various other fishes. **5.** a snapping beetle.
snap·per-up (snap′ər up′), *n.* one that snaps up or seizes upon a thing quickly: *The author's poor deluded customer seems just a greedy snapper-up of ill-considered trifles* (Harper's).
snap·pi·ly (snap′ə lē), *adv.* in a snappy manner.
snap·pi·ness (snap′ē nis), *n.* the quality or condition of being snappy.
snap·ping (snap′ing), *adj.* **1.** making quick attempts to bite, as an animal. **2.** snappish: *to talk in a snapping tone.* **3.** making a sharp, cracking or clicking sound: *a snapping, clicker toy.* **4.** flashing, as eyes. —**snap′ping·ly,** *adv.*
snapping beetle, any of several beetles that jump with a snapping or clicking sound when turned on the back; click beetle.
snapping turtle, any of a group of large, savage turtles of American lakes and rivers that have powerful jaws with which they snap at their prey.
snap·pish (snap′ish), *adj.* **1.** apt to snap: *a snappish dog.* **2.** quick and sharp in speech or manner; impatient: *a snappish person, a snappish reply.* —**snap′pish·ly,**

adv. —**snap′pish·ness,** *n.* —**Syn. 2.** testy, crabbed, cross, irascible, petulant.

snap·py (snap′ē), *adj.*, **-pi·er, -pi·est. 1.** snappish; sharp. **2.** snapping or crackling in sound: *a snappy fire.* **3.** *Informal.* having snap, crispness, smartness, liveliness, pungency, etc.: *a snappy cheese, a snappy new suit.*

snap ring, piston ring.

snap roll, (of an airplane) a fast barrel roll, especially as a maneuver in stunting.

snap·shoot (snap′shüt′), *v.t.*, **-shot, -shoot·ing.** to take a snapshot of or at: *to snapshoot a duck. Tourist Janet Dulles . . . was snapshot as she snapshot Geneva's lighter side* (Time). —**snap′shoot′er,** *n.*

snap·shot (snap′shot′), *n.*, *v.*, **-shot·ted, -shot·ting.** —*n.* **1.** a photograph taken with a small camera. **2.** a quick shot taken without time for careful aim, usually at game that has just been flushed. —*v.t.*, *v.i.* to take a snapshot (of): *As domestic comedy, "The Male Animal" snapshots some familiar poses, strikes some reminiscent chords* (Time).

snap·shot·ter (snap′shot′ər), *n.* **1.** a person who practices or is skilled in snapshotting. **2.** a person who takes snapshots. **3.** a camera suitable for taking snapshots.

snare[1] (snãr), *n.*, *v.*, **snared, snar·ing.** —*n.* **1.** a noose for catching small animals and birds, etc. **2.** a trap: *Popularity is a snare in which fools are caught.* **3.** a loop of wire used to remove tonsils, tumors, etc.

—*v.t.* **1.** to catch with a snare. **2.** to trap: *Russia is greatly expanding . . . its competitive ability to snare underdeveloped lands into its trade orbit* (Newsweek).

[probably < Scandinavian (compare Old Icelandic *snara*)]

—**Syn.** *n.* **1.** See **trap.**

snare[2] (snãr), *n.* one of the strings of gut, rawhide, or wire stretched across the bottom of a snare drum. [probably < Middle Dutch *snare*]

snare drum, a small drum with strings of gut or rawhide stretched across the bottom to make a rattling sound.

Snare Drum, showing snares on bottom of drum

snar·er (snãr′ər), *n.* **1.** a person who entangles, or lays snares. **2.** a person who catches animals with snares.

snark (snärk), *n.* an animal imagined by Lewis Carroll as the object of the expedition described in his nonsense poem *The Hunting of the Snark* (1876). [blend of *snake* and *shark*[1]]

snarl[1] (snärl), *v.i.* **1.** to growl sharply and show one's teeth: *The dog snarled at the stranger.* **2.** to speak harshly in a sharp, angry tone.

—*v.t.* to say or express with a snarl.

—*n.* **1.** a sharp, angry growl. **2.** sharp, angry words: *A snarl was his only reply.*

[earlier *snar.* Compare Middle Dutch *snarren* to rattle. Related to SNORE, SNEER.]

snarl[2] (snärl), *n.* **1.** a tangle: *She combed the snarls out of her hair.* **2.** a confusion: *His legal affairs were in a snarl.*

—*v.t.* **1.** to tangle. **2.** to confuse. —*v.i.* to become snarled.

[perhaps frequentative form of *snare*[1]]

snarl[3] (snärl), *v.t.* to raise or emboss (metal) by hammering on a tool held against the opposite surface. [perhaps special use of *snarl*[2] knot]

snarl·er (snär′lər), *n.* **1.** a person who snarls metal. **2.** a snarling iron.

snarl·ing (snär′ling), *adj.* **1.** that growls angrily. **2.** speaking or complaining in a sharp, bad-tempered manner: *The silver snarling trumpets 'gan to chide* (John Keats).

snarling iron, a tool held against the opposite surface of metal when it is snarled.

snarl·ing·ly (snär′ling lē), *adv.* in a bad-tempered or growling manner.

snarl·y[1] (snär′lē), *adj.*, **snarl·i·er, snarl·i·est.** inclined to snarl or growl; bad-tempered; cross. [< *snarl*[1] + *-y*[1]] —**Syn.** peevish, irritable.

snarl·y[2] (snär′lē), *adj.*, **snarl·i·er, snarl·i·est.** tangled; full of snarls: *You're still within a snarly wood where angels and the devil wait for you to prove the advocate of good or evil* (New Yorker). [< *snarl*[2] + *-y*[1]] —**Syn.** jumbled.

snash (snash), *Scottish.* —*n.*, *v.i.* insult.

snatch (snach), *v.t.* **1.** to seize suddenly; grasp hastily; grab: *to snatch up one's hat and coat and run for a train. A thief snatched her purse in the crowd.* **2.** to take suddenly: *He snatched off his hat and bowed. At half past four he had snatched a cup of tea* (John Galsworthy). **3.** to save or attain by quick action: *They snatched victory from what seemed to be sure defeat.* **4.** *Slang.* to kidnap.

—*v.i.* **snatch at, a.** to try to seize or grasp; seize; grasp: *He snatched at the railing as he began to fall down the stairs.* **b.** to take advantage of eagerly: *He snatched at the chance to travel.*

—*n.* **1.** the act of snatching: *The boy made a snatch at the ball.* **2.** a short time: *He had a snatch of sleep sitting in his chair.* **3.** a small amount; bit; scrap: *to overhear snatches of a conversation.* **4.** an exercise in weight lifting in which the weight is raised from the floor to above the head in one continuous motion. **5.** *Slang.* the act of kidnaping.

by or **in snatches,** by fits and starts; intermittently: *I have begun two or three letters to you by snatches, and been prevented from finishing them* (Alexander Pope).

[perhaps < Middle Dutch *snakken;* perhaps influenced by *latch, catch*] —**snatch′er,** *n.*

—**Syn.** *v.t.* **1.** catch, snap. **2.** pluck, wrest.

snatch·a·ble (snach′ə bəl), *adj.* that may be snatched: *The child sees a snatchable object in someone's hands* (William James).

snatch block, a block with an opening in one side to receive the bight of a rope.

snatch·i·ly (snach′ə lē), *adv.* in or by snatches.

snatch·y (snach′ē), *adj.* done or occurring in snatches; disconnected; irregular.

snath (snath), *n.* the long wooden handle of a scythe: *O mower, lean on thy bended snath* (John Greenleaf Whittier). [variant of *snead,* Old English *snǣd*]

snathe (snāᴛʜ), *n.* snath.

snav·el (snav′əl), *v.t. Australian.* to steal; rob; snatch.

snaz·zy (snaz′ē), *adj.*, **-zi·er, -zi·est.** *U.S. Slang.* fancy; flashy; elegant: *With a great gold World Series ring on his finger, and wearing a snazzy blue suit with plaid socks, he looks as sharp as he feels* (Time). [origin unknown]

SNCC (no periods) or **S.N.C.C.,** Student Nonviolent Coordinating Committee (an organization formed by Southern Negro students in 1960 to promote Negro civil rights in the South).

snead (snēd), *n. Dialect.* snath. [Old English *snǣd*]

sneak (snēk), *v.i.* **1.** to move in a stealthy, sly way: *The man sneaked about the barn watching for a chance to steal the dog.* **2.** to act in a mean, contemptible, cowardly way: *See how he cowers and sneaks* (Thoreau).

—*v.t.* **1.** to get, put, pass, etc., in a stealthy, sly way. **2.** to steal: *He sneaked all the cookies he could.*

sneak out of, to avoid by slyness: *He tried to sneak out of paying the fine by using every trick he could think of.*

—*n.* **1. a.** the act of sneaking. **b.** *Informal.* a going quietly away; departure: *How about taking a sneak?* (Sinclair Lewis). **2.** a person who sneaks; sneaking, cowardly, contemptible person. **3.** *U.S. Informal.* a sneak preview: *For the producer sweating out audience reaction, the sneak is the most fiendish torture* (Wall Street Journal).

on or **upon the sneak,** sneakily: *A thief [was] detected in a house which he has entered, upon the sneak, for the purpose of robbing it* (J.H. Vaux).

sneaks, *U.S. Informal.* sneakers: *a pair of old sneaks.*

[origin uncertain. Compare Old English *snīcan.*] —**Syn.** *v.i.* **1.** slink, skulk, lurk.

sneak attack, a surprise attack made before a declaration of war: *In 1941, the Japanese sneak attack crippled Pearl Harbor, but in the age of supersonic planes and nuclear weapons, a sneak attack could wipe out the nation* (Newsweek).

sneak boat, *U.S.* a small, flat, shallow boat used for hunting wild fowl, usually covered with brush or weeds as camouflage.

sneak·box (snēk′boks′), *n. U.S.* sneak boat.

sneak·er (snē′kər), *n.* **1.** *U.S.* a light canvas shoe with a soft rubber sole. **2.** a person who sneaks; sneak.

sneak·ered (snē′kərd), *adj.* having or wearing sneakers: *Sneakered footsteps could be heard running down the stone steps* (Harper's).

sneak·i·ly (snē′kə lē), *adv.* in a sneaky manner: *Spirited arguments are regularly waged over whether the Nazis did or did not capture and sneakily avail themselves of certain Allied DC-3s during the war* (New Yorker).

sneak·i·ness (snē′kē nis), *n.* the character or quality of being sneaky.

sneak·ing (snē′king), *adj.* **1.** cowardly; underhand; concealed. **2.** that one cannot justify or does not like to confess: *to have a sneaking suspicion about something.* —**sneak′ing·ly,** *adv.* —**Syn. 1.** skulking, slinking.

sneak preview, *U.S. Informal.* the showing of a new motion picture without announcement beforehand or to a private audience before the film is released for the general public: *In the first seven months this year, 101 sneak previews were held by five of Hollywood's biggest studios* (Wall Street Journal).

sneaks (snēks), *n.pl.* See under **sneak,** *n.*

sneaks·by (snēks′bē), *n., pl.* **-bies.** a paltry, sneaking fellow; a sneak.

sneak shooting, the act or practice of shooting wild fowl from a sneak boat.

sneak thief, a person who takes advantage of open doors, windows, or other easy opportunities to steal.

sneak·y (snē′kē), *adj.*, **sneak·i·er, sneak·i·est.** cowardly; mean; contemptible: *They dropped their eyes and looked sneaky* (Mark Twain).

sneap (snēp), *Archaic.* —*v.t.* **1.** to nip or pinch: *An envious sneaping frost . . .* (Shakespeare). **2.** to check, reprove, or snub: *She had a tongue for the sneaping of too casual boys* (Arnold Bennett). —*n.* a check; reproof; snub: *My lord, I will not undergo this sneap without reply* (Shakespeare). [< Scandinavian (compare Old Icelandic *sneypa* disgrace)]

sneck (snek), *Scottish.* —*n.*, *v.t.*, *v.i.* latch; catch. [origin uncertain]

sneck·draw (snek′drô′), *n. Scottish.* **1.** a thief; burglar. **2.** a crafty, greedy person: *. . . a skinflint and a sneckdraw, sitting, with his nose in an account book, to persecute poor tenants* (Robert Louis Stevenson).

sneck·draw·er (snek′drô′ər), *n.* sneckdraw.

sned (sned), *v.t.*, **sned·ded, sned·ding.** *Scottish.* **1.** to cut off (branches). **2.** to prune (trees). [Old English *snǣdan*]

sneer (snir), *v.i.* to show scorn or contempt by looks or words: *The other girls sneered at poor Dora's clothes.* —*v.t.* **1.** to say or write with scorn or contempt: *Damn with faint praise, assent with civil leer, And without sneering teach the rest to sneer* (Alexander Pope). **2.** to bring, put, force, etc., by sneering: *to sneer down all who disagree.* —*n.* an act of sneering; look or words expressing scorn or contempt: *He fears sneers more than blows.* [earlier *snere;* origin uncertain] —**sneer′er,** *n.* —**Syn.** *v.i.* jeer, gibe, flout, mock. See **scoff.**

sneer·ful (snir′fəl), *adj.* given to sneering.

sneer·ing·ly (snir′ing lē), *adv.* with a sneering manner.

sneer·y (snir′ē), *adj.* of a sneering or scornful character: *You'd think people'd be used to his . . . sneery philosophy by now* (Time).

sneesh (snēsh), *n.* sneeshing: *In Scotland the kilted Highlander . . . has long been welcoming those who partake of sneesh* (London Times).

sneesh·ing (snē′shing), *n. Scottish.* **1.** snuff. **2.** a pinch of snuff. [perhaps < Scottish Gaelic *snaoisín,* Irish *snaoisean,* alterations of English *sneezing*]

sneeze (snēz), *v.*, **sneezed, sneez·ing,** *n.* —*v.i.* to expel air suddenly and violently through the nose and mouth, by an involuntary spasm.

sneeze at, *Informal.* to treat with contempt; despise; scorn: *If there is no episcopacy, there is certainly a bureaucracy, and its power is not to be sneezed at* (Canadian Saturday Night).

—*n.* a sudden, violent expelling of air through the nose and mouth.

[misreading of Middle English *fnesen,* Old English *fnēosan*]

sneeze gas, a gas, especially a derivative of arsine, used in warfare to produce nasal irritation, sneezing, nausea, etc., among enemy soldiers.

sneez·er (snē′zər), *n.* **1.** one who sneezes. **2.** *British Dialect.* a violent blow; a blow that knocks the breath out.

sneeze·weed (snēz′wēd′), *n.* any of a group

of American composite herbs with yellow flower heads that cause sneezing.

sneeze·wort (snēz′wėrt′), *n.* **1.** a native European composite plant, closely related to the yarrow, that causes sneezing. **2.** sneezeweed.

sneez·ing gas (snē′zing), sneeze gas.

sneez·y (snē′zē), *adj.* sneezing; accompanied by sneezes.

snell[1] (snel), *n.* **1.** a short piece of gut, etc., by which a fishhook is fastened to a longer line. **2.** a short, light leader. —*v.t.* to tie or fasten (a hook) to a line with a snell: . . . *makes it easy for a fisherman to snell hooks anywhere* (Science News Letter). [American English; origin uncertain]

snell[2] (snel), *Scottish.* —*adj.* **1.** quick-moving. **2.** smart; clever. **3.** harsh; severe; unsparing: *Bleak December's winds . . . Baith snell an' keen* (Robert Burns).
—*adv.* quickly; smartly; severely.
[Old English *snell*]

snib (snib), *v.t.*, **snibbed, snib·bing.** *Scottish.* to rebuke; reprimand. [< Scandinavian (compare Middle Swedish *snybba*)]

snick[1] (snik), *v.t.* **1.** to cut, snip, or nick. **2.** to strike sharply. **3.** to give (a cricket ball) a light glancing blow.
—*n.* **1.** a small cut; a nick. **2.** *Cricket.* **a.** a light glancing blow given to the ball by the batsman. **b.** a ball so hit.

snick[2] (snik), *v.i.* to make a clicking sound: *And ye may hear a breech bolt snick where never a man is seen* (Rudyard Kipling). —*v.t.* to cause to make a clicking sound: *Barry Snyder was snicking BBs off the blackboard* (New Yorker). —*n.* a slight sharp sound; click. [perhaps imitative]

snick-a-snee (snik′ə snē′), *n.* **1.** a snickersnee. **2.** a fight with swords or heavy knives. [alteration of earlier *snick and snee, stick or snee* < Dutch *steken* to thrust, stick + *snijen* to cut]

snick·er (snik′ər), *n.* a half-suppressed and usually disrespectful laugh; sly or silly laugh; smothered giggle: *a self-conscious snicker.*
—*v.i.* **1.** to laugh in this way. **2.** (of horses) to neigh. —*v.t.* to utter with a snicker.
[probably imitative] —**snick′er·er,** *n.* —**snick′er·ing·ly,** *adv.*

snick·er·snee (snik′ər snē′), *n.* a short sword or heavy knife: *As I gnashed my teeth, When from its sheath I drew my snickersnee* . . . (W.S. Gilbert). [alteration of earlier *stick or snee;* see SNICK-A-SNEE]

snide (snīd), *adj.* **1.** slyly insinuating. **2.** derogatory: *a snide remark.*
—*n.* **1.** a dishonest person; cheat. **2.** something done dishonestly. **3.** a counterfeit; sham. [origin uncertain] —**snide′ly,** *adv.*

sniff (snif), *v.i.* **1.** to draw air through the nose in short, quick breaths that can be heard: *The man who had a cold was sniffing.* **2.** to smell with sniffs: *The dog sniffed suspiciously at the stranger.* —*v.t.* **1.** to try the smell of; test by sniffing: *He sniffed the medicine before taking a spoonful of it.* **2.** to draw in through the nose with the breath: *He sniffed steam to clear his head.* **3.** to suspect; detect: *to sniff danger. The police sniffed a plot and broke up the meeting.*
sniff at, to scorn; treat with contempt: *Though this French aid can scarcely do much to carry the enormous burden of investment which the Alliance for Progress set itself, there is no need to sniff at it* (Manchester Guardian Weekly).
—*n.* **1.** the act or sound of sniffing: *He cleared his nose with a loud sniff.* **2.** a single breathing in of something; breath. **3.** a smell; odor.
[related to SNIVEL. Compare SNIFFLE.] —**sniff′er,** *n.*

sniff·i·ly (snif′ə lē), *adv.* in a sniffy manner: *The request was sniffily refused until the city could reëstablish its credit* (New York Times).

sniff·ish (snif′ish), *adj.* sniffy: *Politicians . . . consider him starchy, sniffish* (Richard Rovere). —**sniff′ish·ly,** *adv.*

snif·fle (snif′əl), *v.*, **-fled, -fling,** *n.* —*v.i.* **1.** to sniff again and again: *The child stopped crying but kept on sniffling.* **2.** to breathe audibly through a partly clogged nose.
—*n.* a loud sniff; a sniffling.
the sniffles, a. a fit of sniffling; tendency to sniffle: *He suffers from hay fever and is very prone to the sniffles.* **b.** a slight cold in the head: *The President . . . has a slight case of the sniffles* (New York Times).
[apparently frequentative form of *sniff*]

snif·fler (snif′lər), *n.* **1.** a person who sniffles: *Sneezing and coughing, even energetic talking by a sniffler, create a spray of germs* (Sidonie M. Gruenberg). **2.** *Nautical.* a brisk breeze; capful of wind.

sniff·y (snif′ē), *adj.*, **sniff·i·er, sniff·i·est.** *Informal.* **1.** inclined to sniff. **2.** contemptuous; scornful; disdainful: . . . *whether the expression on Mr. Coolidge's face was his natural one or whether it was a shade more sniffy than usual* (New Yorker). —**Syn. 2.** supercilious.

snif·ter (snif′tər), *n.* **1.** a stemmed glass for brandy or other aromatic alcoholic liquor, with a broad bottom and a narrow lip to prevent the aroma from escaping: *swirling his brandy around in a snifter* (New Yorker). **2.** a small drink of alcoholic liquor. [apparently < dialectal *snift* to sniff]

snig (snig), *n. Dialect.* a young or small eel. [origin unknown]

snig·ger (snig′ər), *n., v.i., v.t.* snicker: . . . *to him the subject calls for a hearty laugh, not a prurient snigger* (Saturday Review). —**snig′ger·er,** *n.*

snig·ger·y (snig′ər ē), *adj.* that sniggers; snickering: *Teachers everywhere seem to have kids as sniggery as those of Miss Barrett's* (Time).

snig·gle (snig′əl), *v.*, **-gled, -gling.** —*v.i.* to fish for eels by dropping a baited hook into their lurking place. —*v.t.* to catch (eels) in this way. [apparently related to SNIG]

snip (snip), *v.*, **snipped, snip·ping,** *n.* —*v.t.* **1.** to cut with a small, quick stroke or series of strokes with scissors: *She snipped the thread. His mother was snipping dead leaves from the window plants* (Thomas Hardy). **2.** to cut up or off as if by scissors: *The critics snipped the play into little pieces.* —*v.i.* to make cuts with scissors or as if with scissors.
—*n.* **1.** an act of snipping: *With a few snips she cut out a paper doll.* **2. a.** a small piece cut off: *Pick up the snips of cloth and thread from the floor.* **b.** a small cut made by scissors. **3.** any small piece; bit; fragment. **4.** *Informal.* a small or unimportant person: *a snip of a girl.*
snips, a. hand shears for cutting metal: *Hand shears . . . are often called snips, to distinguish them from bench shears* (Holtzapffel and Holtzapffel). **b.** *Slang.* handcuffs: *The accused did not offer to go quietly till the police had the "snips" on him* (Newcastle Evening Chronicle).
[compare Low German *snippen*]

snipe (snīp), *n., pl.* **snipes** or (*collectively for 1 and 2*) **snipe,** *v.*, **sniped, snip·ing.** —*n.* **1.** any of various marsh birds with long bills, related to the sandpipers, as the common or whole snipe of Europe, and the American or Wilson's snipe. **2.** any of certain similar shore birds, as the jacksnipe of Europe and the dowitcher. **3.** a shot made by or as if by a sniper. **4.** *U.S. Slang.* a cigarette or cigar butt.

Wilson's Snipe
(def. 1—11 in. long)

—*v.i.* **1.** to hunt snipe. **2.** to shoot at an enemy, usually from under cover and at long range. —*v.t.* to shoot at (soldiers) one at a time as a sportsman shoots at game; shoot from a concealed place.
snipe at, to attack suddenly or unexpectedly, especially by words: *In a series of barbed "Sunday speeches" he sniped at the ill-starred plan to "internationalize" the industrially opulent Saar border enclave* (Newsweek).
[< Scandinavian (compare Old Icelandic *snīpa*)]

snipe eel, a slender, eellike, marine fish, up to 3 feet long, with a speckled, pale back, and blackish belly and anal fin.

snipe fish, 1. any of various fish having long, tubular snouts resembling a snipe's beak. **2.** a snipe eel.

snipe fly, a two-winged fly with a long proboscis and long, thin legs; deer fly.

snipe·hunt (snīp′hunt′), *n. U.S.* a prank played on a person by inviting him to a desolate place to hunt snipe with a group, none of whom turns up to join him.

snipe·hunt·er (snīp′hun′tər), *n.* a person who hunts snipe.

snip·er (snī′pər), *n.* a hidden sharpshooter.

snip·er·scope (snī′pər skōp), *n. U.S.* a device using infrared rays that can be mounted on a rifle and used to spot targets at night. [< *sniper* + (tele)*scope*]

snip·per (snip′ər), *n.* a person who snips.

snip·pers (snip′ərs), *n.* a pair of shears or scissors shaped for short or small cuts.

snip·per-snap·per (snip′ər snap′ər), *n.* an insignificant fellow; whipper-snapper.

snip·pet (snip′it), *n.* **1.** a small piece snipped off; bit; scrap; fragment: *That is a poor snippet of malicious gossip* (Robert Louis Stevenson). *A narrow band runs low around the hips; below this is a mere snippet of a flounced skirt* (New York Times). **2.** *Informal.* a small or unimportant person: *Do you suppose these snippets would treat Alice the way they do if she could afford to entertain?* (Booth Tarkington). [< *snip* + *-et*]

snip·pet·y (snip′ə tē), *adj.* scrappy.

snip·pi·ness (snip′ē nis), *n.* the quality or condition of being snippy.

snip·py (snip′ē), *adj.*, **-pi·er, -pi·est. 1.** *Informal.* sharp; curt. **2.** *Informal.* haughty; disdainful. **3.** made up of scraps or fragments.

snips (snips), *n.pl.* See under **snip,** *n.*

snip-snap (snip′snap′), *n.* a smart remark or reply; sharp repartee. [varied reduplication of *snip*]

snip·y (snī′pē), *adj.* having a long, pointed nose like a snipe's bill; resembling a snipe.

snit (snit), *n. Slang.* a state or condition of unrest or excitement; dither: *It [the broadcast] sent the British into a snit, for the 16 member nations . . . had agreed not to broadcast any "entertainment" during the initial tests* (Time).

snitch[1] (snich), *v.t. Slang.* to snatch; steal: *They had snitched too many carrots from the big piles of vegetables that were strewn around there* (New Yorker). —**snitch′er,** *n.* —**Syn.** filch.

snitch[2] (snich), *Slang.* —*v.i.* to be an informer; tell tales; peach: *He was afraid the younger boy would snitch about a burglary they perpetrated* (Tuscaloosa News). —*n.* an informer. [originally, nose; origin unknown] —**snitch′er,** *n.*

sniv·el (sniv′əl), *v.*, **-eled, -el·ing** or (*especially British*) **-elled, -el·ling,** *n.* —*v.i.* **1.** to cry with sniffling. **2.** to put on a show of grief; whine: *sniveling sentiment.* **3.** to run at the nose; sniffle.
—*n.* **1.** pretended grief or crying; whining. **2.** a running from the nose; sniffling.
the snivels, the sniffles: *to take nose drops for the snivels.*
[Middle English *snevelen*, related to Old English *snyflung*, verbal noun, and *snofl* mucus] —**sniv′el·er,** *especially British,* **sniv′el·ler,** *n.*

sniv·el·y (sniv′ə lē), *adj.* **1.** running at the nose; snotty. **2.** whining; sniveling.

snob (snob), *n.* **1. a.** a person who cares too much for rank, wealth, position, etc., and too little for real achievement or merit: *a man of a fine old family, brave and loyal, but a dreadful snob.* **b.** a person who tries too hard to please those above him and too little to please those below him. **2.** a person who is contemptuous of the popular taste in some field, and is attracted to esoteric or learned things for their own sake: *a literary snob.* **3.** *Archaic.* a shoemaker or his apprentice. **4.** *Obsolete.* one of the common people who were supposed to have no breeding. [origin uncertain]

snob appeal, appeal directed to snobbishness; attraction possessed by something because it is expensive, rare, high-class, exotic, etc.: *The factor of snob appeal operates in the world of books, but not to the extent . . . that it does in the other arts* (New York Times).

snob·ber·y (snob′ər ē, snob′rē), *n., pl.* **-ber·ies.** snobbishness: *A potent source of snobbery is the conviction that you know all the answers* (Punch).

snob·bess (snob′is), *n.* a female snob.

snob·bish (snob′ish), *adj.* **1.** of or like a snob: *a snobbish remark. Some writers, even American writers . . . display a snobbish shame of something homespun about these makers of America* (H.G. Wells). **2.** looking down on those in a lower position: *a snobbish person.* —**snob′bish·ly,** *adv.*

snob·bish·ness (snob′ish nis), *n.* the character or conduct of a snob; a being a snob.

snob·bism (snob′iz əm), *n.* the state of being a snob; snobbishness: *I have no prejudice against tourists—I consider that a low form of snobbism* (Katherine Anne Porter).

The crowds interpret his detachment as snobbism (Newsweek).

snob·by (snob′ē), *adj.*, **-bi·er, -bi·est.** of or having to do with a snob; snobbish: *. . . a gloomy lady . . . with a voice like a high-class ship going out to sea, very snobby* (New Yorker).

Sno-cat (snō′kat′), *n. Trademark.* a tractor that can travel over deep, soft snow on its four broad caterpillar treads or on enormous balloon tires that distribute its weight over a large area; snow-cat: *The weather was mostly frightful, as Antarctic weather usually is . . . the Sno-cats . . . kept falling into treacherous crevasses* (Scientific American).

snoek (snük), *n.* an edible fish found off the coasts of Australia, South Africa, and South America, having a narrow body and small scales: *Old Cape Town just the same as ever. Malays and snoek fish everywhere* (R.S. Baden-Powell). [< Afrikaans *snoek* < Dutch]

snol·ly·gos·ter (snol′ē gos′tər), *n. Slang.* an ambitious, boastful, talkative, unprincipled fellow: *We are not going to let the special interests and the snollygosters take over this country and run it as their private property* (Harry S. Truman).

snood (snüd), *n.* **1.** a net or bag worn over a woman's hair. **2.** a baglike hat. **3.** a band or ribbon formerly worn around the hair by young unmarried women in Scotland and northern England.
—*v.t.* to bind (hair) with a snood.
[Old English *snōd*]

snood·ed (snü′did), *adj.* **1.** wearing a snood. **2.** bound with a snood.

snook[1] (snük), *v.i. Scottish.* to pry around.
—*n.* **cock a** or **one's snook,** *Especially British Slang.* to thumb one's nose: *One feels that if the need arose they would defy Washington and Moscow as dauntlessly as they have already cocked their snook at London* (Manchester Guardian).
[variant of Middle English *snoken* snuff about, smell, probably < a Scandinavian word (compare Norwegian dialectal *snōka*)]

snook[2] (snük), *n.* any of a group of edible fishes, as a robalo of the Atlantic with a long body, long lower jaw, and prominent lateral line. [< Dutch *snoek.* Compare SNOEK.]

snook·er (snu̇k′ər), *n.* a variation of pool played with 15 red balls, each counting 1, and 6 of other colors, counting 2 to 7.

snool (snül), *Scottish.* —*v.i.* **1.** to snivel. **2.** to submit tamely. —*v.t.* to keep in subjection. [origin uncertain]

snoop (snüp), *v.i.* to go about in a sneaking, prying way; prowl; pry: *He did not remain . . . where he belonged, but snooped all over the island* (Sinclair Lewis). —*n.* a person who snoops. [American English (originally) take food on the sly < Dutch *snoepen* eat in secret] —**snoop′er,** *n.*

snoop·er·scope (snü′pər skōp), *n. U.S.* an infrared device used especially by soldiers in World War II to see the enemy in the dark.

snoop·er·y (snü′pər ē), *n.* the practice of snooping: *It is a scandalous state of affairs when the snoopery of private wiretapping becomes so well established* (Newsweek).

snoop·y (snü′pē), *adj.*, **snoop·i·er, snoop·i·est.** snooping: *Dogs are faithful, watchful, quick, loud, and dependable, and, while undeniably snoopy, keep their secrets to themselves* (New Yorker).

snoot (snüt), *Informal.* —*n.* **1.** the nose. **2.** the face. **3.** a grimace, especially one of contempt.
—*v.t.* to snub or treat with contempt: *Without meaning to snoot the poor old demoded ice tray, I must say that the basket full of pieces of ice, as easy to pick up as marbles, is quite a sight* (New Yorker).
[originally Scottish variant of *snout*]

snoot·ful (snüt′fu̇l), *n., pl.* **-fuls.** *U.S. Slang.* **1.** a large portion of alcoholic beverage, usually sufficient to cause drunkenness: *It may be a foggy mind controlling careless hands and feet . . . or the too relaxing effects of a snootful* (Birmingham News). **2.** too much or enough of something: *He took it out on me. The chrome was rusty, I drove too slow, . . .—nag, nag, nag. I finally got a snootful* (S. J. Perelman).

snoot·i·ly (snü′tə lē), *adv. Informal.* in a snooty manner; snobbishly.

snoot·i·ness (snü′tē nis), *n. Informal.* the quality of being snooty; snobbishness: *He developed a snootiness calculated to alienate co-workers by the hundreds—which it did* (Time).

snoot·y (snü′tē), *adj.*, **snoot·i·er, snoot·i·est.** *Informal.* snobbish; conceited.

snooze (snüz), *v.*, **snoozed, snooz·ing,** *n. Informal.* —*v.i.* to take a nap; sleep; doze: *. . . solemn, whiskered gentlemen snoozing in deep black-leather armchairs under copies of "The Times"* (Atlantic). —*n.* a nap; doze. [origin uncertain]

snoo·zle (snü′zəl), *v.t.*, **-zled, -zling.** to nestle; snuggle: *A dog . . . snoozled its nose overforwardly into her face* (Emily Brontë).

snore (snôr, snōr), *v.*, **snored, snor·ing,** *n.* —*v.i.* to breathe during sleep with a harsh, rough sound. —*v.t.* to pass in snoring: *The man snored away the afternoon.* —*n.* the sound made in snoring. [Middle English *snoren;* perhaps imitative]

snor·er (snôr′ər, snōr′-), *n.* a person who snores.

snor·kel (snôr′kəl), *n.* **1.** a periscopelike intake and exhaust shaft for Diesel engines which allows submarines to remain submerged for a very long period of time. Also, **schnorkle, schnorkel. 2.** a curved tube often attached to a face mask, used by a swimmer to breathe under water: *They prepared to submerge, some with tanks strapped on their backs, and others equipped, less heavily, with a snorkel* (New Yorker).
—*v.i.* to travel underwater using a snorkel: *Reportedly, the scent of a snorkeling sub can be picked up several miles away and . . . for as long as one hour after the sub has glided by under water* (Newsweek). [< German navy slang *Schnorchel* nose (compare German *schnarchen* snore) (because the *snorkel* is the nose of the submarine, and because the intake valve produces a snoring sound)]

snort (snôrt), *v.i.* **1.** to force the breath violently through the nose with a loud, harsh sound: *The horse snorted.* **2.** to make a sound like this: *The engine snorted . . . and the train moved* (John Masefield). **3. a.** to show contempt, defiance, anger, etc., by snorting. **b.** to laugh loudly or roughly in contempt. —*v.t.* **1.** to say or express with a snort: *"Nonsense!" snorted the old man.* **2.** to force out by, or as if by, snorting.
—*n.* **1.** an act of snorting. **2.** the sound made by snorting: *a loud snort of contempt.* **3.** *Slang.* a drink (of liquor): *a snort of whiskey.* [perhaps < Low German *snorten*] —**snort′er,** *n.*

snot (snot), *n.* **1.** *Vulgar or Dialect.* nasal mucus. **2.** *Slang.* a snotty person or remark. [Middle English *snotte,* probably Old English *gesnot*]

snot·ter (snot′ər), *n. Nautical.* **1.** a rope attached to a yardarm, to pull off the lift and brace. **2.** a becket on a mast to hold the lower end of a sprit. [origin unknown]

snot·ti·ly (snot′ə lē), *adv.* in a snotty manner; impudently; snootily: *Name them, name just one, he said snottily* (London Times).

snot·ty (snot′ē), *adj.*, **-ti·er, -ti·est,** *n., pl.* **-ties.** —*adj.* **1.** *Vulgar or Dialect.* foul with snot. **2.** *Informal.* saucy; impudent; conceited; snooty: *a snotty remark.*
—*n. British Slang.* **1.** *Nautical.* a midshipman. **2.** any very small, insignificant person.

snot·ty-nosed (snot′ē nōzd′), *adj. Informal.* snotty: *Let snotty-nosed fellows . . . approve what I write, or let them flout and fleer* (John Selden).

snout (snout), *n.* **1. a.** the projecting part of an animal's head that contains the nose, mouth, and jaws. Pigs, dogs, and crocodiles have snouts. **b.** a similar projection in certain insects; rostrum. **2.** anything like an animal's snout, as a nozzle. **3.** *Informal.* **a.** a large or ugly nose. **b.** any nose.
—*v.t., v.i.* to root with, or as with, the snout: *They snout the bushes and stones aside* (Rudyard Kipling).
[Middle English *snoute;* origin uncertain]

snout beetle, any of a large family of small beetles that have the head prolonged to form a snout, as the boll weevil. Snout beetles eat plants and stored grain.

snout·ed (snou′tid), *adj.* having a snout: *A group of snouted, slit-eyed, sinister, and yet beautifully modelled Crusaders' helmets . . .* (New Yorker).

snout·y (snou′tē), *adj.*, **snout·i·er, snout·i·est. 1.** resembling a snout or muzzle; having a pronounced or prominent snout: *The nose was ugly, long and big, Broad and snouty like a pig* (Thomas Otway). **2.** overbearing; insolent; snooty: *Her manner was perfectly snouty* (London Times).

snow (snō), *n.* **1.** water vapor frozen into crystals that fall to earth in soft, white flakes and spread upon it as a white layer: *To watch his woods fill up with snow* (Robert Frost). **2.** a fall of snow: *There was a heavy snow early in December.* **3.** *Poetic.* pure whiteness. **4.** something resembling or suggesting snow, as the white hair of old age: *carbon-dioxide snow.* **5.** a pattern of dots on a television screen caused by atmospheric interference with the signals. **6.** *Slang.* cocaine or heroin.
—*v.i.* **1.** to fall as snow: *to snow all day.* **2.** to come down like snow. —*v.t.* **1.** to let fall or scatter as snow. **2.** to cover, block up, etc., with snow, or as if with snow. **3.** *U.S. Slang.* to deceive by artful talk.
snow in, to shut in by snow: *We were snowed in for a whole day after the blizzard.*
snow under, a. to cover with snow: *The sidewalks and streets were snowed under by the storm.* **b.** *Informal.* to overwhelm: *snowed under with work. By margins of more than 3-1, Parliament snowed under motions of nonconfidence* (Wall Street Journal).
[Old English *snāw*] —**snow′like′,** *adj.*

snow apple, a red winter apple with very white flesh; Fameuse.

snow·ball (snō′bôl′), *n.* **1.** a ball made of snow pressed together. **2.** any of various viburnums, especially the guelder-rose, with white flowers in large clusters like balls.
—*v.t.* to throw balls of snow at: *The children snowballed each other.* —*v.i.* **1.** to increase rapidly by additions like a snowball: *The number of signers of the petition for a new school snowballed. African nationalism and the drive for self-government are snowballing* (Atlantic). **2.** to throw snowballs.

Snowball (def. 2) (guelder-rose)

snow·bank (snō′bangk′), *n.* a large mass or drift of snow.

snow·bell (snō′bel′), *n.* any of a group of shrubs or small trees grown for their white flowers; storax.

snow·ber·ry (snō′ber′ē), *n., pl.* **-ries. 1.** a North American shrub of the honeysuckle family, that bears clusters of white berries in the fall. **2.** the berry. **3.** any of various other plants having white berries. [American English]

snow·bird (snō′bėrd′), *n.* **1.** the slate-colored junco: *The slate-colored junco, or snowbird, ranges between Canada, New England, and the Gulf of Mexico* (World Book Encyclopedia). **2.** the snow bunting. **3.** *U.S. Slang.* a person addicted to the use of heroin or cocaine.

snow-blind (snō′blīnd′), *adj.* temporarily or partly blind from exposure of the eyes to the glare of snow.

snow blindness, temporary or partial blindness caused by the reflection of sunlight from snow.

snow·blink (snō′blingk′), *n.* the reflection that arises from fields of snow or ice.

snow blower, a machine to clear an area of snow usually by throwing the snow out of its path with paddles or a screw device that feeds snow into a fan.

snow-bound (snō′bound′), *adj.* shut in by snow.

snow·break (snō′brāk′), *n.* **1.** a melting of snow; thaw. **2.** a rush of loose or melting snow. **3.** a narrow strip of forest or other barrier as a protection against snow.

snow-broth (snō′brôth′, -broth′), *n.* melting or melted snow.

snow bunny, *U.S. Slang.* **1.** a person who is learning to ski: *. . . an ideal environment for ski champs and snow bunnies alike* (Wall Street Journal). **2.** a girl skier.

snow bunting, a small, white finch with black and brownish markings, that inhabits cold northern regions.

snow·bush (snō′bu̇sh′), *n.* any of various shrubs bearing many white flowers.

Snow Bunting (about 7 in. long)

snow-capped (snō′kapt′), *adj.* having its top covered with snow: *Lebanon's mountains, usually snow-capped all winter, are nearly bare today* (New York Times).

snow-cat (snō′kat′), *n.* a Sno-cat.

snow-clad (snō′klad′), *adj.* covered with snow.

snow·craft (snō′kraft′, -kräft′), *n.* a knowledge of the behavior of snow and the best methods of combating it, especially in mountaineering.
snow-crest·ed (snō′kres′tid), *adj.* snow-capped.
snow·drift (snō′drift′), *n.* **1.** a mass or bank of snow piled up by the wind. **2.** snow driven before the wind.
snow·drop (snō′drop′), *n.* **1.** any of several small European plants of the amaryllis family with drooping white flowers that bloom early in the spring. **2.** its bulb or flower. **3.** the common anemone. [American English]
snow dust, fine particles of snow raised from the ground by the wind.
snow eater, a warm, dry west wind which rapidly evaporates snow, similar to a Chinook wind.
snow·fall (snō′fôl′), *n.* **1.** a fall of snow. **2.** the amount of snow falling within a certain time and area.
snow fence, a fence put up to break the force of the wind in snowstorms and to prevent the drifting of snow.
snow·field (snō′fēld′), *n.* a wide expanse of snow, especially in arctic regions.
snow finch, a sparrow of mountainous regions of southern Europe and Asia, resembling the snow bunting but having a brown back, gray head, and black chin.
snow·flake (snō′flāk′), *n.* **1.** a small, feathery piece of snow. **2.** any of a group of European plants of the amaryllis family, resembling the snowdrop, but larger. **3.** the snow bunting.

Snowflake Forms (def. 1)

snow fly, 1. a kind of stone fly which appears on the snow. **2.** any of a group of springtails which inhabit snow.
snow goose, a white goose with black wing tips that nests in arctic regions and migrates to the southern United States in winter.
snow·grass (snō′gras′, -gräs′), *n.* a coarse, tall grass of New Zealand.
snow·house (snō′hous′), *n.* a house built of snow; igloo.
snow ice, white, opaque ice formed by the freezing of slush.
snow·i·ly (snō′ə lē), *adv.* in a snowy manner.
snow·i·ness (snō′ē nis), *n.* **1.** a being snowy. **2.** whiteness.
snow-in-sum·mer (snō′in sum′ər), *n.* a perennial with white, tomentose stems, leaves, and calyx, grown in rock gardens and borders or found in the wild.
snow job, *U.S. Slang.* something designed to snow under or overwhelm a person or his efforts, especially a great deal of fast, persuasive talk: *You described* [*the*] *defense of his tax program as "sophisticated rhetoric." I call it a snow job* (Time).
snowk (snouk, snōk, snük), *v.i. Scottish.* snook[1].
snow knife, a knife of bone, used by Eskimos for cutting blocks of snow in making igloos and for other purposes.
snow leopard, a wild cat of the mountains of central Asia; ounce.
snow·less (snō′lis), *adj.* free of snow: *Their houses were built with pitched roofs, rare in the snowless East* (Science News Letter).
snow lily, a yellow dogtooth violet of the Rocky Mountains.
snow line 1. the limit of distance from the equator beyond which snow never completely melts off. **2.** the line above which a mountain is continually covered with snow.
snow·man (snō′man′), *n., pl.* **-men.** a mass of snow made into a figure somewhat like that of a man.
snow·melt (snō′melt′), *n.* the water resulting from melted snow.
snow·mo·bile (snō′mə bēl), *n.* a tractor or other vehicle for use in snow, as a Sno-cat, some having skis or runners in front: *We took fifty men and ten snowmobiles, and in two months drove thirty-four hundred miles . . . along the Arctic coast, and down the Alaska Highway to Edmonton* (New Yorker).

Snowmobile

snow mold, 1. a fungous growth that appears on wheat, rye, and other grasses in the late winter and early spring, especially under melting snow. **2.** the disease caused by this growth.
snow owl, the snowy owl.
snow·pack (snō′pak′), *n.* a large accumulation of snow, as on a mountainside: *Snowpacks there are at record depths and state officials fear warm weather could send the run-off flooding into rich agricultural sections of the central valley* (Wall Street Journal).
snow pellets, pellets of granular snow; soft hail.
snow plant, a bright-red saprophytic plant related to the shinleaf, that grows in high altitudes in the western United States, often appearing while snow is still on the ground.
snow·plow (snō′plou′), *n.* **1.** a machine for clearing away snow from streets, railroad tracks, etc., often a broad, plowlike blade mounted on a truck or tractor. **2.** *Skiing.* a double stem.
—*v.i.* **1.** to clear streets with a snowplow. **2.** *Skiing.* to execute a snowplow (double stem).
[American English < *snow* + *plow*]
snow pudding, a dessert made of beaten whites of eggs stiffened with gelatin or cornstarch, usually flavored with lemon.
snow·scape (snō′skāp′), *n.* a snow-covered landscape. [< *snow* + *-scape*]
snow·shed (snō′shed′), *n.* a long shed built over a railroad track to protect it from snowslides. [American English < *snow* + *shed*[1]]
snow·shoe (snō′shü′), *n., v.,* **-shoed, -shoe·ing.** —*n.* a light, wooden frame with strips of leather stretched across it. Trappers, hunters, etc., in the far North wear snowshoes on their feet to keep from sinking in deep, soft snow. —*v.i.* to walk or travel on snowshoes. [American English < *snow* + *shoe*]

Snowshoes

snowshoe hare, a brownish hare of northern and mountainous areas of North America that turns white in winter; varying hare.
snow·shoe·ing (snō′shü′ing), *n.* travel on snowshoes.
snow·sho·er (snō′shü′ər), *n.* a person who walks or travels on snowshoes.
snowshoe rabbit, snowshoe hare.
snowshoe sickness, a painful swelling of the feet occurring after long journeys on snowshoes.
snow·slide (snō′slīd′), *n.* **1.** the sliding down of a mass of snow on a steep slope. **2.** the mass of snow that slides. [American English < *snow* + *slide*]
snow·slip (snō′slip′), *n.* snowslide.
snow snake, 1. a game played by North American Indians, of sliding a stick along snow or ice as far as possible with one push. **2.** the stick used to play this game.
snow·storm (snō′stôrm′), *n.* a storm with much snow. [American English < *snow* + *storm*]
snow·suit (snō′süt′), *n.* a warm, winter coat and leggings for children: *Everybody's hollering for snowsuits and ski pants* (Wall Street Journal).
snow·swept (snō′swept′), *adj.* strewn or covered with blowing snow: *Across the snow-swept plains of below-zero Alberta, a grain farmer drove 75 miles* (Time).
snow tire, an automobile tire with heavy treads to grip slippery surfaces: *City council made it law today that—snow or no snow—drivers must have snow tires or chains on their vehicles from Jan. 1 to April 1 each year* (Montreal Star).
snow train, *U.S.* a ski train or similar train going to a winter resort.
snow-white (snō′hwīt′), *adj.* white as snow.
snow·y (snō′ē), *adj.,* **snow·i·er, snow·i·est. 1.** having snow. **2.** covered with snow. **3.** like snow; white as snow: *She has snowy hair.* **4.** having a blurred and dotted pattern: *The TV's picture is snowy.*
snowy egret, a white heron or egret of temperate and tropical America with black legs and yellow feet.
snowy owl, a large owl of arctic and northern regions of both hemispheres, having white plumage with dusky markings.
snowy plover, a small white and light-brown plover of the western and southern United States and South America.
snub (snub), *v.,* **snubbed, snub·bing,** *n., adj.* —*v.t.* **1. a.** to treat coldly, scornfully, or with contempt. **b.** to rebuke in a sharp manner. **c.** to treat this way in order to force a result: *to snub a person into silence.* **2.** to check or stop (a boat, horse, etc.) suddenly. **3.** to check or stop (a rope or cable running out) suddenly.
—*n.* **1.** cold, scornful, or disdainful treatment; affront: *Anatole France was a man of superior abilities who had taken some disagreeable snubs* (Edmund Wilson). **2.** a sharp rebuke. **3.** a sudden check or stop.
—*adj.* short and turned up at the tip: *a snub nose.*
[< Scandinavian (compare Old Icelandic *snubba,* snub, reprove, and *snubbōttr* stumpy, cutoff)]
snub·ber (snub′ər), *n.* **1.** a person who snubs. **2.** a device for snubbing a rope, cable, etc. **3.** an early type of automobile shock absorber.
snub·by (snub′ē), *adj.,* **-bi·er, -bi·est.** short and turned up at the tip.
snub-nosed (snub′nōzd′), *adj.* having a snub nose.
snuck (snuk), *v. Dialect or Informal.* sneaked; a past tense and past participle of **sneak:** *The presidents of Smith and Vassar promptly snuck across the border* (Newsweek).
snudge (snuj), *v.i.,* **snudged, snudg·ing.** *Dialect.* **1.** to walk in a stooping or meditative attitude. **2.** to remain snug and quiet; nestle. [origin uncertain]
snuff[1] (snuf), *v.t.* **1.** to draw in through the nose; draw up into the nose: *He snuffs up salt and water to cure a cold.* **2.** to smell at; examine by smelling: *The dog snuffed the track of the fox.* —*v.i.* **1.** to draw air, etc., up or in through the nose. **2.** to sniff, especially curiously as a dog would. **3.** to take powdered tobacco into the nose by snuffing; use snuff. **4.** *Obsolete.* to express scorn, disdain, or contempt by snuffing.
—*n.* **1. a.** powdered tobacco taken into the nose. **b.** a pinch of this, taken at one time. **2.** the act of snuffing. **3.** a smell; odor; scent.
up to snuff, a. *Informal.* in good order or condition; as good as expected: *The performance was not up to snuff.* **b.** *Slang.* not easily deceived: *You American ladies are so up to snuff, as you say* (William D. Howells).
[< earlier Flemish *snuffen*]
—**Syn.** *v.t.* **2.** scent.
snuff[2] (snuf), *v.t.* **1.** to cut or pinch off the burned wick of. **2.** to put out (a candle); extinguish.
snuff it, *Especially British Slang.* to die: *Josh Heckett isn't going to snuff it just for a crack on the head* (George R. Sims).
snuff out, a. to put out; extinguish: *to snuff out the lights.* **b.** to put an end to suddenly and completely; wipe out: *One by one, the bright hopes of the liberation were snuffed out like candles on an altar* (Newsweek).
—*n.* **1.** the burned part of a candlewick. **2.** anything that is faint, feeble, of no value. [origin uncertain. Compare Middle Dutch *snuffen* blow the nose.]
snuff bottle, a bottle designed or used to contain snuff.
snuff·box (snuf′boks′), *n.* a very small box for holding snuff.
snuff color, a dark yellowish brown.
snuff-col·ored (snuf′kul′ərd), *adj.* dark yellowish-brown.
snuff·er[1] (snuf′ər), *n.* a person who snuffs, especially in disdain.
snuff·er[2] (snuf′ər), *n.* **1.** a person who snuffs (a light). **2.** snuffers.
snuff·ers (snuf′ərz), *n.pl.* small tongs for taking off burned wick or putting out the light of a candle.
snuff·i·ly (snuf′ə lē), *adv.* in a snuffy manner.
snuff·i·ness (snuf′ē nis), *n.* the state of being snuffy.

Snuffers (18th century)

snuf·fle (snuf′əl), *v.,* **-fled, -fling,** *n.* —*v.i.* **1.** to breathe noisily through a partly clogged nose. **2.** to snuff or smell; sniff: *Throughout its halls four-footed things lumber and snuffle, scratch and lurk* (Atlantic). **3.**

a. to speak, sing, etc., through the nose or with a nasal tone. b. to speak or act like a hypocrite.
—*n.* 1. the act or sound of snuffling: *With snuffle and sniff and handkerchief . . .* (Rupert Brooke). 2. the nasal tone of voice of a person who snuffles: *With a hypocritical snuffle and a sly twinkle of his eye . . .* (Scott). 3. whining hypocrisy, sanctimoniousness, etc.
the snuffles, a. a fit of snuffling; stuffed-up condition of the nose, caused by a cold, hay fever, etc.: *First the Queen deserts us; then Princess Royal begins coughing; then Princess Augusta gets the snuffles* (Frances Burney). b. a respiratory disease of animals: *swine afflicted with the snuffles.*
[probably < Dutch or Flemish *snuffelen*] —**snuf′fler,** *n.*

snuf·fling·ly (snuf′ling lē), *adv.* 1. with snuffling; in a snuffling manner. 2. hypocritically.

snuff·y (snuf′ē), *adj.*, **snuff·i·er, snuff·i·est.** 1. like snuff. 2. soiled or stained with snuff. 3. having the habit of using snuff. 4. disagreeable; cross. —**Syn.** 4. cranky.

snug (snug), *adj.*, **snug·ger, snug·gest,** *adv.*, *v.*, **snugged, snug·ging,** *n.* —*adj.* 1. warm; comfortable; sheltered: *The cat has found a snug corner behind the stove. The children were nestled all snug in their beds . . .* (Clement Clarke Moore). 2. a. neat; trim; compact: *The cabins on the boat are snug.* b. well-built; seaworthy: *a snug ship.* 3. fitting closely: *That coat is a little too snug.* 4. hidden; concealed: *He lay snug until the searchers passed by.* 5. small but sufficient: *A snug income enables him to live in comfort.* 6. agreeable, especially because of the absence of unpleasant persons or things: *They did occasionally give snug dinners to three or four literary men at a time* (Washington Irving).
—*adv.* in a snug manner.
—*v.t.* 1. to make snug. 2. to make (a ship) ready for a storm. —*v.i.* to nestle; snuggle.
—*n.* a barroom, especially in an inn.
[originally, trim, well prepared (of a ship) probably < Low German] —**snug′ly,** *adv.* —**snug′ness,** *n.*
—**Syn.** *adj.* 1. **Snug, cozy** mean comfortable. **Snug** emphasizes the comfort and security of a small space, warm and sheltered from the weather, or of a quiet and peaceful life, protected from disturbance or excitement: *The children were snug in their beds.* **Cozy** emphasizes warmth, shelter, and ease, often affection or friendliness, making for comfort and contentment: *The lonely man looked through the window at the cozy family.*

snug·ger·y (snug′ər ē), *n.*, *pl.* **-ger·ies.** a snug place, position, room, etc.: *Primary schools vary hugely as buildings, being anything from an urban glass palace to a two-roomed Gothic-windowed snuggery nestling into a Welsh hillside* (Punch).

snug·gle (snug′əl), *v.*, **-gled, -gling,** *n.* —*v.i.* to lie, press, or draw closely for warmth or comfort or from affection; nestle; cuddle: *to snuggle up in a chair, to snuggle down in bed.* —*v.t.* 1. to draw or press closely to, as for comfort or from affection. 2. to draw closely.
—*n.* an act of snuggling.
[< *snug,* verb + *-le,* frequentative]
—**Syn.** *v.i.* nuzzle.

snuz·zle (snuz′əl), *v.i.*, **-zled, -zling.** *Dialect.* to thrust the nose against; rub closely with the nose; nuzzle.

sny[1] (snī), *n.*, *pl.* **snies.** *U.S. and Canada.* a river channel. [American English; apparently < French (colonial America) *chenail,* variant of *chenal* channel]

sny[2] (snī), *n.* the upward curve of the planking at the bow or stern of a ship. [perhaps < Scandinavian (compare Old Icelandic *snua*)]

sny[3] (snī), *v.i.*, **snied, sny·ing.** *British Dialect.* to abound; swarm; teem.

snye (snī), *n.*, *pl.* **snyes.** *Canadian.* sny[1].

so[1] (sō; *sometimes unstressed before consonants* sə), *adv.* 1. in this way; in that way; in the same way; as shown: *Hold your pen so. He has to be treated just so or he won't cooperate. The English people . . . will not bear to be governed by the unchecked power of the sovereign, nor ought they to be so governed* (Macaulay). *For so the Lord said unto me; I will take my rest . . .* (Isaiah 18:4). *Sadder than owl songs . . . is that portentous phrase, "I told you so," uttered by friends* (Byron). 2. as stated: *Is that really so? If this be all so, is it not reasonable . . .* (Scott). 3. to this degree; to that degree: *Do not walk so fast. Never in the field of human conflict was so much owed by so many to so few* (Sir Winston Churchill). *None is so fierce that dare stir him up* (Job 41:10). 4. to such a degree; to the same degree: *He was not so cold as she was. As in the arts, so also in politics, the new must always prevail over the old* (Benjamin Jowett). 5. very: *You are so kind, Sweet day, so cool, so calm, so bright* (George Herbert). 6. very much: *My head aches so!* 7. for this reason; for that reason; accordingly; therefore: *The dog was hungry; so we fed it. We leave at daybreak for Pekin, so I will wish you goodbye now* (Guy Boothby). 8. likewise; also: *She likes dogs; so does he.*
and so, a. likewise; also: *Dick is here and so is John. So it is, and so it will be* (Edna St. Vincent Millay). b. accordingly: *The bill was signed by the President and so became a law.*
and so on, and more of the same; et cetera: *Surrounded by cumbersome furniture, assorted mementos, an ancestral portrait, and so on, he is left literally and figuratively boxed in* (Robert Mazzocco).
in so far. See under **insofar.**
so as (to), in order (to): *to run so as to escape capture. He goes to bed early so as to get plenty of sleep.*
so be it. See under **be.**
so far, a. to this or that point: *I can walk with you just so far.* b. until now or there: *There's a lot of fever about, but I've only had one dose, and E. Wilson has so far escaped altogether* (Graham Greene).
so far as, to the extent that: *So far as you broke the rules, you will be punished.*
so far so good, up to this time all is well: *Concerning the weather, so far so good but it may rain this afternoon.*
so that, a. with the result or consequence that: *He studies hard so that he gets high marks.* b. with the purpose that: *These measures were taken so that he might escape.* c. provided that; if: *To M. it was . . . indifferent who was found guilty, so that he could recover his money* (Maria Edgeworth).
so what?, *Informal.* what about it? what difference does it make?: *So they lost the first inning; so what?*
—*conj.* 1. with the result that; in order that: *Go away so I can rest.* 2. with the purpose or intention that: *I did the work so he would not need to.* 3. on the condition that; if: *So it be done, I care not who does it.*
—*interj.* 1. well! 2. let it be that way! all right! 3. is that true?
—*pron.* 1. the same: *A miser usually remains so.* 2. whatever has been or is going to be said; this; that.
or so, more or less; approximately that: *a pound or so, a day or so ago. It cost a dollar or so.*
[Old English *swā*]
➔ In comparison, **so . . . as** is often used instead of **as . . . as** after a negative: *It's not so large as the other. It's as large as the other.* Even in literary English, however, *as* frequently occurs in sentences of the first type and in the spoken language it predominates.

so[2] (sō), *n.* the fifth tone of the musical scale; sol. [variant of *sol*[1]; see GAMUT]

s.o., seller's option.

So., 1. South. 2. Southern.

S.O., 1. Special Order or Special Orders. 2. Staff Officer.

soak (sōk), *v.i.* 1. to let remain in water or other liquid until wet clear through. 2. to become very wet; remain until wet clear through. 3. a. to make its way; enter; go: *Water will soak through the earth.* b. to make its way into the mind; penetrate: *The magnitude of the problem finally soaked into their minds.* 4. *Informal.* to drink heavily: *You do nothing but soak with the guests all day long* (Oliver Goldsmith). 5. (in Australia) a. a depression in the ground which holds water, especially after rain. b. any temporary marsh or swampy spot.
—*v.t.* 1. to make very wet; wet through: *It rained very hard all day; I was thoroughly soaked* (Benjamin Franklin). 2. to take in by absorption; suck: *The sponge soaked in the water.* 3. *U.S. Slang.* to punish severely; strike hard. 4. *Informal.* to make pay too much; charge or tax heavily: *He admitted he had been soaked in the deal.* 5. to drink too much.
soak up, a. to absorb: *Mr. Johnson yesterday flew to his Texas ranch . . . to soak up the fresh air and sunshine* (New York Times). b. to take into the mind: *to soak up knowledge. Though they soaked up a basic vocabulary of about 1,500 words, they found it an exhausting experience* (Maclean's).
—*n.* 1. the act or process of soaking. 2. the state of being soaked. 3. the liquid in which anything is soaked. 4. *Informal. Slang.* a heavy drinker; sot.
in soak, *Slang.* in pawn: *to put one's rings in soak.*
[Old English *socian*] —**soak′ing·ly,** *adv.*
—**Syn.** *v.t.* 1. See **wet.**

soak·age (sō′kij), *n.* 1. the act of soaking. 2. the condition of being soaked. 3. the liquid which has filtered or oozed out; seepage. 4. the liquid soaked up; moisture absorbed.

soak·a·way (sōk′ə wā′), *n.* *British.* a place through which water soaks or drains away, as a cesspool: *On an offensive front they [trenches] have vertical sides of unsupported earth and occasional soakaways for rain covered by wooden gratings* (H.G. Wells).

soak·er (sō′kər), *n.* *Informal.* 1. a person or thing that soaks. 2. an immoderate drinker: *a very good dinner among the old soakers* (Samuel Pepys).

soak·ing pit (sō′king), a pit to put steel ingots in to cool evenly before rolling.

so-and-so (sō′ən sō′), *n.*, *pl.* **-sos.** some person or thing not named: *I can't stand that old so-and-so. The president . . . remarked that it would be a fine gift for so-and-so* (Time).

soap (sōp), *n.* 1. a substance used for washing, usually made of a fat and caustic soda or potash. 2. *U.S. Slang.* money, especially money as used for bribery. 3. *Chemistry.* any metallic salt of an acid derived from a fat.
no soap, *U.S. Slang.* a. no; nothing doing: *He wanted me to lend him another two dollars, but I told him "no soap."* b. no results; nothing accomplished: *The chief negotiator summed up the meeting by saying "no soap."*
—*v.t.* to rub with soap: *to soap one's face.*
[Old English *sāpe*]

soap·bark (sōp′bärk′), *n.* 1. a bark that can be used like soap, especially that of a tree of Chile. 2. Also, **soapbark tree.** any tree or shrub bearing this bark, as a Chilean tree of the rose family or several tropical American shrubs of the pea family.

soap·ber·ry (sōp′ber′ē), *n.*, *pl.* **-ries.** 1. a fruit or nut that can be used like soap. 2. Also, **soapberry tree.** any of the tropical or subtropical trees bearing such fruit, as the chinaberry.

soapberry family, a group of tropical, dicotyledonous trees and shrubs, with mostly alternate, pinnate leaves and small, odorless flowers. The family includes the soapberry, litchi, balloon vine, and inkwood.

soap·box (sōp′boks′), *n.*, *pl.* **-box·es.** 1. a box, especially of wood, in which soap is packed. 2. an empty box used as a temporary platform by agitators or other speakers addressing gatherings on the streets: *Rabbi Joseph H. Lookstein . . . declared that "religion has an important contribution to make to political life" but that "a pulpit must never degenerate into a soapbox"* (New York Times).
—*v.i.* to address an audience on the public street: *Excitedly, he joined picket lines and soapboxed at bread lines* (Time).
—*adj.* of or characteristic of a speaker on a soapbox; that agitates: *soapbox oratory. Here soapbox orators were allowed to rant about everything from politics to the government ban on betel-nut chewing* (Newsweek).
[American English < *soap* + *box*] —**soap′box′er,** *n.*

soapbox derby, *U.S.* a coasting race for small motorless cars, originally made from wooden soapboxes.

soap bubble, 1. a bubble made with soapy water. 2. something as thin and filmy as a soap bubble: *The talk has been mere soap bubbles* (Emerson).

soap·er (sō′pər), *n.* *U.S. Slang.* a soap opera: *In outline, the soaper as reborn on TV is not too different from the old radio formula, but video has added a whole new set of visual symbols* (Time).

soap·er·y (sō′pər ē), *n.*, *pl.* **-er·ies.** a place where soap is made.

soap flakes, soap manufactured and sold in the form of fine flakes for use in washing machines, dishwashers, etc.

soap·i·ly (sō′pə lē), *adv.* in a soapy manner:

 PRONUNCIATION KEY: hat, āge, cãre, fär; let, ēqual, tėrm; it, īce; hot, ōpen, ôrder; oil, out; cup, pu̇t, rüle;

The man remains as soapily elusive throughout the book as he was in his quick glory (New Yorker).

soap·i·ness (sōp′ē nis), *n.* the state or quality of being soapy.

soap·less (sōp′lis), *adj.* **1.** lacking soap; free from soap: *a soapless detergent.* **2.** unwashed; dirty.

soap opera, *U.S.* a daytime radio or television drama presented in serial form, usually featuring emotional domestic situations.

soap-op·er·at·ic (sōp′op′ə rat′ik), *adj. U.S.* of or like a soap opera: *A sentimental piece of work, but . . . it nearly always avoids seeming soap-operatic* (New Yorker).

soap plant, any of various plants, some part or parts of which can be used like soap.

soap powder, powdered soap and alkaline salts, used as a cleansing agent or detergent.

soap·root (sōp′rüt′, -rut′), *n.* any of certain European herbs of the pink family whose roots are used like soap.

soap·stone (sōp′stōn′), *n.* a stone that feels somewhat like soap, used for griddles, hearths, etc.; steatite. It is a kind of talc.

soap·suds (sōp′sudz′), *n.pl.* bubbles and foam made with soap and water; suds.

soap·wort (sōp′wėrt′), *n.* any of a group of Old World herbs of the pink family, with white or pink flowers and leaves and roots containing a juice that can be used as soap.

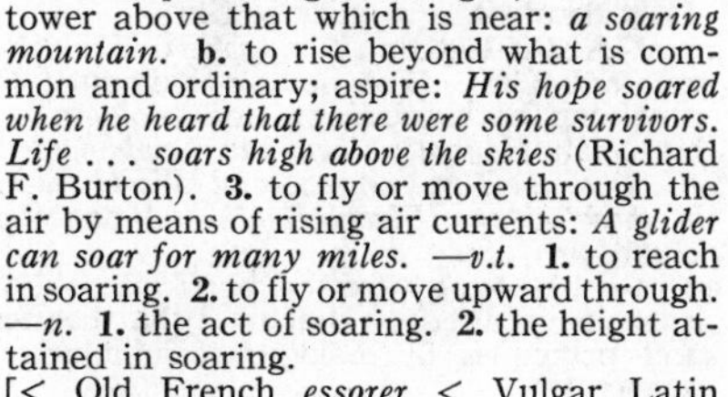
Soapwort (bouncing Bet)

soap·y (sō′pē), *adj.,* **soap·i·er, soap·i·est. 1.** covered with soap or soapsuds. **2.** containing soap. **3.** like soap; smooth; greasy: *to feel soapy.*

soar (sôr, sōr), *v.i.* **1.** to fly at a great height; fly upward: *to soar over the ocean. The hawk soared without flapping its wings.* **2. a.** to rise up to a great height; tower above that which is near: *a soaring mountain.* **b.** to rise beyond what is common and ordinary; aspire: *His hope soared when he heard that there were some survivors. Life . . . soars high above the skies* (Richard F. Burton). **3.** to fly or move through the air by means of rising air currents: *A glider can soar for many miles.* —*v.t.* **1.** to reach in soaring. **2.** to fly or move upward through. —*n.* **1.** the act of soaring. **2.** the height attained in soaring.
[< Old French *essorer* < Vulgar Latin *exaurāre* < Latin *ex-* out + *aura* breeze]
—**soar′er,** *n.*

so·a·ve (sō ä′vā), *adv., adj. Italian.* with sweetness or tenderness (used as a direction in music).

so·a·ve·men·te (sō ä′vā men′tā), *adv. Italian.* soave.

So·ay (sō′ā), *n.,* or **Soay sheep,** a wild sheep native to the island of Soay in the Outer Hebrides: *These apparently wild Soay sheep have bred on the island for centuries, virtually untended by man* (New Scientist).

sob (sob), *v.,* **sobbed, sob·bing,** *n., adj.* —*v.i.* **1.** to cry or sigh with short, quick breaths: *sobbing and crying . . . as if her heart would break* (Laurence Sterne). **2.** to make a sound like a sob: *The wind sobbed in the trees.* —*v.t.* **1.** to put, send, etc., by sobbing: *She sobbed herself to sleep.* **2.** to utter with sobs. —*n.* **1.** a catching of short, quick breaths because of grief, etc.; an act of sobbing. **2.** the sound of this: *The anchor came up with a sob* (Rudyard Kipling).
—*adj. U.S. Informal.* intended to arouse feelings of pity, sadness, etc.: *sob stories.*
[Middle English *sobben;* perhaps ultimately imitative] —**sob′bing·ly,** *adv.*

sob·by (sob′ē), *adj.,* **-bi·er, -bi·est.** soppy: *. . . situations that usually call for sobby sentiment* (Time).

so·be·it (sō bē′it), *conj.* if it be so; provided that.

so·ber (sō′bər), *adj.* **1.** not drunk. **2. a.** temperate; moderate: *The Puritans led sober, hard-working lives.* **b.** avoiding the use of alcoholic liquor altogether. **3.** quiet; serious; solemn; dignified: *a sober expression, sober joy, as sober as a judge.* **4.** calm; sensible: *The judge's sober opinion was not influenced by prejudice or strong feeling. If we read Engel's letters of the nineties . . . we get an old man's soberest effort to state his notion of the nature of things . . .* (Edmund Wilson). **5.** free from exaggeration: *sober facts.* **6.** quiet in color; plain or simple; somber: *dressed in sober gray. The skies were ashen and sober* (Edgar Allan Poe).
—*v.t.* to make sober. —*v.i.* to become sober.
sober down, to make or become quiet, serious, or solemn: *At times . . . solemn speeches sober down a dinner* (Oliver Wendell Holmes).
sober up or **off,** to recover from too much alcoholic drink: *He will sober up after a little nap.*
[< Old French *sobre,* learned borrowing from Latin *sōbrius*] —**so′ber·ly,** *adv.* —**so′ber·ness,** *n.*
—**Syn.** *adj.* **1.** unintoxicated. **3.** See **grave.** —**Ant.** *adj.* **1.** intoxicated, drunk. **3.** lighthearted, gay.

so·ber·ize (sō′bə rīz), *v.t.,* **-ized, -iz·ing.** to make sober.

so·ber-mind·ed (sō′bər mīn′did), *adj.* having or showing a sober mind; self-controlled; sensible. —**so′ber-mind′ed·ness,** *n.* —**Syn.** reasonable.

so·ber·sid·ed (sō′bər sī′did), *adj.* having or showing a serious disposition; sedate: *Since I had known them as sobersided and sensible fellows, I felt their agitation might be worth looking into* (Bulletin of Atomic Scientists). —**so′ber·sid′ed·ness,** *n.*

so·ber·sides (sō′bər sīdz′), *n., pl.* **-sides.** a sedate or serious person: *a melancholy sobersides* (Charlotte Brontë). *The movie is sure to give all but the sobersides in the audience some pleasant moments* (Newsweek).

So·bran·je or **So·bran·ye** (sō brän′ye), *n.* the national assembly of Bulgaria, consisting of a single chamber of elected deputies. [< Bulgarian *sŭbranie* (literally) assembly]

so·bri·e·ty (sə brī′ə tē), *n., pl.* **-ties. 1.** soberness. **2. a.** temperance in the use of strong drink. **b.** avoidance of alcoholic beverages. **3.** moderation. **4.** quietness; seriousness. [< Old French *sobriete,* learned borrowing from Latin *sōbrietās, -ātis* < *sōbrius;* see SOBER] —**Syn. 2. a.** abstemiousness. **b.** abstinence. **4.** sedateness.

so·bri·quet (sō′brə kā), *n.* a nickname: *Because of his daring, energetic research methods, he acquired, and still wears, the sobriquet "Wild Bill"* (Time). Also, **soubriquet.** [< Middle French *sobriquet*]

sob sister, *U.S. Informal.* **1.** a woman reporter who writes with undue sentiment, usually about stories of personal hardship: *The sob sisters of the sentimental magazines are familiar figures of fun, and I do not wish to join their ranks* (Sunday Times). **2.** a person given to telling sob stories.

sob story, *U.S. Informal.* an overly sentimental story or pathetic account, especially of one's own hardship: *When a sob story sounded phony . . . Max . . . could also summon a waiter and say coldly: "Bring Mr. Smith the key to the crying room"* (Time).

soc., society.

Soc., 1. Socialist. **2.** Society.

soc·age or **soc·cage** (sok′ij), *n.* a former way of holding land by which the tenant paid a definite rent or did a definite amount of work, but gave no military service to his lord. [< Anglo-French *socage* < *soc* < Medieval Latin *soca* < Old English *sōcn* jurisdiction, inquiry, (originally) a seeking, hostile visitation]

soc·ag·er or **soc·cag·er** (sok′ə jər), *n.* a person who held land by socage.

so-called (sō′kôld′), *adj.* **1.** called thus. **2.** called thus improperly or incorrectly: *Her so-called friend really dislikes her. The so-called debtor class . . . are not dishonest because they are in debt* (Grover Cleveland). —**Syn. 2.** pseudo, pretended.
➔ **so-called.** *So-called* is usually hyphenated when it precedes its principal word, but not when it follows: *Their so-called liberal views were merely an echo of the conservative attitude. Their justice, so called, smacked of partiality.*

soc·cer (sok′ər), *n.* a game played between two teams of eleven men each, using a round ball; association football. The ball may be struck with any part of the body except the hands and arms. [short for *assoc.,* abbreviation of *association*]

Soccer

➔ **soccer, football.** In American use, these terms have never been synonymous: there is the game of football and the completely different game of soccer. In British use, *soccer* is usually called either "football" or "association football," while Rugby or Rugby football is the name for *football* as played in Great Britain.

so·cia·bil·i·ty (sō′shə bil′ə tē), *n., pl.* **-ties.** social disposition or behavior. —**Syn.** sociableness, sociality.

so·cia·ble (sō′shə bəl), *adj.* **1.** liking company; friendly: *The Smiths are a sociable family and entertain a great deal. Man is said to be a sociable animal* (Joseph Addison). **2.** marked by conversation and companionship: *We had a sociable afternoon together.* **3.** (of animals or plants) naturally inclined to be in company with others of the same species; social.
—*n. U.S.* an informal social gathering: *You'll see her settled down one of these days, and teaching Sunday School and helping at sociables* (Sinclair Lewis).
[< Latin *sociābilis* < *sociāre* to associate < *socius;* see SOCIAL] —**so′cia·ble·ness,** *n.*
—**Syn.** *adj.* **1.** See **social.**

sociable weaverbird or **grosbeak,** the republican grosbeak.

so·cia·bly (sō′shə blē), *adv.* in a sociable manner; conversably; familiarly.

so·cial (sō′shəl), *adj.* **1.** concerned with human beings in their relations to each other: *social justice. A great social and economic experiment, noble in motive and far-reaching in purpose* (Herbert Hoover). *The social state is . . . so natural, so necessary, and so habitual to man* (John Stuart Mill). **2.** of or dealing with the living conditions, health, etc., of human beings: *social problems, social work.* **3.** living or liking to live with others: *Man is a social being.* **4.** for companionship or friendliness; having to do with companionship or friendliness: *a social club, a social engagement.* **5.** liking company: *a social nature; . . . his own friendly and social disposition* (Jane Austen). **6.** connected with fashionable or polite society: *a social leader. Others avoid her company because she has no social grace.* **7. a.** (of animals) living together in organized communities: *Ants and bees are social insects.* **b.** (of plants) growing in wild patches or clumps. **8.** socialistic.
—*n.* a social gathering: *a church social.*
[< Latin *sociālis* < *socius* companion; (originally, adjective) mutual, sharing in, related to *sequī* to follow] —**so′cial·ness,** *n.*
—**Syn.** *adj.* **4, 5. Social, sociable** mean friendly or companionable. In this sense, **social** is now rarely applied to persons, and when it is, suggests fondness for group association rather than personal friendliness: *A man may be social but not at all sociable.* **Sociable,** the term usually ascribed to persons, means liking company and being inclined to seek and enjoy companionship and friendly relations even with strangers: *He is a likable, sociable person.*

social action, 1. *Sociology.* the behavior of an individual in response to his subjective evaluation of the motives of others and the values and goals of the society in which he lives. **2.** organized action taken by a group to improve social conditions.

social anthropology, the branch of anthropology that deals with the social customs, beliefs, and practices of man, especially in primitive and isolated societies.

social climber, a person who tries to gain acceptance or improve his standing in fashionable society by associating with people having more wealth or influence than he has.

social climbing, the actions or conduct of a social climber.

social contract, an agreement to regulate the relations of citizens with one another and with the government.

social control, 1. control of individual behavior by society. **2.** control of social institutions in the interest of the whole society: *Like business corporations, they can be subjected to social control* (Wall Street Journal).

social credit, an economic philosophy that believes in industrial cooperatives in which the consumers share the profits of industry as dividends.

Social Cred·i·ter (kred′ə tər), a member of the Social Credit Party; Socred.

Social Credit Party, a Canadian political party, founded in the 1930's, that advocates social credit.

social Darwinism, the application of the Darwinian theory of evolution to the origin, growth, and development of human society: *Social Darwinism . . . held that human races evolve like animal species and that the non-white races were at the bottom of the evolutionary scale* (Time).

social democracy, the principles of the Social Democrats or of a Social Democratic Party.

Social Democrat, a member or supporter of a Social Democratic Party.

Social Democratic, 1. of or having to do with the Social Democrats. **2.** characterized by or founded on the principles of social democracy.

Social Democratic Party, any of several political parties supporting socialism, especially the political party formed in Russia towards the end of the 1800's which split in 1903 into the Bolshevik (later Communist) and Menshevik parties.

social engineering, the application of the principles of the social sciences to practical social problems: *Colonial administration making use of sociological knowledge about [primitive] peoples is an illustration of social engineering* (Ogburn and Nimkoff).

social evil, 1. anything that is a danger to the welfare of people or opposed to the values of society: *Rat-infested slums and drunkenness are social evils.* **2.** prostitution.

social insurance, insurance of a person against unemployment, illness, etc., through government action: *There are several types of social insurance, such as accident insurance or workman's compensation, sickness and old-age insurance, and unemployment insurance* (Emory S. Bogardus).

so·cial·ism (sō′shə liz əm), *n.* **1.** a theory or system of social organization by which the means of production and distribution are owned, managed, or controlled by the government (state socialism) or by associations of workers (guild socialism). **2.** a political movement advocating or associated with this system. **3.** the practice of such a system. —**Syn. 1.** collectivism.

➔ See **communism** for usage note.

so·cial·ist (sō′shə list), *n.* a person who favors and supports socialism. —*adj.* socialistic.

So·cial·ist (sō′shə list), *n.* a member of a Socialist Party. —*adj.* of or having to do with a Socialist Party.

Socialist and Labor International, an international socialistic organization formed in Germany in 1923 to succeed the Second International, and reorganized in 1948, with headquarters in London.

so·cial·is·tic (sō′shə lis′tik), *adj.* **1.** of or having to do with socialism or socialists. **2.** advocating or supporting socialism.

so·cial·is·ti·cal·ly (sō′shə lis′tə klē), *adv.* in a socialistic manner.

Socialist Party, a political party that favors and supports socialism.

so·cial·ite (sō′shə līt), *n.* **1.** a member of the fashionable society of a community. **2.** a person active in the social life of a community.

so·ci·al·i·ty (sō′shē al′ə tē), *n., pl.* **-ties. 1.** social activity; social intercourse. **2.** social nature or tendencies: *The congregating of people in cities and towns show sociality.*

so·cial·i·za·tion (sō′shə lə zā′shən), *n.* **1.** the act of socializing: *Socialization is a genuine and wholesome identification of a person with the welfare of other persons, of his own group and of other groups* (Emory S. Bogardus). **2.** the state of being socialized. **3.** the act of placing or establishing something on a socialistic basis.

so·cial·ize (sō′shə līz), *v.,* **-ized, -iz·ing.** —*v.t.* **1.** to make social: *to socialize a discussion.* **2.** to make fit for living with others; adapt to life as a social animal. **3.** to adapt to community needs. **4.** to establish or regulate in accordance with socialism: *to socialize transportation.* —*v.i.* to enter social relationships with others: *He has never learned to socialize with his co-workers.*

so·cial·ized medicine (sō′shə līzd), the providing of medical care and hospital services for all classes of society, especially through government subsidization and administration.

social ladder, the levels of society, from lowest to highest: *As an aggressive climber, he rose rapidly on the social ladder.*

so·cial·ly (sō′shə lē), *adv.* **1.** in a social way or manner; in relation to other people: *to be highly developed socially.* **2.** as a member of society or of a social group: *He is an able man, but socially he is a failure.*

so·cial-mind·ed (sō′shəl mīn′did), *adj.* aware of and concerned with social problems and conditions: *In a Communist-riddled see, this active, social-minded cardinal is loved for his generosity and simplicity* (Newsweek). —**so′cial-mind′ed·ness,** *n.*

social pathology, 1. the study of the problems and ills of human society, such as poverty, unemployment, crime, divorce, etc., considered as analogous to bodily disease. **2.** these problems and ills themselves.

social pressure, the force of a group on an individual to make him behave more like the members of the group.

social psychology, the branch of psychology concerned with human beings in their relations to each other.

Social Realism, (in art and literature) an anti-Romantic movement primarily concerned with depicting and commenting upon the social, economic, and political problems of the times.

social register, a list of people who are prominent in fashionable society.

social reg·is·ter·ite (rej′ə stər īt), a person listed in the social register; socially prominent person.

social science, the study of people, their activities, and their customs in relationship to others: *History, sociology, anthropology, economics, and civics are social sciences.*

social scientist, a person skilled in one or more of the social sciences.

social secretary, a secretary who makes arrangements for and keeps track of the social activities of a person or group.

social security, a system of federal old-age pensions for employed persons begun in 1935. The government pays part of the pension, part is deducted from the employee's salary, and part is paid by his employer.

social service, social work.

social settlement, an establishment to improve conditions in a poor neighborhood; settlement.

social studies, *U.S.* subject matter drawn from the social sciences as presented in elementary and high schools; history, civics, economics, anthropology, and other related fields.

social unit, 1. a person or any grouping of people considered as a unit in social organization: *An individual and a family are two different kinds of social units.* **2.** the group of residents in a given area of a community which is being redeveloped.

social wasp, any of various wasps, including hornets and yellow jackets, that live together, usually in large paperlike nests.

social welfare, social work.

social work, work directed toward the betterment of social conditions in a community. Child welfare bureaus, district nursing organizations, free clinics, family counseling services, etc., are forms of social work.

social worker, a person who does social work.

so·cié·taire (sô syā ter′), *n.* an actor in the French national theater in Paris who has a share in the management of the theater and its profits. [< French *sociétaire*]

so·ci·e·tal (sə sī′ə təl), *adj.* of or having to do with society: *Many of the interrelated societal factors . . . have gone into the making of our modern American culture* (Hugh M. Hefner). —**so·ci′e·tal·ly,** *adv.*

so·ci·e·tar·i·an (sə sī′ə tãr′ē ən), *adj.* societal.

so·ci·e·tar·y (sə sī′ə ter′ē), *adj.* societal.

so·cié·té a·no·nyme (sô syā tā′ ȧ nô-nēm′), a business firm in which the liability of each partner or member is limited to the amount of his investment. *Abbr.:* S.A. [< French (literally) anonymous society; because originally the members were silent and anonymous]

so·ci·e·ty (sə sī′ə tē), *n., pl.* **-ties. 1.** a group of persons joined together for a common purpose or by a common interest. A club, a fraternity, a lodge, or an association may be called a society: *a debating society, a legal society. Abbr.:* Soc. **2. a.** all the people; human beings as a group: *The good of society demands that all wrongdoing be punished.* **b.** the people of any particular time or place: *No political society can be, nor subsist without having in itself the power to preserve the property . . . of all those of that society* (John Locke). *A culture is the way of life of a people; while a society is the organized aggregate of individuals who follow a given way of life* (Melville J. Herskovits). **c.** those people thought of as a group because of common economic position, similar interest, etc.: *in cultivated society; the lower, middle, or upper classes of society.* **d.** their activities and customs: *In the earliest stages of society there are many arts, but no sciences* (Henry T. Buckle). **3.** company; companionship: *I enjoy his society. The soul selects her own society, Then shuts the door* (Emily Dickinson). **4. a.** fashionable people. **b.** their doings. **5. a.** an organized community of animals or insects: *a society of wasps.* **b.** an assemblage of plants of the same species not dominant in an ecological community. **6.** *U.S.* (in Congregational churches) the corporation that administers the church property, employs the minister, etc. [< Middle French *société* < Old French *societe,* learned borrowing from Latin *societās* < *socius;* see SOCIAL] —**Syn. 4. a.** élite.

society column, *U.S.* a column in a newspaper devoted to news about socially prominent people.

Society of Friends, the Quakers; a Christian sect opposed to war and to taking oaths, and favoring simple clothes and manners. This sect was founded by George Fox in England about 1650.

Society of Jesus, a Roman Catholic religious order, founded by Saint Ignatius Loyola in 1534. Its members are called Jesuits. *Abbr.:* S.J.

society verse, light, graceful poetry. [translation of French *vers de société*]

So·cin·i·an (sō sin′ē ən), *n.* a person who believes in Socinianism. —*adj.* having to do with Socinianism or its followers.

So·cin·i·an·ism (sō sin′ē ə niz′əm), *n.* the doctrines of Laelius Socinus and his nephew Faustus, Italian theologians of the 1500's. They denied the divinity of Christ.

so·ci·o·bi·o·log·i·cal (sō′sē ō bī′ə loj′ə-kəl, -shē-), *adj.* **1.** of, having to do with, or involving both sociology and biology. **2.** biosocial: *He justly likens the sociobiological effects of the First and Second World Wars to those of the Black Death* (Manchester Guardian).

so·ci·o·bi·ol·o·gy (sō′sē ō bī ol′ə jē, -shē-), *n.* sociological study that uses the theories and principles of biology; sociobiological science.

so·ci·oc·ra·cy (sō′sē ok′rə sē, -shē-), *n.* government by society as a whole.

so·ci·o·crat (sō′sē ə krat, -shē-), *n.* a person who believes in sociocracy.

so·ci·o·cul·tur·al (sō′sē ō kul′chər əl, -shē-), *adj.* of or having to do with both society and culture; social and cultural at the same time: *The question of development is being more and more often treated as a complex sociocultural change where economic development is only one result to be obtained* (Bulletin of Atomic Scientists).

so·ci·o·dra·ma (sō′sē ō drä′mə, -shē-; -dram′ə), *n.* the acting out of real-life situations by a group as a method of instruction or rehabilitation; role-playing.

so·ci·o·e·co·nom·ic (sō′sē ō ē′kə nom′ik, -shē-; -ek′ə-), *adj.* **1.** having to do with phenomena that are both social and economic. **2.** having to do with or involving a person's social and financial status: *By all the evidence, Americans will soon consider at least two years of college a socioeconomic necessity* (Time).

so·ci·o·ge·net·ic (sō′sē ō jə net′ik, -shē-), *adj.* of or having to do with the forces and conditions which create and mold society.

so·ci·og·ra·phy (sō′sē og′rə fē, -shē-), *n.* the observing and descriptive stage or branch of sociology.

sociol., 1. sociological. **2.** sociology.

so·ci·o·log·ic (sō′sē ə loj′ik, -shē-), *adj.* sociological.

so·ci·o·log·i·cal (sō′sē ə loj′ə kəl, -shē-), *adj.* **1.** of or having to do with human society or problems relating to it: *The care of the poor is a sociological concern. . . . the sociological problem of a changing neighborhood* (New York Times). **2.** of sociology: *Sociological concepts already mount upward into the hundreds* (Emory S. Bogardus).

so·ci·o·log·i·cal·ly (sō′sē ə loj′ə klē, -shē-), *adv.* according to sociology; from the standpoint of sociology: *The Tweed Courthouse . . . was somewhat more significant sociologically than aesthetically* (New Yorker).

so·ci·ol·o·gist (sō′sē ol′ə jist, -shē-), *n.* a student of human society and its problems; a person skilled in sociology.

so·ci·ol·o·gy (sō′sē ol′ə jē, -shē-), *n.* the study of the nature, origin, and development of human society and community life; science of social facts. Sociology deals with the facts of crime, poverty, marriage, divorce, the church, the school, etc.: *... sociology, which deals with the relationship of man to his fellowman ...* (Harbaugh and Goodrich). *Sociology as the science of human association in groups has had a century-long history* (Emory S. Bogardus). *Abbr.:* sociol. [< French *sociologie* < Latin *socius* companion + French *-logie* -logy]

so·ci·o·met·ric (sō′sē ō met′rik, -shē-), *adj.* **1.** of or having to do with sociometry. **2.** measuring or indicating the existence, extent, or quality of social relationships: *sociometric tests, sociometric status.*

so·ci·om·e·try (sō′sē om′ə trē, -shē-), *n.* the branch of sociology that measures human relationships.

so·ci·o·path (sō′sē ə path, -shē-), *n.* a person who lacks social or moral responsibility because of mental illness; psychopath: *The sociopath is a person who knows that what he is doing is wrong, but doesn't care* (New York Times). [< *social;* patterned on *psychopath*]

so·ci·o·path·ic (sō′sē ə path′ik, -shē-), *adj.* of a sociopath; like that of a sociopath: *a sociopathic personality.*

so·ci·o·po·lit·i·cal (sō′sē ō pə lit′ə kəl, -shē-), *adj.* of or having to do with both society and politics; social and political at the same time: *The chief manifestation of this dehumanizing process is the constantly increasing sociopolitical pressure on all men to conform in thought, action, and aspiration* (New Yorker).

so·ci·o·psy·cho·log·i·cal (sō′sē ō sī′kə loj′ə kəl, -shē-), *adj.* **1.** social and psychological: *The major focus of our social policies on drug use should be on prevention by eliminating the sociopsychological roots* (New York Times). **2.** of or having to do with social psychology. **3.** psychosocial.

so·ci·us (sō′sē əs), *n. Latin.* a fellow; associate; member.

so·ci·us crim·i·nis (sō′sē us krim′ə nis), *Law.* an accomplice or associate in the commission of a crime. [< Latin *socius* sharer; *crīminis,* genitive of *crīmen* crime]

sock[1] (sok), *n.* **1. a.** a short stocking, especially one that reaches about halfway to the knee. **b.** any article or covering similar to this. **2.** a light, low shoe worn by actors in comedy in ancient Greece and Rome. **3.** comedy. **4.** the comic muse. **5.** *Informal.* a wind sock. —*v.t.* to provide with socks; put socks on.

sock away, *Slang.* to save or hoard (money), as by putting it away in a sock: *Most Americans still aren't convinced the recession is over, so they're still trying to sock a little money away—just in case* (Wall Street Journal).

sock in, *Slang.* to close or restrict because of poor visibility, bad weather, etc.: *Fog and drizzle had socked in the runways* (Time).

[Old English *socc* a light slipper < Latin *soccus*]

sock[2] (sok), *Informal.* —*v.t.* **1.** to strike or hit hard; punch: *to sock a person in the nose.* **2.** to send by hitting: *to sock a ball over the fence.* —*n.* a hard blow. —*adv.* squarely; right. [originally dialectal, probably related to *sockdolager*]

sock·dol·a·ger (sok dol′ə jər), *n. U.S. Slang.* **1.** something unusually large, heavy, etc., of its kind: *The forthcoming safari into Tanganyika ... was destined to be a sockdolager* (New Yorker). **2.** a finishing blow. [American English; perhaps alteration of *doxology;* influenced by *sock*[2]]

sock·er·oo (sok′ə rü′), *n. U.S. Slang.* a smash hit; smasheroo; socko: *Carol Haney ... is one of the major attractions of "The Pajama Game," ... the '53-'54 legit season's sockeroo* (New Yorker).

sock·et (sok′it), *n.* **1.** a hollow part or piece for receiving and holding something: *to screw an electric bulb into a socket. Put paper at the bottom of the candle to make it fit the socket of the candlestick.* **2.** a connecting place for electric wires and plugs: *Please plug the lamp into the socket on the wall.* **3.** *Anatomy.* a hollow place in some part of a bone, tooth, etc., in which another part moves: *The eyes are set in two bony hollows in the head called the eye sockets.* **4.** the part of an iron golf club where the shaft is fitted into the head.
—*v.t.* to put in a socket; fit with a socket.
[< Anglo-French *soket* < Old French *soc* plowshare < Vulgar Latin *soccus,* probably < a Gaulish word]

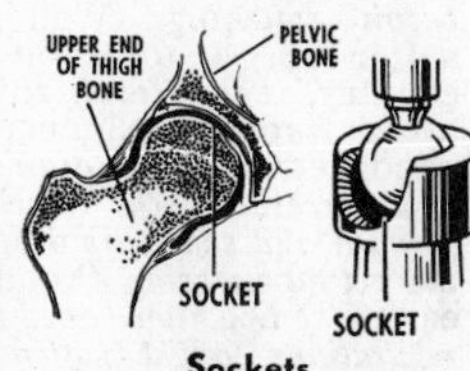

Sockets
Left, hip joint; right, ball and socket

socket chisel, a chisel having a hollow tang in which the handle is inserted.

socket wrench, a wrench having a socket fitted to a particular size and shape of nut or bolthead to be turned or held.

sock·eye salmon (sok′ī′), a salmon of the northern Pacific from Japan to California that ascends rivers to spawn; the blueback salmon. See **nerka** for picture. [American English, alteration of Salishan *sukkegh*]

sock·less (sok′lis), *adj.* lacking socks: *Leonard Lyons left in a dudgeon when the sockless hipsters began to outnumber the quality folk* (Time).

sock·o (sok′ō), *U.S. Slang.* —*n.* a very successful venture or effect, especially in the theater: *It became a sweet socko, an experience that Wodehouse is probably more familiar with than any other humorist* (Newsweek). —*adj.* very successful; wonderful; terrific, especially in reference to a theatrical hit: *For writers, too, the Private Eye shows make a socko source of income* (Time).

so·cle (sok′əl, sō′kəl), *n.* a low, plain block supporting a wall, a pedestal, or the like: *I paused in front of a bust of Alfred de Musset to read again on its socle one of my favorite cheer-up bits of literature* (New Yorker). [< French *socle* < Italian *zoccolo* (originally) a wooden shoe < Latin *socculus* (diminutive) < *soccus* slipper; see SOCK[1]]

soc·man (sok′mən), *n., pl.* **-men.** a person who held land in socage.

soc·man·ry (sok′mən rē), *n., pl.* **-ries.** tenure by socage. [< Medieval Latin *socmanaria* < *socmannus* feudal tenant < Old English *sōcman*]

So·crat·ic (sō krat′ik), *adj.* of or having to do with Socrates, his philosophy, followers, etc.: *My role was a Socratic one, to question them persistently and fairly ruthlessly to force them to consider important problems* (Technology). —*n.* a follower of Socrates.

So·crat·i·cal·ly (sō krat′ə klē), *adv.* **1.** in the Socratic manner. **2.** by the Socratic method.

Socratic irony, pretended ignorance in discussion.

So·crat·i·cism (sō krat′ə siz əm), *n.* **1.** Socratism. **2.** a Socratic peculiarity, trait, etc.

Socratic method, the use of a series of questions to lead a pupil to think, to make an opponent contradict himself, etc. It is based on the assumption that truth is never incompatible with reason.

Soc·ra·tism (sok′rə tiz əm), *n.* the doctrines or philosophy of Socrates.

Soc·red (sok′red), *n.* a member of the Social Credit Party in Canada.

sod[1] (sod), *n., v.,* **sod·ded, sod·ding.** —*n.* **1.** ground covered with grass: *Scores of species of smaller grasses and of colorful wildflowers, all knit together into a deep, tough sod* (Fred W. Emerson). **2.** a piece or layer of this containing the grass and its roots.

the old sod, *Informal.* one's native country or district: *And did ye see old Ireland lately? And how's the poor old sod?* (E. Roper).

under the sod, buried: *I've heard the boys say that he would be under the sod that day* (Anthony Trollope).

—*v.t.* to cover with sods: *a newly sodded grave* (Charlotte Brontë).
[compare Middle Low German *sode*]

sod[2] (sod), *v. Obsolete.* a past tense of **seethe.**

so·da (sō′də), *n.* **1.** any of several substances containing sodium, as sodium carbonate (washing soda or sal soda), sodium bicarbonate (baking soda), and sodium hydroxide (caustic soda). **2.** soda water. **3.** soda water flavored with fruit juice or syrup, and usually containing ice cream: *a chocolate soda.* **4.** (in faro) the top card, shown face up in the dealing box, as play begins. [< Medieval Latin, Italian, or Spanish *soda* < Italian *sodo* firm < Latin *solidus* solid]

soda ash, partly purified sodium carbonate: *Soda ash is used largely by glass makers* (Wall Street Journal).

soda biscuit, 1. a biscuit made with soda and sour milk. **2.** soda cracker.

soda bread, bread made with baking soda and sour milk.

soda cracker, a simple, light, thin cracker made with little or no sugar or shortening.

soda fountain, 1. an apparatus for holding soda water, syrups, ice, etc., and having faucets for drawing off the liquids. **2.** a counter with places for holding soda water, flavored syrups, ice cream, etc. **3.** a store having such a counter.

soda jerk or **jerker,** *Slang.* a person who works behind a soda fountain: *A jumbo-sized banana split Which, when the soda jerk was through, Looked like the Taj Mahal in goo* (Wall Street Journal).

soda lime, a mixture of sodium hydroxide (caustic soda) and calcium hydroxide (slaked lime), used as a reagent and to absorb gases, especially carbon dioxide, and moisture.

so·da·list (sō′də list), *n.* a member of a sodality.

so·da·lite (sō′də līt), *n.* a silicate of sodium and aluminum with chlorine. It occurs in crystals and also massively, is usually blue, and is found in igneous rocks. *Princess marble or sodalite is used for ornamental purposes* (World Book Encyclopedia). *Formula:* $Na_4(AlCl)Al_2(SiO_4)_3$ [< *soda* + *-lite*]

so·dal·i·ty (sō dal′ə tē), *n., pl.* **-ties. 1.** fellowship; friendship. **2.** an association, society, or fraternity: *There were ... military sodalities of musketeers, cross-bowmen, archers, swordsmen in every town* (John L. Motley). **3.** (in the Roman Catholic Church) a lay society with religious or charitable purposes. [< Latin *sodālitās* < *sodālis* companion; (literally) sociable]

so·da·mide (sō′də mīd), *n.* sodium amide.

soda pop, a nonalcoholic carbonated drink: *The folks are gobbling huge quantities of cotton candy, hot dogs, ice cream and soda pop* (Wall Street Journal).

soda water, water charged with carbon dioxide to make it bubble and fizz, often served with the addition of syrup, ice cream, etc., or mixed with an alcoholic drink; carbonated water.

sod·bust·er (sod′bus′tər), *n. Western U.S. Slang.* a farmer: *Its tune was familiar to the lonely "sodbuster"* (Carl Sandburg).

sod·den (sod′ən), *adj.* **1.** soaked through; saturated: *The boy's clothing was sodden with rain.* **2.** heavy and moist; soggy: *This bread is sodden because it was not baked well.* **3.** dull-looking; stupid: *a sodden face, a head sodden with whiskey.* **4.** *Obsolete.* boiled; seethed.
—*v.t., v.i.* **1.** to make or become sodden. **2.** *Obsolete.* a past participle of **seethe.**
—sod′den·ly, *adv.* **—sod′den·ness,** *n.*

sod·dy (sod′ē), *adj.,* **-di·er, -di·est,** *n., pl.* **-dies.** —*adj.* of or like sod; made of sods. —*n.* a house made of sods: *Later, settlers often improved their soddies by whitewashing the walls and hauling in lumber for doors and ceilings* (World Book Encyclopedia).

so·dic (sō′dik), *adj.* **1.** of sodium. **2.** containing sodium. [< *sod*(ium) + *-ic*]

so·di·um (sō′dē əm), *n.* a soft, silver-white, metallic chemical element occurring in nature only in compounds. Salt and soda contain sodium. Sodium is one of the alkali metals which oxidize rapidly in the presence of air and react violently with water. *Sodium is made by distillation and in New York any still—sodium or bourbon—must be okayed by the liquor board* (Wall Street Journal). *Symbol:* Na (for *natrium*); *at.wt.:* (C^{12}) 22.9898 or (O^{16}) 22.991; *at.no.:* 11; *valence:* 1. [< *sod*(a) + New Latin *-ium* element]

sodium acetate, a colorless crystalline or white granular salt of acetic acid, used in dyeing and as a reagent in photography. *Formula:* $C_2H_3NaO_2$

sodium alginate, a cream-colored, powdery salt of algin obtained from kelp, used in making hand lotions and reducing pills, as a food preservative, and to thicken buttermilk, ice cream, etc.

sodium amide, a white, crystalline, flammable powder used in making sodium cyanide and in organic synthesis; sodamide. *Formula:* $NaNH_2$

Sodium Amytal, *Trademark.* a white, odorless, powdery salt, used as a sedative and hypnotic: *Sometimes a patient is so disturbed that the doctors ... use Sodium Amytal ... to help the patient to communicate* (Time). *Formula:* $C_{11}H_{17}N_2NaO_3$

sodium arsenite, a very poisonous, white or grayish-white powdery salt, used as an insecticide against termites and scale insects and as an antiseptic. *Formula:* $NaAsO_2$

sodium benzoate, a white crystalline or powdery salt of benzoic acid, used especially to preserve food and in medicine as an antiseptic. *Formula:* $C_7H_5NaO_2$

sodium bicarbonate, a powdery, white, crystalline salt, with a somewhat alkaline taste, used in cooking, baking powders, medicine, etc.; baking soda; bicarbonate of soda. *Formula:* $NaHCO_3$

sodium bisulfate, a crystalline or white granular salt, used as a strong acid in dyeing, in the manufacture of paper, glue, soap, perfume, etc., as a disinfectant, and as a flux for decomposing metals. *Formula:* $NaHSO_4 \cdot H_2O$

sodium borate, borax.

sodium bo·ro·hy·dride (bôr′ō hī′drīd, -drid; bōr′-), a crystalline salt, used to reduce aldehydes, ketones, and acid halides, and in making fuels for jet airplanes and guided missiles. *Formula:* $NaBH_4$

sodium bromide, a white, crystalline, granular or powdery salt with a somewhat bitter taste, used in photography and in medicine as a sedative. *Formula:* NaBr

sodium carbonate, 1. a salt that occurs in a powdery white form and in a hydrated crystalline form called washing soda. It is used for softening water, making soap and glass, neutralizing acids, as a reagent, in medicine and photography, etc. *Formula:* Na_2CO_3 **2.** sodium bicarbonate.

sodium chlorate, a colorless crystalline salt, used as an oxidizing agent, in fireworks and explosives, in dyeing, and as an antiseptic in toothpaste, mouthwash, etc. *Formula:* $NaClO_3$

sodium chloride, common salt: *Sodium chloride is of first importance as the naturally occurring substance from which most other sodium compounds ... are prepared* (William N. Jones). *Formula:* NaCl

sodium citrate, a white, odorless, crystalline, granular or powdery salt, used in photography, in medicine as a diuretic and expectorant and to prevent stored blood from clotting, and in preserving foods. *Formula:* $C_6H_5Na_3O_7.2H_2O$

sodium cyanide, a very poisonous, white, crystalline salt, used in the cyanide process for extracting gold and silver from ores, in fumigating, etc. *Formula:* NaCN

sodium dichromate, an orange crystalline salt, used as an oxidizing agent, as a reagent, and as an antiseptic. *Formula:* $Na_2Cr_2O_7.2H_2O$

sodium fluoride, a poisonous crystalline salt, used as an insecticide, a disinfectant, in the fluoridation of water, and in treating certain forms of tooth decay. *Formula:* NaF

sodium fluoroacetate, a white, odorless, poisonous powder used as a rodenticide; teneighty.

sodium hydrogen carbonate, sodium bicarbonate.

sodium hydroxide, a white solid that is a strong, corrosive alkali, used in making hard soaps and rayon, in the paper industry, in tanning, and as a bleaching agent; caustic soda. *Formula:* NaOH

sodium hypochlorite, a crystalline salt, used as an antiseptic and disinfectant. Most household bleaches contain a solution of 5 or 6 per cent sodium hypochlorite in water. *Formula:* $NaClO.5H_2O$

sodium hyposulfite, 1. a crystalline salt, used as a bleaching and reducing agent. *Formula:* $Na_2S_2O_4$ **2.** sodium thiosulfate.

sodium iodide, a white, odorless, crystalline or granular salt, used in photography, animal feeds, and in treating respiratory and nervous disorders. *Formula:* NaI

sodium lamp, sodium-vapor lamp.

sodium nitrate, a colorless, crystalline compound, used in making fertilizers, explosives, etc.; Chile saltpeter. *Formula:* $NaNO_3$

sodium nitrite, a white or pale-yellow granular or powdery salt, used in making dyes and organic chemicals, and to treat cyanide poisoning in animals. *Formula:* $NaNO_2$

sodium oxide, a white powder that becomes sodium hydroxide by reaction with water, used especially as a dehydrating agent.

sodium pen·ta·chlo·ro·phe·nate (pen′tə klôr′ə fē′nāt, -klōr′-), a tan, powdery salt, used to destroy fungi, parasitic worms in snails, and as a disinfectant. *Formula:* C_6CL_5ONa

sodium pentothal, thiopental sodium, a barbiturate; Pentothal Sodium.

sodium perborate, perborax.

sodium phosphate, any of various colorless crystalline or white granular salts of sodium and phosphorus occurring in hydrous and anhydrous forms, and used as laxatives, in textile printing, photography, in water softeners, etc. *Formula:* Na_2HPO_4

sodium silicate, a colorless, white or grayish-white crystallike substance, used in preserving eggs, in soap powders, as an adhesive in paper and cardboard products, etc.

sodium sulfate, an odorless, colorless crystalline or white granular salt, used in making glass, dyeing textiles, and in medicine as a strong laxative; Glauber's salt. *Formula:* $Na_2SO_4.10H_2O$

sodium thiosulfate, a colorless or white crystalline salt, used as a fixative in photography, in dyeing, in bleaching, etc.; hypo. *Formula:* $Na_2S_2O_3$

so·di·um-va·por lamp (sō′dē əm vā′pər), an electric street light with two electrodes that cause the sodium vapor in the light to glow when electricity passes through them.

Sod·om (sod′əm), *n.* **1.** an ancient city near the Dead Sea which, according to the account in the Bible, was destroyed by fire from heaven because of the wickedness of its inhabitants. Genesis 18 and 19. **2.** any extremely wicked or corrupt place.

sod·om·ite (sod′ə mīt), *n.* a person who practices sodomy. [< *sodom*(y) + *-ite*[1]]

Sod·om·ite (sod′ə mīt), *n.* an inhabitant of Sodom.

sod·o·mit·ic (sod′ə mit′ik), *adj.* sodomitical.

sod·o·mit·i·cal (sod′ə mit′ə kəl), *adj.* **1.** of, having to do with, or involving sodomy. **2.** given to or guilty of sodomy; grossly wicked.

sod·o·mit·i·cal·ly (sod′ə mit′ə klē), *adv.* in a sodomitical manner.

sod·om·ize (sod′ə mīz), *v.t.*, **-ized, -iz·ing.** to commit sodomy upon.

sod·om·y (sod′ə mē), *n.* unnatural sexual intercourse, especially of one man with another or of a human being with an animal. [< Old French *sodomie* < *Sodom*]

so·ev·er (sō ev′ər), *adv.* **1.** in any case; in any way; in any degree: *to persist no matter how long soever the task may take.* **2.** of any kind; at all: *He has no home soever.*

-soever, *suffix.* in any way; of any kind; at all; ever, as in *whosoever, whatsoever, whensoever, wheresoever, howsoever.*

so·fa (sō′fə), *n.* a long, upholstered seat or couch having a back and usually arms. [perhaps < French *sofa* < Arabic *suffah*] —**Syn.** settee, davenport.

Sofa (Louis XV)

sofa bed, a sofa that can be made into a bed, usually by removing the cushions and pulling the seat forward.

so·far (sō′fär), *n.* a method of locating the position of an underwater explosion by measuring the difference in the time the vibrations of the sound reach three or more distant points. [< *so*(und) *f*(ixing) *a*(nd) *r*(anging)]

so-fa syllables (sō′fä′), syllables used in reading music; sol-fa syllables.

sofa table, a table designed to be placed near the side, back, or front of a sofa.

sof·fio·ni (sōf fyō′nē), *n.pl.* vents from which steam, sulfurous fumes, and other exhalations issue in the dying stages of volcanic action. [< Italian *soffioni* < *soffio* a blowing < *soffiare* to blow upwardly < Latin *sufflāre;* see SUFFLATE]

sof·fit (sof′it), *n.* the undersurface or face of an architrave, arch, or the like. [< Italian *soffitta,* also *soffitto* ceiling, ultimately < Latin *suffigere* < *sub-* under + *figere* to fix, fasten]

Soffits (S)

S. of Sol., Song of Solomon.

soft (sôft, soft), *adj.* **1. a.** not hard; yielding readily to touch or pressure: *a soft tomato, soft ground, a soft bed.* **b.** easily bent without breaking; not stiff; flexible: *Oil keeps leather soft.* **c.** capable of being hammered or pressed into various shapes without being broken; malleable: *soft iron. Copper and lead are softer than steel.* **2.** not hard compared with other things of the same kind: *Pine wood is softer than oak. Chalk is much softer than granite.* **3.** not hard or sharp; gentle and graceful: *soft shadows, soft outlines.* **4.** fine in texture; not rough or coarse; smooth: *a soft skin, soft hair.* **5.** not loud; quiet; subdued: *a soft tap on the door, to speak in a soft voice, to play soft music. The soft rustle of a maiden's gown* (Keats). **6.** quietly pleasant; calm; mild: *a soft breeze. The soft airs that o'er the meadows play* (William Cullen Bryant). **7.** not glaring or harsh: *soft colors, a soft light.* **8.** gentle; kind; tender: *a soft heart. He ... was very soft and gentle with the children* (Thackeray). *He was fond of saying soft things which were intended to have no meaning* (Anthony Trollope). **9.** not strong or robust; weak; unmanly: *muscles which have grown soft from lack of use. The army had become soft from idleness and luxury.* **10.** silly: *soft in the head.* **11.** easy; easy-going: *a soft job, to lead a soft life.* **12.** (of water) good to wash with because comparatively free from certain mineral salts that prevent soap from lathering: *Rain water contains no dissolved solid matter and so is soft* (World Book Encyclopedia). **13.** of or having to do with soft goods: *For many years the chain sold soft lines—clothing—only on a limited basis* (Wall Street Journal). **14.** *Phonetics.* **a.** pronounced as a fricative or an affricate, rather than as a stop. *Example: C* is soft in *city* and hard in *corn; g* is soft in *gentle* and hard in *get.* **b.** (of Slavic consonants) palatalized. **c.** lenis. **d.** voiced. *Example: B* and *d* are soft. **15.** (of photographic prints or negatives) having little contrast between light and shade. **16.** *Physics.* of or having to do with radiation that has low powers of penetration, such as X rays. **17.** (of wheat) containing little gluten.
—*adv.* in a soft manner; quietly; gently: *The wanderer ... Halts on the bridge to hearken How soft the poplar sighs* (A.E. Housman).
—*n.* that which is soft; soft part.
—*interj. Archaic.* hush! stop!
[Old English *sōfte*] —**soft′ly,** *adv.*
—**Syn.** *adj.* **1. b.** pliable. **5.** low. **8.** sympathetic, compassionate.

sof·ta (sof′tə), *n.* in Turkey: **1.** a student at a secondary school. **2.** a student of Moslem theology and sacred law. [< Turkish *softa* < Persian *sūkhtah* afire (with zeal for study)]

soft·back (sôft′bak′, soft′-), *n.* a paperback book.

soft·ball (sôft′bôl′, soft′-), *n.* **1.** a modified kind of baseball that uses a larger and softer ball. **2.** the ball used in this game. [American English < *soft* + *ball*]

soft-bod·ied (sôft′bod′ēd, soft′-), *adj.* having a soft body, as the mollusks.

soft-boiled (sôft′boild′, soft′-), *adj.* (of an egg) boiled only a little so that the yolk is still soft.

soft chancre, chancroid.

soft clam, an edible kind of clam with a long thin shell, found along both coasts of North America; long clam.

soft coal, bituminous coal.

soft-cov·er (sôft′kuv′ər, soft′-), *adj., n.* paperback: *Available in soft-cover and hard-cover bindings* (American Scholar).

soft currency, a currency weakly supported, that cannot be readily converted into other currencies without discount.

soft detergent, a detergent that can be decomposed by bacteria in sewage.

soft drink, a drink that does not contain alcohol.

soft drug, a hallucinogenic drug not considered addictive, such as cocaine, amphetamine, and various cannabis products.

soft·en (sôf′ən, sof′-), *v.t.* to make soft or softer. —*v.i.* **1.** to become soft or softer. **2.** *U.S.* to decrease; decline: *Business was strong until the middle of September, then began softening* (Wall Street Journal).
soften up, a. to lessen the ability of (a country, region, etc.) to resist invasion or attack through preliminary bombing, propaganda, etc.: *In the Indian softening up operations several places in East Pakistan were bombed and saboteurs dropped to prepare for the actual invasion* (London Times). **b.** to ease: *The Governor hoped the stringent Guard regulations might soften up the stubborn resistance of merchants and restaurateurs, who have been adamant in opposing any integration* (New York Times). **c.** to

placate: *I thought, in short, that I was softening up the citizens, and they thought they were softening me up, at least to the point where a dialogue becomes possible* (Atlantic). **d.** to weaken: *Did they in fact lose . . . because they had been softened up by the good life?* (Saturday Review).
—**soft′en·er,** *n.*

soft·en·ing of the brain (sôf′ə ning, sof′-), **1.** a degenerative disease of the brain in which the tissues become soft and fatty, caused by a deficient blood supply. **2.** general paresis. **3.** *Informal.* a weakening of the mental processes.

soft-finned (sôft′find′, soft′-), *adj.* (of fish) not having spines in the fins.

soft focus, intentional diffusion of the light in a photograph or movie film to lessen the sharpness of detail, obtained either by a special lens or attachment on the camera, or by certain methods in processing.

soft-fo·cus (sôft′fō′kəs, soft′-), *adj.* having, characterized by, or causing a soft focus.

soft goods, textiles, clothing, etc.; dry goods.

soft hail, snow pellets.

soft·head (sôft′hed′, soft′-), *n.* a simpleton; fool.

soft-head·ed (sôft′hed′id, soft′-), *adj.* foolish; silly: *He would adopt a middle ground between . . . panicked retreat . . . and . . . soft-headed submission* (New York Times).
—**soft′-head′ed·ness,** *n.*

soft-heart·ed (sôft′här′tid, soft′-), *adj.* gentle; kind; tender: *My grandmother was . . . soft-hearted to children* (Harriet Beecher Stowe). —**soft′-heart′ed·ness,** *n.*

soft·ie (sôf′tē, sof′-), *n. Informal.* a softy.

soft·ish (sôf′tish, sof′-), *adj.* somewhat soft; rather tender: *A bed of softish limestone* (Thomas H. Huxley).

soft-land (sôft′land′, soft′-), *v.t., v.i.* to set down or alight in a soft landing: *A 2,300-pound spacecraft is to soft-land cameras and instruments on the moon* (Wall Street Journal). [back formation < *soft landing*]

soft landing, the landing of a spacecraft, instruments, etc., on a body in outer space at such slow speed as to avoid destruction of the landing object.

soft loan, *U.S.* a loan at a very low rate of interest and a long period in which to repay it, as in foreign aid.

soft money, paper money.

soft·ness (sôft′nis, soft′-), *n.* **1.** the condition or quality of being soft. **2.** mildness; gentleness. **3.** weakness of character or disposition. **4.** ease; comfort; luxury.

soft palate, the fleshy back part of the roof of the mouth.

soft pedal, a pedal for softening the tone of a piano.

soft-ped·al (sôft′ped′əl, soft′-), *v.,* **-aled, -al·ing** or (*especially British*) **-alled, -al·ling.** —*v.t.* **1.** to soften the sound of by means of the soft pedal. **2.** to make quieter, less noticeable, or less strong; tone down: *State Department officials soft-pedal any speculation that dramatic new accords may emerge from the talks* (Wall Street Journal). —*v.i.* **1.** to use a pedal on a piano, organ, etc., to soften musical tones. **2.** to become quieter, less noticeable, or less strong: *Both parties are at present "soft-pedalling" on the world-revolution thesis* (London Daily Express).

soft rays, X rays of low penetrating power, such as are obtained from tubes of low vacuum.

soft rot, a plant disease caused by bacteria or fungi that dissolve the substance cementing the cell walls together. The result is a general decay, or rot, of fleshy tissues.

soft sell, *Informal.* a relaxed way of selling, by suggestion and persuasion rather than by pressure or aggressiveness.

soft-shell (sôft′shel′, soft′-), *adj.* soft-shelled. —*n.* a person or animal that is soft-shelled.

soft-shell or **soft-shelled clam,** soft clam.

soft-shell or **soft-shelled crab,** the common blue crab when it has shed its hard shell and not yet grown another.

soft-shelled (sôft′sheld′, soft′-), *adj.* **1.** having a soft shell: *a soft-shelled lobster.* **2.** *Informal.* **a.** that adopts or is in favor of a moderate policy or temperate course. **b.** that is softhearted.

soft-shelled turtle, any of a family of fresh-water turtles, with flexible, leather-like shells.

soft-shoe (sôft′shü′, soft′-), *v.i.,* **-shoed, -shoe·ing.** *Informal.* to dance or move as if dancing the soft shoe: *We soft-shoed out and, in a corridor adjoining the gym, were introduced to a lady* (New Yorker).

soft shoe, 1. a form of tap dancing in which the dancers wear shoes that have no metal taps. **2.** the type of shoe used for this: *"Sir Galahad" . . . was sung and danced by a trio equipped with straw hats, canes, and the old soft shoe* (New Yorker).

soft soap, 1. a liquid or semiliquid soap. **2.** *Informal.* flattery: *He and I are great chums, and a little soft soap will go a long way with him* (Thomas Hughes).

soft-soap (sôft′sōp′, soft′-), *v.t.* **1.** *Informal.* to flatter; cajole. **2.** to treat or coat with soft soap. —**soft′-soap′er,** *n.*

soft-spo·ken (sôft′spō′kən, soft′-), *adj.* **1.** speaking with a soft voice. **2.** persuasive: *a bland, soft-spoken scoundrel.* **3.** spoken softly: *a soft-spoken reproof.* —**soft′-spo′ken·ness,** *n.*

soft spot, 1. a weak part; condition open to attack; sensitive weakness: *[His] soft spot as a social critic is that, sharp though his critical faculties are, he is of rather too amiable a disposition* (Atlantic). **2.** an area in the atmosphere where the winds are of lesser force than those around it: *a type of radar that can spot rainfall and locate areas of rough air, enabling the pilot to avoid them or to find a "soft spot" through which he could fly safely* (Wall Street Journal). **3.** a fontanel.

soft steel, steel containing only a small percentage of carbon (less than 0.35 per cent); mild steel.

soft top, the folding canvas top of a convertible automobile: *Soft top up against early spring wind . . . you touch the starter and you're gone* (New Yorker).

soft touch, *U.S. Informal.* a person from whom money can easily be obtained for a loan, contribution, or the like: *His neighbors knew him as a soft touch for every charity drive* (Atlantic).

soft·ware (sôft′wãr′, soft′-), *n.* **1.** the design stage or plans of a machine or component. **2.** a program or set of standard procedures for a computer system.

soft wheat, wheat having a soft kernel, used especially for making cakes, crackers, breakfast foods, etc.

soft·wood (sôft′wu̇d′, soft′-), *n.* **1.** any wood that is easily cut. **2.** *Forestry.* a tree that has needles or does not have broad leaves. Pines and firs are softwoods; oaks and maples are hardwoods. **3.** the wood of such trees.
—*adj.* having such wood.

soft·y (sôf′tē, sof′-), *n., pl.* **soft·ies.** *Informal.* **1.** a soft, silly, or weak person: *Our youth seldom walk if they can drive . . . Are we becoming a nation of "softies?"* (Newsweek). **2.** a person who is easily imposed upon: *I'm a sentimental old softy* (Sunday Times).

sog (sog), *v.,* **sogged, sog·ging,** *n. Especially British Dialect.* —*v.i., v.t.* to make or become soggy. —*n.* a bog.

Sog·di·an (sog′dē ən), *n.* **1.** a member of an Iranian group that formerly lived in Sogdiana, now Bokhara, a region in the Soviet Union north of Afghanistan. **2.** the Iranian language of this group.

sog·gi·ly (sog′ə lē), *adv.* in a soggy manner: *People merely called it miserable weather, grumbled, and went soggily about their business* (Newsweek).

sog·gi·ness (sog′ē nis), *n.* the condition or state of being soggy.

sog·gy (sog′ē), *adj.,* **-gi·er, -gi·est. 1.** thoroughly wet; soaked: *a soggy washcloth.* **2.** damp and heavy: *soggy bread, a soggy day.* [< *sog* + *-y*[1]]

soh (sō), *interj.* so.

so·ho (sō hō′), *interj.* ho there! hello! (a shout of hailing, encouragement, discovery, etc., originally used by huntsmen).

soi-di·sant (swȧ′dē zäɴ′), *adj. French.* **1.** calling oneself thus; self-styled: *a soi-disant aristocrat.* **2.** so-called; pretended: *a soi-disant literary classic.*

soi·gné (swȧ nyā′), *adj. French.* **1.** very neat and well-dressed: *Diaghilev had left nothing to chance, including the soigné audience* (Newsweek). **2.** finished or cared for to the smallest detail: *a soigné party. She has a lot of soigné clothes* (New Yorker).

soi·gnée (swȧ nyā′), *adj. French.* the feminine form of **soigné.**

soil[1] (soil), *n.* **1.** the ground; earth; dirt: *A farmer tills the soil. Soil is a well-organized and highly complicated layer of debris covering most of the earth's land surface* (White and Renner). **2.** something thought of as a place for growth or development: *A rich moral soil . . . for aesthetic growth* (G.K. Chesterton). **3.** a land; country; region: *to set foot on foreign soil.* [< Anglo-French *soil* (literally) one's piece (of ground) < Latin *solium* seat, influenced by Latin *solum* soil, ground]

soil[2] (soil), *v.t.* **1.** to make dirty: *He soiled his clean clothes.* **2.** to spot; stain: *The splashing paint soiled the wall.* **3.** to disgrace; dishonor: *His actions have soiled the family name.* **4.** to corrupt morally. —*v.i.* to become dirty: *White shirts soil easily.*
—*n.* **1.** a spot; stain: *The only soil of his fair virtue's gloss . . . Is a sharp wit matched with too blunt a will* (Shakespeare). **2. a.** a soiling. **b.** a being soiled. **3.** dirty or foul matter; filth; sewage; ordure. **4.** manure; compost. [< Old French *soillier,* ultimately < Latin *suile* pigsty < *sus* pig]
—**Syn.** *v.t.* **1.** daub, begrime, besmirch.

soil[3] (soil), *n.* a pool or marshy place in which deer or other animals take refuge. —*v.i.* to take refuge in water or marshy ground. [Middle English *soyle* < Old French *soil* < *soillier;* see SOIL[2]]

soil[4] (soil), *v.t.* **1.** to stallfeed with green fodder to fatten. **2.** to feed green fodder to purge. [origin uncertain, perhaps < *soil*[2] in sense of "manure"]

soil·age (soi′lij), *n.* green fodder.

soil bank, *U.S.* a program adopted by the Federal government in 1956 through which farmers are paid to take land out of production of certain crops to reduce surpluses.

soil binder, a plant which serves to protect a clayey or loamy soil from washing.

soil cap, *Geology.* a layer of soil and detritus covering bed rock.

soil-ce·ment (soil′sə ment′), *n.* a low-cost material for paving roads, etc., consisting of compacted soil, Portland cement, and water.

soil creep, the slow movement or settling of surface soil down a slope.

-soiled, *combining form.* having —— soil or earth: *Black-soiled = having black soil.*

soil·less (soil′lis), *adj.* without soil.

soilless growth, the growing of plants without soil, nutrition being supplied by a water solution; hydroponics.

soil map, a map which shows the distribution of different kinds of soils.

soil mechanics, the study of the physical characteristics of soil and other loose materials on which buildings, highways, etc., may be erected.

soil pipe, a drain pipe for a sink, tub, toilet, etc., or from a house to the sewer line.

soil science, the study of soils; pedology.

soil scientist, an expert in soil science.

soil·ure (soil′yər), *n. Archaic.* **1.** a soiling. **2.** a being soiled. **3.** a stain; spot. [< Old French *soilleure* < *soillier;* see SOIL[2]]

soi·ree or **soi·rée** (swä rā′), *n.* an evening party or social gathering: *Pierre is startling the guests at Anna Pavlovna's soiree by defending Napoleon* (Harper's). [< French *soirée* < *soir* evening < Old French *seir,* ultimately < Latin *sērō* late]

so·ja (sō′jə, -yə), *n.,* or **soja bean,** soybean. [< New Latin *soja,* perhaps < Dutch < Japanese *shōyu;* see SOY]

so·journ (*v.* sō jėrn′, sō′jėrn; *n.* sō′jėrn), *v.i.* to stay for a time: *The Israelites sojourned in the land of Egypt. And that is why I sojourn here, Alone and palely loitering* (John Keats). —*n.* a brief stay: *The entire family enjoyed a sojourn in Europe last month* [Middle English *sojornen* < Old French *sojorner,* ultimately < Latin *sub-* under + *diurnus* of the day < *diū* by day < *diēs* day] —**so·journ′er,** *n.*

So·ka Gak·kai (sō′kä gä′kī), a militant and nationalistic Buddhist sect and political party in Japan, founded in 1936: *Soka Gakkai means "value creating academy" and is an offshoot of the Nichiren . . . sect, itself a thirteenth-century and very Japanese expression of Mahayana Buddhism* (C.L. Sulzberger). [< Japanese *sōka gakkai*]

soke (sōk), *n.* in early English law: **1.** a right to local jurisdiction, as to hold court, collect fines, etc., over a certain district. **2.** a district over which such a right was exercised; a minor local division. [Middle English *sok* < Medieval Latin *soca* < Old English *sōcn;* see SOCAGE]

soke·man (sōk′mən), *n., pl.* **-men.** a tenant holding land in socage; socman.

sol[1] (sōl), *n. Music.* the fifth tone of the scale; G. Also, **so.** [Middle English *sol;* see GAMUT]

sol[2] (sōl), *n., pl.* **sols** (sōlz) or **so·les** (sō′lās). **1.** a unit of money in Peru, worth about 3¾ cents. **2.** a silver coin or piece of paper money having this value. [< Spanish *sol* sun < Latin *sōl, sōlis*]

sol[3] (sol), *n.* a former French silver or copper coin and money of account worth 1/20 of a livre. [< Old French *sol* < Latin *solidus* gold (coin). Doublet of SOU, SOLDO, SOLID.]

sol[4] (sol, sōl), *n.* a colloidal solution.

Sol (sol), *n.* **1.** the Roman god of the sun, identified with the Greek god Helios. **2.** the sun, personified. **3.** *Obsolete.* (in alchemy) gold. [< Latin *sōl, sōlis* (literally) the sun]

sol., **1.** soluble. **2.** solution.

Sol., **1.** Solicitor. **2.** Solomon.

so·la[1] (sō′lə), *adj. Latin.* the feminine form of **solus.**

so·la[2] (sō′lə), *n.* plural of **solum.**

sol·ace (sol′is), *n., v.,* **-aced, -ac·ing.** —*n.* **1.** comfort; relief: *She found solace from her troubles in listening to music.* **2.** something that gives comfort: *Though sight be lost, Life yet hath many solaces* (Milton).
—*v.t.* **1.** to comfort; relieve; soothe: *to solace oneself with a book; . . . fevered with ivy poison and solacing his woes with tobacco and Shakespeare* (Francis Parkman). **2.** *Archaic.* to make (a place) cheerful or pleasant. **3.** *Obsolete.* to entertain. —*v.i. Obsolete.* to give comfort or relief.
[Middle English *solas* < Old French < Latin *sōlācium* < *sōlārī* to console, soothe. Doublet of SOLATIUM.]
—**Syn.** *n.* **1.** consolation, cheer.

sol·ace·ment (sol′is mənt), *n.* **1.** the act of solacing. **2.** the state of being solaced.

sol·ac·er (sol′ə sər), *n.* a person or thing that solaces: *A pipe and some generous port, and King Lear . . . had their effect as solacers* (Charles Lamb).

so·lan (sō′lən), *n.,* or **solan goose,** gannet. [variant of Middle English *soland,* perhaps < Scandinavian (compare Old Icelandic *sūla* gannet, *and-, ond* duck]

sol·a·na·ceous (sol′ə nā′shəs), *adj.* belonging to the nightshade family: *Tobacco, potatoes, tomatoes, and petunias are solanaceous plants.* [< New Latin *Solanaceae* the family (< *Solanum* the typical genus < Latin *sōlānum* nightshade) + English *-ous*]

sol·a·nine (sol′ə nēn, -nin; sō′lə-), *n.* a poisonous alkaloid obtained from the black nightshade and other kinds of solanum. *Formula:* $C_{45}H_{73}NO_{15}$ [< *solan*(um) + *-ine*[2]]

so·la·no (sō lä′nō), *n.* a dry, very warm southeasterly wind that blows in the eastern coastal region of Spain in the summer. [< Spanish *solano* < Latin *Sōlānus* the east wind; properly, adjective, of the sun < *sōl, sōlis* sun]

so·la·num (sō lā′nəm), *n.* any of a large group of erect or climbing herbs, shrubs, or small trees of the nightshade family, as the nightshade, eggplant, and common white potato. [< New Latin *Solanum* the genus name < Latin *sōlānum* nightshade]

so·lar (sō′lər), *adj.* **1.** of the sun: *a solar eclipse.* See **eclipse** for picture. **2.** having to do with the sun: *solar phenomena.* **3.** coming from the sun: *Solar heat is less in winter than in the summer.* **4.** measured or determined by the earth's motion in relation to the sun: *solar time. A solar year is about 365¼ days long.* **5.** working by means of the sun's light or heat: *A solar telegraph uses mirrors to reflect flashes of sunlight.* [< Latin *sōlāris* < *sōl, sōlis* sun]

solar apex, the point in space, situated in the constellation Hercules, toward which the sun is moving.

solar battery, a device that uses silicon crystals to trap sunlight and convert it into electrical energy: *The tiny solar batteries can get all the power they need to run the radio for as long as a year* (Science News Letter).

solar cell, a device that converts solar radiation into electrical energy.

solar constant, the amount of heat from the sun that would reach one square centimeter of the earth's surface in one minute if no heat were lost in the atmosphere and the earth's surface were perpendicular to the sun's rays.

solar day, mean solar day.

solar disk, (in ancient Egyptian art) a disk that stood for the sun, put upright on the head of an idol of a sun god.

Solar Disk on the head of a solar deity

solar flare, a sudden eruption of gases on the surface of the sun, usually associated with sunspots, accompanied by a burst of ultraviolet radiation that travels toward the earth. Solar flares cause ionization in the upper atmosphere and are responsible for the fading of high-frequency radio reception. *. . . the solar flare, the most violent activity on the face of the sun* (Scientific American).

solar furnace, a furnace heated by energy from the sun. It is used especially in research because the usual accompanying impurities of burning fuel are absent. *Solar furnaces, reaching temperatures of 3,000 degrees centigrade, focus the sun's heat by one or more mirrors* (Science News Letter).

so·lar·ism (sō′lə riz əm), *n.* the interpretation of a myth by reference to the sun, especially such interpretation carried to an extreme.

so·lar·i·um (sə lãr′ē əm), *n., pl.* **-i·a** (-ē ə). a room, porch, etc., where people can lie or sit in the sun.

so·lar·i·za·tion (sō′lər ə zā′shən), *n.* **1.** exposure to sunlight. **2.** *Photography.* **a.** overexposure to light. **b.** the effects of this on a print.

so·lar·ize (sō′lə rīz), *v.,* **-ized, -iz·ing.** —*v.t.* **1.** to affect by sunlight. **2.** *Photography.* to overexpose to light. —*v.i.* **1.** to be affected by sunlight. **2.** *Photography.* to be overexposed to light.

solar month, one twelfth of a solar year.

solar physics, the astrophysical study of the sun.

solar plexus, a large network of sympathetic nerves situated at the upper part of the abdomen, behind the stomach and in front of the aorta. [< New Latin *solar plexus* (because of its radial shape)]

solar radiation, radiant energy of the sun.

solar salt, a coarse salt derived from solar evaporation of salt water.

solar still, a device that uses the sun's energy to desalinate water: *The roof-type solar still consists of a blackened tray and a glass roof with condensation troughs along each side* (New Scientist).

solar system, the sun and all the planets, satellites, comets, etc., that revolve around it: *. . . the solar system . . . vast though it is, forms but a speck in the universe of stars and nebulae* (John C. Duncan).

solar time, apparent solar time.

solar wind, a continuous stream of charged particles ejected by the sun, extending well beyond the earth.

solar year, the period of one complete revolution of the earth around the sun, from one vernal equinox to the next; tropical year; astronomical year. The solar year lasts 365 days, 5 hours, 48 minutes, 46 seconds.

so·la·ti·um (sō lā′shē əm), *n., pl.* **-ti·a** (-shē ə). a compensation for suffering, loss, hurt feelings, etc. [< Latin *sōlātium.* Doublet of SOLACE.]

sold (sōld), *v.* the past tense and past participle of **sell:** *He sold his car a week ago.*

sol·dan (sol′dən), *n.* (in the Middle Ages) the supreme ruler of a Moslem country, especially Egypt. [< Old French *soldan* < Arabic *sulṭān.* Compare SULTAN.]

sol·der (sod′ər; *British* sol′dər, sod′ər), *n.* **1.** any metal or alloy that can be melted and used for joining or mending metal surfaces, parts, etc. **2.** anything that unites firmly or joins closely.
—*v.t.* **1.** to fasten, mend, or join with solder: *There have been instances in which two fragments [of old bronze] not belonging to each other have been soldered together to form a complete and spurious object of art* (George Savage). **2.** to unite firmly; join closely; grow together. **3.** to mend; repair; patch. —*v.i.* **1.** to become soldered. **2.** to become united by or as if by soldering: *Their [children's] little brittle bones quickly solder* (W. H. Hudson).
[< Old French *soldure* < *solder* solidify < Latin *solidāre* < *solidus* solid] —**sol′der·er,** *n.*

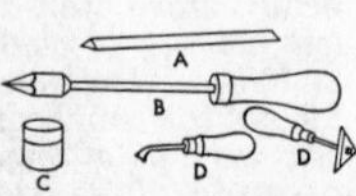

Soldering Tools (def. 1) A, solder bar; B, soldering iron; C, rosin box; D, shavers or scrapers

sol·der·a·ble (sod′ər ə bəl; *British* sol′dər-, sod′ər-), *adj.* that can be soldered.

sol·der·ing iron (sod′ər ing; *British* sol′dər-, sod′ər-), **1.** an electric tool consisting of a long rod in a handle and a pointed copper tip that heats to melt solder: *Soldering irons for the home craftsman heat quickly and are well suited for delicate work or heavy duty* (Wall Street Journal). **2.** a tool like this heated in a flame.

sol·dier (sōl′jər), *n.* **1.** a man who serves in an army. **2.** an enlisted man in the army, not a commissioned officer. **3.** a man having skill or experience in war. **4.** a person who serves in any cause: *soldiers of science, soldiers of Christianity.* **5.** *Zoology.* **a.** (in colonies of certain ants) one of a type of workers with a large head and powerful jaws. **b.** (in colonies of termites) one of a kind of large-headed individuals.
—*v.i.* **1.** to act or serve as a soldier: *Caesar went off to soldier in Asia, at 18, and won both honor and disgrace* (Time). **2.** *Informal.* **a.** to pretend to work but do very little. **b.** to pretend to be ill.
soldier on, *British.* to carry on under adverse conditions, as a soldier would: *The report suggests that some means be found of rewarding specially those who soldier on in the more difficult schools* (London Times).
[Middle English *soudeour* < Old French *soldier* < *solde, soulde* pay, coin < Latin *solidus* a Roman gold coin; see SOLID]

soldier beetle, any of a group of beetles resembling the firefly, whose larva destroys other insects.

soldier bug, any of various hemipterous insects which prey upon cutworms and other destructive larvae, as the stinkbug.

soldier crab, a hermit crab.

sol·dier·like (sōl′jər līk′), *adj.* **1.** having the character or bearing of a soldier: *neat, clean, and soldierlike.* **2.** befitting a soldier. —*adv.* in a manner befitting a soldier.

sol·dier·li·ness (sōl′jər lē nis), *n.* the quality of being soldierly.

sol·dier·ly (sōl′jər lē), *adj.* like a soldier; suitable for a soldier: *a soldierly manner.*

soldier of fortune, a man serving or ready to serve as a soldier under any government for money, adventure, or pleasure; military adventurer.

soldiers' cap, **1.** Dutchman's-breeches. **2.** monkshood.

sol·dier·ship (sōl′jər ship), *n.* **1.** the condition or profession of a soldier. **2.** soldierly qualities or skill.

Soldier's Medal, a military decoration given to a member of the United States armed forces for bravery involving the risk of life on noncombat duty.

sol·dier·y (sōl′jər ē), *n., pl.* **-dier·ies.** **1. a.** soldiers as a group: *the soldiery of the Allies.* **b.** all military personnel as a group. **2.** a body of soldiers: *The mercenaries were . . . a fierce and rapacious soldiery* (Scott). **3.** military training or knowledge.

sol·do (sol′dō), *n., pl.* **-di** (-dē). an Italian copper coin, 1/20 of a lira, formerly worth about 1/4 of a cent. [< Italian *soldo* < Latin *solidus.* Doublet of SOL[3], SOLID, SOU.]

sold-out (sōld′out′), *adj.* being a sellout; having no unsold seats or standing room left: *This spring they played a Beethoven sonata series in Vienna to sold-out houses* (New York Times).

sole[1] (sōl), *adj.* **1. a.** one and only; single: *the sole heir. Is that your sole objection?* **b.** of matchless quality; unique; singular: *The evil time's sole patriot* (Emerson). **2.** only: *We three were the sole survivors.* **3.** of or for only one person or group and not others; exclusive: *the sole right of use.* **4.** alone; without help: *a sole undertaking.* **5.** *Law.* unmarried: *a feme sole.* [< Old French *soul* < Latin *sōlus* alone] —**Syn.** **1. a, 2.** See **single.**

sole[2] (sōl), *n., v.,* **soled, sol·ing.** —*n.* **1.** the bottom or under surface of the foot. **2. a.** the bottom of a shoe, slipper, boot, etc. **b.** a piece cut in the same shape. **3.** the under surface; under part; bottom: *the sole of an iron. The sole of a golf club is the part of the head that comes closest to the ground.*
—*v.t.* **1.** to put a sole on: *I must have my shoes soled.* **2.** *Golf.* to place the sole of (a club) on the ground behind the ball.

[< Old French *sole,* ultimately < Latin *solea* sandal, shoe < *solum* bottom, ground]

sole[3] (sōl), *n., pl.* **soles** or (*collectively*) **sole. 1.** any of a family of flatfishes, as a European variety much esteemed for food. **2.** any of certain related fishes, as some of the flounders. [< Old French *sole* < Vulgar Latin *sola* < Latin *solea;* see SOLE[2]]

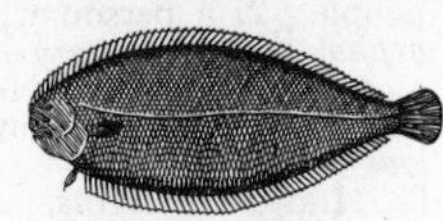
European Sole[3] **(def. 1)**
(10 to 20 in. long)

sol·e·cism (sol′ə siz əm), *n.* **1.** a violation of the grammatical or other accepted usages of a language; mistake in using words: *"I done it" is a solecism.* **2.** a mistake in social behavior; breach of good manners or etiquette: *unused to society and . . . afraid of making herself . . . conspicuous by some solecism or blunder* (Charlotte Brontë). [< Latin *soloecismos* < Greek *soloikismós,* reputedly < *Sóloi,* an Athenian colony in Cilicia, whose form of Attic dialect the Athenians considered barbarous]

sol·e·cist (sol′ə sist), *n.* a person who commits a solecism.

sol·e·cis·tic (sol′ə sis′tik), *adj.* of the nature of a solecism; characterized by solecisms.

sol·e·cis·ti·cal·ly (sol′ə sis′tə klē), *adv.* in a solecistic manner.

sol·e·cize (sol′ə sīz), *v.i.,* **-cized, -ciz·ing.** to commit solecisms.

-soled, *combining form.* having —— soles: *Thick-soled = having thick soles.*

so·le·i·form (sə lē′ə fôrm), *adj.* having the form of a slipper. [< Latin *solea* slipper + English *-form*]

so·leil (sō lā′), *n.* felt, wool, rayon, or other cloth with a silky texture: *Fedoras made of black soleil . . . with headbands of ponyskin* (New Yorker). [< French *soleil* sun]

sole leather, strong, thick hide or leather.

sole·ly (sōl′lē), *adv.* **1.** as the only one or ones; alone: *You will be solely responsible.* **2.** only: *Bananas grow outdoors solely in warm climates. He does it solely for convenience.*

sole Mar·gué·ry (mär′gə rē′), sole served with an elaborate sauce, each portion usually topped with an oyster, a shrimp, and a mushroom. [< French *sole Marguéry*]

sol·emn (sol′əm), *adj.* **1. a.** serious; grave; earnest: *to speak in a solemn tone, solemn meditations. Why do you bend such solemn brows on me?* (Shakespeare). **b.** formal: *to make a solemn promise, to enter into a solemn agreement.* **2.** causing serious or grave thoughts: *The organ played solemn music. There reigned a solemn silence over all* (Edmund Spenser). **3.** done with form and ceremony: *a solemn diplomatic reception.* **4.** connected with religion; observing certain religious rites; sacred: *a solemn Requiem.* **5.** gloomy; dark; somber in color: *These heroes sleep in the land they made free . . . under the solemn pines* (Robert G. Ingersoll). **6.** legally correct. [Middle English *solempne* < Latin *sollempnis,* variant of *sollemnis* established, festal, religious] **—sol′emn·ly,** *adv.* **—sol′emn·ness,** *n.* **—Syn. 2.** impressive.

Solemn High Mass, High Mass.

sol·em·nise (sol′əm nīz), *v.t.,* **-nised, -nis·ing.** *Especially British.* solemnize.

so·lem·ni·ty (sə lem′nə tē), *n., pl.* **-ties. 1.** solemn feeling; seriousness; impressiveness. **2.** a special, formal celebration; solemn observance: *Easter is observed with solemnity.* **3.** *Law.* a formality necessary to make an act or document valid.
solemnities, a solemn, formal ceremony: *The solemnities were concluded with a prayer by the college chaplain.*

sol·em·ni·za·tion (sol′əm nə zā′shən), *n.* **1.** the act of solemnizing. **2.** the state of being solemnized.

sol·em·nize (sol′əm nīz), *v.t.,* **-nized, -niz·ing. 1.** to observe with ceremonies: *Christian churches solemnize the resurrection of Christ at Easter.* **2.** to hold or perform (a ceremony or service): *The marriage was solemnized in the church.* **3.** to make serious or grave. Also, *especially British,* **solemnise.**

sol·em·niz·er (sol′əm nī′zər), *n.* **1.** a person who solemnizes. **2.** a person who performs a solemn rite.

Solemn League and Covenant, the Covenant, an agreement signed by the Scottish Presbyterians in 1643 that established the Presbyterian Church in England.

sole·ness (sōl′nis), *n.* the state or condition of being alone; singleness.

so·le·no·don (sə lē′nə don), *n.* either of two related animals about the size of a squirrel, the almiqui of Cuba and a related variety of Haiti; opossum shrew. They look like the opossum and feed on insects. [< New Latin *Solenodon* the genus name < Greek *sōlēn* channel + *odoús, odóntos* tooth]

so·le·no·dont (sə lē′nə dont), *adj.* **1.** of or having to do with the solenodons. **2.** like the solenodon. —*n.* a solenodon.

so·le·noid (sō′lə noid), *n.* a spiral or cylindrical coil of wire that acts like a magnet when an electric current passes through it, used in circuit breakers, mechanical sorting devices, etc. [< French *solénoïde* < Greek *sōlēn, -ēnos* channel + *eîdos* form]

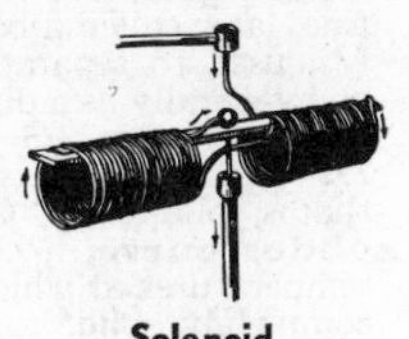
Solenoid
Arrows show path of electricity.

so·le·noi·dal (sō′lə noi′dəl), *adj.* **1.** of or having to do with a solenoid. **2.** of the nature of or resembling a solenoid. **—so′le·noi′dal·ly,** *adv.*

sole·plate (sōl′plāt′), *n.* **1.** the base of a flatiron. **2.** a bedplate. **3.** (in a water wheel) the back part of a bucket. **4.** the casting underneath a large bearing for a shaft. **5.** protoplasm located at the end of several motor nerve fibers, containing their nuclei.

sole·print (sōl′print′), *n.* an impression of the sole of a foot for purposes of identification. Some hospitals take the soleprints of newborn babies.

so·le·ra (sō lā′rä), *adj.* of or having to do with a method of producing sherry, by blending various grades through a system of graded casks to achieve a uniform blend. —*n.* **1.** one of the graded casks used in this process. **2.** the wine produced by these means. [< Spanish *solera*]

sole trader, an unmarried woman who carries on a business.

so·le·us (sō′lē us), *n., pl.* **so·le·i** (so′lē ī). a broad, flat muscle of the calf of the leg, situated immediately in front of and deeper than the gastrocnemius. [< New Latin *soleus* < Latin *solea;* see SOLE[2]]

sol-fa (sōl′fä′), *n., adj., v.,* **-faed, -fa·ing.** —*n.* the system of singing the syllables, *do, re, mi, fa, sol, la, ti, do* to tones of the scale. —*adj.* of or having to do with this system of singing: *sol-fa notation, a sol-fa scale.* —*v.i.* to use the sol-fa syllables in singing. —*v.t.* to sing to the sol-fa scale.
[< Italian *solfa* < *sol* + *fa;* see GAMUT]

sol-fa·ist (sōl′fä′ist), *n.* a person who uses or believes in using the sol-fa syllables in singing.

sol-fa syllables, the sol-fa system of singing; sol-fa.

sol·fa·ta·ra (sōl′fä tä′rä), *n.* a volcanic vent or area that gives off only sulfurous gases, steam, and the like. [< Italian *Solfatara,* a volcano near Naples < *solfo* sulfur < Latin *sulfur, sulphur*]

sol·feg·gio (sol fej′ō, -ē ō), *n., pl.* **-feg·gios** (-fej′ōz, -ē ōz), **-feg·gi** (-fej′ē). *Music.* **1. a.** an exercise for the voice in which the sol-fa syllables are used. **b.** any exercise for voice. **2.** the use of the sol-fa syllables. [< Italian *solfeggio* < *solfa;* see SOL-FA]

sol·fe·ri·no (sol′fə rē′nō), *n.* **1.** a red dyestuff. **2.** a bright purplish pink. [< *Solferino,* Italy, where the French and Sardinians defeated the Austrians in 1859, the year the color was introduced]

so·li (sō′lē), *n.* a plural of **solo.**

so·lic·it (sə lis′it), *v.t.* **1.** to ask earnestly; try to get: *The tailor sent around cards soliciting trade.* **2.** to influence to do wrong; tempt; entice: *To solicit a judge means to offer him bribes.* **3.** to accost with immoral offers. **4.** *Obsolete.* to act as a solicitor for; be a solicitor in. —*v.i.* **1.** to make appeals or requests: *to solicit for contributions.* **2.** to act as a legal solicitor. **3. a.** to solicit orders. **b.** to accost a person with immoral offers. [earlier, manage affairs, disturb < Latin *sollicitāre;* see SOLICITOUS] **—Syn.** *v.t.* **1.** request, beg. See **ask.**

so·lic·i·tant (sə lis′ə tənt), *adj.* soliciting. —*n.* a person who solicits.

so·lic·i·ta·tion (sə lis′ə tā′shən), *n.* **1.** an earnest request; entreaty: *Alumni also can expect more solicitations for such things as gymnasium buildings and fraternity houses* (Wall Street Journal). **2.** an urging to do wrong; temptation; enticement. **3.** the act of soliciting for immoral purposes.

so·lic·i·tor (sə lis′ə tər), *n.* **1.** a person who entreats or requests. **2.** a person who seeks trade or business: *a magazine solicitor.* **3.** a lawyer. In England, a solicitor prepares a case, and a barrister pleads it: *The solicitor is the man of the world who can give the broadest advice to his client at every stage* (London Times). **4.** a lawyer for a town, city, State, etc.

solicitor general, *pl.* **solicitors general. 1.** a law officer who assists the attorney general and ranks next below him in the Department of Justice. **2.** the chief law officer in a State having no attorney general.

so·lic·i·tor·ship (sə lis′ə tər ship), *n.* the office, duty, or calling of a solicitor.

so·lic·i·tous (sə lis′ə təs), *adj.* **1.** showing care or concern; anxious; concerned: *solicitous chiefly for the peace of my own country* (Edmund Burke). *Parents are solicitous for their children's progress.* **2.** desirous; eager: *solicitous to please.* **3.** very careful or attentive; particular: *solicitous in the meeting of an obligation.*
[< Latin *sollicitus* (with English *-ous*) < *sollicitāre* to disturb < Old Latin *sollus* whole, all + Latin *ciēre* arouse] **—so·lic′it·ous·ly,** *adv.* **—so·lic′it·ous·ness,** *n.*

so·lic·i·tress (sə lis′ə tris), *n.* **1.** a female solicitor. **2.** a woman who solicits.

so·lic·i·tude (sə lis′ə tüd, -tyüd), *n.* anxious care; anxiety; concern: *. . . the tender solicitude of a parent* (Lytton Strachey).
solicitudes, cares; troubles; causes of anxiety: *To her the destinies of mankind . . . made the solicitudes of feminine fashion appear an occupation for bedlam* (George Eliot). **—Syn.** See **care.**

so·lic·i·tu·di·nous (sə lis′ə tü′də nəs, -tyü′-), *adj.* full of solicitude.

sol·id (sol′id), *adj.* **1.** not a liquid or a gas: *Water becomes solid when it freezes. A block of stone is solid material . . . no matter where you put it, it keeps its shape* (Beauchamp, Mayfield, and West). **2.** not hollow: *A bar of iron is solid; a pipe is hollow.* **3.** strongly put together; hard; firm: *They were glad to leave the boat and put their feet on solid ground.* **4.** alike throughout: *solid gold, a dress of solid blue. There wasn't a light on; the house was in solid darkness.* **5. a.** firmly united: *The country was solid for peace.* **b.** *U.S. Informal.* regular in attendance; steady in support: *I'm solid for Mr. Peck every time* (William Dean Howells). **6.** serious; not superficial or trifling: *a background of solid study. Chemistry and physics are solid subjects.* **7.** genuine; real; *solid comfort; . . . a debt of solid gratitude* (Edward A. Freeman). **8.** that can be depended on: *He is a solid citizen.* **9.** having or based on good judgment; sound; sensible; intelligent: *a solid book by a solid thinker, a solid argument. These men . . . have some of the solidest information available* (Newsweek). **10.** financially sound or strong: *a solid business. "The gasoline market is the solidest in two years," says one Oklahoma refiner* (Wall Street Journal). **11.** whole; entire; complete: *I waited three solid hours.* **12.** undivided; continuous: *a solid wall, a solid row of houses.* **13.** written without a hyphen: *"Earthworm" is a solid word.* **14.** having length, breadth, and thickness: *A sphere is a solid figure.* **15.** *Printing.* having the lines of type not separated by leads; having few open spaces. **16.** *U.S. Informal.* on a friendly, favorable, or advantageous footing: *to get in solid with one's employer.* **17.** thorough; downright; vigorous; substantial: *a good solid dose of medicine, a good solid blow.* **18.** *U.S. Slang.* good; excellent; first-rate: *"It sounds good!" he shouted. "Solid!"* (New Yorker).
—*n.* **1.** a substance that is not a liquid or a gas: *In a solid, the molecules resist any force that tends to change their relative positions or distances* (John C. Duncan). **2.** a body that has length, breadth, and thickness: *Cubes are solids.*
[< Latin *solidus.* Doublet of SOL[3], SOLDO, SOU.] **—sol′id·ly,** *adv.* **—sol′id·ness,** *n.*
—Syn. *adj.* **3.** compact, stable. See **firm.**

sol·i·da·go (sol′ə dā′gō), *n., pl.* **-gos.** goldenrod. [< New Latin *Solidago* the genus name, ultimately < Latin *solidāre* strengthen < *solidus* solid (because of its supposed healing power)]

solid angle, an angle formed by three or more planes intersecting at a common point.
sol·i·dar·ic (sol′ə dar′ik), *adj.* characterized by solidarity.
sol·i·dar·i·ty (sol′ə dar′ə tē), *n., pl.* **-ties.** unity or fellowship arising from common responsibilities and interests: *Joking and laughter, indicating solidarity and tension release, become more frequent* (Scientific American).
[< French *solidarité* < *solidaire* solid < Latin *solidus;* see SOLID]
sol·i·dar·y (sol′ə der′ē), *adj.* characterized by or involving community of responsibilities and interests. [< French *solidaire* < Latin *solidus;* see SOLID]
sol·id-fu·el (sol′id fyü′əl), *adj.* solid-fueled: *The solid-fuel rocket represents the simplest form of rocket motor and . . . is closely akin to the familiar fourth of July skyrocket* (J. Gordon Vaeth).
solid fuel, 1. rocket fuel in a solid state, usually in the form of a powder or in fine grains, such as a mixture of nitroglycerin and cellulose nitrate: *Solid fuels will propel most military rockets in the future* (Science News Letter). **2.** coal, coke, or other substances in a solid form, used as fuel.
sol·id-fu·eled (sol′id fyü′əld), *adj.* driven by a solid fuel, especially one of the powdered or granulated fuels used in rockets: *A solid-fueled rocket will carry the forthcoming earth satellite on the final stage of its powered journey* (Scientific American).
solid geometry, the branch of mathematics that deals with objects having the three dimensions of length, breadth, and thickness.
sol·id-hoofed (sol′id hůft′, -hüft′), *adj.* having solid hoofs, as the horse.
sol·id-horned (sol′id hôrnd′), *adj.* having solid horns, as deer.
sol·i·di (sol′ə dī), *n.* plural of **solidus.**
so·lid·i·fi·a·ble (sə lid′ə fī′ə bəl), *adj.* that can be solidified.
so·lid·i·fi·ca·tion (sə lid′ə fə kā′shən), *n.* **1.** the act or process of solidifying: *The origin of present practices and beliefs is lost in centuries of sociological solidification* (Atlantic). **2.** the state of being solidified. **3.** *Physics.* the passage of a body from a liquid or gaseous to a solid state, accompanied by loss of heat and a change in volume.
so·lid·i·fy (sə lid′ə fī), *v.,* **-fied, -fy·ing.** —*v.t.* **1.** to make solid; harden: *Extreme cold will solidify water.* **2.** to unite firmly. **3.** to crystallize. —*v.i.* **1.** to become solid; be converted from a liquid to a solid: *Jelly solidifies as it cools.* **2.** to become firmly united: *The opposition in Congress to the President's proposal solidified over the next two weeks.* **3.** to become crystallized. [< *solid* + *-fy*]
so·lid·i·ty (sə lid′ə tē), *n., pl.* **-ties. 1.** a being solid; firmness; hardness; density: *the solidity of marble or steel. Transparency is one goal of the architect, says Breuer, "but transparency needs also solidity"* (Newsweek). **2.** substantial quality, as of a person's learning, judgment, character, etc. **3.** *Geometry.* volume; cubic content.
solid propellant, solid fuel: *Solid propellants are usually in plasticlike, caked forms* (Kenneth F. Gantz).
solid rocket, a rocket using solid fuel. See **rocket** for picture.
Solid South, *U.S.* the Southern states that have usually supported the Democratic Party as a unit since the Reconstruction Period: *The old eleven-state structure of the Solid South, which has stood with Bourbon pride and purpose and faded gallantry for a century or more* (Harper's).
sol·id-state (sol′id stāt′), *adj.* of or having to do with solid-state physics and electronics: *solid-state devices or phenomena.*
solid-state electronics, the branch of electronics that deals with semiconductors, masers, and similar electronic devices developed from studies in solid-state physics.
solid-state maser, a maser that amplifies radio signals by means of a solid material, such as synthetic ruby, surrounded by a magnetic field: *Known as the solid-state maser, the device would amplify the very faint signals received from space* (Science News Letter).
solid-state physics, the branch of physics that deals with the physical properties of solid materials, such as mechanical strength, the movement of electrons, the nature of crystals, etc. Research in solid-state physics has produced the transistor and other semiconductor devices: *In one sense, solid-state physics can be described as a combination of chemistry and electronics* (Wall Street Journal).
sol·id·un·gu·late (sol′ə dung′gyə lit, -lāt), *adj.* belonging to the group of mammals with solid hoofs, such as the horse. —*n.* a solidungulate animal.
sol·i·dus (sol′ə dəs), *n., pl.* **-di** (-dī). **1.** a Roman gold coin introduced by Constantine, later called a bezant. **2.** a sloping line (/), used to separate shillings from pence and generally as a dividing line, as in dates, fractions, etc.: *2/6 (2 shillings, 6 pence); 1/2, 1/3.* [< Latin *solidus* (*nummus*) gold, that is, solid (coin). Compare SOU, SOLDIER.]
solidus curve, a curve which shows the temperatures at which a series of alloys are completely solid.
sol·i·fid·i·an (sol′ə fid′ē ən), *Theology.* —*n.* a person who maintains that faith alone, without works, is all that is necessary for salvation. —*adj.* having to do with the solifidians. [< Latin *sōlus* alone + *fidēs, fideī* faith + English *-an*]
sol·i·fluc·tion or **sol·i·flux·ion** (sol′ə-fluk′shən), *n.* the downward movement of soil and rock on the face of the earth, caused by the action of the weather. [< Latin *solum* ground, earth + English *fluxion*]
so·lil·o·quist (sə lil′ə kwist), *n.* **1.** a person who soliloquizes. **2.** a person who writes soliloquies.
so·lil·o·quize (sə lil′ə kwīz), *v.i.,* **-quized, -quiz·ing. 1.** to talk to oneself: *Soliloquizing with the lucidity of genius* (Harper's). **2.** to speak a soliloquy. —**so·lil′o·quiz′er,** *n.* —**so·lil′o·quiz′ing·ly,** *adv.*
so·lil·o·quy (sə lil′ə kwē), *n., pl.* **-quies. 1.** a talking to oneself. **2.** a speech made by an actor to himself when alone on the stage. It reveals his thoughts and feelings to the audience, but not to the other characters in the play. **3.** a similar speech by a character in a book, poem, etc. [< Late Latin *sōliloquium* (introduced by Saint Augustine) < Latin *sōlus* alone + *loquī* speak]
sol·i·on (sol′ī′ən), *n.* a small electronic device containing ions in solution, that can detect and amplify minute changes in current, pressure, temperature, etc.
sol·i·ped (sol′ə ped), *adj., n.* solidungulate. [< New Latin *solipes, -pedis* < Latin *sōlus* alone + *pēs, pedis* foot]
sol·ip·sism (sol′ip siz əm), *n. Philosophy.* the theory that self is the only object of real knowledge or that nothing but self exists: *In him, personality was more than egotism, more even than egomania; it reached the level of solipsism* (New Yorker). [< Latin *sōlus* alone + *ipse* self + English *-ism*]
sol·ip·sist (sol′ip sist), *n.* a person who believes in solipsism.
sol·ip·sis·tic (sol′ip sis′tik), *adj.* of or characterized by solipsism: *His solipsistic view of the world neatly prevents . . . purposive behaviour because he refuses to admit the initial premise of the existence of anything beyond his own ego* (Manchester Guardian). —**sol′ip·sis′ti·cal·ly,** *adv.*
sol·i·taire (sol′ə tãr), *n.* **1.** a card game played by one person, usually an attempt to put cards in a given order. **2.** a diamond or other gem set by itself. **3.** a solitary; recluse. [< French *solitaire,* Old French, learned borrowing from Latin *sōlitārius.* Doublet of SOLITARY.]
sol·i·tar·i·ly (sol′ə ter′ə lē), *adv.* in a solitary manner; alone.
sol·i·tar·i·ness (sol′ə ter′ē nis), *n.* **1.** the condition or state of being solitary; solitude. **2.** seclusion: *the solitariness of a wood.*
sol·i·tar·y (sol′ə ter′ē), *adj., n., pl.* **-tar·ies.** —*adj.* **1. a.** alone; single; only: *A solitary rider was seen in the distance.* **b.** being the only one; standing by itself; unparalleled: *not a single, solitary exception to the rule. The result, not of solitary conjecture, but of practice and experience* (Samuel Johnson). **2. a.** without companions; lonely: *Secret, and self-contained, and solitary as an oyster* (Dickens). *The life of man solitary, poor, nasty, brutish, and short* (Thomas Hobbes). **b.** away from people; remote; secluded: *The house is in a solitary spot miles from town.* **3. a.** *Zoology.* living alone, rather than in colonies: *the solitary bee.* **b.** *Botany.* growing separately; not forming clusters: *a solitary stipule.*
—*n.* **1.** a person living alone, away from people. **2.** a person who is left alone: *An orphan and a solitary whose mother's death . . . had amounted to a tragedy* (Arnold Bennett). **3.** solitary confinement: *The prisoner was put in solitary.*
[< Latin *sōlitārius,* ultimately < *sōlus* alone. Doublet of SOLITAIRE.]
—**Syn.** *adj.* **1. a.** lone, sole. **2. a.** unattended.
solitary confinement, the separate confinement of a prisoner in complete isolation as a penalty for misbehavior.
solitary greenlet, solitary vireo; the blue-headed vireo of the United States.
solitary sandpiper, a sandpiper with dark wings and back and a white breast, that nests in northern North America and migrates in winter to tropical America.
solitary vireo, the blue-headed vireo of the United States.
solitary wasp, any of various wasps that do not live in communities, but build separate nests.
sol·i·tude (sol′ə tüd, -tyüd), *n.* **1.** a being alone: *He likes company and hates solitude.* **2.** a lonely place: *The river was an awful solitude* (Mark Twain). **3.** loneliness: *to travel through regions of solitude.* [perhaps < Old French *solitude,* learned borrowing from Latin *sōlitūdō* < *sōlus* alone]
—**Syn. 1. Solitude, isolation** mean a state of being alone. **Solitude,** applying to a state of being either where there are no other people for company or cut off voluntarily or involuntarily from those around, emphasizes aloneness, the fact or feeling of being entirely by oneself, without companions: *Both the prospector in the desert and the shy person in the city live in solitude.* **Isolation** emphasizes being separated from others or standing apart from the rest of the world: *A single mountain peak rose in splendid isolation.*
sol·lar or **sol·ler** (sol′ər), *n.* **1.** a loft in a church, especially in a steeple. **2.** *Archaic.* a garret or attic in a house. [Middle English *solar, soler* upper room (exposed to the sun) < Old French *solier* < Latin *sōlārium* solarium + *sōl* sun]
sol·ler·et (sol′ə ret, sol′ə ret′), *n.* a flexible shoe made of steel plates that formed a part of medieval armor. [< Old French *solleret* (diminutive) < *soller* shoe]
sol·mi·zate (sol′mə zāt), *v.,* **-zat·ed, -zat·ing.** *Music.* —*v.t.* to express by solmization. —*v.i.* to use solmization syllables.
sol·mi·za·tion (sol′mə zā′shən), *n.* **1.** a system of singing the syllables *do, re, mi, fa, sol, la, ti, do* to the tones of the scale; sol-fa. **2.** a medieval system of singing plain-song melodies on six syllables, *ut, re, mi, fa, sol, la.* [< French *solmisation* < *sol* + *mi;* see GAMUT]
so·lo (sō′lō), *n., pl.* **-los, -li** (-lē), *adj., v.,* **-loed, -lo·ing.** —*n.* **1.** a piece of music for one voice or instrument. **2.** anything done without a partner, companion, instructor, etc., as a flight made alone in an airplane. **3. a.** any of certain card games in which one person plays alone against others. **b.** a bid to play without discarding.
—*adj.* **1.** arranged for and performed by one voice or instrument: *a solo part.* **2.** playing the solo part: *a solo violin.* **3.** without a partner, companion, instructor, etc.; alone: *a solo flight, a solo dance. Back of the bar, in a solo game, sat Dangerous Dan McGrew* (Robert W. Service).
—*v.i.* to make a solo flight in an airplane.
[< Italian *solo* alone < Latin *sōlus*]
so·lo·ist (sō′lō ist), *n.* a person who performs a solo or solos.
so·lo·is·tic (sō′lō is′tik), *adj.* of or for a soloist or soloists: *. . . thin, transparent soloistic instrumentation* (Harper's).
Solo man, a type of prehistoric man, found near the Solo River in Java, and regarded as more advanced than Pithecanthropus.
Sol·o·mon (sol′ə mən), *n.* **1.** (in the Bible) a king of Israel, in the 900's B.C., a son of David. Solomon was famous for his wisdom and for the great temple which he had built in Jerusalem. I Kings 3:5-28. **2.** a man of great wisdom. **3.** a self-proclaimed wise man; wiseacre: *Solomon of saloons And philosophic diner-out* (Robert Browning).
Sol·o·mo·ni·an (sol′ə mō′nē ən), *adj.* **1.** of or having to do with Solomon, king of Israel. **2.** like that of Solomon; suggesting his wisdom.

Sol·o·mon·ic (sol′ə mon′ik), *adj.* Solomonian: *Children of all ages up to 16 should be fed as often as they are really hungry (a fine point that mother must judge with Solomonic wisdom)* (Time).

Sol·o·mon's-seal (sol′ə mənz sēl′), *n.* any of a group of perennial herbs of the lily family, with small, greenish flowers hanging from the bases of the leaves and a rootstock with seallike scars. See **rhizome** for picture. [translation of Medieval Latin *sigillum Solomonis* (because of scars on its rootstock)]

Solomon's seal, a mystic star-shaped figure formed of two equilateral triangles, one interlaced with or placed upon the other.

Solomon's Seal

So·lon (sō′lən, -lon), *n.* **1.** a wise man; sage. **2.** *U.S. Informal.* a member of a legislature. [< *Solon,* about 638 B.C.-about 558 B.C., the Athenian lawgiver]

so long, *Informal.* good-by; farewell.

So·lo·ni·an (sə lō′nē ən), *adj.* of or having to do with Solon, Athenian lawgiver who lived from about 638 B.C. to about 558 B.C.

So·lon·ic (sə lon′ik), *adj.* Solonian.

solr., solicitor.

sol·stice (sol′stis), *n.* **1.** either of the two times in the year when the sun is at its greatest distance from the celestial equator. In the Northern Hemisphere, June 21 or 22, the summer solstice, is the longest day of the year, and December 21 or 22, the winter solstice, is the shortest. In the Southern Hemisphere the solstices are reversed. **2.** either of the two points reached by the sun at these times. **3.** a turning or culminating point; furthest limit; crisis. [< Old French *solstice,* learned borrowing from Latin *sōlstitium* < *sōl, sōlis* sun + *sistere* stand still, related to *stāre* to stand]

sol·sti·tial (sol stish′əl), *adj.* **1.** having to do with a solstice: *the solstitial heat being over now* (W. H. Hudson). **2.** happening at or near a solstice: *solstitial rains.* **3.** that is like the climate of the summer solstice. [< Latin *sōlstitiālis* < *sōlstitium;* see SOLSTICE]

sol·u·bil·i·ty (sol′yə bil′ə tē), *n., pl.* **-ties. 1.** the quality that substances have of dissolving or being dissolved easily: *the solubility of sugar in water. Solubility is another property which varies with temperature* (William N. Jones). **2.** the quality that problems, difficulties, questions, etc., have of being solved or explained.

sol·u·bil·ize (sol′yə bə līz), *v.t.,* **-ized, -iz·ing.** to make soluble; dissolve: *These dirt-collecting films, which tend to build up on linoleum, tile and other floor surfaces, are solubilized and prevented from re-forming* (Scientific American).

sol·u·ble (sol′yə bəl), *adj.* **1.** that can be dissolved or made into liquid: *Salt is soluble in water.* **2.** that can be solved; solvable: *soluble puzzles. This problem is soluble; but . . . whatever solution is reached it is likely to lead to strong pressures* (Listener). [< Late Latin *solūbilis* < *solvere* dissolve] —**sol′u·ble·ness,** *n.*

soluble glass, water glass.

soluble starch, a product of the hydrolysis of starch, soluble in hot water, obtained by treating with weak acids, heating with glycerine, etc.

sol·u·bly (sol′yə blē), *adv.* in a soluble manner.

so·lum (sō′ləm), *n., pl.* **so·la** (sō′lə). *Law.* ground; a piece of ground. [< Latin *solum*]

so·lus (sō′ləs), *adj. Latin.* by himself; alone (used chiefly as a stage direction). The feminine form is *sola.*

sol·ute (sol′yüt, sō′lüt), *n.* a solid, gas, or liquid that is dissolved in a liquid to make a solution: *Salt is a solute in sea water. Stems . . . act as channels through which water and solutes reach the leaves* (Fred W. Emerson). —*adj.* **1.** dissolved; in solution. **2.** *Botany.* not adhering; free. [< Latin *solūtus,* past participle of *solvere* dissolve, loosen]

so·lu·tion (sə lü′shən), *n.* **1.** the solving of a problem: *The solution of the problem required many hours.* **2.** an explanation; answer: *The police are seeking a solution of the crime.* **3.** the process of dissolving; changing of a solid or gas to a liquid by treatment with a liquid. **4.** a liquid or homogeneous mixture formed by dissolving a solute in a solvent such as water: *Every time you put sugar in lemonade, cocoa, or chocolate, you are making a solution* (Beauchamp, Mayfield, and West). *The components of a solution cannot be distinguished with the aid of a microscope* (Parks and Steinbach). **5.** the condition of being dissolved: *Sugar and salt can be held in solution in water.* **6.** a separating into parts. **7.** *Medicine.* **a.** the termination of a disease. **b.** the crisis of a disease. **8.** *Obsolete, Law.* a payment; discharge (of a contract or obligation). [< Latin *solūtiō, -ōnis* a loosing < *solvere* loosen, dissolve]

so·lu·tion·al (sə lü′shə nəl), *adj.* of, having to do with, or forming a solution.

so·lu·tion·ist (sə lü′shə nist), *n.* **1.** a person who solves problems; problemist. **2.** an expert in solving crossword puzzles.

So·lu·tre·an (sə lü′trē ən), *adj.* of or belonging to the period of the late Pleistocene. —*n.* the late Pleistocene. [< *Solutré,* France, where a cave was discovered containing flint implements of the late Pleistocene + *-an*]

solv·a·bil·i·ty (sol′və bil′ə tē), *n., pl.* **-ties. 1.** solubility: *the solvability of an equation.* **2.** *Obsolete.* solvency.

solv·a·ble (sol′və bəl), *adj.* **1.** that can be solved. **2.** that can be dissolved; soluble.

sol·vate (sol′vāt), *n., v.,* **-vat·ed, -vat·ing.** a chemical substance produced by the combination of the ions or molecules of a solvent and a solute. —*v.i., v.t.* to become or cause to become a solvate.

sol·va·tion (sol vā′shən), *n.* **1.** the combination of a solute with its solvent. **2.** the degree to which this takes place.

Sol·vay process (sol′vā), a process for deriving sodium carbonate from ordinary salt by dissolving carbon dioxide in a solution of salt and ammonia to produce sodium bicarbonate which is converted into sodium carbonate. [< Ernest *Solvay,* 1838-1922, a Belgian chemist, who invented it]

solve (solv), *v.t.,* **solved, solv·ing. 1.** to find the answer to; clear up; explain: *to solve a mystery. He has solved all the problems in the lesson.* **2.** to pay. **3.** to melt. [< Latin *solvere* to loosen, dissolve] —**solv′er,** *n.*

sol·ven·cy (sol′vən sē), *n., pl.* **-cies.** the ability to pay all one owes.

sol·vent (sol′vənt), *adj.* **1.** able to pay all that one owes: *A bankrupt firm is not solvent.* **2.** able to dissolve: *Gasoline is a solvent liquid that removes grease spots.* —*n.* **1.** a substance, usually a liquid, that can dissolve other substances: *Water is a solvent of sugar and salt.* **2.** a thing that solves. [< Latin *solvēns, -entis,* present participle of *solvere* loosen (used in *rem solvere* to free one's property and person from debt)]

so·ma[1] (sō′mə), *n., pl.* **-ma·ta** (-mə tə). all the tissues and organs of an animal or plant except the germ cells: *We need to know more about the interrelationships of the psyche and the soma, the mind and the body* (William C. Menninger). [< New Latin *soma* < Greek *sôma, -atos* body; earlier, corpse]

so·ma[2] (sō′mə), *n.* **1.** an East Indian twining plant of the milkweed family that yields a mildly acid, milky juice. **2.** an intoxicating drink of ancient India used in religious rites, made from the juice of this or related plants. [< Sanskrit *soma*]

So·ma·li (sə mä′lē), *n., pl.* **-li** or **-lis. 1.** a member of a group of people living in eastern Africa, of Negro, Arabian, and other descent. **2.** the Hamitic language of this group.

So·ma·li·an (sə mä′lē ən), *adj.* of or having to do with Somalia, or the Somali Republic, in East Africa, or its people. —*n.* a native or inhabitant of Somalia.

so·ma·lo (sō mä′lō), *n., pl.* **-li** (-lē). a unit of money in Somalia, worth about 14 cents. [< Italian *somalo*]

so·ma·plasm (sō′mə plaz əm), *n.* somatoplasm.

so·ma·scope (sō′mə skōp), *n.* a device used to detect diseases difficult to locate by means of X ray or fluoroscope. It aims very high-frequency sound waves at the body and converts the echoes into visual signals that may be photographed. [< Greek *sôma* body + English *-scope*]

so·mat·ic (sō mat′ik), *adj.* **1.** of or having to do with the body. **2.** having to do with the cavity of the body, or its walls. **3.** having to do with the soma, especially as contrasted with the mind or nervous system. [< Greek *sōmatikós* < *sôma, -atos* body] —**so·mat′i·cal·ly,** *adv.*

somatic cell, any cell of an animal or plant, except a germ cell.

so·mat·ics (sō mat′iks), *n.* somatology.

so·ma·to·chrome (sō′mə tə krōm), *n.* a nerve cell which possesses a well-marked cell body surrounding the nucleus on all sides and staining deeply in basic aniline dyes. [< Greek *sôma, -atos* body + *chrôma* color]

so·ma·to·log·ic (sō′mə tə loj′ik), *adj.* somatological.

so·ma·to·log·i·cal (sō′mə tə loj′ə kəl), *adj.* **1.** of or having to do with somatology. **2.** physical; material.

so·ma·tol·o·gist (sō′mə tol′ə jist), *n.* a person skilled in somatology.

so·ma·tol·o·gy (sō′mə tol′ə jē), *n.* **1.** the science of the human body, especially as a branch of anthropology. **2.** the science of material bodies or substances; physics. [< New Latin *somatologia* < Greek *sôma, -atos* body + *-logíā* -logy]

so·ma·to·phyte (sō′mə tə fīt), *n.* a plant some part of which ceases form growth, thus forming a body. All the higher plants are somatophytes. [< Greek *sôma, -atos* body + English *-phyte*]

so·ma·to·phyt·ic (sō′mə tə fit′ik), *adj.* of the nature of a somatophyte.

so·ma·to·plasm (sō′mə tə plaz′əm), *n.* all the living substance in the cells of the body, except the germ plasm: *Somatoplasm is involved in growth, asexual reproduction, and digestion* (Harbaugh and Goodrich). [< Greek *sôma, -atos* body + *plásma* something molded]

so·ma·to·pleu·ral (sō′mə tə plůr′əl), *adj.* **1.** of or having to do with the somatopleure. **2.** forming somatopleure: *the somatopleural layer or division of mesoderm.*

so·ma·to·pleure (sō′mə tə plůr), *n. Embryology.* the outer of the two layers into which the mesoderm of craniate vertebrates splits, and which forms the body wall. [< Greek *sôma, -atos* body + *pleurā́* side]

so·ma·to·psy·chic (sō′mə tə sī′kik), *adj.* **1.** having to do with or consisting of mind and body. **2.** having to do with a somatic disease which causes secondary psychological symptoms.

so·ma·to·troph·in (sō′mə tə trof′in), *n.* somatotropin.

so·ma·to·trop·in (sō′mə tə trōp′in), *n.* the pituitary hormone that regulates the growth of the body. [< Greek *sôma, -atos* body + *tropē* a turning + English *-in*]

so·ma·to·type (sō′mə tə tīp), *n., v.,* **-typed, -typ·ing.** —*n.* a general classification of human body types within which certain distinct types are arranged. In one classification somatotypes are described as ectomorphic, mesomorphic, and endomorphic: *The Clancys present an interesting contrast in fraternal somatotypes* (New Yorker). —*v.t.* to classify according to body type. [< Greek *sôma, -atos* body + English *type*]

som·ber (som′bər), *adj.* **1.** dark; gloomy: *a cloudy, somber winter day, to dress in somber browns and grays. . . . The somber green of lodge pole pine* (William O. Douglas). **2.** melancholy; dismal: *a somber expression, a somber outlook for the future. His losses made him very somber. He does not understand his more somber-minded colleagues and their preoccupation with the tragic and grotesque* (Time). [< French *sombre;* origin uncertain] —**som′ber·ly,** *adv.* —**som′ber·ness,** *n.* —**Syn. 1.** murky. **2.** depressing, sad.

som·bre (som′bər), *adj. Especially British.* somber: *He showed me into a vast and sombre room, dimly lit at one end* (London Times).

som·bre·ro (som brãr′ō), *n., pl.* **-ros.** a broad-brimmed hat, worn in the southwest United States, Mexico, etc. [< Spanish *sombrero,* ultimately < Latin *sub-* under + *umbra* shade]

Sombrero

som·bre·roed (som-brãr′ōd), *adj.* wearing a sombrero: *The plump señora . . . scolds her sombreroed husband* (Time).

som·brous (som′brəs), *adj. Archaic.* somber.

some (sum; *unstressed* səm), *adj.* **1.** certain, but not known or named: *Some dogs are large; some dogs are small. Some people sleep more than others. Every nation is fitted . . . for some particular employments or manufactures* (John Ruskin). **2.** a number of: *He left the city some years ago.* **3.** a quantity of:

to drink some milk, to wait for some time, some degree of confidence. **4.** a; any: *Ask some girl to come here. Can't you find some kind person who will help you? Some mute inglorious Milton here may rest* (Thomas Gray). **5.** about: *a place some seventy miles distant. Some twenty people saw it.* **6.** *U.S. Informal.* big; good: *That was some storm!*
—*pron.* **1.** certain unnamed persons or things: *Some think so.* **2.** a certain number or quantity: *He ate some and gave the rest away.*
and then some, *U.S. Slang.* and a good deal or a great many in addition: ... *a Western film which is a Western and then some* (Wall Street Journal).
—*adv.* **1.** *Informal.* to some degree or extent; somewhat: *He is some better today.* **2.** *U.S. Informal.* to a great degree or extent: *That's going some!*
[Old English *sum*]

-some[1], *suffix.* **1.** tending to, as in *frolicsome, meddlesome.*
2. causing, as in *awesome, troublesome.*
3. to a considerable degree, as in *lonesome.*
[Middle English *-some,* Old English *-sum*]

-some[2], *suffix.* a group of ——: *Twosome = a group of two. Foursome = a group of four.* [Old English *sum* some (used after numerals)]

-some[3], *combining form.* —— body: *Chromosome = color body. Ribosome = ribose body. Monosome = single body.* [< Greek *sôma*]

some·bod·y (sum′bod′ē, -bə dē), *pron., n., pl.* **-bod·ies.** —*pron.* a person not known or named; some person; someone: *Somebody has taken my pen.* —*n.* a person of importance: *She acts as if she were a somebody since she won the prize.*

some·day (sum′dā′), *adv.* at some future time.

some·deal (sum′dēl′), *n., adv. Archaic.* somewhat.

some·how (sum′hou), *adv.* in a way not known or not stated; in one way or another: *I'll finish this work somehow.*
somehow or other, in one way or another: *His father ... maintained that every pfennig of tax collected was somehow or other returned to the people* (New Yorker).

some·one (sum′wun, -wən), *pron.* some person; somebody. —*n.* somebody.

some·place (sum′plās), *adv.* in or to some place; somewhere: *Let's go someplace for dinner.*

som·er·sault (sum′ər sôlt), *n.* a roll or jump, turning the heels over the head: *I jerked out of the forward somersault into a backward one* (New Yorker).
turn a somersault, to somersault: *I turned a somersault on the lawn.*
—*v.i.* to roll or jump, turning the heels over the head. Also, **summersault.**
[< Middle French *sombresault* < Old Provençal *sobresaut,* ultimately < Latin *suprā* over + *saltus, -ūs* a leaping, jump < *salīre* to leap]

som·er·set (sum′ər set), *n., v.i.,* **-set·ted, -set·ting.** somersault.

so·mes·thet·ic (sō′mes thet′ik), *adj.* of or having to do with bodily sensation. [< Greek *sôma* body; patterned on *anesthetic*]

some·thing (sum′thing), *n.* **1.** some thing; particular thing not named or known: *He has something on his mind. Something there is that doesn't love a wall* (Robert Frost). **2.** a certain amount or quantity; part; little: *Something yet of doubt remains.* **3.** a thing or person of some value or importance: *He thinks he's something. If a man thinketh himself something, when he is nothing, he deceiveth himself* (Galatians 6:3). **4.** a thing or person that is to a certain extent an example of what is named: *There is something of the saint in her. Albert Einstein was something of a violinist.*
something for nothing, that which is sought or obtained without giving something in return: ... *not the fly-by-night variety, looking for something for nothing* (Newsweek).
—*adv.* to some extent or degree; somewhat; rather: *He is something like his father.*

some·time (sum′tīm), *adv.* **1.** at one time or another: *Come over sometime.* **2.** at an indefinite point of time: *It happened sometime last March.* **3.** *Archaic.* sometimes. **4.** *Archaic.* formerly.
—*adj.* former: *a sometime pupil of the school; sometime intelligence officer in the British Royal Navy* ... (Time).

some·times (sum′tīmz), *adv.* now and then; at times: *He comes to visit sometimes. At one time literary, sometimes sanguinary, critic for London's News Chronicle* ... (Time).

some·way (sum′wā), *adv.* in some way: *She was someway clever enough to get the job.*

some·ways (sum′wāz), *adv.* someway.

some·what (sum′hwot), *adv.* to some extent or degree; slightly: *somewhat round, somewhat embarrassed.*
—*n.* **1.** some part; some amount: *somewhat of a musician. A joke loses somewhat of its fun when you hear it the second time.* **2.** a little. **3.** a thing or person of value or importance.

some·when (sum′hwen), *adv.* at some indefinite time: ... *a single tongue, spoken somewhere and somewhen in the past* (William Dwight Whitney).

some·where (sum′hwãr), *adv.* **1.** in or to some place; in or to one place or another: *He lives somewhere in the neighborhood. He said he had to go somewhere to see someone about something* (W.H. Hudson). **2.** at some time: *It happened somewhere in the last century.* **3.** approximately: *The total he owed was somewhere around forty dollars.*
—*n.* some place.

some·while (sum′hwīl), *adv.* **1.** at times. **2.** for some time. **3.** sometime. **4.** formerly.

some·whith·er (sum′hwiᴛʜ ər), *adv.* to some place: *Somewhither would she have thee go with her* (Shakespeare).

some·why (sum′hwī), *adv.* for some reason.

some·wise (sum′wīz), *adv. Obsolete.* someway.

so·mi·tal (sō′mə təl), *adj.* somitic.

so·mite (sō′mīt), *n. Zoology.* any of a longitudinal series of segments into which the body of certain animals, as the earthworm, is divided; metamere. [< Greek *sôma, -atos* body + English *-ite*[1]]

so·mit·ic (sō mit′ik), *adj.* **1.** like a somite: *the somitic divisions of the body.* **2.** of or having to do with somites: *a somitic ring or joint, a somitic appendage.*

som·me·lier (sô mə lyā′), *n. French.* a wine steward in a restaurant: *The sommelier then proffered the wine selected for us* (Maclean's).

som·nam·bu·lance (som nam′byə ləns), *n.* somnambulism.

som·nam·bu·lant (som nam′byə lənt), *adj.* walking in sleep. —*n.* a sleepwalker.

som·nam·bu·lar (som nam′byə lər), *adj.* having to do with a somnambulist or somnambulism.

som·nam·bu·late (som nam′byə lāt), *v.i., v.t.,* **-lat·ed, -lat·ing.** to walk during sleep.

som·nam·bu·la·tion (som nam′byə lā′shən), *n.* somnambulism.

som·nam·bu·la·tor (som nam′byə lā′tər), *n.* a sleepwalker.

som·nam·bule (som nam′byül), *n.* a sleepwalker. [< French *somnambule*]

som·nam·bu·lic (som nam′byə lik), *adj.* somnambular.

som·nam·bu·lism (som nam′byə liz əm), *n.* sleepwalking. [< Latin *somnus* sleep + *ambulāre* walk + English *-ism*]

som·nam·bu·list (som nam′byə list), *n.* a sleepwalker.

som·nam·bu·lis·tic (som nam′byə lis′tik), *adj.* having to do with sleepwalking or sleepwalkers. —**som·nam′bu·lis′ti·cal·ly,** *adv.*

som·ni·al (som′nē əl), *adj.* having to do with or involving dreams. [< Latin *somniālis* < *somnium* a dream < *somnus* sleep]

som·ni·fa·cient (som′nə fā′shənt), *n.* a drug that causes sleep. —*adj.* causing sleep, as some drugs. [< Latin *somnus* sleep + *faciens, -entis,* present participle of *facere* do]

som·nif·er·ous (som nif′ər əs), *adj.* **1.** causing sleep. **2.** sleepy. [< Latin *somnifer* (< *somnus* sleep + *ferre* to bring) + English *-ous*] —**som·nif′er·ous·ly,** *adv.*

som·nif·ic (som nif′ik), *adj.* causing sleep. [< Latin *somnificus* < *somnus* sleep + *facere* do, make]

som·nil·o·quism (som nil′ə kwiz əm), *n.* somniloquy.

som·nil·o·quist (som nil′ə kwist), *n.* a person who talks in his sleep.

som·nil·o·quy (som nil′ə kwē), *n., pl.* **-quies.** the act or habit of talking in one's sleep. [< Latin *somnus* sleep + *loquī* speak]

som·niv·o·len·cy (som niv′ə lən sē), *n., pl.* **-cies.** something that induces sleep; a soporific. [< Latin *somnus* sleep + *volentia* will < *velle* to wish]

som·no·lence (som′nə ləns), *n.* sleepiness; drowsiness.

som·no·len·cy (som′nə lən sē), *n.* somnolence.

som·no·lent (som′nə lənt), *adj.* sleepy; drowsy: *a somnolent expression.* [< Latin *somnolentus* < *somnus* sleep] —**som′no·lent·ly,** *adv.*

Som·nus (som′nəs), *n.* the Roman god of sleep. [< Latin *Somnus* (originally) sleep]

son (sun), *n.* **1.** a male child or person in relation to his parents or parent. **2.** a male descendant: *Adam's sons are my brethren* (Shakespeare). **3.** a son-in-law. **4.** a boy or man attached to country, cause, etc., as a child is to its parents: *sons of liberty. Affliction's sons are brothers in distress* (Robert Burns). **5.** anything thought of as a son in relation to its origin: *Sam Rayburn was a son of Texas.* **6.** a kindly term of address to a boy or from an older person, priest, etc. [Old English *sunu*]

Son (sun), *n.* Jesus Christ.

so·nance (sō′nəns), *n.* **1.** sonant quality or state. **2.** *Obsolete.* **a.** a sound. **b.** a melody; tune.

so·nan·cy (sō′nən sē), *n.* sonance.

so·nant (sō′nənt), *adj.* **1.** of sound; having sound; sounding. **2.** pronounced with the vocal cords vibrating. —*n.* a sound pronounced with the vocal cords vibrating. *Z* and *v* are sonants; *s* and *f* are not. [< Latin *sonāns, -antis,* present participle of *sonāre* to sound < *sonus* a sound]

so·nar (sō′när), *n.* **1.** a device for determining the distance and direction of objects under water by the reflection of sound waves: *Sonar revealed details of lake and ocean coastline bottoms in a new, quick and less costly method of sounding* (Science News Letter). **2.** any device or system using the reflection of sound waves: *In our studies of bats ... we use an apparatus which translates the bats' high-pitched, inaudible sonar signals into audible clicks* (Scientific American). [< *so*(und) *na*(vigation) *r*(anging)]

so·nar·man (sō′när man′), *n., pl.* **-men.** a person who operates sonar: *Sonarmen hunched over their listening posts, monitoring the traffic in the North Atlantic shipping lane overhead* (Newsweek).

so·na·ta (sə nä′tə), *n. Music.* **1.** a piece of music for one or two instruments, having three or four movements in contrasted rhythms but related keys. **2.** (originally) any instrumental composition, as contrasted with a vocal composition or cantata. [< Italian *sonata* (literally) sounded (played on an instrument, contrasted with singing) < Latin *sonāre* to sound]

so·na·ta da ca·me·ra (sə nä′tə dä kä′me rä), an Italian instrumental composition of the 1600's in four movements, performed by two or more stringed instruments with keyboard accompaniment. [< Italian *sonata da camera* (literally) chamber sonata]

so·na·ta da chie·sa (sə nä′tə dä kyā′zä), a composition similar to the sonata da camera but in a more serious, contrapuntal style suitable for performing in a church. [< Italian *sonata da chiesa* (literally) church sonata]

sonata form, a complicated form for a movement, usually the first movement, of a sonata, symphony, concerto, etc., consisting of the exposition, the development, and the recapitulation, often followed by a coda.

son·a·ti·na (son′ə tē′nə), *n., pl.* **-nas, -ne** (-nā). a short or simplified sonata. [< Italian *sonatina* (diminutive) < *sonata;* see SONATA]

so·na·tion (sō nā′shən), *n.* the giving forth of a sound; sounding. [< Medieval Latin *sonatio, -onis* < Latin *sonāre* to sound]

sonde (sond), *n.* a radiosonde.

sone (sōn), *n.* a unit of loudness. One sone is equivalent to a simple tone having a frequency of 1,000 cycles per second, 40 decibels above the listener's threshold. [< Latin *sonus* sound]

son et lu·mière (sôɴ′ā lʏ myãr′), *French.* **1.** a theatrical spectacle or pageant using subtle light effects and recorded music and narrative instead of actors and conventional stage settings. **2.** (literally) sound and light.

song (sông, song), *n.* **1.** something to sing; short poem set to music: *Songs are thoughts, sung out with the breath when people are moved by great forces and ordinary speech no longer suffices* (Beals and Hoijer). **2.** poetry that has a musical sound: *The mightiest chiefs of British song, Scorn'd not such legend, to prolong* (Scott). **3.** a piece of music for, or as if for, a poem that is to be sung. **4.** the act or practice of singing: *The canary burst into song.* **5.** any sound like singing: *the cricket's song, the song of the teakettle, the song of the brook.* **6.** a mere

trifle; low price: *a house offered at a song.* **for a song,** very cheap: *Two men bought them [dogs], harness and all, for a song* (Jack London).
[Old English *sang*]

song and dance, *Informal.* an explanation or account, not necessarily true, and often intended to impress or deceive: *If the Soviet leaders did not make such a song and dance about international trade ...* (Manchester Guardian).

song-and-dance (sông′ən dans′, -däns′; song′-), *adj. U.S.* of or having to do with singing and dancing, especially in a vaudeville act or a musical comedy: *a song-and-dance team.*

song·bird (sông′bėrd′, song′-), *n.* **1.** a bird that sings. **2.** a woman singer.

song·craft (sông′kraft′, song′-; -kräft′), *n.* the art of composing songs; skill in versification.

song cycle, a group of art songs related in style or subject, usually written by one composer, and intended to be performed in a series: *Schubert's "Winterreise" is one of the earliest song cycles, and the greatest of them all* (London Times).

song·fest (sông′fest, song′-), *n. U.S.* an informal gathering or concert where there is much singing, often with members of the audience joining the performers.

song·ful (sông′fəl, song′-), *adj.* full of song; musical; melodious: *... smoothly songful in passages where such sound is indispensable* (Saturday Review). —**song′ful·ly,** *adv.* —**song′ful·ness,** *n.*

song·less (sông′lis, song′-), *adj.* not able to sing; not singing; without song: *a songless bird.*

song·like (sông′līk′, song′-), *adj.* of the nature of song or singing: *The songlike tenderness of her cantabile ...* (London Times).

song·man (sông′mən, song′-), *n., pl.* **-men.** a singer, especially a singer of songs.

song of degrees, any of the fifteen Psalms from 120 to 134, inclusive. [because they were sung by pilgrims as they ascended steps or high places of worship]

Song of Solomon, a book of the Old Testament, attributed to Solomon; Canticles. *Abbr.:* S. of Sol.

Song of Songs, Song of Solomon.

Song of the Three Children, a book of the Old Testament Apocrypha, included in the canon of the Greek and Roman Catholic Bibles as part of Daniel.

song·smith (sông′smith, song′-), *n.* a composer of songs: *The book is realistic in appraising the professional songsmith versus the one-shot wonders* (Saturday Review).

song sparrow, a common North American sparrow having a streaked breast with a dark central spot.

Song Sparrow (6½ in. long)

song·ster (sông′stər, song′-), *n.* **1.** a singer. **2.** a writer of songs or poems. **3.** a songbird: *The place offers good cover and it has water, the two requisites for the peace of mind of small songsters* (New Yorker). [Old English *sangestre* < *sang* song + *-estre* -ster]

song·stress (sông′stris, song′-), *n.* **1.** a woman singer. **2.** a woman writer of songs or poems; poetess. **3.** a female songbird.

song thrush, 1. the wood thrush of eastern North America. See **thrush**[1] for picture. **2.** a common European thrush with a yellowish-brown back, yellowish breast, and white belly, noted for its song; mavis.

song·writ·er (sông′rī′tər, song′-), *n.* a composer of popular songs or tunes.

son·hood (sun′hu̇d), *n.* the condition or relation of being a son.

son·ic (son′ik), *adj.* **1.** of, having to do with, or using sound waves: *a sonic depth finder, sonic impact.* **2.** having to do with the rate at which sound travels in air at sea level (about 1,100 feet per second or 750 miles per hour). [< Latin *sonus* sound + English *-ic;* perhaps patterned on *phonic*]

son·i·cal·ly (son′ə klē), *adv.* with regard to sound or its qualities: *A vigorous, passionate work whose rich coloration took on a special sheen in the sonically clean, echoless hall* (Time).

sonic barrier or **wall,** sound barrier.

sonic boom, a loud noise made by an airplane crossing through the sonic barrier.

sonic depth finder, a device that measures the time for a sound wave to reach the ocean's bottom and be echoed back.

sonic mine, a container holding an explosive charge that is put under water and exploded by propeller vibrations; acoustic mine.

son·ics (son′iks), *n.* **1.** acoustics: *... to reproduce the sonics of the world's foremost concert halls* (New York Times). **2.** the use of acoustic science in solving technical problems of sound; practical or applied acoustics.

sonic speed, the speed of sound.

so·nif·er·ous (sō nif′ər əs), *adj.* carrying or producing sound. [< Latin *sonus* sound + English *-ferous*]

son-in-law (sun′in lô′), *n., pl.* **sons-in-law.** the husband of one's daughter.

son·less (sun′lis), *adj.* having no son; without a son.

son·net (son′it), *n., v.,* **-et·ed, -et·ing** or (*especially British*) **-et·ted, -et·ting.** —*n.* a poem having 14 lines, usually in iambic pentameter, and a certain arrangement of rhymes. Elizabethan and Italian sonnets differ in the arrangement of the rhymes. —*v.i.* to compose sonnets. —*v.t.* to celebrate in a sonnet or sonnets. [< Middle French *sonnet,* or Italian *sonetto* < Old Provençal *sonet* (diminutive) < *son* sound < Latin *sonus*]

son·net·eer (son′ə tir′), *n.* **1.** a writer of sonnets. **2.** an inferior poet: *Our little sonneteers ... have too narrow souls to judge of Poetry* (John Dryden). —*v.i.* to write sonnets.

son·net·ist (son′ə tist), *n.* a sonneteer.

son·net·ize (son′ə tīz), *v.,* **ized, -iz·ing.** —*v.i.* to compose sonnets. —*v.t.* to make the subject of a sonnet; celebrate in a sonnet: *Now could I sonnetize thy piteous plight* (Robert Southey).

sonnet sequence, a series of sonnets by one poet, usually having a single theme.

son·ny (sun′ē), *n., pl.* **-nies.** little son (used as a pet name or as a way of speaking to a little boy or a man younger than the speaker).

son·o·buoy (son′ə boi′, -bü′ē), *n.* a radio device floated in a buoy or dropped from an airplane to receive and transmit underwater sounds, used especially in submarine detection. [< Latin *sonus* sound + English *buoy*]

son of a gun, *Slang.* **1.** a wicked or mischievous person; scoundrel; rascal: *"Why, you son of a gun, you snuck out 11 cabs today"* (New York Times). **2.** a wretched person; unfortunate. *"Them poor son of a guns live the same way ..., eat the same as the kids—slop"* (San Francisco Chronicle). **3.** an exclamation used to greet a friend, express surprise, joy, etc.: *"Mac, old boy!" he shouted heartily. "Beddoes, you ... you son of a gun!"* (New Yorker).

Son of God, Jesus Christ.

Son of Man, Jesus Christ.

son·o·lu·mi·nes·cence (son′ə lü′mə nes′-əns), *n.* light given off when liquid containing dissolved gas is permeated by high-frequency sounds. [< Latin *sonus* sound + English *luminescence*]

So·no·ma oak (sə nō′mə), an oak of the mountains of Oregon and California, of moderate size, valued chiefly as fuel, but furnishing also some tanbark. [< *Sonoma,* a county in California]

so·nom·e·ter (sə nom′ə tər), *n.* **1.** an instrument used in measuring the pitch of musical tones or for experimenting with vibrating strings. **2.** an instrument used for testing a person's hearing; audiometer. [< Latin *sonus* sound + English *-meter*]

son·o·ra·di·o buoy (son′ə rā′dē ō), sonobuoy.

so·no·rant (sə nôr′ənt, -nōr′-), *n. Phonetics.* a sound having more sonority than the stops and fricatives, but less than the vowels, occurring in both syllabic and nonsyllabic position, as *l, m, n, ng,* and *r;* sonant. [< *sonor*(ous) + *-ant*]

so·no·rif·ic (sō′nə rif′ik, son′ə-), *adj.* producing sound or noise, as the organs that a cricket rubs together to make its chirping sound. [< Latin *sonor, -ōris* a sound + *facere* to make]

so·nor·i·ty (sə nôr′ə tē, -nor′-), *n., pl.* **-ties.** sonorous quality or condition: *He has a richer melodic gift than most, ... the ability to invent new sonorities without striving for far-fetched effects* (New York Times).

so·no·rous (sə nôr′əs, -nōr′-), *adj.* **1.** giving out or having a deep, loud sound: *a sonorous bell.* **2.** full and rich in sound: *a round, deep, sonorous voice* (Dickens). **3.** having an impressive sound; high-sounding: *sonorous phrases, a sonorous style.*
[< Latin *sonōrus* (with English *-ous*) < *sonor, -ōris* a sound < *sonāre* to sound < *sonus* sound] —**so·no′rous·ly,** *adv.* —**so·no′rous·ness,** *n.*

sonorous figures, figures which are formed by vibration of a sounding body, as in a layer of fine sand strewn on a disk of glass or metal, which is caused to vibrate by the bow of a violin drawn across its edge.

son·ship (sun′ship), *n.* the condition or relation of being a son.

Sons of Ammon (sunz), (in the Bible) the tribe of Ammon.

Sons of Freedom, a small sect of Doukhobors in Canada.

son·sy or **son·sie** (son′sē), *adj.,* **-si·er, -si·est.** *Scottish and Irish.* **1.** bringing good fortune; lucky. **2.** plump. **3.** comely. **4.** cheerful; jolly. **5.** comfortable-looking. [Middle English *sonse* prosperity < Scottish Gaelic *sonas* < *sona* fortunate]

son·tag (son′tag), *n.* a woman's knitted cape with long ends crossed over the breast and fastened together at the back. [< Henriette *Sontag,* 1806-1854, a German singer]

sool (sül), *v.t. Australian.* **1.** to incite (usually, a dog) to attack someone. **2.** to attack or snap at.

soom (süm), *n., v.,* **soomed, soom·ming.** *Scottish.* swim.

soon (sün), *adv.* **1.** in a short time; before long: *I will see you again soon.* **2.** before the usual or expected time; early: *A diller, a dollar, A ten-o'clock scholar, Why have you come so soon?* (Nursery rhyme). **3.** promptly; quickly: *As soon as I hear, I will let you know.* **4.** readily; willingly: *He would as soon die as yield to such an enemy.* **5.** *Obsolete.* forthwith; straightaway.
had or **would sooner,** would more readily; prefer to: *Why, I'd sooner stay in prison all my life!* (T.A. Guthrie).
sooner or later, at some future time; in the end; inevitably: *sooner or later ... I felt sure that you'd want something out of me* (Graham Greene).
[Old English *sōna* at once, quickly]
—**Syn. 1.** shortly, presently.
➔ **sooner than.** After *no sooner* the connective used is *than,* not *when: The fly had no sooner hit the water than* [not *when*] *a huge trout snapped at it.*

soon·er (sü′nər), *n.* **1.** *U.S. Slang.* a person who settles on government land before it is legally opened to settlers in order to gain the choice of location. **2.** *U.S. Slang.* a person who gains an unfair advantage by getting ahead of others. **3.** a person who acts prematurely.

Soon·er (sü′nər), *n.* a nickname for a native or inhabitant of Oklahoma.

Sooner State, a nickname of Oklahoma.

soot (su̇t, süt), *n.* a black substance in the smoke from burning coal, wood, oil, etc. Soot, caused chiefly by incomplete burning, makes smoke dark and collects on the inside of chimneys. —*v.t.* to cover or blacken with soot. [Old English *sōt*]

soot·fall (su̇t′fôl′, süt′-), *n.* **1.** the fall of soot left in the air by smokestacks, etc., especially in an industrial area. **2.** the amount of soot falling within a certain time and area.

sooth (süth), *Archaic.* —*n.* truth: *He speaks sooth.*
in sooth, in truth; truly; really: *Are you in sooth Lancelot?*
—*adj.* **1.** true. **2.** soothing; soft. **3.** smooth.
[Old English *sōth*]

soothe (süᴛʜ), *v.,* **soothed, sooth·ing.** —*v.t.* **1.** to quiet; calm; comfort: *The mother soothed the crying child. Music hath charms to soothe a savage breast* (William Congreve). **2.** to make less painful; relieve; ease: *Heat soothes some aches; cold soothes others.* **3.** *Obsolete.* to cajole by consenting. —*v.i.* to have or exercise a soothing influence: *Ah, thought which saddens while it soothes* (Robert Browning).
[Old English *sōthian* to verify < *sōth* sooth] —**sooth′er,** *n.*

sooth·fast (süth′fast′, -fäst′), *adj. Archaic.* **1.** true. **2.** truthful. **3.** loyal. [Old English *sōthfæst* < *sōth* sooth + *fæst* fast, firm] —**sooth′fast′ly,** *adv.* —**sooth′fast′ness,** *n.*

sooth·ful (süth′fəl), *adj. Archaic.* **1.** true. **2.** truthful; trustworthy.

sooth·ing (sü′ᴛʜing), *adj.* **1.** that soothes: *soothing words.* **2.** (of various patent medicines) that relieve pain, bring sleep, etc., especially in children: *soothing syrup.* —**sooth′ing·ly,** *adv.* —**sooth′ing·ness,** *n.*

sooth·ly (süth′lē), *adv. Archaic.* truly; in truth: *Soothly, other shores I fain would see* (William Morris).

sooth·say (süth′sā′), *v.,* **-said, -say·ing,** *n.* —*v.i.* to prophesy. —*n.* **1.** a prophecy. **2.** an omen. [back formation < *soothsayer*]

sooth·say·er (süth′sā′ər), *n.* a person who claims to tell what will happen; person who makes predictions: *A soothsayer bids you beware the ides of March* (Shakespeare). [< *sooth* + *sayer*]

sooth·say·ing (süth′sā′ing), *n.* **1.** the foretelling of future events: *Divinations, and soothsayings, and dreams, are vain* (Ecclesiasticus 34:5). **2.** a prediction or prophecy.

soot·i·ly (su̇t′ə lē, sü′tə-), *adv.* in a sooty manner; with soot.

soot·i·ness (su̇t′ē nis, sü′tē-), *n.* the state of being sooty.

soot·less (su̇t′lis, süt′-), *adj.* free from soot.

soot·y (su̇t′ē, sü′tē), *adj.,* **soot·i·er, soot·i·est,** *v.,* **soot·ied, soot·y·ing.** —*adj.* **1.** covered or blackened with soot: *a sooty chimney, sooty hands.* **2.** dark-brown or black; dark-colored. —*v.t.* to black or foul with soot.

sooty albatross, a wide-ranging species of albatross in southern and south temperate seas, of a sooty brown color, with black feet and bill, the latter having a yellow stripe on the side of the under mandible.

sooty shearwater, a black hagden common on the Atlantic coast of North America, of medium size and entirely sooty brown plumage.

sooty tern, a partly white and partly glossy black tern whose eggs are used for food, found in abundance along the coasts of most warm and temperate seas; wideawake.

sop (sop), *n., v.,* **sopped, sop·ping.** —*n.* **1.** a piece of food dipped or soaked in milk, broth, etc. **2.** something given to soothe or quiet; bribe: *Concessions are a sop to the malcontents in the organization.* **3.** a person or thing that is thoroughly soaked. **4.** an accumulation of some liquid: *a great pool and sop of blood* (Hawthorne).
—*v.t.* **1.** to dip or soak: *to sop bread in milk.* **2.** to take up (water, etc.); wipe; mop: *Please sop up that water with a cloth.* **3.** to soak thoroughly; drench. —*v.i.* **1.** to be drenched. **2.** to soak in or through.
[Old English *sopp,* noun]

sop., soprano.

SOP (no periods) or **S.O.P.,** standing or standard operating procedure.

soph (sof), *n. U.S. Informal.* sophomore.

Soph., 1. Sophocles. **2.** Sophomore.

So·pher (sō′fər), *n., pl.* **-pher·im.** a scribe; one of the ancient teachers or expounders of the Jewish oral law. [< Hebrew *sopher*]

So·pher·ic (sō′fər ik), *adj.* pertaining to the Sopherim, or to their teachings or labors.

So·pher·im (sō′fər im), *n.* plural of **Sopher.**

So·phi or **so·phi** (sō′fē, sof′ē), *n.* Sophy.

soph·ic (sof′ik), *adj.* of, having to do with, or teaching wisdom. [< Greek *sophikós* < *sophós* wise, clever]

soph·ism (sof′iz əm), *n.* a clever but misleading argument; argument based on false or unsound reasoning: *But no sophism is too gross to delude minds distempered by party spirit* (Macaulay). [< Latin *sophisma* < Greek *sóphisma, -atos* < *sophízesthai* become wise < *sophós* clever]

soph·ist (sof′ist), *n.* **1.** a person who makes use of a sophism or sophisms, especially intentionally or habitually; a clever but misleading reasoner: *The self-torturing sophist, wild Rousseau* (Byron). *Be neither saint nor sophist led, but be a man* (Matthew Arnold). **2.** Often, **Sophist.** one of a class of teachers of rhetoric, philosophy, ethics, etc., in ancient Greece. **3.** a man of learning.
—*adj.* Also, **Sophist.** of or having to do with sophists or sophism.
[< Latin *sophista* < Greek *sophistḗs* < *sophízesthai* become wise < *sophós* wise, clever]

soph·ist·er (sof′ə stər), *n.* **1.** a student in his second or third year at Cambridge or Oxford universities. **2.** an unsound reasoner; sophist. [< Old French *sophistre,* and *soffistre,* learned borrowing from Latin *sophista;* see SOPHIST]

so·phis·tic (sə fis′tik), *adj.* sophistical.

so·phis·ti·cal (sə fis′tə kəl), *adj.* **1.** clever but misleading; based on false or unsound reasoning: *a sophistical proof. It is a reasoning weak, rotten and sophistical* (Edmund Burke). **2.** using clever but misleading arguments; reasoning falsely or unsoundly: *a sophistical rhetorician, inebriated with the exuberance of his own verbosity* (Benjamin Disraeli). **3.** of or having to do with sophists or sophistry. —**so·phis′ti·cal·ly,** *adv.* —**so·phis′ti·cal·ness,** *n.*

so·phis·ti·cate (*v., adj.* sə fis′tə kāt; *n.* sə-fis′tə kāt, -kit), *v.,* **-cat·ed, -cat·ing,** *n., adj.* —*v.t.* **1.** to make experienced in worldly ways; cause to lose one's natural simplicity and frankness; make artificial. **2.** to mislead: *Books of casuistry, which sophisticate the understanding and defile the heart* (Robert Southey). **3.** to involve in sophistry; misstate: *I have . . . Sophisticated no truth, Nursed no delusion* (Matthew Arnold).
—*v.i. Archaic.* to use sophistry; quibble.
—*n.* a sophisticated person.
—*adj.* sophisticated.
[< Medieval Latin *sophisticare* (with English *-ate*[1]) to cheat, quibble < Latin *sophisticus* sophistical < Greek *sophistikós* < *sophistḗs;* see SOPHIST]

so·phis·ti·cat·ed (sə fis′tə kā′tid), *adj.* **1.** experienced in worldly ways; lacking in natural simplicity or frankness; artificial: *a charming, witty, and thoroughly sophisticated young lady, an empty, sophisticated life.* **2.** appealing to the tastes of sophisticated people: *sophisticated humor.* **3.** that is very advanced and complex: *a sophisticated missile.* **4.** misleading. —**so·phis′ti·cat′ed·ly,** *adv.*

so·phis·ti·ca·tion (sə fis′tə kā′shən), *n.* **1.** a lessening or loss of naturalness, simplicity, or frankness; worldly experience or ideas; artificial ways. **2.** sophistry.

so·phis·ti·ca·tor (sə fis′tə kā tər), *n.* a person who sophisticates, especially one who adulterates.

soph·ist·ry (sof′ə strē), *n., pl.* **-ries. 1.** unsound reasoning. **2.** a clever but misleading argument: *The parson's cant, the lawyer's sophistry* (Alexander Pope). **3.** the art, practice, or learning of the ancient Greek sophists, especially of their type of argument.

Soph·o·cle·an (sof′ə klē′ən), *adj.* of, having to do with, or characteristic of the ancient Greek tragic poet Sophocles, his works, or his style: *a Sophoclean tragedy.*

soph·o·more (sof′ə môr, -mōr; sof′môr, -mōr), *n.* a student in the second year of a four-year college or high school. —*adj.* **1.** of or having to do with second-year students: *the sophomore year.* **2.** of or for sophomores.
[earlier *sophumer* (originally) (one) taking part in dialectic exercises < *sophom, -um,* variant of *sophisme* sophism]

soph·o·mor·ic (sof′ə môr′ik, -mor′-), *adj.* **1.** of, having to do with, or like a sophomore or sophomores. **2.** *U.S.* conceited and pretentious, but crude and ignorant.

Soph·o·ni·as (sof′ə nī′əs), *n.* (in the Douay Bible) Zephaniah.

so·pho·ra (sə fôr′ə, -fōr′-), *n.* any of a group of temperate or semitropical trees and shrubs of the pea family, with odd-pinnate leaves and spikes of white, yellow, or violet flowers. [< New Latin *Sophora* the genus name < Arabic *sofāra* a yellow plant < *asfar* yellow]

So·phy or **so·phy** (sō′fē, sof′ē), *n.* a former title of the ruler of Persia. Also, **Sophi.** [< Persian *ṣafī* < Arabic *ṣafī-d-dīn* purity of religion]

so·pite (sə pīt′), *v.,* **-pit·ed, -pit·ing.**—*v.t.* **1.** to put to sleep; dull. **2.** to put an end to; settle. [< Latin *sōpītus,* past participle of *sōpīre* put to sleep]

so·por (sō′pər, -pôr), *n.* a deep, unnatural sleep. [< Latin *sopor, -ōris* deep sleep]

so·po·rif·er·ous (sō′pə rif′ər əs, sop′ə-), *adj.* bringing sleep; causing sleep. [< Latin *sopōrifer* (< *sopor, -ōris* deep sleep + *ferre* to bring) + English *-ous*] —**so′po·rif′er·ous·ness,** *n.*

so·po·rif·er·ous·ly (sō′pə rif′ər əs lē, sop′ə-), *adv.* in a soporiferous manner; so as to produce sleep.

so·po·rif·ic (sō′pə rif′ik, sop′ə-), *adj.* **1.** causing or tending to cause sleep: *a soporific sermon.* **2.** sleepy; drowsy. —*n.* a drug that causes sleep. [< Latin *sopor, -ōris* deep sleep + *facere* to make]

so·po·rose (sō′pə rōs, sop′ə-), *adj.* characterized by a deep, unnatural sleep.

sopped (sopt), *adj.* soaked; drenched.

sop·pi·ness (sop′ē nis), *n.* the condition of being soppy.

sop·ping (sop′ing), *adj.* soaked; drenched. **sopping wet,** soaked; drenched: *He came out of the rain sopping wet.*

sop·py (sop′ē), *adj.,* **-pi·er, -pi·est. 1.** soaked; very wet: *soppy weather, soppy ground.* **2.** *Informal.* full of insincere sentiment.

so·pra·ni·no (sōp rə nē′nō), *adj., n., pl.* **-nos.** —*adj.* (of a musical instrument) having a higher pitch than the soprano of the same family of instruments: *a sopranino cornet, saxophone, etc.* —*n.* a sopranino instrument. [< Italian *sopranino* little soprano]

so·pran·ist (sə pran′ist, -prä′nist), *n.* a soprano.

so·pran·o (sə pran′ō, -prä′nō), *n., pl.* **-pran·os,** *adj.* —*n.* **1.** the highest singing voice in women and boys. **2.** a singer with such a voice. **3.** a part to be sung by a soprano voice. **4.** an instrument corresponding in compass to this voice.
—*adj.* of, for, or having to do with the soprano.
[< Italian *soprano,* adjective to *sopra* above < Latin *suprā*]

soprano clef, *Music.* a C clef when placed on the bottom line of a staff.

so·ra (sôr′ə, sōr′-), *n.,* or **sora rail,** a small, brown and gray, short-billed North American rail; Carolina rail; ortolan. [American English; origin uncertain]

sorb[1] (sôrb), *v.t.* to absorb or adsorb: *At 78°C (the temperature of solid carbon dioxide) both oxygen and nitrogen are sorbed readily* (New Scientist).

sorb[2] (sôrb), *n.* **1.** either of the two European service trees. **2.** the European rowan. **3.** the fruit of any of these trees. [< Middle French *sorbe* the serviceberry, learned borrowing from Latin *sorbum*]

Sorb (sôrb), *n.* **1.** one of a Slavic people living in central Germany; Wend. **2.** their language; Sorbian.
[< German *Sorbe,* variant (influenced by Medieval Latin *Sorabi* Sorbs) of *Serbe* < Sorbian *Serb*]

sorb apple, 1. the fruit of the service tree. **2.** the tree.

sor·bate (sôr′bāt), *n.* a salt of sorbic acid.

sor·be·fa·cient (sôr′bə fā′shənt), *adj.* promoting absorption. —*n.* a sorbefacient agent.
[< Latin *sorbēre* absorb + *faciens, -entis,* present participle of *facere* to do]

sorb·ent (sôr′bənt), *n.* anything that absorbs or adsorbs: *A mixture of chemical compounds is applied to a stationary sorbent (blotting paper demonstrates the effect) and is then made to migrate along the sorbent* (L.J. Morris).

sor·bet (sôr′bit), *n.* sherbet.

Sor·bi·an (sôr′bē ən), *adj.* of or having to do with the Sorbs or their language. —*n.* **1.** the West Slavic language of the Sorbs; Wendish; Lusatian. **2.** a Sorb.

sor·bic acid (sôr′bik), an acid found in the berries of the mountain ash and produced synthetically, used to prevent mold in yeast, cheese, and other foods, often put into food wrappers. *Formula:* $C_6H_8O_2$

sor·bite (sôr′bīt), *n. Metallurgy.* a granular constituent of steel related to pearlite, formed during the tempering process. [< Henry C. *Sorby,* 1826-1908, an English geologist + *-ite*[1]]

sor·bit·ic (sôr bit′ik), *adj.* **1.** having to do with sorbite. **2.** containing sorbite.

sor·bi·tol (sôr′bə tōl, -tol), *n.* a sweet crystalline substance derived from the berries of the mountain ash, certain other berries and fruits, and corn sugar, used as a softener in candy, as a sugar substitute for diabetics, in making ascorbic acid, and as a moisture conditioner in leather, tobacco, etc. *Formula:* $C_6H_{14}O_6$

Sor·bon·ist (sôr′bə nist), *n.* a student or doctor of the Sorbonne.

Sor·bonne (sôr bon′; *French* sôr bôn′), *n.* **1.** the seat of the faculties of letters and science of the University of Paris. **2.** (formerly) the theological college of the University of Paris.
[< Old French *Sorbonne* < Robert de *Sorbon,* 1201-1274, who founded the original college]

sorb·ose (sôr′bōs), *n.* a monosaccharide sugar produced from sorbitol, used in synthesizing vitamin C. *Formula:* $C_6H_{12}O_6$ [< Latin *sorbum* the serviceberry + English *-ose*[2]]

sor·cer·er (sôr′sər ər), *n.* a person who practices magic with the supposed aid of evil spirits; wizard; magician: *Sorcerer and witch doctor . . . are still an integral part of the African pattern* (Atlantic).

sor·cer·ess (sôr′sər is), *n.* a woman who practices magic with the supposed aid of evil spirits; witch: *Again she [Medea] grew to be the sorceress, Worker of fearful things* (William Morris).

sor·cer·ize (sôr′sə rīz), *v.t.*, **-ized, -iz·ing.** to transform by sorcery: *A Lombard was sorcerized into a goose* (Frederick James Furnivall).

sor·cer·ous (sôr′sər əs), *adj.* using, involving, or resembling sorcery: *sorcerous spells.* —**sor′cer·ous·ly,** *adv.*

sor·cer·y (sôr′sər ē), *n., pl.* **-cer·ies.** magic performed with the aid of evil spirits; witchcraft. [< Old French *sorcerie,* ultimately < Latin *sors, sortis* lot, fate] —**Syn.** necromancy.

sor·da·men·te (sôr′dä men′tā), *adv. Music.* in a muted or muffled manner; softly. [< Italian *sordamente* < *sordo* deaf, dull]

sor·del·li·na (sôr′də lē′nä), *n.* a small bagpipe. [< Italian *sordellina* < *sordo* mute]

sor·des (sôr′dēz), *n.* **1. a.** dirt; filth. **b.** foul matter gathering on the teeth, in the stomach, etc. **2.** *Medicine.* scabs from fever blisters. [< Latin *sordēs*]

sor·did (sôr′did), *adj.* **1.** dirty; filthy: *The poor family lived in a sordid shack.* **2. a.** caring too much for money; meanly selfish: *His ambitions are a little sordid . . . he is too intent upon growing rich* (Winston Churchill). **b.** mean; low; base: *It is through Art . . . that we shield ourselves from the sordid perils of actual existence* (Oscar Wilde). **3.** of a dull or dirty color, as some birds and fishes. [< Latin *sordidus* dirty < *sordēre* be dirty, related to *sordēs, -is* dirt] —**sor′did·ly,** *adv.* —**sor′did·ness,** *n.*
—**Syn. 1.** foul, squalid. **2. b.** ignoble, degraded.

sor·dine (sôr′dēn), *n. Music.* **1.** a mute, as for a trumpet; sourdine. **2.** a trumpet fitted with this. [< Italian *sordina;* see SOURDINE]

sor·di·no (sôr dē′nō), *n., pl.* **-ni** (-nē). *Music.* a mute. [< Italian *sordino* (diminutive) < *sordo* < Latin *surdus* deaf, mute]

sor·dor (sôr′dər), *n.* sordid character: *the sordor of civilisation* (Byron). [< Latin *sordēre* be dirty, related to *sordēs* dirt + English *-or,* as in *squalor*]

sore (sôr, sōr), *adj.,* **sor·er, sor·est,** *n., adv.* —*adj.* **1.** painful; aching; tender; smarting: *a sore finger.* **2.** sad; sorrowful or grieving; distressed: *Why speak I vain words to a heart still sore With sudden death of happiness?* (William Morris). **3.** easily angered or offended; irritable; touchy. **4.** *Informal.* angered; offended; vexed: *He is sore at missing the game.* **5.** causing pain, misery, anger, or offense; vexing: *Their defeat is a sore subject with the members of the team.* **6.** severe; distressing: *For want of money the poor family was in sore need. Your going away is a sore grief to us.*
—*n.* **1.** a painful place on the body where the skin or flesh is infected, broken, or bruised. **2.** a cause of pain, sorrow, sadness, anger, offense, etc.
—*adv. Archaic.* in a sore manner.
[Old English *sār*] —**sore′ly,** *adv.* —**sore′ness,** *n.*
—**Syn.** *adj.* **3.** sensitive. *-n.* **2.** affliction.

so·re·di·al (sə rē′dē əl), *adj. Botany.* having the appearance of a soredium.

so·re·di·um (sə rē′dē əm), *n., pl.* **-di·a** (-dē ə). *Botany.* a gonidium of a lichen that is able to develop into a new thallus when detached from the surface of the thallus. [< New Latin *soredium* < Greek *sōrós* heap]

sore·fal·con (sôr′fôl′kən, -fal′-, -fô′-; sōr′-), *n.* a falcon in the reddish-brown plumage of the first year. [< Anglo-French *sore,* Old French *sor* reddish-brown + English *falcon;* origin uncertain]

sore·hawk (sôr′hôk′, sōr′-), *n. Archaic.* a sorefalcon.

sore·head (sôr′hed′, sōr′-), *U.S. Informal.* —*n.* **1.** a person who is angry or offended. **2.** a disappointed politician. —*adj.* irritable: *In a special issue in 1956, it offered a sorehead view of Harvard and a garish mix of ideas* (Harper's). [American English < *sore* + *head*]

sore·head·ed (sôr′hed′id, sōr′-), *adj. U.S. Informal.* feeling angered or offended: *You were soreheaded about something* (Sinclair Lewis).

sore·hon (sôr′hən), *n.* sorren.

sore spot, something that angers or offends easily: *Everybody has a few sore spots, such as an embarrassing occurrence he would rather not discuss.*

sore throat, inflammation of the throat, causing pain especially when one is swallowing.

sor·ghum (sôr′gəm), *n.* **1.** a tall cereal grass resembling corn. One variety has a sweet juice used for making molasses or syrup, others provide food for livestock either by their grain or as hay, and still others furnish material for brushes or brooms. **2.** *U.S.* molasses or syrup made from a sweet sorghum plant. [< New Latin *Sorghum* the genus name < Italian *sorgo;* see SORGO]

Common Sorghum (def. 1—to 12 ft. high)

sor·go (sôr′gō), *n., pl.* **-gos.** any of the sweet sorghums. [< Italian *sorgo* < Medieval Latin *surgum,* variant of Latin *syricum,* neuter adjective, Syrian]

so·ri (sôr′ē, sōr′-), *n.* the plural of **sorus.**

sor·i·cine (sôr′ə sīn, -sin; sor′-), *adj.* **1.** of or belonging to the family comprising the shrews. **2.** shrewlike. [< Latin *sōricīnus* < *sōrex, -icis* shrew]

so·ri·tes (sō rī′tēz), *n., pl.* **-tes.** a form of argument having several premises and one conclusion. A sorites can be resolved into a number of syllogisms, the conclusion of each being the premise of the next. [< Latin *sōrītēs* < Greek *sōreítēs* < *sōrós* a heap]

so·rit·i·cal (sō rit′ə kəl), *adj.* **1.** having to do with a sorites. **2.** resembling a sorites.

sorn (sôrn), *v.i. Scottish.* to sponge for food or lodging. [< *sorren*]

so·ro·che (sō rō′chē), *n.* (in the Andes Mountains) mountain sickness; puna: *In Peru the Indians, who are the product of centuries of painful adaptation to scarcity of oxygen, are immune to . . . soroche* (White and Renner). [< Quechua *sorochi*]

so·rop·ti·mist or **So·rop·ti·mist** (sə rop′tə mist), *n.* a member of an international organization of service clubs for professional and executive businesswomen. [< *sor*(ority) + *optimist*]

so·ro·ral (sə rôr′əl, -rōr′-), *adj.* **1.** having to do with a sister. **2.** sisterly. [< Latin *soror* sister + English *-al*[1]]

so·ror·ate (sôr′ə rāt, sōr′-), *n.* the custom among some primitive peoples that allows or requires a man to marry his deceased wife's younger sister. [< Latin *soror* sister + English *-ate*[2]]

so·ror·i·cid·al (sə rôr′ə sī′dəl, -ror′-), *adj.* **1.** of or having to do with sororicide. **2.** tending towards sororicide.

so·ror·i·cide[1] (sə rôr′ə sīd, -ror′-), *n.* the act of killing one's sister. [< Latin *sorōricīdium* < *soror, -ōris* sister + *-cīdium* act of killing]

so·ror·i·cide[2] (sə rôr′ə sīd, -ror′-), *n.* a person who kills his sister. [< Latin *sorōricīda* < *soror, -ōris* sister + *-cīda* killer]

so·ror·i·ty (sə rôr′ə tē, -ror′-), *n., pl.* **-ties.** **1.** *U.S.* a club or society of women or girls. There are student sororities in many American colleges. **2.** a sisterhood. [probably < Medieval Latin *sororitas* < Latin *soror, -ōris* sister]

so·ro·sis (sə rō′sis), *n., pl.* **-ses** (-sēz). **1.** *Botany.* a fleshy multiple fruit composed of the ovaries, receptacles, and associated parts of an entire cluster of flowers, as in the pineapple and mulberry. **2.** *U.S.* a society, especially a women's society or club. [< New Latin *sorosis* < Greek *sōrós* a heap]

sorp·tion (sôrp′shən), *n.* **1.** absorption. **2.** adsorption. [apparently back formation < *absorption*]

sorp·tive (sôrp′tiv), *adj.* absorptive.

sor·rel[1] (sôr′əl, sor′-), *adj.* reddish-brown. —*n.* **1.** a reddish brown. **2.** a reddish-brown horse. **3.** a three-year-old buck. [< Old French *sorel* < *sor* yellowish-brown, *sor,* or *sore* hawk with red plumage]

sor·rel[2] (sôr′əl, sor′-), *n.* **1.** any of various small perennial herbs of the buckwheat family, with sour leaves. **2.** any of various plants resembling this. **3.** an oxalis; wood sorrel. [< Old French *surele* < *sur* sour < Germanic (compare Old High German *sūr*)]

Sorrel[2] (def. 1) (to 3 ft. high)

sorrel tree, the sourwood, a tree of the heath family.

sor·ren (sôr′ən, sor′-), *n.* **1.** hospitality formerly due to the lord or his men in Ireland and Scotland. **2.** a tax imposed instead of this. [< obsolete Irish *sorthan*]

sor·ri·ly (sor′ə lē, sôr′-), *adv.* in a sorry manner.

sor·ri·ness (sor′ē nis, sôr′-), *n.* the state or feeling of being sorry.

sor·row (sor′ō, sôr′-), *n.* **1.** grief; sadness; regret: *Sorrow comes with years* (Elizabeth Barrett Browning). **2.** a cause of grief, sadness, or regret; trouble; suffering; misfortune: *Her sorrows have aged her. Call ignorance my sorrow, not my sin* (Robert Browning).
—*v.i.* **1.** to feel or show grief, sadness, or regret; mourn. **2.** to be sad; feel sorry; grieve.
[Old English *sorg*] —**sor′row·er,** *n.*
—**Syn.** *n.* **1. Sorrow, grief, distress** mean sadness or mental suffering caused by loss or trouble. **Sorrow** suggests deep and usually prolonged sadness or anguish: *The dope addict became a criminal and brought great sorrow to his mother.* **Grief** suggests acute but usually not prolonged sorrow: *Her grief when he died was almost unbearable.* **Distress** suggests the strain or pressure of pain (physical or mental), grief, fear, anxiety, etc.: *War causes widespread distress.* **2.** affliction, woe.

sor·row·ful (sor′ə fəl, sôr′-), *adj.* **1.** full of sorrow; feeling sorrow; sad: *a very sorrowful person.* **2.** showing sorrow: *a sorrowful smile.* **3.** causing sorrow: *A funeral is a sorrowful occasion.* —**sor′row·ful·ly,** *adv.* —**sor′row·ful·ness,** *n.* —**Syn. 1, 2.** unhappy, mournful.

sor·row·less (sor′ō lis, sôr′-), *adj.* feeling no sorrow; free from sorrow: *I came to as if with the wearing off of a drug that left me sober and sorrowless in this strange room* (New Yorker).

sor·ry (sor′ē, sôr′-), *adj.,* **-ri·er, -ri·est.** **1.** feeling pity, regret, sympathy, etc.; sad: *I am sorry that you are sick.* **2.** wretched; poor; pitiful: *a sorry excuse for a man. The baron . . . grew fat and wanton, and a sorry brute* (Emerson). *Slipshod handling once the packages reach the grocery can reduce even the finest brand to a sorry and sometimes dangerous mess* (Wall Street Journal). **3.** painful; distressing: *The blind beggar in his ragged clothes was a sorry sight. Nothing dear goes cheap except for a sorry reason* (New Yorker). [Old English *sārig* < *sār* sore] —**Syn. 1.** distressed, sorrowful.

sort[1] (sôrt), *n.* **1. a.** a group of things having common or similar characteristics; kind; class: *This sort of fish is abundant along our coast. The fire shall try every man's work of what sort it is* (I Corinthians 3:13). **b.** a certain class, order, or rank of people: *the meaner sort, the better sort.* **c.** a person or group of a certain kind or quality: *He is a good sort, generous and kind.* **2.** character; quality; nature: *I hate to . . . take the risk of breaking up a friendship of the sort that ours has gotten to be* (Ernest Hemingway). **3.** a particular kind, species, variety, or description, as distinguished by the character or nature: *What sort of work do you do?* **4.** manner; method; fashion; way: *She was named after, or in some sort related to, the Abbey at Westminster* (Dickens).

a sort of, something like; a kind of: *They use a sort of jabber* (Jonathan Swift).

of sorts, a. of one kind or another: *The Alcalde . . . was . . . police officer, petty magistrate of sorts* (W.H. Hudson). **b.** of a poor or mediocre quality: *We've a fountain of sorts; we're very vain of our shabby fountain!* (Leonard Merrick).

out of sorts, slightly ill, cross, or uncomfortable: *We've had a hot day and are all tired and out of sorts* (Robert L. Stevenson).

sort of, *Informal.* somewhat; rather: *sort of*

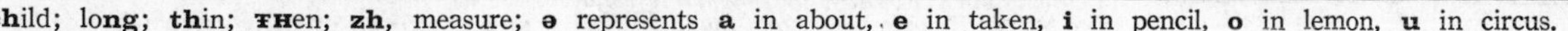

foolish. In spite of her faults I sort of like her. **sorts,** *Printing.* a letter or piece in a font of type: *The expense . . . in casting a fount of letter with such a number of heavy sorts will be considerable* (Charles Stower).
—*v.t.* **1.** to arrange by kinds or classes; arrange in order: *to sort mail. Sort these cards according to their colors.* **2.** to separate from others: *Sort out the best apples for eating and cook the rest. They will sort out the good from the evil* (Edmund Burke). **3.** to rank; class: *I will not sort you with the rest of my servants* (Shakespeare). **4.** *Scottish.* to arrange or put in order; put to rights. —*v.i.* **1.** *Archaic.* to be in harmony; agree; accord (with): *Different styles with different subjects sort* (Alexander Pope). **2.** *Scottish.* to associate; consort: *to sort with queer people.*
[< Old French *sorte* < Vulgar Latin *sorta* < Late Latin *sors, sortis* rank, class < Latin, lot] —**sort′er,** *n.* —**Syn.** *n.* **1. a.** See **kind**[2]. -*v.t.* **1.** assort, classify, select.
➔ See **kind**[2] for usage note.

sort[2] (sôrt), *n. Obsolete.* **1.** destiny; fate; fortune. **2.** lot: *Make a lottery, And by device let blockish Ajax draw the sort to fight with Hector* (Shakespeare). [< Old French *sort,* learned borrowing from Latin *sors, sortis* lot, fortune. Compare SORT[1].]

sort·a·ble (sôr′tə bəl), *adj.* that can be sorted.

sor·ta·tion (sôr tā′shən), *n.* the act or process of arranging or sorting.

sor·tie (sôr′tē), *n.* **1. a.** a sudden attack by troops from a defensive position; sally: *The troops . . . were . . . annoyed by the frequent and vigorous sorties of the besieged* (John F. Kirk). **b.** the group that makes a sortie: *They were a sortie of the besieged* (G. K. Chesterton). **2.** a single round trip of an aircraft against the enemy; combat mission. [< French *sortie* < *sortir* go out < Old French, able, obtain by lot < Latin *sortīrī* cast lots < *sors, sortis* lot]

sor·ti·lege (sôr′tə lij), *n.* divination by the casting or drawing of lots: *They endeavoured by sortilege . . . to find as it were a byroad to the secrets of futurity* (Scott). [< Medieval Latin *sortilegium* < Latin *sortilegus* diviner < *sors, sortis* lot, sort[2] + *legere* choose]

sor·ti·leg·er (sôr′tə li jər), *n.* a person who divines, chooses, or settles by drawing lots or otherwise; diviner; fortuneteller.

sor·ti·le·gious (sôr′tə lē′jəs), *adj.* of, having to do with, or characteristic of sortilege.

sort·ing yard (sôr′ting), a switchyard, a railroad yard where cars are sorted.

sor·ti·ta (sôr tē′tə), *n. Music.* the first aria sung by a principal singer in an opera. [< Italian *sortita* < *sortire* go out]

sor·ti·tion (sôr tish′ən), *n.* **1.** the casting or drawing of lots; determination or selection by lot. **2.** an instance of determining by lot. [< Latin *sortītiō, -ōnis* < *sortīrī;* see SORTIE]

so·rus (sôr′əs, sōr′-), *n., pl.* **-ri.** any of the dotlike clusters of sporangia on the underside of the frond of a fern. [< New Latin *sorus* < Greek *sōrós* heap]

S O S (es′ō′es′), **1.** the letters *s o s* of the international Morse alphabet (...---...), used in wireless telegraphy by ships, aircraft, etc., as a signal of distress. **2.** *Informal.* any urgent call for help.

so-so (sō′sō′), *adj.* neither very good nor very bad, but inclining toward bad; mediocre: *The sermon was only so-so, but they enjoyed the singing* (George W. Cable). —*adv.* in a mediocre manner or degree; passably; indifferently; tolerably.

sos·te·nu·to (sos′tə nü′tō), *adj., adv., n., pl.* **-tos, -ti** (-tē). *Music.* —*adj., adv.* **1.** sustained, as a note held for or over its full time value or a passage whose notes are thus held. **2.** prolonged, as a passage played at a uniformly decreasing rate of speed. —*n.* a movement or passage performed in this manner. [< Italian *sostenuto,* past participle of *sostenere* sustain < Latin *sustinēre*]

sot (sot), *n.* a person made stupid and foolish by drinking too much alcoholic liquor; drunkard. [Old English *sot* < Medieval Latin *sottus* stupid; a fool]

so·te·ri·al (sō tir′ē əl), *adj.* of or having to do with the Saviour or salvation.

so·te·ri·o·log·ic (sō tir′ē ə loj′ik), *adj.* soteriological.

so·te·ri·o·log·i·cal (sō tir′ē ə loj′ə kəl), *adj.* of or having to do with soteriology.

so·te·ri·ol·o·gy (sō tir′ē ol′ə jē), *n.* the branch of theology dealing with salvation through Jesus Christ. [< Greek *sōtēríā* salvation (< *sōtḗr, -ēros* savior < *sṓzein* save)]

So·thi·ac (sō′thē ak), *adj.* Sothic.

So·thic (sō′thik, soth′ik), *adj.* of or having to do with Sothis or Sirius, the Dog Star. [< Greek *Sôthis* Sothis + English *-ic*]

Sothic cycle or **period,** a cycle or period of 1,460 Sothic years.

Sothic year, the fixed year of the ancient Egyptians, comprising 365 days, determined by the annual heliacal rising of Sirius.

So·this (sō′this), *n.* Sirius, the Dog Star. [< Greek *Sôthis*]

So·tho (sō′thō), *n., pl.* **-tho** or **-thos. 1.** Basuto. **2.** Bantu language of the Basuto.

so·tol (sō′tōl, sō tōl′), *n.* any of a group of plants of the lily family, resembling the yucca, and growing in the southwestern United States and in Mexico. [American English < Mexican Spanish *sotol,* also *zotol* < Nahuatl *tzotolli*]

sot·ted (sot′id), *adj.* besotted.

sot·tish (sot′ish), *adj.* **1.** stupid and foolish from drinking too much alcoholic liquor; drunken. **2.** of or like a sot; stupid and coarse. —**sot′tish·ly,** *adv.* —**sot′tish·ness,** *n.*

sot·to vo·ce (sot′ō vō′chē), **1.** in a low tone. **2.** aside; privately: *"She makes herself too cheap," Mrs. Van Buren said sotto voce* (Leonard Merrick). [< Italian *sotto voce* (literally) below (normal) voice < Latin *subter,* and *vōx, vōcis*]

sou (sü), *n., pl.* **sous** (süz; *French* sü). **1. a.** a former French coin, worth 5 centimes or 1⁄20 of a franc. **b.** any of various earlier French bronze, copper, silver, or gold coins, varying in value. **2.** anything of little value. [< French *sou* < Old French *sol.* Doublet of SOL[3], SOLDO, SOLID.]

sou·a·ri nut (sü ä′rē), the large, edible nut of a tall, tropical American tree; butternut. [< Galibi (Guiana) *sawarra*]

sou·bise (sü bēz′), *n.,* or **soubise sauce,** a sauce flavored with a purée of onions. [< French *sauce soubise* < Prince Charles de Rohan *Soubise,* 1715-87, a French general]

sou·bre·saut (sü′brə sō′), *n.* a ballet jump with the body erect and the legs clinging together. [< French *soubresaut* < Middle French *sombresault;* see SOMERSAULT]

sou·brette (sü bret′), *n.* **1.** a maidservant or lady's maid in a play or opera, especially one of a coquettish, pert, and intriguing character; a lively or pert young woman character. **2.** an actress or singer taking such a part. [< French *soubrette* < Provençal *soubreto* coy < *soubrar* to set aside < Latin *superāre* rise above < *super* over]

sou·bret·tish (sü bret′ish), *adj.* of or like a soubrette; coquettish; pert.

sou·bri·quet (sü′brə kā), *n.* sobriquet.

sou·car (sou′kär), *n.* (in India) a Hindu banker or moneylender. Also, **sowcar.** [< Hindustani *sāhūkār* < Sanskrit *sādhu*]

sou·chong or **Sou·chong** (sü′shong′, -shông′), *n.* a fine variety of black tea, originally from China. [< Cantonese *siu chung* small, or fine, sort]

Sou·da·nese (sü′də nēz′, -nēs′), *adj., n.* Sudanese.

souf·fle (sü′fəl), *n.* a murmuring or blowing sound, as heard when listening to the heart with a stethoscope. [< French *souffle* < Old French *souffler;* see SOUFFLÉ]

souf·flé (sü flā′, sü′flā), *n.* a frothy baked dish usually made light by folding in beaten egg whites with the other ingredients and cooking very quickly in a hot oven: *a cheese soufflé, a chocolate soufflé.* —*adj.* made light, as by beating and cooking; puffed up: *potatoes soufflé.* [< French *soufflé,* past participle of *souffler* puff up]

souf·fléed (sü flād′, sü′flād), *adj.* soufflé.

sou·gan (sü′gən, sug′ən), *n.* sugan.

sough (suf, sou), *v.i.* **1.** to make a rustling, rushing, or murmuring sound: *. . . branches soughing with the four winds* (William O. Douglas). **2.** *Scottish.* **a.** to sigh deeply. **b.** to die. —*v.t.* **1.** to express by a soughing sound. **2.** *Scottish.* to utter in a sighing tone. **3.** *Scottish.* to hum (a tune).
—*n.* **1.** a rustling or murmuring sound, as made by wind, water, etc.: *It is the sough of the wind among the bracken* (Scott). **2.** a deep sigh or breath. **3.** *Scottish.* a canting or whining way of speaking, especially in preaching or praying: *I ken the sough o' her texts* (Scott). **4.** *Scottish.* a rumor; vague report. [Middle English *swoghen,* Old English *swōgan*]

sought (sôt), *v.* the past tense and past participle of **seek:** *For days she sought a safe hiding place. He was sought and found.*

sought-af·ter (sôt′af′tər, -äf′-), *adj.* wanted; in demand; popular.

soul (sōl), *n.* **1.** the part of the human being that thinks, feels, and makes the body act; the spiritual part of a person as distinct from the physical. Many religions teach that in death the soul and the body become separated, and the soul lives forever. *For what shall it profit a man, if he shall gain the whole world, and lose his own soul?* (Mark 8:36). *The soul selects her own society, Then shuts the door* (Emily Dickinson). *Breathes there the man, with soul so dead, Who never to himself hath said, This is my own, my native land!* (Scott). **2.** energy or power of mind or feelings; spirit; fervor: *She puts her whole soul into her work.* **3.** the cause of inspiration or energy; leading spirit; prime mover: *Florence Nightingale was the soul of the movement to reform nursing.* **4.** the essential part: *Brevity is the soul of wit* (Shakespeare). **5.** a person; individual: *Don't tell a soul.* **6.** the embodiment of some quality; personification: *He is the soul of honor.* **7.** the spirit of a dead person: *John Brown's body lies a-mouldering in the grave, His soul goes marching on* (Thomas B. Bishop). **8. Soul.** (in the belief of Christian Scientists) God. **9.** the quality that stirs emotion or sentiment, especially in an empathetic response from an audience: *Ray Charles . . . is the quintessence of soul: it's not what he sings but the way he sings it* (Time).
—*adj.* having the quality of arousing a sense of identification with another or with the actions or thoughts of another: *But what emerged beyond question as the mainstream of pop music today was the "soul" sound* (Time).
upon my soul! as I hope to be saved! indeed! well!: *Upon my soul, a lie; a wicked lie* (Shakespeare). [Old English *sāwol*]
—**Syn. 2.** heart. **4.** essence, substance. **5.** mortal, man. **7.** ghost.

soul brother, 1. a Negro or, sometimes, one closely identified with Negro interests, especially in civil rights: *The session was a gathering of "soul brothers"—Negro military men and civilians, including a correspondent* (New York Times). **2.** a person who belongs to the same or a similar group: *. . . even Vancouver's soul brothers, the Toronto Maple Leafs and Montreal Canadiens, turned thumbs down* (Maclean's).

-souled, *combining form.* having a ——— soul: *Great-souled = having a great soul.*

soul food, food or cooking thought of as characteristically eaten by Negroes in the southern United States: *He is . . . just as comfortable with Negro friends eating "soul food", . . . consisting of pig's feet, ham, fried fish, cornbread and greens—to which Brooke sometimes adds champagne* (Time).

soul·ful (sōl′fəl), *adj.* **1.** full of feeling; deeply emotional: *soulful music.* **2.** expressing or suggesting a deep feeling: *a soulful sigh.* —**soul′ful·ly,** *adv.* —**soul′ful·ness,** *n.*

soul house, a small clay model of a house, placed in a tomb by the ancient Egyptians to accommodate a departed soul.

soul·less (sōl′lis), *adj.* **1.** having no life or soul. **2.** without spirit, courage, or noble feelings: *Do you think, because I am poor . . . I am soulless and heartless?* (Charlotte Brontë). **3.** without vivacity, animation, etc.; dull; insipid. —**soul′less·ly,** *adv.* —**soul′less·ness,** *n.*

soul mate, 1. an intimate associate or companion: *. . . a need for an intellectual soul mate* (Newsweek). **2.** a lover.

soul music, 1. music that is a blend of blues and rock'n'roll. **2.** a composition of such music.

soul-search·ing (sōl′sėr′ching), *n.* a close, vigorous, and serious examination of one's motives, beliefs, etc., especially at a critical time: *"There will be a great deal of soul-searching," predicted a retired judge . . . "because there is no retreat from whatever choice we make"* (Newsweek). —*adj.* of, engaged in, or requiring such examination.

soul session, a discussion, usually on civil rights, Negro culture, etc.: *The soul session, which has become a tradition of the movement in the South, is a kind of marathon group therapy, with a dash of mysticism* (New Yorker).

soul-sick (sōl′sik′), *adj.* spiritually depressed; sick at heart; deeply dejected: *. . . the masses made blind and soul-sick by materialism and agnosticism* (Dublin Review).

sou mar·kee or **mar·quee** (sü′ mär kē′),

U.S. **1.** sou marqué. **2.** a trifling sum or amount; little or nothing: . . . *he didn't have a sou markee* (George Ade). [American English < French *sou marqué*]

sou mar·qué (sü′ mär kā′), *French.* a coin of base metal and low value, used in the 1700's.

sound[1] (sound), *n.* **1.** that which is or can be heard; sensation produced in the organs of hearing by stimulation of the auditory nerves. **2.** the vibrations causing this sensation: *Sound travels in waves at a rate of about 1,100 feet per second through air under normal conditions of pressure and temperature.* **3.** a noise, note, tone, etc., whose quality indicates its source or nature: *the sound of music, thunder, or fighting, the sound of a baby or of an ambulance siren.* **4.** the distance within which a noise can be heard; earshot: . . . *in sound of the swallowing sea* (Matthew Arnold). **5.** one of the simple elements composing speech, produced by a single position, movement, or set of movements of the vocal organs of the speaker: *a vowel sound.* **6.** the effect produced on the mind by what is heard: *a warning sound, a queer sound.* **7.** mere noise, without meaning or importance: *A tale told by an idiot, full of sound and fury, signifying nothing* (Shakespeare). **8.** *Archaic.* a report or rumor; news; tidings.

within sound, near enough to hear: *The inbound train was already within sound when we reached the railroad station.*

—*v.i.* **1.** to make a sound or noise: *The alarm began to sound. The whistle of the locomotive . . . sounding like the scream of a hawk sailing over some farmer's yard* (Thoreau). **2.** to be filled with sound: *The street sounds to the soldiers' tread* (A.E. Housman). **3.** to summon: *The trumpet sounds to battle.* **4.** to make a sound on an instrument, etc.: *The singers sang, and the trumpeters sounded* (II Chronicles 29:28). **5.** to be pronounced: *"Rough" and "ruff" sound alike.* **6. a.** to be heard, as a sound: *As if the words of an oracle sounded in his ears* (Scott). **b.** to issue or pass as sound: *From you sounded out the word of the Lord* (I Thessalonians 1:8). **c.** to be mentioned: *Wherever I went my name sounded* (Benjamin Disraeli). **7.** to give an impression or idea; seem; appear: *That excuse sounds queer. Your story sounds improbable.* **8.** *Law.* to be capable of measurement in money for damages: *The action sounds in damages.*

—*v.t.* **1.** to cause to make a sound: *Sound the trumpets; beat the drums* (Thomas Morell). **2.** to give forth (a sound): *When winter's roar Sounded o'er earth and sea its blast of war* (Shelley). **3.** to announce, order, or direct by a sound: *to sound a retreat. I sound my barbaric yawp over the roofs of the world* (Walt Whitman). **4.** to pronounce or express; say so one can hear: *to sound each syllable.* **5.** to make known; announce; utter: *The trumpets sounded the call to arms. Everyone sounded his praises.* **6.** to celebrate; honor: *Nations unborn your mighty names shall sound* (Alexander Pope). **7.** to test by noting sounds: *to sound a person's lungs.*

sound off, *U.S. Informal.* **a.** to talk frankly or complain loudly: *He would sound off on domestic and international issues as he sees fit* (Wall Street Journal). **b.** to give one's name, serial number, etc., especially in military formations: *The soldiers sounded off smartly during the inspection.*

[Middle English *soun* < Old French *son* < Latin *sonus;* the *-d* is a later addition]

sound[2] (sound), *adj.* **1.** free from damage, decay, or defect; in good condition: *a sound ship, sound fruit.* **2.** free from disease or injury; healthy: *a sound body and mind.* **3.** financially strong; safe; secure: *sound investments, sound credit, a sound business.* **4. a.** solid; massive; compact: *sound as a rock, a sound foundation. . . . hewn . . . out of the sound and solid rock* (Scott). **b.** substantial, ample, or thorough: *a sound recovery, a sound investigation.* **5. a.** in accord with or based on fact, reason, or good sense; reasonable; good: *sound advice, a sound objection, sound judgment. Remarks as sound as they are acute and ingenious* (Edmund Burke). **b.** well-grounded in principles or knowledge; well-informed; reliable: *a sound teacher, a sound critic of music.* **6.** free from error or logical defect: *sound reasoning, a sound argument.* **7.** without any legal defects: *a sound title.* **8. a.** having conventional or orthodox ideas or views: *politically sound, a sound conservative.* **b.** theologically correct; orthodox: *He ordinarily preached sound doctrine* (John Evelyn). **9. a.** morally good; honest; upright: *No sounder piece of . . . manhood was put together in that eighteenth century of time* (Thomas Carlyle). **b.** loyal; true; trusty: . . . *the requisites that form a friend, a real and sound one* (William Cowper). *Old soldiers . . . are surest, and old lovers are soundest* (John Webster). **10.** deep; heavy; profound: *a sound sleep.* **11.** vigorous; thorough; hearty: *a sound beating.* —*adv.* deeply; profoundly: *The tired boy slept long and sound.*

[short for Middle English *isund,* Old English *gesund*]

—**Syn.** *adj.* **1.** uninjured, intact, flawless. **2.** robust. **5. a.** just, right. **6.** See **valid. 9. a.** honorable, straightforward.

sound[3] (sound), *v.t.* **1. a.** to measure the depth of (water, etc.) by letting down a calibrated line with a weight on the end or by some similar means; fathom. **b.** to measure (depth) in this way. **2.** to examine or test (the bottom of the sea, etc.) with a line arranged to bring up samples. **3. a.** to try to find out the views or feelings of (a person); examine in an indirect manner; investigate: *He has even sounded me on the subject; but I have given him no encouragement* (Tobias Smollet). **b.** to seek to find out (a person's views, opinions, etc.): *Cardinal Granvelle was instructed to sound the disposition of Francis* (James A. Froude). **4.** *Medicine.* to examine with a sound instrument: *to sound the bladder.* —*v.i.* **1.** to use a sounding device, such as a line and weight, to determine depth, investigate the bottom of the sea, etc.: *Men went overboard with pails . . . sounding for deeper water* (Daniel Defoe). **2.** to sink and reach bottom, as the weight on a line. **3.** to go deep under water; dive: *The whale sounded.* **4.** to make inquiry or investigation: *His thoughts . . . had sounded into the depths of his own nature* (Thomas Carlyle).

—*n. Medicine.* a long, slender instrument used in examining body cavities.

[< Old French *sonder,* perhaps < the Germanic source of *sound*[4]]

—**Syn.** *v.t.* **3. a, b.** probe.

sound[4] (sound), *n.* **1.** a narrow channel or passage of water, larger than a strait, joining two large bodies of water, or between the mainland and an island: *Long Island Sound.* **2.** an arm or inlet of the sea: *Puget Sound.* [partly Old English *sund* water, sea; partly < Scandinavian (compare Old Icelandic *sund* a strait)] —**Syn. 2.** firth.

sound[5] (sound), *n.* the air bladder of a fish, that helps it in floating. [< Scandinavian (compare Old Icelandic *sundmagi,* Norwegian *sund*)]

sound·a·ble (soun′də bəl), *adj.* that can be sounded.

sound and light, son et lumière.

sound barrier, a point approximating the speed of sound (about 760 miles per hour at sea level) at which an aircraft creates a shock wave and is subjected to various stresses; sonic barrier. This point is viewed as a barrier separating subsonic from supersonic speed. *Jet aircraft . . . have already penetrated what was thought only ten years ago to be an insuperable obstacle—the sound barrier* (Bulletin of Atomic Scientists).

sound·board (sound′bôrd′, -bōrd′), *n.* a thin, resonant piece of wood forming part of a musical instrument, as in a violin or piano, to increase the fullness of its tone.

sound bow (bō), the thickest part of a bell, against which the clapper strikes.

sound·box (sound′boks′), *n.,* or **sound box, 1.** a hollow part of a musical instrument, as of a violin, harp, etc., for strengthening the sonority of its tone; sounding box. **2.** the part of a phonograph holding the sound-reproducing apparatus.

sound cage, *Psychology.* an apparatus for testing a person's ability to locate the source of a sound stimulus, originally in the form of a hollow spherical cage to any part of which the sounding device could be moved.

sound effects, sounds, as of thunder, blows, animals, traffic, etc., artificially produced to simulate sounds called for in the script of a play, motion picture, radio or television production, or the like: *He had told some very noisy stories, assuming as many as twelve parts in a single skit and supplying all the sound effects himself as he went along* (Newsweek).

sound·er[1] (soun′dər), *n.* **1.** a person or thing that makes a sound or causes something to sound. **2.** an electromagnetic receiving instrument that converts a telegraphic message into sound.

sound·er[2] (soun′dər), *n.* a person or thing that measures the depth of water.

sound film, 1. a motion-picture film with a sound track. **2.** a sound motion picture.

sound·head (sound′hed′), *n.* a device in a motion-picture projector that converts the sound track of a film into electrical signals which are then amplified and reproduced.

sound-hole (sound′hōl′), *n.* a curvilinear opening, usually in pairs. in the soundboard of stringed instruments; f-hole.

sound·ing[1] (soun′ding), *adj.* **1.** causing, emitting, or producing a sound or sounds, especially loud sounds; resounding; resonant. **2.** sounding fine, but meaning little; pompous; bombastic: *She used to repeat sounding phrases from books* (Charlotte Brontë). —**sound′ing·ly,** *adv.*

sound·ing[2] (soun′ding), *n.* **1.** the act or process of measuring the depth of water by letting down into it a calibrated line with a weight on the end or by echoing sound off the bottom, as with a sonic depth finder: *A further difficulty in deep-sea prospecting lies in our inadequate knowledge of the sea-bed topography. Soundings are widely spaced and numerous features . . . still remain to be found* (Science News). **2.** investigation. **3.** examining with a sound or probe.

soundings, a. depths of water found by a line and weight: *Up to the very brink of the coral rampart there are no soundings* (Herman Melville). **b.** water not more than 100 fathoms (600 feet) deep, which an ordinary sounding line can measure: *We were soon out of soundings, and well into the Bay of Biscay* (Frederick Marryat).

take soundings, to try to find out quietly how matters stand: *Old Dan bears you no malice, I'd lay fifty pounds on it! But, if you like, I'll just step in and take soundings* (Charles J. Lever).

sounding balloon, a small, free balloon containing meteorological equipment, sent up to investigate and record atmospheric conditions.

sounding board, 1. a soundboard. **2.** a structure used to direct sound toward an audience. **3.** a means of bringing opinions, etc., out into the open: *In view of the prolonged and still unsettled wage negotiations in the industry, the convention is expected to be the sounding board for bitter recriminations* (New York Times).

sounding box, soundbox.

sounding lead, the lead or plummet at the end of a sounding line.

sounding line, a line having a weight at the end and marked in fathoms by various colors or materials, used to measure the depth of water; lead line.

sounding machine, any of various machines for taking deep-sea or other soundings.

sounding rocket, a rocket containing scientific instruments for investigating conditions in the high altitudes: *One of the first major tasks of the newly-formed National Aeronautics and Space Agency will be to send up sounding rockets to find out more about the nature of the space which satellite and space vehicles will traverse* (Wall Street Journal).

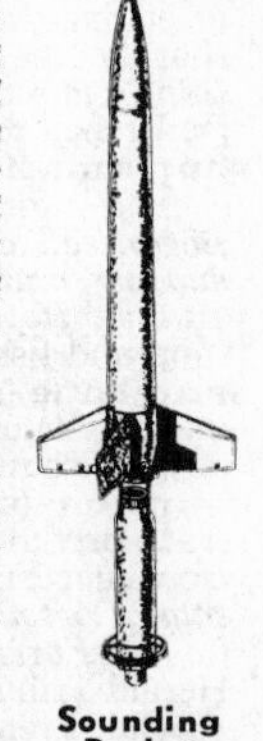

Sounding Rocket
Arcon, lifting 40 lb. payload

sound·ings (soun′dingz), *n. pl.* See under **sounding**[2].

sound·less[1] (sound′lis), *adj.* without sound; making no sound; quiet or silent; noiseless or still: *a soundless waste, a trackless vacancy* (Wordsworth). —**sound′less·ly,** *adv.*

sound·less[2] (sound′lis), *adj.* so deep that the bottom cannot be reached with a sounding line; unfathomable. *the soundless depths of the ocean.* —**Syn.** fathomless.

sound·ly (sound′lē), *adv.* **1.** in a sound manner; deeply; profoundly: *to sleep soundly.* **2.** vigorously; strongly; severely: *to beat, scold, shake, etc., someone soundly.* **3.** thoroughly; completely; properly. **4.** with good judgment or common sense: *He still has the possibility of creating further disasters, but no soundly bottomed hope of raising up his people* (Time).

sound man, sound mixer.

sound mixer, a person who regulates the quality of the sound recorded on films, tapes, etc.

sound motion picture, a motion picture in which the actors can be heard to speak, sing, etc., the speech, music, and other sounds being recorded on a sound track.

sound·ness (sound′nis), *n.* **1.** good health: *soundness of body and mind.* **2.** freedom from weakness or defect. **3.** good judgment: *We have confidence in the doctor's soundness.* —**Syn. 1.** vigor. **2.** perfection. **3.** discernment.

sound perimeter, sound cage.

sound·proof (sound′prüf′), *adj.* that absorbs or deadens sound: *a soundproof room or ceiling.* —*v.t.* to make soundproof.

sound radio, *British.* the medium of broadcasting by radio; radiobroadcast: *He has immense enthusiasm for sound radio, and particularly for what it does best—music and news* (Manchester Guardian Weekly).

sound ranging. See **sofar** and **sonar.**

sound spectrogram, a graphic representation made by a sound spectrograph.

sound spectrograph, an electronic instrument which produces a graphic representation of sound, with vertical marks representing frequency and horizontal marks representing time: *That machine ... is a sound spectrograph, which analyzes sounds made by amphibians, analyzes them visually as well as by ear* (New Yorker).

sound stage, the set on which a sound motion picture is filmed.

sound track, a record of words, music, etc., made along one edge of a motion-picture film and synchronized with the action, which is reconverted into sound by the projector.

sound truck, *U.S.* a truck with one or more loudspeakers, used in making public announcements.

sound waves, the longitudinal progressive vibrations of a material medium by which sounds are transmitted.

soup (süp), *n.* **1.** a liquid food made by boiling meat, fish, vegetables, etc. **2.** *Slang.* a heavy, wet fog or cloud formation: *to fly on instruments through soup.* **3.** *Slang.* power; horsepower.

from soup to nuts, from beginning to end: *The ideal organisation, it is suggested, is integration of production from raw material to the point of sale, doing the whole job from soup to nuts* (Sunday Times).

in the soup, *Informal.* in difficulty: *Hog producers are going to be in the soup by fall ... There'll be overproduction there just as sure as God made little apples* (Maclean's).

—*v.t.* **soup up,** *Informal.* **a.** to increase the horsepower of by adjusting the mechanism, enriching the fuel mixture, adding special parts, etc.: *to soup up an engine.* **b.** to make able to accelerate more quickly, attain a higher speed, etc., by doing this to its engine or engines: *to soup up a car.* **c.** to increase sharply the pace, impact, etc., of (anything): *to soup up a story or song.*

[< French *soupe* < a Germanic word]

soup-and-fish (süp′ən fish′), *n. Informal.* a man's formal evening suit: *Humphrey Bogart, all dressed up in soup-and-fish, is dancing around a huge ballroom set with Audrey Hepburn* (New Yorker). [because soup and fish are served at formal dinners]

soup·bone (süp′bōn′), *n.* a bone (with some meat on it) used for making soup stock, usually the shank of beef.

soup·çon (süp sôɴ′, süp′sôɴ), *n.* a slight trace or flavor; very small amount; suspicion; suggestion: *to add a soupçon of salt to a salad. A soupçon of financial stability came [to the Paris Review] in 1956* (New York Herald Tribune Books). [< French *soupçon* < Old French *sospeçon* < Vulgar Latin *suspectiō, -ōnis,* for Latin *suspīciō;* see SUSPICION] —**Syn.** whit, dash.

soup·fin (süp′fin′), *n.,* or **soupfin shark,** a shark whose fin is used by the Chinese for making soup, especially common on the coast of California.

soup kitchen, a place that serves food free or at a very low charge to poor or unemployed people or to victims of a flood, fire, or other disaster: *The nation was in the full grip of the depression, and on the sidewalks of New York was heard the shuffling of feet at the bread lines and the soup kitchens* (Newsweek).

soup meat, meat used for soup, especially to make the stock of soup.

soup plate, a rather large, deep plate used for serving soup.

soup spoon, a medium-sized, round spoon used for eating soup.

soup·y (sü′pē), *adj.,* **soup·i·er, soup·i·est.** like soup in consistency or appearance: *The weather was soupy and visibility was reduced* (New Yorker).

sour (sour), *adj.* **1.** having a taste like that of vinegar or lemon juice: *Most green fruit is sour.* **2.** fermented; spoiled: *During their absence the food in the cupboard turned sour.* **3.** having a sour or rank smell: *sour breath, a sour medicine.* **4.** disagreeable; bad-tempered; peevish: *a sour face, a sour remark. Sour to them that loved him not; but to those men that sought him, sweet as summer* (Shakespeare). **5.** unusually acid: *sour soil.* **6.** cold and wet; damp: *sour weather.* **7.** possessing contaminating amounts of sulfur: *sour gasoline.*

—*v.i., v.t.* **1.** to become or make sour; turn sour: *Milk is said to sour during a thunder storm.* **2.** to become or make disagreeable, bad-tempered, or peevish: *... such suffering would probably have soured the kindest temper* (William Godwin).

—*n.* **1.** something sour, distasteful, or disagreeable: *the sweets we wish for, turn to loathed sours* (Shakespeare). **2.** a mildly acid bath or steep, used in bleaching, dyeing, etc. **3.** *U.S.* a sour alcoholic drink, such as whiskey and lemon juice: *a whiskey sour.*

—*adv.* in a sour manner; disagreeably; crossly: *to look sour.*

[Old English *sūr*] —**sour′ly,** *adv.* —**sour′ness,** *n.*

—**Syn.** *adj.* **1.** acid, acidulous, tart. **2.** rancid, curdled. **4. Sour, tart, acid,** used figuratively to describe a person, his looks, disposition, words, etc., mean resembling vinegar or lemons in harshness or sharpness. **Sour,** like **acid,** implies unpleasant qualities, suggesting irritability, surliness, or sullenness: *That janitor has a sour face and a sour disposition.* **Tart** suggests sharp and stinging qualities, not necessarily unpleasant: *His tart answer made her cry.* **Acid** suggests biting, sarcastic, severely critical qualities: *I read an acid comment on the political situation in Washington.*

sour·ball (sour′bôl′), *n.* a hard, round piece of candy with a sour taste.

source (sôrs, sōrs), *n.* **1.** the beginning of a brook or river; a spring; fountain. **2.** the place from which anything comes or is obtained; origin: *Mines are the chief source of diamonds. One great original source of revenue ... the wages of labour* (Adam Smith). **3.** a person, book, document, statement, etc., that supplies information or evidence: *A newspaper gets news from many sources. What is the source of your belief?* **4.** a person, company, etc., that pays interest, dividends, etc. [< Old French *sourse* < *sourdre* to rise, spring up < Latin *surgere* rise; see SURGE]

source·book (sôrs′bu̇k′, sōrs′-), *n.* a book of fundamental documents, records, etc., which serve as firsthand or primary sources of information for the study of a subject.

sour cherry, a cherry with tart, edible fruit much used in cooking and baking. The amarelles and morellos are sour cherries.

sour cream, a thick cream made sour by a culturing process, used as a dressing for salads, certain dishes, etc.

sour·dine (su̇r dēn′), *n. Music.* **1.** a mute, as for a trumpet. **2.** a small violin, used formerly by dance teachers. [< French *sourdine* < Italian *sordina* sordino (diminutive) < *sordo, sorda* deaf, muted]

sour·dough (sour′dō′), *n.* **1.** *U.S. and Canadian.* **a.** a prospector or pioneer in Alaska or Canada, especially in the Yukon. **b.** *Informal.* any old resident, experienced hand, etc.; person who is not a tenderfoot. **2.** Also, **sour dough.** fermented dough saved from one baking to start fermentation in the next, such as was used by the original prospectors in the Yukon.

—*adj.* having sourdough as the leavening agent: *sourdough pancakes.*

[American English < the practice of saving sour dough (def. 2) < earlier British, leaven]

sour gourd, 1. the acid fruit of an Australian tree of the bombax family. **2.** the tree itself; bottle tree. **3.** the baobab.

sour grapes, a thing that a person claims to dislike because he cannot have it: *Pearson is also aware ... that too vigorous an attack on the Diefenbaker administration might sound like sour grapes* (Maclean's).

sour gum, any of various tupelos, especially the black gum.

sour·ish (sour′ish), *adj.* somewhat sour.

sour mash, *U.S.* **1.** a fermenting grain mash. **2.** a whiskey made from this.

sour orange, 1. a bitter-tasting orange used in making Eau de Cologne, preserves, etc. **2.** the tree on which it grows, widely cultivated for its rootstock, on which sweet oranges and other citrus fruits are grafted.

sour·puss (sour′pu̇s′), *n. U.S. Informal.* a sullen or surly person; grouch: *One sourpuss ... grumbled ... that the company was probably infiltrated with spies* (Saturday Review).

sour·sop (sour′sop′), *n.* **1.** the large, edible fruit of a tropical American tree of the custard-apple family, having a white, somewhat acid pulp. **2.** the small evergreen tree that bears this fruit.

sour·wood (sour′wu̇d′), *n.* **1.** a tree of the heath family, native to the eastern United States, having a hard, close-grained wood, dark, glossy leaves that turn bright scarlet in the fall, and spikes of small, white, egg-shaped flowers; sorrel tree. **2.** its wood, used to make handles for tools, etc.

sou·sa·phone (sü′zə fōn), *n.* a spiral bass tuba with a wide, flaring bell facing forward, used in brass bands. [American English < John Philip *Sousa,* 1854-1932, an American musical conductor and composer]

souse[1] (sous), *v.,* **soused, sous·ing,** *n.* —*v.t.* **1.** to plunge into liquid: *He soused me head and ears into a pail of water* (Sir Richard Steele). **2.** to drench or soak with, or as if with, water, etc.: *Then the engines arrived and soused the burning houses* (George Meredith). **3.** to dash or pour (a quantity of water, etc.). **4.** to soak in vinegar, brine, etc.; pickle. **5.** *Slang.* to make drunk. —*v.i.* **1.** to be or become soaked or drenched; plunge into water, etc.; soak: *Down I soused into the water* (Thackeray). **2.** *Slang.* to become drunk. [probably < noun]

—*n.* **1.** a plunging into a liquid; drenching: *Keeping her hand on his collar, she gave him two or three good souses in the watery fluid* (Scott). **2.** something soaked or kept in pickle, especially the head, ears, and feet of a pig. **3.** a liquid used for pickling. **4.** *Slang.* a drunkard.

[< Old French *sous, soult* pickled pork < Germanic (compare Old High German *sulza* brine)]

souse[2] (sous), *n., v.,* **soused, sous·ing,** *adv. Archaic.* —*n. Falconry.* **1.** the rise of a bird from the ground, that gives the hawk an opportunity to strike. **2.** the swooping down of a hawk upon a bird.

—*v.i., v.t.* to swoop or pounce (on or upon), as an attacking hawk.

—*adv.* suddenly; without warning.

[apparently alteration of *source,* in obsolete sense "the rise, spring (of a bird)"]

sous-sous (sü′sü′), *n.* a soubresaut performed by springing forward on the toes and bringing the legs tightly together. [< French *sous-sus* < *(des)sous-(des)sus* under-over]

sou·tache (sü′tash, sü tash′), *n.* a narrow ornamental braid of wool, silk, etc., used for trimming. [< French *soutache* < Hungarian *sujtás* soutache, braid, gold lace]

sou·tane (sü tän′), *n.* a cassock, as worn by priests of the Roman Catholic Church. [< French *soutane* < Italian *sottana,* adjective to *sotto* under < Latin *subtus,* adverb < *sub,* preposition]

sou·ter (sü′tər), *n. Scottish.* a shoemaker; cobbler. [Old English *sūtere* < Latin *sūtor, -ōris* cobbler < *suere* to sew, stitch]

sou·ter·rain (sü′tə rān′), *n.* an underground chamber, storeroom, passage, etc. [< French *souterrain* < *sous* under + *terre* earth]

south (*n., adj., adv.* south; *v.* south, south), *n.* **1.** the direction to the left as one faces the setting sun, or to the right as one faces the rising sun; direction in a straight line from any point on earth toward the South Pole. South is one of the four cardinal points of the compass. *Abbr.:* S (no period). **2.** Also, **South.** the part of any country or region toward or at the south.

South (def. 1) on compass

—adj. **1.** toward the south: *the south side of town.* **2.** from the south: *a south wind.* **3.** in the south; facing the south: *A south window catches the noonday sunshine.* **4.** in the southern part; southern.
—adv. **1.** toward the south; southward: *a flock of geese flying south. Drive south forty miles.* **2.** in the south: *The city is south of us.*
—v.i. to move or turn toward the south; blow more from the south: *About sundown the wind southed a point or two* (John M. Falkner).
[Old English *sūth*]
➔ A *south* or *southerly* wind carries a ship sailing before it *north* or on a *northerly* course.

South (south), *n.* **1.** the part of the United States lying south of Pennsylvania, the Ohio River, Missouri, and Kansas. **2.** the Confederacy: *Wherever a Southern woman stood during those four years, there in her small person was a garrison of the South* (Thomas Nelson Page). **3.** (in bridge) the player sitting opposite and in partnership with North. In most written illustrations of bridge hands, South is the declarer. *—adj.* of or having to do with the southern part of a country, region, people, etc.: . . . *the enemy of the South Welsh* (George Borrow).

South African, 1. of or having to do with southern Africa, especially the Republic of South Africa, or its people. **2.** a native or inhabitant of southern Africa or of the Republic of South Africa, especially an Afrikaner.

South African Dutch, 1. Afrikaans. **2.** the Afrikaners; Boers.

South American, 1. of or having to do with South America or its people: *a South American nation.* **2.** a native or inhabitant of South America.

south·bound (south′bound′), *adj.* bound southward; going south.

south by east, the point of the compass or the direction one point or 11 degrees 15 minutes to the east of south.

south by west, the point of the compass or the direction one point or 11 degrees 15 minutes to the west of south.

South Carolinian, 1. of or having to do with South Carolina. **2.** a native or inhabitant of South Carolina.

south celestial pole, the zenith of the southern end of the earth's axis from which every direction is north; South Pole.

South Dakotan, 1. of or having to do with South Dakota. **2.** a native or inhabitant of South Dakota.

South·down (south′doun′), *n.* any of an English breed of small, hornless sheep raised for mutton. [< *South Downs,* an area in Sussex and Hampshire, England, where the breed originated]

south·east (south′ēst′; *Nautical* sou′ēst′), *adj.* **1.** halfway between south and east. **2.** lying toward or situated in the southeast. **3.** coming from the southeast: *a southeast wind.* **4.** facing the southeast: *A southeast window catches the mid-morning sunshine.*
—n. **1.** the point of the compass or the direction midway between south and east. *Abbr.:* SE (no periods). **2.** a place that is in the southeast part or direction.
—adv. **1.** toward the southeast. **2.** from the southeast. **3.** in the southeast.

southeast by east, the point of the compass or the direction one point or 11 degrees 15 minutes to the east of southeast.

southeast by south, the point of the compass or the direction one point or 11 degrees 15 minutes to the south of southeast.

south·east·er (south′ēs′tər; *Nautical* sou′ēs′tər), *n.* a wind or storm coming from the southeast.

south·east·er·ly (south′ēs′tər lē; *Nautical* sou′ēs′tər lē), *adj., adv.* **1.** toward the southeast. **2.** from the southeast.

south·east·ern (south′ēs′tərn; *Nautical* sou′ēs′tərn), *adj.* **1.** in or toward the southeast. **2.** coming from the southeast: *a southeastern wind.* **3.** of or having to do with the southeast.

South·east·ern (south′ēs′tərn), *adj.* of, having to do with, or in the southeastern States of the United States.

south·east·ern·most (south′ēs′tərn mōst; *Nautical* sou′ēs′tərn mōst), *adj.* lying furthest to the southeast.

south·east·ward (south′ēst′wərd; *Nautical* sou′ēst′wərd), *adv., adj.* toward the southeast. *—n.* the southeast.

south·east·ward·ly (south′ēst′wərd lē; *Nautical* sou′ēst′wərd lē), *adj., adv.* **1.** toward the southeast. **2.** from the southeast: *southeastwardly winds.*

south·east·wards (south′ēst′wərdz; *Nautical* sou′ēst′wərdz), *adv.* southeastward.

south·er[1] (sou′ᴛʜər), *n.* a wind or storm coming from the south. [< *south* + *-er*[1]]

sou·ther[2] (sô′ᴛʜər), *n., v. Dialect.* solder. Also, **sowther.**

south·er·li·ness (suᴛʜ′ər lē nis), *n.* the state of being southerly.

south·er·ly (suᴛʜ′ər lē), *adj., adv., n., pl.* **-lies.** *—adj.* **1.** toward the south: *a southerly exposure.* **2.** coming from the south: *a southerly wind.* **3.** of the south. *—adv.* **1.** toward the south; southward: *The windows face southerly.* **2.** from the south.
—n. a southerly wind: *Finally, the fleet got under way with the aid of a light and fluky southerly* (New York Times).
➔ See **south** for a usage note.

south·ern (suᴛʜ′ərn), *adj.* **1.** toward the south: *the southern side of a building.* **2.** coming from the south: *a southern breeze.* **3.** of or in the south: *He has traveled in southern countries.* **4.** *Astronomy.* of or in the southern half of the celestial sphere: *Sirius and Canopus are southern stars.*
—n. **1.** Also, **Southern.** a person living in a southern region; southerner or Southerner: *Both Southern fierce and hardy Scot* (*Scott*). **2.** a south wind; souther.
[Old English *sūtherne*]

South·ern (suᴛʜ′ərn), *adj.* of or in the South of the United States: *Atlanta, Georgia, is a Southern city.*

Southern Baptist, a member of a church belonging to the Southern Baptist Convention, a group of Baptist churches founded in Georgia in 1845.

Southern Cross, a southern constellation with four bright stars in the form of a cross, used in finding the direction south; Crux: *The Southern Cross appears too far south to be seen in the United States, except for a few places* (World Book Encyclopedia).

Southern Crown, a southern constellation near Sagittarius.

south·ern·er (suᴛʜ′ər nər), *n.* a native or inhabitant of the south.

South·ern·er (suᴛʜ′ər nər), *n.* a native or inhabitant of the Southern States of the United States.

Southern Fish, a southern constellation near Aquarius, containing the bright star Fomalhaut.

Southern Hemisphere, the half of the earth that is south of the equator.

South·ern·ism (suᴛʜ′ər niz′əm), *n.* **1.** devotion or attachment to the South, its customs, traditions, etc.: *He has a profound contempt for the slightest touch of professional Southernism* (New York Times). **2.** a word, phrase, or meaning originating or much used in the South. **3.** a custom or trait peculiar to the South.

southern lights, the aurora australis.

south·ern·ly (suᴛʜ′ərn lē), *adj., adv.* southerly.

south·ern·most (suᴛʜ′ərn mōst), *adj.* farthest south.

South·ern·ness (suᴛʜ′ər nis), *n.* the state or quality of being Southern.

Southern Triangle, a small constellation in the south polar zone near the Milky Way, containing three bright stars.

south·ern·wood (suᴛʜ′ərn wu̇d′), *n.* a shrubby wormwood of Europe, grown in gardens for its finely divided, aromatic leaves.

south·ing (sou′ᴛʜing), *n.* **1.** the distance of latitude reckoned southward from the last point of reckoning: *The latest southing was 1 degree 15 minutes from our position at sunrise.* **2.** the distance southward covered by a ship on any southerly course: *On the first day of the voyage the southing was 200 knots.* **3.** *Astronomy.* **a.** declination measured southward. **b.** (of a heavenly body) the act of crossing or approaching the meridian: *the southing of the moon.*

south·land (south′lənd, -land′), *n.* the land in the south; southern part of a country.

south·land·er (south′lən dər, -lan′-), *n.* a native or inhabitant of the southland.

south magnetic pole, the point on the earth's surface toward which one end of a magnetic needle points. Its location varies but is approximately 72 degrees south latitude and 154 degrees east longitude.

south·most (south′mōst), *adj.* farthest south; southernmost.

south·paw (south′pô′), *Slang.* *—n.* **1.** a person who throws with the left hand, especially a left-handed baseball pitcher. **2.** a left-handed person. *—adj.* left-handed, especially in pitching. [American English < *south* "left" as an individual faces west + *paw*]

South Pole, 1. the southern end of the earth's axis; point on the earth's surface from which every direction is north. It was first reached in 1911 by Roald Amundsen, 1872-1928, Norwegian explorer. See diagram under **equator. 2.** the south magnetic pole. **3.** the south celestial pole.

south·ron (suᴛʜ′rən), *adj., n., pl.* **-rons** or **-ron.** *—adj.* southern. *—n.* Also, **Southron. 1.** *U.S.* a Southerner. **2.** a native of the south of Great Britain; Englishman.
the southron, Englishmen: *In Ireland the Scotch and the southron were strongly bound together by their common Saxon origin* (Macaulay).
[Scottish alteration of *southern*]

South Sea arrowroot, pia[2].

South Sea Islander, a native or inhabitant of the South Sea Islands.

South Seas, 1. the southern Pacific Ocean. **2.** all the seas located below the equator.

south-south·east (south′south ēst′; *Nautical* sou′sou ēst′), *n.* the point of the compass or the direction midway between south and southeast, two points or 22 degrees 30 minutes to the east of south. *—adj., adv.* of, from, or toward the south-southeast.

south-south·west (south′south west′; *Nautical* sou′sou west′), *n.* the point of the compass or the direction midway between south and southwest, two points or 22 degrees 30 minutes to the west of south. *—adj., adv.* of, from, or toward the south-southwest.

south·ward (south′wərd), *adv.* toward the south; in a southerly direction: *to sail southward.* *—adj.* toward, facing, or at the south; southerly; south. *—n.* the direction or part that lies to the south; south.

south·ward·ly (south′wərd lē), *adj.* **1.** toward the south. **2.** coming from the south: *southwardly winds.* *—adv.* toward the south.

south·wards (south′wərdz), *adv.* southward.

south·west (south′west′; *Nautical* sou′-west′), *adj.* **1.** halfway between south and west. **2.** lying toward or situated in the southwest. **3.** coming from the southwest: *a southwest wind.* **4.** facing the southwest.
—n. **1.** the point of the compass or the direction midway between south and west. *Abbr.:* SW (no periods). **2.** a place that is in the southwest part or direction.
—adv. **1.** toward the southwest. **2.** from the southwest. **3.** in the southwest.

southwest by south, the point of the compass or the direction one point or 11 degrees 15 minutes to the south of southwest.

southwest by west, the point of the compass or the direction one point or 11 degrees 15 minutes to the west of southwest.

south·west·er (south′wes′tər *or Nautical* sou′wes′tər *for 1;* sou′wes′tər *for 2*), *n.* **1.** a wind or storm coming from the southwest. **2.** a waterproof hat having a broad brim behind to protect the neck, worn especially by seamen. Also, **sou′wester.**

Southwester (def. 2)

south·west·er·ly (south′-wes′tər lē; *Nautical* sou′wes′-tər lē), *adj., adv.* **1.** toward the southwest. **2.** from the southwest.

south·west·ern (south′wes′tərn; *Nautical* sou′wes′tərn), *adj.* **1.** to, toward, or in the southwest: *a southwestern rodeo.* **2.** coming from the southwest: *a southwestern wind.* **3.** of or having to do with the southwest.

South·west·ern (south′wes′tərn), *adj.* of, having to do with, or in a loosely defined area usually including Arizona, New Mexico, Oklahoma, and Texas.

south·west·ern·most (south′wes′tərn-mōst; *Nautical* sou′wes′tərn mōst), *adj.* lying farthest to the southwest.

south·west·ward (south′west′wərd; *Nautical* sou′west′wərd), *adv., adj.* toward the southwest. *—n.* the southwest.

south·west·ward·ly (south′west′wərd lē; *Nautical* sou′west′wərd lē), *adj.* **1.** toward the southwest. **2.** from the southwest. *—adv.* toward the southwest.

south·west·wards (south′west′wərdz; *Nautical* sou′west′wərdz), *adv.* southwestward.

sou·ve·nir (sü′və nir′, sü′və nir), *n.* something to remind one of a place, person, or occasion; token of remembrance; keepsake. [< French *souvenir* (originally, infinitive) to remember < Latin *subvenīre* come to mind < *sub-* up + *venīre* come] —**Syn.** memento, remembrance, reminder, token.

sou′west·er (sou′wes′tər), *n.* southwester.

SOV., sovereign.

sov·er·eign (sov′rən, suv′-), *n.* **1.** the supreme ruler of a people or nation under monarchical government; king or queen; monarch: *It was not for me to bandy civilities with my sovereign* (Samuel Johnson). **2.** a person, group, or nation having supreme control or dominion; ruler; governor; lord; master: *sovereign of the seas.* **3.** a British gold coin, worth 20 shillings, one pound, or about $2.80.
—*adj.* **1.** having the rank or power of a sovereign: *a sovereign prince. Here lies our sovereign lord the king* (John Wilmot). **2.** independent of the control of another government or governments: *a sovereign state.* **3.** greatest in rank, authority, or power: *a sovereign court, sovereign jurisdiction.* **4. a.** above all others; supreme; greatest: *Character is of sovereign importance. The knowledge of Truth . . . is the sovereign good of human nature* (Francis Bacon). **b.** greatest in degree; utmost; extreme: *. . . a sovereign contempt for everyone* (Henry James). **5.** excellent or powerful: *There is no sovereign cure for colds.* **6.** of, belonging to, or characteristic of a sovereign or sovereignty: *sovereign power, a sovereign proclamation.*
[< Old French *soverain* < Vulgar Latin *superānus* < Latin *super* over]
—**Syn.** *adj.* **4. a.** chief, paramount.

sov·er·eign·ly (sov′rən lē, suv′-), *adv.* **1.** exceedingly. **2.** chiefly; especially. **3.** as a sovereign; royally. —**Syn. 1.** eminently. **2.** principally. **3.** regally.

sov·er·eign·ty (sov′rən tē, suv′-), *n., pl.* **-ties. 1.** supreme power or authority; supremacy: *the sovereignty of the sea. State sovereignty was the doctrine that each State was superior to and independent of the United States in power over its own territory.* **2.** a state, territory, community, etc., that is independent or sovereign. **3.** the rank, position, or jurisdiction of a sovereign; royal authority or dominion. **4.** the quality or condition of being sovereign: *Our* [*national*] *sovereignty is not something to be hoarded, but something to be used* (Wendell Willkie).

so·vi·et (sō′vē et, -it; sov′ē-; sō′vē et′), *n.* **1.** a council; assembly. **2.** Often, **Soviet.** in the Soviet Union: **a.** either of two elected assemblies concerned with local government (village soviets, town soviets), composed of representatives of the people. **b.** any of the pyramid of larger assemblies elected by local assemblies, culminating in the Supreme Soviet or Council, the legislature of the Soviet Union. —*adj.* of or having to do with a soviet or soviets. [< Russian *sovet* council < Old Russian *sŭvětŭ* < Old Church Slavonic < *sŭ-* together + *větŭ* counsel, agreement, translation of Greek *symboúlion*]

So·vi·et (sō′vē et, -it; sov′ē-; sō′vē et′), *adj.* of or having to do with the Soviet Union. —*n.* a Russian. [< *soviet*]

so·vi·et·dom (sō′vē it dəm, sov′ē-; sō′vē-et′-), *n.* **1.** the people of the Soviet Union or its satellites. **2.** the realm or sphere of influence of the Soviet Union.

so·vi·et·eer (sō′vē ə tir′, sov′ē-), *n.* an adherent of the Russian or any similar soviet system.

so·vi·et·ism (sō′vē ə tiz′əm, sov′ē-; sō′vē-et′iz əm, sov′ē-), *n.* **1.** a system of government by means of soviets. **2.** communism.

so·vi·et·ist (sō′vē ə tist; sov′ē-; sō′vē et′ist, sov′ē-), *n.* an adherent of a soviet system of government. —*adj.* **1.** of or having to do with sovietists or sovietism. **2.** governed by soviets.

so·vi·et·i·za·tion (sō′vē ə tə zā′shən, sov′-ē-; sō′vē et′ə-, sov′ē-), *n.* the act or process of sovietizing.

So·vi·et·i·za·tion (sō′vē ə tə zā′shən, sō′-vē et′ə-, sov′ē-), *n.* **1.** a Sovietizing. **2.** a being Sovietized.

so·vi·et·ize (sō′vē ə tīz, sov′ē-; sō′vē et′īz, sov′ē-), *v.t.,* **-ized, -iz·ing.** to change to a government by soviets, or to communism: *Just as the most effective antidote to communism in Europe is Eastern Germany, so a gradually sovietized Cuba will be a more effective antidote for the Latin-Americans than any number of broadcasts by the Voice of America* (Manchester Guardian Weekly). —**so′vi·et·iz′er,** *n.*

So·vi·et·ize (sō′vē ə tīz, sov′ē-; sō′vē et′īz, sov′ē-), *v.t.,* **-ized, -iz·ing.** to put under the control or influence of the Soviet Union or its system of government: *The satellite armies vary considerably in strength and capabilities but all of them have been more or less Sovietized* (New York Times).

So·vi·et·ol·o·gist (sō′vē ə tol′ə jist, sov′ē-), *n.* a Kremlinologist.

So·vi·et·ol·o·gy (sō′vē ə tol′ə jē, sov′ē-), *n.* Kremlinology: *The resulting figures will thus be rather like Soviet production statistics and will presumably need a science like Sovietology for their interpretation* (London Times).

sov·khoz (sov koz′; *Russian* sof hôs′), *n., pl.* **-khoz·es** or **-khoz·y** (-hô′zē). (in the Soviet Union) a farm owned by the state, as distinguished from a kolkhoz or collective farm. [< Russian *sovkhoz,* abbreviation of *sovetskoe khozjajstvo* soviet management]

sov·nar·khoz (sov′när koz′; *Russian* sof′-när hôs′), *n., pl.* **-khoz·es, -khoz·y** (-hô′zē). (in the Soviet Union) a regional economic council responsible for the planning and production of all industrial enterprises: *Within a few weeks the theses became law, eliminating all the Soviet Union's industrial ministries and replacing them with a system of regional councils, or sovnarkhozy* (London Times). [< Russian *sovnarkhoz,* abbreviation of *sovnarkom khozjajstvo* council of people's commissars management]

sov·ran (sov′rən, suv′-), *n., adj. Poetic.* sovereign. [introduced by Milton < Italian *sovrano*]

sov·ran·ty (sov′rən tē, suv′-), *n., pl.* **-ties.** *Poetic.* sovereignty.

sow[1] (sō), *v.,* **sowed, sown** or **sowed, sow·ing.** —*v.t.* **1.** to scatter seed on or upon (land, earth, etc.) in order that it may grow; supply with seed: *The farmer sowed the field with oats.* **2.** to scatter (seed) on the ground; plant (a crop) in this way: *He sows more wheat than oats.* **3. a.** to scatter or distribute for development or to produce consequences: *to sow distrust or dissension.* **b.** to try to propagate or extend; disseminate: *to sow the gospel among all nations. The enemy tried to sow discontent in our men.* —*v.i.* to scatter seed on the ground, as for growth: *I resolved . . . to sow but once a year* (Daniel Defoe). [Old English *sāwan*]

sow[2] (sou), *n.* **1.** a fully grown female pig. **2. a.** a large mass of solidified iron or other metal formed in the channel through which the molten metal passes from the smelting furnace to the series of parallel channels in which the pigs form. **b.** the channel in which it is formed. [Old English *sugu*]

so·war (sə wär′, -wôr′), *n.* (in India, formerly) a native soldier in the British service, either as a member of a cavalry unit or as a mounted orderly. [< Hindustani, Persian *sawār* horseman]

sow·bel·ly (sou′bel′ē), *n. U.S. Informal.* salt pork consisting mostly of fat.

sow bug (sou), any of a group of small isopod crustaceans similar to the pill bugs, that lives under stones, bark, etc.; wood louse.

sow·car (sou′kär), *n.* soucar.

sow·ens (sō′ənz, sü′-), *n.pl. Scottish and Irish.* a kind of coarse porridge made from steeped oat husks. [earlier *sowannis* < Gaelic *súghan* broth used in preparing sowens < *súgh* juice, sap]

sow·er (sō′ər), *n.* a person or thing that sows.

sowff (souf), *v.t. Scottish.* sowth.

sowl (soul), *v.t. British Dialect.* **1.** to pull by the ears. **2.** to handle roughly. [origin unknown]

sown (sōn), *v.* a past participle of **sow**[1]: *The field had been sown with oats.*

sowth (south), *v.t. Scottish.* to sing, hum, or whistle softly. [variant of obsolete *solf* < Old French *solfier* to sing a tune to the *sol-fa* syllables. Compare GAMUT.]

sow·ther (sô′ᴛʜər), *n., v. Dialect.* souther[2] (solder).

sow thistle (sou), any of a group of coarse weeds of the composite family, with thistlelike leaves, yellow flowers, and milky juice.

sox (soks), *n.pl. Informal.* socks (stockings).

soy (soi), *n.* **1.** Also, **soy sauce.** a salty, dark-brown sauce made from fermented soybeans, used especially in Chinese and Japanese cooking to give flavor and color to meat, fish, etc. **2.** the soybean. [< Japanese *shōyu* < Chinese (Peking) *chiang -yu*]

soy·a (soi′ə), *n. British.* soy.

soy·bean (soi′bēn′), *n.* **1.** the bean of a plant of the pea family, widely grown in China, Japan, and the United States. Soybeans are used in making flour, an oil, etc., and as food. **2.** the plant that it grows on, used as fodder for cattle. Also, **soja, soja bean.**

Soybean

so·zal (sō′zal), *n.* a crystalline salt of aluminum with a strongly astringent taste, used as an antiseptic. [< Greek *sṓzein* save + English *al*(uminum)]

so·zin (sō′zin), *n.* any protein normally present in the animal body and protecting it against disease. [< Greek *sṓzein* save + English *-in*]

soz·zled (soz′əld), *adj. Slang.* intoxicated; drunk.

sp., an abbreviation for the following:
1. special.
2. species.
3. specific.
4. specimen.
5. spelling.
6. spirit.

s.p., an abbreviation for the following:
1. *Printing.* small pica.
2. *Banking.* supra protest.
3. *Law.* without issue (Latin, *sine prole*).

Sp., 1. Spain. **2.** Spaniard. **3.** Spanish.

SP (no periods), specialist (def. 4).

SP (no periods) or **S.P.,** shore patrol.

spa (spä), *n.* **1.** a mineral spring. **2.** a town, locality, or resort having a mineral spring or springs: *There are fifty spas in England as efficacious and salutary as that of Scarborough* (Tobias Smollett). [< *Spa,* a Belgian resort]

space (spās), *n., v.,* **spaced, spac·ing.** —*n.* **1.** unlimited room or place extending in all directions: *The earth moves through space.* **2.** a part of this in a given instance; area; room: *The larger a house, the more space it occupies. Children need a lot of space to play in.* **3.** outer space: *U.S. spacemen . . . fired a satellite farther into space than any other man-made object* (Time). **4. a.** extent or room in a periodical, book, letter, etc., available for, or occupied by, written or printed matter. **b.** *Advertising.* the part of a page or the number of lines in a periodical, newspaper, etc., available or used for advertising. **5.** a limited place or area: *to find a parking space. Is there space in the car for another person? This brick will fill a space 2¼ by 4 by 8 inches.* **6.** an extent or area of ground, surface, sky, etc.; expanse: *The trees covered acres of space.* **7.** a distance between two or more points or objects: *The two trees are set at equal spaces apart.* **8.** a blank or interval between words or lines in written or printed matter: *Fill in the spaces as directed.* **9.** length, or a length, of time; duration: *The flowers died in the space of a day. Many changes occur within the space of a man's life.* **10.** an interval of time; a while: *After a space, he continued his story.* **11.** *Printing.* one of the small pieces of blank type used to separate words, etc., or to justify a line. **12.** *Music.* one of the intervals or open places between the lines of a staff. **13.** a reserved seat, room, etc., on a train, airplane, ship, etc.; accommodations. **14.** *Telegraphy.* an interval in the transmission of a message in Morse code or a similar system when the key is not in contact and no signal is transmitted. **15.** *Mathematics.* a set of points or elements that usually fulfills certain postulates.
—*v.t.* **1.** to fix the space or spaces of; divide into spaces. **2.** to separate by spaces: *Space your words evenly when you write.* **3.** *Printing.* to extend to a required length by inserting additional space between the words or lines: *to space out a word or a line.*
[< Old French *espace,* learned borrowing from Latin *spatium*]

space age or **Space Age,** the current period in history, as marked by the advances made in the exploration and conquest of outer space through the launching and orbiting of artificial satellites and other space vehicles: *The conquest of space has* *moved ahead with breath-taking speed since the Space Age began on Oct. 4, 1957. On that day, Russian scientists launched the first true space traveler, an artificial satellite called Sputnik I* (World Book Encyclopedia).

space·borne (spās′bôrn′, -bōrn′), *adj.* borne or carried into outer space: *He also suggests applying continuous flight acceleration to the craft once it is spaceborne* (Science News Letter).

space capsule, a spacecraft consisting of a closed receptacle or chamber, designed to contain one or more persons, animals, or special equipment for carrying out an experiment or operation in space: *A space capsule containing both a monkey and a rat would be rocket-launched high above the earth . . . to provide clues to human intellectual reaction caused by weightlessness in space travel* (Wall Street Journal).

Manned Space Capsule, Mercury (cutaway)

space charge, the electric charge distributed through the area between the filament and the plate in a vacuum tube.

space·craft (spās′kraft′, -kräft′), *n.* **1.** any vehicle designed for flight in outer space: *The whole spacecraft would rotate slowly about its long axis to provide artificial gravity, through centrifugal force, for the crew* (Science News Letter). **2.** such vehicles collectively or as a class: *Revealing views of the lunar surface will be made by cameras mounted either in lunar satellites or in spacecraft designed to land on the moon* (Scientific American).

space engineer, a person trained or skilled in astronautics.

space flight, flight in outer space: *A new federal agency . . . will concentrate on . . . the biological and medical problems of space flight* (Bulletin of Atomic Scientists).

space gun, a portable apparatus equipped with a nozzle for jet propulsion, used in space to maneuver oneself in various directions while outside a flying or orbiting spacecraft: *In a series of films they saw the astronaut propel himself with his space gun to the end of his golden, 25-foot tether cord 140 miles above a brilliantly blue earth* (New York Times).

space heater, a gas or electric heater, often portable, for warming an enclosed area, such as a tent or a room.

space lattice, a pattern consisting of a series of points formed by the intersections of three systems of parallel and equally spaced lines, as in the arrangement of the atoms in a crystal.

space law, 1. the law relating to problems growing out of travel and exploration in outer space, as regional rights, ownership, jurisdiction, etc.: *The rapid pace of space exploration since the Soviets fired Sputnik I . . . has abruptly shifted space law out of the category of mere intellectual exercise* (Wall Street Journal). **2.** a projected code of international law that would deal with these problems and govern the use or control of space by different nations.

space·less (spās′lis), *adj.* **1.** independent of space; not limited by space; infinite; boundless: *the spaceless reaches of the universe.* **2.** occupying no space.

space·man (spās′man′), *n., pl.* **-men. 1.** a person skilled in or trained for space navigation. **2.** a person, especially a scientist, engaged in research, projects, etc., concerned with space flight: *U.S. spacemen, reaching for the moon, fired a satellite farther into space than any other man-made object* (Time).

space medicine, the branch of medicine concerned with the study of the body's capacity to endure space flight and the prevention, cure, or alleviation of illnesses or diseases that may be expected to result from space flight.

space-mind·ed (spās′mīn′did), *adj.* interested in outer space and space travel: *Planned as a small confab of space-minded missilemen, the conference ballooned into a crammed mass meeting of engineers and scientists* (Time). —**space′-mind′ed·ness,** *n.*

space platform, a space station: *It would start on its Martian journey from an earth-circling space platform* (Science News Letter).

space·port (spās′pôrt′, -pōrt′), *n.* a place where space ships, satellites, etc., can take off or land: *The U.S. moved another stride toward the day when man will blast into space, and return . . . to land at a chosen spaceport* (Time).

space power, the capacity of a nation to produce and utilize spacecraft and other apparatus for space exploration, military strategy, etc.: *Webb estimated that the Russians are two years ahead of the United States in space power* (Atlantic).

space probe, a rocket with scientific instruments, shot into space to record certain phenomena, carry on research, etc.; probe. See **probe** for picture.

spac·er (spā′sər), *n.* **1.** a device for spacing words, etc., as in a typesetting machine, typewriter, etc. **2.** an instrument that reverses a telegraphic current to increase the speed of transmission.

space race, the competition between the Soviet Union and the United States for first place in the exploration of outer space.

space rate, the rate of payment for space writing: *Our local newspaper pays free-lance writers at space rates.*

space rocket, a space ship: *Even the idea that a space rocket might be propelled by a succession of small nuclear explosions has been taken seriously* (New Scientist).

space satellite, an earth satellite: *The orbit of a space satellite is the most sensitive known tool for studies of the earth and its atmosphere* (Science News Letter). See **satellite** for picture.

space-sav·ing (spās′sā′ving), *adj.* that saves or tends to save available space; that helps to use space more efficiently: *When stationary, on the other hand, the machines are sensationally space-saving; since they have flat tops, they can be set one on top of the other* (New Yorker).

space science, 1. any science dealing with outer space, as astronautics, space medicine, etc. **2.** the group of studies concerned with problems related to the exploration of outer space, including those branches of physics, biology, chemistry, geology, etc., that deal with extraterrestrial phenomena.

space scientist, an expert in or student of space science or any of the space sciences: *A group of space scientists has been on the alert for the past few months, waiting for Mariner 4 to reach Mars* (Science News Letter).

space ship, or **space·ship** (spās′ship′), *n.* an aircraft for interplanetary travel, as between the earth and Mars, or travel beyond the solar system in outer space.

space·shot (spās′shot′), *n.* **1.** the launching of a spacecraft into outer space. **2.** space flight: *Psychologically, it is obvious that no American spaceshot thus far has so captured and fired the public imagination as did the fifteen-minute flight of Commander Shepard* (New York Times).

space stage, a theater stage with little or no scenery, on which the actors perform in lighted spots against a dark background.

space station, a station to be constructed in space and designed to operate as a satellite of the earth. Space stations are intended for scientific observation in meteorology and astronomy or as a supply or stopping point for space ships.

space suit, a pressure suit for use in space flight, that enables the wearer to endure conditions of low pressure: *He designed the ingenious five-layered aluminized space suit that will meet the human needs of space flight* (Newsweek).

Space Suit

space thunder, thunder that follows the arcs of the earth's magnetic field out into space, and that is inaudible except as a whistle on a radio.

space time, 1. the frame of reference within which, according to the theory of relativity, any physical event has particularity of existence, consisting of the three traditional dimensions of physical being (length, breadth, thickness) and the fourth dimension (time). **2.** space-time continuum.

space-time continuum (spās′tīm′), the concept of the universe as a continuum in the four dimensions of space time, within which it is possible to identify or locate physical events only by reference to three spatial coordinates and the temporal coordinate (the fourth dimension).

space travel, travel through outer space, especially in spacecraft: *Satellites and moon rockets promise that space travel will one day be possible* (New Scientist).

space·walk (spās′wôk′), *n.* the act of moving or floating in space while outside a spacecraft; extravehicular motion or activity. —*v.i.* to move or float in space while outside a spacecraft. —**space′walk′er,** *n.*

space·ward (spās′wərd), *adv.* upward or outward into outer space: *The world hopes desperately that Russia and the United States will continue to launch their giant rockets spaceward instead of at each other* (Atlantic).

space·wom·an (spās′wu̇m′ən), *n., pl.* **-wom·en.** a woman astronaut.

space·wor·thy (spās′wėr′ᴛʜē), *adj.* capable of being used in space flight: *Engineers have been turning out better and better experimental rocket planes, but they are by no means ready to launch a really spaceworthy ship* (New Yorker).

space writer, (in newspaper and other literary work) a person who is paid on the basis of the amount of space in type his accepted writing fills.

space writing, in newspaper work: **1.** the system of payment to reporters or other writers in proportion to the space allowed to their articles in print. **2.** writing or work done under this system.

spa·cial (spā′shəl), *adj.* spatial.

spac·ing (spā′sing), *n.* **1.** the fixing or arranging of spaces. **2.** the manner in which spaces are arranged: *even, close, or open spacing in printed matter.* **3.** a space or spaces in printing or other work.

spa·cious (spā′shəs), *adj.* **1.** having or affording much space or room; large; roomy: *the spacious rooms of an old castle.* **2.** of great extent or area; extensive; vast: *the spacious plains of Kansas and Iowa.* **3.** broad in scope or range; not limited or narrow; expansive: *a spacious mind; the spacious times of great Elizabeth* (Tennyson). [< Latin *spatiōsus* < *spatium* space] —**spa′cious·ly,** *adv.* —**spa′cious·ness,** *n.* —**Syn. 1.** capacious, commodious. **2.** wide, broad. —**Ant. 1.** cramped.

spa·cis·tor (spā sis′tər), *n.* a miniature electronic device that can amplify electric signals of a much wider frequency limit than ordinary transistors and vacuum tubes, and at much higher temperatures.

Spack·le (spak′əl), *n. v.t.,* **-led, -ling,** —*n. Trademark.* a powder which when mixed with water to form a paste is used to fill cracks and holes in walls and ceilings before painting or papering. —*v.t.* to apply Spackle paste to (a surface); repair with Spackle.

spade[1] (spād), *n., v.,* **spad·ed, spad·ing.** —*n.* **1.** a tool for digging, having an iron blade which can be pressed into the ground with the foot, and a long handle with a grip or crosspiece at the top. **2.** any of various spadelike knives used by whalers, especially in flensing a whale. **3.** the sharp end of a gun trail sunk into the ground to hold the carriage in place during recoil.

call a spade a spade, to call a thing by its real name; speak plainly and frankly, without mincing words: *If it is absolutely necessary to call a spade a spade then it must be done in a whisper* (Punch).

—*v.i., v.t.* to dig, cut, or remove with a spade: *to spade up a garden, to spade up worms and rocks.*

[Old English *spadu*] —**spad′er,** *n.* —**spade′-like′,** *adj.*

spade[2] (spād), *n.* **1.** a black figure (♠) used on playing cards. **2.** a card bearing such figures: *The spade took the trick.*

in spades, *U.S. Slang.* **a.** to the utmost degree; plentifully: "*Bob Taft did not have political . . . appeal,*" *says a conservative strategist.* "*But Barry has it—in spades*" (Newsweek). **b.** without holding back; with a vengeance: *Tom Vail . . . hopes to reply to his competition not only in kind but in spades* (Time).

spades, the suit of playing cards bearing such figures, usually the highest-ranking suit: "*Let spades be trumps!*" *she said, and trumps they were* (Alexander Pope).

[< Italian *spade,* feminine plural of *spada* sword < Latin *spatha* < Greek *spáthē* sword. Doublet of ÉPÉE, SPATHE.]

spade beard, a beard cut or trimmed to the shape of a pointed or broad spade blade: *Handsome suntanned features, spade beard,* *and arching eyebrows give him the look of a hearty Mephistopheles* (Newsweek).

spade·fish (spād′fish′), *n., pl.* **-fish·es** or (*collectively*) **-fish. 1.** any of a group of deep-bodied, spiny-finned food fish, as a variety found along the eastern coast of the United States. **2.** the paddlefish.

spade·ful (spād′fu̇l), *n., pl.* **-fuls.** as much as a spade can hold.

spade money, an early Chinese bronze coinage made in the form of spades.

spade·work (spād′wėrk′), *n.* **1.** a digging, cutting, or removing with a spade. **2.** preparatory work, such as intensive research, investigation, discussion, etc., serving as a basis for further work or activity.

spadg·er (spaj′ər), *n. British Dialect or Informal.* **1.** a sparrow. **2.** a small boy.

spa·di·ceous (spā dish′əs), *adj.* **1.** *Botany.* **a.** in the form of or like a spadix. **b.** bearing a spadix. **2.** reddish or brownish; chestnut. [< New Latin *spadiceus* (with English *-ous*) < Latin *spādīx, -īcis* date, date-colored, nut-brown; see SPADIX]

spa·dix (spā′diks), *n., pl.* **spa·dix·es, spa·di·ces** (spā dī′sēz). a spike composed of minute flowers set closely on a thick, fleshy stem. A spadix is usually enclosed in a petallike leaf called a spathe, as in the jack-in-the-pulpit and the calla lily. See **spathe** for picture. [< Latin *spādīx, -īcis* < Greek *spádīx, -īkos* any branch (especially a palm) torn off a tree < *spân* pluck off, out]

spae (spā), *v.t., v.i.,* **spaed, spae·ing.** *Scottish.* to foretell; prophesy. [< Scandinavian (compare Old Icelandic *spā*)]

spae·man (spā′mən), *n., pl.* **-men.** *Scottish.* a prophet, soothsayer, or fortuneteller.

spae·wife (spā′wīf′), *n., pl.* **-wives.** *Scottish.* a woman fortuneteller.

spa·ghet·ti (spə get′ē), *n.* **1.** a dried mixture of wheat flour and water shaped into long sticks, thinner than macaroni and not hollow, cooked by boiling in water. **2.** *Electricity.* an insulating cloth tubing used for protecting bare wire. [< Italian *spaghetti,* plural of *spaghetto* cord, twine (diminutive) < *spago* cord < Late Latin *spacus*]

Spa·gnuo·lo (spä nyō′lō), *n., pl.* **Spa·gnuo·li** (spä nyō′lē). a Sephardic Jew of Turkey or the Balkan States.

spa·gyr·ic or **spa·gir·ic** (spə jir′ik), *Obsolete.* —*adj.* having to do with alchemy; alchemical. —*n.* an alchemist. [< New Latin *spagiricus,* perhaps < Greek *spân* draw, separate, pluck + *ageírein* assemble]

spa·gyr·i·cal or **spa·gir·i·cal** (spə jir′ə kəl), *adj. Obsolete.* spagyric.

spa·hi or **spa·hee** (spä′hē), *n.* **1.** a member of a special corps of native Algerian cavalry in the French army. **2.** a member of an élite body of cavalry in the Turkish army from about 1500 to about 1800. [< Turkish *sipahi* < Persian *sipāhī* < *sipāh* army. Compare SEPOY.]

spake (spāk), *v. Archaic.* a past tense of **speak:** *Thus spake the Lord.*

spale or **spail** (spāl), *n. Scottish.* a chip, splinter, or thin strip of wood.

spall (spôl), *n.* a chip, splinter, or small piece of stone or ore. —*v.t.* to chip or break up roughly, as ore, preparatory to sorting. —*v.i.* to chip off. [Middle English *spalle;* origin uncertain]

spal·la·tion (spə lā′shən), *n.* the ejection from a nucleus of protons and neutrons as the result of intense bombardment or excitation by foreign particles.

spal·peen (spal pēn′, spal′pēn), *n. Irish.* a scamp; rascal. [Anglo-Irish < Irish *spailpīn* bully; (originally) migratory laborer]

span[1] (span), *n., v.,* **spanned, span·ning.** —*n.* **1.** the distance between the tip of a man's thumb and the tip of his little finger when the hand is spread out; about 9 inches. **2.** something of the length of a span; very small extent: *There was not a span free from cultivation* (Mountstuart Elphinstone). **3.** a short space of time: *This pupil has a short attention span. His life's span is nearly over. Did many talents gild thy span?* (Robert Burns). **4. a.** the distance between two supports: *The arch had a fifty-foot span.* **b.** the part between two supports: *The bridge crossed the river in three spans.* **5.** the full extent or reach of anything: *the span of a bridge, the span of memory.* **6.** the lateral distance of an airplane, or of a wing, from wing tip to wing tip.
—*v.t.* **1.** to measure by the hand spread out: *This post can be spanned by one's two hands.* **2.** to encircle or encompass (the waist, wrist, etc.) with the hand or hands. **3.** to extend over or across: *A bridge spanned the river.* **4.** to provide with something that stretches over or across: *to span a river with a bridge.* **5.** to reach or extend over: *Memory spans the past.*
[Old English *spann*]

span[2] (span), *n., v.,* **spanned, span·ning.** —*n.* a pair of horses, mules, etc., harnessed and driven together: ... *comfortable carryalls drawn by steady spans* (Booth Tarkington). —*v.t.* to harness (horses, etc.) to a vehicle. [American English, probably < Dutch *span* < *spannen* to stretch, yoke]

span[3] (span), *v. Archaic.* a past tense of **spin:** *When Adam delved, and Eve span, who was then a gentleman?* (John Ball).

Span., Spanish.

span·cel (span′səl), *n. Dialect.* a fetter or hobble, especially, a rope for tying together the hind legs of a cow during milking. [< Dutch *spansel* < *spannen;* see SPAN[2]]

span·dex (span′deks), *n.* a synthetic fiber made from a polymer containing at least 85 per cent polyurethane, used as an elastic.

span·drel (span′drəl), *n.* **1.** the triangular space between the outer curve of an arch and the rectangular molding or framework enclosing the arch. **2.** the space between the outer curves of two adjacent arches and the molding above them. [perhaps < Anglo-French *spaundre,* short for Old French *espandre* expand < Latin *expandere.* Compare EXPAND.]

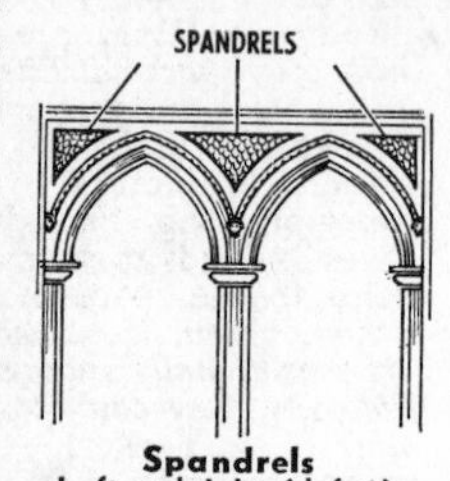

Spandrels
Left and right, (def. 1); center, (def. 2)

span·dy (span′dē), *adj. Especially U.S. Informal.* very good or fine; smart: *My silk stockings and two pairs of spandy gloves are my comfort* (Louisa May Alcott). —*adv.* wholly; perfectly: *At eleven, McAndless threw everybody out, and with a spandy new quart of scotch in his fist, stomped off to his cottage* (Atlantic). [probably variant of dialectal *spander*(-new) < *span-new;* see SPAN-NEW]

spa·ne·mi·a or **spa·nae·mi·a** (spə nē′mē ə), *n.* anemia.

spa·ne·mic or **spa·nae·mic** (spə nē′mik), *adj.* anemic.

spang (spang), *adv. U.S. Informal.* with a sudden spring or impetus; slap; smack.
right spang, a. entirely; quite: *He was good at making up stories right spang out of his own head.* **b.** exactly: *The bullet landed right spang in the middle of the target.*
[American English, perhaps < dialectal *spang* a jerk, sharp rap, smack]

span·gle (spang′gəl), *n., v.,* **-gled, -gling.** —*n.* **1.** a small piece of glittering metal used for decoration: *The dress was covered with spangles.* **2.** any bright bit: *This rock shows spangles of gold.*
—*v.t.* **1.** to decorate with spangles: *The dress was spangled with gold.* **2.** to sprinkle with or as if with small bright bits: *The sky is spangled with stars.* —*v.i.* to sparkle with or as if with spangles; glitter.
[perhaps diminutive form of Old English *spang* clasp, buckle]

span·gly (spang′glē), *adj.,* **-gli·er, -gli·est.** covered with spangles; glittering with or as if with spangles: *a spangly starfish, a spangly flag. Rockefeller Plaza is as spangly and tinkly as ever* (Manchester Guardian).

Span·iard (span′yərd), *n.* a native or inhabitant of Spain.

span·iel (span′yəl), *n.* **1.** any of various breeds of dogs, usually of small or medium size with long, silky hair and drooping ears. Spaniels are divided into three classes: the field spaniels, the water spaniels, the toy spaniels. **2.** a person who yields too easily to others: *Perish shall all which makes a spaniel of the man* (John Greenleaf Whittier). [< Old French *espagneul* (literally) Spanish < Latin *Hispāniolus* < *Hispānia* Spain]

Span·ish (span′ish), *adj.* of or having to do with Spain, a country in southwestern Europe, its people, or their language: *Spanish custom normally puts the father's family name first and the mother's last* (Newsweek). —*n.* **1.** the people of Spain. **2.** the Romance language of Spain. It is also the standard language in Latin American countries (except Brazil, British Honduras, and the Guianas), Mexico, and former colonies of Spain. *Abbr.:* Sp.

Span·ish-A·mer·i·can (span′ish ə mer′ə kən), *adj.* **1.** of or having to do with Spain and America, or with Spain and the United States: *Spanish-American relations.* **2.** of or having to do with the parts of America where Spanish is the standard language: *The President in making appointments* [*must*] *pay due respect to our Spanish-American populace* (Weekly New Mexican Review).

Spanish American, 1. *Southwestern U.S.* a person born in the United States whose parents or forebears were Mexicans. **2.** a native or inhabitant of a Spanish-American country, especially a person of Spanish descent.

Spanish-American War, the war between Spain and the United States in 1898.

Spanish Armada, the great fleet sent by Philip II of Spain to attack England in 1588; Armada; Invincible Armada. It was defeated in the English Channel, and subsequently many of its ships were wrecked by storms.

Spanish bayonet, any of several desert plants or yuccas of the agave family, having narrow, rigid, evergreen leaves with spines at the tips.

Spanish black, a black paint used by artists, made from burnt cork shavings.

Spanish broom, a plant common to the Mediterranean region, with rushlike branches or twigs used in basketwork and in the manufacture of cords, coarse cloths, etc.

Spanish fly, a bright-green European blister beetle whose dried and powdered body is a source of cantharides, used for raising blisters on the skin; cantharis.

Spanish grippe or **influenza,** influenza, especially in the virulent form that was pandemic in the United States and elsewhere in 1918-1919.

Spanish Inquisition, 1. a body of men appointed by the Roman Catholic Church to suppress heresy in Spain. It was put under state control at the end of the 1400's and was very active during the 1500's. **2.** the activities of this body of men.

Spanish jasmine or **jessamine,** a jasmine of India, having large, fragrant, white flowers. See **jasmine** for picture.

Spanish mackerel, any of a group of marine food fishes related to the tuna and mackerel, as the cero.

Spanish Main, 1. (formerly) the mainland of America adjacent to the Caribbean, especially between the mouth of the Orinoco River and the Isthmus of Panama. **2.** (in later use) the Caribbean Sea. Pirates and privateers used to go there in quest of Spanish treasure ships outward bound from Mexico.

Spanish moss, a mosslike plant of the pineapple family, growing on the branches of certain trees, from which it hangs in gray streamers, found in the southern United States and tropical America; Florida moss.

Spanish needles, 1. an annual weed of the composite family, having barbed fruits. **2.** its barbed fruits.

Span·ish·ness (span′ish nis), *n.* the quality or state of being Spanish or of Spanish descent.

Spanish onion, a large, mild, usually red-skinned, juicy onion, often eaten raw in sandwiches and salads.

Spanish paprika, 1. a cultivated pepper of Spanish origin. **2.** its mild red pod.

spank[1] (spangk), *v.t.* to strike, especially on the buttocks, with the open hand, a slipper, etc.: *The father spanked the naughty child.* —*n.* a blow with the open hand, a slipper, etc.; slap; smack. [imitative]

spank[2] (spangk), *v.i. Informal.* to go quickly and vigorously; move at a speedy rate. [probably back formation < *spanking*]

spank·er (spang′kər), *n.* **1. a.** a fore-and-aft sail on the mast nearest the stern. **b.** the mast nearest the stern of a ship having four or more masts. See **sail** for diagram. **2.** *Informal.* a swift horse. **3.** *Informal.* anything fine, large, or unusual for its kind. [apparently < *spanking,* or < *spank*[2] move fast]

spank·ing (spang′king), *adj.* **1.** blowing briskly: *a spanking breeze.* **2.** moving with a quick, lively pace, as a horse. **3.** quick and vigorous, as a pace, rate, etc. **4.** *Informal.* unusually fine, great, large, etc.: *a spanking good time.* [earlier, fast-moving (of horses). Compare Danish *spanke* to strut.]

span·less (span′lis), *adj.* that cannot be spanned.

span loading, the gross weight of an aircraft divided by the span of its wings.

span·ner (span′ər), *n.* **1.** a person or thing that spans: *the spanners of a bridge.* **2.** *Especially British.* a tool for holding and turning a nut, bolt, etc.; wrench. [< German *Spanner* < *spannen* fasten, draw tight]

span-new (span′nü′, -nyü′), *adj.* entirely new; brand-new: *The men were exuberant, sprawling over their tanks, all span-new Shermans* (New Yorker). [< Scandinavian (compare Old Icelandic *spān-nȳr* < *spānn* chip + *nȳr* new)]

span·worm (span′wėrm′), *n.* a measuring worm.

spar[1] (spär), *n., v.,* **sparred, spar·ring.** —*n.* **1.** a stout pole used to support or extend the sails of a ship, such as a mast, yard, gaff, boom, etc. **2.** the main horizontal support of an airplane wing, to which the ribs are attached.
—*v.t.* to equip (a ship) with spars; put a spar or spars on.
[Middle English *sparre* a rafter. Compare Old English *gespearrian* to shut, bar (as a door).]

spar[2] (spär), *v.,* **sparred, spar·ring,** *n.* —*v.i.* **1.** to make motions of attack and defense with the fists; box. **2.** to dispute or argue cautiously, as if to test one's opponent; bandy words. **3.** to fight, as roosters, with the feet or spurs.
—*n.* **1.** a boxing match. **2.** a sparring motion. **3.** a dispute.
[< Middle French *esparer* to kick < Italian *sparare* to fling < *s-*, intensive (< Latin *ex-*) + *parare* to parry, ward off, protect]

spar[3] (spär), *n.* any of various crystalline minerals, more or less lustrous, that split into flakes easily, as calcspar and fluorspar. [< Middle Low German *spar*, related to Old English *spær* in *spærstān* gypsum, *spæren* of plaster]

SPAR or **Spar** (spär), *n.* a member of the SPARS. [< *s*(*emper*) *par*(*atus*) always ready (the motto of the Coast Guard)]

spar·a·ble (spar′ə bəl), *n.* a small, headless, wedge-shaped iron nail used in shoemaking. [alteration of earlier *sparrow-bill*]

spa·ra·da (spə rä′də, -rā′-), *n.* a small surf fish common on the Pacific coast of North America. [origin unknown]

spar buoy, a buoy shaped like a short, thick pole.

spar deck, the upper deck of a ship, extending from one end to the other.

spare (spãr), *v.,* **spared, spar·ing,** *adj.,* **spar·er, spar·est,** *n.* —*v.t.* **1.** to show mercy to; refrain from harming or destroying: *to spare a conquered enemy. He hoped that the squire's life would be long spared* (Anthony Trollope). **2.** to show consideration for; save from labor, pain, etc.: *We walked uphill to spare the horse. Her cruel tongue spares nobody.* **3.** to get along without; do without: *Can you spare a moment to discuss the problem? Father couldn't spare the car; so I had to walk. Caesar and Pompey must each spare a legion for the East* (James A. Froude). **4.** to make (a person, etc.) free from (something); relieve or exempt (a person, etc.) from (something): *He did the work to spare you the trouble. Spare me the gory details.* **5.** to refrain from using; forbear; forego; omit: *to spare the rod and spoil the child.* **6.** to use in small quantities or not at all; be saving of; stint: *to spare no expense.* **7.** to set aside; keep in reserve for a particular use or purpose; have free: *to spare some time for reading, to have an hour to spare, to spare some pasture for a crop.* —*v.i.* **1.** to show mercy; refrain from doing harm: *spare not for spoiling of thy steed* (Scott). **2.** to be saving, economical, or frugal: *I, who at some times spend, at others spare* (Alexander Pope).
—*adj.* **1.** not in actual or regular use; in reserve; extra: *a spare tire, a spare room.* **2.** free for other use; surplus: *spare time.* **3.** not fat or plump; thin; lean: *Lincoln was a tall, spare man.* **4.** small in quantity; meager; scanty; frugal: *a spare meal. Fat people should live on a spare diet.*
—*n.* **1.** a spare thing, part, tire, room, etc. **2.** *Bowling.* **a.** the knocking down of all the pins with two rolls of the ball. **b.** the score for doing this.
[Old English *sparian*] —**spare′ness,** *n.* —**spar′er,** *n.* —**Syn.** *adj.* **3.** lank, gaunt.

spare·a·ble (spãr′ə bəl), *adj.* that can be spared.

spare·ly (spãr′lē), *adv.* **1.** not amply or fully; frugally. **2.** thinly; sparsely.

spare part, a duplicate of a part of a machine kept in readiness to replace a loss or breakage: *The cost of the new planes known as Model 61's will be about $8 million each, without spare parts* (New York Times).

spare·rib (spãr′rib′), *n.* a rib of pork having less meat than the ribs near the loin. [probably alteration of earlier *ribspare* < Middle Low German *ribbespēr* rib cut]

sparge (spärj), *v.,* **sparged, sparg·ing,** *n.* —*v.t., v.i.* **1.** to dash, splash, or sprinkle about. **2.** to bespatter; besprinkle.
—*n.* **1.** a sprinkling or splashing. **2.** a sprinkle; dash (of liquor, etc.).
[earlier, to plaster over, apparently < Old French *espargier* < Latin *spargere* to sprinkle]

sparg·er (spär′jər), *n.* **1.** a sprinkler for dampening paper, clothes, or the like. **2.** (in brewing) a perforated cylinder for discharging a fine shower of hot water over grain falling into a mash tub. **3.** a person who sparges.

spar·hawk (spär′hôk′), *n. Archaic.* a sparrow hawk.

Spar·ine (spãr′ēn), *n. Trademark.* promazine.

spar·ing (spãr′ing), *adj.* **1.** that spares. **2.** economical; frugal: *a sparing use of sugar.* —**spar′ing·ness,** *n.* —**Syn. 2.** parsimonious, stingy.

spar·ing·ly (spãr′ing lē), *adv.* economically; frugally.

spark[1] (spärk), *n.* **1.** a small bit of fire: *The burning wood threw off sparks.* **2.** *Electricity.* **a.** the flash given off when electricity jumps across an open space. **b.** the discharge itself. **c.** (in an internal-combustion engine) the discharge in a spark plug. **d.** the mechanism generating and controlling this discharge. **e.** a spark transmitter or spark transmission. **3.** a bright flash; gleam; sparkle: *a spark of light.* **4.** a small amount; trace; indication: *I haven't a spark of interest in the plan. They still kept alive the sparks of future friendship* (Washington Irving). **5.** a trace of life or vitality: *O speak, if any spark of life remain* (Thomas Kyd). **6.** a glittering bit: *The moving sparks we saw were fireflies.*
—*v.i.* **1.** to send out small bits of fire; produce sparks: *This wood burns steadily with no sparking* (William O. Douglas). **2.** to flash; gleam; sparkle: *Her eyes did spark, at every glance, like diamonds in the dark* (Francis Quarles). **3.** to issue or fall as or like sparks. **4.** to operate properly in forming sparks, as the ignition in an internal-combustion engine. —*v.t.* to stir to activity; stimulate: *to spark a revolt, spark sales, etc.*
[Old English *spearca*]
—**Syn.** *v.t.* animate, excite.

spark[2] (spärk), *n.* **1.** a beau; lover: *A . . . woman . . . daring death just for the sake of thee, her handsome spark!* (Robert Browning). **2.** a gay, showy young man: *A fop came . . . a fine spark, and gave them fine words* (Stanley J. Weyman). —*v.t., v.i. Informal.* to court; woo: *His master was courting, or, as it is termed, 'sparking' within* (Washington Irving). [earlier, a beauty, a wit, perhaps special use of *spark*[1]] —**Syn.** *n.* **2.** dandy.

spark arrester, **1.** anything that keeps sparks from flying, such as a piece of mesh on the top of a chimney. **2.** *Electricity.* a device for preventing or minimizing injurious sparking at points where frequent interruptions of the circuit occur, as in telegraph keys, relays, etc.

spark chamber, a gas-filled chamber containing metal plates connected to a source of electricity. Subatomic particles passing through leave a trail of bright sparks which may be photographed.

spark coil, *Electricity.* an induction coil for producing sparks, used in an internal-combustion engine, wireless telegraphy equipment, etc.

spark·er (spär′kər), *n.* **1.** a person or thing that produces sparks. **2.** *Electricity.* a spark arrester.

spark gap, an open space between two electrodes across which a discharge of electricity travels.

spark generator, an alternating-current generator that uses the electric discharge of a condenser across a spark gap as the power source.

spark·i·ly (spär′kə lē), *adv.* in a sparky manner.

spark·ing plug (spär′king), *British.* a spark plug.

spark·ish (spär′kish), *adj.* of or like a spark; gay and showy.

spark killer, *Electricity.* a spark arrester.

spar·kle (spär′kəl), *v.,* **-kled, -kling,** *n.* —*v.i.* **1.** to shine as if giving out sparks; glitter; flash; gleam: *The diamonds sparkled. Disdain and scorn ride sparkling in her eyes* (Shakespeare). **2.** to be brilliant; be lively: *a conversation sparkled with wit.* **3.** to send out little sparks: *The children's fireworks sparkled.* **4.** to bubble, as champagne, ginger ale, etc. —*v.t.* to cause to sparkle: *The . . . sun . . . sparkling the landscape with a thousand dewy gems* (Washington Irving).
—*n.* **1.** a little spark: *to count the sparkles which flew from the horses' hoofs* (Scott). **2.** a shine; glitter; flash; gleam: *the gay sparkle of her eyes.* **3.** brilliance; liveliness.
[< *spark*, noun + *-le* (frequentative)]
—**Syn.** *n.* **2.** See **flash.**

spar·kler (spär′klər), *n.* **1.** a person or thing that sparkles. **2.** a firework that sends out little sparks. **3.** a sparkling gem, especially a diamond.

spark·less (spärk′lis), *adj.* free from sparks: *sparkless ashes.*

spar·kling (spär′kling), *adj.* **1.** that sparkles: *a sparkling fire.* **2.** flashing; glittering; brilliant: *a sky sparkling with stars, a sparkling gem.* **3.** brilliant; lively: *a sparkling performance, sparkling wit.* **4.** effervescent; bubbling: *Ginger ale and champagne are sparkling drinks.* —**spar′kling·ly,** *adv.*

spark plug, **1.** a device in the cylinder of an internal-combustion engine which explodes the mixture of gasoline and air by an electric spark. **2.** *Informal.* a person who gives energy or enthusiasm to others: *The shortstop is the spark plug of our baseball team.*

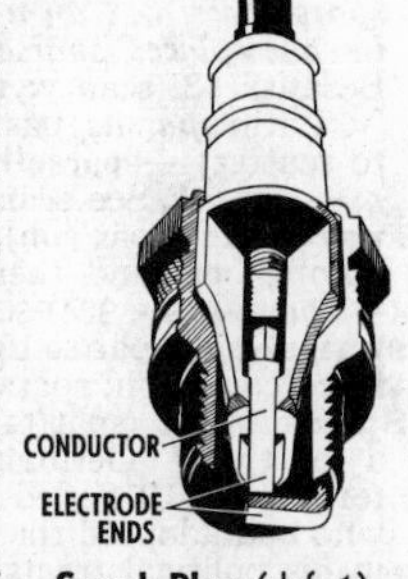

Spark Plug (def. 1) Electric current passes through conductor to electrode ends where it produces a spark which ignites combustion gases.

spark-plug (spärk′plug′), *v.t.,* **-plugged, -plug·ging.** *Informal.* **1.** to be the spark plug of (a group, organization, etc.). **2.** to be the originator of; lead in bringing about: *He spark-plugged the investigation of corruption in the town.*

sparks (spärks), *n. Slang.* a telegraph or radio operator, as on a ship.

spark spectrum, the spectrum a metal or other conduction substance produces by passing an electric spark between electrodes made of the metal or other substance.

spark transmission, radio transmission by means of a spark transmitter.

spark transmitter, a radio transmitter that uses the electric discharge of a condenser across a spark gap to provide its alternating-current power.

spark·y (spär′kē), *adj.,* **spark·i·er, spark·i·est.** **1.** emitting sparks. **2.** lively; vivacious: *It seems to be part of a process, . . . as well as part of a never adjourned discussion brightened by the sparky friction of ideas on ideas* (New Yorker).

spar·ling (spär′ling), *n.* the smelt of Europe. Also, **sperling.** [Middle English *sperlinge* < Old French *esperlinge* < Germanic (compare Low German *spierling*, Middle Dutch *spirlinc*)]

spar·mate (spär′māt′), *n.* sparring partner.

spar·oid (spãr′oid, spar′-), *adj.* **1.** of or belonging to a group of marine fishes related to the grunts and snappers, having spiny fins and deep bodies, including the sea bream, scup, porgy, etc. **2.** like a porgy. —*n.* a sparoid fish. [< Latin *sparus* gilthead (< Greek *spáros* sea bream) + English *-oid*]

spar·rer (spär′ər), *n.* a person who spars or boxes.

spar·ring (spär′ing), *n.* **1.** boxing. **2.** an arguing back and forth; disputing.

spar·ring partner, a boxer hired to keep another in practice while training for a fight.

spar·row (spar′ō), *n.* **1.** any of various small, usually brownish finches most abundant in North and South America, such as the chipping sparrow, song sparrow, field sparrow, sage sparrow, swamp sparrow, and vesper sparrow. **2.** any of a related group of birds native to Europe, Asia, and Africa, as the tree sparrow, Java sparrow, and English sparrow. **3.** any of several similar birds, such as the hedge sparrow or dunnock of Europe (a warbler). [Old English *spearwa*] —**spar′row·like′,** *adj.*

English Sparrow (def. 2) (about 6 in. long)

spar·row·grass (spar′ō gras′), *n. Dialect.* asparagus. [alteration by folk etymology of obsolete *sparagus* < Medieval Latin, short for *asparagus* < Latin]

sparrow hawk, 1. a small North American falcon that feeds on large insects and small animals. **2.** a hawk of Europe and Asia that feeds on small birds.

Sparrow Hawk (def. 1) (about 11 in. long)

spar·ry (spär′ē), *adj.* full of spar; like spar (the mineral).

SPARS or **Spars** (spärz), *n.pl.* the Women's Reserve of the United States Coast Guard Reserve.

sparse (spärs), *adj.*, **spars·er, spars·est. 1.** occurring here and there; thinly scattered: *a sparse population, sparse hair; . . . an unorganised mob—thick in one place, sparse in another* (Walter Besant). **2.** scanty; meager: *a sparse diet.* [< Latin *sparsus,* past participle of *spargere* to scatter] —**sparse′ly,** *adv.* —**sparse′ness,** *n.* —**Syn. 1.** See **scanty.**

spar·sim (spär′sim), *adv.* at scattered points; here and there. [< Latin *sparsim* < *sparsus;* see SPARSE]

spar·si·ty (spär′sə tē), *n.* sparse or scattered condition; sparseness.

Spar·ta·cist (spär′tə sist), *n.* a member of a party of German socialist extremists formed in 1918, led by Karl Liebknecht, who had adopted the pseudonym *Spartakus* in his political tracts. [< German *Spartakist*]

Spar·tan (spär′tən), *adj.* **1.** of or having to do with Sparta or its people. **2.** like the Spartans; simple; frugal; severe, sternly disciplined, brave, and concise: *Spartan fortitude, Spartan taste.*
—*n.* **1.** a native or inhabitant of Sparta. The Spartans were noted for living simply, saying little, being brave, and enduring pain without complaining. **2.** a person who is like the Spartans.

Spartan dog, 1. a bloodhound. **2.** a cruel or bloodthirsty person.

Spar·tan·ic (spär tan′ik), *adj.* Spartan.

Spar·tan·ism (spär′tə niz əm), *n.* **1.** the beliefs and methods of ancient Sparta. **2.** any discipline, method, etc., like that of the ancient Spartans.

spar·te·in (spär′tē in), *n.* sparteine.

spar·te·ine (spär′tē ēn, -in), *n.* a bitter, poisonous liquid alkaloid obtained from certain species of broom and lupine, used in medicine as a heart stimulant. *Formula:* $C_{15}H_{26}N_2$ [< New Latin *Spartium* the broom genus (< Greek *spártos* Spanish broom) + English *-ine*[2]]

spar·te·rie (spär′tər ē), *n.* articles manufactured from esparto, as mats, nets, cordage, and ropes. [< French *sparterie* < Spanish *espartería* < *esparto;* see ESPARTO]

spar varnish, an oleoresinous, weather-resistant varnish used for exterior surfaces, especially on ships.

spasm (spaz′əm), *n.* **1.** a sudden, abnormal, involuntary contraction of a muscle or muscles. A clonic spasm is characterized by alternate contraction and relaxation of the muscles, and a tonic spasm by prolonged contraction without relaxation for some time: *The child in a spasm kept twitching his arms and legs.* **2.** any sudden, brief fit or spell of unusual energy or activity: *As with an earthquake's spasm* (Shelley). *He caused her a spasm of anguish* (George Meredith). *Between the spasms of violence there were long quiet intervals when the ordinary occupations of men went on as usual* (James A. Froude). [< Latin *spasmus* < Greek *spasmós* < *spân* draw (up), tear away] —**Syn. 1.** convulsion.

spas·mat·ic (spaz mat′ik), *adj.* spasmodic.

spas·mod·ic (spaz mod′ik), *adj.* **1.** having to do with, like, or characterized by a spasm or spasms: *a spasmodic cough.* **2. a.** sudden and violent, but brief: *spasmodic rage.* **b.** occurring very irregularly; intermittent: *a spasmodic interest in reading.* **3.** very emotional; excited; agitated: *Miss Tox immediately became spasmodic* (Dickens). **4.** disjointed; choppy: *a spasmodic style, spasmodic writing.* [< Medieval Latin *spasmodicus* < Greek *spasmṓdēs* < *spasmós;* see SPASM]
—**Syn. 2. b.** fitful. **4.** jerky.

spas·mod·i·cal (spaz mod′ə kəl), *adj.* spasmodic.

spas·mod·i·cal·ly (spaz mod′ə klē), *adv.* **1.** by means of or accompanied by a spasm or spasms. **2.** in a spasmodic manner; by fits and starts: *The boy's interest in science was spasmodically aroused whenever new equipment was brought into the laboratory.*

spas·mo·dist (spaz′mə dist), *n.* a person who acts or works in a spasmodic manner.

spas·mo·phil·i·a (spaz′mə fil′ē ə), *n.* a condition of abnormal sensitiveness in which any mechanical or electrical stimulation causes spasms or convulsions. [< New Latin *spasmophilia* < Latin *spasmus* spasm + New Latin *-philia*]

spas·tic (spas′tik), *adj.* **1.** caused by a spasm or spasms: *spastic pain.* **2.** of, having to do with, or characterized by spasms, especially tonic spasms: *a spastic disease.* **3.** having spastic paralysis.
—*n.* a person affected with spastic paralysis. [< Latin *spasticus* < Greek *spastikós* < *spân* draw (up)] —**spas′ti·cal·ly,** *adv.*

spas·tic·i·ty (spas tis′ə tē), *n.* **1.** the tendency to go into spasms. **2.** the state of being spastic: *Elaborate animal experiments have been attempted to try to relate how damage to the brain causes spasticity* (New Scientist).

spastic paralysis, a condition marked by partial or complete inability to control muscular movement, caused by brain damage.

spat[1] (spat), *n., v.,* **spat·ted, spat·ting.** —*n.* **1.** a slight quarrel; tiff: *They got into kind of a spat about which one'd make the best actress* (Booth Tarkington). **2.** a light blow; slap.
—*v.i.* **1.** to quarrel slightly or briefly: *The dogs and cats spat before the dog chased the cat up the tree.* **2.** to give a slap or slaps. —*v.t.* to slap lightly. [American English; perhaps imitative]

spat[2] (spat), *v.* a past tense and a past participle of **spit**[1]: *The cat spat at the dog.*

spat[3] (spat), *n.* See under **spats.**

spat[4] (spat), *n., v.,* **spat·ted, spat·ting.** —*n.* **1.** the spawn of oysters or other shellfish. **2.** a young oyster. —*v.i.* (of oysters) to spawn. [origin uncertain. Perhaps related to SPIT[1].]

spa·tan·goid (spə tang′goid), *adj.* of or like the spatangus; heart-shaped.

spa·tan·gus (spə tang′gəs), *n., pl.* **-gi** (-gē). any of a group of sea urchins, some of which are heart-shaped. [< New Latin *Spatangus* the genus name < Greek *spatángēs* a kind of sea urchin]

spatch·cock (spach′kok′), *n.* a freshly killed fowl, split and broiled. —*v.t.* **1.** to cook as or in the manner of a spatchcock. **2.** *Especially British Informal.* to insert or interpolate; sandwich in: *The new matter consists of long quotations from secondary sources . . . and of over-written descriptive paragraphs, spatchcocked into the old text* (Manchester Guardian). [earlier, to cook hastily < phrase *dispatch cock* (originally) a chicken chosen, killed, and prepared with dispatch]

spate (spāt), *n.* **1.** a sudden outburst; violent outpouring: *a spate of words or of anger.* **2.** *British.* **a.** a sudden flood; freshet: *Is the torrent in spate? He must ford it or swim* (Rudyard Kipling). **b.** a sudden, heavy downpour of rain. [origin uncertain]

spa·tha·ceous (spə thā′shəs), *adj.* **1.** furnished with or enclosed by a spathe. **2.** of or like a spathe.

spa·thal (spā′thəl), *adj.* spathaceous.

spathe (spāᵺ), *n.* a large bract or pair of bracts enclosing a flower cluster: *The calla lily has a white spathe around a yellow flower cluster.* [< Latin *spatha* < Greek *spáthē* broad, flat blade. Doublet of ÉPÉE, SPADE[2].]

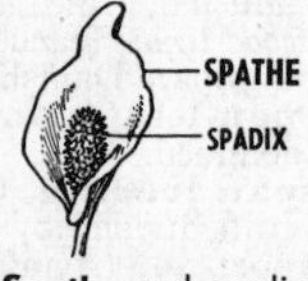

Spathe and **spadix** of calla lily

spathed (spāᵺd), *adj.* having or surrounded by a spathe.

spath·ic (spath′ik), *adj.* spathose. [earlier *spath, spat* spar[3] (< German *Spath*) + *-ic*]

spath·i·form (spath′ə fôrm), *adj.* resembling spar in form: *a spathiform variety of uranite.*

spath·ose[1] (spath′ōs), *adj.* like or consisting of spar; foliated; sparry.

spa·those[2] (spā′thōs, spath′ōs), *adj. Botany.* like or formed like a spathe.

spath·u·late (spath′yə lit, -lāt), *adj. Botany.* spatulate.

spa·tial (spā′shəl), *adj.* **1.** of or having to do with space. **2.** existing or occurring in space. **3.** occupying or taking up space. Also, **spacial.** [< Latin *spatium* space + English *-al*[1]]

spa·ti·al·i·ty (spā′shē al′ə tē), *n.* spatial character.

spa·tial·ly (spā′shə lē), *adv.* in spatial respects; so far as space is concerned; in space.

spa·ti·o·tem·po·ral (spā′shē ō tem′pər əl), *adj.* belonging to both space and time: *linked in a manner transcending the spatio-temporal order, and hence wholly outside the ambit of "the laws of mechanics"* (New Scientist). [< Latin *spatium* space + English *temporal*]

spats (spats), *n.pl.* a short gaiter worn over the instep and reaching just above the ankle, usually fastened by a strap under the foot and buttons on one side. [short for *spatterdash*]

spat·ter (spat′ər), *v.t.* **1.** to scatter or dash in drops or particles; splatter: *to spatter paint, to spatter mud.* **2.** to strike in a shower; strike in a number of places: *Bullets spattered the wall.* **3. a.** to splash or stain with drops of liquid, mud, etc.; bespatter. **b.** to stain with slander, disgrace, etc. —*v.i.* **1.** to send out or throw off drops or particles. **2.** to fall in drops or particles: *Rain spatters on the sidewalk.*
—*n.* **1.** a spattering: *a spatter of bullets.* **2.** the sound of spattering: *the spatter of rain on a roof.* **3.** a splash or spot; splatter. [apparently a frequentative form. Compare Dutch or Low German *spatten* to spout.] —**spat′ter·ing·ly,** *adv.*
—**Syn.** *v.t.* **3. b.** smear.

spat·ter·dash (spat′ər dash′), *n.* Often, **spatterdashes.** a long gaiter or legging of leather, cloth, etc., worn to keep the trousers or stockings from being splashed with mud, as in riding. [< *spatter* + *dash*]

Spatterdashes

spat·ter·dock (spat′ər dok′), *n.* **1.** an aquatic plant of the water-lily family, with large erect leaves and rounded yellow flowers, common in stagnant waters of the eastern United States. **2.** any of various related water plants. [American English, earlier *splatterdock* < *splatter* + *dock*[4]]

spat·ter·ing (spat′ər ing), *n.* **1.** a splash or sprinkling: *a spattering of paint on the floor.* **2.** the act of splashing, sprinkling, etc.

spat·ter·ware (spat′ər wãr′), *n.* earthenware with a design produced by spatterwork.

spat·ter·work (spat′ər wėrk′), *n.* decorative work in which a design is produced on a surface by spattering ink or the like over exposed parts.

spat·u·la (spach′ə lə), *n.* a tool with a broad, flat, flexible blade, used for mixing drugs, spreading paints or frostings, etc. [< Late Latin *spatula* spoon (diminutive) < Latin *spatha* broad, flat blade < Greek *spáthē*]

spat·u·lar (spach′ə lər), *adj.* of or like a spatula.

spat·u·late (spach′ə lit, -lāt), *adj.* **1.** shaped like a spatula; rounded somewhat like a spoon: *a spatulate blade.* **2.** *Botany.* having a broad, rounded end and a long, narrow base: *a spatulate leaf.* **3.** wide at the tips: *spatulate fingers.*

spat·u·la·tion (spach′ə lā′shən), *n.* spatulate condition or form.
spat·ule (spach′ůl), *n.* **1.** spatula. **2.** *Zoology.* a spatulate formation or part, as at the end of the tail feathers of a bird. [< French *spatule* < Late Latin *spatula*]
spat·u·li·form (spach′ə lə fôrm), *adj.* spatulate in form; spoon-shaped.
spat·u·lig·e·rous (spach′ə lij′ə rəs), *adj.* *Zoology.* bearing a spatule. [< Latin *spatula* + *gerere* to carry + English *-ous*]
spa·vie (spā′vi, spav′i), *n. Scottish.* spavin.
spa·viet (spā′vit, spav′it), *adj. Scottish.* spavined.
spav·in (spav′ən), *n.* **1.** a disease of horses in which a bony swelling forms at the hock, causing lameness. **2.** a less serious disease of horses in which the capsule of tissue at the hock fills with fluid. [< Old French *espavain*, probably < a Germanic word]
spav·ined (spav′ənd), *adj.* **1.** having spavin. **2.** lame; crippled: *Even by its own spavined standards the native product is poor* (London Times).
spawl[1] (spôl), *v.i. Archaic.* to spit; expectorate. [origin unknown]
spawl[2] (spôl), *n., v.* spall.
spawn (spôn), *n.* **1. a.** the eggs of fish, frogs, shellfish, etc. **b.** the young that are newly hatched from such eggs. **2.** a swarming brood; offspring. **3.** a person regarded as the offspring of some stock, or as imbued with some quality or principle: *Tyrants are but the spawn of Ignorance, Begotten by the slaves they trample on* (Lowell). **4.** a product, result, or effect. **5.** the mass of white, threadlike fibers (mycelium) from which mushrooms grow. [< verb]
—*v.i.* **1.** (of fish, etc.) to produce spawn. **2.** to increase or develop like spawn; become reproductive.
—*v.t.* **1.** to produce (spawn). **2.** to bring forth; give birth to; produce: *Adenauer himself had spawned a political hassle with a proposed new election law* (Newsweek). **3.** to supply with spawn (mycelium). [< Anglo-French *espaundre*, Old French *espandre* < Latin *expandere* spread out. Doublet of EXPAND.] —**spawn′er,** *n.*
—**Syn.** *n.* **1. a.** roe. **2.** progeny.
spawn·ing bed (spô′ning), a bed or nest made by salmon, trout, etc., in the bottom of a stream to deposit their spawn and milt.
spawning ground, 1. the place where fish spawn or to which they return to spawn. **2.** a place in which something commonly originates; breeding place: *Boxing's spawning grounds, the neighborhood clubs, are . . . unable to compete with the fights on TV* (Newsweek).
spawning screen, a frame or screen on which the spawn of fish is collected.
spay[1] (spā), *v.t.* to remove the ovaries of (a female dog, etc.). [< Anglo-French *espeier* cut with a sword, ultimately < Old French *espee* sword, épée < Latin *spatha;* see SPATHE]
spay[2] (spā), *n. Archaic.* a male red deer in its third year. [origin unknown]
SPC (no periods), South Pacific Commission.
S.P.C.A., Society for the Prevention of Cruelty to Animals.
S.P.C.C., Society for the Prevention of Cruelty to Children.
SPD (no periods), Social Democratic Party, the socialist party of West Germany, founded originally in 1869.
speak (spēk), *v.,* **spoke** or (*Archaic*) **spake, spo·ken** or (*Archaic*) **spoke, speak·ing.** —*v.i.* **1.** to say words: talk; converse: *to speak with a stranger, to speak about something. Speak distinctly. We speak a hundred times for every once we write* (George Herbert Palmer). **2. a.** to make a speech: *Some lecturers speak without notes.* **b.** to deliver an argument, plea, etc.: *to speak against a bill before Congress. Speak softly and carry a big stick* (Theodore Roosevelt). **3.** to state or declare in written or printed words: *The daily press speaks to millions of people.* **4.** to tell; express: *Her eyes speak of suffering.* **5.** to express an idea, feeling, etc.; communicate: *Actions speak louder than words. For the heart must speak when the lips are dumb* (Kate P. Osgood). **6.** to give forth sound: *The violins spoke at the nod of the conductor. The cannons spoke.* **7.** (of dogs) to bark when told: *Speak for the candy, Fido.*
—*v.t.* **1.** to say or utter (a word or words): *No one spoke a word to him.* **2.** to tell or express in words or speech: *to speak nonsense, to speak the truth. On an occasion of this kind it becomes more than a moral duty to speak one's mind. It becomes a pleasure* (Oscar Wilde). **3.** to use (a language): *Do you speak French?* **4. a.** to reveal; indicate; make known: *The loud laugh that spoke the vacant mind* (Oliver Goldsmith). **b.** to indicate by expression: *His face spake hope, while deep his sorrows flow* (John Dryden). **5.** to speak to or with; converse; address: *One is terribly at the mercy of any surgeon-dentist; and I, for one, always speak them fair till I have got my mouth out of their clutches* (Elizabeth Gaskell). **6.** to communicate with (a passing vessel) at sea; hail. **7.** *Archaic.* to show to be; characterize: *His conduct speaks him honorable.*
so to speak, to speak in such a manner; to use that expression: *Pearl . . . was the leading spirit of the pair, and led Maud by the nose, so to speak* (J.S. Winter).
speak for, a. to speak in the interest of; represent: *Why don't you speak for yourself, John?* (Longfellow). *They are slaves who fear to speak For the fallen and the weak* (Lowell). **b.** to ask or apply for: *to speak for reserved seats ahead of time.*
speak of, to mention; refer to: *I shall have occasion to speak again of these books at the next session. Speaking of school, how do you like the new teacher?*
speak out or **up,** to speak loudly, clearly, or freely: *Speak out: what is it thou hast heard, or seen?* (Tennyson).
speak up (or **out**) **for,** to speak strongly on behalf or in defense of: *It's all very well for you to speak up for him . . . You'll get a fortune by him* (Dickens). *Two thirds said in next November's election they would vote for candidates who spoke out for peace* (Maclean's).
speak well for, to give a favorable idea of; be evidence in favor of: *Her behavior speaks well for her.*
to speak of, worth mentioning: *I have no complaints to speak of.*
[Old English *specan*]
—**Syn.** *v.i.* **1. Speak, talk** mean to say or use words. **Speak** suggests more formality than **talk** or, when applied to children, more fluency: *He spoke at the banquet. He talks readily on almost any subject. My little daughter is learning to talk, but she cannot really speak yet.* —*v.t.* **4. a.** betoken, denote. **b.** manifest.
speak·a·ble (spē′kə bəl), *adj.* that can be spoken.
speak·eas·y or **speak-eas·y** (spēk′ē′zē), *n., pl.* **-eas·ies.** *U.S. Slang.* a place where alcoholic liquors are sold contrary to law, especially one that sold such liquor by the drink during the period of national prohibition. [American English < *speak* + *easy* (perhaps because of the quiet nature of the conversation therein)]
speak·er (spē′kər), *n.* **1.** a person who speaks, especially one who speaks formally or skillfully before an audience; orator. **2.** any of various devices for reproducing sound, as in a radio, phonograph, television set, etc. See **phonograph** for picture. **3.** a book containing pieces for recitation or reading aloud.
the Speaker, the presiding officer of a legislative assembly, especially of the United States House of Representatives or the British House of Commons: *The Lord Chancellor need not be a member of the House of Lords of which he is the Speaker* (Law Times).
Speaker of the House, the presiding officer of the United States House of Representatives.
speak·er·ship (spē′kər ship), *n.* the office or position of Speaker in a legislative assembly.
speak·ing (spē′king), *n.* **1. a.** the act of a person who speaks; talking: *Within an hour from the time of my speaking* (Scott). **b.** a speech; talk; discourse: *So sweet his speaking sounded* (William Morris). **2.** the making of speeches: *public speaking, after-dinner speaking.*
—*adj.* **1.** that speaks; giving information as if by speech: *a speaking example of a thing.* **2.** used in, suited to, or involving speech: *within speaking distance, a speaking part in a play.* **3.** permitting conversation: *I hardly know our new neighbors; as a matter of fact I have only a speaking acquaintance with them.* **4.** highly expressive: *speaking eyes.* **5.** lifelike: *a speaking likeness.*
—**Syn.** *adj.* **4.** eloquent.
speaking trumpet, a device, shaped somewhat like a straight trumpet, for amplifying and directing sound, used at sea to communicate between vessel and vessel, to issue orders from the bridge during storms, etc.
speaking tube, 1. a tube or pipe for speaking, communicating orders, etc., from one room, building, etc., to another: *Many ships used to have speaking tubes from the bridge to the engine room.* **2.** a speaking trumpet.
speaking voice, the kind of voice used in speaking, as distinguished from the singing voice: *The man had a very clear speaking voice and could be heard throughout the hall.*
spean (spēn), *v.t. Scottish.* to wean.
spear[1] (spir), *n.* **1.** a weapon with a long shaft and a sharp-pointed head, sometimes barbed. Spears are for throwing or thrusting with the hand in hunting, fishing, warfare, etc. **2.** *Archaic.* a spearman.
—*v.t.* to pierce with a spear: *The Indian speared a fish. I think it a gain to be speared by a foe rather than to be stabbed by a friend* (Cardinal Newman). —*v.i.* to penetrate or pierce like a spear: *His reproachful gaze speared into my heart. Long shafts of light . . . spearing right down into the . . . night below* (Margaret Kennedy).
[Old English *spere*] —**spear′er,** *n.*
spear[2] (spir), *n.* a sprout or shoot of a plant: *asparagus spears. I lean and loaf at my ease observing a spear of summer grass* (Walt Whitman).
—*v.i.* to sprout or shoot into a long stem; germinate: *The first blades of grass speared out of the earth.* [earlier, a church spire, variant of *spire*[1]; perhaps influenced by *spear*[1]]
spear crowfoot, a yellow-flowered spearwort introduced into Newfoundland and Nova Scotia from Europe.
spear·fish (spir′fish′), *n., pl.* **-fish·es** or (*collectively*) **-fish.** any of various large, powerful, ocean fishes having a long, pointed beak or spear, related to the swordfishes, marlins, and sailfishes: *He said the spearfish weighed up to 1,000 lbs. and could travel through the water at 68 miles an hour* (London Times).
spear·fish·er·man (spir′fish′ər mən), *n., pl.* **-men.** a person skilled or engaged in spearfishing: *There is a growing tendency among expert spearfishermen . . . to use powerful spearguns charged with steel springs or compressed CO_2* (Time).
spear·fish·ing (spir′fish′ing), *n.* the sport of fishing with a spear or speargun.
spear grass, any of various grasses with a spearlike leaf, flower cluster, or other part, such as the couch grass.
spear·gun (spir′gun′), *n.* an underwater weapon used to shoot steel darts at fish. It operates by spring action like a crossbow or by the expansion of compressed carbon dioxide gas: *Spearguns are often used by scuba divers.*
spear·head (spir′hed′), *n.* **1.** the sharp-pointed striking end of a spear. **2.** the part that comes first in an attack, undertaking, etc., clearing a way for those that follow: *A spearhead of tanks and fighter planes led the infantry attack.*
—*v.t.* to lead or clear the way for; head: *He commanded the 505th Parachute Infantry Regiment, which spearheaded the allied assault in Sicily* (Newsweek). *The Chesapeake and Ohio Railway . . . is anxious to spearhead any program that will move more goods, more efficiently* (Time).
spear·man (spir′mən), *n., pl.* **-men.** a soldier, warrior, etc., armed with a spear: *Achilles was wounded by a spearman.*
spear·mint (spir′mint′), *n.* a common garden mint, a fragrant herb much used for flavoring, which yields a fragrant oil. [< *spear*[1] (perhaps because of the shape of the flowers) + *mint*[1]]

Spearmint

spear·point (spir′point′), *n.* **1.** the point of a spear; spearhead. **2.** a person or thing that acts as a spearhead: *He was the spearpoint of the new power growing up in the rural areas* (London Times). —*v.t.* to spearhead: *The new musical* *drama . . . will spearpoint the advance of this task force on the world tour* (New York Times).

spear side, the male line of descent: *Such and such qualities he got from a grandfather on the spear side* (Lowell).

spear thistle, the common thistle with lance-shaped leaves.

spear·wort (spir′wėrt′), *n.* any of several crowfoots with lance-shaped leaves, such as the spear crowfoot.

spear·y (spir′ē), *adj.* spearlike; sharp-pointed.

spec (spek), *n. Informal.* speculation (in financial matters).

spec., 1. a. special. **b.** specially. **2.** specification. **3.** specimen. **4.** spectrum.

spe·cial (spesh′əl), *adj.* **1.** of a particular kind; distinct from others; not general; certain: *money set aside for a special purpose, a desk with a special lock, a special edition of a book, special prices for the clearance sale. A play may be violent, full of motion; yet it has that special kind of repose which allows contemplation* (Tennessee Williams). **2.** more than ordinary; unusual; exceptional: *special care, a matter of special importance. Today's topic is of special interest.* **3.** for a particular person, thing, purpose, etc.: *to run special trains on holidays, a letter to be sent by special messenger, special permission to leave school early, a special correspondent from the Congo, a special application of a theory.* **4.** belonging exclusively to a person, thing, etc.: *a scholar's special field of knowledge, the special merits of a plan. Every country has its special attractions.* **5.** held in high regard; great; chief: *a special friend, a special favorite.* **6.** specific: *special instructions.*

—*n.* **1.** a special train, car, bus, etc. **2.** any special person or thing. **3. a.** a special edition of a newspaper. **b.** a special article in or communication to a newspaper: *A Washington special reports that President Kennedy has met with his advisers on the Berlin crisis.* **4.** *U.S.* a specially featured product, service, etc.; sale: *This week's special is ham and eggs.* **5.** a television show, produced especially for a single broadcast, usually out of the pattern of regular daily or weekly programs; spectacular.

[< Latin *speciālis* < *speciēs, -ēī* appearance; see SPECIES. Doublet of ESPECIAL.]

—**Syn.** *adj.* **1. Special, particular** mean not general, but belonging or relating to one person, thing, or group, as distinguished from others. **Special** implies being different from others of its kind: *Babies need special food.* **Particular** implies being or treated as being unique: *This particular brand of milk is sold only in one store. These synonym studies give both the general and particular meanings of words.*

special agent, an agent authorized to act for his principal only in a particular transaction or a particular kind of business, as distinguished from a general agent: *a special agent of the revenue department.*

special checking account, a checking account in which a minimum balance is not required. The depositor is usually charged a small fee for monthly service and for every check he uses.

special creation, the theory that the different species, or higher groups, of animals and plants were brought into existence at different times substantially as they now exist.

special delivery, the delivery of a letter or package by a special messenger rather than by the regular postman. Special delivery mail has much higher rates, but is handled faster and delivered sooner than regular mail.

special effects, illusory effects created by various techniques in a motion picture.

Special Forces, a unit of the U.S. Army whose members are trained in unconventional warfare, especially guerrilla and antiguerrilla fighting. Special Forces men wear green berets.

special handling, the handling and sending of fourth-class postal matter (parcel post) at a faster than normal rate, for an additional fee. It is not sent by special delivery.

spe·cial·ise (spesh′ə līz), *v.i., v.t.,* **-ised, -is·ing.** *Especially British.* specialize.

spe·cial·ism (spesh′ə liz əm), *n.* **1.** devotion or restriction to one particular branch of study, research, business, etc. **2.** a special study or investigation: *The ordinary layman . . . will find it difficult to understand why entrants to a university should not be asked to display how competent they are in a few subjects outside their specialisms* (London Times).

spe·cial·ist (spesh′ə list), *n.* **1.** a person who devotes or restricts himself to one particular branch of study, research, business, etc.: *a specialist in colonial American history.* **2.** a physician or surgeon who limits his practice to the study or treatment of particular diseases or a part of the body: *an eye specialist. Dr. White is a specialist in diseases of the nose and throat.* **3.** a broker on the floor of a stock exchange who is in charge of regulating the supply and demand of a particular security or securities and who executes special orders to buy or sell shares of that security. **4.** (in the U. S. Army) an enlisted man in a technical or administrative position, ranking below a corporal and above a private. —*adj.* specialistic: *specialist skills, products, etc.*

spe·cial·is·tic (spesh′ə lis′tik), *adj.* of or having to do with specialism or specialists.

spé·cia·li·té de la mai·son (spe′syä lē tā′ də lȧ me zôN′), *French.* specialty of the house: *There is also Le Drug Store on the Champs Elysées, where the spécialités de la maison are hamburgers* (Time).

spe·ci·al·i·ty (spesh′ē al′ə tē), *n., pl.* **-ties. 1.** special, limited, or particular character: *In the general ordinances . . . it would have been out of place because of its speciality* (James G. Murphy). **2.** a special quality or characteristic; distinctive property or feature of a thing; peculiarity: *Weather is a literary speciality, and no untrained hand can turn out a good article on it* (Mark Twain). **3.** a special point; particular; detail. **4.** *British.* a special pursuit, branch of study, product, etc.; specialty. [< Latin *speciālitās* < *speciālis;* see SPECIAL]

spe·cial·i·za·tion (spesh′ə lə zā′shən), *n.* **1.** a specializing. **2.** a being specialized.

spe·cial·ize (spesh′ə līz), *v.,* **-ized, -iz·ing.** —*v.i.* **1.** to pursue some special branch of study, research, work, etc.: *to specialize in American history. Many students specialize in engineering.* **2.** *Biology.* to become specialized. **3.** to go into particulars or details. —*v.t.* **1.** to make special or specific; give a special character, function, etc., to: *All the Allied infantrymen tend to become specialized, as machine gun men, and so on* (H. G. Wells). **2.** *Biology.* to adapt to a special function or environment: *a specialized organ. Lungs and gills are specialized for breathing.* **3.** to mention specially; specify. **4.** to endorse (a bill, note, draft, etc.) so that only one payee may receive payment. —**Syn.** *v.t.* **3.** particularize.

spe·cial·iz·er (spesh′ə lī′zər), *n.* a person who specializes; specialist.

spe·cial·ly (spesh′ə lē), *adv.* in a special manner or degree; particularly; unusually: *. . . Writing it almost as though they were creating a new language specially invented for the purposes of their poetry* (Manchester Guardian Weekly). —**Syn.** expressly.

spe·cial·ness (spesh′əl nis), *n.* the state or quality of being special: *As the boys grew up, they were conscious of their specialness and of their parents' earnest . . . attempts to shield them from photographers and other purveyors of publicity* (New Yorker).

special partner, a partner who invests a certain amount in a business and whose liability is no greater than the amount of his investment.

special plea, *Law.* a plea which does not answer the charge, but alleges some new fact on the basis of which the suit should be delayed or dismissed.

special pleading, 1. *Law.* a pleading that does not deny what is alleged by the opposition but claims that other or additional points deriving from the case will offset it. **2.** any pleading or arguing that ignores or sets aside points or features that are unfavorable to one's own side.

special sessions, a sitting or meeting of a court, council, legislature, etc., for an extraordinary purpose and outside of the usually appointed time.

spe·cial·ty (spesh′əl tē), *n., pl.* **-ties. 1. a.** a special line of work or business: *Steel manufacturing is a specialty of that region.* **b.** a special field or subject of study or research: *Linguistics is his specialty.* **2.** a product, article, etc., to which special attention is given, or for which a particular person or place is noted: *Children's clothes are a specialty in this store. Fine linen is a specialty of Ireland.* **3.** special character; special quality: *The specialty of Lincoln's wisdom made him one of the great leaders of history.* **4.** a special or particular characteristic; peculiarity: *A specialty of the tribe was its belief in one supreme god.* **5.** a special point or item; particular; detail. **6.** *Law.* a special contract, bond, obligation, etc., expressed in an instrument under seal. [earlier, special attachments; a mark of favor < Old French *especialte* < Latin *speciālitās;* see SPECIALITY]

specialty shop or **store,** a store, usually small, selling a more or less complete assortment of one kind of thing, as hats, or a limited number of closely related things, as books, cards, and stationery.

spe·ci·ate (spē′shē āt), *v.i.,* **-at·ed, -at·ing.** to form new species by evolutionary process: *Hybridization prevents races speciating* (New Scientist).

spe·ci·a·tion (spē′shē ā′shən), *n.* the formation of species by evolutionary process.

spe·cie (spē′shē), *n.* money in the form of coins, especially gold or silver coins; metal money.

in specie, a. in kind: *The power of the advocate, though . . . less in degree is in specie the same with the power of the judge* (Jeremy Bentham). **b.** in actual coin: *Our coin . . . whether we send it in specie . . . or . . . melt it down here to send it in bullion* (John Locke).

[earlier, coin < *in specie* in the real or actual form; in kind < Latin *in speciē* in kind, ablative of *speciēs* kind, form]

spe·cies (spē′shēz), *n., pl.* **-cies** (-shēz). **1.** *Biology.* a group of animals or plants, ranking next below a genus or subgenus, that have certain permanent characteristics in common: *Wheat is a species of grass.* **2.** a distinct kind or sort; kind; sort: *There are many species of advertisements. That species of writing which is called the marvellous* (Henry Fielding). *He fought for the species of freedom which is the most valuable* (Macaulay). **3.** *Logic.* **a.** a number of individuals having certain common characteristics or essential qualities and a common name. **b.** the individuals belonging to one species. **4. a.** the consecrated bread and wine used in the Mass. **b.** either of these elements.

the species, the human race: *The female of the species is more deadly than the male* (Rudyard Kipling).

[earlier, common properties marking a class < Latin *speciēs* kind, sort; (originally) appearance. Doublet of SPICE.]

spe·cies-spe·cif·ic (spē′shēz spi sif′ik), *adj.* limited in reaction or effect to one species: *Only recently it has become apparent that viruses, which had been thought to be species-specific, can cross from one species to another and thus spread disease* (New Scientist).

specif., specifically.

spec·i·fi·a·ble (spes′ə fī′ə bəl), *adj.* that can be specified: *He cannot even claim that specifiable laws of physics are violated* (Science).

spe·cif·ic (spi sif′ik), *adj.* **1.** definite; precise; particular: *a specific command or request, a specific sum of money. When you describe something, be specific.* **2.** specially belonging to and characteristic of a thing or group of things; peculiar (to): *A scaly skin is a specific feature of snakes.* **3.** *Medicine.* **a.** produced by a special cause or infection: *a specific disease.* **b.** effective in preventing or curing a particular disease: *a specific remedy.* **4.** *Biology.* of, having to do with, or characteristic of a species: *a specific name.*

—*n.* **1.** any specific statement, quality, subject, etc.: *He still doesn't know specifics on all issues, but his general knowledge is sharpening and his instincts are surer* (Birmingham Post-Herald). **2.** a cure for some particular disease; specific remedy: *Quinine is a specific for malaria.*

[< Late Latin *specificus* making up a species < Latin *speciēs* sort, kind + *facere* to make]

—**spe·cif′ic·ness,** *n.*

—**Syn.** *adj.* **1.** explicit. **2.** distinctive.

spe·cif·i·cal (spi sif′ə kəl), *adj.* specific.

spe·cif·i·cal·ly (spi sif′ə klē), *adv.* in a specific manner; definitely; particularly: *The doctor told her specifically not to eat eggs.*

spec·i·fi·ca·tion (spes′ə fə kā′shən), *n.* **1.** the act of specifying; definite mention; detailed statement of particulars: *The want ad made careful specification as to the requirements of the position.* **2. a.** a detailed description of the dimensions, materials, quantities, etc., for a building, road, dam, boat, etc. **b.** the document containing this. **3.** an article, item, or particular specified: *statements unsupported by specifications.* **4.** a description or definition according to specific or particular characters.

specific duty, a duty or tariff on a certain kind of article or on a given quantity of an article, without reference to its value or market price.

specific gravity, *Physics.* the ratio of weight of a given volume of a substance to that of an equal volume of some other substance taken as a standard, usually water at 4 degrees centigrade for solids and liquids, and hydrogen or air for gases. *Abbr.:* sp.gr.

specific heat, *Physics.* **1.** the number of calories of heat needed to raise the temperature of one gram of a given substance one degree centigrade. **2.** the ratio of the thermal capacity per unit mass of a given body to that of some body taken as a standard.

specific impulse, the thrust in pounds of a rocket motor or engine produced by burning one pound of a specified fuel with its oxidizer in one second.

spec·i·fic·i·ty (spes′ə fis′ə tē), *n.* **1.** the quality of having specific character or relation: *There has always been a certain lack of specificity about these fears; people have been bothered . . . without being able to say precisely why* (New Yorker). **2.** the quality of being specific in operation or effect: *It is also known that the protein coat determines the specificity of the virus, i.e., whether or not it will attack a certain bacterium* (Scientific American).

spec·i·fi·er (spes′ə fī′ər), *n.* a person who specifies.

spec·i·fy (spes′ə fī), *v.t.,* **-fied, -fy·ing. 1.** to mention or name definitely; state or describe in detail: *Did you specify any particular time for us to call? He delivered the paper as specified.* **2.** to include in a specification: *The contractor couldn't use shingles for the roof because slate was specified.* **3.** to give as a condition or requisite: *Punctuality was specified as the first requisite for the situation.* [< Old French *specifier,* learned borrowing from Late Latin *specificāre* < *specificus;* see SPECIFIC]

spec·i·men (spes′ə mən), *n.* **1.** one of a group or class taken to show what the others are like; single part, thing, etc., regarded as an example of its kind: *The statue is a fine specimen of Greek sculpture. He collects specimens of all kinds of rocks and minerals. Abbr.:* sp. **2.** a human being; person: *The tramp was a queer specimen.* —*adj.* taken or regarded as a specimen; typical: *a strong desire to see something more of Christendom than a specimen whaler or two* (Herman Melville). [< Latin *specimen, -inis* < *specere* to view] —**Syn.** *n.* **1.** instance. *-adj.* representative.

spe·ci·os·i·ty (spē′shē os′ə tē), *n., pl.* **-ties. 1.** the quality of being specious; speciousness: *Speciosity . . . usurps the place of reality . . . ; instead of performance, there is appearance of performance* (Thomas Carlyle). **2.** a specious act, appearance, remark, etc.

spe·cious (spē′shəs), *adj.* **1.** seeming desirable, reasonable, or probable, but not really so; apparently good or right, but without real merit: *a specious appearance of fair play. This specious reasoning is nevertheless false* (Thomas Hobbes). *The teacher saw through John's specious excuse.* **2.** making a good outward appearance in order to deceive: *His actions showed him to be nothing but a specious hypocrite.* **3.** *Archaic.* showy; beautiful; lovely. [< Latin *speciōsus* < *speciēs, -ēī* appearance] —**spe′cious·ly,** *adv.* —**spe′cious·ness,** *n.*

speck (spek), *n.* **1.** a small spot or mark; stain: *Can you clean the specks off this wall? In beauty faults conspicuous grow, The smallest speck is seen on snow* (John Gay). **2.** a tiny bit; particle: *a speck of dust, to have a speck in one's eye. He has not a speck of humor or of sense.* —*v.t.* to mark with or as with a speck or specks: *This fruit is badly specked.* [Old English *specca*] —**Syn.** *n.* **1.** speckle. **2.** mite.

speck·le (spek′əl), *n., v.,* **-led, -ling.** —*n.* a small spot or mark; speck: *a gray hen with white speckles.* —*v.t.* to mark with or as with speckles: *The Adventure of the Speckled Band* (Sir Arthur Conan Doyle). *That boy is speckled with freckles.* [probably < *speck* + *-le* (frequentative)]

speck·led trout (spek′əld), brook trout.

speckled wood, wood having speckled or mottled markings, as: **a.** the letterwood. **b.** palmyra wood when cut transversely into veneers.

speck·less (spek′lis), *adj.* free from specks; without blemishes: *I am still awed in recalling the perfection of the wine, its deep golden color, its speckless brilliance* (Atlantic).

speck·y (spek′ē), *adj.,* **speck·i·er, speck·i·est.** having specks or spots; slightly or partially spotted.

specs (speks), *n.pl. Informal.* spectacles.

spec·ta·cle (spek′tə kəl), *n.* **1.** a thing to look at; sight: *a charming spectacle of children at play, the spectacle of a storm at sea. A quarrel is an unpleasant spectacle.* **2.** a public show or display: *The big army parade was a fine spectacle.* **3.** a person or thing set before the public view as an object of curiosity, contempt, wonder, or admiration.

make a spectacle of oneself, to behave foolishly or crudely in public: *She was greatly embarrassed when her partner made a spectacle of himself on the dance floor.*

spectacles, a. a pair of glasses to help a person's sight or protect his eyes: *Spectacles and reading glasses are among the simplest and most useful of optical instruments* (David Brewster). **b.** a means or medium through which anything is viewed or regarded; point of view: *Subjects are to look upon the faults of princes with the spectacles of obedience and reverence* (John Donne). **c.** anything like spectacles, such as the device attached to a railway semaphore for displaying lights of different colors by means of colored glass, or the pattern of contrasting scales on the hood of a cobra: . . . *two varieties of cobra, one with the spectacles and the other without them* (E.M. Gordon).

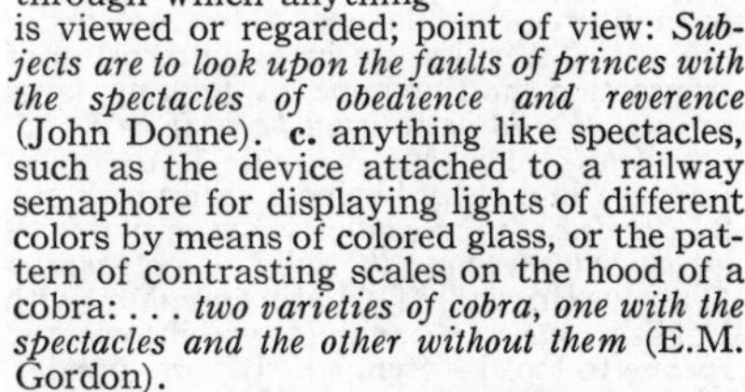

Spectacles (def. a)

[< Latin *spctāculum* < *spectāre* to watch (frequentative) < *specere* to view]
—**Syn. 2.** exhibition, parade, pageant.

spec·ta·cled (spek′tə kəld), *adj.* **1.** provided with or wearing spectacles: *a scholar spectacled and slippered* (Edward G. Bulwer-Lytton). **2.** having markings resembling spectacles: *the spectacled cobra.*

spectacled bear, a small black bear of the Andes, having a light-colored marking that looks like spectacles on the face.

spectacled snake, the cobra of India that commonly has a black and white marking like spectacles on the back of the hood.

spectacled warbler, a small European warbler resembling the whitethroat, with straw-colored legs and white markings around the eyes.

spec·tac·u·lar (spek tak′yə lər), *adj.* **1.** making a great display or show: *a spectacular display of wrath* (Arnold Bennett). *Motion pictures present spectacular scenes like battles, processions, storms, or races.* **2.** having to do with a spectacle or show.
—*n.* **1.** a spectacular display: *Our scientific studies of outer space . . . have easily matched those of the Soviet Union, notwithstanding the greater publicity given to the Soviet technological spectaculars* (Bulletin of Atomic Scientists). **2.** a lengthy television show, usually produced on an extravagant scale; special: *Its big feature . . . will be a series of costly and lavish ninety-minute "spectaculars" —opera, drama, musical comedy, circuses, ice shows, etc.* (New York Times).
—**Syn.** *adj.* **1.** showy. **2.** theatrical.

spec·tac·u·lar·i·ty (spek tak′yə lar′ə tē), *n.* spectacular quality or character.

spec·tac·u·lar·ly (spek tak′yə lər lē), *adv.* **1.** in a spectacular manner or degree. **2.** as a spectacle.

spec·tate (spek′tāt), *v.i.,* **-tat·ed, -tat·ing.** to be a spectator: *Hearing that a big match was under way here, . . . we repaired to the arena, and asked leave to spectate* (New Yorker). [back formation < *spectator*]

spec·ta·tion (spek tā′shən), *n.* spectatorship: *President Kennedy called upon Americans to spend less time in athletic spectation and more time in athletic participation* (George McNickle). [< Latin *spectātiō, -ōnis* < *spectāre;* see SPECTACLE]

spec·ta·tor (spek′tā tər, spek tā′-), *n.* **1.** a person who watches without taking part: *There were many spectators at the game. The Puritan hated bear-baiting, not because it gave pain to the bear, but because it gave pleasure to the spectators* (Macaulay). **2.** spectator pump. [< Latin *spectātor* < *spectāre;* see SPECTACLE] —**Syn.** observer, witness, onlooker, bystander.

spec·ta·to·ri·al (spek′tə tôr′ē əl, -tōr′-), *adj.* having to do with or characteristic of a spectator.

spec·ta·tor·ism (spek tā′tə riz′əm), *n.* the practice of being a spectator or onlooker at sports or games; spectatorship: . . . *a still-to-be-assessed turn from cool spectatorism to active involvement* (Harper's).

spec·ta·tor·i·tis (spek tā′tə rī′tis), *n.* excessive or undue spectatorism: *"Spectatoritis is the nation's No. 1 fitness problem," said Shane McCarthy, executive director of the President's Council on Youth Fitness* (Time).

spectator pump, a woman's sports pump with a medium or high heel, usually white but having a dark-colored heel and toe.

spec·ta·tor·ship (spek tā′tər ship), *n.* **1.** the act of watching as a spectator. **2.** the state or occupation of being a spectator.

spectator sport, a sport which usually attracts a large number of spectators, as distinguished from a sport, such as boating or hunting, in which more people participate than watch: *Baseball, football, and basketball rank high among the most popular spectator sports in the United States* (World Book Encyclopedia).

spec·ter (spek′tər), *n.* **1.** a phantom or ghost, especially one of a terrifying nature or appearance. **2.** a thing that causes terror or dread: *the grim specter of war.* [< Latin *spectrum* appearance; see SPECTRUM] —**Syn. 1.** See **ghost.**

specter of the Brocken, Brocken specter.

spec·tra (spek′trə), *n.* a plural of **spectrum.**

spec·tral (spek′trəl), *adj.* **1.** of or like a specter; ghostly: *the spectral form of a ship surrounded by fog. He saw the spectral form of the headless horseman.* **2. a.** of or produced by the spectrum: *spectral colors.* **b.** carried out or performed by means of the spectrum: *spectral analysis.* —**spec′tral·ly,** *adv.*

spectral class, any of the classes into which stars are divided on the basis of their spectra. Spectral classes range from very hot blue stars to very cool red stars.

spec·tral·i·ty (spek tral′ə tē), *n.* the quality or state of being spectral.

spec·tre (spek′tər), *n. Especially British.* specter.

spectro-, *combining form.* having to do with the spectrum or with spectrum analysis: *Spectroscope = an instrument for spectrum analysis. Spectrogram = a photograph of a spectrum.* [< *spectrum*]

spec·tro·bo·lom·e·ter (spek′trō bō lom′ə tər), *n.* an instrument consisting of a combined spectroscope and bolometer, used in determining the distribution of radiant heat or energy in a spectrum.

spec·tro·chem·i·cal (spek′trō kem′ə kəl), *adj.* of or having to do with spectrochemistry.

spec·tro·chem·is·try (spek′trō kem′ə strē), *n.* the branch of chemistry that deals with the techniques and findings of spectrum analysis.

spec·tro·gram (spek′trə gram), *n.* a photograph of a spectrum: *If the spectroscope is arranged for photographic observation, so the spectral lines can be photographed side by side on a film or plate, the instrument is called a spectrograph, and the picture a spectrogram* (Shortley and Williams).

spec·tro·graph (spek′trə graf, -gräf), *n.* **1.** a spectrogram. **2.** an instrument for photographing a spectrum.

spec·tro·graph·ic (spek′trə graf′ik), *adj.* of or by means of a spectrograph: *A spectrographic analysis of coffee leaves has been initiated to ascertain the specific needs of coffee trees* (New Scientist). —**spec′tro·graph′i·cal·ly,** *adv.*

spec·trog·ra·phy (spek trog′rə fē), *n.* the art of using the spectrograph.

spec·tro·he·li·o·gram (spek′trō hē′lē ə gram), *n.* a photograph of the sun taken with a spectroheliograph.

spec·tro·he·li·o·graph (spek′trō hē′lē ə graf, -gräf), *n.* an apparatus for photographing the sun with light of a single wave length, in order to show the details of various solar phenomena, such as sun spots, as they would appear if only one kind of light were emitted.

spec·tro·he·li·o·scope (spek'trō hē'lē ə-skōp), *n.* **1.** an instrument like the spectroheliograph but used for visual rather than photographic observations of the sun. **2.** a spectroheliograph.

spec·tro·log·i·cal (spek'trə loj'ə kəl), *adj.* of, having to do with, or determined by spectrology: *spectrological analysis.*

spec·trol·o·gy (spek trol'ə jē), *n.* the scientific study of spectra.

spec·trom·e·ter (spek trom'ə tər), *n.* a spectroscope especially adapted to measure deviations in wave lengths of spectra.

spec·tro·met·ric (spek'trə met'rik), *adj.* of or by means of a spectrometer.

spec·trom·e·try (spek trom'ə trē), *n.* **1.** the science that deals with the use of the spectrometer and the analysis of spectra. **2.** the use of the spectrometer.

spec·tro·pho·tom·e·ter (spek'trō fō-tom'ə tər), *n.* an instrument used to compare the intensities of two spectra, or the intensity of a given color with that of the corresponding color in a standard spectrum.

spec·tro·pho·to·met·ric (spek'trō fō'tə-met'rik), *adj.* of or by means of the spectrophotometer: *Kuiper, on the basis of his infrared spectrophotometric studies, finds that the Mars dusts resemble . . . felsite* (New Astronomy).

spec·tro·pho·to·met·ri·cal·ly (spek'trō-fō'tə met'rə klē), *adv.* by means of the spectrophotometer.

spec·tro·pho·tom·e·try (spek'trō fō-tom'ə trē), *n.* **1.** the science that deals with the use of the spectrophotometer. **2.** the use of the spectrophotometer.

spec·tro·scope (spek'trə skōp), *n.* an instrument for the production and examination of a spectrum of radiation from any source by the passage of rays through a prism or a grating: *With the possible exception of the telescope itself, no astronomical instrument has excelled the simple spectroscope in importance for our knowledge of the material universe* (Harlow Shapley).

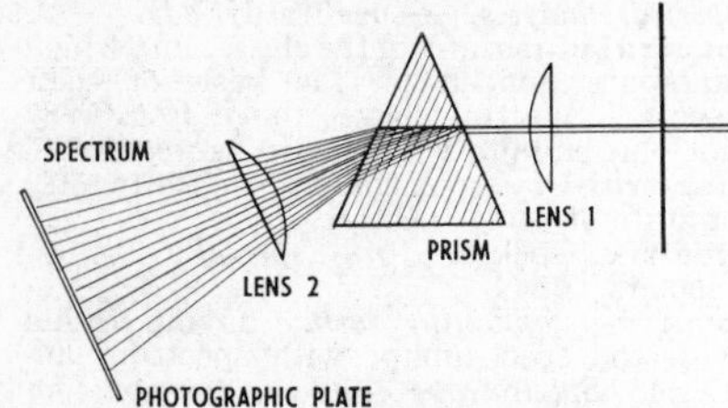

Spectroscope
Light ray enters spectroscope, where it passes through lens 1 and is refracted by prism and lens 2. The spectrum (red, orange, yellow, green, blue, indigo, and violet) is recorded on photographic plate.

spec·tro·scop·ic (spek'trə skop'ik), *adj.* of or having to do with the spectroscope or spectroscopy: *a spectroscopic prism. The principal results of the use of the spectroscopic method at Mount Wilson are contained in a list of the parallaxes of 1646 stars published recently* (Walter S. Adams). **—spec'tro·scop'i·cal·ly,** *adv.*

spec·tro·scop·i·cal (spek'trə skop'ə kəl), *adj.* spectroscopic.

spectroscopic binary, *Astronomy.* a binary whose two components are so close that they cannot be separated with a telescope and are known to exist only through spectrum analysis: *. . . examples of spectroscopic binaries among the brighter stars are Capella, Castor, and Algol* (Robert H. Baker).

spec·tros·co·pist (spek tros'kə pist, spek'-trə skō'-), *n.* a person skilled in spectroscopy.

spec·tros·co·py (spek tros'kə pē, spek'trə-skō'-), *n.* **1.** the science having to do with the examination and analysis of spectra. **2.** the use of the spectroscope.

spec·trum (spek'trəm), *n., pl.* **-tra** or **-trums. 1.** *Physics.* the band of colors formed when a beam of white light is broken up by being passed through a prism or by some other means. A rainbow has all the colors of the spectrum: red, orange, yellow, green, blue, indigo, and violet. **2.** the band of colors formed when any radiant energy is broken up. The ends of such a band are not visible to the eye, but are studied by photography, heat effects, etc.: *Unfortunately, the spectra of galaxies provide information only with regard to motion along our line of sight, not at right angles to it* (Sky and Telescope). **3.** the wave-length range between 30,000 meters and 3 centimeters; radio spectrum. **4.** range; scope; compass: *Hear . . . the full spectrum of sound the next time you visit your music dealer* (Atlantic). *This outstanding opportunity requires a scientific mind with a broad spectrum of electronic background* (Wall Street Journal). [< New Latin *spectrum* < Latin; see SPECTER]

spectrum analysis, the examination and study of bodies and substances by means of the spectra they form.

spec·u·la (spek'yə lə), *n.* a plural of **speculum.**

spec·u·lar (spek'yə lər), *adj.* **1.** of or like a mirror; reflecting. **2.** of, having to do with, or like a speculum. **3.** *Medicine.* by means of a speculum: *specular examination.* [< Latin *speculāris* < *speculum* mirror; see SPECULUM]

specular iron, hematite, especially in its brilliant crystalline form.

specular schist, a rock made up chiefly of quartz, specular iron ore, and mica.

spec·u·late (spek'yə lāt), *v.,* **-lat·ed, -lat·ing.** *—v.i.* **1.** to reflect; meditate; consider: *The philosopher speculated about time and space. She . . . speculated without reserve on the coming of many grandsons* (Rudyard Kipling). **2.** to buy or sell when there is a large risk, with the hope of making a profit from future price changes. **3.** to take part or invest in a risky business enterprise or transaction in the hope of making large profits: *Would he be what he is if he hadn't speculated?* (Dickens). *—v.t.* **1.** to invest (money) in a risky business enterprise, etc. **2.** *Obsolete.* to consider; contemplate: *If we do but speculate the folly . . . of avarice* (Thomas Browne). [< Latin *speculārī* (with English *-ate*[1]) < *specula* watchtower < *specere* to look] **—Syn.** *v.i.* **1.** pore, ponder.

spec·u·la·tion (spek'yə lā'shən), *n.* **1.** a speculating; thought; reflection; conjecture: *If the world were good for nothing else, it is a fine subject for speculation* (William Hazlitt). *Former speculations about electricity were often mere guesses. Science carries us into zones of speculation where there is no habitable city for the mind of man* (Robert Louis Stevenson). **2.** a buying or selling when there is a large risk, with the hope of making a profit from future price changes: *His speculations in unsound stocks made him poor.* **3.** a taking part in any risky business enterprise, transaction, etc.

spec·u·la·tist (spek'yə lā'tist), *n.* a person given to speculation or abstract reasoning: *a refining speculatist* (Edmund Burke).

spec·u·la·tive (spek'yə lā'tiv, -lə-), *adj.* **1.** thoughtful; reflective: *a speculative turn of mind.* **2.** theoretical rather than practical: *speculative knowledge.* **3.** risky. **4.** of or involving speculation in land, stocks, commodities, etc.: *speculative ventures in real estate, speculative buying of cotton futures.* **—spec'u·la'tive·ly,** *adv.* **—spec'u·la'tive·ness,** *n.* **—Syn. 2.** academic.

spec·u·la·tiv·ism (spek'yə lā'tə viz əm, -lə-), *n.* the tendency to speculation or theory, as opposed to experiment or practice.

spec·u·la·tor (spek'yə lā'tər), *n.* **1.** a person who speculates, usually in business or financial enterprises. **2.** a person who buys tickets for shows, games, etc., in advance, hoping to sell them later at a higher price. [< Latin *speculātor* explorer, spy < *speculārī;* see SPECULATE] **—Syn. 2.** scalper.

spec·u·la·to·ry (spek'yə lə tôr'ē, -tōr'-), *adj.* **1.** speculative. **2.** serving for observation; giving an outlook or view.

spec·u·lum (spek'yə ləm), *n., pl.* **-la** or **-lums. 1.** a mirror or reflector of polished metal: *A reflecting telescope contains a speculum.* **2.** a surgical instrument for enlarging an opening in order to examine a cavity. **3.** a patch of color on the wing of many ducks and certain other birds. In ducks it is often an iridescent green or blue. [< Latin *speculum* mirror < *specere* to view, look]

sped (sped), *v.* a past tense and a past participle of **speed:** *The police car sped down the road.*

speech (spēch), *n.* **1.** the act of speaking; uttering of words or sentences; talk: *Men . . . express their thoughts by speech* (George Berkeley). **2.** the power of speaking: *Animals lack speech. Pity the man who has no gift of speech* (A. W. H. Eaton). **3.** manner of speaking; dialect, language, or tongue: *His speech showed that he was a Southerner.* **4.** what is said; the words spoken: *We made the usual farewell speeches.* **5.** a public, usually formal, talk or address: *The President gave an excellent speech.* **6.** a number of lines spoken by an actor in a single sequence. **7.** the study and practice of the spoken language: *to take a course in speech.* **8.** *Archaic.* rumor; mention; report: *Dr. Clement, what's he? I have heard much speech of him* (Ben Jonson). [Old English *spǣc*]
—**Syn. 1.** discourse. **4.** utterance, remark, declaration. **5. Speech, address, oration** mean a talk made to an audience. **Speech** is the general word applying to a prepared or unprepared, formal or informal talk made for some purpose: *Most after-dinner speeches are dull.* **Address** means a prepared formal speech, usually of some importance or given on an important occasion: *Who gave your commencement address?* **Oration** means a formal address on a special occasion, and suggests artistic style, dignity, and eloquence: *Daniel Webster's speech defending the Compromise of 1850 is a famous oration.*

speech area, the area in which a particular language or dialect is spoken.

speech clinic, a clinic where speech disorders, such as lisping, stuttering, etc., are treated.

speech community, a group of people who speak the same language or dialect: *A group of people who use the same system of speech signals is a speech community* (Leonard Bloomfield).

speech day, the periodical examination day of an English public school.

speech from the throne or **Speech from the Throne, 1.** a statement of foreign and domestic affairs and of the chief measures to be considered by the British Parliament or any legislative body in the British Commonwealth, read by the sovereign at the opening of parliamentary sessions; King's (or Queen's) speech. **2.** such a parliamentary statement by any sovereign or his representative: *There were no real surprises in the Speech from the Throne read by Hon. J. J. Bowlen, lieutenant-governor of Alberta, at opening ceremonies of the third session of the 12th Alberta legislature* (Grande Prairie, Alberta, Herald-Tribune).

speech·ful (spēch'fəl), *adj.* **1.** full of speech; loquacious. **2.** speaking or expressive. **—speech'ful·ness,** *n.*

speech·i·fi·er (spē'chə fī'ər), *n. Informal.* a person who speechifies.

speech·i·fy (spē'chə fī), *v.i.,* **-fied, -fy·ing.** *Informal.* to make a speech or speeches; orate: *A man always makes a fool of himself speechifying* (George Eliot). **—Syn.** harangue.

speech island, an area in which the people speak a different language from that spoken in the surrounding area.

speech·less (spēch'lis), *adj.* **1.** temporarily unable to speak: *George was speechless with anger.* **2.** not expressed in speech or words; silent: *. . . speechless pride and rapture* (Eugene Field). **3.** unable to speak; mute or dumb: *Today as a result of electronic developments . . . thousands of persons throughout the world who were once speechless can communicate again* (New York Times). **—speech'less·ness,** *n.* **—Syn. 1, 3.** See **dumb.**

speech·less·ly (spēch'lis lē), *adv.* **1.** without speaking. **2.** so as to be speechless.

speech·mak·er (spēch'mā'kər), *n.* a person who makes a speech or speeches, especially in public; orator: *If the speechmakers confined themselves to statements of true fact . . . maybe the ordinary citizen would not become so terribly confused on election day* (Wall Street Journal).

speech·mak·ing (spēch'mā'king), *n.* the act or fact of making or delivering a speech or speeches.

speech reading, lip reading.

speech sound, vocal utterance.

speech·way (spēch'wā'), *n.* a habit or way of speech peculiar to a certain people or region: *For it is a fact that Americans differ from one another in their speechways, as they differ in their modes of life and in their occupations* (Donald J. Lloyd).

speech·writ·er (spēch'rī'tər), *n.* a person

who writes speeches for another: *a presidential speechwriter.*

speed (spēd), *n., v.,* **sped** or **speed·ed, speed·ing.** —*n.* **1.** swift or rapid movement; quickness in moving from one place to another or in doing something: *to work with speed. He could run with the speed of a deer.* **2.** rate of movement: *to regulate the speed of machines. He drove the whole distance at full speed.* **3.** an arrangement of gears to give a certain rate of movement: *An automobile usually has three speeds forward and one backward.* **4.** *Baseball.* the ability of a pitcher to throw balls hard: *So many men are like the pitcher. Plenty of speed but poor control* (H. W. Raper). **5.** *Archaic.* good luck; success; prosperity: *The king wished us good speed* (Daniel Defoe). **6.** *Slang.* methamphetamine.
—*v.t.* **1.** to make go fast: *to speed a horse. Let's all help speed the work.* **2.** to send fast: *to speed reinforcements to the front.* **3.** to further the going or progress of: *Welcome the coming, speed the parting guest* (Alexander Pope). **4.** to help forward or further; promote: *to speed a bill through Congress, to speed an undertaking.* **5.** to give a certain speed to (a machine, etc.). **6.** *Archaic.* to give success or prosperity to: *God speed you.*
—*v.i.* **1.** to go fast; go faster than is safe or legal: *The car sped away at a breakneck clip. He was speeding when they caught up with him.* **2.** *Archaic.* to succeed; prosper; thrive: *The affair speeds well.*
speed up, to go or cause to go faster; increase in speed: *The United States has agreed to speed up delivery of 36 F-104 Starfighters to Jordan* (Manchester Guardian Weekly).
[Old English *spēd* luck, success, advancement]
—**Syn.** *n.* **1.** rapidity, celerity, quickness, haste. See **hurry.**

speed·ball (spēd′bôl′), *n. U.S.* **1.** a game resembling soccer except that a ball caught in the air can be passed or thrown with the hands. **2.** a fast ball pitched in baseball: *He still has his old speedball when he needs it, but he backs it up with a variety of curves* (Time). **3.** *Informal.* a person who moves quickly: *When it comes to work around the house, she isn't exactly a speedball.*

speed·ball·er (spēd′bôl′ər), *n. U.S.* a fast baller: *Ever since Cleveland's Pitcher Bob Feller burst on the baseball scene ... baseball scouts have combed the bushes and sandlots looking for another speedballer* (Time).

speed·boat (spēd′bōt′), *n.* a motorboat built to go fast, especially for use on lakes and rivers.

speed brake, any flap designed for slowing down an airplane in flight.

speed counter or **indicator,** any of various devices for indicating the speed of an engine, such as a tachometer, speedometer, etc.

speed demon, *Informal.* a speedster; one who enjoys moving at high speeds: *The Bonneville Salt Flats of Utah ... have a special fascination for a special kind of fanatic: the speed demon* (Time).

speed·er (spē′dər), *n.* a person or thing that speeds, especially a person who drives an automobile at a higher speed than is legal or safe: *the judge's crackdown on speeders.*

speed·i·ly (spē′də lē), *adv.* with speed; quickly; soon; rapidly.

speed·i·ness (spē′dē nis), *n.* speedy quality; quickness; rapidity.

speed·ing (spē′ding), *n.* the act of a person or thing that speeds, especially of a driver who exceeds the legal speed limit.

speed limit, the speed that a vehicle is forbidden by law or other regulation to exceed on a street, road, or highway, or part of it.

speed·om·e·ter (spē dom′ə tər), *n.* **1.** an instrument for indicating the speed of an automobile or other vehicle. **2.** a similar instrument for indicating distance traveled; odometer. **3.** a tachometer. [< *speed* + *-meter*]

speed reading, any of various systems for teaching or learning how to read rapidly, usually up to 400 words a minute: *In the past few years, "speed reading" has become a widespread technique for the rapid assimilation of the written word* (New Scientist).

speed skating, skating in competition, as in a race against others or as a contest of speed: *Almost as surprising as the sudden Soviet domination of speed skating was the Russian women skiers' performance* (Time).

speed·ster (spēd′stər), *n.* **1.** a person who drives, flies, etc., at high or reckless speed; speeder: *The speedsters, who pass each other on the autobahns at seventy-five and eighty miles an hour, were responsible ... for a tragic 21.7 per cent increase in accidents* (New York Times). **2.** a speedboat, racing or sports car, or the like: *The new ... pleasure line will include a 14-foot outboard, a 17-foot sports speedster ... and a 25-foot deluxe cabin cruiser* (Wall Street Journal). **3.** a very fast runner: *He watched speedsters ... place one-two in the 100-meter dash* (Newsweek).

speed trap, a section of a highway under constant surveillance by concealed patrolmen, electronic devices for measuring speed, etc., along which even the slightest infraction of the speed limit can be penalized.

speed-up (spēd′up′), *n.* an increase in speed as in some process or work: *Among the urgent areas for study, the report included an all-weather landing system ... speed-up of boarding and deplaning procedures, ... and better air traffic control procedures* (Science News Letter).

speed·walk (spēd′wôk′), *n.* a conveyor belt on a level or slight incline used to transport passengers a short distance; moving platform or sidewalk: *The Merrion centre also has a speedwalk 66 feet long for carrying shoppers up to first floor level* (Manchester Guardian).

speed·way (spēd′wā′), *n. U.S.* **1.** a highway over which motorists may drive at a constant, high speed. **2.** a track for motor racing: *Here is how they finished ... in the thirteenth annual 500-mile motor classic on the Indianapolis speedway yesterday* (Kansas City Star). [American English]

speed·well (spēd′wel), *n.* any of a group of small, low plants of the figwort family, with leafy stems and small blue, purple, pink, or white flowers; veronica.

Germander Speedwell (12 to 18 in. high)

Speed·writ·ing (spēd′rī′ting), *n. Trademark.* a shorthand system using letters of the alphabet instead of symbols, in which words are written as they sound. *Examples: You* is written as *u, are* is written as *r,* and *eye* is written as *i.*

speed·y (spē′dē), *adj.,* **speed·i·er, speed·i·est.** **1.** moving, going, or acting with speed: *Most of them [ponies] are small, wiry beasts, not very speedy* (Theodore Roosevelt). **2.** done with or characterized by speed; rapid; fast: *a speedy flight, speedy progress.* **3.** rapidly coming or brought to pass: *a speedy change.* **4.** coming, given, or arrived at quickly or soon; prompt: *a speedy reply, a speedy decision.*

speel (spēl), *Scottish.* —*v.i.* to climb; clamber. —*v.t.* to climb (a hill, tree, etc.): *Sma' heart hae I to speel the steep Parnassus* (Robert Burns). [origin uncertain]

speer or **speir** (spir), *Scottish.* —*v.i.* to make inquiries; ask: *Speer as little about him as he does about you* (Scott). —*v.t.* **1. a.** to make inquiries about. **b.** to ask for (advice). **c.** to beg (leave). **2.** to seek (out) by inquiry: *Oh that people would speer out Christ!* (Samuel Rutherford). Also, **spier.** [Old English *spyrian* ask about; (originally) seek, follow (or make) a track. Related to SPOOR.]

speiss (spīs), *n.* an impure metallic compound of arsenic or antimony, often containing nickel, cobalt, iron, etc., produced in the smelting of certain ores. [< German *Speise* speiss; (originally) food < Vulgar Latin *spēsa* < Latin *exspēnsa,* feminine past participle of *expendere* weigh out; expend]

spe·le·an or **spe·lae·an** (spi lē′ən), *adj.* **1.** having to do with or like a cave: *spelean darkness.* **2.** living in or frequenting caves: *Those primitive spelean people who contended against and trapped the mammoth* (Fraser's). [< Latin *spēlaeum* cave (< Greek *spḗlaion*) + English *-an*]

spe·le·o·log·i·cal or **spe·lae·o·log·i·cal** (spē′lē ə loj′ə kəl), *adj.* of or having to do with speleology.

spe·le·ol·o·gist or **spe·lae·ol·o·gist** (spē′lē ol′ə jist), *n.* a person skilled in speleology.

spe·le·ol·o·gy or **spe·lae·ol·o·gy** (spē′lē ol′ə jē), *n.* the scientific study of caves. [< French *spéléologie* < Greek *spḗlaion* cave + French *-logie* -logy]

spell[1] (spel), *v.,* **spelled** or **spelt, spell·ing.** —*v.t.* **1.** to say, write, or signal the letters of (a word or syllable) in order: *"Cat" is easy to spell; "phthisis" is difficult.* **2.** (of letters) to make up or form (a word or syllable): *"K" "e" double "n" "e" "d" "y" spells Kennedy.* **3.** to amount to; mean: *Delay spells danger. I'd like to talk about five important lessons ... which I feel have made me a better catcher. Any one of them can spell the vital difference in a game* (Del Crandall). **4. a.** to read letter by letter; read very slowly or with difficulty: *to spell out a message. You spell out the words when you read the newspaper still* (Thackeray). **b.** to make (one's way) letter by letter in reading: *to spell one's way through a message.* **5.** to discover or make out by close study or observation: *to spell out the truth of a matter.* —*v.i.* to write or say the letters of a word or syllable in order: *She cannot spell well. A foolish opinion ... that we ought to spell exactly as we speak* (Jonathan Swift).
spell out, to explain thoroughly, step by step, carefully, and in detail: *The Defense Department proposed a new set of rules that would spell out in greater detail the costs a manufacturer may pass along to the Government* (Wall Street Journal).
[< Old French *espeller* < Germanic (compare Old High German *spellōn* to tell). Compare GOSPEL.]
—**Syn.** *v.t.* **3.** signify, imply, involve. **5.** discern.

spell[2] (spel), *n., v.,* **spelled, spell·ing.** —*n.* **1.** a word or set of words supposed to have magical powers; charm; incantation: *I'm a dealer in magic and spells* (William S. Gilbert). **2.** fascination; charm: *We were under the spell of the beautiful music.*
cast a spell on, a. to put under the influence of a spell; hex: *The witch cast an evil spell on Sleeping Beauty.* **b.** to influence or have an effect on someone as if he were put under a spell; fascinate: *The magic of the beautiful ballet cast a spell on the audience.*
under a spell, controlled by a spell; fascinated: *The explorer's story held the children under a spell.*
—*v.t.* to charm; bewitch.
[Old English *spell* story, discourse]

spell[3] (spel), *n., v.,* **spelled, spell·ing.** —*n.* **1.** a period of work or duty: *The sailor's spell at the wheel was four hours.* **2.** a period or time of anything; turn; bout: *a spell of coughing, a spell of crying.* **3.** a period of weather of a specified kind: *a spell of hot or cold weather.* **4.** the relief of one person by another in doing something. **5.** *U.S. Informal.* an attack or fit of illness or nervous excitement: *When Hepsy does get beat out she has spells, and she goes on awful* (Harriet Beecher Stowe). **6.** *U.S. Informal.* a brief period: *to rest for a spell. You hold on ... for a spell, and I'll be back* (Bret Harte). **7.** *Australian.* a rest.
[earlier, the relief gang, perhaps Old English *gespelia* a substitute; perhaps < verb]
—*v.t.* **1.** *Informal.* to work in place of (another) for a while; relieve: *to spell another person at rowing a boat.* **2.** *Australian.* to give a time of rest to; rest: *to spell a horse.*
—*v.i. Australian.* to take a time of rest.
[variant of Middle English *spelen,* Old English *spelian*]

spell·bind (spel′bīnd′), *v.t.,* **-bound, -bind·ing.** to make spellbound; fascinate; enchant.

spell·bind·er (spel′bīn′dər), *n. U.S.* a speaker who can hold his listeners spellbound.

spell·bound (spel′bound′), *adj.* bound by or as if by a spell; too interested to move; fascinated; enchanted; entranced: *There were moments when his wizardry held me spellbound* (New Yorker). [< *spell*[2] + *bound*[1]]

spell·er (spel′ər), *n.* **1.** a person who spells words: *a poor speller.* **2.** a book for teaching spelling; spelling book.

spell·ing (spel′ing), *n.* **1.** the writing or saying of the letters of a word in order. **2.** the way that a word is spelled: *"Ax" has two spellings, "ax" and "axe."* **3.** manner of writing or expressing words with letters; orthography: *An instance of futile classicism ... is the conventional spelling of the English language* (Thorstein Veblen).

spelling bee, *U.S.* a contest in spelling between two or more persons or sides.

spelling book, a book containing exercises or instructions in spelling; speller.

spelling match, *U.S.* spelling bee.

spelling pronunciation, pronunciation that conforms with the written form of a word when that differs from the usual spoken form, as the pronunciation of *often* with a t-sound because of the *t* in the spelling, or of *herb* with the h-sound because of the *h* in the spelling.

spelling reform, the regulation of the spelling of the words of a language according to systematic principles, to secure greater uniformity or simplicity or a more satisfactory representation of the sound of the spoken words.

spelt[1] (spelt), *v.* spelled; a past tense and a past participle of **spell**[1].

spelt[2] (spelt), *n.* a kind of wheat grown chiefly in Europe. It is now used mainly in developing new kinds of wheat. [Old English *spelt* < Late Latin *spelta*]

spel·ter (spel′tər), *n.* zinc, usually in the form of small bars. [origin uncertain. Compare Low German *spialter.*]

spe·lunk·er (spi lung′kər), *n.* a person who explores and maps caves as a hobby: *No spelunker with any respect for his own skill will venture into a perilous cave without . . . a climbing rope* (New Yorker). [< Latin *spelunca* cave (< Greek *spēlaion*)]

spe·lunk·ing (spi lung′king), *n.* the act or hobby of exploring and mapping caves.

spence (spens), *n. Archaic or Dialect.* **1.** a pantry. **2.** a cupboard. Also, **spense.** [short for Old French *despense*]

spen·cer[1] (spen′sər), *n.* a short coat or jacket for men or women, usually knitted. [< George John *Spencer,* second Earl Spencer, 1758-1834]

spen·cer[2] (spen′sər), *n.* a trysail. [origin uncertain]

Spen·ce·ri·an[1] (spen sir′ē ən), *adj.* of or having to do with the English philosopher Herbert Spencer, or his philosophy. —*n.* an adherent of the philosophy of Herbert Spencer.

Spen·ce·ri·an[2] (spen sir′ē ən), *adj.* of or having to do with a system of handwriting characterized by clearly formed, rounded letters that slant to the right. [< Platt R. *Spencer,* 1800-1864, an American penmanship expert, who originated it + *-ian*]

Spen·ce·ri·an·ism (spen sir′ē ə niz′əm), *n.* the philosophical views of Herbert Spencer or his followers. The basic idea is that the universe and all its phenomena can be explained in terms of an evolutionary process that operates mechanistically according to the laws of science.

spend (spend), *v.,* **spent, spend·ing.** —*v.t.* **1.** to pay out: *She spends three dollars a day for lunch and dinner.* **2.** to pass (time, one's life, etc.) in a particular manner, occupation, place, etc.: *to spend one's spare time reading, to spend a day at the beach. All his life had been spent confronting others with the truth about themselves* (Morris L. West). **3.** to use up; exhaust or consume by use; wear out: *The hurricane has spent its force. He spends himself in foolish activities.* **4.** to use (labor, material, thought, etc.) in a specified way: *Why do you spend many words and speak in many ways on this subject?* (Benjamin Jowett). **5.** to waste; squander: *He spent his fortune on horse racing.* **6.** to lose, as for a cause: *To royalize his blood, I spent mine own* (Shakespeare). —*v.i.* **1.** to pay out money: *Earn before you spend.* **2.** *Obsolete.* to be exhausted, consumed, or used up: *The sound spendeth, and is dissipated in the open air* (Francis Bacon). [Middle English *spenden,* Old English *-spendan,* as in *forspendan* use up < Latin *expendere.* Doublet of EXPEND.] —**spend′er,** *n.*

—**Syn.** *v.t.* **1. Spend, expend, disburse** mean to pay out money, time, effort, etc. **Spend** is the common word meaning to pay out money or other resources for some thing or purpose: *He spends all he earns.* **Expend,** more formal, emphasizes the idea of using up by spending sums or amounts, commonly large, that reduce or exhaust a fund: *She expends her energies on parties.* **Disburse,** formal or financial, means to pay out from a fund for expenses: *The treasurer reports what he disburses.*

spend·a·ble (spen′də bəl), *adj.* capable of being spent: *Traveler's checks are safe and spendable anywhere* (New Yorker).

spendable earnings or **income,** the amount left to a worker after taxes, social security, etc., have been deducted from his pay; net earnings.

spend·ing (spen′ding), *n.* expenditure: *Federal spending has become the main issue on which the tax-cut vote in the House will turn next week* (Wall Street Journal).

spending money, money used or available for small, miscellaneous expenses; pocket money.

spend·thrift (spend′thrift′), *n.* a person who spends wastefully or extravagantly; prodigal: *Fie, what a spendthrift is he of his tongue* (Shakespeare). —*adj.* extravagant with money; wasteful: *spendthrift ways.* —**Syn.** *adj.* improvident, thriftless.

Speng·ler·i·an (speng glir′ē ən), *adj.* of or having to do with the philosophy of Oswald Spengler, 1880-1936, who interpreted the history of mankind as a series of cultures completing identical cycles, the last of eight cultures being Western civilization. —*n.* a student or follower of Spengler's philosophy.

spense (spens), *n. Archaic or Dialect.* spence.

Spen·se·ri·an (spen sir′ē ən), *adj.* of, having to do with, or characteristic of Edmund Spenser or his work.
—*n.* **1.** a poet of the school of Spenser. **2.** a Spenserian stanza. **3.** a poem in the meter of the Spenserian stanza.

Spenserian sonnet, a sonnet in which the fourteen lines follow this special rhyme pattern: *ababbcbccdcdee.*

Spenserian stanza, the stanza used by Spenser in his *Faerie Queene,* consisting of eight iambic pentameter lines and a final Alexandrine, with three rhymes arranged thus: *ababbcbcc.*

spent (spent), *v.* the past tense and past participle of **spend:** *Saturday was spent in playing.* —*adj.* used up, exhausted, or worn out: *a spent swimmer, a spent horse.*

spe·os (spē′os), *n. Archaeology.* a temple or tomb excavated in solid rock. [< Greek *speos* cave]

sper·ling (spėr′ling), *n.* sparling.

sperm[1] (spėrm), *n., pl.* **sperm** or **sperms. 1.** the fluid of a male animal that fertilizes the eggs of the female; semen. **2.** one of the male sperm cells in it; spermatozoön. [< Late Latin *sperma* < Greek *spérma, -atos* seed < *speírein* to sow[1]]

sperm[2] (spėrm), *n.* **1.** spermaceti. **2.** a sperm whale. **3.** sperm oil. [short for *spermaceti*]

sper·ma·cet·i (spėr′mə set′ē, -sē′tē), *n.* a pale or whitish, waxy substance obtained from the oil in the head of the sperm whale and used in making fine candles, ointments, cosmetics, etc. [< Medieval Latin *sperma ceti* sperm of a whale < Late Latin *sperma* sperm[1], seed, and Latin *cētus* large sea animal < Greek *kētos*]

sper·ma·duct (spėr′mə dukt), *n.* an organ conveying sperm; a spermatic duct. [< New Latin *spermaductus* < Late Latin *sperma* sperm[1] + Latin *ductus* duct]

sper·ma·go·ni·um (spėr′mə gō′nē əm), *n., pl.* **-ni·a** (-nē ə). spermogonium.

sper·ma·ry (spėr′mər ē), *n., pl.* **-ries.** the organ or gland in which spermatozoa are generated in male animals; testis. [< New Latin *spermarium* < Late Latin *sperma;* see SPERM[1]]

sper·ma·the·ca (spėr′mə thē′kə), *n., pl.* **-cae** (-sē). a receptacle in the oviduct of many female invertebrates, for receiving and holding spermatozoa: *The female ant, along with the wasp and bee, possesses a spermatheca, a receptacle in which the male sperm is stored and kept alive for a lifetime, being withdrawn in infinitesimal quantity as needed* (Alfred L. Kroeber). [< Late Latin *sperma* (see SPERM[1]) + Greek *thḗkē* receptacle]

sper·ma·the·cal (spėr′mə thē′kəl), *adj.* of or having to do with a spermatheca.

sper·mat·ic (spėr mat′ik), *adj.* **1.** of or having to do with sperm; seminal; generative. **2.** containing, conveying, or producing sperm or seed; seminiferous. **3.** of or having to do with a spermary or testis.

spermatic cord, the cord by which the testicle is suspended within the scrotum, enclosing the vas deferens, the blood vessels and nerves of the testicle, etc., and extending to the groin.

spermatic fluid, semen.

sper·ma·tid (spėr′mə tid), *n.* a cell that develops into a spermatozoön. It results from the meiotic division of a secondary spermatocyte.

sper·ma·ti·um (spėr mā′shē əm), *n., pl.* **-ti·a** (-shē ə). **1.** the nonmotile male gamete that fuses with the carpogonium of the red algae. **2.** one of the tiny, cylindrical or rod-shaped bodies in certain lichens and fungi that are produced like spores in spermogonia. The spermatia are conjectured to be the male fertilizing organs. [< New Latin *spermatium* < Greek *spermátion* (diminutive) < *spérma* sperm[1], seed]

spermato-, *combining form.* seed; sperm: *Spermatocyte = a germ cell that produces spermatozoa. Spermatophyte = a plant that produces seeds.* [< Greek *spérma, -atos* sperm[1]]

sper·ma·to·cide (spėr′mə tə sīd, spėrmat′ə-), *n.* a substance that kills spermatozoa.

sper·ma·to·cyte (spėr′mə tə sīt), *n.* a germ cell that gives rise to spermatozoids or to spermatozoa. A primary spermatocyte divides by meiosis to form two secondary spermatocytes which, in turn, undergo meiosis to form spermatids which are converted into spermatozoa.

sper·ma·to·gen·e·sis (spėr′mə tə jen′ə-sis), *n.* the formation and development of spermatozoa.

sper·ma·to·ge·net·ic (spėr′mə tō jə net′-ik), *adj.* of or having to do with spermatogenesis.

sper·ma·to·gen·ic (spėr′mə tə jen′ik), *adj.* spermatogenetic.

sper·ma·tog·e·nous (spėr′mə toj′ə nəs), *adj.* producing spermatozoa.

sper·ma·to·go·ni·al (spėr′mə tə gō′nē əl), *adj.* of or having to do with a spermatogonium or spermatogonia.

sper·ma·to·go·ni·um (spėr′mə tə gō′nē-əm), *n., pl.* **-ni·a** (-nē ə). **1.** one of the primitive germ cells from which spermatocytes develop. **2.** spermogonium. [< New Latin *spermatogonium* < Greek *spérma, -atos* seed + a root *gen-* to bear]

sper·ma·toid (spėr′mə toid), *adj.* like sperm.

sper·ma·toph·o·ral (spėr′mə tof′ər əl), *adj.* of or having to do with a spermatophore.

sper·ma·to·phore (spėr′mə tə fôr, -fōr), *n.* a capsule or case containing many spermatozoa, produced by the male of many insects, mollusks, annelids, and some vertebrate animals.

sper·ma·toph·o·rous (spėr′mə tof′ə rəs), *adj.* spermatophoral.

sper·ma·to·phyte (spėr′mə tə fīt), *n.* any of a large group of plants that produce seeds. The spermatophytes are the most highly developed plants and form the largest division of the plant kingdom. They are divided into two groups, the angiosperms and the gymnosperms. Also, **spermophyte.**

sper·ma·to·phyt·ic (spėr′mə tə fit′ik), *adj.* of or having to do with a spermatophyte.

sper·ma·tor·rhe·a or **sper·ma·tor·rhoe·a** (spėr′mə tə rē′ə), *n.* an involuntary and frequent discharge of semen without orgasm. [< *spermato-* + Greek *rheîn* flow]

sper·ma·to·zo·al (spėr′mə tə zō′əl), *adj.* **1.** of or having to do with spermatozoa. **2.** like a spermatozoön.

sper·ma·to·zo·an (spėr′mə tə zō′ən), *adj.* spermatozoal.

sper·ma·to·zo·ic (spėr′mə tə zō′ik), *adj.* spermatozoal.

sper·ma·to·zo·id (spėr′mə tə zō′id), *n.* one of the tiny motile bodies produced in an antheridium by which the female organs are fertilized; antherozoid. [< *spermatozo*(on) + New Latin *-id,* a suffix meaning "belonging to"]

sper·ma·to·zo·oid (spėr′mə tə zō′oid), *n.* spermatozoid.

sper·ma·to·zo·ön (spėr′mə tə zō′ən), *n., pl.* **-zo·a** (-zō′ə). a male reproductive cell. A spermatozoön unites with an ovum to fertilize it. [< *spermato-* + Greek *zôion* animal]

sperm cell, a spermatozoön.

sper·mic (spėr′mik), *adj.* of or having to do with sperm or seed.

sper·mi·cide (spėr′mə sīd), *n.* spermatocide.

sper·min (spėr′min), *n.* spermine.

sper·mine (spėr′mēn, -min), *n.* a crystalline basic substance found in semen, sputum, yeast, and other substances. *Formula:* $C_{10}H_{26}N_4$

sperm·ism (spėr′miz əm), *n.* the theory or doctrine that the sperm or spermatozoön contains the whole germ of the future animal.

sperm·ist (spėr′mist), *n.* a person who supports or believes in spermism.

sper·mo·go·ni·um (spėr′mə gō′nē əm), *n., pl.* **-ni·a** (-nē ə). one of the cup-shaped cavities or receptacles in which the spermatia of certain lichens and fungi are produced; spermatogonium. Also, **spermagonium.** [< New Latin *spermogonium* < Greek *spérma* seed + a root *gen-* to bear]

sperm oil, a light-yellow oil from the head of the sperm whale, used for lubricating.

sper·mo·phile (spėr′mə fīl, -fil), *n.* any of various squirrellike burrowing rodents, including the ground squirrels and certain related forms that do much damage to crops. [< New Latin *spermophilus* < Greek *spérma* seed + *phílos* loving]

sper·mo·phyte (spėr′mə fīt), *n.* spermatophyte.

sper·mous (spėr′məs), *adj.* of or like sperm; spermatic.

sperm whale, a large, square-headed, toothed whale having a large cavity in its head filled with sperm oil and spermaceti, and sometimes forming ambergris in its alimentary canal; cachalot.

Sperm Whale (to 60 ft. long)

sper·ry·lite (sper′ē līt), *n.* a mineral, an arsenide of platinum, occurring in minute, silvery white, isometric crystals. It is the only compound of platinum known to occur in nature. *Formula:* $PtAs_2$ [< Francis L. *Sperry,* a Canadian scientist of the 1800's who discovered it near Sudbury, Ontario + *-lite*]

spes·sart·ite (spes′ər tīt), *n.* **1.** a variety of garnet that is red or yellowish-red in color. *Formula:* $Mn_3Al_2(SiO_4)_3$ **2.** a basic intrusive igneous rock. [alteration of French *spessartine* < *Spessart,* a district in Bavaria, where it was found]

spetch (spech), *n.* one of the waste pieces or parings of hide, leather, etc., used as a material for making glue, etc. [related to SPECK]

spew (spyü), *v.t., v.i.* to throw out; cast forth; vomit: *A crater-crust which may crack and spew fire any day* ... (Charlotte Brontë). *The encampment began to spew out men* (H. G. Wells). —*n.* something that is spewed; vomit. Also, **spue.** [Old English *spīwan*] —**spew′er,** *n*

spew·y (spyü′ē), *adj.,* **spew·i·er, spew·i·est.** exuding moisture; wet or moist: *spewy ground.*

sp. gr., specific gravity.

sphac·e·late (sfas′ə lāt), *v.t., v.i.,* **-lat·ed, -lat·ing.** to affect or be affected with gangrene; mortify: *Sometimes the ... swelling suddenly inflames and sphacelates* (Samuel Cooper). [< New Latin *sphacelare* (with English *-ate*[1]) < *sphacelus;* see SPHACELUS]

sphac·e·la·tion (sfas′ə lā′shən), *n.* an affecting or being affected with gangrene; mortification.

sphac·e·lous (sfas′ə ləs), *adj.* of or affected with sphacelus; gangrenous.

sphac·e·lus (sfas′ə ləs), *n.* **1.** a gangrenous or mortified tissue or part; slough. **2.** gangrene; mortification. [< New Latin *sphacelus* < Greek *sphákelos*]

sphag·nous (sfag′nəs), *adj.* **1.** consisting of or like sphagnum. **2.** producing sphagnum; full of sphagnum.

sphag·num (sfag′nəm), *n.* **1.** any of a group of soft mosses, found chiefly in boggy or swampy places: *Peat moss is one kind of sphagnum.* **2.** a mass or quantity of this moss used by florists in potting and packing plants, in surgery for making dressings for wounds, etc. [< New Latin *sphagnum* < Latin, a kind of moss < Greek *sphágnos* a spiny shrub]

sphal·er·ite (sfal′ə rīt, sfā′lə-), *n.* a native zinc sulfide, occurring both crystalline and massive; blende; zinc blende; blackjack: *The main ore mineral of zinc is sphalerite, or zinc blende, a compound of zinc with sulfur* (World Book Encyclopedia). *Formula:* ZnS [< Greek *sphalerós* deceptive, slippery (< *sphállein* overthrow, baffle) + English *-ite*[1]]

sphene (sfēn), *n.* the mineral titanite, especially in its yellowish or greenish variety. [< French *sphène* < Greek *sphēn, sphēnós* a wedge (because of its crystalline shape)]

sphe·nic (sfē′nik), *adj.* wedge-shaped.

sphenic number, a number that has three unequal prime factors.

sphe·no·don (sfē′nə don), *n.* a lizardlike reptile native to New Zealand; tuatara. It is the only remaining rhynchocephalian and has much in common with the forerunners of present-day reptiles. [< New Latin *Sphenodon* the genus name < Greek *sphēn* wedge + *odoús, odóntos* tooth]

sphe·no·graph·ic (sfē′nə graf′ik), *adj.* of or having to do with sphenography.

sphe·nog·ra·phy (sfē nog′rə fē), *n.* the study and description of cuneiform writings. [< Greek *sphēn* a wedge + English *-graphy*]

sphe·noid (sfē′noid), *adj.* **1.** wedge-shaped: *a sphenoid crystal.* **2.** of or having to do with a compound bone of the base of the skull.
—*n.* the sphenoid bone. [< New Latin *sphenoides* < Greek *sphēnoeidês* < *sphēn* wedge + *eîdos* form]

sphe·noi·dal (sfi noi′dəl), *adj.* sphenoid.

spher·al (sfir′əl), *adj.* **1.** spherical. **2.** symmetrically rounded, or perfect: *The poet, whose verses are to be spheral and complete* ... (Emerson).

sphe·ral·i·ty (sfi ral′ə tē), *n.* spheral or spherical quality or state; sphericality.

sphere (sfir), *n., v.,* **sphered, spher·ing.** —*n.* **1. a.** a round geometrical body whose surface is equally distant at all points from the center. **b.** any rounded body approximately of this form; globe; ball: *the world's storm-troubled sphere* (Emily Brontë). **2.** any of the stars or planets: *The earth, sun, and moon are spheres.* **3.** a supposed hollow globe, with the earth at its center, enclosing the stars, sun, and planets; celestial sphere. **4. a.** any of a series of such globes, one inside another, in which the stars and planets were supposed by ancient astronomers to be set. Movement of the spheres was believed to cause the stars and planets to revolve around the earth and produce a harmonious sound known as the music of the spheres. **b.** the particular sphere occupied by each of the fixed stars and planets. **5.** the heavens; the sky. **6.** the place or surroundings in which a person or thing exists, acts, works, etc.: *People used to say that woman's sphere was the home.* **7.** the whole province, domain, or range of a quality, thing, action, activity, etc.; extent; region: *Extending principles which belong altogether to building, into the sphere of architecture proper* (John Ruskin). **8.** a place, position, or rank in society: *the sphere of the aristocracy.*
—*v.t.* **1.** to enclose in or as if in a sphere; encircle; surround: *Mourners, sphered by their dark garb in a sacred and touching solitude* ... (William R. Alger). **2.** to make into a sphere. **3.** to place among the heavenly spheres; set aloft: *But thou art as a planet sphered above* (Shelley).
[< Late Latin *sphēra,* in Latin *sphaera* < Greek *sphaîra*] —**sphere′like′,** *adj.*

sphere·less (sfir′lis), *adj.* **1.** without spheres; starless. **2.** having no proper sphere; wandering.

sphere of influence, 1. a small and usually underdeveloped nation or geographical area over which a powerful nation exercises economic or political control, influence, etc.: *Southeast Asia is conceded to be Peking's natural sphere of influence* (New York Times). **2.** such economic or political control, influence, etc.: [*Several nations*] *are thought here to be ... opposing Washington's effort to retain a sphere of influence in Southeast Asia* (New York Times).

spher·ic (sfer′ik), *adj.* spherical: **a.** globular. **b.** formed in or on a sphere. **c.** of or having to do with a sphere or spheres.

spher·i·cal (sfer′ə kəl), *adj.* **1.** shaped like a sphere; globular. **2.** formed in or on a sphere: *spherical lines or figures.* **3.** of or having to do with a sphere or spheres; dealing with the properties of the sphere or spherical figures: *spherical geometry or trigonometry.* **4.** of or having to do with the heavenly spheres. **5.** *Astrology.* planetary.

spherical aberration, *Optics.* aberration of rays of light resulting in a blurred or indistinct image, and arising from the spherical shape of the lens or mirror: *Spherical aberration is found in all lenses bounded by spherical surfaces. The marginal portions of the lens bring rays of light to a shorter focus than the central region* (Scientific American).

spherical angle, *Geometry.* an angle formed by two intersecting arcs of great circles of a sphere.

spherical geometry, the branch of geometry that deals with figures formed on the surface of a sphere.

spher·i·cal·i·ty (sfer′ə kal′ə tē), *n.* spherical state or form.

spher·i·cal·ly (sfer′ə klē), *adv.* **1.** in the form of a sphere, or of part of a sphere. **2.** so as to be spherical.

spherical polygon, *Geometry.* a polygon formed on the surface of a sphere by arcs of great circles.

spherical sailing, the plotting of a ship's course in which allowance is made for the arc of the earth's curvature.

spherical triangle, *Geometry.* a triangle formed on the surface of a sphere by intersecting arcs of three great circles.

spherical trigonometry, the trigonometry of spherical triangles.

sphe·ric·i·ty (sfi ris′ə tē), *n., pl.* **-ties.** spherical form or quality; roundness: *The ideal of the well-rounded man is a meaningless ideal unless this sphericity means a fusion of knowledge to achieve balanced judgment and understanding* (Atlantic).

spher·ics[1] (sfer′iks), *n.* the study of figures, such as circles and triangles, formed on the surface of a sphere, comprising spherical geometry and trigonometry.

spher·ics[2] (sfer′iks), *n.* the study and detection of distant atmospheric disturbances by electronic instruments. [< (atmo)-*spheric* + *-s*[1]]

spher·i·form (sfir′ə fôrm), *adj.* formed or existing as a sphere; spherical.

sphe·roid (sfir′oid), *n.* a body shaped somewhat like a sphere, especially one formed by the revolution of an ellipse about one of its axes. See **prolate** for picture. —*adj.* spheroidal.

sphe·roi·dal (sfi roi′dəl), *adj.* **1.** shaped somewhat like a sphere. **2.** having to do with a spheroid or spheroids. —**sphe·roi′dal·ly,** *adv.*

sphe·roi·dic (sfi roi′dik), *adj.* spheroidal.

sphe·roi·dic·i·ty (sfir′oi dis′ə tē), *n.* the quality or state of being spheroidal.

sphe·roi·di·ty (sfi roi′də tē), *n.* spheroidicity.

sphe·rom·e·ter (sfi rom′ə tər), *n.* an instrument for measuring the curvature of spheres and curved surfaces. [< French *sphéromètre* < Greek *sphaîra* sphere + French *-mètre* -meter]

spher·u·lar (sfer′ů lər), *adj.* **1.** having the form of a spherule; resembling a spherule. **2.** of or having to do with spherulites; spherulitic.

spher·ule (sfer′ül), *n.* a small sphere or spherical body. [< Late Latin *sphērula* (diminutive) < *sphēra* sphere]

spher·u·lite (sfer′ů līt), *n.* a small, spherical, concretionary mass formed in certain igneous rocks. [< Late Latin *sphērula* (see SPHERULE) + English *-ite*[1]]

spher·u·lit·ic (sfer′ů lit′ik), *adj.* **1.** of or containing spherulites. **2.** like a spherulite.

spher·u·li·tize (sfer′ə lə tīz), *v.t.,* **-tized, -tiz·ing.** to change into spherulites; cause to assume a spherulitic form.

spher·y (sfir′ē), *adj.,* **spher·i·er, spher·i·est. 1.** spherical. **2.** like a heavenly body; starlike.

sphex (sfeks), *n.* any of a group of large digging or burrowing wasps. [< New Latin *Sphex* the genus name < Greek *sphēx* wasp]

sphinc·ter (sfingk′tər), *n.* a ringlike muscle that surrounds an opening or passage of the body, and can contract to close it. [< Late Latin *sphincter* < Greek *sphinktēr* < *sphíngein* to squeeze, bind]

sphinc·ter·al (sfingk′tər əl), *adj.* of or like a sphincter.

sphinc·te·ri·al (sfingk tir′ē əl), *adj.* sphincteral.

sphinc·ter·ic (sfingk ter′ik), *adj.* sphincteral.

sphin·gid (sfin′jid), *n.* any of a group of moths including the sphinx, sphinx moth, or hawk moth. —*adj.* of or belonging to this group. [< New Latin *Sphingidae* the family name < Latin *sphinx;* see SPHINX]

sphin·go·my·e·lin (sfing′gō mī′ə lin), *n.* any of a class of phosphatides found in the brain, kidney, liver, etc., consisting of choline, sphingosine, phosphoric acid, and a fatty acid. [< Greek *sphíngein* squeeze, bind + English *myelin*]

sphin·go·sine (sfing′gə sēn, -sin), *n.* a basic amino alcohol found in sphingomyelin, cerebroside, and ganglioside. [< *sphingo-*(myelin) + (cerebro)*si*(de) + *-ine*[2]]

Sphinx (sfingks), *n.* **1.** a huge stone statue with a man's head and a lion's body, near Cairo, Egypt. **2.** *Greek Mythology.* a monster with the head of a woman, the body of a lion, and wings. The Sphinx proposed a riddle to every passer-by and killed those unable to guess it. [< Latin *Sphinx* < Greek *Sphínx, Sphingós* < *sphíngein* squeeze, bind]

Sphinx (def. 2)

sphinx (sfingks), *n., pl.* **sphinx·es, sphin·ges** (sfin′jēz). **1.** a statue of a lion's body with the head of a man, ram, or hawk. Egyptian sphinxes usually have male heads and wingless bodies; in the Greek type the head is female and the body winged. **2.** a puzzling or mysterious person. **3.** a hawk moth. [< *Sphinx*] —**Syn. 2.** enigma.

sphinx·i·an (sfingk′sē ən), *adj.* of, like, or befitting a sphinx.

sphinx moth, a hawk moth; sphinx.

sphrag·ide (sfraj′id), *n.* Lemnian earth. [< Greek *sphrāgís, -îdos* seal, Lemnian earth bearing the seal of the priestess of Lemnos]

sphra·gis·tic (sfrə jis′tik), *adj.* of or having to do with engraved seals or signet rings: *The seals follow and illustrate the . . . successive styles of English sphragistic art* (Allan Wyon). [< Greek *sphrāgistós* stamped with the public seal (< *sphrāgís, -îdos* seal, signet) + English *-ic*]

sphra·gis·tics (sfrə jis′tiks), *n.* the study of engraved seals or signet rings.

sp. ht., specific heat.

sphyg·mic (sfig′mik), *adj.* of or having to do with the pulse. [< New Latin *sphygmicus* < Greek *sphygmikós* < *sphygmós* pulse[1]; see SPHYGMUS]

sphygmo-, *combining form.* the pulse; pulsation: *Sphygmograph = an instrument that records pulse beats.* [< Greek *sphygmós* throbbing, heartbeat; see SPHYGMUS]

sphyg·mo·gram (sfig′mə gram), *n.* a diagram of the pulse beats recorded by a sphygmograph.

sphyg·mo·graph (sfig′mə graf, -gräf), *n.* an instrument that records the rate, strength, etc., of the pulse by means of tracings; pulsimeter.

sphyg·mo·graph·ic (sfig′mə graf′ik), *adj.* of or by a sphygmograph.

sphyg·moid (sfig′moid), *adj.* resembling the pulse; pulselike.

sphyg·mo·ma·nom·e·ter (sfig′mō mə nom′ə tər), *n.* an instrument for measuring blood pressure, especially in an artery. [< *sphygmo-* + Greek *manós* at intervals + English *-meter*]

sphyg·mom·e·ter (sfig mom′ə tər), *n.* sphygmomanometer.

sphyg·mo·phone (sfig′mə fōn), *n.* an instrument that makes pulse beats audible.

sphyg·mo·scope (sfig′mə skōp), *n.* an instrument that makes pulse beats visible.

sphyg·mus (sfig′məs), *n.* the pulse. [< New Latin *sphygmus* < Greek *sphygmós* pulse[1]; a throbbing < *sphýzein* to beat, throb]

spi·ca (spī′kə), *n., pl.* **-cae** (-sē). **1.** *Botany.* a spike. **2.** *Surgery.* a spiral bandage with reversed turns. [< Latin *spīca* spike[2]. Doublet of SPIKE[2].]

Spi·ca (spī′kə), *n.* a bright star in the constellation Virgo: *Follow the curve of the Dipper's handle through Arcturus to Spica* (Zim and Baker). [< Latin *Spīca* (originally) spike[2]]

spic-and-span (spik′ən span′), *adj.* spick-and-span: *. . . handsome men and beautiful women, with their spic-and-span, smiling children* (Edmund Wilson).

spi·cate (spī′kāt), *adj.* **1.** *Botany.* **a.** having spikes: *a spicate plant.* **b.** arranged in spikes: *a spicate flower.* **2.** *Zoology.* having the form of a spike; pointed: *a spicate appendage.* [< Latin *spīcātus,* past participle of *spīcāre* furnish with spikes < *spīca* spike[2]; see SPICA]

spic·ca·to (spi kä′tō), *adj. Music.* separate; distinct; played with short, springing movements of the bow, achieving a staccato effect (a direction for violins, etc., marked with dots or little wedges above or below notes): *The scherzo . . . allowed Mr. Campoli to unfold long stretches of the most prodigious spiccato bowing* (London Times). [< Italian *spiccato,* (literally) past participle of *spiccare* to detach < *picco* peak]

spice (spīs), *n., v.,* **spiced, spic·ing.** —*n.* **1. a.** any of a group of pungent or aromatic vegetable substances, used as seasoning, preservatives, etc.: *Pepper, cinnamon, cloves, ginger, and nutmeg are common spices.* **b.** such substances considered collectively or as a material: *The dead . . . with precious gums and spice fragrant, and incorruptibly preserved* (Robert Southey). **2.** a spicy, fragrant odor. **3.** something that adds flavor or interest: *Variety is the spice of life.* **4.** a slight touch or trace: *The world loves a spice of wickedness* (Longfellow).
—*v.t.* **1.** to put a spice or spices in; season. **2.** to add flavor or interest to: *The principal spiced his speech with stories and jokes. . . . days of adventure, all the pleasanter for being spiced with danger* (W. H. Hudson).
[< Old French *espice, espece,* learned borrowings from Latin *speciēs* kind, sort; produce, especially spices. Doublet of SPECIES.]

spice·ber·ry (spīs′ber′ē, -bər-), *n., pl.* **-ries.** **1.** the North American wintergreen; checkerberry. **2.** a small tree of the myrtle family, grown in Florida and the West Indies for its edible, blackish or orange fruit.

spice box, a box for holding spices, especially a box enclosing several smaller boxes for holding the various spices used in cooking.

spice·bush (spīs′bu̇sh′), *n.* a North American shrub of the laurel family, with yellow flowers and spicy-smelling bark and leaves.

spice cake, a cake flavored with a mixture of spices.

spiced (spīst), *adj.* **1.** seasoned or flavored with spice: *spiced apples, spiced ham.* **2.** fragrant as if with spice; spicy: *spiced groves of ceaseless verdure* (Herman Melville).

spice·less (spīs′lis), *adj.* **1.** without spices: *a salad mixed with a spiceless dressing.* **2.** without flavor or interest: *. . . a little house with a garden, and spiceless bourgeois respectability* (Listener).

spic·er·y (spī′sər ē), *n., pl.* **-er·ies.** **1.** spices. **2.** spicy flavor or fragrance: *The pine forest exhaled the fresher spicery* (Bret Harte). **3.** *Obsolete.* a room or part of a house for keeping spices. [< Old French *espicerie* < *espice;* see SPICE]

spice tree, an evergreen tree of the laurel family, growing in Oregon and California, with aromatic leaves and a hard brown wood used in furniture and building.

spice·wood (spīs′wu̇d′), *n.* the spicebush.

spi·ci·form (spī′sə fôrm), *adj.* having the form of a spike. [< Latin *spīca* (see SPICA) + English *-form*]

spic·i·ly (spī′sə lē), *adv.* in a spicy manner; piquantly.

spic·i·ness (spī′sē nis), *n.* spicy flavor or smell.

spick-and-span (spik′ən span′), *adj.* **1.** neat and clean; spruce or smart; trim: *a spick-and-span room, apron, or uniform.* **2.** fresh or new; brand-new. [short for earlier *spick-and-span-new* new as a recently made spike and chip; *spick,* variant of *spike*[1]; *span-new* < Scandinavian (compare Old Icelandic *spān-nȳr* < *spānn* chip + *nȳr* new)]

spi·cose (spī′kōs), *adj.* spicous.

spi·cos·i·ty (spī kos′ə tē), *n.* the state of being spicous.

spi·cous (spī′kəs), *adj. Botany.* having spikes or ears like corn. [< New Latin *spicosus* < Latin *spīca* spike, ear]

spic·u·la[1] (spik′yə lə) *n., pl.* **-lae** (-lē). **1.** a spicule. **2.** a sharp-pointed crystal, especially of frost or ice. [< New Latin *spicula,* variant of Latin *spīculum* (diminutive) < *spīca;* see SPICA]

spic·u·la[2] (spik′yə lə), *n.* plural of **spiculum.**

spic·u·lar (spik′yə lər), *adj.* spiculate.

spic·u·late (spik′yə lāt, -lit), *adj.* **1.** having, consisting of, or covered with spicules. **2.** like a spicule; slender and sharp-pointed. [< New Latin *spiculatus,* past participle of *spiculare* provide with a spicula; see SPICULA[1]]

spic·ule (spik′yül), *n.* **1.** a small, slender, sharp-pointed piece, usually bony or crystalline. **2.** *Zoology.* one of the small, slender, calcareous or siliceous bodies that form the skeleton of a sponge. **3.** *Botany.* a small spike of flowers; spikelet. **4.** a small solar prominence. [< Latin *spīculum;* see SPICULUM]

spic·u·lum (spik′yə ləm), *n., pl.* **-la.** *Zoology.* **1.** a sharp-pointed process or formation, as a spine of an echinoderm. **2.** a spicule. [< Latin *spīculum* sharp point, dart (diminutive) < *spīca* spica, spike[2]]

spic·y (spī′sē), *adj.,* **spic·i·er, spic·i·est.** **1.** flavored with spice: *The cookies were rich and spicy.* **2.** like spice; sharp and fragrant: *Those apples have a spicy smell and taste.* **3.** lively and keen; spirited: *spicy, free-for-all discussion.* **4.** somewhat improper or indelicate: *a spicy joke.* **5.** producing spices; rich in spices: *on India's spicy shores* (William Cowper). —**Syn. 2.** aromatic. **4.** salacious.

spi·der (spī′dər), *n.* **1. a.** any of the wingless, eight-legged arachnids having an unsegmented cephalothorax and abdomen. Its abdominal spinnerets produce a silky thread for spinning webs to catch insects, making cocoons, etc. **b.** any of various similar arachnids, such as a harvestman (daddy-longlegs). **2.** a person or thing that resembles or suggests a spider in manner of catching prey, wily patience, etc.: *He was one of the kind sports call a spider, All wiry arms and legs* (Robert Frost). **3.** a small frying pan, originally one with short legs. **4.** *U.S.* a frame with three legs to support a pot or pan over a fire. **5.** a device for pulverizing the soil, to be attached to a cultivator. **6.** a highly flexible fiber ring which centers the voice coil of a loud speaker. [Middle English *spither,* unrecorded Old English *spīthra* < *spinnan* to spin] —**spi′der-like′,** *adj.*

Garden Spider (def. 1a) (Line shows actual length.)

spider bug, a heteropterous insect of the United States having a very slender body with threadlike middle and hind legs, and spinous forelegs adapted for seizing; stick bug.

spider crab, any of a group of crabs having long legs and retractable eyes, as a common variety found along the Atlantic Coast of the United States, and the giant crab of Japan. See **lithodid** for picture.

spi·der·let (spī′dər lit), *n.* a spiderling: *What worries me now is that those thick wisps might have contained a nestful of viable spiderlets* (Punch).

spider line, one of the threads of a spider's web used in forming the cross hairs of a telescope or the like.

spi·der·ling (spī′dər ling), *n.* a little or young spider.

spider mite, any of various mites parasitic on insects, birds, and other animals, and on plants.

spider monkey, any of a group of monkeys of South and Central America, having a long, slim body and limbs, a long, prehensile tail, and rudimentary thumbs or none at all. See **prehensile** for picture.

spider orchid, a European orchid with small brown flowers resembling a spider in shape.

spider phaeton, a lightweight, high carriage with a rear seat for a footman and a closed seat in front.

spider plant, spiderwort.

spider wasp, any wasp which stores its nest with spiders for its young.

spider web, **1.** the web spun by a spider; cobweb. See **web** for picture. **2.** any design or construction of interwoven lines or parts similar to a spiderweb: *Driving a rented car from Tempelhof Airport . . . I soon became lost in a spiderweb of new freeways* (New Yorker).

spi·der-web (spī′dər web′), *v.t.,* **-webbed, -web·bing.** to cover with a network resembling a spider web: *The Communists have spider-webbed southern China and Laos with roads leading to the Thai and Burmese borders* (Time).

spi·der·web·by (spī′dər web′ē), *adj.* **1.** covered with or having spider webs: *a spiderwebby old barn.* **2.** like a spider web: *Through the glass they can see the mountains descending, dark green where they are covered with spruce, spiderwebby where tall hardwoods stand leafless* (New Yorker).

spi·der·wort (spī′dər wėrt′), *n.* any of a group of erect or trailing plants that take root at the knots of their stems and bear clusters of blue, purple, or white flowers.

spiderwort family, a group of dicotyledonous herbs growing mostly in tropical or subtropical regions. The family includes the dayflower, wandering Jew, and spiderwort.

spi·der·y (spī′dər ē), *adj.* **1.** like the legs of a spider; long and thin: *a person with* *spidery arms.* **2.** suggesting a spider web or cobweb. **3.** full of, or infested with, spiders: *a spidery attic.*

spied (spīd), *v.* the past tense and past participle of **spy:** *The hunter spied the buck in the distance. Who spied on us?*

spie·gel (spē′gəl), *n.* spiegeleisen.

spie·gel·ei·sen (spē′gəl ī′zən), *n.* a crystalline and lustrous variety of pig iron containing 15 to 30 per cent of manganese, used in making steel. [< German *Spiegeleisen* < *Spiegel* mirror + *Eisen* iron]

spiegel iron, spiegeleisen.

spiel[1] (spēl), *U.S. Slang.* —*n.* **1.** a talk; speech; harangue, especially one of a cheap, noisy nature. **2.** any glib or wordy talk or speech; line: *a salesman's spiel.* [< the verb] —*v.i., v.t.* to talk; speak; say in or as a spiel: *He's always spieling about the "value of languages"* (Sinclair Lewis). [American English < German *spielen* to play]

spiel[2] or **'spiel** (spēl), *n. British, Canadian.* a curling match; bonspiel: *This year's 'spiel has produced the usual number of close contests* (Winnipeg Free Press). [short for *bonspiel*]

spiel·er[1] (spē′lər), *n. Slang.* **1.** *U.S.* a person who spiels. **2.** *Australian.* a card sharper or professional swindler.

spiel·er[2] or **'spiel·er** (spē′lər), *n. British, Canadian.* a player in a spiel or curling match; curler.

spi·er[1] (spī′ər), *n.* a spy.

spier[2] (spir), *v.i., v.t. Scottish.* speer.

spiff (spif), *v.i. Slang.* to make neat, spruce, or fine; dress neatly or smartly: *We flatter ourselves that we are spiffed out; at all events we've got our best dresses on* (William S. Gilbert). [origin unknown]

spiff·ing (spif′ing), *adj. Slang.* excellent; first-rate; very good: *We like to say that if he shaved his [head] he would make a spiffing monk* (Punch).

spif·fli·cate (spif′lə kāt), *v.t.,* **-cat·ed, -cat·ing.** *Informal.* spiflicate.

spiff·y (spif′ē), *adj.,* **spiff·i·er, spiff·i·est.** *Slang.* **1.** very enjoyable: *a spiffy time.* **2.** smart; neat; trim: *a spiffy appearance.*

spif·li·cate (spif′lə kāt), *v.t.,* **-cat·ed, -cat·ing.** *Informal.* **1.** to confound or dismay. **2.** to overcome; destroy; kill. [a coined word]

spif·li·ca·tion (spif′lə kā′shən), *n. Informal.* a spiflicating.

Spi·ge·li·an (spī jē′lē ən), *adj.* of or having to do with Spigelius, a Belgian anatomist and botanist at Padua.

Spigelian lobe, a small lobe on the upper, posterior side of the right lobe of the liver.

spig·ot (spig′ət), *n.* **1.** a valve for controlling the flow of water or other liquid from a pipe, tank, barrel, etc. **2.** *U.S.* a faucet. **3.** a peg or plug used to stop the small hole of a cask, barrel, etc.; bung. [Middle English *spigote;* origin unknown]

spike[1] (spīk), *n., v.,* **spiked, spik·ing.** —*n.* **1.** a large, strong nail or pin usually of iron, used for fastening rails to the ties. **2.** a sharp-pointed piece of metal, wood, etc., fastened in something with the point outward, as at the top of a wall, gate, or the like, for defense or to hinder passage. **3. a.** a young mackerel six or seven inches long. **b.** the antler of a young deer, when straight and without snag or tine. **4.** one of the metal points or sharp cleats, or a plate of them, attached to the sole of a shoe to prevent slipping. **5.** *Physics.* a sudden, sharp uprise or peak in a motion, voltage, current, etc.: *An infinitely sharp spike would have an energy uncertainty of zero* (Scientific American). **6.** any tip or high point on a linear graph: . . . *brain-wave patterns characterized by six- and 14-per-second spikes in the brain-wave tracing* (Science News Letter).

spikes, a pair of shoes fitted with spikes, used in baseball, track, and other sports to prevent slipping: *Wearing spikes is forbidden in football, since in this game spikes can cause serious injuries.*

—*v.t.* **1.** to fasten with spikes: *The men spiked the rails to the ties when laying the tracks.* **2.** to provide or fit with or as if with spikes: *Runners wear spiked shoes to keep from slipping.* **3.** to pierce with or as if with a spike. **4.** to injure (an opponent, player, etc.) with the spikes of one's shoes. **5.** to put (a cannon) out of operation by driving a spike into the opening where the powder is set off. **6.** to put an end or stop to; make useless; block; thwart: *The extra guard spiked the prisoner's attempt to escape.* **7.** *Informal.* to add alcoholic liquor to (a drink, etc.). —*v.i.* to project up or out like a spike. [< Scandinavian (compare Old Icelandic *spīkr*)] —**spike′like′,** *adj.*

spike[2] (spīk), *n.* **1.** an ear of grain. **2.** a long, pointed cluster of sessile flowers. [< Latin *spīca.* Doublet of SPICA.]

Spikes[2] Left, (def. 1); right, (def. 2)

spike buck, *U.S.* a male deer in its first or second year, when its antlers are in the form of straight spikes.

spiked heel (spīkt), spike heel.

spike heel, a high, usually narrow and tapered heel on a woman's dress shoe: *We had to have the floor grille made finer, so spike heels wouldn't get stuck* (New Yorker).

spike horn, 1. a deer's horn in the form of a spike. **2.** a spike buck: *From a few yards away an old ram and a young spike horn stared back at us, alert and curious, but unalarmed* (Atlantic).

spike lavender, a lavender native to the Mediterranean region, having spikes of pale-purple flowers and yielding an oil used in painting.

spike·let (spīk′lit), *n.* a small spike or flower cluster.

spike·nard (spīk′nərd, -närd), *n.* **1.** a sweet-smelling ointment used by the ancients. **2.** the fragrant East Indian plant yielding this substance; nard. **3.** a tall American herb of the ginseng family, having greenish flowers and a fragrant root. [< Medieval Latin *spica nardi* ear of nard < Latin *spīca* spica, and *nardus* nard]

spik·er (spī′kər), *n.* **1.** a person or thing that spikes. **2.** a workman who drives the spikes in the ties in laying railroad tracks.

spike rush, any of a group of plants of the sedge family, having simple stems with a solitary terminal spike and closely overlapping scales.

spikes (spīks), *n.pl.* See under **spike**[1], *n.*

spike team, *U.S.* a team of three draft animals, one leading the other two, that are harnessed abreast.

spik·i·ly (spī′kə lē), *adv.* in a spiky manner; like spikes.

spik·y (spī′kē), *adj.,* **spik·i·er, spik·i·est. 1.** having spikes; set with sharp, projecting points: *Being tough and spiky, cacti are relatively poor fodder* (Science News). **2.** having the shape of a spike.

spile (spīl), *n., v.,* **spiled, spil·ing.** —*n.* **1.** a peg or plug of wood used to stop the small hole of a cask or barrel; spigot; bung. **2.** *U.S.* a small wooden or metal spout for drawing off sap from the sugar maple. **3.** a heavy stake or beam driven into the ground as a support; pile.

—*v.t.* **1.** to stop up (a hole) with a plug. **2.** to provide (a tree) with a spile or spout. **3.** to furnish, strengthen, or support with stakes or piles. **4.** *Dialect.* to draw (liquid) from a cask by broaching.

[compare Middle Dutch *spīle* splinter, peg]

spil·i·kin (spil′ə kin), *n.* spillikin.

spil·ing (spī′ling), *n.* **1.** spiles; piling. **2.** the act of driving in spiles.

spill[1] (spil), *v.,* **spilled** or **spilt, spill·ing,** *n.* —*v.t.* **1.** to let (liquid or any matter in loose pieces) run or fall: *to spill milk or salt.* **2.** to scatter; disperse. **3.** to shed (blood), as in killing or wounding: *blood spilled on the battlefield.* **4.** to cause to fall from a horse, cart, boat, etc.: *The boat upset and spilled the boys into the water.* **5.** *Informal.* to make known; tell: *to spill a secret.* **6.** to let wind out of (a sail). —*v.i.* **1.** to fall or flow out: *Water spilled from the pail.* **2.** to become empty of wind: *The ship turned slowly to the wind, pitching and chopping as the sails were spilling* (Frederick Marryat).

—*n.* **1.** a spilling. **2.** the quantity spilled. **3.** *Informal.* a fall: *He got a bad spill trying to ride that horse.* **4.** *Informal.* a downpour (of rain). **5.** a spillway.

[Old English *spillan* destroy, kill] —**spill′er,** *n.* —**Syn.** *v.t.* **5.** divulge, disclose.

spill[2] (spil), *n.* **1.** a thin piece of wood, or a folded or twisted piece of paper, used to light a candle, pipe, etc.: *candle-lighters, or "spills" . . . of coloured paper* (Elizabeth Gaskell). **2.** a splinter; sliver. **3.** a pin or slender rod upon which anything turns; spindle. **4.** a spile; bung. [Middle English *spille.* Perhaps related to SPILE.]

spill·a·ble (spil′ə bəl), *adj.* that can be spilled.

spill·age (spil′ij), *n.* **1.** a spilling, as of liquid, food, etc.: *The food dishes should be about two inches high and have steep sides to prevent spillage* (Scientific American). **2.** what is spilled; amount spilled: . . . *eating the spillage of grain and fruit manhandled through the port by our laborers* (Harper's).

spil·li·kin (spil′ə kin), *n.* a jackstraw. Also, **spilikin.**

spillikins, the game of jackstraws: *I have heard that the Bishops play spillikins for cups of tea* (Punch).

[apparently a diminutive form of *spill*[2]]

spill·o·ver (spil′ō′vər), *n.* **1.** a spilling or running over, as beyond certain limits: *Inaccurately aimed low-power bombs could cause a spillover of nuclear destruction to civilian areas* (Bulletin of Atomic Scientists). **2.** something that spills over; overflow; overabundance: *Thus the idea of Australia becoming an outlet for the spillover of Asia is chimerical* (Julian Huxley).

spill·way (spil′wā′), *n.* a channel or passage for the escape of surplus water from a dam, river, etc.

spi·lo·site (spī′lə sīt), *n.* a greenish schistose rock resulting from metamorphism of slate. [< Greek *spîlos* spot, speck]

spilt (spilt), *v.* spilled; a past tense and a past participle of **spill**[1]: *Don't cry over spilt milk.* [*We*] . . . *are as water spilt on the ground, which cannot be gathered up again* (II Samuel 14:14).

spilth (spilth), *n. Archaic.* **1.** the act of spilling. **2.** something spilled.

spin (spin), *v.,* **spun** or (*Archaic*) **span, spun, spin·ning,** *n.* —*v.t.* **1.** to draw out and twist (cotton, flax, wool, etc.) into thread, either by hand or by machinery. **2.** to make (thread, yarn, etc.) by drawing out and twisting cotton, flax, wool, etc. **3.** to make (a thread, web, cocoon, etc.) by giving out from the body sticky material that hardens into thread: *A spider spins a web.* **4.** to make (glass, gold, etc.) into thread. **5.** to cause to turn or revolve rapidly: *When you spun tops and snapped marbles* (Emerson). **6. a.** to produce, evolve, or devise in a manner suggestive of spinning: *spinning their dark intrigues* (Benjamin Disraeli). **b.** to tell: *The old sailor used to spin yarns about adventures at sea.* **7.** to shape on a lathe or wheel. —*v.i.* **1.** to draw out and twist the fibers of cotton, flax, wool, etc., into thread. **2.** to produce a thread, web, cocoon, etc., from a sticky material, as spiders do. **3.** to turn or revolve rapidly: *The wheel spins round. Let the great world spin forever down the ringing grooves of change* (Tennyson). **4.** to feel dizzy or giddy: *My head is spinning.* **5.** to run, ride, drive, etc., rapidly: *The automobile spun over the smooth expressway.* **6.** to fish or troll with a spinning hook or lure.

spin off, a. to distribute shares in a new corporation among stockholders of a parent corporation: *Reports persist that Grayson-Robinson will spin off its Klein's stores early in the new year* (Wall Street Journal). **b.** to create or make separate, especially as a by-product or copy: *In fact, Willi Stoph recently replied to an earlier Kiesinger letter with a return missive demanding that Bonn . . . spin off West Berlin as an independent "free city"* (Time).

spin out, to make long and slow; draw out; prolong: *The old fisherman always spun out the tales of his adventures at sea.*

—*n.* **1.** a spinning. **2.** a rapid run, ride, drive, etc.: *Come for a spin on your bicycle.* **3.** a rapid turning around of an airplane as it falls. **4.** a twisting or spinning motion, as of a ball when thrown, struck, or delivered in a certain way. **5.** *Physics.* the angular momentum of an elementary nuclear particle. **6.** (in Australia) experience; fortune; luck: *I know you've 'ad a bad spin and . . . you're all on edge* (Ray Lawlor).

[Old English *spinnan*]

—**Syn.** *v.t.* **5,** *v.i.* **3.** twirl, whirl, rotate.

spi·na bi·fi·da (spī′nə bī′fə də), a congenital gap or cleft in the posterior wall of the spinal canal. [< New Latin *spina bifida* a bifid or cleft spine]

spi·na·ceous (spi nā′shəs), *adj.* **1.** of or like spinach. **2.** belonging to the family of plants that includes spinach. [< New Latin *Spinacia* the spinach family (< Medieval Latin *spinachia;* see SPINACH) + English *-ous*]

spin·ach (spin′ich, -ij), *n.* **1.** a plant of the goosefoot family, with green, succulent leaves that are boiled and eaten as a vegetable or used uncooked in a salad. **2.** the leaves. [< Old French *espinache*, or *espinage* < Medieval Latin *spinachia* < Spanish *espinaca*, probably ultimately < Arabic *'isbānākh*]

spi·nal (spī′nəl), *adj.* **1.** of or having to do with the spine or backbone: *a spinal nerve, a spinal anesthetic.* **2.** resembling a spine in form or function: *a spinal ridge or hill.* **3.** of or having to do with spines or sharp-pointed parts or bodies. —*n. Informal.* a spinal anesthetic: *to administer a spinal.* [< Late Latin *spīnālis* < Latin *spīna;* see SPINE]

spinal anesthesia, anesthesia by injection into the spinal canal, affecting the lower part of the body and the legs.

spinal block, an obstructing of the flow of cerebrospinal fluid by the injection of an anesthetic into the nerves of the spinal canal.

spinal canal, the duct formed by the openings of the articulated vertebrae, containing the spinal cord.

spinal column, the backbone or spine.

spinal cord, the thick, whitish cord of nerve tissue in the backbone or spine, extending from the medulla oblongata through the spinal column. See **brain** for picture.

spinal marrow, the tissue of the spinal cord, found in the cavity running through the chain of vertebrae.

spinal tap, the removal of some cerebrospinal fluid from the base of the spine to analyze it for symptoms of brain or spinal disease or to replace it with an anesthetic.

spi·nate (spī′nāt), *adj.* bearing spines.

spi·na·tion (spī nā′shən), *n.* **1.** the condition of having spines. **2.** the arrangement of spines.

spin·dle (spin′dəl), *n., adj., v.,* **-dled, -dling.** —*n.* **1. a.** (in hand spinning) a round, usually wooden rod, tapering toward each end, that revolves and twists into thread the fibers drawn out from the bunch of wool, flax, etc., on the distaff. See **distaff** for picture. **b.** (on a spinning wheel) the rod used for twisting the thread and then for holding it when it is wound. **c.** (in a spinning machine) one of the many steel rods on which a bobbin is placed to hold the thread as it is spun. **2.** a certain quantity or measure of yarn, as 15,120 yards for cotton, and 14,400 yards for linen. **3. a.** a small axle, axis, shaft, arbor, or mandrel. **b.** either of the two shaftlike parts of a lathe that hold the work. **c.** a small shaft passing through a lock, upon which the knobs or handles are fitted. **4.** an iron rod or post fixed to a rock, reef, etc., to warn navigators. **5.** a hydrometer. **6.** something shaped like a spindle. **7.** *Biology.* the group of achromatic fibers joining the two newly formed nuclei during mitosis, and forming a rounded figure which tapers from the middle toward each end. **8.** one of the turned or circular, supporting parts of a baluster or stair rail.
—*adj.* of or like a spindle; rounded and tapering at each end; fusiform.
—*v.i.* **1.** to grow tall and thin. **2.** (of a plant) to shoot up or grow into a long, slender stalk or stem. —*v.t.* to form into the shape of a spindle.
[Middle English *spindel*, alteration of Old English *spinel*, related to *spinnan* to spin]

spindle cell, a spindle-shaped or fusiform cell: *Spindle cells found in the gill covers, chest and throat regions of the minnow Phoxinus laevis . . . were in fact closely associated with what seemed to be nerve fibers* (New Scientist).

spin·dle·ful (spin′dəl fu̇l), *n., pl.* **-fuls.** as much thread or yarn as a spindle can hold.

spin·dle-leg·ged (spin′dəl leg′id, -legd′), *adj.* having long, thin legs.

spin·dle·legs (spin′dəl legz′), *n.pl.* **1.** long, thin legs. **2.** *Informal.* a person with long, thin legs.
➔ **Spindlelegs,** meaning long, thin legs is plural in form and use: *The spindlelegs of that chair are shaky.* When the meaning is a person with long, thin legs, *spindlelegs* is plural in form and singular in use: *Spindlelegs, as the boys call John, is a good basketball player.*

spin·dle-shanked (spin′dəl shangkt′), *adj.* spindle-legged.

spin·dle·shanks (spin′dəl shangks′), *n.pl.* spindlelegs.

spindle side, the female side, or line of descent, of a family; distaff side.

spindle tree, any of a group of trees and shrubs of the staff-tree family, whose hard, fine-grained, yellowish wood was formerly much used for spindles.

spin·dling (spin′dling), *adj.* very long and slender; too tall and thin: *a weak, spindling plant.* —*n.* a spindling plant, animal, etc.

spin·dly (spin′dlē), *adj.,* **-dli·er, -dli·est.** spindling: *He strengthens his spindly shanks with rolls of white tape before each game* (Time).

spin·drift (spin′drift′), *n.* spray blown or dashed up from the waves: *It . . . began to blow with furious gusts which angrily tore the small waves of the inland sea into spindrift* (Norman Macleod). Also, **spoondrift.** [originally Scottish variant of *spoondrift*, probably < Scottish pronunciation of *spoon*] —**Syn.** scud.

spin dryer or **drier,** a dryer that forces water from washed clothes by centrifugal action.

spine (spīn), *n.* **1.** the series of bones down the middle of the back in man and other vertebrates; backbone. **2. a.** anything like a backbone; long, narrow ridge or support: *the spine of a mountain.* **b.** courage, determination, etc., as that by which a person is supported in the face of danger or adversity: *Threats merely stiffened his spine.* **3.** *Botany.* a stiff, sharp-pointed growth of woody tissue: *The cactus and hawthorn have spines.* **4.** *Zoology.* **a.** a stiff, pointed, thornlike part or projection: *A porcupine's spines are called quills.* **b.** a sharp, rigid fin ray of a fish. **c.** a spicule. **5.** a slender, pointed process, as of a bone. **6.** the supporting back portion of a book cover. [< Latin *spīna* (originally) thorn] —**spine′like′,** *adj.*

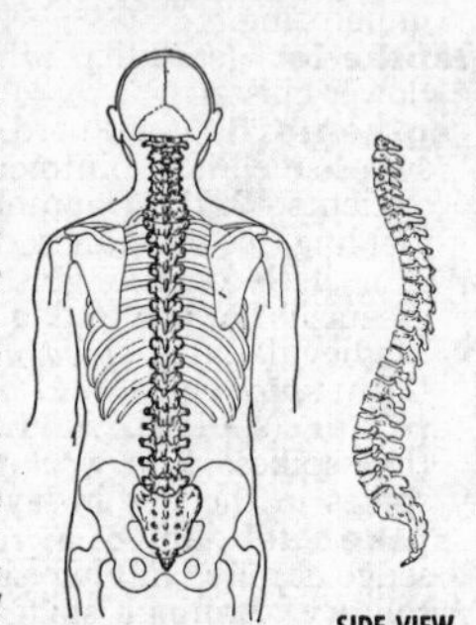

Spine (def. 1) of a human being

spine-chill·ing (spīn′chil′ing), *adj.* that causes the spine to tingle with chilling fright; terrifying; exciting: *Edgar Allan Poe wrote many spine-chilling short stories.*

spined (spīnd), *adj.* having a spine or spines.

spi·nel (spi nel′, spin′əl), *n.* a crystalline mineral, consisting chiefly of oxides of magnesium and aluminum, and occurring in various colors. Transparent spinel is used for jewelry. [< Middle French *spinelle* < Italian *spinella* < *spina* thorn < Latin *spīna;* see SPINE]

spine·less (spīn′lis), *adj.* **1.** without spines or sharp-pointed processes: *a spineless cactus.* **2.** having no spine or backbone: *a spineless animal.* **3.** having a weak or diseased spine; limp. **4.** without moral force, resolution, or courage; weak-willed; feeble: *She's just a poor, spineless creature.* —**spine′less·ly,** *adv.* —**spine′less·ness,** *n.* —**Syn. 4.** irresolute.

spi·nelle (spi nel′, spin′əl), *n.* spinel.

spinel ruby, a deep-red variety of the gem spinel.

spi·nes·cence (spī nes′əns), *n.* the condition of being spinescent.

spi·nes·cent (spī nes′ənt), *adj.* **1.** *Botany.* **a.** developing into, or ending in, a spine or thorn. **b.** bearing or covered with spines. **2.** *Zoology.* coarse and spinelike, as feathers or hair. [< Late Latin *spīnēscēns, -entis*, present participle of *spīnēscere* grow thorny < Latin *spīna;* see SPINE]

spin·et (spin′it, spi net′), *n.* **1.** an old-fashioned musical instrument like a small harpsichord. **2.** a compact upright piano. [< French *espinette* < Middle French < Italian *spinetta*, perhaps < Giovanni *Spinetti*, around 1500, an Italian inventor; perhaps < Latin *spīna;* see SPINE (because the strings were plucked with quills)]

Spinet (def. 1)

spine·tail (spīn′tāl′), *n.* any of various swifts (birds) having tail feathers with stiff, spinelike points.

spine-tailed (spīn′tāld′), *adj.* having stiff, spinelike points on the tail feathers.

spine-tin·gling (spīn′ting′gling), *adj.* spine-chilling: *This mission itself, its spine-tingling dangers* [*and*] *hairbreadth escapes, is worthy of an entire book* (Wall Street Journal).

spin fisherman, a person who engages in spin fishing: *There are large numbers of spin fishermen organized into clubs* (New York Times).

spin fishing, spinning.

spi·nif·er·ous (spī nif′ər əs), *adj.* having or covered with spines; spiny. [< Latin *spīnifer* (< *spīna;* see SPINE; + *ferre* to bear) + English *-ous*]

spin·i·fex (spin′ə feks), *n.* any of a group of Australian grasses with seeds that have elastic spines: *Spinifex is often planted on the seashore to hold down sand. The contest arises when a bunch of American oilmen arrive in Australia's spinifex country* (*so named for its tough desert grass*) (Time). [< New Latin *Spinifex* the genus name < Latin *spīna* thorn, spine + *facere* make]

spi·ni·form (spī′nə fôrm), *adj.* having the form of a spine; spinelike.

spi·nig·er·ous (spī nij′ər əs), *adj.* bearing spines; spiniferous.

spi·ni·grade (spī′nə grād), *adj.* moving by means of spines or spinous parts, as a starfish, sea urchin, etc. [< Latin *spīna* (see SPINE) + *gradī* to walk]

spin·i·ness (spī′nē nis), *n.* spiny quality or state.

spink (spingk), *n. Dialect.* the chaffinch (a European songbird). [imitative]

spin·na·ble (spin′ə bəl), *adj.* that can spin or be spun: *a spinnable fiber.*

spin·na·ker (spin′ə kər), *n.* a large, triangular sail set on the side opposite the mainsail on a yacht, sloop, etc., when sailing with the wind. [origin uncertain]

spinnaker boom, a long, light spar to which the foot of a spinnaker is attached.

spin·ner (spin′ər), *n.* **1.** a person, animal, or thing that spins: *I am a spinner of long yarns* (Hawthorne). **2.** a revolving hook or lure, especially a spoon, used in trolling or casting. **3.** a football maneuver or play in which the player receiving the ball from the center turns with his back to the line to fake or hand the ball to a teammate. **4.** *Aeronautics.* the conical or parabolic sheet of metal attached to and revolving with the propeller hub to reduce drag or air resistance. **5.** a cricket ball bowled with a spin: *Greensmith . . . pitched his spinners to the right spot* (London Times).

spin·ner·et (spin′ə ret), *n.* **1.** the organ by which spiders, and certain insect larvae such as silkworms, spin their threads for webs, cocoons, etc. **2.** Also, **spinnerette.** a small, metal device with tiny holes through which the viscous chemical solution is pressed out to form filaments or threads in the production of synthetic fibers: *The mechanical shaping of the polymer is accomplished by extruding the viscous fluid through minute orifices in a spinneret* (Scientific American). [< *spinner* + *-et*]

spin·ner·u·lar (spi ner′ů lər), *adj.* of or having to do with spinnerules.

spin·ner·ule (spin′ər ül), *n.* one of a number of tubules which collectively form the spinneret of a spider.

spin·ner·y (spin′ər ē), *n., pl.* **-ner·ies.** a mill, factory, etc., for spinning thread or yarn; spinning mill.

spin·ney (spin′ē), *n., pl.* **-neys.** *British.* a small wood with undergrowth, especially one preserved for sheltering game birds; small group of trees; thicket; copse: *He produces other maps . . . of larger and larger scale . . . where you can count every tree in a spinney* (Punch). Also, **spinny.** [< Old French *espinee*, ultimately < Latin *spīna;* see SPINE]

spin·ning (spin′ing), *adj.* that spins: *a spinning mill or machine.* —*n.* **1.** the act of a person or thing that spins. **2.** (in fishing) the sport or technique of casting with a very light line and a spinning reel: *Casting instruction will be available, without charge, for novices interested in fly-casting, bait-casting and spinning* (New York Times).

spinning jenny, an early type of spinning machine having several spindles, set in motion by a band from one wheel, whereby one person could spin a number of threads at the same time; jenny.

spinning reel, (in fishing) a nearly frictionless reel with a spool that points along the rod rather than at right angles to it, and allows the line at the end to run off without the spool revolving.

spinning wheel, a large wheel operated by hand or foot and having a spindle for spinning cotton, flax, wool, etc., into thread or yarn.

Spinning Wheel (early American)

spin·ny (spin′ē), *n., pl.* **-nies.** *British.* a spinney.

spi·node (spī′nōd), *n.* that point on a curve where a point generating the curve has its motion precisely reversed; cusp. [< Latin *spīna* (see SPINE) + English *node*]

spin-off (spin′ôf′, -of′), *n.* **1.** the distribution of the stocks of a new or subsidiary company among the stockholders of the controlling company: *On May 31, 1957, all the capital stock of Republic Industrial Corp. . . . was distributed by Barium Steel Corp. to its shareholders in a tax-free spin-off* (Wall Street Journal). **2.** the attempt to sell a new television series by showing one of its segments on another series. **3.** the by-products or fringe benefits of an operation; fallout: *Yet the reams of medical, astrophysical and even geological data produced as spin-off will probably not be fully analyzed even by the time the first astronauts set foot on the moon* (Science News Letter).

spi·nose (spī′nōs), *adj.* having or full of spines; thorny; spinous. [< Latin *spīnōsus* < *spīna* thorn] —**spi′nose·ly,** *adv.*

spi·nos·i·ty (spī nos′ə tē), *n., pl.* **-ties. 1.** a being spinous or spinose; thorniness; sharpness. **2.** a rude or disagreeable remark. **3.** a difficult argument or theory.

spi·nous (spī′nəs), *adj.* **1.** *Botany.* having or full of spines or thorns; thorny. **2.** *Zoology.* armed with or bearing spines or sharp-pointed processes: *The porcupine has a spinous back.* **3.** slender and sharp-pointed; spinelike; sharp. —**spi′nous·ness,** *n.*

spinous process, a process, especially of a vertebra, shaped like a spine or thorn.

Spi·no·zism (spi nō′ziz əm), *n.* the philosophy of Spinoza, essentially an expression of pantheism in which all reality consists of God (the Substance) in one or the other of two aspects (thought and extension, or mind and matter).

Spi·no·zist (spi nō′zist), *n.* an adherent of Spinozism.

Spin·o·zis·tic (spin′ō zis′tik), *adj.* of, having to do with, or characteristic of Spinoza or his followers: *Spinozistic pantheism.*

spin·ster (spin′stər), *n.* **1.** a woman, often elderly, who has not married; old maid: *a middle-aged spinster. He was a beau of all the elder ladies and superannuated spinsters* (Washington Irving). **2.** *British.* any girl or woman of marriageable age who has yet to marry (used since the 1600's as a legal description): *I, Anthony Lumpkin, Esquire . . . refuse you, Constantia Neville, spinster* (Oliver Goldsmith). **3.** a woman who spins flax, wool, etc., into thread: *the spinsters and the knitters in the sun* (Shakespeare). **4.** *Archaic.* any unmarried gentlewoman.

spin·ster·hood (spin′stər hu̇d), *n.* the state of being a spinster.

spin·ster·ish (spin′stər ish), *adj.* like or befitting a spinster: *a spinsterish high-necked dress* (Sinclair Lewis).

spin·ster·ly (spin′stər lē), *adj.* spinsterish.

spin·ster·ship (spin′stər ship), *n.* spinsterhood.

spin·stress (spin′stris), *n.* **1.** a woman spinner. **2.** a spinster.

spin·stry (spin′strē), *n.* the work or occupation of spinning.

spin·thar·i·scope (spin thar′ə skōp), *n.* an instrument in which the alpha particles emitted by radioactive substances are evidenced by the production of tiny sparks when the particles strike a fluorescent screen. [< Greek *spintharís* a spark + English *-scope*]

spin·thar·i·scop·ic (spin thar′ə skop′ik), *adj.* of or by means of a spinthariscope.

spin the bottle, a children's game of spinning a bottle and calling out the name of a player who must catch the bottle before it stops spinning.

spin·ther·ism (spin′thə riz əm), *n.* the sensation as of points of light dancing before the eyes. [< Greek *spinthḗr* spark + English *-ism*]

spin·u·late (spin′yə lāt, spīn′yə-), *adj.* *Zoology.* covered with little spines: *spinulate hairs.*

spin·u·lat·ed (spin′yə lā′tid, spīn′yə-), *adj.* spinulate.

spi·nule (spī′nyül, spin′yül), *n.* a small, sharp-pointed spine. [< Latin *spīnula* (diminutive) < *spīna* thorn, spine]

spin·u·les·cent (spin′yə les′ənt, spīn′yə-), *adj. Botany.* producing small spines; somewhat spiny. [< *spinul*(e) + *-escent*]

spin·u·lose (spin′yə lōs, spīn′yə-), *adj.* **1.** provided with spinules. **2.** spinulelike. —**spin′u·lose·ly,** *adv.*

spin·y (spī′nē), *adj.,* **spin·i·er, spin·i·est. 1.** covered with spines; having spines; thorny: *a spiny cactus, a spiny porcupine.* **2.** stiff and sharp-pointed; spinelike: *the spiny quills of a porcupine.* **3.** difficult; troublesome; thorny: *His spiny disposition made it difficult to approach him.*

spiny anteater, the echidna.

spiny dogfish, any of a family of small sharks with a spine in front of each dorsal fin.

spin·y-finned (spī′nē find′), *adj.* having fins with sharp, rigid, unsegmented rays: *The bass and perch are spiny-finned.*

spiny lobster, a lobster much like the usual kind but lacking the enlarged pair of claws; sea crayfish.

spin·y-rayed (spī′nē rād′), *adj.* spiny-finned.

spin·y-skinned (spī′nē skind′), *adj.* having or covered with skin consisting of spinelike projections; echinodermatous: *Like the familiar starfish, sea urchins, and sand dollars, they are in the general category of spiny-skinned animals known as echinoderms* (Science News Letter).

spi·ra·cle (spī′rə kəl, spir′ə-), *n.* **1.** an opening for breathing: *Insects take in air through tiny spiracles. A whale breathes through a spiracle in the top of its head. A shark or ray gives off water through a spiracle.* **2.** an opening in the ground by which underground vapors are given off; air hole. [< Latin *spīrāculum* < *spīrāre* to breathe]

spi·rac·u·lar (spī rak′yə lər), *adj.* **1.** of or having to do with spiracles. **2.** serving as a spiracle.

spi·rae·a (spī rē′ə), *n.* any of a group of shrubs of the rose family that have clusters of small white, pink, or red flowers with five petals. The bridal wreath and meadowsweet are two kinds. Also, **spirea.** [< Latin *spīraea* meadowsweet < Greek *speiraíā* privet < *speîra* coil]

spi·ral (spī′rəl), *n., adj., v.,* **-raled, -ral·ing** or (*especially British*) **-ralled, -ral·ling.** —*n.* **1.** a winding and gradually widening curve or coil: *A watch spring, the thread of a screw, and a bedspring are spirals.* **2.** one of the separate circles or coils of a spiral object. **3.** a continuous and expanding increase or decrease in prices, wages, employment, etc.: *an inflationary spiral, a deflationary spiral.* **4.** the descent of an aircraft in a spiral path. **5.** *Football.* a kick or pass in which the ball spins through the air on its longer axis.
—*adj.* **1.** winding or coiling around a fixed center while moving away or toward it; coiled; helical: *A snail's shell has a spiral shape.* **2.** having to do with or like a spiral or coil.
—*v.i.* **1.** to wind or move in a spiral: *There is no security for anyone in a spiraling arms race* (Saturday Review). **2.** (of an airplane) to descend in a spiral course. —*v.t.* to form into a spiral; approach in a spiral: *The plane spiraled the airport before landing.*
[< Medieval Latin *spiralis* < Latin *spīra* a coil < Greek *speîra*] —**spi′ral·ly,** *adv.*

spi·ral-bound (spī′rəl bound′), *adj.* with a binding consisting of a spiral coil of wire looping the pages together: *a spiral-bound notebook.*

spiral galaxy or **nebula,** a galaxy or nebula appearing as one or more spiraling streams issuing from a center: *Our Milky Way system seems to be a spiral galaxy, presumably very much resembling in outline and appearance the Great Spiral in Andromeda* (Bart J. Bok).

spi·ral·i·form (spī ral′ə fôrm), *adj.* **1.** having the form of a spiral. **2.** having to do with a type of decoration based on the spiral, common in primitive art, especially the Mycenaean in Greece and Crete.

spi·ral·i·ty (spī ral′ə tē), *n.* spiral quality; degree of being spiral.

spi·rant (spī′rənt), *n., adj. Phonetics.* fricative. [< Latin *spīrāns, -antis,* present participle of *spīrāre* to breathe]

spire[1] (spīr), *n., v.,* **spired, spir·ing.** —*n.* **1. a.** the top part of a tower or steeple that rises to a point: *The steeple, which has a spire to it, is placed in the middle of the church* (Laurence Sterne). **b.** a tall structure rising from a tower, roof, etc., and ending in a slender point; steeple: *that sweet city with her dreaming spires* (Matthew Arnold). **2.** anything tapered and pointed: *the spire of an icicle, a spire of flame, the spire of a sword.* **3.** the highest point of something; peak; summit: *The sunset shone on the rocky spires of the mountains. And, striving to be man, the worm mounts through all the spires of form* (Emerson). **4. a.** a young or tender shoot or sprout. **b.** a blade or shoot of grass, etc.; spear.
—*v.i.* to shoot up; rise into a spire: *The crowded firs spire from thy shores* (Samuel Taylor Coleridge). —*v.t.* to furnish with a spire or spires.
[Old English *spīr* spike, blade]

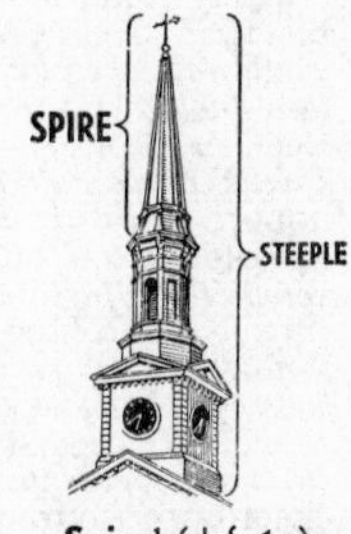

Spire[1] (def. 1a)

spire[2] (spīr), *n.* **1.** a coil; spiral. **2.** a single twist of a coil or spiral. **3.** the upper part of a spiral shell, excluding the body whorl. [< Latin *spīra* < Greek *speîra* coil]

spi·re·a (spī rē′ə), *n.* spiraea.

spired[1] (spīrd), *adj.* **1.** having a tapering, sharp-pointed top; peaked: *the spired roof of a silo.* **2.** having or carrying a spire: *a spired tower.*

spired[2] (spīrd), *adj.* having a spire or coil: *a spired shell.*

spire·like (spīr′līk′), *adj.* like a spire; tall and tapering: *These black spruces are spirelike trees with stiff, flat branches* (William O. Douglas).

spi·reme (spī′rēm), *n.* the chromatin of the nucleus of a cell when it assumes a threadlike form during mitosis. [< German *Spirem* < Greek *speírēma, -atos,* variant of *speirāma* a coiling < *speirâsthai* be coiled < *speîra* a coil]

spi·ri·cle (spī′rə kəl), *n. Botany.* one of the delicate coiled threads on the surface of certain seeds and fruits, which uncoil when wet. [< New Latin *spiricula,* diminutive of Latin *spīra* spire; see SPIRE[2]]

spi·rif·er·ous (spī rif′ər əs), *adj.* **1.** having a spire, as a univalve shell. **2.** having spiral appendages, as a brachiopod. [< Latin *spīra* (see SPIRE[2]) + English *-ferous*]

spi·ril·lum (spī ril′əm), *n., pl.* **-ril·la** (-ril′ə). **1.** any of a group of bacteria having long, rigid, spirally twisted forms and bearing a tuft of flagella. **2.** any of various similar microorganisms. See **microbe** for picture. [< New Latin *spirillum* < Latin *spīra;* see SPIRE[2]]

spir·it (spir′it), *n.* **1.** the immaterial part of man; soul: *He is present in spirit, though absent in body. And the spirit shall return unto God who gave it* (Ecclesiastes 12:7). **2.** man's moral, religious, or emotional nature: *Create in me a clean heart, O God; and . . . renew a right spirit within me* (Psalms 51:10). **3.** a supernatural being, such as a deity, fairy, elf, ghost, etc.: *an evil spirit. . . . the Spirit of Christmas Past* (Dickens). **4.** a person; personality: *He was one of the leading spirits of the New Deal. Robert E. Lee was a noble spirit.* **5.** an influence that stirs up and rouses: *a spirit of reform, the spirit of independence.* **6.** courage; vigor; liveliness: *a horse with great spirit, a man of spirit.* **7.** enthusiasm and loyalty: *school spirit.* **8. a.** the real meaning or intent: *The spirit of a law is more important than its words.* **b.** the prevailing character, quality, or tendency: *To act collectively is according to the spirit of our institutions* (Emerson). **9.** any of various mordant solutions used in dyeing, usually prepared from tin salts. **10.** *Chemistry, Obsolete.* a liquid essence or extract of a substance, especially one obtained by distillation. **11.** *Alchemy.* one of four substances: sulfur, sal ammoniac, mercury, or orpiment. **12. Spirit.** (in the belief of Christian Scientists) God.

out of spirits, sad; gloomy: *Who can be out of spirits in such weather?* (Edward G. Bulwer-Lytton).

spirits, a. a state of mind; disposition; temper; humor; mood: *He is in good spirits.* **b.** vigor; liveliness; cheerfulness: *The horse would roll when he was bringing him up from the stable; he's so full of spirits* (Harriet Beecher Stowe). **c.** a solution in alcohol: *spirits of camphor.* **d.** a strong alcoholic liquor: *He drinks beer and wine but no spirits.*

the Spirit, a. God: *The apostolic power with which the Spirit Has filled its elect vessels* (Shelley). **b.** the Holy Ghost: . . . *if ye through the Spirit do mortify the deeds of the body, ye shall live* (Romans 8:13).

—*v.t.* **1.** to carry (away or off) secretly: *The child has been spirited away.* **2.** to stir or cheer up; encourage; cheer. **3.** to produce as if by magic; conjure (up).

—*adj.* **1.** of or having to do with alcoholic spirits. **2.** of or having to do with spirits or spiritualism: *the spirit world.*

[< Latin *spīritus, -ūs* (originally) breath, related to *spīrāre* to breathe. Doublet of ESPRIT, SPRITE.]

—**Syn.** *n.* **3.** phantom, specter, apparition. **6.** animation, mettle, vivacity. **7.** ardor, zeal.

spir·it·ed (spir′ə tid), *adj.* **1.** having or showing spirit; lively; dashing; bold: *a spirited race horse. He entered into a spirited discussion concerning the relative merits of the imperishable Master of Baker Street* (Anthony Boucher). **2.** having a spirit or spirits: *good-spirited, mean-spirited, low-spirited.* —**spir′it·ed·ly,** *adv.* —**spir′it·ed·ness,** *n.* —**Syn. 1.** animated, mettlesome.

spirit gum, a quick-drying preparation of gum used by actors and others to glue false hair to the head or face.

spir·it·ism (spir′ə tiz əm), *n.* spiritualism.

spir·it·ist (spir′ə tist), *n.* a spiritualist.

spir·it·is·tic (spir′ə tis′tik), *adj.* spiritualistic: *Chicanery in the spiritistic field has long been recognized and long been a bane to those who attempt to examine under controlled conditions the reality of the alleged powers of telepathy and clairvoyance* (Science).

spirit lamp, a lamp in which alcohol is burned.

spir·it·less (spir′it lis), *adj.* without spirit or courage; without vigor; depressed; dejected: *tired, spiritless soldiers. The evening was passed in spiritless conversation* (Fanny Burney). —**spir′it·less·ly,** *adv.* —**spir′it·less·ness,** *n.*

spirit level, an instrument used to find out whether a surface is level. When the bubble of air in the alcohol-filled glass tube of a spirit level is exactly in the middle of the tube, the surface is level.

spir·i·to·so (spir′ə tō′sō), *adj. Music.* spirited; lively. [< Italian *spiritoso* < Vulgar Latin *spīritōsus* < Latin *spīritus;* see SPIRIT]

spir·it·ous (spir′ə təs), *adj.* **1.** *Archaic.* like an essence or distilled product: *One first matter all, Endued with various forms . . . But more refined, more spiritous and pure As nearer to him placed* (Milton). **2.** *Obsolete.* alcoholic; spirituous.

spirit rapping, rapping or knocking, believed to be a form of communication from or with spirits.

spir·its (spir′its), *n.pl.* See under **spirit,** *n.*

spirits or **spirit of hartshorn,** a water solution of ammonia.

spirits or **spirit of turpentine,** oil of turpentine.

spirits or **spirit of wine,** alcohol.

spir·i·tu·al (spir′ə chü əl), *adj.* **1.** of or having to do with the spirit or soul: *an outward and visible sign of an inward and spiritual grace given unto us* (Book of Common Prayer). **2.** caring much for things of the spirit or soul: *Great men are they who see that spiritual is stronger than any material force* (Emerson). **3.** of or having to do with spirits; supernatural: *Millions of spiritual creatures walk the earth unseen* (Milton). **4.** having to do with or belonging to the church: *spiritual lords.* **5.** sacred; religious: *spiritual writings, a spiritual order.* —*n.* a sacred song or hymn as originally created or interpreted by the Negroes of the southern United States: *While the Negro was being assimilated, however, America was adding such Negro contributions as jazz music and spirituals to its cultural store* (Ogburn and Nimkoff).

spirituals, a. matters primarily concerning religion or the church: *The civil power does best absolutely and unreservedly to ignore spirituals* (John Morley). **b.** spiritual matters, affairs, or ideas: *He [Dante] assigns supremacy to the pope in spirituals, and to the emperor in temporals* (James Russell Lowell).

[< Latin *spīrituālis* < *spīritus;* see SPIRIT] —**spir′i·tu·al·ly,** *adv.* —**spir′i·tu·al·ness,** *n.*

spir·i·tu·al·ism (spir′ə chü ə liz′əm), *n.* **1.** the belief that the spirits of the dead can hold communication with the living, especially through persons called mediums; spiritism. **2.** the doctrine that spirit alone is real. **3.** emphasis or insistence on the spiritual: *He often checked Seth's argumentative spiritualism by saying "Eh, it's a big mystery"* (George Eliot).

spir·i·tu·al·ist (spir′ə chü ə list), *n.* **1.** a person who believes that the dead communicate with the living. **2.** a believer in or adherent of spiritualism as a philosophical doctrine. **3.** a person who sees or interprets things from a spiritual point of view.

—*adj.* spiritualistic.

spir·i·tu·al·is·tic (spir′ə chü ə lis′tik), *adj.* of or having to do with spiritualism or spiritualists.

spir·i·tu·al·i·ty (spir′ə chü al′ə tē), *n., pl.* **-ties. 1.** devotion to spiritual instead of worldly things: *Prayer is, undoubtedly, the life and soul of spirituality* (John Jebb). **2.** the fact or quality of being spiritual; being neither corporeal nor material: *That He is invisible is accounted for by His spirituality* (James Tait). **3.** *Archaic.* the clergy: *He blamed both spirituality and laity* (John Strype).

spiritualities, a. spiritual things: *So these pretended successors of Peter . . . have notoriously imitated that example of Simon in buying and selling spiritualities* (Henry More). **b.** properties or revenues of the church or of a clergyman in his official capacity: *Their spiritualities, the tithes and oblations, were not to be taxed* (William Stubbs).

spir·i·tu·al·i·za·tion (spir′ə chü ə lə zā′shən), *n.* **1.** a spiritualizing. **2.** a being spiritualized.

spir·i·tu·al·ize (spir′ə chü ə līz), *v.t.,* **-ized, -iz·ing. 1.** to make spiritual. **2.** to give a spiritual sense or meaning to: *The works of Richardson . . . are romances as they would be spiritualized by a Methodist preacher* (Horace Walpole).

spir·i·tu·al·iz·er (spir′ə chü ə lī′zər), *n.* a person or thing that spiritualizes.

spir·i·tu·al-mind·ed (spir′ə chü əl mīn′did), *adj.* having the mind set on spiritual things; caring much for things of the spirit or soul —**spir′i·tu·al-mind′ed·ness,** *n.*

spir·i·tu·als (spir′ə chü əlz), *n.pl.* See under **spiritual,** *n.*

spir·i·tu·al·ty (spir′ə chü əl tē), *n., pl.* **-ties. 1.** Often, **spiritualties.** the property or revenue of the church or of a clergyman. **2.** the clergy.

spir·i·tu·el (spir′ə chü el′; *French* spē rē tʏ el′), *adj.* showing a refined mind or wit. [< French *spirituel* < Old French, learned borrowing from Latin *spīrituālis;* see SPIRITUAL]

spir·i·tu·elle (spir′ə chü el′; *French* spē-rē tʏ el′), *adj.* **1.** spirituel: *She has such a flow of spirits and of wit; . . . the most spirituelle creature I ever met with* (Mary Delany). **2.** delicate; graceful. [< French *spirituelle,* feminine of *spirituel;* see SPIRITUEL]

spir·i·tu·ous (spir′ə chü əs), *adj.* **1.** having to do with, containing, or like alcohol; alcoholic: *spirituous liquors.* **2.** distilled, not fermented. —**spir′it·u·ous·ness,** *n.*

spir·i·tus as·per (spir′ə təs as′pər), *Greek Grammar.* rough breathing.

spir·i·tus fru·men·ti (spir′ə təs frü men′tī), *Latin.* whiskey. [< New Latin *spiritus frumenti* < Latin *spīritus* (see SPIRIT), *frūmentī,* genitive of *frūmentum* grain]

spir·i·tus le·nis (spir′ə təs lē′nis), *Greek Grammar.* smooth breathing.

spir·it·y (spir′ə tē), *adj.* full of spirit, animation, energy, or vivacity; spirited: *He is a most active, spirity man, and by his great mental exercises keeps himself from anything like a lethargy* (Lord Malmesbury).

spir·ket (spėr′kit), *n.* a space forward or aft between the floor timbers of a ship. [origin unknown]

spir·ket·ing or **spir·ket·ting** (spėr′kə-ting), *n.* the inside planking between the waterways and the ports of a ship.

spi·ro·che·tal or **spi·ro·chae·tal** (spī′-rə kē′təl), *adj.* of or having to do with spirochetes.

spi·ro·chete or **spi·ro·chaete** (spī′rə-kēt), *n.* any of a large group of slender, spiral, very flexible and active microorganisms that are usually classed as bacteria. One kind causes syphilis, and another causes relapsing fever. [< New Latin *Spirochaeta* the genus name < Greek *speîra* a coil + *chaítē* hair]

spi·ro·che·ti·cide or **spi·ro·chae·ti·cide** (spī′rə kē′tə sīd), *n.* an agent for destroying spirochetes. [< *spirochete* + *-cide*[1]]

spi·ro·che·to·sis or **spi·ro·chae·to·sis** (spī′rə kē tō′sis), *n.* an infectious, often fatal, blood disease of poultry and other birds, caused by a spirochete.

spi·ro·gram (spī′rə gram), *n.* a graphic record of a person's lung capacity made by a spirometer. [< Latin *spīrāre* breathe + English *-gram*]

spi·ro·graph (spī′rə graf, -gräf), *n.* an instrument for recording respiratory movements. [< Latin *spīrāre* breathe + English *-graph*]

spi·ro·gy·ra (spī′rə jī′rə), *n.* any of a large group of green algae that grow in scumlike masses in fresh-water ponds or tanks. The cells have one or more bands of chlorophyll winding spirally to the right. See **conjugation** for picture. [< New Latin *Spirogyra* the genus name < Greek *speîra* a coil + *gŷros* circle]

spi·roid (spī′roid), *adj.* tending to be spiral in form; like a spiral: *a spiroid curve, a spiroid shell.* [< New Latin *spiroides* < Greek *speiroeidês* coiled < *speîra* a coil + *eîdos* form]

spi·rom·e·ter (spī rom′ə tər), *n.* an instrument for measuring the capacity of the lungs, by the amount of air that can be breathed out after the lungs have been filled as full as possible: *To tell whether it is safe to operate on a patient with lung trouble, doctors can first have the patient inhale the inert balloon gas, helium, from a spirometer* (Science News Letter). [< Latin *spīrāre* breathe + English *-meter*]

spi·ro·met·ric (spī′rə met′rik), *adj.* of or having to do with the spirometer or spirometry.

spi·rom·e·try (spī rom′ə trē), *n.* **1.** the measurement of breathing power or lung capacity. **2.** the use of the spirometer.

spirt (spėrt), *v.i., v.t., n.* spurt.

spir·u·la (spir′yə lə, -ə-), *n., pl.* **-lae** (-lē). any of a group of small cephalopods having an internal, chambered, spiral shell and ten tentacles. [< New Latin *spirula* (diminutive) < Latin *spīra;* see SPIRE[2]]

spir·y[1] (spīr′ē), *adj.* **1.** having the form of a spire; tapering: *a spiry turret or steeple, spiry grass or rocks.* **2.** having many spires: *The spiry habitable city* (Robert Louis Stevenson).

spir·y[2] (spīr′ē), *adj.* spiral; coiled; curving.

spis·sat·ed (spis′ā tid), *adj.* made thick, dense, or compact; inspissated. [< Latin *spissātus,* past participle of *spissāre* thicken (< *spissus* thick) + English *-ed*[2]]

spis·si·tude (spis′ə tüd, -tyüd), *n.* thickness; density; compactness. [< Latin *spissitūdo, -inis* < *spissus* thick]

spit[1] (spit), *v.,* **spat** or **spit, spit·ting,** *n.* —*v.t.* **1.** to throw out (saliva, etc.) from the mouth; expectorate. **2.** to throw out as if by spitting: *The gun spits fire. He spat curses.* **3.** to light (a fuse). —*v.i.* **1.** to throw out saliva from the mouth: *Stalky spat on to the back of a young rabbit sunning himself far down* (Rudyard Kipling). **2.** to spit (at, on, etc.) a person or thing to express hatred or contempt: *The wit of fools that slovenly will spit on all things fair* (George Chapman). *You call me misbeliever . . . And spit upon my Jewish gabardine* (Shakespeare). **3.** to make a spitting noise: *The cat spits when angry.* **4.** to sputter: *The sausage began to spit* (Charles Reade). **5.** to rain or snow suddenly or lightly, as in a brief flurry.

—*n.* **1.** the liquid produced in the mouth; saliva. **2.** the noise or act of spitting. **3. a.** the frothy or spitlike secretion given off by a spittle insect. **b.** a spittle insect. **4.** a light rain or snow.

spit and image, the exact image: *My mother was the spit and image of Queen Wilhelmina* (New Yorker).

the spit of, *Informal.* just like: *He is the very spit of his father.*

[< Old English *spittan*] —**spit′like′,** *adj.*

➔ See **expectorate** for usage note.

spit[2] (spit), *n., v.,* **spit·ted, spit·ting.** —*n.* **1.** a sharp-pointed, slender rod or bar on which meat is roasted or broiled. **2.** a narrow point of land running into the water. **3.** a long, narrow reef, shoal, or sandbank extending from the shore.

—*v.t.* **1.** to run a spit through; put on a spit: *He lighted a fire, spitted a leg of mutton* (Tobias Smollett). **2.** to pierce or stab with a sharp-pointed weapon, etc.; impale on something sharp: *The hunters spitted two rabbits.*

[Old English *spitu*]

Spit[2] (def. 1)

spit·al (spit′əl), *n.* **1.** a shelter or other place of refuge, as for travelers, paupers, etc. **2.** a hospital for the poor or diseased, especially for lepers; lazaretto. [alteration (influenced by *hospital*) of earlier *spittle,* Middle English *spitell,* ultimately < Medieval Latin *hospitale.* Doublet of HOSPITAL, HOSTEL, HOTEL.]

spit and polish, 1. the act of cleaning up or furbishing, especially as part of the work of a sailor or soldier: *The army concentrated on spit and polish, retreat formations, and parades* (Dwight D. Eisenhower). **2.** superficial neatness or smart appearance: *They looked weather-beaten, there was little spit and polish to them* (New Yorker).

spit-and-pol·ish (spit′ən pol′ish), *adj.* characterized by great attention to superficial neatness, orderliness, and smart appearance; fussy: *What with all these spit-and-polish young pianists, to whom a wrong note would be inconceivable, it is almost with a sense of relief that one turns to a more modest type of playing* (Harper's).

spit·ball (spit′bôl′), *U.S.* —*n.* **1.** a small ball of chewed-up paper, used as a missile. **2.** *Baseball.* an illegal curve thrown by the pitcher after wetting one side of the ball with saliva.

—*v.i.* **1.** to throw a spitball: *Birdie Tebetts, the Cincinnati manager, accused Burdette of spitballing* (Newsweek). **2.** *Slang.* to express one's immediate ideas without thought or preparation; brainstorm: *We're just spitballing, of course, but here are a few* [*ideas*] *we'll hand along* (New Yorker). —*v.t. Slang.* to say or express without thought or preparation: *"Never mind—spitball some dialogue to give the general idea," said Gallwise* (S.J. Perelman).

[American English < *spit*[1] + *ball*[1]]

spit·ball·er (spit′bô′lər), *n. U.S.* a baseball player who throws spitballs.

spitch·cock (spich′kok′), *n.* an eel split, cut up into pieces, and broiled or fried. —*v.t.* to split, cut up, and broil or fry (an eel). [origin uncertain]

spit curl, *U.S. Informal.* a small lock of hair dampened, originally with saliva, and curled flat on the cheek, forehead, etc.: *Her face was firm and strong, but heavily rouged and framed with spit curls* (New Yorker).

spite (spīt), *n., v.,* **spit·ed, spit·ing.** —*n.* **1.** desire to annoy or harm another; ill will or malice, or an instance of it; grudge: *That girl stayed away from May's party out of spite.* **2.** *Obsolete.* misfortune; insult; injury: *The time is out of joint: O cursed spite, That ever I was born to set it right!* (Shakespeare).

in spite of, not prevented by; notwithstanding: *The children went to school in spite of the rain.*

—*v.t.* to show ill will toward; annoy; irritate: *He left his yard dirty to spite the people next door.*

[short for Middle English *despit* despite]

—**Syn.** *n.* **1. Spite, malice, grudge** mean ill will against another. **Spite** suggests envy or mean disposition, and applies to active ill will shown by doing mean, petty things to hurt or annoy: *She ruined his flowers out of spite.* **Malice** emphasizes actual wish or intention to injure, and suggests hatred or, especially, a disposition delighting in doing harm or seeing others hurt: *Many gossips are motivated by malice.* **Grudge** suggests wishing to get even for real or imagined injury, and applies to ill will nursed for a long time: *She bears grudges.*

spite·ful (spīt′fəl), *adj.* full of spite; eager to annoy; behaving with ill will and malice: *a spiteful remark. The spiteful girl tore up her sister's papers.* —**spite′ful·ly,** *adv.* —**spite′ful·ness,** *n.* —**Syn.** malicious, malevolent.

spite·less (spīt′lis), *adj.* free from spite.

spit·fire (spit′fīr′), *n.* **1.** a person, especially a woman or girl, who has a quick and fiery temper. **2.** something that sends forth fire, such as a cannon or certain fireworks.

spit·rack (spit′rak′), *n.* an iron rack formerly used to support a spit before a fire.

spit·ter (spit′ər), *n.* **1.** a person who spits. **2.** *Baseball.* a spitball: *"I gotta laugh at the players which favor the return of the spitter," said the cynical Stengel* (New York Times).

spit·ting image (spit′ing), *Informal.* the exact likeness; spit and image: *The hero is the spitting image of the author* (Harper's).

spit·tle (spit′əl), *n.* **1.** saliva; spit. **2.** the secretion produced by a spittle insect. [alteration of obsolete *spattle* (influenced by *spit*[1]), Old English *spātl* saliva < *spittan* spit]

spittle insect, any of a group of homopterous insects whose larvae cover themselves with a protective foamy secretion.

spit·toon (spi tün′), *n.* a container to spit into; cuspidor. [American English < *spit*[1]]

spitz (spits), *n.,* or **spitz dog,** a small dog with pointed muzzle and ears and a tail curled up over its back, a white variety of Pomeranian. [< German *Spitz* < *spitz* pointed]

spitz·en·berg or **Spitz·en·berg** (spit′sən bėrg), *n.* spitzenburg.

spitz·en·burg or **Spitz·en·burg** (spit′sən bėrg), *n.* any of several varieties of fine-flavored winter apple. They are red, sometimes streaked with yellow. [American English; origin uncertain; perhaps < Dutch *spits* pointed + *berg* mountain (because of its shape)]

spitz·flute (spits′flüt′), *n.* an organ stop having conical pipes of metal, which give a thin, somewhat reedy tone. [half-translation of German *Spitzflöte* < *spitz* pointed + *Flöte* flute]

spiv (spiv), *n. British Slang.* a man who makes his living by petty thievery, blackmail, pimping, etc. [probably < *SPIV,* abbreviation of *Suspected Person Itinerant Vagabond* (a police charge)]

spiv·ver·y (spiv′ər ē), *n. British Slang.* the activities or practices of spivs.

SPIW (no periods) or **S.P.I.W.,** Special Purpose Individual Weapon (a gun equipped with separate barrels for firing fléchettes and grenades).

splake (splāk), *n., pl.* **splakes** or (*collectively*) **splake.** a Canadian trout developed in 1946 from a cross between the brook or speckled trout and the lake trout. [blend of *speckled* trout and *lake* trout]

splanch·nic (splangk′nik), *adj.* of, having to do with, or in the region of the viscera; visceral. [< New Latin *splanchnicus* < Greek *splanchnikós* < *splánchnon,* singular of *splánchna* the inward parts, viscera < *splēn, splēnós;* see SPLEEN]

splanch·nol·o·gy (splangk nol′ə jē), *n.* the scientific study of the viscera. [< Greek *splánchnon* (see SPLANCHNIC) + English *-logy*]

splanch·no·pleure (splangk′nə plůr), *n. Embryology.* the inner layer of the mesoderm combined with the endoderm. It gives rise to the connective and muscle tissue of most of the intestinal tracts, etc. [< Greek *splánchnon* (see SPLANCHNIC) + *pleurā́* side]

splanch·not·o·my (splangk not′ə mē), *n., pl.* **-mies.** the dissection or anatomy of the viscera. [< Greek *splánchnon* (see SPLANCHNIC) + *-tomiā* a cutting]

splash (splash), *v.t.* **1.** to cause (water, mud, etc.) to fly about. **2.** to cause to scatter a liquid about: *He splashed the oars as he rowed.* **3.** to wet; spatter; soil: *Our car is all splashed with mud.* **4.** to make (one's way) with splashing: *The . . . vessel ploughed and splashed its way up the Hudson* (Washington Irving). **5.** to mark with spots or patches: *The careless painter splashed the furniture.* **6.** to move (logs) by opening a dam and releasing a flood of water. —*v.i.* **1.** to dash water, mud, etc., about: *The baby likes to splash in his tub.* **2.** to fall, move, or go with splashing: *The dog splashed across the brook.* **3.** to dash in scattered masses or drops: *Muddy water splashed on our windshield.*

—*n.* **1.** the act, result, or sound of splashing: *The splash of the wave knocked him over. The boat upset with a loud splash.* **2.** a spot of liquid splashed upon a thing: *She has splashes of grease on her dress. The cleaner could not remove the splashes on her dress.* **3.** a large or uneven patch or spot: *The dog is white with brown splashes.* **4. a.** the moving of logs by splashing. **b.** the water released from a dam in order to splash logs.

make a splash, *Informal.* to attract attention; cause excitement: *He is free from the desire to make a splash, or the impulse of some academics to bite their former mentors in the leg* (Marcus Cunliffe).

[probably alteration of *plash*[2]]

splash·back (splash′bak′), *n.* a guard in the back of a cookstove or on a wall to protect against splashes.

splash·board (splash′bôrd′, -bōrd′), *n.* **1.** a guard in front of the driver's seat, or one over or beside a wheel, to prevent mud, water, etc., from splashing into the vehicle; dashboard; mudguard. **2.** a screen rising from the deck of a boat to block off water or spray. **3.** a plank for closing the sluice or spillway of a dam.

splash dam, a dam built to store a head of water for driving logs.

splash·down (splash′doun′), *n.* the landing of a spacecraft in the ocean after reëntry.

splash·er (splash′ər), *n.* **1.** a person or thing that splashes. **2.** something that protects from splashes; splashboard.

splash·i·ness (splash′ē nis), *n.* the state or quality of being splashy; gaudiness; ostentation: *It was evident that Mr. Ross's instinct for theatrical splashiness had far outrun his powers of invention* (New Yorker).

splash·y (splash′ē), *adj.,* **splash·i·er, splash·i·est. 1.** making a splash. **2.** full of irregular spots or streaks; done in splashes. **3.** *Informal.* attracting attention; causing excitement or comment; showy: *The star of the show made a splashy entrance. Around the World in 80 Days — a big, splashy, funny review of the Jules Verne fantasy* (New Yorker).

splat[1] (splat), *n.* a broad, flat piece of wood, especially one forming the central upright part of the back of a chair. [origin uncertain, apparently < Middle English *splat* to split open, cut up]

splat[2] (splat), *v.,* **splat·ted, splat·ting.** —*v.t.* to cause to shatter against a hard surface; splatter: *He splats lemons against a wall* (Harper's). —*v.i.* to make a dull, flat sound, as of splattering: *A full wallet splatted to the sand* (Barnaby Conrad). [back formation < *splatter*]

splatch (splach), *n., v.t.* splotch.

splat·ter (splat′ər), *v.t., v.i., n.* splash; spatter: *The cotton is . . . white, splattered with stylized red and black snowflakes* (New Yorker). [perhaps blend of *spatter* and *splash*]

splay (splā), *v.t.* **1.** to spread out; expand; extend. **2.** to make slanting, as the jambs or sides of a window; bevel. **3.** to dislocate, as a horse's shoulder.

—*v.i.* **1.** to have or lie in a slanting direction; slope. **2.** to spread out; flare.

—*n.* **1.** a spread; flare. **2.** a surface that makes an oblique angle with another, as the beveled jamb of a window or door; a slanting surface.

—*adj.* **1.** spread out; wide and flat; turned outward: *splay feet.* **2.** awkward; clumsy; ungainly. **3.** oblique; awry.

[Middle English *splayen,* short for *displayen* display]

SPLAY

Splayed Doorway (def. 2)

splay·foot (splā′fůt′), *n., pl.* **-feet,** *adj.* —*n.* a broad, flat foot, especially one turned outward. —*adj.* splay-footed.

splay-foot·ed (splā′fůt′id), *adj.* **1.** having splayfeet. **2.** awkward; clumsy.

splay-kneed (splā′nēd′), *adj.* having the knees turned outward.

splay-leg·ged (splā′leg′id, -legd′), *adj.* bow-legged.

splay-toed (splā′tōd′), *adj.* having the toes spread out.

spleen (splēn), *n.* **1.** a ductless gland at the left of the stomach in man, and near the stomach or intestine in other vertebrates, that stores blood and helps filter foreign substances from the blood. It was once believed to cause low spirits, bad temper, and spite. **2.** bad temper; spite; anger: *This is the land where hate should die, No feuds of faith, no spleen of race* (Denis A. McCarthy). **3.** *Archaic.* low spirits; moroseness; melancholy. **4.** *Obsolete.* a whim; caprice: *A thousand spleens bear her a thousand ways* (Shakespeare). [Middle English *splen,* and *splene* < Latin *splēn* < Greek *splḗn*] —**spleen′like′,** *adj.*

spleen·ful (splēn′fəl), *adj.* irritable or peevish; spiteful. —**spleen′ful·ly,** *adv.*

spleen·less (splēn′lis), *adj.* having no spleen.

spleen·wort (splēn′wėrt′), *n.* any of a group of ferns having oblong spore cases situated obliquely on the upper surface of small veins. [< *spleen* + *wort* (because it was believed to be medically helpful)]

spleen·y (splē′nē), *adj.* full of or characterized by spleen; spleenful.

splen·da·cious (splen dā′shəs), *adj.* very splendid; gorgeous; magnificent: *The room is papered with some splendacious pattern in blue and gold* (Blackwood's Magazine). [< *splend*(id) + (viv)*acious*]

splen·dent (splen′dənt), *adj. Archaic.* **1.** shining brightly; brilliant: ... *splendent planets* (Sir Thomas Browne). **2.** gleaming; lustrous: ... *splendent Parian marble* (Thackeray). **3.** splendid; gorgeous: ... *splendent in gold lace* (Thomas Carlyle). [< Latin *splendēns, -entis,* present participle of *splendēre* be bright]

splen·did (splen′did), *adj.* **1.** brilliant; glorious; magnificent; grand: *a splendid sunset, splendid clothes or jewels, a splendid victory or achievement. Give me the splendid silent sun with all his beams full-dazzling* (Walt Whitman). **2.** very good; fine; excellent: *a splendid chance, a splendid time, etc.* [< Latin *splendidus* < *splendēre* be bright] —**splen′did·ly,** *adv.* —**splen′did·ness,** *n.* —**Syn. 1.** See **magnificent.**

splen·dif·er·ous (splen dif′ər əs), *adj. Informal.* splendid; magnificent: *The splendiferous hotel was surely the set where the Marx brothers had gambolled through "A Night in Casablanca"* (Sunday Express). [< Late Latin *splendifer,* for Latin *splendōrifer* (< *splendor, -ōris* splendor + *ferre* to bear) + English *-ous*]

splen·dor (splen′dər), *n.* **1.** great display of riches or costly things; magnificent show; pomp: *the splendor of a royal wedding.* **2.** brilliant distinction; eminence; glory: *How the grand band-wagon shone with a splendor all its own* ... (James Whitcomb Riley). **3.** great brightness; brilliant light or luster: *The sun set in a golden splendor.* ... *splendor of coral seas* (William O. Douglas). [< Latin *splendor, -ōris* < *splendēre* be bright]

splen·dor·ous (splen′dər əs), *adj.* full of splendor: *A light that spreads a finer joy, Than cloudless noon-tide splendorous o'er the world* (George MacDonald).

splen·dour (splen′dər), *n. Especially British.* splendor.

splen·dour·ous (splen′dər əs), *adj. Especially British.* splendorous.

splen·drous (splen′drəs), *adj. Especially British.* splendorous.

sple·nec·to·my (spli nek′tə mē), *n., pl.* **-mies.** the surgical removal of the spleen. [< Greek *splḗn, splēnós* spleen + *ektomḗ* a cutting out]

sple·net·ic (spli net′ik), *adj.* **1.** of or having to do with the spleen. **2.** bad-tempered; irritable; peevish; irascible: *a splenetic woman, who must have someone to find fault with* (Samuel Richardson).
—*n.* a person who is splenetic in disposition. [< Late Latin *splēnēticus* < Latin *splēn;* see SPLEEN] —**sple·net′i·cal·ly,** *adv.*

sple·net·i·cal (spli net′ə kəl), *adj.* splenetic.

sple·ni·al (splē′nē əl), *adj.* of or having to do with the splenius.

splen·ic (splen′ik, splē′nik), *adj.* of, having to do with, or in the region of the spleen. [< Latin *splēnicus* < Greek *splēnikós* < *splḗn, splēnós* spleen]

sple·ni·tis (spli nī′tis), *n.* inflammation of the spleen. [< Greek *splēnîtis* < *splḗn, splēnós* spleen]

splen·i·tive (splen′ə tiv), *adj.* **1.** splenetic; ill-humored; irritable. **2.** spleenful; impetuous; passionate: *I am not splenitive and rash* (Shakespeare).

sple·ni·us (splē′nē əs), *n.* a broad, flat muscle extending from the upper vertebrae to the neck and base of the skull. It serves to move the head and neck. [< New Latin *splenius* < Greek *splēnion* bandage, compress (especially, one used for the spleen) < *splḗn, splēnós* spleen (because of its shape)]

sple·ni·za·tion (splē′nə zā′shən), *n. Medicine.* a change produced in the lungs by inflammation, in which they resemble the form of the spleen.

sple·noid (splē′noid), *adj.* spleenlike.

sple·no·meg·a·ly (splē′nō meg′ə lē, splen′ō-), *n.* enlargement of the spleen. [< Greek *splḗn, splēnós* spleen + *mégas, megálou* big + English *-y*[3]]

sple·not·o·my (spli not′ə mē), *n., pl.* **-mies.** a surgical incision into the spleen. [< Greek *splḗn, splēnós* spleen + *-tomiā* a cutting]

spleu·chan (splü′Hən), *n. Scottish and Irish.* a pouch for holding tobacco, sometimes used as a purse. [< Gaelic *spliùchan*]

splice (splīs), *v.,* **spliced, splic·ing,** *n.* —*v.t.* **1.** to join together (ropes, etc.) by weaving together ends that have been pulled out into separate strands. **2.** to join together (two pieces of timber) by overlapping. **3.** to join together (film, tape, wire, etc.). **4.** *Informal.* to marry: *We never meant to be spliced in the humdrum way of other people* (Charlotte Brontë).

Short Splice (def. 1a) for mending broken rope and splicing two ropes

—*n.* **1. a.** a joining of ropes or timbers by splicing: *How neat a splice can you make?* **b.** the joint so formed. **2.** *Slang.* a marriage; wedding. [perhaps < Middle Dutch *splissen*]

splic·er (splī′sər), *n.* a person who splices.

spline (splīn), *n., v.,* **splined, splin·ing.** —*n.* **1.** a long, narrow, relatively thin strip of wood or metal; slat. **2.** a long, flexible strip of wood, etc., used as a guide in drawing curves. **3.** *Machinery.* **a.** a flat, rectangular key fitting into a groove or slot between parts, as in a shaft, wheel, etc. **b.** the groove for this key.

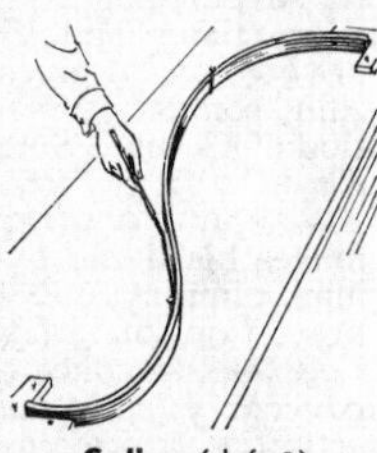
Spline (def. 2)

—*v.t.* **1.** to fit with a spline or key. **2.** to provide with a groove for a spline or key. [origin uncertain]

splint (splint), *n.* **1.** an arrangement of wood, metal, plaster, etc., to hold a broken or dislocated bone in place: *The man's broken arm was set in splints to hold it in position.* **2.** a thin, flexible strip of wood, such as is used in making baskets: *My basket is woven from splints.* **3.** a thin metal strip or plate: *Old armor often had overlapping splints to protect the elbow, knee, etc., and allow easy movement.* **4.** a hard, bony growth on the splint bone of a horse, mule, etc. **5.** *Dialect.* a splinter of wood or stone; chip.
—*v.t.* **1.** to secure, hold in position, or support by means of a splint or splints. **2.** to support as if with splints.
[probably < Middle Low German *splinte*]

splint·age (splin′tij), *n.* the application or use of splints.

splint armor, armor made of overlapping plates or strips of metal.

splint bone, one of the two smaller bones on either side of the large bone between the hock and the fetlock of a horse, mule, etc.

splint-bot·tomed (splint′bot′əmd), *adj.* having the bottom or seat made of splints, usually interwoven: *a splint-bottomed chair.*

splint coal, a hard, bituminous coal with a dull, grayish-black color and a splintery structure, producing a hot fire.

splin·ter (splin′tər), *n.* **1.** a thin, sharp piece of wood, bone, stone, glass, etc.; sliver: *He got a splinter in his hand. The mirror broke into splinters.* **2.** a splinter group.
—*adj.* of or having to do with dissenting groups that break away from regular political groups, religious organizations, etc.: *A few other splinter Socialist groups exist* (Harper's).
—*v.t.* to break or split into splinters: *He splintered the locked door with an ax.* —*v.i.* to be broken or split into splinters; break off in splinters: *The mirror splintered. There were few men in the room who did not remember 1931, when the Labor Party ... splintered hopelessly* (Time).
[< Middle Dutch *splinter*]

splinter bar, **1.** a crossbar between the shafts of a carriage, etc., to which the traces are attached. **2.** a singletree.

splin·ter·proof (splin′tər prüf′), *adj.* proof against splinters, as of bursting shells, etc.

splin·ter·y (splin′tər ē), *adj.* **1.** apt to splinter: *splintery wood.* **2.** of or like a splinter. **3.** rough and jagged, as if from splintering: *The ridgy precipices ... showed their splintery and rugged edges* (Scott). **4.** full of splinters. **5.** characterized by the production of small splinters.

split (split), *v.,* **split, split·ting,** *n., adj.* —*v.t.* **1.** to break or cut from end to end, or in layers; cleave: *to split logs for the fireplace, a tree split by lightning. She split the cake and filled it with jelly.* **2.** to separate into parts; divide: *to split the cost. The old farm has been split up into house lots.* **3.** to divide into different groups, factions, parties, etc.: *Disagreements split the club into rival factions.* **4.** to cast (a vote or a ballot) for candidates of different political parties in the same election: *He split his vote by voting for a Democratic mayor and a Republican sheriff.* **5. a.** to divide (a molecule) into two or more individual atoms or atomic groups. **b.** to remove by such a process. **c.** to divide (an atomic nucleus) into two portions of approximately equal mass by forcing the absorption of a neutron. **6.** to issue a certain number of new shares of (stock) for each share currently held: *American Tobacco Co. directors voted to split its common stock two-for-one* (Wall Street Journal).
—*v.i.* **1. a.** to come apart or break open by or as if by being split: *The rock split into two. She complains that her head is splitting from the noise. I laughed till I thought I should split* (Jonathan Swift). **b.** to be capable of being split: *Birch splits easily.* **2.** to separate into parts; divide. **3.** to divide into different groups, factions, parties, etc. **4.** *British Slang.* to turn informer; peach: *I might have got clear off, if I'd split upon her* (Dickens).
split hairs. See under **hair,** *n.*
—*n.* **1.** a splitting; break; crack; fissure: *a split in the door. Frost caused the split in the rock.* **2.** division in a group, party, etc.: *There was a split in the church for a time but harmony was soon restored.* **3.** *Slang.* a share; portion: *to get a split of the profits.* **4.** an issuing of a certain number of new shares of stock for each currently held. **5.** *Informal.* a bottle of a drink half the usual size; about 7 fluid ounces. **6.** a sweet dish made of ice cream, sliced fruit, syrup, nuts, etc.: *a banana split.* **7.** Often, **splits.** an acrobatic feat of sinking to the floor with the legs spread far apart in opposite directions. **8.** the wide separation of two or more standing pins after the first roll in bowling, making a spare very difficult. **9.** one of the thin sheets of leather into which a skin is sometimes sliced before or during tanning. **10.** one of the strips into which osiers are cut in basketmaking.
—*adj.* **1.** broken or cut from end to end; divided; cleft: *a split log, a split door.* **2.** (of a stock market quotation) given in sixteenths rather than eighths (the usual way of quoting stock).
[apparently < Middle Dutch *splitten*]

split-bot·tomed (split′bot′əmd), *adj.* splint-bottomed.

split decision, a decision that is not unanimous, as in a boxing match: *Ezzard Charles ... got off the canvas after a second-round knockdown to gain a ten-round split decision over Paul Andrews in the Chicago Stadium* (New York Times).

split-hair (split′hãr′), *adj.* extremely narrow or close; very precise; hairline: *a split-hair distance away, split-hair timing, split-hair accuracy.*

split infinitive, an infinitive with a word between *to* and the verb. *Example:* He wants to never work, but to always play.

➔ **split infinitive.** Awkward split infinitives should be avoided. Awkward: *After a while I was able to, although not very accurately, distinguish the good customers from the sulky ones.* Improved: *After a while I was able to*

 PRONUNCIATION KEY: hat, āge, cãre, fär; let, ēqual, tėrm; it, īce; hot, ōpen, ôrder; oil, out; cup, pu̇t, rüle;

distinguish—though not very accurately—the good customers from the sulky ones.

split jump, a jump in the air made in dancing with the legs spread far apart in opposite directions.

split-lev·el house, or **split-lev·el** (split′lev′əl), *n.* a one-story house with an upper level about half a floor above the main level.

split-off (split′ôf′, -of′), *n.* **1.** something that is split or divided from something else: *Split-offs from the parent clumps are best planted four inches apart* (Punch). **2.** the distribution of stock in a new corporation to stockholders of the parent corporation in partial exchange for old stock: *Company officials declined to explain the split-off other than to say "it is for good business reasons"* (Wall Street Journal).

split page, the front page of the second section of a newspaper.

split peas, husked peas split for making pea soup.

split personality, 1. schizophrenia: *Split personality, or schizophrenia, is a psychosis characterized by a personality which is split, or separated, from reality* (Atlantic). **2.** a person whose personality shows markedly inconsistent or contradictory qualities.

split-phase (split′fāz′), *adj.* of or having to do with an alternating single-phase current in a divided circuit where there is a difference of phase between the currents in the two branches.

split·saw (split′sô′), *n.* a kind of ripsaw.

split second, a very brief moment of time; instant: *It disappears in a split second* (Science News Letter).

split-sec·ond (split′sek′ənd), *adj.* instantaneous; very quick: *split-second timing.*

split stroke or **shot,** *Croquet.* a stroke or shot made in such a way that two balls placed in contact are driven in different directions.

split·tail (split′tāl′), *n.* a cyprinoid fish of California rivers. The upper lobe of its caudal fin is much more developed than the lower.

split·ter (split′ər), *n.* **1.** a person or thing that splits. **2.** a person who splits hairs.

split·ting (split′ing), *adj.* **1.** that splits. **2. a.** very severe; extreme; violent: *a splitting headache.* **b.** aching severely: *a splitting head.*

split·tism (split′iz əm), *n.* fractionalism: *Mr. Khrushchev's "revisionism and great power chauvinism and splittism" were wrong* (London Times).

split-up (split′up′), *n.* **1.** division; separation; breakup: *a family split-up.* **2.** an issuing of a number of new shares of stock for each currently held; split: *a stock split-up.* **3.** the exchange of all the stocks of a parent corporation for the stocks of one or more newly formed or subsidiary corporations, resulting in the dissolution of the parent corporation.

splodge (sploj), *n.* a thick, heavy, or clumsy splotch. [compare SPLOTCH]

splodg·y (sploj′ē), *adj.*, **splodg·i·er, splodg·i·est.** full of splodges; showing coarse splotches of color: *Ninety per cent of them are in the depth of fashion—abstract, splodgy, drip-laden, and untitled* (Manchester Guardian).

splore (splôr, splōr), *n. Scottish.* **1.** a frolic; merrymaking; revel. **2.** an embroilment; scrape. [origin unknown]

splosh (splosh), *n.* **1.** splash: *the gentle thud and splosh of surf* (Punch). **2.** *Slang.* money: *The gentleman in the Old Kent Road . . . came into a little bit of splosh* (Westminster Gazette).

splotch (sploch), *n.* a large, irregular spot; splash: . . . *instead of wiping away the tomato splotch he . . . put out a tasting finger* (Frederic Morton). —*v.t.* to make a splotch or splotches on; splash. [origin uncertain. Compare Middle English *splotty* spotty.]

splotch·y (sploch′ē), *adj.*, **splotch·i·er, splotch·i·est.** marked with splotches.

splurge (splėrj), *n., v.,* **splurged, splurg·ing.** —*n.* **1.** a showing off; ostentatious display: *a splurge of wealth.* **2.** an outburst: *a sudden splurge of energy.*
—*v.i.* **1.** to show off. **2.** to spend lavishly; be extravagant.
[American English; origin uncertain]

splut·ter (splut′ər), *v.i.* **1.** to talk in a hasty, confused way; speak quickly and with spitting or sputtering sounds: *People sometimes splutter when they are excited.* **2.** to make spitting or popping noises; sputter.
—*v.t.* to utter in a spluttering manner; say with spluttering: *to splutter out an apology.*
—*n.* a spluttering.
[perhaps variant of *sputter*] —**splut′ter·er,** *n.*

Spode or **spode** (spōd), *n.* fine china or porcelain of the type perfected by Josiah Spode (1754-1827), one of the first great potters of Staffordshire, England: *to buy a set of Spode.* —*adj.* of such china or porcelain: *a Spode platter.*

spod·o·man·cy (spod′ə man′sē), *n.* divination by means of ashes. [< Greek *spodós* ashes + *manteíā* divination]

spod·o·man·tic (spod′ə man′tik), *adj.* divining by ashes.

spod·u·mene (spoj′ů mēn), *n.* a mineral, a silicate of aluminum and lithium, usually occurring in flat prismatic crystals. It is hard, transparent to translucent, and varies in color from grayish-, yellowish-, or greenish-white to emerald-green and purple. Some varieties are used as gems. *Formula:* $LiAlSi_2O_6$ [< French *spodumène* < German *Spodumen* < Greek *spodoúmenos*, past participle of *spodoûsthai* be burned to ashes < *spodós* ashes, powder (because it powders under the blowtorch)]

spof·fish (spof′ish), *adj. British Slang.* bustling; fussy; officious. [origin unknown]

spoil (spoil), *v.,* **spoiled** or **spoilt, spoil·ing,** *n.* —*v.t.* **1.** to damage, impair, or injure (something) so as to make it unfit or useless; destroy: *He spoils a dozen pieces of paper before he writes a letter.* **2.** to injure the character or disposition of, especially by overindulgence or undue lenience: *That child is spoiled by too much attention.* **3.** *Archaic.* **a.** to strip (a person, country, house, etc.) of goods, possessions, or valuables by force; plunder; despoil; sack: *to spoil a poor widow of her savings.* **b.** to seize (goods) by force; carry off as plunder; rob; steal. —*v.i.* **1.** to be damaged or injured; become bad or unfit for use; deteriorate; decay: *The fruit spoiled because I kept it too long.* **2.** *Archaic.* to plunder; ravage; rob.

spoil for, *Informal.* to long for (a fight, etc.); desire: *He is not spoiling for a fight, though he would probably give as good as he got if a fight were forced on him* (Manchester Guardian).

—*n.* **1.** Often, **spoils. a.** the plunder taken from an enemy or captured city in time of war; booty; loot: *The soldiers carried the spoils back to their own land.* **b.** any goods, property, etc., seized by force or similar means after a struggle. **2.** objects of art, books, etc., which have been acquired by special effort. **3.** an object of plundering; prey. **4.** the act or practice of plundering; spoliation. **5.** earth or refuse matter from excavating, mining, dredging, etc.

spoils, *Especially U.S.* government offices and their advantages regarded as at the disposition of a political party when it comes to power: *The post of policeman is "spoils," . . . but spoils equally divided between the parties* (James Bryce).

[< Old French *espoillier* < Latin *spoliāre* < *spolium* booty, spoil]

—**Syn.** *v.t.* **1. Spoil, ruin** mean to damage beyond repair or recovery. **Spoil** emphasizes damage that so reduces or weakens the value, strength, beauty, usefulness, etc., of something as to make the thing useless or bring it to nothing: *Her friend's unkind comments spoiled her pleasure in her new dress.* **Ruin** emphasizes bringing to an end the value, soundness, beauty, usefulness, health and happiness, etc., of someone or something through a destructive force or irretrievable loss: *He ruined his eyes by reading in a poor light.* **3. a.** pillage. *-v.i.* **1.** rot.

spoil·a·ble (spoi′lə bəl), *adj.* that can be spoiled: *If on occasion you . . . doll yourself up in spoilable clothing . . .* (Harper's).

spoil·age (spoi′lij), *n.* **1.** the act of spoiling. **2.** the fact of being spoiled: *Lower grades of rubber will be purchased to replace material in the stockpile that has been damaged by spoilage* (Wall Street Journal). **3.** something that is or has been spoiled.

spoil·a·tion (spoi lā′shən), *n.* the act of spoiling or damaging something: *The opponents contend that the [construction of a] playground . . . will cause a considerable wastage of funds . . . and the destruction and spoilation of a very valuable parkland property* (New York Times).

spoil·bank (spoil′bangk′), *n.* a bank or mound of refuse earth, stone, or other waste material: *Owners of colliery spoilbanks are required to take all practicable steps to minimize the emission of smoke and fumes* (London Times). [< *spoil*, noun + *bank*[1]]

spoil·er (spoi′lər), *n.* **1.** a person or thing that spoils. **2.** a person who takes spoils. **3.** a movable flap on or under the wing of an airplane, to help in slowing down or in decreasing lift, as in descending or landing: *Even stranger are the spoilers—large squarish flap-type panels that rise out of the wings top and bottom* (New York Times).

spoil·five (spoil′fīv′), *n.* a card game for from three to ten players having five cards each. The game is said to be "spoiled" if no player can take three tricks.

spoils (spoilz), *n.pl.* See under **spoil,** *n.*

spoils·man (spoilz′mən), *n., pl.* **-men. 1.** a person who gets or tries to get a government office or job as a reward for his service to the successful party. **2.** a person who supports the spoils system. [American English < *spoils* + *man*]

spoil·sport (spoil′spôrt′, -spōrt′), *n.* a person who acts so as to spoil or hinder the enjoyment or plans of others: *It is unusual for a candidate to win first time around, and if one does, he arouses a certain amount of resentment as a spoilsport* (New Yorker). *What harm will it do, just for once . . . ? Don't let us be spoilsports* (George Bernard Shaw).

spoils system, *U.S.* the system or practice in which public offices with their salaries and advantages are at the disposal of the victorious political party for its own purposes and in its own (rather than the public) interest: *Adams was a remarkable President in many ways (such as his iron refusal to adopt the spoils system) but he failed in his chief aims* (Newsweek).

spoilt (spoilt), *v.* spoiled; a past tense and a past participle of **spoil.**

spoke[1] (spōk), *v.* **1.** a past tense of **speak:** *She spoke about that yesterday.* **2.** *Archaic.* spoken; a past participle of **speak.**

spoke[2] (spōk), *n., v.,* **spoked, spok·ing.** —*n.* **1.** one of the set of staves, bars, or rods projecting radially from the hub of a wheel and supporting the felloe or rim. See **felloe** for picture. **2.** one of the set of handles projecting radially from the wheel by which the rudder of a ship or other vessel is controlled. **3.** any of various sets of radially projecting pieces similar to either of these in appearance or function. **4.** a rung of a ladder.

put a spoke in one's wheel, to stop or hinder one: *Capitalists . . . were trying to put a spoke in the wheel of Socialism* (Manchester Examiner).

—*v.t.* to furnish or provide with spokes.
[Old English *spāca*] —**spoke′like′,** *adj.*

spo·ken (spō′kən), *v.* a past participle of **speak:** *They have spoken about having a picnic.*
—*adj.* **1.** (of language, words, etc.) expressed or uttered in speech; oral: *the spoken word.* **2.** (of an opinion, view, etc.) made known by any utterance; expressed.

-spoken, *combining form.* speaking in a ____ way: *Blunt-spoken = speaking in a blunt way.*

spoke·shave (spōk′shāv′), *n.* a cutting tool having a blade with a handle at each end, used for planing curved work.

spokes·man (spōks′mən), *n., pl.* **-men.** a person who speaks for another or others, especially one who is chosen or deputed to represent the views of a body, party, etc.: *Mr. Smith was the spokesman for the factory workers.*

spokes·man·ship (spōks′mən ship), *n.* the office or position of a spokesman: *He felt there was some fitness in his spokesmanship that evening, for he was the representative of an institution* (London Daily News).

spokes·wom·an (spōks′wům′ən), *n., pl.* **-wom·en.** a woman who speaks for another or others; a female advocate or representative; woman speaker: *The frosty comment of a spokeswoman for Brighton's Roedean School: "We have absolutely no intention of modifying our uniform"* (Time).

spoke·wise (spōk′wīz), *adv.* in the manner of, or like the movements of, spokes of a wheel: *The sun's rays pour spokewise over the distant mountain rim* (New Yorker).

spo·li·a o·pi·ma (spō′lē ə ō pī′mə), *Latin.* rich spoils; valuable booty (with allusion to the arms taken from the defeated enemy's general by the victorious general, considered by the ancient Romans to be the noblest and choicest spoils of battle).

spo·li·ate (spō′lē āt), *v.t.*, **-at·ed, -at·ing.** to spoil, plunder, or despoil. [< Latin *spoliāre* (with English *-ate*[1]) < *spolium* booty]

spo·li·a·tion (spō′lē ā′shən), *n.* **1.** a plundering or pillaging; robbery; despoliation: *The history of the place is such a record of iconoclasms, massacres, persecutions, spoliations, demolitions* . . . (George Bernard Shaw). **2.** the authorized plundering of neutrals at sea during a war. **3.** *Law.* **a.** the act of destroying a document, or of tampering with it so as to destroy its value as evidence. **b.** the destruction of a ship's papers, as to conceal an illegal act. —**Syn. 1.** brigandage.

spo·li·a·tive (spō′lē ā′tiv), *adj.* (of a disease, etc.) diminishing the quantity of blood.

spo·li·a·tor (spō′lē ā′tər), *n.* a person who commits spoliation; a spoiler or despoiler.

spo·li·a·to·ry (spō′lē ə tôr′ē, -tōr′-), *adj.* of the nature of or characterized by spoliation.

spon·da·ic (spon dā′ik), *adj.* **1.** of a spondee. **2.** consisting of spondees. **3.** having a spondee where a different foot is normal, especially in the fifth foot of a hexameter line. [< Latin *spondaicus*, variant of *spondīacus* < Greek *spondeiakós* < *spondeîos*; see SPONDEE]

spon·dee (spon′dē), *n. Prosody.* a foot having two accented syllables: **a.** (in English verse) two stressed syllables. *Example* (in the first two metrical feet): So′ strode′/he′ back′/slow′/to the wound′/ed king′ (Tennyson). **b.** (in Greek and Latin verse) two long syllables. *Example: hērōs.* [< Latin *spondēus* < Greek *spondeîos* the meter originally used in chants accompanying libations < *spondḗ* libation < *spéndein* make a drink offering]

spon·du·licks or **spon·du·lix** (spon dü′liks), *n. Slang.* money; cash: *Then she boarded a bus for Reno, presumably to spend the spondulicks* (Daily Express). [American English; origin unknown]

spon·dy·li·tis (spon′də lī′tis), *n.* inflammation of the vertebrae. [< New Latin *spondylitis* < Latin *spondylus* (< Greek *spóndylos* vertebra) + New Latin *-itis* -itis]

spon·dy·lo·lis·the·sis (spon′də lō lis thē′sis), *n.* a pain in the back caused by the displacement of a lumbar vertebra, especially the fifth lumbar vertebra over the sacrum. [< Greek *spóndylos* vertebra + *olísthēsis* a slipping and falling]

sponge (spunj), *n., v.,* **sponged, spong·ing.** —*n.* **1.** any of a group of aquatic, usually marine animals, characterized by a tough, elastic skeleton of interlaced fibers. Sponges are free-swimming as larvae but soon become attached to stones, plants, etc., where they exist in large, complex colonies: . . . *sponges . . . for a long time were thought to be plants because they spend most of their life attached in one place and are not active in the sense that most animals are* (A.M. Winchester). **2.** the soft, light, porous, and easily compressible framework which remains after the living matter has been removed from these animals, characterized by readily absorbing liquids and yielding them on pressure, and much used in bathing, cleansing surfaces, etc. **3.** a piece of this or a similar substance, especially as used for wiping surfaces, bathing, etc.: *cellulose sponges.* **4.** the act of bathing with a sponge, especially in a small amount of water. **5. a.** a person or thing that absorbs, drains, or sucks up in the manner of a sponge: *His active mind was a sponge, soaking up impressions and information.* **b.** a person who drinks heavily: *I will do any thing, Nerissa, ere I will be married to a sponge* (Shakespeare). **6.** *Informal.* a person who continually lives at the expense of others; parasite. **7.** something having the appearance or consistency of a sponge. **8.** metal, as platinum or iron, in a porous or spongelike form, usually obtained by reduction without fusion: [*Titanium Corp.*] *expects to be in full production this fall at the rate of 3,600 tons of sponge a year* (Wall Street Journal). **9.** a sterile pad, usually of cotton gauze, used to absorb blood, etc., during surgical operations. **10.** a mop for cleaning the bore of a cannon. **11.** in cookery: **a.** the soft, fermenting dough of which bread is made. **b.** a fluffy pudding made with gelatin, egg whites, flavoring, etc. **c.** a sponge cake.

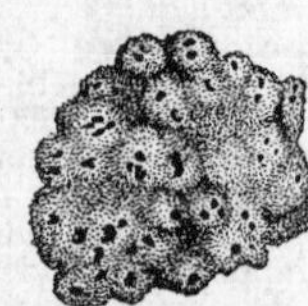
Sponge (def. 2)

throw in (or **throw up**) **the sponge,** to abandon a contest or struggle; admit defeat; give up (from the practice of a boxer's seconds' tossing a sponge into the ring in acknowledgment of defeat): *The tax-reform program was so badly battered that the administration threw in the sponge* (Harper's).

—*v.t.* **1.** to wipe or rub with a wet sponge in order to clean or dampen: *Mrs. Hansen sponged herself, dressed, and had a quiet breakfast* (New Yorker). **2.** to remove or wipe (away or off) with a sponge: *Sponge the mud spots off the car.* **3.** to absorb or take (up) with a sponge: *Sponge up the spilled water.* **4.** to rub or wipe (out) as if with a sponge; remove all traces of; obliterate; efface: *Time . . . That sponges out all trace of truth* (Eliza Cook). **5.** *Informal.* to get from another or at another's expense in a mean or parasitic way; cadge: *He sponges all his smokes.* **6.** to preshrink (cloth) before making it into clothing. —*v.i.* **1.** to absorb or take up, as a sponge. **2.** to gather sponges. **3.** *Informal.* to live or profit at the expense of another: *The lazy good-for-nothing man won't work, but sponges on his family.*

[Old English *spynge* < Latin *spongia* < Greek *spongiā*, variant of *sphóngos*] —**sponge′like′,** *adj.*

sponge·a·ble (spun′jə bəl), *adj.* that can be sponged without damage: *Jackson . . . always wore a spongeable celluloid collar* (Manchester Guardian).

sponge·bag (spunj′bag′), *n. British.* a waterproof bag used to carry a bath sponge and other toilet articles.

sponge cake, or **sponge·cake** (spunj′kāk′), *n.* a light, spongy cake made with eggs, sugar, flour, etc., but no shortening.

sponge cloth, a cotton fabric of loose texture, used for women's clothing.

sponge glass, a bucket with a glass bottom, used in searching for sponges.

sponge gourd, 1. the fruit of the loofah. **2.** the plant itself.

sponge iron, iron ore rendered light and porous by the removal of foreign matter.

sponge mop, a mop consisting of a sponge fastened at the end of a stick, usually with a wringing device: . . . *a "mechanical blotter" that soaks up excess moisture in much the same way as a household sponge mop* (Newsweek).

spon·geous (spun′jəs), *adj.* spongy.

spong·er (spun′jər), *n.* **1.** a person who sponges. **2. a.** a machine for sponging cloth. **b.** a person who sponges cloth. **3.** a person or vessel engaged in sponge fishing. **4.** *Informal.* a person who gets on at the expense of others.

sponge rubber, rubber similar to foam rubber, used for cushions, insulators, etc. It is made from dried natural rubber or latex by adding chemicals that release air bubbles inflating the rubber into a spongy mass.

spon·gin (spun′jin), *n.* the horny or fibrous substance of some sponges, related chemically to silk: *Certain sponges develop a framework consisting of fibers composed of a protein compound termed spongin* . . . (Harbaugh and Goodrich).

spon·gi·ness (spun′jē nis), *n.* spongy character: *The sponginess of ordinary springs and shock absorbers is replaced with a new firmness* (Atlantic).

spong·ing house (spun′jing), a building formerly maintained by a sheriff's officer in England for the temporary confinement of debtors, from which a person could obtain release through the satisfaction of his creditor or creditors, or be committed to prison: *Peter Quennell . . . is . . . a knowing and fascinating guide among . . . the . . . sponging houses of 18th century London* (Time).

spon·gi·ose (spun′jē ōs), *adj.* spongy; porous.

spon·gi·ous (spun′jē əs), *adj.* spongiose.

spon·goid (spong′goid), *adj.* spongelike; spongy. [< Greek *spongoeidēs* < *spongiā* sponge + *-oeidēs* -oid]

spon·gy (spun′jē), *adj.,* **-gi·er, -gi·est. 1.** having a soft, elastic texture; readily compressible: *a spongy dough, spongy soil.* **2.** having an open, porous structure; full of small holes: *spongy ice.* **3.** *Obsolete.* having much rain; wet: *I saw . . . the Roman eagle wing'd From the spongy South* (Shakespeare).

spon·sing (spon′sing), *n.* a sponson.

spon·sion (spon′shən), *n.* **1.** a solemn or formal engagement, promise, or pledge, often one entered into or made on behalf of another person. **2.** (in international law) a promise or act on behalf of a state by an agent without definite authority for it. [< Latin *spōnsiō, -ōnis* < *spondēre* promise solemnly]

spon·son (spon′sən), *n.* **1.** a structure built out from the side of a vessel for support or shelter, especially a platform for handling gear or an armored structure containing a turret and gun, such as was common on large naval vessels built in the late 1800's: *The new tugs will have a length of 145 ft. between perpendiculars and a beam of 58 ft. across the paddle sponsons* (London Times). **2.** a projecting structure to increase stability: **a.** an air-filled compartment on either side of the hull of a canoe. **b.** a short, winglike protuberance on either side of the hull of a seaplane, by which the craft is steadied while on the water. [origin uncertain]

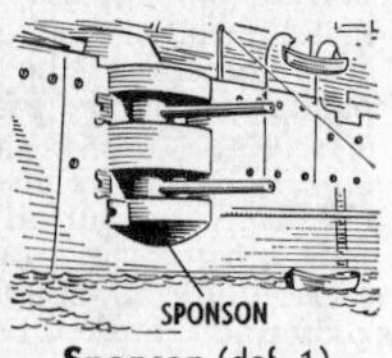

Sponson (def. 1)

spon·sor (spon′sər), *n.* **1.** a person or group that formally endorses or supports another: *the sponsor of a law, the sponsor of a student applying for a scholarship.* **2.** a person who makes a formal promise or pledge on behalf of another; surety. **3.** a person who takes vows for an infant at baptism; godfather or godmother. **4.** a business or other organization that pays the costs of a radio or television program advertising its products: *A television sponsor is shopping for a replacement for "My Favorite Husband"* (New York Times). **5.** a person or group that arranges or promotes an organization, meeting, etc. **6.** a person who pledges or gives a certain amount of financial assistance to an organization: *A contribution of $25 entitles you to be a sponsor; $15 to be a sustaining member.*

—*v.t.* to act as sponsor for; be the sponsor of: *A local jeweler who had been confined to a wheelchair for 16 years, sponsored the troop* (Time).

[< Latin *spōnsor* < *spondēre* give assurance, promise solemnly]

spon·so·ri·al (spon sôr′ē əl, -sōr′-), *adj.* of or having to do with a sponsor: *a sponsorial grant.*

spon·sor·ship (spon′sər ship), *n.* the position, duties, etc., of a sponsor: *FM radio stations increased in importance . . . with many classical music and cultural programs gaining local sponsorship* (World Book Annual).

spon·ta·ne·i·ty (spon′tə nē′ə tē), *n., pl.* **-ties. 1.** the state, quality, or fact of being spontaneous: *Mr. Rosen's quartet was . . . possessed more of expert workmanship than any great feeling of spontaneity* (New York Times). **2.** a spontaneous action or movement on the part of a living organism, especially activity of physical organs in the absence of any external stimulus.

spon·ta·ne·ous (spon tā′nē əs), *adj.* **1.** caused by natural impulse or desire; not forced or compelled; not planned beforehand: *Both sides burst into spontaneous cheers at the brilliant play.* **2.** taking place without external cause or help; caused entirely by inner forces: *The eruption of a volcano is spontaneous.* **3.** growing or produced naturally without cultivation or labor; not planted, cultivated, etc.

—*adv.* in a spontaneous manner.

[< Late Latin *spontāneus* (with English *-ous*) < Latin *sponte* of one's own accord] —**spon·ta′ne·ous·ly,** *adv.* —**spon·ta′ne·ous·ness,** *n.* —**Syn.** *adj.* **1.** See **voluntary.**

spontaneous combustion, the bursting into flame of a substance without anyone's having set it on fire. In spontaneous combustion, the heat produced by chemical action within the substance itself causes it to catch fire: *Spontaneous combustion is self-initiating combustion* (W.N. Jones).

spontaneous generation, the supposed production of living organisms from nonliving matter; abiogenesis; autogenesis: . . . *worms from mud, maggots from decaying meat. . . . This is the view that came to be called spontaneous generation* (Scientific American).

spontaneous pneumothorax, pneumothorax produced by internal causes.

spon·toon (spon tün′), *n.* a type of pike, having a short shaft, carried by officers, especially officers up to the rank of captain, in the British infantry from about 1740 until the early 1800's. [< French *esponton* < Italian *spontone,* and *spuntone,* variant of *puntone* < *punto* a point < Latin *pungere* to pierce]

spoof (spüf), *Informal.* —*n.* a trick, joke, or hoax, especially in satire: . . . *to the Imperial Theatre to see "Silk Stockings," a musical spoof of a Soviet woman commissar's trip to Paris* (New York Times). —*v.t., v.i.* to treat or offer as a spoof; joke; fool: *The most successful part of the show is his spoofing of TV programs and commercials* (Newsweek). [earlier, a game involving hoaxing (invented and named by Arthur Roberts, 1852-1913, a British comedian)]

spoof·er (spü′fər), *n. Informal.* a person or thing that spoofs: *Noel Coward, an agile spoofer of mad dogs and Englishmen . . .* (Newsweek).

spoof·er·y (spü′fər ē), *n. Informal.* **1.** cheating; deceit. **2.** a making fun (of); mockery; parody: *Their affectionate tributes to Bohr on his 70th birthday take the form of playful spoofery of physics today* (Scientific American).

spook (spük), *Informal.* —*n.* a ghost; specter: *There did I see a spook, sure enough—milk-white and moving round* (E. G. Paige). —*v.t.* **1.** to haunt (a person or place). **2.** to scare; frighten: *Lights on the water during night fishing are apt to spook the fish away* (Wall Street Journal). [American English < Dutch *spook*] —**Syn.** *n.* wraith, apparition.

spook·er·y (spü′kər ē), *n., pl.* **-er·ies.** that which is spooky or characteristic of spooks: *The writer drags in sundry hauntings and spookeries of a mild nature* (Athenaeum).

spook·i·ly (spü′kə lē), *adv.* in a spooky manner: *The owl hooted spookily from the dark woods.*

spook·i·ness (spü′kē nis), *n.* the quality or condition of being spooky: *"All the spookiness began on the afternoon of Feb. 3," [she] said with a frown* (Newsweek).

spook·ish (spü′kish), *adj. Informal.* **1.** like a spook or ghost; ghostly. **2.** given over to spooks; haunted: *a spookish house.* **3.** affected by a sense or fear of ghosts; suggestive of the presence or agency of spooks: *a spookish sensation.*

spook·y (spü′kē), *adj.,* **spook·i·er, spook·i·est.** *Informal.* like a spook; suited to spooks; suggesting spooks: . . . *the view from the North Church belfry of the spooky and moonlit harbor* (New Yorker).

spool (spül), *n.* **1.** a small cylinder of wood or other material on which thread or yarn is wound as it is spun, especially for use in weaving; bobbin; quill. **2.** a similar piece of wood with a rim or wider part at each end, on which sewing thread is wound; reel. **3.** any cylinder on which cord, wire, tape, etc., is wound for convenience or for a special purpose. **4.** something like a spool in shape or use.
—*v.t.* to wind on a spool.
[< Middle Dutch *spoele*] —**spool′er,** *n.*

spoom (spüm), *v.i. Archaic.* to run or scud, as a ship before the wind: *When virtue spooms before a prosp'rous gale, My heaving wishes help to fill the sail* (John Dryden). [variant of earlier *spoon;* origin unknown]

spoon (spün), *n.* **1.** a utensil consisting of a small, shallow bowl at the end of a handle, used to take up or stir food or drink: *a coffee spoon.* **2.** something shaped like a spoon or the bowl of a spoon. **3.** a golf club with a wooden head, having a slightly shorter and more rigid shaft and a face with greater slope than a driver or brassie. **4.** spoon bait. **5.** a curved projection at the top of a torpedo tube to keep the torpedo going in a horizontal path.
born with a silver spoon in one's mouth, born lucky or rich: *There never was a child so plainly born with the traditional silver spoon in his mouth as Waller* (Edmund W. Gosse).
—*v.t.* **1.** to take up or transfer with or as if with a spoon: *She negligently spooned her soup, and then, after much parade, sent it away untouched* (Benjamin Disraeli). **2.** to hollow out or form in the shape of the bowl of a spoon. **3.** *Informal.* to make love to in a sentimental manner: *He's spooning our schoolmarm* (Owen Wister). **4.** to push (a croquet ball) with the mallet instead of hitting it. **5.** to hit (a golf ball) feebly with a lifting motion, as in a sand trap. **6.** *Cricket.* to hit (the ball) into the air weakly. **7.** to troll for or catch (fish) with a spoon bait.
—*v.i.* **1.** to spoon a croquet, golf, or cricket ball. **2.** to fish or troll with a spoon bait. **3.** *Informal.* to make love in a silly or sentimental way.
[Old English *spōn* chip, shaving; meaning probably influenced by Scandinavian (compare Old Icelandic *spōnn, spānn* chip; wooden spoon)] —**spoon′like′,** *adj.*

spoon back, the back of a chair slightly curved to fit the sitter's form: *Taylor gave 650 gns. for a set of six Queen Anne walnut chairs with spoon backs* (London Times).

spoon bait, a bright, spoon-shaped piece of metal swiveled just in front of the hook or hooks, used as a lure in casting or trolling for fish.

spoon·bill (spün′bil′), *n.* **1.** any of a group of longlegged wading birds closely related to the ibises, having a long spatulate or spoon-shaped bill. **2.** any of certain other birds having such a bill. **3.** a paddlefish.

Roseate Spoonbill (def. 1—30 in. long)

spoon·billed (spün′bild′), *adj.* **1.** (of birds) having a spoonlike or spatulate bill, dilated at the end. **2.** (of fishes) duckbilled; shovel-nosed; having a long, spatulate snout, as a sturgeon.

spoon bread, a mixture of corn meal, and sometimes rice, with milk, eggs, shortening, etc., cooked by baking but always soft enough to be served with a spoon.

spoon·drift (spün′drift′), *n.* spindrift. [< obsolete *spoon* to sail before the wind (origin unknown) + *drift,* noun]

spoon·er·ism (spü′nə riz əm), *n.* an accidental transposition of sounds, usually the initial sounds, of two or more words, as "well-boiled icicle" for "well-oiled bicycle." [< Reverend William A. *Spooner,* 1844-1930, of New College, Oxford, who was famous for such mistakes + *-ism*]

spoon·ey (spü′nē), *adj.,* **spoon·i·er, spoon·i·est,** *n., pl.* **spoon·eys.** spoony.

spoon-fash·ion (spün′fash′ən), *adv.* like spoons put close together; with the face of one to the back of the other and with the knees bent: *to lie spoon-fashion.*

spoon-fed (spün′fed′), *adj.* **1.** protected and coddled, like a child who must be fed with a spoon; pampered: *a spoon-fed industry.* **2.** discouraging or minimizing independence of thought and action, especially by avoiding what is difficult, controversial, unpleasant, etc.: *spoon-fed education.*

spoon-feed (spün′fēd′), *v.t., v.i.,* **-fed, -feed·ing.** to feed with or as if with a spoon; coddle; pamper: *Nobody has yet come up with a solution of how to spoon-feed an industry without stifling it* (Time).

spoon·ful (spün′fu̇l), *n., pl.* **-fuls.** as much as a spoon can hold.

spoon hook, a hook with a spinning lure (spoon) attached.

spoon·i·ly (spü′nə lē), *adv. Informal.* in a silly or spoony manner.

spoon·i·ness (spü′nē nis), *n. Informal.* spoony character or state; silly fondness.

spoon meat, food taken with a spoon; soft or liquid food, especially for infants or invalids.

spoon oar, an oar which is slightly curved lengthwise at the end of its broad blade.

spoon·y (spü′nē), *adj.,* **spoon·i·er, spoon·i·est,** *n., pl.* **spoon·ies.** *Informal.* —*adj.* foolish or silly in lovemaking; demonstratively fond: *I was never in love myself, but I've seen many others spoony* (Frederick Marryat). —*n.* **1.** a sentimental or overfond lover. **2.** a simpleton: *What the deuce can she find in that spoony . . . ?* (Thackeray).

spoor (spůr), *n.* the trail of a wild animal or person; track: *The spoor of every species of game could be found* (V. Pohl). *Only . . . Bushmen . . . could have made that spoor* (London Times). —*v.t.* to track (an animal) by its spoor. —*v.i.* to follow a spoor. [< Afrikaans *spoor* < Middle Dutch] —**spoor′er,** *n.*

spor-, *combining form.* the form of **sporo-** before vowels, as in *sporulate.*

spo·rad·ic (spə rad′ik), *adj.* **1.** appearing, happening, etc., now and again or at intervals; occasional: *sporadic outbreaks.* **2.** being or occurring apart from others; isolated: *The sporadic meteors, which appear to be independent travelers, seem to be divided between stony and metallic . . .* (Robert H. Baker). **3.** occurring in scattered instances; not epidemic: *sporadic cases of scarlet fever.* **4.** occurring singly or widely apart in locality; scattered; dispersed: *sporadic genera of plants.* [< Medieval Latin *sporadicus* < Greek *sporadikós* scattered < *sporás, -ados* scattered < *sporá;* see SPORE]

spo·rad·i·cal (spə rad′ə kəl), *adj.* sporadic.

spo·rad·i·cal·ly (spə rad′ə klē), *adv.* here and there; now and then; separately: *There are any number of uncatalogued diseases that crop up sporadically* (Scientific American).

spo·ra·dic·i·ty (spôr′ə dis′ə tē, spōr′-), *n.* sporadic quality.

spo·ra·do·sid·er·ite (spôr′ə dō sid′ə rīt, spōr′-), *n.* a stony meteorite containing grains of iron. [< Greek *sporás, -ados* scattered + English *siderite*]

spo·ral (spôr′əl, spōr′-), *adj.* of or having to do with spores.

spo·ran·gi·a (spə ran′jē ə), *n.* the plural of **sporangium.**

spo·ran·gi·al (spə ran′jē əl), *adj.* **1.** of or relating to the sporangium: *the sporangial layer.* **2.** containing spores. **3.** having the character of a sporangium.

spo·ran·gi·o·phore (spə ran′jē ə fôr, -fōr), *n.* the structure or receptacle which bears the sporangia.

spo·ran·gi·um (spə ran′jē əm), *n., pl.* **-gi·a.** *Botany.* a receptacle or case in which asexual spores are produced; spore case. The sporangium receives different names according to the kind of spores produced, as *macrosporangium, microsporangium,* etc. In mosses *sporangium* is usually the same as *capsule.* The little brown spots sometimes seen on the under side of ferns are groups of sporangia. [< New Latin *sporangium* < Greek *sporá* seed (see SPORE) + *angeîon* vessel]

spore (spôr, spōr), *n., v.,* **spored, spor·ing.** —*n.* **1.** *Biology.* a single cell which becomes free and is capable of developing into a new plant or animal. The name is given to all the reproductive bodies of flowerless plants, which are the analogues of the seeds of the higher or flowering plants, from which they further differ by having no embryo, and to the reproductive bodies of some protozoans. Spores are produced asexually (asexual spores) or sexually (sexual spores) by the fusion of gametes. *These organisms not only flourish without oxygen, but also form resistant spores which survive pasteurization* (J. A. Barnett). **2.** a germ; seed. —*v.i.* (of a plant) to form or produce spores. [< New Latin *spora* < Greek *sporá* seed; a sowing < *speírein* to sow]

spore case, a receptacle containing spores; sporangium: *Each spore case, or sporangium, is about the size of a pinhead* (World Book Encyclopedia).

spore fruit, any part of a plant that produces spores, such as an ascocarp.

spore·ling (spôr′ling, spōr′-), *n. Botany.* a young plant, such as a fern, developed from a spore: *Hans Mohr has demonstrated that fern sporelings show a marked phototropic response to red light* (Scientific American).

spo·ri·cid·al (spôr′ə sī′dəl, spōr′-), *adj.* destructive of spores: *The agency now proposes to use . . . sporicidal agents on exposed surfaces, and special handling methods to minimise contamination* (New Scientist). [< *spore* + *-icidal,* as in *fungicidal*]

spo·rif·er·ous (spə rif′ər əs), *adj.* bearing or producing spores. [< New Latin *spora* (see SPORE) + English *-ferous*]

sporo-, *combining form.* spore or spores: *Sporogenesis = the formation of spores.* Also, **spor-** before vowels. [< Greek *sporá,* or *spóros* seed; a sowing < *speírein* to sow]

spo·ro·carp (spôr′ə kärp, spōr′-), *n. Botany.* **1.** a multicellular body serving essentially for the formation of spores, as in red algae and ascomycetous fungi. **2.** (in mosses) sporogonium. **3.** a sorus in certain aquatic ferns. [< *sporo-* + Greek *karpós* fruit]

spo·ro·cyst (spôr′ə sist, spōr′-), *n.* **1.** a cyst formed by sporozoans during reproduction, in which sporozoites develop. **2.** an encysted sporozoan. **3.** a capsule or sac containing germ cells, that develops from the embryo of trematode worms, usually within the body of a snail. **4.** *Botany.* a resting cell which produces asexual spores, as in algae.

spo·ro·cyte (spôr′ə sīt, spōr′-), *n. Botany.* a cell from which a spore is derived.

spo·ro·duct (spôr′ə dukt, spōr′-), *n.* a duct in which spores are lodged or through which they pass.

spo·ro·gen·e·sis (spôr′ə jen′ə sis, spōr′-), *n. Biology.* **1.** the formation of spores: *... in the mosses, ferns and seed plants [meiosis] occurs ... during sporogenesis* (Harbaugh and Goodrich). **2.** reproduction by means of spores.

spo·rog·e·nous (spə roj′ə nəs), *adj.* **1.** reproducing or reproduced by means of spores. **2.** bearing or producing spores: *There is an operculum, as usual, but the sporogenous cells form a dome-shaped mass* (Fred W. Emerson).

spo·ro·go·ni·um (spôr′ə gō′nē əm, spōr′-), *n., pl.* **-ni·a** (-nē ə). (in mosses) the asexual generation that produces the spores; sporocarp. [< New Latin *sporogonium* < Greek *sporá* (see SPORE) + a root *gen-* to bear]

spo·rog·o·ny (spə rog′ə nē), *n.* reproduction by spore formation, as in sporozoans.

spo·ront (spôr′ont, spōr′-), *n.* (in sporozoans) a cell or zygote which forms spores by encystment and subsequent division. [< *spor*(e) + Greek *ṓn, ontós* being, present participle of *eînai* to be]

spo·ro·phore (spôr′ə fôr, spōr′ə fōr), *n. Botany.* **1.** the branch or portion of the thallus (plant body) which bears spores. In fungi, it is a single hypha or branch of a hypha. **2.** (in ferns and mosses) sporophyte.

spo·roph·o·rous (spə rof′ə rəs), *adj.* **1.** bearing spores. **2.** of or having to do with the sporophore.

spo·ro·phyll or **spo·ro·phyl** (spôr′ə fil, spōr′-), *n. Botany.* a leaf or leaflike organ, usually more or less modified, which bears receptacles containing spores (sporangia). [< *sporo-* + Greek *phýllon* leaf]

spo·ro·phyte (spôr′ə fīt, spōr′-), *n. Botany.* the individual plant or the generation of a plant which produces asexual spores, in a plant which reproduces both sexually and asexually: *In other words, the moss sporophyte acts as a parasite on the gametophyte* (Fred W. Emerson). [< *sporo-* + Greek *phytón* plant]

spo·ro·phyt·ic (spôr′ə fit′ik, spōr′-), *adj.* having to do with, resembling, or characteristic of a sporophyte.

spo·ro·tri·cho·sis (spôr′ō tri kō′sis, spōr′-), *n.* a fungous disease of horses, dogs, cats, and man, characterized by cutaneous lesions along the lymph vessels. [< New Latin *Sporotrichum* the genus name (< Greek *sporá* spore + *thríx, trichós* hair)]

spo·ro·zo·an (spôr′ə zō′ən, spōr′-), *n.* any of a class of minute parasitic protozoans which absorb food through the body wall and reproduce sexually and asexually in alternate generations. Certain sporozoans cause diseases of man and animals, such as malaria. —*adj.* of or belonging to the sporozoans. [< New Latin *Sporozoa* the class name (< Greek *sporá* spore + *zôion* animal)]

spo·ro·zo·ite (spôr′ə zō′īt, spōr′-), *n.* any of the minute, immature bodies, often infective, produced by the division of the spore of certain sporozoans, each of which develops into an adult sporozoan.

spo·ro·zo·ön (spôr′ə zō′on, spōr′-), *n., pl.* **-zo·a** (-zō′ə). a sporozoan: *Of particular interest is the malaria-like disease ... Texas fever; this is caused by a sporozoön ... which parasitizes the red blood cells* (Hegner and Stiles). [< *sporo-* + Greek *zôion* animal]

spor·ran (spôr′ən, spor′-), *n.* a large purse or pouch, usually covered with fur and ornamental tassels, worn in front of the kilt by Scottish Highlanders. [< Scottish Gaelic *sporan*]

Sporran

sport (spôrt, spōrt), *n.* **1.** a game or other form of pastime involving some amount of bodily exercise and carried on either in the open air, as football, baseball, tennis, hunting, or fishing, or indoors, as basketball or bowling: *Of all sports, only mountain-climbing, bullfighting, and automobile racing really tried a man ... the rest were recreations* (Atlantic). **2.** any activity providing entertainment or recreation; pastime; diversion: *After love, book collecting is the most exhilarating sport of all* (A.S.W. Rosenbach). **3.** playful joking; fun: *There is no sport in hate* (Shelley). **4.** ridicule. **5.** an object or subject of amusement, jesting, laughter, derision, etc.; laughingstock: *Don't make sport of the lame boy.* **6.** something driven or whirled about, especially by the wind or waves, as in sport; plaything: *the sport of chance. His hat blew off and became the sport of the wind.* **7.** a person who follows or participates in sports or a particular sport; sportsman. **8.** *Informal.* a young man; fellow. **9.** a good fellow; one who behaves in a sportsmanlike manner: *to be a sport, to be a good sport.* **10.** *Informal.* a betting man; gambler. **11.** *Informal.* a flashy person; one who wears showy clothes, pursues gay pastimes, or the like. **12.** *Biology.* an animal, plant, or part of a plant that varies suddenly or in a marked manner from the normal type or stock: *These differences were not the slight variations emphasized by Darwin but were wide differences, known among plant and animal breeders of today as sports* (Harbaugh and Goodrich). **13.** *Obsolete.* amorous dalliance.

for or **in sport,** for fun; in jest or as a joke; not seriously: *to say a thing in sport.*

turn to sport, to turn into or take as a matter for jesting or mirth: *Thrice I deluded her, and turn'd to sport Her importunity* (Milton).

—*v.i.* **1.** to amuse or entertain oneself; frolic; gambol; play: *See the children sport upon the shore* (Wordsworth). *If all the year were playing holidays, to sport would be as tedious as to work* (Shakespeare). **2.** to participate in or follow a sport or sports, especially an open-air sport. **3.** to deal (with) in a light or trifling way; dally: *To sport with Amaryllis in the shade* (Milton). *It was selfishness which made him sport with your affections* (Jane Austen). **4.** *Biology.* to vary abnormally from the normal type; exhibit spontaneous mutation. **5.** *Botany.* to show bud variation. —*v.t.* **1.** *Informal.* to wear, display, or use: *to sport a new hat. If a man ... sports loose views on morals at a decent dinner party, he is not asked again* (James A. Froude). **2.** *Obsolete.* to amuse or entertain (oneself).

—*adj.* **1.** of or suitable for outdoor sports. **2.** designed for informal, outdoor, or athletic wear.

[ultimately short for *disport*] —**sport′er,** *n.*

—**Syn.** *n.* **1.** See **play.**

sport·cast (spôrt′kast′, -käst′; spōrt′-), *n. Informal.* a sportscast.

sport·cast·er (spôrt′kas′tər, -käs′-; spōrt′-), *n. Informal.* a sportscaster: *From listening to these sportcasters ... I know that their eyes are not so much on the field below as on their score cards and record books* (Atlantic).

sport fish, a fish caught for sport, as a game fish.

sport·ful (spôrt′fəl, spōrt′-), *adj.* **1.** playful; sportive. **2.** diverting; entertaining; recreational. —**sport′ful·ly,** *adv.* —**sport′ful·ness,** *n.*

spor·tif (spôr tēf′), *adj. French.* sportive: *Models in the latest après-ski creations were strolling about looking appropriately sportif* (New Yorker).

sport·i·ly (spôr′tə lē, spōr′-), *adv. Informal.* in a sporty fashion or manner: *We were joined by an elderly gentleman who was dressed rather sportily in a brown silk suit, a pink shirt, and a black tie* (New Yorker).

sport·i·ness (spôr′tē nis, spōr′-), *n. Informal.* sporty quality or tendency.

sport·ing (spôr′ting, spōr′-), *adj.* **1.** of, interested in, or engaging in sports. **2.** playing fair. **3.** willing to take a chance. **4.** *Informal.* involving risk; uncertain: *a sporting chance.* —**sport′ing·ly,** *adv.*

sporting goods, clothing and equipment used in sports.

spor·tive (spôr′tiv, spōr′-), *adj.* **1.** playful; frolicsome; merry; gay: *The old dog seemed as sportive as the puppy.* **2.** not earnest or serious; jesting: *a sportive remark.* **3.** sporting: *It was now not a sportive combat, but a war to the death* (Macaulay). **4.** *Archaic.* very amorous; wanton: *Where sportive ladies leave their doors ajar* (Robert Browning). —**spor′tive·ly,** *adv.* —**spor′tive·ness,** *n.*

sport of kings, horse racing: *It is often called the sport of kings because at one time only kings and noblemen took part in it* (World Book Encyclopedia).

sports (spôrts, spōrts), *adj.* **1.** of or having to do with athletic sports: *the sports column or page, the sports editor of a paper.* **2.** designed or suitable for outdoor, athletic, or casual wear: *a sports shirt, a sports coat. Everyone wore leather patches on the elbows of perfectly new Harris tweed sports jackets* (Punch).

sports car, any of various small, low, fast cars that usually have open tops: *The Mille Miglia is a race for sports cars, not racing cars, but in recent years the distinction between the two has narrowed almost to the vanishing point* (Atlantic).

Sports Car

sports·cast (spôrts′kast′, -käst′; spōrts′-), *n. Informal.* a broadcast or telecast of a sporting event: *With his three radio sportscasts a day, five TV shows a week ... [he] is the most-listened-to broadcaster in the west* (Maclean's).

sports·cast·er (spôrts′kas′tər, -käs′-; spōrts′-), *n. Informal.* a person who does the spoken part of a sportscast: *He received a clamorous standing ovation from 600 radio and TV men who cited him as their "counselor, dean of sportscasters, and the architect of our profession"* (Newsweek).

sports·cast·ing (spôrts′kas′ting, -käs′-; spōrts′-), *n. Informal.* **1.** the occupation or work of a sportscaster. **2.** the making of a sportscast: *It amounts to the most spectacularly accurate piece of reportage in the history of sportscasting* (Newsweek).

sport shirt, a comfortable shirt designed for informal wear, usually without a tie: *He was barefoot and barelegged, wearing only floppy khaki shorts and a checked sport shirt, its tail tumbling outside* (Atlantic).

sport-shirt·ed (spôrt′shėr′tid, spōrt′-), *adj.* wearing a sport shirt: *He led us up to a ... group of sport-shirted moviemakers sitting around on canvas chairs* (New Yorker).

sports·man (spôrts′mən, spōrts′-), *n., pl.* **-men. 1.** a man who takes part in a sport or sports, especially hunting, fishing, riding, or racing. **2.** a man who likes sports: *Martin, a more sedentary sportsman, occasionally goes on a boat ride ... but mostly to be affable* (New Yorker). **3.** a person who plays fair. **4.** a person who is willing to take a chance.

sports·man·like (spôrts′mən līk′, spōrts′-), *adj.* like or befitting a good sportsman; fair and honorable: *That was a sportsmanlike gesture from a great pilot* (Atlantic).

sports·man·ly (spôrts′mən lē, spōrts′-), *adj.* like a good sportsman; sportsmanlike.

sports·man·ship (spôrts′mən ship, spōrts′-), *n.* **1.** the qualities or conduct of a good sportsman, especially insistence on fair play accompanied by the capacity to win or lose gracefully, without arrogance in victory or whining in defeat: *She would have been raised by solid people ... and would respect all the ... virtues: courage, good sportsmanship ... and honor* (New Yorker). **2.** ability in sports.

sports·wear (spôrts′wãr′, spōrts′-), *n.* a type of casual, usually tailored apparel originally designed to be worn for active participation in sports, now also used by men and women for informal wear: *Men became ... fonder of wash-and-wear fabrics, and more daring in their approach to colorful sportswear* (World Book Encyclopedia).

sports·wom·an (spôrts′wu̇m′ən, spōrts′-), *n., pl.* **-wom·en.** a woman who engages in or is interested in a sport or sports.

sports·writ·er (spôrts′rī′tər, spōrts′-), *n.* a journalist who specializes in writing about sports: *Sportswriters ... speculating on the possibility of some new kind of rabbit ball* ... (Time).

sports·writ·ing (spôrts′rī′ting, spōrts′-), *n.* the occupation or work of writing about sports: *He dissects the drama ... with a racy enthusiasm that is nowadays more likely to be found in sportswriting* (New Yorker).

sport·y (spôr′tē, spōr′-), *adj.,* **sport·i·er, sport·i·est.** *Informal.* **1.** gay or fast; flashy: *... she knew he was associating with ... "a sporty crowd"* (Sinclair Lewis). **2.** smart in dress, appearance, manners, etc. **3.** sportsmanlike; sporting. —**Syn.** **1.** showy. **2.** natty.

spor·u·late (spôr′yə lāt, spōr′-), *v.*, **-lat·ed, -lat·ing.** *Biology.* —*v.i.* to form spores or sporules. —*v.t.* to convert into spores.

spor·u·la·tion (spôr′yə lā′shən, spōr′-), *n. Biology.* the formation of or conversion into spores or sporules: *Propagation by sporulation is characteristic of a class of the Protozoa known as the Sporozoa . . .* (Harbaugh and Goodrich).

spor·ule (spôr′yül, spōr′-), *n. Biology.* **1.** a spore. **2.** a small spore. [< French *sporule* < New Latin *sporula* (diminutive) < *spora;* see SPORE]

sposh (sposh), *n. U.S.* slush; watery matter; mud. [probably imitative]

spot (spot), *n., v.,* **spot·ted, spot·ting,** *adj.* —*n.* **1.** a small discoloring or disfiguring mark made by a foreign substance; stain; speck: *a spot of ink on the paper.* **2.** a stain or blemish on character or reputation; moral defect; fault; flaw: *Sublimely mild, a spirit without spot* (Shelley). **3.** a small part of a surface differing in some way from the rest, as in color, material, or finish; dot: *a blue tie with white spots, a leopard's spots.* **4.** a small extent of space; place; site; locality: *From this spot you can see the parade. A lonely spot by a woodside* (George Gissing); *the most pleasant spot in Italy* (John Evelyn). **5.** *Especially British Informal.* a small amount or quantity; little bit: *a spot of lunch.* **6.** *Informal.* a position or place with reference to employment, radio or television scheduling, or the like: *Its time spot . . . put it in head-on competition with the season's most popular show* (Newsweek). **7.** *Informal.* a spotlight: *Hung from perches . . . above the stage and in the wings . . .* [*are*] *vertical pipes . . . which support clusters of spots* (New Yorker). **8.** a small sciaenoid food fish of the Atlantic Coast of North America, having a dark marking on each side. **9.** a variety of domestic pigeon, having white plumage with a spot of another color above the beak. **10.** a sunspot: *A complete and fully formed spot shows a central portion, known as the umbra, surrounded by a not-so-dark area called the penumbra* (Wasley S. Krogdahl). **11.** *Botany.* a plant disease; leaf spot. **12.** *U.S. Slang.* a piece of paper money; bill: *a five spot, a ten spot.* **13.** a pip or dot on a playing card or die.

hit the spot, *Informal.* to be just right; be satisfactory: *A cool drink on a hot day is always certain to hit the spot.*

in spots, a. in one spot, part, place, point, etc., and another: *an argument weak in spots.* **b.** at times; by snatches: *Mammy has a kind of obstinacy about her, in spots, that everybody don't see as I do* (Harriet Beecher Stowe).

on or **upon the spot, a.** at the very place in question: *You know in business there's nothing like being on the spot* (Lord Dunsany). **b.** immediately; at once; straightway: *He expected his orders to be carried out on the spot.* **c.** *Informal.* in trouble or difficulty; in an awkward or embarrassing position: *A tall, gray-haired man, obviously enjoying his opportunity to try to put the Prime Minister on the spot, opened with a question on post-war credits* (New York Times).

put on the spot, *Slang.* to mark (someone) for death by assassination: *You get rid of inconvenient subordinates . . . by putting them on the spot—that is, deliberately sending them to their death* (Punch).

—*v.t.* **1.** to make spots on; stain: *to spot a dress.* **2.** to stain, sully, or tarnish (character, reputation, etc.): *He spotted his reputation by lying repeatedly.* **3.** to mark, cover, or decorate with spots. **4.** to catch sight of; recognize or detect: *I spotted my sister in the crowd. The teacher spotted every mistake. To CONAD's Colorado control center come instantaneous reports on every unidentified aircraft spotted over North America* (Newsweek). **5.** to place in a certain spot or area: *to spot a billiard ball. Lookouts were spotted all along the coast.* **6.** to locate (an enemy position, weapon, etc.) exactly on the ground or a map. **7.** *Informal.* to give or allow a lead or handicap to: *Wisconsin spotted Illinois a first-period touchdown, then turned loose a sharp ground attack to down the nation's third ranking football team, 34-7, today* (New York Times). —*v.i.* **1.** to make a spot or stain. **2.** to be subject to spots; become spotted, as a fabric: *Silk will spot with rain.* —*adj.* **1.** on hand; ready: *a spot answer.* **2.** for immediate cash payment and delivery: *a spot sale.* **3.** having to do with or specializing in cash transactions: *A leading spot firm said there was a decided improvement in mill buying* (Wall Street Journal). **4.** *Informal.* produced by and broadcast from a local station: *There are many variations of this procedure, allowing for the placing of national and local "spot" commercials* (London Times).

[compare Middle Dutch *spot* speck]

—**Syn.** *n.* **1.** fleck, blotch, blot.

spot announcement, a short advertisement or other announcement inserted by a local radio or television station before or during a regular network program.

spot cash, money paid just as soon as goods are delivered or work is done.

spot check, 1. a brief, rough sampling: *The number of people waiting in line to make withdrawals or deposits was normal in most banks around the city, a spot check and talks with bankers showed* (Wall Street Journal). **2.** a checkup made without warning: *Russian negotiators at Geneva have made a special point of trying to limit . . . the numbers of spot checks* (Manchester Guardian).

spot-check (spot′chek′), *v.t.* to make a spot check of: *Tons of gold — and silver too — are being spot-checked for purity and weight* (New York Times).

spot·face (spot′fās′), *v.t.,* **-faced, -fac·ing.** to face (a spot) around a hole drilled for a bolt or screw: *The heads . . . drill and countersink holes, spotface them . . . and face the outer surfaces* (Newsweek).

spot lamp, *Especially British.* spotlight: *To study the fuel distribution before combustion, the chamber is lit by intense spot lamps* (New Scientist).

spot·less (spot′lis), *adj.* **1.** without a spot; absolutely clean; immaculate: *a spotless kitchen. She wore a spotless white apron.* **2.** without a stain or blot; unblemished: *a spotless reputation.* —**spot′less·ly,** *adv.* —**spot′less·ness,** *n.*

spot·light (spot′līt′), *n., v.,* **-light·ed** or **-lit, -light·ing.** —*n.* **1.** *Theater.* **a.** a spot or circle of strong light thrown upon a particular person or object, leaving the rest of the stage more or less unilluminated. **b.** a lamp that gives such a light: *The single overhead spotlight, which once was extensively used to throw a sharp ray onto a darkened stage . . . is regarded as an antiquated cliché* (New Yorker). **2.** any of various somewhat similar lamps, as an electric lamp of the type mounted on certain police cars, having a powerful, narrowly focused beam that can be pointed in any desired direction. **3.** conspicuous attention; public notice.

—*v.t.* **1.** to light up with a spotlight or spotlights: *At night, red lights flash; the launching pad is spotlighted like a baseball field* (Newsweek). **2.** to call attention to; highlight: *The investigation, too, will spotlight an industry that, despite its importance, remains much of a mystery to most Americans* (Wall Street Journal). —**Syn.** *n.* **3.** publicity.

spot news, news reported at once from where it happens: *The newspapers, wire services, and networks sent their best men, top-seasoned hands to handle the fast-breaking spot news* (Harper's).

spot pass, *Football.* a pass timed to meet a receiver at a certain spot on the field: *Fullback Homer Williams prepares to take a spot pass from* [*the*] *quarterback* (Birmingham News).

spot·ta·ble (spot′ə bəl), *adj.* that can be spotted.

spot·ted (spot′id), *adj.* **1.** stained with or as if with spots, especially morally stained; blemished: *a spotted reputation.* **2.** marked with spots: *a spotted dog.* —**Syn. 2.** speckled, dappled.

spotted adder, the milk snake.

spotted cavy, the paca.

spotted cowbane, a North American water hemlock with mottled stems and poisonous roots.

spotted crake, a small European rail related to the American sora; water crake.

spotted crane's-bill, the common wild geranium of North America, with purplish or white flowers.

spotted deer, the axis deer of southeast Asia.

Spotted Dog or **Dick,** *British.* **1.** a white or light-colored dog with black or dark spots, as the Dalmatian. **2.** a suet pudding made with currants or raisins showing outside.

spotted fever, a fever characterized by the appearance of spots on the skin, especially cerebrospinal meningitis, typhus, or Rocky Mountain spotted fever: *Spotted fever is a serious disease that infects cattle, and expensive dipping of cattle for tick eradication is a necessity in many of the cattle-raising regions of the country* (A.M. Winchester).

spotted hemlock, the spotted cowbane.

spotted hyena, a grayish hyena with dark spots, found throughout most of Africa.

spotted jewfish, a large edible grouper of warm American seas.

spotted moray, a kind of moray common in West Indian waters.

spot·ted·ness (spot′id nis), *n.* the quality or state of being spotted: *There are some birds who do not seem to care about the size or spottedness of the egg* (Science News Letter).

spotted salamander, a bluish-black salamander with two rows of yellow spots along the back and tail, common in the eastern United States and Canada.

spotted sandpiper, a North American sandpiper with large spots on a white breast. See **sandpiper** for picture.

spotted skunk, a small North American skunk with white spots on the head, narrow white stripes on the body and a white-tipped tail.

Spotted Swine, any of an American breed of swine, similar to the Poland China hog breed.

spotted wilt, a variety of wilt disease characterized by the inward and downward curling of the youngest leaves and reddish spotting or metallic bronzing of the foliage.

spot·ter (spot′ər), *n.* **1.** a person who makes or removes spots: *After drying, the garment goes to a highly-skilled worker called a spotter . . . to remove any stains* (World Book Encyclopedia). **2.** a device for making or removing spots. **3.** a person who observes a wide area of enemy terrain, as from an aircraft or high point on the ground, in order to locate, and direct artillery fire against, any of various targets, as enemy gun emplacements, troop concentrations, etc. **4.** a person who watches for and reports the presence of unidentified aircraft. **5.** a person employed to watch employees, customers, etc., for evidence of dishonesty or other misconduct, usually one who watches from a hidden place or whose identity is concealed. **6.** a person or airplane whose job is to watch for or spot any situation which may require attention: *Crevasse spotters at the MacMurdo Sound base tragically missed a perfect score* (Newsweek). **7.** a machine that automatically sets up the pins in a bowling alley; pinspotter.

spot test, 1. a spot check. **2.** a chemical analysis in which a drop of the sample to be analyzed is mixed with a reagent on a filter paper, glass plate, etc., used to identify the presence of metals, alkaloids, etc.

spot·ti·ly (spot′ə lē), *adv.* in a spotty manner; without uniformity.

spot·ti·ness (spot′ē nis), *n.* the quality or state of being spotty: *Spottiness has developed in appliance manufacturers' buying of steel* (Wall Street Journal).

spot·ting scope (spot′ing), a small, portable telescope used in hunting, target shooting, etc.: *Old-time ornithologists shot birds to identify them . . .. The modern school relies on superior knowledge of field marks, binoculars or spotting scope, and/or camera* (Time).

spot·ty (spot′ē), *adj.,* **-ti·er, -ti·est. 1.** having spots; spotted. **2.** not of uniform quality; irregularly good and bad: *spotty work.*

spot-weld (spot′weld′), *v.t.* to weld by passing electric current through the contacting spots and applying pressure: *It has also proved possible to spot-weld electrically studs and stiffener brackets to the steel back of the laminate without damaging the film on the surface* (New Scientist).

spot weld, a weld made by spot-welding.

spous·al (spou′zəl), *Archaic.* —*n.* Often, **spousals.** the ceremony of marriage; nuptials. —*adj.* of or having to do with marriage; nuptial. [short for Old French *espousaille* espousal]

spouse (spous, spouz), *n.*, *v.*, **spoused, spous·ing.** —*n.* a husband or wife; married person: *The family plan allows the purchaser of a full-fare, first-class ticket to take his spouse and children ... along at half the one-way fare* (Wall Street Journal). —*v.t. Archaic.* to marry; wed. [< Old French *espous, espouse* < Latin *spōnsus* bridegroom, *spōnsa* bride (in Medieval Latin, spouse) < *spondēre* bind oneself, promise solemnly]

spouse·less (spous′lis, spouz′-), *adj.* having no spouse; unmarried or widowed: *The spouseless Adriatic mourns her lord* (Byron).

spout (spout), *n.* **1.** a pipe, tube, or trough through which water or other liquid flows and is discharged, as the pipe for carrying rain water off a roof. **2.** a tube or lip through or over which liquid is poured, as on a teakettle, coffeepot, sprinkling can, etc. **3.** a chute for grain, coal, flour, etc. **4.** a discharge of water or other liquid, in some quantity and with some force, from or as if from a pipe, etc.; jet; stream. **5.** a waterspout. **6.** a column of spray thrown into the air by a whale in breathing: *When the whale surfaces after a dive and empties its lungs, the foam expelled is the visible spout* (Time). **7.** a lift or shaft formerly used by pawnbrokers to take up pawned articles for storage. **8.** *Slang.* a pawnshop.

go up the spout, *Slang.* to be hopelessly lost; ruined: *Everything I owned has gone up the spout.*

put up the spout, *Slang.* to put in pawn: *I put my watch up the spout last week.*

[apparently < verb]

—*v.t.* **1.** to throw out (a liquid) in a stream or spray: *A whale spouts water when it breathes.* **2.** to pour forth in quantity: *Machines now in operation spout quotations at a 500-character clip* (Wall Street Journal). **3.** *Informal.* to speak in loud tones with affected emotion; declaim: *The old-fashioned actor used to spout his lines.* **4.** *Slang.* to pawn. —*v.i.* **1.** to throw out a liquid in a jet or stream: *The fountain spouted up high.* **2.** to flow out with force: *Water spouted from a break in the pipe.* **3.** *Informal.* to spout or declaim words, lines in a play, etc.: *There he took his stand in a vacant lot ... and spouted to the rustic crowd* (Newsweek). [Middle English *spouten* < Middle Dutch *spouten*] —**spout′er,** *n.*

—**Syn.** *v.i.* **2.** gush, jet, squirt, spurt.

spout hole, a blowhole or spiracle of a whale or other cetacean.

spout·less (spout′lis), *adj.* having no spout, as a pitcher.

spout shell, 1. the shell of any of a group of snaillike marine gastropods. **2.** the animal itself, so called from the spoutlike aperture.

spp., species (plural of *specie*).

S.P.Q.R., the Roman Senate and People (Latin, *Senatus Populusque Romanus*).

S.P.R., Society for Psychical Research.

Sprach·ge·fühl (shpraH′gə fyl′), *n. German.* feeling for language; sensitivity to what is right or proper in speech: *It doesn't take much Sprachgefühl to recognize that Mr. Wilder is ... being a mite folksy* (New Yorker).

sprack (sprak), *adj. Especially British Dialect.* active; lively; brisk; smart. [origin unknown]

sprad·dle (sprad′əl), *v.*, **-dled, -dling.** —*v.i.* to sprawl. —*v.t.* **1.** to spread or stretch (one's legs) wide apart: *He stood with legs spraddled over a large grass basket* (Jack London). **2.** to stretch over or across; straddle: *Overnight, refineries spraddled the shore of the Persian Gulf* (Time). [compare SPRAWL, STRADDLE]

sprad·dle-foot·ed (sprad′əl fu̇t′id), *adj.* with feet spread wide apart: *Rolling into a Town Hall luncheon with his familiar spraddle-footed gait, Khrushchev settled down at a table* (Time).

sprad·dle-leg·ged (sprad′əl leg′id, -legd′), *adj.* with legs spread wide apart: *He runs spraddle-legged, his trainer says, throwing his legs every which way* (New Yorker).

sprag[1] (sprag), *n.*, *v.*, **spragged, sprag·ging.** —*n.* a device to keep a carriage, wagon, etc., from rolling backwards on a hill, especially: **a.** a piece of wood placed under the wheel or between the spokes. **b.** a rod or bar attached to the rear axle and lowered against the ground as needed. —*v.t.* to check or stop (a wheel) by using a sprag. [origin unknown]

sprag[2] (sprag), *n.* a young cod. [earlier, a lively fellow; origin unknown]

sprag[3] (sprag), *adj. Archaic.* lively; smart; clever. [perhaps altered pronunciation of *sprack*]

Sprague's pipit (sprāgz), a buff-colored pipit of the North American plains, with a streaked back and white-edged tail.

sprain (sprān), *v.t.* to injure (the ligaments or muscles of a joint) by a sudden twist or wrench: *He sprained his ankle.* —*n.* **1.** a sudden twist or wrench of the ligaments or muscles of a joint: *He got a bad sprain in his ankle when he missed the lower step.* **2.** the painful condition caused by this: *What with climbing and falling, running and throwing, and general zestful physical activity, almost all children suffer a sprain sometime or other* (Sidonie M. Gruenberg). [perhaps < Old French *espreindre* force out < Vulgar Latin *expremere*, for Latin *exprimere.* Compare EXPRESS.]

sprang (sprang), *v.* a past tense of **spring:** *The tiger sprang at the man.*

sprat (sprat), *n.* **1.** a small herring of the Atlantic Coast of Europe. **2.** any of certain similar herrings [variant of earlier *sprot*, Old English *sprott*]

sprat·tle (sprat′əl), *n.*, *v.*, **-tled, -tling.** *Scottish.* struggle or scramble. [origin uncertain]

sprau·chle (spräH′əl), *v.i.*, **-chled, -chling.** *Scottish.* to clamber. [origin unknown]

sprawl (sprôl), *v.i.* **1.** to toss or spread the limbs about, as an infant or an animal lying on its back. **2.** to lie or sit with the limbs spread out, especially ungracefully or awkwardly: *The people sprawled on the beach in their bathing suits.* **3.** to crawl in a struggling or ungraceful manner; move awkwardly; scramble. **4.** to spread out in an irregular or awkward manner, as vines, handwriting, etc.; straggle: *He wrote in a large handwriting that sprawled across the page.*

—*v.t.* to spread or stretch (out something) in a wide, straggling, or ungraceful manner: *to sprawl out one's legs.*

—*n.* **1.** the act or position of sprawling: *Any kind of a sprawl is ungraceful.* **2.** a straggling array or display (of something): *London's great sprawl* ... (London Times). [Old English *sprēawlian*] —**sprawl′er,** *n.*

sprawl·ing (sprô′ling), *adj.* spread out in an irregular or rambling fashion: ... *New York's sprawling apparel industry* (New York Times).

sprawl·y (sprô′lē), *adj.*, **sprawl·i·er, sprawl·i·est.** of a sprawling character; straggly: *Why is my alphabet so much more sprawly than yours?* (Jane Austen).

spray[1] (sprā), *n.* **1. a.** liquid going through the air in small drops: *We were wet by the sea spray.* **b.** small drops of medicine, insecticide, disinfectant, etc., blown on something by compressed air or gas: *Big advantage of the internal poison is that it protects the whole young plant, while sprays ... may leave some parts unprotected* (Time). **2.** something like this: *a spray of bullets.* **3. a.** an instrument that sends a liquid out as spray. **b.** an aerosol bomb.

—*v.t.* **1.** to throw in the form of spray; scatter in small drops: *to spray paint on a cupboard.* **2.** to sprinkle with spray; wet with small drops or particles: *to spray a lawn with water.* **3.** to direct numerous small missiles, etc., upon: *to spray the enemy with bullets.* —*v.i.* **1.** to throw up or scatter spray. **2.** to issue or rise as spray. [apparently < Middle Dutch *sprayen, spraeien* to sprinkle] —**spray′er,** *n.*

spray[2] (sprā), *n.* **1.** a single, graceful shoot, twig, or branch of some plant with its leaves, flowers, or fruit, especially when used for decoration or ornament: *a spray of lilacs, ivy, or berries.* **2.** any ornament, pattern, or design resembling this: *a spray of diamonds.* **3.** small or slender twigs of trees or shrubs collectively, either still growing or cut off. [compare Danish *sprag*]

spray·a·ble (sprā′ə bəl), *adj.* that can be sprayed: *A spray gun will apply all sprayable materials* ... (Science News Letter).

spray drain, a drain formed in grassland, etc., by burying in the earth brush, or the spray of trees, to keep open a channel.

spray·dry (sprā′drī′), *v.t.*, **-dried, -dry·ing.** to dehydrate (food, etc.) by spraying and drying in powdery particles.

spray·ey[1] (sprā′ē), *adj.* forming or scattering spray; in the form of spray.

spray·ey[2] (sprā′ē), *adj.* **1.** consisting of sprays, as of a plant. **2.** resembling sprays.

spray gun, a device that works by compressed air to spray paints, insecticides, or other liquids over a surface: *The nylon, 8-ounce spray gun handles all types of paints and can easily be cleaned for spraying insecticides* (Newsweek).

spray nozzle, an attachment to the nozzle of a hose for spreading liquid insecticides and fungicides in the form of a fine spray.

spray-on (sprā′on′), *adj.* applied in the form of a spray: *a spray-on deodorant, spray-on paint.*

spread (spred), *v.*, **spread, spread·ing,** *n.*, *adj.* —*v.t.* **1.** to cause to cover a large or larger area; stretch or draw out (anything folded, piled, rolled up, etc.) to a greater or its greatest extent; open out; lay out: *to spread out a rug, to spread papers on a table.* **2.** to unfurl: *to spread all possible sails.* **3.** to unfold or raise and hold sideways from the body; extend outward: *to spread wings, to spread one's arms.* **4.** to cause to be protracted in time; break down the total of into parts distributed (over a period of time): *to spread a shipment over two months, to spread the repayment of a debt over a year.* **5.** to move the sides of outward by force, especially: **a.** to extend the circumference of: *He spread the head of the rivet with a hammer.* **b.** to displace and push outward from the line of vertical thrust: *walls spread by too much weight.* **6.** to cause to lie on, as a cover; extend (something over): *to spread a blanket over a child.* **7.** to make widely or generally known; diffuse; disseminate: *to spread the rumor of victory. He spread the news.* **8.** to make widely or generally prevalent; propagate: *to spread a religion.* **9.** to distribute by or as if by strewing over an area; scatter: *to spread seed, to spread fertilizer.* **10.** to cover with a thin layer; coat or overlay (with): *to spread a slice of bread with butter.* **11.** to put as a thin layer; smear (on): *to spread jam on bread.* **12.** to prepare (a table) for a meal or other purpose; set; lay. **13.** to put food on (a table). **14.** to make a written record of; enter in or as if in minutes.

—*v.i.* **1.** to cover a large or larger area; expand; unfold; open: *a fan that spreads when shaken.* **2.** to move outward or further apart: *The rails of the track have spread.* **3.** to extend or grow outward from a trunk or center: *The roots of the tree spread.* **4.** to lie; extend: *Fields of corn spread out before us. The evening is spread out against the sky Like a patient etherized upon a table* (T.S. Eliot). **5.** to become widely or generally known or prevalent; be distributed: *The disease spread rapidly.* **6.** to be or to be able to be put on as a thin layer: *This paint spreads evenly.*

spread oneself, *Informal.* **a.** to exert oneself: *He had promised ... to spread himself in the preparation of this meal* (S.H. Hammond). **b.** to make a display; show off: *The gentleman who had just spread himself was very angry at having the effect of his speech thus spoiled* (Edward Kinglake).

—*n.* **1.** the act or process of spreading: *to fight the spread of an infection, to encourage the spread of knowledge, etc.* **2.** the amount of or capacity for spreading; extent of expanding or ability to expand outward; width when opened, unfolded, etc.: *the great spread of an eagle's wings, the spread of elastic.* **3.** the wing span of an aircraft. **4.** a stretch; expanse: *a great spread of green fields.* **5. a.** the difference between what something is bought for and what it is sold to another for: *a 30-cent spread in the buying and selling prices of wheat.* **b.** the difference between any two prices, rates, etc.: *a serious spread between actual and scheduled production.* **6.** a cloth covering for a bed or table; tablecloth, blanket, etc. **7.** *Informal.* food for a meal put on the table, especially in abundance; feast; banquet. **8.** an article of food intended to be spread on bread, crackers, etc., as butter, jam, etc.: *Our beefsteaks are homogenized into hamburger, and Roquefort cheese is now a "spread"* (Atlantic). **9.** a piece of advertising, a news story, etc., occupying a large (and now usually specified) number of adjoining columns: *The advertisement was a three-column spread.* **10.** two facing pages of a newspaper, magazine, etc., viewed as a single unit in makeup. **11.** *Commerce.* a contractual privilege, usually purchased, of

both a put and a call, similar to a straddle except that the price of the put is different from the price of the call.
—*adj.* stretched out; expanded; extended: *Front and low vowels are more easily pronounced with lips unrounded, that is, spread or neutral* . . . (Simeon Potter).
[Middle English *spreden,* Old English *-sprǣdan* (compare *sprǣdung* spreading)]
—**Syn.** *v.t.* **1.** unroll. **7.** circulate.

spread eagle, 1. a representation of an eagle with body, legs, and both wings displayed, used as an emblem of the United States and certain other countries. **2.** a boastful, self-assertive person, especially an American with an excess of national or regional pride. **3.** a figure executed in skating, consisting of a sideways glide with the arms outstretched and the legs widely opened.

spread-ea·gle (spred′ē′gəl), *adj., v.,* **-gled, -gling.** —*adj.* **1.** having or suggestive of the form or appearance of a spread eagle. **2.** boastful or high-sounding, especially in praise of the United States: *spread-eagle oratory. It wasn't a spread-eagle speech, but he* [*Daniel Webster*] *made you see it* (Stephen Vincent Benét).
—*v.t.* **1.** to stretch out flat and sprawling as if in a spread eagle: *The man . . . fell and lay spread-eagled on the snow* (New Yorker). **2.** to tie (a person) with the arms and legs spread widely to the sides as a form of punishment or torture. **3.** to beat thoroughly, as by lapping one's opponents: [*He*] *virtually spread-eagled the field with a perfect start and lengthy strides* (New York Times). —*v.i.* to do a spread eagle or spread eagles in skating.
—**Syn.** *adj.* **2.** grandiloquent, bombastic.

spread-ea·gle·ism (spred′ē′gəl iz əm), *n.* patriotic boasting and grandiloquence.

spread·er (spred′ər), *n.* a person or thing that spreads: *After the fabrics dry, spreaders pile them on a large table* (World Book Encyclopedia). *More expensive than all of these tools put together is a spreader for lawn seed, fertilizer and weedkiller* (New York Times).

spread·ing adder (spred′ing), hognose snake: *The spreading adder becomes very gentle after being handled a little and makes a nice pet* (A. M. Winchester).

spreading decline, a disease affecting citrus trees, caused by a nematoid worm: *America's citrus industry was declared seriously threatened by . . . spreading decline* (Science News Letter).

spreading dogbane, a perennial herb of North America, having light-green leaves and clusters of pale pink flowers.

Sprech·ge·sang (shpreн′gə zäng′), *n. German.* **1.** (in music) a vocal utterance halfway between speaking and singing, similar to recitative, but less sustained: [*The*] *drama is considerably enhanced by Meller's use of Sprechgesang . . . and ordinary speech as well as song* (London Times). **2.** (literally) speaking song.

Sprech·stim·me (shpreн′shtim′ə), *n. German.* **1.** (in music) Sprechgesang. **2.** (literally) speaking voice.

spree (sprē), *n.* **1.** a lively frolic; boisterous time. **2.** a prolonged bout of drinking; a drunken carousal: *He described both . . . as excessive drinkers who would leave the children alone while they went on sprees* (New York Times). [origin uncertain]

sprent (sprent), *adj. Archaic.* sprinkled: *the brown hair sprent with grey* (Matthew Arnold). [past participle of obsolete *spreng,* Old English *sprengan* sprinkle]

sprew (sprü), *n.* sprue[1].

spri·er (sprī′ər), *adj.* spryer; a comparative of **spry.**

spri·est (sprī′ist), *adj.* spryest; a superlative of **spry.**

sprig (sprig), *n., v.,* **sprigged, sprig·ging.** —*n.* **1.** a shoot, twig, or small branch: *a sprig of holly. He wore a sprig of lilac in his buttonhole.* **2.** an ornament or design shaped like a sprig or spray: *glasses covered with little gold sprigs* (Henry James). **3.** a scion or offspring of some person, class, institution, etc. **4.** a young fellow; youth; stripling: *a sprig whom I remember with a whey face and a satchel not so very many years ago* (Scott). **5.** a small wedge of tin or zinc, used to hold glass in a sash until the putty dries. **6.** a small, headless nail or brad.
—*v.t.* **1.** to decorate (pottery, fabrics, etc.) with designs representing sprigs. **2.** to strip a sprig or sprigs from (a plant, tree, etc.). **3.** to fasten with sprigs or brads.
[Middle English *sprigge;* origin uncertain]
—**sprig′ger,** *n.*

sprigged (sprigd), *adj.* adorned or ornamented with sprigs (used especially of fabrics, etc.): *some friendly flounces of sprigged muslin . . .* (Lytton Strachey).

sprig·ging (sprig′ing), *n.* the planting or repair of a lawn by means of grass sprigs rather than seed: *Sprigging is . . . used where the grass being planted is a poor-seeding or non-seeding species* (Roy Wiggans).

sprig·gy (sprig′ē), *adj.,* **-gi·er, -gi·est. 1.** full of sprigs: *spriggy underbrush.* **2.** consisting of or like sprigs.

spright (sprīt), *n. Obsolete.* sprite.

spright·ful (sprīt′fəl), *adj. Obsolete.* full of spirit; spirited: *Spoke like a sprightful noble gentleman* (Shakespeare).

spright·li·ness (sprīt′lē nis), *n.* **1.** liveliness; briskness; vigor. **2.** gaiety; vivacity.

spright·ly (sprīt′lē), *adj.,* **-li·er, -li·est,** *adv.* —*adj.* lively; gay: *a sprightly bounce to one's walk. This brought a sprightly note into the conversation* (Atlantic). —*adv.* in a sprightly manner; vivaciously.
—**Syn.** *adj.* spirited, animated, vivacious.

sprig·tail (sprig′tāl′), *n. U.S.* **1.** the pintail duck. **2.** the ruddy duck.

sprig-tailed (sprig′tāld′), *adj.* having a sprigged or sharp-pointed tail.

spring (spring), *v.,* **sprang** or **sprung, sprung, spring·ing,** *n., adj.* —*v.i.* **1.** to move with or as if with a sudden jerk or bound; leap; jump: *to spring to attention. He sprang to his sleigh, to his team gave a whistle* (Clement C. Moore). **2.** to rise with a springing motion; leap or jump up: *The boy sprang to his feet.* **3.** to go forward suddenly; dart; fly: *The dog sprang at the thief.* **4.** to go suddenly to the position of nature or rest as if by elastic force; fly back or away: *The branch sprang up when I dropped from it. The door sprang to.* **5.** to be flexible, resilient, or elastic; be able to spring: *This branch springs enough to use as a snare.* **6.** to come from some source; arise; grow: *A wind sprang up. Plants sprang up from the seeds we planted.* **7.** to derive by birth or parentage; be descended; be the issue of: *to spring from New England stock.* **8.** to begin to move, act, grow, appear, etc., suddenly; burst forth: *Towns sprang up where oil was discovered.* **9.** to have its ground or cause; originate: *an alliance springing from mutual peril.* **10.** to pour or burst forth; gush; flow; issue: *blood springing from a severed artery. Sparks sprang from the fire.* **11.** to give way, by or as if by bending or warping. **12.** to crack, split, or break: *Cracks all along the concrete wall showed where it had sprung.* **13.** to extend upward; rise; tower: *a cliff springing sheer to a height of 2,000 feet.* **14.** (of arches, vaults, rafters, etc.) to take a curving or slanting upward course from some point of support. **15.** to rise from cover, as partridges. **16.** of a mine: **a.** to explode. **b.** to be exploded.
—*v.t.* **1.** to cause to spring; cause to act by a spring: *to spring a trap.* **2.** to bring out, produce, or make suddenly: *to spring a surprise on someone.* **3.** to announce or reveal suddenly and usually unexpectedly: *to spring the news of an engagement.* **4.** to cause to move from its proper position, by or as if by warping or bending: *Miles of travel along rocky roads had sprung the wagon shaft.* **5.** to crack, split, or break: *Frost had sprung the rock wall.* **6.** to force to open, slip into place, etc., by or as if by bending: *The burglar was able to spring the lock quite easily.* **7.** to jump over: *to spring a distance of 12 feet, to spring a wall.* **8.** to cause (partridges, etc.) to rise from cover: *I would throw her off, wait until she was up, and spring the birds* (T.H. White). **9.** *Slang.* to secure the release of (a person) from prison by bail or otherwise: *After a stretch in a Parma jail,* [*he*] *was sprung conditionally, time off for good behavior* (Time).
spring a leak. See under **leak,** *n.*
spring a mine. See under **mine**[2], *n.*
—*n.* **1.** a bound; leap; jump: *a sudden spring for safety.* **2.** the distance covered or that can be covered by a spring. **3.** an elastic device consisting of one or more strips, plates, etc., usually of metal, bent, coiled, or otherwise shaped or adjusted, which, when compressed or forced out of its normal shape, possesses the property of returning to it, and is variously used, as to communicate or regulate motion, lessen concussion, etc.: *Beds have wire springs. The springs in a watch make it go.* **4.** elastic quality or capacity; elasticity: *There is no spring left in these old rubber bands. The old man's knees have lost their spring.* **5.** a flying back or recoil from a compressed or strained position: *the bow well bent, and smart the spring* (William Cowper). **6.** the season of the year when plants begin to grow in the temperate and colder regions of the earth (in North America, the months of March, April, and May; in Great Britain, February, March, and April): *O, Wind, If Winter comes, can Spring be far behind?* (Shelley). **7.** *Astronomy.* the three months between the vernal equinox and the summer solstice. **8.** the first and freshest or most vigorous stage of anything, especially of life; period of youth: *You are blighted for ever in the very spring of your life* (Benjamin Disraeli). **9.** a flow of water rising or issuing naturally out of the earth. **10.** a source of anything; origin; cause; wellspring: *the springs of emotion.* **11.** a crack, bend, strain, or break, especially a vertical split or transverse crack in a mast, spar, etc., of a ship or other vessel. **12.** the point at which an arch or vault springs or rises from its abutment or impost; the rise of an arch: *It was just under five feet above the floor at the spring of the vaulting, a little over seven feet down the middle* (Oliver LaFarge). **13.** *Scottish.* a quick or lively tune: *Robin took the pipes, and played a little spring* (Robert Louis Stevenson).

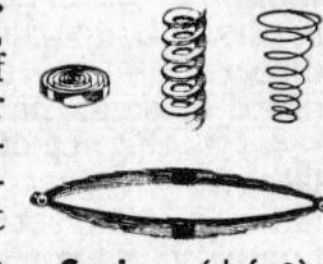
Springs (def. 3)

—*adj.* **1.** fitted with a spring or springs; operating by means of springs: *a spring balance, a spring lock.* **2.** hung or suspended on springs: *a spring cart.* **3.** of or having to do with the season of spring: *Probably the most colorful of all flowers are the spring flowers.* **4.** characteristic of or suitable for the season of spring: *spring weather, new spring hats.* **5.** from a spring: *spring salts.*
[Old English *springan* to move suddenly; come to sight; grow up]
—**Syn.** *v.i.* **2.** bound, vault. **4.** rebound, recoil. **6.** emerge. **9.** emanate. **10.** shoot, rush, dart. –*n.* **1.** vault. **4.** resiliency, buoyancy.

spring·al[1] (spring′əl), *n. Archaic.* a youth; springald.

spring·al[2] (spring′əl), *n. Archaic.* a kind of catapult; springald.

spring·ald[1] (spring′əld), *n. Archaic.* a young man; youth; stripling.

spring·ald[2] (spring′əld), *n.* a machine of war used in the Middle Ages for throwing stones, etc.
[apparently < Anglo-French *springalde,* Old French *espringalle* < *espringuer* to spring < Germanic (compare Old English *springan* to spring)]

spring beauty, 1. any of a group of North American herbs of the purslane family producing small pink or white flowers in early spring. **2.** the small pink or white flowers of any of these plants.

spring-blade knife (spring′blād′), a switchblade knife.

spring·board (spring′bôrd′, -bōrd′), *n.* **1.** a projecting board from which persons dive. **2.** an elastic board used in vaulting, etc., mounted at one or both ends. **3.** anything that serves as a way to get to something else: *Hard work is the only sure springboard to success. This will give us among other things entry into the British market and a springboard to the Continent* (Wall Street Journal).

spring·bok (spring′bok′), *n., pl.* **-boks** or (*collectively*) **-bok.** a small antelope of South Africa, that leaps almost directly upward when excited or disturbed: *If you are lucky you will see a springbok standing still and graceful before he leaps away* (Allan Gordon). [< Afrikaans *springbok* < *springen* to leap (< Dutch) + *bok* antelope (< Dutch)]

Springbok
(about 2½ ft. high at the shoulder)

spring·buck (spring′buk′), *n., pl.* **-bucks** or (*collectively*) **-buck.** springbok.

spring chicken, 1. a young chicken, especially one only a few months old, used for frying or broiling because of its tenderness. 2. *Slang.* a young woman: *"She's no spring chicken," she would say of another woman* (New Yorker).

spring-clean (spring′klēn′), *v.t.* to clean thoroughly when mild weather sets in: *It's time to spring-clean the office and open up a few more windows* (Punch).

spring-clean·ing (spring′klē′ning), *n.* 1. the general cleaning of a house, etc., when mild weather sets in. 2. a thorough cleaning; cleanup: *Lord Montgomery . . . has called for "a good spring-cleaning" within the N.A.T.O. alliance* (Manchester Guardian Weekly).

springe (sprinj), *n., v.,* **springed, spring·ing.** —*n.* a snare for catching small game, especially a noose attached to a twig bent over and released by a trigger. —*v.t.* to catch in a springe; snare. —*v.i.* to set a springe or springes. [apparently < Old English *sprengan* burst, crack; (in unrecorded sense "cause to spring")]

spring·er (spring′ər), *n.* 1. a person or thing that springs. 2. the support or impost from which an arch springs. 3. the stone at each end of an arch next to this. 4. a springer spaniel. 5. springbok. 6. grampus. 7. spring chicken. 8. a spring lamb: *Lamb prices touched a three months' low at Chicago, with most springers selling mostly 50 cents lower* (Wall Street Journal). 9. a tin can containing spoiled food that has forced the ends of the can to bulge.

Spring·er·le (shpring′ər lə), *n. German.* a Christmas cooky with a design, in relief, pressed onto its top.

springer spaniel, any of certain of the larger breeds of field spaniels used to spring or flush game, as the English springer spaniel and the Welsh springer spaniel. See **English springer spaniel** for picture.

spring fever, a listless, lazy feeling felt by some people during the first sudden warm weather of spring: *It's spring fever . . . when you've got it you want—oh, you don't quite know what it is you do want, but it just fairly makes your heart ache, you want it so* (Mark Twain).

Spring·field rifle (spring′fēld), a type of breechloading rifle, .30 caliber, in which the bolt is operated by hand to eject the spent shell and reload from the magazine after each firing, adopted by the U.S. Army in 1903 and used until the early part of World War II (when it was replaced by the Garand rifle). [< *Springfield,* a city in Massachusetts, where a United States Army arsenal is located]

spring garden, *Especially British.* a public pleasure garden, as formerly in Hyde Park and at Vauxhall, London.

spring gun, 1. a gun fixed in place as a booby trap to fire at the person or animal who touches a trip wire attached to the trigger: *So it went on, a gripping chronicle of folly and ill-fortune . . . gamekeepers tripping over their own spring guns* (Punch). 2. a gun in which the missile is discharged by the release of a spring: *They wore rubber flippers, underwater goggles, and carried spring guns with which to slaughter anything submarine* (Manchester Guardian).

spring·haas (spring′häs′), *n.* the jumping hare of South Africa. [< Afrikaans *springhaas* < *spring* jump + *haas* hare]

spring·halt (spring′hôlt′), *n.* a diseased condition of the hind legs of a horse; stringhalt.

spring hare, springhaas.

spring·head (spring′hed′), *n.* a fountainhead; wellspring.

spring-heeled (spring′hēld′), *adj. Especially British.* 1. having a spring in one's step; light-footed: *Kath is forty-one but gallivants about the sitting room . . . like a spring-heeled eurhythmics teacher* (Punch). 2. sprightly; jaunty: *The orchestra sounded both suave and spring-heeled* (Charles Reid).

spring house, *U.S.* a small outbuilding constructed over a spring or brook, used as a dairy or a place to keep meat, etc., cool.

spring·i·ly (spring′ə lē), *adv.* in a springy manner; with a springy movement or step.

spring·i·ness (spring′ē nis), *n.* the state or property of being springy.

spring·ing (spring′ing), *n.* 1. the spring of an arch. 2. an arrangement of springs; fitting of a spring or springs: *Many auto men consider independent front springing . . . as the last major advance in softening auto riding* (Wall Street Journal).

springing line, springing (def. 1).

spring lamb, a young and tender lamb, originally one born after January 1st and brought to market in April.

spring·less (spring′lis), *adj.* 1. without spring or elasticity: . . . *an unheated dormitory on a wooden, springless bed covered with a thin mattress* (Time). 2. without elastic springs, as a vehicle: *big springless carts* (W. H. Hudson). 3. without springs of water. 4. having no spring season.

spring·let (spring′lit), *n.* a little spring (of water): *Out from the little hill Oozes the slender springlet still* (Scott).

spring·like (spring′līk′), *adj.* of or characteristic of the spring; vernal: *A drowsy springlike sultriness pervaded the air* (Francis Parkman). *A land where mild, springlike days were beginning to soften winter's deep freeze* (Time).

spring-load·ed (spring′lō′did), *adj.* held in place or operated by a spring: *Safety . . . is a prime factor with these machines and most are fitted with a spring-loaded switch lever which cuts out automatically when the grip is released* (Sunday Times).

spring lock, a lock that fastens automatically by a spring.

spring peeper, a small, brown tree frog with a dark patch across the face, whose peeping call is heard early in the spring: *The first faint, hesitant announcement by the spring peeper that the earth's sleep is not the sleep of death* (Atlantic).

spring salmon, the chinook salmon, a large salmon of the Pacific Coast.

spring·tail (spring′tāl′), *n.* any of a group of small, wingless insects having a pair of partially fused appendages at the end of the abdomen under the body which act as a spring, giving them great jumping ability.

spring-tailed (spring′tāld′), *adj.* 1. springing by means of the tail. 2. having a spring on the tail, as a collembolous insect.

spring·tide (spring′tīd′), *n.* springtime.

spring tide, 1. a tide occurring on the days shortly after the new and full moon, when the high-water level reaches its maximum; highest level of high tide: *Approximately twice monthly the sun, moon, and earth are nearly in line and at these times the sun and moon combine their tide-raising forces to produce the greatest tides, called spring tides* (Wasley S. Krogdahl). 2. any great flood, swell, or rush; copious flow: *With Kleist we are on the spring tide of German romanticism* (London Times).

spring·time (spring′tīm′), *n.* 1. the season of spring. 2. the first or earliest period: *the springtime of life.*

spring water, water issuing or obtained from a spring: *Spring water usually reaches the surface through either hydrostatic pressure or gravity flow* (White and Renner).

spring wheat, a variety of wheat sown in the spring: *If spring wheat is planted in the fall, it will not live through the winter except in mild climates or during unusually warm winters* (World Book Encyclopedia).

spring·wood (spring′wu̇d′), *n.* 1. a light ring or layer of wood formed around a tree each spring. It has large open spaces and thin cell walls to allow for the rapid passage of water to the growing parts. 2. a wood or thicket of young trees: *the wide expanse of country beyond the cypress groves and springwoods* (Sir Osbert Sitwell).

spring·y (spring′ē), *adj.,* **spring·i·er, spring·i·est.** 1. that springs; resilient; elastic: *His step was springy. Curves in the backbone give it a springy quality.* 2. having many springs of water. 3. spongy with moisture, as soil in the area of a subterranean spring or springs.

sprin·kle (spring′kəl), *v.,* **-kled, -kling,** *n.* —*v.t.* 1. to scatter in drops; let fall in small particles here and there; strew: *He sprinkled ashes on the icy sidewalk.* 2. to spray or cover with small drops or particles: *to sprinkle flowers with water.* 3. to dot or vary with something scattered here and there: *a countryside sprinkled with farmhouses.* 4. to distribute here and there; disperse. —*v.i.* 1. to scatter something in drops or small particles. 2. to rain a little. —*n.* 1. the act of sprinkling: *Baptizing the Christian infant with a solemn sprinkle* (Milton). 2. a sprinkling; a small number or quantity: *a sprinkle of salt. The cook put a sprinkle of nuts on the cake.* 3. a light rain. [compare Dutch *sprenkelen*]
—**Syn.** *v.t.* 1. spatter, besprinkle.

sprin·kler (spring′klər), *n.* 1. a person who sprinkles. 2. a device or apparatus for sprinkling.

sprin·klered (spring′klərd), *adj.* equipped with a sprinkler system: *Modern, 6 story heavy-duty, fireproof manufacturing building, 100 per cent sprinklered* (Wall Street Journal).

sprinkler head, the nozzle of a water sprinkler.

sprinkler system, a system of pipes with nozzles spaced regularly apart to carry water, etc., especially as used to spray lawns and orchards or to help control fire by releasing water as the temperature rises: *Fire departments encourage the use of automatic sprinkler systems . . .* (World Book Encyclopedia).

sprin·kling (spring′kling), *n.* 1. a small number scattered or distributed here and there: *a sprinkling of gray hairs.* 2. a small or slight quantity or amount: *a sprinkling of knowledge.* 3. a small quantity sprinkled: *a sprinkling of rain.* 4. the act of a person or thing that sprinkles: *regular sprinkling of a lawn.* —**Syn.** 2. dash.

sprint (sprint), *v.i.* to run, gallop, etc., at full speed, usually for a short distance.
—*n.* 1. a race over a short distance run at top speed: *The first of the added-money runs was the $22,725 Autumn Day Handicap, a sprint for fillies and mares* (New York Times). 2. any short spell of running, rowing, etc., at top speed. 3. anything resembling this: *to finish the job with a sprint of very hard work.*
[Middle English *sprenten,* probably < Scandinavian (compare Old Icelandic *spretta*)] —**sprint′er,** *n.*

sprit (sprit), *n.* a light pole running from the foot of a mast diagonally up to the top corner of a fore-and-aft sail, which supports the sail and holds it open. [Old English *sprēot* pole]

Sprit

sprite (sprīt), *n.* 1. an elf; fairy; goblin. 2. a white crab. 3. *Obsolete.* a ghost; spirit. [< Old French *esprit* spirit < Latin *spīritus.* Doublet of ESPRIT, SPIRIT.]
—**Syn.** 1. pixie.

sprite·li·ness (sprīt′lē nis), *n.* sprightliness.

sprite·ly (sprīt′lē), *adj.,* **-li·er, -li·est.** *Especially British.* sprightly: *This spritely account of the first Cook's excursion to Switzerland . . .* (Manchester Guardian Weekly).

sprit·sail (sprit′sāl′; *Nautical* sprit′səl), *n.* any fore-and-aft sail supported and held open by a sprit: *It is beamy, with a rounded bow, and it carries a broad mainsail—spritsail rigged* (Listener).

spritz·er (sprit′sər), *n.* a cold drink made with syrup or wine and carbonated water. [< German *Spritzer* < *spritzen* squirt, splash]

sprock·et (sprok′it), *n.* 1. a projection on the rim of a wheel, engaging with the links of a chain to keep the chain from slipping. 2. a sprocket wheel: *The pedals and the front sprocket* [*of a bicycle*] *make a wheel and axle* (Beauchamp, Mayfield, and West). [origin uncertain]

sprocket wheel, a wheel with sprockets that engage with the links of a chain: *In the projector, sprocket wheels with small teeth move the film past a powerful beam of light* (World Book Encyclopedia).

Sprocket Wheel

sprog (sprog), *n. British Slang.* a green or raw recruit: *I was twenty-two then —a sprog . . . and this was to be my first operational mission* (Maclean's). [origin unknown]

sprout (sprout), *v.i.* 1. to put forth a shoot or shoots; begin to grow; bud; germinate: *Buds sprout in the spring.* 2. to bring forth or produce shoots or shootlike growths: *After a shower a meadow sprouts with the yellow buds of the dandelion* (Theodore Winthrop). 3. to shoot forth or develop rapidly or naturally: *A straggling black moustache sprouted on his upper lip* (Robert

S. Hichens). —*v.t.* **1.** to cause to sprout; produce by sprouting; grow: *to sprout wings. The rain sprouted the corn.* **2.** *Informal.* to remove sprouts from: *He sprouted the potatoes twice every winter.*
—*n.* **1.** a shoot from a branch, root, or stump of a tree, shrub, or other plant. **2.** the young shoot from a germinating seed, or from a rhizome, tuber, etc.: *bean sprouts. The gardener was setting out sprouts.* **3.** something like a sprout in appearance, formation, or growth.
a course of sprouts. See under **course,** *n.*
sprouts, Brussels sprouts: *sprouts served in cream sauce.*
[Old English *-sprūtan,* as in *āsprūtan*]
sprout·ling (sprout′ling), *n.* a little or young sprout.
sprouts (sprouts), *n.pl.* See under **sprout,** *n.*
spruce[1] (sprüs), *n.* **1.** any of a group of coniferous evergreen trees of the pine family, having narrow, needle-shaped leaves arranged spirally around the branches, and bearing drooping cones, as the Norway spruce or black spruce: *The favorite Christmas tree in America is the spruce* (Science News Letter). **2.** any of various other coniferous trees, as the Douglas fir or Douglas spruce, the hemlock spruce, the balsam spruce, etc. **3.** the wood of any of these trees.

Red Spruce[1] Branch (def. 1) with cones

[earlier, adjective < Middle English *Spruce,* variant of *Pruce* Prussia (perhaps because the trees first came from there)]
spruce[2] (sprüs), *adj.,* **spruc·er, spruc·est,** *v.,* **spruced, spruc·ing.** —*adj.* smart in appearance; neat; trim: *to make oneself spruce for a party. A good-looking man; spruce and dapper and very tidy* (Anthony Trollope).
—*v.t.* to make spruce: *He spruced himself up for dinner.* —*v.i.* to become spruce. [perhaps special use of Middle English *Spruce* Prussia. Compare *spruce leather (jerkin),* a popular style in the 1500's (made in Prussia and considered smart-looking)]
—**spruce′ly,** *adv.* —**spruce′ness,** *n.*
—**Syn.** *adj.* dapper, jaunty.
spruce beer, a fermented beverage made from an extract of spruce needles and twigs boiled with molasses or sugar, formerly used especially as a diuretic and antiscorbutic.
spruce budworm, the larva of a small, thick-bodied moth that feeds on the bud tips of spruce, fir, and related trees.
spruce fir, a spruce, especially the Norway spruce.
spruce grouse, a grouse of the coniferous forests of northern North America; Canada grouse.
spruce gum, a resinous exudation from various spruces and firs, used as a chewing gum, or as an ingredient of chewing gum.
spruce partridge, the spruce grouse: *There are more spruce partridges in the woods than I have seen anywhere in this country* (Canadian Historical Review).
sprue[1] (sprü), *n. Metallurgy.* **1.** an opening or passage through which molten metal is run into the gate and then into the mold. **2.** the waste piece of metal cast in this passage. [origin uncertain]
sprue[2] (sprü), *n.* **1.** a chronic disease characterized by emaciation, anemia, inflammation of the mouth, and digestive upsets, occurring especially in tropical countries: *Many sufferers of sprue and celiac disease, a digestive illness, cannot digest ordinary bread* (Science News Letter). **2.** thrush, a disease. [probably < Dutch *spruw*]
sprui·ker (sprü′kər), *n. Australian.* a fluent speaker who urges people to buy a product, see an exhibit, etc.; barker; spieler.
spruit (sprīt, sproit, sprœ′it), *n.* (in South Africa) a small stream or watercourse, usually dry except after rain: *Instead of riding up the opposite bank of the spruit . . . we galloped along the bed under cover of the high banks* (Deneys Reitz). [< Afrikaans *spruit*]
sprung (sprung), *v.* a past tense and the past participle of **spring:** *The trap was sprung.*
—*adj.* **1.** that has worked loose from a fastening, as a part of a tool. **2.** split or cracked, as a mast. **3.** bent or warped, as a board. **4.** *Slang.* tipsy or drunk.
sprung rhythm, *Prosody.* rhythm which has feet that vary greatly in the number of syllables, usually having between one and four, but that always have equal time length, the stress being on the first syllable. It was much used by both Gerard Manley Hopkins and Dylan Thomas.
spry (sprī), *adj.,* **spry·er** or **spri·er, spry·est** or **spri·est.** full of health and spirits; active; lively; nimble; brisk: *The spry old lady traveled everywhere.*
[origin uncertain] —**spry′ly,** *adv.* —**spry′·ness,** *n.* —**Syn.** sprightly.
spt., seaport.
spud (spud), *n., v.,* **spud·ded, spud·ding.** —*n.* **1.** a spadelike implement with a narrow blade for digging up weeds or cutting their roots. **2.** a tool something like a wide chisel, used for removing bark. **3.** *Informal.* a potato: *Spuds and yams show some price recovery* (Wall Street Journal).
—*v.t.* **1.** to remove or dig up by means of a spud. **2.** to drill (a hole) as part of the preliminary stages of sinking an oil well: *The third well was down 4,000 feet at last report and the fourth had just been spudded in* (Wall Street Journal).
[Middle English *spudde* a short knife; origin uncertain]
spud·der (spud′ər), *n.* **1.** a spud. **2.** a machine for spudding oil wells: . . . *a completely portable cable tool "spudder" . . . capable of drilling to a maximum of 10,000 feet* (Wall Street Journal).
spud·dy (spud′ē), *adj.,* **-di·er, -di·est.** short and fat or thick: *spuddy hands.*
spue (spyü), *v.t., v.i.,* **spued, spu·ing,** *n.* spew.
spume (spyüm), *n., v.,* **spumed, spum·ing.** —*n.* frothy matter, as that on the crest of a wave; foam; froth. —*v.i.* to foam or froth: *No longer do all the raging rivers spume untamed down to the fiords* (Newsweek). [< Latin *spūma*]
spu·mo·ne or **spu·mo·ni** (spə mō′nē), *n.* an Italian ice cream, usually containing candied fruit, nuts, etc. [< Italian *spumone,* singular, *spumoni,* plural < *spuma* foam < Latin *spūma*]
spu·mous (spyü′məs), *adj.* consisting of froth or scum; foamy: *a crazy boat, which made a spumous track upon the water* (Dickens).
spum·y (spyü′mē), *adj.,* **spum·i·er, spum·i·est.** covered with foam; foamy.
spun[1] (spun), *v.* a past tense and the past participle of **spin:** *The thread was spun from silk.*
spun[2] (spun), *n.* a fabric made of spun rayon: *Cottons and spuns in this category continue to receive substantial reorders* (New York Times). [apparently short for *spun rayon*]
spun-dyed (spun′dīd′), *adj.* dyed before being spun or pulled out into filaments: *Spun-dyed rayon and acetate yarn hold colors fast.*
spun glass, glass drawn into fine threads while in a liquid state.
spunk (spungk), *n.* **1.** *Informal.* courage; pluck; spirit; mettle. **2.** *Scottish.* **a.** a spark. **b.** a match. **3.** touchwood; punk.
get one's spunk up, *Informal.* **a.** to show courage, pluck, or spirit: *How a woman got her spunk up and left the country* (M. Thompson). **b.** to become angry: *My spunk is getting up a little about it* (Jamestown Journal).
spunk of fire, a small fire; bit of flame: *Ye might light a spunk of fire in the red room* (Scott).
—*v.i.* **spunk up, a.** *U.S.* to show spunk or spirit: *Just spunk up to the old codger—let him know you are not afraid of him* (Elbridge G. Paige). **b.** *Scottish.* to flare up with anger: *He spunked up like tinder. "Do you call me a liar?" he said* (Neil Munro).
[< Scottish Gaelic *spong* tinder, pith; (churlish) spirit, perhaps ultimately < Latin *spongia;* see SPONGE]
—**Syn.** *n.* **1.** nerve.
spunk·ie (spung′kē), *n. Scottish.* **1.** a will-o'-the-wisp. **2.** whiskey or other strong drink. [< *spunk* + *-ie*]
spunk·i·ly (spung′kə lē), *adv. Informal.* in a spunky manner; courageously.
spunk·i·ness (spung′kē nis), *n. Informal.* spunky quality; spunk: *Young Joe showed early signs of his father's spunkiness* (Time).
spunk·y (spung′kē), *adj.,* **spunk·i·er, spunk·i·est.** *Informal.* courageous; plucky; spirited: *He is a spunky fellow and I'll be his second* (Frederick Marryat). —**Syn.** mettlesome.
spun rayon, 1. any of various rayon fabrics made to resemble linen, wool, cotton, or silk. **2.** the yarn, made from rayon, used for these.
spun silk, silk waste spun into yarn: *Short fibers spun from the silk from pierced cocoons is called spun silk* (Bernice G. Chambers).
spun sugar, sugar drawn out or worked up into a threadlike form, used in making cotton candy, and as an ornament and frosting for desserts: *The dessert was soufflé glacé with raspberries and spun sugar* (Craig Claiborne).
spun yarn, a line composed of two or more rope yarns loosely twisted together.
spur (spėr), *n., v.,* **spurred, spur·ring.** —*n.* **1.** a pricking instrument consisting of a small spike or spiked wheel, worn on a horseman's heel for urging a horse on. **2.** anything that urges on; stimulus; incentive; incitement: *Ambition was the spur that made him work.* **3.** any sharp or short projection, point, or spike suggestive of a spur. **4.** a protuberance on the inner side of the leg of a fowl, either knotlike or pointed, according to the age and sex of the fowl. **5.** a piercing or cutting device fastened to each of a gamecock's legs; gaff. **6.** a sharp-pointed, bony growth on some part of the body, especially on the heel or in the nose: *Because there is no swelling, pain or tenderness to show the spur, team mates and coaches may think the player is shirking* (Science News Letter). **7.** a short or stunted branch or shoot of a tree. **8.** a slender, generally hollow, projection from a flower part, as from the calyx of columbine; calcar. **9.** a fungous disease of cereal plants; ergot. **10.** a climbing iron used in mounting telephone poles or the like. **11.** a range, ridge, mountain, hill, or a part of one of these, projecting from the main mass: *The spurs between the valley bends are often trimmed on the upstream side, as if undercut by a large river* (G. H. Dury). **12.** *Architecture.* **a.** a short strut or stay set diagonally to support an upright timber; shore; prop. **b.** a sloping buttress. **c.** an ornament at the base of a column; griffe. **13.** a spur track, line, etc. **14.** a buttress or platform of masonry strengthening an outwork of a fortification.

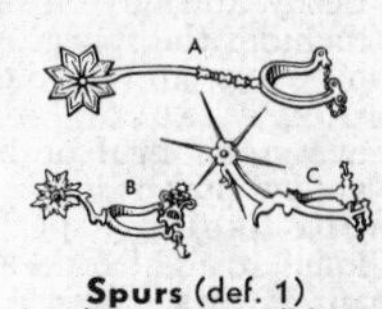

Spurs (def. 1) A, brass spur (Henry VII); B, rowel spur (Edward IV); C, steel spur (Henry VIII)

on the spur of the moment, on a sudden impulse; without previous thought or preparation: *He went in on the spur of the moment and was taken on as an English translator* (Manchester Guardian Weekly).
set or **put spurs to,** to start or impel by or as if by applying spurs: *Hawker . . . set spurs to his noble chestnut horse* (Henry Kingsley).
win one's spurs, to make a reputation for oneself; attain distinction: *The painter . . . executed his task with a patience . . . worthy of one who had to win his spurs* (George Walter Thornbury).
—*v.t.* **1.** to prick (a horse) with spurs; urge on with spurs: *The rider spurred his horse on.* **2.** to urge on; stimulate; incite: *Pride spurred the boy to fight. He had spurred his party till he could no longer curb it* (Thackeray). **3.** to provide with a spur or spurs. **4.** to strike or wound with a spur or gaff.
—*v.i.* **1.** to ride quickly by urging on one's horse with a spur. **2.** to hasten.
[Old English *spura*] —**spur′like′,** *adj.*
spur·dog (spėr′dôg, -dog), *n., pl.* **-dogs** or (*collectively*) **-dog.** spur dogfish: *The spurdogs, the commonest of the British dogfishes, are the mini-sharks of the high latitudes* (New Scientist).
spur dogfish, a variety of the common dogfish with two pectinated spurs on its upper and under sides; spiny dogfish.
spur·gall (spėr′gôl′), *n.* a gall or sore on the side of a horse or other animal, due to the use of the spur.
spurge (spėrj), *n.* any of a group of plants, many of which are characterized by an acrid, milky juice possessing purgative or medicinal properties, as the poinsettia; euphorbia. [< Old French *espurge* < *espurgier* to purge < Latin *expūrgāre* < *ex-* out + *pūrgāre* to purge, cleanse]

spur gear, 1. a simple gearwheel, having teeth on its rim set radially and with faces parallel to the axis: *Spur gears have the teeth parallel to the shaft, while helical gear teeth are at an angle* (Purvis and Toboldt). See also **gear** for picture. 2. Also, **spur gearing.** gearing using such gearwheels.

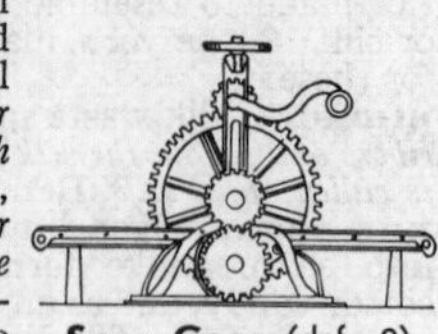
Spur Gear (def. 2)

spurge family, a group of dicotyledonous herbs, shrubs, and trees, some of which are fleshy and have a milky juice. The family includes the spurge, croton, cassava, castor-oil plant, and candlenut.

spurge laurel, an Old World laurellike evergreen shrub of the mezereum family with yellow flowers.

spur-heeled (spėr′hēld′), *adj.* having a long, straight hind claw, as certain birds.

spu·ri·ous (spyůr′ē əs), *adj.* 1. not genuine or authentic, especially: a. not having the source, origin, or author claimed for it; forged; counterfeit: *a spurious painting, a spurious document.* b. false; sham: *spurious anger.* 2. *Botany.* superficially resembling but differing in form and structure. 3. illegitimate. [< Latin *spurius* (with English *-ous*) illegitimate child] —**spu′ri·ous·ly,** *adv.* —**spu′ri·ous·ness,** *n.*

spurious fruit, *Botany.* a pseudocarp.

spur·less (spėr′lis), *adj.* without a spur or spurs.

spurn (spėrn), *v.t.* 1. to refuse with contempt or disdain; reject contemptuously: *to spurn an offer of friendship. The judge spurned the bribe.* 2. to strike with the foot or feet; kick away; trample: *With flying foot the heath he spurned* (Scott). —*v.i.* 1. to oppose with scorn; protest strongly or rebel: *to spurn at restraint.* 2. *Obsolete.* to kick (at something). —*n.* 1. disdainful rejection; contemptuous treatment. 2. a kick. [Old English *spurnan* strike (the foot) on something; reject. Related to SPUR.] —**spurn′er,** *n.* —**Syn.** *v.t.* 1. scorn, despise, contemn.

spur-of-the-mo·ment (spėr′əv ᴛʜə mō′mənt), *adj.* made or occurring suddenly, without deliberation: *In the Dominican crisis and others, Mr. Johnson was forced to act hastily and saw spur-of-the-moment decisions turn sour* (Atlantic).

spurred (spėrd), *adj.* 1. having a spur or spurs attached: *a spurred boot, spurred feet.* 2. having sharp spines, as those on the legs of a gamecock. 3. *Botany.* calcarate.

spur·rer (spėr′ər), *n.* a person or thing that spurs.

spur·rey (spėr′ē), *n., pl.* **-reys.** spurry.

spur·ri·er (spėr′ē ər), *n.* a person who makes spurs.

spur royal, an English gold coin of the time of James I, worth fifteen shillings, named from a figure on the reverse suggesting the rowel of a spur.

spur·ry (spėr′ē), *n., pl.* **-ries.** 1. a small European herbaceous weed of the pink family, having white flowers and very narrow, whorled leaves. 2. any of several related or similar herbs. [< Dutch *spurrie,* earlier Flemish *speurie,* perhaps related to Medieval Latin *spergula*]

spurt (spėrt), *v.i.* 1. to flow suddenly in a stream or jet; gush out; squirt: *Blood spurted from the wound.* 2. to come forth as if by spurting; spring: *Dust spurted out from the wall when the bullets struck.* 3. to put forth great energy for a short time; run, work, etc., very hard and fast for a brief period: *The runners spurted near the end of the race.* —*v.t.* to send forth in a spurting manner; squirt: *to spurt blood.*
—*n.* 1. a sudden rushing forth; jet: *Spurts of flame broke out all over the building.* 2. a sudden outbreak or brief spell of activity, exertion, etc. 3. a sudden outburst of feeling, etc.: *He had ceased to be aggressive except in momentary spurts* (H. G. Wells). 4. a sudden rise in prices, improvement in business, etc. 5. the period of this. Also, **spirt.** [earlier *spirt,* variant of *sprit,* Old English *spryttan*]

spur·tle (spėr′təl), *n. Scottish.* a wooden stick for stirring porridge, etc.

spur track or **line,** a branch railroad track or line connected with the main track or line at one end only.

spur wheel, a spur gear.

spur-winged (spėr′wingd′), *adj.* (of a bird) having one or more horny spurs projecting from the bend of the wing, as the plectropterus.

sput·nik (sput′nik, spůt′-), *n.* a small artificial earth satellite containing instruments to record and report natural phenomena: *If the speed is below a certain value the rocket moves in an ellipse: it is in fact a sputnik* (New Scientist). *The Russians last week launched the heaviest sputnik yet into an orbit which is larger than any so far achieved by a Russian satellite* (Manchester Guardian). [< Russian (*Iskusstvennyj*) *Sputnik* (*Zemli*) (Artificial) Satellite (of the Earth)]

Sputnik III (Russian)

sput·ter (sput′ər), *v.i.* 1. to spit out food or saliva with some force and in a noisy, explosive manner; splutter. 2. to speak so rapidly and vehemently as to seem to spit out the words; speak confusedly and indistinctly. 3. to throw out small particles with some crackling or noise: *fat sputtering in the frying pan. The firecrackers sputtered.* —*v.t.* 1. to spit out (bits of food, saliva, etc.) in small particles and with an explosive sound, as in excitement or talking too fast. 2. to utter in a confused, indistinct, or uncontrolled manner, especially from anger or excitement: *He would sputter uneasy protest* (Sinclair Lewis). 3. to emit in small amounts with slight explosions: *A burning green stick sputters out smoke.* 4. to coat (a surface) with a thin film of metal by bombarding with particles of the metal moving at high speed.
—*n.* 1. a sputtering; sputtering noise: *When he began working with the torch . . . a few window-watchers seemed annoyed at the glare and sputter* (Newsweek). 2. noisy and confused speech or discourse; splutter. 3. matter ejected in or by sputtering. [probably related to SPOUT] —**sput′ter·er,** *n.*

spu·tum (spyü′təm), *n., pl.* **-ta** (-tə). 1. saliva; spittle; spit. 2. what is coughed up from the lungs and throat and spat out. [< Latin *spūtum,* neuter past participle of *spuere* to spit]

spy (spī), *n., pl.* **spies,** *v.,* **spied, spy·ing.** —*n.* 1. a person who keeps a constant and secret watch upon the action of others. 2. a person employed by a government to enter other countries, secretly or under false pretenses, to obtain information concerning military or naval affairs or other intelligence: *One feels again a chilled amazement at the achievements of this shrewd, fearless, and determined spy* (New Yorker). 3. the act of spying; secret observation or watching. [< Old French *espie* < *espier;* see the verb]
—*v.t.* 1. to watch (someone) in a secret or stealthy manner; keep under constant observation. 2. to look at or examine closely or carefully, as with a telescope. 3. to catch sight of; descry; discover; see: *He was the first to spy the rescue party in the distance.* —*v.i.* 1. to make secret or stealthy observations; be a spy: *The Russians think inspection is spying. . . . And so we watch each other spy and arm on the brink of disaster* (R. S. Emrich). 2. to be on the lookout; keep watch, especially with a telescope. 3. to examine or inspect something carefully.
spy out, a. to watch or examine secretly or carefully: *Peder Pederson and a lieutenant . . . slipped out Sunday to spy out the situation* (Harper's). b. to find out by watching secretly or carefully: *She spies out everything that goes on in the neighborhood.*
[< Old French *espier* < Germanic (compare Old High German *spehōn*)]

spy·glass (spī′glas′, -gläs′), *n.* a small telescope, especially one not requiring a tripod or other mount in order to be used: *This type of instrument was very common before the invention of the prism binocular and is well known to everyone as the spyglass of the old-time sea captain* (Hardy and Perrin).

spy·hole (spī′hōl′), *n.* a hole for spying; peephole: *There are, of course, bars over every window, locks and spyholes in every door* (Manchester Guardian Weekly).

spy·mas·ter (spī′mas′tər, -mäs′-), *n.* a person who directs the activities of, and acts as a clearing agent for, an organized group of spies (spy ring): *Wilhelm Stieber, spymaster to Bismarck, boasted that he had some 40,000 agents in France at the outbreak of the Franco-Prussian War in 1870* (Time).

spy·plane (spī′plān′), *n.* a high-altitude aircraft for secret reconnaissance of foreign defense installations by means of aerial photographs and tape recordings of radio and radar emissions.

sq., 1. sequence. 2. square. 3. the following (Latin, *sequens,* singular, or *sequentia,* plural).

Sq., 1. squadron. 2. square (street).

sq. ft., square foot or square feet.

sq. in., square inch or square inches.

sq. km., square kilometer or square kilometers.

sq. mi., square mile or square miles.

squab (skwob), *n.* 1. a very young pigeon, such as is preferred for eating. 2. any very young bird; fledgling. 3. a short, stout person. 4. a thick or soft cushion: *Deeper, softer seats and squabs on both models give extra comfort* (Economist). 5. a sofa or couch. —*adj.* 1. newly hatched; still unfledged: *a squab turkey.* 2. (of persons) short and stout. [origin uncertain. Compare Swedish dialectal *sqvabb* loose or fat flesh, Norwegian dialectal *skvabb* soft, wet mass.]

squab·ble (skwob′əl), *n., v.,* **-bled, -bling.** —*n.* a petty, noisy quarrel: *Family squabbles are very unpleasant. Children's squabbles annoy their parents.* —*v.i.* to take part in a squabble; wrangle or argue disagreeably: *I won't squabble over a nickel.* —*v.t. Printing.* to throw (type) out of line; disarrange or mix (lines of type). [perhaps imitative. Compare German *schwabbeln* babble, prate.]

squab·bler (skwob′lər), *n.* a person who squabbles or quarrels.

squab·by (skwob′ē), *adj.,* **-bi·er, -bi·est.** short and stout; squat; thick-set.

squac·co (skwak′ō), *n.* a small, crested heron of Africa, southern Europe, and parts of Asia. [< Italian dialectal *sguacco;* probably imitative]

squad (skwod), *n., v.,* **squad·ded, squad·ding.** —*n.* 1. the smallest tactical unit of infantry and certain other elements of the ground forces, usually consisting of eleven men and a squad leader, and composing the basic unit for drill, duty, etc. There are usually four squads in a platoon. 2. any small group of persons working, training, or acting together: *a squad of police. He hired a squad of boys to work for him.* —*v.t.* to form into a squad or squads. [< earlier French *esquade,* variant of *escadre* < Italian *squadra* battalion; (literally) square, ultimately < Latin *ex-* out + *quadrāre* to quarter. Compare CADRE, SQUARE.] —**Syn.** *n.* 2. corps.

squad car, a police patrol car that keeps in communication with headquarters by radio-telephone equipment: *They got us out of there with billy clubs swinging, bundled us into squad cars and hustled us to the police station* (Maclean's).

squad·ron (skwod′rən), *n.* 1. a tactical subdivision of a fleet consisting of two or more divisions, usually of the same type of ship: *a destroyer squadron.* 2. a tactical unit of cavalry or armored cavalry, usually having from 120 to 200 men, consisting of two or more troops, a headquarters troop, and attached units, corresponding to a battalion in the infantry. 3. *U.S.* a tactical unit of the Air Force, consisting of a formation of airplanes, usually two or three flights, that fly or fight together. 4. any group: *A stately squadron of snowy geese were riding in an adjoining pond* (Washington Irving).
—*v.t.* to form into a squadron or squadrons. [< Italian *squadrone* < *squadra* squad; see SQUARE]

squad·ron·al (skwod′rə nəl), *adj.* of or having to do with a squadron or squadrons.

squads·man (skwodz′mən), *n., pl.* **-men.** a member of a squad: *Vice squadsmen arrested thirteen persons in a . . . New Orleans apartment* (Newsweek).

squail (skwāl), *n.* 1. one of a number of disks or counters in a table game, driven by snapping toward a mark in the center of the table. 2. the game itself. [origin uncertain]

squal·ene (skwol′ēn, skwā′lēn), *n.* a colorless oil, first found in shark liver, occurring in vegetable and animal fats including human sebum: *Recent researches suggest a material called squalene has an ameliorating effect on the ability of particular materials (called carcinogens) to cause cancer* (New York Times). *Formula:* $C_{30}H_{50}$ [< New Latin *Squalus* the shark genus]

squal·id (skwol′id), *adj.* 1. foul through neglect or want of cleanliness; repulsively mean and dirty; filthy: *squalid tenements.*

It is futile to expect a hungry and squalid population to be anything but violent and gross (T.H. Huxley). **2.** morally repulsive or wretched; degraded: *His life had been squalid and mean. The squalid belief in witchcraft* (James Harvey Robinson). [< Latin *squālidus* < *squālēre* be filthy] **—squal'id·ly,** *adv.* **—squal'id·ness,** *n.*

squall[1] (skwôl), *n.* **1.** a sudden, violent gust of wind, often with rain, snow, etc. **2.** a disturbance or commotion; trouble: *The squall of criticism which has blown around the Administration's ten-year $101 billion road-building program . . .* (Newsweek). *—v.i.* to undergo or give rise to a squall or squalls. [compare Swedish *skval* impetuous rush of water < *skvala* to stream, gush] **—Syn.** *n.* **1.** blast.

squall[2] (skwôl), *v.i.* to cry out loudly; scream violently: *The baby squalled. —v.t.* to cry (out) in a loud, discordant tone. *—n.* a loud, harsh cry: *The parrot's squall was heard all over the house.* [perhaps imitative. Compare Old Icelandic *skvala* cry out, Swedish *skvaller* idle talk.] **—squall'er,** *n.*

squall line, a line of thunderstorms preceding a cold front, characterized by severe thunder, strong wind squalls, and heavy rains and lightning, and very often productive of tornadoes: *At Chicago, a huge freak wave, formed by a sudden change in pressure at a squall line on Lake Michigan, swept a 25-mile stretch of shoreline* (Newsweek).

squall·y (skwô'lē), *adj.,* **squall·i·er, squall·i·est. 1.** characterized by squalls: *squally weather.* **2.** (of the wind) blowing in squalls; gusty: *It was raining again with a squally wind* (Arnold Bennett). **3.** *Informal.* threatening; troublous.

squa·loid (skwā'loid), *adj.* **1.** sharklike. **2.** having to do with sharks. [< New Latin *Squalus* (see SQUALUS) + English *-oid*]

squal·or (skwol'ər), *n.* **1.** misery and dirt; filth: *By modern standards people in medieval Europe lived in indescribable squalor. Hovel piled upon hovel—squalor immortalized in undecaying stone* (Hawthorne). **2.** the quality of being morally squalid. [< Latin *squālor* < *squālēre* be filthy; see SQUALID]

squa·lus (skwā'ləs), *n., pl.* **-li** (-lī). any of a group of sharks comprising many of the spiny dogfishes. [< New Latin *Squalus* the genus name < Latin *squalus* a sea fish]

squam (skwom), *n. U.S.* a waterproof, oilskin hat with a broad brim in the back; southwester. [< *Annisquam,* Massachusetts]

squa·ma (skwā'mə), *n., pl.* **-mae** (-mē). a scale or scaly part, especially the thin vertical portion of the temporal bone in man and other vertebrates: *a squama of bone.* [< Latin *squāma*]

squa·ma·ceous (skwə mā'shəs), *adj.* scaly.

squa·mate (skwā'māt), *adj.* provided or covered with squamae or scales. [< Latin *squāmātus* < *squāma* squama]

squa·ma·tion (skwə mā'shən), *n.* **1.** the condition of being covered with scales. **2.** the arrangement or pattern of the scales covering an animal. **3.** the scales covering an animal.

squa·mel·late (skwə mel'āt), *adj.* squamulose.

squa·mi·form (skwā'mə fôrm), *adj.* having the shape of a scale; squamous.

squa·mo·sal (skwə mō'səl), *adj.* **1.** of or having to do with the squama of the temporal bone. **2.** scaly. *—n.* the squama of the temporal bone.

squa·mose (skwā'mōs), *adj.* squamous. **—squa'mose·ly,** *adv.* **—squa'mose·ness,** *n.*

squa·mous (skwā'məs), *adj.* **1.** furnished with, covered with, or formed of scales. **2.** characterized by the development of scales; scalelike: *An epithelium is designated cubical, columnar, or squamous, according to the shape of its component cells . . .* (A. Franklin Shull). *Immense, of fishy form and mind, Squamous . . .* (Rupert Brooke). **3.** having to do with the squama of the temporal bone. [< Latin *squāmōsus* < *squāma* scale, squama] **—squa'mous·ly,** *adv.* **—squa'mous·ness,** *n.*

squam·u·late (skwam'yə lāt, -lit), *adj.* squamulose.

squam·u·lose (skwam'yə lōs, skwā'myə-), *adj. Botany.* provided or covered with small scales. [< Latin *squāmula* (diminutive) < *squāma* scale + English *-ose*[1]]

squan·der (skwon'dər), *v.t.* **1.** to spend or employ foolishly; waste: *to squander a fortune in gambling. Do not squander time* (Benjamin Franklin). **2.** to cause to scatter; disperse. *—v.i.* to be squandered: *Youth was made to squander.* *—n.* **1.** the act of squandering. **2.** an instance of squandering.
—squan'der·er, *n.* **—squan'der·ing·ly,** *adv.*
—Syn. *v.t.* **1.** dissipate.

squan·tum (skwon'təm), *n. U.S. Dialect.* a good time; merrymaking; picnic.

squar·a·ble (skwãr'ə bəl), *adj.* capable of being squared.

square (skwãr), *n., adj.,* **squar·er, squar·est,** *v.,* **squared, squar·ing,** *adv. —n.* **1.** a plane figure with four equal sides and four right angles (□). **2.** anything of or near this shape: *a square of light, a square of chocolate.* **3.** a usually rectangular area in a city or town that is bounded by streets on four sides; block: *The automobile factories fill several squares.* **4.** the length of one side of such a space: *to walk six squares.* **5.** an area of this or another shape, as a triangle formed by the intersection of two converging main streets and a third street, left free of buildings and sometimes planted with trees or shrubs: *Times Square, Berkeley Square. Abbr.:* Sq. **6.** any similar open space, such as at the meeting of streets. **7.** the buildings surrounding such an area: *to tear down Washington Square.* **8.** a body of troops drawn up in a square formation, such as was common before the development of automatic weapons. **9.** an L- or T-shaped instrument, for laying out or testing right angles, drawing parallel lines, etc., in carpentry, drawing, etc. **10.** the product obtained when a number is multiplied by itself; the second power of a number or quantity: *16 is the square of 4.* **11.** the bracts subtending a cotton blossom: *White flowers blossom from the squares, or buds* (World Book Encyclopedia). **12.** *Slang.* a person who is not familiar with the latest fashions in popular entertainment, culture, etc.: *Junior, of course, is a square* (Wall Street Journal). **13.** *Informal.* a square meal: *The animals are seen performing their customary tasks, which mostly consist of making certain that they obtain three squares daily* (New Yorker).

Square (def. 9)

back at or **to square one,** *British Informal.* back where or to where one began; at an impasse: *The argument over the rise in mortgage rates seems to be back to square one* (London Sunday Times).

on or **upon the square, a.** face to face; directly: *He is awkward, and out of place . . . He cannot meet you on the square* (Charles Lamb). **b.** justly; fairly; honestly: *He had played on the square with them* (Tobias Smollett).

out of square, out of order or proportion: *Something must be wrong in the inner man of the world, since its outer man is so terribly out of square!* (Thomas Carlyle).

[Middle English *squyr* (originally) a carpenter's square < Old French *esquire,* ultimately < Latin *ex-* out of + *quadrāre;* see the verb]

—adj. **1.** having four equal sides and four right angles. **2.** that is square or rectangular in cross section: *a square file.* **3.** that is square or rectangular in both vertical and lateral section; having six sides, each one of which is at a right angle to the four that adjoin it: *a square box.* **4.** (of an area) equal to a square having the length of the side specified: *a room ten feet square.* **5.** having breadth more nearly equal to length or height than is usual: *a square jaw.* **6.** forming a right angle; turning at 90 degrees: *a square corner.* **7.** (of a yard) at right angles to the mast and keel. **8.** plumb and level in its vertical and horizontal surfaces, respectively; straight and proper; even. **9.** correctly built, finished, etc. **10.** having no unbalanced amount on either side; even; balanced: *Five dollars more and our accounts will be square.* **11.** just; fair; honorable; honest: *You will get a square deal at this shop.* **12.** straightforward; plain; direct: *a square refusal. His ideas being square, solid and tangible* (Hawthorne). **13.** satisfying and solid; substantial; plentiful: *a square meal.* **14.** (of units of length) designating an area each of whose dimensions is that unit of length; squared: *a square yard.* **15.** based on such units; in square measure: *square measurement.* **16.** multiplied by itself; squared: *3 square equals 9.* **17.** solid and strong; sturdy. **18.** *Slang.* not up to date; old-fashioned: *He thought we had flipped our beanies. He was real square* (Time). **19.** having the same number of warp ends and picks of filling yarn in each inch of cloth: *The price of 80-square print cloth . . . has remained steady* (Wall Street Journal).

all square, *U.S. Informal.* **a.** having paid what is owing, done what is needed, etc.: *Am I all square now, or do I still owe you something?* **b.** even; tied: *two teams all square at the end of the second quarter.*

—v.t. **1.** to make square, rectangular, or cubical: *to square a block of granite.* **2.** to mark out as a square or in squares: *The children squared the sidewalk off to play hopscotch.* **3.** to bring to the form of a right angle: *to square a corner.* **4.** to make straight, level, or even; place accurately in position: *to square up a gun mount.* **5.** to test with a square or other instrument for deviation from a right (or the desired) angle, line, etc. **6.** to adjust; settle; balance: *Let us square our accounts.* **7.** to settle (a debt); pay up: *At present the Italian balance of payments is squared only because of the offshore orders and other dollar expenditures in Italy of the United States Government* (New York Times). **8.** to guide or regulate: *I cannot square my conduct to time, place, or circumstance* (Keats). **9.** in mathematics: **a.** to calculate the number of square units of measure in. **b.** to multiply (a number or quantity) by itself. **10.** *Sports.* to bring (the score of a game or contest) to equality; tie: *to square the score with a touchdown in the third quarter.* **11.** *Slang.* to win over, conciliate, or secure the silence or consent of, especially by bribery; bribe: *Is there a word of truth in the suggestion that you paid Stevenson £200 to "square" him?* (London Times). *—v.i.* **1.** to fit, accord, or agree; conform: *His acts do not square with his promises.* **2.** *Sports.* to equalize the scores; become equal in score.

square away, a. to sail with the yards square before the wind: *We squared away to a spanking breeze* (Frank T. Bullen). **b.** to take, or cause to take, a new course; make a new start: *He said if I didn't get squared away I'd get into combat some day and come back in a wooden coffin* (New York Times).

square off, to put oneself in a position of defense or attack; prepare to fight, especially with the fists: *As usual, the extremists square off and argue about everything but the root cause of the trouble* (Wall Street Journal).

square oneself, a. to make up for something one has said or done: *She decided to square herself with her mother after their quarrel.* **b.** to get even: *He angrily departed, vowing to square himself before long.*

square up, to pay what one owes; settle an account: *Square up everything whatsoever that it has been necessary to buy* (Dickens).

—adv. **1.** fairly or honestly: *to speak fair and square.* **2.** so as to be square; in a square or rectangular form. **3.** at right angles; perpendicularly. **4.** directly; precisely: *to hit someone square between the eyes.* **5.** firmly; solidly.

[< Old French *esquarer,* ultimately < Latin *ex-* out + *quadrāre* make square < *quadrus* a square < *quattuor* four]

—Syn. *adj.* **11.** equitable.

square·bash (skwãr'bash'), *v.i. British Slang.* to do military foot drill: *When he wasn't squarebashing, young Private Lowery was swotting* (London Times). **—square'-bash'er,** *n.*

square·bash·ing (skwãr'bash'ing), *n. British Slang.* military foot drill.

square bracket, the mark [or].

square dance, a dance performed by an even number of couples (a set) arranged in a particular form, as the quadrille and Virginia reel: *The square dances are socially stimulating, and recently have been recovering some of their lost popularity* (Emory S. Bogardus).

square-dance (skwãr'dans', -däns'), *v.i.,* **-danced, -danc·ing.** to do a square dance. **—square'-danc'er,** *n.*

squared circle or **ring** (skwãrd), *Informal.* a ring for boxing bouts; prize ring.

square deal, 1. fair and honest treatment. **2.** an honest deal (in cards).

square·dom (skwãr'dəm), *n. Slang.* **1.** the condition of being a square: *a hero, who . . . wears . . . clothes so well cut that you can tell he is doomed to ultimate squaredom* (New Yorker). **2.** all those who are squares.

square·flip·per (skwãr'flip'ər), *n.* a large gray and yellowish seal of arctic regions with a bristly beard and weighing up to 1,000 pounds.

square foot, a unit of square measure, equal to an area 1 foot by 1 foot. *Abbr.:* sq. ft.

square·head (skwãr′hed′), *n. U.S. Slang.* **1.** a slow-witted person; dolt. **2.** a Scandinavian or a German.

square inch, a unit of square measure, equal to an area 1 inch by 1 inch: *A jet plane traveling 1,500 mph hits the rain drops with a force of 70,000 pounds per square inch* (Newsweek). *Abbr.:* sq. in.

square-jawed (skwãr′jôd′), *adj.* having a square jaw: ... *a square-jawed man with blue eyes and thinning dark hair* (Wall Street Journal).

square John, *U.S. Slang.* a person who obeys the law; an honest or respectable individual: *"Legality is for square Johns," Hanna said, still smiling* (New Yorker).

square kilometer, a unit of square measure, equal to an area 1 kilometer by 1 kilometer. *Abbr.:* sq. km.

square knot, a type of knot tied with two overhand knots so the free ends come out alongside of the standing parts. It will not slip and is easily untied. See **knot**[1] for picture.

square leg, 1. the position in the cricket field to the left of the batsman and nearly on a line with the wicket. **2.** the fielder stationed at this point.

square·ly (skwãr′lē), *adv.* in a square manner: *His approach was thus entirely rational, based squarely on the philosophy of the eighteenth century—anti-clerical, democratic* (Edmund Wilson).

square meal, *U.S.* a substantial or satisfying meal: *Where M. Coulet was, I knew, there would be a square meal, and he did not disappoint me* (New Yorker).

square measure, a system for measuring area:

144 square inches = 1 square foot
9 square feet = 1 square yard
30¼ square yards = 1 square rod
160 square rods = 1 acre
640 acres = 1 square mile or 1 section
36 sections = 1 township

square mile, a unit of square measure, equal to an area 1 mile by 1 mile. *Abbr.:* sq. mi.

square·ness (skwãr′nis), *n.* the quality or state of being square.

square number, the product of a number multiplied by itself, as 25 (5 × 5), or 36 (6 × 6).

square peg, a person or thing that is unfit or unsuitable: *You can't put a square peg in a round hole.*

square piano, a rectangular piano having horizontal strings parallel to the keyboard.

squar·er (skwãr′ər), *n.* a person who reduces wood, stone, etc., to a square form.

square-rigged (skwãr′rigd′), *adj.* having the principal sails set at right angles across the masts.

square-rig·ger (skwãr′rig′ər), *n.* a square-rigged ship: *In Boston ... you could look over the harbor at the big square-riggers anchored in the stream* (Atlantic).

Square-rigged Sails on the foremast of a barkentine

square root, a number that produces a given number when multiplied by itself: *The square root of 64 is 8. The genius of William Hamilton sought the square root of minus one* (Walter de la Mare).

square sail, any four-sided sail carried on a yard across the line of the keel.

square set, a set of four couples forming a square in square-dancing: *"Drop hands," Mr. Gordon instructed them. "Take a step next to your partner. Now. That's a square set"* (New Yorker).

square shake, a square deal: *We never got a square shake* (New York Times).

square shooter, *Informal.* a fair and honest person: *I trust businessmen and their wives, who buy annually, as square shooters* (Wall Street Journal).

square shooting, *Informal.* the behavior or activities of a square shooter.

square-shoul·dered (skwãr′shōl′dərd), *adj.* having shoulders that are high, not sloping, and well braced back: *She was ... tall, square-shouldered, and erect* (Harper's).

square·tail (skwãr′tāl′), *n.* **1.** a brook trout. **2.** a prairie chicken.

square-toed (skwãr′tōd′), *adj.* **1.** (of a shoe) having a broad, square toe. **2.** old-fashioned and homely in habits, ideas, etc.: *We old people must retain some square-toed predilection for the fashions of our youth* (Edmund Burke).

square-toes (skwãr′tōz′), *n.* a precise, formal, old-fashioned person, having strict or narrow ideas of conduct.

square wheel, a flat wheel.

squar·ish (skwãr′ish), *adj.* nearly square; having breadth more nearly equal to length or height than is usual: *A kart is little more than four wheels supporting a squarish frame, one or two engines, and a seat for the driver* (Atlantic).

squar·rose (skwar′ōs, skwo rōs′), *adj.* **1.** *Botany.* **a.** composed of or covered with scales, bracts, or other processes standing out at right angles or more widely, as a calyx or involucre. **b.** standing out at right angles or more widely, as scales, bracts, etc. **2.** rough with spreading scales or other processes. [< Latin *squarrōsus* scurfy, scabby]

squar·rous (skwar′əs), *adj.* squarrose.

squar·ru·lose (skwar′ə lōs), *adj. Botany.* somewhat squarrose. [diminutive form of *squarrose*]

squash[1] (skwosh), *v.t.* **1.** to squeeze or press into a flat mass or pulp; crush: *The boy squashed the bug.* **2.** to put an end to in a summary manner; stop by force; suppress; quash: *The police squashed the riot.* **3.** *Informal.* to silence or disconcert (a person) with a crushing argument, reply, etc. —*v.i.* **1.** to be pressed into a flat mass; flatten out on impact or under pressure: *Cream puffs squash easily.* **2.** to make a splashing sound; move, walk, etc., with a splash: *We heard him squash through the mud and slush.* **3.** to crowd; squeeze.

—*n.* **1.** the act, fact, or sound of something soft being squashed or crushed. **2.** the impact of a soft, heavy body falling on a surface. **3.** the sound produced by this. **4.** something easily squashed: *The grapes are just a squash and not fit to eat.* **5.** squash tennis. **6.** squash rackets. **7.** *British.* a beverage made with fruit juice and (usually) carbonated water: *I'll have a lemon squash if you don't mind* (Graham Greene).

[< Old French *esquasser,* ultimately < Latin *ex-* out + *quassāre* < *quatere* to shake. Compare QUASH[1].] —**squash′er,** *n.*

squash[2] (skwosh), *n., pl.* **squash** or **squashes. 1.** the fruit of any of various annual vinelike plants of the gourd family, often eaten as a vegetable or made into a pie. **2.** any of these plants. [American English, short for earlier *squantersquash* < Algonkian (compare Narragansett *askútasquash* the green things that may be eaten raw)]

squash bug, a large, brownish hemipterous bug having an offensive odor, harmful to squash vines and certain other plants.

squash·i·ly (skwosh′ə lē), *adv.* in a squashy manner.

squash·i·ness (skwosh′ē nis), *n.* the state of being squashy, soft, or miry.

squash rackets, a game similar to rackets but played on a smaller court with a shorter racket.

squash tennis, a game similar to handball and tennis, played with rackets and a hollow rubber ball in a walled court.

squash·y (skwosh′ē), *adj.,* **squash·i·er, squash·i·est. 1.** having a soft or pulpy consistency; easily squashed: *squashy cream puffs.* **2.** soft and wet: *squashy ground.* **3.** having a squashed or flattened look: *a squashy nose.*

squat (skwot), *v.,* **squat·ted** or **squat, squat·ting,** *adj., n.* —*v.i.* **1.** to sit on the heels with the legs closely drawn up beneath the hams or in front of the body; crouch: *He found it difficult to squat on his heels for more than ten minutes.* **2.** to sit on the ground, floor, etc., in this way: *The two of them were squatting on this dirt road, talking the way farmers do* (Newsweek). **3.** to crouch close to the ground to avoid observation or capture, as a hare: *Some tenth-rate poeticule ... now squats in his hole like the tailless fox* (Algernon Charles Swinburne). **4.** to settle on new, uncultivated, or unoccupied land without title or right: *He was a Kentucky man, of the Ohio, where he had "squatted"* (Frederick Marryat). **5.** to settle on public land to acquire ownership of it under government regulation. —*v.t.* to cause to squat; seat (oneself) with the legs drawn up.

—*adj.* **1.** seated in a squatting position. crouching: *A squat figure sat before the fire;* **2.** short and thick, like the figure of an animal squatting; low and broad; flattened: *a squat teapot, a squat building.*

—*n.* **1.** the act of squatting or sitting close to the ground; crouching. **2.** a squatting posture.

[< Old French *esquatir* to crush, ultimately < Latin *ex-* out + *coactāre* constrain < *cogere* drive together < *co-* together + *agere* drive] —**squat′ly,** *adv.* —**squat′ness,** *n.*

—**Syn.** *adj.* **2.** dumpy.

squat·tage (skwot′ij), *n.* **1.** the occupation of land by squatting. **2.** a piece of land occupied or held by a squatter.

squat·ter (skwot′ər), *n.* **1.** a person who settles on land without title or right, especially a person who settles on another's land which is not at the moment occupied or cultivated by its owner: *Judging from the treatment of squatters on similar lands in Manitoba, there need be no fear of settling on lands within the reserves* (Saskatoon Herald). **2.** a person who settles on public land to acquire ownership of it. **3.** a squatting person or animal. **4.** (in Australia) a person who operates a sheep ranch or farm.

squatter or **squatter's right,** *U.S.* the right or claim of a squatter to the land on which he has settled: *Gramp ... took up the land, by squatter's right, about 1892* (Atlantic).

squatter sovereignty, *U.S.* the right claimed by the settlers of new territories to make their own laws, especially in regard to slavery: *the doctrine of "squatter sovereignty" (local determination of the status of slavery)* (R.B. Morris).

squat·toc·ra·cy (skwo tok′rə sē), *n. Australian.* squatters, especially the socially and politically important sheep ranchers: *For England's "county" aristocracy, Australia substituted its own "squattocracy"—men who had carved out for themselves sheep or cattle stations the size of Maryland and sent their sons to Cambridge or Oxford* (Time).

squat·ty (skwot′ē), *adj.,* **-ti·er, -ti·est.** short and thick; low and broad; squat.

squaw (skwô), *n.* **1.** a North American Indian girl or woman. **2.** such a girl or woman as a partner to a male, as wife, concubine, etc. **3.** *Slang.* any girl or woman. **4.** *Slang.* a female spouse; wife. [American English, earlier, an Indian woman or wife < Algonkian (compare Massachusetts *squa*)]

squaw·ber·ry (skwô′ber′ē), *n., pl.* **-ries.** a low-growing shrub of the eastern United States bearing tart, inedible berries; deerberry.

squaw·fish (skwô′fish′), *n., pl.* **-fish·es** or (*collectively*) **-fish.** any of several large, slender carp, common in rivers of the Pacific Coast of North America.

squawk (skwôk), *v.i.* **1.** to call or cry with a loud, harsh note; squall or screech hoarsely: *Hens and ducks squawk when frightened.* **2.** (of things) to give out a discordant sound; creak or squeak harshly. **3.** *Informal.* to complain loudly; give vent to vigorous protests: *Machine tool builders squawk as the Air Force buys $500,000 worth of tools abroad* (Wall Street Journal). —*v.t.* to utter harshly and loudly, with or as if with a squawk. —*n.* **1.** a squawking; a loud, harsh sound. **2.** *Informal.* a loud complaint; vigorous protest. **3.** the American black-crowned night heron.

[probably imitative]

squawk·box (skwôk′boks′), *n.,* or **squawk box,** *U.S. Slang.* a loudspeaker in a public-address system or intercom: *One of Wilson's first acts was to order the squawkbox moved out of his office so that he could do business face to face* (Time).

squawk·er (skwô′kər), *n.* **1.** a person or thing that squawks. **2.** a speaker of intermediate size in a phonograph, tape recorder, etc., designed to reproduce frequencies in the middle range.

squawl (skwôl), *v.i., v.t.* to cry out loudly: *Hardly was the White House meeting over than the Soviet Union started squawling about how the U.S. was "playing with fire" in even considering a step-up in the Vietnamese war effort* (Time). [variant of *squall*[2]]

squaw man, a white man living with an Indian wife or concubine, especially one who has more or less abandoned white customs (used in an unfriendly way).

squaw·root (skwô′rüt′, -růt′), *n.* a fleshy, leafless plant related to the beechdrops, with yellowish flowers, growing as a parasite usually on oak roots. It is found in eastern North America.

squaw winter, a brief period of prematurely cold weather early in autumn: *In my youthful days back in New York, Indian summer never came until we had had a squaw winter* (Newsweek).

squdge (skwuj), *v.t., v.i.,* **squdged, squdging.** to squish; squash. [imitative]

squdg·y (skwuj′ē), *adj.* **squdg·i·er, squdg·i·est.** 1. squishy; squashy: *A pretty squdgy mass you have underfoot at that* (Punch). 2. pudgy; dumpy: *He made haste to shake Joseph Bluett's squdgy hand and escape* (G. Warwick Deeping).

squeak (skwēk), *v.i.* 1. to make a short, sharp, shrill sound: *A mouse squeaks.* 2. *Slang.* a. to turn informer; squeal. b. to confess. 3. *Informal.* to get or pass (by or through) with difficulty: *The Senate will block it even if it squeaks through the House* (Wall Street Journal). —*v.t.* 1. to cause to squeak. 2. to utter in a squeaking manner or with a squeaky voice: *to squeak out an apology.*
—*n.* 1. a short, sharp, shrill sound. 2. *Informal.* a narrow chance or escape.
[probably imitative. Compare Swedish *sqväka* to croak.] —**squeak′ing·ly,** *adv.*

squeak·er (skwē′kər), *n.* 1. a person or thing that squeaks. 2. *Informal.* a contest whose outcome is uncertain until the final moment or period: *The game was a squeaker until the Yankees exploded for three runs in the eighth* (New York Times).

squeak·i·ly (skwē′kə lē), *adv.* with a thin, squeaky sound or voice: *to sing squeakily.*

squeak·i·ness (skwē′kē nis), *n.* (of sound) thin sharpness or shrillness.

squeak·y (skwē′kē), *adj.,* **squeak·i·er, squeak·i·est.** 1. characterized by squeaking sounds; tending to squeak: *a squeaky window.* 2. (of the voice) squeaking; thin and shrill.

squeal (skwēl), *v.i.* 1. to make a prolonged, loud, sharp sound; scream or cry shrilly: *A pig squeals when it is hurt.* 2. *Informal.* to turn informer; inform. 3. *Informal.* to complain loudly; squawk. —*v.t.* to utter sharply and shrilly: *to squeal out a command.*
—*n.* 1. a prolonged, sharp cry; shrill scream or sound: *the squeal of a pig.* 2. *Informal.* an act of informing against another. 3. *Informal.* an act of complaining loudly.
[probably imitative]

squeal·er (skwē′lər), *n.* 1. a person or thing that squeals. 2. the young of the grouse, partridge, quail, or pigeon. 3. a young pig: *This year's new squealers number around 100 million—up 23 per cent in two years* (Wall Street Journal).

squeam·ish (skwē′mish), *adj.* 1. too readily offended by anything approaching immodesty or indecency; easily shocked; prudish: *a squeamish old maid.* 2. excessively fastidious or punctilious; too particular; too scrupulous: *Trifles magnified into importance by a squeamish conscience* (Macaulay). 3. slightly sick at one's stomach; sickish: *He turned squeamish at the sight of blood.* 4. readily affected with nausea; easily turned sick or faint. [Middle English *squaymish,* variant of *scoymous* < Anglo-French *escoymous* disdainful, shy; origin uncertain] —**squeam′ish·ly,** *adv.* —**squeam′ish·ness,** *n.* —**Syn.** 2. fussy.

squee·gee (skwē′jē), *n., v.,* **-geed, -gee·ing.** —*n.* 1. an implement, usually having a straight-edged blade of rubber or the like and a long handle, for sweeping water from wet decks, scraping water off windows after washing, cleaning a sink, etc.: *A small squeegee or an automatic automobile windshield wiper will help in the cleaning job* (Scientific American). 2. any of various similar devices. 3. a device with a roller for pressing water from photographic prints, etc.
—*v.t.* to clean, scrape, or press with a squeegee.
[perhaps < earlier *squeege,* variant of *squeeze.* Compare SQUILGEE.]

squeez·a·ble (skwē′zə bəl), *adj.* that can be squeezed: *It's polyethylene, the plastic that's most familiar to consumers as the material in squeezable bottles* (Wall Street Journal).

squeeze (skwēz), *v.,* **squeezed, squeez·ing,** *n.* —*v.t.* 1. to press hard; compress: *to squeeze a sponge or a lemon. If you squeeze the kitten, you will hurt it.* 2. to force by pressure; thrust or cause to pass forcibly: *to squeeze oneself through a narrow opening. I can't squeeze another thing into my trunk.* 3. to force out or extract by pressure; cause to ooze or flow out by or as if by pressing: *to squeeze juice from a lemon. Lady Kew could . . . squeeze out a tear over a good novel too* (Thackeray). 4. to obtain by force, pressure, or effort; extort: *The dictator squeezed money from the people. When it comes to squeezing a profit out of you . . .* (Dickens). 5. *Informal.* to put pressure on or try to influence (a person or persons) to do something, especially to pay money: *The blackmailer squeezed his victim for more money.* 6. to burden or oppress, as by exactions, heavy taxes, or the like: *Heavy taxes squeezed the people.* 7. to press (the hand) in friendship or affection. 8. to hug; embrace: *She squeezed her child.* 9. to get a facsimile impression of. 10. *Bridge.* to compel (an opponent) to discard or unguard a winning card. —*v.i.* 1. to press hard; exert pressure, especially with the hand. 2. to yield to pressure: *Sponges squeeze easily.* 3. to force a way: *He squeezed through the crowd.*
—*n.* 1. a squeezing; the application of pressure. 2. the state of being squeezed. 3. a friendly or affectionate pressing of another's hand in one's own: *a squeeze of the hand.* 4. a hug; close embrace. 5. a crush; crowd: *It's a tight squeeze to get five people in that little car.* 6. a small quantity or amount squeezed out. 7. a facsimile impression of an inscription, design, etc., made by pressing a plastic substance around or over it. 8. *Informal.* a situation from which escape is difficult, as when a retailer is caught between low prices and high costs: *a cost-price squeeze.* 9. *Informal.* pressure used to extort a favor, money, etc. 10. a squeeze play in baseball or bridge. 11. a shortage or the intense competition resulting from this: *Top manufacturers in all categories are warning that there will be a squeeze on desirable merchandise . . . this fall and winter* (New York Times). 12. the act or state of forcing a short seller to pay a high price, as for securities, etc.
[apparently variant of dialectal *squize, squiss,* and *quease;* all perhaps ultimately Old English *cwȳsan*]
—**Syn.** *v.t.* 8. clasp.

squeeze bottle, a plastic bottle squeezed to force out liquid in a spray or small quantity through a nozzle: *Many cosmetics and lotions are sold in squeeze bottles.*

squeeze·box (skwēz′boks′), *n. Informal.* an accordion.

squeeze cage, a cage having one or more walls that can be moved by a crank from the outside, used to squeeze a wild, injured, or sick animal into a narrow space where it can be controlled and treated: *The baboons . . . fought ferociously when first trapped [and] had to be maneuvered into squeeze cages, where they were compressed into stillness long enough for a doctor to inject an anesthetic* (Time).

squeeze play, 1. (in baseball) a play in which a runner on third base starts for home as soon as the pitcher is legally committed to pitch, the batter trying to protect the runner by bunting the ball away from the catcher to permit the runner to score. It is usually attempted with not more than one man out. 2. (in bridge) a play or series of plays in which the holder of a card that may win a trick is compelled to discard it or to unguard another possible winner. 3. any pressure applied to force a result: *The great Soviet squeeze play for Germany was developing according to plan* (Newsweek).

squeez·er (skwē′zər), *n.* a person or thing that squeezes.

squelch (skwelch), *v.t.* 1. to cause to be silent; crush: *to squelch an annoying child. She squelched him with a look of contempt.* 2. to strike or press on with crushing force; put down; squash; suppress: *to squelch a revolt.* —*v.i.* 1. to walk or tread heavily in water or wet ground, or with water in the shoes, so as to make a splashing sound: *. . . drillers squelching through the mud back to their barges* (London Times). 2. to make the sound of one doing so.
—*n.* 1. *Informal.* something that serves to squelch, as a crushing retort, sharp command, etc. 2. a splashing sound made by walking in mud, water, wet shoes, etc.
[apparently imitative] —**squelch′er,** *n.*
—**Syn.** *v.t.* 2. quell. *-v.i.* 1. slosh.

squelch·y (skwel′chē), *adj.* 1. soft and wet; marshy: *Down there in that squelchy river basin Edward the Confessor was born* (Manchester Guardian). 2. causing or characterized by squelching sounds: *At each stamp his shoes had made a squelchy squeak* (Westminster Gazette).

sque·teague (skwē tēg′), *n., pl.* **-teague.** 1. the weakfish of the Atlantic Coast. 2. any of certain other related fishes. [American English < the Algonkian (Narragansett) name]

sque·tee (skwē tē′), *n., pl.* **-tee.** squeteague.

squib (skwib), *n., v.,* **squibbed, squib·bing.** —*n.* 1. a short, witty or satirical attack in speech or writing; lampoon: *The play was a virulent one-act squib lasting just over an hour* (Kenneth Tynan). 2. a brief item in a newspaper used mainly to fill space. 3. a small firework, about 6 inches long, that burns with a hissing noise and finally explodes: *It's only . . . that people amuse themselves by lighting squibs and throwing rockets* (Atlantic). 4. *British.* a coward.
—*v.i.* 1. to say, write, or publish a squib or squibs. 2. to let off or fire a squib. 3. to move (about) restlessly or swiftly. 4. to make a slight, sharp report like that of a squib. —*v.t.* 1. to assail or attack with squibs; lampoon. 2. to cast, throw, or use like a squib. 3. (in Australia) to evade (an action, issue, etc.) in a cowardly way.
[origin uncertain; perhaps imitative]

squid (skwid), *n., pl.* **squids** or (*collectively*) **squid,** *v.,* **squid·ded, squid·ding.** —*n.* any of certain cephalopods related to the cuttlefish, having ten tentacles. —*v.i.* to fish with a squid as bait. [origin uncertain]

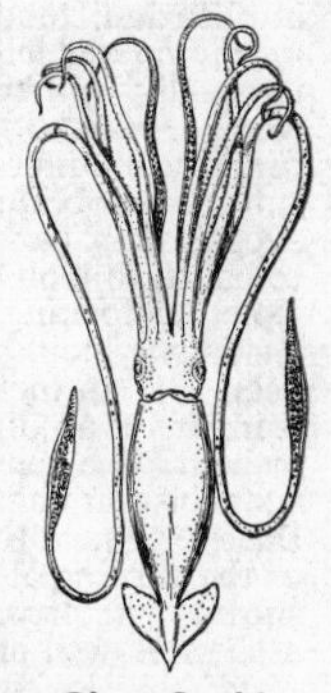
Giant Squid (body, 15 to 18 ft. long)

squidge (skwij), *n.* a large disk used to flick the smaller disks into the cup in the game of tiddlywinks. [origin unknown]

squid-jig·ger (skwid′jig′ər), *n.* a device for catching squids, consisting of a number of hooks soldered together by the shanks so that the points radiate in all directions. It is dragged or jerked through the water.

squid-jig·ging (skwid′jig′ing), *n.* the act of jigging for squids; the use of a squid-jigger.

squiffed (skwift), *adj. Slang.* squiffy: *[He] . . . cannot remember getting squiffed earlier than the age of six* (Time).

squif·fy (skwif′ē), *adj. Slang.* intoxicated; drunk. [origin unknown]

squig·gle (skwig′əl), *n., v.,* **-gled, -gling.** —*n.* a wriggly twist or curve: *He may, for example, point to a squiggle in one corner of the card and say, "That looks like a caterpillar"* (Science News Letter). —*v.t.* to make with twisting or curving lines: *The automatic pens squiggling recordings on numerous graphs traced eminently satisfactory data* (New York Times). —*v.i.* to twist and turn about; writhe; squirm; wriggle: *Then a squiggling, squirming mass of eels made an exodus into the sea* (Science News Letter). [origin unknown]

squig·gly (skwig′lē), *adj.* full of twists and turns: *Students pored over the squiggly lines that are man's first clues to the geography of outer space* (Time).

squil·gee (skwil′jē, skwil jē′), *n., v.,* **-geed, -gee·ing.** —*n.* 1. a squeegee. 2. a line bearing toggles with which a studding sail is set. —*v.t.* to squeegee. Also, **squillgee, squillagee.** [origin uncertain]

squill (skwil), *n.* 1. Often, **squills.** the bulb or root of the sea onion, which is sliced and dried for medicinal use, especially as an expectorant. 2. the plant itself; sea onion. 3. any of a group of Old World plants of the lily family, bearing small flowers on a leafless stalk, as the bluebell or wood hyacinth. [< Latin *squilla,* variant of *scilla* sea onion; prawn < Greek *skilla*]

squil·la (skwil′ə), *n., pl.* **squil·las, squil·lae** (skwil′ē). any of a group of stomatopod crustaceans, somewhat like the mantis, which burrow into the shallow ocean bottom along the shore; mantis shrimp. [< Latin *squilla;* see SQUILL]

squil·la·gee (skwil′ə jē), *n., v.t.,* **-geed, -gee·ing.** squilgee.

squill·gee (skwil′jē, skwil jē′), *n., v.t.,* **-geed, -gee·ing.** squilgee.

squinch[1] (skwinch), *n.* a straight or arched support constructed across an interior angle between walls in order to carry some superstructure, such as the side of an octagonal spire superimposed on a square tower. [short for Middle English *scuncheon* < Old French *escoinson,* apparently < *es-* out (< Latin *ex-*) + *coin* angle < Latin *cuneus* wedge]

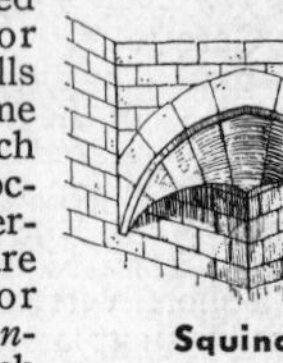
Squinch

squinch[2] (skwinch), *v.t.* to screw or distort (the face, eyes, etc.): *How it will make her squinch her face, won't it?* (Thomas Haliburton). —*v.i.* to squeeze up so as to take up less space: *The bench was crowded so we all squinched together to make more room.* [origin uncertain]

squin·ny (skwin′ē), *v.,* **-nied, -ny·ing,** *n., pl.* **-nies.** *Dialect.* —*v.i.* to squint. —*v.t.* to cause (the eyes) to squint. —*n.* a squint.

squint (skwint), *v.i.* **1.** to look or gaze with the eyes partly closed. **2.** to look sideways; glance obliquely or in other than the direct line of vision. **3.** to glance hastily; peep. **4.** to be cross-eyed or affected with strabismus. **5.** to have an indirect bearing, reference, or implication; tend; incline: *The general's remark squinted towards treason.* **6.** *Grammar.* to modify either a preceding or following word. *Example:* In *A man who runs swiftly tires,* the modifer *swiftly* squints. **7.** to move, run, or go obliquely. —*v.t.* **1.** to hold (the eyes) partly closed, as in a bright light. **2.** to cause to look sideways or obliquely.
—*n.* **1.** a looking with partly closed eyes. **2.** a sidelong look. **3.** a hasty or casual glance; peep. **4.** an inclination or tendency; drift; leaning. **5.** an oblique or perverse tendency or bent. **6.** a tendency to look sideways. **7.** a strabismus characterized by the turning of the eye toward the nose (convergent squint) or the turning of the eye outward (divergent squint). **8.** *Architecture.* a small opening in a chancel arch or wall; hagioscope.
—*adj.* **1.** looking sideways or obliquely; looking askance. **2.** cross-eyed or affected with strabismus.
[short for *asquint*] —**squint′er,** *n.* —**squint′ing·ly,** *adv.*

squint-eyed (skwint′īd′), *adj.* **1.** affected with strabismus; cross-eyed. **2.** narrowly and selfishly vindictive; malicious; spiteful: *squint-eyed jealousy. . . . False and squint-eyed praise, which, seeming to look upwards on his glories, looks down upon my fears* (John Denham).

squint·y (skwin′tē), *adj.,* **squint·i·er, squint·i·est.** having or characterized by a squint: . . . *the young girl with the yellow hair and squinty blue eyes* (Theodore Dreiser).

squin·y (skwin′ē, skwī′nē), *v.i., v.t.,* **squin·ied, squin·y·ing,** *n., pl.* **squin·ies.** *Dialect.* squinny; squint.

squir·arch (skwīr′ärk′), *n.* squirearch.

squir·ar·chy (skwīr′är′kē), *n., pl.* **-chies.** squirearchy.

squire (skwīr), *n., v.,* **squired, squir·ing.** —*n.* **1.** an English country gentleman or landed proprietor, especially one who is the principal landowner in a particular village or district (now often only a title of courtesy, but formerly the formal designation of such a person as the chief personage of his community, having specific legal responsibilities within it, and having the highest status of a gentleman, just below a knight). **2.** *U.S.* a justice of the peace, magistrate, or local judge, especially in a rural community (used as a title of courtesy, especially in the 1700's and 1800's, when such persons were often comparable in community status to the squires of England). **3.** a young man of noble family who attended a knight until he himself was made a knight. **4.** a male personal attendant, especially of a sovereign or noble personage. **5.** a woman's escort; gallant; lover.
—*v.t.* **1.** to attend as squire. **2.** to accompany as a squire; escort: *to squire a pretty girl about town.*
squire it, to act as a squire; play the squire: *Survey the Great, in City, Town, or Court, Who squire or lord it o'er the meaner sort* (Roger Bull).
[< Old French *esquier* < Latin *scūtārius* shield-bearer. Compare ESQUIRE.] —**squire′like′,** *adj.*

squire·arch (skwīr′ärk′), *n.* a member of the squirearchy: *Even the proudest of the neighbouring squirearchs always spoke of us as a very ancient family* (Edward G. Bulwer-Lytton).

squire·ar·chal (skwīr′är kəl), *adj.* of or having to do with a squirearchy.

squire·ar·chi·cal (skwīr′är′kə kəl), *adj.* squirearchal: *A large-built, well-dressed man of military bearing and most squirearchical proportions* (Grant Allen).

squire·ar·chy (skwīr′är kē), *n., pl.* **-chies. 1.** the collective body of squires, or landed proprietors; the country gentry as a class, regarded especially in respect to political or social influence. **2. a.** government dominated by the country gentry, such as generally existed in England from the early 1700's until 1832, when sweeping electoral reforms diminished the representation of the country gentry in the House of Commons. **b.** a country, state, or community having such a government: *We should never have left home, home being something like an eighteenth-century English squirearchy* (Harper's). [< *squir*(e) + *-archy,* as in *hierarchy*]

squir·een (skwī rēn′), *n. Especially Irish.* a petty squire; a small landed proprietor: *Squireens are persons who, with good long leases, or valuable farms, possess incomes from three to eight hundred a year* (Maria Edgeworth). [< *squire* + Irish *-in*]

squire·hood (skwīr′hu̇d), *n.* the state of being a squire; the rank or position of a squire.

squire·ling (skwīr′ling), *n.* **1.** a petty squire. **2.** a young squire.

squire·ly (skwīr′lē), *adj.* **1.** of or having to do with a squire. **2.** befitting a squire: *In recent years Colman led a squirely life in the Santa Barbara hills* (Time).

squire of dames, a man very attentive to women and much in their company: *"I'm not a squire of dames," Harris said with a poor attempt at pride* (Graham Greene).

squire·ship (skwīr′ship), *n.* squirehood.

squir·ess (skwīr′is), *n.* the wife of a squire.

squirm (skwėrm), *v.i., v.t.* **1.** to wriggle; writhe; twist: *The restless boy squirmed in his chair. A rusting, war-built oil tanker squirmed its way into a dry dock* (Wall Street Journal). **2.** to show great embarrassment, annoyance, confusion, etc. —*n.* a wriggle; writhe; twist. [perhaps imitative]

squirm·y (skwėr′mē), *adj.,* **squirm·i·er, squirm·i·est.** squirming; wriggling: *To win the attention of squirmy teen-age audiences, Anita told the story of how she and Fawn were wakened by the sound of screams one night in Chicago's LaSalle Hotel* (Time).

squir·rel (skwėr′əl), *n.* **1.** any of a group of slender, agile rodents that live in trees, have long, bushy tails, furry coats, bright eyes, and feed especially on nuts, shoots, and bark, as the fox squirrel and red squirrel. **2.** any of numerous related rodents, as the ground squirrels, chipmunks, woodchucks or marmots, and flying squirrels. **3.** the grey, reddish, or dark-brown fur of any squirrel. **4.** (in Australia) any of various flying phalangers. **5.** *Slang.* a reckless driver of a hot rod: *There was not a squirrel among them—no juvenile delinquent with wheels to zoom through traffic and terrorize the workaday motorist* (Time).
—*v.t.* to hide (away); bury or store (away): *She is squirreling the stuff away, deep in one of the closets, and I stumbled on her cache this morning* (H. Allen Smith).
[< Anglo-French *esquirel,* Old French *escurel* < Vulgar Latin *sciūriolus* (diminutive) < Latin *sciūrus* < Greek *skíouros* < *skiā́* shadow + *ourā́* tail] —**squir′rel-like′,** *adj.*

Common Gray Squirrel (def. 1—including tail, about 1½ ft. long)

squirrel cage, 1. a cylindrical cage for squirrels, that revolves as they move. **2.** any structure or situation similar to this.

squirrel corn, an American herb of the fumitory family, having finely divided leaves, cream-colored, heart-shaped flowers, and small tubers which resemble kernels of corn.

squir·rel·fish (skwėr′əl fish′), *n., pl.* **-fishes** or (*collectively*) **-fish.** any of a family of nocturnal, usually reddish, tropical fishes with large eyes and sharp spines and scales.

squirrel frog, a small green tree frog found in the southern United States.

squirrel glider, a flying phalanger (marsupial) found in isolated areas of eastern Australia, Papua, and Tasmania. It has a squirrel-like face and a full parachute.

squirrel grass, squirreltail.

squirrel hake, a variety of New England hake.

squirrel hawk, a large hawk of western North America with reddish-brown back and white underparts, so called because it preys extensively on ground squirrels.

squirrel monkey, 1. any of certain small South and Central American monkeys with a bushy, nonprehensile tail: *Although the squirrel monkey possesses a brain that is proportionately larger than man's, the animal is not particularly intelligent* (Science News Letter). **2.** a marmoset.

squir·rel·tail (skwėr′əl tāl′), *n.* any of various wild grasses related to the common barley.

squirt (skwėrt), *v.t.* **1.** to cause (liquid) to issue or stream (out) in a jet, as from a squirt or syringe: *With his trunk, the elephant squirted soft mud over his back.* **2.** to propel in a stream from or through any small opening: *to squirt water through a tube.* —*v.i.* to come out in a jet or jetlike stream; spurt.
—*n.* **1.** the act of squirting. **2.** a jet of liquid, etc. **3.** a small pump, syringe, or other device for squirting. **4.** *Informal.* an insignificant person who is impudent or self-assertive; whippersnapper: *a little squirt of a man* (Sinclair Lewis).
[origin uncertain] —**squirt′er,** *n.*

squirt gun, a kind of squirter or syringe used as a toy by boys.

squirt·ing cucumber (skwėr′ting), a trailing Mediterranean plant of the gourd family whose ripened fruit separates from the stalk and expels the seeds and pulp with considerable force.

squish (skwish), *v.i.* (of water, soft mud, etc.) to make a soft, splashing sound when walked in or on: *the caress of soft mud squishing up between the toes* (Rudyard Kipling). —*v.t. Dialect.* to squeeze or squash. —*n.* a squishing sound. [imitative]

squish·i·ness (skwish′ē nis), *n.* the quality or condition of being squishy: *The degree of squishiness is unpredictable; some years are flood years and others are . . . drought years* (New Yorker).

squish·y (skwish′ē), *adj.* making or characterized by soft, splashing sounds; wet and soft.

sq. yd., square yard or square yards.

Sr (no period), strontium (chemical element).

Sr., 1. senior. **2.** señor. **3.** sir.

S.R., Sons of the Revolution.

Sra., *Spanish.* señora.

sra·dha (srä′də), *n.* a Hindu funeral ceremony in honor of a deceased ancestor, at which food is offered, and gifts are made to Brahmans. Also, **shraddha.**

Sra·nan·ton·go (srä′nən tän′gō), *n.* a pidgin dialect of English spoken in Surinam; Taki-Taki.

S. Rept., Senate Report (used with a number).

S. Res., Senate Resolution (used with a number).

S.R.I., Holy Roman Empire (Latin, *Sacrum Romanum Imperium*).

S.R.N., State Registered Nurse.

S.R.O., standing room only: *The Carnegie Hall box office dusted off its S.R.O. sign* (Harper's).

S.R.S., Fellow of the Royal Society (Latin, *Societatis Regiae Socius*).

Srta., *Spanish.* señorita.

ss (no period) or **ss., 1.** *Law.* scilicet. **2.** sections. **3.** *Baseball.* shortstop.

SS (no periods), **1.** Schutzstaffel. **2.** steamship.

S/S, steamship.

SS., 1. most holy (Latin, *sanctissimus*). **2.** saints. **3.** scilicet. **4.** steamship.

S.S., an abbreviation for the following:
1. secretary of state.
2. Silver Star.
3. steamship.
4. Straits Settlements.
5. Sunday school.

SSA (no periods), Social Security Administration.

SSB (no periods), single sideband.

SSE (no periods) or **S.S.E.,** south-southeast.

S.S.F., standard Saybolt furol (a measure of viscosity for heavy oils).

S.Sgt. or **S/Sgt.,** staff sergeant.

SSM (no periods), surface-to-surface missile.

SSR (no periods) or **S.S.R.,** Soviet Socialist Republic.

SSS (no periods), Selective Service System.

SST (no periods), supersonic transport: *Boeing's SST could take off and land at the same speeds as supersonic jets* (Time).

SS Troops, a select military unit of fanatical Nazis who served as a bodyguard to Hitler; Schutzstaffel.

S.S.U., standard Saybolt universal (a measure of viscosity for fluids).

SSW (no periods) or **S.S.W.,** south-southwest.

st., an abbreviation for the following:
1. stanza.
2. statute or statutes.
3. stere.
4. stet.
5. stitch or stitches.
6. stone (weight).
7. street.
8. strophe.

s.t., short ton.

St (no period), stratus.

St., **1.** saint. **2.** statute or statutes. **3.** strait. **4.** street.

sta., **1.** stationary. **2.** stator.

Sta., **1.** Santa (*Spanish or Italian,* saint; holy). **2.** station.

Staats•rat (shtäts′rät′), *n. German.* **1.** council of state. **2.** councilor of state.

stab (stab), *v.,* **stabbed, stab•bing,** *n.* —*v.t.* **1.** to pierce or wound with a thrust of a pointed weapon, chiefly with a short weapon, as a dagger. **2.** to thrust (a weapon) into a person. **3.** to wound sharply or deeply in the feelings: *The mother was stabbed to the heart by her son's lack of gratitude. Lord, thy most pointed pleasure take And stab my spirit broad awake* (Robert Louis Stevenson). —*v.i.* **1.** to thrust with a pointed weapon; aim a blow. **2.** to penetrate suddenly and sharply; pierce: *She speaks poniards, and every word stabs* (Shakespeare).
—*n.* **1.** an act of stabbing; thrust dealt with a dagger or other sharp-pointed instrument. **2.** any thrust or sudden, sharp blow. **3.** a wound made by stabbing. **4.** an injury to the feelings. **5.** *Informal.* an attempt at something; try: *The conference was primarily an initial, amiable stab at getting acquainted* (Time).
have or **make a stab at,** to try; attempt: *Even if you've never done it before, make a stab at it.*
stab in the back, an act of unexpected treachery: *He absorbed this political stab in the back with the best grace he could muster* (Harper's).
[originally Scottish; apparently variant of *stob,* noun variant of *stub.* Compare Swedish *stabbe* stump, stub.] —**Syn.** *v.i.* **1.** jab.

Sta•bat Ma•ter (stä′bät mä′ter; stā′bat mā′tər), **1.** a celebrated Latin hymn of the 1200's, beginning "Stabat mater dolorosa," about the sorrows of the Virgin Mary at the Crucifixion. **2.** the musical setting of this. **3.** one of several other hymns beginning with the same words. **4.** a musical setting of any of these hymns. [< Medieval Latin *Stabat Mater* the Mother was standing (the first two words of the hymn)]

stab•ber (stab′ər), *n.* a person or thing that stabs.

stab•bing (stab′ing), *adj.* **1.** that stabs: *But still his struggling force he rears, 'Gainst hacking brands and stabbing spears* (Scott). **2.** sharp and sudden: *Unconscious of the stabbing pain in his foot . . .* (Mary Beaumont). **3.** piercing; penetrating; incisive: *This stabbing satire of a playgirl's progress from obscurity to celebrity owes much to Julie Christie's stunning presence* (Time). —**stab′bing•ly,** *adv.*

sta•bile (stā′bəl, stab′əl), *adj.* **1.** *Medicine.* **a.** designating or having to do with treatment by electricity in which an electrode is kept stationary over the part treated. **b.** not affected by an ordinary amount of heat. **2.** having stability; stable. —*n.* a stationary sculpture made of colored spheres, disks, and wires, or of large cut and bent sheets of metal, etc. [< Latin *stabilis;* see STABLE[2]]

sta•bil•i•fy (stə bil′ə fī), *v.t.,* **-fied, -fy•ing.** to render stable, fixed, or firm; establish. [< Latin *stabilis* (see STABLE[2])]

sta•bi•lise (stā′bə līz), *v.t., v.i.,* **-lised, -lis•ing.** *Especially British.* stabilize.

sta•bil•i•tate (stə bil′ə tāt), *v.t.,* **-tat•ed, -tat•ing.** to give stability to; make stable. [< Latin *stabilitāre* (with English *-ate*[1]) < *stabilis;* see STABLE[2]]

sta•bil•i•ty (stə bil′ə tē), *n., pl.* **-ties.** **1.** the capacity to remain in position; ability to resist being dislodged, overturned, etc.: *A concrete wall has more stability than a light wooden fence.* **2.** fixity of position in space; firmness of position. **3.** the capacity to resist destruction or essential change; enduring quality; permanence: *A party of order or stability, and a party of progress or reform, are both necessary elements of a healthy state of political life* (John Stuart Mill). *Every quotation contributes something to the stability or enlargement of the language* (Samuel Johnson). **4.** firmness of character, purpose, resolution, etc.; steadfastness. **5.** the ability of an object to return to its original or normal position, especially the ability of an aircraft, ship, etc., to regain a position of equilibrium when forced from it by the wind, sea, etc. **6.** (in the Roman Catholic Church) a fourth vow, made by a Benedictine, binding him to continuance in his profession and residence for life in the same monastery. **7.** *Obsolete.* solidity. —**Syn.** **1.** steadiness, equilibrium.

sta•bi•li•za•tion (stā′bə lə zā′shən), *n.* the act of making stable.

stabilization fund, a fund established by a country to keep stable the foreign exchange rates of its currency and to influence the domestic currency market.

sta•bi•li•za•tor (stā′bə lə zā′tər), *n.* stabilizer.

sta•bi•lize (stā′bə līz), *v.,* **-lized, -liz•ing.** —*v.t.* **1.** to make stable or firm; confer stability on: *to stabilize a government.* **2.** to prevent changes, especially further changes, in; hold steady: *to stabilize prices.* **3.** to keep in or restore to a position of equilibrium: *to stabilize an aircraft in level flight after hitting an air pocket.* **4.** to give stability to (an aircraft, ship, etc.) by the manner of its design, loading, etc., or by special devices, as gyroscopic controls. —*v.i.* to become stable: *This situation has fairly stabilized and we do not expect such an outbreak next year* (New York Times). [< French *stabiliser* < Latin *stabilis;* see STABLE[2]]

sta•bi•liz•er (stā′bə lī′zər), *n.* **1.** a person or thing that makes something stable. **2.** a device by which an aircraft, ship, etc., is kept in or restored to a position of equilibrium: *a gyroscopic stabilizer. The stabilizers can be rotated on a horizontal axis to fit varying conditions at sea* (New York Times). **3.** *Aeronautics.* the horizontal airfoil in the tail of an aircraft. **4.** a substance added to an explosive to make it less liable to spontaneous decomposition. **5.** a substance such as gelatin, agar, gum, etc., added to commercial foods to produce or retain smoothness or softness, preserve an emulsion, etc.

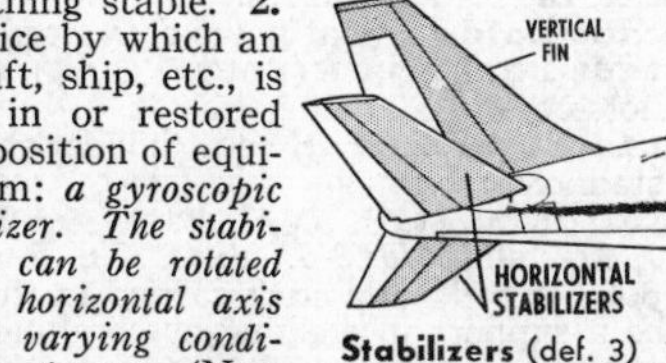

Stabilizers (def. 3)

sta•ble[1] (stā′bəl), *n., v.,* **-bled, -bling.** —*n.* **1.** a building fitted with stalls, rack and manger, etc., in which horses are kept: *She wanted him to stop at the stable where Katherine took riding lessons* (New Yorker). **2.** a barn, shed, or other building in which any domestic animals, as cattle, goats, etc., are kept. **3.** a group of animals housed in such a building. **4.** a group of race horses belonging to one owner. **5.** the grooms, trainers, etc., who work for a racing stable. **6.** *Informal.* a group of people joined for a common purpose, interest, etc., or who work for a particular business: *It was found that the gamble of financing a Broadway production required the assembly of a whole stable of backers* (Times Literary Supplement).
stables, the buildings and grounds where race horses are quartered and trained: *to work at the stables.*
—*v.t.* to put or keep in a stable: *to stable a horse for the night.* —*v.i.* to be lodged in a stable.
[< Old French *estable* < Latin *stabulum* (literally) a standing place < *stāre* to stand]

sta•ble[2] (stā′bəl), *adj.* **1.** that will not, or will not easily, fall, be overturned, etc.: *a stable government. The whole world needs a stable peace.* **2.** not likely to give way; steady; firm: *a stable support. Concrete reinforced with steel is stable.* **3.** not likely to change in nature or purpose; steadfast: *a calm, stable person.* **4.** fixed in nature or purpose; constant; unwavering: *a stable resolve.* **5.** not liable to destruction or essential change; permanent: *a stable design.* **6.** able to maintain or return to its original or normal position: *a stable ship.* **7.** (of a chemical compound) not easily decomposed. [< Old French *estable* < Latin *stabilis* (literally) able to stand < *stāre* to stand] —**sta′ble•ness,** *n.* —**Syn.** **3.** constant, unwavering.

sta•ble•boy (stā′bəl boi′), *n.* a boy or man who works in a stable.

stable fly, a common fly of Europe and North America that resembles the housefly but has a severe bite.

sta•ble•man (stā′bəl man′), *n., pl.* **-men.** a man who is employed in a stable to groom, feed, and otherwise look after the horses.

sta•ble•mate (stā′bəl māt′), *n.* **1.** a horse which shares the same stable as another; horse which belongs to the same stable as another: *Thorpe Hanover, a stablemate of the winner, was third* (New Yorker). **2.** any person, group, or thing sharing the same ownership, purpose, or interest.

sta•bler (stā′blər), *n.* a person who provides stabling for horses, etc.

sta•bles (stā′bəlz), *n.pl.* See under **stable**[1], *n.*

sta•bling (stā′bling), *n.* **1.** the act of placing or accommodating horses in a stable. **2.** stable accommodation: *There's stabling in this place for a dozen horses* (Dickens). **3.** a building, or buildings, comprising a stable: *A cloak of cold silence hung over the stabling area; the racetrack was barren of its customary early morning life* (Harper's).

stab•lish (stab′lish), *v.t. Archaic.* establish.

sta•bly (stā′blē), *adv.* in a stable manner; firmly; fixedly; securely.

stacc., staccato.

stac•ca•to (stə kä′tō), *adj., adv., n., pl.* **-tos** or **-ti** (-tē).
—*adj.* **1.** *Music.* detached; disconnected; with breaks between the successive notes: *His piano Bach is in the approved lighter, percussive, and staccato style* (Harper's). **2.** abrupt: *Her manner to her husband was . . . a little staccato; she was nervous* (Margaret Kennedy).

WRITTEN PLAYED

Staccato Phrase

—*adv.* in a staccato manner.
—*n.* **1.** *Music.* a succession of disconnected or staccato notes; passage played in a staccato manner. **2.** anything of an abrupt or disconnected nature, as speech: *His characters converse with curt clinical efficiency. This staccato creates a delicious undercurrent of venom* (Punch).
[< Italian *staccato* (literally) detached, short for *distaccato,* past participle of *distaccare* to detach]

stach•er (staᴴ′ər, stäᴴ′-), *v.i. Scottish.* stacker.

stack (stak), *n.* **1.** an orderly pile, heap, or group of things: *a stack of wood, a stack of boxes.* **2.** a large, usually round, pile of hay, straw, grain in the sheaf, etc., often coming to a point at the top and thatched to protect it from the weather: *a hay stack or straw stack.* **3.** a number of chimneys, flues, or pipes standing together in one group: *a stack of chimneys.* **4.** a chimney or funnel of a house, factory, etc.; the chimney or funnel of a locomotive or steamship. **5.** a number of rifles hooked together and arranged to support each other on the ground in a cone or pyramid. **6.** a pile of poker chips, usually 20, sold by the banker to a player. **7.** an English unit of measure for cut wood or coal, equal to 108 cubic feet. **8.** a tall pillar of rock, detached from the main part of a cliff, and rising out of the sea. **9.** an arrangement of airplanes at different altitudes above an airport, awaiting landing instructions. **10.** *Informal.* a great quantity or number: *a stack of compliments. Sometimes a stack of people would come there* (Mark Twain).
blow one's stack, *Slang.* to lose one's temper: *It takes . . . three times the normal self-control necessary to keep from blowing your stack over trifles* (Saturday Evening Post).
stacks, in libraries: **a.** a number of bookcases arranged so as to save space: *to return*

borrowed books to the stacks. **b.** a large bookcase, usually accessible from both sides: *the top shelf of the stacks.* **c.** the part of a library in which the main collection of books is shelved: *He is up in the library stacks of our Investment Research department* (New Yorker).
—*v.t.* **1.** to pile, arrange, or build in a stack: *to stack hay, to stack firewood, to stack rifles.* **2.** to fill or load with stacks of: *The left hand half of every step of the stairs was stacked with books* (Arnold Bennett). **3.** to put (the cards in a pack) into a predetermined arrangement, as for cheating. **4.** to arrange in such a way as to force or urge a predisposed result; load: *This committee is one of two or three in the House whose memberships are stacked to give the majority party substantial control* (New York Times).
stack up, a. to pile materials on to make (a fire): *We stacked up the fire* (H. Rider Haggard). **b.** to pile up one's chips at poker: *to stack up before dealing.* **c.** *Informal.* to measure up; compare (against): *Stacked up against what's happening in the industry, these actions point to far-reaching changes* (Wall Street Journal). **d.** to arrange (aircraft) at different altitudes above an airport: *Jet planes cannot be stacked up at the landing site while awaiting landing instructions* (Science News Letter).
[< Scandinavian (compare Old Icelandic *stakkr*)] —**stack'er,** *n.*

stack·a·bil·i·ty (stak'ə bil'ə tē), *n.* the condition of being stackable.

stack·a·ble (stak'ə bəl), *adj.* that can be stacked: *stackable tableware.*

stacked (stakt), *adj. Slang.* well-built; voluptuous: *Can I help it if this Mexican spitfire is fantastically stacked and wears a flimsy blouse?* (S.J. Perelman).

stack·er (stak'ər, stäk'-), *v.i. British Dialect.* to totter or reel; stagger. Also, **stacher.** [< Scandinavian (compare Old Icelandic *stakra* stagger < *staka* push)]

stack·ing (stak'ing), *n.* the circling of an airport by aircraft in a controlled pattern while awaiting landing instructions: [*He*] *had been asked to determine whether tighter scheduling of airliners would eliminate stacking at the airport* (Wall Street Journal).

stack room, a room in a library in which books are stacked.

stacks (staks), *n.pl.* See under **stack,** *n.*

stack·stand (stak'stand'), *n.* a stand or framework for supporting a stack of hay, grain, or the like.

stack·yard (stak'yärd'), *n.* a yard or enclosure for stacks of hay or grain.

stac·te (stak'tē), *n.* (in the Bible) a fragrant, sweet spice used by the Hebrews in the holy incense. Exodus 30:34. [< Latin *stactē* < Greek *staktḗ* sweet spice; oil of myrrh, ultimately < *stázein* to drop]

stac·tom·e·ter (stak tom'ə tər), *n.* an instrument for measuring a liquid in drops. [< Greek *staktós* distilling in drops (< *stázein* to drop) + English *-meter*]

stad·dle (stad'əl), *n.* **1.** the lower part of a stack of hay, straw, etc. **2.** the platform on which this stands. **3.** a supporting framework. Also, **stadle.** [Old English *stathol* foundation, support, base]

stade[1] (stād), *n.* an ancient unit of linear measure; stadium: *Strabo says that the ruins . . . were situated above Demetrias, at seven stades distance from it* (Henry F. Tozer). [shortened form of *stadium*]

stade[2] (stād), *n. Geology.* a subdivision of a glacial stage; the period of time represented by a glacial substratum. [< French *stade* stage < Latin *stadium;* see STADIUM]

stad·hold·er (stad'hōl'dər), *n.* **1.** the chief executive of the former republic of the United Provinces of the Netherlands. **2.** (originally) the viceroy or governor of a province in the Netherlands. Also, **stadtholder.** [< Dutch *stadhouder* < *stad* town, city + *houder* holder]

stad·hold·er·ate (stad'hōl'dər it), *n.* **1.** the office of stadholder. **2.** the rule or government of a stadholder: *The commonwealth which William had liberated . . . continued to exist . . . under the successive stadholderates of his sons and descendants* (John L. Motley). **3.** a province or state governed by a stadholder. Also, **stadtholderate.**

stad·hold·er·ship (stad'hōl'dər ship), *n.* the office of stadholder. Also, **stadtholdership.**

sta·di·a[1] (stā'dē ə), *n.* **1.** an instrument for measuring distances or heights by means of angles: *A surveyor's transit is one kind of stadia.* **2.** a method of measuring distances by using such an instrument. **3.** a stadia rod. **4.** a surveying station. **5.** a crude type of range finder consisting of a graduated rod held vertically at arm's length to indicate the distance of the target.
—*adj.* of or having to do with surveying by means of a stadia.
[apparently < Italian *stadia* lengths < Latin *stadia,* plural of *stadium* stadium]

sta·di·a[2] (stā'dē ə), *n.* a plural of **stadium.**

stadia hairs or **wires,** fine, parallel cross hairs placed at one end of the distance to be measured by a stadia.

sta·di·al (stā'dē əl), *Geology.* —*n.* a subdivision of a glacial stage; stade. —*adj.* of or having to do with such a subdivision.

stadia rod, a staff or graduated rod placed at one end of the distance to be measured by a stadia.

sta·dim·e·ter (stə dim'ə tər), *n.* an optical instrument for measuring distances of objects, especially ships, of which the heights are known.

sta·di·om·e·ter (stā'dē om'ə tər), *n.* **1.** an instrument consisting of a rolling wheel with spaced teeth, used for measuring the length of a line, curve, etc. **2.** a modified theodolite in which the directions are not read off but marked upon a small sheet, which is changed at each station. [< Greek *stádion* + English *-meter*]

sta·di·um (stā'dē əm), *n., pl.* **-di·ums** or **-di·a. 1.** an oval, circular, or U-shaped structure with seats in tiers for spectators around an arena or playing field. **2.** an ancient Greek running track for footraces, with tiers of seats along each side and at one end, as at Athens. **3. a.** *Biology.* a stage of a process. **b.** a stage of a disease. **4.** a unit of linear measure used in various parts of the ancient world, varying according to time and place, but most commonly equal to slightly over 600 feet (607 feet being the approximate length of the stadium at Athens) or 1/8 of a Roman mile. [< Latin *stadium* < Greek *stádion* 607 feet (see definition 4)] —**Syn. 1.** amphitheater.
➔ In the sense of def. 1, the plural is usually *stadiums.* In the senses of defs. 2, 3, and 4, the plural is regularly *stadia.*

stad·le (stad'əl), *n.* staddle.

stadt·hold·er (stat'hōl'dər), *n.* stadholder.

stadt·hold·er·ate (stat'hōl'dər it), *n.* stadholderate.

stadt·hold·er·ship (stat'hōl'dər ship), *n.* stadholdership.

staff[1] (staf, stäf), *n., pl.* **staves** or **staffs** *for 1, 2, 7,* **staffs** *for 3-6, adj., v.* —*n.* **1.** a stick, pole, or rod: **a.** a stick carried in the hand as a support in walking or climbing. **b.** a stick or club used as a weapon; cudgel. **c.** a pole from which a flag is flown. **d.** a rod or wand as an emblem of office, as the crosier of episcopal authority. **e.** a rod used in surveying for measuring distances and heights. **2.** something that supports or sustains: *Bread is called the staff of life.* **3.** a group of people employed under a manager, superintendent, or other leader: *the editorial staff of a paper, a hospital staff, the teaching staff of a college.* **4.** *Military.* a group of officers assisting a commanding officer with administration, planning, etc., but without command or combat duties. **5.** a similar group assisting or attending a governor, president, or other executive. **6.** *Music.* a set of five horizontal lines, and the spaces between, on which notes are placed to indicate pitch; stave. **7.** *Archaic.* the long handle of a spear, lance, poleax, or halberd.
—*adj.* having to do with or belonging to a military or administrative staff: *staff duties. The gate was partly blocked by a staff car* (Harper's).
—*v.t.* to provide with a staff of officers, teachers, servants, etc.: *Staffing the administrative services of the new republic has also been difficult* (Manchester Guardian).
[Old English *stæf*]

staff[2] (staf, stäf), *n.* a building material consisting of plaster of Paris, cement, and fibrous material, used for temporary ornamental work. [apparently < German *staffieren* to trim]

staff angle, a square strip of wood, standing flush with the wall on each of its sides, at the external angles of plastering, to protect them from injury.

Staff College or **School,** a special school of the United States Army to train both staff and command officers for higher duties: *That's the way it is in the book; that's the way they learn it at the Staff School at Fort Leavenworth* (Ralph Ingersoll).

staf·fel·ite (staf'ə līt), *n.* a greenish mineral, a phosphate and carbonate of calcium, occurring in botryoidal forms of a fibrous structure. [< German *Staffelit* < *Staffel,* Prussia, where it was found + *-it* -ite[1]]

staff·er (staf'ər, stäf'-), *n. Informal.* a member of a staff: *Twelve fashion staffers will fly to the Continent on July 17 for the showing of original collections* (New York Times).

staff·ing (staf'ing, stäf'-), *n.* the members of an official or working staff.

staff·man (staf'man', stäf'-), *n., pl.* **-men.** a member of a staff: *Public relations men, whether as corporate staffmen or as hired counsel, are acquiring power and acceptance in America's executive suites* (Vance Packard).

staff officer, 1. a commissioned army or navy officer charged with executive and administrative duties, but having no command over a combat force. **2.** *U.S. Navy.* any commissioned officer, as a surgeon, chaplain, etc., who is not eligible to take over command of a vessel, aircraft, etc.

Staf·ford·shire terrier (staf'ərd shir, -shər), any of a breed of sturdy dogs having a short stiff coat, weighing 35 to 50 pounds, and developed from the bulldog and a terrier. [< *Staffordshire,* a county in England, where the breed originated]

staff ride, a course of instruction in the field for officers of a general staff.

staff·room (staf'rüm', stäf'-), *n. Especially British.* a room for the use of the staff only, as in a school.

staff sergeant, (formerly) a noncommissioned army officer below a technical sergeant and above a sergeant in rank (abolished 1948). *Abbr.:* S. Sgt.

staff tree, any of a group of twining shrubs, especially the bittersweet.

staff-tree family (staf'trē', stäf'-), a group of dicotyledonous, climbing, shrubs or trees including the American bittersweet, strawberry bush, wahoo, and kat.

staff·work (staf'wėrk', stäf'-), *n.* work by a staff; administrative work.

stag (stag), *n., adj., v.,* **stagged, stag·ging.** —*n.* **1.** a full-grown male deer, especially the European red deer; hart. **2.** the male of many other large animals of the group including deer. **3.** the male of various other animals. **4.** an animal, especially a hog, castrated when full grown. **5.** *Informal.* a man who goes to a dance, party, etc., alone or with other men. **6.** *U.S. Informal.* a dinner, party, etc., attended by men only. **7.** *Scottish.* a young horse, especially one that is unbroken. **8.** *Slang.* a person who seeks to buy stocks in a corporation to sell them immediately at a profit: *The stock is obviously a useful investment and expectations are for a higher premium when the stags have finished selling* (Economist).

Stag (def. 1) of English red deer (about 4 ft. high at the shoulder)

—*adj. Informal.* attended by, or for, men only: *a stag dinner, a stag party.*
—*v.t.* **1.** *Slang.* to purchase or deal in (stock) as a stag. **2.** *Obsolete, Slang.* to observe; watch. **3.** *Obsolete, Slang.* to detect.
[Old English *stagga* stag]

stag beetle, any of various large lamellicorn beetles, some of the males of which have mandibles resembling antlers.

stag·bush (stag'bu̇sh'), *n.* the black haw.

stage (stāj), *n., v.,* **staged, stag·ing.** —*n.* **1.** one step or degree in a process; period of development: *at this stage of his life. An insect passes through several stages before it is full grown. Frogs pass through a tadpole stage. The communicable diseases are most contagious in this early stage* (Time). **2.** a raised platform, especially in a theater and on which actors perform: *Like a lone actor on a gloomy stage* (Thomas Hardy). *All the world's a stage And all the men and women merely play-*

ers (Shakespeare). *Thirty feet above its stage floor was the grid—a set of rafters from which hung scenery, lights, and drapes* (New Yorker). **3.** the scene of action: *Bunker Hill was the stage of a great battle.* **4.** a stagecoach. **5.** a place of rest on a journey; a regular stopping place for stagecoaches, etc., where horses were changed. **6.** the distance between two places of rest on a journey; distance between stops. **7.** the small platform on which an object is placed to be viewed through a microscope: *The doctor looked through the microscope at the slide on the stage.* **8.** a scaffold for workmen and their tools, etc.; staging. **9.** a section of a rocket or missile having its own motor and fuel. A three-stage rocket has three motors, one in each stage, which separate one after another from the rocket or missile after use. *Russia said the next to last stage of the vehicle burned up in the atmosphere about 50 miles up* (Wall Street Journal). **10.** *Geology.* two or more sets of related beds of stratified rocks; a subdivision of a series. **11.** *Radio.* one element in some complex apparatus, as one tube and its accessory equipment in an amplifier consisting of several tubes; a stop. **12.** (in a turbine) a single set each of stationary blades or nozzles and of moving blades or rotor buckets. **13.** *U.S.* a level (of water): *During last year's flood, the river rose to record stages at four different locations.*

NOSE-CONE, THIRD STAGE, SECOND STAGE, FIRST STAGE

Stages (def. 9) Construction of a 3-stage rocket

by easy stages, a little at a time; often stopping; slowly: *We proceeded leisurely and by easy stages* (J.B. Crozier).
hold the stage, to be the center of attention: *He held the stage all the time. He went on to say that he had killed three of four people* (London Times).
on stage, on a stage; before the audience or public: *Yet we are on stage, whether we like it or not ... the curtain is about to go up ... and the world is watching* (Harper's).
on the stage, in the acting profession: *If he had gone on the stage he would have made a good actor* (E.F. Adeline Sergeant).
set the stage, to prepare the way; set up the necessary conditions: *The House set the stage for possible widespread grass roots protest* (New York Times). *It's hoped the venture will set the stage for later U.S.-Soviet efforts* (Wall Street Journal).
the stage, the theater; the drama; the actor's profession: *Eugene O'Neill wrote for the stage.*
—*v.t.* **1.** to put (a play, etc.) on a stage; arrange: *The play was excellently staged.* **2.** *U.S.* to arrange to have an effect; plan and carry out: *The angry people staged a riot.* **3.** to burn out and detach from a rocket or missile: *to stage a motor or a fuel tank.* **4.** to carry out or do by stages: *The West called for staged reduction of both atomic and conventional weapons* (New York Times).
—*v.i.* **1.** to be suited to the theater: *That scene will not stage well.* **2.** to travel by stagecoach.
[< Old French *estage* < Late Latin *staticum* < Latin *stāre* to stand] —**stage′like′,** *adj.*
—**Syn.** *n.* **3.** arena. **4.** diligence. **5.** station.

stage·a·ble (stāj′ə bəl), *adj.* that can be staged or put on stage: *The Stratford Festival receives manuscripts of plays: that was to be expected. A pity none of them has proved stageable* (Canadian Saturday Night).

stage box, a box in a theater, in or close to the proscenium arch, seating several spectators.

stage carriage, *British.* stagecoach.

stage·coach (stāj′kōch′), *n.* a horse-drawn coach carrying passengers and parcels over a regular route: *Stagecoaches made the coaching inn, railroads the terminal hotel* (Saturday Review).

Stagecoach

stage·craft (stāj′kraft′, -kräft′), *n.* skill in, or the art of, writing, adapting, or presenting plays: *The theater badly needs workmen who are wise in stagecraft and anxious to use their talents* (Newsweek).

stage direction, a direction in a written or printed play to indicate the appropriate action, arrangement of the stage, etc.

stage director, *Theater.* **1.** *Especially U.S.* a director. **2.** *Especially British.* a stage manager.

stage door, the door giving access to the stage and the parts behind it in a theater; the actors' and workmen's entrance to a theater.

stage-door Johnny (stāj′dôr′, -dōr′), *Informal.* a man who waits at a stage door or goes to a theater to court an actress or showgirl.

stage effect, a striking theatrical effect, as the use of thunder and lightning on the stage.

stage fever, a strong desire to go on the stage, or to be an actor or actress.

stage fright, nervous fear or sudden panic experienced when appearing before an audience, especially for the first time: *She told us that she was still recovering from the stage fright she'd suffered the night before* (New Yorker).

stage·hand (stāj′hand′), *n.* a person whose work is moving scenery, arranging lights, etc., in a theater.

stage·land (stāj′land′), *n.* the stage.

stage-man·age (stāj′man′ij), *v.t.,* **-aged, -ag·ing. 1.** to arrange with a view to dramatic effect; supervise the details of closely: *to stage-manage a Christmas party. But the hours of waiting had their own theatrical shape, a prologue of high expectation splendidly stage-managed by tradition* (Manchester Guardian). **2.** to be the stage manager of.

stage manager, the person who superintends the arrangements of the stage during the preparation and performance of a play, etc.

stage name, a name used by an actor instead of his real name.

stage play, 1. a dramatic performance. **2.** a play adapted for representation on the stage. **3.** dramatic acting.

stag·er (stā′jər), *n.* **1.** a person of long experience or employment in an office, a profession, etc.; an old hand; veteran. **2.** a coach horse.

stage right, the sole and exclusive right of representation of a dramatic composition; the right to perform or authorize the performance of a particular drama.

stage-struck (stāj′struk′), *adj.* extremely interested in acting; wanting very much to become an actor or actress: *He was stage-struck early, and in those days of vaudeville, juggling seemed to be the place to start* (Newsweek).

stage whisper, 1. a loud whisper on a stage, meant for the audience to hear. **2.** a whisper meant to be heard by others than the person addressed. **3.** any loud whisper.

stage-whis·per (stāj′hwis′pər), *v.i., v.t.* to speak or say in a stage whisper: *"Why don't you fellows call this whole thing off," he stage-whispered to the nearby press table* (Time).

stage·wor·thi·ness (stāj′wėr′ᴛʜē nis), *n.* the quality or condition of being stageworthy.

stage·wor·thy (stāj′wėr′ᴛʜē), *adj.* worthy of representation on the stage: *[The] new play is a skillfully stageworthy adaptation of his novel* (London Times).

stag·y (stā′jē), *adj.,* **stag·i·er, stag·i·est.** stagy: *It isn't stagey, and the actors enacted their roles faithfully* (Wall Street Journal).

stag·gard (stag′ərd), *n.* a four-year-old male red deer. [Middle English *stagard* < *stag* stag]

stag·gart (stag′ərt), *n.* staggard.

stag·ger (stag′ər), *v.i.* **1.** to sway from side to side when trying to stand or walk, as from weakness, a heavy load, or drunkenness; move unsteadily; totter; reel: *I saw him staggering up the street in a state of intoxication* (George Borrow). **2.** to begin to doubt or waver; become less confident or determined; hesitate. **3.** to become unsteady; give way, as an army, line of battle, etc.: *The troops staggered under the severe gunfire. A prince's banner wavered, then staggered backward, hemmed by foes* (E. R. Sill). —*v.t.* **1.** to make sway or reel: *The blow staggered him for the moment.* **2.** to confuse or astonish greatly; shock; nonplus; overwhelm; bewilder: *The difficulty of the examination staggered him. The size of the debt staggered him. He was staggered by the news of his friend's death.* **3.** to cause to doubt, waver, or falter: *a fire from the militia which ... staggered the regulars* (James Fenimore Cooper). **4.** to make helpless. **5.** to arrange in zigzag order, or in positions alternately on one side and the other, as spokes in a wheel hub. **6.** to arrange (the wings of a biplane) so that the leading edge of one is set farther forward on the fuselage than the leading edge of the other. **7.** to arrange (times of opening and closing, work, jobs, etc.) at intervals or at other than the normal times, so as to avoid traffic congestion, etc.: *Vacations were staggered so that only one person was away at a time. The school was so crowded they had to stagger the classes.*
—*n.* **1.** an act of staggering; a swaying, tottering, or reeling motion of the body. **2.** a staggered arrangement. **3.** an arrangement of wings of a biplane, one farther forward than the other. **4.** the extent to which one wing is ahead of the other, expressed as a percentage of the vertical distance between the wings.
staggers, any of several nervous diseases of horses, cattle, etc., that make them stagger or fall suddenly: *Staggers is sometimes called "blind staggers."*
[variant of *stacker*] —**stag′ger·er,** *n.*
—**Syn.** *v.i.* **1.** See **reel**[2].

stag·ger·bush (stag′ər bu̇sh′), *n.* a shrub of the heath family with white or pink flowers, growing in the eastern United States. Its foliage is poisonous to stock, and was supposed to cause staggers in animals that ate it.

stag·gered (stag′ərd), *adj.* arranged in a progressing sequence of time, location, etc.: *12 large new plants ... built on a staggered schedule* (Scientific American).

stag·ger·ing (stag′ər ing), *adj.* **1.** causing to stagger; confounding; shocking: *a staggering surprise, thought, etc.* **2.** enormous; immense; stupendous: *From a material standpoint, the achievements of the United States ... have been staggering* (Newsweek). —**stag′ger·ing·ly,** *adv.*

stag·ger·y (stag′ər ē), *adj.* staggering; inclining to stagger or fall.

stag·gy or **stag·gie** (stag′ē), *n., pl.* **-gies.** *Scottish.* a colt.

stag·head (stag′hed′), *n.* a diseased condition of trees in which the topmost branches become dead and bare.

stag-head·ed (stag′hed′id), *adj.* (of a tree) having the upper branches bare and dead.

stag·horn coral (stag′hôrn′), any of various madreporic corals having a branched skeleton that resembles the antlers of a stag.

staghorn sumac, a tall variety of sumac of eastern North America, with branchlets covered with velvety hairs.

stag·hound (stag′hound′), *n.* any of a former breed of large hounds resembling the foxhound but larger, used for hunting deer, wolves, etc.

stag·i·ly (stā′jə lē), *adv.* in a stagy manner; theatrically.

stag·i·ness (stā′jē nis), *n.* **1.** stagy or exaggerated character or style; conventional theatricality: *Balcon's first two productions followed safe patterns of staginess and formality* (Harper's). **2.** a certain stage or state of an animal. **3.** that stage when an animal is out of condition, as when a fur-bearing animal is shedding.

stag·ing (stā′jing), *n.* **1.** a temporary flooring with posts and boards for support, used as a platform by workmen or builders; scaffolding. **2.** the act, process, or art of putting a play on the stage. **3.** a traveling by stages or by stagecoach. **4.** the business of running or managing stagecoaches.

staging area, an area where troops, equipment, or the like are prepared before a military movement.

Stag·i·rite (staj′ə rīt), *n.* a native or inhabitant of ancient Stagira, a city in ancient Macedonia, especially Aristotle, who was born there.

stag line, *U.S. Informal.* the men, or place for men, who have no dancing partners.

stag·nan·cy (stag′nən sē), *n.* stagnant condition.

stag·nant (stag′nənt), *adj.* **1.** not running or flowing; lacking motion or current: *stag-*

nant air. *A fen of stagnant waters* (Wordsworth). **2.** foul from standing still: *a stagnant pool of water.* **3.** not active; sluggish; dull: *There is always a chance that the perfect society might be a stagnant society* (Harper's). [< Latin *stāgnāns, -antis,* present participle of *stāgnāre;* see STAGNATE] —**stag′nant·ly,** *adv.* —**Syn. 1.** stationary. **3.** inactive, quiescent.

stag·nate (stag′nāt), *v.,* **-nat·ed, -nat·ing.** —*v.i.* to be or become stagnant. —*v.t.* to make stagnant. [< Latin *stāgnāre* (with English *-ate*[1]) < *stāgnum* standing water]

stag·na·tion (stag nā′shən), *n.* **1.** a becoming stagnant. **2.** a making stagnant. **3.** stagnant condition: *France . . . is the country of Catholicism and disbelief, tradition and impiety, stagnation and drama, order and anarchy* (Newsweek).

stag party, 1. a party or entertainment for men only. **2.** a party or company consisting of men only.

stag·worm (stag′wėrm′), *n.* the larva of one of several botflies which infest the stag.

stag·y (stā′jē), *adj.,* **stag·i·er, stag·i·est. 1.** of or having to do with the stage. **2.** suggestive of the stage; theatrical in appearance, manner, style, etc. **3.** artificial; pompous; affected: *The play, closing on a lame, stagy note, lacks stature* (Time).

Stahl·helm (shtäl′helm), *n.* a quasi-military organization of German veterans of World War I formed during the 1920's, having strongly nationalistic and monarchistic sympathies, and formally dissolved in the 1930's. [< German *Stahlhelm* < *Stahl* steel + *Helm* helmet]

staid (stād), *adj.* **1.** having a settled, quiet character; sober; sedate: *Most people think of the Quakers as staid people.* **2. a.** (of beliefs, institutions, etc.) permanent; settled; unchanging. **b.** (of a person's gaze) fixed; set. —*v. Archaic.* a past tense and a past participle of **stay**[1]. [earlier *steyed, stayed,* (originally) past participles of *stay*[1] in the sense of "restrain"] —**staid′ly,** *adv.* —**staid′ness,** *n.* —**Syn.** *adj.* **1.** grave, serious, steady, composed.

staig (stāg), *n. Scottish.* a young horse; stag.

stain (stān), *n.* **1.** a discoloration; soil; spot. **2.** a natural spot or patch of color different from the ground. **3.** a cause of reproach, infamy, or disgrace; a moral blemish; stigma: *a stain on one's character or reputation. When you know the dream is true And lovely with no flaw nor stain* (Robert Graves). **4.** a liquid preparation of dye used to color woods, fabrics, etc. **5.** a dye or pigment used to make visible transparent or very small structures, or to differentiate tissue elements by coloring, for microscopic study: *. . . many of the various stains used in microscopic work have a selective effect on bacteria, coloring some species and leaving others more or less unaffected* (Fred W. Emerson).

—*v.t.* **1.** to discolor (something); spot: *The tablecloth is stained where food has been spilled. Let not women's weapons, water-drops, Stain my man's cheeks* (Shakespeare). **2.** to bring reproach or disgrace on (a person's reputation, honor, etc.); blemish; soil: *But thoughtless follies laid him low, And stain'd his name* (Robert Burns). **3.** to corrupt morally; taint with guilt or vice; defile. **4.** to color, as a microscopic specimen. —*v.i.* **1.** to cause a stain or discoloration. **2.** to take a stain; admit of staining. [probably fusion of short form of Middle English *distainen* (< Old French *desteign-,* stem of *desteindre* take out the color, ultimately < Latin *dis-* off + *tingere* to dye), and a Scandinavian borrowing (compare Old Icelandic *steina* to paint)] —**stain′er,** *n.*

stain·a·bil·i·ty (stā′nə bil′ə tē), *n.* the ability of a cell or a part of a cell to take up a stain.

stain·a·ble (stā′nə bəl), *adj.* that can be stained.

stained (stānd), *adj.* discolored; colored by staining: *A French officer in a stained white uniform stood in the bow* (Graham Greene).

stained glass, 1. colored glass as used in sheets or fitted pieces in church windows to form a picture, or as used in mosaic or composite designs. **2.** any enameled or painted glass.

stained-glass (stānd′glas′, -gläs′), *adj.* **1.** having to do with or made of stained glass. **2.** characteristic of a church, cathedral, or the like.

stain·less (stān′lis), *adj.* without stain; spotless. —*n.* stainless steel. —**stain′less·ly,** *adv.* —**stain′less·ness,** *n.*

stainless steel, steel containing a high percentage of chromium (from 10 to 25 per cent), making it especially resistant to rust and corrosion.

stair (stãr), *n.* **1.** one of a series of steps for going from one level or floor to another. **2.** a set of such steps; staircase: *We climbed the winding stair in the tower.* **3.** a means of ascending in rank, power, moral excellence, etc.: *He passed one after another of his associates on the stair to success.*

stairs, the series of steps for going from one level or floor to another: *the head of the stairs.*

[Old English *stǣger* stair, related to *stīgan* to climb]

stair·case (stãr′kās′), *n.* a flight, or a series of flights, of stairs with their supporting framework, balusters, etc.

staircase shell, 1. the shell of any of a group of gastropods of tropical seas, that suggests in its appearance a spiral staircase. **2.** the animal itself.

stair foot, the foot or bottom of a stair or staircase.

stair·head (stãr′hed′), *n.* the top of a staircase or flight of stairs.

stair·less (stãr′lis), *adj.* having no stairs: *. . . rundown apartments with leaking water taps and stairless staircases* (Maclean's).

stair rod, a rod or strip of thin metal used to hold a stair carpet in place.

stair·step (stãr′step′), *n.* **1.** one of the steps in a flight of stairs. **2.** *Informal.* one of a number of siblings differing in age and height by regular intervals. —*adj.* rising or falling in a series of steps: *a stairstep tax reduction.*

stair·way (stãr′wā′), *n.* a way up or down a flight of stairs; staircase.

stair·well (stãr′wel′), *n.,* or **stair well,** the vertical passage or open space containing the stairs of a building.

staith or **staithe** (stāth), *n. British Dialect.* **1.** a landing place, as a wharf, especially one equipped for loading or unloading coal. **2.** an embankment. [partly Old English *stæth* a shore, bank, and partly < Scandinavian (compare Old Icelandic *stāth*)]

stake[1] (stāk), *n., v.,* **staked, stak·ing.** —*n.* **1.** a stout stick or post, usually of wood, pointed at one end for driving into the ground to form part of a fence, mark a boundary, support a plant, or the like. **2.** a post upon which a person is bound and then executed by burning. **3.** each of the posts which fit into sockets on the edge of a wagon, flatcar, boat, etc., to prevent the load from slipping off. **4. a.** a district within the authority of the Mormon Church; diocese. **b.** the see or jurisdiction of a Mormon bishop.

drive stakes, *Informal.* **a.** to pitch one's tent or camp: *We stopped near the river and drove stakes for the night.* **b.** to stake off a claim: *In the gold rush of '49, he succeeded in driving stakes in the San Fernando valley.* **c.** to establish oneself; settle: *After drifting about several years I finally drove stakes on the Spokane River* (Outing).

pull up stakes, *U.S. Informal.* to move on to another place; change the place where one lives: *Many of the South's best educated citizens . . . are among those pulling up stakes* (Wall Street Journal).

the stake, death by being burned at a stake: *I know that I would go to the stake for you* (Thackeray).

—*v.t.* **1.** to mark (out or off) with stakes: *The miner staked out his claim. The surveyor staked off the district boundaries.* **2.** to close (up or in), keep (out), or shut (off) with a barrier of stakes. **3.** to support (a plant, tree, vine, etc.) with a stake or stakes. **4.** to tether (an animal) to a stake. **5.** to fasten with a stake or stakes.

stake out, a. to maintain surveillance over (an area, a person, etc.): *The police staked out his home, hoping he would return to get the money.* **b.** to assign (someone) to maintain surveillance: *Department stores staked out a cameraman in a room across from the store to photograph unloading trucks* (Time). **c.** to set aside for a special purpose; reserve: *Powell is . . . demanding that the office of Borough President of Manhattan be permanently staked out as the inheritance of "a black man or a black woman"* (New York Times).

[Old English *staca,* noun]

stake[2] (stāk), *n., v.,* **staked, stak·ing.** —*n.* **1.** something deposited or guaranteed, to be taken by the winner of a game, race, contest, wager, etc.: *The men played for high stakes.* **2.** the sum of money with which a gambler operates. **3.** something to gain or lose; share in a property, business, etc.; interest. **4.** *U.S. Informal.* a grubstake.

at stake, to be won or lost; in jeopardy; risked: *His honor is at stake.*

stakes, a. the prize in a contest or race: *. . . whose game was empires, and whose stakes were thrones* (Byron). **b.** a race for a prize, usually a sum of money: *He made a two-dollar bet at the stakes.*

—*v.t.* **1.** to risk (money or something valuable) on the result of a game, race, cast of dice, etc. **2.** to risk the loss of; hazard. **3.** *U.S. Informal.* to grubstake: *For the last time he staked the old prospector.* **4.** *Informal.* to assist (a person) with money or other resources (to something): *I'll stake you to a dinner if you'll come.*

—**Syn.** *v.t.* **1.** bet, wager.

stake·boat (stāk′bōt′), *n.* a boat moored or otherwise fixed to serve as a starting point or mark for racing boats.

stake driver, *U.S.* the bittern, a small heron whose cry suggests the sound of a stake being driven into mud.

stake·hold·er (stāk′hōl′dər), *n.* the person who holds the money staked in a wager until the winner is determined.

stake net, a kind of net for catching fish, consisting of netting vertically hung on stakes driven into the ground.

stake·out (stāk′out′), *n.* surveillance of an area where criminal activity is expected: *Detectives . . . got her picture identified, discovered her modus operandi, and put a stakeout on her neighborhood* (Time).

stake presidency, the office of president of a stake of the Mormon Church. The president, with two counselors, presides over the spiritual affairs of the church in the stake locality.

stak·er[1] (stā′kər), *n.* a person or thing that drives in or uses a stake.

stak·er[2] (stā′kər), *n.* a person who stakes money.

stake race or **stakes race,** a horse race in which part or all of the stake is put up by the owners of the horses running in the race.

stakes (stāks), *n.pl.* See under **stake**[2], *n.*

Sta·kha·nov·ism (stə Hä′nə viz əm), *n.* (in the Soviet Union) a system to increase industrial production by voluntary cooperation among workers divided into units or teams, in which each man does a part of the job at which he is most skilled and is paid for the work on a piecework basis. [< Aleksey G. *Stakhanov,* a coal miner whose record output in two shifts in 1935 was taken as a model for the system + *-ism*]

Sta·kha·nov·ite (stə Hä′nə vīt), *n.* (in the Soviet Union) a worker who regularly exceeds his quota of scheduled output and is rewarded for it. —*adj.* of, having to do with, or characteristic of Stakhanovites or Stakhanovism: *One young biochemist . . . regularly works Stakhanovite hours in his Midwestern laboratory* (Harper's).

sta·lac·tic (stə lak′tik), *adj.* having to do with or like stalactites or a stalactite; stalactitic.

sta·lac·ti·cal (stə lak′tə kəl), *adj.* stalactitic; stalactic.

sta·lac·ti·form (stə lak′tə fôrm), *adj.* having the form of a stalactite.

sta·lac·tite (stə lak′tīt, stal′ək-), *n.* **1.** an icicle-shaped formation of calcium carbonate hanging from the roof or sides of a cave and deposited by dripping water: *Perfect stalactites, as thin as straws and untouched by man, have been found in a cave on North Island, New Zealand* (Science News Letter). **2.** any formation shaped like this. [< New Latin *stalactites* < Greek *stalaktós* dripping < *stalássein* to trickle]

Stalactites (def. 1) **and stalagmites**

stal·ac·tit·ic (stal′ək tit′ik), *adj.* **1.** of the nature of or like a stalactite or stalactites. **2.** characteristic or suggestive of stalactites: *the stalactitic structure of some minerals.* **3.** having stalactites: *a stalactitic cave.* —**stal′ac·tit′i·cal·ly,** *adv.*

stal·ac·tit·i·cal (stal′ək tit′ə kəl), *adj.* stalactitic.

sta·lag (stä′läg; *German* shtä′läk′), *n.* a German camp for noncommissioned prisoners of war: *Mr. Philpot . . . spent two years in various . . . stalags in Germany before he broke free* (New Yorker). [< German *Stalag* < *Sta(mm)lag(er)* base camp]

sta·lag·mite (stə lag′mīt, stal′əg-), *n.* **1.** an incrustation or deposit of calcium carbonate, more or less like an inverted stalactite, built up on the floor of a cave by water dripping from the roof of a cave: *A fluffy stalagmite shaped like a knife blade shot skyward* (Newsweek). See **stalactite** for picture. **2.** any formation shaped like this. [< New Latin *stalagmites* < Greek *stalagmós* a dropping, or *stálagma, -atos* a drop, drip < *stalássein* to trickle]

stal·ag·mit·ic (stal′əg mit′ik), *adj.* **1.** of the nature of or like a stalagmite or stalagmites. **2.** characteristic of a stalagmite or stalagmites. —**stal′ag·mit′i·cal·ly,** *adv.*

stal·ag·mit·i·cal (stal′əg mit′ə kəl), *adj.* stalagmitic.

stale[1] (stāl), *adj.*, **stal·er, stal·est,** *v.*, **staled, stal·ing.** —*adj.* **1.** that has lost some or all of its softness, flavor, etc., through age; not fresh: *stale bread.* **2.** (of a carbonated beverage, beer, etc.) flat. **3.** no longer new or interesting; worn-out; hackneyed: *a stale joke. How weary, stale, flat and unprofitable Seems to me all the uses of this world* (Shakespeare). **4.** out of condition through overtraining or too long continued exertion, as an athlete, race horse, etc.: *The team has gone stale from too much practice.* **5.** temporarily lacking in vigor, nimbleness, etc., especially through unremitting application to one kind of thing, as the mind. **6.** *Law.* (of a claim or demand in a court of equity) having been allowed to lie dormant for so long that it has lost validity.
—*v.t.* **1.** to make stale: *These are things which cannot be staled by repetition* (George Gissing). **2.** *Obsolete.* to lower in value, estimation, etc.; cheapen. —*v.i.* to become stale: *To see her was a delight that never staled* (Somerset Maugham).
[Middle English *stale.* Compare STALEMATE, STALL[1].] —**stale′ly,** *adv.* —**stale′ness,** *n.*
—**Syn.** *adj.* **3.** trite, banal.

stale[2] (stāl), *v.*, **staled, stal·ing,** *n.* —*v.i.* (of horses and cattle) to urinate. —*n.* the urine of horses and cattle. [origin uncertain. Compare Old French *estaler*, Dutch and Middle High German *stallen.*]

stale·mate (stāl′māt′), *n.*, *v.*, **-mat·ed, -mat·ing.** —*n.* **1.** *Chess.* a position in which the player whose turn it is to move finds no legal move available to him, his king not being in check. This is now a drawn game. **2.** any position in which no action can be taken; complete standstill; deadlock: *The prolonged stalemate outside Richmond [in 1864] made a sinister impression upon the North* (Sir Winston Churchill). *The military and diplomatic stalemate in Europe had freed Soviet hands for evil work elsewhere* (Newsweek).
—*v.t.* **1.** to put in a position in which no action can be taken; bring to a complete standstill: *House and Senate Republicans have stalemated each other* (Time). **2.** *Chess.* to subject to a stalemate.
[Middle English *stale* stalemate (perhaps < Anglo-French *estale* a standstill < a Germanic word; compare STALE[1]) + *mate*[2]]

Sta·lin·ism (stä′lə niz əm), *n.* the theory or system of Communism as practiced or interpreted by Joseph Stalin: *There was widespread hope of relief from the excesses of Stalinism* (Atlantic). [< Joseph *Stalin*, 1879-1953, a Russian political leader, and premier of Russia 1941-1953 + *-ism*]

Sta·lin·ist (stä′lə nist), *n.* a follower of Stalin or Stalinism: *China's leaders are devoted Marxists. More than that, they are Leninists and Stalinists too* (Edward Crankshaw). —*adj.* of, having to do with, or characteristic of Stalinism: *Soviet police moved in and put the screws on Poland, instituting an era of Stalinist terror* (New Yorker).

stalk[1] (stôk), *n.* **1.** the stem or main axis of a plant, which rises directly from the root, and which usually supports the leaves, flowers, and fruit: *It is a long green reed, like the stalk of the maize* (Fanny Kemble). **2.** any slender, supporting, or connecting part of a plant, especially: **a.** the petiole of a leaf. **b.** the peduncle or pedicel of a flower, fruit, or inflorescence. **c.** the funiculus of an ovary. **3.** a similar slender connecting or supporting process of an animal, as an eyestalk of a crustacean. **4.** a slender, upright support, as the stem of a wine glass. **5.** *Obsolete.* a quill. [Middle English *stalke;* origin uncertain; perhaps diminutive form of Old English *stela* stalk] —**stalk′like′,** *adj.*

stalk[2] (stôk), *v.t.* **1.** to approach (wild animals) without being seen or heard by them: *The hunter stalked the lion.* **2.** to pursue (an animal or person) without being seen or heard: *He stalked his quarry without avail.* —*v.i.* **1.** to spread silently and steadily: *Disease stalked through the land.* **2.** to walk with slow, stiff, or haughty strides: *Offended, she stalked out of the room.* **3.** to hunt or come up to game, etc., stealthily: *He stalked with camera instead of gun.* **4.** *Obsolete.* to walk softly, cautiously, or stealthily.
—*n.* **1.** a stiff or haughty gait. **2.** a stealthy approach to game.
[Old English *-stealcian*, as in *bestealcian* steal along] —**stalk′er,** *n.*

stalked (stôkt), *adj.* having a stalk or stem: *a stalked barnacle or crinoid.*

-stalked, *combining form.* having a —— stalk or stalks: *Tall-stalked = having tall stalks.*

stalk-eyed (stôk′īd′), *adj.* having the eyes set upon stalks, as certain crustaceans.

stalk·ing-horse (stô′king hôrs′), *n.* **1.** a horse, or figure of a horse or some other animal, behind which a hunter conceals himself in stalking game. **2.** anything used to hide plans or acts; something put forward to conceal one's real intentions, desires, etc.; pretext. **3.** *U.S.* a candidate used as a blind to conceal the identity of a more important candidate or to divide the opposition.

stalk·less (stôk′lis), *adj.* having no stalk.

stalk·let (stôk′lit), *n.* a diminutive stalk, especially a secondary stalk; pedicel.

stalk·y (stô′kē), *adj.*, **stalk·i·er, stalk·i·est.** **1.** consisting of stalks. **2.** abounding in stalks. **3.** of the nature of a stalk or stalks; long and slender like a stalk.

stall[1] (stôl), *n.* **1.** a division for one animal in a stable. **2.** a stable or shed for horses or cattle. **3.** *Especially British.* a booth, either in the open air or in a building, in which goods are exposed for sale or in which some business is conducted: *At the public market different things were sold in different stalls under one big roof.* **4.** a fixed seat for the use of the clergy, partly or entirely enclosed at the back and sides, in the choir of a church. **5.** a pew in a church. **6.** *British.* a seat in the front part of a theater; orchestra seat. **7.** one of the sheathes for the fingers in a glove. **8.** any of various other sheaths or receptacles. **9.** a parking space for a vehicle. **10.** the condition resulting from stalling; failure to remain in operation.

Stalls[1] (def. 1)

stalls, *British.* **a.** the orchestra section of an auditorium: *From our places in the stalls we could see our four friends . . . in the loge* (Thackeray). **b.** those who occupy it: *Why should the stalls stand to oblige the pit?* (Sunday Express).
—*v.t.* **1.** to put, keep, or confine (an animal) to a stall. **2.** to stop or bring to a standstill, usually against one's wish: *to stall an engine.* **3.** to cause to become stuck in mud, snow, etc. —*v.i.* **1.** to live in a stall, stable, kennel, etc. **2.** to come to a stop or standstill, especially against one's wish, as an engine: *The car always stalls on this hill.* **3.** to become stuck in mud, snow, etc. **4.** (of an airplane) to lose speed so that controlled flight cannot be maintained.
[Old English *steall*, probably related to *stæl* a place] —**stall′-like′,** *adj.*

stall[2] (stôl), *Informal.* —*n.* any pretext to prevent or delay action, the accomplishment of a purpose, etc. —*v.i.* **1.** to act or speak evasively, deceptively, or hesitantly so as to prevent action, etc.: *Every time I ask her to set the date she stalls.* **2.** *Sports.* to play worse or more slowly than one is capable of, especially to use up the remaining time. —*v.t.* **stall off,** to put off or prevent by evasive tactics, a plausible tale, or the like; evade; deceive: *[He] did his best . . . to . . . stall off the awful truth with discreet shrugs and simpers* (George A. Sala).
[perhaps < Anglo-French *estale* decoy < a Germanic word]

stall·age (stô′lij), *n.* **1.** the right of erecting stalls, as at a fair. **2.** rent paid for a stall.

stall·board (stôl′bôrd′, -bōrd′), *n.* one of a series of floors upon which soil or ore is pitched successively in excavating.

stall end, the end of a stall or seat, as in the choir of a church, often richly carved.

stall-feed (stôl′fēd′), *v.t.*, **-fed, -feed·ing.** to feed (an animal) in a stall, especially to fatten for eating, selling, etc.

stall gate, the gate in front of the row of stalls in which horses stand at the start of a race: *The fourteen three-year-olds put on a thriller from the moment the stall gates flew open* (New Yorker).

stall·hold·er (stôl′hōl′dər), *n. Especially British.* a person who owns, rents, or runs a stall in a market: *I bought . . . an old Italian colored print from one of the artistic little stallholders who set up shop there every day* (Maclean's).

stall-in (stôl′in′), *n.* the deliberate stalling of automobiles on a highway as a form of protest or demonstration: *A proposed stall-in . . . discouraged traffic from the vicinity of the World's Fair when it opened in the spring of 1964* (New York Times).

stal·lion (stal′yən), *n.* an uncastrated male horse, especially one kept for breeding purposes. [Middle English *stalyone*, alteration of *staloun* < Old French *estalon* < Germanic (compare Old High German *stal* stable, stall) (because it was kept in a stall)]

stall·man (stôl′mən), *n.*, *pl.* **-men.** a man who keeps a stall, as for the sale of meat, books, or other commodities.

stalls (stôlz), *n.pl.* See under **stall**[1], *n.*

stall shower, a small enclosure for taking a shower bath.

stal·wart (stôl′wərt, stol′-), *adj.* **1.** strongly and stoutly built; sturdy; robust: *She was proud of her stalwart, good-looking son* (Booth Tarkington). **2.** strong and brave; valiant: *a stalwart knight* (Tennyson). **3.** firm; steadfast; resolute; determined.
—*n.* **1.** a stalwart person. **2.** a loyal supporter of a political party.
[(originally) Scottish variant of Middle English *stalworth*, Old English *stælwierthe* serviceable < *stæl* place, position + *wierthe* worthy. Related to STALL[1].] —**stal′wart·ly,** *adv.* —**stal′wart·ness,** *n.*
—**Syn.** *adj.* **1.** stout, muscular, powerful. **2.** bold.

stal·worth (stôl′wərth, stol′-), *adj. Archaic.* stalwart.

sta·men (stā′mən), *n.*, *pl.* **sta·mens** or **stam·i·na.** the fertilizing organ of a flower, situated within the inner circle of floral envelopes (the corolla or petals), and consisting of a slender, threadlike stem (filament) which supports a double-celled sac (anther) containing the fertilizing dust (pollen): *When the flower is fully open numerous stamens are revealed, forming a circle just inside the ring of petals . . .* (Fred W. Emerson). [< New Latin *stamen* < Latin *stāmen, -inis* warp, thread]

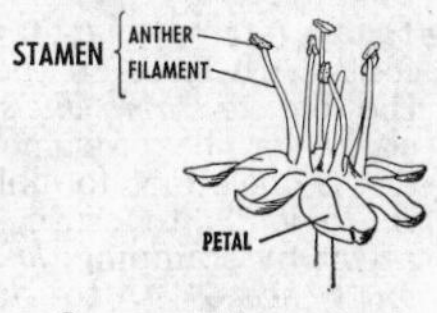

Stamens of an onion flower

sta·mened (stā′mənd), *adj.* having stamens.

stam·i·na[1] (stam′ə nə), *n.* power to resist, sustain, or recover from that which weakens, as fatigue, illness, etc.; strength; endurance: *moral stamina, a man of great physical stamina. Reading aloud requires stamina in the reader as well as in those read to* (London Times). [< Latin *stāmina* threads (of life, spun by the Fates), plural of *stāmen;* see STAMEN]

stam·i·na[2] (stam′ə nə), *n.* stamens; a plural of **stamen.**

stam·i·nal (stam′ə nəl), *adj.* **1.** *Botany.* **a.** having to do with stamens. **b.** consisting of stamens. **2.** *Obsolete.* of or having to do with that which is original, fundamental, or essential in a thing.

stam·i·nate (stam′ə nit, -nāt), *adj.* **1.** having stamens but no pistils. **2.** having a stamen or stamens; producing stamens. [< New Latin *staminatus* < Latin *stāminātus* < *stāmen, -inis* stamen]

sta·min·e·al (stə min′ē əl), *adj. Botany.* staminal.

stam·i·nif·er·ous (stam′ə nif′ər əs), *adj. Botany.* bearing or having stamens. [< Latin *stamēn, -inis* (see STAMEN) + English *-ferous*]

stam·i·nig·er·ous (stam′ə nij′ər əs), *adj.* staminiferous.

stam·i·node (stam′ə nōd), *n. Botany.* staminodium.

stam·i·no·di·um (stam′ə nō′dē əm), *n., pl.* **-di·a** (-dē ə). *Botany.* **1.** a sterile or abortive stamen. **2.** an organ resembling an abortive stamen. [< New Latin *staminodium* < *stamen* (see STAMEN) + *-odium,* a suffix meaning "resembling"]

stam·i·no·dy (stam′ə nō′dē), *n. Botany.* the metamorphosis of various organs of a flower, as a sepal, petal, pistil, or bract, into a stamen. [< Latin *stāmen, -inis* + English *-ody,* as in *phyllody*]

stam·mel (stam′əl), *n.* a coarse woolen fabric or linsey-woolsey, usually dyed red, formerly used for garments. [perhaps < obsolete French *estamel*]

stammel color, the shade of red in which stammel was commonly dyed.

stam·mer (stam′ər), *v.i.* to repeat the same sound in an effort to speak; hesitate in speaking. *Example:* I s-s-see a d-d-dog. *Stammering was relieved when the stammerer was prevented from monitoring his own speech* (Science News Letter).
—*v.t.* to utter or say with stammering: *to stammer an excuse.* —*n.* a stammering; stuttering: *John has a nervous stammer.* [Old English *stamerian*] —**stam′mer·er,** *n.* —**stam′mer·ing·ly,** *adv.*
—**Syn.** *v.i.* **1. Stammer, stutter** mean to speak in a stumbling or jerky way, pausing and repeating sounds. **Stammer** suggests painfully effortful speaking with breaks or silences in or between words, especially through fear, embarrassment, or emotional disturbance. **Stutter** suggests a habit of repeating rapidly or jerkily the same sound, especially initial consonants (*s, p,* etc.).

stamm·tisch (shtäm′tish′), *n.* a reserved table, as in a restaurant, for regular customers or at which a group regularly meets: *He often spoke with pleasure of the frequent seminars round the stammtisch in the famous Thuringer Hof in Leipzig* (London Times). [< German *Stammtisch* < *Stamm* family, clan + *Tisch* table]

stam·nos (stam′nos), *n., pl.* **-noi** (-noi). an ancient Greek vessel or jar for water or wine, resembling a hydria but with a shorter neck. [< Greek *stámnos* < *histánai* cause to stand]

stamp (stamp), *v.t.* **1.** to bring down (one's foot) with force on the ground, a floor, or the like: *to stamp one's foot in anger.* **2.** to strike or beat (something) by bringing down one's foot forcibly: *to stamp the floor in fury.* **3.** to crush, drive, or otherwise affect by stamping: *to stamp the snow from one's boots.* **4.** to mark (paper, fabric, leather, wax, metal, etc.) with an instrument that cuts, shapes, or impresses a design, characters, words, etc. **5.** to impress, mark, or cut out (a design, characters, words, etc.) on something, as to indicate genuineness, quality, inspection, ownership, or the like. **6.** to impress with an official stamp or mark: *to stamp a deed.* **7.** to put postage on. **8.** to fix deeply or permanently; imprint; impress: *an event stamped on one's memory. His words were stamped on my mind.* **9.** to show to be of a certain quality or character; indicate; characterize: *His speech stamps him as an educated man.* **10.** *Dialect.* to crush, pound, or bray. —*v.i.* **1.** to bring down the foot forcibly, as in crushing or beating down something, for emphasis, to express anger, etc.: *to stamp on a spider.* **2.** to walk with a heavy, pounding tread: *The soldier stamped up and down in front of the gate.*
stamp out, a. to put out or extinguish by trampling or stamping: *to stamp out a fire or a cigarette.* **b.** to put an end to or suppress by force or vigorous measures: *to stamp out a rebellion.*
—*n.* **1.** an act of stamping, as with the foot: *"She shall go," said Jos, with another stamp of his foot* (Thackeray). **2.** an instrument, as an engraved block or die, or the like, that cuts, shapes, or impresses a design, characters, words, etc., on paper, wax, metal, etc. **3.** a heavy metal pestle for crushing ores; one of the pestles of a stamp mill. **4.** a mill or machine that crushes rock, etc. **5.** the mark, impression, or imprint made with an engraved block or die, etc. **6.** an official mark certifying quality, genuineness, validity, etc.: *The South wants the stamp of national approval upon slavery* (John Drinkwater). **7.** an official mark required by the government to be stamped on certain things or papers, especially documents which require legal execution or notarization, on which the government charges a fee, duty, or tax, as a sign that the charge has been paid. **8.** an adhesive label of paper issued by the government for a fixed amount of money, which when affixed to a paper or item on which the government charges a fee, duty, or tax indicates that the charge has been paid: *a postage stamp.* **9.** a similar paper issued by a business, organization, or the like to indicate that a charge has been paid or for some other purpose, as a trading stamp. **10.** a distinguishing or distinctive mark; impression; imprint: *Her face bore the stamp of suffering. Man, with all his noble qualities . . . still bears in his bodily frame the indelible stamp of his lowly origin* (Charles Darwin). **11.** character; kind; make; cast; type: *Men of his stamp are rare.*
[Middle English *stampen* stamp with the foot, pound in a mortar, partly unrecorded Old English *stampian,* partly < Old French *estamper* < Germanic (compare Old Frisian *stâmpa* club, cudgel)]

Stamp Act, a revenue act of the British Parliament in 1765, requiring the use of stamped paper and stamps for official and legal documents, commercial papers, etc., in the American colonies, which was so bitterly opposed that it was repealed in March, 1766.

stamp·age (stam′pij), *n.* **1.** the act of stamping. **2.** an impression made by stamping. **3.** the amount charged or paid for stamps; postage.

stamp album, a blank book or album used by collectors for the classification and display of postage stamps.

stamp book, a book in which to collect stamps, such as trading stamps: *The 60-year-old . . concern has . . . 450 stores where housewives can trade their stamp books for premiums* (Wall Street Journal).

stamp collector, a philatelist.

stamp duty, *Especially British.* stamp tax.

stamped (stampt), *adj.* **1.** crushed by stamping. **2.** beaten down with the feet. **3.** impressed with a design, characters, etc. **4.** ornamented with an embossed device or design; cut out or shaped by stamping. **5.** impressed with an official mark or device showing that a duty or charge has been paid. **6.** bearing an adhesive paper stamp, as a revenue stamp or a postage stamp. **7.** impressed on something by means of a stamp, as a device.

stam·pede (stam pēd′), *n., v.,* **-ped·ed, -ped·ing.** —*n.* **1.** a sudden scattering, confused rush, or headlong flight of a frightened herd of cattle, horses, etc. **2.** a headlong flight of any large group: *the panic-stricken stampede of the audience from a burning theater.* **3.** a general rush: *a stampede to newly discovered gold fields. Steel demand is assuming the proportions of a mild stampede* (Wall Street Journal). **4.** *U.S.* a sudden, apparently unconcerted rush of the delegates at a political convention to support a particular candidate. **5.** a rodeo; rodeolike entertainment: *How did you like the Calgary Stampede?* (Maclean's).
—*v.i.* **1.** to scatter or flee in a stampede. **2.** to make a general rush. —*v.t.* to cause to stampede: *Those most trying times when . . . the cattle are stampeded by a thunderstorm at night* (Theodore Roosevelt). *We should not allow ourselves to be stampeded by undue fears into exaggerated positions* (Atlantic).
[American English < Mexican Spanish *estampida* (in Spanish, an uproar) < Spanish *estampar* to stamp, press, ultimately < a Germanic word. Compare STAMP.]
—**stam·ped′er,** *n.*

stamp·er (stam′pər), *n.* **1.** a person who uses a stamp or operates a stamping machine: *a metal stamper, a die stamper.* **2.** a person who applies the postmark and cancels the postage stamps in a post office. **3.** an instrument or machine used in stamping. **4.** a pestle.
stampers, the pestle or each of several pestles in a crushing apparatus, especially in a stamping mill: *It is beat by iron-headed stampers upon an iron bed* (John Smeaton).

stamp·ing (stam′ping), *n.* a part or thing made with a stamper or stamping machine: *Hupp makes stampings and assemblies for the automotive, air conditioning, electrical appliance and other industries* (Wall Street Journal).

stamping ground, *U.S.* a person's or animal's habitual place of resort: *He is back on his old stamping ground doing the thing he loves best* (Time).

stamping mill, an apparatus used to crush ores by means of a pestle (stamp) or series of pestles operated by machinery.

stamp·less (stamp′lis), *adj.* without a stamp.

stamp machine, a machine from which to obtain postage stamps by dropping in a coin.

stamp mill, stamping mill.

stamps·man (stamps′mən), *n., pl.* **-men.** a person who operates a stamping mill.

stamp tax, *U.S.* any tax or duty paid to the government through the purchase of the official stamps that must be affixed to certain products and documents; stamp duty.

stamp weed, the Indian mallow, formerly used to stamp designs on butter.

stance (stans), *n.* **1.** the manner of standing or the position of the feet of a player when making a swing or a stroke with a bat, club, etc.: *He has changed his stance a bit and I think it has helped* (New York Times). **2.** manner of standing; posture: *an erect stance.* **3.** mental or emotional posture; attitude; point of view: . . . *to adopt the stance of the Tammany politician to whom nothing matters but victory* (Saturday Review). **4.** *Scottish.* **a.** a standing place, station, or position. **b.** a site. [< Old French *estance,* ultimately < Latin *stāre* to stand. Doublet of STANZA.]

stanch[1] (stônch, stänch, stanch), *v.t.* **1.** to stop or check the flow of (blood, etc.). **2.** to stop or check the flow of blood from (a wound). **3.** *Obsolete.* to satisfy (thirst, hunger, etc.). **4.** *Obsolete.* to put an end to (strife, rebellion, etc.); quell. —*v.i.* (of blood, etc.) to cease flowing. Also, **staunch.** [< Old French *estanchier* stop, hinder, perhaps ultimately < Vulgar Latin *tancare* to fix, hold < unrecorded Celtic *tanko* I join] —**stanch′er,** *n.*

stanch[2] (stônch, stänch, stanch), *adj.* **1.** able to resist or repel attack; firm; strong: *stanch walls, a stanch defense.* **2.** not to be turned aside; unwavering; loyal; steadfast: *a stanch friend, a stanch supporter of the law.* **3.** soundly built and calked; watertight: *a stanch boat.* Also, **staunch.** [< Old French *estanche,* feminine of *estanc* < *estanchier;* see STANCH[1]] —**stanch′ly,** *adv.* —**stanch′ness,** *n.* —**Syn. 2.** constant, true, faithful, steady, unswerving.

stan·chion (stan′shən), *n.* **1.** an upright bar, post, or pillar used as a support, as for a window, a roof, or the deck of a ship. **2.** the vertical bars of a stall for cattle.
—*v.t.* **1.** to fasten (cattle) by stanchions. **2.** to strengthen or support with stanchions.
[< Old North French *estanchon* < *estance;* see STANCE]

STANCHIONS

Stanchions (def. 2)

stanch·less (stônch′lis, stänch′-, stanch′-), *adj.* that cannot be stanched.

stand (stand), *v.,* **stood, stand·ing,** *n.* —*v.i.* **1.** to be upright on one's feet: *Don't stand if you are tired, but sit down.* **2.** to be of a specified height when erect: *She stands five feet tall.* **3.** to rise to one's feet: *He stood when she entered the room.* **4.** to remain erect on one's feet in a specified place, occupation, position, condition, etc.: *to stand aside. "Stand back!" called the policeman to the crowd.* **5.** to remain motionless on one's feet; stop moving; halt; stop: *"Stand!" cried the sentry.* **6.** to remain steadfast, firm, or secure; take a way of thinking or acting: *to stand for justice.* **7.** to be or remain in a specified condition: *to stand accused, to stand in danger. The door stood ajar.* **8.** (of things) to be in an upright position with the lower part resting on or fixed in the ground or other support: *a chair standing in a corner. Pillars stand on* *each side of the door.* **9.** to be set, placed, or fixed; rest; lie: *Some food stood on the table.* **10.** to be situated in a specified position; be located: *The house stood in a forest.* **11.** to take or hold the office, position, responsibility, etc., indicated: *to stand godfather.* **12.** to be at a particular degree: *The thermometer stands at 32°.* **13.** to remain erect and entire; resist destruction or decay; last: *The old house has stood for a hundred years.* **14.** to collect and remain: *Tears stood in her eyes.* **15.** to collect and remain motionless; be stagnant, as water: *Flood water stands in low-lying fields.* **16.** to become or remain still or motionless; not to move or be operated: *The pumps were allowed to stand.* **17.** to have a certain rank, position, etc.: *He stands first in his class. There are men and classes of men that stand above the common herd* (Robert Louis Stevenson). **18.** to remain valid; be in force: *The rule against lateness will stand.* **19.** (of plants) to grow erect: *corn standing in the fields.* **20.** (of an account, score, etc.) to show a (specified) position of the parties concerned: *The score stands in his favor.* **21.** *Nautical.* to take or remain in a certain course or direction: *The ship stood due north.* **22.** *Hunting.* (of a dog) to point. **23.** *Obsolete.* (in a negative clause) to hesitate; scruple: *He would not stand at stealing.*

—*v.t.* **1.** to cause to stand; place or leave standing; set upright: *to stand a ladder against a wall.* **2.** to bear the brunt of without flinching or retreating; confront; face; encounter: *to stand enemy fire.* **3.** to be submitted to (a trial, test, ordeal, etc.); undergo: *to stand a rigid examination.* **4.** to endure without hurt or damage, or without succumbing or giving way: *This cloth will not stand washing. Those plants cannot stand cold.* **5.** to act as: *to stand guard, stand sentinel.* **6.** *Informal.* to bear the expense of; pay for: *I'll stand you a dinner.*

stand by, a. to be faithful or loyal to; side with; support; defend: *to stand by a friend.* **b.** to adhere to or abide by (a statement, agreement, etc.); keep; maintain: *to stand by one's promise.* **c.** to be near; be present: *His son and daughter stood by him at the bar* (Macaulay). **d.** to be laid aside with disregard: *And now everything stands by for the discussion of Home Rule* (Sketch). **e.** to be or make ready; be prepared to perform some act (used chiefly in the imperative, as a word of command): *The starboard watch . . . left the ship to us for a couple of hours, yet with orders to stand by for a call* (Richard Henry Dana). **f.** *Radio.* (1) to be prepared to transmit signals, etc., but not actually do so: "*Stand by to send message,*" *the captain ordered.* (2) to remain tuned in to a station until it starts sending messages or for the continuance of a program: *The station asked its listeners to stand by for an announcement.*

stand down, a. to step down and leave the witness stand after giving evidence: *I will not trouble the court by asking him any more questions. Stand down, Sir* (Dickens). **b.** to withdraw from a contest or competition: *The coach forced the new runner to stand down in favor of the more experienced senior classman.*

stand easy, *British Military.* to stand completely at ease: *Soldiers standing easy are permitted to talk.*

stand for, a. to represent; be in the place of; mean: *What do the initials stand for? The olive branch stands for peace.* **b.** to be on the side of; take the part of; uphold: *to stand for liberty.* **c.** to be a candidate for: *to stand for mayor.* **d.** *Informal.* to put up with; tolerate: *He won't stand for nonsense.* **e.** to sail or set the course toward: *They hoisted sail and stood for the nearest island.*

stand in, a. *Informal.* to be on good terms; have a friendly or profitable understanding: *to stand in well with the police.* **b.** to cost: *Dinner stood me in a lot of money.* **c.** to take the place of another: *The understudy stood in for the star in one scene.*

stand off, a. *Informal.* to keep off; keep away; evade: *to stand off an angry crowd, to stand off a questioner.* **b.** to hold oneself aloof, as from an offer or appeal, friendship, etc.: *He stood off from her plea.* **c.** *Nautical.* to sail away from the shore: *We tacked about again and stood off to sea* (John Glanville).

stand on, *Nautical.* to keep one's course; remain on the same tack: *The Admiral continued, with a press of sail, standing on close to the wind* (Robert Beatson).

stand on or **upon, a.** to depend on; be based on: *to stand on the facts. Your future stands on your decision. He does not stand on ceremony.* **b.** to demand; assert; claim: *to stand on one's rights.*

stand out, a. to project or protrude; be prominent: *His ears stood out.* **b.** to be conspicuous: *Certain facts stand out.* **c.** to refuse to yield; oppose; resist: *to stand out against popular opinion.* **d.** to refuse to come in or join others: *The ladies proposed a dance . . . . The captain himself stood out* (National Observer). **e.** to endure to the end: *to stand out the war.*

stand over, to be left or reserved for later treatment, consideration, or settlement: *His accounts are balanced at the close of each season, and no bad debts are allowed to stand over* (Saturday Review).

stand to, a. to support or uphold, as a cause, interest, etc.: *We stood to our fellow student right loyally* (Tait's Magazine). **b.** to apply oneself manfully to (a fight, contest, etc.): *The peasants stood to it like men* (Sir Arthur Conan Doyle). **c.** to be or make ready; stand by: *The platoon stood to for battle.*

stand up, a. to get to one's feet; rise: *He stood up and began to speak.* **b.** to endure; last: *The smaller boy, . . . though still standing up pluckily, was getting decidedly the worst of it* (A.E. Houghton). **c.** *Informal.* to break a date with; fail to meet: *To keep the date, Sheridan has to stand up Shelley, the pretty librarian* (Newsweek).

stand up and be counted, to take a public stand (on a controversial issue) as an individual; state one's own position openly and fearlessly: *One can understand the desire of Americans who oppose their government's Vietnam policy to stand up and be counted* (K.H. Hecht).

stand up for, to take the part of; support; defend: *to stand up for a friend.*

stand up to, to meet or face boldly: *to stand up to an enemy.*

stand up with, *Informal.* to act as best man, bridesmaid, etc., to: *I want to tell you . . . about the wedding. . . . We had no one to stand up with us, as we wished to have a simple service* (Chicago Sunday Tribune).

—*n.* **1.** the act of standing. **2.** a coming to a position of rest; pause; halt. **3.** a halt, as of moving troops, for defense or resistance: *to make a last stand against the enemy, to make a stand against oppression.* **4.** a halt made on a theatrical tour to give a performance or performances: *a one-night stand.* **5.** a town where such a halt is made. **6.** a state of arrested progress (of affairs, natural processes, etc.); standstill: *Business was at a stand.* **7.** a place of standing; position; station: *to take one's stand on the stage. The policeman took his stand at the street corner.* **8.** a moral position with regard to other persons, a question, etc.: *to take a new political stand.* **9.** an elevated platform or other structure for spectators at a race course, football field, etc., or for a band or other group of performers: *to watch a parade from a stand.* **10.** the place where a witness stands or sits to testify in court. **11.** a stall, booth, table, etc., for the display of goods for sale or for business: *a vegetable stand.* **12.** a position, site, or building for a business. **13.** the post or station of a soldier, sentinel, watchman, etc. **14.** a station for a row of vehicles available for hire: *a stand for taxis.* **15.** the row of vehicles occupying such a station. **16.** a frame or piece of furniture on or in which to put or hang articles: *Leave your wet umbrella in the stand in the hall.* **17.** a base, bracket, framework, etc., upon which articles may be set for support, exhibition, etc.: *a stand for a microscope.* **18.** a small, light table. **19.** a standing growth or crop, as of wheat, cotton, etc. **20.** a growth of trees, especially those of a particular species on a given area: *We have a fair stand of oaks that covers the path leading up to the top of our ridge* (Atlantic). **21.** *Archaic.* a complete set: *a stand of armor.*

take the stand, to go on the witness stand and give evidence: *The judge called on the witness to take the stand for the cross-examination.*

[Old English *standan*] —**Syn.** *v.t.* **4.** See **bear.** —*n.* **2.** stay. **7.** post.

stand·ard (stan′dərd), *n.* **1.** anything taken as a basis of comparison; model: *They have no general standard of taste, or scale of opinion* (William Hazlitt). **2.** a rule, test, or requirement; criterion: *. . . applying his English standards to the examination of the American system* (James Bryce). **3.** an authorized weight or measure by which the accuracy of all others is determined. **4.** a commodity that is given a fixed value in order to serve in a monetary system as a measure of value for all other commodities, as a metal (monometallic standard), usually gold (gold standard) or silver (silver standard), or gold and silver, in a fixed relationship (bimetallic standard). **5.** the legally prescribed proportion of metal and alloy to be used in coins. **6.** the prescribed degree of fineness for gold or silver. **7.** a level or degree of excellence, attainment, wealth, or the like, considered as a goal or as adequate: *Your work is not up to standard.* **8.** (in commercial use) the lowest level or grade of excellence. **9.** (in British elementary schools) a grade or class. **10.** a flag or other conspicuous object raised on a pole, used to indicate the rallying point of an army, etc., as the distinctive ensign of a king, nobleman, etc., or as the emblem of a nation or city: *The swastika was the standard of Nazi Germany.* **11.** a military or naval flag of a particular kind, usually longer and more tapering than a banner and broader than a pennon. **12.** (in the United States and Great Britain) the flag of a cavalry unit. **13.** an upright support: *The floor lamp has a long standard.* **14.** *Horticulture.* a tree, shrub, or other plant growing on an erect stem of full height, not dwarfed or trained on a wall, trellis, espalier, etc.: *There are bush roses, standards and climbing roses on arches and towers* (New York Times). **15.** *Botany.* a vexillum. **16.** a unit of measure for lumber, equal to $16\frac{2}{3}$ cubic feet or 1,980 board feet. **17.** *U.S.* a grade of beef that is cut from cattle not over four years old, tender, and having a mild flavor and little fat.

—*adj.* **1.** serving as or conforming to the prescribed weight, measure, or fineness. **2.** of the prescribed or normal size, amount, power, quality, etc.: *the standard rate of pay, a standard gauge.* **3.** serving as or fitted to serve as a standard of comparison or judgment: *standard pitch, a standard text.* **4.** of recognized excellence; having permanent rank as an authority: *a standard reference book. Dickens and Mark Twain are standard authors.* **5.** (of pronunciation, grammatical usage, etc.) characteristic of the speech of cultivated persons and of the language used in writing and in the conduct of public affairs, schools, courts, and churches; socially acceptable: *standard spelling.* **6.** *Printing.* (of type) of the usual height, width, or weight. **7.** of the lowest grade or quality: *Canners use brand names that correspond to their best, or fancy, products; their medium, or extra-standard, grades; and their lowest, or standard, products* (World Book Encyclopedia). *Abbr.:* std.

[< Old French *estandart* < a Germanic word]

—**Syn.** *n.* **1. Standard, criterion** mean something used to measure or judge a person or thing. **Standard** applies to a rule, principle, ideal, pattern, or measure generally accepted as a basis of comparison in determining the quality, value, quantity, social or moral or intellectual level, etc., of something: *Our school has high standards of teaching.* **Criterion** applies to a test used in judging the true nature, goodness, or worth of a person, thing, or accomplishment: *Popularity by itself is not a reliable criterion of a good motion picture.*

standard atmosphere, a hypothetical atmosphere having an arbitrarily selected set of atmospheric conditions, used as a standard for purposes of comparing the performance of aircraft, resolving problems in ballistics, designing pressure altimeters, etc.

stand·ard·bear·er (stan′dərd bãr′ər), *n.* **1.** an officer or soldier who carries a flag or standard; colorbearer. **2.** a person who carries a banner in a procession. **3.** a conspicuous leader of a movement, political party, etc.

stand·ard·bred (stan′dərd bred′), *adj.* **1.** bred to the standard of excellence prescribed by some authority. **2.** (of a horse) bred and trained primarily for harness racing, as a trotter or pacer. —*n.* a standardbred horse.

standard candle, candle, a former unit for measuring the intensity of a light.

standard cell, a voltaic cell that is used as a standard of measurement for voltage.

standard deviation, *Statistics.* (in a frequency distribution) the square root of the mean of the deviations from the arithmetic mean; root-mean-square deviation. A distance of one standard deviation on each side of the mean of a normal curve includes 68.27 per cent of the cases in the frequency distribution. *Symbol* σ

standard dollar, the value of a U.S. dollar in gold, being $15\frac{5}{21}$ grains, .900 fine, at present, and 25.8 grains, .900 fine, before 1934.

Standard English, current English, both formal and informal, as it is spoken and written by educated people: *I do not suppose that there are now any linguists who hold that . . . Standard English must fit some logical . . . scheme apart from the test of usage* (Paul Roberts).

standard error, *Statistics.* the standard deviation of the sample in a frequency distribution.

standard gauge, the distance between railroad rails or between the right and left wheels of an automobile, wagon, etc. The standard gauge between rails is 56½ inches.

stand·ard·ise (stan′dər dīz), *v.t., v.i.,* **-ised, -is·ing.** *Especially British.* standardize.

stand·ard·i·za·tion (stan′dər də zā′shən), *n.* **1.** a standardizing. **2.** a being standardized.

stand·ard·ize (stan′dər dīz), *v.,* **-ized, -iz·ing.** —*v.t.* **1.** to make standard in size, shape, weight, quality, strength, etc.: *The parts of an automobile are standardized.* **2.** to regulate by a standard. **3.** to test by a standard. —*v.i.* to establish a standard or standards; adopt something as the standard: *The no-pay interval can be 13, 14, or 15 hours depending on the region of the country. "Where do you standardize?" asks an industry official* (Wall Street Journal).
—**stand′ard·iz′er,** *n.*

standard of living, the way of living that a person or community considers necessary to provide enough material things for comfort, happiness, etc.: *Even those Americans who can't afford to buy all the gadgets that have become synonymous with the American standard of living still are better off than people anywhere else in the world* (Newsweek).

standard star, a star whose position and proper motion are particularly well known, used in determining the positions of other stars, instrumental constants, time, latitude, etc.

standard time, the time officially adopted as the standard for a region or country. Each meridian 15 degrees east or west of Greenwich, England, marks a time difference of one hour. Noon is usually reckoned in a given region as the time the sun apparently passes the meridian closest to that region.

stand·a·way (stand′ə wā′), *adj.* made to stand up straight, curled, or in folds away from the rest of the garment or from the body: *A favorite coat has a broad standaway collar, dropped shoulders, and three-quarter sleeves* (New Yorker).

stand-by (stand′bī′), *n., pl.* **-bys,** *adj.* —*n.* **1.** a person or thing that can be relied upon; chief support; ready resource: *Verdi's music for this old stand-by never fails* (Wall Street Journal). **2.** a ship, boat, or other vessel kept in readiness for emergencies. **3.** an order or signal for a vessel to stand by. **4.** a substitute; stand-in: *He . . . was Phil Silvers's stand-by in "Do Re Mi"* (New York Times).
on stand-by, waiting in readiness or reserve: *During the emergency, nurses and doctors were on stand-by twenty-four hours a day.*
—*adj.* in a position of readiness or reserve.

Stand-by Reserve, *U.S.* the part of the reserve forces that can be called into active service only in case of war or national emergency, as specified by Congress.

stand·ee (stan dē′), *n. U.S. Informal.* a person who has to stand in a theater, on a bus, etc., because he cannot obtain a seat: *The seated audience freely showed its enthusiasm, and the standees were ecstatic* (Wall Street Journal). [American English < *stand* + *-ee*]

stand·er (stan′dər), *n.* a person or thing that stands.

stand·er-by (stan′dər bī′), *n.* a person who stands near or looks on but does not take part; bystander.

stand·fast (stand′fast′, -fäst′), *adj.* that holds stubbornly to an opinion, attitude, etc.; stubborn. —*n.* a fixed or stable position.

stand-in (stand′in′), *n.* **1.** a person whose work is standing in the place of a motion-picture actor or actress while the lights, camera, etc., are being arranged. **2.** anything that takes the place of another for some reason: *Certainly, the New Dealing Advisory Council of the National Democratic Committee has been an inadequate stand-in for a national party leader* (Wall Street Journal). **3.** *Informal.* a favorable position; good standing. **4.** *U.S.* the presence of Negroes in a line of persons waiting to enter a theater, etc., as a protest against racial segregation in a public place.

stand·ing (stan′ding), *n.* **1.** rank or position in society, a profession or business, religion, or the like; social, professional, or commercial reputation; status: *men of good standing. What people say behind your back is your standing in the community* (E.W. Howe). **2.** good or high rank or reputation. **3.** length of service, experience, residence, or the like, especially as determining position, wages, etc. **4.** length of existence; duration: *a feud of long standing between two families.* **5.** the act of one who stands, in any sense. **6.** the time at, in, or during which one stands. **7.** a place in which to stand; post; station.
—*adj.* **1.** straight up; erect; upright: *standing timber.* **2.** done from or in an erect position: *a standing jump.* **3.** that stands up, upright, or on end: *a standing lamp or collar.* **4.** permanent; established: *a standing invitation.* **5.** remaining at rest or in a fixed position: **a.** (of water) not flowing; stagnant. **b.** (of a factory, machine, tool, etc.) not in operation; at a standstill. **c.** remaining stationary, especially while another part moves.
—**Syn.** *adj.* **1.** perpendicular. **4.** lasting, enduring.

standing army, 1. an army, or that part of it, that is under arms and ready for immediate action, especially in time of peace, and now usually including reservists and conscripts as well as members of the regular army. **2.** the regular army, as a permanently organized military force.

standing committee, a permanent committee, as of a legislative body or club, selected or elected to deal with all matters in a particular sphere.

standing ground, 1. ground to stand on. **2.** a basis for operations or argument.

standing order, *Military.* a regulation for operation or procedure mandatory for an entire command, or for specified members of it, and not subject to change by subordinate or temporary commanders.
standing orders, the regular rules for procedure in parliamentary bodies, in force from session to session unless specifically rescinded or repealed: *Both houses have agreed, at various times, to standing orders, for the permanent guidance and order of their proceedings* (Thomas Erskine May).

standing part, a part of a rope, etc., that is made fast to something.

standing rigging, the ropes, stays, etc., supporting the masts and fixed spars.

standing room, 1. space to stand in after all the seats are taken; accommodation for a standee or standees: *standing room at the back of a theater.* **2.** space to stand in, especially space having sufficient headroom for a person to stand erect in.

standing wave, *Physics.* a kind of wave characterized by lack of vibration at certain points (nodes), between which are regions (loops or antinodes) where maximum vibration occurs periodically; stationary wave. Standing waves are produced by the interference of two similar waves traveling at the same time in opposite directions, as in the vibration of a violin string.

stand·ish (stan′dish), *n.* a stand containing ink, pens, and other writing materials and accessories; inkstand: *He wanted pen, ink, and paper. There was an old standish on the high mantel containing a dusty apology for all three* (Dickens). [taken by folk etymology to be < *stand,* verb + *dish,* noun]

stand-off (stand′ôf′, -of′), *n.* **1.** a contest in which the score is tied; tie; draw. **2.** something which counterbalances; that which serves to offset the strength, effect, meaning, etc., of something else: *It is far easier to maintain a stand-off between two superpowers than between three or four* (Bulletin of Atomic Scientists). **3.** a standing off or apart; reserve; aloofness.
—*adj.* stand-offish: *Young Oliver . . . soon lost his stand-off air* (John Galsworthy).
[American English < *stand* + *off*]

stand-off bomb, a guided missile fired from an airplane at a ground target several hundred miles away.

stand-off halfback or **half,** (in Rugby football) the halfback who takes a position between the scrum-half and the three-quarter back: *Risman had a splendid game at stand-off half* (Sunday Times).

stand-off·ish (stand′ôf′ish, -of′-), *adj.* reserved; aloof. —**Syn.** distant, unapproachable.

stand-off·ish·ness (stand′ôf′ish nis, -of′-), *n.* a being stand-offish; aloofness: *We have thus opened the first breach in our stand-offishness* (Atlantic).

stand oil, linseed oil, tung oil, etc., made heavy and thick by heating under pressure, used as a medium in paint, varnish, etc.

stand-out (stand′out′), *n. U.S.* **1.** a person or thing that is outstanding of its kind, especially in excellence: *Kudos . . . to the hostess who is ever on the lookout for goodies to make the cookout a stand-out* (New Yorker). **2.** *Informal.* a person who refuses to act with the others of a group, accept the desires of the majority, etc. —*adj. Informal.* outstanding: *He has written a lot of stand-out stories in his time* (Newsweek).

stand·pat (stand′pat′), *adj. Informal.* standing firm for things as they are; opposing any change: *When a Welsh villager or farmer wants to vote in a standpat manner, he thinks of voting Liberal* (New York Times). [American English < *stand* + *pat*]

stand·pat·ter (stand′pat′ər), *n. Informal.* a person who stands firm for things as they are and opposes any change, especially in politics. —**Syn.** do-nothing.

stand·pat·tism (stand′pat′iz əm), *n. Informal.* the principles or conduct of standpatters; condition of being a standpatter: *The prevailing attitude is one of uneasy standpattism* (Harper's).

stand·pipe (stand′pīp′), *n.* a large vertical pipe or tower to hold water under pressure, especially one used as a reservoir or auxiliary to a reservoir.

stand·point (stand′point′), *n.* the point at which one stands to view something; point of view; mental attitude: *To judge of the total scientific achievement of any age, the standpoint of a succeeding age is desirable* (William Tyndall). *From a material standpoint, the achievements of the United States . . . have been staggering* (Newsweek).

St. An·drew's cross (an′drüz), Saint Andrew's cross.

stand·still (stand′stil′), *n.* **1.** a complete stop; halt; pause: *All activity about the place had come to a standstill at noontime.* **2.** a state of being unable to proceed, owing to exhaustion: *[Robert E.] Lee could not extricate himself and his supply trains without fighting Meade's army to a standstill* (Sir Winston Churchill).
—*adj.* **1.** that is at a standstill: *The old standstill Mexico of mañana and the travel posters is scrambling toward prosperity* (Time). **2.** of the nature of a standstill. **3.** causing a standstill: *The standstill strike forced industry to negotiate a work contract.*
—**Syn.** *n.* **1.** cessation, deadlock.

stand-up (stand′up′), *adj.* **1.** that stands erect; upright: *a stand-up collar.* **2.** performed or taken while standing: *a stand-up dinner.* **3.** designed and built for standing upright: *a stand-up lunch counter. The new plane is designed for full comfort, with a roomy stand-up cabin.* **4.** between opponents who stand up fairly to each other without flinching or evasion: *They wouldn't let us make a stand-up fight of it* (George Bernard Shaw). *A gray fox, casting vulpine caution to the winds, fought a stand-up battle with a dog its own size* (New York Times).

stane (stān), *n., adj., v.t.,* **staned, stan·ing.** *Scottish.* stone.

Stan·ford-Bi·net test (stan′fərd bə nā′), an adaptation of the Binet intelligence test to American problems and situations. [< *Stanford* University, in California, where the revisions were made]

stang[1] (stang), *v. Archaic.* a past tense of **sting.**

stang[2] (stang), *n. British and Scottish Dialect.* a pole, bar, or rail.

ride the stang, to be carried about in public mounted astride on a pole, in an old popular mode of punishment, as for wife beating, the culprit being sometimes represented by an effigy or a proxy: *In some Scottish and northern English villages, one who is found working on New Year's Day has to ride the stang or pay a forfeit.*
[< Scandinavian (compare Old Icelandic *stöng*). Compare Old English *steng* pole.]
stang[3] (stang), *v.t., v.i., n. Especially Scottish.* sting. [< Scandinavian (compare Old Icelandic *stanga* to jab, goad)]
stan·hope (stan′hōp, -əp), *n.* a light, open carriage having one seat and two or four wheels. [< Fitzroy *Stanhope,* 1787-1864, a British clergyman, for whom it was first made]
stan·iel (stan′yəl), *n.* the kestrel. Also, **stannel.** [Old English *stāngella* < *stān* stone + *gellan* yell]
Stan·i·slav·sky method (stan′i släf′skē), a system of acting developed and taught by Stanislavsky (Constantin Sergeyevich Alexeyev, 1863-1938), that stressed the importance of realism in acting and feeling and living the part one is playing.
stank[1] (stangk), *v.* a past tense of **stink:** *The dead fish stank.*
stank[2] (stangk), *n. British Dialect and Scottish.* **1.** a pond or pool. **2.** a ditch of slowly moving water; moat. **3.** a dam or weir. [< Old French *estanc,* ultimately < Latin *stāgnum* standing water]
Stan·ley Cup (stan′lē), the trophy awarded annually to the champion of the National Hockey League in the United States and Canada.
Stanley Steamer, an early make and type of automobile that ran on steam power.

Stanley Steamer
(1906)

stan·na·ry (stan′ər ē), *n., pl.* **-ries. 1.** a region or district where tin is mined. **2.** *British.* a tin mine. [< Medieval Latin *stannaria* < Late Latin *stannum* tin; see STANNUM]
stan·nate (stan′āt), *n.* a salt of stannic acid. [< *stann*(ic) + *-ate*[2]]
stan·nel (stan′əl), *n.* staniel.
stan·nic (stan′ik), *adj.* **1.** of or having to do with tin. **2.** containing tin, especially with a valence of four. [< Late Latin *stannum* tin + English *-ic*]
stannic acid, any of several white or colorless acids of tin, used in making stannates.
stannic chloride, a colorless, caustic liquid made from tin and chlorine, used as a dye and color brightener, for coating objects, as a bleaching agent, etc. *Formula:* $SnCl_4$
stannic oxide, a white powder found in nature as cassiterite and produced synthetically, used to glaze and color ceramics and glass, to polish glass and metal, in making cosmetics, etc. *Formula:* SnO_2
stannic sulfide, mosaic gold.
stan·nif·er·ous (sta nif′ər əs), *adj.* yielding tin. [< Late Latin *stannum* tin + English *-ferous*]
stan·nite (stan′īt), *n.* a mineral, a sulfide of tin, copper, iron, and (sometimes) zinc; tin pyrites. It is a brittle, steel-gray or iron-black mineral with a metallic luster. *Formula:* Cu_2FeSnS_4 [< Late Latin *stannum* tin + English *-ite*[1]]
stan·no·type (stan′ə tīp), *n.* **1.** a tintype. **2.** a photomechanical process of printing in ink from a gelatin plate coated with tinfoil. **3.** the plate itself. **4.** a print made from it. [< Late Latin *stannum* tin + English *-type*]
stan·nous (stan′əs), *adj.* **1.** of or having to do with tin. **2.** containing tin, especially with a valence of two.
stannous chloride, a crystalline compound made by dissolving tin with hydrochloric acid, used to galvanize tin, remove ink stains, silver mirrors, as a reducing agent for various chemicals, etc. *Formula:* $SnCl_2$
stannous fluoride, a fluoride of tin, added to toothpaste or applied topically to prevent tooth decay. *Formula:* SnF_2
stan·num (stan′əm), *n.* tin. *Symbol:* Sn (no period). [< New Latin *stannum* < Late Latin, tin; earlier, an alloy of silver and lead, variant of Latin *stagnum*]
St. An·tho·ny's fire (an′thə nēz, -tə-), **1.** erysipelas. **2.** ergotism.
stan·za (stan′zə), *n.* **1.** a group of lines of verse, commonly four or more, arranged according to a fixed plan. This plan may regulate the number of lines, the meter, the pattern of rhymes, etc. *Abbr.:* st. **2.** a verse of a poem: *They sang the first and last stanzas of "America."* **3.** *Sports.* any period of time in, or division of, a game, as an inning in baseball or a quarter in football. [< Italian *stanza* (originally) a stopping place, ultimately < Latin *stāre* to stand. Doublet of STANCE.]
-stanzaed, *combining form.* having — stanzas: *Two-stanzaed = having two stanzas.*
stan·za·ic (stan zā′ik), *adj.* **1.** of or having to do with a stanza. **2.** forming a stanza. **3.** composed of stanzas. **—stan·za′i·cal·ly,** *adv.*
stan·zic (stan′zik), *adj.* stanzaic.
sta·pe·di·al (stə pē′dē əl), *adj.* of or having to do with the stapes.
sta·pe·li·a (stə pē′lē ə), *n.* any of a group of African plants of the milkweed family, with fleshy, leafless stems and oddly mottled flowers with a fetid odor. [< New Latin *Stapelia* the genus name < Jan Bode van *Stapel,* died 1636, a Dutch botanist]

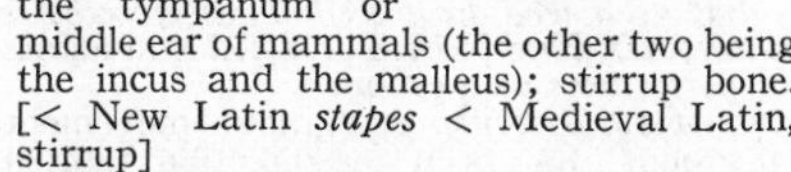
Stapelia
(diameter, to 12 in.)

sta·pes (stā′pēz), *n.* the innermost of the three small bones of the tympanum or middle ear of mammals (the other two being the incus and the malleus); stirrup bone. [< New Latin *stapes* < Medieval Latin, stirrup]
staph (staf), *n. Informal.* staphylococcus or staphylococci: *Staph are among the most common germs ever to bother man* (Wall Street Journal).
sta·phyl·i·on (stə fil′ē on), *n.* the median point of the posterior edge of the hard palate. [< Greek *staphýlion* (diminutive) < *staphylē* uvula]
staph·y·lo·coc·cal (staf′ə lə kok′əl), *adj.* **1.** having to do with staphylococcus. **2.** produced by staphylococcus: *Staphylococcal infections originating in hospitals and spreading to the community are becoming increasingly severe and frequent* (Science News Letter).
staph·y·lo·coc·cic (staf′ə lə kok′sik), *adj.* staphylococcal.
staph·y·lo·coc·cus (staf′ə lə kok′əs), *n., pl.* **-coc·ci** (-kok′sī). *Bacteriology.* any of a group of spherical or eggshaped bacteria that bunch together in irregular masses, as the micrococcus which causes the formation of pus: *The penicillin-resistant staphylococci protect themselves by producing an enzyme, penicillinase, which destroys penicillin* (New Scientist).
[< New Latin *Staphylococcus* the genus name < Greek *staphylē* bunch of grapes + New Latin *coccus* coccus (because of the shape they assume)]
staph·y·lo·ma (staf′ə lō′mə), *n., pl.* **-ma·ta** (-mə tə). a protrusion of the cornea or sclera of the eye. [< New Latin *staphyloma* < Greek *staphýlōma* an eye disease < *staphylē* bunch of grapes (because of the shape of the protrusion)]
staph·y·lo·plas·ty (staf′ə lə plas′tē), *n., pl.* **-ties.** plastic surgery on the soft palate or uvula. [< Greek *staphylē* bunch of grapes; uvula + *plastós* something molded]
staph·y·lor·rha·phy or **staph·y·lor·a·phy** (staf′ə lôr′ə fē, -lor′-), *n.* plastic surgery to unite a cleft palate. [< Greek *staphylē* a bunch of grapes; uvula + *rhaphē* a suture < *rháptein* to stitch]
staph·y·lot·o·my (staf′ə lot′ə mē), *n.* amputation of the uvula. [< Greek *staphylē* uvula + *-tomíā* a cutting]
sta·ple[1] (stā′pəl), *n., v.,* **-pled, -pling.** —*n.* **1.** a U-shaped piece of metal pointed at the ends, driven into a surface to hold hooks, pins, bolts, etc. **2.** a piece of wire of similar shape, used to hold together papers, parts of a book, etc. —*v.t.* to fasten or secure with a staple or staples. [Old English *stapol* post]
sta·ple[2] (stā′pəl), *n., adj., v.,* **-pled, -pling.** —*n.* **1.** the most important or principal article regularly grown or manufactured in a country, region, city, etc.: *Cotton is the staple in many southern states.* **2.** a principal article of commerce or trade; something of recognized quality and in constant demand. **3.** the principal element, ingredient, or constituent of anything; chief item: *Politics is often a staple of conversation.* **4.** the material of which anything is made; raw material. **5.** a fiber of cotton, wool, etc., considered with regard to its length and fineness. **6.** a particular length and degree of fineness in the fiber of cotton, wool, etc. **7.** a staple fiber. **8.** (formerly) a town or place in which a body of merchants was granted by royal authority the exclusive right to buy certain goods for export: *He had borrowed a great sum of money of the merchants of the staple* (Holinshed's "Chronicles"). **9.** *Archaic.* the principal market of a place; chief center of trade.
—*adj.* **1.** principal among the articles regularly grown, manufactured, or consumed in a country, region, etc.; foremost among the exports of a country or place: *Corn is a staple commodity of Iowa.* **2.** established and important in commerce; leading: *a staple trade or industry.* **3.** most important; chief; principal: *The weather was their staple topic of conversation.*
—*v.t.* to sort according to fiber: *to staple wool.*
[< Anglo-French, Old French *estaple* mart < Germanic (compare Dutch *stapel* pile, heap)]
-stapled, *combining form.* having a—— staple: *Long-stapled wool = wool that has a long staple.*
staple fiber, the short fiber lengths of rayon, acetate, or the like that are spun into yarn: *Staple fibers are those used to spin yarns, as distinguished from filament, or continuous, yarns already suitable for weaving into cloth* (Wall Street Journal).
sta·pler[1] (stā′plər), *n.* a machine for fastening together several sheets of paper, parts of a book, etc., with wire staples: *Many magazines are now bound by staplers.*
sta·pler[2] (stā′plər), *n.* a person who sorts and grades fibers of wool, cotton, etc.
stapp (stap), *n.* a unit of measure used in aviation medicine, equal to the force exerted by one G acting on the body for one second. [< John P. *Stapp,* born 1911, a U.S. Air Force medical officer, who did research on rocket sled acceleration and deceleration]
star (stär), *n., v.,* **starred, star·ring,** *adj.* —*n.* **1.** any of the heavenly bodies appearing as bright points in the sky at night. **2.** *Astronomy.* any heavenly body that shines by its own light, except the moon, comets, meteors, and nebulae. The majority of stars, including the sun, fall into one pattern (the main sequence) when plotted on a graph according to luminosity and type of spectrum. **3.** any heavenly body. **4.** *Astrology.* a planet or constellation of the zodiac, considered as influencing people and events. **5.** one's fortune, rank, destiny, or temperament, viewed as determined by the stars; fate: *The fault, dear Brutus, is not in our stars, But in ourselves, that we are underlings* (Shakespeare). **6.** a conventional figure of usually five or six rays or points, taken to represent a star of the sky, as ☆ or ✡. **7.** something having or suggesting this shape. **8.** an asterisk (*). **9.** (in the United States) a representation of a star symbolizing one of the states in the Union. **10.** *U.S.* any of the military medals, awards, etc., having a star-shaped design. **11.** a person of brilliant qualities or talents in some art, science, etc.: *an athletic star.* **12.** *Theater, etc.* an actor, singer, etc., who is exceptionally well known or prominently advertised, or who has the leading part in a particular production; lead: *an opera star, the star of the new musical. All stars have one characteristic in common . . . some magnetic quality which sets them apart on the screen from all other actors* (New York Times). **13.** *Physics.* a star-shaped pattern of lines radiating outward from the nucleus of an atom that is exploded by high-energy particles, as seen in a photograph of this effect produced in a cloud chamber.
see stars, to see flashes of light as a result of a hard blow on one's head: *Quicker than thought, in comes his right, and if you only see stars you are pretty lucky* (John D. Astley).
thank one's (lucky) stars, to be thankful for one's good luck: *You may thank your stars, my lad, that I followed Master Barns tonight* (Joseph Hatton).
with stars in one's eyes, full of idealism, optimism, etc.; starry-eyed: *The depressing thing to one whose entire ancestry, immediate and remote, is British, and who came to*

England with stars in his eyes, is the bleakness of the future (Atlantic).
—*v.t.* **1.** to set, adorn, or ornament with stars; bespangle. **2.** to mark with an asterisk. **3.** to single out for special notice or recommendation. **4.** *Theater, etc.* to give a leading part to (an actor or actress, etc.); present to the public as a star. —*v.i.* **1.** to shine above others; be brilliant or outstanding; excel. **2.** *Theater, etc.* (of an actor, singer, etc.) to be a leading performer; perform the leading part: *She has starred in many motion pictures.*
—*adj.* brilliant or outstanding; excellent; best; leading: *the star player on a football team.*
[Old English *steorra*]

star apple, 1. the apple-shaped, edible fruit of a tropical American evergreen tree of the sapodilla family, whose carpels present a star-shaped figure when cut across. **2.** the tree itself.

star·board (stär′bərd, -bôrd, -bōrd), *n.* the right side of a boat or ship when facing forward.
—*adj.* on, at, or of the right side of a boat or ship.
—*adv.* to or toward the right side of a boat or ship.
—*v.t., v.i.* to turn or move to or in the direction of the right side of a boat or ship.
[Old English *stēorbord* the side from which a vessel was steered. Compare STEER[1], BOARD.]

starch (stärch), *n.* **1.** a white, odorless, tasteless, powdery or granular substance, chemically a complex carbohydrate, found in all parts of a plant which store plant food, as seeds and grains, tubers and rhizomes (the potato and arrowroot), and, in many plants, the stem and pith (the sago). It is an important ingredient of food, reacting with certain enzymes to form dextrose, maltose, etc., and is widely used commercially. *Formula:* $(C_6H_{10}O_5)_n$ **2.** a preparation of this used to stiffen clothes, curtains, etc., to give a finish to certain textiles, to size paper, etc. **3.** a stiff, formal manner; stiffness. **4.** *Informal.* vigor; energy; zest.
starches, foods containing much starch: *to lose weight by avoiding starches.*
take the starch out of, *Informal.* to cause to lose courage, confidence or determination: *This apparently took the starch out of the fast-crumpling opposition* (New York Times).
—*v.t.* to stiffen (clothes, curtains, etc.) with starch; apply starch to.
starch up, *Obsolete.* to make formal or rigid: *She starched up her behaviour with a double portion of reserve* (Tobias Smollett).
[Old English unrecorded *stercan* (in *sterced-ferhth* stouthearted) < *stearc* stiff, strong. Compare STARK.]

Star Chamber, *English History.* a court that existed by statute in England from 1487 until 1641, with full authority for asserting both criminal and civil jurisdiction, and enabled to proceed and act without regard for the common law. Persons were tried by it in secret session, without a jury, and were frequently condemned on the basis of confessions obtained by torture. [Middle English *sterred chambre,* translation of Medieval Latin (England) *camera stellata* a room in Westminster Palace where the king's council first met (probably so called from a decoration of stars on its ceiling). Compare CAMERA, STELLATE.]

star chamber, any court, committee, or group like the Star Chamber in its procedures.

star-cham·ber (stär′chām′bər), *adj.* **1.** of or having to do with a star chamber. **2.** characteristic of a star chamber, especially in holding secret sessions: *His constitutional rights were violated by "star-chamber" proceedings in which he was not allowed to confront or cross-examine his accusers* (New York Times).

star chart, a chart which shows the stars in a certain portion of the sky.

starched (stärcht), *adj.* **1.** stiffened with starch: *a starched collar.* **2.** stiff; rigidly formal: *throwing aside all the starched reserve of her ordinary manner* (Hawthorne).

starch·er (stär′chər), *n.* **1.** a person who starches. **2.** a machine for starching.

starch·i·ly (stär′chə lē), *adv.* in a starchy manner.

starch·i·ness (stär′chē nis), *n.* the quality of being starchy, or of abounding in starch.

starch·ness (stärch′nis), *n.* stiffness of manner; preciseness.

starch syrup, glucose.

starch·y (stär′chē), *adj.,* **starch·i·er, starch·i·est. 1.** of the nature of starch. **2.** composed of starch. **3.** containing starch. **4.** stiffened with starch. **5.** stiff in manner; formal: *Sir William Haley, the starchy editor of The Times, has donned his black cap and passed his savage sentence* (Newsweek).
—**Syn. 5.** prim.

star cluster, a group of stars that are relatively close together, classified as either galactic or globular clusters.

star-con·nect·ed (stär′kə nek′tid), *adj.* having a star connection.

star connection, an arrangement in a polyphase system, as in a transformer, by which the coils or circuits have a common junction while the free ends are connected with the terminals of the line wires.

star coral, any of various stony corals with radiating septa that give the cuplike depression of the skeleton a star-like appearance.

star·craft (stär′kraft′, -kräft′), *n.* knowledge of the stars; astrology.

star-crossed (stär′krôst′, -krost′), *adj.* born under an evil star; ill-fated: *So the star-crossed lovers and the perplexed older people moved step by step into tragedy* (New York Times).

star·dom (stär′dəm), *n.* **1.** a being a star actor or performer: *Woe betide the successful young actor who accepts stardom before he is ready for it* (New York Times). **2.** star actors or performers as a group.

star drift, *Astronomy.* a gradual movement of groups of stars in one direction; motion common to a group of stars.

star dust, 1. masses of stars that look so small as to suggest particles of dust. **2.** particles from meteors falling from space to earth. **3.** *Informal.* glamour; happy enchantment.

stare (stãr), *v.,* **stared, star·ing,** *n.* —*v.i.* **1.** to look long and directly with the eyes wide open; gaze fixedly. A person stares in wonder, surprise, stupidity, curiosity, or from mere rudeness: *The little girl stared at the toys in the window.* **2.** to be very striking or glaring: *His eyes stared with anger.* **3.** to stand on end (now chiefly of hair, feathers, fibers, etc.). —*v.t.* to bring to a (specified) condition by staring: *to stare a person into silence.*
stare down, to confuse or embarrass by staring; abash: *The Colombian government and foreign groups complete formalities for the resumption of aid after almost a year of trying to stare each other down* (New York Times).
stare (a person) **up and down,** to gaze at or survey (a person) from head to foot: *They are staring me up and down like a wild animal* (Henry Seton Merriman).
—*n.* a long and direct look with the eyes wide open: *The doll's eyes were set in an unwinking stare. A stony British stare* (Tennyson). [Old English *starian*]
—**Syn.** *v.i.* **1.** gape. See **gaze.**

sta·re de·ci·sis (stãr′ē di sī′sis), *Latin.* **1.** to abide by things decided. **2.** the legal principle that precedents are, or define law.

star·er (stãr′ər), *n.* a person who stares.

sta·rets (stä′rets), *n.* a saintly religious teacher or holy man in Russia: *Unbounded faith in the powers of his starets may well have helped to halt the Tsarevitsch's haemophilia* (Sunday Times). [< Russian *starets*]

star facet, one of the eight small triangular facets sloping down from the flat top of a gem cut as a brilliant.

star field, the stars in a portion of the sky seen through a telescope: *The axis of the telescope will describe a complicated trajectory through the star field* (New Scientist).

star·fish (stär′fish′), *n., pl.* **-fish·es** or (*collectively*) **-fish.** any of a class of echinoderms, characterized by a flattened body consisting of five arms or rays radiating from a central disk; asteroid. The rays are sometimes very short or altogether absent, the body having the form of a pentagonal disk. Starfishes feed on organic matter; some are carnivorous and do great damage to oyster beds.

Common Starfish (diameter, about 5 in.)

star·flow·er (stär′flou′ər), *n.* any of various star-shaped flowers or the plants bearing them, especially: **a.** the star-of-Bethlehem. **b.** any of a group of low, white-flowered plants of the primrose family.

star·gaze (stär′gāz′), *v.i.,* **-gazed, -gaz·ing. 1.** to gaze at the stars; study the heavens. **2.** to be absent-minded; daydream.

star·gaz·er (stär′gā′zər), *n.* **1.** a person who studies the heavens, as an astronomer or astrologer. **2.** a person given to daydreaming. **3.** any of a family of spiny-finned marine fishes having both eyes on the top of the head.

star·gaz·ing (stär′gā′zing), *n.* **1.** attentive observation and study of the stars; astronomy or astrology. **2.** daydreaming.
—*adj.* **1.** given to the observation and study of the stars. **2.** given to daydreaming; absent-minded.

star grass, any of several grasslike plants with star-shaped flowers or a starlike arrangement of leaves, especially: **a.** any of a group of herbs of the amaryllis family. **b.** the colicroot.

star·ing (stär′ing), *adj.* **1.** very conspicuous; too bright; that cannot be overlooked; glaring: *a staring blunder. . . . printed in great black letters on a staring broad sheet* (Dickens). **2.** gazing with a stare; wide-open.
—**star′ing·ly,** *adv.*

star jelly, any of the gelatinous blue-green algae which appear suddenly upon the surface of the ground after a rain or heavy dew, popularly believed to have fallen from the stars.

stark (stärk), *adj.* **1.** downright; complete; sheer; absolute: *That fool is talking stark nonsense. The boys went swimming stark naked. She moved with the stark simplicity of a Martha Graham dancer* (Newsweek). **2.** stiff, especially from rigor mortis; rigid: *The dog lay stark in death.* **3.** (of a landscape, region, etc.) bare; barren; desolate. **4.** *Dialect.* (of climate or weather) harsh; inclement. **5.** *Archaic.* (of persons) stern; severe: *He is . . . stark as death To those that cross him* (Tennyson). **6.** *Archaic.* strong; sturdy.
—*adv.* **1.** to the fullest extent or degree; entirely; completely; absolutely; utterly: *stark mad.* **2.** in a stark manner.
[Old English *stearc* stiff, strong] —**stark′ly,** *adv.*
—**Syn.** *adj.* **1.** utter. -*adv.* **1.** wholly.

star·less (stär′lis), *adj.* without stars or starlight; having no stars visible: *a cloudy, starless night.*

star·let (stär′lit), *n.* **1.** a young actress or singer who is being trained and publicized for leading roles in motion pictures: *. . . some remote Hollywood starlet's marriage was on the rocks* (J.D. Salinger). **2.** a tiny star.

star·light (stär′līt′), *n.* light from the stars: *By starlight and by candlelight . . . She comes to me* (Herbert Trench). —*adj.* **1.** starlit. **2.** done by starlight.

star·light·ed or **star-light·ed** (stär′lī′tid), *adj.* starlit.

star·like (stär′līk′), *adj.* **1.** shaped like a star: *a pattern of starlike snowflakes.* **2.** shining like a star. —**Syn. 1.** stellate. **2.** sparkling.

star lily, the sand lily.

star·ling[1] (stär′ling), *n.* **1.** any of a group of common Old World perching birds, especially a variety which has been naturalized in America. It is a glossy greenish- or brownish-black, speckled with buff in the winter, often nests about buildings, and is easily tamed. **2.** any of certain North American blackbirds, as the redwing. [Old English *stærling* < *stær* starling]

Common European Starling (def. 1) (about 8 in. long)

star·ling[2] (stär′ling), *n.* a projecting outwork of piles to protect a pier of a bridge.

star·lit (stär′lit′), *adj.* lighted by the stars: *a starlit night. There, by the starlit fences, The wanderer halts* (A. E. Housman).

star·lite (stär′līt′), *n.* a variety of zircon which, on special treatment with heat, becomes a brilliant blue gem.

star map, a projection of part or all of the heavens, showing the fixed stars as they appear from the earth.

star·nose (stär′nōz′), *n.* star-nosed mole.

star-nosed mole (stär′nōzd′), a mole of eastern North America that has a star-shaped circle of small, fleshy processes at the end of its nose.

star-of-Beth·le·hem (stär′əv beth′lē əm, -lə hem), *n.* an Old World plant of the lily family, naturalized in eastern North America, bearing a tall cluster of green-and-white, star-shaped flowers. [because of the shape of its flowers]

Star of Bethlehem, (in Christian use) the star described in Matthew 2:2,9-10, that heralded Christ's birth and was followed by the Three Wise Men to the manger where the Christ child lay.

Star of David, a Jewish emblem, consisting of a six-pointed star formed of two triangles, one interlaced with or placed upon the other; magen-David. See **Solomon's seal** for picture.

star quartz, asteriated quartz.

starred (stärd), *adj.* **1.** (of the heavens, the sky, etc.) full of stars; starry. **2.** marked with a star or stars. **3.** decorated with stars: *Gartered peers and starred ambassadors ...* (Benjamin Disraeli). **4.** marked or distinguished with an asterisk. **5.** presented as a star actor or performer. **6.** influenced by the stars or by fate.

star·ri·ly (stär′ə lē), *adv.* in a starry manner.

star·ri·ness (stär′ē nis), *n.* the state of being starry.

star route, (in the U.S. postal service) a route, other than the ordinary routes, over which mail is carried by special contract with private individuals, rather than by the usual carriers (so called from asterisks used to mark such routes in official papers).

star ruby, a ruby exhibiting asterism, like the more common star sapphire or asteria.

star·ry (stär′ē), *adj.*, **-ri·er, -ri·est. 1.** full of stars: *a starry sky.* **2.** lighted by stars; starlit: *a starry night.* **3.** shining like a star or like stars; very bright: *starry eyes.* **4.** like a star in shape. **5.** of or relating to the stars. **6.** consisting of stars. —**Syn. 4.** stellate. **5.** astral.

star·ry-eyed (stär′ē īd′), *adj.* tending to view too favorably or idealistically; unrealistic; dreamy: *He's no starry-eyed optimist* (Margery Allingham).

Stars and Bars, the first flag of the Confederate States, having two horizontal red stripes with a white stripe between and a blue square containing a circle of seven white stars, one for each of the first seven seceding states.

Stars and Stripes, the flag of the United States, which when first adopted by Congress on June 14, 1777, contained 13 stripes and 13 stars, representing the 13 original states of the Union, and which now contains 13 stripes and 50 stars.

star sapphire, a sapphire which exhibits by reflected light a star of bright rays, resulting from its crystalline structure.

star saxifrage, a small saxifrage found northward in both hemispheres having white starry flowers.

star-shaped (stär′shāpt′), *adj.* shaped like a star; having rays proceeding from, or angular points disposed in a regular outline about, a central point.

star shell, a flare which bursts into bright starlike clusters or a single light, suspended by a parachute, used in war to illuminate enemy positions or, in various colors, as a signal, firework, etc.

star·shine (stär′shīn′), *n.* starlight: *The garden trees looked densely black in the starshine* (John Galsworthy).

star shower, a meteor shower.

star-span·gled (stär′spang′gəld), *adj.* spangled with stars.

Star-Spangled Banner, 1. the national anthem of the United States, the words of which were composed by Francis Scott Key in 1814, during the War of 1812, as he watched the British bombardment of Fort McHenry near Baltimore. **2.** the flag of the United States; Stars and Stripes.

star-stud·ded (stär′stud′id), *adj.* **1.** star-spangled: *a star-studded canopy.* **2.** having or featuring many motion-picture stars or other famous celebrities: *It's a good, spectacular, star-studded thriller* (Punch).

start[1] (stärt), *v.i.* **1.** to begin a journey; get in motion; set out: *The train started on time.* **2.** to begin a course of action, process, etc.: *to start in business, to start from the beginning.* **3.** to begin to go (to school). **4.** to begin or commence, as a process, performance, etc.: *The play started at nine.* **5.** to give a sudden, involuntary jerk or twitch, as from surprise, fright, sudden pain, etc.; move suddenly: *He started in surprise. To start at shadows* (Scott). **6.** to move suddenly or unexpectedly from a position of rest; leap, dart, or rush with sudden quickness; spring; bound: *to start backward, to start from one's seat, to start to one's feet.* **7.** to issue, rise, fly, flow, or appear suddenly: *Tears started from her eyes.* **8.** (of the eyes) to seem to burst out (from their sockets), as in horror or fury. **9.** to be displaced, as by pressure or shrinkage; get loose.
—*v.t.* **1.** to begin; commence: *to start a book, start work, start a song, start an argument.* **2.** to cause to begin moving, going, acting, operating, etc.; set in motion: *to start an automobile, to start a fire.* **3.** to set on foot, initiate, or establish; originate: *to start a business, to start a rumor, to start a club.* **4.** to cause or enable (a person) to begin some course of action or career: *He started his son in business.* **5.** to induce (a person) to begin to talk on some subject. **6.** to introduce (a subject, topic, etc.); broach. **7.** to rouse suddenly into action, motion, or flight, as an animal from its lair: *to start a rabbit.* **8.** to displace, as by pressure; loosen, or cause to loosen or lose hold: *to start a plank, to start an anchor. The huge waves had started the ship's bolts.* **9.** to begin the flow of (a liquid) from a container; empty (a vessel); tap. **10.** to enter in a race, especially a horse race. **11.** to cause (a race or contestants in a race) to begin. **12.** *Obsolete.* to startle.
start in or **out,** to begin to do something: *Some roughs jumped the Catholic bone yard and started in to stake out town lots in it* (Mark Twain).
start up, a. to rise suddenly; spring up: *Chaerephon ... started up and ran to me, seizing my hand* (Benjamin Jowett). **b.** to come suddenly into being or notice: *I am surrounded by difficulties, and as fast as I get the better of one, another starts up* (Earl Carlisle). **c.** to cause (an engine) to begin operating: *Before starting up the engine make sure that the gear lever is in the central or neutral position* (Morris Owner's Manual). **d.** to begin to do something: *They started up at six and finished the job by eight.*
—*n.* **1.** the beginning of a movement, act, journey, race, career, etc.; a starting or setting out: *to see a race from start to finish.* **2.** an act of setting in motion; a signal to start a race, etc. **3.** a sudden, involuntary movement of the body, as from surprise, terror, etc.: *to give someone a start, to wake up with a start.* **4.** a sudden burst or display of energy or activity: *to work by fits and starts.* **5.** *Archaic.* an outburst, sally, or flight of wit, humor, passion, grief, etc.: *some starts of his former ... vivacity break out* (Fanny Burney). **6.** an advantage at the beginning of a race or other contest; a handicap in a contestant's favor: *He got the start of his rivals.* **7.** an advantage in the beginning or first stage of anything. **8.** an opportunity or assistance given for entering on a career or course of action: *to get a start in life. His father gave him a start in business.* **9.** the place at which a race begins. **10.** a part that has started; a displaced or loosened part. **11.** a break, opening, or other condition resulting from this.
[< variant of Old English *styrtan* leap up]
—**Syn.** *v.i.* **1.** embark, leave, go. *-v.t.* **1.** See **begin.**

start[2] (stärt), *n.* the tail of an animal (now used only in compounds). [Old English *steort* tail]

start·er (stär′tər), *n.* **1.** a person or thing that starts. **2.** an official who gives the signal to begin a race. **3.** any contestant who sets out in a race. **4.** an official who is responsible for maintaining the schedule and sequence of departures from a station, and who signals buses, subways, trains, etc., to start out. **5.** the first in a series of things: *Air Force officials had indicated that this request was only a starter* (New York Times). **6.** an apparatus for starting a machine, especially an automobile; self-starter. **7.** a chemical agent or bacterial culture used to start a reaction, as in the formation of acid in making cheese, sour cream, vinegar, etc.
as or **for a starter,** *Informal.* as a beginning; to begin with; for a start.

star thistle, 1. a low, spreading, European composite weed having small heads of purple flowers surrounded by radiating spines; caltrop. **2.** a related weed of more erect habit and having yellow flowers.

star·throat (stär′thrōt′), *n.* a hummingbird having the throat spangled with the scales of the gorget.

start·ing gate (stär′ting), a device by which race horses are aligned at the start of a race; barrier.

starting point, a point from which a person or thing starts; place of starting; beginning: *Inspection is the starting point for any realistic system of disarmament* (Time).

star·tle (stär′təl), *v.*, **-tled, -tling,** *n.* —*v.t.* to frighten suddenly; surprise. —*v.i.* to move suddenly in fear or surprise. —*n.* an experience of being startled; a sudden start or shock of surprise or alarm. [probably Old English *steartlian* to kick, stumble]
—**Syn.** *v.t.* scare, alarm, shock, stun.

star·tler (stär′tlər), *n. Informal.* **1.** a startling thing. **2.** a person who does startling things.

star·tling (stär′tling), *adj.* surprising; frightening: *startling tales.* —**star′tling·ly,** *adv.*

start-up (stärt′up′), *n.* the beginning of an operation or production: *The system is completely automatic after the initial start-up* (Edward H. Owen). —*adj.* of or having to do with the process of beginning an operation or production: *start-up costs.*

star turn, the principal person or item in a show; starred performer or feature: *The return of Ann Corio, as M.C., star turn, and director of an old-time burlesque show ..* (New Yorker).

star·va·tion (stär vā′shən), *n.* **1.** a starving. **2.** a suffering from extreme hunger; being starved: *Kept ... on starvation rations through lack of supplies, the men sickened, and many died of yellow fever and dysentery* (Time).

starve (stärv), *v.*, **starved, starv·ing.** —*v.i.* **1.** to die of hunger; perish from lack or insufficiency of food. **2.** to suffer severely from lack of food; famish: *Let not poor Nellie [Nell Gwyn] starve* (Charles II of England). **3.** to be very hungry. **4.** to suffer extreme poverty and need: *She ended up starving in a New York tenement* (Time). **5.** *Dialect.* to die or suffer from exposure to extreme cold. **6.** *Obsolete.* to die. —*v.t.* **1.** to cause to die of hunger; weaken from lack of food: *They starved the enemy into surrendering.* **2.** to weaken or destroy through lack of something needed: *The powers of their minds are starved by disuse* (John Locke). **3.** *Dialect.* to cause to die or suffer from cold.
starve down or **out,** to force or subdue from lack of food: *After a siege of many weeks the garrison of the castle was starved out.*
starve for, to suffer from the lack of (something); have a strong desire or craving for (a thing): *starved for affection.*
[Old English *steorfan* die]

starve·ling (stärv′ling), *adj.* **1.** starving; hungry: *Women nursed their starveling infants ...* (Katherine Anne Porter). **2.** poverty-stricken. —*n.* a person, animal, etc., that is suffering from lack of food.

starv·er (stär′vər), *n.* a person or thing that starves.

star·ward (stär′wərd), *adv., adj.* toward the stars.

star·wort (stär′wėrt′), *n.* **1.** any of various chickweeds with white star-shaped flowers. **2.** any plant of the group including the asters. **3.** water starwort.

stase (stās), *n.* a fossil plant deposit that has remained in its original position. [< Greek *stásis;* see STASIS]

stash (stash), *v.t. Informal.* **1.** *U.S.* to hide or put away for safekeeping or future use: *Better stash some cash in the bank* (Wall Street Journal). **2.** *British or Archaic.* **a.** to bring to an end; stop. **b.** to quit (a place). [origin uncertain] —**Syn. 1.** cache.

sta·sis (stā′sis, stas′is), *n., pl.* **-ses** (-sēz). a stoppage or stagnation of the flow of any of the fluids of the body, as of the blood in the blood vessels or of the feces in the intestines. [< New Latin *stasis* < Greek *stásis* a standing < *sta-*, a root of *histánai* to stand]

-stat, *combining form.* **1.** a mechanical device or instrument that causes something to be or become stable, as in *rheostat,* and *thermostat.* **2.** any regulating, stabilizing, or controlling center, agent, etc., as in *appestat.* [probably < Greek *-státēs*, a noun agent suffix < *sta-*, a root of *histánai* cause to stand, or stop]

stat., **1. a.** statuary. **b.** statue. **2. a.** statute (miles). **b.** statute or statutes.

stat·a·ble (stā′tə bəl), *adj.* that can be stated: *statable relationships.*

sta·tant (stā′tənt), *n. Heraldry.* (of an animal, especially a lion) standing in profile with all four feet on the ground. [< Latin *status, -ūs* (< *stāre* to stand)]

stat·cou·lomb (stat′kü lom′), *n.* an electrostatic unit equivalent to the charge that repels a like charge, separated from it by one centimeter in a vacuum, and having a force of one dyne. [< *stat*(ic) + *coulomb*]

state (stāt), *n., adj., v.,* **stat·ed, stat·ing.** —*n.* **1.** the condition of a person or thing at a certain time; situation: *the state of the weather, a state of war, the state of our present knowledge of the Russian espionage system. He is in a state of poor health. Let us pray for the whole state of Christ's Church* (Book of Common Prayer). **2.** physical condition with regard to composition, form, structure, phase or stage of existence, or the like: *Ice is water in a solid state.* **3.** the mental or emotional condition of a person at a particular time: *a state of uncertainty or excitement.* **4.** spiritual existence; the mode of existence of a spiritual being: *the state of grace, our mortal state.* **5. a.** a person's position in life; rank: *a humble state.* **b.** high rank; greatness; eminence. **c.** *Archaic.* a person of high status; noble. **6.** high style of living; dignity; pomp: *a coach of state. Kings lived in great state.* **7. a.** a nation. **b.** a State, as of the United States. **c.** the territory, etc., of a State. **d.** the civil government.

be in a state, *Informal.* **a.** to be in a bad or disordered condition: *He leaves things lying around, and look what a state his room is in!* **b.** to be in an agitated or excited condition of mind or feeling: *Don't you remember when she went away, what a state you were in and how you raged?* (Violet Jacob).

lie in state, to lie in a coffin to be seen by people before being buried: *Her Majesty is to lie in state at Hanover* (London Gazette). *It was in this chamber he breathed his last; here he lay in state* (Charlotte Brontë).

states or **States,** the bodies from which a national legislature, such as the States-General, was formed (chiefly in historical use): *The Elector Frederick William III in 1701, in an assembly of the States, was accorded the title of King in Prussia* (F. M. Hueffer).

—*adj.* **1. a.** of, having to do with, or belonging to the civil government or highest civil power or authority: *state control.* **b.** of or having to do with a State of the United States. **2.** used on or reserved for very formal and special occasions; ceremonious; formal: *state robes.* **3.** accompanied with or involving ceremony and pomp: *state occasions, a state banquet.*

—*v.t.* **1.** to tell in speech or writing; express; say: *to state one's reasons.* **2.** to set forth formally or in proper form: *to state a question, to state a case. Every argument was stated with logical precision* (Edward Bulwer-Lytton). **3.** to settle; fix; specify: *to state a price.*

[< Latin *status, -ūs* condition, position < *stāre* to stand; common in Latin phrase *stātus rēī publicae* condition of the republic. Doublet of ESTATE, STATUS.]

—**Syn.** *n.* **1, 2. State, condition** mean the form or way in which something exists, especially as affected by circumstances. **State,** the more general word, applies to the circumstances in which a person or thing exists or to his (its) nature or form at a certain time: *The state of the world today should interest every serious person.* **Condition** applies to a particular state due to given causes or circumstances: *The condition of the patient is critical.* **5. a.** standing, status. *-v.t.* **1.** declare.

➔ See **say**[1] for usage note.

State (stāt), *n.* **1. a.** a nation. **b.** one of several organized political groups of people that form a nation or sovereign state: *The State of Texas is one of the United States.* **2.** the territory, government, or authority of a state: *Never any State was ... so open to receive strangers into their body, as were the Romans* (Francis Bacon). **3.** the civil government; highest civil authority: *affairs of State. The State is properly ... the nation in its collective and corporate capacity* (Matthew Arnold).

the States, the United States (used especially abroad): [*The trend*] *apparently started in the States, where women are now said to own more capital than men* (Punch).

—*adj.* of or having to do with a nation or a State, especially a State of the United States: *a State road, State police.*

[< *state*]

state aid, financial or other assistance given by a federal or State government, especially to a local or private enterprise. —**state′-aid′,** *adj.*

state bank, 1. *U.S.* a bank that has a charter from a State government. **2.** a bank owned or controlled by a government, especially an institution through the agency of which currency is issued or controlled.

state·craft (stāt′kraft′, -kräft′), *n.* **1.** statesmanship. **2.** crafty statesmanship.

stat·ed (stā′tid), *adj.* **1.** said; told: *the stated facts of a case.* **2.** fixed; settled: *at a stated time, for a stated fee.* **3.** (of a rule, penalty, etc.) explicitly set forth; formulated. —**stat′ed·ly,** *adv.*

State Department, an executive division of the United States government, presided over by the Secretary of State, charged with the conduct of foreign affairs.

State flower, a flower adopted or confirmed by official action, especially of the legislature, as the emblem of a particular State of the United States.

state·hood (stāt′hu̇d), *n.* the condition or status of being a State, especially a State of the United States.

State·house or **state·house** (stāt′hous′), *n.,* or **state house,** *U.S.* the building in which the legislature of a State meets; the capitol of a State.

state·less (stāt′lis), *adj.* **1.** having citizenship in no country; without national affiliation: *a stateless refugee. The surviving German Jews were among the persons displaced by World War II who have suffered the most ... In many cases they are stateless and with no chance of acquiring citizenship anywhere* (Emory S. Bogardus). **2.** without national sovereignty or boundaries: *a stateless world.* —**state′less·ness,** *n.*

state·let (stāt′lit), *n.* a small state: *The case of the British-protected statelets along the Persian Gulf has to be distinguished from that of other areas* (Economist).

state·li·ly (stāt′lə lē), *adv.* in a stately manner.

state line, any boundary line between States of the United States.

state·li·ness (stāt′lē nis), *n.* the quality or character of being stately.

state·ly (stāt′lē), *adj.,* **-li·er, -li·est,** *adv.* —*adj.* **1.** dignified; deliberate: *to speak and move in a slow, stately manner.* **2.** imposing; grand; majestic: *the stately music of Handel, a region of stately homes. The Capitol at Washington is a stately building.*

—*adv.* with stately or dignified bearing, movement, or expression.

—**Syn.** *adj.* **2.** See **grand.**

state medicine, a system under which medical care and hospital services are provided by the government for all in the State, the costs being borne by some form of taxation.

state·ment (stāt′mənt), *n.* **1.** the act of stating; manner of stating something: *The statement of an idea helps me to remember it.* **2.** something stated; report: *His statement was correct.* **3.** a summary of an account, showing the amount owed, due, or on hand: *a bank statement.*

State of the Union message, an address by the President of the United States to Congress soon after it convenes early in January, in which he reviews the nation's economic, political, and social developments of the past year and outlines his program for the coming year.

State prison, *U.S.* a prison maintained by and operated under the penal code of the State in which it is situated.

sta·ter (stā′tər), *n.* any of various gold, silver, or electrum coins of the ancient Greek states or cities, varying in value. [< Latin *statēr* < Greek *statḗr* (originally) a weight < *sta-*, a stem of *histánai* cause to stand; place in the balance]

state religion, the official religion of a nation, as Anglicanism in England and Roman Catholicism in Italy.

State rights, States' rights.

state·room (stāt′rüm′, -ru̇m′), *n.* **1.** a private room on a ship affording sleeping and (now usually) toilet facilities for a single person or small group of persons; cabin. **2.** a private room on certain American railroad cars of the late 1800's resembling the drawing room or bedroom of today.

states (stāts), *n.pl.* See under **state,** *n.*

States (stāts), *n.pl.* **the.** See under **State,** *n.*

State's attorney, *U.S.* the law officer responsible for preparation and presentation of the case of the State in a court action.

state's evidence, 1. *U.S.* testimony given in court by one of the accused against one or more of his alleged associates in the crime. **2.** evidence brought forward by the government in a criminal case.

turn state's evidence, *U.S.* to testify in court against one's alleged associates in a crime.

States-Gen·er·al (stāts′jen′ər əl, -jen′rəl), *n.* **1.** the legislative body of France up to 1789, consisting of representatives of the three estates, the clergy, the nobility, and the middle class; Estates-General. **2.** the lawmaking body of The Netherlands.

state·side (stāt′sīd′), *U.S. Informal.* —*adj.* of, having to do with, from, to, or in the continental United States: *a stateside assignment, stateside mail. American soldiers abroad are happy to have stateside magazines.* —*adv.* to or in the continental United States: *to fly stateside.*

state·sid·er (stāt′sī′dər), *n. U.S. Informal.* a person born or living in the continental United States; mainlander.

states·man (stāts′mən), *n., pl.* **-men.** a man skilled in the management of public or national affairs: *Lincoln was a famous American statesman. Wise statesmen ... foresee what time is thus bringing, and endeavor to shape institutions and to mold men's thought and purpose in accordance with the change* (Viscount Morley). —**Syn.** See **politician.**

states·man·like (stāts′mən līk′), *adj.* having the qualities of a statesman.

states·man·ly (stāts′mən lē), *adj.* like, worthy of, or befitting a statesman.

states·man·ship (stāts′mən ship) *n.* the qualities of a statesman; skill in the management of public or national affairs: *One can hardly hope to understand the particular quality of Victorian statesmanship ... without stressing the character of the Iron Duke* [*Wellington*] (Algernon Cecil).

state socialism, a form of socialism involving government control, management, or ownership of all or certain enterprises, especially in the industrial, commercial, and financial realms.

state socialist, an adherent of state socialism.

State's prison, State prison.

States' righter, *U.S. Informal.* an advocate or supporter of States' rights.

States' rights, the rights and powers belonging to the separate States of the United States under the Constitution. The doctrine of States' rights holds that all powers not specifically delegated by the Constitution to the national government, nor denied by it to the States, belong to the States. Some States have interpreted this doctrine further so as to exclude activity on the part of the federal government of the United States in any area, such as education or voting laws, that is normally under the control of the individual States.

states·wom·an (stāts′wu̇m′ən), *n., pl.* **-wom·en.** a woman statesman.

State trooper, *U.S.* a member of the police force of a State.

State university, a university maintained by a State of the United States as a unit of or adjunct to its system of public education.

state-wide or **state·wide** (stāt′wīd′), *adj.* covering an entire State; over all of a State: *a state-wide election campaign.* —*adv.* in an entire State; over a whole State: *McLeod supported Mr. Kennedy in 1960, but now he'll go Republican locally, statewide, and nationally* (Wall Street Journal).

stat·ic (stat′ik), *adj.* **1.** of or in a fixed or stable condition, rather than a state of progress or change; at rest; standing still: *a static character in a novel. Civilization does not remain static, but changes constantly.* **2. a.** of or having to do with stationary electrical charges that balance each other. **b.** producing such electricity, as by rubbing a glass rod with a silk cloth. **3.** of, having to do with, or caused by atmospheric electricity that interferes with radio reception. **4.** *Physics.* **a.** having to do with bodies at rest or forces that balance each other. **b.** acting by weight without producing motion: *static pressure.* **5.** *Economics.* having to do with the conditions, problems, etc., occurring in a relatively stable society.

—*n.* **1.** atmospheric electrical phenomena produced by electrical storms, etc., and causing interference with radio reception; atmospherics. **2.** noises and other interference with radio reception caused by such electrical phenomena; strays: *Thin squeaks of radio static* (Hart Crane).
[< Greek *statikós* causing to stand < *sta-*, a stem of *histánai* cause to stand or stop]
—**stat′i·cal·ly,** *adv.*
—**Syn.** *adj.* **1.** passive, immobile.
stat·i·cal (stat′ə kəl), *adj.* static.
stat·i·ce (stat′ə sē), *n.* **1.** any of a group of small herblike plants related to the leadwort, with rosettes of narrow evergreen leaves on the ground and globular heads of pink, purplish, or white flowers; thrift. **2.** any of a group of related herbs or shrubs growing especially in sandy areas of the Old World; sea lavender. [< New Latin *Statice* the genus name < Latin *staticē* an astringent herb < Greek *statikḗ,* feminine of *statikós;* see STATIC]

Statice (def. 1) (common thrift) (8 to 12 in. long)

static line, a line attached at one end to a closed parachute and at the other end to a cord suspended from a cable inside the aircraft. As the parachutist jumps clear the static line pulls taut and serves as a rip cord to open the parachute. It is used chiefly in dropping paratroopers, supplies, etc.
stat·ics (stat′iks), *n.* the branch of mechanics that deals with objects at rest or forces that balance each other.
static testing, the testing of a rocket, missile, etc., on the ground.
static tube, a small tube for measuring the static pressure of the air or other fluids, used especially on aircraft.
sta·tion (stā′shən), *n.* **1. a.** the place or spot that a person is appointed to occupy in the performance of some duty; assigned post: *The policeman took his station at the corner.* **b.** a locality or post assigned for military duty to a person or unit. **c.** a camp or area assigned to a unit or units; military post. **d.** a place or region to which a naval vessel or fleet is assigned for duty. **e.** a place at which naval vessels or aircraft are regularly located: *a naval air station.* **f.** (formerly, in India) the place of residence of the British officials of a district or officers of a garrison. **2. a.** a place to which men are assigned and where equipment is set up for some particular kind of work, research, or the like: *a postal station, a biological station, a weather station.* **b.** the police headquarters of a district. **c.** the place or equipment for sending out or receiving programs, messages, etc., by radio or television. **3.** social position; rank: *A serf was a man in a humble station in life.* **4.** situation or position, as in a class, scale of estimation, or the like: *The masters told his parents he was dull and advised them to take him out: they were only wasting their money trying to educate him beyond his station* (Edmund Wilson). **5. a.** a regular stopping place: *a bus station.* **b.** the building or buildings erected at such a place; depot: *Father met Kate at the railroad station.* **6.** (in Australia, New Zealand, etc.) a cattle or sheep farm: *Stations either for sheep or cattle were spotted about . . . over the whole country* (Samuel Butler). **7.** *Surveying.* **a.** each of the selected points at which observations are taken. **b.** a fixed uniform distance into which a survey line is divided. **8.** *Biology.* the condition or position of an animal or plant in its habitat, or its relation to its environment (often used synonymously with *habitat,* but *habitat* is the place where an animal or plant lives, *station* the condition under which it lives there). **9.** the act or posture of standing on the feet. **10.** the condition or fact of standing still: *Her motion and her station are as one; She shows a body rather than a life* (Shakespeare).
—*v.t.* to assign a post, position, or station to (a person, troops, ships, etc.); place: *The faithful dog stationed himself at the door behind which his master lay sick in bed. They . . . stationed . . . musicians . . . in the "front hall"* (Booth Tarkington).
[< Latin *statiō, -ōnis* < *stāre* to stand]
—**Syn.** *n.* **1. a.** position, location.
station agent, stationmaster.
sta·tion·al (stā′shən əl), *adj.* of or having to do with a station.
sta·tion·ar·i·ly (stā′shə ner′ə lē), *adv.* in a stationary position; without moving.
sta·tion·ar·i·ness (stā′shə ner′ē nis), *n.* the quality or character of being stationary.
sta·tion·ar·y (stā′shə ner′ē), *adj.* **1. a.** having a fixed station or place; not movable: *A factory engine is stationary.* **b.** residing or established in one place; not itinerant or migratory: *I deemed it advisable to . . . change my late wandering life for a stationary one* (William Godwin). **2.** standing still; not moving. **3.** not changing in size, number, activity, etc.: *The population of this town has been stationary for ten years at about 5,000 people.* [< Latin *statiōnārius* (*mīlitēs*) (soldier) belonging to a military station < *statiō;* see STATION] —**Syn. 1. a.** immovable. **2.** motionless. **3.** invariable.
➤ **Stationary** and **stationery** are usually pronounced identically and as a consequence sometimes carelessly confused in writing.
stationary front, *Meteorology.* a surface between two dissimilar air masses neither of which is displacing the other and usually resulting in mild temperatures and cloudy weather.
stationary wave, standing wave.
station bill, a list posted in a ship containing the appointed station of each member of the ship's company in any emergency.
station break, a pause in a radio or television program, or between programs, to identify the broadcasting station by its call letters or number and location. Station breaks usually occur on the hour or half hour.
sta·tion·er (stā′shə nər), *n.* **1.** a person who sells paper, pens, pencils, etc. **2. a.** a bookseller, especially one dealing primarily in books published by himself, such as was common in England in the early days of publishing. **b.** *Obsolete.* a publisher. [< Medieval Latin *stationarius* shopkeeper, especially, a bookseller; (originally) a stationary seller, as distinct from a roving peddler < Late Latin, a postmaster at a military post-station]
Stationers' Company, a company or guild of the City of London, incorporated in 1556, comprising booksellers, printers, bookbinders, and dealers in writing materials.
Stationers' Hall, the hall or building of the Stationers' Company in London, where formerly copyrights were required to be entered in a register kept for that purpose.
sta·tion·er·y (stā′shə ner′ē), *n.* writing materials, such as paper, cards, and envelopes. —*adj.* of or having to do with stationery.
➤ See **stationary** for usage note.
station house, a building used as a station, especially as a police station.
sta·tion·mas·ter (stā′shən mas′tər, -mäs′-), *n.* the person in charge of a railroad station, usually an employee of a particular railroad by which the station is owned, but sometimes an employee of a separate corporation, as one owning a station used by two or more railroads.
sta·tions of the cross or **Sta·tions of the Cross** (stā′shənz), **1.** a series of representations (usually fourteen) of successive incidents of Christ's Passion, placed in a church or along a road leading to a shrine, to be visited for meditation and prayer. **2.** the devotional exercises appointed to be used at these stations.
sta·tion-to-sta·tion (stā′shən tə stā′shən), *adj.* designating a long-distance telephone call in which the person calling will speak to anyone who answers at the number called.
station wagon, automobile with a rear door that comes down to load and unload the back part, which has folding seats that become part of the floor to permit use as a light truck.
➤ **station wagon, beach wagon.** The latter term, relatively common especially in the eastern United States in the 1920's and early 1930's, now survives for all practical purposes only in the fiction of that period.
stat·ism (stā′tiz əm), *n.* **1.** highly centralized governmental control of the economy, information media, etc., of a state or nation. **2.** advocacy of the sovereignty of a state, especially of a state of a republic.
stat·ist (stā′tist), *n.* **1.** a person who advocates statism. **2.** a statistician.
—*adj.* having to do with or advocating statism.
sta·tis·tic (stə tis′tik), *adj.* statistical. —*n.* **1.** any value, item, etc., used in statistics: *an important statistic.* **2.** statistics.
sta·tis·ti·cal (stə tis′tə kəl), *adj.* of or having to do with statistics; consisting of or based on statistics.
statistical independence, *Statistics.* the absence of correlation between two or more ways of classifying a group.
sta·tis·ti·cal·ly (stə tis′tə klē), *adv.* in a statistical manner; according to statistics.
stat·is·ti·cian (stat′ə stish′ən), *n.* an expert in statistics; person who prepares statistics.
sta·tis·tics (stə tis′tiks), *n.* **1.** numerical facts or data about people, the weather, business conditions, etc.: *Wherever statistics are kept, the numbers of births and of deaths rise and fall in nearly parallel lines* (William R. Inge). *The methods of statistics are so various and uncertain, so apt to be influenced by circumstance, that it is never possible to be sure that one is operating with figures of equal weight* (Havelock Ellis). **2.** the science of collecting and classifying such facts in order to show their significance. [< German *Statistik,* apparently < New Latin *statisticum collegium* lecture course on state affairs < *statista* one skilled in statecraft < Latin *status;* see STATE]
➤ **Statistics** is plural in form and in the sense of def. 1 is plural in use: *Statistics are classified systematically;* but in the sense of def. 2 it is singular in use: *Statistics is taught in many colleges.*
sta·tive (stā′tiv), *adj.* (of certain Hebrew verbs) expressing a state or condition.
Stat. L., Statutes at Large.
stat·o·blast (stat′ə blast), *n.* any of the horny buds developed within certain freshwater bryozoans that are set free when the parent colony dies, remain inactive throughout the winter, and give rise to new individuals in the spring. [< Greek *statós* standing, static + *blastós* sprout, germ]
stat·o·blas·tic (stat′ə blas′tik), *adj.* **1.** having the character or nature of a statoblast; of or having to do with statoblasts. **2.** giving rise to statoblasts; reproduced by means of statoblasts.
stat·o·cyst (stat′ə sist), *n. Zoology.* an organ of balance found in various crustaceans, flatworms, and other invertebrates, consisting of a sac containing particles (statoliths) of sand, lime, etc., suspended in fluid. [< Greek *statós* standing, static + English *cyst*]
stat·o·lith (stat′ə lith), *n.* a particle of sand, lime, etc., suspended in fluid, contained in a statocyst. [< Greek *statós* standing, static + *líthos* stone]
sta·tor (stā′tər), *n.* a stationary portion enclosing rotating parts, as in a steam turbine, or in an electric generator or motor. [< New Latin *stator* < Latin *stātor* sustainer < *sistere* cause to stand < *stāre* to stand]
stat·o·scope (stat′ə skōp), *n.* **1.** a form of aneroid barometer for measuring very small variations of atmospheric pressure. **2.** an instrument for detecting a small rise or fall in the altitude of an aircraft. [< Greek *statós* standing + English *-scope*]
stat·o·spore (stat′ə spôr, -spōr), *n. Botany.* a resting spore. [< Greek *statós* standing + *sporá* seed]
stat·u·ar·y (stach′ü er′ē), *n., pl.* **-ar·ies,** *adj.* —*n.* **1.** statues collectively. **2.** the art of making statues; sculpture. **3.** a sculptor: *He [Byron] had a head which statuaries loved to copy* (Macaulay).
—*adj.* of or having to do with the making of statues; suitable for statues: *statuary marble.*
stat·ue (stach′ü), *n.* a representation of a person or animal in the round, that is carved, molded, or cast in stone, clay, plaster, metal, wood, or the like: *Nearly every city has a statue of some famous man. He sat rigid, immovable, like a statue* (F. Marion Crawford).
statues, a game in which the players become suddenly motionless at a signal after having spun around and are judged on the awkwardness and ridiculousness of their poses.
[< Old French *statue,* learned borrowing from Latin *statua* < *status, -ūs* a standing still, condition < *stāre* to stand]
—**Syn.** sculpture.
stat·ued (stach′üd), *adj.* **1.** adorned with statues. **2.** in the form of a statue or of statuary.

stat·ue·like (stach′ü līk′), *adj.* like a statue; stationary; immovable: *How statuelike I see thee stand, Ah Psyche!* (Edgar Allan Poe).

Statue of Liberty, 1. a colossal figure of the goddess of liberty carrying a torch, on Liberty (formerly Bedloe's) Island in New York harbor, designed by Frédéric Auguste Bartholdi, 1844-1904, and presented in 1884 to the United States by France. It is made of copper on an iron framework and encloses a staircase. The torch is illuminated at night. **2.** Also, **statue of liberty.** a play in football in which a back holds the ball up as if to pass and another back comes around behind him and takes it.

Statue of Liberty (def. 1)

stat·ues (stach′üz), *n.pl.* See under **statue.**

stat·u·esque (stach′ü esk′), *adj.* like a statue in dignity, formal grace, or classic beauty: *the white statuesque immobility of her person* (Joseph Conrad). —**stat′u·esque′ly,** *adv.* —**stat′u·esque′ness,** *n.*

stat·u·ette (stach′ü et′), *n.* a small statue; figurine. [< French *statuette* (diminutive) < Old French *statue;* see STATUE]

stat·ure (stach′ər), *n.* **1.** height: *A man six feet tall is above average stature.* **2.** physical, mental, or moral growth; development: *The men are of meaner moral stature. The very patriots work for lower objects* (William Stubbs). *If we are true to plan, Our statures touch the skies* (Emily Dickinson). [< Old French *stature,* learned borrowing from Latin *statūra* < *stāre* to stand]

stat·ured (stach′ərd), *adj.* **1.** having stature; tall. **2.** having a certain kind of stature: *Man, fair-statured as the stately palm* (Robert Southey).

sta·tus (stā′təs, stat′əs), *n.* **1.** the condition of being; state: *Diplomats are interested in the status of world affairs. The status of the world in 1940 was discouraging to lovers of peace.* **2. a.** the condition of being relative to others; social or professional standing; position; rank: *What is his status in the government? Making way for no one under the status of a priest* (Rudyard Kipling). *Mr. Polly's status was that of a guest pure and simple* (H. G. Wells). **b.** standing, position, or rank considered to be desirable: *to seek status, to lose status.* **3.** legal position of a person as determined by his membership in some class of persons with certain rights or limitations: *the status of the foreign-born in America.* [< Latin *status,* -*ūs* < *stāre* to stand. Doublet of ESTATE, STATE.] —**Syn. 2. a.** footing, station. **3.** classification.

sta·tus asth·mat·i·cus (stā′təs az mat′ə-kəs, stat′əs; as-), an intense and persisting attack of asthma; asthmatic crisis: *The critical threat to life in . . . status asthmaticus is the degree to which carbon dioxide is retained or improperly removed, with consequent increase in blood acid* (Science News Letter). [< New Latin *status asthmaticus* asthmatic state]

sta·tus in quo (stā′təs in kwō′, stat′əs), *Latin.* status quo.

sta·tus-of-forc·es agreement (stā′təs əv fôr′siz, -fōr′-; stat′əs-), an agreement that establishes the legal rights and jurisdiction of a country in which foreign military forces are stationed, especially with reference to unlawful acts committed by servicemen in civilian areas.

status quo (kwō), **1.** the way things are; the existing state of affairs: *The demonstrated truth is that the status quo in Germany is partition* (Walter Lippmann). **2.** status quo ante: *to restore the status quo.* [< Latin *status quō* the state in which; see STATUS]

status quo an·te (an′tē), *Latin.* the way things were previously.

status symbol, something that is supposed to indicate or represent a desirable status in society: *Owning a car has become a status symbol of the successful American family* (Wall Street Journal).

stat·u·ta·ble (stach′ü tə bəl), *adj.* statutory.

stat·ute (stach′üt), *n.* **1. a.** a law enacted by a legislative body of a state or nation and recorded in a formal document: *The statutes for the United States are made by Congress.* **b.** the document recording such a law. *Abbr.:* stat. **2.** a formally established rule; law; decree: *the statutes of a university.* **3.** *International Law.* an instrument annexed or subsidiary to an international agreement, as a treaty. [< Old French *statut,* learned borrowing from Late Latin *statūtum* < Latin *statuere* establish < *stāre* to stand] —**Syn. 1. a.** See **law.**

statute book, a collection or record of statutes.

statute law, law expressed or stated by statutes; written law.

statute merchant, *Obsolete.* a bond of record acknowledged before the chief magistrate of a trading town, on which, if not paid at the appointed time, an execution might be awarded against the body, lands, and goods of the obligor or debtor.

statute mile, 5,280 feet (the standard mile for land measurement throughout the English-speaking world).

statute of limitations, a statute limiting the time during which rights or claims can be enforced by legal action.

statute staple, *Obsolete.* a bond of record acknowledged before the mayor of a staple, operating against a debtor in like manner to the statute merchant.

stat·u·to·ri·ly (stach′ü tôr′ə lē, -tōr′-), *adv.* in a statutory manner; by statutory enactment; in accordance with the provisions of the statutes.

stat·u·to·ry (stach′ü tôr′ē, -tōr′-), *adj.* **1.** having to do with or consisting of statutes. **2.** fixed by statute. **3.** punishable by statute. **4.** conforming to the provisions of a statute.

statutory law, statute law.

statutory rape, *U.S.* sexual intercourse with a girl who has not yet attained the age of consent, with or without the exercise of force by the male.

stat·volt (stat′vōlt′), *n.* an electrostatic unit of charge with a potential of one erg per statcoulomb, equal to about 300 volts.

staum·rel (stôm′rəl), *Scottish.* —*adj.* very stupid; half-witted. —*n.* a very stupid person; half-wit. [< dialectal *staumer,* variant of *stammer*]

staunch[1] (stônch, stänch), *v.t., v.i.* stanch[1].

staunch[2] (stônch, stänch), *adj.* stanch[2]: *Maury . . . was a staunch Southerner but no extremist* (Bruce Catton). —**staunch′ly,** *adv.* —**staunch′ness,** *n.*

staunch·less (stônch′lis, stänch′-), *adj.* stanchless.

stau·ro·lite (stôr′ə līt), *n.* a mineral, a silicate of aluminum and iron, yellowish-brown to dark-brown in color, found frequently twinned in the form of a cross. *Formula:* $FeAl_4Si_2O_{10}(OH)_2$ [< French *staurolite* < Greek *staurós* a cross; (originally) stake + French *-lite* -lite]

stau·ro·lit·ic (stôr′ə lit′ik), *adj.* having to do with, resembling, or characterized by the presence of staurolite.

stau·ro·scope (stôr′ə skōp), *n.* an instrument used in the microscopic examination of crystals, to find the position of planes of light vibration. [< Greek *staurós* cross + English *-scope*]

stau·ro·scop·ic (stô′rə skop′ik), *adj.* of, having to do with, or made by means of the stauroscope: *stauroscopic examination.*

stau·ro·scop·i·cal·ly (stô′rə skop′ə klē), *adv.* by means of the stauroscope: *stauroscopically determined systems of crystallization.*

stave (stāv), *n., v.,* **staved** or **stove, stav·ing.** —*n.* **1.** one of the thin, narrow, curved pieces of wood which, when placed together side by side and hooped, form the side of a barrel, cask, tub, or the like. **2.** a stick, staff, rod, bar, or pole. **3.** a rung of a ladder or a crossbar between the legs of a chair. **4.** a verse or stanza of a poem or song: *After they had played a stave, a small . . . choir . . . broke forth* (Arnold Bennett). **5.** *Music.* staff[1].
—*v.t.* **1.** to break a hole in (a barrel, cask, etc.): *a carman . . . having staved a cask of port . . .* (Tobias Smollett). **2.** to smash (a hole) in a boat, door, etc.: *He [a whale] had . . . been known to turn round suddenly and . . . stave their boat to splinters* (Herman Melville). **3.** to furnish with staves. **4.** to drive off or beat with or as if with a staff or stave. —*v.i.* **1.** to become smashed or broken in, as a boat: *Like a vessel of glass she stove and sank* (Longfellow). **2.** *Dialect.* to go with a rush or dash: *I lost no time, but down through the valley . . . as hard as I could stave* (Stevenson).

stave off, to put off; keep back; prevent; delay: *The lost campers ate birds' eggs to stave off starvation.*
[back formation < *staves,* plural of *staff*]
➤ The variant past tense and past participle form **stove** is used chiefly with reference to the breaking of boats and the like: *The waves stove* (or *staved*) *the boat in,* but *He staved off his creditors.*

staves (stāvz), *n.* **1.** a plural of **staff**[1]. **2.** the plural of **stave.**

staves·a·cre (stāvz′ā kər), *n.* **1.** an Old World larkspur whose seeds are violently emetic and cathartic. **2.** its seeds. [alteration of Middle English *staphisagre* < Medieval Latin *staphisagria* < Greek *staphìs agriā* (literally) wild raisin < *staphís* raisin, and *ágrios* wild]

stave·wood (stāv′wu̇d′), *n.* any of various trees whose wood has been used for making staves, as species of trees of Australia and the East Indies.

stav·ing (stā′ving), *n.* staves collectively.

stay[1] (stā), *v.,* **stayed** or (*Obsolete*) **staid, stay·ing,** *n.* —*v.i.* **1.** to continue in a place or in the company of others, rather than going on or away; remain: *Stay here till I call you. The cat stayed out all night. Shall I go or stay?* **2.** to live in a place for a while, especially as a guest; dwell: *to stay at a hotel. She is staying with her aunt while her mother is ill.* **3.** to continue to be as indicated; keep: *to stay clean, stay thin.* **4.** to pause; wait; tarry; delay: *Time and tide stay for no man.* **5. a.** to last, hold out, or endure in a race or run: *a runner unable to stay to the end of a race.* **b.** to keep up (with a competitor in a race, etc.). **6.** *Poker.* to call or see a bet; continue playing a hand. **7.** to come to a stop; halt (often used as a command to pause or to cease doing something): *Stay, stay, until the hasting day, Hath run but to the evensong* (George Herrick). **8.** to make a stand; stand firm: *Give them leave to fly that will not stay* (Shakespeare). **9.** *Archaic.* to cease or desist: *The little girl was unable to stay from crying.*
—*v.t.* **1.** to stop, detain, or hold back (a person or thing); arrest the progress of; hinder from going on or away: *to stay a boat. If I could stay this letter an hour* (John Donne). **2.** to prevent (a person or thing) from doing something; check; restrain: *Stay, stay thy hands, thou art an Amazon* (Shakespeare). **3.** to stop, delay, or postpone (an action or process which is begun): *The teacher stayed judgment till she could hear both sides.* **4.** to put an end to for a while; satisfy (hunger, appetite, etc.): *Jim ate some bread and butter to stay his hunger until dinner.* **5.** to bring under control or suppress (strife, rebellion, etc.). **6.** to remain for, during, or throughout: *He stayed the night in the spare room* (William De Morgan). **7.** *Informal.* to last for (a certain distance or time): *He cannot stay a mile.* **8.** *Archaic.* to wait for; await: *My father stays my coming* (Shakespeare).

stay out, to remain to the end of or beyond the limit of: *It seemed as if we had stayed our English welcome out* (Hawthorne).

stay put, *Informal.* to remain where or as placed; remain fixed: *[a shirt] with big oversized French cuffs and generous shirttails that really stay put* (New Yorker).
—*n.* **1.** the act or fact of remaining in a place; a stop; time spent: *a pleasant stay in the country, a week's stay.* **2.** the act or fact of stopping; check; restraint: *a stay on his activity.* **3.** a coming to a standstill; halt; pause: *without stop or stay* (Matthew Prior). **4.** *Law.* a delay in carrying out the order of a court: *The judge granted the condemned man a stay for an appeal.* **5.** *Informal.* staying power; endurance. **6.** *Obsolete.* **a.** a cause of stoppage; obstacle; hindrance. **b.** control; restraint.
[probably < unrecorded Anglo-French *estaier,* variant of Old French *ester* stand < Latin *stāre*]
—**Syn.** *v.i.* **1. Stay, remain** mean to continue in (some) stated place, position, state, condition, relation to action, etc. **Stay** emphasizes keeping on in the present or specified place, state, condition, etc., without leaving or stopping: *He decided to stay in school another year.* **Remain,** often used interchangeably with *stay,* emphasizes keeping on in the same place or state, without changing in condition, quality, or form: *This room remains cool all summer.* **2.** lodge, sojourn, abide, reside.

 PRONUNCIATION KEY: hat, āge, cãre, fär; let, ēqual, tėrm; it, īce; hot, ōpen, ôrder; oil, out; cup, pu̇t, rüle;

stay[2] (stā), *n., v.,* **stayed, stay·ing.** —*n.* **1.** a support; prop; brace. **2.** a person who affords support: *The oldest son was the family's stay.*
stays, a corset, especially a stiffened one: *Susan . . . had suddenly become so very upright that she seemed to have put an additional bone in her stays* (Dickens).
[probably < verb]
—*v.t.* **1.** to support; prop; hold up. **2.** to strengthen mentally or spiritually; fix or rest in dependence or reliance.
[probably < Old French *estayer* < a Germanic word]
—**Syn.** *v.t.* **1.** brace. **2.** sustain.
stay[3] (stā), *n., v.,* **stayed, stay·ing.** —*n.* **1.** one of the strong ropes, often of wire, running from a mast to the deck or another mast, that supports the mast of a ship. **2.** any rope or chain similarly used, as one supporting a broadcasting antenna or a flagpole; guy.

Stay[3] **(def. 1)**

in stays, (of a ship) in the act of changing from one tack to another: *"Christabel" was sailed . . . and was remarkably quick in stays* (London Times).
—*v.t.* **1.** to support, secure, or attach (a mast, etc.) by means of a stay or stays. **2.** to incline (a mast) forward, aft, etc., by stays.
—*v.i.* (of a ship) to change to the other tack.
[Old English *stæg*]
stay-at-home (stā′ət hōm′), *n.* a person who would much rather remain at home than travel, go out, etc.: *This stay-at-home was delighted to sit by the fire and watch the Hibiscus Stakes . . . on television* (New Yorker). —*adj.* that is a stay-at-home; characteristic of or befitting a stay-at-home; choosing to remain at home in preference to going out, traveling, etc.: *Then a person traveling at close to light's speed would not age as fast as his stay-at-home twin* (Science News Letter).
stay bar, *Architecture.* a horizontal iron bar extending in one piece from jamb to jamb along the top of the mullions of a traceried window.
stay bolt, a bolt or rod binding together opposite plates, as in a boiler, to enable them to sustain each other against internal pressure.
stay·er[1] (stā′ər), *n.* **1.** a person who stays or remains: *a stayer at home.* **2.** a person or animal having great staying power, especially a race horse. **3.** a person or thing that stops or restrains.
stay·er[2] (stā′ər), *n.* a person who stays or supports.
stay·ing power (stā′ing), the power to hold out and not give in even though weakened or tired; power or will to endure: *The old fellow's staying powers were really extraordinary.* (W. H. Hudson).
stay-in strike, or **stay-in** (stā′in′), *n. British.* a sit-down strike.
stay·lace (stā′lās′), *n.* a lace for drawing together the parts of stays or corsets.
stay of execution, a delay in carrying out a sentence, granted to a prisoner by the court that sentenced him.
stays (stāz), *n.pl.* See under **stay**[2], *n.*
stay·sail (stā′sāl′; *Nautical* stā′səl), *n.* any fore-and-aft sail fastened on a stay. See **sail** for picture.
S.T.B., Bachelor of Sacred Theology (Latin, *Sacrae Theologiae Baccalaureus*).
St. Bernard, a Saint Bernard dog. See **Saint Bernard** for picture.
std., standard.
STD (no periods), Subscriber Trunk Dialing (the British equivalent of DDD or Direct Distance Dialing).
S.T.D., Doctor of Sacred Theology (Latin, *Sacrae Theologiae Doctor*).
Ste. or **Ste** (no period), Sainte.
stead (sted), *n.* **1.** the place or function (of a person or thing) as held by a substitute or a successor: *Our scheduled speaker could not come, but sent a first-rate speaker in his stead.* **2.** *Obsolete or Dialect.* **a.** a tract or property in land. **b.** a farm; homestead.
stand in good stead, to be of advantage or service to: *Ed's ability to swim stood him in good stead when the boat upset.*
—*v.t. Archaic.* to avail, profit, or be of use to (a person): *In my dealing with my child . . . my accomplishments and my money stead me nothing* (Emerson). *There's none but truth can stead you* (Walt Whitman).
[Old English *stede*]
—**Syn.** *n.* **1.** lieu.
stead·fast (sted′fast, -fäst, -fəst), *adj.* **1** loyal; unwavering: *Benjamin Franklin was a steadfast servant of his country.* **2.** (of an object, building, etc.) firmly fixed; immovable: *. . . this tall pile . . . By its own weight made steadfast and immovable* (William Congreve). **3.** (of a law, condition of things, etc.) firmly settled; unchangeable; established. Also, **stedfast.** [Old English *stedefæst* < *stede* a place + *fæst* fast[1], firm] —**stead′fast·ly,** *adv.* —**stead′fast·ness,** *n.*
—**Syn. 1.** unswerving.
stead·i·er (sted′ē ər), *n.* a person or thing that steadies: *She uses her cane for a steadier.*
stead·i·ly (sted′ə lē), *adv.* in a steady manner; with regularity in habits; firmly; evenly; unwaveringly; steadfastly: *[He] saw life steadily and saw it whole* (Matthew Arnold).
stead·i·ness (sted′ē nis), *n.* steady character, quality, or condition: *It will be your duty . . . to set an example of discipline and perfect steadiness under fire* (Horatio H. Kitchener).
stead·ing (sted′ing), *n. Scottish.* a farmhouse and outbuildings. [< *stead* a farm + *-ing*[1]]
stead·y (sted′ē), *adj.,* **stead·i·er, stead·i·est,** *v.,* **stead·ied, stead·y·ing,** *interj., n., pl.* **stead·ies,** *adv.* —*adj.* **1. a.** changing little; regular; uniform: *a steady breeze, a steady price, a steady barometer. John is making steady progress at school.* **b.** regularly doing a particular thing; constant: *a steady worker, a steady playgoer.* **2. a.** firmly fixed; not swaying or shaking; firm: *a steady hand, to hold a ladder steady.* **b.** assured in movement or action; not faltering or tremulous: *a steady aim.* **3.** resolute; steadfast: *a steady belief, a steady purpose, steady friendship.* **4.** not easily excited; calm: *a steady mind or head, steady nerves.* **5.** having good habits; reliable: *a steady young man.* **6.** (of a ship) keeping nearly upright and on course, especially in a heavy sea. **7.** *Informal.* being one's regular sweetheart: *a steady beau. Mary was his steady girl.*
—*v.t.* **1.** to make or keep steady; keep from shaking or swaying: *Steady the ladder while I climb to the roof.* **2.** to make regular in character and conduct.
—*v.i.* to become steady; regain or maintain an upright or stable position or condition: *Our sails filled as the wind steadied from the East.*
—*interj.* **1.** be calm! don't get excited! **2.** *Nautical.* hold the helm as it is! keep on course!
—*n. U.S. Informal.* one's regular boy friend or girl friend: *I heard this Russell was . . . your . . . friend Mildred's steady* (Booth Tarkington).
—*adv.* in a steady manner; steadily: *to steer steady.*
go steady, *Informal.* to keep regular company with a person of the opposite sex: *"Going steady" . . . undoubtedly is a factor in building toward early marriage* (Paul H. Landis).
[< *stead*[1] + *-y*[1]]
—**Syn.** *adj.* **1.a, b. Steady, regular** mean constant or uniform in acting, doing, moving, happening. **Steady** emphasizes the absence of interruption or of change: *He has been unable to find steady work.* **Regular** emphasizes a fixed, usual, or uniform procedure, practice, program, or pattern: *He is a regular subscriber to several magazines.* **3.** unwavering. **5.** trustworthy, dependable.
stead·y-go·ing (sted′ē gō′ing), *adj.* steady in action, habits, etc.
steady motion, motion of a fluid maintained at a velocity constant in magnitude and direction at any point.
stead·y-state (sted′ē stāt′), *adj.* unchanging, or changing very little, in quality or behavior: *a steady-state current.*
steady-state theory, the theory that the universe is in appreciably the same state as it has always been, for, although matter has been and is being lost or dispersed, other matter is continuously created to take its place.
steak (stāk), *n.* **1.** a slice of beef, especially one cut from the hindquarter, for broiling or frying; beefsteak. **2.** a slice of any meat or fish for broiling or frying: *a salmon steak.* **3.** finely ground meat, especially beef but sometimes beef mixed with pork, veal, etc., shaped and cooked somewhat in the fashion of a steak: *hamburger steak, a Salisbury steak.* [probably < Scandinavian (compare Norwegian *steik* < Old Icelandic *steikja* to roast)]
steak hammer, a hammer having a broad face divided into points or projections, used in beating steak.
steak house, or **steak·house** (stāk′hous′), *n.* a restaurant that serves broiled steaks as its specialty; grill.
steak knife, a table knife with a sharp blade for cutting beefsteak.
steak maul, an implement for pounding steaks in order to soften the fiber.
steal (stēl), *v.,* **stole, sto·len, steal·ing,** *n.* —*v.t.* **1.** to take (something) that does not belong to one; take dishonestly: *to steal money. Who steals my purse, steals trash* (Shakespeare). **2.** to take or appropriate (another's work, words, ideas, etc.) without permission or acknowledgment; pass off as one's own: *No man like you for stealing other men's inventions* (Scott). **3.** to take, get, or do secretly: *to steal a kiss, to steal a look at someone. Jane stole time from her lessons to read a story.* **4.** to take, get, or win by art, charm, or gradual means: *The baby stole our hearts.* **5.** to place, move, or convey furtively: *She stole her hand into his.* **6.** (in baseball) to advance to (a base) without being helped by a hit, base on balls, error, passed ball, wild pitch, or balk: *to steal second, to steal home.* **7.** to make (a play, point, etc.) unexpectedly. —*v.i.* **1.** to commit or practice theft: *From childhood she had stolen whenever she had a chance.* **2.** to move, come, or leave secretly or quietly: *to steal out of the house. A mink steals out of the marsh . . . and seizes a frog* (Thoreau). **3.** to move, pass, come, or go slowly, gently, or imperceptibly: *The years steal by. A feeling of drowsiness stole over him.*
—*n.* **1.** *Informal.* **a.** the act of stealing. **b.** the thing stolen. **2.** *Informal.* something obtained at a very low cost or with very little effort: *This table is such a bargain it's a steal.* **3.** *Informal.* a dishonest or unethical transaction at a great profit: *Of all the swindles and steals that have ever been proposed or carried out in our State, this is the largest and boldest* (Daily Gazette [Little Rock, Arkansas]). **4.** (in baseball) a safe advance from one base to another by stealing: *Davis overthrew second in an attempt to nail Hale on a steal* (Oregonian).
[Old English *stelan*] —**steal′er,** *n.*
—**Syn.** *v.t.* **1. Steal, pilfer, filch** mean to take dishonestly or wrongfully and secretly something belonging to someone else. **Steal** is the general and common word: *Thieves stole the silver.* **Pilfer** implies stealing and carrying away in small amounts: *In many supermarkets hidden guards watch for people who pilfer food.* **Filch** implies stealthy or furtive pilfering, usually of objects of little value: *The boys filched some candy from the counter.* -*v.i.* **2.** sneak, skulk, slink.
steal·age (stē′lij), *n.* **1.** what is lost or gained through stealing; stealings. **2.** a stealing.
steal·ing (stē′ling), *n.* the act of one who steals: *Stealing is a crime.*
stealings, what is stolen.
—*adj.* that steals or moves stealthily.
stealth (stelth), *n.* **1.** secret or sly action: *He obtained the letter by stealth. The greatest pleasure I know is to do a good action by stealth, and to have it found out by accident* (Charles Lamb). **2.** *Obsolete.* the act of stealing or going furtively into or out of a place: *I told him of your stealth into this wood* (Shakespeare). [Middle English *stelthe,* apparently unrecorded Old English *stælth* (compare *stælthing* theft), related to *stelan* steal]
stealth·ful (stelth′fəl), *adj.* stealthy.
stealth·i·ly (stel′thə lē), *adv.* in a stealthy manner; by stealth: *Ethelberta breathed a sort of exclamation, not right out, but stealthily, like a parson's damn* (Thomas Hardy).
stealth·i·ness (stel′thē nis), *n.* stealthy character or action.
stealth·y (stel′thē), *adj.,* **stealth·i·er, stealth·i·est.** done in a secret manner;

secret; sly: *The cat crept in a stealthy way toward the bird.* —**Syn.** furtive, sneaking, underhand, surreptitious.

steam (stēm), *n.* **1. a.** (technically) the invisible vapor or gas into which water is converted upon being heated to the boiling point. **b.** (popularly) the white cloud or mist formed by the condensation, when cooled, of the invisible vapor from boiling water. **2. a.** the vapor of boiling water used, especially by confinement in special apparatus, to generate mechanical power and for heating and cooking. **b.** the mechanical power thus generated. **3.** *Informal.* power; energy; force: *That old man still has a lot of steam left in him.* **4.** a vapor or fume; exhalation.

get up steam, *Informal.* to work up the necessary energy: [*He*] *tried to work, but could not get up steam* (Sunday Times).

let or **blow off steam,** *Informal.* **a.** to get rid of excess energy: *The children ran around the playground at recess, letting off steam.* **b.** to relieve one's feelings: *He let off steam by yelling at a clerk.*

—*v.i.* **1.** to give off, emit, or exhale steam or vapor: *steaming hot coffee.* **2.** (of vapor, etc.) to rise or issue in the form of steam: *Several damp gentlemen, whose clothes . . . began to steam* (Dickens). **3.** (of a surface) to become covered with condensed vapor. **4.** (of an engine, boiler, etc.) to generate or produce steam. **5.** to move by steam: *A ship with a cargo of wheat steamed off to Marseilles* (Sinclair Lewis). **6.** *Informal.* to run or go quickly, as if powered by steam; move with speed and vigor: *The runner steamed into second base for a double.* —*v.t.* **1.** to cook, remove, soften, freshen, or disinfect by steam: *to steam a plum pudding, stamps off an envelope, velvet, surgical instruments, etc.* **2.** to give off or emit (steam or vapor); send out in the form of vapor. **3.** to transport or cause to move by steam.

—*adj.* **1.** of, having to do with, or consisting of steam: *steam power. Many large office buildings and apartments have steam heat.* **2.** cooking, softening, washing, heating, treating, etc., by steam: *a steam laundry, a steam kettle.* **3.** propelled by or with a steam engine: *a steam train.* **4.** operated by steam or a steam engine: *a steam hammer.* **5.** containing, conveying, or regulating steam: *a steam pipe, a steam valve.*

[Old English *stēam* vapor, fume] —**steam′like′,** *adj.*

steam bath, 1. a bath taken in a steam room: *He keeps fit by daily visits to the gymnasium for steam baths* (New York Times). **2.** a Turkish bath or a sauna. **3.** a bath of steam, used in a laboratory. **4.** laboratory apparatus containing such a bath.

steam·boat (stēm′bōt′), *n.* a boat moved by steam.

steam·boat·ing (stēm′bō′ting), *n.* traveling by or operating a steamboat or steamboats, especially as a regular means of passenger or freight service.

steam boiler, a boiler in which water is heated to make steam, as for working a steam engine or a steam turbine.

steam·car (stēm′kär′), *n.* **1.** an automobile driven by steam; steamer. **2.** *U.S., Archaic.* a railroad car.

steam chest or **box,** the chamber through which the steam of an engine passes from the boiler to the cylinder.

steam coal, a bituminous coal used in heating steam boilers.

steam cylinder, the cylinder of a steam engine.

steamed-up (stēmd′up′), *adj. Informal.* excited; agitated; angry.

steam engine, an engine operated by steam, typically one in which a sliding piston in a cylinder is moved by the expansive action of steam generated in a boiler. —**steam′-en′gine,** *adj.*

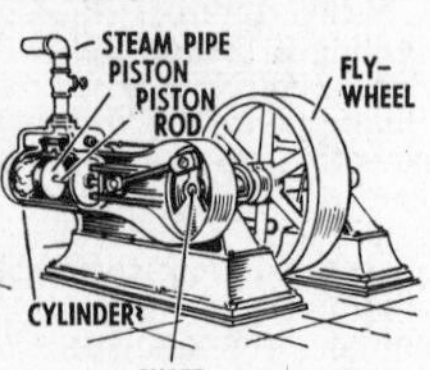

Horizontal Steam Engine
Pressure of steam in cylinder pushes piston forward, causing rod to turn shaft and flywheel.

steam·er (stē′mər), *n.* **1.** a steamboat; steamship. **2.** an engine run by steam. **3.** a container in which something is steamed, as for sterilization or cooking. **4.** a boiler or other vessel for generating steam. **5.** a steamcar.

steamer chair, a kind of reclining chair used by passengers on the deck of a ship.

steamer clam, the soft clam.

steamer rug, a heavy blanket, especially such as is used to keep a person warm in a chair on the deck of a ship.

steamer trunk, a small trunk suitable for use in a ship's stateroom.

steam fitter, a man specially trained or experienced in the installing and repairing of steam pipes, radiators, boilers, etc.

steam fitting, the work of a steam fitter.

steam gauge, an attachment to a boiler to indicate the pressure of steam.

steam generator, a unit for producing high-pressure steam, consisting of a combined boiler and superheater.

steam hammer, a powerful hammer for forging steel, etc., operated by steam power.

steam heat, heat given off by steam in radiators and pipes.

steam·i·ly (stē′mə lē), *adv.* in a steamy manner: *The kettle bubbled steamily on the stove.*

steam·i·ness (stē′mē nis), *n.* steamy or vaporous character or quality; mistiness.

steam·ing (stē′ming), *adj.* emitting steam or vapor: *a steaming glass of tea. He . . . pulled up his steaming horse by the station* (Joseph S. Le Fanu).

steaming hot, piping hot; very hot: *a cup of steaming hot coffee.*

—*n.* travel by steamboat or steamship: *Eight hundred miles of swift steaming down the Coromandel Coast brings us to Madras* (J.H. Morrison).

steam iron, an iron that releases steam from a water tank inside through holes in or near its under surface to dampen cloth while pressing it.

steam jacket, an enclosure or jacket into which steam passes, built round a tank, kettle, or the like, in order to heat it.

steam-jack·et (stēm′jak′it), *v.t.* to apply a steam jacket to or surround with one; furnish with hollow walls within which hot dry steam may be circulated to supply heat.

steam locomotive, a locomotive that moves by means of steam generated in its own boiler: *Steam locomotives are all but extinct* (Wall Street Journal).

steam pipe, a pipe through which steam is conveyed.

steam point, a standard of measurement for temperature, equal to the temperature at which water boils under normal atmospheric pressure; 100 degrees centigrade.

steam power, the power of steam applied to move machinery or produce any other result.

steam radio, *British.* daytime radio programs designed mainly for housewives.

steam-roll (stēm′rōl′), *v.t., v.i.* steam-roller.

steam roller, 1. a heavy roller, formerly run by steam but now usually by a Diesel engine, used to crush and level materials in making and repairing roads. **2.** *Informal.* a means of crushing opposition.

steam-roll·er (stēm′rō′lər), *v.t.* **1.** *Informal.* **a.** to override by crushing power or force; crush: *to steam-roller all opposition.* **b.** to force (into or through) by this means. **2.** to make level, smooth, etc., with a steam roller. —*v.i. Informal.* to override or crush a person or thing that is in opposition.

—*adj. Informal.* crushing as if with a steam roller; overriding: *steam-roller methods, steam-roller relentlessness.*

steam room, a room filled with dry or wet steam for sweating, as in a Turkish bath.

steam·ship (stēm′ship′), *n.* a ship moved by steam. *Abbr.:* SS (no periods).

Steamship

steam shovel, a machine for digging, formerly always operated by steam, but now often by an internal-combustion engine.

steam table, a fixture resembling a shallow tank in which water is heated or into which steam is piped, with holes in its upper surface into which containers are fitted, used by restaurants, institutional kitchens, etc., to keep food warm.

steam-tight (stēm′tīt′), *adj.* impervious to the passage of steam under pressure.

steam trap, a device permitting the passage of condensed water out of pipes, radiators, etc., while preventing the escape of steam.

steam turbine, a rotary engine operated by steam.

steam whistle, a whistle operated by the steam from a boiler.

steam·y (stē′mē), *adj.,* **steam·i·er, steam·i·est. 1.** of steam; like steam: *a steamy vapor.* **2.** full of steam; giving off steam; rising in steam: *a steamy room.*

stean (stēn), *n. Archaic.* a jar, pot, or vessel of earthenware: *In the corner nearest the kitchen was a great stean in which the bread was kept* (Arnold Bennett). Also, **steen.** [Old English *stǣne* < *stān* stone]

ste·ap·sin (stē ap′sin), *n.* a digestive enzyme (alipase) secreted in the pancreatic juice, that changes fat into glycerol and fatty acids. [< *stea*(rin) and (pe)*psin*]

ste·a·rate (stē′ə rāt, stir′āt), *n.* a salt or ester of stearic acid. [< *stear*(ic) + *-ate*[2]]

ste·ar·ic (stē ar′ik, stir′-), *adj.* of, having to do with, or obtained from stearin, suet, or fat. [< *stearic* (acid)]

stearic acid, a white, odorless, tasteless, saturated fatty acid, obtained chiefly from tallow and other hard fats by saponification. Stearic acid exists in combination with glycerol as stearin, in beef and mutton fat, and in several vegetable fats. *Formula:* $C_{18}H_{36}O_2$ [< French *acide stéarique* < *stéarine* stearin]

ste·a·rin (stē′ər in, stir′in), *n.* **1.** a white, odorless, crystalline solid substance, an ester of stearic acid and glycerol, that is the chief constituent of many animal and vegetable fats. *Formula:* $C_{57}H_{110}O_6$ **2.** a mixture of stearic acid and palmitic acid, used for making candles, solid alcohol, etc. **3.** the solid or higher melting parts of any fat. [< French *stéarine* < Greek *stéār, stéātos* fat + French *-ine* -ine[2]]

ste·a·rine (stē′ər in, -ə rēn; stir′in, -ēn), *n.* stearin.

ste·a·rop·tene (stē′ə rop′tēn), *n.* the solid part of an essential oil. [< Greek *stéār* fat + *ptēnós* winged < *pétesthai* to fly (because of its volatility)]

ste·ar·rhe·a or **ste·ar·rhoe·a** (stē′ə rē′ə), *n.* seborrhea. [< Greek *stéār, stéātos* fat, tallow + *rhein* to flow]

ste·a·ryl alcohol (stē′ə rəl, stir′əl), a solid alcohol produced from stearic acid, occurring as white flakes or granules, used in pharmaceuticals and cosmetics, as a lubricant and detergent, etc. *Formula:* $C_{18}H_{38}O$

ste·a·tite (stē′ə tīt), *n.* a rock composed of impure talc, with a smooth, greasy feel; soapstone. [< Latin *steatitis* soapstone < Greek *stéār, stéātos* fat, tallow]

ste·a·tit·ic (stē′ə tit′ik), *adj.* of, having to do with, like, or made of steatite or soapstone.

ste·a·to·py·gi·a (stē′ə tə pī′jē ə, -pij′ē-), *n.* an excessive deposit of fat on the buttocks and thighs, prevalent especially among the women of the Hottentots and certain other native African peoples. [< New Latin *steatopygia* < *steatopyga* a protuberance of the buttocks < Greek *stéār, stéatos* fat, suet + *pȳgḗ* rump, buttocks]

ste·a·to·pyg·ic (stē′ə tə pij′ik), *adj.* having to do with, characterized by, or exhibiting steatopygia.

ste·a·to·py·gous (stē′ə tə pī′gəs), *adj.* steatopygic.

ste·a·top·y·gy (stē′ə top′ə jē), *n.* steatopygia.

ste·a·tor·rhe·a or **ste·a·tor·rhoe·a** (stē′ə tə rē′ə), *n.* **1.** seborrhea. **2.** an abnormally great proportion of fat in the bowel movements, caused by poor absorption of fat in the small intestine. [< Greek *stéār, stéātos* tallow, fat + *rhein* to flow]

ste·a·to·sis (stē ə tō′sis), *n.* **1.** fatty degeneration. **2.** any disease of the sebaceous glands. [< New Latin *steatosis* < Greek *stéār, stéātos* fat, suet + New Latin *-osis* -osis]

sted·fast (sted′fast, -fäst, -fəst), *adj.* steadfast. —**sted′fast·ly,** *adv.* —**sted′fast·ness,** *n.*

steed (stēd), *n.* **1.** a horse, especially a riding horse: *I set her on my pacing steed* (Keats). **2.** a high-spirited horse. **3.** anything, as a person or vehicle, likened to either of these. [Old English *stēda* stallion]

steed·less (stēd′lis), *adj.* without a steed.

steek (stēk), *Scottish.* —*v.t.* **1.** to shut. **2.** to stitch. —*v.i.* **1.** to close a place; lock a door. **2.** to sew.

—*n.* (in needlework or knitting) a stitch. [Middle English *steken,* probably unrecorded Old English *stecan*]

steel (stēl), *n.* **1.** an alloy consisting essentially of iron and varying amounts of carbon (less than about 1.7 per cent, and less than the amount contained in cast iron but more than that in wrought iron), and produced by separating a given amount of carbon from molten pig iron. It has greater hardness and elasticity than iron and hence is much used for tools, machinery, girders, etc. Commercially, steel is commonly divided into three classes: hard steel, containing a relatively large amount of carbon (more than 0.85 per cent); medium steel, containing a relatively small amount of carbon (between 0.85 and 0.3 per cent); and mild or soft steel, containing only a small percentage of carbon (less than 0.3 per cent). **2.** something made from steel: **a.** a sword or knife of steel. **b.** a piece of steel for striking sparks from flint. **c.** a rod of steel for sharpening knives. **d.** a narrow strip of steel used for stiffening and support, as in a corset, dress, etc. **3.** steel-like hardness or strength: *nerves of steel, true as steel.* **4.** the market quotation for stock in a steel company.
steels, shares of stock, bonds, etc., issued by steel companies: *Steels . . . registered substantial gains yesterday* (Wall Street Journal).
—*adj.* **1.** made or consisting of steel. **2.** of, belonging to, or used for the production of steel. **3.** like steel in color, hardness, etc.
—*v.t.* **1.** to point, edge, or cover with steel. **2.** to make hard or strong like steel: *The soldiers steeled themselves to withstand the attack.*
[unrecorded Old English *stēle*] —**steel′like′,** *adj.* —**Syn.** *v.t.* **2.** harden, indurate, inure.

steel band, a West Indian musical band that performs on various percussion instruments usually made from oil drums.

steel blue, a lustrous dark blue, like the color of tempered steel. —**steel′-blue′,** *adj.*

steel engraving, *Graphic Arts.* **1.** the art or process of engraving upon a steel plate. **2.** a print or impression from such a plate.

steel gray, a dull, dark gray color, having a tinge of blue. —**steel′-gray′,** *adj.*

steel·head (stēl′hed′), *n.* rainbow trout that has entered or returned from the sea.

Steel Helmet, 1. Stahlhelm. **2.** a member of the Stahlhelm.

steel·ie (stē′lē), *n.* **1.** a steel marble: *McGurk took all his marbles, including a good steelie* (Harper's). **2.** a steelhead.

steel·i·ness (stē′lē nis), *n.* steely nature or quality.

steel·less (stēl′lis), *adj.* (of an article) containing no steel.

steel·mak·er (stēl′mā′kər), *n.* a manufacturer of steel.

steel·mak·ing (stēl′mā′king), *n.* the manufacture of steel. —*adj.* of or having to do with steelmaking: *a steelmaking furnace, the steelmaking industry.*

steel·man (stēl′man′), *n., pl.* **-men.** *U.S.* **1.** a steelmaker. **2.** a seller of steel.

steel·mas·ter (stēl′mas′tər, -mäs′-), *n. Especially British.* steelmaker.

steel mill, a place where steel is made.

steels (stēlz), *n.pl.* See under **steel,** *n.*

steel trap, a trap with jaws and spring of steel.

steel-trap (stēl′trap′), *adj.* resembling or suggesting a steel trap; sharp and powerful: *steel-trap cunning.*

steel wool, small, fine steel shavings, used for cleaning or polishing surfaces.

steel·work (stēl′wėrk′), *n.* tools, parts, framing, etc., made of steel.

steel·work·er (stēl′wėr′kər), *n.* a person who works in a place where steel is made.

steel·works (stēl′wėrks′), *n.pl. or sing.* a place where steel is made.

steel·y (stē′lē), *adj.,* **steel·i·er, steel·i·est. 1.** made of steel. **2.** like steel in color, strength, or hardness.

steel·yard[1] (stēl′yärd′, stil′yərd), *n.* a type of scale for weighing, with unequal arms, the calibrated longer one having a movable weight and the shorter a hook for holding the object to be weighed. [apparently < *steel* + *yard*[2] rod, beam; probably influenced by *Steelyard*]

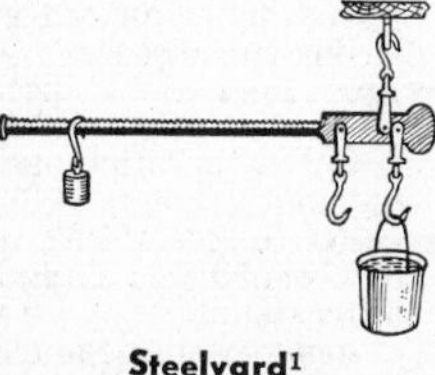
Steelyard[1]

Steel·yard or **steel·yard**[2] (stēl′yärd′), *n.* in English history: **1.** a place in London where the Hanseatic merchants formerly had an establishment. **2.** the merchants themselves. **3.** a similar establishment elsewhere. [mistranslation of Middle Low German *stâlhof* < *stâl* (pronounced "steel") pattern + *hof* courtyard]

steen (stēn), *n.* stean.

steen·bok (stēn′bok′, stān′-), *n.* any of various small African antelopes with straight, slender horns, frequenting grassland or open woodland. Also, **steinbock, steinbok, steinbuck.** [< Afrikaans *steenbok* < *steen* stone + *bok* buck[1]]

Steenbok
(about 1¾ ft. high at the shoulder)

steep[1] (stēp), *adj.* **1. a.** having a sharp slope: *a very steep hill, a steep grade.* **b.** almost straight up and down: *a steep cliff.* **2.** unreasonable: *a steep price.* **3.** *Informal.* (of a story, etc.) exaggerated; incredible. **4.** *Obsolete.* headlong: *from that steep ruin to which he had nigh brought them* (Milton). **5.** *Obsolete.* elevated; lofty.
—*n.* a steep slope, precipitous place, etc.
[Old English *stēap*] —**steep′ly,** *adv.* —**steep′ness,** *n.*
—**Syn.** *adj.* **1. a,b. Steep, abrupt, precipitous** mean having a sharp slope. **Steep** suggests a slope sharp enough to be hard to go up or down: *I do not like to drive up a steep hill. Steep Hill—Use Low Gear.* **Abrupt** suggests a very sharp and sudden slope: *From the rim they made their way down the abrupt sides of the canyon.* **Precipitous** suggests an abrupt and very steep slope, like that of a cliff: *The climbers will attempt to scale the precipitous slope of the peak.*

steep[2] (stēp), *v.i.* to undergo soaking; soak: *Let tea leaves steep in boiling water for five minutes.* —*v.t.* **1.** to permit to steep; soak, especially in order to soften, cleanse, or extract an essence. **2.** to make thoroughly or frequently wet (with); saturate (in): *His sword was steeped in the blood of his enemies.* **3.** to immerse; imbue: *to steep oneself in knowledge of the Middle Ages.*
steep in, to fill with; permeate by: *ruins steeped in gloom, a mind steeped in hatred. The whole of modern thought is steeped in science* (Thomas H. Huxley).
—*n.* **1.** a soaking. **2.** the liquid in which something is soaked. **3.** *Obsolete.* a steeping vessel.
[Middle English *stepen,* perhaps unrecorded Old English *stēpan* (compare *stēap* bowl)]

steep-down (stēp′doun′), *adj.* having a sheer descent; precipitous: *Wash me in steep-down gulfs of liquid fire* (Shakespeare).

steep·en (stē′pən), *v.i.* to become steep or steeper. —*v.t.* to make steep or steeper.

steep·er (stē′pər), *n.* **1.** a person or thing that steeps or soaks. **2.** a vessel used in steeping.

steep·grass (stēp′gras′, -gräs′), *n.* the butterwort, often used like rennet in making cheese, etc.

steep·ish (stē′pish), *adj.* rather steep: *a bare valley . . . with steepish sides* (Theodore Roosevelt).

stee·ple (stē′pəl), *n.* **1.** a high tower on a church, temple, or other public building containing the bells, whether a simple tower or one topped by a spire, cupola, etc.: *spire steeples . . . point as with silent finger to the sky* (Samuel Taylor Coleridge). See **spire** for picture. **2.** such a tower together with the spire or other structure surmounting it. **3.** a spire on the top of the tower or roof of a church or similar building. [Old English *stēpel,* related to *stēap* steep[1]] —**stee′ple-like′,** *adj.*

stee·ple·bush (stē′pəl bu̇sh′), *n. U.S.* a shrub of the rose family; hardhack.

stee·ple·chase (stē′pəl chās′), *n., v.,* **-chased, -chas·ing.** —*n.* **1. a.** a horse race over a course having ditches, hedges, and other obstacles. **b.** a cross-country horse race in which the contestants hurdle such obstacles as fences, brooks, etc. **2.** a cross-country foot race. —*v.i.* to ride or run in a steeplechase. [because formerly it was a race with a church steeple in view as goal] —**stee′ple-chas′er,** *n.*

stee·ple-crowned (stē′pəl kround′), *adj.* having a tall, pointed crown, as a hat: *a man . . . wearing a steeple-crowned hat and a skull-cap beneath it* (Hawthorne).

steeple cup, a tall, ornamental cup, as of silver, having the cover surmounted by a steeplelike part.

stee·pled (stē′pəld) *adj.* having a steeple or steeples or abounding in steeples: *many a steepled town* (John Greenleaf Whittier).

steeple hat, a steeple-crowned hat: *An old doublet and a steeple hat . . .* (Robert Browning).

stee·ple·jack (stē′pəl jak′), *n.* a man specially trained or experienced in climbing steeples, towers, very high chimneys, etc., to make repairs, etc. —*v.i.* to do the work of a steeplejack: *[He] steeplejacked, punched cows in Texas, got married at 21* (Time).

steeple top, 1. the top of a steeple: *David would hang thee on thy steeple top* (Robert Southey). **2.** the Greenland whale (because its spout holes end in a sort of cone).

steep-to (stēp′tü′), *adj.* descending almost perpendicularly into water, as a shore or shoal bordering navigable water; abruptly steep.

steep·wa·ter (stēp′wôt′ər, -wot′-), *n.* the water in which a thing is soaked or macerated: *A recent derivative of [corn] steepwater is a medically important chemical, inositol* (Science News Letter).

steep·y (stē′pē), *adj. Archaic.* steep: *the steepy hill* (Scott).

steer[1] (stir), *v.t.* **1.** to guide the course of: *to steer a sled, steer an automobile, steer an airplane. And all I ask is a tall ship and a star to steer her by* (John Masefield). **2.** to guide; lead; conduct; pilot: *to steer a person through a crowd, steer a horse to victory.* **3.** to set and follow (a certain course): *You must steer a middle course* (William Hazlitt). *He was bravely steering his way across the continent* (Washington Irving). **4.** to direct or guide the course of (something immaterial): *to steer one's plans toward success.* —*v.i.* **1.** to guide the course of a ship, automobile, bicycle, etc.: *The sail collapsed; the pilot steered for the bank* (Amelia B. Edwards). **2.** to admit of being steered; be guided: *This car steers easily.* **3.** to direct one's way or course: *to steer away from flattery. He steered along the street by her side* (Elizabeth Gaskell).
steer clear of, to keep well away from; avoid: *We would have steered clear of them, and cared not to have them see us, if we could help it* (Daniel Defoe).
—*n. U.S. Slang.* an idea or a suggested course of action; tip.
[Old English *stēran*] —**steer′er,** *n.*

steer[2] (stir), *n.* **1.** a young ox, usually two to four years old. **2.** any male of beef cattle. [Old English *stēor*]

steer[3] (stir), *v.t., v.i., n. Dialect* stir.

steer·a·bil·i·ty (stir′ə bil′ə tē), *n.* the quality of being steerable: *Winter sliding toy for children combines the thrill of a toboggan with the steerability of a sled* (Science News Letter).

steer·a·ble (stir′ə bəl), *adj.* that can be steered: *The world's largest steerable telescope is under construction in West Virginia* (Scientific American).

steer·age (stir′ij), *n.* **1.** the part of a passenger ship occupied, especially during the 1800's and early 1900's, by passengers traveling at the cheapest rate, superseded on most lines originally by third class and now by tourist class. **2. a.** the act or process of steering a boat or ship. **b.** the manner in which a ship is affected by the helm. **3.** direction; guidance: *the steerage of a country through war.*

steer·age·way (stir′ij wā′), *n.* the amount of forward motion a ship must have before it can be steered; speed below which a vessel will not answer the helm: *it fell dead calm, the vessel lost her steerageway* (Richard H. Dana).

steer·hide (stir′hīd′), *n.* **1.** the hide of a steer. **2.** leather made from it.

steer·ing column (stir′ing), the cylindrical shaft connecting the steering gear of an automobile with the steering wheel: *To eliminate the hazards of the steering column, Vacante has invented a gear that includes two wheels but no post* (New York Times).

steering committee, *U.S.* (in a law-making or other body) a committee responsible for deciding which items shall be considered and in what order.

steering gear, 1. a. the mechanism by which the front wheels of an automobile are turned to right or left. **b.** the mechanism by which the rudder of a ship is turned to port or starboard. **2.** any apparatus for steering: *the steering gear of a bicycle.*

steering wheel, the wheel by which the steering gear of an automobile, ship, etc., is controlled.

steer·less (stir′lis), *adj.* having no rudder. [Old English *steōrleās* < *steōr* rudder + *-leās* -less]

steers·man (stirz′mən), *n., pl.* **-men.** a person who steers a ship: *By and by . . . nearly every pilot on the river had a steersman* (Mark Twain). —**Syn.** helmsman.

steers·man·ship (stirz′mən ship), *n.* the office or art of a steersman; skill in steering.

steeve[1] (stēv), *n., v.,* **steeved, steev·ing.** —*n.* a long derrick or spar with a block at one end, used in stowing cargo. —*v.t.* to stow (cargo) in the hold or on the deck of a ship: *Each morning we . . . brought off as many hides as we could steeve in the course of the day* (Richard H. Dana). [< Old French *estiver* or Italian *stivare* < Latin *stīpāre* to press, crowd; pack in. Compare STEVEDORE.]

steeve[2] (stēv), *v.,* **steeved, steev·ing,** *n.* —*v.i.* (of a bowsprit) to extend upward at an angle rather than horizontally with the keel. —*v.t.* to set (a bowsprit, etc.) at an angle upward. —*n.* the angle upward of a bowsprit. [origin uncertain]

steev·ing (stē′ving), *n.* steeve[2].

steg·o·ce·pha·li·an (steg′ə sə fā′lē ən), *adj.* of or having to do with a group of extinct tailless amphibians whose skulls were protected by bony plates. [< New Latin *Stegocephalia* the name of the order (< Greek *stégos* roof + *kephalē̂* head)]

steg·o·don (steg′ə don), *n., pl.* **-dons** or (*collectively*) **-don.** any of a group of very large extinct mammals with ridged teeth, related to the elephants and mastodons: *There were bones of deer, boar, tapir, stegodon and rhinoceros, animals known to have lived in China in the Middle Pleistocene Age, some 400,000 to 600,000 years ago* (Science News Letter). [< New Latin *Stegodon* the genus name < Greek *stégos* roof + *odoús, odóntos* tooth (because their teeth are ridged)]

steg·o·my·ia (steg′ə mī′ə), *n.* the former name of any of various mosquitoes that transmit yellow fever. [< New Latin *Stegomyia* a former genus name < Greek *stégos* house, roof < *myîa* fly]

steg·o·saur (steg′ə sôr), *n.* a stegosaurus: *Stegosaurs, the first of the armored dinosaurs, were protected by triangular bony plates standing up along their backs* (World Book Encyclopedia).

steg·o·sau·rus (steg′ə sôr′əs), *n., pl.* **-sau·ri** (-sôr′ī). an extinct, plant-eating reptile of great size (sometimes nearly 40 feet long), with heavy, bony armor. [< New Latin *Stegosaurus* the genus name < Greek *stégos* house, roof + *saûros* lizard]

stein (stīn), *n.* **1.** a mug for beer, usually of earthenware or glass, holding about a pint. **2.** the amount of beer a stein holds. [< German *Stein* stone, short for *Steinkrug* stone jug]

stein·bock or **stein·bok** (stīn′bok′), *n.* **1.** ibex. **2.** steenbok. [< German *Steinbock* < *Stein* stone + *Bock* buck[1]]

stein·buck (stīn′buk′), *n.* steenbok.

Stein·heim man (stīn′hīm′), an early type of pre-Neanderthal man similar to Homo sapiens, identified from the skull bones found at Steinheim am Murr in Germany.

ste·le (stē′lē), *n., pl.* **-lae** (-lē), **-les. 1.** an upright slab or pillar of stone bearing an inscription, sculptured design, or the like. **2.** a prepared surface on the face of a building, a rock, etc., bearing an inscription or the like. **3.** (in ancient Greece and Rome) an upright slab or pillar of stone used to mark a grave. **4.** *Botany.* the central cylinder of conducting (vascular) tissue in the stems and roots of plants. It includes, typically, those tissues within the endodermis, as the pericycle, xylem, phloem, and pith. [< Greek *stē̂lē* slab, pillar]

stel·lar (stel′ər), *adj.* **1.** of or having to do with the stars or a star; like a star: *stellar magnitudes.* **2.** chief; principal: *to play the stellar role in a government.* **3.** of or having to do with a theatrical star: *a stellar part in a play.* [< Latin *stellāris* < *stēlla* star] —**Syn. 1.** astral, sidereal.

stel·la·ra·tor (stel′ə rā′tər), *n.* a device consisting of a series of circular tubes in which highly ionized gas is heated to extremely high temperatures and confined in a powerful magnetic field, used in the study of thermonuclear energy and reactions.

stellar interferometer, an interferometer attached to a telescope for the measurement of the diameters of stars.

stel·late (stel′āt, -it), *adj.* spreading out like the points of a star; star-shaped. [< Latin *stellātus,* past participle of *stellāre* to set or cover with stars < *stēlla* star] —**stel′late·ly,** *adv.*

stel·lat·ed (stel′ā tid), *adj.* stellate.

Stel·ler's jay (stel′ərz), a large, crested jay of western North America with blackish head and foreparts and blue wings, tail and belly: *Lastly, down with a swoop came a Steller's jay out of a fir-tree, probably with the intention of moistening his noisy throat* (John Muir). [< Georg Wilhelm *Steller,* 1709-1745, a German naturalist]

Steller's sea cow, a large, toothless sea mammal similar and related to the manatee, weighing up to four tons. It formerly lived about the Bering Islands, but became extinct in the 1760's.

Steller's sea eagle, a large gray sea eagle of the northern Pacific coast of Asia, with white tail and shoulders.

Steller's sea lion, a large sea lion of the Pacific coast of North America; northern sea lion.

stel·lif·er·ous (ste lif′ər əs), *adj.* abounding with stars. [< Latin *stellifer* (< *stēlla* star + *ferre* to bear) + English *-ous*]

stel·li·form (stel′ə fôrm), *adj.* star-shaped. [< New Latin *stelliformis* < Latin *stēlla* star + *-formis* -form]

stel·li·fy (stel′ə fī), *v.t.,* **-fied, -fy·ing.** to turn into or cause to resemble a star; convert into a constellation; make glorious; glorify.

stel·lion (stel′yən), *n.* any of a group of Old World lizards with the scales of the tail arranged in whorls. [< Latin *stēlliō, -ōnis* < *stēlla* star]

stel·lion·ate (stel′yə nāt, -nit), *n.* (in civil or Scottish law) any fraud not distinguished by a special name and not defined by any written law, especially the sale of the same property to two or more different buyers. [< Late Latin *stēlliōnātus* trickery < *stēlliō, -ōnis* knave; (literally) newt, lizard]

Stel·lite (stel′īt), *n. Trademark.* a very hard alloy consisting chiefly of cobalt, chromium, and tungsten, that resists corrosion and rust, and retains a cutting edge well, used for making metalworking tools, cutlery, and surgical instruments.

stel·lu·lar (stel′yə lər), *adj.* having the form of a small star or small stars. [< Late Latin *stellula* (diminutive) < Latin *stēlla* star + English *-ar*]

St. El·mo's fire or **light** (el′mōz), the ball of light due to a discharge of atmospheric electricity, often seen on masts, towers, etc.; corposant.

stem[1] (stem), *n., v.,* **stemmed, stem·ming.** —*n.* **1. a.** the main part (usually more or less cylindrical) of a tree, shrub, or other plant that is above the ground; trunk; stalk: *The tree's stem supports the branches.* **b.** the ascending axis (whether above or below ground) of a plant, bearing the remaining aerial parts of the plant (distinguished from the root or descending axis). **2.** the stalk supporting a flower, leaf, or fruit: **a.** the peduncle of the fructification. **b.** the pedicel of a flower. **c.** the petiole or stalk of a leaf. **3.** a bunch of bananas. **4.** anything like or suggesting the stem of a plant or of a flower, etc., as: **a.** the tube of a tobacco pipe. **b.** the upright, cylindrical support of a goblet, wineglass, etc. **c.** the shaft connecting the mechanism of a watch to the knob by which the watch is wound. **d.** the cylindrical rod in certain locks, about which the key fits and turns. **e.** (in printing) the upright stroke of a letter. **f.** *Music.* the vertical line forming part of any note smaller than a whole note. **5. a.** the line of descent of a family. **b.** ancestry; pedigree. **6.** *Grammar.* the part of a word to which inflectional endings are added and in which inflectional changes occur. *Run* is the stem of *running, runner, ran,* etc. **7.** the upright at the bow of a ship between the keel and the bowsprit, to which the side planking or plates are joined. **8.** the bow or front end of a ship; prow.

from stem to stern, a. from one end of a ship to the other: *The sea ran high, and swept the little craft from stem to stern* (Charles J. Lever). **b.** along the whole length of anything: *They searched the train from stem to stern, looking for the missing suitcase.*

—*v.t* **1.** to remove the stalk from (a leaf, fruit, etc.). **2.** to provide with a stem.

—*v.i.* **1.** to grow out; develop: *Newspapers stemmed from the invention of the printing press.* **2.** to originate or spring (from).

[Old English *stefn, stemn*] —**stem′like′,** *adj.*

stem[2] (stem), *v.,* **stemmed, stem·ming,** *n.* —*v.t.* **1.** to dam up (a stream, etc.). **2.** to stop or check by or as if by damming up: *It was the Spanish power indisputably which stemmed the Reformation* (James A. Froude). **3.** to plug or tamp (a hole for blasting); make tight (a joint). **4.** *Scottish.* to stop or stanch (bleeding). **5.** (in skiing) to turn (one or both skis) so that the tips converge. —*v.i.* (in skiing) to slow down or stop by turning the back of one or both skis outward so that the tips converge.

—*n.* (in skiing) a maneuver involving stemming with one ski (single stem) or both skis (double stem).

[perhaps < Scandinavian (compare Old Icelandic *stemma*)]

—**Syn.** *v.t.* **2.** hinder, restrain.

stem[3] (stem), *v.t.,* **stemmed, stem·ming. 1.** (of a ship, boat, etc.) to make headway against: *When you swim upstream you have to stem the current.* **2.** to make progress against (opposition of any kind); go counter to. [Middle English *stemmen* to head, or urge, the stem toward < *stem*[1]] —**Syn. 2.** breast.

stem borer, an insect whose larva bores in the stems of plants: *The worst insect enemy of rice is the stem borer, which . . . can reduce the yield of a stand of rice by a couple of thousand pounds an acre* (New Yorker).

stem cell, an embryonic or primitive cell that gives rise to specialized cells: *It is believed that under normal conditions the white blood cells are the mature functional descendants of ancestral . . . stem cells, located in the bone marrow, lymph nodes, spleen, and other parts of the reticuloendothelial system* (New Scientist).

stem eelworm, a minute nematoid which causes stem sickness in certain plants, as clover.

stem-end rot (stem′end′), **1.** a fungus disease infecting the end of the stem of watermelons and other fruit after harvesting. **2.** the fungus causing this disease.

stem leaf, a leaf growing from the stem; a cauline leaf.

stem·less (stem′lis), *adj.* having no stem; having no visible stem.

stem·let (stem′lit), *n.* a little stem.

stemmed (stemd), *adj.* **1.** having or bearing a stem or stems (used chiefly in composition). **2.** having the stem removed, as tobacco leaves.

stem·mer (stem′ər), *n.* a person or thing that removes stems, as from tobacco leaves or grapes.

stem·mer·y (stem′ər ē), *n., pl.* **-er·ies.** a factory where tobacco is stripped from the stem.

stem mother, a female plant louse which, being hatched in the spring from a winter egg, is the foundress of a summer colony of aphids.

stem·ple (stem′pəl), *n.* a small timber driven into the wall or placed crosswise in a mine, to prevent caving, to serve as a support for a platform or as a step, or for other purposes. [compare Dutch *stempel* mark, stamp]

stem rot, 1. a fungus disease attacking the stem of the tomato, banana, sweet potato, and other plants, causing it to wilt. **2.** the fungus causing this disease.

stem rust, 1. a fungus disease attacking the head and stem of wheat, barley, and other grains, robbing the plant of its nutriments and water, and leaving small rust-colored spots on the stem. **2.** the fungus causing this disease.

stem sickness, a disease of clover caused by the stem eelworm, that brings about first a stunted condition and finally the death of the plant.

stem·son (stem′sən), *n.* a curved timber in the bow of a ship extending from the keelson to the stem. [< *stem*[1]; patterned on *keelson*]

stem stitch, a stitch in making bobbin lace

that produces a thick, braidlike stripe for the stems of flowers and sprigs, tendrils, etc.

stem turn, (in skiing) a method of turning in which a skier stems the ski opposite the direction of turn and applies his weight to it.

stem·ware (stem′wãr′), *n.* glasses or goblets with stems, used for wine, alcoholic liquor, liqueur, etc.: *There's true splendor to this beautiful stemware* (New Yorker).

stem·wind·er (stem′wīn′dər), *n.* **1.** *Informal.* a watch with a stem and knob for winding. **2.** *Dialect.* a first-rate person or thing.

stem·wind·ing (stem′wīn′ding), *adj.* (of a watch) wound by turning a knob on the stem.

stench (stench), *n.* a very bad smell; foul odor; stink: *the stench of burning rubber, the stench of gas. A narrow winding street, full of offence and stench* (Dickens). [Middle English *stenche,* Old English *stenc* odor (pleasant or not), related to *stincan* smell] —**Syn.** fetor.

stench bomb, a stink bomb.

stench·ful (stench′fəl), *adj.* full of bad smells; stinking.

stench·y (sten′chē), *adj.* having a stench or offensive smell.

sten·cil (sten′səl), *n., v.,* **-ciled, -cil·ing** or (*especially British*) **-cilled, -cil·ling.** —*n.* **1.** a thin sheet of metal, paper, cardboard, etc., having letters or designs cut through it. When it is laid on a surface and ink or color is spread on, these letters or designs appear on the surface: *to mark packages with a stencil.* **2.** the letters or designs so made.

HANDLE WITH CARE

Stencil (def. 2)

—*v.t.* **1.** to mark or paint (a surface) with a stencil: *The curtains have a stenciled border.* **2.** to produce (letters or designs) by means of a stencil.

[earlier *stanesile* < Old French *estenceler,* ultimately < Latin *scintilla* spark. Doublet of SCINTILLA, TINSEL.] —**sten′cil·er,** *especially British,* **sten′cil·ler,** *n.*

sten·cil·i·za·tion (sten′sə lə zā′shən), *n.* a stenciling or being stenciled.

sten·cil·ize (sten′sə līz), *v.t.,* **-ized, -iz·ing.** to stencil.

Sten·dhal·i·an (stäɴ dál′ē ən), *adj.* of, having to do with, or in the style of Stendhal (Marie Henri Beyle), 1783-1842, French novelist and critic.

sten·gah (steng′gə), *n.* (in the Malay Peninsula) a small whiskey and soda. [< Malay *stengah* half]

Sten gun (sten), a light machine gun of simple design, weighing 8 pounds or less and able to be fired at the rate of 550 rounds per minute either from the hip or mounted. It was a standard weapon of the British and other Commonwealth forces in World War II. [< *S*(heppard) and *T*(urner), *En*(glish) inventors of the 1900's]

sten·o (sten′ō), *n., pl.* **sten·os.** *U.S. Slang.* a stenographer: *My girl friend who got me in there was steno to the boss* (Saturday Evening Post). [< *steno*(grapher)]

steno-, *combining form.* narrow; small: *Stenocephalic = narrow-headed. Stenopetalous = having narrow petals.* [< Greek *stenós*]

sten·o·bath·ic (sten′ə bath′ik), *adj.* having a narrow range of depth, said of animals living in the water between definite limits of depth. [< *steno-* + Greek *báthos* depth + English *-ic*]

sten·o·ce·phal·ic (sten′ə sə fal′ik), *adj.* narrow-headed. [< *steno-* + Greek *kephalḗ* head + English *-ic*]

sten·o·chro·mat·ic (sten′ə krə mat′ik), *adj.* of or having to do with stenochromy.

sten·o·chro·my (sten′ə krō′mē), *n.* the art or process of printing in several colors at one impression. [< *steno-* + Greek *chrôma* color + English *-y*[3]]

ste·nog (stə nog′), *n. Slang.* a stenographer.

sten·o·graph (sten′ə graf, -gräf), *n.* **1.** a writing in shorthand. **2.** any of various keyboard machines, somewhat resembling a typewriter, used for writing in shorthand. —*v.t., v.i.* to write in shorthand. [back formation < *stenographer*]

ste·nog·ra·pher (stə nog′rə fər), *n.* a person who makes or is able to make a record in shorthand of words as they are spoken and subsequently reproduce them, especially by means of the typewriter; one whose work is stenography.

sten·o·graph·ic (sten′ə graf′ik), *adj.* **1.** of or having to do with stenography; written or produced by stenography. **2.** (of style) concise. —**sten′o·graph′i·cal·ly,** *adv.*

sten·o·graph·i·cal (sten′ə graf′ə kəl), *adj.* stenographic.

stenographic machine, a machine for writing in shorthand; stenograph.

ste·nog·ra·phist (stə nog′rə fist), *n.* a stenographer.

ste·nog·ra·phy (stə nog′rə fē), *n.* **1.** shorthand and typing, as the primary skills of the modern stenographer: *to study stenography.* **2.** shorthand: *I bought an approved scheme of the noble art and mystery of stenography . . . and plunged into a sea of perplexity* (Dickens). [< *steno-* + *-graphy*]

sten·o·morph (sten′ə môrf), *n.* a plant that is unusually small due to a cramped habitat, as from crowding by other plants. [< *steno-* + Greek *morphḗ* form]

sten·o·pae·ic (sten′ə pē′ik), *adj.* stenopaic.

sten·o·pa·ic (sten′ə pā′ik), *adj. Optics.* having to do with, characterized by, or of the nature of a small or narrow opening. [< *steno-* + Greek *opḗ* an opening + English *-ic*]

stenopaic slit, a narrow slit in an opaque plate, placed before an eye in testing its astigmatism.

stenopaic spectacles, spectacles in which each lens is covered by an opaque plate with a small central aperture.

sten·o·pet·al·ous (sten′ə pet′ə ləs), *adj.* having narrow petals. [< *steno-* + *petal* + *-ous*]

sten·o·phyl·lous (sten′ə fil′əs), *adj.* having narrow leaves. [< *steno-* + Greek *phýllon* leaf + English *-ous*]

sten·o·rhyn·chous (sten′ə ring′kəs), *adj.* having a narrow beak or bill. [< *steno-* + *rhýnchos* snout + English *-ous*]

ste·nosed (sti nōst′, sten′ōzd), *adj.* affected with stenosis; abnormally narrowed or constricted: *Early in 1948, Dr. Horace G. Smithy, Jr., of South Carolina successfully reopened a patient's stenosed mitral valve* (Harper's). [< *stenos*(is) + *-ed*[2]]

ste·no·sis (sti nō′sis), *n. Medicine.* the contraction or stricture of a passage, duct, or canal. [< New Latin *stenosis* < Greek *sténōsis* a narrowing < *stenoûn* to narrow < *stenós* narrow]

sten·o·ther·mal (sten′ə thėr′məl), *adj. Biology.* incapable of enduring a great range of temperature; not found in places having a broad range of temperatures.

ste·not·ic (sti not′ik), *adj.* having to do with or characterized by stenosis: *a stenotic condition, valve, or duct.*

sten·o·trop·ic (sten′ə trop′ik), *n.* of a plant or animal, having narrow limits of adaptation to changes in environment. [< Greek *stenós* narrow + *tropḗ* a turning + English *-ic*]

sten·o·type (sten′ə tīp), *n.* a letter or group of letters used for a sound, word, or phrase in stenotypy.

Sten·o·type (sten′ə tīp), *n. Trademark.* a kind of small typewriter, used in stenotypy.

sten·o·typ·ist (sten′ə tī′pist), *n.* a person who is skilled in stenotypy, especially one whose work is to write in stenotypy or on a Stenotype.

sten·o·typ·y (sten′ə tī′pē, stə not′ə-), *n.* **1.** a form of shorthand that uses ordinary letters. **2.** the use of a Stenotype machine to record speeches, etc.

stent (stent), *v.t., v.i., n.* stint[1].

Sten·tor (sten′tôr), *n. Greek Legend.* a Greek herald in the Trojan War, whose voice (as described in the *Iliad*) was as loud as the voices of fifty men.

sten·tor[1] (sten′tôr), *n.* a man of powerful voice. [< *Stentor*]

sten·tor[2] (sten′tôr), *n.* one of a group of trumpet-shaped protozoans that are among the largest of all single-celled animals. [< New Latin *Stentor* the genus name < Greek *Sténtōr* Stentor (because it is shaped like a speaking trumpet)]

sten·to·ri·an (sten tôr′ē ən, -tōr′-), *adj.* very loud or powerful in sound: *The stentorian voice . . . rang through the valley* (James Fenimore Cooper). —**sten·to′ri·an·ly,** *adv.* —**Syn.** sonorous, thundering.

sten·to·ri·ous (sten tôr′ē əs, -tōr′-), *adj.* stentorian. —**sten·to′ri·ous·ly,** *adv.*

step (step), *n., v.,* **stepped** or (*Poetic*) **stept, step·ping.** —*n.* **1.** a movement made by lifting the foot and putting it down again in a new position; one motion of the leg in walking, running, dancing, etc.: *to make a long step to the side, walk with short steps, a polka step, a gliding step, a dance with fancy steps.* **2.** the distance covered by one such movement: *She was three steps away when he called her back.* **3.** a short distance; little way: *The school is only a step away.* **4.** a way of walking, dancing, running, etc.; gait; stride: *a brisk step. Light of step and heart was she* (Walter de la Mare). **5. a.** a pace uniform with that of another or others or in time with music: *to keep step.* **b.** a particular marching pace: *a quick step.* **6.** a place for the foot in going up or coming down. A stair or a rung of a ladder is a step. **7.** the sound made by putting the foot down; footstep: *to hear a heavy step on the stairs.* **8.** a footprint: *to see steps in the mud.* **9.** an action: *the first step toward peace.* **10.** a degree in a scale; a grade in rank; stage: *A colonel is three steps above a captain.* **11.** *Music.* **a.** a degree of the staff or scale. **b.** the interval between two adjoining degrees of the scale, called a *half step* (semitone) or a *whole step* (two semitones). **c.** (popularly) a whole step. **12.** an offset, or part of a machine, fitting, etc., resembling a step in outline. **13.** a frame or hole in which the lower end or heel of a mast is set to support it: *the step of a mast.*

change step, to fall into marching step more correctly: *One of the marchers quickly changed step to keep in time with the music.*

in step, a. at a uniform pace with others or in time with music: *She had difficulty keeping in step with the rest of the marchers.* **b.** in harmony or agreement: *The new price increase is in step with the rising costs of production.*

out of step, a. not keeping pace with others or in time with music: *That boy was out of step during most of the parade.* **b.** not in harmony or accord: *People who live solitary lives are often out of step with the times.*

pick one's steps, to move with great care and caution over treacherous ground, a difficult situation, etc.: *The dashing stream stays not to pick his steps among the rocks* (Arthur H. Clough).

step by step, little by little; slowly: . . . *the revolution which human nature desires to effect step by step in many ages* (Benjamin Jowett). *Step by step Wykeham rose to the highest dignities* (George W. Thornbury).

steps, a. a path, route, etc., traversed; course: *to retrace one's steps.* **b.** a stepladder: *Steps, nails, and hammer were quickly at the disposal of the stranger* (F.W. Robinson).

take steps, to adopt, put into effect, or carry out measures considered to be necessary, desirable, etc.: *Steps have already been taken to deal with the emergency.*

watch one's step, to be careful: *The . . . chairman warned that "Congress should watch its step" in trying to regulate economic pressures* (Wall Street Journal).

[Old English *steppa*]

—*v.i.* **1.** to move the legs as in walking, running, dancing, etc.: *to step to the side. Step lively!* **2.** to walk a short distance: *to step across the road, step this way.* **3.** to put the foot down; tread (on, upon): *to step on a worm, step on the accelerator.* **4.** *Informal.* to go fast; move quickly. —*v.t.* **1. a.** to measure (off) by taking steps; pace (off): *Step off the distance from the door to the window.* **b.** to mark (off) with dividers, compasses, etc. **2.** to make or arrange like a flight of steps. **3. a.** to set (a mast); fix or place in a support. **b.** to fit (a deck, rail, etc.) in position on a ship. **4.** to move (the foot) forward in walking, etc.: *to step foot into a room.* **5.** to go through the steps of (a dance); perform: *He stepped a minuet gravely and gracefully.*

step aside, a. to move away a small distance; retire a few steps: *Please step aside to make room for the luggage.* **b.** to withdraw: *Recently he stepped aside from his diplomatic role to speak to a New York audience out of his own Buddhist faith* (Maclean's).

step back, a. to move a little distance to the rear; go backward: *The favorite of the Princess, looking into the cavity, stepped back and trembled* (Samuel Johnson). **b.** to withdraw; retire: *Bobby [Kennedy] stepped back before the overriding claims of Jack's fight for the White House* (Maclean's).

step down, a. to come down: *In robe and crown the king stept down* (Tennyson). **b.** to surrender or resign from an office, position of precedence, etc.: *Last week Editor Hutchinson, 65, announced that he was stepping down to devote all his time to writing* (Time). **c.** to decrease: *Congress voted to step down government spending.*

step in, to come in; intervene; take part: *But where the Federal government must step in, it will* (Newsweek).

step into, to come into, acquire, or receive, especially without particular effort or through the action of fate: *to step into a fortune.*

step on it, *Slang.* to go faster; hurry up: *If you want to catch the train, you'd better step on it.*

step out, *U.S. Slang.* **a.** to go out for entertainment: *We're celebrating by stepping out tonight.* **b.** to withdraw; retire: *He intended to remain as president of the World's Fair. "There is no possibility at all of getting me to step out" [he said]* (New York Times).

step up, a. to go up; ascend: *The instructor stepped up onto the stage to deliver his lecture.* **b.** to increase: *My salary was stepped up last week.* **c.** to increase or raise as if by steps or degrees: *to step up production, demand, spending, etc.* **d.** *Informal.* to come forward (used by a carnival barker): *Step right up, ladies and gentlemen!* [Old English *steppan*]
—**Syn.** *n.* **9.** measure, proceeding.

step-, *prefix.* related by the remarriage of a parent, not by blood, as in *stepmother, stepsister, stepniece.* [Old English *stēop-*, probably meaning "bereaved, orphaned"]

step·broth·er (step′bruᴛʜ′ər), *n.* a stepfather's or stepmother's son by a former marriage: *If John's father marries a widow with a little boy, this boy will be John's stepbrother.*

step·child (step′chīld′), *n., pl.* **-chil·dren.** a child of one's husband or wife by a former marriage; stepson or stepdaughter.

step cut, an ornamental design in gem cutting with long, steplike facets cut into the top and back of the stone. This cut intensifies or darkens the stone's color, and therefore is used especially for the emerald, ruby, etc.; trap cut.

step·dame (step′dām′), *n. Archaic.* a stepmother.

step dance, a dance marked by originality, variety, or difficulty in the steps; a dance in which the steps are more important than the figure.

step·daugh·ter (step′dô′tər), *n.* a daughter of one's husband or wife by a former marriage.

step-down (step′doun′), *adj.* **1.** serving or causing to decrease gradually. **2.** *Electricity.* lowering the voltage of a current, as by means of a transformer.

step·fa·ther (step′fä′ᴛʜər), *n.* a man who has married one's mother after the death or divorce of one's real father.

step fault, 1. one of a series of small, nearly parallel faults by which strata have been dislocated so as to occupy a position resembling a series of steps or stairs. **2.** the compound fault comprising such a series.

steph·a·ne (stef′ə nē), *n. Greek Antiquity.* a bandlike headdress or coronal widest at the front and narrowing toward the sides, often seen on representations of the goddess Hera. [< Greek *stephánē* < *stéphein* put round]

Stephane on Hera

steph·an·ite (stef′ə nīt), *n. Mineralogy.* a soft, brittle, black mineral with a metallic luster, an ore of silver. *Formula:* Ag_5SbS_4 [< German *Stephanit*]

steph·a·nos (stef′ə nos), *n. pl.* **-noi** (-noi). *Greek Antiquity.* **1.** a wreath or crown serving as a prize, a mark of honor, etc. **2.** a coronal like the stephane but of the same width all around. [< Greek *stéphanos* crown]

steph·a·no·tis (stef′ə nō′tis), *n.* any of a group of tropical twining shrubs of the milkweed family, as a variety often grown in greenhouses for its fragrant, waxy, white or cream-colored flowers. [< New Latin *Stephanotis* the genus name < Greek *stephanōtis* fit for a crown < *stéphanos* crown]

Ste·phen (stē′vən), *n.* **Saint,** the first Christian martyr. Acts 6 and 7.

step-in (step′in′), *adj.* (of garments, shoes, slippers, etc.) put on by being stepped into.

step-ins (step′inz′), *n.pl.* a garment, especially a woman's undergarment with short legs, that one may put on by stepping into it and pulling it up over the body.

step·lad·der (step′lad′ər), *n.* a ladder with flat steps instead of rungs, usually four-legged and often hinged at the top.

step·less (step′lis), *adj.* having no step or steps: *You might as well climb the stepless air . . . as overtake my Sylvia* (George Darley).

step·like (step′līk′), *adj.* resembling a step or series of steps.

step·moth·er (step′muᴛʜ′ər), *n.* a woman who has married one's father after the death or divorce of one's real mother.

step·moth·er·ly (step′muᴛʜ′ər lē), *adj.* **1.** having to do with or suitable to a stepmother. **2.** harsh or neglectful.

step-out (step′out′), *n.* **1.** a stepping or getting outside: *In preparation for his step-out into space, White spent sixty hours in vacuum chambers* (Time). **2.** a step-out well.

step-out well, a well dug near another that has been proven to yield oil, gas, etc., as for confirmation of the area's productivity.

step·par·ent (step′pãr′ənt), *n.* a stepfather or stepmother.

steppe (step), *n.* **1.** one of the vast, level, treeless plains in southeastern Europe and Siberia, especially that in southwestern Soviet Union in Asia, north of the Caspian and Aral seas. **2.** any vast, treeless plain. [< Russian *step′*] —**Syn. 2.** savanna, prairie.

stepped (stept), *adj.* having a step or steps; formed in a series of steps: *a stepped pyramid.*

stepped-up (stept′up′), *adj.* increased in size, speed, or extent.

steppe·land (step′land′, -lənd), *n.* any vast treeless plain; steppe.

step·per (step′ər), *n.* a person or animal that steps, especially in a certain way: *a high stepper, a fast stepper.*

step·ping stone (step′ing), **1.** a stone or one of a line of stones in shallow water, a marshy place, or the like, used in crossing. **2.** a stone for use in mounting or ascending. **3.** anything serving as a means of advancing or rising: *I held it truth . . . That men may rise on stepping stones Of their dead selves to higher things* (Tennyson).

step rocket, a multistage rocket.

steps (steps), *n.pl.* See under **step,** *n*

step·sis·ter (step′sis′tər), *n.* one's stepfather's or stepmother's daughter by a former marriage.

step·son (step′sun′), *n.* a son of one's husband or wife by a former marriage.

stept (stept), *v. Poetic.* a past tense and a past participle of **step.**

step·toe (step′tō′), *n. Northwestern U.S.* a hill or mountain surrounded and isolated by a large flow or plain of lava.

step turn, (in skiing) a method of turning in which a skier lifts and turns first the inner ski and then the outer one until the turn is complete.

step-up (step′up′), *adj.* **1.** serving or causing to increase gradually. **2.** *Electricity.* increasing the voltage of a current, as by means of a transformer. —*n.* an increase: *The chief of the Public Health Service said "we can expect to see a gradual step-up in the production and release of vaccine"* (New York Times).

step·way (step′wā′), *n.* a way or passage formed by steps.

step·wise (step′wīz′), *adv.* in the manner of steps; by steps: *Another suggestion, adopted immediately, was to proceed stepwise, starting with a provisional organization devoted to planning and the elaboration of a six or seven years' budget* (Bulletin of Atomic Scientists). —*adj.* occurring step by step; gradual: . . . *the stepwise activation of particular components of the genetic code* (New Scientist).

-ster, *suffix.* **1.** a person who ——s, as in *fibster.*
2. a person who makes or handles ——, as in *maltster, punster, tapster, rhymester.*
3. a person who is ——, as in *youngster, oldster.* **4.** special meanings, as in *gangster, roadster, teamster.*
[Middle English *-estre,* a feminine agent suffix, Old English *-istre, -estre* a feminine suffix]

ster., sterling.

ste·ra·di·an (sti rā′dē ən), *n. Geometry.* a unit of measurement of solid angles. It is the solid angle subtended at the center by the part of a sphere equal to the square of its radius. [< Greek *stereós* solid + English *radian*]

ster·co·ra·ceous (stėr′kə rā′shəs), *adj.,* **1.** of, like, or having to do with dung or feces. **2.** frequenting or feeding on dung, as certain beetles, flies, etc. [< Latin *stercorāceus* (with English *-ous*) < *stercus, -oris* dung]

Ster·co·ra·nism (stėr′kər ə niz′əm), *n.* the doctrine or belief of the Stercoranists.

Ster·co·ra·nist (stėr′kər ə nist), *n.* a person who believes that consecrated elements of the Eucharist are digested just as ordinary food is. [< Medieval Latin *Stercoranistae,* plural < Latin *stercus, -oris* dung]

ster·co·rar·y (stėr′kə rer′ē), *adj., n., pl.* **-rar·ies.** —*adj.* stercoraceous. —*n.* a place for putting or storing dung or manure. [< Latin *stercorārius* < *stercus, -oris* dung]

ster·co·ric·o·lous (stėr′kə rik′ə ləs), *adj.* living in dung or feces. [< Latin *stercus, -oris* dung + *colere* inhabit + English *-ous*]

ster·co·rous (stėr′kər əs), *adj.* stercoraceous.

ster·cu·li·a·ceous (stər kyü′lē ā′shəs), *adj.* belonging to the sterculia family of plants. [< New Latin *Sterculiaceae* the order name < *Sterculia* the typical genus < Latin *stercus, -oris* dung (from the fetid odor of some species)]

ster·cu·li·a family (stər kyü′lē ə), a group of dicotyledonous, chiefly tropical, trees, shrubs and herbs, including the bottle tree, cacao, kola nut, and flame-tree.

stere (stir), *n.* a unit of measure, used especially for firewood, equal to one cubic meter. [< French *stère* < Greek *stereós* solid]

ster·e·o[1] (ster′ē ō, stir′-), *n.* **1.** stereophonic sound reproduction. **2.** the system or apparatus reproducing stereophonic sound: *And so, each Friday night, I flip on Swan Lake and Bolero on the stereo* (Harper's). —*adj.* stereophonic: *Monteux' "Pathetique" was recorded on location in Boston's Symphony Hall on a dual-track stereo tape, then transferred to a dual-track stereo disc* (New York Journal American).

ster·e·o[2] (ster′ē ō, stir′-), *n.* **1.** a stereo camera or a print made with it. **2.** stereophotography: *Stereo, or third dimension photography, has been tested and proved in the laboratories and plants of American science and industry* (Scientific American). —*adj.* stereoscopic: *a stereo image, picture, or viewer.*

stereo-, *combining form.* **1.** hard, firm, or solid: *Stereobate = a solid mass of masonry.* **2.** three-dimensional: *Stereoscopic = seen as three-dimensional.* [< Greek *stereós* solid]

stereo., stereotype.

ster·e·o·bate (ster′ē ə bāt, stir′-), *n.* **1.** a solid mass of masonry serving as a base for a wall, etc.; foundation. **2.** the substructure of a row of columns, including the stylobate. [< Latin *stereobata* a foundation wall or substructure for a colonnade < Greek *stereós* solid + *-bátēs* step(ping); obstructed < *bainein* step]

ster·e·o·bat·ic (ster′ē ə bat′ik, stir′-), *adj.* of, having to do with, or like a stereobate.

stereo camera, a camera with twin lenses that take simultaneous photographs, the resulting pairs of prints or slides giving an effect of three dimensions when seen in a viewer.

ster·e·o·chem·i·cal (ster′ē ō kem′ə kəl, stir′-), *adj.* having to do with stereochemistry.

ster·e·o·chem·is·try (ster′ē ō kem′ə strē, stir′-), *n.* the branch of chemistry dealing with theoretical differences in the relative position in space of atoms in a molecule in relation to differences in the optical and chemical properties of the substances.

ster·e·o·chrome (ster′ē ə krōm, stir′-), *n.* **1.** a process of mural painting in which water glass is used as a vehicle or as a preservative coating. **2.** a picture produced by this process. [< German *Stereochrom* < Greek *stereós* solid + *chrôma* color]

ster·e·o·chro·mic (ster′ē ə krō′mik, stir′-), *adj.* of, having to do with, or produced by stereochrome.

ster·e·o·chro·my (ster′ē ə krō′mē, stir′-), *n.* stereochrome.

ster·e·o·com·pa·ra·tor (ster′ē ō kom′pə-rā′tər, -kəm par′ə-; stir′-), *n.* an instrument on the stereoscopic principle, used to superpose a pair of astronomical photographs taken at an interval of time, and detect any movement of a star or other object which has taken place in that interval.

ster·e·og·no·sis (ster′ē og nō′sis, stir′-), *n. Psychology.* mental apprehension of the forms of solid objects by touch. [< New Latin *stereognosis* < Greek *stereós* solid + *gnôsis* a knowing]

ster·e·og·nos·tic (ster′ē og nos′tik, stir′-), *adj.* having to do with stereognosis.

ster·e·o·gram (ster′ē ə gram, stir′-), *n.* **1.** a diagram representing a solid object on a plane, especially a drawing in which the inequalities or curvature of a surface is indicated by contour lines or shading. **2.** stereograph. [< *stereo-* + *-gram*]

ster·e·o·graph (ster′ē ə graf, -gräf; stir′-), *n.* a pair of nearly identical pictures, giving a three-dimensional effect when viewed in a stereoscope. —*v.t., v.i.* to take a stereograph or stereoscopic photograph (of). [< *stereo-* + *-graph*]

ster·e·o·graph·ic (ster′ē ə graf′ik, stir′-), *adj.* showing the whole of a sphere on the whole of an infinite plane, while preserving the angles. —**ster′e·o·graph′i·cal·ly,** *adv.*

ster·e·o·graph·i·cal (ster′ē ə graf′ə kəl, stir′-), *adj.* stereographic.

ster·e·og·ra·phy (ster′ē og′rə fē, stir′-), *n.* the art of representing the forms of solid bodies on a plane; a branch of solid geometry that deals with the construction of all regularly defined solids.

ster·e·o·i·so·mer (ster′ē ō ī′sə mər, stir′-), *n. Chemistry.* one of two or more isomeric compounds that are held to differ by virtue of a difference in the spatial arrangement (not in the order of connection) of the atoms in the molecule. [< *stereo-* + *isomer*]

ster·e·o·i·so·mer·ic (ster′ē ō ī′sə mer′ik, stir′-), *adj. Chemistry.* characterized by stereoisomerism.

ster·e·o·i·som·er·ism (ster′ē ō ī som′ə riz-əm, stir′-), *n. Chemistry.* a kind of isomerism considered as due to the difference in the spatial arrangement (not in the order of connection) of the atoms in the molecule.

ster·e·om (ster′ē om, stir′-), *n.* stereome.

ster·e·ome (ster′ē ōm, stir′-), *n.* **1.** the elements which give strength to a fibrovascular bundle in plants. **2.** the hard tissue of the body of invertebrates. Also, **stereom.** [< Greek *sterėōma* a solid body < *stereós* solid]

ster·e·o·met·ric (ster′ē ə met′rik, stir′-), *adj.* having to do with or performed by stereometry. —**ster′e·o·met′ri·cal·ly,** *adv.*

ster·e·o·met·ri·cal (ster′ē ə met′rə kəl, stir′-), *adj.* stereometric.

ster·e·om·e·try (ster′ē om′ə trē, stir′-), *n.* the measurement of solid figures; solid geometry.

ster·e·o·mi·cro·scope (ster′ē ə mī′krə-skōp, stir′-), *n.* a microscope with two eyepieces, used to obtain a three-dimensional image of the object viewed; stereoscopic microscope.

ster·e·o·phon·ic (ster′ē ə fon′ik, stir′-), *adj.* **1.** of or having to do with a system of sound reproduction in which the sound reaching each of two or more microphones, placed apart, is reproduced by one of a corresponding number of loudspeakers, also placed apart, giving an effect of depth and direction much like that of the original sound. **2.** of or having to do with the sound thus reproduced. [< *stereo-* + *phonic*] —**ster′e·o·phon′i·cal·ly,** *adv.*

ster·e·oph·o·ny (ster′ē of′ə nē, stir′-), *n.* stereophonic sound reproduction: *The differentiation between the directions of the direct sounds from the musical instruments . . . can be simulated by means of stereophony* (New York Herald Tribune).

ster·e·o·pho·tog·ra·phy (ster′ē ō fə tog′-rə fē, stir′-), *n.* the making of stereoscopic pictures, as with a stereo camera.

ster·e·o·pho·to·mi·crog·ra·phy (ster′ē-ō fō′tō mī krog′rə fē, stir′-), *n.* the art of making stereoscopic or three-dimensional photomicrographs.

ster·e·op·sis (ster′ē op′sis, stir′-), *n.* stereoscopic vision. [< New Latin *stereopsis* < Greek *stereós* solid + *-ópsis* vision]

ster·e·op·ti·can (ster′ē op′tə kən, stir′-), *adj.* of, resembling, or having to do with a stereopticon: *He brings an unusual kind of stereoptican vision to bear upon his subject* (Harper's).

ster·e·op·ti·cian (ster′ē op tish′ən, stir′-), *n.* a person trained in the use of a stereopticon.

ster·e·op·ti·con (ster′ē op′tə kən, stir′-), *n.* a double magic lantern having a powerful light arranged to project two images of the same object or scene upon a screen, so as to produce the appearance of solidity as in a stereoscope. It is also used to cause the image of one object or scene to pass gradually into that of another with dissolving effect. [American English < *stereo-* + Greek *optikón,* neuter of *optikós* relating to vision]

ster·e·o·ra·di·o·graph (ster′ē ō rā′dē ō-graf, -gräf; stir′-), *n.* a stereoscopic X-ray photograph.

ster·e·o·reg·u·lar (ster′ē ō reg′yə lər, stir′-), *adj.* of or having to do with a polymer that has a definite and regular spatial arrangement of the atoms in its repeating units: *stereoregular rubber.*

ster·e·o·reg·u·lar·i·ty (ster′ē ō reg′yə-lar′ə tē, stir′-), *n.* the quality or state of being stereoregular: *Few methods [are] available for studying the stereoregularity of polymers* (New Scientist).

ster·e·o·scope (ster′ē ə skōp, stir′-), *n.* an optical instrument with two eyeglasses, used for obtaining a single image from two pictures (usually photographs) of an object or scene, taken from slightly different points of view (corresponding to the positions of the two eyes). The object or scene thus viewed appears to have three dimensions, as it would if really seen.

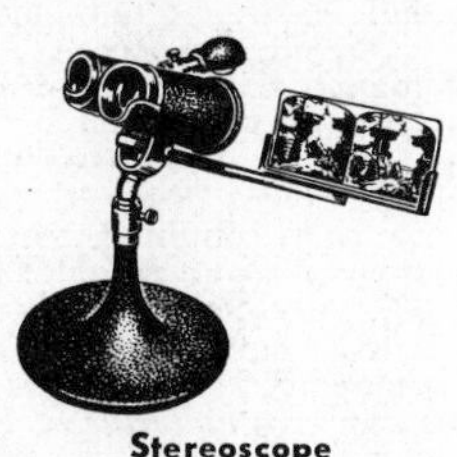
Stereoscope

ster·e·o·scop·ic (ster′ē ə skop′ik, stir′-), *adj.* **1.** seeming to have depth as well as height and breadth; three-dimensional. **2.** having to do with stereoscopes.

ster·e·o·scop·i·cal (ster′ē ə skop′ə kəl, stir′-), *adj.* stereoscopic.

ster·e·o·scop·i·cal·ly (ster′ē ə skop′ə klē, stir′-), *adv.* by means of a stereoscope.

ster·e·os·co·pist (ster′ē os′kə pist, stir′-), *n.* a person skilled in the use or construction of stereoscopes.

ster·e·os·co·py (ster′ē os′kə pē, stir′-), *n.* the use or construction of stereoscopes.

ster·e·o·ski·ag·ra·phy (ster′ē ō skī ag′rə-fē, stir′-), *n.* the taking of several X-ray pictures at different angles in order to produce a stereoscopic effect. [< *stereo-* + *skiagraphy*]

ster·e·o·son·ic (ster′ē ə son′ik, stir′-), *adj. Especially British.* stereophonic.

ster·e·o·spe·cif·ic (ster′ē ō spi sif′ik, stir′-), *adj.* of or having to do with a chemical process in which a steroid, alkaloid, or other product is used to form a specific stereoisomer of related structure, usually with the aid of a catalyst.

ster·e·o·spe·cif·i·cal·ly (ster′ē ō spi sif′ə-klē, stir′-), *adv.* in a stereospecific manner.

ster·e·o·spec·i·fic·i·ty (ster′ē ō spes′ə fis′-ə tē, stir′-), *n.* the quality or state of being stereospecific: *stereospecificity of enzymic reactions.*

ster·e·o·tac·tic (ster′ē ə tak′tik, stir′-), *adj.* of, having to do with, or exhibiting stereotaxis; thigmotactic.

ster·e·o·tax·is (ster′ē ə tak′sis, stir′-), *n. Biology.* a movement of an organism as a result of contact with a solid body; thigmotaxis. [< *stereo-* + Greek *táxis* arrangement]

ster·e·o·trope (ster′ē ə trōp, stir′-), *n.* an optical device based on the same principle as a zoetrope but fitted with a stereoscope, giving solidity to the figures in motion. [< *stereo-* + Greek *-tropos* turned]

ster·e·o·trop·ic (ster′ē ə trop′ik, stir′-), *adj. Biology.* bending or turning under the stimulus of contact with a solid body.

ster·e·ot·ro·pism (ster′ē ot′rə piz əm, stir′-), *n. Biology.* a tendency to bend or turn in response to contact with a solid body or rigid surface. [< *stereo-* + *tropism*]

ster·e·o·type (ster′ē ə tīp, stir′-), *n., v.,* **-typed, -typ·ing.** —*n.* **1.** the method or process of printing in which a solid plate, usually of type metal, is cast from a mold (or matrix) of papier-mâché, plastic, etc., taken from the surface of a form of type and the printing is from the plate instead of the form. **2.** a printing plate cast from a mold. **3.** the making or use of such plates; stereotypy. **4.** a fixed, hackneyed form, expression, character, image, etc.; something stereotyped; convention.
—*v.t.* **1.** to make a stereotype of. **2.** to print from stereotypes. **3.** to give a fixed or settled form to.
[< French *stéréotype* < Greek *stereós* solid + *týpos* type]

ster·e·o·typed (ster′ē ə tīpt, stir′-), *adj.* **1.** cast in the form of, or printed from, a stereotype. **2.** fixed or settled in form; conventional: *stereotyped characters in a novel. "It gives me great pleasure to be with you tonight" is a stereotyped opening for a speech.*

ster·e·o·typ·er (ster′ē ə tī′pər, stir′-), *n.* a person who stereotypes or makes stereotype plates.

ster·e·o·typ·ic (ster′ē ə tip′ik, stir′-), *adj.* of or relating to stereotype or stereotype plates.

ster·e·o·typ·i·cal (ster′ē ə tip′ə kəl, stir′-), *adj.* stereotypic: *In her passionate rejection of all stereotypical thinking she has, in fact, become something of a stereotype herself* (Mary Lowrey Ross). —**ster′e·o·typ′i·cal·ly,** *adv.*

ster·e·o·typ·i·cal·i·ty (ster′ē ə tip′ə kal′ə-tē, stir′-), *n.* the quality or state of being stereotypic: *These magazines are boring in their inevitable stereotypicality of regimented subject matter* (London Times).

ster·e·o·typ·y (ster′ē ə tī′pē, stir′-), *n.* **1.** the process of making, or of printing from, stereotype plates. **2.** persistence of a fixed or stereotyped idea, mode of action, etc., as in certain types of insanity.

ster·ic (ster′ik, stir′-), *adj. Chemistry.* of or having to do with the arrangement in space of the atoms in a molecule. [< Greek *stereós* solid + English *-ic*] —**ster′i·cal·ly,** *adv.*

ster·i·cal (ster′ə kəl, stir′-), *adj.* steric.

ste·rig·ma (stə rig′mə), *n., pl.* **-ma·ta** (-mə-tə). **1.** a ridge extending down a stem below the point of attachment of a decurrent leaf. **2.** a stalk or filament bearing a spore in a fungus. **3.** a branch or outgrowth of a basidium. [< Greek *stērigma* a support < *sterízein* to support]

ster·ig·mat·ic (ster′ig mat′ik), *adj.* having to do with or like a sterigma.

ster·i·lant (ster′ə lənt), *n.* a chemical or other agent that sterilizes, as a chemical that destroys an insect's ability to reproduce.

ster·ile (ster′əl), *adj.* **1.** free from living microorganisms or germs: *The nurse kept the surgeon's instruments sterile.* **2.** not producing crops; not fertile; barren; unproductive: *Sterile soil does not produce good crops.* **3.** not producing seed or offspring: *a sterile cow.* **4. a.** (of a plant) not bearing fruit or spores. **b.** (of a flower) producing only stamens, or producing neither stamens nor pistils. **5.** not producing results: *verbal logic drawing sterile conclusions from untested authority* (John Morley). [< Latin *sterilis*] —**ster′ile·ly,** *adv.* —**Syn. 2.** infertile.

ster·i·lise (ster′ə līz), *v.t.,* **-lised, -lis·ing.** *Especially British.* sterilize.

ste·ril·i·ty (stə ril′ə tē), *n., pl.* **-ties.** a sterile condition or character; barrenness.

ster·i·liz·a·ble (ster′ə lī′zə bəl), *adj.* capable of being sterilized: *sterilizable plastic baby bottles.*

ster·i·li·za·tion (ster′ə lə zā′shən), *n.* **1.** the act or operation of sterilizing: *the sterilization of dishes by boiling them.* **2.** the state of being sterilized.

ster·i·lize (ster′ə līz), *v.t.,* **-lized, -liz·ing.** **1.** to make free from living microorganisms or germs, as by heating or otherwise: *The water had to be sterilized by boiling to make it fit to drink.* **2.** to make incapable of producing offspring by removing the organs of reproduction or by the inhibition of their function. **3.** to make unproductive, unprofitable, or useless. —**Syn. 1.** disinfect, purify.

ster·i·liz·er (ster′ə lī′zər), *n.* any device for destroying microorganisms, as a vessel containing boiling water, with or without disinfecting liquids, through which live steam may be passed to kill the germs.

ster·let (stėr′lit), *n.* a small sturgeon of the Black Sea, Caspian Sea, etc., highly esteemed for its flavor and for the superior caviar from its roe. [< Russian *sterljad'* < German *Störling* (diminutive) < *Stör* sturgeon]

ster·ling (stėr′ling), *n.* **1. a.** British money, especially the pound as the standard British monetary unit in international trade: *to pay in sterling.* **b.** British silver or gold coin, as that which is historically and by law the actual coin of the realm, the standard of fineness for silver being .500 at present, .925 before 1920, and that for gold .9166 at

present, formerly .995. *Abbr.:* stg. **2.** sterling silver or things made of it. **3.** (in Australia) persons born in Great Britain or Ireland.
—*adj.* **1.** of or payable in British money. **2.** of standard quality; containing 92.5 per cent pure silver. *Sterling* is stamped on solid silver knives, forks, etc. **3.** made of sterling silver. **4.** genuine; excellent; dependable: *Everyone admired George Washington's sterling character.*
[Middle English *sterling* silver penny, Old English *steorra* star (which was on certain early Norman coins) + *-ling*]
—**Syn.** *adj.* **4.** sound.

sterling area, a group of countries in the British Commonwealth, protectorates, territories, and certain others that use the British pound sterling as the unit of currency in foreign trade: *Canada, being in the dollar area, is outside the sterling area.*

sterling bloc, a group of countries that have adjusted their currencies and foreign exchange in accordance with the value of the British pound sterling.

sterling silver, solid silver; silver that is 92.5 per cent pure (the original British standard of fineness for silver coin).

stern[1] (stėrn), *adj.* **1.** severe; strict; harsh: *a stern master, a stern look, a stern religion.* **2.** not yielding; hard; firm: *stern necessity, stern reality. . . . ambition should be made of sterner stuff* (Shakespeare). **3.** grim: *a stern climate; . . . a stern and rock-bound coast* (Felicia D. Hemans). [Old English *styrne*] —**stern′ly,** *adv.* —**stern′ness,** *n.* —**Syn. 1.** See **severe.**

stern[2] (stėrn), *n.* **1.** the hind part of a ship or boat, beginning where the sides curve inward. See **aft** for picture. **2. a.** the buttocks. **b.** the hinder part of any creature. —*adj.* of, at, or having to do with the stern. [Compare Old Frisian *stiārne* stern, rudder, Old Icelandic *stjōrn* a steering]

ster·nal (stėr′nəl), *adj.* of, having to do with, or in the region of the breastbone or sternum.

stern board, *Nautical.* a backward motion of a vessel.

stern chase, a chase in which the pursuing ship is directly following in the wake of another: *a stern chase, which proverbially is known as a long chase* (Joseph Conrad).

stern chaser, a gun in the stern of a ship for protection against an enemy ship following in its wake.

-sterned, *combining form.* having a ____ stern: *A high-sterned vessel = a vessel having a high stern.*

stern·er sex (stėr′nər), men.

stern·fore·most (stėrn′fôr′mōst, -məst; -fōr′-), *adv.* **1.** with the stern first; backwards. **2.** clumsily; awkwardly.

ster·nine (stėr′nīn), *adj.* of or like a tern; belonging to a subfamily of birds including the terns. [< New Latin *sterninus* < *Sterna* the tern genus. Compare Old English *stearn* a sea bird.]

stern knee, sternson.

stern·most (stėrn′mōst, -məst), *adj.* **1.** nearest the stern. **2.** farthest in the rear.

ster·no·cla·vic·u·lar (stėr′nō klə vik′yə lər), *adj.* of, having to do with, or connecting the breastbone (sternum) and clavicle.

ster·no·clei·do·mas·toid (stėr′nō klī′dō mas′toid), *adj.* connecting the breastbone (sternum), the clavicle, and the mastoid process of the temporal bone (applied to each of two muscles of the neck that serve to turn and nod the head). [< New Latin *sternum* breastbone + Greek *kleís, kleidós* clavicle + English *mastoid*]

ster·no·cos·tal (stėr′nō kos′təl), *adj.* of, having to do with, or connecting the sternum and the ribs. [< New Latin *sternum* breastbone + English *costal*]

ster·no·mas·toid (stėr′nō mas′toid), *adj.* sternocleidomastoid.

ster·no·scap·u·lar (stėr′nō skap′yə lər), *adj.* of or having to do with the sternum and the scapula: *a sternoscapular muscle.*

stern·post (stėrn′pōst′), *n.* the upright timber or metal bar at the stern of a vessel. Its lower end is fastened to the keel, and it usually supports the rudder.

stern·sheets (stėrn′shēts′), *n.pl.* the space at the stern of an open boat.

stern·son (stėrn′sən), *n.,* or **sternson knee,** a timber or metal bar set in the angle between the keelson and the sternpost to strengthen the joint; stern knee. [< *stern*[2]; patterned on *keelson, stemson*]

ster·num (stėr′nəm), *n., pl.* **-na** (-nə) or **-nums.** a long bone or series of bones, occurring in most vertebrates except snakes and fishes, extending along the middle line of the front or ventral aspect of the trunk, usually articulating with some of the ribs (in man, with the true ribs), and with them completing the wall of the thorax; breastbone. [< New Latin *sternum* < Greek *stérnon* chest]

ster·nu·ta·tion (stėr′nyə tā′shən), *n.* **1.** the act of sneezing: *If she had not sneezed, she would have heard all . . . but that unlucky sternutation routed Dr. John* (Charlotte Brontë). **2.** a sneeze. [< Latin *sternūtātiō, -ōnis* < *sternūtāre* to sneeze (frequentative) < *sternuere* to sneeze]

ster·nu·ta·tive (stər nyü′tə tiv), *adj., n.* sternutatory.

ster·nu·ta·tor (stėr′nyə tā′tər), *n.* any type of gas designed to cause irritation of the nose, coughing, tears, etc.

ster·nu·ta·to·ry (stər nyü′tə tôr′ē, -tōr′-), *adj., n., pl.* **-ries.** —*adj.* having to do with or causing sneezing. —*n.* a substance that causes sneezing, as snuff. [< Medieval Latin *sternutatorius* < Latin *sternūtāre;* see STERNUTATION]

stern·ward (stėrn′wərd), *adv., adj.* **1.** toward or in the direction of the stern. **2.** (of position) astern.

stern·wards (stėrn′wərdz), *adv.* sternward.

stern·way (stėrn′wā′), *n.* the movement of a ship in reverse, with the stern preceding the bow.

stern-wheel (stėrn′hwēl′), *adj.* that is a stern-wheeler.

stern-wheel·er (stėrn′hwē′lər), *n.* a steam-propelled ship with a paddle wheel at the stern.

Stern-wheeler

ster·oid (ster′oid), *n. Biochemistry.* any of a large class of structurally related compounds containing the carbon ring of the sterols, and including the sterols, bile acids, various hormones, and saponins. —*adj.* steroidal: *Steroid chemicals have a profound effect in the body's transformation of food into tissues needed for growth and repair* (Science News Letter). [< *ster*(ol) + *-oid*]

ste·roi·dal (stə roi′dəl), *adj.* **1.** of, resembling, or having to do with a steroid: *The circulation of some steroidal substance in pregnancy and in jaundice might be responsible for the alleviation of the* [*arthritic*] *symptoms* (Beaumont and Dodds). **2.** of, resembling, or having to do with a sterol: *a steroidal ketone.*

ster·ol (ster′ōl, -ol), *n.* any of a group of solid, (chiefly) unsaturated alcohols, as ergosterol, cholesterol, etc., present in animal and plant tissues. [< (chole)*sterol,* (ergo) *sterol*]

ster·tor (stėr′tər), *n.* a heavy snoring sound caused especially by the passage of air through mucus in the trachea. [< New Latin *stertor* < Latin *stertere* to snore]

ster·to·rous (stėr′tər əs), *adj.* making a heavy snoring sound: *stertorous breathing.* [< New Latin *stertor* snoring + English *-ous*] —**ster′to·rous·ly,** *adv.* —**ster′to·rous·ness,** *n.*

stet (stet), *n., v.,* **stet·ted, stet·ting.** *Printing.* —*n.* "let it stand" (do not delete), a direction on printer's proof, a manuscript, or the like, to retain matter that had been marked for deletion. The passage to be retained is underlined with a series of dots. *Abbr.:* st. —*v.t.* to mark (a canceled or deleted passage) for retention by writing "stet" in the margin and underlining the passage with a series of dots. [< Latin *stet* let it stand]

steth·o·graph (steth′ə graf, -gräf), *n.* an instrument for recording the respiratory movements of the chest. [< Greek *stêthos* breast, chest + English *-graph*]

steth·o·graph·ic (steth′ə graf′ik), *adj.* of, having to do with, or obtained by means of the stethograph.

ste·thom·e·ter (ste thom′ə tər), *n.* an instrument for measuring the expansion of the chest in respiration. [< Greek *stêthos* breast, chest + English *-meter*]

steth·o·met·ric (steth′ə met′rik), *adj.* having to do with or obtained by means of a stethometer.

steth·o·phone (steth′ə fōn), *n.* a kind of stethoscope. [< Greek *stêthos* breast, chest + English *-phone*]

steth·o·scope (steth′ə skōp), *n., v.,* **-scoped, -scop·ing.** —*n.* an instrument used by doctors to convey sounds from the heart, lungs, etc., to the ear of the examiner. —*v.t.* to examine with a stethoscope. [< Greek *stêthos* breast, chest + English *-scope*]

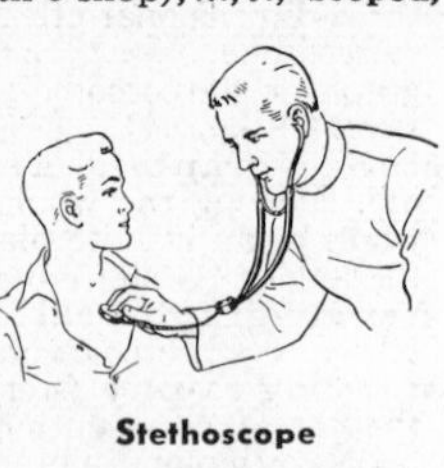
Stethoscope

steth·o·scop·ic (steth′ə skop′ik), *adj.* **1.** having to do with the stethoscope or its use. **2.** made or obtained by the stethoscope —**steth′o·scop′i·cal·ly,** *adv.*

steth·o·scop·i·cal (steth′ə skop′ə kəl), *adj.* stethoscopic.

ste·thos·co·pist (ste thos′kə pist), *n.* a person skilled in the use of the stethoscope.

ste·thos·co·py (ste thos′kə pē), *n.* the art or process of using the stethoscope.

Stet·son (stet′sən), *n.,* or **Stetson hat,** a soft felt hat with a broad brim and high crown, worn especially in the western United States. [< *Stetson,* trademark of a company that manufactures hats]

Steu·ben glass or **glassware** (stü′bən, styü′-; stü ben′, styü-), a handmade American glass or glassware made of heavy lead crystal, that is transparent, basically simple in shape, and either completely unadorned or engraved with designs: *Steuben glass is known throughout the world and in Europe it has never lost its popularity* (Manchester Guardian). [< *Steuben* Glass, Incorporated, a company in Corning, New York, that produces it]

ste·ve·dore (stē′və dôr, -dōr), *n., v.,* **-dored, -dor·ing.** —*n.* a man employed at a port to load and unload ships. —*v.t.* to load or unload (a vessel or cargo). —*v.i.* to work as a stevedore. [American English < Spanish *estibador* < *estibar* to stow cargo < Latin *stīpāre* pack down; press. Compare STEEVE[1].]

stevedore's knot, a type of knot forming a bulge to keep a rope from going through a hole or block.

Ste·ven·so·ni·an (stē′vən sō′nē ən), *adj.* having to do with, characteristic of, or like the Scottish author Robert Louis Stevenson or his writings: *Mr. Muller's dramatization carefully preserved the bright Stevensonian colours* (London Times). —*n.* an admirer of Stevenson or his writings.

ste·vi·o·side (stē′vē ə sīd), *n.* a glucoside obtained from the leaves of a South American composite plant, that is 300 times as sweet as ordinary cane sugar. *Formula:* $C_{38}H_{60}O_{18}$ [< New Latin *Stevia* the genus name + English *-ose*[2] + *-ide*]

stew (stü, styü), *v.t.* to cook by simmering or slow boiling in a closed vessel: *The cook stewed the chicken for a long time.* —*v.i.* **1.** to be or be able to be stewed. **2.** *Informal.* to worry; fret: *to stew about an imagined insult. Retailers still stew about the taxability of a number of items* (Wall Street Journal).
—*n.* **1.** any of the class of dishes consisting typically of pieces of meat, especially beef, veal, lamb, or mutton, and one or more of various vegetables, cooked until tender by slow boiling or simmering and served with the sauce produced in cooking. **2.** *Informal.* a state of worry; fret: *to be in a perpetual stew. She is all in a stew over her lost trunk. You'll be worried and fretted and kept in a stew* (Samuel Dodge).
[< Old French *estuver* < Vulgar Latin *extūfāre* < Latin *ex-* out + Greek *tŷphos* vapor; fever. Compare TYPHUS.]
—**Syn.** *n.* **2.** dither, agitation.

stew·ard (stü′ərd, styü′-), *n.* **1.** a man who has charge of the food and table service for a club, ship, railroad train, etc. **2. a.** any of various persons on a ship who wait upon the passengers: *a dining-room steward, a cabin steward, deck steward, etc.* **b.** an employee of an airline, railroad, etc., with duties similar to any of these. **3.** a man who manages another's property: *He is the steward of that great estate.* **4.** a person appointed to supervise the arrangements or maintain order at a race meeting, dinner, ball, show, etc. **5.** a shop steward. [Middle English *stuard,* and *styward,* Old English *stīgweard* house guardian < *stig* hall, building + *weard* keeper, ward] **—Syn. 3.** manager. **4.** chairman.

stew·ard·ess (stü′ər dis, styü′-), *n.* **1.** a woman steward. **2.** a woman employed on a ship, airplane, etc., to wait upon passengers.

stew·ard·ship (stü′ərd ship, styü′-), *n.* **1.** the position, duties, and responsibilities of a steward. **2.** management for others.

stew·bum (stü′bum′, styü′-), *n. Slang.* a drunkard.

stewed (stüd, styüd), *adj.* **1. a.** cooked by stewing: *stewed meat.* **b.** cooked by boiling until very soft: *stewed fruit.* **2.** *Slang.* drunk: *stewed to the gills.*

stew·pan (stü′pan′, styü′-), *n.* a pot, or a heavy saucepan, used for stewing.

stew·pond (stü′pond′, styü′-), *n. Especially British.* a pond or tank in which fish are kept until needed for the table: *When Henry VIII knocked down the monasteries of England he presumably also took the plugs out of the monks' stewponds, and since then the culture of carp has been a declining craft in Britain* (New Scientist).

stew·pot (stü′pot′, styü′-), *n.* a covered pot for making soups, stews, etc.: *Italian cooking . . . to be at its best, requires a wood or charcoal fire . . . and earthenware stewpots* (Atlantic).

St. Ex., stock exchange.

stey (stā), *adj. Scottish.* (of a mountain, cliff, etc.) steep.

stg., sterling.

stge., storage.

St. George's cross, Saint George's cross.

St. George's Day, April 23, observed by the English in honor of Saint George, the patron saint of England.

sthe·ni·a (sthi nī′ə, sthē′nē-), *n. Medicine.* abnormal or excessive bodily strength or action. [< New Latin *sthenia* < Greek *sthénos* strength; patterned on *asthenia*]

sthen·ic (sthen′ik), *adj.* **1.** having to do with vigor or nervous energy. **2.** (of diseases, symptoms, etc.) characterized by abnormal or excessive action of the vital processes. [< New Latin *sthenicus* < Greek *sthénos* strength]

Sthe·no (sthē′nō, sthen′ō), *n. Greek Legend.* one of the Gorgons.

stiac·cia·to (styät chä′tō), *adj.* (of a relief) very flat or shallow, as on a coin. —*n.* a carving or modeling in very low relief. [< Italian *stiacciato* flattened, past participle of *stiacciare* to crush, variant of *schiacciare* crack a nut, perhaps < a Germanic word]

stib·i·al (stib′ē əl), *adj.* like or having the qualities of antimony; antimonial.

stib·in (stib′in), *n.* stibine.

stib·ine (stib′ēn, -in), *n.* a colorless, poisonous, gaseous compound; a hydride of antimony. *Formula:* SbH_3 [< *stib*(ium) + *-ine*[2]]

stib·i·um (stib′ē əm), *n.* antimony. *Symbol:* Sb [Middle English *stibium* stibnite; kohl < Latin < Greek *stíbi,* variant of *stimmi*]

stib·nite (stib′nīt), *n.* a lead-gray mineral occurring in orthorhombic crystals and also massive. It is the most important ore of antimony. *Formula:* Sb_2S_3 [< *stibine* + *-ite*[1]]

stib·o·phen (stib′ə fen), *n.* a white, crystalline drug used in the treatment of schistosomiasis and leishmaniasis. *Formula:* $C_{12}H_4Na_5O_{16}S_4Sb.7H_2O$

stich (stik), *n.* a line, especially of verse; verse. [< Greek *stíchos* row, line, verse < *steíchein* to walk, march (in a line)]

sti·che·ron (sti kir′on), *n., pl.* **-ra** (-rə). a troparion. [< Medieval Greek *sticheron,* neuter of *sticheros* < Greek *stíchos* verse]

stich·ic (stik′ik), *adj.* having to do with a verse or line; consisting of verses or lines; linear.

stich·o·met·ric (stik′ə met′rik), *adj.* of or having to do with stichometry.

stich·o·met·ri·cal (stik′ə met′rə kəl), *adj.* stichometric.

sti·chom·e·try (sti kom′ə trē), *n.* the writing of a prose text in lines each one of which is a unit of sense or cadence. This was felt to be sometimes necessary before the development of punctuation permitted the separation of phrases, clauses, etc., within the same line. [< Late Greek *stichometríā* < Greek *stíchos* line + *-metríā* a measuring < *métron* measure]

stich·o·myth·i·a (stik′ə mith′ē ə), *n.* dialogue in alternating single lines, as in Greek drama. [< New Latin *stichomythia* < Greek *stíchos* row, line + *mŷthos* word, speech]

sti·chom·y·thy (sti kom′ə thē), *n., pl.* **-thies.** stichomythia.

stich·os (stik′os), *n., pl.* **-oi** (-oi). (in the Greek Church) a verse or versicle as in the psalter or the odes, especially a verse or part of a verse from a psalm, used as a versicle.

stich·wort (stich′wėrt′), *n.* stitchwort.

stick[1] (stik), *n., v.,* **sticked, stick·ing.** —*n.* **1. a.** a long, thin piece of wood: *Put some sticks on the fire.* **b.** such a piece of wood shaped for a special use: *a walking stick.* **2.** a slender branch or twig of a tree or shrub, especially when cut or broken off. **3.** something like a stick in shape: *a stick of candy, a stick of cinnamon.* **4.** a stalk of celery, rhubarb, etc. **5.** *Informal.* a stiff, awkward, or stupid person: *a prig, a stick, a petrified poser* (George Meredith). **6.** the device by which the ailerons, elevator, and rudder of an airplane are manipulated, originally a simple sticklike lever projecting upward between the pilot's knees as he sat in the cockpit. **7. a.** a mast or a section of a mast. **b.** a yard. **8.** *Informal.* a portion of alcoholic liquor added to a drink, especially of tea or coffee. **9.** *Printing.* **a.** a small metal tray in which type is set by hand; composing stick. **b.** the amount of type so set; stickful of type. **10.** a number of bombs capable of being released from an aircraft so as to strike the target in a line. **11. a.** a hockey stick. **b.** (in lacrosse) a crosse. **c.** (in racing) a hurdle. **12.** *Slang.* a group of paratroopers jumping in succession in a single pass over an area: *Two "sticks" of parachutists made drops in which they delayed opening their canopies until they were no more than 1,000 feet from the ground* (London Times).

in a cleft stick, *Especially British.* in a position from which it is impossible either to advance or retreat; in a dilemma: *The other side are in a cleft stick; they cannot go on long as they are, and they cannot stir into any new path without demolishing the . . . Laws* (P. Thompson).

shake a stick at, *U.S. Informal.* to take notice of: *There was not enough snow to shake a stick at.*

sticks, pieces of cut or broken branches or pieces of cut and chopped wood, used as fuel: *Mr. Phillips has laid the paper, the sticks, and the coals neatly in the grate* (Arthur Symons).

the sticks, *U.S. Informal.* the outlying or undeveloped districts; backwoods: *The past theatrical season may have been the worst in living memory, but it was a series of flops in Manhattan, not in the sticks* (Saturday Review).

—*v.t.* **1.** to furnish with a stick or sticks to support or prop. **2.** *Printing.* to arrange (type) in a composing stick.

[Old English *sticca* rod, twig, spoon] **—stick′like′,** *adj.* **—Syn.** *n.* **1. a.** rod, staff.

stick[2] (stik), *v.,* **stuck, stick·ing,** *n.* —*v.t.* **1.** to pierce (flesh, a surface, etc.) with a pointed instrument; thrust (a point) into; stab (a person, animal, etc.): *He stuck his fork into the potato.* **2.** to kill by stabbing or piercing: *stick him like a calf* (Tennyson). **3.** to fasten by thrusting the point or end into or through something: *He stuck a flower in his buttonhole.* **4. a.** to fix on a pointed implement, etc.; impale: *Their heads were stuck upon spears* (Edmund Burke). **b.** to mount by transfixing with pins: *I have not stuck an insect this term* (Charles Darwin). **5.** to put into a position; place: *to stick a finger in the pie. Don't stick your head out of the window.* **6.** to fasten; attach: *to stick a notice on the bulletin board. Stick a stamp on the letter.* **7.** to set into or adorn the surface of: *to stick a ham with cloves.* **8.** to bring to a stop: *Our work was stuck by the breakdown of the machinery.* **9.** *Informal.* to puzzle: *That question still sticks me.* **10.** *Informal.* to smear (with an adhesive, plaster, etc.). **11.** *Informal.* **a.** to impose upon by or as if by fraud; cheat; swindle: *to stick the public with shoddy goods.* **b.** to leave (a person) with, as something to pay: *How much did they stick you for this lot?* (Arnold Bennett). **12.** *Informal.* to stand or put up with; tolerate: *I won't stick his insults much longer.*

—*v.i.* **1.** to be thrust; extend (from, out, through, up, etc.): *His arms stick out of his coat sleeves.* **2.** to keep close: *The little boy stuck to his mother's heels. He sticks here instead of getting out into the world and enjoying the fight* (Sinclair Lewis). **3.** to be or become fastened; become fixed; be at a standstill: *an arrow stuck in a tree. Two pages of the book stuck together. Our car stuck in the ditch.* **4.** to hold one's position; cling: *to stick on a horse's back.* **5.** *Informal.* to remain; stand; last: *McDonald has been unable to make . . . his charges stick* (Maclean's). *It would be just a matter of guessing whether the rise will stick* (Wall Street Journal). **6.** to hesitate; be puzzled: *He always stuck in the middle, everybody recollecting the latter part except himself* (Washington Irving).

stick around, *Informal.* **a.** to stay or wait nearby: *I'll stick around for a while, but then I must go.* **b.** to remain in a place; stay on: *The members of the office staff who stick around long enough to get to know him swear by Adams* (Time).

stick at, to hesitate or stop for: *Roy sticks at nothing in order to get his own way. She's not a woman to stick at trifles* (George Meredith).

stick by or **to,** to remain resolutely faithful or attached to; refuse to desert: *to stick to one's friends when they are in trouble.*

stick it out, *Informal.* to put up with unpleasant conditions, circumstances, etc.; endure: *Try to stick it out for a few more days.*

stick out, a. *Informal.* to put up with until the end: *By this method, companies, and sometimes whole battalions, which had stuck out the shellfire, were overwhelmed and annihilated* (E.W. Hamilton). **b.** to stand out; be plain: *His inefficiency sticks out like a sore thumb.*

stick together, to keep or cling together; stay united; support each other or one another: *While we live we will stick together; one fate shall belong to us all* (Elisha K. Kane).

stick up, *Informal.* to hold up; rob: *The Emerson's long-suffering night clerk . . . has been stuck up three times in the last two months* (Time).

stick up for, *Informal.* to support; defend: *I shall always like him [Whittier] the better for sticking up for old New England* (James Russell Lowell).

—*n.* **1.** a thrust; stab. **2.** sticky condition or quality; adhesiveness. **3.** a standstill; stop. **4.** a cause of delay; obstacle; impediment: *That should be no stick to you* (Stevenson). *When we came to the Hill Difficulty he made no stick at that* (John Bunyan).

[Middle English *stikien,* Old English *stician*]

—Syn. *v.i.* **2,3,4. Stick, adhere** mean to be firmly or closely attached to something. **Stick,** the common and general word, suggests being fastened as if by something gummy: *Flies stick to flypaper. He stuck to his work.* **Adhere,** a more formal word sometimes used as a dignified substitute for *stick,* suggests being firmly attached as if by its own accord: *This adhesive tape will adhere evenly to very smooth surfaces. Churchill firmly adhered to his announced aim of winning the war.*

stick·a·bil·i·ty (stik′ə bil′ə tē), *n.* **1.** capacity for sticking or remaining stuck. **2.** *Informal.* endurance; perseverance: *To be able to take rebuffs happily and still go on requires . . . stickability* (British Weekly).

stick·a·ble (stik′ə bəl), *adj.* **1.** capable of sticking or remaining stuck: *Most people would gladly forgo . . . an advertising promise in exchange for some absolutely stickable glue* (Wall Street Journal). **2.** *Informal.* capable of enduring or persevering.

stick·ball (stik′bôl′), *n.* a form of baseball played in small areas such as streets and vacant back lots, and played with a rubber ball and a stick or broomhandle for a bat.

stick bug, 1. a walking stick. **2.** a spider bug.

stick dance, a folk or ritual dance marked by the symbolic use or beating of sticks, found throughout the world in many forms.

stick·er (stik′ər), *n.* **1.** a person or thing that sticks. **2.** *U.S.* a gummed label. **3.** a bur; thorn. **4.** *Informal.* a puzzle.

stick·ful (stik′fu̇l), *n., pl.* **-fuls.** *Printing.* as much type as a composing stick will hold.

stick·han·dle (stik′han′dəl), *v.i.* (in hockey) to keep control of the puck while skating with it by moving it deceptively in or almost in contact with the stick.

stick·i·ly (stik′ə lē), *adv.* in a sticky manner.

stick·i·ness (stik′ē nis), *n.* the state of being sticky.

stick·ing plaster (stik′ing), a cloth coated with a sticky substance, used to cover and close slight cuts and wounds.

sticking point, **1.** the place in which a thing stops and holds fast: *The nut has been screwed on the bolt to the sticking point. He screwed up his courage to the sticking point.* **2.** any issue over which proceedings, negotiations, etc., are brought to a halt: *The shippers and the union are apart on every issue, with the . . coastwide contract demand the key sticking point* (Wall Street Journal).

stick insect, a walking stick.

stick-in-the-mud (stik′in ŦHə mud′), *Informal.* —*n.* **1.** a person who prefers old methods, ideas, etc., to new; a very dull or conservative person; old fogy: *On the Track of Unknown Animals, in which (not without copious illustrations) he sets about the skeptics, the stick-in-the-muds and the unbelievers* (Punch). **2.** a person who lacks initiative; backward, unresourceful person: *When it comes to handling money, I am an old stick-in-the-mud.* —*adj.* narrow in outlook; backward; provincial: *You have used the standards of some stay-at-home, stick-in-the-mud place to judge those progressive attitudes that have become part of the universally approved heritage of all Americans* (Harper's).

stick·it (stik′it), *adj. Scottish.* **1.** imperfect or bungled; unfinished. **2.** having failed, as in a calling or profession: *[He] was ever after designated as a 'stickit minister'* (Scott). [alteration of *sticked,* adjective < obsolete past participle of *stick*[2], verb]

stick·lac (stik′lak′), *n.* a natural, dark-red, transparent resin deposited on the twigs of trees in India and southern Asia by certain insects; shellac (in its natural state); lac.

stick·le (stik′əl), *v.,* **-led, -ling,** *n.* —*v.i.* **1.** to make objections about trifles; insist stubbornly: *Flying for life, one does not stickle about his vehicle* (Thomas Carlyle). **2.** to feel difficulties about trifles; have objections; scruple.
—*n. Dialect or Informal.* **1.** fuss; ado; disturbance: *Sometimes the victims may feel that the letter-writer's main purpose in . . . reading has been to find cause for a good stickle* (London Times). **2.** an agitated or bewildered state of mind; consternation.
[apparently variant of Middle English *stightlen* to regulate (a contest), mediate, arrange (frequentative) < Old English *stihtan* arrange]
—**Syn.** *v.i.* **2.** demur.

stick·le·back (stik′əl bak′), *n., pl.* **-backs** or (*collectively*) **-back.** any of a group of small fishes, either scaleless or with bony plates along the sides, and with two or three sharp spines on the back. The male builds an elaborate nest for the eggs. [Middle English *stykylbak* < Old English *sticel* a prick, sting + *bæc* back[1]]

Ocean Stickleback in nest (to 7 in. long)

stick·ler (stik′lər), *n.* a person who contends stubbornly, sometimes over trifles: *a stickler for punctuality.*

stick·man (stik′man′), *n., pl.* **-men.** *U.S. Slang.* **1.** a gambling house employee; croupier: *He had made extra money as a nighttime stickman at a casino across the Mississippi in Arkansas* (Time). **2.** a batter in baseball.

stick-out (stik′out′), *Informal.* —*n.* a person or thing that stands out: *He was clearly a stick-out in an otherwise lack-luster, fifteen horse field* (Time). —*adj.* that sticks out; prominent or conspicuous: *a stick-out athlete.*

stick·pin (stik′pin′), *n.* a long, slender pin having a decorated head worn in a necktie or scarf for ornament. [American English < *stick*[2] + *pin*]

sticks (stiks), *n.pl.* See under **stick**[1], *n.*

stick·seed (stik′sēd′), *n.* any of a group of herbs of the borage family with flowers whose prickly seeds stick to clothing, as the burseed.

stick·shift (stik′shift′), *n.* a lever projecting from the floor of an automobile, used to shift or change the speed of gears.

stick·tight (stik′tīt′), *n.* any of a group of weedy herbs of the composite family, having flat barbed seeds (achenes) that stick to clothing; bur marigold; beggar's-tick.

stick-to-it·ive (stik′tü′ə tiv), *adj. U.S. Informal.* persistent; persevering.

stick-to-it·ive·ness (stik′tü′ə tiv nis), *n. U.S. Informal.* perseverance.

stick·um (stik′əm), *n. Slang.* any sticky substance; gum; adhesive: *postage stamp stickum.*

stick-up (stik′up′), *n. Informal.* a holdup; robbery. [American English < *stick up,* idiom]

stick·wa·ter (stik′wôt′ər, -wot′-), *n.* a sticky solution obtained from the steam processing of fish for industrial use: *Stickwater contains many valuable minerals, water-soluble proteins, amino acids, vitamins and other ingredients* (Scientific American).

stick·weed (stik′wēd′), *n.* ragweed.

stick·work (stik′wėrk′), *n.* the way a player manipulates his stick in such sports as hockey and lacrosse.

stick·y (stik′ē), *adj.,* **stick·i·er, stick·i·est.** **1.** having the property of sticking or adhering: *sticky glue.* **2.** that makes things stick; covered with adhesive matter: *sticky fly-paper.* **3.** *Informal.* hot and unpleasantly humid: *sticky weather.* **4.** *Informal.* difficult: *It is, we know, a sticky question* (Wall Street Journal). *A night carrier landing can be a very sticky thing* (Saturday Evening Post). **5.** *Informal.* (of securities, wares, etc.) selling with difficulty: *Used car stocks . . . are somewhat improved, although currently sticky* (Wall Street Journal). **6.** *Slang.* unpleasant; extremely disagreeable: *A few years ago this old peasant would have certainly joined up with wreckers and saboteurs and have reached a sticky end* (London Times). —**Syn. 1.** adhesive, viscous, mucilaginous.

stick·y·beak (stik′ē bēk′), *n. Australian.* a prying, inquisitive person.

stick·y-fin·gered (stik′ē fing′gərd), *adj. Slang.* inclined to steal; thievish: *Sticky-fingered cops . . . protect the numbers racket* (Time).

sticky wicket, **1.** *Cricket.* the condition when the ground around the wicket is wet and sticky, so that the ball bounces low. **2.** *Especially British.* a bad arrangement; difficult situation; unfavorable condition; rough deal: *Could the Commonwealth survive if the British Government decreed a sticky wicket for the West Indies?* (London Times).

stiff (stif), *adj.* **1.** not easily bent: *a stiff collar, a stiff brush.* **2.** hard to move: *a stiff hinge, a stiff gear.* **3.** not able to move easily: *Ed was stiff and sore.* **4.** drawn tight; tense; taut: *a stiff cord, to keep a stiff rein.* **5.** not fluid; firm: *a stiff cake batter. That jelly is stiff enough to stand alone.* **6.** dense; compact: *stiff soil.* **7.** not easy or natural in manner; formal: *a stiff bow, a stiff style of writing.* **8.** lacking grace of line, form, or arrangement: *stiff geometrical designs.* **9.** resolute; steadfast; unyielding: *a stiff resistance. He . . . was as stiff about urging his point as ever you could be* (Charlotte Brontë). **10.** strong and steady in motion: *a stiff breeze.* **11.** hard to deal with; hard; laborious: *a stiff fight, stiff opposition. The teacher gave us a stiff test.* **12.** harsh or severe: *a stiff penalty.* **13.** *Informal.* **a.** more than seems suitable: *a stiff price.* **b.** firm, as prices, a commodity, or market. **14.** (of a ship) carrying a press of canvas in the wind without heeling or veering excessively. **15.** *Scottish.* strongly built; stalwart; sturdy.
—*n. Slang.* **1.** a dead body; corpse: *They piled the stiffs outside the door* (John Hay). **2.** a stiff, formal, or priggish person: *These old stiffs of teachers just give you a lot of junk about literature and economics* (Sinclair Lewis). **3.** a hopeless or incorrigible fellow. **4.** *U.S.* a hobo; tramp: *stiffs riding the rods of Western freight cars* (Time). **5.** an unskilled dockworker. **6.** a person who fails to tip for service. **7.** a drunken person.
—*v.t. Slang.* to leave without giving a tip to: *to stiff a waiter or a bellhop.*
[Old English *stīf*] —**stiff′ly,** *adv.* —**stiff′ness,** *n.*
—**Syn.** *adj.* **1. Stiff, rigid** mean not easily bent. **Stiff** implies being so firm or solid that it does not bend easily or cannot be bent without injury: *Library books need stiff covers.* **Rigid** implies being so stiff and hard that it will not bend at all and cannot be bent without breaking: *The bodies of animals become rigid after death.* **7.** stilted, affected, constrained, ceremonious. **11.** rigorous. **13. a.** immoderate, excessive.

stiff-arm (stif′ärm′), *n., v.t.* straight-arm.

stiff-backed (stif′bakt′), *adj.* **1.** erect or rigid of posture, as a soldier at attention. **2.** stiffly precise; rigid; formal: *There is nothing stiff-backed about the furnishings of her mind* (New Yorker).

stiff·en (stif′ən), *v.t.* to make stiff or stiffer: *She stiffened the shirt with starch.* —*v.i.* to become stiff or stiffer: *The jelly will stiffen as it cools. Pat stiffened with anger.* —**stiff′en·er,** *n.*

stiff·en·ing (stif′ə ning, stif′ning), *n.* **1.** a making or becoming stiff or stiffer. **2.** something used to stiffen a thing.

stiff-heart·ed (stif′här′tid), *adj. Archaic.* stubborn; contumacious.

stiff·ish (stif′ish), *adj.* rather stiff: *The doctor . . . [is] the only adult outside holy orders obliged to follow a stiffish line of Victorian morals* (Richard Gordon).

stiff-lamb disease (stif′lam′), white muscle disease.

stiff-lipped (stif′lipt′), *adj.* showing no emotion; reserved; stoical: *A picture [emerged] of widespread decadence beneath . . . stiff-lipped [British] society* (Washington Post).

stiff-necked (stif′nekt′), *adj.* **1.** having a stiff neck. **2.** stubborn; obstinate: *The stiff-necked old aristocrat . . .* (George Gissing). —**Syn. 2.** mulish, intractable, refractory.

stiff-neck·ed·ness (stif′nek′id nis, -nekt′-), *n.* the property or character of being stiffnecked; stubbornness.

sti·fle[1] (stī′fəl), *v.,* **-fled, -fling.** —*v.t.* **1. a.** to stop the breath of; suffocate; smother: *The smoke stifled the firemen.* **b.** to choke to death. **2.** to keep back or down; suppress; stop: *to stifle a cry, stifle a yawn, stifle business activity, stifle a rebellion.* **3.** to smother or extinguish (a flame, etc.): *The fog . . . stifled the roar of the traffic of London* (Rudyard Kipling). —*v.i.* **1.** to be unable to breathe freely: *I am stifling in this hot room. Brother, the creed would stifle me That shelters you* (Karle Wilson). **2.** to die or become unconscious by being unable to breathe. [Middle English *stufflen* or *stifflen* < *stuffen* to stuff, stifle; perhaps influenced by Scandinavian. Compare Old Icelandic *stīfla* dam up (water).] —**Syn.** *v.t.* **1. a, b.** strangle. **2.** repress. *-v.i.* **1.** choke, strangle.

sti·fle[2] (stī′fəl), *n.,* or **stifle joint,** the joint of the upper hind leg of various animals, as horses, dogs, etc., corresponding to the knee of a human being. [origin unknown]

sti·fler (stī′flər), *n.* a person or thing that stifles, suffocates, smothers, suppresses, etc.

sti·fling (stī′fling), *adj.* that stifles; suffocating; oppressively close: *stifling heat.* —**sti′fling·ly,** *adv.*

stig·ma (stig′mə), *n., pl.* **-mas** or **-ma·ta.** **1.** a mark of disgrace; stain or reproach on one's reputation: *But, in the lapse of . . . years . . . the scarlet letter ceased to be a stigma which attracted the world's scorn* (Hawthorne). *They were suffering from the stigma of a crushing defeat* (John L. Motley). **2.** a distinguishing mark or sign. **3. a.** an abnormal spot or mark in the skin, especially one that bleeds or turns red during hysteria. **b.** an indication of a particular condition, as hysteria. **4.** *Zoology.* **a.** the pigmented eyespot of a protozoan. **b.** a spiracle of an insect. **5.** *Botany.* the part of the pistil in flowering plants that receives the pollen in impregnation, situated either directly on the ovary or at the top (more rarely the side) of the style. **6.** *Archaic.* a special mark burned on a slave or criminal; brand. [< Latin *stigma* < Greek *stígma, -atos* mark, puncture < *stig-,* root of *stízein* to mark, tattoo]

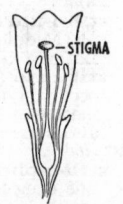

Stigma (def. 5)

stig·mal (stig′məl), *adj.* of or having to do with a stigma; stigmatic.

stig·mas·ter·ol (stig mas′tə rōl, -rol), *n.* a crystalline alcohol, a sterol, occurring in the oil of the Calabar bean and in soybean and other vegetable oils, used in the preparation of some sex hormones. *Formula:* $C_{29}H_{48}O$ [< New Latin (*Physio*)*stigma* the Calabar bean genus + English *sterol*]

stig·ma·ta (stig′mə tə), *n.* **1.** a plural of **stigma. 2.** marks or wounds like the five wounds on the crucified body of Christ, in the hands, feet, and side, said to appear supernaturally on the bodies of certain persons. [< Greek *stígmata*, plural of *stígma;* see STIGMA]

stig·mat·ic (stig mat′ik), *adj.* **1.** of or having to do with a stigma; like that of a stigma; marked by a stigma. **2.** having to do with or accompanying the stigmata. **3.** *Optics.* anastigmatic (applied especially to rays that converge to a single point).
—*n.* a person bearing marks suggestive of the wounds of Christ.

stig·mat·i·cal (stig mat′ə kəl), *adj. Obsolete.* stigmatic.

stig·mat·i·cal·ly (stig mat′ə klē), *adv.* **1.** with stigma. **2.** with a mark of infamy or deformity.

stig·ma·tif·er·ous (stig′mə tif′ər əs), *adj. Botany.* stigma-bearing.

stig·ma·tise (stig′mə tīz), *v.t.,* **-tised, -tis·ing.** *Especially British.* stigmatize.

stig·ma·tism (stig′mə tiz əm), *n.* **1.** a condition characterized by the presence of stigmata. **2.** the absence of astigmatism.

stig·ma·tist (stig′mə tist), *n.* a person on whom the stigmata appear.

stig·ma·ti·za·tion (stig′mə tə zā′shən), *n.* **1.** the act of stigmatizing. **2.** the condition of being stigmatized.

stig·ma·tize (stig′mə tīz), *v.t.,* **-tized, -tiz·ing. 1.** to set some mark of disgrace on; reproach: *He always felt that his father's prison record stigmatized both of them.* **2.** to brand: *As to their white wines, he stigmatizes them as mere substitutes for cider* (Washington Irving). **3.** to produce stigmata on. —**stig′ma·tiz′er,** *n.* —**Syn. 1.** vilify, defame.

stilb (stilb), *n.* a unit of brightness or luminance equal to one candle per square centimeter of a surface. [< Greek *stilbein* to glitter]

stil·bam·i·dine (stil bam′ə din), *n.* a drug used chiefly in the treatment of fungus diseases, especially blastomycosis and actinomycosis. *Formula:* $C_{20}H_{28}N_4O_8S_2$ [< Greek *stílbein* to glitter + English *amid*(e) + *-ine*[2]]

stil·bene (stil′bēn), *n.* a crystalline hydrocarbon, used in the manufacture of dyes. *Formula:* $C_{14}H_{12}$ [< Greek *stílbein* to glitter + English *-ene*]

stil·bes·trol or **stil·boes·trol** (stil bes′trōl, -trol), *n.* diethylstilbestrol. *Formula:* $C_{18}H_{20}O_2$ [< *stilb*(ene) + (o)*estr*(us) + *-ol*[1]]

stil·bite (stil′bīt), *n.* a mineral, a hydrous silicate of aluminum, calcium, and sodium, usually occurring in radiated or sheaflike tufts of crystals with a pearly luster. It varies in color from white to brown or red. [< French *stilbite* < Greek *stílbein* to glitter + French *-ite* -ite[1]]

stile[1] (stīl), *n.* **1.** a step, or an arrangement of steps, rungs, or the like, for getting over a fence or wall, while forming a barrier to the passage of sheep or cattle: *past the village, and down over the stile, into a field path* (John Galsworthy). **2.** a turnstile. [Old English *stigel,* related to *stīgan* climb]

stile[2] (stīl), *n.* a vertical piece in a paneled wall, the side of a door, etc. [perhaps < Dutch *stijl* doorpost, pillar]

sti·let·to (stə let′ō), *n., pl.* **-tos** or **-toes,** *v.,* **-toed, -to·ing.** —*n.* **1.** a type of dagger with a narrow, pointed blade: *a sharp, double-edged stiletto* (Frederick Marryat). **2.** a small, sharp-pointed instrument for making eyelet holes in embroidery. —*v.t.* to stab with a stiletto: *They [robbers] stiletto all the men* (Washington Irving). [< Italian *stiletto* (diminutive) < *stilo* dagger < Latin *stilus* pointed instrument]

stiletto heel, spike heel: *She wore ... black pumps with stiletto heels* (Harper's).

still[1] (stil), *adj.* **1.** remaining in the same position or at rest; motionless; stationary: *to stand, sit, or lie still.* **2. a.** without noise; quiet; tranquil: *a still night. The room was so still that you could have heard a pin drop.* **b.** (of water, the air, etc.) unruffled or undisturbed; free from waves, violent current, winds, or the like: *a pool of still water. The lake is still today.* **3.** making no sound; silent: *to keep still. Peace, and be still* (Shakespeare). **4.** not loud; soft; low; subdued: *a still, small voice.* **5.** not sparkling or bubbling: *a still wine.* **6.** of, having to do with, or used in taking a single photograph, as distinguished from a motion picture: *a still camera.*
—*n.* **1.** a single photograph, as distinguished from a motion picture. **2.** *U.S.* an individual picture or frame of a motion picture, or a photograph of a scene in a play, used in advertising. **3.** *Informal.* **a.** a still-life picture. **b.** a still alarm. **4.** *Poetic.* stillness; hush; calm.
—*v.t.* **1.** to make quiet: *The mother stilled the crying baby.* **2.** to calm; relieve: *The people prayed that the storm might be stilled.* **3.** to stop the movement or activity of. —*v.i.* to become still, calm, or quiet.
—*adv.* **1.** at this or that time: *He came yesterday and he is still here.* **2.** up to this or that time: *Was the store still open? The teacher's question is still unanswered.* **3.** in the future as in the past: *It will still be here.* **4.** even; yet: *still more, still worse. You can read better still if you try.* **5.** in spite of some event, circumstance, statement, etc.; nevertheless; yet: *Proof was given, but they still doubted.* **6.** without moving; quietly. **7.** *Archaic.* steadily; constantly; always: *still achieving, still pursuing* (Longfellow).
still and all, *U.S. Informal.* after all; nevertheless: *Still and all, he's a good man and knows the law* (New Yorker).
—*conj.* nevertheless; notwithstanding; yet: *Though she has new dolls, still she loves her old ones best. Alice has many friends; still she likes to stay home.*
[Old English *stille*]
—**Syn.** *adj.* **1, 2 a. Still, quiet** mean without noise or activity. **Still** suggests being at rest, sometimes implying absence of sound, sometimes absence of motion: *It was very late and the night was still. Her hands are never still.* **Quiet** suggests being calm and peaceful, without disturbance, excited activity, or noise: *He lives in a quiet little town.* -*v.t.* **1.** silence, hush, tranquilize, pacify.

still[2] (stil), *n.* **1.** an apparatus for distilling liquids, especially alcoholic liquors, consisting essentially of a vessel in which the liquid to be distilled is heated and a device to condense the vapor thus produced. **2.** a place where alcoholic liquors are distilled; distillery. **3.** *U.S. Slang.* a heat exchanger. —*v.t. Obsolete.* **1.** to distill. **2.** to give forth in drops. —*v.i. Obsolete.* **1.** to drip. **2.** to issue from something that is being distilled. [short for *distill*]

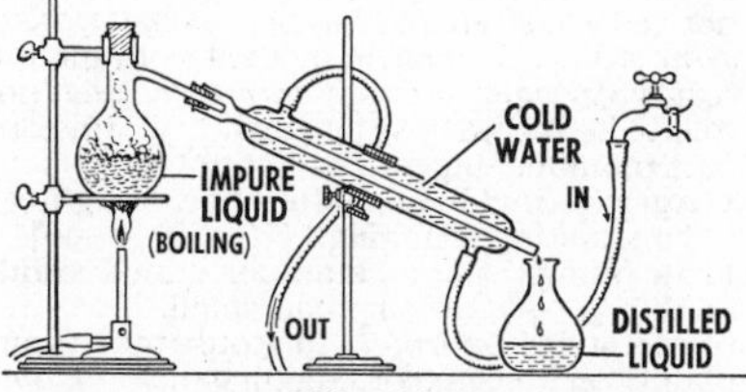

Still[2] (def. 1)

stil·lage (stil′ij), *n.* a low stool or bench in a factory, etc., used to keep manufactured products from coming in contact with the floor. Some stillages can be tilted to allow articles placed on them to slide into packing boxes. [probably < Dutch *stellage* platform, stand]

still alarm, a fire alarm communicated to the fire department by telephone or by any means other than a signal box or other apparatus activating the alarm bell in the fire house.

still·birth (stil′bėrth′), *n.* **1.** the birth of a dead child. **2.** a child dead at birth.

still·born (stil′bôrn′), *adj.* **1.** dead when born. **2. a.** destined never to be realized: *stillborn hopes.* **b.** that fails utterly to attract an audience: *a stillborn book or play.*

still-burn (stil′bėrn′), *v.t.,* **-burned** or **-burnt, -burn·ing.** to burn in the process of distillation: *to still-burn brandy.*

still fishing, fishing from a boat at anchor or from the bank of a stream, by dropping or casting a baited hook into the water and waiting for the fish to bite.

still house, a distillery, or that part of it which contains the still.

still hunt, 1. quiet or secret pursuit. **2.** a pursuit of game stealthily or under cover; stalking.

still-hunt (stil′hunt′), *v.t., v.i.* to stalk.

stil·li·cid·i·um (stil′ə sid′ē əm), *n., pl.* **-i·a** (-ē ə). *Medicine.* a morbid dropping or trickling of a liquid, as of the urine in strangury. [< Latin *stillicidium* < *stilla* a drop + *cadere* to fall]

stil·li·form (stil′ə fôrm), *adj.* drop-shaped. [< Latin *stilla* a drop + English *-form*]

still life, 1. inanimate objects, such as fruit, flowers, furniture, pottery, or dead game, shown in a picture. **2.** a picture containing such things. —**still′-life′,** *adj.*

still·man (stil′mən), *n., pl.* **-men.** a workman employed to attend to a still.

still·ness (stil′nis), *n.* **1.** freedom from noise; quiet; silence: *the stillness of the grave, to listen in sullen stillness. "A Stillness at Appomattox"* (Bruce Catton). **2.** absence of motion; calm: *the stillness of a mill pond.* —**Syn. 1.** hush. **2.** immobility.

still-room (stil′rüm′, -rům′), *n. British.* **1.** (originally) a room in a house in which cordials, etc., were distilled: *A hundred years ago every lady in the country had her still-room* (Thackeray). **2.** (later) a room where cordials, preserves, etc., are kept, and tea, coffee, etc., are prepared. [< *still*[2] + *room*]

Still's disease (stilz), a chronic disease of children, in which the spleen and lymphatic glands become enlarged and many of the joints inflamed. It is a kind of rheumatoid arthritis. [< George F. *Still,* 1868-1941, an English pediatrician]

Still·son wrench (stil′sən), *Trademark.* a wrench with an adjustable L-shaped jaw that tightens as pressure on the handle is increased, used for turning pipes and other round objects.

Stillson Wrench

stil·ly (*adj.* stil′ē; *adv.* stil′lē), *adj.,* **-li·er, -li·est,** *adv.* —*adj. Poetic.* quiet; still; calm. —*adv.* calmly; quietly.

stilp·nom·e·lane (stilp nom′ə lān), *n.* a hydrous silicate of iron and aluminum, occuring as thin scales or as a velvety coating, of a black or bronze color. [< Greek *stilpnós* glittering + *mélas, -anos* black]

stilt (stilt), *n., pl.* **stilts** or (*for 3, collectively*) **stilt,** *v.* —*n.* **1.** one of a pair of poles with a support for the foot at some distance above the ground. Stilts are used for walking in shallow water, or by children for amusement. **2.** a long post or pole used to support a house, shed, etc., above water, swampy land, etc. **3.** any of a widely distributed group of wading birds with very long, slender legs and slender, sharp bills, that live in marshes.
—*v.t.* to raise on or as if on stilts: *A sort of raw curate ... stilted up on his thick-soled high-lows* (Charlotte Brontë).
[Middle English *stilte* a crutch] —**stilt′like′,** *adj.*

stilt·bird (stilt′bėrd′), *n.* the stilt.

stilt·ed (stil′tid), *adj.* **1.** stiffly dignified or formal: *stilted conversation. There were letters of stilted penitence to his father, for some wrong-doing* (Elizabeth Gaskell). **2.** raised above the general level by a course of masonry, as an arch, vault, etc., that does not spring immediately from the top of a pier or other apparent point of impost. **3.** supported on props or posts so as to be raised above the ground. —**stilt′ed·ly,** *adv.* —**Syn. 1.** pompous.

stilted arch, *Architecture.* an arch that does not spring immediately from the apparent imposts, but is raised above them by intervening courses or members.

stilt·er (stil′tər), *n.* a person who walks on or as if on stilts.

Stil·ton cheese, or **Stil·ton** (stil′tən), *n.* a rich white cheese veined with mold when well-ripened, somewhat resembling Roquefort cheese and classed as one of the great cheeses of England. [< *Stilton,* a village in Huntingdonshire, England, where it was sold at a coaching inn]

stilt sandpiper, a long-legged American sandpiper with a gray back and white rump.

stilt·y (stil′tē), *adj.* inflated; pompous; stilted.

sti·lya·ga (sti lyä′gə), *n., pl.* **sti·lya·gi** (stilyä′gē). *Russian.* a young person in the Soviet Union, who seeks to cultivate the style of dress, uninhibited manners, etc., associated with the teddy-boys, zoot-suiters, beatniks, etc., in Western countries: *There have, of course, been unofficial movements of dress reform in recent years among young Russians — such as the bright shirts and drainpipe trousers worn by the stilyagi — but these were condemned by the party because they showed an alien ideology* (Manchester Guardian).

stime (stīm), *n. Scottish.* a glimpse.

stim·u·la·bil·i·ty (stim′yə lə bil′ə tē), *n.* the state or quality of being stimulable.

stim·u·la·ble (stim′yə lə bəl), *adj.* that can be stimulated.

stim·u·lant (stim′yə lənt), *n.* **1.** a food, drug, medicine, etc., that temporarily increases the activity of some part of the body. Tea and coffee are stimulants. **2.** something that spurs one on or stirs one up; motive, influence, etc., that rouses one to action: *Hope is a stimulant.* —*adj.* stimulating. [< Latin *stimulāns, -antis,* present participle of *stimulāre;* see STIMULATE] —**Syn.** *n.* **2.** stimulus.

stim·u·late (stim′yə lāt), *v.,* **-lat·ed, -lat·ing.** —*v.t.* **1.** to spur on; stir up; rouse to action: *Praise always stimulated her to work hard.* **2.** to increase temporarily the functional activity of (an organ or part of the body, especially a nerve). **3.** to excite with alcoholic liquor; intoxicate. —*v.i.* to act as a stimulant or a stimulus. [< Latin *stimulāre* (with English *-ate*[1]) < *stimulus* (originally) a goad] —**Syn.** *v.t.* **1.** prick, goad, incite, encourage, impel, urge.

stim·u·lat·er (stim′yə lā′tər), *n.* stimulator.

stim·u·lat·ing (stim′yə lā′ting), *adj.* rousing to (mental, physical, etc.) action; stirring; inspiring: *a stimulating speech, article.* —**stim′u·lat′ing·ly,** *adv.*

stim·u·la·tion (stim′yə lā′shən), *n.* the act of stimulating or the state of being stimulated: *Lazy children need some stimulation to make them work.*

stim·u·la·tive (stim′yə lā′tiv), *adj.* tending to stimulate; stimulating. —*n.* a stimulating thing; stimulus.

stim·u·la·tor (stim′yə lā′tər), *n.* a person or thing that stimulates.

stim·u·lose (stim′yə lōs), *adj. Botany.* covered with stimuli or stings. [< New Latin *stimulosus* < Latin *stimulus* a goad]

stim·u·lus (stim′yə ləs), *n., pl.* **-li** (-lī). **1.** something that stirs to action or effort: *Ambition is a great stimulus. We need some imaginative stimulus ... to carry us year after year ... through the routine work which is so large a part of our life* (Walter Pater). **2.** something that excites an organ or part of the body to a specific activity or function; something that produces a reaction, as the transmitting of an impulse along a nerve, the movement of a muscle, or a changed state of consciousness, in an organism: *The stimulus of a loud sound, carried by nerves to the brain, made the baby cry.* **3.** *Botany.* a sting, as a stinging hair on a nettle. [< Latin *stimulus* (originally) a goad] —**Syn.** **1.** incentive, spur.

stimulus threshold, *Psychology.* the minimum amount of stimulus required to produce a conscious effect.

sti·my (stī′mē), *n., pl.* **-mies,** *v.,* **-mied, -my·ing.** stymie.

sting (sting), *v.,* **stung** or (*Archaic*) **stang, sting·ing,** *n.* —*v.t.* **1.** to pierce or wound with a sharp-pointed organ (often) bearing a poisonous fluid: *If a honeybee stings you, remove the stinger.* **2.** (of certain plants, etc.) to produce irritation, rash, or inflammation in (a person's skin) by contact. **3.** to affect with a tingling pain, burning sensation, sharp hurt, or the like: *stung by a spark. The bullet stung his leg.* **4.** to affect with a sudden, sharp mental pain; cause to suffer mentally: *Jim was stung by the jeers of the other children.* **5.** to drive or stir up as if by a sting: *Their ridicule stung him into making a sharp reply.* **6.** *Slang.* to impose upon; charge too much; cheat: *Guess I'll have to get down to the office now and sting a few clients* (Sinclair Lewis). —*v.i.* **1.** to use a sting: *Bees, wasps and hornets sting.* **2.** to cause a feeling like that of a sting: *Mustard stings.* **3.** to feel sharp mental or physical pain or distress; smart: *The groans of a person stinging under defeat* (Thackeray).
—*n.* **1.** the act of stinging. **2. a.** a prick; wound: *Put mud on the sting to take away the pain.* **b.** the pain or smart of such a wound. **3.** the sharp-pointed part of an insect, animal, or plant that pricks or wounds and often poisons: *A wasp's sting is not left in the wound.* **4.** *Botany.* a stiff, sharp-pointed, glandular hair that emits an irritating fluid when touched, as on the nettle; stinging hair. **5.** a sharp pain or wound: *the stings of remorse. O death where is thy sting? O grave, where is thy victory?* (I Corinthians 15:55). **6.** something that causes a sharp pain: *The ball team felt the sting of defeat.* **7.** something that spurs to action; stimulus; incitement. **8.** stinging quality; capacity to sting or hurt: *This passage ... has been deprived of half its sting* (Sir George Trevelyan).
[Old English *stingan*] —**sting′ing·ly,** *adv.*

sting·a·ree (sting′ə rē, sting′ə rē′), *n.* sting ray. See **sting ray** for picture. [American English, alteration of *sting ray*]

stinged (stingd), *adj.* having a sting, as an insect.

sting·er[1] (sting′ər), *n.* **1.** the stinging organ of an insect or other animal. **2.** anything, as an insect or other animal or a plant, that stings: *Keep away from yellow jackets; they are stingers.* **3.** *Informal.* a stinging blow, remark, etc.

sting·er[2] (sting′ər), *n.* **1.** *U.S.* a cocktail consisting of brandy and white crème de menthe. **2.** *British Informal.* Scotch whiskey and soda. [alteration of *stengah* < a Malay word meaning "half"]

stin·gi·ly (stin′jə lē), *adv.* in a stingy manner.

stin·gi·ness (stin′jē nis), *n.* the state or quality of being stingy.

sting·ing hair (sting′ing), *Botany.* a sting.

stinging nettle, 1. a variety of Eurasian nettle now naturalized in eastern North America, having bristles on the stems and leaves that irritate the skin when touched. **2.** any nettle that bears stings.

sting·less (sting′lis), *adj.* having no sting.

stin·go (sting′gō), *n. British Slang.* **1.** strong ale or beer. **2.** vigor; energy; zip. [< *sting,* verb (from its sharp taste) + *-o,* perhaps imitative of Spanish or Italian endings]

sting ray, or **sting·ray** (sting′rā′), *n.* any of various groups of rays whose long, flexible, tapering tail is armed near the middle with a flattened, sharp-pointed, bony spine, serrated on both sides, capable of inflicting a severe and painful wound.

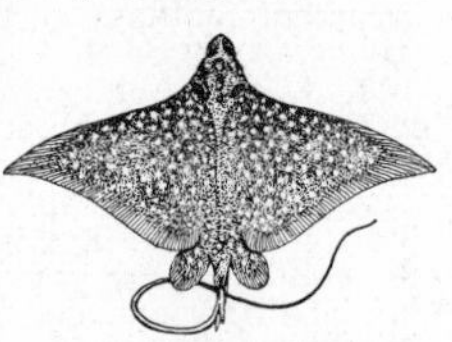

Australian Sting Ray (including tail, 10 to 14 ft. long)

stin·gy[1] (stin′jē), *adj.,* **-gi·er, -gi·est. 1.** (of persons, actions, etc.) mean about spending or giving money; not generous: *He tried to save money without being stingy.* **2.** poor in quantity or amount; scanty; meager: *a stingy helping of pudding.* [related to STING] —**Syn. 1.** miserly, parsimonious, niggardly, penurious.

sting·y[2] (sting′ē), *adj.,* **sting·i·er, sting·i·est.** having a sting; stinging. [< *sting* + *-y*[1]]

stink (stingk), *n., v.,* **stank** or **stunk, stunk, stink·ing.** —*n.* a very bad smell.
raise a stink, *Informal.* to arouse much complaint, criticism, or disturbance: *Homeowners threatened to raise a stink if property taxes were increased again.*
—*v.i.* **1.** to have a very bad smell: *Decaying fish stink.* **2. a.** to have a very bad reputation; be in great disfavor. **b.** to savor offensively (of): *His remark stinks of treason.*
—*v.t.* to cause to have a very bad smell.
stink out, to drive out with stinking smoke or fumes: *He let down by a rope a bag of burning sulphur and pitch, and stunk them* [*rats*] *out* (Charles Reade).
[Old English *stincan* to smell. Related to STENCH.]
—**Syn.** *n.* stench.
➔ **Stunk** as the past tense form was once common, but is now rare in standard English.

stin·kard (sting′kərd), *n.* **1.** any of various ill-smelling animals: **a.** a polecat. **b.** a badger. **2.** a person who stinks (formerly often used as a term of abuse).

stink·ball (stingk′bôl′), *n.* a ball or missile containing explosives, etc., for generating offensive and suffocating vapors, used in warfare for throwing among the enemy.

stink bomb, a can, jar, or other container filled with certain chemicals that gives off a disagreeable smell when exploded or burst: *We used to have some pretty rough times in those days — broken windows in the clubhouse, stink bombs in the piano* (New Yorker).

stink·bug (stingk′bug′), *n.* **1.** any of a family of large, flat bugs that have a very disagreeable odor. **2.** any of certain other bugs having a disagreeable odor. [American English < *stink* + *bug*]

stink·er (sting′kər), *n.* **1.** a thing that stinks, especially: **a.** any of several large ill-smelling petrels. **b.** a stinkpot. **2.** a person who stinks. **3.** *Informal.* a low, mean, contemptible person. **4.** *Slang.* something very difficult: *It is also a very dreary sort of a place and whoever has the job of redeveloping it has his job cut out. It is a real stinker ...* [*but*] *just the place to tackle* (Manchester Guardian).

stink fly, any of a family of green-colored lacewings that are commonly attracted to lights at night, and give off a strong odor when handled.

stink grass, an ill-smelling grass native to Europe and Asia and widely naturalized in the United States.

stink·horn (stingk′hôrn′), *n.* any of a group of ill-smelling basidiomycetous fungi.

stink·ing (sting′king), *adj.* that stinks; having an offensive smell: *a stinking pig pen. It's a stinking shame.* —**stink′ing·ly,** *adv.*

stinking nightshade, henbane, a bad-smelling plant of the nightshade family.

stinking smut, bunt, a disease of wheat kernels.

stink·o (sting′kō), *adj. Slang.* **1.** drunk. **2.** unpleasant; offensive: *Can it be that everything is lovely, nothing is absolutely stinko?* (Bayard Iverson).

stink·pot (stingk′pot′), *n.* a potlike metal vessel filled with combustibles that produce a suffocating, bad-smelling smoke, formerly flung at an enemy, especially in naval warfare, to drive him into the open or overcome his capacity to resist assault.

stink·stone (stingk′stōn′), *n.* any stone that gives out a fetid odor on being scratched or struck, because of rotten organic matter.

stink·weed (stingk′wēd′), *n.* any of several ill-smelling plants, especially the jimson weed.

stink·wood (stingk′wu̇d′), *n.* **1.** any of various trees whose wood has an unpleasant odor. **2.** the wood.

stink·y (sting′kē), *adj.,* **stink·i·er, stink·i·est.** that stinks; stinking: *A dirty, stinky, uncared-for closet-size section of a great city ...* (Claude Brown).

stint[1] (stint), *v.t.* **1.** to keep on short allowance; be saving or careful in using or spending; limit: *The parents stinted themselves of food to give it to their children.* **2.** *Archaic.* to stop; cease. —*v.i.* **1.** to be saving; get along on very little. **2.** *Archaic.* to cease action; desist.
—*n.* **1.** limit; limitation: *That generous man gives without stint.* **2.** an amount or share set aside. **3.** an allotted portion of work; task assigned: *Washing the breakfast dishes was her daily stint.* **4.** *Archaic.* a stop. Also, **stent.**
[Middle English *stinten,* Old English *styntan* to blunt, make dull] —**stint′er,** *n.* —**stint′ing·ly,** *adv.*

stint[2] (stint), *n.* any of various small sandpipers, especially the dunlin or the least sandpiper. [Middle English *stynte*]

stint·less (stint′lis), *adj.* without stint; unstinted; generous: *stintless hospitality.*

stip., stipend.

sti·pate (stī′pāt, -pit), *adj. Botany.* crowded. [< Latin *stīpātus,* past participle of *stīpāre* to stuff, crowd]

stipe (stīp), *n.* **1.** *Botany.* a stalk, especially of some special kind, other than an ordinary leaf or flower stalk: **a.** (in flowering plants) the stalk formed by the receptacle or some part of it, or by a carpel. **b.** the stalk or petiole of a frond, especially of a fern or seaweed. **c.** (in certain fungi) the stalk or stem which supports the pileus or cap: *the stipe of a mushroom.* **2.** *Zoology.* a stalklike part or organ. [< French *stipe* < New Latin *stipes;* see STIPES]

sti·pel (stī′pəl), *n. Botany.* a secondary stipule situated at the base of the leaflets of a compound leaf. [< New Latin *stipella* (diminutive) < Latin *stipula;* see STIPULE]

sti·pel·late (stī pel′āt, -it; stī′pə lāt, -lit), *adj.* having stipels.

sti·pend (stī′pend), *n.* **1.** fixed or regular pay; salary. **2.** a fixed, periodic allowance, as to a student holding a scholarship. [< Latin *stipendium* < *stips, stipis* gift (in small coin), soldier's pay; (originally) coin + *pendere* weigh out]
➔ **Stipend** is the usual word in England for the pay of a curate or other clergyman remunerated at a fixed rate, of a professor, of a judge, and of certain other professional persons. The official income of a minister of state, on the other hand, or that of a civil servant, is more commonly called *salary.*

sti·pen·di·ar·y (stī pen′dē er′ē), *adj., n., pl.*

-ar·ies. —*adj.* **1.** receiving a stipend. **2.** paid for by a stipend. **3.** of or having to do with a stipend. **4.** performing services for regular pay: *the insidious spy, the stipendiary informer* (Henry Hallam). **5.** that renders or is obligated to render services, tribute, etc., especially under feudal or ancient Roman law.
—*n.* **1.** a person who receives a stipend; salaried clergyman, official, or the like. **2.** (in ancient Rome) a stipendiary person or piece of property.
[< Latin *stīpendiārius* < *stipendium;* see STIPEND]

stipendiary magistrate, (in Great Britain and Canada) a salaried official having judicial functions similar to those of the unpaid justices of the peace.

sti·pes (stī′pēz), *n., pl.* **stip·i·tes** (stip′ə tēz). **1.** *Zoology.* a part or organ resembling a stalk, especially the second section of one of the maxillae of a crustacean or insect. **2.** *Botany.* a stipe. [< New Latin *stipes* < Latin *stīpes, -itis* tree trunk, post, stalk]

sti·pi·form (stī′pə fôrm), *adj. Botany, Zoology.* having the form or character of a stipe.

stip·i·tate (stip′ə tāt), *adj. Botany, Zoology.* having or supported by a stipe or stipes.

stip·i·ti·form (stip′ə tə fôrm), *adj.* stipiform.

stip·ple (stip′əl), *v.,* **-pled, -pling,** *n.* —*v.t.* **1.** to paint, draw, or engrave by dots. **2.** to produce a stippled effect on.
—*n.* **1.** the method of painting, drawing, or engraving by stippling. **2.** an effect produced by or as if by this method. **3.** stippled work: *rose-moles all in stipple upon trout that swim* (Gerard Manley Hopkins).
[< Dutch *stippelen* (frequentative) < *stippel* prick, speckle < *stip* a point]

stip·pler (stip′lər), *n.* **1.** a brush or engraving tool used for stippling. **2.** a person who stipples.

stip·pling (stip′ling), *n.* **1. a.** the act, method, or work of a person or thing that stipples. **b.** the design or shading so produced; dotted work. **2.** any natural appearance resembling stippled painting or engraving.

stip·u·la·ceous (stip′yə lā′shəs), *adj.* of the nature of stipules; stipular.

stip·u·lar (stip′yə lər), *adj. Botany.* **1.** of or having to do with stipules. **2.** having stipules; stipulelike. **3.** situated on, near, or in the place of a stipule.

stip·u·late[1] (stip′yə lāt), *v.,* **-lat·ed, -lat·ing.** —*v.t.* to arrange definitely; demand as a condition of agreement: *He stipulated that he should receive a month's vacation every year if he took the job.* —*v.i.* **1.** to make an express demand or arrangement (for): *In accepting the job he stipulated for a raise every six months.* **2.** *Obsolete.* to make a bargain or contract; covenant. [< Latin *stipulārī* (with English *-ate*[1]) stipulate, perhaps related to *stips;* see STIPEND]

stip·u·late[2] (stip′yə lit, -lāt), *adj. Botany.* having stipules.

stip·u·lat·ed[1] (stip′yə lā′tid), *adj.* stated; agreed upon: *a stipulated amount, the stipulated conditions in a contract.*

stip·u·lat·ed[2] (stip′yə lā′tid), *adj. Botany.* having stipules; stipulate.

stip·u·la·tion (stip′yə lā′shən), *n.* **1.** a definite arrangement; agreement; bargain. **2.** a condition in an agreement or bargain: *We rented the house with the stipulation that certain rooms should be papered and painted by the owner.* —**Syn. 1.** contract. **2.** proviso.

stip·u·la·tor (stip′yə lā′tər), *n.* a person who stipulates.

stip·u·la·to·ry (stip′yə lə tôr′ē, -tōr′-), *adj.* having to do with or characterized by stipulation.

stip·ule (stip′yül), *n. Botany.* one of a pair of little leaflike parts at the base of the petiole of many leaves. [earlier *stipula* < New Latin use of Latin *stipula* stem, stalk (of hay). Doublet of STUBBLE.]

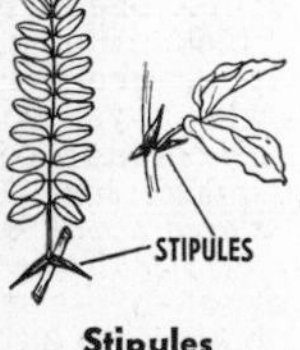

Stipules

stir[1] (stėr), *v.,* **stirred, stir·ring,** *n.* —*v.t.* **1.** to mix by moving around with the hand or an implement: *to stir the fire with a poker, stir one's tea with a spoon, stir sugar into one's coffee.* **2.** to change the position or situation of; move, especially slightly: *Thy companion had been slain by thy side . . . without thy stirring a finger to his aid* (Scott). **3.** to set in motion; shake: *The wind stirs the leaves.* **4.** to excite to feeling, emotion, or passion; affect; move: *Words . . . that really stir the soul . . .* (Anthony Trollope). *Abraham Lincoln was stirred to the depths of his being by the passing of the Kansas-Nebraska Act* (Sir Winston Churchill). **5.** to move to action; incite; instigate: *The untruth of the stories by which they had been stirred to rebellion* (James A. Froude). **6.** to bring into notice or debate.
—*v.i.* **1.** to pass from rest or inaction to motion or action; begin to move, especially slightly; budge: *They dare not stir.* **2.** to move about: *Not a creature was stirring, not even a mouse* (Clement C. Moore). **3.** to be in circulation; be current: *There is no news stirring here now* (William Dean Howells). **4.** to become active, much affected, or excited: *The countryside was stirring with new life.* **5.** to be mixed with the hand or an implement: *This dough stirs hard.*
stir oneself, to move briskly; bestir: *The French ambassador . . . stirred himself not only to keep this project alive, but to bring it to a practical conclusion* (John H. Burton).
stir up, a. to rouse to action, activity, or emotion; incite; stimulate: *John stirs up the other children to mischief.* **b.** to excite; provoke; induce: *to stir up a mutiny.*
—*n.* **1.** movement; action. **2.** a state of motion, activity, briskness, bustle, etc. **3.** excitement: *The coming of the queen made a great stir.* **4.** emotion; impulse; feeling. **5.** the act of stirring: *Mary gave the mixture a hard stir.* **6.** a jog; thrust; poke. **7.** *Archaic.* a public disturbance, tumult, or revolt.
[Old English *styrian*]
—**Syn.** *v.t.* **5.** rouse, animate, agitate. *-n.* **1.** motion, activity. **2, 3. Stir, bustle, ado** mean excitement or excited activity. **Stir** suggests disturbance or excitement, especially where there has previously been quiet: *There was a stir in the courtroom.* **Bustle** suggests an excited, energetic activity: *All the week before the class picnic, studying gave way to the bustle of preparations.* **Ado** suggests much needless or pointless busyness and fuss, especially over something not worth it: *They made much ado about a comfortable bed for the kitten.*

stir[2] (stėr), *n. Slang.* prison: *He's just out of stir.* [origin uncertain]

stir·a·bout (stėr′ə bout′), *n. British.* a porridge made with corn meal or oatmeal.

stir-cra·zy (stėr′krā′zē), *adj. U.S. Slang.* mentally disturbed because of long confinement in prison or subjection to dull, restrictive routine: *They go through little rituals, crouching in a corner and rubbing a hand ceremoniously or sitting motionless for hours in apparent catatonia—"just stir-crazy," as one staff man phrased it* (Scientific American).

stirk (stėrk), *n.* a bullock or heifer between one and two years old. [Old English *stirc*]

stir·less (stėr′lis), *adj.* without stir or movement; not stirring; motionless.

stirp (stėrp), *n. Poetic.* **1.** a stock or family. **2.** lineage: *Some maid Of royal stirp* (Lowell). [< Latin *stirps, stirpis* stem, stock]

stir·pi·cul·tur·al (stėr′pə kul′chər əl), *adj.* of or having to do with stirpiculture.

stir·pi·cul·ture (stėr′pə kul′chər), *n.* the breeding or production of special races, stocks, or strains.

stirps (stėrps), *n., pl.* **stir·pes** (stėr′pēz). **1.** stock; family. **2.** *Law.* the person from whom a family is descended. **3.** *Biology.* the organic units present in a newly fertilized ovum.

stir·rer (stėr′ər), *n.* **1.** a person or thing that stirs. **2.** an implement or device for stirring something.

stir·ring (stėr′ing), *adj.* **1.** moving; active; lively: *stirring times.* **2.** rousing; exciting: *a stirring appeal.* —**stir′ring·ly,** *adv.*
—**Syn. 1.** bustling, brisk. **2.** stimulating, inspiring.

stir·rup (stėr′əp, stir′-), *n.* **1.** a support for a rider's foot, hung from the side of a saddle, usually a loop of metal or wood with the bottom part flattened and often broadened. See **saddle** for picture. **2.** something shaped like a stirrup, especially a U-shaped clamp or support. **3.** *Nautical.* one of the short ropes hanging from a yard, with an eye at the lower end through which a foot rope is passed and thus supported. **4.** the stirrup bone. [Old English *stigrāp,* ultimately < *stige* a climbing, ascent < *rāp* rope] —**stir′rup·like′,** *adj.*

Stirrups (def. 1)

stirrup bone, *Anatomy.* the innermost of the three bones in the middle ear; stapes.

stirrup cup, 1. a drink, especially an alcoholic drink, taken or offered just before leaving or at parting. **2.** a cup of wine or other liquor handed to a man when already on horseback setting out for a journey, or to mounted huntsmen at the beginning of a fox hunt.

stirrup leather or **strap,** the leather strap by which a stirrup hangs from the saddle.

stirrup pump, a hand pump held by the foot in a stirruplike bracket, used to put out fires with water pulled from a bucket, tank, pond, etc.

stir-up (stėr′up′), *n.* the action of stirring up or condition of being stirred up; agitation; commotion: *How it gives the heart and soul a stir-up* (Robert Browning). *The stir-up at Oxford afforded a lesson for the whole country* (London Daily News).

stish·o·vite (stish′ə vīt), *n.* a mineral, a dense form of silica, formed by extreme pressure, as at a meteoritic crater. [< S.M. *Stishov,* a Russian geochemist who produced it artificially + *-ite*[1]]

stitch[1] (stich), *n.* **1.** one complete movement of a threaded needle through cloth in sewing or embroidery, or through skin, flesh, etc. in surgery: *Take long stitches when you baste your skirt hem.* **2.** a loop or portion of thread, yarn, etc., left in the cloth, skin, flesh, etc., by such a movement: *The doctor will take the stitches out of the wound tomorrow.* **3.** a particular method of using the needle in sewing, embroidery, knitting, etc., or the kind of work thus produced: *blanket stitch, buttonhole stitch.* **4.** one complete movement of the needle or other implement in knitting, crocheting, tatting, lacemaking, etc. **5.** the portion of work produced by such a movement. **6.** a piece of cloth or clothing: *He hadn't a dry stitch on.* **7.** *Informal.* a small bit: *The lazy boy wouldn't do a stitch of work.* **8.** a sudden, sharp, stabbing pain, especially a spasmodic one in the intercostal muscles: *a stitch in the side. Laugh yourself into stitches* (Shakespeare).
in stitches, laughing uncontrollably: *With this Latin outburst* [*he*] *had Oxford masters and deans in stitches today* (New York Times).
—*v.t.* **1.** to make stitches in; fasten or ornament with stitches. **2.** to fasten (cartons or the like) by stapling. —*v.i.* to work with a needle and thread; make stitches; sew.
[Old English *stice* a puncture. Related to STICK[1].] —**stitch′er,** *n.* —**stitch′like′,** *adj.*

stitch[2] (stich), *n. Dialect.* a linear or temporal span, viewed as a fragment or part of a whole.
a good stitch, a considerable distance or period: *You have gone a good stitch; you may well be weary; sit down* (John Bunyan).
[Old English *stycce* fragment, piece]

stitch·er·y (stich′ər ē), *n.* the process or the product of stitching or sewing; needlework: *yards of fine stitchery.*

stitch·ing (stich′ing), *n.* **1.** the act or work of a person who stitches: *She continued her stitching.* **2.** stitches collectively.

stitch·work (stich′wėrk), *n.* stitchery; needlework.

stitch·wort (stich′wėrt′), *n.* any of certain plants of the pink family, especially a white-flowered species supposed to cure a stitch in the side. Also, **stichwort.** [< *stitch*[1] a sharp pain + *wort* plant (because of its reputed medicinal value)]

stith·y (stiᴛʜ′ē, stith′-), *n., pl.* **stith·ies,** *v.,* **stith·ied, stith·y·ing.** —*n.* **1.** an anvil. **2.** a forge; smithy. —*v.t. Obsolete.* to forge. [Middle English *stithi* < Scandinavian (compare Old Icelandic *stethi*)]

stive (stīv), *v.,* **stived, stiv·ing.** —*v.t.* **1.** *Scottish.* to pack or stow (cargo, goods, etc.). **2.** *Scottish.* to stuff or cram full. **3.** *Dialect.* to crowd with things or persons. **4.** *Dialectal or Informal.* to shut up in a close or stifling place. —*v.i. Informal or Dialect.* to remain shut up in a close or stifling place. [< Old French *estiver.* Compare STEEVE[1].]

sti·ver (stī′vər), *n.* **1.** a Dutch coin worth about 1½ cents. **2.** anything having small value.

not a stiver, not at all; nothing: *They did not care a stiver if my head was blown off* (Blackwood's Magazine).

[< Dutch *stuiver*, or Middle Flemish *stuver*]

St.-John's-bread (sānt jonz′bred′), *n.* the edible bean of the carob. [< the account of *Saint John* the Baptist's diet while in the wilderness. See Matthew 3:4.]

St. John's Day, June 24, Midsummer Day, named for Saint John the Baptist.

St. John's Eve, the night before St. John's Day, long celebrated with bonfires and other festivities in various countries of Europe, apparently in continuation of an ancient heathen festival of the summer solstice.

St. John's evil, epilepsy.

St.-John's-wort (sānt jonz′wėrt′), *n.* any of a large group of herbs or shrubs that have clusters of showy, mostly yellow flowers and translucent dots in the leaves; hypericum.

stk., stock.

St. Law·rence skiff (lôr′əns, lor′-), a type of small, light boat with a single sail and a centerboard. [< *St. Lawrence* River]

St. Lou·is encephalitis (lü′is), a form of viral encephalitis that first occurred epidemically around St. Louis, Missouri, and is now endemic in America.

St. Luke's Day (lüks), the feast day of St. Luke, October 18.

St. Luke's summer, a period of mild weather occurring about St. Luke's Day.

S.T.M., Master of Sacred Theology (Latin, *Sacrae Theologiae Magister*).

St. Mar·tin's Day (mär′tənz), Martinmas; November 11.

St. Martin's summer, a period of mild weather occurring about St. Martin's Day.

St. Nich·o·las's clerk (nik′ə lə siz), *Obsolete.* a highwayman; thief.

sto·a (stō′ə), *n., pl.* **sto·ae** (stō′ē), **sto·as.** (in ancient Greece) a long portico or roofed colonnade, usually detached and of considerable length, often walled on one side and open on the other, used as a promenade or meeting place: *In the shade of the pine grove . . . are the remains of temples, stoas, treasuries* (Atlantic). [< Greek *stoā́*]

Stoa of Attalos, Athens

Sto·a (stō′ə), *n.* **the,** the Porch, a public walk at Athens, where the Stoic philosopher Zeno taught. He founded the philosophy of Stoicism. [< Greek *stoā́*]

stoat (stōt), *n.* **1.** an ermine in its summer coat of brown. **2.** any weasel. [Middle English *stote;* origin uncertain]

stob (stob), *n. Dialect.* **1.** a stake or post. **2.** a gibbet. [variant of *stub*]

stoc·ca·do (sto kä′dō, -kā′-), *n., pl.* **-dos** or **-does.** *Archaic.* a thrust or stab with a sword or the like. [alteration of *stoccata*]

stoc·ca·ta (sto kä′tə, -kā′-), *n.* a stoccado. [< Italian *stoccata* < *stocca* dagger, sword]

sto·chas·tic (stō kas′tik), *adj. Statistics.* having to do with random variables, processes, etc. [< Greek *stochastikós* conjectural, ultimately < *stóchos* aim, guess]

stock (stok), *n.* **1.** things for use or for sale; supply used as it is needed: *a stock of words, a stock of canned goods. This store keeps a large stock of toys.* **2.** cattle or other farm or ranch animals; livestock: *The farm was sold with all its stock.* **3. a.** the capital of a company or corporation, divided into portions or shares of uniform amount which are represented by transferable certificates. The holder of one of these is considered a part owner, rather than a creditor, of the company. **b.** the shares or portions of one such company or corporation: *Father owns some stock in that railroad.* **4.** the estimation in which a person or thing is held: *to set great stock by a remedy.* **5.** the raw material from which anything is made: *soap stock. Rags are used as a stock for making paper.* **6.** the broth in which meat, fish, or vegetables have been cooked, used as a base for soups, sauces, gravies, etc. **7.** the undistributed remainder of a pack of cards, set of dominoes or anagrams, etc., after the players have taken their allotted number, placed on the table to be drawn from according to the rules. **8.** *Botany.* **a.** the trunk or stem of a tree or other plant, as distinguished from the root and branches. **b.** an underground stem like a root; rhizome. **9.** *Horticulture.* **a.** a stem, tree, or plant that furnishes slips or cuttings for grafting. **b.** a stem in which a graft is inserted and which is its support. **10.** the descendants of a common ancestor; family; race; lineage: *She is of New England stock.* **11.** an original ancestor of a family, tribe, or race: *Their stock was King Alfred.* **12.** a race or other group of closely related animals or plants in a breed or species. **13.** an ancestral type from which various races, species, etc., have diverged. **14.** a large ethnic division; race: *The people who built this house were of Dutch stock with whom thrift was second nature* (Wall Street Journal). **15.** a related group of languages. **16.** the main upright part of anything; the vertical beam. **17.** the main part, serving as a support or handle; the part in which other parts are inserted or to which they are attached, especially: **a.** the wooden or metal piece to which the barrel and firing mechanism of a rifle or other firearm are attached: *The wooden stock of a rifle.* **b.** a similar part on certain automatic weapons. **c.** the trail on the carriage of a field gun. **18.** the handle of a whip, fishing rod, etc. **19.** an adjustable wrench for holding screwcutting dies. **20. a.** a carpenter's boring tool; brace. **b.** the body of a carpenter's plane, consisting of the frame or block which holds the blade. **21.** the part of an anchor across the top of the shank. **22.** the basic part of a plow, to which all the other parts are fastened. **23.** the lower part of a tree trunk left standing; a stump. **24.** an old-fashioned stiff neckcloth, used in place of the modern collar and tie: *Around his throat he had negligently fastened a stock of black silk* (James Fenimore Cooper). **25.** *Theater.* **a.** various plays produced by a company at a single theater. **b.** a stock company, or such companies and their activities as a category or type of theatrical production (used without article): *She is playing in summer stock.* **26. a.** (formerly) the part of a tally that a creditor received as evidence of a debt. **b.** the money represented by this tally. **c.** a debt owed, especially by a nation, city, etc., to individuals who receive a fixed rate of interest. **27. a.** any of a group of garden plants of the mustard family, that have large flowers of various colors, as the gillyflower. **b.** cabbage or colewort. **28.** *Zoology.* a compound organism consisting of a colony of zooids. **29.** *Obsolete.* **a.** a block of wood; a log. **b.** something lifeless, motionless, or void of sensation: *You stocks and stones!* **c.** a person who is senseless and lifeless like a block or log; stupid person. **30.** *Obsolete or Dialect.* a stocking.

in stock, ready for use or sale; on hand: *I intend to dispose of the whole of the goods in stock* (W.J. Greenwood).

on the stocks, a. being built: *In addition to the Britannia, at least one other long-range turboprop airliner was on the stocks* (Edwin C. Shepherd). **b.** being planned; in preparation: *I have had a long letter on the stocks for you for the last fortnight* (Cardinal Newman).

out of stock, no longer on hand; lacking: *The supplies he needs are out of stock, but they should be arriving soon.*

stocks, a. an obsolete instrument of punishment consisting of a heavy wooden frame with holes to put a person's feet and sometimes his hands through: *Since my ordination (it was in 1870) I have seen a man in the stocks as a punishment for drunkenness* (Westminster Gazette). **b.** the framework on which a ship or boat is supported while being built: *One of the galleys [is] planked and completely rigged on the stocks* (New York Mercury). **c.** a frame in which an animal, as a horse, is confined for shoeing: *The frisky horse was put into the stocks when the blacksmith arrived.*

Stocks (def. a)

take stock, a. to find out how much stock one has on hand: *The business of the servant of the company was . . . to take stock* (Macaulay). **b.** to make an estimate or examination: *The end of fifty years is a convenient moment to take stock* (London Times).

take stock in, a. *Informal.* to take an interest in; consider important; trust: *to take little stock in a story.* **b.** to take shares in (a company): *He made money by taking stock in two new airlines.*

take stock of, a. to reckon up; evaluate: *to take stock of one's holdings.* **b.** *Informal.* to look at with suspicion or interest: *to take stock of a stranger.*

—*adj.* **1.** kept on hand regularly: *stock sizes.* **2.** having as one's employment the care or handling of stock: *a stock clerk.* **3.** in common use; commonplace; everyday: *The weather is a stock topic of conversation. He merely got the stock answer that the matter was under consideration* (Time). **4. a.** having to do with, presenting, or acting in a stock or repertoire: *a stock play, a stock company, a stock actor.* **b.** appearing or recurring in various productions because of convention, custom, or unfailing appeal: *a stock character in pantomime, a stock situation in melodrama.* **5.** of, having to do with, or devoted to the raising of livestock: *a stock farm.* **6.** of or having to do with stock or stocks: *a stock certificate.*

—*v.t.* **1.** to lay in a supply of; supply: *Our camp is well stocked with everything we need for a short stay.* **2.** to keep regularly for use or sale: *A toy store stocks toys.* **3.** to furnish with horses, cattle, etc.: *to stock a farm.* **4.** to provide with wild life: *to stock a lake with fish.* **5.** to fasten to or fit with a stock, as a plow, bell, anchor, rifle, etc. **6.** to sow (land) with grass, clover, etc. **7.** *Obsolete.* to put in the stocks, as an offender. —*v.i.* **1.** to lay in a stock or supply: *a store that stocks up yearly, to stock up for the winter.* **2.** (of corn, grass, etc.) to send out shoots.

[Old English *stocc* stump, post]

—**Syn.** *n.* **1.** fund, store, goods, merchandise, wares. *–v.t.* **1.** furnish, store.

stock account, an account in a ledger showing on one side the amount of the original stock with accumulations, and on the other the amount used up.

stock·ade (sto kād′), *n., v.,* **-ad·ed, -ad·ing.** —*n.* **1.** a defensive work consisting of a wall or fence of large, strong posts set upright in the ground: *A heavy stockade round the cabins protected the pioneers from attack.* **2. a.** a pen or other place of confinement for human beings or animals, now especially one enclosed by barbed wire or wire mesh. **b.** *U.S. Military.* a place of confinement on a military post for soldiers awaiting court martial or sentenced to relatively short terms of incarceration.

—*v.t.* to protect, fortify, or enclose with a stockade.

[< French *estocade,* alteration of *estacade,* ultimately < Provençal *estaca* stake < Germanic (compare Dutch *stâke*)]

stock·age (stok′ij), *n.* **1.** the act of stocking up. **2.** stock; store: *I pointed out that, without . . . ample stockages of supplies on hand, there was no possibility of maintaining a force in Germany capable of penetrating to its capital* (Dwight D. Eisenhower).

stock·a·teer (stok′ə tir′), *n. Slang.* a person dealing in fraudulent stocks: *Stockateers sell shares in worthless bushland . . . by telephone campaigns so high-pressured the offices they originate in are called boiler shops* (Maclean's). [< *stock* + (racke)*teer*]

stock·book (stok′bu̇k′), *n. Australian.* a book in which a rancher keeps records of his cattle.

stock·boy (stok′boi′), *n.* a boy who unpacks and puts merchandise in its place in a store: *He often stood at the window looking down at his twenty-five stockboys and wondering which one of them possessed the qualities he needed* (New Yorker).

stock breeder, a person who raises or breeds livestock; stock farmer; stock raiser.

stock breeding, the breeding of livestock; stock farming; stock raising.

stock·bro·ker (stok′brō′kər), *n.* a person who buys and sells stocks and bonds for others for a commission: *As the strike fever spread, even stockbrokers were infected and staged a walk-out of their own against a new law penalizing tax dodgers* (Newsweek).

stock·bro·ker·age (stok′brō′kər ij), *n.* the business of a stockbroker.

stock·bro·king (stok′brō′king), *n.* stockbrokerage.

stock car, 1. a standard passenger car equipped for automobile racing: *A stock car* *racer can be almost anything from a Cadillac convertible to a jig-saw puzzle on wheels* (Newsweek). **2.** a railroad freight car for livestock.

stock certificate, a transferable certificate evidencing ownership of one or more shares of a corporation's capital stock.

stock company, 1. a company whose capital is divided into shares; joint-stock company or corporation. **2.** a theatrical company employed more or less permanently under the same management, usually at one theater but sometimes on tour, to perform many different plays.

stock dividend, 1. a dividend payable in additional shares of the company: *The last payment was a stock dividend of 4% in June* (Wall Street Journal). **2.** any dividend payable in cash to a stockholder.

stock dove, a wild pigeon of Europe.

stock·er (stok′ər), *n.* **1.** a person who makes or fits gunstocks. **2.** *U.S. and Canada.* a young steer or heifer, bought for butchering but kept until fattened or mature: *The movement of stocker and feeder cattle to the corn belt is gaining momentum* (Wall Street Journal).

stock exchange, 1. a place or building where stocks and bonds are bought and sold on an organized basis. **2.** an association of brokers and dealers who buy and sell stocks and bonds in the manner of an auction at a particular place or market according to fixed regulations.

stock farm, a farm where livestock is bred and raised for profit.

stock farmer, a farmer who is chiefly engaged in the breeding and raising of livestock.

stock farming, the business of a stock farmer.

stock·fish (stok′fish′), *n., pl.* **-fish·es** or (*collectively*) **-fish.** fish, such as cod, haddock, hake, etc., preserved by splitting and drying in the air without salt.

stock gillyflower, a common variety of stock grown in flower gardens and greenhouses.

stock·hold·er (stok′hōl′dər), *n.* a person who owns stock; holder of a share or shares in a company.

stock·hold·ing (stok′hōl′ding), *adj.* that owns stock. —*n.* the owning of a share or shares in a company.

stock·horse (stok′hôrs′), *n. Australian.* a horse used in herding cattle.

stock·i·ly (stok′ə lē), *adv.* in a stocky manner.

stock·i·ness (stok′ē nis), *n.* the quality or state of being stocky.

stock·i·net or **stock·i·nette** (stok′ə net′), *n.* an elastic, machine-knitted fabric used for making underwear, etc. [apparently short for earlier *stocking-net*]

stock·ing (stok′ing), *n.* **1.** a close-fitting, usually knitted covering of wool, cotton, nylon, etc., for the foot and leg. **2.** anything suggesting a stocking, as a patch of coloring on an animal's leg: *a chestnut horse with four white stockings.* [< *stock* stocking]

stocking cap, a covering for the head, usually knitted and somewhat resembling a long, tapering stocking, such as is sometimes worn for skating or by children in the winter: *He has a snowball head, big green sequin eyes, and a red felt stocking cap* (New Yorker).

stock·inged (stok′ingd), *adj.* **1.** clad in or furnished with a stocking or stockings: *a hulking, obese Babu whose stockinged legs shook with fat* (Rudyard Kipling). **2.** (of the feet) wearing stockings without shoes.

stocking feet, the feet covered only with stockings: *he . . . being at least six feet three inches in his stocking feet* (Weir Mitchell).

stock·ing·less (stok′ing lis), *adj.* without stockings.

stock-in-trade (stok′in trād′), *n.* **1.** the stock of a dealer or company: *Half its stock-in-trade is glossy paper-backs* (Punch). **2.** a workman's tools, materials, etc. **3.** resources.

stock·ish (stok′ish), *adj.* stupid; dull: *I could never deny . . . that I was eminently stockish* (Robert Louis Stevenson). —**stock′ish·ly,** *adv.* —**stock′ish·ness,** *n.*

stock·ist (stok′ist), *n. British.* a person who keeps a stock of certain goods for sale at retail; merchant; dealer: *Order your spares from the largest stockists of these spares* (Cape Times).

stock·job·ber (stok′job′ər), *n.* **1.** *U.S.* any stockbroker. **2.** *British.* a member of the stock exchange who deals with other members, as in wholesale amounts, but not with the public.

stock·job·ber·y (stok′job′ər ē), *n.* the business or practice of a stockjobber.

stock·job·bing (stok′job′ing), *n.* stockjobbery. —*adj.* that deals in stocks and shares; concerned with stockjobbery.

stock·less (stok′lis), *adj.* without a stock: *a stockless gun, a stockless anchor.*

stock list, a list published daily or periodically in connection with a stock exchange, enumerating stocks dealt in, current prices, actual transactions, etc.

stock·mak·er (stok′mā′kər), *n.* a person who makes gunstocks.

stock·man (stok′mən), *n., pl.* **-men. 1. a.** *U.S.* a man who raises livestock, especially cattle or sheep. **b.** (in Australia) a man employed to look after livestock, especially cattle or sheep. **2.** a man in charge of a stock of materials or goods.

stock market, 1. a place where stocks and bonds are bought and sold; stock exchange: *the New York stock market.* **2.** the buying and selling in such a place. **3.** the trend of prices of stocks and bonds. —**Syn. 1.** bourse.

stock option, an option giving an employee, executive, etc., the right to purchase stock from a corporation at a given price and within a given time: *The handsomest fringe benefit in U.S. business is the stock option, . . . a device that enables a man to buy stock at a fixed price long after the shares have risen above that price* (Time).

stock·pile (stok′pīl′), *n., v.,* **-piled, -pil·ing.** —*n.* **1.** a supply of raw materials, essential items, etc., built up and held in reserve for use during time of emergency or shortage: *the national stockpiles of strategic materials and farm commodities* (Arthur Krock). **2.** a supply of atomic weapons for wartime. —*v.t., v.i.* to collect or bring together as a stockpile. —**stock′pil′er,** *n.*

stock·pot (stok′pot′), *n.* **1.** a large pot in which meat, bones, vegetables, etc., are simmered with water to make stock for soup, sauces, gravies, etc. **2.** any vessel in which a mixture of things is prepared for use by or as if by long, slow cooking.

stock·proof (stok′prüf′), *adj.* that will not let livestock through: *a stockproof fence.*

stock raiser, a person who raises livestock.

stock raising, the raising of livestock.

stock-rid·er (stok′rī′dər), *n.* (in Australia) a mounted stockman.

stock·room (stok′rüm′, -rům′), *n.,* or **stock room, 1.** a room where stock is kept, especially one in which reserve stock is kept: *I was promoted fairly rapidly . . . to stockroom clerk and then to an assistant bookkeeper* (New Yorker). **2.** a room in a hotel, etc., where salesmen can show their samples and receive orders from retailers and wholesalers.

stocks (stoks), *n.pl.* See under **stock,** *n.*

stock split, the division of the shares of stock of a corporation into a larger number of shares, in which the value of the total shares remains the same but each individual share is less. A 3-for-1 stock split of 100 shares worth $12.00 each, would give the stockholder 300 shares worth $4.00 each.

stock-still (stok′stil′), *adj.* as still as a post or log; motionless. —**Syn.** stationary, immobile.

stock·tak·ing (stok′tā′king), *n.* **1.** a periodical examination and inventorying of the stock of goods in a shop, warehouse, etc. **2.** an accounting or reckoning up of resources, weaknesses, achievements, failures, etc.; appraisal; evaluation: *a spiritual stocktaking.*

stock ticker, a telegraphic instrument that prints stock quotations and other market news automatically; ticker: *The stock ticker ran behind as much as three minutes in reporting transactions from the floor of the Exchange* (Wall Street Journal).

stock·turn (stok′tėrn′), *n.* the frequency with which merchandise is replaced during a given period of time, used often as a measure of business efficiency.

stock·whip (stok′hwip′), *n. British.* a herder's whip, having a short handle and long thong.

stock·work (stok′wėrk′), *n.* a deposit of ore which is uniformly distributed through a large mass of rock, so that the excavations are not limited to a certain narrow zone.

stock·y (stok′ē), *adj.,* **stock·i·er, stock·i·est.** having a solid or sturdy form or build; thick for its height: *Ogata is a stocky, round-faced man whose baggy eyes sometimes suggest a Buddha on a bender* (Time).

stock·yard (stok′yärd′), *n.* a place with pens and sheds for cattle, sheep, hogs, or horses. Livestock is kept in a stockyard before being bought, shipped to market, or slaughtered. [American English]

Stod·dard solvent (stod′ərd), a clear, sweet-smelling liquid made by the distillation of petroleum, used as a dry cleaning agent. [< a proper name]

stodge (stoj), *v.,* **stodged, stodg·ing,** *n.* —*v.t., v.i.* to gorge; stuff; cram: *He grabs the Leader and leaves me to stodge myself with his Times* (George Bernard Shaw). —*n.* **1.** a thick, heavy, usually starchy food. **2.** dull, stodgy subjects, articles, composition, etc.: *This symposium devoted to the arts . . . was never planned as a solemn magazine of esoteric stodge* (Punch).

stodg·er (stoj′ər), *n. Informal.* a person who is lacking in spirit and liveliness; stodgy person.

stodg·i·ly (stoj′ə lē), *adv.* in a stodgy manner; heavily; dully.

stodg·i·ness (stoj′ē nis), *n.* the quality or state of being stodgy; heaviness; fullness; dullness.

stodg·y (stoj′ē), *adj.,* **stodg·i·er, stodg·i·est. 1.** dull or uninteresting; tediously commonplace: *a stodgy book, a stodgy mind or character.* **2.** thick and heavy in consistency; very filling: *stodgy food.* **3.** heavily built: *a stodgy person.* **4.** stuffed full: *a stodgy bag.* [< *stodge* to stuff + -y[1]]

stoe·chi·ol·o·gy (stē′kē ol′ə jē), *n.* stoichiology.

stoe·chi·om·e·try (stē′kē om′ə trē), *n.* stoichiometry.

stoep (stüp), *n.* (in South Africa) a raised porch around the front and often the sides of a house: *Tante Let was still sitting on the stoep when Gijs returned from the veld* (L. H. Brinkman). [< Afrikaans *stoep* < Dutch, doorstep]

sto·gie or **sto·gy** (stō′gē), *n., pl.* **-gies. 1.** a long, slender cigar, costing relatively little and usually rather strong in flavor: *Mr. Born listened politely, tilting his stogie this way and that* (New Yorker). **2.** a rough, heavy kind of boot or shoe.
[American English, earlier *stoga,* short for *Conestoga,* a town in Pennsylvania (reputedly because drivers of Conestoga wagons favored them)]

Sto·ic (stō′ik), *n.* a member of the ancient school of philosophy founded at Athens by Zeno (336?-264? B.C.). This school taught that virtue is the highest good and that men should be free from passion and unmoved by life's happenings.
—*adj.* of, having to do with, or belonging to the school of the Stoics or to its system of philosophy.
[< Latin *stōicus* < Greek *stōikós* pertaining to a *stoá* portico (especially the one in Athens where Zeno taught)]

sto·ic (stō′ik), *n.* a person who remains calm, represses his feelings, and is indifferent to pleasure and pain: *A stoic of the woods—a man without a tear* (Thomas Campbell). *The sternest seeming stoic is human after all* (Charlotte Brontë).
—*adj.* stoical: *stoic fortitude.* [< *Stoic*]

sto·i·cal (stō′ə kəl), *adj.* **1.** like a stoic; indifferent to pleasure or pain; self-controlled: *a stoical person.* **2.** of or like that of a stoic: *stoical courage.* —**sto′i·cal·ly,** *adv.* —**sto′i·cal·ness,** *n.*

Sto·i·cal (stō′ə kəl), *adj.* Stoic.

stoi·chei·ol·o·gy (stoi′kī ol′ə jē), *n.* stoichiology.

stoi·chei·om·e·try (stoi′kī om′ə trē), *n.* stoichiometry.

stoi·chi·ol·o·gy (stoi′kē ol′ə jē), *n.* the study of the elements comprising animal tissues. Also, **stoechiology, stoicheiology.** [< German *Stöchiologie* < Greek *stoicheîon* element (< *steíchein* to step, walk) + German *-logie* -logy]

stoi·chi·o·met·ric (stoi′kē ə met′rik), *adj.* having to do with stoichiometry. —**stoi′chi·o·met′ri·cal·ly,** *adv.*

stoi·chi·o·met·ri·cal (stoi′kē ə met′rə kəl), *adj.* stoichiometric.

stoi·chi·om·e·try (stoi′kē om′ə trē), *n.* **1.** the process or art of calculating the equivalent and atomic weights of the elements participating in any chemical reaction. **2.** the branch of science that deals with the relationships between the elements making up substances and the properties of the substances. Also, **stoechiometry, stoicheiometry.** [< German *Stöchiometrie* < Greek *stoicheîon* element (< *steíchein* to step, walk) + German *-metrie* -metry]

Sto·i·cism (stō′ə siz əm), *n.* the philosophy of the Stoics.

sto·i·cism (stō′ə siz əm), *n.* patient endurance; indifference to pleasure and pain: *There is . . . no stoicism, and no philosophy, that a mortal man can evoke, which will stand the final test in a real impassioned onset of Life and Passion upon him* (Herman Melville).

stoit (stoit), *Scottish.* —*v.i.* to move unsteadily; stumble or lurch. —*n.* a lurch; stumble. [perhaps < Dutch *stuiten* rebound, bounce]

stoit·er (stoi′tər), *n. Scottish.* a stoit.

stoke[1] (stōk), *v.,* **stoked, stok·ing.** —*v.t.* **1.** to poke, stir up or shake down, and feed (a fire). **2.** to tend the fire in (a furnace) or under (a boiler). —*v.i.* to stoke or stoke up anything.

stoke up, a. to get or supply with fuel: *Stoke up the furnace. The ship is stoking up.* **b.** to stir up; feed, as if with fire: *Neither the British nor the German soldier has been able to stoke up that virulent hate* (Blackwood's Magazine). **c.** to gird or be girded; prepare: *Now she is stoking up for a personal-appearance tour to promote her biggest and best part yet* (Time).

[back formation < *stoker*]

stoke[2] (stōk), *n.* in the centimeter-gram-second system, a unit for measuring the kinematic viscosity of a fluid (the viscosity of a fluid divided by its density). [< Sir George *Stokes*, 1819-1903, a British mathematician and physicist]

stoke·hold (stōk′hōld′), *n.* **1.** the section of a steamship in which the furnaces, boilers, etc., are set, adjoining or including the engine room, and usually below the water line. **2.** a stokehole.

stoke·hole (stōk′hōl′), *n.* **1.** the hole through which fuel is put into a furnace, especially into a coal-burning furnace. **2.** the space in front of a furnace or rank of furnaces where the stokers stand to shovel in coal and take out ashes.

stok·er (stō′kər), *n.* **1.** a person who feeds and tends a furnace or furnaces. **2.** a mechanical device that automatically feeds coal or other solid fuel into a furnace. [< Dutch *stoker* < *stoken* stoke, feed (a fire)]

Stokes-Ad·ams disease (stōks′ad′əmz), a slow, progressive degeneration of the heart muscle, accompanied by fainting and dizzy spells, convulsions, dropsy, slow pulse, and shortness of breath: *The patients treated suffered heart stand-still from attacks of Stokes-Adams disease* (Science News Letter). [< William *Stokes*, 1804-1878, and Robert *Adams*, 1791-1875, Irish physicians]

sto·ke·si·a (stō kē′zhē ə, -sē-), *n.* a composite perennial herb of the southern United States, that has large terminal heads of blue, purplish, or white flowers. [< New Latin *Stokesia* the genus name < Jonathan *Stokes*, 1755-1831, an English botanist]

STOL (no periods), short take-off and landing (of airplanes).

sto·la (stō′lə), *n., pl.* **-lae** (-lē). a long, ample robe worn by matrons in ancient Rome. [< Latin *stola;* see STOLE[2]]

stole[1] (stōl), *v.* the past tense of **steal:** *He stole the money years ago.*

stole[2] (stōl), *n.* **1.** an ecclesiastical vestment consisting of a narrow strip of silk or other material worn over the shoulders (by deacons over one shoulder) and hanging down in front to the knee or lower. Stoles are worn during certain church functions. **2.** a woman's scarf or similar garment of fur or fabric, worn usually with the ends hanging down in front: *She wore a cloth coat, preferring it to a mink stole she won in a raffle a year ago* (Newsweek). **3.** *Archaic.* a long robe. [Old English *stole* < Latin *stola* < Greek *stolḗ* garment; equipment, related to *stéllein* to place, array]

stoled (stōld), *adj.* wearing a stole.

stole fee, (in the Roman Catholic Church) a fee paid to a priest for a religious service, as a marriage, christening, or funeral.

sto·len (stō′lən), *v.* the past participle of **steal:** *The money was stolen by a thief.*

stol·id (stol′id), *adj.* hard to arouse; not easily excited; showing no emotion; seeming dull: *a stolid person, face, refusal, etc. The Prime Minister is immensely popular among the stolid and dour northerners* (New York Times). [< Latin *stolidus*] —**stol′id·ly,** *adv.* —**stol′id·ness,** *n.* —**Syn.** impassive, stodgy.

sto·lid·i·ty (stə lid′ə tē), *n., pl.* **-ties.** stolid quality or condition: *One is apt to associate the Swiss with solidity, not to say stolidity, rather than with sparkle* (Atlantic).

Stol·len (shtō′lən), *n. German.* a rich, fancy bread, often containing nuts, fruits, and spices.

sto·lon (stō′lon), *n.* **1.** *Botany.* **a.** a reclined or prostrate branch that takes root at the tip and grows into a new plant. A very slender, naked stolon with a bud at the end constitutes a runner. **b.** a rhizome or rootstock of certain grasses, used for propagation. **2.** *Zoology.* a rootlike process of the coenosarc, joining a bud or zooid to the compound organism. [< Latin *stolō, -ōnis* a shoot, sucker of a plant]

STOLON

Stolon (def. 1a)

sto·lo·nate (stō′lə nit, -nāt), *adj.* having a stolon or stolons.

sto·lo·nif·er·ous (stō′lə nif′ər əs, stol′ə-), *adj.* producing stolons.

sto·lo·ni·za·tion (stō′lə nə zā′shən), *n.* the producing of stolons.

sto·ma (stō′mə), *n., pl.* **-ma·ta. 1.** one of the small mouthlike openings in the epidermis of plants, especially of the leaves, occurring as a slit between two (or sometimes more) cells of special structure (guard cells), and opening into intercellular spaces in the interior tissue so as to afford communication with the outer air; breathing pore. **2.** a mouthlike opening in an animal body (chiefly used of small or simple apertures in the lower animals). [< New Latin *stoma* < Greek *stóma, -atos* mouth]

stom·ach (stum′ək), *n.* **1. a.** the part of the human or of a vertebrate body that serves as a receptacle for food and in which early stages of digestion occur. In man, it is a saclike dilation of the alimentary canal, occupying the upper part of the left side of the abdomen. **b.** (in invertebrates) any portion of the body capable of digesting food. **2.** the part of the body containing the stomach; abdomen; belly: *Dick hit Billy in the stomach.* **3.** appetite for food. **4.** desire; liking: *He had no stomach for instruments of warfare and was a profound lover of peace* (Atlantic). **5.** disposition. **6.** *Obsolete.* **a.** spirit; temper; heart. **b.** pride; haughtiness: *He was a man of unbounded stomach, ever ranking himself with princes* (Shakespeare). **c.** anger; irritation.

turn one's stomach, to nauseate; disgust extremely: *This filthy smile . . . Quite turns my stomach* (Alexander Pope).

—*v.t.* **1.** to be able to eat or keep in one's stomach. **2.** to put up with; bear; endure: *He could not stomach such insults. They could stomach even the fugitive slave law if—and only if—they could be sure that some day no such laws would be necessary* (Bruce Catton). —*v.i. Obsolete.* to be offended (at): *What one . . . doth not stomach at such contradiction?* (Richard Hooker).

[< Old French *estomac*, learned borrowing from Latin *stomachus* < Greek *stómachos* (originally) the throat < *stóma* mouth]

stom·ach·ache (stum′ək āk′), *n.* a pain in the stomach or abdomen.

stom·ach·al (stum′ə kəl), *adj.* **1.** having to do with the stomach; gastric. **2.** good for the stomach, as a remedy. **3.** of the nature of a stomach.

-stomached, *combining form.* having a —— stomach: *Large-stomached = having a large stomach.*

stom·ach·er (stum′ə kər; *formerly* stum′ə-chər), *n.* an ornamental covering for the stomach and chest, formerly worn by women under the lacing of the bodice.

Stomacher

stom·ach·ful (stum′ək-fu̇l), *n., pl.* **-fuls.** as much as one desires (of anything); sufficiency and more besides.

sto·mach·ic (stō mak′ik), *adj.* **1.** of or having to do with the stomach; gastric: *He leans on popcorn . . . and he suffers emotional and stomachic disturbances unless he gets his daily ration* (New Yorker). **2.** beneficial to the stomach, digestion, or appetite. —*n.* a medicine for the stomach.

sto·mach·i·cal (stō mak′ə kəl), *adj.* stomachic.

stomach pump, a pump or syringe used for emptying the stomach: *I've used a stomach pump, and I think they'll be all right* (New Yorker).

stomach sweetbread, the pancreas of a young animal, especially a calf, used for food; sweetbread.

stomach tooth, a canine milk tooth of the lower jaw (because gastric disturbance frequently accompanies its appearance).

stomach tube, a long, flexible tube for passing liquids into or out of the stomach.

stomach worm, a nematode worm that infests the stomach of sheep; wireworm.

stom·ach·y (stum′ə kē), *adj. British Dialect.* **1. a.** high-spirited. **b.** irritable. **2.** big-bellied; portly.

sto·ma·ta (stō′mə tə, stom′ə-), *n.* the plural of **stoma.**

stom·a·tal (stom′ə təl, stō′mə-), *adj. Biology.* **1.** having to do with or connected with a stoma or stomata; of the nature of a stoma. **2.** having stomata; stomatous.

sto·mate (stō′māt), *adj.* having stomata or a stoma. —*n.* a stoma.

sto·mat·ic (stō mat′ik), *adj.* **1. a.** of or having to do with the mouth. **b.** curing diseases of the mouth. **2.** *Biology.* stomatal. [< Greek *stóma, -atos* mouth + English *-ic*]

sto·ma·ti·tis (stō′mə tī′tis, stom′ə-), *n.* inflammation of the mouth. [< New Latin *stomatitis* < Greek *stóma, -atos* + New Latin *-itis* inflammation, -itis]

sto·ma·to·log·i·cal (stō′mə tə loj′ə kəl, stom′ə-), *adj.* having to do with stomatology.

sto·ma·tol·o·gy (stō′mə tol′ə jē, stom′ə-), *n.* the branch of medicine dealing with the mouth and the diagnosis and treatment of its diseases.

sto·mat·o·my (stō mat′ə mē), *n., pl.* **-mies.** surgical incision of the mouth of the uterus. [< Greek *stóma, -atos* mouth + *-tomíā* a cutting]

stom·a·to·plas·tic (stom′ə tə plas′tik, stō′mə-), *adj.* having to do with stomatoplasty.

stom·a·to·plas·ty (stom′ə tə plas′tē, stō′mə-), *n.* plastic surgery on the mouth. [< Greek *stóma, -atos* mouth + *plastós* something formed]

stom·a·to·pod (stom′ə tə pod, stō′mə-), *adj.* of or belonging to an order of marine crustaceans having the gills on abdominal appendages. —*n.* a stomatopod crustacean, as the squilla. [< New Latin *Stomatopoda* the order name < Greek *stóma, -atos* mouth + *poús, podós* foot]

stom·a·tous (stom′ə təs, stō′mə-), *adj.* having or furnished with stomata; stomatal.

-stome, *combining form.* mouth; mouthlike part; opening: *Pneumostome = an opening for the passage of air.* [< Greek *stóma* mouth]

sto·mo·dae·al (stō′mə dē′əl, stom′ə-), *adj.* stomodeal.

sto·mo·dae·um (stō′mə dē′əm, stom′ə-), *n., pl.* **-dae·a** (-dē′ə). stomodeum.

sto·mo·de·al (stō′mə dē′əl, stom′ə-), *adj.* having to do with or having the character of a stomodeum.

sto·mo·de·um (stō′mə dē′əm, stom′ə-), *n., pl.* **-de·a** (-dē′ə). the anterior or oral portion of the alimentary canal of the embryo, beginning as an invagination of the ectoderm. [< New Latin *stomodeum* < Greek *stóma, -atos* mouth + *hodaîos* (something) on the way (to) < *hodós* way, road]

stomp (stomp), *v.t., v.i.* to stamp (with the foot): *In Luxembourg we first met the custom of hearing the audience stomp their feet in addition to applauding for numbers they really liked* (Musical America). —*n.* **1.** a stomping. **2.** *U.S.* a form of jazz music and accompanying dance especially popular before and during the 1930's, marked by a spirited rhythm and the stamping of feet. [variant of *stamp*] —**stomp′er,** *n.*

stomp·down (stomp′doun′), *n. U.S. Dialect.* a square dance or a party with square dancing.

stone (stōn), *n., pl.* **stones** (*but for def. 10*

 PRONUNCIATION KEY: hat, āge, cãre, fär; let, ēqual, tėrm; it, īce; hot, ōpen, ôrder; oil, out; cup, pu̇t, rüle;

stone), *adj., v.,* **stoned, ston·ing.** —*n.* **1.** the hard, compact mineral material of which rocks consist; hard substance other than metal. Stone, such as granite and marble, is much used in building. **2.** a particular kind of rock or hard mineral matter. **3.** a piece of rock, especially one of a small or moderate size: *The cruel boys threw stones at the dog.* **4. a.** a piece of rock of definite size, shape, etc., used for some special purpose, as for building or paving: *foundation stones.* **b.** a block, slab, or pillar set up as a monument, boundary mark, or the like: *His grave is marked by a fine stone.* **c.** a shaped piece of rock for grinding or sharpening something; grindstone, millstone, or whetstone. **5.** a precious stone; gem; jewel: *The queen's diamonds were very fine stones.* **6.** a small, hard, rounded object resembling a stone or pebble, as a hailstone. **7.** *Botany.* the hard covering (endocarp) of a stone fruit or drupe, enclosing the seed, and enclosed by soft, pulpy flesh (the mesocarp): *peach stones, plum stones.* **8.** *Medicine.* **a.** a hard, abnormal formation resembling a rounded stone, that sometimes forms in the kidney, urinary bladder, or gall bladder, causing sickness and pain; calculus. **b.** a disease characterized by the presence of such a formation. **9.** one of the pieces used in playing certain games, as backgammon or dominoes. **10.** a British unit of weight, equal to 14 pounds: *He has the best part of a stone in weight to lose before he reaches his fastest and his best* (London Times). **11.** *Printing.* a flat table with a top of stone or (now usually) metal on which type is imposed; imposing stone or table. **12.** the block of fine-grained limestone used in lithography, especially the smooth printing surface of it.

cast the first stone, to be the first to criticize or attack (in allusion to John 8:7): *Let him who is without sin cast the first stone against the accused for the sin he has committed.*

leave no stone unturned, to do everything that can be done to bring about a desired result: *We'll leave no stone unturned to develop workable disarmament* (Wall Street Journal).

throw (or **cast**) **stones (at),** to make an attack (on); bring an accusation (against): *In view of the British record so far, no one in this country is in any position to throw stones at the attitudes of American voters to racial discrimination and civil rights* (Manchester Guardian Weekly).

—*adj.* **1.** made or built of stone; consisting of stone: *a stone wall.* **2.** of, having to do with, or relating to stone or stones: *The stone strength of the past* (Robinson Jeffers). **3.** made of stoneware or coarse clay.

—*v.t.* **1. a.** to throw stones at; drive by throwing stones: *The cruel boys stoned the dogs. They stoned her out of Thrums* (James Barrie). **b.** to put to death by doing this: *Saint Stephen was stoned.* **2.** to put stones on; pave, build, line, etc., with stones. **3.** to rub or polish with a stone; sharpen on a stone. **4.** to take the stones or seeds out of: *to stone cherries or plums.*

[Old English *stān*] —**stone′like′,** *adj.*

—**Syn.** *n.* **3.** pebble, boulder.

Stone Age, a prehistoric period when people used tools and weapons made from stone. The Stone Age is divided into the eolithic, paleolithic, mesolithic, and neolithic periods.

stone-blind (stōn′blīnd′), *adj.* totally blind.

stone·boat (stōn′bōt′), *n. U.S. and Canada.* **1.** a flat-bottomed sled without runners for hauling stones or other heavy objects over short distances: *in 1803, when Toronto was still York, the town of swamp mud, shanties and stoneboats* (Maclean's). **2.** a platform hung below the axles of a wagon, used for similar purposes.

stone-broke (stōn′brōk′), *adj. Slang.* totally without funds; penniless; ruined; stony. Also, **stony-broke.**

stone bruise, a bruise caused by a stone or other hard object, especially one on the sole of the foot.

stone canal, a duct in the water-vascular system of an echinoderm, usually with calcareous walls, leading from the madreporite to the circumoral vessel.

stone·cat (stōn′kat′), *n.* a yellowish-brown, fresh-water catfish of North America that reaches a length of about one foot.

stone cell, *Botany.* a short, hardened cell that serves to support other tissues, found especially in seeds and fruit; sclereid.

stone·chat (stōn′chat′), *n.* a small European songbird related to the thrushes whose alarm note sounds like pebbles striking together: *Stonechats and whinchats have disappeared from many heaths where they used to flourish* (Observer).

[< *stone* + *chat* (reputedly from its note of alarm resembling pebbles striking together)]

stone coal, 1. mineral coal, or coal dug up from the earth, as distinguished from charcoal. **2.** a hard variety of such coal; anthracite.

stone-cold (stōn′kōld′), *adj.* cold as stone; quite cold: *a meal of stone-cold leftovers.* —*adv.* completely; thoroughly; quite: *stone-cold dead. No passion can last forever at boiling point, and . . . men wake up one morning stone-cold middleaged* (New Yorker).

stone color, 1. a dark, dull bluish gray. **2.** a brownish gray.

stone-col·ored (stōn′kul′ərd), *adj.* **1.** dark, dull bluish-gray. **2.** brownish-gray.

stone crab, an edible crab of the Atlantic Coast of the southern United States: *Down in dark little dens on the sea floor lurk the enemies of the whelks—the stone crabs, of massive body and crushing claws that are capable of breaking away a whelk's shell, piece by piece* (New Yorker).

stone·cress (stōn′kres′), *n.* any of a group of woody herbs of the mustard family native to the Mediterranean region, with racemes of usually white or pinkish flowers.

stone·crop (stōn′krop′), *n.* **1.** any of a group of low plants of the orpine family, especially a creeping, mosslike herb with small, fleshy leaves and clusters of small, yellow flowers, that grows in masses on rocks, old walls, etc.; sedum. **2.** any of various allied plants. [Old English *stāncrop* (supposedly from its growing on rocks, old walls, etc.)]

stone curlew, any of a group of brown or grayish birds similar to the plover and curlew, with thick knees and large yellow eyes. They are found in the Old World and tropical America, especially on dry, stony ground.

stone·cut·ter (stōn′kut′ər), *n.* **1.** a person who cuts or carves stones: *Where we did find Romanesque churches in St. Gilles—and in Arles the hands of Roman stonecutters might almost have been at work* (Russell Lynes). **2.** a machine for cutting, shaping, or dressing stone.

stone·cut·ting (stōn′kut′ing), *n.* the business of cutting, shaping, or dressing stone.

stoned (stōnd), *adj.* **1.** having a stone or stones. **2.** having the stones removed, as fruit. **3.** *Slang.* intoxicated.

stone-dead (stōn′ded′), *adj.* dead as stone; lifeless: *This collection finally kills an old legend stone-dead* (Manchester Guardian).

stone-deaf (stōn′def′), *adj.* totally deaf.

stone·face (stōn′fās′), *n.* any of a group of stemless, succulent, South African plants of the carpetweed family, with the leaves forming a stonelike body from the top of which a single yellow or white flower grows.

stone-faced (stōn′fāst′), *adj.* stony-faced: *The affair . . . still draws stone-faced, humorless "no comments" from the celebrities involved* (Barnaby Macleod).

stone·fish (stōn′fish′), *n., pl.* **-fish·es** or (*collectively*) **-fish.** a very poisonous fish, found in shallow water in the tropics of the Indian and Pacific Ocean. It is a scorpionfish that resembles a small rock as it lies partly buried in sand on the ocean floor. *The stonefish . . . must be the ugliest creature in existence—a slimy, discolored fiend with a glaring eye, a skin covered with warts, and 13 quills on its back, each loaded with poison* (New Yorker).

stone fly, any of an order of insects, the nymphs of which are aquatic and frequently found under stones. The adults are much used as fish bait.

stone fruit, a fruit having the seed covered with a hard shell (stone) that is surrounded by a layer of pulp; drupe: *Peaches, cherries, and olives are stone fruits.*

stone·hand (stōn′hand′), *n.* a typesetter who imposes pages of type on a stone and secures them in the chase for electrotyping or printing.

Stone·henge (stōn′henj), *n.* a prehistoric ruin in southern England, near Salisbury, consisting of huge slabs or megaliths of roughly shaped stone in a circular arrangement.

stone·less (stōn′lis), *adj.* having no stone or stones.

stone lily, a fossil flower-shaped sea animal or crinoid.

stone·man (stōn′mən), *n., pl.* **-men. 1.** a stonemason. **2.** a stonehand.

stone marten, 1. a marten of Europe and Asia that has a patch of white fur on the throat and breast. **2.** the fur of this animal.

stone·ma·son (stōn′mā′sən), *n.,* or **stone mason,** a person who cuts stone or uses stone in building walls, etc.

stone·ma·son·ry (stōn′mā′sən rē), *n., pl.* **-ries.** the art of, or work done by, a stonemason.

stone oak, an oak found in Java and other islands, having a thick, bony, ridged acorn.

stone oil, petroleum.

stone parsley, an Old World herb of the parsley family, with aromatic seeds which are used as a seasoning; honewort.

ston·er (stō′nər), *n.* a person who stones or pelts with stones.

stone roller, 1. a fish of the eastern United States and Mexico, related to the carps. **2.** an American sucker.

stone sheep, a wild sheep of British Columbia, a brownish-black variety of the white sheep.

stone's throw, a short distance: *The parson lives only a stone's throw from the church.*

stone-still (stōn′stil′), *adj.* still as a stone; absolutely motionless: *She lay stone-still in a trance of terror* (George Meredith).

stone·wall (stōn′wôl′), *v.i.* **1.** (in cricket) to bat solely to protect the wicket. **2.** *Slang.* to obstruct business, especially parliamentary business, by long speeches, etc. —*v.t. Slang.* to obstruct (parliamentary business) by long speeches, etc. —**stone′wall′er,** *n.*

stone wall, 1. a wall built of stones. **2.** *Slang.* **a.** an obstruction of business, especially parliamentary business, by long speeches, etc. **b.** any insurmountable obstruction or obstacle.

stone·ware (stōn′wãr′), *n.* a hard, dense, vitreous kind of pottery ware, made from very siliceous clay, or a mixture of clay with a considerable amount of flint, sand, prefired clay, or the like to give it greater strength, fired higher (about 2,300 degrees Fahrenheit) than earthenware, and often glazed with salt.

stone·work (stōn′wėrk′), *n.* **1.** work done in or with stone. See **masonry** for picture. **2. a.** a wall or other structure built of stone. **b.** the part of a building made of stone. **3.** artistic work of any kind executed in stone.

stone·work·er (stōn′wėr′kər), *n.* a person who shapes or cuts stone.

stone·works (stōn′wėrks′), *n.pl.* **1.** a factory or shop where stone is cut and shaped for building, etc.; stonecutter's establishment. **2.** a place where stoneware is made.

stone·wort (stōn′wėrt′), *n.* any of a group of green algae, whose jointed stems are frequently encrusted with deposits of lime, commonly growing submerged in fresh water.

stone·yard (stōn′yärd′), *n.* a yard in which stonecutting is carried on.

ston·i·ly (stō′nə lē), *adv.* in a stony manner; stiffly; harshly; frigidly.

ston·i·ness (stō′nē nis), *n.* the quality of being stony.

ston·ish (ston′ish), *v.t. Obsolete.* to astonish.

ston·ish·ment (ston′ish mənt), *n. Obsolete.* astonishment.

ston·ker (stong′kər), *v.t. Australian.* **1.** to strike heavily; beat. **2.** to catch off guard; outwit.

ston·y (stō′nē), *adj.,* **ston·i·er, ston·i·est. 1.** having many stones, outcroppings of rock, etc.: *The beach is stony.* **2.** hard like stone; very hard: *concrete hardened to a stony consistency.* **3. a.** without expression or feeling: *a stony stare.* **b.** cold and unfeeling: *a stony heart.* **c.** (of fear, grief, etc.) petrifying; stupefying. **4.** *Slang.* stone-broke. **5.** *Obsolete.* made of stones or stone. **6.** *Obsolete.* (of a fruit) having a stone.

ston·y-broke (stō′nē brōk′), *adj. British Slang.* stone-broke.

stony coral, any of an order of corals that secrete a hard calcareous skeleton.

ston·y-faced (stō'nē fāst'), *adj.* having or showing a cold, unfeeling expression; expressionless: [*The senator*] *listened, stony-faced, tight-lipped, and angry* (Atlantic).

ston·y-heart·ed (stō'nē här'tid), *adj.* cruel; unfeeling; merciless.

stood (stůd), *v.* the past tense and past participle of **stand.**

stooge (stüj), *n., v.,* **stooged, stoog·ing.** *Informal.* —*n.* **1. a.** a person on the stage who asks questions of a comedian and is the butt of the comedian's jokes. **b.** (in vaudeville) an actor in the audience who heckles a comedian. **2.** a person who follows and flatters another; hanger-on. —*v.i.* to be or act as a stooge (for). [American English; origin uncertain]

stook (stůk, stůk), *n.* a shock (of grain). —*v.t.* to set up in shocks: *the grain was cut and stooked* (Atlantic). [Middle English *stouk;* origin uncertain]

stool (stül), *n.* **1.** a seat without back or arms. **2.** a similar article used to rest the feet on, or to kneel on; footstool. **3. a.** the stump of a felled tree, or a group of stumps. **b.** the stump or base of a tree felled or headed to produce saplings, young timber, etc., or of a plant cut down to produce branches for layering. **c.** the base of plants producing new stems or foliage annually. **d.** a cluster of stems or foliage from a stool or from the same root, or a shoot or layer from a plant. **4.** *Hunting.* **a.** a decoy. **b.** a movable pole to which a bird is fastened as a decoy. **5. a.** an article or place to be used as a toilet. **b.** a movement of the bowels; waste matter from the bowels. **6.** a window sill.

fall between two stools, to make a complete failure by hesitating between two opportunities or trying to use both: *Asked to develop two patterns of thought he may well fall between two stools and develop neither* (Technology).

—*v.i.* **1.** to send out shoots or stems; form a stool. **2.** to evacuate the bowels.

[Old English *stōl*] —**stool'like',** *adj.*

stool end, a part of rock left unworked in a mine to support the rest.

stool pigeon, 1. *Slang.* a spy for the police; informer: *Everybody in the plant was regarding everybody else as a possible stool pigeon* (Maclean's). **2. a.** a pigeon fastened to a stool and used to lead other pigeons into a net or other trap. **b.** *Slang.* a person employed as a decoy, as by gamblers.

stool·y or **stool·ie** (stü'lē), *n., pl.* **stool·ies.** *U.S. Slang.* a stool pigeon.

stoop[1] (stüp), *v.i.* **1.** to bend forward: *He stooped to pick up the money. She stoops over her work.* **2.** to carry the head and shoulders bent forward: *The old man stoops.* **3.** (of trees, precipices, etc.) to bend forward and downward; slope. **4.** to lower oneself; descend: *He stooped to cheating. When lovely woman stoops to folly* (Oliver Goldsmith). **5.** to swoop like a hawk or other bird of prey. **6.** *Archaic.* to submit; yield. **7.** *Obsolete.* to descend from a height. —*v.t.* **1.** to lower by bending forward; bow: *A superb-looking warrior stooped the towering plumes of his head-dress . . . and entered the house* (Herman Melville). **2.** *Archaic.* to humble; subdue; subject.

—*n.* **1.** an act of stooping; a bending forward. **2.** a forward bend. **3.** a forward bend of the head and shoulders: *My uncle walks with a stoop.* **4.** condescension. **5.** the swoop of a bird of prey on its quarry: *The peregrine in its "stoop" attains 175 an hour, the highest speed ever recorded for a bird* (Scientific American).

[Old English *stūpian*] —**stoop'er,** *n.*

—**Syn.** *v.i.* **1.** incline. **4.** condescend, deign.

stoop[2] (stüp), *n. U.S.* a porch or platform at the entrance of a house. [American English < Dutch *stoep*]

Stoop[2]
Van Rensselaer House, Greenbush, New York

stoop[3] (stüp), *n.* stoup.

stoop[4] (stüp), *n. Dialect.* a post or pillar. [< Scandinavian (compare Old Icelandic *stolpe*)]

stoop[5] (stüp), *n. Obsolete.* stupe.

stoop·ball (stüp'bôl'), *n. U.S.* a variation of baseball, usually played in city streets, in which a rubber ball is thrown against the stoop of a house or building and players on the opposing team try to catch the ball before it bounces.

stoop·ing·ly (stüp'ing lē), *adv.* in a stooping manner; with a forward bend.

stoop labor, *U.S.* labor requiring much stooping or bending over, as picking, weeding, or other such farm labor in the fields: *He supports himself and his family by odd jobs and stoop labor in the fields* (New Yorker).

stoop-shoul·dered (stüp'shōl'dərd), *adj.* having a habitual stoop in the shoulders and back.

stop (stop), *v.,* **stopped** or (*Poetic*) **stopt, stop·ping,** *n.* —*v.t.* **1. a.** to keep from moving, acting, doing, being, etc.: *to stop work, stop a speaker, stop a car, stop a clock. The men stopped the boys from teasing the cat.* **b.** to hold back; restrain; prevent: *If anyone wants to go, I shan't stop him.* **2.** to cut off; withhold: *to stop supplies, stop a person's pay.* **3.** to put an end to; interrupt; check: *to stop a noise.* **4.** to close by or as if by filling; fill holes in; close: *to stop a crack, stop a leak, stop a wound. Father stopped up the ratholes.* **5.** to block; obstruct: *A fallen tree stopped traffic.* **6.** to check, counter, or parry (a stroke, blow, weapon, etc.); ward off. **7.** (in boxing) to defeat by a knockout: *He was stopped in the second round.* **8.** (in various games) to defeat. **9.** to bring down or kill by or as if by the action of a weapon. **10.** to punctuate. **11.** *Music.* **a.** to close (a finger hole, etc.) in order to produce a particular tone from a wind instrument. **b.** to press down (a string of a violin, etc.) in order to shorten its vibrating length and thus produce a higher tone than that of the unstopped (open) string. **c.** to produce (a tone or sound) by this means. **12.** to instruct a bank not to honor (a check, bill, etc.) when presented. **13.** to issue a stop order on (a particular security, etc.). **14.** (in bridge) to have (a suit) guarded or blocked by holding a high card and cards to protect it and thus to prevent an opponent from running all the tricks in the suit.

—*v.i.* **1.** to stay; halt: *to stop, look, and listen, to stop for the night at a hotel. Mrs. Blank stopped at the bank for a few minutes. Because I could not stop for Death—He kindly stopped for me* (Emily Dickinson). **2.** to leave off moving, acting, doing, being, etc.; discontinue; cease: *All work stopped. The rain is stopping.* **3.** to be or become plugged or clogged.

stop by or **in,** to stop for a short visit: *He stopped in, not at all sure that on this first occasion he would be able to broach the dangerous subject* (Theodore Dreiser).

stop down, *Photography.* to reduce the aperture of a lens and thus the amount of light reaching the film or plate: *The sharpness of the picture can . . . be greatly improved by the simple expedient of "stopping down"* (J.A. Hodges).

stop off, *Informal.* to stop for a short stay: *Yet would I counsel the traveler whose way lies by Avignon to stop off, if only for an hour, in order to ascend the Rocher des Doms* (Outing).

stop over, a. to make a short stay: *By stopping over at Dalhousie* [*in Canada*] *. . . the following localities may be visited* (J.W. Dawson). **b.** *Informal.* to stop in the course of a trip: *You renewed your ticket after stopping over in Baltimore* (Mark Twain).

—*n.* **1. a.** the act of coming to a halt; cessation of onward movement: *His sudden stop startled us.* **b.** a cessation of an activity or process; end: *The singing came to a stop.* **c.** a stay or halt in the course of a journey: *a short stop for lunch.* **d.** a blocking, hindering, checking, or obstructing: *to be the cause of a complete stop of traffic.* **2.** a being stopped. **3.** a place where a stop is made: *a bus stop.* **4.** a thing that stops; obstacle. **5.** a plug or cork; stopper. **6.** any piece or device that serves to check or control movement or action in a mechanism. **7. a.** a punctuation mark that normally indicates some kind of pause, as a comma or semicolon. **b.** a full stop; period. **8.** a word used in telegrams, cables, etc., instead of a period. **9.** *Music.* **a.** the closing of a finger hole or aperture in the tube of a wind instrument, or the act of pressing with the finger on a string of a violin, etc., so as to alter the pitch of its tone. **b.** a key or other device used for this purpose. **c.** (in an organ) a graduated set of pipes of the same kind, producing tones of the same quality: *One music from a thousand stops and strings* (Henry Augustin Beers). **d.** the handle or knob that is pulled out or pushed in to turn a particular (organ) stop on or off, or to control a coupler; stop knob. See **organ** for picture. **e.** a similar set of reeds in a reed organ. **10. a.** an instruction to a bank or banker not to honor a check, bill, etc. **b.** a stop order. **11.** *Nautical.* any piece of small rope, cloth, etc., used to hold or tie something, especially a furled sail. **12.** *Photography.* the aperture of a lens, or the f/number indicating this: *The next stop smaller than f/3.5 is f/2.* **13.** a high card or group of cards in a suit that protects the holder against an opponent's run in that suit. **14.** *Phonetics.* **a.** a speech sound articulated, with the nasal passage closed, by completely stopping the breath stream either in the glottis, at some point in the mouth, or at the lips, followed by its sudden release, as English *p, b, t, d, k,* and *g.* **b.** (in some classifications) a speech sound articulated, with the nasal passage either open or closed, by completely stopping the breath stream at some point, thus including also the nasals, as English *m, n,* and *ng.* **c.** the actual stoppage of the breath stream.

pull out all (the) stops, to do something in the biggest way possible; exert maximum effort: *But perhaps the best scene in the show is Art Smith's shrewd lawyer pulling out all stops to get Volpone acquitted* (Saturday Review).

put a stop to, to stop; end: *Henry . . . put a stop to this* (M.J. Guest). *The coal trade at Newcastle was for some time put a stop to by a mutiny* (John Brand).

[Old English *-stoppian* (in *for-stoppian*), ultimately < Latin *stuppa* tow[2], oakum < Greek *stýppē.* Doublet of ESTOP.]

—**Syn.** *v.t.* **1. a. Stop, arrest, check** mean to keep someone or something from continuing an action, movement, progress, or the like. **Stop,** the general word, means to bring to an end any kind of advance or movement: *He stopped the car.* **Arrest** means to stop and firmly restrain something that is already advancing: *His case of tuberculosis was arrested early.* **Check** means to stop or arrest suddenly, sharply, or with force, sometimes only temporarily: *An awning over the sidewalk checked his fall and saved his life.* **2.** discontinue, intermit. **3.** hinder, deter, impede, prevent, suspend. *-v.i.* **2. Stop, cease, pause** mean to leave off. **Stop,** the general word, means to leave off doing, acting, moving, or going ahead: *The train stopped. He stopped breathing.* **Cease,** a more formal word, means to come to an end, and therefore is used of things that are existing or lasting, or to emphasize that action or movement has stopped permanently: *All life has ceased. He has ceased to breathe.* **Pause** means to stop for a time, but suggests going on again: *He paused to tie his shoe.*

stop bath, an acid solution used to halt the developing process in photography; short-stop.

stop·cock (stop'kok'), *n.* a device for turning the flow of a liquid or gas on or off; faucet; valve.

stop drill, a drill made with a solid shoulder or attachable collar to limit the depth of its penetration.

stope (stōp), *n., v.,* **stoped, stop·ing.** *Mining.* —*n.* a steplike excavation in a mine to take out the ore after shafts have been sunk: *This stope will be producing at a limited rate only, pending completion of the underground crushing station later in the current year* (London Times).

—*v.t., v.i.* to remove (the contents of a vein) by stopes.

stope out, to stope: *to stope out salt.*

[probably related to STEP, noun]

stop·gap (stop'gap'), *n.* **1.** a thing or person that fills the place of something lacking; temporary substitute: *We ought to send them our surplus food and clothing as a stopgap, until we can do something more permanent for them* (Atlantic). **2.** an utterance intended to fill up a gap or an awkward pause in conversation or discourse: *a mere conversational stopgap, to be dropped now that the real business could be commenced* (H.G. Wells). —*adj.* serving as a stopgap: *U.S. economists consider stabilization plans only short-term, stopgap methods of straightening out world markets* (Time).

stop knob, a handle used to turn an organ stop on or off; stop.

stop·light (stop′līt′), *n.* **1.** a red light on the rear end of a vehicle that turns on automatically when the brakes are applied. **2.** a traffic light: *At the stoplight, a boy in the car alongside yells to his dad to look* (Wall Street Journal).

stop-loss (stop′lôs′, -los′), *adj.* of the nature of or having to do with a stop order: *Stop-loss orders have not been much of a factor in the price decline* (Wall Street Journal).

stop motion, a method of taking motion pictures at extended intervals so that a slow movement or process, such as the opening of a flower, will appear much accelerated; time-lapse photography.

stop·off (stop′ôf′, -of′), *n. U.S. Informal.* a stopover.

stop order, an order to buy or sell (stocks, commodities, etc.) whenever the market reaches a set price, especially to prevent a loss from a further change in the market price: *The council met and determined that we should unload all coupons the following morning if a stop order had not already been issued* (Harper's).

stop·o·ver (stop′ō′vər), *n.* **1.** a stopping over in the course of a journey, especially with the privilege of proceeding later on the ticket originally issued for the journey. **2.** a place where a journey is broken: *We'd have to keep driving steadily if we were to reach our first stopover point in time for a decent night's rest* (New Yorker). [American English < *stop* + *over*]

stop·pa·ble (stop′ə bəl), *adj.* capable of being stopped: *The ICBM will be, as far as man can now foresee, the world's least stoppable weapon* (New York Times Magazine).

stop·page (stop′ij), *n.* **1.** a stopping: *a work stoppage for repairs. Her psychiatrist helped Emma to see how her emotional tensions were linked with fears of drowning and other accidents which involved stoppage of breathing* (Time). **2.** a being stopped. **3.** a block; an obstruction.

stop payment, an instruction to a bank or banker by the maker of a check not to pay that check.

stopped (stopt), *adj.* **1. a.** obstructed; blocked. **b.** (of a hole, crevice, etc.) filled up. **2.** (of a vessel, tube, etc.) closed with a plug or stopper. **3.** brought to a standstill. **4. a.** (of an organ pipe) having the upper end closed, thereby being about an octave lower in pitch than an open pipe of equal length. **b.** (of a violin string, etc.) pressed down with the finger. **c.** (of a tone or note) produced by stopping a string, finger hole, etc., of an instrument. **d.** (of a French horn) having the sound muffled by the placing of the player's hand in the bell. **5.** *Phonetics.* articulated as a stop.

stopped diapason, an organ stop that gives powerful, flutelike tones.

stop·per (stop′ər), *n.* **1.** a plug or cork for closing a bottle, tube, etc. **2.** a person or thing that stops.
—*v.t.* **1.** Also, **stopper down.** to close or secure (a bottle, etc.) with a stopper. **2.** to fit with a stopper.

stop·ple (stop′əl), *n., v.,* **-pled, -pling.** —*n.* a stopper for a bottle, etc.; plug. —*v.t.* to close or fit with a stopper. [partly < *stop;* partly short for *estoppel*]

stop-press (stop′pres′), *British.* —*n.* a newspaper column containing late news inserted after printing has begun: *Look at . . . the racing news in the stop-press* (London Times). —*adj.* containing late or the latest news: *a stop-press newspaper, a stop-press item.*

stops (stops), *n.pl.* any of a group of similar card games in which a player may lay down from his hand as many cards in a sequence as he holds, usually (but not always) played with a deck of cards from which a card has been left out.

stop sign, *U.S.* a traffic sign posted at an intersection to signal motorists going toward it to come to a full stop: *Police believed that the farm workers' truck had run through a stop sign at the intersection and directly into the path of the tractor-trailer* (Newsweek).

stopt (stopt), *v. Poetic.* stopped; a past tense and a past participle of **stop.**

stop watch, a watch having a hand or hands that can be stopped or started at any instant. A stop watch indicates fractions of a second and is used for timing races and other contests.

stop·work (stop′wėrk′), *n.* a device attached to a watch, clock, music box, etc., to prevent overwinding.

stor·a·bil·i·ty (stôr′ə bil′ə tē, stōr′-), *n.* the quality of being storable.

stor·a·ble (stôr′ə bəl, stōr′-), *adj.* that can be stored: *. . . promised to maintain supports under basic storable commodities at 90 per cent parity* (Newsweek).

stor·age (stôr′ij, stōr′-), *n.* **1. a.** the act or fact of storing goods: *room for storage, the storage of clothes in a trunk.* **b.** the condition of being stored: *to remove winter clothes from storage.* **2.** a place for storing: *She has put her furniture in storage.* **3.** the price for storing, especially rent paid for warehousing: *She paid $30 storage on her furniture.* **4.** the production by electric energy of chemical reactions that can be reversed to produce electricity, especially that occurring in and exemplified by the charging of a storage battery.

storage battery, a connected group of electrolytic cells for the production of electrical energy. When the cells have been discharged they may be charged again by the passage through them of a current in a direction opposite to that of the current flow when discharging.

storage cell, a storage battery.

storage tank, a tank for storing water, oil, liquid gas, etc.

sto·rax (stôr′aks, stōr′-), *n.* **1.** a solid resin resembling benzoin, with an odor like that of vanilla, obtained from a small styracaceous tree of Asia Minor and Syria, formerly used in medicine and perfume. **2.** the tree itself. **3.** any other tree or shrub of the same group, found chiefly in warm regions of Asia and America, as the species from which benzoin is obtained. **4.** a fragrant gum resin or balsam obtained from various species of liquidambar, especially the inner bark, used in medicine, perfumery, etc. [< Latin *storax,* variant of *styrax* < Greek *stýrax, -akos*]

store (stôr, stōr), *n., v.,* **stored, stor·ing.** —*n.* **1.** *Especially U.S.* a place where goods are kept for sale; shop. **2.** *Especially British.* a place where supplies are kept for future use; warehouse; storehouse. **3.** *Archaic.* quantity; abundance: *We wish them a store of happy days* (Tennyson).
in store, a. saved for future use; in reserve; on hand: *It was determined . . . that a hundred and seventy thousand barrels of gunpowder should constantly be kept in store* (Macaulay). **b.** awaiting (a person, etc.): *Eight of the nation's leading economic seers . . . let the world know just what was in store . . . for business in the year ahead* (Newsweek).
set store by, to value; esteem: *She sets great store by her heirlooms.*
stores, a. the things needed to equip and maintain an army, ship, household, etc., as food, clothing, arms, etc.; supplies: *naval stores.* **b.** a thing or things laid up for future use; supply; stock: *She puts up stores of preserves and jellies every year.*
[short for Middle English *astore* < Old French *estor,* noun < *estorer;* see the verb]
—*v.t.* **1.** to supply or stock: *These studies . . . store a man's mind with valuable facts* (Washington Irving). **2.** to put away for future use; lay up; accumulate: *He stores old coins in a metal box.* **3.** to put in a warehouse or other place for preserving or safekeeping: *We stored our furs during the summer.*
store away or **up,** to put away for future use; lay up; accumulate: *The squirrel stores away nuts.*
[short for Middle English *astoren* < Old French *estorer* construct, erect, furnish, store, restore < Latin *instaurāre* restore < *in-* in + unrecorded *staurus* pillar]

store·front (stôr′frunt′, stōr′-), *n.* the front or front room of a store: *The façade of the office is a storefront* (New Yorker). —*adj.* situated in a storefront: *a storefront clubhouse.*

store·house (stôr′hous′, stōr′-), *n.* **1.** a place where things are stored; warehouse: *This factory has many storehouses for its product.* **2.** any person or thing viewed as resembling this: *A library is a storehouse of information.*

store·keep·er (stôr′kē′pər, stōr′-), *n.* **1.** *U.S.* a person who has charge of or owns a retail store or stores. **2.** *Especially British.* a person who has charge of receiving and issuing supplies, especially military or naval supplies.

store·keep·ing (stôr′kē′ping, stōr′-), *n.* the keeping of a store; business of a storekeeper.

store·man (stôr′man′, stōr′-), *n., pl.* **-men. 1.** *U.S.* an owner or manager of a store, especially a department store: *But for all the hustle and bustle of this late burst of buying, most storemen figured they would be lucky to merely equal last year's sales mark* (Wall Street Journal). **2.** a man in charge of stores or supplies, as on a ship or in a store: *The deck storeman . . . was a former divinity student and a bridge player of international repute* (New Yorker).

stor·er (stôr′ər, stōr′-), *n.* a person who lays up or accumulates a store.

store·room (stôr′rüm′, -rům′; stōr′-), *n.* a room where things are stored.

stores (stôrz, stōrz), *n.pl.* See under **store, *n.***

store·ship (stôr′ship′, stōr′-), *n.* a government ship detailed to carry naval or military stores.

sto·rey (stôr′ē, stōr′-), *n., pl.* **-reys.** *Especially British.* story[2].

sto·reyed (stôr′ēd, stōr′-), *adj. Especially British.* storied[2].

sto·ri·at·ed (stôr′ē ā′tid, stōr′-), *adj.* historiated. [short for *historiated*]

sto·ried[1] (stôr′ēd, stōr′-), *adj.* **1.** celebrated in story or history: *the storied Wild West.* **2.** ornamented with designs representing happenings in history or legend: *storied tapestry.* [< *story*[1] + *-ed*[2]]

sto·ried[2] (stôr′ēd, stōr′-), *adj.* having stories or floors: *a storied tower, a two-storied house.* [< *story*[2] + *-ed*[2]]

sto·ri·ette (stôr′ē et′, stōr′-), *n.* a very short story. [American English]

sto·ri·o·log·i·cal (stôr′ē ə loj′ə kəl, stōr′-), *adj.* of or having to do with storiology.

sto·ri·ol·o·gist (stôr′ē ol′ə jist, stōr′-), *n.* a person who is versed in folklore.

sto·ri·ol·o·gy (stôr′ē ol′ə jē, stōr′-), *n.* the study of popular tales and legends, their origin, distribution, etc. [< *story*[1] + *-logy*]

stork (stôrk), *n.* any of a family of large wading birds with long legs and a long, stout bill, related to the ibises and herons, as the jabiru and the European white stork. [Old English *storc*] —**stork′like′,** *adj.*

White Stork
(about 3 ft. high)

stork's-bill (stôrks′-bil′), *n.* any of a group of plants that includes most of the cultivated varieties of geraniums; pelargonium. [< the beaklike prolongation of the seed pod]

storm (stôrm), *n.* **1.** a strong wind with rain, snow, hail, or thunder and lightning. In deserts there are storms of sand. *One of the worst storms of the winter suddenly swept down on the Northeast* (Newsweek). **2.** a heavy fall of rain, hail, or snow, or a violent outbreak of thunder and lightning, without strong wind. **3.** *Meteorology.* a wind having a velocity of 64-75 miles per hour (on the Beaufort scale, force 11). **4.** anything like a storm: *a storm of arrows.* **5.** a violent attack: *The castle was taken by storm.* **6.** a violent outburst or disturbance: *a storm of tears, a storm of angry words, a storm of applause.*
storm in a teacup, *Especially British.* a great commotion about a small matter: *[He] described the mystery of his whereabouts at the weekend as "a storm in a teacup"* (London Times).
—*v.i.* **1.** to blow hard; rain; snow; hail: *It stormed last night.* **2.** to be violent; rage: *She curses and storms at me like a trooper* (Samuel Richardson). *Why look you, how you storm, I would be friends with you* (Shakespeare). **3.** to rush to an assault or attack: *troops storming up the hill.* **4.** to rush violently: *He stormed out of the room.* —*v.t.* **1.** to attack or trouble violently, as if with a storm: *He laid siege to her affections and stormed her heart. A fickle maid . . . Storming her world with sorrow's wind and rain* (Shakespeare). **2.** (of loud and angry speech) to affect as if with a storm: *His curses stormed the air.* **3.** to attack violently: *Troops stormed the city.*
[Old English *storm*]

storm and stress, Sturm und Drang.

storm belt, a belt or zone in which storms occur in a regular pattern of frequency.

storm·bird (stôrm′bėrd′), *n.* **1.** the stormy petrel. **2.** any bird that seems to foretell bad weather by its cries or other actions.

storm·bound (stôrm′bound′), *adj.* confined or detained by a storm.

storm cellar, *U.S.* a cellar for shelter during cyclones, tornadoes, etc.: *Throughout this corridor, the storm cellar is a functional unit of residential architecture* (New Scientist).

storm center, **1.** the center of a cyclone; area where the pressure is lowest, characterized by comparative calm. **2.** any center of trouble, tumult, etc.: *She was a troublemaker, a constant storm center at school.*

storm cloud, **1.** a cloud that brings or threatens storm: *Cloud seeding may actually increase ... the amount of hail formed in storm clouds* (Science News Letter). **2.** any threatening sign, as of violence, trouble, etc.: *He ran out of capital ... as the storm clouds of the second world war began to gather* (Harper's).

storm·coat (stôrm′kōt′), *n.* a thick, usually lined and waterproof coat.

storm·cock (stôrm′kok′), *n.* **1.** the fieldfare. **2.** the green woodpecker. [from the belief that they are stormbirds]

storm door, *U.S.* an extra door outside of an ordinary door, to keep out snow, cold winds, etc.

storm drain, a storm sewer.

storm·er (stôr′mər), *n.* **1.** a person who takes by storm; member of a storming party. **2.** a person who rages.

storm·ful (stôrm′fu̇l), *adj.* having or troubled by many storms. —**storm′ful·ness,** *n.*

storm·i·ly (stôr′mə lē), *adv.* in a stormy manner.

storm·i·ness (stôr′mē nis), *n.* the state of being stormy.

storm jib, a small jib made of heavy canvas for use in bad weather.

storm·less (stôrm′lis), *adj.* without storms.

storm·proof (stôrm′prüf′), *adj.* resistant to storms; that can withstand a storm.

storm sewer, a sewer for carrying off rain from paved streets, etc.

storm signal, **1.** a signal displayed along a seacoast or lakeshore to give warning of the approach of high winds and storms. **2.** any sign of trouble or danger to come: *Recession storm signals are going up in Europe even while inflation remains a chronic threat* (Wall Street Journal).

storm tide, an unusually high tide caused by strong onshore winds.

storm track, the path traveled by the center of a cyclonic storm.

storm trooper, **1.** a member of the Sturmabteilung of Nazi Germany. **2.** an extremely brutal or vicious individual.

storm troops, Sturmabteilung.

storm·ward (stôrm′wərd), *adv., adj.* toward the storm.

storm warning, **1.** a display of storm signals or a broadcast predicting a storm and its probable intensity: *The storm warnings that flew Lake Michigan's length changed that night into "whole gale" warnings* (Time). **2.** a sign of trouble to come.

storm wind, **1.** the wind or blast of a storm. **2.** a wind that brings a storm.

storm window, an extra window outside of an ordinary window, to keep out snow, cold winds, etc.

storm·y (stôr′mē), *adj.,* **storm·i·er, storm·i·est.** **1.** having a storm or storms; likely to have storms; troubled by storms: *a stormy sea, a stormy night, stormy weather.* **2.** rough and disturbed; violent: *They had stormy quarrels.* —**Syn. 1.** tempestuous, blustery, windy. **2.** wild.

stormy petrel, **1.** any of a family of small, black-and-white sea birds whose presence is supposed to give warning of a storm. See **petrel** for picture. **2.** anyone believed likely to cause trouble or to indicate trouble: *He [Sinclair Lewis] was a stormy petrel in his life as in his books* (Basil Davenport).

stor·nel·lo (stôr nel′ō), *n., pl.* **-nel·li** (-nel′ē). a simple Italian folksong, usually improvised, and either sentimental or satirical. [< Italian *stornello*]

Stor·thing or **Stor·ting** (stôr′ting′, stōr′-), *n.* the national legislature of Norway. [< Norwegian *Storting, Storthing* < *stor* great + *ting, thing* assembly]

sto·ry¹ (stôr′ē, stōr′-), *n., pl.* **-ries,** *v.,* **-ried, -ry·ing.** —*n.* **1.** an account of some happening or group of happenings: *the story of the boy's disappearance, the story of his life, the story of the gold rush.* **2.** such an account, either true or made-up, intended to interest the reader or hearer; tale: *fairy stories, ghost stories, a speech abounding in good stories, the short stories of Poe, of O. Henry, etc.* **3.** *Informal.* a falsehood: *That boy tells stories.* **4.** stories as a branch of literature: *famous in song and story.* **5.** the plot or succession of incidents of a play, novel, etc.: *If you were to read [Samuel] Richardson for the story, your impatience would be so much fretted that you would hang yourself* (Samuel Johnson). **6.** *U.S.* **a.** a newspaper article. **b.** the subject or material for this. **7.** *Archaic.* history: *well-read in story.*

—*v.t.* **1.** to ornament with sculptured or painted scenes from history or legend. **2.** *Archaic.* to tell the history or story of; relate.

[< Anglo-French *estorie,* learned borrowing from Latin *historia* < Greek *historíā.* Doublet of HISTORY.]

—**Syn.** *n.* **1.** relation, narrative, recital, record, chronicle. **2. Story, anecdote, tale** mean a spoken or written account of some happening or happenings. **Story** applies to any such account, true or made-up, long or short, in prose or verse, intended to interest another: *I like stories about science.* **Anecdote** applies to a brief story about a single incident, usually funny or with an interesting point, often in the life of a famous person: *He knows many anecdotes about Mark Twain.* **Tale** applies to a longer story told as if giving true facts about some happening or situation but usually made-up or exaggerated: *an ancient Persian tale. He reads tales of frontier days.* **3.** fib, lie.

sto·ry² (stôr′ē, stōr′-), *n., pl.* **-ries.** **1.** one of the structural divisions in the height of a building; a floor or the space between two floors: *a house of two stories. There are four rooms on the third story.* **2.** a room or set of rooms on one floor or level: *The third story is for rent.* **3.** each of a number of tiers or rows (of columns, windows, etc.) placed horizontally one above another. Also, *especially British,* **storey.** [perhaps ultimately a special use of *story¹*]

sto·ry·board (stôr′ē bôrd′, -bōrd′; stōr′-), *n.* a series of drawings to show the sequence of a planned motion picture, television program, commercial, etc., each drawing representing a major change of scene or action and usually including script and directions for sound effects: *The ad agency's writer ... worked with us on the storyboard. The agency's own storyboard [was] prepared by its art director* (New Yorker).

sto·ry·book (stôr′ē bu̇k′, stōr′-), *n.* a book containing one or more stories or tales, especially for children. —*adj.* of or like that of a storybook; romantic; fictional: *a storybook hero, a storybook ending.*

sto·ry·less (stôr′ē lis, stōr′-), *adj.* without a story or stories.

story line, the line or plan of development of a story, novel, play, etc.: *The screen writers may have trouble developing a story line and picking a hero* (Harper's).

sto·ry·ol·o·gy (stôr′ē ol′ə jē, stōr′-), *n.* storiology.

sto·ry·tell·er (stôr′ē tel′ər, stōr′-), *n.* **1.** a person who tells stories: *I have often thought that a storyteller is born, as well as a poet* (Sir Richard Steele). **2.** *Informal.* a person who tells falsehoods; liar: *He was ... the greatest liar I had met with ... none of your hesitating, half storytellers* (Charles Lamb).

sto·ry·tell·ing (stôr′ē tel′ing, stōr′-), *n.* **1.** the act or art of relating stories, either true or made-up. **2.** *Informal.* the telling of falsehoods.

—*adj.* **1.** that tells stories: *I hope to gain the double benefits of the energy and inspiration of the live theater combined with the storytelling power of the camera's eye* (Newsweek). **2.** *Informal.* lying.

stoss (stos; *German* shtōs), *adj.* turned toward a former oncoming glacier: *the stoss side of a hill, the stoss end of a rock.* [< German *Stoss* a thrust, push]

stot (stot), *n.* **1.** *Scottish.* a steer, or young ox. **2.** *Obsolete.* a horse. [Old English *stot*]

sto·tin·ka (stō ting′kə), *n., pl.* **-ki** (-kē). a Bulgarian coin, worth 1/100 of a lev. [< Bulgarian *stolinka* < *stotna* one hundredth]

stot·tite (stot′īt), *n.* a mineral with a very high content of germanium, found in southwestern Africa. *Formula:* $FeGeO_3.3H_2O$

stound (stound, stünd, stün), *n.* **1.** *Especially Scottish.* **a.** a sharp pain; a pang. **b.** a fierce attack; a shock. **c.** a thrill of delight. **2.** *Obsolete except Dialect.* **a.** a time; while. **b.** a short time; moment. —*v.i. Scottish.* to smart; throb. [Old English *stund* a time, moment; time of trouble]

stoup (stüp), *n.* **1.** a basin for holy water, usually set in or against the wall at a church entrance. **2.** *Scottish.* **a.** a drinking vessel of varying size for liquids, such as a cup, flagon, or tankard: *Let us hasten to the piazza of yonder village and purchase ... a caste of bread, a flitch or so of smoked halibut, and perhaps a stoup of wine* (New Yorker). **b.** the amount it holds. Also, **stoop.** [Middle English *stowpe* < Scandinavian (compare Old Icelandic *staup*)]

Holy Water Stoup (def. 1) Church of San Miniato, Florence

stour (stu̇r), *n. Scottish* **1.** tumult; uproar. **2.** a storm. **3. a.** flying dust, spray, etc. **b.** a deposit of dust. **4.** a fight. [< Anglo-French *estur,* Old French *estour, estorn* conflict, tumult < Germanic (compare Old High German *sturm*)]

stoush (stoush), *n. Australian Informal.* a battering; beating; brawl.

stout (stout), *adj.* **1.** fat and large: *a stout body. That boy could run faster if he weren't so stout.* **2.** strongly built; firm; strong: *a stout dam, a stout fighting ship. The fort has stout walls.* **3.** brave; bold: *a stout heart. Robin Hood was a stout fellow.* **4.** not yielding; stubborn; resolute; uncompromising: *stout resistance, a stout advocate or enemy.* **5.** characterized by endurance or staying power: *a stout horse, a stout engine.*

—*n.* **1.** a strong, dark-brown variety of beer. **2. a.** a stout person. **b.** a garment designed for such a person. **c.** the size of this garment.

[< Old French *estout,* earlier *estolt* strong < Germanic (compare Middle Dutch *stout*)]

—**stout′ly,** *adv.* —**stout′ness,** *n.*

—**Syn.** *adj.* **1.** stocky, plump, portly. See **fat. 2.** durable, tough, sturdy, hardy. **3.** valiant. **4.** determined.

stout-heart·ed (stout′här′tid), *adj.* brave; bold; courageous: *a stout-hearted person, stout-hearted defense.* —**stout′-heart′ed·ly,** *adv.* —**stout′-heart′ed·ness,** *n.*

stout·ish (stou′tish), *adj.* somewhat stout: *a short, stoutish, almost fat little man* (W.H. Hudson).

Sto·va·ine (stō vā′in), *n. Trademark.* a crystalline drug used as a local anesthetic, similar to cocaine, but less toxic. *Formula:* $C_{14}H_{21}NO_2.HCl$

stove¹ (stōv), *n., v.,* **stoved, stov·ing.** —*n.* **1.** an apparatus, fixed or portable and usually of metal, for cooking food and heating rooms, tools, etc., by means of wood, coal, gas, oil, or electricity. **2.** a heated room or box for some special purpose, as a hothouse or kiln. —*v.t.* to heat in a stove: *Layers were glued, one by one, over moulds in the shapes of boxes and lids, and then stoved at about 100 degrees Fahrenheit* (London Times). [< perhaps Middle Dutch *stove* a hot room < Germanic (compare Old High German *stuba*)]

stove² (stōv), *v.* a past tense and a past participle of **stave:** *The barrel was stove in when it dropped off the truck.*

➔ See **stave** for usage note.

stove bolt, a bolt with a slotted head and coarse thread.

stove·mak·er (stōv′mā′kər), *n.* a manufacturer of stoves.

stove·pipe (stōv′pīp′), *n.* **1.** a pipe of sheet metal serving as the chimney of a stove or to connect a stove with the chimney flue. **2.** *U.S. Informal.* a tall silk hat.

stove plant, a plant cultivated in a hothouse.

sto·ver (stō′vər), *n.* **1.** stalks of grain without the ears, used as fodder. **2.** winter food for cattle. **3.** *British Dialect.* any fodder. [short for Middle English *estovers* in sense of "necessary provisions"]

stove-up (stōv′up′), *adj. Dialect or Informal.* worn-out: *At 30, he was a badly stove-up cowboy, and he knew he would never ride the range again* (Time). [< *stove²* + *up*]

stow¹ (stō), *v.t.* **1.** to put together for storing, moving, etc.; pack: *to stow books in a trunk, to stow cargo in the hold of a ship, etc.* **2.** to pack things closely in; fill by packing: *The boys stowed the little cabin with supplies for the trip.* **3.** *Slang.* to stop. **4.** to have room for; hold.

stow away, a. to hide on a ship, airplane, etc., to get a free ride: *They escaped and reached Gibraltar on a steamer on which they had stowed away* (London Daily Chronicle). **b.** to put away in a safe place or to be out of the way: *The bales of merchandise . . . could not be stowed away before dark* (Harriet Martineau).

[Middle English *stowen* to put in a certain place or position, ultimately < Old English *stōw* a place] —**stow′er,** *n.* —**Syn. 2.** cram.

stow[2] (stō), *v.t. Scottish.* to cut or trim close; crop. [apparently < unrecorded Middle English *stuven,* ultimately < Scandinavian (compare Old Icelandic *stūfr* stump)]

stow·a·ble (stō′ə bəl), *adj.* that can be stowed.

stow·age (stō′ij), *n.* **1.** the act of stowing. **2.** the state or manner of being stowed. **3.** a room for stowing; place for stowing. **4.** what is stowed. **5.** a charge for stowing something.

stow·a·way (stō′ə wā′), *n.* a person who hides on a ship, airplane, train, etc., to get a free passage or to escape secretly.

stown·lins (stoun′linz), *adv. Scottish.* by stealth; secretly. [< Scottish *stown* stolen + Old English *-ling,* an adverbial suffix + adverbial genitive *-s*]

stowp (stōp), *n. Obsolete.* stoup.

str., 1. steamer. **2.** strait. **3.** *Music.* string or strings. **4.** *Mechanics.* stroke.

stra·bis·mal (strə biz′məl), *adj.* strabismic.

stra·bis·mic (strə biz′mik), *adj.* **1.** cross-eyed. **2.** distorted: *The six sprightly clowns who people this excellent revue seem to have no difficulty in adjusting to the author's hopelessly strabismic view of the world* (New Yorker).

stra·bis·mi·cal (strə biz′mə kəl), *adj.* strabismic.

stra·bis·mom·e·ter (strā′biz mom′ə tər), *n.* an instrument for measuring strabismus.

stra·bis·mus (strə biz′məs), *n.* a disorder of vision due to the turning of one eye or both eyes from the normal position so that both cannot be directed at the same point or object at the same time; cross-eye; walleye; cast; squint. [< New Latin *strabismus* < Greek *strabismós* < *strabízein* to squint < *strabós* squint-eyed, related to *stréphein* to turn]

stra·bot·o·my (strə bot′ə mē), *n., pl.* **-mies.** the surgical incision of one or more of the muscles of the eye to cure strabismus. [< New Latin *strabotomia* < Greek *strabós* squint-eyed + *-tomiā* a cutting]

STRAC (no periods), *U.S.* Strategic Army Corps (an emergency force kept ready for duty anywhere on short notice): *STRAC includes 36,000 combat troops poised for quick movement abroad on short notice* (Wall Street Journal).

Strad (strad), *n. Informal.* a Stradivarius.

strad·dle (strad′əl), *v.,* **-dled, -dling,** *n.* —*v.i.* **1.** to walk, stand, or sit with the legs wide apart. **2.** (of the legs) to stand wide apart. **3.** to avoid taking sides; appear to favor both sides: *to straddle on the tariff issue.* **4.** *Commerce.* to buy and sell stocks, etc., so as to balance a long holding against a short holding. —*v.t.* **1.** to spread (the legs) wide apart. **2.** to have a leg on either side of (a horse, bicycle, chair, ditch, etc.); bestride. **3.** to stand or lie across; be on both sides of: *A pair of field glasses straddled his nose.* **4.** to attempt to favor both sides of (a question, etc.).

—*n.* **1.** a straddling. **2.** the distance straddled. **3.** an attempt to favor both sides of a question, especially in politics. **4.** a contractual privilege, usually purchased, covering both a put and a call, allowing the holder either to demand certain securities, commodities, etc., of its issuer, or to deliver certain securities, commodities, etc., to its issuer within a given period, and at the same specified price: *A straddle is the purchase of a commodity for delivery in one month and the simultaneous sale of a commodity (generally the same one) for delivery in another month* (New York Times).

[a frequentative form of a variant of *stride*] —**strad′dling·ly,** *adv.*

—**Syn.** *v.t.* **3.** span.

straddle carrier or **truck,** a vehicle with motor and driver located on a raised frame, so that a load of lumber, pipe, or other material can be straddled and carried beneath it.

strad·dle-legged (strad′əl legd′), *adj.* having the legs set wide apart: *The monstrous straddle-legged figure of that legitimate monarch, Henry VIII* (William Hazlitt). —*adv.* with the legs astride: *The wives . . . who sit straddle-legged on the tiniest of donkeys* (William Howard Russell).

strad·dler (strad′lər), *n.* a person or thing that straddles.

Strad·i·var·i (strad′ə vãr′ē), *n.* Stradivarius.

Strad·i·var·i·us (strad′ə vãr′ē əs), *n.* a violin, viola, or cello made by the Italian violin maker Antonio Stradivari, 1644-1737. [< *Stradivarius,* Latinized form of *Stradivari*]

strafe (strāf, sträf), *v.,* **strafed, straf·ing,** *n.* —*v.t.* **1.** (of an aircraft) to machine-gun and bomb (enemy ground positions) at close range: *to strafe a line of soldiers, to strafe the deck of a ship.* **2.** to shell or bomb heavily. —*n.* a strafing. [originally, to punish, attack < the German World War I slogan *Gott strafe England* God punish England]

straf·er (strā′fər, strä′-), *n.* a person who strafes.

strag·gle (strag′əl), *v.,* **-gled, -gling,** *n.* —*v.i.* **1.** to wander in a scattered fashion: *Cows straggled along the lane.* **2.** to stray from the rest; wander: *to straggle from a herd. Children . . . cannot keep their minds from straggling* (John Locke). **3.** to spread in an irregular, rambling manner: *Vines straggled over the yard.*

—*n.* **1.** a group or body of scattered persons or objects: *A straggle of late Victorian tourists totter over a glacier, umbrellas up against the glare* (Manchester Guardian Weekly). **2.** an irregular or fitful emergence (of something): *Here are some private utterances of his, throwing a straggle of light on those points* (Thomas Carlyle).

[perhaps < unrecorded Middle English *strakelen* (frequentative) < *straken* to move, go, extend. Probably related to STRETCH.]

—**Syn.** *v.i.* **1.** roam, range, rove.

strag·gler (strag′lər), *n.* a person or thing that straggles.

strag·gling (strag′ling), *adj.* **1.** that straggles; wandering or straying: *any such casual accidental landing of straggling people from the main* (Daniel Defoe). **2.** wandering apart from a line of march or a main body: *straggling soldiers.* **3.** spreading irregularly in growth; rambling; spindling: *straggling plants.* **4.** extending or scattered irregularly over an area: *a straggling village, straggling houses.* **5.** winding irregularly: *a straggling road.* —**strag′gling·ly,** *adv.*

strag·gly (strag′lē), *adj.* spread out in an irregular, rambling way; straggling: *On one side of us was a thick dark wood of pine trees and straggly rhododendrons* (London Times).

strag·u·lum (strag′yə ləm), *n.* the back and folded wings of a bird taken together as a distinguishing feature; mantle; pallium. [< Latin *strāgulum* spread, covering]

straight (strāt), *adj.* **1. a.** without a bend or curve; direct: *a straight edge, a straight line, a straight road.* **b.** evenly formed or set; not crooked: *a straight back, a straight nose. Keep your shoulders straight.* **c.** not curly or wavy: *straight hair.* **2.** leading directly or directed to some point, mark, etc.: *a straight course, straight aim, a straight throw.* **3. a.** frank; honest; upright: *straight talking, a straight answer, a man straight in all his dealings.* **b.** right; correct: *straight thinking, a straight thinker.* **4.** in proper order or condition: *to keep one's accounts straight. Set the room straight.* **5. a.** without interruption or break; continuous: *in straight succession.* **b.** in an unbroken series: *straight sets, to lose 15 straight games.* **6.** *U.S.* without reservations or exceptions; thoroughgoing; unreserved: *to vote the straight Democratic ticket, a straight Republican.* **7.** *U.S.* **a.** unmixed; undiluted: *straight whiskey.* **b.** without qualification; unmodified: *a straight comedy.* **8.** *Informal.* reliable; sure; authoritative: *a straight tip, straight information.* **9.** (in poker) made up of a sequence of five cards: *a straight flush.* **10.** serious rather than comic; natural rather than eccentric: *a straight part in a play, a straight performance.* **11.** (of an internal-combustion engine) having its cylinders in one straight line rather than radially or in a V-shaped pattern: *a straight eight.*

—*adv.* **1.** in a straight course; directly to or from a place: *to go straight home, to walk straight ahead.* **2. a.** in a straight line; not crookedly: *to write or walk straight, to hang a picture straight.* **b.** in an erect position; upright: *Stand up straight. Sit straight.* **3.** in a straight direction; directly to a mark or object: *to look someone straight in the eye, to shoot straight at a target.* **4.** continuously to the end; all the way: *a hole straight through a wall, to drive straight on.* **5.** honorably; uprightly; honestly: *to live straight.* **6.** without reservation; frankly; outspokenly: *straight from the shoulder, straight from the horse's mouth. Tell me straight out what you think.* **7.** without delay; immediately; straightway: *The bridge must straight go down* (Macaulay). **8.** *Informal.* selling at a fixed price regardless of quantity: *cigars selling at 10 cents straight.*

straight away or **off,** at once: *Your ma went straight off to see what was needed* (Louisa May Alcott).

—*n.* **1.** straight condition or quality: *to be out of the straight.* **2.** a straight form, part, position, or line. **3.** (in poker) a sequence of five cards, ranking above three of a kind and below a flush. **4.** *Sports.* a series of shots, plays, etc., producing a perfect score. **5.** straight whiskey: *Increasing consumer demand for straights . . . requires the use of more whiskey* (Wall Street Journal).

the straight, the home stretch of a race track: *There was no important change in the order of running until after the turn into the straight* (London Times).

[Middle English *streigt,* Old English *streht,* past participle of *streccan* to stretch] —**straight′ly,** *adv.* —**straight′ness,** *n.*

—**Syn.** *adj.* **1. a.** undeviating, unswerving. **3. a.** honorable. —**Ant.** *adj.* **1. a, b.** crooked, curving.

straight and narrow, conventional standards or requirements of proper behavior: *These flirtations almost prove disastrous but Tung and Chen finally return to the straight and narrow* (Sunday Times).

straight angle, an angle of 180 degrees.

180°

Straight Angle

straight-arm (strāt′ärm′), *v.t.* **1.** to prevent (an opponent) from making a tackle in football by holding one's arm straight out. **2.** to keep (a person) away by or as if by holding one's arm straight out; fend off: *"We're not going to be straight-arming the customers any more," he declared. "We're going to inform everyone what their entitlements are"* (New York Times). —*n.* the act of straight-arming.

straight·a·way (strāt′ə wā′), *n.* a straight course. —*adj.* in a straight course. —*adv.* as quickly as possible; at once; immediately: *The captain read the letter and burned it straightaway.*

straight chain, *Chemistry.* an arrangement of atoms in an organic molecule represented in a structural formula by a straight line with no forks or branches.

straight·edge (strāt′ej′), *n.* **1.** a strip of wood or metal having one edge accurately straight, used in obtaining or testing straight lines and level surfaces. **2.** a straight razor.

straight·en (strā′tən), *v.t.* **1.** to make straight: *Straighten your shoulders. He straightened the bent pin.* **2.** to put in the proper order or condition: *to straighten up a room, to straighten out an account.* —*v.i.* **1.** to become straight: *Suddenly resolved, he straightened and marched out of the room.* **2.** *U.S. Informal.* to mend one's ways; reform. —**straight′en·er,** *n.*

straight face, a face or expression that shows no emotion, humor, etc.: *He kept a straight face while telling the joke. How can you say that with a straight face?*

straight-faced (strāt′fāst′), *adj.* having or told with a straight face: *a straight-faced comedian, a straight-faced joke. He is not a debunker; he achieves his effects not by wisecracks but by straight-faced deadly irony* (Atlantic).

straight flush, (in poker) a sequence of five cards in the same suit, ranking higher than four of a kind.

straight·for·ward (strāt′fôr′wərd), *adj.* **1.** honest; frank: *He has a reputation for being straightforward. He has written for the most part a straightforward and unvarnished* *drama* (Wall Street Journal). **2.** going straight ahead; direct. —*adv.* directly. —**straight′for′ward·ly,** *adv.* —**straight′for′ward·ness,** *n.* —**Syn.** *adj.* **1.** forthright, downright, aboveboard.

straight·for·wards (strāt′fôr′wərdz), *adv.* straightforward.

straight-from-the-shoul·der (strāt′frəm ᴛʜə shōl′dər), *adj.* straightforward; frank; direct: *Mr. Barnes acknowledges this in straight-from-the-shoulder typewritten language* (New York Times).

straight-grained (strāt′grānd′), *adj.* (of timber) having the grain running straight, or parallel to the length, instead of at cross directions.

straight·ish (strā′tish), *adj.* somewhat straight.

straight jacket, a strait jacket.

straight life insurance, a plan of life insurance in which premiums are paid as long as the insured lives.

straight-line (strāt′līn′), *adj.* **1.** having the main parts placed in a straight line, as a machine. **2.** acting or exerted in a straight line: *straight-line movement, a straight-line force.* **3.** producing or transferring motion in a straight line, as a system of rods, etc., so linked as to change rotating or oscillating movement into movement that acts in a straight line.

straight-line depreciation, a method of depreciation in which the original cost of machinery, equipment, etc., less the estimated resale value, is divided evenly over the number of years of expected use, and the percentage thus fixed is periodically charged off.

straight man, a person who serves as a foil for a comedian: *A BBC comedian asked his straight man to read the day's news* (Time).

straight-out (strāt′out′), *adj. U.S. Informal.* out-and-out; complete; thorough: *It was a case of straight-out dishonesty.*

straight razor, a heavy blade fixed to a handle, used chiefly by barbers for shaving.

straight-run gasoline (strāt′run′), gasoline of low octane rating distilled and condensed from crude petroleum.

straight shooter, *Informal.* a person who is honest and free from deceit or fraud: *Are you sure he's a straight shooter?* (Newsweek).

straight-time (strāt′tīm′), *adj.* for or based on regular working hours: *The straight-time base pay in logging camps and sawmills is now $1.80 an hour* (Wall Street Journal). —*adv.* at regular hours: *On this job everyone works straight-time.*

straight-up (strāt′up′), *adj.* having an erect figure or posture; upright: *Jones, a straight-up fighter, stands conventionally* (New Yorker).

straight·way (strāt′wā′), *adv.* at once; immediately; straightaway: *The warning has straightway to be given that this will be no easy gathering* (London Times).

straight whiskey, whiskey distilled and aged without blending either with neutral spirits or with other whiskeys: *He predicted that straight whiskies would gain in favor at the expense of blends* (New York Times).

strain[1] (strān), *v.t.* **1.** to draw tight; stretch: *The weight strained the rope.* **2.** to stretch as much as possible or beyond the proper or reasonable limit: *She strained the truth in telling the story. The political system [in 1860] was being strained beyond its limit* (Bruce Catton). **3.** to use to the utmost: *She strained her eyes to see.* **4. a.** to injure by too much effort or by stretching: *The runner strained his heart. She strained her back in scrubbing the floor.* **b.** to damage or weaken by too much tension, pressure, or force: *The heavy cargo strained the ship's hold.* **5. a.** to press or pour through a strainer: *Strain the soup before serving it. Babies eat strained foods.* **b.** to remove or keep back (dense or solid parts) in this way. **6.** to make excessive demands upon; tax severely: *to strain one's credit.* **7.** to press closely; squeeze; hug: *to strain a person to one's heart.* **8.** *Physics.* to cause alteration of form, shape, or volume in (a solid). **9.** *Obsolete.* to force; constrain: *The quality of mercy is not strain'd* (Shakespeare).

—*v.i.* **1.** to pull hard: *a dog straining at his leash.* **2. a.** to make a very great effort: *Both sides were straining to reconcile the most repulsive difficulties* (Benjamin Disraeli). **b.** to exert oneself to the utmost; strive: *a rower straining against the current.* **3. a.** to be injured or damaged by too much effort, tension, or pressure. **b.** to undergo too much tension or pressure. **4.** to drip through.

strain at, to have difficulty accepting: *Even his best friend strained at such an obvious lie.*

—*n.* **1.** any force or weight that stretches, pulls apart, or drags from a position: *The strain on the rope made it break.* **2. a.** a great muscular or physical effort. **b.** too much effort. **c.** an injury caused by too much effort or by stretching; sprain: *The injury to John's back was only a strain.* **3. a.** any severe, trying or wearing pressure: *the strain of worry, the strain of debts. The strain of sleepless nights made her ill.* **b.** its effect on the body or mind. **4. a.** a manner or style of doing or speaking: *a playful strain, a poem in a melancholy strain.* **b.** mood; tone: *a moralizing or thoughtful strain.* **5.** a passage of poetry. **6.** a flow or burst of language, eloquence, etc. **7.** *Physics.* **a.** alteration of form, shape, or volume caused by external forces; deformation. **b.** stress.

strains, a part of a piece of music complete in itself; melody; song; tune: *In sweet Italian strains our shepherds sing* (William Congreve).

[< Old French *estreind-*, stem of *estreindre* bind tightly < Latin *stringere* draw tight]

—**Syn.** *v.t.* **4. a.** wrench, sprain. *-v.i.* **1.** tug. **4.** filter, trickle, percolate.

strain[2] (strān), *n.* **1. a.** a line of descent; race; stock: *Charlemagne, And the long heroes of the Gallic strain* (Matthew Prior). **b.** ancestry; descent; lineage: *He is of a noble strain* (Shakespeare). **2.** any of various lines of ancestry united in an individual or a family: *His Irish strain gives him a sense of humor.* **3. a.** a group of animals or plants that form part of a race, breed, or variety, and are distinguished from related organisms by some feature: *Certain strains of hybrid corn yield more hardy seed than others.* **b.** a variety developed by breeding. **c.** an artificial variety of a domestic animal. **d.** a variety of microbes, etc., developed by breeding. **4.** an inherited tendency, quality, or character: *a strain of madness in a family.* **5.** a trace or streak: *a horse with a mean strain, a scientist with a strain of superstition.* **6.** a kind, class, or sort: *His ambition was of a noble and generous strain* (Edmund Burke). **7.** *Archaic.* offspring; progeny. **8.** *Obsolete.* a begetting; generation; procreation. [variant of Middle English *strene,* Old English *strēon* a gain, begetting, short form of *gestrēon*]

strained (strānd), *adj.* not natural; forced: *a strained smile. Her greeting was cold and strained.*

strain·er (strā′nər), *n.* **1.** a utensil or device for straining, filtering, or sifting: *A filter, a sieve, and a colander are strainers.* **2.** a device for stretching or tightening.

strain gauge, any of various gauges for measuring strains or pressures, such as stresses exerted on steel. One type consists of a small, flattened coil of fine wire which varies in electrical resistance according to the degree of deformation: *To ensure the precise load, a strain gauge is inserted between the jack and the article under test* (New Scientist).

strain·ing (strā′ning), *n.* the act of a person or thing that strains.

straining arch, *Architecture.* an archlike structure, such as a flying buttress, designed to resist pressure like a strut. See **flying buttress** for picture.

straining beam or **piece,** the horizontal timber or beam in a roof truss between the tops of two queen posts, which holds them in place.

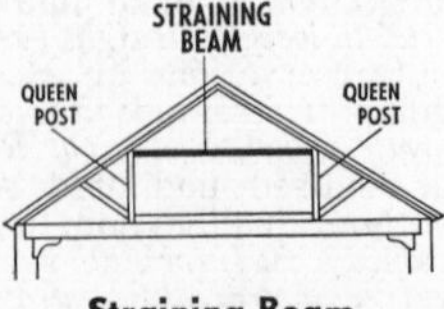

Straining Beam

strain hardening, *Physics.* the hardening of metals or alloys by a change in structure due to strain or deformation: *Strain hardening results from the breakdown of the metal's microscopic grains* (Scientific American).

strains (strānz), *n.pl.* See under **strain**[1], *n.*

strait (strāt), *n.* **1.** a narrow channel or passage connecting two larger bodies of water: *The Strait of Gibraltar connects the Mediterranean Sea and the Atlantic Ocean. Abbr.:* str. **2.** *Archaic.* an isthmus. **3.** *Obsolete.* a narrow, confined place or space.

straits, difficulty; need; distress; crisis; emergency; plight: *He was in desperate straits for money.*

—*adj. Archaic.* **1.** narrow; limited; confining: *It matters not how strait the gate* (W. E. Henley). **2.** strict; rigorous: *The nun took strait vows.*

[< Old French *estreit* < Latin *strictus* drawn tight, bound, past participle of *stringere.* Doublet of STRICT, STRETTO.] —**strait′ly,** *adv.* —**strait′ness,** *n.*

strait·en (strā′tən), *v.t.* **1.** to limit by the lack of something; restrict. **2.** to make narrow; contract. **3.** *Archaic.* to confine within narrow limits; confine. —**Syn. 1.** hamper, impede.

strait·ened (strā′tənd), *adj.* **1.** limited or reduced, especially to insufficiency: *straitened means or income.* **2.** hampered by insufficiency of means; needing money badly: *The day before payday found him in straitened circumstances.* **3.** *Archaic.* narrowed or contracted; narrowly confined. **4.** *Obsolete.* drawn tight.

strait jacket, 1. a strong coat with long sleeves that can be tied to hold the arms close to the sides, used to keep a violent person from harming himself or others. **2.** anything which acts as a restraint upon someone or something: *To help free scientists from the present security strait jacket, the House Committee recommends . . .* (Science News Letter). Also, **straight jacket.**

strait-jack·et (strāt′jak′it), *v.t.* to restrain or confine in or as in a strait jacket: *The campaign is strait-jacketed by lack of funds* (Newsweek). *Scientists suddenly found themselves strait-jacketed by security regulations which limited severely their contacts with fellow scientists, their freedom to publish . . .* (Scientific American).

strait-laced (strāt′lāst′), *adj.* **1.** very strict in matters of conduct; prudish: *I'm not strait-laced, but I tell you we got to have decent women in our schools* (Sinclair Lewis). **2.** *Archaic.* **a.** tightly laced. **b.** wearing tightly laced garments. —**Syn. 1.** stiff, formal.

straits (strāts), *n.pl.* See under **strait,** *n.*

Straits dollar, a silver coin of the Straits Settlements, a former British colony in southeastern Asia.

strait waistcoat, *Especially British.* strait jacket.

strake (strāk), *n.* a single breadth of planks or metal plates along the side of a ship from the bow to the stern. [Middle English *strake* iron rim of a wheel. Apparently related to STRETCH.]

stram (stram), *v.,* **strammed, stram·ming,** *n. U.S Dialect.* —*v.i.* to walk with ungraceful strides; tramp: *Don't go stramming off another afternoon* (Harriet Beecher Stowe). —*n.* a long, hard walk; tramp.

stra·mash (strə mash′, stram′ish), *n. Scottish.* a disturbance; uproar; row. [apparently imitative]

stra·min·e·ous (strə min′ē əs), *adj.* **1.** of or like straw. **2.** *Botany.* straw-colored. [< Latin *strāmineus* (with English *-ous*) < *strāmen, -inis* straw, related to *sternere* to spread, scatter]

stra·mo·ni·um (strə mō′nē əm), *n.* **1.** jimson weed. **2.** a drug made from its dried leaves, used as an antispasmodic, as a sedative, in the treatment of asthma, etc. [< New Latin *stramonium;* origin uncertain]

stram·o·ny (stram′ə nē), *n.* stramonium.

strand[1] (strand), *v.t., v.i.* **1.** to run aground; drive on the shore: *The ship was stranded on the rocks.* **2.** to bring or come into a helpless position: *He was stranded a thousand miles from home with no money.* [< noun] —*n. Poetic.* the land bordering a sea, lake, or river; shore: *wandering on a foreign strand* (Scott). [Old English *strand*] —**Syn.** *n.* beach, coast.

strand[2] (strand), *n.* **1.** one of the threads, strings, or wires that are twisted together to form a rope, cord, line, cable, or electric conductor: *a rope of three strands.* **2.** one of the threads or strips of a woven or braided material. **3.** a string, thread, tress, etc.: *a strand of beads or pearls, a strand of hair.* **4.** a fiber in animal or plant tissue.

—*v.t.* **1.** to break one or more of the strands of (a rope). **2.** to form (a rope) by the twisting of strands.

[perhaps < Old French *estran* < Germanic (compare Old High German *streno*)]

strand·ed[1] (stran′did), *adj.* aground; helpless.

strand·ed[2] (stran′did), *adj.* made of strands; having a certain number of strands: *a three-stranded rope.*

strand·ing (stran′ding), *n.* the act or process of being stranded: *Other victims of the stranding had by now congregated* (London Times).

strand line, *Geology.* the line of contact between a lake or ocean and the land.

strand·loop·er (strand′lü′per), *n.* (in South Africa) a Bushman living on the coast and working largely along the shore. [< Afrikaans *strandlooper* < Dutch *strand* shore + *looper* runner]

strange (strānj), *adj.*, **strang·er, strang·est,** *adv.* —*adj.* **1.** unusual; queer; peculiar: *a strange accident, a strange experience. She wore strange, old-fashioned clothing. 'Tis strange—but true; for truth is always strange; Stranger than fiction* (Byron). **2.** not known, seen, heard of, or experienced before; unfamiliar: *strange faces, a strange language. The custom was strange to them.* **3.** unaccustomed (to); inexperienced (at): *He is strange to this job but will soon learn.* **4.** out of place; not at home: *a strange dog walking down a street. She felt strange in the new school.* **5.** distant or cold; reserved.
—*adv.* in a strange manner.
[< Old French *estrange* < Latin *extrāneus* foreign. Doublet of EXTRANEOUS. Related to ESTRANGE.]
—**Syn.** *adj.* **1. Strange, odd, peculiar,** mean unusual or out of the ordinary. **Strange** applies to anyone or anything unfamiliar, unknown, or unaccustomed: *A strange quiet pervaded the city.* **Odd** applies to anyone or anything irregular or puzzling: *That is an odd color.* **Peculiar** applies to anyone or anything unique or different from others: *Raising frogs is a peculiar way to make a living.* **2.** foreign, alien, new, novel. —**Ant.** *adj.* **1.** usual.

strange·ly (strānj′lē), *adv.* in a strange or peculiar way.

strange·ness (strānj′nis), *n.* **1.** the quality or state of being strange. **2.** *Nuclear Physics.* a property of certain elementary particles, used in explaining their relatively slow rate of decay.

strange particle, *Nuclear Physics.* any of the heavier, unstable elementary particles, comprising the heavy mesons and the hyperons, so called because their relatively long life appeared to be inconsistent with existing atomic theories.

stran·ger (strān′jər), *n.* **1.** a person not known, seen, or heard of before: *She is a stranger to us.* **2.** a person or thing new to a place; newcomer: *He is a stranger in New York.* **3.** a person who is out of place or not at home in something: *He is no stranger to hard work.* **4.** a guest; visitor: *... thy stranger that is within thy gates* (Exodus 20:10). **5.** *Archaic.* a foreigner; alien. **6.** *Law.* a person who has no legal interest or standing in an action or transaction.

stran·gle (strang′gəl), *v.*, **-gled, -gling,** *n.* —*v.t.* **1.** to kill by squeezing the throat to stop the breath: *Hercules strangled a snake with each hand.* **2.** to suffocate; choke: *His high collar seemed to be strangling him.* **3.** to choke down; suppress; keep back: *to strangle a yawn, to strangle an impulse to laugh, to strangle a nation's economy by too many taxes.* —*v.i.* to be strangled: *He strangled before help could reach him.*
—*n.* **strangles,** an acute, infectious disease of horses, mules, etc., caused by a bacterium, and characterized by fever and inflammation of the mucous membranes.
[< Old French *estrangler* < Latin *strangulāre.* Compare STRANGULATE.]
—**Syn.** *v.t.* **2.** throttle, stifle.

stran·gle·hold (strang′gəl hōld′), *n.* **1.** a wrestling hold for stopping an opponent's breath. **2.** anything that suppresses or hinders free movement, development, etc.: *The processes of maturity had me in a grim stranglehold ... and the joys of the intellectual life were beginning to overwhelm me* (Punch).

stran·gler (strang′glər), *n.* a person or thing that strangles.

strangler fig, a fig tree of Florida and the Bahama Islands that begins its growth as a parasite on another tree, reaches its top, and then gradually strangles the existing tree in a mass of roots, finally standing in place of the original tree.

strangler tree, clusia, a tropical American shrub or tree.

stran·gles (strang′gəlz), *n.* See under **strangle,** *n.*

stran·gu·late (strang′gyə lāt), *v.t.*, **-lat·ed, -lat·ing.** **1.** *Medicine.* to constrict or compress so as to stop the circulation in, or hinder the action of. **2.** to strangle; choke. [< Latin *strangulāre* (with English *-ate*[1])]

stran·gu·lat·ed (strang′gyə lā′tid), *adj.* **1.** *Medicine.* compressed or constricted so as to prevent circulation or suppress function: *In a strangulated hernia, the circulation in the protruded part is arrested.* **2.** *Botany.* irregularly contracted and expanded: *a strangulated stem.*

stran·gu·la·tion (strang′gyə lā′shən), *n.* **1.** a strangling or being strangled. **2.** a strangulating or being strangulated: *Today vast urban areas ... suffer from traffic strangulation* (Wall Street Journal).

stran·gu·ri·ous (strang gyůr′ē əs), *adj.* of or affected with strangury.

stran·gu·ry (strang′gyər ē), *n.* a slow, painful emission of urine, drop by drop. [< Latin *strangūria* < Greek *strangouriā* < *stránx, strangós* a drop squeezed out + *oûron* urine]

strap (strap), *n., v.*, **strapped, strap·ping.** —*n.* **1.** a narrow strip of leather or other material that bends easily. **2.** a narrow, flat band or strip of cloth: *The cadet wore shoulder straps.* **3.** a narrow strip for fastening things, holding things together, etc.: *The box was strengthened by straps of steel.* **4.** a narrow strip of leather to sharpen razors on; strop. **5.** a looped band suspended from a bar in a bus, train, car, etc., for passengers to hold on to, to steady themselves. **6.** a looped band attached to a boot to help pull it on.
—*v.t.* **1.** to fasten, bind, or secure with a strap or straps: *We strapped the trunk.* **2.** to beat with a strap. **3.** to sharpen (a razor, knife, etc.) on a strap or strop. **4.** to dress and bandage.
[dialectal variant of *strop,* partly Old English < Latin *stroppus;* partly < Old French *estrop* < Latin *stroppus* < Greek *stróphos* < *stréphein* to turn] —**strap′like′,** *adj.*
—**Syn.** *n.* **1.** thong.

strap·hang (strap′hang′), *v.i.*, **-hung, -hang·ing.** *Informal.* to be a straphanger: *You cannot straphang in an airliner as you can on a London bus* (New Scientist).

strap·hang·er (strap′hang′ər), *n. Informal.* a passenger in a bus, streetcar, train, etc., who cannot get a seat and stands holding on to a strap.

strap hinge, a hinge with a long band of metal on each side, by which it is secured to a door and a post.

strap·less (strap′lis), *adj.* having no strap or straps; not fitted with straps: *a strapless ball gown of white satin with a plain one-button jacket* (New Yorker). —*n.* a strapless garment or undergarment.

stra·pon·tin (strə pon′tin), *n.* **1.** a folding seat as used in automobiles, etc. **2.** a similar type of seat used in theaters, etc.: *I spotted her once on a backless strapontin, lost to the world, her shining face uplifted to the stage* (New Yorker). [< French *strapontin*]

strap·pa·do (strə pā′dō, -pä′-), *n., pl.* **-does.** **1.** a form of human torture in which the victim was raised by a rope and suddenly let fall the length of the rope. **2.** the mechanism for doing this. [alteration of Middle French *estrapade* < Italian *strappata* < *strappare* to drag, snatch < Vulgar Latin *extirpāre* extirpate, fused with Latin *trahere* to drag]

strapped (strapt), *adj.* **1.** fastened or provided with straps. **2.** finished with bands of cloth, etc., as seams or garments. **3.** *Informal.* short of money: *Over the country, banks were more strapped for funds than they have been in the last 10 months* (Wall Street Journal).

strap·per (strap′ər), *n.* **1.** a person or thing that straps. **2.** *Informal.* a tall, robust person.

strap·ping (strap′ing), *adj. Informal.* **1.** tall, strong, and healthy; robust: *a fine strapping girl. There is a strong gleam of didacticism under his rather strapping prose* (Manchester Guardian). **2.** very big; great; whopping: *a strapping lie.* —*n.* thin, narrow steel straps or bands used to reinforce crates, cartons, packages, etc., for shipping.
—**Syn.** *adj.* **1.** sturdy, husky.

strap·work (strap′wėrk′), *n.* architectural design consisting of folded, crossed, and interlaced fillets or bands.

strap·wort (strap′wėrt′), *n.* a coastal herb native to the Mediterranean region and western Europe, with many slender trailing stems and small white flowers in little heads or cymes, the sepals petallike on the margin.

Stras·bourg goose (stras′bėrg), a goose that is specially fattened to enlarge its liver for use in making pâté de foie gras. [< *Strasbourg,* a city in northeastern France where these geese are raised]

strass[1] (stras), *n.* a brilliant glass containing oxide of lead, used in making artificial gems; paste. [< German *Strass,* reputedly < Joseph *Strasser,* who invented it]

strass[2] (stras), *n.* silk waste that remains after working up skeins. [< French *strasse,* earlier *estrasse* or *estrace* < Italian *straccio* a tear, torn cloth, rag < *stracciare* < Vulgar Latin *distractiāre* pull apart]

stra·ta (strā′tə, strat′ə), *n.* a plural of **stratum.**

strat·a·gem (strat′ə jəm), *n.* **1.** a scheme or trick for deceiving an enemy: *The spy got into the castle by the stratagem of dressing as a beggar.* **2.** a trick; trickery. [< Middle French *stratagème,* learned borrowing from Latin *stratēgēma* < Greek *stratēgēma, -atos* < *stratēgeîn* be a general < *stratēgós* general; see STRATEGY]
—**Syn. 1, 2. Stratagem, artifice, ruse** mean a scheme or device to trick or mislead others. **Stratagem** applies to a plan to gain one's own ends or defeat those of others by skillful deception: *The general planned a stratagem to trap the enemy.* **Artifice** applies to a clever trick or device, sometimes mechanical, to gain one's ends by misleading, and usually deceiving, others: *Motion pictures often employ artifices to get realistic effects.* **Ruse** applies to a trick or device to gain one's ends indirectly by deceiving others about one's real purpose: *Her headache was a ruse to leave early.*

stra·tal (strā′təl), *adj.* having to do with a stratum or strata.

strat·e·get·ic (strat′ə jet′ik), *adj.* strategic.

stra·te·gic (strə tē′jik), *adj.* **1.** of or having to do with strategy; based on strategy; useful in strategy: *a strategic retreat.* **2.** important in strategy: *The Panama Canal is a strategic link in our national defense.* **3.** having to do with raw material necessary for warfare which must be obtained, at least partially, from an outside country. **4.** specially made or trained for destroying key enemy bases, industry, or communications behind the lines of battle, rather than for supporting combat units on land or sea: *a strategic bomber. The government plans to continue limited direct purchases of ... lead and zinc for the strategic stockpile* (Wall Street Journal).

Strategic Air Command, *U.S.* a branch of the Air Force concerned with carrying out strategic air operations against an enemy: *Under the new concept the greatest military power of the United States is still offensive in nature but is massed in the Strategic Air Command* (New York Times).

stra·te·gi·cal (strə tē′jə kəl), *adj.* strategic.

stra·te·gi·cal·ly (strə tē′jə klē), *adv.* in a strategic manner; by strategy: *As far as sheer value of territory is concerned ... there is no more strategically important area in the world than the Middle East* (Newsweek).

strategic hamlet, a village fortified militarily against incursions by guerrillas.

stra·te·gios (strə tē′jiks), *n.* strategy.

strat·e·gist (strat′ə jist), *n.* a person trained or skilled in strategy: *a brilliant military, chess, or football strategist.*

strat·e·gy (strat′ə jē), *n., pl.* **-gies.** **1.** the science or art of war; planning and directing military movements and operations: *Tactics are used to win an engagement, strategy to win a campaign or a war* (Bulletin of Atomic Scientists). **2.** a plan based on or involving this. **3.** the planning and management of anything, especially skillful planning: *... the faulty strategy of idealists who have too many illusions when they face realists who have too little conscience* (Reinhold Niebuhr). [< Greek *stratēgiā* < *stratēgós* general < *stratós* army + *ágein* to lead] —**Syn. 1.** strategics. **2.** maneuver. **3.** manipulation.

Strat·ford·i·an (strat fôr′dē ən, -fōr′-), *n.* a supporter of the view that William Shakespeare and not Francis Bacon or some other person was the author of the Shakespearian plays. —*adj.* of, having to do with, or characteristic of the Stratfordians: *... Stratfordian theories* (Manchester Guardian). [< *Stratford*-on-Avon, the town in central

England where Shakespeare was born + *-ian*]

strath (strath), *n. Scottish.* a wide valley. [< Scottish Gaelic *srath*]

strath·spey (strath′spā′, strath′spā′), *n.* **1.** a vigorous Scottish dance, usually in 4/4 time, somewhat like a reel. **2.** the music for this dance. [supposedly < *Strathspey*, a place name in Scotland]

stra·tic·u·late (strə tik′yə lit, -lāt), *adj. Geology.* arranged in thin layers of strata. [< a diminutive form of *stratum* + *-ate*[1]]

stra·tic·u·la·tion (strə tik′yə lā′shən), *n.* arrangement in thin layers.

strat·i·fi·ca·tion (strat′ə fə kā′shən), *n.* **1.** a stratifying; arrangement in layers or strata: *Some people pay too much attention to the stratification of society.* **2.** *Geology.* **a.** the formation of strata; deposition or occurrence in strata. **b.** a stratum.

strat·i·form (strat′ə fôrm), *adj.* **1.** *Geology.* arranged in strata; forming a stratum or layer. **2.** *Anatomy.* occurring in thin layers in bones: *stratiform cartilage.* **3.** having the form of stratus clouds. [< French *stratiforme* < Latin *strātum* (see STRATUM) + *-formis* -form]

strat·i·fy (strat′ə fī), *v.*, **-fied, -fy·ing.** —*v.t.* **1.** to arrange in layers or strata; form into layers or strata: . . . *a sample selected from a population which has been stratified, part of the sample coming from each stratum* (Kendall and Buckland). **2.** *Geology.* to deposit (sediment, etc.) in strata; form strata in. **3.** to preserve (seeds) by putting them between alternate layers of earth or sand. —*v.i.* to form strata: *Already a few of the new settlers are starting to rise in the world, to stratify and to disperse* (Punch). [< Medieval Latin *strātificāre* < Latin *strātum* (see STRATUM) + *facere* to make]

stra·tig·ra·pher (strə tig′rə fər), *n.* a person skilled in stratigraphy.

strat·i·graph·ic (strat′ə graf′ik), *adj.* of or having to do with stratigraphy. —**strat′i·graph′i·cal·ly,** *adv.*

strat·i·graph·i·cal (strat′ə graf′ə kəl), *adj.* stratigraphic.

stra·tig·ra·phy (strə tig′rə fē), *n.* **1.** the branch of geology that deals with the order and position of strata. **2.** the order and position of the strata (of a country, region, etc.): *The stratigraphy of river deposits can pose obdurate problems* (G. H. Dury).

strato-, *combining form.* **1.** horizontal layers: *Stratosphere = area of the atmosphere where the winds are mainly horizontal.* **2.** of the stratosphere; having to do with high altitudes: *Stratotanker = a tanker that refuels at high altitudes.* [< *stratus*]

stra·to·cir·rus (strā′tō sir′əs), *n.* a cloud closely resembling a cirro-stratus, but more compact, and formed at a lower altitude.

stra·toc·ra·cy (strə tok′rə sē), *n., pl.* **-cies.** government by the army; military government. [< Greek *stratós* army + *-kratiā* rule]

strat·o·crat·ic (strat′ə krat′ik), *adj.* of or having to do with stratocracy.

Strat·o·cruis·er (strat′ə krü′zər), *n. Trademark.* a large aircraft for carrying freight or passengers at high altitudes.

stra·to·cu·mu·lus (strā′tō kū′myə ləs), *n., pl.* **-li** (-lī). a cloud layer made up of large, dark, rounded masses above a flat, horizontal base, usually seen in winter.

strat·o·lab (strat′ə lab), *n.* a manned gondola equipped with scientific instruments, suspended from a balloon at high altitudes for meteorological or other investigation.

Strat·o·lin·er (strat′ə lī′nər), *n. Trademark.* a multi-engined commercial jet aircraft for flying at moderately high altitudes.

strat·o·pause (strat′ə pôz′, strā′tə-), *n.* the upper limits of the stratosphere.

strat·o·scope (strat′ə skōp), *n.* a balloon carrying a telescope equipped with a camera for photographing the sun from heights of over 80,000 feet: *In our next venture with the stratoscope . . . we shall attempt to point and focus the instrument by remote control* (Scientific American).

stra·tose (strā′tōs), *adj. Botany.* arranged in strata or layers.

strat·o·sphere (strat′ə sfir, strā′tə-), *n.* **1.** an upper region of the atmosphere between the troposphere and ionosphere, beginning between five and ten miles above the earth. In the stratosphere temperature varies little with changes in altitude, and the winds are chiefly horizontal. See **atmosphere** for diagram. **2.** (formerly) the stratosphere and ionosphere together. **3.** a high or rarefied region: *On one point he seemed to take off into a stratosphere of fancy* (Wall Street Journal). [< French *stratosphère* < Latin *strātus, -ūs* a spreading out (see STRATUS) + French *-sphère,* as in *atmosphère* atmosphere]

strat·o·spher·ic (strat′ə sfer′ik, strā′tə-), *adj.* of or having to do with the stratosphere: *But that would mean tax rates would stay at their present stratospheric height* (Wall Street Journal). —**strat′o·spher′i·cal·ly,** *adv.*

strat·o·tank·er (strat′ə tang′kər), *n.* a military tanker plane that can refuel bombers at high altitudes.

stra·tum (strā′təm, strat′əm), *n., pl.* **-ta** or **-tums. 1.** a layer of material, especially one of several parallel layers placed one upon another: *In digging the well, the men struck first a stratum of sand, then several strata of rock.* **2.** *Geology.* a bed of sedimentary rock, usually consisting of a series of layers of the same kind, representing continuous periods of deposition. **3.** *Sociology.* **a.** a social level or grade: *to rise from a low to a high social stratum. Gladstone tried to find a stratum of society that was more susceptible to Christian doctrine* (Time). **b.** a group having about the same education, culture, development, etc. **4.** *Biology.* a layer of tissue; lamella. **5.** a region of the atmosphere or of the sea assumed as bounded by horizontal planes for purposes of calculation. [< New Latin *stratum* < Latin *strātum* something spread out; coverlet; pavement; neuter past participle of *sternere* to spread out] —**Syn. 3. a.** caste.

Strata (def. 2)

stratum cor·ne·um (kôr′nē əm), the horny outer layer of the skin, consisting of broad, thin cells. [< New Latin *stratum corneum*]

stra·tus (strā′təs), *n., pl.* **-ti** (-tī). a low, uniform, horizontal layer of gray cloud that spreads over a large area. [< Latin *strātus, -ūs* a spreading out < *sternere* to spread out]

Strauss·i·an (strou′sē ən), *adj.* of or having to do with the German musical composer and conductor Richard Strauss, 1864-1949, or his musical style, theories, or compositions. —*n.* a follower of Richard Strauss.

straw (strô), *n.* **1.** the stalks or stems of grain after drying and threshing. Straw is used for bedding for livestock, for making hats, and for many other purposes. **2.** a stem of any cereal plant, such as wheat, rye, barley, etc., when dry and separated from the grain. **3.** a tube of waxed paper, plastic, etc., used for sucking up drinks. **4. a.** a bit; trifle: *He doesn't care a straw.* **b.** a minor thing that indicates how something else may turn out: *Already there are a few straws which the Republican National Committee is eying hopefully* (Harper's). **5.** *Informal.* a straw hat: *I've already talked about her glorious flower-laden straws* (New Yorker).

catch at a straw, to try anything in desperation: *A drowning man will catch at a straw, the proverb well says* (Samuel Richardson).

straw in the wind, something taken as an indication of a trend: *A more specific election straw in the wind can be found in yesterday's heavy buying of steel shares* (Wall Street Journal).

—*adj.* **1.** made of straw: *a straw hat.* **2.** pale-yellow; straw-colored: *a straw coat.* **3.** of little value or consequence; worthless: *a straw bid.*

[Old English *strēaw.* Probably related to STREW.] —**straw′like′,** *adj.*

straw bail, bail furnished by a person not possessing the property he pretends to have.

straw bass, the largemouth bass.

straw·ber·ry (strô′ber′ē, -bər-), *n., pl.* **-ries. 1.** a small, juicy, red, edible fruit. It is covered with tiny, yellow, seedlike achenes. **2.** the low plant of the rose family it grows on.

Strawberry (def. 2) (4 to 8 in. high)

strawberry bass, calico bass.

strawberry blite, a low, weedy plant of the goosefoot family with globular clusters of flowers and bright-red fruit.

strawberry blonde or **blond,** a person, especially a woman, with reddish blonde hair: *The waiting-room door flew open, and a . . . strawberry blonde in a brown-and-white tweed suit came out* (New Yorker).

strawberry bush, 1. a low, upright or straggling North American shrub of the staff-tree family with crimson fruit and seeds with scarlet coverings. **2.** the wahoo.

strawberry finch, a small songbird; amadavat.

strawberry leaf, the trifoliate leaflike ornament on the coronet of a duke, marquis, or earl, commonly taken as the symbol of the rank involved.

strawberry mark, a soft, reddish birthmark slightly raised above the skin.

strawberry shrub, *U.S.* any of various shrubs having brownish or purplish-red flowers with a fragrance like that of strawberries.

strawberry tomato, 1. the small, edible, yellowish or greenish fruit of a ground cherry that looks like a tomato. **2.** the plant it grows on.

strawberry tree, a low evergreen tree of the heath family having a bright-scarlet fruit resembling a strawberry, cultivated for ornament.

straw·board (strô′bôrd′, -bōrd′), *n.* a coarse, yellowish cardboard made of straw pulp, used for boxes, packing, etc.

straw boss, *U.S. Informal.* an assistant foreman.

straw cloth, cloth of natural or synthetic straw, used for hats, handbags, etc.

straw color, the color of straw; pale yellow.

straw-col·ored (strô′kul′ərd), *adj.* of a straw color; pale-yellow: *fine, straw-colored hair.*

straw·flow·er (strô′flou′ər), *n.* any of various flowers that keep their shape and color when dry.

straw-hat (strô′hat′), *adj. U.S.* of or for plays, concerts, etc., performed during the summer in suburban or country areas: *a straw-hat theater. The show tried out with some success on the straw-hat circuits this summer* (Time). [< *straw hat* (because they are worn in the summer)]

straw man, 1. an imaginary opponent or opposing argument, put up in order to be defeated or refuted; man of straw. **2.** a person put up as a surety in a fraudulent action: *The usual procedure . . . is for straw men to set up the Corporation and then resign to turn it over to its directors* (Wall Street Journal). **3.** a puppet.

straw ride, *U.S.* a hayride.

straw·stack (strô′stak′), *n.* a large, outdoor pile of straw.

straw vote, *U.S.* an unofficial vote taken to estimate the amount of support for or strength of opposing candidates or issues, general opinion, etc.: *The continued strength of the Labor party is suggested by straw votes* (New York Times).

straw wine, wine made from grapes dried or partly dried in the sun on straw, usually sweet and rich.

straw·worm (strô′wėrm′), *n.* **1.** the larva of certain chalcid flies, that attacks grain stalks. **2.** a caddis worm.

straw·y (strô′ē), *adj.* **1.** of, containing, or like straw. **2.** strewed or thatched with straw.

straw·yard (strô′yärd′), *n.* **1.** a yard littered with straw, in which horses and cattle are wintered. **2.** *Informal.* a man's straw hat: *With umbrella, strawyard, black vicuña short jacket and striped trousers I was on my way to the office* (Listener).

stray (strā), *v.i.* **1.** to lose one's way; wander; roam: *straying about in a strange city. Our dog has strayed off somewhere.* **2.** to turn from the right course; go wrong: *We have erred and strayed from thy ways like lost sheep* (Book of Common Prayer). *Most of us have . . . a readiness to stray far, ever so far, on the wrong road* (Joseph Conrad). **3.** to wander in mind, purpose, etc.; digress: *I am straying from the question* (Oliver Goldsmith).

—*adj.* **1.** wandering; lost: *a stray cat, dog, or sheep.* **2.** here and there; scattered: *a stray customer or two, stray thoughts. There were a few stray fishermen's huts along the beach.* **3.** separated from the rest; isolated: *a stray copy of a book.*

—*n.* **1.** an animal that has wandered away

from its flock, home, or owner. **2.** any homeless or friendless person or animal. **3.** something that has wandered from its usual or proper place.
strays, *Electronics.* static: *Thomas Edison . . . says, "Marvellous! marvellous! but let us not forget that there are such things as electric strays"* (Westminster Gazette).
[short for Old French *estraier,* (originally) adjective < Vulgar Latin *strātārius* roaming the streets < Late Latin *strāta,* for Latin (*via*) *strāta* paved (street). Compare ESTRAY.] —**stray′er,** *n.*
—**Syn.** *v.i.* **1.** rove; straggle. See **wander. 2.** deviate, err.

streak (strēk), *n.* **1.** a long, thin mark or line: *He has a streak of dirt on his face. We saw a streak of lightning. He gets up at the first streak of daylight. A window, through which the first streaks of light could be seen* (Time). **2. a.** a stratum or vein of ore. **b.** a layer: *Bacon has streaks of fat and streaks of lean.* **3.** an element; vein; strain: *He has a streak of humor though he looks very serious.* **4.** *U.S.* a brief period; spell: *We've had a streak of bad luck* (Bret Harte). **5.** *Mineralogy.* the line of colored powder produced by scratching a mineral or fossil or rubbing it on a harder surface, forming an important distinguishing character. **6.** *Bacteriology.* the distribution of material to be inoculated over the surface of a medium in a line or stripe. **7.** a flash of lightning.
like a streak, very fast; at full speed: *The dog ran like a streak across the lawn.*
—*v.t.* to put long, thin marks or stripes on: *The Indians used to streak their faces with paint.* —*v.i.* **1.** to become streaked or streaky. **2.** *Informal.* to move very fast; go at full speed: *Our man streaked past the others and over the finishing line.*
[Middle English *streke,* Old English *strica*]
—**Syn.** *n.* **3.** trace, touch.

streaked (strēkt), *adj.* **1.** marked or diversified with streaks; streaky. **2.** *U.S. Dialect.* perturbed; uneasy; alarmed. —**Syn. 1.** striated.

streak·i·ly (strē′kə lē), *adv.* in a streaky manner.

streak·i·ness (strē′kē nis), *n.* streaky quality or state.

streak plate, a piece of unglazed porcelain on which to rub or scratch a mineral in testing the streak.

streak·y (strē′kē), *adj.,* **streak·i·er, streak·i·est. 1.** marked with streaks; streaked: *an old man with a streaky gray chin-beard* (Booth Tarkington). **2.** occurring in streaks. **3.** varying; uneven: *The dress has faded so much that the color is streaky.*

stream (strēm), *n.* **1.** a flow of water in a channel or bed; a small river; a large brook. **2.** a steady current of water, as in a river or in the ocean. **3. a.** any current or flow: *a stream of blood pouring from a wound, a stream of tears, a stream of air, gas, or electricity.* **b.** a ray or beam: *a stream of light.* **4.** a steady or continuous flow: *a stream of shoppers, a stream of cars, a stream of words or talk.* **5.** trend; drift; course: *the prevailing stream of opinion.* **6.** (in British secondary schools) any of several divisions into which students of the same grade are placed on the basis of the marks they receive in examinations such as the eleven-plus.
on stream, in full production: *Part of the new plant is now in operation . . . and the remainder will be on stream later this month* (Wall Street Journal).
—*v.i.* **1.** (of liquid) to flow: *Tears streamed down her cheeks.* **2. a.** to move steadily in large numbers: *People streamed out of the theater.* **b.** to move swiftly; streak: *A meteor streamed across the sky.* **3.** to be so wet as to drip in a stream; run; drip; overflow: *a streaming umbrella, eyes streaming with tears, a face streaming with perspiration.* **4.** to wave or float: *Flags streamed in the wind.* **5.** to hang loosely and waving: *streaming hair.* **6.** to be carried or given off in a stream, current, or trail: *dust streaming out behind the car, sun streaming in at the window.* —*v.t.* **1.** to cause to flow; pour out: *to stream water on a fire. The wound streamed blood.* **2.** to cause to stream or float outward, as a flag in the wind.
[Old English *strēam*] —**stream′like′,** *adj.*
—**Syn.** *n.* **1, 2. Stream, current** mean a flow of liquid or something fluid. **Stream** emphasizes a continuous flow, as of water in a river or from a spring or faucet: *Because of the lack of rain many streams dried up.* **Current** emphasizes a strong or rapid, onward movement in a certain direction, and applies particularly to the more swiftly moving part of a stream, ocean, body of air, etc.: *He let his boat drift with the current.* —*v.i.* **1.** See **flow.**

stream·er (strē′mər), *n.* **1.** any long, narrow, flowing thing: *Streamers of ribbon hung from her hat. We saw streamers of snow blowing around the hilltop.* **2.** a long, narrow, pointed flag or pennon streaming in the air. **3.** a newspaper headline that runs all the way across a page. **4.** a ribbonlike column of light shooting across the heavens in the aurora borealis. —**Syn. 2.** pennant.

streamer fly, any of various large artificial fishing flies with long wings extending past the hook, made to imitate a minnow.

stream·flow (strēm′flō′), *n.* the volume of water flowing in a stream at a given time: *Streamflow from snowmelt gives water surveyors a good picture of how much water will be available for irrigation* (Science News Letter).

stream·ing (strē′ming), *n. Biology.* the flowing motion or rotation of protoplasm in a cell.

stream·let (strēm′lit), *n.* a small stream; rivulet. —**Syn.** creek, brook.

stream·line (strēm′līn′), *adj., v.,* **-lined, -lin·ing,** *n.* —*adj.* **1.** of or having to do with a motion or flow that is free from disturbance, as of a particle in a steadily flowing mass of fluid. **2.** streamlined.
—*v.t.* **1.** to give a streamlined shape to (an airplane, automobile, etc.). **2.** to make more up-to-date, efficient, etc.: *to streamline an office.*
—*n.* **1.** a streamlined shape. **2.** *Physics.* the path of a particle in a steadily flowing mass of fluid.

stream·lined (strēm′līnd′), *adj.* **1.** having a shape or body that offers the least resistance to air or water: *a streamlined automobile, airplane, or train. Birds have streamlined bodies* (A. M. Winchester). **2.** brought up-to-date; made more efficient: *One curious little difficulty about streamlined reading . . . is the sluggishness of one's emotional reactions* (Atlantic).

Streamlined Bodies (def. 1)
From top to bottom: racing car, atomic submarine, and supersonic plane

streamline flow, a steady flow of a fluid past a body, in which the fluid remains smooth and relatively unchanged.

stream·lin·er (strēm′lī′nər), *n.* a streamlined railroad train or other vehicle: *Lightweight, low-slung streamliners whisk you from city to city in record time* (Wall Street Journal).

stream of consciousness, the series of mental experiences of an individual moving continuously onward through time: *He can navigate the rapids of a zany stream of consciousness without drowning the reader* (Time).

stream-of-con·scious·ness (strēm′əv-kon′shəs nis), *adj.* of or having to do with a method of storytelling in which the author tells the story through the freely flowing thoughts and associations of one of the characters.

stream·side (strēm′sīd′), *n.* the margin or bank of a stream: *Workers were gathered into factories which moved down to the streamsides for power* (London Times). —*adj.* beside a stream; on the bank of a stream: *Even the beaver would not be able to survive without food and building materials provided by streamside trees* (Fred Emerson).

stream·way (strēm′wā′), *n.* **1.** the shallow bed of a stream; watercourse: *The present meandering course of the river probably follows an ancestral streamway across an old surface now washed and blown away* (William O. Douglas). **2.** the main current of a river.

stream·y (strē′mē), *adj.,* **stream·i·er, stream·i·est. 1.** full of streams or watercourses. **2.** flowing in a stream; streaming.

streek (strēk), *Scottish.* —*v.t.* **1.** to stretch. **2.** to lay out (a corpse). —*v.i.* to stretch. —*n.* extent.

[variant of Middle English *strecchen,* Old English *streccan* stretch]

street (strēt), *n.* **1.** a public road in a city or town, usually with buildings on both sides, and including the sidewalks or paths as well as the roadway. A street is maintained by the city or town, a highway by the county or state. *Abbr.:* St. **2.** such a road, not including the sidewalks, as a place or way for vehicles to go: *Be careful in crossing the street.* **3.** the people who live in the buildings on a street: *All Oak Street welcomed him home.*
be streets ahead, *Especially British.* to be far ahead in a contest; be far superior: *When it came to pure boxing ability, Winstone was streets ahead* (London Times).
on easy street, *Informal.* in comfortable circumstances; financially secure or independent: *He tried one scheme after another, looking for the quickest way to get on easy street.*
the Street, *Informal.* Wall Street: *"They still know me in the Street," he added* (New Yorker).
—*adj.* **1.** of a street: *a street cleaner.* **2.** in a street: *a street scene.*
[Old English *strēt, strǣt* < Late Latin *strāta,* for Latin (*via*) *strāta* paved (road), feminine past participle of *sternere* lay out] —**street′like′,** *adj.*

street Arab, a homeless child who lives by his wits on the streets of a city, as by begging, stealing, etc. —**Syn.** waif.

street·car (strēt′kär′), *n. U.S.* a car that runs on rails in the streets and carries passengers; trolley car.

street club, *U.S.* a juvenile gang in a city block or district, especially one assigned to a street worker. —**street′-club′,** *adj.*

street·ed (strē′tid), *adj.* having streets.

street·ful (strēt′fu̇l), *n., pl.* **-fuls.** as much or as many as a street will hold: *The streetful of villagers turned in a great stirring of sackcloth* (Punch).

street lamp, a lamp that lights a street: *Perhaps . . . the starlings enjoyed the light and warmth from the powerful street lamps* (New Scientist).

street-length (strēt′lengkth′, -length′), *adj.* of a length suitable for everyday wear on the street; not full-length: *The honor attendants wore street-length dresses of lavender shantung* (New York Times).

street light, a street lamp.

street name, *U.S.* the name of a broker or brokerage firm. A person usually buys stocks in a street name for convenience in the safekeeping, handling, and transfer of the stocks. *Most of the stock in favor of the special meeting is held in street name* (Wall Street Journal).

street piano, a small mechanical piano set on wheels and operated by turning a crank, formerly played in the streets for gratuities; hurdy-gurdy.

street railway, 1. a route or routes served by streetcars in a city or town. **2.** a company owning or operating such a route or routes.

street·side (strēt′sīd′), *n.* the side of a street: *Along the streetside were the remains of a narrow building* (John Ward). —*adj.* beside a street: *Carpenters hammered together streetside reviewing stands for his big show* (Time).

street·walk·er (strēt′wô′kər), *n.* a prostitute who frequents the streets or public places in search of customers.

street·walk·ing (strēt′wô′king), *n.* the work or activities of a streetwalker. —*adj.* of or like a streetwalker.

street·ward (strēt′wərd), *adv., adj.* near or toward the street; looking out on the street.

street worker, a social worker who deals directly with street clubs and problems common to poor neighborhoods: *The street worker has become so friendly with them that he can sometimes return stolen goods before the police are even aware of the theft* (Maclean's).

stre·ga (strā′gä), *n.* a yellow Italian liqueur with a sweet, perfumed taste. [< *Strega,* the trademark of the product]

streng·ite (streng′īt), *n.* a purplish or deep pink mineral, a hydrous phosphate of iron, occurring mainly in botryoidal form. *Formula:* $FePO_4.2H_2O$ [< German *Strengit*]

strength (strengkth, strength), *n.* **1.** the quality or condition of being strong; power;

force; vigor: *enough strength to lift a heavy weight, to recover one's strength after sickness. A nation's strength does not lie in material things alone; a rich nation can also be a decaying one* (Newsweek). **2.** mental or moral power: *strength of memory or of judgment, to have strength of character.* **3.** power to resist or endure; toughness: *the strength of a beam, rope, or bridge, tensile strength.* **4.** power or force as measured in numbers; the number or quota of soldiers, warships, etc.: *an army or fleet at full strength.* **5.** power derived from authority, the law, influence, the possession of resources, or the like: *the strength of public opinion, the strength of a leader.* **6.** power or capacity for producing effects; cogency or potency; weight: *the strength of words, arguments, or evidence.* **7.** degree of strength; intensity: *the strength of a wind, fire, stream, or current of electricity, the strength of a color, sound, odor, or light, the strength of a drug, liquor, or solution. Take this cough medicine at full strength. Some flavorings lose their strength in cooking.* **8.** something that makes strong; support: *God is our refuge and strength* (Psalms 46:1). **9.** the existence of a firm or rising level of stock or commodity prices on an exchange, etc.: *Strength in the railroads highlighted last week's stock market* (Wall Street Journal). **10.** energy or vigor of literary or artistic conception or treatment.

by main strength, by using full strength: *It was only by main strength that he was able to raise the cart and save the man trapped beneath its wheels.*

on the strength of, relying or depending on; with the support or help of: *He bought the book on the strength of his teacher's recommendation.*

[Old English *strengthu* < *strang* strong]

—**Syn. 1.** See **power.**

strength·en (strengk′thən, streng′-), *v.t.* to make stronger: *The soldiers strengthened their defenses.* —*v.i.* to grow stronger. —**strength′en·er,** *n.* —**Syn.** *v.t.* reinforce, fortify.

strength·less (strengkth′lis, strength′-), *adj.* lacking strength: *The sun over the Cypress Hills was low and strengthless* (Harper's).

stren·u·os·i·ty (stren′yu̇ os′ə tē), *n., pl.* **-ties. 1.** the quality or state of being strenuous. **2.** a strained effect or a straining for effect.

stren·u·ous (stren′yu̇ əs), *adj.* **1.** very active: *We had a strenuous day moving into our new house. I wish to preach, not the doctrine of ignoble ease, but the doctrine of the strenuous life* (Theodore Roosevelt). **2.** full of energy: *The gym teacher is a strenuous man.* [< Latin *strēnuus* (with English *-ous*)] —**stren′u·ous·ly,** *adv.* —**stren′u·ous·ness,** *n.* —**Syn. 1, 2.** See **vigorous.**

strep (strep), *n. Informal.* streptococcus: *Special attention to "strep" infections is necessary to guard children against rheumatic fever* (Newsweek). [short for *streptococcus*]

Streph·on (stref′on), *n.* a swain or lover in pastoral and other literature (the loved one often called Chloe). [< *Strephon,* a shepherd in *Arcadia,* by Sir Philip Sidney, 1554-1586, an English soldier and author]

streph·o·sym·bo·li·a (stref′ō sim bō′lē ə), *n.* **1.** a reading difficulty in certain children characterized by confusion between similar letters, such as *b* and *d,* or *n* and *u.* **2.** a visual disorder in which objects appear reversed, as in a mirror. [< New Latin *strephosymbolia* < Greek *stréphein* twist + *sýmbolon* symbol]

strep·i·tant (strep′ə tənt), *adj.* strepitous.

strep·i·to·so (strep′ə tō′sō), *Music.* —*adv.* in a noisy manner; accompanied with much noise. —*adj.* noisy. [< Italian *strepitoso* < *strepito* noise < Latin *strepitus, -ūs*]

strep·i·tous (strep′ə təs), *adj.* noisy: *a strepitous movement in a symphony.* [< Latin *strepitus, -ūs* noise, clatter (< *strepere* make a noise) + English *-ous*]

strep·o·gen·in (strep′ə jen′in), *n.* a peptide found in insulin and other proteins that is essential to the growth of mice and certain microorganisms. [< *strep* + *-gen* + *-in*]

strep·sic·e·ros (strep sis′ə rəs), *n.* any of a group of antelopes with twisted or spiral horns, including the kudu and the nyala. [< New Latin *Strepticeros,* the genus name < Greek *strepsikerōs,* an animal with twisted horns]

strep·sir·rhine or **strep·si·rhine** (strep′sə rīn, -sər in), *adj.* having twisted or curved nostrils, as a lemur. —*n.* a strepsirrhine animal. [< Greek *strepsi-* (< *stréphein* to twist, turn) + *rhís, rhinós* nose]

strep throat, septic sore throat.

strepto-, *combining form.* **1.** twisted or linked; resembling chains: *Streptococcus = a group of bacteria that occur in chains.* **2.** streptococcus: *Streptokinase = an enzyme derived from streptococci.* [< Greek *streptós* twisted; a chain or linked collar < *stréphein* to twist, turn]

strep·to·coc·cal (strep′tə kok′əl), *adj.* streptococcic.

strep·to·coc·cic (strep′tə kok′sik), *adj.* having to do with or caused by streptococci.

strep·to·coc·cus (strep′tə kok′əs), *n., pl.* **-coc·ci** (-kok′sī). any of a group of spherical, gram-positive bacteria that occur in chains or as paired cells, and divide in only one direction; strep. Many serious infections and diseases, such as scarlet fever, erysipelas, and septicemia, etc., are caused by streptococci. [< New Latin *Streptococcus* the genus name < Greek *streptós* (see STREPTO-) + *kókkos* a grain, kernel; berry]

strep·to·dor·nase (strep′tō dôr′nās), *n.* an enzyme produced by certain bacteria, used in combination with, and having effects similar to, streptokinase. [< *strepto-* *d*(e)*o*(cy)*r*(ibo)*n*(ucle)*ase*]

strep·to·ki·nase (strep′tō kī nās′), *n.* a protein enzyme that loosens or dissolves blood clots, pus, and other waste matter associated with infections. It is also derived from streptococcal bacteria.

strep·to·my·ces (strep′tə mī′sēz), *n., pl.* **-ces.** any of a group of soil microbes sometimes classified fungi, sometimes bacteria, which are the source of streptomycin and other antibiotics. [< New Latin *Streptomyces* the genus name < Greek *streptós* twisted + *mýkēs* fungus]

strep·to·my·cin (strep′tə mī′sin), *n.* a powerful antibiotic similar to penicillin, obtained from a kind of streptomyces. It is effective against tuberculosis, typhoid fever, tularemia, and certain other bacterial infections. *Formula:* $C_{21}H_{39}N_7O_{12}$

strep·to·nig·rin (strep′tō nig′rin), *n.* a very toxic, dark brown, crystalline antibiotic produced by a variety of streptomyces, and active against various forms of tumors. *Formula:* $C_{24}H_{20}N_4O_8$ [< *strepto-* + Latin *niger* black + English *-in*]

strep·to·thri·cin or **strep·to·thry·sin** (strep′tə thrī′sin), *n.* an antibiotic obtained from a soil microorganism. It is similar to streptomycin in its action. [< New Latin *Streptothrix* the genus name of the fungus (< Greek *streptós*; see STREPTO-; + *thríx, trichós* a hair) + English *-in*]

strep·to·va·ri·cin (strep′tō və rī′sin), *n.* an antibiotic obtained from a kind of streptomyces, used against tuberculosis.

stress (stres), *n.* **1.** pressure; force; strain: *the stress of poverty, war, or weather, to steal food under the stress of hunger. Other animals have like tensions ... know the deadly effects of stress* (William O. Douglas). *My purpose was to teach students how to think under stress* (Time). **2.** great effort. **3.** emphasis; importance: *More high schools today lay stress upon scientific studies.* **4.** *Physics.* **a.** the internal forces interacting between contiguous parts of a body, caused by the external forces, such as tension or shear, which produce the strain. **b.** the intensity of these forces, generally measured in pounds per square inch. **c.** a force or system of forces causing strain. **5.** *Phonetics.* **a.** the relative loudness in the pronunciation of syllables, words in a sentence, etc.; accent. In *hero,* the stress is on the first syllable. **b.** a stressed syllable. **6.** *Prosody.* **a.** the relative loudness or prominence given a syllable or word in a metrical pattern. **b.** any accented syllable in a foot. **7.** *Music.* an accent.
—*v.t.* **1.** to put pressure upon. **2.** to treat as important; emphasize: *The English curriculum should stress both composition and reading.* **3.** to pronounce with stress.
[partly short for Middle English *destresse* distress, partly < Old French *estrece* narrowness, oppression, ultimately < Latin *strictus,* past participle of *stringere* draw tight]
—**Syn.** *n.* **3.** significance, weight.

stressed-skin construction (strest′-skin′), a type of aircraft construction, such as monocoque, in which the skin bears all or part of the stresses arising in the aircraft.

stress·ful (stres′fəl), *adj.* full of stress; subject to strain: *More important than mere aptitude for a mechanical or technical job is the ability to keep on doing the job under stressful conditions* (Newsweek).

stress·less (stres′lis), *adj.* **1.** not under stress or strain: *a stressless life.* **2.** unstressed: *Some languages—Hindi, Marathi, and Japanese—may be described as stressless* (Simeon Potter).

stretch (strech), *v.t.* **1.** to draw (out); extend (oneself, body, limbs, wings, etc.) to full length: *He stretched himself out on the grass and fell asleep.* **2.** to extend so as to reach from one place to another or across a space: *to stretch a clothesline from a tree to a pole, to stretch a carpet on the floor.* **3.** to reach (out); hold (out): *He stretched out his hand for the money.* **4.** to draw out to greater length or width; lengthen or widen: *to stretch shoes or gloves until they fit.* **5.** to draw tight; strain: *to stretch a muscle. He stretched the violin string until it broke.* **6.** to extend beyond proper or natural limits: *to stretch one's credit. He stretched the law to suit his purposes.* **7.** *Informal.* to exaggerate: *to stretch the truth. There was things which he stretched, but mainly he told the truth* (Mark Twain). **8.** *Dialect.* to straighten the limbs of (a dead person). **9.** *Informal.* to hang (a person).
—*v.i.* **1.** to extend one's body, or limbs at full length, as in lying down, yawning, or reaching: *He stretched out on the couch.* **2.** to extend one's hand; reach for something: *to stretch out to get the book.* **3.** to make great effort. **4.** to continue over a distance; fill space; spread: *The forest stretches for miles. The hours stretched by like years* (Alfred Noyes). **5.** to become longer or wider without breaking: *Rubber stretches.* **6.** *Informal.* to go beyond the strict truth. **7.** *Informal.* to be hanged.
—*n.* **1. a.** an unbroken length or extent: *A stretch of sand hills lay between the road and the ocean.* **b.** an uninterrupted period: *to work for a stretch of five hours.* **2.** *Slang.* **a.** a term of imprisonment. **b.** *British.* a year's term in prison. **3.** a stretching or straining something beyond its proper limits: *a stretch of authority or of the law, no great stretch of the imagination.* **4. a.** a stretching or being stretched: *With a sudden stretch John took Tom's cap.* **b.** a stretching of the legs; walk for exercise. **5.** capacity for being stretched; extent to which something can be stretched: *shouted ... at the utmost stretch of his voice* (George Eliot). **6.** *Racing.* one of the two straight sides of a race course. The part between the first and second turns is called the back stretch: the part between the last turn and the finish line is called the home stretch: *Down the back stretch, Needles was still lost in the pack* (Time). **7.** *Mining, Geology.* the course or direction of a seam or stratum. **8.** the ability of an aircraft to be modified and improved in design, performance, etc., after its original construction: [*It*] *is capable of considerable further stretch in power and efficiency, already claimed to equal or exceed that of other engines* (Wall Street Journal).
—*adj.* of a material that stretches easily to fit all sizes, as of certain clothes sizes: *stretch gloves, stretch socks.*
[spelling variant of Middle English *strecchen,* Old English *streccan.* Compare STREEK.]

stretch·a·bil·i·ty (strech′ə bil′ə tē), *n.* the ability to stretch or be stretched.

stretch·a·ble (strech′ə bəl), *adj.* that can be stretched: *Chiefly responsible for the upturn has been the company's introduction of stretchable sheer hosiery for women* (Wall Street Journal).

stretched-out (strecht′out′), *adj.* drawn out beyond the original size; extended; prolonged: *The stretched-out buying pattern will mean financing trouble for some small firms with meager capital resources* (Wall Street Journal).

stretch·er (strech′ər), *n.* **1.** a person or thing that stretches: *A glove stretcher makes gloves larger.* **2.** canvas stretched on a frame for carrying the sick, wounded, or dead. **3. a.** a brick or stone laid with its length in the direction of the face of the wall. **b.** a bar, beam,

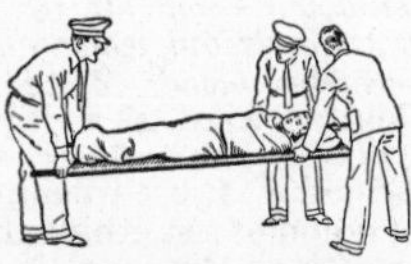

Stretcher (def. 2)

or rod used as a tie or brace, as between the legs of a chair. **4.** a wooden frame on which an artist's canvas is spread and drawn tight, usually by means of tacks along the sides and small wedges in the angles. **5.** *Informal.* an exaggerated tale; yarn: . . . *mostly a true book, with some stretchers* (Mark Twain). —**Syn. 2.** litter.

stretch·er-bear·er (strech′ər bãr′ər), *n.* one of the persons who carry a stretcher, as in moving a sick, injured, or dead person.

stretch·er·man (strech′ər mən), *n., pl.* **-men.** a stretcher-bearer.

stretch nylon, a nylon yarn or fabric specially treated to stretch and retract to its original dimensions.

stretch·out (strech′out′), *n. Informal.* **1.** a postponement, especially of the date for filling defense orders: *Such cuts might take the form of a stretchout of defense goals so that their cost might be distributed over a longer period* (New York Times). **2.** a system in which factory or other workers are required to do additional work without overtime pay. —*adj.* of or having to do with a stretchout.

stretch·y (strech′ē), *adj.,* **stretch·i·er, stretch·i·est.** *Informal.* **1.** elastic; stretchable. **2.** liable to stretch too much.

stretch yarn, any synthetic yarn treated to give it elasticity: *The biggest advances in the apparel field were in "wash-and-wear" fabrics, stretch yarns, and synthetic furs* (Glenn Fowler).

stret·ta (stret′tä), *n., pl.* **-te** (-tā), **-tas.** *Music.* **1.** a passage, especially a final passage, performed in quicker or accelerated time for climactic effect, a device often used in oratorio and opera. **2.** stretto in a fugue or canon. [< Italian *stretta,* feminine of *stretto;* see STRETTO]

stret·to (stret′tō), *n., pl.* **-ti** (-tē), **-tos.** *Music.* **1. a.** (in a fugue or canon) an overlapping of subject and answer so as to produce a rapidly cumulative effect. **b.** the third section of the fugue, after exposition and development, in which this device is often used. **c.** a canon in which this device is used. **2.** a final passage; stretta. [< Italian *stretto* close, narrow < Latin *strictus.* Doublet of STRAIT, STRICT.]

streu·sel (stroi′zəl, strü′-; *German* shtroi′-zəl), *n.* a crumb topping for cake, usually made of flour, sugar, and nuts. [< German *Streusel* (literally) sprinkling]

strew (strü), *v.t.,* **strewed, strewed** or **strewn** (strün), **strew·ing. 1.** to scatter; sprinkle: *She strewed seeds in her garden. The boy strewed his clothes all over the floor.* **2.** to cover with something scattered or sprinkled: *The ground was strewn with leaves. Wild tornadoes strewing yonder sea with wrecks* (William Cowper). **3.** to be scattered over; be sprinkled over: *Photographs strewed the low tables* (Edith Wharton). **4. a.** *Poetic.* to utter: *For so I have strewed it in the common ear* (Shakespeare). **b.** to spread about; disseminate: *All heaven bursts her starry floors, And strews her lights below* (Tennyson). [Old English *strēowian.* Compare STROW. Probably related to STRAW.]

strew·ment (strü′mənt), *n. Archaic.* something strewed, as flowers: *She is allow'd . . . Her maiden strewments* (Shakespeare).

strewn (strün), *v.* strewed; a past participle of **strew.**

stri·a (strī′ə), *n., pl.* **stri·ae** (strī′ē). **1.** a slight furrow or ridge; small groove or channel, as produced on a rock by moving ice, or on the surface of a crystal or mineral by its structure. **2.** a linear marking; a narrow stripe or streak, as of color or texture, especially one of a number in parallel arrangement. **3.** *Architecture.* a fillet between the flutes of columns, etc. [< Latin *stria* a facet or flute (of a column)]

stri·ate (strī′āt), *v.,* **-at·ed, -at·ing,** *adj.* —*v.t.* to mark or score with striae; furrow; stripe; streak. —*adj.* striated. [< Latin *striāre* (with English *-ate*[1]) to furrow, channel < *stria;* see STRIA]

stri·at·ed (strī′ā tid), *adj.* marked with striae; striped; streaked; furrowed: *striated rock, a striated pattern.*

striated muscle, a type of muscle with fibers of cross bands contracted by voluntary action, as the muscles that move the arms, legs, neck, etc.

stri·a·tion (strī ā′shən), *n.* **1.** striated condition or appearance. **2.** one of a number of parallel striae; a stria.

stri·a·ture (strī′ə chər), *n.* **1.** disposition of striae; striation. **2.** a stria. [< Latin *striātūra* < *stria;* see STRIA]

strick (strik), *n.* **1.** a bundle of broken hemp, flax, jute, etc., for hackling. **2.** a bunch of silk fiber for the second combing. [apparently variant of *strike*]

strick·en (strik′ən), *adj.* **1.** affected by (wounds, disease, trouble, sorrow, disaster, etc.): *a stricken deer or whale. a sorrow-stricken face, a poverty-stricken family. Insurance is the magic which provides the means for reconstruction and hope for the stricken people* (Newsweek). **2.** filled level to the top or brim; full but not heaped up: *a stricken measure or container of grain.* —*v.* struck; a past participle of **strike.** —**Syn.** *adj.* **1.** afflicted.

strick·le (strik′əl), *n., v.,* **-led, -ling.** —*n.* **1.** a straight piece of wood used to level a measure of grain in a container. **2.** a piece of wood covered with emery, used for whetting or sharpening scythes; rifle. **3.** *Metallurgy.* **a.** a straightedge used to level off sand in a flask. **b.** a specially shaped piece used in sweeping patterns in sand or loam.

—*v.t.* to sweep off or level (grain, etc.) with a strickle.

[Old English *stricel* wheel, pulley, related to *strīcan* to pass over a surface; strike]

strict (strikt), *adj.* **1.** very careful in following a rule or in making others follow it: *The teacher was strict but not unfair.* **2.** harsh; severe; stern: *strict discipline, strict justice.* **3.** complete; perfect; absolute: *strict neutrality, to tell a secret in strict confidence.* **4.** exact; precise; accurate: *the strict meaning of a word. He told the strict truth.* **5.** careful or minute: *a strict method, a strict inquiry.* **6.** *Botany.* close or narrow and upright: *a strict stem or inflorescence.* **7.** *Archaic.* tight; close. [< Latin *strictus,* past participle of *stringere* bind tight. Doublet of STRAIT, STRETTO.] —**strict′ly,** *adv.* —**strict′ness,** *n.*

—**Syn. 1, 2. Strict, rigid, rigorous** mean severe and unyielding or harsh and stern. **Strict** emphasizes showing or demanding a very careful and close following of a rule, standard, or requirement: *Our teacher is strict and insists that we follow instructions to the letter.* **Rigid** emphasizes being firm and unyielding, not changing or relaxing for anyone or under any conditions: *He maintains a rigid working schedule.* **Rigorous** emphasizes the severity, harshness, or sternness of the demands made, conditions imposed, etc.: *We believe in rigorous enforcement of the laws.*

strict imitation, *Music.* the repetition of a phrase or melody in another part or voice, usually at a different pitch but with the same intervals, rhythm, and melodic outline.

stric·tion (strik′shən), *n.* a drawing tight; constriction. [< Latin *strictiō, -ōnis* < *strictus;* see STRICT]

stric·ture (strik′chər), *n.* **1.** an unfavorable criticism; critical remark: *We may now and then add a few strictures of reproof* (Samuel Johnson). **2.** an abnormal narrowing of some canal, duct, or tube of the body, as of the urethra, esophagus, or intestine. **3.** a binding or tightening; binding restriction; constriction: *A windless stricture of frost had bound the air* (Robert Louis Stevenson). *They are heterodox Moslems, accepting the Prophet's precepts but rejecting some of his strictures, e.g., their women go unveiled* (Time). **4.** *Obsolete.* strictness: *A man of stricture and firm abstinence* (Shakespeare). [< Latin *strictūra* < *strictus;* see STRICT]

stride (strīd), *v.,* **strode** or (*Obsolete*) **strid** (strid), **strid·den** (strid′ən) or (*Obsolete*) **strid, strid·ing,** *n.* —*v.i.* **1.** to walk with long steps: *The tall man strides rapidly down the street.* **2.** to take a long step; pass (over or across) with a long step: *He strode over the brook.* —*v.t.* **1.** to walk with long steps: *to stride the streets.* **2.** to go over or across with one long step: *to stride a brook.* **3.** to sit or stand with one leg on each side of; straddle; bestride: *to stride a fence.*

—*n.* **1.** a striding; long step: *The child could not keep up with his father's stride.* **2.** the distance covered by a stride.

hit one's stride, to reach one's regular speed or normal activity: *At first the comedian's monologue fell flat, but after a few minutes he hit his stride.*

make great or **rapid strides,** to make great progress; advance rapidly: *The Corporation of the Cauca Valley (CVC), is making great strides in bringing ample power, irrigation, and agricultural extension services to the landrich Cauca Valley* (Atlantic).

take in (one's) stride, to deal with in one's normal activity; do or take without difficulty, hesitation, or special effort: *I'd want something that would look more easy and natural, more as if I took it in stride* (Edith Wharton).

[Old English *strīdan*]

—**Syn.** *v.i.* **1.** See **walk.**

stri·dence (strī′dəns), *n.* a being strident.

stri·den·cy (strī′dən sē), *n.* stridence.

stri·dent (strī′dənt), *adj.* **1.** making or having a harsh sound; creaking; grating; shrill: *The strident voice sounded harsher than ever* (Mrs. Humphry Ward). *The details make pretty strident reading* (Atlantic). **2.** having a harsh voice; rasping; shrill: *a strident person.* [< Latin *strīdēns, -entis,* present participle of *strīdere* sound harshly, screech] —**stri′dent·ly,** *adv.* —**Syn. 1.** piercing.

stride piano, *Jazz Slang.* ragtime piano playing consisting of single notes on the first and third beats of the bar and chords on the second and fourth beats. —**stride pianist.**

strid·er (strī′dər), *n.* a person or thing that strides, especially a horse.

stri·dor (strī′dər), *n.* **1.** a harsh, shrill sound; strident noise. **2.** *Medicine.* a harsh respiratory sound, caused by obstruction of the air passages. [< Latin *strīdor, -ōris* < *strīdere* to creak, screech, sound harshly]

strid·u·lant (strij′ə lənt), *adj.* stridulating.

strid·u·late (strij′ə lāt), *v.i.,* **-lat·ed, -lat·ing. 1.** to make a shrill, grating sound, as a cricket or katydid, by rubbing together certain parts of the body. **2.** to shrill; chirr. [< New Latin *stridulare* (with English *-ate*[1]) < Latin *strīdulus;* see STRIDULOUS]

strid·u·la·tion (strij′ə lā′shən), *n.* the act or sound of stridulating.

strid·u·la·to·ry (strij′ə lə tôr′ē, -tōr′-), *adj.* having to do with stridulation; stridulating.

strid·u·lous (strij′ə ləs), *adj.* **1.** making a harsh or grating sound; strident: *She . . . closed her eyes in halcyon tranquillity, enjoying everything—even the stridulous cries of the gulls, even the windless heat* (New Yorker). **2.** *Medicine.* of, having to do with, or characterized by stridor. [< Latin *strīdulus* (with English *-ous*) < *strīdere* creak, sound harshly] —**strid′u·lous·ly,** *adv.* —**strid′u·lous·ness,** *n.*

stri·é (strē ā′), *adj. French.* striated: *strié silks, strié velvets.*

strife (strīf), *n.* **1.** a quarreling; fighting: *bitter strife between rival factions.* **2.** a quarrel; fight. **3.** *Archaic.* rivalry; competition; emulation: *I strove with none, for none was worth my strife* (Walter S. Landor). **4.** *Archaic.* a strong effort; endeavor. [< Old French *estrif* < a Germanic word, related to *estriver* strive] —**Syn. 1.** conflict, contention. **2.** struggle, dispute.

strig·il (strij′əl), *n.* **1.** a scraper for the skin, used after a bath or gymnastic exercise by the ancient Greeks and Romans. **2.** one of a set of curved flutings or reedings, used in Roman architecture. **3.** a brushlike part on the legs or abdomen of certain insects, as the bee. [< Latin *strigilis,* related to *stringere* strip off, scrape; draw tight, bind]

strig·i·la·tion (strij′ə lā′shən), *n.* vigorous friction with a strigil or the like.

strig·il·lose (strij′ə lōs), *adj. Botany.* minutely strigose.

stri·gose (strī′gōs, stri gōs′), *adj.* **1.** *Botany.* covered with stiff and straight bristles or hairs; hispid. **2.** *Zoology.* marked with fine, closely set ridges, grooves, or points. [< New Latin *strigosus* < *striga* stiff bristle < Latin, row of grain cut down, swath, stubble, related to *stringere;* see STRIGIL]

strike (strīk), *v.,* **struck, struck** or **stricken,** or (*Obsolete*) **strook** or **struck·en, strik·ing,** *n.* —*v.t.* **1.** to deal a blow to; hit: *to strike a person in anger. Lightning struck the barn.* **2.** to deal; give. **3.** to cause to hit; dash; knock: *The child struck her head against the crib. He struck his fist against the table and called for order.* **4.** to make by stamping, printing, etc.: *to strike a medal.* **5.** to set on fire by hitting or rubbing: *to strike a spark, to strike a light, to strike a match.* **6.** to impress: *The plan strikes me as silly. That play strikes my fancy.* **7.** to sound: *The clock strikes the hour.* **8. a.** to overcome by death, disease, suffering, etc.: *The town was struck with a flu epidemic.* **b.** to cause to feel; affect deeply: *They were struck with terror.* **9.** to occur to: *An amusing thought struck her.* **10.** to come upon; find: *to strike water, to strike oil, to strike gold.* **11.** to cross; rub; cancel; expunge: *Strike his name from the list.* **12.** to take away by or as if by a blow: *Strike the weapon from his hand.* **13.** to assume: *to strike an attitude.* **14.** (of a plant, cutting, etc.) to send down or out (a root). **15. a.** to balance: *to strike a ledger.* **b.** to get by figuring: *to strike an average.* **16.** to enter upon; make; decide: *to strike a bargain, to strike a compromise, to strike an agreement.* **17. a.** to lower (a flag, sail, etc.) as a salute or sign of surrender: *The ship struck her flag.* **b.** to lower (an object) into a ship's hold with a rope and tackle. **18.** to remove the tents of; break (camp): *to strike camp in the morning.* **19. a.** to make level with the top edge of a measure: *to strike grain.* **b.** to level with a strickle: *to strike up sand.* **20.** to cause to enter; penetrate: *The wind struck a chill into her bones.* **21.** (of a snake, etc.) to wound with fangs or sting. **22. a.** to harpoon (a whale). **b.** to hook (a fish) by pulling or jerking the line. **23.** to alter one's pace into (a faster movement): *The horses struck a canter.* **24.** to collide with: *The car struck a fence.* **25.** to fall on; touch; reach; catch: *The sun struck his eyes. A whistle struck his ear. The waving palm trees struck his view.* **26.** to come across; come upon; find: *to strike an amusing book. We shall strike the main road soon.* **27.** to remove (a scene) from the stage; remove the scenery, etc., of (a play). **28.** to leave off (work) at the close of the day, at meal times, etc. **29.** *Dialect.* to stroke; smooth: *to strike one's beard.* **30.** *Informal.* to make a sudden and pressing demand upon: *to strike a friend for a loan.* **31.** *Obsolete.* to fight (a battle).

—*v.i.* **1.** to deal or aim a blow, as with the fist, a stick, etc.: *to strike at a person with a whip.* **2.** to attack: *The enemy will strike at dawn.* **3.** to use one's weapons; fight: *to strike for freedom.* **4.** (of a snake, etc.) to wound its prey with the fangs or sting. **5.** to tap, rap, or knock: *He struck upon the window.* **6.** to be set on fire by hitting or rubbing: *The match wouldn't strike.* **7.** to sound with or as if with blows; sound: *The clock struck twelve times at noon.* **8.** to stop work to get better pay, shorter hours, certain benefits, etc.: *The coal miners struck.* **9.** to proceed; go: *to strike into a gallop. We walked along the road a mile, then struck across the fields.* **10.** to make a stroke with one's arms or legs in swimming or with one's oar in rowing. **11.** to put forth roots; send or take root: *The roots of oats strike deep.* **12.** to collide: *The car struck against a wall. The ship struck against a reef.* **13.** to fall; catch: *The sunlight struck on his face. A sound struck on his ear.* **14.** to make an impression, as on the mind, senses, etc. **15.** to move quickly; dart; shoot. **16.** to come; light: *to strike upon a new book.* **17. a.** to lower a flag, colors, etc., as a signal of surrender or to honor or salute a dignitary. **b.** to raise a white flag in surrendering. **18.** to seize the bait and the hook: *The fish are striking well today.*

strike off, a. to take off; cancel; remove: *The first person who flouts her shall be struck off my visiting list* (Matilda Betham-Edwards). **b.** to print: *to strike off a hundred copies.*

strike out, a. to cross out; rub out: *His name was struck out of the list of privy councillors* (Macaulay). **b.** (in baseball) to fail to hit three pitches; be called out on strikes: *The batter struck out.* **c.** to cause to fail to hit three pitches: *The pitcher struck out six men.* **d.** to use arms and legs to move forward: *The swimmer struck out across the lake.* **e.** to hit from the shoulder: *He struck out his right arm deprecatingly* (George Meredith).

strike up, a. to begin: *to strike up an acquaintance, a friendship, or a conversation.* **b.** to begin or cause to begin to play, sing, or sound: *to strike up a song. Strike up the band.* **c.** to raise by hammering, etc.: *to strike up metal.*

—*n.* **1. a.** the act or fact of finding rich ore in mining, oil in boring, etc.: *to make a strike. Drilling crews recently have hit at least . . . seven strikes in the same vicinity* (Wall Street Journal). **b.** a sudden success: *He made a strike with his first play.* **2.** a general quitting of work in order to force an employer or employers to agree to the workers' demands for higher wages, shorter hours, or other benefits. **3.** a striking. **4.** (in baseball) the failure of a batter to hit a pitched ball. **5.** in bowling: **a.** an upsetting of all the pins with the first ball bowled: *Some proprietors offer baby sitters while mother seeks a strike or a spare on the alley* (Wall Street Journal). **b.** the score so made. **6.** the number of coins minted at one time. **7.** a taking hold of the bait and the hook: *He got a strike at his first cast in the lake.* **8.** a metal piece in a doorjamb, into which the latch of a lock fits when the door closes. **9.** *Mining, Geology.* the horizontal course of a stratum; direction with regard to the points of the compass. **10.** a strickle for leveling a measure of grain, salt, etc. **11.** an attack by bombers upon a target: *The bombardiers reported clearing weather and "good to excellent" results in both strikes* (New York Times). **12.** *Obsolete.* **a.** the degree of strength of ale or beer. **b.** the unit proportion of malt in ale or beer.

[Old English *strīcan* to pass lightly (over a surface); to rub, stroke[2]; to beat, hit]

—**Syn.** *v.t.* **1.** smite, beat, buffet, slap.

strike-a-light (strīk′ə līt′), *n.* a piece of trimmed flint used with pyrites or steel for producing fire from the sparks: *Strike-a-lights have often appeared among prehistoric findings.*

strike·bound (strīk′bound′), *adj.* having its operations stopped by a labor strike: *The company has been strikebound since August 10, when the old pact expired* (Wall Street Journal).

strike·break·er (strīk′brā′kər), *n.* a person who helps to break up a strike of workers by taking a striker's job or by furnishing persons who will do so. —**Syn.** scab.

strike·break·ing (strīk′brā′king), *n.* forceful measures taken to halt a strike.

strike fault, *Geology.* a fault whose trend is roughly parallel to the strike of the rocks in which it occurs.

strike force, striking force: *In December 1960, the U.S. first proposed to help NATO develop its own nuclear strike force* (Time).

strike·out (strīk′out′), *n.* **1.** in baseball: **a.** an out earned by a pitcher throwing three strikes against a batter. **b.** the act of striking out: . . . *"Casey at the Bat," which builds up to one of the biggest letdowns in all literature—Casey's strikeout with two men on and two out* (Time). **2.** *U.S.* an ex-convict forbidden to work as a longshoreman because of his undesirable associations.

strik·er (strī′kər), *n.* **1.** a worker who is on strike: *The union won't accept any settlement that doesn't return strikers to their old jobs* (Newsweek). **2.** an assistant worker who wields the heavy hammer in working metal. **3.** the hammer that rings the alarm or strikes the hour in certain clocks. **4. a.** *U.S. Army.* an orderly. **b.** *U.S. Navy.* an enlisted man serving an apprenticeship for a petty officer's rating. **5. a.** a person who strikes fish with a spear or harpoon. **b.** a harpoon.

strik·ing (strī′king), *adj.* **1.** that strikes. **2.** engaged in a strike; on strike: *The striking miners will soon return to work.* **3.** attracting attention; very noticeable: *a striking woman, a striking change.* —**strik′ing·ness,** *n.* —**Syn. 3.** remarkable, impressive.

striking distance, the distance within which it is possible to strike effectively: *They can be set up within striking distance of potential enemies* (Newsweek).

striking force, 1. striking power: *The Strategic Air Command's striking force consists of medium bombers . . .* (Newsweek). **2.** an armed force equipped for attack: *a small mobile striking force.* **3.** force de frappe: . . . *a Franco-British atomic striking force* (Atlantic).

strik·ing·ly (strī′king lē), *adv.* in a way that attracts attention: *strikingly handsome.*

striking power, the power or means to attack an enemy: *The Chinese Communists are building up their striking power with artillery bases and airfields* (New York Times).

string (string), *n., v.,* **strung, strung** or (*Rare*) **stringed, string·ing,** *adj.* —*n.* **1.** a thick thread; small cord or wire; very thin rope: *The box is tied with red string.* **2.** a thread, cord, chain, etc., with things on it: *a string of beads or pearls.* **3.** a special cord of gut, silk, fine wire, nylon, etc., as for a violin, guitar, or tennis racket. **4.** anything used for tying: *apron strings.* **5.** a cordlike part of plants, as the tough piece connecting the two halves of a pod in string beans. **6. a.** a number of people, animals, or things in a line or row; file: *a string of cars or pack horses, a string of new houses.* **b.** a continuous series or succession: *a string of questions or stories.* **7.** *Informal.* a condition; proviso: *an offer with strings attached to it. Our aid programs to non-Communist nations must be free of political strings* (Atlantic). **8.** a group of players forming one of the teams of a squad, ranked according to relative skill: *The first string will practice against the second string.* **9. a.** the race horses belonging to a particular stable or owner. **b.** a group of persons or things under the same ownership or management: [*He*] *owns a string of newspapers, radio and television stations in Ohio, along with some manufacturing plants* (Wall Street Journal). **10.** *Architecture.* **a.** a stringcourse. **b.** a sloping board, etc., supporting the ends of the treads and risers in a staircase. **11.** in billiards: **a.** a stroke made to determine the order of play, in which each player attempts to place his ball closest to the head cushion or the string line after bouncing it off the opposite cushion. **b.** the string line. **12.** *Journalism.* a strip of paper used to paste up the printed stories of a part-time correspondent who is paid by the line. **13.** *Obsolete.* a tendon, nerve, muscle fiber, etc.

have two strings to one's bow, to have more than one possible course of action: *As he that has two strings to his bow, And burns for love and money too* (Samuel Butler).

on a string, under someone's control: *Mr. H. said he was not a candidate on a string; he had his own convictions* (Westminster Gazette).

pull strings, to use secret influence: *I pulled strings and got myself into school, but I had to pay a lot of money to do it* (Atlantic).

pull the strings, to control the course of affairs; direct secretly the actions of others: *Persons . . . who pull the strings of the Catholic world in the city of Rome* (John Bright).

strings, a. violins, cellos, and other stringed instruments: *Praise him upon the strings and the pipe* (Book of Common Prayer). **b.** the players on stringed instruments: *With the orchestra little fault could be found beyond the weakness of the strings* (London Daily Telegram).

—*v.t.* **1.** to furnish with a string or strings: *to string a guitar or a tennis racket.* **2.** to put on a string: *to string beads or pearls.* **3.** to tie with a string or strings. **4. a.** to hang with a string, wire, or rope: *to string herbs or tobacco to dry. Lights were strung on the Christmas tree.* **b.** to furnish or ornament with something hanging: *a street strung with Christmas lights.* **5.** to extend or stretch from one point to another: *to string a cable.* **6.** to extend in a line, row, or series: *Cars were strung for miles bumper to bumper.* **7.** to adjust or tighten the strings of; tune: *to string a violin or guitar.* **8.** to make tight; brace; strengthen. **9.** to make tense or excited: *I suppose it was despair that strung my nerves* (Edgar Allan Poe). **10.** to remove the strings from: *to string beans.* —*v.i.* **1.** to move in a line or series. **2.** to form into a string or strings; become stringy. **3.** (in billiards) to make a string in determining the order of play.

string along, *Informal.* **a.** to fool; hoax: *That boy is so easy to string along that you can convince him of just about anything.* **b.** to go along; agree (with): *"I'll string along with your chairman about this being the greatest country," he began* (New Yorker). **c.** to keep (a person) waiting; stall off: *He has been stringing us along for too long, and now we want a decision.*

string out, to prolong; stretch; extend: *The program was strung out too long.*

string up, *Informal.* to hang: *to string up a criminal.*

—*adj.* made up of stringed instruments: *a string band, a string trio. The ovation given the string ensemble was stirring.* [Old English *streng* harp string, rope, sinew] —**string′like′,** *adj.*

—**Syn.** *n.* **1.** twine. **6. a, b.** series, chain.

string bass (bās), double bass; bass viol.

string bean, 1. any of various bean plants bearing yellow or green pods which are used as a vegetable; snap bean. **2.** the pod of any of these plants. **3.** *Informal.* a tall, thin, gangling person: *Phil took one look at the*

happy-go-lucky string bean with the outsize hands, and saw just what he was looking for (Time).
string·board (string′bôrd′, -bōrd′), *n.* a board or facing that covers the ends of steps in a stair.
string-col·ored (string′kul′ərd), *adj.* of a light grayish-brown color, as lace; ficelle.
string correspondent, *U.S.* **1.** a part-time or local correspondent for a newspaper or magazine. **2.** a newspaper correspondent paid on the basis of linage: *His father . . . a string correspondent for a Boston newspaper . . . shifted to the New Bedford paper's news desk* (New Yorker).
string·course (string′kôrs′, -kōrs′), *n.* a decorative horizontal band around a building, often at floor level; cordon.

Stringcourse
Amiens Cathedral, France

stringed (stringd), *adj.* **1.** having a string or strings. **2.** produced by a stringed instrument or instruments: *stringed music.* **3.** held together or caused to close by a string or strings.
—*v. Rare.* a past participle of **string.**
stringed instrument, a musical instrument having strings, played either with a bow or by plucking.
strin·gen·cy (strin′jən sē), *n., pl.* **-cies. 1.** strictness; rigorousness; severity. **2.** lack of ready money; tightness. **3.** convincing force; cogency: *the stringency of a debater's argument.* —**Syn. 1.** harshness. **2.** scarcity.
strin·gen·do (strin jen′dō), *adj., adv. Music.* accelerating the tempo (a direction, used sometimes on a passage approaching a climax). [< Italian *stringendo,* present participle of *stringere* < Latin, draw tight]
strin·gent (strin′jənt), *adj.* **1.** strict; severe: *stringent laws against speeding.* **2.** lacking ready money; tight: *a stringent market for mortgage loans.* **3.** convincing; forcible; cogent: *stringent arguments.* [< Latin *stringēns, -entis,* present participle of *stringere* bind, draw tight] —**strin′gent·ly,** *adv.* —**Syn. 1.** rigid, rigorous, exacting, binding.
string·er (string′ər), *n.* **1.** a person or thing that strings: *a stringer of pearls.* **2. a.** a horizontal timber or girder connecting uprights in a framework, supporting a floor, etc.; tie beam: *There were oak beams connecting the pillars and supporting a criss-crossed network of stringers, made of peeled saplings* (New Yorker). **b.** the string supporting a staircase. **3.** *U.S.* a heavy, horizontal timber or girder supporting the ties of a railroad trestle or bridge or the flooring of a wooden bridge. **4.** *U.S.* a string correspondent: *These stringers (an old newspaper name for correspondents paid on the basis of pasted-up strings of their clippings) might well comprise a bluebook of the U.S. working press* (Time). **5.** *Geology.* a narrow vein of mineral. **6.** a member of a team ranked according to ability; person ranked according to ability: *a defensive first-stringer and offensive second-stringer . . .* (Newsweek).
string figure, 1. a figure or design made with a string passed over the fingers of both hands. **2.** a game in which such figures are made; cat's cradle.
string galvanometer, a galvanometer having a fine conducting fiber for measuring rapidly fluctuating currents.
string·halt (string′hôlt′), *n.* a diseased condition of horses that causes jerking of the hind legs in walking; springhalt. [apparently < *string* tendon + *halt*[2], adjective and noun]
string·halt·ed (string′hôl′tid), *adj.* suffering from stringhalt.
string·halt·y (string′hôl′tē), *adj.* stringhalted.
string·i·ness (string′ē nis), *n.* stringy quality or condition.
string·less (string′lis), *adj.* without a string or strings: *a stringless variety of snap bean.*
string line, (in billiards and pool) a line from behind which the cue ball is played after being out of play.
string·piece (string′pēs′), *n.* a long, heavy, horizontal beam in a framework, used to strengthen or connect other parts.
string player, a person who plays a stringed instrument or instruments, especially in an orchestra.
string quartet, 1. a quartet of stringed instruments, usually consisting of two violins, a viola, and a cello. **2.** a composition for such a quartet.
strings (stringz), *n.pl.* See under **string,** *n.*
string tie, a short, narrow necktie, usually knotted into a bow, sometimes worn with ends dangling: *The Honorary Order of Kentucky Colonels will stage its annual banquet, a traditional, string tie fête* (New York Times).

String Tie

string·y (string′ē), *adj.,* **string·i·er, string·i·est. 1.** like a string or strings; having tough fibers: *a piece of tough, stringy meat, a dry, stringy radish.* **2.** forming strings: *a stringy syrup.* **3.** lean and sinewy: *a man of about sixty, tall, hard, and stringy* (George Bernard Shaw).
stringy bark, 1. any of a group of Australasian gum trees having a strong, fibrous bark. **2.** the bark of such a tree.
stri·o·la (strī′ə lə), *n., pl.* **-lae** (-lē). a small stria. [< New Latin *striola* (diminutive) < Latin *stria* a facet]
stri·o·late (strī′ə lāt), *adj. Biology.* marked with striolae; delicately striated.
strip[1] (strip), *v.,* **stripped** or (*Rare*) **stript, strip·ping.** —*v.t.* **1.** to make bare or naked; undress (a person, thing, etc.). **2.** to remove (the clothes, a garment, etc.) from a person, body, or part of the body: *to strip off one's gloves.* **3.** to take off the covering of: *to strip a banana by taking off the skin, to strip a tree of its bark.* **4.** to remove; tear off; pull off: *to strip paper from a wall, to strip fruit from a tree.* **5.** to make bare; clear out; empty: *to strip a house of its furniture, to strip a forest of its timber.* **6.** to take away the equipment of; dismantle; disassemble: *to strip a car in a junkyard, to strip a ship of its guns.* **7.** to rob; plunder: *Thieves stripped the house of everything valuable.* **8.** to take away the titles, rights, etc., of (a person or thing). **9. a.** to tear off the teeth of (a gear, etc.). **b.** to break the thread of (a bolt, nut, etc.). **10. a.** to separate the leaves from the stalks of (tobacco) after curing. **b.** to remove the midrib and large veins from (tobacco leaves) after curing. **11.** to milk (a cow) thoroughly; draw the last milk from (a cow). **12.** to mine (a mineral) from the surface by removing overlying layers of earth; lay bare (a mineral deposit). —*v.i.* to take off the clothes or covering; undress; uncover; become undressed or uncovered: *Other lads than I Strip to bathe on Severn shore* (A.E. Housman). [Old English *-strīepan,* as in unrecorded *bestrīepan* to plunder] —**Syn.** *v.t.* **3.** skin, peel. **7.** despoil.
strip[2] (strip), *n., v.,* **stripped, strip·ping.** —*n.* **1. a.** a long, narrow, flat piece (of cloth, paper, bark, metal, wood, etc.). **b.** a flat piece of rolled steel less than 24 inches wide: *Galvanized steel sheets are being slit into strips, which in turn will be formed into moulding channels* (Newsweek). **2.** a long, narrow tract of land, territory, forest, etc. **3. a.** a long, narrow runway for aircraft to take off from and land on; landing strip; airstrip. **b.** a flight strip. **4.** a horizontal or vertical row of three or more stamps. **5.** a continuous series of pictures, etc., in a newspaper or magazine: *a comic strip, a cartoon strip.* **6.** a local, minor civil division in Maine. **7.** *U.S.* a special area or course set aside for drag racing: *The strips are scattered through 37 states, according to the National Hot Rod Association* (Wall Street Journal).
tear a strip or **strips off,** *Slang.* to reprimand: *A quiet English girl gave a surprising display of bilingualism herself by tearing strips off Jacques-Robert Rivart in some French no nice English girl should know* (Maclean's).
—*v.t.* to cut into strips.
[apparently variant of *stripe*[1]]
strip cartoon, *British.* comic strip.
strip cropping or **planting,** the growing of rows of crops with strong root systems between rows of crops having weak root systems, along the contour of a slope, in order to prevent excessive erosion of topsoil.
stripe[1] (strīp), *n., v.,* **striped, strip·ing.** —*n.* **1.** a long, narrow band of a different color, material, weave, etc., from the rest of a surface or thing: *the stripes of a tiger. The American flag has thirteen stripes.* **2.** a striped material or cloth. **3.** a strip or narrow piece. **4.** sort; type; class: *a man of quite a different stripe. Of a democratic, liberal stripe* (Edmund C. Stedman). **5.** a narrow line painted or marked as a line of demarcation: *Temple* [*University*], *which gained most of its yardage in its own territory, was unable to get past the midfield stripe in the last quarter* (New York Times).
stripes, a. a number or combination of strips of braid on the sleeve of a uniform to show rank, length of service, etc.: *to earn one's stripes.* **b.** *Slang.* chevrons: *sergeant's stripes.*
—*v.t.* to mark or ornament with a stripe or stripes: *a stick of candy striped with red.*
[< Middle Dutch *strīpe*]
—**Syn.** *n.* **1.** stria. **4.** kind, stamp.
stripe[2] (strīp), *n.* **1.** a stroke or lash with a whip, scourge, rod, etc. **2.** *Archaic.* the mark made by a stroke or lash; weal; welt. [probably special use of *stripe*[1]]
striped (strīpt, strī′pid), *adj.* having stripes; marked with a stripe or stripes: *Zebras are striped.*
striped bass, a sea bass with blackish stripes along the sides, found in North American coastal waters.
striped gopher, striped spermophile.
striped marlin, a small marlin of the Pacific with vertical bars across the back and sides.
striped-pants (strīpt′pants′), *adj. Informal.* **1.** of or having to do with the diplomatic corps: *Pakistan's . . . Mohammed Ali, 45, ambassador to the U.S. for 15 months in 1952-53, was reappointed to his old striped-pants post in the capital* (Time). **2.** of diplomacy; characteristic of diplomacy: *striped-pants formality, protocol, etc.*
striped skunk, the common black skunk or the black-and-white skunk, found throughout the United States and spreading into northern Mexico and southern Canada.
striped snake, the garter snake.
striped spermophile, a common striped ground squirrel of the western plains of North America; striped gopher.
striped squirrel, a chipmunk.
strip·er (strī′pər), *n.* **1.** *Slang.* a naval officer whose rank is indicated by the stripes on his sleeve: *A three-striper is a commander.* **2.** *Slang.* any serviceman whose rank or length of service is indicated by a stripe or stripes on the sleeve. **3.** the striped bass.
stripes (strīps), *n.pl.* See under **stripe**[1], *n.*
strip farming, strip cropping.
strip·film (strip′film′), *n.* a reel of film with still frames; filmstrip.
strip·ling (strip′ling), *n.* a boy just coming into manhood; youth; lad.
strip method, a conservative method of lumbering in which trees are reproduced on cleared strips by self-sown seeds from an adjoining forest.
strip mill, a rolling mill producing strips of steel.
strip mine, a mine which is operated from the surface by removing the overlying layers of earth.
strip-mine (strip′mīn′), *v.t.,* **-mined, -min·ing.** to take (a mineral or ore) from a strip mine: *The ore is near hydro-electric power and can be strip-mined after removal of a small amount of over-burden* (Wall Street Journal).
strip mining, the work or business of operating a strip mine.
strip·pa·ble (strip′ə bəl), *adj.* that can be stripped off: *This strippable sign-paint is particularly useful for outdoor signs on glass* (Science News Letter).
stripped (stript), *adj.* stripped-down.
stripped-down (stript′down′), *adj.* reduced to the bare essentials: *Detroit has found that the stripped-down car is not what most people want* (Newsweek).
strip·per (strip′ər), *n.* **1.** a person or thing that strips. **2.** an oil well that can produce oil only a few hours a day, requiring several hours to rebuild enough pressure for the oil to flow freely through the sand. **3.** *Informal.* a stripteaser.
strip·ping (strip′ing), *n.* **1.** the act of a person or thing that strips. **2.** something removed by this act.
strippings, the last milk drawn from a cow.

strip poker, a form of poker in which the players take off a piece of clothing each time they lose a hand.

strip·tease (strip′tēz′), *n., v.,* **-teased, -teas·ing.** —*n.* a dance in which a woman slowly and coyly removes her clothing piece by piece to music, as in a burlesque show, night club, etc. —*v.i.* to do a striptease.

strip·teas·er (strip′tē′zər), *n.* a performer of the striptease.

strip·teuse (strip tœz′), *n., pl.* **-teuses** (-tœz′). a stripteaser. [< *stript*(ease) + (dans)*euse*]

strip·y (strī′pē), *adj.* **1.** having stripes; striped. **2.** occurring in or suggestive of stripes.

stri·sci·an·do (strē′shē än′dō), *Music.* —*adj.* creeping or gliding. —*adv.* in a creeping or gliding manner. [< Italian *strisciando,* present participle of *strisciare* to creep, glide]

strive (strīv), *v.i.,* **strove** or **strived, striv·en, striv·ing. 1.** to try hard; work hard: *to strive for self-control. Strive to succeed.* **2.** to struggle (with); fight (against): *The swimmer strove against the tide.* **3.** *Obsolete.* to compete. [short for Old French *estriver* < a Germanic word] —**striv′ing·ly,** *adv.* —**Syn. 1.** endeavor. **2.** contend, battle.
➔ Verbs borrowed from Old French normally have been conjugated in English with *-ed* in the past tense and past participle. **Strive,** an exception, was early attracted into the class of *ride, drive,* and the like. Alongside of *strove, striven,* however, the form *strived* is also recorded from the fourteenth century and is still in use. At present it occurs more often as past participle than as past tense.

striv·en (striv′ən), *v.* a past participle of **strive:** *She has striven hard to make the party a success.*

striv·er (strī′vər), *n.* **1.** a person who tries or works hard. **2.** a person who fights, struggles, or contends.

stroan (strōn), *Scottish.* —*v.i.* to urinate. —*n.* urine. Also, **strone.** [origin uncertain]

strob (strob), *n. Physics.* a unit of velocity for bodies moving in a circular path, equal to one radian per second. [< Greek *stróbos;* see STROBOSCOPE]

strobe light (strōb), an electronic flash gun for action photography. Its neon- or xenon-filled tube can be used over and over in contrast to the flash bulb, which must be replaced after each picture. [short for *stroboscope*]

strob·ic (strob′ik), *adj.* spinning or whirling; appearing to spin or whirl. [< Greek *stróbos* (see STROBOSCOPE) + English *-ic*]

strobic circles, a group of concentric circles that appear to spin round or revolve when the paper or object they are drawn on is moved about.

strobic disk, a disk containing strobic circles or the like.

strob·il (strob′əl), *n.* strobile.

stro·bi·la (strə bī′lə), *n., pl.* **-lae** (-lē). **1. a.** the body of a tapeworm, as distinct from the head, consisting of a chain of segments. **b.** the whole body of a tapeworm, including the head and the chain of segments. **2.** a stage in the development of certain jellyfish in which a series of disk-shaped bodies split off to form new individuals. [< New Latin *strobila* < Greek *strobílē* cone-shaped plug of lint < *stróbīlos* pine cone; (originally) any twisting thing < *streblós* twisted, related to *stréphein* to turn, twist]

strob·i·la·ceous (strob′ə lā′shəs), *adj.* **1.** of or like a strobile. **2.** bearing strobiles. [< New Latin *strobilaceus* (with English *-ous*) < Late Latin *strobīlus;* see STROBILE]

strob·i·la·tion (strob′ə lā′shən), *n.* an asexual form of reproduction in which segments of the body separate to form new individuals, as in tapeworms and scyphozoans. [< *strobil*(a) + *-ation*]

strob·ile (strob′əl), *n. Botany.* any seed-producing cone, such as a pine cone, or a compact mass of scalelike leaves that produce spores, such as the cone of the club moss; strobil. [< Late Latin *strobīlus* < Greek *stróbīlos* pine cone; see STROBILA]

strob·i·lus (strob′ə ləs), *n., pl.* **-li** (-lī). strobile.

strob·o·graph (strob′ə graf, -gräf), *n.* a device that makes a record of the phenomena observed with a stroboscope or similar instrument. [< *strobo*(scope) + *-graph*]

strob·o·graph·ic (strob′ə graf′ik), *adj.* of or having to do with a strobograph.

strob·o·ra·di·og·ra·phy (strob′ō rā′dē og′rə fē), *n.* the use of X rays with a special motion-picture camera to take pictures of moving parts inside an object.

strob·o·scope (strob′ə skōp), *n.* an instrument for studying the successive phases of the periodic motion of a body by means of light periodically interrupted. [< German *Stroboskop* < Greek *stróbos* a twisting, whirling, related to *stréphein* to twist, turn + German *-skop* < Greek *skopeîn* look at]

strob·o·scop·ic (strob′ə skop′ik), *adj.* of or having to do with a stroboscope.

strob·o·scop·i·cal (strob′ə skop′ə kəl), *adj.* stroboscopic.

stroboscopic light, a strobe light: *Its action is stopped in mid-flight by using the camera's stroboscopic light* (Science News Letter).

strob·o·tron (strob′ə tron), *n.* an electron tube containing a rare gas, or mixture of such gases, used as a source of light in a stroboscope.

strode (strōd), *v.* a past tense of **stride:** *He strode over the ditch.*

stroke¹ (strōk), *n., v.,* **stroked, strok·ing.** —*n.* **1.** the act of striking; blow: *a stroke of the fist or of an ax, a backhand stroke. He drove in the nail with one stroke of the hammer.* **2.** the sound made by striking, as of a bell, clock, etc.: *We arrived at the stroke of three.* **3.** a piece of luck, fortune, etc.: *a stroke of bad luck.* **4.** *Machinery.* **a.** a single com-

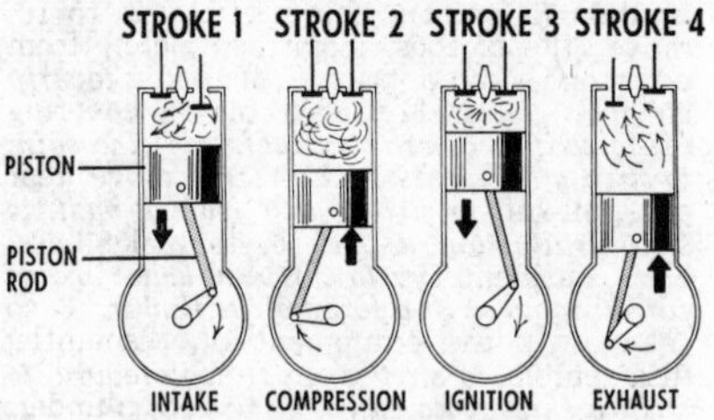

STROKE 1 STROKE 2 STROKE 3 STROKE 4

PISTON

PISTON ROD

INTAKE COMPRESSION IGNITION EXHAUST

Strokes¹ (def. 4a)
4-stroke cycle of an automobile engine

plete movement to be made again and again, especially of a moving part or parts, in one direction. **b.** the distance traveled by this part. **5.** a throb or pulsing, as of the heart; pulsation. **6.** a movement or mark made by a pen, pencil, brush, etc.: *He writes with a heavy down stroke.* **7. a.** a vigorous attempt to attain some object: *a bold stroke for freedom.* **b.** a measure or expedient adopted for some purpose: *a great stroke of politics.* **8. a.** a feat or achievement: *a stroke of wit or genius.* **b.** an effective, clever, or characteristic touch in literary composition. **9.** an act, piece, or amount of work: *a good stroke of business. He will not do a stroke of work.* **10. a.** a sudden attack (of disease). **b.** an attack of paralysis; apoplexy: *With newer therapeutic methods and modern rehabilitation, strokes need no longer be considered a hopeless and helpless condition* (New York Times). **11.** a damaging or destructive discharge: *a stroke of lightning.* **12.** a sudden action like a blow in its effect, as in causing pain, injury, or death: *a stroke of fate, the stroke of death.* **13.** in swimming: **a.** one of a series of propelling movements, involving the pull of one arm (or both together) with one or more kicks. **b.** a style or method of swimming: *He swims a fast stroke.* **14.** in rowing: **a.** a single pull of the oar. **b.** the style or rate of pulling the oars: *He rows with a strong stroke.* **c.** the rower seated nearest the stern of the boat, who sets the time for the other oarsmen. **d.** the position of this rower.
keep stroke, to make strokes at the same time, as in rowing: *I, being unable to keep stroke with the rest, was well beaten* (James Wadsworth).
—*v.t.* **1.** to be the stroke of; set the stroke for: *Who stroked the Yale crew?* **2.** to mark with a stroke or strokes; cancel by drawing a line or lines across. **3.** (of a clock) to sound (the time) by striking. **4.** (in rowing) to make a specified number of strokes per minute: *The winner stroked an average of 28 to Gunther's 30* (London Times). —*v.i.* to execute a stroke; make the motions of stroking: *Fred Delello of Oneonta, N.Y., stroking superbly despite a bleeding ring finger on his bowling hand, rolled a 744* (New York Times).
[unrecorded Old English *strāc.* Compare STROKE².]
—**Syn.** *n.* **1.** See **blow.**

stroke² (strōk), *v.,* **stroked, strok·ing,** *n.* —*v.t.* to move the hand gently or soothingly over: *to stroke a child's hair, to stroke a kitten, etc.* —*n.* a stroking movement: *She brushed away the crumbs with one stroke.* [Middle English *stroken,* Old English *strācian.* Related to STRIKE.]

stroke oar, 1. the oar nearest the stern of a boat. **2.** the rower that pulls the stroke oar. The stroke oar sets the time for the other oarsmen.

stroke play, 1. (in golf) medal play. **2.** the quality or style of one's stroke or stroking movement: *Australians took Pollock to their hearts for his entrancing stroke play* (London Times).

strok·er (strō′kər), *n.* **1.** a person who strokes. **2.** *Archaic.* a person who claims to cure diseases by stroking. **3.** *British.* (in printing) a kind of wood or bone paper folder that brings forward separate sheets of paper to a printing machine.

strokes·man (strōks′mən), *n., pl.* **-men.** the oarsman nearest to the stern of a boat, who sets the stroke for the other oarsmen.

stroll (strōl), *v.i.* **1.** to take a quiet walk for pleasure; walk: *a few . . . soldiers were strolling about under the trees* (William Dean Howells). **2.** to go from place to place: *strolling gypsies.* —*v.t.* to stroll along or through: *He noticed three people strolling the muddy street* (Sinclair Lewis).
—*n.* a leisurely walk: *a stroll through the park. My life is like a stroll upon the beach* (Thoreau).
[origin uncertain]
—**Syn.** *v.i.* **1.** saunter, ramble, roam. **2.** rove. -*n.* saunter.

stroll·er (strō′lər), *n.* **1.** a person who strolls or rambles: *holiday strollers in the park.* **2.** a strolling player or actor. **3.** a wandering vagrant; tramp. **4.** a light baby carriage in which an older baby can sit erect: *Children were everywhere: in strollers, in mothers' arms, and perched on curbs* (Newsweek).

Stroller (def. 4)

stro·ma (strō′mə), *n., pl.* **-ma·ta** (-mə tə). *Anatomy.* **1.** the connective tissue, nerves, and vessels that form the framelike support of an organ or part. **2.** the spongy, colorless framework of a red blood corpuscle or other cell. [< Latin *strōma, -ātis* bed cover < Greek *strôma, -atos* a spread to lie or sit on]

stro·mat·ic (strō mat′ik), *adj.* of or like stroma.

stromb (strom), *n.* **1.** a large marine gastropod of the West Indies whose delicate-pink shell is used for ornament, cameo cutting, etc. **2.** the shell of such a gastropod. [< New Latin *Strombus* the genus name < Latin *strombus* spiral shell < Greek *strómbos,* related to *stréphein* twist]

strom·boid (strom′boid), *adj.* having to do with or resembling a stromb. —*n.* a stromb.

strom·bu·li·form (strom′byə lə fôrm), *adj. Botany.* twisted or coiled into the form of a screw, helix, or spiral. [< New Latin *strombuliformis* < Latin *strombus* (see STROMB) + *forma* form]

stro·mey·er·ite (strō′mī′ə rīt), *n.* a steel-gray mineral, a sulfide of silver and copper, with a metallic luster, occurring massive and in crystals. [< Friedrich *Stromeyer,* died 1835, a German chemist + *-ite*¹]

strone (strōn), *v.i.,* **stroned, stron·ing,** *n. Scottish.* stroan.

strong (strông, strong), *adj.* **1. a.** having much force or power: *strong arms, a strong grip, a strong man, a strong army or nation. A strong wind blew down the trees.* **b.** vigorous; healthy; hale: *He has never been strong since his illness.* **c.** having or showing moral or mental force: *a strong mind. Be strong in faith, bid anxious thoughts lie still* (Wordsworth). **2.** able to last, endure, resist, etc.: *a strong fort, strong walls.* **3.** not easily influenced, changed, etc.; firm: *a strong will.* **4.** of great force or effectiveness: *a strong argument.* **5.** having a certain number: *A group that is 100 strong has 100 in it.* **6.** having much of the quality expected: *a strong rope, a strong acid, strong tea.* **7.** containing much alcohol: *a strong drink.* **8. a.** having much flavor or odor: *strong seasoning, strong perfume, a strong cigar.* **b.** having an unpleasant taste or smell: *strong* *butter.* **9. a.** loud and firm; powerful: *a strong voice.* **b.** vivid or intense: *a strong light, a strong color.* **c.** marked; definite: *a strong resemblance, a strong impression.* **d.** powerful in working effect: *a strong poison, strong glasses.* **10.** vigorous; forceful; emphatic: *a strong speech, a protest in strong terms.* **11.** hearty; zealous; ardent: *a strong dislike, a strong Republican, a strong sense of duty.* **12.** well-skilled; well-versed; proficient: *I am not very strong in spelling* (Thackeray). **13.** *Commerce.* steadily good or advancing; firm; active: *a strong market, strong prices.* **14.** *Grammar.* **a.** inflected for tense by a vowel change within the stem rather than by adding endings; irregular. *Examples:* find, found; give, gave, given. **b.** (of Germanic nouns and adjectives) belonging to the vocalic declensions; having a stem originally ending with a vowel. **15.** *Phonetics.* stressed.

—*adv.* **1.** with force; powerfully. **2.** in a strong manner; vigorously: *When we left, the party was still going strong.*

[Old English *strang*] **—strong′ly,** *adv.* **—strong′ness,** *n.*

—Syn. *adj.* **1. a, b. Strong, sturdy, robust** mean having or showing much power, force, or vigor. **Strong,** the general word, suggests great power or force in acting, resisting, or enduring: *Lumberjacks need strong backs and arms.* **Sturdy** suggests power coming from good, solid construction and unyielding strength: *Children need sturdy clothes.* **Robust** suggests healthy vigor of mind or body and a toughness of muscles or spirit: *Team sports make boys robust.*

strong-arm (strông′ärm′, strong′-), *Informal.* —*adj.* using or involving force or violence: *strong-arm methods.* —*v.t.* to use force or violence on: *to strong-arm an opponent.* [American English]

strong·back (strông′bak′, strong′-), *n.* **1.** *Nautical.* a spar across boat davits, to which the boat is secured at sea. **2.** a piece of wood or iron over the windlass, to haul up and secure the chain when the windlass is ready to be used.

strong·bark (strông′bärk′, strong′-), *n.* any of a group of small trees or shrubs of the borage family growing in the West Indies and southern Florida, having a strong, hard, brown wood streaked with orange.

strong·box (strông′boks′, strong′-), *n.* a strongly made box or safe to hold valuable things.

strong breeze, a wind between 25 and 31 miles per hour.

strong drink, **1.** a drink containing much alcohol: *Whiskey, brandy, and rum are strong drinks compared with wine or beer.* **2.** such drinks as a class.

strong·er sex (strông′gər, strong′-), men.

strong gale, a wind between 47 and 54 miles per hour.

strong-head·ed (strông′hed′id, strong′-), *adj.* **1.** headstrong. **2.** having a strong intellect. **—strong′-head′ed·ness,** *n.*

strong·hold (strông′hōld′, strong′-), *n.* **1.** a strong place; fort; fortress. **2.** a safe place, as of refuge or retreat; fastness: *The robbers have a stronghold in the mountains.* **—Syn. 1.** bulwark.

strong·ish (strông′ish, strong′-), *adj.* somewhat or rather strong: *a simple-minded man, with a strongish will* (Alexander W. Kinglake).

strong·man (strông′man′, strong′-), *n., pl.* **-men. 1.** a strong man, especially one who performs feats of strength in a circus, carnival, etc. **2.** a leader who uses force to obtain and hold power; despot; dictator: *Egypt's strongman Mohammed Naguib seemed likely last week to ... outlaw the tarboosh (fez in Turkey) as a symbol of the Old Order* (Time).

strong-mind·ed (strông′mīn′did, strong′-), *adj.* **1.** having a strong mind; mentally vigorous. **2.** (of women) having or affecting masculine mentality or rights. **—strong′-mind′ed·ly,** *adv.* **—strong′-mind′ed·ness,** *n.*

strong·point (strông′point′, strong′-), *n.* a stronghold: *The attackers seized another strongpoint at the Indo-China post and beat back desperate French attempts to recapture it* (Wall Street Journal).

strong room, or **strong·room** (strông′rüm′, -rům′; strong′-), *n.* a room for keeping valuable things, as at a mint, bank, storage warehouse, etc.

strong suit, a strong point; long suit: *Ireland's strong suit that afternoon was desperate defence, since they were seldom allowed to suggest attack* (London Times).

strong-willed (strông′wild′, strong′-), *adj.* strong-minded; stubborn; obstinate: *His Mother ... was a strong-willed young woman from whom [he] got an obsessive love of music* (Time).

stron·gyle or **stron·gyl** (stron′jəl), *n.* any of a group of roundworms, many of which are disease-producing parasites in men, horses, etc. [< New Latin *Strongylus* the genus name < Greek *strongýlos* round < *strânx, strangós* drop (of liquid)]

stron·gy·lo·sis (stron′jə lō′sis), *n.* a disease due to the presence of strongyles in the organs and tissues.

stron·ti·a (stron′shē ə), *n.* **1.** a grayish-white, amorphous powder resembling lime; strontium oxide: *Formula:* SrO **2.** a colorless powder formed by treating strontium oxide with water; strontium hydroxide. *Formula:* $Sr(OH)_2$ [< *strontian*]

stron·ti·an (stron′shē ən, -shən), *n.* **1.** strontianite. **2.** strontia. **3.** strontium. [< *Strontian,* a parish in Argyllshire, Scotland, location of the lead mines where strontium was first found]

stron·ti·an·ite (stron′shē ə nīt), *n.* a mineral consisting of strontium carbonate, occurring massive, fibrous, etc., and varying in color from white to yellow and pale green. *Formula:* $SrCO_3$ [< *strontian* + *-ite*[1]]

stron·tic (stron′tik), *adj.* having to do with strontium.

stron·ti·um (stron′shē əm, -tē-), *n.* a soft, yellowish metallic chemical element resembling calcium. It is one of the alkaline-earth metals and occurs only in combination, as in strontianite and celestite: *Fall-out contains strontium made radioactive* (New York Times). *Symbol:* Sr; *at. wt.:* (C^{12}) 87.62 or (O^{16}) 87.63; *at. no.:* 38; *valence:* 2. [< New Latin *strontium* < *Strontian;* see STRONTIAN]

strontium carbonate, a white, odorless powder, in its natural state the constituent of strontianite, used in sugar refining and in the making of iridescent glass, fireworks, and salts of strontium.

strontium hydroxide, strontia.

strontium 90, a radioactive isotope of strontium, produced especially by the explosion of a hydrogen bomb, that can cause cancer of the bone if absorbed in sufficient quantities by humans; radiostrontium.

strontium oxide, strontia.

strontium titanate, a crystalline substance almost as brilliant and clear as diamond, made by fusing strontium, titanium, and oxygen, used for lenses, in jewelry, etc.

strook (strůk), *v. Obsolete.* struck; a past participle of **strike.**

strop (strop), *n., v.,* **stropped, strop·ping.** —*n.* **1.** a leather strap used for sharpening razors: *Men who shave with straight-edged razors are always on the lookout for a good strop* (New Yorker). **2.** any band, strip, etc., of leather; strap. —*v.t.* to sharpen on a strop. [Old English *strop* < Latin *stroppus;* see STRAP]

stro·phan·thin (strō fan′thin), *n.* a bitter, poisonous glucoside obtained from the seeds of various tropical African shrubs or small trees of the dogbane family. It is used as a heart stimulant. [< *strophanth*(us) + *-in*]

stro·phan·thus (strō fan′thəs), *n.* **1.** any of a group of tropical African shrubs or small trees of the dogbane family, the seeds of which are used in making strophanthin. **2.** the seeds. [< New Latin *Strophanthus* the genus name < Greek *stróphos* twisted cord (< *stréphein* to turn) + *ánthos* flower (from the twisted sections of the corolla)]

stro·phe (strō′fē), *n.* **1. a.** the part of an ancient Greek choric ode sung during the movement of the chorus from right to left. **b.** the movement itself. **2. a.** a series of lines forming a division of a poem and having metrical structure which is repeated in a second group of lines (the antistrophe), especially in ancient Greek choral and lyric poetry. **b.** one of two or more metrically corresponding series of lines forming divisions of a lyric poem. In modern poetry it is often called a stanza. [< Greek *strophḗ* (originally) a turning; section sung by the chorus while turning and moving in one direction < *stréphein* to turn]

stroph·ic (strof′ik, strō′fik), *adj.* of or having to do with a strophe.

stroph·i·cal (strof′ə kəl, strō′fə-), *adj.* strophic.

stroph·i·o·late (strof′ē ə lāt, strō′fē-), *adj.* bearing a strophiole.

stroph·i·ole (strof′ē ōl, strō′fē-), *n. Botany.* a cellular outgrowth near the hilum in certain seeds; caruncle. [< Latin *strophiolum* (diminutive) < *strophium* chaplet < Greek *stróphion* (diminutive) < *stróphos* twisted band < *stréphein* twist]

stroph·u·lus (strof′yə ləs), *n.* a pimply eruption of the skin of infants; red gum. [< New Latin *strophulus,* apparently alteration of Medieval Latin *scrofulus* red gum, alteration of Latin *scrōfulae* scrofula]

strop·per (strop′ər), *n.* **1.** a person who strops. **2.** a device for stropping.

stroud (stroud), *n.* a large, coarse blanket formerly used in bartering with North American Indians. [origin uncertain]

strove (strōv), *v.* a past tense of **strive:** *They strove hard but did not win the game.*

strow (strō), *v.t.,* **strowed, strown** (strōn) or **strowed, strow·ing.** *Archaic.* to strew.

stroy (stroi), *v.t. Archaic.* to destroy. [short for *destroy*]

struck (struk), *v.* a past tense and past participle of **strike:** *The clock struck four. The barn was struck by lightning.* —*adj.* closed or affected in some way by a strike of workers: *The struck company would be unable to supply its customers at a time when demands for steel are taxing the industry's capacity* (New York Times).

struck·en (struk′ən), *v. Obsolete.* struck; a past participle of **strike.**

struck jury, a special jury selected from a list (usually of 48 persons) by having the lawyers on both sides strike out the same number of names.

struck measure, a stricken or leveled measure of grain, etc.

struc·tur·al (struk′chər əl), *adj.* **1.** of, having to do with, or used in building; constructional: *structural materials. Blue-gray structural glass and stainless steel will be used on the outside of the first three floors* (New York Times). **2.** of or having to do with structure or structures: *the structural unity of a novel.* **3.** *Biology.* of or having to do with the organic structure of an animal or plant; morphological. **4.** *Geology.* having to do with the structure of rock, the earth's crust, etc.; tectonic: *The geologist showed the structural difference in rocks of different ages.* **5.** *Chemistry.* of or showing the placement or manner of attachment of the atoms that make up a particular molecule. **6.** *Economics.* caused by the economic structure: *the structural fluctuation of prices.*

structural formula, a chemical formula that shows the kind of atoms in a molecule, their number, spatial relationships, and bonds or valence electrons.

structural iron or **steel,** **1.** iron or steel in shapes, lengths, etc., for use in building, such as I-beams, girders, etc.: *Structural steel ... is a key item in construction of large industrial and commercial buildings, and bridges* (Wall Street Journal). **2.** the type or composition of iron or steel so used.

struc·tur·al·ism (struk′chər ə liz′əm), *n.* **1.** *Psychology.* the study of the structure of consciousness, or what it consists of, as opposed to its function, or what it does. **2.** structural linguistics: *Structuralism ... forced recognition that there were separate and high levels in the hierarchy of language symbols* (Archibald A. Hill). **3.** any study or theory which regards structure as more important than function.

struc·tur·al·ist (struk′chər ə list), *n.* a follower or believer in structuralism. —*adj.* structuralistic.

struc·tur·al·is·tic (struk′chər ə lis′tik), *adj.* of, having to do with, or characteristic of structuralism.

structural linguistics, the study of linguistic structure to determine and describe patterns and their interrelationships of language.

struc·tur·al·ly (struk′chər ə lē), *adv.* with regard to structure: *The new church is structurally sound, but it is not beautiful.*

struc·tur·als (struk′chər əlz), *n.pl.* heavy steel members, beams, etc. used in construction: *Some steel consumers have ample stocks of sheets, but their supply of structurals or pipe is not enough* (New York Times).

struc·ture (struk′chər), *n., v.,* **-tured, -tur·ing.** —*n.* **1.** something built; a building: *Dams, bridges, tunnels, and office buildings are great and useful structures.* **2.** anything composed of parts arranged to-

gether: *The human body is a wonderful and complex structure.* 3. the manner of building; way parts are made or put together; construction: *The structure of the new school is excellent.* 4. the relation of the parts or elements of a thing, especially as it determines its peculiar nature or character: *the structure of society, man's moral structure, sentence structure, the structure of a language, the structure of a story.* 5. *Biology.* the arrangement of tissues, parts, or organs of a whole organism: *The cytoplasm of plant cells usually exhibits a considerable amount of structure as seen with the microscope* (Fred W. Emerson). 6. *Geology.* a. the character of rocks as determined by stratification, faults, etc. b. the features of rocks that are due to fracture or to the arrangement of heterogeneous components. 7. *Chemistry.* the manner in which the atoms making up a particular molecule are attached to one another.
—*v.t.* to make into a structure; build; fabricate: *Language is not only dependent on its culture, but in turn structures reality for this culture* (Herbert Hackett).
[< Latin *structūra* < *struere* build, arrange]
—**Syn.** *n.* 1. See **building**.

struc·tured (struk′chərd), *adj.* having a definite structure: *Linguists have often been favoured with the most obviously structured material with which to work* (Henry A. Gleason, Jr.).

struc·ture·less (struk′chər lis), *adj.* having no definite structure; amorphous: *It had previously been thought that myelin was a structureless mass* (Science News Letter). *To interpret the scattering of neutrons one idealizes the nucleus as a structureless sphere* (New Scientist).

stru·del (strü′dəl; *German* shtrü′dəl), *n.* a pastry, usually consisting of fruit or cheese covered by a very thin dough: *apple strudel.* [< German *Strudel* (literally) whirlpool]

strug·gle (strug′əl), *v.*, **-gled, -gling,** *n.* —*v.i.* 1. to make great efforts with the body; work hard against difficulties; try hard: *to struggle to make a living, to struggle against the tide.* 2. to get, move, or make one's way with great effort: *to struggle through, to struggle along, to struggle to one's feet.* —*v.t.* 1. to bring, put, do, etc., by struggling. 2. *Obsolete.* to contest (a point) persistently.
—*n.* 1. great effort; hard work. 2. a fighting; conflict.
[Middle English *struglen;* origin uncertain]
—**Syn.** *v.i.* 1. strive, labor, toil, cope, contend. —*n.* 1. exertion, labor, endeavor. 2. strife, contest.

struggle for existence or **life,** *Biology.* the competition between living animals or plants for survival; natural selection. Often, the circumstances helping one form survive cause another to die out.

strug·gler (strug′lər), *n.* a person who struggles.

strug·gling (strug′ling), *adj.* 1. that struggles. 2. having a struggle to make a living: *a struggling professional man, a struggling periodical.* —**strug′gling·ly,** *adv.*

Struld·brug (struld′brug), *n.* one of a class of immortals described in Swift's *Gulliver's Travels* who, after reaching the age of eighty, although regarded as legally dead, live on at the public expense in the imbecility of extreme age. [coined by Swift]

struld·brug (struld′brug), *n.* any person or thing that continues to exist although in a state of extreme decay. [< *Struldbrug*]

Struld·brug·gi·an (struld brug′i ən), *adj.* of or like a Struldbrug; decayed; senile; imbecilic.

strum (strum), *v.*, **strummed, strum·ming,** *n.* —*v.t., v.i.* 1. a. to play on (a stringed musical instrument) carelessly or unskillfully: *to strum a guitar.* b. to play by strumming: *to strum a melody, to strum out a few chords.* 2. to tap against or strike as by strumming: *to strum one's fingers impatiently on a table, to strum on a table with one's fingers.*
—*n.* 1. a strumming. 2. the sound of strumming.
[perhaps imitative]

stru·ma (strü′mə), *n., pl.* **-mae** (-mē). 1. *Medicine.* a. scrofula. b. goiter. 2. *Botany.* a cushionlike swelling or dilatation of or on an organ, as at one side of the base of the capsule in many mosses, or at the tip of the petiole in many leaves. [< New Latin *struma* < Latin *strūma* scrofulous tumor]

stru·mat·ic (strü mat′ik), *adj. Medicine.* strumous.

strum·mer (strum′ər), *n.* a person who strums.

stru·mose (strü′mōs), *adj.* 1. *Medicine.* strumous; strumatic. 2. *Botany.* having a struma or strumae.

stru·mous (strü′məs), *adj. Medicine.* affected with or characteristic of struma.

strum·pet (strum′pit), *n.* a prostitute. [origin uncertain]

strung (strung), *v.* the past tense and a past participle of **string**: *The children strung along after the teacher. The vines were strung on poles.*

strunt (strunt), *Scottish.* —*n.* a fit of ill humor; the sulks.
—*v.i.* 1. to sulk. 2. to strut.
[origin uncertain]

strun·zite (strun′zīt), *n.* a yellowish mineral consisting chiefly of iron, manganese, and phosphorus, with small amounts of magnesium and zinc. [< Hugo *Strunz,* a German mineralogist]

strut[1] (strut), *v.*, **strut·ted, strut·ting,** *n.* —*v.i.* to walk in a vain, self-important, or affected manner: *The rooster struts about the barnyard.* —*v.t.* to walk upon or over with a vain, self-important, or affected manner: *to strut the stage.*
—*n.* a strutting walk: *after our little hour of strut and rave* (Lowell).
[Old English *strūtian* stand out stiffly]
—**Syn.** *v.i.* **Strut, swagger** mean to walk or hold oneself with an air of importance. **Strut** suggests sticking the chest out and holding the head and body stiffly and proudly to show how important one is: *The little boy put on his father's medals and strutted about the room.* **Swagger** suggests showing off how much better one is than others by strutting boldly, rudely, or insultingly: *After being put on probation again, the boys swaggered out of the principal's office.*

strut[2] (strut), *n., v.*, **strut·ted, strut·ting.** —*n.* a bar or rod of wood, iron, etc., for supporting a structure in the direction of its length; brace. —*v.t.* to brace or support by a strut or struts. [ultimately related to STRUT[1]]

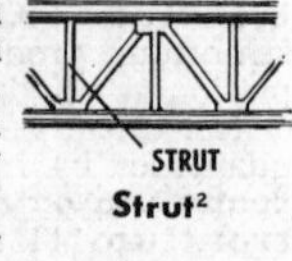

Strut[2]

stru·thi·oid (strü′thē oid), *adj.* struthious.

stru·thi·o·lar·i·a (strü′thē ə lãr′ē ə), *n.* a gastropod mollusk of the southern Pacific waters having a conical shell with an oval aperture and a lip resembling the foot of an ostrich. [< New Latin *Struthiolaria* the genus name < Late Latin *strūthio;* see STRUTHIOUS]

stru·thi·ous (strü′thē əs), *adj.* 1. of or belonging to a large group of flightless birds including the ostriches and, sometimes, other birds with unkeeled sternums, such as the emus, cassowaries, etc. 2. of or like the ostrich: *struthious tactics.* [< Late Latin *strūthio* ostrich, short for Latin *strūthiocamēlus* (< Greek *strouthokámēlos* < *strouthós* sparrow + *kámēlos* camel) + English *-ous;* because of the bird's long neck]

strut·ter (strut′ər), *n.* a person or thing that struts.

strut·ting (strut′ing), *adj.* that struts or is like a strut: *a strutting rooster, a strutting drum major.* —**strut′ting·ly,** *adv.*

strut·ty (strut′ē), *adj.* **-ti·er, -ti·est.** walking with an affected air of dignity; strutting: *A tough, strutty little man said, "I believe in capital punishment"* (Truman Capote).

strych·ni·a (strik′nē ə), *n. Archaic.* strychnine.

strych·nic (strik′nik), *adj.* of, obtained from, or caused by strychnine.

strych·nin (strik′nin), *n.* strychnine.

strych·nine (strik′nin, -nēn, -nīn), *n.* a highly poisonous alkaloid consisting of colorless crystals obtained from the nux vomica and related plants. It is used in medicine in small doses as a stimulant to the central nervous system and as a tonic. *Formula:* $C_{21}H_{22}N_2O_2$
[< French *strychnine* < New Latin *Strychnos* the genus name of the nux vomica plant < Greek *strýchnos* a kind of nightshade; various emetic plants]

strych·nin·ism (strik′nə niz əm), *n.* a disordered condition produced by too great a use of strychnine.

strych·nos (strik′nos), *n.* any of a group of tropical trees and shrubs, with usually poisonous bark, roots, or seeds, such as the nux vomica. [< New Latin *Strychnos;* see STRYCHNINE]

Strychnos Branch (nux vomica)

sts., 1. stanzas. 2. stitches.

stub (stub), *n., v.*, **stubbed, stub·bing,** *adj.* —*n.* 1. a short piece that is left: *the stub of a pencil, the stub of a cigar.* 2. a. the short piece of each leaf in a checkbook, etc., kept as a record. b. a similar part of a motion-picture or theater ticket, etc. 3. something short and blunt; a short, thick piece or part. 4. a pen having a short, blunt point. 5. the stump of a tree, a broken tooth, etc. 6. a stub nail.
—*v.t.* 1. to strike against something: *to stub one's toe against the door sill.* 2. to clear (land) of tree stumps. 3. to dig up by the roots; grub up (roots). 4. to put out (a cigarette) by pressing the lighted end of the stub against a hard object: *He hesitated, took it, smoked it only half way before stubbing it out* (Cape Times).
—*adj.* squat; stubby.
[Old English *stybb* stump]

stub axle, a short axle holding one front wheel of an automobile, pivoted to an end of a fixed front axle or part of the frame to permit steering.

stub·bed (stub′id, stubd), *adj.* 1. reduced or worn down to a stub. 2. cut close to the skin; stubbly: *stubbed hair.* 3. having many stubs. 4. sturdy; hardy. —**stub′bed·ness,** *n.*

stub·bi·ness (stub′ē nis), *n.* stubby state or form.

stub·ble (stub′əl), *n.* 1. the lower ends of stalks of grain left in the ground after the grain is cut: *[fallen apples] spiked with stubble* (Robert Frost). *The stubble hurt the boy's bare feet. The long-lasting stubbles, with their spilled grain, were also the partridge's winter granaries* (London Times). 2. any short, rough growth: *He had a three days' stubble on his unshaven face.* [< Old French *estuble,* ultimately < Late Latin *stupula,* variant of Latin *stipula* stem. Doublet of STIPULE.] —**Syn.** 2. bristle.

stub·bled (stub′əld), *adj.* covered with stubble.

stubble field, a field from which grain has been cut; stubbled piece of ground.

stub·bly (stub′lē), *adj.*, **-bli·er, -bli·est.** 1. covered with stubble: *stubbly waste land* (Sinclair Lewis). 2. like stubble; bristly: *a stubbly gray moustache* (Somerset Maugham).

stub·born (stub′ərn), *adj.* 1. fixed in purpose or opinion; not giving in to argument or requests; unyielding: *a disagreeable and stubborn child.* 2. characterized by obstinacy: *a stubborn refusal to listen to reason, a stubborn defense of a belief.* 3. hard to deal with or manage: *a stubborn cough, a stubborn metal. Facts are stubborn things. Not a plough had ever disturbed a grain of that stubborn soil* (Thomas Hardy). [probably ultimately < *stub*] —**stub′born·ly,** *adv.* —**stub′born·ness,** *n.* —**Syn.** 1, 2. dogged, resolute. See **obstinate.** 3. unruly, ungovernable, refractory.

stub·by (stub′ē), *adj.*, **-bi·er, -bi·est.** 1. a. short and thick or broad: *stubby fingers, a stubby figure. His stubby-fingered, thick-veined hands and his short, corded arms were like steel and leather* (Atlantic). b. short and blunt, as the result of wear: *a stubby pencil.* 2. short, thick, and stiff: *a stubby beard.* 3. having many stubs or stumps.

stu·be or **Stu·be** (shtü′bə, stü′-), *n., pl.* **-bes, -ben** (-bən). bierstube. [< German *Stube* (literally) room]

stub iron, iron made from stubs or scraps, formerly used in making fine gun barrels.

stub nail, 1. a short, thick nail. 2. a worn or broken nail, especially an old horseshoe nail.

stub pen, a stub (def. 4).

stub wing, or **stub·wing** (stub′wing′), *n.* 1. that part of a wing on certain aircraft that lies next to the fuselage, to which the rest of the wing, separately built, is attached. 2. a short wing, especially as used on certain autogiros.

stuc·co (stuk′ō), *n., pl.* **-coes** or **-cos,** *v.*, **-coed, -co·ing.** —*n.* 1. any of various types of plaster used for covering walls. One kind, made of Portland cement, sand, and lime, is used for covering the outer walls of buildings. Another kind, made of lime and pulverized marble, is used for cornices, moldings, and other interior decoration. *The white stucco buildings were trim and gay in the sunlight* (Harper's). **2.** stuccowork. —*v.t.* to cover, coat, or decorate with stucco. [< Italian *stucco* < Germanic (compare Middle High German *stucke* piece)]

stuc·co·er (stuk′ō ər), *n.* a person who covers or decorates with stucco.

stuc·co·work (stuk′ō wėrk′), *n.* work, decoration, etc., done in stucco.

stuck (stuk), *v.* past tense and past participle of **stick**²: *She stuck out her tongue. We were stuck in the mud.*

stuck-up (stuk′up′), *adj. Informal.* too proud; conceited; vain; haughty. —**stuck′-up′ness,** *n.* —**Syn.** egotistical.

stud¹ (stud), *n., v.,* **stud·ded, stud·ding.** —*n.* **1.** a nailhead, knob, or boss standing out from a surface, for ornament or protection: *a belt ornamented with silver studs.* **2.** a kind of small button that fits through eyelets or buttonholes, used as a collar fastener on men's shirts or as an ornament. **3.** a vertical post to which boards, laths, wallboard, etc., are nailed in making walls. **4.** a projecting pin or socket on a machine, as one in which the end of an axle, pin, etc., fits or that serves as a support, axis, or stop. **5.** a crosspiece put in each link of a chain cable to strengthen it. **6.** stud poker.
—*v.t.* **1.** to set or ornament with or as if with studs, nailheads, etc.: *a sword hilt studded with jewels.* **2.** to be set or scattered over: *a city studded with factories. Little islands stud the harbor.* **3.** to set like studs; scatter at intervals: *Shocks of corn were studded over the field.* **4.** to provide, frame, or support (a wall, etc.) with studs.
[Old English *studu* pillar, post]

stud² (stud), *n.* **1.** a collection of stallions and mares kept for breeding, hunting, racing, etc. **2.** a place where such a collection is kept; studfarm. **3.** *U.S.* a studhorse; stallion. **4.** any male animal kept for breeding.
at stud, ready for use in breeding: *a stallion at stud.*
—*adj.* **1.** of or having to do with a studhorse. **2.** kept for breeding purposes.
[Old English *stōd.* Compare STEED.]

stud., student.

stud·book (stud′bu̇k′), *n.,* or **stud book,** a book giving the pedigrees and performance records of thoroughbred horses and dogs: *Dog genealogists can pore cozily over studbooks from twenty-eight nations* (New Yorker).

stud·ded (stud′id), *adj. U.S.* (of a room, story, etc.) having studs or wall uprights: *Have the parlours high-studded ... Have the entrance-story low-studded* (William Dean Howells).

stud·die (stud′ē), *n. Dialect.* stithy.

stud·ding (stud′ing), *n.* **1.** the studs of a wall, house, etc. **2.** lumber for making studs.

stud·ding·sail (stud′ing sāl′; *Nautical* stun′səl), *n.,* or **studding sail,** a light sail set at the side of a square sail, as on a square-rigged ship; stunsail; stuns′le. [origin unknown]

stu·dent (stü′dənt, styü′-), *n.* **1.** a person who studies: *a student of human nature.* **2.** a person who is studying at a school, college, or university: *A student is a person who is learning to fulfill his powers and to find ways of using them in the service of mankind* (Harold Taylor). [< Latin *studēns, -entis,* present participle of *studēre* apply oneself to learning; (originally) be eager]
—**Syn. 1, 2. Student, pupil, scholar** mean a person who is studying or being taught. **Student,** emphasizing the idea of studying, applies to anyone who loves to study or studies a subject, but especially to someone attending a higher school, college, or university: *Several high-school students were there.* **Pupil,** emphasizing personal supervision by a teacher, applies to a child in school or someone studying privately with a teacher: *She is a pupil of an opera singer.* **Scholar** now applies chiefly to a learned person who is an authority in some field or to a student who has a scholarship: *He is a distinguished medieval scholar.*

student body, the collective community of students studying at a school, college, or university.

student council, a group of students elected by their classmates to represent them in the management of school or college activities.

student lamp, an adjustable lamp for reading at a table or desk. The old-fashioned kind burned kerosene.

stu·dent·ship (stü′dənt ship, styü′-), *n.* **1.** the fact or condition of being a student. **2.** a scholarship or fellowship granted to a student in a college or university: *At the end of 1852 he was given first class honors in mathematics and was appointed to a "studentship"* (Scientific American).

student teacher, a college or university student who teaches in a school for a certain period to qualify for a teacher's certificate or diploma.

student union, a building set aside at a college or university for student activities, usually with dining facilities, lounges, etc.: *I would approach them ... at the student union about reading our assignments together* (Atlantic).

stud·farm (stud′färm′), *n.* stud² (def. 2).

stud fee, the fee charged for the use of a male animal for breeding: *When the horse retires ... his stud fee will be $15,000. This is the highest in breeding history* (Newsweek).

stud·fish (stud′fish′), *n., pl.* **-fish·es** or (*collectively*) **-fish.** any of several bluish or greenish killifish found in rivers of central and southern United States.

stud·horse (stud′hôrs′), *n.* a male horse kept for breeding; stallion.

stud·ied (stud′ēd), *adj.* **1.** resulting from or characterized by deliberate effort; done on purpose; carefully planned: *a studied air of simplicity, a studied insult, a studied laugh. While its performances of popular songs and jazz tunes are dexterous, they are a bit too studied for my taste* (New Yorker). **2.** learned. —**stud′ied·ly,** *adv.* —**stud′ied·ness,** *n.* —**Syn. 1.** premeditated, intentional. See **elaborate.**

stud·ies (stud′ēz), *n.pl.* See under **study,** *n.*

stu·di·o (stü′dē ō, styü′-), *n., pl.* **-di·os,** *adj.* —*n.* **1. a.** the workroom of a painter, sculptor, photographer, etc. **b.** a room in which a music teacher, dramatic coach, etc., gives lessons. **2.** a place where motion pictures are made. **3.** a place where a radio or television program is produced or given.
—*adj.* of or having to do with a studio.
[< Italian *studio* a study; study < Latin *studium* study, enthusiasm, related to *studēre;* see STUDENT. Doublet of ÉTUDE, STUDY.] —**Syn.** *n.* **1. a.** atelier, workshop.

studio apartment, a one-room apartment having a bathroom and sometimes a small kitchen or kitchenette.

studio couch, an upholstered couch, without a back or arms, that can be used as a bed.

stu·di·ous (stü′dē əs, styü′-), *adj.* **1.** fond of study: *A studious boy usually likes school.* **2.** giving or showing careful attention or consideration; careful; thoughtful: *She is always studious of her invalid mother's comfort. He made a studious effort to please customers.* **3.** studied; deliberate: *The study was furnished with studious simplicity* (John Galsworthy). **4.** *Archaic.* used for or suited to study: *To walk the studious cloisters ...* (Milton). [< Latin *studiōsus* < *studium;* see STUDY] —**stu′di·ous·ly,** *adv.* —**stu′di·ous·ness,** *n.* —**Syn. 2.** earnest, painstaking, solicitous, zealous, assiduous.

stud poker, a form of poker in which each player is dealt one card face down and another face up. At each round of betting, another card is dealt face up to each remaining player, until five cards are distributed. In another form, each player receives two cards down and a third card up, then three more up and the last card down, giving seven cards to each remaining player.

stud·work (stud′wėrk′), *n.* **1.** building or structures built with or supported by studs. **2.** fabrics or leather set with knobs or studs.

stud·y (stud′ē), *n., pl.* **stud·ies,** *v.,* **stud·ied, stud·y·ing.** —*n.* **1.** the effort to learn by reading or thinking: *After an hour's hard study he knew his lesson. Study to him was pleasure and delight* (George Crabbe). **2.** a careful examination; investigation: *to make a study of a case at law, a man's life or character, or the causes of a depression. Such a study, brought down to date, would show the same expansion going on in the last six years* (Newsweek). **3.** a subject that is studied; branch of learning; thing investigated or to be investigated: *Arithmetic, spelling, and geography are three school studies. The proper study of mankind is Man* (Alexander Pope). **4.** a room for study, reading, writing, etc.: *The minister was reading in his study.* **5.** a work of literature or art that deals in careful detail with one particular subject: *a study of medieval art in Germany. The face of Nature [was] a study in old gold* (Kenneth Grahame). **6.** a sketch for a picture, story, etc. **7.** a piece of music for practice or testing; étude. **8.** earnest effort, or the object of endeavor or effort: *Her constant study is to please her parents.* **9.** deep thought; reverie: *to be in a brown study.* **10.** a person, usually an actor, with respect to his ability to memorize: *a quick or slow study.*
studies, a person's work as a student: *to return to one's studies after a vacation.*
—*v.t.* **1.** to try to learn, by oneself or in school: *to study the rules of a game or contest, to study philosophy, to study law.* **2.** to examine, observe, or investigate carefully or in detail: *to study the customs of society, to study a man's character, to study a poem. We studied the map to find the shortest road home.* **3.** to read carefully to learn or understand: *to study the Bible.* **4.** to memorize or try to memorize: *to study one's part in a play.* **5.** to consider with care; think (out); plan; devise: *to study a suitable answer. The prisoner studied ways to escape.* **6.** to give care and thought to; try hard for; aim at: *The three villains studied nothing but revenge* (Daniel Defoe).
—*v.i.* **1.** to try to learn or gain knowledge by means of books, observation, or experiment: *He is studying to be a doctor.* **2.** to be a student: *to study for a master's degree, to study under a famous musician.* **3.** to think intently; meditate; ponder. **4.** to try hard; endeavor: *The grocer studies to please his customers. I studied to appear calm* (W.H. Hudson).
[< Latin *studium* study; (originally) eagerness, related to *studēre;* see STUDENT. Doublet of ÉTUDE, STUDIO.]
—**Syn.** *v.t.* **2.** scrutinize. **5.** ponder. See **consider.**

study group, a group of people who come together or are appointed to study a particular subject or problem: *The leaders set up study groups, headed by top atomic and defense officials of the U.S. and Britain, to devise quickly some specific plans* (Wall Street Journal).

study hall, a large room in a school or college for studying, reading, preparing assignments, etc.

stu·fa (stü′fä), *n., pl.* **-fas, -fe** (-fā). a jet of steam issuing from a fissure in the earth in a volcanic region. [< Italian *stufa.* Compare STOVE.]

stuff (stuf), *n.* **1. a.** what a thing is made of; material: *There are even greater difficulties in "managing" the stuff of history than in understanding it* (Bulletin of Atomic Scientists). **b.** material used to make something; raw material: *Clay is the stuff of which pottery is made. We are such stuff as dreams are made on* (Shakespeare). **2.** any woven fabric, especially a woolen or worsted one: *She bought some white stuff for curtains.* **3.** a thing or things; substance: *The doctor rubbed some kind of stuff on the burn.* **4.** goods; belongings; possessions: *He was told to move his stuff out of the room.* **5.** worthless material; useless objects; refuse: *The attic is full of old stuff.* **6.** silly words and thoughts: *a lot of stuff and nonsense.* **7.** inward qualities; character; capabilities: *... places where a man has got to show the stuff that's in him* (Joseph Conrad). *He was not naturally of the stuff of which martyrs are made* (Hawthorne). **8.** *Slang.* (in baseball) the ability to throw a variety of pitches with deception: *He's not a fast ball pitcher, but he has lots of stuff. Pitch for pitch, many of his contemporaries have what the trade calls "more stuff"* (Time).
do one's stuff, *Informal.* to perform, especially with skill: *Quite a few people come to our fair city to see the King [a dancer] do his stuff* (New Yorker).
know one's stuff, *Informal.* to be competent or well-informed, especially in a particular field; be knowledgeable: *For all the clarity and originality of his presentation, this is very much a book for those who know their stuff* (Scientific American).

strut one's stuff, *Slang.* to show off one's looks, clothing, abilities, etc.: *A "dandy look" struts its stuff this spring* (New York Times).

—*v.t.* **1.** to pack full; fill: *to stuff a pillow with feathers.* **2.** to stop (up); block; choke (up): *to stuff one's ears with cotton, to stuff a hole with rags, a stuffed nose, a head stuffed up by a cold.* **3.** to fill the skin of (a dead animal) to make it look as it did when alive. **4.** to fill (a chicken, turkey, etc.) with seasoned bread crumbs, meat, chestnuts, etc. **5.** to force; push; thrust: *to stuff clothes into a drawer. He stuffed his hands into his pockets.* **6.** *U.S.* to put more votes in (a ballot box) than there are rightful voters. **7.** to fill with food, information, rubbish, etc.: *He stuffed himself with pie and got sick. Don't stuff up your mind with useless facts. We are the hollow men We are the stuffed men ... Head-pieces filled with straw* (T.S. Eliot). **8.** to fill or pack together tightly: *a box stuffed with old letters, to stuff tobacco in a pipe, people stuffed in an elevator.* **9.** to treat (a hide, etc.) with a compound of tallow and other substances to soften, waterproof, and preserve it. —*v.i.* to gorge oneself with food; eat too much.

[< Old French *estoffe,* perhaps ultimately < Latin *stuppa* tow[2], oakum < Greek *stýppē.* Compare STOP.]

—**Syn.** *n.* **5.** rubbish, trash. *-v.t.* **1, 8.** cram.

stuffed shirt (stuft), *U.S. Informal.* a person who tries to seem more important than he really is: *His [Dylan Thomas's] deliberately offensive behaviour to academic stuffed shirts ...* (David Daiches). *Faculty members ... delighted in the newsman's flair for deflating campus stuffed shirts* (Time).

stuff·er (stuf′ər), *n.* **1.** a person or thing that stuffs. **2.** material used to stuff something.

stuff·i·ly (stuf′ə lē), *adv.* in a stuffy manner.

stuff·i·ness (stuf′ē nis), *n.* the quality or state of being stuffy.

stuff·ing (stuf′ing), *n.* **1.** material used to fill or pack something. **2.** seasoned bread crumbs, meat, chestnuts, etc., used to stuff a chicken, turkey, etc., before cooking. **3.** the act of a person or thing that stuffs.

stuffing box, a chamber through which a piston rod or shaft passes and which is packed with an elastic material impermeable by a particular liquid or gas, in order to prevent leakage of the liquid or gas at the orifice through which the shaft passes: *Their metal bearings are kept lubricated by oil-soaked waste in a stuffing box* (Scientific American).

Cutaway of Stuffing Box

stuffing nut, a nut which when tightened reduces the cubic capacity of a stuffing box, so as to compress the elastic material contained in it and thus seal its orifice against leakage of a particular liquid or gas.

stuff·y (stuf′ē), *adj.,* **stuff·i·er, stuff·i·est.** **1.** lacking fresh air: *a stuffy room.* **2.** lacking freshness or interest; stodgy; dull: *a stuffy conversation. Lewis Cass of Michigan, very old and very dignified and very stuffy, was Secretary of State* (Bruce Catton). **3.** stopped up: *A cold makes one's head feel stuffy.* **4.** *Informal.* easily shocked or offended; prim; strait-laced: *a stuffy chaperone.* **5.** *Informal.* angry; sulky: *They never growl at us or get stuffy* (Rudyard Kipling).

Stu·ka (stü′kə), *n.* a powerful German dive bomber used in World War II. [< German *Stuka* < *Stu(rz)ka(mpfflieger)* < *Sturz* a plunge + *Kampf* battle + *Flieger* flyer]

stull (stul), *n. Mining.* **1.** a heavy timber secured in an excavation to provide support for a mine working. **2.** a platform or framework of timber to support workmen, protect miners from falling stones, etc. [perhaps < German *Stollen* a prop]

stul·ti·fi·ca·tion (stul′tə fə kā′shən), *n.* **1.** a stultifying. **2.** a being stultified: *Our simple survival is not worth so much that it is to be purchased at the cost of intellectual stultification* (Bulletin of Atomic Scientists).

stul·ti·fi·er (stul′tə fī′ər), *n.* a person or thing that stultifies.

stul·ti·fy (stul′tə fī), *v.t.,* **-fied, -fy·ing.** **1. a.** to make worthless, useless, or futile; frustrate: *a program of reform stultified by public indifference. It was infinitely dreary, stultifying, and meaningless* (Harper's). **b.** to make passive or weak by requiring absolute obedience or conformity: *the stultifying atmosphere of a prison or dictatorship.* **2.** to cause to appear foolish or absurd; reduce to foolishness or absurdity: *Many oldline companies ... clinging to their past practices, their stale traditions and stultifying smugness* (Christian Science Monitor). **3.** *Law.* to allege (a person or oneself) to be of unsound mind. [< Late Latin *stultificāre* < Latin *stultus* foolish + *facere* to make]

stul·ti·fy·ing·ly (stul′tə fī′ing lē), *adv.* in a stultifying manner: *Etiquette was stultifyingly elaborate* (Harper's).

stul·til·o·quence (stul til′ə kwəns), *n.* foolish or silly talk; senseless babble. [< Latin *stultiloquentia* < *stultiloquus* speaking foolishly, ultimately < *stultus* foolish + *loquī* speak]

stul·til·o·quent (stul til′ə kwənt), *adj.* given to stultiloquence.

stul·til·o·quy (stul til′ə kwē), *n., pl.* **-quies.** foolish talk; stultiloquence.

stum (stum), *n., v.,* **stummed, stum·ming.** —*n.* **1.** unfermented or partly fermented grape juice, often used for toning up flat wines. **2.** wine toned up with must.

—*v.t.* **1.** to tone up (wine) with unfermented or partly fermented grape juice. **2.** to stop the fermentation of (new wine).

[perhaps < Dutch *stom,* noun use of adjective, stupid, insipid]

stum·ble (stum′bəl), *v.,* **-bled, -bling,** *n.* —*v.i.* **1.** to trip by striking the foot against something: *He stumbled over the stool in the dark kitchen.* **2.** to walk or move unsteadily: *The tired old man stumbled along.* **3.** to speak, act, or proceed in a clumsy or hesitating way; blunder: *to stumble through a recitation.* **4.** to make a mistake; do wrong; err: *The officials stumbled repeatedly in carrying out the new program.* **5.** to come by accident or chance: *to stumble upon some fine antiques in the country.* **6.** to take offense; find an obstacle to belief; falter (at). —*v.t.* **1.** to cause to stumble; trip. **2.** to puzzle; perplex; nonplus.

—*n.* **1.** a wrong act; mistake; blunder. **2.** a stumbling.

[origin uncertain. Compare Swedish dialectal *stambla.*] —**stum′bling·ly,** *adv.*

stum·ble·bum (stum′bəl bum′), *n. Slang.* **1.** a person who moves about awkwardly or unsteadily as if in a daze or drunk. **2.** a person of little ability; unskilled or inept person: *Said one U.S. official: "This conference ought to dispel forever the idea that the Russians are stumblebums in science"* (Time).

stum·bler (stum′blər), *n.* **1.** a person or thing that stumbles. **2.** something that puzzles or perplexes.

stum·bling block (stum′bling), **1.** an obstacle; hindrance; impediment: *A big stumbling block preventing settlement was the union's demand for a cost-of-living escalator clause* (Wall Street Journal). **2.** something that makes a person stumble.

stum·bly (stum′blē), *adj.* **1.** apt to stumble. **2.** apt to cause stumbling.

stu·mer (stü′mər, styü′-), *n. British Slang.* a forged or worthless check; counterfeit banknote, coin, etc.; sham. [origin unknown]

stump (stump), *n.* **1. a.** the lower end of a tree or plant, left after the main part is broken or cut off. **b.** a standing tree trunk from which the upper part and the branches have been removed. **2.** anything left after the main or important part has been removed, cut or broken off, or used up; stub; butt: *the stump of a cigar, pencil, or candle, the stump of a tooth. The dog wagged his stump of a tail.* **3.** a person with a short, thick build. **4. a.** a place from which a political speech is made. It was formerly the stump of a large felled tree. **b.** public speaking around the country as a candidate or in support of a cause: *The senator is on the stump.* **5. a.** a heavy step or gait, as of a lame or wooden-legged person. **b.** a sound made by stiff walking or heavy steps; clump. **6. a.** a wooden leg. **b.** *Slang.* a leg: *to stir one's stumps.* **7.** *U.S. Informal.* a dare; challenge. **8.** a tight roll of paper, soft leather, rubber, or other soft material, pointed at the ends and used to soften or blend pencil, charcoal, or crayon marks in drawing. **9.** *Cricket.* one of the three upright sticks on the tops of which the bails are laid to form a wicket.

go on or **take the stump,** to go on a political campaign tour: *[They] said they would take the political stump to offset any Texas rebellion on the offshore oil issue* (New York Times).

up a stump, *U.S. Informal.* unable to act, answer, etc.; impotent; baffled: *We've got the map ... but we ain't no nearer to finding the valley .... We're up a stump, and no mistake* (K. Munroe).

—*v.t.* **1.** *U.S.* to remove stumps from (land). **2.** to reduce to a stump; cut off; lop. **3.** *U.S.* to make political speeches in: *The candidates for governor will stump the state.* **4.** *U.S. Informal.* to make unable to do, answer, etc.; nonplus; baffle: *Nobody could think of anything to do—everybody was stumped* (Mark Twain). **5.** *U.S. Informal.* to dare or challenge (a person) to do something. **6.** *U.S. Informal.* to stub (one's toe). **7.** to tone or treat (lines or drawings) with a stump. **8.** *Cricket.* (of the wicketkeeper) to put (a batsman) out by dislodging a bail, or knocking down a stump, with the ball held in the hand, when the batsman is out of the area within which he may bat.

—*v.i.* **1.** to walk in a stiff, clumsy, or noisy way: *The lame man stumped along.* **2.** *U.S.* to make political speeches: *The candidate for senator stumped through every county of the state. Stumping it through England for seven years made Cobden a consummate debater* (Emerson).

[compare Middle Low German *stump*] —**stump′like′,** *adj.*

stump·age (stum′pij), *n.* **1. a.** standing timber with reference to its value or quantity. **b.** the monetary value of such timber. **2.** the right to cut such timber. **3.** the price or tax paid for this.

stump·er (stum′pər), *n. U.S. Informal.* **1.** a person or thing that stumps. **2.** a puzzling or baffling question, problem, etc.: *This was a stumper; I had been asked it dozens of times since I had arrived in Britain* (New Yorker). **3.** a stump speaker: *an energetic stumper for the Republican candidate* (New Yorker).

stump·i·ly (stum′pə lē), *adv.* in a stumpy manner.

stump·i·ness (stum′pē nis), *n.* the quality or condition of being stumpy.

stump·jump plough or **plow** (stump′-jump′), (in Australia) a machine by which land can be plowed without clearing it of stumps.

stump·knock·er (stump′nok′ər), *n.* a sunfish of southeastern United States with red or bronze spots on the body.

stump·land (stump′lənd, -land′), *n.* land covered with tree stumps.

stump speaker, a person who makes political speeches from a platform, etc.

stump speech, a political speech: *Mr. Humphrey is no mean speaker himself, but all the editors got was a stump speech that ticked off the glories of the Democratic Party* (Vermont Royster). *Governor Earl Long showed up ... to make the first major stump speech of his campaign for renomination on the Democratic ticket* (New Yorker).

stump tracery, a form of tracery in medieval German architecture, in which the molded bar passes through itself and is cut off short to form a stump.

stump work, a kind of embroidery made in England in the 1600's, in which lace, brocade, satin, corals, feathers, etc., were stitched together and raised on pieces of wood or wool pads in fantastic shapes.

stump·y (stum′pē), *adj.,* **stump·i·er, stump·i·est.** **1.** short and thick; squat and broad: *a stumpy figure, a stumpy person.* **2.** having many stumps: *stumpy ground.*

stun (stun), *v.,* **stunned, stun·ning,** *n.* —*v.t.* **1.** to make senseless; knock unconscious: *He was stunned by the fall.* **2.** to daze; bewilder; shock; overwhelm: *She was stunned by the news of a friend's death.*

—*n.* **1. a.** the act of stunning or dazing. **b.** the condition of being stunned. **2.** a thing that stuns; stunner.

[Old English *stunian* to crash, resound; influenced by Old French *estoner* to resound, stun, ultimately < Latin *ex-* out, from + *tonāre* to thunder]

—**Syn.** *v.t.* **2.** stupefy, dumfound, astound, amaze.

Stun·dism (shtün′diz əm), *n.* the beliefs and practices of Stundists.

Stun·dist (shtůn′dist), *n.* a member of a large Russian religious sect that originated among the peasants of southern Russia about 1860. It takes the New Testament for its rule of faith and rejects the authority and practices of the Orthodox Church. [< Russian *shtundist* < German *Stunde* hour (referring to a particular hour set aside for Bible reading)]

stung (stung), *v.* a past tense and past participle of **sting:** *A wasp stung him. He was stung on the neck.*

stunk (stungk), *v. Rare.* a past tense and past participle of **stink:** *The garbage dump stunk.*

➔ See **stink** for usage note.

stun·ner (stun′ər), *n.* **1.** a person, thing, or blow that stuns. **2.** *Informal.* a very striking or attractive person or thing. **3.** *Informal.* an expert: *The cook . . . was really a stunner for tarts* (Thackeray).

stun·ning (stun′ing), *adj.* **1. a.** very attractive or good-looking; strikingly pretty: *a stunning girl, a stunning new hat.* **b.** excellent or delightful; first-rate; splendid: *a stunning performance.* **2.** that stuns or dazes; bewildering: *a stunning blow, a stunning piece of news.* —**stun′ning·ly,** *adv.*

stun·sail or **stun·s'le** (stun′səl), *n.* a studdingsail.

stunt¹ (stunt), *v.t.* **1.** to check in growth or development: *Lack of proper food often stunts a child.* **2.** to decrease the rate of; retard: *to stunt the growth of a plant.* —*n.* **1.** a stunting. **2.** a stunted animal or plant. [earlier, to bring to a stand, nonplus < Middle English *stunt* foolish, Old English]

stunt² (stunt), *n.* a feat to attract attention; act showing boldness or skill: *to do stunts on horseback, in the water, or with an airplane.* —*v.i.* to perform a stunt or stunts. —*v.t.* to perform a stunt or stunts with: *to stunt an airplane.* [perhaps variant of *stint* a task]

stunt·ed (stun′tid), *adj.* **1.** checked in growth or development; undeveloped; dwarfed: *a knot of stunted hollies* (Thomas Hardy). **2.** disproportionately or abnormally short or small. **3.** (of growth, etc.) checked or arrested. —**stunt′ed·ly,** *adv.* —**stunt′ed·ness,** *n.*

stunt·i·ness (stun′tē nis), *n.* a being stunted or stunty; stuntedness.

stunt·man (stunt′man′), *n., pl.* **-men.** a man who performs stunts as a profession, especially in motion pictures where he often acts as a double for an actor: *He frequently went through hazards that would not be accepted lightly by the doughtiest stuntman* (New York Times).

stunt·y¹ (stun′tē), *adj.* stunted.

stunt·y² (stun′tē), *adj.* done for display; showy: *Writing should be literate but not fine, amusing but not facetious, attractive but not stunty* (Observer).

stu·pa (stü′pə), *n.* (in the Buddhist countries) a dome-shaped monumental structure erected to commemorate some event or to mark a sacred spot. [< Sanskrit *stūpa*]

Great Stupa
Sanchi, India

stupe¹ (stüp, styüp), *n.* **1.** a small compress of soft material, used in dressing a wound. **2.** a piece of flannel or other cloth soaked in hot water and wrung out, applied as a counterirritant to an inflamed area. [< Medieval Latin *stupa* < Latin *stūpa*, variant of *stuppa* coarse flax < Greek *stýppē*]

stupe² (stüp, styüp), *n. Slang.* a stupid person. [< *stupid*]

stu·pe·fa·cient (stü′pə fā′shənt, styü′-), *adj.* stupefying. —*n.* a drug or agent that produces stupor. [< Latin *stupefaciēns, -entis*, present participle of *stupefacere;* see STUPEFY]

stu·pe·fac·tion (stü′pə fak′shən, styü′-), *n.* **1.** dazed or senseless condition; stupor. **2.** overwhelming amazement, consternation, etc. **3.** a stupefying. —**Syn. 1.** torpor. **2.** petrifaction.

stu·pe·fac·tive (stü′pə fak′tiv, styü′-; stü′pə fak′-, styü′-), *adj.* stupefying; stupefacient.

stu·pe·fi·er (stü′pə fī′ər, styü′-), *n.* a person or thing that stupefies.

stu·pe·fy (stü′pə fī, styü′-), *v.t.,* **-fied, -fy·ing. 1.** to make stupid, dull, or senseless: *to be stupefied by a drug.* **2.** to overwhelm with amazement, consternation, etc.; astound: *They were stupefied by the calamity.* [< Latin *stupefacere* < *stupēre* be amazed + *facere* to make] —**Syn. 1.** deaden. **2.** stun.

stu·pe·fy·ing·ly (stü′pə fī′ing lē, styü′-), *adv.* in a manner that is stupefying: *This stupefyingly tedious excursion into the past loses itself in a yawn* (Observer).

stu·pend (stü pend′, styü-), *adj. Archaic.* stupendous.

stu·pen·dous (stü pen′dəs, styü-), *adj.* amazing; marvelous; immense: *Niagara Falls is a stupendous sight. The whole thing was a stupendous, incomprehensible farce* (W. Somerset Maugham). [< Latin *stupendus* to be wondered at, gerundive of *stupēre* be amazed] —**stu·pen′dous·ly,** *adv.* —**stu·pen′dous·ness,** *n.* —**Syn.** astounding, prodigious.

stu·pe·ous (stü′pē əs, styü′-), *adj.* **1.** *Entomology.* covered with long, loose scales, like tow. **2.** *Botany.* woolly. [< Latin *stūpeus* (with English *-ous*) made of tow < *stūpa;* see STUPE¹]

stu·pid (stü′pid, styü′-), *adj.* **1.** not intelligent; dull: *a stupid person, a stupid remark.* **2.** not interesting; tiresome; boring: *a stupid book, to have a stupid time.* **3.** dazed; stunned: *to be stupid with grief.*
—*n. Informal.* a stupid person: *The wrath of the stupid has laid waste the world quite as often as has the craft of the bright* (Time).
[< Latin *stupidus* < *stupēre* be dazed, amazed] —**stu′pid·ness,** *n.*
—**Syn.** *adj.* **1. Stupid, dull** mean having or showing little intelligence. **Stupid,** describing people or what they say or do, suggests a natural lack of good sense or ordinary intelligence: *Driving away from an accident is stupid.* **Dull** suggests a slowness of understanding and a lack of sharpness or alertness, either by nature or because of overwork, poor health, etc.: *The mind becomes dull if the body gets no exercise.* **2.** vapid.
—**Ant.** *adj.* **1.** intelligent. **2.** lively.

stu·pid·i·ty (stü pid′ə tē, styü-), *n., pl.* **-ties. 1.** lack of intelligence; dullness. **2.** a foolish act, idea, etc. —**Syn. 1.** obtuseness. **2.** folly.

stu·pid·ly (stü′pid lē, styü′-), *adv.* **1.** in a stupid manner. **2.** to an extent or degree that is stupid. **3.** so as to appear or sound stupid.

stu·por (stü′pər, styü′-), *n.* **1.** a dazed condition; loss or lessening of the power to feel: *The man lay in a stupor, unable to tell what had happened to him.* **2.** intellectual or moral numbness: *a joyless stupor* (John Woolman). [< Latin *stupor, -ōris* < *stupēre* be dazed, amazed] —**Syn. 1.** lethargy, torpor. **2.** apathy.

stu·por·ous (stü′pər əs, styü′-), *adj.* characterized by or affected with stupor.

stu·pose (stü′pōs, styü′-), *adj. Biology.* bearing tufts or mats of long hairs; composed of matted filaments like tow. [< Medieval Latin *stuposus* < Latin *stūpa;* see STUPE¹]

stur·died (stėr′dēd), *adj.* (of sheep) afflicted with sturdy or gid.

stur·di·ly (stėr′də lē), *adv.* in a sturdy manner.

stur·di·ness (stėr′dē nis), *n.* sturdy quality or condition; strength; firmness.

stur·dy¹ (stėr′dē), *adj.,* **-di·er, -di·est. 1.** strong; stout: *a sturdy child, a sturdy plant, sturdy legs, a sturdy chair.* **2.** not yielding; firm: *a sturdy resistance, sturdy defenders.* **3.** simple and vigorous in character; downright; uncompromising: *sturdy courage, honesty, or common sense.* [Middle English *stourdy* reckless, violent, strong < Old French *esturdi* violent; (originally) dazed, past participle of *estourder* to stun, daze] —**Syn. 1.** hardy, robust, muscular. See **strong. 2.** resolute, indomitable.

stur·dy² (stėr′dē), *n.* a kind of staggers in sheep; gid. [< Old French *estordie* giddiness < *estourder;* see STURDY¹]

stur·geon (stėr′jən), *n., pl.* **-geons** or (*collectively*) **-geon.** any of a family of large food fish whose long body has a tough skin with five rows of bony plates. Caviar and isinglass are obtained from sturgeons. [< Anglo-French *esturgeon,* ultimately < Germanic (compare Old High German *sturion,* accusative)]

Atlantic Sturgeon
(to 10 ft. long)

stur·in (stėr′in), *n.* sturine.

stur·ine (stėr′ēn, -in), *n.* a protamine obtained from sturgeon's sperm.

Sturm·ab·tei·lung (shtůrm′äp′tī lůng), *n. German.* **1.** a paramilitary Nazi Party organization, known as the Brown Shirts and noted for its terroristic activities. After 1934 it was replaced by the Schutzstaffel (SS). **2.** (literally) storm division.

Sturm und Drang (shtůrm′ ůnt dräng′), *German.* **1.** storm and stress; upheaval; turmoil: *The Metropolitan was not the only opera company beset by Sturm und Drang this week* (Newsweek). **2.** a phrase applied to a period of rebellion against convention in German literature during the latter half of the 1700's and typified by a play of the same name, written by F. Klinger in 1776.

sturt (stėrt), *n. Scottish.* contention; quarreling. [alteration of *strut*¹]

Sturt's desert pea (stėrts), a creeping perennial of the pea family, having red flowers streaked with black, which grows in dry sandy soil in Australia.

stuss (stus), *n.* a gambling game with cards, resembling faro. [< German dialectal and Yiddish *shtus* nonsense]

stut (stut), *v.i., v.t.,* **stut·ted, stut·ting.** *British and Scottish Dialect.* to stutter. [Middle English *stutten;* see STUTTER]

stut·ter (stut′ər), *v.i., v.t.* **1.** to repeat (the same sound) in an effort to speak, because of a speech impediment or of tension. *Example:* C-c-c-can't th-th-th-they c-c-come? **2.** to make any sound resembling this: *the stuttering rifles' rapid rattle* (Wilfred Owen). —*n.* the act, habit, or sound of stuttering. [frequentative form of Middle English *stutten* stutter. Compare Dutch *stotteren.*] —**stut′ter·er,** *n.* —**stut′ter·ing·ly,** *adv.* —**Syn.** *v.i., v.t.* **1.** See **stammer.**

STV (no periods), subscription television.

St. Vi·tus dance (sānt vī′təs), St. Vitus's Dance.

St. Vitus's dance, a nervous disorder, which usually affects children, characterized by involuntary twitching of the muscles; chorea. [< *St. Vitus,* legendary martyr during the reign of Diocletian, venerated for his gift of healing]

sty¹ (stī), *n., pl.* **sties,** *v.,* **stied** or **styed, sty·ing.** —*n.* **1.** a pen for pigs. **2.** any filthy or disgusting place: *I see . . . human beings living in sties* (Thoreau).
—*v.t.* to keep or lodge in or as if in a sty: *The most beggarly, vile place that ever pigs were styed in* (Robert Louis Stevenson).
—*v.i.* to live in or as if in a sty.
[Old English *stig* building]

sty² (stī), *n., pl.* **sties.** a small, inflamed swelling on the edge of the eyelid. A sty is like a small boil. [probably < misdivision of Middle English *styanye* (taken as "sty on eye"), ultimately Old English *stīgend* a rising, riser, sty + *ēage* eye]

sty·ca (stī′kə), *n.* a small copper coin used in Northumbria from the 600's to the 900's, weighing about eighteen grains. [Old English (Northumbrian) *stycas*]

stye (stī), *n.* sty².

Styg·i·an (stij′ē ən), *adj.* **1.** of or having to do with the river Styx or the lower world. **2.** black as the river Styx; dark; gloomy: *a Stygian sky. Its Stygian blackness prohibits plant life, which depends on sunlight* (Scientific American). **3.** infernal; hellish. **4.** (of an oath) completely binding; inviolable like the oath by the Styx, which the gods themselves feared to break. [< Latin *Stygius* (< Greek *Stýgios* < *Stýx, Stygós* the river Styx) + English *-an*]

sty·lar (stī′lər), *adj.* of, having to do with, or like a style for writing on wax, etc.

sty·late (stī′lāt, -lit), *adj.* **1.** *Zoology.* **a.** having a style or stylet. **b.** styloid; styliform. **2.** *Botany.* having a persistent style.

style (stīl), *n., v.,* **styled, styl·ing.** —*n.* **1.** fashion: *to dress in the latest style. Paris, London, Rome, and New York set the style of dress for the world.* **2.** a manner, method, or way of speaking, writing, building, doing, living, or appearing: *a lecturer with a free and easy style, the Gothic style of architecture, an opera in the Wagnerian style, styles of swimming or acting, to entertain in a lavish style. Books for children should have a clear, easy style.* **3.** good style; fashionable appearance: *She dresses in style. That otherwise impalpable quality which women call style* (William Dean Howells). **4. a.** literary or artistic excellence: *a model of style. Get your facts right first: that is the foundation of all style* (Time). **b.** writing or speaking with reference to its form and expression as distinct from its subject matter: *Style is the dress of thoughts* (Lord Chesterfield). *Proper words in proper places, make the true definition of a style* (Jonathan

Swift). **5.** an official name; title: *Salute him with the style of King.* **6.** a kind, sort, or type: *There was something in her style of beauty* ... (Jane Austen). **7.** a pointed instrument for writing on wax; stylus. **8.** something like this in shape or use, such as an etching needle, a graver, a pen, or a phonograph needle. **9.** the pointer on a dial, chart, etc., especially the gnomon of a sundial. **10.** *Botany.* the stemlike part of the pistil of a flower containing the stigma at its top. Pollen is passed along the style to the ovules. **11.** *Zoology.* a small, slender, pointed process or part; stylet. **12.** the rules of spelling, punctuation, typography, etc., as used by printers or followed by a particular editorial department or publication. **13.** a method of reckoning time and dates, as Old Style (Julian calendar) and New Style (Gregorian calendar). **14.** a surgical probe with a blunt point; stylet.

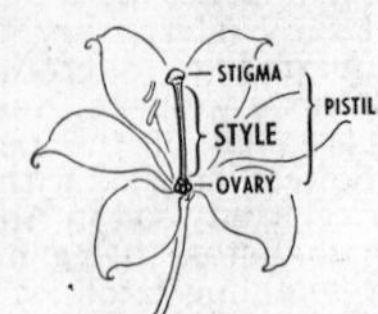

Style (def. 10)

cramp one's style, *Informal.* to keep one from showing his skill, ability, etc.: *The presence of curious onlookers watching him paint cramped his style.*
—*v.t.* **1.** to name; call: *Joan of Arc was styled "the Maid of Orleans."* **2.** to make in or conform to a given or accepted style.
[< Old French *estile* < Latin *stilus* (originally) pointed writing instrument; influenced in modern spelling by Greek *stŷlos* column. Doublet of STYLUS.]
—**Syn.** *n.* **1.** See **fashion.**

style·book (stīl′bu̇k′), *n.* **1.** a book containing the rules of punctuation, capitalization, and other matters of style followed by a printing or editorial office, school or college, etc. **2.** a book showing fashions in dress, etc.

style·less (stīl′lis), *adj.* without style; of no particular style: *Her art deserved a better epitaph than this styleless, half-baked concoction* (Saturday Review). —**style′less·ness,** *n.*

styl·er (stī′lər), *n.* a person who styles.

style·set·ter (stīl′set′ər), *n.* a person or thing that sets a style for others to follow: *Ernest Hemingway was a stylesetter in the short story field in the thirties* (Maclean's).

sty·let (stī′lit), *n.* **1. a.** a slender surgical probe. **b.** a wire inserted in a catheter or cannula to stiffen it. **2.** *Zoology.* a style. **3.** a stiletto or dagger. [< French *stylet* < Italian *stiletto* stiletto]

style·wise (stīl′wīz′), *adv. Informal.* in a manner characteristic of style: *That led to the assumption that corduroy was "dead" stylewise* (Wall Street Journal).

style-wise (stīl′wīz′), *adj.* wise in the ways of style: *It was the first time in Ford history ... that a group of style-wise executives had spontaneously applauded an automobile* (Newsweek).

sty·li (stī′lī), *n.* a plural of **stylus.**

sty·li·form (stī′lə fôrm), *adj.* shaped like a stylus or style: *a styliform bone, a styliform projection of rock.* [< New Latin *styliformis* < *stylus* style + *-formis* -form]

styl·ing (stī′ling), *n.* the way in which something is styled: *It is a conservative car because of the deliberate simplicity of its styling* (Time).

styl·ise (stī′līz), *v.,* **-ised, -is·ing.** *Especially British.* stylize.

styl·ish (stī′lish), *adj.* **1.** in the current fashion of dress, design, etc.; having style; fashionable: *stylish clothes, a stylish woman.* **2.** graceful and polished; skillful and smooth: *a stylish performance.* —**styl′ish·ly,** *adv.* —**styl′ish·ness,** *n.* —**Syn. 1.** modish, chic.

styl·ism (stī′liz əm), *n.* (in art and literature) excessive concern for style, with little consideration of content.

styl·ist (stī′list), *n.* **1.** a writer, speaker, artist, musician, etc., considered to have a good style; person who takes much pains with his style: *an excellent stylist. He did turn out to have qualities as a musician and stylist that shone to advantage in this particular concerto* (New Yorker). **2.** a person who designs or advises concerning interior decorations, clothes, etc.

sty·lis·tic (stī lis′tik), *adj.* of or having to do with style, especially in literature, music, or art: *I should like to hear music ... that is free of self-conscious formulas and tricks of stylistic sleight of hand* (New Yorker).

sty·lis·ti·cal (stī lis′tə kəl), *adj.* stylistic.

sty·lis·ti·cal·ly (stī lis′tə klē), *adv.* as regards style; in matters of style: *The text itself is loaded with clichés, grossly repetitive and stylistically dull* (Scientific American).

sty·lite (stī′līt), *n.* any of various Christian ascetics of the early Middle Ages who lived on the tops of pillars or columns. [< Late Greek *stylītēs* < Greek *stŷlos* a pillar]

sty·lit·ic (stī lit′ik), *adj.* of or like the stylites.

sty·lit·ism (stī′lī tiz əm), *n.* the ascetic principles or way of life of the stylites.

styl·i·za·tion (stī′lə zā′shən), *n.* **1.** a stylizing: *The stage was empty except for fragmentary décors of a roof or a fence as stylizations of a wrecked home and loneliness* (New Yorker). **2.** a being stylized.

styl·ize (stī′līz), *v.t., v.i.,* **-ized, -iz·ing.** to conform to a particular or to a conventional style; conventionalize: *We prefer to stylize and indicate—we do our best to avoid ambiguity* (New Yorker). —**styl′iz·er,** *n.*

sty·lo (stī′lō), *n., pl.* **-los.** a stylograph: *writing down the details of the order with his ivory-handled stylo* (Arnold Bennett). [short for *stylograph*]

sty·lo·bate (stī′lə bāt), *n. Architecture.* a continuous base under a row of columns; the top part or surface of a stereobate. [< Latin *stylobata* < Greek *stylobátēs* < *stŷlos* pillar + *bainein* to walk, step]

sty·lo·glos·sal (stī′lō glos′əl), *adj.* of or having to do with the styloid process of the temporal bone and the tongue. [< *stylo*(id process) + Greek *glôssa* tongue + English *-al*[1]]

sty·lo·graph (stī′lə graf, -gräf), *n.* an old fountain pen similar to a modern ball-point pen, in which the writing point consists of a fine metal tube instead of a nib. [< New Latin *stylus* style (< Latin *stilus*) + English *-graph*]

sty·lo·graph·ic (stī′lə graf′ik), *adj.* of or having to do with a stylograph or stylography.

sty·lo·graph·i·cal (stī′lə graf′ə kəl), *adj.* stylographic.

stylographic pen, a stylograph.

sty·log·ra·phy (stī log′rə fē), *n.* writing, drawing, or engraving with a stylus.

sty·lo·hy·oid (stī′lō hī′oid), *adj.* of or having to do with the styloid process of the temporal bone and the hyoid bone.

sty·loid (stī′loid), *adj.* **1.** like a style; slender and pointed. **2.** of or having to do with a styloid process. [< New Latin *styloides* < Greek *styloeidḗs* < *stŷlos* pillar (sense influenced by Latin *stilus* style) + *eîdos* form]

styloid process, 1. a sharp spine pointing down at the base of the temporal bone in man. **2.** the pointed projection at the lower extremity of the ulna, on the inner and posterior side.

sty·lo·lite (stī′lə līt), *n.* a columnar structure in limestones and certain other rocks, consisting of vertical layers at right angles to the stratification. [< Greek *stŷlos* pillar + English *-lite*]

sty·lo·man·dib·u·lar (stī′lō man dib′yə lər), *adj.* connecting the styloid process of the temporal bone and the lower jawbone: *a stylomandibular ligament.*

sty·lo·mas·toid (stī′lō mas′toid), *adj.* common to the styloid and mastoid processes of the temporal bone.

sty·lo·max·il·lar·y (stī′lō mak′sə ler′ē), *adj.* stylomandibular.

Sty·lo·my·cin (stī′lə mī′sin), *n. Trademark.* an antibiotic derived from certain soil actinomycetes, used in treating African sleeping sickness, amoebic dysentery, etc.; puromycin: *Lederle's new antibiotic, Stylomycin, is being used effectively against many existing cases of African sleeping sickness* (Newsweek). *Formula:* $C_{22}H_{29}N_7O_5$

sty·lo·pha·ryn·ge·al (stī′lō fə rin′jē əl), *adj.* of or having to do with the styloid process of the temporal bone and the pharynx.

sty·lo·po·di·um (stī′lə pō′dē əm), *n., pl.* **-di·a** (-dē ə). *Botany.* one of the double, fleshy disks surmounting the ovary and supporting the styles in plants of the parsley family. [< New Latin *stylopodium* < *stylus* (< Greek *stŷlos* pillar) + *-podium* little foot < Greek *poús, podós* foot]

sty·lus (stī′ləs), *n., pl.* **-lus·es, -li** (-lī). **1.** a pointed instrument for writing on wax; style. **2. a.** a phonograph needle: *If the turntable is shaken by extraneous vibration ... this will be picked up by the stylus and reproduced in mixture with the music* (Atlantic). **b.** a needlelike device for cutting the sound grooves in a phonograph record. The record then can either be played back by itself or used as a mold to make other records. **3.** the lightweight pen that records lines on a moving drum or chart on an oscillograph, galvanometer, and the like. **4.** *Botany, Zoology.* a style. [< New Latin *stylus* < Latin *stilus,* also *stylus;* spelling influenced by Greek *stŷlos* pillar. Doublet of STYLE.]

Stylus (def. 1) and wax tablet

sty·mie (stī′mē), *n., pl.* **-mies,** *v.,* **-mied, -mie·ing.** —*n. Golf.* **1.** the situation when a ball on a putting green is directly between the player's ball and the hole for which he is playing. **2.** (formerly) an opponent's ball on a putting green when it is directly between the player's ball and the hole for which he is playing, and when the distance between the balls is more than six inches. **3.** the occurrence of a ball in either of such positions or either of these positions of the ball.
—*v.t.* **1.** *Golf.* to hinder or block with a stymie. **2.** to stop or halt the progress of; block completely: *to be stymied by a problem or by lack of funds. A brilliant talent, but he, too, stymied himself working in a distasteful environment* (S. J. Perelman). Also, **stimy.** [origin uncertain]

sty·my (stī′mē), *n., pl.* **-mies,** *v.,* **-mied, -my·ing.** stymie.

styph·nic acid (stif′nik), a yellow crystalline compound obtained from resorcinol or the wood of certain trees, used in making explosives. *Formula:* $C_6H_3N_3O_8$

styp·sis (stip′sis), *n.* the application or use of styptics. [< Late Latin *stypsis* < Greek *stŷpsis* < *stýphein* to constrict]

styp·tic (stip′tik), *adj.* able to stop or check bleeding; astringent. —*n.* something that stops or checks bleeding by contracting the tissue: *Alum is a common styptic.* [< Latin *stypticus* < Greek *styptikós* < *stýphein* to constrict]

styp·ti·cal (stip′tə kəl), *adj.* styptic.

styp·tic·i·ty (stip tis′ə tē), *n.* the property of being styptic; astringency.

styptic pencil, a small stick of alum or other styptic substance, used on slight wounds to stop bleeding.

sty·ra·ca·ceous (stī′rə kā′shəs), *adj.* belonging to the family of dicotyledonous shrubs and small trees that includes the storax and silver bell. [< Latin *styrax, -acis* storax + English *-aceous*]

sty·rax (stī′raks), *n.* storax. [< Latin *styrax* < Greek *stýrax, -akos*]

sty·rene (stī′rēn, stir′ēn), *n.* **1.** an aromatic unsaturated liquid hydrocarbon, produced by distilling storax and by other methods, used in making synthetic rubber and plastics. *Formula:* C_8H_8 **2.** polystyrene: *chrome with rich chip-slip proof styrene handle* (Wall Street Journal). [< Latin *styrax, -acis* storax + English *-ene*]

sty·rene-bu·ta·di·ene (stī′rēn byü′tə dī′ēn, -dī ēn′; stir′ēn-), *n.* a common type of synthetic rubber derived from petroleum, capable of withstanding very high temperature and pressure, used in automobile tires, footwear, etc.: *Dow probably will build a plant within the common market area to make a line of styrene-butadiene latexes* (Wall Street Journal).

styrene resin, polystyrene.

Sty·ro·foam (stī′rə fōm′), *n. Trademark.* a polystyrene foam used for insulation, in decorations, etc.: *She led us on a missile-like tour of the workshop, which proved to be a wonderland of papier-mâché Santa Clauses, Styrofoam angels and latex reindeer* (New Yorker).

sty·rol (stī′rol), *n.* styrene.

sty·ro·lene (stī′rə lēn), *n.* styrene.

Sty·ron (stī′ron), *n. Trademark.* a colorless polystyrene material resistant to the effects of weather, sun, acids, etc., used in making plastic products: *He grasps the Lucite handle of his toothbrush and then runs a comb made of Styron through his thick, gray-white hair* (New Yorker).

stythe (stīth), *n. Dialect.* chokedamp. [origin uncertain]
Styx (stiks), *n. Greek Mythology.* a river in the lower world. The souls of the dead were ferried across it into Hades by Charon. [< Latin *Styx* < Greek *Stýx, Stygós*, related to *stygeîn* to hate]
su-, *prefix.* the form of **sub-** before *sp*, as in *suspect.*
Su., Sunday.
su·a·bil·i·ty (sü'ə bil'ə tē), *n.* the state of being suable; liability to be sued.
su·a·ble(sü'ə bəl), *adj.* that can be sued; liable to be sued.
sua·sion (swā'zhən), *n.* an advising or urging; persuasion: *Moral suasion is persuasion exerted through or acting upon the moral nature or sense. The effectiveness of rules must never be based on paper promises or moral suasion* (Bulletin of Atomic Scientists). [< Latin *suāsiō, -ōnis* < *suādēre* to persuade]
sua·sive (swā'siv), *adj.* advising or urging; persuasive. —*n.* a suasive speech, influence, etc. —**sua'sive·ly,** *adv.* —**sua'sive·ness,** *n.*
sua·so·ry (swā'sər ē), *adj.* suasive.
suave (swäv), *adj.* smoothly agreeable or polite: *a suave and slippery scoundrel, a suave manner.* [< Middle French *suave*, learned borrowing from Latin *suāvis* agreeable] —**suave'ly,** *adv.* —**suave'ness,** *n.* —**Syn.** urbane, bland.
sua·vi·ter in mo·do, for·ti·ter in re (swav'ə tər in mō'dō, fôr'tə tər in rē'), *Latin.* gently in manner, vigorously in deed.
sua·vi·ty (swä'və tē, swav'ə-), *n., pl.* **-ties.** smoothly agreeable quality or behavior; smooth politeness; blandness: *These words, delivered with a cutting suavity* (Dickens). *The suavity and elegance of his prose is . . . a little benumbing* (Scientific American).
sub[1] (sub), *n., adj., v.,* **subbed, sub·bing.** —*n., adj.* **1.** substitute. **2.** submarine. **3.** subordinate. **4.** subaltern. **5.** subway. —*v.i.* to act as a substitute; substitute (for). —*v.t.* to subedit.
sub[2] (sub), *n., v.,* **subbed, sub·bing.** *British.* —*n.* an advance of money, especially on account of wages due at the end of a certain period. —*v.t., v.i.* to pay or receive an advance of money: *A workman who was erroneously given a full pay packet when he had already subbed most of his week's wages, did not commit theft when he failed to return the money* (Sunday Times). [< *sub*(sistence) money]
sub-, *prefix.* **1.** under; below, as in *subway, submarine.*
2. down; further; again, as in *subclassify, sublease.*
3. near; nearly, as in *subarctic.*
4. a. lower; subordinate; assistant, as in *subaltern.* **b.** of less importance, as in *subhead.*
5. resulting from further division, as in *subatom.*
6. in a comparatively small degree or proportion; slightly; somewhat, as in *subacid.* Also, **su-**, before *sp;* **suc-**, before *c;* **suf-**, before *f;* **sug-**, before *g;* **sum-**, in some cases before *m;* **sup-**, before *p;* **sur-**, before *r;* **sus-**, in some cases before *c, p, t.*
[< Latin *sub* underneath, under, beneath]
sub., an abbreviation for the following:
1. subaltern.
2. subject.
3. submarine.
4. subscription.
5. substitute.
6. suburb.
7. suburban.
S.U.B. or **SUB** (no periods), supplemental unemployment benefits (money paid by a company to unemployed workers, in addition to their unemployment compensation): *A laid-off American steelworker under SUB (supplemental unemployment benefits) was receiving more income than a fully employed steelworker in any other country* (Harper's).
sub·ac·e·tate (sub as'ə tāt), *n.* an acetate in which there is an excess of the base or metallic oxide beyond the amount that reacts with the acid to form a normal salt; basic acetate: *Verdigris is a subacetate of copper.*
sub·ac·id (sub as'id), *adj.* slightly acid: *An orange is a subacid fruit.*
sub·a·cid·i·ty (sub'ə sid'ə tē), *n.* subacid quality or state.
sub·a·cute (sub'ə kyüt'), *adj.* **1.** somewhat or moderately acute. **2.** *Medicine.* between acute and chronic: *Antibiotics have made possible a recovery rate of better than 75 per cent in subacute bacterial endocarditis, an infection of the lining of the heart that was once invariably fatal* (New York Times). —**sub'a·cute'ly,** *adv.*
sub·a·dult (sub'ə dult', sub ad'ult), *adj.* nearly full grown; approaching adulthood. —*n.* a subimago May fly.
sub·aer·i·al (sub ãr'ē əl), *adj.* taking place, existing, operating, or formed in the open air or on the earth's surface: *. . . they are cut in moraine which was not exposed to subaerial denudation until some 10,000 years ago* (G. H. Dury). —**sub·aer'i·al·ly,** *adv.*
sub·a·gent (sub ā'jənt), *n.* a person employed as the agent of an agent.
su·bah·dar (sü'bä där'), *n.* **1.** (formerly) the chief native officer of a company of native troops in the British Indian service: *an old loyal pensioned subahdar of our former Indian Army* (London Times). *The subahdar recognized the Nana Sahib whom he knew quite well as a boy in Cawnpore before the Mutiny* (London Times). **2.** any of various former high administrative officials under the Mogul emperors in India, especially one appointed as his viceroy by the emperor in a particular province. [Anglo-Indian < Hindustani *ṣūbahdār* < *ṣūbah* province (< Arabic) + *dār* master]
sub·a·late (sub ā'lāt), *adj.* somewhat like a wing; thin and triangular.
sub·al·ka·line (sub al'kə līn, -lin), *adj.* slightly alkaline.
sub·al·pine (sub al'pīn), *adj.* **1.** of, having to do with, or characteristic of mountain regions next in elevation below those called alpine, usually between 4,000 and 5,500 feet in most parts of the North or South Temperate Zones: *a subalpine climate, a subalpine tree or plant.* **2.** of or having to do with regions at the foot of the Alps.
sub·al·tern (sə bôl'tərn, sub'əl-), *n.* **1.** *Especially British.* any commissioned army officer below a captain in rank: *His Majesty presented the Colours to two subalterns* (London Times). **2.** a subordinate. **3.** *Logic.* a subaltern proposition. [< adjective] —*adj.* **1.** *Especially British.* ranking below a captain. **2.** having lower rank; subordinate: *Todd's mode is distinctly romantic; but he is one of those subaltern figures of romanticism who can smile at the main current even while it carries them along* (Hayden Carruth). **3.** *Logic.* (of a proposition) particular, in relation to a universal of the same quality. [< Late Latin *subalternus* < Latin *sub-* under + *alternus* alternate < *alter* other]
sub·al·ter·nate (sub ôl'tər nit), *adj. Botany.* alternate, but with a tendency to become opposite.
sub·ant·arc·tic (sub'ant ärk'tik, -är'tik), *adj.* near or just above the antarctic region; having to do with or occurring in a region just north of the Antarctic Circle: *Chile maintained six stations in the Palmer peninsula area and three stations on subantarctic islands* (Lawrence M. Gould).
sub·ap·os·tol·ic (sub'ap ə stol'ik), *adj.* of, having to do with, or being the period succeeding that of the apostles: *subapostolic literature.*
sub·a·quat·ic (sub'ə kwat'ik, -kwot'-), *adj.* **1.** subaqueous. **2.** partly aquatic, as plants or animals.
sub·a·que·ous (sub ā'kwē əs, -ak'wē-), *adj.* **1.** under water; suitable for use under water: *At the skin-diving stall, a movie was being shown on a TV-size screen of flipper-footed people snaking their way through coral formations as a male voice intoned subaqueous aphorisms* (New Yorker). **2.** *Geology.* existing, formed, or occurring under water. **3.** *Biology.* living or growing under water.
sub·a·rach·noid (sub'ə rak'noid), *adj.* situated or taking place beneath the arachnoid membrane: *subarachnoid hemorrhage.* —*n.* the space between the arachnoid membrane and the pia mater.
sub·arc·tic (sub ärk'tik, -är'-), *adj.* near or just below the arctic region; having to do with or occurring in regions just south of the Arctic Circle: *a subarctic climate, a subarctic exploration. Father . . . took his family to a Saskatchewan crossroads where the northern prairies turn into a subarctic wasteland of muskeg, timber and lakes* (Time).
sub·ar·id (sub ar'id), *adj.* moderately arid.
sub·as·sem·bly (sub'ə sem'blē), *n., pl.* **-blies. 1.** a putting together of parts in subordinate components or structures preparatory to the main or final assembly of the finished product. **2.** a single such component or structure: *A new production technique divides television circuits into 20 subassemblies, each having an electron tube and associated components* (Science News Letter).
sub·as·tral (sub as'trəl), *adj.* situated under the stars or heavens; terrestrial.
sub·as·trin·gent (sub'ə strin'jənt), *adj.* slightly astringent.
sub·at·om (sub at'əm), *n.* a constituent of an atom: *Protons and electrons are subatoms.*
sub·a·tom·ic (sub'ə tom'ik), *adj.* **1.** of or having to do with subatoms or phenomena connected with them: *Like all other subatomic bits of matter, electrons have wave-like as well as particle-like properties* (Scientific American). **2.** of or having to do with the interior of an atom or any phenomenon occurring there.
sub·au·di·ble (sub ô'də bəl), *adj.* slightly or barely audible: *The subaudible electromagnetic radiation has been detected by four Canadian scientists* (Science News Letter).
sub·au·di·tion (sub'ô dish'ən), *n.* **1.** the act of implying something that is not expressed. **2.** something that is inferred or understood. [< Late Latin *subauditiō, -ōnis* < *subaudīre* to supply an ellipsis, understand < Latin *sub-* under, slightly + *audīre* hear]
sub·au·ric·u·lar (sub'ô rik'yə lər), *adj.* below an auricle, especially of the ear.
sub·ax·il·lar·y (sub ak'sə ler'ē), *adj.* **1.** *Botany.* situated or placed beneath an axil. **2.** *Anatomy.* situated beneath the axilla.
sub·base (sub'bās'), *n.* **1.** the lowest part of a base that is divided horizontally. **2.** a base placed under the bottom of a machine or other apparatus to raise it higher from the ground. **3.** subbass. **4.** a secondary base of supplies.
sub·base·ment (sub'bās'mənt), *n.* any basement below the first or main basement of a building: *Beneath the level of obvious fraud . . . was a subbasement of chicanery where we were all fooling one another* (Harper's).
sub·bass (sub'bās'), *n.* a pedal stop producing the lowest tones of an organ; bourdon.
sub·bing (sub'ing), *n.* a very thin layer of gelatin between the emulsion and the supporting layer of a photographic film.
sub·bi·tu·mi·nous coal (sub'bə tü'mə nəs, -tyü'-), a black coal with a dull to glossy luster, lower in quality and value than bituminous coal, but higher than peat and lignite: *The U.S. alone has nearly half of all the bituminous and subbituminous, the most valuable of all coals* (Scientific American).
sub·branch (sub'branch', -bränch'), *n.* **1.** a subdivision of a branch. **2.** a subphylum.
sub·breed (sub'brēd'), *n.* a recognizable strain or subdivision of a breed.
sub·cab·i·net (sub kab'ə nit, -kab'nit), *n.* a subordinate cabinet, chosen by the leader of a government, and acting under the principal cabinet.
sub·cal·i·ber or **sub·cal·i·bre** (sub kal'ə bər), *adj.* **1.** (of a shell, bullet, etc.) having a diameter less than that of the bore of the gun from which it is fired. Subcaliber projectiles are fitted with a disk the size of the bore or fired from a tube attached to the inside or the outside of the gun, and are used in practice firing as a substitute for more costly full-sized projectiles. **2.** using or involving the use of such ammunition: *a subcaliber gun, subcaliber practice.*
Sub·car·bon·if·er·ous (sub'kär bə nif'ər əs), *Geology.* —*adj.* of or having to do with a geological period or a system of rocks of the earlier or lower portion of the Carboniferous period or system; Mississippian. —*n.* the Subcarboniferous period or system.
sub·car·ri·er (sub kar'ē ər), *n.* a carrier wave that is used to modulate another carrier wave.
sub·car·ti·lag·i·nous (sub'kär tə laj'ə nəs), *adj.* **1.** partially or incompletely cartilaginous. **2.** below or beneath cartilage.
sub·caste (sub'kast', -käst'), *n.* a subdivision of a caste: *The whole situation is made far more intricate by the fact that each caste is divided into subcastes with special distinctions and privileges* (Santha Rama Rau).

sub·cat·e·go·ry (sub kat′ə gôr′ē, -gōr′-), *n., pl.* **-ries.** a subordinate category; subdivision of a category: *Under the agreement, quotas apply to subcategories in each of the major classifications* (New York Times).

sub·ce·les·tial (sub′sə les′chəl), *adj.* **1.** situated or existing below the heavens; terrestrial; mundane. **2.** *Astronomy.* directly under the zenith. —*n.* a subcelestial being.

sub·cel·lar (sub′sel′ər), *n.* any cellar beneath another cellar.

sub·cel·lu·lar (sub sel′yə lər), *adj.* smaller in size than ordinary cells: *subcellular particles. In a second set of experiments Weiss was able to watch organization at the subcellular level* (Scientific American).

sub·cen·ter (sub′sen′tər), *n.* a subordinate or secondary center: *The system is highly centered on San Francisco, with Oakland as a subcenter* (Scientific American).

sub·cen·tral (sub sen′trəl), *adj.* **1.** being under the center. **2.** nearly central; a little off center. —**sub·cen′tral·ly,** *adv.*

subch., subchapter.

sub·chas·er (sub′chā′sər), *n.* a submarine chaser: *He sent his PT boats, subchasers and gunboats to blockade the coastline south and west of the mountains* (Time).

sub·chief (sub′chēf′), *n.* an official next in rank to the chief, as of a tribe, clan, etc.: *Below the chief, subchiefs were appointed for certain districts* (New Yorker).

sub·chlo·rid (sub klôr′id, -klōr′-), *n.* subchloride.

sub·chlo·ride (sub klôr′īd, -id; -klōr′-), *n.* a chloride that contains a relatively small proportion of chlorine.

sub·class (sub′klas′, -kläs′), *n. Biology.* a group of animals or plants ranking above an order and below a class; superorder.

sub·cla·vi·an (sub klā′vē ən), *Anatomy.* —*adj.* **1.** beneath the clavicle. **2.** of or having to do with the subclavian artery, vein, groove, or muscle. —*n.* a subclavian artery, vein, groove, or muscle. [< New Latin *subclavius* < *sub-* under (< Latin) + *clavis* clavicle (< Latin *clāvis* key) + English *-an*]

subclavian artery, the large artery forming the trunk of the arterial system of the arm or forelimb.

subclavian groove, either of two shallow depressions on the first rib for the subclavian artery and vein.

subclavian muscle, a small muscle extending from the first rib to the clavicle.

subclavian vein, the part of the main vein of the arm lying under the clavicle.

sub·cli·max (sub klī′maks), *n. Biology.* a climax whose normal development has been arrested by some factor.

sub·clin·i·cal (sub klin′ə kəl), *adj.* having mild symptoms that are not apparent or easily detected: *a subclinical infection.*

sub·com·mis·sion (sub′kə mish′ən), *n.* a subordinate commission chosen from and acting under a larger commission for some special duty: *The bank is being sponsored by ECAFE, a U.N. subcommission* (New York Times).

sub·com·mit·tee (sub′kə mit′ē), *n.* a small committee chosen from and acting under a larger committee for some special duty: *The second week of meetings in the United Nations disarmament subcommittee has ended without any notable advance* (London Times).

sub·con·scious (sub kon′shəs), *adj.* **1.** not wholly conscious; on the border of consciousness. **2.** beneath or beyond consciousness; existing but not felt: *subconscious desires, a subconscious suggestion. Her poor grades caused a subconscious irritation that made her cross.* —*n.* thoughts, feelings, etc., that are present in the mind but not fully perceived or recognized. —**sub·con′scious·ly,** *adv.*

sub·con·scious·ness (sub kon′shəs nis), *n.* **1.** the quality of being subconscious. **2.** the subconscious.

sub·con·ti·nent (sub kon′tə nənt), *n.* **1.** a land mass of great extent, but smaller than that of a continent: *The subcontinent of New Guinea, too, would require separate treatment* (Melville J. Herskovits). **2.** a large section of a continent having a certain geographical or political independence: *A few lady delegates from nations on the Indian subcontinent —India, Pakistan, and Nepal—have appeared in saris* (New Yorker).

sub·con·ti·nen·tal (sub′kon tə nen′təl), *adj.* of, having to do with, or characteristic of a subcontinent: *Arabia, a block of subcontinental size, . . . was formerly a part of Africa* (New Scientist).

sub·con·tract (sub kon′trakt; *also for v.* sub′kən trakt′), *n.* a contract under a previous contract; contract for carrying out a previous contract or a part of it: *The contractor for the new school building gave out subcontracts to a plumber, an electrician, and a steam fitter.* —*v.i., v.t.* to make a subcontract; make a subcontract for.

sub·con·trac·tor (sub kon′trak tər, sub′kən trak′-), *n.* a person who contracts to carry out a previous contract or part of it.

sub·con·tra·oc·tave (sub′kon trə ok′tiv), *n. Music.* the octave below the contra-octave, as on an organ; fourth octave below middle C.

sub·cor·tex (sub kôr′teks), *n., pl.* **-ti·ces** (-tə sēz). the white matter beneath the cortex of the brain.

sub·cor·ti·cal (sub kôr′tə kəl), *adj.* **1.** of or having to do with the subcortex: *The subcortical regions of the brain appear to play a role of equal or even greater importance in the learning process* (Scientific American). **2.** situated beneath the cortex of a sponge, the cortex or bark of a tree, etc.

sub·crit·i·cal (sub krit′ə kəl), *adj.* having less than the amount of fissionable material necessary to sustain a chain reaction: *These machines are complete with uranium and a neutron source, but are what the scientists call subcritical, that is, they are not self-energetic and "hot"* (Science News Letter).

subcritical assembly or **reactor,** a nuclear reactor in which a radioactive substance undergoes fission on a subcritical level, especially for use in research and education.

sub·crust (sub′krust′), *n.* the under portion of the crust of the earth, from about 15 to about 40 miles below the surface.

sub·crus·tal (sub krus′təl), *adj.* happening or located below the earth's crust: *Earth's subcrustal mantle must have a much larger mechanical strength than previously believed in order to support the pear-like shape* (Science News Letter).

sub·cul·tur·al (sub kul′chər əl), *adj.* of or having to do with a subculture.

sub·cul·ture (sub kul′chər), *v.,* **-tured, -tur·ing,** *n.* —*v.t.* to cultivate (a bacteriological culture) from a previous culture: *I subculture the water into a nutrient medium as soon as possible — preferably as soon as we bring the specimens out of the cave* (New Scientist). —*n.* **1.** a bacteriological culture derived from a previous culture. **2.** an element or class within or on the fringe of a culture or society: *Most of his work has been with . . . a youth subculture dominated by gang-joining potentially explosive teen-agers* (Newsweek).

sub·cur·rent (sub′kėr′ənt), *n.* a secondary or subordinate current: *One of the historical subcurrents he believes to be a constant in human development is a tendency to equate the traditional with art* (Harper's).

sub·cu·ta·ne·ous (sub′kyü tā′nē əs), *adj.* **1.** under the skin: *subcutaneous tissue.* **2.** living under the skin: *a subcutaneous parasite.* **3.** placed or performed under the skin: *a subcutaneous injection.* —**sub′cu·ta′ne·ous·ly,** *adv.*

sub·cu·tis (sub′kyü′tis, sub kyü′-), *n.* the deeper part of the cutis.

sub·dea·con (sub dē′kən), *n.* a member of the clergy next below a deacon in rank.

sub·dea·con·ate (sub dē′kə nit), *n.* the office or order of subdeacon.

sub·dean (sub′dēn′), *n.* an official next below a dean in rank, and acting as his deputy.

sub·deb (sub′deb′), *n.* a subdebutante.

sub·deb·u·tante or **sub·dé·bu·tante** (sub deb′yə tänt, -tant; sub deb′yə tänt′), *n.* a young girl soon to make her debut in society. [American English < *sub-* + *debutante*]

sub·del·e·gate (sub del′ə git, -gāt), *n., v.,* **-gat·ed, -gat·ing.** —*n.* a subordinate delegate. —*v.t.* to delegate (powers, etc.) to a subordinate delegate.

sub·del·e·ga·tion (sub′del ə gā′shən), *n.* the act of subdelegating.

sub·de·lir·i·um (sub′di lir′ē əm), *n.* a mild delirium with lucid intervals.

sub·den·tate (sub den′tāt), *adj.* imperfectly dentate; having indistinct notches.

sub·de·pot (sub dep′ō), *n.* a branch military depot, nearer the regiment than a depot.

sub·di·ac·o·nate (sub′dī ak′ə nit), *n.* subdeaconate.

sub·di·a·lect (sub dī′ə lekt), *n.* a division or variety of a dialect: *The variety of subdialects . . . is very great* (William Dwight Whitney).

sub·dis·trict (sub′dis′trikt), *n.* a division or subdivision of a district.

sub·di·vide (sub′də vīd′, sub′də vīd), *v.t., v.i.,* **-vid·ed, -vid·ing. 1.** to divide again; divide into smaller parts. **2.** to divide (land) into lots for houses, buildings, etc.: *A real-estate dealer bought the farm and subdivided it into building lots.*

sub·di·vid·er (sub′də vī′dər, sub′də vī′-), *n.* a person or company that subdivides land for building or other development: *By means of many-laned highways, every acre everywhere is to be made accessible for the real-estate speculator and the subdivider* (New Yorker).

sub·di·vis·i·ble (sub′də viz′ə bəl, sub′də-viz′-), *adj.* that can be subdivided.

sub·di·vi·sion (sub′də vizh′ən, sub′də-vizh′-), *n.* **1.** a division into smaller parts. **2.** a part of a part. **3.** a tract of land divided into building lots.

sub·di·vi·sion·al (sub′də vizh′ə nəl, sub′-də vizh′-), *adj.* of or having to do with subdivision.

sub·do·lous (sub′də ləs), *adj. Obsolete.* crafty; artful; cunning; sly. [< Late Latin *subdolus* < Latin *sub-* under, away + *dolus* cunning] —**sub′do·lous·ly,** *adv.*

sub·dom·i·nant (sub dom′ə nənt), *n. Music.* the tone or note next below the dominant; fourth tone or note from the tonic in ascending scale, and the fifth in descending scale. —*adj.* of or having to do with this tone: *a subdominant chord.*

sub·drain·age (sub drān′ij), *n.* an underground drainage system.

sub·du·a·ble (səb dü′ə bəl, -dyü′-), *adj.* that can be subdued.

sub·du·al (səb dü′əl, -dyü′-), *n.* **1.** the act of subduing. **2.** the state of being subdued.

sub·duct (səb dukt′), *v.t., v.i.* **1.** to draw down or downward. **2.** to take away; subtract; deduct. [< Latin *subductus,* past participle of *subdūcere* to lead away < *sub-* away + *dūcere* to lead]

sub·duc·tion (səb duk′shən), *n.* a taking away or withdrawing; subtraction.

sub·due (səb dü′, -dyü′), *v.t.,* **-dued, -du·ing. 1.** to conquer; overcome by superior force: *The Spaniards subdued the Indian tribes in Mexico. He who . . . subdues mankind Must look down on the hate of those below* (Byron). **2.** to get the better of; prevail over: *Swords conquer some, but Words subdue all men* (Matthew Prior). **3.** to gain control over: *to subdue one's fears, to subdue a desire to laugh.* **4.** to tone down; soften: *The window curtains subdue the light in a room.* **5.** to reduce or allay: *to subdue a fever or a boil.* **6.** to bring (land) under cultivation. [ultimately < Latin *subdūcere* draw, lead away < *sub-* from under + *dūcere* lead; meaning influenced by Latin *subdere* subdue < *sub-* under + *dare* put]

—**Syn. 1.** vanquish, subjugate, enslave. **3.** suppress.

sub·dued (səb düd′, -dyüd′), *adj.* **1.** reduced to subjection; made submissive. **2.** reduced in intensity or force; toned down: *a sort of boudoir, pervaded by a subdued, rose-coloured light* (Henry James). —**sub·dued′ly,** *adv.* —**sub·dued′ness,** *n.*

sub·due·ment (səb dü′mənt, -dyü′-), *n.* subdual.

sub·du·er (səb dü′ər, -dyü′-), *n.* a person or thing that subdues.

sub·du·ple (sub′dü pəl, -dyü-), *adj.* being half of a quantity or number; having a proportion of one to two. [< Late Latin *subduplus* < Latin *sub-* under + *duplus* double]

sub·du·pli·cate (sub dü′plə kit, -dyü′-), *adj.* being that of the square roots of the quantities. *Example:* 2 : 3 is the subduplicate ratio of 4 : 9.

sub·du·ral (sub důr′əl, -dyůr′-), *adj.* situated or existing below the dura mater: *He had suffered a subdural hemorrhage of the right side of the head* (New York Times).

sub·dwarf (sub′dwôrf′), *n.,* or **subdwarf star,** any of a group of stars lying just below the main sequence in the Russell diagram, being relatively small and dim when compared to a main-sequence star of the same spectral class.

sub·e·co·nom·ic (sub′ē kə nom′ik, -ek ə-), *adj.* below what is economically proper or desirable; not up to economic standards: *We still suffer from subeconomic rates of freight* (London Times).

sub·ed·it (sub ed′it), *v.t.* to edit under the direction of a chief editor.

sub·ed·i·tor (sub ed′ə tər), *n.* a subordinate editor.

sub·ed·i·to·ri·al (sub′ed ə tôr′ē əl, -tōr′-), *adj.* of or having to do with a subeditor.

sub·ed·i·tor·ship (sub ed′ə tər ship), *n.* the position or responsibility of a subeditor.

sub·en·try (sub′en′trē), *n., pl.* **-tries.** a subordinate entry, as in a list.

sub·e·qua·to·ri·al (sub′ē kwə tôr′ē əl, -tōr′-), *adj.* near or adjoining the equatorial region.

su·ber·ate (sü′bə rāt), *n.* a salt of suberic acid.

su·be·re·ous (sü bir′ē əs), *adj.* of or like cork; corky. [< Latin *sūbereus* (with English *-ous*) < *sūber, -eris* cork, cork oak, probably < Greek *sŷphar* anything wrinkled]

su·ber·ic (sü ber′ik), *adj.* of or having to do with cork. [< French *suberique* < Latin *sūber, -eris* cork, cork oak]

suberic acid, a crystalline dicarboxylic acid prepared by the action of nitric acid on cork, paper, fatty acids, and various other substances, used in making plastics and dyes. *Formula:* $C_8H_{14}O_4$

su·ber·in (sü′bər in), *n.* a substance in cork tissue that gives cork its waterproof quality. [< Latin *sūber* (see SUBEREOUS) + English *-in*]

su·ber·ine (sü′bər in, -ə rēn), *n.* suberin.

su·ber·i·za·tion (sü′bər ə zā′shən), *n. Botany.* the making of cell walls into cork by the formation of suberin.

su·ber·ize (sü′bə rīz), *v.t.,* **-ized, -iz·ing.** *Botany.* to change (a cell wall) into cork tissue by the formation of suberin. [< Latin *sūber, -eris* (see SUBEREOUS) + English *-ize*]

su·ber·ose (sü′bə rōs), *adj.* of or like cork; corky; subereous.

su·ber·ous (sü′bər əs), *adj.* suberose.

sub·e·so·phag·e·al (sub′ē sə faj′ē əl), *adj.* situated or existing below the esophagus.

sub·fam·i·ly (sub fam′ə lē, sub′fam′-), *n., pl.* **-lies.** *Biology.* a group of plants or animals ranking above a genus and below a family. Organisms are classified into classes, subclasses, orders, suborders, families, subfamilies, genera, subgenera, species, and subspecies.

sub·fer·tile (sub fėr′təl), *adj.* not wholly fertile: *In three to five months the centre is usually able to list a couple as fertile, subfertile (requiring surgery or other special treatment), or sterile* (Maclean's).

sub·floor (sub′flôr′, -flōr′), *n.* an underlying floor used as a base for the finished floor.

sub·floor·ing (sub flôr′ing, -flōr′-), *n.* a flooring of steel or other material forming the base of the floor of a room.

sub·fos·sil (sub fos′əl), *adj.* partly fossilized. —*n.* a subfossil animal or plant.

sub·freez·ing (sub frē′zing), *adj.* below freezing: *After a three-alarm fire . . . subfreezing cold turned the shell of the building into a grotto of ice* (Newsweek).

sub·fusc or **sub·fusk** (sub fusk′), *adj.* somewhat dark or dusky; brownish: *a subfusc hue like that of old furniture* (John Galsworthy). [< Latin *subfuscus* < *sub-* under, away + *fuscus* dark]

sub·fus·cous (sub fus′kəs), *adj.* subfusc.

sub·ge·ner·ic (sub′jə ner′ik), *adj.* of, having to do with, or being a subgenus. —**sub′ge·ner′i·cal·ly,** *adv.*

sub·ge·nus (sub jē′nəs, sub′jē′-), *n., pl.* **sub·gen·er·a** (sub jen′ər ə, sub′jen′-), **sub·ge·nus·es.** *Biology.* a group of plants or animals ranking above a species and below a genus.

sub·gi·ant (sub′jī′ənt), *n.,* or **subgiant star,** any of a group of stars lying just above the main sequence in the Russell diagram, being relatively large and bright when compared to a main-sequence star of the same spectral class.

sub·gla·cial (sub glā′shəl), *adj.* existing or formed beneath a glacier: *a subglacial stream.* —**sub·gla′cial·ly,** *adv.*

sub·grade (sub′grād′), *n.* a layer of earth or rock below the surface, leveled off as a foundation for a road or structure.

sub·grav·i·ty (sub grav′ə tē), *n.* a gravitational effect or state characterized by less than the normal force of gravity (usually less than one G): *I felt a crushing force, and then the ineffable relief of subgravity and the euphoria of zero gravity* (Time).

sub·group (sub′grüp′), *n.* **1.** a subordinate group; subdivision of a group, especially in botany and zoology: *Two subordinate types of this subgroup can be distinguished as far as the English elms are concerned* (R.H. Richens). **2.** *Chemistry.* a division of a group in the periodic table; family.

sub·gum (sub′gum′), *adj.* (of Chinese food) served with mixed vegetables: *subgum fried noodles, subgum chicken chow mein.* [< Chinese pidgin English *subgum*]

sub·head (sub′hed′), *n.* **1.** a subordinate head or title, as in a book, chapter, article, etc. **2. a.** a subordinate division of a head or title. **b.** a short heading used to break up the paragraphs of a long news story. **3.** an official next in rank to the head, as of a college, etc.

sub·head·ing (sub′hed′ing), *n.* subhead.

sub·hu·man (sub hyü′mən), *adj.* **1.** below the human race or type; less than human. **2.** almost human. —*n.* a subhuman creature.

sub·hu·man·i·ty (sub′hyü man′ə tē), *n.* **1.** subhumans taken as a group. **2.** the fact of being subhuman; subhuman character or quality: *What the rescuers of the Nottingham's crew take off Boon Island after nearly a month is ten scarecrows who are close to subhumanity* (Time).

sub·hu·mid (sub hyü′mid), *adj.* having sufficient rainfall to support the growth of tall grass or similar vegetation: *The prairies of the United States and the pampas of South America have subhumid climates.*

sub·i·ma·go (sub′i mā′gō), *n., pl.* **-i·ma·gos, -i·mag·i·nes** (-i maj′ə nēz). a May fly just after it emerges from the nymph stage. The subimago sheds its skin to become an imago. See **May fly** for picture.

sub·in·dex (sub in′deks), *n., pl.* **-di·ces** (-də sēz). a figure or letter following and slightly below a symbol; subscript. *Example:* 2 is the subindex in H_2O and b_2.

sub·in·feud (sub′in fyüd′), *v.t., v.i.* subinfeudate.

sub·in·feu·date (sub′in fyü′dāt), *v.t., v.i.,* **-dat·ed, -dat·ing.** to grant by subinfeudation.

sub·in·feu·da·tion (sub′in fyü dā′shən), *n.* in feudal law: **1.** the granting of lands by a feudal tenant to a subtenant, who held them on terms similar to those of the grant to the tenant. **2.** the tenure so established. **3.** an estate or fief so created.

sub·in·feu·da·to·ry (sub′in fyü′də tôr′ē, -tōr′-), *n., pl.* **-ries.** a person who holds by subinfeudation.

sub·ir·ri·gate (sub ir′ə gāt), *v.t.,* **-gat·ed, -gat·ing.** to irrigate beneath the surface of the ground, as by underground pipes.

sub·ir·ri·ga·tion (sub′ir ə gā′shən), *n.* the act of subirrigating: *These pipes provide subirrigation from flowing wells* (New York Times).

su·bi·ta·ne·ous (sü′bə tā′nē əs), *adj. Obsolete.* sudden; unexpected; hasty. [< Latin *subitāneus* (with English *-ous*); see SUDDEN]

su·bi·to (sü′bi tō), *adv. Music.* quickly; suddenly (a direction): *piano subito.* [< Italian *subito* < Latin *subitō,* ablative of *subitus;* see SUDDEN]

subj., **1.** subject. **2.** subjective. **3.** subjectively. **4.** subjunctive.

sub·ja·cen·cy (sub jā′sən sē), *n.* the state of being subjacent.

sub·ja·cent (sub jā′sənt), *adj.* **1.** situated underneath or below; underlying. **2.** forming the basis or substratum. **3.** lying or situated at a lower level, at or near the base, as of a mountain. [< Latin *subjacēns, -entis,* present participle of *subjacēre* < *sub-* below + *jacēre* to lie]

sub·ject (*n., adj.* sub′jikt, -jekt; *v.* səb jekt′), *n.* **1.** something thought about, discussed, investigated, etc.: *a subject of discussion or negotiation, the subject of a sermon.* **2.** a course of study, field of learning, etc.: *English, history, mathematics, and biology are required subjects in this school. An examination in each subject is held at the end of the semester.* **3. a.** a person under the rule of a state, government, sovereign, etc.: *the subjects of a king. The kings of our own day very much resemble their subjects in education and breeding* (Benjamin Jowett). **b.** a person who is under the power, control, or influence of another. **4.** a person or thing that undergoes or experiences something: *Rabbits and mice are often subjects for medical experiments. The patient of a doctor or psychologist is his subject. Medical students dissect dead bodies which they call subjects.* **5.** *Grammar.* the word or group of words indicating the performer or, when the verb is passive, the receiver of the action of the verb. In "I see" and "I am seen," *I* is the subject. *Abbr.:* subj. **6. a.** the theme of a book, poem, or other literary work. **b.** a figure, scene, object, incident, etc., chosen by an artist for representation. **c.** *Music.* the theme or melody on which a work or movement is based. **7.** *Philosophy.* **a.** the substance of anything, as contrasted with its qualities or attributes. **b.** the mind or self, as contrasted with everything outside the mind. **c.** substance or reality, as contrasted with appearance. **8.** *Logic.* **a.** the term of a proposition of which the other term (predicate) is affirmed or denied. **b.** the thing about which such affirmation or denial is made. **9.** a ground, motive, or cause: *Lateness and carelessness are subjects for complaint.*

—*adj.* **1.** under some power or influence: *We are subject to our country's laws.* **2.** liable to suffer from; likely to have; prone (to): *subject to decay, a person subject to colds. Japan is a country subject to earthquakes.* **3.** liable to receive; exposed or open (to): *subject to criticism, reproach, or contempt.* **4.** liable, as to something that can and often does occur: *Human affairs are all subject to changes and disasters* (Daniel Defoe). **5.** depending on; on the condition of: *I bought the car subject to your approval.*

—*v.t.* **1.** to bring under some power or influence: *Ancient Rome subjected all Italy to her rule.* **2.** to make subordinate or submissive: *to subject the minds of a people.* **3.** to lay open or expose; make liable (to): *Credulity subjects one to impositions.* **4.** to cause to undergo or experience something: *The savages subjected their captives to torture.* **5.** *Obsolete.* to put, lay, or spread under.

[< Latin *subjectus,* past participle of *subicere* place under < *sub-* under + *jacere* throw]

—**Syn.** *n.* **1. Subject, topic** mean the main thing or idea thought, talked, or written about, as in a conversation, lecture, essay, or book. **Subject** is the general word: *He tried to change the subject. Juvenile delinquency is a broad subject.* **Topic** often applies to a subject having to do with a current event or problem, but particularly applies to a limited and definitely stated subject that is, or is to be, discussed in a lecture, essay, etc., or some part of it: *"The need for a recreation center here" is today's topic.*

subject catalogue, a card catalogue, or part of one, in which books are entered by subject.

sub·jec·ti·fi·ca·tion (səb jek′tə fə kā′shən), *n.* **1.** a subjectifying. **2.** a being subjectified.

sub·jec·ti·fy (səb jek′tə fī), *v.t.,* **-fied, -fy·ing.** to make subjective; identify with the subject.

sub·jec·tion (səb jek′shən), *n.* **1.** a bringing under some power or influence; subjugating; conquering: *The subjection of the rebels took years.* **2.** the condition of being under some power or influence; subjugation: *Women used to live in subjection to men.*

sub·jec·tion·al (səb jek′shə nəl), *adj.* **1.** having to do with subjection. **2.** based upon subjection.

sub·jec·tive (səb jek′tiv), *adj.* **1.** existing in the mind; belonging to the person thinking rather than to the object thought of: *Ideas and opinions are subjective; facts are objective.* **2.** about the thoughts and feelings of the speaker, writer, painter, etc.; personal: *Lyric poetry is subjective, expressing the feelings of the poet; narrative poetry is generally objective, telling a story.* **3.** *Psychology.* **a.** originating within or dependent on the mind of the individual rather than an external object. **b.** introspective. **4.** *Philosophy.* **a.** of or relating to reality as perceived by the mind, as distinct from reality as independent of the mind. **b.** influenced by an individual's state of mind: *a subjective perception or apprehension.* **c.** having to do with the substance of anything, as opposed to its qualities and attributes. **5.** *Grammar.* being or serving as the subject of a sentence; nominative. **6.** *Medicine.* (of symptoms) discoverable by the patient only. **7.** *Obsolete.* of or having to do with someone who is subject to rule or control. —**sub·jec′tive·ly,** *adv.* —**sub·jec′tive·ness,** *n.*

sub·jec·tiv·ism (səb jek′tə viz əm), *n.* **1.** the theory that all knowledge is subjective.

2. any theory that emphasizes the subjective elements in experience or learning. **3. a.** the ethical theory that conceives the aim of morality to be the attainment of states of feeling. **b.** the ethical theory that an individual's feelings are a criterion of values.

sub·jec·tiv·ist (səb jek′tə vist), *n.* a person who believes in or advocates a theory of subjectivism. —*adj.* subjectivistic.

sub·jec·ti·vis·tic (səb jek′tə vis′tik), *adj.* having to do with or characterized by subjectivism.

sub·jec·tiv·i·ty (sub′jek tiv′ə tē), *n.* **1.** subjective quality or state; existence in the mind only; absorption in one's own mental states or processes; tendency to view things through the medium of one's own individuality: *Her great charm was her utter subjectivity* (New Yorker). **2.** subjectivism.

sub·jec·tiv·ize (səb jek′tə vīz), *v.t.*, **-ized, -iz·ing.** to make subjective: *The picture seems to me sentimentalized and subjectivized out of all proportion* (Harper's).

sub·ject·less (sub′jikt lis, -jekt-), *adj.* without a subject or subjects: *Big, bold, brightly colored shapes keep turning corners in the most subjectless, unliterary, and unsensual art that the 20th century has up to the present produced* (Time).

subject matter, 1. something thought about, discussed, studied, written about, etc.: *While an ingenious questionnaire might be devised to meet these contingencies, it is usually better, where the subject matter is complex, to use the unguided interview* (Anthony H. Richmond). **2.** the meaning of a talk, book, etc., as distinguished from its form or style: *The lecturer's subject matter was better than his presentation.*

sub·join (sub join′), *v.t.* **1.** to add at the end of something spoken or written; append. **2.** to place in immediate sequence or juxtaposition to something else. [< Middle French *subjoindre* < Latin *subjungere* < *sub-* under + *jungere* to join]

sub ju·di·ce (sub jü′də sē), *Latin.* **1.** still before the court; under consideration; not decided: *The Kastner-Gruenwald case is sub judice, but it will now be ... an election issue* (London Times). **2.** (literally) under judgment.

sub·ju·gate (sub′jə gāt), *v.t.*, **-gat·ed, -gat·ing. 1.** to subdue; conquer. **2.** to bring under complete control; make subservient or submissive: *His love and his hatred were of that passionate fervour which subjugates all the rest of the being* (George Eliot). [< Latin *subjugāre* (with English *-ate*[1]) < *sub-* under + *jugum* yoke]

sub·ju·ga·tion (sub′jə gā′shən), *n.* conquest; subjection: *the subjugation of Greece by the Ottomans.*

sub·ju·ga·tor (sub′jə gā′tər), *n.* a person who subjugates.

sub·junc·tion (səb jungk′shən), *n.* **1.** the act of subjoining. **2.** the state of being subjoined. **3.** something subjoined. [< Late Latin *subjunctiō, -ōnis* < Latin *subjungere;* see SUBJOIN]

sub·junc·tive (səb jungk′tiv), *n.* **1.** the mood of a verb that expresses a state, act, or event as possible, conditional, or dependent, rather than as actual. *Abbr.:* subj. **2.** a verb in this mood. *Examples:* I insist that he *go,* if this *be* treason, if I *were* you. —*adj.* of or having to do with this mood. [< Late Latin *subjunctīvus* < Latin *subjungere;* see SUBJOIN]

sub·king·dom (sub king′dəm, sub′king′-), *n. Biology.* a primary division of the animal or plant kingdom, now usually called a phylum.

sub·lap·sar·i·an (sub′lap sãr′ē ən), *adj.* of or having to do with sublapsarianism or its adherents. —*n.* an adherent of the doctrine of sublapsarianism. [< New Latin *sublapsarius* (< Latin *sub-* under, after + *lapsus, -ūs* a lapse, fall + *-ārius* -ary) + English *-an*]

sub·lap·sar·i·an·ism (sub′lap sãr′ē ə niz′əm), *n.* the Calvinist doctrine that the fall of man, while foreseen by God, was not decreed as part of the plan of creation and that election and damnation are therefore correctives that came after the Fall; infralapsarianism.

sub·la·tion (sub lā′shən), *n. Medicine.* the removal or detachment of a part.

sub·lease (*n.* sub′lēs′; *v.* sub lēs′, sub′lēs′), *n., v.*, **-leased, -leas·ing.** —*n.* a lease granted by a person who rents the property himself. —*v.t.* to grant or take a sublease of.

sub·les·see (sub′le sē′), *n.* the receiver or holder of a sublease.

sub·les·sor (sub les′ər), *n.* the grantor of a sublease.

sub·let (sub let′, sub′let′), *v.*, **-let, -let·ting,** *n.* —*v.t.* **1.** to rent to another (something that has been rented to oneself): *to sublet a house for the summer.* **2.** to give part of (a contract) to another: *The contractor for the whole building sublet the contract for the plumbing.* —*n.* an apartment, building, etc., that has been sublet: ... *the hapless couple's horrid little furnished sublet in the city* (New Yorker).

sub·le·thal (sub lē′thəl), *adj.* not causing death; short of being fatal: *In experimental animals ... sublethal doses of radiation appreciably reduce the life span* (Scientific American).

sub·lev·el (sub′lev′əl), *n.* a lower level; substratum.

sub·lieu·ten·an·cy (sub′lü ten′ən sē; *in general British usage, except in the navy* sub′lef ten′ən sē), *n.* the position or rank of a sublieutenant.

sub·lieu·ten·ant (sub′lü ten′ənt; *in general British usage, except in the navy* sub′lef ten′ənt), *n.* **1.** a subordinate lieutenant. **2.** (in the British Army and Navy) a commissioned officer ranking next below a lieutenant.

sub·li·mate (*v.* sub′lə māt; *adj., n.* sub′lə mit, -māt), *v.*, **-mat·ed, -mat·ing,** *adj., n.* —*v.t.* **1.** to purify; refine: *The heat of Milton's mind may be said to sublimate his learning* (Samuel Johnson). **2.** *Chemistry.* to sublime (a solid substance). **3.** *Psychology.* to change (an undesirable impulse or trait) into a more desirable or acceptable activity. —*v.i.* to become sublimated.
—*adj.* sublimated.
—*n. Chemistry.* material obtained when a substance is sublimed: *Bichloride of mercury is a very poisonous sublimate.*
[< Latin *sublīmāre* (with English *-ate*[1]) to raise < *sublīmis* lofty; see SUBLIME]

sub·li·ma·tion (sub′lə mā′shən), *n.* **1.** the act or process of sublimating or subliming; purification. **2.** the resulting state or product, especially, mental elevation or exaltation: *that enthusiastic sublimation which is the source of greatness and energy* (Thomas L. Peacock). **3.** the highest stage or purest form of a thing. **4.** a chemical sublimate: *This direct transition from solid to vapor is called sublimation* (Sears and Zemansky).

sub·lime (sə blīm′), *adj., n., v.*, **-limed, -lim·ing.** —*adj.* **1.** lofty; grand; noble; majestic: *Mountain scenery is often sublime.* **2.** exalted; excellent; eminent; supreme: *sublime devotion. How sublime a thing it is To suffer and be strong* (Longfellow). **3.** expressing lofty ideas in a grand manner: *The sublime Dante* (Samuel Taylor Coleridge). **4.** *Poetic.* **a.** of lofty bearing or appearance: *In his simplicity sublime* (Tennyson). **b.** *Obsolete.* haughty; proud. **5.** *Archaic.* set or raised aloft. **6.** *Obsolete.* elated.
—*n.* **1.** something that is lofty, noble, exalted, etc., in writing, life, feeling, nature, art, etc.: *No, never need an American look beyond his own country for the sublime and beautiful of natural scenery* (Washington Irving). **2.** the highest degree or example (of): *Your upward gaze at me now is the very sublime of faith, truth, and devotion* (Charlotte Brontë).
from the sublime to the ridiculous, from one extreme to the other: *His writing is very uneven, running the gamut from the sublime to the ridiculous.*
—*v.t.* **1.** to make higher or nobler; make sublime: *A judicious use of metaphors wonderfully raises, sublimes and adorns oratory* (Oliver Goldsmith). **2.** *Chemistry.* **a.** to heat (a solid substance) and condense the vapor given off; purify; refine. **b.** to cause to be given off by this or a similar process. —*v.i.* **1.** to pass off as a vapor and condense as a solid; become purified or refined. **2.** to be changed into a gas directly from the solid state.
[< Latin *sublīmis* (originally) sloping up (to the lintel) < *sub-* up + *līmen, -inis* threshold] —**sub·lime′ly,** *adv.* —**sub·lime′ness,** *n.*

Sublime Porte, Porte.

sub·lim·er (sə blī′mər), *n. Rare.* a person or thing that sublimes.

sub·lim·i·nal (sub lim′ə nəl, -lī′mə-), *Psychology.* —*adj.* **1.** below or beyond the threshold of consciousness; subconscious: *the subliminal self. For years psychologists have been experimenting with subliminal stimulation — exposing subjects to stimuli which are too faint or too fleeting to be noticed consciously but which nevertheless evoke a response* (Scientific American). **2.** too weak or small to be felt or noticed: *a subliminal stimulus.* —*n.* the subconscious. [< *sub-* + Latin *līmen, -inis* threshold + English *-al*[1]] —**sub·lim′i·nal·ly,** *adv.*

subliminal advertising, an advertising technique in which messages are flashed so fast on a television or motion-picture screen that the viewer does not see them consciously but absorbs them through the subconscious mind: *Subliminal advertising's major use will be for "reminder advertising" for a product already known to the public. It could not promote new products where fairly complex explanations are needed* (Wall Street Journal).

sub·lim·i·ty (sə blim′ə tē), *n., pl.* **-ties. 1.** lofty excellence; grandeur; majesty; exalted state: *There was an awful sublimity in the hoarse murmuring of the thunder* (Francis Parkman). **2.** something sublime; sublime person or thing: *The soul ... retains an obscure sense Of possible sublimity* (Wordsworth).

sub·li·mize (sub′lə mīz), *v.t.*, **-mized, -miz·ing.** to make sublime; elevate; exalt.

sub·lin·e·ar (sub lin′ē ər), *adj.* **1.** nearly linear. **2.** placed below a written or printed line: *Hebrew has sublinear vowel signs.*

sub·lin·e·ate (sub lin′ē āt), *v.t.*, **-at·ed, -at·ing.** to underline; underscore. [< *sub-* + *lineate*]

sub·lin·e·a·tion (sub′lin ē ā′shən), *n.* the act of sublineating.

sub·lin·gual (sub ling′gwəl), *Anatomy.* —*adj.* situated under or on the under side of the tongue: *a sublingual gland, artery, cyst, etc.* —*n.* a sublingual gland, artery, etc. [< *sub-* + *lingual*]

sub·lit·er·ar·y (sub′lit′ə rer′ē), *adj.* of, having to do with, or characteristic of subliterature: *Even aficionados of murder fiction will concede, in a moment of honesty, that except in the hands of a few writers it has been a subliterary product* (Charles J. Rolo).

sub·lit·er·ate (sub lit′ər it), *adj.* below the accepted standard of literacy; semi-educated: *Subliterate, they were not in any sense skilled and therefore could not earn good wages* (New Scientist). —*n.* a subliterate person.

sub·lit·er·a·ture (sub′lit′ər ə chůr, -chər; -lit′rə-), *n.* **1.** writings with little or no literary merit; substandard literature: *The Tarzan books ... from a lofty view ... are subliterature* (Edmund Fuller). **2.** written accounts, such as laboratory reports, discussions, etc., that are mimeographed or printed in impermanent form for use within the organization that prints them.

sub·lit·to·ral (sub lit′ər əl), *adj.* **1.** near the seacoast: *a sublittoral plant.* **2.** of or having to do with the area of an ocean from low tide to the edge of the continental shelf.

sub·lu·nar (sub lü′nər), *adj.* sublunary: *He still believed that comets were meteorological (sublunar) phenomena* (New York Times).

sub·lu·nar·y (sub′lü ner′ē, sub lü′nər-), *adj.* beneath the moon; earthly: *the vanity of all sublunary things* (Benjamin Disraeli). *The Van Allen radiation belt is the chief feature of sublunary space and the most important discovery of space research so far* (New Scientist). [< New Latin *sublunaris,* ultimately < Latin *sub-* under + *lūna* moon]

sub·lu·nate (sub lü′nāt), *adj.* almost crescent-shaped: *a sublunate mark.*

sub·lux·ate (sub luk′sāt), *v.t.*, **-at·ed, -at·ing.** to dislocate partially: *The patient is told ... that his troubles are due to just one thing: a subluxated vertebra* (Maclean's).

sub·lux·a·tion (sub′luk sā′shən), *n.* a partial dislocation; sprain: *Do you shrug off shooting pains in the wrist, ascribing them to a mere passing subluxation of the radial head?* (Punch). [< New Latin *subluxatio, -onis* < Latin *sub-* under, away + *luxāre* dislocate]

sub·ma·chine gun (sub′mə shēn′), a small light, automatic or semiautomatic gun, designed to be fired from the shoulder or hip.

sub·mar·gin·al (sub mär′jə nəl), *adj.* **1.** below the margin; not up to the minimum standard: *submarginal housing, submarginal intelligence.* **2.** not productive enough to be worth cultivating, developing, etc.: *submarginal farm land. Lots of Soviet land is submarginal by U.S. standards* (Wall Street Journal). **3.** *Biology.* near the margin or edge of a body or organ. —**sub·mar′gin·al·ly,** *adv.*

sub·ma·rine (*n., v.* sub′mə rēn; *adj.* sub′-mə rēn′), *n., v.,* **-rined, -rin·ing,** *adj.* —*n.* **1.** a boat that can operate under water for discharging torpedoes, often armed also with ballistic missiles: *The submarine may soon become, as Adm. Louis Denfeld put it in 1949: "The dreadnought of the deep . . . the capital ship of the future"* (Newsweek). **2. a.** an organism that lives under water. **b.** anything designed to be used under water, such as a mine or other explosive device.

Atomic Submarine, Nautilus

—*v.t.* to attack, damage, or sink by a submarine. —*v.i. Football.* to charge very low against and upset a lineman.

—*adj.* **1.** of or carried out by a submarine or submarines: *submarine tactics, submarine warfare, a submarine attack.* **2.** placed, growing, or used below the surface of the sea: *submarine plants, a submarine mine.* **3.** of, occurring, or carried on below the surface of the sea: *The continental terrace is one of the main subjects of investigation in submarine geology today* (Scientific American).

submarine chaser, a small, fast warship for pursuing and destroying submarines. It is usually smaller than a destroyer.

submarine pen, an underground shelter along the shore for docking and refueling submarines. Many partly exposed submarine pens are reinforced with concrete. *Russian submarines have been slipping out from submarine pens in nearby Albania* (Newsweek).

sub·ma·rin·er (sub′mə rē′nər; -mar′ə nər), *n.* a member of the crew of a submarine: *Sealed inside a steel prison, the submariner is bored stiff for weeks at a time* (Time).

sub·ma·rin·ism (sub′mə rē′niz əm), *n.* the policy or practice of using submarines, especially on a large scale or without restriction in warfare.

sub·ma·rin·ist (sub′mə rē′nist), *n.* an advocate of the practice of using submarines in warfare.

sub·max·il·la (sub′mak sil′ə), *n., pl.* **-max·il·lae** (-mak sil′ē). the lower jaw or lower jawbone in man and other vertebrates. [< Latin *sub-* under + *maxilla* maxilla]

sub·max·il·lar·y (sub mak′sə ler′ē), *n., pl.* **-lar·ies,** *adj.* —*n.* **1.** the lower jawbone. **2.** a salivary gland situated beneath the lower jawbone on either side.

—*adj.* **1.** of, having to do with, or beneath the lower jaw or lower jawbone: a submaxillary fracture. **2.** having to do with the submaxillary gland.

submaxillary gland, either of a pair of salivary glands beneath the lower jaw.

sub·me·di·an (sub mē′dē ən), *adj.* situated near but not at the middle.

sub·me·di·ant (sub mē′dē ənt), *n. Music.* **1.** the tone next above the dominant in the scale. **2.** a key in which the submediant is the tonic: *The slow movement was in the submediant.*

sub·men·tum (sub men′təm), *n.* the lower part of the labium in insects.

[< New Latin *submentum* < Latin *sub-* under + *mentum* chin]

sub·merge (səb mėrj′), *v.,* **-merged, -merg·ing.** —*v.t.* **1.** to put under water; cover with water: *The flooded river submerged most of the farmland in the valley.* **2.** to cover; bury: *His talent was submerged by his shyness.* —*v.i.* **1.** to sink under water; go below the surface of a body of water: *The submarine submerged to escape enemy attack.* **2.** to sink out of sight; be lost to view. [< Latin *submergere* < *sub-* under + *mergere* to plunge] —**Syn.** *v.t.* **1.** plunge, immerse, submerse.

sub·merged (səb mėrjd′), *adj.* **1.** sunk under water or beneath the surface of something. **2.** living in extreme poverty and misery: *the submerged classes of society.* **3.** *Botany.* growing under water.

sub·mer·gence (səb mėr′jəns), *n.* **1.** the act of submerging. **2.** the state of being submerged.

sub·mer·gi·bil·i·ty (səb mėr′jə bil′ə tē), *n.* submersibility.

sub·mer·gi·ble (səb mėr′jə bəl), *adj., n.* submersible.

sub·merse (səb mėrs′), *v.t., v.i.,* **-mersed, -mers·ing.** to submerge. [< Latin *submersus,* past participle of *submergere;* see SUBMERGE]

sub·mersed (səb mėrst′), *adj.* **1.** submerged. **2.** *Botany.* growing under water, as the leaves of aquatic plants.

sub·mers·i·bil·i·ty (səb mėr′sə bil′ə tē), *n.* the quality or state of being submersible.

sub·mers·i·ble (səb mėr′sə bəl), *adj.* that can be submerged: *To preserve future catches, Millot is designing a large submersible cage* (Scientific American). —*n. Obsolete.* a submarine.

sub·mer·sion (səb mėr′zhən, -shən), *n.* **1.** a submerging. **2.** a being submerged.

sub·me·tal·lic (sub′mə tal′ik), *adj.* imperfectly or partially metallic.

sub·mi·cron (sub mī′kron), *n.* a particle that is smaller than a micron, or 10,000 to 20,000 times smaller than a millimeter: *Finest glass fibers ever made may serve to screen out submicron dust and particles such as would result from atomic explosions* (Science News Letter).

sub·mi·cro·scop·ic (sub′mī krə skop′ik), *adj.* so tiny or minute as to be invisible through the normal microscope: *It is composed of submicroscopic cigar-shaped particles of iron* (Scientific American).

sub·mil·li·me·ter (sub mil′ə mē′tər), *adj.* smaller than a millimeter.

sub·min·i·a·ture (sub min′ē ə chər, min′ə-), *adj.* smaller than the standard small size: *A subminiature radio receiver, small enough to be plugged into an ear* (Science News Letter).

sub·min·i·a·tur·i·za·tion (sub min′ē ə-chər ə zā′shən, -min′ə chər-), *n.* **1.** the act or process of subminiaturizing: *From time to time complete new technologies are evolved —subminiaturization of electronic circuits is a current example* (New Scientist). **2.** the state of being subminiaturized.

sub·min·i·a·tur·ize (sub min′ē ə chə rīz, -min′ə chə-), *v.t.,* **-ized, -iz·ing.** to reduce to subminiature size.

sub·min·i·mal (sub min′ə məl), *adj.* below the minimum; not up to the minimum standard: *Oklahoma, despite ample resources, maintains a subminimal public education program* (New York Times).

sub·miss (səb mis′), *adj. Archaic.* submissive; humble: *In adoration at his feet I fell submiss* (Milton). [< Latin *submissus,* past participle of *submittere;* see SUBMIT]

sub·mis·sion (səb mish′ən), *n.* **1. a.** a submitting; yielding to the power, control, or authority of another: *The defeated general showed his submission by giving up his sword.* **b.** the condition or an instance of having submitted. **2.** obedience; humbleness: *He bowed in submission to the king's order.* **3. a.** a referring or being referred to the consideration or judgment of another or others. **b.** something submitted to another for decision or consideration: *The Government Departments have contributed letters, reports and submissions to the Queen* (Sunday Times). *They spitefully submitted a sonnet by Keats. This was returned as speedily as the other submissions* (Maclean's).

[< Latin *submissiō, -ōnis* a lowering < *submittere;* see SUBMIT]

—**Syn. 1. a.** compliance, acquiescence, surrender.

sub·mis·sion·ist (səb mish′ə nist), *n.* a person who believes in or advocates submission: *It were well for them if they had no contact with the timorous submissionists . . . who abound in these streets* (London Times).

sub·mis·sive (səb mis′iv), *adj.* yielding to the power, control, or authority of another; inclined to submit; obedient; humble: *He was proud, when I praised, he was submissive when I reproved him; but he did never love me* (Charles Lamb). *Between the overstrict and the easygoing fathers, Dr. Block found striking personality differences. The restrictive men were submissive, indecisive, . . . and unconfident* (Newsweek). —**sub·mis′sive·ly,** *adv.* —**sub·mis′sive·ness,** *n.*

sub·mit (səb mit′), *v.,* **-mit·ted, -mit·ting.** —*v.i.* to yield to the power, control, or authority of another or others; surrender; yield: *The thief submitted to arrest by the police. He submitted to the decision of fate with . . . humility* (G. K. Chesterton). —*v.t.* **1.** to refer to the consideration or judgment of another or others: *The secretary submitted a report of the last meeting.* **2.** to represent or urge in a respectful manner: *I submit that more proof is needed to support the case.* **3. a.** to yield (oneself) to the power, control, or authority of a person or agency. **b.** to cause (a thing) to be subordinated to another. [< Latin *submittere* < *sub-* under + *mittere* let go, send]

—**Syn.** *v.i.* comply, succumb, bow. See **yield.** —**Ant.** *v.i.* resist.

sub·mit·tal (səb mit′əl), *n.* the act of submitting.

sub·mit·ter (səb mit′ər), *n.* a person who submits.

sub·mol·e·cule (sub mol′ə kyül), *n.* a particle smaller than a molecule: *DNA molecules are made up of two very long strands connected to each other by hundreds of thousands of short submolecules, which are set in place like the rungs of a ladder* (Time).

sub·mon·tane (sub mon′tān), *adj.* under or beneath a mountain or mountains; of or at the foothills or lower slopes. [< *sub-* + *montane*] —**sub·mon′tane·ly,** *adv.*

sub·mu·co·sa (sub′myü kō′sə), *n., pl.* **-sae** (-sē). the connective tissue lying beneath the mucous membrane.

sub·mu·co·sal (sub′myü kō′səl), *adj.* submucous: *These lesions appeared submucosal in location* (New Yorker).

sub·mu·cous (sub myü′kəs), *adj.* of or having to do with the submucosa; beneath the mucosa.

sub·mul·ti·ple (sub mul′tə pəl), *n.* a number or quantity that divides another without a remainder; factor. —*adj.* being or having to do with such a number or quantity.

sub·mun·dane (sub mun′dān), *adj.* existing under the world; underground; subterranean.

sub·mus·cu·lar (sub mus′kyə lər), *adj.* situated beneath a muscle.

sub·nar·cot·ic (sub′när kot′ik), *adj.* (of a drug) moderately narcotic.

sub·nor·mal (sub nôr′məl), *adj.* **1.** below normal; less than normal: *a subnormal temperature, subnormal sales.* **2.** inferior to the normal, as in mental capacity: *a subnormal person.* —*n.* a subnormal individual: *Most subnormals require schooling to the age of sixteen because of mental and social immaturity* (Sunday Times).

sub·nor·mal·i·ty (sub′nôr mal′ə tē), *n.* the quality or condition of being subnormal.

sub·nu·cle·ar (sub nü′klē ər, -nyü′-), *adj.* smaller than a nucleus; smaller than known nuclear particles: *The restless genius of man, standing midway between the boundless fields of interstellar space and the tiny, teeming jungles of subnuclear particles* (Newsweek).

sub·ob·so·lete (sub ob′sə lēt), *adj. Zoology.* nearly obsolete; almost disappearing.

sub·o·ce·an·ic (sub′ō shē an′ik), *adj.* existing, formed, or occurring beneath the ocean.

sub·oc·tave (sub′ok′tiv, -tāv), *n. Music.* the octave below a given note.

sub·of·fice (sub′ôf′is, -of′-), *n.* a branch office: *After the November presidential election the NAACP announced plans to open many small suboffices in the Negro slums of Northern and Southern cities* (Charles A. Ford).

sub·of·fi·cer (sub′ôf′ə sər, -of′-), *n.* a subordinate officer.

sub·or·bit·al (sub ôr′bə təl), *adj.* **1.** *Anatomy.* situated below the orbit of the eye, or on the floor of the orbit, as a cartilage, nerve, etc. **2.** of less than a full orbit: *a suborbital launch of an astronaut in the nose-cone of a rocket* (Science News Letter). —*n.* a suborbital cartilage, nerve, etc.

sub·or·der (sub′ôr′dər, sub ôr′-), *n. Biology.* a group of plants or animals ranking above a family and below an order. Organisms are classified into classes, subclasses, orders, suborders, families, subfamilies, genera, subgenera, species, and subspecies.

sub·or·di·na·cy (sə bôr′də nə sē), *n.* a subordinate position or state; subordination.

sub·or·di·nal (sə bôr′də nəl), *adj.* of, having to do with, or ranked as a suborder.

sub·or·di·nar·y (sub ôr′də ner′ē), *n., pl.* **-nar·ies.** *Heraldry.* any of various simple charges or bearings regarded as less important than the ordinaries.

sub·or·di·nate (*adj., n.* sə bôr′də nit; *v.* sə-bôr′də nāt), *adj., n., v.,* **-nat·ed, -nat·ing.** —*adj.* **1.** inferior in rank: *In the army, lieutenants are subordinate to captains.* **2.** in-

ferior in importance; secondary; minor: *An errand boy has a subordinate position.* **3.** under the control or influence of something else. **4.** *Grammar.* **a.** dependent. **b.** subordinating. *Because, since, if, as,* and *whether* are subordinate conjunctions. **5.** *Obsolete.* submissive.
—*n.* a subordinate person or thing: *Platoons of subordinates jump when he twitches* (Time).
—*v.t.* to place in a lower order or rank; make subject to or dependent on: *A polite host subordinates his wishes to those of his guests. He to whose will our wills are to be subordinated* (Thomas Carlyle).
[< Medieval Latin *subordinatus,* past participle of *subordinare* < Latin *sub-* under + *ordināre* arrange, put in order < *ōrdō, -inis* order]
—**Syn.** *adj.* **3.** subject, subservient.

subordinate clause, a dependent clause. A complex sentence has one main (independent) clause and one or more subordinate clauses: In "If I go home, my dog will follow me," *If I go home* is a subordinate clause.

sub·or·di·nat·ing (sə bôr′də nā′ting), *adj.* joining a subordinate clause to a main clause: *a subordinating conjunction.*

sub·or·di·na·tion (sə bôr′də nā′shən), *n.* **1.** the act of subordinating. **2.** the state of being subordinated. **3.** subordinate position or importance. **4.** submission to authority; willingness to obey; obedience. —**Syn.** **3.** subjection. **4.** subservience, dependence.

sub·or·di·na·tion·ism (sə bôr′də nā′shə niz əm), *n. Theology.* the doctrine that the second and third persons of the Trinity are inferior to the first.

sub·or·di·na·tion·ist (sə bôr′də nā′shə nist), *n.* a believer in the doctrine of subordinationism. —*adj.* of or having to do with this doctrine.

sub·or·di·na·tive (sə bôr′də nā′tiv), *adj.* tending to subordinate; involving or expressing subordination or dependence.

sub·orn (sə bôrn′), *v.t.* **1. a.** to get by bribery or other unlawful means. **b.** to obtain (evidence) by such means. **2.** to persuade or cause (a witness) to give false testimony in court: *He had no case without suborning witnesses* (George Meredith). **3. a.** to persuade (a person) to do an evil deed. **b.** to make disloyal; corrupt. [< Latin *subornāre* suborn; (originally) equip < *sub-* under + *ornāre* equip] —**sub·orn′er,** *n.*

sub·or·na·tion (sub′ôr nā′shən), *n.* **1.** a suborning: *A perjury as bloody as that of Oates and Bedlow; — a subornation as audacious* (Edmund Burke). **2.** a being suborned.

subornation of perjury, *Law.* the crime of persuading or causing a witness to give false testimony in court.

sub·or·na·tive (sə bôr′nə tiv), *adj.* having to do with subornation.

sub·ox·id (sub ok′sid), *n.* suboxide.

sub·ox·ide (sub ok′sīd, -sid), *n.* a compound of oxygen and another element or radical, containing a small proportion of oxygen.

sub-par (sub′pär′), *adj.* **1.** below average: *A New York importer claims a Turkish trader sent him a shipment of sub-par sunflower seeds; he wants . . . damages* (Newsweek). **2.** (in golf) under par: *Continuing his sub-par play . . . the British open champion had a point total of 22* (New York Times).

subpar., subparagraph.

sub·par·a·graph (sub par′ə graf, -gräf), *n.* a secondary or supplementary paragraph.

sub·pe·na (sə pē′nə), *n., v.,* **-naed, -na·ing.** subpoena.

sub·phy·lum (sub′fī′ləm, sub fī′-), *n., pl.* **-la** (-lə). *Biology.* a main division of a phylum.

sub·plot (sub′plot′), *n.* a minor or subordinate plot in a play, novel, etc.; underplot: *When several of the subplots must somehow be tied together, the work shows strain and becomes contrived* (New Yorker).

sub·poe·na (sə pē′nə), *n., v.,* **-naed, -na·ing.** *Law.* —*n.* an official written order commanding a person to appear in court. A subpoena is delivered by an officer of the court to the person specified in it, who becomes liable to penalty for failure to comply with it. *Mr. Bell has said that if necessary he will call the corporation officers on subpoena* (London Times). —*v.t.* to summon with a subpoena; serve a subpoena on. Also, **subpena.** [< Medieval Latin *sub poena,* the first words of the writ < Latin *sub* under + *poenā,* ablative of *poena* penalty]

sub·po·lar (sub pō′lər), *adj.* **1.** below or adjoining the poles of the earth in latitude. **2.** beneath the pole of the heavens: *the subpolar passage of a star.*

sub-post office (sub′pōst′), *British.* a branch of a post office.

sub·po·ten·cy (sub pō′tən sē), *n. Biology.* a lessening in the power to transmit inherited characteristics.

sub·po·tent (sub pō′tənt), *adj.* having or exhibiting subpotency.

sub·pre·fect (sub prē′fekt), *n.* an assistant or deputy prefect.

sub·pre·fec·ture (sub prē′fek chər), *n.* **1.** the office or position of a subprefect. **2.** a division of a prefecture.

sub·prin·ci·pal (sub prin′sə pəl), *n.* **1.** an assistant or deputy principal of a school, university, etc. **2.** an auxiliary rafter in the framework of a roof. **3.** *Music.* a subbass of the open diapason class in an organ.

sub·pri·or (sub′prī′ər), *n.* the deputy or assistant of a prior. [< Medieval Latin *subprior* < *sub-* sub- + Latin *prior* prior]

sub·pro·fes·sion·al (sub′prə fesh′ə nəl, -fesh′nəl), *adj.* **1.** below what is professional; not up to the professional level: *subprofessional talent. In a number of other schools, parents, student teachers, or other subprofessional personnel are being brought into use* (Wall Street Journal). —*n.* a person who engages in subprofessional work: *Subprofessionals already were functioning in the Department of Labor's . . . project concerned with youth unemployment* (Joel Allison).

sub·pro·gram (sub′prō′gram, -grəm), *n.* in computers: **1.** a part of a program. **2.** subroutine (def. 2).

sub·ra·mose (sub rā′mōs, sub′rə mōs′), *adj. Botany.* branching only slightly.

sub·re·gion (sub′rē′jən), *n.* a division or subdivision of a geographical region, especially with reference to animal distribution.

sub·re·gion·al (sub rē′jə nəl), *adj.* of or having to do with a subregion.

sub·rep·tion (sub rep′shən), *n.* **1.** the suppression of facts in order to obtain something, as ecclesiastical dispensation, preferment, etc. **2.** a fallacious or deceptive representation or an inference derived from it. [< Latin *subreptiō, -ōnis* < *subripere* remove secretly, steal < *sub-* under + *rapere* snatch. Compare SURREPTITIOUS.]

sub·rep·ti·tious (sub′rep tish′əs), *adj.* **1.** obtained by subreption. **2.** clandestine or surreptitious. —**sub′rep·ti′tious·ly,** *adv.*

sub·res·in (sub rez′ən), *n.* the part of a resin which dissolves in boiling alcohol, and is deposited as the alcohol cools.

sub·ro·gate (sub′rə gāt), *v.t.,* **-gat·ed, -gat·ing.** **1.** to put (a person) into the place of another in respect to a legal right or claim. **2.** to substitute (a thing) for another. Also, **surrogate.** [< Latin *subrogāre* (with English *-ate*[1]) < *sub-* under, away + *rogāre* to pray]

sub·ro·ga·tion (sub′rə gā′shən), *n.* the act of subrogating; process by which a person who pays a debt for another acquires the rights of the creditor to whom he pays it.

sub ro·sa (sub rō′zə), in strict confidence; privately: *A few . . . had purchased in a sub rosa sort of way neckties which remained to be exhibited in public* (Harper's). [< Latin *sub* under, *rosā,* ablative of *rosa* rose (because it was apparently an ancient symbol of secrecy)]

sub·rou·tine (sub′rü tēn′), *n.* **1.** a part of a routine. **2.** a sequence of instructions directing an electronic computer to carry out a well-defined mathematical or logical operation.

sub·salt (sub′sôlt′), *n.* a basic salt.

sub·sat·el·lite (sub sat′ə līt), *n.* an object orbited inside an artificial earth satellite and then ejected.

sub·scap·u·lar (sub skap′yə lər), *adj.* beneath, or on the anterior surface of, the scapula: *a subscapular gland or artery.* —*n.* a subscapular muscle, artery, etc.

sub·scrib·a·ble (səb skrī′bə bəl), *adj.* that can be subscribed to: *The new bond is subscribable only by holders of 2⅞ per cent bonds* (New York Times).

sub·scribe (səb skrīb′), *v.,* **-scribed, -scrib·ing.** —*v.t.* **1. a.** to promise to give or pay (a sum of money): *He subscribed $50 to the hospital fund.* **b.** to give or pay (money) in fulfillment of such a promise. **2.** to write (one's name, etc.) at the end of a document, etc.: *The old man subscribed his mark at the end of the will.* **3. a.** to sign one's name to (a document, etc.); show one's consent, approval, etc.: *Thousands of citizens subscribed the petition.* **b.** to attest (a statement, will, etc.) by signing. **4.** *Obsolete.* to give one's consent, approval, or support to; sanction: *Orestes . . . chose rather to encounter the rage of an armed multitude, than to subscribe the ruin of an innocent people* (Edward Gibbon). —*v.i.* **1. a.** to promise to give or pay money: *to subscribe to several charities.* **b.** to give or pay money in fulfillment of such a promise; contribute. **2.** to promise to take and pay for a number of copies of a newspaper, magazine, etc.: *We subscribe to a few magazines. I am subscribing for some of the books of a book club.* **3.** to give one's consent, approval, or support: *He will not subscribe to anything unfair. I do not expect you to subscribe to my opinion.* **4.** to sign one's name to something to show agreement, approval, etc., or as a witness: *John Hancock was the first man to subscribe to the Declaration of Independence.*
[< Latin *subscrībere* < *sub-* under + *scrībere* write]

sub·scrib·er (səb skrī′bər), *n.* a person who subscribes: *The magazines make a special offer to new subscribers.*

sub·script (sub′skript), *adj.* **1.** written underneath or low on the line. **2.** *Mathematics.* of or having to do with a subindex.
—*n.* a number, letter, or other symbol written underneath and usually to one side of the number, letter, or symbol to which it applies. In H_2SO_4 the *2* and *4* are subscripts.
[< Latin *subscrīptus,* past participle of *subscrībere;* see SUBSCRIBE]

sub·scrip·tion (səb skrip′shən), *n.* **1.** a subscribing. **2. a.** the money subscribed; contribution: *His subscription to the Fresh Air Fund was $5.* **b.** *British.* dues for a society, club, etc. **3.** the right to receive a magazine, newspaper, etc., obtained by subscribing a certain sum: *Your subscription expires next week.* **4.** a sum of money raised by a number of persons; fund: *We are raising a subscription for a new hospital.* **5.** something written at the end of a document, etc.; signature. **6.** a signing, as of one's name or a document. **7.** a signed declaration, statement, or other document. **8.** consent, agreement, or support given by signing one's name. **9. a.** assent to a set of articles of faith, principles, or doctrines which are intended to further uniformity. **b.** (in the Church of England) assent to the Thirty-nine Articles of 1563 and the Book of Common Prayer.

subscription book, 1. a book containing the names of subscribers, along with the amounts of their subscription: *Less than 48 hours after brokers opened subscription books on the largest financial dealing in history, the entire issue had been snapped up* (Newsweek). **2.** a book sold by subscription. **3.** a book of tickets for a series of events: *Twenty-five Loft's Candy Shops will sell subscription books for the 1955 series of Stadium Concerts* (New York Times).

subscription television, television broadcasting that is paid for by the viewers. To prevent nonsubscribers from viewing the programs the pictures are transmitted scrambled and decoded by a device on the set of a subscriber.

sub·scrip·tive (səb skrip′tiv), *adj.* **1.** of or having to do with a subscription or signature. **2.** having to do with the subscribing of money. —**sub·scrip′tive·ly,** *adv.*

sub·sea (sub sē′), *adj.* undersea; submarine: *They might have seeped up through the sediments from subsea oil deposits* (Scientific American).

subsec., subsection.

sub·sec·tion (sub′sek′shən), *n.* a part or division of a section.

sub·sen·si·ble (sub sen′sə bəl), *adj.* deeper than the range of the senses; too deep or subtle for the senses to grasp.

sub·sep·tate (sub sep′tāt), *adj.* not perfectly septate; having an incomplete septum.

sub·se·quence (sub′sə kwəns), *n.* **1.** the fact or condition of being subsequent. **2.** a subsequent event or circumstance; sequel.

sub·se·quen·cy (sub′sə kwən sē), *n., pl.* **-cies.** subsequence.

sub·se·quent (sub′sə kwənt), *adj.* coming after; following; later: *Subsequent events proved that he was right. The story will be continued in subsequent issues of the magazine.*
subsequent to, after; following; later than: *on the day subsequent to your visit.*
[< Latin *subsequēns, -entis,* present participle of *subsequī* < *sub-* from under + *sequī* follow] —**sub′se·quent·ness,** *n.*

sub·se·quen·tial (sub′sə kwen′shəl), *adj.* subsequent.

sub·se·quent·ly (sub′sə kwənt lē), *adv.* afterward; later: *At first we thought we would go; subsequently we learned we were needed at home.*

subsequently to, after; following; later than: *In North America ... the large quadrupeds lived subsequently to that period* (Erasmus Darwin).

sub·serve (səb sėrv′), *v.t.*, **-served, -serv·ing.** to be of use or service in helping along (a purpose, action, function, etc.): *Chewing food well subserves digestion. Liberty is to be subserved whatever occurs* (Walt Whitman). *When words no longer subserve thought but are granted a value of their own equal to that of thought itself, the mediocre mind is sorely tempted to use them, to the detriment of constructive thinking* (Atlantic). [< Latin *subservīre* < *sub-* under + *servīre* serve]

sub·ser·vi·ence (səb sėr′vē əns), *n.* **1.** slavish politeness and obedience; tame submission; servility. **2.** a being of use or service.

sub·ser·vi·en·cy (səb sėr′vē ən sē), *n.* subservience.

sub·ser·vi·ent (səb sėr′vē ənt), *adj.* **1.** slavishly polite and obedient; tamely submissive; servile: *The lawyers had been subservient beyond all other classes to the Crown* (John R. Green). **2.** useful as a means to help a purpose or end; serviceable (to): *A street of small shops subservient to the needs of poor people* (W. Somerset Maugham). **3.** subordinate or subject (to). [< Latin *subserviēns, -entis,* present participle of *subservīre;* see SUBSERVE] —**sub·ser′vi·ent·ly,** *adv.*
—**Syn. 1.** obsequious, truckling.

sub·set (sub′set′), *n. Mathematics.* a set that is part of another set or series of terms: *A subset of S is a set every element of which belongs to S.*

sub·shrub (sub′shrub′), *n.* a plant with a somewhat woody base; small shrub; undershrub.

sub·shrub·by (sub′shrub′ē), *adj.* like a subshrub; suffruticose.

sub·side (səb sīd′), *v.i.*, **-sid·ed, -sid·ing. 1.** to grow less; become less active; die down: *The storm finally subsided. Her fever subsided after she took the medicine. Her anger now subsiding into grief* (Frances Burney). **2.** to sink to a low or lower level: *Once the rain stopped, the flood waters subsided.* **3.** to sink or fall to the bottom; settle. **4.** to sink down, as into a chair, etc. [< Latin *subsīdere* < *sub-* down + *sīdere* to settle] —**Syn. 1.** abate, decrease, ebb, wane.

sub·sid·ence (səb sī′dəns, sub′sə-), *n.* the act or process of subsiding: *the subsidence of a flood.*

sub·sid·i·ar·i·ly (səb sid′ē er′ə lē), *adv.* in a subsidiary manner or position; secondarily; subordinately.

sub·sid·i·ar·y (səb sid′ē er′ē), *adj., n., pl.* **-ar·ies.** —*adj.* **1.** useful to assist or supplement; auxiliary; supplementary: *The teacher sold books as a subsidiary occupation.* **2.** subordinate; secondary: *a subsidiary issue. Only as a subsidiary reason does the message advocate more trade to help assure our own economic growth* (Wall Street Journal). **3.** maintained by or depending on a subsidy or subsidies.
—*n.* **1.** a person or thing that assists or supplements. **2.** a company having over half of its stock owned or controlled by another company: *The bus line was a subsidiary of the railroad.* **3.** *Music.* a secondary theme or subject.
[< Latin *subsidiārius* < *subsidium* reserve troops; see SUBSIDY]

sub·si·dise (sub′sə dīz), *v.t.*, **-dised, -dis·ing.** *Especially British.* subsidize: *The Government could tax the excess profits of commercial television and use the money to subsidise another noncommercial programme* (Observer).

sub·si·di·za·tion (sub′sə də zā′shən), *n.* **1.** a subsidizing. **2.** a being subsidized.

sub·si·dize (sub′sə dīz), *v.t.*, **-dized, -diz·ing. 1.** to aid or assist with a grant of money or by guaranteeing a market: *The government subsidizes steamship and air lines that carry mail. Many universities subsidize research and publications.* **2.** to buy the aid or assistance of with a grant of money. **3.** to bribe. [< *subsid*(y) + *-ize*]

sub·si·diz·er (sub′sə dī′zər), *n.* a person who subsidizes.

sub·si·dy (sub′sə dē), *n., pl.* **-dies. 1.** a grant or contribution of money by a government, corporation, individual, etc., in support of an undertaking or the upkeep of a thing: *a subsidy for education. Under the price-support program, the farmer is given a subsidy to encourage him to produce surpluses* (Newsweek). **2.** money formerly granted to the sovereign by the British Parliament to meet special needs. [< Anglo-French *subsidie,* learned borrowing from Latin *subsidium* aid, reserve troops < *sub-* under + *sedēre* to sit]

sub si·len·ti·o (sub sī len′tē ō), *Latin.* in silence; without a remark being made; without notice being taken: *Sometimes passing a thing sub silentio is evidence of consent* (John Bouvier).

sub·sist (səb sist′), *v.i.* **1.** to continue to be; exist: *Many superstitions still subsist. A club cannot subsist without members.* **2.** to keep alive; live: *People in the far north subsist on fish and meat.* **3.** *Philosophy.* **a.** to stand as fact or truth; hold true. **b.** to be logically necessary, probable, or conceivable. **4.** *Obsolete.* to continue in a condition or position; remain as such. —*v.t.* to provide for; feed; support. [< Latin *subsistere* stand firm; support < *sub-* up to + *sistere* to stand < *stāre* to stand]

sub·sist·ence (səb sis′təns), *n.* **1.** continued existence; continuance. **2.** the state or fact of keeping alive; living: *Selling papers was the poor old man's only means of subsistence.* **3.** a means of support; livelihood: *The sea provides a subsistence for fishermen.* **4.** *Philosophy.* **a.** the individualizing of substance, especially as a particular rational (human) being standing apart from all others but possessing certain rights, powers, etc., in common with all others of the same type. **b.** the condition of subsisting. **5.** *Obsolete.* the condition or quality of inhering or residing (in something). [< Late Latin *subsistentia* < Latin *subsistēns, -entis,* present participle of *subsistere;* see SUBSIST]

subsistence farming, farming that produces only the minimum amount of food necessary to sustain the farmer and his family, with little or no surplus or profit: *A settled community now enjoys a cash crop instead of the insecurity of crude subsistence farming* (Manchester Guardian Weekly).

sub·sist·ent (səb sis′tənt), *adj.* existing of or by itself; existing; subsisting.

sub·soil (sub′soil′), *n.* the layer of earth that lies just under the surface soil: *Below this layer is a gradual transition to a yellowish stratum of clay. This layer usually is thick and is called subsoil* (Fred W. Emerson). —*v.t.* to plow, till, or dig so as to cut into the subsoil. —**sub′soil′er,** *n.*

sub·so·lar (sub sō′lər), *adj.* **1.** directly underneath the sun; having the sun in the zenith. **2.** terrestrial; mundane. **3.** between the tropics.

sub·son·ic (sub son′ik), *adj.* **1.** having to do with or designed for use at a speed less than that of sound. **2.** that moves at a speed slower than that of sound: *Supersonic speed propellers for subsonic planes were designed and promise higher speeds for conventional airplanes* (Science News Letter). —**sub·son′i·cal·ly,** *adv.*

sub spe·ci·e ae·ter·ni·ta·tis (sub spē′shē ē ē tėr′nə tā′tis), *Latin.* under the form of eternity; in its essential form or character.

sub·spe·cies (sub′spē′shēz, sub spē′-), *n., pl.* **-cies. 1.** a subdivision of a species: *We include within the Mongoloid subspecies three major races: the Asiatic Mongoloid, the Indonesian-Malay, and the American Indian* (Beals and Hoijer). **2.** *Biology.* a group of plants or animals ranking below a species.

sub·spe·cif·ic (sub′spi sif′ik), *adj.* of, having to do with, or like a subspecies. —**sub′spe·cif′i·cal·ly,** *adv.*

sub·spher·i·cal (sub sfer′ə kəl), *adj.* not completely spherical; spheroidal: *... subspherical curvatures* (Scientific American).

subst., 1. substantive. **2.** substitute.

sub·stage (sub′stāj′), *n.* **1.** a subdivision of a stage: *The specimens come from different substages of the same [geological] formation* (Charles Darwin). **2.** a device beneath the ordinary stage of a compound microscope to support mirrors and other accessories.

sub·stance (sub′stəns), *n.* **1.** what a thing consists of; matter; material: *Ice and water are the same substance in different forms. The wool-gray air is all about him like a living substance* (Thomas Wolfe). **2.** the real, main, or important part of anything; essence: *The substance of an education is its effect on your life, not just learning lessons.* **3.** the real meaning; gist: *Give the substance of the speech in your own words.* **4.** solid quality; body: *Pea soup has more substance than water.* **5.** wealth; property; possessions: *a man of substance. He spent his substance in book stores.* **6.** a particular kind of matter; stuff: *a chemical substance, a pond covered with a green substance. This variety of substances, which compose the internal parts of our globe* (Oliver Goldsmith). **7.** *Philosophy.* **a.** something that underlies all phenomena, and in which accidents or attributes inhere; something that receives modifications and is not itself a mode. **b.** something that subsists by itself; separate or distinct thing.

in substance, a. essentially; substantially; mainly: *In substance, obviously, this is a moving story* (New Yorker). **b.** really; actually: *We know that the monarchy did not survive the hierarchy, no, not even in appearance, for many months; in substance, not for a single hour* (Edmund Burke).

[< Old French *substance,* learned borrowing from Latin *substantia* < *substāre* stand firm; be present < *sub-* up to + *stāre* stand]

—**Syn. 1. Substance, matter, material** mean what a thing consists or is made of. **Substance** means what a thing consists of, as apart from the form in which it exists, and applies both to things existing in the physical world and to those given form only in the mind: *The substance of the plan is good.* **Matter** applies to any substance that occupies space and that physical objects consist of: *Matter may be gaseous, liquid, or solid.* **Material** applies to any matter from which something is made: *Oil is an important raw material.* **3.** purport.

sub·stance·less (sub′stəns lis), *adj.* without substance; unsubstantial.

sub·stand·ard (sub stan′dərd, sub′stan′-), *adj.* **1.** below standard: *Basically furnished quarters (may for a time be substandard but adequate) at low rentals* (London Times). **2.** *Law, U.S.* below the standard required by law and not so labeled. **3.** not conforming to the accepted standards of speech or writing.

sub·stan·tial (səb stan′shəl), *adj.* **1.** real; actual: *People and things are substantial; dreams and ghosts are not.* **2.** large; important; ample: *a substantial profit. He made a substantial improvement in arithmetic.* **3.** providing ample or abundant nourishment: *to eat a substantial breakfast.* **4.** strong; firm; solid: *a house substantial enough to last a hundred years.* **5.** in the main; or for the most part; in essentials: *The stories told by the two boys were in substantial agreement.* **6.** well-to-do; wealthy; influential: *He ... introduced us to a number of substantial-looking middle-aged civilians* (New Yorker). **7.** of real or solid worth or value; weighty; sound: *substantial criticism, substantial evidence. The substantial comforts of a good coal fire* (Mary R. Mitford). **8. a.** being a substance; being real. **b.** essential; material: *the substantial truth of the story* (John Hay). **9.** *Philosophy.* of, having to do with, or inherent in substance, rather than accident.
—*n.* **substantials,** something substantial: *His judgment in substantials, like that of Johnson, is always worth having* (Lowell).
[< Latin *substantiālis* < *substantia;* see SUBSTANCE] —**sub·stan′tial·ness,** *n.*

sub·stan·tial·ism (səb stan′shə liz əm), *n. Philosophy.* **1.** the doctrine that substantial realities or real substances underlie all phenomena. **2.** the doctrine that matter is a tangible substance and is definable in terms of weight and volume, rather than energy, interacting fields of force, etc., even in its smallest particles.

sub·stan·tial·ist (səb stan′shə list), *n.* an adherent of a doctrine of substantialism.

sub·stan·ti·al·i·ty (səb stan′shē al′ə tē), *n., pl.* **-ties. 1.** real existence. **2.** solidity; firmness. **3.** real worth or value. **4.** something substantial; substantial article of food.

sub·stan·tial·ize (səb stan′shə līz), *v.t.*, **-ized, -iz·ing.** to make substantial; give reality to.

sub·stan·tial·ly (səb stan′shə lē), *adv.* **1.** essentially; mainly: *This report is substantially correct.* **2.** really; actually. **3.** strongly; solidly: *a substantially built house.*

sub·stan·tials (səb stan′shəlz), *n.pl.* See under **substantial,** *n.*

sub·stan·ti·ate (səb stan′shē āt), *v.t.*, **-at·ed, -at·ing. 1.** to establish by evidence; prove; verify: *to substantiate a rumor, a claim, or a theory; ... one of the most fully* *substantiated of historical facts* (James H. Robinson). *Many of these theories could be disproved or substantiated* (Saturday Review). **2.** to give concrete or substantial form to; embody. **3.** to give substantial existence to; make physically real. —**Syn. 1.** See **confirm.**

sub·stan·ti·a·tion (səb stan′shē ā′shən), *n.* a substantiating or being substantiated; embodiment; proof: *For those who want to believe in this sort of thing, the case has a number of impressive substantiations* (Newsweek).

sub·stan·ti·a·tive (səb stan′shē ā′tiv), *adj.* serving to substantiate.

sub·stan·ti·a·tor (səb stan′shē ā′tər), *n.* a person who substantiates.

sub·stan·ti·fy (sub′stən tə fī), *v.t.*, **-fied, -fy·ing.** to substantivize.

sub·stan·ti·val (sub′stən tī′vəl), *adj.* of, having to do with, or consisting of a substantive or substantives. —**sub′stan·ti′val·ly,** *adv.*

sub·stan·tive (sub′stən tiv), *n. Grammar.* **1.** a noun. *Abbr.:* subst. **2.** any word or group of words functioning like a noun.
—*adj.* **1.** *Grammar.* **a.** used like a noun. **b.** (of verbs) showing or expressing existence. The verb *to be* is a substantive verb. **2.** standing of or by itself; independent; self-sufficient. **3. a.** real; actual; essential: *The substantive issue of what constitutes forbidden political activity has rarely been faced* (Bulletin of Atomic Scientists). **b.** substantial. **4.** having a firm or solid basis. **5.** (of dyes) not requiring a mordant, but adhering directly to the material. **6.** *Law.* dealing with rights rather than the procedures of obtaining them.
[< Latin *substantīvus* < *substantia;* see SUBSTANCE] —**sub′stan·tive·ness,** *n.*

sub·stan·tive·ly (sub′stən tiv li), *adv.* **1.** independently. **2.** actually; in substance; in effect. **3.** as a substantive.

sub·stan·tiv·ize (sub′stən tə vīz), *v.t.*, **-ized, -iz·ing.** to make a substantive of; use as a substantive

sub·sta·tion (sub′stā′shən), *n.* a branch station; subordinate station: *The main post office in our city has six substations.*

sub·stit·u·ent (səb stich′u̇ ənt), *Chemistry.* —*n.* an atom or group of atoms taking the place of another atom or group in a compound. —*adj.* having to do with such an atom or group of atoms. [< Latin *substituēns, -entis,* present participle of *substituere;* see SUBSTITUTE]

sub·sti·tut·a·bil·i·ty (sub′stə tü′tə bil′ə tē, -tyü′-), *n.* the quality or condition of being substitutable: *There is a high degree of substitutability among types of loans and lending institutions* (New York Times).

sub·sti·tut·a·ble (sub′stə tü′tə bəl, -tyü′-), *adj.* that can be substituted: *It will always bear a regular proportion to that of other substitutable food* (William Taylor).

sub·sti·tute (sub′stə tüt, -tyüt), *n., v.,* **-tut·ed, -tut·ing,** *adj.* —*n.* **1.** a thing used instead of another; person taking the place of another: *Margarine is a substitute for butter. A substitute taught us at school today.* **2.** a person who took the place of a draftee in the army or navy, usually for pay, as in the American Civil War. **3.** *Grammar.* a word or other linguistic form which under certain circumstances replaces any one of a class of other words or linguistic forms.
—*v.t.* **1.** to put in place of: *We substituted brown sugar for molasses in these cookies.* **2.** to take the place of: *For real wit he is obliged to substitute vivacity* (Oliver Goldsmith).
—*v.i.* **1.** to take the place of another; be a substitute: *The retired teacher substituted for our regular teacher, who was sick.* **2.** *Chemistry.* to replace one or more equivalents of an element or radical by a like number of equivalents of another.
—*adj.* put in for or taking the place of another.
[< Latin *substitūtus,* past participle of *substituere* < *sub-* under + *statuere* establish < *stāre* stand]
—**Syn.** *n.* **1.** expedient; alternate. *-v.t., v.i.* **1.** replace.

sub·sti·tu·tion (sub′stə tü′shən, -tyü′-), *n.* **1.** the use of one thing for another; putting (one person or thing) in the place of another; taking the place of another. **2.** *Chemistry.* the replacing of one or more elements or radicals in a compound by other elements or radicals.

sub·sti·tu·tion·al (sub′stə tü′shə nəl, -tyü′-), *adj.* **1.** having to do with or characterized by substitution. **2.** acting or serving as a substitute. —**sub′sti·tu′tion·al·ly,** *adv.*

sub·sti·tu·tion·ar·y (sub′stə tü′shə ner′ē, -tyü′-), *adj.* substitutional.

sub·sti·tu·tive (sub′stə tü′tiv, -tyü′-), *adj.* **1.** having to do with or involving substitution. **2.** serving as, or capable of serving as, a substitute.

sub·stra·ta (sub strā′tə, -strat′ə), *n.* a plural of **substratum.**

sub·stra·tal (sub strā′təl), *adj.* underlying; fundamental.

sub·strate (sub′strāt), *n.* **1.** a substratum. **2.** *Biochemistry.* the material that an enzyme or ferment acts upon.

sub·stra·tive (sub strā′tiv), *adj.* forming a substratum; underlying.

sub·strat·o·sphere (sub strat′ə sfir, -strā′tə-), *n.* the region of the earth's atmosphere just below the stratosphere, an altitude high enough to require special aids for flying, as oxygen masks, pressurized aircraft cabins, and superchargers.

sub·stra·tum (sub strā′təm, -strat′əm), *n., pl.* **-ta** or **-tums. 1.** a layer lying under another: *Beneath the sandy soil there was a substratum of clay ten feet thick.* **2.** a layer of earth lying just under the surface soil; subsoil. **3.** basis; foundation: *The story has a substratum of truth.* **4.** *Biology.* the base or matter on which an organism develops. **5.** *Metaphysics.* something that is regarded as supporting attributes or accidents; substance in which qualities inhere or from which phenomena derive: *Substances (in the phenomenon) are the substrata of all determinations of time* (Immanuel Kant). [< New Latin *substratum,* neuter of Latin *substrātus,* past participle of *substernere* < *sub-* under + *sternere* to spread]

sub·struc·tion (sub struk′shən), *n.* an under structure, as of a building; foundation; substructure. [< Latin *substrūctiō, -ōnis* < *substruere* construct beneath < *sub-* under + *struere* build]

sub·struc·tur·al (sub struk′chər əl), *adj.* of, having to do with, or like a substructure.

sub·struc·ture (sub′struk′chər, sub-struk′-), *n.* **1.** the underlying and supporting structure of a building; foundation. **2.** the base of earth, concrete, stone, etc., upon which the ballast of a railroad is laid or the superstructure of a bridge is built. **3.** anything like this; groundwork; basis: *a substructure for religious belief.*

sub·sul·tive (səb sul′tiv), *adj.* characterized by sudden leaps or starts; jerky; convulsive: *subsultive earthquake shocks.* [< Latin *subsultus,* past participle of *subsilīre* leap up (< *sub-* under + *salīre* leap) + English *-ive*]

sub·sul·to·ry (səb sul′tər ē), *adj.* subsultive.

sub·sume (səb süm′), *v.t.*, **-sumed, -sum·ing. 1.** to bring (an idea, term proposition, etc.) under another; bring (a case, instance, etc.) under a rule. **2.** to take up into, or include in, a larger or higher class or the like. [< New Latin *subsumere* < Latin *sub-* under + *sūmere* assume, take]

sub·sump·tion (səb sump′shən), *n.* **1. a.** a subsuming. **b.** a being subsumed. **2. a.** *Logic.* a proposition subsumed under another; minor premise. **b.** an assumption. [< New Latin *subsumptio, -onis* < *subsumere;* see SUBSUME]

sub·sump·tive (səb sump′tiv), *adj.* of or involving subsumption.

sub·sur·face (sub sėr′fis), *adj.* under the surface; underlying; underground: *subsurface nuclear tests, subsurface rock, water, or oil.* —*n.* the space or matter immediately below the surface.

sub·sys·tem (sub′sis′təm, sub sis′-), *n.* **1.** a part or subdivision of a system. **2.** *Aerospace.* a component system within a major system of a missile or rocket: *Flight tests demonstrate the compatibility of airframe, engine, and autopilot subsystems* (Air Force Report on the Ballistic Missile).

sub·tan·gent (sub tan′jənt), *n. Geometry.* the part of the axis of a curve cut off between the tangent and the ordinate of a given point in the curve.

sub·teen (sub′tēn), *adj. Informal.* of or for subteen-agers: *a subteen dance or party.* —*n.* a subteen-ager.

sub·teen-ag·er (sub tēn′ā′jər), *n. Informal.* a boy or girl nearly thirteen years old.

sub·tem·per·ate (sub tem′pər it), *adj.* of, having to do with, or found in the colder regions of the temperate zone.

sub·ten·an·cy (sub ten′ən sē, sub′ten′-), *n., pl.* **-cies.** the status, right, or holding of a subtenant.

sub·ten·ant (sub ten′ənt, sub′ten′-), *n.* a tenant of a tenant; person who rents land, a house, etc., from a tenant.

sub·tend (səb tend′), *v.t.* **1.** to extend under; stretch across; be opposite to: *The chord of an arc subtends the arc.* **2.** *Botany.* to enclose in the angle between a leaf or bract and its stem. [< Latin *subtendere* < *sub-* under + *tendere* to stretch]

Subtend (def. 1) Chord AC subtends arc ABC.

sub·tense (səb tens′), *n. Geometry.* the chord of an arc or any other subtending line.

subter-, *prefix.* underneath; beneath; below; less than, as in *subterconscious, subterposition.* [< Latin *subter,* related to *sub* under, beneath]

sub·ter·con·scious (sub′tər kon′shəs), *adj.* subconscious. [< *subter-* + *conscious*]

sub·ter·fuge (sub′tər fyüj), *n.* a trick, excuse, or expedient used to escape something unpleasant: *The girl's headache was only a subterfuge to avoid taking the examination.* [< Late Latin *subterfugium* < Latin *subterfugere* to escape < Latin *subter* beneath + *fugere* flee] —**Syn.** artifice, ruse.

sub·ter·nat·u·ral (sub′tər nach′ər əl), *adj.* below what is natural; less than natural. [< *subter-* + *natural*]

sub·ter·po·si·tion (sub′tər pə zish′ən), *n.* the state of being placed or of lying underneath something else; position underneath.

sub·ter·rane (sub′tə rān), *n.* **1.** *Geology.* the bedrock under a deposit. **2.** an underground cave, chamber, or dwelling. [< Latin *subterrāneus* < *sub-* under + *terra* earth]

sub·ter·ra·ne·an (sub′tə rā′nē ən), *adj.* **1.** beneath the earth's surface; underground: *A subterranean passage led from the castle to the cave. Collins had been searching for a new entrance to Mammoth Cave, the biggest of the subterranean caverns in the limestone deposits of central Kentucky* (Newsweek). **2.** carried on secretly; hidden: *subterranean plotting.* —*n.* a person who lives or works underground: *The strange, sad subterraneans who lived and died in the city beneath the sea* (Punch). [< Latin *subterrāneus* (< *sub-* under + *terra* earth) + English *-an*]
—**Syn.** *adj.* **2.** clandestine, surreptitious.

sub·ter·ra·ne·ous (sub′tə rā′nē əs), *adj.* underground. —**sub′ter·ra′ne·ous·ly,** *adv.* —**sub′ter·ra′ne·ous·ness,** *n.*

sub·ter·res·tri·al (sub′tə res′trē əl), *adj.* underground; subterranean.

sub·ter·sur·face (sub′tər sėr′fis), *adj.* lying below the surface; subsurface. [< *subter-* + *surface*]

sub·ter·tian malaria (sub tėr′shən), falciparum malaria.

sub·thresh·old (sub thresh′ōld, -hōld), *adj.* below the point where a given stimulus is perceptible or two stimuli can be differentiated: *The Subliminal Projection process is a method of conveying an advertising message to the subthreshold area of the human mind* (Bulletin of Atomic Scientists).

sub·tile (sut′əl, sub′təl), *adj.* **1.** not dense or heavy; thin; delicate; rare: *a subtile liquid, a subtile fabric, a subtile powder. . . . after living . . . within the subtile influence of an intellect like Emerson's* (Hawthorne). **2.** *Archaic.* subtle: *And with such subtile toils enveloped him* (Robert Southey). [< Middle French *subtil,* learned borrowing from Latin *subtīlis.* Compare SUBTLE.] —**sub′tile·ly,** *adv.* —**sub′tile·ness,** *n.*

sub·til·i·ty (sub til′ə tē), *n., pl.* **-ties.** *Archaic.* subtlety.

sub·til·i·za·tion (sut′ə lə zā′shən, sub′tə-), *n.* **1.** a subtilizing. **2.** a being subtilized.

sub·til·ize (sut′ə līz, sub′tə-), *v.,* **-ized, -iz·ing.** —*v.t.* to make subtle; introduce subtleties into. —*v.i.* to make subtle distinctions; argue or reason in a subtle manner; split hairs: *Men . . . who subtilize upon the commonest duties until they no longer appear binding* (Oliver Goldsmith).

sub·til·ty (sut′əl tē, sub′təl-), *n., pl.* **-ties.** subtlety.

sub·ti·tle (sub′tī′təl), *n., v.,* **-tled, -tling.** —*n.* **1.** an additional or subordinate title of a book or article. **2. a.** a repetition of the

chief words of the full title of a book at the top of the first page of text. **b.** a half title. **3.** a word or words shown on a motion-picture screen rather than spoken, as a line of dialogue, an identification or description of the scene to come, etc.; caption.
—*v.t.* to furnish with a subtitle or subtitles: *This delightful, cheerful collection might easily be subtitled grim fairy tales for adults* (Harper's).

sub·tle (sut′əl), *adj.* **1.** very fine; thin; delicate: *a subtle odor of perfume, subtle distinctions. Subtle humor is hard to understand.* **2.** faint; mysterious: *a subtle smile or wink* **3.** having a keen, quick mind; discerning; acute: *a subtle observer of slight differences* **4.** sly; crafty; tricky: *a subtle scheme to get some money.* **5.** skillful; clever; expert: *a subtle craftsman in gold and silver, a subtle design* **6.** working unnoticeably or secretly; insidious: *a subtle poison or drug.* [< Old French *soutil* < Latin *subtīlis*] —**sub′tle·ness,** *n.* —**Syn. 1.** tenuous, rare. **3.** discriminating. **4.** artful, cunning, insidious, wily.

sub·tle·ty (sut′əl tē), *n., pl.* **-ties. 1.** subtle quality: *Guides cannot master the subtleties of the American joke* (Mark Twain). *His style is artfully simple and flowing, his portraiture full of subtlety and charm* (Atlantic). **2.** something subtle; cunning; craft: *The laws were violated by power, or perverted by subtlety* (Edward Gibbon).

sub·tly (sut′lē), *adv.* in a subtle manner; with subtlety.

sub·ton·ic (sub ton′ik), *n. Music.* the seventh tone of a scale; tone next below the upper tonic; leading tone.

sub·to·pi·a (sub tō′pē ə), *n.* countryside that has developed into an industrial urban area: *Harrow-on-the-Hill is . . . a linear ridge-top town above green fields on either side, a simultaneous oasis of both town and country in a sea of subtopia* (Observer).

sub·to·pi·an (sub tō′pē ən), *adj.* of or characteristic of a subtopia: *. . . subtopian wastes of semidetached houses and bungaloid growths left by the industrialists of the nineteenth century, and the 'spec' builders of the twentieth* (Manchester Guardian).

sub·top·ic (sub′top′ik), *n.* a subordinate or secondary topic, included under a major topic.

sub·tor·rid (sub tôr′id, -tor′-), *adj.* subtropical.

sub·to·tal (sub′tō′təl), *adj., n., v.,* **-taled, -tal·ing** or (*especially British*) **-talled, -tal·ling.** —*adj.* not quite total; less than complete: *Subtotal counts will be handed to the press every 30 minutes* (New York Times).
—*n.* something less than the total; a partial sum: *The figure you see is a subtotal and not the final amount.*
—*v.t.* **1.** to find the subtotal of: *Subtotal the third column of figures.* **2.** to amount to the subtotal of: *This column of figures subtotals 107,963.*

sub·tract (səb trakt′), *v.t., v.i.* **1.** to take away: *Subtract 2 from 10 and you have 8.* **2.** to take away (something) from a whole. [< Latin *subtractus,* past participle of *subtrahere* < *sub-* from under + *trahere* draw] —**sub·tract′er,** *n.*
—**Syn. 1, 2. Subtract, deduct** mean to take away. **Subtract** means to take away from a whole, but in present usage is not very frequently used except in its mathematical sense, commonly meaning to take away one number from another: *He subtracted 89 from 200.* **Deduct** means to take away a quantity or amount from a total or whole: *He deducted the price of the dishes I broke from the amount he owed me. The butcher deducted 89 cents in tax from the delivery boy's wage of $10.*

sub·trac·tion (səb trak′shən), *n.* **1.** the act or process of subtracting one number or quantity (subtrahend) from another (minuend); finding the difference between two numbers or quantities: *10−2=8 is a simple subtraction.* **2. a.** a taking away. **b.** a being taken away.

sub·trac·tive (səb trak′tiv), *adj.* **1.** tending to subtract; having power to subtract. **2.** to be subtracted; having the minus sign (−).

subtractive process, a process in color photography, in which two or more colorants are used to absorb, in varying degree, their complementary colors from white light.

sub·tra·hend (sub′trə hend), *n.* a number or quantity to be subtracted from another number or quantity (minuend): *In 10−2=8, the subtrahend is 2.* [< Latin *subtrahendus* to be subtracted, gerundive of *subtrahere;* see SUBTRACT]

sub·treas·ur·y (sub′trezh′ər ē, -trā′zhər-; sub trezh′-, -trā′zhər-), *n., pl.* **-ur·ies. 1.** a branch treasury. **2.** any branch of the United States treasury.

sub·tribe (sub′trīb′), *n.* a division of a tribe, especially of animals or plants.

sub·trip·li·cate (sub trip′lə kit), *adj.* (of a ratio or proportion) being that of the cube roots of the quantities. *Example:* 2 : 3 is the subtriplicate ratio of 8 : 27.

sub·trop·ic (sub trop′ik), *adj.* subtropical.

sub·trop·i·cal (sub trop′ə kəl), *adj.* **1.** bordering on the tropics. **2.** characteristic of subtropical regions; almost tropical: *swimming in warm, subtropical waters . . .* (London Times).

sub·trop·ics (sub′trop′iks, sub trop′-), *n. pl.* a region or regions bordering on the tropics.

sub·type (sub′tīp′), *n.* a subordinate type; type included in a general type.

sub·typ·i·cal (sub tip′ə kəl), *adj.* **1.** of or having to do with a subtype. **2.** not quite typical, or true to the type.

su·bu·late (sü′byə lit), *adj. Biology.* slender, more or less cylindrical, and tapering to a point; awlshaped: *a subulate leaf.* [< New Latin *subulatus* < Latin *sūbula* awl]

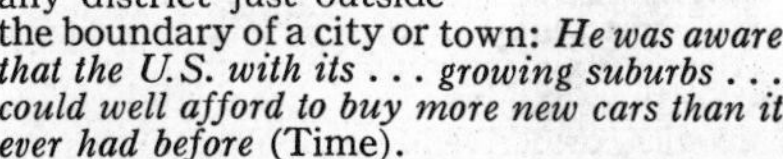
Subulate Leaves of juniper

sub·u·nit (sub yü′nit), *n.* a lower or secondary unit; unit of a unit.

sub·urb (sub′ərb), *n.* **1.** a town, village, or other community just outside a city or larger town. **2.** any district just outside the boundary of a city or town: *He was aware that the U.S. with its . . . growing suburbs . . . could well afford to buy more new cars than it ever had before* (Time).
the suburbs, a residential section or sections near the boundary of a city or town; outlying parts; outskirts: *Many people who work in the city live in the suburbs.*
[< Old French *suburbe,* learned borrowing from Latin *suburbium* < *sub-* below + *urbs, urbis* city]

sub·ur·ban (sə bėr′bən), *adj.* **1.** of, having to do with, or in a suburb: *a suburban school, a suburban shopping center. We have excellent suburban train service.* **2.** characteristic of a suburb or its inhabitants: *suburban life.* —*n.* a suburbanite.

sub·ur·ban·ite (sə bėr′bə nīt), *n.* a person who lives in a suburb: *Suburbanites who get carried away by "do-it-yourself" projects often get carried away, period!* (Newsweek).

sub·ur·ban·i·za·tion (sə bėr′bə nə zā′shən), *n.* the act or process of suburbanizing or being suburbanized: *The suburbanization of American life and growth of the middle class* (Harper's).

sub·ur·ban·ize (sə bėr′bə nīz), *v.t.,* **-ized, -iz·ing.** to make suburban: *to suburbanize a district, suburbanize a rural village.*

sub·ur·bi·a (sə bėr′bē ə), *n.* **1. a.** the suburbs of a particular city or town. **b.** suburbs in general: *In our part of suburbia, there's a get-together somewhere almost every week* (Maclean's). **2.** people who live in the suburbs; suburbanites.

sub·ur·bi·car·i·an (sə bėr′bə kãr′ē ən), *adj.* of or having to do with the dioceses (now six in number) around Rome of which the Pope is metropolitan and whose bishops are cardinals. [< Late Latin *suburbicārius* (< Latin *suburbium;* see SUBURB) + English *-an*]

sub·va·ri·e·ty (sub′və rī′ə tē), *n., pl.* **-ties.** a subordinate or minor variety, especially of a domestic animal or cultivated plant.

sub·vene (səb vēn′), *v.i.,* **-vened, -ven·ing.** to come as a relief, remedy, etc., or in support. [< Latin *subvenīre;* see SUBVENTION]

sub·ven·tion (səb ven′shən), *n.* **1.** money granted to aid or support some cause, institution, or undertaking; subsidy: *A subvention will insure the publication of his doctoral thesis.* **2. a.** the providing of help, support, or relief. **b.** an instance of this. [< Late Latin *subventiō, -ōnis* < Latin *subvenīre* come to one's aid < *sub-* under + *venīre* come]

sub·ven·tion·ar·y (səb ven′shə ner′ē), *adj.* of or like a subvention.

sub ver·bo (sub vėr′bō), *Latin.* under the word; under the heading (directing the reader to a reference). *Abbr.:* s.v.

sub·ver·sal (səb vėr′səl), *n.* subversion.

sub·ver·sion (səb vėr′zhən, -shən), *n.* **1.** a subverting or being subverted; overthrow; destruction; ruin: *They steer clear of harsher reprisals and keep the road open for victory by the more classic means of subversion* (Newsweek). **2.** anything that tends to overthrow or destroy; cause of ruin: *. . . protecting from subversion either from within or without* (E. H. Litchfield). [< Late Latin *subversiō, -ōnis* < Latin *subvertere;* see SUBVERT]

sub·ver·sive (səb vėr′siv), *adj.* tending to overthrow; causing ruin; destructive: *He was rearrested on an old indictment charging him with being a member of a subversive organization advocating the forceful overthrow of the Government* (New York Times). —*n.* a person who seeks to overthrow or undermine a government, etc. —**sub·ver′sive·ly,** *adv.*

sub·vert (səb vėrt′), *v.t.* **1.** to overthrow; ruin; destroy: *Dictators subvert democracy.* **2.** to undermine the principles of; corrupt: *. . . those who would subvert a society* (Key Reporter). *A Red plan to subvert all Africa came to light* (Newsweek). [< Latin *subvertere* < *sub-* under + *vertere* to turn] —**sub·vert′er,** *n.*

sub·vert·i·ble (səb vėr′tə bəl), *adj.* that can be subverted.

sub·ver·ti·cal (sub vėr′tə kəl), *adj.* almost vertical.

sub·vo·cal (sub vō′kəl), *adj.* **1.** having to do with the formulation of words in the mind, with little or no vocal articulation. **2.** subaudible. —**sub·vo′cal·ly,** *adv.*

sub·way (sub′wā′), *n.* **1.** *U.S.* an electric railroad running beneath the surface of the streets in a city. See **third rail** for picture. **2.** an underground passage, tunnel, or way, as for conveying water pipes, gas pipes, telegraph wires, etc., or for pedestrians to pass from one area to another beneath a busy street, railroad station, etc.
➔ **subway** (def. 1). In England it is called an *underground;* in France and certain other European countries, it is called a *Metro.*

sub·ze·ro (sub′zir′ō, sub zir′ō), *adj.* **1.** below zero on the scale of a thermometer: *subzero temperatures.* **2.** characterized by or used in subzero temperatures: *subzero weather, subzero lubricants.*

sub·zone (sub′zōn′), *n.* a subdivision of a zone.

suc-, *prefix.* the form of **sub-** before *c,* as in *succeed.*

Su·car·yl (sü′kər əl), *n. Trademark.* **1.** a sweet-tasting, white, crystalline calcium salt, used as a substitute for sugar; cyclamate calcium: *A slab of strawberry chiffon pie, which, though it stands five inches high, contains fewer calories than an orange. The crust is made of egg white, Sucaryl, and artichoke flour* (New Yorker). *Formula:* $C_{12}H_{24}CaN_2O_6S_2$ **2.** a sweet-tasting, white, crystalline sodium salt, used as a substitute for sugar; cyclamate sodium. *Formula:* $C_6H_{11}NHSO_3Na$

suc·cah (sůk′ə, sů kä′), *n.* sukkah.

suc·ce·da·ne·ous (suk′sə dā′nē əs), *adj.* acting or serving as a substitute.

suc·ce·da·ne·um (suk′sə dā′nē əm), *n., pl.* **-ne·a** (-nē ə), **-ne·ums.** a substitute. [< New Latin *succedaneum,* neuter of Latin *succēdāneus* substituted, succeeding < *succēdere* go near to; see SUCCEED]

suc·ceed (sək sēd′), *v.i.* **1.** to turn out well; do well; have success: *His plans succeeded.* **2.** to accomplish what is attempted or intended: *to succeed in finding an empty seat. The attack succeeded beyond all expectations.* **3.** to come next after; follow another; take the place of another: *When Edward VIII abdicated, George VI succeeded to the throne.* **4.** to have (good or ill) success: *I have succeeded very badly* (George Macdonald). **5.** *Obsolete.* (of an estate, etc.) to devolve. —*v.t.* to come next after; take the place of; follow: *John Adams succeeded Washington as President. Week succeeds week.* [< Latin *succēdere* go after, go near to < *sub-* up or near + *cēdere* go] —**succeed′er,** *n.* —**Syn.** *v.i.* **1.** prosper, thrive, flourish. *-v.t.* See **follow.**

suc·cen·tor (sək sen′tər), *n. Ecclesiastical.* a precentor's deputy. [< Late Latin *succentor, -ōris* < Latin *succinere* sing so as to accompany < *sub-* under + *canere* sing]

suc·cès de scan·dale (sʏk se′ də skäɴ-dȧl′). *French.* **1.** a success due to scandal or notoriety; anything that wins popularity or profit by scandalizing the public or because of its connection with a scandal. **2.** (literally) success of scandal.

suc·cès d'es·time (sʏk se′ des tēm′), *French.* **1.** a play, novel, or other piece of writing that is praised by the critics but largely ignored by the public. **2.** critical acclaim accompanied by popular indifference: *The public's indifference . . . prevented it from having more than a succès d'estime, in spite of the extraordinary music* (Listener). **3.** (literally) success of esteem.

suc·cès fou (sʏk se′ fü′), *French.* **1.** a success marked by wild enthusiasm: *In France, where the antinovel is in, it has been a succès fou* (Punch). **2.** (literally) mad success.

suc·cess (sək ses′), *n.* **1.** a favorable result; wished-for ending; good fortune: *Success in school comes from intelligence and hard work. Success in one field does not assure success in another* (Newsweek). **2.** the gaining of wealth, position, or other advantage: *He has had little success in life.* **3.** a person or thing that succeeds: *The girl from the small village became a social success in the city. The party was a great success.* **4.** outcome; result; fortune: *What success did you have in finding a new apartment?* [< Latin *successus,* past participle of *succēdere;* see SUCCEED]

suc·cess·ful (sək ses′fəl), *adj.* **1.** having success; accomplishing what is desired or intended; ending in success: *a successful writer or book, a successful campaign. Many of these seeds are imperfect, but occasional ones give rise to successful plants* (Fred W. Emerson). **2.** having succeeded in gaining wealth, position, or other advantage; prosperous; fortunate: *a successful business man, a successful match or marriage.* —**suc·cess′ful·ly,** *adv.* —**suc·cess′ful·ness,** *n.*

suc·ces·sion (sək sesh′ən), *n.* **1.** a group of persons or things coming one after another; series: *a rapid succession of victories. A succession of accidents spoiled our automobile trip. Succession thus is the process of migration of one type of people after another into a given area, or the migration of one type of land usage after another into a particular area* (Emory S. Bogardus). **2.** the coming of one person or thing after another. **3.** the act, right, or process of succeeding to an office, property, or rank: *There was a dispute about the rightful succession to the throne.* **4.** a set or arrangement of persons having such a right of succeeding: *The king's oldest son is next in succession to the throne. As the Senate's president pro tem he stood fourth in line of succession to the presidency* (Time). **5.** *Law.* the legal change involved when a person succeeds to the rights and liabilities of a predecessor.

in succession, one after another: *Though she was there several days in succession he was never able to see her* (Edmund Wilson).

[< Latin *successiō, -ōnis* < *succēdere;* see SUCCEED]

—**Syn. 1.** See **series.**

suc·ces·sion·al (sək sesh′ə nəl), *adj.* **1.** of or having to do with succession. **2.** following or occurring in succession. **3.** passing by succession or descent. —**suc·ces′sion·al·ly,** *adv.*

succession duty or **tax,** *Especially British.* a tax on inherited property; inheritance tax.

suc·ces·sive (sək ses′iv), *adj.* **1.** coming one after another; following in order; consecutive: *It has rained for three successive weekends.* **2.** characterized by or involving succession. —**suc·ces′sive·ness,** *n.*

—**Syn. 1. Successive, consecutive** mean following one after another. **Successive** implies coming after one another in regular order: *He has worked on three successive Saturdays.* **Consecutive** implies coming after one another without interruption or a break: *He worked three consecutive days last week.*

suc·ces·sive·ly (sək ses′iv lē), *adv.* one after another; in order.

suc·cess·less (sək ses′lis), *adj.* without success; unsuccessful. —**suc·cess′less·ly,** *adv.* —**suc·cess′less·ness,** *n.*

suc·ces·sor (sək ses′ər), *n.* **1.** a person who follows or succeeds another in office, position, or ownership of property: *Andrew Johnson was Lincoln's successor as President.* **2.** a person or thing that comes next after another in a series. [< Latin *successor, -ōris < succēdere;* see SUCCEED]

suc·ces·sor·ship (sək ses′ər ship), *n.* the position or condition of a successor.

success story, 1. a real or fictitious narrative recounting the rise of someone, usually poor or unknown, to fame and fortune: *The Horatio Alger myth is the American archetype of the success story.* **2.** a person, thing, or event that achieves outstanding, and usually unexpected, success: *Among the major Protestant denominations in Canada, the United Church is the great success story of our times* (Maclean's).

suc·ci·nate (suk′sə nāt), *n.* a salt of succinic acid.

suc·cinct (sək singkt′), *adj.* **1.** expressed briefly and clearly; expressing much in few words; concise: *A tale should be judicious, clear, succinct* (William Cowper). *The memorandum was brief and succinct, with all the major points on one page* (Newsweek). **2.** characterized by brevity or conciseness: *a succinct writer, speaker, or style.* **3.** *Archaic.* (of garments) not full; close-fitting; short; scant. [< Latin *succinctus,* past participle of *succingere* tuck up clothes for action; to gird from below < *sub-* under + *cingere* gird] —**suc·cinct′ly,** *adv.* —**suc·cinct′ness,** *n.* —**Syn. 1.** compressed, condensed. See **concise. 2.** terse, curt.

suc·cinc·to·ri·um (suk′singk tôr′ē əm, -tōr′-), *n., pl.* **-to·ri·a** (-tôr′ē ə, -tōr′-). a vestment worn on solemn occasions by the Pope, similar in shape to a maniple, and hanging on his left side from the girdle or cincture. [< Late Latin *succinctorium* < Latin *sub-* under + *cinctorium* girdle < *cingere* gird]

suc·cinc·to·ry (suk singk′tər ē), *n., pl.* **-ries.** a succinctorium.

suc·cin·ic (suk sin′ik), *adj.* of, having to do with, or derived from amber. [< French *succinique* < Latin *succinum* amber, variant of *sūcinum*]

succinic acid, a colorless, crystalline dicarboxylic acid present in amber, but usually produced synthetically from tartaric acid, used in making dyes, perfumes, etc., and in photography. *Formula:* $C_4H_6O_4$

suc·cin·yl·cho·line chloride (suk′sə nəl-kol′ēn, -kō′lēn), a white, odorless crystalline powder, used to relax the muscles in surgery, treating shock, etc. *Formula:* $C_{14}H_{30}Cl_2N_2O_4.2H_2O$

suc·cin·yl·sul·fa·thi·a·zole (suk′sə nəl-sul′fə thī′ə zōl), *n.* a derivative of sulfathiazole, less toxic than sulfaguanidine, and used orally for the prevention and treatment of bacterial infections of the gastrointestinal tract. *Formula:* $C_{13}H_{13}N_3O_5S_2.H_2O$

suc·cise (sək sīs′), *adj. Botany.* appearing as if cut or broken off at the lower end. [< Latin *succīsus,* past participle of *succīdere* cut below < *sub-* under + *caedere* cut]

suc·cor (suk′ər), *n.* a person or thing that helps, relieves, or assists; help; aid; assistance. —*v.t.* to help, assist, or aid (a person, etc.) in time of need, distress, or danger; support; relieve: *Mr. Harding thought . . . of the worn-out, aged men whom he had succored* (Anthony Trollope). Also, *especially British,* **succour.** [< Anglo-French *succor,* Old French *succurre* < Medieval Latin *succursus, -us* < Latin *succurrere* run to help < *sub-* up (to) + *currere* run] —**suc′cor·er,** *n.*

suc·cor·a·ble (suk′ər ə bəl), *adj.* **1.** capable of being succored or relieved. **2.** *Archaic.* affording succor or relief.

suc·cor·less (suk′ər lis), *adj.* without succor, help, or relief.

suc·co·ry (suk′ər ē), *n.* chicory. [alteration of earlier *sycory* chicory]

Suc·cos (sůk′əs), *n.* Sukkoth.

suc·cose (suk′ōs), *adj.* juicy; succulent. [< Latin *succōsus* < *succus,* or *sūcus* juice]

suc·co·tash (suk′ə tash), *n.* kernels of sweet corn and beans, usually Lima beans, cooked together: *Since corn was their principal product, the Indians devised numerous ways of preparing it . . . They made succotash, a mixture of corn and beans boiled* (Science News Letter). [American English < Algonkian (Narragansett) *m'sickqatash* green corn boiled whole]

Suc·coth (sů kōth′), *n.* Sukkoth.

suc·cour (suk′ər), *n., v.t. Especially British.* succor.

suc·cu·ba (suk′yə bə), *n., pl.* **-bae** (-bē). succubus. [< Late Latin *succuba* strumpet < Latin, supplanter, rival; (literally) one lying under < *sub-* under + *cubāre* lie]

suc·cu·bus (suk′yə bəs), *n., pl.* **-bi** (-bī), **-bus·es. 1.** a demon in female form supposed to have carnal intercourse with men in their sleep. **2.** any evil spirit; demon. [< Medieval Latin *succubus* < Late Latin *succuba;* see SUCCUBA; patterned on *incubus*]

suc·cu·lence (suk′yə ləns), *n.* juiciness.

suc·cu·len·cy (suk′yə lən sē), *n.* succulence.

suc·cu·lent (suk′yə lənt), *adj.* **1.** full of juice; juicy: *a succulent peach.* **2.** interesting; not dull. **3.** *Botany.* having thick or fleshy and juicy leaves or stems, as the houseleek, cactuses, etc.

—*n.* a succulent plant: *Most desert surfaces carry a scattered grass growth, dotted with thorny shrubs and succulents* (White and Renner).

[< Latin *succulentus* < *succus,* or *sūcus* juice] —**suc′cu·lent·ly,** *adv.*

suc·cumb (sə kum′), *v.i.* **1.** to give way; yield: *He succumbed to the temptation and stole the money.* **2.** to die.

succumb to, to die of: *Mr. Picken has since succumbed to his injuries* (Pall Mall Gazette).

[< Latin *succumbere* < *sub-* down + *-cumbere* lie, related to *cubāre*]

suc·cur·sal (sə kėr′səl), *adj.* that is or is like a subsidiary or auxiliary: *A succursal church is dependent on the main church.* [< French *succursale* < Latin *succursus,* past participle of *succurrere;* see SUCCOR]

suc·cus (suk′əs), *n., pl.* **suc·ci** (suk′sī). **1.** the juice in the body. **2.** the extracted juice of a plant for use in medicine. [< Latin *succus* juice]

suc·cuss (sə kus′), *v.t.* **1.** to shake up. **2.** *Medicine.* to subject (a patient) to succussion. [< Latin *succussus,* past participle of *succutere* < *sub-* under + *quatere* shake]

suc·cus·sa·tion (suk′ə sā′shən), *n.* succussion.

suc·cus·sa·to·ry (sə kus′ə tôr′ē, -tōr′-), *adj.* succussive.

suc·cus·sion (sə kush′ən), *n.* **1.** a shaking or being shaken with violence. **2.** *Medicine.* a shaking of the body to detect the presence of fluid in the thorax or other cavity. [< Latin *succusiō, -ōnis* < *succutere;* see SUCCUSS]

suc·cus·sive (sə kus′iv), *adj.* characterized by a shaking motion, especially an up-and-down movement.

such (such), *adj.* **1.** of that kind; of the same kind or degree: *I have never seen such a sight.* **2.** of the kind that; of a particular kind: *She wore such thin clothes it is no wonder she caught cold.* **3.** of the kind already spoken of or suggested: *The ladies took only tea and coffee and such drinks.* **4.** so great, so bad, so good, etc.: *He is such a liar.* **5.** some; certain: *The bank was robbed in such and such a town by such and such persons.*

such as, a. of the kind or degree that; of a particular kind: *Her behavior was such as might be expected of a young child.* **b.** of a particular character or kind: *The food, such as it was, was plentiful.* **c.** for example: *members of the dog family, such as the wolf, fox, and jackal.*

—*pron.* **1.** such a person or thing; such persons or things: *Such as sit in darkness and in the shadow of death* (Psalm 107:10). *Take from the blankets such as you need.* **2.** such a person or thing, or such persons or things, now or before mentioned, described, etc.: *Such was the outcome of the debate.*

as such, a. as being what the name or description implies; in that capacity: *A leader, as such, deserves obedience.* **b.** in or by itself; intrinsically considered: *Mere good looks, as such, will not take you far.*

[Old English *swylc, swelc,* originally a compound of *swā* so + *līc* like. Compare WHICH.]

such·like (such′līk′), *adj.* of such kind; of a like kind; of the before-mentioned sort or character: *dreams, signs, and suchlike fanciful superstitions.* —*pron.* things of such kind; the like: *deceptions, disguises, and suchlike* (Joseph Conrad).

such·ness (such′nis), *n.* **1.** the state or quality of being such; a particular or characteristic quality. **2.** *Buddhism.* the state or quality of nature which transcends reality and is absolute and eternal: *. . . the essential Suchness of the world, which is at* *once immanent and transcendent* (Aldous Huxley).

suck (suk), *v.t.* **1.** to draw (liquid) into the mouth by contracting muscles of the lips, cheeks, and tongue so as to produce a partial vacuum: *Lemonade can be sucked through a straw.* **2. a.** to draw juice, etc., from with the mouth: *to suck an orange.* **b.** to draw with the mouth: *to suck juice from an orange.* **3.** to draw in the mouth and lick: *a baby sucking his thumb. The child sucked a lollipop.* **4.** to drink; take; absorb: *A sponge sucks in water. Plants suck up moisture from the earth.* **5.** to draw in; swallow: *The whirlpool sucked down the boat.* **6.** to render (as specified) by sucking. —*v.i.* **1.** to draw liquid, especially milk from the breast or a bottle, into the mouth by producing a partial vacuum. **2.** to draw or be drawn by sucking: *He sucked at his pipe. The crimson cheeks of the trumpeters sucked in and out* (Arnold Bennett). **3.** (of a pump) to draw air instead of water, as from low water or a defective valve: *The pump sucked noisily.*

suck up to, to curry favor with; toady to: *That* [*his strength*], *and his less enviable gifts for sucking up to the general foreman, got him made a ganger after a month* (Manchester Guardian).

—*n.* **1.** the act of sucking; suction by the mouth or other means: *The baby took one suck at the bottle and pushed it away.* **2.** the sound caused by sucking. **3.** milk or other substance drawn into the mouth by sucking. **4.** *Informal.* a small draft of liquid; sip. [Old English *sūcan*. Ultimately related to SOAK.]

suck·er (suk′ər), *n.* **1.** a person or thing that sucks with the mouth. **2.** a young mammal before it is weaned, especially a suckling pig. **3.** any of a family of North American freshwater fishes that have toothless, fleshy mouths adapted for sucking in food. **4.** an organ adapted for sucking or absorbing nourishment by suction, as the proboscis of an insect. **5.** a part or organ for adhering to an object, as that of a leech or snail: *The animal* [*tapeworm*] *clings to the inner wall of the alimentary canal by means of hooks and suckers . . .* (Hegner and Stiles). **6.** the piston of a suction pump. **7.** the valve of such a piston. **8.** a pipe or tube through which anything is drawn by suction. **9.** *Botany.* **a.** a shoot growing from an underground root. **b.** an adventitious shoot from the trunk or a branch of a tree or plant. **c.** one of the small roots of a parasitic plant; haustorium. **10.** *U.S. Slang.* **a.** a person easily deceived or duped; simpleton; greenhorn. **b.** a sponger; parasite. **11.** *Informal.* a lump of hard candy, especially a lollipop: *She was greeted by two little boys with suckers in their jaws* (New Yorker).

Common Redhorse Sucker (def. 3—about 12 in. long)

—*v.t.* **1.** to strip off suckers or shoots from; remove superfluous young shoots from (tobacco, corn, etc.). **2.** *U.S. Slang.* to treat as a fool or simpleton; deceive; dupe: *. . . suggested that what really surprised the Communists was that the U.N. and U.S. had allowed themselves to be suckered for so long* (Time). —*v.i.* to form or throw up suckers.

sucker bait, *U.S. Slang.* an enticement to attract a person in order to mislead or take advantage of him, especially in monetary matters: *They alluded constantly to bets on long shots and absurd propositions that even yokels recognize as sucker bait* (Saturday Evening Post).

suck·er·el (suk′ər əl), *n.* a long, slender sucker living in large steams and impounded lakes of the Mississippi valley, with a small head and bluish body. [diminutive of *sucker*]

suck·er·fish (suk′ər fish′), *n., pl.* **-fish·es** or (*collectively*) **-fish.** suckfish: *. . . the extraordinary custom of fisherfolk of using suckerfish for catching both green and hawksbill turtles* (Scientific American).

sucker list, *U.S. Slang.* a list of persons who can readily be misled or taken advantage of, especially in monetary matters.

Sucker State, a nickname of Illinois.

suck·fish (suk′fish′), *n., pl.* **-fish·es** or (*collectively*) **-fish. 1.** a fish of the western coast of the United States, having a sucker on the ventral side with which it clings to objects. **2.** any of certain fishes, found especially in tropical waters, which attach themselves to larger sea animals; remora.

suck·ing (suk′ing), *adj.* **1.** that sucks; not yet weaned. **2.** very young; immature; unfledged.

sucking louse, any of an order of wingless, bloodsucking lice that are parasitic on mammals and transmit many diseases, such as typhus fever.

Sucking Louse (Line shows actual length.)

suck·le (suk′əl), *v.,* **-led, -ling.** —*v.t.* **1.** to feed with milk from the breast, udder, etc.; give suck to; nurse: *The cat suckles her kittens.* **2.** to nourish; bring up: *suckled on the literature of Spain* (W. H. Hudson). *A Pagan suckled in a creed outworn* (Wordsworth). —*v.i.* to suck at the breast. [Middle English *sukle*, perhaps back formation < *suckling;* perhaps (frequentative) < Middle English *suken* suck]

suck·ler (suk′lər), *n.* **1.** a young animal not yet weaned; suckling. **2.** an animal that suckles its young; mammal.

sucklers, *British.* the flowering heads of clover: *a pasture of white sucklers.*

suck·ling (suk′ling), *n.* a very young animal or child, especially one not yet weaned: *babes and sucklings* (Psalms 8:2). —*adj.* **1.** very young: *a suckling pig.* **2.** not yet weaned; sucking. —**Syn.** *n.* nursling.

su·crase (sü′krās), *n.* invertase: *Deficiency of sucrase . . . explained the intolerance of some infants to cane sugar which contains sucrose* (Joseph B. Kirsner). [< French *sucre* sugar + English *-ase*]

su·crate (sü′krāt), *n. Chemistry.* a compound of a metallic oxide with a sugar: *calcium sucrate.* [< French *sucrate* < *sucre* sugar + *-ate* -ate[2]]

su·cre (sü′krā), *n.* **1.** the basic Ecuadorian monetary unit, worth 100 centavos, equal to about 5½ cents in U.S. currency. **2.** a silver coin or bank note worth this amount in the currency of Ecuador. [< Antonio José de *Sucre*, 1795-1830, a South American general and liberator]

su·cri·er (sʏ krē ā′), *n. French.* sugar bowl: *An eighteenth-century* [*porcelain*] *sucrier formed as an orange is obviously under oriental influence* (London Times).

su·crose (sü′krōs), *n.* a crystalline disaccharide sugar obtained from sugar cane, sugar beets, etc.; cane sugar; beet sugar; saccharose. Hydrolysis changes sucrose to fructose and glucose. *Formula:* $C_{12}H_{22}O_{11}$ [< French *sucre* sugar + English *-ose*[2]]

suc·tion (suk′shən), *n.* **1.** the production of a vacuum with the result that atmospheric pressure forces fluid into the vacant space or causes the adhesion of surfaces: *Lemonade is drawn through a straw by suction.* **2.** the forcing or drawing upward or inward of the fluid or adhesion of surfaces involved in this. **3.** the force caused by sucking out or removing part of the air in a space. **4.** any part or device, as a pipe, which effects, or operates by, suction, or by pressures less that that of the atmosphere.

—*adj.* **1.** causing a suction; working by suction: *a suction valve.* **2.** in which suction occurs; into or through which something is forced or drawn by suction: *a suction line.* [< Late Latin *sūctiō, -ōnis* < Latin *sūgere* to suck]

suction cup, a cup-shaped piece of rubber, plastic, glass, etc., that can stick to a surface by suction: *Mixing bowls . . . have been provided with a removable suction cup designed to hold them firmly to a table or counter* (Science News Letter).

suction pump, any of various types of pumps in which liquid is drawn into the line to the pump by suction, especially the common hand-operated water pump, in which downward and upward strokes of a piston create a partial vacuum in the line, into which water is forced by atmospheric pressure with each upward stroke. See diagram under **pump.**

suction stop, *Phonetics.* a stop which is released by inward suction, rather than the more usual outward explosion of the checked breath stream. The most familiar suction stops are clicks.

suc·to·ri·al (suk tôr′ē əl, -tōr′-), *adj.* **1.** adapted for sucking or adhering by suction. **2.** having organs adapted for feeding by sucking or adhering by suction. [< New Latin *suctorius* (< Latin *sūgere* to suck) + English *-al*[1]]

suc·to·ri·an (suk tôr′ē ən, -tōr′-), *n.* an animal with a mouth or other organ adapted for sucking or adhering by suction: *The lamprey, leech, and flea are examples of suctorians.*

suc·to·ri·ous (suk tôr′ē əs, -tōr′-), *adj.* suctorial.

sud (sud), *n.* the singular of **suds.**

su·dam·i·na (sü dam′ə nə), *n.pl. Medicine.* minute, whitish vesicles appearing on the skin in various fevers from the accumulation of sweat in the upper layers of the skin. [< New Latin *sudamina* < Latin *sūdāre* to sweat; see SUDATORY]

su·dam·i·nal (sü dam′ə nəl), *adj.* of or having to do with sudamina.

Su·dan (sü dan′), *n. Trademark.* any of a group of yellow, brown, and red dyes used to stain biological specimens and color oils, fats, etc.

Su·dan durra (sü dan′), a grain sorghum used for fodder; feterita.

Su·da·nese (sü′də nēz′), *adj., n., pl.* **-nese.** —*adj.* of or having to do with the Sudan, a country in Africa south of Egypt, or its inhabitants. —*n.* a native or inhabitant of the Sudan. Also, **Soudanese.**

Sudan grass, a variety of sorghum from the Sudan, grown in the United States for hay.

Su·dan·ic (sü dan′ik, -dä′nik), *adj.* of or denoting a grouping of languages of northern Africa, including Tshi, Mandingo, Yoruba, etc. —*n.* the Sudanic language group.

Su·dan·i·za·tion (sü′də nə zā′shən), *n.* the act or process of Sudanizing.

Su·dan·ize (sü′də nīz), *v.t.,* **-ized, -iz·ing.** to make Sudanese: *The British agreed to withdraw from the Sudan as soon as an independent provisional government could "Sudanize" the administration and write its own constitution* (Time).

su·dar·i·um (sü dãr′ē əm), *n., pl.* **-i·a** (-ē ə). **1.** the handkerchief of Saint Veronica miraculously impressed, according to legend, with the features of Christ when He wiped His face with it on the way to Calvary. **2.** a portrait of Christ on a cloth; veronica. **3.** any handkerchief (a humorous use): *The most intrepid veteran . . . dares no more than wipe his face with his cambric sudarium* (Sydney Smith). [< Latin *sūdārium* < *sūdor, -ōris* sweat]

su·da·ry (sü′dər ē), *n., pl.* **-ries.** sudarium. [Middle English *sudary* < Latin *sūdārium* sudarium]

su·da·tion (sü dā′shən), *n.* the process of sweating.

su·da·to·ri·um (sü′də tôr′ē əm, -tōr′-), *n., pl.* **-to·ri·a** (-tôr′ē ə, -tōr′-). a heated room in a bathing establishment, used to induce sweating. [< Latin *sūdātōrium*, noun use of neuter of *sūdātōrius*; see SUDATORY]

su·da·to·ry (sü′də tôr′ē, -tōr′-), *adj., n., pl.* **-ries.** —*adj.* **1.** of or having to do with a sudatorium. **2.** producing sweating. —*n.* a sudatorium. [< Latin *sūdātōrius* < *sūdāre* to sweat, related to *sūdor* sweat]

sudd (sud), *n.* a mass of floating vegetable matter on the White Nile which occasionally obstructs navigation. [< Arabic *sudd* < *sadda* he closed, obstructed]

sud·den (sud′ən), *adj.* **1.** happening or coming without notice, warning, or premonition; not expected: *a sudden stop, a sudden rise to power, a sudden attack. The snake . . . His notice sudden is* (Emily Dickinson). **2.** found or hit upon unexpectedly; abrupt: *a sudden turn in a road, a sudden shift in foreign policy.* **3.** speedy; immediate; quick; rapid: *The cat made a sudden jump at the mouse. The sudden hush as he took his place at the desk on the dais . . .* (James Hilton). **4.** *Archaic.* done or acting without forethought; rash; unpremeditated; hasty: *Jealous in honour, sudden and quick in quarrel* (Shakespeare).

—*adv. Poetic.* suddenly.

—*n. Obsolete.* a sudden need, danger, etc.; an emergency.

(all) of a sudden, without warning or preparation; suddenly; unexpectedly: *As he gazed, he saw of a sudden a man steal forth from the wood* (Arthur Conan Doyle). *Then all of a sudden appears Caligula, and demands that Claudius should be . . . his slave* (Frederic W. Farrar).

on or **upon a sudden,** *Archaic.* suddenly; unexpectedly: *My crop promis'd very well, when on a sudden I found I was in danger of losing it all again* (Daniel Defoe).

[< Anglo-French *sodein,* or *sudein,* Old French *subdain* < Latin *subitāneus* < *subitus* sudden; (originally) past participle of *subīre* < *sub-* under + *īre* come, go] —**sud′den·ness,** *n.*

—**Syn.** *adj.* **1.** See **unexpected.**

sudden death, 1. instant death occurring without warning: *If I were worthy I would pray God for a sudden death . . .* (Scott). **2.** *Sports.* the immediate ending of a game as soon as one team scores in an overtime period to resolve a tie: *He won the sudden death playoff on the first extra hole.*

sud·den·ly (sud′ən lē), *adv.* without warning or preparation; all at once; all of a sudden: *Suddenly he turned from the window and rushed out into the night* (Ernest Hemingway). —**Syn.** abruptly, unexpectedly.

Su·de·ten (sü dā′tən), *n.* a native or inhabitant of the Sudetenland.

su·dor (sü′dôr), *n.* sweat. [< Latin *sūdor, -ōris* sweat]

su·dor·al (sü′dər əl), *adj.* of or having to do with sweat.

su·dor·if·er·ous (sü′də rif′ər əs), *adj.* secreting or causing sweat. [< Late Latin *sūdōrifer* (< Latin *sūdor, -ōris* sweat + *ferre* to bear) + English *-ous*] —**su′dor·if′er·ous·ness,** *n.*

su·dor·if·ic (sü′də rif′ik), *adj.* **1.** causing or promoting sweat. **2.** secreting sweat. —*n.* a sudorific agent or remedy. [< New Latin *sudorificus* < Latin *sūdor, -ōris* sweat + *facere* to make]

su·dor·ip·a·rous (sü′də rip′ər əs), *adj.* secreting sweat. [< New Latin *sudoriparus* (with English *-ous*) < Latin *sūdor, -ōris* sweat + *parere* to bear]

Su·dra (sü′drə), *n.* a member of the lowest of the four major Hindu castes. [< Sanskrit *śūdra*]

suds (sudz), *n.pl.* **1.** soapy water. **2.** bubbles and foam on soapy water; soapsuds. **3.** any froth or foam. **4.** *U.S. Slang.* beer. —*v.t.* to wash with soapy water: *We noticed four New Yorkers carefully sudsing and hosing their cars* (New Yorker).
[perhaps < Middle Dutch *sudse* bog]

suds·er (sud′zər), *n.* something that produces suds: *The washer has a built-in sudser* (Science News Letter).

suds·y (sud′zē), *adj.,* **suds·i·er, suds·i·est.** *U.S.* **1.** full of soapsuds. **2.** full of foam: *sudsy beer.* **3.** *Slang.* soap-operatic: . . . *cloying sentimentality and the pseudodramatic froth typical of sudsy afternoon television dilemmas* (New York Times).

sue (sü), *v.,* **sued, su·ing.** —*v.t.* **1.** to start a lawsuit against (a person, company, etc.); prosecute in court; bring a civil action against: *He sued the railroad because his cow was killed by the engine.* **2.** to appeal to (a court) for legal redress. **3.** to appeal to; petition: *Then will I sue thee to forgive* (Byron). **4.** *Archaic.* to court; woo: *They would sue me and woo me and flatter me* (Tennyson).
—*v.i.* **1.** to take action in law; bring a suit: *to sue for damages.* **2.** to make an appeal; petition; plead: *Messengers came suing for peace.* **3.** *Archaic.* to be a suitor; woo.
sue out, a. to apply before a court for the granting of (a writ or other legal process): *A party detained without any warrant must sue out his habeas corpus at common law* (Henry Hallam). **b.** to proceed with (a legal action) to a decision; gain judicially: *After a man's body was taken in execution, no other process could be sued out against his lands or his goods* (Edward Poste).
[Middle English *suwen* follow, proceed < Anglo-French *suer,* or *siwer,* Old French *sivre,* later *suivre* < Late Latin *sequere,* for Latin *sequī* follow]

suède or **suede** (swād), *n.* a soft leather having a velvety nap, usually on the flesh side of the hide. —*adj.* made of suède: *suède shoes, a suède jacket.* [< French *Suède* Sweden; (originally) in phrase *gants de Suède* Swedish gloves]

suède cloth or **suede cloth,** a fabric with a napped finish resembling suède.

sued·ed or **sued·ed** (swā′did), *adj.* having a napped finish: *suèded calf, a suèded cotton pullover.*

su·er (sü′ər), *n.* a person who sues or petitions.

su·et (sü′it), *n.* the solid, waxy fat about the kidneys and loins of certain animals, especially cattle and sheep, used in cooking and as a source of tallow. [probably < unrecorded Anglo-French *suet* (diminutive) < *sue,* variant of Old French *sieu* tallow < Latin *sēbum*]

suet pudding, a pudding made of flour, chopped suet, bread crumbs, raisins, etc., and usually served with a sauce: *Among the dishes served last Friday were such characteristic Caledonian delicacies as . . . suet pudding* (New Yorker).

su·et·y (sü′ə tē), *adj.* **1.** of or like suet; fat: *his suety face and alderman's stomach* (Time). **2.** full of or made with suet.

suf-, *prefix.* the form of **sub-** before *f,* as in *suffer, suffice.*

suf. or **suff.,** suffix.

suff (suf), *n. Informal.* a suffragist.

Suff., 1. Suffolk. **2.** suffragan.

suf·fer (suf′ər), *v.i.* **1.** to have pain, grief, injury, etc.: *Very sick people may suffer. He suffered from the constant heckling of his guards.* **2.** to experience harm, loss, etc.: *Neither plane nor passengers suffered much from the forced landing.* **3.** to undergo punishment or be executed. **4.** *Obsolete.* to endure patiently: *Charity suffereth long and is kind* (I Corinthians 13:4). —*v.t.* **1.** to have or feel (pain, punishment, disaster, grief, or the like): *to suffer great strain. He suffered harm from being out in the storm.* **2.** to experience (injury, damage, loss, shame, or the like). **3.** to allow; permit: *Suffer the little children to come unto me* (Mark 10:14). **4.** to bear with patiently; endure; tolerate: *I will not suffer such insults. For ye suffer fools gladly, seeing ye yourselves are wise* (II Corinthians 11:19). [< Anglo-French *suffrir,* Old French *sufrir,* < Latin *sufferre* < *sub-* up + *ferre* to bear] —**suf′fer·er,** *n.*

suf·fer·a·ble (suf′ər ə bəl, suf′rə-), *adj.* that can be endured; tolerable; bearable. —**suf′fer·a·ble·ness,** *n.*

suf·fer·a·bly (suf′ər ə blē, suf′rə-), *adv.* in a sufferable manner; tolerably.

suf·fer·ance (suf′ər əns, suf′rəns), *n.* **1.** permission given only by a failure to object or prevent. **2.** power to bear or endure; patient endurance. **3.** *Archaic.* suffering.
on sufferance, allowed or tolerated, but not really wanted; under conditions of passive acquiescence or bare tolerance: *They were a Ministry on sufferance when they appealed to the country* (Justin McCarthy).

suf·fer·ing (suf′ər ing, suf′ring), *n.* **1.** the condition or state of being in pain; pain: *Hunger causes suffering. Motherhood will give the mother much suffering to bear* (Newsweek). *Those little anodynes that deaden suffering* (Emily Dickinson). **2.** the enduring of pain. —*adj.* that suffers or is characterized by the suffering of pain, affliction, distress, etc.: *The suffering human race* (Matthew Arnold). —**suf′fer·ing·ly,** *adv.* —**Syn.** *n.* **1, 2.** distress, agony, misery.

suf·fice (sə fīs′), *v.,* **-ficed, -fic·ing.** —*v.i.* **1.** to be enough; be sufficient: *The money will suffice for one year.* **2.** to have the necessary ability, capacity, or resources (for doing something); be competent or able (to do something). —*v.t.* to meet the desires, needs, or requirements of (a person); make content; satisfy: *A small amount sufficed him.*
suffice it, let it suffice or be sufficient: *Suffice it to say that the party was a success.*
[< Old French *suffis-,* stem of *suffire* < Latin *sufficere* < *sub-* up (next to) + *facere* to make] —**suf·fic′er,** *n.* —**suf·fic′ing·ly,** *adv.* —**suf·fic′ing·ness,** *n.*

suf·fi·cien·cy (sə fish′ən sē), *n., pl.* **-cies. 1.** a sufficient amount; large enough supply: *The car had a sufficiency of fuel for the thousand-mile trip.* **2.** the state or fact of being sufficient; adequacy; ability. **3.** self-confidence. **4.** an income or means adequate for living in a (specified) manner: *a modest sufficiency.* —**Syn. 1.** plenty. **2.** competence, capacity.

suf·fi·cient (sə fish′ənt), *adj.* **1.** as much as is needed; enough: *sufficient proof. The poor child did not have sufficient clothing for the winter.* **2.** *Archaic.* competent; capable; able. [< Latin *sufficiēns, -entis,* present participle of *sufficere;* see SUFFICE] —**Syn. 1.** adequate, ample. See **enough.**

suf·fi·cient·ly (sə fish′ənt lē), *adv.* enough; as much as is needed: *The cost of research was sufficiently low so that it could be met by the universities and private foundations* (New Yorker).

suf·fix (*n.* suf′iks; *v.* sə fiks′, suf′iks), *n.* **1. a.** an addition made at the end of a word to form another word of different meaning or function, as in bad*ly,* good*ness,* spoon*ful,* amaze*ment.* **b.** an inflectional ending, as in talk*s,* talk*ed,* talk*ing.* **2.** *Mathematics.* a subindex.
—*v.t.* **1.** to add at the end; put after. **2.** to fix or place under; subjoin. **3.** to attach as a suffix.
[< New Latin *suffixum,* noun use of Latin, neuter past participle of *suffīgere* < *sub-* upon + *fīgere* fasten]

suf·fix·al (suf′ik səl), *adj.* **1.** having to do with a suffix. **2.** of the nature of a suffix.

suf·fix·a·tion (suf′ik sā′shən), *n.* the forming of suffixes.

suf·fix·ion (sə fik′shən), *n.* **1.** the act of suffixing, especially the attaching of a suffix at the end of a word. **2.** the state of being suffixed.

suf·flate (sə flāt′), *v.t.,* **-flat·ed, -flat·ing.** *Obsolete.* to inflate. [< Latin *sufflāre* (with English *-ate*[1]) < *sub-* up + *flāre* to blow]

suf·fla·tion (sə flā′shən), *n. Obsolete.* inflation.

suf·fo·cate (suf′ə kāt), *v.,* **-cat·ed, -cat·ing.** —*v.t.* **1.** to kill by stopping the breath; choke to death: *The prison may catch fire and he may be suffocated not with a rope, but with common ordinary smoke* (Samuel Butler). **2.** to keep from breathing; hinder in breathing; stifle; choke. **3.** to smother; suppress. —*v.i.* **1.** to become stifled; gasp for breath; choke. **2.** to die for lack of oxygen; be suffocated. [< Latin *suffōcāre* (with English *-ate*[1]) (originally) to narrow up < *sub-* up + *faucēs,* plural, throat, narrow entrance] —**suf′fo·cat′ing·ly,** *adv.*

suf·fo·ca·tion (suf′ə kā′shən), *n.* **1.** the act of suffocating: *aisles crammed almost to suffocation* (Bruce Catton). **2.** the condition of being suffocated: *The body must always be able to take in good air and get rid of bad air; when the body cannot do this, we have suffocation* (Beauchamp, Mayfield, and West).

suf·fo·ca·tive (suf′ə kā′tiv), *adj.* stifling.

Suf·folk (suf′ək), **1.** any of an English breed of hornless sheep raised especially for meat. **2.** any of an English breed of heavy-bodied, chestnut-colored work horses. **3.** any of an English breed of small black swine. [< *Suffolk,* a former county in southeastern England]

Suffr., suffragan.

suf·fra·gan (suf′rə gən), *n.* **1.** a bishop consecrated to assist another bishop. **2.** any bishop considered in regard to his archbishop or metropolitan. —*adj.* assisting. [< Anglo-French *suffragan,* learned borrowing from Medieval Latin *suffraganeus* one owing suffrage < Latin *suffrāgium;* see SUFFRAGE]

suffragan bishop, suffragan.

suf·fra·gan·ship (suf′rə gən ship), *n.* the position of suffragan.

suf·frage (suf′rij), *n.* **1.** the right or privilege of voting, especially the right to vote as a citizen in national or local elections, referendums, etc.; franchise (as a voter): *The United States granted suffrage to women in 1920.* **2.** the exercise of this right; casting of a vote or votes; voting. **3.** a vote in support of or against some particular person or thing; ballot cast in an election, referendum, etc.; vote: *The election of a new emperor was referred to the suffrage of the military order* (Edward Gibbon). **4.** a short prayer or petition. **5.** *Archaic.* approval; assent; sanction; consent. [< Latin *suffrāgium* supporting vote < *sub-* nearby + *fragor* din, crash (as an outbreak of shouts of approval from the crowd), related to *frangere* to break]

suf·fra·gette (suf′rə jet′), *n.* a woman supporter of the cause of suffrage for women.

suf·fra·get·tism (suf′rə jet′iz əm), *n.* the support of suffrage for women.

suf·fra·gism (suf′rə jiz əm), *n.* the advocacy of the grant or extension of political suffrage, especially to women.

suf·fra·gist (suf′rə jist), *n.* a person who favors or actively supports giving suffrage to more people, especially to women. —*adj.* of or having to do with a suffragist or suffragists: *suffragist literature.*

suf·fru·tes·cent (suf′rü tes′ənt), *adj. Botany.* somewhat woody or shrubby at the base. [< New Latin *suffrutescens, -entis* < *sub-* somewhat + Late Latin *frutēscēns, -entis* frutescent]

suf·fru·tex (suf′rü teks), *n., pl.* **suf·fru·ti·ces** (sə frü′tə sēz). *Botany.* **1.** an undershrub, or very small shrub; a low plant with decidedly woody stems, as the trailing arbutus. **2.** a plant having a woody base but a herbaceous annual growth above. [< New Latin *suffrutex* < *sub-* under + *frutex* frutex]

suf·fru·ti·cose (sə frü′tə kōs), *adj. Botany.* **1.** having the character of a suffrutex; small with woody stems. **2.** woody at the base but herbaceous above. [< New Latin *suffruticosus* < *suffrutex, -icis* suffrutex]

suf·fu·mi·gate (sə fyü′mə gāt), *v.t.*, **-gat·ed, -gat·ing.** to fumigate from below: *When we came to burn the bodies of the rats I sprinkled sulphur on the faggots, whereby the onlookers were . . . handsomely suffumigated* (Rudyard Kipling). [< Latin *suffumigāre* (with English *-ate*[1]) < *sub-* from under + *fumigāre* fumigate]

suf·fu·mi·ga·tion (sə fyü′mə gā′shən), *n.* fumigation from below.

suf·fuse (sə fyüz′), *v.t.*, **-fused, -fus·ing.** to overspread (with a color, liquid, dye, etc.): *A broad smile suffused his face. At twilight the sky was suffused with color.* [< Latin *suffūsus*, past participle of *suffundere* < *sub-* under + *fundere* to pour] —**Syn.** cover.

suf·fu·sion (sə fyü′zhən), *n.* **1.** a suffusing. **2.** a being suffused. **3.** that with which anything is overspread. **4.** a flush of color: *There was a healthful suffusion on their cheeks* (Hawthorne). —**Syn. 4.** blush, glow.

suf·fu·sive (sə fyü′siv), *adj.* tending to suffuse.

Su·fi (sü′fē), *n.* **1.** a sect of Moslem mystics and ascetics, especially in Persia, that originated early in the history of Islam. The monastic and ascetic dervishes and fakirs derive from this sect. **2.** an adherent of this sect. [< Arabic *ṣūfī* (literally) man of wool < *ṣūf* wool (probably because of their ascetic garments)]

Su·fic (sü′fik), *adj.* of or having to do with the Sufi or their mystical system.

Su·fism (sü′fiz əm), *n.* the mystical system of the Sufi, using a symbolism popular with Moslem poets.

Su·fis·tic (sü fis′tik), *adj.* Sufic.

sug-, *prefix.* the form of **sub-** before *g*, as in *suggest.*

su·gan (sü′gən, sug′ən), *n.* **1.** *Especially Irish.* **a.** a straw rope. **b.** a saddle of straw or rushes. **2.** *Irish, Western U.S.* a heavy coverlet, as for a bed. Also, **sougan.** [< Irish *sūgān*]

sug·ar (shu̇g′ər), *n.* **1.** a sweet substance, obtained chiefly from sugar cane and beets, and used extensively in food products; sucrose; saccharose. *Formula:* $C_{12}H_{22}O_{11}$ **2.** *Chemistry.* any of a large group of carbohydrates, which are soluble in water, sweet to the taste, and either directly or indirectly fermentable. According to their chemical structure, sugars are classified as monosaccharides (glucose, dextrose or grape sugar, levulose or fruit sugar, etc.), disaccharides (sucrose or cane sugar, lactose or milk sugar, maltose or malt sugar, etc.), and trisaccharides (raffinose). **3.** something resembling sugar in form or taste. **4.** sweet or honeyed words; flattery. **5.** *Slang.* money. —*v.t.* **1.** to put sugar in; sweeten with sugar: *She sugared her tea.* **2.** to cover with sugar; sprinkle with sugar. **3.** to cause to seem pleasant or agreeable; sugar-coat: *The . . . sugared . . . cajoleries that the two women directed upon him* (Arnold Bennett). —*v.i.* to form sugar; granulate: *Honey sugars if kept too long.*
sugar off, to make maple sugar by boiling down the maple sap: *Families that you find up in the hills . . . sugaring off in the spring* (William D. Howells).
[Middle English *sucere*, and *sugure* < Old French *sucre*, and *sukere* < Medieval Latin *succarum* < Arabic *sukkar* < Persian *shakar* < Sanskrit *śarkarā* candied sugar; (originally) grit. Related to SACCHARINE.] —**sug′ar·like′,** *adj.*

sugar apple, sweetsop.

sugar beet, a large, coarse variety of beet, whose white root is a source of sugar.

sug·ar·ber·ry (shu̇g′ər ber′ē), *n., pl.* **-ries.** the hackberry.

sug·ar·bird (shu̇g′ər bėrd′), *n.* **1.** any of various small birds that feed on the nectar of flowers, such as the honey eater, the honeysucker, and certain South African sunbirds. **2.** *U.S.* the evening grosbeak, believed by the Indians to like maple sugar.

sugar bowl, a small, bowl-shaped dish, usually with a cover and often with handles, used for sugar at the table.

sug·ar·bush (shu̇g′ər bu̇sh′), *n. U.S.* **1.** a sugar orchard. **2.** the sugar maples on a particular tract, in a particular area, etc., as distinguished from other kinds of trees.

sugar candy, 1. candy made by boiling pure sugar and allowing it to crystallize. **2.** anything like sugar candy; something sweet, pleasant, or delicious: . . . *Lord John Russell, to whom a rap at the University was always sugar candy* (Frederic E. Gretton).

sug·ar-can·dy (shu̇g′ər kan′dē), *adj.* sugared; honeyed; excessively sweet: *sugar-candy hymns, sugar-candy words.*

sugar cane, a tall, perennial grass, with a strong, jointed stem and long, flat leaves, growing in warm regions. Sugar cane is the chief source of manufactured sugar.

Sugar Cane (about 12 ft. tall)

sug·ar-coat (shu̇g′ər kōt′), *v.t.* **1.** to cover with sugar; put a coating of sugar on: *to sugar-coat pills.* **2.** to cause to seem more pleasant and agreeable: *to sugar-coat discipline with humor. Through front organizations and membership on semi-official committees, they will propagate sugar-coated versions of their main ideas* (New York Times).

sug·ar-coat·ing (shu̇g′ər kō′ting), *n.* **1.** a covering with sugar. **2.** a thing that makes something seem more pleasant or agreeable.

sugar corn, sweet corn.

sugar daddy, *U.S. Slang.* an older man generous with gifts to younger women: *The old sugar daddy who knows he will have to pay plenty for his last fling, but doesn't really mind* (Time).

sugar diabetes, diabetes mellitus.

sug·ared (shu̇g′ərd), *adj.* **1.** containing, impregnated, or coated with sugar; sweetened with sugar. **2.** honeyed: *sugared words of flattery.*

sug·ar·house (shu̇g′ər hous′), *n.* **1.** *U.S.* a building near or in a sugar orchard, in which the sap from the sugar maples is reduced, by boiling, into maple syrup or maple sugar. **2.** a sugar factory; sugarworks.

sug·ar·i·ness (shu̇g′ər ē nis), *n.* sugary quality.

sug·ar·ing off (shu̇g′ər ing), *U.S.* **1.** the making of maple sugar, by boiling off of the free liquid from maple sap. **2.** a gathering of neighbors at a sugar house to help in the making of maple sugar, marked traditionally by much jollity, humor, etc. **3.** a social gathering patterned on this, now often for the entertainment of tourists, visitors, etc.

sug·ar·less (shu̇g′ər lis), *adj.* without sugar: *sugarless soda pop or chewing gum.*

sugar loaf, 1. a cone-shaped mass of hard, refined sugar, the form in which sugar was generally sold during most of the period from the late Middle Ages to the middle of the 1800's. **2.** something shaped like a sugar loaf, especially: **a.** a tall, cone-shaped hat. **b.** a high, cone-shaped hill: *here and there the outline of a wooded sugar loaf in black* (Robert L. Stevenson).

sug·ar-loaf (shu̇g′ər lōf′), *adj.* shaped like a sugar loaf.

sugar maple, a maple tree of eastern North America, highly valued for its heavy, hard, tough wood and for its sweet sap, from which maple sugar and maple syrup are made.

Twig of Common Sugar Maple with double samaras

sugar mill, a machine or factory for making sugar, as by pressing the juice out of sugar cane.

sugar of lead, lead acetate.

sugar of milk, lactose.

sugar orchard, a grove or plantation of sugar maples.

sugar pine, a tall pine of California, Oregon, Nevada, and Mexico, which yields a sugarlike resin when cut deep into the wood. It bears very large cones.

sug·ar·plum (shu̇g′ər plum′), *n.* a small piece of candy; bonbon: *The children were nestled all snug in their beds While visions of sugarplums danced in their heads* (Clement C. Moore). —**Syn.** confection, comfit.

Sugar State, a nickname for Louisiana.

sugar tongs, small tongs for lifting cubes of sugar from a bowl: *A collection of these decorative sugar tongs in the Victoria and Albert Museum contains some seven by one maker* (London Times).

sugar tree, 1. the sugar maple. **2.** any tree from which sugar syrup or sugary sap can be obtained.

sugar vinegar, vinegar made of the waste juice of sugar cane.

sug·ar·works (shu̇g′ər wėrks′), *n.pl.* (*sing. in use*). a place where sugar is made.

sug·ar·y (shu̇g′ər ē), *adj.* **1.** consisting of or containing much sugar. **2.** like sugar; sweet. **3.** outwardly very pleasant or agreeable; deceitfully or flatteringly pleasant: *a sugary greeting.* **4.** excessively or offensively sweet: *The pudding was too sugary for my taste.*

sug·gest (səg jest′, sə-), *v.t.* **1.** to bring to mind; call up the thought of: *The thought of summer suggests swimming, tennis, and hot weather. Democratic Athens, oligarchic Rome, suggest to us Pericles and Brutus* (James Bryce). **2.** to put forward; propose: *John suggested a swim and we all agreed. I suggest that you follow me immediately.* **3.** to provide the motive for; prompt: *Prudence suggested the necessity of a temporary retreat* (Edward Gibbon). **4.** to show in an indirect way; hint; intimate: *His yawns suggested that he would like to go to bed. Bad manners suggest a lack of proper home training. The first* [*report*] *sounded as though the administration was about ready to throw Negro troops into the war, while the later one suggested that the administration was still hesitating* (Carl Sandburg). [< Latin *suggestus*, past participle of *suggere* suggest, supply, put under < *sub-* under, next to + *gerere* bring] —**sug·gest′er,** *n.* —**Syn. 4.** insinuate.

sug·gest·i·bil·i·ty (səg jes′tə bil′ə tē, sə-), *n.* the quality or condition of being suggestible: *Crowd emotionality is perhaps best interpreted in terms of heightened suggestibility, that is the tendency of an individual in a crowd to respond uncritically to the stimuli provided by the other members* (Ogburn and Nimkoff).

sug·gest·i·ble (səg jes′tə bəl, sə-), *adj.* **1.** capable of being influenced by suggestion; readily swayed or influenced: *We are tremendously suggestible. Our mechanism is much better adapted to credulity than questioning* (James Harvey Robinson). **2.** capable of being influenced by hypnotic suggestion. **3.** that can be suggested; capable of suggestion: *a suggestible solution.*

sug·ges·ti·o fal·si (səg jes′tē ō fôl′sī), *Latin.* suggestion of the false; indirect lie; conscious misrepresentation, whether by words, conduct, or artifice: . . . *Despite Mr. Wilson's unqualified denials from Washington which reached London long before the evening papers went to press, the process of suggestio falsi continued, and for obvious political reasons* (Harold Hutchinson).

sug·ges·tion (səg jes′chən, sə-), *n.* **1.** the act of suggesting; the putting into the mind of an idea, course of action, or the like: *The trip was made at his suggestion.* **2.** a thing suggested; proposal: *The picnic was Jane's suggestion.* **3.** the calling up of one idea by another because they are connected or associated in some way. **4.** a very small amount; slight trace; hint; inkling: *There was a suggestion of anger in Father's voice when he called us in from play for the third time. The foreigner spoke English with just a suggestion of his native accent.* **5.** *Psychology.* **a.** the insinuation of an idea, belief, or impulse into the mind, especially a hypnotized person's mind, with avoidance of normal critical thought, contrary ideas, etc. **b.** the idea, belief, or impulse so insinuated. —**Syn. 4.** soupçon, touch.

suggestion box, a box in which written suggestions for improvement are put, as by employees in a factory, business, etc., patrons in a theater or restaurant, etc.: *The majority of employers utilizing suggestion boxes award cash for accepted ideas* (New York Times).

sug·ges·tive (səg jes′tiv, sə-), *adj.* **1.** tending to suggest ideas, acts, or feelings: *The teacher gave an interesting and suggestive list of composition subjects.* **2.** conveying a suggestion or hint (of something): *a tone suggestive of anger.* **3.** tending to suggest something improper or indecent: *Bribery is a suggestive incentive to many weak politicians.*

—**sug·ges′tive·ly,** *adv.* —**sug·ges′tive·ness,** *n.* —**Syn. 1.** See **expressive.**

sugh (süн), *n. Scottish.* sough. [imitative]

su·gi (sü′gē), *n.* a tall Japanese tree of the pine family, whose wood is compact, very white, soft, and much used in construction. [< Japanese *sugi*]

su·i·cid·al (sü′ə sī′dəl), *adj.* **1.** of or having to do with suicide. **2.** leading to or causing suicide: *. . . that war has become so obviously self-defeating and suicidal . . .* (Atlantic). **3.** ruinous to one's own interests; disastrous to oneself or to those involved: *It would be suicidal for a store to sell many things below cost. We still await the arrival of a time of political maturity among candidates and voters in any election campaign when courageous discussion of taxation is not considered suicidal in a bid for public office* (New York Times). —**su′i·cid′al·ly,** *adv.*

su·i·cide[1] (sü′ə sīd), *n., adj., v.,* **-cid·ed, -cid·ing.** —*n.* **1.** the act of deliberately killing oneself: *to commit suicide in a moment of wild despair.* **2.** the destruction of one's own interests or prospects.

—*adj.* **1.** (of a military action or operation) that is certain, or almost certain, to result in the death of the person or persons involved; suicidal: *a suicide attack, suicide missions.* **2.** undertaking such actions or operations: *a suicide pilot, suicide squads.* **3.** used in such actions or operations: *a suicide airplane, suicide bombs.*

—*v.i. Informal.* to commit suicide.

[< New Latin *suicidium* < Latin *suī* of oneself + *-cīdium* -cide²]

su·i·cide[2] (sü′ə sīd), *n.* a person who kills himself intentionally: *Christian burial has usually been denied suicides* (Newsweek). [< New Latin *suicida* < Latin *suī* of oneself + *-cīda* -cide¹]

su·i ge·ne·ris (sü′ī jen′ər is), *Latin.* of his, her, its, or their peculiar kind; unique: *Indeed, society itself is . . . an entity sui generis, something real in itself and unlike a mere sum of the individuals of which it is composed* (Hinkle and Hinkle). —**Syn.** unmatchable.

su·i ju·ris (sü′ī jůr′is), *Law.* that is of age and presumably sane, and therefore legally competent to act and legally responsible for actions: *I made it a rule never to take for treatment anyone who was not sui juris, independent of others in all the essential relations of life* (Sigmund Freud).

[< Latin *suī jūris* (literally) of one's own right; *suus, suī* one's own, *jūs, jūris* (legal) right]

su·il·line (sü′ə līn, -lin), *adj.* of or having to do with swine. [< Latin *suillus* (< *sūs* swine) + English *-ine*¹]

su·i·mate (sü′ə māt′, sü′ī-), *n.* self-mate. [< Latin *suī* of oneself + English *mate*²]

su·ine (sü′in), *n.* a mixture of oleomargarine with lard or other fatty substances, used as a substitute for butter. [< Latin *sūs* swine + English *-ine*² (because it was made from pig lard)]

su·int (sü′int, swint), *n.* dried perspiration found in the natural grease of sheep's wool, containing potash. [< French *suint* < Middle French *suin* < *suer* to sweat < Latin *sūdāre*]

suit (süt), *n.* **1.** a set of clothes, armor, vestments, etc., to be worn at the same time: *A man's suit consists of a coat, vest, and trousers. His suit of ancient black* (Vachel Lindsay). **2.** *Law.* a case in a court of law; application to a court by one party for justice from another: *He started a suit to collect damages for his injuries. The Plaintiff in the suit . . . was adjudged to have not proved his charge* (George Meredith). **3. a.** one of the four sets of cards (spades, hearts, diamonds, and clubs) making up the deck. **b.** all the cards of any one of these sets held in a player's hand at one time: *He had a good heart suit.* **4.** a request; asking; wooing: *His suit was successful and she married him.* **5.** suite: *a suit of furniture.* **6.** (originally) attendance by a tenant at the court of a feudal lord.

follow suit, a. to play a card of the same suit as the leading card: *Having but two or three small trumps, he should never force his partner to trump, if he finds he cannot follow suit* (J. Beaufort). **b.** to follow the example of another: *Kenya and Sierra Leone . . . too must consider the possibility of following suit if Zambia quits the Commonwealth* (Manchester Guardian Weekly).

—*v.t.* **1.** to adapt or accommodate in style, manner, proportion, etc.; make suitable or appropriate: *The teacher suited the punishment to the offense by making Dick sweep up the bits of paper he had thrown.* **2.** to be adapted to; be suitable for; answer the requirements of: *A cold climate suits apples and wheat, but not oranges and tea.* **3.** to be agreeable, convenient, or acceptable to; please; satisfy: *Which date suits you best? It is hard to suit everyone.* **4.** to be becoming to: *Her blue hat suits her fair skin.* **5.** *Archaic.* to provide with a suit of clothes; clothe; attire: *I'll disrobe me Of these Italian weeds and suit myself As does a Briton peasant* (Shakespeare). —*v.i.* **1.** to be suitable, fitting, or convenient. **2.** *Archaic.* to agree or harmonize.

suit oneself, to do as one pleases: *If you will not take my advice, suit yourself.*

suit up, to put on a special suit or uniform: *Two husky football players suited up in the University of Colorado's field house at Boulder* (Time). *He [synthetic man] could be suited up and sent off to war* (Russell Baker).

[Middle English *sywte* attendance at a court; the company attending; then, their livery < Anglo-French *siwte*, or *suite* < Vulgar Latin *sequita,* ultimately < Latin *sequī* follow. Doublet of SUITE.]

—**Syn.** *v.t.* **1.** adjust. **3.** gratify, content.

suit·a·bil·i·ty (sü′tə bil′ə tē), *n.* a being suitable; fitness; appropriateness.

suit·a·ble (sü′tə bəl), *adj.* right for the occasion; appropriate; fitting; proper: *A simple dress is suitable for school wear. The park gives the children a suitable playground.* —**suit′a·ble·ness,** *n.* —**Syn.** See **fit**¹.

suit·a·bly (sü′tə blē), *adv.* in a suitable manner; fitly; agreeably; appropriately.

suit·case (süt′kās′), *n.* a flat, rectangular traveling bag. —**Syn.** valise, grip.

suitcase farmer, *U.S.* a farmer, especially a dry-land farmer, who lives away from the farm most of the year: *They blame the poor condition of the land on suitcase farmers who do not live on their property and therefore do not take care of it* (Wall Street Journal).

suit-dress (süt′dres′), *n.* a woman's outfit consisting of a skirt or dress and matching jacket or coat.

suite (swēt; *also* süt *for* 2), *n.* **1.** a connected series of rooms: *She has a suite of rooms at the hotel — a living room, bedroom, and bath.* **2.** a set of matching furniture: *a dining room suite.* **3.** *Music.* **a.** a series of instrumental movements varying in number and character, sometimes concert arrangements of ballet or stage music. **b.** a series of certain dance tunes in the same or related keys, arranged for one or more instruments; partita. The typical movements are allemande, courante, saraband, and gigue; between saraband and gigue, intermezzos are inserted, the most important being the minuet. **4.** a group of followers, attendants, or servants; retinue: *The queen traveled with a suite of twelve.* **5.** a succession or series of like things. [< French, Old French *suite* < Vulgar Latin *sequita.* Doublet of SUIT.] —**Syn. 1.** apartment. **4.** cortège.

-suited, *combining form.* wearing a —— suit or suits: *Gray-suited = wearing a gray suit.*

suit·ing (sü′ting), *n.* fabric for making suits.

suit·or (sü′tər), *n.* **1.** a man who courts a woman, especially with a view to marriage: *You think that you are Ann's suitor [but] . . . it is you who are the pursued . . . the destined prey* (George Bernard Shaw). **2.** *Law.* a person who brings suit in a court of law. **3.** *Archaic.* anyone who sues or petitions; petitioner; suppliant. —**Syn. 1.** beau. **2.** litigant. **3.** supplicant.

suit·or·ship (sü′tər ship), *n.* the state or condition of being a suitor.

suit·ress (sü′tris), *n. Archaic.* a woman suitor.

suk[1] (sůk), *n., pl.* **suk.** a Korean unit of measure for grain, vegetables, and other dry commodities, equal to about five bushels. [< Korean *suk*]

suk[2] (sük), *n.* suq.

Suk (sük), *n., pl.* **Suk** or **Suks.** a member of a Nilotic people of Kenya: *. . . rival Suk, in elaborate headdress, from the neighboring Kenya frontier territory to the east* (London Times).

su·ki·ya·ki (sü′kē yä′kē, skē yä′-), *n.* a Japanese dish consisting of thin strips of beef, sliced onions, bamboo shoots, shredded spinach, and various other vegetables cooked for a very short time in a mixture of soy sauce, stock, sugar, and white wine. [< Japanese *sukiyaki,* perhaps < *suki* slicing + *-yaki* cooking, roasting]

suk·kah (sůk′ə, sů kä′), *n.* a temporary booth or hut covered with branches, built on the premises of a house or synagogue as a place to eat in and sometimes sleep in during Sukkoth: *Midday meal in the sukkah, the festival tent set up in the quadrangle* (Harper's). Also, **succah.** [< Hebrew *sukkâ* a booth]

Suk·kos (sůk′əs), *n.* Sukkoth.

Suk·koth or **Suk·kot** (sů kōth′), *n.* an eight- or nine-day Jewish festival beginning on the 15th of Tishri (September-October), marked by the building of temporary booths or huts in remembrance of the booths that were used by the Israelites during their wanderings in the desert; Feast of Booths. Leviticus 23:33-44. Also, **Succos, Succoth.** [< Hebrew *Sukkoth,* plural of *sukkâ* a booth]

sul·cate (sul′kāt), *adj.* marked with parallel furrows or grooves, as a stem. [< Latin *sulcātus,* past participle of *sulcāre* to plow, furrow < *sulcus* furrow]

sul·cat·ed (sul′kā tid), *adj.* sulcate.

sul·ca·tion (sul kā′shən), *n.* **1.** a furrow, channel, or sulcus. **2.** a set of sulci collectively. **3.** the state of being sulcated. **4.** the act, manner, or mode of grooving.

sul·cus (sul′kəs), *n., pl.* **-ci** (-sī). *Anatomy.* **1.** a groove or furrow in a body, organ, or tissue. **2.** a shallow groove between two convolutions of the surface of the brain. [< Latin *sulcus* a furrow, trench, wrinkle]

sul·fa (sul′fə), *adj.* of or having to do with a family of drugs containing sulfurous anhydride (SO_2), derived from sulfanilamide, and used in treating various bacterial infections.

—*n.* a sulfa drug. Also, **sulpha.**

[abstracted < *sulfanilamide*]

sul·fa·di·a·zine (sul′fə dī′ə zēn, -zin), *n.* a sulfa drug of the sulfonamide group, a white or yellowish powder, less toxic than sulfanilamide, sulfapyridine, or sulfathiazole, and used against various bacterial infections. *Formula:* $C_{10}H_{10}N_4O_2S$ [< *sulfa* + *diazine*]

sulfa drugs, a family of drugs containing sulfur dioxide (SO_2), especially those derived from sulfanilamide, that are generally powerful in checking the growth of certain bacteria. Members of the group are used (sometimes with antibiotics) chiefly to combat streptococcic, pneumococcic, meningococcic, and staphylococcic infections, but all are more or less toxic and are restricted in use. *Sulfa drugs became available just before World War II and played an important role in preventing deaths from wound infection on the battlefield* (Sidonie M. Gruenberg).

sul·fa·guan·i·dine (sul′fə gwan′ə dēn, -din; -gwä′nə-), *n.* a sulfa drug of the sulfonamide group, a white, crystalline powder, comparatively nontoxic, and used chiefly against bacillary dysentery. *Formula:* $C_7H_{10}N_4O_2S.H_2O$

sul·fa·mer·a·zine (sul′fə mer′ə zēn, -zin), *n.* a sulfa drug of the sulfonamide group, a white or yellowish, crystalline powder similar to sulfadiazine, but more readily absorbed. *Formula:* $C_{11}H_{12}N_4O_2S$ [< *sulfa* + Greek *méros* part, taken as "member of a similar group" + English *azine*]

sul·fa·meth·a·zine (sul′fə meth′ə zēn, -zin), *n.* a sulfa drug used for the treatment of various bacterial infections. *Formula:* $C_{12}H_{14}N_4O_2S$ [< *sulfa* + (di)*meth*(yl) + *azine*]

sul·fam·ic acid (sul fam′ik), a white, crystalline solid obtained by heating urea with sulfuric acid, used for cleaning and electroplating metal, as a fire retardant, in organic synthesis, etc. *Formula:* HSO_3NH_2

sul·fa·nil·a·mide (sul′fə nil′ə mīd, -mid), *n.* a white, crystalline or granular substance, the amide of sulfanilic acid, derived from coal tar. Sulfanilamide was the first sulfa drug to be widely used and is the basis of the sulfonamide group. *Formula:* $C_6H_8N_2O_2S$ [< *sulfanil*(ic acid) + *amide*]

sul·fa·nil·ic acid (sul′fə nil′ik), a grayish-white, crystalline acid produced by heating aniline with sulfuric acid, used especially in the manufacture of dyes. *Formula:* $C_6H_7NSO_3.H_2O$ [< *sulf*(uric acid) + *anil*(ine) + *-ic*]

sul·fa·nil·yl·guan·i·dine monohydrate (sul′fə nil′əl gwan′ə dēn, -din; -gwä′nə-), sulfaguanidine. [< (acetyl)*sulfanilyl* (chloride), a chemical compound + *guanidine*]

sul·fa·pyr·a·zine (sul′fə pir′ə zēn, -zin), *n.* a sulfa drug with uses similar to sulfadiazine. *Formula:* $C_{10}H_{10}N_4O_2S$

sul·fa·pyr·i·dine (sul′fə pir′ə dēn, -din), *n.* a sulfa drug, of the sulfonamide group, used against certain skin infections and pneumonia, but now superseded for general use by less toxic derivatives. *Formula:* $C_{11}H_{11}N_3O_2S$

sul·fa·qui·nox·a·line (sul′fə kwi nok′sə-lēn, -lin), *n.* a synthetic drug used in the treatment of coccidiosis, fowl cholera, dysentery, and other diseases of cattle, sheep, swine, rabbits, and domestic fowl. *Formula:* $C_{14}H_{12}N_4O_2S$

sulf·ar·se·nid (sulf är′sə nid), *n.* sulfarsenide.

sulf·ar·se·nide (sulf är′sə nīd, -nid), *n. Chemistry.* a compound which is a double salt of sulfur and arsenic. [< *sulf*(ide) + *arsenide*]

sulf·ars·phen·a·mine (sulf′ärs fen′ə-mēn′, -min; -fen am′in), *n.* a sulfa drug containing arsenic, used in the treatment of syphilis. *Formula:* $C_{14}H_{14}As_2N_2Na_2O_8S_2$

Sul·fa·sux·i·dine (sul′fə suk′sə dēn, -din), *n. Trademark.* a preparation of succinylsulfathiazole. [< *sulfa* + *succi*(nic anhydride), a chemical compound + *-ide* + *-ine*[2]]

sul·fate (sul′fāt), *n., v.,* **-fat·ed, -fat·ing.** —*n.* a salt or ester of sulfuric acid: *Most sulfates are soluble in water.*
—*v.t.* **1.** to combine or treat with sulfuric acid or a sulfate. **2.** to change into a sulfate. **3.** *Electricity.* to form a scaly deposit of a compound containing lead sulfate on (the plates of a storage battery). —*v.i.* to become sulfated.
[< French *sulphate* < New Latin *sulphatum* (*acidum*) (literally) acid of sulfate < Latin *sulfur*, and *sulphur*]

sulfate paper, any of various grades and types of paper made from pulp produced by the sulfate process, as kraft and other stocks intended for commercial use, certain types of inexpensive typewriter paper, etc.

sulfate process, a papermaking process in which wood chips are converted into pulp by cooking under pressure in a solution of sodium sulfide, sodium hydroxide, and water.

sul·fa·thi·a·zole (sul′fə thī′ə zōl, -zol), *n.* a sulfa drug of the sulfonamide group, used especially in treating gonorrhea and pneumonia, but superseded for general use by sulfadiazine. *Formula:* $C_9H_9N_3O_2S_2$

sul·fa·tion (sul fā′shən), *n.* **1.** the act or process of sulfating: *The additive would . . . ward off the harmful effects . . . of sulfation in lead-acid storage batteries which causes efficiency to drop off* (Wall Street Journal). **2.** the scaly deposit formed on the plates of a storage battery by this process.

sul·fat·i·za·tion (sul′fə tə zā′shən), *n.* the act or process of sulfatizing.

sul·fat·ize (sul′fə tīz), *v.t.,* **-ized, -iz·ing.** to change (sulfide ores, etc.) into sulfates, as by roasting.

sul·fe·trone (sul′fə trōn), *n.* a drug, one of the sulfone compounds, used in the treatment of leprosy. *Formula:* $C_{30}H_{28}N_2O_{14}S_5Na_4$ [< *sulf*(one) + (t)*etr*(a)- fourth (because this is the position of one of the radicals on the chain) + *-one*]

sulf·hy·drate (sulf hī′drāt), *n.* hydrosulfide.

sulf·hy·dric acid (sulf hī′drik), *Chemistry.* hydrogen sulfide. *Formula:* H_2S Also, **sulphydric acid.**

sulf·hy·dryl (sulf hī′drəl), *n.* the univalent radical -SH; thiol. [< *sulf*(ur) + *hydr*(ogen) + *-yl*]

sul·fid (sul′fid), *n.* sulfide.

sul·fide (sul′fīd), *n.* a compound of sulfur and another element or radical; a salt of hydrogen sulfide; sulfuret. [< *sulf*(ur) + *-ide*]

sul·fi·nyl (sul′fə nəl), *n. Chemistry.* a bivalent organic radical, -SO; thionyl. [< *sulf*(ur) + *-in* + *-yl*]

sul·fi·sox·a·zole (sul′fə sok′sə zōl, -zol), *n.* a white or yellowish sulfa drug used to treat various bacterial infections, especially infections of the urinary tract. *Formula:* $C_{11}H_{13}N_3O_3S$

sul·fite (sul′fīt), *n.* a salt or ester of sulfurous acid. [< French *sulfite*, arbitrary alteration of *sulphate;* see SULFATE. Compare -ITE[2].]

sulfite process, a method of producing wood pulp by cooking wood chips in a solution of sulfurous acid and a bisulfite of calcium, magnesium, sodium, or ammonium. It is used mainly with softwoods, such as fir and hemlock.

sul·fit·ic (sul fit′ik), *adj.* of or having to do with a sulfite or sulfites.

Sul·fo·nal (sul′fə nal, sul′fə nal′), *n. Trademark.* sulfonmethane. [< German *Sulfonal* < *Sulfon* sulfone]

sul·fon·a·mide (sul fon′ə mīd; sul′fə nam′-īd, -id), *n.* **1.** any of a group of sulfa drugs, derivatives of sulfanilamide, which check bacterial infections, chiefly by preventing the synthesis in the body of certain substances necessary to the growth of disease-producing bacteria. Their use is governed by factors such as rate of absorption, resistance of the bacteria, etc. Other drugs, such as sodium bicarbonate, are often administered with them to reduce their toxic effects. **2.** *Chemistry.* **a.** an organic compound which contains the univalent radical $-SO_2NH_2$. **b.** the radical itself. [< *sulfon*(yl) + *amide*]

sul·fo·nate (sul′fə nāt), *n., v.,* **-nat·ed, -nat·ing.** *Chemistry.* —*n.* a salt or ester of a sulfonic acid. —*v.t.* to convert into a sulfonic acid.

sul·fo·na·tion (sul′fə nā′shən), *n. Chemistry.* the introduction of one or more sulfonic acid radicals $—SO_2OH$ into an organic compound.

sul·fone (sul′fōn), *n. Chemistry.* any of a group of compounds containing the radical $-SO_2$ united to two hydrocarbon radicals: *Leprosy treatments have developed mostly in the past 15 years. Widespread use of sulfone drugs has made recovery increasingly common* (Time). [< German *Sulfon* < *Sulfur* sulfur + *-on* -one]

sul·fon·ic (sul fon′ik), *adj. Chemistry.* **1.** of or denoting the univalent acid radical $-SO_2OH$ (or $-SO_3H$). **2.** of or having to do with an acid containing this radical. [< *sulfon*(e) + *-ic*]

sulfonic acid, any of a group of organic acids containing the univalent radical $-SO_2-OH$, considered as sulfuric acid derivatives by the replacement of a hydroxyl radical (-OH). They are used in making phenols, dyes, drugs, etc.

sul·fo·ni·um (sul fō′nē əm), *n. Chemistry.* a univalent radical formed by the addition of a proton to hydrogen sulfide. *Formula:* $-H_3S$ [< *sulf*(ur), + *-onium*, on the analogy of *ammonium*]

sul·fon·meth·ane (sul′fōn meth′ān, -fon-), *n.* a soluble, white, crystalline substance used as a hypnotic; Sulfonal. *Formula:* $C_7H_{16}O_4S_2$ [< *sulfon*(e) + *methane*]

sul·fo·nyl (sul′fə nəl, -nēl), *n. Chemistry.* a bivalent radical, $-SO_2$; sulfuryl.

sulfonyl chloride, sulfuryl chloride.

sul·fo·nyl·u·re·a (sul′fə nəl yu̇ rē′ə), *n.* any of a group of drugs, compounds of sulfonyl and urea, related to the sulfa drugs and used as a substitute for insulin in the treatment of diabetes.

sul·fur (sul′fər), *n.* **1.** a light-yellow, nonmetallic chemical element, found abundantly in volcanic regions, and occurring free in nature as a brittle, crystalline solid. It is widely distributed in combination with metals and other substances, and is also present in proteins. Sulfur is highly inflammable and burns in the air with a blue flame and a stifling odor. It is used in making matches and gunpowder, for vulcanizing rubber, in bleaching, in medicine as a laxative and diaphoretic, in ointments for the skin, etc. *Symbol:* S; *at.wt.:* (C^{12}) 32.064 or (O^{16}) 32.066; *at.no.:* 16; *valence:* 2, 4, 6. **2.** a greenish yellow. —*adj.* greenish-yellow. Also, **sulphur.** [Middle English *soufre*, and *sulfre* < Anglo-French *sulfere*, Old French *soufre* < Latin *sulfur*, or *sulphur*]

sul·fu·rate (sul′fə rāt, -fyə-), *v.,* **-rat·ed, -rat·ing,** *adj.* —*v.t.* to combine, impregnate with, or subject to the action of sulfur or a sulfur compound; sulfurize. —*adj.* **1.** made of or consisting of sulfur. **2.** resembling sulfur.
[< Late Latin *sulphurātus* < Latin *sulphur* sulfur]

sul·fu·ra·tion (sul′fə rā′shən, -fyə-), *n.* **1.** the act or process of treating with sulfur. **2.** the state of being treated or impregnated with sulfur.

sul·fu·ra·tor (sul′fə rā′tər, -fyə-), *n.* **1.** an apparatus for treating, impregnating, or sprinkling with sulfur. **2.** an apparatus for fumigating or bleaching with the fumes of burning sulfur.

sul·fur-bot·tom (sul′fər bot′əm), *n.* sulphur-bottom.

sulfur dioxide, a heavy, colorless gas or liquid with a sharp odor, used as a bleach, disinfectant, preservative, and refrigerant, in making sulfuric acid, etc. *Formula:* SO_2

sul·fu·re·ous (sul fyu̇r′ē əs), *adj.* **1.** consisting of or containing sulfur. **2.** having to do with sulfur. **3.** like sulfur. [< Latin *sulphureus* (with English *-ous*) < *sulphur* sulfur] —**sul·fu′re·ous·ly,** *adv.* —**sul·fu′re·ous·ness,** *n.*

sul·fu·ret (sul′fyə ret), *v.,* **-ret·ed, -ret·ing** or (*especially British*) **-ret·ted, -ret·ting,** *n.* —*v.t.* to combine or treat with sulfur. [< noun]
—*n.* (formerly) a sulfide. [< New Latin *sulphuretum*]

sul·fu·ret·ed or **sul·fu·ret·ted** (sul′fyə-ret′id), *adj.* **1.** combined or treated with sulfur. **2.** containing sulfur or a sulfur compound.

sul·fu·ric (sul fyu̇r′ik), *adj.* **1.** of or having to do with sulfur. **2.** containing sulfur, especially with a valence of six.

sulfuric acid, a heavy, colorless, oily, corrosive acid, the dibasic acid of sulfur, formerly produced by the distillation of green vitriol (and therefore called oil of vitriol), now made chiefly from sulfur dioxide. Sulfuric acid is used in making explosives and fertilizers, in refining petroleum, and in many other industrial processes. *Formula:* H_2SO_4

sul·fu·ri·za·tion (sul′fyər ə zā′shən, -fər-), *n.* the act or process of sulfurizing.

sul·fu·rize (sul′fyə rīz, -fə-), *v.t.,* **-rized, -riz·ing. 1.** to cause to combine with, or to be impregnated by, sulfur or a sulfur compound; sulfurate. **2.** to fumigate with burning sulfur.

sul·fur·ous (sul′fər əs, -fyər-; *in Chemistry, also* sul fyu̇r′əs), *adj.* **1.** *Chemistry.* **a.** of or having to do with sulfur. **b.** containing sulfur, especially with a valence of four. **2.** like the fumes or heat of burning sulfur; fiery. **3.** (of language or expression) angry, blasphemous, or profane. **4.** like sulfur in color: *The city, unreal as a mirage in the desert, lay bathed in a sulfurous yellow light* (Edgar Maass). **5.** of or like the fires of hell; hellish. —**sul′fur·ous·ly,** *adv.*

sulfurous acid, a colorless acid, consisting of a solution of sulfur dioxide in water, used as a bleach, reducing agent, etc. It is known chiefly in the form of its salts, the sulfites. *Formula:* H_2SO_3

sulfur trioxide, a chemical compound used chiefly as an intermediate in the production of sulfuric acid. *Formula:* SO_3

sul·fur·y (sul′fər i), *adj.* of or like sulfur; sulfurous.

sul·fur·yl (sul′fər əl, -fə rēl; -fyər əl, -fyə-rēl), *n. Chemistry.* a bivalent radical, $-SO_2$, occurring in sulfuric acid; sulfonyl.

sulfuryl chloride, a colorless, pungent liquid compound, used as a chlorinating agent, as a solvent, in plastics, etc. *Formula:* SO_2Cl_2

sulk (sulk), *v.i.* to keep aloof from others in moody silence; indulge in sullen ill humor; be sulky: *The bride sat crying in one corner of the carriage and the bridegroom sulked in the other* (Samuel Butler). —*n.* a sulking; a fit of sulking.
sulks, ill humor shown by sulking: *The girl has a fit of the sulks.*
[perhaps back formation < *sulky*[1]] —**sulk′er,** *n.*
—**Syn.** *v.i.* mope. *-n.* sullenness.

sulk·i·ly (sul′kə lē), *adv.* in a sulky manner.

sulk·i·ness (sul′kē nis), *n.* the quality or state of being sulky; sullenness; moroseness.

sulk·y[1] (sul′kē), *adj.,* **sulk·i·er, sulk·i·est.** silent and bad-humored because of resentment; sullen: *a sulky silence. She gets sulky and won't play if she can't be leader.* [origin uncertain. Compare Old English *āsolcen* lazy, past participle of *āseolcan* become relaxed, languid.] —**Syn.** See **sullen.**

sulk·y[2] (sul′kē), *n., pl.* **sulk·ies,** *adj.* —*n.* a very light, two-wheeled carriage, sometimes without a body, for one person, having two wheels and pulled by one horse, and now commonly used in trotting races. —*adj.* (of farming equipment) having a seat for the

Sulky[2]

driver: *a sulky plow.* [probably related to *sulky*[1] (because the rider is alone)]

sulky racing, harness racing.

sul·la (sul′ə), *n.* a plant of the pea family, with flowers resembling those of the red clover, cultivated for forage in Mediterranean countries. [< Spanish *sulla*]

sul·lage (sul′ij), *n.* **1.** sewage: *The people themselves feel the misery of having no channels to remove sullage away clear from every habitation* (Florence Nightingale). **2.** the silt washed down and deposited by a stream or flood. **3.** (in founding) the scoria which rises to the surface of the molten metal in the ladle. **4.** *Obsolete.* filth. [earlier *sollage,* perhaps < unrecorded Anglo-French *souillage* < Old French *souiller;* see SOIL[2]. Compare SOILAGE.]

sul·len (sul′ən), *adj.* **1.** silent because of bad humor or anger: *a sullen disposition. The sullen child refused to answer my questions.* **2.** showing bad humor or anger: *a sullen silence.* **3.** gloomy or dismal in aspect: *a gray and sullen sea. The sullen skies threatened rain.* **4.** of a deep, dull, or mournful tone: *sullen thunder.* **5.** *Obsolete.* baleful; malignant. [earlier, also *sollen,* Middle English *soleine* < unrecorded Anglo-French *solain,* and *solein* < Vulgar Latin *sōlānus* < Latin *sōlus* alone] **—sul′len·ly,** *adv.* **—sul′len·ness,** *n.*

—**Syn. 1. Sullen, sulky, glum** mean silent and bad-humored or gloomy. **Sullen** suggests an ill-natured refusal to talk or be cooperative because of anger or bad humor or disposition: *It is disagreeable to have to sit at the breakfast table with a sullen person.* **Sulky** suggests moody or childish sullenness because of resentment or discontent: *Dogs sometimes become sulky because they are jealous.* **Glum** carries less suggestion of bad humor or bad temper, and emphasizes silence and low spirits because of some depressing condition or happening: *He is glum about his failure to be promoted.* **2.** surly.

sul·lens (sul′ənz), *n.pl.* sullen humor: *a fit of sullens.*

sul·ly (sul′ē), *v.t., v.i.,* **-lied, -ly·ing,** *n., pl.* **-lies.** soil; stain; tarnish: *When he had washed his face, which was a little sullied by his fall . . .* (Richard Graves). [probably < Old French *souiller;* see SOIL[2]]

sul·pha (sul′fə), *adj., n.* sulfa.

sul·pha·nil·a·mide (sul′fə nil′ə mīd, -mid), *n.* sulfanilamide.

sulph·ar·se·nid (sulf är′sə nid), *n.* sulfarsenide.

sulph·ar·se·nide (sulf är′sə nīd, -nid), *n.* sulfarsenide.

sul·phate (sul′fāt), *n., v.t., v.i.,* **-phat·ed, -phat·ing.** sulfate.

sul·pha·thi·a·zole (sul′fə thī′ə zōl, -zol), *n.* sulfathiazole.

sul·phat·ize (sul′fə tīz), *v.t.,* **-ized, -iz·ing.** sulfatize.

sul·phe·trone (sul′fə trōn), *n.* sulfetrone.

sul·phid (sul′fid), *n.* sulfide.

sul·phide (sul′fīd), *n.* sulfide.

sul·phite (sul′fīt), *n.* sulfite.

sul·pho·nal (sul′fə nal, sul′fə nal′), *n.* sulfonmethane.

sul·phon·a·mide (sul fon′ə mīd; sul′fə-nam′īd, -id), *n.* sulfonamide.

sul·pho·nate (sul′fə nāt), *n., v.t.,* **-nat·ed, -nat·ing.** sulfonate.

sul·pho·na·tion (sul′fə nā′shən), *n.* sulfonation.

sul·phone (sul′fōn), *n.* sulfone.

sul·pho·ni·um (sul fō′nē əm), *n.* sulfonium.

sul·phon·meth·ane (sul′fōn meth′ān, -fon-), *n.* sulfonmethane.

sul·pho·nyl (sul′fə nəl, -nēl), *n.* sulfonyl.

sul·phur (sul′fər), *n.* **1.** sulfur. **2.** any of a family of yellow or orange butterflies, as the common sulphur of the eastern and midwestern United States. **3.** a pale yellow with a tinge of green; lemon.

—*adj.* pale-yellow with a tinge of green; lemon.

sul·phu·rate (sul′fə rāt, -fyə-), *v.t.,* **rat·ed, -rat·ing,** *adj.* sulfurate.

sul·phur-bot·tom (sul′fər bot′əm), *n.* a whalebone whale, sometimes growing to over 100 feet in length, the largest of all known living creatures, blue-gray with yellowish under parts; blue whale. It lives in the Antarctic and northern Atlantic and Pacific oceans.

sul·phu·re·ous (sul fyůr′ē əs), *adj.* sulfureous. **—sul·phu′re·ous·ly,** *adv.* **—sul·phu′re·ous·ness,** *n.*

sul·phu·ret (sul′fyə ret), *v.t.,* **-ret·ed, -ret·ing** or (*especially British*) **-ret·ted, -ret·ting,** *n.* sulfuret.

sul·phu·ric (sul fyůr′ik), *adj.* sulfuric.

sul·phu·rize (sul′fyə rīz, -fə-), *v.t.,* **-rized, -riz·ing.** sulfurize.

sul·phur·ous (sul′fər əs, -fyər-; *in Chemistry, also* sul fyůr′əs), *adj.* sulfurous. **—sul′phur·ous·ly,** *adv.*

sulphur whale, the sulphur-bottom.

sul·phur·yl (sul′fər əl, -fə rēl; -fyər əl, -fyə-rēl), *n.* sulfuryl.

sul·phy·drate (sul fī′drāt), *n.* hydrosulfide.

sul·phy·dric acid (sul fī′drik), sulfhydric acid.

sul·phy·dryl (sul fī′drəl), *n.* sulfhydryl.

Sul·pi·cian (sul pish′ən), *n.* a priest of a Roman Catholic order established about 1645 to train young men for holy orders. [< French *sulpicien* < St. *Sulpice,* the parish of the founder + *-en* -an]

sul·tan (sul′tən), *n.* **1.** the ruler of any of certain Mohammedan countries, especially of Turkey until 1922. **2.** an absolute ruler. **3.** sultana (bird). [< Arabic *sulṭān* ruler; power]

Sul·tan (sul′tən), *n.* a breed of fowl having white plumage and characterized especially by stiff quill feathers extending backward from the thighs.

sul·tan·a (sul tan′ə, -tä′nə), *n.* **1.** the wife or concubine of a sultan. **2.** the mother, sister, or daughter of a sultan. **3.** a small, seedless raisin produced in the neighborhood of Smyrna. **4.** any of various gallinules having brilliant plumage, especially the purple gallinule. [< Italian *sultana,* feminine of *sultano* sultan < Arabic *sulṭān*]

sultana bird, sultana.

sul·tan·ate (sul′tə nāt), *n.* **1.** the position, authority, or period of rule of a sultan. **2.** the territory ruled over by a sultan: *Egypt was now a Turkish sultanate* (H.G. Wells).

sul·tan·ess (sul′tə nis), *n.* a sultana (def. 1 or 2).

sul·tan·ic (sul tan′ik), *adj.* **1.** of or having to do with a sultan. **2.** suggestive of a sultan: *sultanic luxury.*

sul·tan·ship (sul′tən ship), *n.* the office or dignity of a sultan.

sul·tri·ly (sul′trə lē), *adv.* in a sultry manner; oppressively.

sul·tri·ness (sul′trē nis), *n.* the state of being sultry; heat with moist or close air.

sul·try (sul′trē), *adj.,* **-tri·er, -tri·est. 1.** hot, close, and moist: *We expect sultry weather during July.* **2.** hot; glowing with heat: *beneath the burning sky, And sultry sun . . .* (John Dryden). **3.** characterized by the heat of passion, lust, etc.: *a sultry glance.* [< obsolete *sulter* swelter + *-y*[1]. Related to SWELT.] —**Syn. 1.** muggy. **2.** sweltering.

su·lu (sü′lü), *n.* a sarong worn by men and women of the Fiji Islands: *Sulus for men are often handsome woolen wrap-arounds, and the police wear white ones with saw-tooth edges* (Saturday Review). [< Fijian *sulu*]

Su·lu (sü′lü), *n.* **1.** a member of a native Moslem tribe inhabiting the Sulu Archipelago, a group of islands in the southwestern part of the Philippine Islands. **2.** the Malayan language of these people. [< Malay *Sulu′*]

Su·lu·an (sü′lü ən), *adj.* of or having to do with the natives, inhabitants, or language of the Sulu Archipelago. —*n.* Sulu.

sum (sum), *n., v.,* **summed, sum·ming.** —*n.* **1.** an amount or quantity of money: *He paid a large sum for the house.* **2.** the total of two or more numbers or things taken together; total: *The sum of 20 and 20 is 40.* **3.** a series of two or more numbers or quantities to be added. **4.** *Informal.* a problem in arithmetic: *He can do easy sums in his head but he has to use pencil and paper for hard ones.* **5.** the total amount; aggregate; whole; totality: *an immense sum of misery* (Macaulay). *The sum of human happiness . . .* (Clarence Urmy). **6.** the essence or gist of anything; pith: *That the Sermon on the Mount contains the sum and substance of Christianity* (Frederick W. Robertson). **7.** *Archaic.* a summary; epitome.

in sum, a. in a few words; briefly: *My meaning, in sum, is, that whereas . . .* (F. Hall). **b.** to conclude in a few words; in short: *In sum, I seriously protest, that no man ever had . . . a greater veneration for Chaucer than myself* (Dryden).

—*v.t.* to find the total number or amount of: *Nature's true-born child, who sums his years (like me) with no arithmetic but tears* (Henry King).

sum up, a. to reckon, count, or total: *to sum up the advantages of the offer.* **b.** to bring or collect into a whole or in a small compass: *to sum up strength to deal a final blow.* **c.** to express or tell briefly; summarize; epitomize: *to sum up the week's work. Sum up the main points of the lesson in three sentences.* **d.** to recapitulate the chief points of (the evidence) to a jury before it retires to consider a verdict: *When the evidence is gone through on both sides, the judge . . . sums up the whole to the jury* (William Blackstone). **e.** to form an estimate of the qualities or character of; size up: *They were not obviously staring, but he knew that they were rapidly summing him up* (Hugh Walpole). *Lord Beaverbrook's London Daily Express, which seldom minces words, summed up Sir Anthony Eden's Cabinet shuffle* (Newsweek).

[Middle English *summe,* and *somme* < Anglo-French *summe* < Latin *summa,* noun use of adjective, feminine of *summus* highest]

—**Syn.** *n.* **2.** See **number.**

sum-, *prefix.* the form of **sub-** before *m,* as in *summon.*

su·mac or **su·mach** (sü′mak, shü′-), *n.* **1.** any of a group of shrubs or small trees having divided leaves that turn scarlet in the autumn and cone-shaped clusters (panicles) of small, red, one-seeded fruits (drupes). In some species, as the poison sumac and poison ivy, the foliage is poisonous to the touch. **2.** a preparation of the dried and powdered leaves and shoots of certain of these plants, used in tanning and dyeing. **3.** the wood of any of these plants. [< Old French *sumac,* or Medieval Latin *sumach* < Arabic *summāq*]

Staghorn Sumac (def. 1—30 to 35 ft. tall)

➔ The (sh) of the second pronunciation arose during the Early Modern period, as in *sure* and *sugar.* Today the more common educated pronunciation appears to be the first, where the (s) has been restored, as in *assume, ensue, suit,* and the like, which were also at one time often pronounced with (sh).

sumac family, the cashew family of plants.

Su·ma·tran (sů mä′trən), *adj.* of or having to do with the island of Sumatra, in western Indonesia, its inhabitants, or its language. —*n.* **1.** a native or inhabitant of Sumatra. **2.** the Indonesian language of the Sumatrans.

sum·bul (sum′bəl, sům′bůl), *n.* **1.** any of several aromatic or medicinal plants, as the East Indian spikenard or the Asiatic muskroot. **2.** the root of such a plant. **3.** the root of the muskroot, used as a nerve tonic and antispasmodic. [< French *sumbul* < Arabic *sunbul*]

Su·me·ri·an or **Su·mi·ri·an** (sü mir′ē ən), *adj.* of or having to do with the early inhabitants of Sumer, an ancient region in the valley of the Euphrates River, or their language. —*n.* **1.** one of the ancient non-Semitic inhabitants of Sumer: *In Dr. Gelb's view the Sumerians, that fabled people of Mesopotamia who for at least 1,500 years dominated the culture of the Near East, took the first step toward a "fully developed writing"* (Scientific American). **2.** a non-Semitic language of ancient Sumer, recorded in cuneiform inscriptions.

su·mi (sü′mē), *n.* a black stick made of carbon and glue, dipped in water for writing and drawing by Japanese artists: *Yokoyama's disciplined style produced . . . The Wheel of Life, a 140-ft.-long scroll done in sumi . . . wash* (Time).

[< Japanese *sumi*]

sum·less (sum′lis), *adj. Archaic.* that cannot be summed or reckoned up; incalculable: *Rich . . . As is the ooze and bottom of the sea With sunken wreck and sumless treasures* (Shakespeare).

sum·ma (sům′ə, sum′-), *n., pl.* **-mas, -mae** (-mē). a summary treatise dealing with a particular field or subject, or with the whole of human knowledge: *Although they acknowledged that God was ultimately un-*

knowable, the medieval scholastics devoted page after learned page of their summas to discussions of the divine attributes (Time). [< Latin *summa;* see SUM]

sum·ma·bil·i·ty (sum′ə bil′ə tē), *n.* the condition of being mathematically summable.

sum·ma·ble (sum′ə bəl), *adj.* that can be summed.

sum·ma cum lau·de (sům′ə kům lou′də; sum′ə kum lô′dē), with the highest distinction. These words are added to the diploma of a student who has done unusually good academic work. [< New Latin *summa cum laude* < Latin *summā,* feminine, ablative of *summus* highest, *cum* with, *laude,* ablative of *laus* praise]

sum·mand (sum′and, sum and′), *n.* one of two or more numbers or quantities to be added together. [< Medieval Latin *summandus,* gerundive of *summare* to sum]

sum·ma·ri·ly (sum′ər ə lē, sə mer′-), *adv.* in a summary manner; briefly; without delay.

sum·ma·ri·ness (sum′ər ē nis), *n.* the character of being summary.

sum·ma·rise (sum′ə rīz), *v.t., v.i.,* **-rised, -ris·ing.** *Especially British.* summarize.

sum·ma·rist (sum′ər ist), *n.* the maker of a summary.

sum·ma·ri·za·tion (sum′ər ə zā′shən), *n.* **1.** the act or process of summarizing. **2.** an instance of summarizing.

sum·ma·rize (sum′ə rīz), *v.t., v.i.,* **-rized, -riz·ing.** to make a summary of; give the main points of; express briefly; sum up: *It may be too early as yet to summarize any results* (London Times).

sum·ma·riz·er (sum′ə rī′zər), *n.* a summarist.

sum·ma·ry (sum′ər ē), *n., pl.* **-ries,** *adj.* —*n.* a brief account or statement giving the chief points or substance of a matter; epitome; abstract; abridgment: *The history book had a summary at the end of each chapter.*
[< Latin *summārium* < *summa* sum (in genitive, main points)]
—*adj.* **1.** containing or comprising the chief points; concise and comprehensive; brief: *a summary account.* **2.** without delay or formality; direct and prompt: *The Indian took summary vengeance by killing his enemies. He cleared the table by the summary process of tilting everything upon it into the fireplace* (Dickens). **3.** carried out or determined rapidly, with the omission of certain formalities usually required by law: *summary proceedings.*
[< Medieval Latin *summarius* < Latin *summa* sum]
—**Syn.** *n.* **Summary, digest** mean a brief presentation of facts or subject matter. **Summary** applies to a brief statement, in one's own words, giving only the main points of an article, chapter, book, speech, subject, proposed plan, etc.: *Give a summary of today's lesson.* **Digest** applies to a shortened form of a book, article, etc., leaving out less important details but keeping the original order, emphasis, and words: *Some magazines contain digests of current books.* -*adj.* **1.** terse, succinct.

sum·mate (sum′āt), *v.t.,* **-mat·ed, -mat·ing.** to add; sum; find the total of.

sum·ma·tion (su mā′shən), *n.* **1.** the process of finding the sum or total; addition: *the ... summation of a grotesque assembly of faults* (H.G. Wells). **2.** the total. **3.** *Law.* the final presentation of facts and arguments by counsel for the opposing sides. —**Syn. 2.** aggregate.

sum·ma·tion·al (su mā′shə nəl), *adj.* produced or expressed by summation or addition.

sum·ma·tive (sum′ə tiv), *adj.* involving summation or addition; additive.

sum·mer[1] (sum′ər), *n.* **1.** the warmest season of the year; the season of the year between spring and autumn: *Shall I compare thee to a summer's day? Thou art more lovely and more temperate* (Shakespeare). **2.** anything considered like summer in its warmth, full beauty, healthy maturity, or the like: *a young man in the summer of his life. But thy eternal summer shall not fade ...* (Shakespeare). *I only know that summer sang in me A little while, that in me sings no more* (Edna St. Vincent Millay).
—*adj.* **1.** of summer; in summer: *a summer night, summer flowers, summer heat. Some happy summer isle* (William Morris). **2.** used in summer: *summer clothes, a summer cottage.*
—*v.i.* to pass the summer: *to summer at the seashore.* —*v.t.* to keep or feed during the summer; arrange or manage during the summer: *to summer the stock, to summer cattle in the mountains.*
[Old English *sumor*]

sum·mer[2] (sum′ər), *n.* **1.** a horizontal bearing beam in a building, especially the main beam supporting the girders or joists of a floor (or occasionally the rafters of a roof). **2.** a large stone laid over a column in beginning a cross vault. **3.** a lintel. [< Anglo-French *sumer,* and *somer,* variant of Old French *somier* (originally) beast of burden < Late Latin *saumārius,* for Latin *sagmārius* pack horse < *sagma* pack saddle < Greek *ságma, -atos* < *sáttein* to pack, stuff]

summer camp, a camp for health and recreation, especially for children, open during the summer: *They were forced to send Johnny to a summer camp where he was compelled to concentrate on camp lore ... swimming technique and ... Indian legends* (Wall Street Journal).

summer flounder, a greenish flounder of the Atlantic Coast of North America with white spots on the body and both eyes on the left side of the head.

sum·mer·house (sum′ər hous′), *n.* any of various small, simple structures, typically one resembling a roofed platform with a railing but no walls, built in a park or flower garden to afford shade, shelter from showers, etc., in the summer.

summer house, a home for the summer.

sum·mer·i·ness (sum′ər ē nis), *n.* summery character.

sum·mer·less (sum′ər lis), *adj.* having no summer; without summer weather: *In the high latitudes, in the vicinity of the poles, are the summerless polar regions, where there is a general prevalence of low temperature* (Finch and Trewartha).

sum·mer·like (sum′ər līk′), *adj.* resembling summer; summery.

summer lilac, buddleia, a chiefly tropical, ornamental shrub.

sum·mer·li·ness (sum′ər lē nis), *n.* summeriness.

sum·mer·ly (sum′ər lē), *adj.* summerlike; summery.

summer oil, a thick oil for use in automobile engines during hot weather.

summer resort, a place in the mountains, on a lake, at the seashore, etc., where people go in the summer: *The islands have become summer resorts, and for the most part cottages and metal beach chairs stand where the vineyards once flourished* (New Yorker).

sum·mer·sault (sum′ər sôlt), *n., v.i.* somersault.

summer sausage, uncooked sausage that is smoked or dried by air.

summer savory, an annual European herb of the mint family much used as a flavoring ingredient in cooking.

summer school, a school conducted in the summer, often for training teachers: *I will have to get some credits in summer school if I wish to teach in September.*

sum·mer·set (sum′ər set), *n., v.i.* somersault.

summer solstice, 1. the solstice that occurs about June 21 or 22. It is the time in the Northern Hemisphere when the sun is farthest north from the equator. **2.** the northernmost point of the ecliptic, which the sun reaches at this time. It is now in the constellation Gemini.

summer squash, any of various squashes that ripen quickly and are intended to be eaten while the skins are still tender, as the crookneck squash, the zucchini, etc.

summer stock, 1. a theatrical stock company that performs during the summer: *Many famous actors began their careers as stagehands in summer stock.* **2.** the repertory or theater of such a company.

summer sweet, a shrub of eastern United States with alternate, serrate leaves and racemes of fragrant, white or pink flowers.

summer tanager, a tanager of the southern and eastern United States and Mexico, the male of which has rosy-red feathers.

sum·mer·tide (sum′ər tīd′), *n.* summertime. [< *summer*[1] + *tide*[1] season]

sum·mer·time (sum′ər tīm′), *n.* **1.** the season of summer; summer. **2.** any period in which energy is greatest or talent most productive: *in the summertime of life.*

summer time, *Especially British.* daylight-saving time.

summer wheat, any variety of wheat that is planted in the spring, and ripens in the same summer; spring wheat.

summer White House, a residence occupied in summer by the President of the United States: *He laid down a broad platform of labor reform in an unusual supplemental statement issued from the summer White House at Newport, R.I.* (Wall Street Journal).

sum·mer·wood (sum′ər wůd′), *n.* a dark ring or layer of wood formed around a tree each summer, composed of relatively small, compact cells with thick walls.

sum·mer·y (sum′ər ē), *adj.,* **-mer·i·er, -mer·i·est. 1.** of summer. **2.** for summer: *a summery dress.* **3.** like summer: *a summery day.* —**Syn. 1.** estival.

sum·ming-up (sum′ing up′), *n., pl.* **summings-up. 1.** the act or process of summarizing: *... an opportunity for philosophical reflection or summing-up* (Scientific American). **2.** a summary: *It is read in the Netherlands as a summing-up of the experiences of so many Hollanders* (London Times). **3.** a recapitulation of the chief points of the evidence to a jury before it retires to consider a verdict: *The Judge, resuming his summing-up yesterday, said ...* (Sunday Times). **4.** an estimate of the qualities or character of a person or thing; size-up: *The profile of President Lowell is the fairest, saltiest summing-up I have ever read* (Atlantic).

sum·mist (sum′ist), *n.* a medieval writer of a summary or compendium, especially of theology, as Saint Thomas Aquinas. [< Medieval Latin *summista* < Latin *summa* sum; see SUM]

sum·mit (sum′it), *n.* **1.** the highest point of a mountain, hill, etc.; topmost peak or ridge; top: *the summit of a mountain.* **2.** the topmost part of anything; apex: *The summits of emotion can only be reached at rare intervals* (W. Somerset Maugham). *It is sometimes necessary at the summit of authority ... to remain calm when others panic* (Sir Winston Churchill). **3.** the uttermost objective of ambition, hope, etc., or highest degree of skill, energy, etc.; acme: *The summit of her ambition was to be an actress.* **4.** *Informal.* a conference at the highest level: *A Foreign Ministers' Conference ... might be allowed as much as two months to prepare for a "summit"* (Sunday Times).
at the summit, at the level of diplomacy involving heads of government; at the highest level: *Fruitful negotiations on East-West tension can be achieved only at the summit* (London Times).
—*adj.* of or having to do with a summit meeting: *summit talks, summit decisions.*
[Middle English *somette* < Old French *somete,* feminine, or *somet,* masculine (diminutive) < *som,* or *sum* summit < Latin *summum,* noun use of adjective, neuter of *summus* highest. Compare SUM.]
—**Syn.** *n.* **1, 2, 3.** pinnacle, zenith. See **top.**

sum·mit·al (sum′ə təl), *adj.* of or having to do with a summit.

sum·mit·eer (sum′ə tir′), *n. Informal.* a participant in a summit meeting: *The Western summiteers were determined to make no real concession at all on Berlin* (Time).

sum·mit·less (sum′it lis), *adj.* having no summit.

summit meeting or **conference,** a meeting between heads of governments, especially for the purpose of resolving disagreements and lessening international tensions: *All the big European questions were taken up by the "summit" conference at Geneva* (London Times).

sum·mit·ry (sum′ə trē), *n. Informal.* **1.** the conducting of summit meetings: *He is one of the old hands at Commonwealth summitry, having attended the 1953 conference shortly after succeeding his late father as Prime Minister* (Manchester Guardian). **2.** summit meetings: *warning that the Khrushchev-Eisenhower exchange of visits and summitry does not mean all is well with the world* (Wall Street Journal).

sum·mon (sum′ən), *v.t.* **1.** to call with authority; order to come; send for: *to summon men to defend their country. Summon the children to dinner. A telegram summoned Bill home. It is a knell That summons*

thee to heaven or to hell (Shakespeare). **2.** to call together by authority for action or deliberation; convoke: *to summon a legislative body.* **3.** to order or notify formally to appear before a court or judge, especially to answer a charge. **4.** to call upon to do something: *The church bells summon people to worship.* **5.** to call upon (a fort, army, etc.) to surrender. **6.** to call up; stir to action or effort; arouse: *Jack summoned his courage and entered the deserted house.* [Middle English *sumunen,* or *somenen* < Anglo-French, Old French *sumun-,* stem of *somondre* < Vulgar Latin *summonere* to call, cite, for Latin *summonēre* hint to < *sub-* underneath + *monēre* warn]
—Syn. **1.** See **call.**

sum·mon·a·ble (sum′ən ə bəl), *adj.* that can be summoned: *True, there are bus delivery services and agents—but a free-lance van, summonable by this shop or that and delivering at the door, would be even better* (Punch).

sum·mon·er (sum′ə nər), *n.* **1.** a person who summons. **2.** (formerly) a petty officer whose duty was to warn persons to appear in court.

sum·mons (sum′ənz), *n., pl.* **-mons·es,** *v.* —*n.* **1.** an urgent call for the presence or attendance of a person; a summoning command, knock, message, or the like: *Death is a common friend or foe ... And at his summons each must go* (M.J. Barry). **2.** an authoritative call to appear at a place named, or to attend to some public duty. **3.** *Law.* **a.** an order or notice to a person from an authority to appear before a court or judge on or before a certain date, especially to answer as a defendant to a charge made against him. **b.** the writ (writ of summons) by which such an order is made: *He received a summons for fast driving.* **4.** a call to do something, especially to surrender.
—*v.t. Informal.* to take out a summons against; summon to court: *Say another word and I'll summons you* (Dickens).
[< Anglo-French *somonse* < *somondre;* see SUMMON]

sum·mum bo·num (sum′əm bō′nəm), *Latin.* the highest or ultimate good: *Bentham, the founder of Utilitarianism, ... held as the summum bonum the greatest good for the greatest number and believed that there was no limit to the benefits a good education could confer* (Scientific American).

sum·mum ge·nus (sum′əm jē′nəs), *Latin.* the highest genus or class.

sum·mum jus (sum′əm jus′), *Latin.* the strictest law or legal right.

su·mo (sü′mō), *n.* a Japanese form of wrestling with fewer throws than in jujitsu. [< Japanese *sumō* wrestling]

su·mo·ist (sü′mō ist), *n.* a person who practices sumo: *Kirinji, if you follow the theory, was not lucky to win, he was the superior sumoist* (Manchester Guardian Weekly).

sump (sump), *n.* **1.** a reservoir for oil or other lubricating fluid at the lowest point in a lubricating system, especially that beneath the crankcase of an internal-combustion engine. **2.** the bottom of a mine shaft, where water collects and from which it is pumped. **3.** a shaft or tunnel excavated in front of the main shaft or tunnel of a mine, boring, etc. **4.** any of various pits or reservoirs for collecting water or other fluid, especially fluid waste, as a cesspool, septic tank, etc.: *We have instituted a conservation program of over 400 sumps which are turning back millions of gallons of rain water into the ground, instead of letting it run off into the Atlantic Ocean or Long Island Sound* (New York Times). [< Middle Low German *sump,* or Middle Dutch *somp.* Compare SWAMP.]

sum·pi·tan (sum′pə tən), *n.* a kind of blowgun used by the Dyaks and Malays of Borneo for shooting darts, which are often poisoned. [< Malay *sumpītan* < *sumpit* blowpipe; (originally) narrow]

sump pump, a pump used to remove liquid from a sump.

sump·si·mus (sump′sə məs), *n.* a correct expression for replacing an incorrect but popular one. [< Latin *sumpsimus* (literally) we have taken. Compare MUMPSIMUS.]

sump·ter (sump′tər), *Archaic.* —*n.* a horse or mule for carrying baggage; pack animal. —*adj.* for carrying baggage: *Camels, mules, and horses are sumpter animals.* [Middle English *sumter* < Old French *sommetier* < Vulgar Latin *sagmatārius* < Latin *sagma.* Related to SUMMER².]

sump·tu·ar·y (sump′chủ er′ē), *adj.* having to do with or regulating expenses or expenditure, as for moral or religious reasons, or to avoid extravagance or waste: *Laws forbidding women to wear jewelry would be sumptuary laws.* [< Latin *sūmptuārius* < *sūmptus, -ūs* expense < *sūmere* spend, buy; (originally) take]

sump·tu·os·i·ty (sump′chủ os′ə tē), *n.* expensiveness; costliness.

sump·tu·ous (sump′chủ əs), *adj.* **1.** costly; magnificent; rich: *The king gave a sumptuous banquet.* **2.** splendid or magnificent in appearance: *She spoke and turn'd her sumptuous head* (Tennyson). [< Middle French, Old French *somptueux* (with English *-ous*), learned borrowing from Latin *sūmptuōsus* < *sūmptus, -ūs* expense; see SUMPTUARY] **—sump′tu·ous·ly,** *adv.* **—sump′tu·ous·ness,** *n.*
—Syn. **1.** luxurious, lavish.

sump·weed (sump′wēd′), *n.* the marsh elder.

sum total, the total amount; aggregate; totality; sum: *The sum total of our expenses on the trip came to $55.30.*

sum-up (sum′up′), *n.* a summary; estimate; summing-up: *The sum-up: You can expect a different, more positive U.S. program for dealing with Russia* (Newsweek).

sun (sun), *n., v.,* **sunned, sun·ning.** —*n.* **1.** the brightest of the heavenly bodies as viewed from the earth; the star around which the earth and other planets revolve and which supplies them with light and heat. Its mean distance from the earth is slightly less than 93,000,000 miles, its mean diameter about 864,400 miles, its volume about 1,300,000 times that of the earth, and its mass about 332,000 times that of the earth. The sun is gaseous, consisting chiefly of hydrogen and helium. *... the high temperature of the sun, which is more than sufficient to vaporize all known substances* (George Ellery Hale). **2.** the sun with reference to its position in the sky, its aspect, visibility, heat, etc.: *a tropical sun. The sun lights and warms the earth. The clouds that gather round the setting sun ...* (Wordsworth). **3.** the light and warmth of the sun; sunshine; sunlight: *The cat likes to sit in the sun.* **4.** any heavenly body, especially a star that is the center of a system of planets; luminary; star: *Other suns perhaps with their attendant moons thou wilt descry* (Milton). **5.** something like the sun in brightness or splendor; a source of light, honor, glory, or prosperity: *Knowledge ... is the great sun in the firmament* (Daniel Webster). *Sun of my soul, thou Saviour dear* (John Keble). *But, soft! what light through yonder window breaks? It is the east, and Juliet is the sun* (Shakespeare). **6.** a figure, image, ornament, etc., made to resemble the sun, as a heraldic bearing, usually charged with human features, or a kind of circular firework. **7.** *Archaic.* a day, as being determined by the rising of the sun. **8.** *Archaic.* a year; a revolution of the earth around the sun: *Vile it were For some three suns to store and hoard myself* (Tennyson). *The thoughts of men are widen'd with the process of the suns* (Tennyson).
against the sun, in the direction contrary to the apparent movement of the sun: *When the wind shifts against the sun, trust it not, for back it will run* (Frederick Bedford).
from sun to sun, from sunrise to sunset: *Man's work's from sun to sun, Woman's work's never done* (old rhyme).
under the sun, on earth; in the world: *There is no new thing under the sun* (Ecclesiastes 1:9).
with the sun, in the direction of the apparent movement of the sun: *The starboard cable should be bitted with the sun, and the port cable against the sun* (H. Stuart).
—*v.t.* **1.** to expose to the sun's rays, as to warm, dry, air, etc.; place in the sun: *The swimmers sunned themselves on the beach.* **2.** to bring or get into a specified condition by exposure to the sun. —*v.i.* to expose oneself to the sun's rays; bask in the sun: *We were sunning on the pier* (Arthur S. M. Hutchinson).
[Old English *sunne*]

Sun., Sunday.

sun·back (sun′bak′), *adj.* (of a garment) cut low in the back; allowing exposure of the back to the sun: *Printed voiles and dotted Swiss cotton sleeveless and sunback dresses are particularly strong sellers* (New York Times).

sun-baked (sun′bākt′), *adj.* **1.** baked by exposure to the sun, as bricks, pottery, etc. **2.** excessively heated by the sun; dried up, parched, or hardened by the heat of the sun: *Soil conservationists warn that next year the damaged acreage will be even greater unless enough slow rainfall soaks the sun-baked earth* (Wall Street Journal).

sun bath, 1. the exposure of the body to the direct rays of the sun; basking in the sun. **2.** the exposure of the body to a sunlamp.

sun·bathe (sun′bāᴛʜ′), *v.i.,* **-bathed, -bath·ing.** to bask in the sun; enjoy a sun bath: *You will sunbathe on golden sands beside coral seas* (New Yorker). **—sun′bath′er,** *n.*

sun·beam (sun′bēm′), *n.* a ray of sunlight: *A sunbeam brightened the child's hair to gold.*

sun bear, a small bear of southern Asia, black with white and yellowish markings on the chest.

sun·ber·ry (sun′ber′ē), *n., pl.* **-ries. 1.** the edible berry of a cultivated variety of the black nightshade. **2.** the plant bearing this fruit.

sun·bird (sun′bėrd′), *n.* **1.** any of a family of small birds with brilliant and variegated plumage, found in tropical and subtropical regions of Africa, Asia, and Australia. **2.** sun bittern.

sun bittern, a long-legged, long-necked, tropical American bird, related to the cranes and rails.

Sun Bittern (20 in. long)

sun·bon·net (sun′bon′it), *n.* a woman's large bonnet that shades the face and neck from the sun.

sun·bon·net·ed (sun′bon′ə tid), *adj.* wearing a sunbonnet: *a sunbonneted frontierswoman.*

sun·bow (sun′bō′), *n. Archaic.* an arch of prismatic colors like a rainbow, formed by refraction of sunlight in spray or vapor: *The sunbow's rays still arch The torrent with the many hues of heaven* (Byron). [< *sun* + *bow²;* patterned on *rainbow*]

sun·break (sun′brāk′), *n.* **1.** a burst of sunshine; sunburst. **2.** sunrise.

sun·break·er (sun′brā′kər), *n.* a louvered structure of wood or other material over a window or other opening to keep out direct sunlight, especially during the summer: *To keep cool in summer and warm in winter, each house will have what Le Corbusier calls "sunbreakers"* (Time).

sun·burn (sun′bėrn′), *n., v.,* **-burned** or **-burnt, -burn·ing.** —*n.* **1.** a red and painful inflammation of the skin, caused by overexposure to the sun's rays: *Bad sunburns often cause freckles.* **2.** the color of red or tan resulting from sunburn.
—*v.i.* **1.** to burn the skin by the sun's rays. **2.** to become burned by the sun: *Her skin sunburns very quickly.* —*v.t.* **1.** to affect with sunburn. **2.** to burn (the skin) by exposure to the sun.

sun·burned (sun′bėrnd′), *adj.* burned, scorched, or browned by the sun; tanned: *sunburned grass, sunburned boys.*
—*v.* a past tense and a past participle of **sunburn.**

sun·burnt (sun′bėrnt′), *v.* sunburned; a past tense and a past participle of **sunburn.**

sun·burst (sun′bėrst′), *n.* **1.** a sudden shining of the sun through a break in clouds: *a dazzling sunburst.* **2.** a brooch or other piece of jewelry with jewels arranged to resemble the sun with its rays.

sun clock, 1. a sundial. **2.** a clock which shows solar time.

sun compass, a compass that uses the sun to indicate true north, formerly used in air navigation: *The sun compass is a rather obsolete species of the astro compass.*

sun-cured (sun′kyủrd′), *adj.* dried and prepared by direct exposure to sunlight: *Farms producing both fire-cured Virginia tobacco and sun-cured Virginia tobacco may combine acreage allotments for the two in future years* (Wall Street Journal).

Sund., Sunday.

sun·dae (sun′dē), *n.* a dish of ice cream served with syrup, crushed fruits, nuts, whipped cream, etc. [American English; origin uncertain; probably < *Sunday* (because it was originally sold on this day only)]

sun dance, a religious ceremony in honor of the sun, formerly accompanied by rites of self-torture, etc., performed by North American Indians of the Western prairies at the summer solstice.

Sun·da·nese (sun′də nēz′, -nēs′), *adj., n., pl.* **-nese.** —*adj.* of western Java, its people, or their language.
—*n.* **1.** a native of western Java. **2.** the Malayo-Polynesian language spoken in western Java.

Sun·day (sun′dē, -dā), *n.* **1.** the first day of the calendar week. *Abbr.:* Sun. **2.** this day as one set aside for rest and worship by most Christians; the Christian Sabbath.
—*adj.* **1.** of, taking place on, or characteristic of Sunday: *a Sunday concert, a Sunday picnic.* **2.** not regular or professional; off-and-on; occasional: *a Sunday driver. One may not look to the "Sunday painters" for great art* (London Times).
[Old English *sunnandæg,* ultimately translation of Latin *diēs sōlis* day of the sun, translation of Late Greek *hēmēra hēlíou*]
➔ **Sunday, Sabbath** are not true synonyms. **Sunday** is the name of the first day of the week, which is generally observed among Christians as a day of worship and rest from ordinary business. **Sabbath,** literally meaning a time of rest from work, applies to the seventh day of the week (Saturday) among the Jews and some Christians. But it is commonly applied to Sunday in the religious sense of a day for abstaining from work or activity of any kind except religious: *Some keep the Sabbath going to church—I keep it staying at home* (Emily Dickinson).

Sunday best, *Informal.* best clothes: *O, he was in his Sunday best!* (Robert Southey).

Sun·day-go-to-meet·ing (sun′dē gō′tə mē′ting), *adj. Informal or Dialect.* suitable for use in attending church; best, most presentable, etc.: *Weddings and funerals are for Sunday-go-to-meeting clothes.*

Sun·day·ish (sun′dē ish, -dā-), *adj.* characteristic of or like Sunday: *At the height of the rush hour the London traffic still has a Sundayish leisureliness to it compared with the frantic tempo of Paris* (London Times).

Sunday punch, *Slang.* **1.** a boxer's most powerful blow: *The champion floored his opponent in the second round with a Sunday punch.* **2.** the most powerful measure, weapon, etc., at one's disposal: *Some feel that if air power and our nuclear weapons are to be the main threat, we are not spending enough on aircraft to give us the "Sunday punch" needed* (New York Times).
[probably < *Sunday,* in the informal sense of "best," as in *Sunday best*]

Sunday school, 1. a school held on Sunday for teaching religion. **2.** those who teach and study there. Also, **Sabbath school.**
➔ The word *school* in **Sunday school** is capitalized only when it is part of a proper name, as in *St. Mark's Sunday School.*

sun·deck (sun′dek′), *n.* **1.** the upper deck of a passenger ship: *Around the spacious sundeck, 24 aluminum life boats . . . glisten in the sun* (Time). **2.** a level, terrace, porch, or the like on, alongside, or above a building, swimming pool, etc., for sunbathing, lounging, etc.: *Many of the proposed suites will have sundecks with a view over a wide sweep of the East River* (New York Times).

sun·der (sun′dər), *v.t., v.i.* to separate; part; sever; split: *Time and distance often sunder friends.*
—*n.* **in sunder,** apart; asunder: *Lightning tore the tree in sunder.*
[Old English *syndrian, sundrian* < *sundor* apart. Compare ASUNDER.]
—**Syn.** *v.t., v.i.* divide, disjoin, disconnect.

sun·der·ance (sun′dər əns), *n.* severance; separation.

sun·dew (sun′dü′, -dyü′), *n.* any of a group of small bog herbs whose leaves are covered with glandular hairs secreting viscid drops for capturing and absorbing insects.

Round-leaved Sundew (about 10 in. high)

sun·di·al (sun′dī′əl), *n.* an instrument that marks the hour of the day by the position of a shadow cast by the sun. See picture above in next column.

sun disk, 1. the disk of the sun. **2.** a figure of the sun, used in religious symbolism, especially as an attribute of the Egyptian sun god Ra.

sun·dog (sun′dôg′, -dog′), *n.* **1.** a parhelion. **2.** a fragment of a rainbow. [origin uncertain]

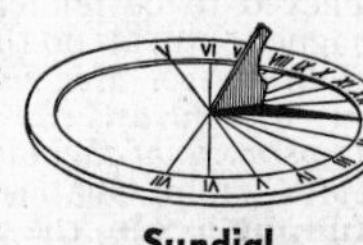
Sundial

sun·down (sun′doun′), *n.* sunset: *We'll be home by sundown.*

sun·down·er (sun′dou′nər), *n.* **1.** *Australian Slang.* a tramp who makes a practice of arriving at a farm, ranch, etc., about sunset under the pretense of seeking work, so as to obtain food and a night's lodging. **2.** (especially in South Africa) a drink of alcoholic liquor taken at sunset: *White settlers of the Salisbury area were comfortably settled on the veranda . . . sipping their customary sundowners* (Time). **3.** *Western U.S.* a person who lives toward the sundown or west.

sun·down·ing (sun′dou′ning), *n.* the practice of a sundowner.

sun-drenched (sun′drencht′), *adj.* overspread with sunlight: *the sun-drenched cane fields of Cuba* (Newsweek).

sun dress, a sleeveless dress with a low-cut neckline in the front and back.

sun-dried (sun′drīd′), *adj.* dried by exposure to the sun: *sun-dried raisins. The Pueblo Indians built with sun-dried bricks.*

sun·dries (sun′drēz), *n.pl.* sundry things; items not named; odds and ends: *My expenses included $36.00 for room and board, $9.50 for shirts, $3.25 for books, and $1.60 for sundries.*

sun·dries·man (sun′drēz mən), *n., pl.* **-men.** *Especially British.* a dealer in sundries.

sun·drops (sun′drops′), *n., pl.* **-drops.** any of various evening primroses having yellow flowers that bloom by day.

sun·dry (sun′drē), *adj.* **1.** a number of; several: *From sundry hints, he guessed he was to be given a bicycle for his birthday.* **2.** composed of diverse elements or items; various in nature; miscellaneous: *a box of sundry trinkets.*
[Old English *syndrig* separate, special, ultimately related to *sundor* separately, apart]

sun·fast (sun′fast′, -fäst′), *adj.* that sunlight will not fade: *sunfast material for a dress.* [< *sun* + *fast*[1] fixed] —**Syn.** sunproof.

SUNFED (no periods), Special United Nations Fund for Economic Development.

sun·fish (sun′fish′), *n., pl.* **-fish·es** or (*collectively*) **-fish. 1.** any of a group of small fresh-water fish of North America, found especially in lakes and ponds, and often caught for food. **2.** a large marine fish having a short, deep, compressed body, sometimes growing as large as 11 feet long, and yielding tough flesh. **3.** any other related fish.

Common Ocean Sunfish (def. 2) (to 11 ft. long)

sun·flow·er (sun′flou′ər), *n.* any of a group of North American plants of the composite family, having conspicuous flower heads with yellow or reddish rays and a yellow, purplish, or brown disk. Sunflowers produce seeds which are used as food for stock and which yield an edible oil. The common sunflower, the state flower of Kansas, is a tall plant with very large, showy flowers.

Common Sunflower (6 to 10 ft. tall)

Sunflower State, a nickname of Kansas.

sung (sung), *v.* a past tense and the past participle of **sing:** *Many songs were sung at the concert.*
➔ See **sing** for usage note.

Sung (sůng), *n.* a Chinese dynasty, 960-1279, noted for its works of art, especially in painting and ceramics.

sun·gar (sung′gər), *n.* a breastwork of stone. Also, **sangar.** [< Hindustani *sàngar*]

sun gear, the central gear around which the planetary gears revolve: *For reverse . . . the front clutch is released and the rear clutch engaged so that the large sun gear is now connected to the turbine* (Jud Purvis). See **planetary** for picture.

sun·glass (sun′glas′, -gläs′), *n.* a lens for concentrating the rays of the sun; burning glass.

sun·glass·es (sun′glas′iz, -gläs′-), *n.pl.* eyeglasses made with tinted lenses to protect against the glare of the sun.

sun·glow (sun′glō′), *n.* **1.** the glow of the sun. **2.** a diffused, hazy light sometimes visible before sunrise or after sunset, due to fine, solid particles in the atmosphere.

sun god, or **sun-god** (sun′god′), *n.* the sun regarded as a deity; a god identified or particularly associated with the sun, as Helios, Apollo, Sol, or Ra.

sun-grebe (sun′grēb′), *n.* a finfoot of Africa or South America, having feet like a grebe's.

sun hat, a broad-brimmed hat worn to protect the head from the sun.

sun helmet, a helmet worn to protect the head from the sun; pith helmet; topi: *Conspicuous in the old-fashioned sun helmet which had accompanied him from Palestine, he led the procession at the head of the 2nd Ethiopian Battalion* (Sunday Times).

sun hemp, sunn: *Sun hemp may furnish a fiber for making paper products* (Wall Street Journal).

sunk (sungk), *v.* a past tense and a past participle of **sink:** *The ship had sunk to the bottom.*

sunk·en (sung′kən), *adj.* **1.** sunk: *a sunken ship.* **2.** submerged: *a sunken rock.* **3.** situated below the general level: *a sunken garden.* **4.** fallen in; hollow: *sunken eyes, sunken cheeks.*
—*v.* a past participle of **sink.**
➔ **Sunken** is now chiefly used as an adjective.

sun·ket (sung′kit, sůng′-), *n. Scottish.* **1.** a dainty; tidbit. **2.** something, especially something to eat. [probably < Scottish *sumquhat* somewhat]

sunk fence, a ha-ha.

sun-kissed (sun′kist′), *adj.* **1.** that has been exposed to sunshine: *Harvesters take the sunkissed grapes into the lagares or wine presses to extract the juice* (New Yorker). **2.** sunshiny: *. . . a sunkissed production of "The Boys from Syracuse"* (New York Times).

sun lamp, 1. a lamp for producing ultraviolet rays similar to those in sunlight, used for therapeutic treatments, as for some skin diseases. **2.** a large lamp used in motion-picture studios which reflects its light by means of parabolic mirrors.

sun·less (sun′lis), *adj.* without sun; without sunlight. —**Syn.** dark, shady.

sun·let (sun′lit), *n.* a little sun.

sun·light (sun′līt′), *n.* the light of the sun. —**Syn.** sunshine.

sun·like (sun′līk′), *adj.* resembling the sun: *A sunlike ball of flame burst last week from a new cylindrical furnace in the Jones and Laughlin Steel Corp. works* (Time).

sun·lit (sun′lit′), *adj.* lighted by the sun.

sun lounge, a sunroom; sun parlor: *Air conditioned suites on tropical patio with sapphire pool, sun lounge . . . and luncheon terrace* (Wall Street Journal).

sunn (sun), *n.,* or **sunn hemp, 1.** an East Indian shrub of the pea family, with long, narrow leaves, slender branches, and bright-yellow flowers. **2.** its inner bark, from which a hemplike fiber is obtained. **3.** the fiber, used for rope, cordage, bags, etc. [< Hindi *san* < Sanskrit *śaṇa* hemp]

Sun·na or **Sun·nah** (sůn′ə), *n.* the traditional part of Moslem law, not directly attributed to Mohammed, but believed to derive from his sayings and actions as recorded by his disciples. As a guide, the Sunna is accepted as being as authoritative as the Koran by the Sunnite or orthodox Moslems but is rejected by the Shiites. [< Arabic *sunna* (literally) form, course, rule]

Sun·ni (sůn′ē), *n., pl.* **-ni** or **-nis. 1.** an orthodox Moslem; a Sunnite. **2.** the Sunnites as a group: *The Sunni . . . compose about 90 per cent of present-day Islam* (Newsweek).

sun·ni·ly (sun′ə lē), *adv.* in a sunny manner.

sun·ni·ness (sun′ē nis), *n.* the state of being sunny.

Sun·nite (sůn′īt), *n.* a Moslem of the majority sect, usually termed orthodox, accepting the Sunna as of equal importance with the Koran and recognizing the first four caliphs as Mohammed's legitimate successors. [< Arabic *sunnī* a believer in *Sunna* + English *-ite*[1]]

sun·ny (sun′ē), *adj.*, **-ni·er, -ni·est. 1.** having much sunshine: *a sunny day, sunny weather.* **2.** exposed to, lighted by, or warmed by the direct rays of the sun: *a sunny room.* **3.** like the sun, especially in color; bright yellow or golden. **4.** bright; cheerful; happy: *a sunny smile.* **5.** (of light) of or proceeding from the sun. —**Syn. 4.** genial.

sunny side, 1. the side that is exposed to sunlight: *the sunny side of the street.* **2.** the pleasant side or aspect of anything: *Then, only looking at the sunny side of things, all was bright* (Edward J. Trelawny).

on the sunny side of, younger than; under the age of: *Mr. [Harold] Wilson, still on the sunny side of 50 himself, wants to lower his Cabinet's average age* (London Times).

sun·ny-side up (sun′ē sīd′), (of an egg) fried only on one side, so that the yolk is on top.

sun parlor, a room or sun porch with many windows, used as a living room or sitting room in sunny weather.

sun porch, a porch enclosed largely by glass.

sun·pow·ered (sun′pou′ərd), *adj.* powered by sunlight or by energy from sunlight: *A sun-powered refrigerator has been developed by two Israeli engineers* (Science News Letter).

sun·proof (sun′prüf′), *adj.* impervious to or unaffected by the rays of the sun: *These sunproof curtains will not fade.*

sun·ray (sun′rā′), *n.* a ray of the sun; sunbeam.

sun·rise (sun′rīz′), *n.* **1.** the apparent rising of the sun above the horizon at the beginning of the day. **2.** the accompanying atmospheric changes: *The scarlet shafts of sunrise* (Tennyson). **3.** the time when the sun rises; the beginning of day. —**Syn. 3.** daybreak, dawn.

sun roof, a section of an automobile roof that can slide open: *Any car can be fitted with this wide-open sun roof* (Observer).

sun·room (sun′rüm′, -rům′), *n.* a room with many windows to let in sunlight; sun parlor.

sun·rose (sun′rōz′), *n.* **1.** a plant often grown in rock gardens, having flowers which expand in sunlight; rockrose. **2.** the flower of this plant.

sun·scald (sun′skôld′), *n.* injury to a plant, such as permanent wilting of the leaves, due to excessive exposure to very bright sunlight.

sun·screen (sun′skrēn′), *n.* a chemical substance that screens ultraviolet rays, used in suntan lotions.

sun·set (sun′set′), *n.* **1.** the apparent setting of the sun below the horizon at the end of the day: *After sunset, the horizon burned and glowed with rich crimson and orange lustre* (Hawthorne). **2.** the accompanying atmospheric changes: *Then in the sunset's flush they went aloft* (John Masefield). **3.** the time when the sun sets; the close of day. **4.** decline or close, especially of a period of prosperity or the like: *the sunset of life* (Thomas Campbell). *The gloom that darkens, or the hope that glorifies the sunset of our days* (John R. Illingworth).
—**Syn. 3.** sundown.

sun·shade (sun′shād′), *n.* **1.** a parasol. **2.** protection against the sun. **3.** an awning, especially one over the outside of a window.

sun·shine (sun′shīn′), *n.* **1.** the shining of the sun; light or rays of the sun: *Occasionally, when the wind opened seams in the roof of cloud, there were brief splashes of . . . sunshine . . .* (Hugh MacLennan). **2.** a place, area, etc., exposed to the shining of the sun. **3.** the warmth, light, etc., deriving from the rays of the sun. **4.** brightness; cheerfulness; happiness. **5.** a source of this.

Sunshine State, a nickname of Florida and of South Dakota.

sun·shin·y (sun′shī′nē), *adj.*, **-shin·i·er, -shin·i·est. 1.** having much sunshine. **2.** bright; cheerful; happy.

sun shower, a summer shower of rain from a passing cumulus cloud, preceded and followed by full sunshine.

sun·sight (sun′sīt′), *n.* an observation of the altitude of the sun, used to determine latitude and longitude, especially at sea: *My position is 40 South, 18.25 East, but this is a rough reckoning as I have been unable to get a sunsight for two days* (Sunday Times).

sun·spot (sun′spot′), *n.* one of the spots that appear periodically in certain zones of the surface of the sun and whose cycle is believed to be related to the frequency of magnetic storms on the earth: *A sunspot is a relatively cool area in the photosphere, dark only by contrast with its surroundings. The temperature of the darkest part . . . is about 4000°C* (John Charles Duncan).

sunspot cycle, the period of about eleven years in which the maximum frequency of sunspots recurs.

sunspot maximum, the period during the sunspot cycle in which sunspots are most frequent: *At sunspot maximum, most of the spots appear at latitudes 10 degrees north and south of the polar equator* (New Astronomy).

sunspot minimum, the period during the sunspot cycle in which sunspots are least frequent.

sun star, any of various starfishes having many rays.

sun·stone (sun′stōn′), *n.* any of several varieties of feldspar showing red or golden-yellow reflections.

sun·stroke (sun′strōk′), *n.* a severe exhaustion, characterized by a very high fever and sometimes fatal, caused by excessive exposure to the infrared rays of the sun.

sun·struck (sun′struk′), *adj.* overcome by the heat of the sun; affected with sunstroke.

sun·suit (sun′süt′), *n.* short pants held up by shoulder straps often attached to a bib and worn without a shirt by children.

sun·swept (sun′swept′), *adj.* swept by the sun; exposed to steady sunlight: . . . *the striking beauty of distant lagoons, ripping hurricanes, and sunswept port towns* (New Yorker).

sun·tan (sun′tan′), *n.* **1.** the reddish-brown color of a person's skin tanned by the sun: *He had collected a walnut suntan from the top of his bald head to practically his toes* (Punch). **2.** a light, brownish-yellow color; khaki: *Sizes 8 to 18 in suntan, white, aqua . . . and black* (New Yorker).

suntans, a khaki military uniform; khaki shirt and trousers: *Tough . . . soldiers in suntans deployed briskly* (Time).
—*adj.* light, brownish-yellow; khaki.

suntan lotion, a lotion containing a chemical substance that screens the sun's ultraviolet rays and prevents sunburn.

sun-tanned (sun′tand′), *adj.* having a suntan: *His blue eyes were startlingly clear, and, like most sun-tanned people, he looked very healthy* (New Yorker).

sun·tans (sun′tanz′), *n.pl.* See under **suntan,** *n.*

sun time, solar time.

sun trap, a place or device for catching sunshine: *As it is protected by the cliffs, this beach is a real sun trap* (Observer).

sun·up (sun′up′), *n.* sunrise.

sun visor, 1. a flap above the windshield of a car, truck, locomotive, etc., that can be lowered to shield the eyes from the sun: *Their automobile has sun visors that can swing from the front to the side.* **2.** a fixed sheet of metal or tinted plastic on the outside of a car, truck, etc., to shield the eyes from the sun.

sun·ward (sun′wərd), *adv., adj.* toward the sun.

sun·wards (sun′wərdz), *adv.* sunward.

sun·wise (sun′wīz′), *adv.* from left to right; clockwise.

sun worship, the worship of the sun, especially as the symbol of the deity or as a source of light and heat.

su·o ju·re (sü′ō jůr′ē), *Latin.* in one's own right.

su·o lo·co (sü′ō lō′kō), *Latin.* in its own or proper place.

sup[1] (sup), *v.*, **supped, sup·ping.** —*v.i.* to eat the evening meal; take supper: *He supped alone on bread and milk.* —*v.t.* to give a supper to or for. [< Old French *souper* < *soupe;* see SOUP]

sup[2] (sup), *v.t., v.i.*, **supped, sup·ping,** *n.* sip: *He supped his soup from a spoon. Who sipped no sup, and who craved no crumb, As he sighed for the love of a lady* (W.S. Gilbert). [Old English *sūpan*]

sup-, *prefix.* the form of **sub-** before *p,* as in *suppress.*

sup., an abbreviation for the following:
1. superior.
2. superlative.
3. supine.
4. **a.** supplement. **b.** supplementary.
5. supply.
6. supra (above).
7. supreme.

Sup. Ct., 1. Superior Court. **2.** Supreme Court.

supe (süp), *n. Slang.* super.

su·per (sü′pər), *n.* **1.** *Informal.* an extra person or thing; supernumerary. **2.** *Informal.* a supernumerary actor; extra: *to use 300 supers for a mob scene.* **3.** *Informal.* a superintendent, especially of an apartment house or office building. **4.** *Commerce.* goods of extremely fine quality, superior grade, very large size, etc. **5.** a thin, starched cotton of open weave used in reinforcing books: *On most sewed books, the machine glues a strip of reinforcing mesh fabric, called super, to the rounded backbone. This super is about two inches wider than the thickness of the book* (Frank B. Myrick). **6.** superhive.
—*adj.* **1.** *Informal.* of superlative quality; excellent: *super-deluxe accommodations.* **2.** superior; extraordinary: *a super gentleman, super elegance.*
—*v.t.* to reinforce (books) with super.
[< *super-*]

super-, *prefix.* **1.** over; above, as in *superimpose, superstructure.*
2. besides, as in *superadd, supertax.*
3. in high proportion; to excess; exceedingly, as in *superabundant, supersensitive.*
4. surpassing, as in *superman, supernatural.*
[< Latin *super,* adverb, preposition]

super., 1. superfine. **2.** superior.

su·per·a·bil·i·ty (sü′pər ə bil′ə tē), *n.* the quality of being superable.

su·per·a·ble (sü′pər ə bəl), *adj.* that can be overcome or vanquished; surmountable. [< Latin *superābilis* < *superāre* to overcome < *super* over] —**su′per·a·ble·ness,** *n.* —**Syn.** conquerable, vincible.

su·per·a·bly (sü′pər ə blē), *adv.* so as to be superable: *a superably built obstacle.*

su·per·a·bound (sü′pər ə bound′), *v.i.* **1.** to be very abundant; occur in great quantity or numbers. **2.** to be too abundant; occur in excessive quantity or numbers.

su·per·a·bun·dance (sü′pər ə bun′dəns), *n.* **1.** a very great abundance: *a superabundance of rain.* **2.** a greater amount than is needed: *a superabundance of evidence* (William Dwight Whitney). —**Syn. 1.** profusion. **2.** superfluity.

su·per·a·bun·dant (sü′pər ə bun′dənt), *adj.* **1.** very abundant; ample. **2.** too abundant; more than enough. —**su′per·a·bun′dant·ly,** *adv.*

su·per·ac·id (sü′pər as′id), *adj.* excessively acid.

su·per·a·cute (sü′pər ə kyüt′), *adj.* excessively acute.

su·per·add (sü′pər ad′), *v.t.* **1.** to add over and above; add to what has been added: *A French war is added to the American; and there is . . . reason . . . to expect a Spanish war to be superadded to the French* (Edmund Burke). **2.** to add besides; add further (to what already exists): *A toothache was superadded to her other troubles. Jealousy was now superadded to a deeply-rooted enmity* (John F. Kirk). [< Latin *superaddere* < *super-* besides, over + *addere* add]

su·per·ad·di·tion (sü′pər ə dish′ən), *n.* **1.** the act of superadding. **2.** the state of being superadded. **3.** something that is superadded.

su·per·aer·o·dy·nam·ics (sü′pər ãr′ō dī nam′iks, -di-), *n.* the branch of aerodynamics that deals with bodies in motion at very high altitudes and speeds, and with the motion of air that contains only a few molecules.

su·per·a·gen·cy (sü′pər ā′jən sē), *n., pl.* **-cies.** a large agency, especially of the government, which is in charge of a group of smaller agencies: . . . *proposed the creation of a superagency that eventually would coordinate all transportation in the tri-state metropolitan area* (New York Times).

su·per·al·loy (sü′pər al′oi), *n.* an alloy with a high percentage of cobalt, nickel, chromium, or certain other elements, capable of withstanding very high temperatures and used in the construction of rockets, jet engines, etc.: *"Superalloys" were developed for the high-temperature jet-engine* (Scientific American).

su·per·al·tar (sü′pər ôl′tər), *n. Ecclesiastical.* **1.** a portable stone slab consecrated for use upon an unconsecrated altar, a table, or the like. **2.** a structure above and at the back of an altar, as a reredos or a gradin. [< Medieval Latin *superaltare* < Latin *super-* over + *altāre* altar]

su·per·an·nu·a·ble (sü′pər an′yů ə bəl),

adj. *Especially British.* qualifying one for a pension: *Posts are superannuable and an allowance of £50 per child is paid* (Economist).

su·per·an·nu·ate (sü′pər an′yů āt), *v.t.*, **-at·ed, -at·ing. 1.** to retire on a pension because of age or infirmity; pension off. **2.** to make old-fashioned or out-of-date: *Each year the new car models superannuate the old.* [back formation < *superannuated*]

su·per·an·nu·at·ed (sü′pər an′yů ā′tid), *adj.* **1.** retired on a pension; pensioned off. **2.** too old for work, service, etc.; old and infirm. **3.** old-fashioned; out-of-date: *Nothing is more tiresome than a superannuated pedagogue* (Henry Adams). [< Medieval Latin *superannuatus* cattle more than a year old < Latin *super annum* beyond a year] —**Syn. 2.** timeworn, decrepit. **3.** passé.

su·per·an·nu·a·tion (sü′pər an′yů ā′shən), *n.* **1.** a superannuating. **2.** a being superannuated. **3.** a pension or allowance granted to a superannuated person.

su·per·a·tom·ic bomb (sü′pər ə tom′ik), the hydrogen bomb.

su·perb (sů pėrb′), *adj.* **1.** grand; stately; majestic; magnificent; splendid: *Mountain scenery is superb.* **2.** grandly and sumptuously equipped, arrayed, or decorated; rich; elegant: *a superb dinner.* **3.** very fine; excellent; first-rate: *The actor gave a superb performance.* [< Latin *superbus* < *super* above] —**su·perb′ly,** *adv.* —**su·perb′ness,** *n.* —**Syn. 1.** imposing. See **magnificent.**

su·per·bi·ty (sů pėr′bə tē), *n.* pride; arrogance: *the superbity of youth.*

su·per·block (sü′pər blok′), *n. U.S.* a large, landscaped city block closed to automobile traffic: *Harvard yard, in Cambridge, is a superblock; indeed, Cambridge is full of mid-nineteenth-century superblocks, with economical cul-de-sacs . . . and spacious gardens that have proved a happy barrier to overcrowding* (New Yorker).

su·per·bomb (sü′pər bom′), *n.* the hydrogen bomb.

su·per·bomb·er (sü′pər bom′ər), *n.* a large, long-range bomber capable of delivering superbombs.

su·per·brain (sü′pər brān′), *n.* an electronic brain.

su·per·cal·en·der (sü′pər kal′ən dər), *v.t.* to subject (paper) to additional calendering, so as to produce a highly glazed surface. —*n.* a roller or machine used in making supercalendered paper.

su·per·cal·en·dered paper (sü′pər kal′ən dərd), paper with a highly glazed surface produced by additional calendering.

su·per·car·go (sü′pər kär′gō), *n., pl.* **-goes** or **-gos.** an officer on a merchant ship who acts for the owner or owners in the acceptance or discharge of cargo, and who serves generally as the business agent of the owner or owners on a particular voyage. [alteration of earlier *supracargo* < Spanish *sobrecargo* < *sobre* over (< Latin *suprā*) + *cargo*]

su·per·car·go·ship (sü′pər kär′gō ship), *n.* the position or business of a supercargo.

su·per·car·ri·er (sü′pər kar′ē ər), *n.* a very large aircraft carrier: *The new Navy is to be a collection of supercarriers, or floating air bases, each attended and guarded by a swarm of supporting surface craft* (Newsweek).

su·per·cav·i·tat·ing propeller (sü′pər-kav′ə tā ting), a type of propeller with square-ended blades that overcome loss of speed due to cavitation, designed especially for ships operating at high speeds.

su·per·cen·ter (sü′pər sen′tər), *n.* a very large shopping center, especially in a suburb.

su·per·charge (sü′pər chärj′), *v.t.*, **-charged, -charg·ing. 1.** to increase the effective power of (an internal-combustion engine) by fitting with a supercharger. **2.** to fit the engine or engines of (a vehicle, aircraft, etc.) with a supercharger or superchargers. **3.** to charge to excess with excitement, emotion, force, etc.

su·per·charg·er (sü′pər chär′jər), *n.* a blower, pump, or similar device fitted to an internal-combustion engine, by which a greater amount of fuel-air mixture is forced into the cylinders than the action of the pistons would draw, used especially on the engines of racing cars and of aircraft designed to fly in the stratosphere.

su·per·cil·i·ar·y (sü′pər sil′ē er′ē), *adj.* **1.** of or having to do with the eyebrow. **2.** in the region of the eyebrow. **3.** designating or having to do with a prominence (superciliary arch) of the frontal bone over the eye. **4.** *Zoology.* **a.** (of a marking) situated over the eye. **b.** having a marking above the eye, as various birds. [< New Latin *superciliaris* < Latin *supercilium* eyebrow; see SUPERCILIOUS]

su·per·cil·i·ous (sü′pər sil′ē əs), *adj.* showing scorn or indifference because of a feeling of superiority; haughty, proud, and contemptuous; disdainful: *a supercilious stare.* [< Latin *superciliōsus* < *supercilium* pride; (originally) brow, eyebrow < *super* above + unrecorded *celium* a cover < *cēlāre* to cover, conceal] —**su′per·cil′i·ous·ly,** *adv.* —**su′per·cil′i·ous·ness,** *n.* —**Syn.** See **proud.**

su·per·civ·i·li·za·tion (sü′pər siv′ə lə zā′shən), *n.* a civilization above or beyond the civilization of the earth: *If the radio transmissions from CTA-21 and CTA-102 are actually attempts to communicate, they must come from supercivilizations with incredibly vast amounts of energy at their disposal* (Time).

su·per·class (sü′pər klas′, -kläs′), *n. Biology.* **1.** a subphylum. **2.** a group of plants or animals comprising two or more classes, ranking below a subphylum.

su·per·cold (sü′pər kōld′), *adj.* **1.** extremely cold: . . . *the eerie world that exists at supercold temperatures two or three degrees Fahrenheit* (Wall Street Journal). **2.** using extremely low temperatures; cryogenic: *Supercold surgery . . . known as cryosurgery, uses extreme cold to replace or supplement traditional methods of surgery in killing and removing diseased tissue* (World Book Year Book).

su·per·co·los·sal (sü′pər kə los′əl), *adj.* extremely large; huge; gigantic; vast: *supercolossal wealth, a supercolossal movie.* —**su′per·co·los′sal·ly,** *adv.*

su·per·co·lum·nar (sü′pər kə lum′nər), *adj. Architecture.* **1.** above a column or columns. **2.** having to do with supercolumniation.

su·per·co·lum·ni·a·tion (sü′pər kə lum′nē ā′shən), *n. Architecture.* the setting of one order of columns upon another.

su·per·con·duct (sü′pər kən dukt′), *v.i.* to act as a superconductor.

su·per·con·duc·tion (sü′pər kən duk′shən), *n.* **1.** the conducting of electric current by means of a superconductor. **2.** superconductivity: *Research into the phenomenon of superconduction at temperatures near absolute zero will be facilitated by a new technique* (New Scientist).

su·per·con·duc·tive (sü′pər kən duk′tiv), *adj.* capable of or having superconductivity: *Strangely, the best electrical conductors, copper and silver, do not become superconductive* (Scientific American).

su·per·con·duc·tiv·i·ty (sü′pər kon′duk-tiv′ə tē), *n.* the ability of some metals, such as lead and tin, to conduct electric current with no resistance at temperatures below —420 degrees Fahrenheit, or near absolute zero: *Physicists today are still hunting for an explanation of . . . superconductivity, which seems to contradict some of our basic ideas about nature* (Scientific American).

su·per·con·duc·tor (sü′pər kən duk′tər), *n.* a superconductive metal.

su·per·con·ti·nent (sü′pər kon′tə nənt), *n.* either of two great land masses, or a single great land mass, that is thought to have covered the earth originally and that later split up into smaller masses which drifted to form the present continents.

su·per·cool (sü′pər kül′), *v.t.* to cool (a liquid) below the normal freezing point without causing it to solidify. —*v.i.* (of a liquid) to undergo supercooling.

su·per·cooled (sü′pər küld′), *adj.* (of a liquid, especially water) cooled below its usual freezing point without solidifying.

su·per·crit·i·cal (sü′pər krit′ə kəl), *adj. Nuclear Physics.* having more than the amount of fissionable material necessary for sustaining a chain reaction: *a supercritical mass, assembly, reactor, etc.*

su·per·dom·i·nant (sü′pər dom′ə nənt), *n. Music.* submediant.

su·per·dread·nought (sü′pər dred′nôt), *n.* any of various very large, heavily armored warships of the battleship class built between about 1910 and the end of World War II, usually having a main armament of eight or more guns of a single caliber in the range from 12 inches upward.

su·per-du·per (sü′pər dü′pər), *U.S. Slang.* —*adj.* very great; most excellent; stupendous; colossal: *Your mileage is calculated for you by roadside signs screaming—"Only ten miles to tupelo honey," . . . or "Twelve miles to Sandy's super-duper jumbo hamburgers"* (Alistair Cooke). —*n.* the greatest or most excellent of its kind.

su·per·e·go (sü′pər ē′gō, -eg′ō), *n. Psychoanalysis.* that part of the personality, comprising rules of conduct, morality, ethics, etc., which is assimilated from parents and others in the environment and which governs the repression or expression by the ego of the drives of the id.

su·per·el·e·va·tion (sü′pər el′ə vā′shən), *n.* the amount of elevation of the outer rail above the inner rail at a curve on a railway, or of one side of a road above another.

su·per·em·i·nence (sü′pər em′ə nəns), *n.* the state of being supereminent; eminence superior to what is common; distinguished eminence: *the supereminence of Demosthenes as an orator* (Milton).

su·per·em·i·nent (sü′pər em′ə nənt), *adj.* of superior eminence, rank, or dignity; standing out or rising above others. [< Latin *superēminēns, -entis,* present participle of *superēminēre* rise above < *super-* above, over + *ēminēre* be prominent, stand out. Compare EMINENT.] —**su′per·em′i·nent·ly,** *adv.* —**Syn.** preëminent, distingué.

su·per·en·ci·pher (sü′pər en sī′fər), *v.t.* to encipher (a message, etc., already in code or cipher): *Codes are often superenciphered: The code words or code numbers are enciphered by some cipher system just as if they were ordinary plain text* (Scientific American).

su·per·en·ci·pher·ment (sü′pər en sī′fər mənt), *n.* **1.** the act of superenciphering. **2.** a message, etc., which has been superenciphered.

su·per·er·o·gate (sü′pər er′ə gāt), *v.i.*, **-gat·ed, -gat·ing. 1.** to do more than is commanded or required. **2.** to make up (for) by excess: *The fervency of one man in prayer cannot supererogate for the coldness of another* (Milton). [< Late Latin *superērogāre* (with English *-ate*[1]); see SUPEREROGATION]

su·per·er·o·ga·tion (sü′pər er′ə gā′shən), *n.* the doing of more than duty or circumstances require. [< Late Latin *superērogātiō, -ōnis* < *superērogāre* pay or do additionally < *super-* above, over + *ērogāre* pay out < *ex-* out + *rogāre* ask (consent)]

su·per·e·rog·a·to·ry (sü′pər ə rog′ə tôr′ē, -tōr′-), *adj.* **1.** characterized by supererogation. **2.** of the nature of supererogation; going beyond what is commanded or required. **3.** unnecessary; superfluous. —**Syn. 3.** needless.

su·per·ette (sü′pə ret′), *n. U.S.* a small supermarket.

su·per·ex·cel·lence (sü′pər ek′sə ləns), *n.* superior excellence.

su·per·ex·cel·lent (sü′pər ek′sə lənt), *adj.* of superior or surpassing excellence: *Tobacco, divine, rare, superexcellent tobacco . . .* (Robert Burton). —**su′per·ex′cel·lent·ly,** *adv.*

su·per·fam·i·ly (sü′pər fam′ə lē), *n., pl.* **-lies.** *Biology.* a group of animals or plants ranking above a family and below an order or, according to some, below a suborder.

su·per·fe·cun·da·tion (sü′pər fē′kən dā′shən, -fek′ən-), *n. Physiology.* the fertilization of two or more ova at the same period of ovulation by two or more acts of coition.

su·per·fe·tate (sü′pər fē′tāt), *v.i.*, **-tat·ed, -tat·ing.** *Physiology.* to conceive during pregnancy. [< Latin *superfētāre* (with English *-ate*[1]) < *super* over, above + *fētāre* to produce, bear < *fētus, -ūs* offspring, fruit]

su·per·fe·ta·tion (sü′pər fi tā′shən), *n.* **1.** *Physiology.* a second conception before the birth of the offspring of the first conception. This occurs normally in some animals. **2.** *Botany.* the fertilization of the same ovule by two different kinds of pollen. **3. a.** additional production; growth or accretion (of one upon another). **b.** an instance of this.

su·per·fice (sü′pər fis), *n.* superficies: *It is not difficult to apprehend the superfices of the music whence interest and deeper satisfaction can begin* (London Times). [< Latin *superficiēs;* see SUPERFICIAL]

su·per·fi·cial (sü′pər fish′əl), *adj.* **1.** of the surface: *a superficial measurement.* **2.** on the surface; at the surface: *His burns were superficial and soon healed.* **3. a.** concerned with or understanding only what is on the surface; not thorough; shallow: *a superficial education, superficial knowledge. Men of superficial understanding and ludicrous fancy* (James Boswell). **b.** not real or genuine: *superficial friendship.* [< Latin *superficiālis* < *superficiēs* surface < *super-* above + *faciēs* (external) form. Compare FACE.] —**su′per·fi′cial·ness,** *n.* —**Syn. 3. a.** cursory.

su·per·fi·cial·ist (sü′pər fish′ə list), *n.* **1.** a person who deals with things superficially. **2.** a person of superficial knowledge or attitudes.

su·per·fi·ci·al·i·ty (sü′pər fish′ē al′ə tē), *n., pl.* **-ties. 1.** superficial quality or condition; shallowness. **2.** something superficial.

su·per·fi·cial·ize (sü′pər fish′ə līz), *v.t.,* **-ized, -iz·ing.** to make superficial; treat superficially.

su·per·fi·cial·ly (sü′pər fish′ə lē), *adv.* in a superficial manner; on the surface; not thoroughly: *superficially attractive.*

su·per·fi·ci·es (sü′pər fish′ē ēz), *n., pl.* **-es. 1.** a surface. **2.** the surface area. **3.** the outward appearance as distinct from the inner or real nature or condition. [< Latin *superficiēs;* see SUPERFICIAL]

su·per·fine (sü′pər fīn′), *adj.* **1.** that is the very best of its kind; extremely fine: *superfine goods.* **2.** excessively refined; too nice, fastidious, or elegant. —**su′per·fine′ly,** *adv.* —**su′per·fine′ness,** *n.*

su·per·flu·id (sü′pər flü′id), *n.* a fluid, especially liquid helium, characterized by the complete disappearance of viscosity at temperatures near absolute zero. —*adj.* extremely fluid; completely lacking viscosity: *The bottom layer, rich in helium-4, is superfluid and can pass through extremely fine cracks that can not be penetrated by other gases and liquids* (Science News Letter).

su·per·flu·id·i·ty (sü′pər flü id′ə tē), *n.* extreme fluidity; lack of viscosity: . . . *the superfluidity of liquid helium, the frictionless flow of entire atoms, demonstrated in the liquid's ability to flow through the tiniest tubes or narrowest slits* (Scientific American).

su·per·flu·i·ty (sü′pər flü′ə tē), *n., pl.* **-ties. 1.** a greater amount than is needed; excess. **2.** something not needed: *Luxuries are superfluities.* —**Syn. 1.** superabundance.

su·per·flu·ous (sů pėr′flů əs), *adj.* **1.** more than is needed or desired: *In writing telegrams, omit superfluous words. Divinely superfluous beauty . . . The incredible beauty of joy* (Robinson Jeffers). **2.** needless: *A raincoat is superfluous on a clear day. Many a poem is marred by superfluous verse* (Longfellow). [< Latin *superfluus* (with English *-ous*) < *super-* over + *fluere* to flow] —**su·per′flu·ous·ly,** *adv.* —**su·per′flu·ous·ness,** *n.* —**Syn. 1.** excessive, surplus. **2.** unnecessary.

su·per·flux (sü′pər fluks), *n.* **1.** an overflowing, or an excessive flow, as of water. **2.** a superabundant amount. **3.** a superfluous amount, or surplus. [< Medieval Latin *superfluxus,* noun use of past participle of Latin *superfluere;* see SUPERFLUOUS]

su·per·foe·ta·tion (sü′pər fi tā′shən), *n.* superfetation.

Su·per·fort (sü′pər fôrt′, -fōrt′), *n.* **1.** a large, heavily armored, American bombing plane used especially against Japan in the latter part of World War II, officially designated as a B-29. **2.** a similar bombing plane officially designated as a B-50. [< *super-* + *fort*(ress), as in *flying fortress*]

Su·per·for·tress (sü′pər fôr′tris, -fōr′-), *n.* Superfort.

su·per·fu·el (sü′pər fyü′əl), *n.* a fuel that surpasses all others in energy, performance, etc.: *This giant booster probably burned the usual kerosene fuel and liquid-oxygen oxidizer rather than some new superfuel* (Newsweek).

su·per·fuse (sü′pər fyüz′), *v.t., v.i.,* **-fused, -fus·ing. 1.** to pour on something. **2.** to be poured on something. **3.** to supercool. [< Latin *superfūsus,* past participle of *superfundere* to flow over or on < *super-* over + *fundere* to pour]

su·per·fu·sion (sü′pər fyü′zhən), *n.* **1.** the act or process of superfusing or pouring liquid, etc., over something. **2.** the cooling of a liquid below its freezing point without solidification taking place.

su·per·ga·lac·tic (sü′pər gə lak′tik), *adj.* of a supergalaxy.

su·per·gal·ax·y (sü′pər gal′ək sē), *n., pl.* **-ax·ies.** a cluster of galaxies: . . . *the supergalaxy of which the Milky Way is a part* (Scientific American).

su·per·gi·ant (sü′pər jī′ənt), *n.,* or **supergiant star,** any of various extremely large and brilliant stars, ranging in luminosity from 100 to 10,000 or more times that of the sun. They are most common in the spiral galaxies and many can be seen in the Large (Magellanic) Cloud. *Supergiant stars are extraordinarily large and luminous giants. Examples are Rigel and Betelgeuse* (Robert H. Baker).

su·per·gla·cial (sü′pər glā′shəl), *adj.* situated or occurring upon a surface of ice, especially of a glacier. —**su′per·gla′cial·ly,** *adv.*

su·per·gov·ern·ment (sü′pər guv′ərn·mənt, -ər-), *n.* **1.** a central organization formed by a group of governments to regulate relations among members and on matters of common interest: *The UN represents not a supergovernment, not a separate institutional personality, but one of a number of forums on which governments communicate with one another* (Atlantic). **2.** a government which has very extensive powers. **3.** rule by a supergovernment: *As long as we expect supergovernment from the UN, we'll remain disillusioned over its "failure"* (Maclean's).

su·per·heat (*v.* sü′pər hēt′, *n.* sü′pər hēt′), *v.t.* **1.** to heat to a very high temperature; make excessively or abnormally hot: *It's hard to manage vapor that's been superheated . . . to five or more times the boiling point of water* (Wall Street Journal). **2.** to heat (a liquid) above its normal boiling point without causing vaporization: *The tracks of particles reveal themselves as lines of bubbles in superheated liquid* (New Scientist). **3.** to heat (steam) apart from its own liquid until it resembles and will remain a dry or perfect gas at the specified pressure.
—*n.* **1.** the excess heat which a vapor acquires when it is superheated from a dry and saturated condition. **2.** the temperature range through which the vapor passes.

su·per·heat·er (sü′pər hē′tər), *n.* a device for superheating steam: *Only 151,000 kilowatts will come from nuclear heat and the remainder from an oil-fired superheater* (Wall Street Journal).

su·per·het (sü′pər het′), *adj., n. Informal.* superheterodyne: *The real heart of a superhet set is the first detector* (Glasgow Herald).

su·per·het·er·o·dyne (sü′pər het′ər ə·dīn), *adj.* of or having to do with a kind of radio reception in which the frequency of the incoming signal is changed by the heterodyne process to some frequency above audibility, but below that of the incoming signal, and in later stages is amplified and rectified to reproduce the sound: *Almost all modern radio sets make use of the superheterodyne principle* (Sears and Zemansky). —*n.* a superheterodyne radio receiving set.

su·per·high frequency (sü′pər hī′), any radio frequency between 3,000 and 30,000 megacycles. *Abbr.:* SHF (no periods).

su·per·high·way (sü′pər hī′wā′), *n.* an express highway, now especially one divided in the middle and having two or more lanes for traffic in each direction: *Thruways and superhighways make industrial parks feasible on the edge of a city rather than in congested downtown areas* (Wall Street Journal).

su·per·hive (sü′pər hīv′), *n.* a removable upper compartment of a beehive.

su·per·hu·man (sü′pər hyü′mən), *adj.* **1.** above or beyond what is human: *Angels are superhuman beings.* **2.** above or beyond ordinary human power, experience, etc.: *a superhuman effort. He has not raised himself to that superhuman level of reason which should correspond to the possession of superhuman strength* (Wall Street Journal). —**su′per·hu′man·ly,** *adv.*

su·per·hu·man·i·ty (sü′pər hyü man′ə tē), *n.* the character of being superhuman.

su·per·hu·man·ize (sü′pər hyü′mə nīz), *v.t.,* **-ized, -iz·ing.** to make superhuman.

su·per·im·pos·a·ble (sü′pər im pō′zə bəl), *adj.* that can be superimposed: *Any compound will theoretically do this if one form is not superimposable on its mirror image* (Ralph C. Dougherty).

su·per·im·pose (sü′pər im pōz′), *v.t.,* **-posed, -pos·ing. 1.** to place (one object on or upon another); lay above or on the top. **2.** to put or join as an addition.

su·per·im·po·si·tion (sü′pər im′pə zish′·ən), *n.* **1.** the act of superimposing. **2.** the state of being superimposed: *Here we have the sudden, more or less complete superimposition of one culture upon an alien one* (Ogburn and Nimkoff).

su·per·in·cum·bence (sü′pər in kum′·bəns), *n.* the state or condition of lying upon something.

su·per·in·cum·ben·cy (sü′pər in kum′·bən sē), *n.* superincumbence.

su·per·in·cum·bent (sü′pər in kum′·bənt), *adj.* **1.** lying or resting on something else; overlying (chiefly in scientific use). **2.** situated or suspended above; overhanging: *It can scarce uplift The weight of the superincumbent hour* (Shelley). **3.** exerted from above: *a superincumbent pressure.* [< Latin *superincumbēns, -entis,* present participle of *superincumbere* rest on < *super-* on, above + *incumbere.* Compare INCUMBENT.]

su·per·in·duce (sü′pər in düs′, -dyüs′), *v.t.,* **-duced, -duc·ing.** to bring in or develop as an addition; introduce in addition: *Their improvement cannot come from themselves, but must be superinduced from without* (John Stuart Mill). [< Late Latin *superindūcere* add, cover over < Latin *super-* over, above + *indūcere.* Compare INDUCE.]

su·per·in·duc·tion (sü′pər in duk′shən), *n.* **1.** a superinducing. **2.** a being superinduced.

su·per·in·fec·tion (sü′pər in fek′shən), *n.* infection caused a second time or more often by the same kind of germ: *Continual superinfection, year in, year out, wet season and dry season . . . kills or renders immune long before childhood has ended* (New Scientist).

su·per·in·tend (sü′prin tend′, -pər in-), *v.t.* to oversee and direct (work or workers); supervise the operation or management of (a place, institution, etc.); supervise; manage. [< Late Latin *superintendere* < Latin *super-* above + *intendere* to direct. Compare INTEND.] —**Syn.** administer.

su·per·in·tend·ence (sü′prin ten′dəns, -pər in-), *n.* guidance and direction; supervision; management. —**Syn.** administration, surveillance.

su·per·in·tend·en·cy (sü′prin ten′dən sē, -pər in-), *n., pl.* **-cies.** the position, authority, or work of a superintendent.

su·per·in·tend·ent (sü′prin ten′dənt, -pər in-), *n.* a person who oversees, directs, or manages: *a superintendent of schools, a superintendent of a factory or apartment house. Abbr.:* Supt. —*adj.* superintending. —**Syn.** *n.* supervisor, controller.

su·per·in·tend·ent·ship (sü′prin ten′·dənt ship, -pər in-), *n.* the position of superintendent.

su·pe·ri·or (sə pir′ē ər, sů-), *adj.* **1.** higher in degree, amount, quality, importance, etc.; of greater value; better: *a superior blend of coffee, a superior legal claim, to win by superior play.* **2.** well above the average in quality, degree, or amount: *to do superior work, a superior intellect. Schools were selected because of their educational provisions for the superior pupil* (Science). **3.** higher in position, rank, or dignity; more exalted in official or social status: *a superior judge, superior officers. The mystic feels . . . sometimes as if he were grasped and held by a superior power* (William James). **4.** showing a feeling of superiority or being above others; proud, supercilious, or dictatorial: *superior airs, superior manners. I resent his superior manner.* **5.** more elevated in place; higher; upper. **6.** *Printing.* set above the main line of type, and often smaller than the body type, as symbols for footnotes, numerals or letters in chemical formulas, etc.: *In* x^2y^3, *the 2 and 3 are superior.* **7.** *Botany.* growing above some other part or organ, as: **a.** the ovary when situated above or free from the (inferior) calyx. **b.** the calyx when adherent to the sides of the (inferior) ovary and thus seeming to rise from its top. **8.** *Astronomy.* **a.** designating those planets whose orbits lie outside that of the earth (originally, according to the Ptolemaic astronomy, as having their spheres above that of the sun). **b.** on the far side of the sun from the earth: *a superior conjunction of Mercury with the sun.* **c.** above the horizon: *the superior passage of a star.*

superior to, a. higher in quality or position than; above: *Man considers himself superior to other animals.* **b.** greater, better, or more inclusive than: *superior in fighter planes to the enemy.* **c.** too great or strong to be overcome or affected by; above yielding to; indifferent to: *A wise man is superior to flattery or revenge.*

—*n.* **1.** a person who is higher or greater than another, as in position, rank, dignity, ability, etc.: *A captain is a lieutenant's superior. As a violin player he has no superior. We return to face our superiors ... those whom we obey* (Joseph Conrad). *Not the least of the marks of a military genius is his capacity to bend both subordinates and superiors to his plans of action* (Newsweek). **2.** the head of a monastery, convent, abbey, etc. **3.** *Printing.* a superior letter or figure. [< Latin *superior, -ōris,* comparative of *superus,* adjective, above < *super,* preposition, above] —**su·pe′ri·or·ly,** *adv.*

superior court, *U.S.* **1.** (in many states) the ordinary court of general jurisdiction. **2.** (in some states) a court above an inferior court, or courts of limited or special jurisdiction, and below the court or courts of appeal.

su·pe·ri·or·ess (sə pir′ē ər is, sů-), *n.* **1.** a woman superior. **2.** a woman who is the head of a convent or order of nuns.

superior general, *pl.* **superiors general.** the head of a religious order or congregation; superior: *It was the first time a Superior General of the Society of Jesus had addressed an audience in the United States* (New York Times).

su·pe·ri·or·i·ty (sə pir′ē ôr′ə tē, -or′-; sů-), *n., pl.* **-ties.** a superior state or quality: *No one doubts the superiority of modern ways of traveling over those of olden times. All nobility in its beginnings was somebody's natural superiority* (Emerson). —**Syn.** preëminence.

superiority complex, an exaggerated feeling of superiority to others, sometimes the result of overcompensation for an inferiority complex.

superior vocal cords, the upper of the two pairs of vocal cords, which do not directly aid in producing voice; false vocal cords.

su·per·ja·cent (sü′pər jā′sənt), *adj.* overlying (now chiefly in technical use). [< Latin *superjacēns, -entis,* present participle of *superjacēre* < *super-* over + *jacēre* to lie, rest]

su·per·jet (sü′pər jet′), *n.* a large jet plane; jetliner.

superl., superlative.

su·per·la·tive (sə pėr′lə tiv, sů-), *adj.* **1.** of the highest kind; above or surpassing all others; supreme; supereminent: *King Solomon was a man of superlative wisdom.* **2.** exaggerated; excessive; hyperbolic: *Such superlative praise could not be sincere.* **3.** *Grammar.* expressing the highest degree of comparison of an adjective or adverb. *Fairest, best,* and *most slowly* are the superlative forms of *fair, good,* and *slowly.*

—*n.* **1.** a person or thing above all others; supreme example. **2.** the highest or utmost degree of something; height; acme. **3.** *Grammar.* **a.** the highest degree of comparison of an adjective or adverb. **b.** a form or phrase in this degree: *Greatest* is the superlative of *great.*

in superlatives, in an exaggerated way: *She overflowed with enthusiasm, describing the school play in superlatives, calling it stupendous and terrific.*

[< Late Latin *superlātīvus* < *superferre* carry over or beyond, or to extremes < *super-* beyond + *ferre* carry] —**su·per′la·tive·ness,** *n.*

su·per·la·tive·ly (sə pėr′lə tiv lē, sů-), *adv.* to the highest degree; above all others; supremely.

su·per·lin·e·ar (sü′pər lin′ē ər), *adj.* placed above a written or printed line: *superlinear punctuation.*

su·per·lin·er (sü′pər lī′nər), *n.* an ocean liner, able to travel at least 10,000 miles without refueling and carrying 3,000 or more passengers and crewmen: *Twenty thousand visitors boarded the new superliner United States Saturday in the first public inspection of the ship* (Birmingham News).

su·per·long (sü′pər lông′, -long′), *adj.* exceedingly long: *The greatest aid to superlong casting is ultra-light line* (Observer).

su·per·lu·nar (sü′pər lü′nər), *adj.* superlunary.

su·per·lu·na·ry (sü′pər lü′nər ē), *adj.* **1.** of or having to do with the heavens beyond the orbit of the moon; situated beyond the moon. **2.** belonging to a higher world; celestial. [< *super-* + Latin *lūna* moon + English *-ary*]

su·per·man (sü′pər man′), *n., pl.* **-men. 1.** a man having more than human powers: *The folk-tale superman really is a superman, a creature of the elements* (New York Times). **2.** a man imagined by Friedrich Nietzsche, the German philosopher, as the ideal human being, achieved by evolution through selection and the elimination of inferior members: *The idea of attaining a race of "supermen" by eugenical selection of mutations in man depends upon the rate of occurrence of mutations in man* (Ogburn and Nimkoff). [translation of German *Übermensch* (coined by Friedrich W. Nietzsche, 1844-1900) literally, above man]

su·per·mar·ket (sü′pər mär′kit), *n.* a large grocery store in which customers select their purchases from open shelves and pay for them on a cash-and-carry basis: *The function of the supermarket is to provide the housewife with all the necessities—for her table, her home, her family* (Time).

su·per·mart (sü′pər märt′), *n.* a supermarket.

su·per·mul·ti·plet (sü′pər mul′tə plit), *n. Physics.* a group of multiplets.

su·per·mun·dane (sü′pər mun′dān), *adj.* being above the world; belonging to a region above the world: *A practical rocket man has worried that his fellow astronauts might someday create serious supermundane traffic problems* (Newsweek). [< Medieval Latin *supermundanus* < Latin *super-* above + *mundus* world]

su·per·nac·u·lum (sü′pər nak′yə ləm), *adv., n., pl.* **-la** (-lə). —*adv.* until no more liquor remains than will rest on the thumbnail: *to drink supernaculum* (a phrase having reference to the custom of turning up the emptied cup or glass on one's thumbnail to show how little liquor remained).

—*n.* **1.** wine or other liquor good enough to be drunk to the last drop; fine liquor. **2.** a draft that empties the cup or glass to the last drop. **3.** a full cup or glass; a bumper.

[< New Latin *super naculum,* translation of German *auf den Nagel* (*trinken*) (drink off) liquor to the last drop; literally, (drink) on the nail]

su·per·nal (sů pėr′nəl), *adj.* **1.** existing in or deriving from the realm above or beyond life on earth; heavenly; divine: *a supernal being. It was a genie whom he had rashly called out of her bottle, and who was now intent upon showing her supernal power* (Lytton Strachey). **2.** of lofty status; very high in rank or dignity; elevated; exalted. **3.** supremely great or excellent: *supernal wisdom, supernal beauty.* **4.** situated in or belonging to the sky; celestial: *the supernal stars.*

[probably < Middle French, Old French *supernal* < Latin *supernus* < *super* above] —**su·per′nal·ly,** *adv.*

su·per·na·tant (sü′pər nā′tənt), *adj.* floating above or on the surface, as a lighter liquid on a heavier: *oil supernatant on water.*

—*n.* a supernatant substance: *Cells from the culture were found 100% effective against the disease while the fluid or supernatant that rises on the culture offered far less protection* (Science News Letter).

[< Latin *supernatāns, -antis,* present participle of *supernatāre* float or swim on the surface < *super-* above + *natāre* to swim, float]

su·per·na·tion·al (sü′pər nash′ə nəl, -nash′nəl), *adj.* above and beyond or independent of national limitations; supranational: *Europe is gradually uniting in extragovernmental and supernational organizations: the Iron and Steel Community, the European Economic Commission, Euratom (for atomic energy), the Common Market* (Harper's).

su·per·na·tion·al·ism (sü′pər nash′ə nə-liz′əm, -nash′nə liz-), *n.* extreme nationalism: *India ... doesn't want supernationalism to scare away the Western capital Asia so badly needs* (Newsweek).

su·per·na·tion·al·ist (sü′pər nash′ə nə-list, -nash′nə-), *n.* an extreme nationalist.

—*adj.* favoring supernationalism; extremely nationalistic: *a supernationalist patriotic organization; ... such uneasy partners as a Buddhist party, a Trotskyite group and the supernationalist Ceylon Freedom Party* (Time).

su·per·na·tion·al·is·tic (sü′pər nash′ə-nə lis′tik, -nash′nə-), *adj.* of supernationalism or supernationalists: ... *members of a supernationalistic organization* (Saturday Review).

su·per·nat·u·ral (sü′pər nach′ər əl, -nach′rəl), *adj.* **1.** belonging to a realm or system above or beyond that of nature: *Angels and devils are supernatural beings.* **2.** relating to, dealing with, or characterized by what is above or beyond nature: *supernatural powers.*

—*n.* **the supernatural,** supernatural agencies, influences, or phenomena: *With the development of the present-day exact scientific methods, beliefs in the "supernatural" gradually faded away and came to be considered superstition* (Bulletin of Atomic Scientists).

[< Medieval Latin *supernaturalis* < Latin *super-* above + *nātūra* nature] —**su′per·nat′u·ral·ly,** *adv.* —**su′per·nat′u·ral·ness,** *n.*

su·per·nat·u·ral·ism (sü′pər nach′ər ə-liz′əm, -nach′rə liz-), *n.* **1.** supernatural character or quality. **2.** a system or collection of supernatural agencies, events, etc. **3.** the belief in the supernatural: *Man must first emancipate himself from supernaturalism before he can see himself as a natural being* (George Simpson). **4.** a theory or doctrine which admits or asserts the reality of supernatural beings, powers, events, etc.

su·per·nat·u·ral·ist (sü′pər nach′ər ə-list, -nach′rə-), *n.* a person who believes in the supernatural; a believer in supernaturalism.

—*adj.* supernaturalistic.

su·per·nat·u·ral·is·tic (sü′pər nach′ər-ə lis′tik, -nach′rə-), *adj.* **1.** of or having to do with supernaturalism. **2.** of the nature of supernaturalism.

su·per·nat·u·ral·ize (sü′pər nach′ər ə līz, -nach′rə-), *v.t.,* **-ized, -iz·ing.** to make supernatural; impart or attribute a supernatural character to.

su·per·nor·mal (sü′pər nôr′məl), *adj.* **1.** exceeding that which is normal: *Hybrid vigour is not anything supernormal: it is rather the degenerate parents which are subnormal* (Eric Ashby). **2.** of or designating phenomena of an extraordinary but not necessarily supernatural kind.

su·per·no·va (sü′pər nō′və), *n., pl.* **-vae** (-vē), **-vas.** *Astronomy.* a nova far brighter than an ordinary nova, as one which appeared in 1885 in the Andromeda galaxy and in a few days radiated more light than the sun does in a million years: *Astronomers observe as a "supernova" the sudden spectacular brightening of a star* (Arthur Beer).

su·per·nu·mer·ar·y (sü′pər nü′mə rer′ē, -nyü′-), *adj., n., pl.* **-ar·ies.** —*adj.* **1.** beyond the usual, regular, or prescribed number; additional; extra. **2.** beyond the number needed or desired; superfluous.

—*n.* **1.** a supernumerary person or thing; one beyond the usual, regular, or prescribed number. **2.** *Theater.* a person who appears on the stage but usually does not speak, as in scenes requiring crowds; extra: *In addition to the regular actors, there were 20 supernumeraries for the mob scene.*

[< Late Latin *supernumerārius* excessive in number (of soldiers added to a full legion) < Latin *super numerum* beyond the number]

su·per·or·der (sü′pər ôr′dər), *n. Biology.* a group of animals or plants ranking above an order and below a class.

su·per·or·di·nal (sü′pər ôr′də nəl), *adj.* of or having to do with a superorder.

su·per·or·di·nar·y (sü′pər ôr′də ner′ē), *adj.* above or beyond the ordinary.

su·per·or·di·nate (sü′pər ôr′də nit), *adj.* superior in rank or importance; not subordinate: *a superordinate position, goal, requirement, etc.*

—*n.* a superordinate person or thing: *Getting along for many of us these days more and more involves the ability to manipulate, to sell, perhaps to con our ... subordinates and superordinates, and perhaps—most of all—ourselves* (New York Times).

su·per·or·gan·ic (sü′pər ôr gan′ik), *adj.* above or outside of the organic realm.

su·per·os·cu·late (sü′pər os′kyə lāt), *v.t.,* **-lat·ed, -lat·ing.** *Geometry.* to osculate at more consecutive points than usually suffice to determine the locus.

su·per·os·cu·la·tion (sü′pər os′kyə lā′-shən), *n. Geometry.* the act or process of superosculating.

su·per·o·vu·la·tion (sü′pər ō′vyə lā′shən), *n.* **1.** the process of inducing the ovaries of animals to greater than normal activity, as by the injection of a hormone serum: *The scientists here claim that superovulation doesn't affect the fertility of the donor animal* (Wall Street Journal). **2.** the greater production of eggs resulting from this treatment: *The agent that is capable of producing this superovulation ... is the pituitary's* *gonad-stimulating hormone* (Scientific American).

su·per·par·a·sit·ic (sü′pər par′ə sit′ik), *n.* having to do with superparasitism.

su·per·par·a·sit·ism (sü′pər par′ə sī tiz′əm), *n.* the infestation of parasites by other parasites.

su·per·pa·tri·ot (sü′pər pā′trē ət; *British* -pat′rē ət), *n.* an extremely or excessively patriotic person.

su·per·pa·tri·ot·ic (sü′pər pā′trē ot′ik; *British* -pat′rē ot′ik), *adj.* extremely or excessively patriotic: *New York City's Society of Tammany adopted its own constitution as a superpatriotic club for 100%-pure Americans* (Time).

su·per·pa·tri·ot·ism (sü′pər pā′trē ə tiz′əm; *British* -pat′rē ə tiz′əm), *n.* extreme or excessive patriotism.

su·per·phos·phate (sü′pər fos′fāt), *n.* *Chemistry.* **1.** a phosphate containing an excess of phosphoric acid; an acid phosphate. **2.** any of various phosphates, as bone, bone-black, etc., which have been treated with sulfuric acid to increase their solubility for use as fertilizers.

su·per·phys·i·cal (sü′pər fiz′ə kəl), *adj.* above or outside of the physical realm; hyperphysical.

su·per·pol·y·mer (sü′pər pol′ē mər), *n.* a polymer having very large molecules.

su·per·pos·a·ble (sü′pər pō′zə bəl), *adj.* that can be superposed; not interfering with one another, or not rendering one another impossible, as two displacements or strains.

su·per·pose (sü′pər pōz′), *v.t.*, **-posed, -pos·ing. 1.** to place above or on something else; superimpose: *Ordinarily, the antennas are vertically superposed a specific distance apart* (L.F.B. Carini). **2.** to add onto something else, by or as if by superimposing. **3.** *Geometry.* to place (a figure) upon another so that the two coincide. **4.** to arrange (the wings of a biplane) one directly over the other. [< French *superposer* < *super-* above (< Latin) + *poser* to place. Compare POSE[1].]

su·per·posed (sü′pər pōzd′), *adj.* *Botany.* situated directly over some other part (used especially of a whorl of organs arranged opposite or over another instead of alternately).

su·per·po·si·tion (sü′pər pə zish′ən), *n.* **1.** the placing of one thing above or on something else: *Such clues as the superposition of later carvings on earlier ones ... helped to determine the sequence of execution* (Scientific American). **2.** the condition of being so placed: *The lattice may be considered as resulting from the superposition of two lattices* [*of atoms*], *say A and B* (P.E. Hodgson). **3.** the thing so placed: *a superposition of gravel on bedrock.* **4.** *Geometry.* the transferring of one figure into the position occupied by another, so as to show that they are coincident.

su·per·pow·er (sü′pər pou′ər), *n.* **1.** power on an extraordinary or extensive scale. **2.** electric power on an extraordinary scale developed by linking together all available power sources in a given area, for providing more efficient and economical power production and distribution. **3.** a world power having such military strength, industrial resources, etc., that no crucial matter involving the community of nations can be acted on or settled without its active support or passive acquiescence: *It marked the beginning of new forms of competition between the superpowers* (New Yorker). **4.** a supernational political entity having authority in the international realm that transcends that of all or most world powers, existing as a concept in political science and reflected to a limited extent in the formal structure of such bodies as the League of Nations and the United Nations.

su·per·pure (sü′pər pyůr′), *adj.* extremely pure: *Demand for "superpure" aluminum (99.99%) has steadily increased* (Harris and Mitchell).

su·per·race (sü′pər rās′), *n.* a race regarded as superior to another or others.

su·per·ra·tion·al (sü′pər rash′ə nəl, -rash′nəl), *adj.* above or beyond what is rational; transcending reason. **—su′per·ra′tion·al·ly,** *adv.*

su·per·re·gen·er·a·tion (sü′pər ri jen′ə rā′shən), *n.* (in wireless telegraphy and telephony) a method of effecting an abnormally great regeneration.

su·per·re·gen·er·a·tive (sü′pər ri jen′ə rā′tiv), *adj.* (in wireless telegraphy and telephony) effecting an abnormally great regeneration.

su·per·sales·man (sü′pər sālz′mən), *n.*, *pl.* **-men.** a very successful salesman; a person who is very skillful and effective in persuading others: *The indomitable Churchill ... put at the head of the party organization no political routineer but a supersalesman, Lord Woolton* (Newsweek).

su·per·sales·man·ship (sü′pər sālz′mənship), *n.* very skillful or effective salesmanship: *Though trained as an architect, Luckman was a slick businessman with a flair for supersalesmanship* (Time).

su·per·salt (sü′pər sôlt′), *n.* *Chemistry.* an acid salt.

su·per·sat·u·rate (sü′pər sach′ə rāt), *v.t.*, **-rat·ed, -rat·ing.** to saturate to excess; dissolve more of a solute in (a solvent) than is sufficient to saturate it. A supersaturated solution is one in which more of a substance is dissolved than the solvent will hold under normal conditions.

su·per·sat·u·ra·tion (sü′pər sach′ə rā′shən), *n.* **1.** the operation of saturating to excess, or of adding to beyond saturation: *supersaturation bombing with nuclear and atomic weapons* (Bulletin of Atomic Scientists). **2.** the state or condition of being supersaturated.

su·per·scribe (sü′pər skrīb′), *v.t.*, **-scribed, -scrib·ing. 1.** to write (words, letters, one's name, etc.) above, on, or outside of something. **2.** *Archaic.* to address (a letter or parcel).
[< Late Latin *superscrībere* write over or above (in Latin, to do this as a correction) < *super-* above + *scrībere* write]

su·per·script (sü′pər skript), *adj.* written above a letter, or above the line of writing. —*n.* a number, letter, etc., placed after and above a number or quantity. *Example:* In x^2 and a^1, 2 and 1 are superscripts. *The superscript ... is the total number of particles in the nucleus, and is the nearest integer to the atomic weight* (Sears and Zemansky). [< Late Latin *superscrīptus*, past participle of *superscrībere;* see SUPERSCRIBE]

su·per·scrip·tion (sü′pər skrip′shən), *n.* **1.** a writing above, on, or outside of something. **2.** something written above or on the outside. **3.** the symbol ℞ (for Latin *recipe*, "take") at the head of a prescription. **4.** *Archaic.* the address on a letter or parcel.

su·per·se·cret (sü′pər sē′krit), *adj.* top-secret: *Administration chiefs plan to keep the wraps on supersecret studies urging vast atomic-shelter construction* (Wall Street Journal).

su·per·sede (sü′pər sēd′), *v.t.*, **-sed·ed, -sed·ing. 1.** to take the place of; cause to be given up or set aside; displace: *Electric lights have superseded gas lights in most homes. Atomic reactors have superseded coal furnaces in many power plants.* **2.** to take the place of (someone removed from an office); succeed and supplant; replace: *A new governor superseded the old one.* **3.** to set aside or ignore in promotion; promote another over the head of.
[< Middle French, Old French *superceder*, learned borrowing from Latin *supersedēre* be superior to, refrain from (in Medieval Latin, succeed to an estate) < *super-* above + *sedēre* sit]
—**Syn. 1, 2.** See **replace.**

su·per·se·de·as (sü′pər sē′dē as), *n.* *Law.* a writ ordering a delay in legal proceedings or suspending the powers of an officer, especially from a court of appeal to a lower court: *The judge also ruled that ... the defendants could file a supersedeas bond* (Wall Street Journal). [< Medieval Latin *supersedeas* you shall stay, present subjunctive of Latin *supersedēre*]

su·per·sed·ence (sü′pər sē′dəns), *n.* supersedure; supersession.

su·per·sed·er (sü′pər sē′dər), *n.* a person or thing that supersedes.

su·per·se·dure (sü′pər sē′jər), *n.* supersession.

su·per·sen·ior·i·ty (sü′pər sēn yôr′ə tē, -yor′-), *n.*, *pl.* **-ties.** seniority not based upon age or length of service: *The Board's five members unanimously found that the award of "superseniority" to replacements for strikers is a form of discrimination against employees engaged in economic walkouts* (Wall Street Journal).

su·per·sen·si·ble (sü′pər sen′sə bəl), *adj.* outside or above the sensory realm; supersensory.

su·per·sen·si·bly (sü′pər sen′sə blē), *adv.* in a supersensible manner.

su·per·sen·si·tive (sü′pər sen′sə tiv), *adj.* extremely or morbidly sensitive: *Sound was supplied by a supersensitive miniature microphone pinned to Philip's lapel* (Newsweek). **—su′per·sen′si·tive·ly,** *adv.* **—su′per·sen′si·tive·ness,** *n.*

su·per·sen·so·ry (sü′pər sen′sər ē), *adj.* outside or above the sensory realm; independent of the organs of sense; extrasensory.

su·per·sen·su·al (sü′pər sen′shů əl), *adj.* **1.** supersensory; extrasensory. **2.** spiritual.

su·per·serv·ice·a·ble (sü′pər sėr′və səbəl), *adj.* **1.** extremely serviceable. **2.** doing or offering service beyond what is desired; officious.

su·per·ses·sion (sü′pər sesh′ən), *n.* **1.** the act of superseding: *The progressive subordination of such* [*military*] *alliances to, and their ultimate supersession by, the collective security system of the United Nations, should be an integral part of the process of general and complete disarmament by stages* (Bulletin of Atomic Scientists). **2.** the condition of being superseded. [< Medieval Latin *supersessio, -onis* < Latin *supersedēre;* see SUPERSEDE]

su·per·ses·sive (sü′pər ses′iv), *adj.* superseding.

su·per·size (sü′pər sīz′), *adj.* supersized.

su·per·sized (sü′pər sīzd′), *adj.* of very great size; oversized.

su·per·son·ic (sü′pər son′ik), *adj.* **1.** of or having to do with vibrations and sound waves beyond the extreme limit of human audibility (above frequencies of 20,000 cycles per second); ultrasonic: *When mutations are induced in fruit flies by ... supersonic vibrations or some other artificial means, most of them are lethal* (Scientific American). **2.** of or having to do with speed which is greater than the speed of sound in air at normal pressure and temperature (about 1,087 feet per second): *The difference in air flow between subsonic and supersonic speeds in turn has created a wholly new branch of aerodynamics* (Scientific American). **3.** that moves or is able to move at a speed greater than the speed of sound: *The supersonic airliner will have immensely more powerful engines than present-day jets* (New Scientist). See **streamlined** for picture.
—*n.* a supersonic wave. **—su′per·son′i·cal·ly,** *adv.*

su·per·son·ics (sü′pər son′iks), *n.* the science dealing with the nature and uses of supersonic waves and the phenomena associated with them.

su·per·spe·cies (sü′pər spē′shēz, sü′pər-spē′-), *n.*, *pl.* **-cies** (-shēz). a group of species which are related, especially on a geographical or ecological basis: *Clancey accepts the concept of the superspecies, but some authorities will certainly disagree with his adoption of the practice of treating subspecies on a specific basis* (New Scientist).

su·per·spec·ta·cle (sü′pər spek′tə kəl), *n.* a very spectacular show or production: *"Spartacus" is a new kind of Hollywood movie: a superspectacle with spiritual vitality and moral force* (Time).

su·per·speed (sü′pər spēd′), *n.* extremely high speed, especially sonic or supersonic speed: *Planes at superspeeds encounter stresses not ordinarily met* (Science News Letter).

su·per·star (sü′pər stär′), *n.* **1.** an exceptionally successful star, as in sports, motion pictures, etc.: *Why don't they wait until he's been in the league for six, seven or eight years before they begin comparing him with the great stars, let alone superstars like Musial* (Birmingham News). **2.** an exceptionally large star or other heavenly body: *If it stemmed from the explosion of a star, it must have been a truly gigantic explosion—the disintegration of a superstar at least 100,000 times more massive than our sun!* (Scientific American).

su·per·state (sü′pər stāt′), *n.* a very large or powerful State: *In our day, when prestige grows out of bigness and physical power, a superstate of unprecedented size which would embrace almost half of humanity is in itself a forceful weapon* (New York Times).

su·per·sti·tion (sü′pər stish′ən), *n.* **1.** unreasoning awe or fear of something unknown, mysterious, or imaginary, especially in connection with religion; worship based on fear or ignorance: *Superstition is the religion of feeble minds* (Edmund Burke). **2.** an irrational religious belief or practice; a tenet, scruple, etc., founded on fear or ignorance. **3.** an irrational or unfounded belief in general: *A common superstition considered it bad luck to sleep in a room numbered 13. New truths . . . begin as heresies and . . . end as superstitions* (Thomas H. Huxley). [< Latin *superstitiō, -ōnis* excessive fear of the gods < *superstāre* stand on, or over < *super-* above + *stāre* stand]

su·per·sti·tious (sü′pər stish′əs), *adj.* **1.** of the nature of or involving superstition. **2.** characterized by superstition: *a superstitious habit, a superstitious belief.* **3.** subject or addicted to superstition; believing or practicing superstitions: *Gamblers and adventurers are generally superstitious* (Bret Harte). —**su′per·sti′tious·ly,** *adv.* —**su′per·sti′tious·ness,** *n.*

su·per·stra·tum (sü′pər strā′təm), *n., pl.* **-ta** (-tə) or **-tums.** a stratum or layer deposited over or upon something. [< New Latin *superstratum,* noun use of neuter past participle of Latin *supersternere* to spread over < *super-* over + *sternere* lay down, strew]

su·per·struct (sü′pər strukt′), *v.t.* to build upon something else; erect as a superstructure: *Those . . . on whose approbation his esteem of himself was superstructed* (Samuel Johnson). [< Latin *superstructus,* past participle of *superstruere* < *super-* over + *struere* to build]

su·per·struc·tur·al (sü′pər struk′chər əl), *adj.* of or having to do with a superstructure.

su·per·struc·ture (sü′pər struk′chər), *n.* **1.** a structure built upon something else as a foundation; structure raised upon something. **2.** the parts of a building above the foundation. **3.** the parts of a ship, especially a naval vessel, above the main deck, exclusive of masts, funnels, antennae, etc.: *The lifeboats, the great funnels, and the bulk of her superstructure are of aluminum* (Newsweek). **4.** the part of a bridge supported by the piers and abutments. **5.** the ties and rails of a railroad line, supported by the ballast.

su·per·sub·ma·rine (sü′pər sub′mə rēn), *n.* a large and powerful type of submarine.

su·per·sub·tle (sü′pər sut′əl), *adj.* extremely or excessively subtle.

su·per·sub·tle·ty (sü′pər sut′əl tē), *n., pl.* **-ties.** excessive subtlety; overnicety of discrimination.

su·per·tank·er (sü′pər tang′kər), *n.* a huge tanker, ranging from 70,000 to 100,000 tons: *Existing supertankers sometimes must transfer their cargo to smaller tankers because harbor facilities are inadequate to handle the giant ships* (Wall Street Journal).

su·per·tax (sü′pər taks′), *n.* a tax in addition to a normal tax; surtax.

su·per·ter·ra·ne·an (sü′pər tə rā′nē ən), *adj.* that is above the earth's surface; not subterranean.

su·per·ter·res·tri·al (sü′pər tə res′trē əl), *adj.* superterranean.

su·per·ton·ic (sü′pər ton′ik), *n. Music.* the second tone or note of a scale; the tone or note next above the tonic.

su·per·vene (sü′pər vēn′), *v.i.,* **-vened, -ven·ing.** to come on or occur as something additional or extraneous; come directly or shortly after something else, either as a consequence of it or in contrast with it: *Those further away are likely to suffer from "radiation sickness," followed by changes in the blood; these changes may continue for up to a month, after which death may supervene* (London Times).
[< Latin *supervenīre* to follow closely < *super-* upon + *venīre* to come]

su·per·ven·ience (sü′pər vēn′yəns), *n.* **1.** the fact of being supervenient. **2.** the act of supervening; supervention.

su·per·ven·ient (sü′pər vēn′yənt), *adj.* supervening.

su·per·ven·tion (sü′pər ven′shən), *n.* a supervening.

su·per·vis·al (sü′pər vī′zəl), *n.* supervision. —*adj.* supervisory.

su·per·vise (sü′pər vīz), *v.t.,* **-vised, -vis·ing.** to look after and direct (work or workers, a process, etc.); oversee; superintend; manage: *Study halls are supervised by teachers.* [< Medieval Latin *supervisus,* past participle of *supervidēre* < Latin *super-* over + *vidēre* to see]

su·per·vi·sion (sü′pər vizh′ən), *n.* **1.** the act or function of supervising or overseeing; management; direction; superintendence: *The house was built under the careful supervision of an architect.* **2.** *U.S.* **a.** the management and evaluation of instruction, especially in a public school or school system. **b.** the authority for this. —**Syn. 1.** oversight.

su·per·vi·sor (sü′pər vī′zər), *n.* **1.** a person who supervises: *The music supervisor had charge of the school band and orchestra.* **2.** *U.S.* an official whose duties are to supervise and assist the teachers of a particular subject, especially in a public school or school system. **3.** *U.S.* (in certain states) an official who is the elected administrative head of a township and a member of the governing board of the county in which the township is located. —**Syn. 1.** administrator, director.

su·per·vi·sor·ship (sü′pər vī′zər ship), *n.* the position or authority of a supervisor.

su·per·vi·so·ry (sü′pər vī′zər ē), *adj.* **1.** of a supervisor; having to do with supervision. **2.** supervising.

su·per·volt·age (sü′pər vōl′tij), *n.* any very high voltage, especially radiation voltage from 500,000 to 2 million volts: *Only a few of the nation's largest hospitals have these big, supervoltage X-ray machines* (Science News Letter).

su·per·weap·on (sü′pər wep′ən), *n.* any military weapon vastly superior to other existing or conventional weapons: *They warn the solid-fuel Minuteman won't be a superweapon, it can't carry as big a warhead as the liquid-fuel jobs* (Wall Street Journal). *The atomic artillery gun is one of the most promising items in Uncle Sam's stable of superweapons* (Newsweek).

su·per·wom·an (sü′pər wu̇m′ən), *n., pl.* **-wom·en.** a woman of extraordinary or superhuman powers: *The novel's heroine, a toothsome superwoman who runs a railroad . . .* (Atlantic).

su·pi·nate (sü′pə nāt), *v.,* **-nat·ed, -nat·ing.** —*v.t.* to hold or turn (the hand or forelimb) so that the palm faces up or forward. —*v.i.* to be supinated; undergo supination. [< Latin *supīnāre* (with English *-ate*[1]) < *supīnus;* see SUPINE, adjective]

su·pi·na·tion (sü′pə nā′shən), *n.* **1.** a rotation of the hand or forelimb so that the palm faces up or forward. **2.** a similar movement of the foot, hind limb, shoulder, etc. **3.** the position which results from this rotation.

su·pi·na·tor (sü′pə nā′tər), *n.* a muscle, especially of the forearm, that effects or assists in supination. [< New Latin *supinator* < Latin *supīnāre* supinate]

su·pine (*adj.* sü pīn′; *n.* sü′pīn), *adj.* **1.** lying flat on the back: *a supine person.* **2.** recumbent with the face or front upward: *a supine position.* **3.** lazily inactive; listless, especially morally or mentally. **4.** not active; passive. **5.** sloping or inclining backwards: *like the young moon supine* (Shelley). **6.** supinated. [< Latin *supīnus,* related to *super* above]
—*n.* **1.** either of two Latin verbal nouns formed from the stem of the past participle, one ending in *-tum* or *-sum* and the other ending in *-tū* or *-sū.* **2.** a verbal form of similar function in another language.
[< Late Latin *supīnum (verbum)* supine (word), noun use of *supīnum,* neuter of *supīnus;* see the adjective] —**su·pine′ly,** *adv.* —**su·pine′ness,** *n.*
—**Syn.** *adj.* **3.** languid, indolent, inert.

supp., supplement.

sup·per (sup′ər), *n.* **1.** the evening meal; meal eaten early in the evening if dinner is near noon, or late in the evening if dinner is at six or later. **2.** the hour at which this is eaten; suppertime. **3.** such a meal made the occasion of a social or festive gathering: *a church supper.*
[Middle English *super,* or *soper* < Old French *soper,* noun use of infinitive, to sup, dine; see SOUP]

supper club, a night club: *The pick of supper clubs awaits the chic after-dinner clique* (Punch).

sup·per·less (sup′ər lis), *adj.* having no supper; going without supper: *The disobedient boy was sent to bed supperless.*

sup·per·time (sup′ər tīm′), *n.* the time at which supper is served: *Then I went back to the hotel and sat around until it got close to suppertime* (New Yorker).

suppl., supplement.

sup·plant (sə plant′, -plänt′), *v.t.* **1.** to take the place of; displace or set aside; supersede: *Machinery has long since supplanted hand labor in making shoes.* **2.** to dispossess and take the place of (another), especially by treacherous or dishonorable means: *A military clique plotted to supplant the president.* **3.** to remove from its position; get rid of; oust.
[< Latin *supplantāre* trip up < *sub-* under + *planta* sole of the foot] —**sup·plant′er,** *n.*
—**Syn. 1, 2.** See **replace.**

sup·plan·ta·tion (sup′lən tā′shən), *n.* **1.** the act of supplanting. **2.** the state of being supplanted.

sup·plant·ment (sə plant′mənt, -plänt′-), *n.* supplantation.

sup·ple (sup′əl), *adj.,* **-pler, -plest,** *v.,* **-pled, -pling.** —*adj.* **1.** bending or folding easily, without breaking or cracking; pliant: *a supple birch tree, supple leather.* **2.** capable of bending easily; moving easily or nimbly: *a supple dancer. "In my youth," said the sage . . . "I kept all my limbs very supple By the use of this ointment"* (Lewis Carroll). **3.** readily adaptable to different ideas, circumstances, people, etc.: **a.** flexible; elastic: *a keen and supple mind. A mind at once supple and copious* (Lytton Strachey). **b.** yielding readily to persuasion or influence; compliant: *Let me be soft and supple to thy will* (George Herbert). **4.** artfully or servilely complaisant or obsequious.
—*v.t.* to make supple: *To set free, to supple and to train the faculties* (Lowell). —*v.i.* to grow supple.
[Middle English *souple* < Old French *souple,* and *supple* < Latin *supplex, -icis* submissive; (literally) bending, related to *supplicāre:* see SUPPLICATE] —**sup′ple·ly,** *adv.* —**sup′ple·ness,** *n.*
—**Syn.** *adj.* **1.** pliable. **3. a.** plastic. —**Ant.** *adj.* **1.** stiff.

sup·ple·jack (sup′əl jak′), *n.* any of various climbing and twining shrubs with tough, pliable stems, found in tropical and subtropical forests.

sup·ple·ment (*n.* sup′lə mənt; *v.* sup′lə-ment), *n.* **1.** something added to complete a thing, or to make it larger or better, especially a part added to complete a literary work or any written account or document. **2.** a part of a newspaper or other periodical issued as an addition to the regular numbers and containing some special item or items: *a travel supplement in a Sunday newspaper.* **3.** something added to supply a deficiency: *a diet supplement.* **4.** the amount needed to be added to an angle or arc to produce an angle or arc of 180 degrees. *Abbr.:* supp.
—*v.t.* to supply what is lacking in; add to; complete: *Bill supplements his regular meals by eating between meals.*
[< Latin *supplēmentum* < *supplēre;* see SUPPLY[1]]
—**Syn.** *n.* **1. Supplement, appendix** mean something added to a book or paper to complete or improve it. **Supplement** applies to a section added later or printed separately to bring the information up-to-date, correct mistakes, or present special features: *This encyclopedia has a supplement covering recent events.* **Appendix** applies to a section added at the end of a book or document to give extra information: *The appendix to this book contains a list of dates.* -*v.t.* See **complement.**

sup·ple·men·tal (sup′lə men′təl), *adj., n.* supplementary: *Appropriations, including two supplementals, for the U.S. Department of Agriculture were increased* (John Kerr Rose).

sup·ple·men·ta·ri·ly (sup′lə men′tər ə lē, -trə lē), *adv.* in a supplementary manner.

sup·ple·men·ta·ry (sup′lə men′tər ē, -trē), *adj., n., pl.* **-ries.** —*adj.* **1.** additional: *a volume supplementary to the original set.* **2.** offered or given to supply what is lacking: *The new members of the class received supplementary instruction.* —*n.* something which is supplementary; supplement: *Mr. Callaghan added a string of supplementaries to Mr. Wilson's simple challenge* (Manchester Guardian Weekly).
—**Syn.** *adj.* **1.** extra, auxiliary. –*n.* addition, appendage.

supplementary angle, an angle needed to be added to another angle to produce an angle of 180 degrees (a straight line): *A 60-degree angle is the supplementary angle of a 120-degree angle.*

A
C B D
Supplementary Angles: ABC and ABD

sup·ple·men·ta·tion (sup′lə men tā′shən), *n.* **1.** the act of supplementing: *Supplementation of the diet with egg-yolk . . . resulted in a fall in recurrences of rheumatic fever* (New Scientist). **2.** a supplementary addition.

sup·plete (sə plēt′), *v.t.*, **-plet·ed, -plet·ing.** *Obsolete.* to supplement. [< Latin *supplētus,* past participle of *supplēre;* see SUPPLY[1]]

sup·ple·tion (sə plē′shən), *n. Grammar.* the occurrence or use of suppletive forms.

sup·ple·tive (sə plē′tiv, sup′lə-), *adj. Grammar.* **1.** (of a word or form) used as the inflected form in a paradigm that lacks one or more inflected forms, as *went* in "go, went, gone," and *better, best* in "good, better, best." **2.** (of a paradigm) containing one or more such words or forms. [< Medieval Latin *suppletivus* < Latin *supplēre;* see SUPPLY[1]]

sup·ple·to·ry (sup′lə tôr′ē, -tōr′-), *adj.* supplementary. [< Late Latin *supplētōrium* a supplement]

sup·pli·ance (sup′lē əns), *n.* supplication.

sup·pli·ant (sup′lē ənt), *adj.* asking or praying humbly and earnestly; supplicating: *lifting suppliant hands in a prayer for mercy. He sent a suppliant message for help.* —*n.* a person who supplicates; humble petitioner: *She knelt as a suppliant at the altar.* [< Middle French, Old French *suppliant* (originally) present participle of *supplier* to pray < Latin *supplicāre;* see SUPPLICATE. Doublet of SUPPLICANT.] —**sup′pli·ant·ly,** *adv.* —**Syn.** *adj.* beseeching. *-n.* supplicant.

sup·pli·cant (sup′lə kənt), *adj., n.* suppliant. [< Latin *supplicāns, -antis,* present participle of *supplicāre;* see SUPPLICATE. Doublet of SUPPLIANT.] —**sup′pli·cant·ly,** *adv.*

sup·pli·cat (sup′lə kat), *n.* a formal petition for a degree or its equivalent at an English university. [< Latin *supplicat* he supplicates < *supplicāre* to beg, supplicate]

sup·pli·cate (sup′lə kāt), *v.,* **-cat·ed, -cat·ing.** —*v.t.* **1.** to implore (a person) humbly and earnestly; address an entreaty to: *The mother supplicated the judge to spare her son.* **2.** to beg humbly for (something); seek by entreaty. —*v.i.* to pray humbly; present a humble petition. [< Latin *supplicāre* (with English *-ate*[1]) beg, beseech < *sub-* under, down + *plicāre* to bend, kneel] —**sup′pli·cat′ing·ly,** *adv.* —**Syn.** *v.t.* **1.** entreat, beseech, petition.

sup·pli·ca·tion (sup′lə kā′shən), *n.* **1.** a supplicating: *He knelt in supplication. Their grave, white faces lifted in a single supplication to the ship* (Thomas Wolfe). **2.** a humble and earnest request or prayer: *Supplications to God arose from all the churches of the besieged town.*

sup·pli·ca·tor (sup′lə kā′tər), *n.* a person or thing that supplicates; suppliant.

sup·pli·ca·to·ry (sup′lə kə tôr′ē, -tōr′-), *adj.* supplicating.

sup·pli·er (sə plī′ər), *n.* a person or thing that furnishes something needed; provider; purveyor: *Ask your supplier to show you how expressive your letterhead looks on Strathmore* (Time).

sup·plies (sə plīz′), *n.pl.* See under **supply**[1], *n.*

sup·ply[1] (sə plī′), *v.,* **-plied, -ply·ing,** *n., pl.* **-plies.** —*v.t.* **1.** to furnish; provide: *to supply power to a factory. The city supplies books for the children. The records did not supply a description of him* (Thomas B. Costain). **2.** to furnish or provide (a person, family, country, etc.) with a commodity, raw material, etc.: *Brazil supplies us with much of our coffee.* **3.** to furnish (a thing) with something needed or desired: *to supply plants with water and sunlight.* **4.** to satisfy (a need, want, etc.) by providing what is needed: *There was just enough to supply the demand.* **5.** to make up for (a loss, lack, absence, etc.); compensate for: *to supply a deficiency.* **6.** to fill (a place, vacancy, pulpit, etc.) as a substitute. **7.** to fill in or add (something that is wanting or necessary): *Rocks and stumps supplied the place of chairs at the picnic. Supply words that are wanting* (Lindley Murray).
—*v.i.* to fill another's place, pulpit, etc., temporarily; be a substitute.
—*n.* **1.** the act of supplying a need, desire, want, loss, lack, vacancy, etc. **2.** a quantity or amount supplied or provided: *a new supply of paper.* **3.** a quantity of goods, etc., required or at hand for use; stock; store: *The school gets its supplies of books, papers, pencils, chalk, etc., from the city. The United States has very large supplies of coal and oil. The amount of the blood supply is therefore all-important to the heart* (Scientific American). **4.** *Economics.* the quantity of any commodity in the market ready for purchase, especially at a given price: *a supply of coffee.* **5.** a sum of money appropriated by a national legislature to meet the expenses of government. **6.** a person who fills a vacancy, pulpit, etc., as a substitute for another. **7.** *Obsolete.* reinforcements. **8.** *Obsolete.* assistance; aid.
supplies, the food, equipment, etc., necessary for an army, expedition, or the like: *The invaders remained until their supplies were exhausted* (Benjamin Jowett).
[< Old French *supplier* < Latin *supplēre* < *sub-* from under + *-plēre* to fill]
—**Syn.** *v.t.* **1.** afford.

sup·ply[2] (sup′lē), *adv.* in a supple manner. [reduction of *supple* + *-ly*[1]]

supply and demand, the interplay of the quantity of goods offered for sale at specified prices and the quantity of goods purchased at those prices in a free market: *The meeting would decide whether . . . export quotas should be changed in the light of supply and demand* (New York Times).

supply pastor, a preacher who fills a pulpit during the temporary absence of the pastor: *He was licensed as a lay preacher, and during his college years he spent his weekends as a supply pastor* (Time).

sup·port (sə pôrt′, -pōrt′), *v.t.* **1.** to keep from falling or sinking; bear the weight of; hold or prop up; sustain: *Crutches supported the injured man. Walls support the roof.* **2.** to give strength, courage, or confidence to; keep up; help: *Hope supports us in time of trouble.* **3.** to endure or undergo, especially with patience or fortitude; bear; tolerate: *She couldn't support life without friends.* **4.** to uphold the rights, claims, authority, validity, etc., of (a person, party, cause, course of action, etc.) by one's aid, approval, or adherence; back; countenance: *His party would not support his campaign for reëlection.* **5.** to second or speak in favor of (a proposition, theory, etc., or one making a proposition): *to support a motion, to support the foreign-aid bill.* **6.** to provide authority for or corroboration of (a statement, etc.); help prove; bear out: *The facts support his claim. The primary assumption made in the theory was supported by evidence* (A.W. Haslett). **7.** to supply with the necessities of life; provide for: *A man should support his family.* **8.** to supply funds or means for; bear the expense of: *to support the expenses of government.* **9.** to maintain, keep up, or keep going: *A town which is able to support two banks* (W.S. Jevons). **10.** to assist or protect (another unit) in a military mission or operation: *Naval fire supported the marine landings.* **11.** *Theater.* **a.** to act with (a leading actor); play a subordinate, though often important, part to; assist. **b.** to sustain (a character) in a dramatic performance; act or play (a part) with success.
—*n.* **2. a.** the act of supporting: *Columns serve for support. He spoke in support of the measure.* **b.** the condition of being supported: *A building must have support. This argument lacks support.* **2.** help; aid: *He needs our support. Inability to enlist informed and enthusiastic public participation and support . . .* (New York Times). **3.** maintenance; means of livelihood: *Her slender earnings were the whole support of the family* (Charles Lamb). **4.** a person or thing that supports; prop; stay: *The neck is the support of the head. Wheat supports are due to fall faster than those on other crops* (Wall Street Journal). **5.** *Military.* **a.** the assistance or protection given by one element or unit to another. **b.** a unit or element which gives such assistance or protection to another unit or element: *Aviation may be used as a support for infantry.* **c.** the part of any unit held in reserve during the initial phase of an attack.
[< Old French *supporter,* learned borrowing from Latin *supportāre* convey, bring up < *sub-* (up from) under + *portāre* carry]
—**sup·port′ing·ly,** *adv.*
—**Syn.** *v.t.* **1, 2. Support, maintain, uphold** mean to hold up or keep up, literally or figuratively. **Support** suggests bearing the weight, serving as a prop, or giving needed strength to prevent something or someone from falling or sinking: *Teammates supported the injured player.* **Maintain** suggests keeping up in a state or condition by providing what is needed to prevent loss of strength, value, etc.: *The state maintains the highways.* **Uphold** chiefly suggests giving aid or moral support to a person, cause, belief, etc.: *He upheld his brother's honor.* **3.** suffer. **6.** verify, confirm, substantiate. **7.** keep. *-n.* **2.** assistance, backing. **3.** See **living.**

sup·port·a·bil·i·ty (sə pôr′tə bil′ə tē, -pōr′-), *n.* the quality or condition of being supportable.

sup·port·a·ble (sə pôr′tə bəl, -pōr′-), *adj.* that can be supported; bearable or endurable: *Future wars must have limited objectives, attainable by limited means and making defeat a painful, but supportable blow to the loser* (Bulletin of Atomic Scientists). —**sup·port′a·ble·ness,** *n.*

sup·port·a·bly (sə pôr′tə blē, -pōr′-), *adv.* in a supportable manner; so as to be supportable or endurable.

sup·port·er (sə pôr′tər, -pōr′-), *n.* **1.** a person who supports, especially one who sides with, backs up, or assists a person, cause, etc.; adherent; partisan. **2.** a thing that supports, especially something worn to hold up a garment, as a garter, or some part of the body, as a jockstrap. **3.** *Heraldry.* either of two figures, as of animals or human beings, standing one on each side of an escutcheon, and often depicted as holding it.

sup·port·ing (sə pôr′ting, -pōr′-), *adj.* **1.** keeping from falling: *The veins and veinlets combine supporting and conductive tissues* (Fred W. Emerson). **2.** keeping from giving way; sustaining; giving assistance or relief: *a strong supporting cast, a topnotch director* (Time). **3.** confirmatory; corroborative.

sup·por·tive (sə pôr′tiv, -pōr′-), *adj.* providing support; supporting; sustaining: *a supportive arch, supportive evidence. Mr. Jones has always played a supportive role at board meetings* (Harper's).

supportive therapy or **treatment, 1.** a moderate form of psychotherapy in which the doctor tries to arrive at a practical solution to a patient's problems by direct and sympathetic discussion with him: *In supportive therapy . . . the doctor merely makes an effort to understand sympathetically the problem, sorting out reactions, and advising the patient about his course of conduct* (Newsweek). **2.** medical therapy that seeks to relieve the symptoms of a disease or disturbance without direct treatment, as the use of blood transfusions in the treatment of shock.

sup·port·less (sə pôrt′lis, -pōrt′-), *adj.* having no support.

sup·por·tress (sə pôr′tris, -pōr′-), *n.* a woman supporter.

sup·pos·a·ble (sə pō′zə bəl), *adj.* that can be supposed.

sup·pos·a·bly (sə pō′zə blē), *adv.* in a supposable degree or way; as may be supposed or presumed.

sup·pos·al (sə pō′zəl), *n.* supposition; assumption; conjecture. [< Old French *supposaille* < *supposer* suppose + *-aille* -al[2]]

sup·pose (sə pōz′), *v.,* **-posed, -pos·ing.** —*v.t.* **1.** to assume, without reference to truth or falsehood, as a basis of argument, or for the purpose of tracing the consequences; frame as a hypothesis; posit: *to suppose that the sum of the angles equals 90 degrees.* **2.** to consider as a suggestion or proposal, or as a hypothetical statement or case: *Suppose we leave early in the morning. Suppose you are late, what excuse will you make?* **3.** to consider as true or probably true, on account of consistency with the known facts; incline to think or believe: *I suppose she will come as usual. I suppose you forgot to return the books. This furniture is supposed to have been in the family for 150 years.* **4.** to consider as true without reflection; take for granted; presume; believe: *Did you suppose that all snakes were poisonous? Happiness depends . . . less on exterior things than most suppose* (William Cowper). **5.** to presume the existence or presence of: *We have no reason to suppose . . . any radical difference of language* (William Ewart

Gladstone). **6.** to require as a condition; involve as necessary; imply; presuppose: *An invention supposes an inventor.* **7.** to have as an opinion; think: *Where do you suppose I left my purse?* **8.** to expect (used in the passive): *I'm supposed to be there early.*
—*v.i.* to conjecture; think; imagine. [< Old French *supposer* < *sub-* under + *poser.* Compare POSE[1].]

sup·posed (sə pōzd′), *adj.* **1.** accepted as true, but without actual or final proof; assumed: *a supposed fact.* **2.** considered as possible or probable; hypothetical: *a supposed limit to human development.* **3.** imaginary: *a supposed insult.*

sup·pos·ed·ly (sə pō′zid lē), *adv.* according to what is supposed or was supposed. —**Syn.** presumably, probably.

sup·pos·ing (sə pō′zing), *conj.* in the event that; if: *Supposing it rains, shall we still go?*

sup·po·si·tion (sup′ə zish′ən), *n.* **1.** the act of supposing: *a policy based on the supposition of continued peace.* **2.** a thing supposed; belief; opinion: *to abandon a basic supposition. The speaker planned his talk on the supposition that his hearers would be school children.*
[< Old French *supposition,* learned borrowing from Latin *suppositiō, -ōnis* a placing under, substitution (in Medieval Latin, a translation of Greek *hypóthesis* hypothesis) < *suppōnere* to substitute < *sub-* under + *ponere* to place]
—**Syn. 2.** assumption, conjecture.

sup·po·si·tion·al (sup′ə zish′ə nəl), *adj.* of or based on supposition; hypothetical; supposed. —**sup′po·si′tion·al·ly,** *adv.*

sup·pos·i·ti·tious (sə poz′ə tish′əs), *adj.* **1.** fraudulently substituted for the genuine or original thing or person. **2.** not genuine; pretended; spurious; counterfeit; false. **3.** involving or based on supposition; hypothetical; supposed. [< Latin *suppositīcius* (with English *-ous*) < *suppōnere;* see SUPPOSITION] —**sup·pos′i·ti′tious·ly,** *adv.* —**sup·pos′i·ti′tious·ness,** *n.*

sup·pos·i·tive (sə poz′ə tiv), *adj.* **1.** of the nature of, implying, or grounded on supposition; supposed. **2.** *Grammar.* expressing a supposition; conditional. —*n. Grammar.* a suppositive word. —**sup·pos′i·tive·ly,** *adv.*

sup·pos·i·to·ry (sə poz′ə tôr′ē, -tōr′-), *n., pl.* **-ries.** *Medicine.* a cone or cylinder of medicinal substance introduced into the rectum to stimulate the bowels to action, or into the vagina or urethra for any of various purposes; bougie. [< Medieval Latin *suppositorium,* noun use of adjective, neuter of *suppositorius* < Latin *suppōnere;* see SUPPOSITION]

sup·press (sə pres′), *v.t.* **1.** to put an end to; stop by force; put down: *The police suppressed a riot. The troops suppressed the rebellion by firing on the mob.* **2.** to prevent or prohibit the publication or circulation of (a book, publication, etc.): *Each nation suppressed news that was not favorable to it. Newspapers had easily gotten copies of the Cameron report and published the suppressed paragraph alongside the final official one* (Carl Sandburg). **3.** to keep in; hold back; keep from appearing: *to suppress a smile. She suppressed a yawn.* **4.** to subdue (a feeling, thought, habit, etc.): *suppressed desires. Gradually the child's unconscious fills more or less deliberately with things forgotten* (*suppressed*) *because they are unpleasant* (Time). **5.** to stop or arrest the flow of; check: *to suppress bleeding.* **6.** to keep secret; refrain from disclosing or divulging: *to suppress the truth.* [< Latin *suppressus,* past participle of *supprimere* < *sub-* down, under + *premere* to press] —**Syn. 1.** subdue, quell, crush. **3.** restrain, repress.

sup·pres·sant (sə pres′ənt), *adj.* that suppresses (an attack, symptom, etc.). —*n.* a suppressant medicine: *cough suppressants.*

sup·pres·sed·ly (sə pres′id lē), *adv.* in a suppressed or restrained manner: *to laugh suppressedly.*

sup·press·er (sə pres′ər), *n.* suppressor.

sup·press·i·ble (sə pres′ə bəl), *adj.* that can be suppressed.

sup·pres·sion (sə presh′ən), *n.* **1.** a putting down by force or authority; putting an end to: *State police were used in the suppression of strike violence.* **2.** a keeping in; holding back: *the suppression of a silly fear. The suppression of facts may be as dishonest as the telling of lies.* **3.** *Psychoanalysis.* **a.** the conscious controlling or inhibiting of a desire or impulse. **b.** repression.

sup·pres·si·o ver·i (sə pres′ē ō ver′ī), *Latin.* suppression of the true; misrepresentation of the truth by concealing facts which ought to be made known: *The English Church Union could hardly subscribe ex animo to an interpretation containing an important suppressio veri* (Spectator).

sup·pres·sive (sə pres′iv), *adj.* having the quality, effect, or intent of suppressing; causing suppression: *The drug, which is synthesized from readily available raw materials, is of the suppressive type, which means it would not provide a cure but would be used to control the disease* (Science News Letter).

sup·pres·sor (sə pres′ər), *n.* **1.** a person or thing that suppresses, crushes, or quells. **2.** a person or thing that represses, checks, or stifles: *Sound suppressors put the finger squarely on the solution of the jet noise problem* (Wall Street Journal). **3.** a person who conceals.

Supp. Rev. Stat., Supplement to the Revised Statutes.

sup·pur·ant (sup′yər ənt), *adj., n.* suppurative.

sup·pu·rate (sup′yə rāt), *v.i.,* **-rat·ed, -rat·ing.** to form pus; discharge pus; fester; maturate: *Some . . . have been found to have gangrenous, suppurating wounds from a previous encounter* (Harper's). [< Latin *suppūrāre* (with English *-ate*[1]) < *sub-* under + *pūs, pūris* pus]

sup·pu·ra·tion (sup′yə rā′shən), *n.* **1.** the formation of pus; discharge of pus; festering; maturation. **2.** pus.

sup·pu·ra·tive (sup′yə rā′tiv), *adj.* **1.** promoting suppuration. **2.** attended or characterized by suppuration. **3.** suppurating.
—*n.* an agent or remedy that promotes suppuration.

supr., supreme.

su·pra (sü′prə), *adv.* **1.** above. **2.** before, in a book or writing. [< Latin *suprā,* related to *super* over]

supra-, *prefix.* on; above; beyond, as in *supraliminal, supramolecular, suprarenal.* [< Latin *suprā,* adverb, preposition, related to *super* over]

su·pra·e·so·phag·e·al (sü′prə ē′sə faj′ē-əl), *adj.* situated above or on the dorsal side of the esophagus: *supraesophageal ganglia.*

su·pra·hu·man (sü′prə hyü′mən), *adj.* superhuman: . . . *the astronomer Johannes Kepler, and his mystical quest for the suprahuman music of the spheres* (London Times).

sup·ra·lap·sar·i·an (sü′prə lap sãr′ē ən), *n.* an adherent of the doctrine of supralapsarianism. —*adj.* of or having to do with supralapsarianism or its adherents.

su·pra·lap·sar·i·an·ism (sü′prə lap-sãr′ē ə niz′əm), *n.* the Calvinist doctrine that the division of mankind into the elect and the damned is God's basic purpose and that the fall of man was an instrumentality to achieve this end, consequent on that original purpose, and formed part of the divinely decreed plan of the creation of the world. [< New Latin *supralapsarius* (< Latin *supra-* + *lapsus, -ūs* a fall + *-ārius* having to do with) + English *-ian* + *-ism*]

su·pra·lim·i·nal (sü′prə lim′ə nəl), *adj.* above the margin or threshold of consciousness; conscious.

su·pra·max·il·la (sü′prə mak sil′ə), *n., pl.* **-max·il·lae** (-mak sil′ē). *Anatomy, Zoology.* **1.** the upper jaw. **2.** the upper jawbone.

su·pra·max·il·lar·y (sü′prə mak′sə ler′ē), *adj., n., pl.* **-lar·ies.** *Anatomy.* —*adj.* of or having to do with the upper jaw or upper jawbone. —*n.* the upper jawbone.

su·pra·mo·lec·u·lar (sü′prə mə lek′yə lər), *adj.* **1.** above, or having more complexity than, a molecule. **2.** made up of more than one molecule.

su·pra·mun·dane (sü′prə mun′dān), *adj.* supermundane: *They were thus tabooed, supramundane days* (Alfred L. Kroeber). *At first it* [*atomic bomb explosion*] *was a giant column that soon took the shape of a supramundane mushroom* (W.L. Laurence).

su·pra·na·tion·al (sü′prə nash′ə nəl, -nash′nəl), *adj.* above or beyond national limitations; supernational: *The conception of a supranational organization solving the world's quarrels . . . is an attractive one* (Punch). —**su′pra·na′tion·al·ly,** *adv.*

sup·ra·na·tion·al·ism (sü′prə nash′ə nə-liz′əm, -nash′nə liz-), *n.* the principle or practice of international coöperation above and beyond national limitations: *In the Council of Ministers, composed of cabinet ministers of all six nations, supranationalism meets nationalism* (Time).

su·pra·na·tion·al·i·ty (sü′prə nash′ə nal′-ə tē), *n.* the state of being supranational: *The* [*European Economic*] *Community was bound to develop supranationality as the six countries agreed to common policies* (New York Times).

su·pra·nat·u·ral (sü′prə nach′ər əl, -nach′-rəl), *adj., n.* supernatural. —**su′pra·nat′u·ral·ly,** *adv.*

su·pra·or·bit·al (sü′prə ôr′bə təl), *adj.* above the socket (orbit) of the eye: *Most apes possess a marked bulge of bone, called a supraorbital ridge, which extends unbroken across the region of the skull just over the eyes* (Beals and Hoijer).

su·pra·per·son·al (sü′prə pėr′sə nəl, -pėrs′nəl), *adj.* above or beyond the personal: *I refer to the needs of adventure, of risk, and hardship in the search for personal significance by way of suprapersonal goals* (Bulletin of Atomic Scientists).

su·pra·pro·test (sü′prə prō′test), *n.* an acceptance or a payment of a bill by a third person to save the reputation of the drawer after protest (official notice) that the drawee has refused to accept or pay it. [Latinization of Italian *sopra protesto* upon protest; *sopra* upon (< Latin *suprā*), *protesto* < *protestare* to protest < Latin *prōtestārī*]

su·pra·ra·tion·al (sü′prə rash′ə nəl, -rash′nəl), *adj.* above or beyond the rational; not comprehensible by reason alone: *Revealed theology, by contrast, is suprarational, and although consonant with reason . . . reason alone could not have attained to it* (Listener).

su·pra·re·nal (sü′prə rē′nəl), *adj.* **1.** situated near or on the kidney; adrenal. **2.** of or from the suprarenal glands. —*n.* a suprarenal gland, body, or capsule. [< New Latin (*capsulae*) *suprarenales,* (literally) suprarenal (capsules) < Latin *suprā* above + *renēs* kidneys]

suprarenal extract, a solution of the hormone secreted by the suprarenal glands, from which commercial Adrenalin is made.

suprarenal gland, body, or **capsule,** one of the two ductless glands on or near the kidneys, which secrete many important hormones, such as adrenalin and cortin; adrenal gland; renal gland.

su·prem·a·cist (sə prem′ə sist, sů-), *n.* a person who believes in the supremacy of one group or person over another: *a male supremacist, a white supremacist.*

su·prem·a·cy (sə prem′ə sē, sů-), *n.* **1.** the state of being supreme: *Nature is loth To yield to art her fair supremacy* (Robert Bridges). **2.** supreme authority or power. **3.** supreme position in achievement, character, or estimation. —**Syn. 2.** domination, predominance, mastery.

su·prem·a·tism (sə prem′ə tiz əm, sů-), *n.* a style in modern art originated in Russia by Kasimir Malevich (1878-1935), characterized by simple geometric shapes painted with a limited selection of colors: *Malevich's suprematism began with a black square on a white ground but soon dealt with very original color effects* (London Times). [< French *suprématie* supremacy + English *-ism*]

su·prem·a·tist (sə prem′ə tist, sů-), *n.* an artist who follows the style of suprematism: *He never joined either of the violent opposing factions in Russian revolutionary art, the suprematists and the constructivists* (London Times).

su·preme (sə prēm′, sů-), *adj.* **1.** holding the highest place in rank or authority: *a supreme ruler, a supreme commander.* **2.** of or belonging to a person or thing that is supreme: *supreme authority. German reunification constituted an obligation on the part of the four Powers who assumed supreme power in Germany* (London Times). **3.** highest in degree; greatest; utmost: *supreme disgust.* **4.** highest in quality: *supreme courage.* **5.** (of persons) highest or greatest in character or achievement. **6.** last; final.
—*n.* suprême (defs. 3 and 4).
[< Latin *suprēmus,* superlative of *superus* a thing above < *super* above] —**su·preme′ly,** *adv.* —**su·preme′ness,** *n.*
—**Syn.** *adj.* **1.** chief, paramount.

su·prême (sə prēm′, -prām′; sů-), *n.* **1.** a white sauce or velouté made from chicken stock; sauce suprême. **2.** a dish made or served with this sauce. **3.** Also, **supreme.**

a shallow bowl or glass on a pedestal. **4.** Also, **supreme.** an appetizer or dessert served in such a bowl or glass: *It was Mrs. Whitney who selected [the] suprême of fresh fruit* (New York Times). [< French *suprême* < Latin *suprēmus;* see SUPREME]

Supreme Being, God.

Supreme Court, 1. *U.S.* **a.** the highest court in the United States, consisting of the chief justice and eight associate justices. It meets at Washington, D.C. *The Supreme Court decision is the law of the land* (Estes Kefauver). **b.** the highest court in most states. **2.** a similar court in certain other countries.

Supreme Soviet, 1. the bicameral legislature of the Soviet Union, consisting of the Soviet of the Union, with deputies elected from electoral districts, and the Soviet of Nationalities, with deputies elected from political divisions (republics, autonomous republics, etc.): *The plan was presented by [the] finance minister ... before a special session of the Supreme Soviet* (Wall Street Journal). **2.** any of certain legislatures patterned on this, as those of the constituent republics of the Soviet Union.

Supt. or **supt.,** superintendent.

suq (sük), *n.* (in Arab countries) a market place. Also, **souk, suk.** [< Arabic *sūq*]

sur-[1], *prefix.* over; above; beyond, as in *surcoat, surcingle, surpass, surrejoinder.* [< Middle French *sur-* < Old French *sour-, sor-* < Latin *super-* super-]

sur-[2], *prefix.* the form of **sub-** before *r*, as in *surreptitious.*

sur., surplus.

su·ra (sůr′ə), *n.* a chapter of the Koran. The 114 suras are arranged, without regard to chronology or subject, according to length, beginning with the longest (after the opening prayer). *He stood in his stocking feet among a crowd of pilgrims and tried to say a sura, or prayer, from the Koran* (New Yorker). [< Arabic *sūra* (literally) row or layer of stones]

su·rah (sůr′ə), *n.* a soft, twilled fabric of silk, or silk and rayon. [earlier *surat* an uncolored cotton fabric < *Surat,* a city in India, where it was produced; pronunciation and form influenced by French *surah*]

su·ral (sůr′əl), *adj.* of or having to do with the calf of the leg: *spasm of the sural muscles.* [< New Latin *suralis* < Latin *sūra* calf of the leg]

sur·base (sėr′bās′), *n. Architecture.* a border or molding above any base, as at the top of wainscoting, a pedestal, etc.

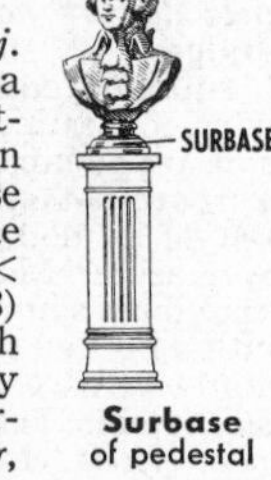

Surbase of pedestal

sur·based (sėr′bāst′), *adj. Architecture.* **1.** having a surbase. **2.** depressed; flattened. **3.** designating an arch, vault, or dome whose rise is less than half the span. [(definition 1) < *surbas*(e) + *-ed*[2]; (definition 3) half-translation of French *surbaissé* < *sur-* exceedingly + *baissé* lowered, past participle of Old French *baisser,* or *baissier* to lower. Compare ABASE.]

sur·base·ment (sėr bās′mənt), *n. Architecture.* the condition of being surbased.

sur·cease (sėr sēs′), *n., v.,* **-ceased, -ceasing.** *Archaic.* —*n.* end; cessation: *Vainly I had sought to borrow from my books surcease of sorrow* (Edgar Allan Poe). —*v.t.* to desist from (a course of action, etc.): *The hobby horse surceased his capering* (Scott). [< Anglo-French *sursise* omission, noun use of Old French, feminine past participle of *surseoir* to refrain < Latin *supersedēre* supersede; spelling influenced by English *cease*]

sur·charge (*n.* sėr′chärj′; *v.* sėr chärj′), *n., v.,* **-charged, -charg·ing.** —*n.* **1.** an extra charge: *The express company made a surcharge for delivering the trunk outside of the city limits.* **2.** an additional mark printed on a postage stamp to change its value, date, etc. **3.** a stamp bearing such a mark. **4.** an additional and usually excessive load, burden, or supply: *The surcharge of the learned, might in time be drawn off to recruit the laboring class of citizens* (Thomas Jefferson). **5.** the act of showing an omission in an account. **6.** a statement showing such an omission.

[< French *surcharge* < Old French *surcharger;* see the verb]

—*v.t.* **1.** to charge extra. **2.** to overcharge. **3.** to overload; oppress; overwhelm: *The widow's heart was surcharged with grief.* **4.** to put an additional and usually excessive physical burden or weight upon; weigh down. **5.** to print a surcharge on (a postage stamp). **6.** to show an omission in (an account) which the accounting party should have charged himself with.

[< Middle French, Old French *surcharger* < *sur-* over + *charger* to charge, load down < Late Latin *carricāre* to load < *carrus* load, wagon. Compare CAR.]

sur·charg·er (sėr chär′jər), *n.* a person who surcharges.

sur·cin·gle (sėr′sing gəl), *n.* **1.** a heavy strap or belt around a horse's body to keep a saddle, blanket, or pack in place. **2.** a girdle or belt for fastening a cassock. [< Old French *surcengle* < *sur-* over + *cengle* a girdle < Latin *cingula,* and *cingulum* < *cingere* to gird]

sur·coat (sėr′kōt′), *n.* **1.** an outer coat or garment of rich material, often worn by knights over their armor, and depicting their heraldic arms. **2.** an outer coat, slightly longer than a jacket, worn by men and boys. [< Old French *surcote* < *sur-* over + *cote* coat, tunic]

Surcoat (def. 1)

sur·cu·lose (sėr′kyə lōs), *adj. Botany.* producing shoots or suckers. [< Latin *surculōsus* woody, twiglike < *surculus* young shoot, twig (diminutive) < *surus* branch]

surd (sėrd), *n.* **1.** *Phonetics.* a sound uttered without vibration of the vocal cords. The sounds of *f, k, p, s* (as in sit), and *t* are surds. **2.** *Mathematics.* an indicated root that cannot be expressed as a whole number or common fraction. *Example:* $\sqrt{2}$.

—*adj.* **1.** *Phonetics.* uttered without vibration of the vocal cords; voiceless. **2.** *Mathematics.* that cannot be expressed as a whole number or common fraction; irrational.

[< Latin *surdus* unhearing; unheard, silent, dull, related to *susurrus* a muttering, whispering]

sure (shůr), *adj.,* **sur·er, sur·est,** *adv., n.* —*adj.* **1.** free from doubt; certain; having ample reason for belief; confident; positive: *He is sure of success in the end. I am sure of his guilt.* **2.** to be trusted; safe; reliable: *a sure messenger.* **3.** never missing, slipping, etc.; unfailing; unerring: *sure aim, a sure touch.* **4.** admitting of no doubt or question: *sure proof.* **5.** *Archaic.* secure or safe.

be sure, to be careful or certain (to do something specified); do not fail: *Be sure to leave plenty of time.*

make sure, a. to act so as to make something certain: *Make sure you have the key.* **b.** to get sure or certain knowledge; ascertain: *That fellow rode up to the house to make sure Tristram was away* (M. Notley).

sure enough, certainly; undoubtedly; of course; to be sure: *And you were so angry with me when you went off—I saw it, sure enough* (J.S. Winter). *Sure enough, just as they prophesied, most of these painters ... became enormously fashionable* (Harper's).

to be sure, certainly; undoubtedly; of course: *The weather, to be sure, was unfavorable.*

—*adv. Informal.* **1.** certainly; undoubtedly; of course: *This year a new 427-inch engine showed up at the track ... and it sure rocked the racing fraternity* (Ray Brock). **2.** without fail; for certain.

—*n.* **for sure,** for certain; undoubtedly: *Who could know for sure how the public was going to respond to color television ...* (Vance Packard).

[< Old French *sur,* and *seür* < Latin *sēcūrus.* Doublet of SECURE, SICKER.]

—**sure′ness,** *n.*

—**Syn.** *adj.* **1. Sure, certain, confident** mean having no doubt about a person, fact, statement, action, etc. **Sure** implies being free from doubt in one's own mind: *Police are sure he was murdered.* **Certain** implies having positive reasons or proof to support one's trust or belief: *They have been certain since they uncovered new evidence.* **Confident** implies having a strong and unshakable belief: *They are confident they will solve the case soon.*

➤ **Sure,** as an adverb, is considered inappropriate in standard written English. In informal English, it is widely used, particularly as a sentence modifier (*Sure, I'm coming*) and not infrequently as an intensifier (*I'm sure tired*).

sure-e·nough (shůr′i nuf′), *adj. U.S. Informal.* genuine; real: *It was at once agreed that he "wasn't the sure-enough bronco-buster he thought himself"* (Theodore Roosevelt).

sure-fire (shůr′fīr′), *adj. Informal.* unfailing; certain: *In the repertoire of the nation's comedians, Hoboken, N.J., ranks almost on a par with Brooklyn, N.Y., and Kokomo, Ind., as a sure-fire laugh-getter* (Newsweek).

sure-foot·ed (shůr′fůt′id), *adj.* not liable to stumble, slip, or fall. —**sure′-foot′ed·ly,** *adv.*

sure-foot·ed·ness (shůr′fůt′id nis), *n.* the quality of being sure-footed: *the sure-footedness of a donkey or of a mountain climber.*

sure-hand·ed (shůr′han′did), *adj.* dexterous; skillful.

sure·ly (shůr′lē), *adv.* **1.** certainly; undoubtedly; assuredly; truly: *Half a loaf is surely better than none.* **2.** as may be confidently supposed; as must be the case: *Surely it will not rain all week.* **3.** without faltering, slipping, etc.; firmly; unerringly: *The goat leaped surely from rock to rock. Surely he hath borne our griefs, and carried our sorrows* (Isaiah 53:4). **4.** without fail: *slowly but surely.*

Sû·re·té (shůr′ə tā′; *French* SYR tā′), *n.* the criminal department of a prefecture of police in France, lower Canada, and other countries where French is spoken: *Across the counter at the Montreal Sûreté the sergeant leaned on his elbow and waited to hear me out* (Maclean's). [< French *Sûreté* < Old French *surtey.* Related to SURETY.]

sure thing, a certainty; safe thing; a bet that one cannot lose: *A host of horseplayers think he's a sure thing* (New Yorker).

sur·e·ty (shůr′ə tē, shůr′tē), *n., pl.* **-ties. 1.** security against loss, damage, or failure to do something: *An insurance company gives surety against loss by fire.* **2.** a ground of certainty or safety; guarantee. **3.** *Law.* a person who agrees to be legally responsible for the debt, default, or failure to perform of another (the principal) who is primarily liable: *He was surety for his brother's appearance in court on the day set.* **4.** *Archaic.* **a.** a sure thing; certainty: *Of a surety he will come.* **b.** the condition of being sure; certain knowledge; sureness. **5.** *Obsolete.* a sponsor at baptism.

[Middle English *sewrte* < Old French *surtey, seurte* < Latin *sēcūritās* < *sēcūrus* sure, secure] —**Syn. 1.** guaranty, pledge. **3.** bondsman, bail, sponsor.

sur·e·ty·ship (shůr′ə tē ship, shůr′tē-), *n.* the obligation of a person to answer for the debt, fault, or conduct of another.

surf (sėrf), *n.* **1.** the waves or swell of the sea rising to a crest and breaking in a heavy foaming mass on the shore, or over a shoal, reef, etc.: *The shooting surf comes hissing in* (John Betjeman). **2.** the deep pounding or thundering sound of this.

—*v.i.* **1.** to travel on the crest of a wave, especially with a surfboard. **2.** to wade or go swimming in the surf.

[alteration of earlier *suff;* origin uncertain. Compare SOUGH.]

sur·face (sėr′fis), *n., adj., v.,* **-faced, -facing.** —*n.* **1.** the outside of anything: *the surface of a mountain. An egg has a smooth surface.* **2. a.** any face or side of a thing: *A cube has six surfaces. The upper surface of the plate has pictures on it.* **b.** the top of the ground or soil, or of a body of water or other liquid: *The stone sank below the surface.* **3.** the outward appearance; what appears on a slight or casual view or without examination: *a meaning that lies below the surface* (Fred A. Paley). *He seems rough, but you will find him very kind below the surface.* **4.** *Geometry.* that which has length and breadth but no thickness: *a plane surface.* **5.** *Aeronautics.* any level part which provides lift, support, or stability, as an airfoil.

—*adj.* **1.** of, on, or carried on at or near, the surface of something: *a surface view.* **2.** superficial; external.

—*v.t.* **1.** to put a surface on; make smooth: *to surface a road.* **2.** to direct or steer (a submarine) to the surface. —*v.i.* **1.** to mine near the surface. **2.** to rise to the surface, as a submarine or fish.

[< French *surface* < *sur-* above + *face* face,

patterned on Latin *superficiēs.* Compare SUPERFICIAL.]

sur·face-ac·tive (sėr′fis ak′tiv), *adj.* of or having to do with a group of chemical substances that have the property of reducing the surface tension of water or other liquid. Certain sulfates or sulfonates made from animal and vegetable fats are surface-active and are used in making household detergents.

surface car, *U.S.* a car moving on the surface of the ground, as distinguished from one moving on an elevated or underground railway.

surface color, an opaque color that is the hued counterpart of any neutral surface.

-surfaced, *combining form.* having a —— surface: *Smooth-surfaced = having a smooth surface.*

surface mail, **1.** mail sent by railroad, ship, etc., as distinguished from air mail. **2.** the system of sending mail by surface transportation.

sur·face·man (sėr′fis mən), *n., pl.* **-men.** a person who works on the surface, as on the roadbed of a railway, or in a mining or military operation: *The average wage at present is 744 francs (£53) a month for pit workers and 550 francs (under £40) for surfacemen* (London Times).

surface mining, mining carried on close to the surface of the earth; shallow mining.

surface plate, a metal plate for testing the accuracy of a flat surface.

sur·fac·er (sėr′fə sər), *n.* **1.** that which produces a smooth or even surface. **2.** a person who mines near the surface.

surface ship, any naval ship that is not a submarine.

surface tension, the tension of the surface film of a liquid that makes it contract to a minimum area. It is caused by molecular forces, and measured in terms of force per unit length.

sur·face-to-air (sėr′fis tü ãr′), *adj.* **1.** launched from the ground or a ship to intercept and destroy flying aircraft and missiles: *surface-to-air missiles.* **2.** between the ground or a ship and an aircraft: *surface-to-air rescue.*

sur·face-to-sur·face (sėr′fis tə sėr′fis), *adj.* **1.** launched from the ground or a ship at a target on the sea or on the ground. **2.** between two ships or two points on the ground: *surface-to-surface communication.*

sur·face-to-un·der·wa·ter (sėr′fis tü-un′dər wôt′ər, -wot′-), *adj.* **1.** launched from the ground or a ship at a target beneath the surface of the sea. **2.** between a surface ship and a submarine, diver, or other object underwater.

surface water, **1.** water that collects on the surface of the ground. **2.** the surface layer of a body of water.

surface wave, a wave created by an earthquake and traveling along the surface of the earth.

sur·fact·ant (sėr fak′tənt), *n.* a surface-active agent or solution, such as a detergent. [< *surf*(ace-)*act*(tive) *a*(ge)*nt*]

surf bird, a shore bird related to the plover, that nests in Alaska and winters along the Pacific Coast of North and South America.

surf·board (sėrf′bôrd′, -bōrd′), *n.* a long, narrow board on which a person may lie or stand and be carried on the crest of a wave as it mounts and breaks as surf on a beach. —*v.i.* to ride the waves on a surfboard; surf. —**surf′board′er,** *n.*

Surfboards

surf·board·ing (sėrf′bôr′ding, -bōr′-), *n.* the act of riding a surfboard.

surf·boat (sėrf′bōt′), *n.* a sturdy, heavily built rowboat designed especially for use in heavy surf.

surf·cast (sėrf′kast′, -käst′), *v.i.,* **-cast, -cast·ing.** to cast a fishing line from the shore into the surf: *Later I tried to teach my oldest son how to surfcast with a drail, but he kept fouling his line and getting sand in the reel, and we had a quarrel* (John Cheever).

surf·cast·er (sėrf′kas′tər, -käs′-), *n.* a fisherman who casts the line from the shore into the surf: *The holiday surfcasters found the striped bass cooperative along the Rhode Island beaches* (New York Times).

surf·cast·ing (serf′kas′ting, -käs′-), *n.* the act of fishing by casting the line from the shore into the surf.

surf duck, a scoter, especially the surf scoter.

sur·feit (sėr′fit), *n.* **1.** a grossly excessive amount of something; too much; excess: *A surfeit of food makes one sick. A surfeit of advice annoys me.* **2.** disgust or nausea caused by this; painful satiety. **3.** gluttonous indulgence, especially gluttonous eating or drinking. **4.** an abnormal condition caused by gluttony; derangement of the digestive system arising from gluttony or intemperance: *He died of a surfeit caused by intemperance* (Oliver Goldsmith).
—*v.t.* to force down or on (a person) in such quantity as to cause nausea, disgust, etc.; feed or supply to excess: *He is weary and surfeited of business* (Samuel Pepys). —*v.i.* to eat, drink, or indulge in something to excess; take one's fill and more (of); feast gluttonously (upon): *They are as sick that surfeit with too much as they that starve with nothing* (Shakespeare).
[< Old French *surfet,* and *surfait* excess; (originally) past participle of *surfaire* overdo < *sur-* over + *faire* do < Latin *facere*] —**sur′feit·er,** *n.*
—**Syn.** *v.t.* glut, gorge. See **satiate.**

surf·er (sėr′fər), *n.* a surf rider: *They do not ride on the surface of the bow wave as a surfer does* (New Scientist).

surf fish, any of a family of small to medium-sized viviparous fishes frequenting shallow water along the Pacific Coast of North America.

surf·ing (sėr′fing), *n.* the act of riding waves on a surfboard; surfboarding.

surf·man (sėrf′mən), *n., pl.* **-men.** **1.** a man skilled in handling boats in surf. **2.** a lifeguard.

surf·man·ship (sėrf′mən ship), *n.* skill in managing a surfboat.

surf rider, a person who rides the surf, especially on a surfboard: *A surf rider moves through the water because his board, perched on the front of a spilling wave, is perpetually sliding downhill* (Scientific American). See **surfboard** for picture.

surf scoter, a North American sea duck, dark with white markings about the head.

surf·y (sėr′fē), *adj.* **1.** having much surf or heavy surf: *a surfy beach.* **2.** forming or resembling surf.

surg., **1.** surgeon. **2.** surgery. **3.** surgical.

surge (sėrj), *v.,* **surged, surg·ing,** *n.* —*v.i.* **1.** to rise and fall, as a ship on the waves; ride at anchor or over the waves. **2.** to rise in great waves or billows; swell with great force: *A great wave surged over us.* **3.** to swell or sweep forward as waves do; move tempestuously: *The mob surged through the streets.* **4.** to rise or swell (up) tempestuously or excitedly, as feelings, thoughts, etc. **5.** *Physics.* to increase or oscillate suddenly or violently, as an electrical current. **6.** *Nautical.* **a.** (of a rope or cable) to slip back or slacken, especially when wound around a capstan or windlass. **b.** (of a ship) to sweep, pull, or jerk in a certain direction. —*v.t.* **1.** to cause to move in, or as in, swelling waves or billows. **2.** *Nautical.* to cause (a rope or cable) to slip back or slacken.
—*n.* **1.** a high, rolling swell of water; a large, heavy, or violent wave; billow: *The sea was rolling in immense surges* (Richard Henry Dana). **2.** such waves or billows collectively; the swelling and rolling of the sea: *Laced with white foam from the eternal surge* (Charles Kingsley). **3.** a swelling or sweeping forward like that of the waves; a swelling volume, as of fire, wind, sound, etc.: *a sudden surge of smoke, the surge of the mob through the streets.* **4.** a tempestuous or excited rising or swelling up of feelings, thoughts, etc.; impetuous onset of actions, events, etc.: *a surge of anger, a surge of public opinion. ... The surge of encouragement* (Sir Winston Churchill); *the surge and thunder of the Odyssey* (Andrew Lang). **5.** *Physics.* **a.** a sudden or violent rush or oscillation of electrical current in a circuit. **b.** a wave of pressure in a liquid system caused by a sudden stoppage of flow. **6.** *Nautical.* **a.** a slipping back or slackening of a rope or cable. **b.** the tapered part of a capstan or windlass, upon which the rope surges.
[probably < Middle French, Old French *sourgeon* a spring < Latin *surgere* to rise < *sub-* (up from) under + *regere* to reach; rule]

surge chamber, a chamber or tank which absorbs surges of flow in a liquid system: *At the outlet of the tunnel there is a surge chamber* (London Times).

surge·less (sėrj′lis), *adj.* free from surges; smooth; calm.

sur·geon (sėr′jən), *n.* a doctor who performs operations; medical practitioner whose specialty is surgery: *A surgeon removed the boy's appendix. Abbr.:* surg. [Middle English *surgeoun* < Anglo-French *surgien,* Old French *cirurgien* < *cirurgie;* see SURGERY. Doublet of CHIRURGEON.]

sur·geon·cy (sėr′jən sē), *n., pl.* **-cies.** the position or duties of a surgeon.

sur·geon·fish (sėr′jən fish′), *n., pl.* **-fish·es** or (*collectively*) **-fish.** any of a group of fishes having long spines growing near the tail, found especially in tropic seas, near coral reefs, etc.; tang.

Surgeon General, *pl.* **Surgeons General.** **1.** the chief medical officer of a particular branch of the armed forces of the United States. **2.** the chief medical officer of the United States Public Health Service (formerly the Bureau of Public Health). **3.** a member of the medical staff of the British army. *Abbr.:* Surg. Gen.

surgeon's knot, any of various knots used by surgeons in tying ligatures, bandages, etc.

sur·ger·y (sėr′jər ē), *n., pl.* **-ger·ies.** **1.** the art and science of treating deformities, diseases, injuries, etc., by operations and instruments: *Malaria can be cured by medicine, but a ruptured appendix requires surgery.* **2.** the office, laboratory, or operating room of a surgeon. **3.** the work performed by a surgeon. **4.** any corrective treatment consisting primarily of cutting out or trimming away something that impairs health, appearance, or quality: *to save a tree by skillful surgery.* **5.** *British.* the office of a doctor or dentist. [< Old French *surgerie,* or *cirurgerie,* earlier *cirurgie,* learned borrowing from Latin *chīrūrgia* < Greek *cheirourgíā* < *cheirourgós* surgeon < *cheír* hand + *érgon* work]

Surg. Gen., Surgeon General.

sur·gi·cal (sėr′jə kəl), *adj.* **1.** of or having to do with surgery: *surgical experience.* **2.** used in surgery: *surgical instruments. Surgical gloves, should, of course, present an impermeable barrier to bacteria on the skin* (New Scientist). **3.** performed by a surgeon. **4.** following or resulting from an operation or other treatment by a surgeon: *surgical fever.* —**sur′gi·cal·ly,** *adv.*

surg·y (sėr′jē), *adj.,* **surg·i·er, surg·i·est.** **1.** surging; swelling; billowy. **2.** produced by surges: *The surgy murmurs of the lonely sea* (Keats).

su·ri·cat (sůr′ə kat), *n.* suricate.

su·ri·cate (sůr′ə kāt), *n.* a small, burrowing, carnivorous mammal of the civet family, found in South Africa. [< French *surikate;* origin uncertain; perhaps influenced by Dutch *surikat* the macaque]

Su·ri·nam toad (sůr′ə nam), an aquatic toad of northern South America, notable for the manner in which the eggs, distributed by the male over the back of the female, are retained there, in cells of the skin which form about them, until fully developed into young. [< *Surinam,* a Dutch territory in South America]

sur·li·ly (sėr′lə lē), *adv.* in a surly manner; crabbedly; morosely.

sur·li·ness (sėr′lē nis), *n.* the state or character of being surly; gloomy moroseness; crabbed ill-nature.

sur·loin (sėr′loin), *n.* sirloin.

sur·ly (sėr′lē), *adj.,* **-li·er, -li·est.** **1.** bad-tempered and unfriendly; rude; gruff: *They got a surly answer from the grouchy old man.* **2.** *Obsolete.* haughty; arrogant: *Be opposite with a kinsman; surly with servants* (Shakespeare). [Middle English *sirly,* perhaps < *sir* lord + *-ly*²] —**Syn.** **1.** sullen, churlish, cross. —**Ant.** **1.** genial.

sur·mise (sər mīz′; *n. also* sėr′mīz), *v.,* **-mised, -mis·ing,** *n.* —*v.t., v.i.* to infer conjecturally; guess: *We surmised that the delay was caused by some accident on the highway.* [< Old French *surmise,* past participle of *surmettre* < *sur-* upon + *mettre* to put < Latin *mittere* send]
—*n.* **1.** a surmising; guessing: *His guilt was a matter of surmise; there was no proof.* **2.** a conjecture; guess: *a shrewd surmise. To*

trust the soul's invincible surmise (George Santayana).
[< Old French *surmise* accusation, verbal noun of *surmettre;* see the verb] **—sur·mis′er,** *n.*
—**Syn.** *v.t., v.i.* suppose. See **guess.**

sur·mount (sər mount′), *v.t.* **1.** to rise above; surpass in height; be higher than; overtop: *Mount Rainier surmounts all the peaks near it.* **2.** to be situated above; rest on top of; top; crown: *a steeple surmounting a church.* **3.** to go up and across; get over: *to surmount a hill.* **4.** to prevail over; get the better of; overcome: *Lincoln surmounted many difficulties before he rose to be President.* [< Old French *surmonter* < *sur-* over + *monter.* Compare MOUNT[1].]

sur·mount·a·ble (sər moun′tə bəl), *adj.* that can be surmounted.

sur·mul·let (sėr mul′it), *n.* the red mullet. [< French *surmulet* < Old French *sormulet,* probably < *sor* reddish-brown + *mulet.* Compare MULLET[1].]

sur·name (sėr′nām′), *n., v.,* **-named, -nam·ing.** *—n.* **1.** that part of a person's full name which he shares with all other members of his immediate family and by which he is identified as belonging to a particular family group, normally (in the English-speaking world) deriving from the father and occurring as the last element of the full name; last name; family name: *Smith is the surname of John Smith.* **2.** *Archaic.* a name added to a person's name or names, especially one derived from the place of his birth or from some outstanding quality, achievement, etc.; epithet; agnomen. *Examples:* Francis (*of Assisi*), Ivan (*the Terrible*), William (*the Conqueror*).
—v.t. **1.** to give a surname to. **2.** to call or identify by the surname of: *Simon was surnamed Peter.*
[Middle English alteration (influenced by *name*) of *surnoun* < Anglo-French *sournoun,* variant of Old French *surnom* < *sur-* over + *nom* name < Latin *nōmen, -inis*]

sur·nom·i·nal (sėr nom′ə nəl), *adj.* of or having to do with surnames.

sur·pass (sər pas′, -päs′), *v.t.* **1.** to do more or better than; be greater than or superior to; excel: *His work surpassed expectations. The sense of accomplishment I felt in actually aiding birth surpassed any feeling I'd had before* (Parents' Magazine). **2.** to be beyond the range, reach, or capacity of; be too much or too great for; transcend; exceed: *beauty that surpasses description.* [< Middle French *surpasser* < *sur-* beyond + *passer* to pass, go by] —**Syn. 1.** outdo, outstrip, outrun, eclipse. See **excel.**

sur·pass·a·ble (sər pas′ə bəl, -päs′-), *adj.* that can be surpassed.

sur·pass·ing (sər pas′ing, -päs′-), *adj.* greatly exceeding or excelling others; of the highest degree or quality: *Helen of Troy was a surpassing beauty.* *—adv. Poetic.* in a surpassing degree; exceedingly: *a gracious damsel and surpassing fair.* **—sur·pass′ing·ly,** *adv.* **—sur·pass′ing·ness,** *n.*

sur·plice (sėr′plis), *n.* **1.** a broad-sleeved, white gown worn by clergymen and choir singers over their other clothes. **2.** an arrangement of folds on a blouse or the bodice of a dress that cross one another from the waist up to the opposite shoulder. [Middle English *surplis* < Anglo-French *surpliz,* contraction of Old French *surpelize* < *sur-* over + *pelice* fur garment < Medieval Latin *pellicia* < Latin *pellis* hide]

Surplice (def. 1)

sur·pliced (sėr′plist), *adj.* wearing a surplice: *Throughout the day, surpliced priests, accompanied by acolytes carrying pots of holy water, visited every business and residential section of Rome, blessing homes and offices* (New York Times).

sur·plus (sėr′pləs, -plus), *n.* **1.** what remains over and above what is needed, taken, or used; quantity left over; excess: *The bank keeps a large surplus of money in reserve.* **2.** *Accounting.* **a.** the total assets of a business, minus the sum of its total liabilities and the face value of its capital stock. **b.** an excess of assets over dividends, interest, and other fixed charges within some given period of time.
—adj. beyond what is needed, taken, or used; excess: *surplus wheat and cotton.*
[< Old French *surplus* < *sur-* over + *plus* more < Latin]—**Syn.** *n.* **1.** residue, remainder.

sur·plus·age (sėr′plu sij), *n.* **1.** a surplus; excess. **2.** an excess or superabundance of words. **3.** *Law.* nonessential or irrelevant language in a pleading or plea.

sur·print (sėr′print′), *v.t.* **1.** to print over (something already printed) with new matter. **2.** to print (new matter) over something already printed. *—n.* surprinted matter.

sur·pris·al (sər prī′zəl), *n.* **1.** a surprising. **2.** a being surprised; surprise.

sur·prise (sər prīz′), *n., v.,* **-prised, -pris·ing,** *adj.* *—n.* **1.** the feeling or emotion caused by something happening suddenly or unexpectedly; astonishment; amazement: *His face showed surprise at the news.* **2.** anything which causes this feeling; a sudden, unexpected, or extraordinary occurrence or event: *Life is a series of surprises* (Emerson). **3.** the act of coming upon one unexpectedly, or of attacking suddenly and without warning; a catching unprepared or taking unawares.
take by surprise, a. to come upon suddenly or unexpectedly; catch unprepared: *That he was taken by surprise is true. But he had twelve hours to make his arrangements* (Macaulay). **b.** to astonish because unexpected; amaze: *This statement, I confess, took me by surprise* (John Tyndall).
—v.t. **1.** to cause to feel surprise, as by something unexpected or extraordinary; astonish. **2.** to come upon suddenly or unexpectedly; take unawares; take or catch in the act. **3.** to attack suddenly and without warning; make an unexpected assault upon (an unprepared place, army, person, etc.): *The enemy surprised the fort.* **4.** to betray (into doing something not intended); lead or bring unawares: *The news surprised her into tears.* **5.** to find or discover (something) by a sudden or unexpected question, attack, etc.; detect or elicit: *to surprise the truth of the matter from him.* **6.** *Obsolete.* to capture by an unexpected assault or attack.
—adj. that is not expected; surprising: *a surprise visit, a surprise party.*
[< Old French *surprise,* noun use of feminine past participle of *surprendre* < *sur-* over + *prendre* to take < Latin *prehendere*]
—**Syn.** *n.* **1.** wonder. *-v.t.* **1. Surprise, astonish, amaze** mean to cause sudden wonder. **Surprise** emphasizes the sudden reaction produced by something unexpected: *His answer surprised her.* **Astonish** emphasizes the wonder caused by something extraordinary or incredible: *He astonished many people by failing in college work after getting high grades in high school.* **Amaze** implies bewildered wonder: *New scientific discoveries constantly amaze us.*

sur·pris·ed·ly (sər prī′zid lē), *adv.* in a manner indicating surprise; with surprise.

sur·pris·er (sər prī′zər), *n.* a person or thing that surprises.

sur·pris·ing (sər prī′zing), *adj.* causing surprise: *a surprising recovery.* **—sur·pris′ing·ly,** *adv.* **—sur·pris′ing·ness,** *n.* —**Syn.** astonishing, amazing.

sur·ra (su̇r′ə), *n.* an acute, infectious blood disease, usually fatal, of horses and other domesticated animals, occurring chiefly in India, China, and the Philippines and caused by a protozoan. [< Marathi *sūra* a wheezing; air breathed through the nostrils]

sur·re·al (sə rē′əl, sėr rē′-), *adj.* **1.** surrealistic. **2.** characterized by a dreamlike distortion of reality; eerie; bizarre. [back formation < *surrealism*]

sur·re·al·ism (sə rē′ə liz əm), *n.* a modern movement in painting, sculpture, literature, etc., that tries to show what takes place in the subconscious mind. In surrealism the pictures, images, etc., often combine the conventional and the unconventional, or the familiar and the bizarre, in order to represent the imagery or thought patterns characteristic of dreams or other activities of the subconscious mind. *Dadaism, the school of determinedly impromptu expression, was giving way to the more rigidly formulated doctrines of surrealism* (New Yorker). [< French *surréalisme* < *sur-* beyond, sur-[1] + *réalisme* realism]

sur·re·al·ist (sə rē′ə list), *n.* an artist or writer who uses surrealism: *The surrealists' intention [in painting] was to discover and explore . . . the world of psychic experience as it had been revealed by psychoanalytical research* (Helen Gardner). *—adj.* of or having to do with surrealism or surrealists.

sur·re·al·is·tic (sə rē′ə lis′tik), *adj.* of or having to do with surrealism or surrealists. **—sur·re′al·is′ti·cal·ly,** *adv.*

sur·re·but (sėr′ri but′), *v.i.,* **-but·ted, -but·ting.** *Law.* (of a plaintiff) to reply to a defendant's rebutter.

sur·re·but·tal (sėr′ri but′əl), *n. Law.* a plaintiff's evidence or giving of evidence to refute the defendant's rebuttal.

sur·re·but·ter (sėr′ri but′ər), *n. Law.* a plaintiff's answer to the defendant's rebutter.

sur·re·join (sėr′ri join′), *v.i. Law.* to reply to a defendant's rejoinder.

sur·re·join·der (sėr′ri join′dər), *n. Law.* a plaintiff's answer to the defendant's rejoinder (the fifth step in ordinary pleadings).

sur·ren·der (sə ren′dər), *v.t.* **1.** to give up (something) to the possession or power of another, upon demand or compulsion; yield (to): *to surrender a town to the enemy.* **2.** to give up, resign, or abandon possession of (something) in favor of or for the sake of another; relinquish: *to surrender an office or privilege.* **3.** to give up or abandon (hope, joy, comfort, etc.): *As the storm increased, the men on the raft surrendered all hope.* **4.** to give (oneself) up to a dominating thing or influence: *He surrendered himself to bitter grief.* **5.** *Obsolete.* to give back or return (thanks, etc.).
—v.i. to yield to the power of another, as a person, body of men, town, etc.; submit: *The captain had to surrender unconditionally to the enemy.*
—n. **1.** the act of surrendering; the giving up of something or of oneself into the possession or power of another: *The surrender of the soldiers saved them from being killed.* **2.** *Insurance.* the abandonment of an insurance policy by the party insured, in return for a sum of money (surrender value), the amount payable depending upon the amount of the premiums paid. **3.** *Law.* the deed by which an estate, lease, etc., is legally surrendered.
[< Anglo-French *surrender,* Old French *surrendre* < *sur-* over, sur-[1] + *rendre.* Compare RENDER.] **—sur·ren′der·er,** *n.*

sur·rep·ti·tious (sėr′əp tish′əs), *adj.* **1.** acting by stealth or secretly; stealthy: *a surreptitious glance* (Arnold Bennett). **2.** taken, obtained, used, done, etc., by stealth; secret and unauthorized; clandestine: *surreptitious meetings.* [< Latin *surreptīcius,* or *surreptītius* (with English *-ous*) < *surripere* seize secretly < *sub-* under + *rapere* to snatch] **—sur′rep·ti′tious·ly,** *adv.* **—sur′rep·ti′tious·ness,** *n.*

sur·rey (sėr′ē), *n., pl.* **-reys.** a light, four-wheeled carriage having two seats facing forward, and sometimes a top. [American English < earlier *surrey cart* < *Surrey,* a county in England]

Surrey

sur·ro·gate (*n., adj.* sėr′ə gāt, -git; *v.* sėr′ə-gāt), *n., adj., v.,* **-gat·ed, -gat·ing.** *—n.* **1.** a substitute; deputy. **2.** the deputy of an ecclesiastical judge, usually of a bishop or his chancellor. **3.** *Law, U.S.* (in certain states) a judge or judicial officer having charge of the probate of wills, the administration of estates, guardianships, etc.
—adj. that takes the place of or stands for something else; representative; substitute: *To support this idea, by now stale, of Communism as a surrogate religion, Chayefsky feels free to rewrite the early history of the Russian Revolution* (Time).
[< Latin *surrogātus,* (originally) past participle of *surrogāre;* see the verb]
—v.t. **1.** *Law.* **a.** to designate (another) to succeed oneself. **b.** to subrogate. **2.** *Obsolete.* to put instead of another; substitute.
[< Latin *surrogāre* (with English *-ate*[1]) to substitute < *sub-* in the place of, under + *rogāre* ask for (by election)]

sur·ro·gate·ship (sėr′ə gāt ship, -git-), *n.* the office or authority of a surrogate.

sur·round (sə round′), *v.t.* **1.** to shut in on all sides; enclose; encompass: *A high fence surrounds the field.* **2.** to go or extend around; encircle: *inscriptions surrounding the base of a monument.* **3.** to make available to in abundance; provide unstintingly: *They surrounded the invalid with every comfort.* **4.** to encompass and beset on all sides with hostile military force, especially so as to cut

off from supplies, reinforcements, etc.: *to surround a city.*
—*n.* a border or edging of a particular material, nearly or completely surrounding a central piece: *the linoleum surround of a carpet, the plastic surround of the television screen.*
[< Anglo-French *surounder* surpass; (originally) overflow, abound < Late Latin *superundāre* overflow < Latin *super-* over + *undāre* to flow (in waves) < *unda* wave; meaning influenced by *round*]
sur·round·ings (sə roun′dingz), *n.pl.* surrounding things, conditions, etc.; environment.
sur·roy·al (sėr roi′əl), *n.* an upper or terminal branch of an antler, above the royal antler.
sur·sum cor·da (sėr′səm kôr′də), *Latin.* **1.** lift up your hearts (words pronounced just before the Preface of the Mass). **2.** words used to incite or encourage.
sur·tax (sėr′taks′), *n.* an additional or extra tax on something already taxed, especially an income tax over and above the normal income tax, levied at progressively higher rates on the amounts by which net incomes exceed a certain sum. —*v.t.* to subject to a surtax. [< French *surtaxe* < *sur-* over, sur-[1] + *taxe* tax]
sur·tout (sėr tüt′, -tü′), *n.* a kind of single-breasted frock coat with pockets cut diagonally in front, especially one of the type worn by men during the latter 1800's. [< French *surtout* < *sur-* over, sur-[1] + *tout* all < Latin *tōtus* everything]
surv., **1.** surveying. **2.** surveyor. **3.** surviving.
sur·veil·lance (sər vā′ləns, -vāl′yəns), *n.* **1.** watch or guard kept over a person, etc., especially over a suspected person, a prisoner, or the like. **2.** supervision: *The teachers promised they would . . . supply exam-room surveillance to guard against cheating* (Newsweek).
under surveillance, subject to a watch or guard: *The police kept the suspected criminal under close surveillance.*
[< French *surveillance* < *surveiller;* see SURVEILLANT]
sur·veil·lant (sər vā′lənt, -vāl′yənt), *n.* a person who keeps watch over another or others. [< French *surveillant,* noun use of present participle of *surveiller* oversee < *sur-* over, sur-[1] + *veiller* to watch < Latin *vigilāre* < *vigil, -ilis* vigil]
sur·veille (sər vāl′), *v.t.,* **-veilled, -veil·ling.** to keep under surveillance; watch or guard closely: *From foregoing, [I] suspect we are surveilling wrong party* (Harper's). [back formation < *surveillance*]
sur·vey (*v.* sər vā′; *n.* sėr′vā, sər vā′), *v., n., pl.* **-veys.** —*v.t.* **1.** to take a broad, general, or comprehensive view of; view, examine, consider, or contemplate as a whole: *to survey the situation, to survey accounts. Grandma surveyed Mary with a stern look. The buyers surveyed the goods offered for sale.* **2.** to determine the form, extent, situation, etc., of (a tract of ground, or any portion of the earth's surface) by linear and angular measurements and by applying geometric and trigonometric principles so as to construct a map, plan, or detailed description: *Men are surveying the land before it is divided into house lots.* —*v.i.* to survey land.
—*n.* **1.** the act of viewing or considering something as a whole; a general or comprehensive view: *We were pleased with our first survey of the house. After a moment's survey of her face . . .* (Dickens). **2.** a comprehensive literary examination, discussion, or description of something: *a survey of contemporary poetry.* **3.** a formal or official examination or inspection of the particulars of something, in order to determine condition, quality, etc.: *a survey of fire hazards in public buildings, a research center for business surveys.* **4.** a statement or description embodying the result of such examination: *a published survey of population trends.* **5.** the process of determining the form, extent, situation, etc., of a tract of ground or any part of the earth's surface, so as to be able to delineate or describe it accurately and in detail: *A survey showed that the northern boundary was not correct.* **6.** a plan or description thus obtained: *He pointed out the route of the railroad on the government survey.*
[< Anglo-French *surveier,* or Old French *sourveeir* < Medieval Latin *supervidere* < Latin *super-* over + *vidēre* to see]
sur·vey·a·ble (sər vā′ə bəl), *adj.* that can be surveyed.
sur·vey·ing (sər vā′ing), *n.* **1.** the process, art, or business of surveying land, etc. **2.** mathematical instruction in the principles and art of making surveys.
sur·vey·or (sər vā′ər), *n.* **1.** a person whose business is surveying land, etc.: *The surveyor set up his instruments and began to make a survey of the road.* **2.** *U.S.* a customs official with the duty of determining the quantity, value, etc., of commodities brought into a port from another country.
surveyor general, *pl.* **surveyors general, 1.** a principal or head surveyor. **2.** an officer of the United States government who supervises the surveys of public lands.
surveyor's chain, a measuring instrument used by surveyors, consisting of 100 interlinked metal rods; Gunter's chain.
sur·vey·or·ship (sər vā′ər ship), *n.* the position of a surveyor.
surveyor's level, an instrument used by a surveyor to determine whether a surface is level.
surveyor's measure, a system of measuring used by surveyors. The unit is usually a chain 66 ft. long with links 7.92 in. long.

625 square links = 1 square pole
16 square poles = 1 square chain
10 square chains = 1 acre
640 acres = 1 section
(or 1 square mile)
36 sections = 1 township

sur·view (sėr′vyü′), *n. Archaic.* a view, especially a mental view, of something; survey. [< Old French *surveue* < *sourveeir;* see SURVEY]
sur·viv·a·bil·i·ty (sər vī′və bil′ə tē), *n.* capability of surviving or lasting: *retaliatory missile systems of high survivability* (Bulletin of Atomic Scientists).
sur·viv·a·ble (sər vī′və bəl), *adj.* capable of surviving or lasting.
sur·viv·al (sər vī′vəl), *n.* **1.** the act or fact of surviving; continuance of life; living or lasting longer than others: *No small number of what the English stigmatize as Americanisms are cases of survival from former good usage* (William D. Whitney). **2.** something that continues to exist after the cessation of something else, or of other things of the kind. **3.** a custom, observance, etc., kept after the circumstances or conditions in which it originated or which gave significance to it have passed away: *Belief in the evil eye is a survival of ancient magic. Thanksgiving Day is a survival from pre-Revolutionary times.*
survival kit, food, water, medicine, etc., in a kit given to the crew of an airplane for use in case of a crash or forced landing: *They wore long cotton underwear . . . winter flying gloves, wool socks, A-13A oxygen masks, B-5 parachutes, and carried A-1 survival kits* (Newsweek).
survival of the fittest, *Biology.* the fact or the principle that those organisms which are best adapted to their environment continue to live and produce offspring, while those of the same or related species which are less adapted perish; the process or result of natural selection.
survival value, *Biology.* usefulness of any part, characteristic, etc., of an organism in enabling the organism to survive: *Over many generations certain genetically controlled characteristics tend to grow scarce within a population as others gradually replace them, owing to a difference in their survival values* (Atlantic).
sur·viv·ance (sər vī′vəns), *n.* survival.
sur·vive (sər vīv′), *v.,* **-vived, -viv·ing.** —*v.t.* **1.** to live longer than; outlive: *He survived his wife by three years.* **2.** to remain alive after; not die during: *He survived the automobile accident, but died in the hospital within a few hours.* **3.** to sustain the effects of and continue to live; outlast: *The crops survived the drought.* —*v.i.* **1.** to continue to live; remain alive; live on: *Yea, though I die, the scandal will survive* (Shakespeare). **2.** to continue to exist; last on: *Books have survived from the time of the Egyptians.* [< Anglo-French *survivre,* Old French *sourvivre* < Latin *supervīvere* < *super-* above + *vīvere* to live]
sur·viv·ing (sər vī′ving), *adj.* that survives: **a.** still living after another's death. **b.** still remaining after the cessation of something else.
sur·vi·vor (sər vī′vər), *n.* **1.** a person, animal, or plant that remains alive; thing that continues to exist. *Law.* **2.** the one of two or more joint tenants or other persons with a joint interest in property who outlives the other or others.
sur·vi·vor·ship (sər vī′vər ship), *n. Law.* **1.** the condition of a survivor, or the fact of one person surviving another or others, considered in relation to some right or privilege depending on such survival or the period of it. **2.** the right of the survivor or survivors of two or more joint tenants or other persons having a joint interest in property, to take the whole on the death of the other or others.
sus-, *prefix.* the form of **sub-** sometimes before *c, p,* or *t,* as in *susceptible, suspend, sustain.*
Sus., Susanna (book of the Apocrypha).
Su·san·na (sü zan′ə), *n.* **1.** (in the Old Testament Apocrypha) a woman accused of adultery who was proved innocent by Daniel's cross-examination of her accusers. **2.** the book of the Old Testament Apocrypha telling her story, included in the canon of the Greek and Roman Catholic Bibles as part of the Book of Daniel. *Abbr.:* Sus.
sus·cep·ti·bil·i·ty (sə sep′tə bil′ə tē), *n., pl.* **-ties. 1.** the quality or state of being susceptible, especially: **a.** a capacity for feeling or emotion; sensibility. **b.** a capacity for receiving mental or moral impressions; sensitiveness. **2.** *Physics.* the capacity of a substance to be magnetized, measured by the ratio of the magnetization to the magnetizing force. *Symbol:* k (written without a period).
susceptibilities, sensitive feelings: *Blunt susceptibilities are very consistent with strong propensities* (Charlotte Brontë).
susceptibility to, capability of receiving, being affected by, or undergoing: *a susceptibility to infection.*
sus·cep·ti·ble (sə sep′tə bəl), *adj.* **1.** capable of being affected by, or easily moved to, feeling; subject to emotional or mental impression; impressionable: *Poetry appealed to her susceptible nature.* **2.** subject to some physical affection, as infection.
susceptible of, a. capable of receiving, undergoing, or being affected by: *Oak is susceptible of a high polish.* **b.** sensitive to: *Her young heart was susceptible only of pleasure and curiosity* (Edward G. Bulwer-Lytton).
susceptible to, easily affected by; liable to; open to: *Vain people are susceptible to flattery. I . . . am peculiarly susceptible to draughts* (Oscar Wilde).
[< Late Latin *susceptibilis* < Latin *suscipere* sustain, support, acknowledge; take on oneself < *sub-* (up from) under + *capere* take]
—**sus·cep′ti·ble·ness,** *n.*
—**Syn. 1.** See **sensitive.**
sus·cep·ti·bly (sə sep′tə blē), *adv.* in a susceptible manner.
sus·cep·tion (sə sep′shən), *n.* **1.** merely passive mental reception. **2.** *Obsolete.* the act of taking up, assuming, or receiving.
sus·cep·tive (sə sep′tiv), *adj.* **1.** having the quality of taking or receiving; receptive. **2.** susceptible; impressionable. —**sus·cep′tive·ness,** *n.*
sus·cep·tiv·i·ty (sus′ep tiv′ə tē), *n.* the capacity of admitting; susceptibility.
su·shi (sü′shē), *n.* a Japanese and Hawaiian dish of cold cooked rice, fish, and vegetables, rolled in pressed seaweed. [< Japanese *sushi*]
Su·sie-Q (sü′zē kyü′), *n.* a kind of shuffling, sideways dance step, especially popular in the 1930's: *. . . where happy feet first stomped out the Lindy Hop, Big Apple, and Susie-Q* (Time). Also, **Susy-Q.** [origin unknown]
sus·lik (sus′lik), *n.* **1.** a small grayish ground squirrel of Europe and Asia. **2.** its fur. [< Russian *suslik*]
sus·pect (*v.* sə spekt′; *n.* sus′pekt; *adj.* sus′pekt, sə spekt′), *v.t.* **1.** to imagine (something) to be possible or likely; imagine to be so; surmise: *The old fox suspected danger and did not touch the trap. I suspect his knowledge did not amount to much* (Charles Lamb). **2.** to imagine something evil, wrong, or undesirable in (a person or thing) on slight or no evidence; believe or fancy to be guilty or faulty, with insufficient proof or knowledge: *The policeman suspected the thief of lying. The hoodlum is the suspected thief.* **3.** to feel no confidence in; be very skeptical of; doubt: *The judge suspected the truth of the thief's excuse.* —*v.i.* to imagine something, especially some evil, as possible or likely.

[< adjective, and < French *suspecter* suspect, ultimately < Latin *suspectus;* see the adjective]
—*n.* a person suspected of some offense, evil intention, or the like; suspicious character: *The police have arrested two suspects in connection with the bank robbery.* [< adjective]
—*adj.* open to or viewed with suspicion; suspected: *As for the aims and ideals of Marxism, there is one feature of them that is now rightly suspect* (Edmund Wilson).
[< Latin *suspectus,* past participle of *suspicere* esteem, look up to < *sub-* under + *specere* to look]
—**Syn.** *v.t.* **1.** conjecture.

sus·pect·a·ble (sə spek′tə bəl), *adj.* that may be suspected; open to suspicion.

sus·pect·ed (sə spek′tid), *adj.* **1.** that one suspects to be such; possible; likely: *The medical aid to expectant mothers is intended to avert premature births, a suspected cause of mental retardation* (Wall Street Journal). **2.** regarded with suspicion; imagined guilty or faulty; suspect: *. . . the search and detention of suspected ships* (London Times).

sus·pect·ful (sə spekt′fəl), *adj. Obsolete.* **1.** inclined to suspect. **2.** causing suspicion.

sus·pend (sə spend′), *v.t.* **1.** to hang down by attaching to something above, especially so as to allow movement about the point of attachment: *The lamp was suspended from the ceiling.* **2.** to hold in place as if by hanging; cause to be held up by gravity, buoyancy, etc.: *We saw the smoke suspended in the still air.* **3.** to hold or cause to be held in suspension. **4.** to put a stop to or bring to a stop, usually for a time: *to suspend work on a road until more funds are voted. The hurricane suspended all ferry service for three days.* **5.** to cause (a law, etc.) to be for a time no longer in force; abrogate or make inoperative temporarily: *The privilege of the writ of habeas corpus shall not be suspended . . .* (Constitution of the United States). **6.** to keep undecided or undetermined; refrain from concluding definitely, especially until more facts are known: *Let us suspend judgment until we know all the facts. The court suspended judgment until next Monday.* **7.** to defer temporarily (sentence on a convicted person). **8.** to remove or exclude from some office, privilege, etc., usually for a time; debar temporarily: *He was suspended from school for a week for bad conduct.*
—*v.i.* **1.** to come to a stop for a time. **2.** (of a bank, company, etc.) to stop payment; be unable to pay debts or claims.
[< Latin *suspendere* < *sub-* down, under + *pendere* hang]
—**Syn.** *v.t.* **1.** dangle, swing. **4.** interrupt, intermit. **6.** defer.

sus·pend·ed animation (sə spen′did), a temporary suspension of breathing, pulse, and other vital functions, especially that due to asphyxia.

sus·pend·er (sə spen′dər), *n.* **1.** *British.* a garter. **2.** a person or thing that suspends. **3.** that by which something is suspended.
suspenders, *Especially U.S.* straps worn over the shoulders and attached to the trousers to keep them up. In British English the term is *braces. He wore red suspenders.*

sus·pense (sə spens′), *n.* **1.** the condition or state of being mentally uncertain, especially: **a.** such a condition or state induced by art or craft in order to hold the attention of a reader, audience, etc.: *The detective story kept me in suspense until the last chapter.* **b.** anxious uncertainty; anxiety: *Mothers feel suspense when their children are very sick.* **2.** the condition or state of being undecided or undetermined; suspending of judgment. **3.** *Obsolete.* suspending of action; suspension.
—*adj.* of suspense; suspenseful: *. . . Mr. Hitchcock . . . revealed that for the first time in a long and illustrious career he will do a remake of one of his successful suspense stories* (New York Times).
[< Anglo-French *suspens,* in phrase (*en*) *suspens* (in) abeyance, or < Old French *suspense,* delay < Medieval Latin *suspensus* a checking or withholding, and Vulgar Latin *suspēnsa* < Latin *suspendere;* see SUSPEND]

suspense account, an account in which sums received or spent are temporarily entered until their proper place in the books is determined.

sus·pense·ful (sə spens′fəl), *adj.* characterized by or full of suspense: *superbly acted suspenseful entertainment* (Saturday Review). *This time there was an even longer and more suspenseful silence before the answer came* (New Yorker).

sus·pen·si·bil·i·ty (sə spen′sə bil′ə tē), *n.* the capability of being suspended.

sus·pen·si·ble (sə spen′sə bəl), *adj.* that can be suspended.

sus·pen·sion (sə spen′shən), *n.* **1. a.** the act of suspending: *the suspension of a boy from school for bad conduct, suspension of judgment or opinion, a suspension of law and order.* **b.** the state of being suspended: *a suspension from office.* **2.** a support on which something is suspended. **3.** the arrangement of springs, shock absorbers, etc., above the axles, for supporting the body of an automobile, railroad car, etc. **4.** *Physics.* **a.** a mixture in which very small particles of a solid remain suspended without dissolving. **b.** the condition of the solid in such a mixture. **c.** a solid in such condition. **5.** inability to pay one's debts; failure: *the suspension of a bank.* **6.** the temporary deprivation of a clergyman of his right to perform his sacred duties or to receive his ecclesiastical dues. **7.** *Electricity.* a wire or filament for supporting the moving part of various instruments. **8.** the method or mechanism by which the pendulum or balance wheel is suspended in a clock or watch. **9.** *Music.* **a.** a prolonging of one or more tones of a chord into the following chord, usually producing a temporary discord until the part or parts prolonged are allowed to proceed. **b.** the tone or tones so prolonged. **10. a.** the act of keeping in suspense. **b.** the state of being kept in suspense.
—**Syn. 1. a, b.** interruption, intermission, stop, postponement, respite.

suspension bridge, a bridge hung on cables and chains between towers.

Suspension Bridge

suspension point, one of a series of dots (...) showing an omission or a longer than usual pause in written or printed matter.

suspension system, the shock absorbers, springs, torsion bars, or similar devices, suspended between the wheels and the frame of an automobile to protect the body and mechanical parts from road shock.

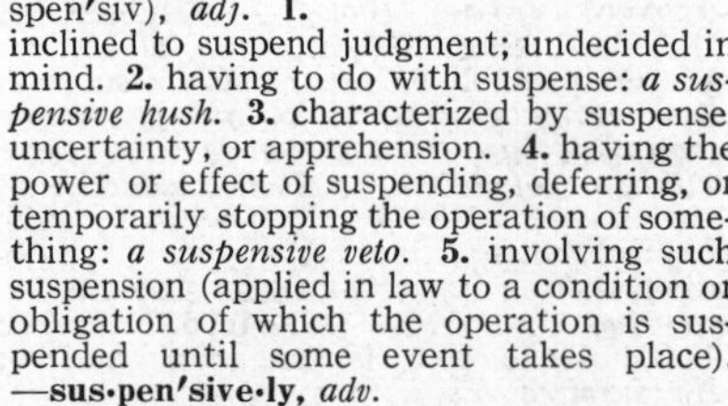

Suspension System at rear wheel of automobile

suspension vase, a vase with a handle or handles by which it may be suspended without spilling the contents.

sus·pen·sive (sə spen′siv), *adj.* **1.** inclined to suspend judgment; undecided in mind. **2.** having to do with suspense: *a suspensive hush.* **3.** characterized by suspense, uncertainty, or apprehension. **4.** having the power or effect of suspending, deferring, or temporarily stopping the operation of something: *a suspensive veto.* **5.** involving such suspension (applied in law to a condition or obligation of which the operation is suspended until some event takes place). —**sus·pen′sive·ly,** *adv.*

sus·pen·soid (sə spen′soid), *n. Chemistry.* a colloidal system in which solid particles are dispersed in a liquid medium.

sus·pen·sor (sə spen′sər), *n.* **1.** a suspensory ligament, bandage, etc. **2.** *Botany.* a group of cells at the extremity of the embryo that help position the embryo in relation to its food supply.
[< Medieval Latin *suspensor* < Latin *suspendere,* see SUSPEND]

sus·pen·so·ry (sə spen′sər ē), *adj., n., pl.* **-ries.** —*adj.* **1.** serving or fitted to hold up or support: *a suspensory bandage.* **2.** stopping for a while; leaving undecided. —*n.* a muscle, ligament, bandage, etc., that holds up or supports a part of the body.

suspensory ligament, a supporting ligament, especially the membrane that holds the lens of the eye in place.

sus. per coll., hanged by the neck (Latin, *suspendatur per collum*): *that lamentable note of sus. per coll. at the name of the last male of her line* (Thackeray).

sus·pi·cion (sə spish′ən), *n.* **1.** the act of suspecting; state of mind of one who suspects: *The real thief tried to turn suspicion towards others.* **2.** an instance of this: *Her suspicions were aroused.* **3.** the condition of being suspected. **4.** a slight or faint trace; very small amount; suggestion: *She spoke with a suspicion of shyness.* **5.** a slight belief or idea; faint notion; inkling: *not a suspicion of danger.*
above suspicion, not to be suspected: *The wife of Caesar must be above suspicion* (Charles Merivale). *The rare red-brown sixpenny Barbados [stamp], unperforated, . . . is not altogether above suspicion* (Philatelist).
on suspicion, because of being suspected: *As the result of a student demonstration in which he had played no important part, he [Lenin] was dismissed from the University of Kazan on suspicion as the brother of the terrorist* (Edmund Wilson).
under suspicion, suspected: *He was under suspicion as an accomplice in the theft.*
—*v.t. U.S. Dialect.* to suspect: *She naturally suspicioned most things she read* (Dayton Rommel).
[< Latin *suspīciō, -ōnis* < Latin *suspicer* to suspect]
—**Syn.** *n.* **1. Suspicion, distrust, doubt** mean lack of trust or confidence in someone. **Suspicion** suggests fearing, or believing without real proof, that someone or something is guilty, wrong, false, etc.: *Suspicion points to him, but the evidence is circumstantial.* **Distrust** suggests lack of confidence or trust, and may suggest certainty of guilt, falseness, etc.: *Even his mother feels distrust.* **Doubt** suggests merely lack of certainty: *He had no doubt about his son's honesty.*
➔ **suspicion.** As a verb *suspicion* is substandard: *Nobody suspicioned who it was. Suspect* is the formal and informal verb.

sus·pi·cion·al (sə spish′ə nəl), *adj.* **1.** of or having to do with suspicion. **2.** having to do with or characterized by morbid or insane suspicions.

sus·pi·cious (sə spish′əs), *adj.* **1.** deserving of or exciting suspicion; causing one to suspect: *A man was hanging about the house in a suspicious manner.* **2.** full of, inclined to, or feeling suspicion; suspecting; mistrustful: *Our dog is suspicious of strangers.* **3.** expressing, indicating, or characterized by suspicion: *The dog gave a suspicious sniff at my leg.* —**sus·pi′cious·ly,** *adv.* —**sus·pi′cious·ness,** *n.* —**Syn. 1.** questionable, doubtful.

sus·pi·ra·tion (sus′pə rā′shən), *n. Poetic.* a sigh: *windy suspirations of forced breath* (Shakespeare).

sus·pire (sə spīr′), *v.,* **-pired, -pir·ing.** *Poetic.* —*v.i.* **1.** to sigh or long; yearn. **2.** to breathe. —*v.t.* to breathe forth: *a bolt from heaven . . . suspiring flame* (Robert Browning). [< Latin *suspīrāre* draw a deep breath < *sub-* (from) under + *spīrāre* breathe]

Suss., Sussex.

Sus·sex (sus′iks), *n.* **1.** any of an English breed of domestic fowl, raised for meat and eggs. It has white skin and light, speckled, or red plumage, and lays eggs with brown shells. **2.** any of an English breed of beef cattle.
[< *Sussex,* a county in England where they were first developed]

sus·tain (sə stān′), *v.t.* **1.** to keep up; keep going; maintain; prolong: *Hope sustains him in his misery. The arts by which he sustains the reader's interest* (Benjamin Jowett). *. . . Sympathy's sustaining bread* (Louisa May Alcott). **2.** to supply with food, provisions, etc.: *to sustain an army. She eats barely enough to sustain life.* **3.** to hold up; support: *Columns sustain the weight of the roof.* **4.** to bear; endure: *The sea wall sustains the shock of the waves.* **5.** to suffer; experience: *to sustain a broken leg. She sustained a great loss in the death of her husband.* **6.** to allow; admit; favor: *The court sustained his suit.* **7.** to agree with; confirm: *The facts sustain his theory.*
[< Anglo-French *sustein-,* stem of *sustenir* < Latin *sustinēre* < *sub-* (from) under + *tenēre* to hold] —**sus·tain′er,** *n.*
—**Syn. 1.** aid, assist, comfort. **4.** stand. **5.** undergo. **7.** corroborate, sanction.

 Pronunciation Key: hat, āge, cãre, fär; let, ēqual, tėrm; it, īce; hot, ōpen, ôrder; oil, out; cup, pu̇t, rüle;

sus·tain·a·ble (sə stā′nə bəl), *adj.* that can be sustained.

sus·tained (sə stānd′), *adj.* **1.** kept up without intermission or flagging: *a sustained attack, sustained illness, Her sustained chatter was unbearable.* **2.** maintained uniformly, especially at a high pitch or level: *the best sustained performance.* **3.** *Music.* of a tone or note: **a.** held to its full time value. **b.** maintained for several beats or measures in one part while the other parts progress.

sus·tain·ed·ly (sə stā′nid lē), *adv.* in a sustained manner: *I think Beethoven is rather spasmodically, than sustainedly, grand* (Edward FitzGerald).

sustained yield, the continuing yield of a forestry or fishery crop by special, controlled harvesting, usually aimed at a steady optimum yield: *Sustained yield management, as the term is most accurately and commonly employed, means continuity of harvest . . . current harvest does not necessarily equal current growth although in the long run and on the average it does* (K.P. Davis).

sus·tain·er engine (sə stā′nər), a rocket engine that maintains the speed reached by a booster engine: *After 120 seconds of flight, the two outrider engines, their job done, dropped away, leaving the sustainer engine to finish the brute task of pushing Atlas to 17,100 mph orbiting velocity* (Newsweek).

sus·tain·ing program (sə stā′ning), a radio or television program having no commercial sponsor but maintained at the expense of a station or network.

sus·tain·ment (sə stān′mənt), *n.* **1.** the act of sustaining. **2.** the state of being sustained. **3.** a person or thing that sustains; means of support; sustenance.

sus·te·nance (sus′tə nəns), *n.* **1.** means of sustaining life; food: *He has gone for a week without sustenance.* **2.** nourishment. **3.** means of living or subsistence; support: *He gave money for the sustenance of his aged relatives.*
[< Anglo-French *sustenaunce* < *sustenir;* see SUSTAIN]

sus·ten·tac·u·lar (sus′ten tak′yə lər), *adj.* *Anatomy.* supporting: *sustentacular muscle fibers.* [< New Latin *sustentaculum* sustaining (in Latin, a prop, stay, support; in Late Latin, sustenance or nourishment) < Latin *sustentāre* (frequentative) < *sustinēre;* see SUSTAIN; + English *-ar*]

sus·ten·ta·tion (sus′ten tā′shən), *n.* **1.** the act of keeping up an establishment, building, etc.; upkeep; maintenance. **2.** preservation of a condition or state, especially human life. **3.** the act of maintaining a person or concrete thing in being or activity (used especially in the 1600's of divine support). **4.** support; sustenance. [< Latin *sustentātiō, -ōnis* < *sustentāre* (frequentative) < *sustinēre;* see SUSTAIN]

sus·ten·ta·tive (sus′ten tā′tiv, sə sten′-tə-), *adj.* having the quality of sustaining.

sus·ten·tion (sə sten′shən), *n.* **1.** the act of sustaining or keeping up a condition, feeling, etc. **2.** the holding on of a musical tone. **3.** the quality of being sustained in argument or style. [< *sustain;* patterned on *retention* < *retain*]

sus·ten·tive (sə sten′tiv), *adj.* having the quality or property of sustaining.

su·sur·rant (sů sėr′ənt), *adj.* softly rustling or murmuring; whispering. [< Latin *susurrāns, -antis,* present participle of *susurrāre* to whisper, hum < *susurrus* susurrus]

su·sur·rate (sů sėr′āt), *v.i.,* **-rat·ed, -rat·ing.** *Obsolete.* to whisper. [< Latin *susurrāre* (with English *-ate*[1]) < *susurrus* susurrus]

su·sur·ra·tion (sü′sə rā′shən), *n.* **1.** whispering. **2.** a rustling murmur. [< Late Latin *susurrātiō, -ōnis* < Latin *susurrāre* to whisper, hum < *susurrus* susurrus]

su·sur·rous (sů sėr′əs), *adj.* susurrant.

su·sur·rus (sů sėr′əs), *n.* a low, soft, whispering sound; whisper: *the soft susurrus and sighs of the branches* (Longfellow). [< Latin *susurrus* a whispering. Compare SURD.]

Su·sy-Q (sü′zē kyü′), *n.* Susie-Q.

sut·ler (sut′lər), *n.* (formerly) a merchant who followed or camped near a body of troops, or outside a military post, and sold tobacco, liquor, etc., on his own account to those who wished to buy. [< early Dutch *soeteler* small tradesman < *soetelen* ply a low trade; do mean duties]

sut·ler·ship (sut′lər ship), *n.* the office or occupation of a sutler.

su·tra (sü′trə), *n.* **1.** any of certain aphoristic rules, consisting typically of one line and dealing with such various realms as grammar, philosophy, and law, that form part of the link between Vedic and later Sanskrit literature. **2.** any of various collections of such rules, from some of which in varying degree both Hinduism and Buddhism derive certain rules of social ceremony, family life, etc. **3.** a division of (Pali) Buddhist sacred literature containing general expositions of doctrine, the sermons of Buddha, etc. [< Sanskrit *sūtra* rule; (originally) thread]

sut·ta (sůt′ə), *n.* sutra.

sut·tee (su tē′, sut′ē), *n.* **1.** the Hindu custom, now forbidden by law but still occasionally practiced, of burning a widow alive with the body of her husband: *He was cremated yesterday in a secret place to prevent demonstrations and perhaps suttee* (London Times). **2.** a woman who dies by suttee; widow who throws herself, or is thrown, on the funeral pyre of her husband and is burned alive. [< Hindustani *satī* < Sanskrit *satī* faithful wife; feminine of *sat* good, wise; (literally) present participle of *as* to be]

sut·tee·ism (su tē′iz əm), *n.* the practice of suttee.

su·tur·al (sü′chər əl), *adj.* **1.** of or having to do with a suture. **2.** *Botany.* taking place at, or otherwise relating to, a suture: *the sutural dehiscence of a pericarp.* —*n.* any of various small, irregular bones sometimes found in the sutures of the skull. —**su′tur·al·ly,** *adv.*

su·ture (sü′chər), *n., v.,* **-tured, -tur·ing.** —*n.* **1.** a seam formed in sewing up a wound, the ends of a severed tendon or nerve, etc. **2.** the act or method of doing this. **3.** one of the stitches or fastenings used. **4.** the material, as gut, linen, or silk, used. **5.** a sewing together or a joining as if by sewing. **6.** a stitch or seam. **7.** the line or seam where two bones, especially of the skull, join in an immovable articulation. **8.** the immovable articulation itself: *All of these [bones] are firmly united by immovable joints called sutures* (Beals and Hoijer). **9.** *Zoology.* the juncture or line of juncture of adjoining parts, as the line of closure of the valves of a shell: *The sutures, the lines of junction of the septa with the wall of the shell, were nearly straight or only slightly curved* (A. Franklin Shull). **10.** *Botany.* the seam or line of junction between two edges, as between the component carpels of a pericarp, that commonly mark the line of dehiscence.
—*v.t.* to unite by suture or as if by a suture.
[< Latin *sūtūra* < *suere* sew]

su·um cui·que (sü′əm kī′kwē, kwī′kwē), *Latin.* his own to each; (render) to each his due: *[He] had invested in it, but I suggested that Irwin invest somewhere else. Suum cuique, as it were* (New Yorker).

su·ze·rain (sü′zər in, -zə rān), *n.* **1.** a feudal lord. **2.** a ruler, state, or government exercising political control over a dependent state. —*adj.* of or like a suzerain; sovereign: *a suzerain power.* [< French *suzerain,* earlier *suserain* < *sus* above < Latin *sūrsum* upward < *sub* (from) under + *versus* turned; patterned on Old French *souverain* sovereign]

su·ze·rain·ty (sü′zər in tē, -zə rān′-), *n., pl.* **-ties.** the position, rank, or power of a suzerain.

s.v., sub verbo or sub voce (under the word or heading).

S.V., Sons of Veterans.

svan·berg·ite (svän′bər gīt), *n.* a mineral occurring in rhombohedral crystals of a yellow, red, or brown color. It consists of sulfate and phosphate of aluminum and calcium. [< Lars F. *Svanberg,* a Swedish chemist + *-ite*[1]]

svelte (svelt), *adj.* slender; lithe; slim; willowy: *This dazzling, svelte charmer . . . wheedles her way into our hearts with stunning brilliance* (London Times). [< French *svelte* < Italian *svelto* (literally) past participle of *svellere* to tear up; probably < Latin *ex-* out + *vellere* to pluck, or < Vulgar Latin *solvitus* free, released < Latin *solvere* loosen]

Sven·ga·li (sven gä′lē), *n.* **1.** a musician who hypnotizes and gains control over the heroine of the novel *Trilby* (1894), by George Du Maurier. **2.** a person with irresistible hypnotic powers.

Sw., **1.** Sweden. **2.** Swedish.

SW (no periods), **1.** short wave. **2.** Southwest. **3.** Southwestern.

s.w., **1.** southwest. **2.** southwestern.

S.W., **1.** South Wales. **2.** Southwest. **3.** Southwestern. **4.** South-Western (postal district of London).

S.W. (2d), Southwestern Reporter, second (series).

swab (swob), *n., v.,* **swabbed, swab·bing.** —*n.* **1.** a long-handled mop for cleaning decks, floors, etc. **2.** a bit of sponge, cloth, or cotton for cleansing some part of the body, for applying medicine to it, etc.: *There are swabs which can be left in the body after an operation to dissolve harmlessly in the blood* (London Times). **3.** a specimen taken with such a bit of sponge, cloth, or cotton. **4.** a patch of cloth, often treated with a fluid, attached to a ramrod for cleaning the bore of a firearm. **5.** *Slang.* an awkward, clumsy person.
—*v.t.* to clean with a swab; apply a swab to: *to swab the deck, to swab a person's throat. Main decks of battleships, which receive rough treatment and constant swabbing, are usually surfaced with teak* (New Yorker). Also, **swob.**
[back formation < *swabber*]

Swab., **1.** Swabia. **2.** Swabian.

swab·ber (swob′ər), *n.* **1.** a person who uses a swab. **2.** a mop; swab. **3.** a kind of mop for cleaning ovens. **4.** *Slang.* swab. [< earlier Dutch *zwabber* < *zwabben* swab]

swab·by (swob′ē), *n., pl.* **-bies.** *U.S. Slang.* a sailor of enlisted rank; gob: *He was, after all, the luckiest swabby in Uncle Sam's Navy* (Time).

Swa·bi·an (swā′bē ən), *adj.* of or having to do with Swabia, a former duchy in southwest Germany. —*n.* a native or inhabitant of Swabia.

swad·dle (swod′əl), *v.,* **-dled, -dling,** *n.* —*v.t.* **1.** to wrap (an infant) in swaddling clothes. **2.** to restrict the action of (any person or thing); halt or hinder the movement of by or as if by binding or enfolding: *[His thoughts] have been cramped and twisted and swaddled into lifelessness and deformity* (William Hazlitt). **3.** to wrap (anything) tightly with clothes, bandages, etc.; envelop; swathe.
—*n.* a cloth used for swaddling; swaddling clothes.
[Middle English *swathelen* < *swethel* a swaddle, Old English *swethel.* Related to SWATHE[1].]

swad·dling clothes, bands, or **clouts** (swod′ling), **1. a.** long, narrow strips of cloth used for wrapping a newborn infant so as to prevent its free movement: *And she brought forth her first born son, and wrapped him in swaddling clothes, and laid him in a manger* (Luke 2:7). **b.** long clothes for an infant. **2. a.** the earliest period of existence of a person or thing, when movement or action is restricted; infancy. **b.** the restrictions so imposed.

Swa·de·shi (swə dā′shē), *n.* that part of the movement for Indian political autonomy (swaraj) involving the boycott of foreign, especially British, commodities in favor of those made or processed in India, intended both to strike an economic blow against Great Britain and to encourage the development of domestic industry. [< Bengali *Swadeshi* (literally) own-country things < Sanskrit *svadeśin* native < *svadeśa* native land]

swag (swag), *n., v.,* **swagged, swag·ging.** —*n.* **1.** *Informal.* **a.** things stolen; booty; plunder: *What'll we do with what little swag we've got left?* (Mark Twain). **b.** a quantity of money or goods unlawfully acquired; dishonest gains, especially dishonest political gains. **2.** *Australian.* a bundle of personal belongings, especially of a traveler in the bush, a tramp, miner, etc. **3.** an ornamental festoon of flowers, leaves, ribbons, etc.: *He got out the stepladder . . . and began to unfasten the crêpe-paper swags* (New Yorker). **4.** a swaying or lurching movement.
[< verb. Compare Middle English *swagge* bag.]
—*v.i.* **1.** to move unsteadily or heavily from side to side or up and down; sway without control; lurch. **2.** to hang loosely or heavily; sag.
—*v.t.* **swag it,** *Australian.* to carry one's swag: *The solitary pedestrian, with the whole of his supplies . . . strapped across his shoulders [was] "swagging it"* (T. M'Combie).
[probably < Scandinavian (compare dialec-

tal Norwegian *svagga* to sway). Related to SWAY.]

swage (swāj), *n., v.,* **swaged, swag·ing.** —*n.* **1.** a tool for bending cold metal to the required shape. **2.** a die or stamp for shaping metal on an anvil, in a press, etc. **3.** a swage block.
—*v.t.* to shape or bend by means of a swage. [earlier, a molding, mounting < Old French *souage,* perhaps < Late Latin *sōca* rope]

swage block, a heavy iron or steel block with holes and grooves of various sizes, for shaping bolts or other objects.

swag·ger (swag′ər), *v.i.* **1.** to walk with a bold, rude, or superior air; strut about or show off in a vain or insolent way: *The bully swaggered into the schoolyard.* **2.** to talk boastfully and loudly; brag noisily: *By swaggering could I never thrive* (Shakespeare). **3.** to bluster; bluff. —*v.t.* to affect by bluster, especially to bring (into or out of a state) by blustering talk; bluster; bluff.
—*n.* the act of swaggering; swaggering way of walking, acting, speaking, etc.: *He . . . moved with a dignified swagger as became a pirate who felt that the public eye was on him* (Mark Twain).
—*adj.* showily or ostentatiously smart or fashionable.
[apparently < *swag,* verb + *-er*[6]] —**swag′ger·er,** *n.* —**swag′ger·ing·ly,** *adv.*
—**Syn.** *v. i.* **1.** See **strut.**

swagger cane, a swagger stick.

swagger coat, a woman's loosely fitting, beltless sportcoat.

swagger stick, a short, light stick or cane, sometimes carried by soldiers: *Like all the Indian Army men of comparable rank, he is a strapping, glittering model of swagger stick smartness* (New Yorker).

swag·gie (swag′ē), *n. Australian.* swagman.

swag·man (swag′mən), *n., pl.* **-men.** *Australian.* a man who travels with a swag: *There the unjolly swagman was—suspended motionless, strangely elongated in the mirage* (Alwyn Lee).

swags·man (swagz′mən), *n., pl.* **-men.** swagman.

Swa·hi·li (swä hē′lē), *n., pl.* **-li** or **-lis,** *adj.* —*n.* **1.** a member of a Bantu people inhabiting Zanzibar and the adjacent coast of Africa. **2.** their Bantu language, which has a large admixture of Arabic and other foreign words, used as a lingua franca throughout most of East Africa: *Swahili . . . is used throughout East Africa and eastern Belgian Congo, and is occasionally heard in all the adjoining countries* (H.A. Gleason, Jr.) —*adj.* of or having to do with the Swahili or their language: *"Simba" is the Swahili word for lion, and the arrogant symbol of the terrorists* (Newsweek). [< Swahili *Swahili* (literally) coastal people < Arabic *sawāḥil,* plural of *sāḥil* coast]

Swa·hi·li·an (swä hē′lē ən), *adj.* Swahili.

swain (swān), *n. Archaic.* **1.** a country gallant or lover. **2.** a lover, wooer, or sweetheart, especially in pastoral poetry. **3.** a young farm laborer or shepherd; rustic: *Thus sang the uncouth swain to th'oaks and rills* (Milton). [Middle English *swein* < Scandinavian (compare Old Icelandic *sveinn* boy)]

swain·ish (swā′nish), *adj.* **1.** having to do with a swain. **2.** resembling a swain; rustic; boorish. —**swain′ish·ness,** *n.*

Swain·son's hawk (swān′sənz), a brownish hawk, often with white throat and abdomen, found in South America and western North America. [< William *Swainson,* 1789-1855, an English naturalist]

Swainson's thrush, the olive-backed thrush.

Swainson's warbler, a warbler of southeastern United States with olive back and dull whitish breast.

swale (swāl), *n.* **1.** a moist or marshy depression in a tract of land: *The bear we spotted in a grassy swale was already fattened after his winter sleep* (Paul Brooks). **2.** *Dialect.* a shady place. [probably < Scottish *swaill* low, hollow place, or < dialectal *swale* or *swell* shady place. Compare Old Icelandic *svalr* cool.]

swal·low[1] (swol′ō), *v.t.* **1.** to take (food, drink, etc.) into the stomach through the mouth, throat, and esophagus: *to swallow food.* **2.** *Informal.* to accept without question or suspicion; believe too easily; drink in: *He will swallow any story.* **3.** to accept without opposition or protest; take meekly or patiently; put up with; bear: *He had to swallow the insult. He doesn't give you more than you can swallow and he makes you feel you are part of the team* (Harper's). **4.** to keep from expressing or giving vent to; repress: *to swallow one's anger. She swallowed her displeasure and smiled.* **5.** to take back; retract; recant: *to swallow words said in anger.* —*v.i.* to take food, drink, etc., into the stomach through the esophagus; perform the act of swallowing, as in trying to suppress emotion.

swallow up, a. to cause to disappear utterly, as if by devouring or absorption; consume; destroy; engulf: *The waves swallowed up the swimmer. Must not all things at last be swallowed up in death?* (Benjamin Jowett). **b.** to absorb or appropriate (a territory or other possession); take for oneself or into oneself: *The French King . . . swallow'd up almost all Flanders* (John Evelyn). **c.** to take up completely: *The first printing was swallowed up before publication* (New Yorker).
—*n.* **1.** an act of swallowing; gulp: *He took the pill at one swallow.* **2.** a quantity swallowed at once; mouthful: *There are only about four swallows left in the bottle.* **3.** the capacity for swallowing; appetite. **4.** the throat; esophagus; gullet. **5.** *Nautical.* the space between the sheave and the shell in a pulley block, through which the rope is passed.
[Middle English *swalewen,* Old English *swelgan*] —**swal′low·er,** *n.*

swal·low[2] (swol′ō), *n.* **1.** any of a family of small, migratory perching birds, having long, pointed wings, weak feet, a swift, curving flight, and a twittering cry, as the bank swallow or sand martin, the barn swallow, the cliff swallow, and the purple martin: *Some listen for the first . . . swallow, but at least one countryman awaits more eagerly the liquid call of the first quail* (London Times). **2.** any of certain swifts that resemble swallows, as the chimney swift (or chimney swallow). [Old English *swealwe*] —**swal′low·like′,** *adj.*

Barn Swallow[2] **(def. 1)**
(about 5 in. long)

swal·low·a·ble (swol′ō ə bəl), *adj.* **1.** that can be swallowed. **2.** that can be believed; credible.

swallow dive, *Especially British.* a swan dive.

swallow hole, *Especially British.* an opening or cavity, common in limestone formations, through which a stream disappears underground; sinkhole.

swal·low·tail (swol′ō tāl′), *n.* **1.** a thing shaped like or suggesting the deeply forked tail of certain swallows. **2.** a tail like that of a swallow; forked tail. **3.** a swallow-tailed coat: *Two carabinieri got up in three-cornered hats and full-dress swallowtails* (Time). **4.** any of a family of large butterflies, having taillike extensions of the hind wings, including the tiger swallowtail and the zebra swallowtail: *Swallowtails . . . include some of the most beautifully colored butterflies* (A.M. Winchester).

swal·low-tailed (swol′ō tāld′), *adj.* **1.** having a tail like that of a swallow. **2.** of the form of a swallow's tail.

swallow-tailed coat, a man's coat for formal wear with an open front and two long, tapering tails.

swallow-tailed kite, a graceful black and white hawk with a long, black, forked tail, found in the southern United States and south to Argentina.

swal·low·wort (swol′ō-wėrt′), *n.* **1.** any of several plants of the milkweed family, especially a European herb whose pods suggest a swallow with outspread wings. It has a root with emetic, cathartic, and diuretic properties. **2.** the greater celandine.

Swallow-tailed Coat

swam (swam), *v.* the past tense of **swim:** *When the boat sank we swam to shore.*

swa·mi (swä′mē), *n., pl.* **-mis.** a title of a Hindu religious teacher. [< Hindi *svāmī* master (used as term of address) < Sanskrit *svāmin* lord, master]

swamp (swomp, swômp), *n.* **1.** a tract of low-lying ground in which water collects; a piece of wet, spongy ground; mire; bog; marsh: *The farmer will drain the swamp so that he can plant crops there.* **2.** (originally) a tract of rich soil having a growth of trees and other vegetation, but too moist for cultivation.
—*adj.* **1.** having to do with a swamp or swamps. **2.** living in a swamp or swamps: *a swamp bird.* **3.** growing in a swamp or swamps: *swamp grass.*
—*v.t.* **1.** to flood, submerge, or soak with water, etc. **2.** to fill (a boat) with water and sink: *The wave swamped the boat.* **3.** to plunge or sink in or as if in a swamp: *The horses were swamped in the stream.* **4.** to overwhelm with difficulties or by superior numbers: *to be swamped by debts. That factory is swamped with orders it cannot fill.* **5.** to clear out underbrush or fell trees in, to make logging roads or to haul out logs on a skidway: *The clearing was swamped in three days.* —*v.i.* **1.** (of a boat) to sink by filling with water: *Their boat swamped.* **2.** to sink or stick in or as if in a swamp or water. **3.** to become involved with difficulties or sink under superior numbers: *Their small force soon swamped amid the onrushing horde of Tartars.*
[American English, apparently variant of *sump*]
—**Syn.** *n.* **1.** morass, fen, slough, quagmire.

swamp azalea or **honeysuckle,** a variety of azalea with white or pinkish flowers, growing in swampy areas of eastern United States.

swamp bay, the sweet bay.

swamp blackbird, the redwing.

swamp cabbage, the skunk cabbage.

swamp cypress, the bald cypress.

swamp·er (swom′pər, swôm′-), *n. U.S.* **1.** a person who lives in a swamp or swampy region: *Everybody thought we were just a state of hillbillies and swampers* (Time). **2. a.** a person who works clearing roads for lumberjacks or clearing fallen trees of limbs, knots, etc., for the men who cut the trunks into logs. **b.** a person who hauls logs out of the woods on a skidway.

swamp fever, 1. malaria. **2.** leptospirosis. **3.** a usually fatal virus disease of horses and other animals, often characterized by anemia: *The regulatory action grew out of a mounting concern by state veterinary agencies throughout the country over the incidence of equine infectious anemia—swamp fever* (New York Times).

swamp·fish (swomp′fish′, swômp′-), *n., pl.* **-fish·es** or (*collectively*) **-fish.** a small striped fish with a transparent skin covering its eyes, found in swamps and streams of the Atlantic coastal plain of southern United States.

swamp hare, swamp rabbit.

swamp hickory, a species of hickory that grows in swamps and bears nuts with a bitter kernel; bitternut.

swamp·i·ness (swom′pē nis, swôm′-), *n.* swampy quality or condition: *. . . studies of tides, rainfall, and swampiness in that area* (New Yorker).

swamp·ish (swom′pish, swôm′-), *adj.* swampy, as land: *when all this flat central country was swampish and hadn't been drained off yet* (Booth Tarkington).

swamp·land (swomp′land′, swômp′-), *n.* a tract of land covered by swamps: *In the swamplands of the southeastern United States there are several . . . important conifers* (Fred W. Emerson).

swamp·less (swomp′lis, swômp′-), *adj.* without a swamp or swamps: *Mountain regions are usually swampless.*

swamp magnolia, the sweet bay.

swamp maple, a common variety of maple of eastern North America often growing in swampy areas; red maple.

swamp oak, pin oak.

swamp ore, bog ore, a variety of limonite.

swamp owl, 1. the barred owl. **2.** the short-eared owl.

swamp rabbit, a large, coarse-haired rabbit, a species of cottontail, most common in wet areas of the lower Mississippi Valley.

swamp robin, 1. the towhee. **2.** any of various American thrushes.

swamp sparrow, a sparrow of the marshes of eastern North America, with a white throat and rusty crown.

swamp spruce, the black spruce.

swamp white oak, an oak having a flaky gray bark, found in swamps in eastern North America.

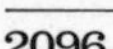

swamp·y (swom′pē, swôm′-), *adj.*, **swamp·i·er, swamp·i·est.** **1.** like a swamp; soft and wet: *swampy ground.* **2.** containing swamps: *a swampy region.* **3.** of swamps. —**Syn. 1.** boggy, marshy.

swa·my (swä′mē), *n., pl.* **-mies.** swami.

swan[1] (swon, swôn), *n.* **1.** any of a group of large, graceful water birds with a long, slender, curving neck and in most species a pure-white plumage in the adult. **2.** a person or thing that is considered faultless and has purity, great beauty, etc. **3.** *Archaic.* a sweet singer; poet; bard: *Sweet swan of Avon* (Ben Jonson). [Old English *swan*] —**swan′like′**, *adj.*

Mute Swan[1] (def. 1) (about 3 ft. long)

swan[2] (swon, swôn), *v.i. U.S. Dialect.* **I swan,** I declare: *If you haven't observed it, I have, and a queer one it is, I swan* (Thomas C. Haliburton).
[American English, perhaps contraction of dialectal (New England) *I s'warn* I shall warrant; *warrant,* in the sense of "swear"]

Swan (swon, swôn), *n.* the northern constellation Cygnus. [translation of Latin *Cygnus* Cygnus]

swan dive, a graceful dive in which the legs are held straight, the back is arched, and the arms are spread like the wings of a gliding bird.

swang (swang), *v. Archaic and Dialect.* swung; a past tense of **swing**[1].

swan·herd (swon′hėrd′, swôn′-), *n.* a person who looks after swans.

swan-hop·per (swon′hop′ər, swôn′-), *n.* swan-upper.

swan-hop·ping (swon′hop′ing, swôn′-), *n.* swan-upping.

swank[1] (swangk), *v.i. Informal.* to show off; bluff; swagger.
—*n. Informal.* **1.** ostentatious or pretentious behavior or talk; showing off: *I do not mind his money, but I do not like his swank* (G. K. Chesterton). **2.** style; smartness; dash.
—*adj.* **1.** *Informal.* stylish; smart; dashing. **2.** *Scottish.* agile; active; nimble.
[origin uncertain; perhaps (originally) variant of *swing*[1], in sense of "swing the body," related to Scottish *swank* active, agile. Compare Old English *swancor* lithe.]

swank[2] (swangk), *v. Archaic.* a past tense of **swink.**

swank·i·ly (swang′kə lē), *adv. Informal.* in a swanky manner.

swank·i·ness (swang′kē nis), *n. Informal.* the state or quality of being swanky.

swank·y (swang′kē), *adj.*, **swank·i·er, swank·i·est,** *n., pl.* **swank·ies.** —*adj.* **1.** *Informal.* **a.** stylish; smart; dashing. **b.** swaggering. **2.** *Scottish.* swank. —*n. Scottish.* a smart, active, strapping young fellow.

swan maiden, a fabulous creature able to appear in the guise of either a young maiden or swan by taking off or putting on a magic garment of swan's feathers, or by invoking the power of a magic ring, golden chain, etc., versions of which are encountered in Teutonic and Asian folklore and myth.

swan-mark (swon′märk, swôn′-), *n. British.* the official mark cut on the beak of a swan in swan-upping.

swan·neck (swon′nek′, swôn′-), *n.* **1.** a neck like that of a swan, as in length, slenderness, or whiteness. **2.** something shaped like or suggesting the neck of a swan, as a curved section of a pipe.

swan-necked (swon′nekt′, swôn′-), *adj.* **1.** having a neck like that of a swan, as in length, whiteness, or slenderness. **2.** shaped or curved like the neck of a swan.

swan·ner·y (swon′ər ē, swôn′-), *n., pl.* **-ner·ies.** a place where swans are kept and reared.

Swans·combe man (swonz′kəm), an early type of pre-Neanderthal man similar to Homo sapiens, identified from skull bones found at Swanscombe, England.

swan's-down (swonz′doun′, swônz′-), *n.* **1.** the soft down of a swan, used for dress trimmings, powder puffs, etc. **2.** Also, **swansdown. a.** a fine, thick, soft fabric, usually made from wool, used for babies' coats, bathrobes, etc. **b.** cotton flannel.

swan shift, a garment made of swan's feathers which the swan maiden put on to assume her guise as a swan.

swan·skin (swon′skin′, swôn′-), *n.* **1.** the skin of a swan, with the feathers on. **2.** any of various soft fabrics, as cotton flannel. —*adj.* made or consisting of swanskin.

swan song, 1. a person's last piece of work, farewell performance, or final statement, especially a last work of literature, music, or art. **2.** the melancholy but surpassingly beautiful song which, according to fable, a swan sings as it is about to die.

swan-up·per (swon′up′ər, swôn′-), *n. British.* an official who takes up and marks swans.

swan-up·ping (swon′up′ing, swôn′-), *n. British.* **1.** the act or practice of taking up swans and marking them with nicks on the beak in token of being owned by the Crown or somebody chartered by the Crown. **2.** the annual expedition to do this on the Thames, carried out under the aegis of the sovereign. [< *swan*[1] + *upping,* gerund of *up,* verb]

swap (swop), *v.t., v.i.,* **swapped, swap·ping,** *n. Informal.* exchange; barter; trade: *He [President Lincoln] had swapped horses in mid-stream* (Sir Winston Churchill). Also, **swop.** [Middle English *swappen* strike, strike the hands together; probably imitative; the modern sense is from the practice of "striking hands" as a sign of agreement in bargaining. Compare the phrase "to strike a bargain."]

swap·per (swop′ər), *n. Informal.* **1.** a person who swaps. **2.** *Especially British.* something very big; whopper.

swa·raj (swə räj′), *n.* political autonomy for India; establishment of India as a self-governing political unit.
—*adj.* of or having to do with swaraj. [< Sanskrit *svarāja* self-ruling < *sva* one's own + *rāj* reign, rule]

Swa·raj (swə räj′), *n.* the party in India primarily devoted to swaraj during the latter period of British domination.
[< *swaraj*]

swa·raj·ism (swə rä′jiz əm), *n.* the swaraj principle or movement.

swa·raj·ist (swə rä′jist), *n.* an advocate of swaraj; a member of the Swaraj party. —*adj.* of or having to do with swaraj.

sward (swôrd), *n.* a grassy surface; turf.
—*v.i.* to form a sward; become covered with grassy turf.
—*v.t.* to cover with a sward (used chiefly in the passive).
[Old English *sweard* skin, rind]

sware (swãr), *v. Archaic.* swore; a past tense of **swear.**

swarf (swôrf, swärf), *n.* **1.** the greasy grit that collects on a knife as it is sharpened on a stone, or on an axle as it revolves in a bearing. **2.** filings or shavings that come from a drilled hole, etc.: *Every "do-it-yourself" driller knows that it is important when drilling a long small diameter hole to withdraw the drill every so often to clear the swarf and debris* (New Scientist). [Old English *geswearf* filings < *sweorfan* to file. Related to SWERVE.]

swarm[1] (swôrm), *n.* **1.** a large group of honeybees which at a particular season leave the hive, gather in a compact mass, and fly off together, under the guidance of a queen, to start a new colony. **2.** a group of honeybees settled together in a hive. **3.** a large group of insects flying or moving about together. **4.** a great number or multitude, especially in motion; crowd; throng: *Swarms of children were playing in the park.* **5.** *Biology.* a cluster of free-swimming or free-floating cells or one-celled organisms, as zoospores, moving in company.
—*v.i.* **1.** (of bees) to gather in a compact cluster and leave the hive in a body to found a new colony. **2.** to fly or move about in great numbers: *The mosquitoes swarmed about us.* **3.** to come together in a dense crowd; collect, assemble, or congregate thickly and confusedly; crowd; throng. **4.** to be crowded or thronged (with); contain great numbers; abound; teem: *The swamp swarms with mosquitoes.* **5.** *Biology.* to escape from the parent organism in a swarm, with characteristic movement.
—*v.t.* to fill or beset, as, or with, a swarm; throng.

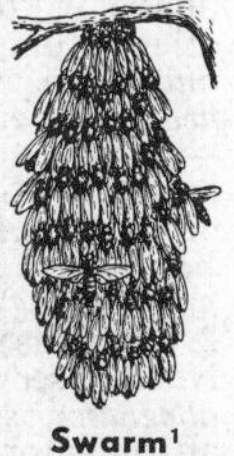

Swarm[1] (def. 1) of honeybees

swarm off, to leave a hive, colony, etc., to start another or others: *The number of monks increased so rapidly that they were soon obliged to swarm off, like bees, into new monasteries of the same Order* (Joseph T. Fowler).
[Old English *swearm*]
—**Syn.** *n.* **4.** See **crowd.**

swarm[2] (swôrm), *v.i., v.t.* to climb; shin: *to swarm up a tree.* [origin uncertain]

swarm cell, swarm spore: *The life cycle is repeated when spores fall in a suitable environment. Free-swimming swarm cells . . . are then released* (Scientific American).

swarm·er (swôr′mər), *n.* **1.** one of a number that swarm; one of a swarm, as of insects. **2.** *Biology.* a swarm spore.

swarm spore, *Biology.* any tiny motile spore produced in great abundance; zoospore.

swart (swôrt), *adj.* dark in color; dusky; swarthy. [Old English *sweart*] —**swart′ness,** *n.*

swarth[1] (swôrth), *adj. Archaic.* swarthy. [variant of *swart*]

swarth[2] (swôrth), *n. Dialect.* turf; sward. [Old English *swearth,* variant of *sweard* sward]

swarth[3] (swôrth), *n. Dialect.* swath.

swarth·i·ly (swôr′ᴛʜə lē, -thə-), *adv.* with a swarthy hue.

swarth·i·ness (swôr′ᴛʜē nis, -thē-), *n.* the state of being swarthy; a dusky or dark complexion; tawniness: *The swarthiness of the fisherman's skin bespoke his days in the sun.*

swarth·y (swôr′ᴛʜē, -thē), *adj.,* **swarth·i·er, swarth·i·est.** having a dark skin; dark in color; dusky (used especially of the skin or complexion, or of persons in respect to these): *The sailor was swarthy from the sun of the tropics.*
[apparently < *swarth*[1] + *-y*[1]. Compare obsolete *swarty* < *swart* + *-y*[1].]
—**Syn.** See **dusky.**

swash (swosh, swôsh), *v.t.* **1.** to dash (water or other liquid) about; splash. **2.** to dash water or other liquid upon; souse. —*v.i.* **1.** to dash with a splashing sound; splash (about, against). **2.** to swagger.
—*n.* **1.** a swashing action or sound: *the swash of waves against a boat.* **2.** a swagger; swashbuckling. **3.** a channel of water through or behind a sandbank. **4.** ground under water or over which water washes.
[probably imitative]

swash·buck·le (swosh′buk′əl, swôsh′-), *v.i.,* **-led, -ling.** to swagger in a noisy, blustering, or boasting manner: *Laurence Olivier sings and swashbuckles in eighteenth-century costume* (Newsweek). [back formation < *swashbuckler*]

swash·buck·ler (swosh′buk′lər, swôsh′-), *n.* a swaggering swordsman, bully, or boaster: *He had a garrison after his own heart . . . guzzling, deep-drinking swashbucklers* (Washington Irving).

swash·buck·ler·ing (swosh′buk′lər ing, swôsh′-), *n., adj.* swashbuckling.

swash·buck·ling (swosh′buk′ling, swôsh′-), *n., adj.* swaggering; bullying; boasting: *He may seek to offset the Kremlin's loss of face . . . by political swashbuckling* (Wall Street Journal).

swash·er (swosh′ər, swôsh′-), *n.* a swashbuckler.

swash·ing (swosh′ing, swôsh′-), *adj.* **1.** (of water or other liquid) dashing and splashing. **2.** swaggering; swashbuckling: *We'll have a swashing and a martial outside, As many other mannish cowards have* (Shakespeare).
—*n.* **1.** a dashing or splashing of water: *A rising tide creates . . . swashings and swirlings and a continuous slapping against the rocky rim of the land* (New Yorker). **2.** *Archaic.* swaggering; ostentatious behavior.

swash letters, italic capital letters of a style characterized by flourishes or tails, as in *𝒜, ℬ, 𝒩.* [< obsolete *swash,* noun, abstracted from obsolete *aswash* aslant; origin uncertain]

swash·plate (swosh′plāt′, swôsh′-), *n.* a rotating circular plate inclined to the plane of its revolution, which gives and receives reciprocal motion to and from other parts of the mechanism: *A swashplate or like system links the pistons to a central shaft* (New Scientist).

swash·y (swosh′ē, swôsh′-), *adj.,* **swash·i·er, swash·i·est.** soft and watery; splashy: *Bulldozers cleared the course in fine style for the reopening last Friday, but . . . the footing was still a little swashy* (New Yorker).

swas·ti·ka or **swas·ti·ca** (swos′tə kə), *n.* **1.** an ancient symbol or ornament supposed to bring good luck, in the form of a cross with equal arms with a limb of the same length projecting at right angles from the end of each arm; fylfot. **2.** such a figure with arms turning clockwise, used as the official emblem of the Nazi Party and Nazi Germany. [< Sanskrit *svastika* < *svasti* luck < *sū* well + *astī*, noun, being < *as* to be]

Swastikas Left, (def. 1); right, (def. 2)

swat[1] (swot), *v.*, **swat·ted, swat·ting,** *n. Informal.* —*v.t.* to hit with a smart or violent blow: *to swat a fly, to swat a home run.* —*n.* a smart or violent blow. Also, **swot.** [apparently imitative]

swat[2] (swot), *v.i.*, **swat·ted, swat·ting,** *n. British Slang.* swot[2].

swat[3] (swot), *v. Obsolete.* sweat; a past tense and past participle of **sweat.**

swatch (swoch), *n.* **1.** a sample of cloth or other material: *a swatch of calico. After picking a model from samples and a fabric from an assortment of swatches ...* (New Yorker). **2.** a specimen of anything: *Over cocktails and frequent swatches of non-dance music, one can take an eagle's-nest gander at New York* (New Yorker). [earlier, a tally or its counterpart; origin uncertain]

swath (swoth, swôth), *n.* **1. a.** the space covered by a single cut of a scythe or by one cut of a mowing machine. **b.** the grass, hay, or standing grain within such a space. **c.** a row of grass, hay, or grain cut by a scythe or mowing machine. **d.** something compared to grass, etc., falling before the scythe or mowing machine. **2.** a strip, belt, or longitudinal extent (of something).

cut a wide swath, to make a showy display; splurge: *You folks been cuttin' a pretty wide swath here in New York* (H.L. Wilson).

[Old English *swæth* track, trace, footprint]

swathe[1] (swāᴛʜ), *v.*, **swathed, swath·ing,** *n.* —*v.t.* **1.** to wrap up closely or fully: *swathed in a blanket.* **2.** to bind; wrap; bandage. **3.** to envelop or surround like a wrapping; enwrap; enfold: *White clouds swathed the mountain.*

—*n.* a wrapping; bandage: *Young men ... disguised with swathes of straw tied over their clothes* (George A. Birmingham).

[Old English *swathian* < *swath-* a band of cloth. Related to SWADDLE.]

swathe[2] (swāᴛʜ), *n.* swath: *The great mower Time, who cuts so broad a swathe* (Thoreau). *I had frankly looked forward to cutting a bit of a swathe at the wedding* (Atlantic). [Middle English *swathe,* Old English *swæth* swath]

swath·er[1] (swā′ᴛʜər), *n.* a device with curved arms extending diagonally backward, fixed to the end of the cutter bar of a reaper or mower to lift up uncut stalks, and throw those that are cut in such a way as to mark a line of separation between the uncut and the cut. [< *swath* + *-er*[1]]

swath·er[2] (swā′ᴛʜər), *n.* a person who swathes.

swath·ing (swā′ᴛʜing), *n.* **1.** the act of a person or thing that swathes. **2.** that with which something is swathed: *Lady Frensham has arrived ... by automobile; she appeared in veils and swathings* (H. G. Wells).

swats (swots), *n.pl. Scottish.* new small beer or ale. [Old English *swātan* beer]

swat·ter (swot′ər), *n. Informal.* **1.** a person or thing that swats. **2.** something to swat with: *a fly swatter.*

S wave, secondary wave: *S waves travel at about two thirds of the speed of P waves* (Scientific American).

sway (swā), *v.i.* **1.** to swing back and forth or from side to side: *Branches sway in the wind. The pail swayed in his hands as he ran.* **2.** to bend or move to one side or downward; lean: *She swayed toward him and then fainted.* **3.** to incline to one side, party, etc., or to one and then the other; vacillate, as in judgment or opinion. **4.** *Poetic.* to have control; rule; govern: *Where still doth sway the triple tyrant* (Milton). —*v.t.* **1.** to make move; cause to swing or move back and forth or from side to side: *The wind sways the grass.* **2.** to cause to incline or bend down on one side. **3.** to cause (a person, his action, conduct, etc.) to be inclined to one side, party, etc.; influence: *to try to sway an election with bribery. The speaker's words swayed his audience. ... an enormously popular man with a quite remarkable ability to sway and lead the masses* (Harper's). **4.** to cause to change, as in judgment or opinion: *Nothing could sway him after he had made up his mind.* **5.** to have control of; direct; govern: *The will of man is by his reason sway'd* (Shakespeare). **6.** *Archaic.* to rule, as a sovereign. **7.** to wield as an emblem of sovereignty: *to sway the scepter.*

sway up, *Nautical.* to raise or set aloft (a yard, topmast, etc.): *Forward there, Jacob, and sway up the mast* (Frederick Marryat).

—*n.* **1.** a swaying; a swinging back and forth or from side to side: *The sway of the truck caused some boxes to spill out. Regardless of the sweeping whirlwind's sway* (Thomas Gray). **2.** influence; control; rule: *Few countries are now under the sway of dictators. They bent before the sway of his vehement and impetuous will* (John F. Kirk).

[Middle English *sweye* to go, sink, probably < Scandinavian (compare Old Icelandic *sveigja*)] —**sway′er,** *n.* —**sway′ing·ly,** *adv.*

—**Syn.** *v.i.* **1.** wave, fluctuate, oscillate. See **swing.**

sway·back or **sway-back** (swā′bak′), *adj.* sway-backed. —*n.* an exaggerated sag or downward curvature of the spinal column of an animal. especially of a horse.

sway-backed (swā′bakt′), *adj.* **1.** of horses and other animals: **a.** strained in the back, as by overwork. **b.** having the back sagged or hollowed to an unusual degree. **2.** that sags in the middle, especially through age or lack of care: *a sway-backed old wagon or barn.*

sway brace, a diagonal brace used on a tower, bridge, etc., to resist side or swaying strains.

swayed (swād), *adj.* sway-backed.

sway·less (swā′lis), *adj.* not swaying; without sway: *Front-wheel drive, combined with ... advanced suspension design, provides swayless directional stability for relaxed driving* (Scientific American).

Swa·zi (swä′zē), *n.* a member of a Bantu people of South Africa, of Zulu origin: *The Swazis are a Zulu offshoot who settled in their present country just over a hundred years ago* (Napier Davitt).

sweal (swēl), *Dialect.* —*v.i.* **1.** of a candle, tallow, etc.: **a.** to melt (away). **b.** to gutter. **2.** to waste away.

—*v.t.* to cause to waste away like a guttering candle: *... the time not spent in study, for the most part swealed away* (C. Mather).

[fusion of Old English *swǣlan* to burn (something), and of *swelan* to burn. Related to SWELTER.]

swear (swãr), *v.*, **swore** or (*Archaic*) **sware, sworn, swear·ing.** —*v.i.* **1.** to make a solemn statement, appealing to God or some other sacred being or object; take an oath. **2.** to promise solemnly; vow (to). **3.** to testify under oath; make a declaration under oath (to or against). **4.** to utter an oath or use profane language, as for emphasis or to express anger, vexation, or other strong feeling; curse: *The pirate raged and swore. It's 'most enough to make a deacon swear* (Lowell).

—*v.t.* **1.** to declare or affirm with an appeal to God or some other sacred being or object: *A witness at a trial has to swear "I promise to tell the truth, the whole truth, and nothing but the truth, so help me God."* **2.** to promise or undertake on oath or solemnly to observe or do (something): *to swear allegiance, swear revenge.* **3.** to declare or affirm emphatically or confidently: *I swear I'll never go near the place again. Major Scobie, when I lent you money, I swear it was for friendship, just friendship* (Graham Greene). **4.** to take an oath as to the fact or truth of; testify under oath: *He swore treason against his friend* (Samuel Johnson). **5.** to take or utter (an oath), either solemnly or profanely. **6.** to bind by an oath; require to promise: *Members of the club were sworn to secrecy.* **7.** to admit to office or service by administering an oath: *to swear a witness.* **8.** to bring, set, take, etc., by swearing: *to swear a person's life away.*

swear by, a. to name (God, or a sacred being or object) as one's witness in taking an oath: *They had sworn by the sacred head of the emperor himself* (Edward Gibbon). **b.** to have great confidence in: *The members of the office staff who stick around long enough to get to know him swear by Adams* (Time).

swear in, to admit to an office or service by giving an oath: *to swear in a jury.*

swear off, *Informal.* to promise to give up: *to swear off smoking.*

swear out, to get by taking an oath that a certain charge is true: *to swear out a warrant for a burglar's arrest.*

[Old English *swerian.* Compare ANSWER.] —**swear′er,** *n.*

—**Syn.** *v.i.* **4.** See **curse.**

swear·word (swãr′wėrd′), *n.* a word used in profane swearing; profane word: *The poor man's supply of swearwords was evidently not enough for the situation and it quickly ran out after his extravagant expenditure* (Atlantic).

sweat (swet), *n., v.,* **sweat** or **sweat·ed, sweat·ing.** —*n.* **1.** moisture coming through the pores of the skin, usually as a result of heat, exertion, emotion, etc.; perspiration: *He wiped the sweat from his face. His brow is wet with honest sweat* (Longfellow). **2.** a fit or condition of giving out moisture through the pores of the skin: *He was in a cold sweat from fear.* **3.** such a condition induced for a purpose, especially a therapeutic purpose. **4.** moisture given out by something or gathered on its surface: *the sweat on a pitcher of ice water.* **5.** an exuding of moisture from something, or the process of producing an exudation, as part of certain industrial processes, as tanning. **6.** *Informal.* a state or fit of suffering, anxiety, impatience, or anything that might make a person sweat: *He was in quite a sweat that his father would find out about the damaged car.* **7.** a run given to a horse as part of his training for a race. **8.** anything that causes sweat; hard work or strenuous exertion; labor: *I have nothing to offer but blood, toil, tears, and sweat* (Sir Winston Churchill). **9.** *Obsolete.* the sweating sickness.

no sweat, *Slang.* no trouble at all; no effort: *For most of those involved in this Strategic Air Command operation it was routine. As Capt. Smith or one of his crew would say, "It's no sweat"* (Birmingham News).

[Middle English *swete* < *sweten;* see the verb]

—*v.i.* **1.** to give out moisture through the pores of the skin; perspire: *We sweated because it was hot.* **2.** to gather moisture from the air by condensation, so that it appears in drops on the surface: *A pitcher of ice water sweats on a hot day.* **3. a.** to give out moisture, as before storage or preparation for use. **b.** (of tobacco) to ferment. **4.** to come out in drops; ooze. **5.** to work very hard: *He sweated over his written reports. Some, lucky, find a flowery spot, for which they never toiled nor sweat* (Robert Burns). **6.** to suffer severely, especially as a penalty: *They will sweat for the wrong they have done.* **7.** to be annoyed or vexed; fume: *to sweat over a delay.*

—*v.t.* **1.** to give out through the pores of the skin, as or like sweat. **2.** to give out or get rid of as by sweating (off, out): *to sweat out a prison sentence.* **3.** to wet, soak, or stain with sweat: *to sweat one's collar.* **4.** to cause (a person or animal) to sweat: *He sweated his horse by riding him too hard.* **5.** to give out (moisture, etc.) in drops or small particles like sweat. **6. a.** to cause to give out moisture; force the moisture out of: *to sweat hides in preparing them for use.* **b.** to ferment (tobacco) by removing moisture. **7.** to cause to work hard and under bad conditions: *That employer sweats his workers.* **8.** *Slang.* to deprive of or cause to give up something, especially money; rob; fleece. **9.** *Informal.* to extract or try to extract information from (a person, especially a prisoner) by long, hard questioning. **10.** to remove bits of metal from (a coin, especially of gold), as by shaking it with others in a bag. **11. a.** to heat (metal) in order to remove an easily fusible constituent. **b.** to heat (solder) until it melts; fasten or join by applying heat after soldering, so as to produce partial fusion.

sweat it out, *Informal.* to wait anxiously or nervously for something to happen: *And they were continuing to tilt it [a rocket] at X minus ten seconds. In the blockhouse, at the control board, Fred Marmo sweated it out* (Saturday Review).

[Middle English *sweten,* Old English *swǣtan* < *swāt* sweat]

—**Syn.** *n.* **1. Sweat, perspiration** mean moisture coming through the pores of the skin. **Sweat** is the direct native English word, used always when speaking of animals or things and often of people, especially when the moisture is flowing freely or is mixed with grime or blood: *Sweat streamed down the horse's flanks, and the rider's shirt was stained with sweat.* **Perspiration** is the more polite word, applicable only when speaking of human beings: *Tiny drops of perspiration formed at her temples.*

sweat·band (swet′band′), *n.* a band, of leather, cloth, etc., around the head or on the inside of a hat or cap, protecting it from perspiration: *The sweatband, which keeps spectacles and goggles clear, is feather-light* (Science News Letter). [American English < *sweat,* noun + *band*[2]]

sweat bee, any of a family of small blackish bees that nest in tunnels in the ground, so called from their habit of alighting on the skin of a perspiring person.

sweat·box (swet′boks′), *n.* **1.** any of various boxlike enclosures within which certain commodities, as hides, figs, etc., are caused to give out or lose moisture preparatory to use or sale. **2.** *Slang.* a very small, narrow cell in which a prisoner is confined as a means of punishment or torture: *Just let me out of this third-degree sweatbox and I'll sign anything you like* (Punch).

sweat·ed (swet′id), *adj.* **1. a.** employed in a sweatshop; overworked and underpaid: *We had all benefited in the past from the cheap food and raw materials produced by . . . sweated labour* (London Times). **b.** utilizing or produced by sweated workers. **2.** sweaty.

sweat·er (swet′ər), *n.* **1.** any of various knitted jackets of wool, nylon, etc., worn for warmth: *She also finds time for social engagements and such normal pastimes as knitting a sweater* (Newsweek). **2.** an agent or remedy that causes sweating; sudorific. **3.** a person or company that grossly overworks and underpays employees; operator of a sweatshop. **4.** a person who perspires, especially one who does so to lose weight or as part of the process of a Turkish bath.

sweat·ered (swet′ərd), *adj.* wearing a sweater: *Sweatered young men sat on stools and jibed at the jaded values of a commercial society* (New York Times).

sweat·ful (swet′fəl), *adj.* abounding in, attended with, or inducing sweat; toilsome.

sweat gland, any of the numerous small, coiled glands that secrete sweat, in man found in the deeper layer (derma) of the skin of most of the body and communicating with the surface through a tube or duct that ends in a pore: *Excretion in the skin is done by the sweat glands, of which there are about two million in man* (A. Franklin Shull).

sweat·i·ly (swet′ə lē), *adv.* in a sweaty manner; with sweat.

sweat·i·ness (swet′ē nis), *n.* the state of being sweaty or moist with sweat.

sweat·ing sickness (swet′ing), miliaria, a febrile disease characterized by profuse sweating, that was epidemic in England at various times during the 1400's and 1500's.

sweating system, a system of employment involving abuse of workers, as by employing them at low wages, during overlong hours, under unsanitary or otherwise unfavorable conditions, or letting work out by contract to middlemen, to be done in inadequate workshops or at the homes of the workers.

sweat·less (swet′lis), *adj.* without sweat.

sweat pants, a pair of baggy pants gathered in at the ankles, worn especially by athletes to keep warm before and after exercise.

sweat room, a room in which tobacco or other agricultural produce is sweated.

sweat shirt, a heavy, long-sleeved, pullover jersey, sometimes with a fleece lining, worn especially by athletes to keep warm before and after exercise.

sweat·shop (swet′shop′), *n.* a place where workers are employed at low pay for long hours under unsanitary, dangerous, or otherwise bad conditions: *A $1.25 minimum wage will help to eliminate unfair competition based on sweatshop wages in the clothing industry* (Wall Street Journal). [American English < *sweat,* noun + *shop,* noun]

sweat suit, a suit consisting of a sweat shirt and sweat pants, used by athletes and by people trying to lose weight by sweating: *A lank-haired boy in a blue sweat suit was wielding dumbbells on the third-floor landing* (New Yorker).

sweat·y (swet′ē), *adj.,* **sweat·i·er, sweat·i·est. 1.** covered or wet with sweat; sweating. **2.** causing sweat: *the sweaty forge* (Matthew Prior). **3.** laborious; toilsome.

Swed., 1. Sweden. **2.** Swedish.

Swede (swēd), *n.* **1.** a native or inhabitant of Sweden. **2.** Also, **swede.** a rutabaga. [< Middle Low German, or Middle Dutch *Swede*]

Swe·den·bor·gi·an (swē′dən bôr′jē ən), *n.* a believer in the theology and religious doctrines of Emanuel Swedenborg, a Swedish philosopher, scientist, and mystic. —*adj.* having to do with Swedenborg, his doctrines, or his followers.

Swe·den·bor·gi·an·ism (swē′dən bôr′jē ə niz′əm), *n.* the religious doctrines and theology of Emanuel Swedenborg, founder of the New Church, not established separately but working within existing churches to spread the new dispensation in which man is morally free.

Swe·den·borg·ism (swē′dən bôrg iz′əm), *n.* Swedenborgianism.

Swed·ish (swē′dish), *adj.* of or having to do with Sweden, a country in northern Europe, its people, or their language. —*n.* **1.** the people of Sweden. **2.** the North Germanic language of Sweden.

Swedish clover, alsike clover.

Swedish massage, a massage in which Swedish movements are used.

Swedish movements, a series of exercises designed to tone up the different muscles, joints, etc.

Swedish turnip, a rutabaga; Swede.

swee·ny (swē′nē), *n.* atrophy of the shoulder muscles of a horse, due to damage to a nerve or disuse of the limb. [probably < dialectal German *Schweine* atrophy (< *schweinen* become emaciated) + English *-y*[3]]

sweep (swēp), *v.,* **swept, sweep·ing,** *n.* —*v.t.* **1. a.** to clean or clear (a floor, etc.) with a broom, brush, etc.; use a broom or something like one to remove dirt; brush: *Sweep the steps.* **b.** to make safe, passable, etc., by or as if by sweeping; clear of what impedes or endangers: *to sweep the sidewalk after a snowfall, to sweep a passage through a minefield.* **2.** to move, drive, or take away with or as with a broom, brush, etc.: *to sweep small change into a bag. The wind sweeps the snow into drifts.* **3.** to remove with a sweeping motion; carry along: *a bridge swept away by a flood, persons swept off the deck of a ship by waves. He kept abreast of the times and was not just swept along with them as his work . . . proved* (London Times). **4.** to trail upon: *Her dress sweeps the ground.* **5.** to pass over with a steady movement: *Her fingers swept the strings of the harp. His eyes swept the sky, searching for signs of rain.* **6.** to range over; scour: *Enthusiasm for the candidate swept the country.* —*v.i.* **1.** to use a broom or something like one to remove dirt; clean a room, surface, etc., by sweeping. **2.** to move swiftly; pass swiftly: *Guerrillas swept down on the town. When the deer sweeps by, and the hounds are in cry* (Scott). **3.** to move with dignity: *Having so spoken she swept out of the room* (Anthony Trollope). **4.** to move or extend in a long course or curve; stretch: *The shore sweeps to the south for miles.*

—*n.* **1.** an act of sweeping; clearing away; removing: *to give a room a good sweep. He made a clean sweep of all his debts.* **2.** a steady, driving motion or swift onward course of something: *The sweep of the wind kept the trees from growing tall. The sheer sweep of dramatic events carried many men along* (Bruce Catton). **3.** a smooth, flowing motion or line; dignified motion: *the regular sweep of an oar, the stately sweep of heroic verse.* **4.** a swinging or curving motion: *He cut the grass with strong sweeps of his scythe.* **5.** a curve; bend: *the sweep of a road.* **6.** a continuous extent: expanse; stretch: *The house looked upon a wide sweep of farming country. The full length of civilization, as we know it, seemed hardly a second in the sweep of geological history unfolded in this painted canyon* (William O. Douglas). **7.** reach; range; extent: *The mountain is beyond the sweep of your eye. The Western plan had sweep and imagination* (Time). **8.** a person who sweeps chimneys, streets, etc.: *The sweep will dump his soot there* (Manchester Guardian). **9.** a long oar used in rowing and sometimes in steering: *Their sweeps were shorter, the oarsmen pulled in shorter arcs* (Time). **10. a.** a long pole used to lower and raise a bucket in a well. **b.** a pump handle. **11.** anything collected by or as by sweeping; refuse. **12.** a sweepstakes. **13. a.** a slam in whist. **b.** a pairing or combining of all the cards on the board, and so taking them, in cassino. **14.** *Physics.* a process of settling, or tending to settle, into thermal equilibrium.

sweeps, gold and silver waste salvaged from the work of goldsmiths and silversmiths; sweepings: *The inhabitants of Africa . . . dress their gold dust in small bowls, after the manner that goldsmiths wash their sweeps* (William Pryce).

[Middle English *swepen* < Old English *geswǣpa* sweepings, related to *swāpan* to sweep]

sweep·back (swēp′bak′), *n.* the acute angle at which the wing of an aircraft slopes or slants backwards from the fuselage to the wing tip: *The wings pivot in such a way that they can be ranged with almost no sweepback for take-off and landing* (Observer).

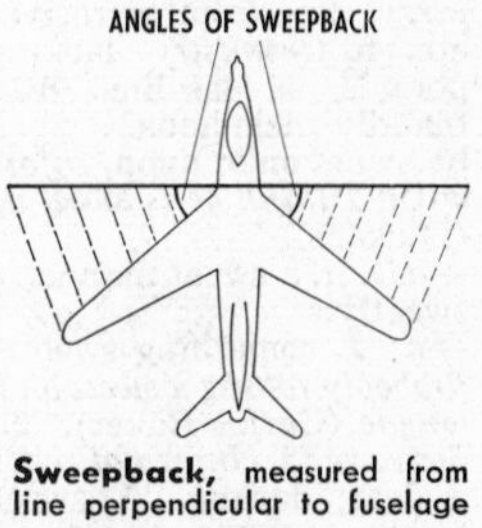

ANGLES OF SWEEPBACK

Sweepback, measured from line perpendicular to fuselage

sweep·er (swē′pər), *n.* **1.** a person or thing that sweeps: *a street sweeper.* **2.** a mine sweeper: . . . *gave aggressive gun-fire support to sweepers working close inshore* (New York Times).

sweep hand, second hand: . . . *the silent inevitability of the sweep hand of a watch* (Punch).

sweep·ing (swē′ping), *adj.* **1.** passing over a wide space: *a sweeping glance.* **2.** having a wide range: *a sweeping victory, a sweeping statement. New York's Senate unanimously voted a sweeping investigation of illegal wire tapping* (Wall Street Journal). *Uncle Billy included the whole party in one sweeping anathema* (Bret Harte). —*n.* the act of a person or thing that sweeps.

sweepings, a. dust, rubbish, scraps, etc., swept out or up: *She just shoved the sweepings into the closet.* **b.** the most worthless people: *the sweepings of the city.* **c.** the metal-yielding scraps of an establishment where precious metals are worked: *Goldsmiths and refiners are wont . . . carefully to save the very sweepings of their shops* (Robert Boyle). —**sweep′ing·ly,** *adv.* —**sweep′ing·ness,** *n.*

sweep net, 1. a large net enclosing a wide space, used in fishing. **2.** a net used for catching insects by sweeping it over herbage, etc.

sweeps (swēps), *n.pl.* See under **sweep,** *n.*

sweep·stake (swēp′stāk′), *n.* **1.** a sweepstakes. **2.** *Obsolete.* **a.** a person who wins all the stakes in a game. **b.** a person who takes all or everything. **3.** *Obsolete.* **a.** a sweeping in or winning of all the stakes in a game. **b.** any total removal or clearance.

sweep·stakes (swēp′stāks′), *n., pl.* **-stakes. 1.** a system of gambling on horses, races, etc. People buy tickets, and the money they pay goes to the drawer or drawers of winning tickets. **2. a.** a race or contest by which the winner or winners are determined under such a system of gambling. **b.** a race or contest in which the prize or prizes derive from a pooling of the stakes of the contestants, with or without additional contributions by the sponsor or sponsors of the contest. **3.** a prize in such a race or contest. [< *sweep,* in obsolete sense of "to win all the stakes in a game" + *stake*[2] + *-s*[1]]

sweep·swing·er (swēp′swing′ər), *n.* an oarsman in a racing crew, especially in scull racing: *Right from the start, Navy's powerful sweepswingers made it clear they intended to get in front and stay there* (Time). [< *sweep* (def. 9) + *swinger*[1]]

sweep ticket, a ticket giving a chance in a sweepstakes.

sweep·y (swē′pē), *adj.* characterized by sweeping movement or form; sweeping.

sweer (swir), *adj. Scottish.* **1.** inactive; indolent; slothful. **2.** reluctant; unwilling. [Old English *swǣr* heavy, oppressive]

sweet (swēt), *adj.* **1.** having a taste or flavor like that of sugar or honey: *Pears are sweeter than lemons.* **2.** having a pleasant taste or smell: *a sweet flower.* **3.** pleasing to the ear; having or giving a pleasant sound;

musical; melodious; harmonious: *a sweet singer, a sweet song. Like sweet bells, jangled out of tune* (Shakespeare). *Jonah Jones, who heads a quartet, keeps his cornet sweet* (New Yorker). **4.** pleasing to the eye; of charming appearance; lovely: *a sweet face, a sweet smile.* **5.** pleasant; agreeable: *a sweet child, sweet sleep, sweet words of praise. What a sweet hat!* **6.** dear; darling: *sweet sir.* **7.** free from disagreeable taste or smell; not sour or spoiled; fresh: *sweet milk.* **8.** not salted or salty: *sweet butter.* **9.** (of wines) having a sweet taste. **10.** (of soil) fertile, not acid or sour; good for farming. **11.** easily managed, handled, or dealt with: *a sweet ship. The clutch is exceptionally sweet in operation* (London Times). **12. a.** *Metallurgy.* free from corrosive salt, sulfur, acid, etc. **b.** *Chemistry.* lacking any sulfur compounds, as gasoline. **13.** (of jazz music) blandly melodious.

be sweet on or **upon,** *Informal.* to be in love with: *I think he is sweet upon your daughter* (Dickens).

—*adv.* in a sweet manner; so as to be sweet; sweetly.

—*n.* **1.** something sweet: *Becky Sharp was probably rolling a sweet on her prettily pointed tongue* (Carlos Baker). **2.** *British.* a sweet dessert. **3.** *Informal.* a sweet potato. **4.** a dear; darling. **5.** sweetness of taste or smell.

sweets, a. candy or other sweet things: *She was carrying a bag of sweets* (London Times). **b.** pleasant or agreeable things: *The Gods have envy'd me the sweets of life* (John Dryden).

[Old English *swēte*]

—**Syn.** *adj.* **1.** saccharine. **2.** fragrant, perfumed. **5.** pleasing, winning. —**Ant.** *adj.* **1.** sour, tart.

sweet alyssum, a common, low-growing garden plant of the mustard family, with clusters of small, fragrant, white or purple flowers.

sweet·bag (swēt′bag′), *n.* a small bag filled with a scented or aromatic substance, used for perfuming the air, clothes, etc.; sachet: *Hast thou no perfumes and sweetbags . . . of the newest mode?* (Scott).

sweet basil, basil, an aromatic plant of the mint family whose leaves are much used in cooking for seasoning.

sweet bay, 1. an American magnolia, a shrub or small tree with round, fragrant, white flowers, common in swamps along the Atlantic coast from Massachusetts southward; bay. **2.** the bay or European laurel.

sweet·bells (swēt′belz′), *n.pl.* a shrub of the heath family growing in eastern United States, having racemes of white or pink flowers.

sweet·bread (swēt′bred′), *n.* the pancreas (stomach sweetbread) or thymus (neck or throat sweetbread) of a young animal, now especially a calf, used as meat. [probably < *sweet* + Middle English *brede,* Old English *brǣd* roasted or grilled meat]

sweet·bri·er or **sweet·bri·ar** (swēt′-brī′ər), *n.* a European and Asiatic wild rose, naturalized in the United States, with strong, hooked prickles on a tall stem, pink, single flowers, and small, aromatic leaves; eglantine; wild brier.

sweet cassava, a variety of cassava of Brazil with starchy, edible roots.

sweet cherry, a kind of wild cherry with sweet, edible, yellow or red fruit; mazzard. The bigarreaus and geans are sweet cherries.

sweet chestnut, 1. a chestnut of Spain and Italy that is larger, and less sweet, than the American variety. **2.** the tree it grows on: *The Romans are thought to have introduced the sweet or Spanish chestnut to Britain* (London Times).

sweet cicely, a European plant of the parsley family, with white flowers, fernlike leaves, and aromatic roots.

sweet cider, unfermented cider.

sweet clover, any of a group of cloverlike herbs of the pea family, that are grown for hay and pasture: *Sweet clover is a quick growing legume valuable for soil improvement, for nutritious pasturage and as a honey plant* (Science News Letter).

sweet corn, 1. a variety of corn, the kernels of which are particularly rich in sugar; sugar corn. The kernels when slightly immature, at the milky stage, are much used as a cooked table vegetable in America and some other parts of the world, being eaten either directly from the ear or after being cut from the ear. *It is better to plant sweet corn in blocks rather than in single rows* (Sunday Times). **2.** an ear or ears of such corn, at the milky stage; green corn.

sweet·en (swē′tən), *v.t.* **1.** to make sweet: *to sweeten the air of a room. He sweetened his coffee with two lumps of sugar. All the perfumes of Arabia will not sweeten this little hand* (Shakespeare). **2.** *Informal.* **a.** to increase the collateral of (a loan) by adding further securities of a high grade. **b.** to improve the terms of (an offer, bid, etc.): *The companies . . . have indicated recently that they are ready to "sweeten" their offer somewhat* (Wall Street Journal). **3.** (in poker) to increase the value of (a pot), especially by an ante of money, chips, etc., additional to that required as a preliminary to play. —*v.i.* to become sweet: *The pears will sweeten as they ripen* [< *sweet* + *-en*[1]] —**sweet′en·er,** *n.*

sweet·en·ing (swē′tə ning, swēt′ning), *n.* **1.** something that sweetens: sweetener. **2.** the act of a person or thing that sweetens.

sweet fern, 1. a small shrub of North America related to the wax myrtle, with fragrant, fernlike leaves. **2.** any of various ferns.

Sweet Fern (def. 1)

sweet flag, a water plant of the arum family, with long, sword-shaped leaves and a thick, creeping rootstock of a pungent, aromatic flavor; calamus; sweetroot. Its rootstock is used in medicine and is sometimes preserved with sugar and eaten as candy.

sweet gale, a low, aromatic shrub of Europe, Asia, and North America with yellowish fruit; gale.

sweet gas, natural gas containing little or no hydrogen sulfide, used for fuel.

sweet grass, any grass that has a sweet taste and is used for fodder: *It is found throughout the Ethiopian region wherever there is water, sweet grass and shelter from the midday heat* (New Scientist).

sweet gum, 1. a large North American tree with shining, star-shaped leaves that turn scarlet in the fall; bilsted; liquidambar. In warm regions it exudes a balsam, used in the preparation of chewing gum and in medicine. **2.** the balsam from this tree.

sweet·heart (swēt′härt′), *n.* **1.** a loved one; lover. **2.** a girl or woman loved: —*that old sweetheart of mine* (James Whitcomb Riley). —**Syn. 1.** suitor, beau, swain.

sweetheart agreement, sweetheart contract.

sweetheart contract, *U.S. Slang.* a secret contract between an employer and an unscrupulous union leader by which workers are made to join a union but receive substandard wages: *Management and union officials who conspire to the detriment of working people, as in "sweetheart contracts," could be punished equally* (Wall Street Journal).

sweet·ie (swē′tē), *n. U.S. Informal.* a sweetheart; darling.

sweeties, *British Informal.* candy; sweets: *Burnt almonds, chocolate, and sweeties of every flavour* (Christina Rossetti).

sweet·ing (swē′ting), *n.* **1.** a sweet apple. **2.** *Archaic.* sweetheart; darling. [Middle English *sweting* < *swete* sweet + *-ing,* a noun suffix that meant "one having the designated quality"]

sweet·ish (swē′tish), *adj.* **1.** somewhat sweet. **2.** too sweet; cloying.

sweet·leaf (swēt′lēf′), *n.* any of a group of shrubs or trees of tropical and subtropical regions sometimes grown for ornament, as the sapphireberry.

sweet·ly (swēt′lē), *adv.* in a sweet manner.

sweet marjoram, the common marjoram, a plant used for flavoring.

sweet·meats (swēt′mēts′), *n.pl.* **1.** candy; sugar-covered nuts; bonbons. **2.** preserves. —**Syn. 1.** confectionery.

sweet·ness (swēt′nis), *n.* a sweet quality: *The sweetness of her manners made everyone like her.*

sweetness and light, 1. a person or thing exhibiting unusual tolerance, understanding, sympathy, etc. (often used ironically when such a display is entirely out of character): *Now that they need us they are suddenly all sweetness and light. Politics is neither "sweetness and light" nor "too dirty to get into," Mrs. Younger said* (New York Times). **2.** a union of moral, intellectual, and aesthetic qualities, regarded as the highest cultural ideal of mankind: *Their ideal of beauty and sweetness and light, and a human nature complete on all its sides* (Matthew Arnold). *Instead of dirt and poison, we have rather chosen to fill our lives with honey and with wax thus furnishing mankind with the two noblest of things, which are sweetness and light* (Jonathan Swift).

sweet nothings, *Informal.* words of endearment between lovers: *And whispered sweet nothings in her ear* (Frank Sullivan). *The sweet nothings that men whisper into my ear don't mean a thing to me* (Wall Street Journal).

sweet oil, any mild or pleasant, edible oil, especially olive oil.

sweet orange, the common orange, an evergreen tree of the rue family with fragrant white blossoms and oval leaves.

sweet pea, 1. an annual climbing plant of the pea family, much grown for its showy, delicate, fragrant flowers of various colors. **2.** the flower.

sweet pepper, 1. any of various mild-flavored pepper plants. **2.** the fruit of any of various mild-flavored pepper plants, used as a vegetable, for stuffing, etc.; green pepper.

sweet potato, 1. the sweet, thick, yellow or reddish root of a creeping vine of the morning-glory family, much used as a vegetable. **2.** the vine that it grows on, much cultivated in tropical and subtropical regions: *The sweet potato, a New World plant, was found by the first white explorers all over Polynesia* (Harper's). **3.** *Music, Informal.* an ocarina.

sweet potato weevil, a weevil whose larva feeds in the stems or roots of sweet potatoes and related plants.

sweet rocket, a perennial garden plant of Europe and Asia with showy white, pinkish, and purplish flowers.

sweet·root (swēt′rüt′, -ru̇t′), *n.* **1.** licorice. **2.** sweet flag.

sweets (swēts), *n.pl.* See under **sweet,** *n.*

sweet scabious, a plant with long, tough stems and dense flower heads, a kind of scabious much cultivated in flower gardens.

sweet-scent·ed (swēt′sen′tid), *adj.* having a sweet scent; sweet-smelling; fragrant.

sweet·shop (swēt′shop′), *n. British.* a candy store.

sweet·sop (swēt′sop′), *n.* **1.** the sweet, edible, pulpy fruit of a tropical American tree of the custard-apple family; sugar apple. It has a thick, green, scaly rind and black seeds. **2.** the tree itself.

sweet sorghum, any of a group of cultivated varieties of sorghum used for making molasses or syrup and as food for livestock.

sweet spirit of niter, an alcoholic solution of ethyl nitrite, used as a diuretic and as a means of increasing sweating.

sweet talk, *Informal.* pleasant, agreeable, usually insincere talk to convince, befriend, set at ease, etc.: *As a man of good will he had to . . . give them a chance to back up their sweet talk with action* (Newsweek).

sweet-talk (swēt′tôk′), *Informal.* —*v.t.* to try to convince, befriend, or set at ease by pleasant, agreeable talk; charm: *But he argues that the most effective tactics of gaining peace don't always consist of sweet-talking our enemies* (Wall Street Journal). —*v.i.* to use sweet talk; be charming or flattering. —**Syn.** *v.t.* mollify.

sweet-tem·pered (swēt′tem′pərd), *adj.* having a gentle or pleasant nature. —**Syn.** amiable, affable.

sweet tooth, a taste or liking for sweet things; fondness for candy, cake, etc.

sweet wil·liam or **sweet Wil·liam** (wil′-yəm), a common garden pink with dense, rounded clusters of small flowers of various shades of white and red, usually variegated or parti-colored.

Sweet William

sweet·wood (swēt′wu̇d′), *n.* **1.** any of various trees and shrubs, chiefly of the laurel family, of the West Indies and tropical America. **2.** the wood of such a tree or shrub.

sweet woodruff, a species of woodruff with a sweet fragrance when dried. It has been used as a flavoring and in perfumes.

swell (swel), *v.*, **swelled, swelled** or **swollen, swell·ing,** *n., adj.* —*v.i.* **1.** to grow bigger: *Bread dough swells as it rises.* **2. a.** to rise above the usual level, as a river. **b.** to rise in waves, as the sea during and after a storm. **c.** to rise to the brim, as a spring; well up, as tears. **3.** to be larger or thicker in a particular place: *A barrel swells in the middle.* **4.** to rise above the general level: *Rounded hills swell gradually from the village plain.* **5.** to increase in amount, degree, or force: *Savings may swell into a fortune. The ranks swelled with volunteers.* **6.** to grow louder or more intense, as sound or music: *Once again the organ swells* (John Greenleaf Whittier). *The murmur gradually swelled into a fierce and terrible clamor* (Macaulay). **7.** to become proud or conceited; behave proudly, arrogantly, or pompously: *to swell with pride or indignation. He would come home and swell around the town in his blackest and greasiest clothes* (Mark Twain).
—*v.t.* **1.** to make larger; increase in size: *The bee sting on the arm had swelled his fingers.* **2.** to cause to rise above the usual level: *The river is swollen by rain.* **3.** to cause to bulge out or protrude. **4.** to make greater in amount, degree, etc.: *Volunteers were swelling the ranks. The government brought four army regiments . . . to swell . . . military strength* (Newsweek). **5.** to make louder: *All joined in to swell the chorus.* **6.** to make proud or conceited: *swollen with pride, swollen with his own importance.*
—*n.* **1.** the act of swelling; increase in size, amount, degree, force, etc.: *The swell of insolence* (Samuel Johnson). **2.** the condition of being swollen or increased in size. **3.** a part that bulges out. **4.** a long, unbroken wave, or waves, as after a storm: *riding out a gale which was accompanied by as big a swell as we have ever seen* (London Times). *The boat rocked in the swell.* **5.** a piece of higher ground; rounded hill. **6.** a sound or succession of sounds gradually increasing in loudness. **7.** *Music.* **a.** crescendo followed by diminuendo. **b.** the sign for this (< >). **c.** a device in an organ, harpsichord, etc., to control the volume of sound. **8.** *Informal.* a fashionable, stylishly dressed, or distinguished person: *I never was a gentleman—only a swell* (Frederick Marryat).
—*adj.* **1.** *Informal.* stylish; grand. **2.** *Informal.* excellent; first-rate: *a swell time, a swell worker. The woman is a lot better. That was swell medicine you gave her* (Sinclair Lewis).
[Old English *swellan*]
—**Syn.** *v.i., v.t.* **1.** inflate, distend, dilate. See **expand.** **3.** bulge. -*v.t.* **1.** dilate, distend.
➔ Both **swelled** and **swollen** are in common use as past participles (*had swelled* or *swollen*); as an attributive adjective *swelled* is occasionally employed, as in the informal phrase *a swelled head,* but *swollen* is usual.

swell box, a swell organ.

swell·dom (swel′dəm), *n. Informal.* swells collectively; the fashionable world.

swelled (sweld), *adj.* **1.** swollen: *a swelled face or ankle.* **2.** *Informal.* having an overdeveloped sense of one's own importance or merits: *a swelled ego. He has a bad case of swelled head.*

swell·fish (swel′fish′), *n., pl.* **-fish·es** or (*collectively*) **-fish.** a fish that can inflate the body by swallowing air; puffer.

swell front, any horizontally convex projection in furniture or architecture, as a bow window.

swell-head·ed (swel′hed′id), *adj. Informal.* conceited; arrogant.
—**swell′-head′ed·ness,** *n.*

swell·ing (swel′ing), *n.* **1.** an increase in size. **2.** a swollen part: *There is a swelling on Dick's head where he bumped it. . . . Inoculation of the virus resulted in the development of a localized swelling of the skin* (Fenner and Day). —*adj.* that swells. —**Syn.** *n.* **2.** protuberance.

swell·ish (swel′ish), *adj. Informal.* characteristic of a swell; fashionable; stylish.

swell mob, *British Slang.* a class of criminals who go about fashionably dressed to avoid suspicion.

swell-mobs·man (swel′mobz′mən), *n., pl.* **-men.** *British Slang.* a fashionably dressed criminal.

swell organ, the chief enclosed section of an organ, containing a set of pipes or reeds, and having shutters somewhat resembling Venetian blinds, that are opened and closed by a pedal, etc., to vary the volume of sound.

swelt (swelt), *Scottish.* —*v.i.* **1.** to die. **2.** to faint or swoon. **3.** to languish or swelter with oppressive heat. —*v.t.* to oppress or overcome with heat; cause to swelter. [Old English *sweltan* to die. Related to SULTRY, SWELTER.]

swel·ter (swel′tər), *v.i.* **1.** to suffer from heat: *We sweltered . . . in the stagnant superheated air* (Joseph Conrad). **2.** to perspire freely; sweat. —*v.t.* **1.** to oppress with heat. **2.** to exude (venom, poison, etc.) like sweat: *A reptile contemporary has recently sweltered forth his black venom* (Dickens).
—*n.* a sweltering condition.
[< *swelt* be faint with heat + *-er*[6]. Related to SWEAL.]

swel·ter·ing (swel′tər ing, -tring), *adj.* **1.** (of heat, weather, or a season) oppressively hot: *The heat was sweltering, and he became very tired* (John Galsworthy). **2.** suffering from or overpowered by oppressive heat.
—**swel′ter·ing·ly,** *adv.*

swel·try (swel′trē), *adj.* oppressively hot; sweltering; sultry: *The fierce heat of the sun had rendered the atmosphere sweltry and oppressive* (Blackwood's Magazine). [< *swelter* + *-y*[1]. Related to SULTRY.]

swept (swept), *v.* the past tense and past participle of **sweep:** *a joint slate of candidates that swept the polls* (Atlantic). —*adj.* sweptback.

swept-back (swept′bak′), *adj.* (of the wings of an airplane) extending outward and sharply backward from the fuselage: *It has swept-back wings to permit high speed, and is equipped with six . . . turbo-jet engines* (Science News Letter). See **sweepback** for picture.

swept·wing (swept′wing′), *n.* a sweptback wing. —*adj.* having sweptback wings: *The R.A.F.'s latest type of Hawker Hunter sweptwing fighter, the Mark IV, is being used for the first time* (London Times).

swerve (swėrv), *v.,* **swerved, swerv·ing,** *n.* —*v.i., v.t.* to turn aside: *to swerve off the road, to be swerved from the path of virtue. The car swerved and hit a tree. The world has swerved from truth and right* (William Morris). —*n.* a turning aside: *The swerve of the ball made it hard to hit.* [Middle English *swerven* go off, turn aside, Old English *sweorfan* to rub, file] —**Syn.** *v.i., v.t.* deviate, diverge, stray.

swerve·less (swėrv′lis), *adj.* unswerving: *His gaze at the preacher had become swerveless* (Owen Wister).

swerv·er (swėr′vər), *n.* a person or thing that swerves.

swev·en (swev′ən), *n.* **1.** *Archaic.* a dream or vision. **2.** *Obsolete.* sleep. [Middle English *sweven,* Old English *swefen* a dream; sleep]

S.W.G., standard wire gauge.

swift (swift), *adj.* **1.** moving with great speed: *a swift horse, a swift automobile.* **2.** made or done at high speed; quick: *a swift pace, the swift clicking of the knitting needles.* **3.** coming, happening, or performed without delay; prompt: *a swift response.* **4.** acting, or ready to act, without delay; ready; alert (to): *swift to suspect.* **5.** *Poetic.* passing quickly; that is soon over; brief: *Swift Summer into the Autumn flowed* (Shelley).
—*adv. Poetic.* swiftly.
—*n.* **1.** any of a family of small birds related to the hummingbirds and goatsuckers, although similar to the swallows, and noted for their rapidity of flight, as the chimney swift of North America, that often builds its nest in an unused chimney: *The swift . . . has a wingspread of some 16 inches, which makes it an incomparable little flying machine* (Scientific American). **2.** any of certain small lizards that run quickly. **3.** any of a family of large moths distinguished by their rapid flight; ghost moth. **4.** a kind of reel, usually adjustable in diameter, used for winding skeins of yarn, silk, etc. **5.** a cylinder in a carding machine. [Old English *swift*] —**swift′ly,** *adv.*
—**Syn.** *adj.* **1.** fleet, speedy, rapid.

Chimney Swift (about 5 in. long)

swift·en (swif′tən), *v.t., v.i.* to make or become swift or swifter; hasten. [< *swift* + *-en*[1]]

swift·er (swif′tər), *Nautical.* —*n.* **1.** a rope passed through holes or notches in the outer ends of capstan bars and drawn taut to keep the bars in their sockets while the capstan is being turned. **2.** the forward shroud of a lower mast, extending to either side of the mast. **3.** a rope encircling a boat or ship lengthwise to strengthen and protect its sides.
—*v.t.* to hold tight or draw together with a swifter.
[apparently < Middle English *swift* to make fast + *-er*[1]]

swift-foot·ed (swift′fu̇t′id), *adj.* able to run swiftly.

Swift·i·an (swif′tē ən), *adj.* of, having to do with, or characteristic of the British satirist Jonathan Swift or his works: *The woodcutter's version of the crime lays bare the meanness of man with Swiftian bitterness and contempt* (Time).

swift·let (swift′lit), *n.* a little or young swift, especially a small species of swift that constructs the edible bird's-nest of southeastern Asia.

swift·ness (swift′nis), *n.* rapid motion; speed: *He turned with the swiftness of a cat.*

swig (swig), *n., v.,* **swigged, swig·ging.** *Informal.* —*n.* a big or hearty drink. —*v.t., v.i.* to drink heartily or greedily: *I am . . . drinking as much tea . . . as I can swig* (John Ruskin). [origin uncertain]

swig·ger (swig′ər), *n.* a person who swigs.

swill (swil), *n.* **1. a.** kitchen refuse, especially when partly liquid; garbage; slops; hogwash: *Swill is sometimes fed to pigs.* **b.** any of various other foods for animals resembling this in consistency, as a mixture of water and used distillery mash, sometimes with added grain, dried waste from slaughter houses, etc. **2.** very unappetizing food. **3.** a deep drink; swig. **4.** the act of eating or drinking greedily; gluttonous ingestion. [< verb]
—*v.t.* **1.** to drink (down) or (sometimes) eat greedily or to excess; guzzle: *a number of well-dressed people . . . devouring sliced beef and swilling port* (Tobias Smollett). *She had seen them swilling down champagne with a couple of unknown Americans* (Atlantic). **2.** to fill with drink: *to swill my belly with wine* (Robert Louis Stevenson). **3.** to wash or rinse out by flooding with water.
—*v.i.* **1.** to drink greedily or to excess; tipple: *Ye eat, and swill, and sleep, and gourmandise* (Richard Brinsley Sheridan). **2.** to move or dash about, as liquid shaken in a vessel; flow freely or forcibly. **3.** to let water wash over soil, gravel, etc., especially as a way of panning gold: *There was a certain glamour about the old gold-rush boys, swilling hopefully away with their little tin pannikins* (Punch).
[Old English *swilian, swillan* to wash]
—**swill′er,** *n.*

swim (swim), *v.,* **swam** or (*Dialect*) **swum, swum, swim·ming,** *n.* —*v.i.* **1.** to move along on or in the water by using arms, legs, fins, etc.: *Fish and dogs swim, cats do not.* **2.** to float: *a leaf swimming on a pond, meat swimming in gravy.* **3.** to move, glide, or be suspended in the air, as if gliding or floating on water: *The white cloud swam across the sky.* **4.** to move or glide smoothly or quietly, especially over a surface: *She . . . swam across the floor as though she scorned the drudgery of walking* (Robert Louis Stevenson). **5.** to be dizzy or feel giddy; whirl or seem to whirl: *The heat and noise made my head swim.* **6.** to be overflowed or flooded (with or in): *Her eyes were swimming with tears.*
—*v.t.* **1.** to go (a certain distance) or do (a certain stroke) by swimming: *to swim a mile, unable to swim a stroke.* **2.** to move in, on, or over by swimming; swim across: *to swim a lake.* **3.** to make swim or float: *He swam his horse across the stream.* **4.** to provide with enough water for (something) to swim in or float on.
—*n.* **1.** an act, time, motion, or distance of swimming: *to go for a swim.* **2.** a smooth gliding motion or movement, especially of the body. **3.** the swim bladder of a fish.
the swim, *Informal.* the popular current in fashion, business, opinion, etc.: *An active and sociable person likes to be in the swim.*
[Old English *swimman* to move in or on the water, to float]

swim bladder, (in fishes) a sac containing air or gas and serving as an organ of flotation; a structure homologous with the lungs of air-breathing animals: *Certain fishes have a swim bladder which aids in diffusion of gases* (Harbaugh and Goodrich).

swim fin, a rubber, paddlelike attachment worn on the foot to increase kicking power in swimming; fin: *The next day I bought a pair of swim fins and I have been skin diving ever since* (Scientific American).

swim-in (swim′in′), *n.* wade-in: *With the temperature at 101 degrees, the leaders of a civil rights protest movement decided against a street march here today and held a "swim-in" instead* (New York Times).

swim·ma·ble (swim′ə bəl), *adj.* that can be swum.

swim·mer (swim′ər), *n.* a person or animal that swims.

swim·mer·et (swim′ə ret), *n.* one of a number of abdominal limbs or appendages of many crustaceans, used in respiration, for carrying eggs (in females), and usually adapted for swimming, and thus distinguished from other limbs adapted for walking or seizing; pleopod. [< *swimmer* + *-et*]

swim·ming (swim′ing), *n.* **1.** the practice or sport of moving along or in water by using arms, legs, fins, etc.: *Tom is an expert at both swimming and diving.* **2.** the act of moving this way: *Can you reach the island by swimming?* **3.** a state of dizziness or giddiness; vertigo.
—*adj.* **1. a.** of or for swimming or swimmers: *a swimming teacher.* **b.** that habitually swims, as some birds and insects. **2.** filled with tears; watery: *swimming eyes.* **3.** faint; dizzy: *a swimming sensation.*
—**Syn.** *adj.* **3.** giddy, vertiginous.

swimming bath, *British.* a swimming pool: *There is a pleasant garden round the house and a beautiful swimming bath* (Cape Times).

swimming crab, any of a family of crabs that includes the blue crab and the lady crab.

swimming hole, a pool, as in a small stream, with sufficient depth of water to swim in: *The boy's love for the water, his affection for the old swimming hole* (J.H. Moore).

swim·ming·ly (swim′ing lē), *adv.* with great ease or success: *Everything went swimmingly at our party. The ... light opera program moves along swimmingly with the current revival* (Wall Street Journal). *I found the association went on swimmingly* (Benjamin Franklin).
—**Syn.** easily, smoothly.

swimming pool, a large tank, usually of concrete, used for swimming, diving, etc.: *to build an outdoor swimming pool.*

swimming pool reactor, a nuclear reactor partly immersed in a tank of water that absorbs heat, slows down nuclear fission, and is a radiation shield: *The first license granted was to Pennsylvania State University for a 100-kilowatt swimming pool reactor already completed* (Bulletin of Atomic Scientists).

swim·my (swim′ē), *adj.*, **-mi·er, -mi·est.** **1.** slightly dizzy or giddy; light-headed: *The blow on the head left him feeling swimmy.* **2.** not seeing clearly; blurred: *Through the smoke his swimmy eyes made out a vague shape.*

swim pool, swimming pool: *The apartment houses are embellished ... with air conditioning, music in laundry room, and elevator and swim pools* (New York Times).

swim·suit (swim′süt′), *n.* a bathing suit: *Women's swimsuits are selling fine and are as eye-catching as ever* (Wall Street Journal).

swim·wear (swim′wãr′), *n.* clothes worn for swimming: *The most exciting collection of coordinated swimwear* (New Yorker).

Swin·burn·i·an (swin bėr′nē ən), *adj.* of, having to do with, or characteristic of the English poet Algernon Charles Swinburne, 1837-1909, or his works: *The poem 'Ad Mariam' [by Gerard Manley Hopkins] is ... thoroughly Swinburnian* (Times Literary Supplement).

swin·dle (swin′dəl), *v.*, **-dled, -dling,** *n.* —*v.t.* **1.** to cheat; defraud: *Honest merchants do not swindle their customers.* **2.** *Obsolete.* to get (something) by fraud. —*v.i.* to be guilty of swindling another or others; practice fraud.
—*n.* an act of swindling; cheat or fraud: *to suspect a swindle.*
[back formation < *swindler*]
—**Syn.** *v.t.* **1.** rook.

swin·dle·a·ble (swin′də lə bəl), *adj.* that can be swindled; easily tricked or cheated.

swin·dler (swin′dlər), *n.* a person who cheats or defrauds. [< German *Schwindler* < *schwindeln* to befog, confuse; cheat]

swindle sheet, *U.S. Slang.* an expense account: *To catch a few suspected swindle sheet artists, the Internal Revenue Service has now decided to crack down on all ... who get so much as a penny of their expenses paid by their employers* (Wall Street Journal).

swin·dling (swin′dling), *n.* the act of a person who swindles or defrauds.

swine (swīn), *n., pl.* **swine. 1. a.** hogs; pigs: ... *and he sent him into his fields to feed swine* (Luke 15:15). **b.** a hog; pig. **2.** a coarse or beastly person. [Old English *swīn.* Related to SOW[2].]

swine fever, hog cholera: *Because of swine fever there will be no pig classes at the Shropshire and West Midland Show at Shrewsbury* (London Times).

swine·herd (swīn′hėrd′), *n.* a person who tends pigs or hogs, especially for hire.

swine plague, an infectious disease of swine, caused by a specific bacterium, and marked by internal hemorrhage, fever, and often pneumonia and pleurisy.

swine pox, 1. an infectious disease of hogs, caused by a virus and characterized by itching skin lesions, especially on the underparts. **2.** *Obsolete.* chicken pox.

swing[1] (swing), *v.*, **swung** or (*Dialect*) **swang, swung, swing·ing,** *n., adj.* —*v.t.* **1.** to move (something) back and forth, especially with a regular motion: *He swings his arms as he walks.* **2.** to hang or suspend so as to turn freely: *to swing a hammock between two trees.* **3.** to cause to turn in alternate directions or in either direction, on or as on an axle or pivot: *to swing a door open.* **4.** to drive or cause to move in a curve: *He swung the automobile around a corner.* **5.** to move, wield, or flourish (something held, as a weapon) with a sweeping, oscillating, or rotating movement: *to swing a lasso, swing a club about one's head.* **6.** to manage or influence successfully: *to swing a business deal. Real estate brokers from all over the country bring him deals they can't afford to swing* (Wall Street Journal). *Princeton's financial-aid officer tells how to swing the high cost of higher education* (Saturday Evening Post). —*v.i.* **1.** to move freely or regularly back and forth, as an object suspended from above; oscillate, as a pendulum. **2.** to move back and forth through the air on a suspended rope as a sport. **3. a.** to be suspended or hang freely. **b.** *Informal.* to be put to death by hanging: *They all lovingly swung together at Execution-Dock* (Daniel Defoe). **4.** to turn in alternate directions or in either direction on or as on an axle or pivot; wheel: *A gate swings on its hinges. He swung around to see who was speaking. The ship, swinging to her anchor with the flood tide* (Herman Melville). **5.** to go along or around in a curve; sweep. **6.** to go along with a free, swaying movement: *soldiers swinging down a street.*
—*n.* **1.** the act or manner of swinging: *a mighty swing.* **2.** the amount of swinging. **3. a.** the act of swinging or flourishing a weapon, etc. **b.** a curving movement such as that made in flourishing a weapon. **4.** a swinging movement or gait: *An easy swing in my walk* (Washington Irving). **5.** a steady, vigorous rhythm or movement characterizing a verse or piece of music: *His poetry lacked the swing of ... Kipling* (Sinclair Lewis). **6.** freedom of action; free scope: *The giving free swing to one's temper and instincts* (Matthew Arnold). **7.** the course of a career, business, period of time, etc., especially as marked by vigorous activity: *to get into the swing of working after a vacation.* **8.** a trip around a country, region, etc.; tour: *The Argentine Minister of Agriculture has just completed a swing through the United States* (Wall Street Journal). **9.** something that swings or is swung, especially a seat hung from ropes, chains, or rods, on which one may sit and swing. **10.** *Archaic.* forcible motion of something; impetus.

in full swing, going on actively or completely; without restraint: *By five the party was in full swing. The Victorian Age was in full swing* (Lytton Strachey).

swing around the circle, *U.S.* a political swing or tour.
—*adj.* **1.** capable of turning to and fro; swinging: *a swing lamp, a swing gate.* **2.** that can influence the outcome of an election or other issue: *swing voters, a swing district.*
[Old English *swingan* to beat, strike; move violently. Related to SWINGE, SWINGLE.]
—**Syn.** *v.i.* **1. Swing, sway, rock** mean to move back and forth or from side to side. **Swing** applies to the movement of something attached at one side or the end or ends, and often but not always suggests a regular or rhythmical movement: *The lantern hanging overhead swung in the wind.* **Sway** suggests the unsteady motion of something that bends or gives easily at any pressure: *The branches sway in the breeze.* **Rock** suggests either a gentle swinging or a violent swaying: *The house rocked in the storm.*

swing[2] (swing), *n., v.*, **swung, swing·ing,** *adj.* —*n.* jazz, especially jazz for dancing, of the type popular between about 1935 and 1944, in which the players improvise on the original melody: *The sextet's style is swing, and it swings in the most dexterous manner imaginable* (New Yorker).
—*v.t.* to play as swing. —*v.i.* **1.** to play, sing, etc., with a lively, swinging rhythm: *There is little that is new or startlingly original in the arrangements themselves, but how they swing!* (Saturday Review). **2.** *Slang.* to be completely satisfying, lively, up-to-date, etc.; be hip: *"The first old-fashioned specialty store around here ... had gotten slightly old ladyish. Now it swings"* (New York Times).
—*adj.* of or having to do with swing or its style: *Tatum ... created "swing" piano and anticipated nearly all the rhythmic and harmonic idioms of the modern period* (John Mehegan). [special use of *swing*[1]]

swing·back (swing′bak′), *n.* **1.** a reversion of opinion, etc.; a turning back to formerly held beliefs or ideas. **2.** the backward swing of the body, a weapon, etc.

swing bridge, a bridge that pivots on its center to open and let ships pass.

swing·by (swing′bī′), *n.* the passing of a spacecraft through the gravitational field of a heavenly body to accelerate momentum, alter course, etc.

swing door, a swinging door.

swinge[1] (swinj), *v.t.*, **swinged, swinge·ing.** **1.** *Archaic.* to beat; flog; whip: *Saint George, that swinged the Dragon* (Shakespeare). **2.** *Obsolete.* to chastise or castigate. [variant of Old English *swengan* (causative) < *swingan;* see SWING[1]]

swinge[2] (swinj), *v.t.*, **swinged, swinge·ing.** *Dialect.* to singe or scorch. [perhaps alteration of *singe*]

swinge·ing (swin′jing), *adj. Informal.* very forcible, excellent, or large of its kind: *He and his editor are swiftly haled before the bench and swingeing penalties ... are demanded* (Punch). —**swinge′ing·ly,** *adv.*

swing·er[1] (swing′ər), *n.* **1.** a person or thing that swings: *a lasso swinger, a good swinger.* **2.** *Slang.* a person who is up-to-date and lively, especially in an unrestrained way: *The go-go spirit of today's glamorized young swingers is hardly conducive to interest in exact and abstract reasoning* (New York Times).

swing·er[2] (swin′jər), *n.* **1.** *Informal.* anything very forcible, great, or large, as a blow, or a lie; whopper. **2.** a person or thing that swinges.

swing·ing (swing′ing), *adj.* **1.** moving freely in either direction upon a fixed center or axis, as a stool or a door. **2.** moving or proceeding with a swing, as a pace or gait, or a rhythm in verse or music. **3.** *Slang.* up-to-date and lively, especially in an unrestrained way: *Miss Shrimpton and a troop of other notable models played host at a champagne luncheon at noon and a swinging party at night* (London Times). —**swing′ing·ly,** *adv.*

swinging door, a door that swings shut by itself and opens from either direction: ... *the swinging door into the butler's pantry gave its old swish and slap* (New Yorker).

swin·gle (swing′gəl), *n., v.*, **-gled, -gling.** —*n.* **1.** a wooden instrument shaped like a large knife, used for beating flax or hemp and scraping from it the woody or coarse portions. **2.** the striking part of a flail; swiple.
—*v.t.* to clean, beat, and scrape (flax or hemp).
[Middle English *swingle,* Old English *swingel* a stroke, whip < *swingan* beat]

swin·gle·bar (swing′gəl bär′), *n.* singletree.

swin·gle·tree (swing′gəl trē′), *n.* whiffletree.

swing·man (swing′man′, -mən), *n., pl.* **-men. 1.** *U.S.* one of the outriders who keeps a moving herd of cattle in order. **2.** a musician who plays swing: *Swingman Benny Goodman, 57, named . . . for his contributions to world culture and American music* (Time). **3.** *Slang.* a person who casts the decisive vote: *The swingman, Justice Harlan, voted to reverse Estes' conviction* (New York Times).

swing music, swing[2].

swing-over (swing′ō′vər), *n.* **1.** a change to an opposite side, position, or opinion: *An odd phenomenon in American postwar life is the swing-over of young women from ambitious career girls to full-time housewives* (London Times). **2.** an acrobatic movement of hanging from one arm and swinging the body in a complete vertical circle: *Victoria Unis . . . is shown doing the rhythmic swing-overs that entitle her to center ring position as a star* (New York Times).

swing shift, the hours between the day and night shifts, usually from 4 p.m. to midnight, designated as a working day in factories, etc., on a 24-hour basis: *In addition to his swing shift job at Douglas, Mr. Nagurski works days as an airplane mechanic* (Wall Street Journal). [American English, perhaps < *swing*[1] (because the shift is the middle one)]

swing shifter, a person who works on the swing shift.

swing tail, an airplane tail that swings open on hinges to facilitate loading and unloading, especially of large and heavy pieces of freight. —**swing′-tail′,** *adj.*

swing·tree (swing′trē′), *n.* singletree.

swing·y (swing′ē), *adj.*, **swing·i·er, swing·i·est.** of or in the style of swing music; lively; jazzy: . . . *an impressive collection of 12 swingy ballads* (Saturday Review).

swing wing, *British.* variable-sweep wing: *When applied to aircraft the terms . . . variable sweep, polymorphism, and swing wings all refer basically to wing mobility* (London Times).

swin·ish (swī′nish), *adj.* **1.** like swine; hoggish; beastly; dirty; greedy. **2.** having to do with or fit for swine: *in swinish sleep* (Shakespeare). —**swin′ish·ly,** *adv.* —**swin′ish·ness,** *n.*

swink (swingk), *n., v.*, **swank** or **swonk, swonk·en, swink·ing.** *Archaic.* —*n.* labor; toil. [Old English *swinc*]
—*v.i.* to labor; toil.
—*v.t.* to weary with toil; overwork. [Old English *swincan.* Ultimately related to SWING[1].] —**swink′er,** *n.*

swinked (swingkt), *adj. Archaic.* wearied with toil: *the swink'd hedger at his supper sat* (Milton).

swipe (swīp), *n., v.,* **swiped, swip·ing.** —*n.* **1.** *Informal.* a sweeping stroke; hard, driving blow: *He made two swipes at the golf ball without hitting it.* **2.** a kind of lever for raising a weight, especially for raising water. **3.** (in barbershop quartet singing) harmony that changes several times on a single note of the melody.
take a swipe at, *Informal.* to seek to hit; deliver a blow at: *A pampered but kindly king . . . takes a good-natured swipe at conformity and some unsuccessful attempts to resist it* (New York Times).
—*v.t.* **1.** *Informal.* to strike with a sweeping blow. **2.** *Slang.* to steal.
[partly variant of *sweep;* partly variant of obsolete *swip* to strike, move hastily, Middle English *swippen,* perhaps Old English *swippan,* variant of *swipian.* Compare Old English *swipu* a stick, scourge.]
—**Syn.** *v.t.* **2.** snatch.

swipes (swīps), *n.pl. British Slang.* **1.** poor, weak beer; small beer. **2.** alcoholic malt beverages in general; beer. [< *swipe,* in obsolete sense of "to drink hastily" + -*s*[1]]

swi·ple or **swip·ple** (swip′əl), *n.* the part of a flail that strikes the grain in threshing; swingle. [Middle English *swepell* a besom, and *swipyll* a swipple. Probably related to SWEEP, SWIPE.]

swirl (swėrl), *v.i.* **1.** to move or drive along with a twisting motion: *dust swirling in the air, a stream swirling over rocks.* **2.** to twist; curl: *a lock of hair swirled against the neck.*
—*v.t.* **1.** to give a whirling motion to: *Add the firm butter to the sauce in little curls, swirling the pan* (New York Times). **2. a.** to give a twisted or curled form to: *Gold is used as an accent to emphasize the swirled pattern on a round table* (New York Times). **b.** to wrap around (with something).
—*n.* **1.** a swirling movement; whirl; eddy. **2.** a twist; curl: *Her hat had a swirl of lace around it.*
[Middle English *swirle* eddy, probably < dialectal Norwegian *svirla.* Compare Dutch *zwirrelen* to whirl.]

swirl·y (swėr′lē), *adj.* **1.** twisted. **2.** knotty; gnarled.

swish[1] (swish), *v.i.* **1.** to move with a thin, light, hissing or brushing sound: *The whip swished through the air.* **2.** to make such a sound: *a long, swishing gown.* —*v.t.* to cause to swish: *She swished the stick.*
—*n.* a swishing movement or sound: *the swish of paddles in dark water* (William O. Douglas). *A few shots and swishes of scimitars and it was all over* (Newsweek).

swish[2] (swish), *adj. British Slang.* elegant; classy; posh: *Her new premises in Bruton Street are swish* (Sunday Times). [special use of *swish*[1]]

swish·y (swish′ē), *adj.* characterized by a swishing sound or motion.

swiss (swis), *n.* Swiss muslin; Swiss.

Swiss (swis), *adj., n., pl.* **Swiss.** —*adj.* **1.** of or having to do with Switzerland, a small country in central Europe, or its people. **2.** characteristic of Switzerland or its people.
—*n.* **1.** a native or inhabitant of Switzerland. **2.** the people of Switzerland. **3.** Swiss muslin: *A short sash curtain of . . . Swiss or dimity is easier to handle* (London Daily Chronicle).
[< French *suisse* < Middle High German *Swiz*]

Swiss chard, any of several varieties of beets whose leaves are often eaten as a vegetable; chard: *For brilliant foliage no other vegetable quite equals the . . . Swiss chard* (New York Times).

Swiss cheese, a firm, pale-yellow or whitish cheese with many large holes.

Swiss franc, the basic Swiss monetary unit and silver coin, worth about 23 cents.

Swiss Guards, a body of Swiss soldiers that acts as a bodyguard to the Pope in the Vatican.

Swiss muslin, a kind of thin muslin with or without raised loose work in various patterns, as dots or figures, used especially for curtains.

Swiss roll, a sponge cake rolled up with a layer of jam or jelly; jellyroll.

Swiss steak, a slice of beef, veal, or lamb, kneaded with flour, browned, and cooked with gravy and tomato sauce: *To stimulate more beef-eating, the Agriculture Department is putting out recipes for . . . ragout of beef and Swiss steak* (Wall Street Journal).

Swit., Switzerland.

switch (swich), *n.* **1.** any of various devices for changing the direction of something, for making or breaking a connection, or other purposes: **a.** a lever, plug or other device for making or breaking an electric circuit or for altering the connections in a circuit, as for connecting a trunk line with any of various other lines. **b.** a device, usually a short movable track pivoted at one end, by which a train can move from one track to another. **2.** the act of operating any of these devices. **3.** a turn; change; shift: *a last-minute switch of plans; . . . so that their [delegates'] timely switch could be properly recorded* (Bruce Catton). *In Peking, the Red Chinese Government pulled another switch* (Newsweek). **4.** (in bridge) a turning to another suit in bidding or play: *Don't double if there is a probability of a switch into some other call which you cannot possibly double* (A.M. Foster). **5.** a slender stick for whipping or beating, especially a riding whip. **6.** a thin, flexible shoot cut from a tree: *Not so long ago, exasperated mothers snatched off a switch from the lilac bush while ushering junior to the shed.* **7.** a blow with or as with a switch; stroke; lash: *The big dog knocked a vase off the table with a switch of his tail.* **8.** a bunch or coil of long hair, often of false hair, worn by a woman in addition to her own hair.
—*v.t.* **1.** *Electricity.* **a.** to connect or disconnect with a battery (a particular line or circuit on a telephone, etc.) by a switch; turn (an electric light, current, etc., on or off): *Switch off the lights before you go to bed.* **b.** to shift to another circuit. **2. a.** to move (a train, railroad car, etc.) from one track to another by a switch; shunt. **b.** to form (a train) by joining or removing cars; join or remove (cars). **3.** to turn, shift, or divert; change: *to switch the subject, to switch places. The Middle East's awakening nations . . . could switch the balance of world power* (Newsweek). **4.** (in bridge) to shift (suits) in bidding or play. **5.** to strike, hit, beat, or whip with or as with a switch. **6.** to swing or flourish like a switch; jerk suddenly; whisk: *The horse switched his tail to drive off the flies.*
—*v.i.* **1.** to shift from or as if from one railroad track to another. **2.** to change or shift in direction, suits in cards, etc.: *At contract he has the additional and highly important duty of raising the opener's bid as far towards a game or slam contract as his hand permits, and if he switches, of deciding whether to make a pre-emptive bid or not* (London Daily Telegraph). **3.** to strike a blow or blows with or as with a switch.
[probably < variant of Low German *swutsche*] —**switch′like′,** *adj.*

switch·back (swich′bak′), *n.* **1.** a section of a railroad or highway built in a zigzag course up a steep grade, as on the side of a mountain, by means of which the rate of climb of the roadbed is held within a tolerable range: *The trail began suddenly to rise in sharp switchbacks from the valley floor* (Paul Brooks). **2.** *Especially British.* a roller coaster. —*v.i.* to take a zigzag course: *For three miles, without either village or cottage, this narrow . . . byroad switchbacked up and down across the high ground* (Geoffrey Household).

switch·blade knife, or **switch·blade** (swich′blād′), *n.* a pocketknife with a blade that springs out at the push of a button or knob on the handle: *A large quantity of guns and switchblade knives were scooped up by police* (Birmingham News).

switch·board (swich′bôrd′, -bōrd′), *n.* a panel or group of panels containing the necessary switches, meters, and other devices for opening, closing, combining, controlling, measuring, and protecting a number of electric circuits. A telephone switchboard has plugs for connecting one line to another.

switch box, a box containing the parts of one or more electric switches.

switched-on (swicht′on′), *adj. Slang.* smart; alert; up-to-date; modern: *Preceding the actual bridal gown, it might appeal to a very switched-on bride-to-be* (New York Times).

switch engine, an engine used in railroad yards for moving and switching trains and railroad cars; switcher: *In Ogden, Utah, police . . . accused them of making off with a 116-ton Diesel heavy-duty switch engine* (Time).

switch·er (swich′ər), *n.* **1.** a person or thing that switches. **2.** *U.S.* a railroad engine used for switching cars, making up trains, etc., in a railroad yard: *The Atchison, Topeka and Santa Fe Railway ordered 25 . . . road switchers* (Wall Street Journal).

switch·er·oo (swich′ə rü′), *n. U.S. Slang.* a sudden, startling change, as in character, appearance, or action; sudden reversal: *As things seem to be moving toward a sordid triangle case, Charlotte Armstrong pulls her switcheroo* (Newsweek).

switch·gear (swich′gir′), *n.* the device operating switches in electric circuits.

switch-hit (swich′hit′), *v.i.*, **-hit, -hit·ting.** to bat either right-handed or left-handed; be a switch-hitter.

switch-hit·ter (swich′hit′ər), *n.* a baseball player who bats either right- or left-handed: *For a while Lloyd talked of baseball . . . how he'd practiced batting left-handed so he could be a switch-hitter like Mickey Mantle* (New York Times).

switch-hit·ting (swich′hit′ing), *n., adj.* hitting right-handed or left-handed; being a switch-hitter.

switch·man (swich′mən), *n., pl.* **-men. 1.** a man in charge of one or more railroad switches, as at a junction, siding, etc. **2.** a man who helps with the shifting of cars, the makeup of trains, etc., as at a sorting yard, freight terminal, etc.

switch·o·ver (swich′ō′vər), *n.* the act of switching or changing over (to); conversion: *Now that the campaign is over, the big problem is the switchover to a new administration* (Newsweek).

switch plant, *Botany.* a plant that bears slender green shoots or rodlike branches with small leaves or without leaves: *Leaves may be omitted altogether and the green food-*

making surface confined to modified stems, as in . . . such switch plants (Science News Letter).

switch plate, a plate for covering a switch box so that the lever, plug, or other switch protrudes.

switch·yard (swich′yärd′), *n.* a railroad yard where cars are switched from one track to another, put together to make trains, etc.; sorting yard.

swith (swith), *Archaic.* —*adv.* **1.** at a rapid rate; very quickly. **2.** instantly; immediately.
—*interj.* quick! hence! away! [Old English *swithe*]

swith·er (swiᴛʜ′ər), *v.i. Scottish.* to falter; hesitate. —*n.* **1.** a state of agitation or excitement; flurry or fluster: *The novelty of having women appear in pants suits has headwaiters across the country in a swither* (Time). **2.** *Scottish.* a state of perplexity or hesitation; doubt or uncertainty: [*He*] *stands some time in jumbled swither, to ride in this road, or that ither* (Allan Ramsay). [origin uncertain. Compare Old English *geswithrian* weaken.]

Switz., Switzerland.

Switz·er (swit′sər), *n.* a Swiss. [ultimately < Middle High German *Switzer,* or < Middle Dutch *Switser,* and *Swytzer* < *Switzen* Switzerland; (literally) the canton of Schwyz]

swiv·el (swiv′əl), *n., v.,* **-eled, -el·ing** or (*especially British*) **-elled, -el·ling.** —*n.* **1. a.** a simple fastening or coupling device that allows the thing fastened to turn freely upon it. **b.** (in a chain) a link having two parts, one of which turns freely in the other. **2.** a support on which a chair can revolve. **3. a.** the flexible support of a swivel gun, by which the weapon is permitted to be elevated, depressed, or to range to right or left. **b.** a gun that turns on such a support; swivel gun: *Mounted high up in the rigging, however, the ships had a few smaller guns, called swivels* (New Yorker).
—*v.i.* **1.** to turn (anything) on a swivel. **2.** to swing around; rotate; turn. —*v.t.* **1.** to turn on a swivel. **2.** to furnish with a swivel; fasten or support by means of a swivel: *Leitzel, as every circus familiar knows, performed on Roman rings and on a swivelled rope in the tent top* (New Yorker). **3.** to swing round; rotate; turn.
[Middle English *swivell,* related to Old English *swīfan* move in a course, sweep]

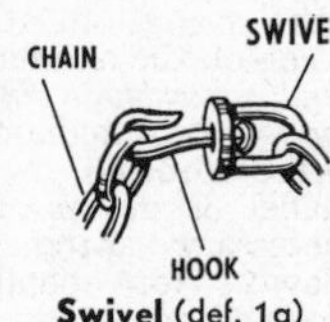

Swivel (def. 1a)
Hook turns freely in swivel.

swivel chair, a chair having a seat that turns on a swivel.

swivel gun, a gun, especially any of various relatively light pieces of artillery formerly used on land and at sea, having a barrel mounted on a swivel so that it can be turned in any direction.

swiv·el-hip (swiv′əl hip′), *v.i.,* **-hipped, -hip·ping.** to walk or move with a swinging motion of the hips: *"Garçon!" he cried, as a waiter swivel-hipped . . . down one of the aisles, holding his tray high overhead* (New Yorker).

swiv·et (swiv′it), *n. U.S. Slang.* great excitement; frenzy; stir; dither: *In Galveston, one Joe Grasso flew into a swivet over the fact that two Texas pelicans died recently in the London zoo* (Time). [origin uncertain]

swizz (swiz), *n. Slang.* a swindle; fraud: *Amanda said, in tones of desperation, "It's a swizz. Michael is never going to die"* (New Yorker). [origin uncertain]

swiz·zle (swiz′əl), *n., v.,* **-zled, -zling.** —*n.* **1.** a drink consisting of rum or other alcoholic liquor, crushed ice, bitters, sugar, and lemon or lime juice. **2.** any other mixed alcoholic drink.
—*v.t. Informal.* to drink habitually and to excess; swill.
[apparently variant of earlier *switchel*]

swizzle stick, a stick used for stirring swizzles or other alcoholic drinks: *Swizzle sticks coated with rock candy are a unique gadget for sweetening old fashioneds, collins drinks, tea or coffee* (New York Times).

swob (swob), *n., v.t.,* **swobbed, swob·bing.** swab.

swob·ber (swob′ər), *n.* swabber.

swol·len (swō′lən), *adj.* enlarged; bulging; swelled: *a swollen ankle. His swollen heart almost bursting* (Dickens). *Swollen mountain streams burst out of the woods like furious brown snakes, swallowing topsoil and drowning animals* (Time).
—*v.* a past participle of **swell:** *The controversy about bomb tests has swollen in the last three years into a torrent of words* (Eugene Rabinowitch).
—**Syn.** *adj.* puffy, tumid.

swollen shoot, a disease of cocoa trees caused by a virus carried by mealy bugs feeding on tree sap: *The swollen shoot virus disease of cocoa trees . . . has cut cocoa bean production by as much as three-fourths in some Gold Coast areas* (Science News Letter).

swoln (swōln), *adj. Archaic.* swollen.

swonk (swungk), *v. Archaic.* a past tense of **swink.**

swonk·en (swung′kən), *v. Archaic.* the past participle of **swink.**

swoon (swün), *v.i.* **1.** to faint: *She swoons at the sight of blood.* **2.** to fade or die away gradually. **3.** to go into a state of great joy; become thrilled with overwhelming delight; become enraptured: *Liszt is a wonderful man: the ladies have been swooning all over him and keeping the dregs from his tea in cologne bottles* (Edmund Wilson).
—*n.* **1.** a faint; syncope. **2.** *Obsolete.* a deep or sound sleep.
[Middle English *swonen,* ultimately < Old English *geswōgen* in a swoon] —**swoon′ing·ly,** *adv.*

swoop (swüp), *v.i.* **1.** to come down with a rush; descend in a sudden, swift attack: *One night the Indians swooped down on an unsuspecting village and burned it.* **2.** to make a rapid sweeping descent through the air, as a bird of prey, in order to seize, kill, destroy, etc.: *The flying death that swoops and stuns* (Dorothy Sayers). —*v.t.* **1.** to pounce upon and catch (up); snatch: *The nurse rushed into the blazing room and swooped the child up in her arms.* **2.** *Obsolete.* to sweep (up, away, off, etc.).
—*n.* a rapid downward rush; sudden, swift descent or attack: *With one swoop the hawk seized the chicken and flew away. Influenza came down upon me with a swoop* (Thomas H. Huxley).
in or **at one fell swoop,** in a single blow or stroke; in one sweeping act: *No longer are the governments, East or West, under any illusion that they can settle all the problems of the world in one fell swoop* (Wall Street Journal).
[apparently dialectal variant of obsolete *swope,* Old English *swāpan* to sweep] —**swoop′er,** *n.*

swoosh (swüsh), *Informal.* —*v.i.* to move very swiftly with a whirling, brushing sound: *Jet planes swooshed overhead* (New York Times). —*v.t.* to cause to swoosh: *to swoosh air through a tunnel. The propellers of the plane swooshed a gale.* —*n.* a swooshing movement or sound: *the shattering swoosh of jets flying past.*
[imitative]

swop (swop), *v.t., v.i.,* **swopped, swop·ping,** *n.* swap: *Stamps, with all the fun of albums and swopping, forgeries and watermarks . . .* (London Times). —**swop′per,** *n.*

sword (sôrd, sōrd), *n.* **1.** a weapon, usually metal, with a long, sharp blade fixed in a handle or hilt. **2.** something that wounds or kills; destroying agency: *He hath loosed the fateful lightning of His terrible swift sword* (Julia Ward Howe). *This avarice . . . hath been the sword of our slain kings* (Shakespeare). **3.** a symbol of power or authority, especially to judge and impose sentence.
be at swords' points, be in a hostile attitude; be avowed enemies: *They were at swords' points as a result of the election.*
cross swords, a. to fight: *Few men ventured to cross swords with him* (Scott). **b.** to quarrel; dispute: *They rarely met without crossing swords on one matter if not another* (Lynn Linton).
draw the sword, to begin a war: *He would not draw the sword against his king.*
measure swords, a. to fight with swords: *You . . . wanted to measure swords with Mohun, did you?* (Thackeray). **b.** to take part in a duel, battle, debate, etc.: *The senator has often measured swords with his colleagues on the issue of foreign relations.*
put to the sword, to kill or slaughter with or as if with the sword: *De Thermes . . . took the fortress of Broughty, and put the garrison to the sword* (David Hume).
sheathe the sword, to end a war: *The sword should not be sheathed till he had been brought to condign punishment as a traitor* (Macaulay).
the sword, a. war: *If I were young again, the sword should end it* (Shakespeare). **b.** military power: *. . . all they that take the sword shall perish with the sword* (Matthew 26:52). *The pen is mightier than the sword* (Edward G. Bulwer-Lytton). **c.** the army: *This influential portion was formed by . . . the sword, the . . . clergy, and the members of the parliaments* (John Austin).
[Old English *sweord*] —**sword′like′,** *adj.*
—**Syn. 1.** rapier, saber, blade, cutlass, scimitar.

sword arm, the arm, usually the right arm, with which the sword is wielded.

sword bayonet, a bayonet with a long, narrow blade able to be used as a sword in close combat, especially one of, or patterned on, those originally used in the French army.

sword·bear·er (sôrd′bãr′ər, sōrd′-), *n.* (formerly) the person by whom the sword of a great or noble warrior was cared for and carried when not in use.

sword·bill (sôrd′bil′, sōrd′-), *n.* a South American hummingbird with a slender bill longer than its body.

sword-billed hummingbird (sôrd′bild′, sōrd′-), swordbill.

sword cane, a weapon resembling a light cane or walking stick, but having a hollow core within which is a steel blade that may be drawn out or snapped out by a spring.

sword·craft (sôrd′kraft′, -kräft′; sōrd′-), *n.* **1.** the art of or skill in using the sword; swordsmanship. **2.** military power.

sword dance, any of various dances in which the performers go through certain motions with swords or dance among naked swords laid on the ground, etc.: *In Syria's Damascus the celebration was wilder. Bedouins whirled through the Arab sword dance* (Time).

sword dancer, a person who performs a sword dance.

sword dollar, a Scottish silver coin of the reign of James VI, with a sword on its reverse.

sword·ed (sôr′did, sōr′-), *adj.* armed with a sword.

sword fern, a tropical or subtropical fern with long, pinnate fronds.

sword·fight (sôrd′fīt′, sōrd′-), *n.* a combat or fight with swords: *. . . where with single swordfight they ended their quarrel, by dying both* (James Hayward).

sword·fish (sôrd′fish′, sōrd′-), *n., pl.* **-fish·es** or (*collectively*) **-fish.** a very large saltwater food fish with a long, swordlike projection from its upper jaw.

Atlantic Swordfish (about 7 ft. long)

sword·fish·ing (sôrd′fish′ing, sōrd′-), *n.* fishing for swordfish: *Swordfishing is the most popular way of spending the day* [*at Block Island*] (The Congregationalist).

sword grass, any of various plants with sword-shaped leaves, as the gladiolus and various grasses and sedges, and, sometimes, the iris.

sword knot, a looped strap, ribbon, or the like attached to the hilt of a sword, serving as a means of supporting it from the wrist or as an ornament.

sword·less (sôrd′lis, sōrd′-), *adj.* without a sword: *His hand fell upon his swordless belt* (William Morris).

sword lily, a gladiolus.

sword·man (sôrd′mən, sōrd′-), *n., pl.* **-men.** *Archaic.* a swordsman.

sword of Damocles, disaster that may occur at any moment (with allusion to the sword suspended by a thread over the head of Damocles): *In old age we live under the shadow of Death, which, like a sword of Damocles may descend at any moment* (Samuel Butler).

sword·play (sôrd′plā′, sōrd′-), *n.* the act, practice, or art of wielding a sword; fencing: *The large Stratford company . . . manage swordplay and panoplied pageantry with great facility* (Newsweek).

sword·play·er (sôrd′plā′ər, sōrd′-), *n.* a person skilled in swordplay; fencer.

swords·man (sôrdz′mən, sōrdz′-), *n., pl.* **-men. 1.** a person skilled in using a sword. **2.** a person using a sword in sport; fencer. **3.** a warrior; soldier.

swords·man·ship (sôrdz′mən ship, sōrdz′-), *n.* the art of a swordsman; skill in using a sword.

sword·stick (sôrd′stik′, sōrd′-), *n.* a sword cane: *His Grace carries a swordstick and you will hear it tapping on the parquet long before he comes into sight* (Punch).

sword swallower, a person who entertains by swallowing or pretending to swallow a sword: *He was traveling through the Balkans with a small circus, doubling as sword swallower and magician* (Time).

sword·tail (sôrd′tāl′, sōrd′-), *n.* any of a group of small tropical American freshwater fishes, the male of which has a long sword-shaped tail, frequently kept in aquariums.

sword-tailed (sôrd′tāld′, sōrd′-), *adj.* having a long and sharp tail or tail fin, as the horseshoe crab and other sea animals.

swore (swôr, swōr), *v.* a past tense of **swear:** *He swore to be a loyal American when he became a citizen.*

sworn (swôrn, swōrn), *v.* the past participle of **swear.** —*adj.* **1.** having taken an oath; bound by an oath. **2.** declared, promised, etc., with an oath: *We have his sworn statement.*

swot[1] (swot), *v.t.,* **swot·ted, swot·ting,** *n.* swat[1].

swot[2] (swot), *v.,* **swot·ted, swot·ting,** *n. British Slang.* —*v.i.* to work hard at one's studies: *He has swotted at his books since the age of eleven* (New Yorker).
—*n.* **1. a.** hard study at school or college: *For three years of sweat and swot I had imagined that my graduation day would be a solemn occasion* (Punch). **b.** labor; toil. **2.** a person who studies hard: *He mischievously incites . . . the innocent swot* (Observer). Also, **swat.**
[apparently Scottish variant of *sweat*]

swound (swound), *v.i., n. Archaic.* swoon; faint. [Middle English *swoune* swoon; the *-d* is a later addition]

'swounds (zwoundz, zoundz), *interj. Archaic.* a shortened form of *God's wounds,* used as an oath.

Swtz., Switzerland.

swum (swum), *v.* **1.** the past participle of **swim:** *He had never swum before.* **2.** *Archaic.* swam; a past tense of **swim.**

swung (swung), *v.* a past tense and past participle of **swing**[1]: *He swung his arms as he walked. The door had swung open.*

swy (swī), *n. Australian.* two-up. [alteration of German *zwei* two]

sy-, *prefix.* the form of **syn-** before *z* or before *s* plus a consonant, as in *syzygy, system.*

S.Y., steam yacht.

Syb·a·rite (sib′ə rīt), *n.* an inhabitant of Sybaris, an ancient Greek city of southern Italy, proverbial for its luxury. [< Latin *Sybarīta* < Greek *Sybarítēs*]

syb·a·rite (sib′ə rīt), *n.* a person who cares very much for luxury and pleasure; voluptuary: *Once the luxurious guest house . . . was a Mecca for starved sybarites from Baghdad* (London Times). [< *Sybarite*]

syb·a·rit·ic (sib′ə rit′ik), *adj.* characterized by or caring very much for luxury; voluptuous: *Meanwhile, the Egyptians mercilessly attack Saudi Arabia's rulers as corrupt and sybaritic* (Time). —**syb′a·rit′i·cal·ly,** *adv.*

Syb·a·rit·ic (sib′ə rit′ik), *adj.* of or having to do with Sybaris or its inhabitants. —**Syb′a·rit′i·cal·ly,** *adv.*

syb·a·rit·i·cal or **Syb·a·rit·i·cal** (sib′ə-rit′ə kəl), *adj.* sybaritic or Sybaritic.

syb·a·rit·ism (sib′ə rī tiz′əm), *n.* sybaritic life, practices, or luxury.

syc·a·mine (sik′ə min, -mīn), *n. Archaic.* a kind of mulberry tree. [< Latin *sycamīnus* mulberry tree < Greek *sykáminos* < Aramaic *shiqmin,* plural]

syc·a·more (sik′ə môr, -mōr), *n.* **1.** (in the United States) the buttonwood or any other plane tree. **2.** Also, **sycamore maple.** a large maple native to Europe and Asia, grown as a shady ornamental tree and for its wood. **3.** a fig tree grown in Egypt, Syria, etc., as a shade tree, with leaves somewhat resembling those of the mulberry, and bearing a sweetish edible fruit. [Middle English *sycomour* a fig tree < Old French *sichamor* < Latin *sȳcomorus* < Greek *sȳkómoros* < *sȳkon* fig + *móron* mulberry]

Sycamore Twig (def. 1)

sycamore fig, a fig tree of Egypt, Syria, etc.

sycamore maple, a variety of maple of Europe and western Asia with leaves similar to those of a sycamore, and a fine hard wood used in making furniture, violins, carvings, etc.

syce (sīs), *n. Anglo-Indian.* **1.** a servant who attends to horses; groom. **2.** an attendant who follows on foot a mounted horseman or a carriage. Also, **sais, sice.** [< Hindustani and Arabic *sā'is* servant; administrator < Arabic *sāsa* he managed]

sy·cee (sī sē′), *n.* fine uncoined silver in lumps of various sizes, usually stamped with a banker's or assayer's seal, formerly used in China as a medium of exchange. [< Cantonese *sai-si* fine silk (because, if pure, it may be drawn out into fine threads)]

sycee silver, sycee.

sych·no·car·pous (sik′nə kär′pəs), *adj. Botany.* capable of bearing fruit many times without perishing, as a tree. [< Greek *sychnós* many + *karpós* fruit + English *-ous*]

sy·co·ni·um (sī kō′nē əm), *n., pl.* **-ni·a** (-nē ə). *Botany.* a multiple fruit developed from numerous flowers embedded in a hollow fleshy receptacle, as in the fig. [< New Latin *syconium* < Greek *sȳkon* fig]

syc·o·phan·cy (sik′ə fən sē), *n., pl.* **-cies.** servile flattery; self-seeking flattery: *The people, like the despot, is pursued with adulation and sycophancy* (John Stuart Mill).

syc·o·phant (sik′ə fənt), *n.* a servile or self-seeking flatterer; toady; lickspittle: *Great men are likely to be surrounded by sycophants who want favors.* [< Latin *sȳcophanta* < Greek *sȳkophántēs* informer, slanderer; probably (originally) one who makes the insulting gesture of the "fig," that is, sticking the thumb between index and middle finger < *sȳkon* fig + *phaínein* to show]
—**Syn.** fawner, parasite.

syc·o·phan·tic (sik′ə fan′tik), *adj.* having to do with, characteristic of, or acting as a sycophant: *one man, surrounded by the constant incense of sycophantic adulation* (Wall Street Journal). —**syc′o·phan′ti·cal·ly,** *adv.*
—**Syn.** parasitical.

syc·o·phan·ti·cal (sik′ə fan′tə kəl), *adj.* sycophantic.

syc·o·phan·tish (sik′ə fan′tish), *adj.* like a sycophant; sycophantic. —**syc′o·phan′tish·ly,** *adv.*

sy·co·sis (sī kō′sis), *n.* an inflammatory disease of the hair follicles, especially of the beard, characterized by the eruption of crust-forming pimples; barber's itch. [earlier, an ulcer < New Latin *sycosis* < Greek *sýkōsis* < *sȳkon* fig (because of its similar shape) + *-ōsis* -osis]

Syd·en·ham's chorea (sid′ən əmz, -hamz), the ordinary, mild form of chorea; St. Vitus's dance.
[< Thomas *Sydenham,* 1624-1689, an English physician]

sy·e·nite (sī′ə nīt), *n.* a gray, crystalline, igneous rock composed of feldspar with certain other minerals, as hornblende. Also, **sienite.** [< Latin *Syēnītēs* (*lapis*) (stone) from *Syēnē* (modern Aswan), a city in Egypt]

sy·e·nit·ic (sī′ə nit′ik), *adj.* **1.** containing syenite. **2.** like syenite, or possessing some of its properties.

syke (sīk), *n. Scottish.* sike.

syl-, *prefix.* the form of **syn-** before *l,* as in *syllogism.*

syl., syllable.

syl·la·bar·i·um (sil′ə bãr′ē əm), *n., pl.* **-bar·i·a** (-bãr′ē ə). syllabary.

syl·la·bar·y (sil′ə ber′ē), *n., pl.* **-bar·ies.** a collection, set, system, list, or table of syllables, especially a list of symbols or characters each of which represents a syllable, used in writing certain languages.
[< New Latin *syllabarium* < Latin *syllaba* syllable]

syl·lab·ic (sə lab′ik), *adj.* **1.** of or having to do with syllables; consisting of syllables. **2.** *Phonetics.* forming a separate syllable by itself. The second *l* in *little* is syllabic. **3.** pronounced syllable by syllable; uttered with distinct separation of syllables. **4.** representing a syllable; consisting of signs representing syllables. **5.** *Prosody.* denoting versification based on the number of syllables in a line rather than on the arrangement of accents or quantities: *English metre, according to many theorists, is neither syllabic nor quantitative, but simply accentual* (Times Literary Supplement).
—*n. Phonetics.* a syllabic speech sound.
—**syl·lab′i·cal·ly,** *adv.*

syl·lab·i·cate (sə lab′ə kāt), *v.t.,* **-cat·ed, -cat·ing.** to form or divide into syllables; syllabify. [back formation < *syllabication*]

syl·lab·i·ca·tion (sə lab′ə kā′shən), *n.* division into syllables. [< Medieval Latin *syllabicatio, -onis,* ultimately < Latin *syllaba* syllable]

syl·lab·i·fi·ca·tion (sə lab′ə fə kā′shən), *n.* division into syllables: *What he said was unintelligible; but . . . the syllabification was distinct* (Edgar Allan Poe).

syl·lab·i·fy (sə lab′ə fī), *v.t.,* **-fied, -fy·ing.** to divide into syllables.

syl·la·bism (sil′ə biz əm), *n.* **1.** the use of syllabic characters. **2.** division into syllables. **3.** syllabic verse.

syl·la·bize (sil′ə bīz), *v.t.,* **-bized, -biz·ing.** **1.** to form or divide into syllables. **2.** to utter with careful distinction of syllables.

syl·la·ble (sil′ə bəl), *n., v.,* **-bled, -bling.** —*n.* **1.** a word or part of a word pronounced as a unit, usually consisting of a vowel alone or with one or more consonants. *A mer i can* and *Al a bam a* are words of four syllables. *Do, this,* and *stretch* are words of one syllable. **2.** a letter or group of characters representing a syllable in writing and printing. **3.** the slightest bit; word: *He promised not to breathe a syllable of the secret to anyone.*
—*v.t.* **1.** to pronounce in syllables; utter distinctly; articulate: *Airy tongues, that syllable men's names On sands and shores and desert wildernesses* (Milton). **2.** to represent by syllables.
—*v.i.* to utter syllables; speak.
[< Anglo-French *sillable,* variant of Old French *sillabe* < Latin *syllaba* < Greek *syllabḗ* (originally) a taking together < *syn-* together + *lab-,* stem of *lambánein* to take]

-syllabled, *combining form.* having —— syllable or syllables: *One-syllabled = having one syllable.*

syl·la·bub (sil′ə bub), *n.* sillabub.

syl·la·bus (sil′ə bəs), *n., pl.* **-bus·es, -bi** (-bī). **1.** a brief, often tabular, statement of the main points of a speech, a book, a course of study, etc. **2.** *Law.* a brief summary, at the beginning of the report of a case, of the rulings of a court on the legal points involved.
[< New Latin *syllabus* < Late Latin, misreading of Greek *síllybos* parchment label]
—**Syn. 1.** abstract, synopsis.

syl·lep·sis (sə lep′sis), *n., pl.* **-ses** (-sēz). *Grammar.* formal grammatical agreement with one word but not with another. *Example:* Neither he nor we are willing. [< Late Latin *syllēpsis* < Greek *sýllēpsis* < *syn-* together + *lêpsis* a taking < *lambánein* to take]

syl·lep·tic (sə lep′tik), *adj.* of, having to do with, or containing syllepsis. —**syl·lep′ti·cal·ly,** *adv.*

syl·lep·ti·cal (sə lep′tə kəl), *adj.* sylleptic.

syl·lo·gism (sil′ə jiz əm), *n.* **1.** a form of argument or reasoning expressed or claimed to be expressible in the form of two propositions (the major premise and the minor premise) containing a common term, and a third proposition (the conclusion) following necessarily from them. *Example:* All trees have roots; an oak is a tree; therefore, an oak has roots. **2.** reasoning or argumentations in this form; deduction. **3.** a specious or very subtle argument; deviously crafty piece of reasoning. [< Latin *syllogismus* < Greek *syllogismós* (originally) inference, conclusion < *syllogízesthai* reckon up < *syn-* together + *logízesthai* to reckon, count < *lógos* a reckoning]

syl·lo·gis·tic (sil′ə jis′tik), *adj.* of, having to do with, of the nature of, or consisting of a syllogism or syllogisms; using syllogisms: *Dottie follows a logical, syllogistic construction; she is more of a technician and a scientist* (Time).
—*n.* syllogistic reasoning; branch of logic dealing with syllogisms. —**syl′lo·gis′ti·cal·ly,** *adv.*

syl·lo·gis·ti·cal (sil′ə jis′tə kəl), *adj.* syllogistic.

syl·lo·gis·tics (sil′ə jis′tiks), *n.* syllogistic.

syl·lo·gi·za·tion (sil′ə jə zā′shən), *n.* a reasoning by syllogisms.

syl·lo·gize (sil′ə jīz), *v.i., v.t.*, **-gized, -giz·ing. 1.** to argue or reason by syllogisms. **2.** to deduce by syllogism: *those who, as Dante says, syllogize hateful truths* (Lowell). —**syl′lo·giz′er,** *n.*

sylph (silf), *n.* **1.** a slender, graceful girl or woman. **2.** any of the beings, typically slender and graceful, supposed by Paracelsus to exist as the elemental denizens of the air, having mortality but lacking souls.
[< New Latin *sylphes,* plural (coined by Paracelsus)]

sylph·id (sil′fid), *n.* a little or young sylph. [< French *sylphide* < *sylphe* sylph < New Latin *sylphes* sylphs]

sylph·id·ine (sil′fə din, -dīn), *adj.* like a sylphid. [< *sylphid* + *-ine*[1]]

sylph·like (silf′līk′), *adj.* like a sylph; slender and graceful; willowy: *I prefer to think that Ethel was not as sylphlike as she thinks, that it was me who was on the cornstalk side* (Tallulah Bankhead).

syl·va (sil′və), *n., pl.* **-vas, -vae** (-vē). silva.

syl·van (sil′vən), *adj.* **1. a.** of or having to do with a wood or forest: *They lived in a sylvan retreat.* **b.** rural; rustic: *sylvan historian* (Keats). **2.** consisting of or formed by woods or trees: *a sylvan scene, a sylvan glade.* **3.** abounding in woods or trees; wooded; woody: *a sylvan region.*
—*n.* **1.** a denizen of the woods; sylvan being. **2.** a person living or working in a woodland region; forester. **3.** a rustic. Also, **silvan.**
[< Latin *sylvānus,* variant of *silvānus* < *silva* forest, grove]
—**Syn.** *adj.* **3.** woodsy.

Syl·van·er (sil vä′nər), *n.* **1.** an aromatic white wine made in the Rhine region and in California. **2.** the grape from which this wine is made. [< German *Sylvaner* < Latin *sylvānus* sylvan]

syl·van·ite (sil′və nīt), *n.* a telluride of gold and silver, occurring in crystals or masses of gray, white, or yellow, with metallic luster. [< *(Tran)sylvania,* a region in Rumania, where it is found + *-ite*[1]]

syl·vat·ic (sil vat′ik), *adj.* **1.** of, belonging to, or found in woods; sylvan: *sylvatic animals, sylvatic trees.* **2.** of, carried by, or transmitted by woodland or jungle animals or insects, as rodents, monkeys, mosquitoes, etc.: *Sylvatic plague is comparable to typhus, [and] relapsing fever . . . which smolder silently and often unnoticed in their reservoir hosts, only flaring into epidemics when they come in contact with vectors that habitually or frequently bite human beings* (Asa C. Chandler). [< Latin *silvāticus* < *silva* forest]

syl·ves·tral (sil ves′trəl), *adj.* belonging to or growing in woods. [< Latin *sylvestris,* or *silvestris* + English *-al*[1]]

syl·vics (sil′viks), *n.* silvics.

syl·vi·cul·tur·al (sil′və kul′chər əl), *adj.* silvicultural.

syl·vi·cul·ture (sil′və kul′chər), *n.* silviculture.

syl·vi·cul·tur·ist (sil′və kul′chər ist), *n.* silviculturist.

syl·vin or **syl·vine** (sil′vin), *n.* sylvite. [< French *sylvine* < New Latin *sal digestivus sylvii;* see SYLVITE]

syl·vi·nite (sil′və nīt), *n.* sylvite.

syl·vite (sil′vīt), *n.* a mineral, potassium chloride, occurring in white or colorless cubes or octahedrons. It is an important source of potassium. *Formula:* KCl [abstracted < New Latin *sal digestivus sylvii* (literally) digestive salt of *Sylvius* (probably François de la Boe *Sylvius,* 1614-1672, a Flemish anatomist) + English *-ite*[1]]

sym-, *prefix.* the form of **syn-** before *b, m,* or *p,* as in *symbol, symmetry, sympathy.*

sym., 1. symbol. 2. *Chemistry.* symmetrical. 3. symphony.

sym·bi·ont (sim′bī ont, -bē-), *n. Biology.* an organism that lives in a state of symbiosis: *Instead of depending on its symbiont only for support, it also takes water and practically all of its food from it* (Fred W. Emerson). [< Greek *symbiôn, -ountos,* present participle of *symbioûn* live together; see SYMBIOSIS]

sym·bi·o·sis (sim′bī ō′sis, -bē-), *n. Biology.* **1.** the association or living together of two unlike organisms (usually two plants, or an animal and a plant) for the benefit of each other, as distinguished from *parasitism,* in which one organism feeds on the body of the other. The lichen, which is composed of an alga and a fungus, is an example of symbiosis; the alga provides the food, and the fungus provides water and protection. *Symbiosis covers those associations where neither is harmed, and one or both benefit* (David Park). **2.** any association of two unlike organisms, as in commensalism or parasitism. [< New Latin *symbiosis* < Greek *symbíōsis* < *symbioûn* live together < *sýmbios* (one) living together (with another); partner < *syn-* together + *bios* life]

sym·bi·ot·ic (sim′bī ot′ik, -bē-), *adj.* having to do with symbiosis; living in symbiosis. —**sym′bi·ot′i·cal·ly,** *adv.*

sym·bi·ot·i·cal (sim′bī ot′ə kəl, -bē-), *adj.* symbiotic.

sym·bol (sim′bəl), *n., v.,* **-boled, -bol·ing** or (*especially British*) **-bolled, -bol·ling.** —*n.* **1.** something that stands for or represents an idea, quality, condition, or other abstraction: *The lion is the symbol of courage; the lamb, of meekness; the olive branch, of peace; the cross, of Christianity . . . Metaphysical myths . . . the symbols of vital beliefs* (Jacques Maritain). *We are symbols and inhabit symbols* (Emerson). *All civilizations have been generated, and are perpetuated, only by the use of symbols* (Beals and Hoijer). *The V sign is the symbol of the unconquerable will of the occupied territories . . .* (Sir Winston Churchill). **2.** a letter, figure, or sign conventionally standing for some object, process, etc., as the figures denoting the signs of the zodiac, or the letters and other characters denoting chemical elements or mathematical quantities, operations, etc.: *The marks* +, −, ×, *and* ÷ *are symbols for add, subtract, multiply, and divide. A symbol not only stands for the name of the element, but it also signifies one atom of that element* (Parks and Steinbach). **3.** *Psychoanalysis.* an object, gesture, action, etc., representing a repressed emotion or impulse: *We call . . . the dream-element itself a symbol of the unconscious dream-thought* (Sigmund Freud).
—*v.t.* to symbolize.
[< Latin *symbolum* < Greek *sýmbolon* token, mark, ticket < *syn-* together + *bállein* to throw]
—**Syn.** *n.* **1.** token. See **emblem.**

sym·bol·a·try (sim bol′ə trē), *n., pl.* **-tries.** symbololatry.

sym·bo·le·og·ra·phy or **sym·bo·lae·og·ra·phy** (sim′bə lē og′rə fē), *n.* the art of drawing up legal documents.
[< Greek *symbolaiographíā* < *symbolaiográphos* notary < *symbólaion* a contract (< *syn-* together + *bállein* to throw) + *-graphíā* -graphy]

sym·bol·ic (sim bol′ik), *adj.* **1.** used as a symbol: *A lily is symbolic of purity.* **2.** of a symbol; expressed by a symbol or set of symbols; using symbols: *Writing is a symbolic form of expression. As far as we know, man is the only animal capable of symbolic behavior* (Beals and Hoijer). **3.** consisting of, denoted by, or involving the use of written symbols: *Shorthand is a symbolic method of writing.* **4.** (in art and literature) having the characteristics of symbolism. **5.** *Semantics.* expressing a mere relation. —**sym·bol′i·cal·ly,** *adv.* —**sym·bol′i·cal·ness,** *n.* —**Syn.** *adj.* **1.** emblematic, representative.

sym·bol·i·cal (sim bol′ə kəl), *adj.* symbolic.

symbolical books, those books containing the fundamental doctrines, creeds, etc., of the several churches, as the Confession of Augsburg of the Lutherans.

symbolic logic, the most recently developed branch of formal logic, deriving from advanced mathematics, and utilizing the methods and symbols of mathematics as its principal tools of inquiry and definition; mathematical logic: *It is possible to translate this problem into the notation of symbolic logic and solve it by appropriate techniques* (Martin Gardner).

sym·bol·ics (sim bol′iks), *n.* the branch of theology that treats of the history and matter of Christian creeds and confessions of faith.

sym·bol·ise (sim′bə līz), *v.,* **-ised, -is·ing.** *Especially British.* symbolize: *They symbolise our essential loneliness and egolism* (Sunday Times).

sym·bol·ism (sim′bə liz əm), *n.* **1.** the use of symbols, or the giving of a symbolic character to objects or acts; the systematic use of symbols. **2.** an organized set or pattern of symbols; system of symbols: *The cross, the crown, the lamb, and the lily are parts of Christian symbolism. Symbolisms developed in the church to add impressiveness to the setting and liturgy* (Matthew Luckiesh). **3.** symbolic meaning or character: *Symbolism, then, is a second and independent factor in dream-distortion, existing side by side with the censorship* (Sigmund Freud). **4.** (in literature or art) the principles or practice of a symbolist or the symbolists: *Their sculpture and architecture glow with color . . . and full-dimensional symbolism* (Time).

sym·bol·ist (sim′bə list), *n.* **1.** a person who uses symbols or symbolism. **2.** any of a school of French and Belgian poets (including Verlaine, Mallarmé, and Maeterlinck) of the late 1800's, who sought to represent ideas and emotions by indirect suggestion, attaching a symbolic meaning to particular objects, words, etc., in a reaction against realism: *The symbols of the symbolist school are usually chosen arbitrarily by the poet to stand for special ideas of his own* (Edmund Wilson). **3.** a painter who aims at symbolizing ideas rather than representing the form or aspect of actual objects, especially one of a recent school of painters who use representations of objects and schemes of color to suggest ideas or states of mind. **4.** a person who has experience in the study or interpretation of symbols or symbolism. **5. a.** a person who uses or advocates the use of symbolism in religious ceremonies. **b.** a person who holds that the elements of the Eucharist are not transubstantiated but are mere symbols.
—*adj.* symbolistic: *Artistic creation, no matter how realistic, has always been and remains symbolist* (Leon Trotsky).

Sym·bol·ist (sim′bə list), *n.* **1.** a symbolist poet or artist: *The outstanding characteristic of the Symbolist movement lay in the fact that it evoked, rather than described; reflected, rather than stated* (Atlantic). **2.** a person who holds that the elements of the Eucharist are symbols.

sym·bol·is·tic (sim′bə lis′tik), *adj.* of or having to do with symbolism or symbolists. —**sym′bol·is′ti·cal·ly,** *adv.*

sym·bol·i·za·tion (sim′bə lə zā′shən), *n.* a representation by symbols; symbolizing: *The more intricate and variable is the situation we wish to describe the more dependent we become upon mathematical systems of symbolization* (George Simpson).

sym·bol·ize (sim′bə līz), *v.,* **-ized, -iz·ing.** —*v.t.* **1.** to be a symbol of; stand for; represent: *A dove symbolizes peace.* **2.** to represent by a symbol or symbols: *to symbolize a nation by its flag.* **3.** to make into or treat as a symbol; regard as symbolic or emblematic.
—*v.i.* to use symbols: *Men symbolize, that is, bestow meanings upon physical phenomena, in almost every aspect of their daily lives* (Beals and Hoijer). —**sym′bol·iz′er,** *n.*

sym·bo·log·i·cal (sim bə loj′ə kəl), *adj.* of or having to do with symbology.

sym·bol·o·gist (sim bol′ə jist), *n.* a person who is versed in symbology; symbolist.

sym·bol·o·gy (sim bol′ə jē), *n.* **1.** the science or study of symbols. **2.** the use of symbols; symbolism: *one not unfamiliar with cartoon symbology* (Carl Rose). [< New Latin *symbologia* < Greek *sýmbolon* (see SYMBOL) + New Latin *-logia* -logy]

sym·bol·ol·a·try (sim′bə lol′ə trē), *n., pl.* **-tries.** worship of or excessive reverence for symbols. [< *symbol* + *-latry,* as in *idolatry*]

sym·bo·lo·pho·bi·a (sim′bə lō fō′bē ə), *n.* an abnormal fear of having one's actions interpreted symbolically.

sym·me·tal·lic (sim′mə tal′ik), *adj.* of or having to do with symmetallism.

sym·met·al·lism or **sym·met·al·ism** (sim met′ə liz əm), *n.* a proposed monetary system in which the standard metal is a combination of two or more precious metals in a fixed proportion, usually a gold-silver alloy: *The arrangement that there should be a joint demand for gold and silver money might, perhaps be called symmetallism, to distinguish it from the arrangement that there should be a composite supply which is called bimetallism* (F.Y. Edgeworth).

sym·met·ric (si met′rik), *adj.* symmetrical: *A symmetric flower is one in which the parts of each whorl are of the same number, or multiples of the same number, as the Lily or Rose* (Heber W. Youngken).

sym·met·ri·cal (si met′rə kəl), *adj.* **1.** having symmetry; regular in form; well-proportioned: *symmetrical figures. . . . Symmetrical as an endless row of lead soldiers* (Newsweek). **2.** *Botany.* **a.** (of a flower) having the same number of parts (sepals, petals, stamens, and carpels) in each whorl; isomerous. **b.** (of a flower) divisible vertically into similar halves either by one plane only (bilaterally symmetrical or zygomorphic) or by two or more planes (radially symmetrical or actinomorphic). **3.** *Chemistry.* **a.** having a structural formula characterized by symmetry. **b.** denoting a derivative of benzene in which hydrogen atoms occupying positions one, three, and five have been replaced. **4.** *Logic, Mathematics.* (of propositions, equations, etc.) so constituted that the value or truth is not changed by interchanging the terms. **5.** *Medicine.* (of a disease) affecting corresponding organs or parts at the same time, as both arms or both lungs or both ears equally. —**sym·met′ri·cal·ly,** *adv.* —**sym·met′ri·cal·ness,** *n.* —**Syn. 1.** balanced.

sym·me·trist (sim′ə trist), *n.* a person who studies or favors symmetry.

sym·me·tri·za·tion (sim′ə trə zā′shən), *n.* the act or process of symmetrizing.

sym·me·trize (sim′ə trīz), *v.t.,* **-trized, -triz·ing.** to make symmetrical; reduce to symmetry.

sym·me·try (sim′ə trē), *n., pl.* **-tries. 1.** a regular, balanced arrangement on opposite sides of a line or plane (bilateral), or around a center or axis (radial): *A swollen cheek spoiled the symmetry of his face. Its asymmetry was deliberate, for the Japanese believe that symmetry stunts the imagination* (Atlantic). **2.** pleasing proportions between the parts of a whole; well-balanced arrangement of parts; harmony: *In a scale passage . . . you have symmetry of timing—whether the notes follow each other at even intervals or not* (Time). **3.** *Botany.* agreement in number of parts among the cycles of organs that compose a flower.
[< Latin *symmetria* < Greek *symmetríā* < *sýmmetros* symmetrical < *syn-* together + *métron* a measure]

Symmetry (def. 1) Top, bilateral; bottom, radial

sym·pa·thec·to·my (sim′pə thek′tə mē), *n., pl.* **-mies.** the surgical removal of a section of a sympathetic nerve: *A nerve-cutting operation called sympathectomy helps many with early cases of severe high blood pressure* (Science News Letter). [< *sympathe*(tic) + Greek *ektomḗ* a cutting out]

sym·pa·thet·ic (sim′pə thet′ik), *adj.* **1.** having or showing kind feelings toward others; sympathizing: *an unselfish and sympathetic friend; an unusually tender and sympathetic audience* (Dickens); *a look of sympathetic concern* (Fanny Burney). **2.** approving; agreeing: *The teacher was sympathetic to the class's plan for a trip to the museum. When the third volume of Das Kapital came out, even economists sympathetic to Marx expressed disillusion and disappointment* (Edmund Wilson). **3.** enjoying the same things and getting along well together. **4.** *Anatomy, Physiology.* **a.** of or having to do with the part of the autonomic nervous system that produces involuntary responses opposite to those produced by the parasympathetic nervous system, as increasing the rate of the heartbeat and slowing down the activity of glands and digestive and reproductive organs. It consists of two groups of ganglia connected by nerve cords, one on either side of the spinal column. **b.** of or having to do with the entire autonomic nervous system. **5.** *Physics.* **a.** (of sounds) produced by responsive vibrations induced in one body by transmission of vibrations of the same period through the air or other medium from another: *The phenomena of resonance are examples of sympathetic sound.* **b.** denoting a vibration induced in one body by transmission of vibrations of the same period from another. —**Syn. 1.** compassionate, commiserating, tender. **3.** harmonious, congenial.

sym·pa·thet·i·cal·ly (sim′pə thet′ə klē), *adv.* in a sympathetic manner; with sympathy: *If one cannot be sure one knows enough to advise, it still is possible to listen . . . sympathetically* (Harper's).

sympathetic ink, any of certain colorless liquid compositions used as ink. The writing done remains invisible until the color is developed by the application of heat or some chemical reagent.

sympathetic magic, contagious magic.

sympathetic ophthalmia, inflammation in one eye due to lesion or other injury to the other eye: *Eye wounds are particularly dangerous because of "sympathetic ophthalmia," a complication in the good eye that usually results in complete blindness, unless the injured eye is removed at once* (New York Times).

sympathetic strike, sympathy strike.

sym·pa·thin (sim′pə thin), *n.* a substance released at the endings of the sympathetic nerves that has an effect on the body similar to that produced by epinephrine.

sym·pa·thique (saN pà tēk′), *adj. French.* likable and pleasant; agreeable; congenial: *He looked smaller somehow than he had been on my last visit, and for that reason, perhaps, more sympathique* (Atlantic).

sym·pa·thise (sim′pə thīz), *v.i.,* **-thised, -this·ing.** *Especially British.* sympathize: *It is tempting to sympathise with his spirited defense of Djilas* (Manchester Guardian).

sym·pa·thize (sim′pə thīz), *v.i.,* **-thized, -thiz·ing. 1.** to feel or show sympathy: *to sympathize with a child who has hurt himself.* **2.** to share in or agree with a feeling or opinion: *My mother sympathizes with my plan to be a doctor.* **3.** to enjoy the same things and get along well together. **4.** to respond sympathetically to some influence or to some disorder of the body.
[< French *sympathiser* < *sympathie* sympathy, learned borrowing from Latin *sympathīa;* see SYMPATHY] —**sym′pa·thiz′ing·ly,** *adv.*
—**Syn. 1.** condole, commiserate.

sym·pa·thiz·er (sim′pə thī′zər), *n.* a person who sympathizes with another; person who feels sympathy: *The issue of whether he was a "sympathizer," a "promoter" or a "follower" of communism involved forbidden inquiry into a man's beliefs* (New York Times).

sym·pa·tho·mi·met·ic (sim′pə thō′mi·met′ik, -mī-), *adj.* that imitates or mimics the action of the sympathetic nervous system: *At present the medical profession is using drugs called "sympathomimetic amines" to treat depression* (Wall Street Journal).

sym·pa·thy (sim′pə thē), *n., pl.* **-thies. 1.** a sharing of another's sorrow or trouble: *We feel sympathy for a person who is ill. Sympathy . . . enables one to put himself in the place of his fellows and to understand them* (Emory S. Bogardus). *The dedicated doctor knows that sympathy and understanding are just as important as scientific knowledge* (New York Times). **2.** agreement in feeling; condition or fact of having the same feeling: *The sympathy between the twins was so great that they smiled or cried at the same things.* **3.** agreement; approval; favor: *He is in sympathy with my plan.* **4. a.** an affinity between certain things, whereby they are similarly or correspondingly affected by the same influence. **b.** an action or response induced by such a relationship. **c.** *Physiology.* a relation between parts or organs such that a disorder or any condition in one produces an effect, often a similar one, on the other. **d.** *Physics.* a relation between two vibratile bodies such that when one is thrown into vibration it transmits its vibration to the other through air or some other medium.
[< Latin *sympathīa* < Greek *sympátheia,* or *sympathḗs* having a fellow feeling < *syn-* together + *páthos* a feeling] —**Syn. 1.** compassion, commiseration. See **pity. 2.** harmony, affinity.

sympathy strike, a strike by workers, not to enforce demands on their own employer, but to help or give moral support to workers on strike against another employer or other employers.

sym·pat·ric (sim pat′rik), *adj.* of or having to do with sympatry; being native to the same region.

sym·pa·try (sim′pə trē), *n.* the existence of plant or animal species in the same area without hybridization through interbreeding.
[< Greek *syn-* together + *pátrā* fatherland, native country + English *-y*[3]]

sym·pel·mous (sim pel′məs), *adj.* (of birds) having the two deep flexor tendons of the toes blended into one before dividing to proceed to the digits. Also, **synpelmous.** [< *sym-* + Greek *pélma* sole of the foot + English *-ous*]

sym·pet·al·ous (sim pet′ə ləs), *adj. Botany.* gamopetalous. Also, **synpetalous.**

sym·phi·lism (sim′fə liz əm), *n.* symphily.

sym·phi·lous (sim′fə ləs), *adj.* of or having to do with symphily.

sym·phi·ly (sim′fə lē), *n.* the occurrence in ant or termite colonies of guest insects which establish a mutually beneficial relation with their hosts; friendly commensalism. [< Greek *symphilía* mutual friendship < *syn-* + *philía* friendship]

sym·pho·nette (sim′fə net′), *n.* **1.** an orchestra similar to a symphony orchestra but having fewer members and playing less elaborate compositions. **2.** a musical composition similar to a symphony but shorter and usually less elaborate: *Morton Gould's Latin-American symphonette is in keeping with the festive mood of the rest of the record* (Atlantic).

sym·phon·ic (sim fon′ik), *adj.* **1.** *Music.* of, having to do with, or having the form or character of a symphony: *Massine, using it frankly as theatre music, made it into a setting for a "symphonic" ballet* (Winthrop Sargeant). **2.** of or having to do with symphony or harmony of sounds; similar in sound: *Nature's symphonic world drowned by man's industrial cacophony.* —**sym·phon′i·cal·ly,** *adv.*

symphonic poem, an orchestral composition similar in character and dimensions to a symphony but freer in form and usually consisting of only one movement. It is a musical description of some story, series of images, or program, poetic in nature, upon which its form depends, often employing leitmotifs to represent each character, sentiment, etc.

sym·pho·ni·ous (sim fō′nē əs), *adj.* harmonious. —**sym·pho′ni·ous·ly,** *adv.*

sym·pho·nist (sim′fə nist), *n.* a composer of symphonies: *The European symphonists have their American counterparts in Harris, Piston and William Schuman* (New York Times).

sym·pho·nize (sim′fə nīz), *v.i.,* **-nized, -niz·ing.** to agree; harmonize.

sym·pho·ny (sim′fə nē), *n., pl.* **-nies. 1.** *Music.* **a.** an elaborate musical composition for an orchestra. It usually has three or four movements in different tempos but related keys. **b.** an instrumental passage in a vocal composition or between movements in an oratorio, etc. **c.** (formerly) sinfonia. **2.** harmony of sound. **3.** harmony of colors: *In autumn the woods are a symphony in red, brown, and yellow.* **4.** anything having a harmonious combination of elements: *What I had experienced was a symphony of the wilderness* (William O. Douglas). [Middle English *symphanye* any of various instruments; harmony < Latin *symphōnia* < Greek *symphōníā* harmony; a concert; orchestra < *sýmphōnos* harmonious < *syn-* together + *phōnḗ* voice, sound] —**Syn. 2.** concord, consonance.

symphony orchestra, a large orchestra suitable for playing symphonies, and having a large string section: *These selections are all thrilling brand-new performances played by world-famous symphony orchestras* (Time).

sym·phys·i·al or **sym·phys·e·al** (sim·fiz′ē əl), *adj.* of, having to do with, situated at, or forming a symphysis.

sym·phy·sis (sim′fə sis), *n., pl.* **-ses** (-sēz). **1.** *Anatomy.* **a.** the union of two bones originally separate, either by the fusion of the bony substance or by intervening cartilage, especially of two similar bones on opposite sides of the body in the median line, as that of the pubic bones or of the two halves of the lower jawbone. **b.** the part or line of junction thus formed. **c.** an articulation in which bones are united by cartilage without a synovial membrane. **d.** a union, line of junction, etc., of other parts either originally or normally separate. **2.** *Botany.* a fusion or coalescence of parts of a plant normally distinct.
[< Greek *sýmphysis* a natural growing together or articulation (especially, of bones) < *symphýein* to unite < *syn-* together + *phýein* grow]

sym·pi·e·som·e·ter (sim′pē ə som′ə tər), *n.* **1.** an instrument formerly used for measuring the pressure of a current of water. **2.** an early form of barometer in which the pressure of the atmosphere is balanced partly by a column of liquid and partly by the pressure of a confined gas above it. [< Greek *sympíesis* compression (< *sympiézein* to compress < *syn-* together + *piézein* to press) + English *-meter*]

sym·plec·tic (sim plek′tik), *adj.* of or having to do with a bone of the lower jaw or mandibular arch of fishes interposed between others.
—*n.* the symplectic bone.
[< Greek *symplektikós* twining together < *symplékein* to twine together < *syn-* together + *plékein* to twine, weave]

sym·po·di·al (sim pō′dē əl), *adj.* having to do with, of the nature of, or producing a sympodium.

sym·po·di·um (sim pō′dē əm), *n., pl.* **-di·a** (-dē ə). *Botany.* an axis or stem that imitates a simple stem, but is made up of the bases of a number of axes that arise successively as branches one from another, as in the grapevine.
[< New Latin *sympodium* < *syn-* syn- + Greek *poús, podós* foot]

sym·po·si·ac (sim pō′zē ak), *adj.* of, suitable for, or like a symposium. —*n.* **1.** a symposiac meeting, or the conversation at it. **2.** an account of such a meeting or conversation. [< Late Latin *symposiacus* < Greek *symposiakós* < *sympósion;* see SYMPOSIUM]

sym·po·si·arch (sim pō′zē ärk), *n.* **1.** the master or director of an ancient symposium. **2.** a toastmaster. [< Greek *symposíarchos* < *sympósion* (see SYMPOSIUM) + *árchein* to rule]

sym·po·si·ast (sim pō′zē ast), *n.* a person who takes part in a symposium or social affair. [< *symposi*(um) + *-ast,* as in *enthusiast*]

sym·po·si·as·tic (sim pō′zē as′tik), *adj.* symposiac.

sym·po·si·um (sim pō′zē əm), *n., pl.* **-si·ums, -si·a** (-zē ə). **1.** a collection of opinions delivered, or a series of articles contributed, by a number of persons on some subject: *This magazine contains a symposium on sports.* **2.** a meeting or conference for the discussion of some subject: *a symposium on American foreign policy. Our next problem . . . is setting up seminars and symposia to digest all the data* (Newsweek). **3. a.** a convivial meeting for drinking, conversation, and intellectual entertainment among the ancient Greeks. **b.** any convivial meeting, dinner, etc., considered as resembling this.
[< Latin *symposium* < Greek *sympósion* < *syn-* together + *pósis* a drinking < *pínein* to drink]

symp·tom (simp′təm), *n.* **1.** a sign; indication: *Fever is a symptom of illness. Quaking knees and paleness are symptoms of fear.* **2.** a noticeable change in the normal working of the body that indicates or accompanies disease, sickness, etc.: *The doctor made his diagnosis after studying the patient's symptoms.*
[< Late Latin *symptōma, -atis* < Greek *sýmptōma, -atos* a happening, accident, disease < *sympíptein* to befall < *syn-* together + *píptein* to fall]
—Syn. **1.** token, mark.

symp·to·mat·ic (simp′tə mat′ik), *adj.* **1.** being a sign; signifying; indicative: *Riots are symptomatic of political or social unrest. The present tendency of scientists to emphasize uncertainty is symptomatic of the times* (Bulletin of Atomic Scientists). **2. a.** indicating or accompanying a disease, etc.: *The infection caused a symptomatic fever. Headaches are sometimes symptomatic.* **b.** relating to or concerned with symptoms of disease, etc.: *symptomatic treatment.* —**symp′to·mat′i·cal·ly,** *adv.*

symp·to·mat·i·cal (simp′tə mat′ə kəl), *adj. Obsolete.* symptomatic.

symp·to·mat·o·log·i·cal (simp′tə mat′ə-loj′ə kəl), *adj.* of or having to do with symptomatology. —**symp′to·mat′o·log′i·cal·ly,** *adv.*

symp·tom·a·tol·o·gy (simp′tə mə tol′ə-jē), *n.* the branch of medicine dealing with symptoms; semeiology. [< New Latin *symptomatologia* < Greek *sýmptōma, -atos* (see SYMPTOM) + *-logíā* -logy]

symptom complex, symptom group.

symptom group, a group of symptoms frequently occurring together, and constituting a syndrome.

symp·tom·ize (simp′tə mīz), *v.t.,* **-ized, -iz·ing. 1.** to be a symptom of: *The condition . . . could also symptomize other ailments, such as kidney block* (New York Times). **2.** to characterize or indicate as a symptom: *Demoniacal possession . . . was symptomized by superhuman manifestations* (James Tait).

symp·tom·less (simp′təm lis), *adj.* **1.** without symptoms. **2.** not attended with the usual symptoms, as a disease: *A symptomless attack [of polio] early in life confers lifetime immunity* (New York Times).

symp·tom·ol·o·gy (simp′tə mol′ə jē), *n.* symptomatology.

syn-, *prefix.* with; together; jointly; at the same time; alike, as in *synagogue, synchronize, syndrome, synonym, synoptic.* Also: **sy-** before *z* and before *s* plus a consonant; **syl-** before *l;* **sym-** before *b, m,* or *p.* [< Greek *sýn* together, with]

syn., 1. synonym. **2.** synonymous. **3.** synonymy.

syn·ac·tic (si nak′tik), *adj.* working together; cooperating; synergetic. [< Greek *synaktikós* able to bring together < *synágein;* see SYNAGOGUE]

syn·aer·e·sis (si ner′ə sis), *n.* **1.** contraction, especially of two vowels, into a diphthong or simple vowel. **2.** *Chemistry.* the loss of liquid and resulting contraction of a gel or clot. **3.** *Grammar, Prosody.* synizesis. Also, **syneresis.**
[< Greek *synaíresis* (literally) contraction, drawing together < *synaireîn* to contract, take as one < *syn-* together + *haireîn* to take]

syn·aes·the·sia (sin′es thē′zhə), *n.* synesthesia.

syn·a·gog (sin′ə gôg, -gog), *n.* synagogue.

syn·a·gog·al (sin′ə gôg′əl, -gog′-), *adj.* synagogical.

syn·a·gog·i·cal (sin′ə goj′ə kəl), *adj.* having to do with or relating to a synagogue.

syn·a·gogue (sin′ə gôg, -gog), *n.* **1.** a building or place of meeting for Jewish worship and religious instruction; temple. **2.** an assembly of Jews for religious instruction and worship apart from the Temple services, constituting, since the destruction of the Temple (70 A.D.), the sole form of Jewish public worship. **3.** the Jewish religion.
[< Latin *synagōga* < Greek *synagōgḗ* (literally) assembly < *synágein* to assemble < *syn-* together + *ágein* bring]

syn·a·loe·pha or **syn·a·le·pha** (sin′ə lē′-fə), *n.* the contraction or coalescence of two syllables into one, especially of two vowels at the end of one word and the beginning of the next.
[< Latin *synaloepha* < Greek *synaloiphḗ,* variant of *synaliphḗ* a coalescing < *synaleíphein* coalesce, gloss over; (literally) smear or melt together < *syn-* together + *aleíphein* anoint]

syn·a·loe·phe or **syn·a·le·phe** (sin′ə lē′-fē), *n.* synaloepha.

Syn·a·non (sin′ə non), *n.* a private association of former drug addicts organized for mutual help and rehabilitation. [< *syn-* together + *anon*(ymous)]

syn·an·ther·ous (si nan′thər əs), *adj. Botany.* characterized by stamens that are coalescent by means of their anthers, as a composite plant. [< *syn-* + *anther* + *-ous*]

syn·an·thous (si nan′thəs), *adj. Botany.* **1.** characterized by the abnormal union of two or more flowers. **2.** having flowers and leaves that appear at the same time.
[< *syn-* + Greek *ánthos* flower + English *-ous*]

syn·an·thy (si nan′thē), *n. Botany.* the abnormal union of two or more flowers.
[< *syn-* + Greek *ánthos* flower + English *-y*[3]]

syn·apse (si naps′, sin′aps), *n., v.,* **-apsed, -aps·ing.** *Physiology.* —*n.* the place where a nerve impulse passes from the axon (process carrying impulses away) of one nerve cell to the dendrite (process carrying impulses in) of another: *Changes at the synapse are thought to be involved in the learning process* (S.A. Barnett).
—*v.i.* to form a synapse: *An inhibitory neuron acts to inhibit all cells with which any of its terminals synapse* (Scientific American).
[< Greek *sýnapsis* conjunction < *synáptein* to clasp < *syn-* together + *háptein* to fasten]

syn·ap·sis (si nap′sis), *n., pl.* **-ses** (-sēz). **1.** *Biology.* the union of paternal and maternal paired (homologous) chromosomes, the first step in meiosis. **2.** *Physiology.* synapse.
[< New Latin *synapsis* < Greek *sýnapsis;* see SYNAPSE]

syn·ap·te (si nap′tē), *n., pl.* **-tai** (-tī). a litany in the Greek Orthodox Church. [< Greek *synaptḗ,* feminine of *synaptós* joined together < *synáptein* to clasp, join together; see SYNAPSE]

syn·ap·tic (si nap′tik), *adj.* having to do with a synapsis or synapse: *Any one neuron may have as many as a thousand synaptic connexions* (Science News). —**syn·ap′ti·cal·ly,** *adv.*

syn·ap·tol·o·gy (sin′ap tol′ə jē), *n.* the study of synapses.

syn·ar·chy (sin′är kē), *n., pl.* **-chies.** joint rule or sovereignty. [< Greek *synarchíā* < *synárchein* to rule jointly with < *syn-* together + *árchein* to rule]

syn·ar·thro·di·a (sin′är thrō′dē ə), *n., pl.* **-di·ae** (-dē ē). synarthrosis. [< New Latin *synarthrodia* < Greek *syn-* together + *arthrōdíā* kind of jointing with slightly concave or convex surfaces < *árthron* a joint]

syn·ar·thro·di·al (sin′är thrō′dē əl), *adj. Anatomy.* having to do with or of the nature of a synarthrosis. —**syn′ar·thro′di·al·ly,** *adv.*

syn·ar·thro·sis (sin′är thrō′sis), *n., pl.* **-ses** (-sēz). *Anatomy.* a kind of articulation admitting of no movement, as in the sockets of the teeth.
[< New Latin *synarthrosis* < Greek *synárthrōsis* immovable articulation < *syn-* together, completely + *árthrōsis* a jointing < *árthron* joint]

syn·ax·is (si nak′sis), *n., pl.* **syn·ax·es** (si-nak′sēz). in the early Church, an assembly for public worship, especially for the Eucharist. [< Late Latin *synaxis* < Late Greek *sýnaxis* a gathering < *synágein* to bring together < *syn-* together + *ágein* to drive, lead]

sync (singk), *n. U.S. Slang.* synchronization of sound and action or of speech and lip movement, as in a television or motion picture.
in sync, synchronized: *When you line up the three . . . then you're in sync* (Harper's).
out of sync, not synchronized: *You're coming in weak and out of sync . . .* (Charles Fowler).

syn·carp (sin′kärp), *n. Botany.* **1.** an aggregate fruit. **2.** a multiple fruit. [< New Latin *syncarpium* < Greek *syn-* together + *karpós* fruit]

syn·car·pous (sin kär′pəs), *adj. Botany.* **1.** of or having the character of a syncarp. **2.** consisting of united or coherent carpels.

syn·car·py (sin′kär pē), *n. Botany.* **1.** the state of having united carpels. **2.** the abnormal union or fusion of two or more fruits.

syn·cat·e·gor·e·mat·ic (sin kat′ə gôr′ə-mat′ik, -gor′-), *adj. Logic.* (of a word) that cannot be used by itself as a term, but must be connected with another word or words, as *all, some,* or *it.*

syn·cer·e·bral (sin ser′ə brəl, -sə rē′brəl), *adj.* of, having to do with, or constituting a syncerebrum.

syn·cer·e·brum (sin ser′ə brəm), *n., pl.* **-brums, -bra** (-brə). the compound brain of an insect. [< New Latin *syncerebrum* < *syn-* + Latin *cerebrum* brain]

syn·chon·dro·si·al (sing′kon drō′sē əl), *adj.* of or having to do with synchondrosis.

syn·chon·dro·sis (sing′kon drō′sis), *n., pl.* **-ses** (-sēz). *Anatomy.* **1.** an articulation in which the bones are so fused by intervening cartilage that the joint has little or no motion. **2.** symphysis.
[< New Latin *synchondrosis* < *syn-* together + Greek *chóndros* lump, cartilage + New Latin *-osis* -osis]

syn·chro (sing′krō), *n., pl.* **-chros,** *adj.* —*n.* **1.** a synchro unit. **2.** flash synchronization. —*adj.* working by or using synchronization: *a synchro mechanism, generator, or motor.* [short for *synchronization*]

syn·chro·cy·clo·tron (sing′krō sī′klə-tron, -sik′lə-), *n. Physics.* a kind of cyclotron to accelerate electrified particles by changing the frequency of the alternating electric field: *A . . . synchro-cyclotron discovered that high-energy proton beams are strongly polarized after being scattered from a hydrogen target* (Scientific American).

syn·chro·flash (sing′krə flash′), *adj. Photography.* using or having an attachment by means of which the shutter of the camera is released at the moment a flash bulb is set off: *a synchroflash camera.*

syn·chro·mesh (sing′krə mesh), *n.* a device in an automobile transmission to regulate the speed of gears so that they can mesh without shock or grinding: *There is no synchromesh on first gear, but it is hardly ever necessary to change to that gear* (London Times).
—*adj.* **1.** having synchromesh: *a synchromesh transmission.* **2.** of, having to do with, or utilizing synchromesh transmission: *synchromesh action, shifting, etc.*

syn·chro·nal (sing′krə nəl), *adj.* synchronous.

syn·chro·ne·i·ty (sing′krə nē′ə tē), *n.* synchronism.

syn·chron·ic (sin kron′ik, sing-), *adj.* **1.** dealing with a subject or event only as it occurs at a given stage, without reference to anything but its own characteristics: *A man may surely make a rational and satisfying synchronic or descriptive study of a language now or for any time in the past, but, if that study is to remain one hundred per cent synchronic, he must at no point ask or state the reason why, for that will ineluctably bring in diachronic or historical factors* (Simeon Potter). **2.** synchronous. —**syn·chron′i·cal·ly,** *adv.*

syn·chron·i·cal (sin kron′ə kəl, sing-), *adj.* synchronic.

syn·chro·nic·i·ty (sing′krə nis′ə tē), *n., pl.* **-ties.** synchronism.

syn·chro·nise (sing′krə nīz), *v.,* **-nised, -nis·ing.** *Especially British.* synchronize: [*His*] *arrival in America today has been so beautifully synchronised with the Russians' space rocket success* (Sunday Times).

syn·chro·nism (sing′krə niz əm), *n.* **1.** occurrence at the same time; agreement in point of time: *Human thought . . . is a complex of relationships that must come out of the knowledge of certain specific facts and synchronisms* (Atlantic). **2.** the arrangement of historical events or persons according to their dates, as in a history: *The laws of synchronism . . . bring strange partners together, and we may pass at once from Luther to Ariosto* (Henry Hallam). **3.** *Physics.* the state of being synchronous.

syn·chro·nis·tic (sing′krə nis′tik), *adj.* having to do with or exhibiting synchronism; synchronous.

syn·chro·nis·ti·cal (sing′krə nis′tə kəl), *adj.* synchronistic.

syn·chro·ni·za·tion (sing′krə nə zā′shən), *n.* **1.** the process or act of making synchronous (used especially of clocks). **2.** the occurrence of events at the same time.

syn·chro·nize (sing′krə nīz), *v.,* **-nized, -niz·ing.** —*v.i.* **1.** to occur at the same time; agree in time. **2.** to move or take place at the same rate and exactly together. —*v.t.* **1.** to make agree in time; cause to go at the same rate: *to synchronize all the clocks in a building* **2.** to assign to the same time or period. **3. a.** to make (dialogue and other sounds) coincide with the action in the preparation of a motion picture. **b.** to make sound and action coincide in (a sound motion picture): *A synchronized picture differs from a true talkie in that the scenes are first taken silent and then accompaniment is added* (B. Brown).
[< Greek *synchronízein* < *sýnchronos;* see SYNCHRONOUS] —**syn′chro·niz′er,** *n.* —**Syn.** *v.i.* **1.** coincide.

syn·chro·nized shifting (sing′krə nīzd), a shifting of gears in a motor vehicle that includes a device that brings both of any pair of gears to the same speed just before meshing; synchromesh shifting.

syn·chron·o·scope (sin kron′ə skōp), *n. Electricity.* an instrument for determining the synchronism between two alternating-current machines.

syn·chro·nous (sing′krə nəs), *adj.* **1.** existing or happening at the same time; simultaneous. **2.** moving or taking place at the same rate and exactly together: *the synchronous movements of the two ballet dancers.* **3.** *Physics.* having coincident periods, or coincident periods and phases, as an alternating electric current: *a synchronous compensator for an open-air hydrogen-cooling installation in Italy* (New Yorker).
[< Late Latin *synchronus* (with English *-ous*) < Greek *sýnchronos* < *syn-* together + *chrónos* time] —**syn′chro·nous·ly,** *adv.* —**syn′chro·nous·ness,** *n.*
—**Syn. 1.** coincident, contemporaneous.

synchronous converter, *Electricity.* a synchronous machine for changing alternating current into direct current, or direct current into alternating current; rotary.

synchronous machine, *Electricity.* a dynamoelectric machine, either a generator, motor, or converter, that operates at a speed exactly proportional to the frequency of the current.

synchronous satellite, an artificial satellite whose movement is synchronous with that of the earth. It orbits the earth once every 24 hours, at an altitude of about 22,300 miles, and thus appears to be stationary.

synchronous speed, *Electricity.* a speed, proportional to the frequency of the supply current, at which an alternating-current machine must operate to produce an electromotive force at a specified frequency.

syn·chro·ny (sing′krə nē), *n.* coincidence in time; synchronism.

syn·chro·scope (sing′krə skōp), *n. Electricity.* an electromagnetic device for indicating the synchronism between two alternating-current machines, or two or more engines, as in aircraft. [< *synchro-*(nism) + *-scope*]

syn·chro·tron (sing′krə tron), *n. Physics.* a device in which electrified particles are accelerated to high speeds by means of a varying magnetic field and an alternating high-frequency electric field: *Synchrotrons accelerate particles by spinning them around a circular path* (Science News Letter). [< *synchro*(nous) + *-tron,* as in *electron*]

synchro unit, *Electricity.* an alternating-current motor for maintaining the rotational angle possessed by the electrically connected rotating element of a similar motor.

syn·clas·tic (sin klas′tik), *adj. Mathematics, Physics.* of or having to do with a surface, as that of a ball or egg, which is curved similarly (either convexly or concavely) in all directions. [< *syn-* alike + Greek *klastós* broken, taken as "bent" (< *klân* to break) + English *-ic*]

syn·cli·nal (sin klī′nəl, sing′klə-), *Geology.* —*adj.* **1. a.** sloping downward from opposite directions so as to form a trough or inverted arch. **b.** of or having to do with a syncline. **2.** inclined or sloping toward each other, or characterized by such inclination.
—*n.* a syncline.
[< Greek *synklînes* inclining together (< *synklînein* to lean, incline < *syn-* together + *klînein* to lean) + English *-al*[1]]

synclinal axis, *Geology.* the axis toward which the slopes of a syncline converge.

synclinal line, *Geology.* the line from which a syncline slopes.

syn·cline (sing′klīn), *n. Geology.* a downward or synclinal fold of rock.

Syncline

syn·cli·no·ri·um (sing′klī nôr′ē əm, -nōr′-), *n., pl.* **-no·ri·a** (-nôr′ē ə, -nōr′-), **-no·ri·ums.** *Geology.* a compound syncline, consisting of a series of subordinate synclines and anticlines, the whole formation having the general contour of an inverted arch. [< New Latin *synclinorium* < Greek *synklinein* (see SYNCLINAL) + *óros* mountain]

Syn·com (sing′kəm), *n. Trademark.* an active synchronous satellite; a communications satellite whose movement is synchronous with that of the earth: *The 150-pound Syncom was designed to relay radio and telephone conversations between North America and South Africa from a synchronous or 24-hour orbit* (Science News Letter). [< *syn*(chronous) + *com*(munications)]

syn·co·pal (sing′kə pəl), *adj. Medicine.* having to do with or marked by syncope.

syn·co·pate (sing′kə pāt), *v.t.,* **-pat·ed, -pat·ing. 1.** *Music.* **a.** to begin (a note) on an unaccented beat and hold it into an accented. **b.** to shift (accents) to regularly unaccented beats. **c.** to introduce syncopation into (a passage, etc.). **2.** to shorten (a word) by omitting one or more syllables or sounds in the middle, as in syncopating *Gloucester* to *Gloster.* [< Late Latin *syncopē* (see SYNCOPE) + English *-ate*[1]. Compare Late Latin *syncopāre* to faint, swoon.]

syn·co·pa·tion (sing′kə pā′shən), *n.* **1.** *Music.* **a.** a shifting or anticipating of the accent to a normally unaccented beat, produced as by beginning a note on a normally unaccented beat and holding it into a normally accented beat, by beginning a note between any two beats and holding it into the following beat, or by using accents (sforzandos) on normally unaccented beats. **b.** music marked by syncopation, as jazz or ragtime. **c.** a rhythm, dance step, etc., based upon syncopation. **2.** *Linguistics.* syncope: *The syncopation of words ending in "ary" and "ory" . . . is an Anglicism which never fails to delight the American ear* (Scientific American).

syn·co·pa·tor (sing′kə pā′tər), *n.* a member of a jazz band; person devoted to jazz.

syn·co·pe (sing′kə pē), *n.* **1.** *Linguistics.* a contraction of a word by omission of one or more syllables or sounds in the middle, as in *ne'er* for *never: Syncope is common in proper names: Bennett* (*Benedict*), *Dennis* (*Dionysus*), *Jerome* (*Hieronymus*) (Scientific American). **2.** *Medicine.* a temporary loss of consciousness caused by cerebral anemia; faint. [< Late Latin *syncopē* < Greek *synkopē* (originally) a cutting off, ultimately < *syn-* together, thoroughly + *kóptein* to cut]

syn·cop·ic (sin kop′ik), *adj.* syncopal.

syn·cop·tic (sin kop′tik), *adj.* syncopal.

syn·cret·ic (sin kret′ik), *adj.* of or having to do with syncretism; characterized by syncretism: *Toynbee's prophetic vision is essentially syncretic—a kind of spiritual Noah's ark carrying a specimen of every "higher religion"* (Time).

syn·cre·tism (sing′krə tiz əm), *n.* **1.** attempted union or reconciliation of diverse or opposite tenets or practices, especially in philosophy or religion. **2.** *Linguistics.* the merging or union of originally different inflectional categories, usually the result of phonetic change. **3.** a process in the growth of religions in which the religious doctrines, rituals, deities, etc., of one creed or belief are adopted, adapted, or identified with its own by another, which thus gains adherents from the first. **4.** the doctrines of the Lutheran, George Calixtus (1586-1656), and his followers, who aimed at harmonizing the Protestant sects and ultimately effecting the union of all Christian denominations.
[< New Latin *syncretismus* < Greek *synkrētismós* (< *synkrētízein* to combine, ally, apparently originally a union or federation of Cretan communities < *Krês, Krētós* Crete) + *-ismos* -ism]

syn·cre·tis·tic (sing′krə tis′tik), *adj.* of, having to do with, or characterized by syncretism: *syncretistic sects which combine elements of several religions, including Confucianism and Taoism* (Atlantic).

syn·cre·tis·ti·cal (sing′krə tis′tə kəl), *adj.* syncretistic.

syn·cre·tize (sing′krə tīz), *v.,* **-tized, -tiz·ing.** —*v.i.* to practice syncretism; attempt to combine different or opposing tenets or systems. —*v.t.* to treat in the way of syncretism; combine, as different systems, etc. [< New Latin *syncretizare* < Greek *synkrētízein;* see SYNCRETISM]

syn·cri·sis (sing′krə sis), *n. Obsolete.* a figure by which opposite things are compared. [< Late Latin *syncrisis* < Greek *sýnkrisis* < *synkrínein* to compound, compare < *syn-* syn- + *krínein* to separate]

syn·cy·tial (sin sish′əl, -sit′ē əl), *adj.* of or having to do with a syncytium.

syn·cy·ti·um (sin sish′ē əm, -sit′-), *n., pl.* **-cy·ti·a** (-sish′ē ə, -sit′-), *Biology.* **1.** a single cell containing several nuclei, formed either by fusion of a number of cells without fusion of the nuclei, or by division of the nucleus without division of the cell substance. **2.** a structure composed of such cells, as one forming the outermost fetal layer of the placenta. [< New Latin *syncytium* < Greek *syn-* syn- + *kýtos* anything hollow, cell]

syn·dac·tyl or **syn·dac·tyle** (sin dak′təl), *adj.* having some or all of the digits wholly or partly fused, as the hind feet of the kangaroo or the feet or certain birds. —*n.* a syndactyl animal. [< French *syndactyle* < Greek *syn-* together + *dáktylos* finger, toe]

syn·dac·tyl·ism (sin dak′tə liz əm), *n.* the condition of being syndactyl: *inherited syndactylism.*

syn·dac·ty·lous (sin dak′tə ləs), *adj.* syndactyl.

syn·dac·ty·ly (sin dak′tə lē), *n.* the condition of having fused or webbed digits.

syn·des·mo·sis (sin′des mō′sis), *n., pl.* **-ses** (-sēz). an articulation in which the bones are connected by ligaments, membranes, etc., other than those which enter into the composition of the joint. [< New Latin *syndesmosis* < Greek *sýndesmos* a fastening, bond, binding together (as of sinews) < *syndeîn;* see SYNDETIC]

syn·des·mot·ic (sin′des mot′ik), *adj.* bound together by a fascia, as two bones; of or having to do with syndesmosis.

syn·det (sin′det), *n.* a synthetic detergent: *Less agitation means less wear; and . . . a good soap of syndet and bluing cleaner, brighter clothes* (Tuscaloosa News).

syn·det·ic (sin det′ik), *adj.* serving to unite or connect; connective; copulative. [< Greek *syndetikós* < *syndeîn* connect, unite < *syn-* together + *deîn* bind. Compare DIADEM.] —**syn·det′i·cal·ly,** *adv.*

syn·det·i·cal (sin det′ə kəl), *adj.* syndetic.

syn·dic (sin′dik), *n.* **1.** a person appointed to manage the business affairs of a corporation, especially of any of various British or European universities designated by charter as corporate bodies. **2.** a government official, as the chief official of certain cities or other communities, especially in Europe. [< Middle French *syndic* chief representative or delegate, learned borrowing from Late Latin *syndicus* < Greek *sýndikos* public advocate < *syn-* together + *díkē* defendant's justice; judgment, right < *deiknýnai* bring to light, prove]

syn·di·cal (sin′də kəl), *adj.* **1.** of or having to do with a craft union. **2.** of or having to do with syndicalism; syndicalist: [*He*] *said that the syndical organization of the people fought for ideals and interests* (London Times). [< French *syndical* < Middle French *syndic;* see SYNDIC]

syn·di·cal·ism (sin′də kə liz′əm), *n.* **1.** a movement to put industry and government under the control of labor unions by means of the general strike, sabotage, and any of various other kinds of violence: *Syndicalism is an extreme form of socialism, which aims at a complete overthrow of society by violent means* (Emory S. Bogardus). **2.** the body of theory and doctrine underlying this movement, certain formal elements of which influenced Mussolini in his structural reorganization of Italian industry and government. [< French *syndicalisme,* ultimately < Middle French *syndic;* see SYNDIC]

syn·di·cal·ist (sin′də kə list), *n.* an adherent or advocate of syndicalism: *The syndicalist would have his syndicate, or unions, assume general control in society* (Emory S. Bogardus). —*adj.* syndical.

syn·di·cal·is·tic (sin′də kə lis′tik), *adj.* syndical: *There was nothing particularly syndicalistic about a request for a minimum wage* (London Daily News).

syn·di·cate (*n.* sin′də kit; *v.* sin′də kāt), *n., v.,* **-cat·ed, -cat·ing.** —*n.* **1. a.** a combination of persons or companies formed to carry out some commercial undertaking, especially one requiring a large capital investment, as the underwriting of an issue of securities. **b.** a combination of persons formed for the promotion or continuation of any enterprise. **2.** an agency that sells special articles, photographs, comic strips, etc., to a large number of newspapers or other periodicals for publication at the same time: *This syndicate supplies stories to a hundred newspapers.* **3.** a council or body of syndics. **4.** *U.S. Slang.* a group of criminals at the head of a city's or country's criminal activity: *Crime reporters in America have* [*been*] *referring to organized crime simply as "the mob" or "the syndicate"* (Canadian Saturday Night).

—*v.t.* **1.** to combine into a syndicate. **2.** to control or manage by a syndicate. **3.** to publish through a syndicate. —*v.i.* to unite in a syndicate.

[< French *syndicat* < Middle French *syndic* (see SYNDIC) + *-at* -ate[3]]

syn·di·ca·tion (sin′də kā′shən), *n.* a syndicating or being syndicated: *Red Smith became, statistically in terms of syndication, the number one sports writer in the country* (Harper's).

syn·di·ca·tor (sin′də kā′tər), *n.* a person who forms or is part of a syndicate: *Syndicators must also file annual reports, including profit and loss statements, with the office and all investors* (Wall Street Journal).

syn·drome (sin′drōm), *n.* a group of signs and symptoms considered together as characteristic of a particular disease: *In many cases of the rheumatoid syndrome the joint structures may be little or not at all involved* (Ralph Pemberton). [< New Latin *syndrome* < Greek *syndromḗ* concurrence of symptoms; concourse < *sýndromos* (literally) running together < *syn-* with + *drómos* course, related to *drameîn* to run]

syn·drom·ic (sin drom′ik), *adj.* of or having to do with a syndrome or syndromes.

syne (sīn), *adv., prep., conj. Scottish.* since. [contraction of *sithen*]

syn·ec·do·che (si nek′də kē), *n. Rhetoric.* a figure of speech by which a part is put for the whole, or the whole for a part, the special for the general, or the general for the special, or the like. *Examples:* a factory employing 500 *hands* (persons); to eat of the *tree* (its fruit); a *Solomon* (wise man); a *marble* (a statue) on its pedestal. [< Late Latin *synecdoche* < Greek *synekdochḗ* < *synekdéchesthai* supply a thought or word; take with (something else) < *syn-* with + *ex-* out + *déchesthai* to receive]

syn·ec·doch·ic (sin′ek dok′ik), *adj.* of the nature of or expressed by synecdoche. —**syn′ec·doch′i·cal·ly,** *adv.*

syn·ec·doch·i·cal (sin′ek dok′ə kəl), *adj.* synecdochic.

syn·ec·do·chism (si nek′də kiz′əm), *n.* **1.** synecdochic style; the use of synecdoche. **2.** the use in contagious magic of a part of an object or person as an equivalent of the whole object or person, so that anything done with the part is held to take effect upon the whole: *One or more pieces of the skull* (*for in synecdochism the piece carries the virtue of the whole*) *of the slain were used as amulets* (Report of the Bureau of American Ethnology).

syn·e·cious (si nē′shəs), *adj.* synoecious.

syn·e·col·o·gy (sin′ə kol′ə jē), *n.* the branch of ecology dealing with a species or group and its surroundings: *Synecology deals with plant communities, as related to soil, light, climate, and other environmental factors* (Heber W. Youngken). [< *syn-* together + *ecology*]

syn·ec·thry (sin′ek thrē), *n.* the occurrence in ant or termite colonies of insects to which the hosts are unfriendly but which remain in the colony as unwelcome guests; hostile commensalism. [< *syn-* + Greek *échthros* hostile + English *-y*[3]]

syn·ed·ri·al (si ned′rē əl), *adj.* of or having to do with the Sanhedrin.

syn·ed·ri·on (si ned′rē ən), *n., pl.* **-ri·a** (-rē ə). a Sanhedrin. [< Greek *synédrion;* see SANHEDRIN]

syn·er·e·sis (si ner′ə sis), *n.* synaeresis: *The losing of liquid by a gel is known as syneresis* (William N. Jones).

syn·er·get·ic (sin′ər jet′ik), *adj.* working together, as a group of muscles for the production of some movement; cooperating; synergistic; synergic. [< Greek *synergētikós* < *synergeîn* cooperate; see SYNERGY]

syn·er·gic (si nėr′jik), *adj.* synergetic.

syn·er·gism (sin′ər jiz əm, si nėr′-), *n.* **1.** a united action of different agents or organs, producing a greater effect than the sum of the various individual actions, as in a medicine composed of several drugs: *Synergism . . . has also been demonstrated in other phases of plant development* (New Scientist). **2.** *Theology.* the doctrine that the human will cooperates with divine grace in the work of regeneration. [< New Latin *synergismus* < Greek *synergeîn;* see SYNERGY]

syn·er·gist (sin′ər jist), *n.* **1.** a bodily organ or a medicine that cooperates with another or others. **2.** *Theology.* a person who holds the doctrine of synergism.

syn·er·gis·tic (sin′ər jis′tik), *adj.* **1.** of or having to do with synergism. **2.** (of an organ or a medicine) cooperating with another; acting as a synergist; synergetic: *The drugs have what is called a synergistic effect, which means they increase each other's effectiveness* (Wall Street Journal). **3.** yielding readily to the energy applied.

syn·er·gis·ti·cal (sin′ər jis′tə kəl), *adj.* synergistic. —**syn′er·gis′ti·cal·ly,** *adv.*

syn·er·gize (sin′ər jīz), *v.,* **-gized, -giz·ing.** *Medicine.* —*v.i.* to act as a synergist. —*v.t.* to cooperate with and enforce the activity of: *The catalyst synergizes chemical reaction.*

syn·er·gy (sin′ər jē), *n., pl.* **-gies.** a combined or correlated action, especially of a group of organs of the body, as nerve centers or muscles, or of two or more drugs or remedies. [< New Latin *synergia* < Greek *synergíā* < *synergós* working together < *synergeîn* work together, help in work < *syn-* together + *érgon* work]

syn·e·sis (sin′ə sis), *n. Grammar.* a construction according to sense, not strictly grammatical. [< Greek *sýnesis* sagacity; comprehension; (originally) quickness at putting together < *syn-* together + *hiénai* to send]

syn·es·the·sia (sin′es thē′zhə, -zhē ə), *n.* **1.** *Physiology.* a sensation in one part of the body produced by a stimulus applied to another part. **2.** *Psychology.* a phenomenon in which the stimulation of one sense produces a mental impression associated with a different sense, as color hearing, in which certain sounds are connected with certain colors: *As I tasted it, a tune came into my head* (*this association of two sensory memories is, I believe, called synesthesia*) (New Yorker). Also, **synaesthesia.**

syn·gam·ic (sin gam′ik), *adj.* having to do with syngamy.

syn·ga·mous (sing′gə məs), *adj.* syngamic.

syn·ga·my (sing′gə mē), *n. Biology.* the union of two cells, as of gametes in fertilization. [< *syn-* + *-gamy*]

syn·ge·ne·sious (sin′jə nē′shəs), *adj. Botany.* (of stamens) united by the anthers so as to form a ring or tube.

syn·gen·e·sis (sin jen′ə sis), *n. Biology.* the formation of the germ by fusion of the male and female elements, so that the substance of the embryo is derived from both parents; sexual reproduction. [< *syn-* + *genesis*]

syn·ge·net·ic (sin′jə net′ik), *adj. Biology.* reproduced by means of both parents; of or having to do with syngenesis.

syn·i·ze·sis (sin′ə zē′sis), *n.* **1.** *Linguistics.* the fusion of two syllables into one by the coalescence of two adjacent vowels (or of a vowel and a diphthong) without the formation of a recognized diphthong. **2.** *Biology.* the clustering of the nuclear chromatin before the maturation division. **3.** *Medicine.* closure of the pupil of the eye. [< Latin *synīzēsis* < Greek *synízēsis* (literally) collapsing < *synizánein* sink down < *syn-* together, completely + *hizánein* to seat oneself, settle down (causative) < *hízein* to sit]

syn·kar·y·on (sin kar′ē on), *n. Biology.* a nucleus produced by the fusion of two nuclei, as in fertilization. [< *syn-* + Greek *káryon* nut, taken as "nucleus"]

syn·ki·ne·sis (sin ki nē′sis), *n.* a reflex or involuntary synergetic movement, especially of muscles. [< New Latin *synkinesis* < *syn-* together + *kinesis* kinesis < Greek *kī́nesis* motion]

syn·ki·net·ic (sin ki net′ik), *adj.* of or having to do with synkinesis.

syn·od (sin′əd), *n.* **1.** an assembly of ecclesiastics or other church delegates called together under authority to discuss and decide church affairs; church council. **2.** a court of the Presbyterian Church ranking next above the presbytery. **3.** an assembly, convention, or council of any kind. [< Late Latin *synodus* < Greek *sýnodos* assembly, meeting, conjunction (of planets) < *syn-* together + *hodós* a going, a way] —**Syn. 3.** convocation, meeting.

syn·od·al (sin′ə dəl), *adj.* having to do with a synod.

syn·od·ic (si nod′ik), *adj.* synodical: *The synodic month is the interval between successive conjunctions of the moon and sun, from new moon to new moon again* (Robert H. Baker).

syn·od·i·cal (si nod′ə kəl), *adj.* **1.** having to do with the conjunction of two heavenly bodies, especially the revolution of a heavenly body with respect to the sun: *The synodical period of the moon is the time between one new moon and the next.* **2.** of, having to do with, or transacted in a synod. [(definition 1) < Late Greek *synodikós* < *sýnodos;* see SYNOD; (definition 2) < Late Latin *synodicus* < Late Greek; + English *-al*[1]] —**syn·od′i·cal·ly,** *adv.*

synodical month, the interval between one new moon and the next, about 29½ days; lunar month.

syn·oe·cious (si nē′shəs), *adj. Botany.* **1.** having male and female flowers in one head, as some composite plants. **2.** having male and female organs in the same receptacle, as some mosses. Also, **synecious.** [< *syn-* + *-ecious,* as in *diecious.* Compare Greek *synoikíā* community of persons living together.]

syn·oe·cism (si nē′siz əm), *n.* the uniting of several towns or villages into one city or community. [< Greek *synoikismós* < *synoikízein* to synoecize < *syn-* together + *oikízein* to found as a community < *oîkos* house]

syn·oe·cize (si nē′sīz), *v.t.,* **-cized, -ciz·ing.** to unite into a city or community. [< Greek *synoikízein,* see SYNOECISM]

syn·oi·cous (si noi′kəs), *adj.* synoecious.

syn·o·nym (sin′ə nim), *n.* **1.** a word having a meaning that is the same or nearly the same as that of another word in the same language. *Keen* is a synonym of *sharp: He needs all his wits about him as well, in quickly finding synonyms for words he can't pronounce* (London Times). *Abbr.:* syn. **2.** a word or expression generally accepted as another name for something; metonym: *George Washington's name has become a synonym for patriotic devotion to one's country. Many people are apt to think that public interest is a synonym for consumer interest* (London Times). **3.** *Biology.* a scientific name discarded as being incorrect or out of date. [< Latin *synōnymum* < Greek *synṓnymon,* (originally) noun use of neuter of *synṓnymos;* see SYNONYMOUS] —**Syn. 2.** equivalent.

syn·o·nym·ic (sin′ə nim′ik), *adj.* synonymous.

syn·o·nym·i·cal (sin′ə nim′ə kəl), *adj.* synonymous.

syn·o·nym·ics (sin ə nim′iks), *n.* the study of synonyms; synonymy.

syn·o·nym·i·ty (sin′ə nim′ə tē), *n.* the quality of being synonymous; synonymy.

syn·on·y·mize (si non′ə mīz), *v.t.,* **-mized, -miz·ing. 1.** to give the synonyms of. **2.** to furnish with lists of synonyms. **3.** to make synonymous.

syn·on·y·mous (si non′ə məs), *adj.* having the character of a synonym; having the same or nearly the same meaning: *Being good was . . . represented to me as synonymous with keeping silence* (Harriet Beecher Stowe). *Americans who can't afford to buy all the gadgets that have become synonymous with the American standard of living still are better off than people anywhere else in the world* (Newsweek). [< Medieval Latin *synonymus* (with English *-ous*) < Greek *synṓnymos* < *syn-* together + dialectal *ónyma* name] —**syn·on′y·mous·ly,** *adv.*

syn·on·y·my (si non′ə mē), *n., pl.* **-mies. 1.** being synonymous; equivalence in meaning. **2.** the study of synonyms. **3.** *Rhetoric.* the use or coupling of synonyms in discourse for emphasis or amplification. **4.** a list or analysis of synonyms. **5.** *Biology.* **a.** a list of the several different scientific names that have been applied to a species or other group by various describers or classifiers. **b.** such names collectively.

synop., synopsis.

syn·op·sis (si nop′sis), *n., pl.* **-ses** (-sēz). a brief statement giving a general view of a subject, book, play, etc.; summary: *Write a synopsis of "Treasure Island" in 200 words or less.* [< Late Latin *synopsis* < Greek *sýnopsis* a general view < *synorân* to see altogether, all at once < *syn-* together + *horân* to see, view] —**Syn.** digest.

syn·op·size (si nop′sīz), *v.t.,* **-sized, -siz·ing.** to make a synopsis of: *The opera was called "Vaiva," and before we went to hear it, we asked an Intourist woman to synopsize the action for us* (New Yorker).

syn·op·tic (si nop′tik), *adj.* **1.** (of a table, chart, etc.) furnishing a general view of some subject: *Nearly 20 agencies . . . combined their facilities to make a great synoptic oceanographic survey* (Science). **2.** (of a mental act or faculty, conduct, etc.) having to do with, involving, or taking a comprehensive view of something. **3.** Often, **Synoptic. a.** having an approximately parallel point of view: *Matthew, Mark, and Luke are called the Synoptic Gospels because they are much alike in contents, order, and statement.* **b.** of or having to do with the Synoptic Gospels. **4.** *Meteorology.* **a.** of or having to do with a chart showing meteorological data from simultaneous observations at many points: *Marks were allotted on a system based on synoptic data, height of cloud-top in relation to freezing level* (A.W. Haslett). **b.** of or having to do with the branch of meteorology that deals with the compilation or analysis of such data.
—*n.* one of the Synoptic Gospels or their authors; Matthew, Mark, or Luke.
[< New Latin *synopticus* < Greek *synoptikós* < *sýnopsis;* see SYNOPSIS]

syn·op·ti·cal (si nop′tə kəl), *adj.* synoptic.

syn·op·ti·cal·ly (si nop′tə klē), *adv.* in a synoptic manner; so as to give a general view.

Synoptic Gospels. See **synoptic,** *adj.* (def. 3) and *n.*

syn·op·tist (si nop′tist), *n.* any one of the writers of the Synoptic Gospels; Matthew, Mark, or Luke.

syn·os·te·o·sis (si nos′tē ō′sis), *n.* synostosis.

syn·os·to·sis (sin′os tō′sis), *n., pl.* **-ses** (-sēz). *Anatomy.* union by means of ossified cartilage or bone; ankylosis. [< New Latin *synostosis* < Greek *syn-* together + *ostéon* bone + New Latin *-osis* -osis]

syn·ou·si·acs (si nü′sē aks), *n.* the branch of knowledge that deals with societies. [< Greek *synousíā* society (< *synoûsa,* feminine, present participle of *syneînai* be with < *syn-* with + *eînai* be) + English -(i)*cs*]

syn·o·vi·a (si nō′vē ə), *n.* a viscid, clear, lubricating liquid secreted by certain membranes, as those lining the joints. [< New Latin *synovia* (coined by Paracelsus) various body fluids; gout]

syn·o·vi·al (si nō′vē əl), *adj.* consisting of, containing, or secreting synovia: *synovial fluid, membrane, or capsule. The ends of the bones are padded with cartilage at the joints and there is a lubricating liquid, the synovial fluid, that further reduces friction* (A.M. Winchester).

syn·o·vi·tis (sin′ə vī′tis), *n.* inflammation of a synovial membrane. [< *synov*(ia) + *-itis*]

syn·pel·mous (sin pel′məs), *adj.* sympelmous.

syn·pet·al·ous (sin pet′ə ləs), *adj.* gamopetalous.

syn·sep·al·ous (sin sep′ə ləs), *adj.* gamosepalous.

syn·sper·mous (sin spėr′məs), *adj.* characterized by synspermy.

syn·sper·my (sin spėr′mē), *n.* union or coalescence of two or more seeds.

syn·tac·tic (sin tak′tik), *adj.* syntactical: *The parts of speech, for example, in any new language under examination, should be determined either by their inflexions or, if completely uninflected, by their syntactic function* (Simeon Potter).

syn·tac·ti·cal (sin tak′tə kəl), *adj.* having to do with syntax; in accordance with the rules of syntax. —**syn·tac′ti·cal·ly,** *adv.*

syn·tac·tics (sin tak′tiks), *n.* **1.** the formal syntactical system or structure of a language without reference to meaning. **2.** the study of such a system or structure.

syn·tax (sin′taks), *n.* **1.** *Grammar.* **a.** the arrangement of words to form sentences, clauses, or phrases; sentence structure: *In syntax and vocabulary the message of the written record is unmistakable, and it exerts a tremendous effect upon the standard language* (Leonard Bloomfield). **b.** the patterns of such arrangement in a given language: *The team wants to analyze the syntax of one pair of languages (German and English) in terms of mathematical symbolism* (Newsweek). **c.** the use or function of a word, phrase, or clause in a sentence. **d.** the part of grammar dealing with the construction of phrases, clauses, and sentences: *The object in syntax is still to discover the relations between the parts of the expression* (Joshua Whatmough). **2.** *Obsolete.* an orderly or systematic arrangement of parts or elements; connected order or system of things: *Concerning the syntax and disposition of studies, that men may know in what order . . . to read* (Francis Bacon). [< Late Latin *syntaxis* < Greek *sýntaxis* < *syntássein* < *syn-* together + *tássein* arrange]

syn·tech·nic (sin tek′nik), *adj.* of or having to do with unrelated animals that resemble each other due to the influence of a similar environment.

syn·the·sis (sin′thə sis), *n., pl.* **-ses** (-sēz). **1. a.** the combination of elements or parts into a whole: *Synthesis analysis. . . . in the opinion of several competent critics the best synthesis of Baudelaire that had appeared in English* (London Times). **b.** the state of being put together thus. **c.** a body of things put together thus: *The happiest synthesis of the divine, the scholar and the gentleman* (Samuel Taylor Coleridge). **2.** the formation of a compound or a complex substance by the chemical union of its elements or by the combination of simpler compounds (applied especially to the production of organic compounds, as rubber, alcohol, and ammonia, formerly obtained by extraction from natural products): *A total synthesis implies that in theory a substance has been elaborated from its elements, in this case carbon, hydrogen and oxygen* (A.J. Birch). **3.** *Philosophy, Logic.* **a.** the combination or unification of particular phenomena, observed or hypothesized, into a general body or abstract whole. **b.** (as used by Immanuel Kant) the action of the understanding in combining and unifying the isolated data of sensation into a cognizable whole. **c.** (as used by Thomas Hobbes, Isaac Newton, and others) deductive reasoning. [< Latin *synthesis* a collection, set; the composition (of a medication) < Greek *sýnthesis* composition (logical, mathematical) < *syntithénai* to combine < *syn-* together + *tithénai* put, place. Compare THESIS.]

syn·the·sise (sin′thə sīz), *v.t.,* **-sised, -sis·ing.** *Especially British.* synthesize: *This approach attempts to synthesise for the pilot a near-realistic picture of the normally perceived world* (New Scientist).

syn·the·sist (sin′thə sist), *n.* a person who uses synthesis or a synthetic method.

syn·the·si·za·tion (sin′thə sə zā′shən), *n.* the act or process of synthesizing: *The . . . basic ingredients are human beings, which no doubt will always defy synthesization* (Wall Street Journal).

syn·the·size (sin′thə sīz), *v.,* **-sized, -siz·ing.** —*v.t.* **1.** to put together or combine into a complex whole. **2.** to make by combining parts or elements: *Gottlieb's . . . effort to synthesize antitoxin* (Sinclair Lewis). **3.** to produce or manufacture by (chemical) synthesis; treat synthetically: *to synthesize rubber.* —*v.i.* to come together or combine into a complex whole: *The other chain took eight days to synthesize and showed a final yield of 37 percent* (Scientific American).

syn·the·siz·er (sin′thə sī′zər), *n.* **1.** a person or thing that synthesizes: *Sir Winston Churchill is the great synthesizer of foreign affairs, a man of global vision and striking phrase* (New York Times). **2.** an electronic device that simulates and blends conventional and ultrasonic sounds: *The synthesizer . . . generates its own sound electronically and, at least in theory, can synthesize from five basic sound-elements any musical effect ever conceived, or imaginable in the future* (Harper's).

syn·thet·ic (sin thet′ik), *adj.* **1.** of, having to do with, consisting in, or involving synthesis: *synthetic chemistry.* **2.** of, having to do with, produced by, or involving chemical synthesis: *synthetic ingredients, synthetic rubber, synthetic diamonds. Synthetic vanillin is chemically indistinguishable from vanillin obtained from the bean* (New York Times). **3.** not real or genuine; artificial: *synthetic affection.* **4.** *Linguistics.* characterized by the use of inflectional endings rather than by the use of separate words, such as auxiliary verbs and prepositions. Latin is a synthetic language, whereas English is analytic. For example, the Latin *amabitur* expresses in one word the English *he will be loved.*
—*n.* a product made by chemical synthesis: *Goodyear used a synthetic called "Natsyn," the molecular duplicate of tree-grown latex* (Charles C. Cain).
[< New Latin *syntheticus* < Greek *synthetikós,* ultimately < *syntithénai;* see SYNTHESIS] —**syn·thet′i·cal·ly,** *adv.*
—**Syn.** *adj.* **2.** See **artificial.**

syn·thet·i·cal (sin thet′ə kəl), *adj.* synthetic.

synthetic fiber, any fiber developed by chemical processes from natural substances such as cellulose, petroleum, and coal: *Rayon, fiberglass, and nylon are well-known synthetic fibers. Some imaginative chemists began to experiment with synthetic fibers, and the non-wovens started to take on a new character* (Science News Letter).

synthetic geometry, Euclidean geometry.

syn·thet·i·cism (sin thet′ə siz əm), *n.* synthetic methods or procedure.

synthetic philosophy, the philosophy of Herbert Spencer, an English philosopher, so called by himself as bringing the various sciences into a systematic whole.

synthetic rubber, any rubberlike substance or elastomer developed by chemical processes chiefly from butadiene as a substitute for natural rubber, usually having special properties, such as resistance to heat, cold, age, and harmful chemicals: . . . *On the basis of usefulness, synthetic rubber is nearing the limits where it can seize a big new piece of the market* (Wall Street Journal).

syn·thet·ics (sin thet′iks), *n.* **1.** products made by chemical synthesis: *Today's synthetics are by and large either better than their natural counterparts or have no counterparts at all* (Newsweek). **2.** the field of science or industry dealing with the making of synthetic products: *Only recently did it [a firm] make a halfhearted attempt to get into synthetics* (Time).

syn·the·tism (sin′thə tiz əm), *n.* **1.** a synthetic system or doctrine. **2.** *Medicine.* the complete treatment of a fracture from its reduction to the removal of the splints and restoration of the function of the limb. **3.** (in art) symbolism.

syn·the·tist (sin′thə tist), *n.* a synthesist.

syn·the·tize (sin′thə tīz), *v.t.*, **-tized, -tiz·ing.** to synthesize.

syn·thet·o·graph (sin thet′ə graf, -gräf), *n.* a composite drawing, as from two or more specimens of a new species.

syn·ton·ic (sin ton′ik), *adj.* **1.** of or having to do with the tuning of a transmitter and receiver, so that the receiver responds only to the vibrations of the transmitter. **2.** of or having to do with resonance, especially of radio frequency. **3.** of or having to do with a personality responding emotionally to the environment readily and appropriately. [< *syn-* + Greek *tónos* tone + English *-ic*] —**syn·ton′i·cal·ly,** *adv.*

syn·ton·i·cal (sin ton′ə kəl), *adj.* syntonic.

syn·to·nism (sin′tə niz əm), *n.* syntony.

syn·to·ni·za·tion (sin′tə nə zā′shən), *n.* the act of making syntonic.

syn·to·nize (sin′tə nīz), *v.t.*, **-nized, -niz·ing.** to make syntonic. —**syn′to·niz′er,** *n.*

syn·to·ny (sin′tə nē), *n.* the condition of being syntonic. [< *synton*(ic) + *-y*[3]]

syn·u·ra (si nůr′ə, -nyůr′-), *n., pl.* **syn·u·rae** (si nůr′ē, -nyůr′-), **syn·u·ras.** a flagellate, fresh-water protozoan (sometimes classed as an alga), occurring in radially arranged, globose clusters in pools, swamp-waters, and sometimes in reservoirs; oil bug. The synura gives off an oily matter of cucumber-like or fishy flavor, which, though harmless, may make the water unpleasant for drinking. [< New Latin *Synura* the genus name < Greek *syn-* together + *ourā́* tail (because of its shape)]

syph (sif), *n. Slang.* syphilis.

sy·pher (sī′fər), *v.t.* to fit together the chamfered edges of (boards, etc.) in a joint so as to form one continuous surface. [variant of *cipher*, verb, in obsolete meaning of "to bevel"]

sypher joint, a joint in which the edges of the boards overlap so as to leave a plane surface.

syph·i·lide (sif′ə lid), *n.* a syphilitic skin eruption.

syph·i·lis (sif′ə lis), *n.* a contagious venereal disease, caused by a spirochete, and characterized first by a painless chancre (sore) at the point of invasion (primary syphilis), then by skin eruptions and sore throat (secondary syphilis), and finally severe lesions affecting the bones, brain, and spinal cord (tertiary syphilis); lues; pox. [< New Latin *syphilis*, apparently < *Syphilis, sive Morbus Gallicus*, the title of a poem by Girolamo Fracastoro, 1483-1553, an Italian physician and poet < *Syphilus*, the hero of the poem who is described as the first sufferer of the disease]

syph·i·lit·ic (sif′ə lit′ik), *adj.* **1.** of, having to do with, or caused by syphilis: *syphilitic lesions.* **2.** affected with syphilis; that is a syphilitic. —*n.* a person who has syphilis.

syph·i·loid (sif′ə loid), *adj.* characteristic of syphilis.

syph·i·lol·o·gist (sif′ə lol′ə jist), *n.* a specialist in syphilology.

syph·i·lol·o·gy (sif′ə lol′ə jē), *n.* the branch of medicine that deals with the diagnosis and treatment of syphilis.

syph·i·lous (sif′ə ləs), *adj.* syphilitic.

sy·phon (sī′fən), *n., v.t., v.i.* siphon.

syr., *Pharmacy.* syrup.

Syr., **1.** Syria. **2.** Syriac. **3.** Syrian.

Syr·a·cu·san (sir′ə kyü′sən, -zən), *adj.* **1.** of or belonging to Syracuse, a city in Sicily: *The Syracusan expedition was the deathblow of the Athenian Empire* (John Buchan). **2.** of or belonging to Syracuse, a city in central New York State. —*n.* **1.** a native or inhabitant of Syracuse, Sicily: *Dionysius . . . obliged the Syracusans to accept his tokens in place of silver coins* (William Stanley Jevons). **2.** a native or inhabitant of Syracuse, New York.

sy·ren (sī′rən), *n., adj.* siren.

Syr·ette (si ret′), *n. Trademark.* a collapsible hypodermic syringe with a hypodermic needle attached, holding one dose of a drug.

Syr·i·ac (sir′ē ak), *adj.* of or having to do with Syria or its language. —*n.* the ancient Semitic language of Syria, a dialect of Aramaic. *Abbr.:* Syr. [< Latin *Syriacus* < *Syriā* Syria]

Syr·i·an (sir′ē ən), *adj.* of or having to do with Syria, a country in southwestern Asia, or its people. —*n.* **1.** a native or inhabitant of Syria. **2.** Zyrian.

sy·rin·ga (sə ring′gə), *n.* **1.** any of a group of shrubs of the saxifrage family, especially a species that has fragrant, creamy-white flowers blooming in early summer, often cultivated as an ornamental shrub; mock orange. The blossom of one kind is the floral emblem of Idaho. **2.** any lilac. [< New Latin *Syringa* the mock orange (because of its use for pipe stems); later, the lilac genus < Greek *sŷrinx, -ingos* shepherd's pipe]

Syringa (def. 1) or mock orange

sy·ringe (sə rinj′, sir′inj), *n., v.*, **-ringed, -ring·ing.** —*n.* **1.** a device fitted with a piston or rubber bulb for drawing in a quantity of fluid and then forcing it out in a stream. Syringes are used for cleaning wounds, injecting fluids into the body, etc. **2.** a similar instrument used for various purposes, as exhausting or compressing air, squirting water over plants, etc. —*v.t.* to clean, wash, inject, etc., by means of a syringe. [Middle English *siryng*, and *searing* < Medieval Latin *sirynga* < Greek *sŷrinx, -ingos* shepherd's pipe; spelling and pronunciation influenced by Greek plural *sŷringes*]

sy·rin·ge·al (sə rin′jē əl), *adj.* of, having to do with, or connected with the syrinx in a bird or birds.

sy·rin·go·my·e·li·a (sə ring′gō mī ē′lē ə), *n.* a chronic disease characterized by the formation of abnormal tubular cavities in the central canal of the spinal cord. [< New Latin *syringomyelia* < Greek *sŷrinx, -ingos* shepherd's pipe + *myelós* marrow, taken as "spinal cord"]

syr·inx (sir′ingks), *n., pl.* **sy·rin·ges** (sə rin′jēz), **syr·inx·es. 1.** a Panpipe: *the syrinx, a set of pipes played by ancient shepherds* (Wall Street Journal). **2.** the Eustachian tube. **3.** the vocal organ of birds, situated where the trachea divides into the right and left bronchi. [< Latin *sȳrinx, -ingis* < Greek *sŷrinx, -ingos* shepherd's pipe. Related to SYRINGA, SYRINGE.]

syr·phi·an (sėr′fē ən), *n., adj.* syrphid.

syr·phid (sėr′fid), *n.* syrphus fly. —*adj.* of or having to do with syrphus flies. [< New Latin *Syrphidae* the family name < *Syrphus;* see SYRPHUS FLY]

syr·phus fly (sėr′fəs), any of a family of flies that feed on the nectar of flowers and often resemble bees, whose larvae live on decaying matter or plant lice. [< New Latin *Syrphus* the genus name < Greek *sŷrphos* gnat, some small insect]

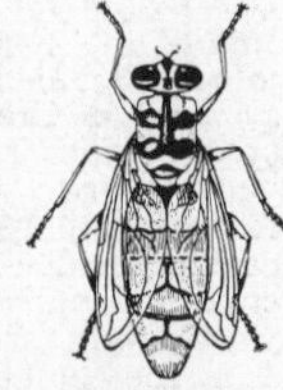
Syrphus Fly (actual size)

syr·tic (sėr′tik), *adj.* having to do with or resembling a syrtis or quicksand.

syr·tis (sėr′tis), *n., pl.* **-tes** (-tēz). *Archaic.* a quicksand: *Quencht in a boggy Syrtis, neither sea, Nor good dry land* (Milton). [< Latin *syrtis* < Greek *Sýrtis* (originally) either of two quicksands (Syrtis Major and Syrtis Minor) off the northern coast of Africa < *sýrein* to drag]

syr·up (sir′əp, sėr′-), *n.* **1.** sugar boiled in water or fruit juice: *cherries canned in syrup.* **2.** a solution of sugar in a medicated liquid: *cough syrup.* **3.** a sweet, thick liquid obtained in the manufacture of sugar, glucose, cornstarch, sorghum, etc., as molasses and corn syrup. Also, **sirup.** [Middle English *sirop* < Old French < Arabic *sharāb* a drink. Compare SHERBET, SHRUB[2].] —**syr′up·like′,** *adj.*

syr·up·y (sir′ə pē, sėr′-), *adj.* **1.** resembling or suggesting syrup in consistency or sweetness: *The solution of the acid . . . is a colorless syrupy liquid* (William H. Jones). **2.** having to do with syrup. Also, **sirupy.**

sys·sar·co·sis (sis′är kō′sis), *n. Obsolete.* the union of bones by means of intervening muscle. [< New Latin *syssarcosis* < Greek *syssárkōsis* < *syssarkóesthai* unite with flesh (< *syn-* + *sárx, sarkós* flesh) + New Latin *-osis* -osis]

syst., system.

sys·tal·tic (sis tal′tik), *adj.* **1.** of the nature of contraction; contracting. **2.** of or having to do with movement in which there is alternate contraction (systole) and dilatation (diastole): *the systaltic action of the heart.* [< Late Latin *systalticus* < Greek *systaltikós* depressing < *syn-* together + *staltikós* astringent < *stéllein* to send; place. Compare SYSTOLE.]

sys·tem (sis′təm), *n.* **1.** a set of things or parts forming a whole: *a mountain system, a railroad system. Title to most of the nation's gold is held by the Federal Reserve System, although the bulk of it is warehoused by the U.S. Treasury* (Wall Street Journal). **2.** an ordered group of facts, principles, beliefs etc.: *a system of government, a system of education. "Uncle Tom's Cabin" . . . presented . . . a succession of simple, poignant incidents inseparable from a system of slavery* (Sir Winston Churchill). **3.** a theory or hypothesis, especially of the arrangement and relationship of the heavenly bodies by which their observed movements and phenomena are explained: *the Copernican system.* **4.** a plan; scheme; method: *a system of classification, a system for betting.* **5.** an orderly way of getting things done: *to read or work without system.* **6.** a group of heavenly bodies forming a whole that obeys certain natural laws: *the solar system.* **7.** the world; universe. **8.** *Biology.* **a.** a set of organs or parts in an animal body of the same or similar structure, or subserving the same function: *the nervous system, the respiratory system. In all the more complex animals the systems are everywhere made up of unlike parts, each contributing a different portion of the general process* (A. Franklin Shull). **b.** the animal body as an organized whole; the organism in relation to its vital processes or functions: *to take food into the system. The living system is essentially an "open" thermodynamic system in which the cells are capable of exchanging energy with outside sources* (Atlantic). **c.** each of the primary groups of tissues or parts in the higher plants. **9.** *Geology.* a major division of rocks including two or more series, and formed during a geological period: *Heterogeneous systems are made up of matter in different states of aggregation* (Parks and Steinbach). *Major segments of the geologic column, which are deemed to have worldwide application, are known as systems* (Raymond C. Moore). **10.** *Chemistry.* **a.** a portion of matter made up of an assemblage of substances which are in, or tend to approach, equilibrium. A system is binary when it is made up of two substances, ternary if made up of three, etc. **b.** a substance, or an assemblage of substances, considered as a separate entity, isolated, at least in mind, for the purpose of restricted study: *Any system, such as a normal atom, containing equal numbers of protons and electrons, exhibits no net charge* (Sears and Zemansky).
[< Late Latin *systēma, -atis* musical interval (in Medieval Latin, the universe) < Greek *sýstēma, -atos* < *synistánai* bring together < *syn-* together + *histánai* stand, place] —**Syn. 4.** arrangement. **5.** organization.

sys·tem·at·ic (sis′tə mat′ik), *adj.* **1.** according to a system; having a system, method, or plan: *systematic work, a systematic investigation. During the time when systematic classification was beginning to develop there was on foot a movement to give precise names to plants* (Fred W. Emerson). **2.** orderly in arranging things or in getting them done: *a systematic person.* **3.** regularly organized, done, or carried on, especially for an evil purpose: *a systematic attack on another person's character.* **4. a.** of, following, or arranged according to a system of classification. **b.** taxonomic. **5.** of, arranged in, containing, or setting forth an orderly system: *The subject matter of all science is essentially the same: systematic observation and systematic presentation of the observations in communicable form* (F.H. George). —**Syn. 1, 2.** See **orderly.** —**Ant. 2.** unsystematic, unmethodical.

sys·tem·at·i·cal (sis′tə mat′ə kəl), *adj.* systematic.

sys·tem·at·i·cal·ly (sis′tə mat′ə klē), *adv.* with system; according to some plan or method.

sys·tem·at·ics (sis′tə mat′iks), *n.* the subject or study of systems, especially of classification: *There are a number of works on the morphology and systematics of many of these animals* (Science).

sys·tem·a·tise (sis′tə mə tīz), *v.t.,* **-tised, -tis·ing.** *Especially British.* systematize. —**sys′tem·a·tis′er,** *n.*

sys·tem·a·tism (sis′tə mə tiz′əm), *n.* systematizing.

sys·tem·a·tist (sis′tə mə tist), *n.* **1.** a person who constructs, or adheres to, a system. **2.** a naturalist who constructs or who is expert in systems of classification; taxonomist: *It has been said that John Ray . . . an Englishman, was the first true systematist* (A. Franklin Shull).

sys·tem·a·ti·za·tion (sis′tə mə tə zā′shən), *n.* the act or process of reducing or forming into a system; systematizing.

sys·tem·a·tize (sis′tə mə tīz), *v.t.,* **-tized, -tiz·ing.** to arrange according to a system; make into a system; make more systematic. —**sys′tem·a·tiz′er,** *n.* —**Syn.** organize, order.

sys·tem·a·tol·o·gy (sis′tə mə tol′ə jē), *n.* the science of systems or their formation.

sys·temed (sis′təmd), *adj.* made into a system; systematized: *Ere systemed suns were globed and lit The slaughters of the race were writ* (Thomas Hardy).

sys·tem·ic (sis tem′ik), *adj.* **1.** of or having to do with a system: *Systemic patterns are blocks or pieces of culture or language sharing a content that is of common origin and is arranged in a common pattern* (Alfred L. Kroeber). **2.** having to do with or affecting a particular system of parts or organs of the body, especially the nervous system: *systemic lesion. A systemic poison is absorbed into the plant itself, not merely sprayed on the outside* (Harper's). **3.** having to do with, supplying, or affecting the body as a whole: *systemic sensations. The circuit . . . from left ventricle through the body to right auricle is called the systemic circulation* (A. Franklin Shull). —*n.* a systemic insecticide.

sys·tem·i·cal·ly (sis tem′ə klē), *adv.* in a systemic manner; in or on the body as a whole.

systemic insecticide, an insecticide that a plant is able to absorb throughout its circulatory system without harm to itself: *These systemic insecticides are all compounds of phosphorus, and by preparing them from radioactive phosphorus the scientists are able to trace their course after they are sprayed onto plants* (Science News Letter).

sys·tem·ist (sis′tə mist), *n.* systematist.

sys·tem·i·za·tion (sis′tə mə zā′shən), *n.* systematization.

sys·tem·ize (sis′tə mīz), *v.t.,* **-ized, -iz·ing.** systematize. —**sys′tem·iz′er,** *n.*

sys·tem·less (sis′təm lis), *adj.* without system.

systems analysis, the overall analysis of any complex operation or activity to determine how an electronic computer or data-processing machine will fit into the operation or activity being analyzed; operations analysis.

systems analyst, an expert in systems analysis: *Management having decided . . . to install a computing system, it is now the task of the systems analyst to transmute general inclination into accomplished fact* (New Scientist).

sys·tems engineer (sis′təmz), an expert in systems engineering.

systems engineering, that branch of engineering that specializes in the technical and economic aspects of production systems.

sys·tem·wide (sis′təm wīd′), *adj.* covering the entire system; over and throughout all of a system: *Mr. Nash will have systemwide responsibility for promoting Central's interest in 50 subsidiary and affiliated companies* (New York Times).

sys·to·le (sis′tə lē), *n.* **1.** the contraction of the heart, rhythmically alternating with its relaxation (diastole), the two together constituting the cardiac cycle. During systole blood is pumped from the heart into the arteries. **2.** (in Greek and Latin prosody) the shortening of a long syllable. [< New Latin *systole* < Greek *systolḗ* contraction < *syn-* together + *stéllein* to put]

sys·tol·ic (sis tol′ik), *adj.* of, having to do with, or characterized by a contraction of the heart.

Sys·tox (sis′toks), *n. Trademark.* an organic phosphate used in agriculture as a systemic insecticide: *Systox, when sprayed on a plant, is absorbed directly into its circulatory system* (Newsweek). *Formula:* $C_8H_{19}O_3PS_2$

syz·y·get·ic (siz′ə jet′ik), *adj.* having to do with a syzygy or syzygies.

syz·y·get·i·cal·ly (siz′ə jet′ə klē), *adv.* with reference to a syzygy or syzygies.

sy·zyg·i·al (si zij′ē əl), *adj.* having to do with or of the nature of a syzygy.

syz·y·gy (siz′ə jē), *n., pl.* **-gies. 1.** *Astronomy.* the conjunction or opposition of two heavenly bodies, or either of the points at which these occur, especially with respect to the sun and the moon: *Cognate problems are the determination of the syzygies, last visibilities of the moon, and eclipses* (I. Bernard Cohen). **2.** (in Greek and Latin prosody) a dipody, or combination of two like feet (or sometimes of two unlike feet). [< Latin *sȳzygia* < Greek *sȳzygíā* yoke (pair); any union (of two) < *syzygeîn* to yoke (in pairs) < *syn-* together + *zygón* yoke]

T Roman 100's A.D. · T Greek 600's B.C. · Phoenician 1000's B.C. · Semitic 1500's B.C. · Egyptian 3000's B.C.

Tt Tt *Tt* *Tt*

T[1], **t** (tē), *n., pl.* **T's** or **Ts, t's** or **ts. 1.** the 20th letter of the English alphabet. **2.** any sound represented by this letter. **3.** the 20th, or more usually the 19th, of a series (either *I* or *J* being omitted).
cross one's or **the t's,** to be minutely exact; emphasize even small points: *Cross his t's and polish up his manuscript* (Manchester Examiner).
to a T, exactly; perfectly: *That suits me to a T.*

T[2] (tē), *n., pl.* **T's** or **Ts,** *adj.* —*n.* something made or fashioned in the form of a T.
—*adj.* shaped like the letter T.

't, *Poetic and Dialect.* contraction of *it* with a verb, as in *'twas, see't.*

-t, *suffix.* a variant of the ending **-ed** in certain verbs, as in *slept, meant, built.* See **-ed**[1] and **-ed**[2].

t (no period), *Statistics.* distribution.

t., an abbreviation for the following:
1. in the time of (Latin, *tempore*).
2. metric ton (French, *tonneau*).
3. tare.
4. teaspoon or teaspoons.
5. telephone.
6. temperature.
7. tempo.
8. tenor.
9. *Grammar.* tense.
10. territory.
11. time.
12. ton or tons.
13. town.
14. township.
15. transitive.
16. volume (French, *tome* or Latin, *tomus*).

T (no period), an abbreviation or symbol for:
1. temperature (absolute).
2. (surface) tension.
3. *Physics.* reduction of the activity of a radioactive product to one-half in the half-life period.
4. *Astronomy.* time of passing perihelion.
5. firing time or launch time, as of a rocket, etc.: *At T minus 139 minutes, wispy white plumes of supercold liquid oxygen will stream out of the Thor's side vents* (Newsweek).

T., an abbreviation for the following:
1. tablespoon or tablespoons.
2. tenor.
3. Territory.
4. Testament.
5. ton; tons.
6. Tuesday.
7. Turkish.
8. Turkish (pounds).

ta (tä), *interj. Especially British Informal.* thank you; thanks. [a child's word]

Ta (no period), tantalum (chemical element).

TA (no periods), therapeutic abortion.

T-A (no periods), toxin-antitoxin.

T.A., 1. *British.* Territorial Army. **2.** toxin-antitoxin. **3.** Transit Authority.

TAA (no periods), Technical Assistance Administration (for projects in economic development, social welfare, and public administration in various countries).

Taal (täl), *n.* Afrikaans, a dialect of Dutch spoken in South Africa; Cape Dutch: *He speaks the Taal better than a Hollander can, and can understand the Boers better* (Westminster Gazette). [< Afrikaans *Taal,* Dutch, language, speech < Middle Dutch *tāle* speech]

tab[1] (tab), *n., v.,* **tabbed, tab·bing.** —*n.* **1.** a small flap, strap, or strip of some material: *He wore a fur cap with tabs over the ears.* **2.** a small extension of or attachment to a card, usually used for labeling, numbering, color-coding, etc., in filing. **3.** a label. **4.** *Aeronautics.* an auxiliary control surface set into or attached to a larger one, as to a rudder. See **aileron** for picture. **5.** *British.* **a.** a colored strap or strip worn by a staff officer: *The officer ... who cannot stand the glory of his tabs* (Newsweek). **b.** a staff officer. **6.** a small, narrow drop curtain in a theater: *... will perform a thrilling twenty-minute excerpt from next week's play, in front of the tabs* (Punch).
—*v.t.* **1.** to put a tab on (something). **2.** to name; mark; identify.

tab[2] (tab), *n.* expense; bill: *The company picked up the tab for the annual picnic.*
keep tab, tabs, or **a tab on** (or **upon**), *Informal.* to keep track of; keep watch on; check: *The foreman kept tab on the workmen.*
—*adj.* tabulating.

tab[3] (tab), *n. Informal.* a tabloid: *a lively, well-edited tab.* [short for *tabloid*]

tab., table or tables.

TAB (no periods), Technical Assistance Board.

tab·ard (tab′ərd), *n.* **1.** a loose coat worn by heralds, emblazoned with the arms of their sovereign. **2.** a mantle worn by knights over their armor, generally embroidered with the arms of the wearer. **3.** *Obsolete.* a cloak of rough and heavy material, formerly worn by the poor during the Middle Ages. [< Old French *tabart,* later *tabar* < Latin *tapēte* figured cloth, tapestry]

Tabard (def. 1) (17th century)

tab·ard·ed (tab′ər did), *adj.* wearing a tabard: *The Queen ... marched ... past lines of tabarded heralds* (Time).

tab·a·ret (tab′ər it), *n.* an upholstery material with alternate satin and watered stripes. [compare TABORET]

Ta·bas·co (tə bas′kō), *n. Trademark.* a kind of peppery sauce, used on fish or meat, prepared from the fruit of a variety of capsicum: *He was ... forced to swallow a large dose of Tabasco sauce mixed with ketchup and cayenne pepper* (Westminster Gazette). [American English < *Tabasco,* a state in Mexico]

tab·a·sheer or **tab·a·shir** (tab′ə shir′), *n.* a siliceous concretion formed in the joints of the bamboo, used in the East as a medicine. [< Arabic, Persian, Hindustani *tabāshīr*]

ta·ba·tière (tȧ bȧ tyer′), *n. French.* a snuffbox: *The Marquis was somewhat disconcerted, and had recourse to his tabatière* (Scott).

tab·by[1] (tab′ē), *n., pl.* **-bies,** *adj.* —*n.* **1.** a brown, gray, or tawny cat with darker streaks and spots. **2.** a female cat. **3.** an old maid; spinster. **4.** a spiteful female gossip: *a lot of old tabbies always busy criticising* (Sinclair Lewis). **5.** *Australian Slang.* a woman or girl.
—*adj.* (of a cat) brown or gray with darker stripes; brindled.
[probably alteration (influenced by the proper name *Tabby* < *Tabitha*) of earlier *tibby,* type name for a female (paired with *Tom* for a male). Compare *Tibbert,* a typical cat name in medieval Reynard stories.]

tab·by[2] (tab′ē), *n., pl.* **-bies,** *adj., v.,* **-bied, -by·ing.** —*n.* any silk cloth with a striped, waved, or watered pattern or marking, as silk taffeta.
—*adj.* **1.** like tabby. **2.** made of the fabric tabby.
—*v.t.* to give a wavy appearance to (silk, etc.) by calendering.
[< French *tabis* < Middle French *atabis* < Arabic *'Attābiy* a section of Bagdad where such cloth was first made]

tab card, a punch card for an electronic tabulator: *To write invoices automatically from existing tab cards ...* (Wall Street Journal).

tab·e·fac·tion (tab′ə fak′shən), *n.* a wasting away or consumption of the body by disease; emaciation; tabes. [< Late Latin *tābefactus,* past participle of *tābefacere* cause to waste away (< Latin *tābēre* waste away + *facere* make) + English *-ion*]

ta·ber (tā′bər), *n., v.i., v.t.* tabor.

Tab·er·nac·le (tab′ər nak′əl), *n.* (in the Bible) the covered wooden framework used by the Israelites as a place of worship during their journey from Egypt to Palestine. Exodus 25-27. [< Latin *tabernāculum* tent, shed, place for religious rites (diminutive) < *taberna* cabin, booth]

tab·er·nac·le (tab′ər nak′əl), *n., v.,* **-led, -ling.** —*n.* **1.** a place of worship for a large audience, as a meeting house used chiefly by Baptists and Methodists in England, or a Congregationalist or Independent place of worship in Scotland. **2.** a Jewish temple; synagogue. **3.** the human body thought of as the temporary dwelling of the soul. **4.** a temporary dwelling; a tent. **5.** a tomb, shrine, etc., with a canopy. **6.** a container for something holy or precious; container for the consecrated bread used in the Mass.
—*v.i.* to dwell for a time; sojourn. —*v.t.* to enshrine: *In thee the light, Creation's eldest born, was tabernacled* (Henry H. Milman).
[< *Tabernacle*]

Tab·er·nac·les (tab′ər nak′əlz), *n.pl.* the Jewish festival of Sukkoth. It is marked by the building of temporary dwellings symbolizing the tabernacles used by the Israelites in their journey to Palestine. *More than any other of the Jewish festivals, Tabernacles claims to be a holy day distinctly commemorative of the harvest* (Westminster Gazette).

tabernacle work, *Architecture.* **1.** ornamental work or tracery used in tabernacles or canopies over tombs, stalls, etc., and in the carved screens of churches. **2.** work in which tabernacles form the characteristic feature.

tab·er·nac·u·lar (tab′ər nak′yə lər), *adj.* **1.** having to do with a tabernacle. **2.** like or characteristic of a tabernacle.

ta·bes (tā′bēz), *n.* **1.** locomotor ataxia; tabes dorsalis. **2.** *Obsolete.* a gradually progressive emaciation; consumption. [< Latin *tābēs, -is* a wasting disease; (literally) a melting away]

ta·bes·cence (tə bes′əns), *n.* a wasting away.

ta·bes·cent (tə bes′ənt), *adj.* wasting away. [< Latin *tābēscēns, -entis,* present participle of *tābēscere* < *tābēre* waste away < *tābēs;* see TABES]

ta·bes dor·sa·lis (tā′bēz dôr sā′lis), a disease of the spinal cord marked by loss of control over walking and other movements; locomotor ataxia. [< New Latin *tabes dorsalis* consumption of the back]

ta·bet·ic (tə bet′ik), *adj.* **1.** having to do with tabes dorsalis. **2.** suffering from tabes dorsalis. —*n.* a person who has tabes dorsalis. [< Latin *tābēs* (see TABES); patterned on *diabetic*]

ta·bi (tä′bē), *n., pl.* **-bi.** *Japanese.* a low, white or blue cotton sock, with a thick sole and a separate part for the big toe, worn with a sandal: *A Japanese in rubber-soled tabi and a workman's short black jacket finished a bottle* (New Yorker).

tab·id (tab′id), *adj.* tabetic: *A gradual and most tabid decline* (Laurence Sterne).

tab·la (tä′blä), *n.* a tuned drum played by hand in India. [< Hindustani *tabla* < Arabic *ṭabl* drum]

Tablas
Drummer plays many at a time.

tab·la·ture (tab′lə chər), *n.* **1.** an old name for musical notation in general, especially for systems differing from ordinary staff notation: *Organ tablature was a system of writing the notes without the stave by means of letters* (Stainer and Barrett). **2.** *Obsolete.* a tabular formation or structure having an inscription or design. **3.** *Obsolete.* a painting; picture: *He prefers the Saracen's head upon a signpost before the best tablature of Raphael* (Henry H. Kames). [< Middle French *tablatura* < Old French *table,* learned borrowing from Latin *tabula* slab for writing or painting]

ta·ble (tā′bəl), *n., v.,* **-bled, -bling.** —*n.* **1.** a piece of furniture having a smooth, flat top on legs: *a dining table, a surgeon's operating table.* **2.** a table upon which food is served: *to set the table.* **3.** food served; fare: *Mrs. Brown sets a good table.* **4.** the entertainment of a family or guests at table; eating; feasting. **5.** the persons seated or gathered around a table to eat, play games, gamble, transact business, etc.: *the contempt of the whole table* (Samuel Johnson). **6.** an arrangement of numbers, words, or other items in columns and lines to show some relation distinctly: *the multiplication table, tables of weights or measure, insurance tables.* **7.** a list of items or particulars: *the table of contents in the front of a book.* **8.** a flat or plane surface like that of a table; level area. **9.** a tableland; plateau. **10.** *Architecture.* **a.** a horizontal molding, especially a cornice. **b.** a panel (of a wall). **11.** the top facet of a jewel. **12.** *Anatomy.* either of the two large bones forming the skull. **13.** a thin, flat piece of wood, stone, metal, etc.; tablet: *The Ten Commandments were written on tables of stone.* **14.** matter inscribed or written on tables. **15.** either of the two leaves of a backgammon board.

lay or **set the table,** to put dishes and silver, but not food, on the table for a meal: *You may as well set the table for two* (J.T. Trowbridge).

on or **upon the table,** (of a report, motion, bill, etc.) on the table of the presiding officer so that the discussion is postponed: *... that for the present this report be received and laid on the table* (Transactions of the Philological Society).

tables, the multiplication table: *She has already memorized her tables.*

the tables, certain collections of ancient Greek and Roman laws cut or carved on thin, flat pieces of stone: *In the comparison of the tables of Solon with those of the Decemvirs, some casual resemblance may be found* (Edward Gibbon).

turn the tables (on), to gain control (over); reverse conditions or circumstances completely: *They had won the first match, though I hoped I might yet turn the tables on them in the return* (Frederick Selous).

under the table, not in the open; secretly; stealthily: *Some money changed hands under the table.*

—*v.t.* **1.** *U.S.* **a.** to postpone discussing (a bill or motion) by voting to leave it on the table of the presiding officer. **b.** to shelve: *a paper dream tabled by legislative inertia* (Time). **2.** *British.* to submit (a bill or motion) for discussion or consideration; bring forward. **3.** to place or lay (a card, money, etc.) on a table. **4.** to tabulate; catalogue. **5.** to provide with meals.

[Old English *tabule, tabele,* ultimately < Latin *tabula* slab for writing or painting]

—**Syn.** *n.* **7.** schedule, synopsis.

tab·leau (tab′lō, tab lō′), *n., pl.* **tab·leaux** (tab′lōz, tab lōz′), *less frequently,* **tab·leaus** tab′lōz, tab lōz′). **1.** a silent, motionless representation of a person, scene, incident, etc., by one person or a group of persons posing in costume; charade without movement: *Those who stumbled through the blackened halls and who could still keep their eyes open were rewarded with wax tableaus on which certain figures suddenly came alive only to freeze again* (Saturday Review). **2.** any picture, usually a scene. **3.** a picturesque or graphic description: *The book starts out with a tableau which in its intellectual irrelevance and mawkish sentimentality is the kind of journalism one has come to expect* (Hans J. Morganthau). [< French *tableau* (diminutive) < Old French *table;* see TABLATURE]

ta·bleau vi·vant (tȧ blō′ vē väɴ′), *pl.* **ta·bleaux vi·vants** (tȧ blō′ vē väɴ′). a tableau. [< French *tableau vivant* (literally) living picture]

table chair, a piece of furniture used either as a table or chair, the top turning back to a vertical position on the hinge.

ta·ble·cloth (tā′bəl klôth′, -kloth′), *n.* a cloth covering for a table.

table cut, a form of ornamentation in diamond cutting in which a usually flat stone is cut with long facets and bordered by beveled edges or smaller facets.

ta·ble d'hôte (tab′əl dōt′, tä′bəl), a meal served at a fixed time and price. In meals table d'hôte, there is one price for the whole meal; but in meals à la carte, a person chooses what he wants and pays for each article. [< French *table d'hôte* (literally) host's table]

ta·ble·ful (tā′bəl fu̇l), *n., pl.* **-fuls. 1.** as many persons as can be seated at a table. **2.** as many things as a table will hold.

ta·ble-hop (tā′bəl hop′), *v.i.,* **-hopped, -hop·ping.** *Informal.* to move from one table to another making brief visits, as in a restaurant or a night club: *An urbane raconteur, [he] spends much of his time happily table-hopping at fashionable restaurants* (Newsweek).

table knife, a knife used while eating, especially to cut meat.

table lamp, a lamp to light the surface of a table, usually placed on the table.

ta·ble·land (tā′bəl land′), *n.* a large, high plain; a plateau: *These lofty plats of table-land seem to form a peculiar feature in the American continents* (Washington Irving). —**Syn.** mesa.

ta·ble·less (tā′bəl lis), *adj.* without a table; not furnished with a table.

table lifting, table rapping.

table linen, tablecloths, napkins, doilies, and mats.

table mat, a table covering, made of fabric, plastic, etc., for an individual place setting; place mat.

table money, *British.* an extra allowance to higher officers of the British Army and Navy for expenses of official hospitality.

table napkin, a napkin used at meals.

table of organization, a table or publication that prescribes the organizational structure and personnel for a military unit.

table rapping, the production of raps or knocking sounds on a table without apparent physical means, used by spiritualists as a supposed means of communicating with departed spirits.

table rock, a flat-topped rock.

ta·bles (tā′bəlz), *n.pl.* See under **table,** *n.*

table salt, ordinary salt for use at table; sodium chloride.

tables of the law, 1. the stone slabs on which the Ten Commandments were inscribed. **2.** the decalogue.

ta·ble·spoon (tā′bəl spün′, -spu̇n′), *n.* **1.** any large spoon used to serve vegetables, etc., at the table; serving spoon. **2.** a spoon used in cookery as a unit of measure and holding three times as much as a teaspoon. **3.** a tablespoonful. *Abbr.:* tbs., tbsp.

ta·ble·spoon·ful (tā′bəl spün fu̇l′, -spu̇n-), *n., pl.* **-fuls. 1.** a standard unit of liquid measure used in cookery, equal to 1/2 fluid ounce; 1/16 cup; 3 teaspoonfuls. **2.** as much as a tablespoon will hold.

tab·let (tab′lit), *n., v.,* **-let·ed, -let·ing** or **-let·ted, -let·ting.** —*n.* **1.** a number of sheets of writing paper fastened together at one edge, often with a stiff back and a cover; pad. **2. a.** a small, flat piece of candy, medicine, etc.; pill; lozenge: *aspirin tablets.* **b.** *British.* a cake of soap. **3.** a small slab, often with an inscription or bas-relief: *Idealism ... is not static, not something writ on tablets, but a constantly developing attitude of heart and mind capable of embracing and giving new meaning to twentieth century society* (Listener). **4.** (in ancient times) a small, smooth plate of stone, wood, ivory, etc., covered with wax or clay to write on, often hinged with another; sheet or slab: *The ancient Romans used tablets as we use pads of paper.* See **stylus** for picture.

—*v.t.* **1.** to make into a tablet: *Their figures did not include the cost of tableting and distributing the bulk powder* (New Yorker). **2.** to furnish with a tablet: *[The] chapel [is] tableted with the names of some who have died in their country's service* (Westminster Gazette).

[< Old French *tablete,* later *tablette* < *table;* see TABLATURE]

table talk, 1. conversation at meals: *The role of family table talk has not been generally appreciated* (Emory S. Bogardus). **2.** the social conversation of famous men or intellectual circles, especially as reproduced in literary form. **3.** a subject for table talk: *To be the table talk of clubs upstairs* (William Cowper).

table tennis, a game played on a large table marked somewhat like a tennis court; miniature tennis; Ping-pong.

ta·ble·top (tā′bəl top′), *n.* **1.** the upper surface of a table. **2.** the flat top of a hill, rock, etc. —*adj.* designed to be used on a tabletop: *a tabletop model.*

ta·ble·ware (tā′bəl wãr′), *n.* the dishes, knives, forks, spoons, and linen used at meals.

ta·ble-wa·ter (tā′bəl wôt′ər, -wot′-), *n.* **1.** a mineral water. **2.** water suitable for drinking at table.

table wine, a wine that is generally served with meals.

ta·ble-work (tā′bəl wėrk′), *n. Printing.* the setting of columns of figures, tables, or other copy in very narrow measure.

ta·bli·er (tȧ bli ā′), *n. French.* **1.** an apron. **2.** an apronlike piece in a woman's dress: *The bride ... wore a dress of striped white satin with pearl tablier in front and net veil* (Pall Mall Gazette).

tab·loid (tab′loid), *n.* **1.** a newspaper, usually of half the ordinary page size, with many pictures, short articles, and large, often sensational, headlines: *He launches another tabloid, "Municipal News," for mayors and civic officials* (Canada Month). **2.** a tablet of medicine or a chemical; pill; pellet: *Burroughs Wellcome registered the word Tabloid years ago, and rise up in reproof whenever they see it spelt with a small T* (Punch). —*adj.* (of writing) in the form of a summary, capsule, or digest; condensed. [originally *Tabloid,* a trademark for compressed or concentrated chemicals < *tabl*(et) + *-oid*]

ta·boo (tə bü′, ta-), *adj., v.,* **-booed, -boo·ing,** *n., pl.* **-boos.** —*adj.* **1.** forbidden; prohibited; banned: *Eating human flesh is taboo in civilized countries. The mention of her neighbours is evidently taboo, since ... she is in a state of affront with nine-tenths of them* (Mary R. Mitford). **2.** (in the South Seas, of certain objects, places, and persons) declared sacred, unclean, or cursed, and forbidden to general use.

—*v.t.* **1.** to forbid; prohibit; ban: *The tabooing of such subjects as Communist China's admission to the United Nations ...* (New York Times). *The Scandinavians, the Dutch and the Swiss all taboo masculine tears ...* (David Gunston). **2.** to forbid social contact with; ostracize; boycott: *You cannot taboo a man who has got a vote* (Lord Bryce).

—*n.* **1.** any ban on a practice or on the use of something; prohibition. **2.** a ban on association with someone; one's exclusion from social relations; ostracism. **3.** in the South Seas: **a.** the system or act of setting things apart as sacred, unclean, or cursed: *The sacred protection of an express edict of the taboo, declaring his person inviolable for ever* (Herman Melville). **b.** the fact or condition of being so placed: *... whoever violates the taboo will presumably be stricken to death by unseen beings* (Emory S. Bogardus). **c.** the prohibition or interdict itself: *Taboos were enforced by invoking fear* (Emory S. Bogardus). Also, **tabu.** [< Tongan *tabu*]

—**Syn.** *v.t.* **1.** proscribe. *-n.* **1.** interdiction.

➤ **taboo, tabu.** *Taboo* is more generally used than *tabu,* except in anthropology.

ta·bor or **ta·bour** (tā′bər), *n.* a small drum used especially to accompany a pipe or fife: *The whole neighbourhood came out to meet their minister ... preceded by a pipe and tabor* (Oliver Goldsmith). —*v.i.* to drum, especially on a tabor. —*v.t. Obsolete.* to beat (anything); thrash. Also, **taber.** [< Old French *tabour, tabur* < Persian *tabīrah* drum] —**ta′bor·er,** *n.*

tab·o·ret or **tab·ou·ret** (tab′ər it, tab′ə-ret′), *n.* **1.** a stool: *He had bought a new easel and two rush-bottomed tabourets* (W.C. Morrow). **2.** a small, low table; stand. **3.** an embroidery frame. **4.** *Archaic.* a small tabor; timbrel. [< French *tabouret* < Middle French (diminutive) < Old French *tabour;* see TABOR]

tab·o·rin, tab·o·rine, or **tab·ou·rine** (tab′ər in), *n. Obsolete.* a drum narrower and longer than the tabor. [< Middle French *tabourin* (diminutive) < Old French *tabour*]

tab·ret (tab′rit), *n. Archaic.* a small tabor.

ta·bu (tə bü′, ta-), *adj., v.,* **-bued, -bu·ing,** *n., pl.* **-bus.** taboo: *South Sea islanders have elaborate tabus governing how and when reef-fish may be eaten* (Scientific American).

➤ See **taboo** for usage note.

tab·u·la (tab′yə lə), *n., pl.* **-lae** (-lē). **1.** in ancient Rome: **a.** a table or tablet, especially a writing tablet. **b.** a writing or document. **c.** a legal instrument or record. **2.** *Ecclesiastical.* a wooden or metal frontal. [< Latin *tabula;* see TABLE]

tab·u·lar (tab′yə lər), *adj.* **1.** having to do with tables or lists. **2.** entered in a table or arranged in columns: *tabular data.* **3.** (of a quantity) read from or calculated by means of tables. **4.** having the form of a tablet, slab, or tablature; flat and usually thin. **5.** tending to split into flat, thin pieces, as a rock. **6.** flat-topped and usually broad, as a hill or crystal: *a tabular rock.* [< Latin *tabulāris* having to do with a slab or plate < *tabula* slab; see TABLE] —**tab′u·lar·ly,** *adv.*

ta·bu·la ra·sa (tab′yə lə rā′sə), *Latin.* **1.** the mind before it is developed and changed by experience: *The mind for [Locke] is entirely passive, a clean blackboard, tabula rasa, on which the experiences of the individual write their own impressions* (Norbert Wiener). **2.** (literally) a wax tablet from which the writing has been erased: *No scientist starts with a tabula rasa, a clean slate* (George Simpson).

tab·u·lar·i·za·tion (tab′yə lər ə zā′shən), *n.* tabulation.

tab·u·lar·ize (tab′yə lə rīz), *v.t.,* **-ized, -iz·ing.** to make tabular; put into tabular form; tabulate.

tab·u·late (*v.* tab′yə lāt; *adj.* tab′yə lit, -lāt), *v.,* **-lat·ed, -lat·ing,** *adj.* —*v.t., v.i.* to arrange (facts, figures, etc.) in columns, lists, or a table. —*adj.* **1.** flat, broad, and usually thin; tabular. **2.** having horizontal partitions: *tabulate corals.* [< Latin *tabula* (see TABLE) + English *-ate*[1]]

tab·u·lat·ing machine (tab′yə lā′ting), a tabulator.

tab·u·la·tion (tab′yə lā′shən), *n.* **1.** the process of arranging in tables or lists: *In 1950, it took 1,400 people a year to prepare the census takers' findings for tabulation* (Newsweek). **2.** the fact or condition of being arranged in tables or lists.

tab·u·la·tor (tab′yə lā′tər), *n.* **1.** a typewriter attachment for spacing figures in neat columns. **2.** any machine for listing or counting. **3.** a person who draws up a table or scheme. **4.** a computing machine that takes in punch cards and instructions and produces lists, totals, and tabulations of the information on separate forms or on continuous paper.

ta·bun (tä bün′), *n.* a toxic nerve gas for military use, first synthesized in Germany. *Formula:* $C_5H_{11}N_2O_2P$ [< German *Tabun*]

TAC (no periods), Tactical Air Command (a branch of the United States Air Force which provides air support for land and sea forces, ready for use in any part of the world).

tac·a·ma·hac (tak′ə mə hak), *n.* **1.** an aromatic resin, used in incense, ointments, and formerly in medicines: **a.** (originally) a resin from a Mexican tree. **b.** (later) any similar resin from various trees of tropical America, Madagascar, or the East Indies. **c.** resin from the buds of the North American balsam poplar. **2.** any of these trees, especially the balsam poplar. Also, **tacmahac, tacmahack.** [< Spanish *tacamahaca* < Nahuatl *tecamaca*]

tac·a·ma·hac·a (tak′ə mə hak′ə), *n.* tacamahac.

TACAN (no periods), or **Tac·an** (tak′an), *n.* Tactical Air Navigation (an electronic unit in an aircraft that supplies a pilot with continuous readings of his distance and bearing from a fixed station, by an emitted pulse and automatic reply).

ta·ces (tā′sēz), *n.pl. Obsolete.* tasses (armor for the thighs).

ta·cet (tā′sit), *v.i. Music.* to be silent (used as an indication that an instrument or voice is to be silent for a time). [< Latin *tacet,* third person singular, present indicative of *tacēre* to be silent]

tache or **tach** (tach), *n. Archaic.* **1.** any device for fastening, as a clasp, buckle, hook and eye, or hook: *Taches of gold . . . connecting together the curtains of the tabernacle* (Hugh Macmillan). **2.** any link or bond: *Finally, the word became . . . a tach between the external object and the internal impression* (Frederic W. Farrar). [< Old French *tache* a pin, brooch, nail < the same root as in *attach, attack, tack*]

tach·e·om·e·ter (tak′ē om′ə tər), *n.* a tachymeter.

tach·i·na fly (tak′ə nə), any of a group of dipterous insects resembling the housefly whose larvae are parasitic in caterpillars and other insects. [< New Latin *Tachina* the genus name < Greek *tachinḗ* swift]

Ta Ch'ing (dä′ ching′), (in China) the Manchu dynasty, 1644-1911.

tach·i·ol (tak′ē ōl, -ol), *n.* a yellowish, crystalline compound, used as an antiseptic; silver fluoride. *Formula:* $AgF.H_2O$

tach·isme or **tach·ism** (tash′iz əm; *French* tȧ shēz′mə), *n.* a style of painting in which colors are splashed or daubed on the canvas, allowing impulse rather than conscious effort to control the form and content of the picture; action painting. [< French *tachisme* < *tache* blot, stain + *-isme, -ism*]

tach·iste (tash′ist; *French* tȧ shēst′), *n.* a painter who uses the style or technique of tachisme. —*adj.* of or having to do with tachisme or tachistes: *The eucalyptus trees with their stringy bark like dribbled tachiste paintings drooped* (Manchester Guardian). [< French *tachiste*]

ta·chis·to·scope (tə kis′tə skōp), *n.* an apparatus which exposes to view, for a selected brief period of time, an object or group of objects, as letters, words, etc. The tachistoscope is used in experimental psychology. *The conference explored every stage of marketing, from blind tests of a new product, from measuring the visual impact of its packaging in a tachistoscope, to surveys to check "brand awareness" of the new name* (London Times).
[< Greek *táchistos* swiftest, superlative of *tachýs* swift + English *-scope*]

ta·chis·to·scop·ic (tə kis′tə skop′ik), *adj.* of or having to do with a tachistoscope: . . . *tachistoscopic flashes on a screen* (Bulletin of Atomic Scientists).

tach·o·gram (tak′ə gram), *n.* a record made by a tachograph.

tach·o·graph (tak′ə graf, -gräf), *n.* **1.** a tachometer which makes a record of its readings over a period of time: *Tachographs . . . record the travelling and stopping times of vehicles* (London Times). **2.** tachogram.

ta·chom·e·ter (tə kom′ə tər), *n.* any of various instruments for measuring or indicating the speed of a machine, a river, the blood, etc. [< Greek *táchos* speed + English *-meter*]

ta·chom·e·try (tə kom′ə trē), *n.* the measurement of velocity.

tachy-, *combining form.* swift; rapid: *Tachycardia = excessively fast heartbeat. Tachygraphy = the art of rapid writing.* [< Greek *tachýs*]

tach·y·car·di·a (tak′ə kär′dē ə), *n. Medicine.* excessively fast heartbeat. [< *tachy-* + Greek *kardíā* heart]

tach·y·car·di·ac (tak′ə kär′dē ak), *Medicine.* —*adj.* of or having to do with tachycardia. —*n.* a person with tachycardia: *One of my tachycardiacs began to ride a bicycle two years ago, and with much advantage* (Thomas C. Allbutt).

tach·y·graph (tak′ə graf, -gräf), *n.* **1.** a tachygraphic writing or manuscript. **2.** a writer of shorthand: *The other tachygraph, Phocas, had also reported this sermon* (Frederic W. Farrar). **3.** a device for measuring the rate of flow of arterial blood.

ta·chyg·ra·pher (tə kig′rə fər), *n.* a writer of shorthand.

tach·y·graph·ic (tak′ə graf′ik), *adj.* **1.** of tachygraphy. **2.** written in shorthand. —**tach′y·graph′i·cal·ly,** *adv.*

tach·y·graph·i·cal (tak′ə graf′ə kəl), *adj.* tachygraphic.

ta·chyg·ra·phist (tə kig′rə fist), *n.* tachygrapher.

ta·chyg·ra·phy (tə kig′rə fē), *n.* **1.** the art or practice of writing quickly. **2.** shorthand, especially the ancient Greek and Roman form. **3.** the art of writing in abbreviations, as in some Greek and Latin written in the Middle Ages. **4.** cursive as letters.

tach·y·lyte or **tach·y·lite** (tak′ə līt), *n.* a black, glassy basalt of volcanic origin that is readily fusible: *Tachylites commonly occur as bombs and cinders, or scoria, thrown out by volcanoes* (Fenton and Fenton). [< German *Tachylit* < Greek *tachýs* swift + *lytós* soluble < *lýein* to loosen (because it is easily fusible)]

tach·y·lyt·ic (tak′ə lit′ik), *adj.* **1.** composed of tachylyte. **2.** resembling tachylyte. **3.** containing tachylyte.

ta·chym·e·ter (tə kim′ə tər), *n.* **1.** an instrument to determine distances, etc., rapidly in a survey. **2.** a tachometer.

tach·y·met·ric (tak′ə met′rik), *adj.* of or having to do with a tachymeter or tachymetry.

ta·chym·e·try (tə kim′ə trē), *n.* the use of the tachymeter.

tach·yp·noe·a (tak′ip nē′ə), *n. Medicine.* excessively rapid respiration. [< New Latin *tachypnoea* < Greek *tachýs* swift + *pneîn* breathe]

ta·chys·ter·ol (tə kis′tə rol), *n. Biochemistry.* a substance formed by irradiating ergosterol, becoming calciferol when further irradiated. *Formula:* $C_{28}H_{44}O$

tac·it (tas′it), *adj.* **1.** not openly stated, but implied; understood: *His eating the food was a tacit admission that he liked it.* **2.** saying nothing; still; silent: *Edward Strachey was . . . a man rather tacit than discursive* (Thomas Carlyle). **3.** unspoken; silent: *a tacit prayer.* **4.** *Law.* existing out of custom or from silent consent but not expressly stated. [< Latin *tacitus,* past participle of *tacēre* be silent] —**tac′it·ly,** *adv.* —**tac′it·ness,** *n.*
—**Syn. 1.** implicit. **3.** unuttered, unexpressed.

Tac·i·te·an (tas′ə tē′ən), *adj.* **1.** of or having to do with Tacitus. **2.** having a graphic, incisive style of writing: *His style is uneven, but redeemed by the occasional Tacitean touch* (Economist). [< *Tacitus,* 55?-117? A.D., a Roman historian, known for this style of writing + *-an*]

Tac·i·tist (tas′ə tist), *n.* a student or follower of Tacitus: *He might like a Tacitist have written the Civil Wars of Flanders* (Earl of Monmouth).

tac·i·turn (tas′ə tėrn), *adj.* in the habit of saying little; not fond of talking; inclined to silence: *At the Council board he was taciturn and . . . never opened his lips* (Thackeray). [< Latin *taciturnus* < *tacitus;* see TACIT] —**tac′i·turn·ly,** *adv.* —**Syn.** reserved. See **silent.** —**Ant.** talkative.

tac·i·tur·ni·ty (tas′ə tėr′nə tē), *n.* the habit of keeping silent; disinclination to talk much: *The secrets of nature Have not more gift in taciturnity* (Shakespeare). —**Syn.** reserve, reticence.

tack[1] (tak), *n.* **1.** a sharp-pointed nail with a flat, broad head: *carpet tacks, thumbtacks.* **2.** a long, loose stitch used as a temporary fastening before thorough sewing. **3.** any very slight, loose fastening: *hanging by a tack.* **4. a.** the act of fastening lightly or temporarily. **b.** the state of being fastened this way. **5.** adhesiveness; tackiness. **6.** *Nautical.* **a.** the direction in which a ship moves in regard to the direction of the wind and the position of her sails: *On port tack, a ship is close-hauled with the wind on her left.* **b.** a slanting or zigzag course against the wind. **c.** one of the straight runs in a zigzag course. **d.** the act of zigzagging; a turn from one straight run to the next. **7.** any zigzag movement. **8.** any line of conduct toward an end; course of action: *They think the House will take a tougher tack on dollar-a-year men* (Wall Street Journal). **9.** *Nautical.* the rope by which the outer lower corner of some sails is held: **a.** that securing a course on a square-rigged ship. **b.** that securing a studding sail to the end of the boom. **c.** the corner held by any such rope, as the forward lower corner of a fore-and-aft sail. **10.** (in gardening) a bar to hold up shoots, etc. **11.** a brace to hold a pipe to a wall.
—*v.t.* **1.** to fasten with tacks (short nails): *to tack up a notice.* **2.** to sew with removable stitches. **3.** to join (any units) together, often artificially without harmonizing them; combine superficially; splice clumsily: *Traditional tales, tacked together without regard to place or chronology* (John Lingard). **4.** to attach (something separate); add (a supplement); append; annex: *She tacked a postscript to the end of her letter.* **5.** *Nautical.* **a.** to sail (a ship) in a zigzag course against the wind. **b.** to turn (a ship) to sail at the same angle to the wind on the other side; change from one leg of a zigzag course to the next: *to tack ship.* —*v.i.* **1.** *Nautical.* of sailors or ships: **a.** to sail zigzag into the wind: *The craft could tack . . . an art unknown to Europeans at the time of Columbus* (Beals and Hoijer). **b.** to turn and sail at the same angle to the wind on the other side. **2.** to move along any zigzag route. **3.** to change one's attitude, conduct, or course of action. **4.** to use indirect methods.
[< Anglo-French *taque* nail, clasp, Old French *tache* < Germanic root] —**tack′er,** *n.*

tack[2] (tak), *n.* **1.** things, especially necessary equipment. **2.** *Slang.* food: *I thought the canteen tack the nastiest stuff I had ever tasted* (D.C. Murray). [origin uncertain]

tack[3] (tak), *n. Scottish.* **1.** tenancy of land, especially leasehold tenure. **2.** the tenure of a benefice. **3.** the period of tenure. [< Scottish *tac, tak* take]

tack-driv·er (tak′drī′vər), *n.* **1.** a machine which automatically places and drives a series of tacks. **2.** a tack-hammer.

tack-ham·mer (tak′ham′ər), *n.* a light hammer for driving tacks.

tack·i·ly (tak′ə lē), *adv.* stickily.

tack·i·ness (tak′ē nis), *n.* stickiness: *No doubt the tackiness of the enamel also helps to hold the tube in place* (Installation News).

tack·le (tak′əl), *n., v.,* **-led, -ling.** —*n.* **1.** any equipment; apparatus; gear, as a fishing rod, line, hooks, etc. **2.** a device consisting of a rope and one or more pulley-blocks, used to obtain a mechanical advantage in moving loads, usually designated as single or double tackle by the number of sheaves in a block, or by the object it moves; block and tackle: *gun tackle, anchor tackle.* **3.** *Nautical.* the rigging of a ship, especially the ropes and blocks by which the sails, yards, etc., are raised and lowered. **4.** a purchase consisting of a rope passed over sheaves or pulleys in two or more blocks. **5.** any arrangement of rope passed through or over several blocks on sheaves. **6.** in football: **a.** the act of throwing the ball carrier to the ground. **b.** the player between either end and the guard. **c.** any act of tackling.

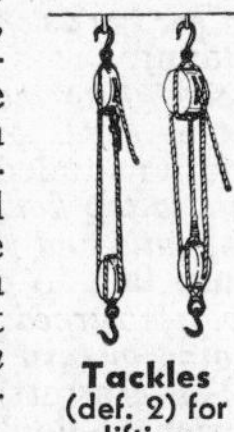
Tackles (def. 2) for lifting

—*v.t.* **1.** to try to deal with, solve, or master (a task, difficulty, etc.); grapple with: *a strange problem to tackle. John tackled his homework before supper.* **2.** to grip (a person or animal) physically; lay hold of; fasten upon; seize or attack: *John tackled the thief and threw him.* **3.** (in football and Rugby) to seize and stop (an opponent who has the ball) by bringing him to the ground. **4.** (in soccer and association football) to obstruct (an opponent) in order to get the ball away from him. **5.** to begin to eat (food). **6.** to harness (a horse): *Go out and tackle the old mare, and have our wagon round to the house* (Harriet Beecher Stowe).
—*v.i.* **1.** (in football) to bring down and stop an opponent who has the ball: *John tackles hard.* **2.** *Especially British Informal.* to set to; grapple: *We'll tackle to* (Anthony Trollope).
tackle up, to harness a horse: *I shall just tackle up and go over and bring them children home agin* (Harriet Beecher Stowe).
[Middle English *takel* gear, especially of a ship; hoisting apparatus, probably < Middle Low German] —**tack′ler,** *n.*

tackle box, a covered box to carry fishing tackle.

tack·ling (tak′ling), *n. Obsolete.* gear; tackle; equipment.

tack·pull·er (tak′pu̇l′ər), *n.* a tool for pulling out tacks or small nails.

tack room, a room for storing gear, supplies, etc., especially for riding.

tacks·man (taks′mən), *n., pl.* **-men.** *Scottish.* a person who holds a tack or lease of land from another; a tenant or lessee: *His grandfather, Malcolm, was "tacksman" of a farm . . . at the extreme north of the island* (Sunday Times). [< *tack's* (possessive of *tack*[3]) + *man*]

tack·y[1] (tak′ē), *adj.,* **tack·i·er, tack·i·est.** very sticky or gummy; adhesive: *A tacky disk surface permits changing the abrasives* (Science News Letter).

tack·y[2] (tak′ē), *adj.,* **tack·i·er, tack·i·est. 1.** *U.S. Informal.* shabby; dowdy; tatty: [*They*] *have the knack of looking tacky even when they are wealthy and titled* (Kansas City Star). **2.** *Slang.* unpleasant; disagreeable: *They are quite tacky about drum beating, horn tooting and other such commercialistic clamor* (New Yorker). [American English; origin uncertain]

tac·ma·hac or **tac·ma·hack** (tak′mə-hak), *n.* tacamahac.

ta·co (tä′kō), *n., pl.* **-cos.** a tortilla filled with chopped meat, chicken, cheese, etc., and served hot. [< Mexican Spanish *taco*]

tac·o·nite (tak′ə nīt), *n.* a variety of chert which is about a third iron ore, occurring especially in the Mesabi Range: *At taconite plants, miners blast the rock from the ground, crush it to talcum fineness and separate a rich, black ore* (Wall Street Journal). [< the *Taconic* range, mountains on the western edge of New England + *-ite*[1]]

tact (takt), *n.* **1.** a keen sense of how to deal with people and difficult situations without giving offense; the ability to say and do the right things; delicacy; diplomacy: *Her tact kept her from talking about things likely to be unpleasant to the guests. Tact consists in knowing how far we may go too far* (Jean Cocteau). **2.** the action, process, or practice of not giving offense. **3.** the sense of touch; touch. **4.** sense. [< Latin *tāctus, -ūs* < *tangere* to touch] —**Syn. 1.** finesse, tactfulness.

tact·ful (takt′fəl), *adj.* **1.** having tact: *a tactful person.* **2.** showing tact: *a tactful reply.* —**tact′ful·ly,** *adv.* —**tact′ful·ness,** *n.* —**Syn. 1.** diplomatic.

tac·tic (tak′tik), *n.* **1.** a detail of military tactics; maneuver. **2.** any skillful move; tack; gambit. **3.** a system of tactics; tactics. **4.** *Mathematics.* (formerly) the study dealing with order and arrangement.
—*adj.* **1.** having to do with arrangement or order. **2.** *Biology.* **a.** having to do with taxis. **b.** characteristic of taxis.
[< Late Latin *tacticus* expert in arms < Greek *taktikós*; see TACTICS]

tac·ti·cal (tak′tə kəl), *adj.* **1.** having to do with tactics. **2.** having to do with the disposal of military or naval forces in action: *a tactical advantage.* **3.** organized for or used in action against enemy troops, rather than against enemy bases, industry, etc., behind the lines of battle: *tactical air force, a tactical bomber. The distinction between tactical nuclear weapons and strategic nuclear weapons is almost entirely one of use* (Manchester Guardian). **4.** of a person, action, etc.: **a.** characterized by skillful procedure, methods, or expedients; adroit; clever. **b.** having to do with ways and means. —**tac′ti·cal·ly,** *adv.*

Tactical Air Command, TAC.

Tactical Air Navigation, TACAN.

tactical unit, a unit of an army activated or organized to fight the enemy.

tac·ti·cian (tak tish′ən), *n.* **1.** an expert in tactics. **2.** any organizer: *He accumulated the experience that made him a political tactician who was useful to his party and to his country* (Wall Street Journal).

tac·tics (tak′tiks), *n.* **1.** the science or skill of directing military and naval forces in battle; the science of disposition and maneuver. **2.** a method or process of doing this. **3.** the actual movements of deployment and maneuver: *Tactics are used to win an engagement, strategy to win a campaign or a war* (Bulletin of Atomic Scientists). **4.** any moves to gain advantage; methods: *When coaxing failed, she changed her tactics and began to cry. To some the obvious answer was to fight fire with fire, to reply in kind if* [*they*] *resorted to bully-boy tactics* (Newsweek). [plural of *tactic* < New Latin *tactica* < Greek *taktikḗ* (*téchnē*) (art of) arrangement, ultimately < *tássein* arrange]
➔ **Tactics,** meaning the science, is plural in form and singular in use: *Tactics differs from strategy, which refers to the overall plans of a nation at war.* Otherwise, it is plural in form and use: *The general's tactics were successful. His tactics in winning the class election were hardly ethical.*

tac·tile (tak′təl), *adj.* **1.** having the sense of touch. **2.** having to do with the sense of touch: *a tactile stimulus.* **3.** that can be touched; tangible.
—*n.* **1.** *Psychology.* a person in whose mind tactile images are predominant or especially distinct. **2.** a work of art designed to appeal to or stimulate the tactile sense: *"The image in my art transcends the visible," he* [*Yaakov Agam*] *said, brushing his hand over one of his "tactiles," a field of silver buttons mounted in springs* (New York Times).
[< Latin *tāctilis* tangible < *tangere* to touch]
—**Syn.** *adj.* **2.** tactual. **3.** palpable.

tactile bud or **corpuscle,** any of numerous minute, oval bodies which occur in sensitive parts of the skin and are involved with the sense of touch.

tac·til·i·ty (tak til′ə tē), *n.* a being tactile.

tac·tion (tak′shən), *n.* the act of touching, or a state of contact: *They neither can speak nor attend to the discourses of others, without being roused by some external taction upon the organs of speech and hearing* (Jonathan Swift).

tact·less (takt′lis), *adj.* **1.** without tact; blunt; gauche: *a tactless person.* **2.** (of an action) showing no tact; undiplomatic: *a tactless reply.* —**tact′less·ly,** *adv.* —**tact′less·ness,** *n.*

tac·tom·e·ter (tak tom′ə tər), *n.* an instrument for determining the acuteness of the sense of touch. [< Latin *tāctus, -ūs* touch + English *-meter*]

tac·tu·al (tak′chu̇ əl), *adj.* **1.** having to do with touch; tactile: *Despite repeated experience of the tactual solidity of the glass, the animals never learned to function without optical support* (Scientific American). **2.** caused by or due to touch. **3.** causing touch; giving sensations of touch. [< Latin *tāctus, -ūs* (< *tangere* to touch) + English *-al*[1]]

tac·tu·al·i·ty (tak′chu̇ al′ə tē), *n.* tactual quality.

tac·tu·al·ly (tak′chu̇ ə lē), *adv.* **1.** by means of touch. **2.** as regards touch.

tad (tad), *n. U.S. Informal.* **1.** a very small boy; chap: *One of the bellboys at the hotel, cute little tad, knew the town like a book* (Sinclair Lewis). **2.** a very small amount.

Ta·djik (tä′jik), *n., pl.* **-djik.** Tadzhik.

tad·pole (tad′pōl′), *n.* one of the aquatic young (larvae) of frogs or toads, having gills, a long tail, and no limbs. Tadpoles gradually adapt to life out of water by developing lungs and limbs, losing gills, and changing internally. [Middle English *taddepol* < *tadde* toad + *pol* (perhaps) poll, head]

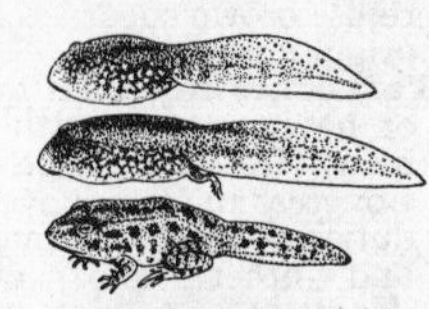
Tadpole, showing different stages of growth

Ta·dzhik (tä′jik), *n., pl.* **-dzhik.** one of an Iranian people living mostly in the Tadzhik Republic of the Soviet Union. Also, **Tadjik, Tajik.**

tae (tā), *prep. Scottish.* to.

tae·di·um vi·tae (tē′dē əm vī′tē), *Latin.* weariness of life; a feeling of unbearable weariness and dissatisfaction with life: *A cloud of vague depression rests on the man, who shuns society, falls off in fat, becomes restless . . . and feels strongly the taedium vitae* (T.S. Clouston).

tael (tāl), *n.* **1.** any of several east Asian units of weight, varying according to locality, especially a liang (1 1/3 ounces avoirdupois). **2.** a former Chinese money of account, originally a tael, in weight, of silver. [< Portuguese *tael* < Malay *tahil*]

ta'en (tān), *v. Poetic.* taken: *The Prince hath ta'en it hence* (Shakespeare).

tae·ni·a (tē′nē ə), *n., pl.* **-ni·ae** (-nē ē). **1.** *Archaeology.* a headband; fillet; hair ribbon. **2.** *Architecture.* a band separating the Doric architrave from the frieze. **3.** *Anatomy.* a ribbonlike structure, as the longitudinal muscles of the colon. **4.** *Zoology.* a tapeworm: *Unbrokenly lay bare each taenia that had sucked me dry of juice* (Robert Browning). Also, **tenia.** [< Latin *taenia* < Greek *tainíā* band, fillet, tapeworm, related to *teínein* to stretch]

tae·ni·a·cid·al (tē′nē ə sī′dəl), *adj.* of or having to do with a taeniacide.

tae·ni·a·cide (tē′nē ə sīd), *n.* an agent or remedy that destroys tapeworms: *A Canadian doctor has recently advocated the use of glycerine as a taeniacide* (Lancet).

tae·ni·a·fuge (tē′nē ə fyüj), *adj.* expelling tapeworms. —*n.* an agent or remedy that expels tapeworms. [< *taenia* tapeworm + Latin *fugere* flee]

tae·ni·a·sis (ti nī′ə sis), *n. Medicine.* an abnormal condition of being infested with taeniae or tapeworms.

tae·ni·cid·al (tē′nə sī′dəl), *adj.* taeniacidal.

tae·ni·cide (tē′nə sīd), *n.* taeniacide.

tae·ni·oid (tē′nē oid), *adj.* **1.** of a ribbonlike shape; like a tapeworm. **2.** related to the tapeworms.

taff (taf), *n.* teff.

Taff (taf), *n.* Taffy.

taf·fa·rel or **taf·fa·ril** (taf′ər əl, -ə rel), *n. Nautical.* taffrail.

taf·fe·rel (taf′ər əl), *n. Nautical.* taffrail.

taf·fe·ta (taf′ə tə), *n.* **1.** (originally) a plain, woven, glossy silk. **2.** a light, stiff silk fabric with a lustrous surface. **3.** a similar fabric of linen, rayon, etc.
—*adj.* **1.** of taffeta. **2.** like taffeta: *taffeta phrases, silken terms* (Shakespeare). **3.** having to do with taffeta.
[< Middle French *taffeta* < Old French *taffetas* < Persian *tāftah* silk, or linen cloth]

taf·fi·a (taf′ē ə), *n.* tafia.

taff·rail (taf′rāl′), *n. Nautical.* **1.** the upper part of the stern of a ship. **2.** the rail around the stern of a ship. [alteration of earlier *tafferel* (carved) panel < Dutch *tafereel* panel (for painting or carving), ultimately < *tafel* table]

Taffrail (def. 2)

taf·fy (taf′ē), *n., pl.* **-fies. 1.** a kind of chewy candy boiled down from brown sugar or molasses, often with butter: *salt-water taffy.* **2.** *Informal.* flattery: *There will be a reaction, and the whole party will unite in an offering of taffy* (New York Tribune). Also, *especially British,* **toffee, toffy.** [originally Scottish, an earlier form of *toffee*] —**Syn. 2.** blarney, blandishment.

Taf·fy (taf′ē), *n., pl.* **-fies.** a nickname for a Welshman; Taff. [< Welsh pronunciation of *Davy* or *David* (in Welsh *Dafydd*)]

taf·i·a (taf′ē ə), *n.* a liquor similar to rum, made in Haiti from low-grade molasses, refuse brown sugar, etc. [American English; origin uncertain]

Taft-Hart·ley (taft′härt′lē), *adj. U.S.* of or having to do with the Labor-Management Relations Act, a law passed by Congress in 1947, governing the rights and duties of labor and management, in strikes and other labor disputes: *The Taft-Hartley Law provides that when the President believes a labor dispute imperils the nation's health and safety, he may appoint the board of inquiry* (Wall Street Journal). [< Senator Robert A. *Taft,* 1889-1953, and Representative Fred A. *Hartley,* born 1902]

tag[1] (tag), *n., v.,* **tagged, tag·ging.** —*n.* **1.** a card or small piece of leather, paper, etc., tied on something, especially as a label: *a price tag.* **2.** a small hanging piece; loosely attached piece; loose end. **3.** a tab or loop by which a coat is hung up. **4.** a binding, usually of metal, on the end of a shoelace, string, etc., to make it pass easily through eyelets. **5.** a quotation, moral, etc., added for ornament or emphasis. **6.** the last words of an actor's speech, or the last lines of a play. **7.** the last lines of a song. **8.** the end of anything, especially a flourish added to a letter. **9.** the tip of an animal's tail, especially when distinct in color. **10.** (in fishing) a small piece of bright material such as tinsel, wrapped around the shank of the hook near the tail of an artificial fly. **11.** a matted lock of wool on a sheep; taglock. **12.** a radioactive tracer. **13.** *Obsolete.* the mob.
—*v.t.* **1.** to add for ornament or emphasis. **2.** to furnish (a speech or composition) with tags, as quotations. **3.** to add on as an afterthought; fasten or tack on: *to tag a moral to a story.* **4.** to mark; label; identify: *to tag suitcases and trunks. A carbon atom can be tagged . . . by substituting the deuterium isotope for one or more of the associated hydrogen atoms* (World Book Encyclopedia). **5.** *Informal.* to follow closely: *The dog tagged them all the way home.* **6.** to cut off tags from (a sheep). —*v.i.* to trail along; follow: *The baby tagged after his brother.*
[origin uncertain]

tag[2] (tag), *n., v.,* **tagged, tag·ging.** —*n.* **1.** a children's game in which the player who is "it" chases the others until he touches one. The one touched is then "it" and must chase the others. **2.** (in baseball) the act of touching a base runner with the ball, or a base with the foot while holding the ball, to make a putout.
—*v.t.* **1.** to touch or tap with the hand. **2.** in baseball: **a.** to touch (a base runner) with the ball, or in making a putout. **b.** to touch (a base) with the foot while holding the ball, as in making a putout.
tag up, (of a runner in baseball) to stay on or return to stay on the base occupied until after a fly ball is caught, before advancing to the next base: *Edwin had no little trouble understanding why a base runner must tag up before running if a fly ball is caught* (New Yorker).
[origin uncertain]

Ta·gal (tä gäl′), *n.* Tagalog.

Ta·ga·la (tä gä′lä, tə gal′ə), *adj.* **1.** having to do with Tagalog, the branch of the Austronesian linguistic family that includes the languages of the Philippines. **2.** having to do with Tagalog, the chief language of the Philippines. —*n.* Tagalog.

Ta·ga·log (tä gä′log, tag′ə-), *n.* **1.** a member of the chief Malay people in the Philippines. **2.** their Indonesian language. **3.** the Austronesian linguistic family that includes the languages of the Philippines.

tag·a·long (tag′ə lông′, -long′), *Informal.* —*n.* a person who follows along: *"And me, I can say something too," said the little tagalong who was never to be outdone by her sisters or brother* (Harper's). —*adj.* that is a tagalong: *For the first time in recent history, the No. 2 man on each ticket will not be a tagalong candidate* (Newsweek).

tag day, *U.S.* a day when contributions to a certain charity are solicited and contributors are each given a tag to wear.

tag end, the very end; last part: *They had been together all season and seemed to resent our coming in on the tag end of it* (Harper's).

tagged (tagd), *adj.* having a tag or tags.

tag·ger (tag′ər), *n.* **1.** a person who tags. **2.** a device for tagging a sheep.

tag·gers (tag′ərz), *n.pl.* iron in very thin sheets, usually coated with tin.

ta·glia·ri·ni (tal′yə rē′nē), *n.* a kind of pasta in the form of flat, broad pieces: *The Bolognese sauce that accompanies the tagliarini is pedestrian* (New York Times). [< Italian *tagliarini* < *tagliare* to cut]

tag line, 1. the last part of an actor's speech or of a play; tag. **2.** a punch line: *An alert member of the audience could often anticipate the tag line of a joke before it was spoken* (Wall Street Journal). **3.** a catch phrase, as in advertising: *The author of the article picks out a few pat tag lines: "Unbelievable—but absolutely true! Nothing like it on any screen! A picture you will never forget . . . "* (New York Times).

tag-lock (tag′lok′), *n.* a tag of wool.

tag·rag (tag′rag′), *n.* **1.** the rabble; the mob. **2.** a shred; tatter.

ta·ha (tä′hä), *n.* **1.** a South African weaverbird, the male of which has yellow and black feathers. **2.** any of various related birds. [< a native name]

Male Taha (def. 1) (4½ in. long)

Ta·hi·ti·an (tə hē′tē ən, -shən), *adj.* of or having to do with the island of Tahiti, its people, their language, or their way of life.
—*n.* **1.** any of the Polynesian people inhabiting Tahiti. **2.** the Polynesian language of Tahiti.

tahr (tär), *n.* any of several beardless wild goats with short curved horns of the Himalayan mountains and southeastern Arabia. Also, **tehr.** [< the native name in the Himalayas]

tah·sil·dar or **tah·seel·dar** (tə sēl′där′), *n.* (in India) a revenue officer. [< Hindustani *taṇṣīldār* < Persian < Arabic *taḥṣīl* collection + Persian *dār* holder]

Tai (tī), *n., adj.* Thai; Siamese.

tai·a·ha (tī′ä hä), *n.* a kind of club or staff about six feet long, carved at one end and frequently ornamented with feathers, used by Maori chiefs as a badge of office, and sometimes for fighting. [< Maori]

Ta·ic (tä′ik, tī′-), *adj.* of or having to do with the Thai race, the principal race of people in Indochina, including the Siamese and others. —*n.* the group of languages or dialects spoken by the Thai race.

tai·ga (tī′gə), *n.* **1.** the swampy, coniferous evergreen forest land of subarctic Siberia between the tundra and the steppes. **2.** the similar forest land in North America. [< Russian *tajga*]

tail[1] (tāl), *n.* **1.** the hindmost part of an animal; the end of the back, on most vertebrates, a separate, flexible appendage to the body. **2.** a thing, part, or appendage resembling the tail of an animal: *the tail of a kite, writing his "g" with a long tail.* **3.** the hind part of anything; back; rear: *the tail of a cart.* **4.** the part of an airplane at the rear of the fuselage, or a tail boom which includes the stabilizers and fins to which the elevators and rudders are hinged. **5.** *Astronomy.* (in most comets) a luminous train from the head, extending away from the sun: *The tail is by far the most spectacular of the comet's features* (Bernhard, Bennett, and Rice). **6.** a long braid or tress of hair. **7.** a part at the end of anything; conclusion: *towards the tail of his letter.* **8.** *Printing.* the end of a page, chapter, or book. **9.** *Prosody.* the lines at the end of certain types of poems, as the sonnet; coda. **10.** the part of a millrace below the wheel; the lower end of a pool or stream; tailrace. **11.** the least valuable part of anything, especially tin scraps; refuse. **12.** any group of followers, as a retinue. **13.** *Slang.* a person who follows another to watch and report on his movements.
at the tail of, following: *She . . . had . . . come to Morocco at the tail of a Spanish embassy* (Hall Caine).
tail of one's eye, the outside corner of one's eye: *Mrs. Westropp watched him with the tail of her eye as she talked to Lady Trevor* (James Payn).
tails, *Informal.* **a.** the reverse side of a coin: *heads or tails.* **b.** Also, **tail coat.** a swallow-tailed coat: *The groom wore tails and a top hat.* **c.** full dress: *The party called for tails and gowns.*
turn tail, to run away; retreat or flee: *The wolves turned tail* (Daniel Defoe). *You are going to turn tail on your former principles* (E.S. Barrett).
twist the lion's tail. See under **lion.**
with one's tail between one's legs, in fear, defeat, or great disappointment; very dejected: *We shall have you back here very soon . . . with your tail between your legs* (William E. Norris).
—*v.t.* **1.** to form the tail of; follow close behind. **2.** to furnish with any kind of tail. **3.** *Slang.* to follow closely and secretly, especially in order to watch or prevent escaping. **4.** to fasten (timber) by an end (in, into, or on a wall, etc.). **5.** to join (any thing) to the end of another. —*v.i.* **1.** to form a tail, especially to move in a file: *Some boys tailed after the parade.* **2. a.** to occur less and less; gradually stop; diminish; subside; die away: *The protests tailed off into only an occasional mutter. . . . a good many numbers, often built round a good idea, that tail away without making an effective point* (Punch). **b.** to fall behind; lag; straggle. **3.** (of a timber) to be held by an end (in, into, or on a wall, etc.). **4.** (of a boat, etc.) to swing its stern or free end away from a wind or current: *tailing upstream in the wind.*
tail off, *Informal.* to run away: *He ducked his head; made a slouching bow; tailed off to his pigs* (Francis E. Paget).
—*adj.* **1.** at the tail, back, or rear. **2.** coming from behind: *a tail wind.*
[Old English *tægel*] —**tail′like′,** *adj.*

tail[2] (tāl), *Law.* —*n.* the limitation of an inheritance or title to a person and the heirs of his body or a specified class of such heirs: *an estate in tail male.* —*adj.* limited as to tenure by an entail.
[< Anglo-French *taile,* variant of Old French *taillie,* past participle of *taillier* allot, cut to shape < Late Latin *tāliāre*] —**Ant.** *n.* fee simple.

tail assembly, the stabilizers and control surfaces at the rear of an aircraft; empennage.

tail·back (tāl′bak′), *n.* (in football) the offensive halfback in the single-wing formation whose position is farthest back from the line of scrimmage.

tail band, *Obsolete.* a crupper.

tail bandage, a bandage divided into strips at the end.

tail bay, 1. the space between a girder and the wall. **2.** the narrow waterspace just below a canal lock, opening out into the lower pond.

tail beam, a tailpiece in building.

tail·board (tāl′bôrd′, -bōrd′), *n.* a board at the rear of a cart or wagon that can be let down when loading or unloading; tailgate.

tail·bone (tāl′bōn′), *n.* **1.** any one of the caudal vertebrae of an animal. **2.** the coccyx.

tail boom, a projecting spar or frame on certain aircraft, connecting the stabilizers and control surfaces of the tail with a main supporting member.

tail coat, swallow-tailed coat.

tail·coat·ed (tāl′kō′tid), *adj.* wearing a tail coat.

tail cone, the cone-shaped assembly behind a turbojet engine through which the exhaust gases are discharged: *When a rocket engine shoots a jet of gas out of its tail cone, Newton's third law takes over* (Time). See **afterburner** for picture.

tail coverts, the feathers concealing the bases of a bird's tail feathers.

-tailed, *combining form.* having a ____ tail: *Bob-tailed = having a bob tail.*

tail end, 1. the hindmost, lowest, or concluding part of anything: *Our plane landed at the new airfield on the tail end of a sandstorm that had swept against us for some hours* (New Yorker). **2.** the end or the tip of a tail.

tail-end·er (tāl′en′dər), *n.* a person or thing at the tail end.

 PRONUNCIATION KEY: hat, āge, cãre, fär; let, ēqual, tėrm; it, īce; hot, ōpen, ôrder; oil, out; cup, pu̇t, rüle;

tail·er (tā′lər), *n.* **1.** *British.* a device for securing a fish by the tail, consisting of a movable loop on a handle. **2.** a fish whose tail breaks the surface of the water.

tail feather, a feather in the tail of a bird.

tail fin, 1. a fin at the tail end of the body of a fish, whale, etc.: *It has two powerful pectoral fins at the front and a tail fin which acts as a skid at the rear* (New Scientist). **2.** any object like this, as that which sticks out on the tail of an airplane or on the rear fenders of an automobile.

tail·first (tāl′fėrst′), *adv.* with the tail leading; backwards: *Ordinarily virus particles attach themselves tailfirst to the cell wall* (Scientific American).

tail·fore·most (tāl′fôr′mōst, -fōr′-), *adv.* tailfirst.

tail·gate (tāl′gāt′), *n., v.,* **-gat·ed, -gat·ing,** *adj.* —*n.* **1.** *U.S.* a tailboard on a truck or station wagon: *They have a leisurely barbecue, using the tailgate of a station wagon as the buffet table* (Sunset). **2.** *Especially British.* the lower gate or pair of gates of a canal lock.
—*v.i.* to drive a truck or car too close to the one ahead of it.
—*adj. Slang.* referring to a style of jazz which consists primarily of the blues and yet is hot: *Sometimes the polyphony is reminiscent of tailgate blues* (Time).

tail·gat·er (tāl′gā′tər), *n.* **1.** *Slang.* a musician who plays tailgate jazz. **2.** a driver who tailgates: *The . . . deliberate tailgater speeds along the lefthand lane, slowing up but three feet from the rear bumper of the car he has overtaken* (New York Times).

tailgate trombone, *U.S. Slang.* a slide trombone played as in tailgate jazz.

tail gun, a gun at the rear of an airplane.

tail·gun·ner (tāl′gun′ər), *n.* a person who operates a tail gun.

tail·gun·ning (tāl′gun′ing), *adj.* having to do with a tail gun. —*n.* the operating of a tail gun.

tail-heav·i·ly (tāl′hev′ə lē), *adv.* (of an airplane) in a tail-heavy manner.

tail-heav·i·ness (tāl′hev′ē nis), *n.* (of an airplane) the state of being tail-heavy.

tail-heav·y (tāl′hev′ē), *adj.* (of an airplane) with the tail tending to pitch down in flight.

tail·ing (tā′ling), *n.* that end of a projecting stone or brick that is built into a wall.
tailings, any residue or rejects; leavings; scraps: *Tailings are a familiar part of any mine landscape; after all, one has to put the stuff somewhere* (New Yorker).

tail lamp, a tail light.

taille (tāl; tä′yə), *n.* (in Old French law) a tax: *The great fiscal grievance of old France was the taille, a tax raised . . . only on the property and income of the unprivileged classes* (John Morley). [< Old French *taille* assessment < *taillier;* see TAIL[2]]

tail·less[1] (tāl′lis), *adj.* having no tail, in any sense; acaudal; anurous: *the tailless ape. A wingless, tailless, propellerless Aerodyne design for jet transports . . .* (Newsweek). —**tail′less·ly,** *adv.* —**tail′less·ness,** *n.*

tail·less[2] (tāl′lis), *adj. Law.* without a tail.

tailless airplane, any type of powered aircraft without a tail, such as a flying wing.

tail·leur (tä yœr′), *n.* a woman's tailor-made suit or dress: *The coolest and most charming summery tailleurs are in crepe de Chine* (Daily Telegraph). [< French *tailleur* tailor, Old French *taillor;* see TAILOR]

tail light, a light, usually red, at the rear of a car, train, etc.: *Sides of the car have been sculptured and round tail lights have been set into the rear* (Wall Street Journal).

tai·lor (tā′lər), *n.* a person whose occupation is making and repairing clothes.
—*v.t.* **1.** to make or fashion (a garment): *to tailor a suit well.* **2.** to fit or furnish (a person) with clothes; outfit. **3.** to make specially to fit; adjust; adapt: *The clinic tailors its treatment to individual needs* (Scientific American). —*v.i.* to make or mend clothes. [< Anglo-French *taillour,* Old French *tailleor* < Late Latin *tāliāre* to cut < *tallia,* for Latin *tālea* rod, cutting]

tai·lor·a·ble (tā′lər ə bəl), *adj.* that can be made into something to wear: *This highly tailorable stuff has been molded into classic clothes* (New Yorker).

tailor bee, any of various bees that cut leaves and line their nests with the pieces.

tai·lor·bird (tā′lər bėrd′), *n.* any of several small passerine songbirds of Asia and Africa that stitch leaves together to form and hide their nests.

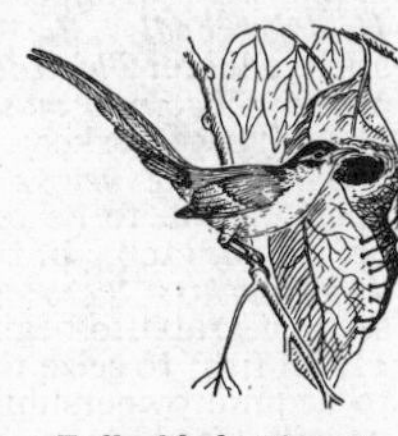
Tailorbird with nest (4 to 5½ in. long)

tai·lored (tā′lərd), *adj.* **1.** cut and sewn: *Paleolithic peoples living at the borders of the great glaciers made tailored skin clothing at least as early as the Solutrean* (Beals and Hoijer). **2.** simple and functional to suit a special purpose: *He sits down with the dealer and a designer and they plan a tailored office* (Wall Street Journal). **3.** of superior fabric, having simple, straight lines and a minimum of ornament: *a tailored suit.*

tai·lor·ess (tā′lər is), *n.* a woman tailor: *At one of the back windows I observed some pretty tailoresses, sewing and chatting* (Nathaniel Hawthorne).

tai·lor·ing (tā′lər ing), *n.* **1.** the business or work of a tailor: *Neither in tailoring nor in legislating does man proceed by mere accident* (Thomas Carlyle). **2.** the clothes or workmanship of a tailor: *British tailoring.*

tai·lor·less (tā′lər lis), *adj.* without a tailor.

tai·lor-made (tā′lər mād′), *adj.* **1.** made by or as if by a tailor; simple and fitting well. **2.** made to fit a certain person, object, or purpose: *Not too many years ago a car would run on most any kind of gasoline, but now engines require fuels that are virtually tailor-made* (Wall Street Journal). **3.** *Informal.* (of a cigarette) manufactured, rather than rolled by hand.
—*n.* a tailor-made article: *She wore English tailor-mades and pale billowy scarves* (New Yorker).

tai·lor-make (tā′lər māk′), *v.t.,* **-made, -mak·ing.** to make especially to fit a person, object, or situation: *We haven't room to list all of the trips they offer or the price ranges, but you can be fairly sure that they'll tailor-make an itinerary to suit you* (Sunset).

tail·piece (tāl′pēs′), *n.* **1.** *Printing.* a small decorative engraving, usually at the end of a chapter. **2.** *Music.* a triangular block, usually of ebony, near the lower end of a violin, viola, etc., to which the strings are fastened. **3.** a short beam, rafter, or joist built into a wall and supported by a header; tail beam. **4.** any piece forming the end; endpiece. **5.** any piece added on; appendage; addition.

tail pin, a slender pin or peg projecting from the lower end of a cello, used to support it on the floor while it is being played.

tail-pipe (tāl′pīp′), *v.t.,* **-piped, -pip·ing.** *Informal.* to fasten something to the back of, so as to annoy: *A party of men and boys . . . having tail-piped a dog for the . . . purpose of making sport of its agonies* (Sporting Magazine).

tail pipe, 1. the intake pipe of a suction pump. **2.** the exhaust pipe of an automobile, bus, truck, or airplane.

tail plane, a horizontal stabilizer. See **stabilizer** for picture.

tail·race (tāl′rās′), *n.* **1.** the part of a millrace, flume, or channel below the water wheel. **2.** any channel that takes water away from a water wheel. **3.** *Mining.* a channel for carrying away refuse (tailings) in water.

tail·rope (tāl′rōp′), *n.* a rope fastened to the back of anything.

tails (tālz), *n.pl.* See under **tail**[1], *n.*

tail·sit·ter (tāl′sit′ər), *n.* an airplane that can take off from or land on its tail.

tail skid, a runner at the back of certain aircraft, used instead of a wheel as a support in landing or on the ground.

tail·slide (tāl′slīd′), *n.* a rearward motion which an airplane may be made to take after having been brought into a stalling position.

tail spin, 1. an airplane's falling with the nose first and the tail circling above it. **2.** *Slang.* mental confusion or agitation; panic.

tail·stock (tāl′stok′), *n.* the adjustable rear frame of a lathe or grinder, carrying the nonrevolving pin.

tail·wag·ging (tāl′wag′ing), *n.* (in skiing) a wide turn at high speed, made with the skis parallel.

tail·walk (tāl′wôk′), *v.i.* (of a fish) to leap repeatedly from the water, as if walking or hopping supported by the tail: *The great fish roars out of the water, sometimes jumping 12 ft. or more, as he goes raging and tail-walking across the ocean* (Time).

tail water, the water running downstream from a millrace, canal, dam, etc.

tail wind, a wind from behind a vehicle, aircraft, etc., helping to move it: *The North Star had picked up a high tail wind and was climbing between the cloud layers at a speed estimated at 240 miles an hour* (Maclean's).

tain (tān), *n.* **1.** a thin tinplate. **2.** tinfoil for silvering mirrors. [< French *tain* tinfoil < Old French *étain* tin < Latin *stagnum* stannum]

Tai·no (tī′nō), *n., pl.* **-nos. 1.** one of the extinct Indian aborigines of the Bahamas and Greater Antilles. **2.** these Indians collectively. **3.** their Arawakan language.

taint (tānt), *n.* **1.** a trace of any harmful or undesirable quality, often: **a.** a condition of contamination, infection, or decay. **b.** a touch of discredit, dishonor, or disgrace; slur: *a taint of bribery. No taint of dishonor ever touched George Washington.* **c.** a touch, shade, or tinge of discoloration; spot; stain; blemish. **2.** an influence toward or cause of any such condition, especially: **a.** a contaminating or corrupting influence; a cause of decay. **b.** a cause of discredit, dishonor, or disgrace. **3.** *Obsolete.* a color, hue, or dye.
—*v.t.* **1.** to tinge, corrupt, or deprave; spoil. **2.** *Obsolete.* to sully (a person's honor); stain; tarnish. **3.** *Obsolete.* to color; dye.
—*v.i.* to become tainted; go bad: *Meat will taint if it is left too long in a warm place.*
[partly short for *attaint;* partly < Old French *teint,* past participle of *teindre* to dye < Latin *tingere.* Doublet of TINT, TINCT.] —**Syn.** *v.t.* **1.** contaminate.

taint·ed (tān′tid), *adj.* **1.** affected with any taint; stained, tinged, contaminated, infected, corrupted, or depraved: *The death toll from tainted liquor in Spain rose to 22 today and officials feared that it would go higher* (New York Times). **2.** *Archaic.* smelling of an animal's scent. —**taint′ed·ly,** *adv.* —**taint′ed·ness,** *n.*

tain·ter gate (tān′tər), a vertically curved dam gate with a horizontal pivotal axis: *Dravo . . . has been awarded a $4,690,050 contract by the U.S. Army Corps of Engineers for fabrication of tainter gates and hoists for four new dams on the Arkansas River* (Wall Street Journal). [< Burnham *Tainter,* an American inventor of the 1800's]

taint·less (tānt′lis), *adj. Poetic.* free from taint or infection. —**taint′less·ly,** *adv.*

taín·ture (tān′chər), *n.* any taint.

tai·pan[1] (tī′pan), *n.* a large poisonous snake of Australia and New Guinea, related to the cobra: *His description of how deadly taipans are milked for their poison by a deft and intrepid snake farmer is hair-raising* (London Times). [< a native Australian name]

tai·pan[2] (tī′pan), *n.* a wealthy Chinese tradesman. [< Chinese *tai pan*]

Tai·wa·nese (tī′wä nēz′, -nēs′), *n., pl.* **-nese.** a native or inhabitant of Taiwan: *Excepting 105,000 Malay aborigines, the Taiwanese are of Chinese stock and have kept their Chinese culture* (Newsweek).

taj (täj), *n.* **1.** a crown or diadem: *He also gave him a taj . . . which kings only were accustomed to wear* (John C. Atkinson). **2.** the conical cap of a Moslem dervish. [< Arabic *taj*]

Ta·jik (tä′jik), *n., pl.* **-jik.** Tadzhik.

tak·a·ble (tā′kə bəl), *adj.* takeable.

ta·ka·he (tə kä′hē), *n.* the notornis: *Believed for many years to be extinct, the takahe was found still to exist when a colony of these handsome birds was discovered in Southland as recently as 1948* (London Times). [< Maori]

tak·a·mak·a (tak′ə mak′ə), *n.* tacamahac: *Mahé . . . is the granite home of a majestic shade tree called the takamaka* (Atlantic).

take (tāk), *v.,* **took, tak·en, tak·ing,** *n.* —*v.t.* **1.** to lay hold of: *He took her by the hand.* **2. a.** to seize; capture: *to take a fortress, to take a man prisoner.* **b.** to catch; snare: *to take a fox in a trap.* **c.** to come upon suddenly: *to be taken by surprise.* **3. a.** to accept; accept and act upon; be guided by; comply with: *to take a hint. Take my advice. The man won't take a cent less for the car.* **b.**

to charge; collect; solicit: *to take money for admission, to take contributions to the Red Cross.* **c.** to accept (a bet). **4. a.** to get; receive; assume the ownership or possession of: *to take a bribe. She took the gifts and opened them. She takes lodgers.* **b.** to obtain in marriage: *He took a wife.* **c.** to bring or receive (a person into some relation): *Take him into your confidence.* **5. a.** to win: *The visiting team took the game 8 to 1. He took first prize.* **b.** to receive (something bestowed, conferred, administered, etc.): *to take a degree in science, to take a sacrament.* **6.** to receive in an indicated manner; react to some or something: *to take it all in good fun. She took the news calmly. He was really good-humoured and kind-hearted if you took him the right way* (Lytton Strachey). **7.** to receive into the body; swallow, inhale, drink: *to take food, to take a drink, to take snuff.* **8.** to absorb: *Wool takes a dye well. Oak takes a high polish.* **9. a.** to have; get: *to take cold, to take a seat, to take cover. Now, in his old age, he takes refuge from his loneliness ... in returning to a vein of childhood memories* (Edmund Wilson). **b.** to obtain from a source; derive: *The town takes its name from George Washington.* **c.** to extract; quote: *a passage taken from Keats.* **10. a.** to make use of; use: *to take medicine, to take an opportunity of leaving, to take the Lord's name in vain.* **b.** to use; use on; beat: *"Take a stick to him!"* (Lewis Carroll). **c.** to use to travel: *to take a train, to take a bus.* **11.** to indulge in: *to take a nap, to take a vacation.* **12. a.** to submit to; put up with: *to take a beating, to take hard punishment, taking things as I found them.* **b.** to study: *to take physiology.* **13. a.** to need; require: *It takes time and patience to learn how to drive an automobile. The trip takes five hours.* **b.** to require as the size that fits: *to take a seven in shoes.* **14.** to pick out; choose; select: *to take sides. Take the shortest way home.* **15.** to carry away; remove: *Please take the wastebasket away and empty it.* **16.** to remove by death: *Pneumonia took him. The devil take him.* **17.** to subtract; deduct: *If you take 2 from 7, you have 5.* **18.** to lead: *Where will this road take me?* **19.** to go with; escort: *Take her home.* **20.** to carry; convey: *Take your lunch. We took flowers to our sick friend.* **21.** to do; make; obtain by some special method: *Please take my photograph.* **22.** to feel; form and hold in mind: *to take it under consideration, to take a dislike to him, to take pride in one's work.* **23.** to find: *The doctor took my temperature.* **24.** to act upon; have effect with. **25. a.** to understand: *I take the meaning.* **b.** to understand the acts or words of; interpret: *How did you take his remark?* **26.** to suppose: *I take that the train is late.* **27.** to consider; regard; view: *to take him as a great man, to take an example.* **28. a.** to assume; undertake (a function, responsibility, right, oath, etc.): *to take all the blame, to take a vow, to take the trouble. She took charge of the household.* **b.** to assume (a form, nature, etc.); develop as: *The cloud took the form of a face.* **29.** to engage; lease; hire: *to take furnished lodgings. We have taken a cottage for the summer.* **30.** to write down; record: *to take dictation, to take minutes at a meeting.* **31.** to receive and pay for regularly: *to take a magazine.* **32.** *Grammar.* to be used with: *A plural noun takes a plural verb.* **33.** to photograph: *to take a scene of a movie.* **34.** to become affected by: *Marble takes a high polish.* **35.** to please; attract; charm: *The new song took our fancy.* **36.** to cause to go: *What takes you into the city today?* **37.** to attempt to get over, through, around, etc.: *My horse took the fence easily.* **38.** (of a batter in baseball) to let (a pitched ball) pass without swinging at it. **39.** *Cricket.* **a.** to catch and to put out: *A minute later Walker was smartly taken at the wicket* (Daily Telegraph). **b.** to capture (a wicket), especially by striking it with the ball. **40.** *Archaic.* to hear and receive (something said to one): *Take our defiance loud and high* (Scott).

—*v.i.* **1.** to catch hold; lay hold: *The fire has taken.* **2.** *Informal.* to become: *He took sick.* **3.** to lessen; remove something; detract: *Her paleness takes from her beauty.* **4.** to act; have effect: *The inoculation took. Skin grafts from donors do not "take" permanently* (Science News Letter). **5.** to make one's way; go: *to take across the fields.* **6.** *Informal.* to appear in one's photographs: *He takes badly.* **7.** to stick to a surface; stick; adhere: *This ink doesn't take on glossy paper. The snow was not taking on the wet street* (New Yorker). **8.** to win favor: *Do you think the new play will take with the public?* **9. a.** to be readily taken (out, off, up, down, etc.). **b.** to be adapted for this: *That machine takes apart.* **10.** (of a plant, seed, or graft) to begin to grow; strike root. **11.** (of fish) to seize the bait; bite. **12.** *Law.* to acquire ownership; inherit: *Since he left no will, his eldest son will take.* **13.** *Archaic.* to accept what is offered: *And when he had given thanks, he brake it, and said, Take, eat: this is my body, which is broken for you: this do in remembrance of me* (I Corinthians 11:24). **14.** *Dialect.* (of a road, a river, etc.) to run in some direction.

take about, to conduct, especially on a round of sightseeing; escort: *He seems to have taken the ... ladies about a good deal* (Annie W. Patterson).

take after, a. to follow (someone's) example: *His followers all take after him in this particular* (Peter Heylin). **b.** to resemble in nature, character, habits, or appearance: *Mary takes after her mother.* **c.** to follow, especially to chase: *The dog took after the rabbit.*

take against, to take sides against; oppose: *The barons took against King John and supported the people in their cause.*

take amiss or take it amiss, to be offended at (something not intended to be offensive): *You ... therefore cannot take it amiss that I have never written* (Samuel Johnson).

take and, *U.S. Dialect.* to proceed to: *I'll take and bounce a rock off'n your head* (Mark Twain).

take apart, a. to dismantle; remove the parts from: *He spent the afternoon taking apart his old Model T Ford.* **b.** to subject to close analysis and usually severe criticism: *The reviewer mercilessly took apart the young writer's first novel.*

take back, a. to withdraw; retract: *I had ... made some complaints of you, but I will take them all back again* (Abigail Adams). **b.** to remind of the past: *The letter took her back ten years.*

take down, a. to write down (what is said): *to take down a speech.* **b.** to lower the pride of; humble: *to take him down a peg.*

take for, to suppose to be: *to be taken for a fool, to be taken for one's sister.*

take in, a. to receive; admit; accept: *to take in boarders, to take in laundry.* **b.** to understand: *Many tragedies on ships and in the air have been due to the failure of a telephone or radio listener to hear or "take in" the message given them* (Science News Letter). **c.** to include: *His jurisdiction now takes in this village. It's too late to take in Helen's party, now.* **d.** to make smaller; tighten: *Sure every one of me frocks must be taken in—it's such a skeleton I'm growing* (Thackeray). **e.** *Informal.* to deceive; cheat; trick: *Some feel he has been taken in by the Administration* (Newsweek). **f.** *Especially British.* to subscribe to (a newspaper, magazine, etc.): *Many of them take in the French paper just as they buy Punch* (Blackwood's Magazine).

take it, a. to suppose: *I take it your own business calls on you* (Shakespeare). **b.** to accept as true or correct; believe (something told one): *Take it from me that he means what he says.* **c.** *Slang.* to endure abuse or punishment: *He can dish it out but he can't take it.*

take it or leave it, to accept or reject without modification: *Too many firms adopt a take it or leave it attitude towards overseas customers* (Economist).

take it out of, a. *Informal.* to exhaust; fatigue: *The sort of day that takes it out of a man* (May Laffan). **b.** to take (something) from a person in compensation; exact satisfaction from: *If any one steals from me, ... and I catch him, I take it out of him on the spot. I give him a jolly good hiding* (Henry Mayhew).

take it out on, *Informal.* to relieve one's anger or annoyance by scolding or hurting: *The nice old lady from Missoula, Montana, who gets hot consommé spilled on her ... shoes, doesn't take it out on the waitress* (Maclean's).

take kindly to, to look favorably upon; be friendly toward: *Freud took kindly to Rank, ... encouraged him to finish Gymnasium ... and get a Ph.D.* (Time).

take lying down, *Informal.* to take without a protest: *He's not going to take this insult lying down.*

take off, a. to leave the ground or water: *Well over a hundred flights a day wing in from or take off for some foreign port* (New York Times). **b.** *Informal.* to give an amusing imitation of; mimic: *to take off a classic.* **c.** *Informal.* to rush away: *He took off at the first sign of trouble.* **d.** *Informal.* to attack: *Committee Democrats ... immediately took off on the Secretary, demanding to know how the loophole got into the ... program* (Wall Street Journal).

take on, a. to acquire: *to take on the appearance of health.* **b.** to show great excitement, grief, etc.: *She took on so about the tiny spot on her dress that we thought she must be extremely vain.* **c.** to engage; hire: *The large manufacturers are ... taking on a considerable number of hands* (Examiner). **d.** to undertake to deal with: *to take on an opponent.*

take one out of oneself, to distract from inner worries; divert: *A drive in the country will take her out of herself.*

take one tardy, *Obsolete.* to surprise in a crime, fault, error, etc.; detect; catch: *He took her tardy with a plain lie* (Nicolas Udall).

take one up on, *Informal.* to accept: *He invited me to dinner and I took him up on it.*

take out, a. to remove: *to take a book out, to take out a stain.* **b.** to apply for and obtain (a license, patent, etc.): *The Bishops were obliged to take out new commissions from the King ... for holding their Bishoprics* (Gilbert Burnet). **c.** to escort: *It was awfully good of you to take the children out, Charlie* (J. Ashby Sterry). **d.** to destroy: *Our initial response might be to take out a couple of Communist airfields by conventional bombing* (Newsweek).

take over, a. to take the ownership or control of: *The company was formed ... for the purpose of taking over the business ... carried on by the plaintiff* (Law Reports). **b.** to adopt; take up: *He had taken over from his father the gift of meeting all sorts of people and dealing with them on their own terms* (Edmund Wilson).

take to, a. to form a liking for; become fond of: *That "instant" coffee so many hurried housewives are taking to lately is exerting a heavy impact* (Wall Street Journal). **b.** to adopt; take up: *If the changes are presented well and explained, then people take to them quite easily* (Maclean's). **c.** make one's way to: *The cat took to the woods.*

take up, a. to soak up; absorb: *A sponge takes up liquid.* **b.** to begin; undertake: *to take up the conversation, to take up residence, to take up law.* **c.** to make smaller: *to take up a dress.* **d.** to pay off: *I am disposed to try and find the money to take up these mortgages* (H. Rider Haggard). **e.** to lift; pry up: *to take up a stone.* **f.** to purchase: *The whole of the limited edition ... was taken up by the booksellers on the day of publication* (Picture World). **g.** to collect: *They take up a collection and bury him* (Mark Twain). **h.** to adopt (an idea, purpose, etc.): *There has, as yet, been no indication whether their resignations will be taken up* (London Times). **i.** to secure the loose end of (a stitch): *This operation of taking up a stitch ... is one of the slowest* (Maria Edgeworth). **j.** to reprove; rebuke: *to take someone up short.* **k.** to reduce or remove (lost motion, etc.); tighten: *to take up the slack.*

take upon oneself, to assume as one's duty or obligation: *This militia must take upon itself to distribute such food as there was* (Edmund Wilson).

take up with, *Informal.* to begin to associate with: *He takes up with younger folks, Who for his wine will bear his jokes* (Jonathan Swift).

—*n.* **1.** the act of taking. **2.** the fact of being taken: *Sometimes there is no "take" on the first vaccination, and it is assumed that the child is immune* (Sidonie M. Gruenberg). **3.** that which is taken. **4.** *Slang.* receipts; profits; *the box-office take.* **5.** act of transplanting or grafting: *Research has demonstrated that permanently successful takes of cross-grafted skin are possible in chicks less than four days old* (Science News Letter). **6.** *Motion Pictures.* **a.** a scene or sequence photographed at one time. **b.** the act of making a photograph or a scene in a motion picture. **7. a.** the act or process of making a recording for a record, tape, etc. **b.** a record or tape of this: *The performance that you buy*

. . . *is as often as not compounded of bits and pieces chosen from a number of takes and edited by a skilled technician* (Punch). **8.** the amount taken: *a great take of fish.* **9.** *Journalism.* any of the portions into which a long story or article is divided to allow the printer to begin preparing it for the press.

on the take, looking for personal gain, usually by illegal means: *When you have a police force of more than 26,000 men there are sure to be some who are on the take* (New York Times).

[Old English *tacan* < Scandinavian (compare Old Icelandic *taka* take, lay hold)]

—**Syn.** *v.t.* **12. a.** endure, undergo, bear.

take·a·ble (tā′kə bəl), *adj.* that can be taken: *We took everything that was takeable.*

take-all (tāk′ôl′), *n.* a fungus disease which attacks wheat and certain other grains, especially in soils which do not have proper nutritional balance: *Take-all in wheat is widely reported, being noted from places as far apart as the East Riding of Yorkshire, Devon, and Essex* (London Times).

take·down (tāk′doun′), *n.* **1.** the act of taking down. **2.** the fact of being taken down. **3.** a rifle or similar firearm that can be taken apart and reassembled readily. **4.** the nut, bolt, joint, etc., between its parts. **5.** *Wrestling.* the act or process of forcing an opponent to the mat. **6.** *Informal.* the act or state of humiliation.

—*adj.* easy to take apart and put back together; collapsible.

take-home pay (tāk′hōm′), the money left after deductions, such as taxes and health insurance, have been made in one's salary or wages: *Based on their current take-home pay, some of the workers probably could spend a good deal more than they do* (Wall Street Journal).

take-in (tāk′in′), *n. Informal.* **1.** any deception, especially a cheat or swindle. **2.** any deceiving thing or person; fraud.

take-leave (tāk′lēv′), *n.* a saying good-by.

tak·en (tā′kən), *v.* past participle of **take.**

take-off (tāk′ôf′, -of′), *n.* **1.** *Informal.* a humorous imitation; caricature; burlesque: *This piece, a take-off on the school and its faculty, is done in typical sophomoric style* (Maclean's). **2.** an airplane's leaving the ground, water, or deck on a flight, especially its move down the runway: *Vertical take-offs and landings long have been a goal of aircraft engineers and builders* (Wall Street Journal). **3.** a leap into the air. **4.** the place from which one leaps. **5.** a disadvantage. **6. a.** a beginning; starting point: *Britain's long-awaited take-off in exports may have arrived at last* (Wall Street Journal). **b.** the act of starting out: *We could try to postpone China's economic take-off* (Manchester Guardian Weekly).

—*adj.* of or for a take-off: *in take-off position. What was required was a massive breakthrough, the achievement of a "take-off" society in contemporary parlance* (Alan Cairns).

take·out (tāk′out′), *n.* **1.** that which is taken out or removed: *The city promised the takeout from the take-home pay will decline to normal* (New York Times). **2.** a magazine article printed on full and successive pages and easily removable as a unit: *There is no doubt that Mailer's journalistic pieces, especially the long takeouts in Esquire, are charged with the energy of art* (Atlantic).

takeout double, (in bridge) an informatory double.

take-o·ver (tāk′ō′vər), *n.* the act of assuming ownership, management, etc.; seizure of control: *An outright Communist take-over would be likely to precipitate civil war* (Manchester Guardian). *In industry there is a continuing healthy ferment of amalgamations and take-overs* (Punch).

take-over bid, *British.* an offer to buy out another company.

tak·er (tā′kər), *n.* **1.** a person or thing that takes. **2.** a person who accepts a bet.

tak·est (tā′kist), *v.* archaic form of the second person singular **take** (used only with *thou*). "Thou takest" means "you take."

tak·eth (tā′kith), *v. Archaic.* takes.

take-up (tāk′up′), *n.* **1.** any taking up, especially forming pleats, a clutch's engaging, or reeling in slack. **2.** a gather in a dress. **3.** *Machinery.* any device for tightening slack ropes, etc., or absorbing waste motion, especially: **a.** a wheel that winds up film, magnetic tape, etc., after use. **b.** (in a sewing machine) a device for tightening the thread in the stitch.

ta·kin (tä′kin), *n.* a goatlike horned antelope found at high altitudes in the eastern Himalayas. [< the native name]

tak·ing (tā′king), *adj.* **1.** *Informal.* attractive; winning; fetching: *a taking smile.* **2.** *Informal.* easy to catch; infectious; contagious. **3.** injurious; harmful: *taking airs* (Shakespeare).

—*n.* **1.** the act or process of one who takes. **2.** capture; seizure: *the taking of game.* **3.** apprehension by the police; arrest. **4.** anything that is taken, especially the fish or animals caught on one trip; a bag or catch.

in a taking, a. in an agitated state of mind: *Lord! what a taking poor Mr. Edward will be in when he hears of it* (Jane Austen). **b.** in unhappy circumstances; in trouble: *The poor boy was in a pitiful taking* (Samuel Pepys).

takings, any money taken in, as receipts, winnings, or profits: *The takings from the Spencer show will go to the church* (Manchester Guardian Weekly).

—**Syn.** *adj.* **1.** captivating, fascinating.

Ta·ki-Ta·ki (tä′kē tä′kē), *n.* a pidgin dialect of English somewhat mixed with Dutch, spoken in Surinam (Dutch Guiana). [a reduplicative variant of *talk*]

tak·y (tā′kē), *adj. Informal.* pleasing; attractive.

ta·la (tä′lə), *n., pl.* **-las.** a set rhythmic pattern used in traditional Hindu music: *Mr. Palghat Raghu . . . undertook to make us aware of triple, quintuple, and septuple rhythmic patterns inside a tala of eight fundamental beats* (London Times). [< Sanskrit *tala*]

tal·a·poin (tal′ə poin), *n.* **1.** a Buddhist monk of southeast Asia. **2.** a small West African monkey. [< Portuguese *talapão* < Talaing (a Burmese language) *tala pôi* (literally) my lord as a title]

talapoin monkey, a talapoin.

tal·a·ri (tal′ər ē), *n.* an Ethiopian silver coin. [< Arabic *talari* (originally) the Maria Theresa dollar < German *Thaler* dollar]

ta·lar·i·a (tə lãr′ē ə), *n.pl. Roman Mythology.* the winged sandals or small wings on the ankles of some gods, especially Mercury (Hermes). [< Latin *tālāria,* neuter plural of *tālāris* relating to the heel or ankle < *tālus* ankle, heel]

Talaria

Ta·la·ve·ra (tä′lä vä′rä), *n.* a variety of spring wheat. [< *Talavera* (*de la Reina*), a town in Spain, in a region where it is grown]

tal·bot (tôl′bət), *n.* a former variety of English hunting hound, with hanging ears and heavy jaws, from which the bloodhound and other hounds were developed. [earlier, the name of a dog, perhaps < *Talbot,* a family whose coat of arms had a dog]

tal·bo·type (tôl′bə tīp), *n.* calotype. [< W.H.F. *Talbot,* 1800-1877, who invented it]

talc (talk), *n., v.,* **talced** (talkt), **talc·ing** (tal′king) or **talcked, talck·ing.** —*n.* a hydrated silicate of magnesium, usually consisting of slippery, translucent, white, apple-green, or yellow sheets, used as filler in paper, a lubricant, and toilet powder; French chalk; soapstone; steatite: *Talc is the softest mineral known* (Frederick H. Pough). *Formula:* $Mg_3Si_4O_{10}(OH)_2$ —*v.t.* to apply talc to, especially to coat (a photographic plate) with talc. [< Medieval Latin *talcum* any of various shiny minerals < Arabic *ṭalq*]

talck·y (tal′kē), *adj.* talcose.

talc·ose (tal′kōs), *adj.* abounding in or consisting largely of talc.

talc·ous (tal′kəs), *adj.* talcose.

tal·cum (tal′kəm), *n.* **1.** talcum powder. **2.** talc.

talcum powder, a powder made of purified white talc, for use on the skin.

tale (tāl), *n.* **1.** a story of an event or incident: **a.** a narrative about a real happening; account: *The old sea captain told the children tales of his adventures. Tales, which are customarily distinguished from myths because of their secular character, are often regarded as an unwritten record of tribal history* (Melville J. Herskovits). **b.** a literary composition cast in narrative form. **2.** a made-up story; fabrication; falsehood; lie. **3.** an improper disclosure of a secret. **4.** idle or mischievous gossip; a rumor. **5.** *Archaic.* **a.** a numerical reckoning; enumeration; counting; numbering: *By measures of forty bushels each, the tale is kept* (Anthony Trollope). **b.** the number counted. **6.** *Obsolete.* conversation; talk.

tell tales, a. to report private or secret matters; spread gossip or scandal: *Dead men tell no tales* (George P.R. James). **b.** to tell lies: *He was punished for telling too many tales.*

tell tales out of school, to reveal confidential matters: *A very handsome . . . supper, at which, to tell tales out of school . . . the guests used to behave abominably* (Thomas A. Trollope).

tell the tale, to tell a tale of woe to evoke pity or sympathy: *We all tell the tale when we want money* (London Daily Express).

[Old English *talu.* Related to TELL.]

—**Syn. 1.** See **story.**

tale·bear·er (tāl′bãr′ər), *n.* a person who repeats harmful gossip, scandal, or rumors: *These words were spoken in private, but some talebearer repeated them to the Commons* (Macaulay). —**Syn.** gossip, scandalmonger.

tale·bear·ing (tāl′bãr′ing), *adj.* spreading gossip or scandal. —*n.* the spreading of gossip or scandal.

tal·ent (tal′ənt), *n.* **1.** a special natural ability; ability: *a talent for music. Genius does what it must, and Talent does what it can* (Owen Meredith). *If a man has a talent and cannot use it, he has failed* (Thomas Wolfe). *Women with the talent for raising the tantrum to an art form and the conniption fit to a way of life* (Time). **2.** a person or people with talent: *Mr. Mayes obviously is a promising talent with something to contribute to TV* (New York Times). **3. a.** an ancient unit of weight or money, varying with time and place. **b.** the value of a talent weight as a money of account. **4.** *Slang.* bookmakers' customers collectively; gamblers. **5.** *Obsolete.* what one prefers; one's liking. [(definition 3) Old English *talente* unit of weight, money < Latin *talentum* < Greek *tálanton;* the obsolete sense < Medieval Latin *talentum* inclination, desire; the other meanings < a figurative sense of money or value. See Matthew 25:14-30.] —**Syn. 1.** faculty, aptitude, capacity, gift. See **ability.**

tal·ent·ed (tal′ən tid), *adj.* having natural ability; gifted: *a talented musician.* —**Syn.** endowed.

tal·ent·less (tal′ənt lis), *adj.* without talent: *a talentless actor, a talentless show.*

talent money, a bonus given to a professional athlete, etc., for an outstanding performance.

talent scout, a person whose work is discovering talented people, as for motion pictures, professional athletics, etc.: *Talent scouts meet frustration in finding the right successor* (Wall Street Journal).

ta·ler (tä′lər), *n., pl.* **-ler.** thaler.

ta·les (tā′lēz), *n.* **1.** *plural in use:* **a.** persons chosen to fill out a jury when the original panel has been depleted because of challenges. **b.** *British.* common jurors summoned to serve on a special jury. **2.** *singular in use:* **a.** one or more people so provided. **b.** the writ ordering them to serve. [< Anglo-French *tales* < Latin *tālēs dē circumstantibus* similar persons from those standing around]

ta·les-book (tā′lēz bu̇k′), *n.* a book recording the names of persons summoned on a tales.

tales·man (tālz′mən, tā′lēz-), *n., pl.* **-men.** a person chosen from among the bystanders or those present in court for jury service when too few of those originally summoned are qualified to be on a jury: *With the consent of the Court, the People will excuse the talesman* (Theodore Dreiser).

tale·tell·er (tāl′tel′ər), *n.* **1.** a talebearer. **2.** a teller of tales or stories; narrator: *You are reminded of those oriental taletellers of the marketplace, whose hands are as eloquent as their voices* (Harper's). **3.** a person who tells a tale or lie with the object of deceiving or misleading.

tale·tell·ing (tāl′tel′ing), *adj., n.* talebearing.

Tal·go (tal′gō), *n.* a lightweight railroad train with a very low center of gravity that enables it to travel at high speed around curves. [< Spanish *t*(ren) *a*(rticulado) *l*(igero) (literally) a light jointed train + *G*(oicoechea), who invented it + *O*(riol), who backed the project in Spain]

ta·li[1] (tā′lī), *n.* the plural of **talus**[1].

ta·li[2] (tä′lē), *n.* a Hindu ornament of gold, engraved with the likeness of the goddess

Lakshmi, and suspended by a consecrated string of many fine yellow threads. It is worn by the wives of Brahmans. *The date had been set . . . when he would clasp the tali around the girl's neck, and the wedding invitations had already been sent out* (New Yorker). [< Hindi]

tal·i·grade (tal′ə grād), *adj.* walking with the weight on the outer side of the foot. [< Latin *tālus* ankle + *gradī* to walk]

tal·i·on (tal′ē ən), *n.* the principle of making the punishment just like the injury; an eye for an eye, a tooth for a tooth; retaliation. [< Middle French *talion* < Latin *tāliō -ōnis* < *tālis,* such, the like]

tal·i·ped (tal′ə ped), *adj.* **1.** having to do with or affected with talipes; clubfooted. **2.** (of a foot) deformed; misshapen. —*n.* a person who has talipes, especially a clubfoot. [< New Latin *talipes, talipedis;* see TALIPES]

tal·i·pes (tal′ə pēz), *n.* **1.** any of various foot defects, especially congenital ones, as clubfoot, characterized by a twisting of the foot to the outside (talipes valgus) or the inside (talipes varus). **2.** a clubfooted condition. [< New Latin *talipes, talipedis* < Latin *tālus* ankle + *pēs, pedis* foot]

tal·i·pom·a·nus (tal′ə pom′ə nəs), *n.* clubhand. [< New Latin *talipes* (see TALIPES) + Latin *manus, -ūs* hand]

tal·i·pot (tal′ə pot), *n.* a tall fan palm of Ceylon, India, and Malaya, with large leaves that are used as fans, umbrellas, wallpaper, and material to write on. [< Singhalese *talapata* < Sanskrit *tālapattra* < *tālas* the fan palm + *pattra* leaf. Compare TODDY.]

Talipot (90 to 100 ft. high)

tal·is·man (tal′is mən, -iz-), *n., pl.* **-mans. 1.** a stone, ring, etc., engraved with figures of occult, astrological significance, usually worn as an amulet to avert evil; charm: *He had stolen from Henry . . . a Talisman, which rendered its wearer invulnerable* (Bishop William Stubbs). **2.** any magic token or charm. **3.** anything that seems to produce extraordinary results. [< French *talisman* < Arabic *tilsam* < Late Greek *télesma, -atos* talisman, religious rite, payment < Greek, consecration ceremony; payment; completion < *teleîn* perform (religious rites) < *télos* services due; completion; tax] —**Syn. 1.** phylactery.

tal·is·man·ic (tal′is man′ik, -iz-), *adj.* **1.** having to do with a talisman. **2.** serving as a talisman: *The name has acquired a talismanic significance* (Harper's). —**tal′is·man′i·cal·ly,** *adv.*

tal·is·man·i·cal (tal′is man′ə kəl, -iz-), *adj.* talismanic.

talk (tôk), *v.i.* **1.** to say words to express feelings or ideas; speak: *A child learns to talk.* **2.** to speak idly; chatter away; prate. **3.** to exchange words; converse. **4.** to consult; confer: *to talk with one's doctor.* **5.** (of animals) to communicate with their voices; make sounds that resemble speech: *The birds were talking loudly.* **6.** to spread rumors; gossip; blab: *to talk behind one's back.* **7.** to spread ideas by other means than speech; communicate: *to talk by signs.* —*v.t.* **1.** to speak (a kind of speech, language, etc.): *to talk French, to talk sense.* **2.** to speak about; discuss: *to talk politics, to talk shop.* **3.** to bring, put, drive, influence, etc., by talk; persuade: *to talk him into waiting.*

talk about, a. to speak in reference to; mention: *Talk about English people being fond of eating, that Canadian party beat all I had ever seen* (E. Roper). **b.** to consider with a view to doing: *He talks about retiring soon from business.*

talk around, to discuss at length without coming to the point or to a conclusion: *The Cabinet members talked around the proposal for several hours before adjourning.*

talk away, to spend (time) in talking; pass by talking: *I am very well content to talk away an evening with you on the subject* (Joseph Addison).

talk back, *U.S. Informal.* to answer rudely or disrespectfully: *The boy was punished for talking back to the teacher.*

talk big, *Slang.* to talk boastfully; brag: *We are able to talk big about light and freedom* (Connop Thirlwall).

talk down, a. to make silent by talking louder or longer; outtalk: *Her that talk'd down the fifty wisest men* (Tennyson). **b.** to give radio instructions for landing an airplane because of instrument failure or poor visibility: *The pilot must rely upon the maintenance staff . . . when it is necessary for him to be talked down by Ground Controlled Approach* (Punch). **c.** to belittle; disparage: *He talks down his competitor's products.*

talk down to, to speak to in a superior tone: *College students resent teachers that talk down to them.*

talk of, a. to speak in reference to; mention: *Talking of Switzerland—have you ever been there in winter?* **b.** to consider with a view to doing: *He talks of moving to a warmer climate.*

talk off (or **out of**) **the top of one's head.** See under **top**[1], *n.*

talk out, a. to discuss thoroughly: *Let's talk this out before we do anything.* **b.** (in the British Parliament) to discuss (a bill) until the time for adjournment and so prevent its being put to a vote: *. . . a form of filibustering to keep all rival records off the air as a politician talks out his opponent* (Punch).

talk over, a. to discuss; consider together: *We will talk over the matter as we go* (Frederick Marryat). **b.** to persuade or convince by arguing: *He talked over Trevittick, who sulkily acquiesced* (Henry Kingsley).

talk up, to talk earnestly in favor of; campaign for: *Two years ago he went to the federal-provincial conference in Ottawa and talked up the idea of a centennial project in Charlottetown* (Maclean's).

—*n.* **1.** the act or process of speaking; using words; speech: *We had talk enough, but no conversation; there was nothing discussed* (Samuel Johnson). **2.** conversation, especially when familiar, empty, or idle: *mere talk.* **3.** mention, especially a rumor; gossip: *There is talk of it.* **4.** an informal speech. **5.** a way of speaking; style; manner: *baby talk.* **6.** a language, dialect, or lingo: *thieves' talk.* **7.** a conference; council: *summit talks. Britain's Prime Minister Harold Macmillan would fly to the U.S. this week for at least two days of top-level talks* (Newsweek). **8.** a subject for conversation or gossip: *She is the talk of the town.*

[Middle English *talken.* Related to TELL.]

—**Syn.** *v.i.* **1.** converse. See **speak.**

➔ See **say** for usage note.

talk·a·thon (tô′kə thon), *n.* **1.** *Informal.* a lengthy period of speaking or debating, similar to a filibuster: *Most Senators agree the Dixie talkathon has been surprisingly successful and the Southerners cannot be worn down physically by round-the-clock sessions* (Wall Street Journal). **2.** a way of political campaigning, by answering questions for an unlimited amount of time before a radio or television audience.

talk·a·tive (tô′kə tiv), *adj.* having the habit of talking a great deal; fond of talking: *He became very talkative over his second bottle of port* (George Eliot). —**talk′a·tive·ly,** *adv.* —**talk′a·tive·ness,** *n.*

—**Syn. Talkative, loquacious** mean talking much. **Talkative,** the common word, emphasizes a fondness for talking and having the habit of talking a great deal: *He is a merry, talkative old man, who knows everybody on our street.* **Loquacious,** a formal word, adds the idea of talking smoothly and easily and suggests a steady stream of words: *The president of the club is a loquacious woman.* —**Ant.** taciturn, reticent, silent.

talk-down (tôk′doun′), *n.* the act of talking down an airplane: *Poor talk-down on the part of the controller, the man in the control tower, contributed to the crash of the plane* (British Broadcasting Company).

talked-a·bout (tôkt′ə bout′), *adj.* discussed: *Certainly she is one of the century's most talked-about authors* (Wall Street Journal).

talked-of (tôkt′uv′, -ov′), *adj.* familiarly or vaguely spoken about.

talk·er (tô′kər), *n.* **1.** any person who talks: *The most fluent talkers . . . are not always the justest thinkers* (William Hazlitt). **2.** a talkative person. —**Syn. 1.** speaker, lecturer. **2.** gossip.

talk·fest (tôk′fest′), *n. Informal.* **1.** a period of light, often aimless discussion: *There must be discipline, because without it classes degenerate into mere talkfests, with the conversation wandering far from the main theme* (Wall Street Journal). **2.** a long or drawn-out discussion: *They saw no reason . . . to propose resumption of the truce conference if it was to be just another futile talkfest* (Newsweek).

talk·ie (tô′kē), *n. Informal.* a sound motion picture; talking picture: *It was not until the talkies came that the cinema divorced itself from reading* (London Times).

talk·ie-talk·ie (tô′kē tô′kē), *n. British.* talky talk.

talk·ing book (tô′king), a phonograph record or tape recording of a book, article, etc., for blind persons.

talking drum, a drum used by certain primitive people for sending messages: *Dressed in native garb, he beat out messages on a pair of African talking drums* (New York Times).

talking machine, *Archaic.* a phonograph.

talking picture, a moving picture with a synchronized sound track: *The "talking picture" . . . sent well-known stars to the scrap heap* (Emory S. Bogardus).

talk·ing-point (tô′king point′), *n.* a subject for talk, especially something to use as an argument: *Many of these tax-free groups can solicit contributions with the powerful talking-point that the gifts are tax-deductible* (Wall Street Journal).

talking stage, a stage or period when some plan has not yet been settled but is still only a matter of discussion: *Also in the talking stage is a plan to link the West Virginia toll road to the Ohio and Pennsylvania Turnpikes* (Wall Street Journal).

talk·ing-to (tô′king tü′), *n., pl.* **-tos.** *Informal.* a scolding; reprimand: *The judge had been kindhearted and let them off without a record . . . though after what a talking-to!* (Atlantic).

talk·y (tô′kē), *adj.,* **talk·i·er, talk·i·est. 1.** talkative. **2.** too full of talk.

talky talk, *Informal.* trivial conversation; small talk: *Probably she'd be called the typical New York girl, if you wanted to talk talky talk* (H.L. Wilson).

tall (tôl), *adj.* **1.** higher than the average; high: *a tall building.* **2.** standing as high as specified: *seven feet tall.* **3.** *Informal.* high or large in amount; extravagant: *a tall price, a tall order.* **4.** *Informal.* hard to believe; exaggerated: *a tall tale.* **5.** *Obsolete.* praiseworthy in various senses; good: **a.** strong in combat; brave. **b.** good-looking; handsome. **c.** proper; fitting; decent. **d.** skillful; dexterous; handy.

—*adv.* **1.** *Slang.* in an exaggerated manner: *to talk tall.* **2.** *Informal.* proudly; with the head high: *to walk tall.*

[Middle English *tall;* Old English *getæl* prompt, active] —**tall′ness,** *n.*

—**Syn.** *adj.* **1.** lofty, towering. See **high.**

tal·lage (tal′ij), *n., v.,* **-laged, -lag·ing.** —*n.* **1.** any tax, toll, or levy. **2.** in English history: **a.** a tax levied by kings on the royal boroughs and crown lands. **b.** a tax levied on feudal dependents by their lords.

—*v.t.* to tax. [Middle English *taillage* < Old French < *taillier* determine the form; (literally) cut to shape; see TAIL[2]]

tall·boy (tôl′boi′), *n.* **1.** *British.* a highboy. **2.** a kind of tall chimney pot. **3.** *Dialect.* a long-stemmed glass; goblet.

tall buttercup, a common, tall, weedy buttercup native to Europe, sometimes grown for its double yellow flowers.

tall copy, a book with wide margins at the top and bottom.

tall fescue, the meadow fescue.

tall folio, a size of paper longer than folio.

tall hat, a silk tophat.

tal·li·a·ble (tal′ē ə bəl), *adj. Archaic.* that can be tallaged; subject to tallage.

tal·li·ate (tal′ē āt), *v.t.,* **-at·ed, -at·ing.** to tax; tallage. [< Medieval Latin *talliare* (with English *-ate*[1]) impose a tax. Compare TAIL[2].]

tal·lied (tal′ēd), *adj.* corresponding; matched; suited.

tal·li·er (tal′ē ər), *n.* **1. a.** a person or thing that tallies. **b.** a person who keeps a tally. **2.** the banker in certain card games. **3.** *Obsolete.* a teller.

tal·lis (tä′lis), *n., pl.* **tal·lei·sim** (tä lā′sim). a prayer shawl; tallith. [< Yiddish *tallis* < Hebrew *tallith;* see TALLITH]

tall·ish (tô′lish), *adj.* **1.** inclining toward tallness; rather tall: [*He*] *is a tallish, vigorous man* (New Yorker). **2.** somewhat exaggerated: *a tallish tale.*

tal·lit (tä′lit), *n., pl.* **tal·li·tim** (tal′ə tim′). a prayer shawl; tallith.

tal·lith (tal′ith, -it; tä′lis), *n., pl.* **tal·liths, tal·li·thim** (tal′ə thim′). a fringed mantle or shawl of wool, silk, or linen, worn by orthodox Jewish men at prayer.
[< Hebrew *tallith* < Aramaic *ṭlal* cover, shelter]

tall oil (täl), a resinous liquid by-product of the manufacture of chemical wood pulp, used in making soap, varnish, etc. [American English, half-translation of German *Tallöl*, a half-translation of Swedish *tallolja* (literally) pine oil]

tall·ol (tä′lôl, -lol), *n.* tall oil. [< German *Tallöl;* see TALL OIL]

tall order, a large requirement, demand, request, or proposal.

tal·low (tal′ō), *n.* **1.** the fat or adipose tissue of an animal; suet. **2.** the hard fat melted down from about the kidneys of sheep, oxen, etc., to make candles and soap, to dress leather, etc. **3.** any of various kinds of grease or greasy substances, especially those obtained from plants.
—*v.t.* to grease with tallow: *I . . . tallowed my nose, and went to bed* (J.K. Jerome). [Middle English *talowe*, oblique case of *talgh*]

tal·low·ber·ry (tal′ō ber′ē), *n., pl.* **-ries. 1.** a small malpighiaceous tree of the West Indies and Florida Keys. **2.** the edible fruit of this tree.

tallow bush, *U.S.* the wax myrtle.

tallow chandler, a person whose business is making and selling tallow candles.

tallow chandlery, chan·dler·ing (chan′dlər ing), or **chan·dling** (chan′dling), **1.** the business or work of a tallow chandler. **2.** his place of work: *Mehevi . . . looking as if he had . . . undergone the process of dipping in a tallow chandlery* (Herman Melville).

tallow dip, a tallow candle.

tallow drop, a gem with the top cut in a smooth, unfaceted curve and the under side the same or flat; tallow-top; carbuncle.

tal·low-faced (tal′ō fāst′), *adj.* (of a person) having a pale, yellowish-white face; pallid (used in an unfriendly way).

tallow gourd, 1. an East Indian climbing plant of the gourd family, that exudes a waxy substance from its fruit when ripe; wax gourd; white gourd. **2.** its edible fruit.

tal·low·ish (tal′ō ish), *adj.* resembling tallow: *The cheeks, formerly tallowish . . ., became ruddy* (Augustus B. Granville).

tallow nut, a thorny tree of tropical America, bearing a plumlike fruit containing a white seed or nut.

tallow nutmeg, a South American nutmeg tree, whose seed yields oil of nutmeg.

tallow shrub, bayberry; candleberry.

tal·low-top (tal′ō top′), *n.* a gem cut as a cabochon; carbuncle.

tal·low-topped (tal′ō topt′), *adj.* **1.** having a slightly rounded or convex surface. **2.** (of a gem) cut as a cabochon.

tallow tree, any of several trees yielding waxy or fatty substances: **a.** a tree of the spurge family of Asia and tropical America, whose seeds are used to make soap and candles. **b.** a tree of tropical Africa whose seeds yield a fat used in cooking and for making soap; butter tree. **c.** the tallowwood tree of Australia.

tal·low·wood (tal′ō wu̇d′), *n.* **1.** a large Australian eucalyptus tree which yields a very hard, greasy, durable wood. **2.** the tallow nut.

tal·low·y (tal′ō ē), *adj.* **1.** like tallow; fat; greasy; sebaceous. **2.** a yellowish-white; pallid; pale. **3.** (of an animal) fat.

tall story or **tale,** *Informal.* an exaggerated, improbable, or highly colored story: *Many tall tales have grown up around the muskies that got away* (Maclean's).

tall talk, far-fetched remarks; exaggeration: *Apocryphal or not, the story is no mere Texan tall talk* (Newsweek).

tal·ly (tal′ē), *n., pl.* **-lies,** *v.,* **-lied, -ly·ing.** —*n.* **1.** a stick in which notches are cut to represent numbers. Tallies were formerly used to show the amount of a debt or payment. **2.** a number or group used in tallying; lot: *The dishes were counted in tallies of 20.* **3.** a notch, stroke, or mark on a tally; mark made for a certain number of objects in keeping account; tally mark. **4.** any board, etc., on which a reckoning is kept. **5.** the account, or score kept; reckoning. **6.** a thing that matches another: **a.** a part that fits; counterpart. **b.** one like it; duplicate. **7.** correspondence; agreement. **8.** any symbol of an amount, as a token, tag, or ticket. **9.** a distinguishing mark on a crate, bale, or case; label. **10.** (formerly in Britain) the charge-account system. **11.** *Sports.* a scoring point; run, goal, etc.
—*v.t.* **1.** to write on a tally; enter; register. **2.** to count; reckon or cast up; inventory. **3.** to mark with an identifying label; tag. **4.** to cause to fit, suit, or correspond. **5.** to score. —*v.i.* **1.** to correspond, match, or answer to; agree; fit: *Your version tallies with mine. It is hard that a man's exterior should tally so little sometimes with his soul* (W. Somerset Maugham). **2.** to duplicate. **3.** to make scoring points: *Larry Jeffrey and Alex Delvecchio tallied in a 49-second span to put Detroit ahead, 4-2* (New York Times). [probably < Anglo-French *tallie* < Medieval Latin *tallia* < Late Latin *tālea* a cutting, rod. Related to TAIL².]
—**Syn.** *v.t.* **1.** record, mark, number, score. *-v.i.* **1.** conform, accord.

tally board, a board on which a tally or score is kept by notches, chalk marks, etc.; scoreboard.

tally clerk, 1. a clerk who checks merchandise against a loading list. **2.** *U.S.* a clerk who helps count votes; teller.

tal·ly·ho (*interj., v.* tal′ē hō′; *n.* tal′ē hō′), *interj., n., pl.* **-hos,** *v.,* **-hoed** or **-ho'd, -ho·ing.** *Especially British.* —*interj.* the huntsman's call when sighting the fox; view halloo. —*n.* **1.** this call. **2.** the act of calling it; a sounding of "tallyho" by a hunter. **3.** a large private or mail coach pulled by four horses.
—*v.t.* **1.** to urge (hounds) by this call. **2.** to cry this upon sighting (a fox). —*v.i.* to call "tallyho." [earlier *tallio*, apparently alteration of French *taïaut* < Old French *taho* or *tielau*]

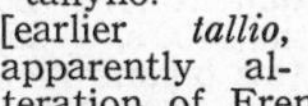

Tallyho (def. 3)

tally keeper, tallyman.

tal·ly·man (tal′ē mən), *n., pl.* **-men. 1.** a man who runs a tally shop; tally-master. **2.** a person who makes entries on a tally.

tally mark, tally.

tal·ly·mas·ter (tal′ē mas′tər, mäs′-), *n.* tallyman.

tally sheet, a sheet on which a record or score is kept: *The TV tally sheet already lists 62 shows . . . devoted to some variation of Cops and Robbers* (Time).

tally shop, (formerly) a shop selling cheap goods on credit.

tally stick, tally.

tal·ma (tal′mə), *n.* a kind of cape or cloak formerly worn by men or women: *He wore a wide hat and a talma—a cloak with full, dashing lines* (New Yorker). [< François *Talma,* 1763-1826, a French tragedian]

Tal·mud (tal′məd), *n.* **1.** the body of Jewish civil and ceremonial traditional law in the Mishnah, 63 books of commentary on and interpretation and expansion of the Old Testament, and the Gemara. **2.** the Gemara, a commentary on the Mishnah, in Palestinian and Babylonian versions, both completed about 500 A.D. [< Hebrew *talmūd* instruction < *lāmad* he taught]

Tal·mud·ic (tal müd′ik), *adj.* of or having to do with the Talmud: *a Talmudic encyclopedia. Chaim Z. Dimitrovsky, 45, professor of Talmudic exegesis at the Jewish Theological Seminary, rested at his home* (New York Times).

Tal·mud·i·cal (tal müd′ə kəl), *adj.* Talmudic.

Tal·mud·ist (tal′mə dist), *n.* **1.** one of the authors or editors of the Talmud. **2.** a person who accepts the doctrines of the Talmud. **3.** a person learned in the Talmud and literature about it.

Tal·mud·is·tic (tal′mə dis′tik), *adj.* Talmudic.

Tal·mud To·rah (täl′mu̇d tôr′ə, tōr′-), *pl.* **Tal·mud To·rahs, Tal·mu·dei To·rah** (täl-mü′dā tôr′ə, tōr′-), a Hebrew school. [< Hebrew *talmūd tōrah* (literally) study of the Torah]

tal·on (tal′ən), *n.* **1.** the claw of an animal, especially a bird of prey. **2.** a clawlike, grasping finger. **3.** cards not dealt; stock; pile. **4.** (in a lock) the projection on the bolt that the key engages; shoulder. **5.** *Architecture.* an ogee molding. **6.** the heel of a sword blade. **7.** *Commerce.* (on a bond) a certificate after the last coupon, to be sent in for more coupons.
talons, clawlike fingers; grasping hands: *the talons of despotism* (Edmund Burke). [< Old French *talon* heel < Medieval Latin *talo, -onis* < Latin *tālus* ankle]

tal·oned (tal′ənd), *adj.* having talons.

tal·pa·ta·te (täl′pä tä′tā), *n.* **1.** a cement-like rock composed chiefly of sand, volcanic ash, etc. **2.** a poor soil composed chiefly of volcanic ash. [< American Spanish *talpatate* < a Nahuatl word]

tal·pe·ta·te (täl′pə tä′tā), *n.* talpatate.

tal·pine (tal′pin), *adj.* **1.** having to do with the mole. **2.** allied to the mole; molelike. [< Late Latin *talpīnus* < Latin *talpa* mole]

ta·luk (tə lük′), *n.* in India: **1.** a subdivision of a tax district, covering several villages, under a collector. **2.** (formerly) the ancestral estate of an Indian family. [Anglo-Indian < Hindustani *ta'alluq* estate, proprietary tract < Arabic *ta'alluq* attachment, dependence]

ta·luk·dar (tə lük′där), *n.* in India: **1.** the holder of a hereditary taluk. **2.** the collector in charge of a taluk.

ta·lus¹ (tā′ləs), *n., pl.* **-li. 1.** the human anklebone; astragalus. **2.** the human ankle. [< Latin *tālus* ankle]

ta·lus² (tā′ləs), *n., pl.* **-lus·es. 1.** a sloping side of a wall, rampart, trench, etc. **2.** *Geology.* a sloping pile of rock that has fallen from a cliff. **3.** any slope. [< Old French *talu* < Latin *talūtium* a sign of gold near the surface]

tam (tam), *n.* a tam-o'-shanter; tammy: *She was smartly dressed in a black velvet jacket with a reddishbrown collar and cuffs, and a bulgy, round tam of the same material* (Theodore Dreiser).

TAM (no periods), *British.* Television Audience Measurement.

tam·a·ble (tā′mə bəl), *adj.* tameable.

tam·a·bly (tā′mə blē), *adv.* tameably.

ta·main (tə mīn′), *n.* tamein.

ta·ma·le (tə mä′lē), *n.* a Mexican food made of corn meal, ground meat, and red peppers, wound in cornhusks, and roasted or steamed. [American English < Mexican Spanish *tamales,* plural of *tamal* < Nahuatl *tamal*]

tam·an·du (tam′ən dü), *n.* tamandua.

ta·man·dua (tä′mən dwä′), *n.* a small arboreal anteater of tropical America, with four toes on the front feet, a prehensile tail, and no teeth. See **anteater** for picture. [< Portuguese *tamanduá* < Tupi (Brazil) *tamanduá*]

tam·a·noir (tam′ə nwär), *n.* the ant bear, or great anteater. [< French *tamanoir,* alteration of *tamanduá* tamandua]

tam·a·rack (tam′ə rak), *n.* **1.** a larch of northern North America with reddish-brown bark, which yields strong, heavy timber; hackmatack. **2.** any of certain similar larches. **3.** the wood of any larch tree. [American English, apparently < an Algonkian word]

ta·ma·rau (tä′mə rou′), *n.* a small, shaggy, black buffalo of Mindoro Island, in the Philippines, with very thick, short horns.

tam·a·rin (tam′ər in), *n.* any of various small South American monkeys allied to the marmosets, having a long, nonprehensile tail and hooked claws. [< French *tamarin,* probably < the Carib name in French Guiana]

tam·a·rind (tam′ər ind), *n.* **1.** a tropical fruit, a brown pod containing one or two seeds in a juicy, spicy pulp, used in medicines, beverages, preserves, etc. **2.** the evergreen tree of the pea family bearing this fruit, also widely grown for its fragrant yellow flowers, streaked with red, and its hard, heavy, yellowish wood. [< Old French *tamarindes,* plural < Arabic *tamr hindī* (literally) date of India]

tam·a·risk (tam′ər isk), *n.* **1.** a small, ornamental evergreen tree or shrub of the Mediterranean region, with fine, feathery branches and minute, scalelike leaves **2.** any other related Old World tree or shrub. [< Late Latin *tamariscus,* variant of Latin *tamarīx, -īcis*]

ta·ma·sha (tə mä′shə), *n.* (in India) a public entertainment, display, or ceremony; function or show. [< Hindustani, Arabic *tamāshā* strolling for fun < Arabic *tamashshā* he walked]

tam·bac (tam′bak), *n.* tombac.

tam·bo (tam′bō), *n., pl.* **-bos.** an end man in a minstrel troupe who plays on the tambourine. [short for *tambourine*]

tam·bo·ri·to (täm′bō rē′tō), *n., pl.* **-tos.** a Panamanian folk dance in which a man and a woman dance together in the center of a circle: *In shirtsleeves and bright native costumes, they waved flags, cheered, sang, wept, and danced the tamborito* (Time). [< Spanish *tamborito* little drum < *tambor* drum]

tam·bour (tam′bůr), *n.* **1.** a drum, especially a bass drum. **2.** a drummer: *Twice a day, the tambour . . . would read aloud the latest dispatches in the village square* (New Yorker). **3.** a pair of hoops, one fitting within the other, for holding cloth stretched for embroidering; pair of embroidery hoops. **4.** embroidery done on this. **5.** (in court tennis) one of the three hazards, projecting from the back wall on the hazard side, to make the ball rebound erratically. **6.** a palisade protecting a gate, road, or entrance. **7.** *Especially British.* a circular vestibule. **8.** *Architecture.* one of the cylindrical stones in a column; drum. **9.** the cylinder on a recording instrument.
—*v.t., v.i.* to embroider on a tambour.
—*adj.* made of strips or slats of wood with half-rounded upper surfaces for sliding easily across rounded surfaces: . . . *a compartment of pigeonholes, which is concealed by a small tambour door* (New Yorker).
[< Middle French *tambour,* variant of Old French *tabour;* see TABOR]

tam·bou·ra (täm bůr′ə), *n.* an oriental musical instrument of the lute family consisting of four strings, and producing a droning sound used as accompaniment to the sitar or sarod: *Even though I had mastered the tamboura in the first three or four lessons, he started showing me all over again how to hold the instrument and rest it on my right shoulder, how to pluck the strings with the forefinger so that they rang as a chord instead of separate notes* (New Yorker). Also, **tambura.** [< Persian *ṭanbūr*]

tam·bou·rin (tam′bůr in; *French* täɴ bü-raɴ′), *n.* **1.** a long, narrow drum or tabor used in Provence. **2.** a Provençal dance, originally accompanied by the tambourin or tabor. **3.** the music for it. [< French *tambourin* (diminutive) < Middle French *tambour;* see TAMBOUR]

tam·bou·rine (tam′bə rēn′), *n.* **1.** a small, shallow drum with only one head, and pairs of loose metal disks (jingles) attached, played by shaking or striking with the knuckles: *The banjos rattled, and the tambourines Jing-jing-jingled in the hands of Queens* (Vachel Lindsay). **2.** an African pigeon with a resonant call. [apparently < French *tambourin;* see TAMBOURIN]

Tambourine (def. 1)

tam·bour-lace (tam′bůr-lās′), *n.* a modern lace of needlework designs on machine-made net, resembling tambour embroidery.

tambour stitch, 1. the loop-stitch used in tambour embroidery. **2.** a stitch used in crochet to make ridges that intersect at right angles.

tam·bu·ra (täm bůr′ə), *n.* tamboura: . . . *the uncanny buzzing drone of a tambura* (Punch).

tame (tām), *adj.,* **tam·er, tam·est,** *v.,* **tamed, tam·ing.** —*adj.* **1.** (of an animal) not wild or savage; obedient; domestic. **2.** (of a wild animal): **a.** taken from the wild state and made obedient: *a tame bear.* **b.** without much fear or shyness; gentle: *The birds are so tame they will eat out of our hands.* **3.** fawning; servile. **4.** without spirit; colorless; insipid; dull: *a tame story.* **5.** not dangerous or harmful: *The reactor was built for tame atomic energy use* (Science News Letter). **6. a.** (of plants or land) cultivated. **b.** (of a fruit) improved by artificial breeding, etc. **7.** not inclined to criticize.
—*v.t.* **1.** to make tame; break in: *The lion was tamed for the circus.* **2.** to take spirit, courage, or interest from; make dull. **3.** to reduce in strength; tone down; subdue; soften; mellow: *The pill will contain living polio virus "tamed" by growing through many generations* (Science News Letter). —*v.i.* to become tame: *She tamed down considerably.* [Old English *tam*] —**tame′ly,** *adv.* —**tame′ness,** *n.*
—**Syn.** *adj.* **1.** domesticated. **2. b.** docile. –*v.t.* **2.** curb, repress.

tame·a·ble (tā′mə bəl), *adj.* **1.** that can be tamed or subdued. **2.** that can be reclaimed from a wild or savage state. Also, **tamable.**

tame·a·bly (tā′mə blē), *adv.* in a tameable manner; so as to tame. Also, **tamably.**

tame cat, *Informal.* a person who is easy to impose upon; tractable person.

tame hay, *Western U.S.* hay made from specially sown grasses or forage plants, such as timothy, clover, and lucerne.

ta·mein or **ta·mehn** (tə mīn′), *n.* a brightly colored silk or cotton garment worn by Burmese women. Also, **tamain, te-mine.** [< a Burmese word]

tame·less (tām′lis), *adj.* **1.** that has never been tamed. **2.** that cannot be tamed. *The leopardess is tameless* (Charlotte Brontë). —**tame′less·ly,** *adv.* —**tame′less·ness,** *n.*

tame-poi·son (tām′poi′zən), *n.* an herb of the milkweed family native to Europe whose root was formerly used as an antidote to poisons.

tam·er (tā′mər), *n.* one that tames.

Tam·il (tam′əl), *n.* **1.** one of the Dravidian people of southern India and Ceylon. **2.** their language. —*adj.* of or having to do with the Tamils or their language.

Tam·il·i·an (tam il′ē ən, tə mil′-), *adj.* Tamil.

tam·is (tam′is), *n.* **1.** a cloth strainer; sieve; tammy. **2.** the fabric used in it. [< French *tamis* sieve of wire, silk, hair]

tam·is-cloth (tam′is klôth′, -kloth′), *n.* tamis (def. 2).

Tam·ma·ny (tam′ə nē), *n.* an influential organization of the Democratic politicians of New York City, founded as a fraternal and benevolent organization in 1789, notorious for corruption in the 1800's. —*adj.* of or having to do with this organization, its politics, methods, or members: *An old Tammany sachem once remarked that he would rather have the "New York Times" against him than for him* (Time). [American English < *Tamanen,* a Delaware Indian chief of the 1600's; (literally) the affable one]

Tammany Hall, Tammany: *Its members are proud of the name Tammany Hall, but the official name . . . is the New York County Democratic Committee* (Time).

Tam·muz (täm′müz; *Biblical* tam′uz), *n.* **1.** (in the Hebrew calendar) the fourth month of the ecclesiastical year and the tenth month of the civil year; June and often part of July. **2.** *Babylonian Mythology.* a god of the springtime and plant growth, who annually returned to earth from the lower world, symbolizing the rebirth of vegetation in spring. Also, **Thammuz.** [< Hebrew *Tammuz*]

tam·my[1] (tam′ē), *n., pl.* **-mies. 1.** *Especially British.* a tam-o'-shanter; tam. **2.** *British Informal.* a Scotsman.

tam·my[2] (tam′ē), *n.* a fine worsted cloth, often with a glazed finish, used in the 1600's and 1700's. [perhaps alteration of obsolete *tamin,* short for French *étamine*]

tam·my[3] (tam′ē), *n., pl.* **-mies.** a strainer; tamis. [apparently < French *tamis;* see TAMIS]

ta·mo·ra (tä mō′rä), *n.* tamure.

ta·mo·re (tä mō′rā), *n.* tamure.

tam-o'-shan·ter (tam′ə shan′tər), *n.* a soft woolen cap of Scottish origin, with a flat, circular crown about twice the circumference of the headband, often with a tassel; tam. [< the hero in Robert Burns's poem]

Tam-o'-shanter

tamp (tamp), *v.t.* **1.** to pack down or in by a series of light blows: *to tamp tobacco into a pipe, to tamp the earth about a newly planted tree.* **2.** (in dynamiting) to fill (the hole containing the explosive) with dirt, etc. [perhaps < *tampin,* variant of *tampion,* taken as *tamping,* present participle; influenced by *stamp*]

tam·per[1] (tam′pər), *v.i.* **1.** to meddle (with); meddle improperly (with): *Do not tamper with the lock. They might not consent to such drastic tampering with the basic structure of the play* (New Yorker). **2.** to work secretly; scheme; plot.

tamper with, a. to influence improperly; bribe; corrupt: *Crooked politicians had tampered with the jury.* **b.** to change so as to damage or falsify: *to tamper with the accounts of a company.*
[earlier, to work clay, apparently variant of *temper,* verb] —**tam′per·er,** *n.*
—**Syn. 1.** see **meddle.**

tamp·er[2] (tam′pər), *n.* **1.** a tool used for tamping concrete. **2.** a person or thing that tamps. **3.** a heavy sheath of lead or tungsten around the explosive elements of a nuclear bomb to prevent the escape of neutrons and to keep the bomb from flying apart too soon.

tam·per·proof (tam′pər prüf′), *adj.* that resists being tampered with: *A tamperproof, nonresettable meter keeps count of checks signed* (Newsweek).

tam·pi·on (tam′pē ən), *n.* **1.** a wooden plug in the muzzle of a gun that is not being used, to protect the bore from dampness, dust, etc. **2.** a plug for the top of a stopped organ pipe. Also, **tompion.** [< Middle French *tampon,* variant of Old French *tapon* < *tape* < *taper* to plug < a Germanic word]

tam·pon (tam′pon), *n.* a pad of cotton, etc., to stop bleeding or absorb secretions. —*v.t.* to apply a tampon to. [< French, Middle French *tampon;* see TAMPION]

tamp work, a surface made hard by tamping.

tam-tam (tum′tum′), *n.* **1.** a large gong, especially one used in a symphony orchestra: *Mahler's Sixth is . . . colored by such exotic instruments as cowbells, chimes, tam-tam, and a special musical hammer devised by Mahler himself* (Atlantic). **2.** a tom-tom. [variant of *tom-tom;* ultimately imitative]

ta·mu·ra (tä mü′rä), *n.* tamure.

ta·mu·re (tä mü′rā), *n.* the schnapper, a New Zealand fish. Also, **tamore, tamora.** [< a Maori word]

Tam·worth (tam′wėrth′), *n.* an English breed of pigs of a reddish color with darker spots, raised chiefly for bacon. [< *Tamworth,* a town in Staffordshire where this breed was developed]

tan (tan), *v.,* **tanned, tan·ning,** *n., adj.* —*v.t.* **1.** to make (a hide) into leather by soaking in a special liquid, especially one containing tannic acid, extracted from the bark of oak or hemlock trees. **2.** to brown (the skin) by exposure to sun or wind. **3.** *Informal.* to whip; thrash; beat. —*v.i.* to become brown.
—*n.* **1.** a yellowish-brown color; light brown or darkish buff. **2.** the somewhat reddish-brown color of a person's skin after being in the sun or wind. **3.** the liquid used in tanning hides, usually containing an acid (tannin) extracted from the bark of oaks, hemlocks, etc. **4.** the bark used in tanning hides and also for covering riding tracks and circus rings; tanbark. **5.** the astringent acid in it; tannin.
—*adj.* **1.** light yellowish-brown in color. **2.** having to do with tanning. **3.** (of a method or substance) used in tanning.
[Old English *tannian* < Medieval Latin *tannare* < *tannum* oak bark, probably < Celtic (compare Breton *tann* oak tree)]

tan (no period) or **tan.,** tangent.

ta·na[1] (tä′nə), *n.* in India: **1.** a police station. **2.** (formerly) a military station or fortified post. Also, **thana.** [< Hindi *thāna*]

ta·na[2] (tä′nä), *n.* the singular of **tanaim.**

ta·na·dar (tä′nə där′), *n.* the head officer of a tana. Also, **tannadar, thanadar.** [< Hindi *thānadār* < *thāna* tana[1] + *-dar* agent]

tan·a·ger (tan′ə jər), *n.* any of a family of small songbirds related to the finches, as the scarlet tanager, the summer tanager, the hepatic tanager, and the western or Louisiana tanager of North America. The male tanager usually has brilliant plumage. [< New Latin *tanagra,* alteration of Portuguese *tángara* < Tupi (Brazil) *tangara*]

Tan·a·gra figurine (tan′ə grə), a terra cotta figurine: *It is very difficult . . . to determine the exact date of the Tanagra figurines* (E.R. Perkins). [< *Tanagra,* an ancient town in Greece]

tan·a·grine (tan′ə grin), *adj.* of or having to do with the tanagers.

ta·na·im (tä nä′im), *n.pl., sing.* **ta·na.** tannaim.

tan·bark (tan′bärk′), *n.* **1.** the crushed bark of oak, hemlock, etc., used in tanning hides. Riding tracks and circus rings are often covered with used tanbark. **2.** a riding track or circus ring so covered: *Out on the tanbark the show will go on much as usual,*

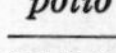

with the frivolous fun of cavorting clowns (Wall Street Journal).

tan·bay (tan′bā′), *n.* the loblolly bay.

tan·dem (tan′dəm), *adv.* one ahead of the other; in single file: *to drive horses tandem.* —*adj.* having animals, seats, parts, etc., placed one ahead of the other: *A tandem helicopter has one overhead rotor in the front of the long narrow fuselage and another in the back* (New York Times).

Tandem (def. 2)

—*n.* **1.** two horses harnessed one ahead of the other. **2.** a high, two-wheeled open carriage, pulled by two horses harnessed in tandem. **3.** a bicycle built with two seats, one behind the other. **4.** a truck or other vehicle with two attached units, as a cab for pulling and a trailer to carry the load.

Tandem (def. 3)

in tandem, a. one ahead of the other; in tandem formation: *mounted in tandem.* **b.** closely together; in cooperation: *The original charge against Oppenheimer was made by Mrs. Crouch (who works in tandem with her husband in the informer's trade)* (Birmingham News).

—*v.i., v.t.* to harness or drive in tandem.

[< a pun on Latin *tandem* at length < *tam* so]

tandem play, (in football) a play in which one player runs close behind another to try to break through the opponent's line.

tan·dem-ro·tor (tan′dəm rō′tər), *n.* a helicopter with two main rotors one behind the other powered by the same engine.

tan·dem-ro·tored (tan′dəm rō′tərd), *adj.* having tandem-rotors.

tan·dour (tan′dúr), *n.* (in the Middle East) a heater consisting of a square table with a brazier under it, to warm those who sit around it. [< French *tandour* < Turkish *tandir* < Arabic *tannūr* < Hebrew < Assyrian *tinūru* furnace, oven]

ta·ne·ka·ha (tä′ne kä′hä), *n.* an evergreen tree of New Zealand with strong wood and a bark containing tannic acid and a red dye. [< a Maori word]

tang[1] (tang), *n.* **1.** a penetrating taste or flavor, often an aftertaste: *the tang of mustard.* **2.** a disagreeable taste absorbed from something else: *a strong tang of onion in the butter.* **3.** the distinctive and indispensable quality of a thing; flavor; nature; characteristic: *The substance of it was pure Russian but the flavor of it had an international tang* (Wall Street Journal). **4.** a slight touch or suggestion; trace: *The language has a tang of Shakespeare* (Thomas Gray). **5.** a penetrating smell. **6.** a characteristic odor: *the salt tang of sea air.* **7.** the long, slender projection, tongue, strip, or prong on a chisel, file, etc., that fits into the handle. **8.** a surgeonfish.

—*v.t.* **1.** to provide with a spike, flange, or other tang. **2.** to give a distinct taste or flavor to: *tanged with orange* (New Yorker).

[< Scandinavian (compare Old Icelandic *tangi* point)] —**tang′er,** *n.*

—**Syn.** *n.* **1.** pungency.

tang[2] (täng), *n.* a ringing sound. —*v.i., v.t.* to ring; clang. [imitative]

tang[3] (täng), *n. Dialect.* any of several large, coarse seaweeds; sea wrack tangle. [< Scandinavian (compare Danish *tang*)]

Tang or **T'ang** (täng), *n.* a Chinese dynasty, 618-906, under which China expanded toward central Asia, Buddhism gained its political influence, printing was invented, and poetry reached its finest development.

tan·ga (tang′gə), *n.* any of various coins in south and central Asia, especially one still used in Goa, worth about 2 cents. [perhaps < Portuguese *tanga,* ultimately < Sanskrit *taṅka* a weight, and a coin]

tan·ga·lung (tang′gə lung), *n.* a civet of Sumatra and Java. [< Malay *tanggālung*]

Tan·gan·yi·kan (tan′gən yē′kən, tang′-), *n.* a native or inhabitant of Tanganyika: *Millions of Africans who had never before been conscious of their national entity or of the very substance of independence now think and act as Nigerians, Tanganyikans, Algerians* (Atlantic). —*adj.* of or having to do with Tanganyika or its people.

tan·ge·lo (tan′jə lō), *n., pl.* **-los. 1.** a hybrid tree of the tangerine orange and the grapefruit (pomelo). **2.** its fruit.

tan·gen·cy (tan′jən sē), *n.* a being tangent.

tan·gent (tan′jənt), *adj.* **1.** *Geometry.* (of a line or surface) touching a curved line or surface at one point only and not intersecting. These circles are tangent: ∞. **2.** in contact; touching; contiguous. **3.** (of a bicycle or tricycle wheel) having the spokes tangent to the hub.

—*n.* **1.** a tangent line, curve, or surface. **2.** *Trigonometry.* (of an acute angle in a right triangle) the ratio of the length of the side opposite it to the length of the shorter of the other sides. The tangent, sine, and secant are the three fundamental trigonometric functions. **3.** *Geometry.* the part of a line tangent to a curve from the point of tangency to the axis of abscissas. **4.** *Music.* the upright metal pin or wedge at the back of a clavichord key, which presses up against the string to produce its sound. **5.** the straight part of a survey line between curves, as on a railroad or highway curve. *Abbr.:* tan (no period).

fly or **go off at** or **on a tangent,** to change suddenly from one line of action or thought to another: *Then his mind went off at a tangent in another direction* (H.G. Wells).

[< New Latin *linea tangens* tangent line < Latin *tangens, -entis,* present participle of *tangere* to touch]

tan·gen·tal (tan jen′təl), *adj.* tangential.

tangent balance, a balance in which the weight is shown on a graduated arc by a pointer attached to the beam.

tan·gen·tial (tan jen′shəl), *adj.* **1.** of or having to do with a tangent or tangency. **2.** having the nature of a tangent; being a tangent: *The two halves of the chamber are connected by a tangential throat* (New Scientist). **3.** (of a motion or force) acting in the direction of a tangent. **4.** wandering off the subject; erratic; digressive. **5.** barely connected with a subject; scarcely relevant or pertinent; marginal. —**tan·gen′tial·ly,** *adv.*

tan·ge·rine (tan′jə rēn′), *n.* **1.** a small, flattened, deep-colored orange with a sweet, spicy pulp and a thin, easily-peeled rind; a variety of mandarin. **2.** a deep, slightly reddish-orange color. [< French *Tanger* Tangier, a seaport in North Africa + English *-ine*[1]]

Tan·ge·rine (tan′jə rēn′), *n.* a native of Tangier. —*adj.* of or having to do with Tangier or its people.

tang·ey (tang′ē), *adj.,* **tang·i·er, tang·i·est.** tangy.

tang fish, *British Dialect.* the seal.

tan·ghan (täng′gən, tang′-), *n.* tangun.

tan·ghin (tang′gin), *n.* **1.** an evergreen shrub of Madagascar. **2.** its fruit. **3.** a poison made from its kernels. [< French *tanghin* < Malagasy *tangena*]

tang·i[1] (tang′ē), *n. New Zealand.* a formal ceremony, poem, or song of lamentation, as a dirge or coronach. [< Maori *tangi* lament]

tan·gi[2] (tang′gē), *n.* (in Pakistan) a sharp, narrow gorge or defile. [< Pushtu *tangi,* plural of *tangai* < Persian *tang* narrow]

tan·gi·bil·i·ty (tan jə bil′ə tē), *n., pl.* **-ties. 1.** the state or quality of being tangible. **2.** a tangible object or matter; reality.

tan·gi·ble (tan′jə bəl), *adj.* **1.** that can be touched or felt by touch; physical; material: *A chair is tangible.* **2.** that can be detected by touching: *a tangible roughness.* **3.** of some importance, moment, or effect; not imaginary; actual: *There has been a tangible improvement in his work.* **4.** specific enough to be understood and dealt with; not vague; definite; real; actual: *tangible evidence.* **5.** whose value can be accurately appraised: *Real estate is tangible property.*

—*n.* **1.** something tangible: *Fighting hunger [and] disease is a tangible that everybody can understand* (Atlantic). **2.** a tangible property, asset, etc.: *National income comprises both tangibles and intangibles* (Wall Street Journal).

[< Late Latin *tangibilis* < Latin *tangere* touch] —**tan′gi·ble·ness,** *n.*

tan·gi·bly (tan′jə blē), *adv.* in a tangible manner; so as to be tangible.

tan·gle[1] (tang′gəl), *v.,* **-gled, -gling,** *n.* —*v.t.* **1.** to twist and twine (strings, etc.) together in a confused mass; jumble (threads); mat; knot; snarl: *The kitten had tangled the ball of twine.* **2.** to hinder, hamper, or obstruct with anything complicated; involve: *tangl'd in the fold Of dire necessity* (Milton). **3.** to mix up; bewilder; confuse: *He had cut the knot which the Congress had only twisted and tangled* (Macaulay). **4.** to trap in ropes, vines, a snare, or a net; catch and hold. —*v.i.* to be or become tangled.

—*n.* **1.** the condition of being tangled; twistedness; obstructedness; confusion; trapping. **2.** a mass of tangled things; knot or jumble. **3.** anything complicated and confused; muddle; puzzle: *a tangle of words.* **4.** perplexed state of mind; bewilderment: *in a tangle of contradictory statements.*

[apparently variant of Middle English *tagilen* entangle < Scandinavian (compare Swedish dialectal *taggla* to disorder)]

—**Syn.** *v.t.* **1.** entangle, snarl, interweave.

—**Ant.** *v.t.* **1.** disentangle.

tan·gle[2] (tang′gəl), *n.* any of various large seaweeds. [< Scandinavian (compare Old Icelandic *thangulr,* probably < *thang* tang[3])]

tan·gle·ber·ry (tang′gəl ber′ē), *n., pl.* **-ries.** a huckleberry of the northeastern United States.

tan·gled (tang′gəld), *adj.* **1.** thoroughly intertwined; matted; tangly: *the fishermen's tangled nets.* **2.** mixed up; confused; jumbled: *His affairs were hopelessly tangled.* **3.** complicated. **4.** bewildered.

tan·gle·fish (tang′gəl fish′), *n., pl.* **-fish·es** or (*collectively*) **-fish.** the needlefish or pipefish.

tan·gle·foot (tang′gəl fút′), *adj.* complicated; confusing; perplexing. —*n.* **1.** anything tangling or confusing. **2.** *U.S. Slang.* an intoxicating beverage, especially whiskey.

tan·gle·foot·ed (tang′gəl fút′id), *adj.* having tangled feet; stumbling.

tan·gle-legs (tang′gəl legz′), *n. U.S.* **1.** a popular name of the hobblebush. **2.** *Slang.* strong beer or liquor.

tan·gle·ment (tang′gəl mənt), *n.* **1.** being tangled. **2.** a tangle.

tangle net, a gill net: *Both the Russians and the Japanese fish with giant tangle nets, measuring 10 feet wide and about five miles long* (Wall Street Journal).

tangle picker, *British Dialect.* the turnstone.

tan·gler (tang′glər), *n.* one that tangles.

tangle tent, a tent or pledget of seaweed.

tan·gle·toad (tang′gəl tōd′), *n. British Dialect.* a variety of buttercup with double yellow flowers, that sends out long runners which root themselves.

tan·gle·weed (tang′gəl wēd′), *n.* tang[3].

tan·gle·wrack (tang′gəl rak′), *n.* tang[3].

tan·gly (tang′glē), *adj.* **1.** in a tangle. **2.** full of tangles.

tan·go (tang′gō), *n., pl.* **-gos,** *v.,* **-goed, -go·ing.** —*n.* **1.** a Spanish-American ballroom dance in rather slow duple time, with intricate gliding, turning, and dipping steps, adapted from an animated Spanish solo dance. **2.** the music for it. —*v.i.* to do this dance. [< Cuban Spanish *tango*]

Tan·go (tang′gō), *n. U.S.* a code name for the letter *t,* used in transmitting radio messages.

tan·go·ist (tan′gō ist), *n.* a person who dances the tango.

tan·gor (tan′jôr, -jor), *n.* a hybrid between a tangerine and an orange: *They are natural hybrids, almost certainly tangors . . . and they are so sweet that people on diets sometimes eat them before dinner in order to throttle their appetites* (New Yorker). [< *tang*(erine) + *or*(ange)]

tan·gram (tang′grəm), *n.* a Chinese puzzle of five triangles, a square, and a parallelogram to arrange into a large square, then into many other figures: *The Chinese puzzle game called tangram [is] believed to be thousands of years old* (Scientific American).

Tangram

tang sparrow, *British Dialect.* the water pipit.

tan·gun (täng′gən, tang′-), *n.* a strong and sure-footed little Tibetan pony. [< Hindi *ṭāṅghan* < Tibetan *Tāñān* < *Ta* horse]

tang whaup, *British Dialect.* curlew.

tang·y (tang′ē), *adj.,* **tang·i·er, tang·i·est. 1.** having a tang; piquant. **2.** with a disagreeable taste. Also, **tangey.**

tan·house (tan′hous′), *n.* a building in which tanning is carried on: *No one knows in the village when the Welsh world ended or English began. Tanhouse, malthouse, lime pit . . . one by one they have dropped out* (Manchester Guardian Weekly).

tan·ia (tan′yə), *n.* a potatolike plant of the arum family related to the taro, cultivated in tropical America and Africa for its edible tubers and leaves. [< Tupi (Brazil) *taña, taya,* Carib *taya*]

tan·ier (tan′yər), *n.* tania.

tan·ist (tan′ist, thô′nist), *n.* (in Irish history) a Celtic chief's heir apparent, elected by the tribe during his lifetime, usually his most vigorous adult kinsman. [< Irish, Scottish Gaelic *tánaiste*]

tan·is·tic (ta nis′tik, thô-), *adj.* of or having to do with a tanist.

tan·ist·ry (tan′ə strē, thô′nə-), *n.* the practice of electing tanists, usually during the chief's lifetime: *Despite tanistry . . . Scotland managed to have real monarchs when Ireland had none* (Times Literary Supplement).

tan·ist·ship (tan′ist ship, thô′nist-), *n.* the position or function of a tanist.

tank[1] (tangk), *n.* **1.** a large container for a liquid or gas, usually a rectangular or cylindrical structure for storage, testing, etc.; vat: *He always kept plenty of gasoline in the tank of his automobile.* **2.** (in India) a natural pool or lake, especially for irrigation. —*v.t.* to fill a tank with and store.
—*v.i.* **tank up, a.** *Slang.* to drink heavily: *Both of 'em are tankin' up next door, and layin' for you and the whole bunch* (Clinton H. Stagg). **b.** *Informal.* to fill up the fuel tank of an automobile, etc., with gasoline: *We tanked up at the service station before getting onto the turnpike.*
[apparently < Portuguese *tanque* < Latin *stagnum* pool; (definition 2) perhaps < Gujarati *tānkh* cistern]
—**Syn.** *n.* **1.** cistern, reservoir.

tank[2] (tangk), *n.* a heavily armored, combat vehicle carrying machine guns and usually cannon, moving on a caterpillar track on each side. [special use of *tank*[1], a label to disguise the content of crates which housed the vehicles during transport in the first World War] —**tank′like′,** *adj.*

Army Tank[2]

tan·ka[1] (tang′kə), *n.* a descendant of an aboriginal people of Canton, China, who live entirely in the boats (tanka boats) by which they make a living. [< Cantonese *tan* egg + Chinese *ka* family, people]

tan·ka[2] (tang′kə), *n.* a Japanese verse form of 31 syllables arranged in five lines of 5, 7, 5, 7, and 7 syllables. [< Japanese *tanka*]

tan·ka[3] (tang′kə), *n.* a Tibetan religious scroll painting carried as a banner. [< a Tibetan word]

tank·age (tang′kij), *n.* **1.** the capacity of a tank or tanks. **2.** storage tanks collectively. **3.** the cost of such storage. **4.** fertilizer and coarse feed made in slaughterhouses of carcasses after rendering their fat.

tank·ard (tang′kərd), *n.* a large beer mug, usually with a handle and a hinged cover; flagon. [compare Middle Dutch *tanckaert*]

tankard turnip, *British Dialect.* a turnip with a long tuber.

tank·bust·er (tangk′bus′tər), *n. Slang.* an airplane equipped with antitank cannon.

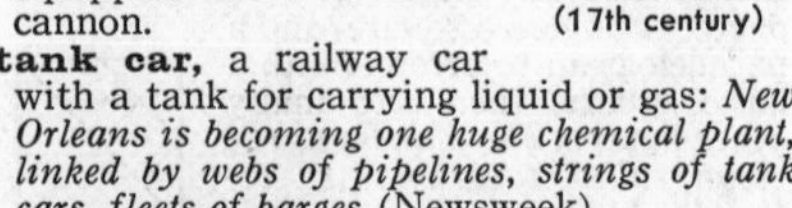
Tankard (17th century)

tank car, a railway car with a tank for carrying liquid or gas: *New Orleans is becoming one huge chemical plant, linked by webs of pipelines, strings of tank cars, fleets of barges* (Newsweek).

tank destroyer, a fast, lightly armored motorized vehicle carrying a heavy gun for destroying tanks.

tank drama, *Slang.* **1.** a sensational play including adventures in a tank of water, especially a drowning rescue. **2.** any sensational melodrama.

tanked (tangkt), *adj. Slang.* drunk.

tank engine, tank locomotive.

tank·er (tang′kər), *n.* **1.** a ship for carrying liquid cargo, especially oil: *The tanker Salem Maritime had just finished taking on 130,000 barrels of gasoline, kerosene, and oil at Lake Charles* (Newsweek). **2.** any vehicle carrying liquid cargo, as a tank truck or tanker plane. **3.** a soldier who fights in a tank: *The Army's tankers are hoping, however, that these tanks . . . will be supplemented eventually* (New York Times).
—*v.t.* to transport in a tanker: *Most of Saudi Arabia's oil is tankered to market* (Wall Street Journal).

tank·er·ing (tang′kər ing), *n.* the loading and unloading of tankers.

tank·er·man (tang′kər mən), *n., pl.* **-men.** the owner or manager of a company that ships oil, etc., by tanker.

tanker plane, an airplane equipped with large tanks to carry fuel: *The Air Force announced today that it had converted a B-47 jet bomber into a tanker plane capable of refueling other B-47's in flight* (New York Times).

tank farm, a group of storage tanks around an oil field or refinery.

tank farming, hydroponics.

tank·ful (tangk′fu̇l), *n., pl.* **-fuls.** as much as a tank will hold: *Florists sometimes release tankfuls of carbon dioxide in greenhouses to promote plant growth* (Scientific American).

tank·ie (tang′kē), *n. British Naval Slang.* an officer or sailor in charge of the freshwater tanks; captain of the hold.

tank·less (tangk′lis), *adj.* without a tank: *a tankless toilet.*

tank locomotive, *U.S.* a railway engine carrying fuel and water itself, not in a separate tender.

tank·man (tangk′mən), *n., pl.* **-men.** **1.** a member of a tank crew. **2.** tankie.

tank runner, a jaçana of Indonesia, Ceylon, etc., with a tail like a pheasant's that lives near watering places and marshes.

tank·ship (tangk′ship′), *n.* an oil tanker.

tank station, a place with tanks, especially to supply water to railway engines.

tank-steam·er (tangk′stē′mər), *n.* an oil tanker run by steam.

tank suit, a one-piece bathing suit for women, of a type popular in the 1920's.

tank top, 1. *U.S.* a woman's loose overblouse: *Her chemise bathing suit combines a black tank top . . . and a maillot* (New Yorker). **2.** *Nautical.* the plating that forms the inner bottom of a ship, creating a watertight space above the outer bottom.

tank town, 1. *U.S.* a small town where trains stopped mainly to get water. **2.** *U.S. Informal.* any small town; hick town. —**tank′town′,** *adj.*

tank trailer, a trailer for transporting liquid cargoes, such as oil, cement, etc.

tank trap, any of a number of obstacles, such as concrete blocks, ditches, mines, etc., put up to stop tanks.

tank truck, a truck for carrying liquids.

tank·ves·sel (tangk′ves′əl), *n.* an oil tanker.

tank·wag·on (tangk′wag′ən), *n.* a tank truck for transporting liquid cargoes.

tank waste, the insoluble sediment from the dissolving tanks in alkali works.

tank·worm (tangk′wėrm′), *n.* a parasitic nematode worm found in the mud in India, probably the young of the guinea worm.

tan·ling (tan′ling), *n. Poetic.* a person tanned or browned by the sun: *hot summer's tanlings* (Shakespeare).

tan·na (tä′nä), *n.* the singular of **tannaim.**

tan·na·ble (tan′ə bəl), *adj.* that can be tanned.

tan·na·dar (tä′nə där′), *n.* tanadar.

tan·na·im (tä nä′im), *n.pl., sing.* **tan·na.** the commentators who wrote the Mishnah, a group of rabbis who lived about 10-200 A.D. [< Hebrew *tannāīm* teachers]

tan·na·ites (tä′nə īts), *n.pl.* the tannaim.

tan·na·it·ic (tä′nə it′ik), *adj.* **1.** of or having to do with the tannaim. **2.** like the tannaim.

tan·nate (tan′āt), *n.* a salt or ester of tannin (tannic acid).

tanned (tand), *adj.* **1.** (of a hide) made into leather. **2.** made brown by the sun or wind. **3.** reddish-brown; tawny color.

tan·ner[1] (tan′ər), *n.* a person whose work is tanning hides.

tan·ner[2] (tan′ər), *n. British Slang.* a sixpence.

tanner's or **tanners' bark,** tanbark.

tanners' sumac, a European sumac whose leaves and shoots are dried and chopped for tanning. Also, **tanning sumac.**

tanners' tree, 1. a low deciduous shrub of southern Europe used in tanning. **2.** tanners' sumac.

tan·ner·y (tan′ər ē), *n., pl.* **-ner·ies.** a place where hides are tanned; tanyard.

Tann·häu·ser (tän′hoi′zər, tan′-), *n. German Legend.* a poet who, after a time of wicked pleasure, was refused pardon by the Pope.

tan·nic (tan′ik), *adj.* **1.** of or like tannin. **2.** derived from tanbark.

tannic acid, 1. any of various astringent organic substances like tannin, especially the principle derived from oak bark. **2.** the white, amorphous, strongly astringent tannin principle derived from nutgalls *Formula:* $C_{14}H_{10}O_9$

tan·nier (tan′yər), *n.* tania.

tan·nif·er·ous (ta nif′ər əs), *adj.* containing or yielding tannin.

tan·nin (tan′ən), *n.* any of various astringent vegetable acids, as common tannin, the whitish tannic acid abundant in nutgalls, or the reddish compound containing the tanning property of oak bark: *Tannin is used in tanning, dyeing, making ink, and in medicine.* [< French *tanin* < *tan* (< Medieval Latin *tannum;* see TAN)] —**tan′nin-like′,** *adj.*

tan·ning (tan′ing), *n.* **1.** the work, process, or art of transforming hide and skins into leather: *True tanning, as opposed to curing with animal fats, is limited to the Old World and to the technologically more advanced cultures* (Beals and Hoijer). **2.** a making brown, as by exposure to the sun. **3.** *Informal.* a beating; thrashing; whipping; flogging.

tannin glycerol, glycerin of tannic acid.

tanning sumac, tanners' sumac.

Ta·no·an (tä′nō ən), *n.* a family of American Indian languages spoken in northern New Mexico. —*adj.* of or having to do with this family of languages.

tan·rec (tan′rek), *n.* tenrec.

tan·sy (tan′zē), *n., pl.* **-sies. 1.** a coarse, strong-smelling weed of the composite family with notched, divided leaves, clusters of small, yellow flowers, and a bitter taste. It was formerly much used in cooking and in medicine as a stomachic. *Equally vivid along the road and in winter bouquets is the pungent herb called tansy* (New York Times). **2.** any other plants of the same genus. **3.** any of various other plants, as the silverweed. **4.** tansy ragwort. **5.** tansy cake.
like a tansy, *Archaic.* perfectly: *I would work . . . like a horse, and make fortifications for you . . . like a tansy* (Laurence Sterne).
[< Old French *tanesie,* short for *athanasie* < Late Latin *athanasia* < Greek *athanasiā* elixir; (originally) immortality < *a-* without + *thánatos* death]

Sprig of Tansy (def. 1)

tansy cake or **pudding,** an Easter cake: *Chester still clings to its Tansy pudding, symbolical of the bitter herb commanded at the paschal feast* (Daily Chronicle).

tansy ragwort, a toxic weed of the composite family native to Europe and naturalized in North America, poisonous to cattle; felonweed.

tan·ta·late (tan′tə lāt), *n.* a salt of tantalic acid.

tan·ta·le·an or **tan·ta·li·an** (tan tā′lē ən), *adj.* **1.** of or having to do with Tantalus. **2.** like that of Tantalus; tantalizing.

tan·tal·ic (tan tal′ik), *adj.* **1.** of or having to do with tantalum. **2.** containing tantalum, especially with a valence of five.

tantalic acid, a colorless, crystalline acid, known mainly in the form of its salts, the tantalates. *Formula:* $HTaO_3$

tan·ta·lise (tan′tə līz), *v.t.,* **-lised, -lis·ing.** *Especially British.* tantalize.

tan·ta·lis·ing (tan′tə lī′zing), *adj. Especially British.* tantalizing. —**tan′ta·lis′ing·ly,** *adv.*

tan·ta·lite (tan′tə līt), *n.* a rare, heavy, black crystalline mineral with a submetallic luster, iron tantalate, rarely found without manganese or columbium. It is the chief ore of tantalum. [< German *Tantalit*]

tan·ta·li·za·tion (tan′tə lə zā′shən), *n.* **1.** a tantalizing. **2.** a being tantalized.

tan·ta·lize (tan′tə līz), *v.t.,* **-lized, -liz·ing. 1.** to torment by showing a desired thing but keeping it out of reach. **2.** to tease by repeatedly raising hopes and deliberately dashing them; frustrate on purpose. —**Syn. 1, 2.** plague, vex. —**Ant. 1, 2.** satisfy, gratify, content, appease.

tan·ta·liz·er (tan′tə lī′zər), *n.* a person or thing that tantalizes.

tan·ta·liz·ing (tan′tə lī′zing), *adj.* exciting desire, curiosity, appetite, etc.; enticing; tempting; provocative: *a tantalizing concept. He lives with the tantalizing knowledge that his late father's millions lie just beyond his reach in a Swiss bank* (Maclean's). —**tan′ta·liz′ing·ly,** *adv.*

tan·ta·lous (tan′tə ləs), *adj.* **1.** of or having to do with tantalum. **2.** derived from tantalum. **3.** containing tantalum, especially with a valence of three.

tan·ta·lum (tan′tə ləm), *n.* a rare metallic chemical element occurring in tantalite, columbite, and other rare minerals. It is hard, ductile, acid-resistant, grayish-white, and of metallic luster. *Symbol:* Ta; *at.wt.:* (C^{12}) 180.948 or (O^{16}) 180.95; *at.no.:* 73; *valence:* (chiefly) 5, 3; *sp.gr.:* 16.6. [< Swedish *Tantalum* < Latin *Tantalus* Tantalus (because it cannot absorb acid though immersed in it)]

Tan·ta·lus (tan′tə ləs), *n. Greek Mythology.* a king of Phrygia, son of Zeus and the nymph Pluto, father of Niobe and Pelops, obliged, for betraying the gods' secrets, to stand in the river Tartarus up to his chin, under branches of fruit. Whenever he tried to drink or eat, the water or fruit withdrew, and a rock continually threatened to fall on him.

tan·ta·lus (tan′tə ləs), *n.* **1.** *British.* a rack of decanters which seem free but must be unlocked to be used. **2. a.** a genus of storks. **b.** a species of these; wood stork. [< *Tantalus*] —**tan′ta·lus·like′,** *adj.*

Tantalus cup, a toy, a siphon in the form of a man whose chin is at the bend in it.

tan·ta·mount (tan′tə mount), *adj.* as much as; equivalent: *The withdrawal of his statement is tantamount to an apology.* [< verb] —*v.i. Obsolete.* to be or become equivalent; amount. [< Anglo-French *tant amunter* amount to as much < *tant* as much (< Latin *tantum*) + *amunter* amount to] —**Syn.** See **equal.**

tan·tar·a (tan tar′ə, -tär′-; tan′tər ə), *n.* **1.** a flourish or blast of a trumpet or horn; fanfare. **2.** any similar sound. [(originally) interjection used as a poetic refrain; imitative (especially of a trumpet)]

tante (tänt), *n. French.* aunt.

Tan·te (tän′tə), *n. German.* aunt.

tan·tiv·y (tan tiv′ē), *interj., n., pl.* **-tiv·ies,** *adv., adj., v.,* **-tiv·ied, -tiv·y·ing.** —*interj.* full gallop! (a cry in hunting).
—*n.* **1.** a ride at full gallop; rush. **2.** a hunting cry when in full gallop. **3.** a High-Churchman or Tory.
—*adv., adj.* at full gallop; headlong.
—*v.i.* to ride at full gallop; rush: *Midnight roundabout riders tantivying under the fairy-lights* (Atlantic). —*v.t.* to call "tantivy." [perhaps imitative of hoofbeats]

tant mieux (tän myœ′), *French.* all the better.

tan·to (tän′tō), *adv. Music.* so; so much; too much (used in a direction). [< Italian *tanto* < Latin *tantum* so much]

tan·to·ny bell (tan′tə nē), **1.** a handbell. **2.** a small church bell. [short for *Saint Anthony,* whose emblem was a bell]

tantony pig, 1. the smallest pig of a litter. **2.** a person who follows another slavishly: *To see you dangling after me everywhere, like a tantony pig* (Isaac Bickerstaffe).

tant pis (tän pē′), *French.* all the worse.

tan·tra (tan′trə), *n.* **1.** one of a class of Hindu religious works in Sanskrit, of comparatively late date, related to the puranas, in which mysticism and magic play a great part. **2.** one of a class of Buddhist works of a somewhat similar character. [< Sanskrit *tantra* loom, warp; principle, doctrine < *tan* to stretch]

tan·tric (tan′trik), *adj.* of or having to do with the tantras.

tan·trum (tan′trəm), *n. Informal.* an outburst of ill-temper intended to get what one wants; fit of petulance. [origin unknown]

Tan·tum Er·go (tan′təm ėr′gō), **1.** the hymn of Saint Thomas Aquinas, "Pange lingua gloriosi Corporis mysterium." **2.** the last two stanzas, sung at Benediction. **3.** a setting of these. [< Latin *tantum* (*sacramentum*) so great (a sacrament); *ergo* therefore (words from the hymn)]

tan·yard (tany′ärd′), *n.* a tannery.

Tan·za·ni·an (tan zə nē′ən), *adj.* of or having to do with the republic of Tanzania (formed in 1964 by the union of Tanganyika and Zanzibar) or its people: *The Arabs and Indians heard the President repeat several times: "The Tanzanian Government does not intend to have slaves"* (Manchester Guardian Weekly). —*n.* a native or inhabitant of Tanzania: *The charge . . . reportedly stemmed from a monitored conversation wrongly interpreted by the Tanzanians* (Geoffrey Godsell).

taoi·seach (tē′shok), *n.* a prime minister of Ireland. [< Irish *taioseach*]

Tao·ism (tou′iz əm, dou′-), *n.* a pantheistic religion and philosophy, ranking with Buddhism and Confucianism as one of the three great religions of China, founded on the principles of the ancient philosopher Lao-tse. Taoism seeks to avoid complexity in life by conforming with nature. [< Chinese *tao* the right way, or path, in the title *Tao te Ching* (*The Way and Its Power*) by Lao-tse, born 604? B.C., a philosopher]

Tao·ist (tou′ist, dou′-), *n.* a believer in Taoism. —*adj.* of or having to do with Taoists or Taoism.

Tao·is·tic (tou is′tik, dou-), *adj.* Taoist.

Taos (tous), *n.* a Tanoan American Indian language of New Mexico.

tap[1] (tap), *v.,* **tapped, tap·ping,** *n.* —*v.t.* **1.** to strike gently; strike lightly, often audibly: *to tap him on the shoulder.* **2.** to use (one's hand, foot, etc.) in knocking; cause to strike lightly: *She tapped her foot on the floor.* **3.** to make (sounds) by light blows: *to tap a rhythm, to tap time, to tap out a message.* **4.** to move by light blows; shove: *to tap the ashes out of a pipe.* **5.** to repair (the heel or sole of a shoe) with leather. **6.** to select; choose. —*v.i.* to strike a gentle blow or series of blows: **a.** to hit slightly; tamp. **b.** to signal by knocking; rap: *Tap on the door.*
—*n.* **1.** a gentle blow, often audible: *There was a tap at the door.* **2.** the sound itself. **3.** a piece of leather used to repair the bottom of a shoe. **4.** a small steel plate on a shoe to reduce wear or to make a louder tap in tap-dancing. **5.** tap-dancing.

taps, a signal on a bugle or drum at which all lights in the soldiers' or sailors' quarters must be put out. Taps are also sounded when a soldier or sailor is buried. *The customary volleys were fired over the grave, and Bugler Fitzgerald sounded taps, the soldier's last sad farewell* (Cambridge Tribune).
[< Old French *taper,* probably < a Germanic word]

tap[2] (tap), *n., v.,* **tapped, tap·ping.** —*n.* **1.** a simple wooden faucet for a barrel, etc., consisting of a short pipe with a stopper-peg inserted crosswise like a setscrew or cotter pin to stop the flow. **2.** any faucet; spigot; cock. **3.** a hole in a barrel made for a spigot. **4.** any opening cut into a supply of liquid, especially for a branch pipe. **5.** the liquor taken from a certain tap. **6.** a certain variety or quality of liquor; brew. **7.** *Informal.* a room where liquor is sold and drunk; bar. **8. a.** (on a coil) an electric connection somewhere other than at an end. **b.** any place where an electric connection can be made; outlet. **9.** any long, tapering cylinder, especially a taproot: *The tap of the oak will make its way downward* (Charles Marshall). **10.** a tool for cutting internal screw threads. **11.** a wire tapping. **12.** *Especially British.* an issue of notes or securities, usually by a government, that are put on continuous sale and may be purchased in unrestricted quantity.

Tap[2] (def. 1)

on tap, a. ready to be let out of a keg, cask, or barrel and be served: *There is good beer on tap down at the Red Lion.* **b.** ready for use; on hand; available: *Much of* [*television's*] *appeal comes from its being on tap* (Manchester Guardian). **c.** (of a barrel) with a spigot inserted for drawing off; broached: *The tavernkeeper had three barrels on tap for the evening's celebration.* **d.** (of a treasury bill, etc.) obtainable when required at a fixed rate; on call: *It is some time since additional Treasury Bills have been on tap at so low a rate as 1⅞ per cent* (Westminster Gazette).
—*v.t.* **1.** to make a hole in to let out liquid: *They tapped the sugar maples when the sap began to flow.* **2.** to remove the plug from (a cask); pierce: *to tap a cask.* **3.** to let out (liquid) by opening a hole. **4.** to provide (a barrel) with a tap. **5.** to let out liquid from by surgery. **6.** to make (resources, reserves, etc.) accessible; make (any potential) available; penetrate; open up: *This highway taps a large district. Chicago is the only inland port in America which can (and does) tap the two great inland water routes* (Newsweek). **7.** to attach a listening device to (a telephone line) in order to eavesdrop. **8.** to make an internal screw thread in (a pipe, etc.). **9.** *Slang.* to ask (a person) for money, help, etc.
[Old English *tæppa.* Related to TIP[1].]

tap[3] (tap), *n.* (in India) malaria. [< Persian *tap* fever, heat < Sanskrit *tāpa* heat, pain]

ta·pa[1] (tä′pə), *n.* **1.** (in the South Pacific) an unwoven kind of cloth made by soaking and pounding the soft inner bark of the paper mulberry tree. **2.** this bark. [< Polynesian *tapa*]

ta·pa[2] (tä′pə), *n.* an hors d'oeuvre served with a drink: *All the south of Spain drinks sherry, generally . . . accompanied by tapas in the form of olives, anchovies, or strips of raw Serrano ham* (London Times). [< Spanish *tapa* (literally) lid (because tapas were once served on lids placed over the glass)]

tapa cloth, tapa.

tap·a·de·ra (tap′ə dãr′ə), *n., pl.* **-ras.** a heavy leather housing for the front of a stirrup of a Mexican saddle, to keep the foot from slipping forward and to protect it against thorny underbrush. [< Spanish *tapadera* < *tapar* to cover]

tap·a·de·ro (tap′ə dãr′ō), *n., pl.* **-ros.** tapadera.

tap bar, a bar placed in a cementation furnace and withdrawn for testing during the process.

tap bond or **issue,** a United States government bond on sale in unlimited amount for an indefinite period of weeks, intended to attract as capital idle funds from outside the usual sources.

tap cinder, the slag or refuse produced in a puddling furnace.

tap dance, a dance in which the rhythm is accented by sharp taps with small metal plates (taps) on the toe or heel.

tap-dance (tap′dans′, -däns′), *v.i.,* **-danced, -danc·ing.** to do a tap dance.

tap-danc·er (tap′dan′sər, -dän′-), *n.* a person who tap-dances.

tap-danc·ing (tap′dan′sing, -dän′-), *n.* the act or art of a person who tap-dances. —*adj.* **1.** of or having to do with a tap dance. **2.** like a tap dance.

tape (tāp), *n., v.,* **taped, tap·ing.** —*n.* **1.** a woven strip or ribbon of durable cotton, linen, etc., used as a bias binding on seams, to make loops, etc. **2.** any thin, flexible strip, as a cloth or steel tape measure: *Surveyors measure with a steel tape.* **3.** *Sports.* a ribbon stretched across a finish line, especially of a foot race, to be broken by the winner. **4.** a ribbon across the entrance of a new building, bridge, road, etc., cut during the official opening ceremony. **5.** the strip of paper on which a teletypewriter prints messages; ticker tape: *Stock quotations are printed on paper tape.* **6. a.** a thin, narrow strip of paper or plastic coated with magnetized iron oxide to record sound, as for a tape recorder. **b.** a recording thus made. **7.** adhesive tape. **8.** red tape.

breast the tape, *Sports.* (of a runner) to break the ribbon stretched across the finish line ahead and win the race: *Masters was able to sprint ahead and breast the tape.*
—*v.t.* **1.** to fasten, bind, or wind with tape; tie: *The doctor taped up the wound.* **2.** to join the sections of (a book) with tape. **3.** to attach a tape or tapes to. **4.** to measure with a tape measure. **5.** to get the range of (a position); hit and silence. **6.** to record on tape.

have or **get one taped,** *Especially British Slang.* to understand one: *But I guess I had you all pretty well taped* (Mellen Cole).
[Middle English *tape,* variant of *tappe,* Old English *tæppe*] —**tape′like′,** *adj.*

tape-car·ri·er (tāp′kar′ē ər), *n.* a frame in which a tape sprinkled with powdered corundum acts as a cutting or filing instrument.

tape check-ac·tion (chek′ak′shən), (on an upright piano) a tape that pulls back the hammer after it strikes.

tape-con·trolled (tāp′kən trōld′), *adj.* controlled by instructions recorded on a tape.

tape deck, the mechanical component of a tape recorder, used in high-fidelity systems, computers, etc.: *The simplest playback machine is the tape deck* (Harper's).

tape·fish (tāp′fish′), *n., pl.* **-fish·es** or (*collectively*) **-fish.** a fish with a long, flat body like an eel; ribbonfish.

tape grass, 1. an underwater herb of the frogbit family with narrow, grasslike leaves. **2.** (in the southern United States) eelgrass.

tape·less (tāp′lis), *adj.* without tape; without the use of tape.

tape line, tape measure.

tape machine, any machine that uses tape, especially: **a.** a tape recorder. **b.** a teleprinter; teletypewriter. **c.** a ticker-tape machine. **d.** (in weaving) a machine for sizing the cotton warp threads.

tape·man (tāp′mən), *n., pl.* **-men.** (in surveying) one of the two men who measure with the tape measure.

tape measure, a strip of cloth or steel marked as a ruler for measuring, often compactly rolled on a spring when not in use.

tape needle, *British Dialect.* an eyed bodkin.

tap·er[1] (tā′pər), *n.* a person who tapes.

ta·per[2] (tā′pər), *v.i.* **1.** to become gradually narrower toward one end, as a funnel: *The church spire tapers to a point.* **2.** to grow steadily less in amount, force, etc.; diminish by degrees; subside; shrink; decrease. —*v.t.* **1.** to make gradually narrower toward one end. **2.** to shape like an awl or wedge.

taper off, to make gradually less in amount, force, etc.; reduce steadily: *to taper off smoking.* [< noun]

—*n.* **1.** a gradual narrowing in width or girth: *Iron plugs ... upon a very gentle taper* (John Smeaton). **2.** a gradual lessening of activity, force, capacity, etc. **3.** a figure that tapers to a point; slender cone or pyramid; spire. **4.** a very slender candle. **5.** a splinter, waxed length of wick, etc., for lighting a candle, cigarette, etc., from an open fire.

—*adj.* becoming narrowed toward one end. [Old English *tapor*] —**ta′per·ing·ly,** *adv.* —**ta′per·ness,** *n.*

tape·re·cord (tāp′ri kôrd′), *v.t., v.i.* to record on tape: *Unlike many interviews between politicians and reporters it was not off the record; it was taperecorded, and the transcript is now before me* (Harper's).

tape recorder, a machine for recording sound, data, etc., on magnetic tape: *In space missiles, tape recorders provide a record of the speed, stresses, temperatures, and other scientific data encountered during flight* (World Book Encyclopedia).

tape recording, 1. the recording of sound on magnetic tape. **2.** the sound itself: *Tape recordings were played of his conversations with two Seattle gamblers* (Wall Street Journal). **3.** the tape used: *A tape recording, after all, is basically nothing more than an organized magnetic pattern arranged in the iron particles which coat a plastic base* (David Sarser).

tape-siz·ing machine (tāp′sī′zing), a tape machine used in weaving.

tape-stretch·er (tāp′strech′ər), *n.* a device to keep a uniform tension on the measuring line when surveying.

tap·es·tried (tap′ə strēd), *adj.* **1.** adorned with or as if with tapestry: *tapestried walls. Still with pleasure I recall The tapestried school, the bright brown-boarded hall* (Robert Southey). **2.** woven in the manner of tapestry: *Our womenfolk weave with multicoloured threads intricate designs on their elaborately tapestried quilts* (London Times).

tap·es·try (tap′ə strē), *n., pl.* **-tries,** *v.,* **-tried, -try·ing.** —*n.* **1.** a fabric whose weft is woven in a picture or ornamental design, used as a hanging on walls, furniture cover, etc.: *a curtain of old tapestry* (George Eliot). **2.** a similar machine-woven fabric. **3.** a picture in or as if in tapestry: *Bushes are now entering a season in which their foliage acquires its most persuasive tints, a planting of any size presenting a delightful tapestry of softly interwoven colors* (London Times).

—*v.t.* **1.** to work or depict in tapestry. **2.** to cover or hang with tapestry. **3.** to adorn with a pattern like that of tapestry.

[variant of Middle English *tapesery* < Old French *tapisserie* < *tapisser* cover with a carpet < *tapis;* see TAPIS] —**tap′es·try·like′,** *adj.*

tapestry beetle, a dermestid beetle whose larva eats tapestry, woolens, etc.

tapestry carpet, a carpet in which the warp yarn is colored in advance, to produce a pattern when woven.

ta·pe·tal (tə pē′təl), *adj.* of or having to do with a tapetum.

tap·e·ti (tap′ə tē), *n.* a small South American rabbit. [< Tupi (Brazil) *tapeti*]

ta·pe·tum (tə pē′təm), *n., pl.* **-ta** (-tə). **1.** *Botany.* (in a sporangium) a cell or sheath of cells around the archespore, absorbed by the maturing spores: *The tapetum cells disorganize, supplying the nourishment that is used in the development of the pollen mother-cells* (Fred W. Emerson). **2.** any of certain layers of membrane in the eye, such as those that make cats' eyes shine at night. [< New Latin *tapetum,* alteration of Latin *tapēta,* or *tapēte, -is* carpet < Greek *tápēs, -ētos*]

tape·worm (tāp′werm′), *n.* any of various parasite worms (cestodes), with a long body (strobila) consisting of many separable parts, a small, inconspicuous head (scolex), and no digestive tract, living when adult in the intestines of man and other vertebrates, often after a larval period elsewhere: *Man gets his commonest tapeworms from insufficiently cooked pork* (A. Franklin Shull).

tap·house (tap′hous′), *n. Especially British.* **1.** a place where liquor is sold and drunk; bar. **2.** one of the rooms in a tavern; taproom; barroom; bar.

tap-in (tap′in′), *n.* a scoring shot in basketball in which a player leaps up to deflect the ball with his fingers through the hoop.

tap·ing (tā′ping), *n.* **1.** a tape recording: *two recording sessions to polish up rough spots in earlier tapings of Verdi operas* (Time). **2.** data on punched or magnetic tape that regulates an electronic computing machine: *The orders given the machine may be fed into it by a taping which is completely predetermined* (Norbert Wiener).

tap·i·o·ca (tap′i ō′kə), *n.* a starchy, granular food prepared by drying moist cassava starch on hot plates, used especially in puddings, for thickening soups, and as a postage-stamp adhesive. [ultimately < Tupi (Brazil) *tipioca*]

ta·pir (tā′pər), *n.* any of a group of grey, piglike, hoofed, herbivorous mammals with flexible snouts, related to the horse and rhinoceros. It lives in South and Central America and southern Asia. [ultimately < Tupi (Brazil) *tapira*]

South American Tapir (about 3 ft. high at the shoulder)

tap·is (tap′ē, tap′is, ta pē′), *n., pl.* **-is.** *Obsolete.* any rug, tablecloth, hanging, or other tapestry.

on the tapis, being given attention; under discussion: *This view was held by Mr. Stansfield when his successor's bill was on the tapis* (Manchester Guardian).

[< Middle French *tapis* < Old French, ultimately < Greek *tápēs, -ētos* rug]

ta·pis·se·rie (tȧ pē′se rē′), *n. French.* tapestry.

ta·pis·sier (tȧ pē syā′), *n. French.* a maker or weaver of tapestries: *All over Europe looms are clacking busily as tapissiers, working elbow to elbow, ply the warp with bobbin and thread* (Time).

tap-off (tap′ôf′, -of′), *n.* a jump ball: *Budd outjumped Wilt in a tap-off near the Knick basket* (New York Times).

tap·pa·ble (tap′ə bəl), *adj.* capable of being tapped; fit for tapping: *tappable bark. Some members of the pent-up and petulant company may start to beat upon one another's heads for want of a more tappable object* (London Times).

tap·per[1] (tap′ər), *n.* **1.** a telegraph key that makes a contact and breaks another in one motion. **2.** a bell clapper. **3.** a person who taps at a door, etc. **4.** a person who taps train wheels to test their soundness. **5.** a cobbler. **6.** *Dialect.* the lesser spotted woodpecker.

tap·per[2] (tap′ər), *n.* **1.** a person who taps trees for the sap, etc. **2.** a milking machine. **3.** a wire tapper: *The tapper finds the particular wire he wants to cut in on and attaches his wire to it directly* (New York Times). [Old English *tæppere* a tapster < *tæppian* to tap[2] < *taeppe* tap[2]]

tap·pet (tap′it), *n.* (in a machine) a projecting arm, cam, etc., that strikes another part of the machine at intervals to transmit an irregular motion.

tappet rod, *Machinery.* a longitudinally reciprocating rod bearing a tappet.

tap·ping[1] (tap′ing), *n.* **1.** the act of striking gently. **2.** a sound made in this way.

tap·ping[2] (tap′ing), *n.* **1.** the act of a person who taps pipes, electricity, resources, etc. **2.** something that runs from a tap.

tap·pit hen (tap′it), **1.** *Scottish.* a hen having a crest or topknot. **2.** *British Dialect.* a woodpecker. [variant of *topped*]

tap plate, a tool for cutting an outside pipe thread.

tap·poon (ta pün′), *n.* a portable dam of wood, metal, or the like, for temporarily damming the water in an irrigation ditch so that it will overflow the adjacent fields. [< Spanish *tapón* stopper, plug]

tap·room (tap′rüm′, -rům′), *n.* a room where alcoholic liquor is sold; barroom.

tap·root (tap′rüt′, -růt′), *n. Botany.* **1.** a main root growing deep downward from the stem, thick at the top, tapering to a point, and sprouting subsidiary lateral roots: *Trees that have well-developed taproots are especially well equipped to withstand wind storms* (Fred W. Emerson). **2.** the main cause or source of development: *Investment ... is the taproot of economic growth* (Wall Street Journal).

taps (taps), *n.pl.* See under **tap**[1], *n.*

tap·ster (tap′stər), *n. Archaic.* a barman or barmaid. [Old English *tæppestre;* (originally) feminine of *tæppere;* see TAPPER[2]]

tap·stress (tap′stris), *n. Archaic.* a barmaid.

tap-tap (tap′tap′), *n., v.,* **-tapped, -tap·ping.** —*n.* a repeated tap; series of taps: *Mr. Tressle's man ... ceased his tap-tap upon the coffin* (Thackeray). —*v.i.* to make a series of tapping sounds or movements: *Writers ... cannot even indulge in a little mild abuse ... without setting your finger tap-tapping on the script* (Punch).

tap tool, a tool for cutting inside pipe threads.

Ta·pu·ya (tä pü′yə), *n., pl.* **-ya. 1.** a member of a primitive group of tribes, once numerous throughout central South America but now found only in the remote regions of Brazil. **2.** any speaker of Tapuyan. [< Portuguese *Tapuya* < Tupi (Brazil) *tapuya* enemy, savage]

Ta·pu·yan (tä pü′yən), *n.* **1.** a family of American Indian languages formerly widely spoken in central Brazil, now restricted to remote areas. **2.** a Tapuya. —*adj.* of or having to do with the Tapuya or with the Tapuyan family of languages.

tap water, water from a pipe.

tap wrench, a wrench to turn a tap tool.

tar[1] (tär), *n., v.,* **tarred, tar·ring,** *adj.* —*n.* **1.** any of various inflammable, gummy, black liquids and solids obtained from the distillation of organic materials, especially wood and coal, much used for coating and preserving timber. **2.** a brownish-black substance produced by the burning of tobacco: *cigarette tar.* **3.** a pitch distilled from coal tar.

beat, knock, whip, or **whale the tar out of,** *Informal.* to beat unmercifully: *If he was sore at me for something, he'd save up ..., then beat the tar out of me* (New Yorker).

—*v.t.* to cover with tar or soak in tar, as for waterproofing: *to tar a road.*

tar and feather, to punish by covering with heated tar and feathers: *If I escape from town without being tarred and feathered, I shall consider it good luck* (Hawthorne).

tarred with the same brush (or **stick**), having similar faults or defects: *They are all tarred with the same stick—rank Jacobites and Papists* (Scott).

tar with (a specified) **brush,** to disgrace in some way; stigmatize: *Nevertheless, Mr. Howarth intends to tar his opponent with the Tory brush* (London Times).

—*adj.* of, like, or covered with tar.

[Old English *teoru, teru*] —**tar′like′,** *adj.*

tar[2] (tär), *n. Informal.* a sailor or seaman; Jack tar. [probably short for *tarpaulin* (in early meaning) sailor]

tar·a·did·dle (tar′ə did′əl), *n. Especially British Informal.* **1.** a trifling falsehood; petty lie; fib: *Everybody told us it would be very cold, and as usual, everybody told taradiddles* (Thomas H. Huxley). **2.** something of little importance or consequence. Also, **tarradiddle.**

ta·ran·ta·ra (tə ran′tər ə), *n.* tantara: *The pit band played a tired tarantara* (Newsweek).

ta·ran·tass or **ta·ran·tas** (tä′rän täs′), *n.* a large, four-wheeled carriage on long, flexible wooden bars with no springs, used in Russia in the 1800's. [< Russian *tarantas*]

tar·an·tel·la (tar′ən tel′ə), *n.* **1.** a rapid South Italian folk dance originally in 4/4 time, now usually performed in 6/8 time by one couple whirling rapidly, once a supposed cure for tarantism: *Williams' screenplay, like his drama, revolves with the frantic formlessness of a tarantella* (Newsweek). **2.** a ballroom dance based on it. **3.** the music for either. **4.** any music in this rhythm. [< Italian *tarantella* < *Taranto* Taranto, a city in Italy < Latin *Tarentum;* popularly associated with *tarantula,* and supposedly a cure for *tarantism*]

ta·ran·telle (tä räɴ tel′), *n. French.* a tarantella.

tar·ant·ism (tar′ən tiz′əm), *n.* a nervous disorder characterized by an extreme impulse to dance, epidemic in southern Italy from the 1400's to the 1600's and popularly attributed to the bite of the tarantula; dancing mania: *Tarantism . . . occurred at the height of the summer heat, in July and August* (Scientific American). Also, **tarentism.** [< New Latin *tarantismus* < Italian *tarantismo* < *Taranto* Taranto. Compare TARANTULA.]

tar·ant·ist (tar′ən tist), *n* a victim of tarantism.

ta·ran·tu·la (tə ran′chə lə), *n., pl.* **-las, -lae** (-lē). **1.** a large spider of southern Europe, whose slightly poisonous bite was once imagined to cause tarantism: *The tarantula's powerful body is covered with long hairs that transmit a delicate sense of touch* (Science News Letter). **2.** any of a family of large, hairy spiders with a painful but not serious bite, especially a group of spiders in the southwestern United States: *A typical southwestern U.S. tarantula has a body about two inches long and a leg span of about six inches* (Science News Letter). [< Medieval Latin *tarantula* < Italian *tarantola* < *Taranto* Taranto, a city in Italy, near which the spider is found]

Italian Tarantula (def. 1—body, about 1 in. long)

tarantula hawk or **killer,** *Southwestern U.S.* a wasp that preys on tarantulas.

tarantula juice, *U.S. Slang.* rotgut.

Ta·ras·can (tə ras′kən), *n.* **1.** a member of a tribe of Indians living in Mexico. **2.** their language. *—adj.* of or having to do with the Tarascans or their language.

ta·ra·ta (tə rä′tə), *n.* lemonwood. [< Maori *tarata*]

ta·rax·a·cum (tə rak′sə kəm), *n.* **1.** any of a group of composite herbs, as the dandelion. **2.** dried dandelion root, used as a tonic, laxative, and diuretic. [< New Latin *Taraxacum* the genus name < Medieval Latin *tarasacon,* probably misreading of Arabic *ṭarakhshaqōq* < Persian *talkh chakūk* bitter herb]

ta·rax·ein (tə rak′sēn, -sē in), *n.* a protein substance extracted from the blood serum of schizophrenic persons. It can produce the symptoms of schizophrenia or psychosis when injected into normal persons.

tar·board (tär′bôrd′, -bōrd′), *n.* a strong millboard made of tarred rope, etc. *—adj.* made of this.

tar·boosh (tär büsh′), *n.* a cloth or felt cap, usually red, with a tassel on top, usually of dark-blue silk, worn by Moslem men, sometimes inside a turban: *Resplendent in a red tarboosh and black gown, the former Grand Mufti of Jerusalem materialized like a wraith from the past* (Time). Also, **tarbush.** [< Arabic *ṭarbūsh*]

tar·boy (tär′boi′), *n. Australian.* a boy who dabs tar on sheep cut during shearing.

tar brush, any brush for applying tar.

tar·bush[1] (tär′bu̇sh′), *n. U.S.* any of a group of California shrubs of the waterleaf family.

tar·bush[2] (tär büsh′), *n.* tarboosh.

Tar·de·nois·i·an (tär′də noi′zi ən), *adj.* of or having to do with the mesolithic culture, remains of which were first discovered in Tardenois, France: *the Tardenoisian people —a shadowy race who inhabited England some 6,000 years ago* (Time).

tar·di·grade (tär′də grād), *adj.* **1.** moving or walking slowly. **2.** of or having to do with a class or subclass of very small arthropods with little-developed circulatory and respiratory systems and four pairs of short legs, either marine or inhabiting damp places, often found as slime on ponds. *—n.* any tardigrade animal. [< French *tardigrade* < Latin *tardigradus* slow-paced < *tardus* slow + *gradī* to walk]

tar·di·ly (tär′də lē), *adv.* slowly; late; with delay: *The night rolled tardily away* (William Cowper).

tar·di·ness (tär′dē nis), *n.* the quality of being tardy; slowness of action: *A tardiness in nature, Which often leaves the history unspoke That it intends to do* (Shakespeare).

tar·do (tär′dō), *adj. Music.* slow (used as a direction). [< Italian *tardo* < Latin *tardus* slow]

tar·dy (tär′dē), *adj.,* **-di·er, -di·est,** *adv. —adj.* **1.** behind time; late. **2.** *U.S.* late for a meeting, school, or appointment; unpunctual. **3.** taking rather long to make little progress; slow in motion or action; sluggish. **4.** delaying; reluctant.
—adv. **come tardy off.** See under **come.**
[Middle English *tardyve* < Middle French *tardif, -ive,* ultimately < Latin *tardus* slow]
—Syn. *adj.* **1.** behindhand. **3.** dilatory. See **late.**
—Ant. *adj.* **1, 2.** punctual, prompt.

tare[1] (tãr), *n.* **1.** any of various fodder plants, especially the common tare, with light-purplish flowers; vetch. **2.** a vetch seed, often a symbol of smallness. **3.** (in the Bible) a harmful cornfield weed, possibly the darnel. Matthew 13:24-30. [compare Middle Dutch *tarwe* wheat]

tare[2] (tãr), *n., v.,* **tared, tar·ing.** *—n.* **1.** a deduction from the gross weight of goods to allow for the weight of the container or vehicle they are in. **2.** the weight deducted. **3.** the weight of an empty motor vehicle, without passengers, load, fuel, etc. **4.** *Chemistry.* **a.** the weight of a vessel, subtracted from its weight with a substance in it, to determine the weight of the substance. **b.** a counterweight to the vessel.
—v.t. to mark or allow for the tare of.
[< Old French *tare* < Medieval Latin *tara* deduction < Arabic *ṭarḥah* thing rejected]

tare-fitch (tãr′fich′) or **tar-fitch** (tär′fich′), *n.* tarevetch.

tar·ent·ism (tar′ən tiz′əm), *n.* tarantism.

tare·vetch (tãr′vech′), *n. British Dialect.* any of various vetches or tares. Also, **tarvetch.**

targe (tärj), *n. Archaic.* a light, circular shield or buckler. [< Old French *targe* < Germanic (compare Old Icelandic *targe*)]

targe·man (tärj′mən), *n., pl.* **-men.** *Archaic.* a man who carries a targe or shield.

tar·get (tär′git), *n.* **1. a.** *Sports.* a design of a circle or concentric circles to be shot at in practice or competition. **b.** any object shot at, thrown at, etc.; butt. **2.** a butt for criticism, ridicule, abuse, etc.: *His unfamiliar ideas made him the target of their jokes.* **3.** any aim one tries to achieve; goal; objective: *The lower farm production targets in the new plan appeared to be more realistic* (Wall Street Journal). **4.** *Historical.* a light shield or buckler, especially a round medieval shield. **5.** *Surveying.* **a.** the movable sight on a leveling staff; vane. **b.** any marker for leveling a sight on. **6.** *Physics.* **a.** (in an X-ray tube) an anticathode. **b.** any substance bombarded by high-energy neutrons to produce nuclear reactions. **7.** a plate in a television camera tube that receives the image from the screen plate in the form of electrons, the image being picked up for transmission by a scanning beam. **8.** a disk to show whether a railway switch is open or closed. **9.** *Obsolete.* a cymbal.
—v.t. **1.** to make or put up as a target: *In a statement released with the figures, [he] stated the company has targeted a profit for the year* (Wall Street Journal). **2.** to guide to a target.
[Middle English *targat* light shield < Middle French *targuete,* variant of *targete* (diminutive) < Old French *targe;* see TARGE]

Archery Target (def. 1a) The five circles (center outward) are scored as follows: gold, 9; red, 7; inner white or blue, 5; black, 3; outer white, 1.

tar·get-card (tär′git kärd′), *n.* a card used for scoring the shooters' respective hits.

target date, a date set for the beginning or completion of a project: *The idea would be to bring everything into readiness by a target date* (Science News Letter).

tar·get·eer (tär′gə tir′), *n.* **1.** a person who tests the sights for accuracy on small arms. **2.** peltast.

tar·get-fir·ing (tär′git fīr′ing), *n. Especially British.* target practice.

tar·get·less (tär′git lis), *adj.* without a target.

target practice, practice at shooting to improve one's aim.

target ship, a condemned ship used as a practice target.

tar·get-shoot·ing (tär′git shü′ting), *n.* target practice.

Tar·gum (tär′gum; *Hebrew* tär güm′), *n., pl.* **Tar·gums, Tar·gu·mim** (tär′gü mēm′). any of various Judean-Aramaic paraphrases of almost all sections of the Old Testament. [< Hebrew *Targum* < Aramaic, interpretation < *targem* to interpret]

Tar·gum·ist (tär′gə mist), *n.* one of the compilers of the Targums.

Tar·gum·is·tic (tär′gə mis′tik), *adj.* of or having to do with a Targumist or the Targumists.

Tar·heel (tär′hēl′), *n.* a nickname for a native or inhabitant of North Carolina. [American English < *tar*[1] + *heel*]

Tarheel State, a nickname for North Carolina.

tar·iff (tar′if), *n.* **1.** the system of duties or taxes that a government charges on imports or exports. **2.** an official list of the customs duties. **3.** any of the duties, or the rate of any duty, in such a list: *There is a very high tariff on jewelry. Heavy revenue duties . . . have the same effect as protective tariffs in obstructing free trade* (Time). **4.** *Especially British.* the table of prices in a hotel, restaurant, etc.: *The tariff at the Grant Hotel ranges from $10 to $13 a day for a single room.* **5.** any scale of prices; book of rates; schedule: *a revised tariff for passenger travel.* **6.** *Obsolete.* an arithmetical table, especially one used to save calculating discounts, etc.; ready reckoner.
—v.t. **1.** to put a tariff on. **2.** to set a value or price for according to a tariff. **3.** to list the tariff or tariffs on.
[< Italian *tariffa* schedule of customs rates < Arabic *taʿrīf* information, notification]

tar·iff·less (tar′if lis), *adj.* without a tariff.

tariff reform, *U.S.* a reduction of most import duties.

Tariff Reform, *British.* an increase or extension of most import duties.

tariff wall, trade barrier.

tar·iff-walled (tar′if wôld′), *adj.* **1.** of or having to do with a tariff wall. **2.** like a tariff wall.

tar·la·tan (tär′lə tən), *n.* a thin, stiff muslin, transparent and unwashable, formerly glazed and used in ballet skirts, bags for Christmas candy, etc. [< French *tarlatane;* origin uncertain]

tar·mac (tar′mak′), *n. British.* any surface made of tarmacadam, especially a road, runway, or other part of an airfield.

Tar·mac (tär′mak′), *n. Trademark.* tarmacadam.

tar·mac·ad·am (tär′mə kad′əm), *n.* a macadam consisting of crushed rock in a tar and creosote binder; black top.

tarn (tärn), *n.* a small mountain lake or pool. [Middle English *terne* < Scandinavian (compare Old Icelandic *tjörn,* Swedish *tjärn* pool, standing water)]

tar·na·tion (tär nā′shən), *U.S. Slang. —n.* damnation. *—adj.* confounded; damned: *a tarnation fool. —adv.* awfully; inordinately: *Travelling is tarnation bad* (Harriet E. Comstock).

tar·nish (tär′nish), *v.t.* **1.** to dim the luster of (metal); discolor by oxidation, etc.; dull: *Soot in the air tarnishes silver.* **2.** to bring disgrace upon (a reputation, one's honor, etc.); sully; taint: *The expedition's triumph was somewhat tarnished by dissension and subsequent recrimination* (Atlantic). *—v.i.* **1.** (of a metal) to lose its brightness; grow dull or dim; discolor: *The brass doorknob tarnished.* **2.** to grow less appealing; become uninviting; pall; fade.
—n. **1.** a discolored coating, especially on silver. **2.** the fact or condition of being tarnished; loss of luster. **3.** any unattractiveness, especially mild disgrace; blot.
[< Middle French *terniss-,* stem of *ternir* < *terne* dark, dull, perhaps < Germanic (compare Middle High German *tarnen, ternen* darken)] **—Syn.** *v.t., v.i.* **1.** blacken. **—Ant.** *v.t., v.i.* **1.** shine.

tar·nish·a·ble (tär′ni shə bəl), *adj.* liable to tarnish.

ta·ro (tä′rō, tar′ō), *n., pl.* **-ros.** **1.** a tropical food plant of the arum family cultivated in many varieties, with a starchy tuber, and succulent leaves, sprouts, and stems, which are acrid when raw, but not when boiled. **2.** its potatolike root. [< Polynesian *taro*]

tar·oc, tar·ock, or **tar·ok** (tar′ək), *n.* tarot. [< Italian *tarocchi,* plural; origin unknown]

tar·ot (tar′ət), *n.* one of a set of Italian playing cards of the 1300's, consisting of 22 figured trumps added to a deck of 56 in four suits, also used in fortunetelling.
tarots, the game played with such cards: *to win at tarots.*
[< French *tarot,* alteration of Italian *tarocchi;* see TAROC]

tarp (tärp), *n. U.S.* a tarpaulin: *There were tents by the creek, and tarps stretched from cars and wagons to make lean-to shelters* (Dan Cushman).

tar·pan (tär′pan), *n.* **1.** a tan wild horse of central Asia, about the size of a mule. **2.** a wild European horse that became extinct in the 1800's: *Tarpans are extinct; the last herds vanished in the 19th century, after ranging eastward to the steppes of the Ukraine* (Time). [< Tartar *tarpán*]

tar paper, heavy paper covered or impregnated with tar, used especially for waterproofing and windproofing buildings: *a tar paper shack.*

tar·pau·lin (tär pô′lən, tär′pə-), *n.* **1.** canvas or other strong cloth waterproofed by painting, tarring, rubberizing, etc. **2.** a sheet of this, used especially against rain. **3.** a hat made of or covered with it, especially a sailor's hat. **4.** a coat or other garment made of this. **5.** a sailor; seaman; tar: *bandy-legged tarpaulins* (Robert Louis Stevenson).
—*v.t.* to cover with a tarpaulin: *On the dot of the announced time, a green-tarpaulined, mysterious-looking truck arrives* (Newsweek).
—*v.i.* to take shelter under a tarpaulin.
[probably < *tar*¹ + *pall*¹ covering + *-ing*¹]

Tar·pe·ia (tär pē′ə), *n. Roman Legend.* a Roman maiden who agreed to open the Capitoline citadel to the Sabines in exchange for what they wore on their left arms. She wanted their bracelets, but instead they threw their shields on her and crushed her to death.

Tar·pe·ian (tär pē′ən), *adj.* of or having to do with a rock on the Capitoline Hill in Rome, from which persons convicted of treason to the state were hurled. [< Latin *Tarpeianus* < *Tarpeia* Tarpeia]

tar·pon (tär′pon), *n., pl.* **-pons** or (*collectively*) **-pon. 1.** a silvery, marine Caribbean fish, having large scales and weighing over 100 pounds, much sought by anglers; jewfish; elops. **2.** a similar East Indian species. [origin unknown]

tar·ra·did·dle (tar′ə did′əl), *n.* taradiddle.

tar·ra·gon (tar′ə gon), *n.* **1.** a wormwood, native to eastern Europe and temperate Asia. **2.** its leaves, used to flavor vinegar, salads, soups, etc. [probably < Old Spanish *taragoncía,* or Middle French *targon* tarragon < Medieval Greek *tarchon* < Arabic *ṭarkhon,* apparently < Greek *drákōn* dragon]

Tar·ra·go·na (tar′ə gō′nə), *n.* a Spanish red wine of the port type. [< *Tarragona,* a province in Spain]

tar·ras (tar′əs), *Obsolete.* —*n.* trass. —*v.t.* to cement with trass. [probably < French *terrasser* to terrace]

tarred (tärd), *adj.* smeared or covered with tar: *a tarred road.*

tar·rer (tär′ər), *n.* a person who tars.

tar·ri·ance (tar′ē əns), *n. Archaic.* **1.** delay: *I am impatient of my tarriance* (Shakespeare). **2.** a brief stay; sojourn.

tar·ri·er¹ (tar′ē ər), *n. Archaic.* a person who tarries; lingerer.

tar·ri·er² (tar′ē ər), *n.* a borer, especially one used to pull a bung. [< Old French *tarere* < Late Latin *taratrum.* Compare Greek *téretron* borer.]

tar·ri·er³ (tär′ē ər), *adj.* the comparative of **tarry**².

tar·rock (tar′ək), *n. British Dialect.* any of various seabirds, as the Arctic tern, kittiwake, gull, or guillemot.

tar·row (tar′ō), *v.i. Scottish.* to delay; hesitate; tarry. [apparently variant of *tarry*¹]

tar·ry¹ (tar′ē), *v.,* **-ried, -ry·ing,** *n.* —*v.i.* **1.** to delay leaving; remain; stay: *He tarried at the inn two days more. Time and tide tarry for no man* (Scott). **2.** to delay starting any action; be tardy; hesitate: *Why do you tarry so long?* —*v.t. Archaic.* to wait for (a person or event).
—*n. Obsolete.* a tarrying.
[Middle English *tarien;* origin uncertain]
—**Syn.** *v.i.* **1.** linger, loiter.

tar·ry² (tär′ē), *adj.,* **-ri·er, -ri·est. 1.** of tar. **2.** like tar; sticky. **3.** covered with tar; tarred. **4.** black. [< *tar*¹ + *-y*¹]

tar·sal (tär′səl), *adj.* **1.** of or having to do with the tarsus: *The first ants to settle in a new place catch onto a rough or soft surface using these tarsal hooks* (Science News Letter). **2.** of or having to do with the edges (tarsi) of the eyelids. —*n.* a tarsal bone, cartilage, etc.

tarsal joint, a joint of the tarsus: **a.** (in man) the joint between the tibia and fibula and the astragalus or tarsus. **b.** a corresponding joint in other vertebrates. **c.** (in birds) the joint between the tibia and the metatarsus, or, strictly, between the tarsal elements of the tibia and the tarsal elements of the metatarsus.

tar sand, a Canadian sand containing tarry substances: *In addition to coal, oil, and natural gas, the earth's crust contains vast potential resources of oil shale and oil-bearing tar sands* (Scientific American).

tar·sec·to·my (tär sek′tə mē), *n., pl.* **-mies.** the removal of one or more tarsal bones.

tar sheet, a tarpaulin.

Tar·shish (tär′shish), *n.* a region mentioned in the Bible. II Chronicles 9:21. It was probably in southern Spain.

tar·si (tär′sī), *n.* the plural of **tarsus.**

tar·si·a (tär′sē ə), *n.* a kind of inlay in wood of various colors. [< Italian *tarsia* inlay of bone, horn, wood, or ivory]

tar·si·er (tär′sē ər), *n.* any of various small, nocturnal mammals with huge eyes, of Indonesia and the Philippines, related to the lemurs: *The tarsier . . . has a brain and other characteristics which ally it to the lower monkeys* (Scientific American). [< French *tarsier* < *tarse* ankle < Medieval Latin *tarsus* (because of its long anklebones)]

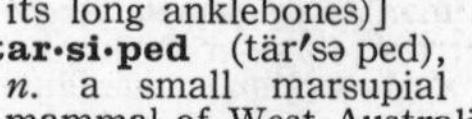
Spectral Tarsier (14½ in. long)

tar·si·ped (tär′sə ped), *n.* a small marsupial mammal of West Australia with a prehensile tail, that feeds on nectar, pollen, and insects. —*adj.* of or belonging to the tarsiped family. [< New Latin *Tarsipes, -pedis* the genus name < *tarsus* tarsus + Latin *pēs, pedis* foot]

tar·si·ped·id (tär′sə ped′id), *n., adj.* tarsiped.

tar·si·ped·ine (tär′sə ped′ēn, -in), *n., adj.* tarsiped.

tar·si·ped·oid (tär′sə ped′oid), *n., adj.* tarsiped.

tar·so·met·a·tar·sal (tär′sō met′ə tär′səl), *adj.* **1.** having to do with the tarsus and the metatarsus. **2.** resulting from a combination of tarsal and metatarsal bones, as a single compound bone. **3.** having parts of the tarsus combined with itself, as a metatarsus. **4.** of the tarsometatarsus.
—*n.* the tarsometatarsal bone.

tar·so·met·a·tar·sus (tär′sō met′ə tär′səs), *n., pl.* **-si** (-sī). **1.** the leg bone or shank in birds and early reptilian types, consisting of united tarsal and metatarsal bones. **2.** the third joint of the limb of a bird.

tar·sus (tär′səs), *n., pl.* **-si. 1. a.** the human ankle. **b.** the group of bones composing it; a collective name for the seven small bones between the tibia and the metatarsus, part of the ankle joint and of the instep, arranged in two transverse series, the proximal, consisting of the talus or anklebone and the calcaneus, and the distal, consisting of the navicular, the cuboid, and the first, second, and third cuneiform. **2.** the corresponding part in most mammals, in some reptiles, and in amphibians. **3.** the shank of a bird's leg; tarsometatarsus. **4.** the last segment of the leg of an arthropod. **5.** the thin plate of condensed connective tissue around the edge of the eyelid. [< New Latin *tarsus* < Greek *tarsós* sole of the foot; rim of the eyelid; (originally) flat basket]

tart¹ (tärt), *adj.* **1.** having a sharp taste; biting, acid, or sour: *tart plums.* **2.** (of words, a speaker, etc.) irritable or biting; cutting; sharp; sarcastic: *A Federal judge, using some tart language, today threw out the $1,000,000 libel suit brought against the A.F.L.-C.I.O. by James R. Hoffa* (New York Times).
—*v.t.* **tart up,** *Especially British.* **a.** to add flavor or interest to: *Joseph Landon has tarted up Dudley Nichols' script* (Canadian Saturday Night). **b.** to improve the appearance of: *. . . galleries and pubs tarted up with driftwood and fishnet* (Atlantic).
[Old English *teart* painful, sharp (of punishment). Probably related to TEAR¹.] —**tart′ly,** *adv.* —**tart′ness,** *n.*
—**Syn.** *adj.* **2.** acrimonious, caustic. See **sour.**

tart² (tärt), *n.* **1.** *U.S.* a small pie for an individual serving, filled with fruit, jam, etc., and without a top crust. **2.** *British.* any fruit pie; pie. [< Old French *tarte;* origin uncertain]

tart³ (tärt), *n. Slang.* a prostitute.

tar·tan¹ (tär′tən), *n.* **1.** a plaid woolen cloth woven in stripes of various colors and breadths crossing at right angles and repeated in a regular pattern. Each Scottish Highland clan has its own pattern, usually both a hunting tartan and a dress tartan, that differ mainly in the background color. **2.** the pattern or design in its particular colors. **3.** any similar plaid design or fabric of silk, cotton, etc.
—*adj.* **1.** of tartan. **2.** like tartan. **3.** having to do with tartan. **4.** made of tartan.
[< Old French *tiretanie* linsey-woolsey; influenced by Old French *tartarin* (cloth) of Tartary]

Tartan¹ (def. 2)

tar·tan² (tär′tən), *n.* a Mediterranean type of boat, having one mast rigged with a lateen sail and a jib. [< French *tartan* < Italian *tartana,* perhaps < Arabic *tarīdah* kind of ship]

tar·taned (tär′tənd), *adj.* **1.** wearing a tartan. **2.** (of cloth) having a tartan pattern.

tar·tar¹ (tär′tər), *n.* **1.** a hard, yellowish substance, chiefly calcium phosphate, with various organic salts, formed on the teeth by the action of saliva on food particles. **2.** an acid solid, potassium bitartrate, present in grape juice and deposited as a reddish crust in wine casks; argol. *Formula:* $KH_5C_4O_6$ **3.** this substance partly purified. When pure as cream of tartar, it is mixed with baking soda to make baking powder. [< Old French *tartre* < Medieval Latin *tartarum* < Late Greek *tártaron,* perhaps < a Semitic word]

tar·tar² (tär′tər), *n.* **1.** a person who has a bad temper; virago: *The old man was an awful tartar* (Dickens). **2.** *Slang.* a person hard to beat or surpass in skill; champion. [< *Tartar*¹]

Tar·tar¹ (tär′tər), *n.* **1.** one of the horde of Mongols, Turks, and other tribes led by Genghis Khan, who overran and devastated most of Asia and eastern Europe in the 1200's and 1300's. **2.** any descendant of these peoples now intermarried with peoples of Asia or Europe, especially one who speaks a Ural-Altaic language of the Turkic branch. **3.** any such language, chiefly in west central Asia, as Turkish or Kirghiz.
catch a Tartar, to attack someone who is too strong; get the worst of it: *You must give up flirting, my boy, or if I mistake not, you'll find you've caught a Tartar* (Florence Marryat).
—*adj.* having to do with any of these peoples or their languages. Also, **Tatar.**
[< Medieval Latin *Tartarus,* probably < Persian *Tātār* < Turkic; influenced by Latin *Tartarus* Tartarus]

Tar·tar² (tär′tər), *n. Archaic.* Tartarus.

tar·tar·at·ed (tär′tə rā′tid), *adj. Chemistry.* made into a tartrate; containing or obtained from tartar.

Tar·tar·e·an or **tar·tar·e·an** (tär tãr′ē ən), *adj.* of or having to do with Tartarus: *Drives the dead to dark, Tartarean coasts* (Alexander Pope).

tartar emetic, a poisonous, white, crystalline, granular salt with a sweetish, metallic taste, used in medicine to cause vomiting and sweating, as a mordant in dyeing, etc. It is a tartrate of potassium and antimony. *Formula:* $K(SbO)C_4H_4O_6 \cdot \frac{1}{2}H_2O$

tar·tar·e·ous (tär tãr′ē əs), *adj.* **1.** of the nature of tartar; tartarlike. **2.** *Botany.* having a rough, crumbling surface.

tar·tar·et (tär′tə ret), *n.,* or **tartaret**

falcon, a small falcon of Africa and Asia. [< Old French *tartaret* < Old French *Tartaire* Tartary (because they were thought to come from there)]

Tar·tar·i·an (tär tãr′ē ən), *adj.* **1.** of or having to do with the Tartars. **2.** savage.

tartarian bread, a vegetable eaten in Hungary with oil, vinegar, and salt. It is the root of an East European perennial herb of the mustard family. [translation of Hungarian *tatár kenyér*]

tartarian lamb, an Asiatic fern with shaggy rhizomes suggesting a small lamb.

tar·tar·ic (tär tar′ik, -tär′-), *adj.* **1.** of or having to do with tartar. **2.** obtained from tartar.

tartaric acid, an acid used in dyeing, medicine, photography, etc., occurring in four isomers; the common colorless, crystalline form is found in unripe grapes and prepared from argol. *Formula:* $C_4H_6O_6$

tar·tar·i·za·tion (tär′tər ə zā′shən), *n.* the act of tartarizing, or of forming tartar.

tar·tar·ize (tär′tə rīz), *v.t.*, **-ized, -iz·ing.** *Chemistry.* to combine or treat with tartar.

tar·tar·ly (tär′tər lē), *adj.* ferocious.

tar·tar·ous (tär′tər əs), *adj. Obsolete.* **1.** consisting of tartar. **2.** containing tartar.

tartar sauce, a sauce, usually for fish, consisting of mayonnaise with chopped pickles, onions, olives, capers, and herbs. [< French *sauce tartare*]

Tar·ta·rus (tär′tər əs), *n. Greek Mythology.* **1.** an abyss of darkness where Zeus punished the Titans, as far below Hades as earth is from heaven. **2.** (later) a place of eternal punishment for the spirits of the worst sinners. **3.** the underworld; Hades; hell.

tar·tine (tär tēn′), *n.* a slice of bread and butter, jam, honey, etc.: *She placidly handed out this decoction, which we took with cakes and tartines* (Thackeray). [< French *tartine* < Old French *tarte* tart[2]]

tart·ish (tär′tish), *adj.* somewhat tart; slightly pungent or acid. **—tart′ish·ly,** *adv.*

tart·let (tärt′lit), *n.* a small tart, two or three inches across. [< Old French *tartelette* (diminutive) < *tarte* tart[2]]

tar·tram·ide (tär′tram′īd, -id), *n.* the amide of tartaric acid. *Formula:* $C_4H_4(NH_2)_2O_4$

tar·trate (tär′trāt), *n.* a salt or ester of tartaric acid. [< French *tartrate*]

tar·trat·ed (tär′trā tid), *adj.* formed into a tartrate; combined with tartaric acid.

tar·tra·zine (tär′trə zēn, -zin), *n.* a yellowish-orange powder used as a dye for cosmetics, wool, etc. *Formula:* $C_{16}H_9N_4Na_3O_9S_2$

tar·tron·ate (tär′trə nāt), *n.* a salt of tartronic acid.

tar·tron·ic acid (tär tron′ik), a dibasic acid occurring in large, colorless crystals. *Formula:* $C_3H_4O_5$

tart-tongued (tärt′tungd′), *adj.* biting or cutting in speech; caustic; sarcastic.

Tar·tuffe or **Tar·tufe** (tär tüf′; *French* tȧr tyf′), *n.* a hypocrite. [< *Tartuffe,* the central character of a French comedy by Molière, produced in 1667, famous for his hypocritical piety]

Tar·tuff·i·an or **Tar·tuf·i·an** (tär tü′fē ən), *adj.* hypocritical; pretentious.

Tar·tuff·ish or **Tar·tuf·ish** (tär tü′fish), *adj.* Tartuffian.

Tar·tuff·ism or **Tar·tuf·ism** (tär tü′fiz əm), *n.* conduct or character like that of Tartuffe.

tart·y (tär′tē), *adj. Informal.* of or like a tart; sharp; snippy.

tar·vetch (tär′vech), *n.* tarevetch.

tar·vi·a (tär′vē ə), *n.* a road-surfacing material made chiefly of asphalt. [< *tar*[1] + Latin *via* road, way]

tar-wa·ter (tär′wôt′ər, -wot′-), *n.* an infusion of tar in cold water, formerly administered as a medicine.

tar·weed (tär′wēd′), *n. U.S.* **1.** any of a group of sticky plants of the composite family with a strong, tarry smell, found especially along the Pacific Coast of America. **2.** any of various similar plants.

Tar·zan or **tar·zan** (tär′zan, -zən), *n.* a man endowed with great physical strength and skill: *Grinda, a tarzan of a Frenchman, with a thunderbolt of a service, was broken three times in all—twice in the opening set and once in the third* (London Times). [< *Tarzan,* the hero of a series of adventure stories by Edgar Rice Burroughs, 1875-1950, an American author]

ta·sa·jo (tä sä′hō), *n.* strips of dried buffalo meat. [< Spanish *tasajo*]

tash·lik or **tash·lich** (täsh lik′), *n. Judaism.* a penitential prayer recited on the afternoon of Rosh Hashana near a stream of water. [< Hebrew *tashlīk* thou shalt cast, future of *shālak* to cast]

ta·sim·e·ter (tə sim′ə tər), *n.* an instrument for measuring differences of temperature, etc., by changes in conductivity and pressure. [< Greek *tásis* tension + English *-meter*]

tas·i·met·ric (tas′ə met′rik), *adj.* of or having to do with the measurement of pressures, or with the tasimeter.

ta·sim·e·try (tə sim′ə trē), *n.* the measurement of pressures.

task (task, täsk), *n.* **1.** a definite job to be done; work assigned or found necessary; duty: *The silk-worm, after having spun her task, lays her eggs and dies* (Joseph Addison). **2.** any piece of work; stint; job. **3.** difficult or heavy work; a chore. **4.** *Obsolete.* tax.

take to task, to blame; scold; reprove: *The Sultan of Johore . . . took his people to task for their apathy toward political murder by terrorists* (London Times).

—*v.t.* **1.** to burden; strain: *Lifting the heavy box tasked him beyond his strength.* **2.** to put a task on; force to work. **3.** *Obsolete.* to levy a tax on.

[< Old North French *tasque* job, tax, Old French *tasche* < Vulgar Latin *tasca,* variant of *taxa* < Latin *taxāre* appraise, evaluate] **—task′er,** *n.*

—Syn. *n.* **1.** assignment, undertaking, responsibility.

task force, 1. a temporary group of military units, especially naval units, assigned to one commander for carrying out a specific operation. **2.** any group temporarily organized for a task: *James L. Farmer, national director of the Congress of Racial Equality, said that a "task force" representing his group had started a "crash program" in Newark* (New York Times).

task·mas·ter (task′mas′tər, täsk′mäs′-), *n.* **1.** a very exacting boss or teacher. **2.** a person who sets tasks for others to do. **—Syn. 2.** supervisor, overseer.

task·mis·tress (task′mis′tris, täsk′-), *n.* a woman who assigns tasks, especially in a household.

task·work (task′wėrk′, täsk′-), *n.* **1.** piecework. **2.** any task, especially a burden: *I feel a dislike to order and to taskwork of all kinds* (Scott).

Tas·ma·ni·an (taz mā′nē ən, -mān′yən), *adj.* of or having to do with Tasmania, an island south of Australia, or with its people. —*n.* a native or inhabitant of Tasmania.

Tasmanian devil, a ferocious-looking, burrowing, carnivorous, black-and-white marsupial mammal of Tasmania, which is like a very small bear and attacks sheep.

Tasmanian myrtle, an evergreen nothofagus tree of Tasmania and Victoria, Australia.

Tasmanian wolf or **tiger,** the thylacine of Tasmania: *The Tasmanian tiger, a marsupial wolf, resembles a dog and has black and brown stripes over its rump* (Science News Letter).

tass (tas, täs), *n. Especially Scottish.* **1.** a small drinking cup, especially of silver; goblet. **2.** the drink in it; a small draft, especially of spirits. [< Old French *tasse* goblet, apparently < Arabic *ṭass* basin, probably < Persian *tast* cup, goblet]

Tass (tas, täs), *n.* a government agency of the Soviet Union which collects, censors, and distributes news: *Tass, the official press agency, said in a commentary that the march focused attention on "the most acute domestic problems of the biggest capitalist power"* (New York Times). [< Russian *T*(elegrafnoe) *A*(genstvo) *S*(ovetskovo) *S*(oyuza) Telegraph Agency of the Soviet Union]

tas·sel[1] (tas′əl), *n., v.*, **-seled, -sel·ing** or (*especially British*) **-selled, -sel·ling.** —*n.* **1.** an ornamental gathering of small cords, threads, beads, etc., fastened together at one end; pendant. **2.** any bunch of hairs, threads, etc., hanging like this. **3.** the sprig at the top of a cornstalk, a staminate inflorescence. **4.** a hanging catkin, blossom, flower, or bud in any tree or plant.

—*v.t.* **1.** to put tassels on, especially as decoration. **2.** to gather into a tassel or tassels. **3.** to remove the tassel from. —*v.i.* (of Indian corn and sugar cane) to grow tassels: *Corn tassels just before the ears form.*

[< Old French *tassel* mantle fastener, probably < Vulgar Latin *tassellus* stick for drawing lots, a die, alteration of Latin *taxillus* a small die]

tas·sel[2] (tas′əl), *n. Archaic.* a short board under the end of a beam where it rests on brickwork or stonework. Also, **torsel, tossel.** [< Old French *tassel* a plug < Latin *taxillus* a small die. Compare TASSEL[1].]

tas·sel[3] (tas′əl), *n. Obsolete.* tercel.

tas·sel-bush (tas′əl bu̇sh′), *n. Especially U.S.* an evergreen shrub with elegant, long, drooping catkins, native to California, Mexico, Cuba, and Jamaica.

tas·sel-eared squirrel (tas′əl ird′), a large squirrel of the southwestern United States and Mexico, with long ear tufts, a reddish-brown back, and a whitish tail.

tas·seled (tas′əld), *adj.* **1.** decorated with a tassel or tassels: *a tasseled cap.* **2.** (of a person) wearing a tassel or tassels. **3.** gathered into tassels. **4.** (of a fern) having divisions like tassels at the apex of each frond.

tas·ses (tas′iz), *n.pl.* armor thigh guards made of narrow, overlapping plates strapped below the waist plates, and forming a sort of kilt. [< Old French *tasse* purse, holster]

tas·sets (tas′its), *n.pl.* tasses.

tast·a·ble (tās′tə bəl), *adj.* **1.** that can be tasted. **2.** pleasant to the taste; savory; relishing. **—tast′a·ble·ness,** *n.*

tast·a·bly (tās′tə blē), *adv.* in a tastable manner; so as to be tasted.

taste (tāst), *n., v.*, **tast·ed, tast·ing.** —*n.* **1.** a quality of a substance which is perceived when it touches the taste buds in the mouth and on the tongue; savor; flavor: *Sweet, sour, salt, and bitter are four important tastes.* **2.** the sensation produced in these organs. **3.** the faculty of perceiving flavor; sense by which the flavor of things is perceived: *Her taste is unusually keen.* **4.** a liking or enthusiasm for something; zest; yen: *a taste for sailing. Suit your own taste.* **5.** the ability to recognize and enjoy what is beautiful and excellent. **6.** a style, manner, or arrangement that shows this ability or lack of it; aesthetic quality or standards: *Her house is furnished in excellent taste.* **7.** the prevailing, typical style in an age, class, or country: *in the Moorish taste.* **8.** a little bit that one takes in the mouth; a morsel or sip; sample: *Take a taste of this cake.* **9.** any little exposure to or experience (of): *brief tastes of joy.* **10.** the act of tasting. **11.** the fact of being tasted. **12.** *Obsolete.* a trying; testing; trial. **13.** *Obsolete.* feeling: **a.** the sense of touch. **b.** a touching.

a bad or **nasty taste in the mouth,** an unpleasant feeling or memory left by a distasteful experience; bad aftertaste: *They [Balzac's novels] leave such a bad taste in my mouth* (Charlotte Brontë).

to one's taste, in harmony with one's preferences; to one's liking; pleasing: *The other girl is more amusing, more to my taste* (Edward G. Bulwer-Lytton).

—*v.t.* **1.** to find out the flavor of by the sense of taste: *When I have a cold I can taste nothing.* **2.** to experience slightly; have or feel; sample: *Having tasted freedom the bird would not return to its cage.* **3.** to taste the quality of (something) by taking a little into the mouth; assess the flavor of: *She tasted the cake.* **4.** to eat or drink a little bit of. **5.** to eat. **6.** *Poetic.* to perceive by any sense, especially smell. **7.** *Archaic.* **a.** to enjoy or like; relish. **b.** to appreciate. **8.** *Obsolete.* to put to the proof; try out; test. **9.** *Obsolete.* to touch: **a.** to feel; handle. **b.** to come into contact with; strike. —*v.i.* **1.** to have or use the sense of taste; tell or distinguish flavors. **2.** to test flavors, as of wines; act as taster. **3.** to have a certain flavor: *The butter tastes rancid.*

taste of, a. to experience; feel; encounter; perceive: *to taste of fame.* **b.** to have the flavor of; smack or savor of: *the soup tastes of onion.* **c.** to eat or drink a little: *I crave . . . that we may taste of your wine* (Shakespeare). **d.** to suggest; smack of: *a sharp word that tastes of envy.*

[Middle English *tasten* to examine by touch, feel < Old French *taster* to feel; taste, probably < Vulgar Latin *tastāre* < *taxitāre* (frequentative) < Latin *taxāre* evaluate. Compare TAX, verb, TASK.]

—Syn. *n.* **1. Taste, flavor** mean the property or quality of a thing that affects the sense organs of the mouth. **Taste** is the general word: *Mineral oil has no taste.* **Flavor** means a characteristic taste belonging to a thing, or a specially noticeable quality in the taste: *These berries have no flavor, but merely a sweet taste.* **4.** inclination, predilection, fondness.

➔ **Taste of** is used in certain dialects for *taste* (verb def. 3). Dialect: *He tasted of the lamb stew and made a face.* General: *He tasted the lamb stew and made a face.*

taste bud, any of certain small, pear-shaped groups of cells, chiefly in the lining (epithelium) of the tongue or mouth, that are sense organs of taste: *In the tongue, taste buds located in different regions conduct specific taste sensations* (Martin E. Spencer).

taste·ful (tāst′fəl), *adj.* **1.** (of persons) having good taste. **2.** (of an act or object) showing or done in good taste. **—taste′ful·ly,** *adv.* **—taste′ful·ness,** *n.* **—Syn. 1.** refined. **2.** tasty, pleasing.

taste·less (tāst′lis), *adj.* **1.** without taste; flavorless; insipid. **2.** uninspiring; dull. **3.** (of persons) having poor taste. **4.** (of things) showing poor taste. **5.** without the sense of taste; unable to taste. **—taste′less·ly,** *adv.* **—taste′less·ness,** *n.*
—**Syn. 1.** flat, vapid.

taste·mak·er (tāst′mā′kər), *n.* a person or thing that sets a style or acts as an indicator to mold popular opinion: *For they are the tastemakers and opinion formers—the one per cent of the population, roughly, who are imitated by the others* (Harper's).

tast·er (tās′tər), *n.* **1.** any person who tastes, especially an expert in flavors of wine, cheese, etc. **2.** (formerly) a person who tasted food to safeguard his master against poison. **3.** a shallow cup, usually metal, to taste wine in. **4.** a utensil like a corer for sampling food, especially cheese. **5.** a small sample, especially of food; taste. **6.** *British Informal.* a portion of ice cream served in a shallow glass.

taste-test (tāst′test′), *v.t.* to test the quality of by tasting: *The commission taste-tested six samples of orange juice concentrate made from freeze damaged fruit last year* (Wall Street Journal).

tast·i·ly (tās′tə lē), *adv. Informal.* in a tasty manner; with good taste.

tast·i·ness (tās′tē nis), *n. Informal.* the quality or state of being tasty.

tast·ing (tās′ting), *n.* **1.** the action of a person or thing that tastes. **2.** a small portion taken to try the taste; sampling.

tasting bone, a bone put into broth to give it flavor.

tast·y (tās′tē), *adj.,* **tast·i·er, tast·i·est.** *Informal.* **1.** pleasant-tasting; delicious; piquant; appetizing. **2.** pleasant; agreeable; attractive: *The members of Harvard's Hasty Pudding Club chose tasty film star Shirley MacLaine ... as their Woman of the Year* (Time). **3.** done in or showing good taste; tasteful; elegant. **—Syn. 1.** palatable, savory.

tat[1] (tat), *v.t., v.i.,* **tat·ted, tat·ting.** to make a kind of lace by looping and knotting (threads) with a shuttle. [probably back formation < *tatting*]

tat[2] (tat), *n. British Slang.* **1.** ragged things, especially shabby furnishings. **2.** a rag. [perhaps < *tatter*[1]]

tat[3] (tat), *n.* **1.** very thick hemp canvas used for mats, sacking, etc. **2.** a strip of it about 10 inches wide, for sewing into mats or screens. **3.** such a mat. Also, **tatty, taut.** [< Hindi *ṭāṭ*]

tat[4] (tat), *n.* a native pony of India; tattoo. Also, **tatt.** [see TATTOO[3]]

TAT (no periods), thematic apperception test.

ta-ta (tä′tä′), *interj.* good-by.

ta·ta·mi (tä tä′mē), *n., pl.* **-mi.** *Japanese.* a mat made of rice straw, used as a floor covering or seat: *In Japan they describe the size of a room as a twelve tatami room or a twenty-four tatami room according to the number of tatami it takes to cover the floor* (Atlantic).

Ta·tar (tä′tər), *n., adj.* Tartar[1].

Ta·tar·i·an (tä tär′ē ən), *adj.* Tartarian.

Ta·tar·ic (tä tar′ik), *adj.* Tartarian.

ta·ter (tā′tər), *n. Dialect.* a potato.

ta·tou (tä tü′), *n.* a large armadillo of South America. Also, **tatu.** [ultimately < Tupi (Brazil) *tatu, tatuaí*]

tat·ou·ay (tat′ů ā, tä′tü ī′), *n.* a tatou.

tatt (tat), *n.* tat, a pony of India; tattoo.

tat·ter[1] (tat′ər), *n.* **1.** a torn or ragged piece dangling from any cloth or garment: *After the storm the flag hung in tatters upon the mast.* **2.** a piece of cloth, paper, etc., torn off; shred; scrap. **3.** useless fragments of anything; pieces; bits.
tatters, torn or ragged clothing: ... *a suit of rags and tatters on my back* (Samuel Rowlands).
—*v.t.* to tear holes in; make ragged; fray.
—*v.i.* to be or become tattered. [ultimately < Scandinavian (compare Old Icelandic *tötturr* rag)]

tat·ter[2] (tat′ər), *n.* a person who tats.

tat·ter[3] (tat′ər), *n. Especially British Slang.* a rag-and-bone man; junkman.

tat·ter·de·mal·ion (tat′ər di māl′yən, -mal′-; -ē ən), *n.* a person in ragged clothes; ragamuffin. —*adj.* tattered; ragged.

tat·ter·ed (tat′ərd), *adj.* **1.** full of tatters; torn; ragged: *a tattered dress.* **2.** dressed in tatters: *This is the man, all tattered and torn* (Nursery Rhyme).

tat·ter·er (tat′ər ər), *n. Especially British Slang.* a tatter[3].

tat·ters (tat′ərz), *n. pl.* See under **tatter**[1], *n.*

Tat·ter·sall or **tat·ter·sall** (tat′ər sôl), *n.* a woven pattern of thin lines of bright or dark colors forming checks on a white or light background. —*adj.* of such a pattern: *a Tattersall vest.* [< *Tattersall's,* a sporting establishment, and horse auction market in London, opened by Richard *Tattersall,* 1724-1795]

tat·ter·y (tat′ər ē), *adj.* tattered.

tat·tie (tat′ē), *n. Scottish Dialect.* a potato.

tat·ti·ly (tat′ə lē), *adv. Especially British.* in a tatty manner; shabbily.

tat·ti·ness (tat′ē nis), *n. Especially British.* the quality or condition of being tatty; shabbiness: *Anyone who had wandered around Whitehall and seen the filthy buildings in which eminent men were supposed to work, or who went inside and saw the tattiness of the curtains, the antiquity of the typewriters, or the state of the carpets would marvel that any work was done at all* (London Times).

tat·ting (tat′ing), *n.* **1.** the process or work of making a netted kind of lace by looping and knotting strong cotton or linen thread on a hand shuttle. **2.** this lace. [perhaps < Scottish *tat* to tangle, *tatty* tangled + *-ing*[1]]

tat·tle (tat′əl), *v.,* **-tled, -tling,** *n.* —*v.i.* **1.** to tell secrets; blab. **2.** to talk idly; chatter; gossip. —*v.t.* **1.** to reveal by tattling; blurt out. **2.** to say idly.
—*n.* **1.** any frivolous talk; idle chatter; gossip: *the tattle of the day.* **2.** the act of tattling. [earlier, stammer, prattle. Compare Middle Dutch *tatelen* to stutter; perhaps imitative.]

tat·tler (tat′lər), *n.* **1.** telltale; tattletale. **2.** any of a group of sandpipers with a noisy cry.

tat·tle·tale (tat′əl tāl′), *U.S. Informal.* —*n.* a telltale. —*adj.* revealing faults; telltale: *tattletale stains.* [American English < *tattle;* patterned on *telltale*]

tat·tling·ly (tat′ling lē), *adv.* in a tattling manner.

tat·too[1] (ta tü′), *n., pl.* **-toos,** *v.,* **-tooed, -too·ing.** —*n.* **1.** in the army or navy: **a.** a call, especially on a bugle, usually a half-hour before taps, a warning to return to quarters for the night. **b.** a drumbeat raising an alarm. **2.** any beating, rapping, or drumming: *The hail beat a loud tattoo on the windowpane.* **3.** *Especially British.* a military display, especially music and parading by show units, usually outdoors in the evening and floodlit: *Producer of the tattoo is retired Brigadier Alasdair MacLean of the Queen's Own Cameron Highlanders* (Time).
—*v.i.* to tap continuously; drum: *Don't tattoo with your fingers.*
[variant of *tap-too* < Dutch *taptoe* < *tap* tap of a barrel + *toe* pull to, shut]

tat·too[2] (ta tü′), *v.,* **-tooed, -too·ing,** *n., pl.* **-toos.** —*v.t.* **1.** to mark (the skin) with designs or patterns by pricking a line of holes and inserting colors. **2.** to put (such a design) on: *The sailor had a ship tattooed on his arm.*
—*n.* **1.** such a picture, design, or motto. **2.** the act or practice of tattooing the skin. [< Polynesian (Marquesan) *tatu*] **—tat·too′er,** *n.*

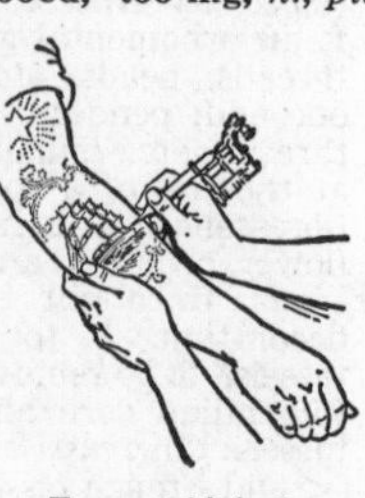

Tattoo[2] (def. 1)

tat·too[3] (tat′ü), *n., pl.* **-toos.** tat; a pony of India. [< Hindi *ṭaṭṭū*]

tat·too·ing (ta tü′ing), *n.* **1.** the practice or art of marking the skin with tattoos. **2.** the marks or pattern so produced.

tat·too·ist (ta tü′ist), *n.* a tattooer.

tat·ty[1] (tat′ē), *adj.,* **-ti·er, -ti·est.** **1.** *Especially British.* ragged or shabby: *The jobber scribbles something in a tatty notebook* (Manchester Guardian Weekly). **2.** *Scottish.* (of hair, an animal, or its coat) tangled; matted; shaggy.

tat·ty[2] (tat′ē), *n., pl.* **-ties.** **1.** a wet grass mat hung up to freshen the room. **2.** tat[3]. [< Hindi *ṭaṭṭī*]

ta·tu (tä tü′), *n.* tatou.

tau (tô, tou), *n.* **1. a.** the 19th letter of the Greek alphabet (*T, τ*), corresponding to English *T, t.* **b.** tav, the last letter of the Hebrew alphabet. **2.** St. Anthony's cross, T-shaped, especially as a sacred symbol and in heraldry. **3.** (as a numeral) 300. **4.** the last letter, as in Hebrew; Z.

tau cross, St. Anthony's cross; tau.

taught (tôt), *v.* the past tense and past participle of **teach.** —*n.* a person who has been taught: *the teacher and the taught.*

taun·gya (tông′gyə), *n.* a Burmese system of cultivation, consisting of clearing a part of the jungle by burning, cultivating a year or two, then leaving it to the jungle again. Also, **toungya.** [< Burmese *taungya* < *taung* hill + *ya* garden]

taunt[1] (tônt, tänt), *v.t.* **1.** to jeer at; reproach; mock; ridicule: *Some mean girls taunted Jane with being poor.* **2.** to get or drive by taunts; provoke: *They taunted him into taking their dare.* —*v.i.* to make mocking or insulting remarks; jeer.
—*n.* **1.** a bitter or insulting remark; sarcasm. **2.** the act of taunting. **3.** (in the Bible) an object of taunts: *So it shall be a reproach and a taunt ... unto the nations* (Ezekiel 5:15). **4.** *Obsolete.* a quip.
[compare French *tant pour tant* tit for tat < Latin *tantus prō tantus* so much for that]
—taunt′er, *n.* **—taunt′ing·ly,** *adv.*
—**Syn.** *v.t.* **1.** deride, gibe, flout.

taunt[2] (tônt, tänt), *adj. Nautical.* unusually high or tall, as a mast. [apparently for *a-taunt* all sails set, perhaps < Middle French *autant* as much < Old French *al* again + *tant* so much < *Latin tantus*]

taupe (tōp), *n.* any of various shades of dark, brownish, moleskin gray, often with yellow flecks. —*adj.* of this color. [< French *taupe* mole < Latin *talpa*]

tau·pie (tô′pē), *n. Scottish.* tawpie.

Tau·ri (tôr′ī), *n.* genitive of **Taurus.**

tau·ri·form (tôr′ə fôrm), *adj.* **1.** having the form of a bull. **2.** shaped like the horns of a bull.

tau·rin (tôr′in), *n.* taurine[2].

tau·rine[1] (tôr′in, -īn), *adj.* **1.** of or having to do with a bull; bovine. **2.** like a bull. **3.** of or having to do with the zodiacal sign Taurus. [< Latin *taurīnus* of a bull < *taurus* bull]

tau·rine[2] (tôr′ēn, -īn, -in), *n.* a neutral, crystallizable substance, found in the fluids of many animals' muscles, lungs, etc., also resulting from the hydrolysis of taurocholic acid. *Formula:* $C_2H_7NO_3S$

tau·ro·cho·lic acid (tôr′ə kō′lik, -kol′ik), a crystalline acid, present as a sodium salt in the bile of man, oxen, and most other animals, and hydrolyzing into taurine and cholic acid. *Formula:* $C_{26}H_{45}NSO_7$

tau·ro·dont (tôr′ə dont), *adj.* (of teeth) having the roots or ridges fused. [< Latin *taurus* bull + Greek *odoús, odóntos* tooth]

tau·ro·ma·chi·an (tôr′ə mā′kē ən), *adj.* of or having to do with tauromachy.

tau·rom·a·chy (tô rom′ə kē), *n., pl.* **-chies.** **1.** bullfighting. **2.** a bullfight. [< Greek *tauromachíā* < *taûros* bull + *máchesthai* to fight]

Tau·rus (tôr′əs), *n., genitive (def. 1)* **Tau·ri.** **1.** a northern constellation between Aries and Gemini, thought of as arranged in the shape of a bull; the Bull. **2.** the second sign of the zodiac, which the sun enters about April 20; the Bull. See **zodiac** for diagram. [< Latin *Taurus* bull, adaptation of Greek *Taûros* (literally) bull]

taut[1] (tôt), *adj.* **1.** pulled tight; tense: *a taut rope.* **2.** in a neat condition; orderly; tidy: *a taut ship.* **3.** (of a person) strict. [earlier *taught,* Middle English *tought*] **—taut′ly,** *adv.* **—taut′ness,** *n.* **—Syn. 1.** See **tight.** **—Ant. 1.** slack, loose.

taut[2] (tat), *n.* tat, a strip of heavy canvas.

taut·en (tôt′ən), *v.t.* to make taut; tighten. —*v.i.* to become taut.

tauto-, *combining form.* the same; identical: *Tautology = repetition of the same word or* *idea.* [< Greek *tautó* < *tò autó* the same]

tau·to·chrone (tô′tə krōn), *n. Mathematics.* the curve joining all points from which gravity takes the same length of time to draw a particle to some fixed point; cycloid. [< *tauto-* + Greek *chrónos* time]

tau·tog (tô tog′, -tôg′), *n.* a dark-colored food fish, a variety of wrasse, common on the Atlantic Coast of the United States; blackfish. [American English < Algonkian (Narragansett) *tautauog* sheepsheads, apparently related to *taut* or *tautau* fish]

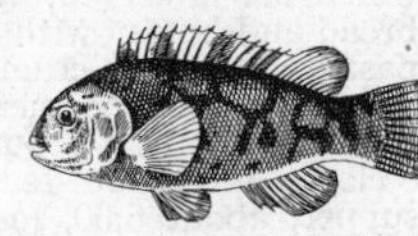
Tautog (about 16 in. long)

tau·to·log·i·cal (tô′tə loj′ə kəl), *adj.* **1.** having to do with tautology. **2.** characterized by tautology. **3.** using tautology. —**tau′to·log′i·cal·ly,** *adv.*

tau·tol·o·gise (tô tol′ə jīz), *v.i.,* **-gised, -gis·ing.** *Especially British.* tautologize.

tau·tol·o·gism (tô tol′ə jiz əm), *n.* **1.** useless repetition. **2.** something so repeated.

tau·tol·o·gist (tô tol′ə jist), *n.* a person who uses repetition or tautology.

tau·tol·o·gize (tô tol′ə jīz), *v.i.,* **-gized, -giz·ing.** to use tautology.

tau·tol·o·gous (tô tol′ə gəs), *adj.* tautological: *Thus mathematical statements are tautologous: they assert nothing more than what is asserted in a statement of the type "All spinsters are unmarried"* (Saturday Review).

tau·tol·o·gy (tô tol′ə jē), *n., pl.* **-gies. 1.** a saying a thing over again in other words without adding clearness or force. *Example:* the *modern* college student of *today.* **2.** *Logic.* a statement, classification, or accounting that overlooks and excludes no possibility. *Example:* She is either married or not. **3.** the stating or believing of a fact to be its own reason; confusion of cause and effect. *Examples:* It's wet because it has water on it. I know because I know. [< Late Latin *tautologia* < Greek *tautologiā* < *tautologeîn* repeat (what has been said) < *tautó* same + *lógos* saying < *légein* speak] —**Syn. 1.** redundancy.

tau·to·mer (tô′tə mər), *n.* one of the isomeric forms exhibited in tautomerism.

tau·to·mer·ic (tô′tə mer′ik), *adj.* **1.** of or having to do with tautomerism. **2.** exhibiting tautomerism.

tau·tom·er·ism (tô tom′ə riz′əm), *n. Chemistry.* the existence of certain organic compounds in equilibrium in two or more structures (isomers or tautomers) that differ in the placement of a hydrogen atom and its double bond, able to react in either structure. [< German *Tautomerie* (< Greek *tautó* the same + *méros* a share + German *-ie* < Greek *-iā* act of) + *-ism*]

tau·tom·er·i·za·tion (tô tom′ər ə zā′shən), *n.* an acquiring of tautomerism.

tau·tom·er·y (tô tom′ər ē), *n.* tautomerism.

tau·to·met·ric (tô′tə met′rik), *adj.* tautometrical.

tau·to·met·ri·cal (tô′tə met′rə kəl), *adj.* **1.** (of verse) in the same meter. **2.** (of syllables) in the same metrical position. [< Greek *tautómetros* the same measure]

tau·to·nym (tô′tə nim), *n. Biology.* a scientific name with the genus and species names alike, now professionally forbidden. *Example: Cygnus cygnus,* the whooper swan. [< Greek *tautṓnymos* the same name]

tau·to·nym·ic (tô′tə nim′ik), *adj. Biology.* (of a scientific name) having the genus and species names alike.

tau·ton·y·mous (tô ton′ə məs), *adj.* tautonymic.

tau·to·phon·i·cal (tô′tə fon′ə kəl), *adj.* repeating the same sound.

tau·toph·o·ny (tô tof′ə nē), *n., pl.* **-nies.** repetition of the same sound, especially a vowel. [< Medieval Greek *tautophonia* < Greek *tautó* the same + *phōnḗ* voice]

tau·to·syl·lab·ic (tô′tə sə lab′ik), *adj.* (of sounds) belonging to the same syllable.

tav (tôf, täv), *n.* the twenty-second and last letter of the Hebrew alphabet. Also, **tau, taw.** [< Hebrew *tāw*]

ta·va·rish (tə vär′ish), *n.* tovarish.

tav·ern (tav′ərn), *n.* **1.** a place where alcoholic drinks are sold and drunk; bar; saloon. **2.** *Archaic.* a small local hotel or public house; inn. [< Old French *taverne* < Latin *taberna* (originally) hut, shed] —**Syn. 2.** hostelry.

tav·er·na (tav′ər nə), *n.* (in Greece) a small, plain restaurant: *In Greece, for instance, many residents will tell you that you can find the best Greek cooking in the basement taverna of the Athens Hilton* (Harper's). [< New Greek *tavérna*]

tav·ern·er (tav′ər nər), *n.* **1.** *Archaic.* a tavernkeeper. **2.** *Obsolete.* a drunkard. [< Anglo-French *taverner,* Old French *tavernier* tavernkeeper < *taverne,* see TAVERN]

tav·ern·keep·er (tav′ərn kē′pər), *n.* the proprietor of a tavern.

tav·ern·less (tav′ərn lis), *adj.* without taverns or inns.

taw[1] (tô), *n.* **1.** a specially fine shooting marble, often streaked or variegated; king marble. **2.** a game in which marbles are hit out of a ring. **3.** the line from which the taw is shot at them.
—*v.i.* to shoot a taw. —**taw′er,** *n.*
—**Syn.** *n.* **1.** agate.

taw[2] (tô), *v.t.* **1.** to prepare (raw material) for further use; dress. **2.** to tan (skins) by soaking in minerals rather than vegetable tanbark. **3.** *Obsolete, Dialect.* to whip; flog; thrash. [Old English *tawian* make ready; harass, insult] —**taw′er,** *n.*

taw[3] (tôf, täv, tou), *n.* tav.

ta·wa (tä′wə, tou′ə), *n.* **1.** a tall New Zealand tree of the laurel family with damson-like fruit. **2.** its light, soft wood, used for making butter kegs. [< Maori *tawa*]

ta·wai (tä′wī), *n.* tawhai.

taw·dri·ly (tô′drə lē), *adv.* in a tawdry manner.

taw·dri·ness (tô′drē nis), *n.* the quality or condition of being tawdry.

taw·dry (tô′drē), *adj.,* **-dri·er, -dri·est. 1.** poor in quality, but showy; flashy. **2.** (of persons) dressed in gaudy and cheap clothes. [short for *tawdry lace,* alteration of *Saint Audrey's lace*] —**Syn. 1.** garish.

ta·whai (tä′hwī), *n.* any of several tall trees of New Zealand, usually called birches. [< Maori *tawhai*]

ta·whi·ri (tä hwē′rē, tä′-), *n.* a small New Zealand tree with fragrant, white blossoms and a tough wood. [< Maori *tawhiri*]

ta·wi·ri (tä wē′rē, tä′-), *n.* tawhiri.

taw·ney (tô′nē), *adj. Obsolete.* tawny.

taw·ni·ly (tô′nə lē), *adv.* in a tawny manner.

taw·ni·ness (tô′nē nis), *n.* the quality of being tawny.

taw·ny (tô′nē), *adj.,* **-ni·er, -ni·est,** *n., pl.* **-nies.** —*adj.* of a rich tan color; brownish-yellow: *A lion has a tawny skin.* —*n.* this color. [Middle English *tauny* < Anglo-French *tauné,* Old French *tane,* past participle of *taner* to tan]

tawny bunting, the snow bunting.

tawny eagle, a brownish-yellow eagle of Africa and India: *Thirty-seven diurnal birds of prey . . . breed in Europe* (*that is, excluding . . . the tawny eagle, whose ranges only just touch the extreme southeast corner of European Russia*) (New Scientist).

tawny emperor, a large, tawny nymphalid butterfly.

tawny owl, a tawny-colored owl of Europe, Asia, and northern Africa.

tawny thrush, a thrush of eastern North America; veery; Wilson's thrush.

taw·pie or **taw·py** (tô′pē), *n. Scottish.* a foolish or thoughtless girl or woman. [compare Danish *taabe* simpleton, Norwegian *taap* half-witted person]

taws or **tawse** (tôz), *n. sing.* or (*especially Scottish*) *pl.* a leather strap divided into narrow strips, formerly much used to punish schoolboys. [apparently plural of *taw*[2]]

Tawny Owl (14 to 16 in. long)

tax (taks), *n.* **1.** money taken from the public by their rulers, as for the cost of government and public works; money paid by people for the support of the government; an assessment; levy. **2.** *U.S.* local taxes; rates: *Our parents pay taxes to the city to pay for our schools.* **3.** any oppressive cost, duty, or demand; burden or strain: *Climbing stairs is a tax on a weak heart.* **4.** *U.S. Informal.* the price for any article or service; charge. **5.** work or goods required from people by the government. [< verb]
—*v.t.* **1.** to require (a person) to pay a tax. **2.** to charge and collect a tax based on the value, cost, or price of: *to tax cigarettes, to tax incomes.* **3.** to put a heavy burden on; make demands on; strain: *Reading in a poor light taxes the eyes.* **4.** to criticize (a person); call to account; censure; accuse: *The teacher taxed Tom for neglecting his work.* **5.** *Law.* to determine the amount of (costs in a lawsuit, etc.). **6.** *U.S. Informal.* in New England: **a.** to price (a thing at so much). **b.** to charge (a price for a thing).
[< Old French *taxer,* learned borrowing from Medieval Latin *taxare* impose a tax; censure, take to task < Latin *taxāre* evaluate, estimate, assess, perhaps < *tangere* to touch. Compare TASK, TASTE.]
—**tax′er,** *n.*
—**Syn.** *n.* **1.** impost, duty, excise. —*v.t.* **3.** task.

tax·a (tak′sə), *n.* the plural of **taxon.**

tax·a·bil·i·ty (tak′sə bil′ə tē), *n.* a being taxable.

tax·a·ble (tak′sə bəl), *adj.* liable to be taxed; subject to taxation: *Churches are not taxable. The basic definition of taxable income* [*is*] *gross income less deductions* (Wall Street Journal). —**tax′a·ble·ness,** *n.* —**Syn.** assessable.

tax·a·bly (tak′sə blē), *adv.* in a taxable manner; so as to be taxable.

tax·a·ceous (tak sā′shəs), *adj.* belonging to the same family of trees and shrubs as the yew.
[< New Latin *Taxaceae* the family name < Latin *taxus* yew tree]

tax·am·e·ter (tak sam′ə tər), *n.* taximeter.

tax·a·tion (tak sā′shən), *n.* **1.** the act or system of taxing: *Taxation is necessary to provide roads, schools, and police.* **2.** the fact of a taxpayer's or commodity's being taxed. **3.** a tax on anything. **4.** the money raised by taxes; the amount people pay for the support of the government; tax revenue.

tax bond, *U.S.* a state bond that may be surrendered in place of taxes.

tax book or **roll,** a list of property subject to taxation and the amount of the taxes.

tax cart, a light delivery cart or farm cart exempt from taxation.

tax certificate, *U.S.* a provisional deed given to the buyer at a tax sale by the authorized official.

tax collector, a government official who collects taxes.

tax cut, a reduction in the rate of a tax.

tax-cut·ting (taks′kut′ing), *n.* a reduction in taxes.

tax-de·duc·ti·ble (taks′di duk′tə bəl), *adj.* that can be taken as a deduction in figuring income tax.

tax deed, *U.S.* the permanent deed delivered to a purchaser of land at a tax sale.

tax-dodg·er (taks′doj′ər), *n.* a person who avoids paying taxes.

tax-dodg·ing (taks′doj′ing), *adj.* legally avoiding paying taxes. —*n.* the act or practice of legally avoiding paying taxes.

tax·eme (tak′sēm), *n. Linguistics.* any device in a language that affects or alters grammatical relationship, as a change of ending (play*ed* — play*ing*), difference in word order (Is he? — He is.), choice of auxiliary verbs (Could be! — Must be!), or change of internal vowel (m*a*n — m*e*n).
[< Greek *táxis* arrangement + English (phon)*eme*]

tax evader, a tax-dodger.

tax evasion, tax-dodging.

tax-ex·empt (taks′ig zempt′), *adj.* free from taxes; not taxed; not taxable. —*n.* a tax-exempt security.

tax farmer, (formerly) a person who bought from his government the privilege of being tax collector in a certain region.

tax-free (taks′frē′), *adj.* **1.** not taxable. **2.** (in Great Britain) having the income tax paid by the corporation and not after being paid to the shareholders.

tax gallon, a standard United States gallon of 231 cubic inches capacity which contains 50 per cent by volume of ethyl alcohol.

tax gatherer, *Archaic.* a tax collector.

tax haven, *U.S.* a foreign country in which a person or company buys property or establishes a subsidiary because of the country's low or nonexistent taxes.

tax·i (tak′sē), *n., pl.* **tax·is,** *v.,* **tax·ied, tax·i·ing** or **tax·y·ing.** —*n.* a taxicab.
—*v.i.* **1.** to ride in a taxi; go by taxi. **2.** (of an aircraft or flier) to move across the ground or water, as before gathering speed to take off. —*v.t.* to make (an airplane) move this way.
[short for *taxicab*]

tax·i·cab (tak′sē kab′), *n.* an automobile for hire with a meter to record the amount to be paid. [short for *taximeter cab*]

tax·i-dance hall (tak′sē dans′, -däns′), *U.S.* a dance hall, cabaret, etc., where women are available as taxi dancers.

taxi dancer, a dance partner paid by the dance, usually a woman.

tax·i·der·mal (tak′sə dėr′məl), *adj.* of or having to do with taxidermy.

tax·i·der·mic (tak′sə dėr′mik), *adj.* taxidermal.

tax·i·der·mist (tak′sə dėr′mist), *n.* a person skilled in taxidermy.

tax·i·der·my (tak′sə dėr′mē), *n.* the art of preparing, embalming, stuffing, and mounting animals' skins to look alive. [< Greek *táxis* taxis + *-dermía* < *dérma, -atos* skin]

tax·i·man (tak′sē man′), *n., pl.* **-men.** a taxicab driver; cabman.

tax·i·me·ter (tak′sē mē′tər, tak sim′ə-), *n.* **1.** a device fitted to a public cab for indicating the fare at any moment. **2.** a taxi with this. [< French *taximètre* < *taxe* fare, tariff + *-mètre* -meter]

tax·in (tak′sin), *n.* taxine.

tax·ine (tak′sēn, -sin) *n.* a light-yellow, resinous, alkaloid poison obtained from the needles and seed of the English yew. *Formula:* $C_{37}H_{51}NO_{10}$ [< New Latin *Taxus* the yew genus + English *-ine*[2]]

tax·ing (tak′sing), *adj.* trying; burdensome; difficult: *The taxing central role ... involves delivering practically nonstop monologues* (New Yorker).

taxing district, a subdivision of a town, county, etc., for assessment.

taxing master, *Especially British.* an officer in a law court who taxes.

tax·i·plane (tak′sē plān′), *n.* an airplane for hire or charter for short trips.

tax·is (tak′sis), *n.* **1.** taxonomy. **2.** *Biology.* movement in a particular direction by a free organism or a cell, as a zoospore, in reaction to an external stimulus, as light. *Taxis* is a change of place, whereas *tropism* is a turning toward a different direction. **3.** *Medicine.* the use of a manipulation rather than surgery to replace a dislodged part, reduce a hernia, etc. **4.** any of various sections or units of ancient Greek troops. [< New Latin *taxis* < Greek *táxis* < *tássein* arrange. Compare TACTIC.]

tax·ite (tak′sīt), *n. Geology.* any lava consolidated from fragments from the same flow having different colors and textures.

tax·it·ic (tak sit′ik), *adj.* **1.** of or having to do with taxite. **2.** like taxite.

tax·i·way (tak′sē wā′), *n.* a path or surface area on an airfield for taxiing to or from the runway, ramp, etc.

tax·less (taks′lis), *adj.* untaxed.

tax lien, *U.S.* the lien of a state on taxable property.

tax·man (taks′man′), *n., pl.* **-men.** a tax collector.

tax·o·di·um family (tak sō′dē əm), a small group of mostly evergreen, gymnospermous trees with scalelike or needlelike leaves, sometimes included in the pine family. The family includes the cryptomeria, bald cypress, redwood, and big tree.

tax·on (tak′sən), *n., pl.* **tax·a.** a taxonomic division, such as a family or order: *Assignment to the taxon is not on the basis of a single property but on the aggregate of properties* (Scientific American). [back formation < *taxonomy*]

tax·on·o·mer (tak son′ə mər), *n.* taxonomist.

tax·o·nom·ic (tak′sə nom′ik), *adj.* of or having to do with taxonomy. —**tax′o·nom′i·cal·ly,** *adv.*

tax·o·nom·i·cal (tak′sə nom′ə kəl), *adj.* taxonomic.

tax·on·o·mist (tak son′ə mist), *n.* a person who knows much about taxonomy: *Thus, in a limited sense, Aristotle was a taxonomist* (New Scientist).

tax·on·o·my (tak son′ə mē), *n.* **1.** classification, especially of plant and animal species. **2.** that branch of a subject which consists in or relates to classification. **3.** the branch of science dealing with classification; study of the general laws and principles of classification.
[< French *taxonomie* < Greek *táxis* arrangement (see TAXIS) + *-nomía*, related to *némein* to distribute]

tax-paid (taks′pād′), *adj.* **1.** paid for by taxes; supported or provided by tax revenues: *tax-paid public officials.* **2.** on which taxes are paid: *It is estimated that Atlanta sells as much "moonshine" as it does tax-paid liquor* (Atlanta Journal).

tax·pay·er (taks′pā′ər), *n.* a person who pays a tax or is required by law to do so.

tax·pay·ing (taks′pā′ing), *n.* the payment of taxes: *Two groups of demonstrators assailed taxpaying* (New York Times). —*adj.* paying taxes: *the taxpaying public.*

tax rate, the rate of taxation on income, etc., especially land.

tax sale, *U.S.* a government sale of property to collect the taxes that are overdue on it.

tax title, *U.S.* the title conveyed by a tax deed.

tax·us (tak′səs), *n.* the yew tree. [< Latin *taxus*]

tax·wise (taks′wīz′), *adv.* with regard to taxes: *It's an axiom that taxwise, an individual house never pays for all the municipal services it requires* (Wall Street Journal).

Ta·yg·e·ta (tā ij′ə tə), *n. Greek Mythology.* one of Atlas's seven daughters who became the Pleiades.

Tay·lor·ism (tā′lə riz əm), *n.* a modified form of Calvinism developed in New England in the 1800's, that placed great emphasis on freedom of the will: *In those days the doctrine of Taylorism was a shadow on the horizon, but the extreme Protestantism of the Exclusive Brethren was well known* (Listener). [< Nathaniel W. *Taylor*, 1786-1858, an American Protestant theologian]

tay·ra (tī′rə), *n.* a small South American carnivorous mammal related to the weasel. It is about two feet long, and has a long tail and black body. [< Tupi *taira*]

Tay-Sachs disease (tā′saks′), amaurotic idiocy. [< Warren *Tay*, 1843-1927, and Bernard *Sachs*, 1858-1944]

ta·zi·a (tə zē′ə), *n.* a model of the tombs of Husain and Hassan carried in the Muharram procession. [< Arabic *ta'zīyat* condolence]

taz·za (tät′sə; *Italian* tät′tsä), *n., pl.* **-zas,** *Italian* **-ze** (-tsā). a shallow, saucer-shaped ornamental bowl or vase, especially one on a pedestal. [< Italian *tazza* gobletlike cup < Arabic *ṭassah* basin]

t.b., 1. trial balance. **2.** *Informal.* tuberculosis of the lungs.

Tb (no period), terbium (chemical element).

TB (no periods), *Informal.* tuberculosis; t.b.

T-band·age (tē′ban′dij), *n.* a T-shaped bandage.

T-bar (tē′bär′), *n.* **1.** a T-shaped girder. **2.** a T-shaped ski lift: *Competition is prodding some ski areas to improve and expand facilities for lifting skiers to the top of slopes. Such facilities range from simple tow ropes, through T-bars, ... to chair lifts and enclosed gondola cars* (Wall Street Journal).

T-beam (tē′bēm′), *n.* a T-bar.

T-bone steak, or **T-bone** (tē′bōn′), *n. U.S.* a steak containing a T-shaped bone, cut from the middle portion of a loin of beef.

tbs. or **tbsp.,** tablespoon or tablespoons.

tc., tierce or tierces (fencing stance).

Tc (no period), technetium (chemical element).

T cart, an open, four-wheeled carriage with two seats, whose body resembles the letter T.

Tchai·kov·ski·an (chī kôf′skē ən), *adj.* of, having to do with, or characteristic of the Russian composer Peter Ilich Tchaikovsky, 1840-1893, his music, or his musical style: *The soloist ... took a certain rhythmic licence more Tchaikovskian than rococo* (London Times).

Tche·ka (che′kə), *n.* Cheka.

tchick (chik), *n.* a sound produced by pressing the tongue against the palate and suddenly withdrawing it with suction or sucking out the air at one side, especially as used to start or quicken the pace of a horse.
—*v.i.* to make the sound of *tchick.*
[imitative]

TCP (no periods), tricresyl phosphate (a gasoline additive).

TD (no periods), *Football.* touchdown.

T.D., *British.* Territorial Officer's Decoration (a medal).

Te (no period), tellurium (chemical element).

tea (tē), *n.* **1.** a common, light-brown drink, slightly bitter, aromatic, and mildly stimulating, made by infusing certain shrub leaves in boiling water, served with milk or lemon, sugar, etc., either hot or iced: *a cup of tea. Love and scandal are the best sweeteners of tea* (Henry Fielding). **2.** the dried and prepared leaves of a shrub from which this drink is made. Tea is raised chiefly in China, Japan, Ceylon, and India. **3.** the shrub it grows on, bearing fragrant, white flowers and oval, evergreen, toothed leaves. **4.** *Especially British.* either of two late afternoon or early evening meals at which tea is served: **a.** tea, bread-and-butter with jam, pastry, scones, crumpets, cake, etc., but no meat or vegetables, at about 4 o'clock; afternoon tea. **b.** supper, about 6:00, instead of afternoon tea and dinner; high tea. **c.** a reception during which afternoon tea is served. **5.** any of various other infusions, usually made from leaves, blossoms, or chopped stems used medicinally or as beverages: *mint tea, beef tea.* **6.** such leaves, blossoms, etc., so used. **7.** such a plant. **8.** *Slang.* marijuana.
cup of tea. See under **cup,** *n.*
[< Chinese (Amoy) *t'e*]

Tea Shrub Branch (def. 3)

tea bag, *U.S.* tea leaves in a little bag of thin cloth or paper for easy, clean removal from the cup or pot after use.

tea ball, *U.S.* **1.** a perforated metal ball for tea leaves in brewing tea. **2.** tea leaves in a little paper bag; tea bag.

tea·ber·ry (tē′ber′ē), *n., pl.* **-ries. 1.** *U.S.* the American wintergreen; Canada tea; mountain tea. **2.** its spicy, red or white berry, used in making tea; checkerberry.

tea biscuit, *British.* a shortbread or cooky, usually served with a cup of tea.

tea boy, a male servant: *Everyone from Director General to the tea boy has been watching election coverage* (Listener).

tea break, *British.* a stopping to have tea.

tea caddy or **canister,** a small can or tin-lined box for keeping tea fresh.

tea cake or **bread,** *British.* a kind of light bread or scone.

tea·cart (tē′kärt′), *n.* a small table on wheels, used in serving foods, as for tea; tea wagon; tea trolley.

teach (tēch), *v.,* **taught, teach·ing,** *n.* —*v.t.* **1.** to give knowledge of, lessons in, or instruction about (a subject). **2.** to give lessons to (a person or animal); help to learn; inform; train; instruct: *to teach a dog tricks.* **3.** to make known to or show (a person) how (to): *Teach me to ride.* **4.** (as a threat) to punish for (to). —*v.i.* to give instruction; act as teacher. —*n. Slang.* teacher: *NBC will also begin a drama series ... with James Franciscus as the muscular teach* (Time). [Old English *tǣcan* show, teach]
—**Syn.** *v.t.* **1, 2. Teach, instruct** mean to convey knowledge or skill to someone. **Teach** implies giving individual guidance and training to the learner: *Some children learn to read by themselves, but most must be taught.* **Instruct** implies providing, in a systematic way, the necessary information or knowledge about a subject: *He instructs classes in chemistry.*
➤ See **learn** for usage note.

teach·a·bil·i·ty (tē′chə bil′ə tē), *n.* the fact or quality of being teachable.

teach·a·ble (tē′chə bəl), *adj.* able to be taught: *Mr. Gatchell believes that anybody can train a teachable dog to learn the meaning of 2,000 words* (New Yorker). —**teach′a·ble·ness,** *n.* —**Syn.** educable.

teach·a·bly (tē′chə blē), *adv.* in a teachable manner; with docility.

teach·er (tē′chər), *n.* **1.** a person who teaches, especially as a profession; instructor: *The teacher trains individuals in developing skills, in doing things, in acquiring information* (Emory S. Bogardus). **2.** any person or event that teaches: *Experience is the best teacher.* —**Syn. 1.** educator, pedagogue.

teach·er·age (tē′chər ij), *n.* a house provided as a residence for a schoolteacher, as in certain rural districts of the United States.

teacher bird, 1. the North American ovenbird. **2.** the red-eyed vireo.

teach·er·ly (tē′chər lē), *adj.* of or like a teacher: *... the teacherly obsession to share all that they can learn* (Time).

teachers college, *U.S.* **1.** a college or university for training teachers. **2.** a normal school.

teach·er·ship (tē′chər ship), *n.* **1.** the office or post of teacher. **2.** an appointment as a teacher.

teachers' institute, a conference for teachers.

tea chest, *Especially British.* a box in which tea is shipped, often 2′x2′x2½′.
teach-in (tēch′in′), *n.* **1.** one of a series of informal, all-night sessions of lectures, debates, and seminars held in the mid-1960's by American college teachers and students to discuss, criticize, or protest against the prevailing American policy on Vietnam: *Comparatively few anthropologists . . . wrote or spoke about human conflict, teach-ins protesting the war in Vietnam . . ., mental health, and campaigns against poverty* (John Joseph Honigmann). **2.** any similar gathering or forum of teachers and students: *"Does Britain need the young?" was the theme of the discussion during a teach-in on community service . . . at Toynbee Hall, London* (London Times).
tea china, china teacups and saucers, etc.
teach·ing (tē′ching), *n.* **1.** the work or profession of a teacher. **2.** the act of one who teaches. **3.** anything taught: **a.** instruction. **b.** a precept or doctrine.
teaching aid, an audio-visual aid.
teaching machine, a device that gives information in a series of units about something and checks how well the information has been learned by a set of questions that often force the pupil to enlarge on the newly acquired facts: *Both education and industry have made increasing use of teaching machines* (Thomas W. Harrell).
tea clam, *U.S.* a very small clam.
tea clipper, (formerly) a fast sailing ship carrying tea.
tea cloth, 1. *Especially British.* a small, ornamental tablecloth for the tea-table. **2.** *British.* dish towel.
tea cooper, *Especially British.* a docker who unloads tea, does necessary repairs to the packing, etc.
tea cozy or **cosy,** a padded jacket to keep the teapot hot.
tea·cup (tē′kup′), *n.* **1.** any cup from which tea is drunk. **2.** a teacupful.
tea·cup·ful (tē′kup′fu̇l), *n., pl.* **-fuls.** as much as a teacup holds.
tea dance, an afternoon tea with dancing.
tea drunkard, a person who habitually drinks so much tea that it makes him ill.
tea equipage, *Especially British.* all the apparatus for making and serving tea.
tea family, a group of dicotyledonous, tropical and subtropical trees and shrubs, including the tea plant, camellia, loblolly bay, and Franklin tree.
tea fight, *British Slang.* a tea party (def. 2).
tea garden, *Especially British.* **1.** an outdoor restaurant for tea and light refreshments, as in a park. **2.** a tea plantation.
tea gown, a loose, long-sleeved, formal gown worn by women in the early part of the 1900's, resembling a modern housecoat, but more formal.
tea-ho (tē′hō′), *n. Australian.* a pause for tea during work, often of 10-20 minutes.
tea·house (tē′hous′), *n.* **1.** a restaurant for tea, light refreshments, and conversation, especially in the Far East. **2.** (in Britain) any café. **3.** *Especially British.* the offices of a firm that imports tea.
teak (tēk), *n.* **1.** a hard, dark-brown, heavy, resinous wood of great strength and durability, used in shipbuilding, fine furniture, etc.; teakwood. **2.** the large East Indian tree it comes from, of the verbena family. **3.** any of various other trees producing strong or durable timber, as a tropical African tree of the spurge family. [< Portuguese *teca* < Malayalam *tēkku*]
tea·ket·tle (tē′ket′əl), *n.* any kettle with a handle and spout for heating water.
teak·wood (tēk′wu̇d′), *n.* teak (def. 1).
teal (tēl), *n., pl.* **teals** or (*collectively*) **teal.** any of various widely distributed, small, fresh-water ducks, as the North American or European green-winged teal, and the North American blue-winged teal. [Middle English *tele*]

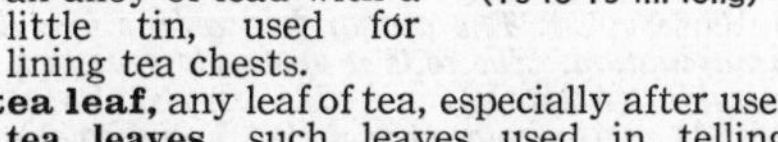

Green-winged Teal
(13 to 15 in. long)

tea-lead (tē′led′), *n.* an alloy of lead with a little tin, used for lining tea chests.
tea leaf, any leaf of tea, especially after use.
tea leaves, such leaves used in telling fortunes.
tea·less (tē′lis), *adj.* **1.** without tea. **2.** not having had one's tea.
team (tēm), *n.* **1.** a group of people working or acting together, especially one of the sides in a game: *a football team, a debating team.* **2.** two or more animals, especially horses, harnessed together for work, as to pull a carriage, wagon, or plow. **3.** one or more draft animals, their harness, and the vehicle they pull. **4.** *British Dialect.* a brood or litter of animals. **5.** *British Dialect.* any chain, as of sausage links. **6.** *Obsolete.* a family line, either of descent or posterity; offspring, lineage, or descendants.
a whole or **full team,** *U.S.* a person who is very capable; expert or champion: [*He*] *was not only a whole team, but a team and a half* (James K. Paulding).
in the team, (of ships) in a line facing outward to watch an enemy: *Nothing can be more dull and monotonous than a blockading cruise in the team* (Frederick Marryat).
—*v.t.* **1.** to combine; join together in a team; yoke. **2.** to work, carry, haul, etc., with a team. —*v.i.* **1.** to combine as a team; join forces. **2.** *U.S.* to drive a team; do teamster's work.
—*adj.* having to do with or performed by a team: *The Americans launched one of the most amazing team rallies on record* (New Yorker).
[Old English *tēam*]
tea·mak·er (tē′mā′kər), *n.* **1.** a person who dries tea leaves and prepares the tea for commercial distribution. **2.** a person or apparatus that makes or infuses tea.
tea·man (tē′man′), *n., pl.* **-men. 1.** a merchant who deals in tea; tea dealer. **2.** *British Slang.* a prisoner who is allowed one pint of tea every evening instead of gruel.
team boat, (formerly) a ferryboat with paddle wheels turned by horses.
team·er (tē′mər), *n. Archaic.* teamster.
team·less (tēm′lis), *adj.* without a team.
team·mate (tēm′māt′), *n.* a fellow member of a team.
team play, joint action; cooperation.
team spirit, esprit de corps.
team·ster (tēm′stər), *n.* anyone who drives horses or a truck, especially for a living; truckdriver: **a.** *U.S.* a member of the transportation workers' union. **b.** *Archaic.* anyone who drives a team of horses.
team teaching, an educational program in which several teachers skilled in particular subjects alternately lecture, instruct, or otherwise meet with a group of students drawn from several regular classes: *Auxiliaries—and . . . team teaching—will have to come soon if the children are to be taught* (Manchester Guardian Weekly).
team·work (tēm′wėrk′), *n.* **1.** joint action by a number of people to make the work of the group successful and effective: *Football requires teamwork even more than individual skill.* **2.** work done with horses. [American English < *team* + *work*] —**Syn. 1.** cooperation.
Te·an (tē′ən), *adj.* Teian.
tea party, 1. an afternoon party at which tea is drunk. **2.** *Slang.* a noisy quarrel; brawl.
tea pavilion, *Cricket.* the pavilion, usually wooden, where players and spectators have tea halfway through the game.
tea·plant·er (tē′plan′tər, -plän′-), *n.* a person whose business is cultivating tea.
tea·plant·ing (tē′plan′ting, -plän′-), *n.* the occupation or business of cultivating tea.
tea·pot (tē′pot′), *n.* a container with a handle and a spout for making and serving tea.
tempest in a teapot. See under **tempest,** *n.*
tea·pot·ful (tē′pot′fu̇l), *n., pl.* **-fuls.** as much as a teapot contains.
tea·poy (tē′poi), *n.* a small, three-legged table for serving tea. [Anglo-Indian < Hindi *tipāi* < *tīn-* (< *tir-* three-) + *pāya* foot]
tear[1] (tir), *n.* **1.** a drop of salty water in the eye, secreted by the lachrymal glands and coming through the tear ducts to moisten the membrane covering the front of the eyeball and the lining of the eyelid. **2.** anything tear-shaped, especially a pendant glass ornament or a kind of English candy. **3.** a bead of liquid condensed on anything. **4.** a small cavity or flaw, especially in glass.
dissolve in tears, to shed many tears: *On hearing the news, she dissolved in tears.*
in tears, crying with grief; weeping: *The people . . . are all in tears and mourning* (John Daus).
[Old English *tēar*] —**tear′like′,** *adj.*
tear[2] (tãr), *v.,* **tore, torn, tear·ing,** *n.* —*v.t.* **1.** to pull apart by force; claw to pieces; rend; sunder: *to tear a box open.* **2.** to make a hole or rent in by a pull; rip: *The nail tore her coat.* **3.** to make (a hole) by pulling: *She tore a hole in her dress.* **4.** to move violently or suddenly by pulling; wrench; wrest: *Tear out the page.* **5.** to wound or lacerate, especially the skin: *The jagged wire tore his skin.* **6.** to produce hostile, dissenting groups in; split: *The party was torn by two factions.* **7.** to plague, as with conflicts: *a person torn by doubts.* **8.** to make miserable; harrow; distract: *His heart was torn by sorrow.* —*v.i.* **1.** to be pulled apart; become torn: *Lace tears easily.* **2.** to make jerking snatches; claw. **3.** *Informal.* to move with great force or haste: *an automobile tearing along.*
be torn between, to find it very hard to choose between (two opposite desires): *Agnes, torn between her interest in what was going on and her desire to get back to her mother, had at last hurriedly accepted this Mrs. Sherwood's offer* (Mrs. Humphry Ward).
tear down, a. to pull down; raze; destroy: *The city tore down a whole block of apartment houses.* **b.** to bring about the wreck of; discredit; ruin: *She tried to tear down his reputation.*
tear into, a. to set upon with great or destructive energy; attack violently: *Last summer's hurricanes killed 200 people . . . as they tore into the coasts and back country* (New York Times). **b.** to attack or criticize severely; lace into: *A legion of critics stand ready to tear into him the moment they can prove him wrong* (Time).
tear it, *Especially British Slang.* to spoil one's chances; wreck one's hopes, plans, etc.: *"Good Lord, that's torn it," she panted. "I am ruined forever"* (Blackwood's Magazine).
tear oneself away or **from,** to leave with great reluctance; go very unwillingly: *They will watch the football* [*game*] *if they can bear to tear themselves away from delights elsewhere* (Manchester Guardian Weekly).
tear up, a. to tear into ragged pieces; rip: *. . . engaged in tearing up old newspapers* (Thomas Hughes). **b.** to cancel by or as if by tearing; destroy: *to tear up a contract.*
—*n.* **1.** a torn place, especially in cloth; rent; hole: *She has a tear in her dress.* **2.** the act of tearing. **3.** the process of being torn. **4.** *Informal.* a hurry; rush. **5.** *Slang.* a spree. **6.** a fit of violent anger.
[Old English *teran*]
—**Syn.** *v.t.* **1. Tear, rip** mean to pull something apart by force. **Tear** means to pull apart or into pieces in such a way as to leave rough or ragged edges: *He tore the letter into tiny pieces.* **Rip** means to tear roughly or quickly, usually along a joining: *She ripped the hem in her skirt by catching her heel in it.*
tear·a·ble (tãr′ə bəl), *adj.* that can be torn. —**tear′a·ble·ness,** *n.*
tear·a·bly (tãr′ə blē), *adv.* in a tearable manner; so as to be torn.
tear·a·way (tãr′ə wā′), *n. British Informal.* a wild, uncontrollable person or animal. —*adj.* impetuous; wild: *It is a very good budget. It avoids the danger of a tearaway boom* (Listener).
tear bomb, shell, or **grenade** (tir), a bomb, shell, or grenade filled with tear gas.
tear bottle (tir), a small bottle or phial, possibly used to hold the mourners' tears, found in an ancient tomb.
tear-down (tãr′doun′), *n.* a tearing down; destruction: . . . *a fast tear-down of all trade boundaries* (Maclean's).
tear·drop (tir′drop′), *n.* **1.** a tear. **2.** something like or suggesting a tear: *crystal teardrops.* **3.** an air bubble in glass, as in a tear glass. —*adj.* of or like a teardrop.
tear·duct (tir′dukt′), *n.* any of several ducts that carry tears from the lachrymals to the eyes or from the eyes to the nose.
tear·er (tãr′ər), *n.* **1.** *U.S. Informal.* any violent person or thing, especially a storm. **2.** tearaway. **3.** anyone who tears.
tear-fall·ing (tir′fô′ling), *adj. Archaic.* tearful.
tear fault (tãr), *Geology.* a big crevice left by a landslide.
tear·ful (tir′fəl), *adj.* **1.** weeping. **2.** inclined to weep. **3.** causing tears; very sad; pathetic. —**tear′ful·ly,** *adv.* —**tear′ful·ness,** *n.* —**Syn. 3.** mournful, melancholy.

tear gas (tir), an irritating gas that temporarily blinds the eyes with tears, used in war and especially against rioters.

tear-gas (tir′gas′), *v.t.*, **-gassed, -gas·sing.** to attack with tear gas; force, subdue, or eject with tear gas.

tear glass (tir), a wineglass with a tear-shaped air bubble in the stem.

tear·ing (tãr′ing), *adj.* **1.** that tears. **2.** *Informal.* headstrong and boisterous; reckless. **3.** *British Slang.* excellent; first-rate. —*adv. British Slang.* extremely; very.

tear-jerk·er (tir′jėr′kər), *n. Slang.* an oversentimental song, film, or story: *Her repertory included such romantic tear-jerkers as "The Lady of Shalott"* (Manchester Guardian Weekly).

tear-jerk·ing (tir′jėr′king), *adj. Slang.* oversentimental.

tear·less (tir′lis), *adj.* **1.** shedding no tears. **2.** dry, as the eyes. **3.** without emotion. —**tear′less·ly,** *adv.* —**tear′less·ness,** *n.*

tear mask (tir), a gas mask worn for protection against tear gas.

tear·proof (tãr′prüf′), *adj.* protected against tearing; resistant to tearing.

tea·room (tē′rüm′, -rům′), *n.* a place where tea, coffee, and light meals are served.

tea·room·y (tē′rü′mē, -rům′ē), *adj.* like a tearoom: *Here, French restaurants quickly become tearoomy, as if some sort of rapid naturalization had taken place* (Harper's).

tea rose, any of several varieties of cultivated rose, derived partly from the China rose, whose flowers have a delicate scent somewhat like that of tea.

tear-shaped (tir′shāpt′), *adj.* pear-shaped.

tear sheet (tãr), *U.S.* a page torn out, as for filing, mounting, or marking.

tear shell (tir), a shell of tear gas.

tear-stained (tir′stānd′), *adj.* stained by tears.

tear strip (tãr), a scored strip, or a band, of paper, tape, etc., that is pulled or wound off to open a can, box top, or wrapper.

tear-up (tãr′up′), *n.* an uprooting.

tear·y (tir′ē), *adj.*, **tear·i·er, tear·i·est. 1.** tearful. **2.** salty.

tea sage, a species or variety of sage whose leaves are used for making sage tea.

tea scrub, *Australian.* a thicket of tea trees.

tease (tēz), *v.*, **teased, teas·ing,** *n.* —*v.t.* **1.** to annoy or worry by jokes, questions, ridiculous requests, etc.; make fun of; bully; plague: *The other boys teased Jim about his curly hair.* **2.** to make a joke of without annoying; make affectionate, good-humored fun of; chaff: *teasing him about all the money he'd won.* **3.** to ask persistently; beg of: *The child teases her for everything he sees.* **4.** to separate the fibers of; pull apart, comb, or card (wool, flax, etc.). **5.** to bring up a nap on (cloth) by combing all the free fibers in one direction; teasel. —*v.i.* to be annoying by making repeated requests; beg.
—*n.* **1.** a person who teases, especially a nagging child: *Don't be a tease.* **2. a.** the act of teasing. **b.** the state of being teased.
[Old English *tǣsan* pluck, pull apart] —**teas′ing·ly,** *adv.*
—**Syn.** *v.t.* **1. Tease, plague, pester** mean to irritate by continuous or persistent annoyance. **Tease** implies causing a person or animal to lose patience and flare up in annoyance or anger, either by persistent begging or by unkind jokes or tricks: *Children teased the dog until he bit them.* **Plague** emphasizes that the irritation is severe: *Her little brother plagues her.* **Pester** emphasizes that the irritation is constantly repeated: *He pesters his mother for candy.* **4.** shred.

tea·sel (tē′zəl), *n.*, *v.*, **-seled, -sel·ing** or (*especially British*) **-selled, -sel·ling.** —*n.* **1.** any of various Eurasian and African herbs with prickly leaves and flower heads, as the fullers' teasel. **2.** the dried flower head or burr of fuller's teasel, used for raising nap on cloth. **3.** a brush with hooked prongs that does this.
—*v.t.* to raise a nap on (cloth) with teasels; dress with teasels. Also **teazel, teazle.**

Fuller's Teasel (def. 1)

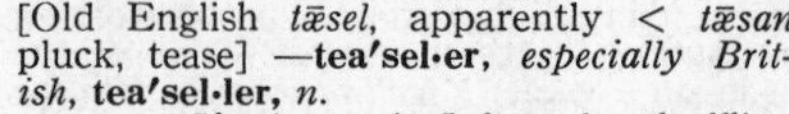

[Old English *tǣsel,* apparently < *tǣsan* pluck, tease] —**tea′sel·er,** *especially British,* **tea′sel·ler,** *n.*

teas·er (tē′zər), *n.* **1.** *Informal.* a baffling problem or difficulty. **2.** one that teases. **3.** a short curtain hung from the top of the proscenium to mask overhead lights and to help frame the stage.

tea service, a tea set.

tea set, a set of china or silver, usually consisting of teapot, sugar bowl, creamer, teacups, and saucers, for use at tea.

tea ship, 1. a ship carrying tea. **2.** a tea stand with two or more shelves.

tea shop, a café; tearoom.

tea·spoon (tē′spün′, -spůn′), *n.* **1.** a small spoon often used to stir tea or coffee, larger in America than in Britain. **2.** a unit of measure holding 1/3 as much as a tablespoon. *Abbr.:* t. **3.** a teaspoonful.

tea·spoon·ful (tē′spün′fůl, -spůn′-), *n.*, *pl.* **-fuls. 1.** a teaspoon. **2.** as much as any teaspoon will hold. *Abbr.:* tsp.

tea stand, a stand where the china is placed for use at tea.

tea stick, a stick cut from the Australian tea tree.

tea stone, a Chinese rose quartz resembling the cairngorm stone.

teat (tēt, tit), *n.* **1.** the nipple of a female's breast or udder, through which the young suck milk. **2.** a rubber or plastic nipple on a baby's feeding bottle: *American goods . . . included rat poison, grain to feed pigeons, chewing gum, and teats for babies' bottles* (Listener). [< Old French *tete,* probably < a Germanic word (compare Old English *titt*)]

tea-ta·ble (tē′tā′bəl), *n.* **1.** a table for tea. **2.** the people who eat at it.
—*adj.* **1.** of or having to do with the tea-table. **2.** frivolous; trivial: *tea-table talk.*

tea-tast·er (tē′tās′tər), *n.* a person whose business is testing the quality of tea by tasting samples; a tea expert.

tea-tast·ing (tē′tās′ting), *n.* the occupation or business of a tea-taster. —*adj.* of or having to do with tea-tasting.

tea things, *Especially British.* the teacups, teapot, etc., of a tea service.

tea time, *Especially British.* the time in the afternoon at which tea is taken.

tea·tow·el (tē′tou′əl), *n.* dishtowel: . . . *teatowels, locally designed but made in Manchester* (Manchester Guardian Weekly).

tea tray, a tray on which tea is brought from the kitchen.

tea tree, 1. the shrub that yields tea. **2.** any of various trees or shrubs that belong to the myrtle family, having a heavy, durable wood, and leaves used as a substitute for tea. **3.** an African shrub of the nightshade family, with violet flowers and spiny branches. **4.** (in Great Britain) a flowering shrub related to the boxthorn, a native of China. **5.** (in southern Asia) a native tree of Ceylon and Coromandel with leaves like those of the tea shrub.

tea trolley, *Especially British.* a teacart.

tea urn, samovar.

tea wagon, *Especially U.S.* a teacart.

tea·zel (tē′zəl), *n.*, *v.*, **-zeled, -zel·ing** or (*especially British*) **-zelled, -zel·ling.** teasel. —**tea′zel·er,** *especially British,* **tea′zel·ler,** *n.*

tea·zle (tē′zəl), *n.*, *v.*, **-zled, -zling.** teasel. —**tea′zler,** *n.*

te·bel·di (tə bel′dē), *n.* the baobab: *A stout tebeldi can hold up to a thousand gallons of water in its hollow trunk, and when it rains in Kordofan, all hands turn to, form a bucket brigade, and fill as many trees as possible* (New Yorker). [< Arabic]

Te·bet or **Te·beth** (tā vāth′, tā′ves), *n.* the tenth month of the Hebrew ecclesiastical, and the fourth of the civil, year, corresponding to December and sometimes part of January. [< Hebrew *ṭebeth* < Babylonian *ṭibitu*]

tec (tek), *n. British Slang.* a detective.

tec·bir (tek bir′), *n.* tekbir.

Tech or **Tec** (tek), *n. Slang.* a technical institute, etc.: *Georgia Tech.*

tech., 1. a. technical. **b.** technically. **2. a.** technological. **b.** technologically. **c.** technology.

teched (techt), *adj.* tetched: *As the pressure mounted, some of the entrants seemed a bit teched* (Time).

tech·i·ly (tech′ə lē), *adv.* tetchily.

tech·i·ness (tech′ē nis), *n.* tetchiness.

tech·ne (tek′nē), *n.* technology: *Barzun . . . calls them "traitors," who have surrendered art to the temptations of science and techne* (American Scholar). [< Greek *technē* art, skill]

tech·ne·ti·um (tek nē′shē əm), *n.* a radioactive metallic chemical element produced artificially, especially by fission of uranium. *Symbol:* Tc; *at. wt.:* (C^{12}) 99 or (O^{16}) 99; *at. no.:* 43. [< Greek *technētós* artificial (< *téchnē* an art, skill) + New Latin *-ium,* a suffix meaning "element"]

tech·nic (tek′nik), *n.* **1.** any technique. **2.** *Especially U.S.* a technical detail, point, term, etc.; technicality. **3.** the science of technics. —*adj.* technical. [< Latin *technicus* < Greek *technikós* of art < *téchnē* art, skill, craft]

tech·ni·ca (tek′nə kə), *n.pl.* technical details, methods, or skills; technics. [< Greek *techniká,* neuter plural of *technikós;* see TECHNIC]

tech·ni·cal (tek′nə kəl), *adj.* **1.** of or having to do with an art, science, discipline, or profession: *a word's technical sense.* **2.** typical of, characteristic of, or special to a subject: *"Electrolysis," "tarsus," and "protein" are technical words.* **3.** of or having to do with industrial arts, applied sciences, mechanical trades, and crafts; technological: *This technical school trains engineers, chemists, and architects.* **4.** using technical terms; treating a subject technically: *a technical lecture.* **5.** judged strictly by the rules; strictly interpreted. **6.** of or having to do with technique: *Her singing shows technical skill, but her voice is weak.* **7.** (of a stock market, its prices, etc.) abnormally high or low because of heavy speculation.
[< *technic* + *-al*[1]] —**tech′ni·cal·ness,** *n.*

tech·ni·cal·ise (tek′nə kə līz), *v.t.*, **-ised, -is·ing.** *Especially British.* technicalize.

tech·ni·cal·ism (tek′nə kə liz′əm), *n.* **1.** technical style, method, or treatment. **2.** overuse of technicalities.

tech·ni·cal·ist (tek′nə kə list), *n.* **1.** an expert in technicalities. **2.** a person addicted to technicalities.

tech·ni·cal·i·ty (tek′nə kal′ə tē), *n.*, *pl.* **-ties.** a technical matter, point, detail, term, expression, etc.

tech·ni·cal·i·za·tion (tek′nə kə lə zā′shən), *n.* **1.** the act or process of technicalizing: *He [Dr. Erhard] said this cooperation was necessary as a balance against the growing "technicalization" of the Common Market* (London Times). **2.** the state of being technicalized.

tech·ni·cal·ize (tek′nə kə līz), *v.t.*, **-ized, -iz·ing.** to make technical.

technical knockout, a knockout scored in a boxing match when the referee decides that a fighter is too hurt or dazed to continue fighting, although he has not been knocked out.

tech·ni·cal·ly (tek′nə klē), *adv.* in a technical manner or respect; in relation to a particular art or the like, or to the arts and applied sciences; in accordance with technical methods; in technical terms; in a technical sense.

technical officer, *Especially British.* an industrial official engaged in investigation, research, and development work.

technical sergeant, (in the U.S. Air Force, Marine Corps, and formerly in the Army) a noncommissioned army officer who is above a staff sergeant and below a master sergeant. *Abbr.:* T.Sgt.

tech·ni·cian (tek nish′ən), *n.* **1.** an expert in the details of a subject or skill, especially a mechanical one. **2.** any artist, musician, etc., with skilled technique. **3.** (formerly) one of three specialists' ratings (third, fourth, and fifth grades) in the United States Army, ranking as staff sergeant, sergeant, and corporal respectively.

tech·ni·cist (tek′nə sist), *n.* technician.

tech·ni·co·log·ic (tek′nə kə loj′ik), *adj.* technological.

tech·ni·co·log·i·cal (tek′nə kə loj′ə kəl), *adj.* technological.

tech·ni·col·o·gy (tek′nə kol′ə jē), *n.* technology.

Tech·ni·col·or (tek′nə kul′ər), *n. Trademark.* a special process by which three-color photographs are combined in one film. [American English < *techni*(cal) + *color*]

tech·ni·col·or (tek′nə kul′ər), *n.* bright, intense color: *The author has a fine visual imagination. She rolls it on in glorious technicolor* (Atlantic). —*adj.* very colorful; vivid: *a technicolor sunset.* [< *Technicolor*]

Tech·ni·col·ored (tek′nə kul′ərd), *adj.* made in Technicolor: *a Technicolored western.*

tech·ni·col·ored (tek′nə kul′ərd), *adj.* technicolor.

tech·nics (tek′niks), *n.* **1.** a study or

science of the arts, especially the mechanical or industrial arts. **2.** technic or technique.

tech·ni·cum or **tech·ni·kum** (tek′nə kəm), *n.* a secondary school in the Soviet Union that prepares students for semiprofessional jobs such as nursing. [< Russian *tekhnikum*]

tech·nique (tek nēk′), *n.* **1.** the skill of a composing artist, as a musician, painter, sculptor, poet, etc. **2.** the method or way of performing the mechanical details of an art; technical skill: *The pianist's technique was excellent, though his interpretation of the music was poor.* **3.** any special method or system of doing something. [< French *technique,* noun use of adjective < Greek *technikós;* see TECHNIC]

techno-, *combining form.* the arts and crafts, especially industrial arts; technics; technology: *Technocracy = government by technological principles.* [< Greek *téchnē* an art, method, system; skill]

tech·noc·ra·cy (tek nok′rə sē), *n., pl.* **-cies.** **1.** governmental, social, and industrial management according to the findings of engineers and usually administered by technologists: *The French Government is determined, however, to fight any attempt at uniting Europe under a "technocracy"* (New York Times). **2.** the theory popular in the 1930's that such management would benefit everyone. **3.** advocacy of this theory.

tech·no·crat (tek′nə krat), *n.* a supporter of technocracy: *In top positions there are too many technocrats—men of tremendous ability in their own sphere, but who lack the essential quality of being able to lead men* (London Times).

tech·no·crat·ic (tek′nə krat′ik), *adj.* of or having to do with technocracy.

tech·nog·ra·pher (tek nog′rə fər), *n.* an expert in technography.

tech·no·graph·ic (tek′nə graf′ik), *adj.* of or having to do with technography.

tech·nog·ra·phy (tek nog′rə fē), *n. Anthropology.* the study of the geographical distribution of arts and crafts.

technol., 1. technological. **2.** technology.

tech·no·lith·ic (tek′nə lith′ik), *adj. Archaeology.* of or having to do with a group of stone implements made according to a particular design or pattern. [< *techno-* + Greek *líthos* stone + English *-ic*]

tech·no·log·ic (tek′nə loj′ik), *adj.* technological.

tech·no·log·i·cal (tek′nə loj′ə kəl), *adj.* **1.** of or having to do with technology. **2.** used in technology. **—tech′no·log′i·cal·ly,** *adv.*

technological gap, the difference in technological advancement between two nations or groups of nations.

technological unemployment, unemployment caused by technical advances and inventions eliminating jobs or industries: *Automatic power looms in the textile industry and great improvements in making finished steel also contributed to technological unemployment in many countries* (Robert D. Patton).

tech·nol·o·gist (tek nol′ə jist), *n.* a person skilled in technology.

tech·nol·o·gy (tek nol′ə jē), *n.* **1.** the science of the mechanical and industrial arts; applied science; engineering: *He studied engineering at a school of technology.* **2.** technical words, terms, or expressions; technical terminology or nomenclature. [< Greek *technologiā* < *téchnē* art, craft, or technique + *-logos* systematic treating of, -logy]

tech·no·nom·ic (tek′nə nom′ik), *adj. Archaic.* of or having to do with technonomy.

tech·non·o·my (tek non′ə mē), *n. Archaic.* the science of technology.

tech·y (tech′ē), *adj.,* **tech·i·er, tech·i·est.** tetchy.

tec·nol·o·gy (tek nol′ə jē), *n.* the study of children. [< Greek *téknos* child + *-logy*]

tec·non·y·mous (tek non′ə məs), *adj.* practicing tecnonymy.

tec·non·y·my (tek non′ə mē), *n. Anthropology.* the practice of identifying a person as the parent of his named child rather than by his personal name. [< Greek *téknos* child + *ónyma* name + English *-y*[3]]

te·co·ma (ti kō′mə), *n. Botany.* **1.** any of various plants of the bignonia family, consisting chiefly of erect, climbing, or twining shrubs with showy, trumpet-shaped flowers, mostly red or yellow. **2.** any of several related tall trees with digitate leaves, used for timber and in medicine. [< New Latin *Tecoma* the genus name < Nahuatl *tecomaxochitl* < *tecomatl* calabash tree, earthen pot + *xochitl* rose, flower]

tec·ta (tek′tə), *n.* the plural of **tectum.**

tec·tal (tek′təl), *adj.* of or having to do with a tectum; tectorial.

tec·ti·branch (tek′tə brangk), *Zoology.* —*adj.* belonging to the marine gastropod mollusks, having the gills covered by the mantle, and small shells often concealed by the mantle. —*n.* such a gastropod. [< Latin *tectus, -ī* covered + *branchiae* gills]

tec·ti·bran·chi·an (tek′tə brang′kē ən), *adj.* tectibranch.

tec·ti·bran·chi·ate (tek′tə brang′kē it), *n.* tectibranch.

tec·ti·form (tek′tə fôrm), *adj. Zoology.* **1.** sloping down on each side from a ridge, as a wing. **2.** serving as a covering or lid. [< Latin *tectus, -ī* covered + *forma* form]

tec·to·log·i·cal (tek′tə loj′ə kəl), *adj.* of or having to do with tectology.

tec·tol·o·gy (tek tol′ə jē), *n. Biology.* that branch of morphology which regards an organism as composed of morphons of different orders. [< German *Tektologie* < Greek *téktōn* builder + German *-logie* -logy]

tec·ton·ic (tek ton′ik), *adj.* **1.** of or having to do with the structure of buildings; constructional; architectural. **2.** *Geology.* **a.** belonging to the structure of the earth's crust and to general changes in it, as folding, faulting, etc. **b.** resulting from these: *a tectonic ridge.* [< Late Latin *tectonicus* < Greek *tektonikós* of building < *téktōn, -onos* builder] **—tec·ton′i·cal·ly,** *adv.*

tec·ton·ics (tek ton′iks), *n.* **1.** the science or art of assembling, shaping, or ornamenting materials in construction; construction. **2.** tectonic geology; structural geology (of the earth's crust). **3.** the branch of zoology that deals with structure.

tec·ton·ism (tek′tə niz əm), *n. Geology.* tectonic activity; diastrophism: *Climatic and geologic aspects control slopes and gradients as well as tectonism* (Lawrence Ogden).

tec·to·no·phys·ics (tek′tə nə fiz′iks), *n.* the application of the principles of physics to tectonic geology.

tec·to·ri·al (tek tôr′ē əl, -tōr′-), *adj.* covering like a roof; forming a protective structure over something: *the tectorial membrane of the ear.* [< Latin *tectōrium* a covering (< *tegere* to cover) + English *-al*[1]]

tec·tri·cial (tek trish′əl), *adj.* having to do with the tectrices.

tec·trix (tek′triks), *n., pl.* **tec·tri·ces** (tek trī′sēz, tek′trə-). a feather covering the base of wing and tail quills. [< New Latin *tectrix,* feminine of Latin *tector* one who covers < *tegere* to cover]

tec·tum (tek′təm), *n., pl.* **-ta.** any rooflike structure in the human or animal anatomy: *Anatomical studies had shown that not all the frog's optic nerve fibers pass to the tectum; some go instead to a secondary visual center in the dorsal thalamus* (Scientific American). [< Latin *tectum* roof < *tegere* to cover]

ted (ted), *v.t.,* **ted·ded, ted·ding.** to spread or scatter (new-mown grass) for drying. [compare Old Icelandic *tethja* spread manure]

Ted (ted), *n. British Slang.* teddy-boy.

ted·der (ted′ər), *n.* a machine that spreads out hay for drying.

ted·dy or **Ted·dy** (ted′ē), *n., pl.* **-dies.** *British Slang.* a teddy-boy.

teddy bear, a child's furry toy bear.

ted·dy-boy or **Ted·dy-boy** (ted′ē boi′), *n. British Slang.* an uncouth, rough, idle, usually low-class young tough (about 15 to 25 years old), often violent; juvenile delinquent. [< their fancy suits, cut in the style of *Edward VII*]

ted·dy-girl or **Ted·dy-girl** (ted′ē gėrl′), *n. British Slang.* a teddy-boy's girl friend.

Te De·um (tē dē′əm), **1.** an ancient hymn of praise and thanksgiving sung at morning prayers or on special occasions in the Roman Catholic Church in Latin, and in the Anglican Church in English. **2.** a musical setting for this hymn. **3.** a thanksgiving service in which this hymn is prominent. [< Late Latin *Te Deum Laudamus* we praise thee, God (the first words of the hymn)]

te·di·ous (tē′dē əs, tē′jəs), *adj.* **1.** tiresomely long; boring; irksome: *Life is as tedious as a twice-told tale* (Shakespeare). **2.** writing or talking on and on; wordy; wearying; long-winded. [< Late Latin *taediōsus* < Latin *taedium* tedium] **—te′di·ous·ly,** *adv.* **—te′di·ous·ness,** *n.* **—Syn. 1.** wearisome. **2.** prolix. See **tiresome. —Ant. 1.** engaging, spellbinding.

te·di·um (tē′dē əm), *n.* **1.** the state of being tedious; wearisomeness. **2.** ennui; boredom. [< Latin *taedium* < *taedet* it is wearisome] **—Syn. 1.** irksomeness.

te·di·um vi·tae (tē′dē əm vī′tē), taedium vitae.

tee[1] (tē), *n., v.,* **teed, tee·ing.** —*n. Golf.* **1.** the starting place in the play for each hole, often slightly elevated. **2.** an inch-high stand, as of wood or plastic, on which the ball is set for the first drive.
—*v.t.* to set (a golf ball) on a tee.

tee off, *Especially U.S.* **a.** *Golf.* to drive (a ball) from a tee: *A field of 134 will tee off tomorrow . . . for the Professional Golfers Association championship* (New York Times). **b.** to begin any series of actions: *He will tee off this year's new ten-week course next Sunday with tips on "how to read a Shakespeare play"* (New York Times). **c.** *Slang.* to make angry: *Missing the train teed him off.*

tee up, a. to set (a golf ball) on a tee: *The golfer teed up his ball on the grass.* **b.** *Especially British.* to tee off: *You tee up first. They teed up to launch the ship. Most ratepayers . . . have been teed up to get whatever relief was going* (London Times).
[origin uncertain]

tee[2] (tē), *n.* the mark or peg aimed at in curling, quoits, etc. [perhaps < *tee*[3]]

tee[3] (tē), *n.* **1.** the letter *T, t.* **2.** anything T-shaped, especially a pipe fitting with three openings, one at right angles to the other two. **3.** a T-bar.

to a tee, to a T; exactly: *Politicians . . . are calculating to a tee how to extract the maximum advantage* (London Times).
—*adj.* with a crosspiece on top; T-shaped. [< Latin *tē* the letter T]

tee[4] (tē), *n.* an umbrella-shaped decoration, usually gilded and hung with bells on top of pagodas, especially in Burma. Also, **htee.** [< Burmese *h'ti* umbrella]

tee-hee (tē hē′), *interj., n., v.,* **-heed, -hee·ing.** te-hee.

teel (tēl), *n.* til[1].

teem[1] (tēm), *v.i.* **1.** to be full; abound; swarm: *The swamp teemed with mosquitoes.* **2.** to be fertile, fruitful, or prolific: *His mind teemed with large schemes* (William E. H. Lecky). **3.** *Obsolete.* to be or become pregnant; give birth. [Old English *tēman, tieman* < *tēam* progeny] **—teem′er,** *n.*

teem[2] (tēm), *v.t.* **1.** to empty (a vessel). **2.** to pour off (the contents); decant. —*v.i.* to flow out. [< Scandinavian (compare Old Icelandic *tœma* to empty < *tōmr* empty)]

teem·ful (tēm′fəl), *adj.* **1.** fruitful; teeming. **2.** *British Dialect.* full to the top.

teem·ing (tē′ming), *adj.* **1.** full (of); alive (with). **2.** fruitful; prolific. **—teem′ing·ly,** *adv.* **—teem′ing·ness,** *n.*

teem·less (tēm′lis), *adj.* barren: *Such fiery tracks of dearth Their zeal has left, and such a teemless earth* (John Dryden).

teen[1] (tēn), *n.* **1.** *Archaic.* grief. **2.** *Archaic.* pains; care. **3.** *Obsolete.* revenge. [Old English *tēona* injury, damage, trouble]

teen[2] (tēn), *adj.* of or having to do with the teens or teen-agers.

teen-age (tēn′āj′), *adj.* of, for, or being a teen-ager: *a teen-age club, a teen-age girl.*

teen-aged (tēn′ājd′), *adj.* being in the teens; in one's teens: *a teen-aged athlete.*

teen-ag·er (tēn′ā′jər), *n.* a person in his or her teens.

teens (tēnz), *n.pl.* the years of life from 13 to 19 inclusive; adolescence.

teen·sy (tēn′sē), *adj.,* **-si·er, -si·est.** *Informal.* very small; tiny: *Of course, Max was not, or only a teensy bit, to blame* (W.H. Auden).

teen·sy-ween·sy (tēn′sē wēn′sē), *adj. Informal.* teensy: *There were even loyal Administration men who nervously prayed for a teensy-weensy touch of recession to settle the tax brawl* (Manchester Guardian Weekly).

teent·sy (tēnt′sē), *adj.,* **-si·er, -si·est.** *Informal.* very small; tiny

tee·ny (tē′nē), *adj.,* **-ni·er, -ni·est.** *Informal.* very small; tiny.

tee·ny-wee·ny (tē′nē wē′nē), *adj. Informal.* teeny.

tee·pee (tē′pē), *n.* tepee.

tee shirt, T shirt.

tee·soo or **tee·so** (tē′sü), *n.* in India: **1.** the brilliant orange-red flowers of the dhak or palas. **2.** the yellow dye they yield. [< Hindi *tēsū*]

tee·tee (tē′tē), *n.* titi[1]. [< Tupi *titi*]

tee·ter (tē′tər), *v.i., v.t.* **1.** to rock unsteadily; sway. **2.** to balance on a seesaw. —*n.* **1.** a swaying movement; reeling. **2.** *Especially U.S.* a seesaw. **3.** hesitation between two alternatives; vacillation. [American English < Middle English *titeren* < Scandinavian (compare Old Icelandic *titra* shake, totter)]

tee·ter-board (tē′tər bôrd′, -bōrd′), *n. Especially U.S.* a seesaw: *We were having a grand time with our teeter-boards upon the highest fence* (Knickerbocker Magazine).

tee·ter·ing-board (tē′tər ing bôrd′, -bōrd′), *n. Especially U.S.* a seesaw.

tee·ter-tot·ter (tē′tər tot′ər), *n. Especially U.S.* a seesaw: *Ford ... passed the hat around for money to buy swings, teeter-totters, and soccer balls* (Maclean's).

tee·ter·y (tē′tər ē), *adj. U.S.* unsteady; shaky: *The orchestra spieled some teetery music* (Rex Beach).

teeth (tēth), *n.* the plural of **tooth.**

cut one's teeth, a. to have the teeth begin to grow through the gums; begin teething: *Their first child is just now cutting his teeth.* **b.** to get one's first training; have one's first experience: *The National Cinema School has been training a fine and aggressive group of young directors who are allowed to cut their teeth on short films and pictures made for TV* (Bosley Crowther).

get or **sink one's teeth into,** to become deeply involved with, as a problem; take hold of; come to grips with: *When [he] gets his teeth into a good, meaty, high-calorie political issue, he does not let go easily* (New York Times). *Mr. Woodbridge is struggling valiantly to discover something that he can sink his teeth into* (London Times).

in the or **one's teeth, a.** in direct opposition or conflict: *Others ... met the enemy in the teeth* (William Whiston). **b.** to one's face; openly: *Dost thou jeer and flout me in the teeth?* (Shakespeare).

in the teeth of, a. straight against; in the face of: *They came on in the teeth of our men, fearless of danger* (Daniel Defoe). **b.** in defiance of; in spite of: *Why do you continue to live here in the teeth of these repeated warnings?* (Leigh Hunt).

kick in the teeth, *Informal.* to insult; betray; reject: *Is it not time to be more realistic, ... and, when a country kicks you in the teeth, withdraw aid?* (London Times).

lie in one's teeth, to lie brazenly and boldly: *He also accused [the] general secretary-treasurer of the union, of "lying in his teeth" in asserting the 30-day rule had been in practice 45 years* (Wall Street Journal).

put teeth in or **into,** to put force into: *[His] efforts help to put the strongest possible teeth into whatever the UN does* (Manchester Guardian Weekly).

set one's teeth, to prepare (for a struggle) with firmness: *"I think not!" replied Mr. Sawyer, setting his teeth for a catastrophe* (G.J. Whyte-Melville).

set one's teeth on edge, to be so unpleasant or annoying as to cause physical discomfort: *The screenplay is so arty that it constantly sets one's teeth on edge* (Brendan Gill).

show one's teeth, to show anger; threaten: *When the law shows her teeth, but dares not bite ...* (Edward Young).

throw in one's teeth, to blame or reproach for (especially something shameful): *This neglect of family devotions is often thrown in our teeth* (Francis Bragge).

to the teeth, completely: *Everybody in Spain travels armed to the teeth* (Richard Ford). *I'm not trying to excuse the salesman, but I am fed up to the teeth with seeing him picked on all the time* (Colm Hogan).

teethe (tēᴛʜ), *v.i.,* **teethed, teeth·ing.** to cut teeth.

teeth·ing (tē′ᴛʜing), *n.* **1.** the growing or cutting of teeth; dentition. **2.** any often painful or upsetting early development: *Progress thus far has exceeded expectations with unusually few teething troubles* (Wall Street Journal).

teething ring, a ring of plastic, bone, or ivory for a teething baby to bite on.

teeth·ridge (tēth′rij′), *n.* alveoli.

tee·to·tal (tē tō′təl), *adj.* **1.** of or having to do with total abstinence from alcoholic liquor. **2.** urging total abstinence from alcoholic liquor. **3.** pledged to drink no alcoholic liquor. **4.** *Informal.* without exception; complete; entire. [apparently formed < *total,* with repetition of initial *t;* influenced by *teetotum*] —**tee·to′tal·ly,** *adv.*

tee·to·tal·er (tē tō′tə lər), *n.* a person who more or less formally pledges or binds himself to drink no alcoholic liquor. —**Syn.** abstainer.

tee·to·tal·ing (tē tō′tə ling), *adj.* abstaining completely from the use of alcoholic liquor; abstemious.

tee·to·tal·ism (tē tō′tə liz əm), *n.* the principle or practice of total abstinence from alcoholic liquor.

tee·to·tal·ist (tē tō′tə list), *n.* a teetotaler: *Is Mr. Wood, the builder, not a teetotalist, but a firm and sensible man?* (Pall Mall Gazette).

tee·to·tal·ler (tē tō′tə lər), *n. Especially British.* teetotaler.

tee·to·tum (tē tō′təm), *n.* a top spun with the fingers: *She'll waltz away like a teetotum* (W.S. Gilbert). [for earlier *totum,* the original name (< Latin *tōtum* all), with *tee* = T, a letter stamped on one side of the toy]

teff or **tef** (tef), *n.* the principal cereal of Ethiopia, producing minute black or white grains from which bread is made, introduced elsewhere for fodder. Also, **taff.** [< Amharic *ṭēf*]

te·fil·lin (tə fil′ən), *n.pl.* phylacteries. [< Aramaic *təphillīn,* perhaps irregular plural of *təphillāh* prayer]

Tef·lon (tef′lon), *n. Trademark.* polytetrafluoroethylene, a plastic.

teg or **tegg** (teg), *n. Especially British.* a sheep from its weaning till its first shearing in its second year. [perhaps < Scandinavian (compare Swedish *tacka* ewe)]

teg·men (teg′men), *n., pl.* **-mi·na** (-mə nə). **1.** *Biology.* a cover, covering, or coating; integument. **2.** *Botany.* the thin, soft, delicate inner coat of a seed, surrounding the embryo; integument. **3.** *Entomology.* a forewing of an insect when modified to serve as a covering for the hind wings. [< Latin *tegmen, -minis* a covering < *tegere* to cover]

teg·men·tal (teg men′təl), *adj.* having to do with the tegmentum.

teg·men·tum (teg men′təm), *n., pl.* **-ta** (-tə). *Botany.* **1.** the scaly coat which covers a leaf bud. **2.** one of the scales of such a coat. [< Latin *tegmentum,* variant of *tegumentum* < *tegere* to cover]

teg·mi·nal (teg′mə nəl), *adj.* tegumentary.

te·guex·in (te gwek′sin), *n.* a large South American lizard resembling a monitor. [< New Latin *teguexin* the species name < Nahuatl *tecoixin* lizard]

teg·u·lar (teg′yə lər), *adj.* **1.** having to do with a tile. **2.** like a tile. **3.** consisting of or made of tiles. **4.** arranged or fitted like tiles. [< Latin *tēgula* tile (< *tegere* to cover) + English *-ar*] —**teg′u·lar·ly,** *adv.*

teg·u·ment (teg′yə mənt), *n.* a natural covering; a shell, capsule, or cocoon; integument: *He [a suckling pig] must be roasted. I am not ignorant that our ancestors ate them seethed or boiled—but what a sacrifice of the exterior tegument!* (Charles Lamb). [< Latin *tegumentum* < *tegere* to cover]

teg·u·men·tal (teg′yə men′təl), *adj.* tegumentary.

teg·u·men·ta·ry (teg′yə men′tər ē), *adj.* **1.** of or having to do with integument. **2.** composed or consisting of skin or other covering or investing part or structure.

te-hee (tē hē′), *interj., n., v.,* **-heed, -hee·ing.** —*interj.* a word representing the sound of a tittering laugh.
—*n.* **1.** the sound of a tittering laugh. **2.** a titter; snicker; snigger; giggle.
—*v.i.* to titter; snicker; snigger; giggle. Also, **tee-hee.** [Middle English *tihi, tehee;* imitative]

tehr (tãr), *n.* tahr.

Te·huel·che (te wel′chā), *n.* **1.** a tribe of Indians in Patagonia, renowned for their tallness. **2.** any of various neighboring tribes.

Tei·an (tē′ən), *adj.* **1.** of Teos, in ancient Ionia, Greece. **2.** of the poet Anacreon, who was a native of Teos. Also, **Tean.**

te ig·i·tur (tē ij′ə tər), the first prayer of the canon of the Mass according to the Roman Catholic and some other Latin rites. [< Latin *te igitur* (literally) thee, therefore (the prayer's first words)]

teil (tēl), *n.,* or **teil tree, 1.** the linden tree. **2.** (in the Bible) the terebinth. [partly < Medieval Latin *tilia* linden; partly < Old French *til, teil* < Latin *tiliolus* (diminutive) < *tilius* lime]

teind (tēnd), *Scottish.* —*n.* a tithe. **teinds,** property assessed for tithes: *The teinds are the kirk's patrimony* (John Row).
—*v.i.* to pay teinds. —*v.t.* to take a tithe of. [Middle English *tende* tenth] —**teind′er,** *n.*

teis·tie (tēs′tē), *n. British Dialect.* the black guillemot. [< Scandinavian (compare Old Icelandic *theist,* Norwegian *teist*)]

te·ja·no (tā hä′nō), *n., pl.* **-nos.** *Southwestern U.S.* a Texan: *The term tejano is pejorative in New Mexico, intended to conjure up an image of an ignorant and vicious cowhand* (Harper's). [< Spanish *tejano* < *Tejas* Texas]

tek·bir (tek bir′), *n.* an Arab cry of victory, "Allah Akbar" ("God is greater"). [< Arabic *tekbīr* to exalt < *kabura* to be great]

tek·ke or **tek·keh** (tek′ke), *n.* tekkieh.

tek·ki·eh (tek′kē ə), *n.* a Moslem monastery. [< Arabic *takīyah*]

tek·tite (tek′tīt), *n. Geology.* any of various kinds of rounded, glassy objects found in Australia and elsewhere but of unknown origin. [< Greek *tēktós* molten (< *tḗkein* to melt) + English *-ite*[1]]

tek·tit·ic (tek tit′ik), *adj. Geology.* of or having to do with tektites: *If the glass chemist were asked to formulate a material which would survive both hypersonic entry through the atmosphere and prolonged geological weathering, he could not improve upon the tektitic formula* (New Scientist).

tel-, *combining form.* a variant of **tele-,** as in *telelectric, teloptic.*

tel., 1. telegram. **2.** telegraph. **3.** telephone.

TEL (no periods), tetraethyl lead (an antiknock additive for gasoline).

tel·aes·the·sia (tel′əs thē′zhə; -zhē ə, -zē-), *n.* telesthesia; telepathy.

tel·aes·thet·ic (tel′əs thet′ik), *adj.* telesthetic; telepathic.

Tel·a·mon (tel′ə mon), *n. Greek Mythology.* the father of Ajax and Teucer, and king of the island of Salamis.

tel·a·mon (tel′ə mon), *n., pl.* **tel·a·mo·nes** (tel′ə mō′nēz). *Architecture.* a figure of a man used as a column; atlas. [< *Telamon*]

tel·an·gi·ec·ta·sis (te lan′jē ek′tə sis), *n., pl.* **-ses** (-sēz). *Medicine.* a disorder in which the capillaries are permanently dilated, as in red-faced alcoholics, or persons who spend much time out of doors: *Congenital hemorrhagic telangiectasis ... is hereditary and marked by enlargement of small blood vessels in such various parts of the body as the nose, throat, and intestines* (Science News Letter). [< New Latin *telangiectasis* < Greek *télos* end + *angeîon* vessel + *éktasis* dilation < *ek-* out + a root of *teínein* to stretch]

tel·an·gi·ec·tat·ic (te lan′jē ek tat′ik), *adj.* **1.** having to do with telangiectasis. **2.** showing telangiectasis.

Tel·an·thro·pus (tel′an thrō′pəs), *n.* an extinct man, fragments of whom were discovered in 1952 near Johannesburg, South Africa. [< New Latin *Telanthropus* the genus name < Greek *télos* end + *ánthrōpos* man]

tel·au·to·gram (tel ô′tə gram), *n.* the record produced by a TelAutograph.

Tel·Au·to·graph (tel ô′tə graf, -gräf), *n. Trademark.* a telegraph for reproducing handwriting, pictures, etc. The movements of a pen at one end are produced in facsimile by a pen at the other end.

tel·au·to·graph·ic (tel ô′tə graf′ik), *adj.* having to do with the TelAutograph.

tel·au·tog·ra·phy (tel′ô tog′rə fē), *n.* the use of the TelAutograph.

tele-, *combining form.* **1.** having to do with operating over long distances: *Telegraph = an instrument to send messages over a long distance.*
2. having to do with television: *Telecast = to broadcast on television.*
3. telescopic: *Tele-camera = a telescopic camera.* Also, **tel-** before vowels.
[< Greek *tēle* far off]

Tel·e·bit or **tel·e·bit** (tel′ə bit), *n.* a device in space satellites to store scientific data and transmit it to earth.

tel·e·cam·er·a (tel′ə kam′ər ə), *n.* a telescopic camera. [< *tele-* + *camera*]

tel·e·cast (tel′ə kast′, -käst′), *v.,* **-cast** or **-cast·ed, -cast·ing,** *n.* —*v.t., v.i.* to broadcast on television. —*n.* **1.** a television program. **2.** a television broadcast. —**tel′e·cast′er,** *n.*

tel·e·chir·ic (tel′ə kir′ik), *adj.* of or having to do with telechirics: *The job of patrolling ... would seem suited for a telechiric vehicle* (New Scientist). —**tel′e·chir′i·cal·ly,** *adv.*

tel·e·chir·ics (tel′ə kir′iks), *n.* the study, design, and operation of remote-control machines and processes: *Telechirics ... seems likely to find a wide variety of applications in industry, beneath the sea, and in space* (John W. Clark). [< *tele-* + Greek *cheír, -os* hand + English *-ics*]

tel·e·cine (tel′ə sin), *n. British.* the transmitting of motion pictures by television.

tel·e·com (tel′ə kom), *n.* telecommunication.

tel·e·com·mu·ni·ca·tion (tel′ə kə myü′nə kā′shən), *n.* the electrical and electronic transmission of messages, as by telegraph. **telecommunications,** the study of this: *to read up on telecommunications.*

tel·e·con (tel′ə kon), *n.* **1.** a device that flashes teletyped messages on a screen. **2.** a conference held by means of a telecon.

tel·e·con·trol (tel′ə kən trōl′), *n.* remote control.

tel·e·cop·ter (tel′ə kop′tər), *n.* a helicopter equipped with a television camera and transmitter, to televise news and events.

tel·e·course (tel′ə kôrs′, -kōrs′), *n.* a televised course of study offered by a college or university.

tel·e·dra·ma (tel′ə drä′mə, -dram′ə), *n.* a drama written or adapted for television; teleplay: *By year's end, well over 1,000 teledramas will have been shown* (Time).

tel·e·du (tel′ə dü), *n* a small carnivorous mammal of Indonesia, which is related to and resembles the skunk, except for a short tail, and can give off a very strong, unpleasant smell. [< Malay]

Teledu (about 15 in. long)

tel·e·fe·rique (tel′ə fə rēk′), *n.* a ski lift. [< French *téléférique* < *téléphérage* transportation by telphers < English *telpherage*]

tel·e·film (tel′ə film′), *n.* a motion picture produced especially for television.

teleg., **1.** telegram. **2.** telegraph. **3.** telegraphy.

te·le·ga (te le′gə), *n.* a primitive, four-wheeled, springless Russian wagon. [< Russian *telega*]

Telega

tel·e·gen·ic (tel′ə jen′ik), *adj. Especially U.S.* appearing attractive on television; suitable for telecasting.

tel·e·gon·ic (tel′ə gon′ik), *adj.* of or having to do with telegony.

te·leg·o·ny (tə leg′ə nē), *n. Genetics.* the sire's supposed influence on the dam's offspring by later sires. [< *tele-* + Greek *-goniā* a begetting]

tel·e·gram (tel′ə gram), *n.* a message sent by telegraph.

tel·e·gram·mat·ic (tel′ə grə mat′ik), *adj.* telegrammic: *... the telegrammatic neatness of Whistler or Wilde* (London Times).

tel·e·gram·mic (tel′ə gram′ik), *adj.* **1.** of or having to do with a telegram. **2.** brief; concise; succinct.

tel·e·graph (tel′ə graf, -gräf), *n.* an electrical apparatus, system, or process for sending messages. *—v.t.* **1.** to send (a message) by telegraph. **2.** to send a message to (a person, etc.) by telegraph. *—v.i.* to signal or communicate by telegraph. [(originally) a semaphore < French *télégraphe* < Greek *tēle* at a distance + *-graphos* writer < *gráphein* to write] —**Syn.** *v.t., v.i.* wire.

telegraph boy, *Especially British.* a boy who personally delivers telegrams.

te·leg·ra·pher (tə leg′rə fər), *n. Especially U.S.* telegraph operator.

telegrapher's cramp, painful cramps in the muscles of the arm and fingers, an occupational disorder of telegraphers.

tel·e·graph·ese (tel′ə gra fēz′, -fēs′), *n.* the concise and elliptical style in which telegrams are worded: *Another colleague rewrote the paper in telegraphese, leaving out most adjectives, inserting the word "stop" for periods* (Time).

tel·e·graph·ic (tel′ə graf′ik), *adj.* **1.** of or having to do with a telegraph. **2.** sent as a telegram. **3.** extremely concise; contracted: *a telegraphic style.* —**tel′e·graph′i·cal·ly,** *adv.*

tel·e·graph·i·cal (tel′ə graf′ə kəl), *adj.* telegraphic.

te·leg·ra·phist (tə leg′rə fist), *n. Especially British.* a telegrapher; telegraph operator.

telegraph key, a small lever to tap out messages by telegraph.

te·leg·ra·phone (tə leg′rə fōn), *n.* a form of telephone which receives and magnetically records the spoken message.

tel·e·graph·o·scope (tel′ə graf′ə skōp), *n.* a telegraphic device for transmitting and reproducing a still picture, as a wirephoto.

telegraph plant, an East Indian tick trefoil plant, whose leaflets, spontaneously jerking up and down and rotating on their own axes, suggest a semaphore.

telegraph pole, *Especially British.* telephone pole.

telegraph printer, a ticker.

te·leg·ra·phy (tə leg′rə fē), *n.* the making or operating of telegraphs.

Tel·e·gu (tel′ə gü), *n., pl.* **-gu** or **-gus,** *adj.* Telugu.

tel·e·guide (tel′ə gīd′), *v.t.,* **-guid·ed, -guid·ing.** to guide by remote control: *The Russians were able to teleguide the last stage of their moon rocket* (New York Herald Tribune).

tel·e·ki·ne·sis (tel′ə ki nē′sis), *n.* psychokinesis. [< *tele-* + Greek *kīnēsis* motion]

tel·e·ki·net·ic (tel′ə ki net′ik), *adj.* **1.** like telekinesis. **2.** having to do with telekinesis.

tel·e·lec·tric (tel′i lek′trik), *n.* transmission by electrical means. *—adj.* having to do with transmission by electrical means.

tel·e·lec·tro·scope (tel′i lek′trə skōp), *n.* an electrical transmitter of motion pictures.

tel·e·lens (tel′ə lenz′), *n.* a telephoto lens.

Te·lem·a·chus (tə lem′ə kəs), *n. Greek Legend.* the son of Penelope and Odysseus. When Odysseus returned from the Trojan War, Telemachus helped him slay Penelope's insolent suitors.

Tel·e·mark (tel′ə märk, tā′lə-), *n.,* or **Telemark turn,** a method of turning or stopping skis by advancing the outside ski.

tel·e·me·chan·ics (tel′ə mə kan′iks), *n.* the science of transmitting electric power by radio, without wires.

te·lem·e·ter (tə lem′ə tər), *n.* **1.** a device or devices, usually at least in part electronic, used in telemetry. **2.** any of various range finders used in surveying and gunnery. **3.** *Physics.* a device to measure strains. *—v.t.* to measure and transmit by telemeter.

tel·e·met·ric (tel′ə met′rik), *adj.* having to do with telemetry.

tel·e·met·ri·cal (tel′ə met′rə kəl), *adj.* telemetric.

te·lem·e·try (tə lem′ə trē), *n.* the automatic taking of measurements, as of temperature, humidity, pressure, number of charged particles, etc., and transmission of the data by wire, radio, or other means to a point distant from the data's source.

tel·e·mo·tor (tel′ə mō′tər), *n.* a hydraulic or electric system of remote control, especially of a ship's rudder.

tel·en·ce·phal·ic (tel′en sə fal′ik), *adj.* of or having to do with the telencephalon.

tel·en·ceph·a·lon (tel′en sef′ə lon), *n.* the anterior part of the forebrain (prosencephalon) in vertebrates, comprising mainly the cerebral hemispheres; endbrain.

te·len·gi·scope (tə len′jə skōp), *n.* an instrument which combines the functions of a telescope and a microscope. [< *tel-* + obsolete *engyscope* a microscope < Greek *engýs* near + English *-scope*]

tel·e·o·log·i·cal (tel′ē ə loj′ə kəl, tē′lē-), *adj.* **1.** of, having to do with, or relating to teleology. **2.** having to do with a design or purpose. **3.** of the nature of a design or purpose. —**tel′e·o·log′i·cal·ly,** *adv.*

teleological argument, the doctrine that teleology proves the existence of a Creator.

tel·e·ol·o·gist (tel′ē ol′ə jist, tē′lē-), *n.* a person who believes in or studies teleology.

tel·e·ol·o·gy (tel′ē ol′ə jē, tē′lē-), *n.* **1.** the fact or quality of being purposeful. **2.** purpose or design as shown in nature: *Either the world shows a teleology or it does not* (William R. Inge). **3.** the doctrine that mechanisms alone cannot explain the facts of nature and that purposes have causal power. **4.** the doctrine that all things in nature were made to fulfill a plan or design. [< New Latin *teleologia* < Greek *télos, -eos* end, goal + *-logiā* -logy]

tel·e·ost (tel′ē ost, tē′lē-), *adj.* of or having to do with a group of fishes with bony skeletons, including most common fishes, as the perch, flounder, etc., but not the sharks, rays, and lampreys. *—n.* a teleost fish. [< New Latin *Teleostei* the order name < Greek *téleios* finished, complete + *ostéon* bone]

tel·e·os·te·an (tel′ē os′tē ən, tē′lē-), *adj., n.* teleost.

tel·e·path (tel′ə path′), *n.* a telepathist: *With a powerful and imaginative insight he turns on the inward world of the telepath and produces a fantastically rich tapestry of ideas* (New Scientist).

tel·e·path·ic (tel′ə path′ik), *adj.* **1.** of or having to do with telepathy. **2.** by telepathy.

tel·e·path·i·cal·ly (tel′ə path′ə klē), *adv.* by telepathy.

te·lep·a·thist (tə lep′ə thist), *n.* **1.** a person who has telepathic power. **2.** a student of or believer in telepathy.

te·lep·a·thize (tə lep′ə thīz), *v.,* **-thized, -thiz·ing.** *—v.i.* to practice telepathy: *He guessed or telepathized to what I was imagining rather than what I was saying* (New Scientist). *—v.t.* to communicate with or affect by telepathy.

te·lep·a·thy (tə lep′ə thē), *n.* the communication of one mind with another by means other than the five senses.

teleph., **1.** telephone. **2.** telephony.

tel·e·phe·rique (tel′ə fə rēk′), *n.* teleferique.

tel·e·phone (tel′ə fōn), *n., v.,* **-phoned, -phon·ing.** *—n.* **1.** an instrument for transmitting sound or speech by electricity. **2.** the process of, or system for, doing this. *Abbr.:* tel. *—v.t.* **1.** to talk to or summon by telephone: *He decided ... to telephone her and free himself from the engagement* (Sinclair Lewis). **2.** to send (a message) by telephone. *—v.i.* to speak on the telephone: *We can telephone to your mother for a car* (John Galsworthy). [American English < *tele-* + Greek *phōnḗ* sound, voice]

telephone book, a telephone directory.

telephone booth, a public booth with a telephone and coin box for making prepaid calls.

telephone box, *Especially British.* a telephone booth.

telephone directory, a list of the names, telephone numbers, and addresses of people or businesses with telephones in a certain area.

telephone pole, a pole to carry telephone wires, usually wooden and about 30 feet tall.

tel·e·phon·er (tel′ə fō′nər), *n.* a person who telephones.

telephone receiver, the earpiece of a telephone set, which changes electrical impulses into sound.

tel·e·phon·ic (tel′ə fon′ik), *adj.* **1.** of or having to do with the telephone. **2.** by the telephone. —**tel′e·phon′i·cal·ly,** *adv.*

te·leph·o·nist (tə lef′ə nist), *n. Especially British.* a telephone switchboard operator: *Even the telephonist at a ministry switchboard seems to convey an atmosphere of small print and chipped cups* (Punch).

tel·e·pho·ni·tis (tel′ə fə nī′tis), *n.* an excessive or abnormal urge to make telephone calls (humorous use): *All the young ladies had telephonitis* (New York Times).

tel·e·pho·no·graph (tel′ə fō′nə graf, -gräf), *n.* a device to record and reproduce telephone messages.

tel·e·pho·no·graph·ic (tel′ə fō′nə graf′ik), *adj.* **1.** having to do with a telephonograph. **2.** by a telephonograph.

te·leph·o·ny (tə lef′ə nē), *n.* the science of making or of operating telephones.

tel·e·pho·to (tel′ə fō′tō), *adj., n., pl.* **-tos.** *—adj.* telephotographic: *I climbed the barbed wire fence ... and made ready my eight-millimeter telephoto movie camera* (Harper's). *—n.* a wirephoto.

tel·e·pho·to·graph (tel′ə fō′tə graf, -gräf), *n.* **1.** a picture taken through a telephoto lens. **2.** a picture sent by telegraphy. *—v.t.* **1.** to photograph with a telephoto lens. **2.** to send by telegraphy or radio. *—v.i.* **1.** to take a picture with a telephoto lens. **2.** to send a picture by telegraphy or radio.

tel·e·pho·to·graph·ic (tel′ə fō′tə graf′ik), *adj.* **1.** of or having to do with telephotography. **2.** used in telephotography.

tel·e·pho·tog·ra·phy (tel′ə fə tog′rə fē), *n.* **1.** the method or process of photographing distant objects by using a camera with a telephoto lens. **2.** the method or process of sending and reproducing pictures by radio or telegraph.

telephoto lens, a lens used in a camera for producing an enlarged image of a distant object.

tel·e·plasm (tel′ə plaz əm), *n.* the ectoplasm of a medium in a trance. [< *tele-* + Greek *plásma* something formed]

tel·e·plas·mic (tel′ə plaz′mik), *adj.* of, having to do with, or like teleplasm.

tel·e·play (tel′ə plā′), *n.* a play produced especially for television: *The first was a well-written teleplay ... about the development of a Confederate submarine* (Time).

tel·e·print·er (tel′ə prin′tər), *n. Especially British.* a teletype machine: *Up-to-the-minute reports on aircraft movements throughout the country ... are relayed in by teleprinter from central operations control in Wellington and other branch offices* (Auckland Star).

tel·e·proc·ess·ing (tel′ə pros′əs ing), *n.* the use of a computer that can process data which the computer collects from distant points by radio or wire: *Earlier computer networks involving high-speed teleprocessing have been limited to such applications as the Mercury control system for space flight and defense and industrial installations* (Science News Letter).

Tel·e·Promp·Ter (tel′ə promp′tər), *n. Trademark.* a device consisting of a moving band that gives a prepared speech line for line, used by speakers who are being televised.

tel·e·ran (tel′ə ran), *n.* an aid to landing aircraft which sends radar maps of the sky, an airfield, etc., by television. [< *Tele*(vision) *R*(adar) *A*(ir) *N*(avigation)]

tel·e·re·cord (tel′ə ri kôrd′), *v.t.* to record on film for televising; make a telerecording of: *a telerecorded performance.*

tel·e·re·cord·ing (tel′ə ri kôr′ding), *n.* **1.** a film to be televised. **2.** a television program broadcast from this.

tel·e·scope (tel′ə skōp), *n., v.,* **-scoped, -scop·ing,** *adj.* —*n.* an instrument for making distant objects appear nearer and larger. It consists of an arrangement of lenses, and sometimes mirrors, in one or more tubes. In a refracting telescope the image is produced by a lens and magnified by the eyepiece. In a reflecting telescope the image is produced by a concave mirror or speculum and magnified. Both these kinds are used by astronomers: *After the invention of the telescope in 1609, observatories were established in many European cities* (Helmut Abt).

Refracting Telescope used in observatory

—*v.t.* **1.** to force together one inside another, like the sliding tubes of some telescopes: *When the trains crashed into each other, the cars were telescoped.* **2.** to bring together and shorten; splice and condense. —*v.i.* to fit or be forced together, one part inside another, like the parts of some telescopes.

—*adj.* collapsible.

[< New Latin *telescopium* < Greek *tēleskópos* far-seeing < *têle* far + *skopeîn* to watch]

telescope carp, a variety of goldfish with protruding eyes and a double caudal fin.

telescope fish, telescope carp.

telescope sight, a small telescope used for aiming a gun.

tel·e·scop·ic (tel′ə skop′ik), *adj.* **1.** of or having to do with a telescope. **2.** obtained or seen by means of a telescope: *a telescopic view of the moon.* **3.** visible only through a telescope. **4.** far-seeing: *a telescopic lens.* **5.** making distant things look clear and close. **6.** consisting of parts that slide inside another like the tubes of some telescopes.

tel·e·scop·i·cal (tel′ə skop′ə kəl), *adj.* telescopic.

tel·e·scop·i·cal·ly (tel′ə skop′ə klē), *adv.* **1.** in a telescopic manner. **2.** by means of a telescope; as seen through a telescope.

telescopic rifle, a rifle with a telescopic sight. See **rifle**[1] for picture.

Tel·e·sco·pi·i (tel′ə skō′pē ī), *n.* genitive of **Telescopium.**

te·les·co·pist (tə les′kə pist), *n.* a person skilled in telescopy.

Tel·e·sco·pi·um (tel′ə skō′pē əm), *n., genitive* **Tel·e·sco·pi·i.** a southern constellation near Sagittarius. [< New Latin *telescopium*]

te·les·co·py (tə les′kə pē), *n.* **1.** the science or practice of using telescopes. **2.** the science or practice of making telescopes.

tel·e·screen (tel′ə skrēn′), *n.* a television screen.

tel·e·seism (tel′ə sī′zəm), *n.* an earth tremor remote from a place where it is recorded or indicated by a seismograph or the like. [< *tele-* + Greek *seismós* earthquake]

tel·e·seis·mic (tel′ə sīz′mik), *adj.* of or having to do with a teleseism: *A network of 20 to 30 teleseismic recording stations ... could just about determine whether it was an earthquake or an explosion* (New Scientist).

tel·e·sis (tel′ə sis), *n.* the policy of using the forces of nature and society to accomplish a chosen end. [< New Latin *telesis* < Late Greek *télesis* event, fulfillment < Greek *teleîn* to finish, complete, related to *télos* end, goal]

tel·e·spec·tro·scope (tel′ə spek′trə skōp), *n.* an instrument consisting of a telescope with a spectroscope attached.

tel·e·ster·e·o·scope (tel′ə ster′ē ə skōp, -stir′-), *n.* **1.** an instrument for viewing distant objects in three dimensions as in a stereoscope, consisting of two pairs of mirrors arranged to produce this effect; binoculars. **2.** an optical range finder.

tel·es·the·sia (tel′əs thē′zhə; -zhē ə, -zē-), *n.* telepathy. Also, **telaesthesia.** [< New Latin *telesthesia* < Greek *têle* far off + *aísthēsis* perception]

tel·es·thet·ic (tel′əs thet′ik), *adj.* telepathic. Also, **telaesthetic.**

te·les·tich (tə les′tik, tel′ə stik), *n.* a short poem in which the final letters of the lines, in order, spell a word or words. [< Greek *télos* end + *stíchos* line]

tel·e·ther·a·py (tel′ə ther′ə pē), *n.* radiotherapy of a high intensity, applied at a distance from the body or affected organ: *Teletherapy is much like present radium-X-ray treatment* (New York Times).

tel·e·ther·mo·graph (tel′ə thėr′mə graf, -gräf), *n.* **1.** a telethermometer. **2.** a record made by such a device.

tel·e·ther·mom·e·ter (tel′ə thər mom′ə tər), *n.* any of various thermometers whose readings are automatically transmitted.

tel·e·ther·mom·e·try (tel′ə thər mom′ə trē), *n.* the use of a telethermometer.

tel·e·thon (tel′ə thon), *n.* a television program lasting many hours, often soliciting contributions.

Tel·e·type (tel′ə tīp), *n. Trademark.* teletypewriter.

tel·e·type (tel′ə tīp), *n., v.,* **-typed, -typ·ing.** —*n.* a communication system of Teletype machines, circuits, etc. —*v.t.* to send by Teletype. [< *Teletype*] —**tel′e·typ′er,** *n.*

tel·e·type·set·ter (tel′ə tīp′set′ər), *n.* a telegraphic device for sending signals by teletype. The signals make another machine punch holes in a tape that is put into a typesetting machine that sets printing type automatically.

tel·e·type·writ·er (tel′ə tīp′rī′tər), *n.* a telegraphic device sending and receiving signals by means of two instruments resembling typewriters.

tel·e·typ·ist (tel′ə tī′pist), *n.* a person who operates a teletypewriter.

te·leu·to·spore (tel yü′tə spôr, -spōr), *n. Botany.* a teliospore. [< Greek *teleutḗ* end (< *teleîn* to complete) + English *spore*]

te·leu·to·spor·ic (tel yü′tə spôr′ik, -spōr′-), *adj. Botany.* teliosporic.

tel·e·view (tel′ə vyü′), *v.t., v.i.* to look at (a television program). —**tel′e·view′er,** *n.*

tel·e·vise (tel′ə vīz), *v.,* **-vised, -vis·ing.** —*v.t.* **1.** to send by television: *Ed Sullivan, on a trip to Moscow, taped some of the circus acts and televised them on his show here* (New York Times). **2.** to receive or see by television. —*v.i.* to broadcast television programs.

tel·e·vi·sion (tel′ə vizh′ən), *n.* **1.** the process of transmitting the image of an object, scene, or event by radio or wire so that a person in some other place can see it at once. In television, waves of light from an object are changed into electric waves which are transmitted by radio or wire, and then changed back into waves of light that produce an image of the object on a screen. **2.** a view of scenes transmitted thus. **3.** an apparatus for receiving and making visible the images so sent; a television receiver. **4.** the broadcasting of television programs. *Abbr.:* TV (no periods).

tel·e·vi·sion·al (tel′ə vizh′ə nəl), *adj.* of or having to do with television.

tel·e·vi·sion·ar·y (tel′ə vizh′ə ner′ē), *adj.* televisional.

tel·e·vi·sion·ist (tel′ə vizh′ə nist), *n. Especially British.* a television fan.

television set, an apparatus for receiving and making visible television broadcasts; television receiver: *Probably before the end of the 1960's, we will have television sets that hang on the wall like pictures* (Stanley L. Englebardt).

tel·e·vi·sor (tel′ə vī′zər), *n.* the television receiver designed in 1928 by J. L. Baird: *The scene in front of the televisor is turned into electrical impulses* (Glasgow Herald).

tel·e·vis·u·al (tel′ə vizh′ü əl), *adj. Especially British.* of or suitable for television: *a televisual subject. What we got ... was a televisual parable: a didactic drama of the suburbs* (Observer).

tel·ex (tel′eks), *n. British.* a teleprinter service that the Post Office rents to subscribers, as bookmakers.

tel·fer (tel′fər), *n, v.t., adj.* telpher.

tel·fer·age (tel′fər ij), *n.* telpherage.

tel·ford (tel′fərd), *n.* a pavement consisting of layers of rolled stones. —*adj.* **1.** of or having to do with such a pavement. **2.** made by layers of rolled stones. [< Thomas *Telford,* 1757-1834, a Scottish engineer]

tel·ford·ize (tel′fər dīz), *v.t.,* **-ized, -iz·ing.** to pave with telford (pavement).

telford pavement, telford.

tel·har·mo·ni·um (tel′här mō′nē əm), *n.* an electrical keyboard instrument to produce music at a distance over an electrical circuit.

tel·har·mo·ny (tel här′mə nē), *n.* telharmonium music.

te·li·al (tē′lē əl, tel′ē-), *adj. Botany.* **1.** of or having to do with a telium. **2.** like a telium.

telial stage, *Botany.* the last phase in the life cycle of certain rust fungi, in which teliospores are produced.

tel·ic (tel′ik), *adj.* **1.** *Grammar.* (of a conjunction or clause) expressing end or purpose. *Example:* He asked in order to find out. **2.** done for a purpose; teleological. [< Greek *telikós* final < *télos* end, goal]

tel·ics (tel′iks), *n.* a branch of sociology dealing with planned and directed progress. [< Greek *télos* goal + English *-ics*]

te·li·o·spore (tē′lē ə spôr, -spōr; tel′ē-), *n. Botany.* a thick-walled spore produced by certain rust fungi generally in autumn, remaining in the tissues of the host during winter and germinating in the spring to produce basidia.

te·li·o·spor·ic (tē′lē ə spôr′ik, -spōr′-; tel′ē-), *adj. Botany.* having to do with or characterized by teliospores.

te·li·o·stage (tē′lē ə stāj′, tel′ē-), *n. Botany.* the telial stage.

te·li·um (tē′lē əm, tel′ē-), *n., pl.* **te·li·a** (tē′lē ə, tel′ē-). *Botany.* a sorus bearing teliospores, formed by certain rust fungi. [< New Latin *telium* < Greek *télos* end, goal]

tell[1] (tel), *v.,* **told, tell·ing.** —*v.t.* **1.** to give an account of (a sequence of actions or events); narrate; relate; report: *to tell a story, to tell the truth.* **2.** to make (a fact, news, information, ideas, etc.) known in words; communicate: *Tell him the news. He said much but told little.* **3.** to inform; let know: *They told us the way at the station.* **4.** to find a way of expressing; put in words; utter; express: *I can't tell you how much I liked it.* **5.** to disclose (private matters); reveal (a secret): *Promise not to tell this.* **6.** to order (a person to do something); direct; command: *Tell him to wait.* **7.** to say with assurance; be positive about: *I couldn't tell exactly when he came.* **8.** to recognize well enough to identify; discern: *He couldn't tell which house it was.* **9.** to understand the difference between; distinguish; discriminate: *He can't tell one twin from another.* **10.** to name one by one; count off; count over: *The nun tells her beads.* **11.** to count (votes or voters). **12.** *Archaic.* to declare formally or state publicly; announce; proclaim; publish: *Tell it not in Gath* (II Samuel 1:20). **13.** *Archaic.* to reckon up the number of; count up: *He could not tell twenty in English* (Daniel Defoe). **14.** *Obsolete.* to reveal.

—*v.i.* **1.** to report secrets; act as talebearer; blab; tattle: *Promise not to tell on me.* **2.** to be effective; count for something; have a decided effect: *Every blow told.* **3.** to be a strain; be weakening or damaging: *The continued effort told on his heart. The strain was telling on the man's health.* **4.** *British Dialect.* to talk idly without acting.

don't tell me, an expression of incredulity or impatience: *Error of judgment! don't tell me. I know how these things happen quite well* (Cardinal Newman).

I (can) tell you, yes, indeed; I emphasize: *I tell you, it got on my nerves* (F. Young).

let me tell you, yes, indeed; I emphasize: *Let me tell you, I am not to be persuaded by metaphysical arguments* (Bishop Berkeley).
tell me another, an expression of incredulity, irony, etc.: *You lost your money. Indeed! Tell me another.*
tell of, to be an indication or sign of; show: *His hard hands and sinewy sunburnt limbs told of labour and endurance* (Charles Kingsley).
tell off, a. to count off; count off and detach for some special duty: *Ten knights were then told off, and ten followers for every knight, to ride down to Doncaster* (James A. Froude). **b.** to reprimand; scold; reprove: *Monty came to see me and I had to tell him off for falling foul of both the King and the Secretary of State* (Maclean's).
tell good-by, *U.S.* to say good-by to: *She told me to tell you good-by* (Booth Tarkington).
[Old English *tellan*, related to *talu* tale]
—**Syn.** *v.t.* **1.** utter. **2.** mention. **5.** divulge.

tell[2] (tel), *n.* an artificial hillock or mound, usually one covering the ruins of an ancient city: *Some Palestinian tells are 70 ft. thick and contain dozens of different layers of debris* (Time). [< Arabic *tall* hillock]

tell·a·ble (tel′ə bəl), *adj.* that can be told; worth telling. —**tell′a·ble·ness,** *n.*

tell·a·bly (tel′ə blē), *adv.* in a manner that is tellable; so as to be tellable.

tell·er (tel′ər), *n.* **1.** a person who counts, especially: **a.** a bank cashier who accepts deposits and pays out withdrawals. **b.** an official who counts votes, especially in a legislature. **2.** a person who tells, especially a story; narrator.

tell·er·ship (tel′ər ship), *n.* the office or post of teller; a position as teller.

tel·lies (tel′ēz), *n.pl.* See under **telly,** *n.*

tell·ing (tel′ing), *adj.* having effect or force; striking: *a telling blow. He is a master of a singularly lucid ... and telling style* (Times Literary Supplement). —*n.* **1.** the act of relating or making known: *something beautiful beyond all telling. The narrative loses nothing in the telling* (Athenaeum). **2.** the act of counting: *This mixed telling did not mean mixed voting* (Scotsman). —**Syn.** *adj.* effective, potent, forceful.

tell·ing·ly (tel′ing lē), *adv.* effectively; forcefully: *How tellingly the cool lights and warm shadows are made to contrast* (Thackeray).

tell·ing-off (tel′ing ôf′, -of′), *n. Informal.* a scolding; rebuke.

tell·tale (tel′tāl′), *n.* **1.** a person who tells on others; person who reveals private or secret matters from malice. **2.** a warning sign; indication. **3.** any of various indicators or recording instruments, as a time clock. **4.** *Music.* (on an organ) an indicator of the pressure of the air supply. **5.** *Nautical.* a device above deck to indicate the rudder's position. **6.** a row of ribbons hung over a track before a tunnel, low bridge, etc., to warn trainmen off the roofs of cars.
—*adj.* **1.** telling what is not supposed to be told; revealing: *a telltale fingerprint.* **2.** showing, signaling, or warning of something.
—**Syn.** *n.* **1.** talebearer, tattler.

tell·truth (tel′trüth′), *n.* a truthful or candid person: *Telltruths in the service of falsehood we find everywhere* (Samuel Taylor Coleridge).

tel·lu·rate (tel′yə rāt), *n. Chemistry.* a salt of telluric acid with a maximum of oxygen.

tel·lu·ri·an[1] (te lůr′ē ən), *adj.* **1.** having to do with the earth. **2.** earthly; terrestrial. —*n.* an inhabitant of the earth: *Our own case, the case of poor mediocre tellurians* (Thomas DeQuincey). [< Latin *tellūs, -ūris* earth + English *-an*]

tel·lu·ri·an[2] (te lůr′ē ən), *n.* tellurion.

tel·lu·ric[1] (te lůr′ik), *adj.* **1.** of the earth; terrestrial. **2.** arising from the soil; of earth. [< Latin *tellūs, -ūris* earth + *-ic*]

tel·lu·ric[2] (te lůr′ik), *adj. Chemistry.* **1.** having to do with tellurium. **2.** containing tellurium, especially with a valence of six.

telluric acid, an acid containing tellurium with a valence of six, obtained by oxidizing tellurium or its oxide. *Formula:* H_6TeO_6

tel·lu·rid (tel′yər id), *n.* telluride.

tel·lu·ride (tel′yə rīd, -yər id), *n.* a compound of tellurium with an electropositive element or radical.

tel·lu·rif·er·ous (tel′yə rif′ər əs), *adj.* containing or yielding tellurium.

tel·lu·ri·on (te lůr′ē ən), *n.* a model of the moving earth and the sun, showing how day and night and the changes in the seasons result from the earth's revolution about the sun. [< Latin *tellūs, -ūris* earth + Greek *-ion*, a neuter diminutive suffix]

tel·lu·rite (tel′yə rīt), *n.* **1.** *Chemistry.* a salt of tellurous acid, containing less oxygen than a tellurate. **2.** a mineral, a native dioxide of tellurium, usually found in clusters of minute, whitish or yellowish crystals. *Formula:* TeO_2

tel·lu·ri·um (te lůr′ē əm), *n.* a rare, tin-white, metalloid chemical element, poisonous, brittle unless extremely pure, and similar to sulfur and selenium chemically, usually combined with gold or silver. *Symbol:* Te; *at. wt.:* (C^{12}) 127.60 or (O^{16}) 127.61; *at.no.:* 52; *valence:* 2, 4, 6. [< New Latin *Tellurium* < Latin *tellūs, -ūris* earth]

tel·lu·rize (tel′yə rīz), *v.t.*, **-rized, -riz·ing.** to combine or treat with tellurium.

tel·lu·rom·e·ter (tel′yə rom′ə tər), *n.* an electronic device for measuring distances by the time it takes a radio microwave to travel from one point to another and back.

tel·lu·rous (tel′yər əs, te lůr′-), *adj.* **1.** of tellurium. **2.** containing tellurium, especially with a valence of four.

tellurous acid, an acid containing tellurium with a valence of four. It is a white, water-soluble powder. *Formula:* H_2TeO_3

Tel·lus (tel′əs), *n. Roman Mythology.* an ancient goddess who blessed crops and marriage.

tel·ly (tel′ē), *n. British Slang.* television.

tel·ma·tol·o·gy (tel′mə tol′ə jē), *n.* the science that deals with the formation and contents of peat bogs. [< Greek *télma, -atos* marsh + English *-logy*]

tel·o·dy·nam·ic (tel′ō dī nam′ik, -di-), *adj.* of or having to do with the transmission of power, especially by cables on pulleys. [< Greek *tēloû* far off + English *dynamic*]

tel·o·lec·i·thal (tel′ō les′ə thəl), *adj.* (of eggs) having the yolk in one end and the cytoplasm in the other end. [< Greek *télos* end + English *lecith*(in) + *-al*[1]]

tel·o·mer (tel′ə mər), *n.* a reduced polymer formed by the reaction between a substance capable of being polymerized and an agent that arrests the growth of the chain of atoms: *Du Pont chemists found how to limit the number of atoms that link together to form a long-chain molecule, creating telomers in contrast to the long-chain polymers of earlier plastics* (Science News Letter). [< Greek *télos* end + English (poly)*mer*]

tel·o·phase (tel′ə fāz), *n.* the final stage of mitosis, when a membrane forms around each group of chromosomes in the cell and a nucleus is produced in each group, just before the cytoplasm of the cell constricts and the two new cells appear. See **mitosis** for picture. [< Greek *télos* end + English *phase*]

tel·o·phas·ic (tel′ə fā′zik), *adj.* of or having to do with the telophase.

te·los (tē′los, tel′os), *n., pl.* **-loi** (-loi). end; purpose; ultimate object or aim: ... *a clash between the laws of the inorganic which has no telos, and the behavior of living creatures who have one* (New Yorker). [< Greek *télos* end]

tel·pher (tel′fər), *n.* **1.** a car or other unit running from electric cables. **2.** a system using these; telpherage. —*v.t.* to carry or convey by a telpher. —*adj.* **1.** of or having to do with telpherage. **2.** used in telpherage. Also, **telfer.** [short for earlier *telephore* < *tele-* + Greek *phoreîn* to bear]

tel·pher·age (tel′fər ij), *n.* **1.** a transportation system using telphers supplied with electric current by the cable. **2.** a similar system in which cars are pulled by an endless cable worked by a motor. Also, **telferage.**

tel·son (tel′sən), *n.* the rearmost segment of the abdomen in certain crustaceans and arachnids, as the middle flipper of a lobster's tail or the sting of a scorpion. [< Greek *télson* limit; headland]

Tel·star (tel′stär′), *n. Trademark.* a small artificial earth satellite to amplify and relay microwave signals of television, telephone, etc.: *Overseas transmission of television's straight-line wave was prevented by the earth's curvature. Telstar, in line-of-sight relationship with stations on two sides of the Atlantic, overcame the problem by relay* (New York Times).

Tel·u·gu (tel′ə gü), *n., pl.* **-gu** or **-gus,** *adj.* —*n.* **1.** a Dravidian language spoken on the Coromandel Coast of Hyderabad, in eastern India. **2.** one of the Dravidian people who speak this language. —*adj.* of or having to do with this Dravidian people, or their language. Also, **Telegu.**

TEM (no periods), triethylene melamine.

tem·blor (tem blôr′), *n., pl.* **-blors, -blo·res** (-blôr′ās). *U.S.* a tremor; earthquake. [American English < Spanish *temblor* a trembling < *temblar* to tremble < Vulgar Latin *tremulāre* < Latin *tremulus* trembling]

Tem·bu (tem′bü), *n., pl.* **-bu** or **-bus.** a member of a Kaffir tribe that lives in Tembuland, a region in Cape of Good Hope Province, South Africa: *The Tembu [comprise] possibly the largest tribe in Transkei territory which is to become the first Bantustan* (London Times).

tem·e·nos (tem′ə nos), *n., pl.* **-ne** (-nē). (in ancient Greece) a piece of ground surrounding or adjacent to a temple; a sacred enclosure or precinct: *Tradition says that this square formed in very early ages the temenos of a temple* (T.S. Hughes). [< Greek *témenos* < *témnein* to cut off]

tem·er·ar·i·ous (tem′ə rãr′ē əs), *adj.* characterized by temerity. [< Latin *temerārius* (with English *-ous*) rash; fortuitous < *temere* heedlessly] —**tem′er·ar′i·ous·ly,** *adv.*

te·mer·i·ty (tə mer′ə tē), *n.* reckless boldness; rashness: *What preposterous temerity—to analyze what happened in a half hour five billion years ago!* (Atlantic). [< Latin *temeritās* < *temere* heedlessly] —**Syn.** foolhardiness, audacity. —**Ant.** caution, wariness.

te·mine (tə mīn′), *n.* tamein.

Tem·ne (tem′nā), *n.* **1.** a tribe that inhabits part of Sierra Leone, a republic in West Africa. **2.** their Niger-Congo language.

temp., **1.** in the time of (Latin, *tempore*). **2.** temperature. **3.** temporary.

tem·per (tem′pər), *n.* **1.** state of mind; disposition; condition: *to be in a good temper, a man of even temper.* **2.** an angry state of mind: *In her temper she broke a vase.* **3.** a calm state of mind: *He became angry and lost his temper.* **4.** the toughness, hardness, etc., of a mixture, given by tempering: *The temper of the clay was right for shaping.* **5.** a substance added to something to modify its qualities. **6.** *Archaic.* **a.** a regulation; adjustment. **b.** a middle course; mean. **7.** *Obsolete.* the temperament. [< verb]
—*v.t.* **1.** to moderate; soften: *Temper justice with mercy.* **2.** to check; restrain; curb. **3.** to bring to a proper or desired condition by mixing or preparing: *A painter tempers his colors by mixing them with oil.* **4.** to tune or adjust the pitch of (a musical instrument, a voice, a note, etc.). **5.** *Obsolete.* to fit, adapt, or make suitable (to). —*v.i.* to be or become tempered.
[Middle English *tempren*, Old English *temprian* < Latin *temperāre* (originally) observe due measure < *tempus, -oris* time. Compare TAMPER[1].] —**tem′per·er,** *n.*
—**Syn.** *n.* **1.** mood, humor. See **disposition.** -*v.t.* **1.** qualify, modify.

tem·per·a (tem′pər ə), *n.* **1.** a method of painting in which colors are mixed with white or yolk of egg, the whole egg, or other substances instead of oil. **2.** the paints used. [< Italian *tempera* < *temperare* to temper < Latin *temperāre.* Compare DISTEMPER[2].]

tem·per·a·ble (tem′pər ə bəl, -prə-), *adj.* that can be tempered.

tem·per·a·ment (tem′pər ə mənt, -prə-), *n.* **1.** a person's nature or disposition: *a nervous temperament. Her highly strung temperament made her uncertain ... capricious ... enchanting* (George Bernard Shaw). **2.** an unusual nature or disposition that is not inclined to submit to ordinary rules or restraints: *An artist, singer, or actress often has temperament.* **3.** in medieval physiology: **a.** animal temperament. **b.** the bodily habit attributed to this. **4.** *Music.* **a.** the adjustment of the intervals of the natural scale by slightly varying the pitch. **b.** a system according to which this is done. **5.** *Archaic.* **a.** moderation. **b.** mitigation. **c.** due regulation. **6.** *Obsolete.* consistency; composition. **7.** *Obsolete.* climate. **8.** *Obsolete.* temperature. [< Latin *temperāmentum* mixture < *temperāre* to mix, temper] —**Syn.** **1.** See **disposition.**

tem·per·a·men·tal (tem′pər ə men′təl, -prə-), *adj.* **1.** due to temperament; constitutional: *Cats have a temperamental dislike for water.* **2.** showing a strongly marked individual temperament. **3.** subject to moods and whims; easily irritated; sensitive.

tem·per·a·men·tal·ly (tem′pər ə men′tə lē, -prə-), *adv.* in temperament; as regards temperament.

tem·per·ance (tem′pər əns, -prəns), *n.* **1.** moderation in action, habits, or speech. **2.** moderation in the use of alcoholic drinks: *Abstinence is as easy to me as temperance would be difficult* (Samuel Johnson). **3.** the principle or practice of not using alcoholic drinks at all. [< Anglo-French *temperaunce,* learned borrowing from Latin *temperantia* moderation < *temperāre* to temper] —**Syn.** **3.** abstinence.

tem·per·ate (tem′pər it, -prit), *adj.* **1.** not very hot and not very cold: *a temperate climate.* **2.** self-restrained; moderate: *He spoke in a temperate manner, not favoring either side especially.* **3. a.** moderate in using alcoholic drinks. **b.** abstemious. **4.** *Music.* tempered. **5.** of or having to do with the Temperate Zone: *New Zealand supported . . . the orderly marketing . . . of temperate agricultural products* (London Times).
[< Latin *temperātus* restrained; duly regulated, past participle of *temperāre* (originally) observe due measure; see TEMPER] —**tem′per·ate·ness,** *n.* —**Syn.** **2.** calm, dispassionate. See **moderate.**

tem·per·ate·ly (tem′pər it lē, -prit-), *adv.* **1.** with moderation. **2.** without overindulgence. **3.** without violence or extravagance.

Temperate Zone or **temperate zone,** either of the two parts of the earth between the tropics and the polar circles. See **zone** for diagram.

tem·per·a·ture (tem′pər ə chər, -chůr; -prə-), *n.* **1.** the degree of heat or cold: *The temperature of freezing water is 32 degrees Fahrenheit. The colour of a glowing opaque body depends only on its temperature and not on its composition* (Bondi and Bondi). *Abbr.:* temp. **2.** the degree of heat contained in a human or other living body: *The temperature of a person who has a fever is over 98.6 degrees Fahrenheit.* **3.** the excess of this degree of heat above the normal; fever: *The child is running a temperature.* **4.** *Obsolete.* **a.** moderation. **b.** temperament. [< Latin *temperātūra* a tempering < *temperāre* to temper]

temperature gradient, the rate of change in temperature: *Though an intriguing possibility the use of temperature gradients in the oceans does not appear to be an important source of useful power* (J.J. William Brown).

temperature-humidity index, discomfort index; humiture.

temperature inversion, an atmospheric condition in which a layer of warm air develops above a layer of cool air, often resulting in mirages of light in the night sky, or in smog: *In December, 1952, the Civil Aeronautics Administration reported that flying saucers seen on radar screens were caused by temperature inversions* (Willy Ley).

tem·pered (tem′pərd), *adj.* **1. a.** softened; moderated. **b.** seasoned: *tempered wisdom.* **2.** having a (specified) state of mind: *a good-tempered person.* **3.** treated so as to become hard but not too brittle. **4.** *Music.* tuned or adjusted in pitch according to equal temperament.

temper pin, *Scottish.* **1.** the wooden screw used in regulating a spinning wheel. **2.** a peg for a violin string.

temper tantrum, a tantrum.

tem·pest (tem′pist), *n.* **1.** a violent wind storm, usually accompanied by rain, hail, or snow. **2.** a violent disturbance.
tempest in a teapot, *Especially U.S.* a great disturbance over a small matter: *To Ferger the whole fracas was "a tempest in a teapot" and his major accuser "emotionally unstable"* (Time).
—*v.t.* to affect by or as if by a tempest: *The huge dolphin tempesting the main* (Alexander Pope).
[< Old French *tempeste* < Vulgar Latin *tempestus,* or *tempesta,* variants of Latin *tempestās* storm; weather; season, related to *tempus, -oris* time, season]
—**Syn.** *n.* **1.** gale. **2.** uproar, tumult.

tem·pes·tu·ous (tem pes′chů əs), *adj.* **1.** stormy: *a tempestuous night.* **2.** violent: *a tempestuous argument.* —**tem·pes′tu·ous·ly,** *adv.* —**tem·pes′tu·ous·ness,** *n.*

tem·pi (tem′pē), tempos; a plural of **tempo.**

Tem·plar (tem′plər), *n.* **1.** a member of a religious and military order founded among the Crusaders about 1118 to protect the Holy Sepulcher and pilgrims to the Holy Land. **2.** a member of an order of Masons in the United States. **3.** Also, **templar.** *British.* a barrister, etc., who has chambers in the Inner or Middle Temple in London. [< Medieval Latin *templarius* < Latin *templum* temple (because the order occupied a building in Jerusalem near the site known as Solomon's Temple)]

tem·plate (tem′plit), *n.* **1.** a pattern, gauge, or mold of a thin, flat piece of wood or metal, used in shaping a piece of work. **2. a.** a horizontal piece under a girder, beam, etc., to distribute downward thrust. **b.** a piece for supporting joists or rafters over a doorway, window, etc. **3.** a wedge supporting the keel of a ship under construction. **4.** any model on which something is formed or based; pattern: *There seems little doubt that . . . only one strand of the DNA molecule serves as a template for RNA synthesis* (Scientific American). [variant of *templet;* probably influenced by *plate*]

tem·ple[1] (tem′pəl), *n.* **1.** a building used for the service or worship of a god or gods. **2.** Often, **Temple. a.** any of three buildings built at different times on the same spot in ancient Jerusalem by the Jews. **b.** Also, **Temple of Solomon.** the first of these three buildings, built by Solomon and destroyed by the Babylonians. I Kings 6 and 7. **3.** a building set apart for Christian worship; church. **4. a.** a synagogue. **b.** the services conducted there. **5.** a place in which God specially dwells. **6.** a Mormon church. **7. a.** a building occupied by a local unit of a secret order. **b.** a local unit of certain secret orders. [Old English *tempel* < Latin *templum.* Doublet of TEMPLE[3], TEMPLON.] —**Syn.** **1.** sanctuary, tabernacle.

Temple[1] **(def. 1)**
Maison Carée,
Nimes, France

tem·ple[2] (tem′pəl), *n.* **1.** the flattened part on either side of the forehead. **2.** *U.S.* the bow of eyeglasses. [< Old French *temple* < Vulgar Latin *tempula,* feminine < Latin *tempora,* neuter plural of *tempus, -oris* temple (of the head)]

tem·ple[3] (tem′pəl), *n.* an apparatus in a loom for keeping cloth stretched to its proper width. [< Middle French *temple* weaver's stretcher, learned borrowing from Latin *templum* small timber; temple. Doublet of TEMPLE[1], TEMPLON.]

Tem·ple (tem′pəl), *n.* either of two English legal societies (the Inner Temple and Middle Temple).

temple block, any of various hollowed-out wooden vessels of different sizes and pitches, used with a stick as a percussion instrument in Korean and Chinese ritual music and sometimes in modern bands and orchestras.

tem·pled (tem′pəld), *adj.* furnished or adorned with a temple or temples.

tem·ple·less (tem′pəl lis), *adj.* having no temple or temples.

tem·plet (tem′plit), *n.* template.

tem·plon (tem′plon), *n.* (in the Greek Church) an iconostasis. [< Late Greek *témplon* < Latin *templum.* Doublet of TEMPLE[1], TEMPLE[3].]

tem·po (tem′pō), *n., pl.* **-pos, -pi** (-pē). **1.** *Music.* the time or rate of movement; proper or characteristic speed of movement: *Hundreds of people identified themselves with the conductor, standing in front of their screens with rulers and pencils in their hands and giving the beat and tempo* (Time). **2.** rhythm; characteristic rhythm: *the fast tempo of modern life.* [< Italian *tempo* time < Latin *tempus.* Doublet of TENSE[2].]

tem·po·ral[1] (tem′pər əl, -prəl), *adj.* **1.** of time. **2. a.** lasting for a time only. **b.** of this life only: *The things which are seen are temporal; but the things which are not seen are eternal* (II Corinthians 4:18). **3.** not religious or sacred; worldly. **4.** *Grammar.* **a.** expressing time, as an adverb or a clause. **b.** of tense.
—*n.* Often, **temporals.** that which is temporal; a temporal thing or matter: *. . . trying by some other way than through these homely temporals, to learn the spiritual life* (H. Drummond).
[< Latin *temporālis* < *tempus, -oris* time]
—**Syn.** *adj.* **2. a.** temporary, transient. **b.** earthly, terrestrial.

tem·po·ral[2] (tem′pər əl, -prəl), *adj.* of the temples or sides of the forehead. [< Late Latin *temporālis* < Latin *tempora,* plural of *tempus, -oris* temple]

temporal bone, a complex bone that forms part of the side and base of the skull.

tem·po·ral·i·ty (tem′pə ral′ə tē), *n., pl.* **-ties. 1.** temporal character or nature; temporariness. **2.** something temporal; temporal matter or affair. **3.** the laity.
temporalities, the property, revenues, etc., of a church or clergyman: *The Pope . . . gave to the said Nicholas the said Abbey, with all the said spiritualities and temporalities* (Roger Coke).

tem·po·ral·ly (tem′pər ə lē, -prə-), *adv.* in a temporal manner; as regards temporal matters.

tem·po·rar·i·ly (tem′pə rer′ə lē, tem′pə-rãr′-), *adv.* for a short time; for the present: *The work is postponed temporarily.*

tem·po·rar·i·ness (tem′pə rer′ē nis), *n.* the state or character of being temporary.

tem·po·rar·y (tem′pə rer′ē), *adj., n., pl.* **-rar·ies.** —*adj.* lasting for a short time only; used for the time being; not permanent: *temporary housing, temporary relief from pain.* —*n.* a person employed, enrolled, etc., temporarily; casual: *He entered the army as a temporary* (London Times).
[< Latin *temporārius* of seasonal character; lasting a moment of time < *tempus, -oris* time, season]
—**Syn.** *adj.* **Temporary, transient** mean lasting or staying only for a time. **Temporary** applies either to something meant to last only for the time being or to something liable to come to an end at any time: *He has a temporary job. Our school is a temporary building.* **Transient** applies to something that is passing and hence will not stay long: *His panic was transient, and ceased when he began to speak.* —**Ant.** permanent, abiding, lasting.

tem·po·ri·za·tion (tem′pər ə zā′shən), *n.* a temporizing; compromise: *Charges of temporization and compliance had somewhat sullied his reputation* (Samuel Johnson).

tem·po·rize (tem′pə rīz), *v.i.,* **-rized, -rizing. 1.** to evade immediate action or decision in order to gain time, avoid trouble, etc. **2.** to fit one's acts to the time or occasion. **3.** to make or discuss terms; negotiate. [< Middle French *temporiser,* learned borrowing from Medieval Latin *temporizare* pass time, perhaps < Vulgar Latin *temporāre* to delay < Latin *tempus, -oris* time] —**tem′po·riz′er,** *n.* —**Syn.** **1.** hedge. **2.** trim. **3.** parley.

tem·po·riz·ing·ly (tem′pə rī′zing lē), *adv.* in a temporizing manner; in a way designed to gain time: *I wrote temporizingly in reply to the invitation* (Punch).

tem·po·ro·man·dib·u·lar (tem′pər ō-man dib′yə lər), *adj.* having to do with the temporal bone and the mandible.

tempt (tempt), *v.t.* **1.** to make or try to make a person do something: *The sight of the food tempted the hungry man to steal.* **2.** to appeal strongly to; attract: *That candy tempts me.* **3.** to provoke: *It is tempting Providence to go in that old boat.* **4.** *Archaic.* to test: *God tempted Abraham by asking him to sacrifice his son.* [< Anglo-French *tempter,* learned borrowing from Latin *temptāre,* later *tentāre* to try (intensive) < *tendere* to stretch (oneself), strive]
—**Syn.** **1.** lure, inveigle, decoy. **2.** allure, entice.

tempt·a·ble (temp′tə bəl), *adj.* that can be tempted.

temp·ta·tion (temp tā′shən), *n.* **1.** a tempting. **2.** the fact or state of being tempted: *Lead us not into temptation . . .* (The Lord's Prayer). **3.** a thing that tempts: *But in spite of all temptations he remains an Englishman* (W. S. Gilbert).
—**Syn.** **3.** attraction, lure, enticement, inducement.

tempt·er (temp′tər), *n.* a person or thing that tempts. —**Syn.** seducer.

Tempt·er (temp′tər), *n.* the Devil; Satan.

tempt·ing (temp′ting), *adj.* that tempts; alluring; inviting: *a tempting offer.* —**tempt′ing·ly,** *adv.* —**tempt′ing·ness,** *n.*

tempt·ress (temp′tris), *n.* a woman who tempts. —**Syn.** siren.

tem·pu·ra (tem pu̇r′ə; *Japanese* tem′pu̇ rä), *n.* a dish of fried shrimps and vegetables. [< Japanese *tempura*]

tem·pus e·dax re·rum (tem′pəs ē′daks rir′əm), *Latin.* time the devourer of (all) things.

tem·pus fu·git (tem′pəs fyü′jit), *Latin.* time flies.

tem·u·len·cy (tem′yə lən sē), *n.* drunkenness; intoxication.

tem·u·lent (tem′yə lənt), *adj.* **1.** drunken; intoxicated. **2.** intoxicating. [< Latin *tēmulentus,* related to *tēmētum* intoxicating drink]

ten (ten), *n.* **1.** one more than nine; 10. **2.** set of ten persons or things. **3.** a playing card, throw of the dice, etc., with ten spots. **4. a.** a ten-dollar bill. **b.** a ten-pound note. —*adj.* being one more than nine.
[Old English *tēn, tīen*]

ten., 1. tenor. **2.** *Music.* tenuto.

ten·a·bil·i·ty (ten′ə bil′ə tē), *n.* the fact or quality of being tenable.

ten·a·ble (ten′ə bəl), *adj.* that can be held or defended: *a tenable position, a tenable theory.*
[< Middle French *tenable* < Old French *tenir* hold (< Latin *tenēre*)] —**Syn.** defensible, unassailable.

ten·a·bly (ten′ə blē), *adv.* in a tenable manner.

ten·ace (ten′ās), *n.* a holding of two cards lacking a third between them to form a sequence, as ten and queen.
[probably < Spanish *tenaza* (literally) pincers < Latin *forcipes tenāces* gripping forceps. Compare French *demeurer tenace* to have the tenace.]

te·na·cious (ti nā′shəs), *adj.* **1.** holding fast: *the tenacious jaws of a bulldog, a person tenacious of his rights.* **2.** stubborn; persistent: *a tenacious salesman.* **3.** able to remember: *a tenacious memory.* **4.** holding fast together; not easily pulled apart. **5.** sticky.
[< Latin *tenax, -ācis* (with English *-ous*) < *tenēre* to hold] —**te·na′cious·ly,** *adv.* —**te·na′cious·ness,** *n.*
—**Syn. 2.** obstinate. **3.** retentive.

te·nac·i·ty (ti nas′ə tē), *n.* **1.** firmness in holding fast. **2.** stubbornness; persistence. **3.** ability to remember. **4.** firmness in holding together; toughness. **5.** stickiness. **6.** *Physics.* tensile strength. —**Syn. 1.** adhesion, grip. **2.** obstinacy. **3.** retentiveness. **4.** cohesion. **5.** viscosity.

te·nac·u·lum (ti nak′yə ləm), *n., pl.* **-la** (-lə). a long-handled surgical instrument with a sharp hook, used to pick up parts, draw edges of wounds together, etc. [< New Latin *tenaculum* (in Latin, a holder) < Latin *tenēre* to hold]

te·naille or **te·nail** (te nāl′), *n.* a low defensive structure built outside a main fortification between two bastions: *A second party of forty or fifty men ... attacked a tenaille which by its fire flanked one of the breaches* (N.L. Walford). [< Middle French *tenaille* < Old French, forceps, < unrecorded Latin *tenācula,* plural of *tenāculum;* see TENACULUM]

te·nailled or **te·nailed** (te nāld′), *adj.* furnished with tenailles.

ten·an·cy (ten′ən sē), *n., pl.* **-cies. 1.** the state of being a tenant; occupying and paying rent for land or buildings: *Tenancy is the human condition in Manhattan* (New Yorker). **2.** the property so held. **3.** the length of time a tenant occupies a property. —**Syn. 1.** occupancy. **2.** holding. **3.** tenure.

ten·ant (ten′ənt), *n.* **1.** a person paying rent for the temporary use of land or buildings of another person: *That building has apartments for one hundred tenants.* **2.** a person or thing that inhabits or occupies any place: *Birds are tenants of the trees or, if more fortunate, birdhouses.*
—*v.t.* to hold or occupy as tenant; inhabit: *That old house has not been tenanted for many years.*
—*v.i.* to reside; dwell; live (in).
[< Old French *tenant,* (originally) present participle of *tenir* to hold < Latin *tenēre*]
—**Syn.** *n.* **2.** inhabitant, occupant, dweller.

ten·ant·a·ble (ten′ən tə bəl), *adj.* fit for being tenanted or occupied.

tenant farmer, a farmer who raises crops on and lives on land belonging to another, to whom he pays as rent a share of the crops: *More than half the decrease occurred in the South, largely because sharecropper and tenant farmers left the farm and turned to the rapidly growing opportunities in industry* (Time).

ten·ant·less (ten′ənt lis), *adj.* vacant: *a dreary and tenantless mansion* (Longfellow).

tenant right, a right that a person has as a tenant, as the right to receive a compensation from the landlord for crops left in the ground or produce left on the farm.

ten·ant·ry (ten′ən trē), *n., pl.* **-ries. 1.** all the tenants on an estate: *The old Squire's visits to his tenantry were rare* (George Eliot). **2.** tenancy.

ten·ant·ship (ten′ənt ship), *n.* tenancy; occupancy.

tench (tench), *n., pl.* **tench·es** or (*collectively*) **tench.** a fresh-water fish of Europe, related to the carp, and noted for the length of time it can live out of water: *Tench are partial to foul and weedy waters* (William Bingley). [< Old French *tenche* < Late Latin *tinca*]

Ten Commandments, (in the Bible) the ten rules for living and for worship that God revealed to Moses on Mount Sinai, according to the Bible. Exodus 20:2-17; Deuteronomy 5:6-22.

tend[1] (tend), *v.i.* **1.** to be apt; incline (to): *Modern industry tends toward consolidation. Homes tend to use more mechanical appliances now.* **2.** to move or be directed (toward): *The coastline tends to the south here.*
[< Old French *tendre* < Latin *tendere* to aim, stretch out. Doublet of TENDER[2].]

tend[2] (tend), *v.t.* **1.** to take care of; look after; attend to: *A shepherd tends his flock. He tends shop for his father.* **2.** to wait upon. **3.** *Nautical.* to stand by and watch over (a line, anchor cable, etc.). —*v.i.* **1.** to serve (upon). **2.** move (toward); be directed. **3.** *Informal.* to pay attention. **4.** *Obsolete.* to wait in expectation or readiness: *The time invites you, go, your servants tend ...* (Shakespeare). [short for *attend,* or *intend* apply oneself to. Compare TENT[3].]

Ten·dai (ten′dī), *n.* a Buddhist sect of Japan noted for its synthesis of all Buddhist doctrines: *Buddhism in Japan today has five major divisions: Tendai and Shingon, which came from China early in the ninth century, Zen, Jodo, and Nichiren* (Atlantic).

tend·ance (ten′dəns), *n.* attention; care.

ten·den·cious (ten den′shəs), *adj.* tendentious: *A false and tendencious account of what had taken place* (Contemporary Review). —**ten·den′cious·ly,** *adv.* —**ten·den′cious·ness,** *n.*

tend·en·cy (ten′dən sē), *n., pl.* **-cies. 1.** a leaning; inclination: *Boys have a stronger tendency to fight than girls.* **2.** a natural disposition to move, proceed, or act in some direction or toward some point, end, or result: *Wood has a tendency to swell if it gets wet.*
[< Medieval Latin *tendentia* < Latin *tendere* tend, incline]
—**Syn. 1.** bent, bias, proneness, propensity. **2.** See **direction.**

ten·den·tial (ten den′shəl), *adj.* **1.** marked by a tendency. **2.** tendentious.

ten·den·tious (ten den′shəs), *adj.* **1.** troublemaking; rebellious: *a spoiled, tendentious child.* **2.** that argues on behalf of some particular cause: *Nothing is known of them save what can be learned from patronizing and tendentious references in the records of their Hittite enemies* (Scientific American). [< *tendency* + *-ous*] —**ten·den′tious·ly,** *adv.* —**ten·den′tious·ness,** *n.*

ten·der[1] (ten′dər), *adj.* **1.** not tough or hard; soft: *tender meat.* **2.** not strong and hardy; delicate: *tender young grass.* **b.** soft; subdued: *a tender blue.* **3.** kind; affectionate; loving: *She spoke tender words to the child.* **4.** not rough or crude; gentle: *He patted the dog with tender hands.* **5.** young; immature: *Two years old is a tender age.* **6.** sensitive; painful; sore: *a tender wound.* **7. a.** feeling pain or grief easily: *She has a tender heart and is easily moved to tears.* **b.** sensitive to insult or injury; ready to take offense: *a man of tender pride.* **8.** considerate; careful: *He handles people in a tender manner.* **9.** requiring careful or tactful handling: *a tender situation.* **10.** (of a ship) crank.
—*v.t. Archaic.* **1.** to make tender. **2.** to weaken. **3.** to feel or act tenderly toward.
—*v.i. Obsolete.* to become tender.
—*n. Obsolete.* care; regard; concern.
[Middle English *tendre* soft, delicate < Old French, earlier *tenre* < Latin *tener*] —**ten′der·ly,** *adv.*
—**Syn.** *adj.* **2. a.** weak. **3.** compassionate, merciful. **4.** mild, sympathetic. —**Ant.** *adj.* **1.** tough. **3.** cruel. **4.** harsh, rough.

ten·der[2] (ten′dər), *v.t.* **1.** to offer formally: *to tender thanks, to tender one's resignation.* **2.** *Law.* to offer (money, goods, etc.) in payment of a debt or other obligation.
—*n.* **1.** a formal offer: *She refused his tender of marriage.* **2.** the thing offered: *Money that must be accepted as payment for a debt is called legal tender.* **3.** *Law.* an offer of money, goods, etc., to satisfy a debt or liability. **4.** *Commerce.* a bid to supply or purchase: *All tenders must be enclosed in sealed envelopes* (Cape Times).
[< Middle French *tendre* to offer < Latin *tendere* extend. Doublet of TEND[1].] —**ten′der·er,** *n.*
—**Syn.** *v.t.* **1.** proffer, present. See **offer.** —*n.* **1.** proposal, proffer, overture.

tend·er[3] (ten′dər), *n.* **1.** a person or thing that tends another: *a machine tender.* **2. a.** a boat or small ship used for carrying supplies and passengers to and from larger ships. **b.** a small boat carried on or towed behind a larger boat or a ship for similar use. **3.** the small car attached behind a locomotive and used for carrying coal, oil, water, etc. [probably < *tend*[2] + *-er*[1]]

ten·der·a·ble (ten′dər ə bəl), *adj.* that can be tendered.

ten·der·foot (ten′dər fu̇t′), *n., pl.* **-foots** or **-feet.** *U.S.* **1.** a newcomer to pioneer life. **2.** a person not used to rough living and hardships: *The tenderfoot, new to the sounds and solitude of the Canadian timber belt, wondered if indeed an occasional hot-dog stand or friendly filling station might not be desirable when the night closed in* (Wall Street Journal). **3.** an inexperienced person; beginner. **4. a.** a beginning member of the Boy Scouts. **b.** an equivalent member of the Girl Scouts. —**Syn. 3.** tyro, novice.

ten·der-heart·ed (ten′dər här′tid), *adj.* kindly; sympathetic: *a tender-hearted smile.* —**ten′der-heart′ed·ly,** *adv.* —**ten′der-heart′ed·ness,** *n.* —**Syn.** compassionate.

ten·der·ize (ten′də rīz), *v.t.,* **-ized, -iz·ing.** to make soft or tender: *Meat processors use cold storage to tenderize meat* (John T.R. Nickerson).

ten·der·iz·er (ten′də rī′zər), *n.* **1.** any substance which tenderizes meat by breaking down the meat fibers: *The tenderizers sold in grocery stores are commonly used by housewives not only on steaks but on such other cuts as pot roast and chuck* (Wall Street Journal). **2.** a small, ridged mallet for pounding meat to make it tender before cooking.

ten·der·loin (ten′dər loin′), *n.* **1.** a tender part of the loin of beef or pork. **2.** a cut of beef or pork consisting of this part.

Ten·der·loin (ten′dər loin′), *n. U.S. Slang.* **1.** a city district or section that includes the great mass of theaters, hotels, etc., and that is noted for the graft paid to the police for protection of vice; red-light district: *His precinct is known as the Tenderloin, because of its social characteristics* (Harper's). **2.** (originally) a police district in New York City where the large amount of graft available was supposed to enable a corrupt policeman to live on a diet of tenderloin.

tenderloin district or **section,** Tenderloin: *I had a cousin and an uncle who were playtime boys and they used to take me downtown to the tenderloin section with them* (New Yorker).

ten·der-mind·ed (ten′dər mīn′did), *adj.* **1.** impractical: *He belongs in William James's well-known division of the human race, to the tender-minded* (Manchester Guardian). **2.** tender-hearted: *To be tender-minded does not become a sword* (Shakespeare).

ten·der·ness (ten′dər nis), *n.* **1.** the quality or state of being tender. **2.** a tender feeling: *She has a tenderness for cats.*

ten·der·om·e·ter (ten′də rom′ə tər), *n.* an instrument for measuring the tenderness of various types of foods: *The percentages of intramuscular fat were then related to tenderness, as measured both objectively, using a tenderometer, and subjectively, using a panel of tasters* (New Scientist).

ten·di·ni·tis (ten′də nī′tis), *n.* tenonitis: *Russ has bursitis in his elbow, tendinitis in his knee, and strained ligaments in his ankle* (Time).
[< Medieval Latin *tēndo, -inis* tendon + English *-itis*]

ten·di·nous (ten′də nəs), *adj.* **1.** of or like a tendon. **2.** consisting of tendons.

ten·don (ten′dən), *n.* a tough, strong band or cord of tissue that joins a muscle to a bone or some other part; sinew: *They transplant tendons to enable the crippled to walk, and graft skin over tissue mutilated by fire, gunshot, and auto accident* (Arthur J. Snider). [< Medieval Latin *tendo, -inis,* alteration of Late Latin *tenōn, -ontis* < Greek *ténōn, -ontos* tendon; influenced by Latin *tendere* to stretch]
—**Syn.** ligament.

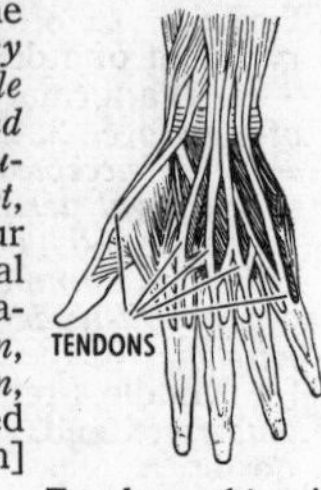

Tendons of hand

tendon of Achilles, the tendon that connects the muscles of the calf of the leg to the bone of the heel; Achilles' tendon.
ten·drac (ten′drak), *n.* tenrec.
ten·dresse (tän dres′). *n. French.* tender regard; tenderness: *The fair Truffi, for whom I still cherish a certain degree of tendresse* (Washington Irving).
ten·dril (ten′drəl), *n.* **1.** *Botany.* a thread-like part of a climbing plant that attaches itself to something and helps support the plant. **2.** something similar: *tendrils of hair curling about a child's face.* [< Middle French *tendrillon* bud, shoot (diminutive) < *tendron* bud, tendril; (literally) clasper, < Old French *tendre;* see TENDER[1]; influenced by Middle French *tendre* to stretch]

Tendrils (def. 1)

ten·dril·lar (ten′drə lər), *adj.* **1.** full of tendrils. **2.** resembling a tendril.
ten·dril·ous (ten′drə ləs), *adj.* tendrillar.
Ten·e·brae (ten′ə brē), *n.pl.* in the Roman Catholic Church: **1.** the office of matins and lauds for the following day sung the afternoon or evening before each of the three days preceding Easter. **2.** a public service at which this office is sung. [< Medieval Latin *Tenebrae* < Latin *tenebrae,* plural, darkness]
ten·e·brif·ic (ten′ə brif′ik), *adj.* causing or producing darkness; obscuring. [< Latin *tenebrae,* plural, darkness + English *-fic*]
ten·e·bri·o·nid (ten′ə brē ə nid), *adj.* of or having to do with a group of beetles living in arid places on decaying matter, and producing larvae that feed on grain and meal in storage. [< New Latin *Tenebrionidae* the family name < Latin *tenebrio, -onis* one who lurks in the dark < *tenebrae* darkness]
ten·e·brous (ten′ə brəs), *adj.* dark; gloomy; dim: *... the library of the club, a tenebrous chamber some seventy-five feet long and eighteen feet wide* (New Yorker). [< Latin *tenebrōsus* < *tenebrae,* plural, darkness] —**ten′e·brous·ness,** *n.* —**Syn.** somber, murky, dusky.
ten-eight·y (ten′ā′tē), *n.* a poisonous compound, used as a rat poison (usually written *1080*). *Formula:* $C_2H_2FNaO_2$
ten·e·ment (ten′ə mənt), *n.* **1.** a tenement house. **2.** any house or building to live in; dwelling house. **3.** the part of a house or building occupied by a tenant as a separate dwelling. **4.** an abode; habitation.
tenements, *Law.* anything permanent that one person may hold of another, as land, buildings, franchises, rents, etc.: *The Sheriffs of London [in] those days might lawfully enter into the ... tenements that the Abbot had within Middlesex* (Richard Grafton).
[earlier, tenure of immovable property < Anglo-French, Old French *tenement,* learned borrowing from Medieval Latin *tenementum* < Latin *tenēre* to hold]
—**Syn. 3.** apartment, flat.
ten·e·men·tal (ten′ə men′təl), *adj.* having to do with a tenement or tenements.
ten·e·men·ta·ry (ten′ə men′tər ē), *adj.* **1.** that can be leased. **2.** held by tenants.
tenement house, a building divided into sets of rooms occupied by separate families, especially such a building in the poorer sections of large cities.
ten·ent (ten′ənt), *n. Obsolete.* tenet.
te·nes·mus (ti nez′məs, -nes′-), *n. Medicine.* the continual inclination to void the contents of the bladder or bowels, with little or no discharge. [< Medieval Latin *tenesmus,* alteration of Latin *tēnesmos* < Greek *teinesmós* (literally) straining < *teínein* to strain, stretch]

ten·et (ten′it; *especially British* tē′nit), *n.* a doctrine, principle, belief, or opinion held as true: *The practical consequences of any political tenet go a great way in deciding upon its value* (Edmund Burke). [< Latin *tenet* he holds, third person singular of *tenēre* to hold] —**Syn.** dogma, persuasion.
ten·fold (ten′fōld′), *adj., adv., n.* ten times as much or as many.
ten-gal·lon hat (ten′gal′ən), *Western U.S.* a large, broad-brimmed hat, usually worn by cowboys.
te·ni·a (tē′nē ə), *n., pl.* **-ni·ae** (-nē ē). taenia.
te·ni·a·cide (tē′nē ə sīd), *n.* taeniacide.
te·ni·a·fuge (tē′nē ə fyüj), *adj., n.* taeniafuge.
te·ni·a·sis (ti nī′ə sis), *n.* taeniasis.
Ten·ite (ten′īt), *n. Trademark.* any of various thermoplastic materials used in packaging, in making pipes, coatings, etc.
Ten·ku (teng′kü), *n.* Tunku.
Tenn., Tennessee.
ten·nant·ite (ten′ən tīt), *n.* a gray to black mineral, a sulfide of arsenic with copper and usually iron. It is an ore of copper. *Formula:* Cu_3AsS_3 [< Smithson *Tennant,* 1761-1815, an English chemist]
ten·né (ten′ē), *n.* (in heraldry) the tawny color in coats of arms. [< Middle French *tenné,* variant of *tanné.* Compare TAWNY.]
ten·ner (ten′ər), *n. Informal.* **1.** a ten-dollar bill or a ten-pound note. **2.** anything that counts as ten.
Ten·nes·se·an (ten′ə sē′ən), *adj.* of or having to do with Tennessee. —*n.* a native or inhabitant of Tennessee.
Ten·nes·see Valley Authority (ten′ə-sē), TVA.
Tennessee walking horse, an easy-gaited saddle horse originally bred from Morgan and standard-bred stock by Southern plantation owners to obtain a horse with a comfortable mount: *The passage of this legislation ... would greatly reduce the number of "Tennessee walking horses," whose gait is obtained by cutting the forefeet, blistering them with chemicals, and adding chains which rub up and down on the inflamed area* (New York Times).
Tennessee warbler, a warbler with an olive-green back and white breast, that nests in coniferous forests of northeastern North America.
ten·nis (ten′is), *n.* **1.** a game played by two or four players on a special court, in which a ball is knocked back and forth over a net by a tennis racket; lawn tennis. **2.** court tennis. [Middle English *teneys,* apparently alteration of earlier *tenets* < Anglo-French *tenetz,* Old French *tenez* hold!, imperative of *tenir* < Latin *tenēre*]
tennis ball, a ball used in tennis, made of rubber with a cloth covering.
tennis court, a level, rectangular area prepared and marked out for playing the game of tennis.
tennis elbow, inflammation or bursitis of the elbow, commonly associated with tennis and certain other sports.
tennis racket, the racket used in tennis.
tennis shoes, any of various shoes worn for tennis.
ten·ny (ten′ē), *n.* tenné.
Ten·ny·so·ni·an (ten′ə sō′nē ən), *adj.* of or having to do with Alfred, Lord Tennyson, English Victorian poet, his style, or his works: *"Lohengrin" has a few strokes of magic and many pages of idyllic Tennysonian rapture* (Desmond Shawe-Taylor).
ten·on (ten′ən), *n.* the end of a piece of wood cut so as to fit into a hole (mortise) in another piece and so form a joint. See **mortise** for picture. —*v.t., v.i.* **1.** to cut in such a way as to form a tenon. **2.** to fit together with tenon and mortise. [< Middle French *tenon* < Old French *tenir* to hold < Latin *tenēre*]
ten·o·ni·tis (ten′ə nī′tis), *n.* inflammation of a tendon. [< Late Latin *tenōn, -ontis* tendon + English *-itis*]
ten·or (ten′ər), *n.* **1.** the general tendency; course: *The calm tenor of her life has never been disturbed by excitement or trouble.* **2.** the general meaning or drift: *I understand French well enough to get the tenor of his speech.* **3.** *Music.* **a.** the highest adult male voice. Bass and tenor are two parts of men's voices. **b.** a part sung by, or written for, such a voice. **c.** a man who sings this part; singer with such a voice. **d.** an instrument corresponding in compass to this voice. **e.** the largest bell of a peal, having the lowest tone. **4.** *Law.* an exact copy of a document. **5.** *Obsolete.* **a.** nature. **b.** condition. —*adj. Music.* of or for the tenor: *a tenor part.*
[< Latin *tenor* contents, course; (originally) a holding on < *tenēre* to hold; (definition 3) < Middle French, or Medieval Latin *tenor* holding (the melody)]
—**Syn.** *n.* **1.** direction. **2.** gist, purport.
tenor clef, *Music.* the C-clef when placed on the second from the top line of the staff.
te·no·re di gra·zi·a (te nō′rā dē grät′sē ä), *n.* a tenor with a light, flexible, lyrical voice: *Tito Schipa ... was the outstanding tenore di grazia of his day, a singer of marvellous refinement and musicianship* (London Times). [< Italian *tenore di grazia* (literally) tenor of grace]
te·no·re ro·bus·to (te nō′rā rō büs′tō), a tenor with a vigorous, powerful voice. [< Italian *tenore robusto* (literally) robust tenor]
ten·or·ite (ten′ə rīt), *n.* a black oxide of copper, found in thin, iron-black scales in lava. *Formula:* CuO
ten·or·oon (ten′ə rün), *n.* **1.** an obsolete wooden reed instrument intermediate in pitch between the oboe and the bassoon: *The tenoroon ... has entirely gone out of use* (W.H. Stone). **2.** a reed stop in an organ, resembling the oboe stop, but not extending below tenor C. **3.** any stop not extending below tenor C. [< *tenor* + (bass)*oon*]
te·nor·rha·phy (tə nôr′ə fē, -nor′-), *n., pl.* **-phies.** the surgical suture of a tendon. [< Greek *ténōn* + *rhaphḗ* a seam or suture]
ten·o·syn·o·vi·tis (ten′ō sin′ə vī′tis), *n.* inflammation of the synovial membrane of a tendon. [< Late Latin *tenōn, -ontis* tendon + English *synovitis*]
te·not·o·my (tə not′ə mē), *n., pl.* **-mies.** surgical incision into or through a tendon. [< Greek *ténōn* + *-tomíā* a cutting]
ten·pence (ten′pəns), *n.* **1.** a sum of ten (English) pennies. **2. a.** a coin worth ten pennies (as one issued by the Bank of Ireland in the early 1800's). **b.** *Archaic.* any of various foreign coins worth about ten pennies.
ten·pen·ny (ten′pen′ē, -pə nē), *adj.* **1.** worth 10 (English) pennies, or a little less than 12 cents in United States money. **2.** designating a kind of large-sized nail: *I drove a couple of tenpenny nails in the ground* (New Yorker).
ten-per·cent·er (ten′pər sen′tər), *n. Slang.* **1.** an agent of an actor, writer, etc.: *The ... ten-percenters retired to several of the town's toney hangouts* (Manchester Guardian Weekly). **2.** any person whose commission is ten percent of the profit or merchandise.
ten·pin (ten′pin′), *n.* one of the pins in tenpins.
ten·pins (ten′pinz′), *n. sing. or pl.* **1.** a game played with ten wooden pins at which a ball is bowled to knock them down. **2.** the pins used in this.
➔ **Tenpins,** the game (def. 1.), is plural in form and singular in use: *Tenpins is similar to ninepins. Tenpins,* the pins used in the game (def. 2), is plural in form and in use: *The tenpins were all knocked down.*

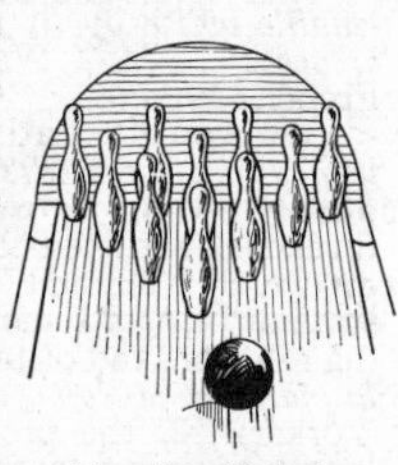
Tenpins (def. 1)

ten-point (ten′point′), *n.* a size of type.
This sentence is set in ten-point.
ten·rec (ten′rek), *n.* any of certain insectivorous, quilled mammals of Madagascar, especially one that is tailless. Also, **tanrec, tendrac.** [< French *tanrec* < Malagasy *tàndraka,* variant of *tràndraka*]
tense[1] (tens), *adj.,* **tens·er, tens·est,** *v.,* **tensed, tens·ing.** —*adj.* **1.** stretched tight; strained to stiffness: *a tense rope, a face tense with pain.* **2.** keyed up; strained: *tense nerves, a tense moment.* **3.** *Phonetics.* pronounced with the muscles of the speech organs relatively tense.
—*v.t., v.i.* to stretch tight; tighten; stiffen: *He tensed his muscles for the leap.*
tense up, to make or become tense: *You're all tensed up* (Atlantic).
[< Latin *tēnsus,* past participle of *tendere* to stretch] —**tense′ly,** *adv.* —**tense′ness,** *n.*
—**Syn.** *adj.* **1.** taut, rigid. —**Ant.** *adj.* **1.** loose, lax, relaxed.
tense[2] (tens), *n. Grammar.* **1.** the form of a verb that shows the time of the action or state expressed by a verb. *Examples: He*

obeys is in the present tense. *He obeyed* is in the past tense. *He will obey* is in the future tense. **2.** a set of such forms for the various persons. *Example:* The present tense of *obey* is: *I obey, thou obeyest; he obeys, we obey, you obey, they obey.* [< Old French *tens* time < Latin *tempus.* Doublet of TEMPO.]

tense·less (tens′lis), *adj.* having no tense: *a tenseless verb.*

ten·si·ble (ten′sə bəl), *adj.* that can be stretched. [< Late Latin *tēnsibilis* capable of tension < Latin *tendere* to stretch]

ten·sile (ten′səl), *adj.* **1.** of or having to do with tension: *Steel has great tensile strength.* **2.** that can be stretched; ductile: *tensile metals.* [< New Latin *tensilis* < Latin *tendere* to stretch]

ten·sil·i·ty (ten sil′ə tē), *n.* ductility.

ten·sim·e·ter (ten sim′ə tər), *n.* an instrument for measuring the pressure or tension of vapor, as a manometer. [< Latin *tēnsus* past participle of *tendere* stretch + *-meter*]

ten·si·om·e·ter (ten′sē om′ə tər), *n.* an instrument for testing the tautness of wire. Also, **tensometer.** [< Latin *tēnsiō, -ōnis* tension + *-meter*]

ten·sion (ten′shən), *n.* **1.** stretching. **2.** a stretched condition. **3.** mental or nervous strain: *A mother feels tension when her baby is sick.* **4.** a strained condition: *political tension.* **5.** stress caused by the action of a pulling force: *An elevator exerts tension on the cables supporting it.* **6.** a device to control the pull or strain on something: *The tension in a sewing machine may be adjusted to hold the thread tight or loose.* **7.** voltage: *high-tension wires.* **8.** the pressure of a gas.

—*v.t.* to make tense; tighten; draw out: *tensioned steel rods.*

[< Latin *tēnsiō, -ōnis* < *tendere* to stretch] —**Syn.** *n.* **3.** anxiety, uneasiness.

ten·sion·al (ten′shə nəl), *adj.* of or having to do with tension.

ten·sion·er (ten′shə nər), *n.* a device to control the pull or strain on something: *The overhead wire is strung with special tensioners to remain at a constant height above the track* (Bruce H. Frisch).

ten·sion·less (ten′shən lis), *adj.* without tension; unstrained.

ten·si·ty (ten′sə tē), *n.* a being tense: *It braced him into such a tensity of spirit* (Thomas Carlyle).

ten·sive (ten′siv), *adj.* **1.** causing tension. **2.** denoting a sensation of tension in any part of the body.

ten·som·e·ter (ten som′ə tər), *n.* tensiometer.

ten·son (ten′sən), *n.* **1.** a contest in verse between rival troubadours. **2.** verse composed for or sung at such a contest. [< French *tenson* < Latin *tēnsiō, -ōnis*]

ten·sor (ten′sər, -sôr), *n.* **1.** a muscle that stretches or tightens some part of the body. **2.** *Mathematics.* a vector that can only be defined by reference to more than three components: *The gravitational equations of the general theory of relativity are written in a form of mathematics that deals with quantities called tensors* (Harper's). [< New Latin *tensor* < Latin *tendere* to stretch]

ten spot, *Informal.* a ten-dollar bill.

ten-strike (ten′strīk′), *n.* **1.** a stroke that knocks down all ten pins in bowling. **2.** *Informal.* any completely successful stroke or act.

tent[1] (tent), *n.* **1.** a movable shelter made of canvas supported by a pole or poles. **2.** a tentlike device to regulate the temperature and humidity of the air in treating certain respiratory diseases.

—*v.i.* to live in or as in a tent: *We're tenting tonight on the old campground* (Walter Kittredge). —*v.t.* **1.** to cover with or as with a tent. **2.** to put up or lodge in a tent or tents.

[< Old French *tente* < Latin *tenta,* (originally) plural of *tentum,* variant past participle of *tendere* to stretch] —**tent′like′,** *adj.*

tent[2] (tent), *Medicine.* —*n.* **1.** a roll of gauze that increases in size when wet, used to dilate an opening. **2.** *Obsolete.* a probe.

—*v.t.* to keep open with a tent. [< Old French *tente* < *tenter* to try, examine < Latin *temptāre;* see TEMPT]

tent[3] (tent), *Scottish.* —*n.* heed; care.

—*v.t.* **1.** to take or have charge and care of. **2.** to heed. **3.** to hinder. **4.** to teach.

[short for Middle English *attent* intent]

ten·ta·cle (ten′tə kəl), *n.* **1.** one of the long, slender, flexible processes on the head or around the mouth of an animal, used to touch, hold, or move; feeler. **2.** any power or influence that has a far-reaching or strangling hold: *He began as the chairman of a Senate investigating committee to trace the tentacles of organised crime in the U.S.* (Alistair Cooke). **3.** a sensitive hairlike growth on a plant. [< New Latin *tentaculum* < Latin *tentāre,* earlier *temptāre;* see TEMPT]

ten·ta·cled (ten′tə kəld), *adj.* having a tentacle or tentacles: *She worked with hydra, the small fresh-water animal which consists of a wormlike trunk and a tentacled head* (Scientific American).

ten·tac·u·lar (ten tak′yə lər), *adj.* of, forming, or resembling tentacles: *We checked in with Roger L. Stevens, the busiest producer of the era, as well as a real-estate man of tentacular scope* (New Yorker).

ten·tac·u·late (ten tak′yə lit, -lāt), *adj.* having tentacles.

tent·age (ten′tij), *n.* equipment of tents.

ten·ta·tion (ten tā′shən), *n.* tentative operation.

ten·ta·tive (ten′tə tiv), *adj.* done as a trial or experiment; experimental: *a tentative plan.* —*n.* a trial; experiment: *I had even made some tentatives for . . . a reconciliation* (H. G. Wells). [< Medieval Latin *tentativus* < Latin *tentāre;* see TEMPT] —**ten′ta·tive·ly,** *adv.* —**ten′ta·tive·ness,** *n.*

tent caterpillar, a caterpillar that spins tentlike silken webs.

tent dress, a loose-fitting dress having the shape of a tent.

tent·ed (ten′tid), *adj.* covered with tents: *A tented camp was set up, with facilities for journalists, photographers, and publicity agents* (Punch).

tent·er[1] (ten′tər), *n.* a framework on which cloth is stretched so that it may set or dry evenly without shrinking.

—*v.t.* to stretch (cloth) on a tenter. —*v.i. Obsolete.* to be able to be tentered, as cloth.

[ultimately < Latin *tentus,* variant past participle of *tendere* to stretch]

tent·er[2] (ten′tər), *n. British Dialect.* a tender; person or thing that tends another.

tent·er[3] (ten′tər), *n.* a person who lives or stays in a tent.

ten·ter·hook (ten′tər hůk′), *n.* one of the hooks or bent nails that hold cloth stretched on a tenter.

on tenterhooks, in painful suspense; anxious: *The parties here are on tenterhooks about the way the vote will go* (London Times).

tenth (tenth), *n.* **1.** next after the ninth; last in a series of 10. **2.** one of 10 equal parts: *A dime is a tenth of a dollar.* **3.** *Music.* **a.** a tone or note ten degrees from a given tone or note. **b.** the interval between such tones or notes. **c.** the combination of such tones or notes.

—*adj.* **1.** next after the ninth; last in a series of 10. **2.** being one of 10 equal parts.

tenth·ly (tenth′lē), *adv.* in tenth place.

tenth Muse, 1. a goddess of some aspect of human effort not protected by the nine classical Muses. **2.** a woman of considerable literary talent.

tent·mak·er (tent′mā′kər), *n.* **1.** a person who makes tents, as for a traveling circus. **2.** any moth whose larvae spin large silken webs in trees.

tent meeting, *U.S.* a camp meeting held in a tent.

tent peg or **pin,** a stake driven into the ground, to fasten a tent rope.

tent pole, a pole used to hold up a tent.

tent show, a show performed in a tent, usually in rural areas where no theater is available: *Although it is described as a musical comedy it is really an old-fashioned tent show* (New Yorker).

tent stitch, petit point.

tent·y (ten′tē), *adj.,* **tent·i·er, tent·i·est.** *Scottish.* watchful; observant: *Never, a gun or sword left . . . but what tenty folk have hidden in their thatch* (Robert Louis Stevenson).

ten·u·i·ros·tral (ten′yů ə ros′trəl), *adj.* (of birds) slender-billed. [< Latin *tenuis* thin, slender + *rostrum* beak + English *-al*[1]]

ten·u·is (ten′yů is), *n., pl.* **-u·es** (-yů ēz). *Phonetics.* a voiceless stop, as English *p, t,* and *k.* [< Latin *tenuis* thin, fine; translation of Greek *psīlós* unaspirated, bare]

te·nu·i·ty (ten yü′ə tē, ti nü′-), *n.* rarefied condition; thinness; slightness.

ten·u·ous (ten′yů əs), *adj.* **1.** thin; slender: *The tenuous thread of a spider's web.* **2.** not dense; rare; rarefied: *Air ten miles above the earth is very tenuous.* **3.** having slight importance; not substantial: *a tenuous claim.* [< Latin *tenuis* thin] —**ten′u·ous·ly,** *adv.* —**ten′u·ous·ness,** *n.*

ten·ure (ten′yər), *n.* **1.** a holding; possessing. **2.** length of time of holding or possessing: *The tenure of office of the president of our club is one year.* **3.** the manner of holding land, buildings, etc., from a feudal lord or superior: *The military tenure of land had been originally created as a means of national defence* (Macaulay). **4.** conditions, terms, etc., on which anything is held or occupied. **5.** permanent status, especially on a faculty after a period of trial. [< Anglo-French, Old French *tenure* < Medieval Latin *tenitura* < Latin *tenēre* hold]

ten·ured (ten′yərd), *adj.* having tenure: *The power of the central administration is offset by the counterweight of the tenured faculty who are safe from interference and dismissal* (New York Times).

ten·u·ri·al (te nyůr′ē əl), *adj.* of or having to do with a tenure. —**ten·u′ri·al·ly,** *adv.*

te·nu·to (te nü′tō), *adj., adv. Music.* (of a tone or chord) held or sustained to its full time value. [< Italian *tenuto,* past participle of *tenere* to hold < Latin *tenēre*]

te·o·cal·li (tē′ə kal′ē; *Spanish* tā′ō kä′yē), *n., pl.* **-lis.** an Aztec temple, constructed on top of a high pyramid, the remains of some of which survive in parts of Mexico and Central America. [< Spanish *teocalli* < Nahuatl, temple (literally) house of a god < *teotl* god + *calli* house]

te·on·a·na·ca·tl (tē on′ə nə ka′təl), *n.* **1.** a drug that induces hallucination. **2.** a mushroom from which the drug is derived. [< Nahuatl *teonanacatl*]

te·o·sin·te (tē′ə sin′tē), *n.* a tall, annual grass related to corn, native to Mexico and Central America, used for fodder and sometimes as a cereal: *Some botanists conjecture that the ancestor of the corn was the Mexican grass teosinte* (Science News Letter). [< Mexican Spanish *teosinte* < Nahuatl *teosintli,* the name of a wild grass]

Te·o·ti·hua·can (ta′ō tē′wä kän′), *adj.* of or having to do with the period of Mexican history when the Toltec civilization was predominant (approximately 900-1200 A.D.).

[< *Teotihuacán,* a town in southern Mexico where remains of this civilization are found]

TEPA (no periods), triethylene phosphoramide.

tep·a·ry (tep′ər ē), *n., pl.* **-ries.** an annual, drought-resistant bean, native to the southwestern United States and Mexico: *The only indigenous North American vegetables are the tepary and the Jerusalem artichoke* (New Yorker). [< Mexican Spanish *tepari* < a Piman word]

te·pee (tē′pē), *n.* a tent of the American Indians, especially of certain of those west of the Mississippi, formed of bark, mats, skins, etc., stretched over a conical frame of poles fastened together at the top; wigwam: *In a strict sense, a wigwam is a dome-shaped wooden American Indian house, the skin structures . . . being tepees* (New York Times). Also, **teepee, tipi.** [American English < Siouan (Dakota) *tipi* dwelling]

Tepees

tep·e·fac·tion (tep′ə fak′shən), *n.* the act or process of making tepid.

tep·e·fy (tep′ə fī), *v.t., v.i.,* **-fied, -fy·ing.** to make or become tepid. [< Latin *tepefacere* < *tepēre* to be tepid + *facere* to make]

Tep·ex·pan Man (tep′eks pän′), a very early form of man whose remains were discovered in Mexico, believed to have existed between 10,000 and 12,000 years ago. [< *Tepexpán,* a village in Mexico]

te·phil·lin (tə fil′ən), *n.pl.* tefillin.

teph·ra (tef′rə), *n.* volcanic material, as ash, dust, cinders, scoria, pumice, etc., given off in an eruption. [< Greek *téphra* ashes]

teph·rite (tef′rīt), *n.* any of a group of volcanic rocks related to basalt. [< Greek *tephrós* ash-colored]

teph·rit·ic (tef rit′ik), *adj.* of the nature of tephrite; having to do with tephrite.

tep·id (tep′id), *adj.* moderately or slightly warm; lukewarm: *tepid soup, a tepid bath.*

[< Latin *tepidus* < *tepēre* be warm] —**tep′id·ly,** *adv.* —**tep′id·ness,** *n.*

tep·i·dar·i·um (tep′ə dãr′ē əm), *n., pl.* **-i·a** (-ē ə). a warm room in an ancient Roman bath, between the cold room and the hot room. [< Latin *tepidārium* < *tepidus;* see TEPID]

te·pid·i·ty (ti pid′ə tē), *n.* tepid condition.

TEPP (no periods), tetraethyl pyrophosphate.

te·qui·la (tə kē′lə, tā kē′lä), *n.* **1.** a Mexican agave. The juices of its roasted stems are made into a distilled liquor. **2.** this liquor. [American English < American Spanish *tequila* < *Tequila,* a town in Mexico]

ter., **1.** terrace. **2.** territory.

tera-, *combining form.* one trillion ______: *Teravolt = one trillion volts.* [< Greek *téras, -atos* monster; marvel]

ter·a·cy·cle (ter′ə sī′kəl), *n.* one trillion cycles per second.

te·rai (tə rī′), *n.,* or **terai hat,** a wide-brimmed felt hat, perforated at the sides for ventilation. [< Hindi *tarāī* moist land < *tar* moist]

ter·a·phim (ter′ə fim), *n.pl., sing.* **ter·aph** (ter′əf). (in the Bible) images or idols of the household gods used as oracles by the ancient Hebrew and kindred peoples. Genesis 31:19. [< Late Latin *theraphim* < Hebrew *tərāfim* images]

ter·a·to·gen (ter′ə tə jən, -tō′-), *n.* a drug or other agent that causes teratogenesis: *Thalidomide's effect classified it as a teratogen, a substance which can alter a developing embryo and lead to malformations* (Malcolm A. Holliday).

ter·a·to·gen·e·sis (ter′ə tə jen′ə sis), *n. Biology.* the production of monsters or misshapen organisms. [< Greek *téras, -atos* monster; marvel + English *genesis*]

ter·a·to·ge·net·ic (ter′ə tə jə net′ik), *adj.* of or having to do with teratogenesis.

ter·a·to·gen·ic (ter′ə tə jen′ik), *adj.* teratogenetic: *Recent reports from England indicate that preparations made from mandrake may be teratogenic, i.e., capable of deforming babies* (Maclean's).

ter·a·tog·e·ny (ter′ə toj′ə nē), *n.* teratogenesis.

ter·a·toid (ter′ə toid), *n.* like a monster. [< Greek *téras, -atos* monster + *-oid*]

ter·a·to·log·i·cal (ter′ə tə loj′ə kel), *adj.* of or having to do with teratology.

ter·a·tol·o·gist (ter′ə tol′ə jist), *n.* an expert in teratology.

ter·a·tol·o·gy (ter′ə tol′ə jē), *n.* the study of abnormal formations. [< Greek *téras, -atos* monster; marvel + English *-logy*]

ter·a·to·ma (ter′ə tō′mə), *n., pl.* **-mas, -ma·ta** (-mə tə). a complex congenital tumor, often containing many different tissues, as skin, hair, teeth, connective tissue, cartilage, bone, muscles, and glands, and found at the lower end of the spine, about the head and neck, and in the generative organs. [< Greek *téras, -atos* monster + English *-oma*]

ter·bi·a (tėr′bē ə), *n.* terbium oxide. [< New Latin *terbia* < *terbium;* see TERBIUM]

ter·bic (tėr′bik), *adj.* of or having to do with terbium.

ter·bi·um (tėr′bē əm), *n.* a rare-earth metallic chemical element found in gadolinite, monazite, and other minerals. *Symbol:* Tb; *at. wt.:* (C^{12}) 158.924 or (O^{16}) 158.93; *at. no.:* 65; *valence:* 3, 4. [< New Latin *terbium* < (Yt)*terby,* a town in Sweden. Compare ERBIUM, YTTRIUM.]

terbium oxide, a brown powder, one of the rare earths. *Formula:* Tb_4O_7

terce (tėrs), *n.* tierce.

ter·cel (tėr′səl), *n.* a male falcon or goshawk. [< Old French *tercel,* and *terçuel* < Vulgar Latin *tertiolus* (diminutive) < Latin *tertius* third]

terce·let (tėrs′lit), *n.* tercel.

ter·cen·te·nar·y (tėr sen′tə ner′ē, tėr′senten′ər-; *especially British* -sen tē′nər ē), *adj., n., pl.* **-nar·ies.** —*adj.* of or having to do with a period of 300 years: *a tercentenary anniversary.* —*n.* **1.** a 300th anniversary. **2.** a period of 300 years. [< Latin *ter* three times + English *centenary*]

ter·cen·ten·ni·al (tėr′sen ten′ē əl), *adj., n.* tercentenary.

ter·cet (tėr′sit, tėr set′), *n.* **1.** a group of three lines rhyming together, or connected by rhyme with the adjacent group or groups of three lines. **2.** *Music.* a triplet. [< French *tercet,* Middle French *tiercet* < Italian *terzetto* (diminutive) < *terzo* third < Latin *tertius.* Doublet of TERZETTO.]

ter·e·bene (ter′ə bēn), *n.* a liquid mixture of terpenes obtained from turpentine, used as an antiseptic and expectorant.

te·reb·ic (te reb′ik, -rē′bik), *adj.* of or having to do with terebic acid.

terebic acid, a crystalline acid obtained from oil of turpentine. *Formula:* $C_7H_{10}O_4$

ter·e·binth (ter′ə binth), *n.* a tree of the cashew family, growing in the Mediterranean region, a source of crude turpentine. [< Latin *terebinthus* < Greek *terébinthos,* variant of earlier *térbinthos*]

ter·e·bin·thic (ter′ə bin′thik), *adj.* terebinthine.

ter·e·bin·thi·na (ter′ə bin′thə nə), *n. Pharmacology.* turpentine. [< Medieval Latin *terebinthina*]

ter·e·bin·thi·nat·ed (ter′ə bin′thə nā′tid), *adj.* containing turpentine.

ter·e·bin·thine (ter′ə bin′thin), *adj.* **1.** of or having to do with turpentine. **2.** of or having to do with the terebinth.

ter·e·brate (ter′ə brāt), *v.t., v.i.,* **-brat·ed, -brat·ing.** to bore or perforate. [< Latin *terebrāre* (with English *-ate*[1])]

ter·e·bra·tion (ter′ə brā′shən), *n.* the act of boring or piercing: *Terebration of Trees doth make them prosper better* (Sir Francis Bacon).

te·re·do (tə rē′dō), *n., pl.* **-dos, -di·nes** (-də nēz). a small, wormlike marine clam that bores into and destroys the wood of ships, etc.; shipworm. [< Latin *terēdo* < Greek *terēdōn* < *teírein* to rub away, weaken, bore]

te·rel·la (tə rel′ə), *n. Obsolete.* terrella.

ter·eph·thal·ate (ter′ef thal′āt), *n.* a salt or ester of terephthalic acid.

ter·eph·thal·ic acid (ter′ef thal′ik), a white, crystalline acid obtained from petroleum, used chiefly in making Dacron and other polyester fibers. *Formula:* $C_8H_6O_4$

te·rete (tə rēt′, ter′ēt), *adj.* **1.** having a cylindrical or slightly tapering form. **2.** rounded and smooth. [< Latin *teres, -etis* rounded off < *terere* to rub, wear away]

Te·reus (tir′yüs, -ē əs), *n. Greek Mythology.* an evil king, the husband of Procne.

ter·gal (tėr′gəl), *adj. Zoology.* dorsal.

ter·gem·i·nate (tėr jem′ə nit, -nāt), *adj.* (of a compound leaf) having at the base a pair of leaflets and then forking, with a pair on each branch. [< Latin *tergeminus,* variant of *trigeminus* triple + English *-ate*[1]]

ter·gi·ver·sate (tėr′jə vər sāt), *v.i.,* **-sat·ed, -sat·ing.** **1.** to change one's attitude or opinions with respect to a cause or subject; turn renegade. **2.** to shift or shuffle; evade. [< Latin *tergiversārī* evade < *tergum* the back + *versāre* < *vertere* to turn]

ter·gi·ver·sa·tion (tėr′jə vər sā′shən), *n.* **1.** change of attitude or opinions. **2.** a backing out; an evasion.

ter·gi·ver·sa·tor (tėr′jə vər sā′tər), *n.* a person who tergiversates.

ter·gum (tėr′gəm), *n., pl.* **-ga** (-gə). *Zoology.* the back. [< Latin *tergum* the back]

ter·i·ya·ki (ter′i yä′kē), *n.* a Japanese dish consisting of fish or meat with onions, green peppers, etc., and soy sauce, often broiled and served on a skewer. [< Japanese *teriyaki.* Compare SUKIYAKI.]

term (tėrm), *n.* **1.** a word or phrase used in a recognized and definite sense in some particular subject, science, art, business, etc.: *medical terms.* **2.** an expression: *an abstract term, a term of reproach.* **3.** a set period of time; length of time that a thing lasts: *the term of a lease; a president's term of office.* **4.** one of the long periods into which the school year is divided: *the fall term.* **5.** one of the periods of time during which a court is in session. **6.** *Mathematics.* **a.** one of the members in a proportion or ratio. **b.** one of the parts of a compound algebraic expression. In $13ax^2—2bxy+ y$, $13ax^2$, $2bxy$, and y are the terms. **c.** a point, line, or surface that limits in geometry. **7.** *Logic.* **a.** the word or words that form the subject or predicate of a proposition. **b.** one of the three parts of a syllogism. **8.** a terminal or end figure. **9.** *Archaic.* a boundary; end limit.

bring to terms, to compel to agree, assent, or submit; force to come to an agreement: *The company found out that the union could not be brought to terms without the promise of a new contract.*

come to terms, **a.** to accept a situation; become resigned: *Somehow the British public has never really come to terms with the phenomenon of women in politics* (Manchester Guardian Weekly). **b.** to agree upon conditions; reach an understanding: *The Chinese accuse the Soviets of planning to betray the cause of revolution by coming to terms with the United States* (Atlantic).

in terms of, **1.** in the phraseology or mode of thought belonging to: *Criticisms of M.I.T.'s warm embrace of business are often couched in terms of conflict of interest* (New York Times). **2.** with regard to: *The book [is] a big success in terms of the interest it aroused* (New Yorker).

terms, **a.** conditions; stipulations; provisions: *the terms of a treaty, board and lodging on reasonable terms, the lowest terms offered.* **b.** a way of speaking: *flattering terms.* **c.** personal relations: *on good terms, on speaking terms.*

—*v.t.* to name; call: *He might be termed handsome.*

[< Old French *terme* limit < Latin *terminus* end, boundary line. Doublet of TERMINUS.]

—**Syn.** *n.* **3.** duration. **4.** semester.

term., **1.** terminal. **2.** termination. **3.** terminology.

ter·ma·gan·cy (tėr′mə gən sē), *n.* shrewishness.

Ter·ma·gant (tėr′mə gənt), *n.* a deity, supposed in medieval Europe to have been worshiped by the Moslems, appearing in morality plays as a violent, ranting, overbearing personage. [alteration of Middle English *Tervagant* < Old French *Tervagan,* origin uncertain]

ter·ma·gant (tėr′mə gənt), *n.* a violent, quarreling, scolding woman: *Tom's wife was a tall termagant, fierce of temper, loud of tongue, and strong of arm* (Washington Irving). —*adj.* violent; quarreling; scolding. [< *Termagant*] —**Syn.** *n.* shrew, virago. *-adj.* shrewish.

term day, **1.** quarter day. **2.** each of a series of days appointed for taking systematic scientific observations, as of meteorological phenomena.

term·er (tėr′mər), *n.* **1.** a person who is serving a term as a public official: *a fourth-termer.* **2.** *Obsolete.* termor.

ter·mi·na·bil·i·ty (tėr′mə nə bil′ə tē), *n.* the fact or quality of being terminable.

ter·mi·na·ble (tėr′mə nə bəl), *adj.* **1.** that can be ended: *The contract was terminable by either party.* **2.** coming to an end after a certain term: *a loan terminable in 10 years.* —**ter′mi·na·ble·ness,** *n.*

ter·mi·na·bly (tėr′mə nə blē), *adv.* in the way of being terminable.

ter·mi·nal (tėr′mə nəl), *adj.* **1. a.** at the end; forming the end part. **b.** *Botany.* growing at the end of a branch or stem, as a bud or flower. **2.** coming at the end: *a terminal examination.* **3.** having to do with a term. **4. a.** at the end of a railroad line. **b.** having to do with or for the handling of freight at a terminal. **5.** marking a boundary, limit, or end.

—*n.* **1.** end; the end part. **2. a.** either end of a railroad line, airline, shipping route, etc., where sheds, hangars, garages, offices, etc., and stations to handle freight and passengers are located; terminus. **b.** a station at a junction or other central point along a railroad, bus route, etc. **3.** a device making an electrical connection: *the terminals of a battery.*

[< Latin *terminālis* < *terminus* terminus]

—**Syn.** *adj.* **2.** final, ultimate. *-n.* **1.** extremity.

Ter·mi·na·li·a (tėr′mə nā′lē ə), *n.pl.* an ancient Roman festival in honor of Terminus, the god of boundaries. [< Latin *Terminālia* < *Terminus* Terminus]

terminal leave, a leave of absence given to a member of the armed forces before discharge, amounting to the remaining days of leave due.

ter·mi·nal·ly (tėr′mə nə lē), *adv.* **1.** at the end. **2.** with respect to termination.

terminal moraine, a moraine deposited at the end of a glacier.

terminal rocket, a rocket designed to put a space vehicle into the final course desired.

terminal velocity, the constant velocity of a falling body, attained when the resistance of air, water, or other surrounding fluid has become equal to the force of gravity acting upon the body: *[The] terminal velocity for a man is about 120 m.p.h.* (*e.g. for a parachutist delaying the opening of his chute*);

the corresponding velocity for a cat is probably 40 m.p.h. at the most (New Scientist).

ter·mi·nate (tėr′mə nāt), *v.*, **-nat·ed, -nat·ing.** —*v.t.* **1.** to bring to an end; put an end to: *to terminate a partnership.* **2.** to occur at or form the end of; bound; limit. —*v.i.* **1.** to come to an end: *His contract terminates soon.* **2.** to result. **3.** to stop short. [< Latin *termināri* (with English *-ate*[1]) < *terminus* end, terminus] —**Syn.** *v.t.* **1.** conclude.

ter·mi·na·tion (tėr′mə nā′shən), *n.* **1.** an ending; end: *All human power has its termination sooner or later* (Cardinal Newman). **2.** an end part. **3.** the ending of a word. *Example:* In *gladly,* the adverbial termination is *-ly.* —**Syn. 1.** conclusion. **2.** bound.

ter·mi·na·tion·al (tėr′mə nā′shə nəl), *adj.* **1.** closing; final. **2.** forming or formed by an inflected ending or suffix.

ter·mi·na·tive (tėr′mə nā′tiv), *adj.* tending to terminate. —**ter′mi·na′tive·ly,** *adv.*

ter·mi·na·tor (tėr′mə nā′tər), *n.* **1.** a person or thing that terminates. **2.** *Astronomy.* the line separating the light and dark parts of the disk of the moon or a planet: *The spacecraft flipped over on its back and snapped the earth from a distance of 240,000 miles, giving a good picture of the terminator —the division of the sunlit and shadowed areas of our planet* (Science News Letter).

ter·mi·ner (tėr′mə nər), *n. Law.* a determining or deciding.

ter·mi·nism (tėr′mə niz əm), *n.* nominalism.

ter·mi·nist (tėr′mə nist), *n.* a person who believes in terminism.

ter·mi·no·log·i·cal (tėr′mə nə loj′ə kəl), *adj.* of or having to do with terminology: *The work offers several hundred brief encyclopedic articles which comment on groups of related terms and terminological problems* (Scientific American). —**ter′mi·no·log′i·cal·ly,** *adv.*

ter·mi·nol·o·gist (tėr′mə nol′ə jist), *n.* a person skilled in terminology.

ter·mi·nol·o·gy (tėr′mə nol′ə jē), *n., pl.* **-gies. 1.** the special words or terms used in a science, art, business, etc.: *medical terminology, the terminology of engineering.* **2.** *Obsolete.* the doctrine or scientific study of terms. [< German *Terminologie* < Medieval Latin *terminus* term (in Latin, end, terminus) + German *-logie* -logy]

term insurance, insurance expiring at the end of a period of time.

ter·mi·nus (tėr′mə nəs), *n., pl.* **-ni** (-nī), **-nus·es. 1.** either end of a railroad line, bus line, etc.; terminal. **2.** a city or station at the end of a railroad line, bus line, etc.: *The Eastern Region termini in London ran 79 extra trains* (London Times). **3.** an ending place; final point; goal; end. **4.** a stone, post, etc., marking a boundary or limit; boundary marker. [< Latin *terminus.* Doublet of TERM.]
—**Syn. 3.** finale.

Ter·mi·nus (tėr′mə nəs), *n. Roman Mythology.* the god presiding over boundaries or landmarks. [< Latin *Terminus*]

ter·mi·nus ad quem (ter′mən əs ad kwem′), *Latin.* the end to which; finishing point.

terminus a quo (ā kwō′), *Latin.* the end from which; starting point.

ter·mi·tar·i·um (tėr′mə tãr′ē əm), *n., pl.* **-tar·i·a** (-tãr′ē ə). **1.** a termites' nest. **2.** a cage or vessel for studying termites. [< New Latin *termitarium* < *termites* termites]

ter·mi·tar·y (tėr′mə tãr′ē), *n., pl.* **-tar·ies.** termitarium: *The formicary, the termitary, the vespiary, and the beehive send forth their thousands* (Kirby and Spence).

ter·mite (tėr′mīt), *n.* any of various insects having a soft, pale body and a dark head, and living in colonies. Termites look like white ants and are very destructive to buildings, furniture, provisions, etc. [< New Latin *termites,* plural of *termes, -mitis* < Late Latin, woodworm (in Latin, *tarmes, -itis*), related to *terere* to rub, wear]

ter·mit·ic (tėr mit′ik), *adj.* of, having to do with, or formed by termites.

term·less (tėrm′lis), *adj.* **1.** not dependent on or limited by any terms or conditions; unconditional. **2.** having no limit; boundless; endless: *infinite and termless complication of detail* (John Ruskin).

term·or (tėr′mər), *n. Law.* a person who has an estate for a specified period of years. [alteration of Middle English *termur,* also *termer* < Anglo-French *termer* < Old French *terme;* see TERM]

term paper, a required essay written for a course in a school term.

terms (tėrmz), *n.pl.* See under **term,** *n.*

terms of reference, *Especially British.* the terms which define the scope of an inquiry: *The committee's terms of reference . . . cover examination of the origins, purpose, and operations of the French agrément system* (London Times).

term time, *Especially British.* **1.** the period of study at a university or school. **2.** the period during which the law courts are in session.

tern[1] (tėrn), *n.* any of a group of sea birds, related to the gulls but with a more slender body and bill, long, pointed wings, and a long, forked tail. [< Scandinavian (compare Danish *terne*)]

Common Tern[1]
(about 15 in. long)

tern[2] (tėrn), *n.* **1.** a ternary; trio; triad. **2. a.** a combination of three winning numbers drawn in a lottery. **b.** a prize won by the holder of such a combination. [< French *terne* < Old French *terne* or *ternes,* plural, double three in dice, ultimately < Latin *ternī* three each < *ter* thrice]

ter·na (tėr′nə), *n.* a list of three candidates for a bishopric or benefice submitted to the Pope or other authority from which to choose. [< Latin *terna*(*nomina*) three (names) at once]

ter·na·ry (tėr′nər ē), *adj., n., pl.* **-ries.** —*adj.* **1.** consisting of three; involving three; triple. **2.** third in rank, order, or position. **3.** *Mathematics.* **a.** having three for the base: *a ternary scale.* **b.** involving three variables. **4.** *Metallurgy.* consisting of three elements or components: *a ternary alloy.* —*n.* **1.** a set or group of three; trio; triad. **2.** a number that is a multiple of three. [< Latin *ternārius* < *ternī* three each < *ter* thrice]

ter·nate (tėr′nit, -nāt), *adj.* **1.** consisting of three. **2.** arranged in threes. **3.** *Botany.* **a.** having or consisting of three leaflets. **b.** having leaves in whorls of three. —**ter′nate·ly,** *adv.*

terne (tėrn), *v.,* **terned, tern·ing,** *n.* —*v.t.* to plate with an alloy of tin and lead. —*n.* terneplate.

terne·plate (tėrn′plāt′), *n.* a thin sheet of iron or steel coated with an alloy of lead and a small percentage of tin: *Terneplate . . . is used in air cleaners and fuel tanks* (Wall Street Journal). [probably < obsolete *terne,* adjective, dull, dark + *plate*]

tern·er·y (tėr′nər ē), *n., pl.* **-er·ies.** a place where terns congregate to breed.

ter·ni·on (tėr′nē ən), *n.* **1.** a ternary. **2.** a section of paper for a book, containing twelve pages. [< Latin *terniō, -ōnis* a triad < *ternī* three each < *ter* thrice]

Ter·on (ter′on), *n. Trademark.* a polyester fiber similar to Dacron.

ter·pene (tėr′pēn), *n.* **1.** any of a group of isomeric hydrocarbons, as pinene, limonene, etc., many of which are produced by distilling the volatile oils of plants, especially conifers. *Formula:* $C_{10}H_{16}$ **2.** any of various alcohols derived from or related to terpene.

ter·phen·yl (tėr fen′əl, -fē′nəl), *n.* a crystalline organic compound used as a moderator and coolant in certain nuclear reactors. *Formula:* $C_{18}H_{14}$ [< Latin *ter* three times (because it contains three benzene rings) + English *phenyl*]

ter·pin (tėr′pin), *n.* **1.** a compound like alcohol, whose hydrate is prepared from oil of turpentine. *Formula:* $C_{10}H_{20}O_2$ **2.** a compound isomeric with it. [< German *Terpin* < *Terpentin* turpentine]

ter·pin·e·ol (tėr pin′ē ōl, -ol), *n.* a tertiary colorless alcohol, found in essential oils, and also produced synthetically. It is used as a solvent and in making perfumes. *Formula:* $C_{10}H_{18}O(OH)$

ter·pin·ol (tėr′pə nōl, -nol), *n.* a mixture of the isomeric forms of terpineol.

ter·pol·y·mer (ter pol′i mer), *n. Chemistry.* a compound formed by the polymerization of three different compounds, each of which usually is able to polymerize alone. [< Latin *ter* thrice + English *polymer*]

Terp·sich·o·re (tėrp sik′ə rē), *n. Greek Mythology.* the Muse of dancing.

Terp·si·cho·re·an (tėrp′sə kə rē′ən), *adj.* of or having to do with Terpsichore.

terp·si·cho·re·an (tėrp′sə kə rē′ən), *adj.* of or having to do with dancing: *the terpsichorean art.* —*n.* a dancer (now usually humorous in use).

terr., 1. terrace. **2.** territory.

Terr., Territory.

ter·ra (ter′ə; *Italian* ter′rä), *n.* **1.** the earth. **2.** earth; soil. [< Italian and Latin *terra* earth, land]

Ter·ra (ter′ə), *n. Roman Mythology.* a goddess of the earth.

ter·ra al·ba (ter′ə al′bə), pipe clay. [< Latin *terra alba* (literally) white earth]

ter·race (ter′is), *n., v.,* **-raced, -rac·ing.** —*n.* **1. a.** a flat, raised piece of land, with a vertical or sloping front, or sides, faced with masonry, turf, etc., especially any of a series of such levels placed one above the other. **b.** such a raised piece of land and the masonry, turf, etc., collectively. **2. a.** a street along the side or top of a slope. **b.** a row of houses on such a street. **3.** an outdoor space usually paved or tiled, adjoining a house, used for lounging, dining, etc. **4.** the flat roof of a house, especially of an Oriental or Spanish house. *Abbr.:* ter.
—*v.t.* to form into a terrace or terraces; furnish with terraces: *to terrace a hillside. Hundreds of terraced flats are being built, going back into the hillside* (Listener).
[< Middle French *terrace* (originally) a heap of rubble (used to underlie a platform) < Vulgar Latin *terrācea* < Latin *terra* earth]

ter·raced (ter′ist), *adj.* **1.** furnished with a terrace or terraces. **2.** arranged or constructed in the form of a terrace.

ter·rac·ing (ter′ə sing), *n.* **1.** the formation of terraces. **2.** a terraced surface or formation. **3.** a platform or stand with rows of seats rising in tiers behind each other: *In Argentina, Brazil, and elsewhere on that continent deep moats and wire netting separate the players and the pitch from the terracings* (London Times).

ter·ra cot·ta (ter′ə kot′ə), **1.** a kind of hard, brownish-red earthenware, used for vases, statuettes, decorations on buildings, etc. **2.** an object made of this substance. **3.** a dull brownish red. [< Italian *terra cotta* < *terra* earth + *cotta* baked; (literally) cooked, feminine past participle of *cuocere* < Latin *coquere* to cook.]

ter·ra-cot·ta (ter′ə kot′ə), *adj.* **1.** having to do with or made of terra cotta: *The floor was made of terra-cotta tiles* (Atlantic). **2.** of the color of terra cotta.

ter·rae fi·li·us (ter′ē fil′ē əs), *pl.* **ter·rae fi·li·i** (ter′ē fil′ē ī). **1.** a student at Oxford University formerly appointed to make jesting satirical speeches: *To appreciate Mr. Stewart fully, you really have to . . . understand the spleen of the little magazines and blush for anyone who doesn't know the meaning of terrae filius* (London Times). **2.** *Archaic.* a person of obscure birth or low origin. [< Latin *terrae fīlius* a son of the earth, a man of unknown origin]

ter·ra fir·ma (ter′ə fėr′mə), solid earth; dry land. [< Latin *terra firma*]

ter·rain (te rān′, ter′ān), *n.* **1. a.** the land of an area or region: *the hilly, rocky terrain of parts of New England.* **b.** any tract of land considered as to its extent and natural features in relation to its use in warfare. **2.** *Geology.* terrane. [< French *terrain* < Old French *terain* < Vulgar Latin *terrānum,* for Latin *terrēnum,* noun use of adjective, earthy < *terra* earth, land]

ter·ra in·cog·ni·ta (ter′ə in kog′nə tə), *pl.* **ter·rae in·cog·ni·tae** (ter′ē in kog′nə tē). an unknown or unexplored region: *Hungarian fiction since World War II is likely to constitute a sort of terra incognita for most English-speaking readers* (Saturday Review). [< Latin *terra incognita* (literally) unknown land]

ter·ra Ja·pon·i·ca (ter′ə jə pon′ə kə), *pl.* **ter·rae Ja·pon·i·cae** (ter′ē jə pon′ə sē). gambier or catechu. [< New Latin *terra Japonica* (literally) Japanese land]

Ter·ra·my·cin (ter′ə mī′sin), *n. Trademark.* an antibiotic derived from a soil microorganism, used in the treatment of syphilis, rheumatic diseases, bacterial infections, etc. *Formula:* $C_{22}H_{24}N_2O_9.2H_2O$ [< Latin *terra* earth + Greek *mýkēs* fungus + English *-in*]

ter·rane (te rān′, ter′ān), *n. Geology.* a formation or a connected series of formations. [apparently alteration of *terrain*]

ter·ra·pin (ter′ə pin), *n.* **1.** any of certain edible North American turtles that live in fresh or brackish water, especially any of the diamondback terrapins of the Atlantic and Gulf coasts. **2.** any of certain other turtles. [American English, alteration of Algonkian (Abnaki) *turepé* or (Delaware) *turpa*]

Diamondback Terrapin (def. 1—7½ in. long)

ter·ra·que·ous (te rā′kwē əs), *adj.* **1.** consisting of land and water: *the terraqueous globe.* **2.** living in land and water, as a plant. [< Latin *terra* land, earth + English *aqueous*]

ter·rar·i·um (tə rãr′ē əm), *n., pl.* **-i·ums, -i·a** (-ē ə). an enclosure in which small land animals are kept. [< New Latin *terrarium* < Latin *terra* land. Compare Late Latin *terrārius* earthly.]

ter·ra ros·sa (ter′ə rôs′ə, ros′ə), a red soil formed by the weathering of limestone. [< Italian *terra rossa* (literally) red earth]

ter·ra sig·il·la·ta (ter′ə sij′ə lā′tə), sphragide. [< New Latin *terra sigillata* (literally) sealed earth]

ter·rasse (te räs′), *n. French.* terrace.

ter·ra ver·de (ter′ə ver′dā), any of certain mineral substances used as green pigments in painting. [< Italian *terra verde* (literally) green earth. Doublet of TERRE-VERTE.]

ter·raz·zo (te rät′sō), *n.* a floor made of small pieces of marble and cement. [< Italian *terrazzo* floor of broken stone and cement < Vulgar Latin *terrāceum* rubble, useless earth, noun use of neuter adjective < Latin *terra* earth. Compare TERRACE.]

terre-à-terre (ter′ə ter′), *adj.* **1.** (of a kind of dance) performed close to the ground; performed with the feet on the ground. **2.** matter-of-fact; unimaginative: *He is content with such terre-à-terre foods as chicken salad and hamburger* (New Yorker). [< French *terre à terre* (literally) earth to earth]

ter·rel·la (tə rel′ə), *n.* **1.** a space capsule with an environment of the earth: *Sanitary engineers . . . are figuring out how to dispose of wastes and insure the cleanliness of the terrella* (New Yorker). **2.** a magnetic globe or other spherical object so placed that its poles, equator, etc., correspond exactly to those of the earth, and often marked with lines representing meridians, parallels, etc., for illustrating magnetic phenomena of the earth. **3.** *Obsolete.* a little earth; small planet. [< New Latin *terrella* (diminutive) < Latin *terra* earth, world]

ter·rene (te rēn′), *adj.* **1.** belonging to the earth; earthly; worldly. **2.** of the nature of earth; earthy.
—*n.* **1.** the earth. **2. a.** a land. **b.** terrain. [< Latin *terrēnus* earthly, worldly < *terra* earth, land. Compare TERRAIN.]

terre·plein (ter′plān′), *n.* **1.** the top of a rampart, on which cannon are placed. **2.** the surface of a fortification in the field, especially for cannon. [< French *terreplein* < Italian *terrapieno*, ultimately < Latin *terra* earth + *plēna*, feminine of *plēnus* full]

ter·res·tri·al (tə res′trē əl), *adj.* **1.** of the earth; having to do with the earth: *this terrestrial globe.* **2.** of the land, not water: *Islands and continents make up the terrestrial parts of the earth.* **3.** living on the ground, not in the air, water, or trees: *terrestrial animals. These animals are now able to crawl out on land and take their place as terrestrial vertebrates* (A.M. Winchester). **4.** growing on land; growing in the soil: *terrestrial plants.* **5.** worldly; earthly.
—*n.* a terrestrial being, especially a human. [< Late Latin *terrestria* earthly things (< Latin *terrestris* earthly, worldly < *terra* earth) + English *-al*[1]]
—**Syn.** *adj.* **5.** mundane. See **earthly.**

terrestrial globe, ball, or **sphere, 1.** the earth. **2.** a sphere with a map of the earth on it.

terrestrial magnetism, geomagnetism.

terrestrial space, a zone from the earth's surface to about 4,000 miles into space, within which the earth's magnetic and electric influences are strongest.

ter·ret (ter′it), *n.* **1.** one of the round loops or rings on the saddle of a harness, through which the driving reins pass. **2.** a round loop or ring, especially one turning on a swivel, by which a string or chain is attached to anything.
[Middle English *tyret*, variant of *toret*, probably < Old French *touret* (diminutive) < *tour* a circuit, tour]

terre-verte (ter′vert′), *n.* any of certain native minerals, used as green pigment. [< French *terre-verte*, earlier *terre verde* (literally) green earth. Doublet of TERRA VERDE.]

ter·ri·bi·li·tà (ter′ri bi li tä′), *n. Italian.* **1.** terribleness. **2.** *Fine Arts.* an awesome quality of power or grandeur: *The terribilità that frightened those who met him* [*Michelangelo*] *fills us with awe immediately we are faced with any work of his* (Nikolaus Pevsner).

ter·ri·ble (ter′ə bəl), *adj.* **1.** causing great fear; dreadful; awful: *a terrible leopard, the terrible weapons of warfare.* **2.** distressing; severe: *the terrible suffering caused by war.* **3.** *Informal.* extremely bad, unpleasant, etc.: *a terrible temper, a terrible student.* [< Old French *terrible*, learned borrowing from Latin *terribilis* < *terrēre* to terrify] —**ter′ri·ble·ness,** *n.* —**Syn. 1.** frightful, appalling, horrible, shocking.

ter·ri·bly (ter′ə blē), *adv.* **1.** in a terrible manner. **2.** *Informal.* extremely: *I'm terribly sorry.*

ter·ric·o·lous (te rik′ə ləs), *adj. Biology.* living on or in the ground. [< Latin *terricola* < *terra* earth + *colere* inhabit]

ter·ri·er[1] (ter′ē ər), *n.* any of certain breeds of small, active, intelligent dogs, having either a short-haired, smooth coat or a long-haired, rough coat, formerly used to pursue prey into its burrow, including the bull, fox, Irish, Scottish, Sealyham, Skye, and Welsh terriers, the airedale, the Dandie Dinmont, and the schnauzer. [Middle English *terrere* < Old French (*chien*) *terrier* terrier (dog) < Medieval Latin *terrārium*, noun use of adjective, neuter of Late Latin *terrārius* earthly < Latin *terra* earth] —**ter′ri·er·like′,** *adj.*

Dandie Dinmont Terrier[1] (8 to 11 in. high at the shoulder)

ter·ri·er[2] (ter′ē ər), *n.* **1.** a list of land owners and a description of their land. **2.** (formerly) a register of property listing vassals and tenants, their holdings, services, and rents. [< Old French *terrier* rent roll, noun use of adjective < Medieval Latin (*liber*) *terrarius* (book) of the landed estates < Late Latin *terrārius* earthly < Latin *terra* land, earth]

ter·rif·ic (tə rif′ik), *adj.* **1.** causing great fear; terrifying: *a terrific storm.* **2.** *Informal.* very great, severe, etc.: *terrific applause, a terrific student.* [< Latin *terrificus* < *terrēre* to terrify + *facere* to make] —**Syn. 1.** awful. **2.** extraordinary.

ter·rif·i·cal·ly (tə rif′ə klē), *adv.* in a terrific manner; to a terrific degree: *Debussy . . . believed that Beethoven had terrifically profound things to say* (Atlantic).

ter·rif·ic·ly (tə rif′ə klē), *adv.* terrifically.

ter·ri·fied (ter′ə fīd), *adj.* filled with great fear; frightened: *Elizabeth . . . hastened . . . along the principal alley of the Pleasance, dragging with her the terrified Countess* (Scott). —**Syn.** See **afraid.**

ter·ri·fied·ly (ter′ə fīd lē), *adv.* in a terrified manner: *She is still terrifiedly clutching his hand* (Temple Bar Magazine).

ter·ri·fi·er (ter′ə fī′ər), *n.* a person or thing that terrifies.

ter·ri·fy (ter′ə fī), *v.t.,* **-fied, -fy·ing.** to fill with great fear; frighten very much. [< Latin *terrificāre* < *terrēre* terrify + *facere* to make] —**Syn.** scare, alarm, horrify, appall.

ter·ri·fy·ing·ly (ter′ə fī′ing lē), *adv.* in a terrifying manner: *Aunt Kate yelled terrifyingly from the back of the hall "I'm going to tell your mother"* (Time). *It includes some terrifyingly vivid writing* (Anthony West). *Much refuse from fission is low-level and short-lived but about one-third of it is terrifyingly radioactive* (Newsweek).

ter·rig·e·nous (tə rij′ə nəs), *adj.* **1.** produced by the earth. **2.** *Geology.* of or having to do with marine deposits from the neighboring land. [< Latin *terrigenus* (with English *-ous*) < *terra* earth + *gen-*, root of *gignere* beget]

ter·rine (te rēn′), *n.* **1.** a bowllike earthenware vessel with a cover, and handles on either side: *As the waitress brought in a great terrine of potato soup, the boss asked me if I had eaten* (New Yorker). **2.** the contents of such a vessel. [early form of *tureen*]

ter·ri·to·ri·al (ter′ə tôr′ē əl, -tōr′-), *adj.* **1.** of or having to do with territory or land: *The purchase of Louisiana was a valuable territorial addition to the United States. An actual invasion of our territorial rights* (George Washington). **2.** of a particular territory or district; restricted to a particular district: *The gods . . . were local and territorial divinities* (Joseph Priestley). —**Syn. 2.** local, sectional.

Ter·ri·to·ri·al (ter′ə tôr′ē əl, -tōr′-), *adj.* **1.** of a United States Territory: *a Territorial legislature, Territorial laws.* **2.** *British.* organized for home defense. —*n. British.* a soldier of the Territorial Army.

Territorial Army, 1. the portion of the British Army auxiliary to the regular army, especially for home defense. **2.** of the Territorial Army.

ter·ri·to·ri·al·ism (ter′ə tôr′ē ə liz′əm, -tōr′-), *n.* **1.** a theory that gives predominance in a state to the landed class; landlordism. **2.** the theory of church government holding that ecclesiastical supremacy is inherently a prerogative of the civil power; territorial system.

ter·ri·to·ri·al·ist (ter′ə tôr′ē ə list, -tōr′-), *n.* an advocate of territorialism.

ter·ri·to·ri·al·i·ty (ter′ə tôr′ē al′ə tē, -tōr′-), *n.* territorial quality, condition, position, or status.

ter·ri·to·ri·al·i·za·tion (ter′ə tôr′ē ə lə zā′shən, -tōr′-), *n.* **1.** a territorializing. **2.** a being territorialized.

ter·ri·to·ri·al·ize (ter′ə tôr′ē ə līz, -tōr′-), *v.t.,* **-ized, -iz·ing. 1.** to make territorial. **2.** to associate with or allocate to a particular territory or district. **3.** to make larger by increasing the territory of.

ter·ri·to·ri·al·ly (ter′ə tôr′ē ə lē, -tōr′-), *adv.* in respect to territory; as to territory.

territorial system, territorialism.

territorial waters, the waters off the coastline of a state over which the state exercises jurisdiction: *Canada proposed that the limit of territorial waters should be six miles, with an additional six miles of exclusive fishing rights for the coastal State* (Manchester Guardian Weekly).

ter·ri·to·ry (ter′ə tôr′ē, -tōr′-), *n., pl.* **-ries. 1.** land; region: *to map an unexplored territory from the air. Much territory in Africa is desert.* **2.** land belonging to a government; land under the rule of a distant government: *Gibraltar is British territory.* **3.** a region assigned to a salesman or agent. **4.** the facts investigated by some branch of science or learning: *the territory of biochemistry.* **5.** an area within definite boundaries, such as a nesting ground, in which an animal lives and from which it keeps out others of its kind. [< Latin *territōrium*, apparently < *terra* land] —**Syn. 1.** tract, area. **2.** dominion. **4.** field.

Ter·ri·to·ry (ter′ə tôr′ē, -tōr′-), *n., pl.* **-ries. 1.** *U.S.* a district not admitted as a State but having its own lawmaking body: *Hawaii and Alaska were once Territories.* **2.** a district with a somewhat similar status elsewhere, as in Australia or Canada. *Abbr.:* Terr. [< *territory*]

ter·ror (ter′ər), *n.* **1.** great fear: *a child's terror of the dark.* **2.** a cause of great fear: *Pirates were once the terror of the sea. There is no terror, Cassius, in your threats* (Shakespeare). **3.** *Informal.* a person or thing that causes much trouble and unpleasantness: *What an awful person! She must be a holy terror to live with* (Sinclair Lewis). [< Latin *terror* < *terrēre* to terrify] —**Syn. 1.** fright, alarm, dread, consternation.

Ter·ror (ter′ər), *n.* **1.** a period when a community lives in fear of death or violence because of the methods used by a political party or group to win or keep power, as the Reign of Terror in France. **2.** a group or movement using such methods. [< *terror*]

ter·ror·ise (ter′ə rīz), *v.t.,* **-ised, -is·ing.** *Especially British.* terrorize.

ter·ror·ism (ter′ə riz əm), *n.* **1.** a terrorizing; the use of terror. **2.** a condition of fear and submission produced by frightening people. **3.** a method of opposing a government internally through the use of terror.

Ter·ror·ist (ter′ər ist), *n.* **1.** any of various political extremists in Russia during the latter 1800's and early 1900's. **2.** an agent or active supporter of the revolutionary tribunal during the Reign of Terror in France. [< French *terroriste* < Latin *terror* terror + French *-iste* -ist]

ter·ror·ist (ter′ər ist), *n.* a person who uses or favors terrorism: *Venezuelan terrorists attacked a prison in Caracas and about 600 prisoners were said to have escaped* (Wall Street Journal). —*adj.* of or by terrorists; terroristic: *Kaunda is already facing terrorist opposition from the African National Congress* (Time). [< *Terrorist*]

ter·ror·is·tic (ter′ə ris′tik), *adj.* using or favoring methods that inspire terror: *We can use our power in these incidents with fine discrimination and refrain from bombings the world could consider terroristic* (Newsweek).

ter·ror·i·za·tion (ter′ər ə zā′shən), *n.* a terrorizing or being terrorized; rule by terror.

ter·ror·ize (ter′ə rīz), *v.t.*, **-ized, -iz·ing. 1.** to fill with terror. **2.** to rule or subdue by causing terror. —**ter′ror·iz′er,** *n.* —**Syn. 1.** terrify. **2.** browbeat, intimidate.

ter·ror·less (ter′ər lis), *adj.* **1.** free from terror. **2.** without terrors.

ter·ror-strick·en (ter′ər strik′ən), *adj.* terrified.

ter·ry (ter′ē), *n., pl.* **-ries.** a rough cotton cloth made of uncut looped yarn. [perhaps < French *tiré* drawn]

terry cloth, terry.

terse (tėrs), *adj.*, **ters·er, ters·est.** brief and to the point (said of writing, speaking, writers, or speakers): *a terse reply.* [< Latin *tersus* clean-cut, burnished, past participle of *tergere* to rub, polish, wipe] —**terse′ly,** *adv.* —**terse′ness,** *n.* —**Syn.** See **concise.**

ter·tial (tėr′shəl), *adj.* of or having to do with the flight feathers on the basal section of a bird's wing. —*n.* a tertial feather. [< Latin *tertius* third + English *-al*[1]]

ter·tian (tėr′shən), *n.* a fever or ague with a bad spell recurring every other day. —*adj.* recurring every other day. [Middle English *(fever) tercian* < Latin *tertiāna (febris)* < *tertius* third]

ter·tian·ship (tėr′shən ship), *n.* the last of three stages or periods of probation, which prepares a member of the Society of Jesus for admission to the final vows. [< Latin *tertiānus* of the third + English *-ship*]

ter·ti·ar·y (tėr′shē er′ē, -shər-), *adj., n., pl.* **-ar·ies.** —*adj.* **1.** of the third order, rank, or formation. **2.** *Chemistry.* **a.** of or having to do with a carbon atom joined to three other carbon atoms in a chain or ring. **b.** resulting from the replacement of three atoms or groups. **3.** tertial.
—*n.* **1.** a tertial feather. **2.** a lay member of the third order of certain monastic fraternities of the Roman Catholic Church, not subject to the strict rule of the regulars. [< Latin *tertiārius,* adjective, of or having to do with a (or the) third < *tertius* third]

Ter·ti·ar·y (tėr′shē er′ē, -shər-), *n., pl.* **-ar·ies,** *adj.* —*n.* **1.** the earlier of the two periods making up the Cenozoic era, immediately following the Mesozoic. During this time the great mountain systems, such as the Alps, Himalayas, Rockies, and Andes, appeared, and rapid development of mammals occurred. **2.** the rocks formed during this period. —*adj.* of or having to do with this period or its rocks.

tertiary root, a branch of a secondary root.

tertiary syphilis, the last stage of syphilis, with severe lesions of skin, bones, brain, etc.

ter·ti·um quid (tėr′shē əm kwid′), a third something; something related in some way to two things but distinct from both; something intermediate between two opposite things. [< Latin *tertium quid* some third thing; translation of Greek *tríton ti*]

ter·ti·us (tėr′shē əs), *adj.* **1.** third (used in prescriptions). **2.** (in some English schools) designating the youngest of three boys of the same surname: *Smith tertius hit the ball* (London Times). [< Latin *tertius* third]

ter·va·lent (tėr vā′lənt), *adj. Chemistry.* **1.** trivalent. **2.** having three valences. [< Latin *ter* thrice + English *-valent*]

Ter·y·lene (ter′ə lēn), *n. British Trademark.* Dacron.

ter·za ri·ma (ter′tsä rē′mä), an Italian form of iambic verse consisting of ten-syllable or eleven-syllable lines arranged in tercets, the middle line of each tercet rhyming with the first and third lines of the following tercet (*aba, bcb, cdc,* etc.). Dante's *Divine Comedy* and Shelley's *Ode to the West Wind* are in terza rima. [< Italian *terza rima* < *terza* third + *rima* rhyme]

ter·zet (tert′set), *n.* terzetto.

ter·zet·to (ter tset′tō), *n., pl.* **-ti** (-tē). *Music.* a trio, especially a vocal trio. [< Italian *terzetto.* Doublet of TERCET.]

Tes·la coil (tes′lə), an air-core transformer used to produce high-frequency alternating or oscillating currents. [< Nikola *Tesla,* 1856-1943, an American electrician and inventor born in Croatia]

Tesla current, a current generated by the Tesla coil.

tes·sel·la (tes′ə lə), *n., pl.* **-lae** (-lē). a small tessera or block, as in mosaic. [< Latin *tessela,* variant of *tessera;* see TESSERA]

tes·sel·late (*v.* tes′ə lāt; *adj.* tes′ə lit, -lāt), *v.,* **-lat·ed, -lat·ing,** *adj.* —*v.t.* to make of small squares or blocks, or in a checkered pattern. —*adj.* made in small squares or blocks or in a checkered pattern. [< Medieval Latin *tessellare* (with English *-ate*[1]) < Latin *tessella,* variant of *tessera;* see TESSERA]

Tessellated Floor

tes·sel·la·tion (tes′ə lā′shən), *n.* **1. a.** the act or art of tessellating. **b.** tessellated condition. **2.** a piece of tessellated work.

tes·ser·a (tes′ər ə), *n., pl.* **tes·ser·ae** (tes′ə-rē). **1.** a small piece of marble, glass, or the like, used in mosaic work. **2.** a small square of bone, wood, or the like, used in ancient times as a token, tally, ticket, die, etc. [< Latin *tessera* (originally) a cube < Greek *téssera* four (because of the four corners)]

tes·si·tur·a (tes′ə tůr′ə), *n. Music.* the part of the total compass of a melody or voice part in which most of its tones lie; range. [< Italian *tessitura* texture]

test[1] (test), *n.* **1.** an examination; trial: *People who want to drive an automobile must pass a test.* **2.** a means of trial: *Trouble is a test of character.* **3.** *Chemistry.* **a.** the examination of a substance to see what it is or what it contains. **b.** the process or substance used in such an examination. **4.** a cupel used in assaying or refining precious metals. **b.** examination by a test or cupel. **5.** *British.* a test match.
—*adj.* **1.** of or having to do with a test: *There are other test issues* (New York Times). **2.** taken, done, or made as a test: *a test specimen, test laws.*
—*v.t.* to put to a test; try out: *He tested Al's honesty by leaving money on the table.* [< Old French *test* vessel used in assaying < Latin *testū* earthen vessel, variant of *testa;* see TESTA]
—**Syn.** *n.* **1.** See **trial.**

test[2] (test), *n.* **1.** *Zoology.* the shell; hard covering of certain animals. **2.** *Botany.* testa. [< Latin *testa;* see TESTA]

Test., Testament.

tes·ta (tes′tə), *n., pl.* **-tae** (-tē). **1.** *Botany.* the hard outside coat of a seed. See **embryo** for picture. **2.** *Zoology.* test[2]. [< Latin *testa;* earthenware (pot)] —**Syn. 1.** integument.

test·a·bil·i·ty (tes′tə bil′ə tē), *n.* the quality or state of being testable.

test·a·ble (tes′tə bəl), *adj.* that can be tested: *The higher-powered institutions are committed to testable information and techniques* (Harper's).

tes·ta·cean (tes tā′shən), *adj.* of or belonging to an order of shell-covered rhizopods. —*n.* a testacean animal. [< New Latin *Testacea* the order name (< Latin *testāceus* covered with a shell < *testa* testa) + English *-an*]

tes·ta·ceous (tes tā′shəs), *adj.* **1.** of the nature or substance of a shell or shells. **2.** having a hard shell. **3.** *Biology.* of a dull brownish-red, brownish-yellow, or reddish-brown color. [< Latin *testāceus* (with English *-ous*); see TESTACEAN]

tes·ta·cy (tes′tə sē), *n.* the leaving of a will at death.

Tes·ta·ment (tes′tə mənt), *n.* **1.** a main division of the Bible; the Old Testament or the New Testament. **2.** the New Testament. **3.** a copy of the New Testament. [< Latin *testāmentum* < *testārī;* see TESTATE]

tes·ta·ment (tes′tə mənt), *n.* **1.** written instructions telling what to do with a person's property after his death. **2.** expression; manifestation: *There is here no . . . reflection of his tender regard for Thomas Hardy, though there is many a testament of friendship* (Canadian Forum). **3.** a statement of beliefs or principles: [*He*] *laid down his personal testament of what Canadian Conservation meant to him* (Maclean's). **4.** (in the Bible) a covenant between God and man; dispensation. [< *Testament*]

tes·ta·men·ta·ry (tes′tə men′tər ē, -trē), *adj.* **1.** of or having to do with a testament or will. **2.** given, done, or appointed by a testament or will. **3.** in a testament or will.

tes·tate (tes′tāt), *adj.* having made and left a valid will: *He clearly desired when he died to die testate and not intestate* (London Times). —*n.* a person who has left a valid will. [< Latin *testātus,* past participle of *testārī* make a will < *testis* witness]

tes·ta·tor (tes′tā tər, tes tā′-), *n.* **1.** a person who makes a will. **2.** a person who has died leaving a valid will.

tes·ta·trix (tes tā′triks), *n., pl.* **-tri·ces** (-trə sēz). **1.** a woman who makes a will. **2.** a woman who has died leaving a valid will.

test ban, a ban on testing, especially of nuclear weapons.

test bed, 1. a base to hold equipment for testing: . . . *the difficulties . . . uncovered by operating experience with prototype reactors in ground test beds* (Scientific American). **2.** an aircraft, rocket, etc., to test engines.

test blank, a form containing a test and blank spaces to fill in answers.

test case, a legal case whose outcome will be used as precedent: *He had been one of the most active in pushing a test case that established the right of Negroes to vote in the Georgia primaries* (New Yorker).

test drive, a ride taken in an automobile to test its performance: *It's not easy to choose, we know, but take your choice—and then let a test drive convince you that here is everything that you want in a car* (Cape Times).

test-drive (test′drīv′), *v.t.*, **-drove, -driv·en, -driv·ing.** to drive (a motor vehicle) for testing purposes: *Every . . . engine is run for seven hours at full throttle before installation, and each car is test-driven for hundreds of miles over varying road surfaces* (Harper's).

tes·te (tes′tē), *n.* the witness being (the person or authority specified). [< Latin *testē,* ablative of *testis* witness]

test·ee (tes tē′), *n.* a person who takes a test.

test·er[1] (tes′tər), *n.* a person or thing that tests. [< *test*[1], verb + *-er*[1]] —**Syn.** examiner.

tes·ter[2] (tes′tər), *n.* a canopy, especially one over a bed. [Middle English *testere,* probably < Old French *testre* headboard of a bed < *teste* head < Vulgar Latin *testa* head (in Latin, earthen pot)]

tes·ter[3] (tes′tər), *n.* **1.** the teston of Henry VIII, especially as debased or depreciated. **2.** *British Informal.* a sixpence. [earlier *testor* < *testorne,* alteration of *teston*]

tes·tes (tes′tēz), *n.* the plural of **testis.**

test-fire (test′fīr′), *v.t.*, **-fired, -fir·ing.** to fire (a rocket, nuclear weapon, etc.) as a test: *The Navy has been test-firing guided missiles from subs since 1955* (Newsweek).

test flight, a flight in which the performance of an aircraft, rocket, etc., is tested: *The experimental plane, the X-15, designed to carry man to the edge of outer space, began its series of power test flights* (Science News Letter).

test-fly (test′flī′), *v.t.*, **-flew, -flown, -fly·ing.** to subject to a test flight: *Dr. Wernher von Braun . . . proudly announced . . . that the test was "100 per cent successful," and the first Saturn will be test-flown in the summer* (Newsweek).

tes·ti·cle (tes′tə kəl), *n.* one of the glands of a male animal that secrete the fertilizing element; testis. [< Latin *testiculus* (diminutive) < *testis* testis]

tes·tic·u·lar (tes tik′yə lər), *adj.* of or having to do with a testicle or testis.

tes·tic·u·late (tes tik′yə lit, -lāt), *adj.* formed like a testicle.

tes·ti·fi·ca·tion (tes′tə fə kā′shən), *n.* a testifying; testimony. [< Latin *testificātiō, -ōnis* < *testificārī;* see TESTIFY]

tes·ti·fi·er (tes′tə fī′ər), *n.* a person who gives testimony; witness: *Because he understands, the testifier is involved in the life around him* (London Times).

tes·ti·fy (tes′tə fī), *v.,* **-fied, -fy·ing.** —*v.i.* **1.** to give evidence; bear witness: *The excellence of Shakespeare's plays testifies to his genius.* **2.** to give evidence under oath in a court of law. **3.** to bear testimony: *In vain thy creatures testify of thee* (Cowper). —*v.t.* **1.** to give evidence of; bear witness to: *The firm testified their appreciation of her* *work by raising her pay.* **2.** to declare under oath in a law court. **3.** to declare solemnly; affirm. [< Latin *testificārī* < *testis* witness + *facere* to make]

tes·ti·ly (tes′tə lē), *adv.* in a testy manner.

tes·ti·mo·ni·al (tes′tə mō′nē əl), *n.* **1.** a certificate of character, conduct, qualifications, value, etc.; recommendation: *The boy looking for a job has testimonials from his teachers and former employer. Advertisements of patent medicines often have testimonials from people who have used them.* **2.** something given or done to show esteem, admiration, gratitude, etc.: *The members of the church collected money for a testimonial to their retiring pastor.*
—*adj.* given or done as a testimonial: *a testimonial letter, a testimonial dinner.*
—**Syn.** *n.* **1.** credential, voucher.

tes·ti·mo·ni·al·ize (tes′tə mō′nē ə līz), *v.t.*, **-ized, -iz·ing. 1.** to furnish with a recommendation. **2.** to honor with a testimonial: *Georgia Political Boss Roy V. Harris . . . was being testimonialized for 35 years of service to his state* (Time).

tes·ti·mo·ny (tes′tə mō′nē), *n., pl.* **-nies. 1.** a statement used for evidence or proof: *A witness gave testimony that Mr. Doe was home at 9 p.m.* **2.** evidence: *The pupils presented their teacher with a watch in testimony of their respect and affection.* **3.** an open declaration or profession of one's faith. **4.** *Archaic.* the Ten Commandments.
testimonies, the precepts of God; the divine law: *to keep the Lord's testimonies and statutes.*
[< Latin *testimōnium* < *testis* witness]
—**Syn. 1, 2.** proof. See **evidence.**

tes·ti·ness (tes′tē nis), *n.* the quality or state of being testy.

test·ing (tes′ting), *n.* the act of subjecting to a test of any kind: *A philosophy, which has for its object the trial and testing of the weights and measures themselves* (Samuel Taylor Coleridge). —*adj.* **1.** having to do with or used for experimentation: *a testing station, testing mechanisms.* **2.** that tests or puts to the test: *a testing crisis.*

tes·tis (tes′tis), *n., pl.* **-tes.** testicle. [< Latin *testis* (originally) witness (because it bears witness to man's virility)]

test-mar·ket (test′mär′kit), *v.t.* to test by putting on sale or distributing in certain areas: *Margarine made from one-third butter and two-thirds safflower oil is being test-marketed* (Wall Street Journal).

Test or **test match,** *British.* a contest or tournament for a cricket or Rugby championship.

tes·ton (tes′tən), *n.* **1.** any of various silver coins usually bearing a head, as one of certain early French silver coins or the English shilling of Henry VIII. **2.** *Obsolete.* a sixpence. [< Middle French *teston* < Italian *testone* (augmentative) < *testa* head < Vulgar Latin, shell, (in Latin, testa, pot) (because the coin had a head or portrait on one face). Compare TESTER[3].]

tes·toon (tes tün′), *n.* teston.

tes·tos·ter·one (tes tos′tə rōn), *n.* a hormone obtained from the testicles of bulls or produced synthetically. *Formula:* $C_{19}H_{28}O_2$

test paper, 1. *U.S.* a paper on which a person taking a test has written his answers. **2.** *Chemistry.* litmus paper.

test pattern, a standard, fixed picture, usually of straight lines and circles, broadcast by a television transmitter to test and aid in the adjustment of broadcasting or receiving devices.

test pilot, a pilot employed to test new or experimental aircraft by subjecting them to greater than normal stress: *The American test pilot Scott Crossfield will take a brand-new missile on the first flight of a series in which it will eventually reach 3,600 miles per hour* (New Scientist).

test-pi·lot (test′pī′lət), *v.t.* to test (aircraft) as a test pilot: *He was soon recalled to test-pilot single-seater fighter planes* (New York Times). —*v.i.* to be a test pilot; work as a test pilot: *Men risk and sometimes find death in many ways . . . mountain climbing, test-piloting, and war* (Wall Street Journal).

test range, 1. an area set aside for tests. **2.** the extent of any test.

test site, a place where anything is tested.

test stand, a device to hold something that is being tested, as a rocket engine.

test track, 1. a course for testing motor vehicles: *A jet-powered car will roar down a cement test track at more than 200 miles per hour* (Science News Letter). **2.** rails on which a vehicle moves at high speed to imitate flying conditions, such as rapid acceleration.

test tube, a thin glass tube closed at one end, used in making chemical tests: *When we think of a scientist today, we imagine a person surrounded with test tubes, delicate measuring instruments, and bottles of strange substances* (Beauchamp, Mayfield, and West).

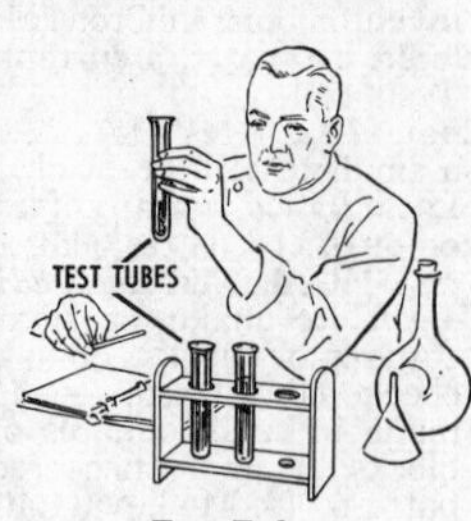

Test Tubes

test-tube (test′tüb′, -tyüb′), *adj.* **1.** of, having to do with, or contained in a test tube: *a test-tube experiment, test-tube cultures.* **2.** of or by chemical synthesis; synthetic: *a test-tube product.* **3.** born through artificial insemination: *test-tube cattle.*

tes·tu·di·nal (tes tü′də nəl, -tyü′-), *adj.* of, having to do with, or resembling a tortoise or tortoise shell.

tes·tu·di·nar·i·ous (tes tü′də nãr′ē əs, -tyü′-), *adj.* testudinal.

tes·tu·di·nate (tes tü′də nit, -nāt; -tyü′-), *adj.* **1.** arched; vaulted. **2.** of or having to do with a tortoise or tortoises. —*n.* a tortoise or turtle. [< Latin *testūdinātus* arched, vaulted (of a roof) < *testūdō, -inis* tortoise; see TESTUDO]

tes·tu·do (tes tü′dō, -tyü′-), *n., pl.* **-di·nes** (-də nēz). **1. a.** (among the ancient Romans) a movable shelter with an arched roof, for protection in siege operations. **b.** a shelter formed by troops overlapping their shields above their heads. **2.** some other shelter. [< Latin *testūdō, -inis* (literally) tortoise < *testa* shell, testa]

test well, a well made to test a site for oil.

tes·ty (tes′tē), *adj.*, **-ti·er, -ti·est.** easily irritated; impatient: *a very unpleasant and testy old man.* [Middle English *testyf* headstrong < Anglo-French *testif* < *teste* head < Vulgar Latin *testa* pot] —**Syn.** irascible, peevish, petulant, cross.

Tet (tet), *n.* (in Vietnam) the lunar New Year. [< Annamese *tet*]

te·tan·ic (ti tan′ik), *adj.* having to do with tetanus.

tet·a·nize (tet′ə nīz), *v.t.*, **-nized, -niz·ing.** to cause (a muscle) to have tetanic spasms.

tet·a·nus (tet′ə nəs), *n.* **1. a.** a disease caused by certain bacilli usually entering the body through wounds, characterized by violent stiffness of many muscles, and even death. Tetanus of the lower jaw is called lockjaw. **b.** the bacillus that causes this disease. **2.** a condition of prolonged contraction of a muscle. [< Latin *tetanus* < Greek *tetanós* < *teínein* to stretch. Doublet of TETANY.]

tet·a·ny (tet′ə nē), *n.* a disease characterized by spasms of the muscles. [< French *tétanie,* or new Latin *tetania* < Latin *tetanus.* Doublet of TETANUS.]

te·tar·to·he·dral (ti tär′tō hē′drəl), *adj.* (of a crystal) having one fourth of the number of faces required by the highest degree of symmetry belonging to its system. [< Greek *tétartos* fourth (< *tetra-;* see TETRA-) + *hédra* side, base + English *-al*[1]]

tetched (techt), *adj. U.S. Dialect.* slightly crazy; touched. Also, **teched.**

tetch·i·ly (tech′ə lē), *adv.* in a tetchy manner; irritably.

tetch·i·ness (tech′ē nis), *n.* the state of being tetchy; irritability.

tetch·y (tech′ē), *adj.*, **tetch·i·er, tetch·i·est.** irritable; touchy. Also, **techy.**

tête-à-tête (tāt′ə tāt′, tet′ə tet′), *adv.* two together in private: *They dined tête-à-tête.*
—*adj.* of or for two people in private.
—*n.* **1.** a private conversation between two persons. **2.** an S-shaped seat built so that two people can sit facing one another: *And between the columns which ranged away toward three separate entrances . . . were lamps, statuary, rugs, palms, chairs, divans, tête-à-têtes—a prodigal display* (Theodore Dreiser).
[< French *tête-à-tête* (literally) head to head; *tête* < Vulgar Latin *testa* (in Latin, pot)]

tête-bêche (tet′besh′), *adj.* (of two adjacent stamps) printed upside down or sideways in relation to each other. [< French *tête* head + *bêche,* reduction of *béchevet* double head of a bed < *bes-* twice (< Latin *bis*) + *chevet* head of a bed]

tête-de-nè·gre (tet′də ne′grə), *n.* **1.** a curled or knotted woolen cloth. **2.** a dark brown. [< French *tête-de-nègre* (literally) Negro head]

tête-de-pont (tet′də pôN′), *n., pl.* **têtes-de-pont** (tet′də pôN′). a bridgehead. [< French *tête de pont* (literally) bridge head]

teth (teth), *n.* the ninth letter of the Hebrew alphabet. [< Hebrew *ṭēth*]

teth·er (teᴛʜ′ər), *n.* **1.** a rope or chain for fastening an animal so that it can graze only within certain limits: *The cow had broken her tether and was in the cornfield.* **2.** something that acts as a chain or rope to limit ability, resources, action, etc.: *We soon find the shortness of our tether* (Alexander Pope).
at the end of one's tether, at the end of one's resources or endurance: *She is capable also of doing a little mothering of her son when he seems at the end of his tether* (London Times).
—*v.t.* to fasten with a tether: *The horse is tethered to the stake.*
[< Scandinavian (compare Old Icelandic *tjothr*)]

teth·er·ball (teᴛʜ′ər bôl′), *n.* **1.** a game played by two persons with a ball fastened by a cord to the top of a tall post. The object of each person is to hit the ball so as to wind the cord around the post, in one direction or the other. *Among the other standard sports recommended for women and girls by the American Recreation Society were . . . soccer, speedball, tetherball* (Stacy V. Jones). **2.** the ball used in this game.

Te·thys (tē′this), *n. Greek Mythology.* the wife of Oceanus, daughter of Uranus and Gaea.

tetr-, *combining form.* the form of **tetra-** sometimes before vowels, as in *tetrarch.*

tet·ra (tet′rə), *n.* any of a group of small, brilliantly colored fishes of the upper Amazon region, such as the neon tetra. [< New Latin *Tetra(gonopterus),* genus name < Greek *tetrágōnon* tetragon + *pterón* wing]

tetra-, *combining form.* four: *Tetrahedron = a plane figure having four sides.* Also, sometimes **tetr-** before vowels. [< Greek *tetra-,* for *téttares,* variant of *téssares*]

tet·ra·ba·sic (tet′rə bā′sik), *adj. Chemistry.* **1.** (of an acid) having four hydrogen atoms that can be replaced by basic atoms or radicals. **2.** having four atoms or radicals of a univalent metal. **3.** containing four basic hydroxyl (-OH) radicals.

tet·ra·brach (tet′rə brak), *n.* (in Greek and Latin prosody) a word or foot of four short syllables. [< Greek *tetrábrachys* < *tetra-* tetra- + *brachýs* short (syllable)]

tet·ra·bran·chi·ate (tet′rə brang′kē it, -āt), *adj.* of or belonging to an order of cephalopods that have two pairs of gills and an external shell, as the pearly nautilus and certain fossil mollusks.
—*n.* a tetrabranchiate cephalopod.
[< New Latin *Tetrabranchiata* the order name (< Greek *tetra-* tetra- + *bránchia* gills)]

tet·ra·caine hydrochloride (tet′rə kān), a drug used as a local anesthetic in the eye, nose, throat, and spinal canal; Pontocain Hydrochloride. *Formula:* $C_{15}H_{24}N_2O_2 \cdot HCl$

tet·ra·car·pel·lar·y (tet′rə kär′pə ler′ē), *adj. Botany.* having four carpels.

tet·ra·chlo·rid (tet′rə klôr′id, -klōr′-), *n.* tetrachloride.

tet·ra·chlo·ride (tet′rə klôr′īd, -id; -klōr′-), *n.* a compound containing four atoms of chlorine combined with another element or radical.

tet·ra·chlo·ro·eth·yl·ene (tet′rə klôr′ō-eth′ə lēn, -klōr′-), *n.* perchlorethylene.

tet·ra·chord (tet′rə kôrd), *n. Music.* **1.** a diatonic scale series of four notes, the first and last being a perfect fourth apart (the most important unit of Greek melody and music theory); half an octave. **2.** an ancient instrument with four strings. [< Latin *tetrachordon* < Greek *tetráchordon* < *tetrachordós* producing four tones < *tetra-* tetra- + *chordḗ* string; (originally) gut]

tet·ra·chor·dal (tet′rə kôr′dəl), *adj.* having to do with a tetrachord; consisting of tetrachords.

tet·ra·chot·o·mous (tet′rə kot′ə məs), *adj.* **1.** divided or dividing into four parts. **2.**

branching into four parts; giving off shoots by fours.

tet·ra·chot·o·my (tet′rə kot′ə mē), *n., pl.* **-mies.** division into four parts, classes, branches, etc. [< Greek *tétracha* in four parts (< *tetra-* tetra-) + *tomíā* a cutting, division]

tet·ra·chro·mat·ic (tet′rə krō mat′ik), *adj.* **1.** having or showing four colors. **2.** having to do with four colors. **3.** using four colors.

te·trac·id (te tras′id), *Chemistry.* —*adj.* **1.** (of a base or alcohol) having four hydroxyl (-OH) groups that may react with the hydrogen of an acid to form water, leaving a salt or ester. **2.** having four acid atoms of hydrogen per molecule. —*n.* a base or an alcohol having four replaceable hydroxyl (-OH) groups.

tet·ra·cy·clic (tet′rə sī′klik, -sik′lik), *adj.* **1.** passing through or having four cycles. **2.** *Chemistry.* having four rings in the structural formula. **3.** *Botany.* having four whorls of floral organs.

tet·ra·cy·cline (tet′rə sī′klin), *n.* an antibiotic used in treating a wide variety of diseases, including pneumonia, tuberculosis, meningitis, and dysentery: *Severe disorders of the liver and pancreas attributed to the antibiotic tetracycline have been discovered in the United States in five pregnant women being treated for inflammation of the kidney* (Observer). *Formula:* $C_{22}H_{24}N_2O_8$ [< *tetra-* + *cycl-* + *-ine*[2] (because it contains four benzene rings)]

Tet·ra·cyn (tet′rə sin), *n. Trademark.* tetracycline.

tet·rad (tet′rad), *n.* **1.** a sum, group, or set of four. **2.** *Chemistry.* an element, atom, or radical with a valence of four. **3.** *Biology.* a group of four chromosomes formed in various organisms when a pair of chromosomes splits longitudinally during meiosis. **4.** *Botany.* a group of four cells, as of spores or pollen grains. [< Greek *tetrás, -ádos* (a group of) four < *tetra-* tetra-]

tet·ra·dac·tyl (tet′rə dak′təl), *adj.* having four fingers, claws, toes, etc., on each limb. [< Greek *tetradáktylos* < *tetra-* tetra- + *dáktylos* finger, toe]

te·trad·ic (te trad′ik), *adj.* of or having to do with a tetrad.

tet·ra·drachm (tet′rə dram′), *n.* a silver coin of ancient Greece, of the value of four drachmas: *Baldwin gave £105 for three Greek silver tetradrachms* (London Times).

te·trad·y·mite (te trad′ə mīt), *n. Mineralogy.* a telluride of bismuth, found in pale, steel-gray laminae with a bright, metallic luster. *Formula:* Bi_2Te_3 [< German *Tetradymit* < Greek *tetrádymos* fourfold + German *-it* -ite[1]]

tet·ra·dy·na·mous (tet′rə dī′nə məs, -din′ə), *adj. Botany.* having six stamens, four longer, arranged in opposite pairs, and two shorter, inserted lower down (characteristic of flowers of the mustard family). [< New Latin *Tetradynamia* the class name (< Greek *tetra-* tetra- + *dýnamis* power, strength) + English *-ous*]

tet·ra·eth·yl·am·mo·ni·um chloride (tet′rə eth′ə lə mō′nē əm), a crystalline salt used as a drug to block the sympathetic nervous system during surgery, lower blood pressure in treating hypertensive conditions, etc. *Formula:* $C_8H_{20}ClN$

tet·ra·eth·yl lead (tet′rə eth′əl), a poisonous, colorless liquid, used in gasoline to reduce knocking. *Formula:* $Pb(C_2H_5)_4$

tetraethyl pyrophosphate, a crystalline compound, or a solution of it, used as an insecticide against mites and aphids, and in medicine as a stimulant in the treatment of certain diseases of the ocular, bulbar, and sacral nerves. *Formula:* $C_8H_{20}P_2O_7$

tet·ra·flu·o·ride (tet′rə flü′ə rīd, -ər id), *n.* a fluoride with four atoms of fluorine.

tet·ra·fluo·ro·eth·yl·ene (tet′rə flôr′ō-eth′ə lēn, -flü′ər ō-), *n.* a colorless, nonflammable gas used in making heat-resistant and acid-resistant plastics, such as Teflon. *Formula:* $F_2C{:}CF_2$

tet·ra·gon (tet′rə gon), *n.* a figure, especially a plane figure, having four angles and four sides, as a square or diamond. [< Greek *tetrágōnon* quadrangle < *tetra-* tetra- + *gōníā* angle]

te·trag·o·nal (te trag′ə nəl), *adj.* **1.** of or having to do with a tetragon; having four angles. **2.** designating or having to do with a system of crystallization (tetragonal system) in which the three axes are at right angles, the two lateral axes being equal and the vertical of a different length; dimetric.

tet·ra·gram (tet′rə gram), *n.* **1.** a word of four letters, especially the Tetragrammaton. **2.** *Geometry.* a figure formed by four straight lines in a plane and their six points of intersection; quadrilateral. [< Late Greek *tetrágrammon* < Greek *tetra-* tetra- + *grámma* letter]

Tet·ra·gram·ma·ton (tet′rə gram′ə ton), *n.* the mysterious and sacred Hebrew word of four consonants, transliterated YHWH, YHVH, JHWH, or JHVH, standing for the Ineffable Name of God. The vowel points of *Adonai* (Lord) or *Elohim* (God) are assigned to these consonants to indicate that, in pronouncing the word in text, one of the two less sacred names is substituted (though some hold that the vowels properly belong to the name). The name is usually transcribed in English as *Yahweh* or *Jehovah.* [< Greek (*tò*) *tetragrámmaton* (literally) (the word) of four letters < *tetra-* tetra- + *grámma, -atos* letter]

tet·ra·gram·ma·ton (tet′rə gram′ə ton), *n.* a word of four letters used as a symbol. [< *Tetragrammaton*]

tet·ra·he·dral (tet′rə hē′drəl), *adj.* **1.** of or having to do with a tetrahedron; having four sides. **2.** *Crystallography.* belonging to a division of the isometric system of which the regular tetrahedron is the characteristic form. —**tet′ra·he′dral·ly,** *adv.*

tet·ra·he·drite (tet′rə hē′drīt), *n. Mineralogy.* native sulfide of antimony and copper, with various elements sometimes replacing one or the other of these, often occurring in tetrahedral crystals. [< German *Tetraëdrit* < Greek *tetráedron* (see TETRAHEDRON) + German *-it* -ite[1]]

tet·ra·he·dron (tet′rə hē′drən), *n., pl.* **-drons, -dra** (-drə). *Geometry.* a solid bounded by four plane sides. The most common tetrahedron is a pyramid whose base and three sides are equilateral triangles. [< Greek *tetráedron* < *tetra-* tetra- + *hédra* seat, base]

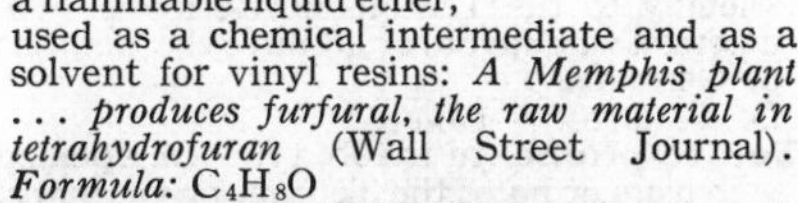
Tetrahedron

tet·ra·hy·dro·fu·ran (tet′rə hī′drō fyůr′an), *n.* a flammable liquid ether, used as a chemical intermediate and as a solvent for vinyl resins: *A Memphis plant . . . produces furfural, the raw material in tetrahydrofuran* (Wall Street Journal). *Formula:* C_4H_8O

te·tral·o·gy (te tral′ə jē), *n., pl.* **-gies. 1.** a series of four connected dramas, operas, etc. **2.** (in ancient Greece) a series of four dramas, three tragic (the trilogy) and one satiric, exhibited at Athens at the festival of Dionysus. [< Greek *tetralogíā* < *tetra-* tetra + *logíā* -logy]

tetralogy of Fallot, Fallot's tetralogy.

tet·ra·mer (tet′rə mər), *n.* a chemical compound in which four molecules of the same substance are produced by polymerization.

te·tram·er·al (te tram′ər əl), *adj.* tetramerous.

te·tram·er·ous (te tram′ər əs), *adj.* **1.** having, consisting of, or characterized by four parts. **2.** *Botany.* (of a flower) having four members in each whorl (generally written *4-merous*). **3.** *Zoology.* having tarsi with four joints.
[< New Latin *tetramerus* (with English *-ous*) < Greek *tetramerḗs* < *tetra-* tetra- + *méros* part]

te·tram·e·ter (te tram′ə tər), *Prosody.* —*adj.* consisting of four measures or feet. —*n.* **1.** a line of verse having four measures or feet. *Example:* "The stág / at éve / had drúnk / his fíll." **2.** (in Greek and Latin verse) a line having four dipodies (eight feet), in trochaic, iambic, or anapestic meter. [< Latin *tetrametrus* < Greek *tetrámetron* < *tetra-* tetra- + *métron* measure, -meter]

tet·ra·morph (tet′rə môrf), *n.* a composite figure combining the symbols of the four Evangelists. It is represented as having wings covered with eyes, and standing on fiery winged wheels. [< Greek *tetrámorphos,* adjective, of or having four forms < *tetra-* tetra- + *morphḗ* form]

tet·ra·mor·phic (tet′rə môr′fik), *adj.* occurring in four distinct forms; exhibiting tetramorphism.

tet·ra·mor·phism (tet′rə môr′fiz əm), *n.* the occurrence in four different forms of a crystalline substance.

te·tran·drous (te tran′drəs), *adj. Botany.* (of a flower) having four stamens. [< *tetra-* + Greek *anḗr, andrós* male, man + English *-ous*]

tet·ra·ni·tro·meth·ane (tet′rə nī′trə-meth′ān), *n.* a colorless, poisonous liquid insoluble in water, derived from the combination of fuming nitric acid with benzene, acetic anhydride, or acetylene, and used for rocket fuel, as an oxidant, etc. *Formula:* $C(NO_2)_4$

tet·ra·on·id (tet′rə on′id), *adj.* belonging to a family of gallinaceous birds including the grouse and allied forms.
—*n.* a tetraonid bird.
[< New Latin *Tetraonidae* the family name < Latin *tetrāō, -ōnis* grouse < Greek *tetráōn*]

tet·ra·pet·al·ous (tet′rə pet′ə ləs), *adj. Botany.* having four petals.

tet·ra·phyl·lous (tet′rə fil′əs), *adj. Botany.* having four leaves or leaflets. [< *tetra-* + Greek *phýllon* leaf + English *-ous*]

tet·ra·ploid (tet′rə ploid), *adj.* having a chromosome number that is four times the haploid number: *Tetraploid snaps* [*snapdragons*] *are those that have been treated with colchicine to give them extremely large flowers, husky growth habit and good foliage* (New York Times). —*n.* an organism or cell having four times the haploid number of chromosomes: *Tetraploids are the result of recent genetic research and practical flower breeding* (Gordon Morrison). [< *tetra-* + *-ploid,* as in *haploid*]

tet·ra·pod (tet′rə pod), *n.* **1.** an animal having four limbs; a quadruped. **2.** a very large concrete block with four legs that can be interlocked with another, used especially in building breakwaters and jetties.
—*adj.* having four limbs; quadruped: *tetrapod mammals.*
[< Greek *tetrápous, -podos,* adjective, having four feet < *tetra-* tetra- + *poús, podós* foot]

tet·ra·pod·ic (tet′rə pod′ik), *adj.* having four metrical feet.

te·trap·o·dy (te trap′ə dē), *n., pl.* **-dies.** *Prosody.* **1.** a group of four metrical feet in a line of verse. **2.** a line of verse having four metrical feet. [< Greek *tetrapodíā* < *tetrápous, -podos;* see TETRAPOD]

te·trap·o·lis (te trap′ə lis), *n.* a group of four cities or towns; political division consisting of four cities. [< Greek *tetrápolis* < *tetra-* tetra- + *pólis* city]

tet·ra·pol·i·tan (tet′rə pol′ə tən), *adj.* of or having to do with a tetrapolis, or group of four cities.

Tetrapolitan Confession, a confession of faith presented at the Diet of Augsburg in 1530 by the representatives of the four cities of Constance, Lindau, Memmingen, and Strassburg.

te·trap·ter·ous (te trap′tər əs), *adj.* **1.** *Entomology.* having four wings. **2.** *Botany.* having four winglike appendages, as certain fruits. [< New Latin *tetrapterus* (with English *-ous*) < Greek *tetrápteros* < *tetra-* tetra- + *pterón* wing]

tet·ra·py·lon (tet′rə pī′lon), *n.* a pylon or arch with four gates, marking the intersection of two avenues, especially in ancient Rome.

tet·rarch (tet′rärk, tē′trärk), *n.* **1.** the ruler of a part (originally a fourth part) of a subject country or province in the ancient Roman Empire. **2.** any of various subordinate rulers. **3. a.** a ruler of a fourth part. **b.** one of four joint rulers, directors, or heads.
[< Latin *tetrarchēs* < Greek *tetrárchēs* < *tetra-* tetra- + *árchein* to rule]

tet·rar·chate (tet′rär kāt, tē′trär-), *n.* the office, jurisdiction, government, or territory of a tetrarch.

te·trar·chic (te trär′kik), *adj.* of, having to do with, or belonging to a tetrarch or tetrarchy.

tet·rar·chy (tet′rär kē, tē′trär-), *n., pl.* **-chies. 1.** the government or jurisdiction of a tetrarch; territory governed by a tetrarch. **2.** government by four persons. **3.** a set of four rulers. **4.** a country divided into four governments.

tet·ra·seme (tet′rə sēm′), *n.* a metrical foot consisting of four short syllables. —*adj.* tetrasemic.
[< Greek *tetrásēmos* < *tetra-* tetra- + *sêma, -atos* a sign]

tet·ra·se·mic (tet′rə sē′mik), *adj.* **1.** consisting of four morae or short syllables. **2.** equivalent to four morae or short syllables.

tet·ra·sep·al·ous (tet′rə sep′ə ləs), *adj. Botany.* having four sepals.

tet·ra·sper·mous (tet′rə spėr′məs), *adj. Botany.* four-seeded.

tet·ra·spo·ran·gi·um (tet′rə spô ran′jē əm, -spō-), *n., pl.* **-gi·a** (-jē ə). *Botany.* a sporangium producing or containing a group of four asexual spores, resulting from the division of a mother cell.

tet·ra·spore (tet′rə spôr, -spōr), *n. Botany.* one of a group of four asexual spores, resulting from the division of a mother cell, in certain algae.

tet·ra·stich (tet′rə stik, te tras′tik), *n.* a stanza or poem of four lines. [< Latin *tetrastichon* < Greek *tetrástichon,* neuter of *tetrástichos* having four rows < *tetra-* tetra- + *stíchos* row, line of verse]

tet·ra·stich·ic (tet′rə stik′ik), *adj.* having to do with or constituting a tetrastich or tetrastichs.

te·tras·ti·chous (te tras′tə kəs), *adj. Botany.* **1.** (of flowers) arranged in a spike having four vertical rows. **2.** (of a spike) having the flowers arranged in four vertical rows. [< New Latin *tetrastichus* (with English *-ous*) < Greek *tetrástichos;* see TETRASTICH]

tet·ra·style (tet′rə stīl), *adj.* having four columns in front, as a temple or a portico. —*n.* a tetrastyle structure. [< Latin *tetrastȳlos* < Greek *tetrastȳlos* < *tetra-* tetra- + *stȳlos* pillar, column]

Tetrastyle North Porch of Erechtheum, Athens

tet·ra·syl·lab·ic (tet′rə sə lab′ik), *adj.* consisting of four syllables.

tet·ra·syl·lab·i·cal (tet′rə sə lab′ə kəl), *adj.* tetrasyllabic.

tet·ra·syl·la·ble (tet′rə sil′ə bəl), *n.* a word of four syllables.

tet·ra·tom·ic (tet′rə tom′ik), *adj. Chemistry.* **1.** containing four atoms; consisting of molecules containing four atoms each. **2.** (incorrectly) quadrivalent. **3.** having four atoms or groups that can be replaced. [< *tetr-* + *atomic*]

tet·ra·va·lent (tet′rə vā′lənt, te trav′ə-), *adj. Chemistry.* **1.** having a valence of four; quadrivalent: *An element like carbon whose atom can hold four monovalent atoms in combination is called a tetravalent element* (Parks and Steinbach). **2.** having four different valences; quadrivalent.

te·trax·i·al (te trak′sē əl), *adj.* having four axes. [< *tetra-* + *axial*]

te·trax·ile (te trak′səl, -sīl), *adj.* tetraxial. [< *tetra-* + *axile*]

tet·rode (tet′rōd), *n.* a vacuum tube containing four elements, commonly a cathode, anode (plate), and two grids: *Tetrodes . . . are able to operate at extremely high frequencies* (William C. Vergara). [< *tetr-* + (electr)*ode*]

te·trox·id (te trok′sid), *n.* tetroxide.

te·trox·ide (te trok′sīd, -sid), *n. Chemistry.* an oxide containing four atoms of oxygen in each molecule with another element or radical.

tet·ryl (tet′rəl), *n.* **1.** an explosive used especially to detonate the propelling or bursting charge of artillery shells. *Formula:* $C_7H_5N_5O_8$ **2.** *Chemistry.* butyl.

tet·ter (tet′ər), *n.* any of various itching skin diseases, as eczema and psoriasis. [Old English *teter*]

Teu·cer (tü′sər, tyü′-), *n. Greek Legend.* **1.** the first king of Troy. **2.** the son of Telamon and half brother of Ajax, famous as an archer.

Teu·cri·an (tü′krē ən, tyü′-), *adj.* of or having to do with Teucer or the Trojans. —*n.* a Trojan. [< Latin *Teucer, -crī* Teucer + English *-an*]

teugh (tyüH), *adj. Scottish.* tough. —**teugh′ly,** *adv.* —**teugh′ness,** *n.*

Teut., **1.** Teuton. **2.** Teutonic.

Teu·ton (tü′tən, tyü′-), *n.* **1.** a German. **2.** any member of the group of northern Europeans that speak Germanic languages, including the Germans, Dutch, and Scandinavians. **3.** a member of the Teutones, an ancient Germanic tribe. —*adj.* German; Teutonic; Germanic. [< Latin *Teutonēs,* or *Teutonī,* plural, (originally) a tribe in northern Europe]

Teu·to·nes (tü′tə nēz, tyü′-), *n. pl.* an ancient people of Jutland who in the 100's B.C. devastated Gaul and threatened the Roman republic. [< Latin *Teutonēs;* see TEUTON]

Teu·ton·ic (tü ton′ik, tyü-), *adj.* **1.** of or having to do with the ancient Teutones. **2.** of or having to do with the Germanic languages; Germanic. **3.** of or having to do with the Teutons; German. **4.** of or having to do with the northern European peoples that speak Germanic languages. **5.** Nordic. —*n.* Germanic.

Teu·ton·i·cal·ly (tü ton′ə klē, tyü-), *adv.* in the manner of a Teuton or German; in German style: *Italy is filled with Germans, huddling Teutonically over beer* (New York Times).

Teu·ton·i·cism (tü ton′ə siz əm, tyü-), *n.* **1.** a Teutonic or German character or practice. **2.** a Teutonic or German idiom or expression; Germanism.

Teutonic Knights or **Order,** a military and religious order of German knights founded in Jerusalem about 1190 to spread Christianity and help the needy. Later they helped bring the Baltic Coast and what became Prussia under German rule.

Teu·ton·ism (tü′tə niz əm, tyü′-), *n.* **1.** Teutonic or German feeling and action; spirit of Germany or the Germans. **2.** a Teutonicism.

Teu·ton·ist (tü′tə nist, tyü′-), *n.* **1.** a person versed in the history of the Teutonic races or languages. **2.** a person whose writings have a Teutonic character or style.

Teu·ton·i·za·tion (tü′tə nə zā′shən, tyü′-), *n.* the act of Teutonizing.

Teu·ton·ize (tü′tə nīz, tyü′-), *v.t., v.i.,* **-ized, -iz·ing.** to make or become Teutonic or German.

Teu·to·phil (tü′tə fil, tyü′-), *adj., n.* Teutophile.

Teu·to·phile (tü′tə fīl, tyü′-; -fil), *adj.* friendly to the Teutons or Germans. —*n.* a person who favors or admires the Teutons or Germans. [< *Teuto*(n) + *-phile*]

Teu·to·phobe (tü′tə fōb, tyü′-), *n.* a person who fears or hates the Teutons or Germans. [< *Teuto*(n) + *-phobe*]

tew (tyü), *Obsolete.* —*v.i.* **1.** to work hard; toil. **2.** to bustle (about). —*n.* **1.** constant work and bustling. **2.** a state of worry or excitement. [Middle English *tewen* (originally) to taw leather, to prepare by beating or pounding, apparently variant of *taw*²]

Tex., **1.** Texan. **2.** Texas.

Tex·an (tek′sən), *adj.* of or having to do with Texas, a Southern State of the United States, or its people. —*n.* a native or inhabitant of Texas.

Tex·as (tek′səs), *n.* an Indian of a Caddoan tribe.

tex·as (tek′səs), *n.* a structure on the hurricane deck of a river steamer where officers' cabins are situated. It has the pilot house in front or on top. [< *Texas,* one of the States of the United States]

Texas armadillo, the nine-banded armadillo.

Texas fever, an infectious disease of cattle caused by a protozoan parasite and transmitted by cattle-infesting ticks.

Texas Armadillo (including tail, about 2 ft. long)

Texas leaguer, (in baseball) a fly falling between the infielders and outfielders.

Texas longhorn, longhorn: *Texas longhorn cattle, close to extinction less than 25 years ago, were found to number more than 500* (Science News Letter).

Texas Rangers, **1.** a group of mounted men in the state police of Texas. **2.** a group of United States citizens who tried to maintain order during the early years of settling in Texas.

Texas sparrow, an olive-green finch of southern Texas and Mexico, with two brown stripes on the crown; greenfinch.

Texas Tower or **tower,** *U.S.* a platform built about 100 miles off shore on pilings sunk into the ocean floor and used as a radar station: *Radar-equipped ships, planes, blimps and Texas towers—offshore platforms modeled after oil drilling rigs—complete a warning fence that circles the continent* (Wall Street Journal). [< *Texas,* the state (because of its resemblance to the offshore oil derricks or rigs found there)]

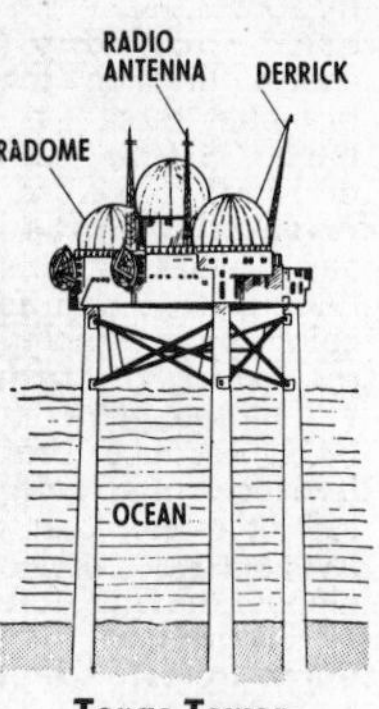

Texas Tower

text (tekst), *n.* **1.** the main body of reading matter in a book, as distinct from the notes, supplements, indices, etc.: *This history contains 300 pages of text and about 50 pages of notes, explanations, and questions for study.* **2.** the original words of a writer, especially a work in the original language, as distinct from a translation or rendering: *A text is often changed here and there when it is copied.* **3. a.** the wording adopted by an editor as (in his opinion) most nearly representing an author's original work. **b.** a book or edition containing this. **4.** a short passage from the Scriptures, used as the subject of a sermon or as proof of some belief: *The minister preached on the text "Judge not, that ye be not judged."* **5.** a topic; subject: *Town improvement was the speaker's text.* **6.** a textbook. **7. a.** the letter of Scripture. **b.** the Scriptures themselves. **c.** a reading of the Scriptures or a wording of a Scriptural passage taken as correct and authoritative. **8.** text hand. [< Middle French *texte* < Old French, learned borrowing from Medieval Latin *textus* the Scriptures; an authority; a treatise (in Late Latin, written account, content, characters) < Latin *textus, -ūs* style or texture of a work; (originally) a thing woven < *texere* to weave] —**text′less,** *adj.*

text·book (tekst′bu̇k′), *n.* a book read or referred to as an authority and standard in the study of a particular subject, especially one written specially for this purpose; manual of instruction: *Most arithmetics and geographies are textbooks.* —*adj.* of or belonging in a textbook; accepted; standard; typical: *Two classic, textbook examples of this difficulty occurred a few weeks ago* (Maclean's). *There are special conditions everywhere. The textbook answer can often be very wrong* (Ralph Allen).

text·book·ish (tekst′bu̇k′ish), *adj.* of the nature of a textbook: *He has put nearly everything into double columns, which I find textbookish and uninviting* (New Yorker).

text hand, **1.** a style of handwriting in which large, bold letters are formed. **2.** (originally) one of the larger and more formal hands in which the text of a book was often written, as distinct from the smaller or more cursive hand used for the gloss, etc.

tex·tile (teks′təl, -tīl), *adj.* **1.** woven: *Cloth is a textile fabric.* **2.** suitable for weaving: *Linen, cotton, silk, and wool are common textile materials.* **3.** of or having to do with weaving: *the textile art.* —*n.* **1.** a woven fabric; cloth. **2.** any fibrous material suitable for weaving. [< Latin *textilis* woven < *texere* to weave]

tex·tile·man (teks′təl man′, -tīl-), *n., pl.* **-men.** a man engaged in the textile industry; a weaver or seller of cloth: *The firm that has contributed most to the prosperity of Hong Kong's textile industry, and profited most from it is . . . the creation of a sprightly textileman named P.Y.* (*for Ping Yan*) *Tang* (Time).

textile mill, place where textiles are made.

tex·tu·al (teks′chu̇ əl), *adj.* **1.** of, having to do with, or contained in the text: *A misprint is a textual error.* **2.** based on, following, or conforming to the text, especially of the Scriptures. [alteration of Middle English *textuel,* probably < Anglo-French, Old French, learned borrowing from Medieval Latin *textualis* < Latin *textus, -ūs;* see TEXT]

textual criticism, lower criticism.

tex·tu·al·ism (teks′chu̇ ə liz′əm), *n.* a strict adherence to the text, especially of the Scriptures.

tex·tu·al·ist (teks′chü ə list), *n.* **1.** a person who adheres strictly to, and bases his doctrine upon, the text of the Scriptures. **2.** a person learned in the text of the Bible.
tex·tu·al·ly (teks′chü ə lē), *adv.* in regard to the text.
tex·tu·ar·y (teks′chü er′ē), *adj., n., pl.* **-ar·ies.** —*adj.* of or belonging to the text; textual. —*n.* textualist.
tex·tur·al (teks′chər əl), *adj.* of or having to do with texture: *They express, in varying degrees, the feeling for color, textural interest, and balanced design that marks a sensitive and imaginative artist* (New Yorker). —**tex′tur·al·ly,** *adv.*
tex·ture (teks′chər), *n.* **1.** the arrangement of threads in a woven fabric: *A piece of burlap has a much coarser texture than a linen handkerchief.* **2. a.** the arrangement of parts of anything; structure; constitution; make-up: *the granular texture of sandy soil, the obvious difference between sandstone and granite in texture. Her skin has a fine texture.* **b.** the structure or minute molding (of a surface). **3.** (in painting, sculpture, etc.) the representation of the structure and minute molding of a surface, especially of the skin, as distinct from its color. **4.** the musical quality of combined voices, instruments, etc.: *the harsh texture of brass instruments.* **5.** *Archaic.* a textile fabric. [earlier, the process of weaving < Latin *textūra* a web; texture; structure < *texere* to weave]
—**Syn. 2. a.** composition.
tex·tured (teks′chərd), *adj.* **1.** having a specified texture: *Open-textured = having an open texture. Rochberg's Symphony No. 2 . . . was thickly textured, darkly intense work that moved in a riptide of conflicting rhythms and clashing dissonances* (Time). **2.** given a bulky, soft texture by adding air to the filament strands to form kinks and loops: *textured yarn.*
tex·ture·less (teks′chər lis), *adj.* having no visible or obvious texture or structure.
tex·tur·ize (teks′chə rīz), *v.t.,* **-ized, -iz·ing.** to provide with texture: *Nylon makers work with yarn processors to give the fiber greater bulk and better feel by texturizing it* (Wall Street Journal).
tex·tus re·cep·tus (teks′təs ri sep′təs), the accepted text, especially the received text of the Greek New Testament: *Henceforth I suggest this version may be regarded as the textus receptus* (London Times). [< Latin *textus, -ūs* text, and *receptus,* past participle of *recipere* receive]
T.F., Territorial Force.
T-for·ma·tion (tē′fôr mā′shən), *n.* (in football) an offensive formation with the quarterback directly behind the center and the other three backs in a horizontal line a few yards behind him, in the general shape of a T.
tfr., transfer.
TFX (no periods), Tactical Fighter, Experimental (warplane).
t.g., type genus.
TGWU (no periods) or **T.G.W.U.,** Transport and General Workers' Union (of Great Britain).
-th, a suffix that forms ordinal numbers (from *fourth* on) when it is attached either to the cardinal number, as in *sixth, hundredth,* or to its altered stem, as in *fifth, twelfth.* [Old English *-tha,* or *-the*]
Th (no period), thorium (chemical element).
Th., **1.** Thomas. **2.** Thursday.
T.H., Territory of Hawaii (the official abbreviation before Hawaii became a State).
tha (ᴛʜə), *pron. British* (*Northern*) *Dialect.* **1.** thee. **2.** thou. **3.** thy.
thack (thak), *n., v.t., v.i. Scottish.* **1.** thatch. **2.** roof. [Old English *thæc.* Compare THATCH.]
Thack·er·ay·an (thak′ə rē ən), *adj.* of, having to do with, or characteristic of the English novelist William Makepeace Thackeray or his works: *A certain cynical humor which is almost Thackerayan in quality* (Scottish Leader).
Thad., Thaddeus.
Thad·dae·us (tha dē′əs), *n.* Jude, or Saint Judas, one of the Apostles.
thae (ᴛʜā), *adj., pron. Scottish.* the plural of **that.** [< Old English *thā.* Compare THOSE.]
Thai (tī), *n.* **1.** the language of Thailand; Siamese. **2. a.** a family of languages spoken in Thailand and parts of Burma, Indochina, and China, including Shan, Lao, and the language of Thailand. **b.** any of the people who speak these languages: *Most Thais also still believe . . . that the elephant is a "great and ample demonstration of the power and wisdom of almighty God"* (Time).
—*adj.* **1.** of or having to do with the Thai language family or the peoples that speak languages of this family. **2.** of or having to do with Thailand (Siam); Siamese. Also, **Tai.**
thairm (thärm), *n. Dialect.* tharm.
thal·a·men·ce·phal·ic (thal′ə men sə fal′ik), *adj.* diencephalic.
thal·a·men·ceph·a·lon (thal′ə men sef′ə lon), *n., pl.* **-la** (-lə). diencephalon. [< *thalam*(us) + *encephalon*]
tha·lam·ic (thə lam′ik), *adj.* of or having to do with the thalamus.
thal·a·mot·o·my (thal′ə mot′ə mē), *n., pl.* **-mies.** a surgical incision into the thalamus, as in the treatment of severe emotional disturbance. [< *thalam*(us) + Greek *-tomiā* a cutting]
thal·a·mus (thal′ə məs), *n., pl.* **-mi** (-mī). **1.** a large, oblong mass in the diencephalon of the forebrain, from which nerve fibers pass to the sensory parts of the cortex and which is connected with the optic nerve; optic thalamus: *Most physiologists believe that the site of salicylic acid's analgesic action is the thalamus, the chief sensory reception center, located in the forebrain* (New Yorker). **2.** *Botany.* **a.** the receptacle of a flower; torus. **b.** thallus.
[< New Latin *thalamus* (in Latin, inner room) < Greek *thálamos*]
thal·as·se·mi·a (thal′ə sē′mē ə), *n.* a hereditary blood disorder in which the red blood cells are misshapen and easily destroyed, leading to anemia; Mediterranean anemia. One form is often fatal in childhood. *A team of New York Medical College physicians reported in New York that the folic acid deficiency frequently occurring in patients with . . . thalassemia major, can be managed by folic acid therapy* (Science News Letter). [< New Latin *thalassemia* < Greek *thálassa* sea; Mediterranean Sea + *haîma* blood (because it was originally thought that the disease was confined to those of Mediterranean origin)]
tha·las·si·an (thə las′ē ən), *adj.* of or having to do with the sea; marine. —*n.* any sea turtle. [< Greek *thalássios* marine (< *thálassa* sea) + English *-an*]
tha·las·sic (thə las′ik), *adj.* **1.** of or having to do with the sea. **2.** of or having to do with the smaller or inland seas, as distinct from the pelagic waters or oceans. **3.** growing or living in, or formed in or by, the sea; marine.
thal·as·soc·ra·cy (thal′ə sok′rə sē), *n., pl.* **-cies.** **1.** mastery at sea; sovereignty of the sea. **2.** a kingdom having such mastery: *The Aegean was the nursery of thalassocracies, that is to say the sea kingdoms that grew fat and then split up through internal dissension or invasion, forming new colonies elsewhere* (New Scientist). [< Greek *thalassokratiā* < *thálassa* sea + *krátos* rule, power]
tha·las·so·crat (thə las′ə krat), *n.* a ruler or master of the sea.
thal·as·sog·ra·phy (thal′ə sog′rə fē), *n.* the science of the ocean; oceanography. [< Greek *thálassa* sea + English *-graphy*]
tha·ler (tä′lər), *n., pl.* **-ler.** **1.** a former German silver coin, worth about 7½ cents; taler. **2.** the Levant dollar. [< German *Thaler.* Compare DOLLAR.]
Tha·li·a (thə lī′ə), *n. Greek Mythology.* **1.** the Muse of comedy and idyllic poetry. **2.** one of the three Graces. [< Latin *Thalia* < Greek *Tháleia* (literally) blooming, luxuriant < *thállein* to bloom]
tha·lic·trum (thə lik′trəm), *n.* any of a group of plants of the crowfoot family; meadow rue. [< Latin *thalictrum* < Greek *tháliktron* meadow rue]
tha·lid·o·mide (thə lid′ə mīd′), *n.* a tranquilizing drug formerly used as a sedative and hypnotic. Its use during early pregnancy usually causes malformation of the fetus, especially the failure of development of the limbs. *Formula:* $C_{13}H_{10}N_2O_4$
thalidomide baby, a malformed baby born to a woman who had taken thalidomide during pregnancy: *Because thalidomide babies have above average intelligence, Dr. Hauberg is theorizing about some mysterious process of natural compensation* (Time).
thal·lic (thal′ik), *adj. Chemistry.* **1.** of thallium. **2.** containing thallium, especially with a valence of three.
thal·line (thal′in, -ēn), *n.* a white, crystalline base yielding salts used as antipyretics. *Formula:* $C_{10}H_{13}NO$ [< Greek *thallós* a green shoot + English *-ine*[2] (because its spectrum is marked by a green band)]
thal·li·ous (thal′ē əs), *adj.* **1.** *Botany.* of a thallus. **2.** *Chemistry.* thallous.
thal·li·um (thal′ē əm), *n.* a rare, metallic chemical element, bluish-white in color with leaden luster, extremely soft and malleable, and almost devoid of tenacity and elasticity. It occurs in small quantities in iron and copper pyrites and in various minerals, and is used in rat poisons and in making glass of high refractive power. *Symbol:* Tl; *at.wt.:* (C^{12}) 204.37 or (O^{16}) 204.39; *at.no.:* 81; *valence:* 1, 3. [< New Latin *thallium* < Greek *thallós* green shoot < *thállein* to bloom (because its spectrum is marked by a green band)]
thallium sulfate, a colorless, crystalline poison absorbed through the skin, used as a rodenticide and insecticide. *Formula:* Tl_2SO_4
thal·lo·gen (thal′ə jən), *n.* a thallophyte.
thal·loid (thal′oid), *adj. Botany.* of, resembling, or consisting of a thallus. [< *thall*(us) + *-oid*]
thal·lo·phyte (thal′ə fīt), *n. Botany.* any of a division of plants in which the plant body usually consists of a thallus that shows no differentiation into stem, leaf, and root. The simpler unicellular forms reproduce by cell division or by asexual spores; the higher forms reproduce both asexually and sexually. *Bacteria, algae, fungi, and lichens are thallophytes.* [< New Latin *Thallophyta* the division name < Greek *thallós* green shoot + *phytón* plant]
thal·lo·phyt·ic (thal′ə fit′ik), *adj.* of or having to do with the thallophytes.
thal·lous (thal′əs), *adj. Chemistry.* **1.** of thallium. **2.** containing thallium, especially with a valence of one.
thal·lus (thal′əs), *n., pl.* **thal·li** (thal′ī), **thal·lus·es.** *Botany.* a vegetable structure or plant body without vascular tissue, not divided into leaves, stem, and root; the plant body characteristic of thallophytes: *Mushrooms, toadstools, and lichens are thalli.* [< New Latin *thallus* < Greek *thallós* green shoot < *thállein* to bloom]
thal·weg (täl′vāk), *n.* the line of greatest slope along the bottom of a valley, forming the natural direction of a watercourse. [< German *Thalweg* bottom path of a valley < *Thal* valley, dale + *Weg* path, way]
Tham·muz (täm′müz; *Biblical* tam′uz), *n.* Tammuz.
than (ᴛʜan; unstressed ᴛʜən), *conj.* **1.** in comparison with; compared to that which: *This train is faster than that one. He has more money than he needs.* **2.** except; besides: *How else can we come than on foot?* —*prep.* compared to; except: *Present also was Sheridan, than whom there was no abler speaker in the group.*
[Old English *thanne, thænne,* or *thonne;* (originally) the same word as *then*]
➤ **a.** In clauses consisting of **than** plus a personal pronoun, the form of the latter is determined by its function as subject or object: *He is older than I* [am]. *I like his cousin better than* [I like] *him.* In sentences like the first of these, *than* is often treated as a preposition and the object form of the pronoun is substituted: *He is older than me.* This construction, although very common in familiar speech, is regarded as nonstandard. **b.** In comparison, the standard idiom is *other than* (not *different than*): *It was other than* (or *different from*) *what he expected.* See **then** for another usage note.
tha·na (tä′nə), *n.* tana[1].
tha·na·dar (tä′nə där′), *n.* tanadar.
than·age (thā′nij), *n.* **1.** the tenure by which a thane held land. **2.** the land so held. **3.** the rank, office, or jurisdiction of a thane. [< *than*(e) + *-age.* Compare Anglo-French *thaynage.*]
tha·nah (tä′nə), *n.* tana[1].
than·a·tism (than′ə tiz əm), *n.* the belief that at death the human soul ceases to exist.
than·a·toid (than′ə toid), *adj.* **1.** resembling death; apparently dead: *We carted the old man into the restaurant and propped him up at a table. He looked exactly the same—thanatoid* (Truman Capote). **2.** deadly, as a venomous snake. [< Greek *thánatos* death + English *-oid*]
than·a·to·log·i·cal (than′ə tə loj′ə kəl), *adj.* of or having to do with thanatology: *Undertakers have organized a thanatological association* (Time).

than·a·tol·o·gy (than′ə tol′ə jē), *n.* the scientific study of death and its causes and phenomena. [< Greek *thánatos* death]

than·a·to·pho·bi·a (than′ə tə fō′bē ə), *n.* an abnormal fear of death. [< Greek *thánatos* death]

than·a·top·sis (than′ə top′sis), *n.* a contemplation of death; meditative viewing of the end of life. [< Greek *thánatos* death + *ópsis* a view of]

Than·a·tos (than′ə tos), *n. Greek Mythology.* death personified as a god, identified with the Roman Mors.

thane (thān), *n.* **1.** (in early English history) a man who ranked between an earl and an ordinary freeman. Thanes held lands of the king or lord and gave military service in return. **2.** (in Scottish history) a person, equal in rank to an earl's son, who held lands of the king; the chief of a clan, who became one of the king's barons: *All hail, Macbeth! hail to thee, thane of Glamis!* (Shakespeare). Also, **thegn.** [alteration of Middle English *thaine* king's baron, Old English *thegn* a military follower. Compare THEGN.]

thane·ship (thān′ship), *n.* **1.** the office, dignity, or character of a thane. **2.** thanes collectively.

thank (thangk), *v.t.* **1.** to say that one is pleased and grateful for something given or done; express gratitude to. **2.** to consider or hold responsible, especially (in ironical use) to blame.

[Old English *thancian* < *thanc;* see the noun]

—*n.* **1.** *Archaic.* grateful thought; gratitude. **2.** *Obsolete.* favorable thought or feeling; good will.

thanks, a. I thank you: *Thanks for your good wishes.* **b.** an expression of gratitude and pleasure for something given or done: *I return the book to you with my sincere thanks.* **c.** a feeling of kindness received; gratitude: *He expressed his thanks for their help.*

thanks to, a. owing to; as a result of; because of: *The passengers—thanks, I expect, to the bitter cold—behaved more quietly at night than in the morning* (Westminster Gazette). **b.** thanks be given to, or are due to: *But (thanks to Homer) . . . I live and thrive, Indebted to no prince or peer alive* (Alexander Pope).

[Old English *thanc* (originally) a thought; an expression of gratitude. Related to THINK[1].] —**thank′er,** *n.*

thank·ful (thangk′fəl), *adj.* feeling or expressing thanks or gratitude; grateful. —**Syn.** See **grateful.**

thank·ful·ly (thangk′fə lē), *adv.* with thanks; gratefully.

thank·ful·ness (thangk′fəl nis), *n.* a thankful feeling; gratitude. —**Syn.** gratefulness.

thank·less (thangk′lis), *adj.* **1.** not feeling or expressing thanks; not grateful: *The thankless boy did almost nothing for his mother. How sharper than a serpent's tooth it is To have a thankless child* (Shakespeare). **2.** not likely to be rewarded with thanks; not appreciated: *Giving advice is usually a thankless act.* —**thank′less·ly,** *adv.* —**thank′less·ness,** *n.* —**Syn. 1.** ungrateful. **2.** unrewarded, unrequited.

thank offering, 1. an offering made according to the Levitical law as an expression of gratitude to God. **2.** any offering made by way of thanks or grateful acknowledgment.

thanks (thangks), *n.pl.* See under **thank,** *n.*

thanks·giv·er (thangks′giv′ər), *n.* a person who gives thanks.

thanks·giv·ing (thangks′giv′ing), *n.* **1.** the giving of thanks, especially the act of giving thanks to God. **2.** an expression of thanks: *They offered a thanksgiving to God for their escape.* **3. a.** a public celebration, often with religious services, held as a solemn acknowledgment of God's favor. **b.** a day set apart for this purpose.

Thanks·giv·ing (thangks′giv′ing), *n.* the fourth Thursday in November, a day set apart as a legal holiday in the United States in commemoration of and deriving from the harvest feast of the Pilgrims in 1621, by which thanks were given to God for the bounteous crops and survival of the colony during the first year of its existence.

Thanksgiving Day, Thanksgiving, the fourth Thursday in November.

thank·wor·thy (thangk′wėr′ŦHē), *adj.* worthy of thanks; deserving gratitude.

thank-you (thangk′yü′), *n.* a saying of "thank you"; an expression of thanks: *You wouldn't have got a thank-you for that service in the old days* (Punch).

thank-you-ma'am (thangk′yə mam′), *n. U.S. Informal.* **1.** a ridge or hollow in a road causing persons riding over it in a vehicle to nod the head suddenly as if making a bow of acknowledgment. **2.** such a ridge or hollow in a road on the face of a hill, designed to throw to one side descending rain water. [referring to the bob of the head, as if to say *"thank you, ma'am"*]

than·na or **than·nah** (tä′nə), *n.* tana[1].

thar (ŦHär), *adv. British* (*Northern*) *Dialect.* there.

tharm (thärm), *n. Dialect.* **1.** an intestine. **2.** gut, especially catgut for violin strings, etc. Also, **thairm.**

tharms, intestines; entrails.

[Old English *tharm*]

tha·ros (thãr′os), *n.* a small North American butterfly with black, orange, and white coloration. [< New Latin *Tharos* the species name]

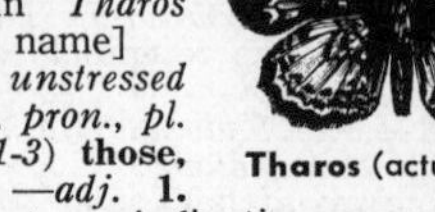

Tharos (actual size)

that (ŦHat; *unstressed* ŦHət), *adj., pron., pl.* (*for defs. 1-3*) **those,** *conj., adv.* —*adj.* **1.** pointing out or indicating some person, thing, idea, etc., already mentioned, understood, or to be emphasized: *Isn't that book the one we discussed last night? Who is that lovely girl in the chair by the fire?* **2.** indicating the farther of two or farthest of most things: *Shall I buy this dress or that one we saw yesterday? What is the name of that mountain beyond the others to the east?* **3.** showing contrast: *This hat is prettier but that one costs less.*

—*pron.* **1.** some person, thing, idea, etc., already mentioned, understood, or to be emphasized: *That is the right way. That's a good boy!* **2.** the farther of two or farthest of most things: *I like that better. I like that best.* **3.** something contrasted: *Which hat do you want, this or that?* **4.** who; whom; which: *Is he the man that sells dogs? She is the girl that you mean. Bring the box that will hold most.* **5.** at or in which; when: *1960 was the year that we went abroad.* **6.** *Archaic.* the former.

at that, *Informal.* **a.** with no more talk, work, etc.: *If I'm invited to have a drink I just say "A fruit juice please" and leave it at that* (Manchester Guardian Weekly). **b.** considering everything: [*He was*] *a shoemaker, and a poor one at that* (Francis Crawford).

in that, because: *I prefer his plan to yours, in that I think it is more practical.*

that is, that is to say; in other words: *Look at me, that is, look on me, and with all thine eyes* (Ben Jonson).

that's that, *Informal.* that is settled or decided: *"Well," he exclaimed, "that's that. At least I know where I'm going"* (P. Marks).

with that, when that occurred; whereupon: *The train reached the station, and, with that, our long trip ended.*

—*conj. That* is used: **1.** to introduce a noun clause and connect it with the verb: *I know that 6 and 4 are 10.* **2.** to show purpose, end, aim, or desire (often with *may, might,* or *should,* rarely *shall*): *He ran fast so that he would not be late.* **3.** to show result: *He ran so fast that he was five minutes early.* **4.** to show cause: *I wonder what happened, not that I care.* **5.** to express a wish: *Oh, that she were here!* **6.** to show anger, surprise, sorrow, indignation, or the like: *That one so fair should be so false!*

—*adv.* to such an extent or degree; so: *He cannot stay up that late. I didn't know you cared that much.*

[Old English *thæt* (originally) neuter of *sē,* demonstrative pronoun and adjective. Compare THE[1], THIS.]

➔ The relative pronouns **that, who,** and **which** are distinguished in present use as follows: (1) *That* may refer to persons, animals, or things, *who* only to persons (or personified abstractions of animals when thought of as having personality, as in children's stories), *which* to animals, things, or groups of people regarded impersonally: *the man that* (or *who*) *answered; the concert that* (or *which*) *was scheduled; the animals that* (or *which*) *are native to this region.* (2) *That* is used chiefly in restrictive clauses: *the man that answered. The book that she selected for her report was the longest on the list. Who* and *which* are used in both restrictive and nonrestrictive clauses. Restrictive: *the man who answered; the parcel which I received.* Nonrestrictive: *the parcel, which had been badly wrapped; Mr. Ross, who is an accountant. The privilege of free speech, which we hold so dear, is now endangered.* (3) *That* is not used as the object of a preposition; it cannot be substituted in *the man to whom I spoke* or *the size for which he asked* (or *which he asked for*). See **this** for another usage note.

that·a·way (ŦHat′ə wā′), *adv. U.S. Dialect.* in that direction: *He went thataway.*

thatch (thach), *n.* **1.** straw, rushes, palm leaves, etc., used as a roof or covering. **2.** a roof or covering made of thatch. **3.** *Informal.* the hair covering the head. **4.** any of various palms whose leaves are used for thatching.

—*v.t.* to roof or cover with or as with thatch.

Thatch (def. 2)

[variant of *thack;* Old English *thæc*] —**thatch′er,** *n.*

thatch·ing (thach′ing), *n.* **1.** thatch. **2.** the act or process of covering with thatch.

thatch·less (thach′lis), *adj.* having the thatch of the roof missing or destroyed: *Hingeless doors and shutters, crooked and thatchless roofs* (Century Magazine).

thatch palm, thatch.

thatch·y (thach′ē), *adj.,* **thatch·i·er, thatch·i·est.** composed of, full of, or like thatch.

thau·ma·tol·o·gy (thô′mə tol′ə jē), *n.* the description or discussion of the miraculous; miracles, as a subject of study or systematic inquiry. [< Greek *thaûma, -atos* a marvel + English *-logy*]

thau·ma·trope (thô′mə trōp), *n.* an optical device for illustrating the persistence of visual impressions, consisting of a card or disk with different figures on each side, that are apparently combined into one when the disk or card is rotated rapidly about one of its diameters. [< Greek *thaûma, -atos* a marvel + *-tropos* a turning]

thau·ma·turge (thô′mə tėrj), *n.* a worker of marvels or miracles; wonder-worker. [< Medieval Latin *thaumaturgus* < Greek *thaumatourgós;* see THAUMATURGY]

thau·ma·tur·gic (thô′mə tėr′jik), *adj.* having to do with a thaumaturge or thaumaturgy; having the powers of a thaumaturge.

thau·ma·tur·gi·cal (thô′mə tėr′jə kəl), *adj.* thaumaturgic.

thau·ma·tur·gist (thô′mə tėr′jist), *n.* thaumaturge.

thau·ma·tur·gy (thô′mə tėr′jē), *n.* the working of wonders or miracles; wonder-working; magic: *Romans put a good deal of faith in thaumaturgy; sophisticated and ignorant citizens alike* (New Yorker). [< Greek *thaumatourgíā* < *thaumatourgós* (one) conjuring < *thaûma, -atos* marvel + *érgon* work]

thaw (thô), *v.t.* **1.** to melt (ice, snow, or anything frozen): *This warm weather should thaw the ice on the roads very quickly.* **2.** to make no longer frozen: *to thaw a frozen chicken, to thaw a package of frozen peas.* **3.** to make less stiff and formal in manner; soften. —*v.i.* **1.** to become warm enough to melt ice and snow; rise above a temperature of 32 degrees Fahrenheit (said of the weather, and used impersonally): *If the sun stays out, it will probably thaw today.* **2.** to become free of frost, ice, etc.: *Our sidewalk thawed yesterday. The pond freezes up in November and thaws out in April. Frozen peas thaw quickly in boiling water.* **3.** to become less stiff and formal in manner; soften: *His shyness thawed under her kindness.*

—*n.* **1.** a thawing. **2.** a condition or period of weather above the freezing point (32 degrees Fahrenheit); time of melting: *a January thaw.* **3.** a becoming less stiff and formal in manner; softening. **4.** a relaxation of authority or control; a lessening in rigidity or severity: *the exceptional freedoms*

granted to the Roman Catholic Church in Poland during the 1956 political "thaw" (London Times).
[Old English *thawian*] —**thaw′er,** *n.*
—**Syn.** *v.t.* **1.** See **melt.**

thaw·less (thô′lis), *adj.* without thawing.

thaw·y (thô′ē), *adj.* characterized by thawing.

Th.D., Doctor of Theology (Latin, *Theologiae Doctor*).

the[1] (*unstressed before a consonant* ᴛʜə; *unstressed before a vowel* ᴛʜi; *stressed* ᴛʜē), *definite article.* The word *the* shows that a certain one (or ones) is meant. Various special uses are: **1.** to mark a noun as indicating something well-known or unique: *the prodigal son, the Alps.* **2.** denoting the time in question or under consideration, now or then present: *the hour of victory. Was that the moment to act?* **3.** with or as part of a title: *the Duke of Wellington, the Right Honorable the Earl of Derby, the Reverend John Smith.* **4.** to mark a noun as indicating the best-known or most important of its kind: *the place to dine, not any book, but the book.* **5.** to mark a noun as being used generically: *The dog is a quadruped.* **6.** to indicate a part of the body or a personal belonging: *to hang the head in shame, to clutch at the sleeve of one's father.* **7.** before adjectives used as nouns: *to visit the sick, a love of the beautiful.* **8.** distributively, to denote any one separately: *candy at one dollar the pound, so much by the day.* [Old English *thē, the,* reduction of oblique forms of *sē*, demonstrative pronoun and adjective. Compare THAT, THIS.]

the[2] (ᴛʜə, ᴛʜē), *adv.* The word *the* is used to modify an adjective or adverb in the comparative degree: **1.** signifying "in or by that," "on that account," "in some or any degree": *If you start now, you will be back the sooner.* **2.** used correlatively, in one instance with relative force and in the other with demonstrative force, and signifying "by how much . . . by so much," "in what degree . . . in that degree": *the more the merrier, the sooner the better.* [Old English *thē*, variant of *thȳ*, instrumental case of demonstrative *thæt* that]

the-, *combining form.* the form of **theo-** before vowels. as in *theanthropism.*

The·a (thē′ə), *n. Greek Mythology.* the wife of Hyperion and mother of Eos, Helios, and Selene.

the·a·ceous (thē ā′shəs), *adj.* belonging to the tea family. [< New Latin *Theaceae* the family name (< *Thea* the former genus name < source of English *tea*)]

T-head (tē′hed′), *n.* a bar, beam, etc., with a crosspiece at the end.
—*adj.* having the shape or form of a T: *a T-head bolt.*

the·an·throp·ic (thē′an throp′ik), *adj.* having to do with or having the nature of both God and man; both divine and human.

the·an·thro·pism (thē an′thrə piz əm), *n.* **1.** *Theology.* **a.** the doctrine of the union of divine and human natures in Christ. **b.** the manifestation of God as man in Christ. **2.** the attribution of human character to the gods; anthropomorphism. [< Late Greek *theánthrōpos* (< Greek *theós* god + *ánthrōpos* man) + English *-ism*]

the·an·thro·pist (thē an′thrə pist), *n.* a person who advocates the doctrine of theanthropism.

the·ar·chic (thē är′kik), *adj.* divinely sovereign or supreme.

the·ar·chy (thē′är kē), *n., pl.* **-chies. 1.** theocracy. **2.** an order or system of deities. [< Greek *thearchiā* < *theós* god + *árchein* to rule, lead]

theat., theatrical.

the·a·ter (thē′ə tər), *n.* **1.** a place where plays, dance programs, or similar kinds of entertainment are presented; place where motion pictures are shown. **2.** the audience; the house. **3.** a place that looks like a theater in its arrangement of seats: *The surgeon performed an operation before the medical students in the operating theater.* **4.** a natural formation or other place suggesting a theater, as a bowllike indentation of the ground with naturally terraced sides. **5.** a place where some action proceeds; scene of action: *Belgium and France were the theater of the First World War.* **6. a.** writing and producing plays; plays; the drama; the stage: *He was interested in the theater and tried to write plays himself.* **b.** a play, situation, dialogue, etc., considered as to its effectiveness on the stage: *This scene is bad theater.* [< Latin *theātrum* < Greek *théātron* < *theâsthai* to behold < *théā* a view]
➤ **Theater** is the preferred American spelling, but **theatre** is very commonly used in the names of theater houses.

the·a·ter·go·er or **the·a·tre·go·er** (thē′ə tər gō′ər), *n.* a person who attends the theater, especially one who goes often: *She is a devoted theatergoer, and loves musicals* (Newsweek).

the·a·ter·go·ing or **the·a·tre·go·ing** (thē′ə tər gō′ing), *n.* the practice or habit of attending the theater: *Ordinarily, my theatergoing . . . does not extend . . . far off Broadway* (New Yorker). —*adj.* attending the theater.

the·a·ter-in-the-round (thē′ə tər in ᴛʜə-round′), *n. Especially U.S.* a theater in which the stage is surrounded by seats on all sides, whether in a permanent building, a tent, or out of doors.

Theater of the Absurd, plays by a group of 20th-century writers, including Samuel Beckett and Eugene Ionesco, who use fantasy, surrealism, etc., to dramatize their belief in the irrationality of life.

the·at·ral (thē at′rəl), *adj.* of or connected with the theater; theatrical; dramatic: *Homer had gathered up his audience and led it off to view the theatral area* (Atlantic).

the·a·tre (thē′ə tər), *n. Especially British.* theater.
➤ See **theater** for usage note.

theatre sister, *British.* a nurse who works in an operating room: *The surgeon had been told by the theatre sister that the swab count was correct* (London Times).

the·at·ric (thē at′rik), *adj.* theatrical.

the·at·ri·cal (thē at′rə kəl), *adj.* **1.** of or having to do with the theater, actors, or dramatic presentations: *theatrical performances, a theatrical company. Dark stools, placed on an unadorned stage, took on theatrical effectiveness* (Christian Science Monitor). **2.** suggesting a theater or acting; showy; spectacular: *a theatrical flourish.* **3.** artificial; affected: *a theatrical manner.*
—*n.* **theatricals, a.** dramatic performances, especially as given by amateurs: *private theatricals.* **b.** matters having to do with the stage and acting: *He . . . dedicated his mind to the study of theatricals* (W. H. Ireland). **c.** actions of a theatrical or artificial character: *It's only the usual theatricals, because he's ashamed to face us* (Ethel Voynich). —**the·at′ri·cal·ly,** *adv.* —**the·at′ri·cal·ness,** *n.*
—**Syn.** *adj.* **1.** histrionic. **2.** See **dramatic.**

the·at·ri·cal·ism (thē at′rə kə liz′əm), *n.* **1.** the theory and methods of scenic representations. **2.** theatrical practice, style, or character; staginess: *Director Victor Vicas has tilted the picture with such suave restraint that an air of deliberate theatricalism pervades most of it* (New York Times).

the·at·ri·cal·ist (thē at′rə kə list), *n.* a person who takes part in theatricals.

the·at·ri·cal·i·ty (thē at′rə kal′ə tē), *n.* the quality or state of being theatrical: *He has a gift for the theatricality of nothing happening, for small sudden changes of key, for the humor of despair* (Time).

the·at·ri·cal·i·za·tion (thē at′rə kə lə zā′shən), *n.* the process of making theatrical; dramatization.

the·at·ri·cal·ize (thē at′rə kə līz), *v.t.,* **-ized, -iz·ing.** to make theatrical; put in dramatic form; dramatize: *Folk-dance purists, therefore, may find his dances too . . . theatricalized for their tastes* (Newsweek).

the·at·rics (thē at′riks), *n.* **1.** the art of producing plays. **2.** doings of a theatrical or artificial character; histrionics: *Pike's return to religion was quiet and without theatrics* (Saturday Evening Post).

the·at·ro·ma·ni·a (thē at′rə mā′nē ə), *n.* a mania or excessive fondness for theatergoing. [< *theatre* + *mania*]

The·ba·ic (thi bā′ik), *adj.* of or having to do with Thebes, an ancient city on the Nile and formerly a center of Egyptian civilization. [< Latin *Thēbaicus* < Greek *Thēbaikós* < *Thêbai*, or *Thêbē* Thebes]

The·ba·id (thē′bā id, -bē-), *n.* the area surrounding Thebes (especially in Greece, rarely in Egypt). [< Greek *Thēbaís, -ídos* < *Thêbai;* see THEBAIC]

the·ba·in (thē′bə in, thi bā′-), *n.* thebaine.

the·ba·ine (thē′bə ēn; thi bā′-; -in), *n.* a highly poisonous alkaloid, obtained in colorless leaflets or prisms from opium. It produces spasms like those caused by strychnine. *Formula:* $C_{19}H_{21}NO_3$ [< Greek *Thêbai* Thebes, Egypt (because it was a chief source of opium) + English *-ine*[2]]

The·ban (thē′bən), *adj.* of or having to do with Thebes in ancient Greece or Thebes in ancient Egypt. —*n.* a native or inhabitant of Thebes. [< Latin *Thēbānus* < Greek *Thêbai;* see THEBAIC]

the·ca (thē′kə), *n., pl.* **-cae** (-sē). **1.** *Botany.* **a.** a sac, cell, or capsule. **b.** a vessel containing spores in various lower plants. **2.** *Anatomy, Zoology.* a case or sheath enclosing some organ or part, as the horny case of an insect pupa. [< Latin *thēca* < Greek *thḗkē* case, cover < *tithénai* to place]

the·cal (thē′kəl), *adj.* having to do with or of the nature of a theca.

the·cate (thē′kit, -kāt), *adj.* having a theca; sheathed.

the·co·dont (thē′kə dont), *n.* any of a group of extinct, carnivorous reptiles with long hind legs, teeth lodged in alveoli, and ribs hollowed on both ends. It is regarded as the ancestor of the dinosaurs. [< New Latin *Thecodontes* the family name < Greek *thḗkē* case, cover + *odoús, odóntos* tooth]

thé dan·sant (tā′ dän sän′), *pl.* **thés dansants** (tā′ dän sän′). *French.* an afternoon tea with dancing; tea dance.

thee (ᴛʜē), *pron. Archaic.* Objective case of **thou;** you: *"The Lord bless thee, and keep thee."* [Old English *thē*, dative of *thū* thou]
➤ **Thee** is generally used as the nominative by members of the Society of Friends (Quakers), and in some of the local dialects of England. In this use, especially by the Quakers, it always takes a verb in the third person: *Is thee going to Meeting?* Among Quakers, especially in the United States, the form is not now generally used in speaking to persons of other religious sects, except by some members of the older generation who use it very much as the French use *tu,* in speaking to close friends and young children. See **thou** for another usage note.

thee·lin (thē′lin), *n. Biochemistry.* the former name of estrone. [< Greek *thēlys* female (< *thēlḗ* nipple) + English *-in*]

thee·lol (thē′lōl, -lol), *n. Biochemistry.* the former name of estriol. [< *theel*(in) + *-ol*[1]]

theft (theft), *n.* **1.** the act of stealing: *The man was put in prison for theft.* **2.** an instance of stealing: *The theft of the jewels caused much excitement.* **3.** something stolen. [Middle English *thefte*, Old English *thēofth* < *thēof* thief] —**Syn. 1.** thievery, pilfering, larceny, robbery.

theft·less (theft′lis), *adj.* **1.** that is not a theft. **2.** not liable to be stolen.

theft·proof (theft′prüf′), *adj.* invulnerable to theft; safe from thievery: *The safe is theftproof.*

thef·tu·ous (thef′chu̇ əs), *adj. Scottish.* thievish. [alteration of Middle English *thiftwis* < *thift* theft + *wis* wise, noun]

thegn (thān), *n.* thane. [modern use of Old English *thegn.* Compare THANE.]

the·in (thē′in), *n.* theine.

the·ine (thē′ēn, -in), *n.* a vegetable alkaloid, originally thought to be a principle peculiar to tea, but found to be identical with caffein. [< New Latin *thea* tea (see THEACEOUS) + English *-ine*[2]]

their (ᴛʜãr), *adj. Possessive form of* **they. 1.** of, belonging to, or having to do with them: *They like their school and do their lessons well.* **2.** of or linked to a (particular or specified) group as something shared in the fact or capacity of doing or being done to: *Those fellows certainly know their physics. Such mistakes will lead to their defeat.* [< Scandinavian (compare Old Icelandic *theirra*, genitive plural)]
➤ **Their, theirs** are the possessive forms of *they. Their* is the adjectival form; *theirs* is the absolute (or substantive) form: *This is their farm. This farm is theirs.*

theirs (ᴛʜãrz), *pron. Possessive form of* **they.** the one or ones belonging to them: *Our house is white; theirs is brown. Those books are theirs.*
➤ See **their** for a usage note.

the·ism (thē′iz əm), *n.* **1.** monotheism: **a.** belief in one God (the Deity), the creator and ruler of the universe. **b.** belief in (any) one god rather than many. **2.** belief in a deity or deities; religious faith or conviction. [< Greek *theós* god + English *-ism.* Compare DEISM.]

the·ist (thē′ist), *n.* a believer in theism: *No one is to be called a theist who does not believe in a personal God* (Cardinal Newman). —*adj.* theistic.

the·is·tic (thē is′tik), *adj.* having to do with theism or a theist; according to the doctrine of theists. —**the·is′ti·cal·ly,** *adv.*

the·is·ti·cal (thē is′tə kəl), *adj.* theistic.

the·li·tis (thi lī′tis), *n.* inflammation of the nipple. [< New Latin *thelitis* < Greek *thēlē* nipple + *-ītis* -itis]

them (ᴛʜem; *unstressed* ᴛʜəm), *pron.* Objective case of **they:** *The books are new; take care of them.* [< Scandinavian (compare Old Icelandic *theim*)]

➔ In many nonstandard dialects **them** is used as a demonstrative adjective, often strengthened by *there: them bales, them there bales.*

Th-Em (no periods), thorium emanation; thoron (chemical element).

the·mat·ic (thē mat′ik), *adj.* **1.** of or having to do with a theme or themes. **2.** *Grammar.* of or having to do with the theme of a word. —**the·mat′i·cal·ly,** *adv.*

the·mat·i·cal (thē mat′ə kəl), *adj.* thematic.

thematic apperception test, a psychological test to reveal traits of personality by a story written or told about a picture or the like.

thematic vowel, a vowel occurring between the root and the inflectional ending of a verb or noun in some Indo-European languages.

theme (thēm), *n.* **1.** a topic; subject: *Patriotism was the speaker's theme.* **2.** a short piece of prose written as an exercise for school. **3.** in music: **a.** the principal melody or subject in a composition or movement. **b.** a short melody or tune repeated in different forms or developed, as in an elaborate musical composition, especially as theme and variations. **4.** a melody used to identify a particular radio or television program. **5.** *Grammar.* the inflectional base or stem of a word, consisting of the root with modifications or additions, but without the inflectional endings. **6.** *Obsolete.* **a.** the text of a sermon. **b.** a proposition to be discussed. [< Latin *thema* < Greek *théma, -atos* (literally) something set down < *tithénai* to put down, place] —**Syn. 1.** text. **2.** essay.

theme·less (thēm′lis), *adj.* without a theme: *The themeless babble of his idiot child* (John Galt).

theme song, 1. a melody repeated so often in a stage play, musical comedy, motion picture, or operetta as to dominate it or establish its character. **2.** a melody used to identify a particular radio or television program; theme.

The·mis (thē′mis), *n. Greek Mythology.* the goddess of law and justice, daughter of Uranus and Gaea and thus a Titaness.

them·selves (ᴛʜem selvz′, ᴛʜəm-), *pron.* **1.** the intensifying or emphatic form of **they** or **them:** *They did it themselves. They were ill and not themselves. The teachers themselves said the test was too hard.* **2.** the reflexive form of **them:** *They injured themselves.*

➔ **Theirselves,** composed of the possessive pronoun *their* plus *selves,* parallels *myself, yourself, ourselves, yourselves.* The form is old but in modern English is found only in the nonstandard dialects.

then (ᴛʜen), *adv.* **1.** at that time: *Prices were then lower. Will prices then be higher?* **2.** soon afterwards: *The noise stopped, and then began again.* **3.** next in time or place: *First comes spring, then summer.* **4.** at another time: *Now one boy does best and then another.* **5.** also; besides: *The dress seems too good to throw away, and then it is very becoming.* **6.** in that case; therefore: *If Harry broke the window, then he must pay for it.*

but then, but at the same time; but on the other hand: *There was . . . some difficulty in keeping things in order, but then Vivian Grey was such an excellent manager!* (Benjamin Disraeli).

then and there, at that precise time and place; at once and on the spot: *The Constable DeLacy . . . was then and there to deliver to the Flemings a royal charter of their immunities* (Scott).

what then? See under **what,** *pron.*

—*n.* that time: *By then we shall know the result.*

—*adj.* being at that time; existing then: *the then President.*

[Middle English *thenne,* variant of Old English *thanne, thonne;* (originally) the same word as *than*]

➔ **then, than.** *Then* is an adverb of time, *than* a conjunction in clauses of comparison: *Then the whole crowd went to the drugstore. I think that book was better than any other novel I read last year.*

the·nar (thē′när), *Anatomy.* —*n.* **1.** the palm of the hand. **2.** the fleshy prominence at the base of the thumb. **3.** the sole of the foot.

—*adj.* of or having to do with the palm or thenar.

[< New Latin *thenar* < Greek *thénar, -aros* palm (of the hand), sole (of the foot)]

the·nard·ite (thə när′dīt, tə-), *n.* a mineral, an anhydrous sulfate of sodium, occurring in white or brown, translucent crystals. *Formula:* Na_2SO_4 [< Louis J. *Thénard,* 1777-1857, a French chemist + *-ite*[1]]

thence (ᴛʜens, thens), *adv.* **1.** from that place; from there: *A few miles thence is a river. Homeward from thence by easy stages* (George Eliot). **2. a.** for that reason; therefore: *You didn't work, thence no pay.* **b.** (as an inference) from those premises or data; therefrom: *He has given his decision and thence there is no appeal.* **3.** from that time; after that; from then: *a few years thence.* [Middle English *thannes, thennes* < *thanne, thenne* (Old English *thanone*) + adverbial genitive *-s*]

thence·forth (ᴛʜens′fôrth′, -fōrth′; thens′-), *adv.* from then on; from that time forward: *Women were given the same rights as men. Thenceforth they could vote.*

thence·for·ward (ᴛʜens′fôr′wərd, thens′-), *adv.* thenceforth.

thence·for·wards (ᴛʜens′fôr′wərdz, thens′-), *adv.* thenceforth.

theo-, *combining form.* a god or gods; God: *Theogony = the origin of the gods. Theocentric = centering in God. Theology = the study of God.* Also, **the-** before vowels. [< Greek *theós* god]

Theo., 1. Theodore. **2.** Theodosia.

the·o·bro·min (thē′ə brō′min), *n.* theobromine.

the·o·bro·mine (thē′ə brō′mēn, -min), *n.* a bitter, volatile, poisonous alkaloid, resembling caffeine, contained in the seeds of the cacao, in kola nuts, and in tea. It is used medicinally (in the form of its salts) to stimulate the nerves and as a diuretic. *Formula:* $C_7H_8N_4O_2$

[< New Latin *theobroma* (*cacao*) the cacao tree; *theobroma* (literally) food of the gods (< Greek *theós* god + *brôma* food) + English *-ine*[2]]

the·o·cen·tric (thē′ə sen′trik), *adj.* centering or centered in God; having God as its center.

the·oc·ra·cy (thē ok′rə sē), *n., pl.* **-cies. 1.** a government in which God, or a god, is recognized as the supreme civil ruler and divine or religious laws are taken as the laws of the state: *In the little theocracy which the Pilgrims established . . . the ministry was the only order of nobility* (Harriet Beecher Stowe). **2.** a government by priests. **3.** a country or nation having such a government.

[< Greek *theokratíā* < *theós* god + *krátos* a rule, regime]

the·oc·ra·sy (thē ok′rə sē), *n., pl.* **-sies. 1.** a mixture of several gods in one deity or of the worship of different gods. **2.** the intimate union of the soul with God in contemplation. [< Greek *theokrāsíā* a mingling with God < *theós* god + *krâsis* a mingling. Compare CRASIS.]

the·o·crat (thē′ə krat), *n.* **1.** a person who rules in a theocracy, alone or as a member of a governing body. **2.** a person who favors theocracy.

the·o·crat·ic (thē′ə krat′ik), *adj.* **1.** of, having to do with, or of the nature of theocracy. **2.** having a theocracy: *On the face of it, the answer of a theocratic state seems cut and dried because 90 per cent of the Indonesian People are said to profess the Moslem Faith* (Harper's). —**the′o·crat′i·cal·ly,** *adv.*

the·o·crat·i·cal (thē′ə krat′ə kəl), *adj.* theocratic.

The·oc·ri·tan (thē ok′rə tən), *adj.* Theocritean: *This bucolic, but far from Theocritan, idyll* (Observer).

The·oc·ri·te·an (thē ok′rə tē′ən), *adj.* of, having to do with, or in the manner of Theocritus, the ancient Greek poet of country life and scenes; pastoral; idyllic: *Berlioz's "L'Enfance du Christ" is a Theocritean idyll of the Nativity* (London Times).

the·od·i·cy (thē od′ə sē), *n., pl.* **-cies.** a vindication of the justice and holiness of God in establishing a world in which evil exists: *Basically Toynbee's work was a theodicy finally assessable only by the trained theologian, . . . Christian or non-Christian, as the case may be* (Howard Becker). [< French *Théodicée,* the title of a work of Leibnitz < Greek *theós* god + *díkē* justice]

the·o·di·dact (thē′ə di dakt′, -dī-), *adj.* taught by God: *Owing nothing to church or schools he [St. Francis] was truly theodidact* (Louise S. Houghton).

—*n.* a person taught by God.

[< Greek *theodídaktos* < *theós* god + *didáskein* teach] .

the·od·o·lite (thē od′ə līt), *n.* a surveying instrument for measuring horizontal and vertical angles. [earlier *theodelitus,* probably coined by Leonard Digges, an English mathematician of the 1500's who reputedly invented it]

Theodolite

the·od·o·lit·ic (thē od′ə lit′ik), *adj.* of or having to do with a theodolite; made by means of a theodolite.

the·o·gon·ic (thē′ə gon′ik), *adj.* of or relating to theogony.

the·og·o·nist (thē og′ə nist), *n.* a person skilled in theogony; person who writes about theogony.

the·og·o·ny (thē og′ə nē), *n., pl.* **-nies. 1.** the origin of the gods. **2.** an account of this; genealogical account of the gods. [< Greek *theogoníā* < *theós* god + *gónos* begetting, descent < *gígnesthai* beget]

theol., 1. theologian. **2.** theological. **3.** theology.

the·o·log (thē′ə lôg, -log), *n. U.S. Informal.* theologue.

the·ol·o·gas·ter (thē ol′ə gas′tər), *n.* a shallow theologian; pretender in theology: *The like measure is offered unto God himself by a company of theologasters* (Robert Burton). [< *theolog*(ian) + Latin *-aster,* a diminutive suffix]

the·ol·o·gate (thē ol′ə gāt), *n.* a theological college or seminary: *At the present theologate of the Servites six theologians, all with doctorates, have only twenty students* (New York Times). [< New Latin *theologatus* < Latin *theológus* theologue + *-ātus* -ate[3]]

the·o·lo·gian (thē′ə lō′jən, -jē ən), *n.* a person skilled or trained in theology, especially Christian theology; divine.

the·o·log·ic (thē′ə loj′ik), *adj.* theological: *thelogic doctrine.*

the·o·log·i·cal (thē′ə loj′ə kəl), *adj.* **1.** of, having to do with, or dealing with theology: *A theological school trains young men for the ministry.* **2.** of or having to do with the word of God; referring to the nature and will of God; scriptural.

the·o·log·i·cal·ly (thē′ə loj′ə klē), *adv.* according to theology: *It is clear then that the religions of Japan are, both theologically and institutionally, quite different from those of the Western world* (Atlantic).

theological virtues, faith, hope, and charity. I Corinthians 13:13.

the·ol·o·gist (thē ol′ə jist), *n.* a theologian: *the Rev. Mr. M'Corkendale, and all the theologists and saints of that persuasion* (Tobias Smollett).

the·ol·o·gi·za·tion (thē ol′ə jə zā′shən), *n.* the act of theologizing.

the·ol·o·gize (thē ol′ə jīz), *v.,* **-gized, -gizing.** —*v.i.* to reason theologically; theorize or speculate on theological subjects. —*v.t.* to make theological; treat theologically. —**the·ol′o·giz′er,** *n.*

the·o·logue (thē′ə lôg, -log), *n. U.S. Informal.* a theological student. Also, **theolog.**

[< Latin *theológus* < Greek *theológos* < *theós* God + *-logos* treating of]

the·ol·o·gy (thē ol′ə jē), *n., pl.* **-gies. 1.** the study of God, His nature and attributes, and His relations with man and the universe. **2.** the study or science of religion and religious beliefs. **3.** a system of religious beliefs: *Calvinistic theology. Abbr.:* theol. [< Late Latin *theologia* < Greek *theologiā* < *theológos* one discoursing on god; see THEOLOGUE]

the·om·a·chy (thē om′ə kē), *n., pl.* **-chies.** a battle or strife among the gods (especially in reference to that narrated in Homer's *Iliad*). [< Late Latin *theomachia* < Greek *theomachíā* < *theós* god + *máchesthai* to fight]

the·o·mor·phic (thē′ə môr′fik), *adj.* **1.** having the form or likeness of God. **2.** of or having to do with the doctrine that man is formed in God's image. [< Greek *theómorphos* (< *theós* god + *morphḗ* form) + English *-ic*]

the·o·pa·thet·ic (thē′ə pə thet′ik), *adj.* responsive to divine influence; emotionally sensitive to feelings inspired by contemplation of God. [< *theopathy;* patterned on *pathetic*]

the·o·path·ic (thē′ə path′ik), *adj.* theopathetic.

the·op·a·thy (thē op′ə thē), *n., pl.* **-thies.** piety or a sense of piety. [< *theo-* + *-pathy.* Compare Greek *theopátheia* the divine suffering.]

the·oph·a·gy (thē of′ə jē), *n.* the symbolic eating of a god in a religious ritual or ceremony. [< Greek *théos* god + *phageîn* eat]

the·oph·a·ny (thē of′ə nē), *n., pl.* **-nies.** an appearance of God or a god to man. [< Late Latin *theophānia* < Greek *theophānīā* vision of God, apparently variant of *theopháneia* a festival at Delphi at which statues of Apollo and other gods were shown to the public < *theós* god + *phaínein* to show]

the·o·pho·bi·a (thē′ə fō′bē ə), *n.* the fear or dread of God.

the·o·phyl·lin (thē′ə fil′in), *n.* theophylline.

the·o·phyl·line (thē′ə fil′ēn, -in), *n.* a poisonous, crystalline alkaloid, isomeric with theobromine, contained in tea leaves in very small amounts and used to treat hypertension and various heart conditions. *Formula:* $C_7H_8N_4O_2.H_2O$ [< New Latin *thea* tea (see THEACEOUS) + Greek *phýllon* leaf + English *-ine*[2]]

theor., theorem.

the·or·bo (thē ôr′bō), *n., pl.* **-bos.** an obsolete kind of lute having two necks. [< French *théorbe* < Italian *tiorba,* probably < Turkish *torba*]

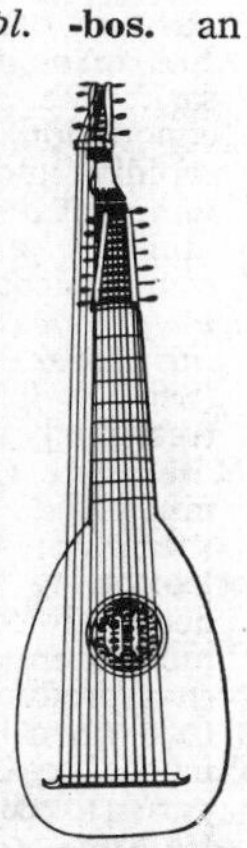

Theorbo (17th century)

the·o·rem (thē′ər əm, thir′əm), *n.* **1.** *Mathematics.* **a.** a statement to be proved. **b.** a rule or statement of relations that can be expressed by an equation or formula: *Geometrical theorems grew out of empirical methods* (Herbert Spencer). **2.** a universal or general statement, not self-evident, that can be proved to be true. [< Latin *theōrēma* < Greek *theṓrēma, -atos* < *theōreîn* to consider; see THEORY]

the·o·re·mat·ic (thē′ər ə mat′ik, thir′ə-), *adj.* having to do with, by means of, or of the nature of a theorem: *theorematic truth.*

the·o·ret·ic (thē′ə ret′ik), *adj.* theoretical: *Distinguished . . . as a theoretic and practical farmer* (George Eliot).
—*n.* **theoretics,** theoretical matters; theory: *Morals come before contemplation, ethics before theoretics* (H. B. Wilson).
[< Late Latin *theōrēticus* < Greek *theōrētikós* < *theōrētós* perceivable < *theōreîn* to consider; see THEORY]

the·o·ret·i·cal (thē′ə ret′ə kəl), *adj.* **1.** planned or worked out in the mind, not from experience; based on theory, not on fact; limited to theory. **2. a.** dealing with theory only; not practical: *City boys can get a theoretical knowledge of farming.* **b.** having the object of knowledge as its end; concerned with knowledge only, not with accomplishing anything or producing anything; purely scientific.
—**Syn. 1.** hypothetical. **2. b.** speculative.

theoretical arithmetic, the theory of numbers.

the·o·ret·i·cal·ly (thē′ə ret′ə klē), *adv.* in theory; according to theory; in a theoretical manner.

the·o·re·ti·cian (thē′ər ə tish′ən), *n.* a person who knows much about the theory of an art, science, etc.

the·o·rist (thē′ər ist, thir′ist), *n.* **1.** a person who forms theories. **2.** one who is adept in the theory (contrasted with practice) of a subject.

the·o·ri·za·tion (thē′ər ə zā′shən), *n.* the formation of a theory or theories; speculation.

the·o·rize (thē′ə rīz), *v.i.,* **-rized, -riz·ing.** to form a theory or theories; speculate: *It is a capital mistake to theorize before one has data* (Sir Arthur Conan Doyle).

the·o·riz·er (thē′ə rī′zər), *n.* a person who theorizes.

the·o·ry (thē′ər ē, thir′ē), *n., pl.* **-ries. 1. a.** an explanation; explanation based on thought; explanation based on observation and reasoning: *the theory of evolution, Einstein's theory of relativity. There were several theories about the way in which the fire started.* **b.** a hypothesis proposed as an explanation; reasonable guess: *Whether I am right in the theory or not . . . the fact is as I state it* (Edmund Burke). **2.** the principles or methods of a science or art rather than its practice: *the theory of music, the theory of modern warfare.* **3. a.** systematic conception or statement of the principles of something; abstract knowledge (often used in implying more or less unsupported hypothesis): *Veneer'd with sanctimonious theory* (Tennyson). **b.** thought or fancy as opposed to fact or practice. **4.** *Mathematics.* a set of theorems which constitute a connected, systematic view of some branch of mathematics: *the theory of probabilities.* **5.** *Obsolete.* mental view; contemplation.
in theory, according to theory; theoretically: *In theory the plan should have worked.* [< Late Latin *theōria* < Greek *theōríā* a looking at, thing looked at < *theōreîn* to consider, look at < *theōrós* spectator < *théā* a sight + *horán* to see]
—**Syn. 1. a, b. Theory, hypothesis** mean an explanation based on observation and thought. **Theory** applies to an explanation that has been tested and confirmed as a general principle explaining a large number of related facts, occurrences, or other phenomena in nature, mechanics, etc.: *Einstein's theory of relativity explains the motion of moving objects.* **Hypothesis** applies to a proposed explanation for a certain group of facts, admittedly unproved but accepted for the time being as highly probable or as an experimental guide: *Archeological discoveries strengthened the hypothesis that Troy existed.*

theory of games, a theory dealing with the strategies used by the competitors in games or other situations involving the interplay of chance and skill in determining action or choice, and the mathematical probabilities associated with these.

theory of numbers, the study of integers and their relationships; number theory.

theos. or **Theos., 1.** theosophical. **2.** theosophist. **3.** theosophy.

the·o·soph (thē′ə sof), *n.* a theosophist.

the·o·soph·ic (thē′ə sof′ik), *adj.* of or having to do with theosophy. —**the′o·soph′i·cal·ly,** *adv.*

the·o·soph·i·cal (thē′ə sof′ə kəl), *adj.* theosophic.

the·os·o·phism (thē os′ə fiz əm), *n.* theosophy.

the·os·o·phist (thē os′ə fist), *n.* a person who believes in theosophy.

the·os·o·phy (thē os′ə fē), *n.* any system of philosophy or religion that claims to have a special insight into the divine nature through spiritual self-development. [< Medieval Latin *theosophia* < Late Greek *theosophíā* < Greek *theósophos* one wise about God < *theós* god + *sophós* wise]

The·os·o·phy (thē os′ə fē), *n.* the modern philosophical system expounded by the Theosophical Society, founded in 1875, drawing inspiration from Buddhism and Brahmanism, and investigating or assuming to possess the tradition claimed to underlie the several historical religions.

the·o·tech·nic (thē′ə tek′nik), *adj.* of or having to do with the action or intervention of the gods; operated or carried on by or as by the gods.

the·o·tech·ny (thē′ə tek′nē), *n.* **1.** the introduction of divine or supernatural beings into a literary composition. **2.** such beings collectively. [< *theo-* + Greek *téchnē* art]

therap., 1. therapeutic. **2.** therapeutics.

ther·a·peu·sis (ther′ə pyü′sis), *n., pl.* **-ses** (-sēz). therapeutic treatment. [< New Latin *therapeusis* < Greek *therapeúein* to cure]

ther·a·peu·tic (ther′ə pyü′tik), *adj.* of or having to do with the treatment or curing of disease; curative: *Heat has therapeutic value.* [< New Latin *therapeuticus* < Greek *therapeutikós* < *therapeutḗs* one ministering < *therapeúein* to cure, treat < *théraps, -apos* attendant] —**ther′a·peu′ti·cal·ly,** *adv.*
—**Syn.** remedial, healing.

ther·a·peu·ti·cal (ther′ə pyü′tə kəl), *adj.* therapeutic.

ther·a·peu·tics (ther′ə pyü′tiks), *n.* the branch of medicine that deals with the treatment or curing of disease.

ther·a·peu·tist (ther′ə pyü′tist), *n.* a person who specializes in therapeutics.

ther·a·pist (ther′ə pist), *n.* therapeutist.

ther·ap·sid (thə rap′sid), *n.* any of a group of reptiles first appearing in the Permian period, that had differentiated teeth and skulls much like the mammals of which they are thought to be the ancestors. [< New Latin *Therapsidae* the family name < *théraps* attendant]

ther·a·py (ther′ə pē), *n., pl.* **-pies. 1.** the treatment of diseases (used especially in compounds): *physical therapy, electrotherapy.* **2.** curative power; healing quality. [< New Latin *therapia* < Greek *therapeíā* < *therapeúein;* see THERAPEUTIC]

Ther·a·va·da (ther′ə vä′də), *n.* the form of Buddhism predominant in southeastern Asia; Hinayana: *At least half a dozen religions or sects were represented by scholars at the center—Buddhism* (*both Mahayana and Theravada*), *Christianity* (*Catholic and Protestant*), *Hinduism, Judaism, Mohammedanism, and the Parsi, or Zoroastrian, faith* (New Yorker). [< Pali *theravāda* (literally) way of the elders]

there (ŦHãr; *unstressed* ŦHər), *adv.* **1.** in or at that place: *Sit there.* **2.** to or into that place: *How did that get there? Go there at once.* **3.** at that point or stage in action, proceeding, speech, or thought: *You have done enough, you may stop there. If you hadn't stopped there, you could have won in a few moves.* **4.** in that matter, particular, or respect: *You are mistaken there.* **5.** *There* is also used in sentences in which the verb comes before its subject: *There comes a time when. . . . There was heard a rumbling noise. There are three new houses on our street. Is there a drugstore near here?* **6.** *There* is used to call attention to some person or thing: *There goes the bell. There comes the mail.*
all there. See under **all,** *adv.*
—*n.* that place; place yonder: *From there we went on to New York.*
—*interj.* an expression of satisfaction, triumph, dismay, encouragement, comfort, etc.: *There, there! Don't cry.*
[Old English *thǣr*]
➤ **there** (*adv.* def. 5). When *there* is used as a temporary substitute for the real subject, the verb agrees in number with the real subject: *There was much work to be done. There are many answers in the back of the book.*

there·a·bout (ŦHãr′ə bout′), *adv.* thereabouts.

there·a·bouts (ŦHãr′ə bouts′), *adv.* **1.** near that place. **2.** near that time: *to leave on June 3 or thereabouts.* **3.** near that number or amount: *to use 50 gallons of oil or thereabouts, to fall to zero or thereabouts.*

there·af·ter (ŦHãr af′tər, -äf′-), *adv.* **1.** after that; afterwards: *He was very ill as a child and was considered delicate thereafter.* **2.** accordingly.
—**Syn. 1.** subsequently.

there·a·gainst (ŦHãr′ə genst′), *adv. Archaic.* against or in opposition to that.

there·a·mong (ŦHãr′ə mung′), *adv.* among that, those, or them.

there·at (ŦHãr at′), *adv.* **1.** when that happened; at that time. **2.** because of that; because of it. **3.** at that place.

there·a·way (ŦHãr′ə wā′), *adv.* **1.** in that region; in those parts. **2.** about that time, amount, etc.: *for five or six months or thereaway* (Scott). **3.** *Obsolete.* away thither; in that direction.

there·by (ŦHãr bī′, ŦHãr′bī), *adv.* **1.** by means of that; in that way: *He wished to travel and thereby study other countries.* **2.** in connection with that: *George won the game, and thereby hangs a tale.* **3.** by or near that place; near there: *a farm lay thereby.* **4.** *Scottish.* thereabouts (in number, quantity, or degree). **5.** *Obsolete.* with reference thereto; apropos of that.

there·for (ᴛʜãr fôr′), *adv.* for that; for this; for it: *He promised to give a building for a hospital and as much land as should be necessary therefor.*

there·fore (ᴛʜãr′fôr, -fōr), *adv.* for that reason; as a result of that; consequently: *Helen went to a party and therefore did not study her lessons.* [Middle English *therfore* < *ther*, Old English *thǣr* there + *fore*, variant of *for* for]

—**Syn. Therefore, consequently,** when used to connect two grammatically independent but logically related clauses, indicate that the second follows as a conclusion from the first. **Therefore** implies that the conclusion is inevitable; **consequently** implies that it is reasonable but not inevitable: *He was the only candidate; therefore, he was elected. He is the popular candidate; consequently, he will be elected. I overslept and, consequently, was late.*

there·from (ᴛʜãr from′, -frum′), *adv.* from that; from this; from it: *He opened his bag and took therefrom an apple.*

there·in (ᴛʜãr in′), *adv.* **1. a.** in that place, time, or thing: *God created the sea and all that is therein.* **b.** into that place or thing. **2.** in that matter; in that way: *The captain thought all danger was past. Therein he made a mistake.*

there·in·af·ter (ᴛʜãr′in af′tər, -äf′-), *adv.* after in that document, statute, etc.; later in the same contract, deed, or other legal instrument.

there·in·be·fore (ᴛʜãr′in bi fôr′, -fōr′), *adv.* before in that document, statement, etc.

there·in·to (ᴛʜãr in′tü, ᴛʜãr′in tü′), *adv.* **1.** into that place; into it. **2.** into that matter.

Ther·e·min (ther′ə min), *n. Trademark.* a musical instrument whose sound is produced by two high-frequency electric circuits, the pitch of the tone and the volume depending upon the distance of the player's outstretched hands from two antennas, without touching them. [< Leon *Theremin*, born 1896, the Russian inventor]

there·ness (ᴛʜãr′nis), *n.* the quality of having location, situation, or existence in a particular point or place: *Giotto was ultimately responsible for the thereness of the figures in Sassetta's painting* (Listener).

there·of (ᴛʜãr ov′, -uv′), *adv.* **1.** of that; of it. **2.** from it; from that source.

there·on (ᴛʜãr on′, -ôn′), *adv.* **1.** on that; on it: *A swan Swims on a lake, with her double thereon* (Thomas Hood). **2.** immediately after that; thereupon.

there·out (ᴛʜãr out′), *adv. Archaic.* thence.

there·o·ver (ᴛʜãr ō′vər), *adv. Archaic.* over or above that.

there's (ᴛʜãrz), there is.

there·through (ᴛʜãr thrü′), *adv.* **1.** through that, it, etc. **2.** by means of that; thereby.

there·to (ᴛʜãr tü′), *adv.* **1.** to that; to it: *The castle stands on a hill, and the road thereto is steep and rough.* **2.** in addition to that; besides; also; moreover.

there·to·fore (ᴛʜãr′tə fôr′, -fōr′), *adv.* before that time; until then: *Its author was a man I had theretofore known only through references in the writings of others* (New Yorker). —**Syn.** previously.

there·un·der (ᴛʜãr un′dər), *adv.* **1.** under that; under it. **2.** under the authority of; according to that. **3.** under or less than that (number, age, etc.).

there·un·to (ᴛʜãr un′tü, ᴛʜãr′un tü′), *adv.* **1.** to that; to it. **2.** *Obsolete.* in addition to that; thereto.

there·up·on (ᴛʜãr′ə pon′, -pôn′), *adv.* **1.** immediately after that: *The President appeared. Thereupon the people clapped.* **2.** because of that; therefore: *The stolen jewels were found in his room; thereupon he was put in jail.* **3.** on that; on it: *The knight carried a shield with a cross painted thereupon.* **4.** *Archaic.* on that subject or matter.

there·with (ᴛʜãr wiᴛʜ′, -with′), *adv.* **1.** with that; with it. **2.** immediately after that; then. **3.** besides; withal. **4.** against that (or those).

there·with·al (ᴛʜãr′wiᴛʜ ôl′), *adv.* **1.** with that; with this; with it. **2.** in addition to that; also.

the·ri·ac (thir′ē ak), *n.* theriaca.

the·ri·a·ca (thi rī′ə kə), *n.* **1.** treacle or molasses. **2.** *Obsolete.* an antidote for poisonous bites or for poisons, made up of many ingredients. [< Latin *thēriaca* < Greek *thēriakē* (*antídotos*), or *thēriakòn* (*phármakon*). Doublet of TREACLE.]

the·ri·a·cal (thi rī′ə kəl), *adj.* having to do with theriaca; medicinal.

the·ri·an·throp·ic (thir′ē an throp′ik), *adj.* **1.** part human and part animal, as a mermaid, sphinx, or centaur. **2.** of or having to do with a deity or deities combining the form of a beast with that of a man. [< Greek *thēríon* (diminutive) < *thēr, thērós* wild beast + *ánthrōpos* man; + English *-ic*]

the·ri·an·thro·pism (thir′ē an′thrə piz əm), *n.* the worship of therianthropic deities.

the·rid·i·id (thə rid′ē id), *n.* one of a group of spiders, most of whom spin webs consisting of irregularly intersecting threads: *In a completely dark basement I have ... seen many sheets spun by theridiids* (Scientific American). —*adj.* of or belonging to the theridiids. [< New Latin *Theridium* the genus name < Greek *thēríon* (diminutive) < *thēr, thērós* wild beast]

the·ri·o·mor·phic (thir′ē ə môr′fik), *adj.* of or having to do with a deity worshiped in the form of a beast. [< Greek *thēriómorphos* < *thēríon* (diminutive) < *thēr* wild beast + *morphḗ* form; + English *-ic*]

the·ri·o·mor·phous (thir′ē ə môr′fəs), *adj.* theriomorphic.

therm (thėrm), *n. Physics.* any of various units of heat: **a.** the small calorie. **b.** the large or great calorie. **c.** a unit equivalent to 1,000 large calories. **d.** a unit equivalent to 100,000 British thermal units, used as a basis of charge for gas supplied. Also, **therme.** [< Greek *thérmē* heat]

therm-, *combining form.* the form of **thermo-** before vowels, as in *thermal.*

therm., **1.** thermometer. **2.** thermometric.

ther·mae (thėr′mē), *n.pl.* **1. a.** a public bathing establishment of the ancient Greeks or Romans, originally built over or near a natural hot spring or springs but later using water heated by artificial means. **b.** the baths of such an establishment. **2.** *Obsolete.* hot springs. [< Latin *thermae* < Greek *thérmai*, plural of *thérmē* heat]

ther·mal (thėr′məl), *adj.* **1.** of or having to do with heat; determined, measured, or operated by heat; thermic: *The thermal balance of the earth is being upset by the carbon dioxide produced by burning coal and oil and already the concentration has been increased 10 per cent* (Science News Letter). **2. a.** of, having to do with, or of the nature of thermae or hot springs. **b.** (of a spring) naturally hot or warm. **c.** having hot springs.

—*n.* a rising current of warm air: *Like gliding, ballooning depends for movement on luck with thermals* (New Yorker). —**ther′mal·ly**, *adv.*

thermal barrier, heat barrier.

ther·mal·i·za·tion (thėr′mə lə zā′shən), *n.* the act or process of thermalizing.

ther·mal·ize (thėr′mə līz), *v.t.*, **-ized, -iz·ing.** to lower the kinetic energy of (an atom or other particle) until it reaches the energy characteristic of the temperature of a particular medium: *These "hot" atoms have such kinetic energy that any molecule they may form by chemical reaction is likely to be instantly fragmented; but if they are "thermalized" ... they will then react in a chemically intelligible manner* (New Scientist).

thermal noise, noise generated in a radio receiver or amplifier by the agitation of electrons in a conductor as a result of heat.

thermal shock, a drastic change in temperature that affects the composition or properties of some organic and inorganic matter: *Severe thermal shock introduces into the metal small plastic strains which result in a slight permanent distortion of the component* (New Scientist).

thermal spring, hot spring.

thermal unit, a unit adopted for measuring and comparing quantities of heat.

therm·an·es·the·sia or **therm·an·aes·the·sia** (thėrm′an əs thē′zhə, -zhē ə), *n.* thermoanesthesia.

therm·an·ti·dote (thėrm an′tə dōt), *n.* a rotating wheellike apparatus, usually enclosed in wet tatties, fixed in a window, and used in India to cool the air: *Will you bring me to book on the Mountains, or where the thermantidotes play?* (Rudyard Kipling). [< *therm-* + *antidote*]

therme (thėrm), *n. Physics.* therm.

therm·es·the·sia or **therm·aes·the·sia** (thėrm′es thē′zhə, -zhē ə), *n. Medicine.* sensitiveness to heat or cold; sensitivity to degree of heat. [< *thermo-* + *esthesia*]

ther·mic (thėr′mik), *adj.* of or having to do with heat; thermal. —**ther′mi·cal·ly**, *adv.*

Ther·mi·dor (thėr′mə dôr; *French* ter mē dôr′), *n.* the eleventh month of the French Revolutionary Calendar, beginning July 19. [< French *Thermidor* < Greek *thérmē* heat + *dôron* gift]

Ther·mi·do·ri·an (thėr′mə dôr′ē ən, -dōr′-), *n.* (in French history) a member of or sympathizer with the more moderate party that overthrew Robespierre and his adherents on the 9th Thermidor (July 27), 1794, thus ending the Reign of Terror.

therm·i·on (thėrm′ī′ən, thėr′mē-), *n. Physics.* an electrically charged particle, either positive (an ion) or negative (an electron), given off by a heated body. [< *therm-* + *ion*]

therm·i·on·ic (thėrm′ī on′ik, thėr′mē-), *adj. Physics.* of or relating to thermionics or thermions: *A thermionic generator is a vacuum or gas-filled device with two elements or electrodes insulated from one another* (J.J. William Brown). —**therm′i·on′i·cal·ly**, *adv.*

thermionic converter, an electronic device that changes heat directly into electricity. It consists of two metallic electrodes held in a tube at different temperatures and separated by a gas at low pressure. When the electrons on the surface of one electrode are heated, they pass to the other electrode and produce electric current.

thermionic current, **1.** an electric current produced by movements of thermions. **2.** a movement of thermions.

thermionic emission, the freeing of electrons by heat, as from a metal: *Thermionic emission was first disclosed in 1883 by Thomas A. Edison* (J.J. William Brown).

therm·i·on·ics (thėrm′ī on′iks, thėr′mē-), *n.* the science of thermionic phenomena.

thermionic tube, **1.** a vacuum tube in which (usually) the cathode is heated to produce electron emission. **2.** thermionic valve.

thermionic valve, *Especially British.* vacuum tube.

ther·mis·tor or **ther·mist·er** (thėr mis′tər), *n.* a small electronic resistor whose conduction of electric current increases rapidly and predictably with a rise in temperature, used especially in heat measurement, and as a voltage regulator in communication circuits: *When the scanning mirror crosses the horizon of a planet, the increase or decrease registers on the thermister* (Science News Letter). [< *therm-* + (res)*istor*]

Ther·mit (thėr′mit), *n. Trademark.* thermite. [< German *Thermit* < *thermo-* thermo- + *-it* -ite[1]]

ther·mite (thėr′mīt), *n.* a mixture of powdered aluminum and the oxide of one or more chemically weak metals, usually iron, that produces an extremely high temperature when ignited, used in welding and in incendiary bombs. [< *therm-* + *-ite*[1]. Compare THERMIT.]

thermo-, *combining form.* **1.** heat, as in *thermodynamics.*
2. thermoelectric, as in *thermocurrent.* Also, **therm-** before vowels.
[< Greek *thermós* hot, and *thérmē* heat]

ther·mo·an·es·the·sia or **ther·mo·an·aes·the·sia** (thėr′mō an′əs thē′zhə, -zhē ə), *n. Medicine.* loss of thermesthesia; inability to feel heat or cold. [< *thermo-* + *anesthesia*]

ther·mo·bar·o·graph (thėr′mō bar′ə graf, -gräf), *n.* an instrument that simultaneously records temperature and atmospheric pressure.

ther·mo·ba·rom·e·ter (thėr′mō bə rom′ə tər), *n.* **1.** a thermometer that indicates the pressure of the atmosphere by the boiling point of water, used in the measurement of altitudes; hypsometer. **2.** a siphon barometer that may be reversed for use as a thermometer.

ther·mo·bat·ter·y (thėr′mō bat′ər ē), *n., pl.* **-ter·ies.** a thermoelectric battery.

ther·mo·cau·ter·y (thėr′mō kô′tər ē), *n., pl.* **-ter·ies.** a cautery in which the metal end of the instrument is heated.

ther·mo·chem·i·cal (thėr′mō kem′ə kəl), *adj.* of or having to do with thermochemistry.
ther·mo·chem·ist (thėr′mō kem′ist), *n.* a person who is skilled in thermochemistry.
ther·mo·chem·is·try (thėr′mō kem′ə strē), *n.* the branch of chemistry dealing with the relations between chemical action and heat.
ther·mo·chro·mic (thėr′mə krō′mik), *adj.* of or having to do with thermochromy.
ther·mo·chro·my (thėr′mə krō′mē), *n.* a change of color occurring in a substance due to varying temperatures: *Thermochromy may well be a general property of solids containing trivalent chromium ions* (New Scientist).
ther·mo·cline (thėr′mə klīn), *n.* a layer within a large body of water sharply separating parts of it that differ in temperature, so that the temperature gradient through the layer is very abrupt. [< *thermo-* + Greek *klīnein* to slope]
ther·mo·cou·ple (thėr′mō kup′əl), *n.* a thermoelectric couple.
ther·mo·cur·rent (thėr′mō kėr′ənt), *n.* the electric current produced in a thermoelectric battery.
ther·mo·dif·fu·sion (thėr′mō di fyü′zhən), *n.* diffusion of heat.
thermodyn., thermodynamics.
ther·mo·dy·nam·ic (thėr′mō dī nam′ik), *adj.* **1.** of or having to do with thermodynamics. **2.** using force due to heat or to the conversion of heat to mechanical energy. —**ther′mo·dy·nam′i·cal·ly,** *adv.*
ther·mo·dy·nam·i·cal (thėr′mō dī nam′ə kəl), *adj.* thermodynamic.
ther·mo·dy·nam·i·cist (thėr′mō dī nam′ə sist), *n.* a person skilled in thermodynamics: *Thermodynamicist required ... for the design study and experimental analysis of compressors, turbines, etc.* (London Times).
ther·mo·dy·nam·ics (thėr′mō dī nam′iks), *n.* the branch of physics that deals with the relations between heat and mechanical energy or work, and of the conversion of one into the other: *The Meteorological Office has now begun a detailed study of the dynamics and thermodynamics of frontal systems and of the quantitative prediction of precipitation* (New Scientist).
ther·mo·e·lec·tric (thėr′mō i lek′trik), *adj.* of or having to do with thermoelectricity: *The voltage output of a single thermoelectric junction is extremely low, about 0.01 volt (direct current) per 100° C. (212° F.) temperature difference between the hot and cold junctions* (J.J. William Brown). —**ther′mo·e·lec′tri·cal·ly,** *adv.*
ther·mo·e·lec·tri·cal (thėr′mō i lek′trə kəl), *adj.* thermoelectric.
thermoelectric couple or **pair,** two dissimilar metallic conductors joined end to end, whose junction, when heated, produces a thermoelectric current in the circuit of which they form a part; thermocouple.
ther·mo·e·lec·tric·i·ty (thėr′mō i lek′tris′ə tē, -ē′lek-), *n.* **1.** electricity produced directly by heat, especially that produced in a closed circuit composed of two dissimilar metals when one of the points of union is kept at a temperature different from that of the rest of the circuit. **2.** the branch of electrical science that deals with such electricity.
thermoelectric thermometer, an electric thermometer consisting essentially of a thermoelectric couple and an indicator.
ther·mo·e·lec·trom·e·ter (thėr′mō i lek′trom′ə tər, -ē′lek-), *n.* an instrument for measuring the heating power of an electric current, or for determining the strength of a current by the heat produced.
ther·mo·e·lec·tro·mo·tive (thėr′mō i-lek′trə mō′tiv), *adj.* of or having to do with electromotive force produced by heat.
ther·mo·el·e·ment (thėr′mō el′ə mənt), *n.* a thermoelectric couple as an element of a battery: *A layer of silica on the silicon-germanium alloy ... protects the thermoelements and renders them chemically inert* (New Scientist).
ther·mo·gal·va·nom·e·ter (thėr′mō gal′və nom′ə tər), *n.* a thermoelectric instrument for measuring small electric currents.
ther·mo·gen·e·sis (thėr′mō jen′ə sis), *n.* the generation or production of heat, especially in an animal body.
ther·mo·ge·net·ic (thėr′mō jə net′ik), *adj.* of or having to do with thermogenesis.
ther·mo·gen·ic (thėr′mə jen′ik), *adj.* thermogenetic.
ther·mog·e·ny (thėr moj′ə nē), *n.* thermogenesis.
ther·mo·ge·og·ra·phy (thėr′mō jē og′rə fē), *n.* the study of the geographical distribution and variation of temperature.
ther·mo·gram (thėr′mə gram), *n.* a measurement recorded by a thermograph: *In medicine, infrared is a supplement to X-ray diagnosis, providing doctors with a thermogram—a photograph that shows not what our eyes would see but what hundreds of thermometers would sense* (Science News Letter).
ther·mo·graph (thėr′mə graf, -gräf), *n.* an automatic, self-registering thermometer.
ther·mo·graph·ic (thėr′mə graf′ik), *adj.* of, having to do with, or obtained by a thermograph or thermography: *The thermographic method, which has become quite popular, is not, strictly speaking, a photocopying method, since it uses the heat of infrared rays, instead of light, for exposure* (R.F. Beckwith). —**ther′mo·graph′i·cal·ly,** *adv.*
ther·mog·ra·phy (thėr mog′rə fē), *n.* the measurement of temperature by means of a thermograph, especially one that uses a photographic process in which infrared rays emitted by the body automatically register temperature changes: *A Canadian breast surgeon, Ray Lawson, working at the Royal Victoria Hospital, Montreal, was the first to use pictorial heat scanning medically, for which he coined the name "thermography"; the year was 1957* (New Scientist).
ther·mo·jet (thėr′mō jet), *n.* a jet engine that forces gas out under great pressure. It is the commonest type of jet engine.
ther·mo·junc·tion (thėr′mō jungk′shən), *n.* the point of union of the two metallic conductors of a thermoelectric couple.
ther·mo·kin·e·mat·ics (thėr′mō kin′ə-mat′iks), *n.* the study of motion caused by heat.
ther·mo·la·bile (thėr′mō lā′bəl), *adj. Biochemistry.* liable to destruction or loss of characteristic properties at moderately high temperatures, as certain toxins.
ther·mol·o·gy (thėr′mol′ə jē), *n.* thermotics.
ther·mo·lu·mi·nes·cence (thėr′mō-lü′mə nes′əns), *n.* the emission of light produced by heat or exposure to high temperature: *Pottery and other heat-treated artifacts up to 500,000 years old can be accurately dated by means of thermoluminescence* (Scientific American).
ther·mo·lu·mi·nes·cent (thėr′mō lü′mə nes′ənt), *adj.* having or showing thermoluminescence.
ther·mol·y·sis (thər mol′ə sis), *n.* **1.** *Physiology.* the dispersion or dissipation of heat from the body. **2.** *Chemistry.* decomposition or dissociation by heat. [< *thermo-* + Greek *lýsis* a loosening; patterned on German *Thermolyse*]
ther·mo·lyt·ic (thėr′mə lit′ik), *adj.* having to do with or producing thermolysis.
thermom., **1.** thermometer. **2.** thermometric.
ther·mo·mag·net·ic (thėr′mō mag net′ik), *adj.* of or having to do with the effect of heat as modifying the magnetic properties of bodies.
ther·mo·me·chan·i·cal (thėr′mō mə-kan′ə kəl), *adj.* having to do with the use of heat to do mechanical work.
ther·mom·e·ter (thər mom′ə tər), *n.* an instrument for measuring the temperature of a body or of space, usually by means of the expansion and contraction of mercury or alcohol in a capillary tube and bulb. [< French *thermomètre* < Greek *thérmē* heat + *métron* measure]

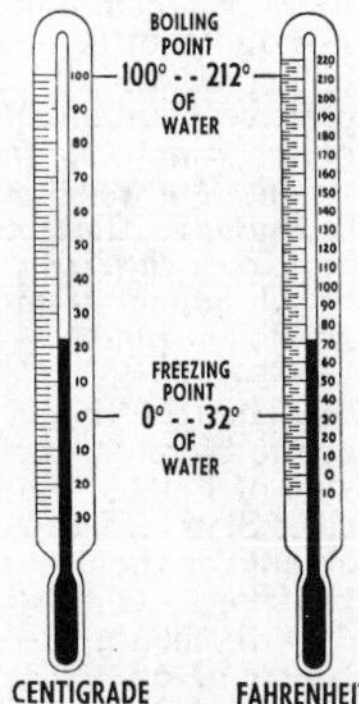

Thermometers

ther·mo·met·ric (thėr′mə met′rik), *adj.* **1.** of or having to do with a thermometer: *the thermometric scale.* **2.** made by means of a thermometer: *thermometric observations.* —**ther′mo·met′ri·cal·ly,** *adv.*
ther·mo·met·ri·cal (thėr′mə met′rə kəl), *adj.* thermometric.
ther·mom·e·try (thər mom′ə trē), *n.* **1.** the measurement of temperature. **2.** the science that deals with the construction of thermometers and their use.
ther·mo·mo·tive (thėr′mō mō′tiv), *adj.* **1.** of, having to do with, or caused by heat applied to produce motion. **2.** relating to a thermomotor.
ther·mo·mo·tor (thėr′mō mō′tər), *n.* an engine driven by the expansive power of heated air or gas.
ther·mo·nu·cle·ar (thėr′mō nü′klē ər, -nyü′-), *adj.* of or having to do with the fusion of atoms through very high temperature, as in the hydrogen bomb: *a thermonuclear reaction, a thermonuclear weapon; an intolerably dangerous jungle of thermonuclear sovereign states* (Observer).
ther·mo·nuke (thėr′mə nük, -nyük), *n. U.S. Informal.* a thermonuclear weapon: *Strategic bombing with "thermonukes" may no longer be a valid military solution* (Bulletin of Atomic Scientists).
Ther·mo·pane (thėr′mə pān), *n. Trademark.* a double insulating glass for windows, doors, etc.
ther·mo·phil·ic (thėr′mə fil′ik), *adj.* (of certain bacteria) requiring high temperatures for development: *He is engaged in research ... on thermophilic bacteria, which flourish at temperatures up to a hundred and seventy-two degrees Fahrenheit, or hot enough to be the death of most bugs* (New Yorker).
ther·mo·pile (thėr′mō pīl), *n. Physics.* a device consisting of several thermoelectric couples acting together for the production of a combined effect, as for generating currents or for ascertaining minute temperature differences. [< *thermo-* + *pile*[1]]
ther·mo·plas·tic (thėr′mō plas′tik), *adj.* becoming soft and capable of being molded when heated, as certain synthetic resins. —*n.* a thermoplastic material.
ther·mo·plas·tic·i·ty (thėr′mō plas tis′ə-tē), *n.* thermoplastic property or condition: *There is one drawback in plastic piping—thermoplasticity* (Science News Letter).
ther·mo·reg·u·la·tion (thėr′mə reg′yə lā′shən), *n.* regulation of body temperature: *mammalian thermoregulation.*
ther·mo·reg·u·la·to·ry (thėr′mō reg′yə-lə tôr′ē, -tōr′-), *adj.* of or having to do with thermoregulation: *The thermoregulatory behaviour of mice was influenced by the intensity and duration of the heat they received* (New Scientist).
Ther·mos bottle, flask, or **jug** (thėr′məs), *Trademark.* a bottle, flask, or jug made with a vacuum between the inner and outer walls so that its contents remain at their original temperature for hours. [< Greek *thermós* hot]

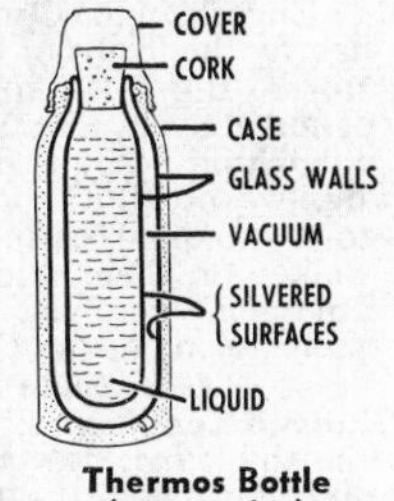

Thermos Bottle (cross section)

ther·mo·scope (thėr′mə skōp), *n.* an instrument or device for indicating variations in temperature without measuring their amount.
ther·mo·scop·ic (thėr′mə skop′ik), *adj.* having to do with or made by means of the thermoscope.
ther·mo·scop·i·cal (thėr′mə skop′ə kəl), *adj.* thermoscopic.
ther·mo·set (thėr′mə set), *adj., n.* thermosetting: *Examples of such randomly connected network polymers are the ... "thermoset" plastics such as Bakelite, most epoxy, urethane, and polyester resins, and vulcanized rubber* (John F. Brown, Jr.).
ther·mo·set·ting (thėr′mō set′ing), *adj.* becoming hard and permanently shaped under the continued application of heat, as certain synthetic resins. —*n.* thermosetting action or quality.
ther·mo·si·phon (thėr′mō sī′fən), *n.* a siphon attachment by which the circulation in a system of hot-water pipes is increased or induced.
ther·mo·sphere (thėr′mə sfir); *n.* the region of the atmosphere above the mesopause, in which temperature increases with height: *The outermost part of the thermosphere is the fringe region where the earth's atmosphere merges with interplanetary gases* (Knudsen and McGuire).

ther•mo•sta•bil•i•ty (thėr′mō stə bil′ə tē), *n.* the quality of being thermostable.

ther•mo•sta•ble (thėr′mō stā′bəl), *adj. Biochemistry.* able to undergo heat without loss to characteristic properties, as certain ferments or toxins.

ther•mo•stat (thėr′mə stat), *n.* **1.** an automatic device for regulating temperature, especially one in which the expansive and contractive action of a metal or gas opens and closes an electric circuit, by which in turn an oil furnace, air conditioner, etc., is caused to operate or cease to operate. **2.** any device that responds automatically to conditions of temperature, as an automatic fire alarm or sprinkler system. [< *thermo-* + *-stat*]

ther•mo•stat•ic (thėr′mə stat′ik), *adj.* of, having to do with, or like a thermostat.

ther•mo•stat•i•cal•ly (thėr′mə stat′ə klē), *adv.* by means of a thermostat.

ther•mo•stat•ics (thėr′mə stat′iks), *n.* the science dealing with the equilibrium of heat.

ther•mo•tax•ic (thėr′mō tak′sik), *adj.* of or having to do with thermotaxis.

ther•mo•tax•is (thėr′mō tak′sis), *n.* **1.** *Biology.* the movement of an organism in response to changes in temperature. **2.** *Physiology.* the regulation of body temperature.

ther•mo•ten•sile (thėr′mō ten′səl), *adj.* relating to tensile strength as affected by variations of temperature.

ther•mo•ther•a•py (thėr′mō ther′ə pē), *n.* therapy in which heat is used.

ther•mot•ic (thər mot′ik), *adj.* **1.** of or having to do with heat. **2.** of or having to do with thermotics.

ther•mot•ics (thər mot′iks), *n.* the science of heat. [< Greek *thermōtikós* warming (< *thermós* warm, hot) + English *-ics*]

ther•mot•o•nus (thər mot′ə nəs), *n. Botany.* the relation between temperature and irritability or movement; responsiveness to heat. [< New Latin *thermotonus* < *thermo-* thermo- + Greek *tónos* tension]

ther•mo•trop•ic (thėr′mə trop′ik), *adj.* of, having to do with, or exhibiting thermotropism.

ther•mot•ro•pism (thər mot′rə piz əm), *n. Biology.* a tendency to bend or turn toward or away from the sun or other source of heat.

ther•mo•vol•ta•ic (thėr′mō vol tā′ik), *adj.* of or having to do with the thermal effects of voltaic electricity, or heat and voltaic electricity.

the•roid (thir′oid), *adj.* like or having the form of a brute; of a bestial nature or character. [< Greek *thḗr, thērós* wild beast + English *-oid.* Compare Greek *thēroeidḗs* having the forms of beasts.]

the•rol•o•gy (thi rol′ə jē), *n.* the science of mammals; mammalogy. [< Greek *thḗr, thērós* wild beast + English *-logy*]

ther•o•pod (thir′ə pod), *adj.* of or belonging to a group of carnivorous dinosaurs that walked on their hind legs. —*n.* a theropod dinosaur. [< New Latin *Theropoda* the suborder name < Greek *thḗr, thērós* wild beast + *poús, podós* foot]

Ther•si•tes (thər sī′tēz), *n. Greek Legend.* (in the *Iliad*) the most vindictive, ugly, and abusive of the Greeks at the siege of Troy, killed by Achilles (who was, with Ulysses, a chief target of his abuse).

ther•sit•i•cal (thər sit′ə kəl), *adj.* abusive; reviling; scurrilous: *There is a pelting kind of Thersitical satire, as black as the very ink 'tis wrote with* (Laurence Sterne). [< Greek *Thersítēs* Thersites + English *-ic* + *-al*[1]]

the•sau•ro•sis (thi sə rō′sis), *n.* a disease in which the cells of the body store an excessive amount of exogenous or endogenous substances: *Fifteen cases of thesaurosis pointing to abnormal inhalation of hair spray have been reported* (Science News Letter). [< Greek *thēsaurós* storehouse + English *-osis*]

the•sau•rus (thi sôr′əs), *n., pl.* **-sau•ri** (-sôr′ī). **1.** a dictionary, encyclopedia, or other book that is a storehouse of information: *This work is one of five thesauri published under the auspices of Kang Hsi, the second Emperor of the present dynasty* (Westminster Gazette). **2.** a treasury; storehouse. [< Latin *thēsaurus* < Greek *thēsaurós* storehouse, treasure. Doublet of TREASURE.]

these (ᴛʜēz), *adj., pron.* the plural of **this:** *These days are cold* (*adj.*). *These two problems are hard* (*adj.*). *These are my books* (*pron.*). [Old English *thes* this, pronoun + *-e,* apparently patterned on the plural form of adjectives. Compare THOSE.]

➔ For *these kind, these sort,* see **kind.**

➔ See **this** for another usage note.

The•se•an (thi sē′ən), *adj.* of or belonging to Theseus.

The•sei•on (thi sī′on), *n.* Theseum. [< Greek *Thēseîon*]

The•se•um (thi sē′əm), *n.* **1.** a temple or shrine dedicated to Theseus, the legendary hero and king of Athens. **2.** a so-called temple of Theseus (now regarded as a temple of Hephaestus) at Athens, a beautiful Doric structure of Pentelic marble and the best-preserved of the Greek temples. [< Latin *Thēsēum* < Greek *Thēseîon* Thesion < *Thēseús* Theseus]

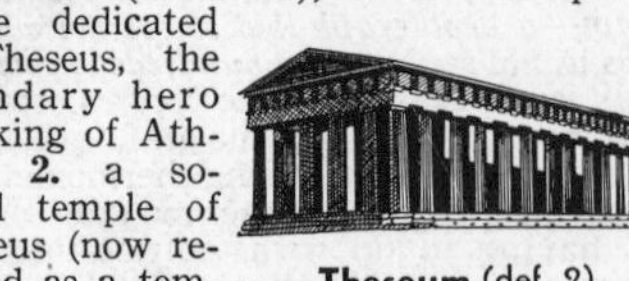

Theseum (def. 2)

The•se•us (thē′sē əs, -süs), *n. Greek Legend.* the most important hero of Attica, son of Aegeus, King of Athens. He killed Procrustes and other robbers, made his way through the Labyrinth at Crete (with Ariadne's help) and killed the Minotaur, united the various states of Attica, fought the Amazons and married their princess, joined the Argonauts, and took part in the Calydonian boar hunt.

the•sis (thē′sis), *n., pl.* **-ses** (-sēz). **1. a.** a proposition or statement to be proved or maintained against objections. **b.** a necessary preliminary assumption, whether to be proved or taken for granted; postulate. **2. a.** an essay. **b.** an essay presented by a candidate for a diploma or degree: *a master's thesis.* **3.** *Music.* the strong or downward beat in a measure. **4.** *Prosody.* **a.** the accented (strong) part of a foot. **b.** the unaccented (weak) syllable or syllables of a foot, the use originating in a misunderstanding of the Greek word. [< Latin *thesis* < Greek *thésis* a proposition, the downbeat (in music); (originally) any setting down or placing < *tithénai* to place]

Thes•pi•an or **thes•pi•an** (thes′pē ən), *adj.* **1.** of or having to do with the drama or tragedy; dramatic; tragic. **2.** of or having to do with Thespis, a Greek tragic poet. —*n.* an actor or actress: *Theatrical agents handle the affairs of all . . . kinds of Thespians* (Punch). [< Greek *Théspis* Thespis, a Greek poet of the 500's B.C., the traditional founder of Greek tragedy + English *-an*]

Thess., Thessalonians.

Thes•sa•li•an (the sā′lē ən), *adj.* of or having to do with Thessaly, a district in eastern Greece, or its people. —*n.* a native or inhabitant of Thessaly.

Thes•sa•lo•ni•an (thes′ə lō′nē ən), *adj.* of or having to do with Thessalonica (Salonika), a seaport in northeastern Greece, or its people. —*n.* a native or inhabitant of Thessalonica (Salonika).

Thes•sa•lo•ni•ans (thes′ə lō′nē ənz), *n.pl.* (*sing. in use*). either of two epistles, books of the New Testament, I Thessalonians and II Thessalonians, written by the Apostle Paul to the Christians of Thessalonica. Full title, *The First* (or *Second*) *Epistle of Paul the Apostle to the Thessalonians. Abbr.:* Thess.

the•ta (thā′tə, thē′-), *n.* the eighth letter (Θ, θ,) of the Greek alphabet, corresponding to the English *th* in *thin.* [< Greek *thêta*]

thet•ic (thet′ik), *adj.* **1.** characterized by laying down or setting forth; involving positive statement: *His* [*Mohammed's*] *genius was not thetic but synthetic, not creative but constructive* (A.M. Fairbairn). **2.** *Prosody.* that bears the thesis; stressed. [< Greek *thetikós* positive; (literally) fit to be placed < *thetós* placed < *tithénai* to set down, place] —**thet′i•cal•ly,** *adv.*

thet•i•cal (thet′ə kəl), *adj.* thetic; positive.

The•tis (thē′tis), *n. Greek Mythology.* one of the Nereids, the mother of Achilles and wife of Peleus. She dipped Achilles in the river Styx and thus made him invulnerable except for the heel by which she held him.

the•ur•gic (thē ėr′jik), *adj.* of or having to do with theurgy. —**the•ur′gi•cal•ly,** *adv.*

the•ur•gi•cal (thē ėr′jə kəl), *adj.* theurgic.

the•ur•gist (thē′ėr jist), *n.* a person who believes in or practices theurgy.

the•ur•gy (thē′ėr jē), *n., pl.* **-gies. 1.** a system of magic, originally practiced by certain members of the Egyptian school of Neoplatonism, to procure communication with beneficent spirits, and by their aid produce miraculous effects. **2. a.** the operation of a divine or supernatural agency in human affairs, especially at the behest of a human being. **b.** an instance of this; divine or supernatural act; miracle. [< Late Latin *theūrgia* < Greek *theourgíā* sorcery < *theós* god + *érgon* work]

thewed (thyüd, thüd), *adj.* having thews; muscled.

thew•less (thyü′lis, thü′-), *adj.* without energy; inert; spiritless.

thews (thyüz, thüz), *n.pl.* **1.** muscles; sinews. **2.** physical power or force; might; strength; vigor. [Middle English *thewe* good qualities, virtues, Old English *thēaw* habit + *-s*[1]]

thew•y (thyü′ē, thü′-), *adj.* sinewy; brawny; muscular.

they[1] (ᴛʜā), *pron., pl. nom.; poss.,* **their, theirs;** *obj.,* **them. 1.** the nominative plural of **he, she,** or **it:** *Where are they? They are on the kitchen table.* **2.** *Informal.* people in general; some people; any people; persons. [< Scandinavian (compare Old Icelandic *their*)]

➔ Indefinite **they,** common in spoken English, is regularly avoided in standard written English: *There have been* (not *They have had*) *no serious accidents at that crossing for over two years. Germany was completely prostrate at the end of the war, but it has* (not *they have*) *made an amazing recovery.*

they[2] (ᴛʜā), *adv. Dialect.* there: *"They'll be work; they's got to be"* (Atlantic).

they'd (ᴛʜād), **1.** they had. **2.** they would.

they'll (ᴛʜāl), **1.** they will. **2.** they shall.

they're (ᴛʜãr), they are.

they've (ᴛʜāv), they have.

THI (no periods), temperature-humidity index.

thi-, *combining form.* a variant of **thio-,** as in *thiamine.*

thi•a•ben•da•zole (thī′ə ben′də zōl), *n.* a drug used in the treatment of trichinosis and other parasitic diseases, especially of animals. [< *thia*(zolyl)*ben*(zimi)*dazole*]

thi•al•dine (thī al′dēn, -dīn), *n.* a white basic compound that has a powerful action on the heart. *Formula:* $C_6H_{13}NS_2$ [< *thi-* + *ald*(ehyde) + *-ine*[2]]

thi•am•ide (thī am′īd, -id), *n.* any of a class of compounds formed by replacing the oxygen of an amide by sulfur.

thi•a•min (thī′ə min), *n.* a crystalline organic compound present in whole-grain cereals, yeast, meats, etc., or prepared synthetically; vitamin B_1; aneurin. It aids in preventing beriberi and neuritis. *Formula:* $C_{12}H_{17}ClN_4OS$ [< *thi-* + *amin*(e)]

thi•a•mine (thī′ə min, -mēn), *n.* thiamin.

Thian-shan sheep (tyän′shän′), Marco Polo sheep.

thi•a•zin (thī′ə zin), *n.* thiazine.

thi•a•zine (thī′ə zin, -zēn), *n.* any of a group of compounds, each having a ring composed of four carbon atoms, one sulfur atom, and one nitrogen atom. The thiazines are the parent substances of certain dyes.

thi•a•zol (thī′ə zōl, -zol), *n.* thiazole.

thi•a•zole (thī′ə zōl), *n.* **1.** a colorless basic liquid that has a pungent odor. It is the parent substance of certain dyes. *Formula:* C_3H_3NS **2.** any of various compounds derived from this substance.

Thi•bet•an (ti bet′ən), *adj., n.* Tibetan.

Thich (tik), *n.* (in Vietnam) a Buddhist honorific title equivalent to reverend or venerable: *Thich Thieu Minh, head of the Buddhist Youth Movement, a close ally of the militant Buddhist leader, Thich Tri Quang . . .* (New York Times).

thick (thik), *adj.* **1.** with much space from one side to the opposite side; not thin: *a thick wall, a thick plank, a thick layer of paint.* **2.** measuring (so much) between two opposite sides: *a board two inches thick.* **3.** set close together; dense: *thick hair, a thick woods, thick foliage.* **4.** many and close together; abundant: *bullets thick as hail.* **5.** filled; covered: *a room thick with flies.* **6.** like glue or syrup, not like water; rather dense or viscid of its kind: *Thick liquids pour much more slowly than thin liquids.* **7.** not clear; foggy: *to land in thick weather, the thick blackness of a moonless night.* **8.** not clear in sound; hoarse: *a thick voice.* **9.** stupid; dull: *He has a thick head.* **10.** *Informal.* very friendly; intimate: *Those two boys are as thick as thieves.* **11.** *Informal.* too much to be endured: *That remark is a bit thick.*

—*adv.* in a thick manner; thickly.

lay it on thick, *Slang.* to praise or blame too much: *Isn't the bloke laying it on a bit* *thick, even for the American tourists?* (Maclean's).

thick and fast, in close or rapid succession; quickly: *Now things started to happen thick and fast* (Jonathan Eberhart). *Thick and fast indeed came the events* (Edward A. Freeman).

—*n.* the thickest part: *in the thick of the fight.*

through thick and thin, in good times and bad: *There's five hundred men here to back you up through thick and thin* (Hall Caine).

—*v.t., v.i. Archaic.* to thicken: *The nightmare Life-in-Death was she, Who thicks men's blood with cold* (Samuel Taylor Coleridge). [Old English *thicce*]

—**Syn.** *adj.* **3.** close, compact, crowded. **4.** plentiful, numerous. **7.** misty, hazy. **8.** indistinct, inarticulate, muffled. **9.** slow, obtuse.

thick-and-thin (thik′ən thin′), *adj.* **1.** that is ready to follow in good times and bad; loyal; steadfast; unwavering: *a thick-and-thin admirer, a thick-and-thin supporter of democracy.* **2.** (of a tackle-block) having one sheave larger than the other.

thick·en (thik′ən), *v.t.* to make thick or thicker: *to thicken a wall, gravy, etc.* —*v.i.* **1.** to become thick or thicker: *The weather has thickened over the Atlantic.* **2.** (of a plot) to become more complex or intricate. —**thick′en·er,** *n.* —**Syn.** *v.t., v.i.* **1.** coagulate, congeal, condense.

thick·en·ing (thik′ə ning, thik′ning), *n.* **1.** a material or ingredient used to thicken something: *to use cornstarch as thickening for a sauce.* **2.** a thickened part or substance. **3.** the act or process of making or becoming thick or thicker.

thick·et (thik′it), *n.* **1.** a number of shrubs, bushes, or small trees growing close together: *We crawled into the thicket and hid.* **2.** a thick, dense mass; jumble: *a thicket of cables.* [Old English *thiccet* < *thicce* thick]

—**Syn. 1.** shrubbery, copse, brake.

thick·et·ed (thik′ə tid), *adj.* covered with thick shrubs, bushes, or small trees.

thick·et·y (thik′ə tē), *adj.* thicketed.

thick·head (thik′hed′), *n.* a person who is dull of intellect; stupid fellow; blockhead.

thick-head·ed (thik′hed′id), *adj.* stupid; dull. —**thick′-head′ed·ness,** *n.* —**Syn.** doltish.

thick·ish (thik′ish), *adj.* somewhat thick: *a faded woman and thickish* (Sinclair Lewis).

thick-knee (thik′nē′), *n.* the stone curlew: *Thick-knees ... were ungainly things, appearing to be something of a cross between a lean chicken and a huge moth* (New York Times).

thick·leaf (thik′lēf′), *n., pl.* **-leaves.** any of a group of mostly South African herbs or shrubs of the orpine family, with thick, succulent leaves.

thick·ly (thik′lē), *adv.* **1.** in a thick manner; closely; densely: *Most of New Jersey is a thickly settled region.* **2.** in great numbers; in abundance: *Weeds grow thickly in rich soil.* **3.** frequently. **4.** with thick consistency. **5.** hoarsely.

thick·ness (thik′nis), *n.* **1.** the quality or state of being thick: *The thickness of the walls shuts out all sound.* **2.** the distance between opposite surfaces; the third measurement of a solid, not length or breadth: *The length of the board is 10 feet, the width 6 inches, the thickness 2 inches.* **3.** the thick part. **4.** a fold or layer: *a bandage made up of three thicknesses of gauze.*

thick·set (thik′set′), *adj.* **1.** growing or occurring closely together; thickly set: *a thick-set hedge.* **2.** thick in form or build: *a short, thick-set man.*

—*n.* **1.** a thicket. **2.** a thick hedge.

thick·skin (thik′skin′), *n.* **1.** a person with a thick skin. **2.** a person who is not sensitive in feeling, as to criticism, rebuff, or the like.

thick-skinned (thik′skind′), *adj.* **1.** having a thick skin or rind: *a thick-skinned orange.* **2.** not sensitive to criticism, reproach, rebuff, or the like.

thick-skulled (thik′skuld′), *adj.* **1.** having a thick skull. **2.** slow or dull; stupid.

thick-sown (thik′sōn′), *adj.* sown or scattered thickly: *thick-sown seeds, thick-sown metaphors.*

thick-wit·ted (thik′wit′id), *adj.* stupid; dull: *He is ... thick-witted enough to adopt any belief that is thrust upon him* (Scott).

thief (thēf), *n., pl.* **thieves.** a person who steals, especially one who steals secretly and without using force; one who commits theft or larceny. [Old English *thēof*]

—**Syn. Thief, robber** mean someone who steals. **Thief** applies to one who steals in a secret or stealthy way: *A thief stole the little boy's bicycle from the yard.* **Robber** applies to one who steals by force or threats of violence: *The robbers bound and gagged the night watchman.*

thieve (thēv), *v.i., v.t.,* **thieved, thiev·ing.** to steal. [Old English *thēofian* < *thēof* thief]

thieve·less (thēv′lis), *adj. Scottish.* **1.** ineffectual; aimless. **2.** spiritless. **3.** cold, especially in manner.

thiev·er·y (thē′vər ē, thēv′rē), *n., pl.* **-er·ies. 1.** the act of stealing; theft. **2.** something stolen.

thieves (thēvz), *n.* the plural of **thief.**

thieves' kitchen, *British Slang.* an area where thieves congregate: *Detectives on a search for illegal gambling are reported to have stumbled on to a thieves' kitchen in Brooklyn* (London Times).

thiev·ish (thē′vish), *adj.* **1.** having the habit of stealing; inclined to steal. **2.** of, having to do with, or like a thief; stealthy; sly: *The cat has a thievish look.* —**thiev′ish·ly,** *adv.* —**thiev′ish·ness,** *n.* —**Syn. 1.** predatory. **2.** furtive.

thig (thig), *v.t., v.i.,* **thigged, thig·ging.** *Scottish.* **1.** to beg; cadge. **2.** to borrow. [Middle English *thiggien* < Scandinavian (compare Old Icelandic *thiggja* receive, related to Old English *thicgean* accept; consume food)]

thig·ger (thig′ər), *n. Scottish.* a person who thigs.

thigh (thī), *n.* **1. a.** the part of the human leg between the hip and the knee. **b.** the corresponding part of the leg of any other primate, as an ape or monkey. **2.** the similar but not corresponding part of a four-legged vertebrate animal, as the horse; upper part of the hind leg. **3.** the second segment of the leg of a bird, containing the tibia and the fibula. **4.** the third segment of the leg of an insect. [Old English *thēoh, thēh*]

thigh·bone (thī′bōn′), *n.* the bone of the thigh in man, the other primates, and four-legged vertebrate animals; femur.

thigh·boot (thī′büt′), *n.* a boot with uppers reaching to the thigh: *The adjutant was pacing up and down in his dark thigh-boots* (Punch).

thighed (thīd), *adj.* having thighs.

thig·mo·tac·tic (thig′mə tak′tik), *adj.* of, having to do with, or exhibiting thigmotaxis.

thig·mo·tax·is (thig′mə tak′sis), *n. Biology.* stereotaxis. [< Greek *thígma, -atos* a touch + *táxis* arrangement]

thig·mo·trop·ic (thig′mə trop′ik), *adj. Biology.* bending or turning in response to a touch stimulus.

thig·mot·ro·pism (thig mot′rə piz əm), *n. Biology.* a tendency of some part of any organism to bend or turn in response to a touch stimulus. [< Greek *thígma, -atos* a touch + English *tropism*]

thill (thil), *n.* either of the shafts between which a single animal drawing a vehicle is placed. [Middle English *thille;* origin uncertain. Compare Old English *thille* board, boarding.]

thim·ble (thim′bəl), *n.* **1.** a small cap of metal or plastic, with many small indentations on its head, worn on the finger to protect it when pushing the needle in sewing. **2.** any of various short metal tubes, rings, sleeves, bushings, or other fittings for machines. **3.** a metal ring fitted within a ring of rope, an open splice, a perforation in a sail, etc., to reduce wear or protect against chafing. [Middle English *thymbyl,* alteration (with intrusive *b*) of Old English *thӯmel* thumbstall < *thūma* thumb] —**thim′ble·like′,** *adj.*

thim·ble·ber·ry (thim′bəl ber′ē), *n., pl.* **-ries.** any of various American raspberries with a thimble-shaped fruit, especially a thornless variety with large, white flowers.

thim·bled (thim′bəld), *adj.* wearing a thimble: *a thimbled finger* (Arnold Bennett).

thim·ble·fish (thim′bəl fish′), *n., pl.* **-fish·es** or (*collectively*) **-fish.** a jellyfish of tropical or warm seas, named from its shape.

thim·ble·ful (thim′bəl fu̇l), *n., pl.* **-fuls. 1.** as much as a thimble will hold; a very small quantity, especially of wine or alcoholic liquor; dram: *Could I trouble you for another thimbleful of brandy?* (H.G. Wells). **2.** a very small amount of anything.

thim·ble·rig (thim′bəl rig′), *n., v.,* **-rigged, -rig·ging.** —*n.* **1.** a form of the shell game using cups shaped like thimbles. **2.** a person who cheats by or as if by the shell game; deft swindler. —*v.t.* to cheat by or as if by the shell game; swindle deftly. [< *thimble* + *rig*[3]] —**thim′ble·rig′ger,** *n.*

thim·ble·rig·ger·y (thim′bəl rig′ə rē), *n.* thimblerigging.

thim·ble·weed (thim′bəl wēd′), *n.* any of various plants whose fruiting heads have the form and markings of a thimble, as an anemone and a rudbeckia.

thin (thin), *adj.,* **thin·ner, thin·nest,** *adv., n., v.,* **thinned, thin·ning.** —*adj.* **1.** with little space from one side to the opposite side; not thick: *a thin book, thin paper, thin wire. The ice on the pond is too thin for skating.* **2.** having little flesh; slender; lean: *a very thin person.* **3.** not set close together; scanty: *thin hair, a thin stand of timber, thin foliage.* **4.** not dense; not rich in oxygen; rarefied: *The air on the top of those high mountains is thin.* **5.** few and far apart; not abundant: *The actors played to a thin audience.* **6.** not like glue or syrup; like water; of less substance than usual: *a thin soup, thin milk, etc.* **7.** not deep or strong: *a shrill, thin voice.* **8.** having little depth, fullness, or intensity: *a thin color, thin applause.* **9. a.** (of liquor) without body; not strong of its kind; of low alcoholic strength; weak. **b.** (of diet or supplies) not full or rich; meager. **10.** easily seen through; flimsy: *It was a thin excuse that satisfied no one.* **11.** *Photography.* (of a negative) relatively transparent, usually as a result of being underexposed or underdeveloped. **12.** *Obsolete.* (of the members of a collective group or class) scarce; rare; few.

—*adv.* **1.** in a thin manner; thinly. **2.** *Obsolete.* in a poor or sparing manner.

—*n.* **1.** something which is thin: *The forms have tentatively been christened thins* (New Scientist). **2.** the thinnest part: *in the thin of things.*

—*v.t.* **1.** to make thin or thinner: *Hunger had thinned her cheeks.* **2.** to make less crowded or close by removing individuals: *to thin a row of beets.* —*v.i.* **1.** to become thin or thinner: *The smoke clouds were thinning away* (Rudyard Kipling). **2. a.** (of a place) to become less full or crowded. **b.** (of a crowd) to become less numerous. [Old English *thynne*] —**thin′ly,** *adv.* —**thin′ness,** *n.*

—**Syn.** *adj.* **1.** narrow, slim, attenuated. **2. Thin, lean, gaunt** mean having little flesh. **Thin,** neither favorable nor unfavorable in connotation, suggests lack of the normal or usual amount of flesh: *She has a thin face.* **Lean,** favorable in connotation, suggests lack of fat: *The forest ranger is lean and brown.* **Gaunt,** unfavorable in connotation, suggests a bony, starved or worn look: *Gaunt, bearded men stumbled into camp.* **5.** sparse.

thine (ᴛʜīn), *Archaic.* —*pron. Possessive case of* **thou.** the one or ones belonging to thee; yours: *My heart is thine.* —*adj. Possessive form of* **thou.** thy; your (used only before a vowel or *h*): *thine enemies.* [Old English *thīn,* genitive of *thū* thou. Compare THY.]

➔ See **thou** for a usage note.

thing[1] (thing), *n.* **1.** any object or substance: *All the things in the house were burned. Put those things away. Food is a nourishing thing. Some drugs are dangerous things.* **2.** whatever is done or to be done; act; deed; fact; event; happening: *It was a good thing to do. A strange thing happened. The shipwreck was a tragic thing.* **3.** whatever is spoken or thought of; idea; opinion: *a dangerous thing to repeat, a mind filled with the oddest things.* **4.** matter; subject; affair; business: *How are things going? Is that thing settled yet?* **5.** an attribute, quality, or property of an actual being or entity: *It is the small things about him that puzzle me.* **6.** something which the speaker is not able or does not choose to particularize, or which is incapable of being precisely described; a something; a somewhat. **7.** (in emphatic use) that which has separate or individual existence (as distinct on the one hand from the totality of being, on the other hand from attributes or qualities). **8.** *Informal.* a person or creature. **9.** *Law.* anything over which a person may exercise possession and control; property.

a thing or two, *Informal.* **a.** things that one should know or find out about; wisdom; experience; knowledge: *Does anyone ... feel inclined to tell me that those old palm-oil*

chiefs have not learnt a thing or two during their lives? (Mary Kingsley). **b.** an example or experience serving as a warning; lesson: *The accident taught him a thing or two about carelessness.*
for one thing, as one point to be noted; in the first place: *For one thing, no one in these hospitals ever seems to do anything* (New Yorker).
have a thing about, *Informal.* to have a phobia about: *They have a thing about opening letters, and never do* (Punch).
make a good thing of, *Informal.* to profit from: *These dealers in ragged merchandise make a good thing of it* (St. Paul's Magazine).
see things, to have hallucinations: *Under the influence of the drug he began to see things.*
(the) first thing, at the earliest possible moment: *He is going first thing in the morning.*
the thing, a. the fashion or style: *The silk is at once rich, tasty, and quite the thing* (Oliver Goldsmith). **b.** the important fact or idea: *The thing about Michelangelo is this: he is not . . . at the head of a class, he stands apart by himself* (John A. Symonds).
things, a. belongings; possessions: *She packed up all her things* (Anthony Trollope). **b.** clothes: *I know every part of their dress, and can name all their things by their names* (Sir Richard Steele). **c.** outdoor clothes: *But having her things on, . . . she thought it best to go* (Samuel Richardson). **d.** implements or equipment for some specified use: *cooking things.*
[Old English *thing* entity, fact; action, a legal case before a court; (originally) a judicial or deliberative assembly. Related to THING².]

thing² (thing, ting), *n.* (in Scandinavian countries) a legislative assembly, court of law, or other public meeting (used especially as the last element of a name): *Storthing, Landsting.* Also, **ting.** [< Scandinavian (compare Icelandic *thing,* Swedish *ting*). Related to THING¹.]

thing·am·a·bob (thing′ə mə bob), *n.* thingumbob.

thing·am·a·jig (thing′ə mə jig), *n.* thingumjig: *He'll send you a little green thingamajig for being so nice* (New Yorker).

thing-in-it·self (thing′in it self′), *n. Philosophy.* a thing regarded apart from its attributes; noumenon. [translation of *Ding an sich,* a phrase used by Kant]

thing·ness (thing′nis), *n.* the quality of a material thing; objectivity; actuality; reality.

thing·stead (thing′sted, ting′-), *n.* a place where a thing (assembly) meets. [Old English *thingstede* < *thing* thing, assembly + *stede* stead, place]

thing·um·a·bob (thing′ə mə bob), *n. Informal.* thingumbob.

thing·um·a·jig (thing′ə mə jig), *n. Informal.* thingumbob.

thing·um·bob (thing′əm bob), *n. Informal.* something whose name one forgets or does not bother to mention: *The boom in continuing education is biggest in the aerospace industry, where landing a Government contract requires a bidder to design the thingumbob in the first place* (Time). [< *thing*¹ + arbitrary suffix]

thing·um·my (thing′ə mē), *n., pl.* **-mies.** *Informal.* thingumbob: *There's no What's-his-name but Thingummy, and What-you-may-call-it is his prophet* (Dickens).

think¹ (thingk), *v.,* **thought, think·ing,** *n., adj.* —*v.t.* **1.** to form (a thought or idea) in the mind: *He thought that he would go. To think so base a thought* (Shakespeare). *O poor hapless nightingale thought I* (Milton). **2.** to form or have an idea, notion, or mental conception of (a thing, action, circumstance, etc.); picture in one's mind; imagine: *You can't think how surprised I was. We think the ocean as a whole* (William James) **3.** to have one's thoughts full of: *He thinks nothing but sports.* **4.** to reflect upon; consider: *I am afraid, to think what I have done* (Shakespeare). **5.** to bring into or out of some specified condition by thinking: *to think one's way out of trouble.* **6.** to intend or plan (to do something); contemplate: *He thinks to escape punishment.* **7.** to believe or suppose (something) to be (as stated); look upon: *Thinking his prattle to be tedious* (Shakespeare). **8.** to believe possible or likely; expect: *I did not think to find you here. Do you think it will rain?* —*v.i.* **1.** to have ideas; use the mind: *to learn to think clearly, to think about a problem.* **2.** to have an idea: *He had thought of her as still a child.* **3.** to consider the matter; reflect: *I must think before answering.* **4.** to call to mind; remember: *I cannot think of the answer. I can't think of his name.* **5.** have regard or consideration (of); consider: *Nothing was thought of, but how to save ourselves* (Samuel Johnson). **6.** to have an opinion; believe: *Do what you think fit.* **7.** to have a (good, bad, etc.) opinion (of a person or thing): *to think well of a person's abilities.* **8.** to have an expectation; look for.
think aloud or **out loud,** to say what one is thinking: *Often, he becomes a sounding board as the President walks about his desk, peers out the window, and "thinks out loud" on upcoming issues* (Newsweek).
think better of, a. to think more favorably or highly of (a person, a plan, etc.), as upon further knowledge: *I think better of him for his present conduct.* **b.** to think more widely or sensibly of, as by a change of mind on reconsideration: *They began an attack, but thought better of it and stopped.*
think for, to expect or suppose: *It will be better than you think for.*
think out, a. to plan or discover by thinking: *He meditated deeply on the philosophy of trade, and thought out by degrees a complete . . . theory* (Macaulay). **b.** to solve or understand by thinking: *to think out a puzzle, problem, etc.* **c.** to think through to the end: *Oh, don't bother me . . . I don't want to be uncivil, but I've got to think this out* (F. Anstey).
think over, to consider carefully: *He would think the matter over* (Frederick Marryat).
think through, to think about until one reaches an understanding or conclusion: *Had he been given time to think the question through, he would have come up with a better answer.*
think twice, to think again before acting; hesitate: *Scientists ought to think twice before venturing into the marts of trade* (New Yorker).
think up, to plan, discover, or compose by thinking: *The idea was a simple one, thought up (so the story goes) at a supper party* (Manchester Guardian Weekly).
—*n. Informal.* a thought: *Each country in the Six will have to have a long think about . . . foreign trade* (Wall Street Journal).
—*adj. Informal.* devoted to thought; engaged in intellectual or theoretical work, study, research, etc.: *The Institute of Defense Analysis is one of the think companies working for the Pentagon* (Jerry E. Bishop).
[Middle English *thinken,* variant of *thenchen,* Old English *thencan.* Related to THANK.]
—**think′er,** *n.*
—**Syn.** *v.t.* **6.** purpose, mean. *-v.i.* **1. Think, reflect, meditate** mean to use the powers of the mind. **Think** is the general word meaning to use the mind to form ideas, reach conclusions, understand what is known, etc.: *I must think about your offer before I accept it.* **Reflect** suggests quietly and seriously thinking over a subject, by turning the thoughts (back) upon it: *They need time to reflect on their problems.* **Meditate** suggests focusing the thoughts on a subject from every point of view, to understand all its sides and relations: *He meditated on the nature of happiness.* **2.** conceive. **4.** recollect, recall.

think² (thingk), *v.i.,* **thought, think·ing.** it seems (used impersonally, with an indirect object; now obsolete except in *methinks, methought*). [Middle English *thinken* variant of *thinchen,* Old English *thyncan*]

think·a·ble (thing′kə bəl), *adj.* capable of being thought; conceivable: *It is hardly thinkable that he could have behaved as he did.* —**Syn.** imaginable.

think·a·bly (thing′kə blē), *adv.* in a thinkable manner; conceivably: *Hideko Takamine . . . deprives him of not only his freedom, but a zealously guarded 80,000 yen which she thinkably banks* (John L. Wasserman).

think factory, *Informal.* a center of scientific or technological research: *The engine comes out of Dr. Farrington Daniels's think factory at the University of Wisconsin* (New Scientist).

think·ing (thing′king), *adj.* **1.** that thinks; reasoning: *Whatever withdraws us from the power of our senses . . . advances us in the dignity of thinking beings* (Samuel Johnson). **2.** given to thinking; thoughtful or reflective. —*n.* mental action or activity; thought: *Thinking . . . in its higher forms . . . is a kind of poetry* (Havelock Ellis).
—**think′ing·ly,** *adv.*
—**Syn.** *adj.* **2.** contemplative, pensive, cogitative.

thinking cap,
put on one's thinking cap, to take time for thinking over something: *No expense has been spared; clearly everyone connected with the enterprise put on his thinking cap, and thought big* (New Yorker).

thinking machine, electronic brain: . . . *a new type of computer that will rival the human brain better than any of the present thinking machines* (Science News Letter).

think piece, a magazine or newspaper article devoted to an extensive analysis or discussion of current news.

think tank, *Informal.* a center of scientific and technological research, usually engaged in government and defense projects; think factory.

thin·ner (thin′ər), *n.* **1.** a liquid, especially turpentine, used to make paint more fluid. **2.** a person or thing that thins.

thin·ning (thin′ing), *adj.* that thins: *thinning hair.* —*n.* a decrease in thickness, closeness, density, etc.
thinnings, slivers, particles, etc., removed in decreasing the thickness of wood or the like: . . . *a fir paling of the horizontal kind, made from the thinnings of trees of that kind* (R. W. Dickson).

thin·nish (thin′ish), *adj.* somewhat thin: *Together, in Chekhov, they could do no more than eke out a thinnish run in New York and a few disappointing weeks on the road* (Harper's).

thin-skinned (thin′skind′), *adj.* **1.** having a thin skin or rind: *a thin-skinned orange.* **2.** sensitive to criticism, reproach, rebuff, or the like; touchy: *When Mr. Hyams gets after the Americans the amusement turns sour and not, one thinks, because an American reader is necessarily thin-skinned* (Wall Street Journal).

thio-, *combining form.* sulfur (replacing oxygen atoms in the designated oxygen compound) as in *thioarsenate, thiocyanate.* Also, sometimes **thi-** before vowels.
[< Greek *theîon* sulfur]

thi·o·a·ce·tic acid (thī′ō ə sē′tik, -set′ik), a liquid produced by heating glacial acetic acid with a sulfide of phosphorus, used as a reagent. *Formula:* C_2H_4OS

thi·o·ac·id (thī′ō as′id), *n.* an acid in which sulfur partly or wholly takes the place of oxygen.

thi·o·al·de·hyde (thī′ō al′də hīd), *n.* any of a group of compounds produced by treating aldehydes with hydrogen sulfides, and considered as aldehydes with sulfur substituted for the oxygen.

thi·o·an·ti·mo·nate (thī′ō an′tə mə nāt), *n.* a salt of thioantimonic acid (corresponding to thiosulfate).

thi·o·an·ti·mo·ni·ate (thī′ō an′tə mō′nē-āt), *n.* thioantimonate.

thi·o·an·ti·mon·ic acid (thī′ō an′tə-mon′ik), an acid known only in the form of its salts (thioantimonates). *Formula:* H_3SbS_4

thi·o·an·ti·mo·ni·ous acid (thī′ō an′ti-mō′nē əs), any of a group of hypothetical acids. *Formulas:* $HSbS_2$, H_3SbS_3, $H_4Sb_2S_5$, and $H_2Sb_4S_7$

thi·o·an·ti·mo·nite (thī′ō an′tə mə nīt), *n.* a salt of a thioantimonious acid, occurring only in solution.

thi·o·ar·se·nate (thī′ō är′sə nāt), *n.* a salt of a thioarsenic acid.

thi·o·ar·se·ni·ate (thī′ō är sē′nē āt), *n.* thioarsenate.

thi·o·ar·sen·ic acid, (thī′ō är sen′ik), any of a group of acids existing only in the form of their salts. *Formulas:* H_3AsS_4, $HAsS_3$, and $H_4As_2S_7$

thi·o·ar·se·ni·ous acid (thī′ō är sē′nē əs), any of a group of hypothetical acids. *Formulas:* H_3AsS_3, $HAsS_2$, $H_4As_2S_5$, and $H_6As_4S_9$

thi·o·ar·se·nite (thī′ō är′sə nīt), *n.* a salt of a thioarsenious acid.

thi·o·car·bam·id (thī′ō kär bam′id), *n.* thiocarbamide.

thi·o·car·bam·ide (thī′ō kär bam′id, -īd), *n.* thiourea.

thi·oc·tic acid (thī ok′tik), one of the vitamins of the vitamin B complex, important in releasing sugar for conversion into energy, and in the proper functioning of the liver; lipoic acid. *Formula:* $C_8H_{14}O_2S_2$ [< *thi-* + *oct-* + *-ic* (because of the eight carbon atoms)]

thi·o·cy·a·nate (thī′ō sī′ə nāt), *n.* a salt or ester of thiocyanic acid, containing the radical -SCN. [< *thio-* + *cyanate*]

thi·o·cy·an·ic acid (thī′ō sī an′ik), a colorless, unstable liquid with a penetrating odor. *Formula:* HSCN

Thi·o·kol (thī′ə kol), *n. Trademark.* any of a group of synthetic rubbers produced from organic halides and metallic polysulfides, especially resistant to gasoline, oils, and typical organic solvents.

thi·ol (thī′ōl, -ol), *n.* **1.** any of a series of organic compounds resembling the alcohols and phenols, but containing sulfur in place of oxygen; mercaptan. **2.** the univalent radical -SH; sulfhydryl. [< *thio-* + *-ol*[1]]

thi·ol·a·ce·tic acid (thī′ōl ə sē′tik, -ol; -set′ik), thioacetic acid.

thi·o·nate (thī′ə nāt), *n.* a salt or ester of a thionic acid.

thi·on·ic (thī on′ik), *adj. Chemistry.* **1.** of or containing sulfur. **2.** having oxygen replaced by sulfur. [< Greek *theîon* sulfur + English *-ic*]

thionic acid, any of a group of unstable acids represented by the formula $H_2S_nO_6$, where *n* equals two, three, four, five, and perhaps six.

thi·o·nin (thī′ə nin), *n.* thionine.

thi·o·nine (thī′ə nēn, -nin), *n.* **1.** a dark crystalline, basic compound derived from thiazine, used as a violet stain in microscopy. *Formula:* $C_{12}H_9N_3S$ **2.** any of several allied dyes. [< Greek *theîon* sulfur + English *-ine*[2]]

thi·o·nyl (thī′ə nəl), *n.* a bivalent inorganic radical -SO; sulfinyl. [< Greek *theîon* sulfur + English *-yl*]

thi·o·pen·tal sodium (thī′ō pen′tal), a yellowish-white barbiturate similar to pentobarbitol sodium, used as an anesthetic; Pentothal Sodium. *Formula:* $C_{11}H_{17}N_2O_2SNa$ [< *thio-* + *pent*(oth)*al*]

thi·o·pen·tone (thī′ō pen′tōn), *n.* thiopental sodium.

thi·o·phen (thī′ə fən), *n.* thiophene.

thi·o·phene (thī′ə fēn), *n.* a colorless liquid compound, present in coal tar, with an odor like that of benzene, and with properties similar to those of benzene. *Formula:* C_4H_4S

thi·o·phe·nic (thī′ə fē′nik), *adj.* derived from thiophene.

thi·o·phe·nol (thī′ə fē′nōl, -nol), *n.* a colorless mobile liquid with the odor of garlic, regarded as phenol with the oxygen replaced by sulfur. *Formula:* C_6H_6S [< *thio-* + *phenol*]

thi·o·sem·i·car·ba·zone (thī′ō sem′ē kär′bə zōn), *n.* a toxic, pale-yellow, crystalline compound, used in treating leprosy and pulmonary tuberculosis. *Formula:* $C_{10}H_{12}N_4OS$ [< *thio-* + *semi-* + *carb*(on) + *az*(o) + *-one*]

thi·o·sin·am·in (thī′ə si nam′in), *n.* thiosinamine.

thi·o·sin·am·ine (thī′ə si nam′in, -sin′ə-mēn′), *n.* a colorless crystalline compound having a garlicky odor, produced by heating mustard oil and alcohol with ammonia. It is used in medicine and in photography. *Formula:* $C_4H_8N_2S$ [< *thio-* + Latin *sināpis* mustard (< Greek *sínāpi*) + English *amine*]

thi·o·sul·fate (thī′ō sul′fāt), *n.* a salt of thiosulfuric acid; (formerly) hyposulfite.

thi·o·sul·fu·ric acid (thī′ō sul fyůr′ik), an unstable acid, considered as sulfuric acid in which one atom of oxygen is replaced by sulfur; (formerly) hyposulfurous acid. It occurs only in solution or in the form of its salts (thiosulfates). *Formula:* $H_2S_2O_3$

thi·o-TE·PA (thī′ō tē′pə), *n.* a crystalline drug derived from nitrogen mustard, used in arresting the growth of cancerous tissue by inhibiting cell division, as in the alleviation of leukemia. [< *thio-* + *TEPA*]

thi·o·u·ra·cil (thī′ō yůr′ə səl), *n.* a white crystalline powder used in treating hyperthyroidism. *Formula:* $C_4H_4N_2OS$ [< *thio-* + *ur*(ic) *ac*(id) + *-il*, a variant of *-yl*]

thi·o·u·re·a (thī′ō yů rē′ə, -yůr′ē-), *n.* a bitter, colorless crystalline substance, considered as urea with sulfur substituted for the oxygen; thiocarbamide. It is used especially in photography. *Formula:* CH_4N_2S

thir (ᴛʜir, ᴛʜėr), *pron., adj. Scottish.* these.

thi·ram (thī′ram), *n.* a white crystalline compound used as a fungicide, seed disinfectant, and bacteriostat. *Formula:* $C_6H_{12}N_2S_4$ [< (tetramethyl) *thi*(u)*ram* disulfide]

third (thėrd), *adj.* **1.** next after the second; last in a series of three. **2.** being one of three equal parts. **3.** *U.S.* of, having to do with, or designating the gear used for ordinary driving in an automobile with a standard transmission; high: *to shift into third gear.*
—*n.* **1.** the next after the second; last in a series of three. **2.** one of three equal parts into which a unit or total may be divided: *to divide a cake into thirds.* **3.** the third of the subdivisions of any standard measure or dimension that is successively subdivided in a constant ratio; subdivision next below seconds. **4.** *Music.* **a.** a tone or note three diatonic degrees from a given tone or note. **b.** the interval of two tones between such tones or notes. **c.** the harmonic combination of such tones or notes. **d.** the third tone or note of a scale, three diatonic degrees above the tonic; mediant. **5.** *U.S.* third gear; high. **thirds, a.** one third of the property of a deceased husband, to which the widow is entitled if there is a child or children. **b.** a widow's dower.
—*v.t.* **1.** to divide (anything) into three equal parts; reduce to one third the number or bulk. **2.** to speak in favor of (a motion, proposition, etc.) as third speaker; support the seconder: *A motion of the lord Wharton, seconded and thirded by the lords Somers and Halifax* (N. Luttrell).
[apparently Middle English alteration of Old English *thridda* < *thrēo* three]

third·bor·ough (thėrd′bėr′ō), *n.* formerly in England: **1.** the head of a frankpledge or tithing. **2.** the peace officer of a tithing; petty constable of a township or manor.

third class, 1. a. the lowest (now usually) or next to the lowest (formerly) class of accommodations on any of various railroads in Europe, Great Britain, and elsewhere. **b.** (formerly) the lowest class of accommodations on a passenger vessel; tourist class. **2.** *Especially British.* **a.** the class next below the second in an examination list. **b.** a place in this class.

third-class (thėrd′klas′, -kläs′), *adj.* of or belonging to the third class. —*adv.* in or by a third-class conveyance, accommodations, etc.: *to travel third-class.*

third-class matter, (in the postal system of the United States) printed matter other than newspapers or periodicals, sent through the mails by the publishers at special rates.

third degree, 1. *Especially U.S. Informal.* the use of severe treatment by the police to force a person to give information or make a confession. **2.** (in Freemasonry) the degree of master mason.

third-de·gree burn (thėrd′də grē′), a deep burn, with charring and actual destruction of the skin and tissue: *In treating patients who suffer extensive third-degree burns . . . physicians must deal not only with great pain and the loss of body fluid, but also with the invasion of bacteria that frequently cause surface infection and blood poisoning* (John Barbour).

third-di·men·sion·al (thėrd′də men′shə-nəl), *adj.* three-dimensional: *The mural is slightly curved, there is a balustrade and the lighting is so deftly placed that the effect is third-dimensional* (New York Times).

third estate, persons not in the nobility or clergy, especially in French history; common people.

third eyelid, the nictitating membrane.

third force, any person or group that tries to hold a middle course between extreme factions, especially a political group trying to hold such a position: *New York's Liberal Party—a powerful third force in New York politics—also demanded that Stark and Gerosa be left off the ticket* (Time).

third-hand (thėrd′hand′), *adj.* **1.** obtained, copied, or imitated from a second-hand source; further away from the original source, and so more stale, less authoritative, etc., than the second-hand source: *Second-hand and third-hand opinions and views . . . are buzzing around this camp like flies* (J.D. Salinger). **2.** dealing in third-hand goods. —*adv.* from a source twice removed from the original: *Details from a Canadian reporter's firsthand description of a royal tour turn up third-hand in a biography* (Maclean's).

Third House, *U.S.* a body of lobbyists; group that tries to influence legislators: *And the power of the so-called "Third House"—the special interest lobbies that had long ruled Sacramento—was waning* (Harper's).

Third International, an organization formed by the Communist Party in Moscow in 1919 to promote communism outside Russia; Communist International; Comintern. It was officially dissolved in 1943.

third·ly (thėrd′lē), *adv.* in the third place.

third party, 1. *U.S. and Canada.* a political party organized as an independent rival of the two major parties: *One of the major functions of third parties in Canada has always been to introduce imaginative ideas into our political life* (Canadian Forum). **2.** a party or person besides the two primarily concerned, as in a law case.

third person, *Grammar.* **1.** the person used when referring to someone or something spoken of. **2.** the form of a pronoun or verb thus used. *He, she, it,* and *they* are pronouns of the third person. In *he walks* and *they walk,* the verbs are in the third person.

third quarter, 1. the period between full moon and second half moon. **2.** the phase of the moon represented by the second half moon, after full moon.

third rail, a rail paralleling the ordinary rails of a railroad. It carries a powerful electric current and is used on some railroads instead of an overhead wire. The power is picked up by a device (shoe) that extends out from the locomotive or car and fits over the rail.—**third′-rail′,** *adj.*

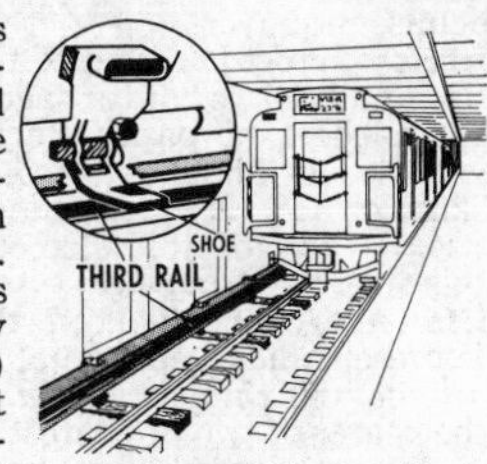

Subway Third Rail
Circle shows an enlargement of the shoe fitting over third rail.

third-rate (thėrd′rāt′), *adj.* **1.** of the third class. **2.** distinctly inferior: *a third-rate hotel.*

third-rat·er (thėrd′rā′tər), *n.* a third-rate person or thing.

Third Reich, the totalitarian state in Germany (from 1933 to 1945) under Adolf Hitler.

Third Republic, the government of France from 1875 to 1946.

third sex, homosexuals.

third stream, a form of musical composition that attempts to combine the harmonic qualities of classical music with the rhythmic and improvisational elements of jazz. —**third′-stream′,** *adj.*

third world, the world of neutral or non-aligned nations; the countries taking neither side in the cold war between Communist and Western nations: *Because he [John F. Kennedy] understood their political problems he had personal rapport with most of the leaders of the third world* (Harper's).

thirl[1] (thėrl), *v.t., v.i. British Dialect.* **1.** to pierce; perforate. **2.** to thrill. [Old English *thyrlian* < *thȳrel* hole, bore, ultimately < *thurh* through. Compare NOSTRIL.]

thirl[2] (thėrl), *n. Scottish.* thirlage. [alteration of obsolete *thrill* bondage, English *thræl.* Compare THRALL.]

thirl·age (thėr′lij), *n.* in Scots and feudal law: **a.** a requirement that tenants have their grain ground at a certain mill. **b.** the charge for this grinding. [alteration of obsolete *thrillage* bondage < *thrill,* verb, to hold as thrall < *thrill,* noun; see THIRL[2]]

thirst (thėrst), *n.* **1.** a dry, painful feeling caused by having nothing to drink: *The traveler in the desert suffered from thirst. He satisfied his thirst at the spring.* **2.** a strong desire; craving: *Many boys have a thirst for adventure.*
—*v.i.* **1.** to feel thirst; be thirsty. **2.** to have a strong desire or craving: *It is not necessary to teach men to thirst after power* (Edmund Burke).
[Old English *thurst*] —**thirst′er,** *n.*

thirst·i·ly (thėrs′tə lē), *adv.* in a thirsty manner.

thirst·i·ness (thėrs′tē nis), *n.* the state of being thirsty; thirst.

thirst·less (thėrst′lis), *adj.* having no thirst.

thirst·y (thėrs′tē), *adj.,* **thirst·i·er, thirst·i·est. 1.** feeling thirst; having thirst. **2.** (of earth or plants) without water or moisture; dry, parched, or arid: *The land seemed thirstier than a desert.* **3.** having a strong desire or craving; eager: *The fellow was evidently thirsty for my blood* (W.H. Hudson). **4.** *Informal.* that causes thirst.

thir·teen (thėr′tēn′), *n., adj.* three more than ten; 13: *She thinks thirteen is an unlucky number.* [Middle English *thirttene,* alteration of earlier *thrittene,* Old English *thrēotēne*]

thir·teenth (thėr′tēnth′), *adj., n.* **1.** next after the 12th; last in a series of 13. **2.** one, or being one, of 13 equal parts.

thir·ti·eth (thėr′tē ith), *adj., n.* **1.** next after the 29th; last in a series of 30. **2.** one, or being one, of 30 equal parts.

thir·ty (thėr′tē), *n., pl.* **-ties,** *adj.* —*n.* **1.** three times ten; 30. **2.** the figure "30" as a symbol placed at, and designating the end of, a news story or other piece of copy. —*adj.* three times ten; 30. [Middle English *thyrty,* alteration of *thrytty,* Old English *thrītig* < *thrī-* three + *-tig* -ty[1]]

thir·ty·fold (thėr′tē fōld′), *adj., adv.* thirty times as great or as much; increased thirty times.

thir·ty-sec·ond note (thėr′tē sek′ənd), *Music.* a note calling for one thirty-second the duration of a sound of a whole note; a demisemiquaver.

thir·ty-two·mo (thėr′tē tü′mō′), *n.* **1.** a size of a book, or of its pages, made by folding a sheet of paper thirty-two times to form leaves about 3½ x 5½ inches. *Abbr.:* 32mo or 32°. **2.** a book having pages of this size. —*adj.* of this size; having pages of this size. [< *thirty-two* + *-mo,* as in *decimo*]

this (ᴛʜis), *adj., pron., pl.* **these,** *adv.* —*adj.* **1.** present; near; spoken of; referred to: *this minute, this child, this idea.* **2. a.** indicating the nearer of two or more things or of several things in time or space: *Do you prefer this tie or that one in the closet?* **b.** indicating one thing as distinct from another or others: *You may have this one, this next one, or that one, but not all three.*

—*pron.* **1.** the person, thing, event, quality, condition, idea, etc., that is present, mentioned, or referred to now: *This is the best. After this you must go home.* **2.** the one emphasized or contrasted with another called "that": *Take this, or this, but not that. This is newer than that.*

—*adv.* to this extent or degree; so: *You can have this much.*

[Old English *this,* neuter demonstrative pronoun and adjective. Compare THESE.]

➔ **a. This,** like *that,* is regularly used to refer to the idea of a preceding clause or sentence: *He had always had his own way at home, and this made him a poor roommate.* **b. This, these, that, those** are called *demonstrative adjectives* when they modify substantives: *this company, that magazine.* When they stand alone, they are called *demonstrative pronouns: This is the one. That's what I want.*

this-a-way (ᴛʜis′ə wā′), *adv. U.S. Dialect.* in this fashion or direction: *It happened this-a-way* (New York Times).

This·be (thiz′bē), *n. Greek Legend.* a maiden loved by Pyramus. Pyramus killed himself thinking that Thisbe had been devoured by a lion, and she killed herself when she found him dead.

this·ness (ᴛʜis′nis), *n.* the state or quality of being this; the particular reality of a thing: *Each community has its particular identity, a thisness that makes it different from other places* (New Yorker).

this·tle (this′əl), *n.* **1.** any of various composite plants that have the stems, leaves, and involucres thickly armed with prickles, the flower heads usually globular, and the flowers most commonly purple, as the bull thistle, a species whose blossom is the heraldic and national emblem of Scotland, and the Canada thistle. See also **decurrent** for picture. **2.** any of several other prickly plants. [Old English *thistel*] —**this′tle·like′,** *adj.*

Thistle (def. 1)

this·tle·down (this′əl doun′), *n.* the down (pappus) that crowns the seeds (achenes) of the thistle, and by means of which they are carried along by the wind.

thistle tube, a funnel-shaped glass tube used by chemists, having a large bulb like the head of a thistle between the conical flaring part and the rest of the tube.

this·tly (this′lē), *adj.* **1.** of the nature of a thistle or thistles; thistlelike; prickly. **2.** abounding in thistles.

this-world·li·ness (ᴛʜis′wėrld′lē nis), *n.* devotion to the things of this world: *She speaks of four modern revolutions—of equality, of this-worldliness, of rising birth rates, and of driving scientific change* (Atlantic).

this-world·ly (ᴛʜis′wėrld′lē), *adj.* of or concerned with the present world or state of existence: *The guests were always this-worldly, and often profane* (Mark Twain).

thith·er (thiᴛʜ′ər, ᴛʜiᴛʜ′-), *adv.* **1.** to that place; toward that place; there. **2.** *Obsolete.* to or toward that end, purpose, result, or action. —*adj.* on that side; farther. [variant of Middle English *thider, thedir,* Old English *thider,* variant of earlier *thæder;* influenced by Old English *hider* hither]

thith·er·to (thiᴛʜ′ər tü′, ᴛʜiᴛʜ′-; thiᴛʜ′ər-tü′, ᴛʜiᴛʜ′-), *adv.* up to that time; until then.

thith·er·ward (thiᴛʜ′ər wərd, ᴛʜiᴛʜ′-), *adv.* toward that place; in that direction; thither: *Were thy vocation in truth thitherward!* (Scott).

thith·er·wards (thiᴛʜ′ər wərdz, ᴛʜiᴛʜ′-), *adv.* thitherward.

thix·o·trop·ic (thik′sə trop′ik), *adj.* exhibiting or characterized by thixotropy: *Certain clays suspended in solutions of alkali chloride of molar strength or greater will give gels that are thixotropic* (Science News).

thix·ot·ro·py (thik sot′rə pē), *n. Chemistry.* the property of becoming fluid when stirred or agitated, as exhibited by gels. [< Greek *thíxis* a touching + *-tropos* a turning + English *-y*[3]]

Th. M., Master of Theology.

tho or **tho′** (ᴛʜō), *conj., adv.* though.

thole[1] (thōl), *n.* a peg or pin, often one of a pair, on the gunwale of a boat to hold an oar in rowing. [Middle English *tholle,* probably Old English *thol*]

thole[2] (thōl), *v.,* **tholed, thol·ing.** *Archaic.* —*v.t.* to be subjected or exposed to (something evil); be afflicted with. —*v.i.* to be patient; wait patiently. [Old English *tholian* to bear (a burden)]

Tholes[1] Top, single; bottom, double

thole·pin (thōl′pin′), *n.* thole.

thol·o·bate (thol′ə bāt), *n.* the circular substructure on which a dome or cupola rests. [< Greek *thólos* dome, cupola + *-batēs* one that goes < *baínein* to go]

tho·los (thō′los), *n., pl.* **-loi** (-loi), **-li** (-lī). **1.** a circular domed building or structure; dome; cupola: *. . . the painted tholos of Kazanlik in Bulgaria, whose colors were flaking off in layers* (Harold J. Plenderleith). **2.** (in Ancient Greece) a circular tomb of the Mycenaean Age, domed and lined with masonry. [< Greek *thólos*]

Thom·as (tom′əs), *n.* (in the Bible) one of the twelve disciples chosen by Jesus as His Apostles. He at first doubted the Resurrection. In the Gospel of John he is surnamed Didymus. John 11:16; 20:24-29.

Tho·mism (tō′miz əm, thō′-), *n.* the doctrines of Saint Thomas Aquinas (1225?-1274), Italian philosopher and theologian of the Roman Catholic Church: *During the fifteenth century Thomism was reaching the position of ascendancy which it has held ever since in Catholic thinking* (Listener).

Tho·mist (tō′mist, thō′-), *n.* a follower of Saint Thomas Aquinas. —*adj.* Thomistic: *He belonged to the . . . Thomist tradition in which he was formed as a philosopher but he was no uncritical disciple of Aquinas* (London Times).

Tho·mis·tic (tō mis′tik, thō′-), *adj.* of or having to do with the Thomists or Thomism.

Thomp·son seedless (tomp′sən), a variety of a light green or pale yellow grape much grown in California for use in the raisin industry.

Thompson submachine gun, *Trademark.* a small, light, air-cooled, automatic firearm using .45-caliber ammunition that can be carried by one man, fired either from the hip or the shoulder. It is accurate to a range somewhat greater than that of a pistol but much less than that of a carbine or rifle; Tommy gun. [American English < General John T. *Thompson,* 1860-1940, U.S. Army, one of the inventors]

thong (thông, thong), *n.* **1.** a narrow strip of hide or leather, especially used as a fastening. **2.** the lash of a whip, especially one made of plaited strips of leather. [Middle English *thonge,* variant of *thwonge,* Old English *thwang.* Related to TWINGE, WHANG[3].]

Thor (thôr), *n.* the ancient Scandinavian god of thunder and war, bringer of rain to the crops. He destroyed the giants, foes of the gods, with his magic hammer made by the dwarfs. [Old English *Thōr* < Scandinavian (compare Old Icelandic *thōrr*). Compare THURSDAY.]

tho·ra·cec·to·my (thôr′ə sek′tə mē, thōr′-), *n., pl.* **-mies.** surgical removal of part of a rib. [< Latin *thōrāx, -ācis* thorax + Greek *ektomē* a cutting out]

tho·rac·ic (thô ras′ik, thō-), *adj.* of, having to do with, or in the region of the thorax: *The thoracic cavity contains the heart and lungs.*

thoracic duct, the main trunk of the lymphatic system, that passes through the thoracic cavity in front of the spinal column and empties lymph and chyle into the blood through the left subclavian vein.

tho·rac·i·co·lum·bar (thô ras′ə kō lum′-bər, thō-), *adj.* of or having to do with the thoracic and lumbar regions.

tho·ra·co·lum·bar (thôr′ə kō lum′bər, thōr′-), *adj.* of or having to do with the thoracic and lumbar regions, especially of the spine or the sympathetic nervous system. [< Greek *thṓrāx, -ākos* thorax + English *lumbar*]

tho·ra·co·plas·ty (thôr′ə kō plas′tē, thōr′-), *n., pl.* **-ties.** plastic surgery on the thorax, especially removal of all or part of some of the ribs to collapse the chest wall, used in some cases of tuberculosis. [< Greek *thṓrāx, -ākos* thorax + *-plastós* something molded]

tho·ra·cot·o·my (thôr′ə kot′ə mē, thōr′-), *n., pl.* **-mies.** surgical incision into the thorax.

tho·rax (thôr′aks, thōr′-), *n., pl.* **tho·rax·es, tho·ra·ces** (thôr′ə sēz, thōr′-). **1.** the part of the body of a mammal between the neck and the abdomen, comprising the cavity enclosed by the ribs and breastbone (sternum), and containing the chief organs of circulation and respiration; chest. **2.** the corresponding part in the lower vertebrates, as birds and fishes. **3.** the second of the three main divisions of an insect's body, between the head and the abdomen. See **abdomen** for picture. [< Latin *thōrāx, -ācis* < Greek *thṓrāx, -ākos* chest]

Tho·ra·zine (thôr′ə zēn, -zin), *n. Trademark.* a drug used as a tranquilizer, in preventing and stopping nausea and vomiting, and in controlling fits of hiccups; chlorpromazine. *Formula:* $C_{17}H_{19}ClN_2S$

Tho·reau·vi·an (thə rō′vē ən), *adj.* of or having to do with the American author and naturalist Henry David Thoreau or his works: *The Garden City enthusiasts drank a bit too deeply at nature's bosom and intoxicated themselves with Thoreauvian ideals* (Harper's). —*n.* a follower of Thoreau, his ideas, or practices: *The small-town Thoreauvian, the walker in the country* (Atlantic).

tho·ri·a (thôr′ē ə, thōr′-), *n.* a heavy white powder, an oxide of thorium, obtained from monazite, and used in making ceramics, as a catalyst, etc. *Formula:* ThO_2 [< New Latin *thoria* < *thorium* thorium]

tho·ri·a·nite (thôr′ē ə nīt, thōr′-), *n.* a radioactive mineral consisting chiefly of the oxides of thorium, uranium, and other rare metals, found in small brownish-black crystals having a resinous luster.

tho·ric (thôr′ik, thōr′-), *adj.* of, having to do with, or derived from thorium.

tho·rite (thôr′it, thōr′-), *n.* **1.** a mineral, a silicate of thorium, occurring crystalline or massive, in color orange-yellow to brownish-black or black. *Formula:* $ThSiO_4$ **2.** an explosive formerly used in artillery shells as a bursting charge. [< Swedish *thorit* < *Thor* Thor + *-it* -ite[1]]

tho·ri·um (thôr′ē əm, thōr′-), *n.* a radioactive, metallic chemical element present in thorite, monazite, and various other rare minerals. It is a heavy gray substance that fuses with difficulty. *Symbol:* Th; *at.wt.:* (C^{12}) 232.038 or (O^{16}) 232.05; *at.no.:* 90; *valence:* 4. [< New Latin *thorium* < Swedish *Thor* Thor]

thorium emanation, thoron.

thorn (thôrn), *n.* **1. a.** a stiff, sharp-pointed, straight or curved, woody process on a stem or branch of a tree or other plant.

A thorn usually grows from a bud. *Hawthorns have thorns.* **b.** a plant that bears thorns or prickles, especially any shrubs or small trees of the hawthorns, as the Washington thorn, a species native to the southern United States. **c.** the wood of any of these plants. **2.** a spine or spiny process in an animal. **3. a.** a letter (þ, capital Þ), originally a rune, used in Old English interchangeably with *edh* to represent either the voiced or voiceless dental fricatives now spelled *th*, as in *then* and *thin*, and still used in the Icelandic alphabet for the voiceless sound. **b.** the symbol þ used in phonetic transcriptions to represent the voiceless dental fricative, as in *thin*.
thorn in the flesh or **side,** a constant affliction; a source of continual grief, trouble, or annoyance: *The sharpest thorn in television's side is its own mammoth audience* (Listener).
—v.t. to vex: *The perplexities with which . . . I have been thorned* (Samuel Taylor Coleridge).
[Old English *thorn*] **—thorn′like′,** *adj.*
—Syn. *n.* **1. a.** spine, prickle.

thorn apple, 1. a. the fruit of the hawthorn; haw. **b.** the hawthorn. **2.** the jimson weed or any other datura (so called from the prickly capsules).

thorn·back (thôrn′bak′), *n.* **1. a.** a spiny-backed European ray. **b.** any of certain similar American rays. **2.** a large spider crab of Europe.

thorn·bush (thôrn′bu̇sh′), *n.* a shrub that produces thorns, such as the hawthorn or bramble: *one mud cabin fenced about with cactus and thornbush* (Manchester Guardian).

thorned (thôrnd), *adj.* having thorns.

thorn·i·ly (thôr′nə lē), *adv.* in a thorny manner.

thorn·i·ness (thôr′nē nis), *n.* thorny quality or condition; prickliness: *The most characteristic feature of the jungle was its thorniness* (A.R. Wallace).

thorn·less (thôrn′lis), *adj.* without thorns.

thorn letter, thorn, a letter used in Old English.

thorn·y (thôr′nē), *adj.*, **thorn·i·er, thorn·i·est. 1.** full of thorns or spines; spiny; prickly: *He scratched his hand on the thorny bush.* **2.** abounding in thorn-bearing or prickly plants; overgrown with brambles: *He tried to make his way through the thorny thicket.* **3.** troublesome; annoying: *The boys argued about the thorny points in the lesson. Life is thorny* (Samuel Taylor Coleridge).
—Syn. 3. vexatious, difficult.

thor·o (thėr′ō), *adj., adv., prep.* thorough.

tho·ron (thôr′on, thōr′-), *n.* a radioactive, gaseous, chemical element; thorium emanation. It is an isotope of radon, formed by the disintegration of thorium. *Symbol:* Tn or Th-Em; *at.wt.:* 220; *at.no.:* 86; *half-life:* 54.5 seconds. [< *thor*(ium) + *-on*]

thor·ough (thėr′ō), *adj.* **1. a.** being all that is needed; complete: *Please make a thorough search for the lost money.* **b.** that is fully what is expressed by the noun; thoroughgoing: *a thorough scoundrel.* **2.** doing all that should be done and slighting nothing; painstaking: *a thorough person. The doctor was very thorough in his examination of the patient.* **3.** going, passing, or extending through (now only in special applications, chiefly with nouns of action or position, being a kind of elliptical use of the adverb).
—adv., prep. Archaic. through. Also, **thoro.**
[Old English *thuruh,* variant of *thurh* through] **—thor′ough·ness,** *n.*
—Ant. *adj.* **1. a.** partial. **2.** superficial, cursory.

Thor·ough (thėr′ō), *n.* a thoroughgoing action or policy, especially that of Thomas Wentworth Strafford and William Laud, ministers of Charles I of England.

thorough bass (bās), *Music.* **1.** a bass part extending throughout a piece, having written figures indicating the intended harmony; figured bass. **2.** the system or method of so indicating harmonies. **3.** the science of harmony in general.

thorough brace, or **thor·ough·brace** (thėr′ō brās′), *n.* either of a pair of two strong braces or bands of leather connecting the front and back springs and supporting the body of a coach, carriage, etc.

thor·ough·bred (thėr′ō bred′), *adj.* **1.** of pure breed or stock; bred from pure stock; purebred. **2.** of, having to do with, or designating a breed of horses, used especially in racing, that derives originally from an admixture of domestic English stock in the female line with Arabian (or Turkish) stock in the male line. **3.** well-bred; thoroughly trained. **4.** having those qualities that are traditionally associated with the thoroughbred horse; high-spirited; mettlesome.
—n. **1.** a thoroughbred horse or other animal. **2.** a well-bred or thoroughly trained person.

thor·ough·fare (thėr′ō fãr′), *n.* **1.** a passage, road, or street open at both ends. **2. a.** any road, street, etc.: *the busy thoroughfares of a great city.* **b.** a main road; highway: *The Lincoln Highway is one of the main thoroughfares of the United States.* **3.** a passage or way through. **4.** *Obsolete.* a going or passing through; passage.
no thoroughfare, no public way through or right of way here: *The sign said "no thoroughfare," so instead of driving through the road we took the detour.*
[Middle English *thurghfare* < Old English *thurh* through + *faru* passage, way]

thor·ough·go·ing (thėr′ō gō′ing), *adj.* thorough; complete: *Perhaps no coronary patient in medical annals ever had more thoroughgoing treatment than that given the President* (Newsweek).

thor·ough·ly (thėr′ō lē), *adv.* in a thorough manner or degree; fully; completely.

thor·ough·paced (thėr′ō pāst′), *adj.* **1.** (of a horse) trained in all paces. **2.** thoroughly trained or accomplished (in something): *A hearty thoroughpaced liar* (Charles Lamb).

thor·ough·pin (thėr′ō pin′), *n.* a swelling in the sheath of a tendon above a horse's hock, appearing on both sides of the leg as if a pin were passing through, sometimes causing lameness.

thor·ough·wort (thėr′ō wėrt′), *n.* **1.** a North American composite herb that has opposite leaves, each pair united at the base so that the stem appears to grow through them, and large corymbs of numerous white flowers; boneset; agueweed; trumpetweed. It is valued for its tonic and diaphoretic properties. **2.** any of several other plants of the same group.

thorp or **thorpe** (thôrp), *n. Obsolete.* a hamlet, village, or small town. [Middle English *thorp,* alteration of Old English *throp;* perhaps influenced by Scandinavian (compare Old Icelandic *thorp*)]

Thos., Thomas.

those (ᴛʜōz), *adj., pron.* the plural of **that:** *That is his book; those are my books.* [Middle English *thos* < *thō,* Old English *thā,* nominative plural of *sē*]
➤ For *those kind, those sort,* see **kind.**
➤ See **this** for another usage note.

Thoth (thōth, tōt), *n.* the ancient Egyptian god of speech, wisdom, and magic, and, as the scribe of the gods, inventor of letters and numbers, identified with the Greek god Hermes. He is represented with a human body and the head of an ibis or a dog.

thou (ᴛʜou), *pron., sing., nom.* **thou;** *poss.* **thy** or **thine;** *obj.* **thee;** *pl. nom.* **you** or **ye;** *poss.* **your** or **yours;** *obj.* **you** or **ye;** *v. Archaic. —pron.* the one spoken to; you: *Thou, God, seest me. —v.t., v.i.* to use the pronoun *thou* to a person, especially familiarly, to an inferior, in contempt or insult, etc. [Old English *thū.* Compare THEE, THY.]
➤ **Thou, thy, thine, thee,** and **ye** are archaic pronouns for the second person, used now chiefly in the formal language of church services.

thou., thousand.

though (ᴛʜō), *conj.* **1.** in spite of the fact that; notwithstanding the fact that; although: *Though it was raining, no one went indoors.* **2.** yet; still; nevertheless; however: *He is better, though not yet cured.* **3.** even if; granting or supposing that: *Though I fail, I shall try again.*
as though, as if; as would or might be the case if: *You look as though you were tired.*
—adv. however; nevertheless: *I am sorry about our quarrel; you began it, though.*
Also, **tho, tho'.**
[Middle English *thoh* < Scandinavian (compare Old Icelandic *thō*)]

thought[1] (thôt), *n.* **1.** what one thinks; idea; notion: *Her thought apparently was to have a picnic.* **2.** the power or process of thinking; mental activity: *Thought helps us solve problems.* **3.** reasoning: *He applied thought to the problem.* **4.** the intellectual activity or mental product characteristic of the thinkers of a (specified) group, time, or place: *in modern scientific thought, 16th century thought.* **5.** consideration; attention; care; regard: *Show some thought for others than yourself. The old man was lost in thought and did not hear us come in.* **6.** an intention; design; purpose: *His thought was to avoid controversy. He doesn't have a thought of leaving.* **7.** conception, imagination, or fancy: *a pretty thought.* **8.** a very small amount; little bit; trifle: *Just a thought more sugar, please. Be a thought more polite.* [Old English *thōht.* Related to THINK[1].] **—Syn. 1.** concept. See **idea. 2.** cogitation, deliberation, meditation.

thought[2] (thôt), *v.* the past tense and past participle of **think:** *We thought it would snow yesterday.*

thought control, the strict limiting or regimentation of ideas, reasoning, etc., in all persons so as to conform to that of a particular group, government, etc.

thought·ful (thôt′fəl), *adj.* **1. a.** full of thought; thinking: *He was thoughtful for a while and then replied, "No."* **b.** indicating thought: *a thoughtful expression or reply.* **2.** careful; heedful: *to be thoughtful of danger.* **3.** showing regard or consideration for others; considerate: *She is always thoughtful of her mother.* **—thought′ful·ly,** *adv.* **—thought′ful·ness,** *n.*
—Syn. 1. a. reflective, meditative, contemplative. **3. Thoughtful, considerate** mean giving careful attention to the comfort or feelings of others. **Thoughtful** emphasizes concerning oneself with the comfort and welfare of others and doing, without being asked, things that will add to their well-being or happiness: *A thoughtful neighbor, knowing the girl was sick and alone, took her food.* **Considerate** emphasizes concerning oneself with the feelings and rights of others and trying to spare them from discomfort, pain, or unhappiness: *She is considerate enough to tell her parents where she goes.*

thought·less (thôt′lis), *adj.* **1.** without thought; doing things without thinking; careless: *a thoughtless person or remark. A thoughtless boy makes blunders.* **2.** not thinking; unmindful: *thoughtless of danger.* **3.** showing little or no care or regard for others; not considerate: *It is thoughtless of her to keep us waiting so long.* **4.** stupid. **—thought′less·ly,** *adv.* **—thought′less·ness,** *n.* **—Syn. 1.** remiss, heedless.

thought-out (thôt′out′), *adj.* arrived at or developed by thinking; thoroughly considered: *It is heartening to see such a well-organized and thought-out project* (New York Times).

thought reading, mind reading.

thought transference, telepathy.

thou·sand (thou′zənd), *n., adj.* ten hundred; 1,000. *Abbr.:* thou. [Old English *thūsend*]

thou·sand·fold (thou′zənd fōld′), *adj., adv., n.* a thousand times as much or as many.

thou·sand-leg·ger (thou′zənd leg′ər), *n.* thousand-legs: *The thousand-leggers or millipedes never have as many as a thousand legs* (Science News Letter).

thou·sand-legs (thou′zənd legz′), *n.* a myriapod, especially a chilopod or centipede, as a species common in the southern United States, that infests houses and preys upon household insects.

thou·sandth (thou′zəndth), *adj., n.* **1.** last in a series of a thousand. **2.** one, or being one, of a thousand equal parts.

thow·less (thou′lis), *adj. Scottish.* **1.** inert; inactive. **2.** spiritless; listless. [origin uncertain. Apparently related to THEWLESS.]

THPC (no periods), *Trademark.* a crystalline compound used in making cotton and rayon fabrics flame-resistant. *Formula:* $C_4H_{12}O_4PCl$

Thra·cian (thrā′shən), *adj.* of or having to do with ancient Thrace, a region in the eastern part of the Balkan Peninsula, or its people. *—n.* **1.** a native or inhabitant of ancient Thrace: *The Thracians were the most musical of the peoples of Greece. But Orpheus had no rival there* (Edith Hamilton). **2.** the Indo-European language of the ancient Thracians, related to Illyrian.

Thra·co-Il·lyr·i·an (thrā′kō i lir′ē ən), *adj.* of or having to do with a branch of the Indo-European language family of which Albanian is the only surviving member. *—n.* a Thraco-Illyrian language, especially Albanian.

Thra·co-Phryg·i·an (thrā′kō frij′ē ən, -frij′ən), *adj.* of or having to do with Thracian and Phrygian, two ancient Indo-European languages. —*n.* either of those languages.

thrall (thrôl), *n.* **1.** a person in bondage; bondman; slave: *The thralls did the work of the castle.* **2.** a person who is a slave to something: *a thrall to alcohol. Slaves of drink and thralls of sleep* (Shakespeare). *I am . . . made up of likings and dislikings—the veriest thrall to sympathies, apathies, antipathies* (Charles Lamb). **3.** bondage; slavery; thralldom: *to be in thrall to drink. An enchantress had the prince in thrall.*
—*adj. Archaic.* that is a thrall; in thrall.
—*v.t. Archaic.* to put or hold in thralldom or bondage; enslave.
[Old English *thrǣl* < Scandinavian (compare Old Icelandic *thrǣll*)]
—**Syn.** *n.* **1.** serf.

thrall·dom or **thral·dom** (thrôl′dəm), *n.* bondage; slavery; servitude.

thrang (thrang), *n., v., adj. Scottish.* throng.

thrap·ple (thrap′əl), *n.* thropple.

thrash (thrash), *v.t.* **1.** to beat as punishment; flog: *The man thrashed the boy for stealing apples.* **2.** to move, swing, or beat vigorously to and fro or up and down: *to thrash one's arms against one's body to keep warm, to thrash one's legs in the water.* **3.** to thresh (wheat, etc.). **4.** *Nautical.* to force (a ship) to move forward against a wind, sea, etc. —*v.i.* **1.** to move violently; toss; lash: *to thrash about in bed unable to sleep, children thrashing about in the water, branches thrashing against a window.* **2.** to thresh grain. **3.** *Nautical.* to make way against the wind, tide, etc.; beat.
thrash out, to settle by thorough discussion: *. . . the problem has not always been fully and adequately thrashed out* (Manchester Guardian).
thrash over, to go over again and again: *The jurors kept thrashing over the evidence without being able to reach a verdict.*
—*n.* **1.** a thrashing or threshing; beating. **2.** *Nautical.* a making way against the wind, etc. **3.** a swimming movement in which the legs are moved alternately and rapidly up and down; flutter kick.
[variant of Middle English *threshen* to thresh]
—**Syn.** *v.t.* **1.** trounce.

thrash·er[1] (thrash′ər), *n.* **1.** a person or thing that thrashes. **2.** a shark; thresher.
[< *thrash* + *-er*[1]]

thrash·er[2] (thrash′ər), *n.* any of several American long-tailed, thrushlike birds related to the mocking-bird, such as the brown thrasher of eastern North America. [American English, apparently variant (influenced by *thrasher*[1]) of English dialectal *thresher, thrusher,* probably < *thrush*[1]]

Brown Thrasher[2] (11½ in. long)

thrasher shark, a thresher (def. 3).

thrash·ing (thrash′ing), *n.* a beating or flogging.

thra·son·ic (thrə son′ik), *adj.* thrasonical.

thra·son·i·cal (thrə son′ə kəl), *adj.* boasting; bragging: *Caesar's thrasonical brag of "I came, saw, and overcame"* (Shakespeare).
[< Latin *Thrasō, -ōnis,* a braggart soldier in Terence's *Eunuchus* (< Greek *Thrásōn* < *thrasýs* bold) + English *-ic* + *-al*[1]]
—**thra·son′i·cal·ly,** *adv.*

thrave (thrāv), *n. Scottish.* **1.** two shocks of grain, usually containing twelve sheaves each, used as a measure of straw, fodder, etc. **2.** a large number; crowd; multitude. **3.** *Obsolete.* a sheaflike bundle.
[Middle English *thrave, threve,* apparently < Scandinavian (compare Old Icelandic *threfi*)]

thraw[1] (thrô, thrä), *n. Scottish.* **1.** a turn or twist around, to one side, etc.; wrench; crook; warp. **2.** throe.
[variant of *throe*]

thraw[2] (thrô, thrä), *v.t., v.i., n. Scottish.* throw.

thrawn (thrôn, thrän), *adj. Scottish.* **1. a.** twisted; crooked. **b.** misshapen; distorted. **2. a.** perverse; contrary. **b.** crabbed; peevish.
[variant of *thrown*]

thread (thred), *n.* **1. a.** cotton, silk, flax, etc., spun out into a fine cord: *You sew with thread.* **b.** each of the lengths of yarn that form the warp and woof of a woven fabric. **c.** an article of clothing; garment; stitch: *not a thread fit to wear.* **2.** something long and slender or fine like a thread, such as a fine ligament, strand, stream, line, or streak: *a spider hanging by a thread, a thread of sand pouring down an hourglass, a thread of light coming through the crack in the door, a thread of gold in a piece of ore.* **3.** something that connects the parts of a story, speech, a train of thought, etc.; continuous or repetitious theme: *I return to the thread of my story* (Edward G. Bulwer-Lytton). **4.** the spiral ridge winding around the shank of a screw or bolt, the end of a pipe joint, the inside of a nut, etc. **5.** the thread of life: *pure grief shore his old thread in twain* (Shakespeare).
hang by, on or **upon a thread,** to be in a precarious condition (often with reference to the legend of Damocles): *The old man's life hung by a thread.*

Thread (def. 4)

—*v.t.* **1.** to pass a thread through: *She threaded her needle.* **2.** to string on or as if on a thread: *She threaded a hundred beads in a pattern to make a necklace.* **3.** to pass like a thread through; pervade. **4. a.** to make (one's way) carefully or skillfully: *to thread one's way through heavy traffic.* **b.** to find one's way through: *A labyrinth of narrow streets . . . rarely threaded by the stranger* (George Eliot). **5.** to form a thread or threads on or in: *Screws and nuts are threaded by special machines.* **6.** *Electricity.* to cause the formation of lines of force around (a conductor). —*v.i.* **1.** to go in a winding course; weave in and out; wind: *He threaded through the forest. The speedy halfback threaded through the field for a touchdown.* **2.** to form into a thread: *Cook the syrup until it threads.*
—*adj.* of, made of, or like thread or a thread.
[Old English *thrǣd* fine cord. Related to THROW.] —**thread′er,** *n.* —**thread′like′,** *adj.*

thread·bare (thred′bãr′), *adj.* **1.** having the nap worn off; worn so much that the threads show: *a threadbare coat. Nail to the mast her holy flag, Set every threadbare sail* (Oliver Wendell Holmes). **2.** wearing clothes worn to the threads; shabby; seedy: *a threadbare beggar.* **3.** very poor; hard up. **4.** old and worn; stale: *a threadbare joke or excuse.*
—**Syn. 4.** hackneyed, trite.

thread·en (thred′ən), *adj. Archaic or Dialect.* made of thread: *A thin, threaden cloak* (Ben Jonson).

thread·fin (thred′fin′), *n.* any of a group of fishes having threadlike rays extending beyond the pectoral fins, as the barbudo.

thread·i·ness (thred′ē nis), *n.* thready quality or condition.

thread lace, lace made of linen thread, as distinguished from cotton and silk laces.

thread mark, a thin, highly-colored thread put into paper money to make counterfeiting difficult.

thread·nee·dle (thred′nē′dəl), *n.* **1.** a children's game in which the players stand in a row holding hands, and the player at one end runs between the others under their uplifted arms, followed by the rest in turn. **2.** a dance figure in which the female partner passes under the male's arm, their hands joined.

thread of life, the, the imaginary thread spun and cut by the fates. It is supposed to symbolize the course and termination of one's existence.

thread-the-nee·dle (thred′ᴛʜə nē′dəl), *n.* threadneedle.

thread·worm (thred′wėrm′), *n.* any of various threadlike nematode worms, especially the pinworm or a filaria.

thread·y (thred′ē), *adj.,* **thread·i·er, thread·i·est. 1.** consisting of or like a thread; threadlike. **2. a.** composed of fine fibers; stringy; fibrous. **b.** (of a liquid) forming strings; viscid; ropy. **3.** (of the pulse) thin and feeble: *The pulse becomes quick . . . and so thready, it is not like a pulse at all, but like a string vibrating just underneath the skin* (Florence Nightingale). **4.** (of the voice, etc.) lacking in fullness.

threap (thrēp), *v.t. Scottish.* **1.** to rebuke; chide; scold. **2.** to assert or maintain obstinately. [Old English *thrēapian*]

threat (thret), *n.* **1.** a statement of what will be done to hurt or punish someone: *The boys stopped playing ball in the classroom because of the janitor's threats to report it to the principal.* **2.** a sign, cause, or source of possible evil or harm: *Those black clouds are a threat of rain. Poverty and disease are threats to society. Germany had been a threat, a menace* (H. G. Wells). —*v.t., v.i. Archaic.* to threaten.
[Old English *thrēat* crowd, troop; oppression]
—**Syn.** *n.* **1.** commination, intimidation.

threat·en (thret′ən), *v.t.* **1.** to make a threat against; say what will be done to hurt or punish: *to threaten a person with imprisonment. The farmer threatened to shoot any dog that killed one of his sheep.* **2.** to be a sign, cause, or source of (possible evil or harm, etc.): *Black clouds threaten a storm.* **3.** to be a cause of possible evil or harm to: *A flood threatened the city.* —*v.i.* **1.** to be or pose a threat. **2.** to utter a threat or threats: *Do you mean to threaten? She threatens and scolds too much.* **3.** to allow oneself to be threatened: *Say what you will, I don't threaten easily.*
[Old English *thrēatnian* press; urge on; afflict < *thrēat;* see THREAT] —**threat′en·er,** *n.* —**threat′en·ing·ly,** *adv.*
—**Syn.** *v.t.* **1. Threaten, menace** mean to indicate the intention of harming someone. **Threaten** applies when one is trying to force someone to do (or not to do) something and warns him of the consequences if he does not obey: *He threatened to hit her if she misbehaved.* **Menace** applies when one tries to frighten someone by means of a look, movement, or weapon: *He menaced her with a gun.* **2.** portend, presage, forebode, augur.

three (thrē), *n.* **1.** one more than two; 3. **2.** a set of three persons or things: *to arrive in threes.* **3.** a card domino, throw of dice, etc., with three spots; trey.
—*adj.* one more than two; 3.
[Old English *thrēo,* feminine and neuter of *thrie*]
—**Syn.** *n.* **2.** trio, threesome, triplet.

three-bag·ger (thrē′bag′ər), *n. Slang.* (in baseball) a three-base hit; triple.

three-ball (thrē′bôl′), *adj.* played with three balls, as a golf match: *Whereas six matches have been played, some of them singles, eight remain to be played, all of them three-ball* (London Times).

three-base hit (thrē′bās′), (in baseball) a safe hit for three bases; triple.

three-card monte (thrē′kärd′), a Mexican gambling game, in which three cards are thrown on the table face down, the opposing players betting on the position of one of the cards.

three-col·or (thrē′kul′ər), *adj.* of or having to do with a photomechanical process of printing in which a colored picture or letterpress is produced by the superposition of the three primary colors or their complementaries.

three-cor·nered (thrē′kôr′nərd), *adj.* **1.** having three corners; tricornered: *He wore . . . a black three-cornered hat* (New Yorker). **2.** of, having to do with, or involving three persons or parties: *Mr. Victor Montagu . . . prospective Conservative candidate for the forthcoming three-cornered general election contest* (London Times).

three-D or **3-D** (thrē′dē′), *n.* a three-dimensional (motion picture).

three-deck·er (thrē′dek′ər), *n.* **1. a.** a ship having three decks. **b.** a warship that used to carry guns on three decks. **2.** a thing having three stories, layers, or parts, such as a novel in three volumes or a sandwich made with three slices of bread.

three-di·men·sion·al (thrē′də men′shə-nəl), *adj.* **1.** having three dimensions. **2.** seeming to have depth as well as height and breadth; appearing to exist in three dimensions: *a three-dimensional photograph.* —**three′-di·men′sion·al·ly,** *adv.*

three-di·men·sion·al·i·ty (thrē′də men′-shə nal′ə tē), *n.* the condition or quality of having three dimensions: *By test with models he established further that shading creates an illusion of three-dimensionality for birds, as it does for us in a painting* (Scientific American).

three-dimensional sound, sound by stereophonic reproduction.

three·fold (thrē′fōld′), *adj.* **1.** three times as much or as many. **2.** having three parts.

—*adv.* in a threefold manner; trebly; triply. —*n.* three times as much or as many; three: *to increase by threefold.*
—**Syn.** *adj.* **1.** treble.
three-four (thrē′fôr′, -fōr′), *adj. Music.* with three quarter notes in a measure or bar: *a three-four time or rhythm.*
three-leg·ged race (thrē′leg′id, -legd′), a race run by couples, the right leg of one person being bound to the left leg of the other.
three-line whip (thrē′līn′), *British.* the strongest form of directive issued by a political party to its members to attend a parliamentary debate. It is underlined three times to emphasize its urgency.
three-mast·er (thrē′mas′tər, -mäs′-), *n.* a ship having three masts.
three-mile belt or **zone** (thrē′mīl′), the strip of water within three miles of a country's coast, included within that country's jurisdiction by international law.
three-mile limit, the distance from the shore that, according to international law, is included within the jurisdiction of the state possessing the coast.
three-part time (thrē′pärt′), *Music.* three beats, or a multiple of three beats, to the measure.
three·pence (thrip′əns, threp′-, thrup′-), *n.* **1.** three British pennies; three pence. **2.** a British coin of this value, worth about 3 cents. Also, **thrippence.**
three·pen·ny (thrip′ə nē, thrip′nē; threp′-, thrup′-; thrē′pen′ē), *adj.* **1.** worth, costing, or amounting to threepence. **2.** *Especially British* of little worth; cheap; paltry.
threepenny bit or **piece,** a threepence.
three-phase (thrē′fāz′), *adj.* **1.** of or having to do with a combination of three electric currents caused by alternating electromotive forces differing in phase by one third of a cycle (120 degrees). **2.** having three phases.
three-piece (thrē′pēs′), *adj.* having three pieces. A three-piece suit has trousers, jacket, and vest (for men), or skirt, jacket, and topcoat (for women).
three-ply (thrē′plī′), *adj.* having three thicknesses, layers, folds, or strands.
three-point landing (thrē′point′), a landing of an aircraft at an angle with the ground that is the same as that of the craft when at rest on the ground. Both wheels of the main landing gear and the wheel or skid under the tail touch the ground at the same time.
three-port (thrē′pôrt′, -pōrt′), *adj.* of or having to do with a type of two-cycle internal-combustion engine having three ports for the intake, transfer, and exhaust.
three-quar·ter (thrē′kwôr′tər), *adj.* consisting of or involving three quarters of a whole. A three-quarter portrait usually shows three quarters of the figure. —*n.* a three-quarter back: *A man swerved and jinked his way like a Rugby three-quarter through the streets of North Kensington* (London Daily Express).
three-quarter back, (in Rugby) one of the four backs whose normal position is in front of the fullback and behind the halfbacks.
three-quarter binding, a book binding using the same material for the back, about one third of each cover, and sometimes the corners, the remainder of the covers having different material.
three-ring circus (thrē′ring′), **1.** a very large circus that has three rings in which separate acts can be presented at the same time. **2.** *Informal.* any activity or undertaking having a great variety of things going on at the same time.
three R's, reading, writing, and arithmetic.
three·score (thrē′skôr′, -skōr′), *adj.* three times twenty; 60.
three·some (thrē′səm), *n.* **1.** a group or set of three people. **2. a.** a game or match played by three people. **b.** (in golf) a match of three players using only two balls in which one player plays against the other two, each of whom takes alternate strokes at the second ball. **c.** the players.
—*adj.* consisting or composed of three; performed by three together; threefold; triple.
[originally, Scottish adjective < Old English *thrēo* three + *-sum* -some[2]]
three-square (thrē′skwãr′), *adj.* having three equal sides; equilaterally triangular.
three-toed sloth (thrē′tōd′), a variety of sloth with three toes on each foot.
three-toed woodpecker, either of two woodpeckers of northern North America that lack the inner hind toe and have a yellow crown.

Three-toed Woodpecker (8¾ in. long)

three-wheel·er (thrē′hwē′lər), *n.* a tricycle or other vehicle running on three wheels: *The schedule referred to motor vehicles, three-wheelers, bubble cars, and certain types of pedestrian controlled vehicles* (London Times).
Three Wise Men, three men who came from the East to honor the infant Jesus; the Magi. In medieval legend they became three kings, named Gaspar (or Kaspar), Melchior, and Balthasar.
threm·ma·tol·o·gy (threm′ə tol′ə jē), *n.* the science of breeding or propagating animals and plants under domestication. [< Greek *thrémma, -atos* nursling (< stem of *tréphein* nourish) + English *-logy*]
threne (thrēn), *n. Archaic.* a threnody: *Whereupon it made this threne To the phoenix and the dove* (Shakespeare).
[< Greek *thrênos*; see THRENODY]
thre·net·ic (thri net′ik), *adj.* having to do with a threnody; mournful. [< Greek *thrēnētikós*]
thre·net·i·cal (thri net′ə kəl), *adj.* threnetic.
thre·node (thrē′nōd, thren′ōd), *n.* threnody.
thre·no·di·al (thri nō′dē əl), *adj.* having to do with or like a threnody.
thre·nod·ic (thri nod′ik), *adj.* threnodial.
thren·o·dist (thren′ə dist), *n.* the composer of a threnody: *Peace, then, rhetoricians, false threnodists of false liberty!* (Thomas DeQuincey).
thren·o·dy (thren′ə dē), *n., pl.* **-dies.** a song of lamentation, especially at a person's death; dirge: *Cyrus Sulzberger's "My Brother Death" is a profoundly moving threnody on man's fate* (New York Times). [< Greek *threnoidiā* < *thrênos* a lament (< *threîsthai* to shriek, cry aloud) + *ōidē* song, ode]
thre·o·nin (thrē′ə nin), *n.* threonine.
thre·o·nine (thrē′ə nēn, -nin), *n.* a crystalline amino acid considered essential to human nutrition. It is a product of the hydrolysis of proteins. *Formula:* $C_4H_9NO_3$
thresh (thresh), *v.t.* **1.** to separate the grain or seeds from (wheat, etc.); thrash: *Nowadays most farmers use a machine to thresh their wheat.* **2.** to toss about; move violently; thrash. —*v.i.* **1.** to thresh grain. **2.** to thrash.
thresh out, to settle by thorough discussion; thrash out: *All this could have been threshed out in private, without a court of inquiry* (Maclean's).
thresh over, to go over again and again; thrash over: *They threshed over the problem all night long.*
—*n.* a threshing.
[Middle English *thresshen,* variant of Old English *therscan* to beat; thresh with a flail; (originally) to tread, tramp]
—**Syn.** *v.t.* **1.** sift.
thresh·er (thresh′ər), *n.* **1.** a person or thing that threshes. **2.** a machine for separating the grain or seeds from wheat, etc. **3.** a large shark of the Atlantic, having a long, curved tail with which it supposedly beats the water to round up the small fish on which it feeds; thrasher; thrasher shark.
thresher shark, a thresher (def. 3).
thresher whale, a killer whale; grampus.
thresh·old (thresh′ōld, -hōld), *n.* **1.** a piece of wood or stone across the bottom of a door frame; doorsill. **2.** the entrance to a house or building; doorway. **3.** a point of entering; beginning point: *to be at the threshold of war. The scientist was on the threshold of an important discovery. I was on the threshold of a surprising adventure* (W. Somerset Maugham). **4.** *Psychology, Physiology.* the limit below which a given stimulus ceases to be perceptible, or the point beyond which two stimuli cannot be differentiated; limen. [Old English *threscold.* Apparently related to THRESH in the sense "to tread, tramp".]
threw (thrü), *v.* past tense of **throw:** *He threw a stone and ran away.*
thrice (thrīs), *adv.* **1.** three times: *He knocked thrice.* **2.** in threefold quantity or degree: *The giant was thrice as strong as an ordinary man.* **3.** very; greatly; extremely. [Middle English *thriës,* Old English *thriwa* < *thrīe* three + adverbial genitive *-s*]
thrid (thrid), *v.,* **thrid·ded, thrid·ding.** *Archaic.* to thread.
thrift (thrift), *n.* **1.** absence of waste; saving; economical management; habit of saving: *By thrift she managed to get along on her small salary. A bank account encourages thrift.* **2.** any of a group of low plants with pink, white, or lavender flowers that grow on mountains and along seashores; statice. **3.** vigorous growth, as of a plant. **4.** *Archaic or Dialect.* industry; labor; employment. **5.** *Obsolete.* prosperity; success. [Middle English *thrift* < *thriven* to thrive; perhaps influenced by Scandinavian (compare Old Icelandic *thrift,* variant of *thrif* prosperity)] —**Syn. 1.** economy, frugality.
thrift·i·ly (thrif′tə lē), *adv.* in a thrifty manner; with thrift; economically: *A blind beggar . . . with a needle and thread thriftily mending his stockings* (Richard Steele).
thrift·i·ness (thrif′tē nis), *n.* the quality or state of being thrifty.
thrift·less (thrift′lis), *adj.* without thrift; wasteful. —**thrift′less·ly,** *adv.* —**thrift′less·ness,** *n.* —**Syn.** improvident.
thrift shop, *U.S.* a shop in which secondhand articles in good condition are sold at low prices and usually paid for by the shopkeeper after he has sold them: *The entire proceeds from the sale of donated articles at the thrift shop have gone to charity* (New York Times).
thrift·y (thrif′tē), *adj.,* **thrift·i·er, thrift·i·est. 1.** careful in spending; economical; saving. **2.** thriving; vigorous; flourishing: *a thrifty plant.* **3.** prosperous; well-to-do; successful: *The countryside had many fine, thrifty farms.* —**Syn. 1.** provident, frugal, sparing. See **economical.**
thrill (thril), *n.* **1.** a shivering, exciting feeling: *a thrill of pleasure or fear, the thrill of adventure or discovery, to get thrills from the movies.* **2.** a vibration or quivering; throbbing; tremor. **3.** an abnormal vibration or fine tremor that can be heard with a stethoscope when listening to the heart or lungs. [< verb]
—*v.t.* **1.** to give a shivering, exciting feeling to: *Stories of adventure thrilled him.* **2.** to cause to tremble or quiver; make vibrate: *to thrill the air with music.*
—*v.i.* **1.** to have a shivering, exciting feeling: *The children thrilled with joy at the sight of the Christmas tree.* **2.** to quiver; tremble: *Her voice thrilled with terror.*
[variant of *thirl*[1]]
—**Syn.** *v.i.* **2.** vibrate, throb.
thrill·er (thril′ər), *n.* **1.** a person or thing that thrills: *still smarting under the sting of losing last night's ten-inning thriller* (New York Times). *For 75 minutes the plane circled. The final landing was a thriller* (Time). **2.** *Informal.* a sensational play or story, especially one involving murder or other violence: *There has been no better thriller in London since the war than "Dial M for Murder," produced at the Westminster Theatre three years ago* (London Times).
thrill·er-dill·er (thril′ər dil′ər), *n. Slang.* a sensational story; thriller: *Not the least pleasurable sort of reading is the good old thriller-diller* (Wall Street Journal).
thrill·ing (thril′ing), *adj.* **1.** affecting with a thrill of emotion: *wild thrilling sounds* (Herman Melville). **2.** vibrating or quivering. **3.** *Obsolete.* piercing or penetrating. —**thrill′ing·ly,** *adv.* —**thrill′ing·ness,** *n.*
thrip·pence (thrip′əns), *n.* threepence.
thrips (thrips), *n.sing.* (*occasionally plural with singular* **thrip**). any of a group of small insects with usually four narrow wings fringed with hair. Some varieties are destructive to crops and spread virus and fungus. [< Latin *thrips* < Greek *thrîps, thripós* woodworm]

Onion Thrips or Tobacco Thrips (Line shows actual length.)

thrive (thrīv), *v.i.,* **throve** or **thrived, thrived** or **thriv·en** (thriv′ən), **thriv·ing. 1.** to grow or develop well; grow vigorously: *Most plants* *will not thrive without sunshine.* **2.** to be successful; grow rich; turn out well; prosper: *He that would thrive Must rise at five He that hath thriven May lie till seven* (John Clarke). [Middle English *thrifen,* perhaps < Scandinavian (compare Old Icelandic *thrīfa*)] —**thriv′ing·ly,** *adv.* —**Syn. 1.** flourish. **2.** succeed.

thrive·less (thrīv′lis), *adj.* not thriving; unsuccessful.

thriv·er (thrī′vər), *n.* a person or thing that thrives.

thro′ or **thro** (thrü), *prep., adv., adj.* through.

throat (thrōt), *n.* **1.** the front of the neck, containing the passages from the mouth to the stomach and lungs. **2.** the passage from the mouth to the stomach or the lungs: *A bone stuck in his throat.* **3.** any narrow passage: *The throat of the mine was blocked by fallen rocks.*

cut one's throat, to defeat; destroy; put an end to: *Arab leaders . . . have been actively trying to cut each other's throats* (Time).

jump down one's throat, *Informal.* to attack or criticize a person with sudden violence: *The fact that he has made a mistake is no excuse for jumping down his throat.*

lie in one's throat, to lie brazenly and boldly: . . . *whoever charged him with the plot lied in his throat* (Washington Irving).

lump in one's throat. See under **lump**[1], *n.*

ram (force, shove, etc.) **down one's throat,** to force (an opinion, etc.) on one's acceptance: *The referendum proposal had to be rammed down the throats of De Gaulle's unhappy ministers* (Atlantic).

stick in one's throat, to be hard or unpleasant to say: *Amen stuck in my throat* (Shakespeare).

[Old English *throte.* Related to THROTTLE.]

throat-cut·ting (thrōt′kut′ing), *n.,* or **throat cutting, 1.** a cutting of the throat to maim or kill. **2.** *Informal.* a deliberate attempt to harm or ruin another or others for personal advantage in a competitive situation.

-throated, *combining form.* having a ___ throat: *White-throated = having a white throat.*

throat·i·ly (thrō′tə lē), *adv.* in a throaty manner.

throat·i·ness (thrō′tē nis), *n.* a being throaty; guttural or velar quality.

throat·latch (thrōt′lach′), *n.* a strap that passes under a horse's throat and helps to hold the bridle in place.

throat sweetbread, the thymus gland of an animal used for food.

throat·y (thrō′tē), *adj.,* **throat·i·er, throat·i·est. 1.** produced or modified in the throat; guttural or velar: *a throaty sound.* **2.** low-pitched and resonant: *The young girl had a throaty voice.*

throb (throb), *v.,* **throbbed, throb·bing,** *n.* —*v.i.* **1.** to beat rapidly or strongly: *a heart throbbing with joy. The long climb up the hill made her heart throb. His wounded arm throbbed with pain.* **2.** to beat steadily: *propellers or engines that throb.* **3.** to quiver; tremble. —*n.* **1.** a rapid or strong beat: *A sudden throb of pain shot through his head.* **2.** a steady beat: *the throb of a pulse.* **3.** a quiver; tremble. [probably imitative] —**throb′bing·ly,** *adv.* —**Syn.** *v.i.* **1.** pulsate, palpitate.

throb·ber (throb′ər), *n.* a person or thing that throbs.

throe (thrō), *n.* a violent spasm or pang; great pain.

throes, a. anguish; agony: . . . *in the very throes of its fell despair* (Benjamin Disraeli). **b.** a desperate struggle; violent disturbance: *When a nation is in the throes of revolution, wild spirits are abroad in the storm* (James Froude). **c.** labor pangs (in childbirth): *My womb . . . Prodigious motion felt and rueful throes* (Milton).

[variant of Middle English *throwe*; origin uncertain]

throm·base (throm′bās), *n.* thrombin.

throm·bi (throm′bī), *n.* plural of **thrombus.**

throm·bin (throm′bin), *n.* an enzyme in blood serum which reacts with fibrinogen to form fibrin, causing blood to clot.

throm·bo·cyte (throm′bə sīt), *n.* platelet, a cellular element of blood. [< Greek *thrómbos* a clot + English *-cyte*]

throm·bo·cy·to·pe·ni·a (throm′bə sī′tə-pē′nē ə), *n.* an abnormal decrease of thrombocytes in the blood. [< *thrombocyte* + Greek *peniā* poverty]

throm·bo·em·bol·ic (throm′bō em bol′ik), *adj.* of, having to do with, or characterized by thromboembolism.

throm·bo·em·bo·lism (throm′bō em′bə-liz əm), *n.* the obstruction of a blood vessel by a clot that has broken loose from its site of formation, a common and very serious complication of coronary thrombosis.

throm·bo·gen (throm′bə jen), *n.* prothrombin.

throm·bo·kin·ase (throm′bō kin′ās, -kī′nās), *n.* a complex substance found in the blood and tissues, which is thought to promote the conversion of prothrombin into thrombin and therefore be active in the clotting of blood. [< Greek *thrómbos* a clot + English *kinase*]

throm·bo·phle·bi·tis (throm′bō fli bī′tis), *n.* the formation of a thrombus in an injured or infected blood vessel, especially in one of the veins of an arm or leg. [< Greek *thrómbos* a clot + English *phlebitis*]

throm·bo·plas·tic (throm′bō plas′tik), *adj.* promoting or having to do with the clotting of blood. [< Greek *thrómbos* a clot + English *plastic*]

throm·bo·plas·tin (throm′bō plas′tin), *n.* **1.** a complex substance found in the blood and in tissues, which is thought to contribute to the formation of prothrombin. **2.** thrombokinase.

throm·bo·sis (throm bō′sis), *n.* the formation of a thrombus; coagulation of blood in a blood vessel or in the heart during life. [< New Latin *thrombosis* < Greek *thrómbōsis,* ultimately < *thrómbos* a clot]

throm·bot·ic (throm bot′ik), *adj.* **1.** of or like thrombosis. **2.** caused by or having to do with thrombosis.

throm·bus (throm′bəs), *n., pl.* **-bi** (-bī). a fibrinous clot which forms in a blood vessel or within the heart and obstructs the circulation: *Coronary thrombosis is the result of a . . . thrombus, forming in a coronary artery and shutting off part of the blood supply of the heart muscles* (Nathan W. Shock). [< New Latin *thrombus* < Greek *thrómbos* a clot]

throne (thrōn), *n., v.,* **throned, thron·ing.** —*n.* **1.** the chair on which a king, queen, pope, bishop, or other person of high rank sits during ceremonies: *Ye also shall sit upon twelve thrones, judging the twelve tribes of Israel* (Matthew 19:28). **2.** the position, power, or authority of a king, queen, etc.: *a tottering throne, to gamble for a throne.* **3.** the person who sits on a throne; sovereign: *to address oneself to the throne.*

ascend the throne, to become king, queen, etc.: *Elizabeth II ascended the British throne in 1952.*

take the throne, to become king or reigning queen; succeed to the throne: *Upon the death of his father the young prince took the throne.*

thrones, the third order of angels, in the highest of the three hierarchies: *Thrones, who God's Judgments hear, and then proclaim* (Thomas Ken).

—*v.t.* to enthrone: *Where Venice sat in state, throned on her hundred isles* (Byron). —*v.i.* to be enthroned.

[< Latin *thronus* < Greek *thrónos*]

—**Syn.** *n.* **2.** sovereignty, dominion.

throne·less (thrōn′lis), *adj.* without a throne; dethroned.

throne room, a palace room in which a sovereign formally receives visitors from his throne.

throne speech, speech from the throne.

throng (thrông, throng), *n.* **1.** a crowd; great number; multitude: *The streets were filled with throngs of people* (Charles Dickens). *Not in the shouts and plaudits of the throng, But in ourselves are triumph and defeat* (Longfellow). **2.** a pressing or crowding; crowded condition: *Went the summons forth Into all quarters, and the throng began* (William Cowper).

—*v.t.* **1.** to fill with a crowd; crowd: *People thronged the theater to see the famous actress.* **2.** to crowd around and press upon; jostle. —*v.i.* to come together in a throng or throngs; go or press in large numbers: *The people thronged to see the king. A thousand fantasies Begin to throng into my memory* (Milton).

—*adj. Especially Scottish.* crowded; thronged. Also, *Scottish,* **thrang.**

[Middle English *throng, thrang,* probably Old English *gethrang,* related to *thringan* to crowd] —**throng′er,** *n.*

—**Syn.** *n.* **1.** host, mass, pack. See **crowd.** —*v.t.* **1.** cram, stuff.

throp·ple (throp′əl), *n. Scottish and British Dialect.* the throat; gullet; windpipe. [origin uncertain]

thros·tle (thros′əl), *n. Dialect.* **1.** a thrush, especially, the song thrush. **2.** a kind of spinning machine that draws, twists, and winds cotton, wool, etc., in one continuous action. [Old English *throstle*]

throt·tle (throt′əl), *n., v.,* **-tled, -tling.** —*n.* **1.** a valve regulating the flow of steam, gasoline vapor, etc., to an engine: *He slowed down the motorcycle and closed the throttle.* **2.** a lever or pedal working such a valve. **3.** *Dialect.* the throat or windpipe.

—*v.t.* **1.** to stop the breath of by pressure on the throat; strangle. **2.** to choke; suffocate. **3.** to check or stop the flow of; suppress: *High tariffs throttle trade between countries.* **4.** to silence or check as if choking. **5. a.** to check, stop, or regulate the flow of (fuel) to an engine. **b.** to lessen the speed of (an engine) by closing a throttle: *to throttle a steam engine.* —*v.i.* to be choked; strangle; suffocate.

[Middle English *throtel* < *throte* throat + frequentative suffix *-le*]

—**Syn.** *v.t.* **1.** garrote. **3.** obstruct.

Throt·tle·bot·tom (throt′əl bot′əm), *n. U.S.* a harmlessly ineffective holder of public office: *Nixon has fulfilled Eisenhower's idea of what a Vice-President should be—not a Throttlebottom but a hard-working member of the Administration* (Atlantic). [< *Throttlebottom,* a character in the musical comedy *Of Thee I Sing* (1932) by George S. Kaufman and Morris Ryskind]

throt·tle·hold (throt′əl hōld′), *n.* a strangling hold; suppressive or stifling control: *a throttlehold on free speech.*

throttle lever or **pedal,** a throttle.

throt·tler (throt′lər) *n.* a person or thing that throttles.

throttle valve, a throttle.

through (thrü), *prep.* **1.** from end to end of; from side to side of; between the parts of; from beginning to end of: *The soldiers marched through the town. The men cut a tunnel through a mountain. The carpenter bored holes through a board. Fish swim through the water.* **2.** here and there in; over; around: *to stroll through the streets of a city, to travel through New England.* **3.** because of; by reason of; on account of; owing to: *to refuse help through foolish pride, to fail through ignorance.* **4.** by means of: *to become rich through hard work and ability.* **5.** having reached the end of; finished with; done with: *We are through school at three o'clock.* **6. a.** during the whole of; throughout: *to work from dawn through the day and into the night.* **b.** during and until the finish of: *to help a person through hard times.*

—*adv.* **1.** from end to end; from side to side; between the parts: *The bullet hit the wall and went through.* **2.** completely; thoroughly: *He walked home in the rain and was wet through.* **3.** from beginning to end: *She read the book through.* **4.** along the whole distance; all the way: *The train goes through to Boston.*

through and through, completely; thoroughly; wholly; entirely: *a scoundrel through and through.*

—*adj.* **1. a.** going all the way without change: *a through train from New York to Chicago.* **b.** for the whole distance, journey, etc.: *a through ticket to Los Angeles.* **2.** having reached the end; at an end; finished: *I am almost through.* **3.** passing or extending from one end, side, surface, etc., to the other. Also, **thro, thro′, thru.**

[Middle English *thrugh,* variant of Old English *thurh.* Compare THOROUGH.]

—**Syn.** *prep.* **4.** See **with.**

through·ly (thrü′lē), *adv. Archaic.* fully; completely; thoroughly.

through-oth·er (thrü′uᴛʜ′ər), *adv. Scottish.* (mingled) through each other or one another; indiscriminately.

through·out (thrü out′), *prep.* all the way through; through all; in or to every part of: *He worked hard throughout his life. The Fourth of July is celebrated throughout the United States.* —*adv.* in or to every part: *This house is well built throughout.* —**Syn.** *adv.* everywhere.

through·put (thrü′pu̇t′), *n.* **1.** the production and distribution of a product: *the throughput of crude oil, the throughput of canned meats.* **2.** the quantity produced: *The average daily throughput was 1,370 short tons of ore* (Cape Times).

through·way (thrü′wā′), *n.* an express highway; thruway: *On the New York State throughway the right of way is often 1,200 feet wide* (Observer).

throu·ther (thrü′ᴛʜər), *adv. Scottish.* through-other.

throve (thrōv), *v.* a past tense of **thrive.**

throw (thrō), *v.*, **threw, thrown, throw·ing,** *n.* —*v.t.* **1. a.** to cast; toss; hurl; fling: *to throw a stone or a ball, to throw water on a blazing rug, to throw spray against a window, to throw caution to the winds. The tree throws a shadow on the grass.* **b.** to fire (a projectile); shoot: *A cannon throws shells.* **2.** to bring to the ground; cause to fall or fall off: *to throw one's opponent in wrestling, to be thrown by a horse.* **3. a.** to put carelessly or in haste: *to throw a sweater over one's shoulders.* **b.** to put or move quickly or by force: *to throw oneself into a fight, to throw a man into prison, to throw reserve troops into a battle.* **c.** to put into a certain condition: *to throw a person into confusion.* **4.** to turn or direct, especially quickly: *to throw a questioning look at a stranger, to throw a glance at passing cars.* **5. a.** to move (a lever, etc.) to connect or disconnect parts of a switch, clutch, or other mechanisms. **b.** to connect or disconnect thus. **6.** to cast off: **a.** to shed: *A snake throws its skin.* **b.** to lose; drop: *The horse threw a shoe.* **7.** (of some animals) to bring forth (young); bear: *The cow threw a healthy calf.* **8.** *Informal.* to let an opponent win (a race, game, etc.), often for money: *Ronald Howells, aged 29, pleaded Not Guilty to conspiring with Gould and others to defraud bookmakers by "throwing" the Scunthorpe v. Darby County match* (London Times). **9.** to make (a specified cast) with dice. **10.** to twist (silk) into threads. **11.** to shape on a potter's wheel: *to throw a bowl from a ball of clay.* **12.** *Especially Scottish.* **a.** to twist; turn. **b.** to strain; wrench. **13.** *Informal.* to give (a party, etc.).

—*v.i.* to cast, toss, or hurl something: *How far can you throw?*

throw away, a. to get rid of; discard: *They will . . . throw away the blessings their hands are filled with because they are not big enough to grasp everything* (John Locke). **b.** to waste: *Advice . . . would be but thrown away upon them* (Spectator). **c.** to fail to use: *Don't throw away this chance of a lifetime.*

throw back, to revert to an ancestral type: *He and his ideas throw back to the Middle Ages* (John Galsworthy).

throw in, a. to put in as a supplement; add, especially as a bargain: *[The] story turns . . . on murder and revenge, with a little love thrown in* (Black & White). **b.** to interpose or contribute (a remark, etc.); put in: *"Not a grain," threw in Julian, hotly* (Sabine Baring-Gould). **c.** to share (one's lot, interests, etc.) with: *He willingly threw in his fortune with theirs* (English Illustrated Magazine).

throw off, a. to get rid of; cast off: *The Spanish colonies . . . have thrown off the yoke of the mother country* (Examiner). **b.** to divest oneself of (a garment, a quality, a habit, etc.); discard: *He throws off his gown and hypocrisy together* (E. Ward). **c.** to give off; emit: *to throw off wastes with perspiration.* **d.** to cause to lose: *to throw a hound off the scent.* **e.** *Informal.* to produce (a poem, etc.) in an offhand manner: *The new articles . . . "thrown off at a heat," stood particularly in want of re-revision* (J. Badcock).

throw oneself at, to try very hard to get the love, friendship, or favor of: *As for the girls, Claire, they just throw themselves at a man* (Walter Besant).

throw oneself on or **upon, a.** to commit oneself entirely to (someone's generosity, etc.): *The criminal threw himself upon the mercy of the court.* **b.** to attack with violence or vigor; fall upon: *He threw himself upon the ragout, and the plate was presently [empty]* (Scott).

throw open, a. to open suddenly or widely: *I had ordered the folding doors to be thrown open* (Joseph Addison). **b.** to remove all obstacles or restrictions from: . . . *labouring to throw open the gates of commerce* (Tait's Magazine).

throw out, a. to get rid of; discard: *When the contract expires, this newspaper will throw out its linotype machines* (Indianapolis Typographical Journal). **b.** to reject: *The Ballot Bill . . . was thrown out by the Lords* (P.V. Smith). **c.** to expel: *The servants threw out the intruder. He has been thrown out from his job.* **d.** to put or send forth (a signal, question, suggestion, etc.): *Athens unhesitatingly accepted the challenge thrown out* (A.W. Ward). *He began to throw out questions about our plans the following day* (George Woodcock). **e.** (in baseball) to put out (a base runner) by throwing the ball to a base.

throw over, a. to give up; discard; abandon: *Mr. Freeman . . . throws over the latter part of Palgrave's theory* (William Stubbs). **b.** to overthrow: *The government was thrown over by a rebel group.*

throw up, a. *Informal.* to vomit: *It is easy to judge . . . the cause by the substances which the patient throws up* (John Arbuthnot). **b.** to give up; abandon: *He had felt tempted to throw up public life in disgust* (James A. Froude). **c.** to build rapidly: *The Greeks threw up a great intrenchment to secure their navy* (Sir Richard Steele).

—*n.* **1.** a throwing; cast, toss, etc.: *a good throw.* **2.** the distance a thing is or may be thrown: *a long throw.* **3.** a scarf; light covering, blanket, etc.: *a knitted throw.* **4.** a cast at dice; venture: *a lucky throw.* **5. a.** the reciprocating motion generated by a cam, eccentric, etc. **b.** the motion of a cam, eccentric, etc. **c.** the extent of this, measured on a straight line passing through the axis of motion. **d.** any of the cranks of the crankshaft of a gasoline engine. **6.** *Geology.* **a.** a fault. **b.** the extent of vertical displacement produced by a fault. **7.** *Obsolete.* a fall.

[Old English *thrāwan* to twist, turn; torture]

—**throw′er,** *n.*

—**Syn.** *v.t.* **1. a. Throw, toss, cast** mean to send something through the air by a sudden twist or quick movement of the arm. **Throw** is the general word: *The children threw pillows at each other.* **Toss** means to throw lightly or carelessly with the palm up: *Please toss me the matches.* **Cast** is now literary except figuratively or in special uses, as in games, voting, fishing, sailing: *They cast anchor. She cast dignity to the wind, and ran.*

throw·a·way (thrō′ə wā′), *n.* a handbill, pamphlet, etc., intended to be thrown away after reading.

—*adj.* that can be thrown away or discarded: *a throwaway bottle.*

throwaway line, a casually or carelessly delivered line from a dialogue or script: *It takes a certain nerve for a comedian to try a throwaway line* (Time).

throw·back (thrō′bak′), *n.* **1.** a throwing back. **2.** a setback or check. **3. a.** a reversion to an earlier ancestral type or character. **b.** an example of this: *The boy seemed to be a throwback to his great-grandfather.*

throw-in (thrō′in′), *n.* the act of putting the ball in play by throwing it into fair territory, as in basketball, soccer, and rugby.

throw·ing (thrō′ing), *n.* a step in the processing of textiles in which the yarn is twisted and doubled without drawing it out or stretching it to give it greater strength.

thrown (thrōn), *v.* the past participle of **throw:** *She has thrown her old toys out.*

throw-out (thrō′out′), *n.* **1.** an act of throwing out; ejection: *The land areas . . . must be controlled to avoid hazard from throw-out of material, dust, air blast, and ground shock* (Science News Letter). **2.** a person or thing that is thrown out; discard: *Ursula is reminded of what she has lost by the sight of a heap of throw-outs* (Punch).

throw rug, a scatter rug: *Wool throw rugs from Mexico, three feet by five and a half, are hand-woven with colorful primitive motifs* (New Yorker).

throw·ster (thrō′stər), *n.* a person who throws silk.

thru (thrü), *prep., adv., adj.* through: *Thru these portals pass the Broadway hopefuls* ('Teen).

thrum[1] (thrum), *v.*, **thrummed, thrum·ming,** *n.* —*v.i.* **1.** to play on a stringed instrument by plucking the strings, especially in an idle, mechanical, or unskillful way; strum: *to thrum on a guitar.* **2.** to sound when thrummed on, as a guitar, etc., or its strings. **3.** to drum or tap idly with the fingers: *to thrum on a table.* **4.** to drone; mumble: *Boswell . . . has thrummed upon this topic till it is threadbare* (Scott). **5.** *Dialect.* (of a cat) to purr. —*v.t.* **1.** to play (a stringed instrument, or tune on it) idly, mechanically, or unskillfully. **2. a.** to recite or tell in a monotonous way. **b.** to hum over (a melody).

—*n.* the sound made by thrumming.

[apparently imitative]

thrum[2] (thrum), *n., v.*, **thrummed, thrum·ming.** —*n.* **1.** an end of the warp thread left unwoven on the loom after the web is cut off. **2.** any short piece of waste thread or yarn. **3.** a tuft, tassel, or fringe of threads at the edge of a piece of cloth. **4.** *Scottish.* a tangle.

thrums, a. the row or fringe of warp threads left unwoven on the loom when the web is cut off: *to cut off the thrums for use as frills.* **b.** odds and ends; scraps: *It is this, which . . . makes life a whole instead of a parcel of thrums bound together by an accident* (John Morley). **c.** *Nautical.* short pieces of coarse woolen or hempen yarn: *thrums used for mops in the cabins.*

—*v.t.* **1.** *Nautical.* to sew or fasten bunches of rope yarn over (a mat or sail) to produce a rough surface to prevent chafing or stop a leak. **2.** *Obsolete* or *Dialect.* to furnish or adorn with thrums; cover with small tufts; make shaggy.

[Old English *-thrum,* in *tungethrum* tongue ligament]

thrum·mer (thrum′ər), *n.* **1.** a person who thrums or strums on a stringed instrument. **2.** an idle or indifferent player.

thrush[1] (thrush), *n.* **1.** any of a large group of migratory songbirds that includes the robin, the bluebird, the wood thrush, and veery. **2.** any of various similar birds, as the Louisiana water thrush. [Old English *thrysce*]

Song Thrush[1] (def. 1) (about 9 in. long)

thrush[2] (thrush), *n.* **1.** a disease often attacking children, characterized by white specks on the inside of the mouth and throat, and caused by a parasitic fungus. **2.** a diseased condition of the horn of the central cleft of the frog in a horse's foot. [perhaps < Scandinavian (compare Swedish *trosk*)]

thrust (thrust), *v.*, **thrust, thrust·ing,** *n.* —*v.t.* **1.** to push with force; shove; drive: *He thrust a chair against the door. He thrust his hands into his pockets. A soldier thrusts himself into danger. Some men are born great, some achieve greatness, and some have greatness thrust upon them* (Shakespeare). **2.** to pierce; stab: *to thrust a knife into an apple. We thrust the tent pole deep into the ground.* **3.** to put forth; extend: *The tree thrust its roots deep into the ground.* —*v.i.* **1.** to push with force; make a thrust. **2.** to make a stab or lunge. **3.** to push or force one's way, as through a crowd, between persons, or against obstacles: *Sarah thrust past me into the room.*

thrust out, to expel; eject: *They were now, without any accusation, thrust out of their house* (Macaulay).

—*n.* **1.** a push with force; drive: *She hid the book behind the pillow with a quick thrust.* **2.** a stab; lunge: *A thrust with the sword killed him.* **3.** a sudden, sharp attack; thrusting assault: *a sarcastic thrust at a prevailing foible* (William Dean Howells). **4.** *Architecture.* the lateral force exerted by an arch, etc., against an abutment or support. It must be counteracted to prevent the structure from collapsing. **5. a.** the endways push exerted by the rotation of a propeller, that causes an aircraft, ship, etc., to move. **b.** the force exerted by the rearward ejection of gases, etc., as in a jet engine, a rocket, etc., that produces forward movement: *Rocket engine thrust depends on the speed of the gases and particles shot out of the tail. The higher this speed, the greater the thrust provided by the exhaust gases which push the rocket in one direction while they rush away in the other* (Christian Science Monitor). **6.** *Geology.* **a.** a compressive strain in the earth's crust. **b.** a thrust fault. **7.** the object, purpose, or goal: *Dr. Stanton said the practical thrust of the rules would be to create an incentive for the networks themselves* (New York Times).

[Middle English *thrusten* < Scandinavian (compare Old Icelandic *thrȳsta*)]

—**Syn.** *n.* **1.** shove, punch.

thrust·er (thrus′tər), *n.* **1.** a person or thing that thrusts or exerts thrust. **2.** thrustor: *The spheres at the rear contain fuel for the thrusters controlling the attitude and orbit of the craft* (Walter Sullivan).

thrust fault, *Geology.* a reversed fault, produced by horizontal compression. See **overthrust** for picture.

thrust·ful (thrust′fəl), *adj.* full of thrust; forceful: *Now at last there is the prospect of some thrustful competition . . . in one vitally important part of the work of the airlines.* (New Scientist).

thrus·tor (thrus′tər), *n.* an electrical engine or similar device for producing thrust in a rocket, spacecraft, etc.: *On the second day in orbit, Conrad reported to ground control in Houston that No. 8 thrustor (out of 16) was "not up to snuff"* (Science News Letter). Also, **thruster.**

thru·way (thrü′wā′), *n. U.S.* an express highway; throughway.

Thu., Thursday.

thud (thud), *n., v.,* **thud·ded, thud·ding.** —*n.* **1.** a dull, heavy sound: *The book hit the floor with a thud.* **2.** a heavy blow; thump. —*v.i., v.t.* to hit, move, or strike with a thud: *We didn't hear the five bullets that thudded into the wall a few feet from our heads until they arrived* (Maclean's). [earlier, blast of wind; origin uncertain. Compare Old English *thyddan* to strike.]

thug (thug), *n.* **1.** a ruffian; cutthroat: *One thug with a pistol struck the druggist on the head* (New York Times). **2.** a member of a former religious organization of robbers and murderers in India, who strangled their victims: *The thugs committed murders and robbed their victims in honor of Kali, the Hindu goddess of destruction and wife of Siva* (George N. Mayhew).
[< Hindi *ṭhag* < Sanskrit *sthaga* rogue]

thug·gee (thug′ē), *n.* the system of robbery and murder practiced by the thugs of India. [< Hindi *ṭhagī* < *ṭhag*; see THUG]

thug·ger·y (thug′ər ē), *n., pl.* **-ger·ies. 1.** the activities or practices of a thug or thugs: *Warehouses . . . in the movies . . . figure as shadowed scenes of thuggery, where cat men swing through skylights and towers of crates topple on persistent flatfoots* (New Yorker). **2.** thuggee.

thug·gish (thug′ish), *adj.* of or like a thug or thugs; ruffianly; cutthroat.

thug·gism (thug′iz əm), *n.* thuggee.

thu·ja (thü′jə, thyü′-), *n.* any of a group of coniferous evergreen trees of the cypress family; arbor vitae. A common American kind yields an aromatic oil (oil of thuja) that is used in medicine. Also, **thuya.** [< New Latin *Thuja* the genus name, ultimately < Greek *thȳiā, thŷā* an African tree]

Thu·le (thü′lē), *n.* the part of the world that the ancient Greeks and Romans regarded as farthest north; some island or region north of Britain, sometimes identified as Iceland, a part of Denmark or Norway, or Mainland (largest of the Shetland Islands). [Old English *Tyle* < Latin *Thūlē,* or *Thȳlē* < Greek *Thoúlē*]

thu·li·a (thü′lē ə), *n.* a greenish-white, amorphous powder, an oxide of thulium. *Formula:* Tm_2O_3 [< *thulium*]

thu·li·um (thü′lē əm), *n.* a rare-earth metallic chemical element of the yttrium group, present in gadolinite and various other minerals. *Symbol:* Tm; *at.wt.:* (C^{12}) 168.934 or (O^{16}) 168.94; *at.no.:* 69; *valence:* 3. [< New Latin *thulium* < Latin *Thūlē* Thule]

thumb (thum), *n.* **1.** the short, thick finger of the human hand, next to the forefinger. **2.** the corresponding part of the paw of an animal; pollex. **3.** the part of a glove or mitten covering the thumb. **4.** *Architecture.* a convex molding; ovolo.
all thumbs, very clumsy, awkward, etc.: *If Jennings—too often all thumbs in his uncertain handling—had been under the Forest crossbar, there might have been a deluge* (London Times).
stick out like a sore thumb, to appear unpleasantly conspicuous: *Wearing a sports coat at the formal dance, he stuck out like a sore thumb.*
thumbs down, a sign of disapproval or rejection: *There are expressions of surprise when many workers, as in the aerospace industry, turn thumbs down on a prime form of union security, the union shop* (Wall Street Journal).
thumbs up, a sign of approval or acceptance: *As the trial progressed, he would leave court each day to the smiles and thumbs up signs of the crowd* (New York Times).
twiddle one's thumbs, a. to keep turning one's thumbs idly about each other: *The bishop was sitting in his easy chair, twiddling his thumbs* (Anthony Trollope). **b.** to have nothing to do; be idle: *You'd have all the world do nothing half its time but twiddle its thumbs* (D. Jerrold).
under the thumb of, under the power or influence of: *Her son-in-law was under the thumb of his womenfolk* (Rudyard Kipling).
—*v.t.* **1.** to soil or wear by handling with the thumbs: *The books were badly thumbed.* **2.** to turn pages of (a book, etc.) rapidly, reading only portions. **3.** to handle awkwardly or clumsily. **4.** *U.S. Informal.* to ask for or get (a free ride) by or as if by holding up one's thumb to motorists going in one's direction; hitchhike: *Some commuters abandoned the trains and thumbed rides* (New York Times).
[Middle English *thoumbe,* Old English *thūma*] —**thumb′like′,** *adj.*
—**Syn.** *v.t.* **2.** skim. **3.** fumble.

thumb index, a series of grooves cut along the front edges of the pages of a book to show initial letters or titles, so that any division may be turned to by placing the thumb or finger on the proper initial or title.

thumb-in·dex (thum′in′deks), *v.t.* to furnish (a book) with a thumb index.

thumb·kins (thum′kinz), *n.pl. Scottish.* a thumbscrew, an instrument of torture.

thumb·nail (thum′nāl′), *n.* **1.** the nail of the thumb. **2.** something very small or short. —*adj.* very small or short: *a thumbnail sketch.*

thumb·piece (thum′pēs′), *n.* **1.** a part of a handle made to receive the thumb: *I fetched the heavy scissors with the queerly shaped thumbpiece* (New Yorker). **2.** a lever, button, or other part of a mechanism operated by pressure of the thumb: *The lid opened on a three-lug hinge with a scroll or corkscrew thumbpiece* (London Times).

thumb·print (thum′print′), *n.* **1.** an impression of the markings on the inner surface of the last joint of the thumb: *In the second century before Christ, the clever Chinese were already using thumbprints as a means of identification* (New Yorker). **2.** an impression; stamp: *He is tall, athletic and handsome, but his soul bears the thumbprint of his ruthless wife* (Time).

thumb·ring (thum′ring′), *n.,* or **thumb ring, 1.** a ring, especially one with a seal, to be worn on the thumb. **2.** a ring for the thumb on the guard of a dagger or sword.

thumb·screw (thum′skrü′), *n.* **1.** a screw with a flattened or winged head that can be turned with the thumb and a finger. **2.** an old instrument of torture that squeezed the thumbs.

thumb·stall (thum′stôl′), *n.* **1.** a kind of thimble worn over the thumb by shoemakers, etc., for pushing a needle. **2.** a protective sheath, as of leather, worn over an injured thumb.

thumb-suck·ing (thum′suk′ing), *n.* the habit of sucking one's thumb: *Fingernails must be kept short and clean, and thumb-sucking and nail-biting discouraged* (Thomas C. Allbutt).

thumb·tack (thum′tak′), *n.* a tack with a broad, flat head, that can be pressed into a wall, board, etc., with the thumb. —*v.t.* to fasten with a thumbtack: *Thumbtacked to another wall [was] a postcard mailed from Vienna* (New Yorker). [American English < *thumb* + *tack*[1]]

Thum·mim (thum′im), *n.pl.* (in the Old Testament) certain objects worn in or upon the breastplate of the Jewish high priest. See **Urim.** [< Hebrew *thummīm*]

thump (thump), *v.t.* **1.** to strike with something thick and heavy; pound: *He thumped the table with his fist.* **2.** to strike against (something) heavily and noisily: *The shutters thumped the wall in the wind.* **3.** *Informal.* to beat or thrash severely. —*v.i.* **1.** to make a dull, somewhat hard sound; pound heavily: *a fist thumping against the door, a hammer thumping against the wood. He thumped on the piano.* **2.** to beat violently; throb heavily: *His heart thumped as he walked past the graveyard at night.* **3.** to move heavily and noisily; bump or jolt along: *to thump across a room. The car thumped along on a flat tire.*
—*n.* **1.** a blow with something thick and heavy; heavy knock: *He hit the thief a thump on the head.* **2.** the dull sound made by a blow, knock, or fall: *We heard the thump as he fell.* [imitative] —**thump′er,** *n.*
—**Syn.** *n.* **1.** whack, bang.

thump·ing (thum′ping), *Informal.* —*adj.* very large; great; excellent: *a thumping fellow.* —*adv.* very: *a thumping good time, a thumping big man.*

thun·der (thun′dər), *n.* **1.** the loud noise that accompanies or follows a flash of lightning. It is caused by a disturbance of the air resulting from the discharge of electricity. **2.** any noise like thunder; very loud or resounding noise: *the thunder of Niagara Falls, a thunder of applause.* **3.** a threat. **4.** a denunciation. **5.** a thunderbolt.
steal one's (or **the**) **thunder, a.** to use another's weapons, method, etc., so as to reduce or annul the effect of his words or actions: *"I'll be damned if he isn't stealing . . . my thunder," thought Mason to himself at this point. "He's forestalling most of the things I intended to riddle him with"* (Theodore Dreiser). **b.** to gain the success, applause, etc., that was meant for or belonged to another: *Although the result . . . of England's final trial at Twickenham suggested [a draw], the junior team stole most of the thunder* (London Times).
—*v.i.* **1.** to give forth thunder: *It is thundering.* **2. a.** to make a noise like thunder; roar: *The cannon thundered.* **b.** to rush or fall with great noise and commotion: *The waterfall thundered over the rocks.* **3.** to utter threats or denunciations: *From his pulpit he thundered against the ungodly.* —*v.t.* **1.** to utter very loudly; roar: *to thunder a reply.* **2.** to threaten. **3.** to denounce.
[Middle English *thunder,* Old English *thunor*]

thun·der·a·tion (thun′də rā′shən), *U.S. Dialect or Informal.* —*n.* the deuce; the devil: *Everybody wants to know who in thunderation Rache will marry* (Century Magazine). —*interj.* an exclamation of surprise or annoyance: *"Thunderation!" he muttered indignantly* (Time). [< *thunder* + *-ation*]

thun·der·bird (thun′dər bėrd′), *n.* a huge bird in the folklore of certain North American Indians, that produces thunder by flapping its wings and lightning by opening and closing its eyes.

thun·der·bolt (thun′dər bōlt′), *n.* **1.** a flash of lightning and the thunder that accompanies or follows it. **2.** something sudden, startling, and terrible: *The news of his death came as a thunderbolt.* **3.** a person with great energy and drive. **4.** a bolt or dart formerly believed to destroy when lightning strikes anything. **5.** a fossil, stone, etc., formerly thought to have fallen from heaven with the lightning.
—*v.t.* to strike with or as if with a thunderbolt; startle; terrify: *It will not be long before he is thunderbolted to the quick by the physical similarities between East Anglia and China* (Punch).

thun·der·burst (thun′dər bėrst′), *n.* a thunderclap.

thun·der·clap (thun′dər klap′), *n.* **1.** a loud crash of thunder. **2.** something sudden or startling.

thun·der·cloud (thun′dər kloud′), *n.* a dark, electrically charged cloud that brings thunder and lightning.

thun·der·er (thun′dər ər), *n.* a person or thing that thunders.

Thun·der·er (thun′dər ər), *n.* Jupiter; Zeus. [< *thunder* + *-er*[1] (because Jupiter is frequently represented with a thunderbolt in his hand)]

thun·der·flash (thun′dər flash′), *n.* **1.** a loud explosion accompanied by a flash. **2.** a tin can, blank artillery shell, etc., filled with powder, that makes such an explosion: *Commanders were warned not to use even blank artillery or thunderflashes in the vicinity of towns or villages* (Maclean's).

Thunder God vine, a climbing perennial plant of the staff-tree family, imported into the United States from China for the insecticidal property of its roots.

thun·der·head (thun′dər hed′), *n.* one of the round, swelling masses of cumulus clouds often appearing before thunderstorms and frequently developing into thunderclouds: *Each towering thunderhead is the top of a huge current of rising, moist air* (Beauchamp, Mayfield, and West).

thun·der·ing (thun′dər ing, -dring), *adj.* **1.** that thunders; very loud and deep: *a thundering voice, a thundering herd of cattle.* **2.** *Informal.* very great or big; immense; too great: *a thundering lie.* —*adv. Informal.* very: *a thundering high price.* —**thun′der·ing·ly,** *adv.*

thun·der·less (thun′dər lis), *adj.* without thunder.

thun·der·ous (thun′dər əs, -drəs), *adj.* **1.** producing thunder. **2.** making a noise like thunder; loud like thunder. —**thun′der·ous·ly,** *adv.* —**Syn. 2.** deafening.

thun·der·pump (thun′dər pump′), *n. U.S.* the bittern, a heron with a peculiar booming cry.

thun·der·peal (thun′dər pēl′), *n.* a clap of thunder; thunderclap.

thun·der·sheet (thun′dər shēt′), *n.* a sheet of metal that produces the sound of thunder when struck or shaken, used in sound effects.

thun·der·show·er (thun′dər shou′ər), *n.* a shower with thunder and lightning.

thun·der·squall (thun′dər skwôl′), *n.* a squall with thunder and lightning.

thunder stick, 1. a bull-roarer. **2.** a musket, as supposedly called by the American Indians when they first saw firearms.

thun·der·stone (thun′dər stōn′), *n.* **1.** any of various stones, fossils, etc., formerly identified with thunderbolts, such as belemnites, meteorites, etc. **2.** *Archaic.* a thunderbolt.

thun·der·storm (thun′dər stôrm′), *n.* a storm with thunder and lightning, and usually, heavy rain.

thun·der·strick·en (thun′dər strik′ən), *adj.* thunderstruck.

thun·der·stroke (thun′dər strōk′), *n.* a stroke of lightning.

thun·der·struck (thun′dər struk′), *adj.* **1.** overcome, as if hit by a thunderbolt; astonished; amazed: *We were thunderstruck by the death of the President.* **2.** *Obsolete.* struck by lightning. —**Syn. 1.** confounded, astounded.

thun·der·y (thun′dər ē), *adj.* thunderous: *sultry thundery weather* (Gilbert White).

thun·drous (thun′drəs), *adj.* thunderous.

Thur., Thursday.

thu·ri·ble (thůr′ə bəl, thyůr′-), *n.* a censer. [< Latin *thūribulum* < *thūs, thūris* incense < Greek *thýos, thýeos* incense; (originally) burnt sacrifice < *thýein* to sacrifice]

Thur·i·cide (thůr′ə sīd, thyůr′-), *n. Trademark.* an insecticide harmless to people, animals, or plants, made from the living spores of a microorganism. [< New Latin (*Bacillus*) *thuri*(*ngiensis*)]

thu·ri·fer (thůr′ə fər, thyůr′-), *n.* an altar boy or acolyte who carries the censer. [< New Latin *thurifer* < Latin *thūrifer* incense-bearing < *thūs, thūris* incense + *ferre* to bear, carry]

thu·rif·er·ous (thů rif′ər əs, thyů-), *adj.* producing or bearing frankincense. [< Latin *thūrifer* (see THURIFER) + English *-ous*]

thu·ri·fi·ca·tion (thůr′ə fə kā′shən, thyůr′-), *n.* a burning or perfuming with incense.

thu·ri·fy (thůr′ə fī, thyůr′-), *v.t.*, **-fied, -fy·ing.** to burn incense before or about; perfume with incense; cense. [< Old French *thurifier* < Late Latin *thūrificāre* < *thūs, thūris* incense + *facere* to make]

Thu·rin·gi·an (thů rin′jē ən, thyů-), *adj.* **1.** of or having to do with Thuringia, a state in southern East Germany, or its people. **2.** *Geology.* of or having to do with the upper division of the Permian in Europe. —*n.* **1.** a native or inhabitant of Thuringia. **2.** a member of a Germanic tribe that established a kingdom in central Germany that was conquered by the Franks in the 500's A.D.

Thurs., Thursday.

Thurs·day (thėrz′dē, -dā), *n.* the fifth day of the week, following Wednesday: *Thanksgiving is always the fourth Thursday in November. Abbr.:* Thurs., Thur., Thu. [Old English *Thuresdæg, Thurresdæg,* perhaps variation of *Thunresdæg* (< *Thunor* god of thunder + *dæg* day), translation of Late Latin *diēs Jovis* day of Jupiter, or Jove]

thus (ᴛʜus), *adv.* **1.** in this way; in the way just stated, indicated, etc.; in the following manner: *He spoke thus.* **2.** accordingly; consequently; therefore: *Thus we decided that he was wrong.* **3.** to this extent, number, or degree: *Yet you can speak thus calmly of unsaying All we have said* (Walter C. Smith). **thus far, a.** until now or then: *Thus far, we haven't heard from him.* **b.** to this or that point: *Thus far you may go and no farther.* [Old English *thus.* Related to THIS.] —**Syn. 2.** hence.

thus-and-so (ᴛʜus′ən sō′), *n.* any of several things not named: *If the local authorities don't do thus-and-so, and at once, they will choke the streets with bigger mobs* (Wall Street Journal).

thus·ly (ᴛʜus′lē), *adv. Informal.* thus: *A Pisa pizza pie peddler we contacted commented thusly: "Balderdash!"* (Maclean's).

thus·ness (ᴛʜus′nis), *n. Informal.* the state of being thus: *What is the reason for this thusness?* (Artemus Ward).

thus·wise (ᴛʜus′wīz), *adv.* thus.

thu·ya (thü′yə), *n.* thuja.

thwack (thwak), *v.t.* to strike vigorously with a stick or something flat; whack: *Take all my cushions down and thwack them soundly* (Thomas Middleton). —*n.* a sharp blow with a stick or something flat; whack: *The man . . . with his open palm gave the animal a resounding thwack* (Joseph Conrad). [probably ultimately imitative] —**thwack′er,** *n.*

thwart (thwôrt), *v.t.* **1.** to oppose and defeat; keep from doing something: *The boy's family thwarted his plans for college.* **2.** to go against; oppose; hinder. **3.** *Obsolete.* to pass or extend across from side to side of; traverse; cross. [< adverb]
—*n.* **1.** a seat across a boat, on which a rower sits. **2.** a brace between the gunwales of a canoe. [< adjective or adverb]
—*adj.* **1.** lying or passing across. **2.** obstinate; stubborn. [< adverb]
—*adv.* across; crosswise; athwart.
[Middle English *thwert* < Scandinavian (compare Old Icelandic *thvert* across, neuter of *thverr* transverse)] —**thwart′er,** *n.*
—**Syn.** *v.t.* **1.** baffle, balk, foil. See **frustrate.**

thy (ᴛʜī), *adj. Possessive form of* **thou.** *Archaic.* your: *Thy kingdom come. Thy will be done* (Matthew 6:10). [Middle English *thi, thin,* Old English *thīn* thine]
➔ See **thou** for usage note.

Thy·es·te·an (thī es′tē ən), *adj.* of or having to do with Thyestes.

Thyestean banquet or **meal,** a repast at which human flesh is served; cannibal feast.

Thy·es·tes (thī es′tēz), *n. Greek Legend.* a son of Pelops, brother of Atreus, and father of Aegisthus. When Thyestes seduced Atreus' wife and plotted his murder, Atreus pretended reconciliation, but killed three sons of Thyestes and served them to him at a banquet.

Thy·es·ti·an (thī es′tē ən), *adj.* Thyestean.

thy·ine (thī′in), *adj.* of or having to do with a precious wood mentioned in the Bible, supposed to be that of the sandarac tree. Revelation 18:12. [< Late Latin *thyīnus* < Greek *thýinos* < *thýā* thuja]

thy·la·cine (thī′lə sīn, -sin), *n.* a doglike, carnivorous, marsupial mammal of Tasmania, with stripes on its back, now almost extinct; Tasmanian wolf or tiger. [< French *thylacine* < Greek *thýlax, -akos* pouch, sack]

Thylacine (about 2 ft. high at the shoulder)

thyme (tīm), *n.* any of a group of herbs of the mint family, with fragrant, aromatic leaves. The leaves of the common garden thyme are used for seasoning. The common wild thyme is a creeping evergreen. [< Latin *thymum* < Greek *thýmon* < *thýein* burn as a sacrifice]

thy·mec·to·my (thī mek′tə mē), *n., pl.* **-mies.** surgical removal of the thymus gland: *Sauerbruch . . . in 1912 introduced the operation of thymectomy for myasthenia gravis* (Beaumont and Dodds). [< *thymus* + Greek *ektomḗ* a cutting out]

thym·e·lae·a·ceous (thim′ə lē ā′shəs), *adj.* belonging to the mezereum family of trees and shrubs. [< New Latin *Thymelaeaceae* the family name (< Greek *thymelaíā* < *thýmon* thyme + *elaíā* olive tree) + English *-ous*]

thy·mic[1] (tī′mik), *adj.* having to do with or derived from thyme. [< *thym*(e) + *-ic*]

thy·mic[2] (thī′mik), *adj.* of or having to do with the thymus gland. [< *thym*(us) + *-ic*]

thymic acid, thymol.

thy·mi·dine (thī′mə din, -dēn), *n.* a nucleoside of thymine occurring in deoxyribonucleic acid that stimulates growth in cells. *Formula:* $C_{10}H_{14}N_2O_5$

thy·mine (thī′min, -mēn), or **thy·min** (thī′min), *n.* a colorless, crystalline compound prepared by hydrolysis of deoxyribonucleic acid and other means. It sublimes in plates and melts above 250°C. *Formula:* $C_5H_6N_2O_2$ [< *thym*(us) + *-ine*[2]]

thy·mol (thī′mōl, -mol), *n.* an aromatic, white or colorless, crystalline phenol obtained from the volatile oil of thyme and various other plants or made synthetically, used chiefly as an antiseptic. *Formula:* $C_{10}H_{14}O$ [< *thym*(e) + *-ol*[1]]

thy·mus (thī′məs), *adj.* of or having to do with the thymus gland. —*n.* the thymus gland. [< New Latin *thymus* < Greek *thýmos* (originally) a warty excrescence]

thymus gland, a small, ductless gland of uncertain function near the base of the neck. It disappears or becomes rudimentary in the human adult. The thymus of lambs and calves is used for food and called sweetbread.

thymus nucleic acid, deoxyribonucleic acid, usually extracted from the thymus gland.

thym·y (tī′mē), *adj.* having to do with or like thyme; full of thyme: *thymy hills.*

thy·ra·tron (thī′rə tron), *n.* a gas-filled, three- or four-element vacuum tube containing a hot cathode, in which the grid initiates, but does not limit, the current. It is used mainly as an electronic switch.

thy·re·oid (thī′rē oid), *n., adj.* thyroid.

thy·ro·ac·tive (thī′rō ak′tiv), *adj.* stimulating the activity of thyroxine and other secretions of the thyroid gland: *The iodine treatment followed large doses of thyroactive substances* (Science News Letter).

thy·ro·ar·y·te·noid (thī′rō ar′ə tē′noid), *adj.* having to do with or connecting the thyroid and arytenoid cartilages of the larynx. [< *thyro*(id) + *arytenoid*]

thy·ro·glob·u·lin (thī′rō glob′yə lin), *n.* a protein of the thyroid gland that contains iodine, found in the colloid substance of the gland. [< *thyro*(id) + *globulin*]

thy·roid (thī′roid), *n.* **1.** the thyroid gland. **2.** a medicine made from the thyroid glands of certain domestic animals, used in the treatment of goiter, obesity, etc. **3.** the thyroid cartilage. **4.** a part of the body, such as a vein, near the thyroid gland.
—*adj.* of or having to do with the thyroid gland or the thyroid cartilage: *Cortisone and thyroid extract . . . can be taken by mouth* (New York Times).
[< Greek *thyreoeidḗs* shield-shaped < *thyreós* oblong shield (< *thýrā* door) + *eîdos* form]

thy·roi·dal (thī roi′dəl), *adj.* thyroid: *Thyroidal deficiency often makes for a flat face and nose but a bulging forehead* (Alfred Kroeber).

thyroid body, the thyroid gland.

thyroid cartilage, the principal cartilage of the larynx, which forms the Adam's apple in man.

thy·roid·ec·to·mize (thī′roi dek′tə mīz), *v.t.*, **-mized, -miz·ing.** to subject to thyroidectomy: *This photomicrograph . . . shows the pituitary region in a thyroidectomized . . . tadpole* (Scientific American).

thy·roid·ec·to·my (thī′roi dek′tə mē), *n., pl.* **-mies.** the surgical removal of all or part of the thyroid gland.

thyroid extract, a medicine made from the thyroid glands; thyroid.

thyroid gland, an important ductless gland in the neck of vertebrates, near the larynx and upper windpipe, that affects growth and metabolism. Goiter is an enlargement or a disorder of the thyroid gland.

thy·roid·i·tis (thī′roi dī′tis), *n.* inflammation of the thyroid gland.

thy·ro·tox·ic (thī′rō tok′sik), *adj.* of or having to do with thyrotoxicosis.

thy·ro·tox·i·co·sis (thī′rō tok′sə kō′sis), *n. Medicine.* any kind of hyperthyroidism.

thy·ro·tro·phic (thī′rō trō′fik), *adj.* thyrotropic.

thy·ro·tro·phin (thī′rō trō′fin), *n.* thyrotropin.

thy·ro·trop·ic (thī′rō trop′ik, -trō′pik), *adj.* stimulating the thyroid gland; regulating thyroid activity.

thy·ro·tro·pin (thī′rō trō′pin), *n.* a hormone produced by the pituitary gland, that regulates the activity of the thyroid gland.

thy·rox·in (thī rok′sin), *n.* thyroxine.

thy·rox·ine (thī rok′sēn, -sin), *n.* a white, crystalline substance, the principal secretion of the thyroid gland. It is also prepared synthetically and used to treat goiter and other thyroid disorders. *Formula:* $C_{15}H_{11}I_4NO_4$

thyrse (thėrs), *n. Botany.* thyrsus.

thyr·soid (thėr′soid), *adj. Botany.* having somewhat the form of a thyrsus.

thyr·soi·dal (thėr soi′dəl), *adj.* thyrsoid.

thyr·sus (thėr′səs), *n., pl.* **-si** (-sī). **1.** *Greek Mythology.* a staff or spear tipped with an ornament like a pine cone and sometimes wrapped round with ivy and vine branches. It was carried by Dionysus (Bacchus) and his followers. **2.** *Botany.* a form of mixed inflorescence, a contracted panicle, in which the main ramification is indeterminate and the secondary or ultimate is determinate, as in the lilac and horse chestnut. [< New Latin *thyrsus* < Latin < Greek *thýrsos* (literally) staff, stem]

thy·sa·nu·ran (thī′sə nůr′ən, -nyůr′-; this′ə-), *adj.* of or belonging to a large group of wingless insects including the bristletails, having two or three slender caudal appendages. —*n.* a thysanuran insect. [< New Latin *Thysanura* the order name (< Greek *thýsanos* tassel, fringe + *ourá* tail) + English *-an*]

thys·a·nu·rous (thī′sə nůr′əs, -nyůr′-; this′ə-), *adj.* thysanuran.

thy·self (ᴛʜī self′), *pron. Archaic.* yourself.

ti[1] (tē), *n. Music.* the seventh note or tone of the diatonic scale; si. [*ti* replaced earlier *si,* to avoid confusion with *sol;* see GAMUT]

ti[2] (tē), *n., pl.* **tis.** any of various Polynesian and Asiatic palmlike shade trees and shrubs of the agave family; ti palm. The elongated leaves of one species are often used for food wrappers, hula skirts, etc. [< Polynesian *ti*]

Ti (no period), titanium (chemical element).

Tian-shan sheep (tyän′shän′), Marco Polo sheep.

ti·ar (tī′ər), *n. Poetic.* tiara.

ti·ar·a (tī ãr′ə, tē-; tē är′-), *n.* **1.** a band of gold, jewels, or flowers worn by women around the head as an ornament. **2. a.** the triple crown worn by the Pope as a symbol of his position. **b.** the position or authority of the Pope. **3.** an ancient Persian headdress worn by men. [< Latin *tiara* < Greek *tiārā*] —**Syn. 1.** coronet.

Tiara (def. 2a)

ti·ar·aed (tī ãr′əd, tē-; tē-är′-), *adj.* adorned with a tiara or tiaras: *In velvet and ermine, tiaraed and beribboned, Europe's royalty turned out in Athens . . . for the wedding of Greece's Princess Sophie* (Time).

ti·bet (ti bet′, tib′ət), *n.,* or **tibet cloth,** a soft, smooth, twilled woolen cloth. [< *Tibet,* a country in central Asia, where it was produced]

Ti·bet·an (ti bet′ən), *adj.* of or having to do with Tibet, an autonomous region in southwestern China, its people, or their language. —*n.* **1.** a member of the native Mongoloid people of Tibet. **2.** the Sino-Tibetan language of Tibet. Also, **Thibetan.**

Ti·bet·o-Bur·man (ti bet′ō bėr′mən), *n.* a subdivision of the Sino-Tibetan language family, including Tibetan and Burmese.

tib·i·a (tib′ē ə), *n., pl.* **-i·ae** (-ē ē) or **-i·as. 1.** the inner and thicker of the two bones of the leg, from the knee to the ankle; shinbone (in man). **2.** a corresponding bone in animals or birds. **3.** the fourth joint of the leg of an insect. **4.** an ancient Roman flute. **5.** one of several organ stops, mostly of the flute family; flageolet. [< Latin *tībia* shinbone, pipe, or flute]

tib·i·al (tib′ē əl), *adj.* of or having to do with the tibia.

tic (tik), *n.* **1.** a habitual, involuntary twitching of the muscles, especially those of the face. **2.** tic douloureux. [< French *tic,* ultimately < a Germanic word]

ti·cal (ti käl′, -kôl′; tē′kəl), *n., pl.* **-cals** or **-cal. 1.** a former Siamese (Thai) monetary unit and silver coin, worth 100 satang, now replaced by the baht. **2.** a former Siamese (Thai) unit of weight, equal to 231.5 grains, or about half an ounce troy. [< Thai *tical* < Malay *tikal*]

tic dou·lou·reux (tik′ dü′lü rü′; *French* tēk dü lü rœ′), a severe facial neuralgia, especially of the trigeminal nerve, accompanied by twitching. [< French *tic douloureux* (literally) painful tic]

tick[1] (tik), *n.* **1.** the quick, light, dry sound made by a watch or clock. **2.** a sound like it: *the tick of a moth against the window pane.* **3.** *Informal.* a moment or second; instant. *I'll be with you in a tick.* **4.** a small mark, such as √, made to check or mark something. —*v.i.* **1.** to make a tick or ticks: *The clock ticks louder and louder in a quiet room.* **2.** *Informal.* to function; work; go.
—*v.t.* **1.** to mark off: *The clock ticked away the minutes.* **2.** to mark with a tick or ticks; check: *He ticked the items with a check mark one by one.*

tick off, to reprove severely: *[He] tried to tick me off, once; and I lost my temper* (M. Cole).

tick over, *British.* **a.** to run slowly without transmitting power; idle. A motor ticks over when it is out of gear and running slowly: *The engines were started and allowed to tick over for about 10 minutes or so, to warm up gradually* (C.F.S. Gamble). **b.** *Slang.* to work; function; operate: *Students . . . would keep the place ticking over in the evening* (London Daily Telegraph).
[Middle English *tek* (originally) a light touch or tap; probably ultimately imitative]
—**Syn.** *n.* **3.** jiffy.

tick[2] (tik), *n.* **1.** any of a group of oval-shaped arachnids related to the mites, that suck the blood of mammals, birds, and reptiles: *Meanwhile certain wise old Western cattle growers . . . had a notion that Texas fever was caused by an insect living on the cattle and sucking blood . . . called a tick* (Paul de Kruif). **2.** any of various bloodsucking, parasitic, dipterous insects, such as the sheep tick. [Middle English *tyke,* perhaps unrecorded Old English *tīca*]

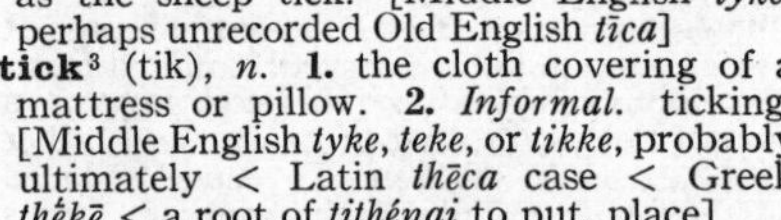

Seed Tick[2] (def. 1—Line shows actual length.)

tick[3] (tik), *n.* **1.** the cloth covering of a mattress or pillow. **2.** *Informal.* ticking. [Middle English *tyke, teke,* or *tikke,* probably ultimately < Latin *thēca* case < Greek *thēkē* < a root of *tithénai* to put, place]

tick[4] (tik), *n. Slang.* credit; trust: *to buy something on tick. This villainous habit of living upon tick* (Robert L. Stevenson). [apparently short for *on (the) tick*(et)]

tick·bird (tik′bėrd′), *n.* a bird that feeds on ticks that infest cattle and other animals, as the cuckoo and the ani.

tick·er (tik′ər), *n.* **1.** a person or thing that ticks. **2.** a telegraphic instrument that prints market reports or news on a paper tape; stock ticker. **3.** *Slang.* a watch or clock. **4.** *Slang.* the heart.

ticker tape, a cellophane or paper tape on which a ticker prints stock market reports or news.

tick·er-tape parade (tik′ər tāp′), a parade through the streets of a city in honor of a visiting celebrity or dignitary, accompanied by showers of ticker tape or the like thrown from buildings.

tick·et (tik′it), *n.* **1.** a card or piece of paper that gives its holder a right or privilege: *a theater ticket, a railroad ticket, a lottery ticket, a laundry ticket.* **2.** *Informal.* a summons given to an offender to pay a fine or appear in court, usually with reference to traffic violations: *a ticket for speeding, a parking ticket.* **3.** a card or piece of paper, etc., attached to something to describe it, show its price, etc. **4.** *U.S.* the list of candidates for various offices that belong to one political party: *to vote the Republican ticket.* **5.** *Banking.* a temporary record of transactions, etc., before their recording in a more permanent form. **6.** *Slang.* a certificate: *a chief engineer's ticket.* **7.** *Obsolete.* a notice posted in a public place; placard.
the ticket, *Informal.* the correct or proper thing: *They ought to be hanged, sir, that's the ticket* (Thomas Haliburton).
—*v.t.* **1.** to put a ticket on; mark with a ticket: *All articles in the store are ticketed with the price.* **2.** to describe or mark as if by a ticket; label; designate; characterize. **3.** *U.S.* to furnish with a ticket, especially a railroad ticket: *We were 'ticketed through to the depot'* (Longfellow). **4.** *Informal.* to serve with a summons: *ticketed for careless driving* (Time).
[short for Middle French *etiquet* ticket < *estiquette* < *estiquer* to affix, stick < Dutch *stikken.* Compare ETIQUETTE.]
—**Syn.** *n.* **1.** voucher, coupon **4.** slate.

ticket chopper, *Informal.* **1.** a machine for chopping or destroying tickets put in it, as by passengers entering the gate to a railroad platform. **2.** an attendant who works such a machine.

tick·et·less (tik′it lis), *adj.* having no ticket: *Hundreds of ticketless hopefuls lined up on the sidewalk outside Manhattan's rundown Hudson Theater on the outside chance that a bona fide ticket holder might not show up* (Newsweek).

ticket of leave, *British.* a permit giving a convict his liberty before his sentence has expired, provided he obeys certain conditions. —**tick′et-of-leave′,** *adj.*

tick·et-of-leave man (tik′it əv lēv′), *British.* a convict released on parole.

tick·et·y-boo (tik′ə tē bü′), *adj. Especially British.* all right; fine; OK: *On the surface, everything seemed tickety-boo, as vacationers crowded the beaches from Brighton to Belfast* (Time).

tick·ey (tik′ē), *n., pl.* **-eys.** (in South Africa) a threepenny piece; threepence. Also, **ticky.**

tick fever, 1. a fever attacking people or cattle, transmitted by ticks, especially Rocky Mountain spotted fever. **2.** an infectious blood disease of cattle, often fatal when acute, caused by an animal parasite that is carried by certain ticks, and characterized by fever, destruction of red blood corpuscles, and emaciation; Texas fever. It was formerly prevalent in the southwestern United States, but has been virtually eradicated.

tick·ing (tik′ing), *n.* a strong cotton or linen cloth, used to cover mattresses and pillows and to make tents and awnings.

tick·le (tik′əl), *v.,* **-led, -ling,** *n., adj.* —*v.t.* **1. a.** to touch lightly, causing little thrills, shivers, or wriggles: *He tickled the baby's feet and made her laugh.* **b.** to cause to have such a feeling: *Don't tickle me.* **2.** to excite pleasurably; please; amuse: *The child was tickled with his new toys. This joke will really tickle you.* **3.** to play, stir, get, or move with light touches or strokes: *to tickle a piano or guitar, to tickle a fire.* **4.** to refresh or jog (the memory). —*v.i.* to have a tickling feeling: *My nose tickles and I want to scratch it.*
—*n.* **1.** a tingling or itching feeling. **2.** a tickling.
—*adj. Dialect.* easily upset or overthrown; insecure; tottering.
[Middle English *tikelen;* origin uncertain]
—**Syn.** *v.t.* **2.** divert.

tick·ler (tik′lər), *n.* **1.** a person or thing that tickles, especially a small feather brush used to tickle the faces of others, as at a carnival, party, etc. **2.** *U.S.* a memorandum book, card index, or the like, kept as a reminder of engagements, payments due, etc. **3.** *Informal.* a difficult or puzzling problem; teaser; puzzler. **4.** *Electronics.* tickler coil.

tickler coil, *Electronics.* a small coil in a vacuum tube that couples inductively the plate circuit with the grid circuit, so that a portion of the amplified signal is returned for additional amplification.

tick·lish (tik′lish), *adj.* **1.** sensitive to tickling: *The bottoms of the feet are ticklish.* **2.** requiring careful handling; delicate; risky: *the ticklish job of telling a person his faults, a ticklish assignment.* **3.** easily upset; unstable: *A canoe is a ticklish craft.* **4.** easily offended; touchy: *a very proud and ticklish fellow.* —**tick′lish·ly,** *adv.* —**tick′lish·ness,** *n.* —**Syn. 2.** precarious. **3.** unsteady, shaky.

tick·seed (tik′sēd′), *n.* **1.** any of various plants with seeds that look like ticks, such as a coreopsis or a bugseed. **2.** tick trefoil.

tickseed sunflower, any of various bur marigolds having conspicuous yellow flowers.

tick-tack (tik′tak′), *n.* **1.** a device for making a ticking or tapping sound, as against a window or door in playing a practical joke. **2.** tick-tock. [apparently imitative]

tick-tack-toe (tik′tak tō′), *n.* **1.** a game in which two players alternately put their marks on a figure, each player trying to be the first to fill three spaces in a row with his mark. **2.** a children's game in which the players, without looking, bring a pencil down on a slate or sheet of paper with a set of numbers drawn on it, the number hit being scored. **3.** the practical joke of using a tick-tack. Also, **tit-tat-toe.** [apparently extension of earlier *tick-tack* backgammon]

tick-tack-too (tik′tak tü′), *n.* tick-tack-toe.

tick-tock (tik′tok′), *n.* the sound made by a clock or watch. —*v.i.* to make this sound; tick: *A tall clock tick-tocked on the stair.*

tick trefoil, any of a group of plants of the pea family, having leaves consisting of three leaflets and jointed pods that stick like ticks to the fur of animals.

tick·y[1] (tik′ē), *n., pl.* **tick·ies.** tickey: *I'll give you each a ticky if you're good children* (Beatrice M. Hicks).

tick·y[2] (tik′ē), *adj.* full of or infested by ticks: *He [a turkey] becomes . . . emaciated and ticky* (Blackwood's Magazine).

tic·po·lon·ga (tik′pə long′gə), *n.* a poisonous snake of India and Ceylon. [< Singhalese *tik* spot + *polongā* viper]

tic-tac-toe (tik′tak tō′), *n.* tick-tack-toe.

tid·al (tī′dəl), *adj.* **1.** of, having, or caused by tides: *A tidal river is affected by the ocean's tide.* **2.** dependent on the state of the tide as to time of arrival and departure: *a tidal steamer.* —**tid′al·ly,** *adv.*

tidal wave, 1. a large, destructive ocean wave caused by an earthquake, hurricane, etc. **2.** either of two great swellings of the ocean surface (caused by the attraction of the moon and sun) that move around the globe on opposite sides and cause the tides. **3.** any great movement or manifestation of feeling, opinion, or the like; overwhelming outburst: *a tidal wave of popular indignation.*

tid·bit (tid′bit′), *n.* a very pleasing bit of food, news, etc. Also, **titbit.** [< earlier *tid* delicate + *bit* morsel]

tid·dle·dy·winks (tid′əl dē wingks′), *n.* tiddlywinks.

tid·dler (tid′lər), *n.* **1.** *Informal.* something or somebody small: **a.** a fish of small size, especially a stickleback: *I could see that such a tiddler did not count for very much with the two Turkana fishermen who were with me* (New Yorker). **b.** a small submarine, rocket, etc.: *But these would have a payload of only 150 lb.; . . . scientists are apt to look contemptuously at tiddlers like this* (New Scientist). **c.** a little child; tot. **2.** a person who plays tiddlywinks.

tid·dley or **tid·dly** (tid′lē), *adj. Especially British. Slang.* intoxicated: *Well, this hairy Dane comes staggering back to camp late one night, tiddly as a newt* (Punch). [origin uncertain]

tid·dly·winks (tid′lē wingks′), *n.* a game in which the players try to make small colored disks jump from a flat surface into a cup by pressing on their edges with larger disks. [origin uncertain]

tide[1] (tīd), *n., v.,* **tid·ed, tid·ing,** *adj.* —*n.* **1. a.** the rise and fall of the ocean about every twelve hours, caused by the attraction of the moon and the sun: *We go swimming at high tide; at low tide we dig for clams.* **b.** the inward or outward flow or current resulting from this on a coast, in a river, etc. **2.** anything that rises and falls like the tide: *the tide of popular opinion. There is a tide in the affairs of men, Which, taken at the flood, leads on to fortune* (Shakespeare). **3.** stream; current; flood: *Feel this arm of mine—the tide within . . .* (Tennyson). *Faith . . . Stands a sea-mark in the tides of time* (Algernon Charles Swinburne). **4.** a season; time: *Christmastide, springtide.* **5.** flood tide: *There is that at work in England which, taken at the tide, may lead on to fortune* (Benjamin Disraeli). **6.** *Archaic.* the right moment or occasion; opportune time.

turn the tide, to change from one condition to the opposite: *The appearance of Joan of Arc turned the tide of war* (Henry Hallam).

—*v.t.* to carry as the tide does. —*v.i.* **1.** to float or drift with the tide. **2.** to flow or surge as the tide. **3.** *Nautical.* to navigate a ship by taking advantage of favoring tides, and anchoring when the tide turns.

tide over, a. to help along for a time: *This money will tide him over his illness.* **b.** to overcome (a difficulty, etc.): *We . . . believe that for the moment the difficulty is tided over* (Manchester Examiner).

—*adj.* tidal.

[Old English *tīd* (originally) a point or portion of time]

tide[2] (tīd), *v.i.,* **tid·ed, tid·ing.** *Archaic.* to betide; happen; befall. [Old English *getīdan* < *tīd* tide[1]]

tid·ed (tī′did), *adj.* having tides: *I see . . . The tided oceans ebb and flow* (John Greenleaf Whittier).

tide·gate (tīd′gāt′), *n.* **1.** a gate through which water flows when the tide is in one direction but which closes when the tide is in the other direction. **2.** a channel in which a tidal current runs.

tide·land (tīd′land′), *n.* **1.** submerged coastal land within the historical boundaries of a state and belonging to that state (according to an act passed by the Congress of the United States in May, 1953). **2.** land flooded at high tide.

tide·less (tīd′lis), *adj.* having no tide; without ebb and flow.

tide·line (tīd′līn′), *n.* the line left or reached by the tide at high or (rarely) low water: *The gray-headed urubu or black vulture . . . picks silently at the refuse on the tideline* (New Yorker).

tide mill, a mill driven by the flow of the tide against a water wheel: *It is natural that man should look for means of harnessing some of the power of the tides for his own benefit, and small tide mills have been operated in a few suitable localities for centuries* (New Scientist).

tide·race (tīd′rās′), *n.* a strong tidal current, especially one that flows in a tideway: *He steered . . . through the torrential tideraces of the Burra Sound* (London Times).

tide rip, a heavy wave or rough current caused by opposing tides or currents.

tide·wait·er (tīd′wā′tər), *n.* a customs officer who formerly waited for and boarded ships to prevent the evasion of the customs regulations.

tide·wa·ter (tīd′wôt′ər, -wot′-), *n.* **1.** water affected by the ordinary ebb and flow of the tide. **2.** water that is brought by the flood tide and overflows land. **3.** the seacoast or a region along a seacoast.

—*adj.* of or along tidewater.

tide·way (tīd′wā′), *n.* **1.** a channel in which a tidal current runs. **2.** a strong current running in such a channel.

ti·di·er (tī′dē ər), *n.* a person who tidies: *a most serviceable cleaner and tidier of things* (H. G. Wells).

ti·di·ly (tī′də lē), *adv.* in a tidy manner; neatly; orderly: *It was like a patient in a hospital with the sheets drawn tidily up to the chin* (Graham Greene).

ti·di·ness (tī′dē nis), *n.* neatness; orderliness.

ti·ding (tī′ding), *n. Obsolete.* a piece of news.

ti·dings (tī′dingz), *n.pl.* news; information: *joyful tidings. The messenger brought tidings from the battle front.* [Old English *tīdung* < *getīdan* to happen, tide[2]] —**Syn.** word, message.

ti·dy (tī′dē), *adj.,* **-di·er, -di·est,** *v.,* **-died, -dy·ing,** *n., pl.* **-dies.** —*adj.* **1.** neat and in order; orderly; trim: *a tidy room.* **2.** inclined to keep things neat and in order: *a tidy person.* **3.** *Informal.* considerable; fairly large: *a tidy sum of money.* **4.** *Informal.* fairly good.

—*v.t., v.i.* to put in order; make tidy: *She tidied up her room before going out.*

—*n.* a small cover to keep the back of a chair, etc., from becoming dirty or worn.

[Middle English *tidy* < *tide* time]

—**Syn.** *adj.* **1.** See **neat.**

ti·dy·tips (tī′dē tips), *n. sing. and pl.* any of a group of California annual composite herbs with flower heads that have yellow rays tipped with white.

tie (tī), *v.,* **tied, ty·ing,** *n.* —*v.t.* **1.** to fasten with string, cord, rope, etc.; bind: *to tie a package, to tie a dog to a tree.* **2.** to arrange to form a bow or knot: *to tie a ribbon in the hair, to tie the strings of an apron.* **3.** to tighten and fasten the string or strings of: *to tie one's shoes, to tie an apron.* **4. a.** to fasten, join, or connect in any way; link: *to be tied to the mainland by an isthmus.* **b.** to connect and make fast by a rod or beam; place a tie beam between. **5.** to restrain; restrict; confine; limit: *to be tied to a steady job.* **6.** to make the same score as: *Harvard tied Yale in football.* **7.** *Music.* to connect (notes) by a tie or ligature. **8.** *Slang.* to offer or think of (something) to equal or surpass: *He eats my food, borrows my car, and thinks he's done me a favor. Can you tie that?* **9.** *Informal.* to unite in marriage. —*v.i.* **1.** to fasten by tying; form a bow or knot: *a rope too heavy to tie. That ribbon doesn't tie well.* **2.** to join or fasten together; make a bond or connection: *Where does this beam tie with the roof?* **3.** to make the same score; be equal in points: *The two teams tied.*

tie down, a. to limit; confine; restrict: *a hard man to tie down. She is tied down by her home and five children.* **b.** to fasten or hold down by tying: *The dogs were accustomed to be tied down separately every night* (Daniel Johnson).

tie in, a. to connect or be connected: *Where does this line tie in with the main circuit?* **b.** to make or have a connection; relate: *How does that remark tie in with what you said yesterday?* **c.** to make subject to a tie-in sale: *Their advertised bargains are usually tied in with some product that's not on sale.*

tie into, *Slang.* to attack; lace into: *They girded up their loins, an' tied into him* (R. A. Wason).

tie one on, *Slang.* to drink heavily; go on a binge: *I'll tell you how you can tell . . . any morning, whether I went and tied one on the night before* (John McNulty).

tie up, a. to tie firmly or tightly: *They had tied up the luggage* (Dickens). **b.** to wrap up: *You tie up the present while I make out the card.* **c.** to hinder; stop: *Death that hath taken her hence . . . ties up my tongue, and will not let me speak* (Shakespeare). **d.** to keep (money or property) from being used, sold, or given away: *He left the money tied up, so that his family could use only the interest on it.* **e.** to complete (a sale, etc.); conclude an agreement with: *to tie up a deal.* **f.** to have one's program full; be very busy, etc.: *I can't go tomorrow; I'm all tied up.* **g.** to connect: *I tried to tie up all that had happened with the inexplicable quietness in Lena's eyes* (P. Perera). **h.** to associate: *There are . . . well over one hundred booksellers who are tying up with the national advertising campaign* (Publishers' Weekly). **i.** to delay: *They've tied us up for these two weeks* (S. Merwin). *Traffic west of Springfield was tied up until about midnight* (Springfield Republican). **j.** to moor; anchor: *Dale . . . eased us into a dock, where we tied up* (Anthony Bailey).

—*n.* **1.** anything connecting or holding together two or more things or parts; link. **2.** a cord, chain, etc., used for tying. **3.** an ornamental knot, bow of ribbon, etc.; knot. **4.** a necktie. **5.** a thing that unites; bond; obligation: *family ties, ties of duty.* **6.** heavy piece of timber or iron: *The rails of a railroad track are fastened to ties about a foot apart.* **7.** a connecting beam, rod, or the like; tie beam. **8. a.** equality in points, votes, etc. **b.** a match or contest in which this occurs; draw: *The game ended in a tie, 3 to 3.* **9.** *Music.* a curved line set above or below two notes of the same pitch, indicating that they are to be played or sung continuously.

TIES

Railroad Ties (def. 6)

ties, *Informal.* low, laced shoes: *to wear Oxford ties.*

[Old English *tīgan* < *tēag* a tie, rope]

—**Syn.** *v.t.* **1.** secure. **4. a.** tether. -*n.* **5.** See **bond.**

tie·back (tī′bak′), *n.* **1.** a strip of material used to tie a curtain back from a window: *Draperies were trimmed with fringe, elaborate tiebacks, and swags* (G. McStay Jackson). **2.** a curtain having such a strip of material.

tie beam, a timber or piece serving as a beam, especially, a horizontal beam connecting the lower ends of two opposite principal rafters, thus forming the base of a roof truss. See **king post** for picture.

tie clasp or **clip,** a clasp or clip for holding a necktie in place by fastening it to the shirt front.

tied house (tīd), *British.* an inn or public house owned by or under contract to a brewery and from which all its liquor is purchased: *The company's forceful management . . . has been active in modernising its tied houses, in selling bottled beers on a national scale and in acquiring interests in other breweries* (Economist).

tie-in (tī′in′), *n.* **1.** a connection; link; relationship: *Police suspected a tie-in between the murder and the international narcotics ring. Work is proceeding on . . . installations of equipment and tie-ins with the main boiler plant* (New York Times). **2. a.** a tie-in sale. **b.** advertising promotion associated with tie-in sales.

—*adj.* having to do with or characteristic of a tie-in or tie-in sales: *Liquor dealers claim they must make tie-in purchases of plentiful rum, cordials, and vodka to get scarce scotch* (Wall Street Journal).

tie-in sale (tī′in′), *U.S.* the sale of something desired or scarce on the condition that the buyer buy something else, often unneeded or of lesser value.

tie·less (tī′lis), *adj.* not having or wearing a necktie.

tie·man·nite (tē′mə nīt), *n.* a mineral, a selenide of mercury, occurring in dark-gray masses or granules with a metallic luster. *Formula:* HgSe [< W. *Tiemann,* a German mineralogist of the 1800's + *-ite*[1]]

Tien-shan sheep (tyen′shän′), Marco Polo sheep.

tie·on (tī′on′, -ôn′), *adj.* that is fastened on by tying: *tie-on labels, a tie-on headband.*

tie·pin (tī′pin′), *n.,* or **tie pin,** a stickpin.

tie plate, a steel plate that supports a rail on a tie.

tier[1] (tir), *n.* one of a series of rows arranged one above another: *tiers of seats at a baseball game.* —*v.t., v.i.* to arrange, or be arranged, in tiers. [< Middle French *tire,* Old French, rank, sequence, order < *tirer* to draw.]

ti·er[2] (tī′ər), *n.* a person or thing that ties.

tierce (tirs), *n.* **1. a.** an old unit of liquid measure, equal to 42 wine gallons; one third of a pipe. **b.** a cask holding this amount. **2.** a sequence of three playing cards. **3.** *Fencing.* the third of a series of eight parries. The wrist of the hand holding the foil is faced inward with the fingernails downward, so that the foil is pointed upward and slightly to the right. **4. a.** the third of the seven canonical hours. **b.** the service for this hour, following prime. Tierce is usually said about 9 A.M. **5.** *Obsolete.* a third; third part. Also, **terce.** [< Old French *tierce,* noun use of feminine of *tiers* third < Latin *tertius* third, related to *trēs* three]

tierce de Pic·ar·die (tirs′ də pik′ər dē), *Music.* Picardy third. [< French *tierce de Picardie*]

tier·cel (tir′səl), *n.* tercel, a male falcon. [< Old French *tercel, tiercel;* see TERCEL]

-tiered, *combining form.* having___tiers: *Three-tiered = having three tiers.*

tie rod, 1. one of the rods connecting the front wheels of an automobile, moved by the steering mechanism when turning the wheels to the left or right. **2.** a tie beam.

tier·ra ca·lien·te (tyer′ə ka lyen′tə), a very warm region or climatic zone, especially in high plateaus of tropical South America, extending from sea level to about 3,000 feet. [< Spanish *tierra caliente* hot land]

tier·ra frí·a (tyer′ə frē′ə), a cold region or climatic zone lying between 6,000 and 10,000 feet above sea level. In the mountains of tropical South America, it lies above the tierra templada. [< Spanish *tierra fría* cold land]

tier·ra tem·pla·da (tyer′ə tem plä′də), a temperate region or climatic zone lying between 3,000 and 6,000 feet above sea level, or midway between the tierra caliente and tierra fría of tropical South America. [< Spanish *tierra templada* temperate land]

tiers é·tat (tyer zā tä′), *French.* the third estate; common people.

tie tack, a decorative pin for holding a necktie in place, the point of which pierces the tie and shirt and is gripped by a small button on the inside.

tie-up (tī′up′), *n.* **1.** a stopping of work or action on account of a strike, storm, accident, etc.: *The heavy snowstorm caused a tie-up of traffic.* **2.** *Informal.* a connection; relation. —**Syn. 1.** halt.

tiff[1] (tif), *n.* **1.** a little quarrel: *a boy and a girl . . . having a bit of a tiff* (Arnold Bennett). **2.** a slight outburst of ill humor.
—*v.i.* **1.** to have a little quarrel. **2.** to be in a huff; be slightly peevish.

tiff[2] (tif), *n.* a little drink, as of punch, beer, or other mild liquor. [probably imitative]

tiff[3] (tif), *v.i.* (in India) to lunch; tiffin. [< British slang *tiffing,* verbal noun of *tiff* to sip, drink. Compare TIFF[2].]

tif·fa·ny (tif′ə nē), *n., pl.* **-nies. 1.** a thin, transparent silk. **2.** a gauzy muslin. [< Old French *tifinie* Epiphany < Latin *theophania* theophany, Epiphany; allusion is uncertain]

Tiffany glass, a favrile glass with rich colors and a silky surface. [< Louis C. *Tiffany,* 1848-1933, an American painter]

tif·fin (tif′ən), *n., v.i., v.t.* (in India) lunch. [Anglo-Indian, probably < *tiffing;* see TIFF[3]]

tig (tig), *v.,* **tigged, tig·ging,** *n.* —*v.i. Scottish.* **1.** to give light or playful touches; trifle; dally. **2.** to interfere or meddle. —*v.t.* to touch in the game of tig or tag.
—*n.* **1.** *Scottish.* a touch or tap. **2.** the children's game of tag. **3.** *British Informal.* a quarrel: *The spectacle of a man in a tig, even of two men in a tig, is not as a rule wholly entertaining* (Punch).

ti·ger (tī′gər), *n.* **1. a.** a large, fierce, carnivorous Asiatic mammal of the cat family that has dull-yellow fur striped with black. See picture under **Bengal. b.** any of various related animals, such as the jaguar of South America, the leopard of South Africa, or the thylacine of Tasmania. **2.** a fierce, cruel, grasping, or bloodthirsty person. **3.** a figure of a tiger, used as a badge or crest: *the Tammany tiger, the Princeton tiger.* **4.** *U.S. Informal.* an extra yell at the end of a cheer: *Let's have three cheers and a tiger!* **5.** *U.S. Slang.* the game of faro. **6.** *Obsolete.* a boy in livery acting as groom or footman.

buck or **fight the tiger,** *U.S. Slang.* **a.** to play faro: *A third amused the company by informing them as to the luck he had had that day bucking the tiger* (Police Gazette). **b.** (in faro, roulette, etc.) to play against the bank: . . . *bucking the tiger, which we wouldn't advise any one to do* (Rocky Mountain News).

ride a tiger, to attempt to use something that one may not be able to control and so endanger oneself: *De Gaulle's insistence on the prolongation of nationalism does not extend to the economic sphere . . . There are uncertainties: one may wonder whether he expects to ride the German economic tiger, and how* (Manchester Guardian).

[partly Old English *tigras,* plural < Latin *tigris;* partly < Old French *tigre,* learned borrowing from Latin *tigris* < Greek *tígris*] —**ti′ger·like′,** *adj.*

tiger beetle, a beetle whose larvae live in burrows in sandy soil and catch insects that come near.

tiger cat, 1. a wildcat smaller than a tiger, but similar in markings and ferocity. **2.** a domestic cat with cross stripes like those of a tiger.

ti·ger-eye (tī′gər ī′), *n.* tiger's-eye.

tiger fish, a ferocious, fresh-water fish of southeastern Africa, having sharp teeth that slant backward and resembling a shark but smaller.

ti·ger·ish (tī′gər ish), *adj.* like a tiger; fierce; cruel; bloodthirsty. —**ti′ger·ish·ly,** *adv.* —**ti′ger·ish·ness,** *n.*

tiger lily, 1. a tall garden lily, native to China, having nodding, dull-orange flowers spotted with black. It produces bulblets in the axils of the leaves. See **lily** for picture. **2.** any of various other lilies with similar flowers.

tiger mosquito, aëdes.

tiger moth, any of a group of moths having a hairy body and brightly colored, striped or spotted wings.

tiger salamander, a large salamander of North America with tigerlike stripes on its back. Some tiger salamanders retain the gills of the larval stage, spending their adult lives in water.

ti·ger's-eye (tī′gərz ī′), *n.* a yellowish-brown stone with a changeable luster, composed chiefly of quartz colored by iron oxide, and used as a gem.

tiger shark, a large shark of the warmer parts of the Atlantic and Pacific oceans having yellow streaks on their grayish black bodies.

tiger snake, a poisonous snake of Australia, having a brownish body with cross bands of different colors.

tiger swallowtail, a large, yellow, swallow-tailed butterfly streaked with black, common in the United States.

tight (tīt), *adj.* **1.** firm; held firmly; packed or put together firmly: *a tight grip, a tight knot.* **2.** drawn; stretched: *a tight canvas, a tight cable. He performed on the tight rope.* **3.** fitting closely; fitting too closely: *tight clothing, a tight fit.* **4.** *Dialect.* well-built; trim; neat: *For she is such a smart little craft . . . a bright, little, tight, little . . . slim little craft* (W.S. Gilbert). **5.** not letting water, air, or gas in or out: *a tight boat, a tight roof.* **6.** not wasteful of words; terse; concise: *tight writing, a tight style.* **7.** *Informal.* hard to deal with or manage; difficult: *to have tight going for a few years. His lies got him in a tight place.* **8.** *Informal.* almost even; close: *a tight race.* **9. a.** hard or expensive to get; scarce: *Money for mortgages is tight just now.* **b.** characterized by scarcity or eager demand: *a tight money market.* **10.** *Informal.* stingy; close-fisted; *a man tight in his dealings, rich but tight.* **11.** *Slang.* drunk; tipsy; intoxicated: *If you get tight, the policemen are told to take you home rather than to prison* (Time). **12.** strict; severe: *to rule with a tight hand.* **13.** *Obsolete.* **a.** competent; capable. **b.** alert; lively.

up tight, *Slang.* in a state of anxiety; tense; keyed-up: *A 21-year-old hippie . . . said that the East Villagers are "up tight and frightened"* (New York Times).

—*adv.* firmly; closely; securely: *holding tight on with both hands* (Dickens). *He . . . shut his lips tight* (Joseph Conrad).

—*n.* *U.S. Informal.* a tight place; position of difficulty: *He will work all day, He will work all night, He will work much harder when he gets in a tight* (Gene Roberts).

in the tight, *British.* in close formation or play, as in rugby: *Instead of being pushed, Cambridge themselves now did the pushing, and they had an advantage in the tight until their numbers were reduced* (London Times).

tights, a close-fitting garment, usually covering the lower part of the body and the legs, worn by acrobats, dancers, etc.

[apparently alteration of Middle English *thight,* perhaps < Scandinavian (compare Old Icelandic *thēttr* watertight)] —**tight′ly,** *adv.* —**tight′ness,** *n.*

—**Syn.** *adj.* **1.** close, compact. **2. Tight, taut** mean drawn or stretched so as not to be loose or slack. **Tight,** the more general word, applies to anything drawn over or around something so firmly that there is no looseness: *You need a tight string around that package.* **Taut** emphasizes stretching until the thing described would break, snap, or tear if pulled more tightly, and is used chiefly as a nautical or mechanical term or to describe strained nerves or muscles: *The covering on a drum must be taut.* **3.** snug, close-fitting. **10.** parsimonious.

-tight, *combining form.* not allowing the passage of___, as in *airtight, watertight.*

tight·en (tī′tən), *v.t.* to make tight or tighter: *He tightened his belt.* —*v.i.* to become tight or tighter: *The rope tightened when I pulled on it.* —**tight′en·er,** *n.*

tight-fist·ed (tīt′fis′tid), *adj.* somewhat miserly; stingy; close-fisted. —**Syn.** parsimonious.

tight·ish (tī′tish), *adj.* **1.** rather tight or close-fitting: *Ken Reskitt was wearing a red open-neck check shirt, blue suede shoes, and tightish trousers* (Punch). **2.** somewhat difficult.

tight-knit (tīt′nit′), *adj.* intimately connected; close-knit: *a tight-knit community.*

tight-laced (tīt′lāst′), *adj.* **1.** tightly laced. **2.** strait-laced.

tight-lipped (tīt′lipt′), *adj.* **1.** keeping the lips firmly together. **2.** saying little or nothing. —**Syn. 2.** taciturn.

tight-mouthed (tīt′mouᴛʜd′, -moutht′), *adj.* **1.** close-mouthed. **2.** tight-lipped: *At 2:40, Walter Croen, an executive of Marquise, emerged tight-mouthed* (New York Times).

tight·rope (tīt′rōp′), *n.* **1.** a raised rope or cable stretched tight, on which acrobats perform. **2.** a difficult or dangerous situation: *The increasingly elaborate structure of the economy balances on the tightrope of international trade* (New York Times).

walk a tightrope, to maneuver in a difficult or dangerous situation: *The West has walked a tightrope on Trieste since then, trying to keep both Italy's and Yugoslavia's friendship and say nothing to alienate either* (Wall Street Journal).

—*adj.* of, having to do with, or done on a tightrope.

tights (tīts), *n.pl.* See under **tight,** *n.*

tight squeeze, a difficult situation; narrow escape.

tight·wad (tīt′wod′), *n.* *U.S. Slang.* a stingy person; skinflint: *I don't want to be a tightwad but after all, a dollar is a dollar* (Sinclair Lewis). [American English < *tight* + *wad*[1] roll of money]

tight·wire (tīt′wīr′), *n.* a wire tightrope: *On a tightwire thirty six feet long . . . Bird Millman . . . danced and trilled popular songs . . . without balancing pole or umbrella* (New Yorker).

tig·lic acid (tig′lik), a poisonous, unsaturated liquid or crystalline acid obtained from croton oil, used in medicine. *Formula:* $C_5H_8O_2$ [< New Latin *tiglium* species name of the croton-oil plant < Medieval Latin *tiglia, tilli*]

tig·lin·ic acid (tig lin′ik), tiglic acid.

ti·glon (tī′glon, -glən), *n.* an offspring of a tiger and a lioness. [< *tig*(er) + *l*(i)*on*]

ti·gon (tī′gon, -gən), *n.* a tiglon. [< *tig*(er) + (li)*on*]

Ti·gré (ti grā′), *n.* one of the two Semitic languages spoken in the north of Ethiopia. The other is Tigrinya.

ti·gress (tī′gris), *n.* **1.** a female tiger. **2.** a fierce, cruel woman.

Ti·gri·ña (ti grē′nyə), *n.* Tigrinya.

ti·grine (tī′grin, -grīn), *adj.* like a tiger, especially in coloring or marking. [< Latin *tigrīnus* < *tigris;* see TIGER]

Ti·gri·nya (ti grē′nyə), *n.* a Semitic language spoken in the north of Ethiopia. Also, **Tigriña.**

ti·grish (tī′grish), *adj.* tigerish.

tike (tīk), *n.* tyke.

ti·ki (tē′kē), *n.* **1.** a Polynesian deity, regarded as the creator of man. **2.** an image of wood or stone representing this deity. [< Maori *tiki*]

til[1] (til, tēl), *n.* sesame. Also, **teel.** [< Hindi *til* < Sanskrit *tila* sesamum plant]

til[2] (tēl), *n.* tilde.

ti·la·pi·a (ti lā′pē ə), *n.* any of a genus of fresh-water cichlid fishes important as a source of food in Africa and Asia. [< New Latin *Tilapia*]

til·bu·ry (til′bər ē), *n., pl.* **-ries.** a light, two-wheeled carriage without a top, fashionable in the early 1800's. [< *Tilbury,* a British coach designer of the 1800's]

til·de (til′də), *n.* **1.** a diacritical mark (~) used over *n* in Spanish when it is pronounced *ny,* as in *cañon* (kä nyōn′). **2.** the same mark, used over certain Portuguese vowels to indicate that they are nasal, as in São (souɴ). The Portuguese name for this mark is *til.* **3.** (in the pronunciations in this book) a mark used over *a* to show that it is pronounced as in *fare* (fãr). [< Spanish *tilde,* ultimately < Latin *titulus* title. Doublet of TITLE, TITTLE, TITER.]

tile (tīl), *n., v.,* **tiled, til·ing.** —*n.* **1. a.** a thin piece of baked clay, often glazed and decorated, used for covering roofs, paving floors, lining walls, and ornamenting. **b.** any of various similar thin pieces of plastic, rubber, linoleum, or cement, used for similar purposes. **2.** a baked clay pipe for draining lands, roads, etc. **3.** tiles; tiling. **4.** *Informal.* a stiff hat; a high silk hat: *Afore the brim went, it was a very handsome tile* (Dickens). —*v.t.* to build, cover, or decorate with tiles: *to tile a floor.* [Old English *tigele,* ultimately < Latin *tēgula,* related to *tegere* cover] —**tile′like′,** *adj.*

tile·fish (tīl′fish′), *n., pl.* **-fish·es** or (*collectively*) **-fish.** a large, blue marine food fish with yellow markings.

til·er (tī′lər), *n.* a person who makes or lays tiles.

til·i·a·ceous (til′ē ā′shəs), *adj.* belonging to the basswood family of plants. [< New Latin *Tiliaceae* the basswood family (< Latin *tiliāceus,* adjective < *tilia* the linden, or lime tree) + English *-ous*]

til·ing (tī′ling), *n.* **1.** tiles. **2.** the work of covering with or laying tiles. **3.** anything consisting of or covered with tiles.

till[1] (til), *prep.* **1.** up to the time of; before; until: *The child played till eight.* **2.** *Especially Scottish.* to or unto; as far as.
—*conj.* up to the time when; until: *Walk till you come to a white house.*
[Old English *til* < Scandinavian (compare Old Icelandic *til* < *-tili,* as in *aldertili* life's end)]

➔ **till, until.** These two words are not distinguishable in meaning. *Till* is more usual except at the beginning of sentences: *Until he went to college, he never had thought of his speech. He had never thought of his speech till* [*or until*] *he went to college.*

till[2] (til), *v.t., v.i.* to cultivate (land), as by plowing, harrowing, manuring, etc.; cultivate; plow: *Farmers till the land.* [Old English *tilian* cultivate, tend, work at; (originally) strive after, probably ultimately < *till* fixed point, goal]

till[3] (til), *n.* **1.** a small drawer for money under or behind a counter: *A cash register is sometimes called a till.* **2.** *Informal.* any place or thing that contains or stores money: *Do we have enough in the till for a vacation?* [origin uncertain] —**Syn. 2.** coffer.

till[4] (til), *n.* **1.** glacial drift or deposit of clay, gravel, and boulders. **2.** *British.* a stiff clay. [origin unknown]

till·a·ble (til′ə bəl), *adj.* that can be tilled; arable.

till·age (til′ij), *n.* **1.** the cultivation of land. **2.** the fact or condition of being tilled. **3. a.** tilled or plowed land. **b.** crops growing on it. —**Syn. 1.** agriculture, husbandry.

til·land·si·a (ti land′zē ə), *n.* any of a large group of herbaceous plants of the pineapple family, found in tropical and subtropical America, most of which grow on trees for support, as the Florida moss. [< New Latin *Tillandsia* < Elias *Tillands,* 1640-1693, a Swedish professor of medicine and botanist]

till·er[1] (til′ər), *n.* a bar or handle at the stern used to turn the rudder in steering a boat. [< Anglo-French *teiler,* Old French *telier* (originally) weaver's beam, learned borrowing from Medieval Latin *telarium* < Latin *tēla* web, loom]

till·er[2] (til′ər), *n.* a person who tills land; farmer. [Middle English *tiliere* < Old English *tilian* till[2] + *-ere* -er[1]]

till·er[3] (til′ər), *n.* **1.** *Dialect.* a shoot that springs from the root or base of the original stalk. **2.** *Dialect.* a young tree; sapling. —*v.i.* to sprout new shoots from the root or base of the original stalk, as corn and certain other plants. [probably Old English *tealgor, telgra* a shoot (especially, a root sucker) < *telga* branch, twig]

till·ite (til′īt), *n.* a sedimentary rock composed of glacial till compacted into hard rock: *Their search is for tillites, formations derived from rocky debris left by ancient glaciers* (New York Times). [< *till*[4] + *-ite*[1]]

til·ly seed (til′ē), the seed of the croton. [apparently < French *tilli* < Medieval Latin; see TIGLIC ACID]

til·ly-val·ly (til′ē val′ē), *interj. Archaic.* nonsense! [origin unknown]

tilt[1] (tilt), *v.t.* **1.** to slope; slant; lean; tip: *You tilt your head forward when you bow. You tilt your cup when you drink.* **2.** to point or thrust (a lance). **3.** to rush at; charge. **4.** to forge or hammer with a heavy pivoted hammer.

Tilt[1] (def. 2)
Knights Tilting

—*v.i.* **1.** to be tilted; slope; slant; lean; tip: *This table tilts.* **2.** to rush, charge, or fight with lances: *Knights used to tilt on horseback.*
tilt at, to attack; fight; protest against: *I'm too discreet To run amuck and tilt at all I meet* (Alexander Pope).
—*n.* **1.** a being tilted; sloping position; slope; slant. **2. a.** a fight between two men on horseback with lances. They charge at each other and try to knock each other off the horse. **b.** the exercise of riding with a lance or the like at a mark, as the quintain. **3.** a thrust of a weapon, as at a tilt. **4.** any dispute or quarrel. **5.** a seesaw. **6.** a tilt hammer.
[Middle English *tilten* push over, fall over, apparently unrecorded Old English *tieltan* < *tealt* unsteady] —**tilt′er,** *n.*

tilt[2] (tilt), *n.* an awning or canopy over a boat, wagon, etc. —*v.t.* to cover with a tilt or tilts. [Middle English *telte* a covering of coarse cloth, variant of *tilde* and *telde,* Old English *geteld*]

tilt·a·ble (til′tə bəl), *adj.* that can be tilted: *Basically, an inboard-outboard includes an engine mounted inside the boat, joined to a steerable, tiltable, outboard drive unit mounted at the stern of the boat* (Wall Street Journal).

tilt·board (tilt′bôrd′, -bōrd′), *n.* an apparatus used especially in the study of kinesthetic senses, consisting of a horizontal board, pivoted at the center upon a transverse axis in such a way that the subject, lying at full length upon it, may be tilted up or down: *He was placed on a tiltboard, and his pulse and blood pressure were checked in both horizontal and vertical positions* (Time).

tilt cart, a tipcart.

tilth (tilth), *n.* **1.** the state of being tilled: *a garden in bad tilth, to put a field into good tilth.* **2.** the cultivation of land; tillage. **3.** tilled land. [Old English *tilth* < *tilian* till[2]]

tilt hammer, a heavy hammer used in forging, etc., alternately tilted up and allowed to drop.

tilt·me·ter (tilt′mē′tər), *n.* an instrument used by seismologists to detect and measure a tilt in the earth's surface. [< *tilt*[1] + *-meter*]

tilt roof, a roof with a generally semicircular section inside and out, like a canopy over a wagon.

tilt-top table (tilt′top′), tip table: *You are fortunate to own this excellent example of curled-maple, Chippendale-type, tripod, tilt-top table* (Maclean's).

tilt-wing (tilt′wing′), *adj.* (of an aircraft) having wings which can be tilted upwards for vertical take-off and landing.

tilt·yard (tilt′yärd′), *n.* a place where tilting with lances was done.

Tim., Timothy (referring to either of two books of the New Testament).

ti·ma·rau (tē′mə rou′), *n.* tamarau.

tim·bal (tim′bəl), *n.* **1.** a kettledrum. **2.** a vibrating membrane like a drumhead, by which a shrill or chirping sound is produced, as in the cicada and certain other insects. Also, **tymbal.** [< Middle French *timbale,* alteration of *tamballe,* alteration of Spanish *atabal* Moorish drum < Arabic *aṭ-ṭabl* the drum. Compare ATABAL.]

tim·bale (tim′bəl), *n.* **1.** minced meat, fish, vegetables, etc., prepared with a sauce and cooked in a mold. **2.** a mold of pastry containing various ingredients, often cooked by frying. [< French *timbale* (originally) timbal (because of the resemblance)]

timbale iron, a cup-shaped iron mold for cooking a timbale.

tim·ber (tim′bər), *n.* **1.** *U.S.* wood used for building and making things. Houses, ships, and furniture are made from timber. **2.** a large, sturdy piece of wood used in building. Beams and rafters are timbers. **3.** a curved piece forming a rib or frame of a ship. **4.** *U.S.* growing trees; wooded land; forests: *Half of his land is covered with timber.* **5. a.** trees suitable for providing wood for building: *to mark timber for felling. Canada is rich in timber.* **b.** logs, green or cured, cut from such trees: *a vessel loaded with timber from Sweden.* **6.** *British.* **a.** a piece of lumber larger than 4½ inches by 6 inches in cross section. **b.** lumber. **7.** worth or value as a man; quality; character: *The country needs more men of his timber.*
shiver my timbers, a mock oath attributed to sailors: *I won't thrash you . . . Shiver my timbers if I do* (Frederick Marryat).
—*v.t.* to cover, support, build, or furnish with timber.
—*adj.* **1.** made or consisting of wood; wooden. **2.** of or for timber.
[Old English *timber* a building; building material, trees suitable for building]
—**Syn.** *n.* **1.** lumber. **4.** timberland.

timber and a half hitch, a knot tied with a half hitch and a timber hitch.

timber cruiser, *U.S.* a man who estimates the amount of timber ready to be felled on a tract of timberland.

tim·bered (tim′bərd), *adj.* **1.** made of or furnished with timber; covered or supported with logs or beams. **2.** covered with growing trees; forested: *the timbered slopes of the Rockies* (Theodore Roosevelt).

tim·ber·head (tim′bər hed′), *n. Nautical.* **1.** the top part of a rib or frame, rising above the deck, and serving for belaying ropes, etc. **2.** a bollard or upright post similar to this in placement and use.

timber hitch, a hitch or knot used to tie a rope around a spar, post, etc. See **hitch** for picture.

tim·ber-hitch (tim′bər hich′), *v.t.* to make fast with a timber hitch.

tim·ber·ing (tim′bər ing), *n.* **1.** building material of wood, especially logs and beams. **2.** timbers. **3.** work made of timbers.

tim·ber·land (tim′bər land′), *n.* **1.** land covered with trees that are, or will be, useful for timber. **2.** any land with many trees; forest; woods.

timber line, the line beyond which trees will not grow on mountains and in polar regions because of the cold.

tim·ber-line (tim′bər līn′), *adj.* of or having to do with the timber line.

tim·ber·man (tim′bər mən), *n., pl.* **-men.** *Mining.* a man who prepares and takes care of the timbers used for supports, etc.

timber rattlesnake, a large rattlesnake found in most of the United States from the Mississippi valley eastward; banded rattlesnake.

timber tongue, actinomycosis in cattle.

timber tree, a tree yielding wood suitable for building or construction.

timber wolf, the gray wolf, a large gray, black, or white wolf of northern and western North America; lobo.

Timber Wolf (including tail, about 5 ft. long)

tim·ber·work (tim′bər wėrk′), *n.* work made with timbers, especially logs and beams.

tim·bre (tim′-bər, tam′-), *n.* **1.** *Music.* the quality in sound that distinguishes a certain voice, instrument, etc., from other voices, instruments, etc., regardless of pitch and volume. **2.** *Phonetics.* the quality in the resonance of a sound, distinct from loudness and pitch, that gives it its identity. [< Old French *timbre* hemispherical bell without a clapper; heraldic crest, seal or stamp; (originally) a drum, timbrel, ultimately < Greek *týmpanon* kettledrum. Doublet of TIMPANI, TYMPAN, TYMPANUM.]

tim·brel (tim′brəl), *n.* a tambourine or the like. [diminutive form of Middle English *timbre* a timbrel, (kettle) drum < Old French *timbre;* see TIMBRE]

tim·breled or **tim·brelled** (tim′brəld), *adj.* accompanied by the playing of timbrels.

time (tīm), *n., v.,* **timed, tim·ing,** *adj.* —*n.* **1.** all the days there have been or ever will be; the past, present, and future: *a rose-red city half as old as time* (John William Burgon). *Time present and time past Are both perhaps present in time future* (T.S. Eliot). **2.** a part of time: *A minute is a short time. He was away from home for a long time. Remember that time is money* (Benjamin Franklin). **3. a.** a period of time; epoch; era; age: *in the time of the Stuart kings of England.* **b.** a period of life; years of living; lifetime: *achievements that will outlast our time.* **c.** a period in the existence of the world; unit of geological chronology. **4. a.** any specified or defined period; period in question: *He was with us the whole time.* **b.** time that is or was present; prevailing period: *to change with the times.* **5.** a term of imprisonment, enlistment, apprenticeship, etc.: *to complete one's time.* **6.** a long time: *What a time it took you!* **7. a.** a particular point in time; hour of the clock: *What time is it? At what time do you go to bed?* **b.** a particular season; date or span of the calendar: *Summer is the time of hot weather. Autumn is a good time of year to be in the country.* **8.** the fit, due, or proper time: *It is time for us to be going. It is time to eat.* **9.** chance; occasion; opportunity: *to bide one's time. Now's your time to strike! This time we will succeed. She got the right answer every time.* **10.** a system of measuring or reckoning the passage of time: *sidereal time, solar time, daylight-saving time.* **11.** the conditions of a certain period; condition or state of life, affairs, etc.: *Wars and lack of work bring hard times.* **12.** an amount of time required or desired; available time: *I need time to rest. I could multiply witness upon witness . . . if I had time* (John Ruskin). **13.** experience during a certain time or on a certain occasion: *The wounded soldier had a bad time for three hours. She had a good time at the party.* **14.** *Music.* **a.** the rhythm or measure of a piece of music, marked by division of the music into bars, and usually denoted by a fraction (time signature), the numerator indicating the number of beats to the measure, and the denominator indicating the time value of the note receiving one beat. **b.** the characteristic rhythm, form, and style of a particular class of compositions; tempo: *waltz time, march time.* **c.** the time value or length of a note or rest. **15. a.** the period for which one works or should work: *His normal time is 8 hours a day.* **b.** the pay for a period of work: *to collect one's time. Pay was due to him—'time' as it was called* (Owen Wister). **c.** the rate of pay: *We offer straight time for work up to 40 hours and time and a half for Saturdays.* **16.** spare time; leisure: *to have time to read, to find time for hobbies.* **17.** one of the three unities (unity of time). **18.** *Prosody.* a unit or a group of units in metrical measurement, especially a short syllable or mora. **19.** *Military.* a rate of stepping; pace: *to march in quick time.* **20. a.** the period of gestation. **b.** the natural ending of gestation; time of giving birth. *Abbr.:* t.

about time, at or near the proper time: *It's about time to go home. It's about time you came!*

against time, so as to finish before a certain time: *. . . A man who . . . was often . . . compelled to write against time for his living* (Swinburne).

at a time, at one time; simultaneously: *. . . an utter aversion to speaking to more than one man at a time* (Spectator).

at the same time, a. at one time; not before or after: *In two of Shakespeare's tragedies are introduced, at the same time, instances of counterfeit madness and of real* [*madness*] (London Mirror). **b.** while saying this; nevertheless; however: *Give them my best wishes. At the same time I must say I do not envy the girl* (John Strange Winter).

at times, now and then; once in a while: *I believe most men have, at times, wished to be . . . possessed of the power of moulding the world to their fancy* (London Mirror).

behind the times, old-fashioned; out-of-date: *A newspaper cannot afford to be behind the times.*

bide one's time, to wait for a good chance: *. . . a bitter heart that bides its time . . .* (Robert Browning).

buy time, to gain time by stalling, postponing, etc.; put off or delay a course of action: *The Africans . . . are not here to buy time while their governments operate behind the scenes, the way Western diplomats are* (New Yorker).

do or **serve time,** *Informal.* to be imprisoned as a criminal: *a man doing time for bank robbery.*

fill in the time, to occupy oneself during a period of inaction: *He filled in the time of waiting by reading a magazine.*

for the time being, for the present; for now: *The member for Nuneaton undertakes to stay in Parliament for the time being* (Manchester Guardian Weekly).

from time to time, now and then; once in a while: *Statesmen are bound to make mistakes from time to time* (Manchester Guardian Weekly).

have the time of one's life, to enjoy oneself to the utmost: *You could tell by his voice that he was having the time of his life out there* (New York Times).

in good time, a. at the right time: *Every true-hearted follower shall, in good time, arrive at the desired goal* (James Gilmour). **b.** soon; quickly: *My aunt wants to be back in good time* (Punch).

in no time, shortly; before long: *We hurried and reached the boys in no time.*

in time, a. after a while: *I think in time she may be won* (Henry Willobie). **b.** soon enough: [*He*] *. . . returned . . . in time to assume the custody of the seal in September 1238* (English Historical Review). **c.** in the right rate of movement in music, dancing, marching, etc.: *They were trained to march in time.*

keep time, a. (of a watch or clock) to go correctly: *The clock is ready . . . with every probability of going and keeping time for two or three years* (Paul Hasluck). **b.** to sound or move at the right rate: *The marchers kept time to the martial music.*

kill time, *Informal.* to spend time so as to bring it to an end, as in activities of merely passing interest or entertainment: *He did not want to stay and filled in the puzzle "only to kill time"* (New York Times).

make time, to go with speed: *We'll have to make time to catch that early train.*

mark time, a. to move the feet as in marching, but without advancing: *The soldiers marked time until the sergeant gave the order to march.* **b.** to suspend progress temporarily: *Others plan on marking time for a couple of years for another stab at Congress* (Wall Street Journal). **c.** to go through motions without accomplishing anything: *He's bored with his job, and merely marking time at it.*

once upon a time, long ago; once: *Once upon a time there were gods only, and no mortal creatures* (Benjamin Jowett).

on time, a. at the right time; not late: *. . . my endeavors to get the family out of the house and into our pew on time* (Scribner's Magazine). **b.** with time in which to pay; on credit: *Like all young marrieds starting from . . . scratch, my niece bought an apartment full of expensive furniture on time, a TV set on time, and a car on time* (Goodman Ace).

out of time, after the prescribed period has elapsed; too late: *Counsel for the respondent took a preliminary objection that the appeal was out of time* (Law Times).

pass the time away, to occupy oneself during the day: *She passed the time away by knitting.*

take one's time, to be in no hurry; proceed slowly; dally: *Mr. Mumford does this in his last paragraph, I know, but he certainly takes his time getting there* (New Yorker).

take time by the forelock, to plan ahead; do things in plenty of time; anticipate: *We must take time by the forelock; for when it is once past, there is no recalling it* (Jonathan Swift).

tell time, *U.S.* to read the clock; tell what time it is by the clock: *to teach a child to tell time.*

time after time or **time and again,** again and again: *Time after time we have warned you* (Benjamin Jowett). *The importance of the vote in helping Negroes gain equality has been shown time and again in recent years* (New York Times).

time of life, age: *a foolish thing to do at his time of life.*

time out of mind, beyond memory or record: *The barber's shop in a country town has been, time out of mind, the grand office of intelligence* (Richard Graves).

times, multiplied by; ×: *four times three, five times as much.*

time was, there was a time; at one time; once: *Time was when we had a national style* (John T. Micklethwaite).

—*v.t.* **1.** to measure the time or rate of speed of: *to time a worker on a new job, to time a race.* **2.** to fix, set, or regulate the length of in time: *to time an exposure correctly.* **3.** to set, regulate, or adjust: *to time an alarm clock, to time all the clocks in an office according to the radio.* **4. a.** to do in rhythm with; set the time of: *The dancers time their steps to the music.* **b.** to mark the rhythm or measure of, as in music. **c.** to fix or assign the metrical quantity of (a syllable) or the length of (a note). **5.** to choose the moment or occasion for: *The lady timed her entrance so well that she went in when the prince did.* —*v.i.* to keep time; sound or move in unison or harmony: *Timing to their stormy sounds, his stormy lays are sung* (Whittier). *Beat, happy stars, timing with things below* (Tennyson).

—*adj.* **1.** of or having to do with time. **2.** having to do with purchases to be paid for at a future date or dates. **3.** *Commerce.* payable at a specified future date or at a certain length of time after presentation.

[Old English *tīma*]

time and a half, payment for overtime work at one and a half times the usual rate of pay: *Labor bills . . . would . . . recommend that employees receive double time rather than time and a half for overtime work* (New York Times).

time and motion study, an examination by an efficiency expert of the manner and time taken to do a job to find out if there is a quicker and easier way to do it; time study.

time ball, a ball suspended on a pole on top of an observatory or other tall building for the purpose of indicating an exact moment of mean time, such as noon, by dropping from the top to the bottom of the pole, usually by the closing of an electric circuit at the predetermined moment.

time belt, time zone.

time bill, a bill to be paid at the future time stated in the bill.

time bomb, a bomb that can be set to go off at a certain time.

time capsule, a container of things sealed to preserve a record of a civilization or some aspect of it: *A torpedo-shaped time capsule containing current news and literature in microfilm form, and also many objects of everyday use, was buried at the New York World's Fair in 1940* (World Book Encyclopedia).

time·card (tīm′kärd′), *n.* **1.** a card for recording the amount of time that a person works. **2.** a card showing the times of trains, buses, airplanes, etc.; timetable.

time charter, 1. a contract for the hiring of a ship, or part of a ship, for a certain period of time, usually to carry cargo: *Most recent time charters have been for the next 8 to 10 months* (Wall Street Journal). **2.** the terms of such a contract. **3.** a document embodying such a contract.

time clock, a clock with a device to record

the time when workers arrive and leave or to release locks on the doors of bank vaults, etc.

time-con·sum·er (tīm′kən sü′mər), *n.* something that is time-consuming.

time-con·sum·ing (tīm′kən sü′ming), *adj.* taking up much or too much time: *At present the only way to detect hog cholera is to inject a healthy pig with fluid from a diseased one, a time-consuming and expensive process* (Science News Letter). *For the whole House to engage in discussion of the minor details of bills is not only time-consuming but inefficient* (Manchester Guardian).

time deposit, a deposit in a bank that must remain for a definite period of time, or can be withdrawn only after the depositor has given an advance notice to the bank.

time depth, *Anthropology.* the period of internal development or continuity of a culture, language, etc.: *I thought about the probable age of this dance . . . and hence came again to the time depth of the inward-turned, castellated quality of Pueblo life down the ages* (Oliver La Farge).

time discount, an amount deducted from an invoice price for payment within a given time.

time draft, a draft to be paid at the future time stated in the draft.

time exposure, **1.** the exposure of a photographic film, plate, etc., for a certain time, longer than a half second. **2.** a photograph taken in this way.

time fuse, a fuse that will burn for a certain time, used to set off a charge of explosive.

time-hon·ored (tīm′on′ərd), *adj.* honored, revered, or respected because old and established: *a time-honored custom.* —**Syn.** venerable.

time-hon·oured (tīm′on′ərd), *adj. Especially British.* time-honored.

time immemorial, **1.** a date or period in time beyond memory or historic record; age or year before the beginning of known chronology: *a tradition observed from time immemorial.* **2.** *Law.* a time beyond legal memory. In England it is fixed by law as time before 1189, the beginning of the reign of Richard I.

time·keep·er (tīm′kē′pər), *n.* a person or thing that keeps time: *The factory timekeeper keeps account of the hours of work done. A timekeeper at a horse race or track meet measures and records the minutes and seconds taken by the winner and other contestants. My watch is an excellent timekeeper.*

time·keep·ing (tīm′kē′ping), *n.* **1.** the work or duties of a timekeeper. **2.** the measuring or recording of time.

time killer, *Informal.* **1.** a pastime: *Touch football is a favorite time killer* (Time). **2.** a person seeking to pass the time away: *. . . those time killers who stroll beneath a marquee, read the ecstatic quotes, and, on a whim, go in* (Harper's).

time killing, *Informal.* the act of passing the time away; diversion: *Some of it is time killing for the lonely and some of it is refreshment for the intellectually hungry* (Harper's).

time lag, the amount of time between two related events one of which is usually the result of or dependent upon the other.

time-lapse (tīm′laps′), *adj.* of or by means of time-lapse photography: *an arrangement for showing a bean plant growing by time-lapse movies* (Science News Letter).

time-lapse photography, the use of motion pictures to take a sequence of photographs at regular intervals to show the condensed progress in a process that is often too long to watch or too slow for the mind and the eye to observe.

time·less (tīm′lis), *adj.* **1.** never ending; eternal. **2.** referring to no special time. **3.** *Archaic.* untimely; unseasonable. —**time′less·ly,** *adv.* —**time′less·ness,** *n.* —**Syn. 1.** unending.

time limit, a time at which something must be done or completed: *We were not working to a rigid syllabus or preparing for an examination; there was no time limit and hence there was a certain leisurely and even playful atmosphere* (New Scientist).

time·li·ness (tīm′lē nis), *n.* a being timely or in good time.

time loan, a loan with a fixed date for payment.

time lock, a lock controlled by clockwork so that when locked it cannot be unlocked before the expiration of a certain interval of time.

time·ly (tīm′lē), *adj.*, **-li·er, -li·est,** *adv.* —*adj.* **1.** at the right time: *The timely arrival of the police stopped the riot.* **2.** *Archaic.* early.

—*adv.* **1.** at the right time; opportunely; seasonably. **2.** *Archaic.* early; soon.

—**Syn.** *adj.* **1. Timely, opportune** mean well-timed or especially suited to the time or occasion. **Timely** describes something perfectly suited to the time or circumstance, coming or happening just when it will be most useful or valuable: *Sunday's paper contained a timely article on wise buying and foolish spending.* **Opportune** describes either the moment or occasion most favorable for doing something, or an event or action happening or done at exactly the right and most advantageous moment: *The invitation came at an opportune moment.*

time machine, an imaginary machine for carrying passengers back and forth in time.

time measure, a system of units used in measuring time. *Examples:* 60 seconds = 1 minute; 60 minutes = 1 hour; 24 hours = 1 day; 7 days = 1 week; 4 weeks, 30 days, or 28, 29, 30, or 31 days = 1 month; 12 months, or 365 or 366 days = 1 year.

time money, a time loan.

time note, a note to be paid at the future time stated in the note.

ti·me·o Da·na·os et do·na fe·ren·tes (tim′ē ō dan′ā ōs et dō′nə fə ren′tēz), *Latin.* I fear the Greeks even when bringing gifts.

time of day, **1.** the hour or exact time as shown by the clock. **2.** a point or stage in any course or period. **3.** *Informal.* **a.** the current state of affairs. **b.** the current fashion; latest thing.

give one the time of day, to pay attention to; acknowledge: *Ten years ago a big company like Frigidaire wouldn't give us the time of day* (Maclean's). *He's just an engineer; if we were home the Secretary of State wouldn't give him the time of day* (Harper's).

know the time of day, to be aware of the current state of affairs; know what is going on or what is fashionable: *"She knows the time of day," said the other* (Ouida).

pass the time of day, to exchange words in greeting; converse with briefly in passing: *Instead of closing the Vatican gardens when he takes a walk, the new Pope will often pause and pass the time of day with workmen, gardeners, and such* (Harper's).

time·ous (tī′məs), *adj.* timely. —**time′ous·ly,** *adv.*

time out, **1.** a period when play is suspended during the course of a game, at the request of one team, a player, a referee, umpire, etc. **2.** any period of suspension of activity; respite: *to take time out from work to smoke a cigarette.*

time·piece (tīm′pēs′), *n.* a clock or watch.

time·pleas·er (tīm′plē′zər), *n.* a time-server.

tim·er (tī′mər), *n.* **1.** a person or thing that times; timekeeper. **2.** a device for indicating or recording intervals of time, such as a stop watch. **3.** a clockwork device for indicating when a certain period of time has elapsed: *Many stoves have timers for baking.* **4.** an automatic device in an internal-combustion engine that causes the spark for igniting the charge to occur just at the time required.

times (tīmz), *n.pl.* See under **time,** *n.*

time·sav·er (tīm′sā′vər), *n.* a person or thing that saves time.

time·sav·ing (tīm′sā′ving), *adj.* that reduces the time previously required to do something: *a timesaving appliance or idea.*

time scale, any sequence of events used as a measure of the length or duration of a period of time: *an atomic time scale, the evolutionary time scale. The standard geologic column is the basis for the geologic time scale* (Gilluly, Waters, and Woodford).

time sense, a sense or perception of time and time relations; the faculty of perceiving length or lapse of time: *Hers was the unerring time sense that got her to the bus stop when the bus was due* (Punch).

time·serv·er (tīm′sėr′vər), *n.* a person who for selfish purposes shapes his conduct to conform with the opinions of the time or of the persons in power: *. . . deserted by all the timeservers who, in his prosperity, had claimed brotherhood with him* (Macaulay). —**Syn.** opportunist.

time·serv·ing (tīm′sėr′ving), *adj.* shaping one's conduct to conform with the opinions of the time or of persons in power, especially for selfish reasons. —*n.* the act or conduct of a timeserver.

time-share (tīm′shãr′), *v.*, **-shared, -shar·ing.** —*v.i.* (of a computing system or program) to allocate divisions of the total operating time to two or more functions. —*v.t.* to share the operations of (a time-sharing computer or program).

time sheet, a sheet for recording the amount of time that a person works: *He asked Mr. Jennings if he had any recollection of the missing batch of time sheets of workmen at 10 Rillington Place* (London Times).

time-shift (tīm′shift′), *n.* deviation from strict chronological order, as in a narrative: *His [William Faulkner's] books are filled with bewildering time-shifts* (Newsweek).

time signature, *Music.* a sign showing the time of a piece. It is usually put at the beginning or where the time changes.

time spirit, the spirit of the time or period; Zeitgeist.

time study, time and motion study.

time·ta·ble (tīm′tā′bəl), *n.* **1.** a schedule showing the times when trains, ships, buses, airplanes, etc., arrive and depart: *I would sooner read a timetable or a catalogue than nothing at all . . . They are much more entertaining than half the novels that are written* (W. Somerset Maugham). **2.** any list or schedule of the times at which things are to be done or happen.

time-test·ed (tīm′tes′tid), *adj.* proven by repeated tests over a long period of time.

time-tried (tīm′trīd′), *adj.* time-tested.

time value, the duration of a musical note in relation to the tempo involved.

time-wast·er (tīm′wās′tər), *n.* a person or thing that wastes time.

time-wast·ing (tīm′wās′ting), *adj.* using time to no value or purpose: *a time-wasting method. Octavian . . . classed fishing with drinking and revelling among Antony's time-wasting activities in Egypt* (Punch).

time·work (tīm′wėrk′), *n.* work paid for by the hour, day, or week.

time·work·er (tīm′wėr′kər), *n.* a worker paid by the hour, day or week.

time·worn (tīm′wôrn′, -wōrn′), *adj.* **1.** worn by long existence or use: *timeworn steps.* **2.** worn out by use; trite: *a timeworn excuse.* **3.** very old; ancient; antiquated: *a timeworn superstition.*

time zone, a zone bounded by lines approximating meridians within which the same standard time is used, especially any one of the series of 24 that begins and ends with the International Date Line.

tim·id (tim′id), *adj.* **1.** easily frightened; shy: *The timid child was afraid of the dark. Deer are timid animals.* **2.** characterized by or indicating fear: *a timid reply.* [< Latin *timidus* < *timēre* to fear] —**tim′id·ly,** *adv.* —**tim′id·ness,** *n.*

—**Syn. 1. Timid, cowardly** mean lacking courage. **Timid** emphasizes being always ready to be afraid, especially of anything new, different, uncertain, or unknown: *He does not like his job, but is too timid to try to find another.* **Cowardly** emphasizes a weak and dishonorable lack of courage in the presence of danger or trouble: *Leaving his wife because she was hopelessly sick was a cowardly thing to do.*

ti·mid·i·ty (tə mid′ə tē), *n.* a being timid; timid behavior; shyness.

tim·ing (tī′ming), *n.* **1. a.** the regulation of the speed or tempo of the parts of any musical, dramatic, or rhetorical performance to secure the greatest possible effect. **b.** the effect produced. **2.** (in sports) the physical and mental coordination necessary to achieve the greatest effect by a throw, blow, stroke, or other maneuver.

timing chain, a chain by means of which the camshaft and accessory shafts of an engine are driven: *It is common to find a timing chain worn so badly that it will "jump" a tooth before it is replaced* (Toboldt and Purvis).

ti·moc·ra·cy (tī mok′rə sē), *n., pl.* **-cies. 1.** a form of government in which love of honor is the dominant motive of the rulers (used in this sense by Plato). **2.** a form of government in which the ownership of property is a requirement for holding office (used in this sense by Aristotle). [< Medieval Latin *timocratia* < Greek *tīmokratiā* < *tīmē* valuation; honor + *-kratiā* a rule, reign < *kratein* to rule]

ti·mo·crat·ic (tī′mə krat′ik), *adj.* of or having to do with timocracy.

ti·mo·crat·i·cal (tī′mə krat′ə kəl), *adj.* timocratic.

Ti·mon (tī′mən), *n.* **1.** the hero of Shakespeare's play *Timon of Athens,* noted for his dislike of mankind. **2.** a hater of mankind; misanthrope.

tim·or·ous (tim′ər əs), *adj.* **1.** easily frightened; timid: *The timorous rabbit ran away.* **2.** characterizing or indicating fear: *a timorous approach to reality.* [< Old French *temerous, timoureus* < Medieval Latin *timorosus* < Latin *timor, -ōris* fear] **—tim′or·ous·ly,** *adv.* **—tim′or·ous·ness,** *n.* **—Syn. 1.** fearful, fearsome.

tim·o·thy (tim′ə thē), *n.,* or **timothy grass,** a coarse grass with long, cylindrical spikes, often grown for hay. [American English, apparently < *Timothy* Hanson, who cultivated it in America around 1720]

Timothy
Left, plant (15 in. high); right, stalk

Tim·o·thy (tim′ə thē), *n.* **1.** a disciple of the Apostle Paul. **2.** either of the books of the New Testament (I Timothy and II Timothy) written as letters by the Apostle Paul to Timothy. Full title, *The First* or *Second Epistle of Paul the Apostle to Timothy. Abbr.:* Tim.

tim·pa·ni (tim′pə nē), *n., pl. of* **tim·pa·no.** kettledrums. Also, **tympani.** [< Italian *timpani,* plural of *timpano* < Latin *tympanum.* Doublet of TIMBRE, TYMPAN, TYMPANUM.]

tim·pa·nist (tim′pə nist), *n.* a person who plays the kettledrums; tympanist.

tim·pa·no (tim′pə nō), *n.* singular of **timpani.**

tin (tin), *n., adj., v.,* **tinned, tin·ning.** *—n.* **1.** a metallic chemical element like silver in color and luster but softer and cheaper. Tin is used in plating, and in making alloys such as bronze, pewter, Britannia metal, etc. *Symbol:* Sn; *at.wt.:* (C^{12}) 118.69 or (O^{16}) 118.70; *at.no.:* 50; *valence:* 2, 4. **2.** thin sheets of iron or steel coated with tin; tin plate. **3.** any can, box, pan, or other container made of or plated with tin: *a pie tin.* **4.** *British.* a can: *to buy two tins of peas.* **5.** *Slang.* money; cash.
—adj. made of or plated with tin: *a tin bucket.*
—v.t. **1.** to cover or plate with tin. **2.** *British.* to put up in tin cans or tin boxes; can: *to tin peas.*
[Old English *tin*]

tin·a·mou (tin′ə mü), *n.* any of various birds of South and Central America and Mexico that look somewhat like a quail or grouse and have a body structure similar to the rhea. [< French *tinamou* < Carib (South America) *tinamu*]

Tinamou
(about 14 in. long)

tin·cal (ting′käl, -kôl, -kəl), *n.* crude borax, found in lake deposits in Tibet, Iran, and certain other Asian countries. [< Malay *tingkal* < Sanskrit *tankana*]

tin can, 1. a can. **2.** *U.S. Naval Slang.* a destroyer. [(definition 2) because of the relatively thin armor plate]

tinct (tingkt), *adj. Archaic.* tinged; flavored: *lucent syrops tinct with cinnamon* (Keats).
—n. Archaic. tint; tinge.
—v.t. Obsolete. **1.** to tinge; tint. **2.** to tincture.
[< Latin *tīnctus,* past participle of *tingere* tinge. Doublet of TAINT, TINT[1].]

tinct., tincture.

tinc·to·ri·al (tingk tôr′ē əl, -tōr′-), *adj.* of, having to do with, or used in dyeing or coloring. [< Latin *tinctōrius* (< *tinctor* dyer < *tingere* dye) + English *-al*[1]]

tinc·ture (tingk′chər), *n., v.,* **-tured, -turing.** *—n.* **1.** a solution of medicine in alcohol or in a mixture that is chiefly of alcohol. **2.** a trace; tinge; flavor: *His stern face showed for a moment a slight tincture of amusement.* **3.** a color; tint: *Her usually pale cheeks showed a faint tincture of pink.* **4.** *Heraldry.* any of the nine colors, eight furs, or two metals used or represented in coats of arms, etc. **5.** *Alchemy.* a supposed spiritual principle or immaterial substance whose character or quality may be infused into material things, which are then said to be tinctured; quintessence, spirit, or soul of a thing. **6.** *Obsolete.* a dye or pigment.
—v.t. **1.** to give a trace or tinge to: *Everything he says is tinctured with conceit.* **2.** to color; tint. [< Latin *tīnctūra* < *tingere;* see TINGE] **—Syn.** *n.* **2.** whit, soupçon.

tind (tind), *v.t., v.i. British Dialect and Scottish.* to kindle; light. [related to TINDER]

tin·der (tin′dər), *n.* **1.** anything that catches fire easily. **2.** a material used to catch fire from a spark. [Old English *tynder*]

tin·der·box (tin′dər boks′), *n.* **1.** a box for holding tinder, flint, and steel for making a fire. **2.** a very inflammable or excitable thing or person.

tin·der·y (tin′dər ē), *adj.* of or like tinder; inflammable.

tine[1] (tīn), *n.* **1.** a sharp, projecting point or prong: *the tines of a fork.* **2.** a pointed branch of a deer's antler. [Old English *tind*]

tine[2] (tīn), *v.,* **tint, tint, tin·ing.** *Especially Scottish. —v.t.* to have or enjoy no longer; lose. *—v.i.* to be lost or destroyed; perish. Also, **tyne.** [Middle English *tinen* to fail; lose, ruin < Scandinavian (compare Old Icelandic *tȳna*)]

tin·e·a (tin′ē ə), *n.* any of various contagious skin diseases caused by fungi, especially ringworm. [< Latin *tinea* a gnawing worm, moth]

tin ear, *U.S. Slang.* **1. a.** inability to perceive small differences in sounds. **b.** tone-deafness. **c.** a tone-deaf person. **2.** a cauliflower ear.

tin·e·id (tin′ē id), *adj.* of or having to do with a family of clothes moths whose larvae are very destructive to woolen fabrics, etc. *—n.* a tineid moth. [< New Latin *Tineidae* a family of moths < *Tinea* the genus name < Latin *tinea* worm, moth]

tin fish, *Slang.* a torpedo.

tin foil, or **tin·foil**[1] (tin′foil′), *n.* **1.** a very thin sheet of tin, or of an alloy of tin and lead, used as a wrapping for candy, tobacco, etc. **2.** tin hammered or rolled into a thin sheet and coated with mercury, used for backing mirrors and other purposes.

tin-foil or **tin·foil**[2] (tin′foil′), *adj.* of, made of, or wrapped in tin foil.

ting[1] (ting), *v.i., v.t.* to make or cause to make a clear ringing sound. *—n.* a clear ringing sound. [ultimately imitative]

ting[2] (ting), *n.* thing[2].

ting-a-ling (ting′ə ling′), *n.* a clear, ringing sound, as of a small bell.

tinge (tinj), *v.,* **tinged, tinge·ing** or **ting·ing,** *n. —v.t.* **1.** to color slightly: *A drop of ink will tinge a glass of water.* **2.** to add a trace of some quality to; change slightly: *Sad memories tinged their present joy. Her remarks were tinged with envy.*
—n. **1.** a slight coloring or tint: *There is a tinge of red in her cheeks.* **2.** a very small amount; trace: *She likes just a tinge of lemon in her tea. There was a tinge of blame in his voice.*
[< Latin *tingere* to dye, color. Compare TAINT, TINCT, TINT.]

ting·er (tin′jər), *n.* a person or thing that tinges.

ting·i·ble (tin′jə bəl), *adj.* that can be tinged or colored.

tin·gis fly (tin′jis), any of a group of small, delicate, heteropterous insects whose wings and body are covered with a lacy network of lines; lacebug. [< New Latin *Tingis* the genus name]

tin·gle (ting′gəl), *v.,* **-gled, -gling,** *n. —v.i.* **1. a.** to have a feeling of thrills or a pricking, stinging feeling: *He tingled with excitement on his first train trip. His ears were tingling with cold after ice-skating on the pond.* **b.** to smart; blush: *cheeks tingling with shame.* **2.** to be thrilling; pass with a thrill: *The newspaper story tingled with excitement. Every note ... tingled through his huge frame* (Thackeray). **3.** to tinkle; jingle. *—v.t.* to cause to tingle; cause to feel thrills or a pricking, stinging feeling: *Shame tingled his cheeks.*
—n. **1.** a pricking, stinging feeling: *The cold caused a tingle in my ears.* **2.** a tinkle; jingle. [probably originally a variant of *tinkle*] **—tin′gling·ly,** *adv.*

tin·gler (ting′glər), *n.* something that causes tingling, as a blow or slap.

tin god, an inferior or mediocre person who assumes an autocratic or omnipotent role; a tin-pot ruler or authority: *People like that* [*become*] *tin gods in the neighborhood —people known for their habitual lawlessness* (New York Times).

tin hat, *Slang.* a metal helmet of the type worn by the British and American soldiers in World War I.

tin·horn (tin′hôrn′), *Slang. —adj.* cheap and showy; noisy and pretentious; pretending to be wealthy, skillful, or influential, but lacking what is required: *a tinhorn sport, a tinhorn gambler or lawyer. —n.* a tinhorn person.

ti·ni·ly (tī′nə lē), *adv.* in a tiny degree; minutely; diminutively: *Most of the action takes place in an enormous chamber containing a miniature of the establishment, in which everything that happens in Miss Alice's big house is tinily reënacted* (New Yorker).

ti·ni·ness (tī′nē nis), *n.* the quality of being tiny; extreme smallness; minuteness.

tink (tingk), *v.i.* to make a short, light, metallic sound; clink. *—n.* a tinking sound. [Middle English *tinken;* imitative]

tink·er (ting′kər), *n.* **1.** a man who mends pots, pans, etc., usually wandering from place to place. **2.** unskilled or clumsy work; activity that is rather useless. **3.** a person who does such work. **4.** any of various fishes or birds, such as a small or young mackerel, a silversides, or a kind of auk.
—v.t. to mend, patch, or repair, especially in an unskilled or clumsy way. *—v.i.* **1.** to work in an unskilled or clumsy way. **2.** to work or keep busy in a rather useless way; potter.
[Middle English *tynekere,* perhaps ultimately < *tin,* or *tink* to mend pots, solder] **—tink′er·er,** *n.*

tinker's damn or **dam,** a tinker's curse; something worthless or useless: *He doesn't care a tinker's damn what others think.*

tin·kle (ting′kəl), *v.,* **-kled, -kling,** *n. —v.i.* **1.** to make short, light, ringing sounds: *The sleigh bells tinkled.* **2.** to move or flow with a tinkling sound. *—v.t.* **1.** to cause to tinkle. **2. a.** to make known, call attention to, or express by tinkling: *The little clock tinkled out the hours.* **b.** to summon or attract by tinkling.
—n. a series of short, light, ringing sounds: *the tinkle of sleigh bells.*
[perhaps frequentative < Middle English *tinken* to ring, jingle; apparently ultimately imitative]

tin·kling (ting′kling), *adj.* that tinkles or jingles. *—n.* **1.** a tinkling noise. **2.** a blackbird of Jamaica that makes a tinkling sound. **—tin′kling·ly,** *adv.*

tin·kly (ting′klē), *adj.* **1.** full of tinkles; characterized by tinkling: *a tinkly toy. The tinkly temple bells* (Rudyard Kipling). **2.** sounding weak, cheap, or childish: *a tinkly tune, a tinkly title, tinkly sentiments.*

tin liz·zie (liz′ē), *U.S. Slang.* a very old car, such as a Model T or the like; jalopy.

tin liz·zy (liz′ē), *pl.* **tin liz·zies.** tin lizzie.

tin·man (tin′mən), *n., pl.* **-men. 1.** a man who works with tin; tinsmith. **2.** a dealer in tinware.

tinned (tind), *adj.* **1.** covered or coated with tin. **2.** put up or preserved in tins; canned.

tin·ner (tin′ər), *n.* **1.** a person who works with tin; tin-plater; tinsmith. **2.** *British.* a canner (of food). **3.** a person who works in a tin mine.

tin·ni·ly (tin′ə lē), *adv.* in a tinny manner.

tin·ni·ness (tin′ē nis), *n.* tinny quality.

tin·ni·tus (ti nī′təs), *n.* a ringing or hissing sensation in the ears, due to a defect of the auditory nerve. [< Latin *tinnītus, -ūs* < *tinnīre* to ring, tinkle]

tin·ny (tin′ē), *adj.,* **-ni·er, -ni·est. 1.** of, containing, or yielding tin. **2.** like tin in looks, sound, or taste: *These sardines have a tinny flavor.* **3.** *Fine Arts.* hard; metallic.

tin opener, *British.* can opener.

tin-pan (tin′pan′), *adj.* like tin; tinny.

tin-pan alley, 1. a district frequented by musicians, song writers, and song publishers. **2.** these people as a group.

tin-pan·ny (tin′pan′ē), *adj.* **1.** tin-pan. **2.** characteristic of tin-pan alley and the music it produces.

tin pants, *U.S.* lined canvas trousers soaked in paraffin to make them waterproof, worn by lumbermen, fishermen, etc.

tin plate, thin sheets of iron or steel coated with tin. Ordinary tin cans are made of tin plate.

tin-plate (tin′plāt′), *v.t.*, **-plat·ed, -plat·ing.** to plate or coat (sheets of iron or steel) with tin.

tin-plat·er (tin′plā′tər), *n.* a workman who makes tin plates.

tin-pot (tin′pot′), *adj.* suggesting a tin pot in worth; of inferior quality; small-time; paltry: *Trujillo had been the model for every tin-pot, medal-jingling dictator that ever rifled a Latin American treasury* (Time).

tin pyrites, stannite.

tin·sel (tin′səl), *n., v.*, **-seled, -sel·ing** or (*especially British*) **selled, -sel·ling,** *adj.* —*n.* **1.** glittering copper, brass, etc., in thin sheets, strips, threads, etc., used to trim Christmas trees, etc. **2.** anything showy but having little value: *That poverty of ideas which had been hitherto concealed under the tinsel of politeness* (Samuel Johnson). **3.** a thin cloth of silk or wool woven with threads of gold, silver, or copper: *She wore a beautiful dress of gold tinsel.*
—*v.t.* **1.** to trim with tinsel. **2.** to make showy or gaudy; cover the defects with or as if with tinsel.
—*adj.* of or like tinsel; showy but not worth much.
[apparently short for Middle French *estincelle* spark < Vulgar Latin *stincilla*, alteration of Latin *scintilla*. Doublet of SCINTILLA, STENCIL.] —**tin′sel·like′,** *adj.*

tin·sel·ly (tin′sə lē), *adj.* **1.** of or like tinsel. **2.** showy without real worth; tawdry.

tins·man (tinz′mən), *n., pl.* **-men.** a tinsmith.

tin·smith (tin′smith′), *n.* a person who works with tin; maker or repairer of tinware.

tin·smith·ing (tin′smith′ing), *n.* the work or trade of a tinsmith.

tin soldier, 1. a toy soldier made of tin. **2.** a person who plays at being a soldier.

tin spirit, a solution of tin in acid used as a mordant in dyeing.

tin·stone (tin′stōn′), *n.* cassiterite.

tint[1] (tint), *n.* **1.** a color or variety of a color; hue: *The picture was painted in several tints of blue.* **2.** a delicate or pale color. **3.** a variety of a color produced by mixing it with white. **4. a.** *Engraving.* an even and uniform shading produced by a series of fine parallel lines. **b.** *Printing.* a light-colored background, as for an illustration.
—*v.t.* to put a tint on; color slightly: *The walls were tinted gray.*
[alteration of *tinct* < Latin *tīnctus, -ūs* a dyeing < *tingere* to dye, tinge. Doublet of TAINT, TINCT.] —**tint′er,** *n.*

tint[2] (tint), *v.* the past tense and past participle of **tine**[2].

tin·tin·nab·u·lar (tin′tə nab′yə lər), *adj.* tintinnabulary: *a brisk . . . kind of tintinnabular alarm at the great gate* (Edward G. Bulwer-Lytton).

tin·tin·nab·u·lar·y (tin′tə nab′yə ler′ē), *adj.* of or having to do with bells or bell ringing; like a bell. [< Latin *tintinnābulum* bell (< *tintinnāre* jingle, ring < *tinnīre* to resound, tinkle) + English *-ary*]

tin·tin·nab·u·la·tion (tin′tə nab′yə lā′shən), *n.* the ringing of bells: *The tintinnabulation that so musically wells From the bells* (Edgar Allan Poe).
[American English < Latin *tintinnābulum* bell + English *-ation*]

tin·tin·nab·u·lous (tin′tə nab′yə ləs), *adj.* tintinnabulary.

tin·tom·e·ter (tin tom′ə tər), *n.* an instrument or apparatus for the exact determination of tints or colors.

tint·y (tin′tē), *adj.* **1.** full of tints. **2.** tinted or colored, as a painting.

tin·type (tin′tīp′), *n.* a photograph taken as a positive on a sheet of enameled tin or iron; ferrotype. [American English < *tin* + *type*]

tin·ware (tin′wãr′), *n.* articles made of tin, or an alloy of tin, such as dippers, pans, etc.

tin white, bluish white; silvery white. —**tin-white,** *adj.*

tin·work (tin′wėrk′), *n.* work done in tin or with tin.

tin·works (tin′wėrks′), *n.pl.* (*sing. in use*). a place where tin is mined or tinware is made.

ti·ny (tī′nē), *adj.*, **-ni·er, -ni·est,** *n.* —*adj.* very small; wee: *She settled in two tiny rooms* (W. Somerset Maugham). *From the hugest nebula to the tiniest atom* (James Harvey Robinson). —*n.* something tiny; a tiny child: *just like when you were a tiny* (John Galsworthy). [Middle English *tine;* origin uncertain] —**Syn.** *adj.* little, minute, microscopic.

-tion, *suffix.* **1.** act, process, or state of ____ing, as in *addition, fruition, opposition.* **2.** condition or state of being ____ed, as in *exhaustion, perfection.*
3. result of ____ing; thing that was ____ed, as in *inflection.*
4. thing or process that is ____ing, as in *apparition, attraction.*
[< Latin *-tiō, -ōnis* < *-t-*, stem ending of past participle + *-iō*, a noun suffix; or alteration of Old French *-cion* < Latin *-tiō*]

tip[1] (tip), *n., v.*, **tipped, tip·ping.** —*n.* **1.** the end part; end; point; top: *the tips of the fingers or toes, the tip of a hill or a baseball bat.* **2.** a small piece put on the end of something: *a new tip for a billiard cue, shoes with steel tips.*
—*v.t.* **1.** to put a tip or tips on; furnish with a tip: *spears tipped with steel.* **2.** to cover or adorn at the tip: *mountains tipped with snow. Sunlight tips the steeple.*
[origin uncertain]
—**Syn.** *n.* **1.** extremity.

tip[2] (tip), *v.*, **tipped, tip·ping,** *n., adj.* —*v.t.* **1.** to cause to have a slanting or sloping position; slant; slope: *She tipped the table toward her.* **2.** to upset; overturn: *He tipped over a glass of water.* **3.** to take off (a hat) in greeting. **4.** to empty out; dump: *She tipped the money in her purse onto the table.* —*v.i.* **1.** to slant; slope. **2.** to upset; overturn.
—*n.* **1.** a tipping or tilting; slope; slant. **2.** a place where vehicles are tipped and their contents dumped, as into the hold of a ship, into a railroad car, etc.
—*adj.* that empties itself by tipping: *a tip car, truck, or wagon.*
[Middle English *typpen;* origin uncertain]
—**Syn.** *v.t., v.i.* **1.** tilt, incline, lean. **2.** capsize.

tip[3] (tip), *n., v.*, **tipped, tip·ping.** —*n.* **1.** a small present of money; gratuity: *He gave the waiter a tip.* **2.** a piece of secret or confidential information: *a tip on a horse or on a stock.* **3.** a useful hint, suggestion, etc.: *a tip on how to save money, a tip on removing stains from clothing. Father gave me a helpful tip about pitching the tent where trees would shade it.*
—*v.t.* **1.** to give a tip or tips to: *to tip the doorman, waiter, and chambermaid at a hotel.* **2.** to give secret or confidential information to. **3.** *Slang.* to let have; give: *He tipped me an impudent wink* (Washington Irving). —*v.i.* to give a tip or tips.
tip off, *Informal.* **a.** to give secret or confidential information to: *to tip off a person about a good restaurant.* **b.** to warn: *The gamblers were tipped off that there would be a police raid.*
[origin uncertain]

tip[4] (tip), *n., v.*, **tipped, tip·ping.** —*n.* **1.** a light, sharp blow; tap. **2.** *Sports.* **a.** a glancing blow. **b.** a ball so hit: *a foul tip.*
—*v.t.* **1.** to hit lightly and sharply; tap. **2.** *Sports.* to hit (a ball) lightly with the edge of the bat; hit with a glancing blow.
[origin uncertain. Compare Low German *tippen* poke, touch lightly. Probably related to TIP[1].]

ti palm (tē), any of various Asian shade trees and shrubs; ti[2].

tip and run, a form of cricket in which the batsman must run for every hit.

tip-and-run (tip′ən run′), *adj. British.* characterized by fleeing immediately after attacking; hit-and-run: *The Dominican Republic provided a useful base for tip-and-run raids mounted by refugees against Cuba* (Graham Greene).

tip·burn (tip′bėrn′), *n.* a disease of potato, lettuce, and other plants in which excessive heat, humidity, etc., causes the tips of the leaves to turn brown: *Greenhouse experiments have shown that ozone concentrations of only four-tenths of a part per million can cause tipburn in onions* (Science News Letter).

tip·cart (tip′kärt′), *n.* a cart that can be tipped endwise or sideways for dumping.

tip·cat (tip′kat′), *n.* **1.** a game in which a short piece of wood (the cat), tapering at both ends, is hit with a stick so as to spring up, and then is hit to a distance by the same player. **2.** the tapered piece of wood used in this game; cat.

tiph·i·a (tif′ē ə), *n.* a digger wasp common in the eastern United States. [< New Latin *Tiphia* the genus name < Greek *típhē* a kind of insect]

ti·pi (tē′pē), *n., pl.* **-pis.** tepee.

tip-in (tip′in′), *n.* a scoring shot in basketball made by tipping a rebounding ball into the basket; tap-in.

tip·off (tip′ôf′, -of′), *n. Informal.* **1.** a piece of secret or confidential information. **2.** a warning. **3.** a tipping off.

tip·pa·ble[1] (tip′ə bəl), *adj.* that can be tipped, tilted, or overturned. [< *tip*[2] + *-able*]

tip·pa·ble[2] (tip′ə bəl), *adj.* that can be tipped, or given a gratuity. [< *tip*[3] + *-able*]

Tip·pe·ca·noe (tip′ə kə nü′), *n.* a campaign nickname given to William H. Harrison, ninth president of the United States. [< *Tippecanoe*, a river in Indiana (because Harrison led victorious American troops in a battle with the Indians near this river in 1811)]

-tipped, *combining form.* having a ____ tip: *Cork-tipped = having a cork tip.*

tip·per (tip′ər), *n.* a person who gives a tip or tips: *a good tipper, a heavy tipper, a cheap tipper.*

tip·pet (tip′it), *n.* **1.** a scarf for the neck and shoulders, usually with the ends hanging down in front. **2.** a long, narrow, hanging part or section of a hood, sleeve, or scarf. **3.** a band of silk or other material worn around the neck with its ends hanging down in front, worn by certain clergymen. [probably diminutive form of *tip*[1]]

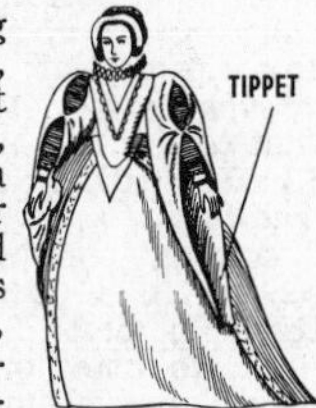

Tippet (def. 2)

tip·ple[1] (tip′əl), *v.*, **-pled, -pling,** *n.* —*v.t., v.i.* to drink (alcoholic liquor) often or too much: *I took to the bottle and tried to tipple away my cares* (Washington Irving). —*n.* alcoholic liquor; strong drink. [origin uncertain. Compare Norwegian *tipla* drip, tipple.]

tip·ple[2] (tip′əl), *n. U.S.* **1.** a mechanism by which freight cars, mining carts, etc., are tipped and emptied. **2.** a place where such vehicles are emptied by tipping, as in a coal yard, at or near a mine shaft, etc. [American English apparently < *tip*[2]]

tip·ple[3] (tip′əl), *v.t., v.i.*, **-pled, -pling.** *Dialect.* to tip over. [frequentative of *tip*[2]]

tip·pler[1] (tip′lər), *n.* a habitual drinker of alcoholic liquor: *You know the illusion habitual tipplers are subject to, that each appeal to the bottle is an exceptional occurrence* (William De Morgan).

tip·pler[2] (tip′lər), *n.* **1.** a person or thing that tips over. **2.** a mechanism for tipping and emptying; tipple. **3.** a kind of tumbler pigeon.

tip·py (tip′ē), *adj. Informal.* liable to tip, upset, or tilt: *a tippy canoe, a tippy table.*

tip·py-toe (tip′ē tō′), *n., v.i.*, **-toed, -toe·ing,** *adj., adv. Informal.* tiptoe.

tip sheet, *Informal.* a bulletin or newsletter furnishing tips for use in betting, speculation, etc.

tip·si·fy (tip′sə fī), *v.t.*, **-fied, -fy·ing.** to make tipsy; intoxicate slightly: *He tipsifies (with that filthy sherry-type) into indiscretion Othello's buddy and underling, Cassio* (Punch).

tip·si·ly (tip′sə lē), *adv.* in a tipsy manner.

tip·si·ness (tip′sē nis), *n.* tipsy quality or condition.

tip·staff (tip′staf′, -stäf′), *n., pl.* **-staves** or **-staffs. 1.** a staff tipped or capped with metal, formerly carried as a badge of office by certain officials. **2.** an official who carried such a staff, as a sheriff's officer, bailiff, or constable. **3.** an attendant or crier in a court of law.

tip·ster (tip′stər), *n. Informal.* a person who makes a business of furnishing private or secret information for use in betting, speculation, etc. [< *tip*[3] a hint + *-ster*]

tip·sy (tip′sē), *adj.*, **-si·er, -si·est. 1.** somewhat intoxicated, but not thoroughly drunk: *He was so tipsy that he wept upon my shoulder* (Robert Louis Stevenson). **2.** tipping easily; unsteady; tilted. [probably < *tip*[2]]

tipsy cake or **parson,** a dry cake soaked with wine and served with custard sauce.

tip table, a small table with a hinged top that can be tipped down when the table is out of use.

tip·toe (tip′tō′), *n., v.,* **-toed, -toe·ing,** *adj. adv.* —*n.* the tips of the toes.
on tiptoe, a. on one's toes: *to stand or walk on tiptoe.* **b.** eager: *The children were on tiptoe for vacation to begin.* **c.** in a secret manner: *He followed his cousin on tiptoe* (Thomas Hughes).
—*v.i.* to go or walk on tiptoe; step lightly: *She tiptoed quickly up the stairs.*
—*adj.* **1.** on tiptoe. **2.** eager; expectant. **3.** tripping; dancing. **4.** silent; stealthy.
—*adv.* on tiptoe: *I stood tiptoe upon a little hill* (Keats).

tip·top (tip′top′), *n.* **1.** the very top; highest point or part. **2.** the highest pitch or degree; the finest or best; acme.
—*adj.* **1.** at the very top or highest point. **2.** *Informal.* first-rate; excellent: *He is a tiptop man and may be a bishop* (George Eliot).
—*adv.* in the highest degree; superlatively.

tip·top·per (tip′top′ər), *n. Informal.* a tiptop person or thing: *Dryden . . . has shown himself such a tiptopper. I didn't think he had such grit in him* (William B. Maxwell).

tip-up (tip′up′), *adj.* designed to tip or tilt up, as a seat when not occupied: *Inside, most cars have . . . poor seat anchorage, dangerous tip-up seats* (Sunday Times). —*n.* **1.** a tip-up seat: *. . . theater with . . . fixed tip-ups to seat 700* (Punch). **2.** anything that tips or tilts up.

ti·rade (tī′rād, tə rād′), *n., v.,* **-rad·ed, -rad·ing.** —*n.* **1.** a long, vehement speech. **2.** a long, scolding speech. **3.** a passage or section in a poem dealing with a single theme or idea.
—*v.i.* to utter or write a tirade; inveigh or declaim vehemently: *They tirade against the influence of dogma* (R.B. Vaughan).
[< French *tirade* speech; a continuation; a drawing out < Italian *tirata* a drawing out < *tirare* to shoot < Vulgar Latin *tirāre*]
—**Syn.** *n.* **1.** harangue. **2.** diatribe.

ti·rage (ti räzh′), *n.* a printing or impression of a book. [< French *tirage* < Old French *tirer* to draw; origin uncertain]

ti·rail·leur (tē rä yœr′), *n.* a soldier trained as a skirmisher and sharpshooter. [< French *tirailleur* < Old French *tirer* shoot; (originally) draw a bow; origin uncertain]

tire[1] (tīr), *v.,* **tired, tir·ing,** *n.* —*v.t.* **1.** to make weary: *He tired his eyes by too much reading. The long walk tired her.* **2.** to wear down the patience, interest, or appreciation of because of dullness, excess, etc.: *Monotonous filing tired the office boy.* —*v.i.* to become weary: *He tires easily. The teacher tired of answering foolish questions. You think I shall tire of her!* (George Bernard Shaw).
tire out, to make very weary: *William, tired out by the voyage . . . determined to land in an open boat* (Macaulay).
—*n. Dialect or Informal.* tiredness; fatigue.
[Old English *tēorian*]
—**Syn.** *v.t.* **1.** exhaust, fatigue, fag. **2.** jade, satiate, bore. —**Ant.** *v.t.* **1.** refresh, revive.

tire[2] (tīr), *n., v.,* **tired, tir·ing.** —*n.* **1.** a hooplike band of rubber on the rim of a wheel, as of an automobile, bicycle, etc.: *Tires are either tubular and inflated with air, or solid.* **2.** a band of iron or steel fitted on the rim of a wheel, as of a wagon, railroad car, etc. —*v.t.* to furnish with a tire or tires. Also, *British,* **tyre.** [apparently < *tire*[3] covering]

tire[3] (tīr), *n., v.,* **tired, tir·ing.** *Archaic.* —*n.* **1.** attire; apparel; raiment. **2.** a covering or ornament for a woman's head; headdress: *She . . . braided the hair of her head, and put a tire on it* (Judith 10:3). —*v.t.* to attire or adorn. [short for *attire*]

tire[4] (tīr), *v.,* **tired, tir·ing.** *Obsolete.* —*v.i.* **1.** to pull, tug, or tear in feeding, as a falcon, hawk, or other bird of prey. **2.** to be engaged or intent (on or upon). —*v.t.* to tear at; pull; draw. [< Old French *tirer;* origin uncertain]

tire[5] (tīr), *n. Obsolete.* a simultaneous firing of a group of guns. [Middle French *tir* < Old French *tirer;* origin uncertain]

tire cord, rayon or nylon yarn corded and coated with rubber to reinforce the casing of a pneumatic tire.

tired (tīrd), *adj.* **1.** weary; wearied; exhausted: *The team was tired but each boy continued to play as hard as he could.* **2.** sick (of); impatient (with): *Oh, you make me tired!* (Sinclair Lewis). [originally, past participle of *tire*[1]] —**tired′ly,** *adv.* —**tired′ness,** *n.*
—**Syn. 1. Tired, weary, exhausted** mean having physical or mental strength, energy, and power of endurance lowered or drained by hard or long-continued work, strain, etc. **Tired** is the general word: *I am tired, but I must get back to work.* **Weary** means feeling worn out and unable or unwilling to go on: *Weary shoppers wait for buses and streetcars.* **Exhausted** means without enough energy or endurance left to be able to go on: *Exhausted by near starvation and bitter winds, the man lay in a stupor.*

-tired, *combining form.* having —— tires: *A rubber-tired vehicle = a vehicle having rubber tires.*

tire·less (tīr′lis), *adj.* **1.** never becoming tired; requiring little rest: *a tireless worker.* **2.** never stopping; unceasing: *tireless efforts.* —**tire′less·ly,** *adv.* —**tire′less·ness,** *n.* —**Syn. 1.** indefatigable.

tire·man (tīr′man′, -mən), *n., pl.* **-men.** a person who manufactures or deals in tires: *Tiremen now expect total passenger tire shipments will be 82.5 million or more* (Wall Street Journal).

Ti·re·si·as (tī rē′sē əs, -shē-; tə-), *n. Greek Legend.* a seer of Thebes who saw Athena bathing. She blinded him for it, but in compensation gave him a staff to serve as eyes, understanding of birds' language, and prophetic vision.

tire·some (tīr′səm), *adj.* tiring; boring: *a tiresome speech.* —**tire′some·ly,** *adv.* —**tire′some·ness,** *n.* —**Syn.** wearisome, irksome.
—**Syn. Tiresome, tedious** mean tiring or boring, or both. **Tiresome** implies being dull and uninteresting: *Our neighbor is goodhearted, but I find her tiresome.* **Tedious** implies being too long, slow, or repetitious: *Weeding a garden is tedious work. His sermons are tedious.*

tire·wom·an (tīr′wům′ən), *n., pl.* **-wom·en.** *Archaic.* a lady's maid. [< *tire*[3] + *woman*]

tir·ing glass (tīr′ing), *Archaic.* a mirror used in dressing, combing the hair, etc.

tiring house, (formerly) a small structure in which actors dressed for the stage: *an Elizabethan tiring house.*

tiring room, a dressing room, especially in a theater.

tirl (tėrl), *Scottish.* —*v.t., v.i.* to thrill; quiver. —*n.* a thrill; tremor.

tirl·ing pin (tėr′ling), *Scottish.* a door knocker.

ti·ro (tī′rō), *n., pl.* **-ros.** tyro.

Ti·ro·le·an (tə rō′lē ən), *adj., n.* Tirolese. Also, **Tyrolean.**

Tir·o·lese (tir′ə lēz′, -lēs′), *adj.* of or having to do with the Tirol, a region in the Alps, chiefly in Austria and partly in Italy, or its inhabitants. —*n.* a native of the Tirol. Also, **Tyrolese.**

Ti·ro·ni·an (tī rō′nē ən), *adj.* of or having to do with Tiro, the learned freedman and amanuensis of Cicero, who introduced a system of shorthand used by the ancient Romans.

tir·ra·lir·ra (tir′ə lir′ə), *n.* **1.** the note of the lark. **2.** a similar sound uttered as an exclamation of delight or gaiety. [imitative]

tir·ri·vee (tėr′ə vē), *n. Scottish.* a fit or show of ill temper; angry outburst. [origin unknown]

tis (tēz), *n.* plural of **ti**[2].

'tis (tiz), it is: *That he is mad, 'tis true . . . And pity 'tis 'tis true* (Shakespeare).

ti·sane (ti zan′; French tē zȧn′), *n.* a decoction used or to be used as medicine: *an herb tisane.* [< Middle French *tizanne* < Latin *ptisana* < Greek *ptisánē* peeled barley; drink of barley water < *ptíssein* to peel, winnow]

Tish·ah B'Ab (tish′ä bə äv′, bäv′), a Jewish fast day, the 9th day of Ab, in remembrance of the destruction of the first Temple by the Babylonians in 586 B.C. and the destruction of the second Temple by Titus in 70 A.D. [< Hebrew *tish'āh bě'ābh*]

Tish·ah bov (tish′ä bôv′), Tishah B'Ab.

Tish·ri (tish′rē), *n.* the seventh month of the Hebrew ecclesiastical year or the first of the civil year, corresponding to October and sometimes part of September. [< Hebrew *Tishrī* < Babylonian *tashritu*]

Ti·siph·o·ne (ti sif′ə nē), *n. Greek Mythology.* one of the three Furies or Erinyes (Alecto and Megaera being the other two).

tis·sue (tish′ü), *n., v.,* **-sued, -su·ing.** —*n.* **1.** *Biology.* the substance forming the parts of animals or plants; mass of cells. The chief kinds of tissue in higher animals are the epithelial, connective, muscular, and nervous tissues. **2.** a thin, light, or delicate cloth: *Her dress was of silk tissue.* **3.** a web; network: *Her whole story was a tissue of lies.* **4.** tissue paper. **5.** a thin, soft, absorbent paper used to wipe the face, etc.; facial tissue.
—*v.t.* **1.** to make into a tissue; weave. **2.** to clothe or adorn with tissue.
[< Old French *tissu,* (originally) past participle of *tistre* to weave < Latin *texere.* Compare TEXTILE, TEXTURE.]

tissue culture, 1. the science of keeping bits of animal tissue alive and growing in an artificial medium. **2.** the process of doing this.

tissue paper, a very thin, soft, unsized paper, used for wrapping, making carbon copies, etc.

tit[1] (tit), *n.* **1.** a titmouse. **2.** any of certain other small birds. **3.** a runty or worthless horse; nag. **4.** *Slang.* a girl or young woman of loose character; hussy; minx. [compare Old Icelandic *tittr* titmouse; small peak, pin]

tit[2] (tit), *n.* a nipple; teat. [Old English *titt.* Related to TEAT.]

tit[3] (tit), *n. Obsolete.* a blow. [apparently variant of earlier *tip for tap*]

tit., title.

Tit., Titus (book of the New Testament).

Ti·tan (tī′tən), *n.* **1.** *Greek Mythology.* **a.** one of a family of giants, children of Uranus (Heaven) and Gaea (Earth), who ruled the world before Zeus, the son of the Titan Cronus, overthrew them and founded the Olympian dynasty. Prometheus and Atlas were Titans. **b.** the sun god, Helios (Sol), son of the Titan Hyperion. **2.** the largest satellite of Saturn, the only satellite in the solar system known to have an atmosphere. **3.** Also, **titan.** a person or thing having enormous size, strength, power, etc.; giant.
—*adj.* Also, **titan. 1.** of or having to do with the Titans. **2.** very powerful; gigantic; huge.

ti·tan·ate (tī′tə nāt), *n.* a salt or ester of titanic acid.

Ti·tan·esque (tī′tə nesk′), *adj.* Titanic.

Ti·tan·ess (tī′tə nis), *n.* a female Titan; giantess.

ti·ta·ni·a (tī tā′nē ə), *n.* **1.** titanium dioxide; titanic oxide. **2.** a synthetic gem as brilliant but not as hard as a diamond, made by heating titanic oxide at a very high temperature.

Ti·ta·ni·a (ti tā′nē ə, tī-), *n.* the queen of the fairies and wife of Oberon, in Shakespeare's *Midsummer Night's Dream.*

ti·tan·ic (tī tan′ik, ti-), *adj.* of or containing titanium, especially with a valence of four. [< *titan*(ium) + *-ic*]

Ti·tan·ic (tī tan′ik), *adj.* **1.** of or like the Titans: *The figure of Napoleon was Titanic* (Thomas Carlyle). **2.** Also, **titanic.** having great size, strength, or power; gigantic; colossal; huge: *Titanic energy. Here once, through an alley Titanic, Of cypress I roamed* (Edgar Allan Poe).

titanic acid, 1. titanic oxide. **2.** any of several weak acids derived from titanic oxide.

titanic oxide, a compound, the dioxide of titanium, occurring in nature in rutile, anatase, and brookite, or prepared artificially as a white powder. It is used in paints and dyes. *Formula:* TiO_2

ti·tan·if·er·ous (tī′tə nif′ər əs), *adj.* containing or yielding titanium. [< *titani*(um) + *-ferous*]

Ti·tan·ism (tī′tə niz əm), *n.* the spirit or quality typical of the Titans, especially that of revolt against the established order, defiance of convention, etc.

ti·tan·ite (tī′tə nīt), *n.* a mineral, a silicate and titanite of calcium, occurring in igneous rocks; sphene. *Formula:* $CaTiSiO_5$ [< German *Titanit* < *Titanium* titanium + *-it* -ite[1]]

ti·tan·it·ic (tī′tə nit′ik), *adj.* of or having to do with titanium.

ti·ta·ni·um (tī tā′nē əm, ti-), *n.* a metallic chemical element with properties similar to those of silicon, occurring in rutile, ilmenite, brookite, and various other minerals. When isolated it is a dark-gray powder with a metallic luster. It is used in making steel and alloys. *Symbol:* Ti; *at.wt.:* (C^{12}) 47.90 or (O^{16}) 47.90; *at.no.:* 22; *valence:* 2, 3, 4. [< German *Titanium* < Latin *Tītan* Titan]

titanium dioxide, titanic oxide.

titanium oxide, any oxide of titanium, especially titanic oxide.

titanium tetrachloride, a colorless liquid with a sharp acid odor, used in the production of titanium metal from the ore.

When combined with water or moist air, it yields titanic oxide. In the presence of ammonia and moist air it yields a dense white smoke used for smoke screens and skywriting. *Formula:* $TiCl_4$

Ti·tan·o·ma·chy (tī′tə nom′ə kē), *n. Greek Mythology.* the war between the Titans and the gods of Olympus, led by Zeus. [< Greek *tītáno-* (< *Tītā́n* Titan) + *-machiā́* < *máchesthai* fight]

ti·tan·o·saur (tī′tə nə sôr), *n.* a Titanosaurus.

Ti·tan·o·sau·rus (tī′tə nə sôr′əs), *n.* any of a group of large herbivorous dinosaurs present in the Cretaceous era, especially in South America. [< New Latin *Titanosaurus* the genus name < Greek *Tītā́n* a Titan + *saûros* lizard]

ti·tan·o·there (tī′tə nə thir), *n.* an extinct, hoofed mammal like a rhinoceros, with a long, broad skull, very small brain, and a pair of horns over the nose. Its remains were found in the Tertiary formations of North America. [< Greek *tītáno-* (< *Tītā́n* a Titan) + *thēríon* beast]

ti·tan·o·the·ri·um (tī′tə nə thir′ē əm), *n.* a titanothere. [< New Latin *Titanotherium*]

ti·tan·ous (tī tan′əs, tī′tə nəs), *adj.* containing titanium, especially with a valence of three.

tit·bit (tit′bit′), *n.* a tidbit. [variant of *tidbit*]

ti·ter (tī′tər, tē′-), *n. Chemistry.* **1.** the weight of a pure substance which is contained in, would react with, or would be equivalent to, a unit volume of a reagent solution, usually expressed in milligrams of solute per milliliter of solution. **2.** the amount of a standard solution necessary to produce a certain result in titration. Also, *especially British,* **titre.** [< French, Old French *titre,* proportions in alloyed metal; quality, (originally) inscription, learned borrowing from Latin *titulus.* Doublet of TILDE, TITLE, TITTLE.]

tit·fer (tit′fər), *n. British Slang.* **1.** a derby hat; bowler. **2.** any hat: *I was naturally thinking of the Pope's tiara. Here we have a jewelled titfer of great beauty* (Punch). [short for *tit for tat,* rhyming slang for *derby hat*]

tit for tat, blow for blow; like for like: *She hasn't the courage to give him tit for tat* (Maria Edgeworth). [perhaps alteration of earlier *tip for tap* blow for blow]

tith·a·ble (tī′ᴛʜə bəl), *adj.* subject to the payment of tithes: *tithable land, produce, or income.*

tithe (tīᴛʜ), *n., v.,* **tithed, tith·ing.** —*n.* **1.** a tenth part; one tenth. **2.** a very small part; fraction. **3.** any small tax, levy, etc.
tithes, *British.* a tax of one tenth of the yearly produce of land, animals, and personal work, paid for the support of the church and the clergy: *The whole tithes of the diocese were then paid to the bishop* (Richard Burn).
—*v.t.* **1.** to put a tax of a tenth on. **2.** to pay a tithe on. **3.** to exact or collect a tithe from. —*v.i.* to give one tenth of one's income to the church or to charity.
[Old English *tēotha* tenth]

tithe barn, (in Great Britain) a barn built formerly to hold the tithes received by a parson or parish church: *There's a tithe barn on my farm which was built a couple of centuries ago when labour was cheap, and slates and timber even cheaper* (Punch).

tithe pig, a pig due or given as a tithe.

tith·er (tī′ᴛʜər), *n.* **1.** a payer or a receiver of tithes. **2.** a supporter of a system of ecclesiastical tithes.

tithes (tīᴛʜz), *n.pl.* See under **tithe,** *n.*

tith·ing (tī′ᴛʜing), *n.* **1.** the payment or exacting of tithes. **2.** one tenth given to the church; tithe. **3. a.** a company of ten householders in the old system of frankpledge in England. **b.** an administrative unit in parts of rural England, descended from this system.

tith·ing·man (tī′ᴛʜing mən), *n., pl.* **-men.** a former town officer in England whose duties were like those of a policeman.

Ti·tho·nus (ti thō′nəs), *n. Greek Mythology.* the son of Laomedon, King of Troy, and beloved of Eos (Aurora, the Dawn), who secured from the gods immortality for himself but not immortal youth, so that he shriveled up and finally was changed into a grasshopper by Eos.

ti·ti[1] (ti tē′), *n.* any of certain small monkeys of South America, such as the squirrel monkey. Also, **teetee.** [< Spanish *tití* < the Tupi (perhaps Brazil) name]

ti·ti[2] (tē′tē), *n.* any of several shrubs or small trees of the southern United States, having glossy leaves and spikes of fragrant white flowers. [American English; origin unknown]

ti·tian (tish′ən), *n., adj.* auburn; golden red. [< *Titian,* about 1477-1576, a Venetian painter who favored this color in his pictures]

tit·il·late (tit′ə lāt), *v.t., v.i.,* **-lat·ed, -lat·ing. 1.** to excite pleasantly; stimulate agreeably. **2.** to tickle. [< Latin *tītillāre* (with English *-ate*[1]) to tickle]

tit·il·lat·ing (tit′ə lā′ting), *adj.* that titillates; pleasantly exciting or stimulating: *The result is interesting but somehow less titillating than an old Kirby fan might have anticipated* (New Yorker). —**tit′il·lat′ing·ly,** *adv.*

tit·il·la·tion (tit′ə lā′shən), *n.* **1.** pleasant excitement; agreeable stimulation: *Thrills and titillations from games of hazard* (Thomas Hardy). **2.** a tickling.

tit·il·la·tive (tit′ə lā′tiv), *adj.* tending to titillate or tickle.

tit·il·la·tor (tit′ə lā′tər), *n.* a person or thing that titillates; tickler.

tit·i·vate (tit′ə vāt), *v.t., v.i.,* **-vat·ed, -vat·ing.** *Informal.* to make smart or spruce; dress up; prink. Also, **tittivate.** [earlier *tiddivate,* perhaps < *tidy* + a pretended classical ending]

tit·i·va·tion (tit′ə vā′shən), *n. Informal.* a titivating; dressing or sprucing up.

tit·lark (tit′lärk′), *n.* a small bird somewhat like a lark; pipit. [< *tit*[1] + *lark*[1]]

ti·tle (tī′təl), *n., v.,* **-tled, -tling.** —*n.* **1. a.** the name of a book, poem, play, picture, song, etc. **b.** a printing of this at the beginning of a book. **c.** a title page. **d.** a descriptive heading or caption, as of a chapter or section of a book, etc. **2.** a name showing rank, occupation, or condition in life: *King, duke, lord, countess, doctor, professor, Madame and Miss are titles.* **3.** any descriptive or distinctive name: *Horatio in Shakespeare's Hamlet deserved the title of a true friend.* **4.** a first-place position; championship: *to win the heavyweight title.* **5.** in law: **a.** a legal right to the possession of property. **b.** the legal evidence, especially a document, showing such a right. When a house is sold, the seller gives title to the buyer. **c.** all of the things that make up legal ownership. **d.** a subdivision of a statute or law book. **e.** the descriptive or formal heading of a legal document, statute, etc. **f.** the heading that names the cause of or right to the action. **6.** an alleged or recognized right; claim: *What title does he have to my gratitude?* **7.** *Ecclesiastical.* **a.** evidence of an assured benefice, or of a definite source of income, required by a bishop before he ordains a candidate. **b.** any of the principal Roman Catholic churches of Rome whose incumbents are cardinals. **8.** *Obsolete.* **a.** an inscription placed on or over an object, giving its name or describing it. **b.** a placard hung up in a theater giving the name of the piece, etc.
—*v.t.* **1.** to call by a title; term. **2.** to furnish with a title; name; entitle.
[< Old French *title,* learned borrowing from Latin *titulus* inscription (in Late Latin, title of a book). Doublet of TILDE, TITER, TITTLE.]
—**Syn.** *n.* **1. a.** See **name.**

➔ **titles.** In formal usage the titles of books, long poems, plays published as separate volumes, and the names of magazines and newspapers are underlined (italics in print). Capitals are used for the first and last words, for all nouns, pronouns, verbs, adjectives, and adverbs, and for prepositions of more than five letters: *Smarter and Smoother; Marching On; Life Behind Bars; A Streetcar Named Desire; The Atlantic Monthly.* Titles of short stories, short poems, songs, essays, and magazine articles are usually put in quotation marks: "Weep No More, My Lady"; "Atomic Power in Tomorrow's World."

ti·tled (tī′təld), *adj.* having a title, especially a title of rank: *She married a titled nobleman.*

title deed, a document showing that a person owns certain property.

ti·tle·hold·er (tī′təl hōl′dər), *n.* the holder of a championship; champion: *the heavyweight titleholder.*

title page, the page at the beginning of a book that contains the title, the author's or editor's name, and usually the publisher and place and date of publication.

title rôle or **part,** the part or character for which a play, opera, operetta, etc., is named. Hamlet and Othello are title rôles.

ti·tlist (tī′tlist), *n.* a titleholder.

tit·mouse (tit′mous′), *n., pl.* **-mice.** any of certain small birds with short bills and dull-colored feathers, related to the nuthatches and found throughout the Northern Hemisphere. A chickadee is one kind of titmouse. [Middle English *titemose* < *tit* titmous + Old English *māse* titmouse; influenced by *mouse*]

Common Bush Titmouse (4½ in. long)

Ti·to·ism (tē′tō iz əm), *n.* the principles and practices of Marshal Tito, Yugoslav premier, especially the stressing of a form of Communism that places national above international interests.

Ti·to·ist (tē′tō ist), *adj.* of or having to do with Titoism. —*n.* a supporter of Titoism.

ti·trant (tī′trənt), *n.* the substance added in titration.

ti·trate (tī′trāt, tit′rāt), *v.,* **-trat·ed, -trat·ing,** *n.* —*v.t., v.i.* to analyze or be analyzed by titration. —*n.* a solution to be analyzed by titration. [< French *titrer* (with English *-ate*[1]) < *titre;* see TITER]

ti·tra·tion (tī trā′shən, ti-), *n.* the process or method of determining the amount of some substance present in a solution by measuring the amount of a different substance that must be added to cause chemical change.

ti·tra·tor (tī′trā tər, tit′rā-), *n.* an instrument used in titration.

ti·tre (tī′tər, tē′-), *n. Especially British.* titer.

ti·tri·met·ric (tī′trə met′rik), *adj.* of or having to do with measurement by titration: *titrimetric analysis.*

tit-tat-toe (tit′tat tō′), *n.* tick-tack-toe.

tit·ter (tit′ər), *v.i.* to laugh in a half-restrained manner, because of nervousness or silliness; giggle. —*n.* a tittering; tittering laugh. —**tit′ter·er,** *n.* —**tit′ter·ing·ly,** *adv.*

tit·ter-tot·ter (tit′ər tot′ər), *n. Dialect.* the sport of seesaw; seesaw. [varied reduplication < *titter* or *totter*]

tit·tie (tit′ē), *n. Scottish Informal.* titty.

tit·ti·vate (tit′ə vāt), *v.,* **-vat·ed, -vat·ing.** *Informal.* titivate.

tit·ti·va·tion (tit′ə vā′shən), *n. Informal.* titivation.

tit·tle (tit′əl), *n.* **1.** a very little bit; particle; whit. **2.** a small stroke or point in writing or printing, as a comma, the dot over the letter *i,* etc. **3.** a very small part, originally of something written: *one jot or one tittle shall in no wise pass from the law* (Matthew 5:18). [< Medieval Latin *titulus* diacritical mark, vowel point, point of a letter < Latin, title, superscription. Doublet of TILDE. TITER, TITLE.]

tit·tle-tat·tle (tit′əl tat′əl), *n., v.,* **-tled, -tling.** gossip. [varied reduplication of *tattle*]

tit·tle-tat·tler (tit′əl tat′lər), *n.* a gossip.

tit·tup (tit′əp), *v.,* **-tuped, -tup·ing** or (*especially British*) **-tupped, -tup·ping,** *n.* —*v.i.* **1.** to walk in an affected or prancing manner. **2.** (of a horse or other animal) to canter or gallop easily; prance; caper. **3.** (of a boat) to toss with abrupt or jerky movements. —*n. Dialect.* a prancing.

tit·tup·y (tit′ə pē), *adj. British Dialect.* **1.** tittuping; prancing or lively. **2.** shaky or unsteady, as furniture.

tit·ty (tit′ē), *n., pl.* **-ties.** *Scottish Informal.* sister (referring to a young woman or girl). [probably imitation of infantile pronunciation of *sissie* sister]

tit·u·bate (tich′ú bāt), *v.i.,* **-bat·ed, -bat·ing. 1.** to stagger; totter; stumble. **2.** to falter in speaking; stammer. [< Latin *titubāre* (with English *-ate*[1])]

tit·u·ba·tion (tich′ú bā′shən), *n.* an unsteady gait or a tottering, associated with spinal and cerebral disorders. [< Latin *titubātiō, -ōnis* < *titubāre* to stagger]

tit·u·lar (tich′ə lər, tit′yə-), *adj.* **1.** in title or name only; nominal: *He is a titular prince without any power. In Australia . . . chancellors are but titular heads of universities* (Manchester Guardian). **2.** having a title; titled. **3.** having to do with a title. **4. a.** of

or having to do with certain Roman Catholic churches called titles. **b.** deriving title from a see, etc. (now only nominal): *a titular bishop.*
—*n.* **1.** a person or clergyman who holds a title. **2.** a person or thing that a title or name, especially of a church, is taken from. [< Latin *titulus* (see TITLE) + English *-ar*]
tit·u·lar·ly (tich′ə lər lē, tit′yə-), *adv.* with respect to title; nominally.
tit·u·lar·y (tich′ə ler′ē, tit′yə-), *adj., n., pl.* **-lar·ies.** titular.
Ti·tus (tī′təs), *n.* **1.** a convert and companion of Saint Paul. **2.** an epistle of the New Testament written to Titus by Saint Paul. Full title, *The Epistle of Paul to Titus.*
Titus An·dron·i·cus (an dron′ə kəs), a tragedy by Shakespeare, published in 1594.
Ti·u (tē′ü), *n.* the Teutonic god of war and of the sky, identified with the Norse god Tyr.
Tiv (tiv), *n.* **1.** a member of an agricultural people of central Nigeria. **2.** the language of this people, related to Efik and Bantu.
tiv·y (tiv′ē), *v.,* **tiv·ied, tiv·y·ing,** *interj.* —*v.i.* to rush headlong, as a hunter on horseback. —*interj.* tantivy. [short for *tantivy*]
tiz·zy[1] (tiz′ē), *n., pl.* **-zies.** *Slang.* a very excited state; dither. [origin uncertain]
tiz·zy[2] (tiz′ē), *n., pl.* **-zies.** *British Slang.* a sixpenny piece; sixpence. [origin unknown]
tk., 1. track. **2.** truck.
T.K.O., TKO (no periods), or **t.k.o.,** (in boxing) a technical knockout.
Tl (no period), thallium (chemical element).
T.L. or **TL** (no periods), trade-last.
T.L.C. or **TLC** (no periods), *Informal.* tender loving care: *Babies who get T.L.C. probably will be better able to stand stresses and less likely to develop heart trouble . . . when they grow up than babies not so gently handled* (Science News Letter).
Tlin·git (tling′git), *n. sing. and pl.* **1.** (*sing. in use*) an American Indian linguistic family comprising languages spoken by a number of tribes in southeastern Alaska and adjacent British Columbia. **2.** (*pl. in use*) the Indians of these tribes. —*adj.* of or having to do with these Indians or their languages.
Tlin·kit (tling′kit), *n.* Tlingit.
t.l.o., total loss only (a condition of marine insurance covering the total destruction of a vessel).
t.m., true mean.
Tm (no period), thulium (chemical element).
T-man (tē′man′), *n., pl.* **-men.** *Informal.* an agent or investigator of the United States Treasury. [American English; abbreviation for *Treasury man*]
T-maze (tē′māz), *n.* a maze used in experimental psychology, consisting of one or more sections shaped like a T, at the intersection of which the subject has to choose whether to go right or left: *They were repeating a well-known experiment with rats selectively bred for good ("maze-bright") or bad ("maze-dull") performances in a T-maze* (New Scientist).
tme·sis (tmē′sis), *n. Grammar.* the separation of the elements of a compound word or a phrase by the interposition of another word or words, as *chit and chat* for *chit-chat; to us-ward* (II Peter 3:9) for *toward us.* [< Late Latin *tmēsis* < Greek *tmēsis* (originally) a cutting < *témnein* to cut]
TMV (no periods), tobacco mosaic virus.
tn., 1. ton. **2.** town.
Tn (no period), thoron (chemical element).
tng., training.
TNT (no periods) or **T.N.T.,** trinitrotoluene, a colorless solid used as an explosive in hand grenades, torpedoes, etc.
to (tü; *unstressed* tů, tə), *prep.* **1.** in the direction of; toward: *Stand with your back to the wall. Go to the right.* **2.** as far as; until: *wet to the skin, rotten to the core, from dawn to dusk, a fight to the bitter end.* **3.** for; for the purpose of; for use with: *a means to an end, a horse bred to the plow. Mother came to the rescue.* **4.** toward or into the position, condition, or state of: *He went to sleep.* **5.** so as to produce, cause, or result in: *To my amazement, he jumped.* **6.** into: *She tore the letter to pieces.* **7.** by: *a fact known to few.* **8.** along with; with: *We danced to the music.* **9.** compared with: *The score was 9 to 5.* **10.** in agreement or accordance with: *a decision not to my liking.* **11.** as seen or understood by: *a symptom alarming to the doctor. To my mind, the situation is not yet hopeless.* **12.** belonging with; of: *the key to my room.* **13.** in honor of: *The soldiers drank to the king.* **14.** on; against: *Fasten it to the wall.* **15.** about; concerning: *What did he say to that?* **16.** included, contained, or involved in: *four apples to the pound, a book without much to it.* **17.** *To* is used to show action toward: *Give the book to me. Speak to her.* **18.** *To* is used with the infinitive form of verbs: *He likes to read. The birds began to sing. To err is human; to forgive . . . divine* (Alexander Pope).
—*adv.* **1.** forward: *He wore his cap wrong side to.* **2.** together; touching; closed: *The door slammed to.* **3.** to action or work: *We turned to gladly.* **4.** to consciousness: *She came to.*
to and fro, first one way and then back again; back and forth: *And the Lord said unto Satan, Whence comest thou? Then Satan answered . . . From going to and fro in the earth* (Job 1:7).
[Old English *tō*]
t.o., 1. table of organization. **2.** turn over. **3.** turnover.
T/O, table of organization.
toad (tōd), *n.* **1.** any of a group of small, tailless amphibians somewhat like a frog, living most of the time on land rather than in water. **2.** any tailless amphibian; any frog. **3.** any of certain other animals, such as the horned toad. **4.** a person or thing regarded as disgusting, contemptible, etc. [Middle English *tode,* Old English *tāde, tādige*]

Common American Toad (def. 1)
(1¾ to 4¼ in. long)

toad·eat·er (tōd′ē′tər), *n.* a fawning flatterer; sycophant; toady. [originally, a charlatan's attendant who pretended to eat toads, so his master might "cure" him of their poison]
toad·eat·ing (tōd′ē′ting), *n.* fawning flattery; sycophancy. —*adj.* sycophantic.
toad·fish (tōd′fish′), *n., pl.* **-fish·es** or (*collectively*) **-fish. 1.** any of various fishes with thick heads, wide mouths, and slimy skin without scales. **2.** a puffer.
toad·flax (tōd′flaks′), *n.* **1.** a common weed of the figwort family with yellow-and-orange flowers; butter-and-eggs; flaxweed. **2.** any other plants of the same genus.
toad-in-the-hole (tōd′in ᴛʜə hōl′), *n. British.* a dish consisting of meat baked in batter.
toad spit or **spittle,** a frothy secretion found on plants, exuded by the nymphs of certain insects; cuckoo spit.
toad·stone (tōd′stōn′), *n.* any of various stones or stonelike objects once believed to have been formed in the head or body of a toad, formerly worn as jewels or amulets.
toad·stool (tōd′stül′), *n.* **1.** any of various fungi, especially the agarics, that have a round, disklike top and a slender stalk, and grow on decaying vegetable matter; mushroom. **2.** any poisonous mushroom. **3.** any of various other fungi, such as a puffball, morel, etc.

Toadstools (def. 1)

toad·y (tō′dē), *n., pl.* **toad·ies,** *v.,* **toad·ied, toad·y·ing.** —*n.* **1.** a fawning flatterer; sycophant. **2.** a humble dependent. —*v.i.* to be or act like a toady. —*v.t.* to fawn upon; flatter. [perhaps alteration of *toadeater*]
toad·y·ish (tō′dē ish), *adj.* of or like a toady. —**toad′y·ish·ly,** *adv.*
toad·y·ism (tō′dē iz əm), *n.* the behavior of a toady; interested flattery; mean servility.
to-and-fro (tü′ən frō′), *adj.* back-and-forth. —*n.* a back-and-forth movement: *She, like some wild creature newly-caged, commenced a to-and-fro* (Tennyson).
toast[1] (tōst), *n.* a slice or slices of bread browned by heat. [< verb]
—*v.t., v.i.* **1.** to brown by heat: *We toasted the bread.* **2.** to heat thoroughly: *He toasted his feet before the open fire.* [< Old French *toster* < Vulgar Latin *tostāre* < Latin *torrēre* to parch]
toast[2] (tōst), *n.* **1. a.** a person whose health is proposed and drunk: *"The King" was the first toast drunk by the officers.* **b.** an event, institution, or sentiment in honor of which a group is requested to drink. **2.** a popular or celebrated person, especially a beautiful or socially prominent woman: *The young pianist was the reigning toast of the town.* **3.** the act of drinking to the health of a person or thing. **4.** a call on another or others to drink to some person or thing.
—*v.t.* to propose a toast; drink to the health or in honor of: *The men toasted the general.*
—*v.i.* to drink toasts.
[< *toast*[1], from the use of spiced toast to flavor drinks]
toast·er[1] (tōs′tər), *n.* **1.** a person who toasts something. **2.** an electric appliance for toasting bread, etc.
toast·er[2] (tōs′tər), *n.* a person who proposes or joins in a toast.
toast·ing fork (tōs′ting), **1.** a long-handled fork used to toast cheese, bread, marshmallows, etc. over live coals. **2.** a sword; rapier.
toast·mas·ter (tōst′mas′tər, -mäs′-), *n.* **1.** a person who presides at a dinner and introduces the speakers: *I was at the cattle show on the 6th, and executed the delegated task of toastmaster* (Scott). **2.** a person who proposes toasts.
toast·mis·tress (tōst′mis′tris), *n.* a woman toastmaster.
toast·y (tōs′tē), *adj.,* **toast·i·er, toast·i·est. 1.** of or like toast; having a slightly burnt flavor. **2.** comfortably warm: *. . . a trim hip-length jacket—toasty wool fleece in a very bright plaid—with a snug turtle neck* (New Yorker).
Tob., Tobit.
to·bac·co (tə bak′ō), *n., pl.* **-cos** or **-coes. 1. a.** the prepared leaves of certain plants of the nightshade family, used for smoking or chewing or as snuff. **b.** any of these plants. **2.** things made from or containing such leaves, such as cigars, cigarettes, etc.: *For thy sake, Tobacco, I Would do anything but die* (Charles Lamb). **3.** the smoking of a pipe, cigars, cigarettes, etc.: *He gave up tobacco for the sake of his children.*
[alteration of earlier *tabaco* < Spanish < Arawak (Haiti) *tabako* a Y-shaped pipe for inhaling smoke through the nostrils; also, a small cigar of rolled tobacco leaves]
tobacco heart, a heart disorder characterized by a rapid or irregular pulse, caused by excessive use of tobacco.
tobacco hornworm, tobacco worm.
to·bac·co·man (tə bak′ō man′, -mən), *n., pl.* **-men.** a man engaged in the business of producing or selling tobacco.
tobacco mosaic, a mosaic disease of the tobacco plant, caused by a virus which attacks the leaves, producing spots, curling, shrinking, etc.
tobacco mosaic virus, the virus that causes tobacco mosaic, a disease of the tobacco plant. *Abbr.:* TMV (no periods).
to·bac·co·nist (tə bak′ə nist), *n.* **1.** a dealer in tobacco; manufacturer of tobacco. **2.** the business of such a person.
Tobacco Road, *U.S.* a run-down, depressed rural area, especially in the Southern United States where poor whites live. *Her childhood was spent . . . in dreary sawmill towns at the dead ends of Tobacco Road* (Time). [< *Tobacco Road,* a novel by Erskine Caldwell (1932) dealing with a family of poor whites in the cotton-growing region of Georgia]
tobacco worm, the large, green caterpillar of either of two species of hawk moths, having white markings and a hornlike process near the end of the body. It feeds on tobacco, tomato, and related plants.
To·ba·go·ni·an (tō′bə gō′nē ən), *n.* a native or inhabitant of Tobago, an island in the West Indies.
to-be (tə bē′), *adj.* that is yet to be or to come; future: *to-be biologists. A wide selection of articles for the mother-to-be.*
tobe (tōb), *n.* a length of cotton cloth worn as an outer garment by natives of northern and central Africa: *The . . . sheiks were dressed in tobes and jibbahs—the loose, swirling dress of the Arab* (New Yorker). [< Arabic *thawb*]
To·bi·as (tə bī′əs), *n.* **1.** in the Douay Bible: **a.** Tobit. **b.** the book of Tobit, included in the canon. **2.** the son of Tobit, hero of the Apocryphal book of Tobit.
To·bit (tō′bit), *n.* **1.** a book of the Protestant Old Testament Apocrypha, included in the canon of the Roman Catholic Bible as Tobias. *Abbr.:* Tob. **2.** an Israelite exile in Nineveh.

to·bog·gan (tə bog′ən), *n.* a long, narrow, flat sled without runners. —*v.i.* **1.** to slide downhill on a toboggan. **2.** *Informal.* to decline sharply and rapidly in value. [American English < Canadian French *tabagane* < Algonkian (probably Micmac) *tobâkun*] —**to·bog′gan·er,** *n.*

Toboggan

to·bog·gan·ist (tə bog′ə nist), *n.* a person who toboggans.

to·break (tə brāk′), *v.t., v.i.,* **-broke** or **-brake, -bro·ken** or **-broke, -break·ing.** *Obsolete.* to break to pieces. [Old English *tobrecan* < *to-* (intensive) + *brecan* break]

to·by[1] (tō′bē), *n.,pl.* **-bies.** *U.S. Slang.* a long, slender, cheap cigar. [American English; origin unknown]

To·by or **to·by**[2] (tō′bē), *n., pl.* **-bies.** a small, fat jug or mug in the form of a fat man wearing a long coat and three-cornered hat, used for drinking ale or beer. [< *Toby,* a proper name, short for *Tobias*]

Toby jug or **mug,** a Toby.

toc·ca·ta (tə kä′tə), *n. Music.* a composition for the piano or organ intended to exhibit the technique of the performer. [< Italian *toccata* (literally) a touching, noun use of past participle of *toccare;* ultimately imitative]

To·char·i·an (tō kãr′ē ən, -kär′-), *n.* **1.** an extinct Indo-European language or group of languages of which records from about 600 A.D. have been discovered in Turkestan. **2.** one of the people of Central Asia who spoke this language. —*adj.* of or having to do with this language or people.

toch·er (toʜ′ər), *Scottish.* —*n.* a dowry. —*v.t.* to furnish with a tocher; dower. [< early Scottish Gaelic and Middle Irish *tochar* dowry, portion < Old Irish *to-chuirim* I assign]

to·col·o·gy (tō kol′ə jē), *n.* obstetrics. Also, **tokology.** [< Greek *tókos* offspring (< *tíktein* give birth to) + English *-logy*]

to·coph·er·ol (tō kof′ə rōl, -rol), *n.* any of four closely related alcohols associated with, or one of the components of, vitamin E, important as an antisterility factor in the diet, present in wheat germ and certain other vegetable oils, milk, and lettuce and other plant leaves. [< Greek *tókos* offspring + *phérein* to bear, produce + English *-ol*[1]]

toc·sin (tok′sən), *n.* **1.** an alarm sounded by ringing a bell or bells; warning signal: *the tocsin of the soul—the dinner-bell* (Byron). **2.** a bell used to sound an alarm: *Oh, what a tocsin has she for a tongue* (Walter De la Mare). [< Middle French *tocsin* < Provençal *tocasenh* < *tocar* to strike, touch + *senh* bell, bell note < Late Latin *signum* bell, ringing of a bell < Latin, sign]

tod[1] (tod), *n. Scottish.* **1.** a fox. **2.** a crafty person: *Take care of the old tod; he means mischief* (Robert Louis Stevenson).

tod[2] (tod), *n.* **1.** an old British unit of weight, usually for wool, equal to about 28 pounds: *a tax of five . . . shillings upon the exportation of every tod of wool* (Adam Smith). **2.** a bushy mass, especially of ivy. [Middle English *todde.* Perhaps related to East Frisian *todde* bundle]

To·da (tō′də), *n., pl.* **-da** or **-das. 1.** a member of a Dravidian people of southern India and Ceylon whose culture centers on the care and cult of the buffalo: *Amongst the Toda, several men, usually brothers, share the wife* (Manchester Guardian Weekly). **2.** the language of this people.

to·day or **to-day** (tə dā′), *n.* **1.** this day: *Today is Sunday.* **2.** the present time or age: *Today is the space age.*
—*adv.* **1.** on this very day: *What are you doing today?* **2.** at the present time; now; nowadays: *Many girls wear their hair short today.*
[Old English *tō dæge* on (the) day]
➤ **Today** (like *tonight* and *tomorrow*) is rarely hyphenated now.

tod·dle (tod′əl), *v.,* **-dled, -dling,** *n.* —*v.i.* to walk with short, unsteady steps, as a baby does: *When his health enabled him to toddle abroad* (Thackeray). —*n.* a toddling way of walking. [origin unknown]

tod·dler (tod′lər), *n.* a child just learning to walk.

tod·dy (tod′ē), *n., pl.* **-dies. 1.** a drink made of whisky, brandy, rum, etc., with hot water, sugar, and spices. **2.** a beverage made of fermented palm sap. [alteration of *tarrie* < Hindustani *tāṛī* palm sap < *tāṛ* palm tree < Sanskrit *tālī* palm tree]

toddy palm, any palm with sap that can be used for toddies.

to-do (tə dü′), *n., pl.* **-dos.** *Informal.* a fuss; bustle: *to make a great to-do over nothing.*

to·dy (tō′dē), *n., pl.* **-dies.** any of various small, brilliantly colored, insect-eating birds of the West Indies, related to the motmots and kingfishers. [< French *todier* < New Latin *Todus* the genus name, special use of Latin *todus* a small bird]

toe (tō), *n., v.,* **toed, toe·ing.** —*n.* **1. a.** one of the five end parts of the human foot. **b.** a corresponding part in a vertebrate animal. **2.** the part of a stocking, shoe, etc., that covers the toes. **3.** the forepart of a foot or hoof. **4.** anything like a toe or the toes in shape or position: *the toe and heel of a golf club.* **5.** a part of a machine placed vertically in a bearing, or a part projecting from a shaft, rod, or belt. **6.** the part beyond the point of a frog in a railroad track.
dig in one's toes, *Especially British.* to take a firm or inflexible position: *If the African leaders dig in their toes, the Government may give way* (London Times).
on one's toes, ready for action; alert: *Leading the Youth Symphony of New York,* [*he*] *offered a program fit to keep a top professional orchestra on its toes* (New York Times).
step or **tread on one's toes,** to offend or annoy one: *. . . stepping on the toes of vested interests* (Bulletin of Atomic Scientists).
stub one's toe, to fumble; blunder: *The scientist as the visionary bungler stubbing his toe over the most obvious facts of life certainly has his counterpart in everyday experience* (Wall Street Journal).
toe to toe, facing one another at close quarters: *to fight it out toe to toe.*
—*v.t.* **1.** to touch or reach with the toes. **2.** to furnish with a toe or toes; make or put a new toe on: *to toe a stocking.* **3. a.** to drive (a nail) in slantwise. **b.** to fasten (boards, etc.) with nails driven in such a way. **4.** to hit or kick with the toe. —*v.i.* **1.** to turn the toes in walking, standing, etc.: *to toe in, to toe out.* **2.** to move on or tap with the toes in dancing.
[Old English *tā*] —**toe′like′,** *adj.*

toe·board (tō′bôrd′, -bōrd′), *n.* **1.** a board for the feet to rest upon, as on the floor of an automobile; floorboard: *The three forward speeds were selected by depressing three interlocked pedals on the toeboard* (New York Times). **2.** a board marking the limit of the thrower's run in putting the shot and similar feats.

toe·cap (tō′kap′), *n.* a caplike piece of leather or metal covering the toe of a shoe, boot, etc.

toe crack, a sand crack, as on the toe of a horse's hoof.

toed (tōd), *adj.* **1.** (of a nail) driven into wood, etc., on a slant. **2.** (of a board) fastened with nails driven in this way.

-toed, *combining form.* having —— toes: *Three-toed = having three toes.*

toe dance, a dance or dancing on the tips of the toes, usually with special slippers, as in ballet.

toe-dance (tō′dans′, -däns′), *v.i.,* **-danced, -danc·ing.** to do a toe dance; be a toe dancer.

toe dancer, a person who does a toe dance, especially a professional dancer.

toe hold, or **toe·hold** (tō′hōld′), *n.* **1. a.** a small crack, projection, ridge, etc., just large enough for the toes in climbing: *a cliff without a toehold.* **b.** the position of being supported by a toehold. **2.** any means of entering, overcoming, expanding, etc. **3.** a hold in wrestling in which the opponent's foot is held and twisted.

toe-in (tō′in′), *n.* a slight inward tilt of the wheels of an automobile, trailer, etc.

toe·less (tō′lis), *adj.* having no toes.

toe·nail (tō′nāl′), *n.* **1.** the nail growing on a toe of the human foot. **2.** a nail driven on a slant. —*v.t.* to fasten with toed nails; toe.

toe-out (tō′out′), *n.* a slight outward tilt of the wheels of an automobile, trailer, etc.

toe·shoe (tō′shü′), *n.* a ballet shoe reinforced at the toe for toe-dancing.

toe strap, a strap which passes over the toes and helps to hold a sandal, ski, etc. on one's foot, or gives one a firm footing or hold and prevents slipping.

toff (tôf, tof), *n. British Slang.* **1.** a stylishly dressed man; swell; dandy. **2.** a well-to-do person; nob. [perhaps alteration of *tuft,* formerly a gentleman commoner at Oxford who wore a gold tassel in his cap]

tof·fee (tôf′ē, tof′-), *n., pl.* **-fees.** a hard, chewy candy; taffy. [variant of *taffy*]

tof·fee-nosed (tôf′ē nōzd′, tof′-), *adj. British Slang.* conceited; pompous; stuck-up: *"Donovan's Reef" may be foolish, but only the irretrievably toffee-nosed will deny it is fun* (London Times).

tof·fy (tôf′ē, tof′-), *n., pl.* **-fies.** toffee.

toft (tôft, toft), *n.* **1.** *British Dialect.* a homestead. **2.** a knoll or hillock. [Old English *toft* < Scandinavian (compare Old Icelandic *topt* ground attached to a house)]

to·fu (tō′fü), *n.* bean curd. [< Japanese *tōfu*]

tog (tog), *n., v.,* **togged, tog·ging.** *Informal.* —*n.* a garment.
togs, clothes: *"Look at his togs, Fagin!" said Charley . . . "Look at his togs!—Superfine cloth, and the heavy swell cut!"* (Dickens).
—*v.t., v.i.* to clothe; dress (out, up).
[apparently short for *togmans,* an obsolete thieves' cant word, perhaps ultimately < Latin *toga* toga]

to·ga (tō′gə), *n., pl.* **-gas, -gae** (-jē). **1.** a loose outer garment worn in public by men of ancient Rome, especially in time of peace. **2.** robe of office: *the toga of royalty.* [< Latin *toga,* related to *tegere* to cover]

Toga (def. 1)

to·gaed (tō′gəd), *adj.* wearing a toga or togas.

to·gat·ed (tō′gā tid), *adj.* **1.** togaed. **2.** Latinized: *togated words or language.* **3.** stately; majestic. [< Latin *togātus* wearing a toga < *toga* (see TOGA) + English *-ed*[2]]

to·ga vi·ri·lis (tō′gə və rī′lis), *Latin.* the toga of manhood. Roman boys began to wear it at the age of fourteen to sixteen.

to·geth·er (tə geᴛʜ′ər), *adv.* **1. a.** with each other; in company: *to eat together. They were standing together. The girls were walking together.* **b.** with united action; in cooperation: *to work together for peace.* **2.** into one gathering, company, mass, or body: *to come together as friends, to call the people together, to sew the pieces of a dress together.* **3.** at the same time; at once: *rain and snow falling together.* **4.** without a stop or break; on end; continuously: *He worked for several days and nights together.*
together with, along with: *Simon . . . entered Persia, together with Thaddeus* (John Jackson).
[Old English *tōgædere* < *tō* to + *gædere* together. Related to GATHER.]
➤ **together with.** Adding *together with* to a singular subject does not change the grammatical number of the subject. Formal English uses a singular verb to agree with the singular subject: *The general, together with his staff, is dining here tonight.* Informal English, however, often uses a plural verb, treating the construction as a compound subject: *The coach together with his players are attending a banquet.*

to·geth·er·ness (tə geᴛʜ′ər nis), *n.* the condition of being together or united in social, educational, or other activity, especially such activity regarded as beneficial to the participants: *The American family is expected to revel in close communal existence, what one national magazine idealises as "togetherness"* (London Times).

tog·ger·y (tog′ər ē), *n., pl.* **-ger·ies.** *Informal.* garments; clothes.

tog·gle (tog′əl), *n., v.,* **-gled, -gling.** —*n.* **1.** a pin, bolt, or rod put through the eye of a rope or the link of a chain to keep it in place, to hold two ropes together, to serve as a hold for the fingers, etc. **2. a.** a toggle joint. **b.** a device furnished with a toggle joint. —*v.t.* to provide, hold, or attach with a toggle or toggles. [apparently variant of earlier *tuggle* to catch, entangle]

toggle bolt, a bolt whose nut is flanged to work a spring and spread out when the bolt has gone through a wall or other surface. It is used to support heavy mirrors, etc., hanging on thin walls.

toggle iron, a harpoon with a pivoted crosspiece near the point, instead of fixed barbs.

toggle joint, a kneelike joint that transmits pressure at right angles. It has two arms that meet at an angle and are joined on a swivel.

Toggle Joint

toggle switch, an electric switch with a projecting lever that is pushed through a small arc to open or close the circuit.

To·go·land·er (tō′gō lan′dər), *n.* a native or inhabitant of the former German protectorate Togoland, in western Africa on the Gulf of Guinea, of which a part is now the Republic of Togo and part incorporated in Ghana.

To·go·lese (tō′ gō lēz′,-lēs′), *adj.* of or having to do with the former Togoland, the region it included, or its people. —*n.* a native or inhabitant of the former Togoland; Togolander.

togs (togz), *n.pl.* See under **tog,** *n.*

togue (tōg), *n., pl.* **togues** or (*collectively*) **togue.** (in Canada, especially the Maritimes) lake trout. [< Canadian French *togue* < Algonkian]

to·he·ro·a (tō′hə rō′ə), *n.* an edible green marine clam of New Zealand. [< Maori *toheroa*]

to·hu·bo·hu (tō′hü bō′hü), *n.* chaos; confusion. [< Hebrew *thōhū wa bhōhu* emptiness and desolation, translated in Genesis 1:2 as "without form and void"]

toil[1] (toil), *n.* **1.** hard work; labor: *to succeed only after years of toil.* **2.** a spell o hard work; laborious task: *All the day's long toil is past* (Thomas Hood). **3.** something made or done by hard work: *the toil Of dropping buckets into empty wells* (William Cowper). **4.** *Archaic.* a fighting; strife.
—*v.i.* **1.** to work hard; labor: *to toil with one's hands for a living.* **2.** to move with difficulty, pain, or weariness: *to toil up a hill.* —*v.t.* to bring, make, or obtain by hard work or effort.
[< Anglo-French *toil* turmoil, contention < *toiler* to agitate, stir up, Old French *toeillier* drag about, make dirty < Latin *tudiculāre* stir up < Latin *tudicula* olive press < *tudes* mallet, related to *tundere* to pound]
—**Syn.** *n.* **1.** drudgery, travail, effort, exertion. See **work.** *-v.i.* **1.** drudge, slave.

toil[2] (toil), *n.* a net; snare: *A lion was caught in the toil.*
toils, something like a net or snare: *The fly was caught in the toils of the spider.*
[< Old French *toile* and *teile* hunting net; cloth; web < Latin *tēla* web, related to *texere* to weave]

toile (twäl), *n.* a sheer linen and silk cloth. [< Old French *toile* linen cloth, canvas; see TOIL[2]]

toile de Jouy (twäl′də zhwē′), a cotton or linen cloth having colored patterns on a light-colored background: *C. V. Whitney looks at [a] view of Oyster Bay through loggia windows draped in red toile de Jouy* (New York Times). [< French *toile de Jouy* (literally) cloth of Jouy < *Jouy-en-Josar,* a town in France]

toil·er (toi′lər), *n.* a person who toils; hard worker; laborer.

toi·let (toi′lit), *n.* **1.** a bathroom; lavatory. **2.** a porcelain bowl with a seat attached and with a drain at the bottom to flush the bowl clean; water closet: *Waste matter from the body is disposed of in a toilet.* **3.** the process of dressing: *Washing, bathing, combing the hair, and putting on one's clothes are all parts of one's toilet.* **4.** a set of toilet articles. **5.** a dressing table. **6. a.** a person's dress; costume. **b.** the manner or style of dressing. **7.** *Surgery.* the cleansing of a part after an operation. —*adj.* of or for the toilet: *Combs and brushes are toilet articles.* [originally, a cover for the clothes, especially in hairdressing < French *toilette* (diminutive) < *toile* toil[2]]

toilet paper, a soft, absorbent, cleansing paper, usually rolled up, for use in a lavatory.

toi·let·ry (toi′lə trē), *n., pl.* **-ries.** a toilet article such as soap, face powder, perfume, etc.

toi·lette (toi let′; *French* twä let′), *n.* toilet. [variant of *toilet*]

toilet training, the training of a child to control his bladder and bowel movements and to use the toilet: *A baby gets off to a better start if his mother is relaxed about toilet training and allows him to be relaxed, too* (Sidonie M. Gruenberg).

toilet water, a fragrant liquid, weaker than perfume, used after bathing, as a cologne in grooming, etc.

toil·ful (toil′fəl), *adj.* characterized by or involving hard work; laborious; toilsome: *We behold the patient train of the toilful muleteer, slowly moving along the skirts of the mountain* (Washington Irving). —**toil′ful·ly,** *adv.*

toil·less (toil′lis), *adj.* free from toil.

toils (toilz), *n. pl.* See under **toil**[2], *n.*

toil·some (toil′səm), *adj.* requiring or characterized by hard work; laborious; wearisome; tiring: *a long, toilsome climb up the mountain.* —**toil′some·ly,** *adv.* —**toil′some·ness,** *n.* —**Syn.** fatiguing, onerous.

toil·worn (toil′wôrn′, -wōrn′), *adj.* worn by toil; showing the effects of toil.

to·ing and fro·ing (tü′ing ən frō′ing), a moving to and fro; restless activity; bustle; fuss: *The toing and froing about the biological dangers of fallout continues* (New Scientist).

toise (toiz), *n.* an old French linear measure equal to 1,949 meters or 6,395 English feet. [< Middle French *toise,* Old French *teise* < Late Latin *tēsa* (*brachia*) outstretched arms < Latin *tendere* to stretch]

To·kay (tō kā′), *n.* **1.** a rich, sweet Hungarian wine, golden in color. **2.** any of various wines made elsewhere in imitation of this. **3.** the large, firm, reddish, sweet grape from which such wine is made, used also as a table grape. [< *Tokay,* a town in Hungary, where it was originally made]

to·ken (tō′kən), *n.* **1. a.** a mark or sign: *Black is a token of mourning.* **b.** something that serves to prove; an evidence: *His actions are a token of his sincerity.* **c.** a characteristic mark or indication: *the tokens of a good horse, the tokens of a disease.* **2.** a sign of friendship; keepsake: *a parting token, birthday tokens.* **3.** a piece of metal, somewhat like a coin, stamped for a higher value than the metal is worth and used for some special purpose, as bus or subway fares. **4.** a piece of metal, plastic, etc., indicating a right or privilege: *This token will admit you to the swimming pool.* **5.** something that is a sign of genuineness or authority; password. **6.** *Archaic.* a signal.
by the same token, for the same reason; in the same way; moreover: *. . . to receive letters from people whom they do not know, and are, by the same token, never likely to know* (Phyllis Dare).
in token of, as a token of; to show: *He sits down in token of submission* (George Bernard Shaw).
—*adj.* having only the appearance of; serving as a symbol; nominal; partial: *a token resistance, a token fleet.*
[Old English *tācen* sign, mark. Related to TEACH.]
—**Syn.** *n.* **1.** symbol. See **mark. 2.** memento, memorial.

to·ken·ism (tō′kə niz əm), *n. U.S.* the policy or practice of making token gestures of eliminating racial segregation and discrimination.

token payment, a nominal payment made to acknowledge an obligation or agreement.

to·kol·o·gy (tō kol′ə jē), *n.* tocology.

to·ko·no·ma (tō′kə nō′mə), *n.* an alcove in a Japanese house for the decorative display of scrolls, prints, and flowers. [< Japanese *tokonoma*]

to·la (tō′lä), *n.* (in India) a unit of weight equal to 180 grains troy. [< Hindi *tola* < Sanskrit *tulā* weight < *tul* to weigh]

to·lan (tō′lan), *n.* a colorless, crystalline, unsaturated hydrocarbon produced synthetically. *Formula:* $C_{14}H_{10}$ [< *tol*(uene) + *-an*(e)]

to·lane (tō′lān), *n.* tolan.

tol·booth (tōl′büth′, -büᴛʜ′), *n. Scottish.* a town prison; jail. Originally, the cells were under the town hall. Also, **tollbooth.** [Middle English *tolbothe* < *toll* toll[2] + *bothe* booth]

tol·bu·ta·mide (tol byü′tə mīd), *n.* a sulfonamide drug taken orally as a substitute for insulin in the treatment of mild diabetes; Orinase. *Formula:* $C_{12}H_{18}N_2O_3S$ [< *tol*(u) + *but*(yric) + *amide*]

told (tōld), *v.* the past tense and past participle of **tell:** *You told me that last week.*
all told, altogether; in all: *a cost of $250 all told.*

tole[1] or **tôle** (tōl), *n.* lacquered and enameled metalware used in the 1700's, imitated today in trays, etc. It often has a dark green or black field with gilt designs on it. [< French *tôle* plate work, sheet iron, probably dialectal variant of *table;* see TABLE]

tole[2] (tōl), *v.t.,* **toled, tol·ing.** toll[3].

To·le·do (tə lē′dō; *Spanish* tō lā′ᴛʜō), *n.* a sword of fine temper made in Toledo, Spain, or elsewhere in imitation of this.

tol·er·a·bil·i·ty (tol′ər ə bil′ə tē), *n.* tolerable state or condition; tolerableness.

tol·er·a·ble (tol′ər ə bəl), *adj.* **1.** able to be borne or endured; bearable; endurable: *a tolerable burden. The pain has become tolerable.* **2.** fairly good; not bad; passable: *to be in tolerable health.* [< Latin *tolerābilis* bearable; able to bear < *tolerāre;* see TOLERATE] —**tol′er·a·ble·ness,** *n.* —**Syn. 1.** sufferable, supportable. **2.** mediocre, ordinary, indifferent.

tol·er·a·bly (tol′ər ə blē), *adv.* **1.** in a tolerable manner. **2.** moderately.

tol·er·ance (tol′ər əns), *n.* **1.** a willingness to be tolerant and patient toward people whose opinions or ways differ from one's own. **2.** the power of enduring or resisting the action of a drug, poison, etc. **3.** the act of tolerating; toleration. **4. a.** an allowable amount of variation from a standard weight or fineness in the minting of coins. **b.** an allowable amount of variation in the dimensions of a machine or part. **5.** *Obsolete.* endurance. —**Syn. 1.** forbearance. See **toleration.**

tol·er·ant (tol′ər ənt), *adj.* **1.** willing to let other people do as they think best; willing to endure beliefs and actions of which one does not approve: *The United States government is tolerant toward all religious beliefs.* **2.** able to endure or resist the action of a drug, poison, etc. —**tol′er·ant·ly,** *adv.*

tol·er·ate (tol′ə rāt), *v.t.,* **-at·ed, -at·ing. 1.** to allow; permit: *The teacher won't tolerate any disorder. A free nation tolerates all religions.* **2.** to bear; endure; put up with: *They tolerate the grouchy old man only because he is their employer.* **3.** to endure or resist the action of (a strong drug, poison, etc.): *He is one of those people who cannot tolerate penicillin.* [< Latin *tolerāre* (with English *-ate*[1]), related to *tollere* to bear]

tol·er·a·tion (tol′ə rā′shən), *n.* **1.** a willingness to put up with beliefs and actions of which one does not approve. **2.** the recognition of a person's right to worship as he thinks best without loss of civil rights or social privileges; freedom of worship.
—**Syn. 1, 2. Toleration, tolerance** mean permitting others to do, say, or think as they wish. **Toleration** means putting up with actions, beliefs, or people one does not like or approve of, often because of indifference or a desire to avoid conflict: *Toleration of dishonest officials encourages corruption.* **Tolerance** means being willing to let others think, live, or worship according to their own beliefs and to refrain from judging harshly or with blind prejudice: *Through tolerance we learn to understand people.*

tol·er·a·tion·ism (tol′ə rā′shə niz′əm), *n.* the principle of tolerating religious differences.

tol·er·a·tion·ist (tol′ə rā′shə nist), *n.* a person who supports or advocates toleration, especially in religious matters.

tol·er·a·tive (tol′ə rā′tiv), *adj.* tending to tolerate or be tolerant; permissive.

tol·er·a·tor (tol′ə rā′tər), *n.* a person who tolerates.

tole·ware (tōl′wãr′), *n.* tole[1]: *It is this type of painted tinware, sometimes called japanned ware or toleware . . . that has immense appeal to collectors of today* (London Times).

tol·i·din (tol′ə din), *n.* tolidine.

tol·i·dine (tol′ə dēn, -din), *n.* a base, a toluene derivative, found in several isomeric forms, one of which is used in the manufacture of dyestuffs. Another is important in testing for chlorine in public water supplies. *Formula:* $C_{14}H_{16}N_2$

toll[1] (tōl), *v.t.* **1.** to cause to sound with single strokes slowly and regularly repeated: *Bells were tolled all over the country at the President's death.* **2.** to call, announce, etc., by tolling. —*v.i.* to sound with single strokes slowly and regularly repeated: *Any man's death diminishes me because I am involved in mankind; And therefore never send to know for whom the bell tolls; it tolls for thee* (John Donne).
—*n.* **1.** a stroke or sound of a bell being tolled. **2.** the act or fact of tolling.
[perhaps special use of *toll*[3] to pull]

toll[2] (tōl), *n.* **1.** a tax or fee paid for some right or privilege: *We pay a toll when we cross that bridge.* **2.** the right to collect tolls. **3.** a charge for a certain service: *There is a toll on long-distance telephone calls.* **4.** something paid, lost, suffered, etc.: *Automobile accidents take a heavy toll of human lives.* **5.** *Obsolete.* **a.** a charge for the transport of goods by railway or canal. **b.** a part of the grain or flour taken by the miller in payment for grinding.
—*v.t.* to collect tolls from; take as toll.
—*v.i.* to take or collect toll; exact or levy toll.
[Old English *toll,* variant of *toln,* apparently < Vulgar Latin *tolōnium,* for Latin *telōnium* < Greek *telōneîon* tollhouse < *telṓnēs* tax collector < *télos* tax]

toll[3] (tōl), *v.t. Dialect.* **1.** to attract; entice; allure. **2.** to lure (animals, ducks, etc.) by arousing curiosity; decoy. Also, **tole.** [Middle English *tollen, tullen,* apparently related to Old English *-tyllan* draw, as in *betyllan* to lure]

toll·a·ble (tō′lə bəl), *adj.* subject to the payment of toll.

toll·age (tō′lij), *n.* **1.** a toll. **2.** the exaction or payment of toll.

toll bar, a barrier, especially a gate, across a road, bridge, etc., where toll is collected.

toll·booth (tōl′büth′, -büŧʜ′), *n.* **1.** a small structure or one of several small structures at the entrance to or exit from a bridge or tunnel, or across a turnpike, throughway, etc., to shelter a toll collector. **2.** *Scottish.* a tolbooth.

toll bridge, a bridge at which a toll is charged.

toll call, any telephone call for which a higher rate is charged than for a local call.

toll collector, 1. a person who collects the tolls on a turnpike, bridge, etc. **2.** a device for collecting tolls, such as a turnstile with a slot into which a coin is dropped.

toll·er[1] (tō′lər), *n.* **1.** a person who tolls a bell. **2.** a bell for tolling.

toll·er[2] (tō′lər), *n.* a dog trained to decoy ducks.

toll·gate (tōl′gāt′), *n.* a gate at a road, bridge, etc., where tolls are collected.

toll·gath·er·er (tōl′gaŧʜ′ər ər), *n.* a person who collects tolls; toll collector.

toll·house (tōl′hous′), *n.* a building beside a tollgate or on a toll bridge, occupied by the toll collector.

toll·keep·er (tōl′kē′pər), *n.* the keeper of a tollgate or tollhouse; toll collector.

toll line, a line for long-distance telephone calls.

toll·man (tōl′man′), *n., pl.* **-men.** a toll collector.

toll plaza, the wide area on a tollway where tollbooths are situated.

toll road, a road on which tolls are charged; turnpike.

toll station, a place where tolls are collected, such as a tollhouse or tollgate.

toll television, subscription television.

toll·way (tōl′wā′), *n.* a toll road; turnpike.

Tol·stoy·an (tol stoi′ən), *adj.* of or having to do with the Russian novelist Leo Tolstoy (1828-1910), his writings, or his philosophy.

Tol·tec (tol′tek), *n.* a member of an Indian people that ruled the central Mexican highlands from about A.D. 900 to 1200, and whose culture influenced the Aztecs, who followed them. —*adj.* of or having to do with the Toltecs or their culture.

Tol·tec·an (tol tek′ən), *adj.* Toltec.

to·lu (tō lü′), *n.,* or **tolu balsam,** a fragrant balsam obtained from the bark of a tropical South American tree of the pea family, used in medicine, perfume, etc. [< Spanish *tolú* < (*Santiago de*) *Tolú,* a city in Colombia, where it was originally obtained]

tol·u·ate (tol′yu̇ āt), *n.* a salt or ester of toluic acid.

tol·u·ene (tol′yu̇ ēn), *n.* a colorless, mobile, aromatic, liquid hydrocarbon with a smell like that of benzene, obtained from coal tar and coal gas. It is used as a solvent and for making explosives, dyes, etc. *Formula:* C_7H_8 [< *tolu*(ol) + *-ene*]

to·lu·ic acid (tə lü′ik, tol′yu̇-), a colorless carboxylic acid homologous with benzoic acid, found in four isomeric forms, derived from toluene or xylene. *Formula:* $C_8H_8O_2$

tol·u·ide (tol′yu̇ īd, -id), *n.* any of a group of compounds homologous with the anilides. The toluides are toluidine derivatives formed by replacement of the hydrogen in the amino radical with an acid radical.

to·lu·i·did (tə lü′ə did), *n.* toluide.

to·lu·i·dide (tə lü′ə dīd, -did), *n.* toluide.

to·lu·i·din (tə lü′ə din), *n.* toluidine.

to·lu·i·dine (tə lü′ə dēn, -din), *n.* a compound analogous to aniline, found in three isomeric forms. Toluidine is a toluene derivative used especially in making dyes. *Formula:* C_7H_9N

tol·u·ol (tol′yu̇ ōl, -ol), *n.* toluene, especially the form used commercially. [< German *Toluin* (< *tolu;* see TOLU) + English *-ol*[2]]

tol·u·ole (tol′yu̇ ōl), *n.* toluol.

tol·u·yl (tol′yu̇ əl), *n.* a univalent radical, C_7H_7CO-, occurring in toluic acid. [< *tolu*(ol) + *-yl*]

tol·yl (tol′əl), *n.* a univalent hydrocarbon radical, C_7H_7-, occurring in toluene. [< *tol*(u) + *-yl*]

tom or **Tom** (tom), *n.* **1.** a male cat; tomcat. **2.** the male of various other animals, such as the turkey. [< *Tom,* used as a type name for a common man]

tom·a·hawk (tom′ə hôk), *n.* a light ax used by North American Indians as a weapon and a tool.

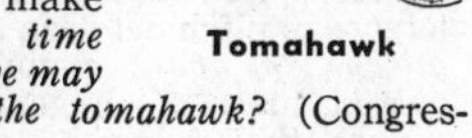
Tomahawk

bury the tomahawk, to stop fighting; make peace: *Will the time never come when we may honorably bury the tomahawk?* (Congressional Globe).
—*v.t.* to strike, kill, or wound with a tomahawk.
[American English < Algonkian (probably Powhatan) *tamahack* a striking instrument]

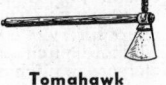

tom·al·ley (tom′al′ē), *n.* the liver of the lobster, regarded as a delicacy. It turns green when cooked. [apparently < Carib *taumali* (originally) the inner part of a crab]

to·man (tə män′), *n.* **1.** in Iran and Turkey: **a.** ten thousand. **b.** military division of 10,000 men. **2.** an Iranian gold coin, not now in circulation, equal to 10 krans or 10,000 dinars, and worth about $1.72. **3.** an Iranian money of account equivalent to 10 krans, or about 80 cents. [< Persian *tuman*]

Tom and Jer·ry (jer′ē), *U.S.* a hot drink made of rum, sugar, beaten eggs, spices, and water or milk. [< two chief characters in *Life in London,* by Pierce Egan, 1772-1849]

to·marc·tus (tə märk′təs), *n.* an extinct mammal of the late Miocene period, believed to be the ancestor of dogs, wolves, foxes, jackals, etc. It had a wedge-shaped head, long, low body, thick coat, and long, furry tail. [< New Latin *Tomarctus*]

to·mat·i·dine (tə mat′ə dēn, -din), *n.* a steroid alkaloid derived from tomatin, used in the synthesis of progesterone and testosterone, and in the treatment of certain fungus diseases. *Formula:* $C_{27}H_{45}NO_2$

to·mat·in (tə mat′in), *n.* an alkaloid extract of the juice of the tomato plant, used in antibiotics for the treatment of certain skin and stomach diseases, and as the source of tomatidine. *Formula:* $C_{50}H_{83}NO_{21}$

tom·a·tine (tom′ə tēn), *n.* the crystalline form of tomatin.

to·ma·to (tə mā′tō, -mä′-), *n., pl.* **-toes. 1.** the juicy, slightly acid fruit of a plant of the nightshade family, eaten as a vegetable: *Most tomatoes are red when ripe. A tomato is technically called a berry.* **2.** the plant it grows on: *Tomatoes are spreading plants with hairy stems and leaves, and small yellow flowers.* **3.** any related plant. **4.** *U.S. Slang.* a girl or woman, especially one who is good-looking. [alteration of earlier *tomate* < Spanish < Nahuatl *tomatl*]

tomato catchup, a catchup made with tomatoes, onions, salt, sugar, and spices.

tomato fruit worm, the bollworm or corn earworm; a moth larva which feeds on tomatoes and parts of other plants.

tomb (tüm), *n.* **1.** a grave, vault, mausoleum, or other place of burial, often above ground: *The greedy sea, The mighty tomb of mariners and kings* (William Morris). **2.** death. —*v.t.* to put in a tomb; shut up as if in a tomb; entomb; bury. [< Anglo-French *tumbe,* Old French *tombe* < Late Latin *tumba* < Greek *týmbos* burial mound] —**tomb′like′,** *adj.*

tom·bac, tom·back, or **tom·bak** (tom′bak), *n.* an alloy consisting essentially of copper and zinc, used for cheap jewelry, bells and gongs, etc. Also, **tambac.** [< French *tombac* < Portuguese *tambaca* < Malay *tambāga* copper < Sanskrit *tāmrāka*]

tomb·less (tüm′lis), *adj.* without a tomb.

tom·bo·la (tom′bə lə), *n. British.* bingo. [< French *tombola* < Italian < *tombolare* turn a somersault, tumble]

tom·bo·lo (tom′bə lō), *n., pl.* **-los.** a sand bar which connects an island to the mainland or to another island: *In time the tombolo will form on the leeward side of the island in line with the advancing wave front* (Scientific American). [< Italian *tombolo* < Latin *tumulus;* see TUMULUS]

tom·boy (tom′boi′), *n.* a girl who likes to play boys' games; boisterous, romping girl.

tom·boy·ish (tom′boi′ish), *adj.* like or characteristic of a tomboy: *tomboyish games or activities.* —**tom′boy·ish·ly,** *adv.* —**tom′boy·ish·ness,** *n.*

tomb·stone (tüm′stōn′), *n.* a stone or other marker, usually having an inscription, placed over a tomb or grave; gravestone: *mossy, tumbledown tombstones, one with a skull and crossbones upon it* (H. G. Wells).

tom·cat (tom′kat′), *n.* a male cat.

tom·cod (tom′kod′), *n.* any of various small salt-water fishes related to the cod. [American English < *tom* + *cod*[1]]

Tomcod (10 in. long)

Tom Collins, *U.S.* a cold drink made of gin, lemon or lime juice, sugar, and carbonated water. [compare COLLINS]

Tom, Dick, and Harry, people in general; everyone: *He was not the hearty pre-election politician who runs around greeting every Tom, Dick, and Harry* (Canada Month).

tome (tōm), *n.* **1.** a book, especially a large, heavy book: *She directed Sir Arthur Helps to bring out a collection of the Prince's speeches and addresses, and the weighty tome appeared in 1862* (Lytton Strachey). **2.** *Obsolete.* a volume forming part of a larger work. [< Middle French *tome,* learned borrowing from Latin *tomus* < Greek *tómos* (originally) piece cut off < *témnein* to cut]

to·men·tose (tō men′tōs, tō′men-), *adj.* **1.** *Anatomy.* fleecy; flaky. **2.** *Botany.* closely covered with down or matted hair. [< New Latin *tomentosus* < Latin *tōmentum* cushion stuffing]

to·men·tum (tō men′təm), *n., pl.* **-ta** (-tə). **1.** *Botany.* a soft down consisting of longish, soft, entangled hairs, pressed close to the surface. **2.** *Anatomy.* a downy covering, especially the flocculent inner surface of the pia mater, consisting of numerous minute vessels entering the brain and spinal cord. [< New Latin *tomentum* < Latin *tōmentum* cushion stuffing]

tom·fool (tom′fül′), *n.* a very foolish or stupid person; dolt. —*adj.* very foolish. [< *Tom Fool,* a personification of stupidity]

tom·fool·er·y (tom′fü′lər ē), *n., pl.* **-er·ies.** foolish, silly, or absurd behavior; nonsense.

Tom·my[1] or **tom·my** (tom′ē), *n., pl.* **-mies. 1.** *Informal.* a British soldier, especially a private soldier. **2.** *British Slang.* **a.** a heavy, dark bread formerly supplied as rations to the enlisted men in the British army; brown tommy. **b.** a loaf or chunk of any bread. **c.** food or provisions carried by workmen each day. **d.** provisions supplied to workmen under the truck system. **e.** a store run by the employer, where vouchers given to workers instead of money wages can be exchanged for goods; tommy shop; truck shop. [< *Tommy,* apparently originally personified as *Tommy Brown* (for brown bread)]

Tom·my[2] (tom′ē), *n., pl.* **-mies.** *Informal.* a Thompson submachine gun.

Tommy At·kins (at′kinz), *Informal.* a British soldier. [< *Thomas Atkins,* name used in the sample forms for privates given in the official regulations of the British Army from 1815 on]

Tommy gun or **tommy gun,** *Informal.* a Thompson submachine gun.

Tom·my-gun or **tom·my-gun** (tom′ē-gun′), *v.t.,* **-gunned, -gun·ning.** to shoot with a Tommy gun: *He and his aide were ambushed and Tommy-gunned to death by four young officers* (Time).

Tom·my-gun·ner or **tom·my-gun·ner** (tom′ē gun′ər), *n.* a person skilled in operating a Tommy gun.

tom·my·rot (tom′ē rot′), *n. Slang.* nonsense; rubbish; foolishness; bosh; twaddle.

tommy shop, *British Slang.* a tommy (store).

to·mo·gram (tō′mə gram), *n.* a photograph made by tomography.

to·mo·graph (tō′mə graf, -gräf), *n.* an X-ray machine used in tomography.

to·mo·graph·ic (tō′mə graf′ik), *adj.* of or having to do with tomography.

to·mog·ra·phy (tə mog′rə fē), *n. Medicine.* X-ray photography of a structure in a certain layer of tissue in the body, in which images of structures in other layers are eliminated. [< Greek *tómos* a cutting, section + English *-graphy*]

to·mor·row or **to·mor·row** (tə môr′ō, -mor′-), *n.* **1.** the day after today; the morrow: *One today is worth two tomorrows* (Benjamin Franklin). **2.** the near future. —*adv.* on or for the day after today; very soon. [Middle English *to morowe*, Old English *tō morgen* < *tō* to + *morgen* morn]
➤ See **today** for usage note.

tom·pi·on (tom′pē ən), *n.* tampion.

Tom Thumb, 1. a diminutive hero popular in English folk tales. **2.** anything that is very small; any dwarf. **3.** a petty or insignificant person.

Tom Tiddler's ground, 1. a children's game in which one player guards a marked-off area over which the other players run and from which he chases them until he catches one who will take his place. **2.** a place or area in which easy profits can be made: *What saddens me is the thought of all the fellows in my circle who have got on this Tom Tiddler's ground without putting me wise* (Sunday Times). **3.** no man's land: *The frontier must not become a Tom Tiddler's ground* (London Times).

tom·tit (tom′tit′), *n.* **1.** a small bird, especially a titmouse. **2.** *British Dialect.* any of various other small birds, such as the wren and the tree creeper. [< *tom* + *tit*[1]]

tom-tom (tom′tom′), *n., v.,* **-tommed, -tomming.** —*n.* **1.** a drum usually beaten with the hands, originally of the East Indies, but common also in Africa, the Caribbean, and elsewhere. **2.** a monotonous, rhythmic beat. —*v.i., v.t.* to beat on or as if on a tom-tom. [< Hindustani *tam-tam;* probably ultimately imitative]

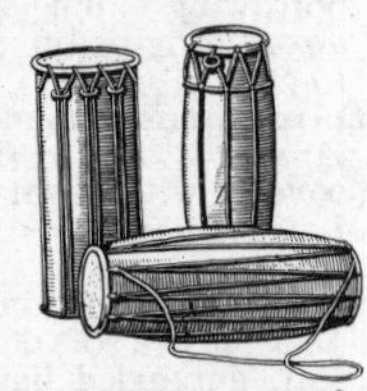
Tom-toms (def. 1)

tom-tom·mer (tom′tom′ər), *n.* a person who beats on or as if on a tom-tom.

-tomy, *combining form.* **1.** a cutting or casting off: *Autotomy = a casting off of part of the body.* **2.** surgical incision or operation: *Lobotomy = surgical incision into a lobe.* [< Greek *-tomiā* a cutting]

ton[1] (tun), *n.* **1. a.** a unit of weight equal to 2,000 pounds, standard in the United States and Canada; short ton. **b.** a unit of weight equal to 2,240 pounds, standard in Great Britain; long ton. **c.** a metric ton (1000 kilograms). **2.** a unit of cubic measure that varies with the thing measured; freight ton. It is about equal to the space occupied by a ton's weight of the particular stuff. Thus a ton of stone is 16 cubic feet; a ton of lumber is 40 cubic feet; a ton of wheat is 20 bushels. **3. a.** a unit of measure of the internal capacity of a ship; 100 cubic feet. **b.** a unit of measure of the carrying capacity of a ship; 40 cubic feet; shipping ton. **c.** a unit of measure of the weight by volume of water a ship will displace; 35 cubic feet (the weight of a long ton of sea water); displacement ton. *Abbr.:* tn. **4.** *Slang.* a motorcycle speed of 100 miles per hour. [spelling variant of *tun*[1]]

ton[2] (tôN), *n.* the prevailing fashion; style. [< French *ton* manner, learned borrowing from Latin *tonus.* Doublet of TONE, TUNE.]

ton·al (tō′nəl), *adj.* **1.** of or having to do with tones or tone. **2.** characterized by tonality: *tonal music.*

tonal center, *Music.* a note around which a passage, movement, or composition is based; tonic.

ton·al·ist (tō′nə list), *n.* **1.** a painter who aims at effect through color harmonization rather than by contrasts. **2.** a composer whose music is characterized by tonality rather than atonality.

to·nal·ite (tō′nə līt), *n.* a granular igneous rock, a variety of diorite, containing quartz and biotite. [< *Tonale,* a pass in Tyrol, where it is found + *-ite*[1]]

to·nal·i·ty (tō nal′ə tē), *n., pl.* **-ties. 1.** *Music.* **a.** the relation, or sum of relations, between the notes or tones of a scale or musical system. **b.** a key or system of tones. **c.** any stressing of a particular tone or note as the basis of a passage, movement, or composition: *The first movement of the Bartók concerto is in the tonality of C.* **2.** the general tone or color scheme of a painting, etc.

ton·al·ly (tō′nə lē), *adv.* with respect to tone.

to-name (tü′nām′), *n. Scottish.* **1.** a name added to another name; surname; nickname. **2.** a name added to a Christian name and surname to distinguish a person from others having the same name; by-name. [Old English *tō-nama* < *tō* to + *nama* name]

ton·do (ton′dō), *n., pl.* **-di** (-dē) or **-dos. 1.** a painting in circular form. **2.** a carved relief in circular form. [< Italian *tondo* (literally) plate < *tondo* round, ultimately < Latin *rotundus;* see ROUND, ROTUND]

tone (tōn), *n., v.,* **toned, ton·ing.** —*n.* **1.** any sound considered with reference to its quality, pitch, strength, source, etc.: *sweet, shrill, or loud tones.* **2.** quality of sound: *a voice silvery in tone.* **3.** *Music.* **a.** a sound of definite pitch and character. **b.** the difference in pitch between two notes: *C and D are one tone apart.* **c.** any of the nine melodies or tunes in Gregorian music, used in singing the psalms; Gregorian tone. **4.** a manner of speaking or writing: *a moral tone. We disliked the haughty tone of her letter.* **5. a.** spirit; character; style: *A tone of quiet elegance prevails in her home.* **b.** mental or emotional state; mood; disposition: *These hardy exercises produce also a healthful tone of mind and spirits* (Washington Irving). **6.** normal healthy condition; vigor: *He exercised regularly to keep up his tone.* **7.** the effect of color and light and shade in a painting, etc.: *a painting with a soft green tone.* **8. a.** the quality given to one color by another color: *blue with a greenish tone.* **b.** shade of color: *a room furnished in tones of brown.* **9.** *Linguistics.* **a.** the pitch of the voice as it is high or low, or as it rises and falls, regarded as a distinctive feature of a language. **b.** any of the tonal levels distinctive in a language: *Mandarin Chinese has four phonemic tones.* **c.** the pronunciation characteristic of a particular person, group of people, area, etc.; accent. **10.** *Phonetics.* **a.** the sound produced by the vibration of the vocal cords; voice. **b.** the stress or emphasis on a syllable. —*v.i.* to harmonize: *This rug tones in well with the wallpaper and furniture.* —*v.t.* **1. a.** to soften or change the color or value contrasts in (a painting, photograph, etc.). **b.** *Photography.* to alter the color of (a print), especially from gray to some other color. **2.** to give the proper or desired tone to (a musical instrument); tune. **3.** to utter with a musical or other tone; intone.
tone down, to soften; moderate: *to tone down one's voice, tone down the colors in a painting.*
tone up, to give more sound, color, or vigor to; strengthen: *Bright curtains would tone up this dull room.*
[< Latin *tonus* < Greek *tónos* vocal pitch, raising of voice; (originally) a stretching, taut string, related to *teínein* to stretch. Doublet of TUNE, TON[2].]

-tone, *combining form.* having —— tones or colors: *Two-tone = having two colors.*

tone arm, the arm of a phonograph, holding the needle and pickup. See **phonograph** for picture.

tone cluster, a large number of musical notes played together, especially on the piano, to produce a dense and dissonant effect.

tone color, *Music.* timbre.

-toned, *combining form.* having a ——tone: *Sweet-toned = having a sweet tone.*

tone-deaf (tōn′def′), *adj.* not able to distinguish between different musical tones.

tone-deaf·ness (tōn′def′nis), *n.* the inability to distinguish between musical tones of different pitch. It is an inborn defect, like color blindness.

to·ne·la·da (tō′nə lä′də; *Spanish* tō′nā-lä′ᴛʜä; *Portuguese* tü′nə lä′ᴛʜə), *n.* a unit of weight equal to about 2,029 pounds in Spain and most of South America and to about 1,749 pounds in Brazil. [< Spanish and Portuguese *tonelada* < *tonel* cask, tun, ancient ship measure < Old French *tonel,* (diminutive) < *tonne* large tun, cask]

tone·less (tōn′lis), *adj.* **1.** without modulation or expression: *a toneless voice, a toneless reading.* **2.** (of color) dull. **3.** without tone; soundless; mute. —**tone′less·ly,** *adv.* —**tone′less·ness,** *n.*

tone painting, 1. the art of musical description or suggestion, as in instrumental music. **2.** such a composition, characteristic of most program music.

tone poem, *Music.* an orchestral composition intended to suggest a train of sentiments such as are contained in a poem.

tone poet, a composer of tone poems.

ton·er (tō′nər), *n.* a person or thing that tones.

ton·ey (tō′nē), *adj.,* **ton·i·er, ton·i·est.** tony: *Some Texas motels dispense with the familiar "Vacancy" signs which, they feel, aren't toney* (Wall Street Journal).

tong[1] (tông, tong), *n.* **1.** a Chinese association or club. **2.** *U.S.* a secret Chinese organization or club in the United States. [American English < Chinese *t'ang, t'ong* (originally) meeting hall]

tong[2] (tông, tong), *v.t.* to grasp, gather, hold or handle with tongs, as clams, oysters, or logs. —*v.i.* to use tongs; work with tongs. —**tong′er,** *n.*

ton·ga (tong′gə), *n.* (in India) a light, small, two-wheeled carriage or cart. [< Hindi *tāngā*]

Ton·gan (tong′gən), *adj.* of or having to do with the Tonga Islands, a group of islands northeast of New Zealand in the South Pacific under British control, their people, or their language. —*n.* **1.** a native or inhabitant of these islands. **2.** their Polynesian language.

tong·man (tông′mən, tong′-), *n., pl.* **-men. 1.** a person whose occupation is the catching of oysters with tongs; tonger. **2.** a member of a Chinese tong: *Amid the inscrutable intrigue of old-fashioned tongmen and new-fangled business operators in San Francisco's Chinatown, tiny Dolly Gee, 64, was empress of finance* (Time).

tongs (tôngz, tongz), *n.pl.* **1.** a tool with two arms that are joined by a hinge, pivot, or spring, for seizing, holding, or lifting: *He changed the position of the burning logs with tongs.* See also **lazy tongs** for picture. **2.** a tool for curling hair. [Old English *tong* + *-s*[1]]

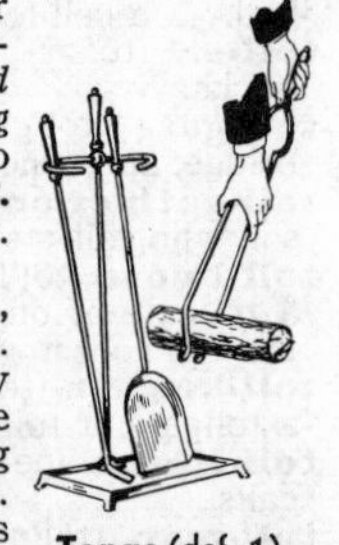
Tongs (def. 1) used to lift log

tongue (tung), *n., v.,* **tongued, tongu·ing.** —*n.* **1. a.** the movable fleshy organ in the mouth. The tongue is used in tasting and, by people, for talking. Most vertebrate animals have tongues. **b.** a similar organ or part in an invertebrate animal. **c.** the tongue of an animal, as a calf, used for food: *cold tongue and salad.* **2.** power of speech; speech: *Have you lost your tongue? Give thy thoughts no tongue* (Shakespeare). **3.** a way of speaking; talk: *a flattering tongue.* **4. a.** the language of a people or nationality: *the English tongue.* **b.** the speech of a particular class or locality; dialect. **c.** language: *a book written in one's native tongue. For he that speaketh in an unknown tongue speaketh not unto men, but unto God: for no man understandeth him* (I Corinthians 14:2). **5.** something shaped or used like a tongue. **6.** the strip of leather, etc., under the laces of a shoe, boot, etc. **7.** a narrow strip of land running into the sea or between two branches of a river. **8.** a tapering jet of flame, light, etc. **9.** the hinged pin of a buckle, brooch, etc. **10.** a long wooden bar attached to the front axle of a carriage, wagon, etc., and extending between the horses or animals that are harnessed to it; pole. **11.** a projecting strip along the edge of a board for fitting into a groove in the edge of another board: *tongue and groove boards.* **12.** the pointer of a dial, balance, etc. **13.** a movable piece inside a bell that swings and rings; clapper. **14.** the vibrating reed or the like in a musical instrument. **15.** the short movable rail of a switch in a railroad or other track. It is tapered at the end to pick up and guide the wheels passing over it when the switch is closed. **16.** *Machinery.* a projecting flange, rib, or strip for any purpose.
at one's tongue's end, in readiness for saying or reciting at any time: *to have names or dates at one's tongue's end.*
give tongue, to bark, as hounds at the sight

of game: *Coonhounds and other breeds bay, or give tongue, when trailing game* (World Book Encyclopedia).
hold one's tongue, to keep still: *Here is your father who knows . . ., though he thinks it best to hold his tongue* (Georgiana Craik).
on one's tongue, almost or ready to be spoken: *The words had been on his tongue all the evening* (Edith Wharton).
on (or **at**) **the tip of one's tongue,** on the point of being spoken; ready to be spoken: *His name is on the tip of my tongue, but I can't seem to remember it. She had arguments at the tip of her tongue* (Daniel Defoe).
wag one's tongue, to chatter; gossip: *Every one who owed him a grudge would eagerly begin to wag his tongue* (William H. Dixon).
with (one's) tongue in (one's) cheek, with sly humor; not to be taken seriously or literally; mockingly: *He enjoys needling the wrong kind of reader by occasionally overwriting with his tongue in his cheek* (Punch). *He painted his apparently flippant still life arrangements with his tongue in his cheek* (Observer).
—*v.t.* **1.** to modify the tones of (a flute, cornet, etc.) with the tongue. **2. a.** to provide with a tongue. **b.** to join (boards) by fitting a tongue into a groove. **3.** to touch with the tongue or with a tongue: *The horse tongued the bit.* **4.** to scold: *Falstaff tongued the barmaid for spilling the ale.* **5.** to utter; pronounce; voice: *What avails . . . to tongue mute misery* (Joel Barlow). —*v.i.* **1.** to use the tongue. **2.** to modify the tones of an instrument by tonguing. **3.** to talk volubly; prattle: *Quiet, ye tonguing gossips!* **4.** to project, as a strip of land, ice, etc. **5.** to throw out jets of flame, light, etc.
[Old English *tunge*]

tongue-and-groove joint (tung′ən grüv′), a joint made by fitting a projecting strip along the edge of one board into a groove cut along the edge of another board, as in matchboard.

tongue-and-groove plane, a carpenter's plane for making tongues and grooves.

-tongued, *combining form.* having a —— tongue or tongues: *Many-tongued = having many tongues.*

tongue depressor, a thin blade of wood used to hold down the tongue in an examination of the mouth and throat.

tongue graft, *Horticulture.* a whip graft.

tongue-in-cheek (tung′in chēk′), *adj.* not to be taken seriously or literally; mockingly ironical or satirical: *All the stories are . . . amusing, mildly racy, and acted with a tongue-in-cheek seriousness that adds up to a rib of Hollywood* (Time).

tongue-lash (tung′lash′), *v.i., v.t.* to reprove loudly or severely; scold: *He . . . personally tongue-lashed employees who fell below his lofty standards* (Time).

tongue-lash·ing (tung′lash′ing), *n.* a loud or severe reprimand; a scolding: *An awkward, excitable man who could never remember his left from his right, and shouldered arms when he should have presented them . . . had to listen to tongue-lashings from a sergeant* (Frank O'Connor).

tongue·less (tung′lis), *adj.* **1.** having no tongue. **2.** speechless; mute.

tongue·let (tung′lit), *n.* a little tongue.

tongue·ster (tung′stər), *n.* a talker; gossip.

tongue-tie (tung′tī′), *n., v.,* **-tied, -ty·ing.** —*n.* impeded motion of the tongue caused by abnormal shortness of the frenum of the tongue. —*v.t.* to make (a person) unable to speak, because of amazement, fear, or timidity, etc.: *The ligaments, which tongue-tied him, were loosened* (Charles Lamb).

tongue-tied (tung′tīd′), *adj.* **1.** having the motion of the tongue hindered. **2. a.** unable to speak because of shyness, embarrassment, etc.; speechless; silent: *to be tongue-tied with rage.* **b.** reserved; reticent.

tongue twister, a series of words, usually alliterative, difficult to say quickly and correctly. *Example:* She sells seashells at the seashore.

tongue-twist·ing (tung′twis′ting), *adj.* of or like a tongue twister; difficult to say quickly and rapidly: *tongue-twisting lyrics.*

tongue worm, 1. any of a group of small tongue-shaped parasites which reach the adult stage in the nasal passages and sinuses of animals. **2.** a small, soft-bodied sea animal; hemichordate.

tongue·y (tung′ē), *adj.* **1.** *Informal.* talkative; loquacious; garrulous. **2.** of or like a tongue; produced by the tongue; lingual.

tongu·ing (tung′ing), *n. Music.* the process or result of modifying or interrupting the tone by rapidly repeated strokes of the tongue, in playing a wind instrument.

ton·ic (ton′ik), *n.* **1. a.** anything that gives strength, invigorates, or braces: *The clean country air was a tonic to the tourists.* **b.** a medicine or remedy: *Cod-liver oil and sassafras tea are tonics.* **2.** *Music.* the first note or fundamental tone of a scale; keynote. **3.** *Phonetics, Obsolete.* a voiced sound. **4.** *U.S.* flavored carbonated water: *celery tonic.* [< adjective]
—*adj.* **1. a.** restoring to health and vigor; giving strength; bracing: *The mountain air is tonic.* **b.** refreshing to the mind or spirit: *Since most bands playing Chicago at the time were of the Dixieland persuasion, to hear Lombardo's restrained melodies over the air was a strange and tonic experience for many residents of the region* (New Yorker). **2. a.** having to do with muscular tension. **b.** characterized by continuous contraction of the muscles: *a tonic convulsion.* **3.** *Music.* **a.** having to do with a tone or tones. **b.** of or based on a keynote: *a tonic chord.* **4.** *Linguistics.* **a.** of or having to do with tone or accent in speaking. **b.** (of a language) using tone distinctively. **5.** *Phonetics.* **a.** stressed; accented. **b.** (formerly) voiced. **6.** of or having to do with the effect of color, or of light and shade, in a picture.
[< Greek *tonikós* of stretching < *tónos* tension; see TONE]

tonic accent, 1. accent given to a syllable in pronunciation as distinct from written accent. **2.** accent featuring pitch rather than loudness.

ton·i·cal·ly (ton′ə klē), *adv.* **1.** as a tonic. **2.** in a tonic manner.

to·nic·i·ty (tō nis′ə tē), *n.* **1.** tonic quality or condition. **2.** the property of possessing bodily tone; the normal elastic tension of living muscles, arteries, etc.

tonic sol-fa, a system of teaching music, especially sight singing, that emphasizes tonality or key relationship. The seven notes of any major scale are sung to the sol-fa syllables, with *do* always denoting the tonic or keynote, and the remaining syllables indicating the relation to it of the other notes of the scale.

tonic spasm, a prolonged contraction of a muscle or muscles without relaxation for some time.

to·night or **to-night** (tə nīt′), *n.* the night of this day; this night.
—*adv.* **1.** on or during this very night: *Do you think it will snow tonight?* **2.** on or during the night following this day. **3.** *Obsolete or Dialect.* on or during the night just past; last night.
[Old English *tō niht*]
➤ See **today** for usage note.

to·nite[1] (tō′nīt), *n.* an explosive consisting of guncotton and barium nitrate, used in blasting or in small bombs. [< Latin *tonāre* to thunder + English *-ite*[1]]

to·nite[2] (tə nīt′), *n., adv. Informal.* tonight.

ton·ka bean (tong′kə), **1.** the black, fragrant, almond-shaped seed of any of various large trees of the pea family, of Brazil, Guiana, and adjacent regions, used in snuff and perfumes. **2.** any of these trees.

ton·kin (ton′kin′), *n.* a high grade of bamboo, used for ski and fishing poles. [< *Tonkin,* a former French protectorate in Indochina, now in North Vietnam]

Ton·kin·ese (ton′kə nēz′, tong′-, tông′-; -nēs′), *n., pl.* **-ese,** *adj.* —*n.* **1.** a native or inhabitant of Tonkin, a former French protectorate in northern Indochina, now part of North Vietnam. **2.** the Vietnamese dialect of the Tonkinese. —*adj.* of or having to do with Tonkin, its people, or their dialect.

ton mile, 1. one ton of freight carried a distance of one mile, a unit of measurement in transportation statistics: *Ton miles of freight moved by trucks today are four times greater than before the war* (New York Times). **2.** a unit of measurement in estimating automobile economy. The loaded weight of the car in tons is multiplied by the miles traveled, and divided by the number of gallons of gasoline consumed.

tonn., tonnage.

ton·nage (tun′ij), *n.* **1. a.** the carrying capacity of a ship, expressed in tons of 100 cubic feet: *A ship of 50,000 cubic feet of space for freight has a tonnage of 500 tons.* **b.** the amount of a commodity or other cargo shipped, loaded, unloaded, etc., expressed in tons of 40 cubic feet. **2.** the total amount of shipping in tons; ships considered with reference to their carrying capacity or together with their cargoes. **3.** a duty or tax on ships for each ton of cargo, as at a wharf, on a canal, etc. **4.** weight in tons.

ton·neau (tu nō′), *n., pl.* **-neaus** or **-neaux** (-nōz′). **1.** the rear part of an automobile body, with seats for passengers and its own doors. **2.** an automobile body having such a rear part. **3.** a metric ton. [< French *tonneau* (literally) cask < *tonne* cask < a Germanic word]

ton·neaued (tu nōd′), *adj.* having a tonneau.

-tonner, *combining form.* something that weighs —— tons: *A 48,000-tonner = a ship that weighs 48,000 tons.*

ton·o·graph (ton′ə graf, -gräf; tō′nə-), *n.* a tonometer.

ton·o·graph·ic (ton′ə graf′ik, tō′nə-), *adj.* tonometric.

to·nog·ra·phy (tə nog′rə fē), *n.* tonometry.

to·nom·e·ter (tō nom′ə tər), *n.* **1.** an instrument, especially a tuning fork or a graduated set of tuning forks, for determining the pitch of tones. **2.** an instrument for measuring the tension of the eyeball, or for measuring blood pressure within the blood vessels. **3.** *Chemistry.* an instrument for measuring strains within a liquid, or for measuring vapor pressure. [(definition 1) < Latin *tonus* tone + English *-meter;* (definition 2, 3) < Greek *tónos* tension]

ton·o·met·ric (ton′ə met′rik, tō′nə-), *adj.* **1.** of or with a tonometer. **2.** of or having to do with tonometry.

to·nom·e·try (tō nom′ə trē), *n.* measurement with a tonometer.

ton·qua bean (tong′kə), tonka bean.

ton·sil (ton′səl), *n.* either of the two oval masses of glandular tissue on the sides of the throat, just back of the mouth. [< Latin *tōnsillae,* plural, related to *tōlēs* goiter]

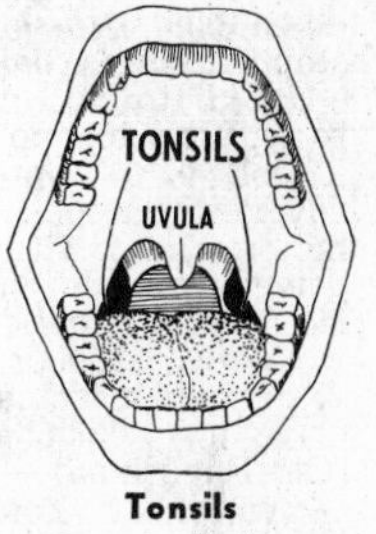

Tonsils

ton·sil·lar or **ton·sil·ar** (ton′sə lər), *adj.* of or having to do with the tonsils.

ton·sil·lec·to·my (ton′sə lek′tə mē), *n., pl.* **-mies.** the surgical removal of the tonsils. [< *tonsil* + Greek *ektomē* a cutting out]

ton·sil·lit·ic (ton′sə lit′ik), *adj.* of or affected with tonsillitis.

ton·sil·li·tis (ton′sə lī′tis), *n.* inflammation of the tonsils. [< Latin *tōnsillae* tonsils + English *-itis*]

ton·sil·lo·scope (ton sil′ə skōp), *n.* an instrument for examining the tonsils.

ton·sil·lo·scop·ic (ton sil′ə skop′ik), *adj.* of or with a tonsilloscope.

ton·sil·lot·o·my (ton′sə lot′ə mē), *n., pl.* **-mies.** the surgical removal of all or part of a tonsil. [< Latin *tōnsillae* tonsils + Greek *-tomiā* a cutting]

ton·so·ri·al (ton sôr′ē əl, -sōr′-), *adj.* of or having to do with a barber or his work (often used humorously). [< Latin *tōnsōrius* having to do with a *tōnsor, -ōris* barber < *tondēre* shear, shave]

ton·sure (ton′shər), *n., v.,* **-sured, -sur·ing.** —*n.* **1.** a clipping of the hair or shaving of the head or a part of the head of a person entering the priesthood or an order of monks. **2.** the shaved part of the head of a priest or monk. **3.** the state of being so shaved.
—*v.t.* to shave the head of, especially as a religious ritual.
[< Latin *tōnsūra* < *tondēre* shear, shave]

ton·sured (ton′shərd), *adj.* having undergone tonsure, especially ecclesiastical tonsure.

ton·tine (ton′tēn, ton tēn′), *n.* **1.** a system of annuity or insurance in which subscribers share a fund. The shares of survivors increase as members die, until the last gets all that is left. **2.** the total of money involved in such a system. **3.** the share or right of each member in such system. **4.** the members as a group. —*adj.* of, having to do with, or like a tontine: *a tontine policy.* [< French *tontine* < Lorenzo *Tonti,* an Italian banker who introduced it into France around 1653]

ton-up (tun′up′), *adj. British Slang.* **1.** traveling in motorcycles at high or reckless speeds; doing a ton: *ton-up boys.* **2.** having to do with or used by ton-up boys: *a ton-up road, black-leather ton-up outfits.*

to·nus (tō′nəs), *n.* **1.** bodily or muscular tone. **2.** a tonic spasm. [< Latin *tonus* < Greek *tónos* tension, tone]

ton·y (tō′nē), *adj.,* **ton·i·er, ton·i·est.** *Slang.* high-toned; fashionable; stylish. [< *ton*[2] + *-y*[1]]

To·ny (tō′nē), *n., pl.* **-nys.** an award presented annually in the United States for outstanding achievements in the theater: *The "Tony" awards . . . were established in 1947 to honor the memory of Antoinette Perry, well-known actress* (New York Times).

too (tü), *adv.* **1.** besides; also: *The dog is hungry, and very thirsty too. We, too, are going away.* **2.** beyond what is desirable, proper, or right; more than enough: *My dress is too long for you. He ate too much. The summer passed too quickly.* **3.** exceedingly; very: *I am only too glad to help.*
[spelling variant of *to,* Old English *tō* to, too]

took (tu̇k), *v.* the past tense of **take**: *She took the car an hour ago.*

tool (tül), *n.* **1.** a knife, hammer, saw, shovel, or any instrument used in doing work: *a carpenter's tools. Most boys like to work with tools.* **2.** anything used like a tool; constituting an instrument of work: *Books are a scholar's tools.* **3.** a person or group used by another like a tool: *He is the tool of the party boss.* **4. a.** a part of a machine that cuts, bores, smooths, etc. **b.** the whole of such a machine. **5.** *Law.* any implement or apparatus needed to carry on one's business or profession: *tools of trade.* **6. a.** a small stamp or roller used to impress designs on book covers. **b.** the design so impressed.
down tools, *British.* to lay down one's tools; stop working: *to down tools for the holiday.*
—*v.t.* **1.** to work or shape with a tool or tools; use a tool on. **2. a.** to ornament with a tool. **b.** to impress a design on (a book cover) with a tool. **3.** to provide or equip (a factory, etc.) with tools. **4.** *Informal.* to drive (a vehicle) in a certain way: *to tool a car smoothly down the street.* —*v.i.* **1.** to work with a tool or tools, as in bookbinding. **2.** to equip a factory, etc., with tools. **3.** to drive in a vehicle: *to tool through the town.*
[Old English *tōl*] —**tool′er,** *n.*
—**Syn.** *n.* **1. Tool, implement** mean an instrument or other article used in doing work. **Tool** means an instrument or simple device especially suited or designed to make a particular kind of work easier, but traditionally applies particularly to something held and worked by the hands in doing manual work: *Plumbers, mechanics, carpenters, and shoemakers need tools.* **Implement** is a general word meaning a tool, instrument, utensil, or mechanical device needed to do something: *Hoes and tractors are agricultural implements.*

tool box, a box in which tools and sometimes small parts, accessories, etc., are kept.

tool·hold·er (tül′hōl′dər), *n.* **1.** a detachable handle used with different tools. **2.** a device for holding the tool of a machine in position for work.

tool house, a building in which tools are kept.

tool·ing (tü′ling), *n.* **1.** work done with a tool. **2.** ornamentation made with a tool: *leather tooling.* **3.** the assembly of machine tools in a factory.

tool·mak·er (tül′mā′kər), *n.* **1.** a machinist who makes, repairs, and maintains machine tools. **2.** any maker of tools: *Prehistoric men were the first toolmakers.*

tool·mak·ing (tül′mā′king), *n.* the work of a toolmaker. —*adj.* that is a toolmaker; involved in making tools.

tool pusher, *Slang.* the person in charge of drilling operations at an oil well: *Operations will be directed in principle by a "tool pusher," an engineer, and a geologist* (London Times).

tool·room (tül′rüm′, -ru̇m′), *n.* a department in a machine shop in which tools are made, kept, and handed out to the workers.

tool·shed (tül′shed′), *n.* tool house.

tool subject, an educational subject taught for its usefulness in other fields, not for its own sake, such as arithmetic, spelling, etc.

toom (tüm), *Scottish.* —*adj.* empty. —*v.t.* to empty. [Old English *tōm*]

too-much·ness (tü′much′nis), *n.* excessiveness: *Indeed, what his book tends particularly to suffer from is a sense of too-muchness, of a larger framework, a fuller commentary, than the subject seems happy with* (Atlantic).

toon (tün), *n.* **1.** a tree of the mahogany family of the East Indies and Australia, that yields a red wood like mahogany, but softer and lighter. **2.** the wood itself, used for furniture, cabinetwork, etc. [< Hindi *tun, tūn* < Sanskrit *tunna*]

toot[1] (tüt), *n.* **1.** the sound of a horn, whistle, etc.; short blast: *The factory gives three toots of the whistle at noon.*
—*v.i.* **1.** to give forth a short blast: *He heard the train whistle toot three times.* **2.** to sound or blow a whistle, horn, etc. **3.** (of a grouse) to utter its call.
—*v.t.* to sound (a horn, whistle, etc.) in short blasts.
[probably ultimately imitative] —**toot′er,** *n.*

toot[2] (tüt), *n. U.S. Slang.* a spree, especially a drinking spree: *to go on a toot.* [earlier, a large drink < obsolete *toot,* verb, to drink copiously; origin unknown]

tooth (tüth), *n., pl.* **teeth,** *v.* —*n.* **1. a.** one of the hard, bonelike parts in the mouth, attached in a row to each jaw, used for biting and chewing. Animals use their teeth as weapons of attack or defense. A tooth in man and most vertebrates is usually composed of dentine surrounding a hollow filled with pulp, through which run blood vessels and nerves, and coated at the root with cementum and at the crown and exposed parts with enamel. See **incisor** for picture. **b.** any of certain hard parts or processes in the mouth or digestive tract of invertebrates. **2.** something like a tooth: *Each one of the pointed projections of a comb, saw, file, rake, harrow, fork, etc., is a tooth.* **3.** one of the series of projections on the edge of a gearwheel, pinion, etc., that engage with others to transmit or convert motion; cog. **4.** a taste; liking: *to have no tooth for fruit.* **5.** a hurtful, gnawing, or destructive power: *'gainst the tooth of time* (Shakespeare). **6.** *Botany.* **a.** (in mosses) one of the delicate, pointed processes surrounding the mouth of the spore case that together form the peristome. **b.** one of the projections at the margin of certain leaves or petals.
tooth and nail or **claw,** with all one's force; fiercely: *to fight or resist tooth and nail.*
—*v.t.* **1.** to furnish with teeth; put teeth on. **2.** to cut teeth on the edge of; indent. —*v.i.* to interlock.
[Old English *tōth*] —**tooth′like′,** *adj.*

tooth·ache (tüth′āk′), *n.* a pain in or around a tooth or the teeth.

tooth·brush (tüth′brush′), *n.* a small, stiff brush for cleaning the teeth.

toothbrush mustache, a small, bristly mustache: *On a face so boyish, the small toothbrush mustache seems almost an affectation* (Harper's).

toothed (tütht, tüᴛʜd), *adj.* having teeth; notched.

toothed whale, a whale or related sea mammal with true teeth in one or both jaws, as the sperm whale, narwhal, bottlenose, dolphin, or porpoise.

tooth·i·ly (tü′thə lē), *adv.* in a toothy manner: *Paul Eddington's toothily genial Mr. Puff is a delightful comic creation* (London Times).

tooth·less (tüth′lis), *adj.* without teeth: *a toothless old man.*

toothless whale, a whale or related sea mammal that has horny plates of whalebone in place of teeth, as the right whale, gray whale, humpback and sulphur-bottom; whalebone whale.

tooth ornament, *Architecture.* a projecting ornament of a pyramidal or flowerlike form, often repeated in a series in a hollow molding; dogtooth.

tooth·paste (tüth′pāst′), *n.* a paste used in cleaning the teeth. [American English]

tooth·pick (tüth′pik′), *n.* a small, pointed piece of wood, sharpened quill, etc., used for removing bits of food from between the teeth.

tooth·pow·der (tüth′pou′dər), *n.* a powder used in cleaning the teeth.

tooth shell, **1.** the long, tubular, toothlike shell of any of certain mollusks. **2.** any of these mollusks.

tooth·some (tüth′səm), *adj.* **1.** pleasing to the taste; tasty. **2.** pleasing in appearance; comely: *a toothsome girl.* —**tooth′some·ly,** *adv.* —**tooth′some·ness,** *n.* —**Syn. 1.** savory, delicious.

tooth·wort (tüth′wėrt′), *n.* **1.** a European and Asian parasitic herb of the figwort family with a rootstock that is covered with toothlike scales. **2.** any of a group of plants of the mustard family having toothlike projections upon its creeping rootstock.

tooth·y (tü′thē), *adj.,* **tooth·i·er, tooth·i·est.** **1.** showing many teeth prominently: *a toothy smile.* **2.** having teeth.

too·tle (tü′təl), *v.,* **-tled, -tling,** *n.* —*v.i.* to toot continuously; produce a succession of toots. —*v.t.* to play by tooting; toot steadily. —*n.* a tootling. [frequentative of *toot*[1]]

too·tler (tüt′lər), *n.* **1.** a person or thing that tootles. **2.** a writer of verbiage or twaddle.

too-too (tü′tü′), *adj.* excessive; extreme: *The piece is nowhere; but my frocks are too-too!* (Mrs. A. Kennard). —*adv.* excessively; extremely: *The too-too painfully ceremonious manners . . . of the French* (Notes and Queries). [reduplication of *too*]

toot·sy (tüt′sē), *n., pl.* **-sies.** *Informal.* **1.** a foot, especially a child's or woman's small foot. **2.** a toe.

toot·sy-woot·sy (tüt′sē wüt′sē), *n., pl.* **-sies.** *Informal.* tootsy.

top[1] (top), *n., adj., v.,* **topped, top·ping.** —*n.* **1.** the highest point or part; peak; summit: *the top of a tree, the top of a mountain.* **2.** the upper end or surface: *the top of a book, the top of a table.* **3.** the highest or leading place, rank, etc.: *He is at the top of the class.* **4.** a person or thing that occupies the highest or leading position; head; chief: *a conference with the tops of government. He is the top in his profession.* **5.** the highest point, pitch, or degree: *the top of the market, at the top of one's voice, the top of fashion.* **6.** the best or most important part: *the top of the morning, a hotel serving the top of society.* **7. a.** the part of a plant growing above ground, as distinct from the root: *carrot tops, turnip tops.* **b.** one of the tender tips of branches or shoots. **8.** the head, especially the crown of the head: *a shaved top.* **9.** a lid or cover; cap: *a top for a kettle, a new top for an automobile, the top of a can.* **10.** the upper part of a shoe or boot. **11.** a bunch of hair, fibers, etc.; tuft; crest. **12. a.** a platform around the head of a lower mast on a ship, and serving as a foothold for sailors, a means of extending the upper rigging, etc. **b.** a similar part of the superstructure of a warship, for firing light guns, observation, etc. **13. a.** the highest card of a suit in a hand. **b.** the highest score made on a particular hand by any team at duplicate bridge. **c.** an ace or a king. **14.** (in golf) a stroke above the center of a ball. **15.** a bundle of combed wool prepared for spinning; sliver. **16.** a tent used as a covering for a circus or other performance. **17.** (in baseball) the first half of an inning: *the top of the seventh.* **18.** *Chemistry.* the part in a distillation that volatilizes first.

TOP

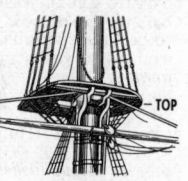

Top[1] (def. 12a)

blow one's top, *Slang.* **a.** to lose one's temper; get very excited: *It is no secret that he often resents criticism, . . . and that he blows his top from time to time* (Harper's). **b.** to become insane: *A prisoner blew his top and tried to kill one of the guards.*
from top to toe, a. from head to foot: *She was dressed in brown from top to toe.* **b.** completely: *[They were] English from top to toe* (James Russell Lowell).
off (or **out of**) **the top of one's head,** *Informal.* without consideration; in an impromptu manner; spontaneously: *The Bishop was such an easy mark for criticism, and the comments of his detractors had been so abundant, making so many points (some of them off the top of their heads), and yet the congregation at large had been so nearly silent* (New Yorker).
on top, with success; with victory: *Which of the two fighters came out on top?*
on top of, a. in addition to: *On top of everything else, it's raining* (Manchester Guardian Weekly). **b.** in control of: *The conductor was always on top of the music, keeping it alive and moving* (New York Times). **c.** following closely: *Hot on top of [him] came Hyndman, struggling to [pass] his . . . opponent* (London Times).

over the top, a. over the front of a trench to make an attack: *Some fellows asked our captain when we were going over the top* (War Illustrated). **b.** over a goal or quota: *The salesman who goes over the top this month will get a bonus.*
top of the morning, a very good morning (used as a greeting): *Captain, my darling, the top of the morning to you!* (Charles J. Lever).
—*adj.* **1.** having to do with, situated at, or forming the top: *the top shelf of a cupboard.* **2.** highest in degree; greatest: *The runners set off at top speed. We pay top prices for used cars.* **3.** chief; foremost: *top honors.*
—*v.t.* **1.** to put a top on: *to top a box.* **2. a.** to be on top of; be at the top of; crown: *A church tops the hill.* **b.** to be or form the top of: *A steeple tops the church.* **3.** to reach the top of: *They topped the mountain.* **4.** to rise above: *The sun topped the horizon.* **5.** to be higher than; be greater than: *That bid tops the best I can afford.* **6.** to do or be better than; surpass; outdo; excel: *His story topped all the rest.* **7.** in golf: **a.** to hit (a ball) above center. **b.** to make (a shot) in this way, usually causing a foozle: *He topped his drive.* **8.** to cut off the top of (a plant, tree, etc.); crop; prune. **9.** *Chemistry.* (in distillation) to remove the part that volatilizes first; skim. **10.** to treat (material, fabric, etc.) with a final dye to improve the color.
top and tail, *British.* to take off both ends of; pull off the greens and roots of (turnips, carrots, etc.): *A gentleman . . . was topping and tailing gooseberries for wine* (L. M. Hawkins).
top off, a. to finish; end: *The market has been broadly hinting that the longlived business boom is topping off* (Wall Street Journal). **b.** to put the finishing touch to: *to top off dinner with a fine cigar.*
top out, a. to reach the top; end: *Real estate values across the country generally topped out during the past year, according to a survey by Chase Manhattan Bank* (Wall Street Journal). **b.** to complete the skeletonic structure of (a building being erected): *The building has been topped out and brickwork now is under way* (New York Times).
top up, to refill: *The terphenyl undergoes slow decomposition in the reactor, and has to be topped up at the rate of 1 or 2 per cent per day* (New Scientist).
[Old English *topp*]
—**Syn.** *n.* **1. Top, summit, crown** mean the highest point or part of something. **Top** is the general word: *It is now easy to drive to the top of Grandfather Mountain.* **Summit** means the topmost point that can be reached, and when used figuratively means the highest level attainable: *The road does not go to the summit. At last he attained the summit of his ambition.* **Crown,** used figuratively, means the highest degree of perfection or completion or highest state or quality: *A Nobel prize is the crown of success.* -*v.t.* **1.** cap.
top[2] (top), *n.* a toy that spins on a point.
sleep like a top, to sleep soundly: *No noisy window [air conditioning] units . . . you sleep like a top* (New Yorker).
[origin uncertain. Compare Old High German *topf,* Old French *topoie.*]

Top[2]

top-, *combining form.* the form of **topo-** before vowels, as in *topectomy.*
to·parch (tō′pärk, top′ärk), *n.* the ruler of a small district or state. [< Greek *topárchēs* < *tópos* place + *árchein* rule]
to·par·chy (tō′pär kē, top′är-), *n., pl.* **-chies.** a little district or state.
to·paz (tō′paz), *n.* **1.** a hard crystalline mineral, a compound of aluminum, silica, and fluorine, that occurs in various forms and colors: *Transparent yellow, pink, and blue topaz are used as gems.* **2.** either of two South American hummingbirds that have bright feathers. **3.** a clear, light brown with a trace of yellow. [Middle English *topace,* or *topaze* < Old French *topace,* learned borrowing from Latin *topazus* < Greek *tópazos* the "Oriental topaz"]
to·paz·o·lite (tō paz′ə līt), *n.* a kind of garnet that looks like topaz in color.
top banana, *Slang.* **1.** the leading comedian, as in burlesque: *He is the top banana. He is, indeed, the whole film* (New York Times). **2.** a leader in any field: *Playing to the hilt his role as top banana on the world diplomatic circuit, Nikita Khrushchev last week took his road show to Asia* (Time).

top boot, 1. a high boot having the upper part of different material and made to look as if turned down. **2.** any boot with a high top.

Top Boot (def. 1)

top-boot·ed (top′bü′tid), *adj.* wearing top boots.
top brass, *U.S. Slang.* **1.** high-ranking military officers: *How long will this careless attitude of some of the troops be tolerated by the top brass?* (Time). **2.** high officials: *CBS hired Silvers after his now-famous appearance before the assembled top brass of the government* (Harper's).
top·coat (top′kōt′), *n.* **1.** a lightweight overcoat. **2.** a loose overcoat.
top cover, 1. air cover at high altitude for a military force or flying mission: *The other four MIG's engaged the Saberjets that were flying top cover for the reconnaissance craft* (New York Times). **2.** the airplanes making up such protection.
top cross, *Genetics.* the offspring produced when a variety is crossed with one inbred line.
top dog, 1. the dog uppermost or on top in a fight. **2.** *Informal.* the victorious group or dominant person; highest, best, or most successful individual: *Norway has been top dog of the whaling business for more than half a century* (Wall Street Journal).
top drawer, *Informal.* the highest level of importance, excellence, etc.: *a family in the top drawer of Washington society.*
top-drawer (top′drôr′), *adj. Informal.* of the highest level of excellence, importance, etc.: *This matter is top-drawer; keep it in mind at all times.*
top-dress (top′dres′), *v.t.* **1.** to spread manure or other fertilizer on the surface of (a piece of land), as before planting or between the rows after planting: *Country which it was difficult or impossible to top-dress by traditional methods can now be treated from the air* (London Times). **2.** to put crushed rock on (a road).
top-dress·ing (top′dres′ing), *n.* **1.** fertilizer applied to the surface and not worked in. **2.** crushed rock, gravel, etc., put on a road without working it in. **3.** the application of such material.
top-dyed (top′dīd′), *adj.* (of fibers, as worsted) dyed as a top or sliver to allow for the blending of colors before the final spinning: *top-dyed woolen or worsted yarn.*
tope[1] (tōp), *v.,* **toped, top·ing.** —*v.t.* to drink (alcoholic liquor) to excess or as a habit. —*v.i.* to be a toper. [perhaps < obsolete *tope,* interjection, used in drinking, apparently in sense "done!," for accepting a toast or a wager < French *toper* < Spanish *topar* accept a wager; (originally) collide; imitative]
tope[2] (tōp), *n.* a small European shark. [origin uncertain]
tope[3] (tōp), *n.* an ancient, dome-shaped monument in Buddhist countries for preserving relics or commemorating some event. [< Hindi *tōp,* perhaps < Pali *thūpo,* ultimately < Sanskrit *stūpa.* Doublet of STUPA.]
tope[4] (tōp), *n.* (in India) a clump, grove, or plantation of trees. [< Tamil *tōppu*]
top-ech·e·lon (top′esh′ə lon), *adj.* high-ranking; of a high level of command or authority: *Top-echelon administrators argued that the people would have to be told the facts if our military defenses were to be bolstered* (Bulletin of Atomic Scientists).
to·pec·to·mize (tə pek′tə mīz), *v.t.,* **-mized, -miz·ing.** to perform a topectomy on.
to·pec·to·my (tə pek′tə mē), *n., pl.* **-mies.** a surgical incision into the cortex of the brain to relieve the symptoms of psychosis. [< *top-* + Greek *ektomē* a cutting out]
to·pee (tō pē′, tō′pē), *n.* topi[1].
top·er (tō′pər), *n.* a person who drinks alcoholic liquor too much or as a habit.
top flight, the highest level or rank: *In the top flight of Britain's Quality Cars—at £2,645* (Sunday Times).
top-flight (top′flīt′), *adj. Informal.* excellent; first-rate; foremost: *The prophet Ezekiel was a top-flight scientific observer and recorder of important meteorological phenomena* (Science News).
top·full (top′fu̇l′), *adj.* full to the top; brimful.
top·gal·lant (top′gal′ənt; *Nautical* tə-gal′ənt), *n.* a mast, sail, yard, etc., next above a topmast, topsail, topsail yard, etc., of any mast. See **sail** for picture.
—*adj.* **1.** of or belonging to a topgallant; next above the topmast. **2.** (of a deck, rail, etc.) situated above a corresponding adjacent part: *topgallant forecastle.* **3.** lofty; grand; first-rate: *To have a new planet swim into one's ken . . . this is topgallant delight* (Clifton Fadiman).
[< *top*[1] + *gallant* (because it makes a brave or gallant show in comparison with the other rigging)]
top gear, *British.* high gear.
top-grade (top′grād′), *adj.* of the highest grade or quality: *Prices for top-grade steers fell to the lowest levels as cattle producers flooded stock yards with huge supplies* (Wall Street Journal).
top grafting, the insertion of a graft in the top or branches of a tree or plant to obtain an improved variety.
toph (tōf), *n.* tophus.
top·ham·per (top′ham′pər), *n.,* **1. a.** the upper masts, sails, rigging, etc., on a ship. **b.** all the spars and rigging above the deck. **2.** any unnecessary weight or rigging aloft or on the deck; hamper.
top hat, a tall, black silk hat worn by men in formal clothes; high hat.
top-hat (top′hat′), *adj. Informal.* high-class; top-drawer: *top-hat executives.*
top-hat·ted (top′hat′id), *adj.* wearing a top hat: [*He*] *is not the kind of big-business man cartoonists portray as fat and top-hatted* (Newsweek).
tophe (tōf), *n.* tophus.
top-heav·i·ness (top′hev′ē nis), *n.* a being top-heavy.
top-heav·y (top′hev′ē), *adj.* **1.** too heavy at the top. **2.** liable to fall or fail as from too great weight above; unstable. **3.** overcapitalized, as a business corporation. **4.** having too many officials of high rank: *a department top-heavy with full professors.*
To·phet or **To·pheth** (tō′fit), *n.* **1.** hell; Gehenna. **2.** a place in the valley of Hinnom, near Jerusalem, where human sacrifices were offered to Moloch. It was later used as a garbage dump and came to symbolize the place of eternal torment. [< Hebrew *tōpheth*]
top-hole (top′hōl′), *adj. British Slang.* first-rate; top-notch.
to·phus (tō′fəs), *n., pl.* **-phi** (-fī). **1.** a small, hard, chalklike growth in the tissues and joints of the feet and hands, around the teeth, etc., in severe cases of gout; chalkstone. **2.** tufa. [< Latin *tōphus,* variant of *tōfus* loose stones. Compare TUFA.]
to·pi[1] (tō pē′, tō′pē), *n.* a helmet made of pith to protect the head against the sun. Also, **topee.** [Anglo-Indian < Hindi *ṭopī,* perhaps related to *top* helmet or hat]
to·pi[2] (tō′pē), *n.* a large African antelope, a variety of hartebeest. [origin uncertain. Compare Swahili *tope.*]
to·pi·a·rist (tō′pē ər ist), *n.* a person skilled in topiary art.
to·pi·ar·y (tō′pē er′ē), *adj., n., pl.* **-ar·ies.** —*adj.* **1.** trimmed or clipped into ornamental shapes: *topiary shrubs and trees.* **2.** of or having to do with such trimming: *topiary art.*
—*n.* **1.** topiary art. **2.** a topiary garden.
[< Latin *topiārius* < *topia* ornamental gardening < Greek *tópia,* plural of *tópion* (originally) a field (diminutive) < *tópos* place]
top·ic (top′ik), *n.* **1.** a subject that people think, write, or talk about: *Newspapers discuss the topics of the day. The main topics at Mother's party were the weather and clothes.* **2.** a short phrase or sentence used in an outline to give the main point of a part of a speech, writing, etc. **3.** *Rhetoric and Logic.* a class of considerations or arguments suitable for debate or discourse. **4.** a general rule or maxim.
[singular of *topics* < Latin *topica* < Greek (*tà*) *topiká,* a work by Aristotle of logical and rhetorical generalities or commonplaces; *topiká* < *tópoi* commonplaces; (literally) plural of *tópos* place] —**Syn. 1.** See **subject.**
top·i·cal (top′ə kəl), *adj.* **1.** of or having to do with topics of the day; of current or local interest: *topical news.* **2.** of or using topics; having to do with the topics of a speech, writing, etc.: *Some books have topical outlines for each chapter.* **3. a.** of or having to do with a place or locality; local. **b.** limited or applied to a certain spot or part of the body; not general.

—*n.* one of the stamps in a stamp collection based on a topic or theme, such as airplanes, world's fairs, etc.: *Nobody collects miscellaneously anymore. Let me show you some of my topicals* (Scientific American). —**top'i·cal·ly,** *adv.*

top·i·cal·i·ty (top'ə kal'ə tē), *n., pl.* **-ties.** **1.** the quality of being topical: *I think there are some situations that a writer dare not turn into adventure stories without running the risk of opportunistic topicality* (Paul Pickrel). **2.** a topical reference or allusion: *The only thing wrong with the operas is Gilbert's outrageous puns and outdated topicalities* (Sunday Times).

top·i·nam·bour (top'ə nam'bər), *n.* the Jerusalem artichoke. [< French *topinambour,* alteration of Middle French *topinambou,* (originally) the name of a tribe in Brazil]

top kick, *U.S. Slang.* **1.** a top or first sergeant. **2.** a person in authority; leader; boss: *The Democratic top kick said he checked with the State Department before dispatching the note* (Wall Street Journal). [< *top*[1] + *-kick,* as in *side-kick*]

top·knot (top'not'), *n.* **1.** a knot or tuft of hair on the top of the head of a person or animal. **2.** a plume or crest of feathers on the head of a bird. **3. a.** a knot or bow of ribbon worn by women as a headdress. **b.** a bow of ribbon worn in a lace cap.

top·less (top'lis), *adj.* **1.** having no top; immeasurably high: *The abysses we skirted ... seemed bottomless, and the mountain itself topless* (New Yorker). **2.** lacking an upper part or piece, as a garment: *a topless bathing suit.* **3.** lofty; exalted: *Topless honours be bestowed on thee* (George Chapman). —**top'less·ness,** *n.*

top-lev·el (top'lev'əl), *adj. Informal.* at the highest level of authority, rank, quality, etc.: *a top-level committee meeting* (Wall Street Journal). *His book is therefore a top-level narrative of the development of the bomb* (Atlantic). *Top-level competition to select from the nation's high school seniors those giving promise of being the creative scientists of tomorrow* (Science News Letter).

top line, the headline of a newspaper, etc.

top-line (top'līn'), *adj. Informal.* of the highest rank or quality; leading; foremost; headline: *The Cavour and the Kaiserhof might be top-line hotels, but the manager was going to show ... the humble Moderno was not to be despised* (Atlantic).

top-lin·er (top'lī'nər), *n. Informal.* a person or thing that is top-line; at the head, or in the first or principal place: *Unfortunately only an hour and a half could be given for the debate, which meant that only the top-liners were likely to be called* (Maclean's).

top·loft·i·ly (top'lôf'tə lē, -lof'-), *adv. Informal.* in a toplofty manner: *He ... declines toploftily a publisher's advance and then can't finish his article because he is too hungry to write* (Time).

top·loft·i·ness (top'lôf'tē nis, -lof'-), *n. Informal.* a being toplofty.

top·loft·y (top'lôf'tē, -lof'-), *adj. Informal.* lofty in character or manner; high and mighty; haughty; pompous; pretentious.

top·mak·er (top'mā'kər), *n.* a person who makes or deals in woolen or worsted tops.

top making, the process of making woolen or worsted tops on a machine by combing the sliver to make the fibers lie parallel to one another.

top·man (top'mən), *n., pl.* **-men.** *Nautical.* a man stationed for duty in a top.

top·mast (top'mast', -mäst'; *Nautical.* top'məst), *n.* a smaller mast fixed at the top of a lower mast; the second section above the deck. See **masthead** for picture.

top minnow, any of various small, soft-finned fishes that feed on the surface of the water and bring forth their young alive.

top·most (top'mōst), *adj.* highest; uppermost: *The best cherries always seem to grow on the topmost branches.*

top-notch or **top·notch** (top'noch'), *adj. Informal.* first-rate; best possible: *A comedy about romance and confusion in a pajama factory that makes an absolutely top-notch musical* (New Yorker). —**Syn.** supreme, incomparable.

top·notch·er (top'noch'ər), *n. Informal.* a first-rate person or thing: *It gave me exceptional opportunities to meet the topnotchers in the theatre at benefits* (Tallulah Bankhead).

topo-, *combining form.* place: *Toponym = a place name.* Also, **top-** before vowels. [< Greek *tópos*]

top-of-the-world (top'əv ᴛʜə wėrld'), *adj.* of or having to do with the north polar regions: *United States-Canadian strategists planning defenses in today's top-of-the-world cold war ...* (New York Times).

topog., **1.** topographical. **2.** topography.

to·pog·ra·pher (tə pog'rə fər), *n.* **1.** a person skilled in topography. **2.** a person who accurately describes the surface features of a place or region.

top·o·graph·ic (top'ə graf'ik), *adj.* topographical.

top·o·graph·i·cal (top'ə graf'ə kəl), *adj.* of or having to do with topography: *In explaining the formation of those topographical features ... it is essential not only to know their structure but also the common features of the earth's crust from which they are derived* (Science News Letter).

top·o·graph·i·cal·ly (top'ə graf'ə klē), *adv.* in reference to topography: *Topographically, the tour ran downhill for the remaining five laps* (Newsweek).

topographic or **topographical map,** a map that shows elevations as well as the positions of points, often in color and with contour lines.

to·pog·ra·phy (tə pog'rə fē), *n., pl.* **-phies.** **1.** the science of making an accurate and detailed description or drawing of places or their surface features. **2.** a detailed description of the surface features of a place or region. **3.** the surface features of a place or region: *The topography of a region includes hills, valleys, streams, lakes, bridges, tunnels, roads, etc.* **4.** topographic surveying. [< Late Latin *topographia* < Greek *topographíā* < *topográphos* topographer < *tópos* place + *gráphein* to write]

top·o·log·ic (top'ə loj'ik), *adj.* of or having to do with topology.

top·o·log·i·cal (top'ə loj'ə kəl), *adj.* topologic.

top·o·log·i·cal·ly (top'ə loj'ə klē), *adv.* in reference to topology: *Surfaces may not only have one or two sides; they may also differ topologically in the number and structure of their edges* (Scientific American).

to·pol·o·gist (tə pol'ə jist), *n.* a person skilled in topology.

to·pol·o·gy (tə pol'ə jē), *n.* **1.** the scientific study of a particular locality in order to learn about its history. **2.** the anatomy of a certain area of the body. **3.** *Geometry.* the study of the properties of figures or solids that are not normally affected by changes in size or shape.

top·o·nym (top'ə nim), *n.* **1. a.** a place name; regional name. **b.** a name derived from the name of a place or location. **2.** *Obsolete.* any area of the body of an animal, as distinguished from any organ. [< *top-* + dialectal Greek *ónyma* name]

to·pon·y·mal (tə pon'ə məl), *adj.* toponymic.

top·o·nym·ic (top'ə nim'ik), *adj.* of or having to do with toponymy.

top·o·nym·i·cal (top'ə nim'ə kəl), *adj.* toponymic.

to·pon·y·my (tə pon'ə mē), *n.* **1.** the place names of a country or district as a subject of study. **2.** *Obsolete.* the naming or the names of areas of the body.

top·o·phone (top'ə fōn), *n.* an instrument for determining the direction from which any sound comes. [< *topo-* + *-phone*]

top-out (top'out'), *n.* the completion of the skeletonic structure of a building being erected: *Theoretically, a top-out can occur at any part of the working day, but, frankly, contractors like to arrange things so it falls toward the end of the afternoon* (New Yorker).

top·per (top'ər), *n.* **1.** *Slang.* an excellent, first-rate person or thing. **2.** *Informal.* a top hat. **3.** *Informal.* a topcoat. **4.** a loose-fitting, short, usually lightweight coat, worn by women. **5.** a person or thing that tops.

top·ping (top'ing), *adj.* **1.** *Especially British Informal.* excellent; first-rate. **2. a.** chief; principal. **b.** fine; pretty (often used ironically). **3.** *Obsolete.* that exceeds in height; surpassingly high.

—*n.* **1.** the cutting off of the top (of a tree or plant). **2. a.** the forelock of the hair of the head. **b.** the forelock of a horse or other animal. **c.** the crest of a bird. **d.** the erect tassel of a Scotch cap. **e.** the head (a humorous use). **3.** something put on the top of anything to complete it; top layer. **4.** the distillation of crude oil to separate it into its fractions.

toppings, branches, stems, etc., cut off in topping trees or plants: *to use toppings to make a fire.*

topping lift, *Nautical.* a rope used to support or raise the outer end of a spanker boom or a lower studdingsail boom.

top·ple (top'əl), *v.,* **-pled, -pling.** —*v.i.* **1.** to fall forward; tumble down: *The chimney toppled over on the roof.* **2.** to lean or hang over in an unsteady way: *beneath toppling crags.* —*v.t.* to throw over or down; overturn: *The wrestler toppled his opponent.* [< *top*[1], verb + *-le*] —**Syn.** *v.i.* **2.** teeter.

top-pri·or·i·ty (top'prī ôr'ə tē, -or'-), *adj.* having the highest priority: *The productive capacity of this country is sure to be the enemy's top-priority target in any future war* (Wall Street Journal).

top-qual·i·ty (top'kwol'ə tē), *adj.* of the highest or best quality: *Its heartening feature is that the few top-quality papers are going up in circulation even though they may raise their prices a bit from time to time* (New Yorker).

top-rank (top'rangk'), *adj.* of the highest rank or recognition: [*He*] *had to be drafted on short notice to conduct the première before a tough audience of top-rank musicians, critics and composers* (Time).

top-ranked (top'rangkt'), *adj.* given the highest rank or rating: *Some sponsors seem to be disenchanted about the selling power of even top-ranked shows* (Time).

top-rank·ing (top'rang'king), *adj.* holding the highest rank or rating: *The 40 trip winners were chosen after a nation-wide competition in which top-ranking seniors in all the public, parochial and private schools were invited to participate* (Science News Letter).

top-rat·ed (top'rā'tid), *adj.* holding the highest rating: *There, in their first race, they recorded another remarkable triumph, a one-and-a-half length victory over the top-rated Soviet eight* (Maclean's).

tops (tops), *Slang.* —*adj.* of the highest degree in quality, excellence, etc.

—*n.* **the tops,** an excellent or outstanding person or thing: *That teacher is the tops.*

top·sail (top'sāl'; *Nautical* top'səl), *n.* **1.** a sail, or either of two sails (upper and lower topsail), attached to a yard or yards on a topmast of a square-rigged vessel. See **sail** for picture. **2.** a square sail on the topmast of certain schooners, especially on the foremast. **3.** a gaff-topsail.

top sawyer, **1.** the sawyer who works the upper handle of a pitsaw. **2.** *Informal.* a person who holds a higher position than another; person of consequence or importance.

top secret, *U.S.* a most important and highly guarded secret.

top-se·cret (top'sē'krit), *adj. U.S.* of utmost secrecy; extremely confidential: *The estimate of Communist intent is based on an observable military buildup and on corroborating intelligence from top-secret sources* (Time).

top-seed·ed (top'sē'did), *adj.* given the best position in a seeded list, as in a tennis or other tournament; top-ranked: *The two top-seeded teams advanced to the semifinals* (New York Times).

top-sell·ing (top'sel'ing), *adj. Informal.* best-selling: *The top-selling 80-square print cloth ... dropped to a new 12-year low* (Wall Street Journal).

top sergeant, *U.S. Informal.* the first sergeant of a military company; top kick.

top shell, any of a group of marine mollusks with a spiral, regularly conical, shell.

top·side (top'sīd'), *n.* **1.** Also, **topsides. a.** the upper part of a ship's side, especially the part above the water line. **b.** the upper part of a ship, especially the part above the main deck, as distinct from the engine room, hold, etc. **2.** *British.* the outer side of a round of beef.

—*adv.* **1.** to, toward, or on the bridge or upper deck. **2.** *Informal.* on the top; above.

top·soil (top'soil'), *n.* **1.** the upper part of the soil; surface soil. **2.** loam or other earth from or in this part of the soil, usually consisting of sand, clay, and decayed organic matter: *a load of good topsoil.* —*v.t.* to remove the topsoil from (land).

top·spin (top'spin'), *n.* a forward rolling

motion given to a ball in the direction of its flight or roll, as in tennis or billiards. A baseball pitcher who throws a drop gives the ball topspin to make it curve down. *His game, emphasizing tricky forehand topspin and an undersliced backhand, still had an unorthodox look* (Newsweek).

Top·sy (top′sē), *n. Informal.* **grow like Topsy,** to grow or expand rapidly; burgeon: *The tax relationship between the provincial and dominion governments has grown like Topsy* (Canada Month). [< *Topsy,* a little slave girl in Harriet Beecher Stowe's *Uncle Tom's Cabin*]

top·sy-tur·vi·ly (top′sē tėr′və lē), *adv.* in a topsy-turvy manner.

top·sy-tur·vi·ness (top′sē tėr′vē nis), *n.* a topsy-turvy quality or state.

top·sy-tur·vy (top′sē tėr′vē), *adv., adj., n., pl.* **-vies.** —*adv., adj.* **1.** upside down. **2.** in confusion or disorder: *A lively child is a godsend, even if she turns the whole house topsy-turvy* (Harriet Beecher Stowe). —*n.* confusion; disorder. [earlier *topsi-tervy,* probably ultimately < *top*[1] + obsolete *terve* overturn, related to Old English *tearflian* roll over]

top·sy-tur·vy·dom (top′sē tėr′vē dəm), *n.* a state of affairs or a place in which everything is topsy-turvy.

top weight, the horse carrying the heaviest weight in a race: *Fair Astronomer, the top weight, is my selection for the richest-ever Lincolnshire Handicap tomorrow* (Daily Telegraph).

top-weight·ed (top′wā′tid), *adj.* (of a horse) carrying the heaviest weight as a handicap in a race: *The top-weighted Determine, with 129 pounds, was fourth in the field of contenders* (New York Times).

toque (tōk), *n.* **1.** a bonnet, cap, or hat without a brim, or with a very small brim, worn by women. **2.** a small, round cap or bonnet of velvet, etc., usually with a plume, formerly worn by men and women. [< Middle French *toque,* perhaps < Spanish *toca,* or Portuguese *touca* kerchief, coif, perhaps < Basque *taika* kind of cap, or perhaps < Arabic *ṭāq* < Persian]

to·quil·la (tō kē′yä, -kēl′yä), *n.* the jipijapa of South and Central America, whose palmlike leaves are used for Panama hats. [< Spanish *toquilla* (diminutive) < *toca;* see TOQUE]

tor (tôr), *n.* a high, rocky, or craggy hill, knoll, etc. [Old English *torr,* apparently < Celtic (compare Welsh *twr* heap, pile, Gaelic *tòrr* conical hill, burial mound)]

to·rah or **to·ra** (tôr′ə, tōr′-), *n., pl.* **to·roth.** **1.** (in Jewish usage) instruction, doctrine, law, or judicial decision. **2.** divine revelation, as manifested in teaching and judicial decisions. **3.** Also, **Torah** or **Tora. a.** the Old Testament. **b.** the body of Jewish doctrinal literature, including the Talmud, etc. **the Torah, a.** the Mosaic law; the Pentateuch: *to study the Torah.* **b.** a scroll on which this is written: *to read the Torah in the Synagogue.*
[< Hebrew *tōrāh* (literally) instruction, law]

tor·ban·ite (tôr′bə nīt), *n.* a deep-brown shale, related to cannel coal, from which paraffin, oils, and gas are extracted. [< *Torban*(e) Hill, a place in Wales, where it is found + *-ite*[1]]

tor·bern·ite (tôr′bər nīt), *n.* a mineral, a hydrated phosphate of uranium and copper, found in bright-green, tabular crystals. It is a minor ore of uranium. *Formula:* $CuU_2P_2O_{12} \cdot 12H_2O$ [< German *Torbernit* < *Torbernus,* a Latinization of *Torbern* Bergmann, 1735-1784, a Swedish chemist + German *-it* -ite[1]]

torc (tôrk), *n.* torque (def. 2).

torch (tôrch), *n.* **1. a.** a light to be carried around or stuck in a holder on a wall: *A piece of pinewood, or anything that burns easily makes a good torch.* **b.** a lamp carried or supported on a pole. **2.** a device for producing a very hot flame, used especially to burn off paint, to solder metal, and to melt metal. **3.** *British.* a flashlight. **4.** something thought of as a source of enlightenment or guidance: *the torch of civilization, the torch of liberty.*
carry a or **the torch,** *Slang.* **a.** to be in love, especially, to suffer unrequited love: *He has been carrying the torch for her for months.* **b.** to crusade (for); campaign (for a cause): *Oddly enough, it is Coronel's younger brother, Rafael, who is carrying the torch for a new Mexican art* (Saturday Review).
hand on the torch, to pass on the tradition; continue or perpetuate the custom, practice, etc.: *Those [sonnets] handed on the torch of courtly love for good and ill to the Elizabethans* (C. C. Abbott).
—*v.t.* **1.** to furnish, or light, with or as if with a torch: . . . *we sit, watching sunlight torch the wooded west* (New York Times). **2.** (in plastering) to point the inside joints of (slating) with a mixture of lime and hair.
—*v.i.* **1.** to flare like a torch; rise like smoke from a torch: "*Law! how them clouds torch up, we shall have rain*" (James Halliwell). **2.** *U.S.* to catch fish, etc., by torchlight.
[< Old French *torche* (originally) a twisted thing; a torch formed of a wick dipped in wax, probably < Vulgar Latin *torca* < Latin *torquēre* to twist] —**torch′like′,** *adj.*
—**Syn.** *n.* **1. a.** firebrand. **4.** lodestar.

torch·bear·er (tôrch′bãr′ər), *n.* a person who carries a torch.

torched (tôrcht), *adj.* furnished with or lighted by torches.

tor·chère (tôr′shãr′), *n.* a tall, ornamental candlestick or lamp stand: *On each side of the doorway I noted the bronze torchères holding big globes of pale milky light* (Guy Endore).
[< French *torchère* < Old French *torche;* see TORCH]

torch·fish (tôrch′fish′), *n., pl.* **-fish·es** or (*collectively*) **-fish.** a deep-sea fish with a dorsal spine carrying a shiny bulb like a torch above the head.

torch·light (tôrch′līt′), *n.* the light of a torch or torches.
—*adj.* carrying or lighted by torchlights: *torchlight parades the night before football games* (Harper's); *the whole congregation singing the old songs of peace and of Christmas, and the torchlight procession home afterward* (Newsweek).

tor·chon lace (tôr′shon), **1.** a handmade linen lace with loosely twisted threads in simple, open patterns. **2.** a machine-made imitation of this in linen or cotton. [< French *torchon* dish or dust cloth < Old French *torche;* see TORCH]

torch singer, a woman singer of sad love songs: *So began a four-year career as a torch singer, which took her into the spotlights of Manhattan's flossiest nightclub* (Time).

torch song, a sad love song: *singing in deep and straightforward tones, a collection of oldtime torch songs* (New Yorker).

torch·wood (tôrch′wu̇d′), *n.* **1.** any of various resinous woods for making torches. **2.** a tree yielding such wood.

torch·y (tôr′chē), *adj.,* **torch·i·er, torch·i·est.** of, having to do with, or characteristic of a torch song or a torch singer: . . . *Pop tunes of a torchy temper, sung with a fine ear for theatrical effect* (Time).

tore[1] (tôr, tōr), *v.* the past tense of **tear**[2]: *She tore her dress on a nail yesterday.*

tore[2] (tôr, tōr), *n. Architecture, Geometry.* torus.
[< Middle French *tore,* learned borrowing from Latin *torus.* Doublet of TORUS.]

tor·e·a·dor (tôr′ē ə dôr), *n.* a bullfighter, especially one mounted on a horse (a term no longer used in Spanish bullfighting). [< Spanish *toreador* < *torear* to fight in a bullfight < *toro* bull < Latin *taurus*]

toreador pants, snug-fitting trousers ending at mid-calf, worn by women: *She looks as well in tight toreador pants as in an ankle-length ball dress* (Harper's).

to·re·ra (tō rā′rä), *n., pl.* **-re·ras** (-rā′räs). a woman bullfighter. [< Spanish *torera,* feminine of *torero* torero]

to·re·ro (tō rā′rō), *n., pl.* **-re·ros** (-rā′rōs). a bullfighter who is not mounted, such as a matador or a banderillero. [< Spanish *torero* < *torear;* see TOREADOR]

to·reu·tic (tə rü′tik), *adj.* of or having to do with the ancient art of working in metal or ivory, including embossing, chasing, working in relief, etc. [< Greek *toreutikós* < *toreúein,* variant of *torneúein* to work in relief, chase < *tórnos* a carpenter's tool or lathe]

to·reu·tics (tə rü′tiks), *n.* the toreutic art.

to·ri (tôr′ī, tōr′-), *n.* plural of **torus.**

tor·ic (tôr′ik, tor′-), *adj.* **1.** of or having to do with a toric lens. **2.** *Geometry.* of or having to do with a torus; shaped like a torus.

toric lens, an optical lens with a surface forming a part of a geometrical torus, used in eyeglasses because it refracts differently in different meridians.

to·ri·i (tôr′ē ē, tōr′-), *n., pl.* **-ri·i.** a gateway at the entrance to a Japanese Shinto shrine, built of two uprights and two crosspieces. [< Japanese *torii* < *tori* bird + *i* a roost (because the structure was a roosting spot for birds)]

Torii

to·ril (tō rēl′), *n.* an enclosed stall where the bull is kept before a bullfight: *Before anyone realized it, the toril gate was open and shut, and one of the ferocious bulls . . . stood in the sun* (Atlantic). [< Spanish *toril*]

tor·ment (*v.* tôr ment′; *n.* tôr′ment), *v.t.* **1.** to cause very great pain to: *Headaches tormented him. Like a hedgehog rolled up the wrong way Tormenting himself with his prickles* (Thomas Hood). **2.** to worry or annoy very much: *He torments everyone with silly questions.* **3.** to torture. [Middle English *turmenten* < Old French *tormenter,* and *turmenter* < *torment;* see the noun]
—*n.* **1.** a cause of very great pain: *A bad burn can be a torment. Instruments of torture were torments.* **2.** very great pain; agony: *years Dark with torment and with tears* (Emily Brontë). *He suffered torments from his aching teeth.* **3.** a cause of very much worry or annoyance.
[Middle English *turment* torture, pain; torsion machine < Old French *torment,* learned borrowing from Latin *tormentum* twisted sling, rack, related to *torquēre* to twist]
—**Syn.** *v.t.* **1. Torment, torture** mean to cause physical or mental pain. **Torment** implies repeated punishment or incessant harassment: *He is tormented by a racking cough.* **Torture** implies the infliction of acute and protracted suffering: *The civilized nations do not believe in torturing prisoners.* **2.** tease, plague, harass. -*n.* **2.** anguish, misery, distress.

tor·ment·er (tôr men′tər), *n.* a tormentor.

tor·men·til (tôr′men təl), *n.* a low European and Asiatic herb of the rose family, with yellow flowers having four petals, and a strongly astringent root used in medicine, tanning, and dyeing; bloodroot. [< Old French *tormentille,* learned borrowing from Medieval Latin *tormentilla,* apparently (diminutive) < Latin *tormentum;* see TORMENT (because it supposedly relieved the gripes). Doublet of TORMENTILLA.]

tor·men·til·la (tôr′men til′ə), *n.* tormentil. [< Medieval Latin *tormentilla.* Doublet of TORMENTIL.]

tor·ment·ing (tôr men′ting), *adj.* that torments. —**tor·ment′ing·ly,** *adv.* —**tor·ment′ing·ness,** *n.*

tor·men·tor (tôr men′tər), *n.* **1.** a person or thing that torments. **2.** a curtain, flat, etc., on either side of the stage at the front, filling the space between the proscenium arch and the scenery and blocking the audience's view into the wings. **3.** a screen covered with special material and used in motion-picture studios to prevent echo in sound recording. Also, **tormenter.**

tor·men·tress (tôr men′tris), *n.* a woman tormentor.

torn (tôrn, tōrn), *v.* the past participle of **tear**[2]: *He has torn up the plants by the roots. His coat was torn.*

tor·nad·ic (tôr nad′ik), *adj.* of or like a tornado: *The tornadic winds raked 12 square blocks in Galveston, demolishing houses and strewing debris* (Wall Street Journal).

tor·na·do (tôr nā′dō), *n., pl.* **-does** or **-dos.** **1. a.** an extremely violent and destructive whirlwind. A tornado moves forward as a whirling funnel extending down from a mass of dark clouds. **b.** any extremely violent windstorm. **2.** a violent, whirling squall occurring during the summer on the west coast of Africa. **3.** any violent outburst: *a tornado of anger. In the fifteenth century a last tornado of nomadism arose in Western Turkestan* (H.G. Wells). **4.** *Obsolete.* a violent thunderstorm of the tropical Atlantic, with torrential rain. [probably alteration of Spanish *tronada* < *tronar* to thunder < Latin *tonāre;* apparently influenced by Spanish *tornar* to turn, twist < Latin *tornāre*]

tornado lantern, a hurricane lamp.

tor·nil·lo (tôr nil′ō, -nē′yō), *n., pl.* **-los.** the screw bean. [American English < American Spanish *tornillo* (in Spanish, a screw, diminutive) < *torno* a turn < *tornar* to turn < Latin *tornāre*]

to·ro (tō′rō), *n.* a bull. [< Spanish *toro* < Latin *taurus*]

to·roid (tôr′oid, tōr′-), *n. Geometry.* **1.** a surface described by the revolution of any closed plane curve about an axis in its own plane. **2.** the solid enclosed by such a surface. [< *tor*(e)[2] + *-oid*]

to·roi·dal (tô roi′dəl, tō-), *adj.* of, having to do with, or characteristic of a toroid: *In this twisted toroidal field the effect of particle drift is much reduced* (Scientific American). **—to·roi′dal·ly,** *adv.*

To·ron·to·ni·an (tə ron′tō′nē ən, tor′on-), *n.* a native or inhabitant of Toronto, Canada: *He was no more a former Torontonian, or Chicagoan . . . than he was a former newspaperman* (Atlantic).

to·rose (tôr′ōs, tōr′-; tô rōs′, tō-), *adj.* **1.** *Botany.* cylindrical, with bulges or constrictions at intervals; swelling in knobs at intervals. **2.** bulging; protuberant; knobbed: *torose muscles.* [< Latin *torōsus* bulging, brawny < *torus* a torus, bulge]

to·roth (tô rōth′, tō-), *n.* the plural of **torah** and **tora.**

to·rous (tôr′əs, tōr′-), *adj.* torose.

tor·pe·do (tôr pē′dō), *n., pl.* **-does,** *v.,* **-doed, -do·ing.** *—n.* **1.** a large, cigar-shaped shell that contains explosives and travels by its own power. Torpedoes are sent under water from a submarine, surface vessel, or low-flying aircraft to blow up enemy ships. **2.** a submarine mine, shell, etc., that explodes when hit. **3.** an explosive put on a railroad track that makes a loud noise for a signal when a wheel of the engine runs over it. **4.** an explosive and gravel wrapped in thin paper, that makes a bang when it is thrown against something hard. **5.** a fish that can give an electric shock; electric ray. **6.** *U.S.* an explosive enclosed in a tube and set off in an oil well to renew or increase the flow. **7.** *Slang.* a hired gunman. **8.** *U.S.* (formerly in military use) any of various encased charges of explosive, especially an underground mine.

—v.t. **1.** to attack, hit, or destroy with a torpedo or torpedoes. **2.** to set off a torpedo in or against. **3.** to bring completely to an end; destroy: *to torpedo a peace conference.*

[< Latin *torpēdō* the electric ray (a fish); (originally) numbness (because of the ray's effect) < *torpēre* be numb or torpid] **—tor·pe′do·like′,** *adj.*

torpedo boat, a small, fast, surface warship for attacking with torpedoes.

tor·pe·do-boat destroyer (tôr pē′dō-bōt′), a ship larger, faster, and more heavily armed than a torpedo boat, used to destroy torpedo boats, or as a more advanced form of torpedo boat. The modern destroyer is a development of this.

torpedo body, a style of automobile body in which all side surfaces including fenders are flush.

tor·pe·do·man (tôr pē′dō man′), *n., pl.* **-men.** a U.S. Navy warrant officer in charge of the maintenance and repair of torpedoes, submarine equipment, etc.

torpedo plane, an airplane for carrying and releasing self-propelled torpedoes.

torpedo tube, a tube through which a torpedo is sent out from a submarine, torpedo boat, etc., either by an explosive charge or by compressed air.

tor·pid[1] (tôr′pid), *adj.* **1.** dull; inactive; sluggish: *It is a man's own fault . . . if his mind grows torpid in old age* (Samuel Johnson). **2.** not moving or feeling; dormant: *Animals that hibernate become torpid in winter.* **3.** numb. [< Latin *torpidus* < *torpēre* be numb] **—tor′pid·ly,** *adv.* **—tor′pid·ness,** *n.* **—Syn. 1.** lethargic, apathetic.

tor·pid[2] (tôr′pid), *n.* **1.** an eight-oared, clinker-built boat rowed in the Lent races at Oxford. **2.** a member of the crew of such a boat.

torpids, the Lent races at Oxford: *A suggestion of cancelling the torpids was defeated, although a further meeting of the captains will be called in the event of flooding or another freeze-up* (London Times).

[< earlier *torpid*[1] *(boat)* the second boat of a college (because it was slower than the varsity boat)]

tor·pid·i·ty (tôr pid′ə tē), *n., pl.* **-ties.** torpid condition.

tor·por (tôr′pər), *n.* **1.** torpid condition or quality; lethargy; apathy; listlessness; dullness: *My calmness was the torpor of despair* (Charles B. Brown). **2.** the absence or suspension of movement or feeling, as of a hibernating animal; dormancy. [< Latin *torpor, -ōris* < *torpēre* be numb] **—Syn. 1.** stupor.

tor·por·if·ic (tôr′pə rif′ik), *adj.* causing torpor.

tor·quate (tôr′kwit, -kwāt), *adj. Zoology.* ringed with hair or feathers around the neck; collared. [< Latin *torquātus* wearing a torque < *torquēs;* see TORQUE]

torque (tôrk), *n.* **1.** a force causing rotation; the moment of a system of forces causing rotation. **2.** a necklace of twisted metal: *The ancient Gauls and Britons wore torques.* **3.** *Optics.* the rotational effect produced by certain liquids or crystals on the plane of polarization of plane-polarized light passing through them. [< Latin *torquēs* twisted neck chain < *torquēre* to twist]

torque converter or **convertor,** a hydraulic device for altering the torque and speed delivered by a driving shaft to the ratio required by a driven shaft. Certain automobiles with automatic transmission use torque converters.

torqued (tôrkt), *adj.* twisted; convoluted; formed like a torque.

Tor·que·ma·da (tôr′kə mä′də), *n.* an intolerant and cruel inquisitor or prosecutor: *[He] was considered safe at the outset but turned into a hyper-aggressive Torquemada* (New Yorker). [< *Torquemada,* 1420-1498, a leader in the Spanish Inquisition]

tor·ques (tôr′kwēz), *n. Zoology.* a ringlike band or marking around the neck of an animal, as of hair, feathers, etc., of a special color or texture; collar. [< Latin *torquēs;* see TORQUE]

torr (tôr), *n.* a unit of pressure equivalent to the amount of pressure that will support a column of mercury one millimeter high. [< Evangelista *Torr*(icelli), 1608-1647, an Italian scientist]

tor·re·fac·tion (tôr′ə fak′shən, tor′-), *n.* **1.** the act or process of torrefying. **2.** the state of being torrefied.

tor·re·fy (tôr′ə fī, tor′-), *v.t.,* **-fied, -fy·ing.** to dry or parch with heat; dry out; roast: *torrefied drugs, torrefied metallic ores.* [< Latin *torrēfacere* < *torrēre* to parch + *facere* make] **—Syn.** bake.

tor·rent (tôr′ənt, tor′-), *n.* **1.** a violent, rushing stream of water. **2.** a heavy downpour: *The rain came down in a torrent during the thunderstorm.* **3.** any violent, rushing stream; flood: *a torrent of lava from a volcano, a torrent of abuse, a torrent of words.*

—adj. rushing like a torrent; torrential.

[< Latin *torrēns, -entis* a rushing stream; boiling; (originally) present participle of *torrēre* to parch] **—Syn.** *n.* **3.** inundation.

tor·ren·tial (tô ren′shəl, to-), *adj.* of, caused by, or like a torrent: *torrential rains.* **—Syn.** raging, tumultuous.

tor·ren·tial·ly (tô ren′shə lē, to-), *adv.* like a torrent; violently; overwhelmingly: *The climate of Bombay . . . is hot and dry for nine months of the year and . . . rains torrentially for the remaining three* (Atlantic).

tor·rid (tôr′id, tor′-), *adj.* **1.** very hot; burning; scorching: *torrid weather.* **2.** exposed or subject to great heat: *torrid deserts.* **3.** very ardent; passionate: *a torrid love scene.* [< Latin *torridus* < *torrēre* to parch] **—tor′rid·ly,** *adv.* **—tor′rid·ness,** *n.*

tor·rid·i·ty (tô rid′ə tē, to-), *n.* extreme heat.

Tor·ri·do·ni·an (tôr′ə dō′nē ən), *Geology.* *—n.* the sedimentary Pre-Cambrian sandstone occurring in northwestern Scotland. *—adj.* of or having to do with this sandstone. [< Loch *Torridon,* Scotland]

Torrid Zone, the very warm region between the tropic of Cancer and the tropic of Capricorn. The equator divides the Torrid Zone. *Most of Brazil is in the Torrid Zone.*

tor·ri·fac·tion (tôr′ə fak′shən, tor′-), *n.* torrefaction.

tor·ri·fy (tôr′ə fī, tor′-), *v.t.,* **-fied, -fy·ing.** to torrefy.

tor·ro·ne (tô rō′nā), *n.* a nougat filled with almonds. [< Italian *torrone*]

tor·sade (tôr sād′), *n.* **1.** a twisted fringe, cord, or ribbon, used as an ornament in headdresses, curtains, etc. **2.** a carved or molded ornament like this. [< French *torsade* < Old French *tors* twisted, ultimately < Latin *torquēre* to twist]

torse (tôrs), *n.* torso. [< Middle French *torse* < Italian *torso.* Doublet of TORSO.]

tor·sel (tôr′səl), *n.* tassel[2].

tor·si·bil·i·ty (tôr′sə bil′ə tē), *n.* **1.** the capability of being twisted. **2.** the tendency to straighten out after being twisted.

tor·sion (tôr′shən), *n.* **1.** the act or process of twisting. **2.** the state of being twisted. **3.** the twisting or turning of a body by two equal and opposite forces. **4.** the tendency of a twisted object to straighten out. [< Old French *torsion,* learned borrowing from Late Latin *torsiō, -ōnis* torture, torment < Latin *tortiō, -ōnis* < *torquēre* to twist]

tor·sion·al (tôr′shə nəl), *adj.* of, having to do with, or resulting from torsion: *The makers state that torsional rubber spring suspension eliminates most of the ride vibration* (Newsweek). **—tor′sion·al·ly,** *adv.*

torsion balance, an instrument for measuring small, horizontal forces by the amount of torsion they cause in a wire.

torsion bar, a type of suspension used in an automobile, resembling a coiled spring that has been straightened out into a rod. When the automobile goes over a bump, the shock is absorbed along the line of the bar by a series of twisting motions.

tor·sion·less (tôr′shən lis), *adj.* free from torsion.

torsk (tôrsk), *n., pl.* **torsks** or *(collectively)* **torsk. 1.** the cusk (fish). **2.** the cod (fish). [< Scandinavian (compare dialectal Norwegian *torsk,* or *tosk*)]

tor·so (tôr′sō), *n., pl.* **-sos, -si** (-sē). **1.** the trunk or body of a statue without any head, arms, or legs. **2.** the trunk of the human body. **3.** something left mutilated or unfinished. [< Italian *torso* (originally) stalk, stump < Vulgar Latin *tursus,* for Latin *thyrsus* stalk < Greek *thýrsos.* Doublet of TORSE.]

tort (tôrt), *n. Law.* a civil (not criminal) wrong (except a breach of contract): *If a man's automobile breaks the glass of a shopwindow, he has committed a tort.* [< Old French *tort* < Medieval Latin *tortum* injustice < Latin *torquēre* turn awry, twist]

tor·te (tôr′tə, tôrt), *n., pl.* **tor·ten** (tôr′tən). **1.** a rich cake made with beaten egg whites, nuts, fruit, and little flour. **2.** a cake with thin layers of custard, preserved fruit, chocolate, etc. [< German *Torte* < Late Latin *tōrta* flat cake]

tor·tel·li·ni (tôr′tə lē′nē), *n.pl.* small, round pieces of dough filled with chopped meat and cooked in boiling water. [< Italian *tortellini,* ultimately < Late Latin *tōrta* flat cake]

tort·fea·sor (tôrt′fē′zər), *n. Law.* a person who is guilty of a tort; wrongdoer. [< Old French *tortfesor, tortfaiseur,* < *tort* tort + *faiseur* doer < *fais-,* stem of *faire* do < Latin *facere*]

tor·ti·col·lis (tôr′tə kol′is), *n.* a muscular disorder in which the neck is twisted and the head turned to one side; wryneck. [< New Latin *torticollis* < Latin *torquēre* to twist + *collum* neck]

tor·tile (tôr′təl), *adj.* **1.** twisted; coiled; winding. **2.** that can be twisted. [< Latin *tortilis* < *torquēre* to twist]

tor·til·la (tôr tē′yə), *n.* a thin, flat, round corn cake, commonly eaten in Spanish America. It is baked on a flat surface and served hot. [American English < American Spanish *tortilla* (diminutive) < Spanish *torta* cake < Late Latin, round loaf < Latin *torquēre* to twist]

tor·tious (tôr′shəs), *adj. Law.* having to do with, like, or involving a tort. [earlier, injurious, hurtful < Anglo-French *torcious,* apparently < Old French *torsion,* or *tortion;* see TORSION; influenced by English *tort*]

tor·tive (tôr′tiv), *adj. Archaic.* twisting; twisted; tortuous. [< Latin *tortīvus* < *torquēre* to twist]

tor·toise (tôr′təs), *n., pl.* **-tois·es** or **-toise. 1. a.** any of a family of turtles that live only on land, especially in arid regions, and have stumpy legs and a high, arched carapace. **b.** any turtle. **2.** a very slow person or thing. [alteration of Middle English *tortuca* < Medieval Latin, also *tortua,* variant of Vulgar Latin *tartarūca* hellish

American Gopher Tortoise (def. 1) (about 15 in. long)

beast of Tartary; the symbol for heretics; spelling influenced by Latin *tortus* twisted (because of the shape of its feet)]

tortoise beetle, a small beetle shaped somewhat like a tortoise.

tortoise shell, 1. the mottled, yellow-and-brown shell of a turtle or tortoise, especially the hawksbill turtle, used for combs and ornaments. **2.** any of a group of butterflies spotted with yellow and black. **3.** a tortoise-shell cat.

tor·toise-shell (tôr′təs shel′), *adj.* **1.** made of tortoise shell. **2.** having the colors or look of tortoise shell.

tortoise-shell cat, a domestic cat with mottled colors like those of tortoise shell.

tortoise-shell turtle, hawksbill turtle.

tor·tri·cid (tôr′trə sid), *adj.* of or belonging to a family of small, thick-bodied moths. —*n.* a tortricid moth. [< New Latin *Tortricidae* the family name < *tortrix, -icis* (literally) twister, ultimately < Latin *torquēre* twist (because of the habit of the larvae of rolling leaves up)]

tor·tu·os·i·ty (tôr′chü os′ə tē), *n., pl.* **-ties. 1.** the quality or condition of being tortuous; twistedness; sinuosity. **2.** a twisted or crooked part, passage, or thing. **3.** a twist, bend or crook in something.

tor·tu·ous (tôr′chü əs), *adj.* **1.** full of twists, turns, or bends; twisted; winding; crooked: *We wind through tortuous ravines* (John Tyndall). **2.** not direct or straightforward; mentally or morally crooked: *tortuous reasoning.* **3.** *Geometry.* (of a curve) having no two successive parts in the same plane. [< Latin *tortuōsus* < *tortus, -ūs* a twisting < *torquēre* to twist] —**tor′tu·ous·ly,** *adv.* —**tor′tu·ous·ness,** *n.*
—**Syn. 1.** sinuous, serpentine, zigzag, circuitous. —**Ant. 1.** direct.

tor·ture (tôr′chər), *n., v.,* **-tured, -tur·ing.** —*n.* **1.** the act or fact of inflicting very severe pain: *Torture was formerly used to make people give evidence about crimes, or to make them confess.* **2. a.** a very severe pain or suffering: *She suffered tortures from a toothache.* **b.** a cause of severe pain or suffering: *The sight of his sick brother was torture to him.* **3.** a violent and continuous twisting, pushing, or shaking that taxes a thing to the limit: *the torture of a boat by pounding waves.*
—*v.t.* **1.** to cause very severe pain or suffering to: *That cruel boy tortures animals.* **2.** to twist the meaning of. **3.** to strain, twist, or force out of its natural form: *Winds tortured the trees. An early Victorian room . . . full . . . of twisted and tortured mahogany* (Arnold Bennett). **4.** to puzzle or perplex greatly.
[< Middle French *torture,* learned borrowing from Late Latin *tortūra* < Latin *torquēre* to twist] —**tor′tur·er,** *n.*
—**Syn.** *n.* **2. a.** agony, anguish, misery, distress. *-v.t.* **1.** rack, persecute, distress. See **torment.**

torture chamber, a room or chamber where persons are subjected to torture.

tor·ture·some (tôr′chər səm), *adj.* characterized by or causing torture; extremely painful or distressing: *The morrow dawned after an all but sleepless night, harrowed by the most torturesome dreams* (Theodore Dreiser).

tor·tur·ing (tôr′chər ing), *adj.* that causes anguish; torturous: *Keep me from torturing jealousy* (Keats). *Daughter of Jove . . . Whose iron scourge and torturing hour The bad affright* (Thomas Gray). —**tor′tur·ing·ly,** *adv.*

tor·tur·ous (tôr′chər əs), *adj.* full of, involving, or causing torture; tormenting.
—**Syn.** excruciating.

tor·u·la (tôr′ə lə, -yə-; tor′-), *n., pl.* **-lae** (-lē), or **torula yeast,** a yeast rich in vitamins and minerals, grown in a medium made from waste products of papermaking, fruit canning, etc., and used as a supplement in animal and poultry feeds, and in pharmaceuticals. [< New Latin *torula,* feminine (diminutive) < Latin *torus* torus]

to·rus (tôr′əs, tōr′-), *n., pl.* **tori. 1.** *Architecture.* a large, convex molding, commonly forming the lowest member of the base of a column. It resembles the astragal, but is much larger; tore. **2.** *Botany.* the receptacle of a flower. **3.** *Anatomy.* a smooth, rounded ridge. **4.** *Geometry.* **a.** a surface described by the revolution of a conic section, especially a circle, about an axis in its own plane; tore. **b.** the solid enclosed by such a surface; tore. [< Latin *torus* (originally) cushion, swelling. Doublet of TORE².]

torus pal·a·ti·nus (pal′ə tī′nəs), a smooth, rounded ridge sometimes present on the hard palate. [< New Latin *torus palatinus*]

To·ry (tôr′ē, tōr′-), *n., pl.* **-ries,** *adj.* —*n.* **1.** (in Great Britain) a member of the political party that favored royal power and the established church and opposed change. Strictly speaking, there is no Tory party in modern England, although members of the Conservative Party are often called Tories. **2.** a member of the Conservative Party in Canada. **3.** an American who favored British rule over the colonies at the time of the American Revolution; Loyalist. **4.** Also, **tory.** a very conservative person. **5.** Also **tory. a.** an Irish outlaw in the 1600's. **b.** any armed Irish Roman Catholic or Royalist.
—*adj.* Also, **tory.** of or having to do with Tories or tories: *Tory policy, a Tory convention.*
[< Irish *tōraidhe,* persecuted person; later, Irishmen dispossessed by the English in the 1600's; (originally) pursuer < Old Irish *tóirighim* I pursue]

To·ry·ism (tôr′ē iz əm, tōr′-), *n.* **1.** a being a Tory. **2.** the doctrines or behavior of a Tory.

tosh (tosh), *n. British Slang.* bosh; nonsense: *You can't deal with all the tosh if you are going to do justice to the good films* (Sunday Times). [origin uncertain. Compare BOSH.]

Tosk (tosk), *n.* **1.** an Albanian living south of the river Shkumbi. **2.** the dialect spoken by such a person.

toss (tôs, tos), *v.,* **tossed** or (*Poetic*) **tost, toss·ing,** *n.* —*v.t.* **1.** to throw lightly with the palm upward; cast; fling: *to toss a ball.* **2.** to throw about; pitch about: *a ship tossed by the waves.* **3.** to lift or move quickly; throw upward: *She tossed her head. He was tossed by the bull.* **4.** to shake up or about, especially in order to mix the ingredients of: *to toss a salad.* **5.** to disturb; agitate; disquiet. **6.** *Informal.* to throw (a party, etc.).
—*v.i.* **1.** to throw, pitch, or move about. **2.** to throw a coin or some object in the air to bet on which side it will fall, or to decide something by this: *Let's toss to see who pays the bill.* **3.** to throw oneself about in bed; roll restlessly: *He tossed in his sleep all night.* **4.** to fling oneself: *He tossed out of the room in anger.*
toss off, a. to do or make quickly and easily: *Archer . . . usually tossed off half a dozen papers with his morning coffee* (Edith Wharton). **b.** to drink all at once: *He tossed off a glass of brandy* (Thackeray).
—*n.* **1.** the distance to which something is or can be tossed. **2.** a throw; tossing. **3.** a pitching about. **4.** a tossing of a coin, or a decision made by this: *A toss of a coin decided who should play first.* **5.** *Obsolete.* agitation; commotion.
[perhaps < Scandinavian (compare dialectal Norwegian *tossa* to strew)] —**toss′er,** *n.*
—**Syn.** *v.t.* **1.** See **throw.**

toss·a·ble (tôs′ə bəl, tos′-), *adj.* capable of being tossed.

toss bombing, loft-bombing.

tos·sel (tôs′əl, tos′-), *n.* tassel².

toss·pot (tôs′pot′, tos′-), *n.* a heavy drinker; toper; drunkard.

toss-up or **toss·up** (tôs′up′, tos′-), *n.* **1.** a tossing of a coin to decide something. **2.** *Informal.* an even chance: *It's a toss-up whether or not he'll accept.*

tost (tôst, tost), *v. Poetic.* a past tense and a past participle of **toss.**

tos·ta·da (tôs tä′ᴛʜä), *n.* a tortilla fried in deep fat until it becomes crisp. [< Mexican Spanish *tostada,* ultimately < Latin *torrēre* parch. Compare TOAST.]

tot¹ (tot), *n.* **1.** a little child. **2.** *Especially British.* **a.** a small portion of drink; dram. **b.** a small quantity of anything. [origin uncertain. Compare Middle English *totte* a fool, Danish *tommel-tot* Tom Thumb.]

tot² (tot), *v.,* **tot·ted, tot·ting,** *n. Informal.* —*v.t.* to find the total or sum of; add or sum (up). —*v.i.* to amount (to).
—*n.* the total of an addition; sum.
[shortening of *total*]

tot., total.

TOT (no periods), time on target; time over target: *The TOT . . . for both raids was 3:45 P.M.* (New York Times).

to·tal (tō′təl), *adj., n., v.,* **-taled, -tal·ing** or (*especially British*) **-talled, -tal·ling.** —*adj.* **1.** whole; entire: *The total cost of the house and land will be $25,000.* **2.** complete; absolute; utter: *He is a total failure. We were in total darkness.*
—*n.* the whole amount; sum: *His expenses reached a total of $100.*
—*v.t.* **1.** to find the sum of; add: *Total that column of figures.* **2.** to reach an amount of; amount to: *The money spent yearly on chewing gum totals millions of dollars.* —*v.i.* to amount (to).
[< Medieval Latin *totalis* < Latin *tōtus* all]
—**Syn.** *adj.* **1.** See **whole.** *-n.* aggregate.

total abstinence, a complete refraining from drinking alcoholic liquor.

total depravity, the theological doctrine of the total unfitness of man for his moral purpose on earth until the stain of original sin is removed by his spiritual rebirth through the influence of the Spirit of God.

total eclipse, an eclipse of the sun or moon in which the whole of the disk is obscured.

total heat, *Physics.* the quantity of heat required to raise a unit mass of a liquid from a standard or convenient temperature, usually its freezing point, to a given temperature, and then to turn it into vapor at that temperature under constant pressure.

to·tal·i·tar·i·an (tō tal′ə tãr′ē ən), *adj.* of or having to do with a government controlled by one political group that permits no other political groups, as in Communist Russia, Nazi Germany, and Fascist Italy: *In a totalitarian state the goal is to serve the needs of an expanding industrial order and the complexities of a bureaucratic government* (Science News Letter). —*n.* a person who favors totalitarian principles.

to·tal·i·tar·i·an·ism (tō tal′ə tãr′ē ə niz′-əm), *n.* a system under which a government is controlled by one political party exclusively and no other political groups are permitted to exist. —**Syn.** autocracy, dictatorship.

to·tal·i·ty (tō tal′ə tē), *n., pl.* **-ties. 1.** the total number or amount; total; whole. **2.** the quality or state of being total; entirety. **3. a.** total obscuration of the sun or moon in an eclipse. **b.** the time or duration of this.

to·tal·i·za·tion (tō′tə lə zā′shən), *n.* **1.** the act or process of totalizing. **2.** the state of being totalized.

to·tal·i·za·tor (tō′tə lə zā′tər), *n.* an apparatus for registering and indicating totals of operations, measurements, etc., especially one used for pari-mutuel betting at horse races.

to·tal·ize (tō′tə līz), *v.t.,* **-ized, -iz·ing.** to make total; combine into a total.

to·tal·iz·er (tō′tə lī′zər), *n.* **1.** something that totalizes, as an adding machine. **2.** a totalizator.

to·tal·ly (tō′tə lē), *adv.* wholly; completely; entirely; altogether: *We were totally unprepared for the test.*

total recall, the ability to recall things to mind with absolute accuracy: *Summoning his talent for something very like total recall, he began an account of the long ride* (Truman Capote).

total theater, a play or other stage production using any combination of theatrical techniques and other mediums, such as motion pictures, to emphasize an effect.

total war, war in which all the resources of a nation, such as manpower, industry, and raw materials, are used in the national interest, and in which attack is made not only on the armed forces of the enemy, but also (subject to certain limitations) on all its people and property.

to·ta·qui·na (tō′tə kē′nə), *n.* totaquine.

to·ta·quine (tō′tə kwēn, -kwin, -kēn, -kin), *n.* a mixture of alkaloids from certain kinds of cinchona, sometimes used against malaria as a substitute for quinine. [< Latin *tōtus* all (the series of alkaloids of quinine) + English *qu*(inine) + *-ine*²]

to·ta·ra (tō′tər ə, tō tär′-), *n.* a New Zealand timber tree, a variety of podocarpus, valued for its reddish wood. [< Maori *tótāra*]

tote¹ (tōt), *v.,* **tot·ed, tot·ing,** *n. U.S. Informal.* —*v.t.* to carry; haul.
—*n.* **1.** a carrying or hauling. **2.** the distance of this; a haul: *a long tote.* **3.** a tote bag.
[American English; origin uncertain]

tote² (tōt), *n. Slang.* a totalizator.

tote bag, a large handbag somewhat like a shopping bag in shape and size: *Buyer Babs whips her order book out of what she calls a tote bag, but which to male eyes looks more* *like a Pony Express letter pouch* (Wall Street Journal).

tote board, *Slang.* the display board of a totalizator on which the odds and results of horse races are flashed: *Watching the tote board as it recorded the wagering in the Peter Pan was as fascinating as watching the race* (New Yorker).

tote box, a box or container for carrying or storing materials: *Smaller orders are drawn from bins in tote boxes* (Wall Street Journal).

to·tem (tō′təm), *n.* **1.** (among American Indians) a natural object, often an animal, taken as the emblem of a tribe, clan, family, etc.: *The clan usually considers the totem holy and prays to it. Sometimes the group considers the totem as an ancestor of the clan* (Fred Eggan). **2.** the image of a totem, often carved and painted on a pole. **3.** any venerated object: *Someone has suggested that every community has its totems and its taboos* (Emory S. Bogardus). [American English < Algonkian (probably Ojibwa) *ototeman* (literally) his sibling kin]

to·tem·ic (tō tem′ik), *adj.* **1.** of a totem; having to do with totems. **2.** having a totem or totems. —**to·tem′i·cal·ly,** *adv.*

to·tem·ism (tō′tə miz əm), *n.* the use of totems to distinguish tribes, clans, families, etc.

to·tem·ist (tō′tə mist), *n.* a person who belongs to a clan having a totem.

to·tem·is·tic (tō′tə mis′tik), *adj.* of or having to do with totemism or totemists.

totem pole or **post,** a pole carved and painted with representations of totems, erected by the Indians of the northwestern coast of North America, especially in front of their houses.

Totem Pole

To·ten·tanz (tô′tən tänts′), *n. German.* dance of death; danse macabre.

tote road, a rough, temporary road for carrying goods to or from a settlement, camp, etc.: *Next morning I followed the tote road into the woods, pausing now and then* (Atlantic).

toth·er or **t'oth·er** (tuᴛʜ′ər), *adj., pron. Dialect.* the other. [Middle English *the tother,* misdivision of *that other* the other]

to·ti·dem ver·bis (tot′ə dem vėr′bis), *Latin.* in so many words; in these very words.

to·ti·pal·mate (tō′tə pal′māt, -mit), *adj.* having all four toes completely webbed, as a pelican. [< Latin *tōtus* whole + English *palmate*]

to·ti·pal·ma·tion (tō′tə pal mā′shən), *n.* the condition of being totipalmate.

to·tip·o·tence (tō tip′ə təns), *n.* the quality of being totipotent.

to·tip·o·ten·cy (tō tip′ə tən sē), *n.* totipotence.

to·tip·o·tent (tō tip′ə tənt), *adj. Biology.* (of a cell, etc.) capable of developing into a complete organism. [< Latin *tōtus* whole + English *potent*]

to·tis vi·ri·bus (tō′tis vir′ə bəs), *Latin.* with all one's powers.

to·to cae·lo (tō′tō sē′lō), *Latin.* **1.** as far apart as the poles; diametrically opposite. **2.** (literally) by the whole heavens.

tot·ter (tot′ər), *v.i.* **1.** to stand or walk with shaky, unsteady steps: *The old man tottered across the room. It is charming to totter into vogue* (Horace Walpole). **2.** to be unsteady; shake as if about to fall or collapse: *The old wall tottered in the gale.* **3.** to shake; tremble.
—*n.* a tottering: *I . . . had his bend in my shoulders, and his totter in my gait* (Samuel Johnson).
[Middle English *toteren* swing back and forth on a rope, perhaps < Scandinavian (compare dialectal Norwegian *totra* to quiver)]
—**tot′ter·er,** *n.*
—**Syn.** *v.i.* **1.** wobble, stagger, reel.

tot·ter·ing (tot′ər ing), *adj.* that totters. —**tot′ter·ing·ly,** *adv.*

tot·ter·y (tot′ər ē), *adj.* tottering; shaky. —**Syn.** unsteady, wobbly.

tot·ty (tot′ē), *adj. Dialect.* shaky or unsteady; dizzy or dazed; fuddled.

Toua·reg (twä′reg), *n.* Tuareg.

tou·can (tü′kan, tü kän′), *n.* any of a group of tropical American birds that feed on fruit and have very large beaks and bright feathers. [< French *toucan* < Tupi (Brazil) *tucana*]

Toucan (1 to 2 ft. long)

Tou·can (tü′kan, tü kan′), *n., genitive* **Tou·ca·nis.** a southern constellation. [< *toucan*]

Tou·ca·nis (tü kā′nis), *n.* the genitive of **Toucan.**

touch (tuch), *v.t.* **1.** to put the hand, finger, or some other part of the body on or against: *She touched the pan to see whether it was still hot.* **2.** to put against; make contact with: *He touched the post with his umbrella.* **3.** to be against; come against: *Your sleeve is touching the butter. Water touched the dock.* **4. a.** to border on: *a country that touches the mountains on the north.* **b.** *Geometry.* to be tangent to. **5.** to strike lightly or gently: *to touch a doorbell.* **6.** to injure slightly: *The flowers were touched by the frost.* **7.** to affect with some feeling: *The sad story touched us.* **8.** to affect in some way by contact: *a metal so hard that a file cannot touch it.* **9.** to wound; hurt: *No soldiers were touched in the skirmish.* **10. a.** to strike the keys, strings, etc., of (a musical instrument) so as to make it sound: *She touched the strings of the harp.* **b.** to play (an air). **11.** to make slightly insane or crazy: *to be touched in the head.* **12.** to have to do with; concern: *The matter touches your interest. The new law does not touch his case.* **13.** to speak of; deal with; refer to; treat lightly: *Our conference touched many points.* **14.** to take or taste; handle; use: *The tired man couldn't touch a bit of dinner. He won't touch liquor or tobacco.* **15.** to have to do with in any way; be a party to: *I won't touch that business —it's crooked.* **16.** to come up to; reach: *His head almost touches the ceiling. The mercury touched 90 degrees.* **17.** to stop at; visit in passing: *The ship touched many ports.* **18.** *Slang.* **a.** to borrow from: *to touch a friend for a dollar.* **b.** to get by underhanded means; steal. **19.** to compare with; rival: *No one in our class can touch her in music.* **20.** to mark slightly or superficially, as with some color: *a sky touched with pink.* **21.** to mark, draw, or delineate, as with strokes of the brush, pencil, etc. **22.** to mark (metal) as of standard purity, etc., with an official stamp, after it has been tested. **23.** to lay the hand upon (a diseased person) for the cure of scrofula, as formerly practiced by French and English sovereigns.
—*v.i.* **1.** to put the hand, finger, or some other part of the body on or against something: *These glasses are delicate—don't touch!* **2.** to come or be in contact: *Their shoulders touched.* **3.** to arrive and make a brief stop: *a ship that touches at many ports.* **4.** to speak or write briefly or in passing. **5.** to approach closely; verge. **6.** to concern or relate: *an event that touches on his career.*

touch down, a. (of an airplane) to land: *At New York's expanding Idlewild airport last week, a Seaboard and Western air freighter touched down with a $50,000 consignment* (Newsweek). **b.** (in Rugby) to touch the ground with (the ball) behind the opposing team's goal line: *A young member of the visiting pack was able to touch down a try in the follow-up* (London Times).

touch off, a. to cause to go off; fire: *The only delay . . . is due to a fear that a dispatch of the troops will touch off the magazine* (London Daily Chronicle). **b.** to set off; ignite; instigate: *Colombian troops pleaded with students, who touched off anti-government demonstrations Saturday, to return to their classes* (Wall Street Journal).

touch on or **upon, a.** to treat lightly; mention: *Our conversation touched on many subjects.* **b.** to come close to: *a sermon that touches on heresy.*

touch up, to change a little; improve: *to touch up a photograph, to touch up a play.*
[< Old French *touchier* hit, knock < Vulgar Latin *toccāre* strike (as a bell). Compare TOCCATA.]
—*n.* **1.** a touching or being touched: *A bubble bursts at a touch. The touch of the cold water made her shiver.* **2. a.** the sense by which a person perceives things by feeling, handling, or coming against them: *The blind develop a keen touch. Some wool is rough to the touch.* **b.** the feeling caused by touching something; feel: *Worms and fish have a slimy touch.* **3.** a coming or being in contact: *the touch of their hands.* **4.** a slight amount; little bit: *a touch of frost, a touch of sarcasm, a touch of salt.* **5. a.** a stroke with a brush, pencil, pen, etc.: *The artist finished my picture with a few touches.* **b.** any light stroke or blow. **6.** a detail in any artistic work: *a story with charming poetic touches.* **7.** a close relation of communication, agreement, sympathy, or interest: *Mental patients often lose touch with daily life.* **8. a.** the act or manner of playing a musical instrument, striking the keys on the keyboard of a machine, etc.: *a pianist with a light touch, a typist's uneven touch.* **b.** the way the keys of a musical instrument or machine work: *a piano with a stiff touch.* **9. a.** a distinctive manner or quality; skill in style: *The work showed an expert's touch.* **b.** a mental or moral perception or feeling: *a delicate, intellectual touch.* **10.** a slight attack: *a touch of fever.* **11. a.** an official mark or stamp put on gold, silver, etc., to show it has been tested and is of standard fineness. **b.** a die, stamp, or punch for impressing such a mark. **c.** the quality or fineness so tested and indicated. **12.** quality, kind, or sort: *friends of noble touch.* **13.** any testing or test; trial; criterion: *to put a new product to the touch.* **14.** (in change ringing) any series of less than a complete set of changes. **15.** *Slang.* **a.** a borrowing or getting money from a person. **b.** money borrowed or gotten. **c.** a person borrowed or to be borrowed from: *He is a soft touch.* **16.** (in Rugby and soccer) the part of the field, including the sidelines, lying outside of the field of play.

in touch, in a close relation of communication, agreement, sympathy, or interest: *A newspaper keeps one in touch with the world.*

out of touch, lacking close relation of communication, agreement, sympathy, or interest: *a Governor of the old type, who is completely out of touch with the spirit of contemporary British colonial policy* (London Times).
[< Old French *touche* a blow, hit < *touchier;* see the verb] —**touch′er,** *n.*
—**Syn.** *v.t.* **5.** tap. **7.** move. –*n.* **4.** trace, tinge, shade, dash.

touch·a·ble (tuch′ə bəl), *adj.* that can be touched.

touch and go, 1. an uncertain, risky, or precarious situation: *It was touch and go whether he would live or die.* **2.** the act of touching for an instant and at once quitting; something done quickly or instantaneously.

touch-and-go (tuch′ən gō′), *adj.* uncertain; risky; precarious: . . . *the touch-and-go international situation* (Wall Street Journal).

touch·back (tuch′bak′), *n.* the act of touching the football to the ground by a player behind his own goal line when the impetus of the ball came from the other team.

touch·down (tuch′doun′), *n.* **1.** the act of a player in putting the football on the ground behind the opponents' goal line. **2.** the score of six points made in this way. **3.** the act of landing an aircraft: *Some 2,000 touchdowns have been executed at Bedford using partial or complete automatic control* (New Scientist).

tou·ché (tü shā′), *n.* a touch, as by the weapon of an opponent in fencing. —*interj.* an exclamation acknowledging an effective point in an argument or a clever reply. [< French *touché,* past participle of *toucher* < Old French *touchier;* see TOUCH, verb]

touched (tucht), *adj.* **1.** *Informal.* not quite normal mentally; slightly crazed; daft. **2.** stirred emotionally; moved.

touch football, a form of American football in which a ball carrier is downed by touching with the hand or hands rather than by tackling. The players usually have little or no protective equipment and the teams consist of fewer than eleven players.

touch·hole (tuch′hōl′), *n.* a small opening in an old-time gun through which the gunpowder inside was set on fire.

touch·i·ly (tuch′ə lē), *adv.* in a touchy manner; irritably; peevishly.

touch·i·ness (tuch′ē nis), *n.* the quality of being touchy; irritability; peevishness.

touch·ing (tuch′ing), *adj.* arousing tender feeling or sympathy: *"A Christmas Carol" is a touching story.* —*prep.* concerning; about: *He asked many questions touching my house and school.* —**touch′ing·ly,** *adv.* —**touch′ing·ness,** *n.* —**Syn.** *adj.* moving, pathetic.

touch judge, (in Rugby) an umpire who marks when and where the ball goes into touch.

touch·less (tuch′lis), *adj.* **1.** lacking the sense of touch. **2.** intangible.

touch·line (tuch′līn′), *n.* (in Rugby and soccer) the boundary of the playing field on either side; sideline.

touch-me-not (tuch′mē not′), *n.* **1.** any of a group of plants whose ripe seed pods burst open when touched; impatiens; jewelweed. **2.** *Obsolete.* the squirting cucumber.

Touch-me-not (def. 1)

touch paper, a paper fuse for fireworks, explosives, etc., made by soaking in potassium nitrate.

touch·piece (tuch′pēs′), *n.* a coin or medal formerly given by the king or queen of England to a person touched for the king's evil (scrofula).

touch·stone (tuch′stōn′), *n.* **1.** any means of testing; test; criterion: *an era . . . in which success is the only touchstone of merit* (Anthony Trollope). *Adversity is the touchstone of friendship. Calamity is man's true touchstone* (Beaumont and Fletcher). **2.** a smooth, fine-grained stone used to test the purity of gold or silver by the color of the streak made on the stone by rubbing it with the metal. —**Syn. 1.** standard.

touch system, the system of touch-typing.

touch-tone (tuch′tōn′), *adj.* using push buttons in place of a rotary dial that activate a system of distinct tones at a central to call a telephone number.

touch-type (tuch′tīp′), *v.i.,* **-typed, -typ·ing.** to type on a typewriter by the sense of touch alone, without having to look at the keyboard: *In writing it, he can already touch-type and, for note-taking, will learn Braille* (Time).

touch-typ·ist (tuch′tī′pist), *n.* a person skilled in touch-typing.

touch-up (tuch′up′), *n.* a touching up; a retouching: *Acting as color guinea pigs, . . . they keep coming back for touch-ups* (Walter Carlson). —*adj.* of or for touching up: *touch-up dabs of paint, a touch-up kit.*

touch·wood (tuch′wu̇d′), *n.* **1.** wood decayed by fungi so that it catches fire easily, used as tinder; punk. **2.** a fungus found on old tree trunks, used as tinder; amadou.

touch·y (tuch′ē), *adj.,* **touch·i·er, touch·i·est. 1.** apt to take offense at trifles; too sensitive. **2.** requiring skill in handling; ticklish; precarious. **3.** very sensitive to touch. **4.** catching fire very readily. —**Syn. 1.** tetchy. **2.** risky.

tough (tuf), *adj.* **1.** bending without breaking: *Leather is tough; cardboard is not.* **2.** hard to cut, tear, or chew: *The steak was so tough he couldn't eat it.* **3.** stiff; sticky: *tough clay.* **4.** strong; hardy: *Donkeys are tough little animals and can carry big loads.* **5.** hard; difficult: *a tough job. Dragging the load uphill was tough work for the horses.* **6.** hard to bear; bad; unpleasant: *A spell of tough luck discouraged him.* **7. a.** hard to influence; firm: *a tough mind.* **b.** stubborn; obstinate: *a tough customer.* **8.** severe; violent; strenuous: *Football is a tough game.* **9.** *U.S.* rough; disorderly: *a tough neighborhood.*
—*adv. Informal.* in a tough manner: *[He] talked tough about America's ideal approach to Communists* (New York Times).
—*n. U.S.* a rough person; rowdy: *A gang of toughs attacked him.*
[Old English *tōh*] —**tough′ly,** *adv.* —**tough′ness,** *n.*
—**Syn.** *adj.* **4.** sturdy, stout. **5.** laborious, arduous. **6.** trying. **7. a.** steadfast, persistent.

tough·en (tuf′ən), *v.t.* to make tough or tougher. —*v.i.* to become tough or tougher. —**tough′en·er,** *n.*

tough·ie (tuf′ē), *n. Slang.* **1.** a tough person or thing: *It's a great old hotel . . . but a real toughie to run* (Canada Month). **2.** a rough person; tough: *In the City of Angels today, the toughie's uniform is a leather jacket* (Newsweek).

tough·ish (tuf′ish), *adj.* somewhat tough.

tough-mind·ed (tuf′mīn′did), *adj.* having firm convictions; not easily influenced or diverted by sentiment; hard-boiled: *The nation's purchasing agents are a tough-minded, down-to-earth group of business men* (Newsweek).

tough-mind·ed·ly (tuf′mīn′did lē), *adv.* in a tough-minded manner or style: *a powerful and convincing novel written tough-mindedly [about] the old-time city boss* (New Yorker).

tough-mind·ed·ness (tuf′mīn′did nis), *n.* the state or quality of being tough-minded.

tough sledding, *Informal.* a difficult time: *House dresses as a rule sell better when more expensive lines have tough sledding* (New York Times).

tough spot, *Informal.* a difficult position.

tough·y (tuf′ē), *n., pl.* **tough·ies.** toughie.

tou·jours (tü zhür′), *adv. French.* always.

tou·jours gai (tü zhür′ gā′), *French.* always gay; forever happy.

tou·jours per·drix (tü zhür′ per drē′), *French.* **1.** too much of a good thing. **2.** (literally) always partridge.

toun·gya (toung′gyə), *n.* taungya.

tou·pee (tü pā′), *n.* **1.** a wig or patch of false hair worn to cover a bald spot. **2.** a curl or lock of false hair formerly worn on the top of the head as a crowning feature of a periwig. [variant of obsolete *toupet* < French, tuft of hair, forelock < Old French *toupe* tuft, perhaps < Germanic (compare Middle Low German *top, toup*). Compare TOP[1].]

tour (tu̇r), *v.i.* **1.** to travel from place to place: *Many Americans tour by car every summer.* **2.** (of actors, shows, etc.) to travel from town to town fulfilling engagements. —*v.t.* **1.** to travel through: *Last year they toured Europe.* **2.** to walk around in: *to tour the museum.* **3.** *Theater.* to take (a play, etc.) on tour. [< noun]
—*n.* **1.** a traveling around from place to place; a long journey: *a tour through Europe.* **2.** a short journey; a walk around: *a tour of the boat.* **3.** a tour of duty: *We . . . present this petition with the one plea that [he] be not returned for yet a third tour as Chief Justice to this Colony* (London Times).
on tour, touring: *A show on tour travels around the country giving performances in a number of different places.*
[< Old French *tour,* probably back formation from *tors* < *torner, tourner* to turn < Latin *tornāre* < *tornus* turner's wheel, lathe < Greek *tórnos.* Related to TURN.]

tou·ra·co (tu̇r′ə kō′), *n., pl.* **-cos.** any of various large African birds with brilliant feathers and a crest, related to the cuckoo. [perhaps < West African native name]

tour·bil·lion (tu̇r bil′yən), *n.* **1.** a kind of firework that spins in a spiral as it rises. **2.** *Obsolete.* a whirling mass or system; vortex. **3.** *Obsolete.* a whirlwind. [alteration of Middle English *turbilloun* < Old French *torbillon,* apparently < Latin *turbō, -inis* whirlwind]

tour de force (tür′ də fôrs′), *pl.* **tours de force** (tür′də fôrs′). **1.** a notable feat of strength, skill, or ingenuity. **2.** something done that is merely clever or ingenious: *His later work showed that his first novel was little more than a tour de force.* [< French *tour de force* (literally) feat of strength]

Tour de France (tür′ də fräns′), a French national sporting event in which professional cyclists compete to circle the entire country in a month. [< French *tour de France* (literally) tour of France]

tour d'ho·ri·zon (tür′ dô rē zôn′), *French.* **1.** a general review: *A student beginning to read a course in French literature at a university will find it [a book] helpful as an initial tour d'horizon* (Manchester Guardian). **2.** (literally) tour of the horizon.

tou·relle (tu̇ rel′), *n.* a turret. [< French *tourelle* (diminutive) < *tour* a tower]

tour·er (tu̇r′ər), *n. Especially British.* a touring car.

tour·ing (tu̇r′ing), *adj.* of or for tourists or making tours: *a touring guide, touring clothes.*

touring car, an open automobile with a folding top and no glass side windows, for four or more passengers.

tour·ism (tu̇r′iz əm), *n.* **1.** a touring or traveling for pleasure. **2.** tourists as a group. **3.** the business of serving tourists: *In many parts of the world tourism is providing the fastest growing source of dollars which in turn provide new funds for local investment in industries* (Wall Street Journal).

tour·ist (tu̇r′ist), *n.* a person who travels for pleasure. —*adj.* **1.** of or for tourists: *the tourist business, tourist accommodations.* **2.** tourist class: *First-class summer-rate fare is now $792; tourist rate $522* (Newsweek). —**Syn.** *n.* excursionist.

tourist camp or **court,** a camp providing such accommodations as tourists need; motel.

tourist class, 1. the least expensive class of accommodations on a ship, airplane, etc. **2.** a class of accommodations on some railroads that offers certain first-class or Pullman facilities at a lower rate.

tour·is·tic (tu̇ ris′tik), *adj.* of or for tourists; having to do with tourism: *For Sardinians, traditional costumes are daily dress and not a holiday or touristic get-up* (Atlantic). —**tour·is′ti·cal·ly,** *adv.*

tourist trap, an establishment that overcharges tourists: *They cite the tourist traps of Greenwich Village and to them Macdougal Street is a danger that "can happen here" if they relax their vigilance* (New York Times).

tour·ist·y (tu̇r′ə stē), *adj. Informal.* like a tourist or tourists: *There was also a gaggle of housewives from Exurbia, Conn., two more couples looking as touristy as we did, and a greyhaired man* (Maclean's).

tour je·té (tür zhə tā′), *French.* (in ballet) a high turning leap: *The steps are modern and functional with never a tour jeté, never an entrechat* (Time).

tour·ma·lin (tu̇r′mə lin), *n.* tourmaline.

tour·ma·line (tu̇r′mə lin, -lēn), *n.* a semiprecious colored mineral (black, brown, red, pink, green, blue, or yellow), a silicate of boron and aluminum with varying amounts of calcium, sodium, etc. The transparent varieties are used in jewelry. Also, **turmaline.** [< French *tourmaline* < Singhalese *tòramalli* a carnelian]

tour·na·ment (tėr′nə mənt, tu̇r′-), *n.* **1.** a contest of many persons in some sport or game: *a golf tournament, a chess tournament, a bridge tournament.* **2. a.** a medieval exercise in which two mounted groups of knights in armor fought each other with blunted weapons, according to certain rules, for a prize. **b.** a meeting at which knightly contests, exercises, and sports took place. **c.** the activities at such a meeting. **3.** any contest of strength or skill. [Middle English *turnement* < Old French *torneiement* < *torneier* to tourney]

tour·nay (tu̇r nā′), *n.* a printed worsted fabric used for upholstery. [< *Tournay,* a town in Belgium]

tour·ne·dos (tu̇r′nə dō′), *n., pl.* **-dos** (-dō′). one of several small slices cut from the center of the fillet of beef. [< French *tournedos*]

tour·ney (tėr′nē, tu̇r′-), *n., pl.* **-neys,** *v.,* **-neyed, -ney·ing.** —*n.* a tournament. —*v.i.* to take part in a tournament. [< Old French *tornei* < *torneier* to tourney < Vulgar Latin *tornidiāre* < Latin *tornus;* see TOUR]

tour·ni·quet (tu̇r′nə ket, -kā; tėr′-), *n.* any device for stopping bleeding by compressing a blood vessel, such as a bandage tightened by twisting with a stick, a pad pressed down by a screw, an inflated rubber tube, etc. [< French *tourniquet* < Old French *tourner* to turn]

tour·nure (tu̇r nyu̇r′; *French* tür nyr′), *n.* **1.** turn, contour, or form. **2.** figure; appearance; bearing. [< French *tournure* < Old French *tourner* to turn]

tour of duty, 1. a period or turn of military duty at a certain place or station. **2.** any spell of work; shift.

touse (touz), *n., v.,* **toused, tous·ing.** *Dialect.* —*n.* **1.** rough or noisy play. **2.** a commotion; fuss. —*v.t.* to tousle. [Middle English *-tousen,* in *betousen* to touse; origin uncertain. Related to TEASE, TOSS.]

tous frais faits (tü fre fe′), *French.* all expenses paid.

tou·sle (tou′zəl), *v.,* **-sled, -sling,** *n.* —*v.t.* to put into disorder; make untidy; muss: *The baby tousled his mother's hair.* —*n.* a disordered mass: *hair or sheets in a tousle.* Also, **touzle.** [< *tous*(e) + *-le.* Compare TUSSLE.] —**Syn.** *v.t.* dishevel, rumple.

tous-les-mois (tü′lā mwä′), *n.* **1.** a starch obtained from the edible rootstocks of a West Indian canna, used in baby food and cocoa. It is like arrowroot. **2.** the plant itself. [< French (West Indies) *tous-les-mois* (literally) all the months; probably by folk etymology < *toloman* the name of the plant, perhaps < the native name]

tout (tout), *Informal.* —*v.t.* **1.** to try to get (customers, jobs, votes, etc.). **2.** *U.S.* to urge betting on (a race horse) by claiming to have special information. **3.** *Especially British.* to spy out (information about race horses) for use in betting. **4.** to praise highly and insistently. —*v.i.* to engage in touting; be a tout.
—*n.* **1.** a person who touts. **2.** a thieves' scout or watchman.
[earlier, spy on, Middle English *tuten* to peep, peer; origin uncertain]

tout à fait (tü tȧ fe′), *French.* entirely; completely; wholly; quite.

tout à vous (tü tȧ vü′), *French.* wholly yours; sincerely yours.

tout com·pren·dre, c'est tout par·don·ner (tü kôN präN′drə, se tü pȧr dô nā′), *French.* to understand all is to forgive all.

tout court (tü kür′), *French.* in short; briefly; simply: *The Icelandic poet Harmer, known to his friends tout court as Iceland . . . was missing* (Sir Osbert Sitwell).

tout de suite (tüt swēt′), *French.* **1.** at once. **2.** consecutively.

tout en·sem·ble (tü täN säN′blə), *French.* **1.** all together. **2.** the general effect of the various parts, as of a work of art, taken as a whole.

tout·er (tou′tər), *n.* a person who touts; tout.

tout le monde (tü lə môNd′), *French.* the whole world; everyone.

tou·zle (tou′zəl), *v.t.,* **-zled, -zling,** *n.* tousle.

to·va·rish, to·va·rich, or **to·va·risch** (tə vä′rish), *n.* comrade. [< Russian *tovarishch*]

tow[1] (tō), *v.t.* to pull by a rope, chain, etc.: *to tow a car from a ditch to a garage. The tug is towing three barges.*
—*n.* **1.** the act of towing. **2.** condition of being pulled along by a rope, chain, etc.: *The launch had the sailboat in tow.* **3.** something that is towed, as a ship taken in tow or a string of boats or barges being towed: *Each tug had a tow of three barges.* **4.** the rope, chain, etc., used for towing; towline. **5.** a ship that tows; tugboat; tug. **6.** a ski tow.
in tow, a. in one's company or charge: *Arizona Democrat Morris "Mo" Udall . . . happened by with three constituents in tow* (Harper's). **b.** under one's care or influence: *The boy had his little brother in tow for the day.*
[Old English *togian* drag]
—**Syn.** *v.t.* haul, drag, tug, draw.

tow[2] (tō), *n.* **1.** the fiber of flax, hemp, or jute prepared for spinning by scutching. **2.** the coarse, broken fibers of flax, hemp, etc., that are separated after hackling: *This string is made of tow.* —*adj.* made of tow. [Old English *tōw-* spinning, as in *tōwlīc* fit for spinning, perhaps related to Old Icelandic *tō* unworked fiber]

tow[3] (tō), *n. Scottish.* a rope; halter. [perhaps < Scandinavian (compare Old Icelandic *tog* rope, cable, or *taug* string, rope)]

tow·a·ble (tō′ə bəl), *adj.* that may be towed: *The dock is towable to any part of Australia* (Glasgow Herald).

tow·age (tō′ij), *n.* **1.** a towing. **2.** a being towed. **3.** a charge for towing. [< Medieval Latin *towagium*]

to·ward (*prep.* tôrd, tōrd, tə wôrd′; *adj.* tôrd, tōrd), *prep.* **1.** in the direction of: *He walked toward the north.* **2.** turned or directed to; facing: *to lie with one's face toward the wall.* **3. a.** with respect to; regarding; about; concerning: *What is his attitude toward war?* **b.** against: *Do you have any malice toward him?* **4.** shortly before; near: *It must be toward four o'clock.* **5.** as a help to; for: *Will you give something toward our new hospital? The United Nations' work is toward peace.*
—*adj.* **1.** about to happen; impending; imminent. **2.** in progress; going on; being done. **3.** *Archaic.* promising, hopeful, or apt.
[Old English *tōweard* < *tō* to + *-weard* -ward]

to·ward·li·ness (tôrd′lē nis, tōrd′-; tō′ərd-), *n.* a readiness to do or learn; aptness; docility.

to·ward·ly (tôrd′lē, tōrd′-; tō′ərd-), *adj.* **1.** ready to do or learn; docile. **2.** promising; advantageous; propitious.

to·wards (tôrdz, tōrdz, tə wôrdz′), *prep.* toward.

tow·boat (tō′bōt′), *n.* a tugboat.

tow car, a wrecker.

tow·el (tou′əl), *n., v.,* **-eled, -el·ing** or (*especially British*) **-elled, -el·ling.** —*n.* a piece of cloth or paper for wiping and drying something wet: *a face towel, a dish towel.*
throw or **toss in the towel,** *Informal.* to admit defeat: *The city made futile efforts to work out a peace formula before the strike deadline, but officials finally tossed in the towel at 6:45 P.M. and confessed that a tie-up was certain* (New York Times).
—*v.t.* to rub or dry with a towel.
[Middle English *towele, towaille* < Old French *toaille* < Medieval Latin *toacula* < Germanic (compare Middle High German *twahele*)]

towel bar, rack, or **rail,** a bar, rod, or frame on which to hang towels.

tow·el·ing (tou′ə ling), *n.* material used for towels, especially cotton.

tow·el·ling (tou′ə ling), *n. Especially British.* toweling.

tow·er (tou′ər), *n.* **1.** a high structure. A tower may stand alone or form part of a castle, church, or other building. *Some towers are forts or prisons.* **2.** a means of defense or protection. **3.** a person or thing that is like a tower in some way: *a tower of strength.*
—*v.i.* to stand or rise high up.
[partly Old English *torr* < Latin *turris;* partly Middle English *ture,* or *tour* < Old French *tur,* and *tour* < Latin]
—**Syn.** *n.* **1.** spire, steeple, turret. **2.** citadel, fortress, stronghold.

Tow·er (tou′ər), *n.* the Tower of London.

tow·ered (tou′ərd), *adj.* **1.** having a tower or towers. **2.** ornamented or defended with towers: *towered battlements.* **3.** rising like a tower.

tow·er·ing (tou′ər ing), *adj.* **1.** very high; lofty: *a towering peak.* **2.** very tall: *a towering basketball player.* **3.** very great: *towering ambition, a towering achievement.* **4.** very violent: *a towering rage.* —**tow′er·ing·ly,** *adv.*

tow·er·man (tou′ər mən), *n., pl.* **-men. 1.** *U.S.* a man in charge of a signal box on a railway. **2.** a man who operates the control tower of an airport: *Both towermen and an enlisted man on the field saw a single, round, orange light drifting in the southern sky* (Time).

Tower of Babel. See under **Babel.**

tow·er·y (tou′ər ē), *adj.* **1.** having towers. **2.** towering; lofty.

tow·head (tō′hed′), *n.* **1.** a person having very light, pale-yellow hair. **2.** a head of light-colored hair. [< *tow*[2] + *head*]

tow·head·ed (tō′hed′id), *adj.* having very light, pale-yellow hair.

tow·hee (tou′hē, tō′-), *n.,* or **towhee bunting,** any of various American finches related to the sparrows but larger, as the Oregon towhee of western North America and the red-eyed towhee, also called chewink or ground robin, of eastern North America. [American English; apparently imitative of its call]

tow·ing tank (tō′ing), a tank of water in which scale-model ships can be tested for seaworthiness and design.

tow·line (tō′līn′), *n.* a line, rope, chain, etc., for towing.

town (toun), *n.* **1.** a large group of houses and other buildings, smaller than a city but larger than a village: *a growing town, an abandoned town.* **2.** any large place with many people living in it: *Chicago is his favorite town.* **3.** the people of a town: *The whole town was having a holiday.* **4.** the part of a town or city where the stores and office buildings are: *Let's go into town.* **5.** the particular town or city under consideration: *to be in town, to have to leave town.* **6.** *U.S.* **a.** (in New England) a local administrative unit consisting of a division of a county and exercising self-government through town meetings. It is similar to a township. **b.** (in other states) a township. **7.** *British.* any village or hamlet: *a market town.*
go to town, *Informal.* **a.** to achieve success: *In Europe, he really went to town with his personal diplomacy; his friends were in the capitals of the Western, "civilized" world* (New Yorker). **b.** to do or go through thoroughly: *The hungry boys really went to town on the pie.*
on the town, a. on a pleasure tour of a city: *The group of tourists went out on the town.* **b.** supported by a town; on charity: *the unemployed who had been a long time on the town.*
paint the town red, *Slang.* to go on a wild spree or party; celebrate in a noisy manner: *Mere horseplay; it is the cowboy's method of painting the town red, as an interlude in his harsh monotonous life* (Century Magazine).
—*adj.* **1.** of, having to do with, or characteristic of a town or towns; urban. **2.** of or belonging to a certain town: *the town clock.*
[Old English *tūn* enclosure; enclosed land with its buildings; a village]

town and gown, the townspeople and the academic community.

town-bred (toun′bred′), *adj.* born and raised in a town rather than in the country: *The original forest dweller does not do . . . these things, because they are really inventions of the recent town-bred generations* (Manchester Guardian Weekly).

town clerk, an official who keeps the records of a town.

town crier, a man in former times who called out the news on the streets of a city or town.

town·ee (tou nē′), *n. Informal.* a townsman.

town father, one of the officials or leading citizens of a town.

town gas, *British.* gas piped to the buildings of a village or town.

town hall, a building belonging to a town, used for the town's business, and often also as a place for public meetings.

town·house (toun′hous′), *n.* **1.** a town hall. **2.** a town prison or poorhouse.

town house, a house in town, belonging to a person who also has a house in the country.

town·ie (tou′nē), *n.* towny.

town·ish (tou′nish), *adj.* **1.** of or having to do with a town or city; urban. **2.** characteristic of the town as distinguished from the country; having the manners or habits of town dwellers.

town·land (toun′lənd), *n.* (in Ireland) a division of a parish; township: *He was born and reared in the townland of Drung, thirteen miles north of Athenry* (New Yorker).

town·let (toun′lit), *n.* a little town.

town meeting, 1. a general meeting of the inhabitants of a town. **2.** (in New England) a meeting of the qualified voters of a town for the transaction of public business.

town planner, a person who is in charge of directing the work of town planning.

town planning, the regulation of the development of a town by controlling the location of buildings, parks, streets, etc., and the type of occupancy permitted in various areas.

town·scape (toun′skāp), *n.* a scene or view of a town, whether pictured or natural: *In Amsterdam, the parked cars so effectively line the canals of the central city that they completely spoil the townscape* (New Yorker). [< *town* + *scape*[3]]

Town·send Plan (toun′zənd), a plan originated in 1934 by Dr. Francis Townsend, but never put into effect, under which all citizens 60 years of age or older would receive a monthly pension of $200, which would be paid out of the receipts from a 2 per cent tax on business transactions.

Townsend's solitaire, a songbird of western North America related to the thrush and resembling a mockingbird, having a gray body with a white ring around the eye. [< John Kirk *Townsend,* 1809-1851, an American ornithologist]

Townsend's warbler, a warbler of western North America with yellow and black markings about the head and breast.

towns·folk (townz′fōk′), *n.pl.* the people of a town: *Townsfolk gathered to see the fire.*

town·ship (toun′ship), *n.* **1.** (in the United States and Canada) a part of a county having certain powers of local government, such as responsibility for schools, poor relief, and maintenance of the roads. *Abbr.:* tp., twp. **2.** (in United States surveys of public land) a region or district six miles square, subdivided into 36 sections. **3.** in English history: **a.** a local administrative division of a large parish, containing a village, and usually having its own church. **b.** a manor, parish, or division of a hundred, as a territorial division. **c.** the inhabitants of such a community as a group. [Old English *tūnscipe* < *tūn* town + *-scipe* -ship]

town·site (toun′sīt′), *n.* **1.** the site of a town. **2.** (in the United States and Canada) a tract of land set apart by law to be occupied by a town, usually surveyed and laid out with streets, etc.

towns·man (tounz′mən), *n., pl.* **-men. 1.** a person who lives or has been raised in a town. **2.** a person who lives in one's own town; fellow citizen. **3.** a selectman of any of certain New England towns.

towns·peo·ple (tounz′pē′pəl), *n.pl.* the people of a town; townsfolk.

towns·wom·an (tounz′wu̇m′ən), *n., pl.* **-wom·en. 1.** a woman who lives in a town. **2.** a woman who lives in one's own town.

town talk, 1. the common talk or gossip of a town. **2.** the subject of gossip.

town·ward (toun′wərd), *adv., adj.* toward the town: *On Sunday evenings in the fall the cars roll back townward* (Harper's).

town·wards (toun′wərdz), *adv.* townward.

town·y (tou′nē), *n., pl.* **town·ies. 1.** *Informal.* a townee. **2.** a citizen of a town, as contrasted with a student or teacher at a college there.

tow·path (tō′path′, -päth′), *n.* a path along the bank of a canal or river for use in towing boats.

tow·rope (tō′rōp′), *n.* a rope, hawser, cable, etc., used in towing.

tow target, an object towed behind a plane for target practice by anti-aircraft weapons or fighter planes.

tow truck, a wrecker.

tow·y (tō′ē), *adj.* of or like tow.

tox., toxicology.

tox·ae·mi·a (tok sē′mē ə), *n.* toxemia.

tox·ae·mic (tok sē′mik), *adj.* toxemic.

tox·al·bu·min (tok′səl byü′min), *n.* a toxic protein, such as snake venom.

tox·a·phene (tok′sə fēn), *n.* a powerful insecticide derived from camphene and chlorine, used chiefly against cotton and forage crop parasites, but not on fruits or vegetables, for it cannot be washed off easily. *Formula:* $C_{10}H_{10}Cl_8$ [< *tox*(ic) + (cam)*phene*]

tox·e·mi·a (tok sē′mē ə), *n.* blood poisoning, especially a form in which the toxins produced by pathogenic bacteria enter the blood stream from a local lesion and are distributed throughout the body. Also, **toxaemia.** [< *tox*(ic) + *-emia*]

tox·e·mic (tok sē′mik), *adj.* **1.** of or having to do with toxemia. **2.** suffering from toxemia.

tox·ic (tok′sik), *adj.* **1.** of, having to do with, or caused by a toxin or poison. **2.** like a poison; poisonous: *It is relatively easy to find a chemical which, when tested in the glasshouse, is more toxic to one species than another* (New Scientist). [< Late Latin *toxicus* < Latin *toxicum* poison < Greek *toxikón* (*phármakon*) (poison) for use on arrows < *tóxon* bow] **—tox′i·cal·ly,** *adv.* **—Syn. 2.** noxious.

tox·i·cal (tok′sə kəl), *adj.* toxic.

tox·i·cant (tok′sə kənt), *adj.* poisonous; toxic. **—***n.* **1.** a poison. **2.** an intoxicant. [< Medieval Latin *toxicans, -antis,* present participle of *toxicare* to poison < Late Latin *toxicus;* see TOXIC]

tox·i·ca·tion (tok′sə kā′shən), *n.* poisoning.

tox·ic·i·ty (tok sis′ə tē), *n., pl.* **-ties.** a toxic or poisonous quality; poisonousness: *Plants are convenient means of assessing the toxicity of smog* (Scientific American).

tox·i·co·den·drol (tok′sə kō den′drol), *n.* a nonvolatile, poisonous oil found in poison ivy, oak, and sumac. It can be washed off with alcohol but not with water. [< Greek *toxikón* poison (see TOXIC) + *déndron* tree + English *-ol*[2]]

tox·i·co·gen·ic (tok′sə kə jen′ik), *adj.* **1.** producing toxins or poisons. **2.** caused by toxins or poisons. [< Greek *toxikón* poison (see TOXIC) + English *-gen* + *-ic*]

toxicol., 1. toxicological. **2.** toxicology.

tox·i·co·log·i·cal (tok′sə kə loj′ə kəl), *adj.* of or having to do with toxicology. **—tox′i·co·log′i·cal·ly,** *adv.*

tox·i·col·o·gist (tok′sə kol′ə jist), *n.* a person skilled in toxicology.

tox·i·col·o·gy (tok′sə kol′ə jē), *n.* the science that deals with poisons, their effects, antidotes, detection, etc. [< Greek *toxikón* poison (see TOXIC) + English *-logy*]

tox·i·co·pho·bi·a (tok′sə kə fō′bē ə), *n.* toxiphobia.

tox·i·co·sis (tok′sə kō′sis), *n., pl.* **-ses** (-sēz). a diseased condition caused by a poison. [< New Latin *toxicosis* < Greek *toxikón* poison (see TOXIC) + *-ōsis* -osis]

tox·i·gen·e·sis (tok′sə jen′ə sis), *n.* the creation or production of toxins.

tox·i·gen·ic (tok′sə jen′ik), *adj.* creating or producing toxins.

tox·in (tok′sən), *n.* any poisonous product of animal or vegetable metabolism, especially one of those produced by bacteria. The symptoms of a disease caused by bacteria, such as diphtheria, tetanus, etc., are due to toxins. [< *tox*(ic) + *-in*]

tox·in-an·ti·tox·in (tok′sən an′tē tok′sən), *n.* a mixture of a toxin, as a diphtheria toxin, with enough of the corresponding antitoxin to almost neutralize it. Inoculation with it causes future immunity to the toxin.

tox·ine (tok′sin, -sēn), *n.* toxin.

tox·i·pho·bi·a (tok′sə fō′bē ə), *n.* an abnormal fear of being poisoned.

tox·oid (tok′soid), *n.* a toxin, as of diphtheria or tetanus, so treated as to lose its toxicity but retain its ability to help produce antibodies when injected. [< *tox*(in) + *-oid*]

tox·oph·i·lite (tok sof′ə līt), *n.* a person who is very fond of archery. [apparently < *Toxophilus,* probably coined by Roger Ascham, 1515-1568, an English scholar and writer, as the title of his book on archery; (literally) lover of the bow (< Greek *tóxon* bow + *phílos* loving) + *-ite*[1]]

tox·oph·i·lit·ic (tok sof′ə lit′ik), *adj.* of or having to do with archers or archery.

tox·oph·i·ly (tok sof′ə lē), *n.* the practice of, or liking for, archery.

tox·o·plas·mic (tok′sə plaz′mik), *adj.* of or having to do with toxoplasmosis.

tox·o·plas·mo·sis (tok′sə plaz mō′sis), *n.* a disease attacking people, dogs, cats, and other animals, caused by a protozoan. Children develop an inflammation of the brain and spinal cord; adults develop a condition similar to Rocky Mountain spotted fever. [< New Latin *toxoplasmosis* < Greek *toxikón* poison + *plásma* plasm, plasma + *-ōsis* -osis]

toy (toi), *n.* **1.** something for a child to play with; plaything. **2.** a thing that has little value or importance: *a toy, a thing of no regard* (Shakespeare). *Love and all his pleasures are but toys* (Thomas Campion). **3.** any of certain breeds of very small animals, especially dogs and pigeons. **4.** *Scottish.* a close-fitting cap of linen or wool, with flaps coming down to the shoulders, formerly worn by lower-class women. **5.** *Obsolete.* **a.** amorous sport; dalliance. **b.** a light caress. **6.** *Obsolete.* an antic; trick.
—*adj.* of, made as, or like a toy.
—*v.i.* to amuse oneself; play; trifle: *She toyed with her beads. Don't toy with matches.* [Middle English *toye* playing, sport; origin uncertain] **—toy′like′,** *adj.*
—Syn. *n.* **2.** trifle, knickknack, trinket.

toy dog, any of certain very small breeds of dogs, especially poodles, spaniels and terriers.

to-year (tə yir′), *adv. Dialect.* this year. [< *to* on + *year.* Compare TODAY, TONIGHT.]

toy·land (toi′land′), *n.* an imaginary place inhabited by toy characters and full of romantic adventure.

toy·mak·er (toi′mā′kər), *n.* **1.** a manufacturer of toys: *Toymakers looked forward to sprucing up their sales from the growing interest in things scientific, ranging from dinosaurs to rockets* (Newsweek). **2.** a craftsman of toys: *Vladimir was not only a great clown; he was also a great scholar, painter, musician, toymaker* (Niccolò Tucci).

toy·man (toi′mən), *n., pl.* **-men.** a maker or seller of toys: *Looking ahead to Christmas, the toymen were already well-stocked* (Time).

toy Manchester terrier, a small variety of Manchester terrier, weighing up to 12 pounds.

to·yo (tô′yō), *n.* **1.** a straw made of rice paper, used for women's hats: *His Pan caps are deep, smooth turbans of toyo or some other straw* (New Yorker). **2.** a hat made of such straw: *Liked particularly was a natural toyo, high-crowned and with medium brim* (New York Times). [< Japanese *toyo*]

to·yon (tō′yən), *n.* a shrub of the rose family found on the Pacific coast of North America, whose evergreen leaves and scarlet berries look much like holly. [American English < American Spanish *tollón,* perhaps < an American Indian name]

toy·shop (tôy′shop′), *n.* a shop where toys or playthings are sold.

tp., township.

t.p., title page.

TPI (no periods), treponema pallidum immobilization (designating a test for the presence of syphilis).

TPN (no periods) or **T.P.N.,** triphosphopyridine nucleotide.

T.P.O., traveling post office.

tr., an abbreviation for the following:
1. trace.
2. transitive.
3. a. translated, **b.** translation, **c.** translator.
4. transpose.
5. treasurer.

Tr (no period), terbium (chemical element).

T.R., Theodore Roosevelt, President of the United States, 1901-1909.

tra·be·a (trā′bē ə), *n.* a toga with horizontal purple stripes, worn as a robe of state by consuls, augurs, etc., in ancient Rome. [< Latin *trabea*]

tra·be·ate (trā′bē it, -āt), *adj.* trabeated.

tra·be·at·ed (trā′bē ā′tid), *adj. Architecture.* **1.** constructed with beams; having a lintel or entablature, instead of an arch: *a trabeated doorway.* **2.** of or having to do with this type of construction.

tra·be·a·tion (trā′bē ā′shən), *n.* **1.** construction with a lintel or entablature. **2.** something constructed in this way. [< Latin *trabs, trabis* beam + English *-ation*]

tra·bec·u·la (trə bek′yə lə), *n., pl.* **-lae** (-lē). **1.** a structure in an animal or plant like a small beam or bar. **2.** *Botany.* a projection extending across the cell cavity in the ducts of some plants, or across the cavity of the sporangium in mosses. [< Latin *trabecula* (diminutive) < *trabs, trabis* beam]

tra·bec·u·lar (trə bek′yə lər), *adj.* **1.** of or having to do with a trabecula. **2.** forming or formed by trabeculae.

tra·bec·u·late (trə bek′yə lit, -lāt), *adj.* having a trabecula or trabeculae.

trace[1] (trās), *n., v.,* **traced, trac·ing. —***n.* **1.** a mark, token, or evidence indicating the former existence, presence, or action of something; vestige; sign: *The explorers found traces of an ancient city.* **2. a.** the track made by the passage of a person, animal, or thing: *We saw traces of rabbits on the snow.* **b.** a beaten path, as through a wild region; trail; track: *the Natchez Trace.* **3.** a very small amount; little bit: *There wasn't a trace of color in her cheeks. The trace of rainfall in the desert is too small to be measured.* **4. a.** a line or figure marked out or drawn; a tracing, drawing, or sketch of something. **b.** a record made by a self-registering instrument. **5.** *Chemistry.* an indication of an amount of some constituent in a compound, usually too small to be measured. **6.** *Psychology.* an engram. **7.** *Obsolete.* the way or path which anything takes. [< Old French *trace* < *tracier;* see the verb]
—*v.t.* **1.** to follow by means of marks, tracks, or signs: *to trace deer. The dog traced the fox to its den. The counterfeit money was traced to a foreign printer.* **2.** to follow the course, development, or history of: *to trace a river to its source, to trace the meanings of a word. The Aldens trace their family back to John Alden, one of the Pilgrims.* **3.** to find signs or proof of; observe; discover: *I could never trace in her one spark of jealousy* (Robert Louis Stevenson). **4.** to draw an outline of; mark out; draw; sketch: *The spy traced a plan of the fort.* **5.** to copy by following the lines of: *He put thin paper over the map and traced it.* **6.** to decorate with tracery. **7.** to write, especially by forming the letters carefully or laboriously: *The old man seized the pen and traced his name* (Francis M. Crawford). **8.** to copy, impress, or imprint with a tracer. **9.** to record in the form of a curving, wavy, or broken line, as a cardiograph, seismograph, etc. **10.** *Obsolete.* to pass along or over; traverse. **—***v.i.* **1.** to trace the origin or history of; go back in time. **2.** *Obsolete.* to make one's way; go; proceed; travel.
[< Old French *trasser,* and *tracier* < Vulgar Latin *tractiāre* < Latin *tractus, -ūs* a drawing < *trahere* to drag]
—Syn. *n.* **1. Trace, vestige** mean a mark or sign of what has existed or happened. **Trace** applies to any noticeable indication left by something that has happened or been present: *The campers removed all traces of their fire.* **Vestige** applies particularly to an actual remnant of something that existed in the past: *Some of our common courtesies are vestiges of very old cultural customs.*

trace[2] (trās), *n.* **1.** either of the two straps, ropes or chains by which an animal pulls a wagon, carriage, etc. See **harness** for picture. **2.** a connecting rod.
kick over the traces, to throw off controls or

restraints: *I could not help thinking that Mr. Finney might produce something really worth listening to if he could kick over the traces of the serial system of composition* (New Yorker). [new singular of Middle English *trays,* collective plural < Old French *traiz,* plural of *trait* < Latin *tractus, -ūs* a drawing, a track < *trahere* to drag, draw. Doublet of TRACT[1], TRAIT, TRET.]

trace·a·bil·i·ty (trā′sə bil′ə tē), *n.* the fact or property of being traceable.

trace·a·ble (trā′sə bəl), *adj.* that can be traced. —**trace′a·ble·ness,** *n.*

trace·a·bly (trā′sə blē), *adv.* in a traceable manner; so as to be traced.

trace element, a chemical element, especially a metallic one, used in small amounts by an organism, but considered necessary to the organism's proper functioning.

trace·less (trās′lis), *adj.* leaving or showing no traces: *This is the sort of thing which, like the traceless sinking of the "News Chronicle" and the "Star," makes the journalist feel that he writes in sand* (Punch). —**trace′less·ly,** *adv.*

trac·er (trā′sər), *n.* **1.** a person or thing that traces. **2.** a machine for making tracings of drawings, plans, etc. **3.** *U.S.* an inquiry sent from place to place to trace a missing person, article, letter, parcel, etc.: *We'll put out a tracer on your stolen car.* **4.** a person whose business is tracing missing persons, property, etc. **5. a.** a burning substance put in a tracer bullet. **b.** a tracer bullet. **6.** *Chemistry.* an element or atom, usually radioactive, that can be traced and observed in a biological process or used to detect small quantities of its isotope in analysis.

tracer bullet, 1. a bullet with a substance in it that burns when the bullet is fired, leaving a trail that can be followed with the eye. **2.** a shell containing such a substance.

trac·er·ied (trā′sər ēd, trās′rēd), *adj.* ornamented with tracery: *a traceried window.*

trac·er·y (trā′sər ē, trās′rē), *n., pl.* **-er·ies. 1.** ornamental work or designs consisting of very fine lines, as in certain kinds of embroidery. **2.** a pattern of intersecting bars or a plate with leaflike decorations in the upper part of a Gothic window, in the ribs of a vault, in carved panels, etc. [< *trac*(e)[1], verb + *-ery*]

Tracery (def. 2)

trace tug, a strap supporting a trace of a harness.

tra·che·a (trā′kē ə, trə kē′-), *n., pl.* **tra·che·ae** (trā′kē ē, trə kē′-). **1.** the tube in air-breathing vertebrates extending from the larynx to the bronchi, by which air is carried to and from the lungs; windpipe. See **lung** for picture. **2.** *Zoology.* one of the air-carrying tubes of the respiratory system of insects and other arthropods. **3.** *Botany.* **a.** a vessel or duct formed by a row of cells that have lost their intervening partitions and have become a single long canal for the carrying of water and dissolved minerals. Tracheae are covered with various markings or thickenings, the spiral being the common type. **b.** one of these cells. [< Medieval Latin *trachea* (*arteria*) trachea (artery), for Late Latin *trāchīa* < Greek *trācheîa artēríā* windpipe; (literally) rough air vessel]

tra·che·al (trā′kē əl, trə kē′-), *adj.* of or having to do with the trachea.

tracheal tissue, 1. tissue making up the tracheae or vessels in the xylem of plants. **2.** conductive tissue in plants, composed of tracheae (vessels), tracheids, or both.

tra·che·id (trā′kē id), *n.* an elongated, more or less lignified cell, usually having bordered pits on its walls, and tapering ends whose walls have not been absorbed. Tracheids are characteristic of the wood of conifers and other gymnosperms and function in both conduction and support. [< German *Tracheide* < *Trachea* trachea]

tra·che·i·dal (trə kē′ə dəl, trā′kē ī′-), *adj.* of, having to do with, or like tracheids.

tra·che·i·tis (trā′kē ī′tis), *n.* inflammation of the windpipe. [< New Latin *tracheitis* < *trachea* trachea + *-itis* -itis]

tra·che·o·bron·chi·al (trā′kē ō brong′kē-əl), *adj.* having to do with the trachea and the bronchi.

tracheobronchial tree, *Anatomy.* the part of the breathing apparatus consisting of the trachea and the bronchi, resembling a tree and its branches.

tra·che·o·bron·chi·tis (trā′kē ō bron kī′-tis, -brong-), *n.* inflammation of the trachea and bronchia.

tra·che·o·e·so·phag·e·al (trā′kē ō ē′sə-faj′ē əl), *adj.* having to do with the trachea and the esophagus.

tra·che·ole (trā′kē ōl), *n.* one of the tiny branches of the trachea of an insect.

tra·che·o·scop·ic (trā′kē ə skop′ik), *adj.* of or having to do with tracheoscopy.

tra·che·os·co·pist (trā′kē os′kə pist), *n.* a person skilled in tracheoscopy.

tra·che·os·co·py (trā′kē os′kə pē), *n., pl.* **-pies.** examination of the interior of the trachea, as with a laryngoscope.

tra·che·ot·o·mist (trā′kē ot′ə mist), *n.* a surgeon who performs a tracheotomy.

tra·che·ot·o·my (trā′kē ot′ə mē), *n., pl.* **-mies.** surgical incision into the trachea. [< *trachea* + Greek *-tomiā* a cutting]

tra·chle (trä′ʜəl), *v.t.,* **-chled, -chling.** *Scottish.* **1. a.** to dishevel. **b.** to disorder or injure by trampling. **2. a.** to exhaust. **b.** to distress. Also, **trauchle.** [origin uncertain. Compare Flemish *tragelen* to go with difficulty, dialectal Swedish *traggla* to worry.]

tra·cho·don (trā′kə don), *n.* a trachodont.

tra·cho·dont (trā′kə dont), *n.* a very large dinosaur with a broad, flat skull, lower jaws like a duck's bill, and as many as 2,000 teeth. Some kinds had webbed feet. [< Greek *trāchýs* rough + *odoús, odóntos* tooth]

Trachodont (about 25 ft. long)

tra·cho·ma (trə kō′mə), *n.* **1.** a contagious inflammation of the eyelids. **2.** granular eyelids, a much less serious condition. [< Late Latin *trāchōma* < Greek *trāchōma* roughness < *trāchýs* rough]

tra·chom·a·tous (trə kom′ə təs, -kō′mə-), *adj.* of or affected with trachoma.

tra·chy·car·pous (trā′kē kär′pəs, trak′ē-), *adj. Botany.* having rough-skinned fruit. [< Greek *trāchýs* rough + *karpós* fruit + English *-ous*]

tra·chy·sper·mous (trā′kē spėr′məs, trak′ē-), *adj. Botany.* having rough-skinned seeds. [< Greek *trāchýs* rough + English *spermous*]

tra·chyte (trā′kīt, trak′īt), *n.* a light, volcanic rock with a rough surface, consisting of feldspars and augite or biotite. [< French *trachyte* < Greek *trāchýs* rough, or < *trāchýtēs, -ētos* roughness]

tra·chyt·ic (trə kit′ik), *adj.* (of rock) having densely packed prisms of feldspar lying parallel to each other.

trac·ing (trā′sing), *n.* **1.** a copy of something made by marking or drawing over it. **2.** a line made by marking or drawing. **3.** one of a series of lines or marks made by an electrical apparatus, such as a lie detector, electrocardiograph, electroencephalograph, etc., that records waves or impulses.

tracing paper, a thin, almost transparent paper for tracing or copying an original design, etc.

track (trak), *n.* **1.** a line of metal rails for cars to run on: *A railroad line has tracks.* **2.** a mark left by anything: *The dirt road showed many automobile tracks.* **3.** a footprint: *There were bear and deer tracks near the camp.* **4. a.** a path; trail; road: *A track runs through the woods to the farmhouse.* **b.** a line of travel or motion: *the track of an eagle to a mountain nest, the track of a comet or hurricane.* **5.** a way of doing or acting: *to go on in the same track year after year.* **6.** a course for running or racing: *a race track.* **7. a.** the sport of running, jumping, throwing, etc. **b.** track and field sports as a group: *Sprinters, polevaulters, and shot-putters are engaged in track.* **8.** a sequence or succession of events, thoughts, etc.: *My pen goes in the track of my thoughts* (Edmund Burke). **9.** the groove or channel of a phonograph record which contains the actual sound recording. **10.** the trace or mark left in a cloud chamber or on a photographic plate by the passage of an electrified subatomic particle. **11.** the distance between the front or rear wheels of an automobile, etc. **12.** one of the endless belts on which a caterpillar tractor moves. **13.** *Obsolete.* a vestige; trace.

in one's tracks, *U.S. Informal.* right where one is; on the spot: *The rifle was fired . . . and he fell dead in his tracks* (R. Carlton).

jump the track, to run off the rails suddenly; derail without warning: *The train jumped the track.*

keep track of, to keep within one's sight, knowledge, or attention: *The noise of the two crowds . . . made it difficult to keep track of what was going on* (James Gilmour).

lose track of, to fail to keep track of: *Day after day passes in precisely the same manner . . ., until one loses all track of the days of the week* (Outing).

make tracks, *Informal.* to go very fast; make rapid progress: *Considering that she started with $5,000 in 1960, Miss Capriotti is making tracks* (New York Times).

off the beaten track, a. not what might be expected; unusual: *This novel has a surprise ending that is definitely off the beaten track.* **b.** remote; little used: *Airlines* [*that*] *fly into primarily rural areas off the beaten track of the big trunk airlines linking the nation's major cities* (Wall Street Journal).

off the track, off the right or proper course: *The speaker was a long way off the track.*

on the track, on the right or proper course: *"If they* [*the Chinese*] *use some sense in managing their . . . farms they will probably get back on the track," says one U.S. farm expert here* (Wall Street Journal).

the wrong side of the tracks, *U.S.* the poor or run-down section of a town or city; the slums: *There are plenty of children from the wrong side of the tracks whose test scores surpass the average* (Saturday Review).

—*v.t.* **1.** to follow by means of footprints, marks, smell, etc.: *The hunter tracked the bear and killed it.* **2.** to trace in any way: *to track down a criminal.* **3.** to find and follow (a track, course, etc.). **4.** to make one's way through or over; traverse. **5.** *U.S.* **a.** to make footprints or other marks on (a floor, etc.): *to track up a rug.* **b.** to bring into a place on one's feet: *to track mud into the house.* **6.** to provide (trains, etc.) with tracks. **7.** to tow (a vessel) from the shore. **8.** to follow and plot the course of, as by radar.

—*v.i.* **1.** to follow a track or trail. **2. a.** (of wheels) to run in the same track; be in alignment. **b.** (of opposite wheels, runners, etc.) to be a certain distance apart.

[< Middle French *trac,* probably < Germanic (compare Middle Low German *trecken* to draw, pull)]

track·age (trak′ij), *n.* **1.** all the tracks of a railroad; lines of track: *10,000 miles of single trackage.* **2.** the right of one railroad to use the tracks of another. **3.** the fee for this. [American English]

track and field, the sports or events of running, jumping, vaulting, throwing, etc., as a group. —**track′-and-field′,** *adj.*

tracked (trakt), *adj.* having tracks like those of a caterpillar tractor: *Troops are learning to cross the frozen tundra with tracked weasels and big-tired snowmobiles* (Time).

track·er (trak′ər), *n.* **1.** a person or thing that tracks or trails. **2.** an apparatus for tracking objects moving in the air, such as radar. **3.** a person or device that tracks or tows a vessel.

tracker dog, a dog used for tracking; trackhound: [*He*] *made his escape just before 9 p.m. by scaling a wall. Police set up roadblocks and tracker dogs were brought out* (Manchester Guardian).

track·hound (trak′hound′), *n.* a dog which hunts or tracks by scent, especially the bloodhound.

track·ing (trak′ing), *n.* a following, trailing, or tracing of the movements of something: *They intensified their tracking of the swirling tropical storms that have ripped a path of destruction up the east coast of the United States* (World Book Annual).

tracking shot, (in motion pictures and television) a shot taken from a moving dolly.

tracking station, one of a series of stations set up to track part of the orbit of a satellite: *Seventeen minutes after launching, its first radio signals beeped to the tracking station in Manchester, England* (Time).

track·lay·er (trak′lā′ər), *n.* a railroad worker who lays track.

track·lay·ing (trak′lā′ing), *n.* the laying of railway track: *Tracklaying began on a . . . 430-mile railway running from northern Alberta to Great Slave Lake* (David M. L. Farr).

track·less (trak′lis), *adj.* **1.** without a track. **2.** without paths or trails: *The region near the South Pole is a trackless wilderness.*

trackless trolley, a trolley bus.

track·man (trak′mən), *n., pl.* **-men. 1.** a railroad worker who lays, inspects, or repairs tracks. **2.** a trackwalker. **3.** an athlete who participates in track-and-field events: *Fullbacks can run the hundred-yard dash as fast as trackmen* (New Yorker).

track meet, a series of contests in running, jumping, throwing, etc.: *to run a relay race in a track meet.*

track shoe, a light, leather shoe worn by trackmen. On a cinder or dirt track shoes with sharp spikes in the sole are used; on a board track the shoes have no spikes.

Track Shoe

track·side (trak′sīd′), *n.* the area adjacent to a railway track: *Dozens of commuters were leaping out of their trains on to the trackside and walking to the nearest station* (London Times). —*adj.* of, having to do with, or located on the trackside: *a trackside rail, trackside equipment.*

track suit, a heavy, fleece-lined suit worn by track-and-field athletes to keep warm before and after exercise.

track·walk·er (trak′wô′kər), *n.* a railroad worker who walks along railroad tracks to inspect a certain section.

track·way (trak′wā′), *n.* **1.** a path beaten by the feet of passers; track. **2.** *Obsolete.* a wooden pathway or track built in ancient times across a peat bog to link various portions of solid ground or rock within the bog which might be inhabited.

tract[1] (trakt), *n.* **1.** a stretch of land, water, etc., extent; area: *A tract of desert land has little value.* **2. a.** a system of related parts or organs in the body: *The stomach and intestines are parts of the digestive tract.* **b.** a bundle of nerve fibers, or one pathway of the central nervous system. **3.** a period of time. **4.** an anthem consisting of verses from the Bible, sung in the Roman Catholic Mass instead of the alleluia from Septuagesima to Easter Eve. **5.** *Obsolete.* course (of time); duration.
[< Latin *tractus, -ūs* track, course, space, duration; (literally) a drawing out or hauling < *trahere* to drag. Doublet of TRACE[2], TRAIT, TRET.] —**Syn. 1.** expanse.

tract[2] (trakt), *n.* **1.** a little book or pamphlet on a religious subject. **2.** any little book or pamphlet. [apparently short for Latin *tractātus* a handling; see TRACTATE] —**Syn. 1.** homily.

trac·ta·bil·i·ty (trak′tə bil′ə tē), *n.* the quality of being tractable; manageableness; docility.

trac·ta·ble (trak′tə bəl), *adj.* **1.** easily managed or controlled; easy to deal with; docile: *a tractable child. Dogs are more tractable than mules.* **2.** easily handled or worked: *Copper and gold are tractable.* [< Latin *tractābilis* < *tractāre;* see TREAT] —**trac′ta·ble·ness,** *n.*
—**Syn. 1.** compliant, manageable. **2.** malleable.

trac·ta·bly (trak′tə blē), *adv.* in a tractable manner; manageably.

Trac·tar·i·an (trak târ′ē ən), *n.* an adherent of Tractarianism. —*adj.* of or belonging to the Tractarians; having to do with Tractarianism.

Trac·tar·i·an·ism (trak târ′ē ə niz′əm), *n.* a system of religious opinion published at Oxford between 1833 and 1841 in a series of papers called *Tracts for the Times.* It opposed the liberalizing tendencies within the Church of England and favored the High-Church doctrines of the dogmatic basis of sacrament and ritual and the apostolic succession of bishops, a position much like that of the Roman Catholic Church; Oxford Movement; Puseyism. [< *tract*[2] + *-arian* + *-ism*]

trac·tate (trak′tāt), *n.* a tract; treatise. [< Latin *tractātus, -ūs* a handling, treatise; treatment < *tractāre* to treat, handle]

trac·tile (trak′təl), *adj.* that can be drawn out in length; ductile.

trac·til·i·ty (trak til′ə tē), *n., pl.* **-ties.** the quality or property of being tractile.

trac·tion (trak′shən), *n.* **1. a.** a drawing or pulling. **b.** a being drawn. **2.** the drawing or pulling of loads along a road, track, etc. **3.** the kind of power used for this: *Electric traction is used on some railroads.* **4.** friction: *Wheels slip on ice because there is too little traction.* **5.** *Medicine.* a pulling or drawing of a muscle, organ, etc., especially as a surgical technique for healing a fracture, dislocation, etc. [< Medieval Latin *tractio, -onis* a drawing out < Latin *trahere* to drag]

trac·tion·al (trak′shə nəl), *adj.* of or having to do with traction.

traction engine, a steam-engine tractor.

trac·tive (trak′tiv), *adj.* drawing or pulling; used for drawing or pulling.

trac·tor (trak′tər), *n.* **1.** an engine used to pull wagons and plows, cultivate crops, etc. **2.** a vehicle having a powerful gasoline or Diesel engine and a cab for the driver, used to pull a freight trailer along the highway. **3.** any of various other machines or devices for drawing, moving earth, etc. **4. a.** an airplane with the propeller or propellers in front of the wings. **b.** the propeller of such an airplane. [< Medieval Latin *tractor* something that pulls < Latin *trahere* to drag] —**trac′tor·like′,** *adj.*

Tractor (def. 1)

tractor airplane, a tractor (def. 4a).

tractor propeller, a tractor (def. 4b).

trac·tor-trail·er (trak′tər trā′lər), *n.* a large highway freight vehicle consisting of a tractor and a detachable trailer: *Freight from out of town comes to one side of the depot, and small carts operating from an overhead track transfer merchandise from the big tractor-trailers to local trucks* (New York Times).

tractor train, a train of vehicles pulled by a tractor.

trad (trad), *adj. British Informal.* traditional: *trad music, trad religion. Trad jazz attracted a new public* (Listener).

trad·al (trā′dəl), *adj.* of or having to do with trade; commercial.

trade (trād), *n., v.,* **trad·ed, trad·ing,** *adj.* —*n.* **1.** a buying and selling; exchange of goods; commerce: *wholesale trade, retail trade, foreign trade, domestic trade.* **2.** exchange: *room and board in trade for doing the chores, an even trade.* **3.** *Informal.* a bargain; business deal: *He made a good trade.* **4.** a kind of work; business, especially one requiring skilled mechanical work: *the carpenter's trade, the plumber's trade, the weaver's trade.* **5.** the people in the same kind of work or business: *the book trade, the building trade.* **6.** *Informal.* customers: *That store has a lot of trade.* **7.** *Obsolete.* a regular course of action, movement, etc. **8.** *Obsolete.* a course; way; path. **9.** *Obsolete.* dealings.

the trades, a. the trade winds: *We caught the southeast trades and ran before them for nearly three weeks* (Richard Henry Dana). **b.** *Informal.* trade journals or newspapers: *You can't possibly know what's going on unless you read the trades* (Time).

—*v.i.* **1.** to buy and sell; exchange goods; be in commerce: *Some American companies trade all over the world. The early settlers traded with the Indians. Some speculators trade heavily in wheat and corn futures.* **2.** to make an exchange: *If you don't like your book, I'll trade with you.* **3.** to bargain; deal. **4.** to be a customer: *We've been trading at that grocery store for years.* —*v.t.* to exchange: *to trade seats.*

trade down, *Informal.* to buy or sell goods of a lower price or grade: *The stores traded down during the slow season.*

trade in, to give (an automobile, refrigerator, television set, etc.) as payment or part payment for something, especially for a newer model: *Yes, I can trade in your old refrigerator irrespective of condition for one of these luxurious models* (Cape Times).

trade off, to get rid of by trading: . . . *to see what chance I could find to trade off my ax handles* (J. Downing).

trade on or **upon,** to make use of for one's own ends; take advantage of: *They . . . still trade on the fears and fancies of their fellows* (Edward Clodd).

trade up, *Informal.* to buy or sell goods of a higher rather than lower price or grade: *The decision to trade up was prompted by demand evidenced by upper income customers* (Wall Street Journal).

—*adj.* **1.** having to do with, used in, or characteristic of trade: *trade goods.* **2.** of or having to do with a trade or calling.
[< Middle Dutch or Middle Low German *trade* trade, track, course (apparently originally, of a trading ship). Related to TREAD.]
—**Syn.** *n.* **1. Trade, commerce** mean the buying and selling or exchanging of goods or other commodities. **Trade** applies to the actual buying and selling, or exchange, between countries or within a country: *The Government has drawn up new agreements for trade with various countries.* **Commerce,** a more general term, applies to the whole business of exchange of commodities, including both trade and transportation, especially as conducted on a large scale between different states or countries: *The Interstate Commerce Commission sets the rates railroads charge for freight.* **4.** occupation, craft, profession. *-v.i.* **1.** barter. **2.** swap.

trade·a·ble (trā′də bəl), *adj.* that can be traded: *Drug stores, new car dealers, laundries flock to offer stamps (usually tradeable for catalog merchandise)* (Wall Street Journal).

trade acceptance, a bill of exchange drawn by the seller of goods on the purchaser for the price of the goods, and payable in cash. The acknowledgment is written across its face by the purchaser.

trade agreement, 1. a contract between an employer and a labor union covering the conditions of employment for the length of the contract. **2.** an agreement to promote trade between two or more nations: *The Benelux countries are about to enter upon their first trade agreement as a unit* (New York Times).

trade area, trading area.

trade association, an association to promote trade, usually of firms within one industry or a group of closely related industries.

trade balance, the difference between the value of all the imports and that of all the exports of a country; balance of trade: *Every foreign trader knows that we have an unfavourable trade balance* (London Times).

trade barrier, anything that hinders or restricts international trade, such as tariffs, or embargoes: *As trade barriers are progressively reduced many established firms will come under serious pressure* (Manchester Guardian).

trade book, a book published for and sold to the general public.

trade card, *British.* a business card.

trade deficit, an unfavorable balance of trade: *Latest figures show Canada's trade deficit with the U.S. was only $589 million compared with $983 million a year earlier* (Newsweek).

trade discount, an amount or percentage deducted from the retail or list price by a manufacturer for a wholesaler or retailer.

trade dollar, a silver dollar formerly issued by the United States for trade in eastern Asia.

trade fair, a fair to display new products, demonstrate industrial processes, and promote trade: *A British trade fair is to be held in Moscow from May 19 to June 4, and there will be a Russian fair in London from July 7 to 29* (Manchester Guardian).

trade gap, an unfavorable balance of trade; trade deficit.

trade-in (trād′in′), *n.* an automobile, refrigerator, television set, etc., given or accepted as payment or part payment for something, especially for a newer model. —*adj.* having to do with such an item or such a means of paying: *We make this exceptional bonus trade-in offer because we need used cars for customers we have waiting* (Cape Times).

trade journal, a magazine published by or for some special trade or business.

trade-last (trād′last′, -läst′), *n. Informal.* a compliment paid to a person without his knowledge but overheard by an acquaintance, who offers to tell it to the person involved in return for a compliment about himself. *Abbr.:* T.L.

trade magazine, a trade journal.

trade·mark or **trade-mark** (trād′märk′), *n.* a mark, picture, name, word, symbol, or letters owned and used by a manufacturer or merchant to distinguish his goods from the goods of others. The registration and protection of trademarks now are provided for by law. —*v.t.* **1.** to distinguish by means of a trademark. **2.** to register the trademark of. —**Syn.** *n.* brand.

trade mission, a group of businessmen sent by their government to a foreign country to negotiate trade agreements: *Recently, an Argentine trade mission traveling behind the Iron Curtain signed up to buy $27 million worth of oil drilling equipment* (Wall Street Journal).

trade name, 1. a name used by a manufacturer or merchant for some article that he sells. **2.** a special name used for anything by those who buy and sell it. **3.** the name under which a company does business.

trade-name (trād′nām′), *v.t.,* **-named, -nam·ing.** to give a trade name to; register under a trade name: *Some pharmacists blame doctors for prescribing trade-named drugs when a prescription with only the drug's generic name would allow them to offer lower-priced products* (Wall Street Journal).

trade pact, a trade agreement.

trade paper, a newspaper published by or for some special trade or business.

trad·er (trā′dər), *n.* **1.** a person who trades; merchant: *The trappers sold furs to traders.* **2.** a ship used in trading. **3. a.** a member of a stock exchange, commodity exchange, etc., who trades for himself and not as an agent of another or others. **b.** a speculator in stocks, commodities, etc.

trade reference, a person or firm whom an applicant gives as a reference for his credit standing.

trade route, a route followed by traders or trading ships.

trades (trādz), *n.pl.* See under **trade,** *n.*

trad·es·can·ti·a (trad′es kan′shē ə), *n.* any of a group of perennial American herbs; spiderwort. [< New Latin *Tradescantia* the genus name < John *Tradescant,* died about 1638, a British naturalist and gardener to Charles I]

trade school, a school where a trade or trades are taught.

trade secret, information about a commercial product kept secret to prevent competitors from duplicating the product: *A trade secret may consist of any formula, pattern, device . . . which is used in one's business* (New Yorker).

trades·folk (trādz′fōk′), *n.pl.* tradespeople.

trades·man (trādz′mən), *n., pl.* **-men. 1.** a person engaged in trade; merchant; storekeeper; shopkeeper. **2.** *Dialect.* a person skilled in a particular trade. [< *trade's* + *man.* Compare SALESMAN.] —**Syn. 1.** dealer, trader.

trades·peo·ple (trādz′pē′pəl), *n.pl.* people engaged in trade; storekeepers; shopkeepers.

trades union, or **trades-un·ion** (trādz′yün′yən), *n. Especially British.* a trade union.

Trades Union Congress, (in Great Britain) TUC (no periods).

trades unionism, or **trades-un·ion·ism** (trādz′yün′yə niz əm), *n. Especially British.* trade unionism.

trades unionist, or **trades-un·ion·ist** (trādz′yün′yə nist), *n. Especially British.* trade unionist.

trades·wom·an (trādz′wu̇m′ən), *n., pl.* **-wom·en.** a woman engaged in trade.

trade union, or **trade-un·ion** (trād′yün′yən), *n.* **1.** an association of workers in any trade or craft to protect and promote their interests. **2.** a labor union; union.

trade unionism, or **trade-un·ion·ism** (trād′yün′yə niz əm), *n.* **1.** the system of having trade unions. **2.** the principles or practices of trade unions.

trade unionist, or **trade-un·ion·ist** (trād′yün′yə nist), *n.* **1.** a member of a trade union. **2.** a supporter of trade unionism.

trade war, intense competition for trade: *The sellers of machinery, wool or copper get benefits which hardly square with calling such deals part of a trade war against the West* (Wall Street Journal).

trade wind, 1. a wind blowing steadily over the ocean toward the equator from about 30 degrees north latitude or from about 30 degrees south latitude. North of the equator, it blows from the northeast; south of the equator, from the southeast. **2.** *Obsolete.* any wind that blows steadily in the same direction at sea. [< *trade* in obsolete sense of "habitual course"]

TRA·DIC (trā′dik), *n.* a transistor digital computer (a small transistorized computer used to make rapid calculation in aerial navigation, gunnery, etc., to meet the demands of supersonic flight).

trad·ing area (trā′ding), the area in which a manufacturer, distributor, or retailer conducts business regularly and profitably; trade area.

trading bank, (in Australia) a commercial bank.

trading post, 1. a store or station of a trader or trading company, especially in uncivilized or unsettled country. **2.** any of a number of posts or booths on the floor of a stock exchange which serves as the headquarters for transactions in certain specific stocks.

trading stamp, a stamp given by certain merchants as a bonus to customers for patronizing them. The stamps have a fixed value and may be exchanged for merchandise at a store of the company issuing such stamps or, rarely, redeemed for cash.

tra·di·tion (trə dish′ən), *n.* **1.** the handing down of beliefs, opinions, customs, stories, etc., from parents to children: *She has been bred up . . . by a very worldly family, and taught their traditions* (Thackeray). **2.** what is handed down in this way: *According to the old tradition, the first American flag was made by Betsy Ross.* **3. a.** (among the Jews) the unwritten laws and doctrines, or any of them, believed to have been received by Moses from God and handed down orally from generation to generation. **b.** (in the Christian Church) the unwritten teachings and doctrines, or any one of them, held to have been received from Jesus and his apostles and handed down orally since then. **4.** *Law.* the delivery of something material to another; transfer. **5.** the delivery, especially oral delivery, of information or instruction. **6.** *Obsolete.* **a.** a giving up; surrender. **b.** betrayal. [< Latin *trāditiō, -ōnis* < *trādere* hand down < *trāns-* over + *dare* give. Doublet of TREASON.] —**Syn. 2.** folklore, legend.

tra·di·tion·al (trə dish′ə nəl, -dish′nəl), *adj.* **1.** of tradition. **2.** handed down by tradition. **3.** according to tradition; conforming to earlier styles or customs: *traditional furniture. An Egyptian architect has designed a traditional building, with fountains for washing before worshipping* (Manchester Guardian). **4.** customary. —**Syn. 2.** legendary.

tra·di·tion·al·ism (trə dish′ə nə liz′əm, -dish′nə liz-), *n.* **1.** adherence to the authority of tradition, especially in matters of religion, morality, etc. **2.** a philosophical system according to which all religious knowledge is derived from divine revelation and received by traditional instruction.

tra·di·tion·al·ist (trə dish′ə nə list, -dish′nə-), *n.* a traditionist. —*adj.* traditionalistic: *His (de Gaulle's) personal background is sternly traditionalist* (Observer).

tra·di·tion·al·is·tic (trə dish′ə nə lis′tik, -dish′nə-), *adj.* of or having to do with traditionalists or traditionalism.

traditional logic, Aristotelian logic.

tra·di·tion·al·ly (trə dish′ə nə lē, -dish′nə-), *adv.* according to tradition: *It is the traditionally correct cognac, unchanging in quality, matchless in flavor and aroma* (New Yorker).

tra·di·tion·ar·y (trə dish′ə ner′ē), *adj., n., pl.* **-ar·ies.** —*adj.* traditional. —*n.* a traditionist.

tra·di·tion·ist (trə dish′ə nist), *n.* **1.** a person who accepts or maintains the authority of tradition. **2.** a person who records, preserves, or hands down tradition.

tra·di·tion·less (trə dish′ən lis), *adj.* having no traditions; lacking a sense of tradition: *They have a lot of new, efficient but traditionless towns* (Punch).

trad·i·tive (trad′ə tiv), *adj.* traditional. [apparently < earlier French *traditive,* ultimately < Latin *trādere;* see TRADITION]

trad·i·tor (trad′ə tər), *n., pl.* **trad·i·to·res** (trad′ə tôr′ēz, -tōr′-). one of the early Christians who, in order to avoid persecution under Diocletian, gave up their sacred books, vessels, etc., or betrayed their fellow Christians. [< Latin *trāditor, -ōris* giver up, betrayer. Doublet of TRAITOR.]

tra·duce (trə düs′, -dyüs′), *v.t.,* **-duced, -duc·ing.** to speak evil of (a person) falsely; slander. [earlier, to alter, change over, transport < Latin *trādūcere* parade in disgrace; (originally) lead along, across, transfer < *trāns-* across + *dūcere* to lead] —**Syn.** defame, malign, vilify, asperse, calumniate.

tra·duce·ment (trə düs′mənt, -dyüs′-), *n.* a traducing; defamation; slander.

tra·duc·er (trə dü′sər, -dyü′-), *n.* a person who traduces; slanderer; calumniator.

tra·du·cian·ism (trə dü′shə niz əm, -dyü′-), *n.* the doctrine that both the body and soul of man are propagated by the human parents. [< earlier *traducian* an adherent of this doctrine (< Late Latin *trāduciānus* a transmitter < Latin *trādux, -ducis* shoot or layer for propagation < *trādūcere* propagate; transmit; see TRADUCE) + *-ism*]

tra·du·cian·ist (trə dü′shə nist, -dyü′-), *n.* a believer in traducianism. —*adj.* traducianistic.

tra·du·cian·is·tic (trə dü′shə nis′tik, -dyü′-), *adj.* of or having to do with traducianism or traducianists.

tra·duc·ing·ly (trə dü′sing lē, -dyü′-), *adv.* in a traducing or defamatory manner; slanderously; by way of defamation.

tra·duc·tion (trə duk′shən), *n.* **1.** *Logic.* the transfer or transition from one classification or order of reasoning to another. **2.** the act of traducing or maligning. **3.** *Obsolete.* a translation, as into another language. **4.** *Obsolete.* a transmission by generation. **5.** *Obsolete.* a bringing over, transferring, or transmitting. [< Latin *trāductiō, -ōnis* < *trādūcere;* see TRADUCE]

traf·fic (traf′ik), *n., v.,* **-ficked, -fick·ing.** —*n.* **1.** people, automobiles, wagons, ships, etc., coming and going along a way of travel: *Police control the traffic in large cities.* **2.** a buying and selling; trade; commerce: *traffic by sea.* **3. a.** the business done by a railroad line, steamship line, etc. **b.** the number of passengers or amount of freight carried. **c.** the revenue from this. **4.** the total amount of business done by any company or industry within a certain time. **5.** the transportation of goods, merchandise, etc., for the purpose of trade: *ships of traffic.* **6.** commercial intercourse; business dealings. **7.** a dealing in something wrong or illegal: *traffic in slaves. An extensive traffic in stolen goods* (George Borrow).

—*v.i.* **1.** to carry on trade; buy and sell; exchange: *The men trafficked with the natives for ivory.* **2.** to have illicit dealings: *to traffic in narcotics.*

[< Middle French *trafficque* < Italian *traffico* < *trafficare* < *tras-* across (< Latin *trāns-*) + *ficcare* shove, poke, ultimately < Latin *fīgere* fix, set]

traf·fic·a·bil·i·ty (traf′ə kə bil′ə tē), *n.* suitability for traffic or passage to and fro: *The practical needs of construction, water supply, sewage disposal, trafficability, and other engineering problems must be solved* (Science News Letter).

traf·fic·a·ble (traf′ə kə bəl), *adj.* suitable for traffic or passage to and fro.

traf·fi·ca·tor (traf′ə kā′tər), *n. British.* a turn indicator on an automobile; turn signal. [< *traffic* + (indic)*ator*]

traffic circle, *U.S. and Canada.* a junction of roads in which the merging traffic passes around a central circular plot in one direction only; rotary.

traffic cop, *Informal.* a policeman who directs the traffic of motor vehicles and pedestrians.

traffic court, a court in charge of the administration of traffic laws.

traffic engineer, an engineer who specializes in traffic engineering.

traffic engineering, a branch of civil engineering dealing with highway design and the efficient control of vehicular traffic.

traffic island, a safety zone in the center of a traffic circle or between traffic lanes.

traffic jam, an overcrowding of vehicles in an area, hindering or stopping free movement.

traf·fic-jammed (traf′ik jamd′), *adj.* **1.** having a traffic jam: *It was hot and muggy that June evening on Detroit's traffic-jammed Belle Isle Bridge* (Newsweek). **2.** having much traffic; crowded with vehicles: *It is a busy highway of commerce, a traffic-jammed link between the east and west coasts of America* (Newsweek).

traf·fick·er (traf′ə kər), *n.* **1.** a person who buys and sells; trader, merchant, or dealer: *. . . an itinerant trafficker in broken glass and rags* (George Eliot). **2.** a person who carries on underhand or illicit dealings: *Clandestine manufacture of morphine . . . near opium-growing areas of the Far East and Middle East indicated a network of well-organized*

international traffickers (Harry J. Anslinger).
traf·fic·less (traf′ik lis), *adj.* without traffic or trade.
traffic light, a signal or set of signal lights placed at a corner or intersection to control traffic. Usually, a red light ("stop") and a green light ("go") are flashed alternately at definite intervals.
traffic pattern, the positions of aircraft above an airport before landing or after take-off, as assigned by the control tower.
traffic sign, a sign along a street or road indicating speed limits, directions, right or left turns, etc.
traffic signal, traffic light.
traffic ticket, a summons issued to a motorist for a violation of a traffic law.
traffic warden, *British.* an official who controls vehicular traffic and parking: *A police officer or traffic warden can use his judgement in using summons, rather than a ticket, for an offence which seems unusually bad* (Manchester Guardian).
trag., **1.** tragedy. **2.** tragic.
trag·a·canth (trag′ə kanth), *n.* **1.** a sticky substance obtained from certain Asiatic shrubs or herbs of the pea family, used for stiffening cloth and for giving firmness to pills, lozenges, etc. **2.** any of these shrubs. [< Latin *tragacantha* < Greek *tragákantha* (literally) goat's-thorn < *trágos* goat + *ákantha* thorn]
tra·ge·di·an (trə jē′dē ən), *n.* **1.** an actor of tragedy. **2.** a writer of tragedies: *Under this curled marble . . . sleepe, rare tragedian, Shakespeare, sleepe alone* (John Donne). [< Old French *tragediane* < *tragedie* tragedy]
tra·ge·di·enne (trə jē′dē en′), *n.* an actress of tragedy. [< French *tragédienne,* feminine of *tragédien,* Old French *tragediane* tragedian < *tragedie* tragedy]
trag·e·dy (traj′ə dē), *n., pl.* **-dies.** **1.** a serious play or other literary work having an unhappy ending. In classical drama a tragedy showed the conflict of man with fate or the gods and the unhappy ending brought about by some weakness or error on the part of the central character. Sophocles' *Oedipus* and Shakespeare's *Hamlet* are tragedies. **2. a.** the branch of drama that includes such plays. **b.** the art or theory of writing or presenting such plays. **3.** a very sad or terrible happening; calamity or disaster: *The father's sudden death was a tragedy to his family.* [< Medieval Latin *tragedia* < Latin *tragoedia* < Greek *tragōidiā* < *trágos* goat (connection uncertain) + *ōidē* song] —**Syn. 3.** catastrophe.
trag·ic (traj′ik), *adj.* **1.** of tragedy; having to do with tragedy: *a tragic actor, a tragic poet.* **2.** very sad; dreadful: *a tragic death, a tragic accident.*
—*n.* **the tragic,** the tragic side of the drama or of life; tragic style or manner.
[< Latin *tragicus* < Greek *tragikós* tragic] —**Syn.** *adj.* **2.** calamitous, disastrous.
trag·i·cal (traj′ə kəl), *adj.* tragic.
trag·i·cal·ly (traj′ə klē), *adv.* in a tragic manner; dreadfully.
trag·i·cal·ness (traj′ə kəl nis), *n.* tragical quality.
tragic irony, speeches or actions in a tragedy that lead toward the doom of the main character, unknown to him but known by the audience.
trag·i·com·e·dy (traj′i kom′ə dē), *n., pl.* **-dies.** **1.** a play having both tragic and comic elements: *"The Merchant of Venice" is a tragicomedy.* **2.** an incident or situation in which serious and comic elements are blended. [< Middle French *tragicomédie* < Latin *tragicōmoedia,* reduction of *tragicocōmoedia* < *tragicus* (see TRAGIC) + *cōmoedia.* Compare COMEDY.]
trag·i·com·ic (traj′i kom′ik), *adj.* having both tragic and comic elements: *The clown is a tragicomic universal, the image of man himself, a sad and ridiculous creature, the gaiety of his tinsel earthly surroundings mocked by his godly consciousness of sin* (Newsweek).
trag·i·com·i·cal (traj′i kom′ə kəl), *adj.* tragicomic.
trag·o·pan (trag′ə pan), *n.* any of a group of brilliantly colored Asiatic pheasants, the male having a pair of upright, fleshy horns on the head. [< New Latin *Tragopan* the former genus name < Latin *tragopān* < a reputed Ethiopian bird < Greek *tragópān* < *trágos* goat + *pân* Pan]
tra·gus (trā′gəs), *n., pl.* **-gi** (-jī). the bulge that partially conceals the external opening of the ear. [< Latin *tragus* < Greek *trágos* (originally) goat (because of the bunch of hairs on it)]
traik (trāk), *v.i., n. Scottish.* stroll. [origin uncertain. Compare Swedish *tråka* to tug, drudge.]
trail (trāl), *n.* **1.** anything that follows along behind: *The car left a trail of dust behind it.* **2. a.** a track or smell: *The dogs found the trail of the rabbit.* **b.** a mark left where something has been dragged or has passed along: *the trail of a snail or a snake.* **3.** a path across a wild or unsettled region: *a mountain trail, the Oregon trail.* **4.** the train of a skirt or gown. **5.** the part of a gun carriage that rests or slides on the ground when the carriage is unlimbered. **6.** the command or position of trail arms.
blaze the trail, to pioneer or prepare the way for something new: *The Treaty blazes the trail to full-scale political federation in Western Europe* (London Times).
hit the trail, *U.S.* **a.** to set out; depart: *Men can pass out the church door, shoulder their packs . . ., and unconcernedly hit the trail to the lower [regions]* (Outing). **b.** *Slang.* to go away at once; get out: *The sheriff ordered the suspicious-looking stranger to hit the trail.*
[< verb]
—*v.t.* **1. a.** to pull, drag, or draw along behind: *She trailed her gown through the mud. The child trailed a toy horse after him.* **b.** to draw along wearily or with difficulty: *The bird trailed its broken wing.* **2.** to carry or bring by or as if by dragging: *to trail snow into a house.* **3.** to bring or have floating after itself: *a car trailing dust.* **4.** to lengthen in time; protract. **5.** to follow the trail or track of; track: *to trail a bear or a thief.* **6. a.** to follow along behind; follow: *The dog trailed its master constantly.* **b.** to follow in a long, uneven line: *The campers trailed their leader down the mountainside.* **7. a.** to mark out (a trail or track). **b.** *U.S.* to make a path by treading down (grass, etc.). **8.** to bring, hold, or carry (a rifle, etc.) at trail arms.
—*v.i.* **1.** to draw along behind; drag: *Her dress trails on the ground.* **2.** to hang down or float loosely from something. **3.** to grow along: *Poison ivy trailed by the road.* **4.** to go along slowly, idly, or with difficulty, as if dragged along: *children trailing to school.* **5.** to move or float from and after something moving, as dust, smoke, etc. **6.** to extend in a long, uneven line; straggle: *refugees trailing from their ruined village.* **7.** to follow, fall, or lag behind, as in a race. **8.** to follow a trail, track, or scent. **9.** to pass little by little: *Her voice trailed off into silence.*
[< Old North French *trailler* to tow, ultimately < Latin *trāgula* dragnet]
trail arms, 1. the military command to bring or hold a weapon at the side with the butt nearly on the ground and the muzzle tilted forward. **2.** the position in the manual of arms in which a weapon is thus held.
trail·bas·ton (trāl′bas′tən), *n.* one of a class of lawless ruffians in England against whom ordinances were issued in the 1300's. [< Anglo-French *traille-baston* (literally) one who trails or carries a cudgel < *traille,* imperative of *trailler* to trail + *baston* stick]
trail·blaz·er (trāl′blā′zər), *n.* a person or thing that pioneers or prepares the way to something new: *In the field of art, he has been a veritable trailblazer* (Saturday Review). *The tests . . served as an invaluable trailblazer for other tests* (Newsweek).
trail·blaz·ing (trāl′blā′zing), *adj.* that prepares or shows the way, especially to something new; innovating; pioneering: *trailblazing projects or exploits. He has written five trailblazing books on education* (Time).
trail board, a curved piece on each side of the prow of a ship, extending to the figurehead.
trail·break·er (trāl′brā′kər), *n.* trailblazer.
trail·er (trā′lər), *n.* **1.** a person or animal that follows a trail; tracker. **2.** a trailing plant or branch; vine that grows along the ground. **3.** a cargo vehicle to be pulled along the highway. There are small two-wheeled trailers pulled by automobiles, and large trailers pulled by trucks, especially by trucks that lack bodies of their own. **4.** a small, furnished house on either two or four wheels, pulled by an automobile. **5.** a few scenes shown to advertise a forthcoming motion picture or television program. —**Syn. 2.** creeper, runner.
trailer coach, a trailer used as a place to live.
trailer court, camp, or **park,** a site equipped with running water, electricity, and other facilities, for accommodating trailers: *The families began to cultivate the little twelve-by-fifty foot plots of ground allotted to them in the trailer court* (Harper's).
trail·er·ite (trā′lə rīt), *n.* a person who travels or lives in a trailer: *Trailerites, of course, buy less furniture and kitchen appliances than most householders* (Newsweek).
trail·er·ship (trā′lər ship′), *n.* a ship designed to carry loaded truck trailers as cargo.
trail·er·ship·ping (trā′lər ship′ing), *n.* the work or business of shipping by trailership.
trail handspike, a lever used to move the trail of a gun carriage in pointing the gun.
trail·ing arbutus (trā′ling), arbutus. See **arbutus** for picture.
trailing edge, the rearward edge of an airfoil or propeller blade.
trail·less (trāl′lis), *adj.* having no trails; trackless; pathless.
trail rope, 1. a rope trailed on the ground to check the speed of a balloon. **2.** a prolonge.
trail spade, a projection at the lower end of the trail of a gun carriage, that is driven into the ground by the recoil and thus checks it.
train (trān), *n.* **1.** a connected line of railroad cars moving along together: *a very long freight train of 100 cars.* **2.** a line of people, animals, wagons, trucks, etc., moving along together; caravan: *While I was in the town, a train of emigrant wagons . . . passed through* (Francis Parkman). **3.** a collection of vehicles, animals, and men accompanying an army to carry supplies, baggage, ammunition, or any equipment or materials. **4.** a part that hangs down and drags along behind: *the train of a lady's gown.* **5.** something that is drawn along behind; a trailing part; tail: *the train of a peacock, the train of a comet.* **6.** a group of followers; retinue: *the king and his train, a train of admirers.* **7. a.** a series; succession; sequence: *a long train of misfortunes.* **b.** a continuous course: *Now where was I when you interrupted? I seem to have lost my train of thought.* **c.** a succession of results or conditions following some event: *The flood brought starvation and disease in its train.* **8.** a line of gunpowder that acts as a fuse to fire a charge or mine. **9.** a series of connected parts, such as wheels and pinions, through which motion is transmitted in a machine. **10.** *Physics.* a series of wave cycles, pulses, etc., such as one caused by a short periodic disturbance.
in train, in proper order, arrangement, or sequence; in process: *Arrangements are also in train for us to borrow a further $500 million from the American Export-Import Bank* (Sunday Times).
[< Old French *train* < *trainer;* see the verb]
—*v.t.* **1.** to bring up; rear; teach: *He trained his children to respect their parents and teachers.* **2.** to make skillful by teaching and practice: *to train women as nurses.* **3.** to discipline and instruct (an animal) to be useful, obedient, perform tricks, race, etc.: *to train a horse. Saint Bernard dogs were trained to hunt for travelers lost in the snow.* **4.** to make fit for a sport, etc., as by proper exercise and diet: *to train a boxer.* **5.** to bring into a particular position: *Train the vine around this post.* **6.** to direct, point, or aim: *to train cannon upon a fort.* **7.** to trail or drag. **8.** *Archaic.* to allure; entice; take in.
—*v.i.* **1.** to be trained; undergo training. **2.** to train some person, group or thing. **3.** to make oneself fit, as by proper exercise, diet, etc.: *to train for a prizefight. Runners train for races.*
[< Old French *trainer* < Vulgar Latin *traginare* < *tragere,* for Latin *trahere* drag, draw]
—**Syn.** *n.* **2.** row, chain, file, procession. -*v.t.* **1.** educate.
train·a·bil·i·ty (trā′nə bil′ə tē), *n.* the ability to be trained: *The authors concluded that trainability in most occupations may be reasonably well predicted* (E.G. Williamson).
train·a·ble (trā′nə bəl), *adj.* that can be trained.
train·band (trān′band′), *n.* an organized group of trained citizen soldiers not in the regular army, such as existed in England in the 1500's, 1600's, and 1700's. [short for earlier *trained band*]
train·bear·er (trān′bãr′ər), *n.* a person who holds up the train of a robe or gown,

especially one appointed to attend a sovereign on a ceremonial occasion.

train case, a small case for carrying the essential articles needed for travel by train.

trained (trānd), *adj.* **1.** formed or made proficient by training; educated; practiced: *a trained eye, a trained teacher.* **2.** having a train: *a trained skirt.*

trained nurse, graduate nurse.

train·ee (trā nē′), *n.* **1.** a person who is receiving training, especially for a particular kind of work in a company, for the government, etc. **2.** *U.S.* a person undergoing basic training in a branch of the Armed Forces, especially in the Army.

train·ee·ship (trā nē′ship), *n.* **1.** the condition or time of being a trainee. **2.** the position or sum of money given to a trainee: *He also urged the establishment by the Public Health Service of traineeships for graduate nurses* (New York Times).

train·er (trā′nər), *n.* **1.** a person or thing that trains, especially a person who trains or prepares men, horses, etc., for athletic or sporting competition. **2.** a member of a gun's crew on a ship who brings the gun or turret laterally to the correct direction. **3.** an aircraft used in training pilots: *The new order brings scheduled production for the two-seat trainer to over 5,000 aircraft* (Wall Street Journal). —**Syn. 1.** coach.

train·ing (trā′ning), *n.* **1.** practical education in some art, profession, or occupation: *training for teachers.* **2.** the development of strength and endurance, as by proper diet and exercise. **3.** good condition maintained by exercise, diet, etc.
—*adj.* that trains; of or for training: *training exercises.*
—**Syn.** *n.* **1.** schooling, discipline. **2.** practice. **3.** fitness.

training camp, 1. a military camp for basic training. **2.** a camp where boxers or other athletes train and practice before the regular playing season, a match, etc.

training college, *British.* a college for training persons for some particular profession, especially one for training teachers.

training school, 1. a school for giving training in some art, profession, etc.: *a training school for teachers or nurses, a training school for mechanics.* **2.** a house of correction for young offenders or criminals: *At least two of the state training schools for delinquent boys, the New York State Training School for Boys in 1937 and the Illinois Training School for Boys, have tried using foster homes for the placement of certain children committed to them* (Clyde B. Vedder).

training ship, a ship equipped and used for practical training in seamanship.

training table, a special dining table or tables set aside for athletes in training, usually providing a special diet.

train·less (trān′lis), *adj.* having no train or trains: *a trainless gown.*

train·load (trān′lōd′), *n.* as much as a train can hold or carry: *It has a positive significance for railways in extreme climates, where maximum permitted trainloads have to be reduced in winter* (New Scientist).

train·man (trān′mən), *n., pl.* **-men.** *U.S.* **1.** a brakeman or railroad worker in a train crew, of lower rank than a conductor. **2.** any member of a train crew other than the engineer and fireman.

train·mas·ter (trān′mas′tər, -mäs′-), *n.* an official of a railroad line who directs trains through a railroad division or the switching operations in a terminal, station, or yard.

train oil, oil obtained from the blubber of whales, especially the right whale, seals, and certain fishes. [< obsolete *trane,* or *train* train oil < Middle Low German *trâne* or Middle Dutch *traen* exuded oil; apparently (originally) teardrop]

train shed, a large, open structure for sheltering railroad trains, especially one covering the tracks, adjacent platforms, etc., at a station or terminal.

train·time (trān′tīm′), *n.* the scheduled time of a train's departure: *He took me inside and showed me where it waited, on a baggage truck pushed up against the wall; he said it would be kept there until traintime* (New Yorker).

traipse (trāps), *v.,* **traipsed, traips·ing,** *n. Informal.* —*v.i.* to walk about aimlessly, carelessly, or needlessly. —*v.t.* to walk or tramp over; tread: *The idle boys traipsed the streets looking for excitement.* —*n.* a traipsing. Also, **trapes.** [origin unknown]

trait (trāt), *n.* **1.** a quality of mind, character, etc.; distinguishing feature; characteristic: *Courage, love of fair play, and common sense are desirable traits. This reliance on authority is a fundamental primitive trait* (James Harvey Robinson). **2.** a stroke of wit, skill, cunning, etc. [< Middle French *trait* < Latin *tractus, -ūs* a draft, a drawing, a drawing out; line drawn, feature < *trahere* to drag. Doublet of TRACE[2], TRACT[1], TRET.] —**Syn. 1.** See **feature.**

trai·tor (trā′tər), *n.* **1.** a person who betrays his country or ruler: *He is a traitor and betray'd the state* (Byron). **2.** a person who betrays a trust, duty, friend, etc.: *Judas Iscariot, which was . . . the traitor* (Luke 6:16).
—*adj.* traitorous. [< Anglo-French, Old French *traitour* < Latin *trāditor, -ōris* < *trādere* transmit < *trāns-* over + *dare* give. Doublet of TRADITOR.] —**Syn.** *n.* **2.** turncoat, renegade.

trai·tor·ous (trā′tər əs), *adj.* of, like, or befitting a traitor; treacherous; faithless. —**trai′tor·ous·ly,** *adv.* —**trai′tor·ous·ness,** *n.* —**Syn.** disloyal, false, perfidious. —**Ant.** faithful, loyal, constant.

trai·tress (trā′tris), *n.* a woman traitor.

tra·ject (*v.* trə jekt′; *n.* traj′ekt), *v.t.* **1.** to throw across; cast over: *A persistent temptation to administer the sacramental wafer to his parishioners' lips by standing back two or three feet and trajecting it in a lovely arc over his left shoulder* (J.D. Salinger). **2.** to pass across; cross (a river, etc.). **3.** to transmit (thoughts, words, etc.).
—*n.* **1.** a way or place for crossing over; means of passage; route: *The motorcade followed the logical traject: straight along Main Street* (Time). **2.** an act of crossing over; passage: *During the whole traject I met with no living thing* (Edmund O'Donovan).
[< Latin *trājectus,* past participle of *trājicere* < *trāns-* across + *jacere* to throw]

tra·jec·tion (trə jek′shən), *n. Archaic.* **1.** a trajecting. **2.** a being trajected.

tra·jec·to·ry (trə jek′tər ē, -trē), *n., pl.* **-ries. 1.** the curved path of a projectile, comet, planet, etc. **2.** *Geometry.* a curve or surface that passes through a given set of points or intersects a given series of curves or surfaces at a constant angle. [< Medieval Latin *trajectorius* for throwing across < Latin *trājectus;* see TRAJECT]

tra-la-la (trä′lä lä′), *interj.* a gay utterance sung as a musical phrase or representing a short instrumental flourish.

tral·a·ti·tious (tral′ə tish′əs), *adj.* **1.** transferred; metaphorical or figurative, as words, etc. **2.** repeated by one person after another, as a statement. **3.** handed down from one generation to another. [< Latin *trālātītius,* variant of *trālātīcius* (with English *-ous*) for *trānslātīcus* < *trānslātus;* see TRANSLATE]

Tral·li·an (tral′ē ən), *adj.* of or having to do with the ancient Greek city of Tralles or its inhabitants: *the Trallian school of sculpture.*

tram[1] (tram), *n., v.,* **trammed, tram·ming.** —*n.* **1.** *Especially British.* a streetcar. **2.** a tramway. **3.** a truck or car for carrying loads in mines. **4.** an overhead or suspended carrier traveling on a cable.
—*v.t.* **1.** to carry (coal, ore, etc.) by a tram or trams. **2.** to push (a car or truck) to and from the shaft in a mine.
[originally, Scottish *tram,* the beams or shafts of a barrow or sledge; a barrow or truck body. Compare Middle Dutch or Middle Low German *trame* beam.]

tram[2] (tram), *n.* silk thread consisting of two or more single strands loosely twisted together, used for the woof in weaving fine silk goods, velvet, etc. Also, **trame.** [earlier *tramme* mechanical contrivance; plot < French *trame,* Old French *traime* cunning device, plot; (originally) woof < Latin *trāma* woof]

tram[3] (tram), *n., v.,* **trammed, tram·ming.** —*n.* **1.** an instrument used in drawing ellipses. **2.** (of machinery) the correct position or adjustment of one part to another: *in tram, out of tram.* **3.** a trammel.
—*v.t., v.i.* to adjust, measure, or align with a tram or trammel. [short for *trammel*]

tram·car (tram′kär′), *n.* **1.** *British.* a streetcar. **2.** *Mining.* a tram.

trame (tram), *n.* tram[2].

tram·line (tram′līn′), *n.* tramway.

tram·mel (tram′əl), *n., v.,* **-meled, -mel·ing** or (*especially British*) **-melled, -mel·ling.**
—*n.* **1.** a fine net to catch fish, birds, etc. **2.** a hook, bar, chain, etc., in a fireplace, to hold pots, kettles, etc., over the fire. **3.** an instrument for drawing ellipses; tram. **4.** a gauge used in adjusting and aligning mechanical parts. **5.** a shackle for controlling the motions of a horse and teaching him to amble; hobble.
trammels, anything that hinders or restrains: *A large bequest freed the artist from the trammels of poverty.*
—*v.t.* **1.** to hinder; restrain. **2.** to catch in or as if in a trammel; entangle.
[earlier, a three-layer net < Old French *tramail* < Medieval Latin *trimaculum* < Latin *tri-* three + *macula* mesh] —**tram′mel·er,** *especially British* **tram′mel·ler,** *n.*
—**Syn.** *v.t.* **1.** fetter, hamper, impede.

tra·mon·ta·na (trä′môn tä′nä), *n.* the north wind, as blowing over Italy or the Mediterranean from across the Alps. [< Italian *tramontana;* see TRAMONTANE]

tra·mon·tane (trə mon′tān, tram′ən-), *adj.* **1.** being or situated beyond the mountains, especially beyond the Alps as viewed from Italy; having to do with the other side of the mountains. **2.** (of the wind) coming across or from beyond the mountains, especially blowing over Italy, etc., from beyond the Alps. **3.** foreign.
—*n.* **1.** a person who lives beyond the mountains, especially beyond the Alps. **2.** a foreigner. **3.** any cold wind from a mountain range.
[< Italian *tramontana* north wind, polestar; in plural, foreigners < Latin *trānsmontānus* beyond the mountains < *trāns-* across + *mōns, montis* mountain]

tramp (tramp), *v.i.* **1.** to walk heavily: *He tramped across the floor in his heavy boots.* **2.** to step heavily (on); trample: *He tramped on the flowers.* **3.** to go on foot; walk: *We tramped through the streets.* **4.** to walk steadily; march: *The soldiers tramped mile after mile.* **5.** to go or wander as a tramp. —*v.t.* **1.** to step heavily on; trample upon. **2.** to travel on or through on foot: *to tramp the streets, to tramp the city night after night.*
—*n.* **1.** the sound of a heavy step or steps: *The steady tramp of marching feet.* **2.** a long, steady walk; march; hike: *a tramp through the woods.* **3.** a person who travels from place to place on foot, living by begging, doing odd jobs, etc.: *A tramp came to the door and asked for food.* **4.** a freighter without a regular route or schedule, that takes a cargo when and where it can; tramp steamer. **5. a.** an iron or steel plate worn under the shoe or boot to protect it in digging, etc. **b.** an iron or steel plate with spikes, worn on a shoe or boot to give a firm foothold on ice. **6.** *Informal.* a woman of low morals.
[perhaps < Low German or Flemish *trampen* to stamp, tread] —**tramp′er,** *n.*
—**Syn.** *n.* **3.** vagabond, hobo, vagrant, beggar.

tramp iron or **metal,** bits of odd or loose metal found in grain, textile fibers, and unpackaged materials, that drop off from machinery in manufacturing.

tram·ple (tram′pəl), *v.,* **-pled, -pling,** *n.* —*v.t.* **1.** to tread heavily on; crush: *The herd of wild cattle trampled the man to death.* **2.** to treat cruelly, harshly or scornfully. —*v.i.* to tread or walk heavily; stamp.
trample on or **upon,** to treat cruelly, harshly or scornfully; regard with contempt: *The dictator trampled on the rights of the people. Wit tramples upon rules* (Samuel Johnson).
—*n.* the act or sound of trampling; tramp: *We heard the trample of many feet.*

tram·pler (tram′plər), *n.* **1.** a person who tramples. **2.** *Obsolete.* a lawyer.

tram·po·lin (tram′pə lin), *n.* trampoline.

tram·po·line (tram′pə lēn′, tram′pə lin), *n.* a gymnastic apparatus consisting of a piece of canvas or other sturdy fabric stretched on a metal frame, used for tumbling, acrobatics, etc. [< Italian *trampolino* < *trampoli* stilts < Low German *trampeln* trample]

Trampoline

tramp steamer or **ship,** a freighter that takes a cargo when and where it can; tramp.

tram·road (tram′rōd′), *n.* **1.** a road or track of parallel lines of wood, stone, or iron rails, for trams or wagons in a mining area. **2.** a railroad in a mine.

tram·way (tram′wā′), *n.* **1.** *Especially British.* a track for streetcars. **2.** *Mining.* **a.** a track or roadway for carrying ores from mines. **b.** *U.S.* a cable or system of cables on which suspended cars carry ore, etc.

trance[1] (trans, träns), *n., v.,* **tranced, tranc·ing.** *—n.* **1.** a state or condition of unconsciousness somewhat like sleep: *a hypnotic trance.* **2.** a dazed or stunned condition. **3.** a dreamy, absorbed, or hypnotic condition: *The old man sat before the fire in a trance, lost in dreams of the past.* **4.** a high emotion; rapture.
—v.t. to throw into or hold in a trance; enchant: *I trod as one tranced in some rapturous vision* (Shelley).
[< Old French *transe* fear of coming evil < *transir* be numb with fear; (originally) die, pass on < Latin *trānsīre* cross over < *trāns-* across + *īre* go] **—trance′like′,** *adj.*
—**Syn.** *n.* **1.** coma. **4.** ecstasy. *-v.t.* entrance.

trance[2] (trans, träns), *n. Scottish.* a passageway. [origin uncertain]

tranc·ed·ly (tran′sid lē, trän′-), *adv.* in a trancelike manner; as if in trance.

tranche (träNch), *n.* **1.** a piece cut off; slice. **2.** a block or series of bonds of a government issue. [< French *tranche* < *trancher* to cut]

tran·quil (trang′kwəl, tran′-), *adj.,* **-quil·er, -quil·est** or (*especially British*) **-quil·ler, -quil·lest.** calm; peaceful; quiet: *the tranquil air of morning* (Longfellow).
[< Latin *tranquillus* < *trāns-* (intensive) + a root related to *quiēs* quiet] **—tran′quil·ly,** *adv.* **—tran′quil·ness,** *n.*
—**Syn.** placid, serene, undisturbed.

tran·quil·ise (trang′kwə līz, tran′-), *v.t., v.i.,* **-ised, -is·ing.** *Especially British.* tranquilize.

tran·quil·i·ty (trang kwil′ə tē, tran-), *n.* tranquillity.

tran·quil·i·za·tion (trang′kwə lə zā′shən, tran′-), *n.* **1.** a tranquilizing. **2.** a being tranquilized.

tran·quil·ize (trang′kwə līz, tran′-), *v.,* **-ized, -iz·ing.** *—v.t.* to make calm, peaceful, or quite; render tranquil; calm; soothe: *Although "The Maltese Falcon" at long last settled Huston professionally, it did not tranquilize his personal life* (Newsweek). *—v.i.* to become tranquil. —**Syn.** *v.t.* pacify, compose, allay, still.

tran·quil·iz·er (trang′kwə lī′zər, tran′-), *n.* any of various drugs for reducing physical or nervous tension, lowering blood pressure, etc.; an ataractic.

tran·quil·iz·ing agent or **drug** (trang′kwə lī′zing, tran′-), a tranquilizer.

tran·quil·lise (trang′kwə līz, tran′-), *v.,* **-lised, -lis·ing.** *Especially British.* tranquilize.

tran·quil·li·ty (trang kwil′ə tē, tran-), *n.* calmness; peacefulness, quiet. —**Syn.** stillness.

tran·quil·lize (trang′kwə līz, tran′-), *v.t., v.i.,* **-lized, -liz·ing.** tranquilize.

trans (trans, tranz), *adj. Chemistry.* of or having to do with an isomeric compound that has certain atoms on the opposite side of a plane: *a trans configuration or structure.*

trans-, *prefix.* **1.** across; over; through, as in *transcontinental, transmit.*
2. beyond; on the other side of, as in *transcend.*
3. across; and also beyond, on the other side of, as in *transarctic, transequatorial, transoceanic,* and many other geographical terms, such as *trans-African, trans-Algerian.*
4. into a different place, condition, etc., as in *transform, transmute.*
[< Latin *trāns,* preposition]

trans., an abbreviation for the following:
1. transactions.
2. transferred.
3. transitive.
4. a. translated, **b.** translation. **c.** translator.
5. transparent.
6. transportation.
7. transpose.
8. transverse.

trans·act (tran zakt′, -sakt′), *v.t.* to attend to; carry on; manage; do: *A lawyer will transact many affairs connected with the purchase of a home.* *—v.i.* to carry on business; have dealings; deal. [< Latin *trānsāctus,* past participle of *trānsigere* accomplish < *trāns-* through + *agere* to drive] —**Syn.** *v.t.* perform, conduct.

trans·ac·tion (tran zak′shən, -sak′-), *n.* **1.** the carrying on (of business, etc.): *The manager attends to the transaction of important matters himself.* **2.** a piece of business: *A record is kept of every transaction of the firm.*
transactions, a record of what was done at the meetings of a society, club, etc.: *What the club says has an audience far beyond Manchester, because its transactions are sent to libraries in this country and to American libraries, including Harvard, the Library of Congress, and the main library in New York* (Manchester Guardian). *Abbr.:* trans.
[< Latin *trānsāctiō, -ōnis* < *trānsigere;* see TRANSACT]
—**Syn. 2.** proceeding, deal, matter, affair.

trans·ac·tion·al (tran zak′shə nəl, -sak′-), *adj.* of or having to do with a transaction. **—trans·ac′tion·al·ly,** *adv.*

trans·ac·tor (tran zak′tər, -sak′-), *n.* a person who transacts business affairs, etc. —**Syn.** dealer, manager.

trans·al·pine (tranz al′pīn, -pin; trans-), *adj.* across or beyond the Alps, especially as viewed from Italy. *—n.* a native or inhabitant of a country across or beyond the Alps. [< Latin *trānsalpīnus* < *trāns-* across + *alpīnus* Alpine < *Alpēs* the Alps]

trans·am·i·nase (trans am′ə nās), *n.* an enzyme that catalyzes the reversible transfer of an amino group from one amino acid to another.

trans-An·de·an (trans′an dē′ən, tranz′;- trans an′dē ən, tranz-), *adj.* across or beyond the Andes, especially as viewed from Argentina or some other country east of the Andes.

trans·an·i·ma·tion (trans′an ə mā′shən, tranz′-), *n.* transmigration of the soul; metempsychosis.

trans·arc·tic (trans ärk′tik, -är′tik; tranz-), *adj.* across or beyond the arctic or north polar region.

trans·at·lan·tic (trans′ət lan′tik, tranz′-), *adj.* **1.** crossing the Atlantic: *a transatlantic liner, a transatlantic cable.* **2.** on the other side of the Atlantic, as viewed from either side: *a transatlantic ally.* **—trans′at·lan′ti·cal·ly,** *adv.*

trans·bor·der (trans bôr′dər, tranz-), *adj.* lying or living beyond the border: *a transborder village.*

trans·ca·len·cy (trans kā′lən sē), *n.* the property of being transcalent.

trans·ca·lent (trans kā′lənt), *adj.* freely permitting the passage of heat. [< *trans-* + Latin *calēns, -entis,* present participle of *calēre* be warm]

trans·cau·ca·sian (trans′kô kā′zhən, -shən; -kazh′ən, -kash′-), *adj.* across or beyond the Caucasus Mountains in southern Soviet Union, between the Black and Caspian Seas.

Trans·cau·ca·sian (trans′kô kā′zhən, -shən; -kazh′ən, -kash′-), *adj.* of or having to do with Transcaucasia, a region of southwestern Soviet Union, in and south of the Caucasus Mountains. *—n.* a native or inhabitant of Transcaucasia.

trans·ceiv·er (trans sē′vər, tran-), *n. Electronics.* a combined transmitter and receiver. [< *trans*(mitter) + (re)*ceiver*]

tran·scend (tran send′), *v.t.* **1.** to go beyond the limits or powers of; exceed: *The beauty of Niagara Falls transcends description.* **2.** to be higher or greater than; surpass; excel: *The speed of airplanes transcends that of any previous form of transportation.* **3.** (of God) to be above and independent of (the physical universe). *—v.i.* to be superior or extraordinary. [< Latin *trānscendere* < *trāns-* beyond + *scandere* to climb]

tran·scend·ence (tran sen′dəns), *n.* a being transcendent.

tran·scend·en·cy (tran sen′dən sē), *n.* transcendence.

tran·scend·ent (tran sen′dənt), *adj.* **1.** going beyond ordinary limits; excelling; superior; extraordinary. **2.** above and independent of the physical universe. **3.** *Philosophy.* **a.** transcending the Aristotelian categories or predicaments, especially as considered by the medieval scholastics. **b.** (in Kantian philosophy) not realizable in human experience. **—tran·scend′ent·ly,** *adv.* **—tran·scend′ent·ness,** *n.* —**Syn. 1.** unequaled, unrivaled, peerless, supreme.

tran·scen·den·tal (tran′sen den′təl), *adj.* **1.** transcendent; surpassing; excelling. **2.** supernatural. **3.** beyond the limits of ordinary human experience; obscure; incomprehensible; fantastic: *an unmeaning and transcendental conception* (Benjamin Jowett). **4.** *Philosophy.* **a.** explaining matter and objective things as products of the mind that is thinking about them; idealistic. **b.** implied in and necessary to human experience. **5.** transcendentalist. **6.** *Mathematics.* that cannot be produced by algebraic operations of addition, subtraction, multiplication, division, and the extraction of roots, each repeated only a finite number of times.
—n. Mathematics. a transcendental term, quantity, or number. **—tran′scen·den′tal·ly,** *adv.*

tran·scen·den·tal·ism (tran′sen den′tə liz əm), *n.* **1.** transcendental quality, thought, language, or philosophy. **2.** any philosophy based upon the doctrine that the principles of reality are to be discovered by a study of the processes of thought, not from experience. **3.** the religious and philosophical doctrines of Emerson and others in New England about 1840. It emphasized the importance of individual inspiration and had an important influence on American thought and literature. **4.** obscurity; incomprehensibility; fantasy.

tran·scen·den·tal·ist (tran′sen den′tə list), *n.* a person who believes in transcendentalism: *Emerson and Thoreau were transcendentalists.* *—adj.* of or having to do with transcendentalism.

tran·scen·den·tal·ize (tran′sen den′tə līz), *v.t.,* **-ized, -iz·ing.** to make transcendental; idealize.

tran·scen·sion (tran sen′shən), *n.* transcendence. [< Late Latin *trānscensiō, -ōnis* < Latin *trānscendere* to transcend]

trans·con·ti·nen·tal (trans′kon tə nen′təl), *adj.* **1.** crossing a continent. **2.** on the other side of a continent.

trans·cor·ti·cal (trans kôr′tə kəl), *adj.* crossing the cortex of the brain.

tran·scribe (tran skrīb′), *v.,* **-scribed, -scrib·ing.** *—v.t.* **1. a.** to copy in writing or in typewriting: *to transcribe an ancient manuscript.* **b.** to write out in ordinary letters, words, etc.: *The account of the trial was transcribed from the stenographer's shorthand notes.* **2.** to set down in writing or print: *His entire speech was transcribed in the newspapers, word for word.* **3.** *Music.* to arrange (a composition) for a different voice or instrument. **4.** to make a recording or phonograph record of (a program, music, etc.) for playing back or broadcasting. **5.** *Phonetics.* to record (speech) in a system of phonetic symbols; represent (a speech sound) by a phonetic symbol. *—v.i.* to broadcast a phonograph record.
[< Latin *trānscrībere* < *trāns-* over + *scribere* write]

tran·scrib·er (tran skrī′bər), *n.* a person who transcribes; a copier or copyist.

tran·script (tran′skript), *n.* **1.** a written or typewritten copy. **2.** *Law.* a copy of a legal record. **3.** a copy or reproduction of anything. [< Latin *trānscriptum,* neuter past participle of *trānscrībere;* see TRANSCRIBE]

tran·scrip·tion (tran skrip′shən), *n.* **1.** a transcribing; copying. **2.** a transcript; copy. **3.** *Music.* the arrangement of a composition for a different instrument or voice. **4. a.** an arrangement of music, etc., on a phonograph record, tape, wire, etc., for use in broadcasting. **b.** the act or fact of broadcasting such a record, etc. **5.** *Phonetics.* a written representation of speech in a system of phonetic symbols.

tran·scrip·tion·al (tran skrip′shən əl), *adj.* of, having to do with, or occurring in transcription: *a transcriptional error.* **—tran·scrip′tion·al·ly,** *adv.*

tran·scrip·tive (tran skrip′tiv), *adj.* **1.** of or having to do with transcribing, copying, or reproducing. **2.** of or like a transcript.

trans·crys·tal·line (trans kris′tə lin, -līn; tranz-), *adj.* through the crystals of a substance: *transcrystalline fissures.*

trans·cul·tur·al (trans kul′chər əl, tranz-), *adj.* **1.** common to all cultures: *transcultural phenomena.* **2.** cutting across cultures; intercultural: *transcultural activities.*

trans·cur·rent (trans kėr′ənt), *adj.* extending or running across. [< Latin *trānscurrēns, -entis,* present participle of *trānscurrere* < *trāns-* across + *currere* to run] —**trans·cur′rent·ly,** *adv.*

trans·di·a·lect (trans dī′ə lekt), *v.t.* to translate from one dialect into another: *to transdialect Doric into Attic Greek.*

trans·duce (trans düs′, -dyüs′; tranz-), *v.t.,* **-duced, -duc·ing.** to convert (energy) from one form to another, as from heat energy to electric energy: *Industrial measurement and control systems . . . integrate fluctuating light, velocity, flow, and other factors which can be transduced to electrical current* (Science). [< Latin *trānsdūcere* < *trāns-* across + *dūcere* to lead. Compare TRADUCE.]

trans·duc·er (trans dü′sər, -dyü′-; tranz-), *n.* a device for converting energy from one form to another.

trans·duc·tion (trans duk′shən, tranz-), *n.* **1.** *Biology.* **a.** the transfer of a gene or chromosome particle from one cell to another. **b.** such a transfer conducted by a bacterial virus in the cells of bacteria. **2.** *Physics.* the conversion of energy from one form to another: *Transduction occurs when a loudspeaker changes electrical into acoustical energy.*

tran·sect (*v.* tran sekt′; *n.* tran′sekt′), *v.t.* to cut across; divide by passing across. —*n.* **1.** a cross section of the vegetation of an area: *For the botanist a brisk 15 miles between, say, Mumbles Head to Rhossili Bay in Glamorganshire is an eventful transect, abounding in rare flora* (New Scientist). **2.** a representation of such a cross section. [< *trans-* + Latin *sectus,* past participle of *secāre* to cut]

tran·sec·tion (tran sek′shən), *n.* a transecting; cross section.

trans·el·e·ment (tranz el′ə mənt, trans-), *v.t.* to transform the elements of.

trans·em·pir·i·cal (tranz′em pir′ə kəl, trans′-), *adj.* beyond the range of experience; metempirical.

tran·sept (tran′sept), *n.* **1.** the shorter part of a cross-shaped church. See **nave**[1] and **apse** for pictures. **2.** either end of this part. [< Medieval Latin *transeptum,* ultimately < Latin *trāns-* across + *saeptum* fence]

tran·sep·tal (tran sep′təl), *adj.* of, having to do with, or like a transept. —**tran·sep′tal·ly,** *adv.*

trans·e·qua·to·ri·al (trans ē′kwə tôr′ē əl, -tōr′-; -ek′wə-; tranz-), *adj.* **1.** situated on the other side of the equator. **2.** crossing the equator.

trans·e·unt (tran′sē ənt), *adj.* passing outward; producing an effect outside; transient: *a transeunt action.* [< Latin *trānsiēns, transeuntis;* see TRANSIENT]

transf., transferred.

trans·fash·ion (trans fash′ən), *v.t.* to transform.

trans·fer (*v.* trans fėr′, trans′fėr; *n.* trans′fėr), *v.,* **-ferred, -fer·ring,** *n.* —*v.t.* **1.** to convey or remove from one person or place to another; hand over: *This farm has been transferred from father to son for generations. Please have my trunks transferred to the Union Station.* **2.** to convey (a drawing, design, pattern, etc.) from one surface to another, as to a lithographic stone, earthenware, glass, etc., by any of various special means or processes: *You transfer the embroidery design from the paper to cloth by pressing it with a warm iron.* **3.** to make over (a title, right, or property) by deed or legal process: *to transfer a bond by endorsement.*
—*v.i.* to change from one streetcar, bus, train, etc., to another.
—*n.* **1. a.** the act of transferring. **b.** the fact of being transferred. **2.** a thing transferred; a writing, drawing, or pattern conveyed from one surface to another, as in lithography, photography, etc. **3.** a ticket allowing a passenger to continue his journey on another streetcar, bus, train, etc. **4.** a point or place for transferring. **5. a.** the act of turning the ownership of a share of stock or registered bond over to someone else. **b.** a document ordering this. **6.** the making over to another of title, right, or property by deed or legal process.
[< Latin *trānsferre* < *trāns-* across + *ferre* to bear]

trans·fer·a·bil·i·ty (trans′fər ə bil′ə tē, trans fėr′-), *n.* the quality of being transferable.

trans·fer·a·ble (trans fėr′ə bəl, trans′fər-), *adj.* **1.** that can be transferred. **2.** that can be made over to another; negotiable: *The currencies of most countries were still not freely convertible into dollars but they were made transferable over a steadily increasing area* (Samuel S. Shipman).

trans·fer·al (trans fėr′əl), *n.* transference; transfer.

trans·fer·ase (trans′fə rās), *n.* any of various enzymes that transfer a radical from one molecule to another, as transaminase and kinase.

transfer book, a register of transfers of shares of stock kept by a joint-stock company.

trans·fer·ee (trans′fə rē′), *n.* **1.** a person who is transferred or removed, as from one place, position, or grade to another. **2.** *Law.* the person to whom a transfer of title, right, or property is made.

trans·fer·ence (trans fėr′əns, trans′fər-), *n.* **1.** a transferring or being transferred. **2.** *Psychoanalysis.* a revival of emotions previously experienced and repressed, as toward a parent, with a new person as the object.

trans·fer·en·tial (trans′fə ren′shəl), *adj.* of or having to do with transference.

transfer machine, a grouping of simpler machines to produce a larger machine that functions as a unit, for automatically performing a series of operations, passing the work along from one machine to the next.

trans·fer·or (trans fėr′ər), *n. Law.* a person who makes a transfer of title, right, or property.

transfer paper, any of various kinds of specially prepared paper for transferring drawings, designs, etc.

transfer payment, money spent by government or business without any return in the form of goods or services: *Such transfer payments as Social Security and veterans' benefits increased only slightly* (Wall Street Journal).

transfer printing, **1.** any process of printing by transfer. **2.** a method of decorating pottery by applying to the ware impressions taken on paper from a copperplate engraving.

trans·fer·ra·ble (trans fėr′ə bəl, trans′fər-), *adj.* transferable.

trans·fer·ral (trans fėr′əl), *n.* transferal.

trans·fer·rer (trans fėr′ər), *n.* a person or thing that transfers.

trans·fer·ri·ble (trans fėr′ə bəl), *adj.* transferable.

trans·fer·rin (trans fer′in, tranz-), *n.* an iron-bearing protein of the blood plasma. [< *trans-* + Latin *ferr(um)* iron + English *-in*]

transfer RNA, a form of ribonucleic acid that delivers amino acids to the ribosomes during protein synthesis: *There is at least one transfer RNA for each of the 20 common amino acids* (Scientific American).

transfer table, a traverse table on a railroad.

transfer tax, a tax levied, usually in the form of a stamp tax, upon the transfer of property, documents, securities, etc.

Trans·fig·u·ra·tion (trans fig′yə rā′shən), *n.* **1.** (in the Bible) the change in the appearance of Christ on the mountain. Matthew 17:2; Mark 9:2-3. **2.** the church festival on August 6 in honor of this. [< Latin *trānsfigūrātiō, -ōnis* < *trānsfigūrāre;* see TRANSFIGURE]

trans·fig·u·ra·tion (trans fig′yə rā′shən), *n.* a change in form or appearance; transformation. [< *Transfiguration*]

trans·fig·ure (trans fig′yər), *v.t.,* **-ured, -ur·ing.** **1.** to change in form or appearance; transform: *New paint and furnishings had transfigured the old house.* **2.** to change so as to glorify; exalt; idealize. [< Latin *trānsfigūrāre* < *trāns-* across + *figūra* figure]

trans·fi·nite (trans fī′nīt), *Mathematics.* —*adj.* beyond or surpassing any finite number or magnitude: *a transfinite cardinal number.* —*n.* a transfinite number.

trans·fix (trans fiks′), *v.t.* **1.** to pierce through: *The hunter transfixed the lion with a spear. An arrow . . . transfixed him* (Scott). **2.** to fasten or fix by piercing through with something pointed; impale. **3.** to make motionless or helpless (with amazement, terror, grief, etc.). [< Latin *trānsfixus,* past participle of *trānsfigere* < *trāns-* through + *fīgere* to fix, fasten]

trans·fix·ion (trans fik′shən), *n.* **1.** a transfixing. **2.** a being transfixed.

trans·flu·ent (trans′flü ənt), *adj.* flowing or running across or through. [< Latin *trānsfluēns, -entis,* present participle of *trānsfluere* < *trāns-* across + *fluere* to flow]

trans·flux (trans′fluks), *n.* a flowing across, through, or beyond. [< *trans-* + Latin *fluxus, -ūs* < *fluere* to flow]

trans·form (*v.* trans fôrm′; *n.* trans′fôrm′), *v.t.* **1.** to change in form or appearance: *The blizzard transformed the bushes into mounds of white.* **2.** to change in condition, nature, character: *The witch transformed men into pigs. To Samarcand . . . we owe the art of transforming linen into paper* (Cardinal Newman). **3.** *Physics.* to change (one form of energy) into another: *A dynamo transforms mechanical energy into electricity.* **4.** to change (an electric current) into one of higher or lower voltage. **5.** *Mathematics.* to change (a figure, term, etc.) to another differing in form but having the same value or quantity. —*v.i.* to be transformed; change: *A tadpole transforms into a frog.*
—*n. Mathematics.* an expression derived from another by changing a figure, term, etc., without changing its quantity or value.
[< Latin *trānsformāre* < *trāns-* across + *formāre* to form < *forma* form]
—**Syn.** *v.t.* **1, 2. Transform, transmute, convert** mean to change the form, nature, substance, or state of something. **Transform** suggests a thoroughgoing or fundamental change in the appearance, shape, or nature of a thing or person: *Responsibility transformed him from a happy-go-lucky boy into a capable leader.* **Transmute** suggests a complete change in nature or substance, especially to a higher kind: *He thus transmuted disapproval into admiration.* **Convert** suggests a change from one state or condition to another, especially for a new use or purpose: *to convert boxes into furniture.*

trans·form·a·ble (trans fôr′mə bəl), *adj.* that can be transformed.

trans·for·ma·tion (trans′fər mā′shən), *n.* **1.** a transforming or being transformed: *the transformation of a caterpillar into a butterfly.* **2.** a wig worn by women. **3.** a transformation scene. **4.** *Linguistics.* the rearrangement of the elements of a sentence to produce an equivalent or more complex sentence. Example: *John hit him. He was hit by John. Has John been hitting him?* —**Syn. 1.** metamorphosis.

trans·for·ma·tion·al (trans′fər mā′shə nəl), *adj. Linguistics.* having to do with or using transformations: *Transformational grammar* [assumes] *that language consists of irreducible kernel utterances, plus transformational laws, plus lexicon* (Harper's).

trans·for·ma·tion·al·ist (trans′fər mā′shə nə list), *n.* a person who uses or teaches transformational grammar or linguistics.

transformation scene, a scene in which the appearance of performers or the setting is transformed in view of the audience, as in English pantomime.

trans·form·a·tive (trans fôr′mə tiv), *adj.* tending or serving to transform.

trans·form·er (trans fôr′mər), *n.* **1.** a person or thing that transforms. **2.** *Electricity.* a device for changing an alternating current into one of higher or lower voltage. The first is called a step-up transformer, and the second a step-down transformer.

trans·form·ism (trans fôr′miz əm), *n.* *Biology.* **1.** the doctrine that species transform into other species by descent with modification through many generations. **2.** such transformation itself. **3.** any form of the doctrine of evolution of species.

trans·form·ist (trans fôr′mist), *n.* an advocate of transformism.

trans·fuse (trans fyüz′), *v.t.,* **-fused, -fus·ing.** **1.** to transfer (blood) from the veins or arteries of one person or animal to those of another. **2.** to inject (a solution) into a blood vessel. **3.** to pour (a liquid) from one container into another. **4.** to infuse; instill: *The speaker transfused his enthusiasm into the audience.* [< Latin *trānsfūsus,* past participle of *trānsfundere* < *trāns-* across + *fundere* to pour]

trans·fus·er (trans fyü′zər), *n.* a person or thing that transfuses.

trans·fus·i·ble (trans fyü′zə bəl), *adj.* that can be transfused.

trans·fu·sion (trans fyü′zhən), *n.* the act or fact of transfusing: *a blood transfusion.* [< Latin *trānsfūsiō, -ōnis* < *trānsfūsus;* see TRANSFUSE]

transfusion cell, a thin-walled plant cell that permits the passage of water to adjacent tissues.

trans·fu·sion·ist (trans fyü′zhə nist), *n.* a person who is trained or skilled in blood transfusion.

trans·fu·sive (trans fyü′siv), *adj.* tending to transfuse or be transfused.

trans·gress (trans gres′, tranz-), *v.i.* to break a law or command; sin (against). —*v.t.* **1.** to go contrary to; sin against. **2.** to go or pass beyond (a limit or bound); exceed: *His manners transgressed the bounds of good taste.* [< Latin *trānsgressus,* past participle of *trānsgredī* go beyond < *trāns-* across + *gradī* to step] —**Syn.** *v.i.* trespass, offend. *-v.t.* **1.** violate, break.

trans·gres·sion (trans gresh′ən, tranz-), *n.* **1.** a transgressing; breaking a law, command, etc.; sin: *A miracle [is] . . . a transgression of a law of nature . . . by the interposition of some invisible agent* (David Hume). **2.** *Geology.* the spread of the sea over the land along a subsiding shoreline, producing an overlap by deposition of new strata upon old. [< Latin *trānsgressiō, -ōnis* (originally) a going over < *trānsgredī;* see TRANSGRESS] —**Syn. 1.** violation, offense, fault, misdeed, trespass.

trans·gres·sive (trans gres′iv, tranz-), *adj.* transgressing; inclined to transgress; involving transgression. —**trans·gres′sive·ly,** *adv.*

trans·gres·sor (trans gres′ər, tranz-), *n.* a person who transgresses; sinner: *The way of transgressors is hard* (Proverbs 13:15).

tran·shape (tran shāp′), *v.t.,* **-shaped, -shap·ing.** transshape.

tran·ship (tran ship′), *v.t., v.i.,* **-shipped, -ship·ping.** transship.

tran·ship·ment (tran ship′mənt), *n.* transshipment.

tran·ship·per (tran ship′ər), *n.* transshipper.

trans·hu·man (trans hyü′mən), *adj.* superhuman.

trans·hu·mance (trans hyü′məns), *n.* the seasonal migration under the care of shepherds of herds and flocks between regions of different climates. [< French *transhumance* < *transhumer* to migrate seasonally < Spanish *trashumar* < Latin *trāns-* across + *humus* ground, soil]

trans·hu·mant (trans hyü′mənt), *adj.* migrating between regions of different climates: *transhumant flocks.*

tran·sience (tran′shəns), *n.* transiency.

tran·sien·cy (tran′shən sē), *n.* the quality or condition of being transient; transitoriness: *Oliver . . . didn't love life, because he hadn't the animal Epicurean faculty of enjoying it in its arbitrariness and transiency* (Atlantic).

tran·sient (tran′shənt), *adj.* **1.** passing quickly or soon; not lasting; fleeting: *Joy and sorrow are often transient.* **2. a.** passing through and not staying long: *a transient guest in a hotel.* **b.** *U.S.* serving transient guests, customers, etc.: *a transient hotel.* **3.** *Music.* introduced in passing but not necessary to the harmony: *a transient modulation.* **4.** transeunt.
—*n. U.S.* a visitor, boarder, customer, etc., who stays for a short time: *This hotel does not accept transients.*
[< Latin *trānsiēns, transeuntis,* present participle of *trānsīre* to go across < *trāns-* across + *īre* to go. Compare TRANSEUNT.] —**tran′sient·ly,** *adv.* —**tran′sient·ness,** *n.*
—**Syn.** *adj.* **1.** transitory, evanescent, momentary, ephemeral. See **temporary.**
—**Ant.** *adj.* **1.** abiding.

tran·sil·i·ence (tran sil′ē əns), *n.* an abrupt passing from one thing to another.

tran·sil·i·ent (tran sil′ē ənt), *adj.* leaping or passing from one thing or condition to another. [< Latin *trānsiliēns, -entis,* present participle of *trānsilīre* < *trāns-* across + *salīre* to leap]

trans·il·lu·mi·nate (trans′i lü′mə nāt, tranz′-), *v.t.,* **-nat·ed, -nat·ing.** to cause light to pass through (an organ or part) as a means of medical diagnosis.

trans·il·lu·mi·na·tion (trans′i lü′mə nā′shən, tranz′-), *n.* the act or process of transilluminating.

trans·i·re (trans ī′rē), *n.* a permit issued by a custom house to let merchandise pass through the port. [< Latin *trānsīre* to go across; see TRANSIENT]

trans·i·sonde (tran′sə sond), *n.* transosonde.

trans·isth·mi·an (trans is′mē ən, tranz-), *adj.* passing or extending across an isthmus.

tran·sis·tor (tran zis′tər), *n. Electronics.* a small crystal device containing semiconductors such as germanium and silicon, that amplifies electricity by controlling the flow of electrons: *The transistor's small size and low power requirements make it an electronic engineer's dream gadget* (Watson Davis). [< *tran*(sfer) < (re)*sistor*]

tran·sis·tor·ise (tran zis′tə rīz), *v.t.,* **-ised, -is·ing.** *Especially British.* transistorize.

tran·sis·tor·i·za·tion (tran zis′tər ə zā′shən), *n.* an equipping or reducing in size with transistors.

tran·sis·tor·ize (tran zis′tə rīz), *v.t.,* **-ized, -iz·ing.** to equip or reduce in size with transistors: *With a new silicon transistor . . . it is now possible to transistorize radio transmitters* (Wall Street Journal).

transistor radio, a usually small, battery-powered radio equipped with transistors: *. . . the music which came from a transistor radio in [his] pocket* (Manchester Guardian).

trans·it (tran′sit, -zit), *n., v.,* **-it·ed, -it·ing.** —*n.* **1.** a passing across or through. **2. a.** a carrying or being carried across or through: *The goods were damaged in transit.* **b.** the carrying of people from one place to another by trains, buses, etc.: *All transit systems are crowded in rush hours.* **3.** a transition or change, especially the passage from this life to the next by death. **4.** an instrument used in surveying to measure horizontal and vertical angles; a theodolite with a telescope that can be rotated through a full circle. **5.** *Astronomy.* **a.** the apparent passage of a heavenly body across the meridian of a place, or through the field of a telescope. **b.** the passage of a heavenly body across the disk of a larger one.
—*v.t.* **1.** to pass across or through; traverse; cross. **2.** to turn (the telescope of a transit) around its horizontal transverse axis to point in the opposite direction. —*v.i.* to pass through or over; pass away.
[< Latin *trānsitus, -ūs* < *trānsīre;* see TRANSIENT]

Transit (def. 4)

trans·it·a·ble (tran′sə tə bəl, -zə-), *adj.* offering means of transit or passage.

transit circle, an astronomical instrument consisting of a telescope carrying a finely graduated circle, used for observing the transit of a heavenly body across the meridian.

transit duty, a duty paid on goods passing through a country.

transit instrument, 1. *Astronomy.* a telescope mounted with its east-west axis fixed so that it can move only in the plane of the local meridian, used to find the time of transit of a heavenly body. **2.** a surveyor's transit.

tran·si·tion (tran zish′ən), *n.* **1.** a change or passing from one condition, place, thing, activity, topic, etc., to another: *The time between two distinct periods of history, art, literature, etc., is called a period of transition. Abrupt transitions in a book confuse the reader.* **2.** *Music.* **a.** a passing from one key to another; modulation. **b.** a transient modulation. [< Latin *trānsitiō, -ōnis* < *trānsīre;* see TRANSIENT]

tran·si·tion·al (tran zish′ə nəl), *adj.* of, characterized by, or involving transition; intermediate: *The "transitional" style incorporates features of both traditional and modern furniture types* (Wall Street Journal). —**tran·si′tion·al·ly,** *adv.*

tran·si·tion·ar·y (tran zish′ə ner′ē), *adj.* transitional.

tran·si·tive (tran′sə tiv), *adj.* **1.** (of verbs) taking a direct object. *Bring, raise, hit* and *tie* are transitive verbs. **2.** transitional.
—*n.* a transitive verb. *Abbr.:* trans. [< Late Latin *trānsitīvus* < Latin *trānsīre;* see TRANSIENT] —**tran′si·tive·ly,** *adv.* —**tran′si·tive·ness,** *n.*
➤ See **verb** for usage note.

tran·si·tiv·i·ty (tran′sə tiv′ə tē), *n.* the condition of being transitive: *The idea of transitivity eludes seven-year-olds* (Time).

tran·si·to·ri·ly (tran′sə tôr′ə lē, -tōr′-), *adv.* in a transitory manner; briefly.

tran·si·to·ri·ness (tran′sə tôr′ē nis, -tōr′-), *n.* the quality or condition of being transitory.

tran·si·to·ry (tran′sə tôr′ē, -tōr′-), *adj.* passing soon or quickly; lasting only a short time; momentary; brief: *We hope this hot weather will be transitory.* —**Syn.** fleeting, transient.

transit theodolite or **compass,** a surveyor's transit. See **transit** for picture.

Trans·jor·da·ni·an (trans′jôr dā′nē ən), *adj.* of or having to do with Transjordan (former name of the kingdom of Jordan); Jordanian. —*n.* a native or inhabitant of Transjordan; Jordanian.

Trans·kei·an (trans kā′ən, -kī′-), *adj.* of or having to do with the Transkei, a Bantustan of the Cape of Good Hope province, in South Africa or its people: *the Transkeian territory, legislature, constitution, etc.* —*n.* a native or inhabitant of the Transkei.

transl., 1. translated. **2.** translation.

trans·lat·a·ble (trans lā′tə bəl, tranz-), *adj.* that can be translated: *At last they are being decoded, following the recent discovery . . . of a stone lion bearing parallel inscriptions in hieroglyphics and translatable Phoenician* (Newsweek). —**trans·lat′a·ble·ness,** *n.*

trans·late (trans lāt′, tranz-; trans′lāt, tranz′-), *v.,* **-lat·ed, -lat·ing.** —*v.t.* **1.** to change from one language into another: *to translate a novel from French into English.* **2.** to change into other words. **3. a.** to explain the meaning of; interpret. **b.** to express (one thing) in terms of another: *to translate words into action.* **4.** to change from one place, position, or condition to another: *She was translated to the fairy palace in a second.* **5.** to take to heaven without death: *By faith Enoch was translated that he should not see death* (Hebrews 11:5). **6.** to remove (a bishop) from one see to another. **7.** to remove (a bishop's see) from one place to another. **8.** *Physics.* to move (a body) from one point or place to another without rotation. **9.** to retransmit (a telegraphic message), as by a relay. **10.** *Archaic.* to enrapture: *their souls, with devotion translated* (Longfellow).
—*v.i.* **1.** to change something from one language or form of words into another. **2.** to bear translation; allow to be translated: *Many foreign expressions do not translate well into English.*
[< Latin *trānslātus,* past participle of *trānsferre;* see TRANSFER] —**Syn.** *v.t.* **2.** paraphrase, render. **4.** transfer, transport.

trans·la·tion (trans lā′shən, tranz-), *n.* **1.** the act of translating; change into another language; change from one position or condition to another. **2.** the result of translating; version: *He would have the original and all the translations* (James Boswell). *Abbr.:* trans. **3.** the automatic retransmission of a long-distance telegraph message by means of a relay. **4.** *Physics.* motion in which there is no rotation; onward movement that is not rotary or reciprocating. —**Syn. 2.** interpretation, rendering.

trans·la·tion·al (trans lā′shə nəl, tranz-), *adj.* of or having to do with translation.

trans·la·tive (trans lā′tiv, tranz-), *adj.* translational.

trans·la·tor (trans lā′tər, tranz-; trans′lā-, tranz′-), *n.* a person who translates.

trans·la·tor·ese (trans lā′tər ēz, tranz-; trans′lā-, tranz′-; -ēs), *n.* the style of language or writing characteristic of translators.

trans·la·to·ry (trans′lə tôr′ē, -tōr′-; tranz′-), *adj. Physics.* consisting in onward motion, as distinct from rotation: *rotatory and translatory motion.*

trans·la·tress (trans lā′tris, tranz-), *n.* a woman translator.

translit., transliteration.

trans·lit·er·ate (trans lit′ə rāt, tranz-), *v.t.,* **-at·ed, -at·ing.** to change (letters, words, etc.) into corresponding characters of another alphabet or language: *to transliterate the Greek χ as ch and φ as ph, to transliterate Arabic words into English letters.* [< *trans-* + Latin *littera* letter]

trans·lit·er·a·tion (trans lit′ə rā′shən, tranz-), *n.* the act of transliterating; the rendering of a letter or letters of one alphabet by equivalents in another.

trans·lit·er·a·tor (trans lit′ə rā tər, tranz-), *n.* a person who transliterates.

trans·lo·cate (trans lō′kāt), *v.t.,* **-cat·ed, -cat·ing. 1.** to remove from one place to another; displace; dislocate. **2.** *Botany.* to cause to undergo translocation.

trans·lo·ca·tion (trans′lō kā′shən), *n.* **1.** *Botany.* the conduction of food from one part of a plant to another. **2.** a being displaced; displacement.

trans·lu·cence (trans lü′səns, tranz-), *n.* translucent quality or condition.

trans·lu·cen·cy (trans lü′sən sē, tranz-), *n.* translucence.

trans·lu·cent (trans lü′sənt, tranz-), *adj.* **1.** letting light through without being transparent: *Frosted glass is translucent.* **2.** *Archaic.* **a.** transparent. **b.** that shines through. [< Latin *trānslūcēns, -entis,* present participle of *trānslūcēre* < *trāns-* through + *lūcēre* to shine] **—trans·lu′cent·ly,** *adv.*

trans·lu·cid (trans lü′sid, tranz-), *adj.* translucent. [< Latin *trānslūcidus* < *trānslūcēre* < *trāns-* through + *lūcēre* to shine]

trans·lu·nar (trans lü′nər, tranz-), *adj.* translunary.

trans·lu·na·ry (trans lü′nər ē, tranz-), *adj.* **1.** situated beyond or above the moon; superlunary. **2.** celestial, rather than earthly; ideal; visionary: *[Marlowe] had in him those brave translunary things that the first poets had* (Michael Drayton). [< *trans-* + Latin *lūna* moon; patterned on *lunary*]

trans·make (trans māk′, tranz-), *v.t.,* **-made, -mak·ing.** to make into something different; reshape.

trans·ma·rine (trans′mə rēn′, tranz′-), *adj.* across or beyond the sea; overseas. [< Latin *trānsmarīnus* < *trāns-* across + *mare* sea]

trans·me·di·al (trans mē′dē əl, tranz-), *adj.* transmedian.

trans·me·di·an (trans mē′dē ən, tranz-), *adj.* passing or lying across a median line, as of the body: *a transmedian muscle.*

trans·me·rid·i·o·nal (trans′mə rid′ē ə nəl, tranz′-), *adj.* crossing the meridional lines or meridians; running east and west.

trans·meth·yl·a·tion (trans′meth ə lā′shən, tranz′-), *n. Chemistry.* the transfer of methyl groups between compounds.

trans·mi·grant (trans mī′grənt, tranz-), *n.* a person passing through a country or place on his way from his own country to a country in which he intends to settle. —*adj.* transmigrating. [< Latin *trānsmigrāns, -antis,* present participle of *trānsmigrāre;* see TRANSMIGRATE]

trans·mi·grate (trans mī′grāt, tranz-), *v.i.,* **-grat·ed, -grat·ing. 1.** (of the soul) to pass after death into another body. **2.** to move from one place or country to another; migrate. [< Latin *trānsmigrāre* (with English *-ate*[1]) < *trāns-* across + *migrāre* to move]

trans·mi·gra·tion (trans′mī grā′shən, tranz′-), *n.* **1. a.** the passing of a soul at death into another body; metempsychosis. **b.** the doctrine of reincarnation of the soul in a human or an animal body after death. Many people in India believe in the transmigration of souls. *That peculiar feeling . . . of having once been someone else, which accounts for so much belief in the transmigration of souls* (John Galsworthy). **2.** the going from one place or country to another; migration.

trans·mi·gra·tor (trans mī′grā tər, tranz-), *n.* a person or thing that transmigrates.

trans·mi·gra·to·ry (trans mī′grə tôr′ē, -tōr′-; tranz-), *adj.* having to do with transmigration; transmigrating.

trans·mis·si·bil·i·ty (trans mis′ə bil′ə tē, tranz-), *n.* the quality of being transmissible.

trans·mis·si·ble (trans mis′ə bəl, tranz-), *adj.* that can be transmitted: *Scarlet fever is a transmissible disease.*

trans·mis·sion (trans mish′ən, tranz-), *n.* **1.** a sending over; passing on; passing along; letting through: *the transmission of money by telegraph. Mosquitoes are the only means of transmission of malaria. Alphabetical writing made . . . the transmission of events more easy and certain* (Samuel Johnson). **2.** something transmitted. **3. a.** the part of an automobile, truck, etc., that transmits power from the engine to the rear axle or sometimes the front axle. **b.** the sets of gears that determine the relative speed. **4.** the passage through space of electromagnetic waves from a transmitting station to a receiving station or stations: *When transmission is good, foreign radio stations can be received.* [< Latin *trānsmissiō, -ōnis* < *trānsmittere,* see TRANSMIT]

trans·mis·sive (trans mis′iv, tranz-), *adj.* **1.** transmitting; having to do with transmission. **2.** obtained by transmission; transmitted; derived.

trans·mis·siv·i·ty (trans′mi siv′ə tē, tranz′-), *n.* the quality of being transmissible: *The transmission of solar heat through the atmosphere at a particular time and under particular conditions is expressed as a percentage. A transmissivity of 100 per cent would mean no atmospheric interference at all* (Scientific American).

trans·mis·som·e·ter (trans′mi som′ə tər, tranz′-), *n.* an electronic apparatus that determines the degree of visibility, as on the runway of an airfield, by measuring the amount of light that comes through the atmosphere to a fixed point from a fixed transmitting point. [< *transmiss*(ion) + *-meter*]

trans·mit (trans mit′, tranz-), *v.t.,* **-mit·ted, -mit·ting. 1.** to send over; pass on; pass along; let through: *I will transmit the money by special messenger. Rats transmit disease.* **2.** *Physics.* **a.** to cause (light, heat, sound, etc.) to pass through a medium. **b.** to convey (force or movement) from one part of a body or mechanism to another. **c.** (of a medium) to allow (light, etc.) to pass through; conduct: *Glass transmits light.* **3.** to send out (signals) by means of electromagnetic waves. [< Latin *trānsmittere* < *trāns-* across + *mittere* send]

trans·mit·ta·ble (trans mit′ə bəl, tranz-), *adj.* transmissible.

trans·mit·tal (trans mit′əl, tranz-), *n.* **1.** a transmitting; transmission. **2.** something transmitted.

trans·mit·tance (trans mit′əns, tranz-), *n.* transmittal.

trans·mit·ter (trans mit′ər, tranz-), *n.* **1.** a person or thing that transmits: *a disease transmitter.* **2.** the part of a telegraph or telephone by which messages are sent; sender. The transmitter converts movements or sound waves into impulses or electrical waves. **3.** an apparatus for sending out signals by means of electromagnetic waves; transmitting set. The term generally refers to the part of the broadcasting equipment that generates and modulates the radiofrequency waves, and sends them to the antenna to be sent out through space.

trans·mit·ti·ble (trans mit′ə bəl, tranz-), *adj.* transmissible.

trans·mit·ting set (trans mit′ing, tranz-), a transmitter.

trans·mog·ri·fi·ca·tion (trans mog′rə fə kā′shən, tranz-), *n.* **1.** a transmogrifying. **2.** a being transmogrified.

trans·mog·ri·fy (trans mog′rə fī, tranz-), *v.t.,* **-fied, -fy·ing.** to change in form or appearance; transform in a surprising or grotesque manner: *Gascar feels no need to transmogrify his humans into animals: World War II and its aftermath, the setting for most of the stories, has already reduced both species to a state of competitive coexistence* (Time). [perhaps a fanciful coinage]

trans·mon·tane (trans mon′tān, tranz-), *adj.* beyond the mountains; tramontane.

trans·mun·dane (trans mun′dān, tranz-), *adj.* beyond the world; beyond this world.

trans·mu·ral (trans myůr′əl, tranz-), *adj.* that is or passes beyond the walls of a city, institution, etc.

trans·mut·a·bil·i·ty (trans myü′tə bil′ə tē, tranz-), *n.* the quality of being transmutable.

trans·mut·a·ble (trans myü′tə bəl, tranz-), *adj.* that can be transmuted.

trans·mut·a·ble·ness (trans myü′tə bəl nis, tranz-), *n.* transmutability.

trans·mut·a·bly (trans myü′tə blē, tranz-), *adv.* in a transmutable manner; so as to be transmutable.

trans·mu·ta·tion (trans′myü tā′shən, tranz′-), *n.* **1.** the change from one nature, substance, or form into another. **2.** the transformation of one species into another; mutation. **3.** *Chemistry, Physics.* the change of one atom into another atom of a different element, occurring naturally, as by radioactive disintegration, or artificially, as by bombardment with neutrons, etc. **4.** (in alchemy) the (attempted) conversion of a baser metal into gold or silver. **5.** *Archaic.* a change of condition, attitude, etc. **—Syn. 1.** alteration, transformation.

trans·mu·ta·tion·al (trans′myü tā′shə nəl, tranz′-), *adj.* of or having to do with transmutation.

trans·mu·ta·tion·ist (trans′myü tā′shə nist, tranz′-), *n.* a person who believes in a theory of transmutation.

trans·mu·ta·tive (trans myü′tə tiv, tranz-), *adj.* serving to transmute.

trans·mute (trans myüt′, tranz-), *v.t.,* **-mut·ed, -mut·ing. 1.** to change from one nature, substance, or form into another: *to transmute water power into electrical power.* **2.** *Chemistry, Physics.* to subject to transmutation. [< Latin *trānsmūtāre* < *trāns-* thoroughly + *mūtāre* to change] **—Syn. 1.** convert. See **transform.**

trans·mut·er (trans myü′tər, tranz-), *n.* a person or thing that transmutes.

trans·na·tion·al (trans nash′ən əl, -nash′nəl; tranz-), *adj.* extending beyond national frontiers or bounds: *a transnational economy, a transnational culture.* **—trans·na′tion·al·ly,** *adv.*

trans·nat·u·ral (trans nach′ə rəl, -nach′rəl; tranz-), *adj.* that is beyond nature; supernatural.

trans·na·ture (trans nā′chər, tranz-), *v.t.,* **-tured, -tur·ing.** to change the nature of: *to transnature the human mind.*

trans·nep·tu·ni·an (trans′nep tü′nē ən, -tyü′-; tranz′-), *adj. Astronomy.* on the other side of the planet Neptune.

trans·o·cean (trans ō′shən, tranz-), *adj.* transoceanic.

trans·o·ce·an·ic (trans′ō shē an′ik, tranz′-), *adj.* **1.** crossing the ocean. **2.** on the other side of the ocean.

tran·som (tran′səm), *n.* **1.** *U.S.* a small window over a door or other window, usually hinged for opening. **2.** a crossbar separating a door from the window over it. **3.** a horizontal bar across a window. **4.** a window divided by a transom. **5.** one of the beams or timbers attached across the sternpost of a ship between the two sides. [perhaps < Latin *trānstrum* (originally) crossbeam, related to *trāns* across]

Transom (def. 1)

tran·somed (tran′səmd), *adj.* having a transom or transoms.

transom window, 1. a window divided by a transom. **2.** a window over the transom of a door.

tran·son·ic (tran son′ik), *adj.* of, having to do with, or designed for operation at speeds between 600 and 800 miles per hour, in the range just below or above the speed of sound. Also, **transsonic.**

trans·o·sonde (tran′sə sond), *n.* a transoceanic balloon equipped with radiosonde for the transmission of meteorological data: *Cost of operating the constant-level balloons, called transosondes, can be as low as $75 for each wind reading* (Science News Letter). [< *transo*(ceanic) (radio)*sonde*]

transp., transportation.

trans·pa·cif·ic (trans′pə sif′ik), *adj.* **1.** crossing the Pacific: *a transpacific liner, a transpacific cable.* **2.** on the other side of the Pacific: *a transpacific ally.*

trans·pa·dane (trans′pə dān, trans pā′-), *adj.* on the farther (or north) side of the river Po, as viewed from Rome. [< Latin *trānspadānus* < *trāns-* across + *Padānus* of the *Padus,* the river Po]

trans·par·ence (trans pãr′əns), *n.* transparent quality or condition; transparency.

trans·par·en·cy (trans pãr′ən sē), *n., pl.* **-cies. 1.** transparent quality or condition. **2.** something transparent. **3.** a picture, design, etc., on glass, celluloid, etc., made visible by light shining through from behind.

trans·par·ent (trans pãr′ənt), *adj.* **1.** transmitting light so that bodies beyond or behind can be distinctly seen: *Window glass is transparent.* **2.** easily seen through or detected; obvious: *a transparent excuse, a transparent lie.* **3.** free from pretense or deceit; frank: *a man of transparent good will toward all. An ingenuous, transparent life* (Thomas Hardy). **4.** *Archaic.* shining through; penetrating: *Like to the glorious sun's transparent beams* (Shakespeare). [< Medieval Latin *transparens, -entis,* present participle of unrecorded *transparere* show light through < Latin *trāns-* through + *pārēre* appear] **—trans·par′ent·ly,** *adv.* **—trans·par′ent·ness,** *n.* **—Syn. 1.** limpid, pellucid, translucent. **2.** manifest, evident. **3.** open, candid.

tran·spic·u·ous (tran spik′yů əs), *adj.* **1.** transparent. **2.** easy to understand; plain; clear. [< New Latin *transpicuus* (with

English *-ous*) < Latin *trānspicere* see through < *trāns-* through + *specere* look at]

trans·pierce (trans pirs′), *v.t.*, **-pierced, -pierc·ing.** to pass through; penetrate; pierce. [< *trans-* + *pierce*, patterned on French *transpercer*, alteration of *trespercier* < *tres-* (< Latin *trāns-* through) + *percier* to pierce]

tran·spi·ra·tion (tran′spə rā′shən), *n.* **1.** a transpiring. **2.** a passing or sending off of vapor, moisture, etc., through a wall or surface, as from the human body or from leaves or other parts of plants.

tran·spir·a·to·ry (tran spīr′ə tôr′ē, -tōr′-), *adj.* transpiring; having to do with transpiration.

tran·spire (tran spīr′), *v.*, **-spired, -spir·ing.** —*v.i.* **1.** to take place; happen; occur: *I heard later what transpired at the meeting.* **2.** to leak out; become known. **3.** to pass off or send off vapor, moisture, etc., through a wall or surface, as from the human body or from leaves, etc. —*v.t.* to pass off or send off in the form of a vapor or liquid, as waste matter through the skin or moisture through the leaves of a plant. [< Middle French *transpirer* < Latin *trāns-* through + *spīrāre* breathe]

➔ **transpire.** The meaning happen, take place was once regarded as not being in good use, but *transpire* is fairly common in cultivated English in this sense today.

tran·spi·rom·e·ter (tran′spə rom′ə tər), *n.* an apparatus for recording the amount of water vapor exuded by a plant.

trans·place (trans plās′, tranz-), *v.t.*, **-placed, -plac·ing.** to transpose.

trans·plant (*v.* trans plant′, -plänt′; *n.* trans′plant, -plänt), *v.t.* **1.** to plant again in a different place: *We start the flowers indoors and then transplant them to the garden.* **2.** to remove from one place to another; transport: *A group of farmers was transplanted to the island by the government.* **3.** to transfer (skin, an organ, etc.) from one person, animal, or part of the body to another. —*v.i.* to bear moving: *Poppies do not transplant well and should be planted where they are to grow.*
—*n.* **1.** a seedling transplanted once or several times. **2.** the transferring of bacterial organisms from one medium to another for culture. **3. a.** the transferring of skin, an organ, etc., from one body, or part of the body, to another. **b.** the part so transferred.
[< Late Latin *trānsplantāre* < Latin *trāns-* across + *plantāre* to plant < *planta* a sprout] —**trans·plant′er,** *n.*

trans·plant·a·bil·i·ty (trans plan′tə bil′ə tē, -plän′-), *n.* the quality of being transplantable.

trans·plant·a·ble (trans plan′tə bəl, -plän′-), *adj.* that can be transplanted: *The suspicion grew stronger on the basis of a Syrian master found to have a transplantable liver cancer* (Science News Letter).

trans·plan·ta·tion (trans′plan tā′shən, -plän-), *n.* **1.** a transplanting or being transplanted. **2.** something that has been transplanted.

trans·po·lar (trans pō′lər, tranz-), *adj.* across the north or south pole or polar region: *a transpolar flight.*

tran·spond·er (tran spon′dər), *n.* an electronic device that can receive a radar or other signal and automatically transmit a response.

trans·po·ni·ble (trans pō′nə bəl), *adj.* transposable. [< Latin *trānspōnere* transpose (< *trāns-* across + *pōnere* to place) + English *-ible*]

trans·pon·tine (trans pon′tin, -tīn), *adj.* across or beyond a bridge, especially on the south side of the Thames in London. [< *trans-* + Latin *pōns, pontis* bridge + English *-ine*[1]. Compare earlier French *transpontin.*]

trans·port (*v.* trans pôrt′, -pōrt′; *n.* trans′pôrt, -pōrt), *v.t.* **1.** to carry from one place to another: *Wheat is transported from the farms to the mills.* **2.** to carry away by very strong feeling: *She was transported with joy by the good news.* **3.** to send away to another country as a punishment: *Convicts of some countries were once transported to remote penal colonies like Devil's Island.* **4.** to kill.
—*n.* **1.** a carrying from one place to another; transporting: *Trucks are much used for transport of freight.* **2.** a ship used to carry soldiers, equipment, supplies, etc. **3.** an airplane that transports passengers, mail, freight, etc. **4.** a very strong feeling: *a transport of joy or rage.* **5.** a transported convict.
[< Latin *trānsportāre* < *trāns-* across + *portāre* carry]
—Syn. *v.t.* **1.** remove, convey. See **carry.** **3.** banish, deport.

trans·port·a·bil·i·ty (trans pôr′tə bil′ə tē, -pōr′-), *n.* the fact or property of being transportable.

trans·port·a·ble (trans pôr′tə bəl, -pōr′-), *adj.* **1.** that can be transported. **2.** involving, or liable to, punishment by transportation: *a transportable offense.*

trans·por·ta·tion (trans′pər tā′shən), *n.* **1. a.** a carrying from one place to another; transporting: *The railroad gives free transportation for a certain amount of baggage.* **b.** the carrying of people or goods, especially as a business: *Without transportation, our modern society could not exist* (World Book Encyclopedia). **2.** the state of being transported. **3.** a means of transport. **4.** the cost of transport; ticket for transport. **5.** a sending away to another country as a punishment: *a set of rascals and rebels whom transportation is too good for* (Dickens).

trans·por·ta·tion·al (trans′pər tā′shən əl), *adj.* of, belonging to, or having to do with transportation.

trans·port·a·tive (trans pôr′tə tiv, -pōr′-), *adj.* serving to transport.

trans·port·ee (trans′pôrtē′, -pōr-), *n.* **1.** a transported convict. **2.** an animal that has been transported from its habitat.

trans·port·er (trans pôr′tər, -pōr′-), *n.* **1.** a person or thing that transports. **2.** a device for transporting coal, etc., from a quay or from one vessel to another.

transporter bridge, a bridge carrying a suspended platform or car which travels from bank to bank of the waterway to transport the traffic. It is built high enough not to interfere with navigation.

trans·por·tive (trans pôr′tiv, -pōr′-), *adj.* transportative.

trans·pos·a·bil·i·ty (trans pō′zə bil′ə tē), *n.* the quality of being transposable.

trans·pos·a·ble (trans pō′zə bəl), *adj.* that can be transposed.

trans·pos·al (trans pō′zəl), *n.* transposition.

trans·pose (trans pōz′), *v.t.*, **-posed, -pos·ing.** **1.** to change the position or order of; interchange: *Transpose the two colors to make a better design.* **2.** to change the usual order of (letters or words). *Example:* Then *comes he* with *horses many* the *road along.* **3.** *Music.* to change the key of (a composition). **4.** *Algebra.* to transfer (a term) to the other side of an equation, changing plus to minus or minus to plus. *Abbr.:* tr. **5.** *Archaic.* to transform; transmute; convert: *Things base and vile ... Love can transpose to form and dignity* (Shakespeare). [< French *transposer* < *trans-* across + *poser* to put. Compare POSE[1].] —**trans·pos′er,** *n.*

trans·po·si·tion (trans′pə zish′ən), *n.* **1.** a transposing or being transposed. **2.** *Music.* a composition transposed into a different key.

trans·po·si·tion·al (trans′pə zish′ə nəl), *adj.* of or involving transposition.

trans·pos·i·tive (trans poz′ə tiv), *adj.* characterized by transposition.

trans·ra·tion·al (trans rash′ə nəl, tranz-), *adj.* beyond what is rational; transcending reason: *They stress the fact that theology deals with myths and symbols which speak to the deeper, transrational levels of the human being* (Manchester Guardian Weekly).

trans·rhe·nane (trans rē′nān, tranz-), *adj.* on the other (the eastern) side of the river Rhine. [< Latin *trānsrhēnānus* < *trāns-* across + *Rhēnānus* of the *Rhēnus*, the river Rhine]

trans·sex·u·al (trans sek′shu̇ əl), *n.* a person affected with transsexualism.

trans·sex·u·al·ism (trans sek′shu̇ ə liz′əm), *n.* a psychological condition in which a person longs to belong to the opposite sex though anatomically normal.

trans·shape (trans shāp′), *v.t.*, **-shaped, -shap·ing.** to change into another shape or form; transform. Also, **transhape.**

trans·ship (trans ship′), *v.t., v.i.*, **-shipped, -ship·ping.** to transfer from one ship, train, car, etc., to another.

trans·ship·ment (trans ship′mənt), *n.* a transshipping. Also, **transhipment.**

trans·ship·per (trans ship′ər), *n.* a person who transships. Also, **transhipper.**

trans·son·ic (trans son′ik), *adj.* transonic.

tran·sub·stan·ti·ate (tran′səb stan′shē āt), *v.t.*, **-at·ed, -at·ing.** **1.** to change (bread and wine) into the body and blood of Christ. **2.** to transmute or transform (any substance).

tran·sub·stan·ti·a·tion (tran′səb stan′shē ā′shən), *n.* **1. a.** the changing of the bread and wine of the Eucharist into the substance of the body of Christ, only the appearance of the bread and wine remaining. **b.** the doctrine that this change occurs. **2.** a changing of one substance into another; transmutation. [< Medieval Latin *transubstantiatio, -onis* < *transubstantiare* to transmute < Latin *trāns-* over + *substantia* substance]

tran·sub·stan·ti·a·tion·al·ist (tran′səb stan′shē ā′shə nə list), *n.* a person who believes in the doctrine of transubstantiation.

tran·su·date (tran′su̇ dāt), *n.* a transudation (a liquid).

tran·su·da·tion (tran′su̇ dā′shən), *n.* **1.** the passing off or oozing out of a liquid through the pores of a substance; transuding. **2.** a liquid that has transuded. [< *trans-* + Latin *sūdātiō, -ōnis* a sweating < *sūdāre* to sweat]

tran·su·da·to·ry (tran sü′də tôr′ē, -tōr′-), *adj.* transuding; characterized by transudation.

tran·sude (tran süd′), *v.i.*, **-sud·ed, -sud·ing.** to ooze through or out like sweat; exude through pores. [< French *transuder* < Latin *trāns-* through, across + *sūdāre* to sweat]

trans·u·ra·ni·an (trans′yu̇ rā′nē ən), *adj.* of or characteristic of a transuranic element.

trans·u·ran·ic element (trans′yu̇ ran′ik), any of a group of radioactive chemical elements whose atomic numbers are higher than that of uranium (92). The group includes neptunium, plutonium, americium, curium, berkelium, californium, einsteinium, fermium, mendelevium, nobelium, and lawrencium.

trans·u·ra·ni·um (trans′yu̇ rā′nē əm), *n.* a transuranic element.

Trans·vaal·er (trans vä′lər, tranz-), *n.* a native or inhabitant of the Transvaal, a province in the Republic of South Africa.

trans·val·u·a·tion (trans′val yu̇ ā′shən), *n.* a change of values; revaluation.

trans·val·ue (trans val′yü), *v.t.*, **-ued, -u·ing.** to change the value of.

trans·vase (trans vās′, tranz-), *v.t.*, **-vased, -vas·ing.** to pour from one vessel into another. [< French *transvaser* < Latin *trāns-* across + *vās* vessel]

trans·ver·sal (trans vėr′səl, tranz-), *adj.* lying or passing across; transverse. —*n. Geometry.* a line intersecting two or more other lines. [< Medieval Latin *transversalis* < Latin *trānsversus;* see TRANSVERSE] —**trans·ver′sal·ly,** *adv.*

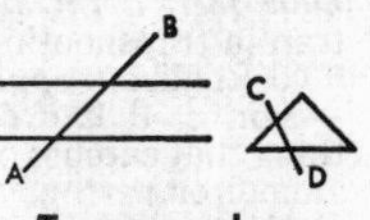

Transversals are AB and CD.

trans·verse (trans vėrs′, tranz-; trans′vėrs, tranz′-), *adj.* **1.** lying or passing across, usually at right angles; placed crosswise; crossing from side to side: *transverse beams.* **2.** *Geometry.* of or having to do with the axis of a conic section that passes through the foci. **3.** (of a flute) having a mouth or opening on the side.
—*n.* **1.** something transverse. **2.** *Geometry.* a transverse axis; the longer axis of an ellipse.
[< Latin *trānsversus*, past participle of *trānsvertere* < *trāns-* across + *vertere* to turn]

transverse colon, the part of the large intestine that crosses under the liver.

trans·verse·ly (trans vėrs′lē, tranz-), *adv.* across; athwart; crosswise; from side to side.

transverse process, a process projecting laterally from a vertebra.

transverse vibrations, *Physics.* periodic disturbances in which the particles of the medium move at right angles to the direction of propagation.

trans·vert·er (trans vėr′tər, tranz-), *n.* a device for changing alternating electric current of low voltage into direct current of high voltage or for changing direct current of high voltage into alternating current of low voltage. [< *trans*(former) + (con)*verter*]

trans·ves·tism (trans ves′tiz əm, tranz-), *n.* the practice of dressing in the clothing of the opposite sex: *The plot, with its elements of transvestism* (*Achilles is disguised as a girl because his father does not want him to be killed in the Trojan war*), *cannot avoid humor* (London Times). [< obsolete *transvest* to clothe in garments, especially of the opposite sex (< *trans-* + Latin *vestīre* to clothe)]

trans·ves·tite (trans ves′tīt, tranz-), *n.* a person who has a desire to dress in the clothing of the opposite sex. —*adj.* of or having to do with transvestism: *the sort of transvestite comedy that has made such a durable commodity of "Charley's Aunt"* (New Yorker).

trans·ves·tit·ism (trans ves′tə tiz əm, tranz-), *n.* transvestism.

Tran·syl·va·ni·an (tran′səl vā′nē ən, -vān′yən), *adj.* of or having to do with Transylvania, a region in western Romania, or its people. —*n.* a native or inhabitant of Transylvania.

trap[1] (trap), *n., v.,* **trapped, trap·ping.** —*n.* **1.** a device or means for catching animals. Most traps have a spring or snare which when touched seizes, kills, or imprisons the animal: *to set a trap for beaver or rats.* **2. a.** a trick or other means for catching someone off guard, making him show his guilt, reveal a secret, etc.: *The police set traps to make the thief tell where the money was.* **b.** anything that attracts because it seems easy but proves to be difficult. **3. a.** the opening covered by a trap door. **b.** a trap door. **4. a.** a device in a pipe to prevent the escape of air, water, steam, gas, etc. **b.** a ventilation door in a mine. **5.** a speed trap. **6.** *British.* a light, two-wheeled carriage, such as a gig. **7.** a device for throwing clay pigeons, etc., into the air to be shot at. **8. a.** a piece of wood, shaped like a shoe with a hollow at the heel and moving on a pivot, used in trapball. **b.** trapball. **9.** a trap net. **10.** *Slang.* the mouth: *Shut your trap!*

Traps[1] (def. 4a)

traps, a group of percussion instruments, such as drums, cymbals, bells, gongs, etc.: *You jazzmen, bang ... drums, traps* (Carl Sandburg).

—*v.t.* **1.** to catch in or as if in a trap: *The bear was trapped.* **2.** to provide with a trap. **3.** to stop and hold with a trap, as water, air, gas, or heat in a pipe. —*v.i.* **1.** to set traps for animals. **2.** to make a business of catching animals in traps for their furs: *Some men make their living by trapping.* **3.** to work a trap in trapshooting.

[Old English *træppe* a snare, trap]

—**Syn.** *n.* **1, 2. a. Trap, snare** mean something that catches or is contrived to catch an animal or person. **Trap,** literally usually a mechanical device springing shut, figuratively suggests a situation deliberately set to catch someone by surprise and destroy him or trick him into doing or saying something: *Suspecting a trap, the detachment of soldiers withdrew.* **Snare,** literally a noose tightening around an animal's foot or neck, figuratively applies to a situation someone gets entangled in unawares, or a device to lure him into getting caught: *The detectives used marked money as a snare for the thief.* -*v.t.* **1.** entrap, ensnare.

trap[2] (trap), *v.,* **trapped, trap·ping,** *n.* —*v.t.* to cover or ornament with trappings. —*n.* *Obsolete.* trappings for a horse.

traps, *Informal.* personal effects; baggage; belongings: *I packed my traps and went on shore* (Frederick Marryat).

[Middle English *trappe* saddle cloth, caparison; origin uncertain; perhaps alteration of Old French *drap,* or Medieval Latin *drappus*]

trap[3] (trap), *n. Geology.* basalt or other fine-grained, dark, igneous rock having a more or less columnar structure. [earlier *trapp* < Swedish < *trappa* stair < Low German (because of its appearance)]

tra·pan (trə pan′), *n., v.t.,* **-panned, -panning.** *Archaic.* trepan[2]. —**tra·pan′ner,** *n.*

trap·ball (trap′bôl′), *n.* **1.** an old game in which a player strikes a trap to throw the ball into the air and then hits the ball to some distance. **2.** the ball used in this game.

trap cut, a step cut.

trap door, 1. a door flush with the surface of a floor, ceiling, or roof. It opens on hinges or by sliding in grooves. **2.** the opening covered by such a door.

Trap Door

trap-door spider (trap′dôr, -dōr′), any of a group of large, hairy spiders that live in underground burrows covered by hinged lids that open and shut like a trap door.

trapes (trāps), *v.i., v.t., n. Informal.* traipse.

tra·peze (tra pēz′), *n.* **1.** a short, horizontal bar hung by ropes like a swing, used in performing acrobatic stunts and exercises. **2.** *Geometry.* a trapezium. **3.** a loose, unbelted dress that flares from the shoulders to the hem: *Araminta is glimpsed through the rain wearing her off-the-peg trapeze in a giant cabbage rose print* (Punch).

[< French *trapèze* < Late Latin *trapezium* < Greek *trapézion* an irregular quadrilateral; small table (diminutive) < *trápeza* table < *tetra-* four + *péza* foot. Doublet of TRAPEZIUM.]

trapeze dress, trapeze.

tra·pe·zi·form (trə pē′zə fôrm), *adj.* shaped like a trapezium or trapezoid.

tra·pez·ist (tra pē′zist), *n.* a performer on the trapeze: *We think of him as a supremely skillful trapezist endowed with an unerring instinct for survival* (Manchester Guardian).

tra·pe·zi·um (trə pē′zē əm), *n., pl.* **-zi·ums, -zi·a** (-zē ə). **1.** *Geometry.* **a.** a four-sided plane figure having no two sides parallel. **b.** *British.* a trapezoid. **c.** a plane figure with two parallel and two nonparallel sides. **2.** *Anatomy.* the greater multangular. [< Late Latin *trapezium.* Doublet of TRAPEZE.]

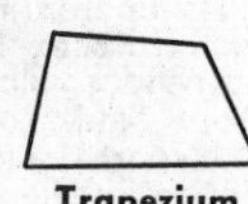

Trapezium (def. 1a)

tra·pe·zi·us (trə pē′zē əs), *n., pl.* **-zi·i** (-zē ī). *Anatomy.* each of a pair of large, flat, triangular muscles of the back of the neck and the upper part of the back and shoulders, together forming a somewhat diamond-shaped figure. [< New Latin *trapezius* < Late Latin *trapezium:* see TRAPEZE]

trap·e·zo·he·dral (trap′ə zō hē′drəl, trə-pē′zō-), *adj.* of or in the form of a trapezohedron.

trap·e·zo·he·dron (trap′ə zō hē′drən, trə-pē′zō-), *n.* a solid whose faces are all trapeziums or trapezoids. See **replacement** for picture. [< *trapezium* + Greek *hédra* base, side + *-on,* as in English *dodecahedron*]

trap·e·zoid (trap′ə zoid), *n.* **1.** *Geometry.* **a.** a four-sided plane figure having two sides parallel and two sides not parallel. **b.** *British.* a four-sided plane figure having no sides parallel; trapezium. **2.** *Anatomy.* the lesser multangular bone. —*adj.* trapezoidal. [< New Latin *trapezöides* < Late Greek *trapezoidēs* (in Greek, shaped like a trapezium) < Greek *trápeza* table + *eîdos* form]

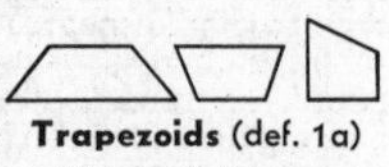

Trapezoids (def. 1a)

trap·e·zoi·dal (trap′ə zoi′dəl), *adj.* in the form of a trapezoid.

trap fishing, fishing with a trap line or net.

trap line, 1. the route along which traps are set in trapping: *All trappers dread the possibility of fires burning their trap lines, for after the flames have gone there is little left in the burned-over area for carnivorous furbearers to track down and kill* (Maclean's). **2.** a line of baited fishing hooks to be anchored in place. **3.** the filament in a spider's web that ensnares the prey.

trap net, an oblong net with one end in the shape of an inverted funnel, for catching fish.

trap·pe·an (trap′ē ən, trə pē′-), *adj. Geology.* of, like, or consisting of trap (rock). [< *trap*[3] + *-ean,* as in *marmorean*]

trap·per (trap′ər), *n.* a person who traps, especially a man who traps wild animals for their furs.

trap·pings (trap′ingz), *n.pl.* **1.** things worn; ornaments: *the gay trappings of the young king and his court, the trappings of a house at Christmas.* **2.** ornamental coverings for a horse; caparisons. [< *trap*[2]]

Trap·pist (trap′ist), *n.* a monk belonging to an extremely austere branch of the Cistercian order established in 1664. The Trappists are vowed to almost complete silence and hard labor. —*adj.* of or having to do with the Trappists. [< French *trappiste* < the abbey *La Trappe* (< the village of *Soligny-la-Trappe,* in France) + *-iste* -ist]

trap·py (trap′ē), *adj.,* **-pi·er, -pi·est.** of the nature of or containing a trap or traps; treacherous: ... *to permit trappy off balls to pass by in such close proximity to his wicket as to make his admirers hold their breath* (London Daily Chronicle).

trap·rock (trap′rok′), *n.* trap[3].

traps (traps), *n.pl.* See under **trap**[1], *n.,* and **trap**[2], *n.*

trap·shoot·er (trap′shü′tər), *n.* a person who shoots at clay pigeons, etc., thrown into the air.

trap·shoot·ing (trap′shü′ting), *n.* the sport of shooting at clay pigeons or other targets thrown or released from traps into the air.

trap shot, a half volley in tennis, etc.

tra·pun·to (trə pün′tō, -pün′-), *n.* embroidery in which a design outlined on one side is padded with cotton, yarn, etc., on the other side. [< Italian *trapunto* < Vulgar Latin *trapūnctus* < Latin *intrā* within + *pūnctum* a point, prick]

trash[1] (trash), *n.* **1.** worthless stuff; rubbish: *Please take the basket of trash to the garbage can. Many books and magazines are filled with cheap, sensational, and lurid trash.* **2.** broken or torn bits, such as leaves, twigs, husks, etc.: *Rake up the trash in the yard and burn it.* **3.** worthless or disreputable people; riffraff: *His father hated him travelling with trash like them* (Owen Wister). **4.** the refuse of sugar cane after the juice has been pressed.

—*v.t.* **1.** to free from trash or refuse, especially to strip the outer leaves from (growing sugar cane) so it can ripen more quickly. **2.** to treat or discard as worthless.

[< Scandinavian (compare dialectal Norwegian *trask,* and Old Icelandic *thraska* to rummage)]

—**Syn.** *n.* **1.** debris, litter, refuse, garbage.

trash[2] (trash), *n.* **1.** a leash for a dog. **2.** anything that checks or restrains; hindrance. —*v.t.* **1.** to check by or as if by a trash or leash. **2.** to hold back; restrain; hinder. [origin uncertain]

trash can, a metal or plastic receptacle for the disposal of trash.

trash·er·y (trash′ər ē), *n.* trash; rubbish.

trash·i·ly (trash′ə lē), *adv.* in a trashy manner.

trash·i·ness (trash′ē nis), *n.* the quality or condition of being trashy.

trash·y (trash′ē), *adj.,* **trash·i·er, trash·i·est.** like or containing trash; worthless: *a trashy novel.*

trass (tras), *n.* a rock consisting largely of consolidated fragments of pumice or other volcanic material, used for making mortar or hydraulic cement. It is common along the Rhine. [< Dutch *tras,* earlier *tarasse,* ultimately < Vulgar Latin *terrācea.* Compare TERRACE.]

trat·to·ri·a (trät′tō rē′ä), *n., pl.* **-ri·e** (-rē′ā). an inexpensive Italian restaurant: *I found a small trattoria behind the Duomo where we could eat for practically nothing* (Atlantic). [< Italian *trattoria*]

trau·chle (trä′ʜəl), *v.t.,* **-chled, -chling.** *Scottish.* trachle.

trau·ma (trô′mə, trou′-), *n., pl.* **-mas, -ma·ta** (-mə tə). **1. a.** a physical wound; injury. **b.** the condition produced by this; traumatism. **2.** *Psychiatry.* an unpleasant experience that affects the mind or nerves, inducing hysteria or the like. [< Greek *traûma, -atos* wound]

trau·mat·ic (trô mat′ik, trou-), *adj.* **1.** of, having to do with, or produced by a wound, injury, or shock. **2.** for or dealing with treatment of wounds or injuries. [< Late Latin *traumaticus* < Greek *traumatikós* of a wound < *traûma, -atos* wound, trauma]

trau·mat·i·cal·ly (trô mat′ə klē, trou-), *adv.* in a traumatic manner; so as to cause a trauma or traumatic neurosis: *The hero ... attends an Ivy League college ... where he is traumatically snubbed because he lacks good looks or money* (Time).

traumatic neurosis, any neurosis brought on by an injury or severe shock.

trau·ma·tism (trô′mə tiz əm, trou′-), *n.* **1.** any abnormal condition caused by a trauma. **2.** a trauma or wound.

trau·ma·tize (trô′mə tīz, trou′-), *v.t.,* **-tized, -tiz·ing.** to wound or injure (the mind or part of the body).

trau·ma·to·log·i·cal (trô′ma tə loj′ə kəl, trou′-), *adj.* of or having to do with traumatology: . . . *a number of burns units and traumatological institutes were established* (Manchester Guardian Weekly).

trau·ma·tol·o·gy (trô′mə tol′ə jē, trou′-), *n.* the scientific study of traumas or physical injuries.

trav., 1. travel or travels. 2. traveler.

trav·ail (trav′āl), *n.* **1.** toil; labor. **2. a.** trouble, hardship, or suffering: *Faint and sick with travail and fear* (Jeremy Taylor). **b.** severe pain; agony; torture. **3.** the labor and pain of childbirth.
—*v.i.* **1.** to toil; labor. **2.** to suffer the pains of childbirth; be in labor.
[< Old French *travail* < Late Latin *trepālium* torture device, ultimately < Latin *tri-* three + *pālus* stake]

trave (trāv), *n. Dialect.* **1. a.** a crossbeam. **b.** a part of a ceiling, etc., between crossbeams. **2.** a frame or enclosure for keeping a restive horse to be shod. [(definition 1) < Old French *trave* < Latin *trabs, trabis* beam; (definition 2) probably short for Old French *entrave* a fetter]

trav·el (trav′əl), *v.,* **-eled, -el·ing** or (*especially British*) **-elled, -el·ling,** *n.* —*v.i.* **1.** to go from one place to another; journey: *to travel across the country. He travels the fastest who travels alone* (Rudyard Kipling). **2** to go from place to place selling things: *He travels for a large firm.* **3.** to move; pass; proceed: *Light and sound travel in waves.* **4.** to walk or run: *A deer travels far and fast when chased.* **5.** to move in a fixed course, as a piece of mechanism. —*v.t.* **1.** to pass through or over: *to travel a road.* **2.** to walk or run along or over: *narrow ledges traveled only by mountain goats.*
—*n.* **1.** a going in trains, ships, cars, etc., from one place to another; journeying: *to spend a summer in travel.* **2.** movement in general. **3.** the length of stroke, speed, way of working, etc., of a part of a machine. **travels, a.** journeys: *Soon after we find him on his travels in Italy* (Samuel Taylor Coleridge). **b.** a book about one's experiences, visits, etc., while traveling: *We possess the travels of a native of . . . India in the fourth century* (Mountstuart Elphinstone).
[variant of *travail* in its sense of "labor, fatigue"]

trav·el·a·ble (trav′ə lə bəl, trav′lə-), *adj.* that can be traveled over: *Icy roads are not travelable.* Also, *especially British,* **travellable.**

travel agency or **bureau,** a business that arranges accommodations for travelers: *Intourist, the Soviet state travel agency, on Friday announced substantial reductions in the costs of Russian holidays for Britons* (Manchester Guardian).

travel agent, a person who arranges for travel accommodations, in a travel agency.

trav·eled (trav′əld), *adj.* **1.** that has done much traveling; experienced in travel. **2.** much used by travelers: *a well-traveled road.* **3.** *Geology.* (of blocks, boulders, etc.) moved to a distance from the original site. Also, *especially British,* **travelled.**

trav·el·er (trav′ə lər, trav′lər), *n.* **1.** a person or thing that travels. **2.** *Especially British.* a traveling salesman; commercial traveler. **3.** a piece of mechanism constructed to move in a fixed course. **4.** a sales slip that a customer takes with him for the recording of two or more purchases, as in different parts of a store. **5.** *Nautical.* **a.** an iron ring or thimble running freely on a rope, rod, or spar. **b.** the rope, rod, or spar on which such a ring slides. Also, *especially British,* **traveller.**

traveler's check, a check issued by a bank for a specified amount and signed by the buyer, who may use it as cash by signing it again in the presence of a witness, as a clerk in a store, hotel, etc.

trav·el·er's-joy (trav′ə lərz joi′, trav′lərz-), *n.* an Old World clematis with woody stems, often growing over wayside hedges, etc.

trav·el·er's-tree (trav′e lərz trē′, trav′lərz-), *n.* a large palmlike plant of the banana family native to Madagascar, so called because the base of its large leaf holds water which a passer-by may drink.

trav·el·ing crane (trav′ə ling, trav′ling), any crane for moving loads from one place to another, such as a bridge crane.

traveling salesman, a person whose work is going from place to place selling things for a company.

trav·el·ing-wave tube (trav′ə ling wāv′), a vacuum tube to amplify microwaves through a coil of wire. The electric field produced in the wire interacts with a beam of electrons to make the microwave stronger.

trav·el·la·ble (trav′ə lə bəl, trav′lə-), *adj. Especially British.* travelable.

trav·elled (trav′əld), *adj. Especially British.* traveled.

trav·el·ler (trav′ə lər, trav′lər), *n. Especially British.* traveler.

travelling post office, *British.* a railroad car in which mail in transit is sorted and classified.

travel of a projectile, (in a loaded cannon) the distance from the base of the projectile to the muzzle.

trav·e·logue or **trav·e·log** (trav′ə lôg, -log), *n.* a lecture describing travel, usually accompanied by pictures, or a motion picture depicting travel. [American English < *trave*(l) + *-logue,* as in *dialogue*]

trav·els (trav′əlz), *n.pl.* See under **travel,** *n.*

travel sickness, motion sickness.

tra·vers·a·ble (trav′ər sə bəl, trə vėr′-), *adj.* **1.** that can be passed across or through. **2.** *Law.* that can be denied.

tra·vers·al (trav′ər səl, trə vėr′-), *n.* a traversing or being traversed; traverse.

trav·erse (*v., adv.* trav′ərs, trə vėrs′; *n., adj.* trav′ərs), *v.,* **-ersed, -ers·ing,** *n., adj., adv.* —*v.t.* **1.** to pass across, over, or through: *We traversed the desert.* **2.** to lie, extend, or stretch across; cross; intersect: *Deeply worn footpaths . . . traversing the country* (Washington Irving). **3.** to go to and fro over or along (a place, etc.); cross: *The Duke traversed the apartment . . . in much agitation* (Scott). **4.** to ski diagonally across (a slope). **5.** to read, examine, or consider carefully: *A field too wide to be fully traversed* (Daniel Webster). **6.** to turn or bring (a thing) across; move sideways. **7.** to turn (a cannon, etc.) to the right or left. **8.** to go counter to; oppose; hinder; thwart. **9.** *Law.* (in pleading) to contradict or to deny formally. To traverse an indictment means to deny or disagree with an indictment. To traverse an office means to deny the validity of an inquest of office (a writ of inquiry into a question of property of the British crown). **10.** *Nautical.* to secure (a yard) fore and aft.
—*v.i.* **1.** to move, pass, or go across or back and forth; cross. **2.** to ski diagonally across a slope. **3.** (in the manège) to move or walk crosswise, as a horse that throws his croup to one side and his head to the other. **4.** to turn on or as if on a pivot; swivel. **5.** (in fencing) to glide the blade along that of the opponent's foil, toward the hilt, while applying pressure.
—*n.* **1.** the act of traversing; a passing across, over, or through; crossing. **2.** something put or lying across, as a crossbeam, transom, rung of a ladder, etc.; crosspiece. **3. a.** a screen, railing, or other barrier. **b.** an earth wall protecting a trench or an exposed place in a fortification. **4.** a gallery or loft from side to side in a church or other large building. **5.** a single line of survey carried across a region; distance across. **6.** a sideways motion of a ship, part in a machine, mountain climbers, etc. **7. a.** the zigzag course taken by a ship because of contrary winds or currents. **b.** any of the straight parts of such a course. **8.** a line that crosses other lines. **9.** a passage or way by which to cross: *This traverse may the poorest take Without oppress of toll* (Emily Dickinson). **10.** an obstacle; hindrance; opposition. **11. a.** a changing the direction of a gun to the right or left. **b.** the amount of such change. **12.** *Law.* a formal denial of something alleged to be a fact by the opposing side.
—*adj.* lying, passing, or extending across; cross; transverse.
—*adv.* across; crosswise.
[< Old French *traverser* < Late Latin *trānsversāre* < Latin *trānsversus;* see TRANSVERSE]

tra·vers·er (trav′ər sər, trə vėr′-), *n.* a person or thing that traverses.

traverse table, 1. a platform moving sideways on wheels, used on a railroad to shift cars from one set of rails to another parallel to it; transfer table. **2.** a table used in navigation to determine the difference of latitude and departure corresponding to any given course and distance.

trav·er·tin (trav′ər tin), *n.* travertine.

trav·er·tine (trav′ər tin, -tēn), *n.* a white or light-colored form of limestone deposited by springs in caves, etc., used in Italy as building material. [< Italian *travertino,* variant of *tivertino* < Latin *tīburtīnus* < *Tībur,* an ancient town of Latium (now Tivoli)]

trav·es·ty (trav′ə stē), *n., pl.* **-ties,** *v.,* **-tied, -ty·ing.** —*n.* **1. a.** an imitation of a serious novel, play, poem, or other literary work, arranged or worded in such a way as to make it seem ridiculous. Travesty is a form of literary burlesque. **b.** writing of this kind: *to be skilled in travesty.* **2.** any treatment or imitation that makes a serious thing seem ridiculous: *The trial was a travesty of justice, since the judge and jury were prejudiced.*
—*v.t.* to make (a serious subject or matter) ridiculous; imitate in an absurd or grotesque way. [(originally) adjective < French *travesti* disguised, past participle of *travestir* to disguise < Latin *trāns-* over + *vestīre* to dress < *vestis* garment. Compare TRANSVESTISM.]

tra·vois (trə voi′), *n., pl.* **-vois.** a primitive conveyance, originally used by North American Plains Indians, consisting of two long poles harnessed at one end to a horse or dog and trailing on the ground at the other, with crossbars, a platform, or a net for carrying loads. [American English < Canadian French *travois,* a pronunciation of *travails* spaces between the two bars in which a horse runs, plural of French *travail,* perhaps ultimately < Latin *trabs, trabis* beam. Compare TRAVE.]

tra·voise (trə voiz′), *n., pl.* **-vois·es.** travois.

trawl (trôl), *n.* **1.** a large, strong net dragged along the bottom of the sea, used in commercial fishing, dredging for deep-sea scientific specimens, etc. **2.** *U.S.* a strong line supported by buoys and having many short lines with baited hooks attached to it.
—*v.i.* **1.** to fish with a net by dragging it along the bottom of the sea: *to trawl for herring.* **2.** to fish with a line supported by buoys and having many hooks attached. **3.** to troll. —*v.t.* **1.** to catch (fish) with a trawl or trawls. **2.** to troll (fish).

trawl·a·ble (trô′lə bəl), *adj.* capable of being trawled: . . . *trawlable stocks of unused fish in the Great Lakes* (A. L. Newman).

trawl·er (trô′lər), *n.* **1.** a person who trawls. **2.** a boat used in trawling.

trawl·er·man (trô′lər man′, -mən), *n., pl.* **-men.** a man who fishes with a trawl or works on a trawler: *It is difficult to find a trawlerman, who has fished off Iceland in the last few months who has not a few well-chosen words to say in its favor* (London Times).

trawl line, a trawl (*n.* def. 2).

trawl net, a trawl (*n.* def. 1).

tray (trā), *n.* **1.** a flat, shallow holder or container with a low rim around it: *to carry dishes on a tray.* **2.** a tray with dishes of food on it: *The nurse brought a breakfast tray to the sick man.* **3.** a shallow box that fits into a trunk, cabinet, etc.: *to keep instruments in trays.* **4.** *Dialect.* any of various shallow open vessels. [Old English *trēg*]

tray agriculture, hydroponics.

tray·ful (trā′fu̇l), *n., pl.* **-fuls.** as much or as many as a tray will hold: *a trayful of sandwiches.*

treach·er·ous (trech′ər əs), *adj.* **1.** not to be trusted; not faithful; disloyal: *The treacherous soldier carried reports to the enemy.* **2.** having a false appearance of strength, security, etc.; not reliable; deceiving: *Thin ice is treacherous.* —**treach′er·ous·ly,** *adv.* —**treach′er·ous·ness,** *n.* —**Syn. 1.** traitorous, perfidious. **2.** deceptive, unstable.

treach·er·y (trech′ər ē), *n., pl.* **-er·ies. 1.** a breaking of faith; betrayal of trust; treacherous behavior; deceit: *Arthur's kingdom was destroyed by treachery.* **2.** treason. [< Old French *trecherie,* and *tricherie* < *trechier,* and *trichier* to cheat, perhaps < Germanic. Compare TRICK.] —**Syn. 1.** See **disloyalty.**

trea·cle (trē′kəl), *n.* **1.** *British.* molasses, especially that produced during the refining of sugar. **2.** anything too sweet or cloying, especially excessive sentimentality: *Hortense Calisher . . . has concocted something far richer and immeasurably rarer than the usual dreadful treacle of youthful domestic odyssey* (Time). **3.** *Obsolete.* a sovereign remedy; panacea. **4.** *Obsolete.* an antidote for poison or poisonous bites. [< Old French *triacle* antidote < Latin *thēriaca* < Greek *thēriakḗ* (*antidotos*) (antidote against) poisonous reptiles < *thērion* (diminutive) < *thēr* beast. Doublet of THERIACA.]

trea·cli·ness (trē′klē nis), *n.* treacly quality; excessive sweetness or sentimentality:

Admittedly we have to suffer a few songs of a treacliness that I am convinced must be as obnoxious to children as they are to me (Punch).

trea·cly (trē′klē), *adj.* **1.** excessively sweet or sentimental; sugared; honeyed: *Mrs. Snow has written a pleasant, better than usual, not too treacly life of the man* (Scientific American). **2.** sweet or sticky like treacle: *"Open your mouth," she said pouring out the treacly liquid* (Punch).

tread (tred), *v.,* **trod** or (*Archaic*) **trode, trod·den** or **trod, tread·ing,** *n.* —*v.i.* **1.** to set the foot down; walk; step: *to tread through the meadow.* **2.** to step heavily (on or upon); trample: *Don't tread on the flower beds.* **3.** (of male birds) to copulate. —*v.t.* **1.** to put the foot or feet on; walk on or through; step on: *to tread the streets.* **2.** to press under; trample on; crush: *to tread grapes. Tread out the fire before you go away.* **3.** to make, form, or do by walking: *Cattle had trodden a path to the pond.* **4.** to follow; pursue: *to tread the path of virtue.* **5.** to treat with cruelty; oppress. **6.** (of male birds) to copulate with (the hen).
—*n.* **1.** the act or sound of treading: *the tread of marching feet.* **2.** a way of walking: *to walk with a heavy tread. Were it ever so airy a tread, My heart would hear her and beat* (Tennyson). **3. a.** the part of stairs or a ladder that a person steps on: *The stair treads were covered with rubber to prevent slipping.* **b.** the width of a step from front to back, measured between risers. **4. a.** the part of a wheel or tire that touches the ground. **b.** the pattern left by the grooves or ridges in a tire: *The new tire left a deep tread in the snow.* **5.** the part of a rail or rails that the wheels touch. **6.** either of the tracks of a caterpillar tractor or similar vehicle. **7.** the distance between opposite wheels of an automobile. **8.** the sole of the foot or of a shoe. **9.** the cicatricle or chalaza of an egg. **10.** a footprint.
treads, injuries at the coronet of a horse's foot, caused by the shoe on the opposite foot or on the foot of the adjacent horse in a team: *A quittor . . . arises often from treads* (J. Bartlet).
[Old English *tredan*] —**tread′er,** *n.*

trea·dle (tred′əl), *n., v.,* **-dled, -dling.** —*n.* **1.** a lever worked up and down by the foot to operate a machine: *the treadle of a sewing machine.* **2.** *British.* a pedal of a bicycle. —*v.i.* to work a treadle. [probably Old English *tredel* step, stair < *tredan* to tread]

tread·mill (tred′mil′), *n.* **1.** an apparatus to turn something by having a person or animal walk on the moving steps of a wheel or of a sloping, endless belt. **2.** any wearisome or monotonous round of work or life: *a kind of mental treadmill, where you are perpetually climbing, but never rise an inch* (Scott).

Treadmill Train (def. 1)

treads (tredz), *n. pl.* See under **tread,** *n.*

treas., 1. treasurer. **2.** treasury.

trea·son (trē′zən), *n.* **1.** the betrayal of one's country or ruler. Treason by a citizen of the United States, as defined in the Constitution, consists of ". . . only in levying war against them, or in adhering to their enemies, giving them aid and comfort" (Article 3, Section 3). An act against any individual does not constitute treason. **2.** the betrayal of a trust, duty, friend, etc.; treachery: *and in trust I have found treason* (Queen Elizabeth I of England). [< Anglo-French *treson* < Latin *trāditiō, -ōnis.* Doublet of TRADITION.] —**Syn. 1.** See **disloyalty.**

trea·son·a·ble (trē′zə nə bəl, trēz′nə-), *adj.* of or involving treason; traitorous: *He virtually accused the Truman Administration of treasonable delay in making the super-weapon* (Newsweek). —**trea′son·a·ble·ness,** *n.*

trea·son·a·bly (trē′zə nə blē, trēz′nə-), *adv.* in a treasonable manner.

trea·son·ous (trē′zə nəs, trēz′nəs), *adj.* treasonable. —**trea′son·ous·ly,** *adv.*

treas·ur·a·ble (trezh′ər ə bəl, trā′zhər-), *adj.* fit or worthy to be treasured; valuable; precious: *a treasurable book.*

treas·ure (trezh′ər, trā′zhər), *n., v.,* **-ured, -ur·ing.** —*n.* **1.** wealth or riches stored up; valuable things: *The pirates buried treasure along the coast. The palace contains treasures.* **2.** any thing or person that is much loved or valued: *The silver teapot was the old lady's chief treasure. The human heart has hidden treasures* (Charlotte Brontë). —*v.t.* **1.** to value highly: *She treasures that doll more than all her other toys.* **2.** to put away for future use; store up: *The patient search and vigil long Of him who treasures up a wrong* (Byron). [< Old French *tresor* < Latin *thēsaurus.* Doublet of THESAURUS.]
—**Syn.** *v.t.* **1.** cherish, prize. **2.** hoard.

treasure house, any place that contains something valuable: *The sea is a treasure house of minerals and food. Salamanca . . . is an architectural treasure house, with its sumptuous buildings, twin cathedrals . . . and its vast Baroque main square* (Charles J. Rolo).

treasure hunt, 1. a search for something of value: *Last week he ended a nine year treasure hunt, exhumed the first complete fossil skeleton of an Oreopithecus (mountain ape)* (Time). **2.** a game, the winner being the one who first finds what has been hidden: *The main event of the morning . . . would be a treasure hunt, for which Kieser and a diving companion would hide a dozen aluminum pie plates on the channel bottom, to represent the treasure* (New Yorker).

treas·ur·er (trezh′ər ər, trā′zhər-), *n.* a person in charge of the money of a club, society, corporation, government body, etc. *Abbr.:* treas.

treas·ur·er·ship (trezh′ər ər ship, trā′-zhər-), *n.* the position or term of office of a treasurer.

Treasure State, a nickname of Montana.

treas·ure-trove (trezh′ər trōv′, trā′zhər-), *n.* **1.** money, jewels, or other treasure that a person finds, especially if the owner of it is not known. **2.** (in English law) gold or silver, money, bullion, etc., found hidden in the ground or other place, the owner of it not known. **3.** any valuable discovery. [< Anglo-French *tresor trove* treasure found; *trove,* past participle of *trover* find]

treas·ur·y (trezh′ər ē, trā′zhər-), *n., pl.* **-ur·ies. 1.** a building, room, or other place where money or valuables are kept for security. **2.** money owned; funds: *We voted to pay for the party out of the club treasury.* **3.** Also, **Treasury.** the department that has charge of the income and expenses of a country. **4.** a place where treasure is kept. **5.** a book or person thought of as a valued source: *a treasury of modern poetry, a treasury of wisdom.*

treasury bill, an instrument of credit issued by a government when money is needed. These bills are drawn for three or six months, bear no interest, and are sold at a discount which varies with the rate current in the money market.

treasury note, a note or bill issued by the Treasury of the United States and receivable as legal tender for all debts.

Treas·ur·ys (trezh′ər ēz, trā′zhər-), *n.pl. U.S.* bonds or other securities issued by the treasury.

treat (trēt), *v.t.* **1.** to act or behave toward; deal with: *to treat a car with care. We must treat our elders with respect.* **2.** to think of; consider; regard: *He treated his mistake as a joke.* **3.** to deal with to relieve or cure: *The dentist is treating my tooth.* **4.** to deal with to bring about some special result: *to treat a metal plate with acid in engraving.* **5.** to deal with; discuss: *This magazine treats the progress of medicine.* **6.** to express in literature or art; represent: *to treat a theme realistically.* **7.** to entertain with food, drink, or amusement: *He treated his friends to ice cream.* —*v.i.* **1.** to deal with a subject. **2.** to discuss terms; arrange terms: *Messengers came to treat for peace.* **3.** to pay the cost of a treat or entertainment: *I'll treat today.*
treat of, to deal with; discuss: *"The Medical Journal" treats of the progress of medicine.*
—*n.* **1.** a gift of food, drink, or amusement: *"This is my treat," she said.* **2.** anything that gives pleasure; pleasure; delight: *Being in the country is a treat to her. It was a treat to see the joy in her face.*
[Middle English *tretien* < Old French *traitier* < Latin *tractāre* (originally) drag violently, handle (frequentative) < *trahere* to drag] —**treat′er,** *n.*
—**Syn.** *v.t.* **7.** regale, feast. *-v.i.* **2.** negotiate.

treat·a·ble (trē′tə bəl), *adj.* that can be treated; suitable to be treated: *Parkinsonism is one of the most treatable of all central nervous system diseases, the doctors state* (Science News Letter).

trea·tise (trē′tis), *n.* **1.** a book or writing dealing with something. A treatise is more formal and systematic than most books or writings. *Never literary attempt was more unfortunate than my Treatise of Human Nature. It fell dead-born from the press* (David Hume). **2.** *Archaic.* a story; tale; narrative; description. [Middle English *tretis* < Anglo-French *tretiz* < Old French *traitier;* see TREAT]

treat·ment (trēt′mənt), *n.* **1.** the act or process of treating: *My cold won't yield to treatment.* **2.** a way of treating: *This cat has suffered from bad treatment.* **3.** a thing done or used to treat something else, such as a disease. **4.** a detailed outline of a proposed motion picture, television script, etc.

trea·ty (trē′tē), *n., pl.* **-ties. 1. a.** an agreement, especially one between nations, signed and approved by each nation. **b.** the document embodying such an agreement: *The peace treaty was signed in Paris.* **2.** *Archaic.* **a.** negotiation: *The treaty was conducted very orderly* (Benjamin Franklin). **b.** any agreement; covenant; compact. **c.** entreaty; persuasion; request. [< Old French *traite,* or *traitie* < Latin *tractātus* discussion < *tractāre;* see TREAT]

treaty Indian, *U.S. and Canada.* a member of a tribe or group of Indians who live on reserves and receive treaty money and other treaty rights.

treaty money, *U.S. and Canada.* an annual payment made by the federal government to treaty Indians.

treaty port, any of various ports in China, Japan, and Korea, formerly required by treaty to be kept open to foreign commerce.

treaty rights, *U.S. and Canada.* the rights enjoyed through treaty with the government by treaty Indians, including the right to hold land on a reserve and to receive treaty money.

tre·ble (treb′əl), *adj., v.,* **-bled, -bling,** *n.* —*adj.* **1.** three times as much or as many; triple: *His salary is treble mine.* **2.** *Music.* **a.** of, having to do with, or for the treble; soprano: *a treble voice.* **b.** high-pitched; shrill: *treble tones.*
—*v.t., v.i.* **1.** to make or become three times as much or as many; triple: *He trebled his money by buying a dog for $5 and selling it for $15.* **2.** *Obsolete.* to sing the treble part.
—*n.* **1.** *Music.* **a.** the highest part in harmonized composition; soprano. **b.** a voice, singer, or instrument that takes this part. **c.** (in change ringing) the highest-pitched and smallest bell of a peal. **2.** a shrill, high-pitched voice, sound, or note.
[< Old French *treble* < Latin *triplus.* Doublet of TRIPLE.]

treble clef, *Music.* a symbol indicating that the pitch of the notes on a staff is above middle C.

treble staff, *Music.* a staff with the treble clef.

tre·bly (treb′lē), *adv.* three times; triply.

treb·u·chet (treb′yu̇ shet), *n.* a machine of war used in the Middle Ages for hurling stones, etc., somewhat like a catapult. [< Old French *trebuchet* < *trebuchier* to stumble, fall < *tres* over (< Latin *trāns*) + *buc* trunk of the body < Germanic (compare Frankish *būk* belly, Old High German *būh*)]

tre·buck·et (trē′buk it), *n.* trebuchet.

tre·cen·tist (trā chen′tist), *n.* **1.** an admirer of Italian art and literature of the trecento. **2.** a follower of the style of the trecento.

tre·cen·to (trā chen′tō), *n.* the 1300's, with reference to Italy, and especially to the Italian art and literature of that period. [< Italian *trecento,* short for *mille trecento* one thousand three hundred]

treck (trek), *v.i., v.t., n.* trek.

tree (trē), *n., v.,* **treed, tree·ing.** —*n.* **1.** a large perennial plant with a woody trunk, branches, and leaves. **2.** any of certain bushes, shrubs, or perennial herbs that resemble trees in form or size, such as the banana and plantain. **3.** a piece or structure of wood for some special purpose: *a clothes tree, a shoe tree.* **4.** anything like a tree with its branches: *A family or genealogical tree is a diagram with branches, showing how the members of a family are descended and related.* **5.** a treelike mass of crystals forming from a solution. **6.** *Archaic.* a gallows. **7.** *Archaic.* the cross on which Christ was crucified. **8.** *Scottish.* a staff; cudgel.

bark up the wrong tree, to pursue the wrong object or use the wrong means to attain it: *If you think to run a rig on me, you have made a mistake . . . and barked up the wrong tree* (Thomas C. Haliburton)

up a tree, *Informal.* in a difficult position: *He was deploring the dreadful predicament in which he found himself, a house full of old women . . . "Reg'larly up a tree, by jingo!" proclaimed the modest boy, who could not face the gentlest of her sex* (Thackeray).

—*v.t.* **1.** to furnish with a tree (beam, bar, wooden handle, etc.): *to tree the roof of a coal mine, to tree a spade or a pick.* **2.** to stretch or shape (a shoe or boot) on a tree. **3.** to chase up a tree; force to take refuge in a tree: *The cat was treed by a dog. The hiker was treed by a bull.* **4.** *Informal.* to put into a difficult position. —*v.i.* **1.** to take refuge in a tree. **2.** to assume a treelike or branching form.

[Old English *trēo*]

tree asp, any of a group of poisonous African snakes, such as the mamba.

tree celandine, plume poppy.

tree crab, a palm crab.

tree creeper, any of various small birds that creep up and down the branches of trees and bushes looking for food, as the brown creeper.

tree farm, *Especially U.S.* any place where trees are grown as a business.

tree fern, any of several groups of ferns of tropical and subtropical regions that grow to the size of a tree, with a woody, trunklike stem and fronds at the top.

Tree Fern (20 to 30 ft. tall)

tree frog, any of a family of mostly small frogs with sticky disks on their feet that enable them to climb trees, as the spring peeper; tree toad.

tree heath, a shrubby heath of southern Europe; brier.

tree hopper, any of a group of insects that live in trees and have mouth parts adapted to sucking. Some tree hoppers are very small and oddly shaped, and can leap long distances.

tree house, a platform, with or without sides and roof, built in a tree, now usually a playhouse.

tree kangaroo, a kangaroo of northern Australia and New Guinea that lives in trees.

tree·less (trē′lis), *adj.* without trees.

tree·like (trē′līk′), *adj.* like a tree in structure or appearance; arboraceous.

tree line, the line or level on a mountain above which no trees grow.

tree·lined (trē′līnd′), *adj.* with trees lining the side or sides: *This treelined village street, charmingly unaware of the passage of time, is one of the most perfect in New England* (New Yorker).

tree moss, **1.** any moss or lichen that grows on trees. **2.** any mosslike plant of branched form like a miniature tree, as the club moss.

tre·en (trē′ən, trēn), *n., pl.* **-en,** *adj.* —*n.* woodenware, especially bowls, dishes, or the like; treenware. —*adj.* wooden: . . . *a treen paten of ancient date* (Athenaeum). [Old English *trēowen* made of wood < *trēo* tree]

tree·nail (trē′nāl′; tren′əl, trun′-), *n.* a round pin of hard, dry wood for fastening timbers together. Also, **trenail, trunnel.** [Middle English *trenayl* < *tree* wood + *nail* nail]

tre·en·ware (trē′ən wãr′, trēn′-), *n.* treen.

tree of heaven, the ailanthus.

tree of knowledge, (in the Bible) the tree in Eden whose fruit, though forbidden, was eaten by Adam and Eve through the tempting of the serpent; knowledge of good and evil. Genesis 2:9, 16-17; 3:1-7.

tree of life, in the Bible: **1.** a tree in the center of Eden whose fruit gave immortality. Genesis 2:9; 3:22. **2.** a tree in the heavenly Jerusalem, the leaves of which were for the healing of the nations. Revelation 22:2. **3.** arbor vitae.

Tree Planters' State, a nickname of Nebraska.

tree ring, an annual ring.

tree-rip·ened (trē′rī′pənd), *adj.* allowed to ripen on the tree: *You begin with slices of grapefruit, melon, banana, papaya, and pineapple, all trucked in, tree-ripened, from Mexico's tropical lowlands* (Maclean's).

tree·scape (trē′skāp), *n.* a landscape full of trees or a painting of this.

tree shrew, any of a group of squirrellike, insect-eating mammals that live in trees, found in India, Borneo, etc.

tree sparrow, **1.** a sparrow with reddish-brown crown and a dark spot on the breast, that nests in northern North America and winters in the United States. **2.** a European sparrow related to the English sparrow.

tree surgeon, a person who practices tree surgery.

tree surgery, the treatment of diseased or damaged trees by filling cavities, cutting away parts, etc.

tree swallow, a North American swallow with a bluish or bluish-green back and a white breast, that nests in a hole in a tree or in a birdhouse.

tree toad, a tree frog; hyla. It has adhesive disks or suckers on its toes.

tree·top (trē′top′), *n.* the top or uppermost part of a tree.

Tree Toad (about 3 in. long)

tref (trāf), *adj.* forbidden by Jewish law; not kosher: *Pork and clams are tref foods.* [< Yiddish *tref* < Hebrew *ṭrēphāh* (literally) that which is torn (see Leviticus 17:15) < *ṭāraf* to tear]

tre·foil (trē′foil), *n.* **1.** any of various plants of the pea family having three leaflets to each leaf, as the clover, black medic, and tick trefoil. **2.** an ornament like a threefold leaf. [< Anglo-French *trifoil* < Latin *trifolium* three-leaved plant < *tri-* three + *folium* leaf. Doublet of TRIFOLIUM.]

Trefoils (def. 2)

tre·foiled (trē′foild), *adj.* of or having ornaments shaped like threefold leaves.

tre·ha·la (tri hä′lə), *n.* the substance of the cocoons of a beetle, weevil, or other coleopterous insect of Asia Minor. [< New Latin *trehala,* ultimately < Persian *tīghāl*]

tre·ha·lose (trē′hə lōs), *n.* a white crystalline sugar obtained from trehala, various fungi, yeast, etc. *Formula:* $C_{12}H_{22}O_{11}$

treil·lage (trā′lij), *n.* a lattice or trellis to support climbing plants, vines, etc. [< earlier French *treillage* < *treille* trellised arbor; latticework < Latin *tricla,* earlier *trichila* arbor, summerhouse, short for *triclīnium*]

trek (trek), *v.,* **trekked, trek·king,** *n.* —*v.i.* **1.** to travel slowly; travel; migrate: *to trek to California.* **2.** *Informal.* to go; proceed: *to trek down to the office.* **3.** (in South Africa) to travel by ox wagon. —*v.t.* (in South Africa) to draw (a vehicle or load), as an ox. —*n.* **1.** a trekking; journey. **2.** a stage of a journey between one stopping place and the next. **3.** (in South Africa) a traveling in a group, as pioneers into undeveloped country. Also, **treck.**

[< Afrikaans *trek,* verb < Dutch *trekken* to march, journey; (originally) to draw, pull]

trek Boer or **boer,** (in South Africa) a Boer who wanders from place to place with his livestock according to the condition of the veld: *Beyond the Orange on the fringe of the Kalahari desert moved . . . poverty-stricken trek boers* (Eric Walker).

trek·ker (trek′ər), *n.* a person who treks.

trel·lis (trel′is), *n.* **1.** a frame of light strips of wood or metal crossing one another with open spaces in between; lattice, especially one supporting growing vines. **2.** a summerhouse or other structure with sides of lattice, used as a shady retreat in summer. —*v.t.* **1.** to furnish with a trellis; enclose with lattice. **2.** to support or train (vines, etc.) on a trellis. **3.** to cross or interweave as in a trellis. [< Old French *trelis* < Vulgar Latin *trilīcius* < Latin *trilīx, -icis* triple-twilled < *tri-* three + *līcium* thread]

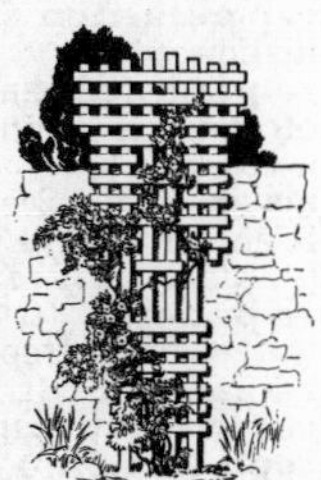
Trellis (def. 1)

trel·lis·work (trel′is wėrk′), *n.* work made of crossed or interwoven strips with open spaces in between; latticework.

trem·a·tode (trem′ə tōd, trē′mə-), *n.* any of various flatworms that live as parasites in or on other animals, as a variety which infests the lungs of sheep and a variety that lives in the blood vessels of man, causing schistosomiasis; fluke. —*adj.* of or belonging to the trematodes. [< New Latin *Trematoda* the class name < Greek *trēmatōdēs* with holes; having a vent to the intestinal canal < *trêma, -atos* hole + *eîdos* form]

trem·a·toid (trem′ə toid, trē′mə-), *n., adj.* trematode.

trem·ble (trem′bəl), *v.,* **-bled, -bling,** *n.* —*v.i.* **1.** to shake because of fear, excitement, weakness, cold, etc.: *The old woman's hands trembled. Her voice trembled with emotion.* **2.** to feel fear, anxiety, etc.: *Don't go out in that storm—I tremble for your safety.* **3.** to move gently: *The leaves trembled in the breeze.* —*v.t.* **1.** to cause to tremble or shake: . . . *joined by an old man who pumped his knees and trembled his hands* (New Yorker). **2.** to utter tremulously or falteringly: . . . *and trembling out prayers, and wailing to die* (Adah Menken).

—*n.* a trembling: *There was a tremble in her voice as she began to recite.*

trembles, a. *U.S.* a disease of cattle and sheep in the western and central United States, caused by a poison in white snakeroot and rayless goldenrod, and characterized by weakness and trembling. **b.** *U.S.* this disease transmitted to man in milk, butter, etc.; milk sickness. **c.** any disease or condition characterized by an involuntary shaking, as louping ill.

[< Old French *trembler* < Medieval Latin *tremulare* < Latin *tremulus;* see TREMULOUS]

—**Syn.** *v.i.* **1.** shiver, quake, shudder, quiver, vibrate. See **shake.**

trem·ble·ment (trem′bəl mənt), *n.* **1.** a trembling. **2.** a tremor.

trem·bler (trem′blər), *n.* **1.** a person or thing that trembles. **2.** an automatic vibrating device which alternately makes and breaks an electric circuit.

trem·bles (trem′bəlz), *n.pl.* See under **tremble,** *n.*

trem·bling·ly (trem′bling lē), *adv.* in a trembling manner; tremulously.

trem·bly (trem′blē), *adj.* trembling; tremulous.

trem·el·lose (trem′ə lōs), *adj. Botany.* shaking like jelly; of a jellylike consistency, as certain fungi. [< New Latin *Tremella* the genus name (diminutive) < Latin *tremula,* feminine of *tremulus* + English *-ose*[1]; see TREMULOUS]

tre·men·dous (tri men′dəs), *adj.* **1.** very great; enormous; immense: *a tremendous house, a tremendous sum, a wrestler of tremendous strength.* **2.** *Informal.* excellent; memorable; wonderful; extraordinary: *to have a tremendous time.* **3.** dreadful; awful: *The army suffered a tremendous defeat.* [< Latin *tremendus* (with English *-ous*) to be trembled at, gerundive of *tremere* to tremble] —**tre·men′dous·ly,** *adv.* —**tre·men′dous·ness,** *n.*

—**Syn. 3.** frightful, horrible.

trem·o·lan·do (trem′ə län′dō), *adj., adv., n., pl.* **-dos, -di** (dē). *Music.* —*adj., adv.* with a tremolo (a direction to perform a tremolo). —*n.* a note or passage rendered with a tremolo. [< Italian *tremolando,* present participle of *tremolare* tremble; warble < Medieval Latin *tremulare* < Latin *tremulus* tremulous]

trem·o·lant (trem′ə lənt), *adj.* having a tremulous or quavering sound, as certain organ pipes. —*n.* **1.** an organ pipe having a tremolant sound. **2.** a tremolo. [< Italian *tremolante* < *tremolare;* see TREMOLANDO]

trem·o·lite (trem′ə līt), *n.* a white or gray mineral, a variety of amphibole, consisting chiefly of a silicate of calcium and magnesium, occurring in fibrous masses or thin-bladed crystals. *Formula:* $Ca_2Mg_5Si_8O_{22}(OH)_2$ [< *Tremola,* valley in the Swiss Alps]

trem·o·lo (trem′ə lō), *n., pl.* **-los,** *adj. Music.* —*n.* **1.** a trembling or vibrating quality in musical tones. A tremolo in the voice is produced by a wavering of pitch and is used to express emotion. A bowed tremolo is produced on a violin, cello, etc., by rapidly repeating a tone with fast up-and-down strokes of the bow. A fingered tremolo on a stringed instrument is an effect very much like a trill or stroke. **2.** a device in an organ to produce this quality. —*adj.* of or like a tremolo. [< Italian *tremolo* < Latin *tremulus.* Doublet of TREMULOUS.]

trem·or (trem′ər), *n.* **1.** an involuntary shaking or trembling: *a nervous tremor in the voice.* **2. a.** a thrill of emotion or excitement. **b.** a state of emotion or excitement: *He went about all day in a tremor of delight* (Dickens). **3.** a tremulous or vibrating movement. An earthquake is called an earth tremor. [< Latin *tremor* a trembling < *tremere* to tremble] —**Syn. 1.** quaking, quivering.

trem·u·lant or **trem·u·lent** (trem′yə-lənt), *adj.* tremulous; trembling. [< Medieval Latin *tremulans, -antis,* present participle of *tremulare* < Latin *tremulus* tremulous]

trem·u·lous (trem′yə ləs), *adj.* **1.** trembling; quivering; quavering: *the tremulous flutter of young leaves, a voice tremulous with sobs.* **2.** timid; fearful: *tremulous beliefs* (Lionel Johnson). **3.** (of writing) wavering; shaky. [< Latin *tremulus* (with English *-ous*) < *tremere* to tremble. Doublet of TREMOLO.] —**trem′u·lous·ly,** *adv.* —**trem′-u·lous·ness,** *n.* —**Syn. 1.** shaking, vibrating.

tre·nail (trē′nāl′; tren′əl, trun′-), *n.* treenail.

trench (trench), *n.* **1.** a long, narrow ditch with earth, sandbags, etc., put up in front to protect soldiers against enemy fire and attack. **2.** a deep furrow; ditch: *to dig a trench around a tent to drain off water.* **3.** a cut, scar, or deep wrinkle.

trenches, a system of ditches built as a military defense line: *After World War I, the canard spread that France had even collected rent for the use of trenches on its soil* (Time).

[< Old French *trenche* < *trenchier;* see the verb]

—*v.t.* **1.** to dig a trench or trenches in (the ground). **2.** to fortify or surround with a trench or trenches. **3. a.** to cut up; slice. **b.** to cut off. **c.** to cut into. **d.** to cut (one's way). —*v.i.* to dig ditches or trenches.

trench on or **upon, a.** to trespass upon: *Though I squandered my own property, I have not trenched on yours* (Mrs. H. Wood). *This scheme . . . may seem to trench on the liberty of individuals* (J. Robertson). **b.** to come close to; border on: *a remark that trenched closely on slander.*

trench to or **unto,** *Obsolete.* to extend in effect to: *In law it is said the demise of the King, and a gift unto the King, without saying more, trenches to his successors* (Sir H. Finch).

[< Old French *trenchier* to cut, apparently ultimately < Latin *truncāre* lop off < *truncus* mutilated]

trench·an·cy (tren′chən sē), *n.* trenchant quality; sharpness.

trench·ant (tren′chənt), *adj.* **1.** sharp; keen; cutting: *trenchant wit, a trenchant remark.* **2.** vigorous and effective: *a trenchant policy.* **3.** clear-cut; distinct: *in trenchant outline against the sky.* **4.** *Archaic.* having a keen edge; sharp: *the trenchant blade* (Samuel Butler). [< Old French *trenchant,* present participle of *trenchier* to cut; see TRENCH, verb] —**trench′ant·ly,** *adv.*

trench coat, a kind of belted raincoat with epaulets on the shoulder, usually made of cotton gabardine or poplin.

trench·er[1] (tren′chər), *n.* **1. a.** a wooden platter, on which meat or other food was formerly served and carved. **b.** such a platter with the food on it. **2.** *Obsolete.* a slice of bread used instead of a plate or platter. **3.** *Obsolete.* a knife.

—*adj.* of or having to do with a trencher.

[< Anglo-French *trenchour,* Old North French *trencheor* knife < Vulgar Latin *truncatōrium* place for cutting, slicing < Latin *truncāre* lop off; see TRENCH, verb]

trench·er[2] (tren′chər), *n.* **1.** a person who makes trenches. **2.** *Obsolete.* a person who carves.

trencher cap, a mortarboard (academic cap). [< *trencher*[1] flat piece + *cap*]

trench·er·man (tren′chər mən), *n., pl.* **-men. 1.** a person who has a hearty appetite; eater. **2.** a hanger-on; parasite.

trench·es (tren′chiz), *n.pl.* See under **trench,** *n.*

trench fever, an infectious fever caused by a rickettsia and transmitted by lice. It affected many soldiers in the trenches during World War I.

trench foot or **feet,** a foot disease like frostbite, caused by prolonged exposure to cold and wet, chiefly affecting soldiers.

trench knife, a knife with a long, double-edged blade, for use in close combat.

trench mortar, a small mortar firing shells at high angles over short ranges.

trench mouth, 1. a contagious, painful inflammation of the mouth accompanied by sores and ulcers on the lining of the gums, cheeks, and tongue; Vincent's stomatitis; Vincent's infection. **2.** any inflammation of the mouth and gums.

trench warfare, hostilities carried on by means of or in trenches.

trend (trend), *n.* **1.** the general direction; course: *The hills have a western trend.* **2.** the general course or drift; tendency: *a trend toward smaller cars. The trend of modern living is away from many old customs.* **3.** fashion; style; vogue: *the latest trend in clothes, to set or spot a new trend.* [< verb]

—*v.i.* **1.** to turn off or bend in a certain direction; run: *a road trending to the north.* **2.** to have a general tendency; tend: *events that trend toward a reconciliation.*

[Middle English *trenden* roll about, turn, Old English *trendan*]

—**Syn.** *n.* **1, 2.** See **direction.**

trend line, a line on a graph representing a trend: *Despite some selective strengthening of prices in the chemical industry, the overall downward trend line will continue in 1965* (Wall Street Journal).

trend·set·ter (trend′set′ər), *n.* a person, or thing that establishes a new style or vogue: *The salon is the trendsetter for future shows in Britain, and many products and ideas make their debut there before being launched in Britain* (London Times).

trend·y (tren′dē), *adj. British Informal.* voguey.

Trent (trent), *n.* **Council of,** a general council of the Roman Catholic Church, held at Trent, Italy, from 1545 to 1563. It settled important points of church doctrine and rules and organized the Roman Catholic opposition to Protestantism.

tren·tal (tren′təl), *n.* a service of thirty requiem masses said either on the same day or on different days. [< Old French *trental* < Medieval Latin *trentale,* ultimately < Latin *trīgintā* thirty]

trente et qua·rante (träN′ tā kȧ räNt′), the card game of rouge et noir (thirty and forty being the winning and losing numbers). [< French *trente et quarante* (literally) thirty and forty]

Tren·tine (tren′tin, -tīn), *adj.* Tridentine: *. . . the decrees of the Trentine doctors which declared the attendances of Catholics at the Protestant services to be unlawful* (Charles Butler).

tre·pan[1] (tri pan′), *n., v.,* **-panned, -pan·ning.** —*n.* **1.** an early form of the trephine. **2.** a boring instrument, used for sinking shafts.

—*v.t.* **1.** to operate on with a trepan (trephine). **2.** to bore through with a trepan; cut a disk out of with a trepan or similar tool.

[< Medieval Latin *trepanum* < Greek *trýpanon* < *trýpē* hole < *trŷpân* to bore]

tre·pan[2] (tri pan′), *n., v.,* **-panned, -pan·ning.** *Archaic.* —*n.* **1.** a person who entraps or decoys others to his advantage and their ruin or loss. **2.** a trick; trap; snare.

—*v.t.* **1.** to entrap; ensnare. **2.** to do out of; cheat; swindle. Also, **trapan.**

[earlier *trapan* < *trap*[1]; spelling influenced by *trepan*[1]]

trep·a·na·tion (trep′ə nā′shən), *n.* trephination.

tre·pang (tri pang′), *n.* **1.** the dried flesh of any of a group of wormlike sea animals, used in China and the East Indies for making soup. See **sea cucumber** for picture. **2.** any of these animals.

[< Malay *tĕripang*]

tre·pan·ner[1] (tri pan′ər), *n.* a person who works with a trepan.

tre·pan·ner[2] (tri pan′ər), *n. Archaic.* a person who trepans; decoy; swindler.

treph·i·na·tion (tref′ə nā′shən), *n.* the operation of trephining: *Some examples of the art of . . . trephination in ancient and modern times are reviewed in the current issue of Man* [*a magazine*] (New Scientist).

tre·phine (tri fīn′, -fēn′), *n., v.,* **-phined, -phin·ing.** —*n.* a cylindrical saw with a removable center pin, used to cut out circular pieces from the skull. —*v.t.* to operate on with a trephine. [earlier *trafine,* alteration of *trapan,* variant of *trepan*[1]; spelling influenced by Latin *trēs fīnēs* three ends]

trep·id (trep′id), *adj.* scared; perturbed; agitated. [< Latin *trepidus*]

trep·i·da·tion (trep′ə dā′shən), *n.* **1.** nervous dread; fear; fright. **2.** a trembling; especially, a trembling of the limbs, as in palsy. **3.** a vibrating movement; vibration. [< Latin *trepidātiō, -ōnis* < *trepidāre* to tremble, be afraid < *trepidus* alarmed, trepid]

trep·o·ne·ma (trep′ə nē′mə), *n.* any of a group of spirochete bacteria parasitic in man and other warm-blooded mammals, including the bacterium that causes syphilis and relapsing fever. [< New Latin *Treponema* the genus name < Greek *trépein* to turn + *nêma* thread, yarn < *neîn* to spin thread]

trep·o·ne·ma·to·sis (trep′ə nē′mə tō′sis), *n., pl.* **-ses** (-sēz). a disease caused by a treponema: *Treponematoses mean infections with treponema. This big group of germs includes the spirochetes that cause syphilis, the germ that causes yaws, and various other related germs* (Science News Letter). [< New Latin *treponematosis* < *Treponema* treponema + *-osis* -osis]

tres·pass (tres′pəs, -pas), *v.i.* **1. a.** to go on somebody's property without any right: *The farmer put up "No Trespassing" signs to keep people off his farm.* **b.** *Law.* to commit any trespass. **2.** to go beyond the limits of what is right, proper, or polite: *I won't trespass on your time any longer.* **3.** to do wrong: sin: *as we forgive those who trespass against us* (Lord's Prayer).

—*n.* **1.** the act or fact of trespassing. **2.** a wrong; sin. **3.** *Law.* **a.** an unlawful act done by force against the person, property, or rights of another. **b.** an action to recover damages for such an injury.

[< Old French *trespasser* to trespass < *tres-* across (< Latin *trāns-*) + *passer* to pass (< *pas* a step < Latin *passus, -ūs*). Compare PACE[1].] —**tres′pass·er,** *n.*

—**Syn.** *v.i.* **1. a, 2.** encroach, infringe, invade. See **intrude.** —*n.* **1.** encroachment, infringement. **2.** transgression, offense.

tress (tres), *n.* a lock, curl, or braid of hair, especially of a woman or girl.

tresses, a. locks of long, flowing hair of a woman or girl: *. . . her loose falling tresses* (George Meredith). **b.** long shoots or tendrils, rays of the sun, etc.: *. . . luxuriant tresses of maidenhair fern* (Henry B. Tristram).

[< Old French *tresce,* and *trece* < Medieval Latin *trecia;* origin uncertain]

tressed (trest), *adj.* (of the hair) arranged in tresses; braided.

tress·es (tres′iz), *n.pl.* See under **tress,** *n.*

tres·sure (tresh′ər), *n. Heraldry.* a diminutive of the orle, consisting of a narrow band one fourth the width of the bordure, usually decorated with fleurs-de-lis. [< Old French *tressure* and *tresseor* hair band; braid < *tresser* to plait < *tresce* a plait; see TRESS]

tres·tine (tres′tīn′), *n.* the third tine from the base of an antler; royal antler. [< Latin *trēs* three + English *tine*]

tres·tle (tres′əl), *n.* **1.** a frame similar to a sawhorse, used as a support for a table top, etc. **2. a.** a supporting framework of timber, steel, etc., for carrying railroad tracks, a road, etc., across a gap. It is usually made of uprights or slanting pieces with diagonal braces, etc. **b.** a bridge, etc., having such a framework. [< Old French *trestel* crossbeam < Vulgar Latin *transtellum* < Latin *trānstrum* beam; see TRANSOM]

trestle table, a movable table made of boards laid upon trestles.

tres·tle·tree (tres′əl trē′), *n.* either of two horizontal, fore-and-aft timbers or bars secured to a masthead, one on each side, to support the crosstrees.

tres·tle·work (tres′əl wėrk′), *n.* any structure or construction consisting of a trestle or trestles; a support, bridge, or the like made of such structures.

tret (tret), *n.* an allowance formerly made to purchasers on goods sold by weight, after deduction for tare. [< Anglo-French *tret,* Old French *trait* a pull of the scale < *traire* to pull, draw < Latin *trahere.* Doublet of TRACE[2], TRACT[1], TRAIT.]

tre·val·ly (trə väl′ē), *n., pl.* **-lies** or (*collec-*

tively) **-ly.** a food fish of the carangoid family found in the waters around Australia. [origin uncertain]

trews (trüz), *n.pl. Scottish.* close-fitting trousers, or breeches combined with stockings, formerly worn by Irishmen and Scottish Highlanders, and still worn by certain Scottish regiments. [variant of earlier *trouse;* see TROUSERS]

trey (trā), *n.* a card, die, or throw of dice showing three spots; a three. [< Old French *trei* < Latin *trēs* three. Related to THREE.]

t.r.f., tuned radio frequency.

T.R.H., Their Royal Highnesses.

tri-, *combining form.* **1.** three; having three parts; having three ——: *Triangle = a plane figure having three angles. Trilogy = a group of three novels, plays, etc.*
2. three times; into three parts; in three directions: *Trisect = to divide into three parts.*
3. occurring once every third; three times in a ——; lasting for three ——: *Trimonthly = occurring every three months.*
4. containing three atoms, radicals, etc., of the substance specified, as in *trioxide, trisulfate.*
[< Latin, Greek *tri-*; < Latin *trēs, tria* or Greek *treîs, tría* three, or *trís* thrice]

tri·a·ble (trī′ə bəl), *adj.* **1.** that can be ascertained, tested, or proved. **2.** *Law.* that can be tried in a court of law. [< Anglo-French *triable* < *trier* to try (legally), Old French, to cull; origin unknown] **—tri′a·ble·ness,** *n.*

tri·ac·e·tate (trī as′ə tāt), *adj.* having three acetate radicals in the molecule. *—n.* **1.** a triacetate compound. *Formula:* $(CH_3COO-)_3$ **2.** something made from it, especially a fiber, film, etc., made from a triacetate cellulose acetate.

tri·ac·e·tin (trī as′ə tin), *n.* an oily liquid found in cod-liver oil, butter, and other fats, or derived by the action of acetic acid on glycerol, used in treating athlete's foot and other fungous diseases, in making celluloid, as a fixative for perfumes, and as a solvent of basic dyes. *Formula:* $C_9H_{14}O_6$ [< *triacet*(ate) + *-in*]

tri·ac·id (trī as′id), *adj.* **1.** (of a base or alcohol) having three hydroxyl (-OH) groups which may replace the hydrogen of an acid to form a salt or ester. **2.** having three replaceable acid atoms of hydrogen per molecule. *—n.* an acid of which one molecule contains three hydrogen atoms which may be replaced by basic atoms or groups.

tri·ad (trī′ad, -əd), *n.* **1.** a group or set of three, especially of three closely related persons or things. **2.** *Music.* a chord of three notes, especially one consisting of a given note (called the root) with its third (either major or minor) and fifth (either perfect, augmented, or diminished). **3.** *Chemistry.* an element, atom, or radical with a valence of three. [< Late Latin *trias, -adis* < Greek *triâs, -ados* < *treîs* three] **—Syn. 1.** trio, trinity.

tri·ad·ic (trī ad′ik), *adj.* **1.** of or having to do with a triad. **2.** constituting a triad. **3.** consisting of triads. **4.** *Chemistry.* that is a triad; trivalent.

tri·age (trī′ij), *n.* **1.** the act of sorting, as according to kind or quality. **2.** something sorted out, as the broken coffee beans separated from the whole coffee in sorting. [< Old French *triage* < *trier* to pick, cull]

tri·ag·o·nal (trī ag′ə nəl), *adj.* triangular. [alteration of *trigonal;* patterned on *tetragonal*]

tri·a junc·ta in u·no (trī′ə jungk′tə in yü′nō), *Latin.* three joined in one (the motto of the Order of the Bath).

tri·a·kai·dek·a·phobe (trī′ə kī dek′ə fōb), *n.* a person having an abnormal fear of the number 13: *Attention, all triakaidekaphobes! Next Friday is, b-r-r-r, the 13th* (Family Weekly). Also, **triskaidekaphobe.**

tri·a·kai·dek·a·pho·bi·a (trī′ə kī dek′ə-fō′bē ə), *n.* an abnormal fear of the number 13. [< Greek *triakaídeka,* neuter of *treiskaídeka* thirteen (< *treîs* three + *kaí* and + *déka* ten) + English *-phobia*] Also, **triskaidekaphobia.**

tri·al (trī′əl), *n.* **1. a.** the examination and determination of the facts and issues in a civil or criminal case by a court. **b.** the determination of the guilt or innocence of an accused person by a court. **2.** the act or process of trying or testing; a trying out; test: *He gave the motor another trial to see if it would start. Democracy is on trial in the world on a more colossal scale than ever before* (Charles F. Dole). **3.** experimentation by investigation, tentative action, use, etc.; experiment: *to learn by trial and error.* **4.** the fact or condition of being tried or tested; probation: *He is employed for two weeks on trial.* **5.** trouble; hardship; affliction: *the trials of pioneer life.* **6.** a cause of trouble or hardship: *to be a trial to one's parents.* **7.** an attempt to do something; endeavor; effort: *I proposed to make a trial for landing if the weather should suit* (John Smeaton). **8.** a preliminary competition in field or track events at a track meet.
—adj. **1.** made, done, used, or taken for or as a trial: *a trial model, a trial trip.* **2.** that is on trial: *a trial employee.* **3.** of or having to do with a trial in a law court: *trial testimony.*
[< Anglo-French *trial* < *trier* to try]
—Syn. *n.* **2. Trial, test, experiment** mean the process or way of discovering or proving something. **Trial** means the process of discovering the qualities of someone or something and establishing its (his) worth, genuineness, strength, effect, etc.: *He gave the soap a trial.* **Test** applies to a trial to end uncertainty about quality, genuineness, or presence, as by thorough examination, experiment, etc.: *The new plane passed all tests.* **Experiment** applies to a process to find out something still unknown or to test conclusions reached: *Experiments indicate the new drug will cure infections.* **5.** misfortune.

trial and error, a method of arriving at a desired result by repeated experiments until past errors are eliminated. **—tri′al-and-er′ror,** *adj.*

trial balance, a comparison of the items on each side of a double-entry ledger, in which the sum of the debits should equal the sum of the credits. If they are not equal, there is an error.

trial balloon, 1. something announced to be done or as likely to be done, especially on a small scale, in order to determine its acceptability to the general public or some particular group, body, etc. **2.** (originally) a small balloon launched to determine atmospheric conditions, especially direction and velocity of wind.

trial by jury, a courtroom trial in which a jury decides the facts in a case instead of a judge or judges.

trial court, a lower or district court in which the first hearing of a case is decided, as contrasted with an appellate court.

trial horse, a person, craft, or animal used as an opponent or competitor to keep another in practice while training for a race, etc.: *Workouts against a trial horse are not as good training as real trials* (London Times).

tri·al·ism (trī′ə liz əm), *n.* **1.** the doctrine of three distinct, ultimate substances or principles. **2.** a union of three countries or states.

tri·al·ist (trī′ə list), *n.* **1.** *Sports.* a person who takes part in a trial or preliminary match. **2.** an advocate or supporter of trialism.

trial judge, a judge who hears a case in a trial court.

trial jury, a jury consisting usually of 12 persons, chosen to decide a case in court; petit jury.

trial lawyer, a lawyer who specializes in presenting cases in court: *Clarence Darrow was one of America's greatest trial lawyers.*

trial marriage, companionate marriage for the purpose of testing the compatibility of the partners over a specific period of time.

trial run, a preliminary or experimental test of performance: *[A new] train . . . has been sidelined to eliminate some of the clatter and bounce observed during trial runs* (Newsweek).

tri·am·cin·a·lone (trī′əm sin′ə lōn), *n.* a steroid drug similar to cortisone, used in the treatment of arthritis, psoriasis, and other inflammatory conditions. *Formula:* $C_{25}H_{31}FO_8$

tri·an·gle (trī′ang′gəl), *n.* **1.** a figure, usually plane, having three sides and three angles. **2.** something having the form of a triangle; any three-cornered body, object, or space. **3.** a group or set of three; triad. **4.** a percussion instrument consisting of a steel rod bent into the form of a triangle, but open at one corner, struck with a small steel rod held in the hand. **5.** a flat, right-angled, straight-edged, triangular object of wood, vulcanite, etc., used with a T-square in drawing parallel, perpendicular, or diagonal lines. [< Latin *triangulum* < *tri-* three + *angulus* corner]

Triangles (def. 1) From left to right: equiangular, right, scalene

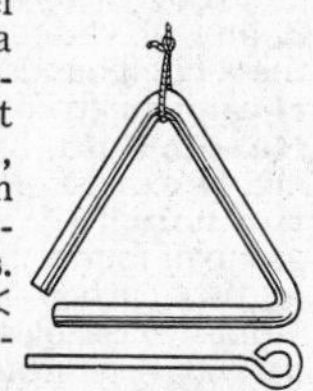

Triangle (def. 4)

tri·an·gu·lar (trī ang′gyə lər), *adj.* **1.** shaped like a triangle; contained by three sides and angles; three-cornered. **2.** relating to or taking place between three persons or parties; three-sided. **3.** constituting a triad or set of three; threefold. **4.** having to do with or relating to a triangle. **5. a.** of or having to do with a pattern of organization formerly standard in the infantry and certain other combat branches of the Armed Forces of the United States and some other countries, in which a division consisted of three regiments, a regiment of three battalions, and so on. **b.** characterized by such a pattern of organization. **—tri·an′gu·lar·ly,** *adv.*

tri·an·gu·lar·i·ty (trī ang′gyə lar′ə tē), *n.* the state or condition of being triangular; triangular form.

tri·an·gu·late (*v.* trī ang′gyə lāt; *adj.* trī-ang′gyə lit, -lāt), *v.,* **-lat·ed, -lat·ing,** *adj.* *—v.t.* **1.** to mark out or divide into triangles. **2.** to survey, measure, and map out (a region) by dividing (it) into triangles and measuring (their) angles and sides. **3.** to find out by trigonometry: *to triangulate the height of a mountain.* **4.** to make triangular; mark out or draw as a triangle.
—adj. **1.** composed of or marked with triangles. **2.** triangular.

tri·an·gu·la·tion (trī ang′gyə lā′shən), *n.* **1. a.** survey or measurement done by means of trigonometry. **b.** the series or network of triangles laid out for such measurement. **2.** division into triangles.

Tri·an·gu·li (trī ang′gyə lī), *n.* genitive of **Triangulum.**

Trianguli Aus·tra·lis (ôs trā′lis), genitive of **Triangulum Australe.**

Tri·an·gu·lum (trī ang′gyə ləm), *n., genitive* **Tri·an·gu·li.** a northern constellation near Andromeda. [< Latin *triangulum;* see TRIANGLE]

Triangulum Aus·tra·le (ôs trā′lē), *genitive* **Tri·an·gu·li Aus·tra·lis.** a southern constellation near Centaurus.

tri·ap·sal (trī ap′səl), *adj.* triapsidal.

tri·ap·si·dal (trī ap′sə dəl), *adj.* having three apses. [< *tri-* + Latin *apsis, -idis* apse + English *-al*[1]]

tri·ar·chy (trī′är kē), *n., pl.* **-ar·chies. 1.** a government by three persons. **2.** three persons ruling jointly; triumvirate. **3.** a group of three districts or states, each under its own ruler. [< Greek *triarchíā* < *tri-* three + *archíā* a rule]

Tri·as (trī′əs), *n.* the Triassic system or period.

Tri·as·sic (trī as′ik), *n. Geology.* **1.** the earliest period of the Mesozoic era, before the Jurassic, characterized by the domination of the earth by reptiles and much volcanic activity. **2.** the system of rocks of this time. *—adj.* of or having to do with this period or system of rocks. [< German *Trias,* a certain series of strata containing three types of deposit < Late Latin *trias;* see TRIAD]

tri·at·ic stay (trī at′ik), *Nautical.* **1.** a stay, usually of wire, between the head of a topmast and the head of the lower section of the next mast toward the stern. **2.** either of two ropes or cables, one attached to the head of the foremast and the other to the head of the mainmast, joined by a shackle and used in hoisting cargo from a hold. [origin uncertain]

tri·a·tom·ic (trī′ə tom′ik), *adj. Chemistry.* **1.** containing three atoms; consisting of molecules each containing three atoms. **2.** having three atoms or groups which can be replaced. **3.** trivalent.

tri·ax·i·al (trī ak′sē əl), *adj.* having three axes.

tri·a·zin (trī′ə zin, trī az′in), *n.* triazine.

tri·a·zine (trī′ə zēn, -zin; trī az′ēn, -in), *n.* **1.** one of three isomeric compounds, each having a ring of three carbon atoms and three nitrogen atoms. *Formula:* $C_3H_3N_3$ **2.** any of various substances derived from these compounds. [< *tri-* + *az*(o)- + *-ine*[2]]

tri·a·zo·ic (trī′ə zō′ik), *adj.* hydrazoic.

triazoic acid, hydrazoic acid, a poisonous, highly explosive acid. *Formula:* HN_3

tri·a·zole (trī′ə zōl, trī az′ōl), *n.* one of a group of four compounds, each having a ring of two carbon atoms and three nitrogen atoms. Triazoles are considered as pyrrole derivatives formed by the substitution of two nitrogen atoms for -CH groups. *Formula:* $C_2H_3N_3$

trib., tributary.

trib·ade (trib′əd), *n.* a woman who is homosexual; Lesbian. [< Latin *tribas, -adis* < Greek *tribás, -ádos* < *tríbein* to rub]

trib·al (trī′bəl), *adj.* **1.** of or having to do with a tribe or tribes. **2.** characteristic of a tribe.

trib·al·ism (trī′bə liz əm), *n.* **1.** the state of existing in separate tribes: *Touré tackled the tribalism that plagues all of Africa* (Time). **2.** tribal relation or feeling.

trib·al·ist (trī′bə list), *n.* a person who favors or supports tribalism: *Udomo discovers that he cannot survive politically without the support of the tribalists* (Harper's).

trib·al·is·tic (trī′bə lis′tik), *adj.* of or having to do with tribalism or tribalists.

trib·al·ize (trī′bə līz), *v.t.,* **-ized, -iz·ing.** to make or divide into tribes; give a tribal character to.

trib·al·ly (trī′bə lē), *adv.* according to tribe; by tribe or tribes.

tri·ba·sic (trī bā′sik), *adj. Chemistry.* **1.** (of an acid) having three hydrogen atoms which can be replaced by basic atoms or radicals. **2.** having three atoms or radicals of a univalent metal. **3.** containing three basic hydroxyl (-OH) radicals.

tribe (trīb), *n.* **1.** a group of people united by race and customs under the same leaders; ethnic group: *America was once the home of many Indian tribes.* **2.** a group of persons forming a community and claiming descent from a common ancestor. **3.** a class of persons; fraternity; set; lot (now often contemptuous): *the whole tribe of gossips. Society is . . . formed of two mighty tribes, the Bores and Bored* (Byron). **4.** *Biology.* a group in the classification of plants or animals, usually forming a subdivision of an order, and containing a number of genera (sometimes used as superior and sometimes as inferior to a family). **5.** any group or series of animals or plants: *the feathery tribe.* **6.** a class, group, kind, or sort of things. **7.** any of the twelve divisions of the ancient Hebrews, each claiming descent from a son of Jacob (Joshua 4:8): *the tribe of Judah, the ten lost tribes.* **8.** (in stock breeding) the descendants of a certain female animal through female offspring. **9.** in ancient Rome: **a.** one of the three divisions (Latins, Sabines, and Etruscans) of the Roman people. **b.** (later) one of the 30 political divisions of the Roman people, increased to 35 in 241 B.C. **10.** (in ancient Athens) the largest political subdivision; phyle. [< Latin *tribus, -ūs*]
—**Syn. 1, 2.** clan.

tribe·let (trīb′lit), *n.* a small tribe.

tribe·ship (trīb′ship), *n.* **1.** the condition of being a tribe. **2.** the territory of a tribe.

tribes·man (trībz′mən), *n., pl.* **-men.** a member of a tribe.

tribes·peo·ple (trībz′pē′pəl), *n.pl.* persons constituting a tribe; the members of a tribe: *China . . . has, living in adjacent border areas, tribespeople similar in stock to those on the Burma side* (Atlantic).

tribes·wom·an (trībz′wu̇m′ən), *n., pl.* **-wom·en.** a woman belonging to a tribe.

trib·o·e·lec·tric·i·ty (trib′ō i lek′tris′ə tē, -ē′lek-), *n.* static electricity. [< Greek *tríbos* a rubbing (< *tríbein* rub) + English *electricity*]

trib·o·lu·mi·nes·cence (trib′ō lü′mə nes′əns), *n.* the quality of emitting light under friction or violent pressure. [< Greek *tríbos* a rubbing (< *tríbein* rub) + English *luminescence*]

tri·bom·e·ter (trī bom′ə tər), *n.* an apparatus for measuring the force of friction in sliding surfaces. [< French *tribomètre* < Greek *tríbein* rub + *métron* measure]

tri·brach (trī′brak, trib′rak), *n. Greek and Latin Prosody.* a foot of three short syllables. [< Latin *tribrachys* < Greek *tríbrachys* < *tri-* three + *brachýs* short]

tri·brach·ic (trī brak′ik, tri-), *adj.* **1.** consisting of three short syllables; constituting a tribrach. **2.** having to do with a tribrach or tribrachs. **3.** consisting of tribrachs.

tri·bro·mo·eth·a·nol (trī brō′mō eth′ə nōl, -nol), *n.* a crystalline substance, used in solution as an anesthetic; Avertin. *Formula:* $C_2H_3Br_3O$

trib·u·la·tion (trib′yə lā′shən), *n.* great trouble or misery; severe trial; affliction: *The early Christians suffered many tribulations. The fiery furnace of domestic tribulations* (Washington Irving). [< Latin *tribulātiō, -ōnis* < *trībulāre* to oppress, press < *trībulum* threshing sledge, related to *terere* to rub] —**Syn.** oppression, distress.

tri·bu·nal (tri byü′nəl, trī-), *n.* **1.** a court of justice; place of judgment or judicial assembly: *He was brought before the tribunal for trial.* **2.** the place where judges sit in a law court. **3.** something by or in which judgment is rendered; judicial or deciding authority: *the tribunal of the polls, the tribunal of the press.* [< Latin *tribūnal* < *tribūnus;* see TRIBUNE[1]] —**Syn. 1.** judicature. **2.** bench.

trib·u·nate (trib′yu̇ nit, -nāt), *n.* **1.** the office of tribune. **2.** government by tribunes. [< Latin *tribūnātus* < *tribūnus;* see TRIBUNE[1]]

trib·une[1] (trib′yün; *see usage note below*), *n.* **1.** any of various officials of ancient Rome. The tribune of the people was an administrative official appointed by the plebeians to protect their rights and interests from arbitrary action by the patricians. A military tribune was one of six officers, each of whom in turn commanded a legion in the course of a year. **2.** any person, especially a government official, who is formally charged with or asserts responsibilities as a defender of the people or their rights. [< Latin *tribūnus* < *tribus, -ūs* tribe]
➤ **Tribune** in the name of a newspaper is often pronounced (tri byün′).

trib·une[2] (trib′yün), *n.* **1.** a raised platform or pulpit. **2.** a raised area or gallery containing seats, especially in a church: *The church was crowded; not a chair nor a tribune vacant* (Benjamin Disraeli). **3.** an apse. [< Italian *tribuna* tribunal < Latin *tribūnus;* see TRIBUNE[1]] —**Syn. 1.** rostrum.

trib·une·ship (trib′yün ship), *n.* the office, or term of office, of a tribune.

trib·u·ni·tial or **trib·u·ni·cial** (trib′yə nish′əl), *adj.* of, having to do with, or characteristic of a tribune or his office or function. [< Latin *tribūnītius* (< *tribūnus;* see TRIBUNE[1]) + English *-al*[1]]

tri·bu·ni·tian or **tri·bu·ni·cian** (trib′yə nish′ən), *adj.* tribunitial.

trib·u·tar·i·ly (trib′yə ter′ə lē), *adv.* in a tributary manner.

trib·u·tar·y (trib′yə ter′ē), *n., pl.* **-tar·ies,** *adj.* —*n.* **1.** a stream that flows into a larger stream or body of water: *The Ohio River is a tributary of the Mississippi River.* **2.** a person or country that pays tribute.
—*adj.* **1.** (of a river or stream) flowing into a larger stream or body of water. **2.** paying tribute; required to pay tribute. **3.** paid or offered as tribute; of the nature of tribute. **4.** contributing; helping. **5.** subsidiary; auxiliary.

trib·ute (trib′yüt), *n.* **1.** money or some other valuable consideration paid by one state or ruler to another for peace or protection, in acknowledgment of submission, or in fulfillment of some agreement: *A large portion of the tribute was paid in money* (Edward Gibbon). **2.** a payment exacted of a subject or vassal, especially in excess of the sum required for such an international tribute. **3.** the obligation or necessity of paying this or something similar to it; condition of being tributary: *Millions for defence but not a cent for tribute* (Robert G. Harper). **4.** any forced payment. **5.** an acknowledgment of thanks or respect; compliment: *Memorial Day is a tribute to our dead soldiers.* [< Latin *tribūtum* < *tribuere* to allot < *tribus, -ūs* tribe]

tri·car·pel·lar·y (trī kär′pə ler′ē), *adj. Botany.* having or consisting of three carpels.

trice[1] (trīs), *v.t.,* **triced, tric·ing.** *Nautical.* **1.** to haul (up) and secure (a sail, boom, etc.) with a rope: *to trice up a sail.* **2.** to pull with an attached rope. [< Middle Dutch *trīsen* hoist < *trīse* pulley]

trice[2] (trīs), *n.* a very short time; moment; instant.
in a trice, in an instant; instantly; immediately: *That structure which was so many years annearing was dashed . . . in a trice* (James Howell).
[abstracted from phrase *at a trice* at a pull; see TRICE[1]]
—**Syn.** twinkling.

tri·cen·ni·al (trī sen′ē əl), *adj.* **1.** of or having to do with thirty years. **2.** occurring every thirty years. [< Late Latin *trīcennium* thirty years (< Latin *triciēs* thirty times + *annus* year) + English *-al*[1]]

tri·cen·te·nar·y (trī sen′tə ner′ē, trī′sen ten′ər-; *especially British* trī′sen tē′nər ē), *adj., n., pl.* **-nar·ies.** tercentenary.

tri·cen·ten·ni·al (trī′sen ten′ē əl, -ten′yəl), *adj., n.* tercentenary.

tri·ceps (trī′seps), *n.* the large muscle at the back of the upper arm which extends or straightens the arm. [< New Latin *triceps* three-headed < Latin *triceps, -cipitis* three-headed < *tri-* three + *caput, capitis* head]

tri·cer·a·tops (trī ser′ə tops), *n.* a dinosaur of the Cretaceous period of western North America, with a huge skull, a large horn above each eye, and a smaller horn on the nose. Its large, bony collar extended from the neck, and the triceratops had a long and powerful tail. [< New Latin *Triceratops* the genus name < Greek *trikératos* three-horned + *ôps* face]

Triceratops
(about 25 ft. long)

trich-, *combining form.* the form of **tricho-** before vowels, as in *trichiasis, trichite.*

tri·chi·a·sis (tri kī′ə sis), *n.* **1.** an abnormal condition characterized by the turning in of the eyelashes. **2.** a disease characterized by the presence of hairlike filaments in the urine. **3.** a disease of the breasts occurring in women during lactation. [< New Latin *trichiasis* < Greek *trichíāsis* (originally) any hairy condition < *trichiân* be hairy < *thríx, trichós* a hair]

tri·chi·na (tri kī′nə), *n., pl.* **-nae** (-nē). a small, slender, nematode worm which infests man, hogs, and various other animals, the adult inhabiting the intestinal tract, and the larvae migrating to and becoming encysted in the muscular tissue, causing trichinosis. Trichinae usually get into the human body from pork which is infected with the larvae and is not cooked long enough to destroy them. See **roundworm** for picture. [< New Latin *Trichina* the genus name < Greek *trichínē*, feminine of *tríchinos* of or like hair < *thríx, trichós* a hair]

trich·i·nel·la (trik′ə nel′ə), *n., pl.* **-lae** (-lē). trichina. [< New Latin *trichinella* (diminutive) < *Trichina* trichina]

trich·i·ni·a·sis (trik′ə nī′ə sis), *n.* trichinosis.

trich·i·ni·za·tion (trik′ə nə zā′shən), *n.* infection with trichinae; the state of being trichinized; trichinosis.

trich·i·nize (trik′ə nīz), *v.t.,* **-nized, -niz·ing.** to infect with trichinae.

trich·i·nosed (trik′ə nōzd, -nōst), *adj.* affected with trichinosis; infected with trichinae.

trich·i·no·sis (trik′ə nō′sis), *n.* a disease characterized by headache, chills, fever, and soreness of muscles, caused by the presence of trichinae in the intestines and muscular tissues. [< New Latin *trichinosis* < *Trichina* trichina + *-osis* -osis]

trich·i·not·ic (trik′ə not′ik), *adj.* of or having to do with trichinosis.

trich·i·nous (trik′ə nəs), *adj.* of or having trichinosis; infected with trichinae: *The average American pork eater consumes three servings of trichinous pork each year* (Science News Letter).

trich·ite (trik′īt), *n.* a very minute, dark-colored, hairlike crystal occurring in some vitreous rocks. [< Greek *thríx, trichós* a hair + English *-ite*[1]]

tri·chlo·rid (trī klôr′id, -klōr′-), *n.* trichloride.

tri·chlo·ride (trī klôr′īd, -id; -klōr′-), *n.* a chemical compound containing three atoms of chlorine combined with another element or radical.

tri·chlo·ro·eth·yl·ene (trī klôr′ō eth′ə lēn, -klōr′-), *n.* a liquid derived from ethylene or acetylene, used in anesthesia, as a grease solvent for dry cleaning, and in chemical manufacturing. *Formula:* C_2HCl_3

tricho-, *combining form.* hair; hairs; hairlike: *Trichology = the study of hair. Trichosis = any disease of the hair.* Also, **trich-** before vowels. [< Greek *thríx, trichós* a hair]

trich·o·car·pous (trik′ə kär′pəs), *adj. Botany.* having hairy fruit. [< *tricho-* + Greek *karpós* fruit + English *-ous*]

trich·o·cyst (trik′ə sist), *n. Zoology.* a stinging organ on the body of certain infusorians, consisting of a hairlike filament in a small sac.

trich·o·cyst·ic (trik′ə sis′tik), *adj.* **1.** having to do with trichocysts. **2.** having the character of trichocysts: *a trichocystic formation.*

trich·o·gyne (trik′ə jin, -jīn), *n.* a hairlike process forming the receptive part of the female reproductive organ in certain algae and fungi. [< *tricho-* + Greek *gynḗ* woman, female]

trich·oid (trik′oid), *adj.* resembling hair; hairlike.

tri·chol·o·gist (tri kol′ə jist), *n.* an expert in trichology.

tri·chol·o·gy (tri kol′ə jē), *n.* the study of the structure, functions, and diseases of the hair. [< *tricho-* + *-logy*]

tri·chome (trī′kōm, trik′ōm), *n.* an outgrowth from the epidermis of plants (a general term including hairs, prickles, etc.) [< Greek *tríchōma, -atos* growth of hair < *thríx, trichós* a hair]

tri·chom·ic (tri kom′ik), *adj.* **1.** of or having to do with a trichome. **2.** like a trichome.

trich·o·mon·ad (trik′ō mon′ad), *n.* any of a group of parasitic flagellate protozoans found in man and certain other animals, having several flagella and a tapering body. [< New Latin *Trichomonas, -adis* the genus name < Greek *thríx, trichós* a hair + Late Latin *monas* monad]

trich·o·mo·ni·a·sis (trik′ō mə nī′ə sis), *n.* the condition of being infected with the parasite trichomonad. Bovine trichomoniasis will cause miscarriage in cattle, and avian trichomoniasis is usually fatal in young chicks.

tri·chop·ter·ous (tri kop′tər əs), *adj.* **1.** having hairy wings. **2.** belonging to an order of insects comprising the caddis flies. [< Greek *thríx, trichós* a hair + *pterón* wing + English *-ous*]

tri·chord (trī′kôrd), *n.* a musical instrument with three strings, as a form of lyre or lute. [< Greek *tríchordos* having three strings < *tri-* three (< *treîs*) + *chordḗ* string]

tri·cho·sis (tri kō′sis), *n., pl.* **-ses** (sēz). any disease of the hair. [< *trich-* + *-osis*]

trich·o·tom·ic (trik′ə tom′ik), *adj.* **1.** divided or dividing into three parts. **2.** branching into three parts; giving off shoots by threes.

tri·chot·o·mous (trī kot′ə məs), *adj.* trichotomic.

tri·chot·o·my (trī kot′ə mē), *n., pl.* **-mies.** **1.** division into three parts, classes, or categories; tripartite arrangement. **2.** *Theology.* division into body, soul, and spirit. [< Greek *trícha* triple, triply (< *tri-* < *treîs* three) + *-tomíā* a cutting, division]

tri·chro·ic (trī krō′ik), *adj.* possessing the property of trichroism.

tri·chro·ism (trī′krō iz əm), *n.* the property of some crystals of exhibiting three different colors when viewed in three different directions. [< Greek *tríchroos* (< *tri-* three + *chróā*, for *chroiā́* skin, color of skin) + English *-ism*]

tri·chro·mat·ic (trī′krō mat′ik), *adj.* **1.** having or showing three colors. **2.** having to do with three colors. **3.** using three colors, as in printing.

tri·chro·ma·tism (trī krō′mə tiz əm), *n.* **1.** the quality of being trichromatic. **2.** the combination of three different colors, as in color photography.

tri·chro·mic (trī krō′mik), *adj.* trichromatic.

tri·cit·y (trī′sit′ē), *n., pl.* **-cit·ies,** *adj.* —*n.* **1.** a group of three adjoining and mutually dependent cities. **2.** a city in such a group: *Fine [industrial] facilities are . . . already in existence in the tri-cities* (Scott R. Schmedel). —*adj.* of, belonging to, or involving such a group of cities: *Calgary, Edmonton, and Red Deer studied the possibility of a tricity project . . . for a large thermoelectric system* (John E. Dutton).

trick (trik), *n.* **1.** something done to deceive or cheat: *The false message was a trick to get him to leave the house.* **2.** something pretended or unreal; illusion: *Those two lines are really the same length, but a trick of the eyesight makes one of them look longer.* **3.** a clever act; feat of skill: *We enjoyed the tricks of the trained animals.* **4.** the best way of doing or dealing with something; knack: *the trick of making pies, to learn the tricks of the trade.* **5.** a piece of mischief; practical joke; prank: *Stealing John's lunch was a mean trick.* **6.** a peculiar habit or way of acting; practice; mannerism: *He has a trick of pulling at his collar.* **7.** the cards played in one round: *When in doubt, win the trick* (Edmund Hoyle). **8.** a turn or period of duty, as at steering a ship. **9.** *U.S. Informal.* a child, especially a young girl.

do or **turn the trick,** to do what one wants done; accomplish the purpose: *Pail of whitewash and box of paints will do the trick* (Punch).

—*adj.* **1.** of, like, or done as a trick or stunt: *trick riding, trick shooting.* **2.** skilled in or trained to do tricks: *a trick dog.* **3.** made or used for doing tricks: *a trick chair.*

—*v.t.* **1.** to deceive by a trick; cheat: *We were tricked into buying a poor car. He was tricked out of his share of the reward. She was tricked into approving the scheme.* **2.** to dress. —*v.i.* **1.** to practice trickery. **2.** to play tricks; trifle.

trick out, a. to dress up; ornament: *I must trick out my dwellings with something fantastical* (Scott). **b.** to disguise: *I mention it only as an example of the frivolous speculation tricked out to look like scholarship with which the Holmes cult defrauds the reading public* (Harper's).

[< Old North French *trique* < *trikier,* Old French *trichier* to trick, cheat, perhaps < Dutch *trekken* to draw, swindle]—**trick′er,** *n.*

—**Syn.** *n.* **1.** ruse, subterfuge, artifice, stratagem. **3.** exploit, stunt. —*v.t.* **1.** defraud, delude, cozen. See **cheat.**

trick·er·y (trik′ər ē, trik′rē), *n., pl.* **-er·ies.** the use of tricks; deceitful conduct or practice; deception. —**Syn.** artifice, cheating, stratagem, imposture, duplicity.

trick·i·ly (trik′ə lē), *adv.* in a tricky manner.

trick·i·ness (trik′ē nis), *n.* the quality of being tricky or trickish; trickishness: *He went off chuckling at his own guile and trickiness* (Sunday Times).

trick·ing (trik′ing), *n.* **1.** the act of deceiving; trickery. **2.** ornamentation: *Go get us properties And tricking for our fairies* (Shakespeare).

trick·ish (trik′ish), *adj.* rather tricky. —**trick′ish·ly,** *adv.* —**trick′ish·ness,** *n.*

trick·le (trik′əl), *v.,* **-led, -ling,** *n.* —*v.i.* **1.** to flow or fall in successive drops: *Tears trickled down her cheeks.* **2.** to flow in a very scanty or halting stream: *The brook trickles through the valley. Salt trickled from a hole in the box.* **3.** to come, go, pass, etc., slowly and unevenly: *An hour before the show, people began to trickle into the theater.* —*v.t.* to cause to trickle; pour drop by drop, or in a fitful stream: *He trickled the water out of the bottle.*

—*n.* **1.** a small flow or stream. **2.** a trickling. [Middle English *triklen;* origin uncertain] —**Syn.** *v.i.* **1.** drip, dribble, ooze.

trick·less (trik′lis), *adj.* without a trick or tricks; involving no tricks.

trick·let (trik′lit), *n.* **1.** a little trickle. **2.** a small trickling stream.

trick·ly (trik′lē), *adj.,* **-li·er, -li·est.** trickling: *The heron is ever on the lookout to use its long neck for . . . a trickly gulp* (Westminster Gazette).

trick or treat, 1. the act of going from door to door on Halloween demanding handouts of candy, fruit, etc., or inflicting mischief, practiced by children dressed in costume: *The "trick or treat" custom is now departing much further from the old Indian way as . . . costumed children . . . beg for a worthy cause, such as UNICEF . . . instead of for goodies to eat or carry away in a big paper bag* (Science News Letter). **2.** such a demand: *candies or pennies on hand to dole out to the oddly dressed midgets, doubling for goblins, who ring his doorbell and demand "trick or treat"* (Scientific American).

trick-or-treat·er (trik′ər trē′tər), *n.* a person who engages in trick-or-treating.

trick-or-treat·ing (trik′ər trē′ting), *n.* the act of demanding a trick or treat.

trick·si·ly (trik′sə lē), *adv.* in a tricksy manner.

trick·si·ness (trik′sē nis), *n.* the quality or state of being tricksy.

trick·some (trik′səm), *adj.* full of tricks; mischievous; frolicsome; playful.

trick·ster (trik′stər), *n.* a person who practices trickery; cheat; deceiver.

trick·sy (trik′sē), *adj.* **1.** mischievous; playful; frolicsome: *a frolicsome and tricksy creature, full of wild fantastic humours* (W. H. Hudson). **2.** tricky: *The chopping about has begun to seem tricksy and ornamental* (New Statesman). **3.** spruce; smart. —**Syn.** **2.** crafty, cunning.

trick·track (trik′trak′), *n.* a variety of backgammon: *Her husband . . . was continuously out of a job and into every small cafe, playing tricktrack and smoking hubble-bubble* (Atlantic). Also, **trictrac.** [< French *trictrac;* ultimately imitative]

trick·y (trik′ē), *adj.,* **trick·i·er, trick·i·est.** **1.** full of tricks; characterized by trickery; deceiving; cheating: *A fox is trickier than a sheep.* **2.** not doing what is expected; dangerous or difficult to handle: *The back door has a tricky lock.* **3.** skilled in performing clever tricks or dodges. —**Syn.** **1.** deceptive, deceitful.

tri·clin·ic (trī klin′ik), *adj.* designating or belonging to a system of crystallization in which the three axes are unequal and obliquely inclined. [< *tri-* + Greek *klī́nein* bend, lean + English *-ic*]

tri·clin·i·um (trī klin′ē əm), *n., pl.* **-i·a** (-ē ə). **1.** a couch or couches extending around three sides of a dining table, on which in ancient Rome the host and his guests reclined while eating, especially during a banquet or other formal meal. **2.** a dining room containing such a couch or couches. [< Latin *triclīnium* < Greek *triklī́nion* (diminutive) < *tríklīnos* a (dining) room with three couches < *tri-* threefold, triply + *klī́nē* couch < *klī́nein* to lean, recline]

tri·col·or (trī′kul′ər), *adj.* having three colors; three-colored. —*n.* **1.** the national flag of France adopted at the Revolution, consisting of equal vertical stripes of blue, white, and red. **2.** any of certain other flags consisting of three equal stripes or blocks each of a different color, as that of Italy which is green, white, and red. [< French *(drapeau) tricolore* tricolored (flag)]

tri·col·ored (trī′kul′ərd), *adj.* having three colors: *a tricolored flag.*

tri·col·our (trī′kul′ər), *adj., n. Especially British.* tricolor.

tri·corn (trī′kôrn), *adj.* having three horns or hornlike projections (applied especially to a cocked hat with the brim turned up on three sides). —*n.* a tricorn hat. [< French *tricorne* < Latin *tricornis* < *tri-* three + *cornū* horn]

tri·corne (trī′kôrn), *n.* a tricorn hat: *It was Washington who wore a tricorne; Napoleon wore a bicorne* (Atlantic).

tri·cor·nered (trī′kôr′nərd), *adj.* three-cornered.

tri·cor·po·rate (trī kôr′pər it), *adj. Especially Heraldry.* having three bodies. [< Latin *tricorpor* (< *tri-* three + *corpus, -oris* body) + English *-ate*[1]]

tri·cos·tate (trī kos′tāt), *adj. Botany, Zoology.* having three ribs or riblike parts (costae). [< *tri-* + Latin *costa* rib + English *-ate*[1]]

tri·cot (trē′kō), *n.* **1.** a knitted fabric of wool, cotton, rayon, nylon, etc., made by hand or machine. **2.** a kind of woolen fabric. **3.** a close-fitting garment worn by ballet dancers. [< French *tricot* < Old French *tricoter* to stir, move about, variant of *estriquier,* probably < Low German *strikken* move about]

tric·o·tine (trik′ə tēn′), *n.* a kind of twilled woolen fabric. [< French *tricotine* < *tricot* tricot]

tri·cres·yl phosphate (trī kres′əl), TCP (no periods).

tri·crot·ic (trī krot′ik), *adj.* (of a pulse or a tracing of it) having or showing a threefold beat. [< Greek *tríkrotos* rowed with a triple stroke (< *tri-* triply + *krótos* noise made by striking hands or feet) + English *-ic*]

tri·cro·tism (trī′krə tiz əm, trik′rə-), *n.* tricrotic condition.

tric·trac (trik′trak′), *n.* tricktrack.

tri·cus·pid (trī kus′pid), *adj.* **1.** having three points or cusps. **2.** denoting or having to do with the tricuspid valve of the heart.
—*n.* **1.** a tricuspid tooth. **2.** the tricuspid valve.
[< Latin *tricuspis, -idis* three-pointed < *tri-* three + *cuspis* tip]

tri·cus·pi·dal (trī kus′pə dəl), *adj.* tricuspid.

tri·cus·pi·date (trī kus′pə dāt), *adj.* three-pointed; tricuspid.

tricuspid valve, the valve of three segments at the opening from the right auricle into the right ventricle of the heart. It prevents blood from being forced back into the right auricle during contraction of the ventricles.

tri·cy·cle (trī′sə kəl, -sik′əl), *n., v.,* **-cled, -cling.** —*n.* **1.** a small, light vehicle having three wheels (one in front, used for steering, and two smaller ones behind, one on each side), caused to move by the action of pedals or handles, now used especially by small children. **2.** a three-wheeled motorcycle. —*v.i.* to ride a tricycle. [< French *tricycle* < *tri-* three + *cycle*, ultimately < Greek *kýklos* ring, circle]

Tricycle (def. 1)

tri·cy·cler (trī′sə klər, -sik′lər), *n.* a person who rides on a tricycle; tricyclist.

tri·cy·clic (trī sī′klik, -sik′lik), *adj.* **1.** passing through or having three cycles. **2.** (of a carbon compound) having three rings or closed chains of atoms in its structural formula.

tri·cy·clist (trī′sə klist, -sik′list), *n.* a person who rides on a tricycle.

tri·dac·tyl (trī dak′təl), *adj.* having three digits (fingers, claws, toes, etc.) on each limb. [< Greek *tridáktylos* < *tri-* three, triple + *dáktylos* finger, toe]

tri·dec·ane (trī dek′ān), *n.* a colorless, liquid hydrocarbon of the methane series. *Formula:* $C_{13}H_{28}$ [< *tri-* + *dec-* ten + *-ane* (because it contains 13 atoms of carbon)]

tri·dent (trī′dənt), *n.* **1.** a three-pronged spear used for fishing. **2.** a three-pronged spear that is the identifying attribute of Poseidon (Neptune) as the ancient Greek and Roman god of the sea, usually represented in sculpture, painting, etc., as being carried in the right hand. See **Poseidon** for picture. **3.** a three-pronged spear that was one of the two weapons (the other being a net) of a retiarius in ancient Roman gladiatorial combat.
—*adj.* three-pronged.
[< Latin *tridēns, -dentis* < *tri-* three + *dēns* tooth]

tri·den·tate (trī den′tāt), *adj.* having three teeth or toothlike points; three-pronged.

tri·den·tat·ed (trī den′tā tid), *adj.* tridentate: *This animal (the leopard seal) is a solitary, large-headed predator, its jaws armed behind sharp canines with rows of magnificent tridentated teeth* (Scientific American).

Tri·den·tine (trī den′tin, -tīn; tri-), *adj.* **1.** of or having to do with Trent, Italy (formerly Austria), or the Council of Trent. **2.** conforming to the doctrine of the Council of Trent. [< Medieval Latin *Tridentinus* pertaining to *Tridentum*, the city of Trent, Italy]

tri·di·men·sion·al (trī′də men′shə nəl), *adj.* having or exhibiting three dimensions; three-dimensional.

tri·di·men·sion·al·i·ty (trī′də men′shə-nal′ə tē), *n.* the condition or quality of having three dimensions; three-dimensionality.

trid·u·um (trij′ů əm), *n.* **1.** a period of three days. **2.** (in the Roman Catholic Church) a three days' period of prayer or devotion, usually preceding some feast. [< Latin *triduum* < *tri-* three + *diēs* day]

trid·y·mite (trid′ə mīt), *n.* a crystallized form of silica found in igneous rocks, usually in twinned groups of three crystals: *Tridymite occurs in small hexagonal tables, colorless and transparent* (James Dwight Dana). [< Greek *trídymos* threefold + English *-ite*[1]]

tri·e·cious (trī ē′shəs), *adj. Botany.* trioecious. —**tri·e′cious·ly,** *adv.*

tried (trīd), *adj.* **1.** proved or tested by experience or examination; proven: *a man of tried abilities.* **2.** (of fat) rendered. **3.** *Obsolete.* freed from impurities; refined.
—*v.* the past tense and past participle of **try.**
—**Syn.** *adj.* **1.** dependable, reliable, trustworthy.

tried-and-true (trīd′ən trü′), *adj.* tested and found to be true over a period of time; proven; dependable: *He believed in the tried-and-true American virtues of honesty, thrift, and opportunity* (Newsweek). *The producer —rather than speculate on something risky and new—sticks to a tried-and-true formula based on the successes of the past* (Harper's).

tri·en·ni·al (trī en′ē əl), *adj.* **1.** occurring every three years: *triennial elections.* **2.** existing or lasting for three years.
—*n.* **1.** an event that occurs every three years. **2.** the third anniversary of an event.
[< Latin *triennium* (see TRIENNIUM) + English *-al*[1]]

tri·en·ni·al·ly (trī en′ē ə lē), *adv.* once every three years.

tri·en·ni·um (trī en′ē əm), *n., pl.* **-en·ni·a** (-en′ē ə). a space or period of three years. [< Latin *triennium* < *tri-* three + *annus* year]

tri·er (trī′ər), *n.* a person or thing that tries.

tri·er·arch (trī′ə rärk), *n.* in ancient Greece: **1.** the commander of a trireme. **2.** (in Athens) a citizen who, singly or in conjunction with others, was charged with fitting out a trireme for the state. [< Latin *triērarchus* < Greek *triērarchos* < *triērēs* trireme + *archós* chief, leader]

tri·er·ar·chic (trī′ə rär′kik), *adj.* of or having to do with a trierarch or the trierarchy.

tri·er·ar·chy (trī′ə rär′kē), *n., pl.* **-chies.** **1.** the command over a trireme. **2.** trierarchs collectively. **3.** (in Athens) the system of requiring citizens to equip triremes for the state. [< Greek *triērarchíā* < *triērarchos;* see TRIERARCH]

tri·e·ter·ic (trī′ə ter′ik), *adj.* (in ancient Greece) occurring or held every third year (in the ancient reckoning, every alternate year), as certain festivals. —*n.* a trieteric festival. [< Latin *trietēricus* < Greek *trietērikós*, ultimately < *tri-* three + *étos* year]

tri·eth·yl·a·mine (trī eth′ə lə mēn′, -lam′-in), *n.* a colorless liquid with a strong smell like that of ammonia, used as a catalyst in organic reactions, as a solvent, and in certain propellants. *Formula:* $C_6H_{15}N$

tri·eth·yl·ene melamine (trī eth′ə lēn), a poisonous, crystalline compound used in manufacturing certain resins, in textile finishing, and as a drug in the treatment of malignant lymphomas and chronic leukemia. *Formula:* $C_9H_{12}N_6$

triethylene phos·phor·a·mide (fos′-fə rə mīd′, -rə mid′; -ram′īd, -id), a drug used in the treatment of certain forms of carcinoma, malignant melanoma and lymphoma, and chronic leukemia; TEPA. *Formula:* $C_6H_{12}N_3OP$

tri·fa·cial (trī fā′shəl), *adj., n. Obsolete.* trigeminal.

tri·far·i·ous (trī fãr′ē əs), *adj.* **1.** threefold; triple. **2.** in three rows. [< Latin *trifārius* (with English *-ous*)]

tri·fid (trī′fid), *adj.* divided into three by clefts. [< Latin *trifidus* < *tri-* three, triply + *fid-*, a root of *findere* to split, cleave]

tri·fi·lar (trī fī′lər), *adj.* consisting of or furnished with three filaments or threads. [< *tri-* + Latin *fīlum* thread + English *-ar*]

tri·fle (trī′fəl), *n., v.,* **-fled, -fling.** —*n.* **1.** a thing having little value or importance: **a.** a matter of little significance; trivial affair. **b.** a small article of little intrinsic value; trinket; bauble; knickknack. **2.** an insignificant quantity or amount; very small sum: *to buy something for a trifle.* **3.** a slight extent; a small degree: *to move something a trifle to the right. He was a trifle late.* **4.** *Especially British.* a rich dessert made of sponge cake soaked in wine or liqueur, and served with whipped cream, custard, fruit, etc. **5.** a kind of moderately hard pewter, used for beer mugs, etc., containing a slightly greater proportion of lead than pewter, used for plates and dishes.
trifles, articles made of moderately hard pewter: *antique trifles.*
—*v.i.* **1.** to spend time idly or frivolously; waste time; dally: *Stop trifling and get to work.* **2.** to act or speak in an idle or frivolous way; be flippant: *Don't trifle with serious matters. Stop trifling now—I want a serious answer.* **3.** to handle or finger a thing idly; fiddle or fidget: *He trifled with his pencil.*
—*v.t.* to spend (time, effort, money, etc.) on things having little value; waste; fritter: *She had trifled away the whole morning.*
[< Old French *trufle* mockery (diminutive) < *truffe* deception; origin uncertain]
—**Syn.** *n.* **1. a.** triviality. *-v.i.* **1.** dawdle, idle. **2. Trifle, dally** mean to treat a person or thing without seriousness. **Trifle,** the more general term, suggests lack of earnestness or serious purpose: *He is not a man to be trifled with.* **Dally** suggests thinking vaguely of something to amuse oneself or to pass the time: *I have dallied with the idea of taking a trip.*

tri·fler (trī′flər), *n.* a person who trifles; frivolous, shallow person.

tri·fles (trī′fəlz), *n.pl.* See under **trifle,** *n.*

tri·fling (trī′fling), *adj.* **1.** of little significance or value; not important; very small; paltry; insignificant: *To a philosopher no circumstance, however trifling, is too minute* (Oliver Goldsmith). **2.** behaving idly or frivolously; shallow. —*n.* the act of a person who trifles. —**tri′fling·ly,** *adv.* —**tri′fling·ness,** *n.*
—**Syn.** *adj.* **1.** trivial, petty. **2.** foolish, vain.

tri·flu·o·ride (trī flü′ə rīd, -ər id), *n.* a chemical compound containing three atoms of fluorine combined with another element or radical.

tri·fo·cal (trī fō′kəl, trī′fō′-), *adj.* **1.** having three focuses. **2.** designating a lens for eyeglasses which has three parts, one for near, one for intermediate (arm's length), and one for distant vision.
—*n.* a trifocal lens.
trifocals, a pair of eyeglasses having trifocal lenses: *old trifocals in a leather case.*
[< *tri-* + *focal;* patterned on *bifocal*]

tri·foil (trī′foil), *n.* trefoil: *Trifoil, a legume which does well in such northern States as Vermont, has a feeding value equal to alfalfa* (Science News Letter).

tri·fo·li·ate (trī fō′lē it, -āt), *adj.* **1.** consisting of three leaves or leaflets (used chiefly, in the latter sense, of compound leaves, as a shortened form of *trifoliolate*). **2.** (of a plant) having such leaves: *Clover is trifoliate.* [< *tri-* + Latin *foliātus* leaved < *folium* leaf]

Trifoliate Leaf (def. 1)

tri·fo·li·at·ed (trī fō′lē ā′tid), *adj.* trifoliate.

tri·fo·li·o·late (trī fō′lē ə lāt), *adj.* **1.** consisting of three leaflets. **2.** having leaves of this form; trifoliate.

tri·fo·li·um (trī fō′lē əm), *n.* any of a group of herbs of the pea family; clover. [< Latin *trifolium* three-layered grass, trefoil < *tri-* three + *folium* leaf. Doublet of TREFOIL.]

tri·fo·ri·um (trī fôr′ē əm, -fōr′-), *n., pl.* **-fo·ri·a** (-fôr′ē ə, -fōr′-). (in some large churches) the wall over the arches at the sides of the nave and choir, and sometimes of the transepts, occupying the space between the vaulting and roofs of the aisles, below the clerestory, usually consisting chiefly of an arcade, either blind or opening into a gallery. See **clerestory** for picture. [< Medieval Latin *triforium* arcade, also, trefoil, apparently < Latin *tri-* three + *foris* door]

tri·form (trī′fôrm), *adj.* having a triple form; combining three different forms; formed or composed in three parts. [< Latin *triformis* < *tri-* three + *forma* form]

triformed (trī′fôrmd), *adj.* triform.

tri·fur·cate (*adj.* trī fėr′kit, -kāt; *v.* trī-fėr′kāt), *adj., v.,* **-cat·ed, -cat·ing.** —*adj.* divided into three branches like the prongs of a fork. —*v.t., v.i.* to divide into three parts. [< Latin *trifurcus* (< *tri-* three + *furca* a (two-pronged) fork) + English *-ate*[1]]

tri·fur·cat·ed (trī fėr′kā tid), *adj.* trifurcate.

tri·fur·ca·tion (trī′fər kā′shən), *n.* **1.** the state of being trifurcate. **2.** a trifurcate shape, formation, or arrangement.

trig[1] (trig), *adj., v.,* **trigged, trig·ging.** —*adj.* **1.** trim or neat in dress; smartly dressed. **2.** (of clothing) smart; stylish: *Trotteur dresses with trig leather belts* (New Yorker). **3.** strong; sound; well. **4.** precise; exact. **5.** smug.
—*v.t.* to make trim or smart: *He has rigged*

and trigged her with paint and spar (Rudyard Kipling).

trig out, *Especially Scottish.* to dress or deck out: *She had gotten me into her room to see that I was trigged out as I should be* (W. Beatty).

[Middle English *trigg* trustworthy, steady, in firm condition < Scandinavian (compare Old Icelandic *tryggr* trusty, true)] **—trig′ly,** *adv.* **—trig′ness,** *n.*

—Syn. *adj.* **1.** tidy, spruce.

trig[2] (trig), *n., v.,* **trigged, trig·ging.** *—n.* a wedge, block, or other obstacle used to keep a wheel, cask, etc., from rolling.

—v.t. **1.** to keep (a wheel, etc.) from rolling by a trig. **2.** to prop up or support with a trig.

[perhaps < Scandinavian (compare Old Icelandic *tryggja* to secure, make firm < *tryggr* firm, trusty)]

trig., 1. trigonometric. **2.** trigonometry.

trig·a·mist (trig′ə mist), *n.* **1.** a person who has three wives or three husbands at the same time. **2.** (formerly) a person who has been married three times. [< *trigam*(y) + *-ist*]

trig·a·mous (trig′ə məs), *adj.* **1.** having three wives or three husbands at the same time; guilty of trigamy. **2.** involving trigamy. **3.** *Botany.* having male, female, and hermaphrodite flowers in the same head.

[< Greek *trígamos* (with English *-ous*) thrice married < *tri-* three + *gámos* wedding]

trig·a·my (trig′ə mē), *n.* the state or offense of having three wives or three husbands at the same time.

[< Late Latin *trigamia* < Greek *trígamos;* see TRIGAMOUS]

tri·gas·tric (trī gas′trik), *adj. Anatomy.* having three fleshy bellies, as certain muscles. [< *tri-* + Greek *gastḗr, gastrós* stomach, belly + English *-ic*]

tri·gem·i·nal (trī jem′ə nəl), *adj.* of or denoting the fifth pair of cranial nerves, each of which divides into three branches. *—n.* a trigeminal nerve. [< Latin *trigeminalis* < Latin *trigeminus* born three at a birth < *tri-* three, triply + *geminus* born together]

trigeminal neuralgia, tic douloureux: [*For*] *patients with the excruciatingly painful condition known as trigeminal neuralgia . . . merely stroking the face or hair on the affected side may bring on a paroxysm of intense pain. Cause of the condition is unknown* (Science News Letter).

trig·ger (trig′ər), *n.* **1.** the small lever on the underside of a gun, which is pulled back by the finger to fire the gun. See also **flintlock** for picture. **2.** a lever pulled or pressed to release a spring or catch and set some force or mechanism in action, as in the springing of a trap. **3.** anything that sets off or initiates something else: *Received from a senate subcommittee a report that violent movies are potential triggers for juvenile delinquency* (Time). *The U.S. set off one of the smallest atomic devices it has ever fired, and some speculated it was designed as a trigger for an H-bomb* (Wall Street Journal).

TRIGGER

Trigger (def. 1) of revolver

quick on the trigger, a. quick to shoot: *He is reported so quick on the trigger, that all the other "shootists" in the country have an awe of him* (J. H. Beadle). **b.** *Informal.* very quick to act or respond; mentally alert: *A born musical leader, fertile in ideas, quick on the trigger* (London Daily Chronicle).

—v.t. to set off; bring about; initiate; activate: *An A-bomb would be needed to "trigger" an H-bomb* (Joint Committee on Atomic Energy). *At present we cannot make rain. We can only trigger it off from suitable clouds* (Science News). *Triggered by moist tropical air, a tremendous downpour began at midnight* (Time).

[earlier *tricker* < Dutch *trekker* < *trekken* to pull]

trigger finger, the finger that presses the trigger of a gun, usually the forefinger.

have an itchy trigger finger, to be overanxious to shoot or gun down: *The fugitive was a reckless outlaw with the reputation of having an itchy trigger finger.*

trig·ger·fish (trig′ər fish′), *n., pl.* **-fish·es** or (*collectively*) **-fish.** any of various plectognath fishes, having several strong spines on the dorsal fin.

trigger guard, a protective device enclosing the trigger of a firearm.

trig·ger-hap·py (trig′ər hap′ē), *adj. Informal.* shooting or inclined to shoot at the slightest provocation: *This tiny community is being threatened by the high-spirited lawlessness of a lot of trigger-happy cowboys* (Sunday Times). *The image is that of a trigger-happy, warlike power, ready to drop its hydrogen bombs* (Newsweek).

trig·ger·man (trig′ər man′), *n., pl.* **-men.** *Informal.* a gunman, especially a hired assassin.

tri·glot (trī′glot), *adj.* using or containing three languages; trilingual. *—n.* a triglot book or edition. [< *tri-* + Greek *glōtta* tongue]

tri·glyc·er·ide (trī glis′ə rīd, -ər id), *n.* any of a group of fatty compounds formed when three acid radicals replace the three hydrogen atoms of the -OH (hydroxyl) groups in glycerol: *Studies indicated that triglycerides may be a cause of coronary artery disease* (Science News Letter).

tri·glyph (trī′glif), *n.* a part of a Doric frieze between two metopes, consisting typically of a rectangular block with two vertical grooves and a half groove at each side. See **metope** for picture.

[< Latin *triglyphus* < Greek *tríglyphos* < *tri-* three + *glyphḗ* a carving < *glýphein* to carve]

tri·glyph·ic (trī glif′ik), *adj.* **1.** having to do with a triglyph or triglyphs. **2.** consisting of a triglyph or triglyphs. **3.** containing three sets of characters or sculptures.

tri·glyph·i·cal (trī glif′ə kəl), *adj.* triglyphic.

tri·go (trē′gō), *n.* wheat. [< Spanish *trigo* < Latin *trīticum* wheat, related to *terere* to rub]

tri·gon (trī′gon), *n.* **1.** in astrology: **a.** a set of three signs of the zodiac, distant 120 degrees from each other, as if at the angles of an equilateral triangle; triplicity. **b.** the aspect of two planets distant 120 degrees from each other; trine. **2.** trigonon. **3.** triangle.

[< Latin *trigōnum* < Greek *trígōnon* triangle < *tri-* three + *-gōnos* angled < *gōníā* angle]

trigon., 1. trigonometric. **2.** trigonometry.

trig·o·nal (trig′ə nəl), *adj.* **1.** (in astrology) of the nature of or having to do with a trigon. **2.** (of a crystal) having triangular faces. **3.** triangular.

trig·o·nom·e·ter (trig′ə nom′ə tər), *n.* an instrument for measuring sides and angles in a plane right triangle.

trig·o·no·met·ric (trig′ə nə met′rik), *adj.* of or having to do with trigonometry; based on or resulting from trigonometry: *trigonometric measurements. These relations* [*between the sides of a right triangle*] *are called trigonometric ratios* (World Book Encyclopedia).

trig·o·no·met·ri·cal (trig′ə nə met′rə kəl), *adj.* trigonometric.

trig·o·no·met·ri·cal·ly (trig′ə nə met′rəklē), *adv.* by or according to trigonometry.

trig·o·nom·e·try (trig′ə nom′ə trē), *n., pl.* **-tries. 1.** the branch of mathematics that deals with the relations between the sides and angles of triangles, particularly with certain functions, as the sine, secant, and tangent, of their angles, and with the determining of measurements involving triangles by means of these functions and relations. *Abbr.:* trig. **2.** a book on this subject. [< New Latin *trigonometria* < Greek *trígōnon* (see TRIGON) + *métron* a measure]

tri·go·non (trī gō′non), *n.* a kind of many-stringed psaltery or harp, triangular in form, originated by the ancient Greeks and borrowed by the Romans. [< Greek *trígōnon;* see TRIGON]

trig·o·nous (trig′ə nəs), *adj.* having three prominent angles, as a plant stem or ovary. [< Greek *trígōnos* (< *tri-* three + *gōníā* angle) + English *-ous*]

tri·gram (trī′gram), *n.* trigraph.

tri·graph (trī′graf, -gräf), *n.* a combination of three letters used to spell a single sound, as *eau* in *beau.*

[< *tri-* + *-graph*]

tri·graph·ic (trī graf′ik), *adj.* having to do with a trigraph.

tri·he·dral (trī hē′drəl), *adj. Geometry.* **1.** having, or formed by, three planes meeting in a point: *a trihedral angle.* **2.** having, or formed by, three lateral planes: *a trihedral prism.*

[< *tri-* + Greek *hédra* seat, base + English *-al*[1]]

tri·he·dron (trī hē′drən), *n., pl.* **-drons, -dra** (-drə). *Geometry.* a figure formed by three planes meeting at a point. [< *trihedr*(al) + *-on,* as in *polyhedron*]

tri·hy·dric (trī hī′drik), *adj.* trihydroxy: *trihydric alcohol, trihydric phenol.*

tri·hy·drox·y (trī′hī drok′sē), *adj. Chemistry.* having three hydroxyl (-OH) radicals.

tri·ju·gate (trī′jü gāt; trī jü′git, -gāt), *adj. Botany.* (of a pinnate leaf) having three pairs of leaflets. [< Latin *trijugus* threefold (< *tri-* three + *jugum* yoke) + English *-ate*[1]]

tri·ju·gous (trī′jü gəs, trī jü′-), *adj.* trijugate.

tri·lat·er·al (trī lat′ər əl), *adj.* having three sides. [< Latin *trilaterus* (< *tri-* three + *latus, -eris* side) + English *-al*[1]] **—tri·lat′er·al·ly,** *adv.*

tri·lat·er·a·tion (trī lat′ə rā′shən), *n.* (in surveying, mapping, etc.) the establishment of a network of triangles by measuring all sides of each, rather than one side and two angles as in triangulation.

tril·by (tril′bē), *n., pl.* **-bies.** a trilby hat: *I tried on every kind of headdress, from billy-cocks to . . . trilbies* (New Yorker).

trilby hat, a soft felt hat, especially one of the Homburg type, with a narrow brim and indented crown. [< *Trilby,* the heroine of the novel by George Du Maurier, published in 1894]

tri·lem·ma (trī lem′ə), *n.* **1.** a form of argument resembling the dilemma, but involving three alternatives instead of two. **2.** a situation requiring a choice of one of three alternatives. [< *tri-* + *-lemma,* as in *dilemma*]

tri·lin·e·ar (trī lin′ē ər), *adj. Mathematics.* **1.** of, having to do with, or involving three lines. **2.** contained by three lines.

tri·lin·gual (trī ling′gwəl), *adj.* **1.** able to speak three languages: *a trilingual person.* **2.** using three languages: *Switzerland is a trilingual country.* **3.** written or expressed in three languages: *a trilingual text.* [< Latin *trilinguis* trilingual (< *tri-* three + *lingua* language, tongue) + English *-al*[1]]

tri·lit·er·al (trī lit′ər əl), *adj.* **1.** consisting of three letters. **2.** consisting of three consonants.

—n. a triliteral word or root.

[< *tri-* + Latin *lītera* letter + English *-al*[1]]

tri·lit·er·al·ism (trī lit′ər ə liz′əm), *n.* the use of triliteral roots, as in Semitic languages.

tri·lith (trī′lith), *n.* a prehistoric structure or monument consisting of two large, upright stones with another stone resting upon them like a lintel. [< Greek *trílithon,* neuter of *trílithos* of three stones < *tri-* three + *líthos* stone]

tri·lith·ic (trī lith′ik), *adj.* **1.** having to do with a trilith. **2.** of the nature of a trilith.

tri·li·thon (trī′lə thon), *n.* trilith.

trill[1] (tril), *v.t., v.i.* **1.** to sound or speak with a tremulous, vibrating, high-pitched sound: *The child burst in, trilling with laughter* (Rudyard Kipling). **2.** to sing with a tremulous vibration of sound: *to trill an aria. Some birds trill their songs.* **3.** to play so as to make such a sound: *to trill on a flute.* **4.** *Phonetics.* to pronounce as a trill: *He trilled his "r's" when he spoke.*

—n. **1.** the act or sound of trilling: *the trill of a wren.* **2.** *Music.* **a.** a rapid alternation of a given musical tone with the tone above or below it; shake. **b.** tremolo or vibrato. **3.** *Phonetics.* **a.** a sound articulated by causing the breath stream to produce rapid vibration of one of the elastic organs of the mouth (the lips, tongue, or uvula), as in certain pronunciations of *r.* **b.** the vibration of one of these organs. **c.** a consonant so pronounced: *Spanish "rr" is a trill.*

[< Italian *trillare;* probably imitative]

trill[2] (tril), *v.t., v.i. Archaic.* to trickle. [perhaps < Scandinavian (compare Norwegian, Swedish *trilla* to roll, trundle)]

tril·lion (tril′yən), *n., adj.* **1.** (in the United States and France) 1 followed by 12 zeros; one thousand billions. **2.** (in Great Britain) 1 followed by 18 zeros; one million billions.

[Middle English *trillion* < *tri-* three; patterned on *million* million]

tril·lionth (tril′yənth), *adj.* **1.** being last in order of a series of a trillion. **2.** being one of a trillion parts. *—n.* one of a trillion parts; the quotient of unity divided by a trillion.

tril·li·um (tril′ē əm), *n.* any of a group of perennial herbs of the lily family, bearing a whorl of three thin, short-stalked or stalkless leaves at the summit of an unbranched stem, with a solitary flower in the middle; wake-robin. [< New Latin *trillium* < Latin *tri-* three]

Large-flowered Trillium (8 to 12 in. high)

tri·lo·bal (trī lō′bəl, trī′-lə-), *adj.* trilobate.

tri·lo·bate (trī lō′bāt, trī′lə-), *adj.* having or divided into three lobes: *a trilobate leaf.*

tri·lo·bat·ed (trī lō′bā-tid), *adj.* trilobate.

tri·lobed (trī′lōbd′), *adj.* trilobate.

tri·lo·bite (trī′lə bīt), *n.* any of a large group of extinct arthropods, believed to be related to the crustaceans, characterized by jointed legs and a segmented body divided into three lobes by furrows running lengthwise on the dorsal surface. Small fossil trilobites, about one or two inches long, are widely found in Paleozoic rocks; larger ones, up to two feet long, are rare. [< New Latin *trilobita,* plural < Greek *tri-* three + *lobós* lobe]

tri·lo·bit·ic (trī′lə bit′ik), *adj.* **1.** of or having to do with trilobites. **2.** having the character of trilobites or affinity with them. **3.** containing trilobites.

tri·loc·u·lar (trī lok′yə lər), *adj.* having three cells or compartments, as the capsule of a plant, or the heart of a reptile.

tril·o·gy (tril′ə jē), *n., pl.* **-gies. 1.** three novels, each formally complete in itself, that are intentionally related by the author to each other in basic theme or subject. **2.** three plays, operas, etc., written by the same person and more or less closely related in theme or subject. **3.** a group of three tragedies by the same author, originally always closely related in subject, written for performance in series during the festival of Dionysus in ancient Athens. [< Greek *trilogíā* < *tri-* three + *lógos* story]

trim (trim), *v.,* **trimmed, trim·ming,** *adj.,* **trim·mer, trim·mest,** *n., adv.* —*v.t.* **1.** to make neat in appearance or reduce to a proper shape by cutting off untidy growth, unwanted projections, etc.: *The gardener trimmed the hedge.* **2.** to put in good order; tidy: *to trim up a room.* **3.** to dress or shape (lumber): *The carpenter trimmed the lumber with a plane.* **4.** to remove by or as if by clipping, pruning, paring, etc.; cut: *to trim off dead branches.* **5.** to decorate; adorn: *to trim a dress with braid. The children trimmed the Christmas tree.* **6.** to cause (a vessel) to float on an even keel by arrangement of cargo, ballast, etc. **7.** to distribute or arrange (cargo, ballast, or people) in a vessel to make it float evenly. **8.** to balance (an aircraft) so that it maintains level flight with main controls in neutral positions. **9.** to adjust (the controls of an aircraft) so as to bring this about. **10.** to adjust (sails, yards, etc.) to fit the direction of the wind and the course to be sailed. **11.** to change (opinions, etc.) to suit circumstances. **12.** *Informal.* to defeat, especially overwhelmingly; beat; thrash. **13.** *Informal.* to cheat; fleece. **14.** *Informal.* to scold; rebuke. **15.** *Obsolete.* to equip.
—*v.i.* **1.** to be or keep in balance, especially to assume a specified position in the water, owing to the distribution of cargo, ballast, etc. **2.** to adjust yards and sails to fit the direction of the wind and the course of the ship. **3.** to maintain a middle course or balance between opposing interests; adapt oneself to prevailing opinions, etc.
—*adj.* **1.** in good condition or order; tidy and pleasing to the eye; neat: *A trim maid greeted us.* **2.** that is or appears to be well designed and maintained: *a trim little ketch.* **3.** *Obsolete.* pretty; handsome.
—*n.* **1.** proper condition: *to get in trim for a race.* **2.** good order: *to put one's affairs in trim.* **3.** general state or condition; order: *That ship is in poor trim for a voyage.* **4.** trimming: *the trim on a dress.* **5.** equipment; outfit. **6.** the condition, manner, or degree of horizontal balance of a ship in the water. **7.** the difference in the draft at the bow from that at the stern of a ship. **8.** the fitness or readiness of a ship for sailing as affected by the cargo, masts, sails, etc. **9.** the position or angle of the sails, yards, etc., in relation to the direction of the wind. **10.** the relative buoyancy of a submarine, controlled by taking in or expelling water from tanks in the hull: *to submerge to 100 feet and correct the trim.* **11.** the attitude of an aircraft relative to the horizontal plane when it is balanced in flight at a particular altitude with regard to prevailing winds. **12.** the visible woodwork inside a building, especially that around doors, windows, and other openings. **13.** the woodwork on the outside of a building used as ornamentation or finish. **14.** the upholstery, handles, and accessories inside an automobile. **15.** the chrome, color scheme, etc., decorating the outside of an automobile. **16.** a display in a store window; window display. **17.** film that is trimmed away and discarded, as in editing.
—*adv. Archaic.* in a trim manner; neatly; accurately.
[probably Old English *trymman* strengthen, make ready] —**trim′ly,** *adv.* —**trim′ness,** *n.*
—**Syn.** *v.t.* **4.** clip, prune. **5.** deck, garnish. -*adj.* **1, 2.** See **neat.**

tri·ma·ran (trī′mə ran′), *n.* a boat with three hulls side by side. [< *tri-* + (cata)-*maran*]

tri·mer (trī′mər), *n. Chemistry.* **1.** a molecule formed by combining three identical smaller molecules. *Example:* C_6H_6 or $(C_2H_2)_3$ is a trimer formed by combining three molecules of C_2H_2. **2.** a compound consisting of trimers. [< *tri-* + Greek *méros* part]

trim·er·ous (trim′ər əs), *adj.* **1.** having or consisting of three parts. **2.** characterized by three parts. **3.** *Botany.* (of a flower) having three members in each whorl (generally written *3-merous*). **4.** *Zoology.* having three segments to each tarsus, as certain insects. [< New Latin *trimerus* (with English *-ous*) < Greek *trimerḗs* < *tri-* three + *méros* part]

tri·mes·ter (trī mes′tər), *n.* **1.** a period or term of three months. **2.** a division (usually one third) of a school year. [< French *trimestre,* learned borrowing from Latin *trimēstris* of three months' duration < *tri-* three + *mēnsis* month]

tri·mes·tral (trī mes′trəl), *adj.* **1.** consisting of or containing three months. **2.** occurring or appearing every three months.

tri·mes·tri·al (trī mes′trē əl), *adj.* trimestral.

trim·e·ter (trim′ə tər), *Prosody.* —*n.* **1.** a verse having three feet. *Example:* "Below/ the light/house top." **2.** (in Greek and Latin poetry) a verse containing three dipodies (six feet). —*adj.* consisting of three feet or three dipodies. [< Latin *trimetrus* < Greek *trímetros* < *tri-* three + *métron* a measure]

tri·meth·yl (trī meth′əl), *adj. Chemistry.* having three methyl ($-CH_3$) radicals.

tri·meth·yl·a·mine (trī meth′ə lə mēn′, -lam′in), *n.* a colorless gas or liquid with a strong odor of ammonia, used in organic synthesis and as an insect attractant. *Formula:* C_3H_9N

tri·met·ric (trī met′rik), *adj.* **1.** consisting of three measures; trimeter. **2.** *Crystallography.* orthorhombic.

tri·met·ri·cal (trī met′rə kəl), *adj.* trimetric.

trimetric projection, *Geometry.* the projection of a solid using different scales at arbitrarily chosen angles for its three dimensions.

tri·met·ro·gon (trī met′rə gon), *n.* a system of photographic mapping from the air, in which one camera photographs the area vertically and two obliquely, operating simultaneously at regular intervals. [< *tri-* + Greek *métron* measure + *gōníā* angle]

trim·mer (trim′ər), *n.* **1.** a person or thing that trims: *a hat trimmer, a window trimmer, a hedge trimmer.* **2.** a person who changes his opinions, actions, etc., to suit the circumstances: *One of the trimmers who went to church and chapel both* (Thomas Hardy). **3.** a machine for trimming edges, as of lumber. **4.** a long beam or timber to which the end of a header is attached in the frame around a window, chimney, or other opening. —**Syn. 2.** timeserver.

trim·ming (trim′ing), *n.* **1.** decoration; ornament: *trimmings for a Christmas tree, trimming for a dress.* **2.** *Informal.* a defeat, especially an overwhelming defeat; beating; thrashing. **3.** *Informal.* a scolding.
trimmings, a. parts cut away in trimming; scraps: *The trimmings of any game . . . may be used for making the . . . sauce* (Alexis Soyer). **b.** *Informal.* additional or special items such as make a festive meal or occasion: *turkey with all the trimmings, a banquet with all the trimmings.*
—*adj.* that trims.

trimming tab, an auxiliary surface hinged at the trailing edge of a control surface of an aircraft, used to make small adjustments in stabilizing flight. See **empennage** and **aileron** for pictures.

tri·mo·lec·u·lar (trī′mə lek′yə lər), *adj. Chemistry.* of or made out of three molecules.

tri·month·ly (trī munth′lē), *adj.* occurring every three months.

tri·morph (trī′môrf), *n. Crystallography.* **1.** a trimorphic substance. **2.** any one of its three different forms.

tri·mor·phic (trī môr′fik), *adj.* existing in or assuming three distinct forms; exhibiting trimorphism.

tri·mor·phism (trī môr′fiz əm), *n.* **1.** the occurrence in three different forms of a crystalline substance. **2.** *Zoology.* the occurrence of three forms distinct in color, size, structure, etc., in different individuals of a species. **3.** *Botany.* the occurrence of three distinct forms of flowers, leaves, or other parts, on the same plant or in the same species. [< Greek *trímorphos* three-formed (< *tri-* three + *morphḗ* form) + English *-ism*]

tri·mor·phous (trī môr′fəs), *adj.* trimorphic.

tri·mo·tor (trī′mō′tər), *n.* an airplane fitted with three motors: *The old Ford trimotor, the . . . monoplane with the corrugated aluminum sides, was perhaps the first truly modern air transport* (Newsweek).

Tri·mur·ti (tri mu̇r′tē), *n.* the three chief Hindu divinities (Brahma, Vishnu, and Siva) as a trinitarian unity, or threefold manifestation of the primary essence of divinity. [< Sanskrit *trimūrti* < *tri* three + *mūrti* shape]

Tri·nac·ri·an (tri nak′rē ən, trī-), *adj.* of Sicily; Sicilian. [< Latin *Trīnacria* Sicily (< Greek *Trīnakríā* < *thrînax, -akos* trident, but taken as < *tri-* three + *ákra* point, cape[2]) + English *-an*]

tri·nal (trī′nəl), *adj.* composed of three parts; threefold; triple: *Trinal Unity* (Milton). [< Late Latin *trīnālis* < Latin *trīnus;* see TRINE]

tri·na·ry (trī′nər ē), *adj.* ternary.

trin·dle (trin′dəl), *n., v.,* **-dled, -dling.** *Obsolete or Dialect.* —*n.* **1.** the wheel of a wheelbarrow. **2.** any small wheel, caster, etc.; trundle. **3.** something of rounded form, as a ball.
—*v.t., v.i.* to trundle.
[variant of Old English *trendel* a wheel, anything round, related to *trendan* to turn. Compare TRUNDLE.]

trine (trīn), *adj.* **1.** threefold; triple. **2.** in astrology: **a.** of or denoting the aspect of two heavenly bodies distant from each other 120 degrees, or the third part of the zodiac. **b.** connected with or relating to this aspect, and therefore benign or favorable.
—*n.* **1.** a group of three; a triad. **2.** (in astrology) the trine aspect, supposed to be benign; trigon.
[< Latin *trīnus* triple < *trēs, tria* three]

Trine (trīn), *n.* the Trinity: *Eternal One, Almighty Trine* (John Keble). [< *trine*]

trin·gle (tring′gəl), *n.* **1.** a curtain rod. **2.** any long, slender rod. **3.** *Architecture.* a narrow, straight molding. [< Middle French *tringle,* Old French *tingle* beam; origin uncertain]

Trin·i·dad·i·an (trin′ə dad′ē ən), *adj.* of or having to do with Trinidad, an island in the West Indies near Venezuela, or its people.
—*n.* a native or inhabitant of Trinidad: *Trinidadians may well be the world's most musical people* (Time).

Trin·i·tar·i·an (trin′ə tãr′ē ən), *adj.* **1.** maintaining the nature and existence of the Trinity; orthodox in Christian belief. **2.** of or having to do with the Trinity. **3.** of or having to do with those who maintain the doctrine of the Trinity.
—*n.* **1.** a person who believes in the doctrine

of the Trinity. **2.** a friar or nun of the Roman Catholic Order of the Holy Trinity, a teaching and nursing fraternity originally founded in 1198 to ransom Christian captives from the Moslems.
[< New Latin *trinitarius* (< Latin *trīnitās;* see TRINITY) + English *-an*]

trin·i·tar·i·an (trin′ə târ′ē ən), *adj.* forming a trinity; consisting of or involving three in one; triple; threefold.

Trin·i·tar·i·an·ism (trin′ə târ′ē ə niz′əm), *n.* the doctrine of Trinitarians; belief in the Trinity.

tri·ni·tro·ben·zene (trī nī′trō ben′zēn, -ben zēn′), *n.* a yellow, crystalline compound used as an explosive. *Formula:* $C_6H_3N_3O_6$ [< *tri-* + *nitro-* + *benzene*]

tri·ni·tro·cre·sol (trī nī′trō krē′sōl, -sol), *n.* a soluble, yellow, crystalline substance, used in the manufacture of certain antiseptics and explosives. *Formula:* $C_7H_5N_3O_7$

tri·ni·tro·tol·u·ene (trī nī′trō tol′yů ēn), *n.* a powerful explosive, known as TNT. *Formula:* $C_7H_5N_3O_6$ [< *tri-* three + *nitro-* + *tolu*(ol) + *-ene*]

tri·ni·tro·tol·u·ol (trī nī′trō tol′yů ōl, -ol), *n.* trinitrotoluene.

Trin·i·ty (trin′ə tē), *n., pl.* **-ties.** **1.** *Theology.* the union of the Father, the Son, and the Holy Ghost in one divine nature; the triple person, separate but united, composed of these three persons; God: *the Holy Trinity.* **2.** Trinity Sunday. [< Old French *trinite,* learned borrowing from Latin *trīnitās* < *trīnus;* see TRINE]

trin·i·ty (trin′ə tē), *n., pl.* **-ties.** **1.** a group of three; triad. **2.** a being three. **3.** a picture or sculpture of the Trinity, usually a symbol like the triangle or trefoil. [< *Trinity*]

Trinity Season, the season of the church year between Trinity Sunday and Advent Sunday.

Trinity Sunday, the eighth Sunday after Easter and the first after Pentecost, observed by Christians as a feast in honor of the Trinity.

trin·ket (tring′kit), *n.* **1.** any small fancy article, bit of jewelry, or the like: *There was nothing personal anywhere: no photographs, no books, no trinkets of any kind* (Graham Greene). **2.** a trifle: *The world's a jest and joy's a trinket* (James K. Stephens).
trinkets, *Obsolete.* the tools, implements, or tackle of an occupation; paraphernalia; accouterments: *The poorer sort of common soldiers have every man his leather bag or satchel well sewn together, wherein he packs up all his trinkets* (Richard Hakluyt).
[origin uncertain]
—**Syn. 1.** knickknack. **2.** bagatelle.

trin·kum (tring′kəm), *n. Dialect.* trinket. [alteration of *trinket*]

tri·nod·al (trī nō′dəl), *adj.* having three nodes or joints. [< Latin *trinōdis* (< *tri-* three + *nōdus* knot, node) + English *-al*[1]]

tri·no·mi·al (trī nō′mē əl), *n.* **1.** *Algebra.* an expression consisting of three terms connected by plus or minus signs: $a + bx^2 - 2$ *is a trinomial.* **2.** *Zoology, Botany.* the name of an animal or plant consisting of three terms, the first indicating the genus, the second the species, and the third the subspecies or variety, as *Malus prunifolia robusta.*
—*adj.* **1.** *Algebra.* **a.** of or having to do with three terms. **b.** consisting of three terms connected by plus or minus signs. **2.** *Zoology, Botany.* having or characterized by three names.
[< *tri-* + *-nomial;* patterned on *binomial*]
—**tri·no′mi·al·ly,** *adv.*

tri·no·mi·al·ism (trī nō′mē ə liz′əm), *n. Biology.* the trinomial system of nomenclature; the use of trinomial names.

tri·o (trē′ō), *n., pl.* **tri·os.** **1.** *Music.* **a.** a composition for three voices or instruments. **b.** three singers or players who perform together. **c.** the second or subordinate division of a scherzo, march, minuet, or other dance movement, usually in a different key or style. The main division is usually repeated after it. **2.** any group of three: . . . *a trio of rusted tools bound by a funereal ribbon* (Esquire). [< Italian *trio* < *tre* three < Latin *trēs, tria* three]

tri·ode (trī′ōd), *n.* a vacuum tube containing three elements, commonly a cathode, anode (plate), and control grid. [< *tri-* + *-ode,* as in *cathode*]

tri·oe·cious (trī ē′shəs), *adj. Botany.* (of a genus, etc.) having male, female, and hermaphrodite flowers, each on different plants. Also, **triecious.** [< New Latin *Trioecia* the order name < Greek *tri-* three + *oîkos* house] —**tri·oe′cious·ly,** *adv.*

tri·oi·cous (trī oi′kəs), *adj.* trioecious.

tri·o·let (trī′ə lit), *n.* a poem having eight lines and only two rhymes. Lines 1, 4, and 7 are the same. Lines 2 and 8 are the same. [< Middle French *triolet* (diminutive) < *trio* three < Italian; see TRIO]

Tri·o·nal (trī′ə nəl), *n. Trademark.* a hypnotic resembling sulfonmethane, with highly toxic properties. *Formula:* $C_8H_{18}O_4S_2$ [< *tri-* + (sulph)*onal*]

tri·o·nym (trī′ə nim), *n.* a name consisting of three terms; trinomial. [< Greek *triṓnymos* having three names < *tri-* three + *ónyma* name]

tri·ose (trī′ōs), *n.* any of a class of sugars containing three atoms of carbon, and produced from glycerin by oxidation.

tri·ox·id (trī ok′sid), *n.* trioxide.

tri·ox·ide (trī ok′sīd, -sid), *n. Chemistry.* a compound containing three atoms of oxygen combined with another element or radical.

trip[1] (trip), *n., v.,* **tripped, trip·ping.** —*n.* **1.** a traveling about; journey; voyage; excursion: *a trip to Europe.* **2.** a journey or run made by a ship, train, airplane, etc., between two places, or to a place and back again (a round trip). **3.** the act of catching a person's foot to throw him down, especially in wrestling. **4.** a stumble or misstep caused by striking the foot against an object. **5.** a mistake or blunder; slip; lapse. **6.** the act of stepping lightly and quickly; a light, quick tread. **7.** of machinery: **a.** a contrivance that releases a catch, lever, etc. **b.** a projecting part which comes into contact with another part so as to start or stop a movement. **c.** a starting or stopping of a movement in this way. **8.** the mental state or experience induced by hallucinogenic drugs, such as LSD. [< verb]
—*v.i.* **1.** to strike the foot against something so as to stagger or fall; stumble: *to trip on the stairs, to trip over a toy.* **2.** to make a mistake or blunder, as in conduct, etc.; be inconsistent or inaccurate, as in a statement; err: *He tripped on that difficult question.* **3.** to take light, quick steps; move with a light, quick tread: *She tripped across the floor.* **4.** to tilt or tip up. **5.** to move past or be released by the pallet, as a cog on an escapement wheel of a watch or clock. **6.** to journey.
—*v.t.* **1.** to cause to stumble or fall: *The loose board tripped him.* **2.** to cause to make a mistake or blunder: *The difficult question tripped him.* **3.** to overthrow by catching in a mistake or blunder; outwit. **4.** to detect in an inconsistency or inaccuracy: *The examining board tripped him up several times.* **5.** to perform (a dance) with a light, quick step. **6.** to tread lightly and quickly. **7.** *Nautical.* **a.** to lift (an anchor) free of the bottom. **b.** to turn (a yard) into a vertical position before lowering. **c.** to lift (an upper mast) enough to remove the pin before lowering to the deck or into its housing. **8.** of machinery: **a.** to release (a catch, lever, or the like), as by contact with a projection. **b.** to operate (a mechanism) in this way.
[< Old French *tripper* strike with the feet < Germanic (compare Middle Dutch *trippen*)]
—**Syn.** *n.* **1. Trip, journey, voyage** mean a traveling from one place to another. **Trip** is the general word, usually suggesting return to the starting place, but not suggesting the length, purpose, manner, or means of travel: *How was your trip? He took a trip to Honolulu.* **Journey** suggests a long or tiring trip by land to a place for a definite purpose: *He decided to make the journey to Mexico by car.* **Voyage** suggests a long trip by water: *The voyage to the Islands will be restful.* -*v.i.* **3.** skip, caper.

trip[2] (trip), *n.* a small group of certain animals: *a trip of goats or seals.* [origin uncertain]

tri·part·ed (trī pär′tid), *adj.* divided into three parts.

tri·par·tite (trī pär′tīt), *adj.* **1.** divided into or composed of three parts or kinds; threefold; triple. **2.** involving division into three parts. **3.** *Botany.* divided into three parts nearly to the base, as a leaf. **4.** made in three corresponding parts or copies, as an indenture drawn up between three persons or parties, each of whom preserves one of the copies. **5.** consisting of or involving three parties: *a tripartite league.* **6.** concluded between three parties: *a tripartite treaty between the United States, England, and France.* [< Latin *tripartītus* < *tri-* three + *partītus,* past participle of *partīrī* to divide < *pars, partis* share, portion] —**tri·par′tite·ly,** *adv.*

tri·par·ti·tion (trī′pär tish′ən), *n.* **1.** division into three parts. **2.** partition among three. **3.** *Obsolete.* arithmetical division by three.

tripe (trīp), *n.* **1.** the walls of the first and second stomachs of a ruminant animal, especially a steer or cow, used as food, the first stomach or rumen being plain tripe and the second or reticulum being honeycomb tripe. **2.** *Informal.* something foolish, worthless, offensive, etc.; nonsensical rubbish; trash. [< Old French *tripe* entrails, perhaps ultimately < Arabic *tharb* suet]

tri·pe·dal (trī′pə dəl, trī pē′-; trip′ə-), *adj.* having three feet. [< Latin *tripedālis* of three feet (in length) < *tri-* three + *pēs, pedis* foot]

tripe-de-roche (trēp′də rôsh′), *n.* any of various edible lichens of arctic, subarctic, and north temperate regions. [< French *tripe-de-roche* (literally) rock tripe (because of its appearance)]

tri·per·son·al (trī pėr′sə nəl), *adj.* **1.** consisting of or existing in three persons (used of the Godhead). **2.** relating to the three persons of the Godhead.

tri·pet·al·ous (trī pet′ə ləs), *adj.* having three petals.

trip·ham·mer (trip′ham′ər), *n.* a heavy iron or steel block which is raised by machinery and then tripped by a cam or the like and allowed to drop, used in foundries, machine shops, etc. —*adj.* of or like a triphammer, especially with regard to power of impact: *a triphammer blow.*

tri·phen·yl (trī fen′əl, -fē′nəl), *adj.* having three phenyl radicals in the molecule. —*n.* a triphenyl compound. *Formula:* $(—C_6H_5)_3$

tri·phen·yl·meth·ane (trī fen′əl meth′ān, -fē′nəl-), *n.* a colorless hydrocarbon, used in the manufacture of many synthetic dyes. *Formula:* $C_{19}H_{16}$

tri·phib·i·an (trī fib′ē ən), *adj.* triphibious.

tri·phib·i·ous (trī fib′ē əs), *adj.* **1.** involving land, sea, and air forces in a single action. **2.** operating on land, water, and in the air: *a triphibious vehicle or craft.* [< *tri-* + (am)*phibious*]

tri·phos·phate (trī fos′fāt), *n.* a substance whose molecule contains three phosphate (PO_4) radicals.

tri·phos·pho·py·ri·dine nucleotide (trī fos′fō pir′ə dēn), a coenzyme that speeds the oxidation of living plant and animal tissues. It is similar in function to diphosphopyridine nucleotide. *Formula:* $C_{21}H_{28}N_7O_{17}P_3$ *Abbr.:* TPN (no periods).

triph·thong (trif′thông, -thong; trip′-), *n.* **1.** a combination of three vowel sounds in one syllable. **2.** a trigraph. [< *tri-,* patterned on *diphthong*]

triph·y·line (trif′ə lin, -lēn), *n.* triphylite.

triph·y·lite (trif′ə līt) *n.* a phosphate of iron, manganese, and lithium, occurring in greenish-gray or bluish crystals. [< *tri-* three + Greek *phȳlḗ* tribe + English *-ite*[1] (because it has three bases)]

tri·phyl·lous (trī fil′əs), *adj. Botany.* having or consisting of three leaves. [< *tri-* + Greek *phýllon* leaf + English *-ous*]

tri·pin·nate (trī pin′āt), *adj. Botany.* triply pinnate (applied to a bipinnate leaf whose divisions are also pinnate). —**tri·pin′nate·ly,** *adv.*

tri·pin·nat·ed (trī pin′ā tid), *adj. Botany.* tripinnate.

Tri·pit·a·ka (tri pit′ə kə), *n.* a sacred book of Buddhism, divided into three sections, Discipline, Discourse, and Metaphysics. It is based on the actual teachings of Gautama and written in Pali. [< Sanskrit *Tripitaka* (literally) three baskets < *tri* three + *pitaka* basket]

tri·plane (trī′plān′), *n.* an airplane having three sets of wings, one above another.

tri·ple (trip′əl), *adj., n., v.,* **-pled, -pling.** —*adj.* **1.** three times as much or as many; of three times the measure or amount; multiplied by three. **2.** having three parts; threefold. **3.** consisting of or involving three parties.
—*n.* **1.** a quantity, sum, or number that is three times as much or as many. **2.** (in

baseball) a hit by which a batter gets to third base.

—*v.t.* to make three times as much or as many; multiply by three: *to triple one's income.*

—*v.i.* **1.** to become three times as much or as many: *The price of bread has nearly tripled since 1940.* **2.** to serve three purposes; play three parts: *Chiffon middy ties can triple as scarves, stoles, and sashes* (New Yorker). **3.** (in baseball) to hit safely for three bases.

[< Latin *triplus* < *tri-* three + *-plus* -fold. Doublet of TREBLE.]

tri·ple-A (trip′əl ā′), *adj.* (in financial rating) of the highest rank: *a triple-A credit rating, triple-A securities.*

triple bond, *Chemistry.* a bond in which three pairs of electrons are shared between two atoms, characteristic of unsaturated compounds such as acetylene.

triple crown, **1.** the tiara worn by the Pope. **2.** any group of three championships, honors, etc.

Triple Crown, *U.S.* first place in the Kentucky Derby, the Preakness, and the Belmont Stakes, races for three-year-old horses.

tri·ple-deck·er (trip′əl dek′ər), *n.* three-decker: *The cost of the sandwiches is from about 65 cents . . . to $2 for an oversize triple-decker* (New York Times).

tri·ple-ex·pan·sion engine (trip′əl ek-span′shən), a steam engine in which the steam passes into three cylinders in succession, so that the expansive force is used in three stages.

tri·ple-head·er (trip′əl hed′ər), *n.* three games played in the same sports arena one after another on the same day: *a basketball triple-header.*

triple measure, triple time.

tri·ple-nerved (trip′əl nėrvd′), *adj. Botany.* designating a leaf in which two principal nerves emerge from the middle one a little above its base.

triple play, (in baseball) a play that puts three men out.

triple point, *Physics.* the point at which the three phases (gas, liquid, and solid) of a substance exist in equilibrium.

tri·plet (trip′lit), *n.* **1.** one of three children born at the same birth to one mother. **2.** a group of three; trio. **3.** *Music.* a group of three notes to be performed in the time of two of the same time value. **4.** three successive lines of verse, usually rhyming and equal in length.

triplets, a. three children at a birth: *Triplets may result from the formation of a pair of twins and the simultaneous development of an additional egg* (Sidonie M. Gruenberg). **b.** three of a kind in certain card games: *He came up with a straight to beat my triplets.*

[< *triple;* perhaps patterned on *doublet*]

tri·ple·tail (trip′əl tāl′), *n.* a large food fish of warm seas, having long dorsal and anal fins which extend backward, appearing to be lobes of the tail.

Tripletail
(to 3 ft. long)

triple threat, 1. a back in football who can pass, kick, and run with the ball adeptly. **2.** a person who has three skills, fields of competence, etc. —**triple-threat,** *adj.*

triple time, *Music.* **1.** time in which each measure contains three beats, with the first beat accented. **2.** the rhythm of this. Also, **triple measure.**

triple tree, *Archaic.* the gallows (with allusion to the two posts and crossbeam comprising it).

tri·plets (trip′lits), *n.pl.* See under **triplet,** *n.*

tri·plex (trip′leks, trī′pleks), *adj.* triple; threefold. —*n.* **1.** something triple or threefold. **2.** *Music.* triple time or measure. [< Latin *triplex, -plicis* < *tri-* three + *-plex, -plicis,* related to *plaga* flat(ness)]

trip·li·cate (*v.* trip′lə kāt; *adj., n.* trip′lə kit), *v.,* **-cat·ed, -cat·ing,** *adj., n.* —*v.t.* **1.** to multiply by three; increase threefold; triple. **2.** *Linguistics.* to form (a word) by triple repetition of an element.

—*adj.* triple; threefold.

—*n.* one of three things exactly alike, especially one of three copies of a document.

in triplicate, in three copies exactly alike: *The constitutions were written in triplicate* (Walter Hook).

[< Latin *triplicātus,* past participle of *triplicāre* to triple < *triplex;* see TRIPLEX]

trip·li·ca·tion (trip′lə kā′shən), *n.* **1.** a triplicating. **2.** a being triplicated. **3.** something triplicated. **4.** *Linguistics.* **a.** the formation of a word by triple repetition of an element. **b.** a word thus formed.

tri·plic·i·ty (tri plis′ə tē), *n., pl.* **-ties. 1.** the quality or condition of being triple; threefold character or existence. **2.** a triad; trio. **3.** (in astrology) a combination of three of the twelve signs of the zodiac, each sign being distant 120 degrees from the other two; trigon.

trip·lite (trip′līt), *n.* a phosphate of iron and manganese containing fluorine, of a brown or blackish color. [< German *Triplit* < Greek *triploûs* threefold + German *-it* -ite[1] (because of its cleavage in three directions)]

trip·loid (trip′loid), *Biology.* —*adj.* having three times the number of chromosomes characteristic of germ cells of the species. —*n.* a triploid organism. [< New Latin *triploides* < Greek *triplóos*]

trip·loi·dy (trip loi′dē), *n. Biology.* the state of having three times the number of chromosomes characteristic of germ cells of the species.

tri·ply (trip′lē), *adv.* in a triple degree or manner; three times. —**Syn.** trebly, thrice.

tri·pod (trī′pod), *n.* **1.** a three-legged support or stand for a camera, transit, or other instrument. See **transit** for picture. **2.** (formerly) a seat, table, or other similar structure with three legs, especially a three-legged stool. **3.** in ancient Greece and Rome: **a.** a three-legged pot or cauldron. **b.** an ornamental vessel on the pattern of this, often presented as a prize, or as a votive offering. [< Latin *tripūs, -podis* < Greek *trípous, -podos* (literally) three-footed < *tri-* three + *poús, podós* foot]

trip·o·dal (trip′ə dəl), *adj.* three-footed; three-legged.

tri·pod·ic (trī pod′ik), *adj.* designating a method of walking in which two legs on one side and one on the other move together, used by certain insects.

trip·o·dy (trip′ə dē), *n., pl.* **-dies.** *Prosody.* a group or verse of three feet. [< Greek *tripodiā* < *trípous, -podos* three-footed; see TRIPOD]

tri·po·lar (trī pō′lər), *adj.* having three poles.

trip·o·li (trip′ə lē), *n.* any of several light, soft earths or rocks, especially infusorial earth and rottenstone, used in polishing, etc. [< French *tripoli* < *Tripoli,* a city in Africa, where it was originally found]

Tri·pol·i·tan (tri pol′ə tən), *adj.* of or having to do with Tripoli, a region in northern Africa, now included in Libya, or its people. —*n.* a native or inhabitant of Tripoli.

Tri·pol·i·ta·ni·an (tri pol′ə tā′nē ən, trip′ə lə-), *n.* a native or inhabitant of Tripolitania, a province of Libya. —*adj.* of or having to do with Tripolitania or the Tripolitanians.

tri·pos (trī′pos), *n., pl.* **-pos·es. 1.** (at Cambridge University) a final honors examination, especially in mathematics. **2.** *Obsolete.* tripod. [originally (at Cambridge), an official who composed humorous commencement verses and joked with degree candidates (because of his tripod stool) < Greek *trípos,* variant of *trípous;* see TRIPOD]

trip·per (trip′ər), *n.* **1.** a person or thing that trips. **2.** a device or mechanism that releases a catch in a machine, a railroad signal, or other mechanism. **3.** *Especially British.* a person who takes a trip; tourist: *Fares will probably be a lot cheaper, perhaps cheap enough to tempt the week-end tripper* (Sunday Times). —**Syn. 3.** excursionist.

trip·per·y (trip′ər ē), *adj. Especially British.* like a tripper or trippers; touristy: *Venice in its most trippery and least attractive garb . . .* (London Daily Express).

trip·pet (trip′it), *n.* a cam, projection, etc., intended to strike some object at regularly recurrent intervals. [< *trip,* verb]

trip·ping (trip′ing), *adj.* moving quickly and lightly; light-footed; nimble. —*n.* **1.** the act of a person or thing that trips. **2.** a light dance. —**trip′ping·ly,** *adv.*

tripping line, a line or cable used to trip (free from the bottom) an anchor.

trip·tane (trip′tān), *n.* a liquid motor fuel noted for its antiknock qualities. It is used chiefly in aviation gasolines, especially to provide additional power. [< *tri-* + *p*(en)*tane*]

trip·ter·ous (trip′tər əs), *adj. Botany.* having three wings or winglike expansions. [< *tri-* + Greek *pterón* wing + English *-ous*]

Trip·tol·e·mus or **Trip·tol·e·mos** (trip-tol′ə məs), *n. Greek Mythology.* a favorite of Demeter, said to have revealed the secrets of successful agriculture to man.

trip·tych (trip′tik), *n.* **1.** a set of three panels side by side, having pictures, carvings, or the like on them. The side panels are usually subordinate, and are hinged to fold over the central panel. Triptychs are commonly used or designed to be used as altarpieces. **2.** a hinged, three-leaved writing tablet, used in ancient times. [< Greek *tríptychos* three-layered < *tri-* three + *ptýx* fold]

trip·tyque (trip tēk′), *n.* an international pass through customs for temporarily importing an automobile, as for touring. [< French *triptyque* (literally) triptych]

trip wire, a wire which, when pulled or disturbed, releases a catch and starts a process, as the explosion of a mine, the sounding of an alarm, etc.: *Trip wires, connected to field transmitters buried underground, supply continuous knowledge of avalanches and smaller slips of snow which observers may then correlate with weather conditions* (New Scientist).

tri·que·trous (trī kwē′trəs, -kwet′rəs), *adj.* three-sided; triangular. [< Latin *triquetrus* (with English *-ous*) three-cornered < *tri-* three + *-quetrus,* related to *quadra* square]

tri·que·trum (trī kwē′trəm), *n., pl.* **-tra** (-trə). a bone of the human carpus (wrist) in the proximal row of carpal bones; the cuneiform or pyramidal. [< New Latin *triquetrum,* neuter of Latin *triquetrus;* see TRIQUETROUS]

tri·ra·di·ate (trī rā′dē āt), *adj.* having or consisting of three rays; radiating in three directions from a central point.

tri·ra·di·at·ed (trī rā′dē ā′tid), *adj.* triradiate.

tri·ra·di·ate·ly (trī rā′dē it′lē), *adv.* in a triradiate manner.

tri·ra·di·us (trī rā′dē əs), *n., pl.* **-di·i** (-dē ī), **-di·us·es. 1.** a junction of three lines at the base of each finger on the palm of the hand. **2.** a tiny triangle formed in fingerprints by ridges meeting at the corners: *Ridges, loops, and triradius points form the basis of fingerprint analysis both for criminal investigation and, diagnostically, for spotting certain kinds of hereditary defects (like mongolism) in humans* (New Scientist).

tri·reg·num (trī reg′nəm), *n.* the triple crown worn by the Pope as a symbol of his position; tiara: *The triregnum evolved in the 13th century, and its original meaning has been lost* (Time). See picture under **tiara.** [< Latin *tri-* three + *regnum* reign]

tri·reme (trī′rēm), *n.* (in ancient Greece and Rome) a ship, usually a warship, with three rows of oars, one above the other, on each side. —*adj.* having three rows of oars. [< Latin *trirēmis* < *tri-* three + *rēmus* oar]

tri·sac·cha·rid (trī sak′ər id), *n.* trisaccharide.

tri·sac·cha·ride (trī sak′ə rīd, -ər id), *n.* any of a class of carbohydrates, as raffinose, which on hydrolysis yields three molecules of simple sugars (monosaccharides).

tri·sect (trī sekt′), *v.t.* **1.** to divide into three parts. **2.** *Geometry.* to divide into three equal parts. [< *tri-* + Latin *sectus,* past participle of *secāre* to cut]

tri·sec·tion (trī sek′shən), *n.* **1.** the division of a thing into three parts. **2.** *Geometry.* the division of a straight line or an angle into three equal parts.

tri·sec·tor (trī sek′tər), *n.* a person or thing that trisects.

tri·seme (trī′sēm), *n.* a metrical foot consisting of three short syllables. —*adj.* trisemic. [< Greek *trísēmos* < *tri-* three + *sêma, -atos* a sign]

tri·se·mic (trī sē′mik), *adj.* **1.** having three morae or short syllables. **2.** equivalent to three morae or short syllables.

tri·sep·al·ous (trī sep′ə ləs), *adj. Botany.* having three sepals.

tri·sep·tate (trī sep′tāt), *adj. Biology.* having three septa (partitions).

tri·se·ri·al (trī sir′ē əl), *adj.* **1.** arranged in three series or rows. **2.** *Botany.* having three floral whorls. [< *tri-* + *serial*]

tri·shaw (trī′shô), *n.* a pedicab: *I flagged a trishaw and told the boy to take me to Wing Yan's silk shop* (S. J. Perelman).

tris·kai·dek·a·phobe (tris′kī dek′ə fōb), *n.* a person having an abnormal fear of the number 13.

tris·kai·dek·a·pho·bi·a (tris′kī dek′ə fō′bē ə), *n.* an abnormal fear of the number 13: *Probably ... the most common phobia is triskaidekaphobia* (Time). [< Greek *treiskaídeka* thirteen (< *treîs* three + *kaí* and + *déka* ten) + English *-phobia*]

tris·kele (tris′kēl), *n.* triskelion.

tris·kel·i·on (tris kel′ē on), *n.* a symbolic figure consisting of three legs or lines radiating from a common center. [< New Latin *triskelion* < Greek *triskelês* three-legged < *tri-* three + *skélos* leg]

tris·mic (triz′mik, tris′-), *adj.* **1.** of or having to do with lockjaw. **2.** having lockjaw.

tris·mus (triz′məs, tris′-), *n.* lockjaw. [< New Latin *trismus* < Greek *trismós*, alteration of *trigmós* a grating, grinding < *trízein* to creak, crack, grate]

tris·oc·ta·he·dral (tris ok′tə hē′drəl), *adj.* **1.** bounded by twenty-four equal faces. **2.** having to do with a trisoctahedron. **3.** having the form of a trisoctahedron.

tris·oc·ta·he·dron (tris ok′tə hē′drən), *n., pl.* **-drons, -dra** (-drə). a solid bounded by twenty-four equal faces, every three of which correspond to one face of an octahedron. A trigonal trisoctahedron has twenty-four triangular faces, and a tetragonal trisoctahedron has twenty-four quadrilateral or trapezoidal faces. [< Greek *trís* (< *trís* thrice) + English *octahedron*]

tri·so·di·um phosphate (trī sō′dē əm), a crystalline compound used as a detergent, metal cleaner, water softener, and in the manufacture of paper and photographic developers. *Formula:* Na_3PO_4

tri·some (trī′sōm), *n. Biology.* a trisomic condition.

tri·so·mic (trī sō′mik), *adj. Biology* diploid except for one chromosome which is triploid. [< *tri-* + Greek *sôma* body + English *-ic*]

tri·so·my (trī′sō mē), *n. Biology.* trisome: *From the present findings it follows that trisomy ... is associated with various congenital defects* (Science News Letter).

tri·sper·mous (trī spėr′məs), *adj. Botany.* containing three seeds. [< *tri-* + Greek *spérma* seed + English *-ous*]

tri·spor·ic (trī spôr′ik, -spor′-), *adj. Botany.* having three spores.

tri·spor·ous (trī spôr′əs, -spōr′-), *adj. Botany.* trisporic.

trist (trist), *adj. Archaic.* sad; sorrowful; melancholy. [< Old French *triste*, learned borrowing from Latin *trīstis* sad]

Tris·tan (tris′tən), *n.* Tristram.

tri·state (trī′stāt′), *adj.* of, belonging to, or involving three adjoining states or the adjoining parts of three such states: *The [New Jersey] legislature refused to grant legal status to a tri-state transportation committee which had already been approved by New York and Connecticut* (Harper's).

triste (trēst), *adj. French.* sad; melancholy; gloomy: *Mrs. Knatchbull, triste as only one persecuted by the Fates can be, shook her head* (New Yorker).

tris·tesse (trēs tes′), *n. French.* sadness; melancholy; gloom.

tris·te·za (tris tā′zə), *n.* a virus disease of citrus trees that attacks sweet orange, tangerine, and scions of certain other related trees grafted on the rootstalks of the sour orange. [< Spanish and Portuguese *tristeza* grief, affliction < Latin *trīstitia* < *trīstis* sad]

trist·ful (trist′fəl), *adj. Archaic.* **1.** sad; sorrowful. **2.** dreary; dismal. —**trist′ful·ly,** *adv.*

tris·tich (tris′tik), *n.* three lines of verse forming a stanza or group. [< *tri-;* patterned on *distich*]

tris·tich·ous (tris′tə kəs), *adj.* **1.** arranged in three rows or ranks. **2.** characterized by three rows or ranks. **3.** *Botany.* arranged in three vertical rows or ranks. [< Greek *trístichos* (with English *-ous*) < *tri-* three + *stíchos* row, line, stich]

Tris·tram (tris′trəm), *n.* one of the most famous knights of the Round Table. His love for Iseult, wife of King Mark, is the subject of many stories and poems and of an opera by Wagner.

tri·sty·lous (trī stī′ləs), *adj. Botany.* having three styles.

tri·sul·cate (trī sul′kāt), *adj.* **1.** *Botany.* having three sulci or grooves. **2.** *Zoology.* divided into three digits, as a foot. [< Latin *trisulcus* having three clefts (< *tri-* tri- + *sulcus* furrow) + English *-ate*[1]]

tri·sul·fid or **tri·sul·phid** (trī sul′fid), *n.* trisulfide.

tri·sul·fide or **tri·sul·phide** (trī sul′fīd, -fid), *n.* a compound containing three atoms of sulfur combined with another element or radical.

tris·yl·lab·ic (tris′ə lab′ik, trī′sə-), *adj.* having three syllables.

tris·yl·lab·i·cal (tris′ə lab′ə kəl, trī′sə-), *adj.* trisyllabic.

tris·yl·lab·i·cal·ly (tris′ə lab′ə klē, trī′sə-), *adv.* as or in three syllables.

tri·syl·la·ble (tri sil′ə bəl, trī-), *n.* a word having three syllables. *Educate* is a trisyllable.

trit., triturate.

tri·tag·o·nist (trī tag′ə nist, tri-), *n.* (in ancient Greece) the third actor in a tragedy, next in importance after the deuteragonist. [< Greek *tritagōnistês* < *trítos* third + *agōnistês* combatant, actor]

trit·a·nope (trit′ə nōp, trī′tə-), *n.* a person who suffers from tritanopia.

trit·a·no·pi·a (trit′ə nō′pē ə, trī′tə-), *n.* a form of color blindness, the inability to distinguish violet, blue, green, and to some extent, yellow. [< New Latin *tritanopia* < Greek *trítos* third + *an-* without + *ôps* eye (referring to the lack of a third constituent of vision necessary for color awareness)]

trit·a·no·pic (trit′ə nō′pik, trī′tə-), *adj.* of or having to do with tritanopia: *tritanopic vision.*

trite (trīt), *adj.,* **trit·er, trit·est.** worn out by constant use or repetition; no longer new or interesting; hackneyed; commonplace: *"Cheeks like roses" is a trite expresssion.* [< Latin *trītus*, past participle of *terere* rub] —**trite′ly,** *adv.* —**trite′ness,** *n.* —**Syn.** stereotyped, banal, stale. —**Ant.** original, new, fresh.

tri·the·ism (trī′thē iz əm), *n.* belief in three Gods, especially the doctrine that the Father, the Son, and the Holy Ghost of the Christian Trinity are three distinct Gods. [< *tri-* + Greek *theós* god + English *-ism*]

tri·the·ist (trī′thē ist), *n.* a person who believes in tritheism.

tri·the·is·tic (trī′thē is′tik), *adj.* **1.** of or having to do with tritheism. **2.** believing in tritheism.

tri·the·is·ti·cal (trī′thē is′tə kəl), *adj.* tritheistic.

tri·thing (trī′THing), *n. Obsolete.* riding[2], an administrative division.

trit·i·ate (trit′ē āt, trish′-), *v.t.,* **-at·ed, -at·ing.** to mix, infuse, or coat with tritium.

trit·i·um (trit′ē əm, trish′-), *n.* an isotope of hydrogen, with an atomic weight of 3. It is the explosive used in a hydrogen bomb. *Symbol:* T or H^3 [< New Latin *tritium* < Greek *trítos* third < *treîs* three]

Tri·ton (trī′tən), *n. Greek Mythology.* **1.** a sea god, son of Poseidon and Amphitrite, having the head and body of a man and the tail of a fish and carrying a trumpet made of a conch shell. **2.** (later) any of a group of minor sea gods by whom Poseidon and the other major sea gods were served. **3.** the larger of the two satellites of Neptune.

tri·ton[1] (trī′tən), *n.* **1.** any of a family of marine gastropods, especially any of a group having a brightly colored, spiral, trumpet-shaped shell. **2.** the shell of such an animal. [< *Triton*]

tri·ton[2] (trī′ton), *n.* the nucleus of a tritium atom. [< *trit*(ium) + *-on*, as in *electron*]

tri·tone (trī′tōn′), *n. Music.* an interval consisting of three whole tones; augmented fourth. [< Greek *trítonos* < *tri-* three + *tónos* a tone]

Tri·ton·ess (trī′tə nis), *n.* a female Triton.

trit·u·ra·ble (trich′ər ə bəl), *adj.* capable of being triturated.

trit·u·rate (trich′ə rāt), *v.,* **-rat·ed, -rat·ing,** *n.* —*v.t.* **1.** to rub, crush, grind, or pound into fine particles or a very fine powder; pulverize. **2.** *Archaic.* to masticate (food). —*n.* **1.** a triturated substance. **2.** *Pharmacology.* a trituration. [< Late Latin *trītūrāre* (with English *-ate*[1]) thresh < Latin *terere* to rub]

trit·u·ra·tion (trich′ə rā′shən), *n.* **1.** a triturating. **2.** a being triturated; pulverization. Trituration is a dry process, and thus distinguished from levigation. **3.** *Pharmacology.* **a.** a powder obtained by triturating 10 grams of a powdered drug, etc., with 90 grams of powdered lactose. **b.** a powder produced, or medicine prepared, by triturating.

trit·u·ra·tor (trich′ə rā′tər), *n.* **1.** a person or thing that triturates. **2.** an apparatus for grinding drugs.

tri·tyl·o·dont (trī til′ə dont), *n.* a small, mammallike reptile of the late Triassic and early Jurassic periods, having a long body and short legs, multiple bones in the lower jaw and cusped teeth. It is regarded as an evolutionary link between reptiles and mammals. [< New Latin *Tritylodon, -ontis* the genus name < Greek *tri-* + *týlos* knob + *odoús, odóntos* tooth (because their teeth had three rows of cusps)]

tri·tyl·o·don·toid (trī til′ə don′toid), *n.* a tritylodont. —*adj.* of or having to do with the tritylodonts.

tri·umph (trī′umf), *n.* **1.** the act or fact of being victorious; victory: *final triumph over the enemy. But in ourselves are triumph and defeat* (Longfellow). **2.** a signal success or achievement: *The use of atomic energy is a triumph of modern science.* **3.** the exultation of victory or success; victorious joy: *a smile of triumph.* **4.** a Roman procession in honor of a victorious general. **5.** *Obsolete.* a spectacle or pageant, especially a tournament.

in triumph, a. triumphant: *to return, in triumph, with the spoils of victory.* **b.** triumphantly: *He brought home the prize in triumph.*

—*v.i.* **1.** to gain victory; win success; prevail: *to triumph over adversity.* **2.** to rejoice because of victory or success; exult; glory. **3.** to celebrate a Roman triumph. —*v.t. Obsolete.* to conquer.

[< Old French *triumphe*, learned borrowing from Latin *triumphus* < Greek *thríambos* a hymn to Dionysus] —**tri′umph·er,** *n.*

—**Syn.** *n.* **1.** conquest. See **victory. 3.** elation. —*v.i.* **1.** conquer.

tri·um·phal (trī um′fəl), *adj.* **1.** of or having to do with a triumph. **2.** of the nature of a triumph; celebrating a victory: *a triumphal procession.* —**tri·um′phal·ly,** *adv.*

tri·um·phal·ism (trī um′fə liz′əm), *n.* the preaching of ultimate victory over one's rivals or enemies, especially as an ideological doctrine or policy: *Nothing is surprising in the Communist triumphalism* (Manchester Guardian Weekly).

tri·um·phant (trī um′fənt), *adj.* **1.** victorious; successful. **2.** rejoicing because of victory or success: *O come all ye faithful, Joyful and triumphant* (Frederick Oakley). **3.** triumphal. **4.** *Obsolete.* splendid; glorious. [< Latin *triumphāns, -antis*, present participle of *triumphāre* to have a triumph] —**tri·um′phant·ly,** *adv.*

—**Syn. 2.** jubilant, exultant.

tri·um·vir (trī um′vər), *n., pl.* **-virs, -vi·ri** (-və rī). **1.** one of three men who shared the same public office in ancient Rome, especially a member of a committee responsible for the administration of a particular department of the government. **2.** one of any three persons sharing power or authority. [< Latin *triumvir*, abstracted from phrase *trium virōrum* of three men, genitive plural of *trēs* three and *vir* man]

tri·um·vi·ral (trī um′vər əl), *adj.* of or having to do with a triumvir or a triumvirate.

tri·um·vi·rate (trī um′vər it, -və rāt), *n.* **1.** government or rule by three men together. **2.** any association of three in office or authority. **3.** the position or term of office of a Roman triumvir. **4.** any group of three; trio. [< Latin *triumvirātus* < *triumvir;* see TRIUMVIR]

Tri·um·vi·rate (trī um′vər it, -və rāt), *n.* **1.** the coalition of Pompey, Caesar, and Crassus; First Triumvirate. **2.** the coalition of Octavian, Antony, and Lepidus; Second Triumvirate.

tri·une (trī′yün), *adj.* consisting of three in one, especially the Trinity: *the triune God.* —*n.* any united group of three; triad. [< *tri-* + Latin *ūnus* one]

Tri·une (trī′yün), *n.* the Trinity.

tri·u·ni·tar·i·an (trī yü′nə tãr′ē ən), *n.* Trinitarian.

tri·u·ni·ty (trī yü′nə tē), *n.* a being three in one.

tri·va·lence (trī vā′ləns, triv′ə-), *n.* the state or quality of being trivalent.

tri·va·len·cy (trī vā′lən sē, triv′ə-), *n., pl.* **-cies.** trivalence.

tri·va·lent (trī vā′lənt, triv′ə-), *adj.* having a valence of three; tervalent.

tri·valve (trī′valv′), *adj.* having three valves, as certain shells.

triv·et (triv′it), *n.* **1.** a small iron frame on short legs, usually three in number, for

use under a hot dish to protect the surface of a table. **2.** any of various iron contrivances similar to this, formerly used to support a pot or kettle over coals in an open fireplace. **3.** a tripod.
as right as a trivet, entirely or perfectly right (in allusion to a trivet's standing firm on its three legs): *"I hope you are well, sir." "Right as a trivet, sir," replied Bob Sawyer* (Dickens).
[Old English *trefet,* probably ultimately < Latin *tripūs, -podis* (see TRIPOD); influenced by Latin *trifidus;* see TRIFID]

triv·i·a (triv′ē ə), *n.pl.* **1.** things of little or no importance; trifles; trivialities. **2.** the plural of **trivium.** [< New Latin *trivia,* neuter plural of Latin *trivium* crossways; influenced by English *trivial*]

triv·i·al (triv′ē əl), *adj.* **1.** not important; trifling; insignificant: *Fred's composition had only a few trivial mistakes.* **2.** of or having to do with the trivium: *the trivial arts.* **3.** *Biology.* (of a taxonomic designation) specific. **4.** *Archaic.* not new or interesting; ordinary; commonplace: *the trivial round, the common task* (John Keble).
[< Latin *triviālis* vulgar; (originally) of the crossways < *trivium* crossways < *tri-* three + *via* road, way] **—triv′i·al·ly,** *adv.* **—triv′i·al·ness,** *n.*
—Syn. 1. paltry, slight, small, unimportant, inconsequential. **—Ant. 1.** important, momentous.

triv·i·al·ise (triv′ē ə līz), *v.t.,* **-ised, -is·ing.** *Especially British.* trivialize.

triv·i·al·ism (triv′ē ə liz′əm), *n.* a triviality; trifle.

triv·i·al·i·ty (triv′ē al′ə tē), *n., pl.* **-ties. 1.** trivial quality. **2.** a trivial thing, remark, affair, etc.; trifle: *completely engulfed in the trivialities of suburban life* (H. G. Wells).
—Syn. 1. unimportance, insignificance.

triv·i·al·i·za·tion (triv′ē ə lə zā′shən), *n.* the act or process of trivializing: *There has to be a halt to the trivialization of scholarship, the rage to publish* (Harper's). *The mass media lend themselves to the trivialization of knowledge and experience* (George Barnes).

triv·i·al·ize (triv′ē ə līz), *v.t.,* **-ized, -iz·ing.** to make trivial; render commonplace or trifling: *We trivialize Lent if we see it merely as a time for giving up smoking* (Manchester Guardian Weekly).

triv·i·um (triv′ē əm), *n., pl.* **-i·a.** (in ancient Rome and in the Middle Ages) grammar, rhetoric, and logic, the first three of the seven liberal arts. The other four, the quadrivium, were arithmetic, music, geometry, and astronomy. [< Medieval Latin *trivium* (literally) a triple road or way < Latin; see TRIVIAL]

tri·week·ly (trī wēk′lē), *adv., n., pl.* **-lies,** *adj.* **—***adv.* **1.** once every three weeks. **2.** three times a week.
—*n.* a publication issued triweekly.
—*adj.* occurring or appearing triweekly.

Tro·bri·and·er (trō′brē ən dər, -an′-), *n.* a native or inhabitant of the Trobriand Islands, near New Guinea: *Trobrianders eventually succeed in distributing goods locally produced throughout the islands* (Beals and Hoijer).

tro·car (trō′kär), *n.* a surgical instrument used to puncture cavities and draw fluid out, as in dropsy. Also, **trochar.** [< French *trocart,* for *troisquarts* (literally) three quarters < *trois* three (< Latin *trēs*) + *carre* side of a sword or knife (because of its triangular form)]

tro·cha·ic (trō kā′ik), *adj.* **1.** consisting of trochees. **2.** characterized by or based on trochees: *trochaic verse.* **3.** of the nature of a trochee: *a trochaic foot.* **—***n.* **1.** a trochaic poem or line of verse. **2.** trochee. [< Latin *trochaicus* < Greek *trochāïkós* < *trochaîos;* see TROCHEE]

tro·chal (trō′kəl), *adj. Zoology.* resembling a wheel, as the ciliated disk of a rotifer. [< Greek *trochós* a wheel (< *tréchein* to run) + English *-al*[1]]

tro·chan·ter (trō kan′tər), *n.* **1.** a protuberance or process on the upper part of the thighbone of many vertebrates. **2.** the second section of the leg of an insect. [< Middle French *trochanter* < Greek *trochantḗr, -êros* protuberance on the thigh; earlier head of the femur; (literally) runner < *tréchein* to run]

tro·char (trō′kär), *n.* trocar.

tro·che (trō′kē), *n.* a small medicinal tablet or lozenge, usually round and often sweetened, especially one to be dissolved in the mouth to medicate or soothe the throat: *cough troches.* [alteration of earlier *trochisk* < Middle French *trochisque,* learned borrowing from Medieval Latin *trochiscus* < Latin, small wheel < Greek *trochískos* (diminutive) < *trochós* wheel]

tro·chee (trō′kē), *n.* **1.** a foot or measure in poetry consisting of two syllables, the first accented and the second unaccented or the first long and the second short. *Example:* "Sińg a / sońg of / siẋpence." **2.** (in Greek and Latin verse) a long syllable followed by a short syllable. *Example: pātĕr.* [< Middle French *trochée,* learned borrowing from Latin *trochaeus* < Greek *trochaîos* (literally) running < *tréchein* to run]

troch·el·minth (trok′el minth), *n.* any of a group of invertebrate animals, including the rotifers and gastrotrichans. [< Greek *trochós* a wheel + English *helminth* (because of the shape)]

tro·chil·ic (trō kil′ik), *adj.* **1.** having to do with rotary motion. **2.** characterized by rotary motion. [< Greek *trochílos,* taken as *trochós* wheel + English *-ic*]

tro·chil·ics (trō kil′iks), *n.* the science of rotary motion.

troch·i·lus (trok′ə ləs), *n., pl.* **-li** (-lī). **1.** any of certain small European warblers. **2.** the crocodile bird. **3.** a hummingbird. [< Latin *trochilus* < Greek *trochílos* an Egyptian bird < *tréchein* to run]

troch·le·a (trok′lē ə), *n., pl.* **-le·ae** (-lē ē). *Anatomy.* a pulleylike structure or arrangement of parts with a smooth surface upon which another part glides, as the part of the humerus with which the ulna articulates. [< New Latin *trochlea* < Latin, pulley block < Greek *trochiliā* (diminutive) < *trochós* a wheel < *tréchein* to run]

troch·le·ar (trok′lē ər), *adj.* **1.** *Anatomy.* **a.** having to do with a trochlea. **b.** connected with a trochlea. **c.** forming a trochlea. **2.** *Botany.* circular and narrowed in the middle, like the wheel of a pulley.

tro·choid (trō′koid), *n.* a curve traced by a point on or connected with a circle which rolls on a straight line, or on the inside or outside of another circle (used especially in naval engineering).
—*adj.* **1.** *Anatomy.* (of a pivot joint) having one bone turning upon another with a rotary motion. **2.** *Zoology.* shaped like a top, as certain shells.
[< Greek *trochoeidēs* round, wheel-shaped < *trochós* a wheel (< *tréchein* to run) + *eîdos* form]

tro·choi·dal (trō koi′dəl), *adj.* **1.** having the form or nature of a trochoid. **2.** of or having to do with trochoids. **3.** trochoid. **—tro·choi′dal·ly,** *adv.*

troch·o·phore (trok′ə fôr, -fōr), *n.* a free-swimming, ciliated larval form constituting a stage in the development of most mollusks and of certain bryozoans, brachiopods, and marine worms. [< Greek *trochós* wheel (< *tréchein* to run) + English *-phore*]

troch·o·sphere (trok′ə sfir), *n.* trochophore.

tro·chus (trō′kəs), *n.* a top shell, especially a large variety of the tropical Pacific having a valuable nacreous shell. [< New Latin *Trochus,* the genus name < Latin *trochus* hoop < Greek *trochós* wheel]

trod (trod), *v.* a past tense and a past participle of **tread:** *The path was trod by many feet.*

trod·den (trod′ən), *v.* a past participle of **tread:** *The cattle had trodden down the corn.*

trode (trōd), *v. Archaic.* a past tense of **tread.**

trog·lo·dyte (trog′lə dīt), *n.* **1.** a cave dweller; cave man. **2.** a person living in seclusion; hermit. **3.** a person of a degraded type or brutish nature, especially one who dwells in and is seemingly indifferent to an environment of filth, vice, etc. **4.** an anthropoid ape, as a gorilla or chimpanzee. [< Latin *trōglodyta* < Greek *trōglodýtēs* < *trōglē* a cave (< *trōgein* gnaw) + *dýein* go in]

trog·lo·dyt·ic (trog′lə dit′ik), *adj.* of, having to do with, or characteristic of troglodytes: *I remember two troglodytic types—an Arab and a Frenchman from some part of the Mediterranean littoral—locked in unfraternal combat* (New Yorker).

trog·lo·dyt·i·cal (trog′lə dit′ə kəl), *adj.* troglodytic.

trog·lo·dyt·ism (trog′lə dī tiz′əm), *n.* the condition of a troglodyte; the habit of living in caves.

tro·gon (trō′gon), *n.* any of a group of tropical or subtropical birds having soft, brilliantly colored plumage. [< New Latin *Trogon* the genus name < Greek *trṓgōn,* present participle of *trṓgein* to gnaw]

troi·ka (troi′kə), *n.* **1.** a Russian carriage, wagon, sleigh, etc., pulled by three horses harnessed abreast. **2.** such a vehicle together with the horses pulling it: *Reveling in normal Moscow winter weather (10°), a troika from Tambov thunders over a fast, slippery track* (Life). **3.** (in Russia) a team of three horses. **4.** a triumvirate: *By the time Lenin died in 1924, Stalin was powerful enough to become with Zinoviev and Kamenev a member of the troika which seized power* (Newsweek). [< Russian *trojka* team of three horses abreast; any group of three; three, noun < *tri* three]

tro·i·lite (trō′ə līt, troi′līt), *n.* a sulfide of iron found in meteorites: *Troilite is a good conductor of heat* (New Scientist). *Formula:* FeS [< Dominico *Troili,* an Italian scientist who in 1766 described a meteorite containing it + English *-ite*[1]]

Troi·lus (troi′ləs, trō′i-), *n.* **1.** *Greek Legend.* a warrior, the son of King Priam of Troy, killed by Achilles. **2.** *Medieval Legend.* this warrior represented as the lover of Cressida.

troilus butterfly, a large, spotted black butterfly of North America. [< *Troilus*]

Tro·jan (trō′jən), *adj.* of or having to do with Troy, an ancient city in northwestern Asia Minor, or its inhabitants.
—*n.* **1.** a native or inhabitant of Troy. **2.** a person of great energy, endurance, pluck, etc.; one who is vigorous and indomitable: *They all worked like Trojans.* **3.** *Archaic.* **a.** a roistering or dissolute fellow. **b.** (in later use) a good fellow.
[< Latin *Trōjānus* < *Trōja* or *Trōia* Troy < Greek *Troiā* < *Trōs,* its mythical founder]

Trojan asteroids or **group,** a group of asteroids that revolve to form an equilateral triangle with Jupiter and the sun. Most of them were named after heroes of the Trojan war.

Trojan horse, 1. *Greek Legend.* a huge wooden horse in which the Greeks concealed soldiers and brought them into Troy during the Trojan War. **2.** an enemy group stationed inside of a country to sabotage its industry and defense preparations.

Trojan War, *Greek Legend.* a ten-year war carried on by the Greeks against Troy, to get back Helen, wife of King Menelaus of Sparta, who was carried off by Paris, son of King Priam of Troy.

tro·land (trō′lənd), *n.* a unit of measure of the retinal response to illumination. The illumination on the retina is one troland when a surface with a brightness of one candle per square meter is seen through an area of the pupil of one square millimeter. [< Leonard T. *Troland,* 1889-1932, an American psychologist and physicist]

troll[1] (trōl), *v.t.* **1.** to draw (the line, baited hook, lure, etc.) continuously through the water, especially from the stern of a moving boat. **2.** to fish in (a body of water) by trolling. **3.** *Archaic or Dialect.* **a.** to sing in a full, rolling voice. **b.** to sing (something) in the manner of a catch or round. When three people troll a round or catch, the soprano sings one line, the alto comes in next with the same line, and then the bass sings it, and so on, while the others keep on singing. **4.** *Obsolete.* to roll. **5.** *Obsolete.* to entice; allure. **6.** *Obsolete.* to move (the tongue) volubly. **7.** *Obsolete.* to cause to pass from one to another; hand around among the company present.
—*v.i.* **1.** to fish by trolling: *to troll for bass.* **2.** *Archaic.* to sing in a full, rolling voice; sing merrily or jovially. **3.** *Obsolete.* to move nimbly, as the tongue in speaking; wag. **4.** *Obsolete.* to ramble; saunter; stroll.
—*n.* **1.** a fishing reel, especially one used for trolling. **2.** a fishing lure, especially a spinning lure or spoon for trolling. **3.** such a lure together with the line by which it is drawn through the water. **4.** *Archaic.* a song whose parts are sung in succession; catch; round: *"Three Blind Mice" is a well-known troll.*
[< Old French *troller* wander, search for game < Germanic (compare Middle High German *trollen* walk with short steps)] **—troll′er,** *n.*

troll[2] (trōl), *n.* (in Scandinavian folklore) an ugly dwarf or giant with supernatural powers, living underground or in caves. [< Scandinavian (compare Old Icelandic *troll* giant, fiend, demon)]

trol·ley (trol′ē), *n., pl.* **-leys,** *v.* —*n.* **1.** a grooved metallic pulley which travels along, and receives current from, an overhead electric wire (trolley wire), the current being then conveyed by a hinged pole (trolley pole) or other conductor to a motor, usually that of an electric car or locomotive. **2.** a trolley car. **3.** a pulley running on an overhead track, used to support and move a load. **4.** any of several devices used to receive and convey current to a motor, as a bow or shoe used in underground railways. **5.** *British.* any of various small carts, especially handcarts.

off one's trolley, *U.S. Slang.* insane: *Among the minor issues with which he tries to cope are a psychology professor who goes off his trolley . . . and the romantic confusions of his own youthful daughter* (Newsweek).

—*v.t.* to convey by trolley. —*v.i.* to travel by trolley.

[probably < *troll*[1] in sense of "to roll"] —**trol′ley·er,** *n.*

trolley bus or **coach,** a passenger bus drawing power from overhead electric wires.

trolley car, a streetcar propelled electrically. The current is often taken from an overhead wire by means of a trolley.

trol·ley·man (trol′ē man′), *n., pl.* **-men.** a man employed in operating a trolley car, as a motorman or a conductor.

troll-mad·am (trōl′mad′əm), *n. Obsolete.* an old game resembling bagatelle, played especially by women. [apparently alteration of French *trou-madame*]

troll-my-dame (trōl′mī dām′), *n. Obsolete.* troll-madam.

trol·lop (trol′əp), *n.* **1.** a morally loose woman; slut. **2.** prostitute. **3.** a very untidy or slovenly woman; slattern. [probably < *troll*[1] in sense of "to trail, draggle"]

Trol·lop·e·an or **Trol·lop·i·an** (trə lop′ē ən, -lō′pē-), *adj.* having to do with, characteristic of, or like the English novelist Anthony Trollope, 1815-1882, or his writings: . . . *a Trollopian background of great houses and grouse moors* (Mollie Panter-Downes).

trol·lop·y (trol′ə pē), *adj.* like a trollop; slovenly; morally loose: *Olympia Dukakis is especially good* [*playing*] *the lusty, trollopy Widow Begbick* (New Yorker).

trol·ly (trol′ē), *n., pl.* **-lies,** *v.t., v.i.,* **-lied, -ly·ing.** *Especially British.* trolley.

trom·ba (trōm′bä), *n.* trumpet. [< Italian *tromba*]

tromba marina, a large, medieval bowed instrument with one long gut string, fingered only to produce natural harmonics. [< Italian *tromba marina;* Latin *marīna* marine]

trom·bi·di·a·sis (trom′bə dī′ə sis), *n.* the state of being infested with chiggers. [< New Latin *Trombidium* the chigger genus + English *-iasis*]

trom·bone (trom′bōn, trom bōn′), *n.* a large, loud-toned, brass wind instrument consisting of a long, cylindrical tube bent twice upon itself, and expanding into a bell at one end. The U-shaped bend nearer the cup mouthpiece usually is of double telescoping tubes that slide one upon the other to vary the length of the sounding tube and thus produce different tones. [< Italian *trombone* < *tromba* trumpet]

Trombone

trom·bon·ist (trom′bō nist, trom bō′-), *n.* a player on the trombone.

trom·mel (trom′əl), *n. U.S.* a rotating cylindrical sieve used for washing and sizing ore. [< German *Trommel* a drum; any of various drum-shaped apparatuses; a sieve]

tro·mom·e·ter (trō mom′ə tər), *n.* an instrument for measuring or detecting very slight earthquake tremors. [< Greek *trómos* a trembling (< *trémein* tremble) + English *-meter*]

tromp[1] (tromp), *U.S. Informal.* —*v.i.* to move with heavy, noisy steps; tramp. —*v.t.* **1.** to pound; thump; stamp: *Satchmo mopped his brow, tromped his foot, lit into a two-beat tune* (Newsweek). **2.** to trample: *If we've got to get out you go fast or you'll get tromped to death in the rush* (Maclean's). [perhaps blend of *tramp* and *stomp*]

tromp[2] (tromp), *n. Archaic.* trump[2].

trompe (tromp), *n.* an apparatus for producing a blast, as for a forge, in which water falling in a pipe carries air into a receiver, where it is compressed, and thence led to the blast pipe. [< French, Old French *trompe;* see TRUMP[2]]

trompe-l'oeil (trôɴp′lœ′yə), *n.* **1.** an optical illusion, especially as an extreme style of realism in painting, sculpture, or architecture: *Trompe-l'oeil mimics architectural elements: startling, lifelike dwarfs open false doors; the long balconies missing from the palace facades are supplied in fresco in the interior* (New Yorker). *Trompe-l'oeil goes back to the legendary Greek, Zeuxis, who was said to have painted grapes so realistically that birds swooped down to peck at them* (Time). **2. a.** something done in trompe-l'oeil. **b.** a school of art emphasizing this. —*adj.* of or in the style of trompe-l'oeil: *trompe-l'oeil perspective, a trompe-l'oeil painting, painter, or school.* [< French *trompe-l'oeil* (literally) it deceives the eye]

tron (tron), *n. Scottish.* trone.

-tron, *combining form.* **1.** a device for directing the movement of subatomic particles, as in *cyclotron, synchrotron, magnetron.* **2.** a device for controlling physical conditions, as in *biotron, phytotron, climatron.* [< Greek *-tron* device, instrument]

tro·na (trō′nə), *n.* a white, gray, or yellow mineral, a native hydrous sodium carbonate, used as a source of various sodium compounds. [< Swedish *trona* < Arabic *ṭrōn,* short for *naṭrūn* natron, soda]

trone (trōn), *n. Scottish.* a weighing machine, especially one for weighing merchandise in bulk. [< Old French *trone* < Latin *trutina* pair of scales < Greek *trȳtánē*]

troop (trüp), *n.* **1.** a number of persons collected together; a group or band: *a troop of boys.* **2.** (of animals) a herd, flock, or swarm: *a troop of deer.* **3.** a great number; a lot; multitude. **4.** a tactical unit of cavalry or armored cavalry, consisting of 80 to 200 men, usually commanded by a captain. A troop corresponds to a company in other branches of the army. *Abbr.:* trp (no period). **5.** a unit of 32 (or 16) Boy Scouts, comprising four (or two) patrols. **6.** *Obsolete.* a company of performers; troupe.

troops, soldiers: *a city filled with foreign troops. The government sent 1500 troops to put down the revolt.*

—*v.i.* **1.** to gather in a group or groups; move or come together; flock; assemble: *The children trooped around the teacher.* **2.** to walk; go; go away: *throngs trooping into a store. The young boys trooped after the older ones.* **3.** to associate (with). —*v.t.* to carry (the colors) before a formation of troops as part of an official ceremony.

[< Old French *troupe* < Late Latin *troppus* herd; origin uncertain]

—**Syn.** *n.* **1.** crowd, throng.

troop carrier, 1. an airplane or ship used to carry soldiers. **2.** a half-track to carry personnel.

troop·er (trü′pər), *n.* **1.** a soldier in the cavalry, especially one with the rank of private attached to a troop of mounted cavalry. **2.** *U.S.* a member of any of certain state police forces which were originally mounted and which are organized on the pattern of the cavalry (used both generically and as a specific designation): *a New York state trooper, Trooper Jones, etc.* **3.** (in Australia) any mounted policeman. **4.** a cavalry horse. **5.** a troopship. **6.** a paratrooper. —**Syn. 1.** dragoon. **4.** charger.

troop·i·al (trü′pē əl), *n.* troupial.

troop·ing (trü′ping), *n.* the transporting of troops.

troops (trüps), *n.pl.* See under **troop,** *n.*

troop·ship (trüp′ship′), *n.* a seagoing vessel used to carry soldiers, especially one specially designed or modified for such use; military transport.

troost·ite (trüs′tīt), *n.* a variety of willemite, with admixture of manganese, occurring in reddish hexagonal crystals. [< Gerard *Troost,* an American geologist of the 1800's + *-ite*[1]]

trop (trō), *adv. French.* too many; too much.

trop., 1. tropic. **2.** tropical.

tro·pae·o·lin (trō pē′ə lin), *n.* any of a group of orange or yellow azo dyes, of complex composition, belonging to the class of sulfonic acids. [< *tropaeol*(um) + *-in* (because its color resembles that of certain species)]

tro·pae·o·line (trō pē′ə lin, -lēn), *n.* tropaeolin.

tro·pae·o·lum (trō pē′ə ləm), *n., pl.* **-lums, -la** (-lə). any of a group of native South American trailing or climbing herbs; nasturtium. [< New Latin *Tropaeolum* the genus name < Greek *trópaion;* see TROPHY (because its leaf resembles a shield, its flower a helmet)]

tro·par·i·on (trō pär′ē ən), *n., pl.* **-i·a** (-ē ə). in the Greek Church: **1.** a short hymn. **2.** a stanza of a hymn. [< Greek *tropárion* (diminutive) < *trópos* trope]

trope (trōp), *n.* **1.** a figure of speech which consists in the use of a word or phrase in a sense different from its ordinary meaning. **2.** the use of such a figure of speech. **3.** any figure of speech; figurative language. *Example:* "All in a hot and *copper* sky, The *bloody* sun at noon." **4.** (formerly, in the Western Church) a phrase, sentence, or verse interpolated into some part of the liturgy. **5.** a subject heading. [< Latin *tropus* figure of speech < Greek *trópos* or *tropḗ* a turn(ing) < *trépein* to turn] —**Syn. 1.** metonymy.

tro·pe·o·lin (trō pē′ə lin), *n.* tropaeolin.

tro·pe·o·line (trō pē′ə lin, -lēn), *n.* tropaeolin.

troph·al·lax·is (trof′ə lak′sis), *n., pl.* **-lax·es** (-lak′sēz). the reciprocal exchange of food among social insects: [*In*] *some groups of termites . . . an adult worker caste takes charge of nest building and trophallaxis, or mutual feeding* (New Yorker). [< Greek *trophḗ* nourishment + *állaxis* exchange]

troph·ic (trof′ik), *adj.* of or having to do with nutrition (used especially of certain nerves). [< Greek *trophḗ* nourishment (< *tréphein* to feed) + English *-ic*] —**troph′i·cal·ly,** *adv.*

troph·i·cal (trof′ə kəl), *adj.* trophic.

tro·phied (trō′fēd), *adj.* decorated with trophies: *trophied walls.*

troph·o·blast (trof′ə blast), *n.* a layer of cells external to the embryo in many mammals, having the function of supplying it with nourishment. [< Greek *trophós* feeder (< *tréphein* to feed) + *blastós* germ, sprout]

tro·phol·o·gy (trō fol′ə jē), *n.* the branch of physiology that deals with nutrition. [< Greek *trophḗ* nourishment (< *tréphein* to feed) + English *-logy*]

Tro·pho·ni·an (trō fō′nē ən), *adj.* of or having to do with Trophonius, the legendary builder of the original temple of Apollo at Delphi, who after his death was worshiped as a god, and had a famous oracle in a cavern in Boeotia. This oracle was said to affect those who entered with such awe that they never smiled again.

tro·phop·a·thy (trō fop′ə thē), *n.* any derangement of nutrition, especially of a tissue. [< Greek *trophḗ* nourishment (< *tréphein* to feed) + English *-pathy*]

troph·o·plasm (trof′ə plaz əm), *n. Biology.* **1.** the nutritive protoplasm of a cell. **2.** a constituent of the cytoplasm. [< Greek *trophḗ* nourishment (< *tréphein* to feed) + *plásma* something formed]

troph·o·zo·ite (trof′ə zō′īt), *n.* a sporozoan during its growing stage. [< Greek *trophḗ* nourishment (< *tréphein* to feed) + *zōion* animal + English *-ite*[1]]

tro·phy (trō′fē) *n., pl.* **-phies. 1.** a spoil or prize of war, hunting, etc., especially if kept or displayed as a memorial: *The hunter kept the lion's skin and head as trophies.* **2.** a memorial or token of victory, valor, power, skill, etc. **3.** (in ancient Greece and Rome) a structure consisting of arms or other spoils taken from the enemy and hung on a tree, pillar, etc., originally on a battlefield, later in any public place, as a memorial of a victory in war. **4.** any of various similar monuments or memorials in later times. **5.** a prize. **6.** anything serving as a remembrance; memento. **7.** *Architecture.* a carved representation of a group of weapons, etc. [< Middle French *trophée,* learned borrowing from Latin *trophaeum,* for *tropaeum* < Greek *trópaion* (things) of a defeat < *tropḗ* a rout; (originally) a turning of the enemy < *trépein* to turn]

trop·ic (trop′ik), *n.* **1.** either of the two circles around the earth, one 23.45 degrees north and one 23.45 degrees south of the equator. The tropic of Cancer is the northern circle, and the tropic of Capricorn is the southern circle. **2.** either of two circles in the celestial sphere, the limits reached by the sun in its apparent journey north and south. *Abbr.:* trop.

tropics or **Tropics,** the zone between latitudes 23.45 degrees north or south or between 30 degrees north and south, the hottest part of the earth; the Torrid Zone and regions immediately adjacent. The tropics have no winter and, except at high altitudes, are almost always very warm: *The tropics are one vast garden* (Emerson).

—*adj.* of, belonging to, or like that of the tropics; tropical: *the unwarning tropic gale* (John Greenleaf Whittier); *the lost days of our tropic youth* (Bret Harte).

[< Latin *tropicus* < Greek *tropikós* pertaining to a turn < *tropḗ* a turn, change < *trépein* to turn]

trop·i·cal[1] (trop′ə kəl), *adj.* **1.** having to do with the tropics: *tropical studies.* **2.** occurring in the tropics: *tropical diseases.* **3.** native to the tropics: *Bananas are tropical fruit.* **4.** of or having to do with the tropics of Cancer and Capricorn, or either one. **5.** like the climate of the tropics; very hot; burning or fervent. **6.** like the growth in those parts of the tropics having abundant rainfall; luxuriant.

—*n. Informal.* a man's lightweight suit for warm or hot weather: *Stay cool yet look neat in tropicals of "Dacron" polyester fiber and worsted* (New Yorker).

[< *tropic* + *-al*[1]] —**trop′i·cal·ly,** *adv.*

—**Syn.** *adj.* **5.** torrid, fiery.

trop·i·cal[2] (trop′ə kəl), *adj.* **1.** having to do with or involving a trope or tropes. **2.** of the nature of a trope or tropes; metaphorical; figurative. [< Latin *tropicus* (see TROPIC) + English *-al*[1]]

tropical fish, any of certain small fishes native to the tropics, commonly kept in home aquariums, as the guppy, scalare, swordtail, etc.

trop·i·cal·ize (trop′ə kə līz), *v.t.,* **-ized, -iz·ing.** to make tropical; make suitable for tropical climates: *I slid down the bank and settled myself, my typewriter (my faithful old tropicalized typewriter), my notebook, my cameras beside him* (Punch).

tropical sprue, a wasting disease, occurring especially in tropical countries; sprue.

tropical worsted, a lightweight worsted fabric, used for men's summer suits.

tropical year, solar year.

tropic bird, any of a group of sea birds resembling the tern, found in tropical regions, swift in flight, and having webbed feet, varied coloration, and a pair of long central tail feathers.

tropic of Cancer, circle around the earth, 23.45 degrees north of the equator. It is the northern boundary of the Torrid Zone.

tropic of Capricorn, circle around the earth, 23.45 degrees south of the equator. It is the southern boundary of the Torrid Zone.

trop·ics or **Trop·ics** (trop′iks), *n.pl.* See under **tropic,** *n.*

tro·pin (trō′pin), *n.* tropine.

tro·pine (trō′pēn, -pin), *n.* a poisonous, white, crystalline, basic alkaloid, obtained by the hydrolysis of atropine or hyoscyamine. *Formula:* $C_8H_{15}NO$

tro·pism (trō′piz əm), *n.* the tendency of an animal or plant to turn or move in response to a stimulus. [abstracted from *geotropism, heliotropism,* ultimately < Greek *tropḗ* a turning < *trépein* to turn]

tro·pist (trō′pist), *n.* **1.** a person who uses tropes. **2.** a person who explains Scripture, or a Scriptural text, figuratively.

tro·pis·tic (trō pis′tik), *adj.* of or having to do with a tropism.

trop·o·log·ic (trop′ə loj′ik), *adj.* figurative: *tropologic interpretation.*

trop·o·log·i·cal (trop′ə loj′ə kəl), *adj.* tropologic.

trop·o·log·i·cal·ly (trop′ə loj′ə klē), *adv.* in a tropologic manner.

tro·pol·o·gy (trō pol′ə jē), *n., pl.* **-gies. 1.** the use of metaphor; figurative language. **2.** the figurative rendition of a text. **3.** the use of a Scriptural text to bring out a moral significance implied but not stated in its direct reading. [< Late Latin *tropologia* < Greek *tropologíā* < *trópos* a turning; see TROPE]

tro·po·my·o·sin (trō′pə mī′ə sin, trop′ə-), *n.* one of the major protein elements of muscle tissue.

tro·po·pause (trō′pə pôz), *n.* the area of atmospheric demarcation between the troposphere and the stratosphere.

tro·poph·i·lous (trō pof′ə ləs), *adj. Botany.* adapted to a climate which is alternately dry and moist or cold and hot. [< Greek *trópos* a turning (< *trépein* to turn) + *phílos* (with English *-ous*) loving]

trop·o·phyte (trop′ə fīt), *n.* a plant which is adapted for growth in a climate which is alternately dry and moist or cold and hot, as the deciduous trees. [< Greek *tropḗ* a turning, change + *phytón* plant]

trop·o·phyt·ic (trop′ə fit′ik), *adj. Botany.* **1.** of or having to do with a tropophyte. **2.** like a tropophyte.

tro·po scatter (trō′pə), tropospheric scatter.

tro·po·sphere (trō′pə sfir), *n.* the lowest region of the atmosphere, between the earth and the stratosphere, within which there is a steady fall of temperature with increasing altitude. Turbulence of the air and most cloud formations occur in the troposphere. See **atmosphere** for diagram. [< French *troposphère* < Greek *tropḗ* a turn, a change + *sphaîra* sphere]

tro·po·spher·ic (trō′pə sfer′ik, -sfir′-), *adj.* of or having to do with the troposphere: *The tropospheric fall-out occurs within two or three weeks or a month after the firing* (Bulletin of Atomic Scientists).

tropospheric scatter, a way of transmitting radio, television, and telephone signals over long distances by bouncing the signals off the troposphere: *To the communications engineer the important fact is that for a route between 100 and 250 miles tropospheric scatter has unrivalled capacity* (New Scientist).

trop·po (trop′ō; *Italian* trôp′pō), *adv. Music.* too much; excessively. *Example: allegro ma non troppo,* fast, but not too fast. [< Italian *troppo* (literally) too much]

trot[1] (trot), *v.,* **trot·ted, trot·ting,** *n.* —*v.i.* **1.** (of a horse) to move at a gait faster than a walk but slower than a canter by raising the front leg on one side and the rear leg on the other side at about the same time. **2.** (of any of certain other animals) to move at a similar gait: *a trotting dog.* **3.** to ride or drive (a horse) at a trot. **4.** to run, but not fast; go briskly or busily: *The child trotted along after its mother.* —*v.t.* **1.** to ride or drive (a horse) at a trot; cause to trot. **2.** to conduct or escort (a person to or around a place). **3.** to jog (a child) on one's knee.

trot out, *Informal.* to bring out for others to see: *Charles trots out his little bit of scientific nomenclature* (William De Morgan).

—*n.* **1.** a gait of a horse or other four-legged animal between walking and running in which the legs move in diagonal pairs almost together. In a slow trot there is always at least one foot on the ground, but in a fast trot all four feet may be momentarily off the ground at once. **2.** a brisk, steady movement. **3.** the sound of trotting. **4.** a single race in a program of harness racing. **5.** *Informal.* **a.** a toddling child; toddler. **b.** a small or young animal. **6.** *U.S. Slang.* a translation used illicitly by a student instead of doing the lesson himself; pony: *A lazy student can dispense with the original and use the English text as a trot* (New York Times Book Review).

[< Old French *trotter* < Germanic (compare Old High German *trottōn*)]

trot[2] (trot), *n.* **1.** one of the short lines suspended from a trotline. **2.** a trotline. [origin unknown]

trot[3] (trot), *n.* an old woman (usually contemptuous); hag: *an old trot with ne'er a tooth in her head* (Shakespeare). [origin unknown]

troth (trôth, trōth), *n. Archaic.* **1.** faithfulness; fidelity; loyalty. **2.** promise. **3.** truth. **4.** betrothal.

in troth, truly; verily: *In troth I think she would* (Shakespeare).

plight one's troth, a. to promise to marry: *and thereto I plight thee my troth* (Book of Common Prayer). *These two young people loved, and plighted their troth* (Frederick Marryat). **b.** to pledge one's faith; give one's word.

—*v.t.* **1.** to promise. **2.** to betroth.

[Middle English *trowthe,* Old English *trēowth* good faith. Doublet of TRUTH.]

troth·plight (trôth′plīt′, trōth′-), *Archaic.* —*n.* a solemn promise or engagement, especially of marriage; betrothal. —*adj.* engaged; betrothed; affianced. —*v.t.* to engage oneself to; betroth; affiance.

trot·line (trot′līn′), *n.* a long fishing line tied or anchored at one end and buoyed or tied at the other, from which short lines with baited hooks are suspended at regular intervals.

Trot·sky·ism (trots′kē iz əm), *n.* the political principles or economic policy of Leon Trotsky, especially the doctrine that revolution and the spread of communism throughout the world must take precedence over everything else, even the internal development of the Soviet Union. [< Leon *Trotsky,* 1879-1940, a leader in the Russian Revolution of 1917 + *-ism*]

Trot·sky·ist (trots′kē ist), *n., adj.* Trotskyite.

Trot·sky·ite (trots′kē īt), *n.* a person who believes in or advocates Trotskyism; follower of Leon Trotsky. —*adj.* of or having to do with Trotskyism or Trotskyites.

trot·ter (trot′ər), *n.* **1.** a horse that trots. **2.** a horse bred and trained for such a gait in harness racing: *At Roosevelt Raceway, the trotters and pacers are working out with the same diligence as the thoroughbreds* (New York Times). **3.** a person who moves or goes about briskly and constantly.

trotters, the foot of a sheep, pig, etc., used for food.

trot·teur (trô tœr′), *adj.* (of women's clothing) simple and tailored, and appropriate for outdoor use: *cashmere flannels and jerseys, including trotteur dresses, with trig leather belts* (New Yorker). —*n.* a garment of this kind: *flannel trotteur done up with white piqué at the neckline and wrists* (New Yorker). [< French *trotteur* (literally) trotter]

trot·ting race (trot′ing), a harness race using trotters: *The first public trotting race that attracted much notice was on a course . . . on Long Island in 1818* (Frank A. Wrensch).

trot·toir (trô twär′), *n.* a sidewalk. [< French *trottoir* < *trotter* to trot]

trot·ty (trot′ē), *adj.,* **-ti·er, -ti·est.** trotting; brisk: *Her speech, with its trotty Jamaican rhythm, brings every syllable to life* (Norma Rosen).

tro·tyl (trō′təl, -tēl), *n.* trinitrotoluene.

trou·ba·dour (trü′bə dôr, -dōr, -důr), *n.* one of a class of knightly poets and composers of southern France, eastern Spain, and northern Italy from the 1000's to the 1200's. The troubadours wrote mainly about love and chivalry and composed ecstatic, lyrical love songs. [< French *troubadour* < Old Provençal *trobador* < *trobar* to find; (probably earlier) to compose in verse, ultimately < Late Latin *tropus* song; musical mode < Greek *trópos* mode, style; see TROPE. Doublet of TROUVÈRE.]

trou·ble (trub′əl), *n., v.,* **-bled, -bling.** —*n.* **1.** distress; worry; difficulty: *a time of great trouble.* **2.** an instance of this; a distressing or vexatious circumstance, occurrence, or experience: *a life containing many troubles. So I was ready When trouble came* (A.E. Housman). **3.** an occasion or cause of affliction, distress, vexation, etc.: *Is she a trouble to you?* **4.** social disturbance; disorder: *political troubles.* **5.** an instance of this; disturbance. **6.** pains or exertion, especially in accomplishing or attempting something; care; bother; effort: *Can't he at least take the trouble to write a note of thanks? Take the trouble to do careful work.* **7.** an ailment; disease: *She suffers from heart trouble.*

ask for trouble, to court danger; be careless of one's welfare or safety: *Oh, Major Scobie, what made you write such a letter? It was asking for trouble* (Graham Greene).

borrow trouble, to worry about something before there is reason to: *Forget about it; why borrow trouble?*

—*v.t.* **1.** to be a source of trouble to; distress; worry: *The lack of business troubled him.* **2.** to distress (with something disagreeable and unwelcome); vex; annoy; bother: *to be troubled with poor eyesight.* **3.** to put to inconvenience; require extra work or effort of: *May I trouble you to pass the sugar?* **4.** to cause pain to; hurt; pain: *His wound troubles him.* **5.** to agitate or ruffle (water, air, etc.), especially so as to make it cloudy, muddy, etc.: *For an angel went down . . . into the pool and troubled the water* (John 5:4). —*v.i.* **1.** to trouble oneself; take the trouble: *Don't trouble to come to the door.* **2.** *Obsolete.* to be troubled.

[< Old French *truble, trouble* < *trubler,*

troubler to trouble, disturb < Vulgar Latin *turbulāre* < Latin *turbula* (diminutive) < *turba* turmoil] —**trou′bling·ly,** *adv.*
—**Syn.** *n.* **1.** anxiety, affliction. *-v.t.* **2.** afflict. *-v.i.* **1.** bother.

trou·bled (trub′əld), *adj.* disturbed; disordered; agitated: *troubled thoughts, a troubled sleep, medicine for a troubled mind.* —**trou′bled·ly,** *adv.*

troubled waters, a situation or state of agitation or disquiet: *An inadvertent inquiry would have brought us into troubled waters* (George Musgrave).
fish in troubled waters, to take advantage of trouble or agitation to gain one's end: *The Mafia has at all times delighted in fishing in troubled waters* (New Yorker).

trou·ble·mak·er (trub′əl mā′kər), *n.* a person who often causes trouble for others: *The police arrest and arraign and deport suspected Red troublemakers before a lawyer can say habeas corpus* (Time).

trou·ble-mak·ing (trub′əl mā′king), *n.* the activities of a troublemaker: *Stalin never lost sleep over adverse U.N. votes; that cynical leader knew how powerless they were to halt him in his trouble-making* (Wall Street Journal). —*adj.* making or causing trouble: *Brazil's trouble-making Communists, who could never have brought off such a coup by themselves, whooped with delight* (Time).

trou·bler (trub′lər), *n.* a person or thing that troubles.

trou·ble-shoot·er (trub′əl shü′tər), *n. U.S.* a person who discovers and eliminates causes of trouble, especially one trained or qualified to do so in a particular field or with a particular kind of apparatus: *He . . . went wandering as an international banker and economic trouble-shooter* (Time).

trou·ble-shoot·ing (trub′əl shü′ting), *n.* the work of a trouble-shooter: *the U.S. Foreign Service officer whose profession is preventing trouble — and trouble-shooting* (Time).
—*adj.* of or having to do with a trouble-shooter or his work: *Sometimes he is sent elsewhere on trouble-shooting errands of one sort or another* (Edward Newhouse).

trou·ble·some (trub′əl səm), *adj.* **1.** giving trouble; causing annoyance; distressing. **2.** *Obsolete.* disturbed; unsettled. —**trou′ble·some·ly,** *adv.* —**trou′ble·some·ness,** *n.*
—**Syn. 1.** disturbing, vexatious, harassing, annoying, bothersome.

trouble spot, a troublesome area or locality; place in which trouble is occurring or is likely to occur: *A high level of unemployment was the chief domestic economic trouble spot* (William B. Franklin). *Another trouble spot, Berlin, was the subject of a gravely worded statement by the West German government* (New York Times).

trou·blous (trub′ləs), *adj.* **1.** disturbed; unsettled; restless: *troublous times.* **2.** (of the sea, wind, etc.) tempestuous; stormy; violent. **3.** troublesome.

trou-de-loup (trü′də lü′), *n., pl.* **trous-de-loup** (trü′də lü′). one of a series of pits having a pointed stake in the center, used to obstruct the progress of an enemy. [< French *trou-de-loup* (literally) wolf pit]

trough (trôf, trof), *n.* **1.** a narrow, open, boxlike container for holding food or water, especially for farm stock or other animals: *He led the horses to the watering trough.* **2.** something shaped like this: *The baker uses a trough for kneading dough.* **3.** a channel for carrying water; gutter: *A wooden trough under the eaves of the house carries off rainwater.* **4.** a long hollow between two ridges, especially the hollow between two waves. **5.** *Meteorology.* a long, narrow area of relatively low barometric pressure. **6.** *Geology.* a basin-shaped depression; the lowest part of a synclinal fold. [Old English *trog*] —**trough′like′,** *adj.* —**Syn. 1.** manger. **3.** conduit. **4.** furrow.

trounce (trouns), *v.t.,* **trounced, trounc·ing. 1.** to beat; thrash; belabor; flog. **2.** to beat by way of punishment; inflict physical chastisement upon. **3.** *Informal.* to defeat in a contest or match: *Hungary's Kanizi soccer team today trounced the Tottenham Hotspurs, an English First Division Club* (New York Times). [origin uncertain]

troupe (trüp), *n., v.,* **trouped, troup·ing.** —*n.* a company, band, or troop, especially a company of actors, dancers, or the like: *a troupe of strolling actors* (Henry James). —*v.i.* to tour or travel with a troupe. [American English < French *troupe* < Old French; see TROOP]

troup·er (trü′pər), *n.* **1.** a member of a theatrical troupe. **2.** an experienced actor (used especially as a term of praise). **3.** any stalwart person.

troup·i·al (trü′pē əl), *n.* any of a family of American birds, including blackbirds, orioles, grackles, cowbirds, etc., especially any tropical American oriole with bright plumage. Also, **troopial.** [< French *troupiale* < *troupe* flock < Old French; see TROOP (because they live in flocks)]

trou·sered (trou′zərd), *adj.* wearing trousers.

trou·ser·ing (trou′zər ing), *n.* cloth for trousers.

trou·sers (trou′zərz), *n.pl.* **1.** a two-legged, loose-fitting outer garment reaching from the waist to the ankles or to the knees, worn especially by men and boys. **2.** the loose, baglike drawers or pantaloons that are a part of the native dress of both men and women in certain Moslem countries. **3.** the lower part of any of certain two-piece garments, especially pajamas. [< earlier *trouse* < Scottish Gaelic *triubhas,* probably < Old French *trebus* boot]
—**Syn. 1.** breeches, pants, knickerbockers, slacks.
➤ See **pants** for usage note.

trousse (trüs), *n.* **1.** a number of small implements carried together, as in a receptacle or case. **2.** a receptacle containing such implements: *a surgeon's trousse.* [< French *trousse* < Old French *trousser;* see TRUSS]

trous·seau (trü sō′, trü′sō), *n., pl.* **trousseaux** or **trous·seaus** (trü sōz′, trü′sōz). **1.** a bride's outfit of clothes, linen, etc. **2.** *Obsolete.* a bundle. [< French *trousseau* (originally) bundle (diminutive) < *trousse* bundle < Old French *trousser* pack into a bundle; see TRUSS]

trout (trout), *n., pl.* **trouts** or (*collectively*) **trout. 1.** any of a group of food fishes of the same family as the salmon, chiefly of fresh waters, although some migrate from the sea to spawn, as the rainbow trout or steelhead, the cutthroat trout, and the brown trout. **2.** any of a group of similar and related fishes as the Dolly Varden, the brook trout, and the lake trout. **3.** any of certain fishes which resemble a trout to some extent, as the trout perch.
[partly Old English *trūht* < Late Latin; partly < Old French *troite, truite* < Late Latin *tructa,* or *trocta,* probably < Greek *trṓktēs* a kind of fish (literally) gnawer < *trṓgein* to gnaw] —**trout′like′,** *adj.*

Brook Trout (def. 2)
(about 10 in. long)

trout fly, a fishing fly used in trout fishing.

trout·less (trout′lis), *adj.* without trout: *I catch a few trout now and then, so I am not left troutless* (Charles Kingsley).

trout·let (trout′lit), *n.* a little trout: *In some sleek restaurant . . . ladies of fashion peck their way through bird or troutlet* (Punch).

trout lily, the yellow dogtooth violet or adder's-tongue: *Bright yellow trout lilies and pale pink spring beauties bloomed along the Appalachian Trail* (Atlantic).

trout·ling (trout′ling), *n.* troutlet.

trout perch, either of two North American fishes having certain striking similarities to both the trouts and the perches.

trou·vaille (trü vä′yə), *n.* something found unexpectedly; windfall; godsend: *We find all these trouvailles, and more, in the correspondence of T. E. Lawrence, now handsomely presented by his brother* (Punch). [< French *trouvaille* a find < *trouver* to find]

trou·vère (trü ver′), *n.* one of a class of poets who flourished in northern France from the 1000's to the 1300's, and whose works were chiefly epic in character. [< French *trouvère* < Old North French *trouvere* < *trouver* to compose, ultimately < Late Latin *tropus.* Doublet of TROUBADOUR.]

trou·veur (trü vœr′), *n.* trouvère.

trove (trōv), *n.* something of value found; a find: *delighted as a child at each new trove* (Rudyard Kipling). [< (treasure) *trove*]

tro·ver (trō′vər), *n. Law.* the finding and taking possession of any personal property.
action of trover, an action for the recovery of the value of personal property illegally converted by another to his own use: *In this sense the author of a dictionary might bring an action of trover against every other author who used his words* (James Russell Lowell).
[noun use of Anglo-French, Old French *trouver* to find; see TROUVÈRE]

trow (trō), *v.i., v.t. Archaic.* to believe; think. [Old English *trēowian.* Related to TROTH, TRUE, TRUTH.]

trow·el (trou′əl), *n., v.,* **-eled, -el·ing** or (*especially British*) **-elled, -el·ling.** —*n.* **1.** a tool having a broad, flat blade, used for spreading or smoothing plaster, mortar, etc. **2.** a tool having a scooplike blade, used in gardening for loosening earth, taking up small plants, etc.

Trowels
Top (def. 1);
bottom (def. 2)

lay it on with a trowel, to be lavish or excessive in expression of praise, apology, etc.: *Everyone likes flattery; and when you come to Royalty you should lay it on with a trowel* (Benjamin Disraeli).
—*v.t.* **1.** to spread (a substance) or smooth (a surface) with or as with a trowel; form or mold with a trowel. **2.** to put, place, or move (something) with or as with a trowel, especially thickly or clumsily: *to trowel mud into a hole, to trowel butter onto bread.*
[< Old French *troele, truele* < Late Latin *truella* a vessel (diminutive) < Latin *trua* a skimmer] —**trow′el·er,** or *especially British,* **trow′el·ler,** *n.* —**trow′el·like′,** *adj.*

trowel bayonet, a bayonet with a short and broad but sharp-pointed, trowellike blade, intended to serve also as an entrenching tool.

trow·el·beak (trou′əl bēk′), *n.* a broad-beaked bird, or broadbill, of Sumatra.

troy (troi), *adj.* in, of, or by troy weight. —*n.* troy weight. [apparently < Middle French *Troyes,* a city in France, former site of a fair, at which this weight may have been used]

troy weight, a standard system of weights used for gems and precious metals. In the United States:
24 grains = 1 pennyweight
20 pennyweight = 1 ounce
12 ounces or 5,760 grains = 1 pound
In Great Britain the ounce and decimal units of the ounce are used.

trp (no period), troop.

tru·an·cy (trü′ən sē), *n., pl.* **-cies.** truant conduct; the habit or practice of playing truant.

tru·ant (trü′ənt), *n.* **1.** a child who stays away from school without permission. **2.** a person who neglects his duty or business.
play truant, to be or behave as a truant: *The boys played truant to go to see the parade.*
—*adj.* **1.** of or having to do with a truant: *a truant report.* **2.** characteristic of a truant: *truant behavior.* **3.** being a truant: *a truant child. That truant dog won't stay home.*
—*v.i.* to be a truant, especially from school.
[< Old French *truant* beggar, vagabond, probably < a Celtic word]
—**Syn.** *n.* **1.** absentee. **2.** shirker.

truant officer, *U.S.* an official whose job is to locate and return truants to school.

tru·ant·ry (trü′ən trē), *n., pl.* **-ries.** truancy.

truce (trüs), *n.* **1.** a suspension of hostilities for a (specified) period between warring armies, countries, etc.; temporary peace or cessation from arms: *A truce was declared between the two armies. There is never an instant's truce between virtue and vice* (Thoreau). **2.** an agreement or treaty effecting this; armistice: *to sign a truce.* **3.** a rest from trouble or pain; respite from something irksome, painful, or oppressive: *The hot weather gave the old man a truce from rheumatism.* [Middle English *trewes,* plural of *trewe,* Old English *trēow* faith, treaty. Compare TRUE.]

Truce of God, a cessation of all active warfare, personal feuding, etc., such as was generally practiced on holy days by Christians during the 1000's and 1100's.

tru·cial (trü′shəl), *adj.* of, having to do with, or bound by a truce (used especially in reference to a truce between the British government and certain sheikdoms in southeastern Arabia, made in 1853): *the trucial states.*

truck[1] (truk), *n.* **1.** *U.S.* a motor vehicle designed primarily for the carrying of things rather than people, ranging in size from small vehicles used to carry tools, deliver parcels, etc., to large vehicles used to carry very heavy objects, commodities in bulk, etc. **2.** (formerly) any of various strongly

built carts, wagons, etc., used for a similar purpose. **3.** a frame with two wheels at the front and handles at the back, used for moving trunks, etc. **4.** a strongly built, rectangular platform resting on four wheels, used to move heavy or bulky objects, as in a warehouse, factory, etc. **5.** any of various small, light, four-wheeled conveyances used in stores, libraries, etc., moved by pushing or pulling. **6.** a swiveling frame with two or more pairs of wheels by which the front end of a locomotive or each end of a railroad car is supported, and by the action of which the vehicle is guided on the rails, through switches, around curves, etc. **7.** *British.* a flatcar, gondola, or other railroad freight car without a top. **8.** a small wooden wheel or roller, such as was formerly used on gun carriages. **9.** a wooden disk at the top of a flagpole or mast having holes through which the ropes for hoisting a flag or pennant are passed. **10.** the ornament at the top of a flagstaff, sometimes used as an indication of rank of a military officer or government official: *The spread eagle is the truck for the personal flag or pennant of an officer or official who rates a 19-gun salute, or better* (Arthur E. DuBois).
—*v.t.* to carry or move by a truck or trucks: *to truck freight to Chicago.*
—*v.i.* **1.** to drive a truck. **2.** to engage in trucking goods, especially as a business; operate a trucking business. **3.** to dance the trucking.
—*adj.* **1.** of a truck. **2.** for a truck; used on trucks: *a truck tire, a truck license.*
[perhaps < Latin *trochus* iron hoop < Greek *trochós* wheel < *tréchein* to run]

truck[2] (truk), *n.* **1.** *U.S.* vegetables grown for the market. **2.** small articles of little value; odds and ends. **3.** *Informal.* rubbish; trash. **4.** *Informal.* dealings: *to have no truck with fools.* **5.** exchange; barter. **6.** the payment of wages in goods, etc., rather than in money. **7.** the system or practice of such payment. [< verb]
—*v.t., v.i.* to exchange; barter: *Liberty's too often truck'd for Gold* (Daniel Defoe).
—*adj.* of truck; having to do with truck.
[Middle English *trukien* < Old North French *troquer* to barter, exchange < Medieval Latin *trocare*; origin uncertain]

truck·age (truk′ij), *n.* **1.** the carrying of goods, etc., by a truck or trucks. **2.** the charge for or cost of such carrying.

truck crane, a crane mounted on a truck.

truck crop, *U.S.* a crop grown on a truck farm.

truck·driv·er (truk′drī′vər), *n.* a person who drives a truck; trucker: *Illegal sales of amphetamine drugs, pep pills, to truck-drivers and motorists are adding to the dangers of highway travel* (Science News Letter).

truck·er[1] (truk′ər), *n.* **1.** a person who drives a truck. **2.** a person who owns or manages a trucking business.

truck·er[2] (truk′ər), *n.* **1.** *U.S.* a person who grows garden produce for market; truck farmer. **2.** a barterer; bargainer.

truck farm or **garden,** a farm where vegetables are grown for market.

truck farmer or **gardener,** a person who operates a truck farm: *A very important event in Noumea is the early morning (5 a.m.) market, where the Javanese truck gardeners sell vegetables from small carts* (Sunset).

truck farming or **gardening,** the business of operating a truck farm.

truck·ing[1] (truk′ing), *n.* **1.** the act or business of carrying goods, etc., on a truck or trucks. **2.** truckage. **3.** a slow, shuffling cakewalk, danced with the index finger of one hand pointed upward.

truck·ing[2] (truk′ing), *n.* the raising of vegetables for market; truck farming.

truck·le[1] (truk′əl), *v.*, **-led, -ling.** —*v.i.* **1.** to yield meanly or obsequiously; act with servility: *That man got his position by truckling to his superiors and flattering them.* **2.** to submit or give way timidly. **3.** *Obsolete.* to trundle. —*v.t. Obsolete.* to trundle. [< *truckle bed,* formerly used by servants and inferiors]
—**Syn.** *v.i.* **1.** cringe, fawn.

truck·le[2] (truk′əl), *n.* **1.** a small wheel, especially a grooved wheel of a pulley. **2.** *Dialect.* a small roller; caster. **3.** a trundle bed. [< Anglo-French *trocle* < Latin *trochlea* < Greek *trochileiā;* see TROCHLEA]

truckle bed, trundle bed.

truck·ler (truk′lər), *n.* a person who truckles or acts with servility.

truck·ling·ly (truk′ling lē), *adv.* in a truckling manner.

truck·load (truk′lōd′), *n.* as much or as many as a truck can carry: *truckloads of fish.*

truck·man (truk′mən), *n., pl.* **-men.** a man who drives a truck; trucker.

truck shop or **store,** a store at which vouchers given to workers can be exchanged for goods.

truck system, the system of paying wages in goods, etc., rather than in money.

truck tractor, a motor truck consisting of a cab and engine, used to pull a truck trailer; tractor.

truck trailer, a trailer designed to be pulled by a motor truck, especially by a truck tractor. See picture under **semitrailer.**

truc·u·lence (truk′yə ləns, trü′kyə-), *n.* savage threatening or bullying; fierceness and cruelty: *There was a jaunty truculence in the President's voice as he spelled out what the order would mean* (Reporter).

truc·u·len·cy (truk′yə lən sē, trü′kyə-), *n.* truculence.

truc·u·lent (truk′yə lənt, trü′kyə-), *adj.* **1.** savagely threatening or bullying; violent or savage in nature or temper: *a truculent bully, a truculent defense of one's rights.* **2.** ruthless and scathing in attack; harsh and cruel: *truculent satire. Voltaire is never either gross or truculent* (Viscount Morley) **3.** *Obsolete.* (of a disease) very dangerous; deadly. [< Latin *truculentus* < *trux, trucis* fierce] —**truc′u·lent·ly,** *adv.* —**Syn. 1.** brutal, fierce.

trudge (truj), *v.,* **trudged, trudg·ing,** *n.* —*v.i.* **1.** to walk heavily, wearily, or with effort, but steadily and persistently: *Let's . . . shoulder our bundles and trudge along* (Louisa May Alcott). **2.** to go or move through anything in a manner similar to this; plod: *to trudge through a dull book.* **3.** to go on foot; walk. —*v.t.* to travel (a distance) by trudging; trudge along or over.
—*n.* **1.** the act of trudging; hard or weary going; plodding. **2.** a hard or weary walk: *It was a long trudge up the hill.* **3.** a person who trudges; trudger. [origin unknown]

trudg·en stroke, or **trudg·en** (truj′ən), *n.* a swimming stroke in which the arms, alternately, are raised over the head and brought down and back parallel with the body, usually done with a scissors kick. [< John *Trudgen,* 1852-1902, a British swimmer, who introduced the stroke from Argentina]

trudg·er (truj′ər), *n.* **1.** a person who trudges. **2.** a swimmer who uses the trudgen stroke.

true (trü), *adj.,* **tru·er, tru·est,** *n., v.,* **trued, tru·ing** or **true·ing,** *adv.* —*adj.* **1.** agreeing with fact; not false: *It is true that 6 and 4 are 10.* **2.** real; genuine: *true gold, true kindness.* **3.** faithful; loyal: *a true patriot.* **4.** agreeing with a standard; right; proper; correct; exact; accurate: *a true copy, a true voice, true to type.* **5.** representative of the class named: *A sweet potato is not a true potato.* **6.** rightful; lawful: *the true heir to the property.* **7.** reliable; sure: *a true sign.* **8.** accurately formed, fitted, or placed: *a true angle.* **9.** steady in direction, force, etc., unchanging: *The arrow made a true course through the air.* **10.** *Archaic.* truthful. **11.** honest.
come true, to happen as expected; become real: *To patch up fragments of a dream, Part of which comes true* (Shelley).
—*n.* **1.** that which is true. **2.** accurate position or adjustment: *A slanting door is out of true.*
—*v.t.* to make true; shape or make in the exact position, place, form, etc., wanted or called for: *If the combination is a lens, it must be trued* (Hardy and Perrin).
true up, to make true; shape or make in the exact position, place, form, etc., wanted or called for: *The clerks, figuring that the weapons had been damaged during the trip over, immediately set about straightening them. The unbending was interrupted by a merchandise manager, but not before* [*they*] *had trued up quite a number of blades* (New Yorker).
—*adv.* **1.** in a true manner; truly; exactly: *His words ring true.* **2.** in agreement with the ancestral type: *to breed true.*
[Middle English *trewe,* Old English *trēowe.* Compare TROTH, TRUTH.] —**true′ness,** *n.*
—**Syn.** *adj.* **1.** See **real. 3.** constant, stanch.

true bill, a bill of indictment found by a grand jury to be supported by enough evidence to justify hearing the case.

true blue, 1. an especially nonfading blue dye or coloring matter. **2.** the blue taken as their badge by the Scottish Covenanters of the 1600's. **3.** a Scottish Covenanter. **4.** the faith of the Scottish Covenanters; Presbyterianism.

true-blue (trü′blü′), *adj.* stanch and unwavering in one's faith, principles, etc.; unchanging; loyal: *Tom's true-blue. He won't desert* (Mark Twain).
—**Syn.** faithful.

true-born (trü′bôrn′), *adj.* born of a pure stock; legitimately born; having the sterling qualities associated with such descent: *The man behind it is quite likely to be the true-born, hire-purchasing Briton* (Manchester Guardian).

true-false (trü′fôls′), *adj.* having to do with or containing statements which must be marked as either true or false: *a true-false test, true-false questions.*

true-heart·ed (trü′här′tid), *adj.* **1.** faithful; loyal. **2.** honest; sincere.

true level, an imaginary line or plane perpendicular at all points to the plumb line.

true-life (trü′līf′), *adj.* **1.** of or belonging to life; not fictitious; actual: *a true-life hero. A brief true-life story is used sometimes as a third feature and presented as an interview* (London Times). **2.** true-to-life: *a true-life novel.*

true·love (trü′luv′), *n.* **1.** a faithful lover; loyal sweetheart. **2.** a person to whom love is pledged; eternal sweetheart; beloved: *My truelove hath my heart and I have his* (Philip Sidney). **3.** the herb Paris, whose whorl of four leaves with a single flower or berry in the midst suggests the figure of a truelove knot.

truelove knot, a complicated bowknot, not easily untied, used as a token or symbol of eternal love.

true-lov·er's knot (trü′luv′ərz), truelove knot.

true·pen·ny (trü′pen′ē), *n., pl.* **-nies.** *Archaic.* an honest person; trustworthy fellow.

true ribs, ribs which articulate with the sternum or breastbone, in man the first seven pairs.

true time, mean time; solar time.

true-to-life (trü′tə līf′), *adj.* consistent with, exactly agreeing with, or faithful to life; realistic: *true-to-life illustrations. He . . . gives an entertaining and true-to-life account of how an orchestra does its work* (Manchester Guardian).

true viper, a poisonous, Old-World snake, that has no pit between the eye and nostrils.

true vocal cords, the lower pair of vocal cords, which produce the sound of voice.

truf·fle (truf′əl, trü′fəl), *n.* **1.** an edible fungus that grows underground, a native of central and southern Europe. **2.** a soft, creamy chocolate candy, often filled with finely ground filberts. [< Old French *truffe* < Old Provençal *truffa* < Late Latin *tūfera,* alteration of Latin *tūber* tuber[1]]

truf·fled (truf′əld, trü′f-; trü′fəld), *adj.* cooked, garnished, or stuffed with truffles.

truffle hound, a dog or pig trained to find truffles by their scent.

trug (trug), *n. British.* **1.** a shallow, oblong basket made of wooden strips for carrying fruit, vegetables, etc. **2.** a shallow, wooden tray or pan to hold milk. **3.** a tray or hod for mortar. **4.** an old local measure for wheat equal to two thirds of a bushel. [perhaps dialect variant < *trough*]

tru·ism (trü′iz əm), *n.* a statement so obviously true as not to require discussion; self-evident truth, especially one that has been needlessly repeated: *The original thought of one age becomes the truism of the next* (Henry Hallam). —**Syn.** axiom.

tru·is·tic (trü is′tik), *adj.* having the character of a truism; trivially self-evident.

trull (trul), *n.* a prostitute. [< German *Trulle* fat, sloppy female; prostitute]

tru·ly (trü′lē), *adv.* **1.** in a true manner; exactly; rightly; faithfully: *Tell me truly what you think.* **2.** in fact; really; genuinely: *It was truly a beautiful day.* **3.** indeed; verily.

Tru·man Doctrine (trü′mən), a declaration made by President Harry S Truman in 1947, that the United States would intervene and help other nations resist "attempted subjugation by armed minorities or by outside pressure."

tru·meau (trü mō′; *French* trʏ mō′), *n., pl.* **-meaux** (-mōz′; *French* -mō′). **1.** a portion of wall between two openings, as doors or windows. **2.** a central pier dividing a wide doorway, as in medieval churches. **3.** a mirror or any piece of decorative work covering the space between two openings or above a mantelpiece or the like. [< French *trumeau;* origin uncertain]

trump[1] (trump), *n.* **1. a.** any card of a suit having the power during the play of a hand to beat any card of another suit: *He did not object . . . to Gladstone's always having the ace of trumps up his sleeve, but only to his pretence that God had put it there* (Henry Labouchere). **b.** the suit itself: *Martin, if dirt were trumps, what hands you would have* (Charles Lamb). **2.** *Informal.* a fine, dependable person; first-rate fellow.
—*v.t.* **1.** to play a trump to and usually thereby take (a trick, card, etc., of another suit). **2.** to be better than; surpass; beat.
—*v.i.* **1.** to play a card of the trump suit when another suit has been led. **2.** to win a trick with a trump.
[alteration of *triumph* < French *triomphe*]

trump[2] (trump), *n.* **1.** *Archaic.* **a.** a trumpet. **b.** the sound of a trumpet. **2.** *Scottish, Northern Irish.* a jew's-harp. Also, **tromp.** —*v.i., v.t. Archaic.* to trumpet. [< Old French *trompe,* perhaps < Germanic (compare Old High German *trumpa, trumba*). Compare TROMBONE.]

trump[3] (trump), *v.t.* to make (up) in order to deceive; fabricate: *to trump up new excuses.* [perhaps special use of *trump*[1], or < French *tromper* to deceive] —**Syn.** concoct, falsify.

trump card, 1. any card in the suit of trumps; trump. **2.** anything decisive held in reserve for use at a critical time: *The government can count on the support of the military, a possible trump card in any showdown* (Wall Street Journal).

trumped-up (trumpt′up′), *adj.* made up in order to deceive; fabricated; spurious: *The Old Mafia leader had to be tried on a trumped-up charge, for lack of anything better* (Norman Lewis).

trump·er·y (trum′pər ē, trump′rē), *n., pl.* **-er·ies,** *adj.* —*n.* something showy, but with little or no value; worthless ornaments; useless stuff; rubbish; nonsense. —*adj.* showy but without value; trifling; worthless; useless; nonsensical. [< Old French *tromperie* < *tromper* to deceive] —**Syn.** *n.* frippery, trash. -*adj.* trashy.

trum·pet (trum′pit), *n.* **1. a.** a wind instrument of bright, powerful, and penetrating tone, consisting of a cylindrical or conical tube, usually of metal, commonly curved or bent upon itself once or twice, with a cup-shaped mouthpiece and a flaring bell at opposite ends. **b.** a powerful reed organ stop with a tone resembling that of a trumpet. **c.** a trumpeter. **2.** a thing shaped like a trumpet: *The deaf old lady has an ear trumpet to help her hearing.* **3.** a sound like that of a trumpet, especially the loud cry of certain animals, as the elephant.

Trumpet (def. 1a)

blow one's own trumpet, *Especially British.* to sound one's own praises; boast; brag: *There is still some British feeling that there is something slightly disreputable about selling and promoting, about getting out and blowing our own trumpet* (Brendan M. Jones).
trumpets, (in the southern United States) any of various pitcher plants with leaves shaped like a trumpet: *a yellow trumpets.*
—*v.i.* **1,** to blow a trumpet. **2.** to make a sound like a trumpet: *The elephant trumpeted.* —*v.t.* **1.** to sound on a trumpet. **2.** to utter with a sound like that of a trumpet. **3.** to announce or publish as by sound of trumpet; proclaim loudly: *She will trumpet the news all over town.*
[< Old French *trompette* (diminutive) < *trompe;* see TRUMP[2]]

trumpet creeper, any of a group of woody climbing plants of the bignonia family, especially a native of the southern United States having clusters of large, scarlet, trumpet-shaped flowers and pinnate leaves; Virginia trumpet flower; trumpet vine.

trum·pet·er (trum′pə tər), *n.* **1.** a person who blows or plays a trumpet. **2.** a soldier who blows calls on a trumpet; bugler. **3.** a large wild swan of western North America with a sonorous call. **4.** any of a group of South American birds having long legs and neck, related to the cranes. **5.** a variety of domestic pigeon having a shell crest and heavily feathered feet.

trumpeter swan, trumpeter.

trumpet flower, 1. any of certain plants with large or showy, trumpet-shaped flowers, especially the trumpet creeper and the trumpet honeysuckle. **2.** the flower of one of these plants.

trumpet honeysuckle, a North American honeysuckle, grown for its large, handsome tubular flowers, which are red on the outside and yellowish within.

trumpet marine, tromba marina.

trum·pets (trum′pits), *n.pl.* See under **trumpet,** *n.*

trum·pet-shaped (trum′pit shāpt′), *adj.* tubular, with one end dilated.

trumpet tree, the trumpetwood.

trumpet vine, trumpet creeper.

trum·pet·weed (trum′pit wēd′), *n.* any of various eupatoriums, especially: **a.** the boneset or thoroughwort. **b.** the joe-pye weed.

trum·pet·wood (trum′pit wu̇d′), *n.* a West Indian and South American tree of the mulberry family, whose hollow stems and branches are used for wind instruments.

trun·cate (trung′kāt), *v.,* **-cat·ed, -cat·ing,** *adj.* —*v.t.* to cut off a part of; cut short: *In the end, my adventure . . . was unexpectedly truncated* (New Yorker). —*adj.* **1.** appearing as if cut off at the tip or base by a transverse line, as the leaf of the tulip tree; abrupt. **2.** having no apex, as some spiral shells. [< Latin *truncāre* (with English *-ate*[1]) < *truncus* maimed, cut off] —**trun′cate·ly,** *adv.*

Truncate Leaf (def. 1) of tulip tree

trun·cat·ed (trung′kā tid), *adj.* **1.** (of a crystal, etc.) having its angles or edges cut off or replaced by a plane face. **2.** (of an edge or angle) cut off or replaced by a plane face. **3.** truncate.

truncated cone or **pyramid,** a cone or pyramid whose apex or vertex has been cut off by a plane.

Truncated Cone (left) and pyramid (right)

trun·ca·tion (trung kā′shən), *n.* **1.** the act of truncating. **2.** the state of being truncated. **3.** a truncated part. **4.** *Crystallography.* the replacement of an angle (or edge) by a crystalline face.

trun·cheon (trun′chən), *n.* **1.** *Especially British.* a stick cut and shaped for use as a weapon; short club: *a policeman's truncheon.* **2.** a staff of office or authority; baton: *a herald's truncheon.* **3.** a length cut from a plant, especially one used for grafting or planting. **4.** *Obsolete.* the stem or stock of a tree. **5.** *Obsolete.* the shaft of a spear.
—*v.t.* to beat with a truncheon; club.
[< Old French *tronchon* < Vulgar Latin *trunciō, -ōnis* < Latin *truncus* stem, trunk; (originally) mutilated]
—**Syn.** *n.* **1.** cudgel. **2.** mace.

trun·dle (trun′dəl), *v.,* **-dled, -dling,** *n.* —*v.t.* **1.** to draw or push along on a wheel or wheels: *The workman trundled a wheelbarrow hour after hour.* **2.** to cause to rotate; twirl; spin; whirl. **3.** *British Informal, Cricket.* to make (a bowl). —*v.i.* **1.** to move or be moved by trundling. **2.** to whirl; revolve. **3.** *British Informal, Cricket.* to bowl: [*He*] *is reported to be the best of his type now trundling* (Punch). [probably < Old French *trondeler* roll < Germanic (compare Middle High German *trendeln* to turn, rotate < *trendel* top)]
—*n.* **1.** the act of trundling or rolling; rolling along: *Our caboose took up again its easy trundle* (Owen Wister). **2.** a small wheel, roller, or revolving disk, especially a small but massive wheel adapted for supporting a heavy weight; caster. **3.** a trundle bed. **4. a.** a lantern pinion. **b.** one of its staves. **5.** *Obsolete.* a low cart or wagon on small wheels.
[perhaps alteration of earlier *trendle,* Old English *trendel* ring, disk]

trundle bed, a low bed moving on small wheels, which can be pushed under another bed when not in use; truckle bed.

trun·dler (trun′dlər), *n.* **1.** a person who trundles. **2.** *British Informal, Cricket.* a bowler.

trun·dle·tail (trun′dəl tāl′), *n.* *Archaic.* a low-bred dog; mongrel; cur.

trunk (trungk), *n.* **1.** the main stem of a tree, as distinct from the roots and branches; bole; stock. **2.** the main part of anything. **3.** a large boxlike container, usually with a hinged cover, for carrying clothes, etc., while traveling. **4.** an enclosed compartment in an automobile for storing baggage, a spare tire, tools, etc. **5.** a human or animal body without the head, arms, and legs. **6.** the thorax of an insect. **7.** the main body of a blood vessel, nerve, or similar structure, as distinct from its branches. **8.** an elephant's proboscis or snout. **9.** trunk line. **10.** a telephone circuit between two central offices or exchanges, used to make connections between individual subscribers. **11. a.** the shaft of a column. **b.** the dado or die of a pedestal. **12.** *Nautical.* **a.** a large, enclosed shaft passing through the decks between the bulkheads of a vessel, for coaling, loading, ventilation, etc. **b.** a watertight casing in a boat or ship, as the vertical box above the slot for the centerboard. **c.** the part above deck of a cabin that is partly above and partly below deck. **13.** any of various box-like passages for light, air, water, or solid objects, usually made of or lined with boards; a wooden shaft, conduit, or chute. **14.** the piston rod of a trunk engine.
trunks, a. very short trousers or breeches worn by athletes, swimmers, acrobats, etc.: *Black velvet trunks cover his* [*the wrestler's*] *hips and thighs* (Archibald Gunter). **b.** trunk hose: *The appearance of Mr. Snodgrass in blue satin trunks and cloak, white silk tights and shoes, and Grecian helmet . . .* (Dickens).
—*adj.* **1.** of or having to do with a trunk line, principal artery, channel, etc. **2.** main; chief: *a trunk highway.* **3.** of or having to do with a trunk engine: *a trunk piston.*
—*v.t.* to shut up or enclose in a trunk or casing.
[< Latin *truncus* (originally) mutilated]

trunk·back (trungk′bak′), *n.* the leatherback, a large sea turtle of tropical waters.

trunk call, *British.* a long-distance telephone call: *It has extended the period for cheap rate trunk calls . . .* (Economist).

trunked (trungkt), *adj.* having a trunk.

trunk engine, any of various reciprocating internal-combustion or steam engines having a piston rod or piston open at one end and tubular. The tubular opening is large enough to permit a connecting rod connected directly to make its lateral motion within the diameter of the opening.

trunk·fish (trungk′fish′), *n., pl.* **-fish·es** or (*collectively*) **-fish.** any of a family of plectognath fishes of tropical seas, having the body encased in bony, armorlike plates, so that only the appendages can be moved.

trunk·ful (trungk′fu̇l), *n., pl.* **-fuls.** as much or as many as a trunk will hold: *a trunkful of old books and letters.*

trunk hose, full, baglike breeches reaching halfway down the thigh, or lower, worn in the 1500's and early 1600's.

Trunk Hose

trunk line, 1. the main line of a railroad, canal, etc., or other system connecting important commercial areas with each other or with the sea. **2.** any main line, as between telephone exchanges.

trunk·load (trungk′lōd′), *n.* as much or as many as a trunk can hold or carry: *Saud had brought fifteen trunkloads of gifts to America* (Newsweek).

trunks (trungks), *n.pl.* See under **trunk,** *n.*

trun·nel (trun′əl), *n.* treenail.

trun·nion (trun′yən), *n.* **1.** either of the two round projections from the barrel of certain cannons, one on each side, which support it on its carriage and act as a pivot in elevation. **2.** either of any similar pair of opposite supporting pins or pivots. **3.** a single projecting pivot. [< Middle French *trognon* trunk < Latin *truncus;* influenced by Old French *moignon* stump of an amputated limb]

trun·nioned (trun′yənd), *adj.* provided with trunnions.

truss (trus), *v.t.* **1.** to tie; fasten; bind: *to truss up a bundle of plants. We trussed the burglar up and called the police.* **2.** to fasten the wings or legs of (a fowl, etc.) with skewers or twine in preparation for cooking: *The cook trussed up the chicken before cooking it.* **3.** to give firm support to (a roof, bridge, etc.) with trusses; strengthen or hold together with trusses. **4.** *Archaic.* to fasten or tighten (a garment). **5.** *Obsolete.* to bundle or pack.
—*n.* **1.** a structure or system of beams or other supports forming a framework of particular design or shape, usually triangular, which strengthens or holds together a roof, bridge, etc. **2.** a bandage, pad, etc., used for support, especially one equipped with a belt or spring and used in cases of hernia. **3.** a bundle of hay or straw, especially (in England) a bundle weighing 56 pounds of old hay, or 60 pounds of new hay, or 36 pounds of straw. **4.** any bundle; pack. **5.** *Nautical.* an iron fitting at the center of a heavy lower yard by which it is fastened to the mast. **6.** a compact cluster or head of flowers of any kind, growing upon one stalk, as an umbel or corymb. **7.** *Architecture.* a large corbel or modillion.
[< Old French *trusser, trousser,* perhaps ultimately < Late Latin *torcere,* for Latin *torquēre* to twist] —**truss′er,** *n.*

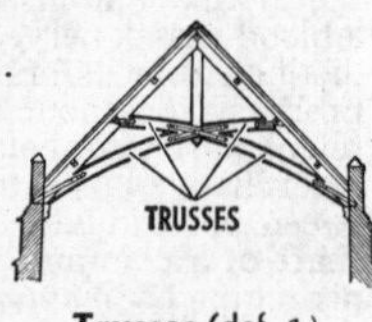

Trusses (def. 1)

truss bridge, a bridge supported wholly or chiefly by trusses.

truss·ing (trus′ing), *n.* **1.** the timbers, girders, etc., forming a truss. **2.** a brace or support consisting of a truss or trusses. **3.** trusses collectively. **4.** the act or process of strengthening or supporting with a truss or trusses.

trust (trust), *n.* **1.** a firm belief in the honesty, truthfulness, justice, or power of a person or thing; faith: *A child puts trust in his mother.* **2.** person or thing trusted: *God is our trust.* **3.** confident expectation or hope: *Our trust is that she will soon be well.* **4.** a group of men or companies that controls much of a certain kind of business: *a steel trust.* **5.** a group of businessmen or firms having a central committee that controls stock of the constituent companies, thus simplifying management and defeating competition. **6.** something managed for the benefit of another; something committed to one's care. **7.** obligation or responsibility imposed on one in whom confidence or authority is placed. **8.** condition of one in whom trust has been placed; being relied on: *A guardian is in a position of trust.* **9.** keeping; care: *The will was left in my trust.* **10.** *Law.* **a.** a confidence reposed in a person by making him nominal owner of property, which he is to hold, use, or dispose of for the benefit of another. **b.** an estate, etc., committed to a trustee or trustees. **c.** the right of a person to enjoy the use or profits of property held in trust for him. **11.** confidence in the ability or intention of a person to pay at some future time for goods, etc.; business credit.
in trust, as something which is entrusted to another: *His sealed commission, left in trust with me* (Shakespeare).
on trust, a. with confidence without investigation or evidence: *I am content to be beloved on trust for what I feel* (Byron). **b.** on business credit; with payment later: *My master lived on trust at an alehouse* (Samuel Johnson).
—*adj.* **1.** managing property for an owner: *a trust company.* **2.** *Law.* **a.** of or having to do with trusts. **b.** held in trust.
—*v.t.* **1.** to believe firmly in the honesty, truth, justice, or power of; have confidence or faith in: *He is a man to be trusted.* **2.** to rely or depend on: *A forgetful man should not trust his memory.* **3.** to expect with confidence; hope: *I trust this is the key you wanted. I trust you will soon feel better.* **4.** to believe (a person or statement): *if you trust my story.* **5.** to supply (a person) with goods on credit; give business credit to: *The butcher will trust us for the meat.* **6.** to commit or consign (something) to another's care with confidence; leave without fear; entrust: *Can I trust the money to him?* **7.** to confide or entrust something to the care of; invest: *Can I trust him with a large sum of money?* **8.** to allow to go somewhere or do something without misgiving or fear of consequences.
—*v.i.* **1.** to have or place confidence or faith (in): *Trust in God.* **2.** to hope (for). **3.** to sell on credit.
trust to, to rely or depend on: *to trust to luck.*
[< Scandinavian (compare Old Icelandic *traust*)] —**trust′er,** *n.*
—**Syn.** *n.* **1.** confidence, credence, reliance. **7.** charge, commission, duty, office. *-v.t.* **6.** confide.

trust·a·ble (trus′tə bəl), *adj.* that can be trusted: *At least one trustable, sympathetic person had been with her mother at the last* (Edna Lyall).

trust·bust·er (trust′bus′tər), *n. U.S.* a person who breaks up or tries to break up, combinations of companies restraining competition: *The trustbusters have not been reluctant in the past to prosecute on the basis of oral agreements* (Wall Street Journal).

trust·bust·ing (trust′bus′ting), *U.S.* —*n.* the activities of a trustbuster: *The politics of a flurry of trustbusting in an election year isn't lost on Justice Department politicians* (Wall Street Journal). —*adj.* breaking up, or trying to break up companies combined to restrain competition.

trust company, a bank or other business concern formed primarily for the purpose of administering trusts, but also often engaging in other financial activities normally performed by banks.

trust deed, a deed to property, held in trust to secure payment of a debt. It is in the nature of a mortgage.

trus·tee (trus tē′), *n., v.,* **-teed, -tee·ing.** —*n.* **1.** a person or one of a group of persons appointed to manage the affairs of an individual, institution, business firm, etc. **2.** a person who holds property in trust for another: *A trustee will manage the children's property until they grow up. The Youth of a nation are the trustees of Posterity* (Benjamin Disraeli). **3.** *U.S.* a person who holds property attached from a debtor.
—*v.t.* **1.** *U.S.* to attach by garnishment. **2.** to turn over to the care of a trustee or trustees.
—**Syn.** *n.* **1.** steward.

trustee process, *U.S., Law.* the attachment of property, etc., by garnishment.

trus·tee·ship (trus tē′ship), *n.* **1.** the office or function of a trustee. **2.** the supervision and control by a country of a trust territory, approved by the United Nations, usually with the idea that the trust territory will be developed toward self-government or independence. **3.** a trust territory.

Trusteeship Council, an agency of the United Nations whose duty it is to supervise the manner of governing and the administration of the various trust territories under United Nations mandate.

trust·ful (trust′fəl), *adj.* ready to confide; ready to have faith; trusting; believing: *Trustful birds have built their nests* (Robert Bridges). —**trust′ful·ly,** *adv.* —**trust′ful·ness,** *n.*
—**Syn.** confiding, credulous, unsuspicious, naïve.

trust fund, money, securities, or similar property of value held by one person in trust for another.

trust·i·ly (trus′tə lē), *adv.* in a trusty manner.

trust·i·ness (trus′tē nis), *n.* the quality of being trusty, especially that quality of a person by which he deserves the confidence of others; fidelity; faithfulness; honesty.

trust·ing (trus′ting), *adj.* that trusts; trustful. —**trust′ing·ly,** *adv.* —**trust′ing·ness,** *n.*

trust territory, any of certain territories, regions, or small countries, administered for the United Nations by various countries, especially former colonial possessions or League of Nations mandates in Africa, Asia, or the Pacific.

trust·wor·thi·ly (trust′wėr′ᴛʜə lē), *adv.* in a trustworthy or reliable manner.

trust·wor·thi·ness (trust′wėr′ᴛʜē nis), *n.* the state or character of being trustworthy.

trust·wor·thy (trust′wėr′ᴛʜē), *adj.* that can safely be depended on or trusted; deserving confidence; reliable: *a trustworthy guide, a trustworthy report. The memory strengthens . . . and becomes trustworthy as you trust it* (Thomas DeQuincey).
—**Syn.** dependable, faithful. See **reliable.**

trust·y (trus′tē), *adj.,* **trust·i·er, trust·i·est,** *n., pl.* **trust·ies.** —*adj.* **1.** trustworthy; reliable: *The master left his money with a trusty servant.* **2.** trustful.
—*n.* **1.** *U.S.* a convict who is given special privileges or responsibilities because of his good behavior. **2.** any person or thing that is trustworthy.

truth (trüth), *n., pl.* **truths** (trüᴛʜz, trüths). **1.** that which is in accordance with the fact or facts: *to speak truth. Is he telling the truth?* **2.** the fact or facts; matter or circumstance as it really is: *to suspect the truth.* **3.** a fixed or established principle, law, etc.; proven doctrine; verified hypothesis: *a basic scientific truth. It is the customary fate of new truths to begin as heresies and to end as superstitions* (Thomas H. Huxley). *All great truths begin as blasphemies* (George Bernard Shaw). **4.** that which is true, real, or actual, in a general or abstract sense; reality: *to find truth in God.* **5.** the quality or nature of being true, exact, honest, sincere, or loyal: *His friends his truth proclaim* (John Dryden). **6. Truth.** (in the belief of Christian Scientists) God.
in truth, in fact; truly; verily; really: *These people pretend to blame him, whereas in truth they ought only to blame themselves* (Daniel Defoe).
[Old English *trēowth* < *trēowe* true. Doublet of TROTH.]

truth drug, truth serum: *In the last war, . . . truth drugs were injected and soldiers were often greatly helped by being made to relive emotionally their horrifying battle experiences* (Atlantic).

truth·ful (trüth′fəl), *adj.* **1.** disposed to tell, or habitually telling, the truth; free from deceitfulness: *a truthful child.* **2.** telling the truth; correct in statement: *a truthful witness.* **3.** conforming to truth; factually accurate: *a truthful report of the accident.* —**truth′ful·ly,** *adv.* —**truth′ful·ness,** *n.*
—**Syn. 1.** veracious, honest, candid. **3.** exact, correct.

truth·less (trüth′lis), *adj.* **1.** untruthful or mendacious, as a person. **2.** untrue or false, as a statement. **3.** *Archaic.* unfaithful.

truth serum, any of various drugs, especially scopolamine or a compound containing it, under the influence of which a person will reveal inner thoughts or emotions that he has been suppressing.

try (trī), *v.,* **tried, try·ing,** *n., pl.* **tries.** —*v.i.* **1.** to make an attempt or effort; endeavor; attempt: *He tried hard but could not succeed.* **2.** to make an experiment. —*v.t.* **1.** to attempt to do or accomplish: *It seems easy until you try it.* **2.** to experiment on or with; make a trial of: *Try this candy and see if you like it.* **3.** to find out about; put to the proof; test: *We try each car before we sell it.* **4.** to investigate in a court: *The man was tried and found guilty.* **5.** to subject to trials; afflict: *Job was greatly tried.* **6.** to put to severe test; strain: *Her mistakes try my patience. Don't try your eyes by reading in poor light.* **7.** to purify by melting or boiling; render: *The lard was tried in a big kettle.* **8.** to shave or smooth the surface of, so as to fit with or to an adjoining surface, especially by planing. **9.** to ascertain the truth or right of (a matter, a quarrel, etc.) by test or endeavor; thrash or fight out.
try on, to test the fit or style of (a garment) by putting it on: *Miss Barton was trying on her new dress* (Maria Edgeworth).
try out, a. to test the effect or result of: *The new rules have been but partially tried out* (New York Evening Post). **b.** to test to find out about: *Picked pilots of proved experience . . . volunteer to try out new types* (Aeroplane). **c.** to appear as a contestant; compete: *One recent afternoon we watched* [*them*] *pass judgment on the merits of a couple of hundred dancers and showgirls who were assembled to try out for the weekly program* (New Yorker).
try over, *Especially British.* to go through (a performance, etc.) by way of experiment: *Let's try it over before we decide.*
—*n.* **1.** an attempt; endeavor; effort. **2.** a trial; test; experiment. **3.** (in Rugby) a play scoring three points, made by holding the ball on or beyond the opponents' goal line.
[< Old French *trier* to cull; origin uncertain]
—**Syn.** *v.i.* **1. Try, attempt, endeavor** mean to make an effort to or at. **Try** is the general word: *I tried to see him.* **Attempt,** a more

formal word, suggests making a real effort, trying hard: *I attempted to obtain an interview.* **Endeavor,** also formal, suggests both great effort and greater obstacles to be overcome: *The United Nations is endeavoring to establish peace.* *-v.t.* **7.** purify, refine, assay.
➔ **try and** or **try to.** The standard English idiom is *try to,* not *try and: Let us try to* (not *try and) get permission.*

try·ing (trī′ing), *adj.* hard to endure or bear; annoying; distressing: *a trying day, a trying person.*
—**Syn.** severe, difficult, vexing.

trying plane, a type of large plane used in trying a surface.

try·lon (trī′lon), *n.* a very tall, three-sided shaft, one of the features of the World's Fair of 1939-1940 in New York. [< *tr*(i)- + (p)*ylon*]

try·ma (trī′mə), *n., pl.* **-ma·ta** (-mə tə). a fruit resembling a drupe, but formed from an originally compound ovary, and having a fleshy or fibrous outer covering (epicarp) which ultimately dehisces, as in the walnut and hickory; a kind of drupaceous nut. [< New Latin *tryma* < Greek *trŷma* hole < *trŷein* wear through by rubbing, rub down]

try-on (trī′on′, -ôn′), *n.* the act of trying on a garment: *Finally you have try-ons of your partly finished garments* (Wall Street Journal).

try·out (trī′out′), *n. U.S. Informal.* **1.** a test made to determine fitness for a specific purpose; experimental trial. **2.** *Sports.* a selective trial to eliminate contestants or candidates not sufficiently capable to compete: *Olympic tryouts, a tryout for the varsity.* **3.** the showing of a play before the opening. [American English < *try out,* idiom]

tryp·a·fla·vine (trip′ə flā′vin, -vēn), *n.* acriflavine.

tryp·a·no·so·ma (trip′ə nə sō′mə), *n.* trypanosome.

tryp·a·no·so·mal (trip′ə nə sō′məl), *adj.* **1.** of or having to do with trypanosomes. **2.** caused by trypanosomes.

tryp·a·no·so·mat·ic (trip′ə nō sō mat′ik), *adj.* trypanosomal.

tryp·a·no·some (trip′ə nə sōm, tri pan′ə-), *n.* any of a group of minute, parasitic, flagellate protozoans inhabiting the blood of vertebrates, usually transmitted by bloodsucking insects or leeches and causing serious diseases, such as African sleeping sickness and nagana. [< New Latin *Trypanosoma* the genus name < Greek *trŷpanon* a borer, auger (< *trŷpân* to bore) + *sôma* a body]

tryp·a·no·so·mi·a·sis (trip′ə nō sō mī′ə-sis), *n.* any of various diseases caused by infection by trypanosomes.

tryp·ars·am·ide (trip′ärs am′id, -īd; trip-är′sə mid, -mīd), *n.* a crystalline drug used to treat syphilis and sleeping sickness. *Formula:* $C_8H_{10}O_4N_2AsNa.\frac{1}{2}H_2O$

tryp·sin (trip′sən), *n.* **1.** an enzyme in the digestive juice secreted by the pancreas, which changes proteins into peptones by hydrolysis. **2.** any of various enzymes having a similar function. [< German *Trypsin* < Greek *trîpsis* a rubbing (< *tríbein* to rub) + German *-in* -in (because it was originally obtained by rubbing down the pancreas with glycerine)]

tryp·sin·o·gen (trip sin′ə jən), *n.* an inactive form of the pancreatic enzyme trypsin, that is converted into trypsin by enterokinase in the small intestine.

tryp·ta·mine (trip′tə mēn), *n.* a crystalline substance closely related to serotonin, formed in the tissues from tryptophan. Various hallucinogenic substances have been derived from it. Formula: $C_{10}H_{12}N_2$

tryp·tic (trip′tik), *adj.* of or having to do with trypsin: *tryptic action.*

tryp·to·phan (trip′tə fan), *n.* a colorless, solid, indispensable amino acid formed from proteins by the digestive action of trypsin, and occurring naturally in the seeds of various plants. *Formula:* $C_{11}H_{12}N_2O_2$ [< *tryptic* + Greek *phainein* to appear]

tryp·to·phane (trip′tə fān), *n.* tryptophan.

try·sail (trī′sāl′; *Nautical* trī′səl), *n.* any small fore-and-aft sail, either a triangular sail or a four-sided sail attached to a gaff, on the foremast, mainmast, or a small extra mast, and used in stormy weather; spencer.

trysail mast, a small mast behind the foremast, on which a trysail is set.

try square, an instrument consisting of two straight pieces attached at right angles to each other, used for drawing right angles or for testing the squareness of anything.

tryst (trist, trīst), *n.* **1.** an appointment or engagement to meet at a specified time and place. **2.** an appointed place of meeting; rendezvous. **3.** *Scottish.* a market or fair, especially for cattle.
—*v.i. Especially Scottish.* to make an agreement (to do something with a person), especially to fix a time and place of meeting (with someone). —*v.t. Especially Scottish.* **1.** to engage with (a person) to meet at a given place and time; agree to meet. **2.** to appoint or fix (a time, place, etc.).
[< Old French *triste;* origin uncertain] —**tryst′er,** *n.*

tryst·ing place (tris′ting, trīs′-), an appointed meeting place; place where a tryst is to be kept.

tsa·di (tsä′dē), *n.* sadhe.

tsar (zär, tsär), *n.* czar: *Even when the Tartar yoke was finally broken, the first Russian Tsar carried on the oriental tradition and ruled as an autocrat* (J. V. Davidson-Houston).

tsar·dom (zär′dəm, tsär′-), *n.* czardom.

tsar·e·vitch (zär′ə vich, tsär′-), *n.* czarevitch.

tsa·rev·na (zä rev′nə, tsä-), *n.* czarevna.

tsa·ri·na (zä rē′nə, tsä-), *n.* czarina.

tsar·ism (zär′iz əm, tsär′-), *n.* czarism.

tsar·ist or **Tsar·ist** (zär′ist, tsär′-), *adj., n.* czarist.

tsa·rit·za or **tsa·rit·sa** (zä rēt′sə, tsä-), *n.* czarina.

tses·se·be (sas′ə bē), *n., pl.* **-bes** or (*collectively*) **-be.** sassaby, a South African antelope.

tset·se fly, or **tset·se** (tset′sē), *n.* any of a group of bloodsucking African flies. One kind of tsetse fly transmits the protozoan parasite causing sleeping sickness, and another kind carries a disease of horses and other domestic animals. Also, **tzetze fly, tzetze.** [< a Bantu word]

Tsetse Fly (Lines show actual length and width.)

tsetse fly disease, nagana.

T. Sgt., technical sergeant.

TSH (no periods) or **T.S.H.,** thyroid stimulating hormone; thyrotropin.

Tshi (chwē, chē), *n.* the principal language of the Negroes of the West African Gold Coast. —*adj.* of or having to do with the Negroes speaking this language.

T-shirt (tē′shėrt′), *n.* **1.** a collarless, close-fitting cotton shirt, usually white, with short sleeves, which pulls over the head, worn by men and boys as an undershirt. **2.** a collarless polo shirt. Also, **tee shirt.** [because of the shape]

Tsim·shi·an (tsim′shē ən), *n.* **1.** a member of an American Indian tribe of the northwestern coast of British Columbia. **2.** the language of this tribe, related to Penutian. —*adj.* of or having to do with the Tsimshians or their language.

tso·tsi (tsō′tsē), *n.* (in South Africa) a young Bantu scamp or hoodlum: *There are people who point to the Rand and its tsotsis, to London, to New York, and say that violence in the teens is just a sign of the times* (Cape Argus). [< Bantu *tsotsi*]

tsp., teaspoonful.

T square, a T-shaped ruler used for making parallel lines, etc. The shorter arm slides along the edge of the drawing board, serving as a guide.

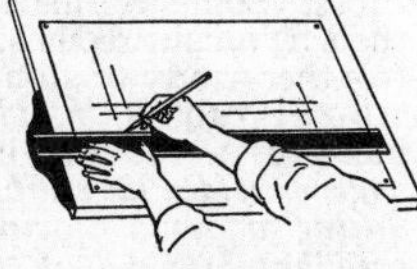
T Square

T-strap (tē′strap′), *n.* a woman's shoe with a vertical center strap that fastens to another strap around the ankle. —*adj.* having such straps: *T-strap sandals or pumps.*

tsu·na·mi (tsü nä′mē), *n.* a tidal wave in the Pacific caused by a submarine earthquake: *Tsunami waves are slowed down and quickly reduced in size when they enter an area of continental shelf studded with islands* (Science News Letter). [< Japanese *tsunami* (literally) storm wave]

tsu·tsu·ga·mu·shi disease (tsü tsü′gə-mü′shē), scrub typhus. [< Japanese *tsutsugamushi* the bug that transmits the disease < *tsutsuga* itching + *mushi* insect]

Tswa·na (tswä′nə, chwä′-), *n., pl.* **-na** or **-nas.** **1.** Bechuana: *The most important economic activity of the Tswana after stock rearing is wage labour in the Republic of South Africa* (London Times). **2.** the language of the Bechuana.

T.T., Tanganyika Territory.

T Tauri star, any of a group of very distant, variable stars found between clouds of dust and gas, usually associated with nebulae. [< *T Tauri,* a star in the constellation *Taurus,* the prototype of these stars]

TTS (no periods), teletypesetter.

Tu (no period), thulium (chemical element). The accepted abbreviation today is *Tm.*

Tu., Tuesday.

T.U., trade union or trade unions.

tu·an or **Tu·an** (tü än′), *n.* a title of respect, equivalent to sir, master, or lord in certain areas of southeastern Asia: *They called him Tuan Jim: as one might say — Lord Jim* (Joseph Conrad). [< Malay *tuan*]

Tua·reg (twä′reg), *n.* **1.** a Moslem nomad of the Sahara speaking a Hamitic language of the Libyan or Berber group. **2.** this language. Also, **Touareg.**

tu·a·ta·ra (tü′ə tä′rə), *n.* a large reptile of New Zealand, the only surviving rhynchocephalian; sphenodon. [< Maori *tuatara*]

tu·a·te·ra (tü′ə tā′rə), *n.* tuatara.

tub (tub), *n., v.,* **tubbed, tub·bing.** —*n.* **1.** any of various large containers, open at the top and having a flat bottom, used for washing, bathing, etc. **2.** a bathtub. **3.** *Informal.* bath: *He takes a cold tub every morning.* **4.** a round, wooden container for holding butter, lard, etc., in bulk, especially one made of staves and hoops. **5.** as much as a tub can hold; contents of a tub. **6.** a thing or person resembling a tub, especially in clumsy squatness of line, bulkiness of form, etc.: **a.** *Informal.* a clumsy, slow boat or ship, especially one which is too broad in proportion to its length. **b.** *Slang.* a fat person. **7.** a small cask or keg containing about four gallons, especially of brandy, rum, or other liquor (a smugglers' term). **8. a.** a car for carrying ore in a mine; tram. **b.** a bucket, box, etc., in which coal or ore is sent up from or conveyed in a mine. **c.** the lining of a mine shaft. **9.** *Obsolete.* **a.** a sweating tub, formerly used in the treatment of venereal disease. **b.** the use of this.
—*v.t.* **1.** to wash or bathe in a tub. **2.** to put or pack in a tub. **3.** to plant in a tub.
—*v.i.* to be washed or bathed in a tub.
[compare Middle Dutch *tubbe* (originally) a vessel with two handles]
—**Syn.** *n.* **4.** firkin, kit.

tu·ba[1] (tü′bə, tyü′-), *n., pl.* **-bas, -bae** (-bē). **1.** a large, brass, wind instrument of the trumpet class, of low pitch. **2.** a very powerful, 8-foot, organ reed stop. **3.** a long, straight war trumpet of the ancient Romans. [< Latin *tuba* war trumpet]

Tuba[1] **(def. 1)**

tu·ba[2] (tü′bä, tü bä′), *n.* an alcoholic drink of the Philippines, made of the fermented sap of the coconut palm. [< Malay *tuba*]

tub·al (tü′bəl, tyü′-), *adj.* **1.** of or having to do with a tube. **2.** occurring in a tube, especially a Fallopian tube: *tubal pregnancy.* —*n.* a Fallopian tube.

Tu·bal-cain (tü′bəl kān′, tyü′-), *n.* (in the Bible) a pioneer in making things out of iron and brass. Genesis 4:22.

tu·bate (tü′bāt, tyü′-), *adj. Botany.* **1.** forming a tube; tubiform. **2.** having a tube or tubes.

tub·ba·ble (tub′ə bəl), *adj.* that can be bathed or put in a tub.

tub·ber (tub′ər), *n.* **1.** a person who makes tubs; cooper. **2.** a person who uses a tub in any industrial process. **3.** a person who tubs; bather.

tub·bi·ness (tub′ē nis), *n.* tubby quality or condition: *Very low frequencies were reproduced cleanly, with no tubbiness* (Hi Fi Stereo Review).

tub·bing (tub′ing), *n.* a bath; washing.

tub·by (tub′ē), *adj.,* **-bi·er, -bi·est.** **1.** stout or broad in proportion to height or length; short and fat; corpulent: *a short, tubby fellow.* **2.** having a sound like that of an empty tub when struck. —**Syn. 1.** chunky.

tub chair, *British.* a barrel chair.

tube (tüb, tyüb), *n., v.,* **tubed, tub·ing.** —*n.* **1.** a hollow body, usually cylindrical, and long in proportion to its diameter, of metal, glass, rubber, etc., used especially to carry or contain a liquid or gas; slender pipe. **2.** a small, collapsible container of thin, easily bent metal with a cap that screws on the open end, used for holding toothpaste, shaving cream, pigment, etc. **3.** a pipe or tunnel through which something is sent, especially by means of compressed air. **4.** a railroad tunnel, especially one bored through rock or under a body of water: *the Hudson tubes.* **5.** *Especially British Informal.* subway. **6.** anything like a tube, especially any of certain tubular or cylindrical animal organs: *the Eustachian tube, the bronchial tubes.* **7.** an electron or vacuum tube. **8.** *Botany.* the lower united portion of a gamopetalous corolla or a gamosepalous calyx. **9.** *Physics.* tube of force. **10.** an electron tube. **11.** *Informal.* television, especially a television set.
—*v.t.* **1.** to furnish or fit with a tube or tubes; insert a tube in. **2.** to pass through or enclose in a tube. **3.** to make tubular.
[< Latin *tubus* tube, pipe]

tube foot, one of the many tubular organs of locomotion of a starfish, sea urchin, or other echinoderm.

tube·less (tüb′lis, tyüb′-), *adj.* having no tube or tubes: *a tubeless telescope.*

tubeless tire, a pneumatic tire with butyl rubber bonded directly to the inside of the casing, sealing the tire to the rim of the wheel and eliminating the need for a separate inner tube: *If punctured, many tubeless tires seal themselves when the object is removed* (World Book Encyclopedia).

tube·like (tüb′līk′, tyüb′-), *adj.* resembling a tube.

tube-nosed (tüb′nōzd′, tyüb′-), *adj.* having nostrils formed into a tube or tubes on the base of the bill, as a petrel: *The albatrosses [are] the kings of the tube-nosed tribe* (New Scientist).

tube of force or **induction,** *Physics.* a space, generally considered as being tubular, bounded by a number of lines of force or induction.

tu·ber[1] (tü′bər, tyü′-), *n.* **1.** *Botany.* a solid, thickened portion of an underground stem or rhizome, of a more or less rounded form, and bearing modified axillary buds (eyes) from which new plants may arise: *A potato is a tuber.* **2. a.** a rounded swelling or projecting part in an animal body. **b.** an abnormal swelling or enlargement. [< Latin *tūber, -eris* lump, bump]

tub·er[2] (tü′bər, tyü′-), *n.* **1.** a person who fits or replaces tubes, as in a boiler. **2.** a person who uses a tube or tubes (in any industrial process). [< *tub*(e) + *-er*[1]]

tube railway, *Especially British.* subway.

tu·ber·cle (tü′bər kəl, tyü′-), *n.* **1.** a small, wartlike swelling or protuberance on a plant. **2.** a nodule, as on the root of a legume. **3.** a small, hard, rounded swelling in or on the body; nodule. **4.** one of the small, soft lesions characteristic of tuberculosis. **5.** a knob (tuberculum costae) near the head of a rib at the point of articulation with the transverse process of a vertebra. [< Latin *tūberculum* small swelling, pimple (diminutive) < *tūber* lump]

tubercle bacillus, the bacillus that causes tuberculosis.

tu·ber·cled (tü′bər kəld, tyü′-), *adj.* characterized by or affected with tubercles.

tu·ber·cu·lar (tü bėr′kyə lər, tyü-), *adj.* **1.** of or having to do with tuberculosis: *tubercular symptoms.* **2.** having tuberculosis; tuberculous. **3.** having tubercles. **4.** having to do with tubercles. **5.** characterized by tubercles. —*n.* a tuberculous person. —**tu·ber′cu·lar·ly,** *adv.*

tu·ber·cu·late (tü bėr′kyə lit, -lāt; tyü-), *adj.* **1.** having or affected with tubercles. **2.** tubercular; tuberculous. [< New Latin *tuberculatus* < Latin *tūberculum;* see TUBERCLE]

tu·ber·cu·lat·ed (tü bėr′kyə lā′tid, tyü-), *adj.* **1.** tuberculate. **2.** characterized by tubercles.

tu·ber·cu·la·tion (tü bėr′kyə lā′shən, tyü-), *n.* **1.** the formation of tubercles. **2.** the disposition or arrangement of tubercles. **3.** a growth or set of tubercles.

tu·ber·cule (tü′bər kyül, tyü′-), *n. Botany.* a tubercle; nodule.

tu·ber·cu·lin (tü bėr′kyə lin, tyü-), *n.* a sterile liquid prepared from the proteins of the tubercle bacillus, or products of these proteins, used in the diagnosis and treatment of tuberculosis, especially in children and animals. [< German *Tuberkulin* < Latin *tūberculum;* see TUBERCLE]

tu·ber·cu·line (tü bėr′kyə lin, -lēn; tyü-), *n.* tuberculin.

tuberculin test, a test to determine the presence of tuberculosis, made by injecting tuberculin into the skin.

tu·ber·cu·li·za·tion (tü bėr′kyə lə zā′shən, tyü-), *n.* **1.** the formation of tubercles. **2.** the condition of becoming tubercled.

tu·ber·cu·lize (tü bėr′kyə līz, tyü-), *v.t.,* **-lized, -liz·ing.** **1.** to affect with tubercles; infect with tuberculosis; make tuberculous. **2.** to treat with tuberculin.

tu·ber·cu·loid (tü bėr′kyə loid, tyü-), *adj.* resembling a tubercle.

tu·ber·cu·lo·sis (tü bėr′kyə lō′sis, tyü-), *n.* an infectious disease that can affect any organ or part of the body, characterized by an acute inflammation or the formation of tubercles on the tissues, and caused by the tubercle bacillus. The most common form, pulmonary tuberculosis, attacks the lungs. *Tuberculosis of the lungs was formerly called consumption. Abbr.:* TB (no periods). [< New Latin *tuberculosis* < Latin *tūberculum* (see TUBERCLE) + New Latin *-osis* -osis]

tu·ber·cu·lo·ther·a·py (tü bėr′kyə lō-ther′ə pē, tyü-), *n.* treatment of tuberculosis.

tu·ber·cu·lous (tü bėr′kyə ləs, tyü-), *adj.* **1.** of or having to do with tuberculosis. **2.** having tuberculosis. **3.** tubercular.

tube·rose[1] (tüb′rōz′, tyüb′-), *n.* a plant of the agave family that grows from a tuber, much grown for its spike of creamy-white, funnel-shaped, very fragrant flowers. [< Latin *tūberōsa,* feminine of *tūberōsus;* see TUBEROUS; often taken as if < *tube* + *rose*]

tu·ber·ose[2] (tü′bə rōs, tyü′-), *adj.* tuberous.

tu·ber·os·i·ty (tü′bə ros′ə tē, tyü′-), *n., pl.* **-ties.** **1.** the quality or condition of being tuberous. **2.** a rounded swelling, protuberance, or prominence. **3.** a large, irregular protuberance of a bone, especially for the attachment of a muscle or ligament.

tu·ber·ous (tü′bər əs, tyü′-), *adj.* **1.** (of a plant) producing or bearing tubers. **2.** of or like a tuber or tubers. **3.** of the nature of tubers or abnormal swellings. **4.** affected with or characterized by tubers or abnormal swellings: *tuberous acne.* [< Latin *tūberōsus* < *tūber, -eris* lump]

tuberous root, *Botany.* a true root (usually one of a cluster) thickened so as to resemble a tuber, but bearing no buds, as in the lesser celandine and the dahlia.

tu·ber·ous-root·ed (tü′bər əs rü′tid, tyü′-; -rut′id), *adj. Botany.* having a tuberous root or roots.

tube well, a device for obtaining water from under the ground, consisting of an iron pipe having a solid steel point with perforations around it, that is driven into the earth until a water-bearing stratum is reached, when a suction pump is applied to the upper end: *The waterlogged land must be drained to avoid salinity, and this means digging tube wells and installing power-operated pumps to lower the water table* (New Scientist).

tube·worm (tüb′wėrm′, tyüb′-), *n.* any of a group of annelids that live in hard, flexible tubes. Some worms make these tubes of their own calcareous secretions; others glue together sandy or stony grit.

tub·ful (tub′fu̇l), *n., pl.* **-fuls.** as much or as many as a tub will hold: *A tubful of hot water provided the simplest way to keep warm during a London winter* (Harper's). *She eyed the tubful of dirty clothes fretfully, "What is wrong with the machine?"* (Atlantic).

tu·bic·o·lous (tü bik′ə ləs, tyü-), *adj. Zoology.* inhabiting a tube, as a mollusk with a tubular shell, an annelid with a tubular case, or a spider which spins a tubular web. [< Latin *tubus, -ī* tube + *colere* inhabit + English *-ous*]

tu·bi·corn (tü′bə kôrn, tyü′-), *adj.* hollow-horned; cavicorn. [< Latin *tubus, -ī* tube + *cornū* horn]

tu·bi·form (tü′bə fôrm, tyü′-), *adj.* having the form of a tube; tube-shaped; tubular. [< Latin *tubus, -ī* tube + *forma* form]

tub·ing (tü′bing, tyü′-), *n.* **1.** material in the form of a tube: *rubber tubing.* **2.** tubes collectively. **3.** a piece of tube. **4.** the act of furnishing with a tube or tubes.

tu·bo·cu·ra·rine chloride (tü′bō kyu̇-rä′rēn, -rin; tyü′-), an alkaloid derived from the South American vine that yields curare, used as a muscle relaxant and antispasmodic. *Formula:* $C_{38}H_{44}N_2O_6Cl_2.5H_2O$ [< Latin *tubus* tube + English *curare* + *-in* (because the curare is packed in tubes)]

Tu B'she·bat (tü′bish bät′), a Jewish arbor day celebrated on the 15th day of Shebat (the fifth month of the Jewish year, beginning in January). [< Hebrew *tu* (< *t,* the ninth letter of the alphabet + *u,* the sixth letter) + *bə* in + *Shabāṭ* Shebat]

tub thumper, *Informal.* **1.** a speaker or preacher who for emphasis thumps the desk or pulpit; a violent or declamatory speaker or orator. **2.** *U.S.* a spokesman or press agent: *Red tub thumpers are promising "business deals with no strings attached," credit terms that would shame the most liberal "buy now, pay later" scheme* (Newsweek).

tub thumping, *Informal.* **1.** loud and emotional oratory; declamatory speaking: *In the face of all that poverty and destruction, it is all he can do to preserve a balance between pity and indignation and shock, without lapsing into tub thumping or sentiment* (Observer). **2.** *U.S. Informal.* sensational advertising or publicity; ballyhoo: *Each year, to the accompaniment of much tub thumping, they pour out a stream of new models designed to make the old ones seem obsolete* (New Yorker).

tub-thump·ing (tub′thum′ping), *adj. Informal.* ranting; loud and emotional; declamatory: *tub-thumping oratory.*

tu·bu·lar (tü′byə lər, tyü′-), *adj.* **1.** shaped like a tube; round, hollow, and open at one or both ends. **2.** that is a tube; consisting of a tube: *a tubular corolla or calyx.* **3.** of or having to do with a tube or tubes. **4.** performed by means of a tube or tubes. **5.** constructed with or consisting of a number of tubes: *a tubular boiler.* **6.** *Medicine.* of or denoting a high-pitched respiratory murmur that sounds as if made through a tube. [< Latin *tubulus* (diminutive) < *tubus* tube, pipe + English *-ar*] —**tu′bu·lar·ly,** *adv.*

tu·bu·late (*adj.* tü′byə lit, -lāt; tyü′-; *v.* tü′byə lāt, tyü′-), *adj., v.,* **-lat·ed, -lat·ing.** —*adj.* tubular. —*v.t.* **1.** to form into a tube. **2.** to furnish with a tube. [< Latin *tubulātus* < *tubulus;* see TUBULE]

tu·bu·lat·ed (tü′byə lā′tid, tyü′-), *adj.* **1.** tubulate; tubular. **2.** furnished with a tube.

tu·bu·la·tion (tü′byə lā′shən, tyü′-), *n.* **1.** the formation of a tube or tubule. **2.** the disposition or arrangement of a set of tubes.

tu·bule (tü′byül, tyü′-), *n.* a small tube, especially a minute tubular structure in an animal or plant body: *the uriniferous tubules of the kidney, the dentinal tubules of the teeth.* [< French *tubule,* learned borrowing from Latin *tubulus* (diminutive) < *tubus* tube, pipe]

tu·bu·li·flo·rous (tü′byə lə flôr′əs, -flōr′-; tyü′-), *adj. Botany.* having all the perfect flowers of a head with tubular corollas, as certain composites.
[< Latin *tubulus, -ī* tubule + *flōs, flōris* flower + English *-ous*]

tu·bu·lose (tü′byə lōs, tyü′-), *adj.* tubular.

tu·bu·lous (tü′byə ləs, tyü′-), *adj.* **1.** tubular. **2.** *Botany.* having florets shaped like tubes. [< New Latin *tubulosus* < Latin *tubulus;* see TUBULE]

tu·bu·lure (tü′byə lər, tyü′-), *n.* a short tube, or projecting opening for the insertion of a tube, in a retort or receiver. [< French *tubulure* < *tubule;* see TUBULE]

T.U.C. or **TUC** (no periods), *British.* Trades Union Congress (the federation of the largest and most important trade unions.

tu·chun (dü′jYN′), *n.* (in China, during the period 1916-1923) the title of the military head of a province.
[< Chinese (Pekingese) *tu-chün* (literally) overseer of troops]

tuck[1] (tuk), *v.t.* **1.** to thrust or put (an object) into some narrow space or into some retired place: *She tucked her purse under her arm. He tucked the letter into his pocket. The little cottage is tucked away under the hill.* **2.** to thrust the edge or end of (a garment, covering, etc.) closely into place: *Tuck your shirt in. Jack tucked a napkin under his chin.* **3.** to cover snugly: *to tuck a child in bed.* **4.** to pull or gather (up) in a fold or folds; fold or turn up: *The man tucked up his trousers before wading across the stream.* **5.** to sew a fold in (a garment) for trimming or to make it shorter or tighter:

The baby's dress was beautifully tucked with tiny stitches.
—*v.i.* **1.** to sew a tuck or tucks. **2.** to draw together; contract; pucker.
tuck away or **in,** *Slang.* to eat or drink heartily; consume with gusto: *to tuck away a big meal.*
—*n.* **1.** a fold sewed down with stitches parallel to the line of the fold, made to shorten or ornament a garment, etc. **2.** *U.S. Dialect.* heart; spirit: . . . *I've got the stuff here that'll take the tuck out of him* (Mark Twain). **3.** the part of a ship where the after ends of the outside planks or plates come together, at or just beneath the stern post. **4.** the position assumed by a diver while in the air in executing a somersault, in which the knees are folded under the chest and the ankles are grasped in the hands. **5.** *British Slang.* eatables, especially candy, pastry, etc.: *Parents at home and abroad. Let us send your child's tuck each week . . . anywhere in U.K.* (London Times).
[Middle English *tukken* gather up, pluck out; stretch (cloth); earlier, upbraid, Old English *tūcian* disturb, chastise, torment]

tuck[2] (tuk), *n. Archaic.* a rapier. [perhaps variant of obsolete *stock* < Old French *estoc,* ultimately < Germanic (compare Old High German *stoc* staff, stick, tree trunk)]

tuck[3] (tuk, tük), *Especially Scottish.* —*n.* a blow, stroke, or tap: *a tuck of drum.* [< verb] —*v.t., v.i.* to beat the drum. [< Old North French *touker,* Old French *toucher;* see TOUCH]

Tuck (tuk), *n.* **Friar,** the jolly friar of Robin Hood's band.

tuck·a·hoe (tuk′ə hō), *n.* the edible food-storage body (sclerotium) of an underground fungus occurring on the roots of trees in the southern United States. [American English, apparently < Algonkian (Powhatan) *p'tûkweu* it is round]

tuck box, *British Slang.* a box in which children at a boarding school, etc., keep the food brought or sent from home: . . . *the new boys, their tuck boxes lost in transit, whistling to keep up their courage* (London Times).

tucked (tukt), *adj.* **1.** drawn up, as in folds; sewed in or ornamented with tucks. **2.** *Informal or Dialect.* cramped, as in position, space, etc. **3.** *Dialect.* wearied or exhausted: *"You're looking tucked up," he concluded* (Rudyard Kipling).

tuck·er[1] (tuk′ər), *n.* **1.** a piece of muslin, lace, etc., worn by women around the neck or over the chest in the 1600's and 1700's. **2.** a chemisette or dicky. **3.** a person or thing that tucks. **4.** a device on a sewing machine for making tucks. **5.** *Australian Slang.* food; a meal. [< *tuck*[1], verb]

tuck·er[2] (tuk′ər), *v.t. U.S. Informal.* to tire; weary; exhaust.
tucker out, to make utterly exhausted; wear out: *She's clean tuckered out, and kind o' discouraged* (Harriet Beecher Stowe).
[American English; origin uncertain. Compare *tucked* worn out, exhausted.]

tucker bag, *Australian Slang.* a bag for carrying food.

tuck·et (tuk′it), *n. Archaic.* a flourish on a trumpet, especially as a marching signal for cavalry. [related to TUCK[3]]

tuck·in (tuk′in′), *n. British Slang.* a hearty meal; feast: *One good tuckin won't give you an ulcer* (Scottish Sunday Express). [< *tuck*[1] eatables + *-in*]

tuck-in (tuk′in′), *adj.* that can or should be tucked in: *a tuck-in blouse or shirt.* —*n.* an edge or end to be tucked in, as of a garment, etc. *It* [*the cummerbund*] *was too tight and it was badly creased, and the tuck-in came too near the front, so that it was not hidden by the jacket* (Graham Greene).

tuck·shop (tuk′shop′), *n. British Slang.* a shop that sells pastry, candy, fruit, etc., especially to schoolboys: *Arm in arm and happily paired, the two friends went down to the tuckshop for tea* (Punch).

Tu·dor (tü′dər, tyü′-), *n.* **1.** a member of the royal house which ruled England from 1485 to 1603. Henry VII, Henry VIII, Edward VI, Mary I, and Elizabeth I were Tudors. **2.** a person who lived in England under the Tudors.
—*adj.* **1.** of or having to do with a style of architecture developed in England during the reign of the Tudors. It was characterized by flat arches, shallow moldings, and elaborate paneling. The principal development was in domestic architecture, typified by the large manor house with regular plan, inner courts, and many windows, gables, and chimneys. **2.** of or having to do with the Tudors.

Tudor arch, a flat, pointed arch.

Tu·dor·esque (tü′də resk′, tyü′-), *adj.* **1.** of or resembling Tudor style in art or architecture: *a Tudoresque hotel.* **2.** of or having to do with the Tudors.

tu·e·bor (tü ē′bôr, tyü-), *Latin.* I will defend (one of Michigan's mottoes).

Tues., Tuesday.

Tues·day (tüz′dē, -dā; tyüz′-), *n.* the third day of the calendar week, between Monday and Wednesday. *Abbr.:* Tues., Tu. [Old English *Tīwesdæg* day of Tiu (god of war), translation of Late Latin *Martis diēs* day of Mars (the planet)]

tu·fa (tü′fə, tyü′-), *n.* **1.** any of various porous rocks formed of powdery matter consolidated and often stratified. **2.** tuff. [< Italian *tufo* < Latin *tōfus.* Doublet of TUFF.]

tu·fa·ceous (tü fā′shəs, tyü-), *adj.* of the nature of or resembling tufa.

tuff (tuf), *n.* a tufa produced by the consolidation of volcanic ashes and other erupted material: *Nuclear devices have been exploded . . . in a spongy, volcanic rock called tuff* (Wall Street Journal). [< Middle French *tuf* < Italian *tufo* tufa. Doublet of TUFA.]

tuff·a·ceous (tu fā′shəs), *adj.* **1.** having the properties of volcanic tuff. **2.** composed of volcanic tuff.

tuft (tuft), *n.* **1.** a bunch, natural or artificial, of small things, usually soft and flexible, as hairs, feathers, etc., fixed or attached at the base: *A goat has a tuft of hair on its chin.* **2.** a bunch of short-stalked leaves or flowers growing from a common point, of stems growing from a common root, etc. **3.** a clump of bushes, trees, etc. **4.** a cluster of threads sewn tightly through a mattress, comforter, etc., so as to keep the padding in place. **5.** a button by which such a cluster is attached. **6.** a gold tassel formerly worn on the cap by titled undergraduates at Oxford and Cambridge. **7.** *Slang.* the wearer of such a tassel.
—*v.t.* **1.** to furnish with a tuft or tufts; put tufts on. **2.** to divide into tufts. —*v.i.* to form a tuft or tufts; grow in tufts.
[alteration of Middle English *tuffe,* perhaps < Old French *touffe* < Late Latin *tūfa* helmet crest]

tuft·ed (tuf′tid), *adj.* **1.** having or adorned with a tuft or tufts: *a tufted quilt.* **2.** (of a bird) having a tuft of feathers on the head; crested. **3.** formed into or forming a tuft.

tufted duck, an old-world crested duck. The male has mostly black plumage.

tufted titmouse, a titmouse of the eastern United States, bluish-gray with white and rust under parts, and a crest.

tuft·er (tuf′tər), *n.* **1.** a hunting dog trained to drive deer out of cover: *Ahead roamed the tufters seeking out the stag which had been located the night before in a thicket* (Newsweek). **2.** a person who tufts mattresses, cushions, etc.

tuft·hunt·er (tuft′hun′tər), *n. Especially British.* a person who tries to become acquainted with persons of rank and title.

tuft·hunt·ing (tuft′hun′ting), *n.* the practice of a tufthunter: *He had kept the letters sent him by the many notable figures of the time whom he "collected" in his long career of tufthunting* (Richard D. Altick). —*adj.* **1.** that is a tufthunter. **2.** that is characteristic of a tufthunter.

tuft·y (tuf′tē), *adj.* **1.** abounding in tufts or knots. **2.** growing in tufts.

tug (tug), *v.,* **tugged, tug·ging,** *n.* —*v.t.* **1.** to move by pulling forcibly; pull with force or effort; drag; haul: *We tugged the boat out of the water.* **2.** to pull at with force; strain at: *to tug a jammed window until it opens.* **3.** to pull or push by tugboat. —*v.i.* **1.** to pull with effort or force; pull hard; strain (at): *to tug at a jammed window. The child tugged at his mother's hand.* **2.** to strive hard; toil; labor; struggle.
—*n.* **1.** an act or the act of tugging; hard pull: *a sudden tug on the line. The baby gave a tug at Mary's hair.* **2.** a hard strain, struggle, effort, or contest. **3.** tugboat. **4.** one of a pair of long leather straps by which a horse pulls a wagon, cart, etc.; trace. See **harness** for picture. **5.** *U.S.* a rope.
[Middle English *toggen* to pull playfully. Related to TOW[1].]
—**Syn.** *v.t.* **1, 2.** See **pull.**

tug·boat (tug′bōt′), *n.* a small, powerful vessel used to pull or push a barge or barges, to tow large ships into berths, etc.; towboat.

Tugboat

tug·boat·man (tug′bōt′mən), *n., pl.* **-men.** a man who works on a tugboat: *Against union advice, Liverpool tugboatmen decided to continue their strike* (London Times).

tug·ger (tug′ər), *n.* **1.** a person who tugs or pulls with force. **2.** *Informal.* a person who pulls in a tug of war.

tug·ging·ly (tug′ing lē), *adv.* with tugging.

tu·ghrik or **tu·grik** (tü′grik), *n.* the monetary unit of the Mongolian People's Republic (Outer Mongolia), equal to one Soviet ruble. [< Mongol *tugrik*]

tug·man (tug′mən), *n., pl.* **-men.** a tugboatman: *The strikes of Yorkshire miners and tugmen on the Mersey River continued* (New York Times).

tug of war, 1. a contest between two teams who haul at opposite ends of a rope, each trying to drag the other over a line marked between them. **2.** any hard struggle, especially for a decision, supremacy, etc.; stubbornly fought contest: *Rural-urban tug of war . . . characterizes most Louisiana elections* (Wall Street Journal).

tu·i (tü′ē), *n.* a New Zealand bird having dark plumage with white neck feathers; parson bird. [< Maori *tui*]

Tui·ler·ies (twē′lər ēz; *French* twēl rē′), *n.* a former royal palace in Paris, France, adjoining the Louvre, burned in 1871, now the site of famous gardens.

tuille (twēl), *n.* **1.** one of the two or more plates of steel hanging below the tasses in a suit of armor. **2.** the lowermost part of the tasses.
[Middle English *toile* < Middle French *teuille,* Old French *tuile* (literally) plaque, tile < Latin *tēgula*]

tu·i·tion (tü ish′ən, tyü-), *n.* **1.** the act of teaching a pupil or pupils; teaching; instruction. **2.** money paid for this; instruction fee or fees. **3.** *Obsolete.* **a.** safekeeping; custody. **b.** guardianship. [< Latin *tuitiō, -ōnis* protection < *tuērī* watch over]

tu·i·tion·al (tü ish′ə nəl, tyü-), *adj.* of or having to do with tuition.

tu·i·tion·ar·y (tü ish′ə ner′ē, tyü-), *adj.* tuitional.

tu·la·re·mi·a or **tu·la·rae·mi·a** (tü′lə rē′mē ə), *n.* an infectious disease of wild rabbits, rodents, and of certain birds, caused by a bacterium that may be carried by ticks and insects and transmitted to man; rabbit fever.
[American English < New Latin *tularemia* < *Tulare,* a county in California + *-emia* -emia]

tu·la work (tü′lə), niello work. [< *Tula,* a town in Russia, where it is made]

tu·le (tü′lē), *n.* either of two large bulrushes abundant in lowlands along riversides in California and neighboring regions. [American English < Mexican Spanish *tule* < Nahuatl *tullin*]

tu·lip (tü′lip, tyü′-), *n.* **1.** any of a group of Old World bulbous plants of the lily family, with long, narrow leaves, much grown in many varieties for their spring-blooming, bell- or cup-shaped, showy flowers, of various colors and markings. **2.** the flower or bulb of any of these plants. [< obsolete Dutch *tulipa* < French *tulipe* < Turkish *tülbent* gauze, muslin < Persian *dulband* turban. Doublet of TURBAN.]

tulip ear, an erect or pricked ear in dogs.

tu·lip-eared (tü′lip ird′, tyü′-), *adj.* prick-eared, as a dog.

tu·lip·o·ma·ni·a (tü′li pə mā′nē ə, tyü′-), *n.* a craze for tulips, as that which prevailed in Holland in the 1600's.

tu·lip·o·ma·ni·ac (tü′li pə mā′nē ak, tyü′-), *n.* a person who is affected with tulipomania.

tulip poplar, a tulip tree: *Ancient tulip poplars and lindens all over the place* (New Yorker).

tulip tree, **1.** a large North American tree of the magnolia family, with greenish-yellow flowers, resembling large tulips, and truncate leaves; yellow poplar; whitewood. Its soft wood is much used in cabinetwork, etc. **2.** any of certain other trees whose flowers resemble tulips.

Tulip Tree Branch (def. 1)

tu·lip·wood (tü′lip wu̇d′, tyü′-), *n.* **1.** the soft wood of the tulip tree; whitewood; white poplar. **2.** any of various other colored and striped woods. **3.** any tree producing such wood.

tulle (tül), *n.* a thin, fine net, usually of silk, used for veils, etc. [< *Tulle,* a town in France, where it was first made]

tul·li·bee (tul′ə bē), *n., pl.* **-bees** or (*collectively*) **-bee.** any of a group of fishes of the Great Lakes area, related to the whitefishes. [American English < Canadian French *toulibi* < Algonkian (Cree, Ojibwa) *otonabi* mouth water < *oton* mouth + *abi* water (because of the watery flesh of this fish)]

tul·war (tul′wär), *n.* a kind of saber used by the peoples of northern India. [< Hindi *talwār*]

tum·ble (tum′bəl), *v.,* **-bled, -bling,** *n.* —*v.i.* **1.** to fall in a helpless way, as from stumbling or violence; be precipitated; fall headlong: *The child tumbled down the stairs.* **2.** to fall prone; fall (down) to the ground. **3.** to stumble by tripping (over an object). **4.** (of a building or structure) to fall in ruins; collapse. **5.** to fall rapidly in value, amount, or price (used especially of stocks). **6.** to throw oneself about in a restless way; toss: *The sick child tumbled restlessly in his bed.* **7.** to roll about on the ground, or in the water or air; pitch; wallow. **8.** to move in a hurried or awkward way; proceed hastily, without apparent order or premeditation: *The occupants tumbled out of the burning building. Tumble into bed and go to sleep* (Charles J. Lever). **9.** to perform leaps, springs, somersaults, or other feats demonstrating physical agility, without the aid of gymnasium apparatus. **10.** *Obsolete.* to dance with posturing, balancing, contortions, etc. —*v.t.* **1.** to throw over or down; cause to tumble: *Unruly wind . . . which . . . tumbles down steeples* (Shakespeare). **2.** to upset the arrangement of (anything neat or orderly) by turning over; disorder; rumple; muss: *to tumble bedclothes.* **3.** to mix, cleanse, or polish in a tumbling box or tumbler.
—*n.* **1.** a fall: *The tumble hurt him badly.* **2.** tumbled condition; confusion; disorder. [Middle English *tumbelen* (frequentative) < Old English *tumbian* to dance about]

tum·ble·bug (tum′bəl bug′), *n.* any of various beetles that roll up a ball of dung in which to lay their eggs.

Tumblebug (actual size)

tum·ble-down (tum′bəl doun′), *adj.* falling or fallen into ruin; dilapidated: *a tumble-down shack in the mountains.* —**Syn.** rickety, ramshackle.

tum·ble-dry (tum′bəl drī′), *v.t., v.i.,* **-dried, -dry·ing.** to dry in a tumble dryer: *The treated wool . . . can be safely . . . tumble-dried without danger of shrinking* (New Scientist).

tumble dryer or **drier,** a dryer in which hot air is blown through the clothes while they are tumbled inside a revolving barrel; tumbler.

tum·ble·dung (tum′bəl dung′), *n.* tumblebug.

tum·bler (tum′blər), *n.* **1.** a person who performs leaps, springs, somersaults, and other feats; acrobat. **2.** a drinking glass without a foot or stem, and with a heavy, flat bottom. **3.** the contents of a tumbler: *to drink a tumbler of water.* **4.** (in a lock) a pivoted piece kept in position by a spring, with projections which drop into notches in the bolt and hold it until lifted by the proper key. **5.** the part of a gunlock acting on a spring which forces the hammer forward when the trigger is pulled. **6.** any of a variety of domestic pigeons that perform aerial acrobatics including backward somersaults during flight; roller. **7.** a toy figure with a low center of gravity and rounded base, that rocks when touched but rights itself. **8. a.** a revolving box or barrel in which things are mixed, cleansed, etc.; tumbling box. **b.** a person who operates such an apparatus. **9.** any of a breed of dogs similar to small greyhounds, formerly used to catch rabbits. **10.** a part in an automobile transmission that moves a gear into place. **11.** a piece projecting from a shaft and actuating a cam, etc. **12.** a tumble dryer. **13.** *Dialect.* tumbrel.

tum·bler·ful (tum′blər fu̇l), *n., pl.* **-fuls.** a quantity sufficient to fill a tumbler: *We drank it through clenched teeth, but after the third tumblerful it was easier to swallow* (Punch).

tum·ble·weed (tum′bəl wēd′), *n. U.S.* any of several plants of the western United States, as an amaranth, the bugseed, etc., forming a globular bush which in autumn is broken off from its roots and is blown about by the wind, scattering its seeds. [American English < *tumble* + *weed*]

tum·bling box or **barrel** (tum′bling), a revolving box or barrel, used for polishing small objects, especially of metal, by shaking them about with abrasives.

tum·brel or **tum·bril** (tum′brəl), *n.* **1.** any of various two-wheeled carts, especially: **a.** a cart formerly used for hauling and dumping manure on a farm, collecting garbage, etc. **b.** such a cart as the vehicle that carried prisoners to the guillotine during the French Revolution. **c.** a covered cart formerly used to carry ammunition, tools, etc., especially one belonging to a particular battery or other artillery unit. **2.** (formerly) an instrument of punishment, especially a ducking stool. [probably < Old French *tumberel, tomberel* dump cart < *tomber* (let) fall or tumble, probably < a Germanic word]

tu·me·fa·cient (tü′mə fā′shənt, tyü′-), *adj.* producing or tending to produce swelling. [< Latin *tumefaciēns, -entis,* present participle of *tumefacere;* see TUMEFY]

tu·me·fac·tion (tü′mə fak′shən, tyü′-), *n.* **1.** a swelling. **2.** a being swollen. **3.** a swollen part. [< French *tuméfaction* < Latin *tumefacere;* see TUMEFY]

tu·me·fy (tü′mə fī, tyü′-), *v.t., v.i.,* **-fied, -fy·ing.** to swell. [< Latin *tumefacere* < *tumēre* to swell + *facere* make]

tu·mes·cence (tü mes′əns, tyü-), *n.* **1.** the state of growing tumid; tumefaction. **2.** a swelling, tumid part, or tumor; intumescence.

tu·mes·cent (tü mes′ənt, tyü-), *adj.* **1.** becoming swollen; swelling. **2.** somewhat tumid. [< Latin *tumēscēns, -entis,* present participle of *tumēscere* begin to swell < *tumēre* to swell]

tu·mid (tü′mid, tyü′-), *adj.* **1.** of a swollen or protuberant form; swelling; bulging. **2.** characterized by swelling; enlarged; swollen. **3.** swollen with big words; pompous; turgid; bombastic: *His letters were tumid, formal and affected* (William E. H. Lecky). **4.** teeming. [< Latin *tumidus* < *tumēre* to swell] —**tu′mid·ly,** *adv.* —**tu′mid·ness,** *n.*

tu·mid·i·ty (tü mid′ə tē, tyü-), *n.* **1.** the state or character of being tumid or swollen. **2.** a pompous or bombastic style; turgidness; fustian.

tum·my (tum′ē), *n., pl.* **-mies.** *Informal.* the stomach; abdomen: *Flat tummies and fetching contours need exercises as rigorous as a prizefighter's workout* (Maclean's). [< children's pronunciation of *stomach*]

tu·mor (tü′mər, tyü′-), *n.* **1.** a benign or malignant growth arising in any part of the body and exhibiting laws of growth independent of the surrounding tissue, characterized by gradual development, and due to unknown causes. **2.** a swollen part or object; swelling. **3.** *Obsolete.* a swollen condition. [< Latin *tumor, -ōris* < *tumēre* to swell]

tu·mor·ous (tü′mər əs, tyü′-), *adj.* **1.** of or having to do with a tumor or tumors. **2.** having a tumor or tumors.

tu·mour (tü′mər, tyü′-), *n. Especially British.* tumor.

tump (tump), *n. British Dialect.* **1.** a hillock; mound. **2.** a clump of trees, grass, etc., especially one marking or forming a dry spot in a bog or fen. **3.** a heap (of anything); pile. [origin unknown]

tump·line (tump′līn′), *n. U.S. and Canada.* a strap across the forehead and over the shoulders, used to carry loads on the back: *The women of the Hupa and their neighbors in northwest California wear a tight-fitting basketry skullcap at times. This headgear apparently was developed to protect the head when carrying weights with the aid of the tumpline* (Beals and Hoijer). [perhaps < Algonkian (compare Massachusetts *tàmpàn* pack strap)]

tu·mu·lar (tü′myə lər, tyü′-), *adj.* **1.** having to do with a mound or tumulus. **2.** consisting of a mound or tumulus. [< Latin *tumulus* (see TUMULUS) + English *-ar*]

tu·mu·lar·y (tü′myə ler′ē, tyü′-), *adj.* **1.** tumular. **2.** having to do with a tomb; sepulchral: *a tumulary stone.*

tu·mu·lose (tü′myə lōs, tyü′-), *adj.* full of little hills or knobs. [< Latin *tumulōsus* hilly < *tumulus;* see TUMULUS]

tu·mu·lous (tü′myə ləs, tyü′-), *adj.* tumulose.

tu·mult (tü′mult, tyü′-), *n.* **1.** noise; uproar; commotion: *The sailors' voices could not be heard above the tumult of the storm.* **2.** the commotion of a multitude, usually with confused speech or uproar; public disturbance; disorderly or riotous proceeding: *The tumult and the shouting dies* (Rudyard Kipling). **3.** an instance of this; riot; insurrection: *There is much bloodshedding in Spain . . . and violent wars and tumults* (George Borrow). **4.** great disturbance or agitation of mind or feeling; confused and violent emotion: *The quarrel left her in a tumult.* [< Latin *tumultus, -ūs,* related to *tumēre* to swell] —**Syn. 3.** brawl, outbreak.

tu·mul·tu·ar·y (tü mul′chu̇ er′ē, tyü-), *adj.* **1.** disposed to or marked by riotous tumult or public disorder. **2.** of the nature of riotous tumult or public disorder.

tu·mul·tu·ous (tü mul′chu̇ əs, tyü-), *adj.* **1.** characterized by or causing tumult; very noisy or disorderly; violent and clamorous: *a tumultuous celebration. Fifty feet from the door a dozen headlights illuminated a bizarre and tumultuous scene* (F. Scott Fitzgerald). **2.** greatly disturbed; agitated and confused: *tumultuous emotions.* **3.** large and violent; rough; stormy: *Tumultuous waves beat upon the rocks.* [< Latin *tumultuōsus* < *tumultus, -ūs;* see TUMULT] —**tu·mul′tu·ous·ly,** *adv.* —**tu·mul′tu·ous·ness,** *n.* —**Syn. 1.** boisterous, turbulent.

tu·mu·lus (tü′myə ləs, tyü′-), *n., pl.* **-lus·es, -li** (-lī). a mound of earth, especially one marking the site of an ancient grave; barrow. [< Latin *tumulus* < *tumēre* to swell]

tun[1] (tun), *n.* **1.** a large cask or barrel, usually for liquids, especially wine, ale, or beer. **2.** a unit of liquid measure for wine, liquor, etc., formerly used in England, equal to eight barrels or two pipes (or approximately 252 gallons, in the measurement of the period). [Old English *tunne*]

tun[2] (tün), *n.* a year in the calendar of the Mayas, consisting of 360 days. [< Mayan *tun*]

tu·na[1] (tü′nə), *n., pl.* **tu·nas** or (*collectively*) **tu·na.** **1.** any of various large marine food fishes related to the mackerel and bonito, having coarse oily flesh that is widely used as food; tunny. **2.** the flesh of such a fish. [American English < American Spanish *tuna* < Spanish *atún* < Arabic *tun* < Latin *thunnus;* see TUNNY]

tu·na[2] (tü′nə), *n.* **1.** any of several prickly pears, especially a treelike pear of tropical America with an edible fruit. **2.** the fruit itself. [< Spanish *tuna* < Arawak (Haiti)]

tun·a·ble (tü′nə bəl, tyü′-), *adj.* **1.** that can be tuned. **2.** in tune; concordant. **3.** *Archaic.* harmonious; tuneful; melodious. Also, **tuneable.** —**tun′a·ble·ness,** *n.*

tun·a·bly (tü′nə blē, tyü′-), *adv.* in a tunable manner; harmoniously; musically. Also **tuneably.**

tuna fish, tuna[1].

tun·dish (tun′dish), *n.* a funnel-shaped receptacle used in brewing, casting steel, etc.: *The glowing bars of 2 in.-square steel have come from a single ladle containing 7½ tons, through two tundishes into reciprocating copper moulds* (New Scientist). [< *tun*[1] + *dish*]

tun·dra (tun′drə), *n.* **1.** a vast, level, treeless plain so far north that the ground never completely thaws but south of the region of perpetual snow and ice. **2.** any of various tracts and areas similar to this, as certain plateaus in the Andes and elsewhere. [< Russian *tundra*]

tune (tün, tyün), *n., v.,* **tuned, tun·ing.** —*n.* **1.** a piece of music; a rhythmical succession of musical tones; melody or air: *A tune is more lasting than the voice of the birds* (Padraic Colum). *To see her is a picture, To hear her is a tune* (Emily Dickinson). **2.** a musical setting of a psalm or hymn, usually in four-part harmony, to be used in public worship: *hymn tunes.* **3.** the state

of being in the proper pitch: *The piano is out of tune. He can't sing in tune.* **4.** agreement in pitch, unison, or harmony: *to keep a violin in tune with one's piano.* **5.** agreement or harmony in vibrations other than those of sound. **6. a.** harmony or agreement with (some person or thing): *A person out of tune with his surroundings is unhappy.* **b.** proper condition: *a horse in good tune.* **7.** frame of mind; temper; mood. **8.** *Obsolete.* a sound or tone.
call the tune, to declare authoritatively what will be or what will happen; dictate: *Dow recognized that when the bears were calling the tune, it was time to be long, not on stocks, but on money* (Wall Street Journal).
change one's tune, to change one's way of speaking or attitude, as from insolence to respect: *He'll soon change his tune.*
sing another or **a different tune,** to speak or act in a very different manner; change one's tune: *I imagine he would sing a different tune if the bluecoats ever get to Richmond* (George A. Henty).
to the tune of, *Informal.* in the amount or sum of: *Britain has been in the red on international trade to the tune of £28 million a month* (Manchester Guardian Weekly).
—*v.t.* **1.** to adjust the tones of (a musical instrument) to a standard of pitch; put in tune: *A man is tuning the piano.* **2.** to adapt (the voice, a song, etc.) to a particular tone or to the expression of a particular feeling or subject. **3.** to adapt or adjust so as to be in harmony, as a circuit into resonance with a different circuit. **4.** to bring into a proper or desirable state or mood or into a condition for producing an effect: *to tune public opinion.* **5.** to bring into harmony or accord; attune. **6.** *Archaic.* to utter or express musically. **7.** *Archaic.* to play upon (an instrument). —*v.i.* **1.** to put in tune, as a musical instrument. **2.** to give forth a musical sound; sound: *In came a fiddler—and tuned like fifty stomachaches* (Dickens). **3.** to sing or sound in tune with; be in tune; be in harmony; harmonize. **4.** accord.
tune in, to adjust a radio or television receiver to receive (a transmission or station): *[He] jots down such entries as "Dworshak Symphony #2," a reminder to tune it in on the radio* (New York Times). **b.** to be attuned: *. . . a genuine gift for tuning in to the spirit of the times* (Punch).
tune out, to adjust a radio or television receiver to get rid of or not receive (an unwanted transmission or station): *The operator . . . has it in his power to tune out either of these two stations* (J.A. Fleming).
tune up, a. to bring musical instruments to the same pitch; put in tune: *The band began to tune up, and a general feeling of expectation pervaded the building* (Violet Jacob). **b.** to put (a motor, racing vessel, etc.) into the best working order: *The system is functioning properly—tuned up, properly greased and oiled* (New York Times). **c.** *Informal.* to begin to play, sing, cry, etc.: *I have heard an old cow tune up in like manner* (John Millais).
[variant of *tone*]
tune·a·ble (tü′nə bəl, tyü′-), *adj.* tunable. —**tune′a·ble·ness,** *n.*
tune·a·bly (tü′nə blē, tyü′-), *adv.* tunably.
tune·ful (tün′fəl, tyün′-), *adj.* **1.** melodious; musical: *That canary has a tuneful song.* **2.** producing musical sounds. —**tune′ful·ly,** *adv.* —**tune′ful·ness,** *n.* —**Syn. 1.** euphonious.
tune·less (tün′lis, tyün′-), *adj.* **1.** unmelodious; unmusical: *The tuneless yet sweet humming of the low, worn voice* (Elizabeth Gaskell). **2.** giving no sound or music. —**tune′less·ly,** *adv.*
tun·er (tü′nər, tyü′-), *n.* **1.** a person who tunes pianos, organs, or other musical instruments. **2.** a device for adjusting a radio receiver to accept a given frequency and reject other frequencies: *an FM tuner.*
tune·smith (tün′smith′, tyün′-), *n. U.S. Informal.* a composer of popular music; songwriter: *He still needs a tunesmith and a lyricist and he hasn't any special stars in view* (New York Times). *"There's Music in You" is by none other than those two preëminent Broadway tunesmiths, Rodgers and Hammerstein* (New Yorker).
tune-up (tün′up′, tyün′-), *n. U.S.* **1.** a series of checks and adjustments made on parts of an engine to put it into efficient order. **2.** a game, match, race, etc., of lesser importance preparatory to a major contest; warm-up: *The Daniels fight was to have been the first of two tune-ups for the Valdez bout* (New York Times).
tung nut (tung), the seed of the tung tree, yielding tung oil: *Tung nuts are grown in Alabama, Florida, Georgia, Louisiana, Mississippi, and Texas* (Wall Street Journal).
tung oil, a poisonous oil obtained from the seeds of the tung tree and related trees of the spurge family, grown in China and in the southern United States. It is much used in varnishes, as it surpasses all other known oils in drying quality. [< Chinese (Pekingese or Cantonese) *t'ung-yu* tung oil]
tung·state (tung′stāt), *n.* a salt or ester of a tungstic acid.
tung·sten (tung′stən), *n.* a rare, heavy, steel-gray, ductile, very infusible, metallic chemical element, occurring in scheelite, wolframite, tungstite, and various other minerals; wolfram; wolframium. Its melting point (3410 degrees centigrade) is higher than that of any other metal. Tungsten is used in making steel and for electric-lamp filaments. *Symbol:* W; *at. wt.:* (C^{12}) 183.85 or (O^{16}) 183.86; *at. no.:* 74; *valence:* 2, 3, 4, 5, 6.
[< Swedish *tungsten* < *tung* heavy + *sten* stone]
tung·sten·ic (tung sten′ik), *adj.* **1.** of or having to do with tungsten. **2.** obtained from tungsten.
tungsten lamp, an incandescent electric lamp whose filament is made of metallic tungsten. See **filament** for picture.
tungsten steel, a hard, heat-resistant steel containing tungsten, used for making lathe tools, etc.: *Machine tools of tungsten steel do not lose their hardness or their sharp cutting edges even if they are red-hot when used* (George L. Bush).
tung·stic (tung′stik), *adj.* **1.** of tungsten. **2.** containing tungsten, especially with a valence of five or of six.
tungstic acid, 1. a yellow powder, a hydrate of tungstic trioxide, used in making textiles and plastics. *Formula:* H_2WO_4 **2.** any of various acids formed by the hydration of the trioxide of tungsten.
tung·stite (tung′stīt), *n.* a yellow or yellowish-green mineral, tungsten trioxide, usually occurring in powdery form and the chief source of tungsten. *Formula:* WO_3
tung tree, a tree of the spurge family, native to China and cultivated in other areas, from which tung oil is obtained.
Tun·gus (tůn gůz′), *n., pl.* **-gus·es** or **-gus,** *adj.* —*n.* **1.** a member of any of a group of Mongolian tribes of Tungusic speech, including the Manchus, in eastern Siberia. **2.** the language of this people. —*adj.* Tungusic. [< the native name]
Tun·gus·i·an (tůn gůz′ē ən), *adj.* Tungusic.
Tun·gus·ic (tůn gůz′ik), *n.* a linguistic family of Siberia and Manchuria, including Tungus and Manchu.
—*adj.* **1.** of or having to do with the Tunguses or their language. **2.** of or denoting the linguistic family to which Tungus and Manchu belong.
Tun·guz (tůn gůz′), *n., pl.* **-guz·es** or **-guz,** *adj.* Tungus.
tu·nic (tü′nik, tyü′-), *n.* **1.** a garment resembling a shirt or gown, usually reaching to the knees, worn by both men and women among the ancient Greeks and Romans. **2.** any garment like this. **3.** a woman's garment, usually belted, extending below the waist, as a blouse, or over the skirt, as a short overskirt. **4.** a short, close-fitting coat reaching below the waist but never below the thighs, worn by soldiers, policemen, etc. **5.** *Botany.* a natural covering or integument. **6.** a membranous sheath enveloping or lining an organ of the body; tunica. **7.** a tunicle (vestment). [< Latin *tunica*]

Roman Tunic (def. 1)

tu·ni·ca (tü′nə kə, tyü′-), *n., pl.* **-cae** (-sē). *Anatomy.* a covering or enveloping membrane or fold of tissue. [< New Latin *tunica* < Latin *tunica* tunic]
Tu·ni·ca (tü′nə kə, tyü′-), *n., pl.* **-ca** or **-cas. 1.** a member of an American Indian tribe that formerly lived along the Yazoo River in Mississippi and was noted for its alliance with the French in the 1700's in fighting against neighboring tribes. **2.** the language of this tribe.
tu·ni·cate (tü′nə kit, -kāt; tyü′-), *adj.* **1.** *Botany.* having or consisting of a series of concentric layers: *An onion is a tunicate bulb.* **2.** *Zoology.* having a tunic or mantle; belonging to the tunicates.
—*n. Zoology.* any of a group of marine chordates, including the ascidians and allied forms, characterized by a saclike body enclosed in a tough, leathery membrane (tunic), with a single or double aperture through which the water enters and leaves the pharynx.
[< Latin *tunicātus,* past participle of *tunicāre* clothe with a tunic < *tunica* tunic]
tu·ni·cat·ed (tü′nə kā′tid, tyü′-), *adj.* tunicate.
tu·ni·cle (tü′nə kəl, tyü′-), *n.* **1.** a vestment worn by subdeacons and bishops over the alb at the Eucharist. **2.** *Obsolete.* an integument or enclosing membrane; tunic. [< Latin *tunicula* (diminutive) < *tunica* tunic]
tun·ing fork (tü′ning, tyü′-), a small, two-pronged steel instrument used in tuning musical instruments. When struck, it vibrates at a fixed, constant, known rate and so makes a musical tone of a certain pitch.

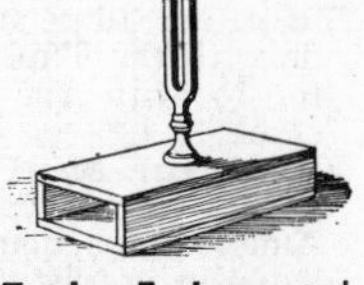
Tuning Fork mounted on sounding box

Tu·ni·sian (tü nish′ən, tyü-; -nē′shən), *adj.* of or having to do with the North African country of Tunisia or its inhabitants. —*n.* a native or inhabitant of Tunisia.
Tun·ku (tůng′kü), *n.* the Malayan title of Prince: *. . . the Malaysian Premier, Tunku Abdul Rahman* (Scotsman). Also, **Tenku.** [< Malay *tunku*]
tun·nage (tun′ij), *n. Obsolete.* tonnage.
tun·nel (tun′əl), *n., v.,* **-neled, -nel·ing** or (*especially British*) **-nelled -nel·ling.** —*n.* **1.** an underground passageway for automobiles, trains, etc., or persons on foot: *The railroad passes under the mountain through a tunnel.* **2.** any of certain other subterranean passageways or borings, as for the passage of water, sewage, etc. **3.** a nearly horizontal passageway in a mine (often used loosely for any drift, level, etc.). **4.** a passageway dug into the earth by any of certain animals, as a means of access to or exit from its burrow. **5.** the burrow itself. **6.** *Obsolete, Dialect.* a funnel. **7.** *Obsolete.* the shaft or flue of a chimney.
—*v.i.* to make a tunnel; excavate a passageway (through some body or substance): *A mole tunneled in the ground about the terrace.*
—*v.t.* **1.** to make a tunnel through or under: *to tunnel a hill or river.* **2.** to make (one's way or a way) by digging. **3.** *Obsolete.* to form into or like a tube or pipe.
[< Old French *tonnelle* tunnel net, *tonel* cask < *tonne;* see TUN[1]] —**tun′nel·er** or, *especially British,* **tun′nel·ler,** *n.* —**tun′nel·like′,** *adj.*
tunnel diode, *Electronics.* a very small semiconductor that uses less power and achieves high frequency faster than a transistor, and is relatively insensitive to temperature changes and nuclear radiation: *The tunnel diode is so named because of the manner in which electrons seem to "tunnel" through the device with the speed of light* (Wall Street Journal).
tunnel of love, a dark, winding tunnel or waterway in a carnival, amusement park, etc., through which couples ride in small cars or boats: *Mild amusements such as tunnels of love and ghost trains are on their way out* (Economist).
tunnel vision, a disorder of the eyes in which the range of vision is contracted so that only objects in the direct line of are seen clearly.
tun·ny (tun′ē), *n., pl.* **-nies** or (*col*
-ny. 1. any of a family of lar
game and food fishes; tuna. **2.** ar
related fishes. [apparently alte
French *thon* < Old Proven
thunnus, or *thynnus* < Greek
haps < Hebrew *tannīn*]
tup (tup), *n., v.,* **tupped**
a male sheep; ram. **2.**
as the head of a stean
weight of a pile dri
—*v.t.* (of a ram) t
[origin uncertai
cock[1].]

tu·pe·lo (tü′pə lō, tyü′-), *n., pl.* **-los. 1.** any of a group of large trees growing in moist places in the southern United States, especially the black gum or the sour gum. **2.** the light, tough wood of any of these trees, used for furniture, pulpwood, crates, boxes, etc. [American English, apparently < Algonkian (Cree) *ito* tree + *opilwa* swamp]

Tupelo (def. 1) or black gum
Left, flowers; right, berries

tupelo gum, tupelo.

Tu·pi (tü pē′), *n., pl.* **-pis. 1.** a member of a group of Indians of the Tupi-Guarani linguistic stock in Brazil, Paraguay, and Uruguay. **2.** their language, constituting the northern branch of the Tupi-Guarani linguistic stock.

Tu·pi·an (tü pē′ən), *adj.* **1.** of or having to do with the Tupi Indians. **2.** of or having to do with the Tupi-Guarani linguistic stock.

Tu·pi-Gua·ra·ni (tü pē′gwä′rä nē′), *n.* a native linguistic stock of central South America, particularly along the lower Amazon, consisting principally of Tupi, the northern branch, and Guarani, the southern branch.

tu·pik (tü′pik), *n.* a hut or tent of animal skins in which Eskimos live during the summer: *When they move from the winter igloo to the summer tupik, they escape the dirt* (White and Renner). [< Eskimo *tupik*]

tup·pence (tup′əns), *n.* twopence: *The only theory worth tuppence in my experience is that if you say a thing fifty thousand times three boys out of ten may remember it* (Punch).

tup·pen·ny (tup′ə nē), *adj.* twopenny.

tuque (tük, tyük), *n.* a kind of knitted cap tapered and closed at both ends, with one end tucked into the other to form the cap, originally worn especially by French-Canadian trappers, farmers, etc., but now also widely by skiers, skaters, etc. [< Canadian French variant of French, Middle French *toque* cap; see TOQUE]

tu quo·que (tü kwō′kwē, tyü), *Latin.* thou, too; you're the same (a retort accusing one's accuser of the same charge that he has made): *Much of the "managed news" debate has been conducted in a tu quoque manner* (Columbia University Forum).

tu·ra·koo (tůr′ə kü), *n.* any of a family of African birds notable for their large size, brilliant plumage, and helmetlike crest. [< a native name in West Africa]

Tu·ra·ni·an (tů rā′nē ən, tyů-), *adj.* **1.** (originally) of, having to do with, or denoting a group or supposed family of languages, including all or nearly all Asiatic languages that are neither Indo-European nor Semitic. **2.** (later) Ural-Altaic.
—*n.* **1.** a member of any of the peoples that speak Turanian or Ural-Altaic languages. **2.** the so-called Turanian languages, collectively.
[< Persian *Tūrān*, a district north of the Oxus River, probably < a Turkic word]

tur·ban (tėr′bən), *n.* **1.** a headdress for a man or boy consisting of a scarf wound around a cap, or worn directly on the head, originally Moslem, but now worn also by Sikhs and certain others who are of Asian origin but not of the Moslem faith. **2.** any headdress resembling this, as a large handkerchief tied around the head. **3.** a small hat with little or no brim, worn by women and children.

Turbans (def. 1)

—*v.t.* to envelop with or as if with a turban: *My hat is off to them—with the lengths of surgical gauze currently turbaning my brow, I can't wear it anyway* (Peter DeVries).
[< obsolete French *turbant*, or Portuguese *turbante* < Turkish *tülbent* muslin, gauze. Doublet of TULIP.]

r·baned (tėr′bənd), *adj.* wearing a turn: *Her high-borne turban'd head she wags* Walt Whitman).

ba·ry (tėr′bər ē), *n., pl.* **-ries. 1.** land e turf or peat may be dug for fuel; peat **2.** *Law.* the right to cut turf or peat for n a common or on another's land: *Then when dipping into the manorial rolls I find I have the right of turbary over ground that is now the Commonwealth Turf Research Station* (Punch). [< Anglo-French *turberie*, Old French *tourberie* < *tourbe* a peat turf < Germanic (compare Low German *turf* or *turv*)]

tur·bel·lar·i·an (tėr′bə lãr′ē ən), *n.* any of a class of flatworms (platyhelminths), including the planarians, which inhabit fresh or salt water or damp earth. The bodies are covered with vibratile cilia which produce minute whirls in the water.
—*adj.* belonging to the turbellarians.
[< New Latin *Turbellaria* the class name (< Latin *turbellae*, plural, a bustle, stir; (literally) little crowd < *turba* crowd, disturbance) + English *-an*]

tur·beth (tėr′bith), *n.* turpeth.

tur·bid (tėr′bid), *adj.* **1.** (of liquid) not clear; cloudy; muddy: *a turbid river.* **2.** (of air, smoke, etc.) thick; dense; dark. **3.** characterized by or producing confusion or obscurity of thought, feeling, etc.; confused; disordered: *a turbid imagination. Clear writers, like fountains, do not seem so deep as they are; the turbid look the most profound* (Walter S. Landor). [< Latin *turbidus* < *turba* turmoil, crowd] —**tur′bid·ly,** *adv.* —**tur′bid·ness,** *n.*

tur·bi·dim·e·ter (tėr′bə dim′ə tər), *n.* an instrument for determining the turbidity of liquids, as a nephelometer. [< Latin *turbidus* (see TURBID) + English *-meter*]

tur·bi·di·met·ric (tėr′bə də met′rik), *adj.* **1.** of or having to do with a turbidimeter. **2.** of or having to do with turbidimetry.

tur·bi·dim·e·try (tėr′bə dim′ə trē), *n.* the act or process of determining the turbidity of liquids with a turbidimeter.

tur·bid·i·ty (tėr bid′ə tē), *n.* the state of being turbid: *Water beetles provide clues to the acidity and turbidity of water* (New Scientist).

turbidity current, *Geology.* an underwater stream of silt, mud, etc., usually along the bottom of a slower-moving body of water: *When a turbidity current flows along a channel on the sea floor it will deposit some of its load at any point where the velocity of the flow decreases* (New Scientist).

tur·bi·nal (tėr′bə nəl), *adj.* shaped like a top; turbinate. —*n.* a turbinate bone. [< Latin *turbō, -inis* a top[2], whirling object or motion, related to *turba* turmoil]

tur·bi·nate (tėr′bə nit, -nāt), *adj.* **1.** resembling a spinning top in shape. **2.** *Botany.* inversely conical; having a narrow tapering base and a broad rounded apex. **3.** *Zoology.* spiral or whorled, as the shells of certain mollusks. **4.** of, having to do with, or denoting one of the nasal conchae (scroll-like, spongy bones of the nasal passages in higher vertebrates).
—*n.* **1.** a turbinate shell. **2.** one of the nasal conchae.
[< Latin *turbinātus* < *turbō, -inis* whirling object or motion]

tur·bi·nat·ed (tėr′bə nā′tid), *adj.* turbinate.

tur·bi·na·tion (tėr′bə nā′shən), *n.* a top-like or turbinate form.

tur·bine (tėr′bin, -bīn), *n.* **1.** any of a class of high-speed, rotary engines or motors consisting essentially of a wheel or spindle set with projecting vanes, or a group of these, caused to operate by the force of a current of liquid, as water, or of a gas, as steam, acting on the vanes. **2.** any of various rotary engines or motors operating on a principle similar to this, as the water wheel. [< French *turbine*, learned borrowing from Latin *turbō, -inis* whirling object or motion, related to *turba* turmoil, crowd]

turbine generator, a turbogenerator.

tur·bit (tėr′bit), *n.* any of a breed of domestic pigeons having a stout, rounded body, a short beak, and a ruffle or frill on the neck and breast. [apparently < Latin *turbō* top[2]; see TURBINE (because of its plump, round build)]

tur·bith (tėr′bith), *n.* turpeth.

tur·bo (tėr′bō), *n., pl.* **-bi·nes** (-bə nēz) *for 1,* **-bos** *for 1 and 2.* **1.** a turbinate shell. **2.** *Informal.* a turbine.

turbo-, *combining form.* **1.** a machine coupled to a turbine which drives it: *Turbogenerator = a generator coupled to and driven by a turbine.*
2. a machine that is a turbine: *Turbomotor = a motor that is a turbine.*
[< *turbine*]

tur·bo·al·ter·na·tor (tėr′bō ôl′tər nā′tər, -al′-), *n.* an alternating-current generator connected to and driven by a turbine.

tur·bo·car (tėr′bō kär′), *n.* an automobile powered by a turbine.

tur·bo·charge (tėr′bō chärj′), *v.t.,* **-charged, -charg·ing.** to equip or operate with a turbocharger.

tur·bo·charg·er (tėr′bō chär′jər), *n.* a supercharger operated by a turbine driven by exhaust gases from the engine.

tur·bo-com·pound engine (tėr′bō kom′-pound), a turbosupercharged aircraft engine: *The Super Constellation can cruise 350 miles an hour, powered by four turbo-compound engines that create 13,000 horsepower* (Science News Letter).

tur·bo·drill (tėr′bō dril′), *n.* a high-speed drill for boring oil or gas wells, in which the bit is rotated inside the well by a turbine powered by mud or water: *Some engineers think that a promising method for drilling the hard rock in the deep part of the hole would be to use a diamond-coring bit on a turbodrill driven by sea water pumped from the surface at high pressure* (Scientific American).

tur·bo·e·lec·tric (tėr′bō i lek′trik), *adj.* of or having to do with an electric generator driven by a turbine: *turboelectric power or machinery.*

tur·bo·fan (tėr′bō fan′), *n.,* or **turbofan engine,** a turbojet engine in which a propeller or fan forces low-pressure air through ducts directly into the hot turbine exhaust at the pressure of the turbine exhaust. See **jet engine** for picture.

tur·bo·gen·er·a·tor (tėr′bō jen′ə rā′tər), *n.* a generator that produces electrical power by means of a steam or gas turbine: *The heat removed from the converter by the collector coolant would be used to generate steam to drive a conventional turbogenerator* (Atlantic).

tur·bo·jet (tėr′bō jet′), *n.* **1.** Also, **turbojet engine.** a type of jet engine having a turbine-driven air compressor attached to the combustion chamber, the power for the turbine being supplied as an auxiliary function by the jet of hot gases that produces the thrust of the engine. See **combustion chamber** for picture. **2.** an aircraft having such an engine.

tur·bo·prop (tėr′bō prop′), *n.* **1.** Also, **turboprop engine.** a type of jet engine in which the principal thrust is provided by a propeller driven by a turbine, to the operation of which the jet of hot gases produced by the engine is primarily devoted, although some additional thrust is normally provided by the ejection of combusted gases from the rear. **2.** an aircraft having such an engine.

tur·bo·ram·jet (tėr′bō ram′jet′), *n.* **1.** Also, **turbo-ramjet engine.** a type of turbojet in which there is a secondary combustion of fuel behind the turbine to produce exhaust gases at a higher temperature than the turbine can withstand. **2.** an aircraft having such an engine.

tur·bo·su·per·charge (tėr′bō sü′pər-chärj′), *v.t.,* **-charged, -charg·ing.** to equip or operate with a turbosupercharger.

tur·bo·su·per·charg·er (tėr′bō sü′pər-chär′jər), *n.* a type of supercharger for an aircraft engine, operated by a turbine driven by the exhaust gases from the engine. With a turbosupercharger piston engines can operate at higher altitudes than would otherwise be possible.

tur·bot (tėr′bət), *n., pl.* **-bots** or (*collectively*) **-bot. 1.** a large European flatfish, an important food fish. **2.** any of numerous similar fishes, such as certain flounders. **3.** a triggerfish. [< Anglo-French *turbut*, variant of Old French *tourbout*, perhaps < Scandinavian (compare Old Swedish *törnbut* < *törn* thorn + *but* butt)]

tur·bu·lence (tėr′byə ləns), *n.* **1.** turbulent condition; disorder; tumult; commotion. **2.** *Meteorology.* an eddying motion of the atmosphere, interrupting the flow of wind.

tur·bu·len·cy (tėr′byə lən sē), *n.* turbulence.

tur·bu·lent (tėr′byə lənt), *adj.* **1.** given to or causing disturbance or commotion; unruly; violent: *a turbulent nature, a turbulent mob.* **2.** characterized by violent disturbance or commotion; violently disturbed or agitated; disorderly; troubled: *turbulent times.* **3.** (of weather, the sea, etc.) stormy; tempestuous. **4.** *Obsolete.* disturbing. [< Latin *turbulentus* < *turba* turmoil, crowd] —**Syn. 1.** boisterous, uproarious. **2.** tumultuous. —**tur′bu·lent·ly,** *adv.*

turbulent flow, flow in a fluid characterized by constant changes in direction and velocity at any particular point.

Tur·co (tėr′kō), *n., pl.* **-cos.** a native soldier of a former body of light infantry commanded by French officers in the French service in Algeria. [< French *Turco* < Italian or Spanish *turco* a Turk]

Turco-, *combining form.* a variant of **Turko-.**

Tur·co·man (tėr′kə mən), *n., pl.* **-mans.** Turkoman.

Tur·co·phil (tėr′kə fil), *n.* Turkophile.

Tur·co·phile (tėr′kə fil, -fīl), *n.* Turkophile.

tur·di·form (tėr′də fôrm), *adj.* having the form or appearance of a thrush; thrushlike. [< Latin *turdus, -ī* thrush + English *-form*]

tur·dine (tėr′dīn, -din), *adj.* of or belonging to the true thrushes. [< New Latin *Turdinae* the subfamily name < Latin *turdus* thrush]

tu·reen (tů rēn′), *n.* a deep, covered dish, usually with two handles and an opening in the cover for the handle of a dipper, for serving soup, etc., at the table. [alteration of French *terrine* earthen vessel < *terrin,* adjective, earthen, ultimately < Latin *terrēnus* of the earth < *terra* earth]

turf (tėrf), *n., pl.* **turfs** or **turves,** *v.* —*n.* **1.** the upper surface of the soil covered with grass and other herbage, including their roots and the soil clinging to them; sod. **2.** a piece of this: *We cut some turfs from a field and covered a bare spot in the lawn with them.* **3.** peat, especially a slab or block of peat dug for use as fuel. **4.** *U.S. Slang.* a city block or district regarded as the exclusive territory of a gang: *They had, he maintained, entered forbidden Dragon "turf" . . . and made threatening gestures* (Newsweek).

the turf, a. a track for horse races: *Have you any horses on the turf?* (Edward G. Bulwer-Lytton). **b.** the sport or business of horse racing: *Already there was among our nobility and gentry a passion for the amusements of the turf* (Macaulay).

—*v.t.* to cover with turf or sod.

[Old English *turf*]

-turfed, *combining form.* having ____ turf: *Short-turfed = having short turf.*

turf·en (tėr′fən), *adj.* **1.** consisting or made of turf. **2.** covered with turf; turfy.

turf·i·ness (tėr′fē nis), *n.* the state or quality of being turfy.

turf·ite (tėr′fīt), *n. Informal.* a frequenter of the turf or of horse races; turfman.

turf·less (tėrf′lis), *adj.* without turf, as ground.

turf·man (tėrf′mən), *n., pl.* **-men.** a person interested or engaged in horse racing.

turf·y (tėr′fē), *adj.,* **turf·i·er, turf·i·est. 1.** covered with turf; grassy. **2.** like turf. **3.** like peat; full of peat. **4.** of or having to do with horse racing.

tur·gent (tėr′jənt), *adj. Obsolete.* turgid. [< Latin *turgēns, -entis,* present participle of *turgēre* to swell]

tur·ges·cence (tėr jes′əns), *n.* **1.** the act or fact of swelling. **2.** a swollen condition. —**Syn. 1.** turgidness. **2.** distention.

tur·ges·cen·cy (tėr jes′ən sē), *n.* turgescence.

tur·ges·cent (tėr jes′ənt), *adj.* becoming swollen; growing bigger; swelling. [< Latin *turgēscēns, -entis,* present participle of *turgēscere* begin to swell < *turgēre* to swell]

tur·gid (tėr′jid), *adj.* **1.** swollen; bloated; distended. **2.** using or characterized by long words and elaborate constructions; bombastic; inflated; pompous; grandiloquent: *turgid, scholarly harangues* (Baron Charnwood). [< Latin *turgidus* < *turgēre* to swell] —**tur′gid·ly,** *adv.* —**tur′gid·ness,** *n.*

tur·gid·i·ty (tėr jid′ə tē), *n.* **1.** the state of being turgid or swollen; tumidity. **2.** bombast; pomposity: *Turgidity, and a false grandeur of diction* (Joseph Warton).

tur·gite (tėr′jīt), *n.* a hydrous oxide of iron, allied to limonite but containing less water. [< *Turginsk,* a mine in the Ural Mountains, where it was found + *-ite*[1]]

tur·gor (tėr′gər, -gôr), *n.* **1.** the normal bulging or rigid condition of plant cells, caused by the pressure of the water within the cells against the cell walls. **2.** the normal swollen condition of blood vessels or of living cells. **3.** the condition or quality of being turgescent or turgid. [< Late Latin *turgor* a swelling up < Latin *turgēre* to swell]

tu·ri·on (tůr′ē ən, tyůr′-), *n. Botany.* a scaly shoot growing from a subterranean bud and becoming a new stem, as in the asparagus. [< Latin *turiō, -ōnis*]

Turk (tėrk), *n.* **1.** a native or inhabitant of Turkey, especially a Moslem who lives in Turkey. **2.** a member of the dominant ethnic group of Turkey; an Osmanli or Ottoman. **3.** a member of any group of people speaking a Turkic language. **4.** a person who fits the Christian conception of the Turk when Turkey was the spearhead of Islam in Europe; a cruel, barbarous person; tyrant. **5.** a very bad-tempered or unmanageable man. **6.** a Turkish horse, especially any of a breed of horses related to the Arabian horse, from at least one of which most modern race horses are descended. **7.** *Historical.* any Moslem; Saracen. [< Old French *Turc* < Medieval Latin *Turcus* < Medieval Greek *Toûrkos* < Persian *turk* < a native Turkic name]

Turk., **1.** Turkey. **2.** Turkish.

tur·key (tėr′kē), *n., pl.* **-keys. 1.** either of two large wild American birds that nest on the ground and fly only short distances. One variety lives in Mexico and Central America; the other in eastern America. **2.** any of various domesticated birds developed from the wild turkey and raised for food. **3.** the flesh of the turkey. **4.** *Archaic.* any of certain birds somewhat resembling a turkey. **5.** *Slang.* a play, motion picture, or other creative work that is a hopeless failure. **6.** *Obsolete.* the guinea fowl.

Turkey (def. 1)
(about 3 ft. long)

talk turkey, *Informal.* to talk frankly and bluntly: *With the U.S. . . . preparing to talk turkey with Red leaders, the political opportunity is obvious* (Time).

[earlier *turkey cock* (originally) a guinea fowl, apparently imported by way of Turkey; later confused with the American bird]

turkey buzzard, a vulture found in South and Central America and the southern United States, having a bare, reddish head and dark plumage.

Turkey Buzzard
(about 3 ft. long)

Turkey carpet, 1. a carpet manufactured in or imported from Turkey made in one piece of richly colored wools, without any imitative pattern, and having a deep pile cut so as to resemble velvet. **2.** any carpet made in imitation of this style.

turkey cock, 1. a male turkey. **2.** a strutting, conceited person.

Turkey red, 1. a brilliant and permanent red color produced in cotton cloth by means of alizarin or (formerly) madder in combination with oil or fat and an aluminum mordant. **2.** a cotton fabric having this color.

turkey trot, a ballroom dance resembling the one-step, with swinging up-and-down movements, popular in the early 1900's.

tur·key-trot (tėr′kē trot′), *v.i.,* **-trot·ted, -trot·ting.** to dance the turkey trot.

turkey vulture, turkey buzzard.

turkey wing, a marine bivalve mollusk with a thick, boat-shaped shell.

Turkey work, Turkish tapestry work or an imitation of it.

Tur·ki (tůr′kē), *adj.* **1.** of or having to do with two typical groups of Turkic languages (East Turki and West Turki) spoken in west central Asia, Persia, Turkey, etc. **2.** of or having to do with the peoples speaking them. [< Persian *Turkī* Turkish < *turk* a Turk]

Tur·kic (tėr′kik), *adj.* **1.** of or having to do with a branch of the Ural-Altaic language family comprised of Eastern Turki or Uigur, and West Turki or Seljuk and Osmanli, Kirghiz, Nogai, Yakut, etc. **2.** Turkish. —*n.* the Turkic group of languages.

Turk·i·fi·ca·tion (tėr′kə fə kā′shən), *n.* a making Turkish.

Turk·i·fy (tėr′kə fī), *v.t.,* **-fied, -fy·ing.** to make Turkish; bring into conformity with Turkish standards or ideas.

Turk·ish (tėr′kish), *adj.* **1.** of or having to do with the Turks, Turkey, a country in western Asia and southeastern Europe, or the language of Turkey. **2.** belonging to the Turks, Turkey, or the language of Turkey. —*n.* the Turkic language of the Turks. *Abbr.:* Turk.

Turkish bath, a kind of bath in which the bather is kept in a heated room until he sweats freely and then is bathed and massaged.

Turkish crescent, a jingling device used in military bands; Jingling Johnny.

Turkish delight or **paste,** a jellylike candy made, usually in cubes dusted with powdered sugar, of sugar, water, gelatin, and flavoring.

Turkish pound, a Turkish gold coin; the Turkish lira. Symbol: £T.

Turkish tobacco, a dark, very fragrant tobacco raised in Turkey, Greece, and neighboring regions of the eastern Mediterranean, used especially in cigarettes.

turkish or **Turkish towel,** a thick, cotton towel with a long nap made of uncut loops.

turkish or **Turkish toweling,** material for Turkish towels.

Turk·ism (tėr′kiz əm), *n.* **1.** Turkish institutions, ways, beliefs, etc. **2.** *Obsolete.* Islam.

Turk·man (tėrk′mən), *n., pl.* **-men. 1.** a native or inhabitant of the Turkmen Soviet Socialist Republic in western Asia. **2.** a native or inhabitant of Turkey; Turk.

Turk·men (tėrk′men), *n.* **1.** an East Turkic language of Turkestan. **2.** the plural of **Turkman.**

Turk·me·ni·an (tėrk mē′nē ən), *adj.* of or having to do with Turkomans.

Turko-, *combining form.* Turkey or Turkish: *Turkophilia = admiration of Turkey, Turkish methods, etc.* Also, **Turco-.** [< French, Italian *Turco-* < Medieval Latin *Turcus;* see TURK]

Tur·ko·man (tėr′kə mən *for 1;* tėrk′mən *for 2*), *n., pl.* **-mans. 1.** a member of any of various nomadic and pastoral Turkic tribes inhabiting the region about the Aral Sea and parts of Iran and Afghanistan. **2.** the Turkic language of this people; Turkmen. Also, **Turcoman.** [< Persian *turkumān* one like a Turk < *turk* + *māndan* to resemble]

Tur·ko·phil (tėr′kə fil), *n.* Turkophile.

Tur·ko·phile (tėr′kə fil, -fil), *n.* a person who greatly admires or favors Turkey, Turkish methods, etc. [< *Turko-* + *-phile*]

Tur·ko·phil·i·a (tėr′kə fil′ē ə), *n.* great admiration of Turkey, Turkish methods, etc.

Tur·ko·phobe (tėr′kə fōb), *n.* a person who greatly dreads or hates Turkey, Turkish methods, etc.

Tur·ko·pho·bi·a (tėr′kə fō′bē ə), *n.* great dread or hatred of Turkey, Turkish methods, etc.

Tur·ko-Ta·tar (tėr′kō tä′tər), *adj., n.* Turkic.

Turk's-cap lily (tėrks′kap′), either of two lilies with nodding flowers whose petals turn sharply backward.

Turk's-head (tėrks′hed′), *n.* a type of ornamental knot tied by winding small cord around a larger rope, used especially by sailors.

tur·ma·line (tėr′mə lin, -lēn), *n.* tourmaline.

tur·mer·ic (tėr′mər ik), *n.* **1.** a yellow powder prepared from the aromatic, pungent rhizome of an East Indian plant of the ginger family, used as a seasoning, especially as an ingredient in curry powder, as a yellow dye, in medicine, etc. **2.** the plant itself. **3.** its rhizome. **4.** any of several similar plants, as the bloodroot. **5.** any of several similar products. [variant of earlier *tarmaret* turmeric < Middle French *terre-mérite* < Medieval Latin *terra merita* (literally) worthy earth < Latin *terra* earth + *merere* to deserve, be worth]

turmeric paper, unsized paper tinged a yellow color with a solution of turmeric, used as a test for alkalis, which turn it brown, or for boric acid, which turns it reddish-brown.

tur·moil (tėr′moil), *n.* **1.** a state of agitation or commotion; disturbance; tumult. **2.** *Obsolete.* harassing labor; toil. [origin uncertain]

turn (tėrn), *v.t.* **1.** to cause to move around on an axis or about a center; cause to rotate or revolve, as a wheel: *I turned the crank* *three times.* **2.** to do by turning; open, close, make lower, higher, tighter, looser, etc., by moving around: *She turned the key in the lock.* **3.** to perform by revolving, as a somersault. **4.** to shape, especially into a rounded form, by cutting with a chisel or similar tool while rotating in a lathe. **5.** to shape, form, or fashion artistically or gracefully: *to turn a pretty compliment.* **6.** to reverse the position or posture of; invert; reverse: *to turn a page.* **7.** to reverse the position of (the turf, soil, etc.) in plowing or digging, so as to bring the under parts to the surface: *to turn a furrow.* **8.** to reverse (a garment, etc.) so that the inner side becomes the outer. **9.** to alter or remake (a garment, etc.) by putting the inner side outward. **10.** to alter the position or posture of, by rotating; move into a different position. **11.** to consider in different aspects; revolve (over) in the mind: *to turn a problem in one's mind.* **12.** to cause (the stomach) to reject food; nauseate: *The sight of blood turned his stomach.* **13.** to give a curved or crooked form to; bend; twist. **14.** to bend back (the edge of a sharp instrument) so as to make it useless for cutting. **15.** to change the course of; cause to go another way; divert; deflect: *to turn a stream.* **16.** to go or pass around (a corner, etc.); get to the other side of; go round: *to turn the corner.* **17.** to pass or get beyond (a particular age, time, or amount): *a man turning sixty.* **18.** to cause to go aside or retreat; drive back; stop; repel: *to turn a blow, to turn an attacker.* **19.** to cause (money or commodities) to circulate steadily. **20.** to direct, present, or point (toward or away from some specified person or thing, or in a specified direction): *to turn a searchlight on a person. He turned his steps to the north.* **21.** to cause or command to go; drive; send: *to turn a person from one's door.* **22.** to change the direction of (especially the eyes or face); avert: *to turn one's face.* **23.** to direct or set (thought, desire, speech, action, etc., to, toward, or away from something): *to turn one's efforts to a new job. He turned his thoughts toward home.* **24.** to apply, as to some use or purpose; make use of; employ: *to turn everything to advantage, to turn money to good use.* **25.** to cause to recoil: *His argument was turned against himself.* **26.** to make antagonistic; prejudice: *to turn friends against friends.* **27.** to change, transform, or convert (into or to): *to turn rain into snow.* **28.** to exchange for; get something else instead of; convert (into or to): *to turn stock into cash.* **29.** to change from one language or form of expression to another; translate; render: *Turn this sentence into Latin.* **30.** to change the color of: *Fall turned the leaves.* **31.** to change so as to make; render: *The bitter cold turned him blue.* **32.** to change for or to a worse condition; make sour; taint; ferment: *Warm weather turns milk.* **33.** to disturb the mental balance of; put out of order; unsettle; distract: *Flattery has turned her head.* **34.** *Obsolete.* to convert. **35.** *Obsolete.* to pervert.

—*v.i.* **1.** to move around on an axis or about a center; rotate; revolve, as a wheel: *The merry-go-round turned.* **2.** to move partly around in this way, as a door on a hinge, a key, etc. **3.** to have a sensation as of whirling; be affected with giddiness; become dizzy: *The height made her head turn.* **4.** to change the position or posture of the body; shift the body from side to side: *Turn over on your back.* **5.** to assume a curved form; become blunted by bending. **6.** (of the stomach) to be affected with nausea. **7.** to reverse course; begin to go, or to tend, in the opposite direction: *It is time to turn and go home.* **8.** to take a new direction: *The wind turned. The road turns to the left here.* **9.** *Nautical.* to beat to windward; tack. **10.** to change one's position so as to face in the contrary, or a different, direction: *He turned and walked away.* **11.** to change one's position so as to face toward or away from some specified person or thing, or in a specified direction: *All faces turned toward him.* **12.** to change one's position in order to attack or resist: *The worm will turn.* **13.** to take up an attitude of opposition (usually implying a change from previous friendliness): *The people turned against their leader.* **14.** to adopt a different religion. **15.** to be changed, transformed, or converted (into or to): *Water turns to ice.* **16.** to change so as to be; become: *She turned pale.* **17.** to become sour or tainted: *That milk has turned.* **18.** to change color; become different in color, as leaves, hair in old age, etc. **19.** to work with a lathe. **20.** *Archaic.* to desert, as to another side or party.

turn down, a. *U.S. Informal.* to refuse to accept; reject: *to turn down an offer.* **b.** *U.S. Informal.* to reject the plan, request, etc., of: *to turn a person down.* **c.** to lower by turning something: *to turn down the gas.* **d.** to fold down: *to turn down the covers on the bed.* **e.** to bend downward: *He turned down the brim of his hat.* **f.** to place with face downward: *The played cards were solemnly turned down* (George Fenn).

turn in, a. *Informal.* to go to bed: *It's late and quite time we turned in* (Nathaniel Gould). **b.** to turn and go in: *Hearing your stable clock strike as I turned in at your gate . . .* (Sarah Tytler). **c.** to point inward: *His feet turn in; he's pigeon-toed.* **d.** to give back: *The soldier turns in his equipment on leaving the Army* (A.J. Worrall). **e.** to exchange: *to turn in an old-style washing machine for a new model.*

turn loose, to free from restraint and allow to go where, or do as, one will: *to turn a prisoner loose.*

turn off, a. to stop the flow of (water, gas, electric current, etc.) by turning a tap, etc., shut off: *She did not turn the gas off at the meter* (Leslie Keith). **b.** to put out (a light): *Turn off the lamp as you leave.* **c.** to turn aside: *Where with noise the waters . . . turn off with care, for treacherous rocks are nigh* (John Norris). **d.** to do: *The German official or man of business is always appalled at the quantity of work his compeer can turn off in a given time* (Granville Hall). **e.** to discharge: *Pay him his wages and turn him off* (Oliver Goldsmith).

turn on, a. to start the flow of (water, gas, electric current, etc.) by turning a tap, etc.: *He turned on the gas in his back room to an unusual brightness* (Harriet Martineau). **b.** to put on (a light): *Turn on the flashlight.* **c.** to attack; resist; oppose: *The man turned on his pursuer.* **d.** to depend on: *The success of the picnic turns on the weather. The election will turn on this one point.* **e.** to be about; have to do with: *The conversation turned on literature.* **f.** *Slang.* to take or cause to take marijuana, heroin, etc.: *A female addict who was sweet on John told others that the two of them had "turned on" together* (Maclean's). **g.** *Slang.* to excite or capture the imagination: *The hero also must touch people's emotions. In modern jargon, that means someone who "turns people on"* (Time).

turn out, a. to put out; extinguish (a lamp, light, etc.): *Turn out that big spotlight.* **b.** to let go out: *to turn the cows out.* **c.** to drive out, expel: *The noisy boys were turned out.* **d.** to make; produce: *to turn out two novels in a year.* **e.** to equip; fit out: *to be smartly turned out in a new suit.* **f.** to come about in the end; result: *The deal turned out successfully.* **g.** to come to be; become ultimately: *He turned out a successful lawyer.* **h.** to be ultimately found or known; prove: *He turned out to be the son of an old friend.* **i.** to come or go out; sally forth: *Everyone turned out for the parade.* **j.** *Informal.* to get out of bed: *The next morning on turning out, I had the first glimpse of old England* (Washington Irving).

turn over, a. to give; hand over; transfer: *to turn over a job to someone.* **b.** to think carefully about; consider in different ways: *to turn a proposition over in one's mind.* **c.** to employ in business; invest and realize (capital): *Some capital is turned over ten times in a year.* **d.** to buy and later sell: *Will he be able to turn over all of those cameras this year?* **e.** to sell or dispose of goods to the amount of (a specified sum): *a business turning over $200,000 yearly.* **f.** to convert to different use: *That house . . . is turned over for a shelter to sheep* (William Lithgow).

turn to, a. to refer to: *He took up a local paper and turned to the list of visitors* (K. S. Macquoid). **b.** to go to for help: *You are the one man . . . that I should turn to in such a time* (Clark Russell). **c.** to get busy; set to work: *I found that no time was allowed for daydreaming, but that we must turn to at the first light* (Richard Henry Dana).

turn up, a. to make (a lamp) burn more brightly: *Turn up the gas a little, I want to go on reading* (Rudyard Kipling). **b.** to make louder; increase the volume of: *Turn up the radio so I can hear it better.* **c.** to fold over (a garment or part of one) so as to shorten; give an upward turn to; bring the underside up: *to turn up a hem.* **d.** to turn and go up: *She turned up the corridor to the left.* **e.** to direct or be directed upwards: *She turned up her eyes in horror at the idea.* **f.** to appear: *An old friend has turned up.*

[partly Old English *turnian* < Latin *tornāre* turn on a lathe < *tornus* lathe < Greek *tórnos;* partly < Old French *torner* < Latin. Related to TOUR.]

—*n.* **1.** a movement of rotation; motion like that of a wheel: *At each turn the screw goes in further.* **2.** a single revolution, as of a wheel. **3.** a movement around something; a twist, as of rope around a mast: *Give that rope a few more turns round the tree.* **4.** the condition of being, or direction in which something is, twisted. **5.** a single coil or twist; a round of coiled rope, etc. **6.** the act of turning or facing another way; a change of direction or posture: *a turn of the eye.* **7.** the act of turning so as to face about or go in the opposite direction; reversal of position or course: *the turn of the tide.* **8.** the act of turning aside from one's course; deflection: *a turn to the left.* **9.** a place or point at which a road, river, etc., changes in direction: *a turn in the road.* **10.** a walk, drive, or ride: *a turn in the park, to take a turn in the garden.* **11.** a change in affairs, conditions, or circumstances: *Matters have taken a turn for the worst. The sick man has taken a turn for the better.* **12.** the time at which such a change takes place: *the turn of the year, the turn of a fever.* **13.** a momentary shock caused by sudden alarm, fright, etc.: *to give someone a bad turn.* **14.** a deed; act: *One good turn deserves another.* **15.** a stroke or spell of work; job; performance: *a hand's turn.* **16.** a spell or bout of action: *to have a turn at a thing. Take a turn at the oars.* **17.** an attack of illness, faintness, or the like. **18.** a time or chance to do anything, which comes round to each individual of a series in succession: *My turn comes after yours. It's my turn to play.* **19.** *British.* the time during which one workman or body of workmen is at work in alternation with another or others; shift. **20.** *Especially British.* one of the performances or acts in a variety show. **21.** requirement; need; exigency; purpose: *This will serve your turn.* **22.** natural inclination, disposition, or bent; aptitude: *He has a turn for mathematics.* **23.** a distinctive or particular style, as of language, arrangement of words in a sentence, etc.; form: *a happy turn of expression.* **24.** direction; tendency; drift; trend: *What turn did the discussion take?* **25.** form; mold; cast: *the turn of her arms.* **26.** *Music.* a melodic ornament or group of grace notes, consisting of a principal tone (the written note) and two auxiliary tones, one degree of the scale above and usually one below it. In the common type, the tone above precedes, and that below follows, the principal tone. In the inverted turn, the tone below precedes and that above follows. In either case, the principal tone is repeated at the end, and sometimes also precedes. **27.** (in military drill) a prescribed movement by which a column or other formation changes direction to the right or left. **28.** (of stocks, bonds, etc.) a complete transaction.

at every turn, on every occasion; without exception; constantly: *He had no tact and insulted people at every turn.*

by turns or **by turn,** one after another in regular succession; successively; in rotation: *They slept by turns, to guard against wild beasts.*

in turn, in due order, course, or succession: *He that shuts Love out, in turn shall be shut out from Love* (Tennyson).

out of turn, a. not in proper order: *playing out of turn.* **b.** not appropriately; at the wrong time: *to speak out of turn.*

take turns, to follow one after another in proper order; alternate: *They took turns watching the baby.*

to a turn, exactly to the proper degree: *meat done to a turn.*

turn about or **turn and turn about,** one after another in proper order: *We took it turn and turn about to sit up and rock the baby* (Elizabeth Gaskell).

[partly < Anglo-French *tourn,* Old French *tour* tour, turn; (originally) a lathe < Latin *tornus* (see the verb); partly < the verb]

—**Syn.** *v.i.* **1. Turn, revolve, rotate** mean to move round in a circle. **Turn** is the general and common word meaning to move in a circle or in circle after circle, either on a pivot or axis or around a center: *That wheel turns freely now.* **Revolve** means to turn round and round on a pivot or, especially, in a circular path around something that serves as a center: *The merry-go-round revolves. Their whole life revolves about their only child.* **Rotate** also means to turn round and round, but usually on its own axis or around its own center: *The earth rotates (on its axis) once every 24 hours and revolves round the sun once each year.* **8.** shift, veer. —*n.* **1.** revolution, rotation.

turn·a·bout (tėrn′ə bout′), *n.* **1.** the act or an act of turning about, especially of turning so as to face the other way. **2.** a person or thing that does this. **3.** a change to an opposite position, view, course, etc.; reversal: *The turnabout did not come out of a feeling of charity. It was purely a business proposition* (Newsweek). **4.** *U.S.* a merry-go-round.

turn·a·round (tėrn′ə round′), *n.* **1.** a reversal: *Most economists agree that there will be no strong turnaround in the economy until business starts building up its inventories again* (Time). **2.** the time that a ship spends in a port before the outgoing voyage; turnround: *With a minimum reorganization the quick loading and turnaround will save us at least 20% on handling alone* (Wall Street Journal). **3.** a place for a vehicle to turn around: *Build us a road with a turnaround at the farther end* (New Yorker).

turn·back (tėrn′bak′), *n.* **1.** a person who retreats or gives up an enterprise; quitter. **2.** that part of anything that is folded or turned back: *He spread his hands on his chest, and touched the turnback of the sheet, and then the blanket* (New Yorker). —*adj.* that is folded back: *a turnback collar, a turnback brim.*

turn·buck·le (tėrn′buk′əl), *n.* any of various types of couplings having internal screw threads, or nuts with opposite threads, etc., at the ends and used for connecting metal rods, wires, etc., lengthwise or for regulating their length or tension.

Turnbuckle

turn·coat (tėrn′kōt′), *n.* a person who changes his party or principles; renegade; apostate. —**Syn.** traitor.

turn·down (tėrn′doun′), *adj.* that is or can be turned down; folded or doubled down: *a turndown collar.*

—*n.* **1.** a turning down; rejection: *turndowns on loan applications* (Wall Street Journal). **2.** a decline; downturn: *Finance companies and commercial paper dealers ascribe the turndown in rates to recent declines in short-term borrowing costs on Treasury bills* (Wall Street Journal).

turned comma (tėrnd), *Printing.* an inverted comma (‘), such as is used (as one of a pair or singly) at the beginning of a quotation.

turn·er[1] (tėr′nər), *n.* **1.** a person who forms things or shapes a substance on a lathe: *a turner of metal spindles, a turner of wood.* **2.** a person or thing that turns. [Middle English *turner* < *turnen* to turn]

turn·er[2] (tėr′nər), *n.* **1.** a member of a Turnverein. **2.** a member of one of the gymnastic societies from which the modern Turnverein derives, instituted in Germany by F. L. Jahn (1778-1852). [American English < German *Turner* < *turnen* perform gymnastics < French *tourner* < Old French *torner;* see TURN, verb]

Tur·ner·esque (tėr′nə resk′), *adj.* in or resembling the style of the English landscape painter Joseph M. W. Turner, 1775-1851: *The sun . . . was going down in an explosive, Turneresque brilliance above the sand hillocks* (New Yorker).

Turner's syndrome, a congenital condition in which sexual development and general growth are retarded. [< Henry H. *Turner,* born 1892, an American physician]

turn·er·y (tėr′nər ē), *n., pl.* **-er·ies. 1.** the art or work of a turner. **2.** objects fashioned on the lathe; turner's work. **3.** a place where articles are made on a lathe; turner's workshop.

turn·hall (tėrn′hôl′), *n.* the building, or part of a building, used by an American Turnverein. [American English < German *Turnhalle* gymnastic hall < *Turner* (see TURNER[2]) + *Halle* hall]

turn indicator, 1. a gyroscopic device that indicates in degrees per unit of time any turning movement about the vertical axis of an airplane. **2.** one of the lights on the front and rear of a motor vehicle for signaling turns; turn signal.

turn·ing (tėr′ning), *n.* **1.** a movement about an axis or center; rotation. **2.** a place or point where a road, path, etc., turns, or turns off. **3.** the act or art of shaping things on a lathe. **4.** shaping, molding, or fashioning (of an epigram, literary work, etc.).

turning point, 1. a point at which a decisive change of any kind takes place; critical point; crisis. **2.** (in surveying) a temporary bench mark, the exact elevation of which is determined in leveling before the instrument is advanced, as a starting point for determining its height after resetting.

tur·nip (tėr′nəp), *n.* **1.** the large, fleshy, roundish, edible root of either of two biennial plants, the white turnip or the rutabaga, Swede, or Swedish turnip, of the mustard family. **2.** one of these plants. **3.** the root of either of these plants, as an item of food for human beings or animals. [earlier *turnepe,* probably ultimately Middle English *turn* turn (from its rounded shape) + *nepe* turnip, neep, Old English *nǣp* < Latin *nāpus* < Greek *nâpy*]

tur·nix (tėr′niks), *n.* any of a group of small, three-toed, quaillike birds related to the bustards, found in southern Europe, northern Africa, and Australia. [< New Latin *Turnix* the genus name < Latin *cōturnīx* quail]

turn·key (tėrn′kē′), *n., pl.* **-keys.** a person who has charge of the keys of a prison, jail, etc.; keeper of a prison; jailer.

turn·off (tėrn′ôf′, -of′), *n.* a place at which a road, path, etc., turns off to another: *They led their horses well past the turnoff* (New Yorker).

turn of the century, the period marking the end of the nineteenth and the beginning of the twentieth century: *The possession of any kind of bath with running water was, until the turn of the century, something to brag about* (Punch).

turn·out (tėrn′out′), *n.* **1.** a gathering or assembling of people; assemblage: *a good turnout for a political rally.* **2.** that which is turned out or produced by an industry, shop, machine, etc.; total product; output. **3.** (in a narrow road) a part wider than the rest, or a short side road, to enable vehicles to pass one another. **4.** a similar place in a canal. **5.** a railroad siding. **6.** the way in which somebody or something is equipped; style of equipment. **7.** equipment; outfit. **8.** a horse or horses and carriage; driving equipage. **9.** *Especially British.* **a.** a strike. **b.** a worker on strike; striker. **10.** a getting out (of bed, etc.). **11.** a call to duty, especially during one's period of rest.

turn·o·ver (tėrn′ō′vər), *n.* **1.** a turning over; upset. **2.** the buying, selling, and replacing of a stock of goods, or the investing, realizing, and reinvesting of capital, in a business: *The store reduced prices to make a quick turnover.* **3.** the number of times this takes place in a given period of time. **4.** the total amount of business done in a given time: *He made a profit of $6,000 on a turnover of $90,000.* **5.** the amount of changing from one job to another: *Employers wish to reduce labor turnover.* **6.** a small pie made by putting a filling on half of a circular or square crust and folding the other half over it. **7.** *Especially British Slang.* a transfer of votes, shifting of allegiance, etc., from one party, group, or faction to another.

—*adj.* **1.** having a part that turns over. **2.** that turns or is turned over.

turnover tax, 1. a tax paid on every sale of a given commodity: *Far more important are the so-called turnover taxes leveled at every stage of the production process* (Wall Street Journal). **2.** *British.* a tax levied on receipts from the gross volume of sales.

turn·pike (tėrn′pīk′), *n.* **1.** Also, **turnpike road.** a road that has, or used to have, a gate where toll is paid. **2.** a tollgate: *I consider supper as a turnpike through which one must pass in order to get to bed* (Oliver Edwards). **3.** *Obsolete.* a turnstile. [< *turn* + *pike*[2] a sharp point (referring to a spiked barrier across a road, turning on a vertical axis)]

turn·plate (tėrn′plāt′), *n. Especially British.* a turntable for locomotives.

turn·round (tėrn′round′), *n.* the time that a ship spends in a port taking on passengers, cargo, and supplies for the outgoing voyage; turnaround: *Refuelling would be less frequent and the turnround of vessels expedited* (R. F. Harrod).

turn signal, a turn indicator: *They do include such normally optional equipment items as cigaret lighter, turn signals and deluxe steering wheel* (Wall Street Journal).

turn·sole (tėrn′sōl′), *n.* **1.** any of various plants whose flowers or leaves turn so as to follow the sun, especially the heliotrope and (formerly) the sunflower. **2.** an annual herb of the spurge family, growing in the Mediterranean region, formerly valued for the blue dyestuff which it yields. **3.** a deep-purple dye obtained from this plant. [< Middle French *tournesol* < *tourner* to turn (< Old French *torner;* see TURN) + Latin *sōl, sōlis* sun]

turn·spit (tėrn′spit′), *n.* **1.** a person or animal, especially a dog, that turns roasting meat on a spit. **2.** any of a breed of small, long-bodied, short-legged dogs originally kept and trained especially as turnspits.

turn·stile (tėrn′stīl′), *n.* a post with bars that turn, set in an entrance or exit.

turn·stone (tėrn′stōn′), *n.* either of two small migratory shore birds of the Old and New Worlds, that turns over stones to get at the worms, insects, etc., beneath them.

turn·ta·ble (tėrn′tā′bəl), *n.* **1.** a revolving circular platform used for turning things around. A turntable with a track is used for turning locomotives around. **2.** the rotating disk on a phonograph upon which records are placed. See **phonograph** for picture.

turntable ladder, an aerial ladder that can be rotated as desired on a turntable mounted on a truck: *All the nine people escaped down a turntable ladder . . . used by the fire brigade to bring the fire under control* (London Times).

turn·up (tėrn′up′), *adj.* that is turned up or turns up. —*n.* **1.** the turned-up part of anything, especially of a garment. **2.** *British.* a trouser cuff.

Turn·ver·ein (tůrn′fer īn′), *n.* any of certain fraternal organizations of gymnasts in Germany, in the United States, and elsewhere in regions of considerable German immigration. [American English < German *Turnverein* < *turnen* to exercise (see TURNER[2]) + *Verein* club]

tur·pen·tine (tėr′pən tīn), *n., v.,* **-tined, -tin·ing.** —*n.* **1.** a volatile oil obtained from various cone-bearing trees; oil or spirits of turpentine. Turpentine is used in mixing paints and varnishes, in medicine, etc., and is usually prepared by distilling crude turpentine. *Formula:* $C_{10}H_{16}$ **2.** the mixture of oil and resin from which the prepared oil is made, now obtained especially by tapping any of certain pine trees; crude turpentine.

—*v.t.* **1.** to treat, mix, or smear with turpentine. **2.** to obtain crude turpentine from (trees).

[alteration of Middle English *terebentine* < Old French < Latin *terebinthina* (*rēsīna*) terebinth (resin) < Greek (*rhētínē*) *terebinthínē.* Compare TEREBINTH.]

tur·peth (tėr′pith), *n.* **1.** a preparation of the roots of an Asiatic plant of the morning-glory family, similar to jalap, formerly used as a cathartic. **2.** the plant itself. **3.** its root. **4.** Also, **turpeth mineral.** a basic mercuric sulfate obtained as a lemon-yellow powder, formerly used as a cathartic. *Formula:* $HgSO_4.2HgO$ Also, **turbeth, turbith.** [alteration of Old French *turpet* < Persian *turbid* < Arabic *turbath*]

tur·pi·tude (tėr′pə tüd, -tyüd), *n.* shameful character; baseness; wickedness: *He could laugh over the story of some ingenious fraud . . . and seem insensible to its turpitude* (Edward G. Bulwer-Lytton). [< Latin *turpitūdō, -inis* < *turpis* vile] —**Syn.** depravity, villainy.

tur·quoise (tėr′koiz, -kwoiz), *n.* **1.** a semiprecious stone of a sky-blue to apple-green color, almost opaque or sometimes translucent, consisting of hydrous phosphate of aluminum and copper. **2.** Also, **turquoise blue.** a greenish blue, like that of the turquoise. —*adj.* greenish-blue.

[< Old French (*pierre*) *turqueise* Turkish (stone)]

tur·ret (tėr′it), *n.* **1.** a small or subordinate tower, often on the corner of a building. **2.** a rounded addition to an angle of a building, sometimes beginning at some height above the ground, and frequently containing a spiral staircase. **3.** a low, armored structure within which a heavy gun, or set of two or three guns, is mounted, and by which the gunners are protected. **4.** a similar structure within which is mounted the heavy gun of a tank, now usually comprising the entire upper portion of the tank. **5.** a gunner's station in a military aircraft, usually enclosed by a domelike structure of strong, transparent plastic projecting from the fuselage, in which is mounted a single heavy machine gun, or set of machine guns. **6.** an attachment on a lathe, drill, etc., to hold cutting tools. **7.** a tall tower on wheels, formerly used to scale the walls of castles, forts, etc. [< Old French *touret* (diminutive) < *tour* tower < Latin *turris* < Greek *týrsis*]

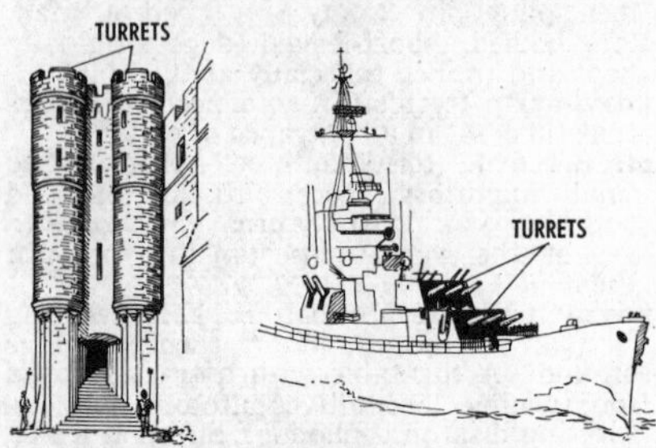

Turrets
Left, (def. 1); right, (def. 3) on battleship

turret camera, a motion picture camera with a plate for holding lenses that can be rotated to a position in front of the shutter.

tur·ret·ed (tėr′ə tid), *adj.* **1.** having a turret or turrets. **2.** *Zoology.* having whorls in the form of a long spiral: *turreted shells.*

Turreted Shell (def. 2)

tur·ret·head (tėr′it hed′), *n.* turret (an attachment to a lathe).

turret lathe, a lathe fitted with a turret.

tur·ret·less (tėr′it lis), *adj.* without a turret or turrets.

tur·ri·cal (tėr′ə kəl), *adj.* of or like a turret.

tur·ric·u·late (tə rik′yə lit, -lāt), *adj.* turreted. [< Latin *turricula* (diminutive) < *turris* tower + English *-ate*[1]]

tur·ric·u·lat·ed (tə rik′yə lā′tid), *adj.* turreted.

tur·ri·lite (tėr′ə līt), *n.* any of a group of fossil cephalopods allied to the ammonites but having a long, spiral, turreted shell, found in Cretaceous formations. [< New Latin *Turrilites* the genus name < Latin *turris* tower + New Latin *-lites* -lite]

tur·rum (tėr′əm), *n.* a large carangoid fish found in the waters around Australia. [< a native Australian name]

tur·tle[1] (tėr′təl), *n., pl.* **-tles** or (*collectively*) **-tle,** *v.,* **-tled, -tling.** —*n.* **1.** any of an order of reptiles, living in fresh or salt water or on land and having a toothless, horny beak and a rounded body encased in a shell, from which the head, tail, and limbs protrude and, in some kinds, into which they can be retracted for protection: *Turtles living on the land are often called tortoises.* **2.** a marine turtle, as distinguished from one of a kind living in fresh water or on land. **3.** the flesh of turtles, especially the terrapin, used as food.

Green Sea Turtle[1] **(def. 2)**

turn turtle, to turn bottom side up; capsize: *An engine and two trucks had turned turtle on the embankment* (London Daily News).

—*v.i.* to catch or seek to catch turtles.

[< French *tortue* tortoise; influenced by *turtle*[2] turtledove]

tur·tle[2] (tėr′təl), *n. Archaic.* turtledove. [Old English *turtle, turtla* < Latin *turtur*]

tur·tle·back (tėr′təl bak′), *n.* **1.** Also, **turtle deck.** an arched frame built over the deck of a steamer at the bow, and often at the stern, as a protection against damage from heavy seas. **2.** the back (carapace) of a turtle.

tur·tle·dove (tėr′təl duv′), *n.* **1.** any of a group of Old World doves, especially the common European kind, noted for its graceful form, harmonious coloring, and affection for its mate. **2.** *U.S. Dialect.* any of various doves of other groups, as the North American mourning dove. [< *turtle*[2] + *dove*[1]]

Turtledove (def. 1)
(about 7 in. long)

turtle grass, 1. a marine plant of the West Indies with long, narrow, grasslike leaves. **2.** the grass wrack.

tur·tle·head (tėr′təl hed′), *n.* any of a group of North American perennial herbs of the figwort family; snakehead.

turtle neck, a round, high, closely fitting collar on a sweater, etc., usually turned down over itself when the garment is worn.

tur·tle-neck (tėr′təl nek′), *adj.* (of a garment) having a turtle neck.

turtle peg, a prong fastened to a pole or cord used for harpooning large turtles, especially marine turtles.

tur·tler (tėr′tlər), *n.* a person or a vessel engaged in catching turtles.

turves (tėrvz), *n.* a plural of **turf.**

Tus·can (tus′kən), *adj.* **1.** of or having to do with Tuscany, a district in central Italy, or its people. **2.** *Architecture.* denoting or belonging to the simplest of the five classical orders, developed by the Romans, and similar in its proportions to the Doric, but having plain, round columns and no decoration. —*n.* **1.** a native or inhabitant of Tuscany. **2.** the dialect of Tuscany, regarded as the classical and standard form of Italian.

Tus·ca·ro·ra (tus′kə rôr′ə, -rōr′-), *n., pl.* **-ra** or **-ras.** a member of a tribe of Iroquoian Indians that formerly lived in what is now the State of North Carolina.

tush[1] (tush), *interj., n.* an exclamation expressing impatience, contempt, etc.: *Tush! we have nothing to fear* (Hawthorne). —*v.i.* to make the sound of "tush."

tush[2] (tush), *n. Archaic.* **1.** a tusk. **2.** a canine tooth, especially of a horse. [Middle English *tusch,* Old English *tusc.* Related to TOOTH.]

tush·er·y (tush′ər ē), *n., pl.* **-er·ies.** a style of writing, especially in historical novels, characterized by excessive use of affected archaisms and other expressions, such as "tush!": *In this witty and urbane story, quite free from romantic tushery, a scholarly author shows us the third century from an unfamiliar point-of-view* (Punch).

Tu·si (tü′sē), *n., pl.* **-si** or **-sis.** Watusi.

tusk (tusk), *n.* **1.** a very long, pointed, projecting tooth. The elephant, walrus, and wild boar have two tusks; the narwhal has only one tusk. **2.** any tusklike tooth or part. **3.** (in woodworking) a bevel or sloping shoulder on a tenon, for additional strength.

—*v.t.* **1.** to wound with a tusk; gore. **2.** to root or dig (up) or tear (off) with the tusks.

[Middle English *tusk,* Old English *tusc, tux;* see TUSH[2]]

Tusks (def. 1)
of a walrus

tusked (tuskt), *adj.* having tusks: *tusked boars* (William Morris).

tusk·er (tus′kər), *n.* an animal, especially a male animal, having well-developed tusks, such as a full-grown elephant, walrus, or wild boar.

tusk·less (tusk′lis), *adj.* having no tusks.

tusk tenon, (in woodworking) a tenon with a tusk or tusks.

tusk·y (tus′kē), *adj.* having tusks, as an animal.

tus·sah or **tus·sa** (tus′ə), *n.* **1.** Also, **tussah silk.** a coarse, brown silk made especially in India. **2.** an Asiatic silkworm from the cocoons of which this is made. [earlier *tessar* < Hindi *tasar* shuttle < Prakrit *tasara* < Sanskrit *trasara* shuttle]

tus·sal (tus′əl), *adj.* of or having to do with a cough. [< Latin *tussis* cough + English *-al*[1]]

tus·sar or **tus·ser** (tus′ər), *n.* tussah.

tus·seh (tus′ə), *n.* tussah.

Tus·si (tü′sē), *n., pl.* **-si** or **-sis.** Watusi.

tus·sis (tus′is), *n. Medicine.* a cough. [< Latin *tussis*]

tus·sive (tus′iv), *adj.* **1.** having to do with a cough. **2.** caused by a cough. [< Latin *tussis* cough + English *-ive*]

tus·sle (tus′əl), *v.,* **-sled, -sling,** *n.* —*v.i.* to struggle; wrestle; scuffle. —*n.* a vigorous or disorderly conflict; severe struggle or hard contest: *The cold war, then, is not a short, sharp tussle* (Manchester Guardian). [apparently variant of *tousle*]

tus·sock (tus′ək), *n.* **1.** a tuft or clump forming a small hillock of grass, sedge, or the like. **2.** a tuft or bunch of hair.

tussock caterpillar, the larva of a tussock moth.

tus·socked (tus′əkt), *adj.* **1.** covered with tussocks: *Its two towers guard a narrow gate set in the rose-pink walls, folded stiffly along a tussocked rise* (Harold Brodkey). **2.** formed into tussocks: *Sunlight filters through to promote the growth of the tussocked grass* (London Times).

tussock moth, any of a family of dull-colored moths having larvae with tufts of hair along the back, as the gypsy moth.

tus·sock·y (tus′ə kē), *adj.* **1.** abounding in tussocks. **2.** forming tussocks.

tus·sor, tus·sore, or **tus·sur** (tus′ər), *n.* tussah.

tut (tut), *interj., n., v.,* **tut·ted, tut·ting.** —*interj., n.* an exclamation of impatience, contempt, or rebuke. —*v.i., v.t.* to say or exclaim "tut" in contempt, rebuke, etc. (of): *There was much tutting and disgusted head shaking on this afternoon* (Robin Marlar). [imitative]

tu·tee (tü tē′, tyü′-), *n.* a person being tutored: *Late in the afternoon, when he met with his tutees, he was patient and meticulous with clever pupils, impatient and hasty with the plodders* (New Yorker).

tu·te·lage (tü′tə lij, tyü′-), *n.* **1.** the office or function of a guardian; guardianship; protection. **2.** instruction. **3.** the state of being in the charge of a guardian or tutor. [< Latin *tūtēla* a watching (< *tuērī* to watch) + English *-age*]

tu·te·lar (tü′tə lər, tyü′-), *adj.* tutelary.

tu·te·lar·y (tü′tə ler′ē, tyü′-), *adj., n., pl.* **-lar·ies.** —*adj.* **1.** having the position of protector, guardian, or patron, especially protecting or watching over a particular person, place, or thing: *a tutelary saint.* **2.** of or having to do with protection or a protector; used as a guardian; protective: *a tutelary charm. Great acts of tutelary friendship* (William Ewart Gladstone). —*n.* a tutelary deity, angel, saint, etc. [< Latin *tūtēlārius* < *tūtēla* protection, watching; see TUTELAGE]

tu·te·nag or **tu·te·nague** (tü′tə nag, tyü′-), *n.* **1.** a whitish alloy of chiefly zinc, copper, and nickel. **2.** zinc. [< Portuguese *tutenaga* < Marathi *tuttināg* < Tamil *tuttanāgam* impure zinc, probably < Sanskrit *tuttha* blue vitriol + *nāga* tin, lead]

tu·tor (tü′tər, tyü′-), *n.* **1.** a person who is attached to a household or employed by a family as a private teacher: *a child educated entirely by tutors.* **2.** a person (not necessarily professionally connected with a college, university, or school) engaged by students to help them prepare for examinations. **3.** *U.S.* (at some colleges and universities) a teacher below the rank of instructor. **4.** (in English universities) a college official to whom students are assigned for advice, supervision, etc. **5.** (in Roman, civil, and Scots law) the guardian of a person legally incapable of managing his own affairs, especially a child under the age of puberty.

—*v.t.* **1.** to give special or individual instruction to; teach; instruct. **2.** to instruct under discipline; school: *The world, however it may be taught, will not be tutored* (Shakespeare). **3.** to admonish or reprove. **4.** *Obsolete.* to take care or charge of. —*v.i.* **1.** *U.S. Informal* to study under a tutor: *He is tutoring in algebra.* **2.** to act as tutor.

[< Latin *tūtor, -ōris* guardian < *tuērī* watch over]

tu·tor·age (tü′tər ij, tyü′-), *n.* **1.** tutorship. **2.** the cost of educational tutoring.

tu·tor·ess (tü′tər is, tyü′-), *n.* a woman tutor.

tu·to·ri·al (tü tôr′ē əl, -tōr′-; tyü-), *adj.* **1.** of or having to do with a tutor: *tutorial fees.* **2.** exercised by a tutor: *tutorial authority.* **3.** using a tutor: *a tutorial system of education.*

—*n.* a period of individual instruction given in some colleges by a tutor either to a single student or a small group: *The smallness of the tutorial encourages maximum participation* (Benjamin Fine).

tutorial system, 1. an educational system, usually at college level, in which each student is assigned, as one of a group, to a tutor, who advises and directs him. **2.** an educational system, at any level, in which each student is taught individually or as one of a small group.

tu·tor·ship (tü′tər ship, tyü′-), *n.* the position, rank, or duties of a tutor.

tu·toy·er (tʏ twä yā′), *v.t.* to treat as an intimate; address with familiarity. [< French *tutoyer* < *tu*, familiar address for *vous* you + *toi* yourself]

Tut·si (tüt′sē), *n., pl.* **-si** or **-sis.** Watusi: *The Tutsi, a tall, Amharic people from the Ethiopian Highlands, settled in Rwanda and Burundi four centuries ago* (London Times).

tut·ta (tüt′tä), *adj. Music.* the feminine of **tutto.**

tut·ti (tü′tē; *Italian* tüt′tē), *adj., n., pl.* **-tis.** *Music.* —*adj.* **1.** all; all (voices or instruments) together. **2.** written for or performed by all voices or instruments together. —*n.* a passage or movement performed by all voices or instruments together. [< Italian *tutti* all < Vulgar Latin *totti*, for Latin *tōtī*, plural of *tōtus* all. Compare TOTAL.]

tut·ti-frut·ti (tü′tē frü′tē), *n* **1.** a preserve of mixed fruits. **2.** ice cream or other confection containing a variety of fruits or fruit flavorings. —*adj.* flavored with or containing mixed fruits. [American English < Italian *tutti frutti* all fruits]

tut·to (tüt′tō), *adj. Music.* all; entire. [< Italian *tutto* < Vulgar Latin *tottus*, for Latin *tōtus* all, whole]

tut-tut (tut′tut′), *interj., n., v.,* **-tut·ted, -tut·ting.** —*interj., n.* tut. —*v.i., v.t.* to say or exclaim "tut-tut" in contempt, rebuke, etc. (of).

tut·ty (tut′ē), *n.* a crude oxide of zinc found adhering in flakes to the flues of smelting furnaces, used chiefly as a polishing powder. [< Old French *tutie* < Arabic *tūtiyā* oxide of zinc, perhaps < Sanskrit *tuttha* blue vitriol]

tu·tu[1] (tü′tü; *French* tʏ tʏ′), *n.* a very short, full, stiff skirt worn by a ballet dancer. [< French *tutu*, alteration of *cucu*, infantile reduplication of *cul* rump < Latin *cūlus*]

Tutu[1]

tu·tu[2] (tü′tü), *n. Hawaiian.* grandma; grandpa.

tu·um (tü′əm, tyü′-), *pron. Latin.* thine; that which is thine.

tu-whit (tu̇ hwit′), *v.i.* **-whit·ted, -whit·ting.** to hoot, as an owl.

tu-whit tu-whoo (tu̇-hwit′tu̇ hwü′), an imitation of the call of an owl: *Then nightly sings the staring owl tu-whit to-whoo—a merry note* (Shakespeare).

tux (tuks), *n. U.S. Informal.* tuxedo.

tux·e·do or **Tux·e·do** (tuk sē′dō), *n., pl.* **-dos** or **-does.** *U.S.* **1.** a man's semiformal suit for evening wear, with a tailless coat or jacket, usually black with satin lapels. **2.** (originally) the jacket of such a suit; dinner coat or jacket. [American English < earlier *tuxedo coat* < *Tuxedo* Park, New York, where it was reputedly first worn]

tux·e·doed (tuk sē′dōd), *adj. U.S. Informal.* dressed in a tuxedo or tuxedos.

tu·yère (twē yãr′, twir), *n.* an opening through which the blast of air is forced into a blast furnace, forge, etc. [< French *tuyère* < Old French *toiere* < a Germanic word]

TV (no periods), **1.** television. **2.** terminal velocity.

TVA (no periods) or **T.V.A.,** Tennessee Valley Authority, a United States government organization for developing the resources of the Tennessee Valley region, started in 1933.

TV dinner, a frozen meal on a tray ready to be heated and served.

T.V.R., *Physics.* temperature variation of resistance.

twa (twä), *n., adj. Scottish.* two.

Twad., Twaddell (hydrometer).

Twad·dell (twod′əl), *n.* a hydrometer used for densities greater than that of water, the excess of density above unity being found by multiplying the number of divisions (degrees) of the scale by 5 and dividing by 1,000. [< the name of the inventor]

twad·dle (twod′əl), *n., v.,* **-dled, -dling.** —*n.* **1.** silly, feeble, tiresome talk or writing: *garrulous twaddle of old men on club sofas* (William B. Maxwell). **2.** *Obsolete.* a person who talks or writes twaddle.

—*v.i., v.t.* to talk or write twaddle.

[alteration of *twattle*, variant of *tattle*]

twad·dler (twod′lər), *n.* a person who talks or writes twaddle.

twain (twān), *n., adj. Archaic or Poetic.* two. Old English *twēgen* two]

twang (twang), *n.* **1.** a sharp, ringing sound, such as is produced when a tense string is sharply plucked or suddenly released: *The bow made a twang when I shot the arrow.* **2.** the modification of vocal sound by its passage through the nose; nasal intonation: *to speak with a Yankee twang.*

—*v.t.* **1.** to cause to make a sharp, ringing sound. **2.** to play, pluck, shoot, etc., with a twang: *He twanged an arrow into the target.* **3.** to speak (words, etc.) with a sharp nasal tone. —*v.i.* **1.** to make a sharp, ringing sound: *The banjos twanged.* **2.** to shoot with a bow. **3.** (of an arrow) to leave the bowstring with a twang. **4.** to speak with a sharp nasal tone. [imitative]

twang·i·ness (twang′gē nis), *n.* twangy quality: *the twanginess of the guitar.*

twan·gle (twang′gəl), *n., v.,* **-gled, -gling.** —*n.* a continuous or repeated resonant sound, usually lighter or thinner than a twang; jingle. —*v.i.* to twang lightly; jingle. [apparently frequentative of *twang*, verb]

twang·y (twang′gē), *adj.,* **twang·i·er, twang·i·est.** having a twang: *The folk element is expressed largely in the choice of tunes and in a twangy banjo* (Harper's).

Twan·kay (twang′kā), *n.,* or **Twankay tea,** a kind of green tea, originally one consisting solely of leaves from a particular part of China, but later simply a designation of a blend of leaves of a particular size. [< Cantonese *t'wen-k'ai*]

'twas (twoz, twuz; *unstressed* twəz), it was.

tway·blade (twā′blād′), *n.* any of a group of terrestrial orchids, having two nearly opposite broad leaves springing from the stem or the root. [< earlier *tway* two, Middle English *tweien* (see TWAIN) + *blade*]

tweak (twēk), *v.t., v.i.* to seize and pull sharply with a twisting movement; pull at with a jerk: *to tweak a person's ear.* —*n.* a sharp pull and twist; twitch; pluck. [variant of *twick*, Old English *twiccian* to pluck. Related to TWITCH.]

twee (twē), *adj. British Slang.* sweet; cute: *You look very twee tonight* (Punch). [< child's pronunciation of *sweet*]

tweed (twēd), *n.* **1.** a twilled woolen fabric with a rough surface, usually woven of yarns of two or more colors. **2.** a suit, etc., made of this fabric.

tweeds, clothes made of tweed: *We do look disreputable enough in our rough tweeds* (George Fenn).

[apparently misreading of *tweel*, Scottish variant of *twill;* probably influenced by the name of the river *Tweed*]

tweed·ed (twē′did), *adj.* dressed in tweeds; wearing tweedy clothes: . . . *elegantly tweeded women shoppers* (Manchester Guardian).

tweed·i·ness (twē′dē nis), *n.* a tweedy appearance, character, or quality.

twee·dle (twē′dəl), *v.i.,* **-dled, -dling.** *Especially British Dialect and Scottish.* **1.** to produce thin or shrill, modulated sounds by playing on a fiddle, bagpipe, or the like. **2.** to pipe or whistle, as a bird. [apparently imitative]

twee·dle·dum and twee·dle·dee (twē′-dəl dum′ ən twē′dəl dē′), two things or parties that are identical or nearly identical. [< *tweedle* + *-dum, -dee*, suffixes suggesting musical notes; originally applied to a pair of musicians]

tweeds (twēds), *n.pl.* See under **tweed,** *n.*

tweed·y (twē′dē), *adj.* **1.** consisting of or like tweed: *a tweedy jacket.* **2.** characterized by or given to wearing tweeds.

'tweel (twēl), *adv. Scottish.* atweel.

tween (twēn), *n. U.S.* a boy or girl between childhood and adolescence, especially between the ages of 10 and 13: *The youngsters choose . . . games . . . tailored to the various levels of teens, tweens, and tots* (Marion K. Sanders). [short for *between*]

'tween (twēn), *prep. Archaic.* between.

tween-deck (twēn′dek′), *adj.* being or lodging between decks of a ship: *tween-deck passengers. Among the changes predicted . . . [was] more complex tween-deck structure* (London Times).

tween·y (twē′nē), *n., pl.* **tween·ies.** *British.* a between maid.

tweet (twēt), *n., interj.* **1.** the note of a young bird; chirp. **2.** any similar sound. —*v.i.* to utter a tweet or tweets; twitter; chirp. [imitative]

tweet·er (twē′tər), *n.* a high-fidelity loudspeaker for reproducing the higher frequency sounds, usually those above 6,000 cycles per second. [< *tweet* + *-er*[1]]

tweeze or **tweese** (twēz), *n. Obsolete.* **1.** a case of small instruments, as of a surgeon. **2.** tweezers. [earlier, plural of *twee* < Old French *etui* a keeping safe < Old French *estuier* to keep. Compare ETUI.]

tweez·ers (twē′zərz), *n.pl.* small pincers for pulling out hairs, picking up small objects, etc. [alteration of *tweeze;* see TWEEZE]

Tweezers

twelfth (twelfth), *adj., n.* **1.** next after the 11th; last in a series of 12: *Lincoln's birthday comes on February twelfth.* **2.** one, or being one, of 12 equal parts: *Two is a twelfth of twenty-four.*

Twelfth-day (twelfth′dā′), *n.* the twelfth day after Christmas, January 6, the festival of the Epiphany, marking the traditional close of the Christmas season.

Twelfth-night (twelfth′nīt′), *n.* the evening (or sometimes the eve) of Twelfth-day or Epiphany, often celebrated as the end of the Christmas season festivities.

Twelfth·tide (twelfth′tīd′), *n.* **1.** the festive time of Twelfth-day and Twelfth-night. **2.** Twelfth-day.

twelve (twelv), *n.* **1.** one more than 11; 12: *A year has twelve months.* **2.** a set of twelve things.

strike twelve, a. to strike twelve times, as a clock does: *We sat down to lunch just as the clock struck twelve.* **b.** to display one's full powers especially in a first or early performance: *Mr. Avery ain't the kind of man that strikes twelve the first time. He's a man that'll wear* (Harriet Beecher Stowe).

—*adj.* one more than 11; 12.

[Old English *twelf*]

Twelve (twelv), *n.* the Twelve Apostles.

Twelve Apostles, the twelve disciples and associates of Jesus (Peter, James, John, Andrew, Thomas, James the Less, Jude, Philip, Bartholomew, Matthew, Simon, and Judas), who were chosen as His Apostles.

twelve·fold (twelv′fōld′), *adj.* **1.** twelve times as much or as many. **2.** having 12 parts. —*adv.* twelve times as much or as many.

twelve·mo (twelv′mō), *n., pl.* **-mos,** *adj.* duodecimo.

twelve·month (twelv′munth′), *n.* a period of twelve months; year.

twelve-note (twelv′nōt′), *adj. British.* twelve-tone.

Twelve Tables, the early code of Roman law, drawn up in 451 and 450 B.C., containing the most important rules and serving as a basis for later legislation.

twelve-tone (twelv′tōn′), *adj.* **1.** of or having to do with the system of atonal music, established by Arnold Schönberg in 1924, which is based on all twelve semitones of the chromatic scale in an arbitrarily selected order without any tone center (tonic). **2.** using such a system: *a twelve-tone composer.* [translation of German *Zwölfton(musik)*]

twen·ti·eth (twen′tē ith), *adj., n.* **1.** next after the 19th; last in a series of 20. **2.** one, or being one, of 20 equal parts.

twen·ty (twen′tē), *n., pl.* **-ties,** *adj.* two times ten; 20. [Old English *twēntig*]

twen·ty·fold (twen′tē fōld′), *adj.* **1.** twenty times as much or as many. **2.** having 20 parts. —*adv.* twenty times as much or as many.

twen·ty-one (twen′tē wun′), *n.* a gambling game in which the players draw cards from the dealer in trying to come as close to a count of twenty-one (in adding the spots on the cards) as possible without going past it. [American English; translation of French *vingt-et-un*, the card game]

twen·ty-three (twen′tē thrē′), *interj.,* or **twenty-three skiddoo,** *U.S. Slang.* be off; go away; get out.

twen·ty-twen·ty or **20/20 vision** (twen′-tē twen′tē), the vision of the normal human eye, being that which can distinguish a character ⅓ inch in diameter from a distance of 20 feet. For vision less acute than this, the latter figure is a multiple of 20 and the amount by which the character seen exceeds ⅓ inch, taken as an arithmetical base of 1. For example, an eye which can distinguish only characters ten times this size at 20 feet is said to have 20/200 vision.

'twere (twėr; *unstressed* twər), it were.

twerp (twėrp), *n. Slang.* a stupid, undesirable, or inferior person.

twi-, *prefix.* two; in two ways; double; twice, as in *twilight.* [Old English *twi-* two-, double]

Twi (twē), *n.* **1.** a member of the chief tribe of Ghana. **2.** the language of this tribe, a Sudanic dialect of Kwa.

twi·bill or **twi·bil** (twī′bil′), *n. Archaic.* a battle-ax having a double-edged head. [Old English *twibill* < *twi-* two-, double + *bill* ax, sword, bill[3]]

twice (twīs), *adv.* **1.** two times; on two occasions: *twice a day, twice in a lifetime. They say, an old man is twice a child* (Shakespeare). **2.** two times in number, amount, or value: **a.** two times as much as; double of: *twice two is four.* **b.** in a twofold degree; two times as much; doubly: *twice as much. It's as large as life and twice as natural* (Lewis Carroll). [Middle English *twies, twiges,* Old English *twiga* twice + adverbial genitive *-es*]

twice-born (twīs′bôrn′), *adj.* **1.** born twice; reincarnated. **2.** that has experienced a second, spiritual birth; regenerate. **3.** of or having to do with the three upper Hindu castes, the boys of which undergo spiritual rebirth in an initiation ceremony.

twice-laid (twīs′lād′), *adj.* **1.** (of a rope) woven of strands of used rope. **2.** made from leftovers, scraps, remnants, etc.

twic·er (twī′sər), *n.* a person who does two things, especially (in England) a typographer who works at both composition and presswork.

twicet (twīst), *adv. U.S. Dialect.* twice.

twice-told (twīs′tōld′), *adj.* **1.** told twice: *Life is as tedious as a twice-told tale* (Shakespeare). **2.** told many times before; hackneyed; trite.

twid·dle (twid′əl), *v.,* **-dled, -dling,** *n.* —*v.t.* **1.** to cause to rotate lightly or delicately; twirl: *to twiddle one's pencil.* **2.** to adjust or bring into some place or condition by twirling or handling lightly. **3.** to play with idly or absently. —*v.i.* **1.** to be busy about trifles; trifle. **2.** to move in a twirling manner; turn about in a light or trifling way.

twiddle one's thumbs. See under **thumb,** *n.*

twiddle with or **at,** to turn, twirl, or play with idly or absently: *Even in the midst of his terror he began mechanically to twiddle with his hair* (Thackeray).

—*n.* a twirl; twist.

[origin uncertain] —**twid′dler,** *n.*

twid·dly (twid′lē), *adj.* trifling; trivial: *Masons [must be] able to make the . . . twiddly bits which any self-respecting mock Gothic architect would insist on putting into his design* (Manchester Guardian).

twi·er (twī′ər), *n.* tuyère.

twi·fold (twī′fōld′), *adj. Archaic.* twofold; double. Also, **twyfold.** [Old English *twifeald* < *twi-* two + *-feald* -fold]

twig[1] (twig), *n.* **1.** a small shoot of a tree or other plant; very small branch. **2.** a small branching division of a blood vessel or nerve. [Old English *twigu,* plural of *twig* twig]

twig[2] (twig), *v.t.,* **twigged, twig·ging.** *British Informal.* **1.** to look at; watch. **2.** to perceive; discern. **3.** to understand; comprehend. [originally underworld slang, perhaps < Scottish Gaelic *tuig,* Irish *tuigim* I perceive, understand]

twig[3] (twig), *n. Obsolete.* style; fashion.

twig blight, *U.S.* a disease of the apple and quince.

twig borer, an insect larva which injures the tender twigs of certain trees, especially fruit trees.

twig gall, an abnormal enlargement of a twig, due to the action of insects, fungi, or bacteria.

twigged (twigd), *adj.* having twigs.

twig·gen (twig′ən), *adj. British Dialect.* made of or covered with twigs or osiers.

twig·gy (twig′ē), *adj.,* **-gi·er, -gi·est.** of, having to do with, or resembling a twig or twigs; slender; slim: *Their Chinese and Korean conquerors, by comparison, were uniformly twiggy and streamlined* (Manchester Guardian Weekly).

twig·less (twig′lis), *adj.* without twigs.

twi·light (twī′līt′), *n.* **1.** the light diffused by the reflection of the sun's rays from the atmosphere just before sunrise and just after sunset. **2.** the period during which this prevails, especially from sunset to dark night. **3.** a dim light resembling twilight. **4.** a condition or period just after or just before full development, glory, etc.

—*adj.* **1.** of or having to do with twilight: *the twilight hour.* **2.** resembling twilight. **3.** seen or done in the twilight.

[Middle English *twilight* < *twi-* two-, double + *light*[1]]

twi·light·ed (twī′lī′tid), *adj.* twilit.

Twilight of the Gods, the final destruction of the world and the gods in the battle with evil; Ragnarok.

twilight sleep, a semiconscious condition produced by the hypodermic injection of scopolamine and morphine, administered to lessen the pains of childbirth. [translation of German *Dämmerschlaf*]

twilight zone, an area not clearly defined or limited, as that between day and night, right and wrong, etc.: *Meanwhile, the party and its members, while increasingly circumscribed as to what they can and cannot do, will remain in a twilight zone of legality* (New York Times).

twi·lit (twī′lit′), *adj.* **1.** lit by or as if by twilight: *It seems, in looking back, like one long twilit day punctuated by meals that would scarcely stay on the table long enough to be eaten* (Atlantic). **2.** not clearly defined; uncertain: *twilit moods, a twilit allegory.*

twill (twil), *n.* **1.** a fabric woven in raised diagonal lines by passing the woof threads over one and under two or more warp threads: *Serge is a twill.* **2.** a diagonal line or pattern formed by such weaving. —*v.t.* to weave (fabric) in the manner of a twill. [variant of Middle English *twile,* Old English *twilī,* half-translation (with *twi-*) of Latin *bilix, -līcis* with a double thread < *bi-* two + *licium* thread]

'twill (twil), it will.

twilled (twild), *adj.* woven in raised diagonal lines.

twin[1] (twin), *n., adj., v.,* **twinned, twin·ning.** —*n.* **1.** one of two children or animals born at the same time from the same mother. Twins sometimes look just alike. **2.** one of two persons or things exactly alike. **3.** a composite crystal consisting of two crystals, usually equal and similar, united in reversed positions with respect to each other. **4.** a composite crystal consisting of more than two.

Twin[1] (def. 3)

—*adj.* **1.** being twins; born at the same birth: *twin sisters.* **2.** being a twin: *a twin brother.* **3.** being two persons or things which are very much alike or closely associated; forming a pair or couple: *twin beds. These twin truths . . .* (Samuel Taylor Coleridge). **4.** being or forming one of such a pair or couple: *a twin bed.* **5.** having or made up of two similar and equal or two closely connected or related parts or constituents: *Body and spirit are twins: God only knows which is which* (Algernon Charles Swinburne). **6.** *Crystallography.* of or like a twin. **7.** *Biology.* growing or occurring in pairs. **8.** *Obsolete.* consisting of two; twofold; double.

—*v.i.* **1.** to give birth to twins: *Two more ewes have twinned* (Thomas Hardy). **2.** to be born at the same birth (with). **3.** to be coupled or joined. —*v.t.* **1.** to conceive or bring forth as twins, or as a twin (with another). **2.** to join closely; couple; pair. **3.** to unite (crystals) so as to form a twin. **4.** to be or provide a counterpart to; match.

[Old English *twinn*]

twin[2] (twin), *v.t., v.i.,* **twinned, twinning.** *Scottish.* to twine; separate.

twin·ber·ry (twin′ber′ē), *n., pl.* **-ries. 1.** partridgeberry. **2.** a North American shrub, a honeysuckle, whose yellowish-red flowers are subtended by purplish involucres.

twin·born (twin′bôrn′), *adj.* born a twin or twins; born at the same birth.

twin Brethren or Brothers, 1. Castor and Pollux, the Dioscuri. **2.** the constellation Gemini.

twin cities, a pair of cities on opposite banks of a river, lake, etc.

twine[1] (twīn), *n., v.,* **twined, twin·ing.** —*n.* **1.** a strong thread or string of hemp, cotton, etc., made of two or more strands twisted together. **2.** a twisting; twisting together. **3.** a twined or twisted object or part, especially: **a.** a twining or trailing stem or spray of a plant. **b.** a twist or turn in the course of anything; coil; convolution. **c.** a tangle; knot; snarl.

—*v.t.* **1.** to twist together: *She twined holly into wreaths.* **2.** to cause (one thing) to encircle or embrace another; twist or wrap (a thing about or around another). **3.** to insert (one thing in or into another) with a twisting or sinuous movement. **4.** to enfold, wreathe, or encircle (one thing with another): *The child twined her arms about her mother's knees.* **5.** (of a plant, wreath, etc.) to clasp, encircle, or enwrap. —*v.i.* **1.** (of plants, stems, etc.) to grow in a twisting or spiral manner; grow in spiral convolutions: *The vine twines around the tree.* **2.** to extend or proceed in a winding manner; meander. **3.** (of a serpent, etc.) to crawl sinuously.

[Old English *twīn.* Related to TWIST.]

twine[2] (twīn), *v.,* **twined, twin·ing.** *Scottish.* —*v.t., v.i.* to put separate; disjoin. [variant of *twin*[2], verb]

twin-en·gine (twin′en′jin), *adj.* having or powered by two engines: *a twin-engine air-liner, twin-engine transport.*

twin-en·gined (twin′en′jind), *adj.* twin-engine.

twin·er (twī′nər), *n.* **1.** a person or thing that twines. **2.** a twining plant.

twin·flow·er (twin′flou′ər), *n.* either of two slender, creeping evergreen plants of the honeysuckle family, one found in Europe and the other found in America, with pairs of fragrant, pink or white flowers borne on long, thin stems.

twinge (twinj), *n., v.,* **twinged, twing·ing.** —*n.* **1.** a sharp, pinching pain, often a momentary, local one: *a twinge of rheumatism.* **2.** a sharp mental pain; pang: *a twinge of remorse.* **3.** *Obsolete.* a tweak; pinch. [< verb] —*v.i.* to experience a twinge. —*v.t.* **1.** to affect (the body or mind) with a twinge. **2.** *Obsolete.* to tweak. [Old English *twengan* to pinch]

—**Syn.** *n.* **1.** ache, cramp.

twi-night (twī′nīt′), *adj. U.S. Baseball.* starting late in the afternoon and continuing at night under lights: *a twi-night double-header.* [< *twi*(light)*-night*]

twi-night·er (twī′nī′tər), *n. U.S. Baseball.* a twi-night double-header.

twink[1] (twingk), *n.* **1.** a winking of the eye. **2.** the time taken by this: *in a twink, with a twink.* **3.** a twinkle or sparkle.

—*v.i.* **1.** to twinkle; sparkle. **2.** *Obsolete.* to wink; blink.

[Middle English *twinken;* see TWINKLE]

twink[2] (twingk), *v.t.* to cause to clink; chink: *Oh, twink the viol and toot the flute* (Frank Sullivan). —*v.i. Obsolete.* to clink; chink. [probably imitative]

twin·kle (twing′kəl), *v.,* **-kled, -kling,** *n.* —*v.i.* **1.** to shine with quick little gleams; sparkle; glitter: *twinkling stars.* **2.** to reveal keenness of interest, emotion, etc.; be animated: *Jack's eyes twinkled with humor.* **3.** to move quickly, especially up and down, to and fro, in and out, etc.: *the twinkling feet of the dancers.* **4.** *Archaic.* **a.** to close and open the eye or eyes quickly (voluntarily or involuntarily); blink. **b.** to make a signal by this means; wink. —*v.t.* to cause to twinkle.

—*n.* **1.** an intermittent or transient shining; sparkle; scintillation: *He has a merry twinkle in his eye.* **2.** a faint or momentary gleam; glimmer. **3.** a quick motion. **4.** the time it takes to wink: *in a twinkle, in the twinkle of an eye.* **5.** *Archaic.* a wink; blink.

[Old English *twinclian* (apparently frequentative) < unrecorded Old English *twincan* twink[1]]

—**Syn.** *v.i.* **1.** scintillate.

twin·kler (twing′klər), *n.* a person or thing that twinkles.

twin·kling (twing′kling), *n.* **1.** a little, quick gleam. **2.** a very brief period; moment; instant. **3.** *Obsolete.* winking.

in the twinkling of an eye, in an instant: *. . . we shall all be changed, In a moment, in the twinkling of an eye . . .* (I Corinthians 15:51-52).

—*adj.* that twinkles: *twinkling eyes.* —**twin′kling·ly,** *adv.*

twin·kly (twing′klē), *adj.* full of twinkles; twinkling: *a twinkly Christmas card with a Dickens stagecoach on it* (Manchester Guardian).

twin lamb disease, pregnancy disease.

twin·leaf (twin′lēf′), *n.* a North American herb of the barberry family, whose leaves are each divided into two leaflets.

twinned (twind), *adj.* **1.** born two at one birth; twin. **2.** united, as two crystals. **3.** consisting of two crystals united, so as to form a twin.

twin·ning (twin′ing), *n.* **1.** the bearing of twins. **2.** close union or combination; coupling. **3.** the union of two or more crystals so as to form a twin.

Twins (twinz), *n.pl.* a constellation and the third sign of the Zodiac; Gemini.

twin-screw (twin′skrü′), *adj.* equipped with two screw propellers, which revolve in opposite directions.

twin·set (twin′set′), *n.* a matching cardigan and sweater: *Though many of the top quality firms find that the classic twinsets still comprise most of their output, nearly every season sees the introduction of something new* (London Times).

twin·ship (twin′ship), *n.* **1.** the condition of being twin, or a twin. **2.** the relation of a twin or twins: *The two streams of mental and organic life coalesce . . . and begin that marvelous twinship which ends only at death* (Griffith Jones).

twire (twīr), *v.i.,* **twired, twir·ing.** *Archaic or Dialect.* **1.** to glance shyly or slyly; peep; peer: *Which maids will twire . . . 'tween their fingers thus!* (Ben Jonson). **2.** to twinkle; wink: *When sparkling stars twire not, thou gild'st the even* (Shakespeare). [origin uncertain]

twirl (twėrl), *v.t.* **1.** to revolve rapidly; spin; whirl. **2.** to turn around and around idly. **3.** to twist; curl. **4.** to flourish. **5.** *Informal.* (in baseball) to pitch. —*v.i.* **1.** to be twirled. **2.** *Informal.* (in baseball) to be the pitcher; pitch: *to twirl for three innings.*
—*n.* **1.** a twirling; spin; whirl; turn: *a twirl in a dance.* **2.** a twist; curl: *a twirl of hair.* **3.** a flourish: *He signed his name with many twirls.*
[origin uncertain] —**twirl′er,** *n.*

twirp (twėrp), *n.* twerp.

twist (twist), *v.t.* **1.** to turn with a winding motion; revolve; rotate: *to twist a key in a lock. She twisted her ring on her finger.* **2.** to wind; coil: *to twist braids of hair on the head.* **3.** to wind together; entwine; interweave: *This rope is twisted from many threads. Mary twisted flowers into a wreath.* **4.** to connect closely together; associate intimately: *Nor twist our Fortunes with your sinking fate* (John Dryden). **5.** to give a spiral or convolute form to. **6.** to curve; crook; bend: *to twist a piece of wire into a loop.* **7.** to cause to move as on an axis; spin; twirl: *to twist an automobile off the road by pulling at the wheel.* **8.** to force out of shape or place, especially: **a.** to contort: *a face twisted with pain, trees twisted by wintry blasts.* **b.** to sprain or wrench: *to twist an ankle.* **9.** to give a different meaning to; distort the import of: *The lawyer confused the witness by twisting his words.* **10.** to distort the purpose or intent of; pervert: *to seek to twist the law to one's own advantage.* **11.** to mix (something up); confuse; confound: *They had twisted up the story* (H. Rider Haggard). **12.** to make (a ball) go round while moving in a curved direction. **13.** (in cricket) to impart spin to (the ball) in bowling, so that it travels in a curve or jumps to the side on the rebound.
—*v.i.* **1.** to wind together. **2.** to turn around: *She twisted in her seat to see what was happening behind her.* **3.** to have a winding shape, course, etc.; wind; meander; curve; bend: *The path twists in and out among the rocks.* **4.** to spin; twirl: *leaves that twist and turn in the air.* **5.** to move with a spin, as a curve in baseball or a billiard ball with english. **6.** (in cricket) to be twisted in bowling; travel in a curve or jump to the side on the rebound. **7.** to dance the twist.
[< noun]
—*n.* **1.** a curve; crook; bend: *to know every twist in the road.* **2.** a spiral line or pattern; a spiral object: *The tusks . . . have a larger twist . . . towards the smaller end* (Oliver Goldsmith). **3.** a spin; twirl. **4.** a twisting. **5.** a being twisted. **6.** the twisting given to yarn in spinning. **7.** alteration of shape such as is caused by turning the ends of an object in opposite directions: *a girder with a bad twist.* **8.** anything given shape by twisting in its manufacture, especially: **a.** a small loaf or roll made of a twisted piece of dough: *Dainty new bread, crusty twists, cool fresh butter* (Dickens). **b.** pipe tobacco wound or braided into ropelike form: *bring me up a pennyworth of twist* (Scott). **9.** a cord, thread, or strand formed by twisting fibers, yarns, etc.: *A twist of gold was round her hair* (Tennyson). **10.** a strong, tightly twisted silk thread, used for tailoring, millinery, etc. **11.** a strong, tightly twisted cotton yarn, used for the warp in weaving. **12.** a peculiar bias or inclination: *His answer showed a mental twist. [The senator] gave a quite unforeseen twist to the American election tonight by renouncing his aspirations to Democratic nomination for the presidency* (London Times). **13.** torsional strain or stress; torque. **14.** a wrench; sprain: *to suffer a painful twist of the elbow.* **15.** the amount or degree of spiral grooving (rifling) in the barrel of a gun: *a rifle with great twist.* **16.** in sports: **a.** a lateral spin imparted to a ball in throwing or striking it. **b.** a ball thus spun. **17.** a dance in two-beat rhythm, with strong swinging movements from side to side.
[earlier, anything made up of two elements, Old English *-twist,* as in *mæsttwist* mast rope, stay. Related to TWINE[1].]
—**Syn.** *v.t.* **3.** intertwine.

twist·a·ble (twis′tə bəl), *adj.* that can be twisted.

twist drill, a type of drill for metal having one or more deep spiral grooves around the body.

twist·ed (twis′tid), *adj.* **1.** formed by or as by twisting strands together: *a twisted cord, twisted columns.* **2.** bent by twisting; forced awry; distorted. **3.** perverted; warped: *a twisted mind. Hitler had a twisted personality.* **4.** bent spirally; spiral. —**twist′ed·ly,** *adv.*

twist·er (twis′tər), *n.* **1.** a person or thing that twists. **2.** a person whose occupation is to twist together the ends of the yarns of the new warp to those of that already woven. **3.** a mechanical device for spinning yarns, etc. **4.** a ball spinning as it moves, as a curve in baseball, a break in cricket, etc. **5.** *U.S. Informal.* a whirling windstorm; whirlwind; tornado; cyclone.

twist·ing (twis′ting), *adj.* that twists; turning; winding. —**twist′ing·ly,** *adv.*

twist·y (twis′tē), *adj.* full of twists and turns; twisting; winding: *I was so wet and spent after getting lost on those twisty back roads that when I saw your mailbox, I almost sobbed with relief* (New Yorker).

twit (twit), *v.,* **twit·ted, twit·ting,** *n.* —*v.t.* to jeer at; reproach; taunt; tease: *The boys twitted me because I would not fight.* —*n.* a reproach; taunt. [earlier *twite,* short for *atwite,* Old English *ætwītan* < *æt* at + *wītan* blame]

twitch (twich), *v.i., v.t.* **1.** to move with a quick jerk: *The child's mouth twitched as if she were about to cry.* **2.** to pull with a sudden tug or jerk; pull (at): *She twitched the curtain aside.*
—*n.* **1.** a slight, involuntary movement of a muscle, etc.; a quick, jerky movement of some part of the body. **2.** a short, sudden pull or tug; jerk. **3.** a sharp pain; twinge.
[Middle English *twicchen,* related to Old English *twiccian* to pluck] —**twitch′er,** *n.* —**twitch′ing·ly,** *adv.*

twitch grass, couch grass. [earlier *twitch,* alteration of *quitch* (grass)]

twitch·i·ness (twich′ē nis), *n.* the quality or condition of being twitchy: *Hoover's decision caused a general twitchiness in the industry* (London Times). *Angst is twitchiness elevated to a way of life* (Charles Poore).

twitch·y (twich′ē), *adj.* **1.** having a tendency to twitch; jerky: *Faces peculiarly swollen, and twitchy about the nose* (Dickens). **2.** nervous; fidgety; irritable: *He was getting twitchy now. His face had the same flushed and popeyed look it got before a dog race* (New Yorker).

twite (twīt), *n.* a linnet found in hilly and moorland districts of northern Great Britain and Europe. [imitative]

twit·ter[1] (twit′ər), *n.* **1.** a sound made by birds; chirping. **2.** a suppressed laugh; brief or muffled giggle; titter. **3.** an excited condition; flutter: *My nerves are in a twitter when I have to sing in public. In a twitter of indignation* (Thackeray).
—*v.i.* **1.** (of a bird) to utter a succession of light, tremulous notes; chirp: *Swallows and martins skimmed twittering about the eaves* (Washington Irving). **2.** (of a person, especially a woman or child) to sing, talk, or chatter rapidly in a small or tremulous voice. **3.** to titter; giggle. **4.** to tremble with excitement, eagerness, fear, etc.; be in a flutter. —*v.t.* to utter or express by twittering. [probably ultimately imitative]

twit·ter[2] (twit′ər), *v.t. Dialect.* to twit; tease.

twit·ter·er (twit′ər ər), *n.* **1.** a bird that twitters. **2.** a person who twitters.

twit·ter·ing (twit′ər ing), *adj.* **1.** chirping lightly and tremulously. **2.** in a flutter; trembling; quivering: [*He was*] *hardly able to come downstairs for twittering knees* (Stevenson). —**twit′ter·ing·ly,** *adv.*

twit·ter·y (twit′ər ē), *adj.* apt to twitter or tremble; fluttering; shaky: *a twittery old man, a twittery love story.*

'twixt or **twixt** (twikst), *prep. Poetic.* betwixt; between.

two (tü), *n., pl.* **twos,** *adj.* —*n.* **1.** one more than one; 2: *Three may keep a secret if two of them are dead* (Benjamin Franklin). **2.** a set of two persons or things: *Count the class by twos.* **3.** a playing card, throw of the dice, domino, etc., with two spots; deuce.
in two, in two parts or pieces: *At its full stretch as the tough string he drew, Struck by an arm unseen, it burst in two* (Alexander Pope).
put two and two together, to consider several facts together and draw an inference; reason about something so as to come to a conclusion: *Putting two and two together . . . it was not difficult to guess who the expected Marquis was* (Thackeray).
—*adj.* one more than one; 2.
[Old English *twā,* feminine of *twēgen* two. Compare TWAIN.]

two-bag·ger (tü′bag′ər), *n. Slang.* (in baseball) a two-base hit; double.

two-base hit (tü′bās′), (in baseball) a hit where the ball goes far enough for the batter to reach second base; double.

two-beat (tü′bēt′), *adj.* of or having to do with jazz in which two beats of the four in every bar are accented: *It used two-beat rhythms, and its arrangement suggested the collective interplay of the Dixieland ensemble* (New Yorker).

two-bit (tü′bit′), *adj. U.S. Slang.* **1.** worth a quarter of a dollar: *There's a man . . . always got a good story and a two-bit cigar for you* (Sinclair Lewis). **2.** cheap; worthless: *I admit that two-bit judge is short on ritual sense* (Saturday Evening Post).

two bits, *Slang.* a quarter of a dollar: *It was a nickel a ride for pedestrians; two bits for a load of hay* (Maclean's).

two-by-four (tü′bī fôr′, -fōr′), *adj.* **1.** measuring two inches, feet, etc., by four inches, feet, etc. **2.** *U.S. Informal.* **a.** small; narrow; limited: *a two-by-four room.* **b.** small in mind or outlook; petty: *a two-by-four political hanger-on.* —*n.* a length of lumber four inches by two inches in cross section, used especially for framing in building.

two cents' worth, *U.S. Slang.* a statement of opinion or point of view: *He is an expert chairman, keeping the discussion firmly to the point and yet giving each speaker the feeling that he is getting in his two cents' worth* (New Yorker).

two-cy·cle (tü′sī′kəl), *adj.* **1.** completing a series of operations in two cycles or strokes, as an internal-combustion engine. **2.** of or having to do with a two-cycle engine. —*n.* a cycle of two strokes in an internal-combustion engine.

two-di·men·sion·al (tü′də men′shə nəl), *adj.* having only two dimensions; lacking depth; superficial: *The inherent weakness of the American Western novel, according to students of that popular literary theme, is that it is two-dimensional* (Newsweek). —**two′-di·men′sion·al·ly,** *adv.*

two-di·men·sion·al·i·ty (tü′də men′shə-nal′ə tē), *n.* the condition or quality of having two dimensions.

two-edged (tü′ejd′), *adj.* **1.** having two edges, especially having two cutting edges, one on each side of the blade: *a two-edged sword.* **2.** effective either way; double-edged, especially: **a.** that supports or may be used in support of either side: *a two-edged argument.* **b.** that may be reversed or sharply altered in order to achieve a purpose: *a two-edged policy.*

two-faced (tü′fāst′), *adj.* **1.** having two faces. **2.** deceitful; hypocritical.

two-fac·ed·ly (tü′fā′sid lē, -fāst′lē), *adv.* in a two-faced manner; deceitfully; hypocritically.

two·fer (tü′fər), *n. U.S. Slang.* **1. a.** a pair of theater tickets sold for roughly the price of one. **b.** a coupon for obtaining such tickets. **2.** any item sold at two for the price of one: *twofer cigars.* [alteration of *two for*]

two-fist·ed (tü′fis′tid), *adj. Informal.* **1.** having two fists and able to use them: *a two-fisted cowboy.* **2.** strong; vigorous: *a two-fisted attack on crime. You tell him that no two-fisted enterprising Westerner would have New York for a gift* (Sinclair Lewis). **3.** such as appeals to persons of simple and virile taste: *a two-fisted romance of the high seas.*

two·fold (tü′fōld′), *adj.* **1.** two times as much or as many; twice as great; double. **2.** having two parts; dual. *—adv.* two times as much or as many; doubly.

two-forked (tü′fôrkt′), *adj.* having two dimensions or branches like the prongs of a fork; bifurcate; dichotomous: *a two-forked argument.*

two-four (tü′fôr′, -fōr′), *adj.* (of a musical time or rhythm) with two quarter notes to a measure.

2,4-D (tü′fôr′dē′, -fōr′-), *n.* a poisonous, crystalline substance used to kill weeds. *Formula:* $C_8H_6Cl_2O_3$ [< *2,4-d*(ichlorophenoxyacetic acid)]

two-hand·ed (tü′han′did), *adj.* **1.** having two hands. **2.** using both hands equally well; ambidextrous. **3.** skillful with the hands; dexterous. **4.** involving the use of both hands; requiring both hands to wield or manage: *a two-handed sword.* **5.** requiring two persons to operate: *a two-handed saw.* **6.** engaged in or played by two persons: *a two-handed game.* **7.** *Obsolete.* big; bulky; strapping.

two-high (tü′hī′), *adj.* of or having to do with a rolling mill having two rollers, one over the other, or with the rollers themselves.

two-man (tü′man′), *adj.* of, having to do with, or consisting of two persons: *a two-man show. When the two-man Gemini spacecraft first performs* ... (Scientific American). *Their hilarious two-man revue made such a hit* (Martin Gardner).

two-mast·er (tü′mas′tər, -mäs′-), *n.* any sailing vessel with two masts.

two-mind·ed (tü′mīn′did), *adj.* vacillating between two intentions; having ambivalent or conflicting attitudes: *Mr. Johnson himself is two-minded about the current situation* (Wall Street Journal).

two-name (tü′nām′), *adj. Banking.* signed by two people: *a two-name note.*

two-name paper, *Banking.* negotiable paper such as bills, notes, etc., signed by two people, usually a maker and an endorser, both of whom are held liable.

two·ness (tü′nis), *n.* the quality of being two; duality; doubleness.

two-o-cat or **two-o'-cat** (tü′ō′kat′), *n.* a ball game similar to one-o-cat, but with two batters on a side instead of one.

two old cat, two-o-cat.

two-part time (tü′pärt′), *Music.* a time or rhythm with two, or a multiple of two, beats to the measure.

two-par·ty system (tü′pär′tē), the condition or system of political balance that has prevailed historically in the United States, Great Britain (since the 1600's), and certain other countries, especially in the English-speaking world, under which normally in any particular election one or the other of two (although not necessarily always the same two) major political parties is certain to win.

two·pence (tup′əns), *n.* **1.** two British pennies; two pence. **2.** a British silver coin worth two pence (since 1662 minted only on special occasions). **3.** a British copper coin worth two pence (minted in the reign of George III). Also, **tuppence.**

two·pen·ny (tup′ə nē), *adj.* **1.** worth, costing, or amounting to twopence. **2.** of very little value; paltry; trifling; worthless. Also, **tuppenny.**

two·pen·ny-half·pen·ny (tup′ə nē hā′pə-nē, -hāp′nē), *adj. British.* **1.** of the value of or costing two-and-a-half pence: *Hundreds of small twopenny-halfpenny ... cabs were running around the streets* (London Times). **2.** worthless; cheap; petty: ... *some little dirty twopenny-halfpenny piece of roguery* (Robert Southey).

two-phase (tü′fāz′), *adj. Electricity.* diphase.

two-piece (tü′pēs′), *adj.* consisting of two parts made to be worn together: *a two-piece dress, a two-piece bathing suit.*

two-piec·er (tü′pē′sər), *n.* a two-piece garment.

two-ply (tü′plī′), *adj.* having two thicknesses, folds, layers, or strands.

two-port (tü′pôrt′, -pōrt′), *adj.* **1.** having two ports. **2.** of or having to do with a type of two-cycle internal-combustion engine, common in marine use, in which the crankcase admission port of the three-port type of engine is dispensed with, and for it is substituted a kind of suction valve leading to the crankcase.

two·score (tü′skôr′, -skōr′), *adj.* forty: [*They have*] *mounted a massive, direct mail offensive involving twoscore different pieces of literature* (Time).

two-seat·er (tü′sē′tər), *n.* a car or airplane with a seat for two persons: *The tiny two-seater has a two-cycle, two-cylinder engine* (Wall Street Journal).

two-sid·ed (tü′sī′did), *adj.* having two sides; bilateral: [*Theirs*] *was a two-sided friendship* (Scientific American). **—two′-sid′ed·ness,** *n.*

two·some (tü′səm), *n.* **1.** a group of two people; two persons together. **2.** *Sports.* **a.** a game or match, especially in golf, in which two play. **b.** the players. *—adj. Sports.* played by two players, especially two golfers. [< *two* + *-some*[2]]

two-step (tü′step′), *n., v.,* **-stepped, -step·ping.** *—n.* **1.** a ballroom dance in march time or 6/8 time, characterized by sliding steps. **2.** the music for it. *—v.i.* to dance the two-step.

two-suit·er (tü′sü′tər), *n.* **1.** a hand in bridge containing two suits with at least five cards in each. **2.** a man's suitcase that holds two suits and accessories: *His two-suiter ... was adorned with the baggage tags of many airlines* (New Yorker).

two tables, the tables of the law.

two-thirds rule (tü′thėrdz′), *U.S.* a former rule of the Democratic Party which required the vote of two-thirds of the delegates at a convention to nominate a candidate for the presidency.

two-time[1] (tü′tīm′), *v.t.,* **-timed, -tim·ing.** *U.S. Slang.* to betray or be disloyal to.

two-time[2] (tü′tīm′), *adj.* having performed, occurred, been given, etc. twice: *I'm a two-time loser* (New York Times).

two-tim·er (tü′tī′mər), *n. U.S. Slang.* a person who is disloyal or unfaithful.

two-tim·ing (tü′tī′ming), *adj. U.S. Slang.* disloyal; unfaithful; deceitful.

two-toed sloth (tü′tōd′), any of a group of sloths of tropical South and Central America having two toes on the forefeet. See **unau** for picture.

two-tone (tü′tōn′), *adj.* having two colors or shades of color: *a two-tone station wagon, two-tone shoes.*

'twould (twůd; *unstressed* twəd), it would.

two-up (tü′up′), *n. Australian Slang.* a game in which players bet on whether two pennies tossed up will fall heads or tails.

two-up school, *Australian Slang.* a gambling house where two-up is played.

two-way (tü′wā′), *adj.* **1.** having two ways, roads, or channels; permitting traffic in opposite directions: *a two-way street.* **2.** going both ways; extending in two directions: *a two-way relationship.* **3.** used in two ways or for two purposes: *a two-way radio for receiving and transmitting messages. There are seventeen two-way mirrors enabling students to watch doctor and patient without bothering the patient* (New York Times). **4.** having to do with a valve or cock with two outlets which may act together or alternately. **5.** *Mathematics.* capable of varying in two ways: *a two-way progression.*

two-wheel·er (tü′hwē′lər), *n.* a bicycle or other vehicle running on two wheels: *The age at which a youngster can handle a two-wheeler, or "real bike," varies* (Sidonie M. Gruenberg).

twp., township.

T.W.U., Transport Workers' Union.

T.W.U.A., Transport Workers' Union of America.

TWX (no periods), teletypewriter exchange: *TWX is like a telephone system except that its messages are sent and received in written form* (Wall Street Journal).

twy·fold (twī′fōld′), *adj. Archaic.* twifold.

-ty[1], *suffix.* tens; times ten, as in *sixty, seventy, eighty.* [Old English *-tig*]

-ty[2], *suffix.* the fact, quality, state, condition, etc., of being ——, as in *safety, sovereignty, surety; -ity* is often used instead of *-ty*, as in *artificiality, complexity, humidity.* [Middle English *-tee, -tie* < Old French *-te* < *-tet* < Latin *-tās, -tātis*]

Ty., territory.

Ty·che (tī′kē), *n. Greek Mythology.* the goddess of fortune, identified with the Roman goddess Fortuna.

ty·coon (tī kün′), *n.* **1.** a man who is a dominant, or the predominant, figure in a (specified) realm of business, industry, etc.; one having great wealth and power: *a financial tycoon, a gathering of shipping tycoons.* **2.** a man of equivalent importance in any (specified) realm: *a political tycoon, a labor tycoon.* **3.** the title by which the former hereditary commanders in chief (shoguns) of the Japanese army were described to foreigners. [< Japanese *taikun* < Chinese *tai* great + *kiun* lord]

ty·coon·er·y (tī kü′nər ē), *n., pl.* **-er·ies.** domineering behavior or action, as of a tycoon.

Ty·deus (tī′dyüs, tid′ē əs), *n. Greek Legend.* the brother of Meleager, father of Diomedes, and one of the Seven against Thebes.

Ty·di·des (ti dī′dēz), *n. Greek Legend.* Diomedes, son of Tydeus.

ty·ee (tī′ē), *n.* **1.** a person of distinction; leader; chief. **2.** the king salmon; chinook salmon. [< Chinook jargon]

ty·er (tī′ər), *n.* a person or thing that ties. Also, **tier.**

tyg (tig), *n.* a large, flat-bottomed drinking cup with two or more handles: [*The*] *three-handled tyg* ... [*is*] *so handled that three different persons, drinking out of it, and each using a separate handle, bring to their mouths different parts of the rim* (de la Beche and Reeks). [origin unknown]

ty·ing (tī′ing), *v.* the present participle of **tie:** *He is tying his shoes.*

tyke (tīk), *n.* **1.** *Informal.* **a.** a mischievous or troublesome child. **b.** any child: *a friendly little tyke.* **2.** *Scottish.* **a.** a mongrel dog; cur. **b.** any dog. **3.** *Scottish.* a low fellow. Also, **tike.** [< Scandinavian (compare Old Icelandic *tīk* bitch)]

ty·lo·sis (tī lō′sis), *n., pl.* **-ses** (-sēz). **1.** *Botany.* a growth from a cell wall into the cavity of woody tissue: *In some woods the parenchyma cells, before they die, push bladderlike outgrowths called tyloses into the vessels, blocking them and making water conduction impossible* (New Scientist). **2.** *Medicine.* **a.** an inflammatory disease in which the eyelids become thick and hard around the edges. **b.** a disease of the mucous membrane of the lips and mouth, characterized by whitish spots. [< Greek *týlōsis* formation of a callus < *týlē* callus]

tym·bal (tim′bəl), *n.* timbal. [< French *timbale*, ultimately < Arabic *aṭ-ṭabl* the drum]

tymp (timp), *n.* (in some blast furnaces) the top portion or crown of the opening in front of the hearth.

tym·pan (tim′pən), *n.* **1.** a stretched membrane, or a sheet or plate of some thin material, in an apparatus. **2.** an appliance in a printing press, often consisting of a thickness of paper, cloth, cardboard, or the like, placed between the platen or impression cylinder and the paper to be printed, so as to soften and equalize the pressure. **3.** *Architecture.* tympanum. **4.** *Music, Archaic.* a kettledrum. [Old English *timpanum* < Latin *tympanum* < Greek *týmpanon.* Doublet of TIMBRE, TIMPANI, TYMPANUM.]

tym·pa·nal (tim′pə nəl), *adj.* of or having to do with the tympanum or eardrum; tympanic.

tym·pa·ni (tim′pə nē), *n.* the plural of **tympano.** timpani; kettledrums.

tym·pan·ic (tim pan′ik), *adj.* **1.** *Anatomy.* **a.** of or having to do with the tympanum. **b.** in the region of the tympanum. **2.** having to do with a drum. **3.** like a drum.

tympanic bone, (in mammals) a bone supporting the eardrum and enclosing the passage of the external ear.

tympanic membrane, *Anatomy.* the eardrum.

tym·pa·nism (tim′pə niz əm), *n.* tympanites.

tym·pa·nist (tim′pə nist), *n.* timpanist.

tym·pa·ni·tes (tim′pə nī′tēz), *n.* distention of the wall of the abdomen by gas or air in the intestine, etc. [< Late Latin *tympanītēs*

< Greek *tympanítēs* < *týmpanon* drum; see TYMPANUM]

tym·pa·nit·ic (tim′pə nit′ik), *adj.* **1.** having to do with tympanites. **2.** of the nature of tympanites.

tym·pa·ni·tis (tim′pə nī′tis), *n.* inflammation of the tympanum or middle ear. [< *tympan*(um) + *-itis*]

tym·pa·no (tim′pə nō), *n., pl.* **-ni.** timpano; a kettledrum. [< Italian *timpano*]

tym·pa·num (tim′pə nəm), *n., pl.* **-nums, -na** (-nə). **1.** the eardrum. **2.** the middle part of the ear, consisting of a cavity in the temporal bone; middle ear. **3.** the diaphragm in a telephone. **4.** *Architecture.* **a.** the vertical recessed face of a pediment, enclosed by the cornices, usually triangular and often adorned with sculpture. **b.** a slab or wall between an arch and the horizontal top of a door or window below. **5.** a drum, especially a kettledrum; tympano. **6.** the stretched membrane of a drum; drumhead. [< Medieval Latin *tympanum* < Latin, drum < Greek *týmpanon* < *týptein* to beat, strike. Doublet of TIMBRE, TIMPANI, TYMPAN.]

Tympanum (def. 4a)

tym·pa·ny (tim′pə nē), *n., pl.* **-nies. 1.** tympanites. **2.** an abnormal swelling or tumor of any kind. **3.** a swelling, as of pride, arrogance, etc.; condition of being inflated or puffed up. **4.** bombast. **5.** *Music.* **a.** tympanum. **b.** tympan. [< Medieval Latin *tympanias* < Greek *tympanías* < *týmpanon;* see TYMPANUM]

Tyn·dall beam (tin′dəl), the visible path of a light beam that enters a colloid and is scattered by colloidal particles in the Tyndall effect. [< John *Tyndall,* 1820-1893, an English physicist]

Tyndall effect, the scattering of light in different colors by the particles of a colloid: *The bluish appearance of a light beam passing through something like a soap solution is called the "Tyndall effect"* (World Book Encyclopedia).

Tyn·dar·e·us (tin dar′ē əs), *n. Greek Legend.* a Spartan king, husband of Leda and father by her of Clytemnestra.

tyne[1] (tīn), *v.,* **tyned** or **tynt, tyn·ing.** *Especially Scottish.* tine[2].

tyne[2] (tīn), *n. Obsolete.* tine[1].

typ., 1. typographer. **2. a.** typographic. **b.** typographical. **3.** typography.

typ·al (tī′pəl), *adj.* **1.** of the nature of or answering to a type, pattern, etc.; representative; typical. **2.** having to do with or relating to a type or symbol; symbolic; emblematic.

type (tīp), *n., adj. v.,* **typed, typ·ing.** —*n.* **1.** a kind, class, or group having certain common characteristics: *three types of local government. Small pox of the most malignant type* (Macaulay). **2.** kind; sort; order: *He doesn't like that type of work.* **3.** a person or thing having the characteristics of a kind, class, or group; a representative specimen; example; illustration: *The Tahitians are considered . . . as the type of the whole Polynesian race* (James C. Prichard). **4.** a perfect example (of a kind, class, or group); model; pattern; exemplar: *John is a fine type of schoolboy. The Republican form of government is the highest form of government; but, because of this, it requires the highest type of human nature* (Herbert Spencer). **5.** the general form, structure, or character of a particular kind, class, or group: *She is above the ordinary type of servant.* **6.** *Biology.* **a.** a general plan or structure characterizing a group of animals, plants, etc. **b.** a genus, species, etc., which most perfectly exhibits the essential characters of its family or group, and from which the family or group is usually named. **7. a.** the inherited characteristics of an animal or breed which fit it for a certain use: *dairy or beef type.* **b.** an animal or breed having such characteristics. **8.** a group of persons or substances which have certain physiological characteristics, functions, or properties in common, as a blood type. **9.** *Mathematics.* **a.** the simplest of the equivalent forms of a series of transformations, as *10* in *10, 2(3+2),* $\sqrt{100}$. **b.** a standard form. **10.** *Printing.* **a.** a small rectangular block, usually of metal or wood, having on its upper end a raised letter, figure, or other character, for use in printing; a letter (used with an article and having a plural): *a type, the types.* **b.** types collectively; letter (used without article or plural): *to set in type.* **c.** a printed character or characters: *small or large type.* **11. a.** a piece similar to a printing type on a typewriter or like machine. **b.** such types collectively. **12.** a figure, inscription, or design on either side of a coin or medal. **13.** something having symbolical significance; symbol; emblem. **14.** something that foreshadows something to come (the antitype); a prefigurement. **15.** a person, object, or event in the Old Testament regarded as foreshadowing a corresponding reality of the new dispensation. **16.** a distinguishing mark or sign.
—*adj.* **1.** of, having to do with, or relating to a type: *a type specimen, a type animal.* **2.** for a type or types, especially printing types (collectively): *type matter, type face, type composition.* **3.** using or dealing with printing types (collectively): *a type caster.* **4.** making printing types (collectively).
—*v.t.* **1.** to typewrite. **2.** to be the type or symbol of; symbolize; typify. **3.** to foreshadow as a type; prefigure. **4.** to be the pattern or model for. **5.** to classify (a sample of blood) as to type: *to type a person's blood.* —*v.i.* to typewrite.
[< Latin *typus* < Greek *týpos* dent, impression < *týptein* to strike, beat]
—**Syn.** *n.* **3, 4.** prototype.
➔ **type, type of.** The standard English idiom is *type of: this type of* (not *type*) *letter.*

type bar, 1. each of the movable bars carrying the letters or characters in a typewriter. **2.** a line of type cast in a solid bar, as by a linotype.

type·case (tīp′kās′), *n.* a flat, compartmented box for holding sorted printing type.

type·cast (tīp′kast′, -käst′), *v.t.,* **-cast, -cast·ing. 1.** to cast in a rôle that seems to suit one's appearance and personality: *He is also a dignified, patriarchal-looking man, practically typecast for the role of a great composer* (New Yorker). **2.** to cast repeatedly in such a rôle: *to become type-cast as a politician.*

type cutter, a person who engraves the dies or punches from which printing types are cast.

type face, 1. the printing surface of a plate or piece of type. **2.** the style of the printing surface of the type, especially its thickness, serifs, etc.

type founder, a person who casts or makes metal printing type.

type founding, the art or process of manufacturing movable metallic types used by printers.

type foundry, a place where printing types are manufactured.

type genus, *Biology.* the genus from which the name of the family or subfamily is taken, theoretically, the genus most perfectly exhibiting the family characteristics.

type-high (tīp′hī′), *adj. Printing.* of the standard height of type (in the United States, 0.9186 inch; in Great Britain, 0.9175 inch).

type metal, an alloy of lead and antimony, sometimes with tin, etc., of which printing types are cast; metal.

type page, the part of a page covered by type or letterpress.

typ·er (tī′pər), *n.* **1.** a person or thing that types; a person who does typewriting. **2.** a typewriter.

type·script (tīp′skript′), *n.* a typewritten manuscript.

type·set (tīp′set′), *v.t.,* **-set, -set·ting.** to set (copy) in printing type.

type·set·ter (tīp′set′ər), *n.* **1.** a person who sets type; compositor. **2.** a machine which sets type.

type·set·ting (tīp′set′ing), *n.* the act, art, or process of setting type for printing; composition. —*adj.* used or adapted for setting type: *a typesetting machine.*

type species, *Biology.* the species from which the name of the genus is taken, theoretically, the species most perfectly exhibiting the generic characteristics; genotype.

type specimen, *Biology.* an individual or specimen from which the description of the species or subspecies has been prepared and upon which the specific name has been based.

type·write (tīp′rīt′), *v.t., v.i.,* **-wrote, -writ·ten, -writ·ing.** to write with a typewriter; type: *to typewrite a letter, to know how to typewrite.*

type·writ·er (tīp′rī′tər), *n.* **1.** a machine for writing by means of letters similar to those of printers. **2.** a typist. **3.** *Printing.* a style of type that resembles that of a typewriter.

type·writ·ing (tīp′rī′ting), *n.* **1.** the act or art of using a typewriter: *to study typewriting.* **2.** work done on a typewriter: *His typewriting is very accurate.*

type·writ·ten (tīp′rit′ən), *adj.* written with a typewriter: *a typewritten letter.* —*v.* the past participle of **typewrite.**

type·wrote (tīp′rōt′), *v.* the past tense of **typewrite.**

typh·lit·ic (tif lit′ik), *adj.* **1.** having to do with typhlitis. **2.** of the nature of typhlitis. **3.** affected with typhlitis.

typh·li·tis (tif lī′tis), *n.* inflammation of the caecum. [< New Latin *typhlitis* < Greek *typhlón* the caecum + New Latin *-itis* -itis]

typh·lol·o·gy (tif lol′ə jē), *n.* the science dealing with blindness. [< Greek *typhlós* blind + English *-logy*]

typh·lo·sis (tif lō′sis), *n.* blindness. [< Greek *typhlōsis* < *typhloûn* make blind < *typhlós* blind]

typh·lo·sole (tif′lə sōl), *n.* a ridge or fold extending along the inner wall of the intestine and partly dividing the intestinal cavity in lampreys, mollusks, and worms. [< Greek *typhlós* blind + *sōlēn* channel]

Ty·pho·e·an (tī fō′ē ən), *adj.* **1.** of or having to do with Typhoeus. **2.** characteristic of Typhoeus.

Ty·pho·eus (tī fō′yüs), *n. Greek Mythology.* a monster with a hundred serpents' heads each with a terrible voice, slain by Zeus's thunderbolt, and buried in Tartarus under Mount Etna.

ty·pho·gen·ic (tī′fə jen′ik), *adj.* **1.** causing typhoid fever. **2.** causing typhus.

ty·phoid (tī′foid), *adj.* **1.** of or having to do with typhoid fever. **2.** characteristic of typhoid fever. **3.** affected with typhoid fever. **4.** resembling or characteristic of typhus, as a stuporous state in certain fevers. —*n.* typhoid fever. [< *typhus*]

ty·phoi·dal (tī foi′dəl), *adj.* **1.** having to do with typhoid fever. **2.** characteristic of or resembling typhoid fever.

typhoid bacillus, a bacillus that causes typhoid fever.

typhoid fever, an acute, often fatal, infectious disease characterized by intestinal inflammation and sometimes hemorrhage, enlargement of the spleen, eruptions of the skin, fever, nosebleed, disorder of the bowels, and sometimes stupor. It is caused by the typhoid bacillus, which is spread by contaminated food, drink, and clothing; enteric fever. People can be inoculated against typhoid fever.

ty·phoi·din (tī foi′din), *n.* a substance made from typhoid bacilli, used to test for the presence of typhoid.

Typhoid Mary, *U.S. Informal.* **1.** a carrier of a communicable disease: *There is a cure for the menace to the public of Typhoid Marys* (Science News Letter). **2.** a carrier or transmitter of anything harmful or evil. [< the name given to a New York City cook who was a carrier of typhoid fever]

ty·pho·ma·lar·i·al (tī′fō mə lãr′ē əl), *adj.* (of a fever) having the characteristics of both typhoid fever and malaria.

Ty·phon (tī′fon), *n. Greek Mythology.* **1.** a monster, the son of Typhoeus. **2.** Typhoeus. **3.** the Greek name for Set, the Egyptian god of evil.

ty·phon·ic (tī fon′ik), *adj.* like a whirlwind or tornado.

ty·phoon (tī fün′), *n.* **1.** a violent cyclonic storm or hurricane of the western Pacific, especially of the China Sea and adjacent regions, occurring chiefly during the period from July to October. **2.** any of various violent storms or tempests occurring in Asia, especially in or near India. **3.** any violent storm: *My coursers . . . outstrip the Typhoon* (Shelley). [< Cantonese *tai-fung* big wind; influenced by Greek *typhṓn, -ônos* whirlwind; (originally) the mythological father of the winds]

ty·phous (tī′fəs), *adj.* of or relating to typhus.

ty·phus (tī′fəs), *n.*, or **typhus fever,** an acute infectious disease characterized by prostration, a dark-red eruption, and high fever, caused by a rickettsia transmitted by fleas, lice, ticks, or mites, as scrub typhus and murine typhus. [< New Latin *typhus* < Greek *tŷphos* stupor caused by fever; (originally) smoke < *tŷphein* to smoke]

typ·ic (tip′ik), *adj.* typical.

typ·i·cal (tip′ə kəl), *adj.* **1.** having the qualities of a type or specimen; serving as a representative specimen; representative: *a typical American home. The typical Thanksgiving dinner consists of turkey, cranberry sauce, several vegetables, and mince or pumpkin pie.* **2.** of or having to do with a type or representative specimen; characteristic: *the hospitality typical of the frontiersman.* **3.** symbolical; emblematic. **4.** *Biology.* that is the type of the genus, family, etc.
[< Medieval Latin *typicalis* figurative, symbolic < Latin *typicus* typic < *typus;* see TYPE] —**typ′i·cal·ness,** *n.* —**Syn. 1.** illustrative. **2.** distinctive.

typ·i·cal·ly (tip′ə klē), *adv.* **1.** in a typical manner. **2.** to a typical degree. **3.** ordinarily.

typ·i·fi·ca·tion (tip′ə fə kā′shən), *n.* the act or state of typifying.

typ·i·fi·er (tip′ə fī′ər), *n.* a person or thing that typifies.

typ·i·fy (tip′ə fī), *v.t.*, **-fied, -fy·ing. 1.** to have the common characteristics of; exemplify: *Daniel Boone typifies the pioneer.* **2.** to be a symbol of: *The Statue of Liberty typifies the American tradition of freedom. The lamb typifies Christ's sacrifice.* **3.** to indicate beforehand.

typ·ist (tī′pist), *n.* **1.** a person who operates or is able to operate a typewriter: *to be a good typist.* **2.** person whose occupation is typing: *a part-time typist.*

ty·po (tī′pō), *n., pl.* **-pos.** *Slang.* a typographical error.

typo., or **typog., 1.** typographer. **2. a.** typographic. **b.** typographical. **3.** typography.

ty·pog·ra·pher (tī pog′rə fər), *n.* a printer.

ty·po·graph·ic (tī′pə graf′ik), *adj.* typographical.

ty·po·graph·i·cal (tī′pə graf′ə kəl), *adj.* **1.** of or having to do with typography or printing; connected or dealing with printing. **2.** produced or expressed by typography or in print: *typographical symbols. "Catt" and "hoRse" contain typographical errors.* —**ty′po·graph′i·cal·ly,** *adv.*

ty·pog·ra·phy (tī pog′rə fē), *n.* **1.** the art, practice, or process of printing, especially the designing, setting, and arrangement of type and printing from it. **2.** typographical execution; the arrangement and appearance of printed matter. *Abbr.:* typo., typog. [< Medieval Latin *typographia* < Greek *týpos* type + *-graphiā* writing, -graphy]

ty·po·log·i·cal (tī′pə loj′ə kəl), *adj.* of or having to do with typology.

ty·po·log·i·cal·ly (tī′pə loj′ə klē), *adv.* with reference to typology.

ty·pol·o·gist (tī pol′ə jist), *n.* a person skilled in typology.

ty·pol·o·gy (tī pol′ə jē), *n. Archaeology.* **1.** the classification of remains and specimens. **2.** the study of the evolution of types of tools, weapons, ornaments, etc. [< Greek *týpos* type + English *-logy*]

ty·po·script (tī′pō skript′), *n.* a typescript.

ty·poth·e·tae (tī poth′ə tē, ti-; tī′pə thē′-), *n.pl.* printers (used in the names of professional associations). [< New Latin *typothetae* < Greek *týpos* type + New Latin *-thetae,* for Greek *-thétai,* plural of *-thétēs,* an agent noun suffix]

Tyr (tir), *n.* a Norse god of war and victory, son of Odin, identified with the Teutonic god Tiu. Also, **Tyrr.**

ty·ra·mine (tī′rə mēn, tir′ə-; tī ram′in, tə-), *n.* a colorless, crystalline amine produced by bacterial action or by the decarboxylation of tyrosine, found in mistletoe, ripe cheese, and putrefied animal tissue. *Formula:* $HOC_6H_4CH_2CH_2NH_2$

ty·ran·nic (tə ran′ik, tī-), *adj.* tyrannical. [< Latin *tyrannicus* < Greek *tyrannikós* < *týrannos* tyrant]

ty·ran·ni·cal (tə ran′ə kəl, tī-), *adj.* **1.** of or having to do with a tyrant. **2.** befitting a tyrant; severely oppressive in governing; harsh or cruel: *Charles I of England was a tyrannical king.* —**ty·ran′ni·cal·ly,** *adv.* —**ty·ran′ni·cal·ness,** *n.* —**Syn. 2.** despotic, dictatorial, arbitrary, unjust.

ty·ran·ni·cide[1] (tə ran′ə sīd, tī-), *n.* the act of killing a tyrant. [< Latin *tyrannicīdium* < *tyrannus* tyrant + *-cīdium* act of killing, -cide[2]]

ty·ran·ni·cide[2] (tə ran′ə sīd, tī-), *n.* a person who kills a tyrant. [< Latin *tyrannicīda* < *tyrannus* tyrant + *-cīda* killer, -cide[1]]

tyr·an·nize (tir′ə nīz), *v.*, **-nized, -niz·ing.** —*v.i.* **1.** to use power cruelly or unjustly; behave as a tyrant: *Those who are strong should not tyrannize over those who are weak.* **2.** to rule cruelly; be a tyrant. —*v.t.* **1.** to rule cruelly; oppress: *to tyrannize one's family. Poverty, which doth so tyrannize . . . and generally depress us* (Robert Burton). **2.** to rule over as a tyrant.

tyr·an·niz·er (tir′ə nī′zər), *n.* a person or thing that tyrannizes.

ty·ran·no·saur (ti ran′ə sôr, tī-), *n.* tyrannosaurus.

ty·ran·no·sau·rus (ti ran′ə sôr′əs, tī-), *n.* a huge, carnivorous dinosaur of the late Cretaceous period in North America, characterized by its ability to walk erect on its two hind limbs. [< New Latin *Tyrannosaurus* the genus name < Greek *týrannos* tyrant + *saûros* lizard]

tyr·an·nous (tir′ə nəs), *adj.* acting like a tyrant; cruel or unjust; arbitrary; tyrannical: *The Stamp Act seemed tyrannous to the colonists. It is excellent To have a giant's strength, but it is tyrannous To use it like a giant* (Shakespeare). —**tyr′an·nous·ly,** *adv.*

tyr·an·ny (tir′ə nē), *n., pl.* **-nies. 1.** arbitrary or oppressive exercise of power; cruelly or unjustly severe use of one's authority: *The boy ran away to sea to escape his father's tyranny.* [*The Americans*] *snuff the approach of tyranny in every tainted breeze* (Edmund Burke). *Where laws end, tyranny begins* (William Pitt). **2.** an instance of this; tyrannical act: *The colonists rebelled against the king's tyrannies. Bad laws are the worst sort of tyranny* (Edmund Burke). **3.** the government, position, rule, or term of office of a tyrant or absolute ruler. **4.** a state ruled by a tyrant. [< Late Latin *tyrannia* < Greek *tyranníā* < *týrannos* tyrant] —**Syn. 1.** oppression, harshness, despotism.

ty·rant (tī′rənt), *n.* **1.** a person who exercises power or authority oppressively, despotically, or cruelly; one who treats those under his control tyrannically; despot: *Necessity is the argument of tyrants; it is the creed of slaves* (William Pitt). **2.** a king or other ruler who uses his power oppressively, unjustly, or cruelly; despotical ruler. **3.** any of various rulers, not necessarily unjust or cruel, who ruled absolutely in ancient Greece, and who gained office usually by usurpation. [< Old French *tyrant,* earlier *tyran,* learned borrowing from Latin *tyrannus* < Greek *týrannos* tyrant (definition 3)]

tyrant bird, a tyrant flycatcher.

tyrant flycatcher, any of a family of American flycatchers, as the kingbird, phoebe, and least flycatcher.

tyre (tīr), *n., v.,* **tyred, tyr·ing.** *British.* tire[2].

Tyr·i·an (tir′ē ən), *adj.* **1.** of or belonging to Tyre, an ancient seaport in Phoenicia. **2.** made in ancient Tyre. **3.** Tyrian-purple. —*n.* a native or inhabitant of ancient Tyre. [< Latin *Tyrius* (< Greek *Tyriós* < *Týros* Tyre) + English *-an*]

Tyrian purple, 1. Also, **Tyrian dye.** a deep crimson or purple dye used by the ancient Greeks, Romans, and certain other Mediterranean peoples, and known to have been obtained from various shellfish, but the exact formula for which is now unknown. It was primarily because of the high cost of obtaining it that the possession of purple cloth was evidence in ancient times of royalty or wealth. **2.** a bluish red.

Tyr·ian-pur·ple (tir′ē ən pėr′pəl), *adj.* of the color Tyrian purple; bluish-red.

ty·ro (tī′rō), *n., pl.* **-ros.** a beginner in learning or doing anything; novice: *Much practice changed the tyro into an expert.* Also, **tiro.** [< Late Latin *tyro,* variant of Latin *tīrō* recruit] —**Syn.** neophyte.

ty·ro·ci·din (tī′rə sī′din), *n.* tyrocidine.

ty·ro·ci·dine (tī′rə sī′dēn, -din), *n.* an antibiotic contained in tyrothricin, obtained from a soil bacterium. [< *tyro*(sine) + *-cide*[1] + *-ine*[2]]

Ty·ro·le·an (tə rō′lē ən), *adj., n.* Tirolese.

Tyr·o·lese (tir′ə lēz′, -lēs′), *adj., n.* Tirolese.

Ty·ro·lienne (tē rô lyen′), *n.* **1.** a dance of Tirolese peasants, in 3/4 time. **2.** a song for it, or in its style, featuring the yodel. [< French *tyrolienne,* feminine of *tyrolien* Tirolese < *Tyrol* Tirol]

ty·ro·sin (tī′rə sin, tir′ə-), *n.* tyrosine.

ty·ro·sin·ase (tī′rō sə nās, tir′ō-), *n.* an enzyme present in vegetable and animal tissues. It converts tyrosine into melanin and similar pigments by oxidation. [< *tyrosin*(e) + *-ase*]

ty·ro·sine (tī′rə sēn, -sin; tir′ə-), *n.* a white, crystalline amino acid produced by the hydrolysis of a number of proteins, as casein. It is a constituent of cheese. *Formula:* $C_9H_{11}NO_3$ [< German *Tyrosin* < Greek *tyrós* cheese + German *-in* -in (because it was first obtained from cheese)]

ty·ro·thri·cin (tī′rə thrī′sin, -thris′in), *n.* a substance made up of the antibiotics gramicidin and tyrocidine, obtained from a soil bacterium, and used in treating localized infections. [< New Latin *Tyrothrix, -icis* former genus name of the bacterium + English *-in*]

Tyrr (tir), *n.* Tyr.

Tyr·rhe·ni·an (tə rē′nē ən), *adj.* Etruscan. [< Latin *Tyrrhenus* of or having to do with the *Tyrrheni* Etruscans]

tzar (zär, tsär), *n.* czar.

tzar·e·vitch (zär′ə vich, tsär′-), *n.* czarevitch.

tza·rev·na (zä rev′nə, tsä-), *n.* czarevna.

tza·ri·na (zä rē′nə, tsä-), *n.* czarina.

tzar·ism (zär′iz əm, tsär′-), *n.* czarism.

tzar·ist or **Tzar·ist** (zär′ist, tsär′-), *adj., n.* czarist.

tza·rit·za (zä rēt′sə, tsä-), *n.* czarina.

tzet·ze fly, or **tzet·ze** (tset′sē), *n.* tsetse fly.

tzi·gane or **Tzi·gane** (tsē gán′), *n.* **1.** a kind of fast folk dance, performed originally by the Hungarian Gypsies. **2.** the music for such a dance. **3.** a Hungarian Gypsy. —*adj.* of or having to do with a tzigane. [< French *tzigane* < German *Tzigan* < Hungarian *cigány*]

Tzi·ga·ny (tsi′gä nē), *n., adj.* tzigane.

tzim·mes (tsim′is), *n.* **1.** a casserole or stew made from a sweetened combination of carrots and other vegetables and fruits. **2.** *U.S. Slang.* an uproar; commotion: *He would stage a big ceremony in Cawnpone, with painted elephants and sword swallowers and the whole tzimmes* (New Yorker). [< Yiddish *tsimes*]

Medieval Scholars

Roman
100's A.D.

Greek
600's B.C.

Phoenician
1000's B.C.

Egyptian
3000's B.C.

Uu Uu *Uu* *Uu*

U[1] or **u** (yü), *n., pl.* **U's** or **Us, u's** or **us. 1.** the 21st letter of the English alphabet. **2.** any sound represented by this letter. **3.** the twenty-first, or more usually the twentieth, of a series (either *I* or *J* being omitted). **4.** anything shaped like a U.

U[2] (yü), *Especially British Slang. —adj.* upper-class; sophisticated; cultured: *The upper classes . . . do not "take a bath"; the U version is "have one's bath"* (Time). *—n.* a person or thing that is upper-class.

U[3] (ü), *n.* a Burmese title of respect that precedes a man's name: *Commonly known as U Thant, Thant, like many Burmese, has only one name* (Eileen Teclaff).

u., 1. and (German, *und*). **2.** uncle. **3.** university. **4.** upper.

U (no period), uranium (chemical element).

U., 1. uncle. **2.** union. **3.** university. **4.** upper.

U-235, the isotope of uranium having an atomic weight of 235. It makes up about 0.7 per cent of naturally occurring uranium. It is a source of atomic energy.

U-238, the isotope of uranium having an atomic weight of 238. It makes up about 99 per cent of all naturally occurring uranium.

U-239, the isotope of uranium having an atomic weight of 239, formed by the bombardment of U-238 with neutrons.

ua·ka·ri (wä kär′ē), *n., pl.* **-ris.** ouakari.

UAM (no periods), underwater-to-air missile.

u·a ma·u ke e·a o ka a·i·na i ka po·no (ü′ä mä′ü kä ā′ä ō kä ä′ē nä ē kä pō′nō), *Hawaiian.* the life of the land is preserved in righteousness (the motto of Hawaii).

U.A.R. or **UAR** (no periods), United Arab Republic.

UAW (no periods) or **U.A.W.,** United Automobile Workers.

U·ban·gi (yü bang′gē, ü bäng′-), *n., pl.* **-gis.** a female member of a tribe living in tropical western Africa near the Ubangi River. *—adj.* of or characteristic of the Ubangis.

Ü·ber·mensch (Y′bər mensh′), *n., pl.* **-men·schen** (-men′shən). *German.* superman.

u·ber·ri·ma fi·des (yü ber′ə mə fī′dēz), *Latin.* the fullest faith: *Uberrima fides . . . is the principle on which the whole of insurance is based* (J.R.L. Anderson).

u·bi·ca·tion (yü′bə kā′shən), *n.* the state of having place or local relation; location.

u·bi·e·ty (yü bī′ə tē), *n.* **1.** condition in respect of place or location; local relationship. **2.** the quality of occupying a position in space; objective reality. [< New Latin *ubietas* < Latin *ubi* where]

u·biq·ui·tous (yü bik′wə təs), *adj.* being everywhere at the same time; present everywhere: *It is through the ubiquitous donkey that Athens keeps in touch with the countryside* (Atlantic). **—u·biq′ui·tous·ly,** *adv.* **—u·biq′ui·tous·ness,** *n.* **—Syn.** omnipresent.

u·biq·ui·ty (yü bik′wə tē), *n.* **1.** a being everywhere at the same time; omnipresence. **2.** the ability to be everywhere at once. [< New Latin *ubiquitas* < Latin *ubīque* everywhere < *ubi* where]

u·bi su·pra (yü′bī sü′prə), *Latin.* where above; in the place mentioned above.

U-boat (yü′bōt′), *n.* **1.** a German submarine. **2.** any submarine. [half-translation of German *U-Boot,* short for *Unterseeboot* undersea boat]

U bolt, a bolt shaped like a U, each prong of which is threaded at the end to receive a nut.

U Bolt

U-bomb (yü′bom′), *n.* a uranium bomb.

u.c. or **uc.,** upper case; a capital letter or capital letters (especially as an instruction to a typist, typesetter, type founder, etc.).

U.C., 1. Upper Canada. **2.** United Church

U.C.L.A. or **UCLA** (no periods), University of California (Los Angeles division).

U.C.V., United Confederate Veterans.

u·dal (yü′dəl), *n.* land in Orkney or Shetland held by the old native form of freehold tenure; allodium. *—adj.* of or having to do with this form of freehold tenure; allodial: *In Scotland land was held according to the feudal system, in Orkney according to the udal system* (John Gunn). [< Scandinavian (compare Old Icelandic *ōthal* property held by inheritance)]

U.D.C., United Daughters of the Confederacy.

ud·der (ud′ər), *n.* the baglike, downward-hanging mammary gland characteristic of cows, adult female goats, etc., having two or more fingerlike teats or nipples. [Middle English *udder,* Old English *ūder*]

UDI (no periods) or **U.D.I.,** the unilateral declaration of independence proclaimed by the British self-governing territory of Southern Rhodesia on November 11, 1965.

u·do (ü′dō), *n.* a plant grown chiefly in Japan and China for its edible young shoots. [< Japanese *udo*]

u·dom·e·ter (yü dom′ə tər), *n.* a rain gauge. [< Latin *ūdus* wet + English *-meter*]

u·do·met·ric (yü′də met′rik), *adj.* **1.** having to do with a udometer. **2.** made by means of a udometer.

u·dom·e·try (yü dom′ə trē), *n.* the measurement of rain by the use of a udometer.

UFO (no periods) or **U.F.O.,** unidentified flying object.

u·fo·log·i·cal (yü′fə loj′ə kəl), *adj.* of or having to do with ufology: *The ufological definition of a flap is a concentration of sightings in a small area within a short period* (New Yorker).

u·fol·o·gist (yü fol′ə jist), *n.* a person who tracks down unidentified flying objects; an enthusiast or devotee of ufology: *This only increased ufologists' conviction that the Air Force was hiding vital evidence* (Sunday Times).

u·fol·o·gy (yü fol′ə jē), *n.* the practice or hobby of tracking unidentified flying objects, such as flying saucers. [< *UFO* + *-logy*]

UFT (no periods) or **U.F.T.,** United Federation of Teachers.

U·gan·dan (yü gan′dən), *adj.* of or having to do with Uganda, a country in eastern Africa. *—n.* a native or inhabitant of Uganda.

U·ga·rit·ic (yü gə rit′ik, ü-), *adj.* of or having to do with Ugarit, an ancient city on the coast of Syria, its people, or its language. *—n.* the Canaanite language of Ugarit, akin to Phoenician and Hebrew.

UGC (no periods) or **U.G.C.,** University Grants Commission (of Great Britain).

ugh (u̇ʜ, uʜ, u, u̇, ug), *interj.* an exclamation expressing disgust, horror, strong distaste, etc. [probably imitative]

ug·li·fi·ca·tion (ug′lə fə kā′shən), *n.* the process of uglifying or disfiguring.

ug·li·fy (ug′lə fī), *v.t.,* **-fied, -fy·ing.** to make ugly; disfigure: *Especially since the year 1914 every single change in the English landscape has either uglified it or destroyed its meaning or both* (London Times). [< *ugly* + *-fy*]

ug·li·ly (ug′lə lē), *adv.* in an ugly manner.

ug·li·ness (ug′lē nis), *n.* **1.** the quality or condition of being ugly: *Of all these bereft, Nothing but pain and ugliness were left* (Keats). **2.** an ugly thing or feature.

ug·ly (ug′lē), *adj.,* **-li·er, -li·est,** *n., pl.* **-lies.** *—adj.* **1.** offensive or repulsive to the eye; disagreeable to look at: *an ugly house, an ugly face.* **2.** loathsome; vile, especially: **a.** morally offensive or repulsive; base: *an ugly act of treason.* **b.** very bad or disagreeable; offensive to the ear, nose, etc.; nasty: *an ugly task, ugly language.* **3.** likely to cause trouble; threatening; dangerous: *ugly clouds, an ugly wound. Death is the ugly fact which Nature has to hide* (Alexander Smith). **4.** *U.S. Informal.* given to or displaying violence, extreme irritability, etc.; very ill-natured: *an ugly temper, an ugly customer.*

—n. an ugly person or thing: *He led a picket line in 1962 to protest the new uglies on the Columbia campus* (Harper's). *Peers and judges, beauties and uglies—they were all in the highest spirits* (Pall Mall Gazette). [< Scandinavian (compare Old Icelandic *uggligr* dreadful < *uggr* fear)]

—Syn. *adj.* **1. Ugly, homely, unsightly** mean not pleasing in appearance. **Ugly,** the strongest of the three, means positively unpleasant or offensive in appearance: *There are two ugly, gaudy lamps in the room.* **Homely** means lacking in beauty or attractiveness, but does not suggest unpleasant or disagreeable qualities: *A homely child often develops into an attractive girl.* **Unsightly** means unpleasing to the sight through carelessness or neglect: *Trains approach the city through an unsightly section.*

ugly duckling, a young person, especially a girl, who lacks beauty, charm, or grace to a striking degree but later develops some or all of these qualities to a surpassing degree. [< *the ugly duckling,* a swan in a story by Hans Christian Andersen, that is hatched by a duck and sneered at by the ducklings until it suddenly grows into the beauty and grace of an adult swan]

U·gri·an (ü′grē ən, yü′-), *n.* **1.** a member of an ethnic group which includes the Magyars and certain peoples of western Siberia. **2.** their languages, as a division of Finno-Ugric; Ugric. *—adj.* of, having to do with, or designating the Ugrians or their division of Finno-Ugric.

U·gric (ü′grik, yü′-), *n.* a division of the Finno-Ugric linguistic family that includes Hungarian, Ostyak, and Vogul. *—adj.* Ugrian.

U·gro-Al·ta·ic (ü′grō al tā′ik, yü′-), *adj., n.* Ural-Altaic.

U·gro-Finn·ic (ü′grō fin′ik, yü′-), *adj., n.* Finno-Ugric: *Ugro-Finnic languages.*

ug·some (ug′səm, u̇g′-), *adj. Scottish.* horrible; loathsome. [Middle English *ugsome* < *uggen* to fear, loathe < Scandinavian (compare Old Icelandic *ugga*) + *-some*[1]]

UHF (no periods), **U.H.F.,** or **uhf** (no periods), ultrahigh-frequency (of or having to do with the electromagnetic spectrum between 300 and 3,000 megacycles per second).

uh·lan (ü′län, ü län′), *n.* **1.** a mounted soldier of a type first known in Europe in Poland, armed with a lance. **2.** (in the former German army) a member of the heavy cavalry. [< German *Ulan, Uhlan* < Polish *ułan* < Turkic *oğlan* boy]

u·hu·ru (ü hü′rü), *n. Swahili.* freedom: *No, said Kenyatta, Kenya Africans should have nothing less than uhuru* (Time).

Ui·gur (wē′gu̇r), *n.* **1.** a member of the eastern branch of the Turkic people, prominent in central Asia from the 700's to the 1100's. **2.** their Turkic language. *—adj.* Uigurian.

Ui·gu·ri·an (wē gu̇r′ē ən), *adj.* **1.** of or having to do with the Uigurs. **2.** used by the Uigurs.

Ui·gu·ric (wē gu̇r′ik), *adj.* Uigurian.

u·in·ta·ite or **u·in·tah·ite** (yü in′tə īt), *n. Mineralogy.* gilsonite. [American English < the *Uinta* Mountains, Utah, where deposits are found + *-ite*[1]]

u·in·ta·there (yü in′tə thir), *n.* a primitive mammal of the Eocene period in North America, having a long skull with three pairs of horns, similar in appearance and size to a small elephant. It had stout legs and round feet, and, in the male, a pair of tusks projecting downward from the upper jaws. [< the *Uinta* Mountains, Utah, where remains were found + Greek *thērion* wild animal]

UIS (no periods), Unemployment Insurance Service.

uit·land·er or **Uit·land·er** (oit′lan′dər, īt′-; *Dutch* œ′it län′dər), *n.* (in South Africa) a foreigner. [< Afrikaans *uitlander* < *uit* out + *land* land + *-er* -er[1]]

u·ji fly (ü′jē), a dipterous insect of Japan whose larva is parasitic on silkworms. [< Japanese *uji* a worm]

U.K. or **UK** (no periods), United Kingdom.

UKAEA (no periods) or **U.K.A.E.A.,** United Kingdom Atomic Energy Authority.

u·kase (yü kās′, yü′kās), *n.* **1.** (formerly) an order, having the force of law, issued by the ruler of Russia or his government; decree by or in the name of the czar. **2.** any

official proclamation or order; decree by authority. [< Russian *ukaz* < *ukazat'* to show, decree]

u·ki·yo-e (yü kē'yô ā'), *n.* a style of Japanese painting and printmaking showing scenes from ordinary life, prevalent from the 1600's to the 1800's. [< Japanese *ukiyo-e* < *ukiyo* world life + *e* picture]

Ukr., Ukraine.

U·krain·i·an (yü krā'nē ən, -krī'-), *adj.* of or having to do with the Ukraine, a republic in the Soviet Union, its people, or their language. —*n.* **1.** a native of the Ukraine. **2.** the Slavic language spoken in the Ukraine; Little Russian.

u·ku·le·le (yü'kə lā'lē), *n.* a small guitar having four strings. [American English < Hawaiian *'ukulele* (literally) leaping flea < *'uku* flea + *lele* to fly, leap, jump, etc.; the word was originally a nickname for a British army officer of the 1800's who popularized the instrument in Hawaii]

Ukulele

UL (no periods) or **U.L.,** Underwriters' Laboratories.

u·la·ma (ü'lə mä'), *n.* ulema: *The ulamas ruled that devout Moslems should regard Communists as infidels* (London Times).

ul·cer (ul'sər), *n.* **1.** a sore in any of the soft parts of the body that sometimes discharges pus. It is open either to the surface or to some natural cavity. **2.** a moral sore spot; any corroding or corrupting influence. [< Latin *ulcus, ulceris*]

ul·cer·ate (ul'sə rāt), *v.t., v.i.,* **-at·ed, -at·ing. 1.** to affect or be affected with an ulcer: *An ulcerated tooth may be very painful.* **2.** to form or be formed into an ulcer. [< Latin *ulcerāre* (with English *-ate*[1]) < *ulcus* ulcer]

ul·cer·a·tion (ul'sə rā'shən), *n.* **1.** the act or process of forming ulcers or of becoming ulcerated. **2.** the state of being ulcerated. **3.** an ulcer or ulcers.

ul·cer·a·tive (ul'sə rā'tiv, -sər ə-), *adj.* **1.** caused by or causing ulceration: *ulcerative colitis.* **2.** like an ulceration.

ul·cered (ul'sərd), *adj.* ulcerated.

ul·cer·ous (ul'sər əs), *adj.* **1.** having an ulcer or ulcers; exhibiting ulceration. **2.** of the nature of ulcers. **3.** characteristic of ulcers. —**ul'cer·ous·ly,** *adv.* —**ul'cer·ous·ness,** *n.*

-ule, *suffix.* small; little, as in *ferule, granule, veinule.* [< Old French *-ule,* learned borrowing from Latin *-ulus, -ula, -ulum,* a diminutive suffix]

u·le·ma (ü'lə mä'), *n.* **1.** any of several bodies of Moslem officials, scholars in the religion and law of Islam, active within their separate countries as judicial bodies. **2.** a Moslem theologian; scholar in Islamic law; mullah. Also, **ulama.** [< Turkish *ulema* < Arabic *'ulamā* learned men, plural of *'ālim* wise]

u·lig·i·nose (yü lij'ə nōs), *adj.* **1.** marshy; muddy; oozy. **2.** (of animals and plants) living or growing in muddy places. [< Latin *ūlīginōsus* moist < *ūlīgō, -inis* moisture]

u·lig·i·nous (yü lij'ə nəs), *adj.* uliginose.

ul·lage (ul'ij), *n.* **1.** the quantity of wine, brandy, etc., by which a cask or bottle falls short of being completely full. **2.** (originally) such a quantity lost by leakage or absorption, and required to be made good to the buyer. **3.** the quantity of any commodity, as grain, flour, etc., by which a bag or other container falls short of being full; loss through spillage, sifting at the seams, etc. [< Anglo-French *ulliage,* Old French *ouillage* < *ouillier, aouiller* fill a cask to the bunghole (or eye) < *a-* + *ueil* eye < Latin *oculus*]

ul·ma·ceous (ul mā'shəs), *adj.* belonging to the elm family of trees and shrubs. [< New Latin *Ulmaceae* the family name (< Latin *ulmus* elm) + English *-ous*]

ul·na (ul'nə), *n., pl.* **-nae** (-nē), **-nas. 1.** the thinner, longer bone of the forearm, on the side opposite the thumb. **2.** the analogous bone in the forelimb of a vertebrate animal. [< Latin *ulna* elbow]

ul·nar (ul'nər), *adj.* **1.** of or having to do with the ulna. **2.** in or supplying the part of the forearm near the ulna.

ul·no·car·pal (ul'nə kär'pəl), *adj.* of or having to do with the ulna and the wrist (carpus).

ul·no·ra·di·al (ul'nə rā'dē əl), *adj.* of or having to do with the ulna and the thicker and shorter bone of the forearm (radius).

u·loid (yü'loid), *adj.* resembling a scar: *a uloid mark on the skin.* [< Greek *oulē* scar + English *-oid*]

U·lot·ri·chi (yü lot'rə kī), *n.pl.* persons having woolly or kinky hair, as a division of mankind (proposed as an anthropological classification by Bory de St. Vincent and adopted in the classification of Thomas Henry Huxley). [< New Latin *Ulotrichi* the division name < Greek *oulóthrix, -trichos* woolly haired < *oûlos* curly + *thríx, trichós* hair]

u·lot·ri·chous (yü lot'rə kəs), *adj.* having woolly or kinky hair. [< New Latin *Ulotrichi* (see ULOTRICHI) + English *-ous*]

ul·pan (ül'pän), *n., pl.* **ul·pa·nim** (ül'pä-nēm'). *Hebrew.* an Israeli school for new immigrants, providing an intensive course of study in the Hebrew language: *The Africans spend three months at an ulpan, . . . and then are assigned to a kibbutz where they study agriculture in practice* (Saturday Review).

ul·ster (ul'stər), *n.* a long, loose, heavy overcoat, usually belted, originally made of frieze, or other heavy fabric, in Ulster, Ireland: *All superimposed upon their normal attire . . . in winter an ulster or its equivalent* (London Times). [short for *Ulster overcoat* < *Ulster,* a province of the Irish Republic]

Ul·ster·man (ul'stər mən), *n., pl.* **-men.** a native or inhabitant of Ulster, a former province of Ireland and now a province of the northern Irish Republic: *The Protestant Ulsterman will quite certainly cling to his own somewhat unmusical version of the English tongue* (Manchester Guardian).

ult., an abbreviation for the following: **1. a.** ultimate. **b.** ultimately. **2.** ultimo; in the past month: *your order of the 14th ult.*
➔ See **inst.** for usage note.

ul·te·ri·or (ul tir'ē ər), *adj.* **1.** beyond what is openly stated, avowed, or evident; intentionally concealed or kept in the background; hidden: *an ulterior motive, an ulterior purpose.* **2.** more distant; on the farther side. **3.** further; later. [< Latin *ulterior,* comparative of root of *ultrā* beyond; see ULTRA] —**ul·te'ri·or·ly,** *adv.*

ul·ti·ma (ul'tə mə), *n.* the last syllable of a word. [< Latin *ultima (syllaba)* last syllable; see ULTIMATE]

ul·ti·ma·cy (ul'tə mə sē), *n.* the state or character of being ultimate.

ul·ti·ma ra·ti·o re·gum (ul'tə mə rā'shē ō rē'gəm), *Latin.* **1.** war; force of arms. **2.** (literally) the final argument of kings.

ul·ti·mate (ul'tə mit), *adj.* **1.** last possible; final, especially: **a.** coming at the very end (of a process, course of action, etc.): *He never stopped to consider the ultimate result of his actions.* **b.** forming a final stage, point, or limit (of a process, course of action, etc.); beyond which there is no advance or progress: *the ultimate boundaries of human knowledge. Which shall have ultimate dominion, Dream, or dust?* (Don Marquis). **2.** that is an extremity; beyond which there is nothing at all; extreme: *the ultimate limits of the universe.* **3.** beyond which nothing further may be ascertained by investigation or analysis, especially: **a.** fundamental; basic; elemental: *an ultimate particle of matter. The brain is the ultimate source of ideas. The ultimate check to population appears then to be want of food* (Thomas Malthus). **b.** original: *The ultimate source of life has not been discovered.* **4.** of which there is nothing greater; greatest possible: *to give one's life and thereby pay the ultimate price. Described as the ultimate weapon, against which there is no defense . . .* (Newsweek). **5.** beyond which breaking, shearing, etc., is certain or very probable; that is a quantitative maximum: *to design metal plate to withstand an ultimate stress of 4,500 pounds per square inch.*
—*n.* an ultimate point, result, fact, etc.
the Ultimate, God; the Ultimate Reality: *belief in the Ultimate.*
[< Medieval Latin *ultimatus,* past participle of *ultimare* < Italian, bring to an end < Latin *ultimāre* come to an end < *ultimus* last, superlative of root of *ultrā* beyond; see ULTRA] —**ul'ti·mate·ly,** *adv.* —**ul'ti·mate·ness,** *n.*
—**Syn.** *adj.* **1.** See **last.**

ultimate analysis, *Chemistry.* a form of analysis in which the quantity of each element in a compound is determined.

Ultimate Reality, God.

ultimate strength, *Physics.* **1.** the inherent resistance in a piece of material equal but opposed to the ultimate stress. **2.** the load necessary to produce fracture.

ultimate stress, *Physics.* the stress necessary to break or crush a piece of material.

ul·ti·ma Thu·le (ul'tə mə thü'lē), **1.** the farthest limit or point possible. **2.** the uttermost degree attainable. **3.** the farthest north. [< Latin *ultima Thūlē;* see ULTIMATE. Compare THULE.]

ul·ti·ma·tum (ul'tə mā'təm), *n., pl.* **-tums, -ta** (-tə). **1.** a final proposal or statement of conditions, acceptance of which is required under penalty of terminating a relationship, negotiations, etc., or of punitive action: *This follows the ETU's [Electrical Trade Union's] reply to the congress' ultimatum that five of the union members should be debarred from office* (Manchester Guardian). **2.** the final terms presented by one party in an international negotiation, rejection of which may lead to the breaking off of diplomatic relations or sometimes to a declaration of war. **3.** something unanalyzable or fundamental: *certain ultimata of belief not to be disturbed in ordinary conversation* (Oliver Wendell Holmes). [< New Latin *ultimatum,* neuter of Medieval Latin *ultimatus;* see ULTIMATE]

ul·ti·mo (ul'tə mō), *adv.* in or of last month. *Abbr.:* ult. [< Medieval Latin *ultimo (mense)* in the course of last (month)]

ul·ti·mo·gen·i·ture (ul'tə mō jen'ə chər), *n. Law.* the right or principle by which the youngest inherits or succeeds. [< Latin *ultimus* last (see ULTIMATE); patterned on *primogeniture*]

ulto., ultimo.

ul·tra (ul'trə), *adj.* beyond what is usual; very; excessive; extreme. —*n.* a person who holds extreme views or urges extreme measures: *In 1871, a group of ultras in the Quebec Conservative party published . . . an authoritarian and reactionary guide for the electors* (Maclean's). [< Latin *ultrā* beyond, properly ablative feminine of unrecorded *ulter* beyond]

ultra-, *prefix.* **1.** beyond; on the other side of, as in *ultramarine, ultraviolet.*
2. going beyond the limits, or province, of; more than, as in *ultramundane, ultraphysical.*
3. very, excessively, or unusually, as in:

ultra-ambitious	**ultrafashionable**
ultraconfident	**ultraloyal**
ultracredulous	**ultramechanical**
ultrademocratic	**ultramodest**
ultraexclusive	**ultrarefined**

[< Latin *ultra-* < *ultrā* beyond; see ULTRA]

ul·tra·ba·sic (ul'trə bā'sik), *adj.* (of rocks) extremely rich in base-forming elements and poor in silica.

ul·tra·cen·trif·u·gal (ul'trə sen trif'ə-gəl, -yə-), *adj.* of or by means of an ultracentrifuge. —**ul'tra·cen·trif'u·gal·ly,** *adv.*

ul·tra·cen·trif·u·ga·tion (ul'trə sen trif'-ə gā'shən, -yə-), *n.* a subjecting or being subjected to the action of an ultracentrifuge.

ul·tra·cen·tri·fuge (ul'trə sen'trə fyüj), *n., v.,* **-fuged, -fug·ing.** —*n.* a centrifuge that can spin at very high speed, for separating substances of different densities. —*v.t.* to subject to the action of an ultracentrifuge.

ul·tra·cold (ul'trə kōld'), *adj.* extremely low in temperature; excessively cold: *Superconducting materials have been tested in the high vacuum and ultracold conditions they would meet in space* (Science News Letter).

ul·tra·con·serv·a·tism (ul'trə kən sėr'və-tiz əm), *n.* extreme opposition to innovation or change; unreasonable conservatism.

ul·tra·con·serv·a·tive (ul'trə kən sėr'və-tiv), *adj.* conservative in the extreme; excessively conservative. —*n.* a person who is extremely conservative.

ul·tra·crit·i·cal (ul'trə krit'ə kəl), *adj.* excessively critical; overcritical.

Ul·tra·fax (ul'trə faks'), *n. Trademark.* a way of printing pictures or the like by radio or television transmission.

ul·tra·fine (ul'trə fīn'), *adj.* extremely fine: *A photographic plate with ultrafine grains . . . would require a prohibitively long exposure to photograph faint stars* (Julian Huxley).

ul·tra·gas·e·ous (ul′trə gas′ē əs), *adj. Physics.* **1.** (of matter) being in the form of a highly rarefied gas with peculiar electrical and other properties, as that in a vacuum tube exhausted to one millionth of an atmosphere. **2.** of or having to do with such matter: *the most rarefied form of matter — an ultragaseous condition of it* (William Ralph Inge).

ul·tra·high (ul′trə hī′), *adj.* extremely high: *The chemical explodes unless kept at ultracold temperatures and ultrahigh pressures* (Science News Letter).

ul·tra·high-fre·quen·cy (ul′trə hī′frē′kwən sē), *adj.* UHF.

ul·tra·ism (ul′trə iz əm), *n.* **1.** doctrines or beliefs of an extremist, especially a political extremist. **2.** an action, or group of actions, exemplifying such doctrines or beliefs.

ul·tra·ist (ul′trə ist), *n.* an extremist. —*adj.* ultraistic.

ul·tra·is·tic (ul′trə is′tik), *adj.* tending to extremes in opinions or practice.

ul·tra·lib·er·al (ul′trə lib′ər əl, -lib′rəl), *adj.* holding very liberal views, especially in politics. —*n.* an ultraliberal person or group: *Although he is a dyed-in-the-wool New Dealer, Humphrey is more acceptable to most Southerners than other ultraliberals in the party* (Newsweek).

ul·tra·ma·rine (ul′trə mə rēn′), *n.* **1.** Also, **ultramarine blue.** a deep-blue color. **2.** a pigment or coloring matter of various shades of blue, originally made from powdered lapis lazuli. **3.** a similar blue pigment, prepared artificially by grinding together a mixture of kaolin, sulfur, soda ash, and charcoal. **4.** any of certain other pigments prepared artificially.
—*adj.* **1.** deep-blue. **2.** beyond or across the sea, especially beyond or across the Mediterranean or some part of it.
[< Medieval Latin *ultramarinus* < Latin *ultrā* beyond + *mare* sea (referring to Asia, the overseas source of lapis lazuli)]
—**Syn.** *adj.* **2.** overseas.

ul·tra·mi·cro (ul′trə mī′krō), *adj.* ultramicroscopic: *experiments on an ultramicro scale.*

ul·tra·mi·cro·chem·i·cal (ul′trə mī′krō-kem′ə kəl), *adj.* of or having to do with ultramicrochemistry.

ul·tra·mi·cro·chem·ist (ul′trə mī′krō-kem′ist), *n.* an expert in ultramicrochemistry.

ul·tra·mi·cro·chem·is·try (ul′trə mī′krō kem′ə strē), *n.* chemistry which treats of very small amounts of substances.

ul·tra·mi·crom·e·ter (ul′trə mī krom′ə-tər), *n.* a very finely calibrated micrometer.

ul·tra·mi·cro·scope (ul′trə mī′krə skōp), *n.* a powerful instrument for making visible particles too small to be visible in the common microscope, by means of light thrown on the object from one side, over a dark background.

ul·tra·mi·cro·scop·ic (ul′trə mī′krə-skop′ik), *adj.* **1.** too small to be seen with an ordinary microscope. **2.** having to do with an ultramicroscope.

ul·tra·mi·cro·scop·i·cal (ul′trə mī′krə-skop′ə kəl), *adj.* ultramicroscopic.

ul·tra·mi·cros·co·py (ul′trə mī kros′kə-pē, -mī′krə skō′-), *n.* the art or practice of using the ultramicroscope.

ul·tra·min·i·a·ture (ul′trə min′ē ə chər, -min′ə chər), *adj.* done or made on an extremely small scale; smaller than miniature: *With continued research it should be possible . . . to extend ultraminiature circuits and instruments to higher performance levels* (Scientific American).

ul·tra·mod·ern (ul′trə mod′ərn), *adj.* modern to the greatest possible degree: *The B-26's haul men, rockets, and bombs, and ferret out enemy hideouts with ultramodern cameras* (Time).

ul·tra·mod·ern·ism (ul′trə mod′ər niz-əm), *n.* modernism to the greatest possible degree.

ul·tra·mod·ern·ist (ul′trə mod′ər nist), *n.* a person who is ultramodern in ideas, tastes, etc.

ul·tra·mod·ern·is·tic (ul′trə mod′ər nis′-tik), *adj.* in an ultramodern style or fashion.

ul·tra·mon·tane (ul′trə mon′tān), *adj.* **1.** beyond the mountains; transmontane. **2.** south of the Alps; Italian. **3.** supporting the absolute authority of the Pope in matters of faith and morals when he speaks as the head of the Roman Catholic Church.
—*n.* **1.** a person living south of the Alps. **2.** one of a party of the Roman Catholic Church maintaining the absolute authority of the Pope in matters of religious faith and ecclesiastical discipline.
[< Medieval Latin *ultramontanus* < Latin *ultrā* beyond + *mōns, montis* mountain]

ul·tra·mon·ta·nism (ul′trə mon′tə niz-əm), *n.* the doctrine of absolute papal supremacy.

ul·tra·mon·ta·nist (ul′trə mon′tə nist), *n.* a person belonging to the ultramontane party; promoter of ultramontanism.

ul·tra·mun·dane (ul′trə mun′dān), *adj.* **1.** beyond the world; beyond the limits of the known universe. **2.** beyond this present life. [< Latin *ultrāmundānus* < Latin *ultrā* beyond + *mundus* world]

ul·tra·na·tion·al (ul′trə nash′ə nəl, -nash′-nəl), *adj.* ultranationalistic.

ul·tra·na·tion·al·ism (ul′trə nash′ə nə-liz′əm, -nash′nə liz-), *n.* extreme nationalism.

ul·tra·na·tion·al·ist (ul′trə nash′ə nə-list, -nash′nə-), *adj.* ultranationalistic. —*n.* an adherent of ultranationalism: *In the area of foreign policy, most ultraconservatives are ultranationalists* (Harper's).

ul·tra·na·tion·al·is·tic (ul′trə nash′ə-nə lis′tik, -nash′nə-), *adj.* of ultranationalism or ultranationalists; extremely nationalistic: *Since internationalism is highly characteristic of science, no science can prosper under ultranationalistic regimes locked behind a closed door or iron curtain* (Bulletin of Atomic Scientists).

ul·tra-Or·tho·dox (ul′trə ôr′thə doks), *adj.* of or belonging to the extreme or ultrareligious wing of Orthodox Judaism: *The ultra-Orthodox . . . Rabbi Shneurson of the Lubavitch Hasidic dynasty released a circular letter condemning the teaching of the doctrines of evolution* (Jacob B. Agus).

ul·tra·phys·i·cal (ul′trə fiz′ə kəl), *adj.* beyond or transcending what is physical.

ul·tra·pure (ul′trə pyůr′), *adj.* more than pure; containing no visible or microscopic impurities: *ultrapure antiserum, ultrapure germanium.*

ul·tra·rad·i·cal (ul′trə rad′ə kəl), *adj.* excessively radical, especially in politics. —*n.* a person who is extremely radical.

ul·tra·red (ul′trə red′), *adj.* infrared.

ul·tra·re·li·gious (ul′trə ri lij′əs), *adj.* religious in the extreme; excessively religious.

ul·tra·right·ist (ul′trə rī′tist), *n.* a person who holds to an extremely conservative point of view, especially in politics. —*adj.* **1.** holding such a point of view. **2.** of or having to do with those who hold such a point of view.

ul·tra·son·ic (ul′trə son′ik), *adj.* supersonic: *Ultrasonic generators produce sound waves to clean miniature parts* (New York Times). [< *ultra-* + Latin *sonus* sound + English *-ic*]

ul·tra·son·i·cal·ly (ul′trə son′ə klē), *adv.* by means of ultrasonic waves or sound: *Materials such as tool steels and superalloys, although very hard and difficult to machine normally, are too tough to erode ultrasonically* (New Scientist).

ul·tra·son·ics (ul′trə son′iks), *n.* the science that deals with or investigates the energy generated by sound waves of 20,000 or more vibrations per second.

ul·tra·sound (ul′trə sound′), *n.* sound above a frequency of 20,000 vibrations per second; ultrasonic sound: *Williams irradiated a solution of virus with high-frequency sound waves. When he dried the solution and photographed the result, he found that the ultrasound had broken the viruses into little bits* (Scientific American).

ul·tra·struc·tur·al (ul′trə struk′chər əl), *adj.* of or having to do with ultrastructure.

ul·tra·struc·ture (ul′trə struk′chər), *n.* a structure with extremely fine details, invisible to an ordinary microscope: *In my own laboratory at present particular attention is being paid to the ultrastructure of neurosecretory systems in crustaceans and in vertebrates, using the electron microscope* (New Scientist).

ul·tra·trop·i·cal (ul′trə trop′ə kəl), *adj.* **1.** outside of the tropics. **2.** warmer than the tropics; very hot.

ul·tra·vi·o·let (ul′trə vī′ə lit), *adj.* **1.** of or having to do with the invisible part of the spectrum just beyond the violet. **2.** of or having to do with the ultraviolet rays. —*n.* the invisible part or range of the spectrum just beyond the violet: *The visible spectrum from violet to red comprises only a small part of the whole range of wavelengths radiated by a source such as the sun. The spectrum goes on into the ultraviolet in one direction and into the infrared in the other, where it is recorded by photography and other means* (Robert H. Baker). *Abbr.:* UV (no periods).

ultraviolet rays, the invisible rays in the part of the spectrum beyond the violet. They are present in sunlight, light from mercury-vapor lamps, etc., and are used for healing, forming vitamins, etc. Ultraviolet rays are more refrangible than violet rays as diffracted by a grating.

ul·tra vi·res (ul′trə vī′rēz), going beyond the powers granted by authority or by law: *His Lordship made a declaration in this action that the expulsion of the plaintiff . . . was invalid and ultra vires* (London Times). [< New Latin *ultra vires* (literally) beyond the power < Latin *ultrā* beyond, *vīrēs,* plural of *vīs, vīris* strength, force]

ul·tra·vi·rus (ul′trə vī′rəs), *n.* a virus which can go through the finest bacterial filters. [< *ultra*(microscopic) *virus*]

u·lu (ü′lü), *n.* a type of knife used by the Eskimos, especially by the women, for cutting blubber, etc.: *The ulu remains the ideal instrument for skinning seal* (Harper's). [< Eskimo *ulu*]

ul·u·lant (yül′yə lənt, ul′-), *adj.* howling. [< Latin *ululāns, -antis,* present participle of *ululāre;* see ULULATE]

ul·u·late (yül′yə lāt, ul′-), *v.i.,* **-lat·ed, -lat·ing. 1.** to howl, as a dog or wolf. **2.** to lament loudly. [< Latin *ululāre* (with English *-ate*[1]) howl]

ul·u·la·tion (yül′yə lā′shən, ul′-), *n.* **1.** a howl or wail. **2.** the act of howling or wailing.

U·lys·se·an (yü lis′ē ən), *adj.* **1.** of or having to do with Ulysses (or Odysseus), legendary king of Ithaca and hero of Homer's *Odyssey.* **2.** resembling Ulysses, as in craft or deceit, or in extensive wanderings. **3.** characteristic of Ulysses.

U·lys·ses (yü lis′ēz), *n.* **1.** the Latin name of Odysseus, the shrewdest of the Greek leaders in the Trojan War. **2.** a novel by James Joyce, published in 1922.

um (əm), *interj.* a low sound used to express hesitation, doubt, etc. [imitative. Compare HUM.]

U·may·yad (ü mī′ad), *n., pl.* **-yads, -ya·des** (-ə dēz). Omayyad.

um·bel (um′bəl), *n. Botany.* an indeterminate inflorescence consisting of a number of flower stalks or pedicels (rays), nearly equal in length and spreading from a common center, their summits forming a level or slightly curved surface. A simple umbel has only one set of rays, as in the ginseng; in a compound umbel the pedicels or rays each bear an umbel of flowers, as in the carrot and dill. [< Latin *umbella* parasol (diminutive) < *umbra* shade]

Umbel

um·bel·lar (um′bə lər), *adj.* umbellate.

um·bel·late (um′bə lit, -lāt), *adj. Botany.* **1.** of or like an umbel. **2.** having an umbel; forming an umbel or umbels. —**um′bel·late·ly,** *adv.*

um·bel·lat·ed (um′bə lā′tid), *adj.* umbellate.

um·bel·let (um′bə lit), *n.* an umbellule.

um·bel·li·fer (um bel′i fər), *n.* any plant of the parsley family. [< New Latin *umbellifer;* see UMBELLIFEROUS]

um·bel·lif·er·ous (um′bə lif′ər əs), *adj. Botany.* **1.** bearing an umbel or umbels: *The parsley and carrot are umbelliferous.* **2.** belonging to the parsley family. [< New Latin *umbellifer* (< Latin *umbella* parasol + *ferre* to bear) + English *-ous*]

um·bel·lu·late (um bel′yə lit, -lāt), *adj. Botany.* having or arranged in umbellules.

um·bel·lule (um′bəl yül, um bel′-), *n. Botany.* a small or partial umbel; an umbel formed at the end of one of the primary pedicels or rays of a compound umbel. [< New Latin *umbellula* (diminutive) < Latin *umbella;* see UMBEL]

um·ber[1] (um′bər), *n.* **1.** a heavy, brown earth consisting principally of alumina, iron oxide, and magnesium oxide, used in its natural state (raw umber) as a brown pigment, or after heating, in its calcined state (burnt umber), as a reddish-brown pigment.

2. a dark-brown or dark reddish-brown color, like that of either of these pigments. —*adj.* dark-brown or dark reddish-brown. —*v.t.* to stain or paint with umber; make of a dark-brown color. [< Italian (*terra di*) *ombra* (earth of) shade; *ombra* < Latin *umbra* shadow]

um·ber[2] (um′bər), *n.* **1.** a grayling. **2.** Also, **umber bird.** an umbrette. [< Old French *umbre* < Latin *umbra,* perhaps the same word as *umbra* shadow]

um·ber·y (um′bər ē), *adj.* **1.** of or having to do with umber. **2.** of the color of umber; dark brown.

um·bil·i·cal (um bil′ə kəl), *adj.* **1.** of or having to do with the navel or umbilical cord. **2.** formed, placed, or shaped like a navel or umbilical cord: *The Chapter-house is large, supported as to its arched roof by one umbilical pillar* (Daniel Defoe). [< Medieval Latin *umbilicalis* < Latin *umbilīcus* navel]

umbilical cord, 1. a cordlike structure attaching the navel of the embryo or fetus of a mammal to the placenta. **2.** something that binds or unites closely; a strong bond or tie: *He could never break the umbilical cord which held him to nature* (Emerson). **3.** an electric cable, fuel line, or the like, connected to a missile on its launching site and released just before launching.

umbilical hernia, hernia of the intestine at the navel; exomphalos.

um·bil·i·cate (um bil′ə kit, -kāt), *adj.* **1.** navel-shaped. **2.** having an umbilicus or navel.

um·bil·i·cat·ed (um bil′ə kā′tid), *adj.* umbilicate.

um·bil·i·ca·tion (um bil′ə kā′shən), *n.* **1.** a central depression resembling a navel. **2.** the condition of being umbilicate.

um·bil·i·cus (um bil′ə kəs, um′bə lī′-), *n., pl.* **-ci** (-sī). **1.** *Anatomy.* the navel; the depression or scar on the middle of the abdomen, marking the spot where the umbilical cord was attached. **2.** *Biology.* a small depression or hollow suggestive of a navel, such as the hilum of a seed. [< Latin *umbilīcus* navel]

um·bil·i·form (um bil′ə fôrm), *adj.* like a navel. [< *umbilicus* + *-form*]

um·ble pie (um′bəl), *Obsolete.* a pie made from umbles: *Mrs. Turner . . . did bring us an umble pie hot out of her oven* (Samuel Pepys). [< *umbles.* Compare HUMBLE PIE.]

um·bles (um′bəlz), *n.pl. Obsolete.* the heart, liver, lungs, etc., of an animal, especially of a deer, used as food; numbles. [variant of *numbles*]

um·bo (um′bō), *n., pl.* **um·bo·nes** (um bō′nēz), **um·bos. 1.** a projection or knob, often pointed, near or at the center of a shield. **2.** any elevation resembling this, as in the eardrum. **3.** *Zoology.* the oldest and most protuberant portion of a bivalve mollusk shell, located near the hinge. [< Latin *umbō, -ōnis* boss of a shield, knob, projection, related to *umbilīcus* navel]

um·bo·nal (um′bə nəl), *adj.* protuberant.

um·bo·nate (um′bə nit, -nāt), *adj.* **1.** having an umbo or boss. **2.** like an umbo or boss.

um·bo·nat·ed (um′bə nā′tid), *adj.* umbonate.

um·bo·na·tion (um′bə nā′shən), *n.* **1.** umbonate formation. **2.** an umbo.

um·bon·ic (um bon′ik), *adj.* umbonal.

um·bra (um′brə), *n., pl.* **-brae** (-brē). **1.** the completely shaded area where all of the direct light from a luminous body is cut off, as in an eclipse of the sun or moon.

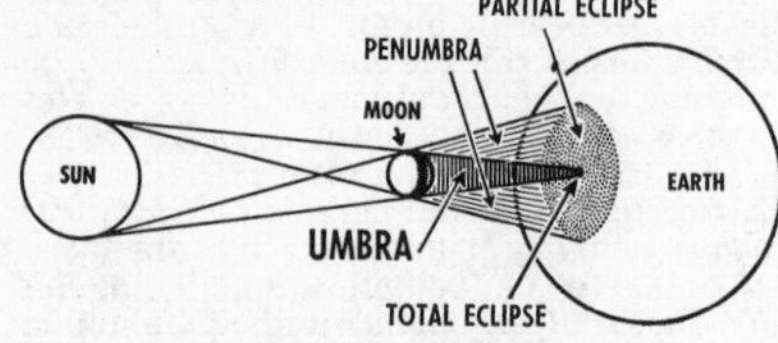

Umbra (def. 1) of solar eclipse

2. the dark inner part (nucleus) of a sunspot. **3.** *Obsolete.* shade; shadow. [< Latin *umbra*]

um·brage (um′brij), *n.* **1.** suspicion that one has been slighted or injured; feeling offended; resentment: *Unless my pacific disposition was displeasing, nothing else could have given umbrage* (George Washington). **2.** the foliage of trees, etc., providing shade: *at the foot of some tree of friendly umbrage* (Charlotte Brontë). **3.** *Archaic.* a faint likeness; shadowy outline or indication. **4.** *Obsolete.* shade; shadow.

take umbrage, to take offense; feel insulted or resentful: *He took umbrage at the slightest criticism.*

[< Old French *ombrage* < Latin *umbrāticum,* neuter of *umbrāticus* shadowy < *umbra* shade]

—**Syn. 1.** offense, pique.

um·bra·geous (um brā′jəs), *adj.* **1.** apt or disposed to take offense; easily insulted. **2.** revealing or displaying umbrage; offended; insulted. **3.** giving shade; shady: *a low-spreading and umbrageous tree* (Charlotte Brontë). **4.** covered over or surrounded by that which cuts off light; somewhat dark; shaded. —**um·bra′geous·ly,** *adv.* —**um·bra′geous·ness,** *n.*

um·bral (um′brəl), *adj.* of or having to do with an umbra: *the umbral shadow of an eclipse.*

um·brel·la (um brel′ə), *n.* **1.** a light, portable, folding frame covered with cloth, used as a protection against rain or sun. **2.** a barrage or screen of aircraft, especially fighter airplanes, to protect ground forces: *to land troops and supplies under an umbrella of fighters and light bombers.* **3.** any protective covering or shelter: *This is just short of the total 256 million bushels put under the Federal price umbrella for the entire season last year* (Wall Street Journal). *Mr. Ben-Gurion looks forward to the time when the American umbrella will be extended as firmly over Israel as it now is over Turkey* (Observer). **4.** the gelatinous disk- or bowl-shaped body of a jellyfish; bell.

—*adj.* **1.** resembling an umbrella. **2.** covering many or diverse elements: *Within this large umbrella framework it should be possible to work out the necessary system of nuclear control* (Listener).

[< Italian *ombrella, ombrello* < *ombra* shade < Latin *umbra*]

umbrella ant, the leafcutter.

umbrella bird, any of a group of tropical American birds, as a kind that is black with a crest of long, curved feathers resembling an umbrella; dragoon bird.

umbrella leaf, a North American plant of the barberry family, having either a large umbrellalike leaf on a stout petiole, or a flowering stem with two similar but smaller leaves.

um·brel·la·like (um brel′ə līk′), *adj.* resembling an umbrella: *an umbrellalike hat, an umbrellalike tree.*

umbrella palm, a palm with pinnate leaves, found on the Solomon Islands.

umbrella pine, a tall, evergreen tree of the taxodium family, shaped like an umbrella, with tufts of stiff, leaflike petioles resembling pine needles. It is native to Japan but is grown in many parts of the world for shade: *Long ago we had spent a week in June at San Sebastian to cool off under the umbrella pines from the heat of Madrid* (Alice B. Toklas).

umbrella tent, a tent made like an umbrella. The covered frame of an umbrella tent consists of ribs attached radially to a central staff or rod.

umbrella tree, 1. an American magnolia tree having long leaves radiating from the ends of the branches, suggesting umbrellas. **2.** any of several other trees whose leaves or habit of growth resemble an open umbrella.

um·brel·la·wort (um brel′ə wėrt′), *n.* any of a group of chiefly American herbs, having opposite leaves, and flower-containing involucres in loose, terminal panicles; four-o'clock.

um·brette (um bret′), *n.* an African and Arabian wading bird with deep-brown plumage, related to the storks and herons; umber; umber bird. [< French *umbrette* < New Latin *umbretta* < Latin *umbra* shade]

Um·bri·an (um′brē ən), *adj.* **1.** of or belonging to Umbria, an ancient region in central and northern Italy, or its inhabitants. **2.** of, having to do with, or designating the Italic dialect of ancient Umbria.

—*n.* **1.** a native or inhabitant of Umbria. **2.** a member of an Italic people who inhabited ancient Umbria. **3.** the Italic dialect, closely related to Oscan, spoken in ancient Umbria.

um·brif·er·ous (um brif′ər əs), *adj.* giving shade; umbrageous. [< Latin *umbrifer* (< *umbra* shade + *ferre* to bear) + English *-ous*] —**um·brif′er·ous·ly,** *adv.*

um·bril (um′brəl), *n.* the visor of a helmet. [variant of earlier *umbrel* < Old French *ombrel* shade, ultimately < Latin *umbra*]

um·brous (um′brəs), *adj.* lying in the shade; shadowed. [< Latin *umbrōsus* (with English *-ous*) < *umbra* shade]

Um·bun·du (əm bün′dü), *n., pl.* **-du** or **-dus. 1.** a member of a Bantu people of central Angola. **2.** the language of this people.

u·mi·ak or **u·mi·ack** (ü′mē ak), *n.* an open Eskimo boat worked by paddles. The umiak is very much broader and usually longer than a kayak and is made by covering a frame of wood or bone with skins. It is used especially by the women of a family or group of families to bring back the meat killed by the men, to transport a family and its possessions from place to place, etc. Also, **oomiac, oomiak.** [< Eskimo *umiaq* an open skin boat]

Umiak

um·laut (úm′lout), *n.* **1.** the partial assimilation of a vowel to another vowel in a preceding or following syllable. **2.** (in the Germanic languages) the partial assimilation of a stem vowel to a following vowel or semivowel, now generally lost but responsible for such pairs as English *man-men, foot-feet,* and *gold-gild* where the vowels of *men, feet,* and *gild* are the result of umlaut. **3.** a vowel that is the result of such partial assimilation, especially one written with the sign (¨) in German. **4.** the diacritic (¨) used over a vowel to indicate that it represents a different sound from the unmarked vowel, generally one resulting from umlaut, used especially in German, as in *Männer, König, süss.*

—*v.t.* **1.** to modify by umlaut. **2.** to write (a vowel) with an umlaut.

[< German *Umlaut* < *um* about (altering) + *Laut* sound]

ump (ump), *n. Slang.* umpire: *For Americans everywhere, there is no thrill like being there when the ump yells, "Play ball!"* (Time).

umph[1] (umf), *interj., n.* humph: *Giving a contemptuous umph, he walked on* (Harriet Beecher Stowe). [imitative]

umph[2] (ümf), *n. U.S. Slang.* oomph.

um·pir·age (um′pīr ij, -pə rij), *n.* **1.** the act of umpiring or arbitrating. **2.** the office or power of an umpire or arbiter. **3.** the decision of an umpire or arbiter.

um·pire (um′pīr), *n., v.,* **-pired, -pir·ing.** —*n.* **1.** a person who rules on the plays in a game and who sees that the rules are not broken: *The umpire called the ball a foul.* **2.** a person chosen to settle a dispute; arbiter, especially one whose decisions are binding on both or all parties to the dispute. —*v.i.* to act as an umpire. —*v.t.* to act as an umpire in (a game, dispute, etc.).

[Middle English *owmpere,* by misdivision < *a noumpere* a third man < Old French *nonper* odd, not even < *non* not (< Latin) + *per* equal < Latin *pār*]

—**Syn.** *n.* **1.** referee. **2.** judge, arbitrator, mediator.

um·pire·ship (um′pīr ship), *n.* the office of an umpire; arbitrament; umpirage.

ump·teen (ump′tēn′), *adj. Informal.* of a great but indefinite number; being one of a long series: *There have been umpteen versions of The Three Musketeers and none of 'em ever lost money* (Time).

ump·teenth (ump′tēnth′), *adj. Informal.* being the last of a great but indefinite number or of a long series: *the umpteenth version of Beauty and the Beast* (New York Times).

ump·ti·eth (ump′tē ith), *adj. Informal.* umpteenth: *Why . . . would anybody venture into the Eiger North face? . . . In July 1938 they tried for the umptieth time* (Canadian Saturday Night).

ump·ty (ump′tē), *adj. Informal.* of an indefinite number; many; umpteen: *umpty months, umpty times.*

UMT (no periods), Universal Military Training.

UMTS (no periods), Universal Military Training Service or System.

UMW (no periods) or **U.M.W.,** United Mine Workers.

un (un, ən), *n., pron. Dialect.* one: "*It [a rose] smells very sweet,*" *he said;* "*those striped uns have no smell*" (George Eliot).

un-[1], *prefix.* not; the opposite of, as in *uncomplimentary, unequal, unfair, unjust.* [Old English *un-*]

➔ **un-.** Although this dictionary lists hundreds of words only a fraction of the possible number of words are entered since *un-* is a prefix freely used in forming new words. The meaning of each of the words in the following list is found by substituting *not* for *un-*. See also **in-**[1], and **a-**[1] for usage notes.

un'a·bat'ing
un'ab·bre'vi·at'ed
un'a·bet'ted
un'a·bid'ing
un'a·bid'ing·ly
un'a·bol'ished
un'ab·rupt'
un·ab'sent
un'ab·solv'a·ble
un'ab·solved'
un'ab·sorbed'
un'ac·cen'tu·at'ed
un'ac·cept'ed
un'ac·cli'mat·ed
un'ac·cli'ma·tized
un'ac·com'plish·a·ble
un'ac·count'ed
un'ac·cu'mu·lat'ed
un'ac·cused'
un'a·chiev'a·ble
un'ac·knowl'edged
un'ac·quit'ted
un·ac'tu·at'ed
un'ad·dict'ed
un'ad·journed'
un'ad·just'a·ble
un'ad·just'ed
un'ad·mir'ing
un'ad·mit'ta·ble
un'ad·mit'ted
un'ad·mon'ished
un'a·dopt'a·ble
un'a·dopt'ed
un'a·dored'
un'ad·van·ta'geous
un·ad'ver·tised
un'aes·thet'ic
un'aes·thet'i·cal
un'af·fec'tion·ate
un'af·flict'ed
un'af·front'ed
un·ag'gra·vat'ed
un'ag·gres'sive
un·aimed'
un·aired'
un'a·larmed'
un'a·larm'ing
un'al·ien·at'ed
un·al'le'vi·at'ed
un'al·lot'ted
un'al·low'a·ble
un·al'pha·bet·ized
un·al'ter·ing
un'a·mazed'
un'a·mend'ed
un·am'pli·fied
un'an·a·lyt'ic
un·an'a·lyz'a·ble
un·an'a·lyzed
un·an'chored
un'an·nealed'
un·an'no·tat'ed
un'an·nounced'
un'a·noint'ed
un'an·tic'i·pat'ed
un·anx'ious
un'a·pol'o·get'ic
un'ap·plaud'ed
un'ap·plied'
un'ap·point'ed
un'ap·prov'ing
un·arched'
un'ar·gu·men'ta·tive
un'ar·rest'ed
un'ar·tic'u·lat'ed
un'ar·ti·fi'cial
un'as·sert'ed
un'as·so'ci·at'ed
un'as·soiled'
un'as·suaged'
un'as·sumed'
un'ath·let'ic
un'a·toned'
un'at·ten'u·at'ed
un'at·tired'
un'at·tract'ed
un·au'dit·ed
un'a·waked'
un·awed'
un·bait'ed
un·band'aged
un·banked'
un·bast'ed
un·bel'li·cose
un'bel·lig'er·ent
un·bend'a·ble
un'be·spok'en
un'be·trayed'
un'be·trothed'
un'be·wailed'
un·billed'
un·blanched'
un·boiled'
un·bombed'
un·boned'
un·bor'rowed
un·both'ered
un·bound'a·ble
un·bowd'ler·ized
un·branch'ing
un·brand'ed
un·breath'a·ble
un·bridge'able
un·bridged'
un-Brit'ish
un·broached'
un·bruised'
un·brushed'
un·bur'nished
un·but'tered
un·but'tressed
un·cal'cined
un·cal'cu·lat'ed
un·cal'cu·lat'ing
un·cal'en·dered
un·cap'i·tal·ized
un·car'bu·ret'ed
un·card'ed
un·car'ing
un·cas'trat·ed
un·catch'a·ble
un·caught'
un·cel'e·brat'ed
un·cen'sored
un·cen'sured
un·cen'tered
un'cer·e·mo'ni·al
un·cham'bered
un·chas'tened
un'chas·tised'
un·check'a·ble
un·cher'ished
un·chew'a·ble
un·chewed'
un·chic'
un·chilled'
un·chol'er·ic
un·chopped'
un·cho'sen
un·chris'tened
un·chron'i·cled
un·churned'
un·cit'ed
un·clar'i·fied
un·classed'
un·clas'sic
un·clas'si·cal
un·cleansed'
un·cleav'a·ble
un·climb'a·ble
un·climbed'
un·clipped'
un·clois'tered
un·cloyed'
un'co·ag'u·lat'ed
un·coat'ed
un·cod'i·fied
un'co·erced'
un·col'lared
un'col·lect'a·ble
un'col·lect'i·ble
un·col'o·nized
un·combed'
un'com·bin'a·ble
un·com'fort·ed
un·com'fort·ing
un'com·mand'ed
un'com·mem'o·rate
un'com·mend'a·ble
un'com·mis'sioned
un'com·pas'sion·ate
un·com'pen·sat'ed
un·com'pli·cat'ed
un'com·ply'ing
un'com·pre·hend'ed
un'com·pressed'
un·com'pro·mised
un'com·put'ed
un·com'rade·ly
un'con·ceal'a·ble
un'con·ced'ed
un'con·cert'ed
un'con·cil'i·at'ed
un'con·clud'ed
un'con·densed'
un'con·ferred'
un'con·fessed'
un'con·fid'ing
un'con·form'ing
un'con·fut'ed
un'con·geal'a·ble
un'con·gealed'
un'con·gest'ed
un'con·sci·en'tious
un'con·soled'
un'con·sol'i·dat'ed
un·con'so·nant
un·con'sti·tut'ed
un'con·strict'ed
un'con·struct'ed
un'con·struc'tive
un'con·sult'ed
un'con·sumed'
un'con·tam'i·nat'ed
un·con'tem·plat'ed
un'con·tend'ing
un'con·tract'ed
un'con·trite'
un'con·tro·ver'sial
un'con·tro·vert'i·ble
un'con·vened'
un'con·vict'ed
un'con·vinced'
un·cooled'
un·cor'dial
un·corked'
un·cor're·lat'ed
un·cor'set·ed
un·court'ed
un·cowed'
un'cre·a'tive
un·cred'it·ed
un·crip'pled
un·crit'i·ciz'a·ble
un·crowd'ed
un·crush'a·ble
un·crys'tal·line
un·crys'tal·liz'a·ble
un·crys'tal·lized
un·cur'dled
un·cured'
un·curled'
un·cur'rent
un·cursed'
un'cur·tailed'
un·cur'tained
un·cush'ioned
un·cus'tom·ar'y
un·cut'ta·ble
un·dan'gered
un·dan'ger·ous
un·dat'a·ble
un·daugh'ter·ly
un·daz'zled
un·dealt'
un'de·bat'a·ble
un'de·cayed'
un'de·cay'ing
un'de·ceived'
un'de·ci'phered
un'de·clared'
un'de·com·posed'
un·dec'o·rat'ed
un·ded'i·cat'ed
un'de·duc'i·ble
un'de·fac'a·ble
un'de·feat'a·ble
un'de·feat'ed
un·de·fen'si·ble
un'de·flect'ed
un'de·formed'
un'de·grad'ed
un'de·lay'a·ble
un'de·layed'
un'de·lin'e·at'ed
un'de·liv'er·a·ble
un'de·liv'ered
un'de·lud'ed
un·dem·o·crat'i·cal·ly
un'de·mon'strat'ed
un'de·nied'
un'de·nounced'
un'de·plored'
un'de·posed'
un'de·put'ed
un'de·rived'
un·der'o·gat'ing
un'de·rog'a·to'ry
un'de·scrip'tive
un·des'ig·nat'ed
un'de·sist'ing
un'de·stroyed'
un'de·tach'a·ble
un'de·tached'
un'de·voured'
un'di·ag·nosed'
un'dif·fused'
un'di·lat'ed
un·dipped'
un'dis·band'ed
un'dis·closed'
un'dis·con·cert'ed
un'dis·cord'ant
un'dis·cour'aged
un'dis·cred'it·ed
un'dis·crim'i·na·tive
un'dis·heart'ened
un'dis·il·lu'sioned
un'dis·man'tled
un'dis·mem'bered
un'dis·missed'
un'dis·patched'
un'dis·pelled'
un'dis·sect'ed
un'dis·sem'bling
un'dis·sem'i·nat'ed
un'dis·so'ci·at'ed
un'dis·tilled'
un'dis·tort'ed
un'dis·traught'
un'dis·tressed'
un·doc'tored
un'dog·mat'ic
un'do·mes'tic
un·dom'i·nat'ed
un·drained'
un·dram'a·tized
un·dried'
un·drilled'
un·dug'
un·dumped'
un·dust'ed
un'ec·cle'si·as'tic
un'e·clipsed'
un·ed'i·fied
un'ef·faced'
un'e·lat'ed
un'e·lec'tri·fied
un·el'e·vat'ed
un'e·lim'i·nat'ed
un'e·luc'i·dat'ed
un'e·man'ci·pat'ed
un'em·balmed'
un'em·bel'lished
un'em·bit'tered
un'em·brac'a·ble
un'e·mend'a·ble
un'e·mend'ed
un'em·phat'ic
un'em·pow'ered
un·emp'tied
un'en·coun'tered
un'en·cour'aged
un'en·dan'gered
un'en·dorsed'
un'en·fran'chised
un'en·gag'ing
un'en·grossed'
un'en·hanced'
un'en·joy'a·ble
un'en·joyed'
un'en·liv'ened
un'en·riched'
un'en·rolled'
un'en·slaved'
un·en'tered
un'en·tic'ing
un'en·ti'tled
un'e·nu'mer·at'ed
un·en'vy·ing
un'e·quipped'
un'e·rased'
un'e·rect'ed
un'e·rupt'ed
un'es·cort'ed
un'es·tab'lished
un'es·teemed'
un'es·thet'ic
un·es'ti·mat'ed
un'e·val'u·at'ed
un'e·vict'ed
un'ex·ag'ger·at'ed
un'ex·alt'ed
un'ex·am'ined
un·ex'ca·vat'ed
un'ex·change'a·ble
un'ex·cit'a·ble
un'ex·clud'ed
un'ex·cused'
un·ex'er·cised
un'ex·ert'ed
un'ex·haust'ed
un'ex·pand'ed
un'ex·pend'a·ble
un'ex·pend'ed
un·ex'pi·at'ed
un'ex·plic'it
un'ex·ploit'ed
un'ex·port'a·ble
un'ex·port'ed
un'ex·punged'
un'ex·ten'u·at'ed
un'ex·ter'mi·nat'ed
un·fad'ed
un·fall'en
un·fas'tened
un'fa·tigued'
un·fa'vored
un·fazed'
un·fear'ing
un·fed'er·at'ed
un'fe·lic'i·tous
un·fes'tive
un·filled'
un·filmed'
un·find'a·ble
un·fired'
un'flam·boy'ant
un·flat'tened
un·flat'tered
un·fla'vored
un·flawed'
un·flick'er·ing
un·flood'ed
un·flus'tered
un·fo'cused
un'for·bear'ing
un·ford'a·ble
un·for'est·ed
un'for·get'ful
un'for·get'ting
un·for'mi·da·ble
un'for·sak'en
un·found'
un'fra·ter'nal
un·freed'
un·freez'a·ble
un-French'
un·fre'quent·ly
un·fright'ened
un·fro'zen
un·furred'
un'gain·say'a·ble
un·gal'va·nized
un·gar'ri·soned
un·gir'dled
un·giv'en
un·gla'ci·at'ed
un·glad'dened
un·glo'ri·fied
un·glossed'
un·glued'
un·gowned'
un·grad'u·at'ed
un·graft'ed
un·grained'
un·grant'ed
un·ground'
un·grouped'
un'guar·an·teed'
un·guess'a·ble
un·gummed'
un·hailed'
un·halved'
un·ham'mered
un·hand'i·capped
un·har'assed
un·harm'ing
un·har'nessed
un·har'rowed
un·har'vest'ed
un·haunt'ed
un·heal'a·ble
un·healed'
un·heal'ing
un·helped'
un·hemmed'
un·hit'
un·hulled'
un·hur'ry·ing
un·husked'
un·hy'phen·at'ed
un·hy'phened
un'i·de·al·is'tic
un'il·lu'mined
un·il'lus·trat'ed
un'im·bued'
un·im'i·tat'ed
un·im'mu·nized
un'im·pair'a·ble
un·im'pli·cat'ed
un·im·preg'nat·ed
un'im·pres'sive
un'im·pris'oned
un'in·au'gu·rat'ed
un'in·ci'sive
un'in·clined'
un'in·clud'ed
un·in'cu·bat'ed
un'in·dem'ni·fied
un'in·dent'ed
un'in·den'tured
un·in'dexed
un·in'di·cat'ed
un'in·dict'a·ble
un'in·dict'ed
un'in·dorsed'
un'in·dus'tri·ous
un'in·fect'ed
un'in·fec'tious
un'in·fest'ed
un'in·flu·en'tial
un'in·fringed'
un'in·quir'ing
un'in·struc'tive
un·in'su·lat'ed
un'in·sur'a·ble
un'in·tel·lec'tu·al
un'in·ter'po·lat'ed
un'in·ter'pret·ed
un'in·terred'
un'in·tim'i·dat'ed
un'in·tox'i·cat'ed
un'in·vad'ed
un'in·vert'ed
un'in·vest'ed
un'in·ves'ti·gat'ed
un'in·voked'
un'in·volved'
un·i'roned
un·ir'ra·di·at'ed
un·ir'ri·gat'ed
un·is'sued
un·jack'et·ed
un·jad'ed
un·joined'
un·joy'ous
un·judged'
un'ju·di'cial
un·killed'
un·kin'dled
un·kink'
un·kissed'
un·knead'ed
un·knot'ted
un·la'beled
un·laced'
un·lac'quered
un·lad'en
un·lashed'
un·lat'ticed
un·laud'a·ble
un·learn'a·ble
un·les'sened
un·let'
un·lev'ied
un'li·bid'i·nous
un·life'like'
un·lift'a·ble
un·lik'a·ble
un·like'a·ble
un·liked'
un·lined'
un·liq'ue·fi'a·ble
un·lit'er·ar'y
un·lit'tered
un·liv'a·ble
un·lived'
un·live'ly
un·lov'a·ble
un·lov'er·like'
un·loy'al
un·lu'bri·cat'ed
un'lux·u'ri·ous
un·ly'ing
un·mag'ni·fied
un·mailed'
un'main·tain'a·ble
un'ma·li'cious
un·malt'ed
un·man'a·cled
un·man'ful
un·man'gled
un·man'i·fest
un·man'i·fest'ed
un·man'nish

un′man·u·fac′tur·a·ble
un·mapped′
un·mar′ket·ed
un·mar′tial
un′ma·ter′nal
un·mat′ted
un′ma·tured′
un′me·chan′i·cal
un·mech′a·nized
un·me′di·at′ed
un·meek′
un·meet′a·ble
un·mel′an·chol′y
un·melt′a·ble
un·melt′ed
un·mem′or·a·ble
un·men′aced
un·mend′a·ble
un·mend′ed
un·men′sur·a·ble
un·men′tion·a·bly
un·mer′ry
un′met·a·phys′i·cal
un·me′tered
un·mil′i·tant
un′mil·i·ta·ris′tic
un·milked′
un·milled′
un·mined′
un·min′is·tered
un·mint′ed
un′mi·rac′u·lous
un·mirth′ful
un·missed′
un′mis·tak′en
un·mix′a·ble
un·mod′ern·ized
un·mod′u·lat′ed
un·mold′ed
un·mol′li·fied
un·mol′ten
un·mon′i·tored
un·moot′ed
un·mort′gaged
un·mo′ti·vat′ed
un·mot′tled
un·mud′dled
un·muf′fled
un·mussed′
un·mut′ed
un′mys·te′ri·ous
un·mys′ti·fied
un·nailed′
un·na′tion·al·ized
un·nau′ti·cal
un′ne·ces′si·tat′ed
un·need′ed
un·net′ted
un·notched′
un·note′wor′thy
un′nu·mer′i·cal
un′o·beyed′
un′o·bliged′
un′o·blig′ing
un′o·blit′er·at′ed
un′ob·scured′
un′ob·tained′
un′ob·trud′ing
un·ob′vi·ous
un′oc·ca′sioned
un′of·fend′ed
un·of′fered
un·of′fi·cered
un·o′pen
un′op·pressed′
un·o′ri·ent·ed
un′or·nate′
un·os′si·fied
un·ox′i·dized
un·ox′y·gen·at′ed
un·pac′i·fied
un·pad′ded
un·paged′
un·pained′
un·paint′a·ble
un·paint′ed
un·pan′eled
un·pa′pered
un·par′a·phrased
un′pa·ren′tal
un·part′ed
un′par·tic′u·lar·ized
un·par′ti·san
un·past′ed
un·pas′teur·ized
un·patched′
un·pa′tron·ized
un·pa′tron·iz′ing
un′pe·dan′tic
un·peeled′
un·pen′e·trat′ed
un·penned′
un′per·fect′ed
un′per·fumed′
un·per′me·at′ed
un′per·suad′ed
un′pe·rused′
un′phil·an·throp′ic
un′phil·o·log′i·cal
un′pho·net′ic
un·pho′to·graphed
un′pic·tur·esque′
un·pig′ment·ed
un·pin′ioned
un·plait′ed
un·planned′
un·plas′tered
un·plat′ed
un·played′
un·pleat′ed
un·pledged′
un·plight′ed
un·ploughed′
un·plowed′
un·po′lar·ized
un′po·lit′i·cal
un·pol′y·mer·ized
un·pon′dered
un·pop′u·lat′ed
un′por·tend′ed
un′por·ten′tious
un′por·tray′a·ble
un·posed′
un·pos′ing
un′pos·sessed′
un′post·pon′a·ble
un·poured′
un·praised′
un′pre·dict′ed
un′pre·oc′cu·pied
un′pre·served′
un·pres′sur·ized
un′pre·sumed′
un·primed′
un·pro′bat·ed
un·probed′
un·proc′essed
un·proc′tored
un′pro·cur′a·ble
un′pro·cured′
un′pro·fessed′
un′pro·fess′ing
un′pro·mot′ed
un·proph′e·sied
un′pro·pi′ti·at′ed
un·propped′
un′pro·tect′a·ble
un′pro·test′ed
un′pro·vok′ing
un·pub′lish·a·ble
un·pul′ver·ized
un·punched′
un·punc′tu·at′ed
un·pur′chas·a·ble
un·pu′ri·fied
un′pur·sued′
un′pur·su′ing
un·quaffed′
un·quail′ing
un·quak′ing
un·qual′i·fy′ing
un·quar′an·tined
un·quar′ried
un·quar′tered
un·quelled′
un·quenched′
un·quiv′er·ing
un·quot′ed
un·ran′somed
un·rat′ed
un·ra′tioned
un·rav′aged
un·razed′
un·reach′a·ble
un·reaped′
un′re·buked′
un′re·called′
un′re·ceiv′a·ble
un′re·cep′tive
un′re·cip′ro·cat′ed
un′re·clined′
un′re·clin′ing
un′re·cord′a·ble
un′re·cruit′ed
un·rec′ti·fied
un′re·deem′a·ble
un′re·dressed′
un′re·duced′
un·reel′a·ble
un′re·flect′ed
un′re·flec′tive
un′re·formed′
un′re·freshed′
un′re·fresh′ing
un′re·frig′er·at′ed
un′re·fund′ed
un′re·fus′a·ble
un′re·fut′ed
un′re·gal
un′re·gard′ful
un·reg′i·ment′ed
un′re·gret′ted
un′re·hearsed′
un′re·ject′ed
un·rel′ished
un·rem′e·died
un′re·mit′ta·ble
un′re·ren′der·a·ble
un·ren′dered
un′re·nounced′
un′re·nowned′
un·rent′a·ble
un′re·peat′a·ble
un′re·peat′ed
un′re·pent′ing
un′re·placed′
un′re·ply′ing
un′re·port′ed
un′re·proach′able
un′re·proached′
un′re·pro·duc′i·ble
un′re·pu′di·at′ed
un′re·quired′
un′re·scind′ed
un′re·sent′ed
un′re·sent′ful
un′re·signed′
un′re·sist′ant
un′re·spect′ful
un′re·spond′ing
un·rest′ed
un′re·stored′
un′re·strain′a·ble
un′re·sumed′
un′re·tired′
un′re·touched′
un′re·tract′ed
un′re·treat′ing
un′re·trieved′
un′re·turned′
un′re·view′a·ble
un′re·viewed′
un′re·vised′
un′rhe·tor′i·cal
un·rhymed′
un·rhyth′mic
un·ribbed′
un·ri′fled
un·right′ed
un·rimed′
un·rinsed′
un·ris′en
un·roast′ed
un·roped′
un·rouged′
un·rubbed′
un·rum′pled
un·rust′ed
un·sac′ri·ficed
un·sad′dled
un′sa·lut′ed
un·sam′pled
un·sapped′
un·sat′ed
un·sa′ti·at′ed
un·sa′ti·at′ing
un·sat′is·fi′a·ble
un·sav′a·ble
un·saved′
un·sa′vored
un·sawn′
un·say′a·ble
un·scab′bard·ed
un·scaled′
un·scan′na·ble
un·scared′
un·scar′i·fied
un·scat′tered
un·scent′ed
un·scep′ti·cal
un·sched′uled
un·schol′ar·like′
un·scorched′
un·scored′
un·scorned′
un·scourged′
un·scraped′
un·scrubbed′
un·scru′ti·nized
un·seamed′
un·seat′ed
un·seg′re·gat′ed
un·seiz′a·ble
un′se·lect′ed
un′se·lec′tive
un′sen·sa′tion·al
un·sen′si·tive
un·sen′su·ous
un·sep′a·rat′ed
un·served′
un·sewed′
un·sewn′
un·sex′u·al
un·sharp′
un·sharp′ened
un·shat′tered
un·shaved′
un·sheathed′
un·shelled′
un·shield′ed
un·shift′ing
un·shock′a·ble
un·shocked′
un·short′ened
un·showed′
un·show′y
un·shroud′ed
un·shrunk′
un·shuf′fled
un·shunt′ed
un·shut′tered
un·si′lenced
un·sim′i·lar
un·sim′pli·fied
un·sim′u·lat·ed
un·singed′
un·skep′ti·cal
un·slacked′
un·slack′ened
un·slaugh′tered
un·sliced′
un·smeared′
un·smoked′
un·smooth′
un·smoothed′
un·smudged′
un·snagged′
un·snob′bish
un·soaked′
un·so′ber
un·sold′
un·sol′dier·like′
un·sol′dier·ly
un′so·lid′i·fied
un·sol′u·ble
un·solv′a·ble
un·soothed′
un·sor′did
un·sound′ed
un·soured′
un·sowed′
un·sown′
un·spe′cial·ized
un·spec′u·la′tive
un·spelled′
un·spiced′
un·splashed′
un·split′
un·spoil′a·ble
un·spoilt′
un·spon′sored
un·sprayed′
un·sprin′kled
un·squan′dered
un·squash′a·ble
un·squeam′ish
un·squeezed′
un·squelched′
un·stain′a·ble
un·stalked′
un·starched′
un·starred′
un·stat′ed
un·stemmed′
un·ster′i·lized
un·stif′fened
un·stig′ma·tized
un·stim′u·lat·ed
un·stim′u·lat·ing
un·stirred′
un·stitched′
un·stocked′
un·stop′pered
un′stra·te′gic
un·stripped′
un·stung′
un·styl′ish
un′sub·mit′ted
un′sub·mit′ting
un′sub·scribed′
un·sub′si·dized
un·sug′ared
un′sug·ges′tive
un·sum′moned
un·sunk′
un·su′per·vised
un′sur·prised′
un′sur·ren′dered
un′sur·ren′der·ing
un·swal′low·a·ble
un·swal′lowed
un·swol′len
un·sys′tem·a·tized
un·tab′u·lat′ed
un·tact′ful
un·tagged′
un·tan′gled
un·ta′pered
un·tapped′
un·tax′a·ble
un·ter′ri·fied
un·teth′ered
un·thatched′
un·thawed′
un′the·at′ri·cal
un·thought′ful
un·thwart′ed
un·tilt′ed
un·tinc′tured
un·toil′ing
un·to′taled
un·trad′ed
un′tra·di′tion·al
un′trans·act′ed
un′trans·ferred′
un′trans·mit′ted
un′trans·port′ed
un′trans·posed′
un·trapped′
un·treas′ured
un·treat′ed
un·trem′bling
un·trust′ing
un·tucked′
un·tune′ful
un·twilled′
un·twist′ed
un·typ′i·cal
un·us′a·ble
un·u′ti·liz′a·ble
un·u′ti·lized
un·vac′il·lat′ing
un·val′i·dat′ed
un·vault′ed
un·vaunt′ed
un·veiled′
un·ven′tured
un′vic·to′ri·ous
un·vin′di·cat′ed
un·vi′o·lent
un·vis′it·ed
un·vi′sored
un·vis′u·al·ized
un·vi′tal
un·vit′ri·fied
un·vo′cal·ized
un·vol′a·til·ized
un·vouched′
un·vul′can·ized
un·walled′
un·wan′ing
un·want′ed
un·warmed′
un·waste′ful
un·wast′ing
un·watched′
un·waxed′
un·wear′a·ble
un·weath′ered
un·weld′ed
un·wet′ted
un·whet′ted
un·whipt′
un·wife′like′
un·wife′ly
un·winc′ing
un·win′dowed
un·with′er·a·ble
un·wom′an·like′
un·won′
un·wood′ed
un·wound′
un·wo′ven
un·wreathed′
un·wrin′kled
un·youth′ful
un·zoned′

un-[2], *prefix.* to do the opposite of; do what will reverse the act, as in *undress, unlock, untie.* [Old English *un-, on-*]

➔ **Un-** is used freely to form verbs expressing the reversal of the action of the verb.

UN (no periods) or **U.N.,** United Nations: **a.** an international organization devoted to peace, to promoting economic and social welfare through special agencies, and to creating cultural understanding between nations. **b.** the nations that belong to this organization.

un·a·bashed (un′ə basht′), *adj.* not embarrassed, ashamed, or afraid; bold; open: *The unabashed nationalism of these aims has aroused the fiercest opposition to Mendès-France* (Harper's). —**Syn.** forward.

un·a·bash·ed·ly (un′ə bash′id lē), *adv.* in an unabashed manner; unashamedly; boldly; openly: *His warm-heartedness was sometimes unabashedly emotional* (London Times). *I should like to hear music that conveys some sort of genuine emotional experience, and does so simply and unabashedly* (New Yorker).

un·a·bat·ed (un′ə bā′tid), *adj.* not abated or lessened.

un·a·ble (un ā′bəl), *adj.* not able; lacking ability or power (to): *A baby is unable to walk or talk.* —**Syn.** incapable, unfit.

un·a·bridged (un′ə brijd′), *adj.* complete; not shortened: *to reissue a book in unabridged form.*

un·ac·a·dem·ic (un′ak ə dem′ik), *adj.* not academic; unconventional, as in literature or art.

un·ac·cent·ed (un ak′sen tid, un′ak sen′-), *adj.* not accented; not stressed.

un·ac·cept·a·ble (un′ak sep′tə bəl), *adj.* not acceptable; unsatisfactory; displeasing; not welcome: *All of the children had behavior problems severe enough to make them socially unacceptable* (Science News Letter). —**un′ac·cept′a·ble·ness,** *n.*

un·ac·cept·a·bly (un′ak sep′tə blē), *adv.* in an unacceptable manner.

un·ac·com·mo·dat·ed (un′ə kom′ə dā′tid), *adj.* **1.** not provided (with): *a few persons still unaccommodated with rooms for the night.* **2.** without accommodation or accommodations: *to leave no one unaccommodated.*

un·ac·com·mo·dat·ing (un′ə kom′ə dā′ting), *adj.* not accommodating or obliging:

She even liked his rugged manners and his rough, unaccommodating speech (Lytton Strachey).

un·ac·com·pa·nied (un′ə kum′pə nēd), *adj.* **1.** not accompanied. **2.** *Music.* without instrumental accompaniment. —**Syn. 1.** unattended, alone.

un·ac·com·plished (un′ə kom′plisht), *adj.* **1.** not accomplished. **2.** incomplete; without accomplishments.

un·ac·count·a·ble (un′ə koun′tə bəl), *adj.* **1.** that cannot be accounted for or explained; inexplicable: *He had an unaccountable foreboding that all was not right* (Frederick Marryat). **2.** that cannot be held to account; not responsible (for): *An imbecile is unaccountable for his actions.* —**un′ac·count′a·ble·ness,** *n.* —**Syn. 1.** incomprehensible.

un·ac·count·a·bly (un′ə koun′tə blē), *adv.* in a way that cannot be explained; strangely: *The chartered jet was roaring down the Orly runway on take-off. Unaccountably, it failed to lift* (Time).

un·ac·count·ed-for (un′ə koun′tid fôr′), *adj.* not accounted for or explained: *an unaccounted-for loss of customers.*

un·ac·cred·it·ed (un′ə kred′ə tid), *adj.* not accredited; not received; not authorized: *an unaccredited minister or consul.*

un·ac·cus·tomed (un′ə kus′təmd), *adj.* **1.** not accustomed (to): *a man unaccustomed to public life.* **2.** not familiar; unusual; strange: *unaccustomed surroundings.* —**Syn. 1.** unused.

un·ac·knowl·edged (un′ak nol′ijd), *adj.* not acknowledged; unrecognized; unavowed; unnoticed.

un·ac·quaint·ance (un′ə kwān′təns), *n.* lack of acquaintance or familiarity; lack of knowledge; ignorance.

un·ac·quaint·ed (un′ə kwān′tid), *adj.* not acquainted. —**un′ac·quaint′ed·ness,** *n.*

un·ac·quir·a·ble (un′ə kwīr′ə bəl), *adj.* not acquirable; not to be acquired or gained. —**un′ac·quir′a·ble·ness,** *n.*

un·ac·quired (un′ə kwīrd′), *adj.* **1.** not acquired. **2.** naturally belonging; innate.

un·act·a·ble (un ak′tə bəl), *adj.* not capable of being acted (on the stage): *"The Cenci" is no more unactable than "Titus Andronicus" or other of Shakespeare's lesser tragedies which, when they have been put on the stage, have turned out to contain wonderful dramatic matter* (Manchester Guardian).

un·act·ed (un ak′tid), *adj.* **1. a.** not acted or carried out in action; unperformed: *The fault unknown is as a thought unacted* (Shakespeare). **b.** not acted (on or upon); undisturbed: *I wish you to peruse it alone and unacted upon by any extraneous influence* (Theodore E. Hook). **2.** not performed on the stage: *His plays went unacted for many years.*

un·a·dapt·a·ble (un′ə dap′tə bəl), *adj.* not adaptable.

un·a·dapt·ed (un′ə dap′tid), *adj.* not adapted; unsuited; unfitted. —**un′a·dapt′ed·ness,** *n.*

un·ad·dressed (un′ə drest′), *adj.* not addressed; bearing no address, as a letter.

un·ad·mired (un′ad mīrd′), *adj.* not admired; not regarded with affection or respect; not admirable.

un·a·dorned (un′ə dôrnd′), *adj.* not adorned; without ornament or embellishment; plain: *Loveliness Needs not the foreign aid of ornament But is when unadorned adorned the most* (James Thomson).

un·a·dul·ter·at·ed (un′ə dul′tə rā′tid), *adj.* not adulterated; pure: *unadulterated flour. Eartha Kitt is an unadulterated delight in the principal role of this fantasy* (New Yorker).

un·ad·ven·tur·ous (un′əd ven′chər əs), *adj.* not adventurous; not bold or resolute.

un·ad·vis·a·ble (un′əd vī′zə bəl), *adj.* inadvisable.

un·ad·vised (un′əd vīzd′), *adj.* **1.** not advised; without advice. **2.** not prudent or discreet; rash: *It is too rash, too unadvis'd, too sudden* (Shakespeare). **3.** ill-advised. —**Syn. 2.** imprudent, unwise.

un·ad·vis·ed·ly (un′əd vī′zid lē), *adv.* in an indiscreet manner; rashly.

un·ad·vis·ed·ness (un′əd vī′zid nis), *n.* the character of being unadvised; imprudence; rashness; indiscretion.

UNAEC (no periods), United Nations Atomic Energy Commission.

un·af·fect·ed[1] (un′ə fek′tid), *adj.* not affected; not influenced; unchanged: *Many of these birds seem unaffected by climate* (Alfred R. Wallace). [< *un-*[1] + *affected*[1]] —**un′af·fect′ed·ly,** *adv.* —**un′af·fect′ed·ness,** *n.* —**Syn.** unmoved, unimpressed.

un·af·fect·ed[2] (un′ə fek′tid), *adj.* simple and natural; without affectation; straightforward; sincere: *easy, unaffected manners* (Jane Austen). [< *un-*[1] + *affected*[2]] —**un′af·fect′ed·ly,** *adv.* —**un′af·fect′ed·ness,** *n.* —**Syn.** unpretentious, artless.

un·af·fil·i·at·ed (un′ə fil′ē ā′tid), *adj.* not affiliated or associated; independent: *an unaffiliated labor union, candidate, or radio station.*

un·a·fraid (un′ə frād′), *adj.* not afraid; fearless: *The menace of the years finds, and shall find, me unafraid* (William Ernest Henley).

un·aid·ed (un ā′did), *adj.* not aided; without aid.

un·al·ien·a·ble (un āl′yə nə bəl, -ā′lē ə-), *adj.* that cannot be given away or taken away; inalienable: *We hold these truths to be self-evident, that all men are created equal, that they are endowed by their Creator with certain unalienable Rights, that among these are Life, Liberty and the pursuit of Happiness* (Declaration of Independence).

un·a·ligned (un′ə līnd′), *adj.* nonaligned.

un·a·live (un′ə līv′), *adj.* **1.** not alive. **2.** not awake or sensitive (to): *Dry, mechanical theorists, unalive to sentiment and fancy* (Leigh Hunt).

un·al·layed (un′ə lād′), *adj.* **1.** not allayed. **2.** *Obsolete.* unalloyed.

un·al·lied (un′ə līd′), *adj.* not allied; unrelated.

un·al·loyed (un′ə loid′), *adj.* that is itself alone; not mixed with or qualified by anything else: *unalloyed generosity.*

un·al·lur·ing (un′ə lůr′ing), *adj.* **1.** not tempting or enticing. **2.** not charming; unattractive: *The catalogue is far from handsome, what with poor photographs, crude color, and unalluring typography* (New Yorker).

un·al·ter·a·ble (un ôl′tər ə bəl), *adj.* that cannot be altered; not changeable; permanent in nature; fixed: *an unalterable policy.* —**Syn.** immutable.

un·al·ter·a·bly (un ôl′tər ə blē), *adv.* in a way that cannot be changed; permanently: *They recognized that they were now unalterably committed to the meeting, whatever its results might be* (New York Times).

un·al·tered (un ôl′tərd), *adj.* not altered; unchanged.

un·am·big·u·ous (un′am big′yů əs), *adj.* not ambiguous; unequivocal; plain; clear. —**un′am·big′u·ous·ly,** *adv.*

un·am·bi·tious (un′am bish′əs), *adj.* not ambitious; unaspiring; unpretending; modest: *Those who . . . pass their days in unambitious indolence* (James Boswell).

un-A·mer·i·can (un′ə mer′ə kən), *adj.* not American; not characteristic of or proper to America; foreign or opposed to the American character, usages, standards, etc.

un-A·mer·i·can·ism (un′ə mer′ə kə niz′əm), *n.* **1.** un-American character, belief, or activity. **2.** an un-American custom or trait.

un·a·mi·a·ble (un ā′mē ə bəl), *adj.* not amiable; ill-natured; ungracious.

un·a·mused (un′ə myüzd′), *adj.* not amused; not entertained; not cheered by diversion or relaxation: *Instead of being unamused by trifles, I am, as I well know I should be, amused by them a great deal too much* (Sydney Smith).

un·a·mus·ing (un′ə myü′zing), *adj.* not amusing. —**un′a·mus′ing·ly,** *adv.*

un·a·neled (un′ə nēld′), *adj.* *Archaic.* without having received extreme unction: *to die unaneled.* [< *un-*[1] + *anele* give extreme unction to + *-ed*[2]]

un·an·i·mat·ed (un an′ə mā′tid), *adj.* **1.** not animated; not possessed of life. **2.** not enlivened; not having spirit; dull; inanimate.

u·na·nim·i·ty (yü′nə nim′ə tē), *n.* complete accord or agreement; being unanimous. —**Syn.** harmony.

u·nan·i·mous (yü nan′ə məs), *adj.* **1.** in complete accord or agreement; mutually agreed: *to be unanimous in rejection of an offer.* **2.** characterized by or showing complete accord; concurred in by all: *He was elected president of his class by a unanimous vote.* [< Latin *ūnanimus* (with English *-ous*) < *ūnus* one + *animus* mind] —**u·nan′i·mous·ness,** *n.*

u·nan·i·mous·ly (yü nan′ə məs lē), *adv.* with complete agreement; without a single opposing vote: *The Committee then voted unanimously to send the bill to the Senate floor* (Wall Street Journal).

un·an·swer·a·ble (un an′sər ə bəl), *adj.* **1.** that cannot be answered; not admitting of any answer or reply: *an unanswerable argument. What remarks he could have made—sarcastic, bitter, unanswerable* (Arnold Bennett). **2.** that cannot be disproved: *an unanswerable proof.* —**un·an′swer·a·ble·ness,** *n.* —**Syn. 2.** irrefutable, irrefragable.

un·an·swer·a·bly (un an′sər ə blē), *adv.* in a manner not to be answered; beyond refutation.

un·an·swered (un an′sərd), *adj.* not answered: *an unanswered argument.*

un·ap·palled (un′ə pôld′), *adj.* not appalled; not daunted; fearless; dauntless.

un·ap·par·ent (un′ə par′ənt), *adj.* **1.** not apparent; obscure: *Bitter actions of despite, too subtle and too unapparent for law to deal with* (Milton). **2.** not visible: *The Zoroastrian definition of poetry, mystical, yet exact, "apparent pictures of unapparent natures"* (Emerson).

un·ap·peal·a·ble (un′ə pē′lə bəl), *adj.* **1.** (of a case) not subject to appeal to a higher court. **2.** (of a judge or a sentence, decision, etc.) that cannot be appealed against.

un·ap·peal·ing (un′ə pē′ling), *adj.* unattractive; devoid of interest or attraction: *Without some correlative understanding in the spectator, Titian's work . . . must be utterly dead and unappealing to him* (John Ruskin). —**un′ap·peal′ing·ly,** *adv.*

un·ap·peas·a·ble (un′ə pē′zə bəl), *adj.* not to be appeased; implacable; insatiable: *unappeasable hatred.*

un·ap·peas·a·bly (un′ə pē′zə blē), *adv.* in an unappeasable manner.

un·ap·peased (un′ə pēzd′), *adj.* not appeased.

un·ap·pe·tiz·ing (un ap′ə tī′zing), *adj.* not appetizing. —**un·ap′pe·tiz′ing·ly,** *adv.*

un·ap·pre·ci·at·ed (un′ə prē′shē ā′tid), *adj.* not appreciated; not properly valued or esteemed.

un·ap·pre·ci·at·ing (un′ə prē′shē ā′ting), *adj.* not appreciating; unappreciative: *drudging at low rates for unappreciating booksellers* (Charles Lamb).

un·ap·pre·ci·a·tive (un′ə prē′shē ā′tiv, -shə tiv), *adj.* not appreciative; wanting in appreciation; inappreciative: *He was a cold-blooded, unappreciative stick* (Leonard Merrick).

un·ap·pre·hend·ed (un′ap ri hen′did), *adj.* **1.** not apprehended; not taken. **2.** not understood, perceived, or conceived of.

un·ap·pre·hen·sive (un′ap ri hen′siv), *adj.* **1.** not apprehensive; not fearful or suspecting: *Careless of the common danger, and, through a haughty ignorance, unapprehensive of his own* (Milton). **2.** not intelligent; not quick in perception or understanding: *Unlearned, unapprehensive, yet impudent* (Milton). **3.** unconscious; not cognizant.

un·ap·prised (un′ə prīzd′), *adj.* not apprised; not previously informed: *You are not unapprised of the influence of this officer with the Indians* (Thomas Jefferson).

un·ap·proach·a·bil·i·ty (un′ə prō′chə bil′ə tē), *n.* the character or condition of being unapproachable.

un·ap·proach·a·ble (un′ə prō′chə bəl), *adj.* **1.** very hard to approach; distant in character; coolly aloof: *an unapproachable manner, unapproachable seclusion.* **2.** without an equal; unrivaled: *Rembrandt was an artist of unapproachable talent.* —**un′approach′a·ble·ness,** *n.* —**Syn. 2.** peerless, matchless.

un·ap·proach·a·bly (un′ə prō′chə blē), *adv.* so as to be unapproachable.

un·ap·proached (un′ə prōcht′), *adj.* not approached; unrivaled.

un·ap·pro·pri·at·ed (un′ə prō′prē ā′tid), *adj.* not appropriated; not taken possession of; not assigned or allotted: *No contestant qualified, so the prize remained unappropriated.*

un·ap·proved (un′ə prüvd′), *adj.* not approved; not having received approval.

un·apt (un apt′), *adj.* **1.** not fit or appropriate; unsuitable: *an unapt remark.* **2.** not normally likely or inclined; not prone by habit or nature: *a mind unapt to wander.* **3.** not skillful or dexterous; awkward; clumsy: *to be unapt with a hammer.* **4.** not quick to learn; somewhat backward or stupid. —**un·apt′ly,** *adv.* —**un·apt′ness,** *n.*

un·ar·gu·a·ble (un är′gyů ə bəl), *adj.* that cannot be argued with or against; indisputable: *The proposition that talking is better than warring is unarguable* (Wall Street Journal).
un·ar·gu·a·bly (un ar′gyů ə blē), *adv.* indisputably: *Master Sergeant Kakuo Shimada was unarguably in command* (New Yorker).
un·ar·gued (un är′gyüd), *adj.* **1.** not argued or debated. **2.** not argued against.
un·arm (un ärm′), *v.t.* to take weapons or armor from; disarm: *To unarm his people of weapons, money, and all means whereby they may resist his power* (Sir Walter Raleigh). —*v.i.* **1.** to lay down one's weapons. **2.** to take off armor: *Unarm, unarm, and do not fight today* (Shakespeare).
un·armed (un ärmd′), *adj.* **1.** without weapons; not armed: *an unarmed man.* **2.** (of plants and animals) without horns, teeth, prickles, spines, thorns, etc. **3.** *Archaic.* without armor. —**Syn. 1.** weaponless.
un·ar·mored (un är′mərd), *adj.* not armored: *an unarmored cruiser.*
un·ar·moured (un är′mərd), *adj. Especially British.* unarmored.
un·art·ful (un ärt′fəl), *adj.* **1.** not artful; artless; not having cunning; guileless; frank; genuine: *I'm sure unartful truth lies open in her mind* (John Dryden). **2.** wanting in skill; inartistic.
un·ar·tis·tic (un′är tis′tik), *adj.* inartistic.
un·as·cer·tain·a·ble (un′as ər tā′nə bəl), *adj.* not ascertainable; that cannot be certainly known, found out, or determined: *The percentage of American makes among small cars is unascertainable* (Harper's).
un·as·cer·tained (un′as ər tānd′), *adj.* not ascertained; not certainly known or determined.
un·a·shamed (un′ə shāmd′), *adj.* not ashamed; without shame: *Coleridge's words have the unashamed nakedness of Scripture* (Lowell).
un·a·sham·ed·ly (un′ə shā′mid lē), *adv.* in an unashamed manner; openly: *At the first run-through she had such power that a critical audience of theatrical professionals was sobbing unashamedly at the final line* (Time). *The novels or biographies are usually unashamedly hearty, sentimental, virile, particularly in regard to priests* (New York Times).
un·asked (un askt′, -äskt′), *adj.* not asked; unsolicited.
un·as·pi·rat·ed (un as′pə rā′tid), *adj.* not aspirated; pronounced without an aspirate.
un·a·spir·ing (un′ə spīr′ing), *adj.* not aspiring; unambitious. —**un′a·spir′ing·ly,** *adv.* —**un′a·spir′ing·ness,** *n.*
un·as·sail·a·ble (un′ə sā′lə bəl), *adj.* not assailable; safe from attack; incontestable.
un·as·sail·a·bly (un′ə sā′lə blē), *adv.* so as not to be assailed; incontestably: *It [the song] remains unassailably a masterpiece* (London Times).
un·as·sailed (un′ə sāld′), *adj.* not assailed or attacked.
un·as·ser·tive (un′ə sėr′tiv), *adj.* not insistent or forward; reserved in speech or actions: *With the little-known and unassertive Rodger in office, the executive committee would clearly have more authority* (Time). —**un′as·ser′tive·ness,** *n.*
un·as·sign·a·ble (un′ə sī′nə bəl), *adj.* not assignable.
un·as·signed (un′ə sīnd′), *adj.* not assigned.
un·as·sim·i·la·ble (un′ə sim′ə lə bəl), *adj.* that cannot be assimilated: *Major and sometimes marginal uglinesses . . . seem unassimilable in art unless they are caricatured* (Louise Bogan).
un·as·sim·i·lat·ed (un′ə sim′ə lā′tid), *adj.* **1.** not made to resemble; not brought into a relation of similarity. **2.** *Physiology.* not united with and actually transformed into the fluid or solid constituents of the living body; not taken into the system as nutriment: *food still unassimilated.*
un·as·sist·ed (un′ə sis′tid), *adj.* not assisted; unaided.
un·as·sum·ing (un′ə sü′ming), *adj.* not putting on airs; modest: *a quiet, unassuming person.* —**un′as·sum′ing·ly,** *adv.* —**un′as·sum′ing·ness,** *n.* —**Syn.** humble, unaffected.
un·as·sured (un′ə shůrd′), *adj.* **1.** not assured; not sure, confident, or certain. **2.** not securely or safely established. **3.** not insured, as against loss.

un·at·tached (un′ə tacht′), *adj.* **1.** not attached. **2.** not connected or associated with a particular body, group, organization, or the like; independent. **3.** not engaged or married.
un·at·tain·a·ble (un′ə tā′nə bəl), *adj.* not attainable; beyond the possibility of attainment; never to be attained or reached. —**un′at·tain′a·ble·ness,** *n.*
un·at·tain·a·bly (un′ə tā′nə blē), *adv.* in an unattainable manner; so as to be unattainable.
un·at·tained (un′ə tānd′), *adj.* not attained or reached.
un·at·taint·ed (un′ə tān′tid), *adj.* **1.** not attainted legally. **2.** *Archaic.* unsullied, unblemished, or without defect.
un·at·tempt·ed (un′ə temp′tid), *adj.* not attempted; not tried or essayed; not subjected to any attempt.
un·at·tend·ed (un′ə ten′did), *adj.* **1.** without attendants; alone. **2.** not accompanied. **3.** not taken care of; not attended to.
un·at·tend·ing (un′ə ten′ding), *adj.* not attending or giving heed; inattentive.
un·at·test·ed (un′ə tes′tid), *adj.* not attested; not confirmed by witness or testimony.
un·at·trac·tive (un′ə trak′tiv), *adj.* not attractive; plain; homely. —**un′at·trac′tive·ly,** *adv.* —**un′at·trac′tive·ness,** *n.*
u·nau (yü nô′, ü nou′), *n.* the South American two-toed sloth. [< French *unau* < a Brazilian native name *unaü;* origin uncertain]

Unau, carrying young (20 in. long)

un·aus·pi·cious (un′ôs pish′əs), *adj.* inauspicious.
un·au·then·tic (un′ô then′tik), *adj.* not authentic, reliable, or genuine.
un·au·then·ti·cat·ed (un′ô then′tə kā′tid), *adj.* not authenticated; not established as authentic.
un·au·then·tic·i·ty (un′ô then tis′ə tē), *n.* unauthentic character; want of authenticity.
un·au·thor·i·ta·tive (un′ə thôr′ə tā′tiv, -thor′-), *adj.* not authoritative; lacking authority. —**un′au·thor′i·ta′tive·ly,** *adv.* —**un′au·thor′i·ta′tive·ness,** *n.*
un·au·thor·ized (un ô′thə rīzd), *adj.* not authorized; not duly commissioned; not warranted by proper authority.
un·a·vail·a·bil·i·ty (un′ə vā′lə bil′ə tē), *n., pl.* **-ties. 1.** the quality or condition of being unavailable: *Part of the reason for the slow progress with nucleic acids was the unavailability of pure material for analysis* (Scientific American). **2.** that which is unavailable: *Faced with commitments, budget limitations, and unavailabilities, he will often make the fatal compromise* (New York Times).
un·a·vail·a·ble (un′ə vā′lə bəl), *adj.* **1.** not available. **2.** of no avail; ineffectual. **3.** not suitable or ready for use. —**un′a·vail′a·ble·ness,** *n.*
un·a·vail·ing (un′ə vā′ling), *adj.* not successful; futile; useless: *unavailing efforts.* —**un′a·vail′ing·ly,** *adv.* —**Syn.** ineffectual.
un·a·venged (un′ə venjd′), *adj.* not avenged.
un·a·void·a·ble (un′ə voi′də bəl), *adj.* **1.** that cannot be avoided; inevitable: *an unavoidable conclusion.* **2.** *Law, Archaic.* not liable to be voided. —**un′a·void′a·ble·ness,** *n.* —**Syn. 1.** inescapable.
un·a·void·a·bly (un′ə voi′də blē), *adv.* because of something that cannot or could not be avoided or prevented; inevitably.
un·a·vowed (un′ə voud′), *adj.* not avowed; secret.
un·a·vow·ed·ly (un′ə vou′id lē), *adv.* in an unavowed manner; secretly.
un·a·wak·ened (un′ə wā′kənd), *adj.* not awakened.
un·a·wak·en·ing (un′ə wā′kə ning), *adj.* having no awakening: *stretched out . . . in eternal, unawakening sleep* (W. H. Hudson).
un·a·ware (un′ə wãr′), *adj.* **1.** not aware; unconscious: *to be unaware of an approaching storm.* **2.** reckless; rash: *And like the rest I grew desperate and unaware* (Shelley). —**un′a·ware′ness,** *n.*
un·a·wares (un′ə wãrz′), *adv.* **1.** without knowing: *Some have entertained angels unawares* (Hebrews 13:2). **2.** without being expected; by surprise: *The police caught the burglar unawares. Age steals upon us unawares* (Matthew Prior). —**Syn. 1.** unconsciously. **2.** unexpectedly.
un·backed (un bakt′), *adj.* **1.** not backed, helped, or supported; unaided. **2.** not bet on. **3.** *Archaic.* that has never been ridden; not yet broken to the bit, saddle, etc.
un·bail·a·ble (un bā′lə bəl), *adj.* not bailable; not admitting of bail, as an offense.
un·baked (un bākt′), *adj.* **1.** not baked; not yet cooked by baking: *unbaked bread.* **2.** not mature; undeveloped.
un·bal·ance (un bal′əns), *n., v.,* **-anced, -anc·ing.** —*n.* lack of balance; unbalanced condition; imbalance. —*v.t.* to throw out of balance; disorder or derange.
un·bal·anced (un bal′ənst), *adj.* **1.** not balanced. **2.** not entirely sane: *an unbalanced mind.* **3.** not in or brought to an equality of debit and credit; not in balance: *an unbalanced account.*
un·bal·last·ed (un bal′ə stid), *adj.* **1.** not ballasted. **2.** not properly steadied or regulated.
un·band·ed (un ban′did), *adj.* having no band, especially in the sense of being stripped of a band, or lacking one where one is needed: *Your bonnet unbanded* (Shakespeare).
un·bap·tized (un bap′tīzd), *adj.* not baptized.
un·bar (un bär′), *v.t., v.i.,* **-barred, -barring. 1.** to remove the bars from; unfasten the bolts of; unlock. **2.** to make possible entry into (a place) or progress along (a way); open up.
un·barbed (un bärbd′), *adj.* **1.** not having a barb or barbs. **2.** *Obsolete.* not shaved, sheared, or mowed.
un·bar·bered (un bär′bərd), *adj.* not barbered; unshaven; untrimmed.
un·bat·ed (un bā′tid), *adj.* **1.** undiminished; unabated: *with unbated zeal* (Scott). **2.** *Obsolete.* not blunted or dull: *a sword unbated* (Shakespeare).
un·bathed (un bāᴛʜd′), *adj.* **1.** not bathed. **2.** not wet.
un·bear (un bãr′), *v.t.,* **-bore, -borne** or **-born, -bear·ing.** to free (a horse) from the checkrein (bearing rein).
un·bear·a·ble (un bãr′ə bəl), *adj.* that cannot be endured: *The pain from a severe toothache is almost unbearable.* —**un·bear′a·ble·ness,** *n.* —**Syn.** intolerable, insufferable.
un·bear·a·bly (un bãr′ə blē), *adv.* in an unbearable manner; intolerably.
un·beard·ed (un bir′did), *adj.* having no beard; beardless: *the yet unbearded grain* (John Dryden); *th' unbearded youth* (Ben Jonson).
un·bear·ing (un bãr′ing), *adj.* infertile; unproductive; barren: *Fruit trees must be continually lacerated to decrease the growth of unbearing wood* (C.R. Smith).
un·beat·a·ble (un bē′tə bəl), *adj.* that cannot be beaten, overcome, or surpassed: *The hand was unbeatable, declarer losing only one trick* (New York Times). *The immense strength-weight ratio of beryllium makes it unbeatable for aircraft structures* (New Scientist). *As unbeatable in retirement as he was at El Alamein, Monty scores a breakthrough on the autobiography front* (Time).
un·beat·a·bly (un bē′tə blē), *adv.* in an unbeatable manner: *unbeatably fast, unbeatably clever.*
un·beat·en (un bē′tən), *adj.* **1.** not defeated or surpassed. **2.** not trodden; not traveled: *unbeaten paths.* **3.** not struck, pounded, or whipped: *unbeaten eggs.*
un·beau·ti·ful (un byü′tə fəl), *adj.* not beautiful; plain; ugly: *Just south of Sennen there is another site, useful but unbeautiful, a caravan park owned by the National Trust* (Listener).
un·be·com·ing (un′bi kum′ing), *adj.* **1.** not becoming; not appropriate: *unbecoming clothes.* **2.** not fitting; not proper; unseemly: *unbecoming behavior.* —**un′be·com′ing·ly,** *adv.* —**un′be·com′ing·ness,** *n.* —**Syn. 1.** inappropriate. **2.** unsuitable.
un·be·fit·ting (un′bi fit′ing), *adj.* not befitting; unbecoming; unseemly. —**un′be·fit′ting·ly,** *adv.* —**un′be·fit′ting·ness,** *n.*
un·be·friend·ed (un′bi fren′did), *adj.* not befriended; not supported by friends; having no friendly aid: *Alas for Love! And Truth who wanderest lone and unbefriended* (Shelley).
un·be·got·ten (un′bi got′ən), *adj.* not begotten; not born.

un·be·gun (un′bi gun′), *adj.* **1.** not yet begun. **2.** *Obsolete.* having had no beginning; eternal.
un·be·hold·en (un′bi hōl′dən), *adj.* **1.** not beheld; unseen. **2.** not beholden; not under obligation (to).
un·be·known (un′bi nōn′), *adj.* **1.** not known (to): *to arrive unbeknown to anyone.* **2.** without the knowledge of others; in secrecy: *My love rose up so early and stole out unbeknown* (A.E. Housman).
un·be·knownst (un′bi nōnst′), *adj.* unbeknown: *He had planned, . . . unbeknownst to the second Mrs. Mannheim, to go to the tiny Jewish cemetery some ten miles out of town* (James Purdy).
un·be·lief (un′bi lēf′), *n.* lack of belief, especially in matters of religious doctrine or faith: *Belief consists in accepting the affirmations of the soul; unbelief, in denying them* (Emerson).
—**Syn. Unbelief, disbelief** mean lack of belief. **Unbelief** suggests only lack of belief in something offered or held as true, with no positive feelings one way or the other: *Nowadays there is general unbelief in the idea that some people are witches.* **Disbelief** suggests a positive refusal to believe: *He expressed his disbelief in universal military training.*
un·be·liev·a·ble (un′bi lē′və bəl), *adj.* not believable; incredible.
un·be·liev·a·bly (un′bi lē′və blē), *adv.* incredibly: *The last decade has brought the introduction of unbelievably fine petunias* (New York Times).
un·be·lieved (un′bi lēvd′), *adj.* **1.** not believed, credited, or trusted: *As I, thus wrong'd, hence unbelieved go* (Shakespeare). **2.** incredible.
un·be·liev·er (un′bi lē′vər), *n.* **1.** a person who does not believe. **2.** a person who does not believe in a particular religion. **3.** a person who is skeptical of Christ's revelation or mission.
un·be·liev·ing (un′bi lē′ving), *adj.* **1.** not believing; doubting: *an unbelieving smile.* **2.** adhering to or inclined toward agnosticism or atheism; not religious. **3.** not Christian; infidel; heathen. —**un′be·liev′ing·ly,** *adv.* —**Syn. 1.** skeptical, incredulous, suspicious, distrustful.
un·be·loved (un′bi luvd′), *adj.* not beloved.
un·belt (un belt′), *v.t.* **1.** to remove (a sword, etc.) by unfastening the belt. **2.** *Obsolete.* to ungird; unbind.
un·bend (un bend′), *v.,* **-bent** or **-bend·ed, -bend·ing.** —*v.t.* **1.** to remove the curves, bends, etc., from; straighten: *a wire hard to unbend.* **2.** to release from strain; relax or cause to relax: *to unbend a bow. She unbent her mind afterwards—over a book* (Charles Lamb). **3.** *Nautical.* **a.** to untie or loosen (a rope, etc.) from its attachment. **b.** to unfasten (a sail) from its spar or stay. —*v.i.* **1.** to straighten: *The wire was hard and it would not unbend.* **2.** to relax: *Grandpa unbent and behaved like a boy.*
un·bend·ing (un ben′ding), *adj.* **1.** not bending or curving; rigid. **2.** not yielding; stubborn; inflexible; firm: *an unbending attitude.* —*n.* relaxation. —**un·bend′ing·ly,** *adv.* —**un·bend′ing·ness,** *n.*
un·ben·e·ficed (un ben′ə fist), *adj.* not enjoying or having a benefice.
un·ben·e·fit·ed (un ben′ə fit′id), *adj.* having received no benefit or advantage.
un·be·night·ed (un′bi nī′tid), *adj.* not benighted; never visited by darkness.
un·be·nign (un′bi nīn′), *adj.* not benign; malignant.
un·bent (un bent′), *v.* a past tense and a past participle of **unbend.** —*adj.* not bent or curved; unbowed: *her unbent will's majestic pride* (John Greenleaf Whittier).
un·be·seem·ing (un′bi sē′ming), *adj.* not beseeming; unbecoming.
un·be·sought (un′bi sôt′), *adj.* not besought; not sought by petition or entreaty.
un·bi·ased or **un·bi·assed** (un bī′əst), *adj.* not prejudiced; impartial; fair: *an unbiased witness, an unbiased opinion.* —**Syn.** disinterested.
un·bib·li·cal (un bib′lə kəl), *adj.* not of, according to, or in the Bible: *The custom of representing Faith and Reason as opposites, is unbiblical and pernicious* (Edward White).
un·bid (un bid′), *adj.* unbidden.
un·bid·da·ble (un bid′ə bəl), *adj.* **1.** *British.* not to be commanded; not obedient: *The unbiddable spirit of perfection might come or it might not* (Paul Jennings). **2.** (of a hand or suit in cards) not strong enough to justify a bid.
un·bid·den (un bid′ən), *adj.* **1.** without invitation; not invited: *an unbidden guest.* **2.** without being ordered; not commanded: *And beasts themselves would worship; camels knelt unbidden* (Tennyson).
un·bind (un bīnd′), *v.t.,* **-bound, -bind·ing.** to release from bonds or restraint; untie; unfasten; let loose. [Old English *unbindan* < *un-* un-² + *bindan* to bind] —**Syn.** detach, loosen, free.
un·bit·ted (un bit′id), *adj.* **1.** unbridled; unrestrained: *conflicts of unbitted nature with too rigid custom* (Robert Louis Stevenson). **2.** freed of the bit: *an unbitted horse.*
un·blam·a·ble or **un·blame·a·ble** (un blā′mə bəl), *adj.* not blamable; blameless. —**un·blam′a·ble·ness** or **un·blame′a·ble·ness,** *n.*
un·blam·a·bly or **un·blame·a·bly** (un blā′mə blē), *adv.* in an unblamable manner; so as to incur no blame.
un·blamed (un blāmd′), *adj.* not blamed; free from censure; innocent: *So . . . unblamed a life* (Ben Jonson).
un·bleached (un blēcht′), *adj.* not bleached; not made white by bleaching: *unbleached linen.*
un·blem·ished (un blem′isht), *adj.* not blemished; without blemish; flawless; spotless; unsullied: *unblemished integrity* (Macaulay).
un·blenched (un blencht′), *adj.* **1.** unflinching. **2.** not soiled; unstained.
un·blessed or **un·blest** (un blest′), *adj.* **1.** not favored or made happy; not blessed: *unblessed with children, unblessed by laughter.* **2.** that has not been consecrated; not holy: *unblessed ground.* **3.** deprived of or excluded from blessing or benediction: *And there his corpse, unblessed, is hanging still* (John Dryden). **4.** unholy; evil; wicked. **5.** unhappy; miserable; wretched.
un·blink·ing (un bling′king), *adj.* **1.** not blinking; remaining open: *I can still see Mama watching him, her hand pressed tight across her mouth, her eyes wide and unblinking* (Atlantic). *She had watched the world with a solemn, unblinking stare* (New Yorker). **2.** without flinching or wavering; steady: *unblinking opposition. He looks over his twelve Caesars, from Julius to Domitian, with a methodical eye, unblinking in the face of some of the most outrageous spectacles in history* (Newsweek). **3.** forthright; candid: *an unblinking study of two wild days in the dull, woolly middle-class lives of Mark and Antonia Painton* (New Yorker). —**un·blink′ing·ly,** *adv.*
un·bliss·ful (un blis′fəl), *adj.* unhappy.
un·block (un blok′), *v.t.* **1.** to release from obstruction; remove the obstruction from: *to unblock a dam. London was once again the world antiques capital, with relaxed British trade restrictions unblocking the flow of merchandise to and from the highly esteemed London dealers* (Newsweek). **2.** (in bridge) to permit (a suit in another hand) to be run: *By discarding his singleton ace of spades, the declarer unblocked dummy's spades.*
un·blood·ied (un blud′id), *adj.* not made bloody.
un·blot·ted (un blot′id), *adj.* **1.** not blotted. **2.** not blotted out; not deleted; not erased.
un·blown¹ (un blōn′), *adj.* **1.** not driven, tossed, or fanned by the wind: . . . *on fields of unblown mist* (Bayard Taylor). **2.** not sounded, as a wind instrument: *The tents were all silent, the banners alone, the lances unlifted, the trumpet unblown* (Byron).
un·blown² (un blōn′), *adj.* **1.** (of flowers) unopened; still in the bud: *The little flowers which we see unblown in the morning and withered at night* (Arthur Golding). **2.** not matured; young; inchoate: *How yet unripe we were, unblown, unhardened* (John Fletcher).
un·blurred (un blėrd′), *adj.* not blurred; distinct: *The sky was absolutely unblurred, and thick . . . with stars* (Sabine Baring-Gould).
un·blush·ing (un blush′ing), *adj.* **1.** unabashed; shameless: *unblushing servility.* **2.** not blushing or reddening. —**un·blush′ing·ly,** *adv.* —**Syn. 1.** brazen, impudent.
un·boast·ful (un bōst′fəl), *adj.* not boasting; unassuming; modest.
un·bod·ied (un bod′ēd), *adj.* **1.** not having a body; incorporeal. **2.** removed from the body; disembodied.
un·bolt (un bōlt′), *v.t., v.i.* to draw back the bolts of (a door, etc.); unbar; unlock.
un·bolt·ed¹ (un bōl′tid), *adj.* not bolted or fastened; unlocked: *an unbolted door.*
un·bolt·ed² (un bōl′tid), *adj.* **1.** not sifted: *unbolted flour.* **2.** *Obsolete.* rough and dirty; lacking any refinement; coarse: *I will tread this unbolted villain into mortar* (Shakespeare).
un·bon·net (un bon′it), *v.i.* to take off the bonnet; uncover the head, as in respect. —*v.t.* to take off the bonnet from.
un·bon·net·ed (un bon′ə tid), *adj.* wearing no bonnet or cap; bareheaded.
un·booked (un bu̇kt′), *adj.* not engaged; having no engagements: *There was not an unbooked day during the time, and the crowds were enormous and enthusiastic* (Maclean's).
un·book·ish (un bu̇k′ish), *adj.* **1.** not bookish; not given to reading. **2.** unlearned.
un·bore (un bôr′, -bōr′), *v.* the past tense of **unbear.**
un·born (un bôrn′), *adj.* not yet born; still to come; of the future: *unborn generations.* —*v.* a past participle of **unbear.**
un·borne (un bôrn′, -bōrn′), *v.* a past participle of **unbear.**
un·bos·om (un bu̇z′əm, -bü′zəm), *v.t.* to reveal; disclose. —*v.i.* to speak frankly and at length: *the last person to whom he could unbosom* (George Meredith).
unbosom oneself, to tell or reveal one's thoughts, feelings, secrets, etc.: *to unbosom himself of his great secret* (Thackeray).
[< *un-*² + *bosom,* verb] —**un·bos′om·er,** *n.*
un·bot·tomed (un bot′əmd), *adj.* bottomless: *the dark unbottom'd infinite abyss* (Milton).
un·bought (un bôt′), *adj.* **1.** not bought; not acquired by purchase. **2.** not hired or bribed.
un·bound¹ (un bound′), *v.* the past tense and past participle of **unbind.**
un·bound² (un bound′), *adj.* not bound, as a book: *Unbound sheets of music were scattered around the floor.* [< *un-*¹ + *bound*¹]
un·bound·ed (un boun′did), *adj.* **1.** not limited; very great; boundless: *the unbounded reaches of the universe. Unbounded courage and compassion join'd . . . make the hero and the man complete* (Joseph Addison). **2.** not kept within limits; not controlled. —**Syn. 1.** infinite.
un·bowed (un boud′), *adj.* **1.** not bowed or bent. **2.** not forced to yield or submit; not subdued: *Under the bludgeonings of chance My head is bloody but unbowed* (William E. Henley).
un·brace (un brās′), *v.t.,* **-braced, -brac·ing.** **1.** to loosen or untie (a band, belt, etc.); undo. **2.** to loosen and detach (an item of clothing, piece of armor, etc.). **3.** to relax the tension of (a drum, etc.); loosen (a drumhead, etc.). **4.** to free (oneself, the: heart, mind, etc.) from tension; relax. **5.** to render feeble; weaken.
un·braced (un brāst′), *adj.* not braced.
un·braid (un brād′), *v.t.* to unwind or unravel the strands of.
un·branched (un brancht′, -bräncht′), *adj.* not branched; not provided with branches.
un·brave (un brāv′), *adj.* cowardly; fearful: *He was a gentle man but strong and not unbrave* (Truman Capote). *All in all, they are pushing us toward a singularly unbrave new world* (Atlantic).
un·break·a·ble (un brā′kə bəl), *adj.* not breakable: *an unbreakable record.*
un·breathed (un brēᴛʜd′), *adj.* not uttered or whispered; unspoken.
un·bred (un bred′), *adj.* not properly bred or brought up; ill-bred.
un·breeched (un brēcht′), *adj.* **1.** not breeched; wearing no breeches: *a parcel of unbreeched heathen* (Herman Melville). **2.** not yet wearing breeches, as a young boy.
un·brib·a·ble (un brī′bə bəl), *adj.* not bribable.
un·bri·dle (un brī′dəl), *v.t.,* **-dled, -dling.** **1.** to remove the bridle from (a horse). **2.** to free (a person or his faculties) from restraint: *The right approach to mathematics, then, is to unbridle the imagination* (Harper's).
un·bri·dled (un brī′dəld), *adj.* **1.** not having a bridle on. **2.** not controlled; not restrained: *unbridled anger.*
un·broke (un brōk′), *adj.* unbroken: *That deep silence was unbroke* (Byron).
un·bro·ken (un brō′kən), *adj.* **1.** not broken; whole: *an unbroken dish.* **2.** not interrupted; continuous: *He had eight hours of unbroken sleep.* **3.** not tamed; not yet broken to the bit, saddle, etc.: *an unbroken*

colt. —**un·bro′ken·ly,** *adv.* —**un·bro′ken·ness,** *n.* —**Syn. 1.** entire, intact.

un·broth·er·ly (un brutн′ər lē), *adj.* not brotherly; not befitting a brother.

un·buck·le (un buk′əl), *v.,* **-led, -ling.** —*v.t.* **1.** to unfasten the buckle or buckles of: *A miser, who will not unbuckle his purse to bestow a farthing* (Scott). **2.** to unfasten; detach. —*v.i.* to unbend; become less stiff: *Even the captain . . . would unbuckle a bit and tell me of the fine countries he had visited* (Robert Louis Stevenson).

un·budg·ing (un buj′ing), *adj.* not budging; inflexible; unyielding: *What made the thing I saw so specially terrible to me was the metallic necessity, the unbudging fatality which governed it* (Herman Melville). —**un·budg′ing·ly,** *adv.*

un·build (un bild′), *v.t.,* **-built, -build·ing.** **1.** to take apart; dismember. **2.** to pull down; demolish.

un·built[1] (un bilt′), *adj.* not yet or ever built.

un·built[2] (un bilt′), *v.* the past tense and past participle of **unbuild.**

un·bur·den (un bėr′dən), *v.t.* **1.** to free from a burden. **2.** to relieve (one's mind or heart) by talking: *Tomorrow I die, and today I would unburden my soul* (Edgar Allan Poe). **3.** to throw off or disclose (something that burdens).

un·bur·ied[1] (un ber′ēd), *adj.* not buried.

un·bur·ied[2] (un ber′ēd), *v.* the past tense and past participle of **unbury.**

un·burned (un bėrnd′), *adj.* **1.** not burned; not consumed or injured by fire. **2.** not baked, as brick.

un·burnt (un bėrnt′), *adj.* unburned.

un·bur·y (un ber′ē), *v.t.,* **-bur·ied, -bur·y·ing.** to take out of the place of burial; disinter; exhume.

un·busi·ness·like (un biz′nis līk′), *adj.* without system and method; not efficient: *an unbusinesslike filing system. That point of view regards the government as an unbusinesslike business enterprise subsidized by hard-earned taxes* (Bulletin of Atomic Scientists).

un·but·ton (un but′ən), *v.t.* to unfasten the button or buttons of: *I was unbuttoning my coat as I turned into the bedroom* (Maclean's).

un·but·toned (un but′ənd), *adj.* **1.** not buttoned; open: *an unbuttoned shirt or coat.* **2.** open and free; easy; casual: *He had had all too much of the unbuttoned, cozy, secure little world of the university* (New Yorker).

U.N.C. or **UNC** (no periods), United Nations Command.

un·cage (un kāj′), *v.t.,* **-caged, -cag·ing.** **1.** to release from a cage. **2.** to release.

un·called (un kôld′), *adj.* not called; not summoned or invited: *to come uncalled.*

un·called-for (un kôld′fôr′), *adj.* **1.** not called for; not requested. **2.** unnecessary and improper; impertinent: *an uncalled-for remark.*

un·can·celed (un kan′səld), *adj.* not canceled.

un·can·celled (un kan′səld), *adj. Especially British.* uncanceled.

un·can·did (un kan′did), *adj.* not candid; disingenuous.

un·can·ni·ly (un kan′ə lē), *adv.* in an uncanny manner: *He could give uncannily accurate estimates of how long a play would run* (Time).

un·can·ni·ness (un kan′ē nis), *n.* the character of being uncanny.

un·can·ny (un kan′ē), *adj.* **1.** strange and mysterious; eerie; weird: *The trees took uncanny shapes in the half darkness.* **2.** so far beyond what is normal or expected as to have some special power: *an uncanny knack for detecting error.* **3.** *Scottish.* **a.** unpleasantly severe; painful. **b.** unsafe; dangerous. —**Syn. 1.** See **weird.**

un·ca·non·i·cal (un′kə non′ə kəl), *adj.* not belonging to the canon (of Scripture); not canonical: *The popular demand for uncanonical rites and offices is a good theme for meditation* (Manchester Guardian Weekly).

un·cap (un kap′), *v.t.,* **-capped, -cap·ping.** **1.** to take the cap, top, or protective covering off of: *to uncap a bottle.* **2.** to remove the hat from (the head, hair, a person, etc.).

un·ca·pa·ble (un kā′pə bəl), *adj. Obsolete.* incapable.

un·cared-for (un kärd′fôr′), *adj.* not cared for or looked after; neglected.

un·care·ful (un kãr′fəl), *adj.* **1.** careless: *Thus, all that we suspected as likely to happen under an uncareful program of disarmament did happen* (Bulletin of Atomic Scientists). **2.** not taking any thought (of). **3.** free from care; untroubled: *One of the . . . most uncareful interludes of my life* (Hawthorne).

un·car·pet·ed (un kär′pə tid), *adj.* not carpeted.

un·cart (un kärt′), *v.t.* to remove or unload from a cart.

un·case (un kās′), *v.t.,* **-cased, -cas·ing.** **1.** to take out of a case; remove the case or covering from; strip; uncover; lay bare. **2.** to disclose or reveal.

un·cashed (un kasht′), *adj.* **1.** not exchanged for cash; unsettled: *an uncashed check.* **2.** (in bridge) not yet played (said of a card certain to take a trick).

un·cat·a·logued (un kat′ə lôgd, -logd), *adj.* not catalogued: *For the location of . . . an uncatalogued item, your librarian has a ferret's nose* (Atlantic).

un·cate (ung′kāt, -kit), *adj.* hooked; uncinate. [< Latin *uncātus* < *uncus* hook]

un·cath·o·lic (un kath′ə lik, -kath′lik), *adj.* **1.** not catholic or universal; limited: *Paradoxical indeed how many of us Catholics can be so uncatholic in our application of freedom* (Harper's). **2.** not Roman Catholic. —*n.* a person who is not a Roman Catholic.

un·caused (un kôzd′), *adj.* not caused; self-existent.

un·ceas·ing (un sē′sing), *adj.* not or never ceasing; continuous; constant: *unceasing labor, unceasing rain.* —**un·ceas′ing·ly,** *adv.*

un·ce·les·tial (un′sə les′chəl), *adj.* not celestial or heavenly; worldly; mundane: *. . . any uncelestial envy or malice* (Anthony Trollope).

un·cer·e·mo·ni·ous (un′ser ə mō′nē əs), *adj.* **1.** not as courteous as would be expected; somewhat abrupt, peremptory, etc. **2.** not ceremonious; informal. —**un′cer·e·mo′ni·ous·ly,** *adv.* —**un′cer·e·mo′ni·ous·ness,** *n.*

uncert., uncertain.

un·cer·tain (un sėr′tən), *adj.* **1.** not known with certainty; not finally established; in doubt; dubious: *The election results were still uncertain.* **2.** not sure; doubtful: *to be uncertain if a candidate will win.* **3.** likely to change; not reliable: *This dog has an uncertain temper.* **4.** not constant; varying: *an uncertain flicker of light.* **5.** not clearly identified, located, or determined; vague; indefinite: *an uncertain shape.* **6.** not settled or fixed; indeterminate: *a job with an uncertain future.* **7.** that may not happen. —**un·cer′tain·ness,** *n.*

—**Syn. 1, 2. Uncertain, insecure** mean not sure in some way or about something. **Uncertain** implies not knowing definitely or surely about something or not having complete confidence in a thing, person, or oneself, and thus suggests the presence of doubt: *His plans for the summer are uncertain.* **Insecure** implies not being protected from or guarded against danger or loss, and thus suggests the presence of fear or anxiety: *His position at the bank is insecure.*

un·cer·tain·ly (un sėr′tən lē), *adv.* in an uncertain way: *He spoke slowly and uncertainly.* —**Syn.** hesitatingly.

un·cer·tain·ty (un sėr′tən tē), *n., pl.* **-ties.** **1.** uncertain quality or condition; doubt. **2.** something uncertain.

uncertainty principle, *Physics.* the principle that certain coordinates of a single physical object can never be accurately determined simultaneously, as the position and velocity of an electron.

un·cer·tif·i·cat·ed (un′sər tif′ə kā′tid), *adj.* not certificated; without certification: *Scotland has 39,000 teachers, of whom about 2,300 are uncertificated* (London Times).

un·cer·ti·fied (un sėr′tə fīd), *adj.* not certified; without certification.

un·chain (un chān′), *v.t.* to free from chains; let loose; set at liberty; free: *Until the spring Unchains the streams* (William Morris).

un·chain·a·ble (un chā′nə bəl), *adj.* incapable of being chained or held in restraint: *We . . . abide Unchainable as the dim tide* (William Butler Yeats).

un·chained (un chānd′), *adj.* not chained; unfettered; free.

un·chal·lenge·a·ble (un chal′ən jə bəl), *adj.* not capable of being challenged or opposed; certain; secure: *The Soviet Union is now most seriously challenging the supposedly unchallengeable industrial might of the United States* (Time). *Mathematics could be saved from internal discord and from external pressures by becoming part of the unchallengeable science of logic* (Scientific American).

un·chal·lenge·a·bly (un chal′ən jə blē), *adv.* in an unchallengeable way; securely; indisputably: *Our freedom must be buttressed by a homogeny equally and unchallengeably free* (William Faulkner).

un·chal·lenged (un chal′ənjd), *adj.* not challenged; not called in question; not called to account.

un·chanc·y (un chan′sē, -chän′-), *adj. Scottish.* **1.** not safe to meddle with; dangerous. **2.** ill-timed. **3.** ill-fated.

un·change·a·ble (un chān′jə bəl), *adj.* that cannot be changed: *'Tis the immortal thought Whose passion still Makes of the unchanging The unchangeable* (Ford Madox Ford). —**un·change′a·ble·ness,** *n.* —**Syn.** immutable, unalterable, invariable.

un·change·a·bly (un chān′jə blē), *adv.* so as not to suffer change; without change; immutably.

un·changed (un chānjd′), *adj.* not changed; the same.

un·chang·ing (un chān′jing), *adj.* not changing; always the same. —**un·chang′ing·ly,** *adv.*

un·chap·e·roned (un shap′ə rōnd), *adj.* not chaperoned; without a chaperon.

un·char·ac·ter·is·tic (un′kar ək tə ris′tik), *adj.* not characteristic; not typical, natural, or usual in the particular instance: *With uncharacteristic mildness, he admitted that he had cut down his output* (Newsweek). —**un′char·ac·ter·is′ti·cal·ly,** *adv.*

un·charge (un chärj′), *v.t.,* **-charged, -charg·ing.** **1.** to unload (a vessel). **2.** to declare free of guilt; acquit.

un·charged (un chärjd′), *adj.* **1.** not charged or loaded with powder or shot: *You have left me in a fair field standing, and in my hand an uncharged gun* (Francis J. Child). **2.** not charged with electrical energy: *Ordinary matter does not exhibit electrical effects and is said to be . . . neutral or uncharged* (Sears and Zemansky). **3.** not burdened (with): *The national desire [is] to be at any rate uncharged with responsibility* (Westminster Gazette). **4.** not formally accused. **5.** not subjected to a financial charge: *uncharged services.* **6.** unassailed: *Open your uncharged ports* (Shakespeare).

un·char·i·ta·ble (un char′ə tə bəl), *adj.* not generous; not charitable; severe; harsh: *I hated them with the bitter, uncharitable condemnation of boyhood* (H.G. Wells). —**un·char′i·ta·ble·ness,** *n.*

un·char·i·ta·bly (un char′ə tə blē), *adv.* in an uncharitable manner; without charity.

un·char·i·ty (un char′ə tē), *n.* want of charity; uncharitable feeling.

un·charm·ing (un chär′ming), *adj.* lacking charm; unpleasant; disagreeable: *Old, uncharming Catherine . . .* (John Dryden). *[His] contempt for women may strike some people as uncharming* (Punch).

un·chart·ed (un chär′tid), *adj.* not mapped; not marked on a chart.

un·char·tered (un chär′tərd), *adj.* **1.** not chartered; without a charter: *an unchartered company.* **2.** without license or regulation.

un·char·y (un chãr′ē), *adj.* not chary; not frugal; not careful; heedless.

un·chaste (un chāst′), *adj.* not chaste; not virtuous. —**un·chaste′ly,** *adv.*

un·chas·ti·ty (un chas′tə tē), *n.* lack of chastity; unchaste character; lewdness.

un·checked (un chekt′), *adj.* not checked; not restrained.

un·cheer·ful (un chir′fəl), *adj.* not cheerful: **a.** sad; gloomy; melancholy. **b.** not willing; grudging: *uncheerful service.*

un·chiv·al·rous (un shiv′əl rəs), *adj.* not chivalrous; ungallant. —**un·chiv′al·rous·ly,** *adv.*

un·chris·tian (un kris′chən), *adj.* **1.** not professing or converted to Christianity; heathen; pagan. **2.** unworthy of Christians; at variance with Christian principles: *a demand . . . that war might be declared unchristian* (John R. Green). **3.** *Informal.* such as any civilized person would object to; barbarous: *to rout a man out of bed at a most unchristian hour.*

un·church (un chėrch′), *v.t.* **1.** to expel from a church; deprive of participation in a

 PRONUNCIATION KEY: hat, āge, cãre, fär; let, ēqual, tėrm; it, īce; hot, ōpen, ôrder; oil, out; cup, pu̇t, rüle;

church; excommunicate. **2.** to refuse the name or character of church to.

un·churched (un chėrcht′), *adj.* **1.** having no church. **2.** excluded from a church. **3.** not belonging to or affiliated with a church: *Surveys . . . showed that more than half of the population of New York was unchurched* (New York Times).
—*n.* people who do not belong to or affiliate with a church; unchurched people, collectively: *Dr. Gockel became even more convinced of the need to reach the nation's unchurched* (Time).

un·church·ly (un chėrch′lē), *adj.* not suitable or proper in or for a church: *unchurchly conduct, unchurchly decorations.*

un·ci (un′sī), *n.* the plural of **uncus.**

un·ci·al (un′shē əl, -shəl), *n.* **1.** an old style of writing, formed with heavy, rounded strokes. **2.** a letter in this style. **3.** a manuscript written in this style or with such letters.
—*adj.* **1.** of or having to do with this style or such letters. **2.** written in this style or such letters.
[< Late Latin *unciāles* (*litterae*) uncial (letters); the exact sense of *uncia* is not known]

Latin Uncials (def. 2) (8th century)

un·ci·form (un′sə fôrm), *adj.* **1.** hook-shaped. **2.** *Anatomy.* denoting or having to do with the hamate bone, its hooklike process, or any similar hooklike process.
—*n. Anatomy.* the hamate bone. [< New Latin *unciformis* < Latin *uncus* hook + *forma* form]

unciform process, *Anatomy.* **1.** the process projecting from the palmar surface of the hamate bone. **2.** a hook-shaped process of the ethmoid bone.

un·ci·nal (un′sə nəl), *adj.* uncinate.

un·ci·na·ri·a·sis (un′sə nə rī′ə sis), *n.* hookworm disease. [< New Latin *Uncinaria* the hookworm genus (< Latin *uncīnus* hook < *uncus* hook) + *-iasis*]

un·ci·nate (un′sə nit, -nāt), *adj.* hooked, especially at the end. [< Latin *uncīnātus* < *uncīnus* hook, barb (diminutive) < *uncus* hook]

un·ci·nat·ed (un′sə nā′tid), *adj.* uncinate.

UNCIO (no periods), United Nations Conference on International Organization.

un·cir·cum·cised (un sėr′kəm sīzd), *adj.* **1.** not circumcised. **2.** Gentile; not Israelite. **3.** heathen; pagan.

un·cir·cum·ci·sion (un′sėr kəm sizh′ən), *n.* in the Bible: **1.** the condition of not being circumcised. Romans 2:25. **2.** the Gentiles. Romans 2:26.

un·civ·il (un siv′əl), *adj.* **1.** not civil; discourteous; rude; impolite: *I hope it's not uncivil to say that you . . . ought to be in jail* (G.K. Chesterton). **2.** uncivilized: *Man cannot enjoy the rights of an uncivil and a civil state together* (Edmund Burke). —**un·civ′il·ly,** *adv.* —**Syn. 1.** unmannerly. **2.** barbarian.

un·civ·i·lized (un siv′ə līzd), *adj.* not civilized; barbarous; savage.

un·clad[1] (un klad′), *adj.* not dressed; not clothed; naked. [< *un-*[1] + *clad*[1]]

un·clad[2] (un klad′), *v.* a past tense and past participle of **unclothe.**

un·claimed (un klāmd′), *adj.* not claimed.

un·clar·i·ty (un klar′ə tē), *n.* lack of clarity; indistinctness.

un·clasp (un klasp′, -kläsp′), *v.t.* **1.** to unfasten. **2.** to release from a clasp or grasp: *She clasped and unclasped her fingers.* —*v.i.* **1.** to unfasten. **2.** to be released from a clasp or grasp: *I feel my feeble hands unclasp* (Longfellow).

un·clas·si·fi·a·ble (un klas′ə fī′ə bəl), *adj.* not classifiable.

un·clas·si·fied (un klas′ə fīd), *adj.* not classified.

un·cle (ung′kəl), *n.* **1.** the brother of one's father or mother. **2.** the husband of one's aunt. **3.** *Informal.* an elderly man. **4.** *Slang.* a pawnbroker.
—*interj. Informal.* I (or we) surrender!
cry, holler, or **say uncle,** *Informal.* to admit defeat; surrender: *The increasing desire of some businesses to cry uncle when the pinch is on . . .* (Wall Street Journal).
[< Anglo-French *uncle,* Old French *oncle* < Latin *avunculus* one's mother's brother (diminutive) < *avus* (maternal) grandfather]

un·clean (un klēn′), *adj.* **1.** not clean; dirty; soiled; filthy. **2.** not pure morally; evil: *Woe is me! . . . because I am a man of unclean lips* (Isaiah 6:1). **3.** not ceremonially clean: *The Gentiles were no longer common or unclean* (Cardinal Newman). [Old English *unclǣne* < *un-* un-[1] + *clǣne* clean] —**un·clean′ness,** *n.*

un·cleaned (un klēnd′), *adj.* not cleaned.

un·clean·li·ness (un klen′lē nis), *n.* want of cleanliness; filthiness; foulness.

un·clean·ly[1] (un klen′lē), *adj.* not cleanly; unclean. [Old English *unclǣnlīc* < *un-* un-[1] + *clǣnlīc* cleanly[1]]

un·clean·ly[2] (un klēn′lē), *adv.* in an unclean manner. [Old English *unclǣnlīce* < *unclǣne* (see UNCLEAN) + *līce* -ly[1]]

un·clear (un klir′), *adj.* not clear; clouded; obscure; indistinct; uncertain: *unclear words, unclear penmanship.* —**un·clear′ly,** *adv.*

un·cleared (un klird′), *adj.* not cleared.

un·clench (un klench′), *v.t.* to open from a clenched state: *to unclench one's fists.* —*v.i.* to become opened from a clenched state: *I saw her hands clench and unclench spasmodically* (W. Somerset Maugham).

Uncle Sam, *Informal.* the government or people of the United States, often caricatured as a tall, thin man with white chin whiskers, wearing a top hat with a band of stars: *Uncle Sam is rather despotic as to the disposal of my time* (Hawthorne). [American English, an expansion of US, initials of the United States]

Uncle Tom, 1. the central character of Harriet Beecher Stowe's antislavery novel *Uncle Tom's Cabin* (1851-52), a humble, pious, long-suffering Negro slave. **2.** *U.S.* a Negro thought of as having the timid, servile attitude of a slave in his relations with whites (used in an unfriendly way).

Uncle Tom·ism (tom′iz əm), *U.S.* a Negro attitude of compromise, gradualism, or half-hearted interest in the struggle to obtain full civil rights and abolish racial discrimination: *Negroes consider Uncle Tomism their most regressive trait* (Time).

un·clinch (un klinch′), *v.t., v.i.* unclench.

un·cloak (un klōk′), *v.t.* **1.** to remove the coat from; divest of a cloak. **2.** to reveal; expose: *to uncloak a scoundrel.* —*v.i.* to take off the cloak or outer garment.

un·clog (un klog′), *v.t.,* **-clogged, -clog·ging.** to free from a clog or from anything that clogs.

un·close (un klōz′), *v.t., v.i.,* **-closed, -clos·ing.** to open.

un·closed (un klōzd′), *adj.* **1.** not closed: *His unclosed eye yet lowering on his enemy* (Byron). **2.** not finished; not brought to a close. **3.** (of accounts) not balanced; not settled: *I don't love to leave any Part of the Account unclos'd* (Sir Richard Steele).

un·clothe (un klōᴛʜ′), *v.t.,* **-clothed** or **-clad, -cloth·ing. 1.** to strip of clothes; undress. **2.** to lay bare; uncover.

un·clothed (un klōᴛʜd′), *adj.* not clothed; naked; bare.

un·cloud·ed (un klou′did), *adj.* not clouded; free from clouds; clear. —**un·cloud′ed·ness,** *n.*

un·club·ba·ble or **un·club·a·ble** (un-klub′ə bəl), *adj.* unfit to be a member of a club; unsociable: *Sir John was a most unclubable man* (Samuel Johnson).

un·clut·tered (un klut′ərd), *adj.* in order; not littered; neat: *Greece is of all countries the most uncluttered* (Eleanor Perényi).

un·co (ung′kō), *Scottish.* —*adv.* remarkably; very; extremely.
—*adj.* **1.** unknown, strange, or unusual: *It was an unco thing to bid a mother leave her ain house* (Scott). **2.** remarkable, extraordinary, or great. **3.** uncanny: *It was an unco place by night* (Robert Louis Stevenson).
[ultimately variant of *uncouth*]

un·cock (un kok′), *v.t.* to let down the hammer of (a firearm) gently from the position of cock, so as not to explode the charge.

un·coil (un koil′), *v.t., v.i.* to unwind.

un·coined (un koind′), *adj.* not coined; not minted.

un·col·lect·ed (un′kə lek′tid), *adj.* **1.** not collected; not brought to one place; not received: *uncollected taxes, debts uncollected.* **2.** not having one's thoughts collected; not having control of one's mental faculties; not recovered from confusion, distraction, or wandering.

un·col·ored (un kul′ərd), *adj.* **1.** not colored. **2.** not made to appear different from reality; open or undisguised; truthful or unbiased, as a statement or account; not influenced or affected by something. **3.** plain or unadorned.

un·col·oured (un kul′ərd), *adj. Especially British.* uncolored.

un·com·bined (un′kəm bīnd′), *adj.* not combined; separate.

un·come·ly (un kum′lē), *adj.* **1.** not comely; wanting grace: *an uncomely person, uncomely dress.* **2.** unseemly; unbecoming; unsuitable; indecent.

un·com·fort·a·ble (un kumf′tə bəl, -kum′fər-), *adj.* **1.** not comfortable. **2.** uneasy; restless. **3.** disagreeable; causing discomfort: *His loyalty to the revolutionary principles made him conspicuous and extremely uncomfortable to the Bourbon Restoration* (Edmund Wilson). —**un·com′fort·a·ble·ness,** *n.*

un·com·fort·a·bly (un kumf′tə blē, -kum′fər-), *adv.* in a way that is not comfortable; with discomfort and uneasiness; disagreeably.

un·com·mer·cial (un′kə mėr′shəl), *adj.* **1.** not commercial; not engaged in or connected with commerce. **2.** not in accordance with the principles or methods of commerce.

un·com·mit·ted (un′kə mit′id), *adj.* **1.** not bound or pledged to a particular action, course, etc.: *an uncommitted country.* **2.** not committed to prison: *an uncommitted felon.*

un·com·mon (un kom′ən), *adj.* **1.** rare; unusual. **2.** remarkable; noteworthy. —**un·com′mon·ness,** *n.*

un·com·mon·ly (un kom′ən lē), *adv.* **1.** rarely; unusually. **2.** remarkably; especially: *She is an uncommonly good cook.*

un·com·mu·ni·ca·bil·i·ty (un′kə myü′nə kə bil′ə tē), *n.* the quality or condition of being uncommunicable.

un·com·mu·ni·ca·ble (un′kə myü′nə kə-bəl), *adj.* incommunicable.

un·com·mu·ni·ca·tive (un′kə myü′nə kā′tiv, -kə tiv), *adj.* not giving out any information, opinions, etc.; talking as little as possible; disposed to silence. —**un′com·mu′ni·ca′tive·ness,** *n.* —**Syn.** reserved, reticent, taciturn.

un·com·pan·ion·a·ble (un′kəm pan′yə-nə bəl), *adj.* not companionable or sociable: *an uncompanionable hermit.*

un·com·pet·i·tive (un′kəm pet′ə tiv), *adj.* **1. a.** that does not or will not compete: *an uncompetitive member firm, uncompetitive prices.* **b.** not in accord with competition: *the uncompetitive spirit and traditions of Christmas.* **2.** that discourages or prohibits competition. —**un′com·pet′i·tive·ly,** *adv.* —**un′com·pet′i·tive·ness,** *n.*

un·com·plain·ing (un′kəm plā′ning), *adj.* not complaining; not disposed to murmur; submissive. —**un′com·plain′ing·ly,** *adv.*

un·com·plai·sant (un′kəm plā′zənt, un-kom′plə zant), *adj.* not complaisant; not civil; not courteous.

un·com·plet·ed (un′kəm plē′tid), *adj.* not completed; unfinished.

un·com·pli·a·ble (un′kəm plī′ə bəl), *adj.* unready or unwilling to comply.

un·com·pli·ant (un′kəm plī′ənt), *adj.* incompliant.

un·com·pli·men·ta·ry (un′kom plə men′tər ē), *adj.* not complimentary; unflattering; disparaging; derogatory.

un·com·posed (un′kəm pōzd′), *adj.* **1.** not calm; disordered; excited: *. . . sudden, uncomposed, and uncollected thoughts* (Edward Reynolds). **2.** (of music) unwritten: *Schoenberg planned "Moses and Aaron" in three acts, but he left the last act uncomposed* (London Times).

un·com·pound·ed (un′kəm poun′did), *adj.* **1.** not compounded; not mixed; simple. **2.** not intricate or complicated.

un·com·pre·hend·ing (un′kom pri hen′-ding), *adj.* not comprehending or understanding. —**un′com·pre·hend′ing·ly,** *adv.*

un·com·pre·hen·si·ble (un′kom pri hen′-sə bəl), *adj. Obsolete.* incomprehensible.

un·com·pre·hen·sion (un′kom pri hen′-shən), *n.* lack of understanding: *They might as well have come from different worlds, so striking is the uncomprehension between them* (Manchester Guardian).

un·com·pro·mis·ing (un kom′prə mī′-zing), *adj.* unyielding; firm: *a stubborn, uncompromising person. The most honest, fearless and uncompromising republican of his time* (Macaulay). —**un·com′pro·mis′ing·ly,** *adv.* —**un·com′pro·mis′ing·ness,** *n.* —**Syn.** inflexible, rigid, inexorable.

un·con·cealed (un′kən sēld′), *adj.* not concealed; openly shown; manifest: *unconcealed scorn.*

un·con·cern (un′kən sėrn′), *n.* **1.** lack of concern; freedom from care or anxiety; nonchalance. **2.** lack of interest; indifference; apathy. —**Syn. 2.** See **indifference.**

un·con·cerned (un′kən sėrnd′), *adj.* **1.** free from care or anxiety; nonchalant. **2.** not interested; indifferent; apathetic. —**un′con·cern′ed·ness,** *n.*

un·con·cern·ed·ly (un′kən sėr′nid lē), *adv.* in an unconcerned manner; without concern or anxiety.

un·con·demned (un′kən demd′), *adj.* not condemned; not judged guilty; not disapproved; not pronounced criminal: *They have beaten us openly uncondemned* (Acts 16:37).

un·con·di·tion·al (un′kən dish′ə nəl, -dish′nəl), *adj.* without conditions; absolute: *an unconditional refusal, unconditional surrender.* —**Syn.** unqualified, unrestricted.

un·con·di·tion·al·ly (un′kən dish′ə nə lē, -dish′nə-), *adv.* without any conditions.

un·con·di·tioned (un′kən dish′ənd), *adj.* **1.** without conditions; absolute. **2.** unconditional. **3.** *Psychology.* deriving from the innate nature of the organism as such; not learned; instinctive: *an unconditioned response.* **4.** (of a student) accepted or promoted without condition. **5.** *Philosophy.* of the nature of or deriving from that which is absolute in its nature and infinite in its extent; not dependent on or determined by antecedent conditions.

un·con·fi·dent (un kon′fə dənt), *adj.* lacking confidence; uncertain; hesitant; self-conscious: *an unconfident office boy.*

un·con·fin·a·ble (un′kən fī′nə bəl), *adj.* **1.** that cannot be confined or restrained. **2.** *Obsolete.* unbounded.

un·con·fined (un′kən fīnd′), *adj.* not confined; unrestricted; broad; unrestrained; free: *On with the dance! let joy be unconfined* (Byron).

un·con·firmed (un′kən fėrmd′), *adj.* not confirmed; without confirmation: *an unconfirmed report.*

un·con·form·a·ble (un′kən fôr′mə bəl), *adj.* **1.** that does not conform. **2.** *Geology.* having the relation of unconformity to underlying rocks.

un·con·form·a·bly (un′kən fôr′mə blē), *adv.* in an unconformable manner; so as not to be conformable.

un·con·form·i·ty (un′kən fôr′mə tē), *n., pl.* **-ties. 1.** lack of agreement; being inconsistent; nonconformity. **2.** *Geology.* **a.** a break in the continuity of contact between strata, indicating an interruption of deposition. **b.** the plane of contact where such a break occurs.

Unconformity (def. 2b) The lower rock strata were worn down before the upper strata were deposited.

un·con·fused (un′kən fyüzd′), *adj.* **1.** free from confusion or disorder. **2.** not confused or embarrassed.

un·con·geal (un′kən jēl′), *v.i.* to thaw; melt.

un·con·gen·ial (un′kən jēn′yəl), *adj.* not congenial.

un·con·nect·ed (un′kə nek′tid), *adj.* **1.** not connected; separate; distinct. **2.** disconnected; incoherent.

un·con·quer·a·ble (un kong′kər ə bəl), *adj.* **1.** that cannot be defeated: *Thou hast great allies; Thy friends are exultations, agonies, And love, and man's unconquerable mind* (Wordsworth). *I thank whatever gods may be For my unconquerable soul* (William E. Henley). **2.** that cannot be brought under control: *an unconquerable temper. Romola . . . shrank with unconquerable disgust from the shrill excitability of those illuminated women* (George Eliot). —**un·con′quer·a·ble·ness,** *n.* —**Syn. 1.** invincible, insuperable, indomitable. **2.** uncontrollable.

un·con·quer·a·bly (un kong′kər ə blē), *adv.* invincibly; insuperably.

un·con·quered (un kong′kərd), *adj.* not conquered; not vanquished or subdued.

un·con·scion·a·ble (un kon′shə nə bəl), *adj.* **1.** not influenced or guided by conscience: *an unconscionable liar. Sometimes the unconscionable editors will clip our paragraphs* (Washington Irving). **2.** unreasonable; very great: *to wait an unconscionable time, an unconscionable amount of snow.* —**Syn. 1.** unprincipled. **2.** inordinate

un·con·scion·a·bly (un kon′shə nə blē), *adv.* in a manner or degree that conscience and reason do not justify; unreasonably; inordinately: *She chewed each mouthful an unconscionably long time* (New Yorker).

un·con·scious (un kon′shəs), *adj.* **1.** lacking all capacity for sensory perception; not conscious, especially: **a.** not in a conscious state: *a person made unconscious by an anesthetic.* **b.** that is not a conscious being: *an unconscious force.* **2.** not aware (of): *to be unconscious of danger.* **3.** not meant; not intended: *unconscious neglect.* **4.** of or having to do with the part of the mind which cannot be drawn into consciousness.

—*n.* **the unconscious,** *Psychoanalysis.* that part of the personality, or function of the mind, of which a person is not directly aware; one's unconscious (but still active, or dynamic) thoughts, desires, fears, etc., which may become manifest in seemingly groundless obsessions, compulsions, etc.: *The unconscious is a special realm, with its own desires and modes of expression and peculiar mental mechanisms not elsewhere operative* (Sigmund Freud). —**un·con′scious·ly,** *adv.* —**un·con′scious·ness,** *n.*

—**Syn.** *adj.* **2.** oblivious, unmindful.

un·con·se·crat·ed (un kon′sə krā′tid), *adj.* not consecrated.

un·con·sent·ing (un′kən sen′ting), *adj.* not consenting; not yielding consent.

un·con·sid·ered (un′kən sid′ərd), *adj.* **1.** not considered; not reflected on; not taken into consideration; not esteemed: *a snapper-up of unconsidered trifles* (Shakespeare). **2.** unaccompanied by consideration or intention: *his own act of cool, nonchalant, unconsidered courage in a crisis* (Arnold Bennett).

un·con·sid·er·ing (un′kən sid′ər ing), *adj.* not considering; void of consideration; regardless.

un·con·sol·a·ble (un′kən sō′lə bəl), *adj.* inconsolable: *When the blow falls she sits unconsolable through the night, nursing a bottle of gin* (London Times).

un·con·stant (un kon′stənt), *adj.* inconstant.

un·con·sti·tu·tion·al (un′kon stə tü′shə nəl, -tyü′-), *adj.* contrary to the constitution. —**un′con·sti·tu′tion·al·ly,** *adv.*

un·con·sti·tu·tion·al·i·ty (un′kon stə-tü′shə nal′ə tē, -tyü′-), *n.* a being contrary to the constitution.

un·con·strained (un′kən strānd′), *adj.* **1.** not constrained; not acting or done under compulsion; not subject to restraint: *unconstrained freedom.* **2.** free from constraint or embarrassment; easy or unembarrassed: *Maggie's manner . . . had been as unconstrained and indifferent as ever* (George Eliot).

un·con·sum·mat·ed (un kon′sə mā′tid), *adj.* not consummated; uncompleted; unfulfilled: *an unconsummated marriage.*

un·con·test·ed (un′kən tes′tid), *adj.* **1.** not contested or disputed: *an uncontested will.* **2.** indisputable; evident: *an uncontested fact.*

un·con·tra·dict·a·ble (un′kon trə dik′tə-bəl), *adj.* that cannot be contradicted.

un·con·tra·dict·ed (un′kon trə dik′tid), *adj.* not contradicted or denied.

un·con·trived (un′kən trīvd′), *adj.* **1.** not worked out beforehand; unplanned; unpremeditated: *uncontrived events.* **2.** not artificial; natural; artless: *uncontrived mirth.*

un·con·trol (un′kən trōl′), *n.* lack of control.

un·con·trol·la·bil·i·ty (un′kən trō′lə bil′-ə tē), *n.* the quality or condition of being uncontrollable; uncontrollableness: *What in the twenties was beyond government control because of the institutional uncontrollability of free capitalism, threatens in the sixties to outgrow once again the controlling power of government* (New York Times).

un·con·trol·la·ble (un′kən trō′lə bəl), *adj.* not controllable; ungovernable: *His . . . fierce and uncontrollable temper* (Samuel Richardson). —**un′con·trol′la·ble·ness,** *n.*

un·con·trol·la·bly (un′kən trō′lə blē), *adv.* in an uncontrollable manner; without being subject to control.

un·con·trolled (un′kən trōld′), *adj.* not controlled, checked, or governed.

un·con·trol·led·ly (un′kən trō′lid lē), *adv.* without control or restraint; without effectual opposition.

un·con·tro·vert·ed (un kon′trə vėr′tid), *adj.* not controverted or disputed; not liable to be called in question.

un·con·ven·tion·al (un′kən ven′shə nəl), *adj.* not bound by or conforming to convention, rule, or precedent; free from conventionality. —**un′con·ven′tion·al·ly,** *adv.*

un·con·ven·tion·al·i·ty (un′kən ven′shə-nal′ə tē), *n., pl.* **-ties.** a being unconventional; freedom from conventional restraints.

un·con·vers·a·ble (un′kən vėr′sə bəl), *adj.* not free in conversation; repelling conversation; not sociable; reserved.

un·con·ver·sant (un′kən vėr′sənt), *adj.* not conversant; not familiarly acquainted.

un·con·vert·ed (un′kən vėr′tid), *adj.* not converted.

un·con·vert·i·ble (un′kən vėr′tə bəl), *adj.* not convertible; that cannot be changed from one thing or form to another.

un·con·vinc·ing (un′kən vin′sing), *adj.* not convincing; open to doubt or disbelief: *an unconvincing argument, unconvincing testimony.* —**un′con·vinc′ing·ly,** *adv.* —**un′con·vinc′ing·ness,** *n.*

un·cooked (un ku̇kt′), *adj.* not cooked; raw.

un·co·op·er·a·tion (un′kō op′ə rā′shən), *n.* lack of cooperation.

un·co·op·er·a·tive (un′kō op′ə rā′tiv, -op′-rə-), *adj.* not cooperative; unwilling to work with others: *The best constitution is useless when administered by disorderly, uncooperative individuals* (David Schoenbrun). —**un′co·op′er·a·tive·ly,** *adv.* —**un′co·op′er·a·tive·ness,** *n.*

un·co·or·di·nat·ed (un′kō ôr′də nā′tid), *adj.* lacking coordination; not working together; not in harmony: *the uncoordinated movements of a newborn baby.* —**un′co·or′di·nat′ed·ly,** *adv.*

un·cop·i·a·ble (un kop′ē ə bəl), *adj.* that cannot be copied.

un·cork (un kôrk′), *v.t.* **1.** to pull the cork from. **2.** *Informal.* to allow to flow out; unloose: *These proposals immediately uncorked drives for action* (Wall Street Journal).

un·cor·rect·ed (un′kə rek′tid), *adj.* not corrected.

un·cor·rob·o·rat·ed (un′kə rob′ə rā′tid), *adj.* not corroborated; unconfirmed.

un·cor·rupt (un′kə rupt′), *adj.* not corrupt; not depraved; not perverted; incorrupt; pure: *an uncorrupt judgment, an uncorrupt text.*

un·cor·rupt·ed (un′kə rup′tid), *adj.* not corrupted; not debased; not vitiated; not depraved; not decomposed: *the common sense of readers uncorrupted with literary prejudices* (Samuel Johnson).

un·coun·seled (un koun′səld), *adj.* **1.** not having counsel or advice. **2.** *Obsolete.* wrongly counseled; led into error.

un·coun·selled (un koun′səld), *adj. Especially British.* uncounseled.

un·count·a·ble (un koun′tə bəl), *adj.* that cannot be counted; innumerable: *an uncountable number of stars.*

un·count·ed (un koun′tid), *adj.* **1.** not counted; not reckoned. **2.** very many; innumerable.

—**Syn. 1.** indefinite. **2.** myriad.

un·cou·ple (un kup′əl), *v.t., v.i.,* **-pled, -pling.** to disconnect; unfasten: *They uncoupled two freight cars.*

un·cour·te·ous (un kėr′tē əs), *adj.* discourteous; impolite; rude. —**un·cour′te·ous·ly,** *adv.*

un·court·li·ness (un kôrt′lē nis, -kōrt′-), *n.* rudeness. —**Syn.** churlishness.

un·court·ly (un kôrt′lē, -kōrt′-), *adj.* not courtly; rude.

un·couth (un küth′), *adj.* **1.** awkward; clumsy; crude; not refined: *an uncouth person, uncouth manners.* **2.** unusual and unpleasant; strange: *the eerie and uncouth noises of the jungle.* [Old English *uncūth* < *un-* un-[1] + *cūth* known < *cunnan* to know] —**un·couth′ly,** *adv.* —**un·couth′ness,** *n.*

un·cov·e·nant·ed (un kuv′ə nən tid), *adj.* **1.** not promised or secured by a covenant. **2.** not in accordance with a covenant. **3.** not bound by a covenant.

un·cov·er (un kuv′ər), *v.t.* **1.** to remove the cover or covers from. **2.** to make known; reveal; expose. **3.** to remove the hat, cap, etc., of. —*v.i.* **1.** to remove one's hat or cap in respect: *The men uncovered as the flag passed by.* **2.** to remove the cover or covers.

un·cov·ered (un kuv′ərd), *adj.* **1.** without a cover: *an uncovered pot of soup, an uncovered head.* **2.** not protected by collateral or other security: *an uncovered note.*

un·cre·ate (un′krē āt′), *v.t.,* **-at·ed, -at·ing.** to undo the creation of; deprive of existence.

un·cre·at·ed (un′krē ā′tid), *adj.* **1.** not created; not brought into existence. **2.** existing without having been created.

un·crit·i·cal (un krit′ə kəl), *adj.* **1.** not critical; not able or wanting to criticize. **2.** wanting in acuteness of judgment or critical analysis: *an uncritical essay.* —**un·crit′i·cal·ly,** *adv.* —**un·crit′i·cal·ness,** *n.*

un·cropped (un kropt′), *adj.* **1.** not cropped or plucked. **2.** not cropped or cut, as the ears of a dog.

un·cross (un krôs′, -kros′), *v.t.* to change from a crossed position.

un·crossed (un krôst′, -krost′), *adj.* **1.** not thwarted; not opposed. **2.** not limited as regards cashability or negotiability by crossing. **3.** not crossed; not canceled.

un·crown (un kroun′), *v.t.* to take the crown from; lower from high rank.

un·crowned (un kround′), *adj.* **1.** not crowned; not having yet assumed the crown. **2.** having royal power without being king, queen, etc.

UNCSAT (no periods), United Nations Conference on Science and Technology.

UNCTAD (no periods), United Nations Conference on Trade and Development.

unc·tion (ungk′shən), *n.* **1.** an anointing with oil, ointment, or the like, for medical purposes or as a religious rite: *The priest gave the dying man extreme unction.* **2.** the oil, ointment, or the like, used for anointing. **3.** something soothing or comforting: *the unction of flattery.* **4.** a soothing, sympathetic, and persuasive quality in speaking. **5.** fervor, especially religious fervor; earnestness. **6.** affected earnestness, sentiment, etc.; smoothness and oiliness of language, manner, etc. **7.** in the Bible: **a.** a divine or spiritual influence acting upon a person. I John 2:20. **b.** the flowing of this influence. [< Latin *unctiō, -ōnis* < *unguere* to anoint]

unc·tu·os·i·ty (ungk′chü os′ə tē), *n.* **1.** the quality of being unctuous. **2.** unction.

unc·tu·ous (ungk′chü əs), *adj.* **1.** like an oil or ointment in texture; oily; greasy: *Oak, now black with time and unctuous with kitchen smoke* (Hawthorne). **2.** soothing, sympathetic, and persuasive; blandly ingratiating: *the hypocrite's unctuous manner.* **3.** characterized by unction; too smooth and oily: *an offensively unctuous speech.* **4.** tending to or gushing with religious fervor or emotion, especially false or affected emotion; fervid in a shallow, sentimental way. **5.** (of ground or soil) soft and clinging, but easily worked; rich in decayed organic matter, and containing more clay than sand: *an unctuous muck, ideal for celery.* **6.** (of clay) very plastic; somewhat fat, as bentonite. [< Medieval Latin *unctuosus* < Latin *unctus, -ūs* anointment, anointing < *unguere* to anoint] —**unc′tu·ous·ly,** *adv.* —**unc′tu·ous·ness,** *n.*

un·culled (un kuld′), *adj.* **1.** not gathered. **2.** not separated; not selected.

un·cul·ti·va·ble (un kul′tə və bəl), *adj.* that cannot be tilled or cultivated.

un·cul·ti·vat·ed (un kul′tə vā′tid), *adj.* not cultivated; fallow; wild; unrefined; rude; undeveloped: *an uncultivated mind.*

un·cul·tured (un kul′chərd), *adj.* not cultured.

un·cum·bered (un kum′bərd), *adj.* unencumbered.

un·cur·a·ble (un kyůr′ə bəl), *adj.* incurable.

un·curb·a·ble (un kėr′bə bəl), *adj.* that cannot be curbed or checked.

un·curbed (un kėrbd′), *adj.* not curbed.

un·cu·ri·ous (un kyůr′ē əs), *adj.* **1.** not curious or inquisitive; lacking curiosity; incurious. **2.** not curious, odd, or strange.

un·curl (un kėrl′), *v.t., v.i.* to straighten out.

un·cus (ung′kəs), *n., pl.* **un·ci** (un′sī). *Biology.* a hooklike part or process. [< Latin *uncus*]

un·cus·tomed (un kus′təmd), *adj.* not passed through customs; with duty unpaid: *The police fined him . . . ninety dollars for having uncustomed goods in his possession* (Punch).

un·cut (un kut′), *adj.* **1.** not cut, gashed, or wounded with a sharp-edged instrument; not having received a cut. **2.** not cut down, mown, or clipped: *an uncut forest, uncut grass, an uncut hedge.* **3.** not fashioned or shaped by cutting: *an uncut diamond.* **4.** not curtailed or shortened, as by editing: *an uncut novel or movie.* **5.** not having the leaves cut open or the margins cut down: *an uncut book.*

un·dam·aged (un dam′ijd), *adj.* not damaged.

un·damped (un dampt′), *adj.* **1.** not damped; not moistened. **2.** not deadened; not checked or retarded in action. **3.** not depressed or discouraged. **4.** *Physics.* not damped; not reduced gradually in amplitude.

un·dat·ed (un dā′tid), *adj.* not dated; not marked with a date, as a letter.

un·daunt·ed (un dôn′tid, -dän′-), *adj.* not afraid; not dismayed or discouraged; dauntless: *an undaunted leader.* —**un·daunt′ed·ly,** *adv.* —**un·daunt′ed·ness,** *n.* —**Syn.** intrepid, fearless.

un·dé or **un·dée** (un′dā), *adj. Heraldry.* having the form of a wave or waves; wavy. [< Old French *unde* wave < Latin *unda*]

un·dec·a·gon (un dek′ə gon), *n. Geometry.* a polygon, especially a plane polygon, having eleven angles and eleven sides. [< Latin *ūndecim* eleven + English (dec)*agon*]

un·de·ceiv·a·ble (un′di sē′və bəl), *adj.* **1.** that cannot be deceived; not subject to deception. **2.** incapable of deceiving.

un·de·ceive (un′di sēv′), *v.t.,* **-ceived, -ceiv·ing.** to free (a person) from error, mistake, or deception; deliver from an erroneous idea or conception.

un·de·cen·na·ry (un′di sen′ər ē), *adj.* undecennial.

un·de·cen·ni·al (un′di sen′ē əl, -sen′yəl), *adj.* **1.** of or having to do with a period of eleven years. **2.** occurring or observed every eleven years. [< Latin *ūndecim* eleven + *annus* year; patterned on English *decennial*]

un·de·cent (un dē′sənt), *adj.* indecent.

un·de·cid·ed (un′di sī′did), *adj.* **1.** not decided or settled. **2.** not having one's mind made up. —**un′de·cid′ed·ly,** *adv.* —**un′de·cid′ed·ness,** *n.* —**Syn. 2.** irresolute, wavering.

un·de·ci·pher·a·ble (un′di sī′fər ə bəl), *adj.* indecipherable.

un·decked (un dekt′), *adj.* **1.** not decked; not adorned. **2.** not having a deck: *an undecked vessel or barge.*

un·de·clin·a·ble (un′di klī′nə bəl), *adj.* **1.** *Grammar.* indeclinable. **2.** *Obsolete.* not to be declined or avoided.

un·de·clined (un′di klīnd′), *adj.* **1.** *Grammar.* not having cases marked by different terminations. **2.** *Obsolete.* not deviating; not turned from the right way.

un·de·com·pos·a·ble (un′dē kəm pō′zə-bəl), *adj.* not admitting of decomposition; that cannot be decomposed.

un·de·faced (un′di fāst′), *adj.* not defaced; not deprived of its form; not disfigured.

un·de·fend·ed (un′di fen′did), *adj.* **1.** not defended; unprotected. **2.** not assisted by legal defense, as a prisoner. **3.** not contested, as a suit at law.

un·de·filed (un′di fīld′), *adj.* not defiled or polluted.

un·de·fin·a·ble (un′di fī′nə bəl), *adj.* indefinable.

un·de·fined (un′di fīnd′), *adj.* **1.** not defined or explained. **2.** indefinite.

un·del·e·gat·ed (un del′ə gā′tid), *adj.* not delegated; not deputed; not granted: *your assumption of undelegated power.*

un·de·mand·ing (un′di man′ding), *adj.* demanding nothing or very little: *an undemanding job, undemanding parents.*

un·dem·o·crat·ic (un′dem ə krat′ik), *adj.* not democratic; not in accordance with the principles of democracy.

un·de·mon·stra·ble (un′di mon′strə bəl), *adj.* indemonstrable.

un·de·mon·stra·tive (un′di mon′strə-tiv), *adj.* not demonstrative; not given to or characterized by open display or expression of the feelings, etc.; reserved. —**un′de·mon′stra·tive·ly,** *adv.* —**un′de·mon′stra·tive·ness,** *n.*

un·de·ni·a·ble (un′di nī′ə bəl), *adj.* **1.** that cannot be disputed; not to be denied; indisputable. **2.** unquestionably good; excellent. —**un′de·ni′a·ble·ness,** *n.*

un·de·ni·a·bly (un′di nī′ə blē), *adv.* beyond denial or dispute; certainly. —**Syn.** unquestionably.

un·de·nom·i·na·tion·al (un′di nom′ə nā′-shə nəl, -näsh′nəl), *adj.* not connected with any particular religious sect.

un·de·pend·a·bil·i·ty (un′di pen′də bil′ə-tē), *n.* unreliability; untrustworthiness.

un·de·pend·a·ble (un′di pen′də bəl), *adj.* not dependable; unreliable; untrustworthy. —**un′de·pend′a·ble·ness,** *n.*

un·de·praved (un′di prāvd′), *adj.* not depraved or corrupted.

un·de·pre·ci·at·ed (un′di prē′shē ā′tid), *adj.* not depreciated or lowered in value.

un·de·pressed (un′di prest′), *adj.* **1.** not pressed down; not lowered; not sunk below the surface. **2.** not depressed, dejected, or cast down: . . . *disarmed but undepressed* (Byron).

un·der (un′dər), *prep.* **1.** below; beneath: *The book fell under the table.* **2.** below the surface of: *under the ground.* **3.** lower than; lower down than; not so high as: *to hit under the belt.* **4.** less than: *It will cost under ten dollars.* **5.** during the rule, time, influence, etc., of: *England under the four Georges.* **6.** in the position or condition of being affected by: *under the new rules.* **7.** because of: *under the circumstances.* **8.** according to: *under the law.* **9.** represented by: *under a new name.* **10.** required or bound by: *under obligation.*

—*adv.* **1.** below; beneath: *The swimmer went under.* **2.** in or to a lower place or condition.

—*adj.* lower in position, rank, degree, amount, price, etc.: *the under level.*

[Old English *under*]

—**Syn.** *prep.* **1. Under, below, beneath** express a relation in which one thing is thought of as being lower than another in some way. **Under** suggests being directly lower: *A corporal is under a sergeant.* **Below** suggests being on a lower level, but not necessarily straight below nor without anyone or anything in between: *A corporal is below a major.* **Beneath** suggests being under and hence covered or hidden from view: *He lies beneath the ground. He is beneath notice.*

under-, *prefix.* **1.** on the underside; to a lower position; from a lower position; below; beneath, as in *underline.*

2. being beneath; worn beneath, as in *underclothes, underwear.*

3. lower, as in *underlip.*

4. lower in rank; subordinate, as in *undersheriff.*

5. not enough; insufficiently, as in *undercooked, underfed.*

6. below normal, as in *undersized.*

[< *under*]

un·der·a·chieve (un′dər ə chēv′), *v.i.,* **-chieved, -chiev·ing.** to fail to do schoolwork at the level of ability indicated by intelligence tests: *Two to three times as many boys underachieve in schools as do girls* (National Education Association Journal).

un·der·a·chieve·ment (un′dər ə chēv′-mənt), *n.* a failure to achieve; lack of accomplishment, especially in schoolwork.

un·der·a·chiev·er (un′dər ə chē′vər), *n.* a pupil who fails to work at his level of ability.

un·der·act (un′dər akt′), *v.t., v.i.* to act (a part) insufficiently or with less than the usual or expected emphasis; underplay.

un·der·age (un′dər āj′), *adj.* not of full age; less than the usual or required age. —**Syn.** minor.

un·der·a·gent (un′dər ā′jənt), *n.* a subordinate agent.

un·der·arm (un′dər ärm′), *adj.* **1.** in or on that part of the arm that is closest to the body when the arm hangs loose: *an underarm scar.* **2.** of or having to do with the armpit. **3.** for the armpit: *an underarm deodorant.* **4.** *Especially British.* underhand: *an underarm throw.*

—*adv. Especially British.* with an underhand motion.

un·der·bel·ly (un′dər bel′ē), *n., pl.* **-lies. 1.** the part of the belly of a four-legged animal or lower surface of a reptile that is farthest from the spine, analogous to the part of man at the front between the ribs and the pelvis. **2.** anything like the underbelly of an animal; an unprotected or vulnerable part.

un·der·bid (un′dər bid′), *v.,* **-bid, -bid·ding,** *n.* —*v.t.* **1.** to offer to work, supply goods, etc., at a lower price than (another): *to underbid a competitor.* **2.** to bid less than the full point value of: *to underbid a hand in bridge.* —*v.i.* to bid less than another or less than the full value of.

—*n.* an underbidding. —**un′der·bid′der,** *n.*

un·der·bill (un′dər bil′), *v.t.* to bill at less than the actual amount or value.

un·der·bit (un′dər bit′), *n. U.S.* an earmark to show ownership, made on the lower part of the ear of cattle.

un·der·bod·ice (un′dər bod′is), *n.* a bodice worn under an outer bodice.

un·der·bod·y (un′dər bod′ē), *n., pl.* **-bod·ies. 1.** the underside of an animal's body. **2.** the under portion of the body of a vehicle. **3.** the part of a ship's hull below the water line.

un·der·branch (un′dər branch′, -bränch′), *n. Obsolete.* a twig or branchlet.

un·der·breath (un′dər breth′), *n.* a low, subdued tone; whisper. —*adj.* whispered.

un·der·bred (un′dər bred′), *adj.* **1.** of inferior breeding or manners; coarse and vulgar; ill-bred: *a pert little obtrusive underbred creature* (Thackeray). **2.** (of a horse, dog, etc.) not of pure breed; not thoroughbred.

un·der·brush (un′dər brush′), *n.* shrubs, bushes, and small trees growing under large trees in woods or forests. [American English < *under* + *brush*[2]]

un·der·build (un′dər bild′), *v.t.,* **-built, -build·ing. 1.** to build under, as a means of strengthening or supporting; underpin: *to underbuild a pier.* **2.** to build too little or too poorly.

un·der·burn (un′dər bėrn′), *v.t.,* **-burned** or **-burnt, -burn·ing.** to bake (brick, tile, etc.) insufficiently.

un·der·but·ler (un′dər but′lər), *n.* an assistant to a butler; one who works under a butler.

un·der·buy (un′dər bī′), *v.t.,* **-bought, -buy·ing. 1.** to buy at less than the actual value or market price. **2.** to buy for less than someone else. **3.** to buy less of than one should.

un·der·cap·i·tal·i·za·tion (un′dər kap′ə tə lə zā′shən), *n.* the state of being undercapitalized.

un·der·cap·i·tal·ize (un′dər kap′ə tə līz), *v.t.,* **-ized, -iz·ing. 1.** to supply with capital less than sufficient to operate efficiently or to carry out a program. **2.** to issue stock or other securities to an amount small in proportion to assets and earnings.

un·der·car·riage (un′dər kar′ij), *n.* **1.** the lower parts, often retractable, of an aircraft, by which it is supported on the ground or water; landing gear. **2.** the supporting framework of an automobile, carriage, etc., on which the body is mounted or built.

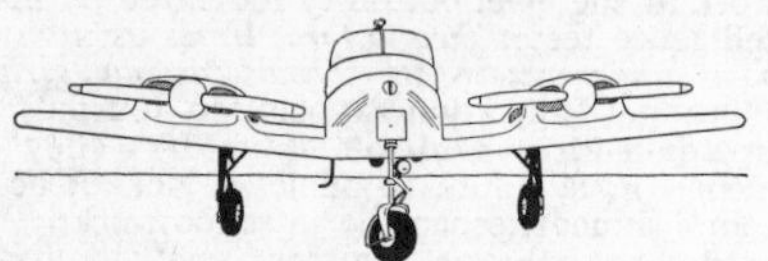

Undercarriage (def. 1)

un·der·cast (un′dər kast′), *n.* **1.** an air passage cut through the rock or coal beneath the floor of a mine. **2.** a layer of clouds beneath a flying airplane: *There's a black cloud of smoke coming up through the undercast* (Time).

un·der·charge (*v.* un′dər chärj′; *n.* un′dər-chärj′), *v.,* **-charged, -charg·ing,** *n.* —*v.t.* **1.** to charge (a person or persons) less than the established or a fair price; charge too little. **2.** to undercharge a person or persons by (so much). **3.** to load (a gun, shell, etc.) with an insufficient amount of explosive.
—*n.* **1.** a charge or price less than is proper or fair. **2.** an insufficient charge or load.

un·der·class·es (un′dər klas′iz, -kläs′-), *n. pl.* the freshman and sophomore classes.

un·der·class·man (un′dər klas′mən, -kläs′-), *n., pl.* **-men.** *U.S.* a freshman or sophomore; lowerclassman.

un·der·clothe (un′dər klōᴛʜ′), *v.t.,* **-clothed, -cloth·ing.** to provide with underclothing. [back formation < *underclothing*]

un·der·clothed (un′dər klōᴛʜd′), *adj.* not sufficiently clothed; not properly clad.

un·der·clothes (un′dər klōz′, -klōᴛʜz′), *n. pl.* underwear.

un·der·cloth·ing (un′dər klō′ᴛʜing), *n.* underclothes; underwear.

un·der·club (un′dər klub′), *v.i.,* **-clubbed, -club·bing.** *Golf.* to use a club of insufficient power to gain the desired distance: *Many British players underclubbed here on Saturday, deceived by the change in weather* (London Times).

un·der·coat (un′dər kōt′), *n.* **1.** a coat (of paint, varnish, etc.) applied before the finishing coats; primer. **2. a.** a heavy, tarlike substance sprayed on the underneath parts of an automobile to protect them from water, dirt, salt, etc., on the road. **b.** a coating of this substance. —*v.t., v.i.* to apply an undercoat to.

un·der·coat·ing (un′dər kō′ting), *n.* **1.** an undercoat. **2.** the process of applying an undercoat.

un·der·cooked (un′dər kůkt′, un′dər-kůkt′), *adj.* not cooked enough; underdone.

un·der·cov·er (un′dər kuv′ər), *adj.* working or done in secret: *The jeweler was an undercover agent of the police.*

un·der·croft (un′dər krôft′, -kroft′), *n.* an underground vault or chamber; crypt, especially a crypt under a church or other place of worship.

un·der·cur·rent (un′dər kėr′ənt), *n.* **1.** a current below the upper currents, or below the surface, of a body of water, air, etc.: *Part of this air then returns as an undercurrent* (Thomas H. Huxley). **2.** an underlying quality or tendency contrary to what is openly avowed or expressed: *There was an undercurrent of melancholy in Lincoln's humor.*

un·der·cut (*v.* un′dər kut′; *n., adj.* un′dər-kut′), *v.,* **-cut, -cut·ting,** *n., adj.* —*v.t.* **1.** to cut under or beneath; cut away or into the substance of from below: *to undercut a stratum of rock.* **2.** to weaken; undermine: *The announcement . . . was timed to undercut attempts . . . to mobilize pressure against the Government* (New York Times). **3.** to cut or shape (an object) so as to leave a portion overhanging, as in carving and sculpture. **4.** to notch (the trunk of a tree, a large limb, etc.) so as to ensure falling in the desired direction or to prevent splitting. **5.** to sell or work, or offer to do so, for less than (another person or persons). **6.** to hit (a ball) slightly under the horizontal axis, thereby usually producing some degree of backspin, a short, loftly, sharply dropping flight, and a minimum of roll or bounce, especially: **a.** to hit (a golf ball) thus, as in getting out of a trap or making a short approach to a hole. **b.** to hit (a tennis ball) thus, as in trapping one's opponent at the net. —*v.i.* to subject anything to undercutting.
—*n.* **1.** a cut, or a cutting away, underneath. **2.** a notch cut in a tree to determine the direction in which the tree is to fall and to prevent splitting. **3.** *Especially British.* a tenderloin or fillet of beef.
—*adj.* **1.** cut away underneath. **2.** done by undercutting.

un·der·de·vel·oped (un′dər di vel′əpt), *adj.* poorly or insufficiently developed, as in technology, medicine, and standard of living: *In the underdeveloped lands, two thirds of the free world's people are underfed, badly housed, illiterate* (Newsweek).

un·der·de·vel·op·ment (un′dər di vel′əp-mənt), *n.* a being underdeveloped.

un·der·do (un′dər dü′), *v.i., v.t.,* **-did, -done, -do·ing.** to cook insufficiently.

un·der·dog (un′dər dôg′, -dog′), *n.* **1.** the dog having the worst of a fight. **2.** the person having the worst of any struggle: *His early experience of poverty made him a champion of the underdog on every possible occasion* (London Times). **3.** a contestant not favored to win: *an outnumbered Army squad that had entered the contest a 4-point underdog* (New York Times). [American English < *under-* + *dog*]

un·der·done (un′dər dun′, un′dər dun′), *adj.* not cooked enough; cooked very little. —*v.* the past participle of **underdo.**

un·der·dose (*n.* un′dər dōs′; *v.* un′dər-dōs′), *n., v.,* **-dosed, -dos·ing.** —*n.* an insufficient dose. —*v.t.* to dose insufficiently; give too small a dose to.

un·der·drain (*v.* un′dər drān′; *n.* un′dər-drān′), *v.t.* to drain by means of drains placed under the ground. —*n.* a drain placed under the ground.

un·der·drain·age (un′dər drā′nij), *n.* the drainage of land by drains buried in it.

un·der·draw (un′dər drô′), *v.t.,* **-drew, -drawn, -draw·ing. 1.** to draw or represent inadequately. **2.** to cover (the inside of a roof, floor, etc.) with boards or with lath and plaster. **3.** to draw from (a bank account) so as to leave a reserve.

un·der·drawers (un′dər drôrz′), *n.pl. U.S.* underpants.

un·der·dress (*v.* un′dər dres′; *n.* un′dər-dres′), *v.t., v.i.* to dress plainly or too plainly: *Well-dressed women often intentionally underdress.* —*n.* **1.** a plain dress worn under an overdress or outer drapery. **2.** a slip.

un·der·dressed (un′dər drest′), *adj.* not dressed well or elaborately enough, as for a state occasion or an entertainment.

un·der·drew (un′dər drü′), *v.* the past tense of **underdraw.**

un·der·drift (un′dər drift′), *n.* a tendency under the surface of things; undercurrent.

un·der·driv·en (un′dər driv′ən), *adj. Machinery.* of or having to do with a driving mechanism in which the power is applied below the place where the work is done.

un·der·earth (un′dər ėrth′), *n.* the regions or matter below the surface of the earth. —*adj.* underground; subterranean.

un·der·eat·en (un′dər ē′tən), *adj.* eaten away or eroded below: *an undereaten rock.*

un·der·ed·u·cat·ed (un′dər ej′ů kā′tid), *adj.* poorly or insufficiently educated: *By overemphasizing courses in "methodology" at the expense of regular academic subjects, they've produced a generation of undereducated teachers* (Wall Street Journal).

un·der·em·pha·sis (un′dər em′fə sis), *n.* insufficient emphasis; lack of importance or stress.

un·der·em·pha·size (un′dər em′fə sīz), *v.t.,* **-sized, -siz·ing.** to emphasize insufficiently; not stress enough: *Basic research is still underemphasized in the United States* (Bulletin of Atomic Scientists).

un·der·em·ployed (un′dər em ploid′), *adj.* **1.** not sufficiently employed: **a.** not put to the fullest or most profitable use: *Lastly, I proceed on the hope . . . that full employment will mean just that and not a body of workers fully paid but underemployed* (Punch). **b.** working only part of the time: *One fourth of the labor force is out of work or underemployed* (Time). **2.** not employing or offering employment to enough people: *Some American railways, at the present time, are underemployed* (Wall Street Journal). —*n.* underemployed people.

un·der·em·ploy·ment (un′dər em ploi′-mənt), *n.* insufficient employment.

un·der·e·quipped (un′dər i kwipt′), *adj.* lacking the necessary equipment; poorly or inadequately equipped: *The great need of the city of New York . . . is the swift rehabilitation of its underequipped and insufficiently used system of rapid mass transportation* (Lewis Mumford).

un·der·es·ti·mate (*v.* un′dər es′tə māt; *n.* un′dər es′tə mit, -māt), *v.,* **-mat·ed, -mat·ing,** *n.* —*v.t., v.i.* to estimate at too low a value, amount, rate, or the like: *to underestimate the power of human endurance* (John Buchan). *Certainly she [Willa Cather] has been radically underestimated* (Manchester Guardian). —*n.* an estimate that is too low.

un·der·es·ti·ma·tion (un′dər es′tə mā′-shən), *n.* **1.** the act or process of estimating at too low a rate. **2.** the state of being so estimated; undervaluation.

un·der·ex·pose (un′dər ek spōz′), *v.t.,* **-posed, -pos·ing.** *Photography.* to expose for a shorter time than required for the best results.

un·der·ex·po·sure (un′dər ek spō′zhər), *n. Photography.* exposure to the light for too short a time. Underexposure makes a photograph look dim.

un·der·fall (un′dər fôl′), *n.* the slope of a foothill.

un·der·feed (un′dər fēd′), *v.t., v.i.,* **-fed, -feed·ing. 1.** to feed too little; not give enough food, fuel, etc., to: *An underfed nation is incapable of the endurance required of first-class soldiers* (William R. Inge). **2.** to stoke with coal or other solid fuel from the bottom.

un·der·fi·nanced (un′dər fə nanst′, -fī-), *adj.* poorly or insufficiently financed: *Every time someone finds a new national need, understaffed, underfinanced schools are pressured to add new courses* (Harper's).

un·der·fired (un′dər fīrd′), *adj.* **1.** not fired or baked enough. **2.** supplied with fuel from below.

un·der·floor (un′dər flôr′, -flōr′), *v.t.* to floor below; make a lower floor for.

un·der·flow (un′dər flō′), *n.* a current flowing beneath the surface, or not in the same direction with the surface current, over a certain region; undercurrent.

un·der·foot (un′dər fůt′), *adv.* **1.** under one's foot or feet; on the ground; underneath: *Katherine, that cap of yours becomes you not . . . throw it underfoot* (Shakespeare). **2.** *U.S.* in the way: *She complained that her six small children were always underfoot.* —*adj.* lying under the foot or feet; downtrodden; abject.

un·der·foot·ing (un′dər fůt′ing), *n.* the ground under one's feet.

un·der·frame (un′dər frām′), *n.* a structure or framework on which a railroad car, the van of a truck, or an automobile engine is supported: *Of 1,380 cars to be built 100 will be 70-ton insulated, damage-free boxcars with cushion underframes and roller bearings* (Wall Street Journal). *In designing a 35-foot trailer, engineers usually allow three to five inches deflection space between the van and the underframe for spring compression* (Science News Letter).

un·der·fur (un′dər fėr′), *n.* the soft, fine hair under the outer coat of coarse hair of various mammals, as seals and beavers.

un·der·gar·ment (un′dər gär′mənt), *n.* a garment worn below another garment, especially next to the skin.

un·der·gird (un′dər gėrd′), *v.t.* to support or secure by a rope or the like passed beneath.

un·der·glaze (un′dər glāz′), *adj.* of or designating a decoration, color, etc., put on a ceramic object, as a piece of majolica, stoneware or china, before a more or less transparent glaze is applied.

un·der·go (un′dər gō′), *v.t.,* **-went, -gone, -go·ing.** **1.** to go or pass through; be subjected to; experience: *to undergo a complete alteration in point of view.* **2.** to bear the burden of; endure; suffer: *Soldiers undergo many hardships.* —**Syn. 1, 2.** See **experience.**

un·der·gone (un′dər gôn′, -gon′), *v.* the past participle of **undergo:** *The town has undergone great change in the last five years.*

un·der·grad (un′dər grad′), *n. Informal.* an undergraduate: *Seton Hall, with fewer than 4,000 undergrads, is noted mainly for its basketball teams* (Time).

un·der·grad·u·ate (un′dər graj′ů it), *n.* a student, especially in a college or university, who has not received a degree for a course of study.
—*adj.* **1.** of or having to do with undergraduates. **2.** for undergraduates. **3.** like undergraduates. **4.** that is an undergraduate.

un·der·grad·u·ate·ship (un′dər graj′ů it ship), *n.* the condition or standing of an undergraduate.

un·der·grad·u·ette (un′dər graj′ů et′), *n. British.* a girl or woman undergraduate; coed: "*It [Oxford] was a male community,*" *says Mr. Waugh.* "*Undergraduettes lived in purdah*" (W. H. Auden).

un·der·ground (*adv.* un′dər ground′; *adj., n., v.* un′dər ground′), *adv.* **1.** beneath the surface of the ground: *to burrow underground. Miners work underground.* **2.** in secrecy or concealment; concealed from the eyes of the public, authorities, etc.; surreptitiously: *Spies work underground.* **3.** into secrecy or concealment: *to go underground.*
—*adj.* **1.** being, working, or used beneath the surface of the ground; subterranean. **2. a.** concealed from the eyes of the public, authorities, etc.; clandestine; secret. **b.** of or having to do with the underground: *an underground headquarters. During the war he had been chosen, it was said, as the underground leader of a very wide area in the event of a successful German invasion* (Geoffrey Household). **3.** resisting tyrannical government, etc., secretly: *an underground movement against the government.*
—*n.* **1.** a place or space beneath the surface of the ground. **2.** *Especially British.* a subterranean railroad; subway. **3.** a secret organization, or grouping of such organizations, working in a country to free it from foreign domination or to overthrow the regime in power: *We ... fought side by side in the anti-Fascist underground* (Atlantic).
—*v.t.* to place or lay underground: *The President's Conference on Natural Beauty specifically recommended widespread undergrounding of low voltage distribution lines* (New York Times). —**un′der·ground′er,** *n.*

underground film or **movie,** a motion picture made outside an ordinary commercial studio, usually at a low cost, and intended for a small or select audience: "*Love Song*" *is a low-pressure, small-scale, highly informal operation, more suggestive of underground movies or off-Broadway theater than ... of commercial television* (New York Times).

underground railroad, 1. *U.S.* a system by which the opponents of slavery secretly helped fugitive slaves to escape to the free states or Canada before the Civil War. **2.** a railroad running through tunnels under the ground or streets; subway.

un·der·grown (un′dər grōn′), *adj.* not fully grown; of low stature.

un·der·growth (un′dər grōth′), *n.* **1.** a growth of plants or shrubs under trees or other tall vegetation; underbrush. **2.** the shorter, finer hair underlying the outer hair of any of various animals.

un·der·hand (un′dər hand′), *adj.* **1.** done with the hand below the level of the shoulder; underarm. **2.** with the knuckles downward: *an underhand hold on a bat.* **3.** underhanded.
—*adv.* **1.** in an underhand manner: *to throw a ball underhand.* **2.** secretly; slyly.

un·der·hand·ed (un′dər han′did), *adj.* not open or honest; basely sly or deceitful: *an underhanded trick.* —**un′der·hand′ed·ly,** *adv.* —**un′der·hand′ed·ness,** *n.*

un·der·housed (un′dər houzd′), *adj.* having poor or inadequate housing: *Yugoslavia is underpopulated, underhoused, underfed* (Atlantic).

un·der·hung (un′dər hung′), *adj.* **1.** resting on a track beneath, instead of being hung from above: *underhung sliding doors.* **2.** (of the lower jaw) projecting beyond the upper jaw; undershot: *A bulldog has an underhung jaw.*

un·der·jaw (un′dər jô′), *n.* the lower jaw; mandible.

un·der·jawed (un′dər jôd′), *adj.* having a protruding lower jaw; undershot.

un·der·keep·er (un′dər kē′pər), *n.* an assistant keeper of a forest, park, etc.

un·der·laid (un′dər lād′), *adj.* **1.** supported, fitted, or supplied underneath (with something). **2.** placed or built beneath; underlying. —*v.* the past tense and past participle of **underlay.**

un·der·lain (un′dər lān′), *v.* the past participle of **underlie.**

un·der·lap (un′dər lap′), *v.t.,* **-lapped, -lap·ping.** to lap under; extend some way below: *The feathers of a bird's wing underlap each other.*

un·der·lay[1] (*v.* un′dər lā′; *n.* un′dər lā′), *v.,* **-laid, -lay·ing,** *n.* —*v.t.* **1.** to lay or place (one thing) under another. **2.** to provide with something laid underneath; raise or support with something laid underneath. **3.** to coat or cover the bottom of.
—*n.* **1.** something laid beneath. **2.** *Printing.* a piece of paper, or a sheet with pieces pasted on it, laid under type to bring it to the proper height for printing.
[Old English *underlecgan* < *under-* under- + *lecgan* to lay]

un·der·lay[2] (un′dər lā′), *v.* the past tense of **underlie.**

un·der·lay·er (un′dər lā′ər), *n.* a lower layer; substratum.

un·der·leaf (un′dər lēf′), *n.* the under surface of a leaf.

un·der·lease (*n.* un′dər lēs′; *v.* un′dər lēs′), *n., v.t., v.i.,* **-leased, -leas·ing.** sublease.

un·der·let (un′dər let′), *v.t.,* **-let, -let·ting.** *Especially British.* **1.** to sublet. **2.** to rent or lease for less than the amount actually worth or able to be obtained.

un·der·lie (un′dər lī′), *v.t.,* **-lay, -lain, -ly·ing. 1.** to lie under; be beneath; subtend. **2.** to form the basis or foundation of, especially: **a.** to give rise to; be the reason behind or origin of: *What underlies that remark?* **b.** to give basic support to; be essential to. **3.** *Finance.* to come before another (privilege or security) in time and order. **4.** *Scottish.* to submit or be required to submit to (a punishment, charge, etc.). [Old English *underlicgan* < *under-* under- + *licgan* lie[1]]

un·der·life (un′dər līf′), *n.* **1.** life below the surface. **2.** a way of living apart and different from the life open to the common knowledge or view.

un·der·line (un′dər līn′, un′dər līn′), *v.,* **-lined, -lin·ing,** *n.* —*v.t.* **1.** to draw a line or lines under; underscore: *In writing we underline titles of books.* **2.** to make emphatic or more emphatic; emphasize.
—*n.* **1.** a line drawn or printed under a word, passage, etc. **2.** the line of the lower part of the body of an animal, especially a sheep.

un·der·lin·en (un′dər lin′ən), *n.* linen (or cotton) undergarments.

un·der·ling (un′dər ling), *n.* a person of lower rank or position; subordinate (usually disparagingly): *The fault, dear Brutus, is not in our stars But in ourselves, that we are underlings* (Shakespeare). [Old English *underling* < *under* under + *-ling* -ling]

un·der·lin·ing[1] (un′dər lī′ning), *n.* the inner lining of a garment.

un·der·lin·ing[2] (un′dər lī′ning), *n.* **1.** the drawing of a line or lines under a word, passage, etc. **2.** the line or lines so drawn.

un·der·lip (un′dər lip′), *n.* the lower lip of a person, animal, or insect.

un·der·load (un′dər lōd′), *v.t.* to put an insufficient load on or in.

un·der·look (*v.* un′dər lůk′; *n.* un′dər-lůk′), *v.t.* **1.** to look at from below. **2.** to miss seeing by looking too low. —*n.* a covert look; secret glance.

un·der·look·er (un′dər lůk′ər), *n.* a person who assists the manager of a mine and is in charge of the miners and workings.

un·der·ly·ing (un′dər lī′ing), *adj.* **1.** lying under or beneath; subtending: *The stones That name the underlying dead* (Tennyson). **2.** forming the basis or foundation of; fundamental; basic; essential: *underlying facts.* **3.** not evident at first glance; present but not apparent except through careful scrutiny. **4.** *Finance.* coming before another in time and order; having priority.
—*v.* the present participle of **underlie.**

un·der·man (un′dər man′), *v.t.,* **-manned, -man·ning.** to furnish with an insufficient number of men: *Our merchant ships are always undermanned* (Richard Henry Dana).

un·der·men·tioned (un′dər men′shənd), *adj.* mentioned below or beneath.

un·der·mine (un′dər mīn′, un′dər mīn′), *v.t.,* **-mined, -min·ing. 1.** to make a passage or hole under; tunnel through or into; dig under: *to undermine a foundation. The soldiers undermined the wall.* **2.** to wear away the foundations of; remove the underlying substance of: *The cliff was undermined by waves.* **3.** to weaken, injure, destroy, or ruin by secret or unfair means: *to undermine a man's reputation by scandal.* **4.** to weaken or destroy gradually; sap: *Her health has been undermined by a starvation diet.* —**Syn. 3, 4.** See **weaken.**

un·der·min·er (un′dər mī′nər, un′dər-mī′-), *n.* **1.** a secret or insidious assailant or destroyer. **2.** *Especially British.* a person who undermines; sapper.

un·der·most (un′dər mōst), *adj., adv.* at the very bottom; lowest.

un·dern (un′dərn), *n. British Dialect.* **1.** the afternoon or evening. **2.** a light meal, especially one taken in the afternoon. [< Middle English *undern* (originally) the third hour of the day, tierce, Old English]

un·der·neath (un′dər nēth′), *prep.* **1.** beneath; below; under: *to sit underneath a tree, a cellar underneath a house.* **2.** under the power or control of; subject to: *underneath the yoke of Government* (Shakespeare). **3.** *Archaic.* under the form or cover of.
—*adv.* **1.** beneath what is on top; down below: *Someone was pushing underneath.* **2.** beneath what is outermost: *to wear wool underneath.* **3.** on the underside; at the bottom or base: *a house rotten underneath.*
—*adj.* lower; under.
—*n.* the lower part or surface.
[Old English *underneothan* < *under-* under + *neothan* below]

un·der·note (un′dər nōt′), *n.* a low or subdued note; undertone; suggestion: *an undernote of gaiety, an undernote of good sense.*

un·der·nour·ish (un′dər nėr′ish), *v.t.* to provide with less food than is necessary for growth, maintenance of vigor, health, etc.; give insufficient nourishment to.

un·der·nour·ished (un′dər nėr′isht), *adj.* not sufficiently nourished; underfed.

un·der·nour·ish·ment (un′dər nėr′ish-mənt), *n.* not having enough food; lack of nourishment.

un·dern·song (un′dərn sông′, -song′), *n. Ecclesiastical, Obsolete.* tierce. [< Old English *undernsang* < *undern* (originally) tierce; noon, forenoon + *sang* song]

un·der·nu·tri·tion (un′dər nü trish′ən, -nyü-), *n.* incomplete or imperfect nutrition; undernourishment: *It is economic unavailability which is the chief reason for the malnutrition and undernutrition which affects two out of three of the world's people* (New Scientist).

un·der·of·fi·cer (*v.* un′dər ôf′ə sər, -of′-; *n.* un′dər ôf′ə sər, -of′-), *v.t.* to furnish inadequately with officers. —*n.* an officer of a lower grade.

un·der·paid (un′dər pād′), *v.* the past tense and past participle of **underpay.**

un·der·paint·ing (un′dər pān′ting), *n.* a plan for a painting, showing the outline, shadows or highlights, and sometimes the color scheme, painted on the canvas: *He paints at times in such very thin washes that the underpainting often shows through, giving a streaky texture that is distracting* (New Yorker).

un·der·pants (un′dər pants′), *n.pl.* pants of various styles and lengths worn as an undergarment by men and women.

un·der·part (un′dər pärt′), *n.* **1.** a secondary or subordinate part; minor rôle: *to play an underpart in a drama.* **2.** the part of an object, animal, etc., that lies below or underneath: *The tree swallow has pure white underparts.*

un·der·pass (un′dər pas′, -päs′), *n.* a passageway for vehicles, pedestrians, or both, under another passageway, as railroad tracks under a main highway. [American English < *under-* + *pass*[2]]

un·der·pay (un′dər pā′), *v.t., v.i.,* **-paid, -pay·ing.** to pay too little.

un·der·peo·pled (un′dər pē′pəld), *adj.* underpopulated.

un·der·pin (un′dər pin′), *v.t.,* **-pinned, -pin·ning. 1.** to support or strengthen (a building or other structure) from beneath, as with props, stones, or masonry: *to underpin a wall.* **2.** to form or provide a base or fundamental support to (anything); support; prop. **3.** to corroborate; vindicate.

un·der·pin·ning (un′dər pin′ing), *n.* **1.** the materials or structure that give support from beneath to a building, wall, etc.: *an outside wall with new underpinning of poured concrete.* **2.** a support; prop.

Underpinning (def. 1)

un·der·plant (un′der plant′, -plänt′), *v.t.* to plant (young trees) under an existing stand of trees.

un·der·play (un′dər plā′), *v.t., v.i.* to underact.

un·der·plot (un′dər plot′), *n.* a dramatic or literary plot subordinate to the principal plot, but connected with it; subplot.

un·der·pop·u·lat·ed (un′dər pop′yə lā′tid), *adj.* not sufficiently or well populated; having too small a population.

un·der·pow·ered (un′dər pou′ərd), *adj.* not sufficiently or well powered: *Early airships were underpowered* (New Scientist).

un·der·price (un′dər prīs′), *v.t.,* **-priced, -pric·ing. 1.** to price lower than the value: *to underprice a car or suit.* **2.** to undercut in price: *to underprice a competitor.*

un·der·print (un′dər print′), *v.t.* to print (a photograph, etc.) with not enough depth or distinctness.

un·der·priv·i·leged (un′dər priv′ə lijd), *adj.* having fewer advantages than most people have, especially because of poor economic or social status: *an underprivileged child, an underprivileged nation.*

un·der·prize (un′dər prīz′), *v.t.,* **-prized, -priz·ing.** to prize too little; put a low value on; underestimate.

un·der·pro·duc·tion (un′dər prə duk′shən), *n.* production that is less than normal or less than there is a demand for.

un·der·pro·mote (un′dər prə mōt′), *v.t.,* **-mot·ed, -mot·ing.** (in chess) to exchange (a pawn) reaching the eighth rank for a rook, bishop, or knight instead of a queen.

un·der·pro·mo·tion (un′dər prə mō′shən), *n.* (in chess) an underpromoting or being underpromoted.

un·der·proof (un′dər prüf′), *adj.* having less alcohol than proof spirit does (in the United States, less than 50 per cent by volume).

un·der·prop (un′dər prop′), *v.t.,* **-propped, -prop·ping.** to prop underneath; support.

un·der·quote (un′dər kwōt′), *v.t.,* **-quot·ed, -quot·ing. 1.** to offer to sell merchandise, a commodity, etc., at a lower price than (another or others); underbid. **2.** to offer (merchandise, a commodity, etc.) for sale at a lower price than someone or anyone else.

un·der·rate (un′dər rāt′), *v.t.,* **-rat·ed, -rat·ing.** to rate or estimate too low; put too low a value on. —**Syn.** underestimate.

un·der·re·port (un′dər ri pôrt′, -pōrt′), *v.t.* **1.** to cover (a news event, etc.) inadequately; underemphasize the importance of: *Africa is very much underreported, even though it is making history every day* (Time). **2.** to report (an amount, etc.) less than the actual: *The totals ... are so low as to suggest considerable underreporting* (Jean A. Flexner).

un·der·rep·re·sent·ed (un′dər rep′ri zen′tid), *adj.* represented inadequately or by less than a proper proportion.

un·der·ripe (un′dər rīp′), *adj.* not fully ripe; partly ripe.

un·der·run (un′dər run′), *v.t.,* **-ran, -run, -run·ning. 1.** to pass or move beneath. **2.** to move along in a boat beneath (a cable, net, etc.) in order to examine, repair, etc.

un·der·score (*v.* un′dər skôr′, -skōr′; *n.* un′dər skôr′, -skōr′), *v.,* **-scored, -scor·ing,** *n.* —*v.t.* **1.** to underline. **2.** to emphasize. —*n.* an underscored line.

un·der·scrub (un′dər skrub′), *n.* underbrush; undergrowth.

un·der·sea (*adj.* un′dər sē′; *adv.* un′dər-sē′), *adj.* being, done, working, or used beneath the surface of the sea: *an undersea cable, undersea exploration. The German submarine was the first dangerous undersea raider of World War II.* —*adv.* underseas.

un·der·seas (un′dər sēz′), *adv.* beneath the surface of the sea: *Submarines go underseas.*

un·der·sec·re·tar·y (un′dər sek′rə ter′ē), *n., pl.* **-tar·ies. 1.** an official of a government department ranking just below the official who is at the head of it, or sometimes just below the official's deputy. **2.** a subordinate secretary.

un·der·sell (un′dər sel′), *v.t.,* **-sold, -sell·ing. 1.** to sell merchandise, a commodity, etc., at a lower price than (someone else); sell for less. **2.** to sell (merchandise, etc.) at less than the actual value; sell at a loss. —**un′der·sell′er,** *n.*

un·der·serv·ant (un′dər sėr′vənt), *n.* a servant who does the simpler or lower tasks.

un·der·set (un′dər set′), *v.t.,* **-set, -set·ting. 1.** to provide or support with something set beneath; underpin; prop. **2.** to set (a thing) under something else.

un·der·sexed (un′dər sekst′), *adj.* having little interest in or capacity for sexual activity.

un·der·shap·en (un′dər shā′pən), *adj.* misshapen.

un·der·sher·iff (un′dər sher′if), *n.* a sheriff's deputy, especially one who acts when the sheriff is not able to act or when there is no sheriff.

un·der·shirt (un′dər shėrt′), *n.* a close-fitting undergarment of knitted cotton, etc., with or without sleeves, for the upper part of the body, worn next to the skin, especially by men, boys, and young children.

un·der·shoot (un′dər shüt′), *v.,* **-shot, -shoot·ing.** —*v.t.* to shoot short of; shoot too low for: *to undershoot a target.* —*v.i.* to shoot too short or low.

un·der·shore (un′dər shôr′, -shōr′), *v.t.,* **-shored, -shor·ing. 1.** to prop up or support with shores. **2.** to support; strengthen.

un·der·shorts (un′dər shôrts′), *n.pl.* underpants for men and boys; shorts.

un·der·shot (un′dər shot′), *adj.* **1.** having the lower jaw or teeth protruding beyond the upper when the mouth is closed; underhung. **2.** driven by water passing beneath: *an undershot water wheel.* —*v.* the past tense and past participle of **undershoot.**

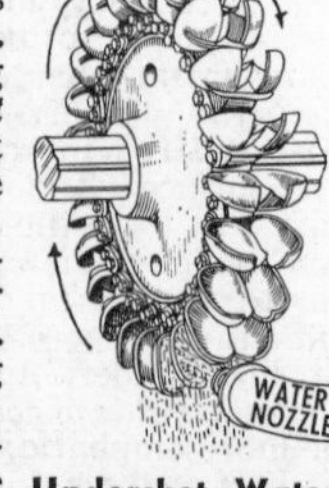

Undershot Water Wheel (def. 2)

un·der·shrub (un′dər-shrub′), *n.* **1.** a small or low-growing shrub. **2.** *Botany.* a plant having a shrubby base.

un·der·side (un′dər-sīd′), *n.* the surface lying underneath; bottom side.

un·der·sign (un′dər sīn′, un′dər sīn′), *v.t.* to sign one's name at the end of (a letter or document); append one's signature to.

un·der·signed (un′dər sīnd′), *adj.* **1.** (of a person) having signed a letter or document; that is a signatory. **2.** (of a name) signed at the end of a letter or document. —*n.* **the undersigned,** the person or persons signing a letter or document: *I, the undersigned, ... am about to-day to lay down my life ... in defence of the Roman Catholic Church* (J. M. Stone).

un·der·size (un′dər sīz′), *adj.* undersized: *My boy looks undersize to me* (McCall's).

un·der·sized (un′dər sīzd′), *adj.* smaller than the usual, required, or specified size: *An undersized fish has to be thrown back.*

un·der·skirt (un′dər skėrt′), *n.* a skirt worn under an outer skirt or overskirt.

un·der·sleep (un′dər slēp′), *v.i.,* **-slept, -sleep·ing.** to sleep less than is necessary.

un·der·sleeve (un′dər slēv′), *n.* a sleeve worn under an outer sleeve, especially an ornamental inner sleeve extending below the other.

un·der·slung (un′dər slung′, un′dər-slung′), *adj.* **1.** (of a vehicle) having the frame suspended below the axles. **2.** (of a jaw) undershot.

un·der·soil (un′dər soil′), *n.* subsoil.

un·der·sold (un′dər sōld′), *v.* the past tense and past participle of **undersell.**

un·der·song (un′dər sông′, -song′), *n.* **1.** a song or strain serving as an accompaniment for another song, such as was common in very old English music. **2.** an underlying meaning; underlying element. [see UNDERNSONG]

un·der·sparred (un′dər spärd′), *adj. Nautical.* **1.** having spars too small for the amount of sail needed. **2.** having too few spars.

un·der·spin (un′dər spin′), *n.* a rolling motion in reverse to the direction of a ball. Underspin checks or reverses the forward motion of a ball when it strikes a surface.

un·der·staffed (un′dər staft′, -stäft′), *adj.* having a staff too small for one's needs and proper functioning: *an understaffed hospital. The major problem is overcrowded and understaffed colleges and universities* (Science News Letter).

un·der·stand (un′dər stand′), *v.,* **-stood, -stand·ing.** —*v.t.* **1.** to be familiar with as a meaningful unit of language; grasp the meaning of; know the meaning of: *I don't understand that word.* **2.** to grasp the meaning, purport, etc., of the words, signs, etc., used by (a person): *What did he say? I couldn't understand him.* **3.** to comprehend by knowing the meaning of the words employed: *I can understand French if it is spoken slowly. A tongue no man could understand* (Tennyson). **4.** to grasp the meaning or idea of; apprehend the import of; comprehend: *to understand the Declaration of Independence, to understand the philosophy of Kant, etc.* **5.** to be more or less thoroughly acquainted or familiar with; know, especially: **a.** to be able to explain, discuss, use, etc.: *to understand human anatomy, to understand the techniques of writing, etc.* **b.** to know how to deal with: *A good teacher understands children.* **6.** to comprehend as a fact; grasp clearly; realize: *You understand, don't you, that I will be away for three weeks?* **7.** to be informed; learn: *I understand that he is leaving town.* **8.** to take as a fact; believe: *It is understood that you will come.* **9.** to interpret; take: *How do you wish that remark to be understood?* **10.** to take as meaning or meant; infer (by); gather (from): *What are we to understand from his words?* **11.** to regard as present in thought, though not expressly stated. In "He hit the tree harder than I," the word *did* is understood after *I.*
—*v.i.* **1.** to have or gain understanding or comprehension; get the meaning; grasp something with the mind: *Don't expect that fool ever to understand. I have told him three times, but he doesn't understand yet.* **2.** to recognize and comprehend with a degree of sympathy, compassion, etc., the difficulties of the position or situation in which another finds himself: *to expect a mother always to understand.* **3.** to believe, assume, or infer: *He intends, as I understand, to leave tomorrow.* **4.** *Obsolete.* to have or get knowledge or information; learn.
understand each other, to know each other's meaning and wishes; agree: *"You trust me," replied Leather, ... with a look as much as to say, "we understand each other"* (R. S. Surtees).
[Old English *understandan*]
—**Syn.** *v.t.* **5.** See **know.**

un·der·stand·a·bil·i·ty (un′dər stan′də-bil′ə tē), *n.* the quality or state of being understandable.

un·der·stand·a·ble (un′dər stan′də bəl), *adj.* that can be understood. —**Syn.** comprehensible, intelligible.

un·der·stand·a·bly (un′dər stan′də blē), *adv.* in a manner that can be understood; conceivably: *an understandably appealing idea* (Wall Street Journal).

un·der·stand·er (un′dər stan′dər), *n.* **1.** a person who understands; one who has knowledge or comprehension: *Some are pleased to be accounted understanders by others, and rest in such high words, as a badge of knowledge* (Richard Gilpin). **2.** one who stands under: . . . *short and muscular, like the understander in a human pyramid* (New Yorker).

un·der·stand·ing (un′dər stan′ding), *n.* **1.** the act of one who understands, especially: **a.** comprehension: *to have a clear understanding of the problem.* **b.** knowledge: *a good understanding of what needs to be done.* **2.** the power or ability to understand; intellect; intelligence: *the limited understanding of a child. Edison was a man of understanding.* **3.** knowledge of each other's meaning and wishes: *a marriage based on true understanding.* **4.** a mutual arrangement or agreement of an informal but more or less explicit nature: *You and I must come to an understanding.*
—*adj.* that understands or is able to understand; intelligent: *an understanding reply.*
—**un′der·stand′ing·ly,** *adv.*

un·der·state (un′dər stāt′), *v.t., v.i.,* **-stat·ed, -stat·ing. 1.** to state too weakly, or less emphatically than most people would; underemphasize the key facts in or crucial nature of. **2.** to say less than the full truth about.

un·der·state·ment (un′dər stāt′mənt, un′dər stāt′-), *n.* **1.** a statement that expresses a fact too weakly. **2.** a statement that says less than could be said truly.

un·der·stock (un′dər stok′), *n.* the plant or part of a plant in which a graft is set.

un·der·stood (un′dər stu̇d′), *v.* the past tense and past participle of **understand:** *Have all of you understood today's lesson?*

un·der·sto·ry (un′dər stôr′ē, -stōr′-), *n., pl.* **-ries.** the low layer of plants forming an underbrush or underwood.

un·der·strap·per (un′dər strap′ər), *n.* a subordinate; inferior; underling. [< *under-* + *strap,* verb + *-er*[1]]

un·der·stra·tum (un′dər strā′təm, -strat′-əm), *n., pl.* **-stra·ta** (-strā′tə, -strat′ə), **-stra·tums.** an underlying stratum or layer; substratum.

un·der·strength (un′dər strengkth′, -strength′), *adj.* having too little strength; not up to the normal or required strength: *After Korea the Army gradually dwindled to 14 understrength divisions* (Time).

un·der·stroke (un′dər strōk′), *v.t.,* **-stroked, -strok·ing.** to underline; underscore.

un·der·struc·ture (un′dər struk′chər), *n.* the base on which a structure rests or is built; foundation: *Underground erosion damaged the understructure of the building. French money supports the whole understructure of the Tunisian economy* (Harper's).

un·der·stud·y (un′dər stud′ē), *n., pl.* **-stud·ies,** *v.,* **-stud·ied, -stud·y·ing.** —*n.* a person who can act as a substitute for an actor, actress, or any other regular performer: *Two of Notre Dame's touchdowns were scored by Worden's understudy, Tom McHugh* (New York Times).
—*v.t.* **1.** to learn (a part) in order to be able to take the place of a principal performer if necessary. **2.** to act as understudy to.
—*v.i.* to act as an understudy.

un·der·suit (un′dər süt′), *n.* a suit worn under or beneath another suit.

un·der·sup·ply (*v.* un′dər sə plī′; *n.* un′dər sə plī′), *v.,* **-plied, -ply·ing,** *n., pl.* **-plies.** —*v.t.* to supply insufficiently or inadequately: *If this should happen, the underdeveloped world will be even more desperately undersupplied with doctors* (Harper's). —*n.* an insufficient or inadequate supply: *The total money market is tight, which means that there is an undersupply of lendable capital and an oversupply of potential borrowers* (New York Times).

un·der·sur·face (un′dər sėr′fis), *n.* the surface lying underneath; underside: *the undersurface of a leaf.*

un·der·take (un′dər tāk′), *v.,* **-took, -tak·en, -tak·ing.** —*v.t.* **1.** to set about; try; attempt: *to undertake to reach home before dark.* **2.** to set about to accomplish; take in hand; begin: *to undertake a journey.* **3.** to agree to do; take upon oneself: *Kate undertook the feeding of my dogs.* **4.** to promise; guarantee: *I will undertake you shall be happy* (Henry Fielding). **5.** *Archaic.* to accept the duty of attending to or looking after; take in charge. **6.** *Obsolete.* to enter into combat with; engage. —*v.i. Archaic.* to make oneself answerable (for a person, fact, etc.); become surety: *I undertake For good Lord Titus' innocence* (Shakespeare).

un·der·tak·er (un′dər tā′kər *for 1;* un′dər-tā′kər *for 2*), *n.* **1.** a person whose business is preparing the dead for burial and arranging funerals. **2.** a person who undertakes something.

un·der·tak·ing (un′dər tā′king *for 1, 2;* un′dər tā′king *for 3*), *n.* **1.** something undertaken; task; enterprise: *a rash undertaking. My uncle engaged afterward in more prosperous undertakings* (Charlotte Brontë). *This is the very ecstasy of love, Whose violent property fordoes itself, And leads the will to desperate undertakings* (Shakespeare). **2.** a promise; guarantee: *Three hundred pounds a year . . . he proposed to pay her on an undertaking that she would never trouble him* (Thackeray). **3.** the business of preparing the dead for burial and arranging funerals.

un·der·ten·ant (un′dər ten′ənt), *n.* a subtenant.

un·der-the-count·er (un′dər ᴛʜə koun′-tər), *adj.* offered or transacted under a counter; hidden and stealthy; secret; unauthorized: *under-the-counter literature, under-the-counter payoffs.*

un·der-the-ta·ble (un′dər ᴛʜə tā′bəl), *adj.* under-the-counter.

un·der·things (un′dər thingz′), *n.pl.* underclothes.

un·der·thrust (un′dər thrust′), *n. Geology.* **1.** the forcing by compression of one rock mass under another, so as to produce a fault or fold. **2.** the condition caused by such a forcing. —*adj.* of or having to do with an underthrust: *an underthrust fault.*

un·der·time (*n., adv., adj.* un′dər tīm′; *v.* un′dər tīm′), *n., adv., adj., v.,* **-timed, -tim·ing.** —*n.* **1.** time less than or below the regular hours. **2.** wages for this period: *Would there not be merit in a scheme to pay undertime to workers?* (Atlantic).
—*adv.* less than or below the average hours: *He worked undertime this week and had to make it up.*
—*adj.* of or for undertime: *undertime pay.*
—*v.t.* to give too little time to: *to undertime a camera exposure.*

un·der·tone (un′dər tōn′), *n.* **1.** a low or very quiet tone: *to talk in an undertone. He dropped his voice to a confidential undertone* (H.G. Wells). **2.** a subdued or underlying tone of color; a color seen through other colors: *There was an undertone of brown beneath all the gold and crimson of autumn.* **3.** an underlying quality, condition, or element: *an undertone of sadness in her gaiety.* **4.** an underlying strength or weakness in the price level of any stock or commodity.

un·der·took (un′dər tu̇k′), *v.* the past tense of **undertake:** *He undertook more than he could do.*

un·der·tow (un′dər tō′), *n.* **1.** any current below the surface of the water, moving in a contrary direction to that of the surface current. **2.** the backward flow from waves breaking on a beach.

un·der·trained (un′dər trānd′), *adj.* insufficiently trained: *Undertrained and overworked sisters in parochial schools have taught hundreds of thousands of Catholic children* (Harper's).

un·der·trick (un′dər trik′), *n.* (in card games) a trick less than the number bid for or needed for game.

un·der·trump (un′dər trump′), *v.* in card games: —*v.t.* to play a trump to (a trick in which the lead is not trumps), lower than a trump already played by (another player). —*v.i.* to play a lower trump than one already played to a trick.

un·der·use (un′dər yüz′), *v.t.,* **-used, -us·ing.** to underutilize.

un·der·u·ti·lize (un′dər yü′tə līz), *v.t.,* **-lized, -liz·ing.** to utilize insufficiently or wastefully: *Children from predominantly Negro and Puerto Rican schools can transfer to underutilized schools* (New York Times).

un·der·val·u·a·tion (un′dər val′yu̇ ā′-shən), *n.* too low a valuation.

un·der·val·ue (un′dər val′yü), *v.t.,* **-ued, -u·ing. 1.** to put too low a value on; underprize. **2.** to esteem too little; appreciate insufficiently: *The Prince never committed the error of undervaluing the talents of his great adversary* (John L. Motley). —**Syn. 1, 2.** underrate, underestimate, depreciate.

un·der·vest (un′dər vest′), *n.* an undershirt.

un·der·vi·tal·ized (un′dər vī′tə līzd), *adj.* insufficiently vitalized; lacking in vitality: *Much of the music sounded starved in emotion, undervitalized, and small-scale* (London Times).

un·der·waist (un′dər wāst′), *n.* a waist worn under another waist.

un·der·wa·ter (un′dər wôt′ər, -wot′-), *adj.* **1.** below the surface of the water. **2.** made for use under the water: *A submarine is an underwater ship.* **3.** situated below the water line of a ship.

un·der·way (un′dər wā′), *adv.* in motion; in progress; going on: *Normally, politicians have a pretty good idea once a campaign gets underway of who is likely to win* (Newsweek).
—*adj.* taking place while in motion or progress: *The student receives training in preparation for sea [and] underway procedures . . . on a submarine* (Submarine Service, U.S. Naval Recruiting).

un·der·wear (un′dər wãr′), *n.* clothes worn below the outer garments, especially next to the skin; underclothes.

un·der·weight (un′dər wāt′), *adj.* having too little weight; not up to the normal or required weight. —*n.* weight that is not up to standard.

un·der·went (un′dər went′), *v.* the past tense of **undergo.**

un·der·wing (un′dər wing′), *n.* one of the hind set of wings of an insect.

underwing moth, any of a group of moths having brightly colored hind wings which are visible only in flight. See also **moth** for picture.

Sappho Underwing Moth
(wingspread, 2¾ in.)

un·der·wit (un′dər-wit′), *n.* a half-witted person; person who is stupid or feeble-minded.

un·der·wit·ted (un′-dər wit′id), *adj.* half-witted.

un·der·wood (un′dər wu̇d′), *n.* **1.** underbrush. **2.** a quantity or stretch of woody undergrowth.

un·der·wool (un′dər wu̇l′), *n.* a fine, soft wool under the coarse outer hair of various mammals.

un·der·work (*n.* un′dər wėrk′; *v.* un′dər-wėrk′), *n., v.,* **-worked** or **-wrought, -work·ing.** —*n.* **1.** subordinate or inferior work. **2.** secret or underhand work. **3.** a structure placed under something; substructure.
—*v.t.* **1.** to put insufficient work or labor on (something). **2.** to exact insufficient work from. **3.** to do the same work at a cheaper price than (another). **4.** *Obsolete.* to injure or weaken by secret or insidious means; undermine. —*v.i.* **1.** to do less work than is required or suitable. **2.** *Obsolete.* to work secretly or insidiously.

un·der·world (un′dər wėrld′), *n.* **1.** the lower, degraded, or criminal part of human society; portion of a community given over to crime and vice. **2.** the lower world; Hades: *The lord of the dark underworld, the king of the multitudinous dead, carried her [Persephone] off when . . . she strayed too far from her companions* (Edith Hamilton). **3.** the earth as distinguished from heaven. **4.** the opposite side of the earth; antipodes.

un·der·world·ling (un′dər wėrld′ling), *n. U.S. Informal.* a racketeer; gangster.

un·der·write (un′dər rīt′, un′dər rīt′), *v.,* **-wrote, -writ·ten, -writ·ing.** —*v.t.* **1. a.** to insure (property, etc.) against loss. **b.** to sign one's name to (an insurance policy), thereby accepting the risk of insuring the person or thing specified against loss. **c.** to assume liability for (a certain amount or risk) by way of insurance. **2. a.** to agree to buy (all the stocks or bonds of a certain issue that are not bought by the public): *The bankers underwrote the steel company's bonds.* **b.** to agree to buy (an entire issue of stocks or bonds). **3.** to agree to meet the expense of: *to underwrite a person's education.* **4.** to write under (other written matter); sign one's name to (a document, etc.); be a signatory to. —*v.i.* to carry on the business of insurance; be an underwriter. [compare Old English *underwrītan,* translation of Latin *subscrībere*]

un·der·writ·er (un′dər rī′tər), *n.* **1.** a person who underwrites an insurance policy or carries on an insurance business; insurer. **2.** an official of an insurance company who determines the risks to be accepted, the premiums to be paid, etc. **3.** a person who underwrites (usually with others) an issue or issues of bonds, stocks, etc. *Abbr.:* u/w

un·der·writ·ten (un′dər rit′ən, un′dər-rit′-), *v.* the past participle of **underwrite.**

un·der·wrote (un′dər rōt′, un′dər rōt′), *v.* the past tense of **underwrite.**

un·der·wrought (un′dər rôt′), *v.* underworked; a past tense and a past participle of **underwork.**

un·de·scribed (un′di skrībd′), *adj.* not described; not depicted, defined, or delineated: *an undescribed species.*

un·de·served (un′di zėrvd′), *adj.* not deserved or merited: *an undeserved reputation for wit* (Eden Phillpotts).

un·de·serv·ed·ly (un′di zėr′vid lē), *adv.* without desert, either good or evil; contrary to desert or what is merited: *athletic brutes whom undeservedly we call heroes* (John Dryden).

un·de·serv·er (un′di zėr′vər), *n.* an undeserving person; an unworthy person.

un·de·serv·ing (un′di zėr′ving), *adj.* not deserving or meriting. **—un′de·serv′ing·ly,** *adv.*

un·de·signed (un′di zīnd′), *adj.* not designed; unintentional.

un·de·sign·ed·ly (un′di zī′nid lē), *adv.* in an undesigned manner; without design or intention.

un·de·sign·ing (un′di zī′ning), *adj.* **1.** having no selfish or ulterior designs; free from designing motives; disinterested. **2.** simple and straightforward; not crafty.

un·de·sir·a·bil·i·ty (un′di zīr′ə bil′ə tē), *n.* the condition or character of being undesirable.

un·de·sir·a·ble (un′di zīr′ə bəl), *adj.* **1.** objectionable; disagreeable: *an undesirable side effect.* **2.** offensive to or subversive of the moral or social standards of an individual or group: *a gathering of criminals and other undesirable persons.* —*n.* an undesirable person or thing. **—un′de·sir′a·ble·ness,** *n.*

un·de·sir·a·bly (un′di zīr′ə blē), *adv.* in an undesirable manner; contrary to what is desirable.

un·de·sired (un′di zīrd′), *adj.* not desired; unwelcome.

un·de·tect·a·ble (un′di tek′tə bəl), *adj.* that cannot be detected.

un·de·tect·ed (un′di tek′tid), *adj.* not detected; unperceived.

un·de·ter·mi·na·ble (un′di tėr′mə nə-bəl), *adj.* indeterminable.

un·de·ter·mined (un′di tėr′mənd), *adj.* not determined; not settled or decided; not definitely fixed or ascertained; uncertain; indefinite; indeterminate.

un·de·terred (un′di tėrd′), *adj.* not deterred.

un·de·vel·op·a·ble (un′di vel′ə pə bəl), *adj.* that cannot be developed: *He's scheduled to take an embassy in an underdeveloped (and probably undevelopable) country* (Harper's).

un·de·vel·oped (un′di vel′əpt), *adj.* **1.** not fully grown; immature. **2.** not put to full use.

un·de·vi·at·ing (un dē′vē ā′ting), *adj.* not deviating; not departing from a line of procedure; unvarying; uniform: *a course of undeviating rectitude* (Oliver Goldsmith). **—un·de′vi·at′ing·ly,** *adv.*

un·de·vout (un′di vout′), *adj.* not devout; having no devotion.

un·did (un did′), *v.* the past tense of **undo.**

un·dies (un′dēz), *n.pl. Informal.* articles of women's underclothing.

un·dif·fer·en·ti·at·ed (un′dif ə ren′shē-ā′tid), *adj.* not differentiated; without clear qualities or distinctive characteristics: *undifferentiated growth of cells. They discovered that both wheat and cotton cloth were "undifferentiated" products—that is, each grain of wheat, each bolt of calico, was like any other grain or bolt* (Wall Street Journal). *The typical student completes his college program with . . . a hodgepodge of undifferentiated knowledge* (Carroll V. Newsom).

un·di·gest·ed (un′də jes′tid, -dī-), *adj.* **1.** not digested in the stomach, intestines, etc.: *undigested food.* **2.** not brought to a mature or proper condition by natural physical change: *undigested metals, undigested blood.* **3.** not understood or absorbed mentally: *undigested facts and figures* (Science News). **4.** not properly arranged or regulated; chaotic; confused: *A crude and undigested mass of useless rubbish* (Manchester Examiner). *The whole was published in an undigested, incoherent, and sometimes self-contradictory paragraph* (Henry Hallam).

un·di·gest·i·ble (un′də jes′tə bəl, -dī-), *adj.* not digestible; indigestible.

un·dig·ni·fied (un dig′nə fīd), *adj.* not dignified; lacking in dignity. **—un·dig′ni-fied′ly,** *adv.*

un·dig·ni·fy (un dig′nə fī), *v.t.,* **-fied, -fy-ing.** to deprive of dignity; make undignified.

un·di·lut·ed (un′də lü′tid, -dī-), *adj.* not diluted or weakened.

un·di·lu·tion (un′də lü′shən, -dī-), *n.* an undiluted state.

un·di·min·ish·a·ble (un′də min′i shə-bəl), *adj.* not diminishable; not subject to lessening or decrease: *Character is of a stellar and undiminishable greatness* (Emerson).

un·di·min·ished (un′də min′isht), *adj.* not diminished or lessened; of full size, amount, etc.; unabated.

un·di·min·ish·ing (un′də min′i shing), *adj.* not diminishing.

un·dimmed (un dimd′), *adj.* not dimmed, as a light or the eyes.

un·di·nal (un dē′nəl), *adj.* **1.** of or having to do with an undine. **2.** of or having to do with the belief in undines.

un·dine (un dēn′, un′dēn), *n.* a female water spirit, who, according to legend, might acquire a soul by marrying a mortal and bearing a child: *She looks, in her moments of . . . loveliness, like an undine sighing in the Seine* (Time). [< New Latin *Undina* < Latin *unda* wave]

un·dip·lo·mat·ic (un′dip lə mat′ik), *adj.* not tactful: *an undiplomatic question, undiplomatic behavior.*

un·dip·lo·mat·i·cal·ly (un′dip lə mat′ə-klē), *adv.* in an undiplomatic manner; tactlessly.

un·di·rect·ed (un′də rek′tid, -dī-), *adj.* **1.** not directed toward some end or on some course; lacking guidance: *undirected energies, undirected children.* **2.** not directed to some person or place; lacking an address: *an undirected letter.*

un·dis·cerned (un′də zėrnd′, -sėrnd′), *adj.* not discerned; unperceived.

un·dis·cern·i·ble (un′də zėr′nə bəl, -sėr′-), *adj.* indiscernible; imperceptible.

un·dis·cern·ing (un′də zėr′ning, -sėr′-), *adj.* not discerning; lacking discernment. **—un′dis·cern′ing·ly,** *adv.*

un·dis·charged (un′dis chärjd′), *adj.* **1.** not dismissed; not freed from obligation: *Hold still in readiness and undischarged* (Ben Jonson). **2.** not fulfilled; not carried out; unexecuted: *an undischarged duty.*

un·dis·ci·plin·a·ble (un dis′ə plin′ə bəl), *adj.* that cannot be disciplined: *. . . a thin, nervous colonel in the undisciplined and seemingly undisciplinable Congolese Army* (New York Times).

un·dis·ci·plined (un dis′ə plind), *adj.* not disciplined; without proper control; untrained. **—Syn.** wild, uncontrolled.

un·dis·cov·er·a·ble (un′dis kuv′ər ə bəl, -kuv′rə-), *adj.* not discoverable; not to be discovered, learned, or found out.

un·dis·cov·er·a·bly (un′dis kuv′ər ə blē, -kuv′rə-), *adv.* in a manner not to be discovered.

un·dis·cov·ered (un′dis kuv′ərd), *adj.* not discovered; not found or known by discovery: *The undiscover'd country from whose bourn No traveller returns* (Shakespeare).

un·dis·crim·i·nat·ing (un′dis krim′ə-nā′ting), *adj.* not discriminating; making no distinctions; lacking discrimination. **—un′-dis·crim′i·nat′ing·ly,** *adv.*

un·dis·cussed (un′dis kust′), *adj.* not discussed; not argued or debated.

un·dis·guised (un′dis gīzd′), *adj.* **1.** not disguised. **2.** unconcealed; open; plain; frank: *undisguised fear, gratitude, or delight.*

un·dis·guis·ed·ly (un′dis gī′zid lē), *adv.* in an undisguised manner; openly; frankly: *Many bars were undisguisedly open after one o'clock, the legal closing hour* (New Yorker).

un·dis·hon·ored (un′dis on′ərd), *adj.* not dishonored; not disgraced.

un·dis·mayed (un′dis mād′), *adj.* not dismayed; undaunted.

un·dis·pensed (un′dis penst′), *adj.* **1.** not dispensed. **2.** not freed from obligation.

un·dis·persed (un′dis pėrst′), *adj.* not dispersed; not scattered.

un·dis·posed (un′dis pōzd′), *adj.* **1.** not disposed (of): *goods remaining undisposed of.* **2.** *Obsolete.* **a.** indisposed. **b.** disinclined.

un·dis·put·a·ble (un′dis pyü′tə bəl, un-dis′pyə-), *adj.* indisputable; incontestable.

un·dis·put·ed (un′dis pyü′tid), *adj.* not disputed; not doubted: *Thou say'st an undisputed thing In such a solemn way* (Oliver Wendell Holmes). **—un′dis·put′ed·ly,** *adv.* **—Syn.** uncontested.

un·dis·put·ing (un′dis pyü′ting), *adj.* not disputing.

un·dis·sem·bled (un′di sem′bəld), *adj.* not dissembled; open; undisguised; unfeigned.

un·dis·si·pat·ed (un dis′ə pā′tid), *adj.* not dissipated or scattered.

un·dis·so·lute (un dis′ə lüt), *adj.* not dissolute; not indulging in evil or foolish pleasures.

un·dis·solv·a·ble (un′di zol′və bəl), *adj.* not dissolvable; insoluble; indissoluble.

un·dis·solved (un′di zolvd′), *adj.* not dissolved.

un·dis·solv·ing (un′di zol′ving), *adj.* not dissolving.

un·dis·tin·guish·a·ble (un′dis ting′gwi-shə bəl), *adj.* not distinguishable; indistinguishable.

un·dis·tin·guished (un′dis ting′gwisht), *adj.* not distinguished: *Though undistinguished from the crowd By wealth or dignity* (William Cowper). *Finding herself undistinguished in the dusk* (Jane Austen).

un·dis·tin·guish·ing (un′dis ting′gwi-shing), *adj.* not distinguishing; undiscriminating. **—un′dis·tin′guish·ing·ly,** *adv.*

un·dis·tract·ed (un′dis trak′tid), *adj.* not distracted; not perplexed by contrariety or variety of thoughts, desires, or concerns.

un·dis·trib·ut·ed (un′dis trib′yə tid), *adj.* not distributed.

undistributed middle term, *Logic.* a middle term which does not include its whole class (*all* or *none*) in either the first or the second premise of a syllogism. It makes the syllogism invalid. *Example:* The middle term "men" or "man" is not distributed to include "all men" or "no man" in: All poets are men; my husband is a man; my husband is a poet.

un·dis·turbed (un′dis tėrbd′), *adj.* not disturbed; not troubled; calm. **—Syn.** unruffled.

un·dis·turb·ed·ly (un′dis tėr′bid lē), *adv.* in an undisturbed or tranquil manner; calmly; peacefully.

un·di·ver·si·fied (un′də vėr′sə fīd, -dī-), *adj.* not diversified; without variety.

un·di·vert·ed (un′də vėr′tid, -dī-), *adj.* **1.** not diverted; not turned aside. **2.** not amused; not entertained or pleased.

un·di·vest·ed (un′də ves′tid, -dī-), *adj.* not divested; not stripped or deprived (of).

un·di·vid·ed (un′də vī′did), *adj.* **1.** not divided; not separated into parts; not separated or parted from each other, or one from another; not portioned out or distributed. **2.** *Botany.* not cleft, lobed, or branched. **—un′di·vid′ed·ly,** *adv.* **—un′di-vid′ed·ness,** *n.*

undivided profits, net profits remaining after the payment of dividends, as by a bank or corporation.

un·di·vorced (un′də vôrst′, -vōrst′), *adj.* not divorced; not separated.

un·di·vulged (un′də vuljd′), *adj.* not divulged; not revealed or disclosed; secret.

un·do (un dü′), *v.t.,* **-did, -done, -do·ing.** **1.** to unfasten and open; unloose and remove the wrapping of: *"Please undo the package," she said.* **2.** to untie: *to undo a knot. I undid the string.* **3.** to do away with; cause to be as if never done, effected, decided, etc.; annul; cancel; rescind: *What's done, cannot be undone* (Shakespeare). **4.** to bring to ruin; destroy; spoil: *We mended the road, but a heavy storm undid our work. Curse on his virtues! they've undone his country* (Joseph Addison). **5.** to unlock the mystery of; explain; solve.
[Old English *undōn* < *un-* un-[2] + *dōn* to do]
—un·do′er, *n.*

un·do·a·ble (un dü′ə bəl), *adj.* that cannot be done: *Schoenberg himself once said that the opera is undoable* (Time).

un·dock (un dok′), *v.t.* **1.** to take (a ship) out of a dock. **2.** to separate (a spacecraft) from a supply satellite, space station, etc., which is docked in space: *Conrad undocked*

Gemini and used his thrusters to back slowly away from the Agena (Time). —*v.i.* (of a spacecraft) to separate from a supply satellite, space station, etc.

un·doc·tri·naire (un dok′trə nãr′), *adj.* not doctrinaire; not dogmatic: *The London group showed the same undoctrinaire attitude which allowed free room for experiment without being tied to a particular theory* (London Times).

un·doc·u·ment·ed (un dok′yə men′tid), *adj.* **1.** without official papers: *an undocumented alien.* **2. a.** without real proof; not supported by facts: *undocumented evidence, undocumented charges.* **b.** without references or sources: *an undocumented book.*

un·do·ing (un dü′ing), *n.* **1.** a bringing to ruin; spoiling; destroying; ruin. **2.** a cause of destruction or ruin: *Gambling was his undoing. Drink was this man's undoing.* **3.** a doing away with; annulment; cancellation.

un·do·mes·ti·cat·ed (un′də mes′tə kā′-tid), *adj.* **1.** not domesticated; not accustomed to a family life. **2.** not tamed, as an animal.

un·done[1] (un dun′), *adj.* **1.** not done; not finished: *Nought done, the Hero deem'd, While ought undone remained* (Matthew Prior). **2.** ruined: *Whichever way I turn I am undone* (Dickens). [< Middle English *undon* < *un-* un-[1] + *don* done] —**Syn. 1.** uncompleted. **2.** destroyed.

un·done[2] (un dun′), *v.* the past participle of **undo.**

un·dou·ble (un dub′əl), *v.t., v.i.,* **-bled, -bling.** to straighten out; unclench.

un·doubt·ed (un dou′tid), *adj.* not doubted; accepted as true; beyond dispute; indisputable.

un·doubt·ed·ly (un dou′tid lē), *adv.* beyond doubt; certainly.

un·doubt·ing (un dou′ting), *adj.* **1.** not doubting; assured; confident. **2.** believing; credulous. —**un·doubt′ing·ly,** *adv.*

un·dra·mat·ic (un′drə mat′ik), *adj.* not dramatic; lacking dramatic effectiveness.

un·dra·mat·i·cal·ly (un′drə mat′ə klē), *adv.* without drama.

un·drape (un drāp′), *v.t.,* **-draped, -draping.** to strip of drapery; bare.

un·draped (un drāpt′), *adj.* not draped; without drapery.

un·draw (un drô′), *v.t.,* **-drew, -drawn, -draw·ing.** to draw back or away; pull open: *She undrew the curtain.*

un·drawn (un drôn′), *adj.* not drawn. —*v.* the past participle of **undraw.**

un·dread·ed (un dred′id), *adj.* not dreaded; not feared.

un·dreamed (un drēmd′), *adj.* not dreamed; undreamed-of: *undreamed wealth, undreamed success.*

un·dreamed-of (un drēmd′uv′, -ov′), *adj.* never thought of, even in the imagination: *undreamed-of advances in science. There we find processes whose regularity makes it possible to measure time with undreamed-of accuracy* (Scientific American).

un·dream·ing (un drē′ming), *adj.* not dreaming.

un·dreamt (un dremt′), *adj.* undreamed.

un·dreamt-of (un dremt′uv′, -ov′), *adj.* undreamed-of.

un·dress (*v.* un dres′; *n.* un′dres′, un dres′; *adj.* un′dres′), *v.t.* **1.** to take the clothes off of; divest of garments; disrobe; strip. **2.** to strip of ornament. **3.** to remove the dressing from (a wound). —*v.i.* to take off one's clothes; strip; disrobe.

—*n.* **1.** loose, informal dress. **2.** clothes proper for ordinary, everyday wear, as distinguished from those worn on formal or ceremonial occasions.

—*adj.* of, having to do with, or designating clothes proper for ordinary, everyday wear: *an undress uniform.*

un·dressed (un drest′), *adj.* **1.** not dressed; unclothed. **2.** of or of the nature of suède: *undressed leather.*

un·drew (un drü′), *v.* the past tense of **undraw.**

un·drink·a·ble (un dring′kə bəl), *adj.* not drinkable.

un·drunk (un drungk′), *adj.* **1.** not swallowed by drinking; not drunk: *In Soviet embassies and legations around the world huge supplies of vodka went undrunk, caviar uneaten* (Time). **2.** not intoxicated.

und so wei·ter (ůnt zō vī′tər), *German.* and so forth. *Abbr.:* usw.

un·due (un dü′, -dyü′), *adj.* **1.** not fitting; inappropriate; unsuitable; improper. **2.** not in accordance with what is just and right; unjustifiable; illegal. **3.** too great; too much; excessive. **4.** not properly owing or payable.

undue influence, *Law.* control over another, making him do in important affairs what he would not do of his free will.

un·du·lan·cy (un′jə lən sē, -dyə-), *n.* wavy state or character.

un·du·lant (un′jə lənt, -dyə-), *adj.* that undulates; waving; wavy: *undulant drapery.*

undulant fever, a disease characterized by an undulating or sometimes continuous fever, disorders of the bowels, enlarged spleen, weakness, anemia, and pain in the joints; brucellosis; Malta fever; Mediterranean fever; Rock fever. It is caused by infection with bacteria usually transmitted from cattle, goats, and hogs in raw milk or milk products.

un·du·late (*v.* un′jə lāt, -dyə-; *adj.* un′jə-lit, -lāt; -dyə-), *v.,* **-lat·ed, -lat·ing,** *adj.* —*v.i.* **1.** to move in or in the manner of waves; rise and fall or come and go with a wavelike motion: *Tall spire from which the sound of cheerful bells Just undulates upon the list'ning ear* (William Cowper). **2.** to have a wavy form or surface. —*v.t.* **1.** to cause to move in or in the manner of waves. **2.** to give a wavy form or surface to.

[< Late Latin *undula* wavelet (diminutive) < Latin *unda* wave + English *-ate*[1]]

—*adj.* wavy.

[< Latin *undulātus* diversified as with waves < *unda* wave]

un·du·lat·ed (un′jə lā′tid, -dyə-), *adj.* undulate.

un·du·lat·ing (un′jə lā′ting, -dyə-), *adj.* **1.** that undulates; having a wavy motion: *undulating hair. The undulating and tumultuous multitude* (Jeremy Bentham). **2.** having a form or surface resembling a series of waves: *an undulating prairie. The country became more undulating* (Samuel Butler). —**un′du·lat′ing·ly,** *adv.*

un·du·la·tion (un′jə lā′shən, -dyə-), *n.* **1.** a wavelike motion; undulating. **2.** wavy form. **3.** one of a series of wavelike bends, curves, swellings, etc. **4.** *Physics.* a wavelike motion in air or other medium, as in the propagation of sound or light; vibration; wave.

un·du·la·to·ry (un′jə lə tôr′ē, -tōr′-; -dyə-), *adj.* undulating; wavy.

undulatory theory, *Physics.* the theory that light is propagated in undulatory movements or waves; wave theory.

un·du·lous (un′jə ləs, -dyə-), *adj.* characterized by undulations or waves; wavy.

un·du·ly (un dü′lē, -dyü′-), *adv.* **1.** in an undue manner; improperly. **2.** to an undue degree; excessively: *unduly harsh, unduly optimistic.*

un·du·pli·cat·ed (un dü′plə kā′tid, -dyü′-), *adj.* **1.** not having a duplicate or duplicates: *an unduplicated set of records.* **2.** not repeated or matched: *an unduplicated performance.*

un·du·ti·ful (un dü′tə fəl, -dyü′-), *adj.* not dutiful; not properly obedient or submissive. —**un·du′ti·ful·ly,** *adv.* —**un·du′ti·ful·ness,** *n.*

un·dyed (un dīd′), *adj.* not dyed; of the natural color.

un·dy·ing (un dī′ing), *adj.* that never dies; deathless; immortal; eternal: *undying beauty, to pledge undying love.* —**un·dy′ing·ly,** *adv.* —**un·dy′ing·ness,** *n.* —**Syn.** perpetual, everlasting.

un·dy·nam·ic (un′dī nam′ik), *adj.* not dynamic; not energetic, forceful, or active: *an undynamic personality. California was only a feeble, undynamic outpost of the Spanish Empire* (New Yorker).

un·earned (un ėrnd′), *adj.* **1.** not earned by labor or service; not worked for: *an unearned gift of nature.* **2.** not earned by merit; not deserved; unmerited: *unearned punishment.* **3.** *Baseball.* scored because of a defensive error or errors: *The Phils tallied two runs, both unearned, in the fourth* (New York Times).

unearned income, income from investments as contrasted with wages.

unearned increment, an increase in the value of property from natural causes, as from growth of population, rather than from the labor, improvements, or expenditures made by the owner.

un·earth (un ėrth′), *v.t.* **1.** to dig out of the earth; exhume: *to unearth a skeleton.* **2.** to disclose by the removal of earth: *to unearth an ancient city.* **3.** to force out of a hole or burrow by or as if by digging: *to unearth a woodchuck.* **4.** to bring to light, especially: **a.** to find out and make public; disclose; reveal: *to unearth a plot.* **b.** to look for and find; discover: *to unearth the answer to a problem.*

un·earth·li·ness (un ėrth′lē nis), *n.* the character or state of being unearthly.

un·earth·ly (un ėrth′lē), *adj.* **1.** not of this world; supernatural: *an unearthly being. In after years, when she looked back upon them a kind of glory, a radiance as of an unearthly holiness, seemed to glow about these golden hours* (Lytton Strachey). **2.** strange; weird; ghostly: *the unearthly wails that sometimes come from the demons* (Santha Rama Rau). **3.** *Informal.* abnormal or unnatural; extraordinary; preposterous: *to rise at an unearthly hour.*

un·ease (un ēz′), *n.* uneasiness: *And to prove God's existence, he ironically cites the unease of those who deny it* (Time).

un·eas·i·ly (un ē′zə lē), *adv.* in an uneasy manner; apprehensively; restlessly.

un·eas·i·ness (un ē′zē nis), *n.* the quality or condition of being uneasy.

un·eas·y (un ē′zē), *adj.,* **-eas·i·er, -eas·i·est. 1.** mentally uncomfortable; disturbed; anxious; apprehensive: *to be uneasy about a decision.* **2.** physically uncomfortable; restless: *uneasy sleep.* **3.** not conducive to ease or comfort; somewhat precarious: *an uneasy peace.* **4.** characterized by absence of ease or comfort: *The benches were hard and uneasy. One or two uneasy sofas* (H.G. Wells). **5.** not easy in manner; stiff; awkward.

un·eat·a·ble (un ē′tə bəl), *adj.* not eatable; unfit to be eaten: *The English country gentleman galloping after a fox—the unspeakable in full pursuit of the uneatable* (Oscar Wilde).

un·eat·en (un ē′tən), *adj.* not eaten.

un·eath (un ēth′), *adj. Obsolete.* not easy; difficult. [Old English *unēathe* < *un-* un-[1] + *ēathe* easy]

un·e·co·nom·ic (un′ē kə nom′ik, -ek ə-), *adj.* not economic; expensive; unprofitable: *The railways are compelled to operate uneconomic lines* (Canada Month).

un·e·co·nom·i·cal (un′ē kə nom′ə kel, -ek-ə-), *adj.* not economical. —**un′e·co·nom′i·cal·ly,** *adv.*

UNEDA (no periods), United Nations Economic Development Administration.

un·ed·i·ble (un ed′ə bəl), *adj.* inedible.

un·ed·i·fy·ing (un ed′ə fī′ing), *adj.* not edifying; not elevating or beneficial morally.

un·ed·it·ed (un ed′ə tid), *adj.* not edited; not changed in any way: *an unedited speech.*

un·ed·u·ca·ble (un ej′ů kə bəl), *adj.* not capable of being educated; ineducable: *Industry finds it . . . difficult to offer employment to uneducated and especially to uneducable young people* (Charles S. Ryckman).

un·ed·u·cat·ed (un ej′ů kā′tid), *adj.* not educated; not taught or trained. —**Syn.** See **ignorant.**

un·ed·u·ca·tion·al (un′ej ů kā′shə nəl), *adj.* not furthering education or the development of the mind.

UNEF (no periods), United Nations Emergency Force.

un·ef·fec·tu·al (un′ə fek′chů əl), *adj. Obsolete.* ineffectual.

un·e·lect·ed (un′i lek′tid), *adj.* not elected; not chosen: *unelected for salvation.*

un·em·bar·rassed (un′em bar′ist), *adj.* not embarrassed or flustered; not confused; composed: *She was frank and unembarrassed toward him, without a trace of boldness or overfamiliarity* (Edgar Maass).

un·em·bod·ied (un′em bod′ēd), *adj.* **1.** not embodied or materialized. **2.** not having a body; incorporeal.

un·em·broi·dered (un′əm broi′dərd), *adj.* not embroidered; without embroidery: *an unembroidered speech.*

un·e·mo·tion·al (un′i mō′shə nəl), *adj.* not emotional; impassive: *an unemotional tone of voice, an unemotional observer.* —**un′e·mo′tion·al·ly,** *adv.*

un·em·ploy·a·bil·i·ty (un′əm ploi′ə bil′ə-tē), *n.* the quality or condition of being unemployable: *Hence, educational inadequacies lead to lack of training, unemployability etc.* (New York Times).

un·em·ploy·a·ble (un′em ploi′ə bəl), *adj.* that cannot be employed, especially that cannot be employed to work because of a physical or mental impediment. —*n.* a person who is unemployable.

un·em·ployed (un′em ploid′), *adj.* **1.** not employed; not in use: *an unemployed skill.* **2.** not having a job; having no work: *an unemployed person.* **3.** earning no interest or dividends; not loaned or invested: *unemployed capital.*
—*n.* **the unemployed,** people out of work: *The employed and the unemployed, taken together, constitute the labour force* (Leon E. Truesdell).
un·em·ploy·ment (un′em ploi′mənt), *n.* lack of employment; being out of work.
unemployment compensation, *U.S.* payment under a system by which eligible workers are guaranteed a small weekly income during a limited period of involuntary unemployment.
unemployment insurance, *U.S.* a Federal insurance program, supported by employer-paid taxes, which provides income for a limited period of time to eligible workers who are involuntarily unemployed.
un·en·closed (un′en klōzd′), *adj.* not enclosed; not shut in or surrounded, as by a fence or wall.
un·en·cum·bered (un′en kum′bərd), *adj.* not encumbered; free from encumbrance.
un·en·deared (un′en dird′), *adj.* not attended with endearment.
un·end·ed (un en′did), *adj.* endless; infinite.
un·end·ing (un en′ding), *adj.* not ending; having no end; endless; ceaseless; eternal. —**un·end′ing·ly,** *adv.* —**un·end′ing·ness,** *n.*
un·en·dowed (un′en doud′), *adj.* not endowed; without an endowment.
un·en·dur·a·ble (un′en dúr′ə bəl, -dyúr′-), *adj.* **1.** not endurable; unbearable; intolerable; insufferable: *unendurable pain, an unendurable braggart.* **2.** that cannot endure; unenduring.
un·en·dur·a·bly (un′en dúr′ə blē, -dyúr′-), *adv.* in an unendurable manner; intolerably.
un·en·dur·ing (un′en dúr′ing, -dyúr′-), *adj.* that does not endure; fleeting: *the unenduring clouds* (Wordsworth).
un·en·force·a·ble (un′en fôr′sə bəl, -fōr′-), *adj.* not enforceable; that cannot be enforced: *The [Chilean] President's hesitancy to legalize the bill was based on the belief that the law would be unenforceable* (Miguel Jorrín).
un·en·forced (un′en fôrst′, -fōrst′), *adj.* not enforced.
un·en·gaged (un′en gājd′), *adj.* not engaged.
un-Eng·lish (un ing′glish), *adj.* **1.** not English; foreign or opposed to the English character, spirit, usages, etc. **2.** not in accordance with the usages of the English language.
un·en·light·ened (un′en lī′tənd), *adj.* not enlightened; without intellectual or moral enlightenment; benighted; ignorant.
un·en·light·en·ing (un′en lī′tə ning), *adj.* not instructive or informative.
un·en·tan·gled (un′en tang′gəld), *adj.* not entangled; not complicated; not perplexed: *unentangled through the snares of life* (Samuel Johnson).
un·en·ter·pris·ing (un en′tər prī′zing), *adj.* not enterprising; lacking enterprise.
un·en·ter·tain·ing (un′en tər tā′ning), *adj.* not entertaining or amusing.
un·en·thralled (un′en thrôld′), *adj.* not enslaved; not reduced to thralldom.
un·en·thu·si·as·tic (un′en thü′zē as′tik), *adj.* not enthusiastic; without enthusiasm.
un·en·thu·si·as·ti·cal·ly (un′en thü′zē-as′tə klē), *adv.* in an unenthusiastic manner.
un·en·vi·a·ble (un en′vē ə bəl), *adj.* not enviable; not such as to excite envy.
un·en·vi·a·bly (un en′vē ə blē), *adv.* so as not to be enviable.
un·en·vied (un en′vēd), *adj.* not envied; exempt from the envy of others.
un·en·vi·ous (un en′vē əs), *adj.* not envious; free from envy.
un·e·qual (un ē′kwəl), *adj.* **1.** not the same in amount, size, number, value, merit, rank, etc.: *unequal sums of money, unequal achievements.* **2.** in which the two sides or parties are not on equal terms or have not an equal advantage, especially: **a.** not balanced; not well matched: *an unequal marriage.* **b.** not fair; one-sided: *an unequal contest.* **3.** not enough; not sufficient; inadequate: *strength unequal to the task.* **4.** not regular; not even; variable: *unequal vibrations.* —**un·e′qual·ly,** *adv.* —**un·e′qual·ness,** *n.*
un·e·qualed (un ē′kwəld), *adj.* **1.** without an equal; matchless: *unequaled beauty, unequaled strength.* **2.** not equaled; unmatched: *beauty unequaled by anything previously seen.*
un·e·qualled (un ē′kwəld), *adj. Especially British.* unequaled.
un·eq·ui·ta·ble (un ek′wə tə bəl), *adj.* inequitable; unfair; unjust.
un·eq·ui·ta·bly (un ek′wə tə blē), *adv.* inequitably; unfairly; unjustly.
un·e·quiv·o·ca·bly (un′i kwiv′ə kə blē), *adv.* unequivocally: *The law unequivocably bars discriminatory state taxation* (Wall Street Journal).
un·e·quiv·o·cal (un′i kwiv′ə kəl), *adj.* **1.** containing no trace of doubt or ambiguity; clear and straightforward in meaning or purpose; blunt and plain: *unequivocal hostility, an unequivocal refusal.* **2.** (of persons) not inclined to temporize, compromise, or equivocate; speaking frankly and bluntly. —**un′e·quiv′o·cal·ly,** *adv.* —**un′e·quiv′o·cal·ness,** *n.*
un·err·ing (un ėr′ing, -er′-), *adj.* **1.** that does not err, especially: **a.** free of error; certain; sure: *unerring aim.* **b.** committing no error; not going or leading astray; infallible: *an unerring guide.* **2.** corresponding exactly to some standard or goal: *unerring precision.* —**un·err′ing·ly,** *adv.* —**un·err′ing·ness,** *n.*
➤ For a note on the pronunciation, see **err.**
un·es·cap·a·ble (un′es kā′pə bəl), *adj.* not escapable; not to be escaped or avoided; inescapable.
un·es·cap·a·bly (un′es kā′pə blē), *adv.* in an unescapable manner.
U·NES·CO, U·nes·co, or **U.N.E.S.C.O.** (yü nes′kō), *n.* the United Nations Educational, Scientific, and Cultural Organization (an independent organization related to and recognized by the United Nations as one of its specialized agencies).
un·es·sayed (un′e sād′), *adj.* not essayed; unattempted.
un·es·sen·tial (un′ə sen′shəl), *adj.* **1.** not essential; not of prime importance. **2.** of little importance; nonessential. —*n.* something not essential.
un·eth·i·cal (un eth′ə kəl), *adj.* not ethical; not in accordance with the rules for right conduct or practice. —**un·eth′i·cal·ly,** *adv.*
un·e·van·gel·i·cal (un′ē van jel′ə kəl, -ev-ən-), *adj.* not evangelical; not in accord with the Gospels: *. . . unevangelical doctrines and practices* (London Times).
un·e·ven (un ē′vən), *adj.* **1.** not level or smooth; having an irregular or broken surface; somewhat bumpy: *uneven ground.* **2.** not equal: *an uneven contest.* **3.** not properly corresponding or agreeing. **4.** not straight or parallel. **5.** (of a number) that cannot be divided by 2 without a remainder; odd: *27 and 9 are uneven numbers.* [Old English *unefen* unequal < *un-* un-[1] + *efen* equal, even] —**un·e′ven·ly,** *adv.* —**un·e′ven·ness,** *n.* —**Syn. 1.** rough, rugged, jagged.
un·e·vent·ful (un′i vent′fəl), *adj.* without important or striking occurrences: *laborious, uneventful years* (H.G. Wells). —**un′e·vent′ful·ly,** *adv.* —**un′e·vent′ful·ness,** *n.*
un·e·volved (un′i volvd′), *adj.* not evolved; undeveloped.
un·ex·act·ing (un′eg zak′ting), *adj.* not exacting; requiring little; easy.
un·ex·am·pled (un′eg zam′pəld, -zäm′-), *adj.* having no equal or like; without precedent or parallel; without anything like it: *Thanking you for your unexampled kindness* (Jane Austen).
un·ex·celled (un′ek seld′), *adj.* not excelled; unsurpassed.
un·ex·cep·tion·a·ble (un′ek sep′shə nə-bəl), *adj.* beyond criticism; wholly admirable. —**un′ex·cep′tion·a·ble·ness,** *n.* —**Syn.** faultless, irreproachable.
un·ex·cep·tion·a·bly (un′ek sep′shə nə-blē), *adv.* in an unexceptionable manner.
un·ex·cep·tion·al (un′ek sep′shə nəl), *adj.* **1.** not exceptional; ordinary. **2.** admitting of no exception. —**un′ex·cep′tion·al·ly,** *adv.*
un·ex·cit·ed (un′ek sī′tid), *adj.* not excited; calm; tranquil.
un·ex·cit·ing (un′ek sī′ting), *adj.* not exciting; quiet; tame; dull.
un·ex·e·cut·ed (un ek′sə kyü′tid), *adj.* **1.** not executed. **2.** *Obsolete.* unemployed; not brought into use; inactive.
un·ex·pect·ant (un′ek spek′tənt), *adj.* not expectant; not expecting, looking for, or eagerly waiting for something. —**un′ex·pect′ant·ly,** *adv.*
un·ex·pect·ed (un′ek spek′tid), *adj.* not expected; not anticipated: *an unexpected difficulty, a sudden and unexpected change in the weather.* —**un′ex·pect′ed·ness,** *n.*
—**Syn. Unexpected, sudden** mean coming, happening, done, or made without advance warning or preparation. **Unexpected** emphasizes the lack of foreknowledge or anticipation: *He made an unexpected visit to the city.* **Sudden** emphasizes the haste and absence of forewarning: *His decision to go was sudden.*
un·ex·pect·ed·ly (un′ek spek′tid lē), *adv.* in a way that is not expected; suddenly.
un·ex·pe·ri·enced (un′ek spir′ē ənst), *adj.* inexperienced.
un·ex·pert (un′ek spėrt′), *adj.* inexpert. —**un′ex·pert′ly,** *adv.*
un·ex·pired (un′ek spīrd′), *adj.* not expired; not having come to an end; having still some time to run, as a lease.
un·ex·plain·a·ble (un′ek splā′nə bəl), *adj.* not explainable; inexplicable.
un·ex·plained (un′ek splānd′), *adj.* not explained.
un·ex·plod·ed (un′ek splō′did), *adj.* not exploded.
un·ex·plored (un′ek splôrd′, -splōrd′), *adj.* not explored.
un·ex·posed (un′ek spōzd′), *adj.* not exposed.
un·ex·pressed (un′ek sprest′), *adj.* not expressed; unuttered.
un·ex·press·i·ble (un′ek spres′ə bəl), *adj.* inexpressible.
un·ex·pres·sive (un′ek spres′iv), *adj.* **1.** inexpressive. **2.** *Obsolete.* ineffable: *So Lycidas . . . hears the unexpressive nuptial Song* (Milton). —**un′ex·pres′sive·ly,** *adv.* —**un′ex·pres′sive·ness,** *n.*
un·ex·pur·gat·ed (un eks′pər gā′tid), *adj.* not expurgated.
un·ex·tend·ed (un′ek sten′did), *adj.* **1.** not extended or stretched out. **2.** not having extension; occupying no assignable space: *a spiritual, that is, an unextended substance* (John Locke).
un·ex·tin·guish·a·ble (un′ek sting′gwi-shə bəl), *adj.* inextinguishable.
un·face·a·ble (un fā′sə bəl), *adj.* not to be faced or approached: *It was as if, by dwelling on these little things, she found relief from the contemplation of the appalling, unfaceable fact that was facing her* (New Yorker).
un·fad·a·ble (un fā′də bəl), *adj.* incapable of fading, perishing, or withering.
un·fad·ing (un fā′ding), *adj.* not or never fading; always fresh or bright. —**un·fad′ing·ly,** *adv.* —**un·fad′ing·ness,** *n.*
un·fail·ing (un fā′ling), *adj.* **1.** never failing or giving way, especially: **a.** never tiring or flagging: *unfailing hope.* **b.** constant in nature; loyal: *an unfailing friend.* **2.** never giving out or running short; endless; continual; unceasing: *an unfailing supply of water.* **3.** sure; certain; infallible: *an unfailing proof.* —**un·fail′ing·ness,** *n.*
un·fail·ing·ly (un fā′ling lē), *adv.* always; without fail.
un·fair (un fãr′), *adj.* **1.** not fair or equitable; unjust: *to have an unfair advantage.* **2.** not right or proper; dishonest: *to win by an unfair trick.* **3.** not complying with the standard of what is honorable or ethical in business relations, as with an employee, employer, competitor, or the general public. [Old English *unfæger* not beautiful or comely < *un-* un-[1] + *fæger* fair] —**un·fair′ly,** *adv.* —**un·fair′ness,** *n.* —**Syn. 1.** partial, prejudiced, biased, one-sided.
un·faith (un fāth′), *n.* want of faith: *Unfaith in aught is want of faith in all* (Tennyson).
un·faith·ful (un fāth′fəl), *adj.* **1.** not faithful, especially: **a.** not true to duty or one's promises; faithless: *an unfaithful servant.* **b.** not true to the vows of matrimony; adulterous: *an unfaithful husband.* **2.** not following the original; not accurate; not exact: *an unfaithful transcript.* —**un·faith′ful·ly,** *adv.* —**un·faith′ful·ness,** *n.* —**Syn. 1.** false, disloyal, inconstant.
un·fal·ter·ing (un fôl′tər ing), *adj.* not faltering; unhesitating; unwavering: *sustained and soothed by an unfaltering trust* (William Cullen Bryant). —**un·fal′ter·ing·ly,** *adv.*
un·fa·mil·iar (un′fə mil′yər), *adj.* **1.** not well known; unusual; strange: *That face is unfamiliar to me.* **2.** not acquainted: *He is unfamiliar with Greek.* —**un′fa·mil′iar·ly,** *adv.*
un·fa·mil·iar·i·ty (un′fə mil′yar′ə tē), *n.* lack of familiarity.
un·fan·cied (un fan′sēd), *adj.* **1.** unimag-

ined: *unfancied joys.* **2.** not liked or favored: *He was beaten decisively by unfancied horses on Saturday* (London Times).

un·fash·ion·a·ble (un fash′ən ə bəl, -fash′-nə-), *adj.* not fashionable; not in good style. —**un·fash′ion·a·ble·ness,** *n.*

un·fash·ion·a·bly (un fash′ə nə blē, -fash′-nə-), *adv.* in an unfashionable manner; not in accordance with fashion: *Both bade me welcome, and if they thought I was unfashionably early, they said nothing* (Maclean's).

un·fash·ioned (un fash′ənd), *adj.* **1.** not modified by art; not molded. **2.** not having a regular form; shapeless.

un·fas·ten (un fas′ən, -fäs′-), *v.t., v.i.* to undo; loose; open.

un·fas·tid·i·ous (un′fas tid′ē əs), *adj.* not fastidious; easily pleased: *Irony, indignation, amusement, an unfastidious acceptance of people—all these . . . make up this very personal account* (Manchester Guardian Weekly). —**un′fas·tid′i·ous·ness,** *n.*

un·fa·thered (un fä′ᴛʜərd), *adj.* **1.** born out of wedlock; illegitimate. **2.** of obscure or dubious origin: *an unfathered rumor.*

un·fa·ther·ly (un fä′ᴛʜər lē), *adj.* not fatherly; unbefitting a father.

un·fath·om·a·ble (un faᴛʜ′ə mə bəl), *adj.* not fathomable; incapable of being fathomed or sounded; impenetrable by the mind; inscrutable; incomprehensible.

un·fath·omed (un faᴛʜ′əmd), *adj.* not fathomed.

un·fa·vor·a·ble (un fā′vər ə bəl, -fāv′rə-), *adj.* **1.** not favorable; contrary to what is desired or needed; adverse: *an unfavorable opinion.* **2.** conducive to bad rather than good; harmful: *an unfavorable environment.* **3.** not pleasing: *an unfavorable appearance.* —**un·fa′vor·a·ble·ness,** *n.*

un·fa·vor·a·bly (un fā′vər ə blē, -fāv′rə-), *adv.* in an unfavorable manner; so as not to countenance or promote; in a manner to discourage.

un·fa·vour·a·ble (un fā′vər ə bəl, -fāv′rə-), *adj. Especially British.* unfavorable. —**un·fa′vour·a·ble·ness,** *n.*

un·fa·vour·a·bly (un fā′vər ə blē, -fāv′rə-), *adv. Especially British.* unfavorably.

un·feared (un fird′), *adj.* **1.** not feared; not dreaded. **2.** *Obsolete.* not afraid; not daunted; intrepid.

un·fea·si·ble (un fē′zə bəl), *adj.* not feasible; impracticable; infeasible.

un·feath·ered (un feᴛʜ′ərd), *adj.* not provided with feathers; featherless.

un·fea·tured (un fē′chərd), *adj.* **1.** without features; featureless: *the starless, unfeatured night* (Robert A. Vaughan). **2.** *Informal.* not featured; not given prominence to: *an unfeatured motion picture.*

un·fed (un fed′), *adj.* not fed; having taken no food.

un·feel·ing (un fē′ling), *adj.* **1.** not kind or compassionate; hard-hearted; cruel: *a cold, unfeeling person. Can it be? That men should live with such unfeeling souls?* (Ben Jonson). **2.** not able to feel; without sensory power or capacity; insensible: *an unfeeling statue for his wife* (William Cowper). —**un·feel′ing·ly,** *adv.* —**un·feel′ing·ness,** *n.* —**Syn. 1.** unsympathetic.

un·feigned (un fānd′), *adj.* not simulated; sincere; real: *unfeigned anger or thanks.* —**Syn.** unaffected, true, genuine.

un·feign·ed·ly (un fā′nid lē), *adv.* really; sincerely; truly: *He pardoneth and absolveth all those who truly repent, and unfeignedly believe in His holy Gospel* (Book of Common Prayer).

un·feign·ed·ness (un fā′nid nis), *n.* the state of being unfeigned; truth; sincerity.

un·fel·lowed (un fel′ōd), *adj.* without a fellow; unmatched; unequaled: *In his meed he's unfellowed* (Shakespeare).

un·felt (un felt′), *adj.* not felt or perceived.

un·fem·i·nine (un fem′ə nin), *adj.* not feminine; unwomanly.

un·fenced (un fenst′), *adj.* **1.** having no fence; not fenced in: *Spreading afar and unfenced o'er the plain* (Longfellow). **2.** without protection, guard, or security; defenseless.

un·fer·ment·ed (un′fər men′tid), *adj.* not fermented.

un·fer·tile (un fėr′təl), *adj.* infertile.

un·fer·ti·lized (un fėr′tə līzd), *adj.* not fertilized.

un·fet·ter (un fet′ər), *v.t.* to remove fetters from; make free; liberate; unchain.

un·fet·tered (un fet′ərd), *adj.* **1.** not fettered. **2.** free from restraint: *unfettered imagination.*

un·filed (un fīld′), *adj.* **1.** not rubbed or polished with a file; not burnished. **2.** not put away in a file, as papers.

un·fil·i·al (un fil′ē əl), *adj.* not filial; unbecoming from a child to a parent; not observing the obligations of a child to a parent.

un·fil·tered (un fil′tərd), *adj.* not filtered.

un·fin·ished (un fin′isht), *adj.* **1.** not finished; not complete. **2.** without some special finish; not polished; rough: *unfinished stone.* **3.** (of fabric) not processed after coming off the loom.

un·fished (un fisht′), *adj.* not fished in: *The main reason why unfished waters are most productive, is that they are then more plentifully stocked* (Charles A. Johns).

un·fit (un fit′), *adj., v.,* **-fit·ted, -fit·ting.** —*adj.* **1.** not fit; not suitable. **2.** not good enough; unqualified. **3.** not adapted. —*v.t.* to make unfit; spoil. —**un·fit′ly,** *adv.* —**un·fit′ness,** *n.*

un·fit·ted (un fit′id), *adj.* **1.** not fitted; unsuited; unfit. **2.** not fitting the body tightly; loose, as a coat or suit: *an unfitted jacket.*

un·fit·ting (un fit′ing), *adj.* not fitting; unbecoming: *an unfitting remark.* —**un·fit′ting·ly,** *adv.* —**un·fit′ting·ness,** *n.*

un·fix (un fiks′), *v.t.* to loosen; detach; unfasten.

un·fixed (un fikst′), *adj.* not fixed; not firmly set; not settled or determined; variable or uncertain.

un·flag·ging (un flag′ing), *adj.* not weakening or failing: *unflagging strength, unflagging efforts.* —**un·flag′ging·ly,** *adv*

un·flap·pa·bil·i·ty (un flap′ə bil′ə tē), *n. Informal.* imperturbability: *Unflappability and golf are almost traditional attributes of Conservative leaders* (Punch).

un·flap·pa·ble (un flap′ə bəl), *adj. Informal.* not easily excited, confused, or alarmed; imperturbable: *His [Macmillan's] unflappable poise was buttressed by arctic sarcasm* (Time).

un·flat·ter·ing (un flat′ər ing), *adj.* not flattering; uncomplimentary. —**un·flat′ter·ing·ly,** *adv.*

un·fledged (un flejd′), *adj.* **1.** too young to fly; not having full-grown feathers: *an unfledged crow.* **2.** undeveloped; immature: *This Society of unfledged Statesmen* (Joseph Addison).

un·flesh·ly (un flesh′lē), *adj.* not in or of the flesh; supernatural; spiritual.

un·flinch·ing (un flin′ching), *adj.* not drawing back from difficulty, danger, or pain; firm; resolute: *unflinching courage, resolve, etc.* —**un·flinch′ing·ly,** *adv.*

un·flur·ried (un flėr′ēd), *adj.* not flurried; without excitement or confusion: *He replaced his cap and continued his unflurried way* (Manchester Guardian).

un·foiled (un foild′), *adj.* not vanquished; not defeated; not baffled.

un·fold (un fōld′), *v.t.* **1.** to open the folds of; open up; spread out: *to unfold a napkin.* **2.** to cause to be no longer bent, coiled, or interlaced; unbend and straighten out: *to unfold one's arms.* **3.** to develop or bring forth the parts or elements of so as to reveal the actual nature or dimensions; lay open to be seen or understood; reveal; show; explain: *to unfold the plot of a story. Briefly and plainly I unfolded what I proposed* (Samuel Butler). **4.** to unwrap. **5.** to let go; release. —*v.i.* to open up or out; spread out or expand; develop: *Buds unfold into flowers.* [Old English *unfealdan* < *un-* un-[2] + *fealdan* to fold[1]] —**un·fold′er,** *n.*

un·fold·ment (un fōld′mənt), *n.* an unfolding; development.

un·for·bid (un′fər bid′), *adj. Dialect.* unforbidden.

un·for·bid·den (un′fər bid′ən), *adj.* not forbidden.

un·forced (un fôrst′, -fōrst′), *adj.* **1.** not forced; not compelled; willing. **2.** natural; spontaneous.

un·fore·bod·ing (un′fôr bō′ding, -fōr-), *adj.* not foretelling; not telling the future; giving no omens.

un·fore·known (un′fôr nōn′, -fōr-), *adj.* not previously known or foreseen.

un·fore·see·a·ble (un′fôr sē′ə bəl, -fōr-), *adj.* not foreseeable; that cannot be foreseen: *an unforeseeable delay.* —**un′fore·see′a·ble·ness,** *n.*

un·fore·see·a·bly (un′fôr sē′ə blē, -fōr-), *adv.* in an unforeseeable manner; so as not to be foreseen.

un·fore·see·ing (un′fôr sē′ing, -fōr-), *adj.* not foreseeing; without foresight.

un·fore·seen (un′fôr sēn′, -fōr-), *adj.* not known beforehand; unexpected: *hoping for some unforeseen turn of fortune* (George Eliot). —**un′fore·seen′ness,** *n.*

un·fore·told (un′fôr tōld′, -fōr-), *adj.* not predicted or foretold.

un·for·feit·ed (un fôr′fə tid), *adj.* not forfeited; maintained; not lost.

un·forged (un fôrjd′, -fōrjd′), *adj.* not forged or counterfeit; genuine.

un·for·get·ta·ble (un′fər get′ə bəl), *adj.* that can never be forgotten: *To smell the unforgettable, unforgotten River smell* (Rupert Brooke).

un·for·get·ta·bly (un′fər get′ə blē), *adv.* in an unforgettable manner.

un·for·giv·a·ble (un′fər giv′ə bəl), *adj.* not to be forgiven; unpardonable.

un·for·giv·a·bly (un′fər giv′ə blē), *adv.* in an unforgivable manner; to an unforgivable degree: *unforgivably bad or rude.*

un·for·giv·en (un′fər giv′ən), *adj.* not forgiven.

un·for·giv·ing (un′fər giv′ing), *adj.* not forgiving; not disposed to forgive; implacable. —**un′for·giv′ing·ly,** *adv.* —**un′for·giv′ing·ness,** *n.*

un·for·got (un′fər got′), *adj.* unforgotten.

un·for·got·ten (un′fər got′ən), *adj.* not forgotten.

un·formed (un fôrmd′), *adj.* **1.** without definite or regular form; shapeless: *an unformed ball of clay.* **2.** not yet shaped by process of growth or schooling; undeveloped: *an unformed mind.* **3.** not formed or made; uncreated: *the yet unformed forefather of mankind* (Byron). **4.** *Biology.* unorganized.

un·for·mu·lat·ed (un fôr′myə lā′tid), *adj.* not formulated.

un·forth·com·ing (un fôrth′kum′ing, -fōrth′-), *adj.* not responsive or obliging; unaccommodating: *. . . the unforthcoming, stiff-upper-lip, monosyllabic Englishman* (Newsweek).

un·for·ti·fied (un fôr′tə fīd), *adj.* not fortified.

un·for·tu·nate (un fôr′chə nit), *adj.* **1.** having, bringing, or accompanied by bad luck or misfortune; not lucky: *an unfortunate person.* **2.** not suitable; not fitting: *an unfortunate choice of words.* —*n.* **1.** an unfortunate person. **2.** a fallen woman; prostitute. **3.** *Irish.* a congenital idiot; halfwit. —**un·for′tu·nate·ly,** *adv.* —**un·for′tu·nate·ness,** *n.*

un·fos·sil·if·er·ous (un′fos ə lif′ər əs), *adj.* bearing or containing no fossils: *The rocks of Scotland are, as a whole, unfossiliferous* (Archibald Geikie).

un·fought (un fôt′), *adj.* not fought: *If they march along unfought withal* (Shakespeare).

un·found·ed (un foun′did), *adj.* **1.** without foundation; unwarranted; baseless: *an unfounded complaint.* **2.** not established. —**un·found′ed·ly,** *adv.* —**un·found′ed·ness,** *n.*

un·framed (un frāmd′), *adj.* **1.** not provided with a frame; not put into a frame: *an unframed picture.* **2.** not formed; not constructed; not fashioned.

un·fran·chised (un fran′chīzd), *adj.* not franchised.

un·fraught (un frôt′), *adj.* not fraught; not filled with a load or burden; unloaded.

un·free (un frē′), *adj.* not free.

un·free·dom (un frē′dəm), *n.* the state of being unfree; want of freedom: *. . . the struggle against injustice and unfreedom* (London Times).

un·freeze (un frēz′), *v.,* **-froze, -fro·zen, -freez·ing.** —*v.t.* **1.** to thaw; loosen: *The company had unfrozen hundreds of pipes by this method* (London Times). *He could not unfreeze himself into hospitality* (George W. Thornbury). **2.** to free from control or restrictions: *The urgent requirement on Capitol Hill is to unfreeze poverty programs, not stall them* (New York Times). **3.** to release (money) for spending: *The Defense Department hopes to unfreeze over $10 billion of funds for new military procurement* (Wall Street Journal). —*v.i.* to thaw; loosen: [*He*] *wanted to know if the weather would unfreeze sufficiently for him to drive to Idlewild the next day* (New Yorker).

un·fre·quent (un frē′kwənt), *adj.* not frequent; not common; infrequent.

un·fre·quent·ed (un′fri kwen′tid), *adj.* not frequented; seldom visited; rarely entered, used, etc.

un·friend·ed (un fren′did), *adj.* without friends: *a raw and unfriended youth* (William Godwin). —**un·friend′ed·ness,** *n.*

un·friend·li·ness (un frend′lē nis), *n.* the quality of being unfriendly; lack of kindness; disfavor.

un·friend·ly (un frend′lē), *adj.* **1.** not friendly; hostile. **2.** not propitious or favorable: *unfriendly stars.* —*adv.* in an unfriendly manner. —**Syn.** *adj.* **1.** See **hostile.**

un·frock (un frok′), *v.t.* **1.** to deprive of priestly or ministerial function or office: *It is not the unfrocking of a priest . . . that will make us a happy nation* (Milton). **2.** to take away a frock from.

un·fruit·ful (un früt′fəl), *adj.* **1.** not fruitful; producing no offspring; barren: *an unfruitful marriage.* **2.** producing nothing worthwhile; unproductive; unremunerative: *an unfruitful line of inquiry.* —**un·fruit′ful·ly,** *adv.* —**un·fruit′ful·ness,** *n.*

un·ful·filled (un′fu̇l fild′), *adj.* not fulfilled.

un·func·tion·al (un fungk′shə nəl), *adj.* not functional; impractical: *There is a certain amount of shoddy, unfunctional, and ugly furniture on sale* (London Times).

un·fund·ed (un fun′did), *adj.* (of a debt, etc.) not funded; floating.

un·fun·ny (un fun′ē), *adj.* not funny; lacking humor: *an unfunny joke.*

un·furl (un fėrl′), *v.t., v.i.* to spread out; shake out; unfold: *to unfurl a sail.*

un·fur·nish (un fėr′nish), *v.t.* to strip of furnishings or furniture; dismantle.

un·fur·nished (un fėr′nisht), *adj.* not furnished; without furniture.

un·fur·rowed (un fėr′ōd), *adj.* not furrowed; not formed into drills or ridges; smooth: *an unfurrowed field.*

un·fused (un fyüzd′), *adj.* **1.** not fused or melted. **2.** not blended or united.

un·fuss·i·ly (un fus′ə lē), *adv.* in an unfussy manner.

un·fuss·y (un fus′ē), *adj.* not fussy: *Mr. Davis, whose editing is exacting and unfussy, deserves our gratitude* (New Yorker).

un·gag (un gag′), *v.t.*, **-gagged, -gag·ging.** to remove a gag from: *Once in the room, they ungagged their hostage.*

un·gained (un gānd′), *adj.* not yet gained; unpossessed.

un·gain·ful (un gān′fəl), *adj.* not producing gain; unprofitable.

un·gain·li·ness (un gān′lē nis), *n.* the state or character of being ungainly; ungainly appearance; awkwardness.

un·gain·ly (un gān′lē), *adj.* ungraceful in form or motion; awkward; clumsy: *his [Lincoln's] ungainly figure, with long arms and large hands* (Baron Charnwood). —*adv.* in an ungainly manner; awkwardly. [Middle English *ungaynly,* adverb, threateningly, improperly < *un-*[1] not + *gainly* fitting, graceful, perhaps < Scandinavian (compare Old Icelandic *ūgegnlig, ōgegnlig* improperly, obstinate < *ūgegn* unreasonable)] —**Syn.** *adj.* uncouth. See **awkward.**

un·gal·lant (un gal′ənt), *adj.* not gallant; unchivalrous. —**un·gal′lant·ly,** *adv.*

un·galled (un gôld′), *adj.* unhurt; not galled; uninjured.

un·gar·nished (un gär′nisht), *adj.* **1.** not garnished or furnished; unadorned. **2.** not properly provided or equipped.

un·gar·tered (un gär′tərd), *adj.* **1.** not held by garters, as the hose or socks. **2.** not having or wearing garters.

un·gath·ered (un gaᴛʜ′ərd), *adj.* **1.** not gathered together; not culled; not picked; not collected. **2.** having to do with printed sheets that have been folded, but not gathered in regular order for binding.

un·gear (un gir′), *v.t.* **1.** to strip of gear. **2.** to throw out of gear.

un·gen·er·ous (un jen′ər əs), *adj.* **1.** not generous; meanly grasping or cruel. **2.** small-minded and cowardly. —**un·gen′er·ous·ly,** *adv.*

un·gen·ial (un jēn′yəl), *adj.* **1.** not favorable to natural growth: *ungenial air, ungenial soils.* **2.** not kindly; unpleasant; disagreeable; harsh; unsympathetic: *an ungenial disposition.* **3.** not congenial; not suited or adapted.

un·gen·teel (un′jen tēl′), *adj.* (of persons or manners) not genteel; impolite; rude.

un·gen·tle (un jen′təl), *adj.* not gentle; harsh; rough. —**un·gen′tle·ness,** *n.*

un·gen·tle·man·li·ness (un jen′təl mən lē nis), *n.* the character of being ungentlemanly.

un·gen·tle·man·ly (un jen′təl mən lē), *adj.* not gentlemanly; not befitting a gentleman; ill-bred; impolite; rude: *It's only if a man's a gentleman that he won't hesitate to do an ungentlemanly thing* (W. Somerset Maugham).

un·gift·ed (un gif′tid), *adj.* not gifted; not endowed with natural gifts.

un·gird (un gėrd′), *v.t.* **1.** to unfasten or take off the belt or girdle of; unbelt. **2.** to loosen, or take off, by unfastening a belt or girdle. [Old English *ongyrdan* < *on-* un-[2] + *gyrdan* to gird[1]]

un·girt (un gėrt′), *adj.* **1.** ungirded: *Now in the ungirt hour, now ere we blink and drowse, Mithras, also a soldier, keep us true to our vows* (Rudyard Kipling). **2.** not braced up or pulled together; loose and shapeless: *an ungirt appearance or style.*

un·giv·ing (un giv′ing), *adj.* not bringing gifts.

un·glam·or·ous (un glam′ər əs, -glam′rəs), *adj.* not glamorous; without charm: *[He] begged Lennie to change his unglamorous name so that his way to success would not be blocked* (Time). —**un·glam′or·ous·ly,** *adv.*

un·glazed (un glāzd′), *adj.* **1.** not provided with glass, as a window. **2.** not coated or covered with a glaze, as earthenware.

un·glove (un gluv′), *v.,* **-gloved, -glov·ing.** —*v.t.* to remove a glove or gloves from: *She ungloved her right hand and signed the papers.* —*v.i.* to take off a glove or gloves: *The gentleman ungloved and shook hands with his rival.*

un·gloved (un gluvd′), *adj.* not gloved; without a glove or gloves.

un·glue (un glü′), *v.t.,* **-glued, -glu·ing.** to separate or open (something fastened with or as with glue).

un·god·li·ly (un god′lə lē), *adv.* in an ungodly manner; impiously; wickedly.

un·god·li·ness (un god′lē nis), *n.* the quality of being ungodly; impiety; wickedness: *The wrath of God is revealed from heaven against all ungodliness* (Romans 1:18).

un·god·ly (un god′lē), *adj.* **1.** not conforming with the law or will of God; wicked; sinful. **2.** not devout; irreligious; impious. **3.** *Informal.* **a.** very annoying; distressing; irritating: *an ungodly noise.* **b.** outrageous; dreadful; shocking: *to pay an ungodly price.* **c.** unbelievable: *to eat an ungodly amount.*

un·got (un got′), *adj.* ungotten.

un·got·ten (un got′ən), *adj.* **1.** not acquired, gained, or won. **2.** unbegotten.

un·gov·ern·a·ble (un guv′ər nə bəl), *adj.* impossible or very hard to control or rule; unruly: *an ungovernable temper.* —**un·gov′ern·a·ble·ness,** *n.* —**Syn.** See **unruly.**

un·gov·ern·a·bly (un guv′ər nə blē), *adv.* in an ungovernable manner; so as not to be governed or restrained.

un·gov·erned (un guv′ərnd), *adj.* not governed; not brought under government or control; unrestrained; unbridled.

un·gown (un goun′), *v.t.* **1.** to divest or strip of a gown. **2.** to deprive of the clerical office.

un·graced (un grāst′), *adj.* not graced; not favored; not honored: *Ungraced, without authority or mark* (Ben Jonson).

un·grace·ful (un grās′fəl), *adj.* not graceful; not elegant or beautiful; clumsy; awkward. —**un·grace′ful·ly,** *adv.* —**un·grace′ful·ness,** *n.*

un·gra·cious (un grā′shəs), *adj.* **1.** not polite; discourteous; rude: *an ungracious remark.* **2.** unpleasant; disagreeable; displeasing. **3.** *Archaic.* ungraceful. —**un·gra′cious·ly,** *adv.* —**un·gra′cious·ness,** *n.*

un·grad·ed (un grā′did), *adj.* not graded; not arranged in grades or classes: *an ungraded school.*

un·gram·mat·ic (un′grə mat′ik), *adj.* ungrammatical.

un·gram·mat·i·cal (un′grə mat′ə kəl), *adj.* not in accordance with, or not observing, the rules of grammar or standard usage. —**un′gram·mat′i·cal·ly,** *adv.*

un·grasp·a·ble (un gras′pə bəl, -gräs′-), *adj.* that cannot be grasped or fully understood: *How ungraspable is the fact that real men ever did fight in real armour* (Mark Twain).

un·grate·ful (un grāt′fəl), *adj.* **1.** not feeling or displaying gratitude; not thankful: *an ungrateful person.* **2.** displaying lack of gratitude: *an ungrateful silence.* **3.** unpleasant; disagreeable; distasteful: *an ungrateful task.* —**un·grate′ful·ly,** *adv.* —**un·grate′ful·ness,** *n.*

un·grat·i·fied (un grat′ə fīd), *adj.* not gratified; not satisfied; not indulged.

un·ground·ed (un groun′did), *adj.* without foundation; without reasons; unfounded.

un·grudg·ing (un gruj′ing), *adj.* willing; hearty; liberal. —**un·grudg′ing·ly,** *adv.*

un·gual (ung′gwəl), *adj.* **1.** of or having to do with a nail, claw, or hoof. **2.** similar to a nail, claw, or hoof. **3.** having a nail, claw, or hoof. [< Latin *unguis* nail, claw, hoof + English *-al*[1]]

un·guard (un gärd′), *v.t.* **1.** to deprive of a guard or guards; lay open to attack. **2.** (in card games) to leave (a possible winning card) unprotected by playing a lower card of the same suit.

un·guard·ed (un gär′did), *adj.* **1.** without a guard or guards; not protected: *an unguarded camp.* **2.** not properly thoughtful or cautious; careless: *in a moment of unguarded frankness.* —**un·guard′ed·ly,** *adv.* —**un·guard′ed·ness,** *n.*

un·guent (ung′gwənt), *n.* an ointment for sores, burns, etc.; salve. [< Latin *unguentum* < *unguere* to anoint]

un·guen·tar·y (ung′gwən ter′ē), *adj.* **1.** of or having to do with unguents. **2.** suitable for unguents. **3.** like unguents.

un·gues (ung′gwēz), *n.* plural of **unguis.**

un·guessed (un gest′), *adj.* not arrived at or attained by guess or conjecture; unsuspected.

un·guic·u·lar (ung gwik′yə lər), *adj.* **1.** of or having to do with a nail or claw. **2.** bearing a nail or claw. [< Latin *unguiculus* (see UNGUICULATE) + English *-ar*]

un·guic·u·late (ung gwik′yə lit, -lāt), *adj.* **1.** (of vertebrate animals) having nails or claws, as distinguished from hoofed animals and cetaceans. **2.** *Botany.* (of a petal) having a clawlike base (unguis). —*n.* an unguiculate animal. [< New Latin *unguiculatus* < Latin *unguiculus* (diminutive) < Latin *unguis* hoof, claw, nail]

un·guic·u·lat·ed (ung gwik′yə lā′tid), *adj.* unguiculate.

un·guid·ed (un gī′did), *adj.* **1.** not guided; not conducted: *a stranger unguided and unfriended* (Shakespeare). **2.** not regulated; ungoverned: *the accidental, unguided motions of blind matter* (John Locke).

un·guif·er·ous (ung gwif′ər əs), *adj.* bearing a nail, claw, or unguis. [< Latin *unguis* (see UNGUIS) + English *-ferous*]

un·guilt·y (un gil′tē), *adj.* not guilty; innocent.

un·gui·nous (ung′gwə nəs), *adj. Obsolete.* oily; fatty; greasy. [< Latin *unguinōsus* < *unguen, -inis* ointment < *unguere* to anoint]

un·guis (ung′gwis), *n., pl.* **-gues** (-gwēz). **1.** a nail, claw, or hoof. **2.** *Botany.* the narrow part of certain petals, by which they are attached to the receptacle; ungula. [< Latin *unguis* hoof, claw, nail]

un·gu·la (ung′gyə lə), *n., pl.* **-lae** (-lē). **1.** a hoof. **2.** a claw or nail. **3.** *Botany.* an unguis. **4.** *Geometry.* a cylinder, cone, etc., the top part of which has been cut off by a plane oblique to the base. [< Latin *ungula* (diminutive) < *unguis* nail, claw, hoof]

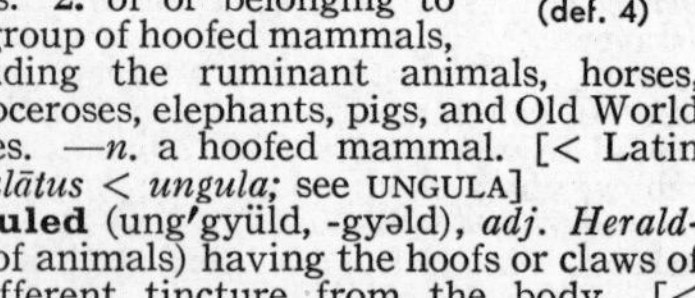

Ungula
(def. 4)

un·gu·lar (ung′gyə lər), *adj.* of or having to do with a hoof, claw, or nail.

un·gu·late (ung′gyə lit, -lāt), *adj.* **1. a.** hoof-shaped. **b.** having hoofs. **2.** of or belonging to the group of hoofed mammals, including the ruminant animals, horses, rhinoceroses, elephants, pigs, and Old World conies. —*n.* a hoofed mammal. [< Latin *ungulātus* < *ungula;* see UNGULA]

un·guled (ung′gyüld, -gyəld), *adj. Heraldry.* (of animals) having the hoofs or claws of a different tincture from the body. [< Latin *ungula* ungula + English *-ed*[2]]

un·gu·li·grade (ung′gyə lə grād), *adj.* walking on the tips of the digits. [< New Latin *unguligradus* < Latin *ungula* claw (see UNGULA) + *gradī* to step]

un·hack·neyed (un hak′nēd), *adj.* **1.** not hackneyed; not trite, commonplace, or stale. **2.** not habituated or experienced: *one unhackneyed in the ways of intrigue* (Scott).

un·hair (un hãr′), *v.t., v.i.* **1.** to divest of or lose the hair. **2.** to remove the hair from (a hide, skin, etc.) as a preliminary to tanning.

un·hal·low (un hal′ō), *v.t.* **1.** to deprive of a holy or sacred character. **2.** to profane.

un·hal·lowed (un hal′ōd), *adj.* **1.** not made holy; not sacred. **2.** wicked; sinful; evil.

un·ham·pered (un ham′pərd), *adj.* not hampered; unimpeded.

un·hand (un hand′), *v.t.* to let go; take the hands from; set free; release.

un·hand·i·ly (un han′də lē), *adv.* in an unhandy manner; awkwardly; clumsily.

un·hand·i·ness (un han′dē nis), *n.* the state or character of being unhandy; want of dexterity; clumsiness.

un·hand·led (un han′dəld), *adj.* **1.** not handled; not touched. **2.** not treated or managed. **3.** not accustomed to being used; not trained or broken in: *youthful and unhandled colts* (Shakespeare).

un·hand·some (un han′səm), *adj.* **1.** not good-looking; plain; ugly. **2.** ungracious; discourteous; unseemly; mean. **3.** not generous; meanly petty or small. **—un·hand′some·ly,** *adv.* **—un·hand′some·ness,** *n.*

un·hand·y (un han′dē), *adj.* **1.** not easy to handle or manage: *an unhandy tool.* **2.** not skillful in using the hands: *an unhandy workman.*

un·hanged (un hangd′), *adj.* not hanged; not punished by hanging: *There goes an unhanged rogue!*

un·hap·pi·ly (un hap′ə lē), *adv.* **1.** in an unhappy manner; miserably: *to live unhappily.* **2.** to one's misfortune; unfortunately: *Unhappily I missed seeing him.* **3.** not suitably or appropriately; not aptly.

un·hap·pi·ness (un hap′ē nis), *n.* **1.** a being unhappy; sadness: *We are erecting a first line of defense against personal maladjustment and unhappiness* (New York Times). **2.** misfortune; bad luck: *It is our great unhappiness, when any calamities fall upon us, that we are uneasy and dissatisfied* (William Wake).

un·hap·py (un hap′ē), *adj.,* **-pi·er, -pi·est. 1.** without gladness; sad; sorrowful: *an unhappy face.* **2.** miserable in lot or circumstances; unlucky: *an unhappy life.* **3.** not appropriate; unsuitable to the occasion or purpose: *an unhappy selection of colors.* **4.** *Obsolete.* mischievous; naughty: *Beat him well, he's an unhappy boy* (Beaumont and Fletcher).

un·hard·ened (un här′dənd), *adj.* not hardened; not indurated.

un·harmed (un härmd′), *adj.* not harmed; uninjured; sound; intact.

un·harm·ful (un härm′fəl), *adj.* not harmful; harmless. **—un·harm′ful·ly,** *adv.*

un·har·mo·ni·ous (un′här mō′nē əs), *adj.* inharmonious.

un·har·ness (un här′nis), *v.t.* **1.** to remove harness from (a horse, etc.); free from harness or gear. **2.** to divest of armor. *—v.i.* to remove harness or gear.

un·hasp (un hasp′), *v.t.* to loose the hasp of.

un·hast·y (un hās′tē), *adj.,* **-hast·i·er, -hast·i·est.** not hasty; not precipitate; not rash; deliberate; slow.

un·hat (un hat′), *v.,* **-hat·ted, -hat·ting.** *—v.t.* to remove the hat from. *—v.i.* to take off one's hat, as in respect.

un·hatched[1] (un hacht′), *adj.* (of a bird, egg, etc.) not hatched; undeveloped.

un·hatched[2] (un hacht′), *adj.* **1.** not hatched or marked with cuts or lines. **2.** not scratched or injured.

UNHCR (no periods) or **U.N.H.C.R.,** United Nations High Commissioner for Refugees.

un·health·ful (un helth′fəl), *adj.* bad for the health. **—un·health′ful·ly,** *adv.* **—un·health′ful·ness,** *n.*

un·health·i·ly (un hel′thə lē), *adv.* in a way that is not healthy.

un·health·i·ness (un hel′thē nis), *n.* **1.** lack of health; sickness. **2.** a condition causing disease or harmful to health.

un·health·y (un hel′thē), *adj.,* **-health·i·er, -health·i·est. 1.** not possessing good health; not well: *an unhealthy child.* **2.** characteristic of or resulting from poor health: *an unhealthy paleness.* **3.** hurtful to health; unhealthful; unwholesome: *an unhealthy climate.* **4.** morally or spiritually harmful. **—Syn. 1.** sickly, frail, ill, diseased. **3.** unsanitary, unhygienic.

un·heard (un hėrd′), *adj.* **1.** not perceived by the ear; not heard: *unheard melodies. The warning shout was unheard.* **2.** without being given a hearing; not listened to: *to condemn a person unheard.* **3.** not heard of; unknown: *Nor was his name unheard . . . In ancient Rome* (Milton).

un·heard-of (un hėrd′uv′, -ov′), *adj.* **1.** that was never heard of; unknown: *Electric stoves were unheard-of 200 years ago.* **2.** such as was never known before; unprecedented: *unheard-of prices. The rude little girl spoke to her mother with unheard-of impudence.*

un·heat·ed (un hē′tid), *adj.* not heated; without heat.

un·heed·ed (un hē′did), *adj.* not heeded; disregarded; unnoticed.

un·heed·ful (un hēd′fəl), *adj.* heedless; unmindful.

un·heed·ing (un hē′ding), *adj.* not heeding; unheedful: *Through the unheeding many he did move, A splendour among shadows* (Shelley).

un·helm (un helm′), *v.t. Archaic.* to deprive of the helm or helmet.

un·help·ful (un help′fəl), *adj.* **1.** affording no aid. **2.** unable to help oneself; helpless.

un·her·ald·ed (un her′əl did), *adj.* not heralded; not announced beforehand.

un·he·ro·ic (un′hi rō′ik), *adj.* not heroic.

un·hes·i·tat·ing (un hez′ə tā′ting), *adj.* prompt; ready. **—un·hes′i·tat′ing·ly,** *adv.*

un·hewn (un hyün′), *adj.* **1.** not hewn; not shaped or fashioned by hewing. **2.** rough; unpolished.

un·hid·den (un hid′ən), *adj.* not hidden or concealed; open; manifest.

un·hin·dered (un hin′dərd), *adj.* not hindered; unimpeded.

un·hinge (un hinj′), *v.t.,* **-hinged, -hing·ing. 1.** to take (a door, etc.) off its hinges. **2.** to remove the hinges from. **3.** to separate from something; detach: *Minds that have been unhinged from their old faith* (George Eliot). **4.** to make unbalanced or disordered; unsettle; disorganize; upset: *Trouble has unhinged this man's mind.*

un·hired (un hīrd′), *adj.* not hired.

un·his·tor·ic (un′his tôr′ik, -tor′-), *adj.* **1.** not famous or important in history: *an unhistoric event.* **2.** unhistorical.

un·his·tor·i·cal (un′his tôr′ə kəl, -tor′-), *adj.* **1.** not in accordance with history: *The thoroughly unhistorical way in which these few subjects are dealt with* (James S. Northcote). **2.** not having actually happened. **3.** not acquainted with the facts of history: *Perhaps the unhistorical prophet had in mind some confused idea* (William G. Palgrave). **—un′his·tor′i·cal·ly,** *adv.* **—un′his·tor′i·cal·ness,** *n.*

un·hitch (un hich′), *v.t.* **1.** to free (a horse, mule, etc.) from being hitched; unloose the hitchings of. **2.** to unloose and make free; unfasten; detach.

un·hive (un hīv′), *v.t.,* **-hived, -hiv·ing.** to drive from or as from a hive.

un·ho·li·ly (un hō′lə lē), *adv.* in an unholy manner.

un·ho·li·ness (un hō′lē nis), *n.* the character or state of being unholy; lack of holiness.

un·ho·ly (un hō′lē), *adj.,* **-li·er, -li·est. 1.** not holy; profane. **2.** ungodly; wicked; sinful. **3.** *Informal.* not seemly; dreadful; fearful: *to charge an unholy price.* [Old English *unhālig* < *un-* un-[1] + *hālig* holy]

un·ho·mo·ge·ne·ous (un′hō mə jē′nē əs), *adj.* not homogeneous; heterogeneous.

un·hon·ored (un on′ərd), *adj.* not regarded with respect or reverence; not famed or renowned; not given marks of esteem.

un·hood (un hu̇d′), *v.t.* **1.** to strip of something that conceals; unmask; unveil. **2.** *Falconry.* to take the hood from the eyes of (a hawk).

un·hook (un hu̇k′), *v.t.* **1.** to loosen from a hook. **2.** to undo by loosening a hook or hooks. *—v.i.* to become loosed from hooks; become undone.

un·hoped (un hōpt′), *adj.* not hoped or looked for.

un·hoped-for (un hōpt′fôr′), *adj.* not expected; in addition to or beyond what is anticipated: *an unhoped-for blessing.*

un·hope·ful (un hōp′fəl), *adj.* not hopeful; leaving no room for hope; hopeless.

un·horse (un hôrs′), *v.t.,* **-horsed, -hors·ing. 1.** to throw from a horse's back; cause to fall from a horse: *When hurdles and brush fences have to be cleared, the jumpers are in danger of spilling and their riders of being unhorsed* (New York Times). **2.** to destroy the power or defenses of; overthrow; discomfit: *There are many striking particulars, such as . . . Douglas completely unhorsed by an alarm clock in his hand which will not stop jangling* (Newsweek). **3.** to deprive of a horse.

un·hos·tile (un hos′təl), *adj.* **1.** not hostile; friendly. **2.** not having to do with an enemy. **3.** not caused by an enemy.

un·housed (un houzd′), *adj.* not housed; houseless.

un·hou·seled (un hou′zəld), *adj.* not having had the Eucharist administered: *He died, unhouseled, in his sins* (Robert Southey).

un·hou·selled (un hou′zəld), *adj. Especially British.* unhouseled.

un·hu·man (un hyü′mən), *adj.* **1.** not human; destitute of human qualities. **2.** inhuman.

un·hu·mor·ous (un hyü′mər əs, -yü′-), *adj.* not humorous; unamusing: *Unfortunately, Chaplin seems to have forgotten that the most unhumorous thing a humorist can do is to lose his sense of humor* (Time).

un·hung (un hung′), *adj.* **1.** not suspended; not hung. **2.** not hanged; unhanged.

un·hur·ried (un hėr′id), *adj.* accomplished without haste; leisurely. **—un·hur′ried·ly,** *adv.*

un·hurt (un hėrt′), *adj.* not hurt; not harmed.

un·hurt·ful (un hėrt′fəl), *adj.* not hurtful; harmless. **—un·hurt′ful·ly,** *adv.*

un·husk (un husk′), *v.t.* to free from or as from a husk.

un·hy·gi·en·ic (un′hī jē en′ik, -jē′nik), *adj.* not hygienic; unhealthful; insanitary. **—un′hy·gi·en′i·cal·ly,** *adv.*

uni-, *combining form.* one; a single; having, or made of, only one: *Unicameral = having one assembly.* [< Latin *ūnus* one]

U·ni·at (yü′nē at), *n.* a member of any Eastern church that is in communion with the Roman Catholic Church and acknowledges the supremacy of the Pope but keeps its own liturgy. *—adj.* of or having to do with such a church or its members. [< Russian *uniat* < obsolete Polish *uniata,* variant of *unita* < Latin *ūnīre* unite < *ūnus* one]

U·ni·ate (yü′nē it, -āt), *n.* a Uniat.

u·ni·ax·i·al (yü′nē ak′sē əl), *adj.* **1.** (of a crystal) having one optic axis. **2.** *Botany.* having but one axis, as when the primary stem of a plant does not branch and terminates in a flower.

u·ni·cam·er·al (yü′nə kam′ər əl), *adj.* having or consisting of one deliberative assembly, especially an assembly with legislative power.

U·NI·CEF (yü′nə sef), *n.* United Nations Children's Fund (an agency of the United Nations, established in 1946 under the name *United Nations International Children's Emergency Fund* to provide food and medical supplies to children and mothers through member nations).

u·ni·cel·lu·lar (yü′nə sel′yə lər), *adj.* comprising a single cell, as an amoeba.

unicellular animals, protozoans.

u·ni·col·or (yü′nə kul′ər), *adj.* of a single color; monochromatic.

u·ni·col·ored (yü′nə kul′ərd), *adj.* unicolor.

u·ni·col·or·ous (yü′nə kul′ər əs), *adj.* unicolor.

u·ni·corn (yü′nə kôrn), *n.* **1.** an animal often mentioned in ancient and medieval fable and legend, resembling a horse with a single, long, (usually) spiral horn in the middle of its forehead: *Neighing far off on the haunted air, The unicorns come down to the sea* (Conrad Aiken). **2.** a figure, picture, or representation of this animal, often used as a heraldic bearing, especially as a supporter (figure beside the escutcheon) of the royal arms of Great Britain. **3.** (in the Bible) a two-horned animal, probably the wild ox or aurochs (a mistranslation of the Hebrew word *re'em*). Numbers 23:22, etc. [< Old French *unicorne,* learned borrowing from Latin *ūnicornis* < *ūnus* one + *cornū* horn]

Unicorn (def. 1)

unicorn fish, a file fish of West Indian and other warm seas, with a hornlike spine upon the head.

unicorn plant, an annual plant of the temperate parts of North America, whose pod ends in two long, curved beaks; double-claw.

u·ni·cos·tate (yü′nə kos′tāt), *adj. Botany.* denoting a leaf which has one large vein,

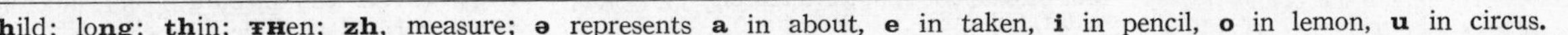

the midrib, running down the center. [< *uni-* + Latin *costa* rib + English *-ate*[1]]

u·ni·cus·pid (yü′nə kus′pid), *adj.* having only one cusp, as an incisor or canine tooth. —*n.* a unicuspid tooth.

u·ni·cy·cle (yü′nə sī′kəl), *n.* a vehicle consisting of a frame mounted on a single wheel, propelled by pedaling, used especially by acrobats, circus performers, etc. [< *uni-* + *-cycle,* as in *bicycle*]

Unicycle

u·ni·cy·clist (yü′nə sī′klist), *n.* a person who rides a unicycle, especially as a circus performer.

un·i·de·aed (un′ī dē′əd), *adj.* without imagination or wit; stupid and dull: *wretched, unideaed girls* (Samuel Johnson).

un·i·de·al (un′ī dē′əl), *adj.* **1.** not ideal: **a.** unimaginative; realistic; material. **b.** coarse. **2.** having no ideas; destitute of ideas, thoughts, or mental action.

un·i·den·ti·fi·a·ble (un′ī-den′tə fī′ə bəl), *adj.* that cannot be identified.

un·i·den·ti·fied (un′ī den′tə fīd), *adj.* not identified.

u·ni·di·men·sion·al (yü′nə də men′shə-nəl), *adj.* having only one dimension; varying in only one way.

un·id·i·o·mat·ic (un′id ē ə mat′ik), *adj.* not idiomatic: *His words in English and German were clear and well matched to his tone, though German vowels sometimes sounded raw and unidiomatic* (London Times). —**un′id·i·o·mat′i·cal·ly,** *adv.*

u·ni·di·rec·tion·al (yü′nə də rek′shə nəl, -dī-), *adj* in only one direction. —**u′ni·di·rec′tion·al·ly,** *adv.*

u·ni·far·i·ous (yü′nə fãr′ē əs), *adj.* single; in one row. [< *uni-* + *-farious,* as in *bifarious*]

u·ni·fi·a·ble (yü′nə fī′ə bəl), *adj.* able to be brought together into a single body or mass; capable of unification.

u·nif·ic (yü nif′ik), *adj.* making one; forming unity; unifying. [< *uni-* + *-fic*]

u·ni·fi·ca·tion (yü′nə fə kā′shən), *n.* **1.** formation into one unit; union. **2.** a making or being made more alike; reduction to a uniform system: *The traffic laws of the different States need unification.* **3.** the result of this; state of being unified.

u·ni·fi·ca·tion·ist (yü′nə fə kā′shə nist), *n.* an advocate of unification.

u·ni·fied field theory (yü′nə fīd), any theory seeking to unify different physical theories or laws, especially a theory developed by Albert Einstein in which electric, magnetic, and gravitational phenomena are treated as parts or phases of a single process.

u·ni·fi·er (yü′nə fī′ər), *n.* a person or thing that unifies.

u·ni·fi·lar (yü′nə fī′lər), *adj.* having, suspended by, or using a single thread or fiber: *a unifilar magnetometer.* [< *uni-* + Latin *fīlum* thread + English *-ar*]

u·ni·flo·rous (yü′nə flôr′əs, -flōr′-), *adj.* having or bearing only one flower. [< New Latin *uniflorus* (with English *-ous*) < Latin *ūnus* uni- + *flōs, flōris* flower]

u·ni·fo·li·ate (yü′nə fō′lē it, -āt), *adj.* **1.** having one leaf. **2.** unifoliolate.

u·ni·fo·li·o·late (yü′nə fō′lē ə lāt), *adj.* **1.** (of a leaf) compound in structure but having only one leaflet, as in the orange. **2.** (of a plant) having such leaves.

u·ni·form (yü′nə fôrm), *adj.* **1.** always the same; not changing: *to follow a uniform policy, to maintain a uniform temperature throughout a house. The earth turns around at a uniform rate.* **2.** all alike; not varying: *uniform hedges before every house. All the bricks have a uniform size.* **3.** not mixed or blended: *lawns of a uniform green.* **4.** free from quantitative fluctuation or variation; regular; even: *a uniform flow of water, a uniform pace.* **5.** in accordance or agreement with one another; conforming to one standard, rule, or pattern: *uniform answers.*
—*n.* the distinctive clothes worn by the members of a group when on duty, by which they may be recognized as belonging to that group: *Soldiers, policemen, and nurses wear uniforms.* —*v.t.* to clothe or furnish with a uniform or uniforms. [< Latin *ūniformis* < *ūnus* one + *forma* form] —**u′ni·form′ly,** *adv.* —**u′ni·form′ness,** *n.* —**Syn.** *adj.* **1, 4.** See **even.**

U·ni·form (yü′nə fôrm), *n. U.S.* a code name for the letter *u,* used in transmitting radio messages.

u·ni·formed (yü′nə fôrmd), *adj.* **1.** wearing a uniform; in uniform: *a uniformed policeman.* **2.** having a uniform: *the army and other uniformed services.*

u·ni·form·i·tar·i·an (yü′nə fôr′mə tãr′ē-ən), *adj.* of or having to do with uniformitarianism or uniformitarians. —*n.* an adherent of uniformitarianism.

u·ni·for·mi·tar·i·an·ism (yü′nə fôr′mə-tãr′ē ə niz′əm), *n.* the theory that geological change is caused by a gradual process rather than sudden upheaval.

u·ni·form·i·ty (yü′nə fôr′mə tē), *n., pl.* **-ties. 1.** uniform condition or character; sameness throughout. **2.** something that is uniform: *Little by little the plain came into view, a vast green uniformity, forlorn and tenantless* (Francis Parkman).

u·ni·fy (yü′nə fī), *v.t., v.i.,* **-fied, -fy·ing.** to make or form into one; bring or come together; unite. [< Late Latin *ūnificāre* < Latin *ūnus* one + *facere* to make]

u·ni·ju·gate (yü′nə jü′git, -gāt; yü nij′ə-gāt), *adj.* (of a pinnate leaf) having only one pair of leaflets. [< *uni-* + *jugate*]

u·ni·lat·er·al (yü′nə lat′ər əl), *adj.* **1.** of, on, or affecting one side only: *It declared itself for "unilateral disarmament," demanding that Britain should take the lead in renouncing the testing, the making, the possessing or using of nuclear weapons, and rejecting guided missile sites and bomber bases* (Bulletin of Atomic Scientists). **2.** having all parts arranged on one side of an axis; turned to one side; one-sided. **3.** *Law.* (of a contract, etc.) affecting one party or person only; done by one side only; putting obligation on one party only. **4.** concerned with or considering only one side of a matter. **5.** *Sociology.* related or descended on only one side. **6.** *Phonetics.* articulated with an opening on one side only: *unilateral l.* —**u′ni-lat′er·al·ly,** *adv.*

u·ni·lat·er·al·ism (yü′nə lat′ər ə liz′əm), *n.* belief in or adoption of a unilateral policy, especially in disarmament.

u·ni·lat·er·al·ist (yü′nə lat′ər ə list), *adj.* of or having to do with unilateralism or unilateralists. —*n.* an adherent of unilateralism.

u·ni·lin·gual (yü′nə ling′gwəl), *adj.* **1.** knowing or using only one language. **2.** having one universal language: *A dream of a unilingual State of the Marathi-speaking peoples became a reality* (Times of India).

u·ni·lin·gual·ism (yü′nə ling′gwə liz əm), *n.* the use of only one language, especially as the official language of a country.

un·il·lu·mi·nat·ed (un′i lü′mə nā′tid), *adj.* **1.** not illuminated; not lighted; dark. **2.** ignorant.

un·il·lu·mi·nat·ing (un′i lü′mə nā′ting), *adj.* unenlightening: *The moments of action are smothered in a fog of unilluminating metaphor* (London Times).

un·il·lu·sioned (un′i lü′zhənd), *adj.* free from illusions; uncolored by illusion.

u·ni·lobed (yü′nə lōbd), *adj.* having or consisting of only one lobe.

u·ni·loc·u·lar (yü′nə lok′yə lər), *adj.* having or consisting of only one chamber or cell.

un·i·mag·i·na·ble (un′i maj′ə nə bəl), *adj.* that cannot be imagined; undreamed-of; inconceivable: *On every side now rose rocks which in unimaginable forms lifted their black and barren pinnacles* (Shelley). —**un′i·mag′i·na·ble·ness,** *n.*

un·i·mag·i·na·bly (un′i maj′ə nə blē), *adv.* in an unimaginable manner; inconceivably: *an unimaginably bad performance. The farthest galaxies we can see are unimaginably remote.*

un·i·mag·i·na·tive (un′i maj′ə nə tiv), *adj.* lacking imagination; literal; prosaic: *an unimaginative person, proposal, or performance.* —**un′i·mag′i·na·tive·ly,** *adv.* —**un′i·mag′i·na·tive·ness,** *n.*

un·i·mag·ined (un′i maj′ənd), *adj.* not imagined; never conceived even in imagination: *unimagined riches.*

un·im·paired (un′im pãrd′), *adj.* not impaired: *unimpaired eyesight. Strong for service still and unimpaired* (William Cowper).

un·im·pas·sioned (un′im pash′ənd), *adj.* not impassioned; not influenced by passion; calm; tranquil.

un·im·peach·a·bil·i·ty (un′im pē′chə-bil′ə tē), *n.* the character of being unimpeachable or blameless.

un·im·peach·a·ble (un′im pē′chə bəl), *adj.* **1.** free from fault, flaw, or error; not able to be doubted or questioned: *an unimpeachable fact, an unimpeachable source. When Parliament met, the leaders of both the parties in both the Houses made speeches in favour of the Prince, asserting his unimpeachable loyalty to the country* (Lytton Strachey). **2.** blameless; irreproachable: *an unimpeachable reputation.*

un·im·peach·a·bly (un′im pē′chə blē), *adv.* in an unimpeachable manner; blamelessly.

un·im·peached (un′im pēcht′), *adj.* not impeached; not called in question.

un·im·ped·ed (un′im pē′did), *adj.* not impeded or hindered.

un·im·plored (un′im plôrd′, -plōrd′), *adj.* not implored; not solicited.

un·im·por·tance (un′im pôr′təns), *n.* unimportant nature or quality.

un·im·por·tant (un′im pôr′tənt), *adj.* not important; insignificant; trifling.

un·im·pos·ing (un′im pō′zing), *adj.* **1.** not imposing; not commanding respect. **2.** not enjoining as obligatory; voluntary.

un·im·pressed (un′im prest′), *adj.* not impressed.

un·im·press·i·ble (un′im pres′ə bəl), *adj.* not impressible; not susceptible; apathetic.

un·im·pres·sion·a·ble (un′im presh′ə-nə bəl), *adj.* not impressionable; not easily impressed or influenced.

un·im·proved (un′im prüvd′), *adj.* **1.** not improved; not turned to account; not cultivated. **2.** not increased in value by betterments or improvements, as real property.

un·in·closed (un′in klōzd′), *adj.* unenclosed.

un·in·cor·po·rat·ed (un′in kôr′pə rā′-tid), *adj.* not incorporated.

un·in·cum·bered (un′in kum′bərd), *adj.* unencumbered.

un·in·flam·ma·ble (un′in flam′ə bəl), *adj.* not inflammable.

un·in·flect·ed (un′in flek′tid), *adj.* not inflected; not subject to inflection: *uninflected languages.*

un·in·flu·enced (un in′flu̇ ənst), *adj.* not influenced; not affected; not persuaded or moved; free from bias or prejudice.

un·in·form·a·tive (un′in fôr′mə tiv), *adj.* not giving information; not instructive: *It does not, however, follow that the truths of logic are of no use simply because they are uninformative* (Scientific American).

un·in·formed (un′in fôrmd′), *adj.* **1.** not informed: **a.** uninstructed, uneducated, or ignorant. **b.** without information on some matter. **2.** not endowed with life or spirit.

un·in·hab·it·a·ble (un′in hab′ə tə bəl), *adj.* not inhabitable; unfit to be inhabited: *an uninhabitable desert or slum.*

un·in·hab·it·ed (un′in hab′ə tid), *adj.* not inhabited; lacking inhabitants: *an uninhabited wilderness.*

un·in·hib·it·ed (un′in hib′ə tid), *adj.* unrestrained; open; free: *an uninhibited person, uninhibited laughter.* —**un′in·hib′i·ted·ly,** *adv.*

un·i·ni·ti·ate (un′i nish′ē it, -āt), *n.* a person who has not been initiated: *Croquet upon the island "lawn" . . . was a pastime to be shunned by the uninitiate* (Alexander Woollcott).

un·i·ni·ti·at·ed (un′i nish′ē ā′tid), *adj.* **1.** not introduced into acquaintance with something. **2.** not having been admitted, as into a society.

un·in·jured (un in′jərd), *adj.* not injured; unharmed.

un·in·quis·i·tive (un′in kwiz′ə tiv), *adj.* not inquisitive; not curious to search or inquire; indisposed to seek information.

un·in·scribed (un′in skrībd′), *adj.* not inscribed; having no inscription.

un·in·spect·ed (un′in spek′tid), *adj.* not examined or investigated, especially by an official inspector.

un·in·spired (un′in spīrd′), *adj.* not inspired: *uninspired writing.*

un·in·spir·ing (un′in spīr′ing), *adj.* not giving or arousing inspiration: *an uninspiring teacher, an uninspiring book.* —**un′in-spir′ing·ly,** *adv.*

un·in·struct·ed (un′in struk′tid), *adj.* **1.** not instructed; not educated. **2.** not informed on some matter. **3.** not furnished with instructions, directions, or orders.

un·in·sured (un′in shu̇rd′), *adj.* not insured; without insurance.

un·in·te·grat·ed (un in′tə grā′tid), *adj.* not integrated; not subjected to a process of integration.

un·in·tel·li·gence (un′in tel′ə jəns), *n.* lack of intelligence; ignorance; unwisdom.

un·in·tel·li·gent (un′in tel′ə jənt), *adj.* **1.** not endowed with intelligence, as an inanimate object. **2.** deficient in intelligence; dull; stupid. **3.** *Obsolete.* having no knowledge (of). —**un′in·tel′li·gent·ly,** *adv.*

un·in·tel·li·gi·bil·i·ty (un′in tel′ə jə bil′ə tē), *n.* the quality or condition of being unintelligible.

un·in·tel·li·gi·ble (un′in tel′ə jə bəl), *adj.* that cannot be understood; not intelligible: *unintelligible patter* (W. S. Gilbert). —**un′in·tel′li·gi·ble·ness,** *n.*

un·in·tel·li·gi·bly (un′in tel′ə jə blē), *adv.* in an unintelligible manner; so as not to be understood.

un·in·tend·ed (un′in ten′did), *adj.* not intended.

un·in·ten·tion·al (un′in ten′shə nəl), *adj.* not intentional; not acting with intention; not done purposely. —**un′in·ten′tion·al·ly,** *adv.*

un·in·ter·est (un in′tər ist, -trist), *n.* disinterest: *The Senator gives an emphatic show of uninterest in such speculation* (New York Times).

un·in·ter·est·ed (un in′tər is tid, -tris-; -tə res′-), *adj.* **1.** showing or having no interest, especially: **a.** inattentive; apathetic; unconcerned: *an uninterested expression.* **b.** not interested (in); indifferent: *to be uninterested in politics.* **2.** having no financial interest (in); not a partner, shareholder, etc. **3.** *Obsolete.* disinterested.

➔ See **disinterested** for usage note.

un·in·ter·est·ing (un in′tər is ting, -tris-; -tə res′-), *adj.* not interesting; not arousing any feeling of interest. —**un·in′ter·est·ing·ly,** *adv.* —**un·in′ter·est·ing·ness,** *n.*

un·in·ter·mit·ted (un′in tər mit′id), *adj.* not intermitted; continuous.

un·in·ter·mit·ting (un′in tər mit′ing), *adj.* not intermitting; continuing. —**un′in·ter·mit′ting·ly,** *adv.*

un·in·ter·pret·a·ble (un′in tėr′prə tə bəl), *adj.* that cannot be interpreted.

un·in·ter·rupt·ed (un′in′tə rup′tid), *adj.* without interruption; continuous. —**un′in·ter·rupt′ed·ly,** *adv.*

un·in·tox·i·cat·ing (un′in tok′sə kā′ting), *adj.* not intoxicating.

u·ni·nu·cle·ate (yü′nə nü′klē it, -nyü′-), *adj.* having a single nucleus.

un·in·vent (un′in vent′), *v.t.* to do away with; cause to be as if never invented: *It may not be possible to uninvent the motor car, but it should not prove difficult to limit its numbers and its uses* (Manchester Guardian).

un·in·vent·ed (un′in ven′tid), *adj.* **1.** not invented. **2.** not found out.

un·in·ven·tive (un′in ven′tiv), *adj.* not inventive; not having the power of inventing, discovering, or contriving: *In every company there is . . . the inventive class of both men and women, and the uninventive or accepting class* (Emerson). —**un′in·ven′tive·ly,** *adv.* —**un′in·ven′tive·ness,** *n.*

un·in·vit·ed (un′in vī′tid), *adj.* not invited.

un·in·vit·ing (un′in vī′ting), *adj.* not inviting; unattractive: *The prospect of a long and damaging fight is uninviting* (Manchester Guardian). —**un′in·vit′ing·ly,** *adv.*

un·ion (yün′yən), *n.* **1.** a uniting: *the union of hydrogen and oxygen in water.* **2.** a being united: *The United States was formed by the union of thirteen states. All your strength is in your union* (Longfellow). **3.** any of various groups of people, states, etc., united for some special purpose: *a credit union, a customs union, the Pan American Union. The American colonies formed a union.* **4.** a group of workers, joined together to protect and promote their interests; labor union; trade union. **5.** marriage. **6.** a flag, or part of one, that is an emblem of union, as the blue rectangle with stars in the American flag. **7.** any of various devices for connecting parts of machinery or apparatus, as a piece to join pipes or tubes; coupling. **8.** a fabric woven of two or more different yarns, especially one containing cotton and another yarn. **9.** *Especially British.* **a.** a number of parishes united for the administration of the poor laws. **b.** a workhouse maintained by such parishes. [< Latin *ūniō, -ōnis* < *ūnus* one; unity; a uniting]

Pipe Union (def. 7)

—**Syn. 1, 2. Union, unity** mean a forming or being one. **Union** emphasizes the joining together of two or more things, people, or groups to form a whole, or the state of being joined together as a unit: *A combat team is formed by the union of infantry and other forces.* **Unity** emphasizes the oneness of the whole thus formed: *The strength of any group is in its unity.* **3.** combination, consolidation, fusion, coalition, confederation, league, merger.

Un·ion (yün′yən), *n.* **1.** *U.S.* the United States of America: *My paramount object is to save the Union, and not either to save or destroy slavery* (Abraham Lincoln). *The Constitution . . . looks to an indestructible Union composed of indestructible States* (Salmon P. Chase). **2.** *British.* the United Kingdom. —*adj.* of or having to do with the Union: *Early in the summer of 1861 he espoused the Union cause* (Nathaniel P. Langford). [< *union*]

union card, a card indicating that one is a member of the labor union by which it is issued.

Union Congress of Soviets, the former name of the Supreme Soviet.

union down, (of a flag or ensign) displaying the union at the lower corner next to the staff, instead of in its normal position (a flag hoisted in this way forming a signal of distress or of mourning): *There was an ensign, union down, flying at her main gaff* (Joseph Conrad).

u·ni·on·id (yü′nē on′id), *n.* any member of a large and widely distributed family of freshwater mollusks, especially numerous in the United States, whose developing larvae are parasitic on fish. [< New Latin *Unionidae* the family name < Latin *ūniō, -ōnis* a single large pearl; (originally) union]

un·ion·ism (yün′yə niz əm), *n.* **1.** the principle of union. **2.** adherence to a union. **3.** the system, principles, or methods of labor unions; trade unionism.

Un·ion·ism (yün′yə niz əm), *n.* adherence to the federal union of the United States, especially at the time of the Civil War.

un·ion·ist (yün′yə nist), *n.* **1.** a person who promotes or advocates union. **2.** a member of a labor union.

Un·ion·ist (yün′yə nist), *n.* **1.** a supporter of the federal government of the United States, especially during the Civil War. **2.** a person who opposed the political separation of Ireland from Great Britain, before the establishment of the Irish Free State.

un·ion·is·tic (yün′yə nis′tik), *adj.* **1.** having to do with or relating to unionism or unionists. **2.** promoting union.

un·ion·i·za·tion (yün′yə nə zā′shən), *n.* **1.** a unionizing. **2.** a being unionized.

un·ion·ize (yün′yə nīz), *v.*, **-ized, -iz·ing.** —*v.t.* **1.** to form into a labor union: *The first big drive of the new organization will be to unionize white collar workers* (Wall Street Journal). **2.** to organize under a labor union; bring under the rules of a labor union. —*v.i.* to join in a labor union.

Union Jack, 1. the national flag of the United Kingdom, formed by combining the crosses of the patron saints of England, Scotland, and Ireland on the blue ground of the banner of Saint Andrew; British national ensign. **2.** (originally) a ship's flag patterned on this. **3.** a ship's flag of any of various other countries, especially that of the United States.

union jack, any small flag, especially a ship's jack, designed with the union of the national flag.

un·ion-made (yün′yən mād′), *adj.* made or produced by unionized labor: *He smoked union-made cigarettes* (New Yorker).

union shop, 1. a business establishment that by agreement employs only members of a labor union but may hire nonmembers provided they join the union within a specified period (30 days). **2.** a business establishment that follows procedures agreed upon with a labor union in all matters concerning employment.

union suit, a suit of underwear in one piece.

u·ni·o·vu·lar (yü′nē ō′vyə lər), *adj.* derived from a single ovum: *Uniovular twins are identical twins.* [< *uni-* + *ovul*(e) + *-ar*]

u·nip·a·rous (yü nip′ər əs), *adj.* **1.** bearing or producing one at a birth. **2.** *Botany.* (of a cyme) developing a single axis at each branching. [< New Latin *uniparus* < Latin *ūnus* one + *parere* to bear]

u·ni·per·son·al (yü′nə pėr′sə nəl), *adj.* **1.** consisting of or existing as a single person. **2.** (of a verb) impersonal.

u·ni·pet·al·ous (yü′nə pet′ə ləs), *adj. Botany.* having but one petal.

u·ni·pla·nar (yü′nə plā′nər), *adj.* **1.** lying or taking place in one plane. **2.** confined to one plane: *uniplanar motion.*

u·ni·pod (yü′nə pod), *n.* a stool, frame, or stand with one leg. —*adj.* having only one leg; being a unipod. [< *uni-* + Greek *poús, podós* foot]

u·ni·po·lar (yü′nə pō′lər), *adj.* **1.** having a single pole. **2.** *Physics.* **a.** produced by or proceeding from one magnetic pole. **b.** having or operating by means of one magnetic pole. **3.** *Anatomy.* (of spinal and cranial nerve cells) having only one fibrous process.

u·ni·po·lar·i·ty (yü′nə pō lar′ə tē), *n.* the character of being unipolar.

u·nique (yü nēk′), *adj.* **1.** having no like or equal; being the only one of its kind; standing alone in comparison with others; unrivaled; unparalleled: *a unique person or work. That which gives to the Jews their unique position among the nations is what we are accustomed to regard as their Sacred History* (Spectator). **2.** single; sole; solitary: *He despised play. His unique wish was to work* (Arnold Bennett). **3.** *Informal.* very uncommon or unusual; rare; remarkable: *The most unique fabric service in the whole wide world* (House and Garden). [< Middle French *unique,* learned borrowing from Latin *ūnicus* single, sole < *ūnus* one] —**u·nique′ly,** *adv.* —**u·nique′ness,** *n.* —**Syn. 1.** unmatched, unequaled.

u·niq·ui·ty (yü nik′wə tē), *n.* uniqueness: *The "Ovid" is of such startling uniquity that I doubt anything comparable will come up again* (Time).

u·ni·sep·tate (yü′nə sep′tāt), *adj. Biology.* having but one septum or partition.

u·ni·se·ri·al (yü′nə sir′ē əl), *adj.* arranged in a single series or row.

u·ni·se·ri·ate (yü′nə sir′ē it, -āt), *adj.* **1.** uniserial. **2.** *Biology.* consisting of a single row of cells: *a uniseriate hair or filament.*

u·ni·sex (yü′nə seks′), *adj.* (of dress) for both men and women: *The "unisex" look arrived . . . and this trend toward a merging of the sexes was emphasized by the wearing of jewelry by men in the form of pendants* (Antony King Deacon).

u·ni·sex·u·al (yü′nə sek′shü əl), *adj.* **1.** that is not a hermaphrodite; having the essential reproductive organs of only one sex in one individual. **2.** *Botany.* diclinous. **3.** having to do with one sex. **4.** restricted to one sex.

u·ni·son (yü′nə zən, -sən), *n.* **1.** harmonious combination or union; concord; agreement: *that unison of sense which marries sweet sound with the grace of form* (Keats). **2.** identity in pitch of two or more sounds, tones, etc. **3.** a combination of tones, melodies, etc., at the same pitch, as performed by different voices or instruments. **4.** the relation of two tones of the same pitch considered as an "interval"; prime. **5.** (loosely) a combination of tones, melodies, etc., one or more octaves apart, as performed by male and female voices.

in unison, as one; together: *to act in unison, soldiers marching in unison. The children sang "happy birthday" in unison.*

—*adj.* **1.** *Music.* **a.** characterized by two or more tones having the same pitch, or pitches an even octave or octaves apart, or both, sounding together: *unison music, a unison phrase or passage.* **b.** done in unison; producing unison music: *unison playing or singing.* **c.** (of strings) tuned to the identical pitch. **2.** (of sounds in general) sounding as one; in unison; unisonous. **3.** done in unison; performed together as one: *a unison movement, unison marching, unison bowing.* [< Medieval Latin *unisonus* sounding the same < Late Latin *ūnisonus* in immediate sequence in the scale, monotonous < Latin *ūnus* one + *sonus* sound]

u·nis·o·nal (yü nis′ə nəl), *adj.* unisonous.

u·nis·o·nance (yü nis′ə nəns), *n.* unison.

u·nis·o·nant (yü nis′ə nənt), *adj.* unisonous.

u·nis·o·nous (yü nis′ə nəs), *adj.* rendered, or composed to be rendered, in unison or in octaves.

u·nit (yü′nit), *n.* **1.** a single thing or person; individual member or part (of a group or number of things or individuals): *to regard husband and wife as the primary units of the family.* **2.** any group of things or persons considered as one; division or section: *The family is a social unit.* **3.** one of the indi-

viduals or groups into which a whole can be analyzed: *The body consists of units called cells. The world . . . so terrible in the mass, is so . . . pitiable in its units* (Thomas Hardy). **4.** a standard division having a certain value, quantity, or amount, devised for measuring: *A foot is a unit of length; a pound is a unit of weight.* **5.** the amount of a drug, vaccine, serum, etc., necessary to produce a specified effect: *international units of vitamins.* **6.** the amount necessary to produce a specified effect upon a particular animal or upon animal tissues: *a rat growth unit.* **7.** the smallest whole number; one; 1. **8.** *Mathematics.* a single magnitude or number considered as the base of all numbers. **9.** *Especially U.S.* a certain number of hours of classroom attendance and the accompanying outside work, or any other determinable amount of instruction or work, used in computing credits, fees, etc. **10.** any of the basic administrative and tactical groups or divisions of an armed force, forming part of a larger group or division.
—*adj.* **1. a.** of, having to do with, or equivalent to a unit. **b.** produced or caused by a unit. **c.** consisting of, containing, or forming a unit or units. **2.** having the distinct or individual existence of a unit; individual: *All things in the exterior world are unit and individual; . . . the mind contemplates these unit realities as they exist* (Cardinal Newman).
[alteration of *unity;* patterned on *digit*]

Unit., Unitarian.

u·nit·age (yü′nə tij), *n.* detailed statement of the quantity making up a unit of measure.

U·ni·tar·i·an (yü′nə tãr′ē ən), *n.* **1.** a Christian who denies the doctrine of the Trinity, maintaining that God is one person, and accepts Christ as a man imbued with the divine spirit but not himself divine. **2.** a member of a Christian group or sect holding this doctrine and maintaining a congregational polity.
—*adj.* **1.** of or having to do with Unitarians or their doctrines. **2.** characteristic of Unitarians or their doctrines. **3.** adhering to Unitarianism.

U·ni·tar·i·an·ism (yü′nə tãr′ē ə niz′əm), *n.* the doctrines or beliefs of Unitarians.

u·ni·tar·y (yü′nə ter′ē), *adj.* **1.** of or having to do with a unit or units. **2.** characterized by, based upon, or directed toward unity: *a unitary policy of government.* **3.** like that of a unit; used as a unit. **4.** of the nature of a unit; undivided or indivisible; single; separate.

U·ni·tas Fra·trum (yü′nə tas frā′trəm), Moravian Brethren. [< Medieval Latin *unitas fratrum* < Latin *ūnitās* unity, *frātrum* of brethren, genitive plural of *frāter* brother]

unit card, a card in a library's card catalogue, duplicated to serve as a unit for other cards, to which only a heading has to be added. The cards of the Library of Congress are used as unit cards.

unit character, a trait caused by one gene, or by a group of inseparable genes; a Mendelian character.

u·nite[1] (yü nīt′), *v.,* **u·nit·ed, u·nit·ing.** —*v.t.* **1.** to join together; make one; combine: *to unite bricks with mortar in a wall.* **2.** to bring together; amalgamate or consolidate into one body; join in action, interest, opinion, feeling, etc.: *to unite one's forces against an enemy. Several firms were united to form one company.* **3.** to join by mutual pledging, covenant, or other formal bond; cause to become a union: *to unite a man and woman in marriage.* **4.** to have or exhibit in union or combination: *a child uniting his father's temper and his mother's red hair.* —*v.i.* to become or act as one; be united: *We united in singing "America."*
[< Latin *ūnītus,* past participle of *ūnīre* < *ūnus* one] —**Syn.** *v.t.* **1,** *v.i.* merge, consolidate, unify, couple. See **join.**

u·nite[2] (yü′nīt, yü nīt′), *n.* an English gold coin, issued by James I after the union of England and Scotland, originally worth 20 shillings. [< obsolete *unite,* adjective, united < Latin *ūnītus;* see UNITE[1] (because of the union of the crowns of Scotland and England in 1603)]

u·nit·ed (yü nī′tid), *adj.* **1.** joined together to make one; combined into a single body or whole; unified. **2.** joined together; closely connected, fastened, etc. **3.** of two or more persons or things. **4.** belonging to two or more persons or things. **5.** produced by two or more persons or things; joint: *united efforts.* **6.** that harmonizes or agrees; in concord. —**u·nit′ed·ly,** *adv.*

United Brethren, 1. Moravian Brethren. **2.** an American Protestant denomination, founded in the early 1800's, Methodist in polity and Arminian in doctrine.

United Church, a Canadian Christian church formed in 1924-1925 as a union of Methodists, Presbyterians, and Congregationalists.

United Empire Loyalist, any of a group of British colonists in America who emigrated to Canada during and after the Revolutionary War because they chose to remain British subjects; Loyalist.

United Greeks, the members of Christian communities which retain the liturgy, rites, etc., of the Greek or Eastern Church but are united to or in communion with the Church of Rome.

United Nations, 1. the UN. **2.** the nations that fought against Germany, Italy, and Japan in World War II.

United Nations Conference on International Organization, a conference held in San Francisco from April 25 to June 26, 1945, to write a charter based on the Dumbarton Oaks proposals.

United Nations Relief and Rehabilitation Administration, UNRRA.

United Press-International, UPI.

United States, 1. a federation or union of states constituting a distinct, sovereign country, usually with territorial integrity: *the United States of Brazil.* **2.** the United States of America. *Abbr.:* U.S.

United States Army, the Regular Army of the United States. *Abbr.:* U.S.A.

u·nit·er (yü nī′tər), *n.* a person or thing that unites; uniting agency or quality.

unit factor, *Biology.* a gene or a group of inseparable genes, causing the inheritance of a unit character.

u·ni·ties (yü′nə tēz), *n.pl.* See under **unity,** *n.*

u·ni·tion (yü nish′ən), *n.* union. [< Late Latin *ūnītiō, -ōnis* < *ūnīre;* see UNITE[1]]

u·ni·tive (yü′nə tiv), *adj.* having or tending toward union. [< Late Latin *ūnītīvus* < Latin *ūnīre;* see UNITE[1]]

u·nit·ize (yü′nə tīz), *v.t.,* **-tized, -tiz·ing. 1.** to make into or reduce to a unit; make as one: *The Rambler's unitized frame construction, in which body and frame are welded into a single unit . . .* (Time). **2.** to make a unit of; treat as an independent unit.

unit magnetic pole, the unit of magnetism exhibited by a magnetic pole which repels a like pole at a unit distance of one centimeter with a force of one dyne, or at a unit distance of one foot with a force of one pound.

unit rule, *U.S.* a rule which requires that members of a delegation at a convention cast their votes in a body for the candidate preferred by the majority of the delegation.

unit trust, a fixed trust.

u·ni·ty (yü′nə tē), *n., pl.* **-ties. 1.** the fact, quality, or condition of being one; oneness; singleness, especially: **a.** being one and indivisible by nature or definition: *divine unity. A circle has more unity than a row of dots. A nation has more unity than a group of tribes.* **b.** being united; union; unification: *unity in marriage, the unity of allies.* **2.** a union of parts forming a complex whole; undivided whole, as distinct from its parts. **3.** concord between two or more persons; harmony: *Brothers and sisters should live together in unity.* **4.** the number one (1). **5.** a quantity or magnitude regarded as equivalent to one in calculation, measurement, or comparison. **6.** oneness of effect; choice and arrangement of material (for a composition, book, picture, statue, etc.) to secure a single effect.
the unities, *Drama.* the three principles of the French classical dramatists, derived from Aristotle, requiring a play to have one plot or course of events (unity of action) occurring on one day (unity of time) and in one place (unity of place): *The unities, Sir . . . are . . . a kind of a universal dovetailedness with regard to place and time* (Dickens).
[< Anglo-French *unité,* learned borrowing from Latin *ūnitās, -ātis* < *ūnus* one]
—**Syn. 1.** See **union.**

Unity of Brethren, Moravian Brethren.

univ., 1. a. universal. **b.** universally. **2.** university.

Univ., 1. Universalist. **2.** University.

U·NI·VAC or **U·ni·vac** (yü′nə vak), *n. Trademark.* an electronic computing device which uses a binary numbering system. [< *Univ*(ersal) *A*(utomatic) *C*(omputer)]

u·ni·va·lence (yü′nə vā′ləns, yü niv′ə-), *n.* a being univalent.

u·ni·va·len·cy (yü′nə vā′lən sē, yü niv′ə-), *n.* univalence.

u·ni·va·lent (yü′nə vā′lənt, yü niv′ə-), *adj.* **1.** *Chemistry.* having a valence of 1; monovalent. **2.** *Biology.* single (applied to a chromosome which lacks, or does not unite with, its homologous chromosome during synapsis).

u·ni·valve (yü′nə valv), *n.* **1.** any mollusk having a shell consisting of one valve: *Snails are univalves.* **2.** its shell.
—*adj.* **1.** (of a mollusk) having a shell consisting of one valve. **2.** (of a shell) composed of a single valve or piece. **3.** having one valve only.

u·ni·valved (yü′nə valvd), *adj.* univalve.

u·ni·val·vu·lar (yü′nə val′vyə lər), *adj.* univalve.

u·ni·ver·sal (yü′nə vėr′səl), *adj.* **1.** of, for, or by all, especially: **a.** not limited to certain individuals or groups within the whole; to which all are subject; shared by all: *Food, fire, and shelter are universal needs. Kings are not born; they are made by universal hallucination* (George Bernard Shaw). **b.** proceeding from the whole body or number; shared in by all: *a universal protest.* **c.** understood or used by all; belonging to all: *the universal language of love.* **2.** of or having to do with the whole universe; existing everywhere: *a universal law of nature.* **3.** covering a whole group of persons, things, cases, etc., within a particular frame of reference; general: *universal adult suffrage.* **4.** of, belonging to, or including all persons, especially consisting of the whole body of Christians. **5.** *Philosophy, Logic.* applicable to all the members of a class; generic. **6.** constituting, existing as, or regarded as a complete whole; complete; entire; whole: *the universal cosmos.* **7.** accomplished in or comprising all, or very many, subjects; wide-ranging: *a universal genius, universal knowledge.* **8.** adaptable to different sizes, angles, kinds of work, etc. **9.** allowing or providing for movement toward any direction: *a universal joint.*
—*n.* **1.** *Philosophy, Logic.* **a.** that which is predicated or asserted of all the individuals or species of a class or genus; universal proposition. **b.** a general term or concept; an abstraction: *The common man is a universal.* **2.** something universal, especially a person or thing that is universally powerful, current, etc.: *He made their pride, pity, love, anguish, glory, and endurance into universals* (Newsweek).
[< Latin *ūniversālis* < *ūniversus;* see UNIVERSE] —**u′ni·ver′sal·ly,** *adv.* —**u′ni·ver′sal·ness,** *n.*

universal coupling, a universal joint.

universal donor, a blood donor who has type O blood, that can be given safely in transfusion to a person of any blood type.

universal gravitation, gravitation conceived as a property of all matter in the universe: *This force [gravitation] exerted by the earth is merely an example of a property possessed by all material bodies, called universal gravitation* (Shortley and Williams).

u·ni·ver·sal·ism (yü′nə vėr′sə liz əm), *n.* **1.** universality: *This is . . . the universalism of Jesus Himself . . . He belongs to humanity, not to Israel* (Andrew M. Fairburn). **2.** the quality of having considerable knowledge of or interest in a great range of subjects. **3.** love or concern for all humanity. **4.** the doctrine of the unification of the world by establishing one religion, nationality, economy, etc., for all mankind.

U·ni·ver·sal·ism (yü′nə vėr′sə liz əm), *n.* the doctrine or beliefs of Universalists.

u·ni·ver·sal·ist (yü′nə vėr′sə list), *n.* a person who believes in or practices universalism. —*adj.* **1.** universalistic. **2.** of or having to do with universalism or universalists.

U·ni·ver·sal·ist (yü′nə vėr′sə list), *n.* **1.** a Christian who believes that all people will finally be saved. **2.** a member of a Christian denomination holding this doctrine.
—*adj.* **1.** of or having to do with Universalists or their doctrines. **2.** characteristic of Universalists or their doctrines. **3.** adhering to Universalism.

u·ni·ver·sal·is·tic (yü′nə vėr′sə lis′tik),

adj. universal in scope or character: *This early, narrow, tribalistic hope was in later centuries to give way to a broad universalistic and all-inclusive concept* (New York Times).

u·ni·ver·sal·i·ty (yü′nə vėr sal′ə tē), *n., pl.* **-ties.** the quality of being universal.

u·ni·ver·sal·i·za·tion (yü′nə vėr′sə lə zā′shən), *n.* the act or process of making universal or general; generalization.

u·ni·ver·sal·ize (yü′nə vėr′sə līz), *v.t.,* **-ized, -iz·ing.** to render universal; make applicable, known, etc., in all places, times, etc., or to all individuals: *Civilization requires a different kind of education to survive, one that humanizes rather than mechanizes man, and one that universalizes rather than nationalizes community* (Saturday Review).

universal joint, 1. a joint that allows or provides for movement or turning toward any direction. **2.** a coupling for transmitting power from one shaft to another when they are not in line, as between the transmission and drive shaft of an automobile.

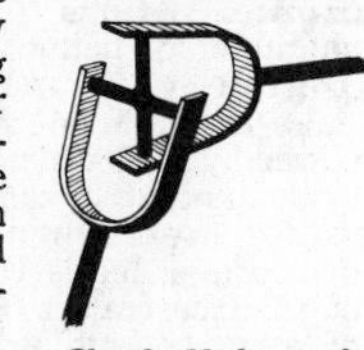

Single Universal Joint (def. 1)

universal language, 1. a language spoken throughout the world: *English and French are universal languages.* **2.** something that can be understood by all: *Love and laughter are universal languages.*

Universal Military Training or **universal military training,** a system in which every qualified man receives a general military training when he reaches a certain age. *Abbr.:* UMT (no periods).

universal recipient, a person having type AB blood, that can receive safely a transfusion of any blood type.

universal solvent, 1. a hypothetical substance, especially the alkahest, that dissolves everything. **2.** a substance that dissolves all or nearly all metals or classes of metals. **3.** water (because it can dissolve many compounds).

universal suffrage, suffrage extended to all the adult men and women of a country other than those disqualified by law.

universal time, Greenwich Time. *Abbr.:* u.t.

u·ni·verse (yü′nə vėrs), *n.* **1.** Also, **Universe.** the whole of existing or created things regarded collectively; everything there is; cosmos, especially: **a.** the whole of reality, as the creation of the Deity: *She had . . . The quest of hidden knowledge, and a mind To comprehend the universe* (Byron). *Roaming in thought over the Universe, I saw the little that is Good steadily hastening towards immortality, And the vast that is Evil I saw hastening to merge itself and become lost and dead* (Walt Whitman). **b.** the whole of observed or hypothesized physical reality; physical universe: *Our world is but a small part of the universe. The Egyptian's conception of the universe was . . . anthropomorphic: the goddess of the heavens, Nut, arched her starry body over the solid Earth and let the ship of the Sun glide over her back* (Rudolf Thiel). **2.** the world, especially as the abode of mankind; earth: *Who all our green and azure universe Threatenedst to muffle round with black destruction* (Shelley). **3.** universe of discourse. [< Latin *ūniversum,* (originally) adjective, whole, turned into one, neuter of *ūniversus* < *ūnus* one + *vertere* to turn]

universe of discourse, all the objects or ideas to which an argument or discussion refers.

u·ni·ver·si·ty (yü′nə vėr′sə tē), *n., pl.* **-ties. 1.** an institution of higher education, usually including several schools, as of law, medicine, theology, and business. In the United States it includes a college for general instruction, and a graduate school or schools, and is empowered to confer various degrees. *Abbr.:* Univ. **2.** a building or buildings occupied by a university. [< Anglo-French *universite,* learned borrowing from Medieval Latin *universitas, -atis* university < Late Latin *ūniversitās, -ātis* corporation, society < Latin, aggregate, whole < *ūniversus;* see UNIVERSE]

university extension, the extending of the advantages of university instruction to adults who are not enrolled as university students, by means of lectures at convenient centers and sometimes also by classwork, homework, and correspondence.

u·ni·ver·sol·o·gist (yü′nə vėr sol′ə jist), *n.* an expert in universology.

un·i·ver·sol·o·gy (yü′nə vėr sol′ə jē), *n.* the science of the universe, or of all created things.

u·niv·o·cal (yü niv′ə kəl), *adj.* having one meaning only; not equivocal; capable of but one interpretation. [< Late Latin *ūnivocus* (< Latin *ūnus* one + *vōx, vōcis* voice) + English *-al*[1]] —**u·niv′o·cal·ly,** *adv.*

un·jaun·diced (un jôn′dist, -jän′-), *adj.* **1.** not affected by jaundice: *an unjaundiced complexion.* **2.** not affected by envy, jealousy, etc.: *His description of the poverty program* [*was*] *all too true; and his strength and courage and unjaundiced eye beautifully evident throughout* (Harper's).

un·jeal·ous (un jel′əs), *adj.* not jealous; not suspicious or mistrustful.

un·jelled (un jeld′), *adj.* not jelled; without a definite form; not fixed: *Its communal character gives the impression of being sketchy, not filled out, unjelled* (New Yorker).

un·joint (un joint′), *v.t.* to take apart the joints of; dismember.

un·joint·ed (un join′tid), *adj.* **1.** having no joints, nodes, or articulations; inarticulate. **2.** unjoined; disjointed; disconnected.

un·joy·ful (un joi′fəl), *adj.* joyless; unpleasant: *this unjoyful set of people* (Sir Richard Steele).

un·just (un just′), *adj.* in opposition to what is morally right; not just; not fair. —**un·just′ly,** *adv.* —**un·just′ness,** *n.*

un·jus·ti·fi·a·ble (un jus′tə fī′ə bəl), *adj.* not justifiable; not defensible or right: *an unjustifiable act. Nor is it unjustifiable to hold that those who owe a superior allegiance to a foreign Government . . . have therefore forfeited the privilege of working for their own Government* (New York Times). —**un·jus′ti·fi′a·ble·ness,** *n.*

un·jus·ti·fi·a·bly (un jus′tə fī′ə blē), *adv.* in a manner that cannot be justified or vindicated: *unjustifiably severe. The organization was launched to an accompaniment of unjustifiably high hopes* (Wall Street Journal).

un·jus·ti·fied (un jus′tə fīd), *adj.* **1.** not proved to be right or proper; unwarranted: *unjustified claims or accusations. The action of the strikers was unjustified.* **2.** *Theology.* not brought into a state of justification; still subject to sin or the penalty of sin.

un·jus·ti·fi·ed·ly (un jus′tə fī′id lē), *adv.* in an unjustified manner; to an unjustified degree: *It is possible that the Soviet leaders . . . however unjustifiedly . . . fear attack from the West* (Times of India).

un·keeled (un kēld′), *adj.* not having a keel: *unkeeled sepals.*

un·kempt (un kempt′), *adj.* **1.** not properly cared for; neglected; untidy: *the unkempt clothes of a tramp.* **2.** (of the hair) not combed; matted or disheveled. [Middle English *unkembed* < *un-* un-[1] + *kempt, kembed,* Old English *cembed* combed, past participle of *cemban* to comb] —**un·kempt′ness,** *n.*

un·kenned (un kend′), *adj. Scottish.* unknown; strange.

un·ken·nel (un ken′əl), *v.,* **-neled, -nel·ing** or (*especially British*) **-nelled, -nel·ling.** —*v.t.* **1.** to let (a hound or hounds) out of the kennel. **2.** to force or drive out from hiding or concealment; bring to light: *to unkennel this knavery* (London Times). —*v.i.* to be unkenneled.

un·kept (un kept′), *adj.* **1.** not kept; not retained; not preserved. **2.** not sustained, maintained, or tended.

un·kind (un kīnd′), *adj.* lacking kindness or compassion; harsh; cruel. —**un·kind′ness,** *n.* —**Syn.** unsympathetic, ungracious.

un·kind·li·ness (un kīnd′lē nis), *n.* the character of being unkindly; unkindness; unfavorableness.

un·kind·ly (un kīnd′lē), *adj.* harsh; unfavorable: *the bleak, unkindly air* (Hawthorne). —*adv.* in an unkind way; harshly.

un·king·ly (un king′lē), *adj.* not kingly; not befitting a king; not royal.

un·knelled (un neld′), *adj.* not having the bell tolled for one at death or funeral; untolled: *Without a grave, unknell'd, uncoffin'd and unknown* (Byron).

un·knight·li·ness (un nīt′lē nis), *n.* the character of being unknightly.

un·knight·ly (un nīt′lē), *adj.* not knightly; unworthy of a knight; not like a knight. —*adv.* in a manner unbecoming to a knight.

un·knit (un nit′), *v.t., v.i.,* **-knit·ted** or **-knit, -knit·ting. 1.** to untie or unfasten (a knot, etc.). **2.** to ravel out (something knitted); unravel. **3.** to smooth out (something wrinkled): *He unknit his black brows* (Charlotte Brontë). [Old English *uncnyttan* < *un-* un-[2] + *cnyttan* to knit]

un·knot (un not′), *v.t.,* **-knot·ted, -knot·ting.** to bring out of a knotted state; free from knots; untie.

un·know·a·bil·i·ty (un′nō ə bil′ə tē), *n.* the quality or state of being unknowable.

un·know·a·ble (un nō′ə bəl), *adj.* that cannot be known; beyond comprehension, especially beyond human comprehension. —*n.* that which cannot be known.

the Unknowable, that which is by its nature beyond man's knowing; ultimate or essential reality, as something outside the realm of that which may be comprehended by man: *We may keep alive the consciousness that it is alike our highest wisdom and our highest duty to regard that through which all things exist as the Unknowable* (Herbert Spencer). —**un·know′a·ble·ness,** *n.*

un·know·ing (un nō′ing), *adj.* not knowing; ignorant or unsuspecting: *an unknowing child.* —*n.* ignorance.

the unknowing, those who do not know or are ignorant: *The pillars would not be recognized immediately by the unknowing as timber* (London Times).

—**un·know′ing·ly,** *adv.* —**un·know′ing·ness,** *n.*

un·known (un nōn′), *adj.* not known; not familiar; strange: *an unknown language. Most of Antarctica was once unknown land. How many ages hence Shall this our lofty scene be acted o'er, In states unborn and accents yet unknown!* (Shakespeare).

—*n.* **1.** a person or thing that is unknown: *a political unknown. The diver descended into the unknown.* **2.** *Mathematics.* an unknown quantity.

the Unknown, something great and unknown or mysterious: *God, the Unknown.*

—**Syn.** *adj.* obscure, nameless, unrenowned.

unknown quantity, *Mathematics.* a quantity whose value is to be found, usually represented by a letter from the last part of the alphabet, as *x, y,* or *z.*

Unknown Soldier, an unidentified soldier killed in combat and buried with honors in a prominent place in his country as a memorial to all the unidentified dead of his country: *The tomb of the American Unknown Soldier is in the Arlington National Cemetery, near Washington.*

UNKRA (no periods) or **U.N.K.R.A.,** United Nations Korean Reconstruction Agency.

un·la·bored (un lā′bərd), *adj.* **1.** not produced by labor or toil: *Unlabored harvests shall the fields adorn* (John Dryden). **2.** not cultivated by labor; not tilled. **3.** spontaneous; voluntary; natural. **4.** not cramped or stiff; easy; free: *an unlabored style.*

un·la·boured (un lā′bərd), *adj. Especially British.* unlabored.

un·lace (un lās′), *v.t.,* **-laced, -lac·ing. 1.** to undo the lace or laces of. **2.** to free or relieve (a person, the body, etc.) of clothing or an article of clothing, especially of clothing that is held on by a lace or laces; undress.

un·lade (un lād′), *v.t., v.i.,* **-lad·ed, -lad·en** or **-lad·ed, -lad·ing.** to unload.

un·la·dy·like (un lā′dē līk′), *adj.* not ladylike; not like or befitting a lady.

un·laid (un lād′), *adj.* **1.** not laid or placed; not fixed: *The first foundations of the world being yet unlaid* (Richard Hooker). **2.** not allayed; not pacified: *Blue meagre hag or stubborn unlaid ghost, That breaks his magic chains at curfew time* (Milton). **3.** not laid out, as a corpse. **4.** *Nautical.* untwisted, as the strands of a rope.

—*v.* the past tense and past participle of **unlay.**

un·la·ment·ed (un′lə men′tid), *adj.* not lamented; whose loss is not deplored; not moaned; unwept: *Thus let me live, unseen, unknown, Thus unlamented let me die* (Alexander Pope).

un·lash (un lash′), *v.t.* **1.** to detach or release by undoing a lashing. **2.** to undo or untie (a lashing).

un·latch (un lach′), *v.t.* to unfasten or open by lifting a latch. —*v.i.* to become or be able to be thus unfastened.

un·laun·dered (un lôn′dərd, -län′-), *adj.* not laundered.

un·law·ful (un lô′fəl), *adj.* **1.** against the law; prohibited by law; not lawful; illegal.

2. (of offspring) bastard; illegitimate. —**un·law′ful·ness,** *n.*

unlawful assembly, *Law.* the meeting of three or more persons to commit an unlawful act, or to carry out some purpose in such manner as to give reasonable ground for apprehending a breach of the peace in consequence of it.

un·law·ful·ly (un lô′fə lē), *adv.* **1.** illegally. **2.** illegitimately.

un·lay (un lā′), *v.i.*, **-laid, -lay·ing.** (of a rope) to have the strands part; untwist; unravel.

un·lead·ed (un led′id), *adj.* **1.** (of type) set without leads between the lines; solid. **2.** not weighted, covered, or furnished with lead.

un·learn (un lėrn′), *v.t.* **1.** to get rid of (ideas, habits, or tendencies); give up knowledge of; forget. **2.** to cause (a person) to unlearn something; teach not to do or to do the opposite of what has been taught.

un·learn·ed (un lėr′nid *for 1, 3;* un lėrnd′ *for 2*), *adj.* **1.** not educated; ignorant: *an audience of unlearned laymen. A man unlearned and poor* (John Greenleaf Whittier). **2. a.** not learned: *an unlearned lesson.* **b.** known without being learned: *an untaught, unlearned, but nevertheless very real appreciation of beauty.* **3.** not showing education.

un·learn·ed·ly (un lėr′nid lē), *adv.* in an unlearned manner; so as to exhibit ignorance; ignorantly.

un·leased (un lēst′), *adj.* not leased.

un·leash (un lēsh′), *v.t.* **1.** to release from a leash: *to unleash a dog.* **2.** to let loose: *to unleash one's temper.*

un·leav·ened (un lev′ənd), *adj.* (of dough, bread, etc.) not leavened: *Unleavened bread is made without yeast.*

un·led (un led′), *adj.* **1.** not led; without guidance. **2.** in command of one's faculties.

un·less (ən les′, un-), *conj.* if it were not that; if not: *We shall go unless it rains.* —*prep.* except: *Nor ever was he known ... [to] Curse, unless against the Government* (John Dryden). [Middle English *onlesse* < *on* + *lesse,* that is, on a less condition (than)]

un·les·soned (un les′ənd), *adj.* untaught; untutored: *an unlesson'd girl, unschool'd, unpractised* (Shakespeare).

un·let·tered (un let′ərd), *adj.* **1.** not educated; unlearned. **2.** not able to read or write; illiterate.

un·lev·el (un lev′əl), *adj., v.*, **-eled, -el·ing** or (*especially British*) **-elled, -el·ling.** —*adj.* not level; uneven. —*v.t.* to make not level or uneven.

un·li·censed (un lī′sənst), *adj.* **1.** not licensed; having no license. **2.** done or undertaken without license; unauthorized.

un·licked (un likt′), *adj.* **1.** not licked. **2.** not brought to the proper shape or condition by or as by licking. **3.** crude, rough, or unpolished.

unlicked cub, a crude or unmannerly young person: *You know, Polly, what an unlicked cub I was when I married you* (Besant and Rice).

un·light·ed (un lī′tid), *adj.* **1.** not lighted; not illuminated. **2.** not kindled or ignited.

un·like (un līk′), *adj.* **1.** having little or no resemblance one to the other; different; dissimilar: *The two problems are quite unlike.* **2.** different in size or number; unequal: *unlike weights.* **3.** *Archaic.* unlikely. —*prep.* different from: *to act unlike others.* —**un·like′ness,** *n.*
—**Syn.** *adj.* **1.** diverse.

un·like·li·hood (un līk′lē hůd), *n.* improbability.

un·like·li·ness (un līk′lē nis), *n.* **1.** the state of being unlikely or improbable; improbability. **2.** the state of being unlike; dissimilarity.

un·like·ly (un līk′lē), *adj.* **1.** not likely; not probable: *He is unlikely to win the race.* **2.** not likely to succeed: *an unlikely undertaking.*

un·lim·ber (un lim′bər), *v.t.* **1.** to detach (a gun) from a limber or towing apparatus in preparation for firing. **2.** to make or get (anything) ready for action or use. —*v.i.* to prepare for action.
—*n.* the act or procedure of unlimbering a gun.

un·lim·it·ed (un lim′ə tid), *adj.* **1.** without limits; boundless. **2.** not restricted: *Unlimited power is apt to corrupt the minds of those who possess it* (William Pitt). **3.** *Mathematics.* indefinite. —**un·lim′it·ed·ness,** *n.*

unlimited policy, an insurance policy which covers every type of a certain risk or contingency.

un·link (un lingk′), *v.t.* **1.** to undo two or more links of (a chain). **2.** to detach or set free by or as if by undoing or unfastening a link or chain. —*v.i.* to become unlinked; part; separate.

un·liq·ue·fied (un lik′wə fīd), *adj.* not dissolved; unmelted.

un·liq·ui·dat·ed (un lik′wə dā′tid), *adj.* not liquidated; not settled: *unliquidated debts or claims.*

un·list·ed (un lis′tid), *adj.* **1.** not on a or the usual (designated) list: *an unlisted telephone number.* **2.** not in the official list of securities that can be traded in a stock exchange.

un·lit (un lit′), *adj.* not lit; unlighted.

un·live (un liv′), *v.t.*, **-lived, -liv·ing.** to reverse, undo, or annul (past life or experience).

un·load (un lōd′), *v.t.* **1.** to take (a load) off or out of; remove (a burden, cargo, etc.). **2.** to take the load off or out of (an animal, vehicle, etc.); discharge the cargo of (a vessel). **3.** to remove (the shell, charge, etc.) from a firearm. **4.** to remove the load from (a firearm). **5.** to get rid of; unburden oneself of: *Alice began to unload her troubles onto her mother.* **6.** to get rid of, dispose of, or sell out (stock, etc.), especially in large quantities. —*v.i.* to be or become unloaded: *The ship is unloading.* —**un·load′er,** *n.*

un·lo·cat·ed (un lō′kā tid), *adj.* **1.** not located or placed. **2.** *U.S.* (of land) not surveyed and marked off: *The disposal of the unlocated lands will hereafter be a valuable source of revenue, and an immediate one of credit* (Alexander Hamilton).

un·lock (un lok′), *v.t.* **1.** to open the lock of: *to unlock a door.* **2.** to open (anything firmly closed). **3.** to disclose; reveal: *to unlock one's heart, one's inmost thoughts. Science has unlocked the mystery of the atom.* —*v.i.* to be or become unlocked.

un·locked (un lokt′), *adj.* not locked: *an unlocked door.*

un·looked-for (un lůkt′fôr′), *adj.* unexpected; unforeseen: *this unlooked-for danger* (William Godwin).

un·loose (un lüs′), *v.t.*, **-loosed, -loos·ing.** to let loose; set free; release: *Something ... seems to have ... unloosed her tongue* (Joseph Conrad).

un·loos·en (un lü′sən), *v.t.* unloose; loosen.

un·love (un luv′), *v.t.*, **-loved, -lov·ing.** to cease to love.

un·loved (un luvd′), *adj.* not loved.

un·love·li·ness (un luv′lē nis), *n.* **1.** unamiableness; lack of the qualities which attract love. **2.** lack of beauty or attractiveness; plainness of feature or appearance.

un·love·ly (un luv′lē), *adj.*, **-love·li·er, -love·li·est.** without beauty or charm; unpleasing in appearance; unpleasant; objectionable; disagreeable.

un·lov·ing (un luv′ing), *adj.* not loving; without love. —**un·lov′ing·ly,** *adv.* —**un·lov′ing·ness,** *n.*

un·luck·i·ly (un luk′ə lē), *adv.* in an unlucky or unfortunate manner; by ill luck; unfortunately; unhappily.

un·luck·i·ness (un luk′ē nis), *n.* the character or state of being unlucky.

un·luck·y (un luk′ē), *adj.*, **-luck·i·er, -luck·i·est.** **1.** having or characterized by misfortune; not lucky; unfortunate. **2.** bringing bad luck; ill-omened; inauspicious. —**Syn. 1.** unsuccessful, ill-fated.

un·made (un mād′), *v.* the past tense and past participle of **unmake.** —*adj.* not made; not yet made: *an unmade bed.*

un·maid·en·li·ness (un mā′dən lē nis), *n.* the character or state of being unmaidenly.

un·maid·en·ly (un mā′dən lē), *adj.* not maidenly; unbefitting a maiden.

un·mail·a·ble (un mā′lə bəl), *adj.* not mailable; that cannot be mailed.

un·make (un māk′), *v.t.*, **-made, -mak·ing.** **1.** to bring to nothing; undo; destroy; ruin: *The machine unmakes the man* (Emerson). **2.** to deprive of rank or station; depose. **3.** to undo the making of; cause to be no longer in being: *The British people will have made a bad bargain, which they will be able to unmake only at great cost* (Manchester Guardian Weekly).

un·mal·le·a·bil·i·ty (un mal′ē ə bil′ə tē), *n.* a being unmalleable.

un·mal·le·a·ble (un mal′ē ə bəl), *adj.* not malleable.

un·man (un man′), *v.t.*, **-manned, -man·ning.** **1.** to deprive of manly courage or fortitude; weaken or break down the spirit of: *to be unmanned by fear.* **2.** to deprive of virility; emasculate. **3.** to deprive of the attributes of man; make no longer human. **4.** to deprive of men: *to unman a ship.*

un·man·age·a·ble (un man′ə jə bəl), *adj.* not manageable; intractable; unruly; incapable of being handled: *an unmanageable horse.* —**un·man′age·a·ble·ness,** *n.*

un·man·age·a·bly (un man′ə jə blē), *adv.* in an unmanageable manner; so as to be unmanageable; uncontrollably.

un·man·like (un man′līk′), *adj.* **1.** unlike man in form or appearance. **2.** unbecoming a man as a member of the human race; inhuman; brutal. **3.** unsuitable to a man; effeminate; childish.

un·man·li·ness (un man′lē nis), *n.* the character of being unmanly; effeminacy.

un·man·ly (un man′lē), *adj.*, **-man·li·er, -man·li·est.** **1.** not manly; effeminate; weak; cowardly: *'Tis unmanly grief* (Shakespeare). **2.** dishonorable; degrading.

un·manned (un mand′), *adj.* **1.** deprived of courage; made weak or timid. **2.** emasculated; castrated. **3.** without a complement of men; lacking a crew, garrison, etc. **4.** without human beings; lacking people; unpopulated. **5.** *Falconry.* not tamed.

un·man·nered (un man′ərd), *adj.* **1.** not affected or pretentious; simple and straightforward. **2.** unmannerly.

un·man·ner·li·ness (un man′ər lē nis), *n.* the state or character of being unmannerly; want of good manners; breach of civility; rudeness of behavior.

un·man·ner·ly (un man′ər lē), *adj.* having bad manners; rude; discourteous: *He called them untaught knaves, unmannerly* (Shakespeare). —*adv.* with bad manners; rudely.
—**Syn.** *adj.* impolite.

un·man·u·fac·tured (un′man yə fak′chərd), *adj.* **1.** not made up; still in its natural state, or only partly prepared for use: *Fiber is unmanufactured before it is made into thread. Thread is unmanufactured before it is woven into cloth.* **2.** not simulated: *unmanufactured grief.*

un·ma·nured (un′mə nůrd′), *adj.* **1.** not manured; not enriched by manure. **2.** *Obsolete.* untilled; uncultivated.

un·marked (un märkt′), *adj.* **1.** not marked; having no mark. **2.** unobserved; not regarded; undistinguished; not noted: *He mix'd, unmark'd, among the busy throng* (John Dryden).

un·mar·ket·a·ble (un mär′kə tə bəl), *adj.* not marketable; unsalable.

un·marred (un märd′), *adj.* not marred or injured: *He had displayed indiscreet valor by provoking Neal, then by sticking his hitherto unmarred face in the way of Big Tom's flying knuckles* (Time).

un·mar·riage·a·ble (un mar′ə jə bəl), *adj.* **1.** not fit to be married. **2.** too young for marriage.

un·mar·ried (un mar′ēd), *adj.* not married; single. —**Syn.** unwed.

un·mar·ry (un mar′ē), *v.*, **-ried, -ry·ing.** —*v.t.* to dissolve the marriage of; divorce. —*v.i.* to become freed from a marriage.

un·mask (un mask′, -mäsk′), *v.t.* **1.** to take off a mask or disguise from. **2.** to expose the true character of; lay bare the actual nature or being of: *to unmask a hypocrite.* **3.** to remove something that hides (a gun or guns) and begin firing: *to unmask a battery of howitzers.* —*v.i.* to be or become unmasked: *The guests unmasked at midnight.*

un·mas·tered (un mas′tərd, -mäs′-), *adj.* **1.** not subdued; not conquered. **2.** not conquerable: *He cannot his unmaster'd grief sustain* (John Dryden).

un·match·a·ble (un mach′ə bəl), *adj.* that cannot be matched or equaled: *an unmatchable color, an unmatchable voice.* —**Syn.** incomparable, peerless.

un·match·a·bly (un mach′ə blē), *adv.* in an unmatchable manner: *His poems are like pebbles—slight and worn, but also unmatchably freaked, hard, compact, accurate* (Manchester Guardian Weekly).

un·matched (un macht′), *adj.* not matched; matchless; unequaled.

un·mat·ed (un mā′tid), *adj.* not mated; not paired.

un·mean·ing (un mē′ning), *adj.* **1.** without meaning; devoid of significance; meaningless: *unmeaning words.* **2.** empty of feeling or thought; without expression or sense; vacant: *an unmeaning stare.* —**un·mean′ing·ly,** *adv.* —**un·mean′ing·ness,** *n.*

un·meant (un ment′), *adj.* not intended; accidental.

un·meas·ur·a·ble (un mezh′ər ə bəl, -mā′-zhər-), *adj.* immeasurable: *Their unmeasurable vanity* (Ben Jonson).

un·meas·ured (un mezh′ərd, -mā′zhərd), *adj.* **1.** not measured; unlimited; measureless. **2.** unrestrained; intemperate: *Lord Melbourne and the Court were attacked by the Tory press in unmeasured language* (Lytton Strachey).

un·med·i·tat·ed (un med′ə tā′tid), *adj.* not meditated; not prepared by previous thought; unpremeditated.

un·meet (un mēt′), *adj.* not fit; not proper; unsuitable. [Old English *unmǣte* < *un-* un-[1] + *gemǣte* suitable, meet] —**un·meet′ly,** *adv.* —**un·meet′ness,** *n.* —**Syn.** unbecoming, unseemly.

un·me·lo·di·ous (un′mə lō′dē əs), *adj.* not melodious; wanting melody; harsh.

un·men·tion·a·ble (un men′shə nə bəl, -mensh′nə-), *adj.* that cannot be mentioned; not fit to be spoken about. —*n.* something unmentionable: *Venereal disease is one of the last unmentionables in conversation today* (Canada Month).

unmentionables, a. underwear (often humorous in use): *a manufacturer of unmentionables.* **b.** (in the 1800's) trousers: *The knees of the unmentionables . . . began to get alarmingly white* (Dickens).
—**un·men′tion·a·ble·ness,** *n.*

un·men·tioned (un men′shənd), *adj.* not mentioned.

un·mer·ce·nar·y (un mėr′sə ner′ē), *adj.* not mercenary; not working or acting for money only.

un·mer·chant·a·ble (un mėr′chən tə bəl), *adj.* not merchantable; unfit for sale.

un·mer·ci·ful (un mėr′si fəl), *adj.* having no mercy; showing no mercy; cruel. —**un·mer′ci·ful·ly,** *adv.* —**un·mer′ci·ful·ness,** *n.* —**Syn.** pitiless, inhuman, merciless.

un·merge (un mėrj′), *v.t.,* **-merged, -merging.** to separate; dissolve: *Under the proposed law, the agency could unmerge corporations that had already consolidated* (New York Times).

un·mer·it·ed (un mer′ə tid), *adj.* not merited; undeserved.

un·mer·it·ing (un mer′ə ting), *adj.* not meriting; undeserving.

un·mer·i·to·ri·ous (un′mer ə tôr′ē əs, -tōr′-), *adj.* undeserving of reward or praise; unworthy: *There are a variety of unmeritorious occupations* (Frederick W. Faber).

un·met (un met′), *adj.* **1.** not met; not encountered: *his yet unmet friend.* **2.** not satisfied; unfulfilled: *unmet needs.*

un·met·alled (un met′əld), *adj. Especially British.* not covered with a surface of crushed stone, cinders, asphalt, etc.: *an unmetalled road.*

un·me·thod·i·cal (un′mə thod′ə kəl), *adj.* not methodical.

un·mew (un myü′), *v.t. Poetic.* to set free; release. [< *un-*[2] + *mew*[3]]

un·mil·i·tar·y (un mil′ə ter′ē), *adj.* not according to military rules or customs; not of a military character.

un·mind·ful (un mīnd′fəl), *adj.* heedless; careless: *to be unmindful of danger.* —**un·mind′ful·ly,** *adv.* —**un·mind′ful·ness,** *n.*

un·min·gled (un ming′gəld), *adj.* not mingled; unmixed; pure.

un·mis·tak·a·ble (un′mis tā′kə bəl), *adj.* that cannot be mistaken or misunderstood; clear; plain; evident: *unmistakable signs of illness.* —**un′mis·tak′a·ble·ness,** *n.* —**Syn.** manifest.

un·mis·tak·a·bly (un′mis tā′kə blē), *adv.* in an unmistakable manner.

un·mi·ter (un mī′tər), *v.t.* to deprive of a miter; depose from the rank of bishop.

un·mit·i·ga·ble (un mit′ə gə bəl), *adj.* not mitigable; not to be softened, lessened, or moderated: *unmitigable rage.*

un·mit·i·ga·bly (un mit′ə gə blē), *adv.* in an unmitigable manner.

un·mit·i·gat·ed (un mit′ə gā′tid), *adj.* **1.** not softened or lessened in severity or intensity: *unmitigated harshness, the unmitigated glare of sun on snow.* **2.** unqualified; absolute: *an unmitigated fraud.* —**un·mit′i·gat′ed·ly,** *adv.* —**Syn. 1.** unallayed. **2.** sheer, utter.

un·mi·tre (un mī′tər), *v.t.,* **-tred, -tring.** *Especially British.* unmiter.

un·mixed or **un·mixt** (un mikst′), *adj.* not mixed; pure: *Marriage is not an unmixed blessing. Good never comes unmixed* (James Russell Lowell).

un·mod·er·at·ed (un mod′ə rā′tid), *adj.* **1.** not having a moderator: *unmoderated debate.* **2.** not moderated, slowed, or reduced: *unmoderated neutrons.*

un·mod·ern (un mod′ərn), *adj.* not modern; old-fashioned: *He makes such surprisingly unmodern things as hourglasses* (Punch).

un·mod·i·fi·a·ble (un mod′ə fī′ə bəl), *adj.* not modifiable; that cannot be modified.

un·mod·i·fied (un mod′ə fīd), *adj.* not modified; not altered in form; not qualified in meaning; not limited or circumscribed.

un·mod·ish (un mō′dish), *adj.* not modish; not according to custom or fashion; not stylish; unfashionable. —**un·mod′ish·ly,** *adv.*

un·moist·ened (un moi′sənd), *adj.* not made moist or humid; not wetted; dry.

un·mold (un mōld′), *v.t.* to remove from a mold: *Unmold the gelatin and place it face down on a plate.*

un·mo·lest·ed (un′mə les′tid), *adj.* not molested; free from molestation. —**un′mo·lest′ed·ly,** *adv.*

un·mon·eyed (un mun′ēd), *adj.* not having money; moneyless: *I wish that unmoneyed fans . . . didn't have to climb to the top ten rows of the upper level to find an unreserved seat* (New Yorker).

un·moor (un mu̇r′), *v.t.* **1.** to release (a ship) from moorings or anchorage. **2.** to raise one anchor of (a ship) when moored by two. —*v.i.* (of a ship) to become free of moorings.

un·mor·al (un môr′əl, -mor′-), *adj.* neither moral nor immoral; not perceiving or involving right and wrong. —**un·mor′al·ly,** *adv.*

un·mo·ral·i·ty (un′mə ral′ə tē), *n.* the absence of morality; unmoral character.

un·mor·tise (un môr′tis), *v.t.,* **-tised, -tising.** to disconnect, remove, or separate (a mortised part, joint, etc.).

un·moth·er·ly (un muᴛʜ′ər lē), *adj.* not resembling or not befitting a mother.

un·mount·ed (un moun′tid), *adj.* **1.** not mounted; not on horseback: *unmounted troops.* **2.** not fixed on or in a support, backing, setting, or the like: *an unmounted photograph.*

un·mourned (un môrnd′, -mōrnd′), *adj.* not mourned or lamented.

un·mov·a·ble (un mü′və bəl), *adj.* immovable. —**Syn.** stationary.

un·moved (un müvd′), *adj.* not moved; unshaken; firm; calm; indifferent.

un·mov·ed·ly (un mü′vid lē), *adv. Obsolete.* in an unmoved manner; without being moved.

un·mov·ing (un mü′ving), *adj.* not moving; motionless. —**un·mov′ing·ly,** *adv.*

un·mown (un mōn′), *adj.* not mowed or cut down.

un·muf·fle (un muf′əl), *v.,* **-fled, -fling.** —*v.t.* to strip of or free from something that muffles: *to unmuffle the face.* —*v.i.* to throw off something that muffles.

un·mur·mur·ing (un mėr′mər ing), *adj.* not murmuring; uncomplaining. —**un·mur′mur·ing·ly,** *adv.*

un·mu·si·cal (un myü′zə kəl), *adj.* **1.** not musical; not melodious or harmonious; harsh or discordant in sound. **2.** not fond of or skilled in music. —**un·mu′si·cal·ly,** *adv.* —**un·mu′si·cal·ness,** *n.*

un·mu·si·cal·i·ty (un′myü zə kal′ə tē), *n.* the quality of being unmusical; lack of musicality: *Dances of poverty-stricken invention and striking unmusicality were performed by dancers obviously more willing than able* (Clive Barnes).

un·muz·zle (un muz′əl), *v.t.,* **-zled, -zling. 1.** to take off a muzzle from (a dog, etc.). **2.** to free from restraint; allow to speak or write freely: *to unmuzzle the press.*

un·muz·zled (un muz′əld), *adj.* not muzzled; without a muzzle.

un·nam·a·ble or **un·name·a·ble** (un-nā′mə bəl), *adj.* that cannot be named; indescribable: *a cloud of unnameable feeling* (Edgar Allan Poe).

un·named (un nāmd′), *adj.* **1.** having no name; not called or known by any name; nameless. **2.** not specified or mentioned by name: *throwing the burden on some unnamed third person* (George Meredith).

un·nat·u·ral (un nach′ər əl, -nach′rəl), *adj.* **1.** not natural, especially: **a.** not in accordance with the usual course of nature; that is an abnormality in nature. **b.** not deriving from nature; synthetic; artificial. **2.** not in accordance with the usual physical nature of a person or animal; that is an abnormality in the individual. **3.** at variance with what is usual or to be expected; not normal; abnormal; unusual: *The cold war . . . is not unnatural* (Manchester Guardian). **4.** at variance with natural feeling or normal decency, morality, etc.; very cruel, wicked, depraved, etc.: *Murder most foul, But this most foul, strange and unnatural* (Shakespeare). —**un·nat′u·ral·ly,** *adv.* —**un·nat′u·ral·ness,** *n.* —**Syn. 3.** irregular, strange.

un·nat·u·ral·ized (un nach′ər ə līzd, -nach′rə-), *adj.* not naturalized.

un·nav·i·ga·bil·i·ty (un nav′ə gə bil′ə tē), *n.* the quality or state of being unnavigable.

un·nav·i·ga·ble (un nav′ə gə bəl), *adj.* not navigable; not admitting of navigation: *an unnavigable river.*

un·nav·i·gat·ed (un nav′ə gā′tid), *adj.* not navigated; not passed over in ships or other vessels; not sailed on or over.

un·nec·es·sar·i·ly (un nes′ə ser′ə lē, un′-nes ə sâr′-), *adv.* in an unnecessary manner; without necessity; needlessly; superfluously: *to be unnecessarily suspicious, to spend money unnecessarily.*

un·nec·es·sar·i·ness (un nes′ə ser′ē nis), *n.* the state of being unnecessary; needlessness.

un·nec·es·sar·y (un nes′ə ser′ē), *adj.* not necessary; needless: *unnecessary haste.*

un·need·ful (un nēd′fəl), *adj.* not needful; not wanted; needless; unnecessary.

un·ne·go·tia·ble (un′nē gō′shə bəl), *adj.* not negotiable.

un·neigh·bor·li·ness (un nā′bər lē nis), *n.* the quality or state of being unneighborly.

un·neigh·bor·ly (un nā′bər lē), *adj.* not neighborly; not kindly, friendly, or sociable.

un·neigh·bour·ly (un nā′bər lē), *adj. Especially British.* unneighborly.

un·nerve (un nėrv′), *v.t.,* **-nerved, -nerving.** to deprive of nerve, firmness, or self-control: *The sight of so much blood unnerved her.*

un·nerv·ing·ly (un nėr′ving lē), *adv.* in a manner or to a degree that is unnerving: *He had unnervingly piercing eyes* (Scientific American).

un·nest (un nest′), *v.t.* to turn out of or as if out of a nest; dislodge: *The earth on its softly-spinning axle never jars enough to unnest a bird or wake a child* (Henry W. Warren).

un·neu·tral (un nü′trəl, -nyü′-), *adj.* not neutral; partial; one-sided: *It is in vain to remind her how very unneutral her armed neutrality is* (Earl Malmesbury).

un·not·ed (un nō′tid), *adj.* **1.** not noted; not observed; not heeded; not regarded; unmarked. **2.** not marked or shown outwardly.

un·no·tice·a·ble (un nō′tə sə bəl), *adj.* not noticeable; not such as to attract notice. —**un·no′tice·a·ble·ness,** *n.*

un·no·tice·a·bly (un nō′tə sə blē), *adv.* in an unnoticeable manner; so as not to be noticed.

un·no·ticed (un nō′tist), *adj.* not noticed; not observed or heeded; unperceived; not receiving any notice or attention: *No more fiendish punishment could be devised . . . than that one should . . . remain absolutely unnoticed* (William James).

un·num·bered (un num′bərd), *adj.* **1.** not numbered; not counted. **2.** too many to count; innumerable. —**Syn. 2.** myriad.

un·nur·tured (un nėr′chərd), *adj.* not nurtured; not educated; untrained; rough.

UNO (no periods) or **U.N.O.,** United Nations Organization.

un·ob·jec·tion·a·ble (un′əb jek′shə nə-bəl), *adj.* not objectionable; not liable to objection. —**un′ob·jec′tion·a·ble·ness,** *n.*

un·ob·jec·tion·a·bly (un′əb jek′shə nə-blē), *adv.* in an unobjectionable manner.

un·ob·li·gat·ed (un ob′lə gā′tid), *adj.* **1.** not set aside or used for a certain purpose: *Congress had directed that no more than $200,000,000 should be carried over unobligated into the new fiscal year* (New York Times). **2.** having no obligations: *The listener, the grown-up, free-riding, unobligated listener, is thrilled, I think, to have it thrown at him* (New Yorker).

un·ob·nox·ious (un′əb nok′shəs), *adj.* **1.** not obnoxious; not offensive or hateful. **2.** not liable; not subject; not exposed to something: *Some apart, In quarters unobnoxious to such chance* (Wordsworth).

un·ob·serv·a·bil·i·ty (un′əb zėr′və bil′-ə tē), *n.* the quality or condition of being unobservable: *The unobservability of abso-*

lute motion was rather a postulate of physics than the result of any particular structure of matter (Norbert Wiener).

un·ob·serv·a·ble (un′əb zėr′və bəl), *adj.* that cannot be observed; imperceptible; unnoticeable: *Two of them sat together on the steel plates of the deck . . . facing forward, and the third faced them from a low seat . . . unobservable from the bridge* (New Yorker). —*n.* something that cannot be observed or perceived by the senses.

un·ob·serv·ant (un′əb zėr′vənt), *adj.* **1.** not observant; not taking notice; not quick to notice or perceive. **2.** disregardful, as of rules or customs.

un·ob·served (un′əb zėrvd′), *adj.* not observed; not noticed; disregarded: *Am I alone, And unobserved? I am* (William S. Gilbert). —**Syn.** unheeded, unnoticed.

un·ob·serv·ing (un′əb zėr′ving), *adj.* not observing; unobservant.

un·ob·struct·ed (un′əb struk′tid), *adj.* not obstructed; not blocked, impeded, or hindered; open or clear: *a wide, unobstructed view of the hills.* —**un′ob·struct′ed·ly,** *adv.*

un·ob·tain·a·ble (un′əb tā′nə bəl), *adj.* not obtainable.

un·ob·tru·sive (un′əb trü′siv), *adj.* not obtrusive; modest; inconspicuous: *Poetry should be . . . unobtrusive, a thing which enters into one's soul and does not startle it* (Keats). —**un′ob·tru′sive·ly,** *adv.* —**un′ob·tru′sive·ness,** *n.*

un·oc·cu·pied (un ok′yə pīd), *adj.* **1.** not occupied; vacant: *an unoccupied house.* **2.** not in action or use; idle: *an unoccupied mind.*

un·of·fend·ing (un′ə fen′ding), *adj.* not offending; inoffensive: *Who . . . could have thought of harming a creature so simple and so unoffending?* (Scott).

un·of·fen·sive (un′ə fen′siv), *adj.* not offensive; harmless; inoffensive.

un·of·fi·cial (un′ə fish′əl), *adj.* not official; without official character or authority. —**un′of·fi′cial·ly,** *adv.*

un·of·fi·cious (un′ə fish′əs), *adj.* not officious; not forward or intermeddling.

un·oiled (un oild′), *adj.* not oiled; free from oil.

un·o·pened (un ō′pənd), *adj.* not opened; closed.

un·op·er·at·ed (un op′ə rā′tid), *adj.* **1.** not operated on: *On the third day the bandage was removed from my unoperated eye* (Harper's). **2.** that is not being operated: *Because of the strike, our elevator is unoperated.*

un·op·posed (un′ə pōzd′), *adj.* not opposed; meeting no opposition.

un·or·dained (un′ôr dānd′), *adj.* **1.** not ordained. **2.** *Obsolete.* inordinate.

un·or·dered (un ôr′dərd), *adj.* **1.** not put in order; disordered; unarranged: *Side by side with the official defined science there appeared a popular science, vague, undisciplined, unordered, and yet extremely influential* (Oscar Handlin). **2.** not ordered or commanded: *He volunteered his services, unordered.*

un·or·di·nar·y (un ôr′də ner′ē), *adj.* not common; rare; unusual: *Here are three excellent and unordinary travel books* (Eliot Fremont-Smith).

un·or·gan·ized (un ôr′gə nīzd), *adj.* **1.** not formed into an organized or systematized whole. **2.** not organized into a labor union or unions: *unorganized workers.* **3.** lacking the characteristics of a living body; not being a living organism; unformed.

unorganized ferment, any of certain compounds of organic origin, as diastase or pepsin, which cause a substance to ferment.

un·o·rig·i·nal (un′ə rij′ə nəl), *adj.* **1.** not original. **2.** having no origin.

un·or·na·men·tal (un′ôr nə men′təl), *adj.* not ornamental.

un·or·na·ment·ed (un ôr′nə men′tid), *adj.* not ornamented; unadorned; not decorated; plain: *[He] was wearing an unornamented uniform and amber sunglasses* (New Yorker).

un·or·tho·dox (un ôr′thə doks), *adj.* not orthodox; heterodox; heretical.

un·or·tho·dox·y (un ôr′thə dok′sē), *n., pl.* **-dox·ies.** the quality or state of being unorthodox; heresy.

un·os·ten·ta·tious (un′os ten tā′shəs), *adj.* not ostentatious; not showy or pretentious; inconspicuous; modest. —**un′os·ten·ta′tious·ly,** *adv.* —**un′os·ten·ta′tious·ness,** *n.*

un·owned (un ōnd′), *adj.* **1.** not owned; having no known owner; not claimed. **2.** not avowed; not acknowledged as one's own; not admitted as done by oneself; unconfessed: *unowned faults.* [< *un-*[1] + *own* + *-ed*[2]]

un·pa·cif·ic (un′pə sif′ik), *adj.* unpeaceful; quarrelsome; belligerent: *East and West ought to be persuaded . . . that it is in their mutual interest to sign a kind of test ban agreement not to use space for unpacific purposes* (New Scientist).

un·pack (un pak′), *v.t.* **1.** to take out (things packed in a box, trunk, etc.): *to unpack a suit.* **2.** to take things out of: *to unpack a trunk.* —*v.i.* to take out things packed.

un·paid (un pād′), *adj.* not paid: *His unpaid bills amounted to $200.*

un·paid-for (un pād′fôr′), *adj.* not paid for: *rustling in unpaid-for silk* (Shakespeare).

un·pain·ful (un pān′fəl), *adj.* not painful; giving no pain: *An easy and unpainful touch* (John Locke).

un·paired (un pārd′), *adj.* not paired.

un·pal·at·a·bil·i·ty (un′pal ə tə bil′ə tē), *n.* the quality or condition of being unpalatable: *Experimental birds had learned to associate color pattern with unpalatability* (Science News Letter).

un·pal·at·a·ble (un pal′ə tə bəl), *adj.* not agreeable to the taste; distasteful; unpleasant: *unpalatable advice* (Washington Irving). —**un·pal′at·a·ble·ness,** *n.* —**Syn.** unappetizing, unsavory.

un·pal·at·a·bly (un pal′ə tə blē), *adv.* in an unpalatable manner; disagreeably; unpleasantly.

un·par·al·leled (un par′ə leld), *adj.* having no parallel; unequaled; matchless: *an unparalleled achievement, an event unparalleled in modern history.* —**Syn.** unmatched, unrivaled.

un·par·don·a·ble (un pär′də nə bəl), *adj.* not pardonable; that cannot be pardoned: *an unpardonable offense or mistake, an unpardonable offender. According to the Bible, the sin of blasphemy against the Holy Ghost is the unpardonable sin.* —**un·par′don·a·ble·ness,** *n.*

un·par·don·a·bly (un pär′də nə blē), *adv.* beyond pardon or forgiveness: *to be unpardonably rude.*

un·par·doned (un pär′dənd), *adj.* not pardoned.

un·par·don·ing (un pär′də ning), *adj.* not pardoning.

un·park (un pärk′), *v.t.* to remove (an automobile, etc.) from a parking place: *The entire operation would be controlled by one customer's man and a push-button operator who'd park and unpark cars throughout the garage without ever leaving his post* (Wall Street Journal). —*v.i.* to move an automobile, etc., from a parking place: *Like the young housewife in Vancouver who found a parking spot all right, but couldn't unpark because other cars fore and aft were snubbed up so tight against hers* (Maclean's).

un·par·lia·men·ta·ri·ly (un′pär lə men′tər ə lē, -men′trə-), *adv.* in an unparliamentary manner.

un·par·lia·men·ta·ri·ness (un′pär lə men′tər ē nis, -men′trē-), *n.* the quality or state of being unparliamentary.

un·par·lia·men·ta·ry (un′pär lə men′tər ē, -men′trē), *adj.* not in accordance with, permitted by, or proper in parliamentary practice, procedure, or usage.

un·passed (un past′, -päst′), *adj.* **1.** not passed or ratified: *The unfinished business included unpassed appropriations for mutual security and public works* (Time). **2.** not crossed: *unpassed barriers.*

un·pas·sioned (un pash′ənd), *adj.* free from passion; dispassionate: *Rupert Brooke wrote of the unpassioned beauty of a great machine* (London Times).

un·pat·ent·a·ble (un pat′ən tə bəl), *adj.* not patentable: *The better mousetraps of today . . . are often unpatentable* (New Yorker).

un·pat·ent·ed (un pat′ən tid), *adj.* not patented; not protected by patent.

un·pathed (un patht′, -pätht′), *adj.* pathless; trackless: *unpathed waters* (Shakespeare).

un·pa·tri·ot·ic (un′pā trē ot′ik), *adj.* not patriotic.

un·pa·tri·ot·i·cal·ly (un′pā trē ot′ə klē), *adv.* in a manner that is unpatriotic: *accused of unpatriotically stabbing the Foreign Secretary in the back in the course of international negotiations* (Time).

un·pa·tri·ot·ism (un pā′trē ə tiz′əm), *n.* the quality or state of being unpatriotic.

un·paved (un pāvd′), *adj.* not paved.

un·pay·a·ble (un pā′ə bəl), *adj.* **1.** that cannot be paid: *The picture often turns out to be a flop, leaving a wake of unpaid and unpayable debts* (Atlantic). **2.** yielding no return; unprofitable; unremunerative: *The wildcat oil well was abandoned as unpayable.*

un·peace (un pēs′), *n.* lack of peace or quiet; constant movement: *The unpopular thesis that the secret of happiness lies in unpeace of mind, that is, fairly continuous, useful mental activity* (Atlantic).

un·peace·a·ble (un pē′sə bəl), *adj.* not peaceable; quarrelsome: *Away, unpeaceable dog, or I'll spurn thee hence!* (Shakespeare).

un·peace·ful (un pēs′fəl), *adj.* not pacific or peaceful; unquiet; disturbed.

un·ped·i·greed (un ped′ə grēd), *adj.* not distinguished by a pedigree.

un·peg (un peg′), *v.t.,* **-pegged, -peg·ging. 1.** to disengage (a rope, line, etc.) from a peg. **2.** to loosen, detach, or dismember (anything) by withdrawal of a peg or pegs. **3.** to discontinue control of the rise or fall of the price of (something): *Government bonds were unpegged a year ago, and interest rates started rising* (Time).

un·pen (un pen′), *v.t.,* **-penned, -pen·ning.** to release from or as from a pen.

un·pen·nied (un pen′ēd), *adj.* not pennied; penniless.

un·pen·sioned (un pen′shənd), *adj.* **1.** not pensioned; not rewarded by a pension: *an unpensioned soldier.* **2.** not kept in pay; not held in dependence by a pension.

un·peo·ple (un pē′pəl), *v.t.,* **-pled, -pling.** to deprive of people; depopulate.

un·peo·pled (un pē′pəld), *adj.* **1.** without inhabitants; not inhabited. **2.** deprived of people; depopulated.

un·per·ceiv·a·ble (un′pər sē′və bəl), *adj.* not perceivable; imperceptible.

un·per·ceived (un′pər sēvd′), *adj.* not perceived; unnoticed.

un·per·ceiv·ing (un′pər sē′ving), *adj.* not perceiving.

un·per·cep·tive (un′pər sep′tiv), *adj.* lacking or incapable of perception or discrimination: *an unperceptive mind, an unperceptive reader.* —**un′per·cep′tive·ness,** *n.*

un·per·fo·rat·ed (un pėr′fə rā′tid), *adj.* **1.** not perforated. **2.** (of a postage stamp) not perforated at the edges; imperforate.

un·per·form·a·ble (un′pər fôr′mə bəl), *adj.* not performable; undoable: *Though the composer grandly pronounced Tristan "the greatest musical drama of all time," opera houses in Dresden, Berlin, Vienna, and Munich rejected it as unperformable* (Time).

un·per·formed (un′pər fôrmd′), *adj.* **1.** not performed; not done; not executed; not fulfilled: *an unperformed promise.* **2.** not represented on the stage; unacted: *The play remained unperformed.*

un·per·ish·a·ble (un per′i shə bəl), *adj.* *Obsolete.* not perishable; imperishable.

un·per·ish·ing (un per′i shing), *adj.* not perishing; lasting; durable.

un·per·plexed (un′pər plekst′), *adj.* **1.** free from perplexity or complication; simple: *simple, unperplexed proposition* (John Locke). **2.** not perplexed; not harassed; not embarrassed: *This [man] throws himself on God, and unperplexed Seeking shall find him* (Robert Browning).

un·per·son (un pėr′sən), *n.* a person who has been removed from public life and set apart in obscurity, as by official decree in a totalitarian state: *Famous men and women in all walks of life have been ruthlessly turned, as in George Orwell's chilling novel "1984," from persons into unpersons* (New York Times).

un·per·suad·a·ble (un′pər swā′də bəl), *adj.* that cannot be persuaded or influenced by motives urged.

un·per·sua·sive (un′pər swā′siv), *adj.* not persuasive; unable to persuade. —**un′per·sua′sive·ly,** *adv.* —**un′per·sua′sive·ness,** *n.*

un·per·turbed (un′pər tėrbd′), *adj.* not perturbed; free from perturbation; undisturbed; calm; composed: *Still with unhurrying chase And unperturbed pace* (Francis Thompson).

un·per·turb·ed·ly (un′pər tėr′bid lē), *adv.* in an unperturbed manner; calmly.

un·per·turb·ed·ness (un′pər tėr′bid nis), *n.* the quality or state of being unperturbed.
un·per·vert·ed (un′pər vėr′tid), *adj.* not perverted; not wrested or turned to a wrong sense or use.
un·phil·o·soph·ic (un′fil ə sof′ik), *adj.* unphilosophical.
un·phil·o·soph·i·cal (un′fil ə sof′ə kəl), *adj.* not philosophical. —**un′phil·o·soph′i·cal·ly,** *adv.*
un·phys·i·cal (un fiz′ə kəl), *adj.* **1.** not physical; immaterial; incorporeal. **2.** not in accordance with the laws of physics: *an unphysical theory of motion.* —**un·phys′i·cal·ly,** *adv.*
un·phys·i·o·log·i·cal (un′fiz ē ə loj′ə kəl), *adj.* not sound or proper physiologically; not in accordance with the laws of physiology: *Fasting is an unphysiological and potentially dangerous practice if continued for more than a few days* (Harper's). —**un′phys·i·o·log′i·cal·ly,** *adv.*
un·pick (un pik′), *v.t.* to pick or take out (stitches, sewing, etc.); pick out the stitches in (a garment, etc.).
un·picked (un pikt′), *adj.* **1.** not picked; not chosen or selected. **2.** unplucked; ungathered, as fruit. **3.** not picked or opened with an instrument, as a lock.
un·pierced (un pirst′), *adj.* not pierced; not penetrated.
un·pile (un pīl′), *v.,* **-piled, -pil·ing.** —*v.t.* **1.** to remove from a pile or heap: *to unpile wood and stack it.* **2.** to cause to be no longer in a pile: *to unpile canned goods.* **3.** to take (a pile, heap, etc.) apart. —*v.i.* to be disengaged from a pile.
un·pi·lot·ed (un pī′lə tid), *adj.* unguided through dangers or difficulties.
un·pin (un pin′), *v.t.,* **-pinned, -pin·ning. 1.** to take out a pin or pins from **2.** to loosen, detach, or dismember (anything) by withdrawal of a pin or pins; unfasten. **3.** to undo the dress by unpinning; undress: *who had the honor to pin and unpin Lady Bellaston* (Henry Fielding).
un·pit·ied (un pit′ēd), *adj.* not pitied.
un·pit·y·ing (un pit′ē ing), *adj.* not pitying; without pity: *The unpitying waters flowed over our prostrate bodies* (Herman Melville). —**un·pit′y·ing·ly,** *adv.*
un·placed (un plāst′), *adj.* **1.** not assigned to, or set in, a definite place: *She is now an unsheltered and unplaced person* (Manchester Guardian). **2.** not appointed to a place or office: *The other fifteen were to be unplaced noblemen and gentlemen of ample fortune* (Macaulay). **3.** not among the first three finishers in a horse race: *After being unplaced in his first start, he won his next ten races* (New Yorker).
un·plagued (un plāgd′), *adj.* not plagued; not harassed; not tormented; not afflicted.
un·plait (un plāt′), *v.t.* to bring out of a plaited state; unbraid, as hair.
un·plant·a·ble (un plan′tə bəl, -plän′-), *adj.* that cannot be planted: *The company also owns in Florida another 10,509 acres of unplanted and in most cases unplantable land* (Wall Street Journal).
un·plant·ed (un plan′tid, -plän′-), *adj.* **1.** not planted; of spontaneous growth. **2.** not cultivated; unimproved.
un·play·a·ble (un plā′ə bəl), *adj.* that cannot be played or played on: *In its 24 years the concerto has gained something of a reputation for being unplayable* (Time). *Hours of heavy rain had rendered the Lawns ground unplayable* (London Times).
un·pleas·ant (un plez′ənt), *adj.* not pleasant; displeasing; disagreeable: *A . . . damp, moist, unpleasant body* (Dickens). —**un·pleas′ant·ly,** *adv.* —**Syn.** objectionable, obnoxious.
un·pleas·ant·ness (un plez′ənt nis), *n.* **1.** unpleasant quality. **2.** something unpleasant. **3.** a fight; quarrel.
un·pleas·ant·ry (un plez′ən trē), *n., pl.* **-ries. 1.** unpleasantness. **2.** an unpleasant circumstance or occurrence.
un·pleased (un plēzd′), *adj.* not pleased; displeased.
un·pleas·ing (un plē′zing), *adj.* not pleasing; not such as to please. —**un·pleas′ing·ly,** *adv.* —**un·pleas′ing·ness,** *n.*
un·pleas·ur·a·ble (un plezh′ər ə bəl), *adj.* not giving pleasure; disagreeable: *Many of our waking hours pass irksome and insipid, unprofitable to others, and unpleasurable to ourselves* (Abraham Tucker)
un·pleas·ure (un plezh′ər), *n.* lack of pleasure; displeasure: *I don't like to use any words that might give you unpleasure* (Samuel Taylor Coleridge).
un·pli·a·ble (un plī′ə bəl), *adj.* not pliable.
un·pli·ant (un plī′ənt), *adj.* **1.** not pliant; not easily bent; stiff. **2.** not readily yielding the will; not compliant.
un·plucked (un plukt′), *adj.* not plucked; not pulled or torn away: *an unplucked chicken.*
un·plug (un plug′), *v.t.,* **-plugged, -plug·ging. 1.** to remove the plug or stopper from: *Unplug your ears and listen to me. Apparently satisfied now that rock-bottom prices have been reached many cautious investors have unplugged their money to buy municipals* (Wall Street Journal). **2.** to disconnect by removing the plug from an electric outlet.
un·plumbed (un plumd′), *adj.* **1.** not fathomed; not measured; of unknown depth: *unplumbed seas. For the readers who seek unplumbed depths of human character the opening scene is discouraging* (Virgilia Peterson). **2.** having no plumbing. **3.** not encased or sealed in lead.
un·po·et·ic (un′pō et′ik), *adj.* not poetic; prosaic; matter-of-fact. —**un′po·et′i·cal·ly,** *adv.*
un·po·et·i·cal (un′pō et′ə kəl), *adj.* unpoetic.
un·point·ed (un poin′tid), *adj.* **1.** not having a point; not sharp. **2.** having no point or sting; wanting point or definite aim or purpose. **3.** unpunctuated. **4.** not having the vowel points or marks: *an unpointed manuscript in Hebrew or Arabic.* **5.** *Obsolete.* having the points unfastened, as a doublet.
un·poised (un poizd′), *adj.* not poised; not balanced.
un·po·liced (un′pə lēst′), *adj.* not supervised or regulated by an agency charged with maintaining the law or the terms of a treaty agreement: *There is no suggestion that the unpoliced test ban be indefinitely continued* (Bulletin of Atomic Scientists).
un·pol·ished (un pol′isht), *adj.* **1.** not polished: *unpolished stone.* **2.** without polish; rough; unrefined; rude: *unpolished manners.*
un·pol·i·tic (un pol′ə tik), *adj.* not politic; impolitic.
un·polled (un pōld′), *adj.* not polled, especially, not voting or not cast at the polls: *an unpolled voter or vote.*
un·pol·lut·ed (un′pə lü′tid), *adj.* not polluted; undefiled; clean; pure.
un·pop·u·lar (un pop′yə lər), *adj.* not popular; not generally liked, accepted, used, etc.; disliked: *an unpopular candidate.* —**un·pop′u·lar·ly,** *adv.*
un·pop·u·lar·i·ty (un′pop yə lar′ə tē), *n.* the state of being unpopular. —**Syn.** disfavor.
un·pos·sess·a·ble (un′pə zes′ə bəl), *adj.* that cannot be possessed: *He did a paper on "The Unpossessable Loved One in Troubadour Poetry"* (New Yorker).
un·post·ed[1] (un pō′stid), *adj.* not bearing signs against trespassing: *He does not mind hunters on the unposted parts of his land.*
un·post·ed[2] (un pōs′tid), *adj.* not having a fixed station or appointment. [< *un-*[1] + *post*[2] + *-ed*[2]]
un·post·ed[3] (un pōs′tid), *adj.* **1.** not sent or delivered by mail: *I stand with an unposted letter before the box of the general post office* (Time). **2.** *Informal.* not informed.
un·prac·ti·cal (un prak′tə kəl), *adj.* not practical; impractical; lacking practical usefulness or wisdom; visionary. —**un·prac′ti·cal·ly,** *adv.* —**un·prac′ti·cal·ness,** *n.*
un·prac·ti·cal·i·ty (un′prak tə kal′ə tē), *n., pl.* **-ties. 1.** the character of being unpractical. **2.** something that is not practical.
un·prac·ticed (un prak′tist), *adj.* **1.** not familiarized or skilled by practice; not expert; inexperienced: *Unpractic'd he to fawn or seek for power By doctrines fashion'd to the varying hour* (Oliver Goldsmith). **2.** not practiced; not used, done, etc., especially: **a.** not put into practice; untried. **b.** no longer current in practice.
un·prec·e·dent·ed (un pres′ə den′tid), *adj.* having no precedent; never done before; never known before: *unprecedented devotion to duty.* —**un·prec′e·dent′ed·ly,** *adv.* —**Syn.** unexampled, new.
un·pre·cise (un′pri sīs′), *adj.* not precise; lacking precision or definiteness; inexact. —**un′pre·cise′ly,** *adv.* —**un′pre·cise′ness,** *n.*
un·pre·dict·a·bil·i·ty (un′pri dik′tə bil′ə tē), *n.* the quality or condition of being unpredictable: *He had an increasing unpredictability of temper and a reputation for violent outbursts that had cost him several good friends* (New Yorker). *The history of the steam engine has been marked by this machine's endearing unpredictability* (Manchester Guardian).
un·pre·dict·a·ble (un′pri dik′tə bəl), *adj.* that cannot be predicted; uncertain: *All the children were emotionally unstable, unpredictable, and unadaptable* (Science News Letter). —*n.* something unpredictable; an uncertainty: *Other unpredictables, such as a switch in Government regulations for the 1964 crop, also could change the outlook* (Wall Street Journal).
un·pre·dict·a·bly (un′pri dik′tə blē), *adv.* in an unpredictable manner: *Prices fluctuate unpredictably from sale to sale* (Punch).
un·prej·u·diced (un prej′ů dist), *adj.* **1.** without prejudice; not biased; impartial: *an unprejudiced observer.* **2.** not impaired: *an unprejudiced right of appeal.* —**Syn. 1.** fair, disinterested. **2.** unimpaired.
un·pre·med·i·tat·ed (un′prē med′ə tā′tid), *adj.* not premeditated; undesigned. —**un′pre·med′i·tat′ed·ly,** *adv.*
un·pre·med·i·ta·tion (un′prē med′ə tā′shən), *n.* absence of premeditation.
un·pre·pared (un′pri pãrd′), *adj.* **1.** not made ready; not worked out ahead: *an unprepared speech.* **2.** not ready: *a person unprepared to answer.* —**Syn. 1.** impromptu, improvised. **2.** unready.
un·pre·par·ed·ness (un′pri pãr′id nis, -pãrd′nis), *n.* a being unprepared.
un·pre·pos·sess·ing (un′prē pə zes′ing), *adj.* not prepossessing; unattractive: *Unprepossessing . . . in feature, gait and manners . . . these poor fellows formed a class apart* (Samuel Butler). —**un′pre·pos·sess′ing·ly,** *adv.* —**un′pre·pos·sess′ing·ness,** *n.*
un·pre·scribed (un′pri skrībd′), *adj.* not prescribed; not authoritatively laid down; not appointed.
un·pre·sent·a·ble (un′pri zen′tə bəl), *adj.* not presentable; not suitable for being introduced into company; not fit to be seen.
un·pressed (un prest′), *adj.* **1.** not pressed. **2.** not enforced.
un·pre·sum·ing (un′pri zü′ming), *adj.* not presuming; modest; humble; unpretentious.
un·pre·sump·tu·ous (un′pri zump′chů əs), *adj.* not presumptuous or arrogant; humble; submissive; modest.
un·pre·tend·ing (un′pri ten′ding), *adj.* unpretentious. —**un′pre·tend′ing·ly,** *adv.*
un·pre·ten·tious (un′pri ten′shəs), *adj.* not given to or characterized by pretention; unassuming; modest. —**un′pre·ten′tious′ly,** *adv.* —**un′pre·ten′tious·ness,** *n.*
un·pret·ty (un prit′ē), *adj.* **1.** without beauty or charm; plain; unattractive: *The only girl in the picture is obliged to look . . . clinical and unpretty* (Brendan Gill). **2.** disagreeable; ugly: *The tougher Novak has an unpretty side* (Time). *Things are coming to a most unpretty pass* (Punch).
un·pre·vail·ing (un′pri vā′ling), *adj.* of no force; unavailing; vain.
un·pre·vent·a·ble (un′pri ven′tə bəl), *adj.* that cannot be prevented.
un·pre·vent·ed (un′pri ven′tid), *adj.* **1.** not prevented; not hindered. **2.** *Obsolete.* not preceded by anything.
un·priced (un prīst′), *adj.* **1.** not having a price assigned: *merchandise still unpriced.* **2.** beyond price; priceless.
un·priest·ly (un prēst′lē), *adj.* not priestly; not befitting a priest.
un·prince·ly (un prins′lē), *adj.* not princely; not becoming a prince.
un·prin·ci·pled (un prin′sə pəld), *adj.* lacking good moral principles; bad. —**un·prin′ci·pled·ness,** *n.* —**Syn.** See **unscrupulous.**
un·print·a·ble (un prin′tə bəl), *adj.* not fit or proper to be printed. —*n.* a word, expression, etc., that is unprintable: *All Maine writers have lamented that so much of what is said up and down the coast runs to unprintables* (John Gould).
un·print·a·bly (un prin′tə blē), *adv.* in a word or words not fit to be printed.
un·print·ed (un prin′tid), *adj.* not, or not yet, printed.
un·priv·i·leged (un priv′ə lijd), *adj.* not privileged; not enjoying a particular privilege, liberty, or immunity.
un·priz·a·ble (un prī′zə bəl), *adj. Obsolete.* **1.** worth little or nothing. **2.** priceless.

un·prized (un prīzd′), *adj.* not prized or valued.

un·pro·duced (un′prə düst′, -dyüst′), *adj.* not yet produced, as a playwright or his work: *He had written several stage and television plays, all unproduced* (Saturday Review).

un·pro·duc·tive (un′prə duk′tiv), *adj.* not productive. **—un′pro·duc′tive·ly,** *adv.* **—un′pro·duc′tive·ness,** *n.*

un·pro·duc·tiv·i·ty (un′prō duk tiv′ə tē), *n.* the quality or state of being unproductive.

un·pro·faned (un′prə fānd′), *adj.* not profaned or desecrated; not polluted or violated.

un·pro·fes·sion·al (un′prə fesh′ə nəl, -fesh′nəl), *adj.* **1.** contrary to or forbidden by professional usage, etiquette, etc.; unbecoming in members of a profession. **2.** not having to do with or connected with a profession. **3.** not belonging to a profession. *—n.* a person who is not a professional: *The secret of his failure in politics . . . is that he was really an unprofessional* (New York Times Book Review). **—un′pro·fes′sion·al·ly,** *adv.*

un·prof·it·a·bil·i·ty (un′prof ə tə bil′ə tē), *n.* the quality or state of being unprofitable: *The milk and fishing industries were on the verge of unprofitability* (London Times).

un·prof·it·a·ble (un prof′ə tə bəl), *adj.* not profitable; producing no gain or advantage: *They proved the most idle and unprofitable [months] of my life* (Edward Gibbon). **—un·prof′it·a·ble·ness,** *n.* **—Syn.** fruitless.

un·prof·it·a·bly (un prof′ə tə blē), *adv.* in an unprofitable manner; without profit, gain, benefit, advantage, or use; to no good purpose or effect: *unprofitably travelling towards the grave* (Wordsworth).

un·prof·it·ed (un prof′ə tid), *adj.* not having profit or gain; profitless.

un·pro·gres·sive (un′prə gres′iv), *adj.* not progressive; conservative; backward. **—un′pro·gres′sive·ly,** *adv.* **—un′pro·gres′sive·ness,** *n.*

un·pro·hib·it·ed (un′prō hib′ə tid), *adj.* not prohibited; not forbidden; lawful.

un·pro·ject·ed (un′prə jek′tid), *adj.* not planned; not projected.

un·pro·lif·ic (un′prə lif′ik), *adj.* not fertile or productive; unfruitful.

un·prom·is·ing (un prom′ə sing), *adj.* not promising; not appearing likely to turn out well. **—un·prom′is·ing·ly,** *adv.*

un·prompt·ed (un promp′tid), *adj.* not prompted; not dictated; not urged or instigated.

un·pro·nounce·a·ble (un′prə noun′sə bəl), *adj.* not pronounceable; difficult to pronounce: *With unpronounceable awful names* (Bret Harte).

un·pro·nounced (un′prə nounst′), *adj.* not pronounced; not uttered.

un·prop·er (un prop′ər), *adj.* not proper; not correct, right, or respectable: *His equally unproper brother . . . shocked purists in the 1930's by building a flat-topped house in Ipswich* (Time).

un·prop·er·tied (un′prop′ər tēd), *adj.* not propertied; not owning property.

un·pro·pi·ti·a·ble (un′prə pish′ē ə bəl), *adj.* that cannot be propitiated.

un·pro·pi·tious (un′prə pish′əs), *adj.* not propitious; not favorable; inauspicious: *On the other hand, unpropitious as the times may be, it is safe to assume that there will be large numbers of serious and talented writers* (Saturday Review). **—un′pro·pi′tious·ly,** *adv.* **—un′pro·pi′tious·ness,** *n.*

un·pro·por·tion·ate (un′prə pôr′shə nit), *adj.* not proportionate; disproportionate.

un·pro·por·tioned (un′prə pôr′shənd), *adj.* not proportioned; not suitable.

un·pro·posed (un′prə pōzd′), *adj.* not proposed; not offered for acceptance, adoption, or the like.

un·pros·per·ous (un pros′pər əs), *adj.* not prosperous; unfortunate; unsuccessful. **—un·pros′per·ous·ly,** *adv.* **—un·pros′per·ous·ness,** *n.*

un·pro·tect·ed (un′prə tek′tid), *adj.* not protected. **—un′pro·tect′ed·ness,** *n.*

un·prov·a·ble (un prü′və bəl), *adj.* that cannot be proved; indemonstrable: *For many years I have been intrigued by a largely unprovable hypothesis about the coexistence of Homo sapiens and Neanderthal man* (Scientific American).

un·proved (un prüvd′), *adj.* not proved.

un·prov·en (un prü′vən), *adj.* unproved: *That politics has a bearing on business confidence is unproven* (Esquire).

un·pro·vid·ed (un′prə vī′did), *adj.* **1.** not provided; not furnished or supplied. **2.** not furnished or supplied with something: *assailants . . . unprovided with regular means of attack* (Alexander W. Kinglake).

un·pro·vid·ed-for (un′prə vī′did fôr′), *adj.* not provided for.

un·pro·voked (un′prə vōkt′), *adj.* not provoked; without provocation.

un·pro·vok·ed·ly (un′prə vō′kid lē), *adv.* in an unprovoked manner; without provocation.

un·pruned (un pründ′), *adj.* not pruned; not lopped or trimmed.

un·pub·li·cized (un pub′lə sīzd), *adj.* not made public; not given publicity: *But, almost unpublicized, another mass escape from behind the Iron Curtain has been going on* (Newsweek).

un·pub·lished (un pub′lisht), *adj.* **1.** not published, especially not issued in print: *an unpublished manuscript.* **2.** that has not yet had a work in print: *an unpublished poet.* **3.** not generally known: *a man of great but unpublished generosity.* **4.** *Law.* designating a literary work which, at the time of registration, has not been made available to the public by general distribution or reproduction in salable form.

un·puck·er (un puk′ər), *v.t.* to straighten out from a puckered condition.

un·punc·tu·al (un pungk′chü əl), *adj.* not punctual; tardy: *a vague, unpunctual star* (Rupert Brooke). **—un·punc′tu·al·ly,** *adv.*

un·punc·tu·al·i·ty (un′pungk chü al′ə tē), *n.* the quality or state of being unpunctual: *Her unpunctuality and light-heartedness drove her husband . . . to the limits of temper* (Manchester Guardian).

un·pun·ish·a·ble (un pun′i shə bəl), *adj.* not punishable; not capable or deserving of being punished.

un·pun·ished (un pun′isht), *adj.* not punished.

un·pure (un pyür′), *adj.*, **-pur·er, -pur·est.** not pure; impure.

un·purged (un pėrjd′), *adj.* **1.** not purified. **2.** not cleared from moral defilement or guilt.

un·pur·posed (un pėr′pəst), *adj.* not intended; not designed.

un·qual·i·fied (un kwol′ə fīd), *adj.* **1.** not qualified; not fitted. **2.** not modified, limited, or restricted in any way: *unqualified praise.* **3.** complete; absolute: *an unqualified failure.* **—un·qual′i·fied′ly,** *adv.* **—un·qual′i·fied′ness,** *n.* **—Syn. 1.** incompetent. **2.** unconditional. **3.** unmitigated.

un·quan·ti·fied (un kwon′tə fīd), *adj.* not quantified; not measured: *According to these criteria, unquantified observations and studies receive little respect* (Saturday Review).

un·quench·a·ble (un kwen′chə bəl), *adj.* not quenchable; inextinguishable: *an unquenchable thirst.*

un·quench·a·bly (un kwen′chə blē), *adv.* in an unquenchable manner; so as to be unquenchable.

un·ques·tion·a·ble (un kwes′chə nə bəl), *adj.* **1.** beyond dispute or doubt; certain: *Size is sometimes an unquestionable advantage.* **2.** impeccable in quality or nature; accepted without question; unexceptionable. **—un·ques′tion·a·ble·ness,** *n.*

un·ques·tion·a·bly (un kwes′chə nə blē), *adv.* beyond dispute or doubt; certainly.

un·ques·tioned (un kwes′chənd), *adj.* **1.** not subjected to interrogation; not questioned. **2.** not inquired into; not examined. **3.** not disputed; unquestionable.

un·ques·tion·ing (un kwes′chə ning), *adj.* not questioning, disputing, or objecting. **—un·ques′tion·ing·ly,** *adv.*

un·qui·et (un kwī′ət), *adj.* **1.** restless: *to pass an unquiet night.* **2.** disturbed; uneasy: *an unquiet mind.* **3.** causing or likely to cause trouble, disturbance, etc.: *an unquiet populace.* **—un·qui′et·ly,** *adv.* **—un·qui′et·ness,** *n.*

un·quot·a·ble (un kwō′tə bəl), *adj.* not quotable.

un·quote (un kwōt′), *v.i.*, **-quot·ed, -quot·ing.** to end a quotation.

U.N.R. or **UNR** (no periods), Union for the New Republic (French, *Union pour la Nouvelle République*); a French political organization favoring the policies of President de Gaulle.

un·raised (un rāzd′), *adj.* **1.** not elevated. **2.** not abandoned, as a siege.

un·raked (un rākt′), *adj.* **1.** not raked. **2.** not raked together; not raked up. **3.** *Obsolete.* not sought or acquired by effort, as by raking.

un·rat·i·fied (un rat′ə fīd), *adj.* not ratified; unsanctioned.

un·rav·el (un rav′əl), *v.*, **-eled, -el·ing** or (*especially British*) **-elled, -el·ling.** *—v.t.* **1.** to separate the threads or strands of; pull apart: *The kitten unraveled the knitting.* **2.** to bring out of a tangled state; work out the problems of; solve: *to unravel a mystery.* *—v.i.* **1.** to come apart: *This sweater is unraveling at the elbow.* **2.** to come out of a tangled state.

un·ra·zored (un rā′zərd), *adj.* unshaven.

un·reached (un rēcht′), *adj.* not reached; not attained to.

un·re·act·ed (un′rē ak′tid), *adj.* that has not taken part in a chemical reaction: *The liquid withdrawn from the reaction vessels contains a higher proportion of unreacted raw materials because some of the incoming liquid finds its way to the outlet before it has time to react* (New Scientist).

un·re·ac·tive (un′rē ak′tiv), *adj.* that cannot take part in a chemical reaction: *Work has been carried out to develop . . . crucibles coated on the inside with an unreactive ceramic* (New Scientist).

un·read (un red′), *adj.* **1.** not read: *an unread book.* **2.** not instructed by reading; not having read much: *an unread person.*

un·read·a·bil·i·ty (un′rē də bil′ə tē), *n.* the quality or state of being unreadable; lack of readability: *The essays themselves . . . are marred, some of them to the point of unreadability, by the dreadful jargon of the specialist* (New Scientist).

un·read·a·ble (un rē′də bəl), *adj.* **1.** that cannot be read or deciphered; illegible: *an unreadable manuscript.* **2.** not suitable or fit for reading; not worth reading: *a dull, unreadable book or poem.*

un·read·i·ly (un red′ə lē), *adv.* in an unready manner: **a.** unpreparedly. **b.** not promptly; not quickly. **c.** awkwardly.

un·read·i·ness (un red′ē nis), *n.* the character of being unready.

un·read·y (un red′ē), *adj.* **1.** not ready; not prepared. **2.** not prompt or quick. **3.** *Obsolete or Dialect.* not dressed or fully dressed.

un·re·al (un rē′əl), *adj.* lacking reality or substance; imaginary; fanciful. **—un·re′al·ly,** *adv.* **—Syn.** fictitious.

un·re·al·is·tic (un′rē ə lis′tik), *adj.* not realistic: *an unrealistic play or novel, an unrealistic education. The President said that it would be unrealistic to expect a miraculous ending of the "cold war" as a result of the conference* (New York Times).

un·re·al·is·ti·cal·ly (un′rē ə lis′tə klē), *adv.* in a manner that is unrealistic: *Well known is Boswell's account of how Johnson unrealistically thought he could complete it [dictionary] in three years' time* (New York Times).

un·re·al·i·ty (un′rē al′ə tē), *n., pl.* **-ties. 1.** lack of reality or substance; imaginary or fanciful quality. **2.** impractical or visionary character or tendency; impracticality. **3.** something without reality; something unreal.

un·re·al·iz·a·ble (un rē′ə lī′zə bəl), *adj.* not realizable.

un·re·al·ized (un rē′ə līzd), *adj.* not realized.

un·rea·son (un rē′zən), *n.* **1.** absence of reason; indisposition or inability to act or think rationally; irrationality: *in some mood of cantankerous unreason* (George Gissing). **2.** that which is contrary to or devoid of reason; an absurdity.

un·rea·son·a·ble (un rē′zə nə bəl, -rēz′nə-), *adj.* **1.** not reasonable, especially: **a.** not acting in accordance with reason or good sense; not reasonable in conduct, demands, etc.: *a capricious, unreasonable child.* **b.** not in accordance with reason; irrational: *unreasonable fears. The unreasonable [man] persists in trying to adapt the world to himself. Therefore all progress depends on the unreasonable man* (George Bernard Shaw). **2.** not moderate; exorbitant; excessive: *an unreasonable price.* **3.** not endowed with reason: *an unreasonable lunatic.* **—un·rea′son·a·ble·ness,** *n.*

un·rea·son·a·bly (un rē′zə nə blē, -rēz′nə-), *adv.* **1.** in a way that is not reasonable; contrary to reason; foolishly. **2.** extremely; immoderately.

un·rea·soned (un rē′zənd), *adj.* not reasoned or based on reasoning.

un·rea·son·ing (un rē′zə ning, -rēz′ning), *adj.* **1.** not reasoning; not using reason;

irrational: *I cannot traffic in the trade of words with that unreasoning sex* (Samuel Taylor Coleridge). **2.** deriving from or yielding to the emotions or instincts without intervention of reason or good sense: *to be the victim of blind, unreasoning terror.* —**un·rea′son·ing·ly,** *adv.* —**Syn. 1.** reasonless.

un·re·buk·a·ble (un′ri byü′kə bəl), *adj.* not deserving rebuke; not open to censure.

un·re·call·a·ble (un′ri kô′lə bəl), *adj.* **1.** that cannot be called back, revoked, or annulled; irrevocable: *You can develop sufficient assurance in the system so that you would do everything short of an unrecallable commitment* (Manchester Guardian). **2.** that cannot be remembered: *Many days of our childhood are unrecallable.*

un·re·ceipt·ed (un′ri sē′tid), *adj.* not receipted.

un·re·ceived (un′ri sēvd′), *adj.* **1.** not taken; not come into possession. **2.** not embraced or adopted.

un·reck·oned (un rek′ənd), *adj.* not reckoned, computed, counted, or summed up.

un·re·claim·a·ble (un′ri klā′mə bəl), *adj.* irreclaimable.

un·re·claimed (un′ri klāmd′), *adj.* **1.** not brought to a domestic state; not tame: *a savageness in unreclaimed blood* (Shakespeare). **2.** not reformed; not called back from vice to virtue: *a sinner unreclaimed.* **3.** not brought into a state of cultivation, as desert or wild land.

un·rec·og·niz·a·ble (un rek′əg nī′zə bəl), *adj.* not recognizable.

un·rec·og·niz·a·bly (un rek′əg nī′zə blē), *adv.* in an unrecognizable manner; without or beyond recognition.

un·rec·og·nized (un rek′əg nīzd), *adj.* not recognized.

un·rec·om·mend·ed (un′rek ə men′did), *adj.* not recommended; not favorably mentioned.

un·rec·om·pensed (un rek′əm penst), *adj.* not recompensed.

un·rec·on·cil·a·ble (un rek′ən sī′lə bəl), *adj.* irreconcilable.

un·rec·on·ciled (un rek′ən sīld), *adj.* not reconciled.

un·re·con·struct·ed (un′rē kən struk′tid), *adj.* **1.** stubborn in adherence to standards, practices, etc., of an earlier day, previous regime, etc.; unashamedly and tenaciously loyal to that which has been overthrown or superseded. **2.** *U.S. History.* not yet subjected to the Reconstruction: *an unreconstructed area.* **3.** *U.S.* not reconciled to the Reconstruction: *an unreconstructed Southerner.*

un·re·cord·ed (un′ri kôr′did), *adj.* not recorded.

un·re·count·ed (un′ri koun′tid), *adj.* not recounted; not related or recited.

un·re·cov·er·a·ble (un′ri kuv′ər ə bəl, -kuv′rə-), *adj.* **1.** that cannot be recovered, found, restored, or obtained again. **2.** not obtainable from a debtor; irrecoverable. **3.** that cannot recover; incurable; irremediable.

un·re·deemed (un′ri dēmd′), *adj.* **1.** not recalled by payment of what is due, as notes or bonds. **2.** not taken out of pawn. **3.** not fulfilled, as a promise. **4.** not ransomed; not delivered or rescued. **5.** not saved spiritually. **6.** not remedied or relieved by any countervailing quality or feature; unmitigated: *unredeemed ugliness* (Thomas Carlyle).

un·reel (un rēl′), *v.t., v.i.* to unwind from or as if from a reel.

un·reeve (un rēv′), *v.,* **-rove** or **-reeved, -reev·ing.** *Nautical.* —*v.t.* to draw (rope) back through a block, thimble, etc. —*v.i.* **1.** (of a rope) to become unreeved. **2.** to draw back a reeved rope.

UNREF (no periods) or **U.N.R.E.F.,** United Nations Refugee Emergency Fund.

un·re·fined (un′ri fīnd′), *adj.* **1.** not purified, as substances. **2.** not free from coarseness or vulgarity; lacking nice feeling, taste, etc.

un·re·flect·ing (un′ri flek′ting), *adj.* unthinking; thoughtless. —**un′re·flect′ing·ly,** *adv.*

un·re·form·a·ble (un′ri fôr′mə bəl), *adj.* not reformable; that cannot be reformed or amended.

un·re·gard·ed (un′ri gär′did), *adj.* **1.** not heeded or noticed; disregarded. **2.** not valued or esteemed.

un·re·gen·er·a·cy (un′ri jen′ər ə sē), *n.* unregenerate condition; enmity toward God; wickedness.

un·re·gen·er·ate (un′ri jen′ər it), *adj.* **1.** not born again spiritually; not turned to the love of God. **2.** not disposed to reform or repent; stubborn and hardened in wickedness, crime, etc. —**un′re·gen′er·ate·ly,** *adv.* —**un′re·gen′er·ate·ness,** *n.*

un·re·gen·er·at·ed (un′ri jen′ə rā′tid), *adj.* unregenerate.

un·reg·is·tered (un rej′ə stərd), *adj.* not registered.

un·reg·u·lat·ed (un reg′yə lā′tid), *adj.* not regulated: *The proposals, sent to Congress Tuesday, would . . . prevent diversion of freight traffic to private, unregulated truck carriers* (Wall Street Journal).

un·re·lat·ed (un′ri lā′tid), *adj.* not related. —**un′re·lat′ed·ness,** *n.*

un·re·laxed (un′ri lakst′), *adj.* **1.** not relaxed. **2.** not made loose or slack. **3.** not slackened or abated.

un·re·lax·ing (un′ri lak′sing), *adj.* not relaxing or slackening: *a time of unrelaxing effort* (John Morley).

un·re·lent·ing (un′ri len′ting), *adj.* **1.** not softening or yielding, especially not giving way to feelings of kindness or compassion; merciless: *an unrelenting enemy.* **2.** not slackening or relaxing in severity, harshness, or determination: *unrelenting anger.* **3.** not slowing down: *an unrelenting pace.* —**un′re·lent′ing·ly,** *adv.* —**un′re·lent′ing·ness,** *n.*
—**Syn. 1.** unyielding, obdurate, relentless. See **inflexible.**

un·re·li·a·bil·i·ty (un′ri lī′ə bil′ə tē), *n.* lack of reliability.

un·re·li·a·ble (un′ri lī′ə bəl), *adj.* not reliable; not to be depended on. —**un′re·li′a·ble·ness,** *n.* —**Syn.** uncertain, irresponsible.

un·re·li·a·bly (un′ri lī′ə blē), *adv.* in an unreliable manner.

un·re·liev·a·ble (un′ri lē′və bəl), *adj.* not relievable.

un·re·lieved (un′ri lēvd′), *adj.* not relieved: *unrelieved monotony, the unrelieved hardships of pioneer life.*

un·re·liev·ed·ly (un′ri lē′vid lē), *adv.* without relief or mitigation: *The tempo is funereal, and throughout the mood is unrelievedly austere* (Time).

un·re·li·gious (un′ri lij′əs), *adj.* **1.** irreligious. **2.** not connected with religion; nonreligious; secular: *The popular poetry . . . became profane, unreligious, at length in some part, irreligious* (Henry H. Milman).

un·re·mark·a·ble (un′ri mär′kə bəl), *adj.* unworthy of remark or notice; not notable or striking: *But how did he make the jump from these unremarkable poems to the later work?* (Punch).

un·re·marked (un′ri märkt′), *adj.* not remarked; not noticed: *The unremarked phenomenon of Herbert Hoover is that he has been so long out of a regular job and has kept himself so busy* (Time).

un·re·mem·ber·a·ble (un′ri mem′bər ə-bəl), *adj.* not rememberable; forgettable: *The smallest flint spark, in a world all black and unrememberable, will be welcome* (Thomas Carlyle).

un·re·mem·bered (un′ri mem′bərd), *adj.* not remembered; forgotten: *little nameless, unremembered acts Of kindness and of love* (Wordsworth).

un·re·mem·ber·ing (un′ri mem′bər ing), *adj.* not remembering; having no memory or recollection: *She went her unremembering way* (Francis Thompson).

un·re·mit·ted (un′ri mit′id), *adj.* **1.** not remitted; not pardoned, forgiven, or canceled. **2.** not slackened or abated: *Our exertions to discover him are unremitted* (Mary Shelley).

un·re·mit·ting (un′ri mit′ing), *adj.* never slackening or relaxing; maintained steadily: *unremitting vigilance. Driving in traffic requires unremitting attention.* —**un′re·mit′ting·ly,** *adv.* —**Syn.** unceasing, incessant, constant.

un·re·morse·ful (un′ri môrs′fəl), *adj.* feeling no remorse; unpitying; remorseless.

un·re·mov·a·ble (un′ri mü′və bəl), *adj.* that cannot be removed; fixed; irremovable.

un·re·moved (un′ri müvd′), *adj.* **1.** not removed; not taken away. **2.** firm; unshaken.

un·re·mu·ner·at·ed (un′ri myü′nə rā′tid), *adj.* not remunerated; without remuneration.

un·re·mu·ner·a·tive (un′ri myü′nə rā′tiv, -nər ə-), *adj.* not remunerative; not affording remuneration; unprofitable. —**un′re·mu′ner·a′tive·ness,** *n.*

un·re·newed (un′ri nüd′, -nyüd′), *adj.* **1.** not made anew: *an unrenewed lease.* **2.** not regenerated; not born of the Spirit: *an unrenewed heart.* **3.** not renovated; not restored to freshness.

un·rent (un rent′), *adj.* not rent; not torn asunder.

un·rent·ed (un ren′tid), *adj.* not rented.

un·re·paid (un′ri pād′), *adj.* not repaid; not compensated; not recompensed; not requited: *a kindness unrepaid.*

un·re·pair (un′ri pãr′), *n.* lack of repair; disrepair; dilapidation.

un·re·pair·a·ble (un′ri pãr′ə bəl), *adj.* that cannot be repaired; irreparable.

un·re·paired (un′ri pãrd′), *adj.* not repaired.

un·re·peal·a·ble (un′ri pē′lə bəl), *adj.* not repealable; irrevocable.

un·re·pealed (un′ri pēld′), *adj.* not repealed.

un·re·pent·ance (un′ri pen′təns), *n.* the state of being unrepentant or impenitent; impenitence.

un·re·pent·ant (un′ri pen′tənt), *adj.* not repentant; impenitent. —**un′re·pent′ant·ly,** *adv.*

un·re·pent·ed (un′ri pen′tid), *adj.* not repented of.

un·re·pin·ing (un′ri pī′ning), *adj.* not repining; uncomplaining. —**un′re·pin′ing·ly,** *adv.*

un·re·plen·ished (un′ri plen′isht), *adj.* not replenished; not filled; not adequately supplied.

un·rep·re·sent·a·tive (un′rep ri zen′tə-tiv), *adj.* not representative; failing to represent adequately; not typical.

un·rep·re·sent·ed (un′rep ri zen′tid), *adj.* not represented.

un·re·pressed (un′ri prest′), *adj.* not repressed; unrestrained.

un·re·priev·a·ble (un′ri prē′və bəl), *adj.* that cannot be reprieved.

un·re·prieved (un′ri prēvd′), *adj.* not reprieved; not respited.

un·re·prov·a·ble (un′ri prü′və bəl), *adj.* not reprovable; not deserving reproof; without reproach; not liable to be justly censured.

un·re·proved (un′ri prüvd′), *adj.* **1.** not reproved; not censured. **2.** not liable to reproof or blame. **3.** *Obsolete.* not disproved.

un·re·quest·ed (un′ri kwes′tid), *adj.* not requested; not asked.

un·re·quit·a·ble (un′ri kwī′tə bəl), *adj.* that cannot be requited; unreturnable: *Britain owes an unrequitable debt to the work of the famous Temporary National Economic Committee* (Manchester Guardian Weekly).

un·re·quit·ed (un′ri kwī′tid), *adj.* not requited; without requital or return: *unrequited love.*

un·re·serve (un′ri zėrv′), *n.* freedom from reserve; candor; frankness: *questions which he will answer with perfect unreserve* (Samuel Butler).

un·re·served (un′ri zėrvd′), *adj.* **1.** frank; open. **2.** not restricted, limited, or qualified; without reservation.

un·re·serv·ed·ly (un′ri zėr′vid lē), *adv.* **1.** frankly; openly. **2.** without reservation or restriction. —**Syn. 1.** straightforwardly. **2.** fully.

un·re·serv·ed·ness (un′ri zėr′vid nis), *n.* the character of being unreserved; freedom of communication; frankness; openness; unlimitedness.

un·re·sist·ed (un′ri zis′tid), *adj.* **1.** not resisted; not opposed. **2.** *Obsolete.* irresistible.

un·re·sist·ing (un′ri zis′ting), *adj.* not resisting; not making resistance; submissive. —**un′re·sist′ing·ly,** *adv.*

un·re·solv·a·ble (un′ri zol′və bəl), *adj.* that cannot be resolved: *I have in the past accused him of both hubris and loss of self-respect, but the paradox is not unresolvable* (Joseph Wood Krutch).

un·re·solved (un′ri zolvd′), *adj.* **1.** not resolved; not determined. **2.** not solved; not cleared: *unresolved doubt.* **3.** not separated into its constituent parts: *an unresolved nebula.* **4.** not reduced to a state of solution.

un·re·spect·a·ble (un′ri spek′tə bəl), *adj.* not respectable; disreputable; dishonorable.

un·res·pit·ed (un res′pə tid), *adj.* **1.** not respited: *Unrespited, unpitied, unreprieved, Ages of hopeless end* (Milton). **2.** *Obsolete.* admitting no pause or intermission.

un·re·spon·sive (un′ri spon′siv), *adj.* not responsive or inclined to respond. —**un′re·spon′sive·ness,** *n.*

un·rest (un rest′), *n.* **1.** lack of ease and quiet; restlessness. **2.** agitation or disturbance amounting almost to rebellion. —**Syn. 1.** inquietude, uneasiness. **2.** disquiet.

un·rest·ful (un rest′fəl), *adj.* **1.** not restful or at rest; restless. **2.** not affording or promoting rest.

un·rest·ing (un res′ting), *adj.* not resting; continually in motion or action; restless: *life's unresting sea* (Oliver Wendell Holmes).

un·re·strained (un′ri strānd′), *adj.* **1.** not kept in check or under control: *unrestrained mirth.* **2.** not subjected to restraint: *unrestrained freedom, an unrestrained movement.* **3.** free from restraint of manner; easy; natural: *an unrestrained greeting.*

un·re·strain·ed·ly (un′ri strā′nid lē), *adv.* in an unrestrained manner; without restraint or limitation.

un·re·straint (un′ri strānt′), *n.* unrestrained quality or condition; lack of restraint.

un·re·strict·ed (un′ri strik′tid), *adj.* not restricted; without limitation. —**un′re·strict′ed·ly,** *adv.*

un·re·tard·ed (un′ri tär′did), *adj.* not retarded; not delayed, hindered, or impeded.

un·re·ten·tive (un′ri ten′tiv), *adj.* not retentive.

un·re·turn·a·ble (un′ri tėr′nə bəl), *adj.* that cannot be returned; impossible to be repaid.

un·re·vealed (un′ri vēld′), *adj.* not revealed; not disclosed.

un·re·venged (un′ri venjd′), *adj.* not revenged.

un·re·versed (un′ri vėrst′), *adj.* not reversed; not annulled by a counter decision; not revoked; unrepealed.

un·re·voked (un′ri vōkt′), *adj.* not revoked; not recalled; not annulled.

un·re·ward·ed (un′ri wôr′did), *adj.* not rewarded; unrequited: *unrewarded kindness.*

un·re·ward·ing (un′ri wôr′ding), *adj.* not rewarding; not affording a reward: *Foremost ... has been a calculated endeavor to develop the Indians' self-reliance and change their own image of themselves—an image of serfs destined to poverty and endless unrewarding work* (Scientific American).

un·rhyth·mi·cal (un riᴛʜ′mə kəl), *adj.* not rhythmical; irregular in rhythm.

un·rid·dle (un rid′əl), *v.t.,* **-dled, -dling.** to work out the answer to (a puzzling matter, mystery, riddle, etc.); solve: *The riddle ... was now unriddled* (Edgar Allan Poe).

un·rig (un rig′), *v.t.,* **-rigged, -rig·ging. 1.** to dismantle and remove the rigging of (a ship). **2.** to take apart and remove (a scaffold, mechanical equipment, etc.); dismantle. **3.** *Archaic or Dialect.* to undress.

un·rigged (un rigd′), *adj.* without rigging; not rigged.

un·right·eous (un rī′chəs), *adj.* **1.** not morally righteous or upright; wicked; sinful. **2.** not justly due; undeserved. [Old English *unrihtwīs* < *un-* un-¹ + *rihtwīs.* Compare RIGHTEOUS.] —**un·right′eous·ly,** *adv.* —**un·right′eous·ness,** *n.* —**Syn. 1.** unprincipled, iniquitous.

un·right·ful (un rīt′fəl), *adj.* **1.** not rightful; unjust; not consonant with justice. **2.** not having right; not legitimate.

un·rip (un rip′), *v.t.,* **-ripped, -rip·ping. 1.** to open up or detach by or as if by ripping; tear or pull open or off. **2.** to lay open by slicing; slit.

un·ripe (un rīp′), *adj.,* **-rip·er, -rip·est. 1.** not ripe; not matured by growth; green: *an unripe peach.* **2.** (of persons, plans, etc.) not fully developed or grown; immature. **3.** *Obsolete.* (of death) too early; premature. —**un·ripe′ness,** *n.*

un·rip·ened (un rī′pənd), *adj.* not ripened; not matured.

un·ri·valed (un rī′vəld), *adj.* having no rival; without an equal; matchless; peerless. —**Syn.** incomparable.

un·ri·valled (un rī′vəld), *adj. Especially British.* unrivaled.

un·robe (un rōb′), *v.t., v.i.,* **-robed, -rob·ing.** to divest or be divested of a robe or robes; undress; disrobe: *The King ... unrobed, took his seat ... and listened ... to the debate* (Macaulay).

un·roll (un rōl′), *v.t.* **1.** to open or spread out (something rolled). **2.** to lay open or spread out so as to be seen; display. **3.** *Obsolete.* to strike from a roll; remove from a roster: *If I make not this Cheat bring out another ... let me be unrolled* (Shakespeare). —*v.i.* to become unrolled. —**Syn.** *v.t.* **1.** unfold, unfurl.

un·ro·man·tic (un′rō man′tik), *adj.* not romantic; prosaic; practical; commonplace. —**un′ro·man′ti·cal·ly,** *adv.*

un·roof (un rüf′, -ru̇f′), *v.t.* to pull or pluck off the roof or upper covering of: *They ... unroofed a great part of the building* (Alexander W. Kinglake).

un·roofed (un rüft′, -ru̇ft′), *adj.* not provided with a roof.

un·root (un rüt′, -ru̇t′), *v.t.* to uproot. —*v.i.* to be uprooted.

un·rough (un ruf′), *adj.* not rough; unbearded; smooth.

un·round (un round′), *v.t. Phonetics.* **1.** to decrease or eliminate the lip rounding in the pronunciation of (a normally rounded sound). **2.** to spread (the lips) during articulation.

un·round·ed (un roun′did), *adj. Phonetics.* pronounced without rounding of the lips, as the vowels in *sit* and *sat.*

un·rove (un rōv′), *adj. Nautical.* unreeved. —*v.* a past tense and a past participle of **unreeve.**

UN·RRA (un′rə), *n.,* or **U.N.R.R.A.,** United Nations Relief and Rehabilitation Administration (an agency established in 1943 by the United Nations to provide food, clothing, medical supplies, etc., to redeveloping nations devastated by war).

un·ruf·fled (un ruf′əld), *adj.* **1.** not ruffled; smooth. **2.** not disturbed; calm: *with contented mind and unruffled spirit* (Anthony Trollope). —**un·ruf′fled·ness,** *n.* —**Syn. 2.** serene, unperturbed.

un·ruled (un rüld′), *adj.* **1.** not kept under control; not governed. **2.** not marked with lines: *unruled paper.*

un·ru·li·ness (un rü′lē nis), *n.* the state or condition of being unruly; disregard of restraint; turbulence: *the unruliness of men.*

un·ru·ly (un rü′lē), *adj.,* **-li·er, -li·est. 1.** hard to rule or control, especially: **a.** not amenable to discipline; ungovernable; unmanageable: *an unruly horse, a disobedient and unruly boy, an unruly lock of hair.* **b.** not amenable to law and order; disorderly; turbulent: *an unruly mob, an unruly section of country.* **2.** stormy; tempestuous: *an unruly sea.*

—**Syn. 1. Unruly, ungovernable** mean hard or impossible to control. **Unruly** means not inclined to obey or accept discipline or restraint, and suggests getting out of hand and becoming disorderly, contrary, or obstinately willful, resisting or defying attempts to bring under control: *The angry mob became unruly.* **Ungovernable** means incapable of being controlled or restrained, either because of never having been subjected to rule or direction or because of escape from it: *One of the circus lions had always been ungovernable.*

UNRWA (no periods) or **U.N.R.W.A.,** United Nations Relief and Works Agency (originally for Palestine refugees in the Near East).

un·sad·dle (un sad′əl), *v.t.,* **-dled, -dling. 1.** to take the saddle off (a horse). **2.** to cause (a person) to fall from a horse; throw; unhorse.

un·safe (un sāf′), *adj.,* **-saf·er, -saf·est.** dangerous. —**un·safe′ly,** *adv.* —**un·safe′ness,** *n.* —**Syn.** perilous, hazardous, precarious.

un·safe·ty (un sāf′tē), *n.* **1.** dangerous quality; lack of safety. **2.** *Archaic.* the state of being in danger; peril.

un·said (un sed′), *adj.* not said or uttered: *All I meant to say remains unsaid* (Wilfred W. Gibson). —*v.t.* the past tense and past participle of **unsay.**

un·saint·ly (un sānt′lē), *adj.* **1.** not saintly; not like a saint. **2.** not befitting a saint.

un·sal·a·bil·i·ty or **un·sale·a·bil·i·ty** (un sā′lə bil′ə tē), *n.* not being of a salable condition or quality: *Unsaleability is almost the hallmark ... of quality in writing* (Logan Pearsall Smith).

un·sal·a·ble or **un·sale·a·ble** (un sā′lə-bəl), *adj.* not salable; not meeting a ready sale. —**un·sal′a·ble·ness, un·sale′a·ble·ness,** *n.*

un·sal·a·ried (un sal′ər id), *adj.* not salaried; not paid, or not provided with, a fixed salary.

un·salt·ed (un sôl′tid), *adj.* not salted; fresh.

un·sanc·ti·fied (un sangk′tə fīd), *adj.* not sanctified; unhallowed; unholy.

un·sanc·ti·mo·ni·ous (un′sangk tə mō′nē əs), *adj.* not making a show of holiness; not putting on airs of sanctity: *Mr. Goodman's unsanctimonious appreciation of the Bible story has some witty and winning scenes* (New York Times).

un·sanc·tioned (un sangk′shənd), *adj.* not sanctioned; not ratified; not approved.

un·san·i·tar·i·ness (un san′ə ter′ē nis), *n.* the state or condition of being unsanitary.

un·san·i·tar·y (un san′ə ter′ē), *adj.* not sanitary; unhealthful.

un·sa·ti·a·ble (un sā′shē ə bəl, -shə bəl), *adj.* incapable of being satiated or appeased; insatiable.

un·sat·is·fac·to·ri·ly (un′sat is fak′tər ə-lē), *adv.* in an unsatisfactory manner.

un·sat·is·fac·to·ri·ness (un′sat is fak′-tər ē nis), *n.* the character or state of being unsatisfactory; failure to give satisfaction.

un·sat·is·fac·to·ry (un′sat is fak′tər ē), *adj.* not good enough to satisfy; inadequate.

un·sat·is·fied (un sat′is fīd), *adj.* not satisfied; not gratified to the full; not contented: *A cigarette ... is exquisite and it leaves one unsatisfied. What more can one want?* (Oscar Wilde).

un·sat·is·fy·ing (un sat′is fī′ing), *adj.* not satisfying; insufficient to meet the desires; inadequate: *an unsatisfying meal.* —**un·sat′-is·fy′ing·ly,** *adv.* —**un·sat′is·fy′ing·ness,** *n.*

un·sat·u·rat·ed (un sach′ə rā′tid), *adj.* **1.** able to absorb or dissolve an additional quantity of a substance (used of a solvent or a solution). **2.** *Chemistry.* (of an organic compound) having a double or triple bond and one or more free valences so that another atom or radical may be taken on without the liberation of other atoms, radicals, or compounds, as acetylene.

unsaturated radical, *Chemistry.* an organic radical having a double or triple bond which joins two atoms of carbon.

un·sat·u·ra·tion (un′sach ə rā′shən), *n.* the state of being unsaturated.

un·sa·vor·i·ly (un sā′vər ə lē, -sāv′rə-), *adv.* in an unsavory manner.

un·sa·vor·i·ness (un sā′vər ē nis, -sāv′rē-), *n.* the character of being unsavory.

un·sa·vor·y (un sā′vər ē, -sāv′rē), *adj.* **1.** unpleasant in taste or smell; distasteful: *a most unsavory medicine.* **2.** morally offensive or dubious: *an unsavory companion.* **3.** *Obsolete.* tasteless; insipid.

un·sa·vour·i·ly (un sā′vər ə lē, -sāv′rə-), *adv. Especially British.* unsavorily.

un·sa·vour·i·ness (un sā′vər ē nis, -sāv′-rē-), *n. Especially British.* unsavoriness.

un·sa·vour·y (un sā′vər ē, -sāv′rē), *adj. Especially British.* unsavory.

un·say (un sā′), *v.t.,* **-said, -say·ing.** to take back (something said or written); withdraw (a statement); retract.

un·scal·a·ble (un skā′lə bəl), *adj.* not scalable; not to be climbed: *the unscalable side of a mountain* (Joseph Conrad).

un·scanned (un skand′), *adj.* not scanned; not measured; not computed.

un·scarred (un skärd′), *adj.* not scarred, as from a wound; having no scars.

un·scathed (un skāᴛʜd′), *adj.* not harmed; uninjured: *He escaped unscathed from the car wreck.*

un·schol·ar·li·ness (un skol′ər lē nis), *n.* the character or state of being unscholarly.

un·schol·ar·ly (un skol′ər lē), *adj.* **1.** not scholarly; lacking scholarly qualities or attainments. **2.** unbefitting a scholar.

un·schooled (un sküld′), *adj.* not schooled; not taught; not disciplined.

un·sci·en·tif·ic (un′sī ən tif′ik), *adj.* **1.** not in accordance with the facts or principles of science: *an unscientific notion. This assumption is unscientific* (Samuel Butler). **2.** not acting in accordance with such facts or principles: *an unscientific farmer.* —**un′-sci·en·tif′i·cal·ly,** *adv.*

un·scoured (un skourd′), *adj.* not scoured; not cleaned by rubbing: *an unscoured sink.*

un·scram·ble (un skram′bəl), *v.t.,* **-bled, -bling. 1.** to reduce from confusion to order; bring out of a chaotic condition: *to unscramble one's neglected affairs.* **2.** to restore to the original condition; make no longer scrambled: *to unscramble a radio message.*

un·scram·bler (un skram′blər), *n.* **1.** a person or thing that unscrambles: *They were also, however, expert unscramblers* (Harper's).

2. a device which unscrambles special broadcasts: *Its figure did not include about $80 for the cost of installation of an unscrambler for subscription TV receivers* (New York Times).

un·scratched (un skracht′), *adj.* not scratched; not torn.

un·screened (un skrēnd′), *adj.* **1.** not screened; not covered; not sheltered; not protected. **2.** not passed through a screen; not sifted: *unscreened coal.* **3.** not made into, or adapted for, a motion picture: *The story as yet is unscreened.*

un·screw (un skrü′), *v.t.* **1.** to take out the screw or screws from. **2.** to detach or remove by doing this: *to unscrew a bracket from the wall.* **3.** to loosen or take off by turning; untwist: *to unscrew an electric bulb.* —*v.i.* to be able to be or become unscrewed: *This fixture won't unscrew.*

un·script·ed (un skrip′tid), *adj. British.* delivered or presented without a script.

un·scrip·tur·al (un skrip′chər əl), *adj.* not scriptural; not in accordance with the Scriptures. —**un·scrip′tur·al·ly,** *adv.*

un·scru·pu·lous (un skrü′pyə ləs), *adj.* not careful about right or wrong; without principles or conscience: *The unscrupulous boy cheated on the test.* —**un·scru′pu·lous·ly,** *adv.* —**un·scru′pu·lous·ness,** *n.*

—**Syn. Unscrupulous, unprincipled** mean without regard for what is morally right. **Unscrupulous** implies a willful disregard of moral principles, a failure to be held back by any doubts of conscience, or by a sense of honor: *He would stoop to any unscrupulous trick to evade the draft.* **Unprincipled** implies a lack of awareness of moral principles: *Only an unprincipled lawyer would defend that criminal.* The distinction is roughly parallel to the difference between *immoral* and *amoral.*

un·sculp·tured (un skulp′chərd), *adj.* **1.** not sculptured; not covered with sculpture or markings. **2.** *Zoology.* without elevated or impressed marks on the surface; smooth.

un·seal (un sēl′), *v.t.* **1.** to break or remove the seal of: *to unseal a letter or a jar.* **2.** to cause to open in speech: *The threat unsealed her lips.*

un·seam (un sēm′), *v.t.* **1.** to undo the seam or seams of. **2.** to rip lengthwise: *Till he unseam'd him from the nave to the chops* (Shakespeare).

un·search·a·ble (un sėr′chə bəl), *adj.* not to be searched into; that cannot be understood by searching; mysterious: *the unsearchable and secret aims Of nature* (Robert Bridges). —**Syn.** inscrutable.

un·search·a·bly (un sėr′chə blē), *adv.* in an unsearchable manner; inscrutably.

un·searched (un sėrcht′), *adj.* not searched.

un·sea·son·a·ble (un sē′zə nə bəl, -sēz′nə-), *adj.* **1.** not suitable to or characteristic of the season: *an unseasonable heat wave.* **2.** coming at the wrong time; not timely. *an unseasonable suggestion.* —**un·sea′son·a·ble·ness,** *n.* —**Syn. 2.** inopportune, untimely.

un·sea·son·a·bly (un sē′zə nə blē, -sēz′nə-), *adv.* in an unseasonable manner; at an inappropriate or awkward time.

un·sea·son·al·ly (un sē′zə nə lē, -sēz′nə-), *adv.* unseasonably: *unseasonally rough weather.*

un·sea·soned (un sē′zənd), *adj.* **1.** not matured, dried, hardened, or prepared by due seasoning, as things. **2.** not inured to a climate, service, work, mode of life, etc., as persons; inexperienced. **3.** not tested and approved by time, as securities. **4.** not flavored with seasoning, as food. **5.** *Obsolete.* unseasonable.

un·seat (un sēt′), *v.t.* **1.** to remove from office: *to unseat a congressman, to unseat a government.* **2. a.** to displace from a seat. **b.** to dislodge from its base: *to unseat a boiler.* **3.** to throw (a rider) from the saddle.

un·sea·wor·thi·ness (un sē′wėr′ᴛʜē nis), *n.* the state of being unseaworthy.

un·sea·wor·thy (un sē′wėr′ᴛʜē), *adj.* not seaworthy, as a ship.

un·sec·tar·i·an (un′sek tãr′ē ən), *adj.* not sectarian; not confined to or dominated by any particular sect; free from sectarian character or aims.

un·sec·tar·i·an·ism (un′sek tãr′ē ə niz′əm), *n.* the character of being unsectarian; freedom from sectarianism; unprejudiced attitude in religious matters.

un·sec·u·lar (un sek′yə lər), *adj.* not secular or worldly.

un·se·cured (un′si kyůrd′), *adj.* **1.** not secured. **2.** not insured against loss, as by a bond, pledge, etc.: *unsecured debts.*

un·see·a·ble (un sē′ə bəl), *adj.* that cannot be seen; invisible: *To see things unseeable, as St. Paul heard things unutterable* (Daniel Defoe).

un·seed·ed (un sē′did), *adj.* **1.** not seeded; not sown. **2.** not having or bearing seed, as a plant. **3.** not ranked in a tournament: *an unseeded player.*

un·see·ing (un sē′ing), *adj.* **1.** not perceiving; unobservant: *We drive to work along a familiar route unseeing and lost in thought* (Scientific American). **2.** blind. —**un·see′ing·ly,** *adv.*

un·seem·li·ness (un sēm′lē nis), *n.* the character of being unseemly; uncomeliness; indecency; indecorum; impropriety.

un·seem·ly (un sēm′lē), *adj.,* **-li·er, -li·est,** *adv.* —*adj.* contrary to what is appropriate, suitable, or decent; not seemly; improper: *to flee with unseemly haste, a joke of a rather unseemly nature.* —*adv.* improperly; unsuitably. —**Syn.** *adj.* unbecoming, unfit.

un·seen (un sēn′), *adj.* **1.** not seen; overlooked by the eye: *an unseen error.* **2.** not capable of being seen; invisible. —**Syn. 1.** unnoticed, unobserved.

un·seg·ment·ed (un seg′men tid), *adj.* not segmented.

un·seized (un sēzd′), *adj.* **1.** not seized; not apprehended; not taken. **2.** *Law.* not possessed; not put in possession.

un·self-con·scious (un′self kon′shəs), *adj.* not self-conscious; uninhibited; natural; spontaneous: *Children and animals make the best movie actors, as Douglas Fairbanks said, because they are unself-conscious and unable to fake* (Harper's). —**un′self-con′scious·ly,** *adv.* —**un′self-con′scious·ness,** *n.*

un·self·ish (un sel′fish), *adj.* considerate of others; generous. —**un·self′ish·ly,** *adv.* —**un·self′ish·ness,** *n.* —**Syn.** charitable, liberal.

un·sell (un sel′), *v.t.,* **-sold, -sell·ing.** *Informal.* to talk out of; persuade not to buy, accept, or undertake something: *Dad unsold me on the idea of going to Seattle this summer.*

un·sell·a·ble (un sel′ə bəl), *adj.* that no one will buy; that cannot be sold; unsalable: *The house which was to provide the mainstay of the trust . . . was proving unsellable* (New Yorker).

un·sent (un sent′), *adj.* not sent; not dispatched; not transmitted: *an unsent letter.*

un·sent-for (un sent′fôr′), *adj.* not summoned or ordered: *unsent-for guests.*

un·sen·ti·men·tal (un′sen tə men′təl), *adj.* not sentimental; hard-headed; practical; matter-of-fact. —**un′sen·ti·men′tal·ly,** *adv.* —**un′sen·ti·men′tal·ness,** *n.*

un·se·ri·ous (un sir′ē əs), *adj.* not serious: *But however serious or unserious the latest warning may be . . . there is no doubt that the Chinese wish it to be seriously regarded* (Manchester Guardian Weekly). —**un·se′ri·ous·ly,** *adv.*

un·serv·ice·a·ble (un sėr′və sə bəl), *adj.* not serviceable; not satisfactory for service or use; not durable. —**un·serv′ice·a·ble·ness,** *n.*

un·serv·ice·a·bly (un sėr′və sə blē), *adv.* not in a serviceable manner; not serviceably.

un·serv·iced (un sėr′vist), *adj.* **1.** not kept fit for service. **2.** not provided with service of any kind.

un·set[1] (un set′), *adj.* **1.** not in a setting; not mounted: *an unset ruby.* **2.** not fixed or settled: *unset jello, unset cement.*

un·set[2] (un set′), *v.t.,* **-set, -set·ting.** to put out of place; undo the setting of: *to unset the hair.*

un·set·tle (un set′əl), *v.,* **-tled, -tling.** —*v.t.* to make unstable; cause to become disordered; disturb greatly: *to unsettle a person's mind.* —*v.i.* to become unsettled. —**Syn.** *v.t.* disorder, upset, disconcert, shake, weaken.

un·set·tled (un set′əld), *adj.* **1.** not in the proper condition or order; disordered: *an unsettled mind. Our house is still unsettled.* **2.** not fixed or firmly established; unstable: *an unsettled government.* **3.** liable to change; uncertain: *The weather is unsettled.* **4.** not adjusted or disposed of: *an unsettled estate, an unsettled bill.* **5.** not determined or decided: *an unsettled question.* **6.** not populated; uninhabited. —**un·set′tled·ness,** *n.*

un·set·tle·ment (un set′əl mənt), *n.* **1.** the act of unsettling. **2.** the state of being unsettled; unsettled or disturbed condition of affairs: *The continuing unsettlement was a call to him that . . . he had still a portion of the Lord's work to do* (John Morley). *Uncertainty as to the scope of the new program added unsettlement in futures* (Wall Street Journal). **3.** an area or region that has not been definitely settled: *It is in the temporary communities and the amorphous unsettlements that conformity and anxiety breed* (Manchester Guardian).

un·set·tling (un set′ling), *adj.* upsetting; disturbing; disconcerting: *In its quiet, pleasant way this is a most unsettling book* (Saturday Review). —**un·set′tling·ly,** *adv.*

un·sev·ered (un sev′ərd), *adj.* not severed; not parted or sundered; not disjoined or separate.

un·sew (un sō′), *v.t.,* **-sewed, -sewed** or **-sewn, -sew·ing. 1.** to undo the sewing of (a garment, etc.); remove the stitches from. **2.** to unwrap or set free by the removal of stitches.

un·sex (un seks′), *v.t.* to deprive of the attributes of one's sex, especially to deprive of womanly character: *Come, you spirits . . . unsex me* (Shakespeare).

un·shack·le (un shak′əl), *v.t.,* **-led, -ling.** to remove the shackles from; set free. —**Syn.** unfetter.

un·shad·ed (un shā′did), *adj.* **1.** without shade, as of trees. **2.** not screened by a shade, as a light. **3.** without shades or gradations of light or color, as a picture.

un·shad·owed (un shad′ōd), *adj.* not shadowed; not darkened or obscured; free from gloom.

un·shak·a·ble or **un·shake·a·ble** (unshā′kə bəl), *adj.* not shakable; not to be shaken: *The rule of unshakeable falsehood and established tyranny . . . was the basis of Orwell's terrible prophecy* (New Statesman).

un·shak·a·bly or **un·shake·a·bly** (unshā′kə blē), *adv.* in an unshakable manner.

un·shak·en (un shā′kən), *adj.* not shaken; firm: *unshaken courage, an unshaken resolve.* —**Syn.** resolute, unwavering.

un·shamed (un shāmd′), *adj.* not shamed; not ashamed; not abashed.

un·shape (un shāp′), *v.t.,* **-shaped, -shap·ing.** *Archaic.* to put out of shape or order; derange: *This deed unshapes me quite* (Shakespeare).

un·shaped (un shāpt′), *adj.* **1.** lacking distinctive shape; formless: *an unshaped thought.* **2.** not yet in final shape; rough and unfinished: *unshaped timber.* **3.** of an ugly shape; misshapen.

un·shape·li·ness (un shāp′lē nis), *n.* unshapely quality or condition.

un·shape·ly (un shāp′lē), *adj.* not shapely; unpleasing in shape; ill-formed: *a foot, unshapely and huge* (Charles Brockden Brown). *The wrong of unshapely things is a wrong too great to be told; I hunger to build them anew* (William Butler Yeats).

un·shap·en (un shā′pən), *adj.* unshaped: *this blind trust in some unshapen chance* (George Eliot).

un·shared (un shãrd′), *adj.* not shared; not partaken or enjoyed in common.

un·shav·en (un shā′vən), *adj.* not shaven.

un·sheathe (un shēᴛʜ′), *v.t.,* **-sheathed, -sheath·ing. 1.** to draw (a sword, knife, etc.) from a sheath: *People . . . as ready to draw a knife on you as a cat was to unsheathe its claws* (W.H. Hudson). **2.** to remove or strip clothing or other covering from.

un·shed (un shed′), *adj.* not shed: *unshed tears.*

un·shell (un shel′), *v.t.* **1.** to take out of the shell. **2.** to remove or release, as from a shell.

un·shel·tered (un shel′tərd), *adj.* not sheltered; without shelter.

un·ship (un ship′), *v.t.,* **-shipped, -ship·ping. 1.** to put off or take off from a ship; discharge (a cargo); unload (goods): *to unship a cargo.* **2.** to detach or remove (a mast, rudder, oar, etc.) from the place or position of use: *to unship an oar or tiller.*

un·shirk·a·ble (un shėr′kə bəl), *adj.* that cannot be shirked: *our unshirkable responsibility . . . to world peace* (Time).

un·shirt·ed (un shėr′tid), *adj. Informal.* unadorned; unreserved; plain: *Unlike his father who gave him unshirted hell in earthy language, Kennedy does not normally use profanity but he can be devastatingly cutting* (Harper's).

un·shod (un shod′), *adj.* without shoes.
un·shorn (un shôrn′, -shōrn′), *adj.* not shorn; not sheared or clipped; unshaven: *an unshorn beard. The unshorn fields, boundless and beautiful ... The Prairies* (William Cullen Bryant).
un·shown (un shōn′), *adj.* not shown; not exhibited.
un·shrink·a·ble (un shring′kə bəl), *adj.* not shrinkable; not liable to shrink: *unshrinkable flannels.*
un·shrink·ing (un shring′king), *adj.* not shrinking: **a.** not drawing up or contracting. **b.** not drawing back or recoiling; unflinching; firm. —**un·shrink′ing·ly,** *adv.*
un·shriv·en (un shriv′ən), *adj.* not shriven: *How about the souls unshriven, the infants unbaptized?* (Time).
un·shroud (un shroud′), *v.t.* to remove the shroud from; divest of something that shrouds; uncover; unveil.
un·shunned (un shund′), *adj.* not shunned; not avoided.
un·shut (un shut′), *v.t.,* **-shut, -shut·ting.** *Obsolete.* to open.
un·shut·ter (un shut′ər), *v.t.* to remove the shutters from; open the shutters of: *Merchants yesterday were beginning to unshutter their stores* (Wall Street Journal).
un·sick·er (un sik′ər), *adj. Scottish.* not to be counted on; uncertain; insecure.
un·sift·ed (un sif′tid), *adj.* **1.** not sifted: *unsifted flour.* **2.** not critically examined; untried: *unsifted evidence.*
un·sight·ed (un sī′tid), *adj.* **1.** not sighted or seen. **2.** not furnished with, or not directed by means of, a sight or sights, as a firearm.
un·sight·li·ness (un sīt′lē nis), *n.* the state of being unsightly; disagreeableness to the sight; deformity; ugliness.
un·sight·ly (un sīt′lē), *adj.* ugly or unpleasant to look at. —**Syn.** See **ugly.**
un·sight unseen (un sīt′), sight unseen.
un·signed (un sīnd′), *adj.* not signed.
un·sing·a·ble (un sing′ə bəl), *adj.* not singable; not suited or adapted for being sung.
un·sink·a·ble (un sing′kə bəl), *adj.* not sinkable.
un·sis·ter·ly (un sis′tər lē), *adj.* not like a sister; unbecoming a sister.
un·sized (un sīzd′), *adj.* not sized; not coated or treated with size.
un·skilled (un skild′), *adj.* **1.** not skilled or expert; not trained: *to be unskilled in logic.* **2.** not involving or requiring skill: *unskilled labor.* **3.** having no special skill; not trained in any craft, trade, etc.
un·skill·ful or **un·skil·ful** (un skil′fəl), *adj.* **1.** displaying lack of skill; awkward; clumsy. **2.** lacking in skill; unskilled. —**un·skill′ful·ly, un·skil′ful·ly,** *adv.* —**un·skill′ful·ness, un·skil′ful·ness,** *n.*
un·slaked (un slākt′), *adj.* **1.** unsatisfied, as thirst; unappeased. **2.** not slaked, as lime. **3.** unrelaxed.
un·sleep·ing (un slē′ping), *adj.* not sleeping; ever wakeful.
un·sling (un sling′), *v.t.,* **-slung, -sling·ing. 1.** to free from the condition of being slung, especially to make no longer slung across the shoulder, back, etc.: *to unsling a rifle.* **2.** *Nautical.* to remove the slings from (a yard, cask, etc.); release from the hoisting slings.
un·slum (un slum′), *v.t.,* **-slummed, -slum·ming.** to rebuild, renovate, or otherwise get rid of (a slum or slum buildings): *Jane Jacobs blasts the urban renewal projects that would destroy the character of cherished neighborhoods in an effort to unslum them* (Saturday Review).
un·slum·ber·ing (un slum′bər ing), *adj.* never sleeping or slumbering; always watching or vigilant.
un·smart (un smärt′), *adj.* not clever, witty, or stylish; not smart.
un·smil·ing (un smī′ling), *adj.* not smiling; grave; serious. —**un·smil′ing·ly,** *adv.*
un·smirched (un smėrcht′), *adj.* not stained; not soiled or blacked; clean.
un·snag (un snag′), *v.t.,* **-snagged, -snag·ging.** to remove or release from a snag.
un·snap (un snap′), *v.t.,* **-snapped, -snap·ping.** to unfasten the snap or snaps of.
un·snarl (un snärl′), *v.t.* to remove the snarls from; untangle.
un·soaped (un sōpt′), *adj.* not soaped; unwashed: *The unsoaped of Ipswich brought up the rear* (Dickens).
un·so·cia·bil·i·ty (un′sō shə bil′ə tē), *n.* unsociable nature or behavior; lack of friendliness.
un·so·cia·ble (un sō′shə bəl), *adj.* **1.** not desiring or welcoming the company of others; aloof and solitary in nature; not companionable: *an ill-tempered, unsociable old man.* **2.** discouraging or repelling those who seek to be sociable: *unsociable behavior.* **3.** incompatible: *very incongruous and unsociable ideas* (Samuel Johnson). —**un·so′cia·ble·ness,** *n.*
un·so·cia·bly (un sō′shə blē), *adv.* in an unsociable manner; with reserve.
un·so·cial (un sō′shəl), *adj.* not social; unsociable: *an unsocial, taciturn disposition* (Jane Austen). *He was now no longer gloomy and unsocial* (Samuel Johnson). —**un·so′cial·ly,** *adv.* —**un·so′cial·ness,** *n.*
un·soft·ened (un sôf′ənd, -sof′-), *adj.* not softened.
un·soiled (un soild′), *adj.* not soiled; not smirched; unsullied; clean.
un·sold (un sōld′), *v.* the past tense and past participle of **unsell.**
un·sol·der (un sod′ər), *v.t.* **1.** to separate (something joined by solder). **2.** to break up; divide; dissolve.
un·so·lic·it·ed (un′sə lis′ə tid), *adj.* not solicited; unasked; unsought: *spontaneous and unsolicited praise.*
un·so·lic·i·tous (un′sə lis′ə təs), *adj.* not solicitous; unconcerned; indifferent. —**un′so·lic′i·tous·ness,** *n.*
un·sol·id (un sol′id), *adj.* **1.** not having the properties of a solid; liquid or gaseous. **2.** not sound, substantial, or firm; empty; weak; vain; ill-founded.
un·solved (un solvd′), *adj.* not solved, explained, or cleared up.
un·son·sy (un son′sē), *adj. Scottish.* **1.** unlucky. **2.** ill-omened. **3.** not handsome; plain. [< *un-*[1] + *sonsy*]
un·so·phis·ti·cate (un′sə fis′tə kāt, -kit), *n.* an unsophisticated person.
un·so·phis·ti·cat·ed (un′sə fis′tə kā′tid), *adj.* not sophisticated; simple; natural; artless. —**un′so·phis′ti·cat′ed·ness,** *n.* —**Syn.** naïve.
un·so·phis·ti·ca·tion (un′sə fis′tə kā′shən), *n.* unsophisticated condition or quality; simplicity; artlessness.
un·sort·ed (un sôr′tid), *adj.* **1.** not sorted; not arranged or put in order; not assorted or classified. **2.** *Obsolete.* ill-sorted; ill-chosen.
un·sought (un sôt′), *adj.* not sought; not looked or searched for; not asked for; unsolicited.
un·sound (un sound′), *adj.* **1.** not in good condition, especially: **a.** not physically sound; unhealthy: *an unsound body.* **b.** poorly built or maintained; likely to fall down or apart: *Unsound walls are not firm. An unsound business is not reliable.* **2.** not entirely sane; mentally incompetent: *an unsound mind.* **3.** not based on truth or fact; not valid: *an unsound doctrine.* **4.** not deep; not restful; disturbed: *an unsound sleep.* —**un·sound′ly,** *adv.* —**un·sound′ness,** *n.*
un·span (un span′), *v.t.,* **-spanned, -span·ning.** to remove (horses, etc.) from their traces; detach (an animal) from a vehicle: *An enthusiastic audience had unspanned the horses from a beloved singer's coach and had drawn it through the town themselves* (Isak Dinesen).
un·spar·ing (un spãr′ing), *adj.* **1.** very generous; lavish; liberal: *to distribute gifts with unsparing hand.* **2.** not merciful; harshly severe; ruthless: *unsparing justice, to forgive others but be unsparing of oneself.* —**un·spar′ing·ly,** *adv.* —**un·spar′ing·ness,** *n.* —**Syn. 1.** bountiful. **2.** rigorous, unmerciful.
un·speak (un spēk′), *v.t.,* **-spoke, -spo·ken, -speak·ing.** to retract (a statement); unsay.
un·speak·a·ble (un spē′kə bəl), *adj.* **1.** that cannot be expressed in words; indescribable: *unspeakable joy, an unspeakable loss.* **2.** bad or objectionable beyond description: *unspeakable manners.* —**un·speak′a·ble·ness,** *n.*
un·speak·a·bly (un spē′kə blē), *adv.* in a manner or degree that cannot be expressed; inexpressibly; unutterably: *unspeakably vile.*
un·speak·ing (un spē′king), *adj.* not speaking; lacking power of speech.
un·spe·cif·ic (un′spi sif′ik), *adj.* not specific; indefinite; vague.
un·spec·i·fied (un spes′ə fīd), *adj.* not specified; not specifically or definitely named or stated: *an unspecified wage.*
un·spec·tac·u·lar (un′spek tak′yə lər), *adj.* not spectacular; modest: *The Council of Europe has provided a broad European forum where many far-reaching if unspectacular achievements have been hammered out* (Bulletin of Atomic Scientists). —**un′spec·tac′u·lar·ly,** *adv.*
un·spent (un spent′), *adj.* not spent; not expended; not used up or exhausted; still active or effective.
un·sphere (un sfir′), *v.t.,* **-sphered, -spher·ing.** to remove (a star, spirit, etc.) from its place or realm of existence: *to unsphere the stars* (Shakespeare).
un·spilled (un spild′), *adj.* not spilled; not shed.
un·spilt (un spilt′), *adj.* unspilled.
un·spir·i·tu·al (un spir′ə chú əl), *adj.* not spiritual; carnal; worldly.
un·spoiled (un spoild′), *adj.* **1.** not ruined or marred. **2.** not impaired in character, or deprived of the original or natural excellences, as by excessive indulgence.
un·spoke (un spōk′), *v.* the past tense of **unspeak.**
un·spo·ken (un spō′kən), *adj.* not spoken; unuttered. —*v.* past participle of **unspeak.**
un·sport·ing (un spôr′ting, -spōr′-), *adj.* not sporting; unsportsmanlike: *He was not a nice man; he had beaten Inchcape Jones at tennis, with a nasty, unsporting serve* (Sinclair Lewis). —**un·sport′ing·ly,** *adv.*
un·sports·man·like (un spôrts′mən līk′, -spōrts′-), *adj.* not sportsmanlike; unbefitting a sportsman; not fair or honorable.
un·spot·ted (un spot′id), *adj.* **1.** without moral stain; unblemished; pure: *an unspotted reputation.* **2.** having no spots.
un·sprung (un sprung′), *adj.* **1.** not sprung: *an unsprung trap.* **2.** having no springs: *an unsprung wagon.* **3.** *Obsolete.* not sprouted: *unsprung seed.*
un·squared (un skwãrd′), *adj.* not squared.
un·sta·ble (un stā′bəl), *adj.* **1.** not firmly fixed or stable in nature, especially: **a.** easily moved or shaken; likely to break down: *an unstable mind.* **b.** easily overthrown: *an unstable government.* **2.** not firm or solid; insecure: *an unstable footing.* **3.** somewhat precarious; unsteady: *an unstable equilibrium.* **4.** not constant; apt to change or alter; wavering; vacillating; fickle; variable: *unstable hopes, an unstable nature.* **5.** *Chemistry.* (of a compound) easily decomposed; readily changing into other compounds, or into elements. —**un·sta′ble·ness,** —**un·sta′bly,** *adv.* —**Syn. 1.** unsettled.
unstable element, *Chemistry.* an element which decomposes because of its radioactive nature; a radioactive element which changes into a radioactive isotope.
un·stack (un stak′), *v.t.* to bring out of a stacked condition; take a stack of (something) down or apart: *to unstack hay.*
un·stained (un stānd′), *adj.* not stained; unsullied; stainless.
un·stamped (un stampt′), *adj.* not stamped; not bearing a stamp.
un·stand·ard·ized (un stan′dər dīzd), *adj.* not standardized.
un·state (un stāt′), *v.t.,* **-stat·ed, -stat·ing. 1.** to deprive of rank or status. **2.** to deprive of the character of a state.
un·states·man·like (un stāts′mən līk′), *adj.* not statesmanlike; unlike or unbefitting a statesman.
un·stead·fast (un sted′fast, -fäst), *adj.* **1.** not steadfast; not firmly fixed. **2.** not firm in purpose, resolution, faith, etc.; inconstant; irresolute. —**un·stead′fast·ly,** *adv.* —**un·stead′fast·ness,** *n.*
un·stead·i·ly (un sted′ə lē), *adv.* in an unsteady manner; without steadiness.
un·stead·i·ness (un sted′ē nis), *n.* the state or character of being unsteady.
un·stead·y (un sted′ē), *adj.,* **-stead·i·er, -stead·i·est,** *v.,* **-stead·ied, -stead·y·ing.** —*adj.* **1.** not steady; shaky. **2.** likely to change; not reliable. **3.** not regular in habits.
—*v.t.* to deprive of steadiness; make unsteady: *I was quite unsteadied by all that had fallen out* (Robert Louis Stevenson).
un·steel (un stēl′), *v.t.* to soften: *Why then should this enervating pity unsteel my foolish heart?* (Samuel Richardson).
un·step (un step′), *v.t.,* **-stepped, -step·ping.** to remove (a mast, especially a lower mast) from its step.
un·stick (un stik′), *v.t.,* **-stuck, -stick·ing.** to make no longer stuck; loosen or free (that which is stuck).
un·stiff·en (un stif′ən), *v.t.* to remove the stiffness from; make limber again; loosen up.
un·stint·ed (un stin′tid), *adj.* not stinted; plentiful. —**un·stint′ed·ly,** *adv.*

un·stint·ing (un stin′ting), *adj.* ungrudging; lavish; liberal: *The critics were unstinting in their praise of the youthful conductor* (New York Times). —**un·stint′ing·ly,** *adv.*
un·stock·inged (un stok′ingd), *adj.* not wearing stockings.
un·stop (un stop′), *v.t.,* **-stopped, -stopping. 1.** to remove the stopper from (a bottle, etc.); uncork. **2.** to free from any obstruction; open: *The ears of the deaf shall be unstopped* (Isaiah 35:5). **3.** to pull out (an organ stop). **4.** to pull out a stop or stops of (an organ).
un·stop·pa·ble (un stop′ə bəl), *adj.* that cannot be stopped: *The opening words of the chairman for the day were drowned by . . . an apparently unstoppable record player* (Sunday Times).
un·stop·pa·bly (un stop′ə blē), *adv.* in an unstoppable manner.
un·stop·per (un stop′ər), *v.t.* **1.** to remove the stopper from; uncork: *There, on the dressing table, was an abandoned glass of brandy, an unstoppered bottle of cologne* (New Yorker). **2.** to free from any obstruction.
un·sto·ried (un stôr′ēd, -stōr′-), *adj.* not yet celebrated in story or history: *To the land vaguely realizing westward, But still unstoried, artless, unenhanced* (Robert Frost).
un·strained (un strānd′), *adj.* **1.** not under strain or tension; not forced; natural. **2.** not separated or cleared by straining.
un·strap (un strap′), *v.t.,* **-strapped, -strapping.** to take off or loosen the strap or straps of (a trunk, box, etc.).
un·strat·i·fied (un strat′ə fīd), *adj.* (of rocks) not deposited in strata.
un·stressed (un strest′), *adj.* not stressed; unaccented.
un·stri·at·ed (un strī′ā tid), *adj.* not striated; nonstriated: *unstriated muscle.*
un·string (un string′), *v.t.,* **-strung, -stringing. 1.** to take off or loosen the string or strings of: *to unstring a guitar.* **2.** to take from a string: *to unstring pearls.* **3.** to weaken the nerves of; make nervous: *I'm told getting married unstrings some men* (Owen Wister).
un·striped (un strīpt′), *adj.* not striped; nonstriated, as muscular tissue.
un·struc·tured (un struk′chərd), *adj.* not structured or organized; lacking a definite structure: *Discussions were unstructured* (Science News Letter).
un·strung (un strung′), *adj.* weakened in the nerves; nervous. —*v.* the past tense and past participle of **unstring.** —**Syn.** *adj.* upset, shaken.
un·stuck (un stuk′), *v.* the past tense and past participle of **unstick.**
un·stud·ied (un stud′ēd), *adj.* **1.** not labored or artificial; natural: *simple and unstudied manners.* **2.** not an object of study; not studied. **3.** not having studied; unversed (in): *I . . . was not unstudied in those authors which are most commended* (Milton).
un·stuffed (un stuft′), *adj.* not stuffed; not crowded.
un·sub·dued (un′səb düd′, -dyüd′), *adj.* not subdued; unconquered.
un·sub·mis·sive (un′səb mis′iv), *adj.* not submissive; unyielding. —**un′sub·mis′sive·ly,** *adv.* —**un′sub·mis′sive·ness,** *n.*
un·sub·stan·tial (un′səb stan′shəl), *adj.* **1.** not based or founded on fact; flimsy; slight; unreal: *these deep but unsubstantial meditations* (Edward Gibbon). *Nor build on unsubstantial hope thy trust* (Robert Southey). **2.** lacking in substance: *a rather unsubstantial meal.* **3.** not of a material substance; intangible: *to man's purer unsubstantial part* (Robert Bridges). —**un′sub·stan′tial·ly,** *adv.*
un·sub·stan·ti·al·i·ty (un′səb stan′shē al′ə tē), *n., pl.* **-ties. 1.** the state or quality of being unsubstantial. **2.** an unsubstantial or illusive thing.
un·sub·stan·ti·at·ed (un′səb stan′shē ā′tid), *adj.* not substantiated; not established by evidence: *an unsubstantiated statement.*
un·sub·stan·ti·a·tion (un′səb stan′shē ā′shən), *n.* a depriving of substantiality.
un·sub·tle (un sut′əl), *adj.* not subtle; coarse; blunt: *He was rugged, unsubtle, passionately sincere and consistent; a headstrong dynamic man of narrow vision and inflexible purpose* (Manchester Guardian Weekly).
un·sub·tly (un sut′lē), *adv.* coarsely; bluntly: *Huston . . . has developed his unsubtly sensational theme into a big, slick composition* (Time).
un·suc·cess (un′sək ses′), *n.* lack of success; failure.
un·suc·cess·ful (un′sək ses′fəl), *adj.* not successful; without success: *The Grimsby trawler "Daniel Quare" ran aground last night. . . . Attempts to refloat the trawler today were unsuccessful* (London Times). —**un′suc·cess′ful·ly,** *adv.* —**un′suc·cess′ful·ness,** *n.* —**Syn.** unavailing.
un·suf·fer·a·ble (un suf′ər ə bəl), *adj. Obsolete.* insufferable; intolerable.
un·suit·a·bil·i·ty (un′sü tə bil′ə tē), *n.* a being unsuitable. —**Syn.** unfitness, inappropriateness.
un·suit·a·ble (un sü′tə bəl), *adj.* not suitable; unfit: *She danced in a highly unsuitable manner* (New Yorker). —**un·suit′a·bleness,** *n.* —**Syn.** inappropriate, incongruous.
un·suit·a·bly (un sü′tə blē), *adv.* in an unsuitable or unfit manner.
un·suit·ed (un sü′tid), *adj.* not suited; unfit.
un·sul·lied (un sul′ēd), *adj.* not sullied; unsoiled; spotless; stainless; untarnished: *The intransigents risked the destruction of the Church in order to keep doctrine unsullied* (Manchester Guardian Weekly).
un·sung (un sung′), *adj.* **1.** not sung: *an unsung note.* **2.** not celebrated in or by song or poetry: *Here . . . not a mountain rears its head unsung* (Thomas Carlyle).
un·sunned (un sund′), *adj.* **1.** not exposed to the sun; not lighted by the sun; dark. **2.** not cheered; gloomy.
un·sup·port·a·ble (un′sə pôr′tə bəl, -pōr′-), *adj.* insupportable: *The tyranny was becoming unsupportable even in Stalin's lifetime* (New Statesman).
un·sup·port·ed (un′sə pôr′tid, -pōr′-), *adj.* not supported; not upheld; not sustained; not maintained; not countenanced; not aided.
un·sup·pressed (un′sə prest′), *adj.* not suppressed; not held or kept under; not subdued; not quelled; not put down: *unsuppressed laughter, unsuppressed rebellion.*
un·sure (un shůr′), *adj.,* **-sur·er, -sur·est.** not sure; uncertain: *What's to come is still unsure* (Shakespeare). —**un·sure′ly,** *adv.* —**un·sure′ness,** *n.*
un·sur·mount·a·ble (un′sər moun′tə bəl), *adj.* insurmountable.
un·sur·pass·a·ble (un′sər pas′ə bəl, -päs′-), *adj.* not surpassable; that cannot be surpassed.
un·sur·pass·a·bly (un′sər pas′ə blē, -päs′-), *adv.* in an unsurpassable manner or degree; so as not to be surpassed: *At his worst, he is unsurpassably tedious* (Observer).
un·sur·passed (un′sər past′, -päst′), *adj.* not or never surpassed; unexcelled: *As a chamber group they [the Budapest String Quartet] stand unsurpassed* (New Yorker).
un·sur·pris·ing (un′sər prī′zing), *adj.* not surprising; expected: *An unsurprising feature of the special new volume: 5,300 of the distinguished women declined to tell their ages* (Newsweek). —**un′sur·pris′ing·ly,** *adv.*
un·sus·cep·ti·ble (un′sə sep′tə bəl), *adj.* not susceptible; unimpressionable.
un·sus·pect·ed (un′sə spek′tid), *adj.* **1.** not suspected; clear of or not under suspicion: *an imperious old dame, not unsuspected of witchcraft* (Hawthorne). **2.** not imagined to exist: *an unsuspected danger.* **3.** not surmised. —**un′sus·pect′ed·ly,** *adv.*
un·sus·pect·ing (un′sə spek′ting), *adj.* not suspecting; having no suspicion; unsuspicious: *the unsuspecting victim.* —**un′sus·pect′ing·ly,** *adv.* —**un′sus·pect′ing·ness,** *n.*
un·sus·pi·cious (un′sə spish′əs), *adj.* **1.** not suspicious; without suspicion; unsuspecting: *to visit them openly as if unsuspicious of any hostile design* (Francis Parkman). **2.** not inclined to suspicion or distrust: *an unsuspicious nature.* **3.** not such as to excite suspicion. —**un′sus·pi′cious·ly,** *adv.* —**un′sus·pi′cious·ness** *n.*
un·sus·tain·a·ble (un′sə stā′nə bəl), *adj.* not sustainable; not to be supported, maintained, upheld, or corroborated.
un·sus·tained (un′sə stānd′), *adj.* not sustained; not maintained; not upheld.
un·swathe (un swāᴛʜ′), *v.t.,* **-swathed, -swath·ing.** to divest of that which swathes or covers; unwrap.
un·sway·a·ble (un swā′ə bəl), *adj.* not to be swayed or influenced.
un·swayed (un swād′), *adj.* not swayed.
un·swear (un swãr′), *v.t., v.i.,* **-swore, -sworn, -swear·ing.** to retract (something sworn or asserted); abjure; recant.
un·sweet·ened (un swē′tənd), *adj.* not sweetened.
un·swept (un swept′), *adj.* not swept.
un·swerv·ing (un swėr′ving), *adj.* not swerving; undeviating; unwavering; firm. —**un·swerv′ing·ly,** *adv.*
un·sworn (un swôrn′, -swōrn′), *adj.* **1.** not bound by an oath; not having taken an oath: *an unsworn witness.* **2.** not solemnly pronounced or taken. —*v.* the past participle of **unswear.**
un·sym·met·ri·cal (un′si met′rə kəl), *adj.* not symmetrical; lacking symmetry; asymmetrical. —**un′sym·met′ri·cal·ly,** *adv.*
un·sym·me·try (un sim′ə trē), *n.* lack of symmetry.
un·sym·pa·thet·ic (un′sim pə thet′ik), *adj.* not sympathetic; without sympathy. —**un′sym·pa·thet′i·cal·ly,** *adv.*
un·sym·pa·thiz·ing (un sim′pə thī′zing), *adj.* not sympathizing; unsympathetic.
un·sym·pa·thy (un sim′pə thē), *n.* lack of sympathy.
un·sys·tem·at·ic (un′sis tə mat′ik), *adj.* not systematic; without system; not methodical. —**un′sys·tem·at′i·cal·ly,** *adv.*
un·tack (un tak′), *v.t.* to unfasten (something tacked); loose or detach by removing a tack or tacks.
un·taint·ed (un tān′tid), *adj.* not tainted; free from taint.
un·tak·en (un tā′kən), *adj.* not taken.
un·tal·ent·ed (un tal′ən tid), *adj.* not talented; not gifted; not accomplished or clever.
un·talked-of (un tôkt′ov′, -uv′), *adj.* not talked or spoken about; not made the subject of talk.
un·tam·a·ble or **un·tame·a·ble** (un tā′mə bəl), *adj.* not tamable; tameless: *an untamable tongue.* —**un·tam′a·ble·ness, un·tame′a·ble·ness,** *n.*
un·tame (un tām′), *adj.,* **-tam·er, -tam·est.** not tame; wild.
un·tamed (un tāmd′), *adj.* **1.** not tamed; not domesticated: *The untamed beauty of mountains.* **2.** unsubdued.
un·tan·gle (un tang′gəl), *v.t.,* **-gled, -gling. 1.** to take the tangles out of; disentangle. **2.** to straighten out or clear up (anything confused or perplexing).
un·tanned (un tand′), *adj.* not tanned.
un·tar·nished (un tär′nisht), *adj.* not tarnished; of unimpaired luster; unstained or unsullied.
un·tast·ed (un tās′tid), *adj.* not tasted.
un·taught (un tôt′), *adj.* **1.** not enlightened or trained by teaching; not educated. **2.** known without being taught; learned naturally: *untaught wisdom. That untaught innate philosophy* (Byron).—*v.* the past tense and past participle of **unteach.**
un·taxed (un takst′), *adj.* not taxed; exempt from taxation.
un·teach (un tēch′), *v.t.,* **-taught, -teaching. 1.** to cause (a person) to forget or discard previous knowledge. **2.** to remove from the mind (something known or taught) by different teaching.
un·teach·a·ble (un tē′chə bəl), *adj.* not teachable; indocile. —**un·teach′a·ble·ness,** *n.*
un·tech·ni·cal (un tek′nə kəl), *adj.* not technical.
un·tem·pered (un tem′pərd), *adj.* not tempered: *untempered steel.*
un·ten·a·ble (un ten′ə bəl), *adj.* not tenable; indefensible: *the untenable proposition that London is as hot as Calcutta* (Thackeray). —**un·ten′a·ble·ness,** *n.*
un·ten·ant·ed (un ten′ən tid), *adj.* not tenanted; not occupied by a tenant.
un·ten·der (un ten′dər), *adj.* not tender; unfeeling: *So young, and so untender?* (Shakespeare).
un·tent·ed (un ten′tid), *adj. Archaic.* without a soft plug or drain: *an untented wound.* [< *un-*[1] + *tent*[2] in obsolete sense "to probe" + *-ed*[2]]
un·test·ed (un tes′tid), *adj.* not tested; untried.
un·teth·er (un teᴛʜ′ər), *v.t.* to loose from a tether.
un·thanked (un thangkt′), *adj.* **1.** not thanked; not repaid with acknowledgments. **2.** not received with thankfulness.
un·thank·ful (un thangk′fəl), *adj.* **1.** ungrateful. **2.** not appreciated; thankless: *One of the most unthankful offices in the world* (Oliver Goldsmith). —**un·thank′ful·ly,** *adv.* —**un·thank′ful·ness,** *n.*
un·think (un thingk′), *v.t.,* **-thought, -thinking. 1.** to put out of the mind; remove from thought. **2.** to reverse one's thinking about; alter one's opinion of.

un·think·a·bil·i·ty (un′thing kə bil′ə tē), *n.* the quality or condition of being unthinkable: *Genuine determinism occupies a totally different ground; not the impotence but the unthinkability of free will is what it affirms* (William James).

un·think·a·ble (un thing′kə bəl), *adj.* **1.** not thinkable; inconceivable: *the unthinkable infinitude of time* (George Bernard Shaw). **2.** not to be thought of or considered: *All wars are really unthinkable till you're in the middle of them* (John Buchan). —*n.* something unthinkable: *In the present crisis a delicate course has to be steered between two unthinkables* (New York Times).

un·think·ing (un thing′king), *adj.* **1.** thoughtless; heedless; careless: *a pert unthinking coxcomb* (Tobias Smollett). **2.** characterized by absence of thought: *blind, unthinking anger.* **3.** not having the faculty of thought; unable to think. —**un·think′ing·ly,** *adv.*

un·thought (un thôt′), *adj.* not thought; not conceived or considered. —*v.* the past tense and past participle of **unthink.**

un·thought-of (un thôt′ov′, -uv′), *adj.* not imagined or considered.

un·thread (un thred′), *v.t.* **1.** to take the thread out of: *to unthread a needle.* **2.** to unravel: *Who can . . . unthread the rich texture of Nature and Poetry?* (Charles Lamb). **3.** to find one's way through.

un·thrift (un thrift′), *n.* **1.** lack of thrift. **2.** a thriftless person. —*adj. Archaic.* unthrifty: *this mad, unthrift world* (James Russell Lowell).

un·thrift·i·ly (un thrif′tə lē), *adv.* **1.** in an unthrifty manner; wastefully; lavishly; prodigally. **2.** poorly.

un·thrift·i·ness (un thrif′tē nis), *n.* **1.** the quality or state of being unthrifty; wastefulness; lavishness. **2.** lack of vigor; poor growth or development: *The chicken mite causes unthriftiness in fowls* (Tracy I. Storer).

un·thrift·y (un thrif′tē), *adj.,* **-thrift·i·er, -thrift·i·est. 1.** wasteful; lavish. **2.** not thriving or flourishing; lacking vigor or promise in growth: *a border of unthrifty grass* (Hawthorne). *Moderate infestations cause sheep to be unthrifty and subject to other diseases* (Tracy I. Storer).

un·throne (un thrōn′), *v.t.,* **-throned, -thron·ing.** to depose; dethrone.

un·ti·di·ly (un tī′də lē), *adv.* in an untidy manner.

un·ti·di·ness (un tī′dē nis), *n.* the character or state of being untidy; lack of neatness; slovenliness.

un·ti·dy (un tī′dē), *adj.,* **-di·er, -di·est.** not neat and orderly; in disorder: *an untidy house.* —**Syn.** disorderly, slovenly, littered.

un·tie (un tī′), *v.,* **-tied, -ty·ing.** —*v.t.* **1.** to loosen; unfasten; undo; unbind: *to untie a knot.* **2.** to undo that which tethers; make free; release: *to untie a horse.* **3.** to make clear; explain (a problem). **4.** to clear away (a difficulty); resolve (a dispute). —*v.i.* to become, or be able to be, untied. [Old English *untīgan* < *un-* un-[2] + *tīgan* to tie]

un·tied (un tīd′), *adj.* **1.** not tied; free from any fastening or bond. **2.** *Obsolete.* morally unrestrained; dissolute.

un·til (ən til′, un-), *prep.* **1.** up to the time of: *It was cold from Christmas until April.* **2.** before: *not to rest until victory. She did not leave until morning.*

—*conj.* **1.** up to the time when: *Wait until the sun sets.* **2.** before: *He did not come until the meeting was half over.* **3.** to the degree or place that: *He worked until he was too tired to do more.*

[Middle English *untill* < *un-* up to (see UNTO) + *till*[1]]

➤ See **till**[1] for usage note.

un·till·a·ble (un til′ə bəl), *adj.* that cannot be tilled or cultivated.

un·tilled (un tild′), *adj.* not tilled or cultivated: *Most will come home to partially or totally destroyed villages, to weed-grown, untilled fields* (Time).

un·time·li·ness (un tīm′lē nis), *n.* the character of being untimely; unseasonableness: *the untimeliness of temporal death* (Jeremy Taylor).

un·time·ly (un tīm′lē), *adj.,* **-li·er, -li·est,** *adv.* —*adj.* **1.** at a wrong time or season; unseasonable: *an untimely refusal. Snow in May is untimely.* **2.** too early or too young: *to die at the untimely age of 18.* —*adv.* too early or young; too soon: *His death came untimely at 32.*

un·time·ous (un tī′məs), *adj. Scottish.* untimely; unseasonable.

un·tim·ous (un tī′məs), *adj. Scottish.* untimeous.

un·tinged (un tinjd′), *adj.* **1.** not tinged; not stained; not discolored. **2.** not infected.

un·tipped[1] (un tipt′), *adj.* not furnished with a tip: *an untipped cane. Laboratory studies have shown that most filter-tip brands are as bad as, in many cases actually worse than, old-fashioned untipped cigarettes* (Time).

un·tipped[2] (un tipt′), *adj.* not presented with a gratuity.

un·tired (un tīrd′), *adj.* not tired; not exhausted.

un·tir·ing (un tīr′ing), *adj.* tireless; unwearying: *untiring energy.* —**un·tir′ing·ly,** *adv.* —**Syn.** indefatigable.

un·ti·tled (un tī′təld), *adj.* **1.** having no title; not named: *an untitled piece of music.* **2.** not distinguished by a title: *an untitled nobility* (Emerson). **3.** not of titled rank: *the gentry and other untitled classes.* **4.** lacking lawful right; not entitled (to rule): *an untitled tyrant* (Shakespeare).

un·to (un′tü; *before consonants often* un′tə), *prep. Archaic or Poetic.* to: *The soldier was faithful unto death.* [Middle English *unto* < *un-* up to (< Scandinavian; compare Old Icelandic *und*) + *to* to]

un·told (un tōld′), *adj.* **1.** not told; not revealed: *an untold story, untold heroism.* **2.** too many to be counted or numbered; innumerable; countless: *to spend untold millions. There are untold stars in the sky.* **3.** very great; immense: *untold wealth. Wars do untold harm.*

un·torn (un tôrn′, -tōrn′), *adj.* not torn; not rent or forced asunder.

un·touch·a·bil·i·ty (un′tuch ə bil′ə tē), *n.* **1.** untouchable quality or state. **2.** the condition or character of being an untouchable.

un·touch·a·ble (un tuch′ə bəl), *adj.* **1.** that cannot be touched, especially: **a.** not composed of a material substance; not tangible; immaterial. **b.** out of reach; unattainable. **c.** unique of its kind; unparalleled. **2.** that must not be touched, especially: **a.** that is defiled by the touch of a human hand, foot, etc. **b.** that defiles if touched, especially if eaten, drunk, etc. **3.** suffering from leprosy; leprous.

—*n.* **1.** a Hindu belonging to the lowest caste in India, whose touch supposedly defiles members of higher castes. Strictly, untouchables are beneath caste. Under the constitution of the Republic of India discrimination is forbidden and the term has been replaced in official use by the phrase "Scheduled Caste." **2.** any person divested of caste; outcaste. **3.** any person rejected by his social group; social outcast; pariah. **4.** a thing or idea that is troublesome or risky to deal with: *The President and his aides are preparing for the Herculean task of trying to cut back that political untouchable known as veterans benefits* (Wall Street Journal).

un·touched (un tucht′), *adj.* not touched: *The cat left the milk untouched. The miser was untouched by the poor man's story.*

un·to·ward (un tôrd′, -tōrd′; -tō′ərd), *adj.* **1.** contrary to what is desired; not propitious; unfavorable: *an untoward wind, untoward weather.* **2.** characterized by misfortune, calamity, etc.; unlucky; unfortunate: *an untoward accident.* **3.** difficult to manage, restrain, or control; perverse; stubborn; willful. **4.** *Obsolete.* awkward; clumsy; ungraceful. [< *un-*[1] + *toward*] —**un·to′ward·ly,** *adv.* —**un·to′ward·ness,** *n.* —**Syn. 1.** inconvenient. **3.** intractable, refractory, contrary.

un·trace·a·ble (un trā′sə bəl), *adj.* that cannot be traced or followed.

un·traced (un trāst′), *adj.* **1.** not traced; not followed. **2.** not marked by footsteps. **3.** not marked out.

un·tracked (un trakt′), *adj.* **1.** not tracked; not marked by footsteps; pathless: *an untracked wilderness.* **2.** not followed by tracking.

un·tract·a·ble (un trak′tə bəl), *adj.* **1.** not tractable; intractible. **2.** *Obsolete.* difficult; rough.

un·trained (un trānd′), *adj.* not trained; without discipline or education: *an untrained mind.*

un·tram·meled (un tram′əld), *adj.* not hindered; not restrained; free. —**Syn.** unimpeded.

un·tram·melled (un tram′əld), *adj. Especially British.* untrammeled.

un·trans·fer·a·ble (un′trans fėr′ə bəl), *adj.* that cannot be transferred or passed from one to another.

un·trans·lat·a·ble (un′trans lā′tə bəl), *adj.* **1.** that cannot be translated. **2.** not fit to be translated.

un·trans·lat·a·bly (un′trans lā′tə blē), *adv.* in an untranslatable manner; so as not to be capable of translation.

un·trans·lat·ed (un′trans lā′tid), *adj.* not translated.

un·trav·eled (un trav′əld), *adj.* **1.** not having traveled, especially to distant places; not having gained experience by travel. **2.** not traveled through or over; not frequented by travelers: *an untraveled road.*

un·trav·elled (un trav′əld), *adj. Especially British.* untraveled: *An untravelled Englishman cannot relish all the beauties of Italian pictures* (Joseph Addison).

un·trav·ers·a·ble (un trav′ər sə bəl), *adj.* not traversable.

un·trav·ersed (un trav′ərst, -trə vėrst′), *adj.* not traversed.

un·tread (un tred′), *v.t.,* **-trod, -trod·den** or **-trod, -tread·ing.** to retrace (one's steps).

un·treat·a·ble (un trē′tə bəl), *adj.* that cannot be treated; unsuitable for treatment: *Difficult to detect, the condition used to be untreatable, and usually caused death before age 20* (Time).

un·tried (un trīd′), *adj.* **1.** not tried or proven by use; not tested: *What is conservatism? Is it not adherence to the old and tried, against the new and untried?* (Abraham Lincoln). **2.** without being given, or not yet given, a trial in court: *to condemn a man untried, an untried case.*

un·trim (un trim′), *v.t.,* **-trimmed, -trim·ming.** to deprive of trimming.

un·trimmed (un trimd′), *adj.* **1.** not trimmed; not decorated with trimming. **2.** not clipped or pruned: *his . . . untrimmed hair and beard* (Scott).

un·trod (un trod′), *adj.* untrodden. —*v.* the past tense and a past participle of **untread.**

un·trod·den (un trod′ən), *adj.* not trodden: *an untrodden forest. Some untrodden region of my mind* (Keats). —*v.* a past participle of **untread.**

un·trou·bled (un trub′əld), *adj.* not troubled; undisturbed; tranquil; calm.

un·trou·ble·some (un trub′əl səm), *adj.* not troublesome; giving no trouble: *The progress of industry is gradually affording other modes of investment almost as safe and untroublesome* (John Stuart Mill).

un·true (un trü′), *adj.,* **-tru·er, -tru·est. 1.** not true to the facts; false; incorrect: *She attributes qualities and characteristics to them that are often obviously untrue* (Saturday Review). **2.** not faithful; faithless; disloyal. **3.** not true to a standard or rule; inaccurate; inexact: *Whose hand is feeble or his aim untrue* (William Cowper). [Old English *untrēowe* < *un-* un-[1] + *trēowe* true] —**un·true′ness,** *n.*

un·tru·ly (un trü′lē), *adv.* **1.** incorrectly; falsely. **2.** inexactly; not in a true course.

un·truss (un trus′), *v.t.* **1.** to unfasten; loose from a truss. **2.** to undress.

un·trust·ful (un trust′fəl), *adj.* **1.** not trustworthy. **2.** not trustful.

un·trust·wor·thi·ness (un trust′wėr′ᴛʜē nis), *n.* the character of being untrustworthy.

un·trust·wor·thy (un trust′wėr′ᴛʜē), *adj.* not trustworthy; unreliable: *He was both skillfully smooth and totally untrustworthy* (Newsweek).

un·trust·y (un trus′tē), *adj.,* **-trust·i·er, -trust·i·est.** not trusty; not worthy of confidence; unfaithful.

un·truth (un trüth′), *n.* **1.** lack of truth; falsity. **2.** a lie; falsehood. **3.** *Archaic.* lack of loyalty; faithlessness. [Old English *untrēowth* < *un-* un-[1] + *trēowth* truth]

un·truth·ful (un trüth′fəl), *adj.* not truthful; contrary to the truth; untrue. —**un·truth′ful·ly,** *adv.* —**un·truth′ful·ness,** *n.*

un·tuck (un tuk′), *v.t.* to undo or free from being tucked up, under, or in.

un·tuft·ed (un tuf′tid), *adj.* without tufts or projecting bunches, as of scales or hairs.

un·tun·a·ble (un tü′nə bəl, -tyü′-), *adj.* **1.** that cannot be tuned or brought to the proper pitch. 2. not harmonious; discordant; not musical.

un·tune (un tün′, -tyün′), *v.t.*, **-tuned, -tun·ing.** 1. to make no longer in tune; render inharmonious. 2. to disorder; upset; discompose.

un·tuned (un tünd′, -tyünd′), *adj.* not tuned.

un·turned (un tėrnd′), *adj.* not turned.

un·tu·tored (un tü′tərd, -tyü′-), *adj.* untaught: *the untutored many* (Jeremy Bentham).

un·twine (un twīn′), *v.t., v.i.*, **-twined, twin·ing.** to untwist.

un·twist (un twist′), *v.t.* to undo or loosen (something twisted); unravel: *Not untwist . . . these last strands of man* (Gerard Manley Hopkins). *—v.i.* to become untwisted.

un·urged (un ėrjd′), *adj.* not urged; of one's own accord; unsolicited; voluntary.

un·used (un yüzd′ *for 1 and 2; for 3, before the word "to,"* un yüst′), *adj.* 1. not made use of; not in use: *unused space, an unused room.* 2. never having been used; still new, clean, etc.: *an unused car, an unused plate.* 3. not accustomed: *hands unused to labor.*

un·u·su·al (un yü′zhü əl), *adj.* not usual; beyond the ordinary; not common; rare. **—un·u′su·al·ly,** *adv.* **—un·u′su·al·ness,** *n.* **—Syn.** strange, singular.

un·ut·ter·a·ble (un ut′ər ə bəl), *adj.* 1. that cannot be expressed in words; indescribable; unspeakable: *General nuclear war, apparently, signals unutterable destruction* (Bulletin of Atomic Scientists). 2. that cannot be articulated; unpronounceable.

un·ut·ter·a·bly (un ut′ər ə blē), *adv.* in a way or to a degree that cannot be expressed or described.

un·ut·tered (un ut′ərd), *adj.* not uttered.

un·vac·ci·nat·ed (un vak′sə nā′tid), *adj.* 1. not vaccinated. 2. having never been successfully vaccinated.

un·val·ued (un val′yüd), *adj.* 1. not valued; not appraised. 2. not esteemed or prized. 3. *Obsolete.* that cannot be valued; of inestimable value: *thy unvalued book* (Milton).

un·van·quished (un vang′kwisht), *adj.* not conquered; not overcome.

un·var·ied (un vãr′ēd), *adj.* not varied; not diversified; not changed or altered.

un·var·nished (un vär′nisht), *adj.* 1. not varnished. 2. plain; unadorned: *the unvarnished truth.*

un·var·y·ing (un vãr′ē ing), *adj.* not varying or changing; uniform. **—un·var′y·ing·ly,** *adv.*

un·veil (un vāl′), *v.t.* 1. to remove a veil from. 2. to remove any covering from; uncover: *to unveil a statue. The sun broke through the mist and unveiled the mountains.* 3. to disclose; reveal: *to unveil a secret. —v.i.* to be or become unveiled; reveal oneself.

un·veil·ing (un vā′ling), *n.* 1. the removal of a veil: *While the Moslem woman suffers slavery from excessive veiling and male domination, her Western sister suffers equally from her unveiling* (Time). 2. the act or ceremony of removing the covering from a statue or monument: *So heavy and persistent was the downpour that the unveiling had to be put off for an hour* (Manchester Guardian).

un·vent·ed (un ven′tid), *adj.* not vented; not uttered; not opened for utterance or emission.

un·ven·ti·lat·ed (un ven′tə lā′tid), *adj.* not ventilated.

un·ve·ra·cious (un′və rā′shəs), *adj.* not veracious; untruthful.

un·ve·rac·i·ty (un′və ras′ə tē), *n.* lack of veracity; untruth; falsehood.

un·ver·i·fi·a·ble (un ver′ə fī′ə bəl), *adj.* not verifiable.

un·ver·i·fied (un ver′ə fīd), *adj.* not verified.

un·versed (un vėrst′), *adj.* not versed; unskilled.

un·vexed (un vekst′), *adj.* not vexed; not troubled; not disturbed; not agitated or disquieted: *A country life unvexed with anxious cares* (John Dryden).

un·vi·o·lat·ed (un vī′ə lā′tid), *adj.* 1. not violated; not injured. 2. not broken; not transgressed.

un·vi·ti·at·ed (un vish′ē ā′tid), *adj.* not vitiated; not corrupted; pure.

un·vo·cal (un vō′kəl), *adj.* 1. not vocal. 2. taciturn.

un·voice (un vois′), *v.t.*, **-voiced, -voic·ing.** *Phonetics.* to stop the vibration of the vocal cords in pronouncing (a normally voiced sound); pronounce without voice: *The "z-" sound at the end of "news" is often unvoiced in the compound "newspaper".*

un·voiced (un voist′), *adj.* 1. not spoken; not expressed in words. 2. *Phonetics.* voiceless; devoiced: *"S" in "sit" and "f" in "fit" are unvoiced sounds.*

un·voic·ing (un voi′sing), *n. Phonetics.* the act of stopping the vibration of the vocal cords in pronouncing a normally voiced sound.

un·wak·ened (un wā′kənd), *adj.* not wakened; not roused from sleep or as from sleep: *unwakened passion.*

un·war·i·ly (un wãr′ə lē), *adv.* in an unwary manner; incautiously; unguardedly.

un·war·i·ness (un wãr′ē nis), *n.* the character or state of being unwary.

un·war·like (un wôr′līk′), *adj.* 1. not fit for war; not military. 2. not used to war.

un·warned (un wôrnd′), *adj.* not warned; not cautioned.

un·warped (un wôrpt′), *adj.* 1. not warped. 2. unbiased; impartial.

un·war·rant·a·ble (un wôr′ən tə bəl, -wor′-), *adj.* 1. not justifiable or defensible; utterly improper: *an unwarrantable conjecture.* 2. without legal warrant; not permitted; illegal. **—un·war′rant·a·ble·ness,** *n.*

un·war·rant·a·bly (un wôr′ən tə blē, -wor′-), *adv.* in an unwarrantable manner; in a manner that cannot be justified.

un·war·rant·ed (un wôr′ən tid, -wor′-), *adj.* 1. not warranted; not assured or certain; not guaranteed, as to fulfillment, reliability, quality, etc. 2. not authorized or justified: *unwarranted interference.* **—un·war′rant·ed·ly,** *adv.*

un·war·y (un wãr′ē), *adj.*, **-war·i·er, -war·i·est.** not cautious; not careful; unguarded. **—Syn.** careless, indiscreet.

un·washed (un wosht′, -wôsht′), *adj.* 1. not washed; not cleansed by water. 2. not washed by waves or flowing water.
—n. **the unwashed** or **the great unwashed,** the lower classes of the people; the rabble: *Gentlemen, there can be but little doubt that your ancestors were the great unwashed* (Thackeray).

un·wast·ed (un wās′tid), *adj.* 1. not wasted or lost by extravagance; not lavished away; not dissipated. 2. not consumed or diminished by time, violence, or other means. 3. not devastated; not laid waste. 4. not emaciated, as by illness.

un·watch·ful (un woch′fəl, -wôch′-), *adj.* not vigilant.

un·wa·tered (un wôt′ərd, -wot′-), *adj.* 1. freed from water; drained, as a mine. 2. not watered; undiluted; unmoistened. 3. not supplied with water; not given water to drink.

un·wa·ver·ing (un wā′vər ing), *adj.* not wavering; steadfast; firm: *an unwavering line of conduct.* **—un·wa′ver·ing·ly,** *adv.*

un·weak·ened (un wē′kənd), *adj.* not weakened; not enfeebled.

un·weaned (un wēnd′), *adj.* 1. not weaned. 2. not withdrawn or disengaged.

un·wea·ried (un wir′ēd), *adj.* 1. not weary; not tired. 2. never growing weary; indefatigable; tireless.

un·wea·ry (un wir′ē), *adj.*, **-ri·er, -ri·est,** *v.*, **-ried, -ry·ing.** *—adj.* not weary. *—v.t.* to relieve of weariness; refresh after fatigue.

un·wea·ry·ing (un wir′ē ing), *adj.* not wearying; not growing weary or tired; untiring: *unwearying efforts.* **—un·wea′ry·ing·ly,** *adv.*

un·weave (un wēv′), *v.t.*, **-wove, -wo·ven, -weav·ing.** to undo, take apart, or separate (something woven); ravel.

un·webbed (un webd′), *adj.* 1. not webbed. 2. not web-footed.

un·wed (un wed′), *adj.* unmarried.

un·wed·ded (un wed′id), *adj.* not wedded; unmarried.

un·weed·ed (un wē′did), *adj.* not weeded; not cleared of weeds.

un·weighed (un wād′), *adj.* 1. not weighed; not having the weight ascertained. 2. not considered and examined; not pondered.

un·wel·come (un wel′kəm), *adj.* not welcome; not gladly received: *an unwelcome guest.* **—un·wel′come·ly,** *adv.* **—un·wel′come·ness,** *n.*

un·well (un wel′), *adj.* ailing; ill; sick.

un·wept (un wept′), *adj.* 1. not wept for; not mourned: *unwept, unhonour'd and unsung* (Scott). 2. not shed: *unwept tears.*

un·whipped (un hwipt′), *adj.* not whipped; not punished.

un·whole·some (un hōl′səm), *adj.* 1. not wholesome, especially: **a.** not conducive to or promoting bodily health, growth, etc.; not physically wholesome; unhealthful: *unwholesome food, a damp, unwholesome climate.* **b.** not conducive to or promoting health of mind or spirit; not morally wholesome: *unwholesome literature. Boys are capital fellows . . . among their mates, but they are unwholesome companions for grown people* (Charles Lamb). 2. not in good health; unhealthy. **—un·whole′some·ly,** *adv.* **—un·whole′some·ness,** *n.*

un·wield·i·ly (un wēl′də lē), *adv.* in an unwieldy manner; cumbrously.

un·wield·i·ness (un wēl′dē nis), *n.* the state of being unwieldy.

un·wield·y (un wēl′dē), *adj.* 1. not easily handled or managed, because of size, shape, or weight; bulky or clumsy: *an unwieldy weapon. The armor worn by knights seems unwieldy to us today.* 2. not graceful; clumsy; awkward: *a fat, unwieldy man.* **—Syn.** 1. unmanageable, cumbersome.

un·willed (un wild′), *adj.* not intended; involuntary; unintentional.

un·will·ing (un wil′ing), *adj.* 1. not willing or ready. 2. not freely or willingly granted or done: *an unwilling acceptance of necessity. The unwilling admiration of his enemies* (Macaulay). **—un·will′ing·ly,** *adv.* **—un·will′ing·ness,** *n.* **—Syn. 1, 2.** reluctant, averse, loath.

un·wind (un wīnd′), *v.*, **-wound, -wind·ing.** *—v.t.* 1. to wind off or uncoil; take from a spool, ball, etc. 2. to disentangle. *—v.i.* 1. to become unwound. 2. to relax: *To unwind from his work, Dykstra likes to raise flowers . . . in the garden of his Georgian colonial home* (Time). [Old English *unwindan* unwrap (clothes) < *un-* un-[2] + *windan* to wind]

un·wink·ing (un wing′king), *adj.* not winking; not shutting the eyes; not ceasing to wake or watch.

un·wis·dom (un wiz′dəm), *n.* absence of wisdom; foolishness; stupidity: *It appears that one officer present knew of the unwisdom of the course adopted, but he was so junior that he did not dare to tell his superiors about it* (Norbert Wiener).

un·wise (un wīz′), *adj.*, **-wis·er, -wis·est.** not wise; not showing good judgment; foolish: *In this climate, delay was unwise* (Graham Greene). [Old English *unwīs* < *un-* un-[1] + *wīs* wise] **—un·wise′ly,** *adv.* **—Syn.** imprudent, indiscreet.

un·wish (un wish′), *v.t.* 1. to take back or cancel (a wish). 2. to make or seek to make not existent by wishing.

un·wished (un wisht′), *adj.* not wished; undesired; unwelcome.

un·wished-for (un wisht′fôr′), *adj.* unwished.

un·with·ered (un wiᴛʜ′ərd), *adj.* not withered or faded.

un·with·er·ing (un wiᴛʜ′ər ing), *adj.* not liable to wither or fade.

un·wit·nessed (un wit′nist), *adj.* not witnessed; not attested by witnesses; wanting testimony.

un·wit·ting (un wit′ing), *adj.* 1. not knowing; unaware; unconscious: *to be unwitting of danger.* 2. unintentional: *an unwitting insult.*

un·wit·ting·ly (un wit′ing lē), *adv.* not knowingly; unconsciously; not intentionally.

un·wom·an·li·ness (un wům′ən lē nis), *n.* unwomanly character or state.

un·wom·an·ly (un wům′ən lē), *adj.* not womanly; unbecoming in a woman; unfeminine: a *woman clad in unwomanly rags* (Thomas Hood).

un·wont·ed (un wun′tid, -wōn′-), *adj.* 1. not customary; not usual: *an unwonted task, unwonted anger. The unwonted jollity that brightened the faces of the people* (Hawthorne). 2. not accustomed; not used: *Then Juno . . . from his unwonted hand received the goblet* (William Cowper). **—un·wont′ed·ly,** *adv.* **—un·wont′ed·ness,** *n.*

un·wooed (un wüd′), *adj.* not wooed.

un·work·a·bil·i·ty (un′wėr kə bil′ə tē), *n.* the quality or condition of being unworkable: *It may have taken a disaster to prove the unworkability of the scheme* (Wall Street Journal).

un·work·a·ble (un wėr′kə bəl), *adj.* 1. that cannot be worked. 2. unmanageable; impracticable, as a scheme.

un·worked (un wėrkt′), *adj.* not worked; not developed or exploited, as a field of operations.

un·work·ing (un wėr′king), *adj.* not working; doing no work.

un·work·man·like (un wėrk′mən līk′), *adj.* not workmanlike; not like or befitting a workman.

un·world·li·ness (un wėrld′lē nis), *n.* the state of being unworldly.

un·world·ly (un wėrld′lē), *adj.* **1.** not caring much for the things of this world, such as money, pleasure, and power: *a gentle, unworldly clergyman.* **2.** belonging to or deriving from a realm above or outside that of mortal life; spiritual; supernatural.

un·worn (un wôrn′, -wōrn′), *adj.* **1.** not worn. **2.** not impaired by wear.

un·wor·shiped or **un·wor·shipped** (un wėr′shipt), *adj.* not worshiped; not adored.

un·wor·thi·ly (un wėr′ᴛʜə lē), *adv.* **1.** in a way that is not worthy or honorable; shamefully. **2.** not according to one's merits.

un·wor·thi·ness (un wėr′ᴛʜē nis), *n.* the condition or character of being unworthy.

un·wor·thy (un wėr′ᴛʜē), *adj.*, **-thi·er, -thi·est,** *n., pl.* **-thies.** —*adj.* **1.** not worthy; not deserving: *Such a silly story is unworthy of belief.* **2.** not befitting or becoming; below the proper level or standard: *a gift not unworthy of a king.* **3.** deserving of contempt; base; shameful; dishonorable: *unworthy conduct.* **4.** lacking value or merit; worthless.
—*n.* an unworthy person: *The worthies of England being your subject, you have mingled many unworthies among them* (Thomas Fuller).
—**Syn.** *adj.* **3.** ignoble, discreditable.

un·wound (un wound′), *v.* the past tense and past participle of **unwind.**

un·wound·ed (un wün′did), *adj.* not wounded.

un·wove (un wōv′), *v.* the past tense of **unweave.**

un·wo·ven (un wō′vən), *v.* the past participle of **unweave.**

un·wrap (un rap′), *v.,* **-wrapped, -wrap·ping.** —*v.t.* to remove the wrapping or wrappings from; open. —*v.i.* to become opened.

un·wreathe (un rēᴛʜ′), *v.t.,* **-wreathed, -wreath·ing.** to bring out of a wreathed condition; untwist; untwine.

un·wrin·kle (un ring′kəl), *v.,* **-kled, -kling.** —*v.t.* to smooth the wrinkles from. —*v.i.* to become smooth.

un·writ·a·ble (un rīt′ə bəl), *adj.* that cannot be written; not suitable or fit for writing: *They insist that . . . the nineteenth-century novel . . . is impossible, over and done with, certainly unwritable, and maybe unreadable* (New Yorker).

un·writ·ten (un rit′ən), *adj.* **1.** not committed to writing; oral; verbal: *an unwritten order.* **2.** not yet written. **3.** understood or customary, but not actually expressed in writing: *the unwritten code of a gentleman.* **4.** not written on; blank.

unwritten law, 1. law that is based on custom or on decisions of judges, rather than on written commands, decrees, statutes, etc.; (English) common law. **2.** the principle that a person who commits certain crimes, especially those which avenge personal or family honor, is entitled to lenient treatment.

un·wrought (un rôt′), *adj.* not wrought; not worked or elaborated into a finished product.

un·wrung (un rung′), *adj.* not pinched; not galled.

un·yield·ing (un yēl′ding), *adj.* not yielding; not giving way; firm; obstinate: *Such is the unyielding nature of his reasoning* (Manchester Guardian). —**un·yield′ing·ly,** *adv.* —**un·yield′ing·ness,** *n.*

un·yoke (un yōk′), *v.,* **-yoked, -yok·ing.** —*v.t.* **1.** to free from a yoke: *to unyoke oxen.* **2.** to make separate; disjoin; disconnect. —*v.i.* to remove a yoke.

un·zeal·ous (un zel′əs), *adj.* not zealous; destitute of fervor, ardor, or zeal.

un·zip (un zip′), *v.t., v.i.,* **-zipped, -zip·ping.** to open or unfasten a zipper or something held by a zipper: *He squatted on his tiny legs to unzip his overshoes* (Atlantic). *When unzipped, the case front drops open and makes the binoculars available for immediate use* (Science News Letter).

U. of S. Afr., (formerly) Union of South Africa.

uo·mo u·ni·ver·sa·le (wō′mō ü′nē ver sä′lā), *Italian.* universal man: *The uomo universale, the man who is omnicompetent, will always demand to be omnipotent* (Sunday Times).

up (up), *adv., prep., adj., n., v.,* **upped, up·ping.** —*adv.* **1.** from a lower to a height place or condition; to, toward, or near her top: *The bird flew up.* **2.** in a higher place or condition; on or at a higher level: *He stayed up in the mountains several days.* **3.** from a smaller to a larger amount: *Prices have gone up.* **4.** to or at any point, place, or condition that is considered higher: *He lives up north.* **5.** above the horizon: *The sun is up.* **6.** in or into an erect position: *Stand up.* **7.** out of bed: *to get up in the morning.* **8.** thoroughly; completely; entirely: *The house burned up.* **9.** at an end; over: *His time is up now.* **10.** in or into being or action: *Don't stir up trouble.* **11.** together: *Add these up.* **12.** to or in an even position; not behind: *catch up in a race, keep up with the times.* **13.** in or into view, notice, or consideration: *bring up a new topic.* **14.** in or into a state of tightness, etc.: *Shut him up in his cage.* **15.** into safekeeping, storage, etc.; aside; by: *store up supplies.* **16.** (in baseball) at bat. **17.** (in tennis, etc.) apiece; for each one.
—*prep.* **1.** to or at a higher place on or in: *The cat ran up the tree.* **2.** to, toward, or near the top of: *They climbed up a hill.* **3.** along; through: *She walked up the street.* **4.** toward or in the inner or upper part of: *We sailed up the river. He lives up state.*
up and down, here and there; at various points; in many or different places throughout an area, etc.: *There are many fine examples of reinforced concrete storage bunkers up and down the country* (London Times).
—*adj.* **1.** advanced; forward. **2.** moving upward; directed upward: *an up trend.* **3.** above the ground: *The wheat is up.* **4.** out of bed. **5.** to or in an even position; not behind. **6.** near; close. **7.** with much knowledge or skill. **8.** (in baseball) at bat. **9.** ahead of an opponent by a certain number: *We are three games up.*
up against, *Informal.* facing as a thing to be dealt with: *First, we are up against a dynamic opponent whose strident anti-Americanism will not soon die away* (New Yorker).
up to, a. doing; about to do: *This may be true of Cage's trick, for it loses its point once we know what he is up to* (New Yorker). **b.** equal to; capable of doing: *up to a task.* **c.** plotting; scheming: *What are you up to?* **d.** before (a person) as a duty or task to be done: *Mr. Kennedy hasn't yet shown public concern about the dispute, but ultimately it may be up to him to determine the Government's policy* (Wall Street Journal).
up and doing, busy; active: *If the Labor party's supporters had been up and doing, the party's losses would not have been so great* (New York Times).
—*n.* **1.** an upward movement, course, or slope. **2.** a piece of good luck.
on the up and up, a. *Informal.* increasing; rising; improving: *Attendances and sales at recent exhibitions of the Royal Academy have been on the up and up* (London Times). **b.** *Slang.* honest; legitimate: *"All my books are open and on the up and up," he declared* (New York Times).
—*v.t.* to put up. —*v.i.* to get up.
[Old English *ūpp* and *uppe*]

up-, *prefix.* up, as in *upland, upkeep, uphold, upstart, upbeat, uplifted, upstanding, uprising.* [< Old English *ūp-*. Related to ᴜᴘ.]

up., upper.

u.p., under proof.

UP (no periods) or **U.P.,** (formerly) United Press. Now, **UPI** (no periods).

U.P., Union Pacific Railroad.

up·an·chor (up′ang′kər), *v.i.* to weigh or heave up the anchor: *Once the cargo is on board the captain will up-anchor* (New York Times).

up-and-com·er (up′ən kum′ər), *n.* an up-and-coming person or thing: *The very best of the Beatles' music was an expression of sheer delight at being a tightly-knit group of attractive young up-and-comers* (Sunday Times).

up-and-com·ing (up′ən kum′ing), *adj. U.S.* **1.** on the way to prominence or success; active; alert; enterprising: *a small but up-and-coming college, an up-and-coming singer or politician. One reason up-and-coming riders are scarce is that the big stables aren't trying to develop them any more* (New Yorker). **2.** gaining or rising in importance: *These three aluminum applications are among the more unusual of the jobs lately undertaken by this up-and-coming metal* (Wall Street Journal).

up-and-down (up′ən doun′), *adj.* **1. a.** directed, occurring, or taking place, alternately upward and downward: *The flapping of an insect's wings is no mere up-and-down motion* (Scientific American). **b.** alternately rising and falling; presenting variations comparable to movement up and down: *The upsurge in farmer benefits will be temporary . . . since an up-and-down trend appears every time the act is extended to a new group* (Wall Street Journal). **2.** perpendicular; straight up; erect: *Still another group involves knit cotton in up-and-down stripes of oyster gray and green-gray* (New Yorker).

U·pan·i·shad (ü pan′ə shad), *n.* any of a group of ancient Sanskrit commentaries, including especially those of the Vedanta. [< Sanskrit *upanishad*]

u·pas (yü′pəs), *n.* **1.** a large, tropical Asian tree of the mulberry family, whose poisonous milky sap is used in making a poison for arrows. **2.** the sap itself. **3.** a climbing plant of Java, a variety of strychnos, whose poisonous sap is also used in making a poison for arrows. **4.** its sap. [< Malay *upas* poison]

Branch of Upas (def. 1)

up·bear (up bãr′), *v.t.,* **-bore, -borne, -bear·ing.** to bear up; raise aloft; support; sustain: *When other actors faltered . . . Julie upbore them* (Time). —**up·bear′er,** *n.*

up·beat (up′bēt′), *n.* **1.** *Music.* the beat of a bar at which the hand is raised; an unaccented beat: *[He] began with the upbeat, an open-string quarter-note G, and I recognized the dearly familiar beginning of Opus 18, No. 4* (New Yorker). **2.** an upswing; upturn; revival: *The economy lags behind last autumn's boom—but it's on the upbeat* (Wall Street Journal).
—*adj.* **1.** upward; rising: *How long will the current upbeat cycle in farm equipment continue?* (Wall Street Journal). *The stock market entered 1958 in an upbeat mood* (Time). **2.** *Informal.* hopeful; optimistic; buoyant: *Each of these [stories] seemed to have everything: dramatic conflict, human interest, and an "upbeat" ending* (Leo Rosten).

up·bind (up bīnd′), *v.t.,* **-bound, -bind·ing.** to bind up.

up·blaze (up blāz′), *v.i.,* **-blazed, -blaz·ing.** to blaze up; shoot up, as a flame.

up·blown (up blōn′), *adj.* blown up; inflated; puffed up.

up·bore (up bôr′, -bōr′), *v.* the past tense of **upbear.**

up·borne (up bôrn′, -bōrn′), *adj.* borne up; raised aloft; supported. —*v.* the past participle of **upbear.**

up·bound[1] (up′bound′), *adj., adv.* upward bound; in an upward direction: *The existing 21-foot depth of the upbound channel bars the way of the largest ocean ships into Lake Huron, Lake Michigan, and Lake Superior* (Atlantic).

up·bound[2] (up bound′), *v.* the past tense and past participle of **upbind.**

up-bow (up′bō′), *n.* a stroke toward the handle or lower end of the bow in playing a violin, cello, or the like.

up·braid (up brād′), *v.t.* to find fault with; censure; reprove: *to upbraid a person for his errors. The captain upbraided his men for falling asleep.* [Old English *ūpbregdan* reproach (with) < *ūp-* up- + *bregdan* to weave, braid] —**up·braid′er,** *n.* —**Syn.** reproach. See **scold.**

up·braid·ing (up brā′ding), *n.* a severe reproof; scolding. —*adj.* full of reproach; reproving. —**up·braid′ing·ly,** *adv.*

up·brake (up brāk′), *v. Archaic.* a past tense of **upbreak.**

up·break (up brāk′), *v.,* **-broke** or (*Archaic*) **-brake, -bro·ken** or (*Archaic*) **-broke, -break·ing,** *n.* —*v.i.* to break or force a way upward; come to the surface; appear. —*n.* a breaking or bursting up; an upburst.

up·breathe (up brēᴛʜ′), *v.t.,* **-breathed, -breath·ing.** *Obsolete.* to breathe up or out; exhale.

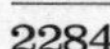

up·bred (up bred′), *v.* the past tense and past participle of **upbreed.**

up·breed (up′brēd′), *v.t.*, **-bred, -breed·ing.** to improve the quality of by mating with superior strains or breeds: *The technique of artificial insemination helps a farmer with poor herds to upbreed his herd only by slow stages* (Time).

up·bring·ing (up′bring′ing), *n.* care and training given to a child while growing up; bringing up; rearing: *to devote care to the upbringing of one's children.*

up·broke (up brōk′), *v.* **1.** a past tense of **upbreak. 2.** *Archaic.* a past participle of **upbreak.**

up·bro·ken (up brō′kən), *v.* a past participle of **upbreak.**

up·build (up bild′), *v.t.*, **-built, -build·ing.** to build up. —**up·build′er,** *n.*

up·built (up bilt′), *v.* the past tense and past participle of **upbuild.**

up·burst (up′bėrst′), *n.* a burst upward; an uprush.

up·cast (up′kast′, -käst′), *adj.* turned or directed upward.
—*n.* **1.** a casting or being cast upward. **2.** something that is cast or thrown up, as in digging a trench, pit, etc. **3.** (in mining) the shaft by which the ventilating air of a mine is returned to the surface.

up·caught (up kôt′, -kot′), *adj.* caught or seized up.

up·chuck (up′chuk′), *v.t., v.i. Informal.* to vomit: *I've painted men and women, drunk and sober, children who upchucked over their best dresses at the sight of me* (Harper's).

up·climb (up klīm′), *v.t., v.i.*, **-climbed** or (*Archaic*) **-clomb, -climb·ing.** to climb up.

up·clomb (up klōm′), *v. Archaic.* a past tense and past participle of **upclimb.**

up·coil (up koil′), *v.t., v.i.* to coil.

up·com·ing (up′kum′ing), *adj.* forthcoming; approaching; impending: *Every upcoming theater season looks exciting on paper; only a few have ever lived up to the great expectations which they arouse* (Newsweek).

up·coun·try (up′kun′trē), *n., pl.* **-tries,** *adv., adj.* —*n.* the interior of a country: *The upcountry is sparsely settled.* —*adv.* toward, in, or into such a section or region: *to go hunting upcountry.* —*adj.* that is in such a section or region; interior: *an upcountry village.*

up·curl (up kėrl′), *v.t., v.i.* to curl up: *Here are Thumbelina's shoes ... with toes upcurled like the roofs of pagodas* (Punch).

up·cur·rent (up′kėr′ənt), *n.* a rising current of air; updraft: *The wind was producing a strong upcurrent as it hit this slope, and a few of the larger birds were taking advantage of it to do some soaring* (Manchester Guardian).

up·curve (up′kėrv′), *n.* an upward curve; upswing: *He's on the upcurve of his political fortunes* (Time).

up·curved (up′kėrvd′), *adj.* curved upward; recurved.

up·date (*v.* up dāt′; *n.* up′dāt′), *v.*, **-dat·ed, -dat·ing,** *n.* —*v.t.* to bring up to or cause to be in accordance with the current date or other (specified) date; make no longer or relatively less out of date: *Though their curriculum is continuously updated, many cadets ... would like to see things tougher* (Harper's). —*n.* a piece of information, instruction, etc., that modifies previous data used in the operation of a computer, spacecraft, etc.; any current or updated information.

up·do (up′dü′), *n.* a hairdo in which the hair is swept upwards and piled on top of the head.

up·draft (up′draft′, -dräft′), *n.* an upward movement of air, wind, gas, etc.: *He parachuted from a plane at 2,500 feet over Alabama, but a thunder storm updraft lifted him to 3,000 feet* (Wall Street Journal).

updraft carburetor, a carburetor below the intake manifold in a motor vehicle.

up·draught (up′draft′, -dräft′), *n. Especially British.* updraft.

up·drawn (up drôn′), *adj.* drawn up.

up·end (up end′), *v.t., v.i.* to set on end; stand on end: *If you upend the box it will take less space.*

up·flare (up′flãr′), *n.* an upward flare.

up·flow (up′flō′), *v.i.* to flow up. —*n.* **1.** an upward flow. **2.** something that flows up.

up·fold (up fōld′), *v.t.* to fold up; fold together.

up·furled (up fėrld′), *adj.* furled or rolled up; upfolded.

up·gath·er (up gaᴛʜ′ər), *v.t.* to gather up or together; contract.

up·go·ing (up′gō′ing), *adj.* going up; moving upward.

up·grade (up′grād′), *n., adv., adj., v.*, **-grad·ed, -grad·ing.** —*n.* **1.** an upward slope or incline. **2.** an increasing in strength, power, value, etc.; improvement.
—*adv., adj.* upward.
—*v.t.* **1.** to raise the status, rating, etc., of; raise to a higher position with a higher salary: *to upgrade a job, to upgrade an employee.* **2.** to sell (a product of lesser worth) as a substitute for a product of greater worth, charging the higher price.

up·grew (up grü′), *v.* the past tense of **upgrow.**

up·grow (up grō′), *v.i.*, **-grew, -grown, -grow·ing.** to grow up.

up·grown (up grōn′), *v.* the past participle of **upgrow.**

up·growth (up′grōth′), *n.* **1.** the process of growing up; development: *To be ashamed with ... noble shame is the very germ and first upgrowth of all virtue* (Charles Kingsley). **2.** something that has grown or is growing up.

up·gush (up gush′), *v.i.* to gush up. —*n.* an upward gush.

up·heap (up hēp′), *v.t.* to pile or heap up; accumulate.

up·heav·al (up hē′vəl), *n.* **1. a.** a heaving up. **b.** a being heaved up. **2.** a sudden or violent agitation in a society; social turmoil: *with post-war social upheaval at its height* (Manchester Guardian). *Tension stayed high in a country torn by a full year of upheaval* (Newsweek). **3.** *Geology.* **a.** a raising above the original level, especially by rapid earth movements. **b.** a being raised above the original level.

up·heave (up hēv′), *v.*, **-heaved** or **-hove, -heav·ing.** —*v.t.* to heave up; lift up; raise: *land ... upheaved by violent volcanic forces* (H. G. Wells). —*v.i.* to rise.

up·held (up held′), *v.* the past tense and past participle of **uphold.**

up·hill (*adj., n.* up′hil′; *adv.* up′hil′), *adj.* **1.** up the slope of a hill; upward: *It is an uphill path all the way.* **2.** situated on high ground; elevated: *an uphill pasture.* **3.** difficult: *an uphill fight.*
—*n.* an upward slope; ascent.
—*adv.* upward: *to go a mile uphill.*

uphill orbit, the orbit of a rocket, satellite, etc., in which it must pull against the sun's gravitational force.

up·hold (up hōld′), *v.t.*, **-held, -hold·ing. 1.** to agree with and give support to; approve and encourage; sustain against opposition or criticism: *The principal upheld the teacher's decision.* **2.** to hold up; keep from falling; support: *Walls uphold the roof.* **3.** to sustain on appeal; approve; confirm: *The higher court upheld the decision of a lower court.* —**up·hold′er,** *n.* —**Syn. 1.** See **support.**

up·hol·ster (up hōl′stər), *v.t.* **1.** to provide (furniture) with coverings, cushions, springs, stuffing, etc. **2.** to furnish (a room) with curtains, rugs, etc. [American English; back formation < *upholsterer*]

up·hol·ster·er (up hōl′stər ər), *n.* a person whose business is to cover furniture and provide it with cushions, springs, stuffing, etc., and sometimes also to furnish and put in place curtains, rugs, etc. [alteration of earlier *upholdster* tradesman < *uphold* + *-ster*]

upholsterer bee, any of various bees which cut small, regularly-shaped pieces of leaves or flower petals to use as a lining for their cells.

up·hol·ster·y (up hōl′stər ē, -hōl′strē), *n., pl.* **-ster·ies. 1.** the fittings or decorations supplied by an upholsterer, especially coverings, cushions, springs, stuffing, etc., for furniture. **2.** the act or occupation of upholstering.

up·hove (up hōv′), *v.* a past tense and past participle of **upheave.**

u·phroe (yü′frō, -vrō), *n. Nautical.* euphroe.

UPI (no periods) or **U.P.I.,** United Press-International (an independent news-gathering agency that distributes news and feature stories to its subscribers).

up·jew·el·ing (up′jü′ə ling), *n.* the addition of jewel bearings to imported watch movements brought in with jewels missing under lower customs duties.

up·keep (up′kēp′), *n.* **1.** maintenance: *the upkeep of a house.* **2.** the expense of maintenance; cost of operation and repair: *The upkeep of a big car is high.* **3.** a being kept up or in good repair, working order, etc.

up·land (up′lənd, -land′), *n.* **1.** elevated or hilly ground; high land. **2.** *Archaic.* upcountry.
uplands, a hilly or mountainous region or section: *the uplands of the American West.*
—*adj.* of high land; living, growing, or situated on high land: *upland vegetation.*

upland cotton, a type of cotton having a short staple, much grown in the United States.

up·land·er (up′lən dər, -lan′-), *n.* **1.** an inhabitant of the uplands. **2.** the upland plover.

upland plover, a large American sandpiper frequenting upland fields, pastures, etc.: *The upland plover breeds from Alaska to Montana and Maine* (George E. Hudson).

up·lands (up′ləndz, -landz′), *n.pl.* See under **upland,** *n.*

up·lift (*v.* up lift′; *n.* up′lift′), *v.t.* **1.** to exalt emotionally or spiritually: *to uplift the mind and soul by prayer.* **2.** to raise socially or economically; improve the status of. **3.** to raise morally or intellectually; improve the quality of. **4.** to lift or move up; raise: *At thy voice her pining sons uplifted Their prostrate brows* (Shelley).
—*n.* **1.** emotional or spiritual exaltation; moral or intellectual improvement: *Now you look here! The first thing you got to understand is that all this uplift ... and settlement work and recreation is nothing in God's world but the entering wedge for socialism* (Sinclair Lewis). **2.** *Geology.* an upward heaving, especially one which is very slow: *Uplift ... turns sea bottoms into land* (Carroll Lane Fenton). —**up·lift′er,** *n.*

up·lift·ment (up lift′mənt), *n.* uplift.

up·look·ing (up′lu̇k′ing), *adj.* looking up; aspiring.

up·ly·ing (up′lī′ing), *adj.* **1.** elevated. **2.** (of land) upland.

up·man·ship (up′mən ship), *n. Informal.* one-upmanship: *Upmanship is the art of being one up on all the others* (London Times).

up·most (up′mōst), *adj.* uppermost.

up·on (ə pon′, -pôn′), *prep.* on. —*adv. Obsolete.* **1. a.** on the surface. **b.** on one's person. **2.** thereafter; thereupon. [< *up* + *on*]

up·per (up′ər), *adj.* **1.** that is the higher of two, especially: **a.** higher in position, location, etc.: *the upper lip, an upper berth.* **b.** higher in rank, office, etc.; superior: *the upper house of a legislature.* **2.** above the bottom or other particular point or place of reference: *the upper notes of a singer's voice, the upper floors of an office building.* **3.** constituting or denoting a geological stratum or series lying nearer the surface and formed later than others of the (designated) group, type, or class. **4.** (of a geological period) more recent: *Upper Cambrian.* **5.** farther from the sea or nearer to the source: *the upper reaches of a river.* **6.** that covers or clothes a part of the body above the waist, especially the chest or shoulders: *an upper garment.* **7.** *Archaic.* worn over another; outer.
—*n.* **1.** the part of a shoe or boot above the sole. **2.** *Informal.* an upper berth. **3.** *U.S., Archaic.* a cloth gaiter.
on one's uppers, *Informal.* **a.** with the soles of one's shoes worn out: *to walk on one's uppers.* **b.** very shabby or poor: *I'm on my uppers ... I want money* (R. Marsh).
uppers, *U.S.* an upper set of false teeth: *The short upper lip ... makes him look like he doesn't have his uppers in* (Time).

upper air or **atmosphere,** the stratosphere and ionosphere.

upper bound, *Mathematics.* a number which is higher than or equal to a given function.

up·per-brack·et (up′ər brak′it), *adj.* of a higher bracket, rank, or level: *As to income, 10 per cent of the total population is rated upper-bracket* (New York Times).

Upper Carboniferous, *Geology.* the name outside of North America for the Pennsylvanian period of Carboniferous time.

upper case, 1. *Printing.* a frame in which types for capital letters are kept for hand setting. **2.** capital letters. *Abbr.:* u.c.

up·per-case (up′ər kās′), *adj., v.*, **-cased, -cas·ing.** *Printing.* —*adj.* **1.** in capital letters. **2.** (of a letter) capital. **3.** kept in or having to do with the upper case.
—*v.t.* to print in capital letters.

up·per-class (up′ər klas′, -kläs′), *adj.* **1.** of or having to do with a superior class or the upper classes of society. **2.** in colleges, universities, high schools, etc. **a.** of or having to do with the junior and senior classes. **b.** like the junior and senior classes.

upper classes, **1.** the classes of society having high status, comprising the gentry, aristocracy, and (now often) some part or all of the middle class. **2.** (in colleges, high schools, etc.) the junior and senior classes.

up·per·class·man (up′ər klas′mən,-kläs′-), *n., pl.* **-men.** a junior or senior in a college, university, high school, etc.

Upper Cretaceous, the most recent of two divisions of the Cretaceous period, characterized by flooding of great areas of the continents by seawater.

upper crust, **1.** *Informal.* the upper classes: *The St. Louis upper crust had looked down their noses at the fair as mere vulgar show and noise* (Harper's). **2.** the upper layer of pastry on a pie.

up·per-crust (up′ər krust′), *adj. Informal.* of or having to do with the upper classes.

up·per·cut (up′ər kut′), *n., v.,* **-cut, -cut·ting.** *Boxing.* —*n.* a blow with the fist that approaches its target from below; punch that is delivered at a sharp upward angle: *a short uppercut to the jaw, a swinging uppercut to the chin.* —*v.t., v.i.* to strike with or deliver such a blow.

Uppercut delivered by boxer on right

upper hand, advantage that is or is likely to prove decisive; control; mastery.

Upper House, **1.** the United States Senate. **2.** the British House of Lords.

upper house, the branch of a bicameral legislature whose members are less numerous and (usually) less subject to direct control by the voters. [< *Upper House*]

up·per·most (up′ər mōst), *adj.* **1.** highest; topmost: *the uppermost reaches of the Amazon.* **2.** having the most force or influence; most prominent.
—*adv.* **1.** in the highest place. **2.** first: *The safety of her children was uppermost in the mother's mind.*

upper register, *Music.* the upper range of a voice or instrument.

up·pers (up′ərz), *n.pl.* See under **upper,** *n.*

upper stage, a second or later stage of a multistage rocket. —**up′per-stage′,** *adj.*

upper story or **storey,** *Humorous.* the head as the seat of the mind or intellect; brain; wits: *He's not overburthen'd i' th' upper storey* (George Eliot).

upper transit, *Astronomy.* the passage of a heavenly body across the upper part of a celestial meridian.

upper works, *Nautical.* the parts of a ship which are above the surface of the water when it is loaded for a voyage.

up·per·world (up′ər werld′), *n.* the respectable portion of society; overworld: *Modern man lives in the upperworld as well as in the underworld, and sometimes he is a reasonably healthy animal and not an animal in an urban zoo* (Atlantic).

up·piled (up pīld′), *adj.* piled up; upheaped.

up·ping (up′ing), *n.* the nicking of the upper part of the beak of a swan to indicate its ownership, especially (in Great Britain) its ownership by the sovereign. [< *up,* verb + *-ing*[1]]

up·pish (up′ish), *adj.* **1.** *Informal.* somewhat arrogant, self-assertive, or conceited. **2.** *British.* upward: *an uppish stroke of the ball.* [< *up,* adverb + *-ish*] —**up′pish·ly,** *adv* —**up′pish·ness,** *n.*

up·pi·ty (up′ə tē), *adj. U.S. Informal.* uppish: *Where she came from, horsewhips were still widely used on uppity servants* (New Yorker). [American English, probably < *uppi*(sh) + *-ty,* as in *haughty*]

up·raise (up rāz′), *v.t.,* **-raised, -rais·ing.** to raise up; lift.

up·rate (up′rāt′), *v.t.,* **-rat·ed, -rat·ing.** **1.** to increase the rate of: *The investment grants will be uprated by 5 per cent during the next two years* (London Times). **2.** to increase in power, efficiency, etc.; improve: *The uprated Saturn 1 booster . . . has almost 140,000 pounds of added thrust in the first stage alone* (Science News).

up·rear (up rir′), *v.t.* to lift up; raise. —*v.i.* to be lifted up.

up·right (up′rīt′, up rīt′), *adj.* **1.** with the principal axis more or less vertical; standing up straight; erect: *a person upright in a chair, a ladder upright against a house, a glass upright on its base.* **2.** morally good; honest; righteous: *a thoroughly honest and upright man.*
—*adv.* straight up; in a vertical position: *Man walks upright on two feet. Hold yourself upright.*
—*n.* **1.** a vertical or upright position. **2.** something upright; vertical part or piece. **3.** an upright piano. **4.** *U.S.* one of the goal posts in football.
[Old English *upriht*] —**up′right′ly,** *adv.* —**up′right′ness,** *n.*
—**Syn.** *adj.* **1. Upright, erect** mean straight up. **Upright** means standing up straight on a base or in a position that is straight up and down, not slanting: *After the earthquake not a lamp or chair was upright.* **Erect** means held or set upright, not stooping or bent: *At seventy she is still erect.*

upright piano, a rectangular piano having vertical strings behind the keyboard.

up·rise (*v.* up rīz′; *n.* up′rīz′), *v.,* **-rose, -ris·en, -ris·ing,** *n.* —*v.i.* **1.** to rise up; rear. **2.** to slope upward; ascend. **3.** to get up from bed; arise. **4.** to increase in volume, amount, etc. —*n.* a rising up; upward rise.

up·ris·en (up riz′ən), *v.* the past participle of **uprise.**

up·ris·ing (up′rī′zing, up rī′-), *n.* **1.** a revolt; rebellion: *a popular uprising against tyranny.* **2.** a rising up. **3.** an upward slope; ascent.

up·riv·er (up′riv′ər), *adj.* **1.** belonging to or situated farther up, or toward the upper end of, a river: *The upriver jetty on the River Thames at Battersea . . . is a particularly interesting structure* (London Times). **2.** leading or directed toward the source of a river: *It finally became necessary to move most upriver freight by wagon, oxcart or muleback along the droughty river roads* (Atlantic). —*adv.* toward or in the direction of the source of a river: *When salmon go upriver to spawn their stomachs contract and their throats shrink so that they lose all desire to return to their sea feeding grounds* (Manchester Guardian).

up·roar (up′rôr′, -rōr′), *n.* **1.** a loud, confused noise; tumultuous sound; clamor: *to hear a sudden uproar in the next room, the thunderous uproar of a passing train.* **2.** a noisy outbreak of violence; tumult.
in an uproar, in a state of great disturbance, confusion, etc.: *Thus it was at Alcamo, where the streets seemed to be in an uproar till after midnight* (Leigh Hunt).
[< Dutch *oproer,* or Middle Low German *oprōr* insurrection, tumult; spelling influenced by English *roar*]
—**Syn. 1.** See **noise. 2.** commotion.

up·roar·i·ous (up rôr′ē əs, -rōr′-), *adj.* **1.** noisy and disorderly; clamorous: *an uproarious crowd.* **2.** very loud, confused, and unrestrained: *uproarious laughter.* —**up·roar′i·ous·ly,** *adv.* —**up·roar′i·ous·ness,** *n.*

up·roll (up rōl′), *v.t.* to roll up.

up·root (up rüt′, -rüt′), *v.t.* **1.** to tear or pull up by the roots: *The storm uprooted many trees.* **2.** to remove or destroy completely; eradicate: *Their system uprooted individual initiative.* —**up·root′er,** *n.*

up·root·al (up rü′təl, -rüt′əl), *n.* **1.** the act of uprooting. **2.** the state of being uprooted.

up·root·ed·ness (up rü′tid ness, -rüt′id-), *n.* the quality or state of being uprooted: *The chief peculiarity of the adolescent's existence is its . . . phase of transition from childhood to manhood, a phase of uprootedness and drastic change* (Harper's).

up·rose (up rōz′), *v.* the past tense of **uprise.**

up·rouse (up rouz′), *v.t.,* **-roused, -rous·ing.** to rouse up; arouse; awake.

up·rush (up′rush′), *v.i.* to rush upward: *It gets a forward push by leaning its tail fluke against the uprushing water of the wave* (Scientific American). —*n.* an upward rush or flow: *the sizzling uprush of a rocket* (New Yorker).

ups-and-downs (ups′ən dounz′), *n.pl.* **1.** changes in fortune, success, etc.; vicissitudes: *the ups-and-downs of a millionaire and a chauffeur's daughter who find themselves in love* (New Yorker). **2.** alternations in condition, quality, etc.; vagaries; variations: *The cycle of ups-and-downs in film-making will always be with us, for its root is in human restlessness* (Saturday Review).

up·set (*v.* up set′; *n.* up′set′; *adj.* up set′, up′set′), *v.,* **-set, -set·ting,** *n., adj.* —*v.t.* **1.** to tip over; cause to capsize; overturn: *to upset the milk pitcher, to upset a boat.* **2.** to disturb greatly; disorder: *The shock upset her nerves. Rain upset our plans for a picnic.* **3. a.** to overthrow; defeat: *to upset a will, to upset an argument.* **b.** to gain an unexpected victory over (the favorite) in a contest. **4.** to force back the end of (a metal bar, etc.) by hammering or beating, especially when heated. **5.** to shorten (a metal tire, etc.) while resetting. —*v.i.* to be or become upset.
—*n.* **1.** a tipping over; overturn. **2.** a great disturbance; disorder. **3.** an unexpected victory over the favorite in a contest. **4.** a swage or other tool used for upsetting. **5.** a bar or rod end, etc., which is upset.
—*adj.* **1.** tipped over; capsized; overturned: *an upset boat.* **2.** greatly disturbed; disordered: *an upset mind, an upset stomach.*
—**Syn.** *v.t.,* **1.** *v.i.* **Upset, overturn** mean to fall, or cause to fall, over or down. **Upset** implies tipping over from an upright or proper position: *He accidentally kicked the table and upset the vase of flowers.* **Overturn** implies turning over from an upright position to one flat on the ground: *He got up too quickly and overturned his chair.*

upset forging, forging in which a heated bar is shortened or thickened on one end by pressure or hammering. In some processes the bar is rammed into a die to achieve a certain shape.

upset price, the lowest price at which a thing offered for sale, especially at auction, will be sold.

up·set·ta·ble (up set′ə bəl), *adj.* capable of being upset; easily upset: *His calm exterior was upsettable by the slightest annoyance.*

up·set·ter (up set′ər), *n.* a person, thing, or event that upsets: *The volunteer driver of the hackney coach . . . and the involuntary upsetter of the whole party* (Dickens).

up·set·ting (up set′ing), *adj.* greatly disturbing; causing disorder: *It was upsetting to have to wait so long for the bus.* —**up·set′ting·ly,** *adv*

up·shoot (up′shüt′), *n.* **1.** a shooting up; something that shoots up. **2.** (in baseball) a curve which shoots or bends up as it approaches home plate.

up·shot (up′shot′), *n.* **1.** conclusion; outcome; result: *The upshot of the affair was that he resigned.* **2.** the conclusion resulting necessarily from the premises of or a summary of the essential facts involved in an argument.
[< the fact that (originally) it was the last shot in an archery match < *up-* + *shot,* noun] —**Syn. 1.** issue.

up·side (up′sīd′), *n.* the upper side; top part or surface.
upside down, a. with what should be on top at the bottom: *The slice of buttered bread fell upside down on the floor.* **b.** in or into complete disorder: *The room was upside down. She turned the room upside down searching for a letter.*
[alteration of earlier *up so down*]

up·side-down cake (up′sīd′doun′), a cake made of batter poured over fruit, baked, and served bottom up.

up·side·down·ness (up′sīd′doun′nis), *n.* topsy-turviness: *Hofstadter is not original if that means turning accepted views upside down for the sake of the upsidedownness* (Manchester Guardian Weekly).

up·si·lon (yüp′sə lon), *n.* the 20th letter of the Greek alphabet, Υ, υ corresponding to the English U, u, or Y, y. [< Greek (*tò*) *y psīlón* (literally) bare *y* (that is, distinguished from *oi,* which had the same pronunciation)]

up·slope (up′slōp′), *adv.* upward toward the top of a slope.

upslope fog, a fog formed by the cooling of stable moist air as it moves from lower to higher elevations.

up·soar (up sôr′, -sōr′), *v.i.* to soar aloft; mount up.

up·sprang (up sprang′), *v.* a past tense of **upspring.**

up·spring (*v.* up spring′; *n.* up′spring′), *v.,* **-sprang** or **-sprung, -sprung, -spring·ing,** *n.* —*v.i.* **1.** to spring up from the soil or into being. **2.** to leap to one's feet; rise suddenly. —*n.* **1.** an upspringing. **2.** an upward jump; spring into the air.

up·sprung (up sprung′), *v.* a past tense and the past participle of **upspring.**

 PRONUNCIATION KEY: hat, āge, cãre, fär; let, ēqual, tėrm; it, īce; hot, ōpen, ôrder; oil, out; cup, pu̇t, rüle;

up·stage (up′stāj′), *adv., adj., v.,* **-staged, -stag·ing.** —*adv.* away from the footlights; toward or at the back of the stage, which was formerly higher than the front.
—*adj.* **1.** having to do with the back part of the stage. **2.** toward or at the back of the stage. **3.** *Informal.* haughty; aloof; supercilious.
—*v.t.* **1.** to stand upstage of (an actor) and force (him) to turn away from the audience while speaking. **2.** to draw attention away from (an actor) by or as if by doing something upstage or in back of him. **3.** *Informal.* to treat rudely or curtly; snub: *If he [a playgoer] wants to see a hit play on Broadway, he is likely to be insulted by the box-office attendant, scalped by a ticket broker, upstaged by the usher and snarled at by a fireman* (Time).

up·stairs (up′stãrz′), *adv.* **1.** up the stairs: *to run upstairs.* **2.** on an upper floor: *to live upstairs.* **3.** *Informal.* to or in a place or rank of greater authority, higher status, etc. **4.** *Informal.* to or at a high or higher altitude, especially in an aircraft: *to avoid a storm by going upstairs.*
—*adj.* on an upper floor: *an upstairs hall.*
—*n.* the upper story or stories: *to hear a cry from upstairs.*

up·stand (up′stand′), *n. British.* an upstanding thing; an upright structure or part.

up·stand·ing (up stan′ding), *adj.* **1.** standing up; erect: *short, upstanding hair.* **2.** straight and tall; well-grown: *a healthy, upstanding plant. Two upstanding, pleasant children* (W. Somerset Maugham). **3.** honorable: *a fine, upstanding young man.*

up·start (up′stärt′), *n.* **1.** a person who is a newcomer to wealth, power, or importance, especially one who is considered to lack the manners, taste, knowledge, etc., requisite or becoming to his position; parvenu. **2.** an unpleasant, conceited, and self-assertive person. **3.** anything considered to resemble either of these: *a culture compared with which that of the West is a mere upstart.*
—*adj.* **1.** suddenly risen from a humble position to wealth, power, or importance: *He dreaded their upstart ambition* (Edward Gibbon). **2.** conceited; self-assertive.
—*v.i.* to rise suddenly up, out, into view, etc.
—*v.t.* to cause to rise suddenly up, out, into view, etc.

up·state (up′stāt′), *U.S.* —*adj.* of, in, or native to the more inland or northern part of any of certain States, especially New York state.
—*n.* the more inland or northern part of any of certain States, especially New York state.

up·stat·er (up′stā′tər), *n.* a person born in, living in, or from an upstate area.

up·stream (up′strēm′), *adv., adj.* against the current of a stream; up a brook, river, etc.: *to paddle upstream (adv.); an upstream camping site (adj.).*

up·stretched (up′strecht′), *adj.* stretched or extended upward: *The length of a ski should equal the height of the skier, plus an upstretched arm* (Punch).

up·stroke (up′strōk′), *n.* **1.** an upward stroke of a pen, pencil, etc. **2.** a stroke delivered upwards: *the upstroke of a piston.*

up·surge (up′sėrj′), *v.,* **-surged, -surg·ing,** *n.* —*v.i.* to surge up. —*n.* **1.** an uprising: *The upsurge in Asia, the most important political event in the world today, is fundamentally a revolt against hunger and poverty* (Scientific American). **2.** a rising upward; rise; upturn: *Business and consumer credit has provided much of the steam behind this year's economic upsurge* (New York Times).

up·sur·gence (up′sėr′jənts), *n.* upsurge.

up·sweep (*v.* up swēp′; *n.* up′swēp′), *v.,* **-swept, -sweep·ing,** *n.* —*v.t.* to cause to be upswept. —*v.i.* to be upswept. —*n.* an upswept thing, part, or arrangement.

up·swell (up swel′), *v.i.,* **-swelled, -swelled** or **-swol·len, -swell·ing.** to swell up.

up·swept (up′swept′), *adj.* **1.** curving or slanting upward, especially in a smooth or regular line: *a dog with an upswept jaw.* **2.** of or designating a style of woman's coiffure in which the hair is brushed upward to or toward the crown of the head: *Her maple brown hair is worn upswept and is held in place by huge pins* (New Yorker).
—*v.* the past tense and past participle of **upsweep.**

up·swing (*n.* up′swing′; *v.* up swing′), *n., v.,* **-swung, -swing·ing.** —*n.* **1.** an upward swing; movement upward: *the upswing of a golf club before driving.* **2.** a marked improvement; strong advance. —*v.i.* to undergo an upswing.

Upswing (def. 1)

up·swol·len (up swō′lən), *v.* a past participle of **upswell.**

up·swung (up-swung′), *v.* the past tense and past participle of **upswing.**

up·sy-dai·sy (up′sē dā′zē), *interj.* an exclamation made to a child on helping it stand up from a fall or when raising it in the arms.

up·take (up′tāk′), *n.* **1.** a line or flue through which a boiler discharges into the smokestack, funnel, or chimney. **2.** a ventilating shaft for the upward discharge of foul air, fumes, etc. **3.** absorption; ingestion: *Patient research work has been carried out . . . on all aspects of the subject — the effect of diet, of mineral uptake during the period in which the teeth are being formed* (New Scientist). **4.** *Informal.* the act of lifting or raising; taking upwards.
on or **in the uptake,** *Informal.* in understanding and response; in perceptive ability: *In touch with some new notions and ways, he has been quick on the uptake* (J. W. R. Scott).

up·tear (up tãr′), *v.t.,* **-tore, -torn, -tear·ing.** to tear up.

up-tem·po (up′tem′pō), *adj.* of rapid or increasing tempo: *They play ballads, blues and up-tempo numbers* (Saturday Review).

up·throw (up′thrō′), *n.* **1.** *Geology.* an upward dislocation, generally due to faulting; upheaval; uplift. **2.** an upward throw or cast.

up·thrust (*n.* up′thrust′; *v.* up thrust′), *n.* **1.** *Geology.* an upward movement of part of the earth's crust. **2.** an upward thrust.
—*v.t.* to push up, as in an upthrust: *The region as a whole consists of a geological anticline, . . . upthrust by an outer ripple of those same Miocene foldings that formed the Alps and the Himalayas* (New Scientist).

up·tick (up′tik′), *n.* **1.** a price higher than that of the immediately preceding one, paid as the condition of a short sale on a stock exchange. **2.** the sale so made.

up-tight (up′tīt′), *adj. Slang.* characterized by anxiety; tense; keyed-up: *He was a genial, relaxed version of the old up-tight campaigner* (Time).

up·tilt (up tilt′), *v.t.* to tilt up.

up-to-date (up′tə dāt′), *adj.* **1.** extending to the present time; based on or inclusive of the latest facts, data, etc.: *an up-to-date textbook, an up-to-date record.* **2.** having modern equipment, utilizing the latest techniques, etc.; not obsolescent: *an up-to-date store, an up-to-date factory.* **3.** keeping up with the times in style, ideas, etc.; modern. —**up′-to-date′ness,** *n.*

up·tore (up tôr′, -tōr′), *v.* the past tense of **uptear.**

up·torn (up tôrn′, -tōrn′), *v.* the past participle of **uptear.**

up-to-the-min·ute (up′tə ᴛʜə min′it), *adj.* latest; most recent; up-to-date: *up-to-the-minute news, styles, or equipment.*

up·town (*adv.* up′toun′; *adj.* up′toun′), *adv., adj.* to or in the upper part of a town: *to go uptown (adv.); an uptown store (adj.).*

up·trend (up′trend′), *n.* an upward tendency or trend; inclination to rise, become better, etc.

up·turn (*v.* up tėrn′; *n.* up′tėrn′), *v.t., v.i.* **1.** to turn or face up. **2.** to turn or roll over, so as to face down. **3.** *Obsolete.* to overturn. —*n.* an upward turn.

up·turned (up tėrnd′, up′tėrnd), *adj.* **1.** turned or facing up. **2.** turned over; overturned. **3.** turned up at the end.

U.P.U. or **UPU** (no periods), Universal Postal Union (an international organization to improve postal services, affiliated with United Nations).

u·pu·poid (yü′pyə poid), *adj.* **1.** resembling the hoopoe. **2.** belonging to a family of Old-World nonpasserine birds including the hoopoes. **3.** having to do with this family. [< New Latin *Upupoideae* the family name < Latin *upupa* hoopoe]

up·waft·ed (up waf′tid, -wäf′-), *adj.* borne up; carried aloft with a waving or undulatory motion: *a kite upwafted by the breeze.*

up·ward (up′wərd), *adv.* **1.** to or toward a higher place; up: *to fly upward. Jack climbed upward till he reached the apple.* **2.** in the higher or highest position; uppermost: *to store baskets with the bottoms upward.* **3.** to or toward a higher rank, amount, age, etc., *to move upward in life.* **4.** to or into the latter or current part of life; onward in years: *to work from the age of 16 upward. From ten years of age upward she had studied French.* **5.** to or toward the source: *to follow a river upward.* **6.** to or toward the upper or topmost part: *to rot from the base upward.* **7.** above; more: *to demobilize soldiers of 35 and upward, hotel rooms at $10 and upward. Children of five years and upward must pay carfare.*
upward of, more than: *Repairs will cost upward of $100.*
—*adj.* directed or moving toward a higher place; in a higher position: *an upward course* (Shakespeare).
[Old English *upweard*]

up·ward·ly (up′wərd lē), *adv.* in an upward manner or direction; upward.

up·wards (up′wərdz), *adv.* upward.
upwards of, more than; upward of: *Its optimum length worked out to upwards of seventy feet* (Fortune).

up·warp (up′wôrp′), *Geology.* —*v.t., v.i.* to fold or bend in an anticlinal or upward manner. —*n.* an upwarped condition or area.

up·well (up wel′), *v.i.* to well or shoot up.

up·whirl (up hwėrl′), *v.t., v.i.* to whirl upward.

up·wind (up′wind′), *adv., adj.* into the wind; against the wind: *to sail a boat upwind (adv.); the upwind side of the island (adj.).*

up·wreathe (up rēᴛʜ′), *v.i.,* **-wreathed, -wreathed** or (*Archaic*) **-wreath·en, -wreath·ing.** to wreathe upward, or rise with a curling motion, as smoke.

up·wreath·en (up rē′ᴛʜən), *v. Archaic.* a past participle of **upwreathe.**

Ur (no period), (formerly) uranium (chemical element). Now, **U** (no period).

u·ra·cil (yůr′ə sil), *n.* a basic compound, constituent of ribonucleic acids: *RNA is a giant molecule built up of nucleotides containing ribose sugar and any one of four bases: adenine, uracil, guanine or cytosine* (Scientific American). *Formula:* $C_4H_4N_2O_2$ [< *ur*(ea) + *ac*(etic) + *-il,* variant of *-yl*]

u·rae·mi·a (yů rē′mē ə), *n.* uremia.

u·rae·mic (yů rē′mik), *adj.* uremic.

u·rae·us (yů rē′əs), *n.* a stylized representation of the sacred asp of ancient Egypt, used especially in the formal headdress of royal persons as a symbol of sovereignty, typically with the forepart of the asp reared and projecting out from the forehead. [< Latin *ūraeus* < Greek *ouraîos* < *ourá* tail]

Uraeus in headdress of Seti I

U·ral (yůr′əl), *adj.* of or having to do with the Ural Mountains or the Ural River.

U·ral-Al·ta·ic (yůr′əl al tā′ik), *adj.* **1.** of the region including the Ural and Altaic Mountains, the people living there, or their language. **2.** of or having to do with a large group of languages spoken in eastern Europe and northern Asia. —*n.* the Ural-Altaic language group.

U·ra·li·an (yů rā′lē ən), *n.* a language family that includes Finno-Ugric and Samoyed.

U·ral·ic (yů ral′ik), *adj.* of the Ural Mountains, the people living in or near them, or their languages. —*n.* Uralian.

u·ral·ite (yůr′ə līt), *n.* a mineral, pyroxene altered to hornblende. [< German *Uralit* < the *Ural* Mountains + *-it* -ite[1]]

u·ral·it·ic (yůr′ə lit′ik), *adj. Mineralogy.* **1.** having the characters of uralite in a greater or less degree. **2.** containing, or consisting wholly or in part of, uralite.

u·ra·nal·y·sis (yůr′ə nal′ə sis), *n., pl.* **-ses** (-sēz). urinalysis.

U·ra·ni·a (yů rā′nē ə), *n. Greek Mythology.* **1.** the Muse of astronomy. **2.** an epithet of Aphrodite (Venus). [< Latin *ūrania* < Greek *Ouraníā*, (originally) feminine of *ouraniós* heavenly < *ouranós* heaven. Compare URANUS.]

U·ra·ni·an (yů rā′nē ən), *adj.* of or having to do with the planet Uranus.

u·ran·ic[1] (yů ran′ik), *adj. Chemistry.* **1.** of uranium. **2.** containing uranium, especially with a valence of six.

u·ran·ic[2] (yů ran′ik), *adj.* of or having to do with the heavens; celestial; astronomical. [< Late Latin *ūranus* (< Greek *ouranós*) + English *-ic*]

u·ra·nif·er·ous (yůr′ə nif′ər əs), *adj.* containing or yielding uranium.

u·ran·i·nite (yů ran′ə nīt), *n.* a black uranium mineral, occurring as crystals, or in veins, when it is called pitchblende. *Formula:* UO_2 [< *uran*(ium) + *-in* + *-ite*[1]]

u·ra·nite (yůr′ə nīt), *n.* a group of minerals, including autunite and torbernite, composed largely of uranium phosphate. [< German *Uranit* < *Uranus*, the planet, which had been discovered shortly before this group + *-it* -ite[1]]

u·ra·nit·ic (yůr′ə nit′ik), *adj.* **1.** of or having to do with uranite. **2.** containing uranite.

u·ra·ni·um (yů rā′nē əm), *n.* a radioactive metallic chemical element occurring in combination in pitchblende, carnotite, and certain other minerals, and isolated as a heavy, white, lustrous substance. Naturally occurring uranium contains three isotopes of atomic weights 234, 235, and 238. The isotope U-235 can sustain efficient chain reaction and is for this reason used in the atomic bomb; U-238 can form plutonium and is thus used as a source of atomic energy. *Symbol:* U; *at. wt.:* (C^{12}) 238.03 or (O^{16}) 238.07; *at. no.:* 92; *valence:* (chiefly) 4, 6; (also) 2, 3, 5. [< New Latin *uranium* < *Uranus*, the planet + *-ium*, a suffix meaning "element"]

uranium 235, U-235.

uranium 238, U-238.

uranium bomb, an atomic bomb that derives its force from the splitting of uranium atoms.

uranium oxide, any of various oxides of uranium obtained from uranium ores, as a black dioxide of uranium, used in ceramics, pigments, etc., and as a nuclear fuel.

u·ra·nog·ra·pher (yůr′ə nog′rə fər), *n.* a person who practices or studies uranography.

u·ra·no·graph·ic (yůr′ə nə graf′ik), *adj.* of or having to do with uranography.

u·ra·no·graph·i·cal (yůr′ə nə graf′ə kəl), *adj.* uranographic.

u·ra·nog·ra·phist (yůr′ə nog′rə fist), *n.* an expert in uranography.

u·ra·nog·ra·phy (yůr′ə nog′rə fē), *n.* the science of describing and mapping the heavens and the position of the heavenly bodies. Also, **ouranography.** [< Greek *ouranographiā* < *ouranós* the heavens, sky + *gráphein* to draw]

u·ra·no·log·i·cal (yůr′ə nə loj′ə kəl), *adj.* of or having to do with uranology.

u·ra·nol·o·gy (yůr′ə nol′ə jē), *n., pl.* **-gies.** **1.** astronomy. **2.** an astronomical treatise. [< Late Latin *ūranus* the heavens, sky (< Greek *ouranós*) + English *-logy*]

u·ra·nom·e·try (yůr′ə nom′ə trē), *n., pl.* **-tries.** **1.** a map or description of the heavens showing the stars with names, magnitudes, relative positions, etc. **2.** the measurement of stellar distances. [< Late Latin *ūranus* the heavens (< Greek *ouranós*) + English *-metry*]

u·ra·nous (yůr′ə nəs), *adj.* **1.** of uranium. **2.** containing uranium, especially with a valence of four.

U·ra·nus (yůr′ə nəs), *n.* **1.** *Greek Mythology.* the personification of Heaven, the husband or son of Gaea (Earth), the father of the Titans, the Cyclopes, the Furies, etc., and the original ruler of the world. He was eventually overthrown by his son Cronus, the youngest of the Titans, at Gaea's instigation in revenge for Uranus' imprisoning his children in Tartarus. **2.** one of the larger planets in the solar system, seventh in distance from the sun. Its orbit lies between those of Saturn and Neptune and takes 84 years to complete, at a mean distance from the sun of about 1,780,000,000 miles. Its mean diameter is about 31,000 miles. It has five satellites. *Symbol:* ♅ [< Late Latin *Ūranus*, the god < Greek *Ouranós* (literally) the heavens, sky]

u·ra·nyl (yůr′ə nəl), *n.* a bivalent radical, UO_2—, existing in many compounds of uranium, and forming salts with acids. [< *uran*(ium) + *-yl*]

u·ra·nyl·ic (yůr′ə nil′ik), *adj.* **1.** of or having to do with uranyl. **2.** containing uranyl.

u·rase (yůr′ās, -āz), *n.* urease.

u·rate (yůr′āt), *n.* a salt of uric acid. [< French *urate* < *urique* uric + *-ate* -ate[2]]

ur·ban (ėr′bən), *adj.* **1.** that is or has the essential characteristics of a city or town: *an urban community, an urban center.* **2.** of or having to do with a city or town, or cities and towns in general: *urban planning.* **3.** living in a city or cities: *urban population.* **4.** characteristic of cities: *urban life.* **5.** accustomed to or inclined toward cities: *a man still urban after 20 years in the country.* [< Latin *urbānus* < *urbs* city]

urban district, (in England, Wales, and Northern Ireland) a subdivision of a county, often containing several towns or cities, governed by a local council but not having the charter of a borough.

ur·bane (ėr bān′), *adj.* **1.** having the elegance of manner, refinement of taste, or sophisticated polish formerly rare outside of the city; courteous; refined; elegant: *His manners were gentle, affable and urbane* (Washington Irving). **2.** smoothly polite; suave: *an urbane but treacherous scoundrel.* [< Latin *urbānus* (originally) urban. Related to URBAN.] —**ur·bane′ly,** *adv.* —**ur·bane′ness,** *n.*

ur·ban·ise (ėr′bə nīz), *v.t.,* **-ised, -is·ing.** *Especially British.* urbanize.

ur·ban·ism (ėr′bə niz əm), *n.* urban character or life: *a study of urbanism — the purpose and utility of cities, town planning* (New Yorker).

ur·ban·ist (ėr′bə nist), *n.* a city planner.

ur·ban·is·tic (ėr′bə nis′tik), *adj.* of or having to do with urbanists or urbanism. —**ur′ban·is′ti·cal·ly,** *adv.*

ur·ban·ite (ėr′bə nīt), *n.* a dweller in a city: *Suburbanites and urbanites have successfully sought relief from the political monopoly of legislative power long exercised by America's rural minorities* (Atlantic).

ur·ban·i·ty (ėr ban′ə tē), *n., pl.* **-ties.** **1.** the character or quality of being urbane; courtesy; refinement; elegance: *When we think of Athens we think . . . of urbanity and clarity and moderation in all things* (James H. Robinson). **2.** smooth politeness. **3.** civilities; courtesies; amenities: *She smiled and murmured urbanities* (Leonard Merrick). **4.** the character or condition of being urban. [< Latin *urbānitās* < *urbānus;* see URBAN]

ur·ban·i·za·tion (ėr′bə nə zā′shən), *n.* **1.** the process of investing with an urban character. **2.** condition of being urbanized.

ur·ban·ize (ėr′bə nīz), *v.t.,* **-ized, -iz·ing.** to make urban: *to urbanize an area.*

ur·ban·ol·o·gist (ėr′bə nol′ə jist), *n.* a person who studies urban culture, society, architecture, and the other aspects of urban life.

urban renewal, improvement of urban areas by removing slums and rebuilding attractive living or industrial areas.

ur·bi·cul·ture (ėr′bə kul′chər), *n.* the care of cities and city people; urban interests.

ur·bi et or·bi (ėr′bī et ôr′bī), *Latin.* to the city (Rome) and to the world; to mankind (used especially in the publication of papal bulls).

ur·ce·o·late (ėr′sē ə lit, -lāt), *adj.* shaped like a pitcher; swelling out like a pitcher and contracted at the orifice, as a calyx or corolla. [< New Latin *urceolatus* < Latin *urceolus* (diminutive) < *urceus* pitcher]

ur·chin (ėr′chən), *n.* **1.** a small boy. **2.** a mischievous boy. **3.** a poor, ragged child: *ragged urchins . . . peeping through the railings* (John L. Motley). **4.** a sea urchin. See **sea urchin** for picture. **5.** *Archaic.* an elf. **6.** *Archaic or Dialect.* a hedgehog. [Middle English *urchun* hedgehog < Old French *irechon* < Latin *ēricius* < *ēr, ēris;* (the term was applied to persons because of a belief that goblins took the shape of a hedgehog)]

urd (ėrd), *n.* a bean, a variety of the mung bean, largely cultivated throughout India. [< Hindustani *urd*]

Ur·da (ůr′dä), *n. Scandinavian Mythology.* one of the three Norns or goddesses of fate, a giantess and the guardian of the past.

Ur·du (ůr′dü, ėr′-; ůr dü′, ėr-), *n.* the Moslem form of Hindustani, spoken in India and Pakistan, using Arabic and Persian loan words and the Arabic alphabet. [< Hindustani (*zaban-i-*)*urdū* (language of the) camp < Persian; *urdū*, ultimately < Turkic *ordu* army, or Tartar *urda.* Compare HORDE.]

-ure, *suffix.* **1.** the act, process, or fact of ——ing, as in *closure, investiture, failure.*
2. the state, rank, or office of that which ——s, as in *judicature, legislature.*
3. the result or product of ——ing, as in *enclosure.*
4. thing that is ——ed, as in *disclosure.*
5. state of being ——ed, as in *pleasure.*
6. other special meanings, as in *procedure, sculpture, denture.*
[< French *-ure* < Latin *-ūra*, or directly < Latin]

u·re·a (yů rē′ə, yůr′ē ə), *n.* a soluble, crystalline nitrogenous solid forming an organic constituent of the urine of mammals, birds, and some reptiles, and also found in the blood, milk, etc.; carbamide. Urea is also produced synthetically, as from ammonium cyanate, for use in making adhesives and plastics, in fertilizers, etc. *Formula:* CH_4N_2O [< New Latin *urea* < French *urée* < *urine*]

u·re·a-for·mal·de·hyde resins (yů rē′ə-fôr mal′də hīd, yůr′ē-), urea resins.

u·re·al (yů rē′əl, yůr′ē-), *adj.* **1.** of or relating to urea. **2.** containing urea.

urea resins, a group of synthetic, thermosetting resins obtained from urea and formaldehyde, used in adhesives, moldings, etc.

u·re·ase (yůr′ē ās, -āz), *n.* an enzyme present in various bacteria, fungi, beans, etc., which promotes the decomposition of urea into ammonium carbonate. Also, **urase.**

u·re·di·al stage (yů rē′dē əl), the uredostage.

u·re·din·i·al stage (yůr′ə din′ē əl), the uredostage.

u·re·din·i·o·spore (yůr′ə din′ē ə spôr, -spōr), *n.* a uredospore.

u·re·din·i·um (yůr′ə din′ē əm), *n., pl.* **-i·a** (-ē ə). a uredium.

u·re·di·um (yů rē′dē əm), *n., pl.* **-di·a** (-dē ə). *Botany.* a pustule bearing uredospores, formed by certain rust fungi. [< *ured*(o) + New Latin *-ium*, a diminutive suffix]

u·re·do (yů rē′dō), *n.* **1.** urticaria. **2.** uredostage. [< Latin *urēdō, -inis* itch, blight < *ūrere* to burn]

u·re·do·so·rus (yů rē′də sôr′əs, -sōr′-), *n., pl.* **-so·ri** (-sôr′ī, -sōr′-). a uredium.

u·re·do·spore (yů rē′də spôr, -spōr), *n. Botany.* a one-celled, orange or brownish spore produced by certain rust fungi. Uredospores appear in the summer after the aeciospores and before the teliospores, and reproduce and extend the fungus rapidly.

u·re·do·stage (yů rē′də stāj′), *n.,* or **uredo stage,** *Botany.* the phase in the life cycle of certain rust fungi in which uredospores are produced.

u·re·id (yůr′ē id), *n.* ureide.

u·re·ide (yůr′ē īd, -id), *n.* a derivative of urea containing acid radicals, as urethane.

u·re·mi·a (yů rē′mē ə), *n.* an abnormal condition resulting from the accumulation in the blood of waste products that should normally be eliminated in the urine. Also, **uraemia.** [< New Latin *uremia* < Greek *oûron* urine + *haîma* blood]

u·re·mic (yů rē′mik), *adj.* **1.** of or having to do with uremia. **2.** suffering from uremia.

u·re·ter (yů rē′tər, yůr′ə-), *n.* a duct that carries urine from a kidney to the bladder or the cloaca. [< Greek *ourētḗr, -ēros* < *oureîn* to urinate < *oûron* urine]

u·re·ter·al (yů rē′tər əl), *adj.* of or having to do with a ureter.

u·re·ter·ec·to·my (yů rē′tə rek′tə mē), *n., pl.* **-mies.** surgical removal of the ureter. [< *ureter* + Greek *ektomḗ* a cutting out]

u·re·ter·ic (yůr′ə ter′ik), *adj.* ureteral.

u·re·than (yůr′ə than′, yů reth′an), *n.* **1.** a compound derived from urethane. **2.** urethane.

u·re·thane (yůr′ə thān′, yů reth′ān), *n.* **1.** any ester of carbamic acid. **2.** a colorless or white crystalline compound, used in medicine and in organic synthesis. *Formula:* $C_3H_7NO_2$ [< French *uréthane* < *urée* (see UREA) + *-thane*]

urethane foam, a foam derived from polyurethane, used for padding, filters, etc.

u·re·thra (yu̇ rē′thrə), *n., pl.* **-thrae** (-thrē), **-thras.** the duct in most mammals through which urine is discharged from the bladder, and through which the male semen is also discharged.
[< Late Latin *ūrethra* < Greek *ourēthra* < *ourein* urinate; see URETER]

u·re·thral (yu̇ rē′thrəl), *adj.* of or having to do with the urethra.

u·re·threc·to·my (yu̇r′ə threk′tə mē), *n., pl.* **-mies.** surgical removal of all or a part of the urethra. [< *urethr*(a) + Greek *ektomē* a cutting out]

u·re·thrit·ic (yu̇r′ə thrit′ik), *adj.* affected with urethritis.

u·re·thri·tis (yu̇r′ə thrī′tis), *n.* inflammation of the urethra.

u·re·thro·scope (yu̇ rē′thrə skōp), *n.* an instrument for examining the urethra. [< *urethra* + *-scope*]

u·re·thros·co·py (yu̇r′ə thros′kə pē), *n.* examination of the urethra with a urethroscope.

u·re·throt·o·my (yu̇r′ə throt′ə mē), *n., pl.* **-mies.** surgical correction of a stricture of the urethra. [< *urethra* + Greek *-tomiā* a cutting]

u·ret·ic (yu̇ ret′ik), *adj.* of or having to do with urine; diuretic. [< Late Latin *ūrēticus* < Greek *ourētikós* < *ourein* urinate; see URETER]

urge (ėrj), *v.,* **urged, urg·ing,** *n.* —*v.t.* **1.** to force or impel forward or onward; push forward with effort or against obstacles; drive (with force, threats, etc.): *The rider urged on his tired horse with whip and spurs.* **2.** to cause to hasten or gather speed; accelerate the pace of; speed up: *to urge a trotting horse into a gallop.* **3.** to try to persuade with arguments; ask or request earnestly; entreat: *They urged him to stay for dinner.* **4.** to press the need of; plead or argue earnestly for; recommend strongly: *to urge a larger budget for education. His doctor urges a change of climate. Motorists urged better roads.* **5.** to press upon the attention; refer to often and with emphasis: *to urge a claim, to urge an argument.* **6.** to use, work, or employ briskly or diligently: *and urge The strokes of the inexorable scourge* (Shelley).
—*v.i.* **1.** to be or act as an impelling force: *Fear urges, reason exhorts* (David Hume). **2.** to press or argue the need, desirability, truth, etc., of something; be ardent in argument, statement, etc., for or against something.
—*n.* **1.** a driving force or impulse: *Always the procreant urge of the world* (Whitman). **2.** the act of urging.
[< Latin *urgēre*]
—**Syn.** *v.t.* **1.** press, incite.

ur·gence (ėr′jəns), *n.* urgency: *the urgence of sleep* (James H. Robinson).

ur·gen·cy (ėr′jən sē), *n., pl.* **-cies. 1.** the state, condition, or fact of being urgent; imperative character; pressing importance: *the urgency to the nation of law and order. A house on fire is a matter of great urgency.* **2.** the need for immediate action or attention; urgent situation: *to be prepared for any urgency. Anxiety to secure the future blunts attention to the urgencies of the present* (John Morley). **3.** insistence; persistence.

ur·gent (ėr′jənt), *adj.* **1.** demanding immediate action or attention; pressing; important: *an urgent duty, an urgent message.* **2.** insistent; persistent. [< Latin *urgēns, -entis,* present participle of *urgēre* to urge] —**ur′gent·ly,** *adv.*
—**Syn. 1.** imperative, necessary. **2.** importunate.

-uria, *combining form.* a state (usually abnormal or morbid) of the urine due to the presence of ____, as in *albuminuria, glycosuria, pyuria.* [< New Latin *-uria* < Greek *-ouria* < *oûron* urine]

U·ri·ah (yu̇ rī′ə), *n.* (in the Bible) a Hittite soldier in David's army, the husband of Bathsheba. David arranged for Uriah to be killed in battle so that he could marry Bathsheba. II Samuel 11:2-27.

u·ri·al (u̇r′ē əl), *n.* a wild sheep of southern Asia, usually reddish-brown, and somewhat like the bighorn. Also, **oorial.** [< a native name]

u·ric (yu̇r′ik), *adj.* **1.** of or having to do with urine. **2.** obtained from urine. [probably < French *urique* < *urine* urine]

uric acid, a white, crystalline acid, only slightly soluble in water, found in the urine of man, certain animals, reptiles, and birds. It is formed as a waste product of the metabolism of nitrogenous bodies, as purines. *Formula:* $C_5H_4N_4O_3$

u·ri·case (yu̇r′ə kās), *n.* a liver enzyme in lower mammals that breaks down uric acid into allantoin before excretion. The presence of uricase prevents the formation of uric acid in the joints. [< *uric* + *-ase*]

u·ri·co·sur·ic (yu̇r′ə kō su̇r′ik), *adj.* aiding or stimulating the passing of uric acid.

u·ri·dine (yu̇r′ə din, -dēn), *n.* a white powder, a nucleoside of uracil, present in ribonucleic acid. *Formula:* $C_9H_{12}N_2O_6$

U·ri·el (yu̇r′ē əl), *n.* (in Hebrew and Christian tradition) one of the archangels.

U·rim (yu̇r′im), *n.pl.* (in the Old Testament) objects whose nature is not known but which were used in connection with the breastplate of the high priest and which served some oracular purpose (usually in the phrase *Urim and Thummim,* as in Exodus 28:30, but sometimes alone, as in Numbers 27:21). [< Hebrew *'urim,* plural, perhaps < *'or* light]

u·ri·nal (yu̇r′ə nəl), *n.* **1.** a container for urine, now especially a plumbing fixture designed for use by men or boys. **2.** a room, building, or other place for urinating. [< Late Latin *ūrinal* chamber pot, ultimately < Latin *ūrīna* urine]

u·ri·nal·y·sis (yu̇r′ə nal′ə sis), *n., pl.* **-ses** (-sēz). chemical analysis of a sample of urine. Also, **uranalysis.**

u·ri·nar·y (yu̇r′ə ner′ē), *adj., n., pl.* **-nar·ies.** —*adj.* **1.** of or having to do with urine. **2.** like urine. **3.** of or having to do with the organs that secrete and discharge urine. **4.** affecting or occurring in the organs that secrete and discharge urine.
—*n.* **1.** a urinal. **2.** *Obsolete.* a reservoir for keeping urine, etc., to be used as manure.

urinary bladder, the bladder.

urinary calculus, a stone formed in any part of the urinary passages; urolith.

u·ri·nate (yu̇r′ə nāt), *v.i.,* **-nat·ed, -nat·ing.** to discharge urine from the body. [< Medieval Latin *urinare* (with English *-ate*[1]) < Latin *ūrīna* urine]

u·ri·na·tion (yu̇r′ə nā′shən), *n.* the act of discharging urine.

u·ri·na·tive (yu̇r′ə nā′tiv), *adj.* provoking the flow of urine; diuretic.

u·rine (yu̇r′ən), *n.* a waste product of the body that is secreted by the kidneys, in man a fluid that passes through the ureters into the bladder and is then discharged through the urethra from the body. Normal human urine is amber in color, slightly acid, and has a specific gravity of about 1.02. [< Latin *ūrīna,* related to Greek *oûron*]

urine analysis, urinalysis.

u·ri·nif·er·ous (yu̇r′ə nif′ər əs), *adj.* conveying urine.

u·ri·no·gen·i·tal (yu̇r′ə nō jen′ə təl), *adj.* urogenital.

u·ri·nose (yu̇r′ə nōs), *adj.* urinous.

u·ri·nous (yu̇r′ə nəs), *adj.* **1.** of or having to do with urine or containing urine. **2.** resembling urine in color, odor, etc.

urn (ėrn), *n.* **1.** a hollow vessel or pot of oval or rounded shape, having a foot or pedestal. Urns were used in Greece and Rome to hold the ashes of the dead. **2.** a place of burial; grave; tomb. **3.** a coffee pot or tea pot with a faucet near the bottom, used for making or serving coffee or tea at the table. **4.** *Botany.* the hollow vessel in which the spores of a moss are produced. [< Latin *urna* a vessel of burned clay < *ūrere* to burn]

German Urn (def. 1) (16th century)

uro-[1], *combining form.* urine; urinary: *Urogenous = secreting urine.* [< Greek *oûron*]

uro-[2], *combining form.* tail; posterior part, as in *urochord, uropod.* [< Greek *ourá* tail]

u·ro·chord (yu̇r′ə kôrd), *n. Zoology.* the notochord of an ascidian larva, usually limited to the caudal region. [< *uro-*[2] + *chord*[2]]

u·ro·chor·dal (yu̇r′ə kôr′dəl), *adj.* **1.** provided with a urochord. **2.** of or having to do with the urochord or larvae having urochords.

u·ro·chrome (yu̇r′ə krōm), *n.* the yellow pigment which colors urine. [< *uro-*[1] + *chrôma* color]

u·rochs (yu̇r′oks), *n.* an aurochs.

u·ro·dele (yu̇r′ə dēl), *adj.* belonging to an order of amphibians which retain the tail throughout life, including the salamanders, newts, etc. —*n.* a urodele amphibian. [< New Latin *Urodela* the order name < Greek *ourá* tail + *dêlos* visible]

u·ro·gen·i·tal (yu̇r′ə jen′ə təl), *adj.* denoting or having to do with the urinary and genital organs; urinogenital.

u·rog·e·nous (yu̇ roj′ə nəs), *adj.* **1.** secreting or producing urine. **2.** obtained from or present in urine. [< *uro-*[1] + *-gen* + *-ous*]

u·rog·ra·phy (yu̇ rog′rə fē), *n., pl.* **-phies.** the examination of the urinary tract, kidneys, bladder, etc., by means of X rays or the like. [< *uro-*[1] + *-graphy*]

u·ro·lith (yu̇r′ə lith), *n.* a urinary calculus.

u·ro·lith·ic (yu̇r′ə lith′ik), *adj.* of or having to do with a urinary calculus.

u·ro·log·ic (yu̇r′ə loj′ik), *adj.* urological.

u·ro·log·i·cal (yu̇r′ə loj′ə kəl), *adj.* of or having to do with urology.

u·rol·o·gist (yu̇ rol′ə jist), *n.* an expert in urology.

u·rol·o·gy (yu̇ rol′ə jē), *n.* the scientific study of the urogenital tract in the male or the urinary tract in the female, their diseases, etc. Also, **ourology.** [< *uro-*[1] + *-logy*]

u·ro·pod (yu̇r′ə pod), *n.* an abdominal appendage of an arthropod, especially one of the last pair of paddlelike appendages of a lobster. [< *uro-*[2] + Greek *poús, podós* foot]

u·ro·pyg·i·al (yu̇r′ə pij′ē əl), *adj.* of or having to do with the uropygium. —*n.* a tail feather, especially a large tail feather.

uropygial gland, a large gland opening on the backs of many birds at the base of the tail, with an oily secretion used in preening the feathers; preen gland.

u·ro·pyg·i·um (yu̇r′ə pij′ē əm), *n.* the rump of a bird, which bears the tail feathers. [< Medieval Latin *uropygium* < Greek *ouropýgion* < *ourá* tail + *pygê* rump]

u·ro·scop·ic (yu̇r′ə skop′ik), *adj.* having to do with the inspection of urine in the diagnosis and treatment of disease.

u·ros·co·pist (yu̇ ros′kə pist), *n.* a person who makes a specialty of urinary examinations.

u·ros·co·py (yu̇ ros′kə pē), *n., pl.* **-pies.** the examination of the urine, especially as a means of diagnosis. Also, **ouroscopy.** [< New Latin *uroscopia* < Greek *oûron* urine + *-scopiā* -scopy]

u·ro·style (yu̇r′ə stīl), *n. Zoology.* the posterior unsegmented portion of the vertebral column in certain fishes and amphibians. [< *uro-*[2] + Greek *stŷlos* pillar]

U·rot·ro·pin (yu̇ rot′rə pin), *n. Trademark.* a colorless, crystalline substance prepared by the action of ammonia on formaldehyde, used chiefly as a urinary antiseptic. *Formula:* $C_6H_{12}N_4$ [< *uro-*[1] + Greek *-tropos* a turning + English *-in*]

u·ro·xan·thin (yu̇r′ə zan′thin), *n.* indican, a substance in the urine. [< German *Uroxanthin* < Greek *oûron* urine + German *Xanthin* xanthin]

Ur·sa (ėr′sə), *n. Astronomy.* **1.** Ursa Major. **2.** Ursa Minor.

Ur·sae Ma·jor·is (ėr′sē mə jō′ris), genitive of **Ursa Major.**

Ur·sae Mi·nor·is (ėr′sē mi nō′ris), genitive of **Ursa Minor.**

Ursa Major, *genitive* **Ur·sae Ma·jor·is.** the most prominent northern constellation, shaped somewhat like a bear with an enormous tail, and including the seven stars of the Big Dipper, two of which (the Pointers) point toward the North Star (Polaris); Great Bear. See **Dipper** for diagram. [< Latin *Ursa Major* (literally) larger bear]

Ursa Minor, *genitive* **Ur·sae Mi·nor·is.** the northern constellation that includes the seven stars of the Little Dipper, with the North Star (Polaris) at the end of its handle (or at the tip of the Little Bear's tail); Little or Lesser Bear; Cynosure. See **Dipper** for diagram. [< Latin *Ursa Minor* (literally) smaller bear]

ur·si·form (ėr′sə fôrm), *adj.* having the form or appearance of a bear. [< Latin *ursus* bear + English *-form*]

ur·sine (ėr′sīn, -sin), *adj.* **1.** of or having to do with a bear; bearlike: *noted for ursine manners* (Robert Southey). **2.** covered with stiff hairlike processes: *ursine caterpillars.* [< Latin *ursīnus* < *ursus* bear]

ursine dasyure, the Tasmanian devil, a carnivorous marsupial resembling a small bear.

ursine howler, a red howler or howling monkey of Brazil.

ur·son (ėr′sən), *n.* the porcupine of forest regions of northern and western North America, of large size with short spines and long hairs. [< Canadian French *ourson* (diminutive) < French *ours* bear < Latin *ursus*]

Ur·spra·che (ür′shprä′ʜə), *n.* an original or parent language, especially proto-Germanic or Indo-European, reconstructed by comparison of common forms in cognate languages. [< German *Ursprache* < *ur-* primitive + *Sprache* language]

Ur·su·line (ėr′sə lin, -līn; -syə-), *n.* a member of a Roman Catholic order of nuns, founded by Saint Angela Merici in 1535 for the teaching of girls and the nursing of the sick. —*adj.* of or having to do with this order. [< New Latin *Ursulinae*, feminine plural < Saint *Ursula*]

ur·ti·ca·ceous (ėr′tə kā′shəs), *adj.* belonging to a family of dicotyledonous herbs, shrubs, and trees, many of which, as the nettle, are covered with stinging hairs. [< New Latin *Urticaceae* the order name (< *Urtica* the typical genus < Latin *urtīca* nettle, probably < *ūrere* to burn) + English *-ous*]

ur·ti·car·i·a (ėr′tə kãr′ē ə), *n.* hives or nettle rash. [< New Latin *urticaria* < Latin *urtīca* nettle; see URTICATE]

ur·ti·car·i·al (ėr′tə kãr′ē əl), *adj.* **1.** having to do with urticaria. **2.** like urticaria. **3.** affected with urticaria.

ur·ti·cate (ėr′tə kāt), *v.,* **-cat·ed, -cat·ing.** —*v.t.* **1.** to sting with or as if with nettles. **2.** to whip (a benumbed or paralyzed limb) with nettles to restore sensation, etc. —*v.i.* to sting as or like a nettle. [< Medieval Latin *urticare* (with English *-ate*[1]) < Latin *urtīca* nettle, probably < *ūrere* to burn]

ur·ti·ca·tion (ėr′tə kā′shən), *n.* **1.** the act or process of urticating, especially in medicine. **2.** a pricking sensation suggestive of stinging with nettles.

Uru., Uruguay.

u·ru·bu (ü′rü bü′), *n.* the black vulture or carrion crow, ranging from Argentina to the southern United States. [< Tupi (Brazil) *urubú*]

Urubu
(about 2 ft. long)

U·ru·guay·an (yůr′ə-gwā′ən, -gwī′-), *adj.* of or having to do with Uruguay or its people. —*n.* a native or inhabitant of Uruguay.

u·rus (yůr′əs), *n. Obsolete.* an aurochs. [< Latin *ūrus* < Germanic (compare Old High German *ūr*)]

u·ru·shi·ol (ü rü′shē-ol, -ōl), *n.* a poisonous, pale, oily liquid derived from catechol. It is the active irritant principle in poison ivy, and is used in making lacquer and for tests as an allergen. *Formula:* $C_{21}H_{32}O_2$ [< Japanese *urushi* lacquer + English *-ol*[2]]

us (us; *unstressed* əs), *pron. Objective case of* **we:** *We learn; the teacher helps us. Please bring us food. Will you go with us? Please don't forsake us.* [Old English *ūs*]

u.s., *Latin.* **1.** ubi supra. **2.** ut supra.

US (no periods), the United States.

U.S., **1.** the United States. **2.** United States Supreme Court Reports.

U.S. or **U.S. No.,** United States Highway: *to turn left on U.S. 40 and follow it into the city.*

U.S.A. or **USA** (no periods), **1.** the Union of South Africa. **2.** the United States Army. **3.** the United States of America.

us·a·bil·i·ty (yü′zə bil′ə tē), *n.* a being usable. Also, **useability.**

us·a·ble (yü′zə bəl), *adj.* **1.** that can be used; capable of use. **2.** fit or proper to be used; suitable for use. Also, **useable.** —**us′a·ble·ness,** *n.*

USAF (no periods) or **U.S.A.F.,** United States Air Force.

USAFI (no periods), United States Armed Forces Institute.

USAFR (no periods) or **U.S.A.F.R.,** United States Air Force Reserve.

us·age (yü′sij, -zij), *n.* **1.** way or manner of being used; act of using; treatment: *The car has had rough usage.* **2.** a long-continued or habitual practice; customary procedure; custom: *Travelers should learn many of the usages of the countries they visit.* **3.** the customary way of using words: *a person familiar with American usage. The usage of the best writers and speakers determines what is good English.* **4.** an instance of such use: *a new usage.* [< Anglo-French, Old French *usage*, ultimately < Latin *ūsus, -ūs;* see USE, verb]

us·ance (yü′zəns), *n.* **1.** *Commerce.* the time allowed, not counting days of grace, by usage or law for the payment of a bill of exchange, etc., especially one drawn in another country. **2.** income in any form derived from the ownership of any kind of wealth. [< Old French *usance* < Vulgar Latin *ūsāre*, see USE, verb]

USAR (no periods) or **U.S.A.R.,** United States Army Reserve.

Us·beg (us′beg), *n.* Uzbek.

Us·bek (us′bek), *n.* Uzbek.

U.S.C., an abbreviation for the following:
1. United States Code.
2. United States of Colombia.
3. University of Southern California.

U.S.C.A., United States Code Annotated.

USCC (no periods), United States Commercial Company.

USCG (no periods) or **U.S.C.G.,** United States Coast Guard.

USCGR (no periods) or **U.S.C.G.R.,** United States Coast Guard Reserve.

U.S.C. Supp., United States Code Supplement.

USDA (no periods) or **U.S.D.A.,** United States Department of Agriculture.

use (*v.* yüz; *n.* yüs), *v.,* **used, us·ing,** *n.*—*v.t.* **1.** to put into action or service; employ (a person, animal, implement, etc.) for a certain end or purpose; utilize: *He used a knife to cut the meat.* **2.** to employ or practice actively; exercise, especially habitually or customarily: *to use one's knowledge, authority, or judgment.* **3.** to employ (words, phrases, etc.); say; utter: *to use bad grammar.* **4.** to avail oneself of; put to one's own purposes: *May I use your telephone?* **5.** to consume or expend by using: *to use most of the available funds, to use water for irrigation. He uses tobacco. We have used most of the money.* **6.** to act or behave toward in a certain way; treat: *He used us well. Use others as you would have them use you.* —*v.i. Archaic.* to go frequently to a place; frequent: *But we be only sailormen That use in London town* (Rudyard Kipling).

used to, a. accustomed to: *used to hardships. Eskimos are used to cold weather.* **b.** was or were accustomed to; formerly did: *He used to come every day.*

use up, to consume or expend entirely: *to use up the available funds. We have used up our sugar.*

[< Old French *user* < Vulgar Latin *ūsāre* < Latin *ūsus, -ūs* act of using < *ūtī* to use]

—*n.* **1.** the act of employing or using a thing for any purpose; application; utilization: *the use of tools.* **2.** the state or condition of being employed or used: *methods long out of use.* **3.** employment or usage resulting in or causing wear, damage, etc. **4. a.** the manner or way of using or employing. **b.** an instance of this: *a proper use of one's time, a poor use of a material.* **5.** a purpose, object, or end that a thing is used for, especially a useful or advantageous purpose: *to find a new use for something.* **6.** the fact or quality of serving the needs or ends (of a person or persons): *a park for the use of all the people.* **7.** function; service; office: *the use of a catalyst in a chemical process.* **8.** the character, property, or quality of being useful or suitable for some purpose; usefulness or utility; advantage or benefit: *a thing of no practical use. There is no use in crying over spilled milk.* **9.** the power or capacity of using; ability to use: *to lose the use of a hand.* **10.** the right or privilege of using: *to have the use of a boat for the summer.* **11.** need or occasion for using; necessity; demand: *He found no further use for it. A hunter often has use for a gun.* **12.** habitual, usual, or customary practice, employment, or procedure; the custom; wont: *It was his use to rise early.* **13.** a custom, habit, or practice: *to learn the uses of the sea.* **14.** the distinctive ritual and form of service, or any liturgical form, of a particular church, diocese, province, etc.: *Sarum use, Roman use.* **15.** *Law.* **a.** the act or fact of employing, occupying, possessing, or holding property so as to derive benefit from it. **b.** the right of a beneficiary to the benefit or profits of land or tenements to which another has legal title in trust for the beneficiary. **c.** a trust vesting title to real property in someone for the benefit of a beneficiary.

have no use for, a. *Informal.* to dislike: *The Marquis had . . . spoken in French, and the Captain had no use for that language* (H.S. Merriman). **b.** not to need or want: *You can have the book; I have no use for it any longer.*

in use, being used; employed or occupied: *All the fashionable phrases and compliments now in use* (Richard Steele).

make use of, a. to put in use; use; employ: *She made much use of milk in her cooking.* **b.** to take advantage of: *Perhaps she had only made use of him as a convenient aid to her intentions* (Thomas Hardy).

put to use, to use; employ: *Every moment may be put to some use* (Lord Chesterfield).

[< Old French *us*, masculine, and *use*, feminine < Latin *ūsus;* see the verb]

—**Syn.** *v.t.* **1. Use, employ, utilize** mean to put into action or service for some purpose. **Use,** the general and common word, suggests any kind of purpose when applied to things but a selfish purpose when applied to persons: *He uses a typewriter for his schoolwork. He uses his friends to get ahead.* **Employ** suggests a special purpose: *That architect frequently employs glass brick.* **Utilize** suggests a practical purpose: *She utilizes every scrap of food.* –*n.* **1.** employment.

➔ **used to.** Before *to, used* is commonly pronounced (yüst) or (yüs).

use·a·bil·i·ty (yü′zə bil′ə tē), *n.* usability.

use·a·ble (yü′zə bəl), *adj.* usable. —**use′a·ble·ness,** *n.*

used (yüzd; yüst, yüs, *for 3, when immediately preceeding "to"*), *adj.* **1.** that has been used, especially: **a.** not new; secondhand: *a used car.* **b.** not clean, fresh, etc.: *to remove used towels from a rack.* **2.** that is used; in use; utilized: *a seldom used room.* **3.** *Obsolete.* accustomed; usual; customary.

used up, *Informal.* tired out; thoroughly exhausted: [*He was*] *barefooted . . .; cleaned out to the last real, and completely used up* (Richard H. Dana).

used-up (yüzd′up′), *adj.* **1.** *Informal.* thoroughly exhausted by physical exertion; tired out. **2.** worn out or made useless, as by hard work, age, dissipation, etc.: *Jim Tyrone is by now a wholly dissipated, used-up drunk, his last reserves gone with the death of his mother* (Time). **3.** reduced, exhausted, or consumed by using; depleted: *Underground salt domes and used-up oil wells are being considered* (Newsweek).

use·ful (yüs′fəl), *adj.* **1.** of use; helpful: *a useful suggestion, to make oneself useful about the house.* **2.** giving or able to give service; serviceable; usable: *an old but still useful pair of shoes.* —**use′ful·ly,** *adv.* —**use′ful·ness,** *n.*

use·less (yüs′lis), *adj.* of no use; worthless: *a useless person, a useless effort.* —**use′less·ly,** *adv.* —**use′less·ness,** *n.*

—**Syn. Useless, ineffectual** mean having or being of no value for a purpose. **Useless** means not serving the purpose one has in mind, not of practical value under the circumstances, or not of value for any purpose at all: *An electric toaster is useless to a man in the woods.* **Ineffectual** means not accomplishing the purpose one has in mind, either not producing the expected or proper results or not having any effect whatever: *His attempts to become friends again after the quarrel were ineffectual.*

us·er (yü′zər), *n.* **1.** a person or thing that puts to use: *a constant user of the telephone, a heavy user of raw cotton.* **2.** *Law.* **a.** a right to use or enjoy property. **b.** the use or enjoyment of property, or of the right to it.

USES (no periods), United States Employment Service.

use tax (yüs), State tax on goods purchased outside the State and later brought in.

U.S.G.A. or **USGA** (no periods), United States Golf Association.

USHA (no periods) or **U.S.H.A.,** United States Housing Authority.

U-shaped (yü′shāpt′), *adj.* having the shape of the letter U.

U·shas (ü′shəs, ů shäs′), *n.* the ancient Indian (Vedic) goddess of the dawn. [< Sanskrit *Ushas*]

ush·er (ush′ər), *n.* **1.** a person who shows people to their seats in a church, theater, etc. **2.** *U.S.* a male friend of the bride or groom serving as an usher at a wedding. **3.**

Especially British. a person who has charge of the door and admits people to a hall, chamber, etc., now especially one who is an official of or employed by a court, college, etc. **4.** *British.* an assistant teacher in an English school: *My companion was a schoolmaster and . . . the youth, one of the bigger boys or the usher* (Charles Lamb).
—*v.t.* **1.** to conduct or guide; escort; show: *He ushered the visitors to the door.* **2.** to go or come before; precede to announce the coming of: *the stars that usher evening* (Milton).
usher in, to inaugurate; introduce: *a winter ushered in by cold rains.*
[< Anglo-French *uissier* < Vulgar Latin *ustiārius* doorkeeper < *ustium,* variant of Latin *ōstium* door, related to *ōs, ōris* mouth]

ush·er·ette (ush′ə ret′), *n.* a woman usher.

USIA (no periods) or **U.S.I.A.,** United States Information Agency (an independent agency of the United States government, established in 1953 to direct the propaganda efforts of the United States.

USIS (no periods) or **U.S.I.S.,** United States Information Service.

U.S.L.T.A. or **USLTA** (no periods), United States Lawn Tennis Association.

USM (no periods), United States Marine or Marines.

U.S.M., 1. United States Mail. **2.** United States Marine or Marines.

U.S.M.A. or **USMA** (no periods), United States Military Academy.

USMC (no periods) or **U.S.M.C.,** United States Marine Corps.

USMCR (no periods) or **U.S.M.C.R.,** United States Marine Corps Reserve.

USN (no periods) or **U.S.N.,** United States Navy.

U.S.N.A. or **USNA** (no periods), **1.** United States National Army. **2.** United States Naval Academy.

us·ne·a (us′nē ə), *n.* any of a group of lichens, commonly found as pendulous, grayish or yellowish, mosslike growths on trees or rocks in temperate or cool climates. [< New Latin *Usnea* the genus name, ultimately < Arabic, or Persian *ushnah* moss]

USNG (no periods) or **U.S.N.G.,** United States National Guard.

us·nic acid (us′nik), a yellow, crystalline substance derived from lichens, used as an antibiotic. *Formula:* $C_{18}H_{16}O_7$ [< *usn*(ea) + *-ic*]

USNR (no periods) or **U.S.N.R.,** United States Naval Reserve.

USO (no periods), United Service Organizations.

USOE (no periods), United States Office of Education.

USOM (no periods), United States Operations Mission.

U.S.P. or **USP** (no periods), United States Pharmacopoeia.

U.S.Pharm., United States Pharmacopoeia.

U.S.P.H.S. or **USPHS** (no periods), United States Public Health Service.

U.S.P.O., United States Post Office.

us·que (us′kwē), *n.* usquebaugh.

us·que ad a·ras (us′kwē ad ā′ras), *Latin.* even to the altars; up to the point where one's religion intervenes.

us·que·baugh or **us·que·bae** (us′kwē-bô, -bä), *n. Obsolete.* whiskey. [< Irish, and Scottish Gaelic *uisge beatha* (literally) water of life]

USS (no periods), United States Ship, Steamer, or Steamship.

U.S.S., 1. United States Senate. **2.** United States Ship, Steamer, or Steamship.

U.S.S.C., United States Supreme Court.

U.S.S.R. or **USSR** (no periods), Union of Soviet Socialist Republics.

USTS (no periods), United States Travel Service (an agency of the Department of Commerce to attract foreign tourists to the United States).

us·tu·late (*v.* us′chə lāt; *adj.* us′chə lit, -lāt), *v.,* **-lat·ed, -lat·ing,** *adj. Obsolete.* —*v.t., v.i.* to scorch. —*adj.* browned or blackened by or as if by scorching. [< Latin *ustulāre* (with English *-ate*[1]) to burn (frequentative) < *ūrere* to burn]

us·tu·la·tion (us′chə lā′shən), *n.* **1.** *Pharmacology.* the roasting or drying of moist substances in preparation for pulverizing. **2.** *Obsolete.* the burning of wine.

usu., 1. usual. **2.** usually.

u·su·al (yü′zhü əl), *adj.* in common use; ordinary; customary: *Snow is usual high up in the Rocky Mountains during winter.*
as per usual, *Humorous or Slang.* as usual: *I shall accompany him, as per usual* (William S. Gilbert).
as usual, in the usual manner; as is customary: *Our conversation opened, as usual, upon the weather* (John Dryden).
[< Late Latin *ūsuālis* < Latin *ūsus;* see USE, verb] —**u′su·al·ly,** *adv.* —**u′su·al·ness,** *n.*
—**Syn. Usual, customary** mean often or commonly seen or found, especially in a certain place or at a given time. **Usual** applies to something of expected occurrence or of familiar nature or quality: *This is the usual weather at this time of year.* **Customary** applies to something that is according to the regular practices or habits of a particular person or group: *He stayed up long past his customary bedtime.* —**Ant.** strange, exceptional, extraordinary.

u·su·cap·tion (yü′zyů kap′shən, -syů-), *n. Law.* the acquisition of the title or right to property by the uninterrupted and undisputed possession of it in good faith for a certain term prescribed by law. [< Old French *usucaption,* learned borrowing from Medieval Latin *usucaptio, -onis,* variant of Latin *ūsūcapiō, -ōnis* < *ūsūcapere* to acquire ownership by prescription]

u·su·fruct (yü′zyů frukt, -syů-), *n.* the legal right to use another's property and enjoy the advantages of it without injuring or destroying it. —*v.t.* to hold or make subject to usufruct. [< Latin *ūsūfrūctū,* ablative of *ūsus-frūctus,* earlier *ūsus* (*et*) *frūctus* use (and) enjoyment]

u·su·fruc·tu·ar·y (yü′zyů fruk′chů er′ē, -syů-), *adj., n., pl.* **-ar·ies.** —*adj.* **1.** of or having to do with a usufruct. **2.** like a usufruct. —*n.* a person who has the usufruct of property. [< Late Latin *ūsūfrūctuārius* < Latin *ūsūfrūctus* < *ūsus-frūctus;* see USUFRUCT]

u·su·rer (yü′zhər ər), *n.* **1.** a person who lends money at an extremely high or unlawful rate of interest. **2.** *Obsolete.* a person who lends money at interest; moneylender. [< Anglo-French *usurer,* Old French *usurier* < Late Latin *ūsūrārius* moneylender < Latin, adverb, at interest, for use < *ūsūra* use, noun < *ūtī* to use]

u·su·ri·ous (yü zhůr′ē əs), *adj.* **1.** taking extremely high or unlawful interest for the use of money. **2.** characterized by or involving usury: *Fifty per cent is a usurious rate of interest.* **3.** of the nature of usury. —**u·su′ri·ous·ly,** *adv.* —**u·su′ri·ous·ness,** *n.*

u·surp (yü zėrp′, -sėrp′), *v.t.* to seize and hold (power, position, authority, etc.) by force or without right: *The king's brother tried to usurp the throne.* —*v.i.* to act as a usurper; be guilty of usurpation. [< Old French *usurper* < Latin *ūsūrpāre* seize possession of (for use) < *ūsū,* ablative of *ūsus* (see USE, verb) + *rapere* seize] —**u·surp′er,** *n.* —**u·surp′ing·ly,** *adv.* —**Syn.** *v.t.* appropriate, arrogate, assume.

u·sur·pa·tion (yü′zər pā′shən, -sər-), *n.* a usurping; the seizing and holding of the place or power of another by force or without right: *the usurpation of the throne by a pretender.*

u·su·ry (yü′zhər ē), *n., pl.* **-ries. 1.** the lending of money at an extremely high or unlawful rate of interest. **2.** an extremely high or unlawful rate of interest. **3.** *Obsolete.* **a.** interest. **b.** the fact or practice of lending money at interest. [< Medieval Latin *usuria,* alteration of Latin *ūsūra;* see USURER]

U.S.V., United States Volunteers.

usw. or **u.s.w.,** and so forth; etc. (German, *und so weiter*).

USW (no periods), United Steelworkers of America (a labor union affiliated with the AFL-CIO).

ut (ut, üt), *n. Music.* the syllable originally used for the keynote of the scale, now commonly called do. [< Latin *ut* (literally) that. See GAMUT.]

u.t. or **U.T.,** universal time.

Ut., Utah (not official).

U·tah·an (yü′tô ən, -tä-), *adj.* of or having to do with the State of Utah or its inhabitants. —*n.* a native or inhabitant of Utah.

ut dict. (ut), as directed (Latin, *ut dictum*).

Ute (yüt, yü′tē), *n., pl.* **Ute** or **Utes. 1.** a member of a group of American Indian tribes now living in Utah and Colorado. **2.** their Shoshonean language. [American English < Shoshonean (Ute) *Ute,* said to mean "person, people"]

u·ten·sil (yü ten′səl), *n.* **1.** a container or implement used for some purpose or in some realm having to do with food: *eating utensils. Pots, pans, kettles, and mops are kitchen utensils.* **2.** an instrument or tool used for any of various practical purposes; implement: *Pens and pencils are writing utensils.* [< Old French *utensile,* learned borrowing from Medieval Latin, noun use of neuter of Latin *ūtēnsilis* usable, that may be used < *ūtī* to use]

u·ter·al·gi·a (yü′tə ral′jē ə), *n.* uterine pain. [< New Latin *uteralgia* < Latin *uterus* womb + Greek *álgos* pain]

u·ter·ec·to·my (yü′tə rek′tə mē), *n., pl.* **-mies.** surgical removal of the uterus; hysterectomy. [< *uter*(us) + Greek *ektomē* a cutting out]

u·ter·ine (yü′tər in, -tə rīn), *adj.* **1.** of or having to do with the uterus (womb). **2.** in the region of the uterus. **3.** having the same mother, but a different father: *Uterine brothers are half brothers born of the same mother.* [< Late Latin *uterīnus* < Latin *uterus* uterus]

u·ter·us (yü′tər əs), *n., pl.* **-ter·i** (-tə rī). the organ of the body in female mammals that holds and usually nourishes the young until birth; womb. It is an enlarged and thickened section of an oviduct. [< Latin *uterus* womb, belly]

Ut·gard (üt′gärd), *n.* Jotunheim.

U·ther (yü′thər), *n.,* or **Uther Pendragon,** a legendary king of ancient Britain, the father of King Arthur and husband of Igraine.

u·tile (yü′təl), *adj.* having utility; useful. [< Old French *utile,* learned borrowing from Latin *ūtilis* < *ūtī* to use]

u·til·i·dor (yü til′ə dôr), *n.* (in Canada) a system of elevated and insulated conduits carrying water, steam, etc., to communities situated on the permafrost. [< *utility;* perhaps patterned on *humidor*]

u·ti·lise (yü′tə līz), *v.t.,* **-lised, -lis·ing.** *Especially British.* utilize.

u·til·i·tar·i·an (yü til′ə tãr′ē ən), *adj.* **1.** of or having to do with utility. **2.** aiming at or designed primarily for practical usefulness rather than beauty, style, etc. **3.** that is a utilitarian; adhering to utilitarianism.
—*n.* an adherent of utilitarianism.

u·til·i·tar·i·an·ism (yü til′ə tãr′ē ə niz′-əm), *n.* **1.** the doctrine or belief that the greatest good of the greatest number should be the purpose of human conduct, especially as proposed by Jeremy Bentham. **2.** the doctrine or belief that actions are good if they are useful.

u·til·i·ty (yü til′ə tē), *n., pl.* **-ties,** *adj.* —*n.* **1.** usefulness; power to satisfy people's wants: *A fur coat has more utility in winter than in summer.* **2.** a useful thing. **3.** a company that performs a public service; public utility: *Railroads, bus lines, and gas and electric companies are utilities.* **4.** the greatest happiness of the greatest number. **5.** a low grade of beef, usually from older animals, as classified by the United States Department of Agriculture. **6.** (in Australia) a motor vehicle with a variety of uses.
utilities, shares of stock issued by a public utility company: *Utilities managed to edge up 0.08%* (Wall Street Journal).
—*adj.* used for various purposes: *a utility shed in the yard, a utility infielder.*
[< Old French *utilite,* learned borrowing from Latin *ūtilitās* < *ūtilis* usable < *ūtī* to use]

utility man, a member of a theatrical company, a baseball team, or the like, who is expected to serve in any capacity when called on.

utility pole, a high wooden pole sunk in the ground, supporting lines or cables carrying electric or telephone wires.

utility room, a room in a house for a furnace, water heater, etc., or for a washing machine, especially in a house with no basement.

u·ti·liz·a·ble (yü′tə lī′zə bəl), *adj.* that can be utilized.

u·ti·li·za·tion (yü′tə lə zā′shən), *n.* **1.** a utilizing. **2.** a being utilized.

u·ti·lize (yü′tə līz), *v.t.,* **-lized, -liz·ing.** to make use of; put to some practical use: *to utilize leftovers in cooking.* —**u′ti·liz′er,** *n.* —**Syn.** See **use.**

ut in·fra (ut in′frə), *Latin.* as below.

u·ti pos·si·de·tis (yü′tī pos′ə dē′tis), the principle of international law under which a belligerent or belligerents may be confirmed by treaty or other formal agreement in possession of all territory controlled at the close of active hostilities. [< Late Latin *utī possidētis* (literally) as you possess]

ut·most (ut′mōst), *adj.* **1.** greatest possible; extreme: *a state of the utmost confusion. Sunshine is of the utmost importance to health.* **2.** most remote; farthest: *the utmost reaches of the universe. He walked to the utmost edge of the cliff.* —*n.* the most that is possible; extreme limit: *to enjoy oneself to the utmost.* [alteration of Old English *ūtemest* < *ūte* outside + *-mest* -most]

U·to-Az·tec·an (yü′tō az′tek ən), *adj.* of, denoting, or having to do with a widespread American Indian linguistic stock that includes Shoshonean, Piman, and Nahuatl. —*n.* this linguistic stock.

U·to·pi·a (yü tō′pē ə), *n.* **1.** an ideal commonwealth where perfect justice and social harmony existed, as described in *Utopia,* by Sir Thomas More. **2.** the island on which this commonwealth existed. [< New Latin *Utopia* < Greek *oú* not + *tópos* place]

u·to·pi·a (yü tō′pē ə), *n.* **1.** an ideal place or state with perfect laws: *the wildest promises of an earthly utopia the day after tomorrow* (William R. Inge). **2.** a visionary, impractical system of political or social perfection: *averse to all enthusiasm, mysticism, utopias and superstition* (William E. H. Lecky). [< *Utopia*]

U·to·pi·an (yü tō′pē ən), *adj.* of or like Utopia. —*n.* an inhabitant of Utopia.

u·to·pi·an (yü tō′pē ən), *adj.* **1.** of or like a utopia. **2.** visionary; impractical: *Many . . . are infused with a passionate utopian faith that it* [*the Party*] *is to redeem mankind* (Manchester Guardian). —*n.* an ardent but impractical reformer; extreme and visionary idealist.

u·to·pi·an·ism (yü tō′pē ə niz′əm), *n.* **1.** the ideas, beliefs, and aims of Utopians. **2.** any ideal schemes for the improvement of life, social conditions, etc.

u·tri·cle (yü′trə kəl), *n.* **1.** a small sac or baglike body, such as a cell filled with air in a seaweed. **2.** a dry, indehiscent, usually one-seeded fruit, similar to an achene, but having a very thin, loose pericarp. **3.** the larger of the two membranous sacs in the labyrinth of the internal ear, the saccule being the smaller. [< Latin *ūtriculus* (diminutive) < *ūter, ūtris* skin bag, skin bottle]

u·tric·u·lar (yü trik′yə lər), *adj.* **1.** of or having to do with a utricle. **2.** like a utricle. **3.** having or composed of a utricle or utricles.

u·tric·u·late (yü trik′yə lit, -lāt), *adj.* utricular.

u·tric·u·li·tis (yü trik′yə lī′tis), *n.* inflammation of a utricle, as of the inner ear.

u·tric·u·lus (yü trik′yə ləs), *n., pl.* **-li** (-lī). a utricle. [< Latin *ūtriculus* utricle]

ut su·pra (ut sü′prə), *Latin.* as above.

ut·ter[1] (ut′ər), *adj.* **1.** complete; total; absolute: *utter defeat, utter surprise, utter darkness.* **2.** that is such to an extreme degree; out-and-out: *an utter fool.* [Old English *ūterra* outer] —**Syn. 1.** entire, unqualified, sheer.

ut·ter[2] (ut′ər), *v.t.* **1.** to speak; make known; express: *the last words he uttered, to utter one's thoughts.* **2.** to give forth; give out; emit: *He uttered a cry of pain.* **3.** to put (especially counterfeit money, forged checks, etc.) into circulation. **4.** *Obsolete.* **a.** to issue or publish: *an order . . . that the . . . translation of Tindal . . . should not be uttered either by printer or bookseller* (John Strype). **b.** to issue or offer for sale or barter; vend: *Such . . . drugs I have; but Mantua's law Is death to any he that utters them* (Shakespeare). [Middle English *utteren,* ultimately < Old English *ūt* out] —**ut′ter·er,** *n.* —**Syn. 1.** deliver, articulate.

ut·ter·a·ble (ut′ər ə bəl), *adj.* that can be uttered.

ut·ter·ance[1] (ut′ər əns), *n.* **1.** an uttering; expression in words or sounds: *The child gave utterance to his grief.* **2.** a way or manner of speaking: *a man of polished utterance. Stammering hinders clear utterance.* **3.** something uttered; a spoken word or words. **4.** the putting into circulation of counterfeit money forged, checks, etc.; uttering. **5.** *Obsolete.* the disposal of goods by sale or barter; vending. [< *utter*[2] + *-ance*]

ut·ter·ance[2] (ut′ər əns), *n.* the utmost extremity of life, strength, etc.; bitter end. [< Old French *oultrance* < *oultrer* pass beyond < *oultre* beyond < Latin *ultrā*]

ut·ter·ing (ut′ər ing), *n. Law.* the act of intentionally putting counterfeit money, forged checks, etc., into circulation.

ut·ter·ly (ut′ər lē), *adv.* completely; totally; absolutely: *I fail utterly to see why* (Sir Winston Churchill).

ut·ter·most (ut′ər mōst), *adj., n.* utmost: *the uttermost parts of the earth* (Psalms 2:8).

ut·ter·ness (ut′ər nis), *n.* the state of being utter; completeness.

U-tube (yü′tüb′, -tyüb′), *n.* a tube shaped like the letter U, used in chemistry experiments, etc.

U-turn (yü′tėrn′), *n.* a U-shaped turn, as by a motor vehicle reversing its direction.

UV (no periods), **1.** ultrahigh vacuum. **2.** ultraviolet.

u·va·rov·ite (ü vä′rə fīt), *n.* an emerald-green variety of garnet containing chromium. *Formula:* $Ca_3Cr_2Si_3O_{12}$ [< Count S.S. *Uvarov,* 1786-1855, president of St. Petersburg Academy + *-ite*[1]]

u·ve·a (yü′vē ə), *n.* **1.** the posterior, colored surface of the iris of the eye. **2.** the middle, vascular coat of the eye, composed of the iris, choroid membrane, and the ciliary muscle and process. [< Medieval Latin *uvea* < Latin *ūva* grape]

u·ve·al (yü′vē əl), *adj.* of or relating to the uvea.

u·ve·it·ic (yü′vē it′ik), *adj.* **1.** affected with uveitis. **2.** resembling uveitis.

u·ve·i·tis (yü′vē ī′tis), *n.* inflammation of the uvea. [< *uve*(a) + *-itis*]

u·ve·ous (yü′vē əs), *adj.* **1.** resembling a grape or a bunch of grapes. **2.** uveal. [< Medieval Latin *uveus* (with English *-ous*) < Latin *ūva* grape]

u·vu·la (yü′vyə lə), *n., pl.* **-las, -lae** (-lē). the small piece of flesh hanging down from the soft palate in the back of the mouth. [< Late Latin *ūvula* (diminutive) < Latin *ūva* (originally) grape]

u·vu·lar (yü′vyə lər), *adj.* **1.** of or having to do with the uvula. **2.** *Phonetics.* **a.** articulated with the extreme back of the tongue raised toward or against the uvula: *One pronunciation of Danish "r" is as a uvular fricative.* **b.** articulated with vibration of the uvula: *Another pronunciation of Danish "r" is as a uvular trill.* —*n. Phonetics.* a uvular sound.

u·vu·li·tis (yü′vyə lī′tis), *n.* inflammation of the uvula. [< *uvul*(a) + *-itis*]

u·vu·lot·o·my (yü′vyə lot′ə mē), *n., pl.* **-mies.** the surgical removal of the whole or a part of the uvula. [< *uvul*(a) + Greek *-tomíā* a cutting]

U/W or **u/w,** underwriter.

ux., wife (Latin, *uxor*).

ux·o·ri·al (uk sôr′ē əl, -sōr′-), *adj.* **1.** of or having to do with a wife. **2.** like that of a wife; wifely: *uxorial affection.* **3.** uxorious. [< Latin *uxor, -ōris* wife + English *-ial*]

ux·or·i·cid·al (uk sôr′ə sī′dəl, -sōr′-), *adj.* **1.** of or having to do with uxoricide. **2.** tending to uxoricide.

ux·or·i·cide[1] (uk sôr′ə sīd, -sōr′-), *n.* a person who kills his wife. [< Latin *uxor, -ōris* wife + English *-cide*[1]]

ux·or·i·cide[2] (uk sôr′ə sīd, -sōr′-), *n.* the act of killing one's wife. [< Medieval Latin *uxoricidium* < Latin *uxor, -ōris* wife + *-cīdium* -cide[2]]

ux·or·i·lo·cal (uk sôr′ə lō′kəl, -sōr′), *adj. Anthropology.* having the focus in the home of the wife's family; matrilocal: *uxorilocal residence, an uxorilocal culture.* [< Latin *uxor, -ōris* wife + *locus* place + English *-al*[1]]

ux·o·ri·ous (uk sôr′ē əs, -sōr′-), *adj.* excessively or foolishly fond of one's wife. [< Latin *uxōrius* (with English *-ous*) < *uxor, -ōris* wife] —**ux·o′ri·ous·ly,** *adv.* —**ux·o′ri·ous·ness,** *n.*

Uz (uz), *n.* (in the Bible) the home of Job. Job 1:1.

Uz·beg (uz′beg), *n.* Uzbek.

Uz·bek (uz′bek), *n.* **1.** a member of a highly civilized Turkic people of Turkestan. **2.** their Turkic language. Also, **Usbeg, Usbek.**

Roman 100's A.D.

Greek 600's B.C.

Phoenician 1000's B.C.

Egyptian 3000's B.C.

V[1] or **v** (vē), *n., pl.* **V's** or **Vs, v's** or **vs. 1.** the 22nd letter of the English alphabet. **2.** the speech sound represented by this letter, usually a voiced labiodental fricative, as in *valve.* **3.** (as a symbol) the 21st, or sometimes the 22nd, in a series. **4.** the Roman numeral for 5. **5.** *Informal.* a five-dollar bill.

V[2] (vē), *n., pl.* **V's** or **Vs,** *adj.* —*n.* something made in the form of a V. —*adj.* shaped like the letter V. [< *V*[1]]

v (no period), volt.

v., an abbreviation for the following:
1. of (German, *von*).
2. see (Latin, *vide*).
3. valve.
4. verb.
5. verse.
6. version.
7. versus.
8. vice-, as in *v.p.* for *vice-president.*
9. vocative.
10. voice.
11. volt.
12. voltage.
13. volume.

V (no period), an abbreviation for the following:
1. vanadium (chemical element).
2. *Mathematics.* vector.
3. velocity.
4. Victory (a symbol of the Allies during World War II).
5. volt.

V., 1. Venerable. **2.** Victoria. **3.** Viscount. **4.** Volunteer.

V-1 (vē′wun′), *n.* a pulsejet flying bomb used by the Germans in World War II in June, 1944; buzz bomb. [abbreviation of German *Vergeltungswaffe eins* vengeance-weapon one]

V-2 (vē′tü′), *n.* a ramjet rocket bomb used by the Germans in World War II after June, 1944. [abbreviation of German *Vergeltungswaffe zwei* vengeance-weapon two]

V-8 (vē′āt′), *n.* a V-8 engine.

V-8 engine, an automobile engine in the shape of a V, with four cylinders on each of the two cylinder heads, opposite each other, instead of all eight cylinders in a single line.

va (no periods), volt-ampere.

v.a., active verb.

Va., the State of Virginia.

VA (no periods), Veterans Administration (an independent agency of the U.S. government, established July 21, 1930, to administer veterans' benefits, such as pensions, hospital care, education, and insurance).

V.A., an abbreviation for the following:
1. Veterans Administration.
2. Vicar Apostolic.
3. Vice-Admiral.
4. *British.* Royal Order of Victoria and Albert.

vac (no period), **1.** vacation. **2.** vacuum.

vac., vacation.

va·ca (vä′kə), *n.* a West Indian fish related to the grouper and sea bass. [< Cuban Spanish *vaca*]

va·can·cy (vā′kən sē), *n., pl.* **-cies. 1.** the state of being vacant; emptiness. **2.** an unoccupied or unfilled position: *The death of two policemen made two vacancies in our police force.* **3.** the state of being or becoming unoccupied: *the vacancy of the bishopric.* **4.** an empty space: *The great arch . . . with the lofty vacancy beneath it* (Hawthorne). **5.** a room, space, or apartment for rent. **6.** a deficiency: *a vacancy in the scheme of knowledge.* **7.** lack of thought or intelligence: *More absolute vacancy I never saw upon the countenances of human beings* (Samuel Butler). **8.** freedom from work, activity, etc.; idleness: *Much time squandered upon trifles, and more lost in idleness and vacancy* (Samuel Johnson). **9.** *Obsolete.* an interval of leisure time.

va·cant (vā′kənt), *adj.* **1.** not occupied: *a vacant house.* **2.** empty; not filled: *a vacant space.* **3.** without thought or intelligence: *a vacant smile.* **4.** free from work, business, etc.: *vacant time.* [< Latin *vacāns, -antis,* present participle of *vacāre* be empty] —**va′cant·ly,** *adv.*
—**Syn. 1.** See **empty. 3.** expressionless, meaningless, inane.

va·cate (vā′kāt), *v.,* **-cat·ed, -cat·ing.** —*v.t.* **1.** to go away from and leave empty or unoccupied; make vacant: *They will vacate the house at the end of the month.* **2.** to leave (a position, office, etc.) empty or unoccupied by death, resignation, or retirement: *His office was automatically vacated when he was judged guilty.* **3.** to make legally void; annul; cancel: *All former agreements were vacated by this contract.*
—*v.i.* **1.** to give up possession or occupancy of a house, etc. **2.** to give up a position, office, etc. **3.** to leave; go away.
[< Latin *vacāre* (with English *-ate*[1]) be empty]

va·ca·tion (vā kā′shən), *n.* **1.** a time of rest and freedom from work; holiday: *a short vacation at the seashore. There is a vacation from schoolwork every year at Christmas.* **2.** the act of vacating: *Immediate vacation of the premises was demanded.* —*v.i.* to take a vacation or holiday: *We vacationed in the Hawaiian Islands.* [< Latin *vacātiō, -ōnis* < *vacāre* have time; be free, empty]

va·ca·tion·er (vā kā′shə nər), *n.* vacationist.

va·ca·tion·ist (vā kā′shə nist), *n.* a person who is taking a vacation: *As the tourist season nears its peak, U.S. vacationists are on the move—about their own country and on record invasions of foreign shores* (Time).

va·ca·tion·land (vā kā′shən land′), *n.* a place with many scenic attractions, lodging, and amusement for vacationists: *There are no more tours to Yugoslavia—the Dalmatian coast, which used to be the Communists' favorite vacationland, is off limits* (Maclean's).

va·ca·tion·less (vā kā′shən lis), *adj.* without a vacation.

vac·ci·nal (vak′sə nəl), *adj.* of or having to do with vaccine; caused by vaccination.

vac·ci·nate (vak′sə nāt), *v.,* **-nat·ed, -nat·ing.** —*v.t.* **1.** to inoculate with a mildly toxic preparation of bacteria or a virus of a specific disease to prevent or lessen the effects of that disease. **2.** to inoculate with the modified virus of cowpox as a protection against smallpox. —*v.i.* to perform or practice vaccination. [< *vaccin*(e) + *-ate*[1]]

vac·ci·na·tion (vak′sə nā′shən), *n.* **1.** the act, practice, or process of vaccinating: *Vaccination has made smallpox a very rare disease.* **2.** the scar where vaccine was injected.

vac·ci·na·tion·ist (vak′sə nā′shə nist), *n.* a person who believes in or advocates vaccination.

vac·ci·na·tor (vak′sə nā′tər), *n.* **1.** a person who vaccinates. **2.** an instrument used in performing vaccination.

vac·cine (vak′sēn, -sin), *n.* **1.** any preparation, especially one of bacteria or a virus of a specific disease, used for preventive inoculation against a disease: *A vaccine is a way to trick the body's natural disease-fighting mechanism into putting up a counterattack immediately and setting up a defense that may last many years* (New York Times). **2.** the virus causing cowpox, prepared for use in preventive inoculation against smallpox.
—*adj.* **1. a.** having to do with a vaccine: *The vaccine test was the most extensive field experiment ever undertaken, and its evaluation was an exceedingly complex task* (Scientific American). **b.** used in vaccine. **c.** connected with vaccination. **2.** characteristic of cowpox. **3.** relating to cows: *vaccine medical knowledge.*
[< Latin *vaccīnus* of or from cows < *vacca* cow]

vaccine point, a sharp-pointed instrument used in vaccinating.

vac·cin·i·a (vak sin′ē ə), *n.* cowpox. [< New Latin *vaccinia* < Latin *vaccīnus;* see VACCINE]

vac·cin·i·a·ceous (vak sin′ē ā′shəs), *adj.* belonging to a group of plants usually placed in the heath family, including the blueberry, huckleberry, and cranberry. [< New Latin *Vaccineaceae* the family name (< *Vaccinium* the typical genus < Latin *vaccīnium* blueberry; (originally) hyacinth) + English *-ous*]

vac·cin·i·al (vak sin′ē əl), *adj.* of or having to do with cowpox.

vac·ci·ni·za·tion (vak′sə nə zā′shən), *n.* a thorough method of vaccination in which repeated inoculations are made until immunity is established.

vac·ci·no·ther·a·py (vak′sə nō ther′ə pē), *n.* treatment of disease by means of vaccines.

vac·il·lant (vas′ə lənt), *adj.* vacillating.

vac·il·late (vas′ə lāt), *v.i.,* **-lat·ed, -lat·ing. 1.** to waver in mind or opinion: *When time came for the final decision, the manager suddenly ceased to vacillate.* **2.** to move first one way and then another; waver. [< Latin *vacillāre* (with English *-ate*[1])] —**Syn. 1.** hesitate. **2.** oscillate, sway.

vac·il·lat·ing (vas′ə lā′ting), *adj.* **1.** tending to hesitate or be uncertain; characterized by hesitation or uncertainty: *A vacillating person finds it hard to make up his mind.* **2.** unsteady; swaying. —**vac′il·lat′ing·ly,** *adv.*

vac·il·la·tion (vas′ə lā′shən), *n.* **1.** a wavering in mind or opinion: *His constant vacillation made him an unfit administrator.* **2.** unsteadiness; a swaying.

vac·il·la·tor (vas′ə lā′tər), *n.* a person who vacillates or wavers: *The Soviet premier is essentially a vacillator, a man who shrinks from unpleasant decisions* (Wall Street Journal).

vac·il·la·to·ry (vas′ə lə tôr′ē, -tōr′-), *adj.* vacillating.

vac·u·a (vak′yu̇ ə), *n.* a plural of **vacuum.**

vac·u·ate (vak′yu̇ āt), *v.t.,* **-at·ed, -at·ing. 1.** to create a vacuum in. **2.** *Obsolete.* to make empty. **3.** *Obsolete.* to annul; nullify. **4.** *Obsolete.* to clear out or discharge. [< Latin *vacuāre* (with English *-ate*[1])]

vac·u·a·tion (vak′yu̇ ā′shən), *n.* the act of emptying; evacuation.

va·cu·i·ty (va kyü′ə tē), *n., pl.* **-ties. 1.** a lack of thought or intelligence: *In indolent vacuity of thought* (William Cowper). **2.** something foolish or stupid: *an undue preoccupation with the vacuities which society has invented* (Arnold Bennett). **3.** an absence or lack (of something specified). **4.** emptiness. **5.** an empty space; vacuum. [< Latin *vacuitās* < *vacuus* vacuous]

vac·u·o·lar (vak′yu̇ ə lər), *adj.* vacuolated.

vac·u·o·late (vak′yu̇ ə lāt), *adj.* vacuolated.

vac·u·o·lat·ed (vak′yu̇ ə lā′tid), *adj.* provided with one or more vacuoles.

vac·u·o·la·tion (vak′yu̇ ə lā′shən), *n.* **1.** the formation of vacuoles. **2.** vacuolated condition.

vac·u·ole (vak′yu̇ ōl), *n.* **1.** a tiny cavity in the protoplasm of a living cell, containing fluid. See **amoeba** for picture. **2.** (formerly) any very small cavity in organic tissue. [< French *vacuole* < Latin *vacuus* empty]

vac·u·ous (vak′yu̇ əs), *adj.* **1.** showing no thought or intelligence; foolish; stupid: *the vacuous smile of an idiot; a vacuous, solemn snob* (Thackeray). **2.** having no meaning or direction; idle; indolent: *a vacuous life.* **3.** empty (of matter or anything solid or tangible). [< Latin *vacuus* (with English *-ous*)] —**vac′u·ous·ly,** *adv.* —**vac′u·ous·ness,** *n.*
—**Syn. 1.** fatuous.

vac·u·um (vak′yu̇m, vak′yu̇ əm), *n., pl.* **vac·u·ums** or (*except for def. 6*) **vac·u·a,** *adj., v.* —*n.* **1.** an empty space without even air in it. **2.** an enclosed space from which almost all the air or other gas has been removed, especially to permit experimentation without atmospheric distortion. **3.** an empty space; void. **4.** the condition or amount of loss in atmospheric pressure within a space. **5. a.** emptiness. **b.** something that needs filling; hiatus; gap: *a political vacuum.* **c.** a condition of seclusion or apartness from others: *to live in a vacuum.* **6.** a vacuum cleaner.
—*adj.* **1.** of or having to do with a vacuum: *a vacuum gauge.* **2.** producing a vacuum: *a vacuum fan.* **3.** using a vacuum: *vacuum canning.* **4.** entirely or partially exhausted of air (or other gas): *a vacuum tube.* **5.** using suction: *vacuum ventilation.* **6.** using gas pressures that are lower than atmospheric pressure, as various processes.
—*v.t. Informal.* **1.** to clean with a vacuum cleaner. **2.** to use any vacuum device on.
[< Latin *vacuum,* neuter of *vacuus* empty]

vacuum bottle or **flask,** a bottle or flask made with a vacuum between its inner and outer walls so that its contents remain hot or cold for long periods of time.
vacuum cleaner, an apparatus for cleaning carpets, rugs, floors, furniture, curtains, etc., by suction.
vacuum cleaning, the act of cleaning with a vacuum cleaner.
vacuum fan, a fan that operates by suction, used to ventilate an enclosed area.
vacuum gauge, a form of pressure gauge for indicating the internal pressure or the amount of vacuum in a container.
vac·u·um·ize (vak′yu̇ mīz, vak′yu̇ ə-), *v.,* **-ized, -iz·ing.** *—v.i.* to produce a vacuum. *—v.t.* to produce a vacuum in (a container, chamber, etc.).
vacuum melting, a method of melting metals or alloys in a sealed furnace to prevent atmospheric oxidation, remove gaseous impurities, and improve purity and physical properties: *To produce stronger and more ductile steel, 17 U.S. companies have adopted another new innovation called vacuum melting* (Time).
vac·u·um-packed (vak′yu̇m pakt′, vak′yu̇ əm-), *adj.* **1.** packed in an airtight can, jar, etc., to retain freshness or as a means of preserving: *vacuum-packed coffee.* **2.** having had all or most of the air removed before sealing: *vacuum-packed cans.*
vacuum pump, 1. a pump or device by which a partial vacuum can be produced. **2.** a pump in which a partial vacuum is utilized to raise water.
vacuum tube, *Electronics.* a sealed glass tube or bulb from which almost all the air has been removed, and into which electrodes from outside project; an electron tube, radio tube, vacuum valve, or thermionic valve. A vacuum tube (typically) consists of three elements: a heated cathode (filament) that emits electrons; a metallic anode (plate) that receives the electrons; and a grid, between the cathode and anode, that controls the flow of electrons. Vacuum tubes are used to control the flow of electric currents in any electronic device, rectify alternating currents, detect radio waves, amplify currents, produce alternating currents of a high frequency range, etc. See also **X ray** for picture.

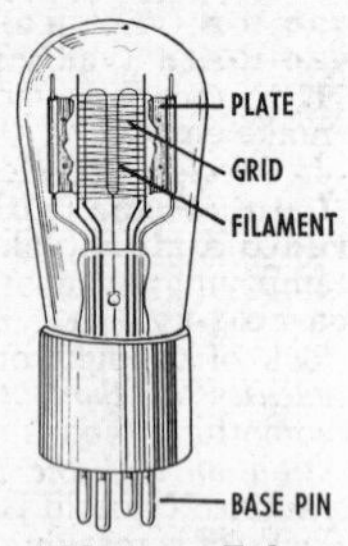

Vacuum Tube

vacuum valve, *Especially British.* vacuum tube.
vacuum ventilation, a system in which the vitiated air is drawn out of the space to be ventilated, and is replaced by the fresh air coming in from the outside because of the decreased pressure.
V.A.D. or **VAD** (no periods), Voluntary Aid Detachment.
va·de me·cum (vā′dē mē′kəm), **1.** anything a person carries about with him because of its usefulness. **2.** a book for ready reference; manual; handbook: *J. K. Lasser's tax guide alone has sold more than thirteen million copies in its eighteen years as the taxpayer's vade mecum* (Harper's). [< Medieval Latin *vade mecum* < Latin imperative of *vādere* go + *mēcum* with me]
V. Adm., Vice-Admiral.
va·dose water (vā′dōs), *Geology.* ground water derived from rain, melted snow, etc., that seeps into rocks and soil from the surface: *By this process the descending vadose water dissolves the soluble minerals and carries them in solution down into the zone of saturation* (White and Renner). [< Latin *vadōsus* shallow < *vadum* a ford]
vae vic·tis (vē vik′tis), *Latin.* woe to the vanquished.
vag·a·bond (vag′ə bond), *n.* **1.** an idle wanderer; wanderer; tramp. **2.** a good-for-nothing person; rascal.
—adj. **1.** wandering: *the Crow chieftain and his vagabond warriors* (Washington Irving). *The gypsies lead a vagabond life.* **2.** good-for-nothing; worthless: *a vagabond tramp.* **3.** moving hither and thither; drifting: *vagabond winds.* **4.** characteristic of a homeless wanderer: *a short book well-suited to vagabond habits.* **5.** not subject to control or restraint; roving; straying: *vagabond thoughts.*
—v.i. to roam or wander about like a vagabond: *the delights and tribulations of vagabonding around the Gulf* (Sunset).
[< Middle French *vagabond,* learned borrowing from Latin *vagābundus* < *vagārī* to wander < *vagus* roving]
—**Syn.** *n.* **1.** vagrant, nomad, hobo. **2.** rogue.
vag·a·bond·age (vag′ə bon′dij), *n.* **1.** the fact, state, or condition of being a vagabond; idle wandering: *to indulge in literary vagabondage.* **2.** vagabonds collectively: *rural vagabondage.* —**Syn. 1.** vagrancy.
vag·a·bond·ism (vag′ə bon diz′əm), *n.* the ways or habits of a vagabond; vagabondage.
vag·a·bond·ize (vag′ə bon dīz), *v.i.,* **-ized, -iz·ing.** to wander as or like a vagabond; roam at will.
va·gal (vā′gəl), *adj.* of or having to do with the vagus nerve: *In 20 more or less sedentary men a 6- to 12-week period of vigorous physical retraining restored the vagal tone toward normal* (Science News Letter).
va·gar·i·ous (və gãr′ē əs), *adj.* having vagaries; whimsical; capricious; erratic: *Bozzy's vagarious search for a wife, described in the previous volume, has succeeded, and for the moment at least he is well-behaved* (Time).
va·gar·y (və gãr′ē, vā′gər-), *n., pl.* **-gar·ies. 1.** an odd fancy; extravagant notion: *the vagaries of a dream.* **2.** odd action; caprice; freak: *the vagaries of women's fashions.* [probably < Latin *vagārī* to wander < *vagus* roving] —**Syn. 1.** whim, fantasy. **2.** fad.
va·gi (vā′jī), *n.* plural of **vagus.**
va·gi·na (və jī′nə), *n., pl.* **-nas, -nae** (-nē). **1.** *Anatomy, Zoology.* **a.** (in female mammals) the membranous canal leading from the uterus to the vulva or external opening. **b.** a sheathlike part, organ, or covering; sheath or theca. **2.** *Botany.* the sheath formed around a stem by the lower parts of some leaves, as the tulip. [< Latin *vagīna* (originally) sheath, scabbard]
vag·i·nal (vaj′ə nəl, və jī′-), *adj.* **1.** of, having to do with, or affecting the vagina of a female mammal. **2.** of, resembling, or serving as a sheath; thecal.
vag·i·na·lec·to·my (vaj′ə nə lek′tə mē), *n., pl.* **-mies.** vaginectomy.
vag·i·nate (vaj′ə nit, -nāt), *adj.* **1.** having a vagina or sheath; invaginate. **2.** like a sheath.
vag·i·nec·to·my (vaj′ə nek′tə mē), *n., pl.* **-mies. 1.** excision of the vagina. **2.** surgical removal of the membrane around the testes. [< *vagin*(a) + Greek *ektomē* a cutting out]
vag·i·ni·tis (vaj′ə nī′tis), *n.* inflammation of the vagina. [< New Latin *vaginitis* < Latin *vagīna* (see VAGINA) + New Latin *-itis* inflammation, -itis]
va·got·o·my (və got′ə mē), *n., pl.* **-mies.** the surgical separation of the vagus nerve. [< *vag*(us nerve) + Greek *-tomíā* a cutting]
va·gran·cy (vā′grən sē), *n., pl.* **-cies. 1.** a wandering idly from place to place without proper means or ability to earn a living: *The tramp was arrested for vagrancy.* **2.** a wandering. **3.** a wandering or digressing in mind, opinion, thought, etc.: *Conscience helps to check the vagrancies of the heart.* **4.** an instance or occasion of wandering or roaming; rambling journey; straying.
va·grant (vā′grənt), *n.* **1.** an idle wanderer; tramp. **2.** a wanderer.
—adj. **1.** leading a wandering or nomadic life; ranging or roaming from place to place: *a vagrant tribe of Indians.* **2.** a wandering without proper means of earning a living: *a town overrun with vagrant beggars.* **3.** of or having to do with a vagrant: *vagrant habits.* **4.** moving in no definite direction or course; wandering: *vagrant thoughts.*
[perhaps alteration of Anglo-French *wacrant* (< a Germanic word); influenced by French *vagant* straying < Latin *vagārī* to wander]
—**va′grant·ly,** *adv.*
va·grom (vā′grəm), *adj. Archaic.* vagrant. [alteration of *vagrant*]
vague (vāg), *adj.,* **va·guer, va·guest. 1.** not definitely or precisely expressed: *a vague statement. He gave a vague assent.* **2.** (of feelings or sensations) indefinite; indistinct: *The vague but strong feeling that her son was a stranger to her* (George Eliot). **3.** indistinctly seen or perceived; formless; obscure; shadowy: *In a fog everything looks vague.* **4.** (of persons, the mind, etc.) lacking clarity or precision: *a vague personality.* **5.** devoid of expression: *his mild, vague old eyes* (Booth Tarkington). [< Old French *vague,* learned borrowing from Latin *vagus* wandering. Doublet of VAGUS.] —**vague′ly,** *adv.* —**Syn. 1.** ambiguous. See **obscure. 3.** hazy.
vague·ness (vāg′nis), *n.* the quality or condition of being vague; indefiniteness: *Vagueness should not be invoked when a precise answer is possible* (Bernard DeVoto).
va·gus (vā′gəs), *n., pl.* **va·gi.** vagus nerve. [< New Latin *vagus* < Latin, wandering. Doublet of VAGUE.]
vagus nerve, either of the tenth pair of cranial nerves, extending from the brain to the heart, lungs, stomach, and other organs: *Production of gastric juices for digesting food results from stimulation of the vagus nerves* (Science News Letter).
va·hi·ne (vä hē′nā), *n. Tahitian.* a woman; female; wife: *Slowly paddling toward us in an outrigger canoe came our host's vahine* (Maclean's).
Vai (vī), *n., pl.* **Vai** or **Vais. 1.** a member of a Mandingo people of Sierra Leone and Liberia: *Classified under the Mandingan group are the Vais, one of the most intellectual communities of West Africa and the only Negroes in the continent who have invented a system of writing* (Walter Fitzgerald). **2.** the language of this people.
vail[1] (vāl), *Archaic.* *—v.t.* **1.** to lower (the eyes, a banner, etc.); cause or allow to fall. **2.** to take off; doff. *—v.i.* to yield; bow. [< Old French *valer,* or short for Middle English *avalen* < Old French *avaler* < *a val* downhill < Latin *ad vallem* to the valley. Compare AVALANCHE.]
vail[2] (vāl), *n. Archaic.* money given to a servant or attendant, especially by a guest on his departure from his host's home. [< Old French *vaille-,* stem of *valoir* be of worth < Latin *valēre.* Compare AVAIL.]
vain (vān), *adj.* **1.** having too much pride in one's looks, ability, accomplishments, etc.: *A good, honest, plain girl, and not vain of her face* (Henry Fielding). **2.** of no use; without effect or success; producing no good result; fruitless: *I made vain attempts to reach her by telephone.* **3.** of no value or importance; worthless; empty. **4.** without sense or wisdom; foolish; senseless: *unruly and vain talkers* (Titus 1:10).
—n. **in vain,** without effect or success: *The drowning man shouted in vain, for no one could hear him.*
take a name in vain. See under **name,** *n.*
[< Old French *vein, vain* < Latin *vānus* idle, empty] —**vain′ness,** *n.*
—**Syn. 1.** conceited, egotistical. **2. Vain, futile** mean without effect or success. **Vain** describes thinking, action, effort, etc., that fails to accomplish a given result: *The principal made another vain appeal for better equipment in the high-school laboratories.* **Futile** adds and emphasizes the idea of being incapable of producing the result, and often suggests that the attempt is useless or unwise: *Without microscopes and other essential equipment, attempts to teach science were futile.*
vain·glo·ri·ous (vān′glôr′ē əs, -glōr′-), *adj.* excessively proud or boastful; extremely vain: *a vainglorious confidence prevailed . . . among the Spanish cavaliers* (Washington Irving). —**vain′glo′ri·ous·ly,** *adv.* —**vain′-glo′ri·ous·ness,** *n.* —**Syn.** vaunting, arrogant, conceited.
vain·glo·ry (vān′glôr′ē, -glōr′-), *n., pl.* **-ries. 1.** an extreme pride in oneself; boastful vanity. **2.** worthless pomp or show. **3.** *Rare.* a vainglorious thing, action, etc.: *What needs these Feasts, pomps and vainglories?* (Shakespeare). [< *vain* + *glory,* translation of Medieval Latin *vana gloria*] —**Syn. 2.** ostentation.
vain·ly (vān′lē), *adv.* **1.** in vain. **2.** with conceit. —**Syn. 2.** arrogantly.
vair (vãr), *n.* **1.** a gray-and-white squirrel fur used for lining and trimming the robes of nobles in the 1200's and the 1300's. **2.** its representation in heraldry by small, shield-shaped figures alternately silver and gold. [< Old French *vair,* oblique of *vairs* < Latin *varius* variegated. Doublet of VARIOUS.]
Vais·ya (vīs′yə), *n.* a member of the mercantile and agricultural caste among the Hindus. [< Sanskrit *Vaiśya* < *viś* settlement; people]
vai·vode (vī′vōd), *n.* voivode.
va·keel (və kēl′), *n.* **1.** (in India) an agent or representative, especially of a person of political importance, as an ambassador or

special commissioner at a court. **2.** a native attorney in a court of law. [< Hindustani *vakīl*]

va·kil (və kēl′), *n.* vakeel.

val·ance (val′əns), *n.* **1.** a short, decorative drapery over the top of a window. **2.** a short curtain, as one hanging from the canopy of a bed or from the mattress to the floor: *An iron bedstead (no valance of course), and hair mattress* (Florence Nightingale). [probably < unrecorded Anglo-French *valance* < Old French *avaler* to descend; see VAIL[1]]

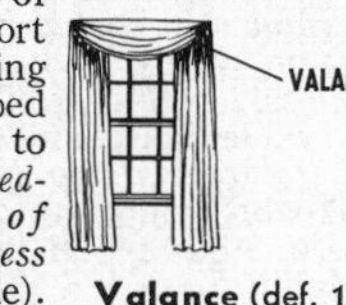

Valance (def. 1)

val·anced (val′ənst), *adj.* provided or furnished with a valance: *an old . . . chair, valanced, and fringed around with worsted bobs* (Laurence Sterne).

Val·div·i·a (val div′ē ə), *adj.* of, having to do with, or belonging to a culture that flourished on the northern coast of Ecuador about 3000 B.C., noted for the similarity of its pottery to that of the Jomon culture of Japan. [< *Valdivia,* a fishing village in northern Ecuador, where remains of this culture were discovered in 1954]

Val·div·i·an (val div′ē ən), *n.* a member of the people who produced the Valdivia culture: *The newcomers from Japan began to instruct the Valdivians, who were such apt students that their pottery soon equaled . . . that of distant Kyushu* (Science News Letter). —*adj.* Valdivia.

vale[1] (vāl), *n.* **1.** *Poetic.* valley: *o'er vale and mountain* (Wordsworth). **2.** the world regarded as a place of sorrow or tears, or the scene of life: *my dear friends and brethren in this vale of tears* (Thackeray). [< Old French *val* < Latin *vallis*]

va·le[2] (vā′lē, vä′lā), *interj.* good-by; farewell. —*n.* **1.** a good-by; a farewell: *I am going to make my vales to you for some weeks* (Shakespeare). **2.** a farewell greeting, letter, etc. [< Latin *valē,* imperative of *valēre* to fare well]

val·e·dic·tion (val′ə dik′shən), *n.* **1.** a bidding or saying farewell: *Their last valediction, thrice uttered by the attendants, was . . . very solemn* (Sir Thomas Browne). **2.** a farewell. [< Latin *valedictus,* past participle of *valedīcere* bid farewell (< *valē* be well! + *dīcere* to say) + English *-ion*]

val·e·dic·to·ri·an (val′ə dik tôr′ē ən, -tōr′-), *n.* (in American colleges and schools) the student who gives the farewell address at the graduation of his class. The valedictorian is often the student who ranks highest in his class. [American English < *valedictory* + English *-ian*]

val·e·dic·to·ry (val′ə dik′tər ē, -dik′trē), *n., pl.* **-ries,** *adj.* —*n.* a farewell address, especially at the graduating exercises of a school or college. —*adj.* bidding farewell: *Sir Winston treated the House of Commons to a stunning valedictory performance* (Newsweek).

va·lence (vā′ləns), *n.* **1.** *Chemistry.* **a.** the quality of an atom or radical that determines the number of other atoms or radicals with which it can combine, indicated by the number of hydrogen atoms with which it can combine or which it can displace. Elements whose atoms lose electrons, such as hydrogen and the metals, have a positive valence. Elements whose atoms add electrons, such as oxygen and other nonmetals, have a negative valence. Atoms or radicals with a valence of one are termed univalent; of two, bivalent; of three, trivalent, etc. In most of their compounds, oxygen has a negative valence of two and hydrogen has a positive valence of one; one atom of oxygen combines with two of hydrogen to form a molecule of water. **b.** a unit of valence. **2.** *Biology.* the ability of chromosomes to unite with or produce a certain effect upon each other. **3.** a somewhat similar capacity of serums, etc. [< Latin *valentia* strength, capacity < *valēns, -entis,* present participle of *valēre* be strong]

valence electron, an electron in the outer shell of an atom. In a chemical change, the atom gains, loses, or shares such an electron in combining with another atom or atoms to form a molecule.

Va·len·ci·a orange, or **Va·len·ci·a** (və-len′shē ə, -shə), *n.* a thin-skinned, yellowish-brown orange that ripens during the summer, grown chiefly in California and Florida. [< *Valencia,* a seaport and former colony in Spain]

Va·len·ci·ennes (və len′sē enz′; *French* vá-läɴ syen′), *n.,* or **Valenciennes lace,** a fine lace in which the pattern and background are made together of the same threads, originally made at Valenciennes, France, but now made elsewhere.

va·len·cy (vā′lən sē), *n., pl.* **-cies.** valence.

-valent, *combining form.* having valence, as in *trivalent.* [< Latin *valēns;* see VALENCE]

val·en·tine (val′ən tīn), *n.* **1.** a greeting card or small gift sent on Saint Valentine's Day, February 14. **2. a.** a sweetheart chosen on this day: *I am also this year my wife's Valentine, and it cost me £5; but that I must have laid out if we had not been Valentines* (Samuel Pepys). **b.** any sweetheart. [< Saint *Valentine* < Late Latin *Valentīnus,* a proper name]

Valentine's Day, Saint Valentine's Day, February 14, the day on which valentines are exchanged.

Val·en·tin·i·an (val′ən tin′ē ən), *adj.* of or having to do with Valentinus, a Gnostic leader who taught at Rome in the middle of the 100's A.D.; of or belonging to the Gnostic system or sect instituted by him. —*n.* a follower of Valentinus; Valentinian Gnostic.

Val·en·tin·i·an·ism (val′ən tin′ē ə niz′əm), *n.* the system of doctrines maintained by the Valentinians.

val·er·ate (val′ə rāt), *n.* a salt of valeric acid.

va·le·ri·an (və lir′ē ən), *n.* **1.** a strong-smelling drug used to quiet the nerves, prepared from the roots of the common variety of valerian. **2.** any of a group of perennial herbs, especially the heliotrope or all-heal, a species that has small pinkish, white, or lavender flowers, cultivated for its medicinal root and often grown in gardens. [< Old French *valeriane* or < Medieval Latin *valeriana* < Latin, adjective, probably ultimately < *valēre* be strong, of worth]

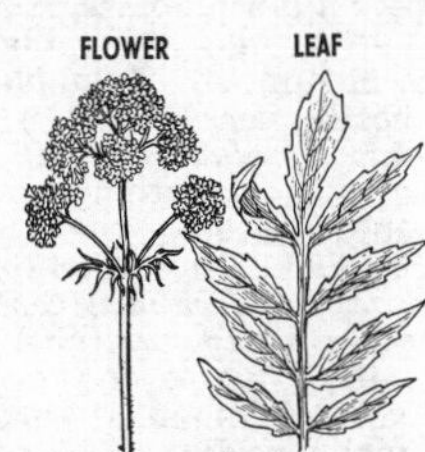

Common Valerian (def. 2)
(garden heliotrope)

va·le·ri·a·na·ceous (və lir′ē ə nā′shəs), *adj.* belonging to a family of dicotyledonous herbs or shrubs typified by the valerian. [< New Latin *Valerianaceae* the family name (< *Valeriana* the typical genus < Medieval Latin *valeriana;* see VALERIAN) + English *-ous*]

va·le·ri·a·nate (və lir′ē ə nāt), *n.* a salt of valeric acid.

va·le·ri·an·ic (və lir′ē an′ik), *adj.* valeric.

valerianic acid, valeric acid.

va·ler·ic (və ler′ik, -lir′-), *adj.* **1.** of, obtained from, or related to the plant valerian. **2.** of or having to do with valeric acid or one of the acids isomeric with it.

valeric acid, 1. an organic acid present in valerian roots or produced synthetically, having a pungent odor and used in making perfumes, in flavoring, and in medicine. *Formula:* $C_5H_{10}O_2$ **2.** any of several acids with the same formula. [short for *valerianic* < *valerian*]

val·et (val′it, -ā; va lā′), *n.* **1.** a servant who takes care of a man's clothes, helps him dress, or performs similar personal services: *No man is a hero to his valet* (Marquise de Sévigné). **2.** a similar servant in a hotel who cleans or presses clothes and performs similar personal services. —*v.t., v.i.* to wait upon or serve as a valet. [< Old French *valet,* variant of *vaslet* (originally) a squire (probably diminutive) < *vasal* vassal. Compare VARLET.] —**Syn.** *n.* **1.** manservant.

va·let de cham·bre (vá le′ də shäɴ′brə), *pl.* **va·lets de cham·bre** (vá le′ də shäɴ′brə). a man's personal servant; valet. [< French *valet de chambre* (literally) chamber servant]

val·e·tu·di·nar·i·an (val′ə tü′də nãr′ē ən, -tyü′-), *n.* **1.** a person in weak health; chronic invalid: *Having been a valetudinarian all his life, without activity of mind or body, he was a much older man in ways than in years* (Jane Austen). **2.** a person who thinks he is ill when he is not; hypochondriac.
—*adj.* **1.** sickly. **2.** thinking too much about the state of one's health.
[< Latin *valētūdinārius* sickly (< *valētūdō, -inis* good or bad health < *valēre* be strong) + English *-an*]

val·e·tu·di·nar·i·an·ism (val′ə tü′də-nãr′ē ə niz′əm, -tyü′-), *n.* valetudinarian condition or habits; invalidism.

val·e·tu·di·nar·y (val′ə tü′də ner′ē, -tyü′-), *n., pl.* **-nar·ies,** *adj.* valetudinarian: *I carry an infirm and valetudinary body* (John Donne).

val·gus (val′gəs), *n.* a form of clubfoot or talipes in which the foot is turned outward. —*adj.* **1.** (of the bones in the foot, knee, hip, etc.) characterized by the abnormal position of turning outward. **2.** knock-kneed.
[< New Latin *valgus* knock-kneed < Latin, bow-legged]

Val·hal·la (val hal′ə), *n.* **1.** *Norse Mythology.* the hall where the souls of heroes slain in battle feast with the god Odin. **2.** a place or sphere assigned to persons worthy of special honor: *Neither Pitt nor Peel lives in my Valhalla* (Lord Acton). Also, **Walhalla.** [< New Latin *Valhalla* < Old Icelandic *valhöll, valhall* < *valr* those slain in battle + *höll, hall* hall]

va·li (vä lē′), *n.* the governor general of a Turkish vilayet. [< Turkish *vali* < Arabic *wālī*]

val·iance (val′yəns), *n.* **1.** bravery; valor; valiancy: *When our affright was over we . . . set out afresh with double valiance* (Elizabeth Gaskell). **2.** *Archaic.* a courageous act or deed. [< Anglo-French *valiance,* Old French *vaillance* < *valiant, vaillant;* see VALIANT]

val·ian·cy (val′yən sē), *n.* the quality of being brave; bravery; valor.

val·iant (val′yənt), *adj.* **1.** having or possessing courage; courageous; brave: *a valiant soldier.* **2.** showing courage; heroic: *a valiant deed.* —*n.* a brave or courageous person: *Wealth . . . is the possession of the valuable by the valiant* (John Ruskin). *Cowards die many times before their deaths; The valiant never taste of death but once* (Shakespeare). [< Anglo-French, Old French *vaillant, valiant,* present participle of *valeir* (originally) be strong < Latin *valēre*] —**val′iant·ly,** *adv.* —**val′iant·ness,** *n.*

val·id (val′id), *adj.* **1.** supported by facts or authority; sound; true: *a valid argument, proof, or assertion.* **2.** having force; holding good; effective: *Illness is a valid excuse for being absent from work.* **3.** having legal authority or force; legally binding: *A contract made by an insane man is not valid.* **4.** *Archaic.* strong; powerful. **5. a.** healthy. **b.** sane. [< Latin *validus* strong < *valēre* be strong] —**val′id·ly,** *adv.* —**val′id·ness,** *n.*
—**Syn. 1. Valid, sound, cogent** mean convincing with respect to truth, rightness, or reasoning. **Valid** implies being based on truth or fact and supported by correct reasoning: *His objections to women doctors are not valid.* **Sound** implies having a solid foundation of truth or right and being free from defects or errors in reasoning: *The author has sound views on opportunities today.* **Cogent** implies being so valid or sound as to be convincing: *He gives cogent advice to young people.*

val·i·date (val′ə dāt), *v.t.,* **-dat·ed, -dat·ing. 1.** to make or declare legally binding; give legal force to. **2.** to support by facts or authority; confirm. —**Syn. 1.** legalize. **2.** corroborate, substantiate.

val·i·da·tion (val′ə dā′shən), *n.* the act of validating or making valid.

va·lid·i·ty (və lid′ə tē), *n., pl.* **-ties. 1.** truth; soundness: *the validity of an argument, the validity of an excuse.* **2.** legal authority, force, or strength; being legally binding: *the validity of a contract.* **3.** effectiveness: *He had . . . too high an opinion of the validity of regular troops* (Benjamin Franklin). —**Syn. 1.** authenticity. **2.** legality. **3.** efficacy.

val·ine (val′ēn, -in), *n.* an amino acid constituent of protein, essential to growth. It can be isolated by hydrolysis of fish proteins for use as a nutrient, in medication, and in biochemical research. *Formula:* $C_5H_{11}NO_2$ [< *val*(eric acid) + *-ine*[2]]

va·lise (və lēs′), *n. U.S.* a traveling bag to hold clothes, etc. [< French *valise* < Italian *valigia;* origin uncertain] —**Syn.** portmanteau, suitcase.

Val·kyr (val′kir), *n.* Valkyrie.

Val·kyr·i·an (val kir′ē ən), *adj.* of or relating to the Valkyries.

Val·kyr·ie (val kir′ē, val′kər ē), *n. Norse Mythology.* one of the twelve handmaidens of Odin, who ride through the air and hover over battlefields, choosing the heroes who are to die in battle and afterward leading them to Valhalla. Also, **Walkyrie.** [earlier *Valkyria* < Old Icelandic *valkyrja* < *valr* those slain in battle + *kyrja* chooser < *kjōsa* to choose]

val·la (val′ə), *n.* the plural of **vallum.**

Val lace (val), Valenciennes lace.

val·late (val′āt), *adj.* surrounded by a ridge or elevation; having a surrounding ridge or elevation. [< Latin *vallātus,* past participle of *vallāre* to surround with a rampart < *vallum* rampart < *vallus* stake]

val·lat·ed (val′ā tid), *adj.* surrounded with or as with a rampart or wall.

val·la·tion (va lā′shən), *n.* a trench; rampart. [< Late Latin *vallātiō, -ōnis* < Latin *vallāre;* see VALLATE]

val·lec·u·la (və lek′yə lə), *n., pl.* **-lae** (-lē). **1.** *Anatomy.* a furrow or fissure. **2.** *Botany.* a groove or channel. [< New Latin *vallecula* < Late Latin *vallicula* depression (diminutive) < Latin *vallis* valley, furrow]

val·lec·u·lar (və lek′yə lər), *adj.* **1.** of or like a vallecula. **2.** having a vallecula or valleculae.

val·lec·u·late (və lek′yə lāt), *adj.* vallecular.

val·ley (val′ē), *n., pl.* **-leys. 1.** a long depression or hollow lying between hills or stretches of high ground and usually having a river or stream flowing along its bottom. **2.** a wide region of generally flat, low country drained by a great river system: *the Mississippi valley.* **3.** any hollow or structure like a valley, especially a trough between waves. **4.** a place or condition marked by depression, darkness, sorrow, etc.: *a valley of tears. Yea, though I walk through the valley of the shadow of death, I will fear no evil* (Psalms 23:4). **5.** *Architecture.* a depression formed by the meeting of two sloping sides of a roof, or a roof and a wall; gutter. [< Old French *valee,* earlier *vallede* < *val* vale[1] < Latin *vallis*] **—val′ley-like′,** *adj.* **—Syn. 1.** vale, dale, glen, dell.

valley fever, a lung disease caused by a fungus, affecting people in hot, dusty areas; coccidioidomycosis: *The long, hot summer apparently cannot completely destroy the soil fungus that causes valley fever in humans* (Science News Letter).

valley flat, a low, level deposit of sediment in the channel of a stream: *Gradually, by undermining and caving the valley wall on one side and depositing on the other, the stream produces the broad valley flat of old age* (Finch and Trewartha).

valley glacier, a glacier that occupies a mountain valley, as in the Alps and the mountains of the western United States.

valley mahogany, feather tree; a tree of the mahogany family, found in valleys of the western United States.

val·lis·ne·ri·a·ceous (val′is nir′ē ā′shəs), *adj.* belonging to the frogbit family of aquatic plants. [< New Latin *Vallisneriaceae* the family name (< Antonio *Vallisneri,* 1661-1730, an Italian naturalist)]

val·lum (val′əm), *n., pl.* **-la.** a wall or rampart of earth, sods, or stone, erected as a permanent means of defense, especially one of those constructed by the Romans in northern England and central Scotland: *He would walk round the ancient vallum . . . and wonder at the mechanical skill which could have moved such ponderous masses* (John Lubbock). [< Latin *vallum* rampart; see VALLATE]

Va·lois (val′wä), *n.* a French royal house that ruled from 1328 to 1589, between the Capetians and Bourbons. *—adj.* of or having to do with Valois, a medieval district in northern France, or the Valois family.

va·lo·ni·a (və lō′nē ə), *n.* the large acorn cups of the valonia oak, used in tanning, dyeing, etc. [< Italian *vallonia* < New Greek *balánia,* plural of *baláni* acorn < Greek *bálanos*]

valonia oak, an oak of Greece and Asia Minor.

val·or (val′ər), *n.* bravery; courage: *The Virginia troops showed great valor* (George Bancroft). [< Old French *valour* < Medieval Latin *valor* < Latin *valēre* be strong] **—Syn.** prowess, intrepidity.

val·or·i·za·tion (val′ər ə zā′shən), *n. U.S.* the actual or attempted maintenance of certain prices for a commodity by a government. [American English < *valor,* in obsolete sense of "value" + *-ize* + *-ation;* perhaps patterned on Portuguese *valorização* < *valor* worth, price]

val·or·ize (val′ə rīz), *v.t., v.i.,* **-ized, -iz·ing. 1.** to assign a value to. **2.** to regulate the price of by valorization.

val·or·ous (val′ər əs), *adj.* **1.** having courage; courageous; valiant; brave: *that host of valorous men who . . . had fought so strenuous a fight for freedom* (John Morley). **2.** marked or characterized by courage and bravery. [< Middle French *valeureux* (with English *-ous*) < Old French *valeur,* earlier *valour;* see VALOR] **—val′or·ous·ly,** *adv.* **—val′or·ous·ness,** *n.*

val·our (val′ər), *n. Especially British.* valor.

Val·po·li·cel·la (väl′pō lē chel′ä), *n.* an Italian red table wine. [< *Valpolicella,* a valley in northern Italy]

valse (väls), *n., v.,* **valsed, vals·ing.** *—n.* a waltz. *—v.i.* to waltz. [< French *valse* < German *Walzer* waltz]

val·u·a·ble (val′yu̇ ə bəl, -yə bəl), *adj.* **1.** having value; being worth something: *valuable jewelry, a valuable old family Bible.* **2.** having great value because of some special trait or quality: *a valuable tool, valuable information, a valuable friend.* **3.** that can have its value measured.

—n. **valuables,** articles of value: *She keeps her jewelry and other valuables in a safe.*

—val′u·a·ble·ness, *n.*

—**Syn.** *adj.* **2. Valuable, precious** mean worth much. **Valuable** applies to anything costly, very useful, or highly esteemed: *He has a valuable stamp collection.* **Precious** applies to anything very valuable, especially to something that is irreplaceable: *The original Declaration of Independence is a precious document kept in Washington.*

val·u·a·bly (val′yu̇ ə blē, -yə-), *adv.* **1.** with valuable or precious articles. **2.** in a valuable manner; so as to be valuable or highly useful.

val·u·a·tion (val′yu̇ ā′shən), *n.* **1.** value estimated or determined: *The jeweler's valuation of the necklace was $10,000.* **2.** an estimating or determining the value of something: *She asked for a valuation of the collection.* **3.** an appreciation or estimation of anything in respect to excellence or merit: *I believe it is difficult to find any two persons, who place an equal valuation on any virtue* (Henry Fielding).

val·u·a·tion·al (val′yu̇ ā′shə nəl), *adj.* of or having to do with valuation.

val·u·a·tor (val′yu̇ ā′tər), *n.* a person who estimates or determines the value of things, especially one appointed or licensed to do so; appraiser.

val·ue (val′yü), *n., v.,* **-ued, -u·ing.** *—n.* **1.** real worth; proper price: *He bought the house for less than its value.* **2.** worth; excellence; usefulness; importance: *the value of education, the value of milk as a food.* **3.** the power to buy: *The value of the dollar has varied greatly.* **4.** an equivalent or adequate return: *We hardly could be said to have received value for our money.* **5.** meaning; effect; force: *the value of a symbol.* **6.** the number or amount represented by a symbol: *The value of XIV is fourteen.* **7.** an estimated worth: *He placed a value on his furniture.* **8.** the relative length of a tone in music indicated by a note. **9.** *Phonetics.* **a.** a special quality of sound in speech. **b.** a speech sound equivalent to a letter or a phonetic symbol: *The symbol* ᴛʜ *represents the value of "th" in "then".* **10. a.** the degree of lightness or darkness of a color, especially in a painting, in relation to other colors and sometimes to black and white; hue; tone: *A certain quantity of cold colours is necessary to give value and lustre to the warm colours* (Joshua Reynolds). **b.** the relationship and effect of an object, spot of color, shadow, etc., to a whole painting.

values, *Sociology.* the established ideals of life; objects, customs, ways of acting, etc., that the members of a given society regard as desirable: *Man lives by values; all his enterprises and activities . . . make sense only in terms of some structure of purposes which are themselves values in action* (Will Herberg).

—v.t. **1.** to rate at a certain value or price; estimate the worth of; appraise: *Appraisers valued the furniture at $5,000.* **2.** to think highly of; regard highly: *to value one's judgment.*

[< Old French *value,* originally past participle of *valeir* be worth < Latin *valēre*] **—val′u·er,** *n.*

—**Syn.** *v.t.* **2. Value, appreciate, esteem** mean to think highly of a person or thing. **Value** means to judge the worth correctly: *I value your friendship.* **Appreciate** means to value wisely and discerningly: *His classmates do not appreciate him.* **Esteem** means to value rightly and therefore highly respect: *One esteems a man like Eisenhower.*

val·ued (val′yüd), *adj.* **1.** having its value estimated or determined. **2.** regarded highly.

valued policy, a policy obliging an insurance company to pay the full face value of the policy in case of total loss, even though the insured property was not worth the full amount.

value engineer, a person who is trained or skilled in value engineering.

value engineering, 1. the analysis of a product, process, etc., to determine the least expensive method of design and production. **2.** the modification of a product, process, etc., as a result of such an analysis.

value judgment, an assessment of someone or something in terms of personal values, such as whether he or it is good or bad, worthwhile or troublesome, etc.; a subjective judgment or appraisal: *Stories about celebrities are only made meaningful through our superimposition of a . . . psychological value judgment which relates the subject's adventures to cause-and-effect experience as the reader himself has observed it* (Harper's).

val·ue·less (val′yü lis), *adj.* without value; worthless: *His quick judgments are valueless.* **—val′ue·less·ness,** *n.*

val·ues (val′yüz), *n. pl.* See under **value,** *n.*

va·lu·ta (vä lü′tä), *n.* **1.** the fixed value of a nation's currency in terms of a foreign currency. **2.** the fixed rate of exchange between a nation's currency and a specified foreign currency. [< Italian *valuta* (literally) value, originally past participle of *valere* be worth < Latin *valēre*]

val·val (val′vəl), *adj.* valvular.

val·var (val′vər), *adj.* valvular.

val·vate (val′vāt), *adj.* **1.** furnished with, or opening by, a valve or valves. **2.** serving as or resembling a valve. **3.** *Botany.* **a.** united by the margins only, and opening as if by valves, as the capsules of regularly dehiscent fruits and certain anthers. **b.** meeting without overlapping, as the parts of a perianth in certain buds. **c.** (of an estivation or vernation) characterized by this arrangement of parts. [< Latin *valvātus* having folding doors < *valvae,* plural, folding door; see VALVE]

valve (valv), *n., v.,* **valved, valv·ing.** *—n.* **1.** a movable part that controls the flow of a liquid, gas, etc., through a pipe or out of an enclosed space by opening or closing the passage. **2.** *Anatomy.* a structure in an organ that works similarly. A valve is usually the fold in a membrane that opens and closes automatically, controlling the flow of blood or other fluid in the body: *the valves of the heart.* **3.** *Music.* a device in wind instruments of the trumpet class, connected with subsidiary loops of tubing, for changing the pitch of a tone by quickly changing the length and direction of the column of air. Cornets and French horns have valves. There are two types of valves, the piston and the rotary cylinder. **4.** *Zoology.* one of the two or more parts of hinged shells like those of oysters and clams, or the whole shell when it is in one piece, as in snails. **5.** *Botany.* **a.** either of the halves of the shell of a diatom. **b.** one of the halves or sections formed when a pod, pericarp, or capsule bursts open (dehisces). **c.** a section that opens like a lid in the bursting open (dehiscence) of certain anthers. **6.** *Electronics.* **a.** any device permitting the passage of electric current in one direction only. **b.** *Especially British.* a vacuum tube or electron tube. **7.** a door or gate controlling the flow of water in a sluice. **8.** *Archaic.* either one of the halves or leaves of a double or folding door.

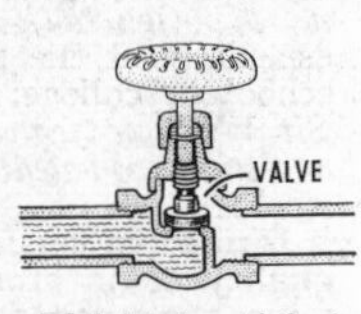

Disk Valve (def. 1) Stopcock is screwed up or down to open or close hole through which water moves.

—v.t. **1.** to furnish with a valve or valves. **2.** to control the flow of (a liquid, gas, etc.)

by a valve. **3.** to discharge (gas) from a balloon by opening a valve. —*v.i.* **1.** to make use of a valve or valves. **2.** to open a valve of a balloon in order to descend.
[< Latin *valva* one of a pair of folding doors; leaf of a door] —**valve′like′**, *adj.*

valve·gear (valv′gir′), *n.* a mechanism which regulates the motions of the valves of an engine or other mechanical apparatus.

valve-in-head engine (valv′in hed′), an internal-combustion engine that has both intake and exhaust valves in the cylinder head.

valve·less (valv′lis), *adj.* having no valve.

valve·let (valv′lit), *n.* a small valve; valvule.

val·vu·lar (val′vyə lər), *adj.* **1.** of, having to do with, or affecting a valve or valves, especially the valves of the heart. **2.** having the form or function of a valve. **3.** furnished with a valve or valves; working by valves.

val·vule (val′vyül), *n.* a small valve; valvelet. [< French *valvule*, learned borrowing from Medieval Latin *valvula* (diminutive) < Latin *valva;* see VALVE]

val·vu·li·tis (val′vyə lī′tis), *n.* inflammation of a valve, especially of a valve of the heart. [< New Latin *valvulitis* < Medieval Latin *valvula* (see VALVULE) + New Latin *-itis* inflammation, -itis]

vam·brace (vam′brās), *n.* defensive armor for the forearm. [alteration of earlier *vantbrace* < Anglo-French *vantbras*, short for *avantbras* < *avant* before + *bras* arm]

va·moose (va müs′), *v.t., v.i.,* **-moosed, -moos·ing.** *U.S. Slang.* to go away quickly. [American English < Spanish *vamos* let's go]

va·mose (va mōs′), *v.t., v.i.,* **-mosed, -mos·ing.** *U.S. Slang.* vamoose.

vamp[1] (vamp), *n.* **1.** the upper front part of a shoe or foot. **2.** a piece or patch added to an old thing to make it look new. **3.** anything that is patched up or restored by a vamp; patchwork. **4.** *Music.* a simple accompaniment, usually an improvised series of chords.
—*v.t.* **1.** to furnish (footwear) with a vamp; repair (a shoe, boot, etc.) with a new vamp. **2.** to make (an old thing) look new; patch up. **3.** to put together (a book, composition, etc.) out of old materials; compile; compose. **4.** to improvise in a simple or crude way to (an accompaniment, song, melody, etc.). —*v.i. Music.* to improvise an accompaniment: *I got a banjo, you know, and I vamp a bit* (H.G. Wells).
vamp up, a. to make (something old) appear new: *The women of the town* [*were*] *vamped up for show with paint, patches, plumpers, and every external ornament that art can administer* (Samuel Johnson). **b.** to make up to deceive: *to vamp up a worthless accusation.*
[short for Old French *avanpie* < *avant* before + *pie* foot < Latin *pēs, pedis*] —**vamp′er**, *n.*

vamp[2] (vamp), *n.* an unscrupulous flirt; adventuress. —*v.t.* to allure or attract (a man) for the purpose of extortion. —*v.i.* to flirt with a man in order to extort from him. [short for *vampire*] —**vamp′er**, *n.*

vamp horn, any of several, variously shaped, valveless horns used in churches in the 1700's and 1800's to amplify the singing or speaking voice.

vamp·i·ness (vam′pē nis), *n.* a vampish quality or condition: *The varnished vampiness of Greta Garbo* (Sunday Express).

vam·pire (vam′pīr), *n.* **1.** a corpse supposed to come to life at night and leave its grave and suck the blood of sleeping people. **2.** a person who preys ruthlessly on others. **3.** a woman who flirts with men to get money or to please her vanity. **4.** an actress known for playing the part of a beautiful woman who is ruthless and vain. **5.** vampire bat. **6.** a trap door with two leaves closed by a string and used for sudden disappearances from the stage. [< French *vampire* < German *Vampir* < Slavic (compare Serbian *vampir*)]

vampire bat, 1. any of several groups of bats of South and Central America that drink blood from animals and sometimes men by piercing the skin with their sharp teeth and lapping the blood as it flows. **2.** any of several large bats of South and Central America, incorrectly reputed to suck blood. **3. a.** any of a group of large, tailless bats of tropical Asia, Africa, and Australia. **b.** the false vampire of tropical America.

vam·pir·ic (vam pir′ik), *adj.* having the character of a vampire; having to do with vampires or the belief in them.

vam·pir·ish (vam′pīr ish), *adj.* vampiric.

vam·pir·ism (vam′pīr iz əm), *n.* **1.** a superstitious belief in the existence of vampires. **2.** the act or practice of bloodsucking. **3.** the practice of extortion or preying on others.

vamp·ish (vam′pish), *adj.* suggestive or characteristic of a vamp: *International stars of vampish wiles . . .* (Observer). —**vamp′ish·ness**, *n.*

vamp·y (vam′pē), *adj.,* **vamp·i·er, vamp·i·est.** vampish: *High fashion has a vampy quality* [*which*] *suggests an aggressiveness with men* (New York Times).

van[1] (van), *n.* **1.** the forward division or detachment of a military or naval force when advancing or set in order for doing so: *Thou, like the van, first took'st the field* (Henry King). **2.** the foremost part of, or the foremost position in, a company or procession of persons moving forward or onward. **3.** vanguard: *to be in the van of industrial nations, to lead the van of modern painting.* [short for *vanguard*]

van[2] (van), *n., v.,* **vanned, van·ning.** —*n.* **1.** a covered truck or wagon for moving furniture, etc., opening from behind. **2.** *British.* **a.** a lightweight vehicle for business, delivery, etc.; pickup truck. **b.** a railroad baggage car or a boxcar.
—*v.t.* to carry or transport in a van: *to van racehorses from track to track.* —*v.i.* to travel by van: *On race days he vans to the track from nearby Tropical Park* (Time).
[short for *caravan*]

van[3] (van; *Dutch* vän), *prep.* of; from (in personal names). [< Dutch *van*]
➤ **Van** in foreign usage is generally written with a small *v;* in American and British usage, it is written with either a small or capital *v*, according to the preference of the person bearing the name.

van[4] (van), *n.* **1.** *Dialect.* a basket or shovel used to catch tossed grain as the chaff is blown away by the wind. **2.** *Poetic.* a wing: *As bats at the wired window of a dairy, They beat their vans* (Shelley). **3.** a sail of a windmill. [probably dialectal variant of *fan*[1]]

van·a·date (van′ə dāt), *n.* a salt or ester of vanadic acid.

va·na·di·ate (və nā′dē āt), *n.* vanadate.

va·nad·ic (və nad′ik, -nā′dik), *adj.* **1.** of, derived from, or having to do with vanadium. **2.** containing vanadium, especially with a valence of three or of five.

vanadic acid, any of a group of acids known only in the form of their salts (vanadates), and considered hydrates, as vanadium pentoxide, V_2O_5.

va·nad·i·nite (və nad′ə nīt), *n.* a mineral consisting of a vanadate and chloride of lead, occurring in brilliant crystals of various colors. *Formula:* $Pb_5ClV_3O_{12}$

va·na·di·ous (və nā′dē əs), *adj.* vanadous.

va·na·di·um (və nā′dē əm), *n.* a rare metallic chemical element occurring in certain iron, lead, and uranium ores, as vanadinite, and isolated as a light-gray, malleable, ductile substance that forms both acidic and basic salts. Vanadium is used especially in making certain kinds of steel. *Symbol:* V; *at.wt.:* (C^{12}) 50.945 or (O^{16}) 50.95; *at.no.:* 23; *valence:* 2,3,4,5. [< New Latin *vanadium* < Old Icelandic *Vanadīs*, a name of the goddess Freya (because it was discovered in Sweden)]

vanadium pentoxide, a yellowish-brown crystalline compound used as a catalyst in oxidation reactions, as a developer in photography, in textile dyeing, and in making certain inks. *Formula:* V_2O_5

vanadium steel, 1. a steel containing some vanadium (from 0.10 to 0.20 per cent) to make it tougher and harder. **2.** a steel containing vanadium, chromium, and various other elements.

van·a·dous (van′ə dəs), *adj.* **1.** of or having to do with vanadium. **2.** containing vanadium, especially with a valence of two or of three.

Van Al·len belt (van al′ən), Van Allen radiation belt.

Van Allen radiation belt, a broad band of radiation surrounding the earth, believed to exist in two general zones, consisting of electrons apparently trapped in the earth's magnetic field. [< James A. *Van Allen*, 1914-1966, an American physicist, who discovered it in 1958]

va·nas·pa·ti (və nes′pə tē), *n.* (in India) a fat made from vegetable oils: *The government in 1965 relaxed restrictions on imported soybean and cottonseed oils and permitted up to 50% of such oils to be used in the manufacture of vanaspati, a hydrogenated vegetable fat used as a butter substitute* (Rose and Sherman). [< Hindustani *vanaspati*]

van·co·my·cin (van′kō mī′sin), *n.* an antibiotic derived from a microorganism found in the soil, used against staphylococcal and other infections.

Van·cou·ver·ite (van kü′və rīt′), *n.* a native or inhabitant of Vancouver, a seaport in British Columbia, Canada: *A Vancouverite who has spent too much of his life stoutly denying that Vancouver weather is strictly for the ducks, now has the proof* (Maclean's).

Van·dal (van′dəl), *n.* a member of a Germanic tribe that invaded western Europe in the 300's and 400's, and ravaged Gaul, Spain, and northern Africa. In 455 A.D. the Vandals took Rome. —*adj.* of or having to do with the Vandals. [< Late Latin *Vandalus* < a Germanic tribal name]

van·dal (van′dəl), *n.* a person who willfully or ignorantly destroys or damages beautiful or valuable things. —*adj.* **1.** destructive. **2.** characterized by vandalism or lack of culture; vandalistic. [< *Vandal* (because of the wanton destruction they carried out)]

Van·dal·ic (van dal′ik), *adj.* **1.** Often, **vandalic.** characteristic of Vandals; destructive; vandalistic. **2.** of, having to do with, or consisting of Vandals.

van·dal·ise (van′də līz), *v.t.,* **-ised, -is·ing.** *Especially British.* vandalize.

van·dal·ism (van′də liz əm), *n.* **1.** willful or ignorant destruction or damaging of beautiful or valuable things. **2.** conduct, spirit, or actions characteristic of the Vandals in respect to culture, especially hostility toward culture. **3.** a vandalistic act.

van·dal·is·tic (van′də lis′tik), *adj.* **1.** characterized by or given to vandalism. **2.** of, having to do with, or consisting of Vandals.

van·dal·ize (van′də līz), *v.t.,* **-ized, -iz·ing.** to destroy willfully or senselessly.

Van de Graaff generator or **accelerator** (van′ də graf′), *Physics.* an electrostatic generator used to produce electric potentials of very high voltages, for accelerating charged particles used in bombarding nuclei. [< Robert *Van de Graaff*, born 1901, an American physicist]

van der Waals forces (van′ dər wôlz′), *Physical Chemistry.* the relatively weak forces of attraction existing between atoms or molecules, caused by the interaction of varying dipoles. [< Johannes *Van der Waals*, 1837-1923, a Dutch physicist]

Van·dyke (van dīk′), *adj.* of or having to do with Anthony Van Dyck, 1599-1641, a Flemish painter, or the style of dress, coloring, etc., characteristic of his portraits. —*n.* Often, **vandyke. 1.** a Vandyke beard. **2.** a Vandyke collar.

Vandyke beard, a short, close-cut, pointed beard.

Vandyke brown, 1. any of various dark-brown pigments, consisting of mixtures of iron oxide and lampblack or other organic substances. **2.** a dark-brown pigment used by Anthony Van Dyck. Its composition is uncertain.

Vandyke Beard

Vandyke collar or **cape,** a wide collar or shoulder covering with a lace or linen border having deep points indenting the edge.

vane (vān), *n.* **1. a.** a flat piece of metal, or some other device, fixed upon a spire or some other high object in such a way as to move with the wind and indicate its direction. **b.** a similar device on the masthead of a boat, consisting of a cloth on a wooden frame. **2.** a blade of a windmill, ship's propeller, etc. **3.** a blade, wing, or similar projection attached to an axis, wheel, etc., so as to be acted upon by a current of air or liquid or to produce a current by rotation. **4.** *Zoology.* the flat, soft part of a feather; web. See **feather** for picture. **5.** *Surveying.* **a.** a target. **b.** a sight on a quadrant, compass, etc. **6.** a feather or strip of feather on an arrow. [dialectal variant of Middle English *fane*, Old English *fana* banner]

vaned (vānd), *adj.* furnished with a vane or vanes.

vane·less (vān′lis), *adj.* having no vane.

va·nes·sa (və nes′ə), *n., pl.* **-sas.** any of a group of butterflies, the members of which have the outer margin of the forewings more or less notched, as the red admiral. [< New Latin *Vanessa* the genus name]

van·ette (və net′), *n.* a small motor van: *A company . . . were sent out, . . . followed . . . by . . . vanettes and an armored car* (Glasgow Herald).

vang (vang), *n.* either of two ropes used for steadying the gaff of a fore-and-aft sail. [apparently variant of *fang*]

van·guard (van′gärd′), *n.* **1.** soldiers marching ahead of the main part of an army to clear the way and guard against surprise. **2.** the foremost or leading position, usually in intellectual and political movements or social reforms. **3.** the leaders of a movement, especially persons who experiment or work with new ideas. [Middle English *vantgarde* < Old French *avangarde* < *avant* before (< Vulgar Latin *abante* < Latin *ab* from + *ante* before) + *garde* guard. Compare AVANT-GARDE.]

van·guard·ism (van′gär′diz əm), *n.* avant-gardism: . . . *the heroic days of Paris vanguardism of the twenties* (Saturday Review).

van·guard·ist (van′gär′dist), *n.* avant-gardist: *Several well-known vanguardists have been represented by old or comparatively conventional works* (London Times). —*adj.* of, having to do with, or characteristic of vanguardism or the vanguardists: *Sunday nights, Jack Elliott's topnotch vanguardist trio is in charge* (New Yorker).

va·nil·la (və nil′ə), *n., pl.* **-las. 1.** any of a group of climbing orchids found in tropical America, especially a species that yields the vanilla bean, used in making vanilla extract. **2.** the bean itself; vanilla bean. **3.** vanilla extract. [< New Latin *Vanilla* the genus name < Spanish *vainilla*, Old Spanish (originally) little pod (diminutive) < *vaina* < Latin *vagīna* sheath]

BEAN

Vanilla Flower and Bean (def. 1)

vanilla bean, the fruit of the vanilla, a slender, pod-like capsule that yields vanilla extract.

vanilla extract, a flavoring extract made from the vanilla bean and used in candy, ice cream, perfumes, etc.

va·nil·lic (və nil′ik), *adj.* of or obtained from vanilla or vanillin.

van·il·lin (van′ə lin, və nil′in), *n.* a white crystalline compound constituting the odoriferous principle of vanilla, used as a substitute for vanilla extract and in making paper pulp. *Formula:* $C_8H_8O_3$

van·il·line (van′ə lin, -lēn; və nil′in, -ēn), *n.* vanillin.

Va·nir (vä′nir), *n. Norse Mythology.* an early race of gods, including Frey, Freya, and Njorth, who preceded the Aesir.

van·ish (van′ish), *v.i.* **1.** to disappear suddenly; disappear: *The sun vanished behind a cloud.* **2.** to pass away; cease to be: *Dinosaurs have vanished from the earth.* **3.** *Mathematics.* to become zero.
—*n. Phonetics.* the brief end sound of phonemes.
[short for Old French *esvaniss-*, stem of *esvanir* < Vulgar Latin *exvānīre*, for Latin *ēvānēscere* < *ex-* out + *vānēscere* vanish < *vānus* empty] —**van′ish·er,** *n.*
—**Syn.** *v.i.* **1.** See **disappear.**

van·ish·ing cream (van′i shing), a facial cream to protect the skin or serve as a base for face powder or other cosmetics.

van·ish·ing·ly (van′i shing lē), *adv.* in a vanishing manner; imperceptibly: *The neutrino is uncharged, has a vanishingly small mass, and has been found to spiral in a left-handed manner* (Science News Letter).

Vanishing Point (def. 1)

vanishing point, 1. the point toward which receding parallel lines seem to converge. **2.** a point of disappearance: *His income had reached the vanishing point.*

van·ish·ment (van′ish ment), *n.* **1.** a vanishing or disappearing: *the overnight vanishment of our "way of life"* (Wall Street Journal). **2.** the state of having vanished.

van·i·to·ry (van′ə tôr′ē, -tōr′-), *n., pl.* **-ries. 1.** a bathroom fixture combining a washbasin and dressing table. **2. Vanitory.** a trademark for this fixture. [< *vani*(ty), def. 7 + (lava)*tory*]

van·i·tous (van′ə təs), *adj.* full of vanity; vain: *French criticism . . . instructs without wounding any but the vanitous person* (George Meredith).

van·i·ty (van′ə tē), *n., pl.* **-ties. 1. a.** too much pride in one's looks, ability, accomplishments, etc.: *The girl's vanity made her look in the mirror often.* **b.** an instance of this; worthless pleasure or display: *In spite of her small vanities, Margaret had a sweet . . . nature* (Louisa M. Alcott). **2.** a lack of real value; worthlessness: *the vanity of wealth.* **3.** a useless, idle, or worthless thing: *I had forsaken the vanities of the world* (Thomas Malory). **4.** a thing of which one is vain: *She was my Vanity, and oh All other vanities how vain!* (Coventry Patmore). **5.** a lack of effect or success: *It is vanity to waste our days in blind pursuit of knowledge* (Sir Thomas Browne). **6.** a vanity case. **7.** a dressing table, usually fitted with a mirror. [< Old French *vanite*, learned borrowing from Latin *vānitās, -ātis* < *vānus* empty]
—**Syn. 1. a.** conceit, egotism, self-esteem.
—**Ant. 1. a.** humility.

vanity case, a small handbag used by women to carry cosmetics and other toilet articles.

Vanity Fair, any place or scene, such as the world, a great city, or the world of fashion, regarded as given over to vain pleasure or empty show. [< *Vanity Fair*, the fair described in John Bunyan's *Pilgrim's Progress*, symbolizing the world of vain pleasure or empty show]

vanity press, a press that publishes books at the expense of the authors.

vanity publisher, a publisher that publishes books at the expense of the authors.

van·load (van′lōd′), *n.* as much as a van can hold or carry: *In Madison Square Garden, huge, fragrant vanloads of flowers were unloaded* (Time).

van·man (van′mən), *n., pl.* **-men.** a man who drives or works on a van.

van·ner (van′ər), *n. Mining.* **1.** a person who separates ore. **2.** an apparatus for separating ores. [< *van*[4] + *-er*[1]]

van·quish (vang′kwish), *v.t.* **1. a.** to conquer, defeat, or overcome in battle or conflict. **b.** to overcome or subdue (a person) by other than physical means: *though vanquished, he could argue still* (Oliver Goldsmith). **2.** to subdue, overcome, or put an end to (a feeling, state of things, etc.); suppress: *thus vanquish shame and fear* (Shelley). [Middle English *vencusen* < Old French *vencus*, past participle of *veintre*, and Middle English *venquisshen*, probably influenced by Old French *vainquiss-*, stem of *vainquir*, both Old French verbs < Latin *vincere* to conquer] —**van′quish·er,** *n.*
—**Syn. 1. a.** See **defeat.**

van·quish·a·ble (vang′kwi shə bəl), *adj.* that can be vanquished.

van·quished (van′kwisht), *adj.* defeated or overcome in conflict or battle; conquered. —*n.* the person, group, army, etc., defeated, subdued, or conquered: *Yet we recognize that another world war in the age of atomic and thermonuclear weapons would be an unparalleled disaster for victor and vanquished alike* (Bulletin of Atomic Scientists).

van·quish·ment (vang′kwish mənt), *n.* the act of vanquishing or overcoming.

van·tage (van′tij, vän′-), *n.* **1.** a better position or condition; advantage: *a station of vantage for introducing him to the public favor* (Thomas De Quincey). **2.** *British.* advantage; the first point scored in a tennis game after deuce. [short for Middle English *avantage* advantage]

vantage ground, vantage point: *No pleasure is comparable to the standing upon the vantage ground of truth* (Francis Bacon).

vantage point, 1. a superior position that gives a person an advantage, as in combat or an argument: *If the manor were attacked, the tower would become a vantage point from which defending archers could pick off attackers who were floundering across the ditch* (Scientific American). **2.** a favorable and sometimes lofty position from which to observe some action or perceive some theory: *The picture he provides of these years is a truthful one, but he gives the impression of looking back from some remote vantage point in order to extract from these fateful events the grim lesson of the spiritual agony of those who endured them* (Atlantic).

van·ward (van′wərd), *adj., adv.* toward or in the front; forward. [< *van*[1] + *-ward*]

vap·id (vap′id), *adj.* **1.** without much life or flavor; tasteless; dull; flat: *table-beer, guiltless of hops and malt, vapid and nauseous* (Tobias Smollett). **2.** lacking interest, zest, or animation; lifeless; insipid: *Conversation would become dull and vapid* (Samuel Johnson). [< Latin *vapidus*, related to *vapor* vapor] —**vap′id·ly,** *adv.* —**vap′id·ness,** *n.*

va·pid·i·ty (va pid′ə tē), *n., pl.* **-ties. 1.** flatness of flavor; insipidity. **2.** a lifeless, uninteresting, or dull remark, idea, feature, etc.

va·por (vā′pər), *n.* **1.** visible moisture such as steam, fog, mist, etc., often forming a cloud suspended or floating in the air, usually due to the effect of heat upon a liquid. **2.** something without substance; empty fancy: *A man to whom Earth and all its glories are in truth a vapor and a dream* (Thomas Carlyle). **3.** *Physics.* a gas formed when a solid or liquid substance is sufficiently heated; a gas. A *gas* is a substance that at ordinary temperatures and pressures exists in the gaseous state, while a *vapor* is the gaseous form of a substance that normally exists in a solid or liquid form. **4. a.** a substance, as alcohol, mercury, or benzoin, that has been changed into vapor for use medicinally, industrially, etc. **b.** a mixture of a vaporized substance and air, as in an internal-combustion engine. **c.** the emission or exhalation of such mixtures or of any substance in gaseous form.
vapors, a. exhalations once considered in medical circles to be injurious to the health, and to originate especially in the stomach: *vapors from an empty stomach* (Daniel Defoe). **b.** a condition once supposed to be caused by the presence of such exhalations: *She had a headache, vapors. They are over* (George Meredith). **c.** *Archaic.* low spirits; hypochondria, hysteria, or other nervous disorder: *I had sent for him in a fit of the vapors* (Stanley J. Weyman).
—*v.t.* **1.** to cause to rise or ascend in the form of a vapor: *Then, upon a gentle heat, vapor away all the spirit of wine* (Francis Bacon). **2.** to give (a person) the vapors; depress or bore. **3.** to boast; swagger; brag.
—*v.i.* **1.** to rise, ascend, or pass off as vapor. **2.** to give or send out vapor, steam, gas, etc.; emit vapors or exhalations. **3.** to use blustering or grandiloquent language; brag or boast: *Strutting and vaporing about his own pretensions* (William Hazlitt). Also, *especially British,* **vapour.**
[< Latin *vapor, -ōris*] —**va′por·er,** *n.*

va·por·a·ble (vā′pər ə bəl), *adj.* that can be converted into vapor.

va·po·rar·i·um (vā′pə rãr′ē əm), *n., pl.* **-rar·i·ums, -rar·i·a** (-rãr′ē ə). an apartment or bath equipped for the application of the vapor of water to the body; vapor bath. [< New Latin *vaporarium* < Latin *vapor, -ōris* vapor]

vapor barrier, a material used to prevent or eliminate condensation and penetration of moisture into a structure: *A new vapor barrier for building construction . . . is made in thin sheets of a pliable material known as polyethylene* (New York Times).

vapor bath, 1. an application of the vapor of water to the body in a close apartment or place. **2.** a vaporarium.

va·por·es·cence (vā′pə res′əns), *n.* the process of changing into vapor.

va·por·es·cent (vā′pə res′ənt), *adj.* changing into vapor; vaporizing.

va·po·ret·to (vä′pô rāt′tō), *n., pl.* **-ti** (-tē). *Italian.* a small steamboat used to carry passengers along a certain route on a canal or canals, especially in Venice: *He stepped with her onto a vaporetto bound from St. Mark's to the Lido* (New Yorker).

va·por·if·ic (vā′pə rif′ik), *adj.* **1.** associated or connected with, producing or causing, vaporization: *vaporific sublimation.* **2.** vaporous: *vaporific form.* [< Latin *vapor, -ōris* vapor, steam + *facere* to make]

va·por·im·e·ter (vā′pə rim′ə tər), *n.* an instrument for measuring vapor pressure or volume.

va·por·ing (vā′pər ing), *adj.* **1.** talking pretentiously or boastfully; bragging: *a vaporing little man.* **2.** pretentious and

foolishly boastful: *vaporing talk.* **3.** vaporous: *vaporing clouds.*
—*n.* boastful talk; pretentious or ostentatious behavior. —**va′por·ing·ly,** *adv.*
va·por·ise (vā′pə rīz), *v.t., v.i.,* **-ised, -is·ing.** *Especially British.* vaporize.
va·por·ish (vā′pər ish), *adj.* **1.** like vapor. **2.** abounding in vapor: *a vaporish cave.* **3.** dim or obscure because of the presence of vapor; vapory: *the vaporish moon.* **4.** in low spirits; depressed; dejected: *Lady Lyndon, always vaporish and nervous ... became more agitated than ever* (Thackeray). **5.** having to do with or connected with low spirits: *vaporish fears.*
va·por·iz·a·ble (vā′pə rī′zə bəl), *adj.* that can be vaporized: *The entire prescription is not large, for the more readily vaporizable material has evanesced during the years of simmering* (Matthew Luckiesh).
va·por·i·za·tion (vā′pər ə zā′shən), *n.* **1.** the act or process of changing or of being changed, into vapor. **2.** the rapid conversion of water into steam with the application of heat, as in a boiler. **3.** *Medicine.* treatment with vapor.
va·por·ize (vā′pə rīz), *v.,* **-ized, -iz·ing.** —*v.t.* to change into vapor by the application of heat, reduction of pressure, or other means; cause to evaporate: *The sun's heat vaporizes the water of the ocean.* —*v.i.* to pass off in vapor; become vaporous: *On the journey some of the liquid will vaporize ...; but this is not expected to exceed more than one-half per cent a day* (New York Times).
va·por·iz·er (vā′pə rī′zər), *n.* **1.** a device for converting a liquid into vapor or mist, such as an atomizer or an apparatus that exhausts steam into a room for medicinal purposes: *There are many preparations that claim to break up respiratory congestion when dissolved in a vaporizer* (Sidonie M. Gruenberg). **2.** a device in the carburetor of an internal-combustion engine for turning liquid fuel into a fine mist.
vapor lamp, an electric lamp that uses a vapor or gas instead of a wire filament to produce light, used chiefly for street and highway lighting. It is similar to a fluorescent lamp. *The more modern ... vapor lamps contain sodium or mercury gas, and provide more light than ordinary electric lights* (Pyke Johnson).
va·por·less (vā′pər lis), *adj.* lacking or free from vapor.
vapor lock, an interruption in the flow of fuel in a gasoline engine, occurring when excessive heat vaporizes the gasoline in the fuel line or carburetor, causing the engine to stall: *Vapor lock occurs most frequently during long, steep climbs on hot days, or when slowing suddenly after a hard drive* (Willard Rogers).
va·por·ole (vā′pə rōl), *n.* a medicinal preparation, as a volatile drug for inhalation, enclosed in a thin glass capsule, to be broken for use.
va·por·os·i·ty (vā′pə ros′ə tē), *n.* vaporous quality.
va·por·ous (vā′pər əs), *adj.* **1.** full of vapor; misty: *vaporous atmosphere.* **2.** covered or obscured with vapor: *vaporous hills.* **3.** like vapor. **4.** soon passing; worthless: *vaporous dreams of grandeur.* **5.** (of fabrics) thin and gauzelike. **6.** (of persons or minds) vague; fanciful; frothy: *vaporous imaginations* (Francis Bacon). **7.** characteristic of vapor: *matter in a vaporous or gaseous state.* —**va′por·ous·ly,** *adv.* —**va′por·ous·ness,** *n.*
vapor pressure or **tension,** *Physics.* the pressure exerted by a vapor in an enclosed space when the vapor is in equilibrium with its liquid at any specified temperature: *The vapor pressure in the container of sea water is lower than in the flask of pure water, because its water molecules, being bound to salt ions, do not evaporate as easily* (Scientific American).
vapor trail, the condensation of water vapor in the exhaust fumes from any aircraft engine, especially those of jet planes and rockets at high altitudes.
va·por·y (vā′pər ē), *adj.* vaporous.
va·pour (vā′pər), *n., v.t., v.i. Especially British.* vapor.
va·pour·ize (vā′pə rīz), *v.t., v.i.,* **-ized, -iz·ing.** *Especially British.* vaporize.
vap·u·la·tion (vap′yə lā′shən), *n. Obsolete.* a flogging or thrashing. [< Latin *vāpulāre* to flog + English *-ation*]
vap·u·la·to·ry (vap′yə lə tôr′ē, -tōr′-), *adj. Obsolete.* of or having to do with vapulation.
va·que·ro (vä kãr′ō), *n., pl.* **-ros.** *Spanish America and Southwestern United States.* a cowboy, a herdsman, or a cattle driver. [American English < American Spanish *vaquero* < Spanish, cowherd < *vaca* cow < Latin *vacca* cow. Compare BUCKAROO.]

Vaquero

var., **1.** variant. **2.** variation. **3.** variety. **4.** various.
VAR (no periods), visual-aural range (a VHF radio-signaling device for both visual and aural reception, used as a navigational aid).
va·ra (vä′rä), *n.* **1.** a measure of length used in Spain, Portugal, and Latin America, usually about 33 inches, but varying from about 32 to about 43 inches. **2.** this measure squared, used as a unit of area. [< Spanish and Portuguese *vara* yardstick, rod < Latin *vāra* forked pole < *vārus* bent (in)]
Va·ran·gi·an (və ran′jē ən), *n.* **1.** one of the Scandinavian rovers who overran parts of Russia, establishing a dynasty there under Rurik in the 800's, and reached Constantinople in the 900's. **2.** Varangian Guard. —*adj.* of or having to do with the Varangians.
[< Medieval Latin *Varangus* < Medieval Greek *Várangos* < Old Russian *varęgŭ* < Scandinavian (compare Old Icelandic *Væringi,* apparently originally, a pledged ally < *vār* plighted faith) + English *-ian*]
Varangian Guard, the bodyguard of later Byzantine emperors, recruited from the Varangians and, later, from Anglo-Saxons.
var·gue·no (vär gān′yō, -gā′nō), *n.* an antique Spanish type of cabinet or desk, consisting of a box-shaped body mounted on columns or a stand, and having the front hinged at the lower edge so as to afford, when let down, a surface for use in writing. [< Spanish *vargueño,* said to be < *Vargas,* a village near Toledo, Spain]
var·i·a·bil·i·ty (vãr′ē ə bil′ə tē), *n.* **1.** the fact or quality of being variable: *The adaptability of man was not, according to Darlington, a matter of individual flexibility or plasticity, but rather one of the genetic variability of the race* (Graham Phillips DuShane). **2.** the tendency to vary.
var·i·a·ble (vãr′ē ə bəl), *adj.* **1.** apt to change; changeable; uncertain: *variable winds. The weather is more variable in New York than it is in California.* **2.** likely to shift from one opinion or course of action to another; inconsistent: *a variable frame of mind.* **3.** that can be varied, changed, or modified: *These curtain rods are of variable length.* **4.** *Biology.* deviating from the normal or recognized species, variety, structure, etc. **5.** likely to increase or decrease in size, number, amount, degree, etc.; not remaining the same or uniform: *a constant or variable ratio.*
—*n.* **1.** a thing or quality that varies: *Temperature and rainfall are variables.* **2.** *Mathematics.* a quantity whose varying amounts are related to known facts: **a.** a quantity (sometimes indistinct) assumed to vary or be capable of varying in value throughout a given calculation or discussion. **b.** a symbol representing any one of a particular set of things. **3.** a shifting wind. **4.** a variable star.
the variables, the region between the northeast and the southeast trade winds: *The meeting of the two opposite currents [of wind] here produces the intermediate space called the ... variables* (Arthur Young).
—**var′i·a·ble·ness,** *n.*
—**Syn.** *adj.* **1.** unsteady, unstable, fluctuating, wavering, mutable. **2.** fickle. **3.** alterable. *-n.* **1.** inconstant.
variable annuity, an annuity in which part of the premium is invested in bonds and the remainder in common stocks, giving the holder an income that varies with the earnings of the stocks.
variable geometry, variable sweep.
var·i·a·ble-pitch propeller (vãr′ē ə bəl-pich′), an aircraft propeller whose pitch can be changed while rotating.
variable star, a star that varies periodically in brightness or magnitude.
variable sweep, a design that allows the angle of aircraft wings to be adjusted so as to give the best conditions for various phases of flight.
var·i·a·ble-sweep wing (vãr′ē ə bəl swēp′), an aircraft wing that can be adjusted in flight. It is set perpendicular to the fuselage during take-off and landing and swung backward when high speeds are reached.
variable time fuse, proximity fuse.
Variable Zone, the Temperate Zone.
var·i·a·bly (vãr′ē ə blē), *adv.* in a variable manner; changeably; inconstantly.
Var·i·ac (vãr′ē ak), *n. Trademark.* an autotransformer which varies and controls voltage, made of a single layer of wire wound on an iron core.
va·ri·a lec·ti·o (vãr′ē ə lek′shē ō), *pl.* **va·ri·ae lec·ti·o·nes** (vãr′ē ē lek′shē ō′nēz). *Latin.* a variant reading.
var·i·ance (vãr′ē əns), *n.* **1.** a difference; disagreement: *variances in the spelling of proper names.* **2.** a difference or discrepancy between two legal statements or documents, as between a writ and a complaint or evidence and an accusation, sufficient to make them ineffectual. **3.** a disagreeing or falling out; discord; quarrel: *to yield without variance.* **4.** a varying; change; variation: *a mean daily variance of eleven degrees.* **5.** *Statistics.* the square of the standard deviation. **6.** *Physical Chemistry.* the number of conditions, as temperature, pressure, etc., which must be fixed in order that the state of the system may be defined; degree of freedom of a system.
at variance, a. in a state of disagreement or difference; conflicting: *Roy's actions are at variance with his promises.* **b.** in a state of discord or dissension: *at variance with the neighbors.*
[< Old French *variance,* learned borrowing from Latin *variantia* < *variāns* variant]
var·i·ant (vãr′ē ənt), *adj.* **1.** varying; different: *"Rime" is a variant spelling of "rhyme".* **2.** variable; changing: *variant results.*
—*n.* **1.** a different form. **2.** a different pronunciation or spelling of the same word. **3.** an edition or translation of a manuscript, book, etc., that differs from the common or accepted version. **4.** a reworking or revising of an original story, song, etc.
[< Latin *variāns, -antis,* present participle of *variāre* change, vary]
var·i·ate (vãr′ē āt), *n.* **1.** *Statistics.* the size or value of a particular character in one specimen. **2.** a variable. [back formation < *variation*]
var·i·a·tion (vãr′ē ā′shən), *n.* **1.** a varying in condition, degree, etc.: *marked variations of dialect.* **2.** the act of changing in condition or degree: *There was no variation in his expression, whatever his mood.* **3.** the amount of change: *There was a variation of 30 degrees in the temperature yesterday.* **4.** a varied or changed form. **5.** *Music.* **a.** a tune or theme repeated with changes; a change, modification, or embellishment with regard to the melody, harmony, or rhythm of a theme, by which on repetition it appears in a new but still recognizable form. **b.** one of a series of such modifications upon a theme. **6.** *Biology.* **a.** a deviation of an animal or plant from type; deviation or divergence in the structure, character, or function of an organism from those typical of or usual in the species or group or from those of the parents. **b.** an animal or plant showing such deviation or divergence. **7.** *Astronomy.* the deviation of a heavenly body, as the moon, from its average orbit or motion. **8.** *Mathematics.* one of the different ways in which the members of any group or set may be combined. **9.** *Geography, Aeronautics.* the angular difference between geographic north and magnetic north from any point.
[< Old French *variation,* learned borrowing from Latin *variātiō, -ōnis* < *variāre* to vary]
var·i·a·tion·al (vãr′ē ā′shə nəl), *adj.* of or having to do with variation, especially in its biological senses.
var·i·cat·ed (var′ə kā′tid), *adj.* having varices, as a shell.
var·i·ca·tion (var′ə kā′shən), *n.* **1.** the formation of a varix. **2.** a set or system of varices.
var·i·cel·la (var′ə sel′ə), *n.* chicken pox. [< New Latin *varicella* (diminutive) < *variola;* see VARIOLA]
var·i·cel·lar (var′ə sel′ər), *adj.* of or relating to varicella.
var·i·cel·late (var′ə sel′āt), *adj.* marked with or having small varices, as some shells.

[< *varices* + Latin *-ella,* a diminutive suffix + English *-ate*[1]]

var·i·cel·loid (var′ə sel′oid), *adj.* resembling varicella or chicken pox: *varicelloid smallpox.* [< *varicell*(a) + *-oid*]

var·i·ces (vãr′ə sēz), *n.* the plural of **varix.**

var·i·co·cele (var′ə kō sēl), *n.* a varicose condition of the veins of the spermatic cord. [< Latin *varix, -icis* dilated vein + Greek *kēlē* tumor]

var·i·col·ored (vãr′ē kul′ərd), *adj.* **1.** having various colors; variegated in color: *varicolored tropical birds.* **2.** different; diverse; diversified: *His varicolored accounts of the accident puzzled the police.* [< Latin *varius* various + English *colored*]

var·i·col·oured (vãr′ē kul′ərd), *adj. Especially British.* varicolored.

var·i·cose (var′ə kōs), *adj.* **1.** (of blood vessels, especially veins) abnormally swollen or dilated; cirsoid: *He has varicose veins on his legs.* **2. a.** having to do with, affected with, or caused by varicose veins. **b.** designed to remedy or be used in the treatment of varicose veins. **3.** *Biology.* unusually enlarged or swollen; resembling a varix. [< Latin *varicōsus* < *varix, -icis* dilated vein]

var·i·cosed (var′ə kōst), *adj.* varicose.

var·i·co·sis (var′ə kō′sis), *n.* **1.** the formation of varicose veins or varices. **2.** varicosity. [< New Latin *varicosis* < Latin *varix, -icis* dilated vein + New Latin *-osis* -osis]

var·i·cos·i·ty (var′ə kos′ə tē), *n., pl.* **-ties. 1.** the state or condition of being varicose or abnormally swollen. **2.** a varicose part; varix.

var·i·cot·o·my (var′ə kot′ə mē), *n., pl.* **-mies.** the surgical removal of a varicose vein. [< Latin *varix, -icis* dilated vein + Greek *-tomiā* a cutting]

var·ied (vãr′ēd), *adj.* **1.** of different sorts or kinds; having variety: *the varied assortment of merchandise in a department store.* **2. a.** characterized by, presenting, or having different forms: *varied shadows at twilight. And changing like that varied gleam is our inconstant shape* (Scott). **b.** changed; altered. **3.** having different colors (used especially in the names of birds or animals): *the varied bunting.* —**var′ied·ly,** *adv.* —**var′ied·ness,** *n.*

varied thrush, a thrush of western North America, similar to a robin but with a black band across the breast.

Varied Thrush (9½ in. long)

var·i·e·gate (vãr′ē ə gāt, vãr′i gāt), *v.t.,* **-gat·ed, -gat·ing. 1.** to vary in appearance; mark, spot, or streak with different colors. **2.** to give variety to. [< Latin *variegāre* (with English *-ate*[1]) < *varius* various + *agere* to drive, make] —**Syn. 2.** diversify.

var·i·e·gat·ed (vãr′ē ə gā′tid, vãr′i gā′-), *adj.* **1.** marked with patches or spots of different colors; many-colored; varicolored: *Pansies are usually variegated.* **2.** having or characterized by variety; diverse. —**Syn. 1.** mottled, dappled.

var·i·e·ga·tion (vãr′ē ə gā′shən, vãr′i gā′-), *n.* **1.** the condition or quality of being variegated; diversity of color. **2.** the act or process of making varied in character.

var·i·e·ga·tor (vãr′ē ə gā′tər, vãr′i gā′-), *n.* a person or thing that variegates.

var·i·er (vãr′ē ər), *n.* a person who varies.

va·ri·e·tal (və rī′ə təl), *adj.* of, having to do with, or indicating a distinct variety of animal or plant; constituting a variety. —*n.* a kind of wine made almost entirely from one variety of grape and bearing its name: *His winery is the only one in the state to make varietals ... like Diana, Elvira, Delaware, or Niagara* (Harper's). —**va·ri′e·tal·ly,** *adv.*

va·ri·e·ty (və rī′ə tē), *n., pl.* **-ties. 1.** the fact, quality, or condition of being varied in nature or character; lack of sameness; difference; variation: *Variety is the spice of life. The variety of her moods kept us guessing.* **2.** a number of different kinds: *The store has a great variety of toys.* **3.** a different form of some quality, condition, or thing; something that differs or varies from others of the same class or kind; sort: *Which variety of cake do you prefer?* **4.** *Biology.* **a.** a plant or animal differing from those of the species to which it belongs in some minor but permanent or transmissible particular. **b.** a group of such individuals constituting a subspecies or other subdivision of a species. **5.** a group of domestic animals or cultivated plants whose modifications have been produced by artificial selection: *a variety of hybrid tea rose.* **6.** *Especially British.* vaudeville. [< Latin *varietās* < *varius* various]

—**Syn. 2. Variety, diversity** mean a number of things of different kinds or qualities. **Variety** emphasizes absence of sameness in form or character, and applies to a number of related things of different kinds or to a number of different things of the same general kind: *A teacher has a wide variety of duties.* **Diversity** emphasizes unlikeness, complete difference, in nature, form, or qualities: *A person who has traveled widely has a diversity of interests.*

variety show, 1. *Especially British.* vaudeville. **2.** a theatrical entertainment produced on radio or television and having the characteristics of vaudeville: *The variety show has won wide popularity because of its high-powered dancing, acrobatic, musical, and wise-cracking performers* (Emory S. Bogardus).

variety store, *U.S.* a store that sells a large variety of low-priced goods; dime store.

var·i·form (vãr′ə fôrm), *adj.* varied in form; having various forms. [< Latin *varius* various + English *-form*]

var·i·hued (vãr′ə hyüd′), *adj.* varicolored: *The varihued deposits resemble brilliant mosaics* (National Geographic).

var·i·o·cou·pler (vãr′ē ō kup′lər), *n. Electricity.* a kind of transformer having within the primary coil a secondary coil that can be rotated to adjust the mutual inductance. [< Latin *varius* various + English *coupler*]

va·ri·o·la (və rī′ə lə), *n.* smallpox. [< Medieval Latin *variola* < Late Latin, any rash, measles; pustule < Latin *varius* various, spotted]

va·ri·o·lar (və rī′ə lər), *adj.* variolous.

var·i·o·late (vãr′ē ə lāt), *v.t.,* **-lat·ed, -lat·ing.** to inoculate with the virus of smallpox. [< *variol*(a) + *-ate*[1]]

var·i·o·la·tion (vãr′ē ə lā′shən), *n.* inoculation with the virus of smallpox.

var·i·ole (vãr′ē ōl), *n.* **1.** a marking or depression resembling the pit left by smallpox; foveola. **2.** a spherulitic concretion of a variolite. [< *variola,* in sense of "pustule, pockmark" (because of its shape)]

var·i·o·lite (vãr′ē ə līt), *n.* a diabasic rock embedded with spherulites that give it a pock-marked appearance when weathered. [< Medieval Latin *variola* pockmark, pustule + English *-ite*[1] (because of its granular surface)]

var·i·o·lit·ic (vãr′ē ə lit′ik), *adj.* having to do with, resembling, or containing variolite.

var·i·o·loid (vãr′ē ə loid), *adj.* having to do with or resembling variola or smallpox. —*n.* a mild form of variola or smallpox, occurring usually in those who are partially protected by vaccination or have had smallpox. [< New Latin *varioloides* < Medieval Latin *variola* (see VARIOLA) + New Latin *-oides* -oid]

va·ri·o·lous (və rī′ə ləs), *adj.* **1.** of, having to do with, or characteristic of variola or smallpox. **2.** affected with or suffering from variola or smallpox. **3.** having marks like the scars of variola or smallpox; pitted.

var·i·om·e·ter (vãr′ē om′ə tər), *n.* **1.** an instrument for comparing the intensity of magnetic forces, especially the magnetic force of the earth at different points. **2.** *Electricity.* an apparatus consisting of a coil of insulated wire connected in series with and designed to turn inside a similar coil and so to vary the inductance. **3.** an instrument used in an airplane, especially a glider, for showing the rate at which it rises or descends, usually in units of 100 feet a minute. [< Latin *varius* various + *-meter*]

var·i·o·rum (vãr′ē ôr′əm, -ōr′-), *n.* **1.** an edition of a book, especially of a classic, that has the comments and notes of several editors, critics, etc. **2.** an edition of a book containing variant versions of the text. —*adj.* of or like a variorum. [< Latin (*editiō cum notīs*) *variōrum* (edition with notes) of various people; genitive plural masculine of *varius* various]

var·i·ous (vãr′ē əs), *adj.* **1.** differing from one another; different: *There have been various opinions as to the best way to raise children.* **2.** several; many: *We have looked at various houses, but have decided to buy this one.* **3.** many-sided; varied: *lives made various by learning.* **4.** varying; changeable: *apparel as gaudy as it is various.* [< Latin *varius* (with English *-ous*). Doublet of VAIR.] —**var′i·ous·ness,** *n.* —**Syn. 1.** diverse, diversified.

➔ It is not always possible to distinguish between senses 1 and 2 as the meaning often blends into *many different.*

var·i·ous·ly (vãr′ē əs lē), *adv.* **1.** in different ways; with variation or variety; differently: *He began to use burlap as a medium, sewing together variously weathered pieces and stretching two or three thicknesses on a frame* (Newsweek). **2.** *U.S.* at different times: *to live variously in town and in the country.*

var·is·cite (var′ə sīt), *n.* a mineral, a hydrous aluminum phosphate, occurring in bright-green, crystalline or kidney-shaped crusts. *Formula:* $AlPO_4.2H_2O$ [< Latin *Variscia,* a part of Saxony + English *-ite*[1] (because it was found there)]

var·i·type (vãr′ē tīp), *v.,* **-typed, -typ·ing.** —*v.t.* to set with a Varityper. —*v.i.* to operate a Varityper.

Var·i·typ·er (vãr′ē tī′pər), *n. Trademark.* a composing machine like a typewriter but with changeable type faces.

var·i·typ·ist (vãr′ē tī′pist), *n.* a person who operates a Varityper.

va·ri·um et mu·ta·bi·le sem·per fe·mi·na (vãr′ē əm et myü tab′ə lē sem′pər fem′ə nə), *Latin.* ever a fickle and changeable thing is woman.

var·ix (vãr′iks), *n., pl.* **var·i·ces. 1. a.** an abnormal dilation or enlargement of a vein or artery, usually accompanied by tortuous development; varicose vein or artery. **b.** the diseased condition characterized by this. **2.** a longitudinal elevation or swelling on the surface of a shell. [< Latin *varix, -icis* dilated vein]

var·let (vär′lit), *n. Archaic.* **1. a.** a man or boy acting as an attendant or servant; groom. **b.** an attendant on a knight or other person of military importance. **2.** a low, mean fellow; rascal: *a little contemptible varlet, without the least title to birth, person, wit* (Jonathan Swift). [< Old French *varlet,* variant of *vaslet* (originally) squire, young man (diminutive) < Old French *vasal* vassal]

var·let·ry (vär′lə trē), *n. Archaic.* a number or crowd of attendants or rascals; varlets: *Shall they hoist me up, And show me to the shouting varletry Of censuring Rome?* (Shakespeare).

var·mint or **var·ment** (vär′mənt), *n. Dialect.* **1.** vermin. **2.** an objectionable animal or person: *skunks, weasels, and suchlike varmints.* [variant of *vermin*]

var·na (vär′nə), *n.* any of the four main castes or classes of Hindu society: *The varnas were the priests* (*Brahmans*), *the warriors* (*Kshatriyas*), *the merchants* (*Vaisyas*), *and the servitors* (*Sudras*) (New Yorker). [< Sanskrit *varna* color; caste]

var·nish (vär′nish), *n.* **1. a.** a thin, transparent liquid that dries into a hard, glossy, and durable or ornamental surface on wood, metal, etc., and is made from resinous substances dissolved in oil, turpentine, or alcohol. **b.** any of various natural or synthetic substances having a similar use. **2.** the smooth, hard surface made by this liquid when dry: *The varnish on the car has been scratched.* **3.** a glossy or lustrous appearance. **4.** a false or deceiving appearance; a pretense: *She covers her selfishness with a varnish of good manners.*

—*v.t.* **1. a.** to put varnish on; to coat with varnish. **b.** to smear or stain with some substance similar to varnish. **2.** to embellish or adorn; improve the appearance of (something). **3.** to give a false or deceiving appearance to.

[Middle English *vernich* < Old French *vernis, verniz* < Medieval Latin *vernix, vernica* odorous resin < Late Greek *verenīkē* < Greek *Berenīkē,* an ancient city in Libya] —**var′nish·er,** *n.*

var·nish·ing day (vär′ni shing), a day before the opening of an exhibition, when exhibitors have the privilege of retouching and varnishing their pictures already hung.

varnish tree, any of several trees yielding a resinous substance used as a varnish or lacquer, especially a Japanese and Chinese tree of the cashew family.

va·room (və rüm′, -rům′), *n.* the sound made by the engine of a speeding sports car or racing car. —*v.i., v.t.* to go or travel at great speed, making such a sound: . . . *va-rooming through town in a new 350-h.p. Corvette Sting Ray* (Time). [imitative]

var·si·ty (vär′sə tē), *n., pl.* **-ties,** *adj.* —*n.* the most important team in a given sport in a university, college, or school. —*adj.* of or having to do with the most important team in any school, college, or university competition. [variant of earlier *versity* < (uni)*versity*]

var·so·via·na (vär′sō vyä′nə), *n.* **1.** a dance which originated in the 1800's, in imitation of the mazurka, polka, and red-owa. **2.** the music for this dance, in triple meter and slow, with a strong accent on the first beat of every second measure. [< Italian *Varsoviana,* feminine of *Varsoviano* of Warsaw < *Varsovia* Warsaw]

var·so·vienne (vär′sō vyen′), *n.* varso-viana. [< French *Varsovienne,* feminine of *Varsovien* of Warsaw]

var·ta·bed (vär′tə bed), *n.* one of an order of clergy in the Armenian church. [< Armenian *vartabed*]

Var·u·na (var′ů nə, vur′-), *n. Hindu Mythology.* the supreme god of the heavens and judge of the earth. [< Sanskrit *Varuna*]

var·us (vãr′əs), *n.* a form of clubfoot or talipes in which the foot is turned inward. —*adj.* **1.** (of the bones in the foot, knee, hip, etc.) characterized by the abnormal position of turning inward. **2.** bowlegged. [< New Latin *varus* foot turned inward < Latin *vārus* knock-kneed, bent in]

varve (värv), *n. Geology.* a stratified layer or band of sediment deposited annually by melting glaciers, used in determining the lapse of time in dating geological phenomena: *Radiocarbon dating of tree rings and clay varves on lake bottoms will permit scientists to determine solar cycles even before 220 B.C.* (Science News Letter). [< Swedish *varv* layer]

varved (värvd), *adj.* deposited in varves.

var·y (vãr′ē), *v.,* **var·ied, var·y·ing.** —*v.t.* **1.** to make different; change: *The driver can vary the speed of an automobile.* **2.** to give variety to (something); introduce changes into (something): *to vary one's style of writing.* **3.** *Music.* to repeat (a tune or theme) with changes and ornament. —*v.i.* **1.** to be different from something, especially by appearing in various forms: *The stars vary in brightness.* **2.** to undergo change or alteration; become different: *The weather varied between cloudy and bright.* **3.** *Mathematics.* to undergo or be subject to a change in value according to some law: *to vary inversely as the cube of y.* **4.** *Biology.* to exhibit or be subject to variation, as by natural or artificial selection. [< Old French *varier* < Latin *variāre* < *varius* varied, spotted, various] —**var′y·ing·ly,** *adv.* —**Syn.** *v.t.* **1.** alter, modify, diversify. *-v.i.* **1.** disagree, deviate.

var·y·ing hare (vãr′ē ing), snowshoe hare.

vas (vas), *n., pl.* **va·sa** (vā′sə). **1.** a duct or vessel conveying blood, lymph, or other fluid through the body. **2.** a tube or conduit in a plant. [< Latin *vās, vāsis* vessel. Doublet of VASE.]

vas·cu·lar (vas′kyə lər), *adj.* **1.** *Zoology.* **a.** having the character or structure of vessels that carry blood, lymph, etc. **b.** affecting the vascular system. **2.** *Botany.* **a.** having a vascular structure. **b.** having the form of or consisting of tubes. [< New Latin *vascularis* < Latin *vāsculum* (diminutive) < *vās* vessel] —**vas′cu·lar·ly,** *adv.*

vascular bundle, *Botany.* a bundle.

vas·cu·lar·i·ty (vas′kyə lar′ə tē), *n.* a vascular form or condition.

vas·cu·lar·i·za·tion (vas′kyə lər ə zā′-shən), *n.* a making or becoming vascular, as by the formation of new blood vessels.

vas·cu·lar·ize (vas′kyə lə rīz), *v.t., v.i.,* **-ized, -iz·ing.** to make or become vascular.

vascular plants, *Botany.* the plants in which the structure is made up in part of vascular tissue or vessels. They comprise the spermatophytes and pteridophytes.

vascular system, **1.** *Zoology.* the vessels and organs that carry and circulate the blood and lymph. **2.** *Botany.* the vascular tissue in a plant.

vascular tissue, *Botany.* the tissue in spermatophytes and pteridophytes composed of tubular vessels or ducts for carrying the sap throughout the plant.

vas·cu·lose (vas′kyə lōs), *n.* the principal constituent of the vascular tissue in plants. —*adj.* vascular.

vas·cu·lous (vas′kyə ləs), *adj.* vascular.

vas·cu·lum (vas′kyə ləm), *n., pl.* **-lums, -la** (-lə). **1.** a long, oval, tin box for carrying newly-collected botanical specimens. **2.** *Botany.* a pitcher-shaped leafy structure; ascidium. [< Latin *vāsculum* (diminutive) < *vās* vessel]

vas de·fe·rens (vas def′ə renz), *pl.* **va·sa de·fe·ren·ti·a** (vā′sə def′ə ren′shē ə). the excretory duct of the testicle, conveying semen from the epididymis to the penis. [< New Latin *vas deferens* < Latin *vās* vessel, *dēferēns* carrying down, present participle of *dēferre* < *dē-* down + *ferre* carry]

vase (vās, vāz; *especially British* väz), *n.* a holder or container used for ornament or for holding flowers. [< French *vase,* learned borrowing from Latin *vās, vāsis* vessel. Doublet of VAS.] —**vase′like′,** *adj.*

Portland Vase (Wedgwood replica)

vas·ec·to·my (va sek′tə mē), *n., pl.* **-mies.** the surgical removal of part or all of the vas deferens. [< Latin *vās* vessel + Greek *ektomē* a cutting out]

Vas·e·line (vas′ə lēn, -lin), *n. Trademark.* a soft petroleum jelly used as an ointment or lubricant. [American English; coined < German *Wasser* water + Greek *élaion* oil + English *-ine*[1]]

vaso-, *combining form.* blood vessel; vascular system: *Vasoconstrictor = a drug, nerve, etc., that constricts blood vessels.* [< Latin *vās, vāsis* vessel]

vas·o·con·stric·tion (vas′ō kən strik′-shən), *n.* constriction of the blood vessels.

vas·o·con·stric·tive (vas′ō kən strik′tiv), *adj.* serving to constrict blood vessels; vasoconstrictor: *a vasoconstrictive drug, a vasoconstrictive nerve.*

vas·o·con·stric·tor (vas′ō kən strik′tər), *adj.* (of drugs, nerves, etc.) constricting blood vessels. —*n.* a drug, nerve, etc., that constricts blood vessels.

vas·o·de·pres·sor (vas′ō di pres′ər), *n.* a drug that lowers blood pressure by artificially relaxing the blood vessels: *A wide variety of vasodepressors of varying effectiveness have now been offered to the physician* (Morris Fishbein).

vas·o·di·lat·ing (vas′ō dī lā′ting, -də-), *adj.* vasodilator: *The drug improved circulation of the scalp by its vasodilating action* (Time).

vas·o·di·la·tion (vas′ō dī lā′shən, -də-), *n.* the dilation of blood vessels by a nerve or drug: *In no case does Dr. Brickner consider vasodilation to be a "cure" for multiple sclerosis; at most, it is a palliative, giving relief, particularly . . . when new symptoms occur* (Newsweek).

vas·o·di·la·tor (vas′ō dī lā′tər, -də-), *adj.* (of drugs, nerves, etc.) dilating blood vessels. —*n.* something that dilates blood vessels, as a nerve or drug.

vas·o·mo·tor (vas′ō mō′tər), *adj.* of or having to do with nerves and nerve centers that regulate the size of blood vessels and so govern circulation.

vas·o·pres·sin (vas′ō pres′in), *n.* **1.** a pituitary hormone that contracts small blood vessels, raises blood pressure, and reduces the excretion of urine by the kidneys. **2.** a synthetic form of this hormone used as an antidiuretic in the treatment of diabetes insipidus; Pitressin. [< *vasopress*(or) + *-in*]

vas·o·pres·sor (vas′ō pres′ər), *adj.* of or having to do with the constriction of blood vessels: *The life-saving vasopressor drugs, used to combat shock after a heart attack, conserve the blood supply to heart and brain at the expense of other less sensitive organs in the body* (Science News Letter). —*n.* a hormone or drug that constricts blood vessels.

vas·o·spasm (vas′ō spaz′əm), *n.* constriction of blood vessels; vasoconstriction.

vas·sal (vas′əl), *n.* **1.** in the European feudal system: **a.** a person who held lands from a superior on conditions of homage and allegiance, usually in the form of military service. A great noble could be a vassal of the king and have many other men as his vassals. **b.** a tenant in fee; retainer. **2. a.** a person who holds a position similar to that of a feudal vassal. **b.** a person devoted to the service of another; servant. **c.** a person completely subject to some influence: *The feeble vassals of wine and anger and lust* (Tennyson). *To You, O Goddess of Efficiency, Your happy vassals bend the reverent knee* (Samuel Hoffenstein). **3.** a bondman; slave.
—*adj.* **1.** like that of a vassal; subject; subordinate: *vassal princes.* **2.** of, having to do with, or like a vassal: *an oath of vassal loyalty.*
[< Old French *vassal* < Medieval Latin *vassallus* retainer < *vassus* < Celtic (compare Old Irish *foss* servant)]
—**Syn.** *adj.* **1.** dependent.

vas·sal·age (vas′ə lij), *n.* **1. a.** the state or condition of being a vassal. **b.** the homage, allegiance, or services due from a vassal to his lord or superior. **c.** the land held by a vassal. **2. a.** dependence; servitude. **b.** subjection to some influence: *the vassalage of strength to the demands of intellect.* **3.** a body or group of vassals.

vas·sal·ize (vas′ə līz), *v.t.,* **-ized, -iz·ing.** to make a vassal or vassals of: *American military aid will vassalize Cambodia and lead it to war* (Time).

vas·sal·ry (vas′əl rē), *n.* a body of vassals.

vast (vast, väst), *adj.* **1.** of great area; of immense extent; extensive; far-stretching: *Texas is a vast state.* **2.** of large dimensions; of very great size; huge; massive: *vast forms that move fantastically* (Edgar Allan Poe). **3.** very great in amount, quantity, or number: *A billion dollars is a vast amount of money. It is a building with a vast collection of chambers and galleries.* **4.** (of the mind, etc.) unusually large or comprehensive in grasp or aims: *the vast and various affairs of government.*
—*n.* **1.** *Poetic.* an immense space: *her return to the unconscious vast* (Eden Phillpotts). **2.** *Dialect.* a very great number or amount: *They had heard a vast of words* (Robert Louis Stevenson).
[< Latin *vastus* immense, empty] —**vast′-ness,** *n.*
—**Syn.** *adj.* **1, 2, 3.** immense, tremendous, colossal.

vas·ti·tude (vas′tə tüd, -tyüd), *n.* **1.** the quality of being vast; immensity. **2.** unusual largeness. **3.** a vast extent or space. [< Latin *vastitūdō* < *vastus* vast]

vas·ti·ty (vas′tə tē), *n., pl.* **-ties. 1.** vastness; immensity; vastitude: *The huge vastity of the world* (Philemon Holland). **2.** wasteness; desolation; void: *Nothing but emptiness and vastity* (Thomas Nashe). [< Latin *vastitās, -ātis* < *vastus* vast]

vast·ly (vast′lē, väst′-), *adv.* **1.** to a vast extent or degree; immensely: *an explosion vastly more rapid and powerful.* **2.** exceedingly; extremely; very: *new housing projects vastly superior to the old slums.*

vast·y (vas′tē, väs′-), *adj.* vast; immense: *I can call spirits from the vasty deep* (Shakespeare).

vat (vat), *n., v.,* **vat·ted, vat·ting.** —*n.* **1.** a large container, as a cask, barrel, or tank, for holding, storing, or maturing liquid. **2.** a large container, often wooden, for fermenting beer, cider, etc. **3.** a container for collecting and evaporating sea water to extract its salt. **4.** a liquid containing a dissolved dye.
—*v.t.* to place, store, or treat in a vat.
[Middle English dialectal variant of *fat*[2], Old English *fæt*]

Vat., Vatican.

vat·ful (vat′fůl), *n., pl.* **-fuls.** the quantity that a vat will hold.

vat·ic (vat′ik), *adj.* of, having to do with, or characteristic of a prophet or seer; prophetic; inspired: *I believe Norman MacCaig's reputation—made slowly and quietly, without any vatic posturing—will prove a durable one* (Manchester Guardian Weekly). [< Latin *vātēs, -is* prophet + English *-ic*]

Vat·i·can (vat′ə kən), *n.* **1. a.** the collection of buildings grouped about the palace of the Pope, built upon the Vatican Hill in Rome. **b.** the artistic or literary treasures preserved there; the Vatican galleries or library. **2.** the government, office, or authority of the Pope. —*adj.* of or having to do with the Vatican or its library. [< Latin *Vāticānus* (*mōns*) Vatican (hill), one of the hills in ancient Rome on which the palace of the Pope was later built]

Vatican Council, **1.** Also, **Vatican I.** the twentieth ecumenical council of the Roman Catholic Church, meeting in the Vatican, which opened in 1869 and was indefinitely suspended in 1870. **2.** Also, **Vatican II.** the twenty-first ecumenical council, which met at the Vatican from 1962 to 1965, and was, in effect, a continuation of Vatican I.

Vat·i·can·ism (vat′ə kə niz′əm), *n.* the doctrine of absolute papal infallibility and supremacy.

Vat·i·can·ist (vat′ə kə nist), *n.* a devoted adherent of the Pope and believer in Vaticanism.

vat·i·cide (vat′ə sīd), *n.* **1.** a person who kills a prophet. **2.** the killing of a prophet. [< Latin *vātēs, -is* prophet + *caedere* kill]

va·tic·i·nal (və tis′ə nəl), *adj.* of the nature of or characterized by prophecy; prophetic.

va·tic·i·nate (və tis′ə nāt), *v.t., v.i.,* **-nat·ed, -nat·ing.** to prophesy. [< Latin *vāticinārī* (with English *-ate*[1]) < *vāticinus* prophetic < *vātēs, -is* seer] —**Syn.** predict.

va·tic·i·na·tion (və tis′ə nā′shən), *n.* **1.** a prophecy or forecast: *The minstrel proceeded with his explanation of the dubious and imperfect vaticinations* (Scott). **2.** the act or fact of vaticinating; utterance of predictions. **3.** the power or gift of prophecies.

va·tic·i·na·tor (və tis′ə nā′tər), *n.* a prophet.

vau·de·ville (vô′də vil, vōd′vil), *n.* **1.** a theatrical entertainment consisting of a variety of acts, such as songs, dances, acrobatic feats, short plays, and trained animals. **2.** a play or stage performance of light character, interspersed with songs. **3.** a light popular song, commonly of a satirical or topical nature.
[< French *vaudeville,* earlier *vau de ville,* alteration of Middle French (*chanson du*) *Vau de Vire* (song of the) valley of Vire in Calvados, Normandy; first applied to the songs of Olivier Basselin, a poet of the 1400's who lived there]

vau·de·vil·lian (vô′də vil′yən, vōd vil′-), *n.* a person who performs in or writes songs, sketches, etc., for vaudeville: *The pros peddle their skill with the peripatetic energy of old-time vaudevillians* (Time). —*adj.* of or having to do with vaudeville: *In these, and the like, he shows a special flair for vaudevillian humor* (Winthrop Sargeant).

Vau·dois (vō dwä′), *n.pl.* the Waldenses. [< Middle French *Vaudois* < Medieval Latin *Valdensis* Waldenian]

vault[1] (vôlt), *n.* **1. a.** an arched masonry or concrete structure built so that the parts support each other, serving as a roof or covering over a space. **b.** an arched roof or ceiling. **c.** something like an arched roof, especially the sky: *Heaven's ebon vault, Studded with stars* (Shelley). **2.** an underground cellar or storehouse: *He went into the inner vault where he kept his choicest wines* (Samuel Butler). **3.** a place for storing valuable things and keeping them safe. Vaults are often made of steel. *A paper currency is employed when there is no bullion in the vaults* (Emerson). **4. a.** *Obsolete.* an arched space under the floor of a church; crypt. **b.** a place for burial: *to be buried in the family vault.* **5.** a natural cavern or cave. **6.** *Anatomy.* an arched structure, especially the skull.
—*v.t.* **1.** to make in the form of a vault. **2.** to set or extend like a vault: *Hateful is the dark-blue sky Vaulted o'er the dark-blue sea* (Tennyson). **3.** to cover with a vault.
[< Old French *voulte, vaulte* < Vulgar Latin *volvita,* noun use of *volvitus,* for Latin *volūtus,* feminine past participle of *volvere* to roll] —**vault′like′,** *adj.*

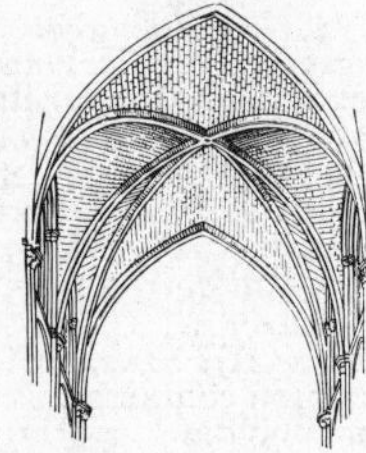

Gothic Vault[1] (def. 1a)

vault[2] (vôlt), *v.i.* to jump or leap: *He vaulted over the wall.* —*v.t.* **1.** to jump or leap over by using a pole or the hands: *He vaulted the fence.* See **pole vault** for picture. **2.** to mount (a horse) by leaping.
—*n.* **1.** the act of vaulting; jump; leap. **2.** (in the manège) the leap of a horse; curvet. [alteration (influenced by *vault*[1]) of Middle French *volter* < Old French < Italian *voltare* < *volta* < Vulgar Latin *volvita;* see VAULT[1]] —**vault′er,** *n.*

vault·ed (vôl′tid), *adj.* **1.** in the form of a vault; arched: *a vaulted ceiling.* **2.** built or covered with a vault: *a vaulted room.* **3.** having vaults or underground passages: *the vaulted catacombs.* —**Syn. 2.** domed.

vault·ing[1] (vôl′ting), *n.* **1.** the art, practice, or operation of constructing vaults. **2.** a vaulted structure. **3.** vaults collectively.

vault·ing[2] (vôl′ting), *adj.* **1.** that vaults or leaps, especially in an overzealous manner: *vaulting ambition.* **2.** used in or for vaulting: *a vaulting horse.* —*n.* the act of leaping with a vault.

vaulting horse, a side horse.

vault of heaven, the sky.

vault·y (vôl′tē), *adj.* like a vault; arched.

vaunt (vônt, vänt), *v.t.* to boast of (something); talk vaingloriously: *Charity vaunteth not itself* (I Corinthians 13:4). —*v.i.* **1.** to brag or boast; use boastful language: *He talked little, never vaunted* (William Temple). **2.** to boast of or praise (oneself).
—*n.* a boasting assertion or speech; brag: *Vainglorious men are . . . the slaves of their own vaunts* (Francis Bacon).
[< Old French *vanter* < Late Latin *vānitāre* < Latin *vānāre* to utter empty words < *vānus* idle, empty]

vaunt-cour·i·er (vônt′kůr′ē ər, vänt′-), *n.* **1.** a person or thing sent in advance to prepare for or announce the approach of another; forerunner. **2.** *Obsolete.* one of the soldiers or horsemen sent before an army or body of troops; an advance guard; scout. [short for Old French *avant-coureur* (literally) forerunner < *avant* forward + *coureur* courier]

vaunt·ed (vôn′tid, vän′-), *adj.* boasted or bragged of; highly praised: *the vaunted triumphs of civilization.*

vaunt·er (vôn′tər, vän′-), *n.* **1.** a boaster or braggart. **2.** a person who boastfully asserts or praises something.

vaunt·ing (vôn′ting, vän′-), *adj.* that vaunts; boasting; bragging; boastful. —**vaunt′ing·ly,** *adv.*

vaunt·y (vôn′tē, vän′-), *adj. British Dialect and Scottish.* boastful; proud; vain.

v. aux., auxiliary verb.

Vaux's swift (vôk′səz), a swift of western North America resembling the chimney swift.

vav (vôv, väv), *n.* the sixth letter of the Hebrew alphabet. [< Hebrew *vāv*]

vav·a·sor (vav′ə sôr, -sōr), *n.* (in the European feudal system) a vassal ranking below a baron, holding land and having other vassals under him: *vavasors subdivide again to vassals* (John L. Motley). [< Old French *vavassour* < Medieval Latin *vasvassor,* apparently reduction of phrase *vassi vassorum* vassals of vassals. Compare VARLET, VALET.]

vav·a·sour (vav′ə sůr), *n.* vavasor.

va·ward (vā′wôrd′), *n. Obsolete.* vanguard: *We that are in the vaward of our youth* (Shakespeare). [variant of *vanward* < earlier *vantward,* short for *avantward* < Old North French, Old French *avant-garde;* see VANGUARD]

vb., **1.** verb. **2.** verbal.

V-belt (vē′belt′), *n.* a belt for running on a pulley with a V-shaped groove, used as the fan belt in automobiles to connect the crankshaft with the fan and generator, and also used to connect a motor to a tool, such as a saw.

V-block (vē′blok′), *n.* a block of metal cut in the shape of the letter V on one side, used for holding cylindrical objects in machining.

V-bomb (vē′bom′), *n.* **1.** a German robot bomb of World War II; V-1. **2.** a German rocket bomb of World War II; V-2. [see V-1]

V-bomb·er (vē′bom′ər), *n.* a British military aircraft capable of carrying nuclear weapons.

V.C., an abbreviation for the following:
1. Veterinary Corps.
2. Vice-Chairman.
3. Vice-Chancellor.
4. Vice-Consul.
5. Victoria Cross.
6. Vietcong: *The V.C. were hardly crushed . . . The Reds attacked through the trees* (Time).

Vd (no period), vanadium (chemical element).

v.d., various dates.

V.D. or **VD** (no periods), venereal disease.

V-Day (vē′dā′), *n.* the day (December 31, 1946) of the presidential proclamation marking the complete victory of the Allied Forces in World War II. [< *v*(ictory)]

VE (no periods), vesicular exanthema.

Ve·a·dar (vē′ə där), *n.* the intercalary month of the Jewish calendar, inserted after Adar during the Hebrew leap years. [< Hebrew *va'ădār* (literally) and Adar; second Adar]

veal (vēl), *n.* **1.** the flesh of a calf, used for food. **2.** a calf, especially as killed or intended for food. [< Anglo-French *vel,* Old French *veel, veal,* earlier *vedel* < Latin *vitellus* (diminutive) < *vitulus* calf, perhaps in the sense of "yearling", related to *vetus* year, weather]

veal·er (vē′lər), *n. U.S.* a milk-fed calf under 12 weeks old.

veal·y (vē′lē), *adj.* like or suggesting veal; having the appearance of veal; immature.

vec·tion (vek′shən), *n. Obsolete.* the act of carrying, especially disease germs. [< Latin *vectiō, -ōnis* a carrying, conveyance < *vehere* carry]

vec·tor (vek′tər), *n.* **1.** *Mathematics.* **a.** a quantity involving direction as well as magnitude. **b.** a line representing both the direction and magnitude of some force, etc. **2.** *Astronomy.* radius vector. **3.** *Biology.* an organism, such as a mosquito or tick, that transmits microorganisms that cause disease.

A B D C

Vectors (def. 1b.) DA and DC are vectors; DB is resultant.

—*v.t.* to guide (a pilot, aircraft, or missile) from one point to another within a given time by means of a vector: *He vectored the pilot back to the base.*
[< Latin *vector* carrier < *vehere* carry]

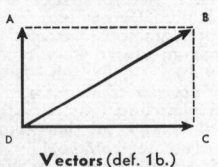

vec·tor·car·di·o·gram (vek′tər kär′dē ə gram), *n.* a tracing of the direction and strength of the electrical forces in the heart.

vector field, a set of vectors each of whose values depend upon a certain point from which the vectors radiate, composing a region of space.

vec·to·ri·al (vek tôr′ē əl, -tōr′-), *adj.* of or having to do with a vector or vectors: *Another new instrument being installed at Palomar is a vectorial recorder which photographs a pattern of the earth's surface motion in two dimensions* (Science News Letter).

vec·to·ri·al·ly (vek tôr′ē ə lē, -tōr′-), *adv.* in a vectorial manner: *We can find the field produced by a number of bodies by adding vectorially all the fields produced by each* (John R. Fields).

vec·tu·rist (vek′chər ist), *n.* a person who collects transportation tokens. [< Latin *vectūra* conveyance (< *vehere* carry) + English *-ist*]

Ve·da (vā′də, vē′-), *n.* any or all of the four collections of sacred Hindu writings in an early form or dialect of Sanskrit. They include *Rig-Veda* or hymns, *Sama-Veda* or chants, *Yajur-Veda* or sacred formulas, and *Atharva-Veda,* later and more superstitious hymns. [< Sanskrit *vēda* (sacred) knowledge < *vid* to know; (literally) to have perceived]

Ve·da·ic (vā dā′ik, vē-), *adj.* Vedic. —*n.* the language of the Veda, an early form of Sanskrit.

Ve·da·ism (vā′də iz əm, vē′-), *n.* the system of religious beliefs and practices contained in the Vedas.

Ve·dan·ta (vi dän′tə, -dan′-), *n.* a leading system of Hindu philosophy founded on the Vedas, and concerned with the relation of the universe and the human soul to the Supreme Spirit. [< Sanskrit *vēdanta* < *vēda* (see VEDA) + *anta* the end]

Ve·dan·tic (vi dän′tik, -dan′-), *adj.* relating to the Vedanta.

Ve·dan·tism (vi dän′tiz əm, -dan′-), *n.* the doctrines or system of the Vedanta.

Ve·dan·tist (vi dän′tist, -dan′-), *n.* a person versed in the doctrines of the Vedanta.

V-E Day (vē′ē′), the day of the Allied victory in Europe in World War II, May 8, 1945.

Ved·da or **Ved·dah** (ved′ə), *n.* a member of a primitive race of Ceylon, an island just off southern India. [< Singhalese *veddā* hunter, archer]

Ved·doid (ved′oid), *n.* a member of a group of Asian people represented by the Vedda of Ceylon, and regarded as intermediate between the Caucasian and Australian types. —*adj.* of or having to do with Veddoids.

ve·dette (vi det′), *n.* **1.** a mounted sentry stationed in advance of the outposts of an army. **2.** vedette boat. Also, **vidette.** [< French *vedette* < Italian *vedetta* sentry post, outlook (alteration of *veletta* < Spanish *vela* watch, vigil) < *vedere* to see < Latin *vidēre*]

vedette boat, a small naval vessel used for scouting.

Ve·dic (vā′dik, vē′-), *adj.* of, having to do with, or contained in the Vedas. —*n.* the language of the Veda, an early form of Sanskrit.

vee (vē), *n.* **1.** the letter V or v. **2.** anything shaped like a V. **3.** *Informal.* a five-dollar bill. —*adj.* V-shaped.

Veep (vēp), *n. Slang.* the vice-president of the United States. [American English < pronunciation of *V.P.*, abbreviation of *Vice President*]

veep (vēp), *n. Slang.* a vice-president. [< *Veep*]

veer[1] (vir), *v.i.* **1.** (of the wind) to change gradually; pass from one point to another by degrees: *The wind veered to the South.* **2.** *Nautical.* **a.** to change course, especially to turn the head away from the wind. **b.** to alter course by swinging the stern to windward so as to sail another tack. **3.** to change in direction; shift; turn: *The talk veered to ghosts.* —*v.t.* to turn (something); to change the direction of: *We veered our boat.*
—*n.* a change of direction; shift; turn.
[< Middle French *virer;* origin uncertain]
—**Syn.** *n.* deviation.

veer[2] (vir), *v.t.* **1. a.** to let out (any line or rope); allow to run out gradually. **b.** to let out or pay out (a cable). **2.** to allow (a boat, buoy, etc.) to drift away or out by letting out line attached to it. [compare Middle Dutch *vieren* to slacken]

veer·ing (vir′ing), *n.* the act or fact of changing course or direction: *The veering of his opinions from day to day kept his supporters in a dither.*
—*adj.* vacillating; variable; changeful.
—**veer′ing·ly,** *adv.*

veer·y (vir′ē), *n., pl.* **veer·ies.** a thrush of eastern North America with tawny head, back, and tail and an almost unspotted white breast; Wilson's thrush; tawny thrush. [American English; probably imitative of its note]

veg (vej), *n.,* or **veg.,** *Especially British Informal.* vegetable or vegetables: *meat with two watery veg and currant roll* (Manchester Guardian).

Ve·ga (vē′gə), *n.* a bluish-white star, the brightest in the constellation Lyra. [< Medieval Latin *Vega* < Arabic (*al-Nasr al-*) *Wāqi'* (the) falling (vulture); the constellation Lyra]

veg·an (vej′ən), *n., adj. British.* —*n.* a strict vegetarian: *The true ... vegan excludes all animal protein from his diet, and he may even forego articles of clothing and household equipment of animal origin* (New Scientist).
—*adj.* strictly vegetarian: *It is difficult for a vegan diet not to result in deficiencies* (J.G. Sutherland). [< *veg*(*etari*)*an*]

veg·e·ta·ble (vej′tə bəl, vej′ə-), *n.* **1.** a plant whose fruit, shoots or stems, leaves, roots, or other parts are used for food. Peas, corn, lettuce, tomatoes, and beets are vegetables. **2.** a living organism belonging to the vegetable kingdom.
—*adj.* **1.** of, having to do with, or like plants: *vegetable substances, vegetable life, the vegetable kingdom.* **2.** consisting of or made from vegetables: *vegetable soup, vegetable oils, a vegetable dinner.* **3.** living and growing as a plant or organism having the lowest form of life.
[< Middle French *vegetable,* learned borrowing from Late Latin *vegetābilis* vivifying, refreshing < Latin *vegetāre* enliven, arouse < *vegetus* vigorous]

vegetable butter, a fixed vegetable oil, solid at ordinary temperatures.

vegetable fat, fat derived from vegetables or vegetable oils: *The main sources of edible oils and fats are vegetable fats* (London Times).

vegetable ivory, 1. the hard endosperm or albumen of the ivory nut, resembling ivory in hardness, color, and texture, used for ornamental work, buttons, etc. **2.** the hard brown shell of the coquilla nut, used similarly.

vegetable kingdom, that division of the natural world that includes all plants.

vegetable lamb, the tartarian lamb, a rhizome which when trimmed and inverted somewhat resembles a small lamb.

vegetable marrow, an oblong squash with a green skin that turns light yellow, used especially in Great Britain as a vegetable; marrow.

vegetable oil, any oil obtained from the fruit or seeds of plants such as olive oil, peanut oil, corn oil, and linseed oil, used in cooking, medicines, and paints, and for lubrication, etc.: *Sunflower seed production is being boosted to provide more vegetable oil* (Wall Street Journal).

vegetable oyster, the salsify, a vegetable with a root that tastes somewhat like an oyster.

vegetable silk, a cottonlike fiber borne on the seeds of a Brazilian tree of the bombax family, used especially for stuffing cushions.

vegetable tallow, a fatty substance obtained from various plants, used in making candles, soap, and lubricants.

vegetable wax, a wax or waxlike substance obtained from plants or vegetable growths.

veg·e·ta·bly (vej′tə blē, vej′ə-), *adv.* in the manner of a vegetable or plant.

veg·e·tal (vej′ə təl), *adj.* **1.** of, having to do with, or derived from plants or vegetables. **2.** of or having to do with the vegetable kingdom. **3. a.** characterized by, exhibiting, or producing plant life and growth. **b.** *Obsolete.* insensible; insensitive; irrational: *All creatures, vegetal, sensible, and rational* (Robert Burton).
—*n.* a plant.
[< Medieval Latin *vegetalis* < Late Latin *vegetāre* to grow; see VEGETATE]

veg·e·tal·i·ty (vej′ə tal′ə tē), *n.* vegetable character or quality.

veg·e·tant (vej′ə tənt), *adj.* **1.** giving life and vigor; invigorating. **2.** vegetating; vegetable; vegetal. [< Latin *vegetāns, -antis,* present participle of *vegetāre* enliven < *vegetus* vigorous]

veg·e·tar·i·an (vej′ə tãr′ē ən), *n.* a person who lives wholly or principally upon vegetable foods; a person who on principle abstains from any form of animal food, especially as obtained by the direct destruction of life.
—*adj.* **1.** eating vegetables but no meat. **2.** devoted to or advocating vegetarianism. **3.** (of animals) living on vegetables: *For the prospective breeder, chinchillas have many advantages; they are very friendly, odourless, and entirely vegetarian* (New Scientist). **4.** containing no meat.
[< *veget*(able) + *-arian,* as in *agrarian, trinitarian,* etc.]

veg·e·tar·i·an·ism (vej′ə tãr′ē ə niz′əm), *n.* the practice or principle of eating vegetables but no meat; abstention from meat, fish, or other animal products: *Vegetarianism is a basic tenet of Hinduism which influences health* (Carl E. Taylor).

veg·e·tate (vej′ə tāt), *v.i.,* **-tat·ed, -tat·ing. 1.** to grow or develop as plants do: *One really lives nowhere; one does but vegetate* (Fanny Burney). **2.** to live an idle, unthinking, useless life; exist without material or intellectual achievement. **3.** *Pathology.* to grow or increase in size as vegetables do. [< Latin *vegetāre* (with English *-ate*[1]) enliven, arouse < *vegetus* lively, vigorous]
—**Syn. 2.** loaf, stagnate.

veg·e·tat·ed (vej′ə tā′tid) *adj.* provided with vegetation or plant life.

veg·e·ta·tion (vej′ə tā′shən), *n.* **1.** plant life; growing plants: *There is not much vegetation in deserts.* **2.** the act or process of vegetating; growth of plants. **3.** an existence similar to that of a vegetable; dull, empty, or stagnant life. **4.** *Pathology.* an abnormal growth occurring on some part of the body.

veg·e·ta·tion·al (vej′ə tā′shə nəl), *adj.* of or having to do with vegetation: [*He*] *studied vegetational areas throughout the world and recognized the role of precipitation in determining the various vegetational types* (Harbaugh and Goodrich).

veg·e·ta·tive (vej′ə tā′tiv), *adj.* **1.** growing as plants do: *a weed so vegetative as to infest the whole land.* **2.** of, having to do with, or characterized by vegetation or growth: *a vegetative season.* **3.** *Botany.* concerned with growth and development rather than reproduction: *The ordinary vegetative organs, such as roots, stems, or leaves of many species, readily form adventitious roots and shoots* (Fred W. Emerson). **4.** causing or promoting growth in plants; productive; fertile: *vegetative mold.* **5.** of or having to do with vegetablelike unconscious or involuntary functions of the body: *the vegetative processes of the body, such as growth and repair.* **6.** having very little action, thought, or feeling. —**veg′e·ta′tive·ly,** *adv.* —**veg′e·ta′tive·ness,** *n.*

vegetative multiplication, 1. artificially induced asexual reproduction by which cuttings, branches, etc., are made to grow independently of the parent plant. **2.** vegetative reproduction.

vegetative pole, the part of an egg's surface located opposite to the animal pole and usually containing the principal mass of yolk.

vegetative reproduction, asexual reproduction by means of budding, fission, etc.

veg·e·tism (vej′ə tiz əm), *n.* vegetal condition or quality.

veg·e·tive (vej′ə tiv), *adj.* vegetative. —*n.* *Obsolete.* **1.** a vegetable or plant. **2.** a vegetable cultivated for food.

ve·he·mence (vē′ə məns), *n.* **1.** great or excessive warmth of emotion or action; passionate force, violence, or excitement; strong personal feeling: *For eighteen months the controversy raged; while the Queen, with persistent vehemence, opposed the Prime Minister and the Foreign Secretary* (Lytton Strachey). **2.** (of physical action or agents) great force or violence; forcefulness. —**Syn. 1.** fervor, ardor.

ve·he·men·cy (vē′ə mən sē), *n.* vehemence.

ve·he·ment (vē′ə mənt), *adj.* **1.** having or showing strong feeling; caused by strong feeling; eager; passionate: *loud and vehement quarrels, vehement partisanship.* **2.** acting with or displaying personal passion or excitement: *a vehement devotee of modern music, a vehement hero.* **3.** characterized by actions of great physical exertion; performed with unusual force or violence; violent: *applause twice as vehement as usual. I announce a life that shall be copious, vehement, spiritual, bold* (Walt Whitman). **4.** with great strength or violence: *vehement deluges of rain.* [< Latin *vehemēns, -entis* impetuous, headlong; carried away, related to *vehere* to carry] —**ve′he·ment·ly,** *adv.* —**Syn. 1.** ardent, fervid.

ve·hi·cle (vē′ə kəl), *n.* **1. a.** any means of carrying, conveying, or transporting: *The Atlas rocket is a space vehicle.* **b.** a carriage, wagon, sled, train, automobile, or other conveyance having wheels or runners and used on land. **2.** the means by which a substance or property, as sound or heat, is conveyed or transmitted from one point to another. **3.** a substance serving as a means for easier use or application of another substance mixed with it: **a.** a medium, especially a liquid, in which strong or unpalatable drugs or medicines are administered. **b.** a liquid into which pigment is mixed to apply color to a surface: *Linseed oil is a vehicle for paint.* **4.** a means or medium by which something is communicated, shown, conveyed, or accomplished: *Language is the vehicle of thought.* [< Latin *vehiculum* (diminutive) < *vehere* to carry]

ve·hic·u·lar (vi hik′yə lər), *adj.* **1.** of or having to do with vehicles: *Merritt-Chapman's construction department ... was awarded an $11 million contract to build a vehicular tunnel at Pittsburgh for the Pennsylvania Department of Highways* (Wall Street Journal). **2.** made, caused, or carried on by a vehicle or vehicles: *a vehicular accident, vehicular homicide. Vehicular traffic was almost entirely suspended* (London Daily News). **3.** of the nature of or serving as a vehicle: *All language is vehicular and ... is good for conveyance* (Emerson).

Vehm·ge·richt (fām′gə riHt′), *n., pl.* **-rich·te** (-riH′tə). one of the medieval tribunals that met (usually in secret) in Germany, especially in Westphalia, in the 1300's and 1400's, and exercised many powers of government. [< obsolete German *Vehmgericht* < *Vehme* judgment + *Gericht* tribunal]

veil (vāl), *n.* **1.** a piece of very thin fabric worn, especially by women, to protect or hide the face, or as an ornament, now especially worn attached to a hat. **2.** a piece of linen, or the like, worn as part of a nun's headdress, and falling over the head and shoulders. **3. a.** the secluded life of a nun. **b.** the vows made by a woman either as a novice, when she takes the white veil, or as a nun, when she pronounces the irrevocable vows and assumes the black veil. **4.** anything that covers or hides: *A veil of clouds hid the sun. A veil of cheerfulness covered her sorrow.* **5.** a piece of fabric serving as a curtain or hanging. **6.** *Biology.* a veillike mem-

brane or membranous appendage or part, serving as a cover or screen; velum. **7.** *Dialect.* a caul.
take the veil, to become a nun: *She never took the veil, but lived and died in severe seclusion, and in the practice of the Roman Catholic religion* (Scott).
—*v.t.* **1. a.** to cover with or as with a veil: *a woman closely veiled.* **b.** to enclose or hang with a veil or curtain. **2.** to bestow the veil of a nun upon (a woman). **3.** to cover; hide: *Fog veiled the shore. The most barefaced action seeks to veil itself under some show of decency* (William H. Prescott).
[< Anglo-French *veil* < Latin *vēla,* plural (taken as feminine singular) of *vēlum* curtain, (sail) covering. Doublet of VELUM, VOILE.]
—**veil′like′,** *adj.*
—**Syn.** *v.t.* **3.** conceal, mask, screen.

veiled (vāld), *adj.* **1.** covered with or wearing a veil: *the veiled figure of a ghost.* **2. a.** concealed, covered, or hidden, as if by a veil: *a magician's veiled hand.* **b.** not clearly expressed; not openly declared or stated: *a veiled threat, veiled insults.*

veil·ing (vā′ling), *n.* **1.** a veil. **2.** material for veils. **3.** a covering or concealing with a veil. **4.** a becoming blurred or dimmed as if covered by a veil.

veil·less (vāl′lis), *adj.* without a veil.

vein (vān), *n.* **1. a.** *Anatomy.* one of the membranous tubes or canals forming part of the system of vessels by which the blood is carried to the heart from all parts of the body. **b.** any blood vessel. **2.** *Botany.* one of the strands or slender bundles of vascular tissue forming the principal framework of the blade of a leaf; nerve or nervure. **3.** *Entomology.* one of the ribs or nervures that strengthen the wing of an insect. **4. a.** a small natural channel within the earth through which water trickles or flows. **b.** a flow of water through such a channel: *a vein of water.* **5.** *Geology.* **a.** a deposit of ore, coal, etc., having a more or less regular development in length, width, and depth; lode: *a vein of copper.* **b.** a continuous crack or fissure filled with matter, especially metallic ore, different from the containing rock. **6.** a streak or stream of a different material or texture from the main substance: *a vein of gristle in the meat.* **7.** an irregular stripe or streak of a different shade or color in wood, marble, glass, etc. **8.** a strain or blend of some quality in conduct, writing, speech, etc.: *a vein of criticism, comedy written in a witty vein.* **9.** a special character or disposition; state of mind; mood: *a vein of cruelty. In the midst of a vein of thought . . . I was interrupted* (Washington Irving).

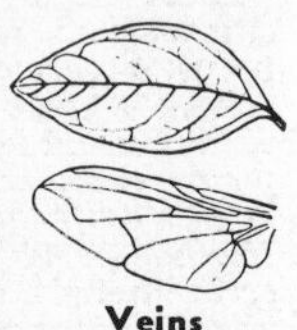
Veins
Top, (def. 2); bottom, (def. 3)

—*v.t.* **1.** to ornament with (lines or streaks) in a manner suggesting veins. **2.** to cover with, spread out over, or run through (something) the way veins do: *Many rivers vein the lowlands.*
[< Old French *veine* < Latin *vēna*] —**vein′like′,** *adj.*

veined (vānd), *adj.* **1.** full of or showing veins: *veined marble.* **2.** *Botany.* having veins, as a leaf; nervate. —**Syn. 1.** streaked.

vein·ing (vā′ning), *n.* the formation or arrangement of veins or veinlike markings on or in something.

vein·less (vān′lis), *adj.* having no veins.

vein·let (vān′lit), *n.* **1.** a small vein. **2.** *Botany.* a branch or subdivision of a vein or venule: *The veins divide and subdivide, making a network, and are so distributed that no part of the mesophyll is far removed from one or more veinlets* (Fred W. Emerson).

vein·ous (vā′nəs), *adj.* **1.** full of, marked with, or having to do with veins. **2.** (of blood) venous.

vein·stone (vān′stōn′), *n.* stone or earth composing a vein and containing ore; gangue; matrix.

vein·ule (vā′nyül), *n.* a small vein; venule. [< French *veinule, venule,* learned borrowing from Latin *vēnula* (diminutive) < *vēna* VEIN. Doublet of VENULE.]

vein·u·let (vā′nyə lit), *n.* veinule.

vein·y (vā′nē), *adj.,* **vein·i·er, vein·i·est. 1. a.** of, having to do with, or full of veins, especially blood vessels. **b.** having prominent veins. **2.** *Geology.* covered with or crossed by veins having different substance or structure. **3.** marked by veins of color. **4.** *Botany.* having many veins, as leaves.

vel., vellum.

ve·la (vē′lə), *n.* the plural of **velum.**

ve·la·men (və lā′mən), *n., pl.* **-lam·i·na** (-lam′ə nə). **1.** *Botany.* the thick, outer, spongy tissue consisting of several layers of cells, covering the aerial roots of epiphytic orchids. **2.** *Anatomy.* a membranous covering or partition; velum. [< Latin *vēlāmen, -inis* < *vēlāre* to cover < *vēlum* covering]

ve·lar (vē′lər), *adj.* **1.** of or having to do with a velum, especially the soft palate: *Velar closure . . . is the closure of the oral passage by the tongue against the lower surface of the velum* (Henry A. Gleason, Jr.). **2.** *Phonetics.* pronounced with the back of the tongue raised toward or against the velum or soft palate; dorsal. *G* in *goose* has a velar sound, *g* in *geese* does not. —*n. Phonetics.* a velar sound. [< Latin *vēlāris* < *vēlum* covering]

ve·lar·i·um (və lãr′ē əm), *n., pl.* **-i·a** (-ē ə). (in ancient Rome) a large awning used to cover a theater or amphitheater as a protection against sun or rain. [< Latin *vēlārium* < *vēlum* covering]

ve·lar·ize (vē′lə rīz), *v.t.,* **-ized, -iz·ing.** *Phonetics.* to pronounce (a sound) or modify (a nonvelar sound) by giving it velar articulation. The second *l* in *lull* is often slightly velarized.

ve·late (vē′lāt), *adj. Biology.* having a veil or velum. [< Latin *vēlātus* veiled, past participle of *vēlāre* to cover < *vēlum* veil]

Vel·cro (vel′krō), *n. Trademark.* a fastener for clothing, carpeting, etc., made usually of a strip of minute nylon hooks that penetrate and catch in a closely woven strip of nylon loops.

veld or **veldt** (velt, felt), *n.* the open plains of South Africa, having grass and bushes but very few trees. [< Afrikaans *veld* < Dutch, earlier *veldt* field]

veld·schoen or **veldt·schoen** (velt′skůn′, felt′-), *n., pl.* **-schoens, -schoen·en** (-skůn′ən). velschoen.

ve·le·ta (və lē′tə), *n.* a round dance for couples, popular in the early 1900's. [< Spanish *veleta* weather vane]

ve·li·ger (vē′lə jər), *n.* **1.** the embryonic stage of a mollusk when it has a ciliated swimming membrane or velum. **2.** the embryo in that stage. [< Latin *vēlum* covering + *-ger* bearing < *gerere* to bear]

vel·i·ta·tion (vel′ə tā′shən), *n.* **1.** a light encounter with the enemy; patrol action; skirmish. **2.** an argument, controversy, or debate; dispute: *He returned to Germany in 1948 after an inconclusive velitation with the Un-American Activities Committee* (New Yorker). [< Latin *vēlitātiō, -ōnis* < *vēlitārī* to skirmish < *vēles, -itis;* see VELITES]

ve·li·tes (vē′lə tēz), *n.pl.* light-armed soldiers used as skirmishers in the Roman armies. [< Latin *vēlitēs,* plural of *vēles,* probably related to *vēlōx* swift]

vel·le·i·ty (və lē′ə tē), *n., pl.* **-ties. 1.** the fact or quality of wishing or desiring, without any action, effort, or resolve toward obtaining fulfillment. **2.** a mere wish or slight inclination, without accompanying action or effort: *He perceived . . . that every wish, every velleity of his had only to be expressed to be at once Victoria's* (Lytton Strachey). [< Medieval Latin *velleitas* < Latin *velle* to wish]

vel·li·cate (vel′ə kāt), *v.,* **-cat·ed, -cat·ing.** *Medicine.* —*v.t. Obsolete.* to pluck, nip, pinch, or tear (the body) with small, sharp points. —*v.i.* to twitch or move convulsively. [< Latin *vellicāre* (with English *-ate*[1]) < *vellere* to pluck (out), twitch]

vel·li·ca·tion (vel′ə kā′shən), *n.* **1.** the act of twitching or causing to twitch. **2.** a twitching or convulsive movement of a muscular fiber.

vel·li·ca·tive (vel′ə kā′tiv), *adj.* having the power of vellicating, plucking, or twitching.

vel·lum (vel′əm), *n.* **1.** the finest kind of parchment, usually prepared from the skins of calves or lambs, used for writing, binding books, or artists' canvas. **2.** a manuscript, testimonial, or degree written or printed on vellum. **3. a.** any superior quality of parchment: *vegetable vellum.* **b.** paper or cloth made to imitate vellum.
—*adj.* made of or resembling vellum.
[Middle English *velym* < Old French *vellin* < *veel* calf; see VEAL]

ve·lo·ce (vā lō′chā), *adv. Music.* with very rapid tempo; presto. [< Italian *veloce* swift < Latin *vēlōx, -ōcis*]

vel·o·cim·e·ter (vel′ə sim′ə tər), *n.* any of various devices for measuring velocity or speed, as an instrument for measuring the initial velocity of a projectile or a ship's log: *The National Bureau of Standards has developed . . . a velocimeter that automatically measures the speed of sound in the sea to depths as great as 300 feet and plots the result as a function of depth or time* (Science). [< Latin *vēlōx, -ōcis* swift + English *-meter*]

ve·loc·i·pede (və los′ə pēd), *n.* **1.** a child's tricycle. See **tricycle** for picture. **2. a.** an early bicycle which the rider straddled and propelled with a walking motion pushing his feet alternately on the ground. **b.** any of the early bicycles or tricycles propelled by pressure from the rider's feet upon pedals usually attached to the front wheel. **3.** a railroad handcar. [< French *vélocipède* < Latin *vēlōx, -ōcis* swift + *pēs, pedis* foot]

ve·loc·i·ty (və los′ə tē), *n., pl.* **-ties. 1.** quickness of motion; speed; swiftness; rapidity: *to fly with the velocity of a bird. [The flood] burst on them . . . whirling great trees and fragments of houses past with incredible velocity* (Charles Reade). **2.** rate of motion: *The velocity of light is about 186,282 miles per second.* **3.** the absolute or relative rate of operation or action: *the rate at which boiled water loses temperature or the velocity of cooling.*
—*adj.* of or having to do with the rapidity or rate of motion or action: *velocity ratio.*
[< Latin *vēlōcitās* < *vēlōx, -ōcis* swift]
—**Syn.** *n.* **1.** celerity. **2.** pace.

ve·lo·drome (vē′lə drōm), *n.* a building having a track for bicycle and motorcycle racing: *The other night a hot-blooded throng went to the velodrome to watch the British cyclists merely rehearse* (Newsweek). [< French *vélodrome* < *vélo,* short for *vélocipède* (see VELOCIPEDE) + Greek *drómos* a running]

ve·lom·e·ter (və lom′ə tər), *n.* velocimeter.

Vel·on (vē′lon), *n. Trademark.* a synthetic fiber derived from petroleum and brine, used in drapery and upholstery materials, shoe fabrics, and industrial cloth.

ve·lours or **ve·lour** (və lůr′), *n.* **1.** a fabric like velvet, made of silk, wool, rayon, or cotton, used for clothing, draperies, upholstery, etc. **2.** a woolen fabric with a velvety pile, used for dresses. [< French *velours* velvet < Old French *velour, velous* < Old Provençal *velos* < noun use of Latin adjective *villōsus* < *villus* shaggy hair]

ve·lou·té (və lü tā′), *n.* a smooth, creamy, white sauce made from meat stock.
—*adj.* made with meat stock, flour, and fat.
[< French *velouté* (literally) velvety < *velours;* see VELOUR]

velouté sauce, velouté.

vel·schoen (vel′skůn′, fel′-), *n., pl.* **-schoens, -schoen·en** (-skůn′ən). (in South Africa) a light shoe made of untanned hide: *From the shapeless roof of his hat to the soft, handmade velschoens he was the human counterpart of the desert* (Harper's). Also, **veldschoen, veldtschoen.** [< Afrikaans *velschoen* < Dutch *vel* hide[2] + *schoen* shoe]

ve·lum (vē′ləm), *n., pl.* **-la. 1.** a membrane or membranous covering or partition resembling a veil. **2.** the soft palate: *Above and behind the velum is the nasal pharynx opening into the cavity of the nose which acts as a resonance chamber* (Simeon Potter). **3.** any of several membranes connected to or in the brain. **4.** a membranous structure or covering in certain fungi. **5.** a ciliated membrane which covers the veliger of a mollusk, serving as an organ of swimming or locomotion: *The free-swimming young teredo hangs in the water from a velum, an extraordinary mobile structure that looks like an animated umbrella and functions as an organ of locomotion* (Scientific American). [< Latin *vēlum* covering, sail. Doublet of VEIL, VOILE.]

ve·lure (və lůr′), *n., v.,* **-lured, -lur·ing.** —*n.* **1.** a soft material like velvet. **2.** a soft pad of silk or plush, used for smoothing and giving a luster to silk hats. —*v.t.* to brush or dress (a hat) with a velure. [earlier, velvet < Old French *velour;* see VELOURS]

ve·lu·ti·nous (və lü′tə nəs), *adj. Biology.* having a hairy surface resembling velvet in texture. [< New Latin *velutinus* (with English *-ous*) < Medieval Latin *velutum,* ultimately < Latin *villus* shaggy hair]

vel·vet (vel′vit), *n.* **1.** a cloth with a thick, short, soft pile on one side, made of silk, rayon, cotton, or some combination of these, in which the warp is pulled over a needle, making loops that are cut (cut velvet) or uncut (pile velvet). **2.** something like velvet

in softness or appearance. **3.** the furry skin that covers the growing antlers of a deer. **4.** *Slang.* clear profit or gain: *Whatever equity the family may build up in the house, no matter how slowly it grows, will be taken as so much velvet* (Wall Street Journal). **5.** *Slang.* money won through gambling.
on velvet, *Slang.* in a position of ease or advantage; in an advantageous or prosperous condition: *Before that we were on velvet; but the instant he appeared everything was changed* (Benjamin Disraeli).
to the velvet, to the good: *Before the whistle blew for dinner I was several hundred to the velvet* (K. McGaffey).
—*adj.* **1.** made of velvet: *She has a velvet hat.* **2.** covered with velvet. **3.** smooth or soft like velvet; velvety: *velvet petals, a cat's velvet paws.*
—*v.t.* to cover with or as if with velvet; cause to resemble velvet: *The back wall is to be velveted in absorbent fiberglass* (Time).
[< Medieval Latin *velvetum,* ultimately < Latin *villus* tuft of hair] —**vel′vet·like′,** *adj.*

velvet ant, any of a group of hymenopterous burrowing insects with soft, hairy coverings, resembling ants and wasps, common in the southern United States.

Velvet Ant (Line shows actual length.)

velvet carpet, a carpet having the loops of the pile cut like Wilton.

vel·vet·ed (vel′və tid), *adj.* covered with or clad in velvet.

vel·vet·een (vel′və tēn′), *n.* a fabric resembling velvet, made of cotton or of silk and cotton.
velveteens, trousers or knickers made of this fabric: *He . . . thought of the fine times coming, when he would . . . wear velveteens* (Charles Kingsley).
—*adj.* made of velveteen.
[< *velvet*]

vel·vet·eened (vel′və tēnd′), *adj.* dressed in velveteen.

vel·vet·leaf (vel′vit lēf′), *n.* any of various plants with soft, velvety leaves, as the Indian mallow and the pareira.

velvet osier, any of various willows with flexible stems used for baskets, wickerwork, furniture, etc.

velvet sponge, horse sponge.

vel·vet-voiced (vel′vit voist′), *adj.* having a deep, rich, mellow voice: *Velvet-voiced contralto Marian Anderson has played to capacity houses at all stops* (Time).

vel·vet·y (vel′və tē), *adj.* smooth and soft like velvet.

Ven., **1.** Venerable. **2.** Venice.

ve·na (vē′nə), *n., pl.* **ve·nae** (vē′nē). *Anatomy.* a vein. [< Latin *vēna*]

ve·na ca·va (vē′nə kā′və), *pl.* **ve·nae ca·vae** (vē′nē kā′vē). *Anatomy.* either of two large veins that form the main trunk of the venous system and discharge blood from the upper and lower halves of the body respectively into the right auricle of the heart. [< Latin *vēna cava* empty vein]

ve·nal (vē′nəl), *adj.* **1.** willing to sell one's services or influence basely; open to bribes; corrupt: *Venal judges are a disgrace to a country.* **2.** influenced or obtained by bribery: *venal conduct.* [< Latin *vēnālis* < *vēnum,* accusative, thing that is for sale] —**ve′nal·ly,** *adv.*

ve·nal·i·ty (vē nal′ə tē), *n.* the quality of being venal: *France and the rest of the world were treated to the spectacle of one set of collaborators trying another set of collaborators with all the venom and venality they could bring to their task* (Observer).

ve·nat·ic (vē nat′ik), *adj.* of, having to do with, or devoted to hunting. [< Latin *vēnāticus* < *vēnārī* to hunt]

ve·nat·i·cal (vē nat′ə kəl), *adj.* venatic.

ve·nat·i·cal·ly (vē nat′ə klē), *adv.* in the chase; in hunting.

ve·na·tion (vē nā′shən), *n.* **1.** *Botany.* the arrangement of the veins in the blade of a leaf; nervation. **2.** *Entomology.* the arrangement of the veins in the wings of insects. **3.** any of these veins collectively. [< Latin *vēna* vein + English *-ation*]

ve·na·tion·al (vē nā′shə nəl), *adj.* of or having to do with venation.

vend (vend), *v.t.* **1.** to sell; peddle: *He vends fruit from a cart.* **2.** to put forward (an opinion, etc.). —*v.i.* to be sold; find a market or purchaser. [< Latin *vendere* < *vēnum dare* offer for sale]

ven·dace (ven′dās), *n.* **1.** a small whitefish found in certain lakes in Scotland. **2.** a closely related species found in England. [apparently < Old French *vendese, vendoise*]

ven·dage (ven′dij), *n.* the harvesting of grapes; vintage. [< Old French *vendange;* see VINTAGE]

Ven·de·an (ven dē′ən), *n.* an inhabitant of La Vendée, in western France, who took part in the insurrection of 1793 against the French Republic.

vend·ee (ven dē′), *n. Especially Law.* the person to whom a thing is sold; buyer.

Ven·dé·miaire (väN dā myer′), *n.* the first month of the French revolutionary calendar, extending from September 22nd to October 21st. [< French *Vendémiare* < Latin *vendēmia* grape gathering]

vend·er (ven′dər), *n.* **1.** a seller, especially a peddler or person who sells on the street: *a flower vender.* **2.** a vending machine. —**Syn. 1.** hawker.

ven·det·ta (ven det′ə), *n.* **1.** a feud in which a murdered man's relatives try to kill the slayer or his relatives, sometimes carried on from one generation to another. **2.** any prolonged or bitter feud, prosecution for private revenge, etc.: *What made the case so obnoxious . . . was the implication that British police were being used to aid a political vendetta in another country* (Bulletin of Atomic Scientists). [< Italian *vendetta* < Latin *vindicta* revenge, related to *vindex, -icis* protector, avenger < *vindicāre;* see VINDICATE]

ven·det·tist (ven det′ist), *n.* a person who takes part in or carries on a vendetta.

ven·deuse (väN dœz′), *n. French.* a saleswoman: *Although customers can change materials, it is wise to take the advice of the vendeuse on this* (London Times).

vend·i·bil·i·ty (ven′də bil′ə tē), *n.* salable quality; quality of being marketable.

vend·i·ble (ven′də bəl), *adj.* **1.** salable; marketable: *Spoiled food is not vendible.* **2.** corrupt; venal: *the vendible favors of some city officials.* —*n.* a salable thing.

vend·ing machine (ven′ding), a machine from which one obtains candy, stamps, etc., when a coin is dropped in.

ven·di·tion (ven dish′ən), *n.* the act of selling or peddling; sale. [< Latin *venditiō, -ōnis* < *vendere* to sell]

ven·dor (ven′dər), *n.* a seller; peddler: *The narcotics vendor is one of society's most dangerous enemies.* [< Anglo-French *vendor,* earlier *vendour* < *vendre* to sell < Latin *vendere;* see VEND]

ven·due (ven dü′, -dyü′), *n.* a public sale or auction. [< Dutch *vendu* < Middle French *vendue* sale < *vendre* to sell; see VEND]

ve·neer (və nir′), *v.t.* **1. a.** to cover (wood) with a thin layer of finer wood or other material to produce an elegant or polished surface: *to veneer a pine desk with mahogany.* **b.** to glue together (thin layers of wood) to make plywood. **2.** to cover (anything) with a layer of something else to give an appearance of superior quality: *A rogue in grain veneer'd with sanctimonious theory* (Tennyson).
—*n.* **1. a.** a thin layer of wood or other material used in veneering: *a panel with a veneer of gold and ivory.* **b.** one of the thin layers of wood used in making plywood. **2.** a surface appearance or superficial show: *a veneer of culture. His treachery was hidden by a veneer of friendship.*
[earlier *fineer, faneer* < German *fournieren* < French *fournir* furnish] —**ve·neer′er,** *n.*

ve·neer·ing (və nir′ing), *n.* **1.** the art or process of applying veneer. **2.** any thin material applied or used as a veneer. **3.** the covering or surface formed by a veneer. **4.** a mere surface appearance or show; outward pretense: *It was not long before his veneering of good will wore through.*

ven·e·nose (ven′ə nōs), *adj.* poisonous; venomous.

ven·e·punc·ture (ven′ə pungk′chər, vē′nə-), *n.* venipuncture.

ven·er·a·bil·i·ty (ven′ər ə bil′ə tē), *n.* the fact or quality of being venerable: *At 57, he was approaching venerability in the eyes of party workers clamoring for younger leadership* (Newsweek).

ven·er·a·ble (ven′ər ə bəl), *adj.* **1.** (of persons) deserving respect because of age, high personal character, and dignity of appearance: *a venerable old man.* **2.** (of things) worthy of reverence or deep respect: *venerable customs.* **3.** (of places) worthy of respect or high regard because of age or historical importance: *the venerable ruins of Athens and Rome.* **4.** designating an archdeacon of the Anglican Church (used as a title of respect). **5.** (in the Roman Catholic Church) designating a person recognized as having attained a degree of virtue but not yet recognized as beatified or canonized: *the Venerable Bede.* [< Latin *venerābilis* < *venerārī;* see VENERATE] —**ven′er·a·ble·ness,** *n.*

ven·er·a·bly (ven′ər ə blē), *adv.* in a venerable manner; so as to excite reverence.

ven·er·ate (ven′ə rāt), *v.t.,* **-at·ed, -at·ing.** to regard with deep respect; revere: *He venerates his father's memory. Holy writers, and such whose names are venerated to all posterity* (Sir Thomas Browne). [< Latin *venerārī* (with English *-ate*[1]) < *Venus, -eris* (goddess of) love] —**Syn.** honor, esteem.

ven·er·a·tion (ven′ə rā′shən), *n.* **1.** a feeling of deep respect; reverence: *to have or hold one's grandfather in veneration.* **2.** the act of showing respect and reverence; worship: *veneration for learning. An important teaching of Confucius was veneration of one's ancestors.* **3.** the condition of being venerated: *Such veneration seems strange to the Western World.*

ven·er·a·tor (ven′ə rā′tər), *n.* a person who venerates or reverences.

ve·ne·re·al (və nir′ē əl), *adj.* **1.** of or having to do with sexual intercourse. **2.** communicated by sexual intercourse. **3.** having to do with diseases communicated by sexual intercourse. **4.** infected with syphilis, gonorrhea, or other venereal disease. **5.** adapted to the cure of venereal disease, as a medicine. [< Latin *venereus* (< *Venus, -eris* Venus; originally, love) + English *-al*[1]] —**ve·ne′re·al·ly,** *adv.*

ve·ne·re·an (və nir′ē ən), *adj.* **1.** inclined to the service of Venus or to sexual desire: *For certain I am venerean in feeling* (Chaucer). **2.** amorous; wanton: *There's nothing wrong with Sir Thomas Urquhart's "venerean ecstasy"* (Anthony Burgess). **3.** of the planet Venus; Venusian. [< Latin *venereus* (see VENEREAL) + English *-an*]

ve·ne·re·ol·o·gist (və nir′ē ol′ə jist), *n.* a person who treats or studies venereal diseases.

ve·ne·re·ol·o·gy (və nir′ē ol′ə jē), *n.* the branch of medicine dealing with venereal diseases. [< *venerea*(l) + *-logy*]

ven·er·er (ven′ər ər), *n. Archaic.* a huntsman. [< *vener*(y)[2] + *-er*[2]]

ven·er·y[1] (ven′ər ē), *n.* the gratification of sexual desire. [< Latin *Venus, -eris* Venus; (originally) love + English *-y*[3]]

ven·er·y[2] (ven′ər ē), *n. Archaic.* the practice or sport of hunting; the chase. [< Old French *venerie* < *vener* to hunt < Latin *vēnārī*]

ven·e·sec·tion (ven′ə sek′shən), *n.* the opening of a vein to let blood: *Venesection was practiced by barbers in the Middle Ages.* [< Medieval Latin *venaesectio, -onis* < Latin *vēnae,* genitive of *vēna* vein + *sectiō, -ōnis* a cutting, section]

Ve·ne·tian (və nē′shən), *adj.* of or having to do with Venice, a city on the northeastern coast of Italy, or its people.
—*n.* **1.** a native or inhabitant of Venice. **2.** Also, **venetian.** *Informal.* a Venetian blind. **3.** a closely woven, twilled woolen fabric, used for dresses, suits, etc.
Venetians, a heavy tape or braid used especially on Venetian blinds: *to use Venetians in decoration.*

Venetian architecture, the style of medieval architecture elaborated in Venice, Italy, combining elements from the Byzantine, Italian, and transalpine European styles, into a new style of high decorative quality and originality.

Venetian blind, a window blind made of many horizontal wooden, steel, or aluminum slats fixed on strong tapes so that the slats can be opened or closed at various angles to regulate the light or air admitted.

ve·ne·tianed (və nē′shənd), *adj.* furnished with Venetian blinds.

Venetian glass, **1.** a very fine, delicate, brittle kind of glass originally manufactured near Venice, Italy. **2.** an article made of this.

Venetian painting, the style of painting distinguished by its mastery and brilliance of coloring, originating in and near Venice, Italy, in the 1400's and reaching its climax in the 1500's: *Those rugged, swart, bald-headed old fisher apostles, with their coppery bare shoulders, are as emblematic of Venetian painting as the sensuous, pensive Madonna with whom they fraternize* (New Yorker).

Venetian red, 1. a red pigment consisting of a mixture of iron oxide and calcium sulfate, produced synthetically. **2.** a dark red with a tinge of orange.

Ve•ne•tians (və nē′shənz), *n.pl.* See under **Venetian,** *n.*

Venetian school, a group of predominantly Italian artists of the 1400's and 1500's who worked in the style of Venetian painting.

Venez., Venezuela.

Ven•e•zue•lan (ven′ə zwē′lən, -zwā′-), *adj.* of or having to do with Venezuela, a country in South America, or its people. —*n.* a native or inhabitant of Venezuela.

venge (venj), *v.t.,* **venged, veng•ing.** *Archaic.* to avenge; revenge. [< Old French *vengier* < Latin *vindicāre*; see VINDICATE]

venge•ance (ven′jəns), *n.* **1.** the inflicting of injury or punishment in return for a wrong; avenging oneself or another: *Vengeance is mine; I will repay* (Romans 12:19). **2.** punishment in return for a wrong; revenge: *The Indian swore vengeance against the man who murdered his father.*

with a vengeance, a. with great force or violence: *It was raining with a vengeance.* **b.** to an unusual extent; much more than expected: *When rebuked for rudeness, Peter turned polite with a vengeance.*

[< Anglo-French *vengeaunce,* Old French *vengeance* < *vengier* to venge]

—**Syn. 2.** retribution.

venge•ful (venj′fəl), *adj.* **1.** inflicting vengeance; serving as an instrument of vengeance: *rebellion's vengeful talons* (Samuel Johnson). **2.** seeking vengeance; inclined to avenge oneself; vindictive: *vengeful enemies.* **3.** arising from or showing a strong desire for vengeance: *vengeful hate.* —**venge′ful•ly,** *adv.* —**venge′ful•ness,** *n.*

ve•ni•al (vē′nē əl, vēn′yəl), *adj.* **1.** that may be forgiven; not very wrong or sinful; pardonable. **2.** of an unimportant nature, as an error or fault; excusable; trivial: *If they do nothing, 'tis a venial slip* (Shakespeare).

[< Latin *veniālis* < *venia* forgiveness, related to *Venus* Venus; (originally) love] —**ve′ni•al•ly,** *adv.* —**ve′ni•al•ness,** *n.*

ve•ni•al•i•ty (vē′nē al′ə tē), *n.* the quality of being venial.

venial sin, (in the Roman Catholic Church) a sin not destroying the soul because it is minor or, if grave, due to inadvertence or not willfully committed.

ven•in (ven′in), *n. Biochemistry.* any of a group of poisonous substances present in the venom of snakes, toads, and scorpions. [< *ven*(om) + *-in*]

ven•i•punc•ture (ven′ə pungk′chər, vē′nə-), *n.* the piercing of a vein, especially with a hypodermic needle for removing blood. Also, **venepuncture.** [< Latin *vēna* vein + English *puncture*]

ve•ni•re (və nī′rē), *n. Law.* a writ issued to a sheriff requiring him to summon persons to serve on a jury. [< Latin *venīre faciās* that you may cause (him) to come]

venire fa•ci•as (fā′shē as), venire.

ve•ni•re•man (və nī′rē mən), *n., pl.* **-men.** *Law.* a person summoned to serve on a jury by a writ of venire. [American English < *venire* (facias) + *man*]

ven•i•son (ven′ə zən, -sən), *n.* **1.** the flesh of a deer, used for food; deer meat. **2.** (formerly) the flesh of any animal killed by hunting, especially a deer, boar, hare, or other game animal. **3.** *Archaic.* any beast or wild animal killed by hunting. [< Old French *venesoun* < Latin *vēnātiō, -ōnis* a hunting < *vēnārī* to hunt]

venison bird, (in Canada) the Canada jay.

Ve•ni•te (vi nī′tē), *n.* **1.** the 95th Psalm (94th in the Vulgate), recited as a canticle at matins or morning prayer. **2.** a musical setting (usually a chant) of this. [< Latin *venīte* come ye! (the first word in the Latin version)]

ve•ni, vi•di, vi•ci (vē′nī vī′dī vī′sī; wā′nē wē′dē wē′kē), *Latin.* I came, I saw, I conquered (a report of victory at Zela made by Julius Caesar to the Roman Senate).

Venn diagram (ven), a diagram using circles and rectangles to represent various types of mathematical sets and to show the relationship between them. In a Venn diagram, separate sets may be represented by two or more separate circles, and overlapping sets by two or more overlapping circles. [< John *Venn,* 1834-1923, an English logician]

ven•om (ven′əm), *n.* **1. a.** the poisonous fluid secreted by some snakes, spiders, scorpions, lizards, etc., and injected into their prey by biting, stinging, etc. **b.** any sort of poison. **2.** bitterness; spite; malice: *the venom of her tongue. She hated the rich and spoke of them with venom.* —*v.t.* to put venom in or on (something); to make venomous: *to venom a refusal with contempt.*

[< Old French *venim,* variant of *venin* < Vulgar Latin *venīmen,* for Latin *venēnum* poison] —**ven′om•er,** *n.* —**Syn.** *n.* **2.** rancor, hate, malignity.

ven•om•less (ven′əm lis), *adj.* without venom.

ven•om•ous (ven′ə məs), *adj.* **1. a.** secreting venom; capable of inflicting a poisonous bite, sting, or wound: *Rattlesnakes are venomous.* **b.** full of or infected with venom, especially so as to be harmful to or destructive of life; poisonous: *the venomous bite of the black widow spider.* **2.** spiteful; malicious; embittered: *a venomous attack. The stings and venomous stabs of public contumely* (Hawthorne). —**ven′om•ous•ly,** *adv.* —**ven′om•ous•ness,** *n.* —**Syn. 2.** malignant.

ve•nose (vē′nōs), *adj.* **1.** *Botany.* having numerous veins or a branching network, as a leaf. **2.** venous. [< Latin *vēnōsus* < *vēna* vein]

ve•nos•i•ty (vē nos′ə tē), *n.* venous or venose quality or condition.

ve•nous (vē′nəs), *adj.* **1.** of, having to do with, or of the nature of a vein or veins; venose. **2.** of or having to do with the blood passing through the capillaries and veins after having given up oxygen and become charged with carbon dioxide, and so having a dark-red color in higher animals: *venous blood.* **3.** having veins: *the venous wings of insects.* [< Latin *vēna* vein + English *-ous*] —**ve′nous•ly,** *adv.* —**ve′nous•ness,** *n.*

vent[1] (vent), *n.* **1.** an opening leading out of or into some enclosed space, especially a small hole or opening made for the passage of air or liquid. **2.** a way out; outlet: *His great energy found vent in hard work.* **3.** expression: *She gave vent to her grief in tears.* **4.** *Zoology.* the anus or excretory opening of animals, discharging both solid and liquid matter, especially in certain nonmammals, as birds, fish, and reptiles. **5.** the small opening in the barrel of a gun by which fire is communicated to the powder; touchhole. **6.** an adjustable opening for indirect ventilation, as a small, often oblong or triangular, window in an automobile.

—*v.t.* **1.** to let out; express freely: *He vented his anger on the dog.* **2.** to make a vent in.

[partly < Middle French *vent* wind < Latin *ventus;* partly short for Middle French *évent* vent, ultimately < Latin *ex-* out + *ventus* wind]

—**Syn.** *n.* **1.** orifice. **2.** escape. **3.** effusion. *-v.t.* **2.** tap.

vent[2] (vent), *n.* an opening or slit in a garment, especially in the back of a coat. [dialectal variant of Middle English *fente* < Middle French, slit, split < Old French *fendre* to split < Latin *findere*]

vent•age (ven′tij), *n.* **1.** a small hole, especially for the escape or passage of air; vent. **2.** a hole in a wind instrument for controlling the pitch of the tone; finger hole.

ven•tail (ven′tāl), *n.* **1.** the lower, movable part on the front of a helmet of armor. **2.** the whole movable part on a helmet including the visor. Also, **aventail.** [< Old French *ventaille* (originally) air hole in a helmet < *vent* wind, air < Latin *ventus;* see VENT[1]]

ven•ter[1] (ven′tər), *n.* **1. a.** the abdomen; belly. **b.** the part of lower forms of animal life corresponding to the belly in function or position. **2. a.** the belly of a bone. **b.** *Obsolete.* the thick, fleshy part of a muscle. **3.** *Obsolete.* the abdomen, thorax, and head. **4.** *Law.* one of two or more wives as sources of one's offspring. **5. a.** the womb as a source of one's birth or origin. **b.** *Obsolete.* a mother in relation to her children. [< Latin *venter, ventris* womb, paunch]

vent•er[2] (ven′tər), *n.* **1.** a person or thing that vents or gives vent. **2.** a person who utters or publishes a statement, doctrine, etc., especially of an erroneous or otherwise objectionable nature.

ven•ti•duct (ven′tə dukt), *n.* a duct or passage bringing cool or fresh air into an apartment or place. [< Latin *ventus* wind + English *duct*]

ven•ti•la•ble (ven′tə lə bəl), *adj.* that can be ventilated.

ven•ti•late (ven′tə lāt), *v.t.,* **-lat•ed, -lat•ing. 1.** to change the air in: *We ventilate a room by opening windows.* **2.** to expose to fresh air so as to keep in, or restore to, good condition: *to ventilate bedding.* **3.** to aerate (blood); oxygenate: *The lungs ventilate the blood.* **4.** (of air) to blow on, pass over, or circulate through so as to purify or freshen. **5.** to make known publicly; discuss openly: *He was glad of an opportunity of ventilating his grievance* (W.H. Hudson). **6.** to furnish with a vent or opening for the escape of air or gas. **7.** *Rare.* to fan or winnow (corn, etc.). [< Latin *ventilāre* (with English *-ate*[1]) to fan, agitate by air < *ventus* wind]

ven•ti•la•tion (ven′tə lā′shən), *n.* **1.** a change of air; act or process of supplying with fresh air: *Ventilation was disregarded in the Middle Ages.* **2.** a means of supplying fresh air: *Ventilation is required in modern house plans.* **3.** a purifying by fresh air: *Air conditioning systems supply regulated temperatures and ventilation.* **4.** an open discussion in public: *The ventilation of one's family affairs is in poor taste.* —**Syn. 1.** aeration.

ven•ti•la•tive (ven′tə lā′tiv), *adj.* of or having to do with ventilation; producing or promoting ventilation.

ven•ti•la•tor (ven′tə lā′tər), *n.* **1.** any apparatus or means, as an opening, shaft, or fan, for changing or improving the air: *A kitchen ventilator does more to make life comfortable than any other single piece of household equipment* (New Yorker). **2.** a person or thing charged with ventilating some enclosure, especially a bee that fans air into a hive with its wings. **3.** a person or thing that brings some matter to public notice.

ven•ti•la•to•ry (ven′tə lə tôr′ē, -tōr′-), *adj.* **1.** of or having to do with ventilation; provided with ventilation. **2.** of or having to do with oxygenation of the blood in the lungs: *Cigarette smoking is associated with a reduction in ventilatory function* (Science News Letter).

vent•less (vent′lis), *adj.* having no vent or outlet.

Ven•tôse (väɴ tōz′), *n.* the sixth month of the French revolutionary calendar, extending from February 19th to March 20th. [< French *Ventôse,* learned borrowing from Latin *ventōsus* windy < *ventus* wind]

ven•trad (ven′trad), *adv. Anatomy.* toward the belly or ventral side of the body. [< Latin *venter, ventris* belly + *ad* toward]

ven•tral (ven′trəl), *adj.* **1.** of, having to do with, or situated in or on the abdomen; abdominal: *To . . . shake . . . with a silent, ventral laughter* (George Eliot). **2.** of, having to do with, or situated on or nearer the surface or part opposite the back. **3.** *Botany.* of or belonging to the anterior or lower surface, as of a carpel.

—*n.* **1.** a ventral fin. **2.** *Entomology.* an abdominal segment.

[< Late Latin *ventrālis* < Latin *venter, ventris* belly, paunch]

ventral fin, (in fishes) either of a pair of fins situated on the fore part of the lower surface of the body, and corresponding to the hind limbs of higher vertebrates.

ven•tral•ly (ven′trə lē), *adv.* in a ventral position or direction; on or toward the abdomen.

ven•tri•cle (ven′trə kəl), *n.* **1.** either of the two lower chambers of the heart that receive blood from the upper chambers and force it into the arteries. See **heart** for picture. **2.** any of a series of connecting cavities in the brain: *These [ideas] are begot in the ventricle of memory* (Shakespeare). **3.** any hollow organ or cavity in an animal body, now chiefly confined to a space between the true and false vocal cords. [< Latin *ventriculus* (diminutive) < *venter, ventris* belly]

ven•tri•cose (ven′trə kōs), *adj.* **1.** *Biology,* swelling out in the middle, or on one side; protuberant. **2.** having an unusually or abnormally large abdomen; big-bellied. [< New Latin *ventricosus* < Latin *venter, ventris* belly]

ven•tri•cous (ven′trə kəs), *adj.* ventricose.

ven•tric•u•lar (ven trik′yə lər), *adj.* **1.** of, having to do with, or like a ventricle. **2.** having to do with the stomach; abdominal; ventral. **3.** swelling out; distended.

ventricular fibrillation, a heart disease, usually fatal, in which the ventricle muscles quiver spasmodically and are unable to pump blood regularly.

ven•tric•u•log•ra•phy (ven trik′yə log′rə fē), *n.* a method of examining the ventricles of the head with X rays after removing the cerebral fluid and replacing it with air or an opaque medium. [< Latin *ventriculus* (see VENTRICLE) + English *-graphy*]

ven•tric•u•lus (ven trik′yə ləs), *n., pl.* **-li** (-lī). **1. a.** the stomach or digestive cavity of certain insects, fish, and reptiles. **b.** the gizzard in birds. **2.** the body cavity of a sponge. [< Latin *ventriculus;* see VENTRICLE]

ven•tri•lo•qui•al (ven′trə lō′kwē əl), *adj.* **1.** having to do with ventriloquism. **2.** using ventriloquism. —**ven′tri•lo′qui•al•ly,** *adv.*

ven•tril•o•quism (ven tril′ə kwiz əm), *n.* the art or practice of speaking or uttering sounds with the lips immobilized so that the voice seems to come from some source other than the speaker. [< *ventriloquy* (< Medieval Latin *ventriloquium* < Latin *ventriloquus* ventriloquist < *venter, ventris* belly + *loquī* speak) + English *-ism*]

ven•tril•o•quist (ven tril′ə kwist), *n.* a person who can make his voice seem to come from some other source. A ventriloquist can talk without any movement of the lips that can be readily observed.

ven•tril•o•quis•tic (ven tril′ə kwis′tik), *adj.* **1.** using or practicing ventriloquism. **2.** of or having to do with ventriloquism.

ven•tril•o•quize (ven tril′ə kwīz), *v.i., v.t.,* **-quized, -quiz•ing.** to speak or utter as a ventriloquist.

ven•tril•o•quous (ven tril′ə kwəs), *adj.* of, having to do with, resembling, or using ventriloquism.

ven•tril•o•quy (ven tril′ə kwē), *n.* ventriloquism.

ven•ture (ven′chər), *n., v.,* **-tured, -tur•ing.** —*n.* **1.** a risky, daring, or dangerous undertaking: *His courage was equal to any venture.* **2.** a speculation to make money: *Ventures in oil stock have made fortunes and beggars.* **3.** something risked, especially in a commercial enterprise or speculation; stake: *to lose an entire venture on the stock market.* **4.** *Obsolete.* the chance or risk of incurring harm or loss; danger; peril.

at a venture, at random; by chance: *'Tis possible that I may several times by guess, or at a venture, hit upon it* (William Whiston).

—*v.i.* **1.** to dare to come, go, or proceed: *He ventured out on the thin ice and fell through.* **2. a.** to dare, presume, or go so far as to do something (to): *to venture to look behind. No one ventured to interrupt the speaker.* **b.** to dare the expression of an opinion, etc.: *to venture to assert the contrary, to venture to offer an opinion.* **3.** to attempt or undertake something difficult or dangerous without assurance of success: *to venture on an arctic expedition.* **4.** to guess (at): *to venture at a reason.* —*v.t.* **1.** to dare to say or make: *to venture a sly joke at matrimony. He ventured an objection.* **2.** to expose to risk or danger: *Men venture their lives in war.* **3.** to run or take the risk of (something dangerous or harmful): *to venture battle in the night, to venture a jail sentence by a crusade against a law.* **4.** *Archaic.* to take the risk of sending: *to venture goods to a distant country.*

[short for *aventure,* an earlier form of *adventure*]

—**Syn.** *n.* **1.** enterprise, adventure, risk. -*v.i.* **1.** See **dare.**

venture capital, risk capital.

ven•tur•er (ven′chər ər), *n.* **1.** a person who ventures; adventurer. **2.** a commercial speculator or trader.

ven•ture•some (ven′chər səm), *adj.* **1.** inclined to take risks; rash; daring: *Venturesome boys hung from rooftops* (Time). **2.** of the nature of or involving risk; hazardous; risky: *A trip to the moon is a venturesome journey.* —**ven′ture•some•ly,** *adv.* —**ven′ture•some•ness,** *n.* —**Syn. 1.** adventurous, bold. —**Ant. 1.** timid.

ven•tu•ri (ven tůr′ē), *n.,* or **venturi tube,** a short, narrow section of a tube in a carburetor or similar device, which lowers the pressure and increases the speed of the air or liquid flowing through it. [< Giovanni B. *Venturi,* 1746-1822, an Italian physicist]

ven•tur•ous (ven′chər əs), *adj.* **1.** rash; daring; adventurous. **2.** risky; dangerous. —**ven′tur•ous•ly,** *adv.* —**ven′tur•ous•ness,** *n.*

ven•ue (ven′yü), *n.* **1.** *Law.* **a.** the place or neighborhood of a crime or cause of action. **b.** the place where the jury is summoned and the case tried: *The prisoner's lawyer asked for a change of venue because the county was so prejudiced against the prisoner.* **c.** the statement on an indictment or complaint designating the place for trial. **d.** the statement indicating where and before whom an affidavit was sworn. **2.** the scene of a real or supposed action or event, especially in a novel or other literary work. [< Old French *venue* coming < *venir* to come < Latin *venīre*]

ven•u•lar (ven′yə lər), *adj.* marked with veins; veined. [< *venul*(e) + *-ar*]

ven•ule (ven′yül), *n.* **1.** a small or minor vein; veinlet. **2.** a small vein in the wing of an insect; nervule. [< Latin *vēnula* (diminutive) < *vēna* vein. Doublet of VEINULE.]

ven•u•lose (ven′yə lōs), *adj.* full of venules.

ven•u•lous (ven′yə ləs), *adj.* venulose.

Ve•nus (vē′nəs), *n.* **1.** the Roman goddess of love and beauty, identified by the Romans with the Greek goddess Aphrodite. **2.** a very beautiful woman: *the Venus of the village.* **3.** *Astronomy.* the most brilliant planet in the solar system, second in distance from the sun, and the planet that comes closest to the earth. Its orbit lies between those of Mercury and the earth and takes 224.7 days to complete, at a mean distance from the sun of about 67,200,000 miles. Its mean diameter is about 7,700 miles. **4.** *Alchemy.* copper.

Ve•nus•berg (vē′nəs bėrg; *German* vā′nůs berk), *n.* in the legends of Tannhäuser, the site of the caverns where Venus held her pagan court. [< *Venusberg,* a mountain in central Germany, between Eisenach and Gotha]

Ve•nu•si•an (və nü′sē ən, -nyü′-), *adj.* of or having to do with the planet Venus: *The little that astronomers can see suggests that the Venusian atmosphere has neither oxygen nor water* (Time). —*n.* a supposed inhabitant of Venus: *In the course of a month the moon would be observed by a Venusian to oscillate to either side of the earth* (Wasley S. Krogdahl).

Ve•nus's-fly•trap (vē′nə siz flī′trap′), *n.* a plant of the coasts of the Carolinas, whose hairy leaves have two lobes at the end that fold together to trap and digest insects. [American English < *Venus*]

Venus's-flytrap
Left, leaves folding to trap fly; right, plant (about 1 ft. high)

Ve•nus's-gir•dle (vē′nə siz gėr′dəl), *n.* a long, transparent, ribbonlike ctenophore that lives in tropical seas.

Ve•nus's-hair (vē′nə siz hãr′), *n.* a maidenhair fern with blackish stipes (frond petioles).

Venus's-shoe (vē′nə siz shü′), *n.* lady's-slipper.

Ve•nu•tian (və nü′shən, -nyü′-), *adj., n.* Venusian. [< *Venus;* patterned on *Martian*]

ven•ville (ven′vil), *n.* a special form of tenure in certain English parishes, by which the tenants enjoy certain privileges in the use of the forest. [origin uncertain]

ver., **1.** verse or verses. **2.** versus.

ve•ra•cious (və rā′shəs), *adj.* **1.** true: *veracious testimony.* **2.** truthful: *The testimony of the two veracious and competent witnesses* (Dickens). [< Latin *vērāx, -ācis* (with English *-ous*) < *vērus* true] —**ve•ra′cious•ly,** *adv.* —**ve•ra′cious•ness,** *n.*

ve•rac•i•ty (və ras′ə tē), *n., pl.* **-ties. 1.** truthfulness: *the unquestioned veracity of a judge. Any fool may write a most valuable book . . . if he will only tell us what he heard and saw with veracity* (Thomas Gray). **2.** truth: *Falsehoods and veracities are separated by so very thin a barrier* (William Stubbs). **3.** correctness; accuracy: *to test the veracity of a scientific instrument. Narratives where historical veracity has no place* (Samuel Johnson). [< Medieval Latin *veracitas* < Latin *vērāx;* see VERACIOUS] —**Syn. 3.** exactitude, precision.

ve•ran•da or **ve•ran•dah** (və ran′də), *n.* a large porch along one or more sides of a house; piazza. [< Hindustani *varandā,* or < Portuguese *varanda* railing] —**ve•ran′da•like′,** *adj.*

ve•ran•daed or **ve•ran•dahed** (və ran′dəd), *adj.* furnished with a veranda or verandas: *We drove . . . to register in the administration building, a verandaed cottage like all the other dwellings of the settlement* (Atlantic).

ve•ra•tri•a (və rā′trē ə, -rat′rē-), *n.* veratrine.

ve•rat•ric acid (və rat′rik), a white crystalline acid present in the seeds of the sabadilla, and also produced by the decomposition of veratrine. *Formula:* $C_9H_{10}O_4$ [< Latin *vērātrum* hellebore]

ve•rat•ri•din (və rat′rə din), *n.* veratridine.

ve•rat•ri•dine (və rat′rə dēn, -din), *n.* **1.** an amorphous alkaloid present in the seeds of the sabadilla. *Formula:* $C_{36}H_{51}NO_{11}$ **2.** veratrine (def. 1).

ver•a•trin (ver′ə trin), *n.* veratrine.

ver•a•tri•na (ver′ə trī′nə), *n.* veratrine.

ver•a•trine (ver′ə trēn, -trin), *n.* **1.** a poisonous mixture containing veratridine and other alkaloids extracted from the seeds of the sabadilla, used medicinally as an ointment for the relief of rheumatism, neuralgia, etc. **2.** veratridine (def. 1). Also, **veratria.** [< French *vératrine* < Latin *vērātrum* hellebore + French *-ine* -ine[2]]

ver•a•trize (ver′ə trīz), *v.t.,* **-trized, -triz•ing.** to drug, poison, or treat with veratrine.

ve•ra•trum (və rā′trəm), *n.* any of a group of plants of the lily family, especially the American hellebore, whose dried roots and stem are used in drugs for the treatment of hypertension, nausea, etc. [< Latin *vērātrum* hellebore]

verb (vėrb), *n.* **1.** a word that expresses action, being, occurrence, etc. *Eat, sit, be, go, going, washed,* etc., are verbs. *Abbr.:* v. **2.** the part of speech or form class to which such words belong. [< Latin *verbum* (originally) word]

➤ **Verbs.** A verb that takes an object (or is used in the passive voice) is said to be *transitive: He washed the car. The car was washed quickly.* A verb that does not take an object is intransitive: *He slept soundly.* Many verbs in English are used both ways, usually with some distinction in meaning. Transitive: *He wrote two books.* Intransitive: *She cannot write.*

ver•bal (vėr′bəl), *adj.* **1.** in words; of words: *A description is a verbal picture.* **2.** expressed in spoken words; oral: *a verbal promise, a verbal message.* **3.** having to do with or affecting words only, rather than things, realities, or context: *a verbal correction not affecting the idea in the sentence.* **4.** word for word; literal: *a verbal translation from the French.* **5.** *Grammar.* **a.** having to do with a verb: *Two common verbal endings are -ed and -ing.* **b.** derived from a verb: *a verbal adjective or noun.* **c.** resembling a verb in function or meaning.

—*n.* **1.** *Grammar.* a word, particularly a noun or adjective, derived from a verb. **2.** *Linguistics.* a word or group of words that functions as a verb.

[< Latin *verbālis* < *verbum;* see VERB]

—**Syn.** *adj.* **4.** verbatim.

➤ See **oral** for usage note.

ver•bal•ism (vėr′bə liz əm), *n.* **1.** a verbal expression; word or phrase. **2.** too much attention to mere words. **3.** a stock phrase or formula in words with little meaning. —**Syn. 2.** literalism.

ver•bal•ist (vėr′bə list), *n.* **1.** a person who is skilled in the use or choice of words. **2.** a person who pays too much attention to mere words.

ver•bal•i•za•tion (vėr′bə lə zā′shən), *n.* **1.** expression in words: *Language can best be thought of as a systematized code of signals involving verbalization* (London Times). **2.** the use of too many words. **3.** the act of changing to a verb. —**Syn. 2.** verbosity, verboseness, verbiage, wordiness.

ver•bal•ize (vėr′bə līz), *v.,* **-ized, -iz•ing.** —*v.t.* **1.** to express in words: *New subjects [who were] shown these pictures usually found them helpful in clarifying their feelings and verbalizing their experiences* (Scientific American). **2.** *Grammar.* to change (a noun, etc.) into a verb. —*v.i.* to use too many words; be wordy.

ver·bal·iz·er (vėr′bə lī′zər), *n.* a person who verbalizes: *Mr. Rexroth ... has preferred instead the role of professional bohemian and iconoclast. And verbalizer* (New York Times).

ver·bal·ly (vėr′bə lē), *adv.* **1.** in words: *to explain verbally.* **2.** in spoken words; orally: *a contract verbally agreed upon. The dumb boy could not reply verbally but used signs.* **3.** word for word: *to translate French verbally. The child reported the conversation verbally.* **4.** in regard to words only: *verbally intelligible.* **5.** as a verb; having the function of a verb: *Breast* is used verbally in *The boat breasts the wave.*

verbal noun. 1. a noun derived from a verb. **2.** an infinitive or gerund functioning as a noun but retaining such characteristics of a verb as being modified by adverbs and taking objects. *Example: To dance* (infinitive) gracefully is fun. *Dancing* (gerund) a polka can be strenuous.
➔ See **gerund** for usage note.

ver·ba·tim (vėr bā′tim), *adv.* word for word; in exactly the same words: *His speech was printed verbatim in the newspaper.*
—*adj.* **1.** corresponding with or following an original, word for word: *a verbatim report.* **2.** of a person who writes or repeats an original, word for word: *verbatim reporters in the Turkish Assembly* (Manchester Guardian).
—*n.* a full or word-for-word report, especially of a speech: *a court reporter taking down a verbatim.* [< Medieval Latin *verbatim* < Latin *verbum* word]
—**Syn.** *adv.* literally, exactly.

ver·ba·tim et lit·te·ra·tim (vėr bā′tim et lit′ə rā′tim), *Latin.* word for word and letter for letter.

ver·be·na (vər bē′nə), *n.* any of a group of low-growing garden plants with elongated or flattened spikes of flowers of various colors; vervain. [< Latin *verbēna* leafy branch. Doublet of VERVAIN.]

Common Garden Verbena

ver·be·na·ceous (vėr′bə nā′shəs), *adj.* belonging to the verbena family of plants. [< New Latin *Verbenaceae* the family name (< *Verbena* the genus < Latin *verbēna;* see VERBENA) + English *-ous*]

verbena family, a group of dicotyledonous trees, shrubs, and herbs of tropical or subtropical regions, having characteristics very similar to those of the mint family. The family includes the verbena, lantana, and teak.

ver·bi·age (vėr′bē ij), *n.* the use of too many words; abundance of useless words or words impossible to understand: *a contract full of legal verbiage.* [< French *verbiage* < Middle French *verbier* to chatter < *verbe* word < Latin *verbum*] —**Syn.** prolixity, diffuseness.

ver·bi·fy (ver′bə fī), *v.t.,* **-fied, -fy·ing.** to convert (a noun, etc.) into a verb; use as a verb; verbalize.

verb·less (vėrb′lis), *adj.* having no verb.

ver·bose (vėr bōs′), *adj.* using too many words; wordy: *a verbose and confused writer, a style verbose to the brink of tediousness.* [< Latin *verbōsus* < *verbum* word] —**ver·bose′ly,** *adv.* —**ver·bose′ness,** *n.* —**Syn.** See **wordy.** —**Ant.** terse, concise, succinct.

ver·bos·i·ty (vėr bos′ə tē), *n., pl.* **-ties. 1.** the use of too many words; wordiness: *verbosity of writing.* **2.** an instance of this: *A ... rhetorician* [*Gladstone*], *inebriated with the exuberance of his own verbosity* (Benjamin Disraeli).

ver·bo·ten (fer bō′tən), *adj. German.* forbidden by authority; prohibited: *The Department of Commerce has made public a list of seven hundred previously verboten items that American exporters may now ship to the Soviet bloc of nations without a special license* (New Yorker).

verb. sap., verbum sap., or **verbum sat.,** verbum sapienti sat est.

ver·bum sa·pi·en·ti sat est (vėr′bəm sap′ē en′tī sat est), *Latin.* a word to the wise is sufficient.

ver·bum sat sa·pi·en·ti (vėr′bəm sat sap′ē en′tī), verbum sapienti sat est.

ver·dan·cy (vėr′dən sē), *n., pl.,* **-cies. 1.** greenness: *the verdancy of the forest.* **2.** inexperience: *the verdancy of youth.*

ver·dant (vėr′dənt), *adj.* **1.** green: *verdant hills. The fields are covered with verdant grass.* **2.** inexperienced: *verdant newcomers.* [< *verd*(ure) + *-ant*] —**ver′dant·ly,** *adv.*

verd an·tique (vėrd′ an tēk′), **1.** an ornamental variety of marble consisting chiefly of serpentine mixed with calcite and dolomite, used especially by the Romans for interior decoration. **2.** a green porphyry; Oriental verd antique. [< obsolete French *verd antique* < Old French *verd* (see VERDURE), *antique* antique]

ver·der·er or **ver·der·or** (vėr′dər ər), *n.* (in English law) a judicial officer responsible for enforcing the law in royal forests and directing their maintenance. [< Anglo-French *verderer,* alteration of *verder* < Late Latin *viridārius* < Latin *viridis* green < *virēre* be green, verdant]

Ver·di·an (vär′dē ən), *adj.* of, having to do with, or characteristic of Giuseppe Verdi, 1813-1901, Italian composer, or his operas: *A sure command of the Italian text and a strong feeling for Verdian line* (Saturday Review). —*n.* an admirer or lover of Verdi's operas.

ver·dict (vėr′dikt), *n.* **1.** *Law.* the decision of a jury in a civil or criminal case on an issue submitted for its judgment: *The jury returned a verdict of "Not Guilty."* **2.** a judgment given by some body or authority acting as or like a jury: *Might we not render some such verdict as this? — 'Worthy of death but not unworthy of love'* (Hawthorne). **3.** a decision or opinion expressed upon some matter or subject; finding; judgment; conclusion: *the verdict of the public, the verdict of history.* [alteration (influenced by Medieval Latin *veredictum*) of Middle English *verdit* < Anglo-French < Old French *ver* true (< Latin *vērus*) + *dit,* past participle of *dire* to speak < Latin *dicere*]

ver·di·gris (vėr′də grēs, -gris), *n.* **1.** a green or bluish coating, usually of a carbonate of copper, that forms on brass, copper, or bronze when exposed to the air for long periods of time. **2.** *Chemistry.* a green or bluish-green poisonous compound obtained by the action of acetic acid on thin plates of copper, used as a pigment, in dyeing, and as an insecticide; basic acetate of copper. **3.** *Chemistry.* a bluish-green poisonous compound used in making synthetic rubber, textiles, etc.; normal acetate of copper. *Formula:* $C_4H_6CuO_4.H_2O$ [< Old French *vert de Grece* (literally) green of Greece; confused with Old French *gris* gray]

ver·di·grised (vėr′də grēst, -grist), *adj.* coated with verdigris: *A forlorn, verdigrised statue of Dante ... will overlook a music and art center rivaling any in the world* (Newsweek).

ver·din (vėr′dən), *n.* a small, yellow-headed titmouse of northern Mexico and southwestern United States. [American English < French *verdin* the yellowhammer, perhaps < Old French *verd* green < Latin *viridis* < *virēre* be green]

ver·di·ter (vėr′də tər), *n.* **1.** one of two pigments usually obtained by grinding azurite (blue verditer) or malachite (green verditer), and consisting of basic carbonate of copper; bice. **2.** *Obsolete.* verdigris. [< Old French *verd de terre* (literally) green of earth < Latin *viridis* green and *terra* land]

ver·dure (vėr′jər), *n.* **1.** a fresh growth of green grass, plants, or leaves. **2.** fresh greenness. **3.** a fresh or flourishing state or condition; vigor: *the verdure of youth.* [< Old French *verdure* < *verd* green < Latin *viridis* < *virēre* be green, verdant]

ver·dured (vėr′jərd), *adj.* covered with verdure or green vegetation; verdant.

ver·dure·less (vėr′jər lis), *adj.* lacking vegetation; bleak; bare.

ver·dur·ous (vėr′jər əs), *adj.* **1. a.** (of vegetation) rich and plentiful; flourishing and green. **b.** covered with rich, green vegetation. **2. a.** of or having to do with verdure or green vegetation. **b.** consisting of verdure; fresh. —**ver′dur·ous·ness,** *n.*

Ver·ein (fer īn′), *n. German.* society; association; club.

Ve·rel (və rel′), *n. Trademark.* an acrylic fiber resembling wool: *Verel ... has the advantage of taking dye very well, is fire-resistant, and withstands chemical action* (Wall Street Journal).

verge[1] (vėrj), *n., v.,* **verged, verg·ing.** —*n.* **1.** the point at which something begins or happens; brink: *on the verge of civil war. His business is on the verge of ruin.* **2.** the extreme edge, margin, or bound of something having definite limits: *the verge of reason and propriety, the verge of a cliff. Give us the eyes to see Over the verge of the sundown The beauty that is to be* (Bliss Carman). **3. a.** a limiting belt, strip, or border of something: *verges of grassy fringes.* **b.** the space within a boundary or limiting border: *a little verge for religious contemplation.* **4. a.** a rod or staff carried as an emblem of authority: *the Bishop's gold verge.* **b.** *Obsolete.* a rod or wand held by a new tenant or vassal swearing loyalty to the lord of a manor. **5.** (in English history) the area extending twelve miles around the royal court, subject to the jurisdiction of the Lord High Steward. **6.** *Architecture.* **a.** that part of a sloping roof which projects over the gable. **b.** the shaft of a column. **7.** the lever or spindle in the escapement of a watch having pallets on the end that lock and release the scape wheel. **8.** *U.S.* the part of a linotype machine carrying the pawls by which the matrices are released.
—*v.i.* to be adjacent to or on the border of; border (on): *Fifth Avenue verges on Central Park. Bill's talk was so poorly prepared that it verged on the ridiculous. Your generosity must have verged on extravagance* (Charlotte Brontë). —*v.t.* to pass along the border or edge of; skirt.
[< Old French *verge* < Latin *virga* staff. Doublet of VIRGA.]

verge[2] (vėrj), *v.i.,* **verged, verg·ing.** to tend; incline: *She was plump, verging toward fatness.* [< Latin *vergere*]

ver·ger (vėr′jər), *n.* **1.** a person who takes care of a church; sexton. **2.** an official who carries a rod, staff, or similar symbol of office before the dignitaries of a cathedral, church, or university. [< Middle French *verger* < *verge;* see VERGE[1]]

ver·ger·ship (vėr′jər ship), *n.* the position, charge, or office of a verger.

Ver·gil·i·an (vėr jil′ē ən), *adj.* Virgilian.

ver·glas (ver glä′), *n.* a hard thin surface of ice over snow: *Verglas ... is formed by precisely the right heaviness of rain falling onto a good bed of snow under precisely the right temperature* (Peter Gzowski). [< French *verglas* < Old French *verre-glaz* < *verre* glass + *glaz* ice]

ve·rid·i·cal (və rid′ə kəl), *adj.* telling the truth; truthful; veracious: *to convert Homer into a veridical historian.* [< Latin *vēridicus* (< *vērum* truth + *dīcere* to speak) + English *-al*[1]] —**ve·rid′i·cal·ly,** *adv.*

veridical hallucination, a hallucination coincident with, corresponding to, or representing real events or persons: *Veridical hallucinations ... do, in fact, coincide with some crisis in the life of the person whose image is seen* (Frederic W. H. Myers).

ver·i·est (ver′ē ist), *adj.* utmost: *the veriest nonsense.* —**Syn.** uttermost.

ver·i·fi·a·bil·i·ty (ver′ə fī′ə bil′ə tē), *n.* the quality of being verifiable: *The honest moralizer labels his statements personal assertions, and he renounces any claim to verifiability* (James B. McMillan).

ver·i·fi·a·ble (ver′ə fī′ə bəl), *adj.* that can be checked or tested and proved to be true. —**ver′i·fi′a·ble·ness,** *n.*

ver·i·fi·ca·tion (ver′ə fə kā′shən), *n.* **1.** proof by evidence or testimony: *verification of the facts.* **2.** a demonstration of truth or correctness by facts or circumstances; confirmation: *to await the verification of time.* **3.** *Law.* an affidavit added to testimony or a statement by the pleading party declaring that his allegations are true.

ver·i·fi·er (ver′ə fī′ər), *n.* a person or thing that verifies.

ver·i·fy (ver′ə fī), *v.t.,* **-fied, -fy·ing. 1.** to prove (something) to be true; confirm: *to verify a theory with examples. The driver's report of the accident was verified by eyewitnesses.* **2.** to test the correctness of; check for accuracy; make sure of: *to verify the spelling of a word by looking it up in a dictionary.* **3.** *Law.* **a.** to testify or affirm to be true, formally or upon oath. **b.** to declare that one's allegations are true. [< Old French *verifier,* learned borrowing from Medieval Latin *verificare* < Latin *vērus* true + *facere* to make]
—**Syn. 1.** substantiate, corroborate, authenticate.

ver·i·ly (ver′ə lē), *adv. Archaic.* in truth; truly; really. [< *very* + *-ly*[1]]

ver·i·sim·i·lar (ver′ə sim′ə lər), *adj.* appearing true or real; probable. [< Latin *vērisimilis* (see VERISIMILITUDE) + English *-ar;* probably patterned on *similar*] —**ver′i·sim′i·lar·ly,** *adv.*
—**Syn.** likely.

ver·i·si·mil·i·tude (ver′ə sə mil′ə tüd, -tyüd), *n.* **1.** an appearance of truth, reality, or fact; probability: *Stories must have verisimilitude to interest most people.* **2.** something having merely the appearance of truth: *They are, in truth, but shadows of fact —verisimilitudes, not verities* (Charles Lamb). [< Latin *vērisimilitūdō, -inis* < *vērisimilis* like truth < *vērus* true + *similis* like]

ver·ism (vir′iz əm), *n.* the literary or artistic style practiced or advocated by verists. [< Italian *verismo*]

ver·is·mo (vār ēs′mō, -ēz′-), *n.* **1.** verism: *The realistic set, costumes, and lighting led beautifully into the whole pattern of true verismo* (Canadian Saturday Night). **2.** the veristic style of Italian opera at the turn of the century: *"Cavalleria Rusticana" is the first flaring excitement of verismo, the style which sought to root Italian opera in everyday life* (London Times). [< Italian *verismo* < *vero* true + *-ismo* -ism]

ver·ist (vir′ist), *n.* a person who believes in or practices the rigid representation of truth and reality in literature or art, especially the use of everyday materials rather than the mythical, legendary, or heroic.

ve·ris·tic (və ris′tik), *adj.* of or having to do with verism; realistic.

ver·i·ta·ble (ver′ə tə bəl), *adj.* **1.** true; real; actual: *veritable proof of honesty. The author himself, the veritable and only genuine author* (Arnold Bennett). **2.** having all the qualities or attributes of the specified person or thing: *The salesman is a veritable fox.* **3.** *Obsolete.* in accordance with the truth or fact, as statements. [< Anglo-French, Old French *veritable* < *verite* verity, learned borrowing from Latin *vēritās;* see VERITY] —**ver′i·ta·ble·ness,** *n.*

ver·i·ta·bly (ver′ə tə blē), *adv.* in truth; truly; really; actually.

ver·i·ty (ver′ə tē), *n., pl.* **-ties.** **1.** truth: *denying the verity of my experiments* (Benjamin Franklin). *In sober verity I will confess a truth to thee* (Charles Lamb). **2.** a true statement, fact, opinion, or doctrine; reality; a truth: *Beliefs that were accepted as eternal verities* (James Henry Robinson). [< Latin *vēritās* < *vērus* true]

ver·juice (vėr′jüs′), *n.* **1.** an acid liquor made from the juice of crab apples, unripe grapes, or other sour fruits, formerly much used in cooking or for medicinal purposes. **2.** sourness, as of temper, expression, or remark. —*adj.* verjuiced. [< Old French *verjus* < *verd* green (< Latin *viridis*) + *jus* juice < Latin *jūs, jūris*]

ver·juiced (vėr′jüst′), *adj.* of or having to do with verjuice; sour.

ver·meil (vėr′məl), *n.* **1.** *Poetic.* the color vermilion. **2.** silver, bronze, or copper coated with gilt.
—*adj.* **1.** *Poetic.* of the color vermilion. **2.** of or like vermeil: *vermeil knives and forks.* [< Old French *vermeil* < Latin *vermiculus* (diminutive) < *vermis* worm]

ver·mi·an (vėr′mē ən), *adj.* **1.** belonging or having to do with a former primary division of the animal kingdom comprising wormlike forms. **2.** wormlike. [< New Latin *Vermes* (< Latin *vermis* worm) + English *-ian*]

ver·mi·cel·li (vėr′mə sel′ē, -chel′-), *n.* a mixture of flour and water, like macaroni and spaghetti, but shaped into long, slender, solid threads thinner than spaghetti. [< Italian *vermicelli* (literally) little worms, plural of *vermicello* (diminutive) < *verme* worm < Latin *vermis*]

ver·mi·cid·al (vėr′mə sī′dəl), *adj.* destroying worms; having the effect of a vermicide.

ver·mi·cide (vėr′mə sīd), *n.* any substance or drug that kills worms, especially parasitic intestinal worms. [< Latin *vermis* worm + English *-cide*[1]]

ver·mic·u·lar (vėr mik′yə lər), *adj.* **1.** of, having to do with, or characteristic of a worm or worms. **2.** like a worm in nature, form, or method of movement. **3.** like the wavy track of a worm. **4.** marked with close, wavy lines. **5.** worm-eaten. [< Medieval Latin *vermicularis* < Latin *vermiculus* (diminutive) < *vermis* worm] —**ver·mic′u·lar·ly,** *adv.*

ver·mic·u·late (*v.* vėr mik′yə lāt; *adj.* vėr-mik′yə lāt, -lit), *v.,* **-lat·ed, -lat·ing,** *adj.* —*v.t.* to ornament with winding and waving lines like the track of a worm. —*v.i.* to become wormeaten.
—*adj.* **1.** vermicular; sinuous: *Subtile, idle, unwholesome, and, (as I may term them) vermiculate questions* (Francis Bacon). **2.** having tortuous excavations as if eaten by worms. [< Latin *vermiculārī* (with English *-ate*[1]) < *vermiculus* (diminutive) < *vermis* worm]

ver·mic·u·la·tion (vėr mik′yə lā′shən), *n.* **1.** the fact or condition of being infested with or eaten by worms. **2.** a marking or boring made by, or resembling the track of, a worm: *The face of the boards is . . . eaten into innumerable vermiculations* (Thomas Hardy). **3.** *Obsolete.* peristaltic movement.

ver·mi·cule (vėr′mə kyül), *n.* **1.** a little worm. **2.** a small wormlike creature or object. [< Latin *vermiculus* (diminutive) < *vermis* worm]

ver·mic·u·lite (vėr mik′yə līt), *n.* a mineral, hydrous micaceous silicate of aluminum, iron, and magnesium, occurring in small foliated scales. It is used as a filler in paint and concrete, as a soil conditioner, insulator, etc. [American English < Latin *vermiculus* (diminutive) < *vermis* worm; + *-ite*[1] (because of its appearance when heated by a blowpipe)]

ver·mi·form (vėr′mə fôrm), *adj.* shaped like a worm; long, thin, and more or less cylindrical. [< New Latin *vermiformis* < Latin *vermis* worm + *forma* form]

vermiform appendix, *Anatomy.* a slender tube, closed at one end, growing out of the large intestine in the lower right-hand part of the abdomen; appendix. Appendicitis is inflammation of the vermiform appendix.

vermiform process, *Anatomy.* **1.** the median lobe of the cerebellum. **2.** the appendix.

ver·mi·fuge (vėr′mə fyüj), *adj.* (of a drug or other agent) causing the expulsion of worms from the intestines. —*n.* a medicine to expel worms from the intestines. [< Latin *vermis* worm + *fugāre* cause to flee]

ver·mil·ion (vər mil′yən), *n.* **1.** a bright red. **2. a.** a bright-red coloring matter consisting of mercuric sulfide; cinnabar. **b.** any of various other bright-red coloring matters.
—*adj.* bright-red; scarlet: *The black strokes of writing thereon looked like the twigs of a winter hedge against a vermilion sunset* (Thomas Hardy).
—*v.t.* to color or paint with, or as with, vermilion: *A blush vermilioned her face.* [Middle English *vermeylion, vermilloun* < *vermeil* < Old French; see VERMEIL]

vermilion flycatcher, a flycatcher found from the southwestern United States to Argentina. The male has a vermilion crown, throat, and breast.

ver·min (vėr′mən), *n. pl. or sing.* **1.** small animals that are troublesome or destructive. Fleas, lice, bedbugs, rats, and mice are vermin. **2.** *British.* animals or birds that destroy game, poultry, etc., in game preserves. **3.** a vile, worthless person or persons. [< Anglo-French *vermin* < Vulgar Latin *vermīnum* < Latin *vermis* worm]

ver·mi·nate (vėr′mə nāt), *v.i.,* **-nat·ed, -nat·ing.** to breed vermin; become infested with parasitic vermin.

ver·mi·na·tion (vėr′mə nā′shən), *n.* **1.** the breeding, growth, or production of vermin, especially parasitic vermin. **2.** a being infested with parasitic vermin.

ver·min·i·cide (vər min′ə sīd), *n.* a preparation for killing vermin: *During the summer months verminicide became a necessary item in the bazar* (Blackwood's Magazine).

ver·min·ous (vėr′mə nəs), *adj.* **1.** consisting of or having to do with vermin. **2.** (of diseases) caused by, due to, or characterized by the presence of parasitic vermin or intestinal worms. **3.** infested with or full of vermin, especially parasitic vermin. **4.** like vermin; vile; worthless. —**ver′min·ous·ly,** *adv.* —**ver′min·ous·ness,** *n.*

ver·miv·o·rous (vėr miv′ər əs), *adj.* eating worms; feeding on worms, as certain birds. [< Latin *vermis* worm + *vorāre* devour + English *-ous*]

Ver·mont·er (vər mon′tər), *n.* a native or inhabitant of Vermont, a State of the United States forming the northwestern part of New England.

Ver·mont·ese (vər mon′tēz′, -tēs′), *n., pl.* **-ese,** *adj.* —*n.* a Vermonter: *Hamilton was a Vermontese* (Thomas G. Fessenden).
—*adj.* of or belonging to Vermont: *Our Vermontese housewives are not a little vain of their knowledge in making homemade wines* (Ira Allen).

ver·mouth (vər müth′, vėr′müth), *n.* a white wine, either dry (yellow) or sweet (usually reddish-brown), flavored with wormwood or other herbs and used as a liqueur or in cocktails. [< French *vermouth* < German *Wermuth* wormwood]

ver·nac·u·lar (vər nak′yə lər), *n.* **1.** the native speech or language used by the people of a certain country or place: *a sixteenth century Saxon of peasant and mining stock, handling a vernacular which has at no period been remarkable for refinement* (C. V. Wedgewood). *Turns of speech that showed they had been that instant translated from the vernacular* (Rudyard Kipling). **2. a.** everyday language; informal speech. **b.** a vernacular word or idiom. **3.** the language of a particular profession, trade, etc.: *There are many strange words in the vernacular of lawyers.* **4.** the common name of a plant or animal, not its scientific name, as *black-eyed Susan* for *Rudbeckia hirta.*
—*adj.* **1.** used by the people of a certain country or district; native: *English is our vernacular tongue.* **2.** of or in the native language, rather than a literary or learned language. **3.** of, having to do with, or forming part of the native language. **4.** (of arts or features of these) native or peculiar to a certain country or locality: *the vernacular style of architecture.* **5.** of or designating the common informal name given to a plant or animal. **6.** *Obsolete.* (of a disease) endemic. [< Latin *vernāculus* domestic, native (< *verna* home-born slave) + English *-ar*] —**ver·nac′u·lar·ly,** *adv.*

ver·nac·u·lar·ism (vər nak′yə lə riz′əm), *n.* **1.** a vernacular word, idiom, or mode of expression. **2.** the use of the vernacular.

ver·nac·u·lar·ist (vər nak′yə lər ist), *n.* a vernacular writer; person who writes in the language of the people or country: *There was ample material . . . which in the hands of a vernacularist of genius could produce a play as striking as "Strife"* (Glasgow Herald).

ver·nac·u·lar·i·za·tion (vər nak′yə lər-ə zā′shən), *n.* the action of making, or fact of being made, vernacular or native to a language: *Thousands of words . . . on their first appearance, or revival, as candidates for vernacularization, must have met with repugnance* (Fitzedward Hall).

ver·nac·u·lar·ize (vər nak′yə lə rīz), *v.t.,* **-ized, -iz·ing.** to make vernacular; express in or translate into the vernacular: *The author undoubtedly felt under obligation to vernacularize his style* (Sidney Ditzion).

ver·nal (vėr′nəl), *adj.* **1. a.** of spring; having to do with spring: *a grass of vernal green, vernal flowers, vernal months.* **b.** like spring; suggesting spring: *vernal rain.* **2.** youthful: *Everyone admired the young girl's vernal freshness.* **3.** (of flowers, plants, etc.) appearing, coming up, or blooming in springtime. [< Latin *vernālis* < *vernus* of spring < *vēr, vēris* spring] —**ver′nal·ly,** *adv.*

vernal equinox, the equinox that occurs about March 21. See **equinox** for diagram.

ver·nal·i·za·tion (vėr′nə lə zā′shən), *n.* the act or process of vernalizing: *Vernalization consists of the transformation of winter cereals into spring varieties by chilling and soaking the seeds* (Laurence H. Snyder).

ver·nal·ize (vėr′nə līz), *v.t.,* **-ized, -iz·ing.** to cause (a plant) to bloom and bear fruit early by subjecting the seed or bulb to a very low temperature; jarovize.

vernal point, vernal equinox.

ver·na·tion (vėr nā′shən), *n. Botany.* the arrangement or formation of the leaves of plants or fronds of ferns in the bud, with reference to their folding, coiling, etc.; foliation. [< New Latin *vernatio, -onis* < Latin *vernāre* bloom, renew foliage, as in spring < *vernus* of spring < *vēr, vēris* spring]

Ver·ner's law (vėr′nərz), a statement by the Danish linguist Karl Verner in 1877, explaining certain apparent exceptions to Grimm's law, by showing that the Germanic voiceless fricatives became voiced between voiced sounds unless the syllable preceding them bore the accent in Indo-European.

ver·neuk (ver nük′), *v.t.* (in South Africa) to cheat; humbug; swindle: *How Hendrich enjoyed verneuking the Boer* (Cape Monthly Magazine). [< Afrikaans *verneuk*]

ver·neuk·er·ing (ver nü′kər ing), *n.* (in South Africa) deception; trickery: *Hence arose the practice of verneukering, by which buyer and seller sought to get the better of each other* (Sir J. Robinson).

ver·neuk·er·y (ver nü′kər ē), *n.* (in South Africa) trickery; verneukering: *We women of South Africa despise such maudlin verneukery* (Westminster Gazette).

ver·ni·cose (vėr′nə kōs), *adj. Botany.* having a shiny surface as if freshly varnished. [< New Latin *vernicosus* < Medieval Latin *vernix* varnish]

ver·ni·er (vėr′nē ər, -nir), *n.* **1.** a small movable scale for measuring a fractional part of one of the divisions of the fixed scale of astronomical, surveying, or other mathematical instruments to which it is attached; vernier scale. **2.** an auxiliary device used to obtain fine adjustments or measurements with another device or mechanism. —*adj.* furnished with a vernier: *a vernier transit.* [< Pierre *Vernier,* 1580-1637, a French mathematician]

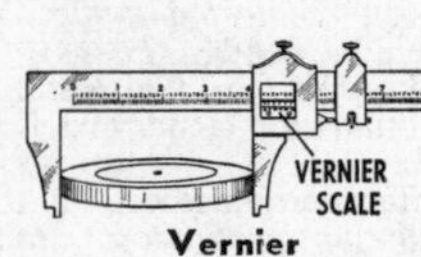

Vernier

vernier engine or **rocket,** a rocket engine of low thrust used to adjust the final velocity and course of a missile or space vehicle just after the last sustainer engine is shut down.

vernier scale, vernier.

ver·nis Mar·tin (ver nē′ mår taN′), a clear, brilliant lacquer used in the decoration of carriages, furniture, fans, etc. [< French *vernis Martin* (literally) Martin varnish < a family of French artificers in the 1700's]

ver·nis·sage (ver nē såzh′), *n.* **1.** varnishing day. **2.** the opening or first showing of an art exhibition: *It was the first time in history that the Vatican had staged a one-man show, or that an artist had been thus honored by the presence of the Pope at his vernissage* (Newsweek). [< French *vernissage* < Old French *vernis;* see VARNISH]

ver·nix (vėr′niks), *n.* a fatty substance covering the skin of the fetus, to prevent its softening by the amniotic fluid. [< New Latin *vernix (caseosa)* (literally) cheesy varnish < Medieval Latin *vernix* varnish, and Latin *caseus* cheese]

vernix ca·se·o·sa (kā′sē ō′sə), vernix. [see VERNIX]

Ver·o·nal (ver′ə nəl, -nôl), *n. Trademark.* barbital. [< German *Veronal* < *Verona,* Italy, where the inventor was going when he proposed the name of the product]

Ver·o·nese (ver′ə nēz′, -nēs′), *adj.* of or having to do with Verona, a city in northern Italy, or its people. —*n.* a native or inhabitant of Verona.

ve·ron·i·ca[1] (və ron′ə kə), *n.* **1.** any of a group of plants of the figwort family; speedwell. **2.** Often, **Veronica.** the sudarium or handkerchief, preserved as a relic at St. Peter's, Rome, and alleged to be the original with which Saint Veronica wiped the face of Christ as He went to Calvary and on which the likeness of Christ's features remained. **3.** a cloth, ornament, etc., bearing a representation of Christ's face. [< Medieval Latin *Veronica,* the saint < Greek *Berenikē*]

ve·ron·i·ca[2] (və ron′ə kə), *n.* a maneuver in bullfighting, in which the matador slowly turns with the cape without moving his feet as the bull rushes toward him: *Cordobano tried a series of curtailed and unsatisfactory veronicas, but the bull had excellent brakes and no acceleration whatever, which made the passes extremely dangerous* (Atlantic). [< Spanish *veronica*]

Veronica[2]

ver·ru·ca (ve rü′kə), *n., pl.* **-cae** (-sē). **1.** *Medicine.* a wart. **2.** *Zoology.* a wartlike growth or prominence. [< Latin *verrūca* wart; excrescence on a stone]

ver·ru·ca·no (ver′ə kä′nō), *n. Geology.* a stratified conglomerate found in the Alps. [< Italian *verrucano* < Mount *Verruca,* near Pisa, Italy]

ver·ru·cose (ver′ú kōs), *adj.* **1.** *Medicine.* covered with or full of verrucae or warts. **2.** *Botany.* studded with small wartlike swellings or protuberances. [< Latin *verrūcosus* < *verrūca;* see VERRUCA]

ver·ru·cos·i·ty (ver′ú kos′ə tē), *n., pl.* **-ties. 1.** verrucose condition. **2.** a wart.

ver·ru·cous (ver′ú kəs), *adj.* verrucose.

ver·ru·ga (ve rü′gə), *n.* a Peruvian skin disease characterized by warty growths and often fatal, caused by a bacillus transmitted by the sandfly. [< Spanish *verruga peruviana* < Latin *verrūca;* see VERRUCA]

vers (no period), *Trigonometry.* versee sine.

ver·sant (vėr′sənt), *n.* **1.** the slope, side, or descent of a mountain or mountain chain. **2.** the area or region covered by a slope. [< French *versant,* noun use of present participle of Middle French *verser* to (make) turn < Latin *versāre* (frequentative) < *vertere* to turn]

ver·sa·tile (vėr′sə təl), *adj.* **1.** able to do many things well: *Theodore Roosevelt was a versatile man; he was successful as a statesman, soldier, sportsman, explorer, and author.* **2.** *Zoology.* **a.** turning forward or backward, as the head of certain insects or the toe of a bird: *the versatile toe of an owl.* **b.** freely moving up and down or from side to side, as antennae. **3.** *Botany.* (of an anther) attached at or near the middle so as to swing freely. **4. a.** changeable; variable: *a versatile taste in reading.* **b.** fickle; inconstant: *a versatile, impressionable woman.* [< Latin *versātilis* turning < *versāre* to turn (frequentative) < *vertere* to turn] —**ver′sa·tile·ly,** *adv.* —**ver′sa·tile·ness,** *n.* —**Syn. 1.** many-sided.

ver·sa·til·i·ty (vėr′sə til′ə tē), *n., pl.* **-ties. 1.** the ability to do many things well: *the versatility of your genius* (Frederick Marryat). **2.** a being changeable; fickleness. **3.** diversity of nature or character; variety of application. **4.** the ability to turn about as on a pivot.

vers de so·cié·té (ver′ də sô syā tā′), light, graceful, entertaining poetry, such as to appeal to polite society. [< French *vers de société* (literally) society verse]

verse (vėrs), *n.* **1.** poetry; lines of words usually with a regularly repeated accent. Verse is sometimes contrasted with poetry by its lighter or more frivolous content and greater emphasis on structure. **2.** a single line of poetry: *And he wrote for them wonderful verses that swept the land like flame* (Rudyard Kipling). *Abbr.:* vs. **3.** a group of lines or short portion in poetry; stanza: *Sing the first verse of "America."* **4.** a type of poetry; meter: *blank verse, iambic verse.* **5.** a short division of a chapter of the Bible: *to cite chapter and verse.* **6.** a certain amount of poetry considered as a whole; the poetry of a particular author: *the minstrel verse* (Scott).
cap verses, to follow one quotation with another in turn, especially as a game in which each verse (usually from the classics) begins with the same letter with which the last ended: *He thinks the Roman poets good for nothing but for boys to cap verses* (The English Theophrastus).
[partly Old English *vers;* partly < Old French *vers;* both < Latin *versus, -ūs* (originally) row, furrow < *vertere* turn around]

versed[1] (vėrst), *adj.* experienced; practiced; skilled; conversant with: *A doctor should be well versed in medical theory.* [< past participle of obsolete *verse* turn over (in the mind) < Latin *versāre* (frequentative) < *vertere* to turn]
—**Syn.** proficient, acquainted.

versed[2] (vėrst), *adj. Mathematics.* turned; reversed. [< Latin *versus,* past participle of *vertere* to turn + English *-ed*[2]]

verse drama, a drama written in verse: *A new verse drama, "Hogan's Goat," by a Harvard professor, . . . proved to be an absorbing tragedy of Irish political life in late 19th-century Brooklyn* (John W. Gassner).

versed sine, *Trigonometry.* unity minus the cosine of an angle. *Abbr.:* vers (no period).

verse·let (vėrs′lit), *n.* a little verse; small or trifling poem: *The pages of this time are crammed with squibs and verselets invaluable to later biographers of the illustrious obscure* (Punch). [< *verse* + *-let*]

Ver·sene (vėr sēn′), *n. Trademark.* a white powdery compound, a chelate, used as a water softener and in the treatment of lead poisoning. *Formula:* $C_{10}H_{12}N_2Na_4O_8$

vers·er (vėr′sər), *n.* versifier: *He [Ben Jonson] thought not Bartas a poet, but a verser, because he wrote not fiction* (William Drummond).

vers·et (vėr′sət), *n.* **1.** a short verse of poetry or prose, especially one from the Bible, the Koran, etc.: *Despite Mr. Shapiro's dismissal of tradition, he must be aware that these versets . . . are very much in a tradition* (Harper's). **2.** a short piece of organ music suitable for use as an interlude or short prelude in a church service.

ver·si·cle (vėr′sə kəl), *n.* **1.** a little verse. **2.** one of a series of short sentences said or sung by the minister during services, to which the people make response. [< Latin *versiculus* (diminutive) < *versus;* see VERSE]

ver·si·col·ored (vėr′sə kul′ərd), *adj.* **1.** changing or varying in color; iridescent. **2.** of various colors; variegated. [< Latin *versus* turned, past participle of *vertere* to turn + English *colored*]

ver·sic·u·lar (vėr sik′yə lər), *adj.* of, having to do with, or consisting of versicles or verses, especially of the Bible.
[< Latin *versiculus* (see VERSICLE) + English *-ar*[1]]

ver·si·fi·ca·tion (vėr′sə fə kā′shən), *n.* **1. a.** the making of verses. **b.** the art or theory of making verses. **2.** the form or style of poetry or verse; metrical structure. **3.** an adaptation in verse of something: *His epigrams are versifications of his own jokes.*

ver·si·fied (vėr′sə fīd), *adj.* written or composed in verse.

ver·si·fi·er (vėr′sə fī′ər), *n.* **1.** a person who makes verses; poet. **2.** poetaster: *Mr. Fitts has contrived hilariously unexpected echoes of Keats, Eliot, Shakespeare, Pound, not to mention parodies of several all too recognizable schools of avant-garde versifiers* (Atlantic).

ver·si·fy (vėr′sə fī), *v.,* **-fied, -fy·ing.** —*v.i.* to write verse: *Miss Arton can versify handsomely enough, and bring things to a happy finish where the necessity of passion does not prohibit sense* (Atlantic). —*v.t.* **1.** to tell in verse; deal with in verse form. **2.** to turn (prose) into poetry; rewrite in verse form. [< Old French *versifier,* learned borrowing from Latin *versificāre* < *versus* (see VERSE) + *facere* to make]

ver·sine or **ver·sin** (vėr′sīn), *n. Trigonometry.* versed sine.

ver·sion (vėr′zhən, -shən), *n.* **1.** a translation from one language to another: *the King James version of the Bible.* **2.** one particular statement, account, or description given by one person or source: *Each of the three boys gave his own version of the quarrel.* **3.** a special form or variant of something: *a Scottish version of the Christmas tree.* **4.** *Obstetrics.* the manipulation or manual turning of the fetus in the uterus so as to facilitate delivery. **5.** an abnormal turning of the uterus so that its axis is deflected without being bent upon itself. [< Latin *versiō, -ōnis* (originally) a turning < *vertere* to turn]

ver·sion·al (vėr′zhə nəl, -shə-), *adj.* of or having to do with a version.

ver·si·tron (vėr′sə tron), *n.* a device that can detect slight temperature changes at great distances: *He told how a versitron could be attached to a radar set, increasing the radiated power of the transmitter 1,000 times* (Science News Letter). [< Latin *versus,* past participle of *vertere* to turn + English *-tron,* as in *electron*]

vers li·bre (ver lē′brə), free verse; verse that follows no fixed metrical form: *His rhythms became more individual as he moved away from conventional metres toward a kind of patterned vers libre* (Louise Bogan). [< French *vers libre*]

vers li·brist (ver lē′brist), a person who writes free verse. [< French *vers-libriste*]

ver·so (vėr′sō), *n., pl.* **-sos** (-sōz). **1.** *Printing.* the back of a leaf in a manuscript or printed book; the left-hand page of an open book. **2.** the reverse side of a coin, medal, etc. [< Latin *versō (foliō)* a turned (leaf), ablative neuter of *versus,* past participle of *vertere* to turn]

verst (vėrst), *n.* a Russian measure of length equal to about 3,500 feet. [< Russian *versta*]

ver·sus (vėr′səs), *prep.* against: *The most exciting game was Harvard versus Yale. Abbr.:* v., ver., or vs. [< Latin *versus* turned toward, past participle of *vertere* to turn]
➔ **Versus** is used especially in legal documents and the like, to denote an action by one party against another: *the State versus Smith,* or in sports writing to signify two contestants: *Army versus Navy.*

vert (vėrt), *n.* **1.** in English forest law: **a.** everything bearing green leaves in a forest. **b.** the right to cut green trees or shrubs in a forest. **2.** (in heraldry) the green color in a coat of arms. [< Old French *vert, verd* green < Latin *viridis* < *virēre* be green]

ver·te·bra (vėr′tə brə), *n., pl.* **-brae** (-brē), **-bras.** **1.** *Anatomy.* any of the bones composing the backbone or spinal column. In man and higher animals a vertebra consists typically of a somewhat cylindrical central body (centrum) and arch (neural arch) supporting seven processes, the whole forming an opening for the passage of the spinal cord. **2.** the vertebral column; the spine or backbone. [< Latin *vertebra* (originally) any joint, a turning place < *vertere* to turn]

ver·te·bral (vėr′tə brəl), *adj.* **1.** of, having to do with, or situated on or near a vertebra or the vertebrae; spinal. **2.** of the nature of a vertebra. **3.** composed of vertebrae. **4.** having vertebrae; backboned. —*n.* a vertebral artery or vein. —**ver′te·bral·ly,** *adv.*

vertebral column, the backbone: *In the higher chordates the notochord is present in the embryo only, since it is replaced by the bony vertebral column in the adult form* (A. M. Winchester).

ver·te·brate (vėr′tə brit, -brāt), *n.* an animal that has a backbone. Fishes, amphibians, reptiles, birds, and mammals are vertebrates: *Vertebrates characteristically have a red blood pigment, rich in iron, known as haemoglobin, which combines readily with oxygen* (Mary Sears).
—*adj.* **1.** having a backbone or spinal column. **2.** of, belonging to, or having to do with the group of animals that have a segmented spinal column and a brain case or cranium enclosing the brain. [< New Latin *Vertebrata* the group name < Latin *vertebrātus* jointed < *vertebra;* see VERTEBRA]

ver·te·brat·ed (vėr′tə brā′tid), *adj.* **1.** having a spinal column; vertebrate. **2.** consisting of or provided with vertebrae. **3.** constructed in a manner suggestive of vertebrae.

ver·te·bra·tion (vėr′tə brā′shən), *n.* division into segments like those of the spinal column; vertebrate formation.

ver·tex (vėr′teks), *n., pl.* **-tex·es** or **-ti·ces.** **1.** the highest point of something, especially a hill or structure; top. **2.** *Anatomy.* the top or crown of the head, especially in man, the part lying between the occiput and the sinciput. **3.** *Astronomy.* the point in the heavens directly overhead; zenith. **4.** *Mathematics.* **a.** the point opposite to and farthest from the base of a triangle, pyramid, or other figure having a base. The vertex of an angle is the point where the two sides meet. **b.** the convex of an angle. **c.** the point in a curve or surface at which the axis meets it. **5.** *Optics.* the point, at the center of a lens, where the axis cuts the surface. [< Latin *vertex, -icis* highest point; (originally) a whirl, whirling < *vertere* to turn] —**Syn. 1.** apex, summit.

ver·ti·cal (vėr′tə kəl), *adj.* **1.** straight up and down; perpendicular to a level surface or to the plane of the horizon; upright: *A person standing straight is in a vertical position.* See **horizontal** for diagram. **2.** of or at the highest point; of the vertex. **3.** directly overhead; at the zenith: *a vertical sighting.* **4.** so organized as to include many or all stages in the production or distribution of some manufactured product: *a vertical union, vertical trusts.* **5.** *Botany.* **a.** having a position at right angles to the plane of the axis, body, or other supporting surface, as the blade of a leaf. **b.** in the direction of the stem or axis; lengthwise.
—*n.* **1.** a vertical line, plane, circle, position, or part. **2.** a vertical angle. **3.** a vertical beam, etc., in a truss.
[< Late Latin *verticālis* < *vertex, -icis* highest point, vertex] —**ver′ti·cal·ly,** *adv.* —**ver′ti·cal·ness,** *n.* —**Ant.** *adj.* **1.** horizontal.

vertical angle, *Geometry.* **1.** an opposite angle. **2.** the angle opposite the base of a triangle or polygon.

vertical circle, *Astronomy.* any great circle of the celestial sphere perpendicular to the plane of the horizon, or passing through the zenith and nadir.

vertical envelopment, attack by airplanes or paratroops, usually combined with operations by ground forces, in an effort to cut off or encircle the enemy.

vertical integration, the overall control by a single company of the making and selling of a product, to insure quality control, a steady supply, etc.: *What is vertical integration as applied to farming? An outstanding example is the modern broiler industry. In this farmers are paid to feed and house in their own buildings chicks usually furnished or financed by feed companies or poultry processors who also market the chickens* (Christian Science Monitor).

ver·ti·cal·i·ty (vėr′tə kal′ə tē), *n.* **1.** *Astronomy.* the fact of being directly overhead or at the zenith. **2. a.** the condition of being vertical; vertical position. **b.** (of buildings) perpendicular quality.

ver·ti·cal·i·za·tion (vėr′tə kə lə zā′shən), *n.* vertical integration.

vertical take-off, a take-off directly upward, as of a helicopter or certain fighter planes designed to take off and land vertically: *With a battery of small jets firing downwards and four nozzles fore and aft and at the wingtips for control, vertical take-off of a new kind becomes possible* (New Scientist).

vertical union, a labor union whose membership includes the workers of an entire industry rather than those employed at a particular craft or task.

ver·ti·ces (vėr′tə sēz), *n.* a plural of **vertex.**

ver·ti·cil (vėr′tə sil), *n. Botany.* a whorl or circle (applied to organs, as leaves or flowers, growing around a stem or central point). [< Latin *verticillus* whorl (diminutive) < *vertex* vertex]

ver·ti·cil·las·ter (vėr′tə si las′tər), *n. Botany.* a determinate inflorescence in which the flowers are arranged in a seeming whorl, consisting in fact of a pair of opposite axillary, usually sessile, cymes, as in many plants of the mint family. [< Latin *verticillus* (see VERTICIL) + *-aster,* a diminutive suffix]

ver·tic·il·late (vėr tis′ə lāt, -lit; vėr′tə sil′āt), *adj.* **1.** disposed in or forming verticils or whorls, as leaves and flowers. **2.** *Obsolete.* (of plants) having leaves, flowers, etc., arranged or produced in circles or whorls around the stem. [< New Latin *verticillatus* < Latin *verticillus;* see VERTICIL] —**ver·tic′il·late·ly,** *adv.*

ver·tic·il·lat·ed (vėr tis′ə lā′tid), *adj.* verticillate.

ver·tic·il·la·tion (vėr tis′ə lā′shən), *n.* **1.** the formation of verticils. **2.** a vertical or verticillate form or structure.

ver·ti·cil·li·um (vėr′tə sil′ē əm), *n.* **1.** a disease of cotton, tomatoes, hops, and other plants, caused by a soil fungus that attacks the entire plant through the roots; verticillium wilt. **2.** the fungus causing this disease: *Verticillium is likely to be present in all old agricultural soils in which potatoes and tomatoes have been grown* (Sunset). [< New Latin *Verticillium* the genus of the fungus < Latin *verticillus;* see VERTICIL]

verticillium wilt, verticillium.

ver·tic·i·ty (vėr tis′ə tē), *n. Obsolete.* a tendency to turn towards a vertex or pole, especially as exhibited by a magnetic needle. [< Latin *vertex, -icis* vertex + English *-ity*]

ver·tig·i·nate (vėr tij′ə nāt′), *v.i.,* **-nat·ed, -nat·ing.** to turn round, spin, or rush dizzily: *Finding where the car is parked once one descends and ceases to vertiginate becomes a real problem* (New York Times). *Surely never did argument vertiginate more* (Samuel Taylor Coleridge).

ver·tig·i·nous (vėr tij′ə nəs), *adj.* **1.** whirling; rotary; revolving: *the vertiginous action of a gyroscope.* **2.** affected with or suffering from vertigo; dizzy: *At the edge of the cliff she grew vertiginous and hastily retreated.* **3.** of the nature of or having to do with vertigo; likely to cause vertigo. **4.** fickle; unstable. [< Latin *vertīginōsus* suffering from dizziness < *vertīgō, -inis;* see VERTIGO] —**ver·tig′i·nous·ly,** *adv.* —**ver·tig′i·nous·ness,** *n.*

ver·ti·go (vėr′tə gō), *n., pl.* **ver·ti·goes, ver·tig·i·nes** (vėr tij′ə nēz). **1.** an abnormal condition characterized by a feeling that the person, or the objects around one, are whirling in space, and by a tendency to lose equilibrium and consciousness; dizziness; giddiness: *Vertigo is caused by changes of the blood supply in the head.* **2.** *Veterinary Medicine.* (sometimes) the staggers in horses, the sturdy or gid in sheep, or a similar disease in dogs. [< Latin *vertīgō, -inis* dizziness; (originally) a turning round < *vertere* to turn]

ver·tim·e·ter (vėr tim′ə tər), *n.* an instrument that measures the rate of climb or descent of an aircraft.

ver·tu (vėr tü′, vėr′tü), *n.* virtu.

Ver·tum·nus (vər tum′nəs), *n.* the Roman god of spring, guardian of gardens and orchards, and husband of Pomona. Also, **Vortumnus.**
[< Latin *Vertumnus* (literally) self-changing < *vertere* to turn]

ver·vain (vėr′vān), *n.* any verbena, especially any species bearing spikes of small white, bluish, or purple flowers, as a common European species and a common American species. [< Old French *verveine, vervainne* < Latin *verbēna* leafy bough. Doublet of VERBENA.]

verve (vėrv), *n.* **1.** enthusiasm; energy; vigor; spirit; liveliness: *full of verve and enjoyment of life.* **2. a.** intellectual vigor or energy, especially as expressed or shown in literary productions; liveliness of ideas and expression. **b.** *Obsolete.* talent in writing. [< French *verve,* Old French, a fancy, caprice, perhaps < Vulgar Latin *verva* < Latin *verba,* in sense of "whimsical words"]

ver·vet (vėr′vit), *n.* a small African monkey of a grayish-green color, one of the guenons. [< French *vervet,* probably fusion of *vert* green + (*gri*)*vet* a grivet]

ver·y (ver′ē), *adv., adj.,* **ver·i·er, ver·i·est.**
—*adv.* **1.** much; greatly; extremely: *The sun is very hot.* **2.** absolutely; exactly: *He stood in the very same place for an hour.*
—*adj.* **1.** same; identical: *The very people who used to love her hate her now.* **2.** even; mere; sheer: *The very thought of blood makes her sick. She wept from very joy.* **3. a.** real; true; genuine: *that very queen and very woman* (Hawthorne). **b.** *Obsolete.* legally valid; rightful; lawful; legitimate. **4.** actual; exact: *He was caught in the very act of stealing. Speak the very truth.* **5.** in the fullest sense; veritable: *Voltaire was the very eye of modern illumination.*
[< Anglo-French *verrai,* Old French *verai* < Vulgar Latin *vērācus,* for Latin *vērāx, -ācis* < *vērus* true]
—**Syn.** *adv.* **1.** exceedingly, surpassingly, excessively.
➤ The use of **very,** in place of *very much* or *much,* to modify past participles, as in *He was very annoyed by the letter,* is regarded as nonstandard. This is not true when the participles function as simple attributive or predicate adjectives: *a very pleased look. He was very tired.*

Very High Frequency or **very high frequency,** VHF.

Very light, a colored flare fired from a pistol at night as a signal: *The commissioner was to reveal his position on the ground by firing a purple Very light into the sky* (New Yorker). [< Edward *Very,* 1847-1910, an American naval officer, who invented it]

Very Low Frequency or **very low frequency,** VLF.

Very pistol, a pistol used to discharge a Very light: *The Very pistol works somewhat like a Roman candle. Both these and rockets are used in signaling* (World Book Encyclopedia).

ve·si·ca (və sī′kə), *n., pl.* **-cae** (-sē). **1.** *Anatomy.* a bladder, especially the urinary bladder; sac. **2.** *Botany.* vesicle. [< Latin *vēsīca* bladder, blister]

ves·i·cal (ves′ə kəl), *adj.* of or having to do with the bladder; formed in the urinary bladder.

ves·i·cant (ves′ə kənt), *n.* **1.** something that raises blisters, as a mustard plaster; vesicatory. **2.** any chemical agent causing burns, inflammation, and destruction of the internal or external tissue of the body. —*adj.* causing or effective in producing blisters, as a medical application; vesicatory. [< New Latin *vesicans, -antis,* present participle of *vesicare* to raise blisters < Latin *vēsīca* blister]

vesica pis·cis (pis′is), a pointed oval figure, formed properly by the intersection of the arcs of two equal circles each of which passes through the center of the other, frequently used in ecclesiastical architecture and art, often to enclose a sacred figure, as that of Christ or the Virgin. [< Latin *vēsīca piscis* (literally) bladder of or like a fish]

ves·i·cate (ves′ə kāt), *v.,* **-cat·ed, -cat·ing.** *Medicine.* —*v.t.* to cause blisters on; blister. —*v.i.* to become blistered. [< Latin *vēsīca* blister + English *-ate*[1]]

ves·i·ca·tion (ves′ə kā′shən), *n. Medicine.* **1.** the formation, development, or result of blistering. **2.** a blister or group of blisters.

ves·i·ca·to·ry (ves′ə kə tôr′ē, -tōr′-), *adj., n., pl.* **-to·ries.** —*adj.* that can raise blisters. —*n.* vesicant.

ves·i·cle (ves′ə kəl), *n.* **1.** a small bladder, cavity, sac, or cyst, especially one filled with fluid, as a blister. **2.** *Botany.* a small bladder or air cavity resembling a bladder. **3.** *Geology.* a small spherical or oval cavity produced by the presence of bubbles of gas or vapor in volcanic rock. [< Latin *vēsīcula* (diminutive) < *vēsīca* bladder, blister]

ve·sic·u·lar (və sik′yə lər), *adj.* **1.** of, having to do with, or connected with vesicles, especially the air cells of the lungs: *vesicular breathing.* **2.** like a vesicle; bladderlike. **3.** having vesicles. [< New Latin *vesicularis* < Latin *vēsīcula,* see VESICLE] —**ve·sic′u·lar·ly,** *adv.*

vesicular exanthema, a contagious virus disease of swine in which blisters appear above the hoof, between the toes, and on the snout and nostrils. It is caused by eating decayed garbage and is similar to foot-and-mouth disease in cattle.

vesicular stomatitis, a noncontagious virus disease of cattle, horses, and hogs, in which small superficial ulcers form on the mucous membrane of the mouth. It is spread by mosquitoes and other insects.

ve·sic·u·late (*v.* və sik′yə lāt; *adj.* və sik′yə lit, -lāt), *v.,* **-lat·ed, -lat·ing,** *adj.* —*v.t., v.i.* to make or become vesicular; develop vesicles (in). —*adj.* vesiculated.

ve·sic·u·lat·ed (və sik′yə lā′tid), *adj.* **1.** full of or having small cavities or air cells. **2.** of the nature of a vesicle or vesicula. **3.** *Medicine.* covered with vesicles.

ve·sic·u·la·tion (və sik′yə lā′shən), *n.* the formation of vesicles, especially on the skin.

ve·sic·u·lose (və sik′yə lōs), *adj.* full of vesicles; vesiculated.

ve·sic·u·lous (və sik′yə ləs), *adj.* vesiculose.

Ves·per (ves′pər), *n.* the evening star, often Venus. [< Latin *Vesper* evening star]

ves·per (ves′pər), *n.* **1.** an evening prayer, hymn, or service. **2.** a vesper bell. **3.** vespers; evensong. **4.** *Obsolete.* evening.
—*adj.* **1.** of, belonging to, or occurring in the evening: *the vesper hours.* **2.** Sometimes, **Vesper.** of, used at, or having to do with vespers. [< Old French *vespre,* variant of *vespres;* see VESPERS]

ves·per·al (ves′pər əl), *n.* **1.** a book containing the psalms, chants, etc., with their music, used at vespers. **2.** a cover used over the altar cloth between services.

vesper bell, the bell that summons to vespers or evensong.

vesper mouse, a mouse having white feet.

ves·pers or **Ves·pers** (ves′pərz), *n.pl.* **1.** a church service held in the late afternoon or evening; evensong. **2. a.** the sixth of the seven canonical hours. **b.** the office or service for this hour, following nones, and said in late afternoon or evening. **c.** (in the Roman Catholic Church) the evening service, often said before a public assembly on Sundays and holy days. [partly < Old French *vespres* < Medieval Latin; partly < Medieval Latin *vesperae,* for Latin, plural of *vespera* evening]

vesper sparrow, a North American sparrow resembling the song sparrow but with its outer tail feathers white; grass finch.

Vesper Sparrow (6 in. long)

ves·per·til·i·o·nid (ves′pər til′ē ə nid), *n.* any of a group of widely distributed insectivorous bats of the temperate regions, as the myotis, pipistrel, hoary bat and evening bat. —*adj.* of or having to do with these bats. [< New Latin *Vespertilionidae* the family name < Latin *vespertīliō, -ōnis* a bat < *vesper* evening]

ves·per·til·i·o·nine (ves′pər til′ē ə nīn, -nin), *adj.* of or having to do with the vespertilionids. [< Latin *vespertīliō, -ōnis* a bat (< *vesper* evening) + *-ine*[1]]

ves·per·ti·nal (ves′pər tī′nəl), *adj.* vespertine.

ves·per·tine (ves′pər tin, -tīn), *adj.* **1.** of or having to do with the evening; occurring in the evening: *vespertine hours.* **2. a.** *Zoology.* flying or appearing in the early evening, as bats and owls. **b.** *Botany.* opening in the evening, as some flowers. **3.** descending toward the horizon in the evening: *a vespertine planet or star.* [< Latin *vespertīnus* < *vesper* evening]

ves·pi·ar·y (ves′pē er′ē), *n., pl.* **-ar·ies.** a nest or colony of social wasps. [< Latin *vespa* wasp; patterned on *apiary*]

ves·pid (ves′pid), *n.* a member of a widely distributed family of insects that includes hornets, yellow jackets, and certain wasps; vespid wasp. Some vespids live in colonies like bees and ants, others are solitary. —*adj.* belonging to or having to do with this family. [< New Latin *Vespidae* the family name < *Vespa* the typical genus < Latin *vespa* wasp]

vespid wasp, vespid.

ves·pi·form (ves′pə fôrm), *adj.* wasplike. [< Latin *vespa* wasp + *forma* form]

ves·pine (ves′pīn, -pin), *adj.* of or having to do with wasps; wasplike. [< Latin *vespa* wasp + English *-ine*[1]]

ves·sel (ves′əl), *n.* **1. a.** any large boat or ship, especially one larger than a canoe or rowboat, designed or equipped for conveying passengers, cargo, etc. **b.** *Law.* any floating structure. **2.** an airship. **3.** a hollow container designed to hold liquid or other substances, as a cup, bowl, pitcher, bottle, barrel, or tub. **4.** a tube or canal carrying and circulating blood, lymph, or other fluid in the body: *Veins and arteries are blood vessels.* **5.** *Botany.* **a.** one of the rows or chains of cells, an essential element of the xylem of plants, that have lost their intervening partitions and have become a long continuous canal permitting the passage of water and dissolved minerals; trachea or duct. **b.** a pericarp. **6.** a person regarded as a container of some quality or as made for some purpose: *a vessel of wrath, the weaker vessel.* [< Old French *vessel* < Latin *vascella,* plural (taken as feminine singular) of *vascellum* (diminutive) < *vās, vāsis* vessel] —**ves′sel·like′,** *adj.*

vest (vest), *n.* **1.** a short, buttoned, sleeveless garment worn by men under a suit coat or a jacket. **2.** a similar garment or part of a dress bodice made to resemble the front of a vest, worn by women. **3. a.** *British.* an undershirt. **b.** an undershirt specifically for a woman. **4.** a man's knee-length, sleeveless garment introduced by Charles II to be worn beneath the coat. **5. a.** a loose outer garment worn by men in Eastern countries or in ancient times; robe or gown. **b.** *Poetic.* a similar garment worn by women. **6.** an ecclesiastical vestment. **7.** *Archaic.* clothing; garment.
close to the vest, with great care and cunning so as to avoid all possible risks: *Modern chess masters, like modern generals, play . . . close to the vest . . ., stressing logistic planning and minutely synchronized attacks* (Newsweek).
[< Old French *veste* < Italian *vesta, veste* < Latin *vestis* garment]
—*v.t.* **1. a.** to clothe, robe, or dress (another person or oneself), especially in ecclesiastical vestments or for a ceremony. **b.** to cover or drape (an altar). **2.** to put in the possession or control of a person or persons: *The management of the hospital is vested in a board of trustees.* **3.** to furnish with powers, authority, rights, etc.: *Congress is vested with the power to declare war.* —*v.i.* **1.** to become vested; pass into possession; descend or devolve on a possessor: *The right of the crown vests upon his heir.* **2.** to dress in ecclesiastical vestment.
[< Old French *vestir* < Latin *vestīre* (literally) clothe < *vestis* garment]

Ves·ta (ves′tə), *n.* **1.** the Roman goddess of the hearth, the hearth fire, and the household, identified with the Greek goddess Hestia. A sacred fire, guarded by the Vestal Virgins, was always kept burning in the temple of Vesta. **2.** *Astronomy.* one of the asteroids or minor planets revolving in an orbit between Mars and Jupiter. It is 240 miles in diameter and the only asteroid visible to the naked eye. [< Latin *Vesta*]

ves·ta (ves′tə), *n.* **1.** a kind of short friction match: *The Skipper scratched a vesta and lit the brass student lamps at either end of the table* (Atlantic). **2.** *British.* a kind of wax match. [< *Vesta*]

ves·tal (ves′təl), *n.* **1.** one of the Vestal Virgins. **2.** a virgin: *She was the most . . . jovial of old vestals, and had been a beauty in her day* (Thackeray). **3.** a nun.
—*adj.* **1.** of or having to do with a vestal; suitable for a vestal. **2.** pure; chaste.

Vestal Virgin, one of the virgin priestesses of the Roman goddess Vesta. Six Vestal Virgins tended an undying fire in honor of Vesta at her temple in ancient Rome.

vest·ed (ves′tid), *adj.* **1.** placed in the possession or control of a person or persons; fixed; settled: *a vested privilege.* **2.** clothed, robed, or dressed, especially in church garments: *a vested choir.*

vested interest, 1. a legally established title to real or personal property. **2.** an interest in something that may be lost by change: *a vested interest in labor, a vested interest in segregation. The U.S. has a deep vested interest in Venezuela's political stability* (Newsweek). **3.** a group that stands to lose by change: *The fulfillment of many of these obligations will mean stepping on the toes of vested interests in both scientific and military spheres* (Bulletin of Atomic Scientists).

vested right, a legally established right to present and prospective enjoyment of a property.
vested rights, rights to pension benefits even if an employee leaves a company before the retirement age; vesting: *Vested rights . . . will vary with different types of plans, and are made available . . . on the basis of years of service, age, or length of participation in the pension program* (New York Times).

vest·ee (ves tē′), *n.* an ornamental vest worn by women as an insert on a dress bodice or between the open edges of a blouse or jacket; dickey. [American English < *vest* + *-ee*]

ves·ti·ar·y (ves′tē er′ē), *adj., n., pl.* **-ar·ies.** —*adj.* of, having to do with, or relating to clothes or dress. —*n.* **1.** a room or building, especially in a monastery or other large establishment, for keeping and storing vestments, clothes, or coats; cloakroom or wardrobe. **2.** a vestry of a church. [< Old French *vestiarie, vestiaire,* learned borrowings from Latin *vestiārium* clothes chest, neuter of *vestiārius* of clothing < *vestis* garment]

ves·tib·u·lar (ves tib′yə lər), *adj.* of, having to do with, or serving as a vestibule.

ves·tib·u·late (ves tib′yə lāt, -lit), *adj.* **1.** *Zoology.* having a vestibule. **2.** vestibular.

ves·ti·bule (ves′tə byül), *n., v.,* **-buled, -bul·ing.** —*n.* **1. a.** a passage, hall, or chamber immediately between the outer door and the inside of a building; an antechamber, entrance hall, or lobby. **b.** (in ancient Greek and Roman buildings) an enclosed or covered area in front of the main entrance; forecourt. **2.** the enclosed platform and entrance at one or both ends of a railroad passenger car, serving as a passage from one car (vestibule car) to another. **3.** *Zoology.* a cavity or hollow regarded as forming an approach or entrance to another (usually larger or more important) cavity. The vestibule of the ear is the central cavity of the internal ear.
—*v.t.* **1.** to replace the open platforms, once universal on railroad trains, by vestibules. **2.** to couple (railroad cars). [< Latin *vestibulum*]

vestibule school, the training department in an industrial plant, teaching new employees the skills necessary to do their work.

vestibule train, a railroad train composed of cars with vestibules.

ves·tige (ves′tij), *n.* **1.** a slight remnant; trace: *A blackened, charred stump was a vestige of a fire. Ghost stories are vestiges of a former widespread belief in ghosts.* **2.** *Biology.* a part, organ, etc., that is no longer fully developed or useful, but performed a definite function in an earlier stage of the existence of the same organism or in lower preceding organisms. **3.** *Rare.* a footprint; track. [< French *vestige,* learned borrowing from Latin *vestīgium* footprint] —**Syn. 1.** See **trace.**

ves·tig·i·al (ves tij′ē əl), *adj.* **1.** remaining as an indication of something that has disappeared. **2.** *Biology.* no longer fully developed or useful. —**ves·tig′i·al·ly,** *adv.*

ves·tig·i·um (ves tij′ē əm), *n., pl.* **-i·a** (-ē ə). **1.** *Biology.* a part, organ, etc., that is no longer fully developed or useful; vestige. **2.** *Obsolete.* a vestige in general. [< Latin *vestīgium* footprint, trace]

ves·ti·men·ta·ry (ves′tə men′tər ē), *adj.* of or having to do with clothes or dress, especially ecclesiastical garments: *The rest of the men ... were in white tie, hatless and gloveless, and with no white carnation—an omission that would have constituted vestimentary impropriety in the old days of the Third Republic* (New Yorker).

vest·ing[1] (ves′ting), *n.* cloth for making vests.

vest·ing[2] (ves′ting), *n.* vested rights: *By vesting is meant the rights given an employee under a pension plan. It usually denotes provisions for vested rights at certain ages and after specified years of service* (New York Times).

vest·less (vest′lis), *adj.* without a vest.

vest·ment (vest′mənt), *n.* **1. a.** one of the garments worn by clergymen, their assistants, the choristers, etc., in performing sacred duties or on some special occasion, and often indicative of the wearer's rank or the ceremony being performed. **b.** one of the garments worn by clergymen at the Eucharist, especially the chasuble. **2.** a garment, especially a robe or gown, worn by an official on a ceremonial occasion. **3.** something that covers as a garment; covering: *the green vestment of the meadow.* [< Old French *vestment,* alteration of Latin *vestimentum* < *vestīre* to clothe < *vestis* garment]

vest·men·tal (vest′mən təl), *adj.* vestimentary.

vest-pock·et (vest′pok′it), *adj.* **1.** able to fit in a vest pocket: *a vest-pocket radio.* **2.** very small: *a vest-pocket industry, a vest-pocket war.*

ves·try (ves′trē), *n., pl.* **-tries. 1.** a room, part of a church, or building attached to a church, where vestments, and often the sacred vessels, altar equipment, parish records, etc., are kept; sacristy. **2.** a similar place used for Sunday School, prayer meetings, etc.; a chapel. **3.** (in the Church of England and the Protestant Episcopal Church of America) an elected committee of church members acting with the churchwardens to manage church business. **4.** (in parishes of the Church of England) a meeting of the parishioners or their representatives on church business. [Middle English *vestrye,* perhaps < unrecorded Anglo-French *vesterie* < Old French *vestir* to vest, clothe + -*(e)rie* -ery]

ves·try·man (ves′trē mən), *n., pl.* **-men.** a member of a committee that helps manage church business.

vestry room, a room forming the vestry of a church.

ves·tur·al (ves′chər əl), *adj.* of or having to do with vesture or clothing.

ves·ture (ves′chər), *n., v.,* **-tured, -tur·ing.** —*n.* **1.** clothing; garments: *Pharaoh ... arrayed him in vestures of fine linen* (Genesis 41:42). **2.** a covering: *a suitable vesture for ideas.* **3.** *British Law.* everything that grows on, covers, or is a product of the land, except trees.
—*v.t.* to put clothing or vesture on; robe; vest.
[< Old French *vesture* < Late Latin *vestītūra* decoration < Latin *vestīre* to clothe < *vestis* garment]

ves·tur·er (ves′chər ər), *n.* **1.** a person who is in charge of the vestments worn in church. **2.** a person who assists the treasurer of a collegiate church or cathedral.

Ve·su·vi·an (və sü′vē ən), *adj.* of, having to do with, or resembling Mount Vesuvius, a volcano southeast of Naples, Italy; volcanic. —*n.* **1.** Sometimes, **vesuvian.** (formerly) a kind of match with a sputtering flame for lighting cigars, etc. **2.** vesuvianite.

ve·su·vi·an·ite (və sü′vē ə nīt), *n.* a mineral, a silicate of aluminum, calcium, iron, and magnesium, sometimes with other elements, occurring in massive or, more frequently, in square crystals of various colors; idocrase. [< *Vesuvian* (< *Vesuvius,* a volcano near Naples, Italy) + *-ite*[1]]

vet[1] (vet), *n., v.,* **vet·ted, vet·ting.** *Informal.* —*n.* a veterinarian. —*v.t.* **1.** to submit to examination or treatment by a veterinarian: *to vet a sick calf. I'd as soon vet a hippopotamus for nerves as you* (John Buchan). **2.** to subject to careful examination; scrutinize; check; test: *Every application for membership is carefully vetted, in such a way as to make it nearly impossible for anyone with no experience of fair business to enter it* (Economist). —*v.i.* to practice veterinary medicine.

vet[2] (vet), *n. Informal.* a veteran. [American English, short for *veteran*]

vet., 1. veteran. **2. a.** veterinarian. **b.** veterinary.

ve·tan·da (vē tan′də), *n.pl.* things to be forbidden. [< Latin *vetanda,* neuter plural gerundive of *vetāre* forbid]

vetch (vech), *n.* **1.** any of a group of (chiefly) climbing herbs of the pea family, species of which are much grown as food for cattle and sheep. **2.** any of several related plants, as the milk vetch. **3.** the beanlike fruit of certain of these plants. [< Old North French *veche* < Latin *vicia*]

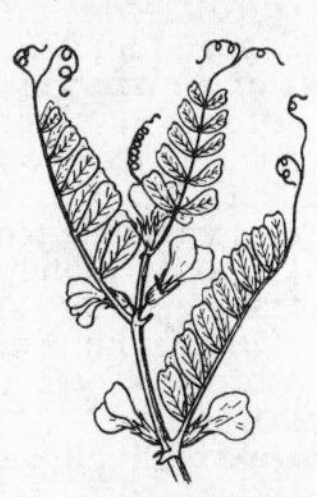
American Vetch (def. 1)

vetch·ling (vech′ling), *n.* any of a group of vetchlike herbs of the pea family, especially a common meadow weed.

veter., veterinary.

vet·er·an (vet′ər ən, vet′rən), *n.* **1.** a soldier or sailor who has had much experience in war; old soldier or sailor. **2. a.** a person who has served in the armed forces: *There are millions of American veterans from the second World War and the Korean War.* **b.** *U.S. Law.* a former member of any branch of the military service who meets the requirements for the extension of some benefit or privilege provided by law to honorably discharged servicemen. **3.** a person who has had much experience in some position or occupation: *He is a veteran in the printing trade.*
—*adj.* **1.** having had much experience in war: *Veteran troops fought side by side with new recruits.* **2.** grown old in service; having had much experience: *a veteran farmer.* **3.** (of things) old; long-continued: *veteran wines.*
[< Latin *veterānus* of old (that is, long) experience < *vetus, -eris* old]

Vet·er·ans Day (vet′ər ənz, vet′rənz), November 11, formerly Armistice Day. The name was changed by Congress in 1954.

vet·er·i·nar·i·an (vet′ər ə nãr′ē ən, vet′rə-), *n.* a doctor who treats animals; doctor of veterinary medicine.

vet·er·i·nar·y (vet′ər ə ner′ē, vet′rə-), *adj., n., pl.* **-nar·ies.** —*adj.* of or having to do with the medical or surgical treatment of animals. —*n.* a veterinarian. [< Latin *veterīnārius* < *veterīnus* having to do with beasts of burden, probably < *vetus, veteris* old (good for nothing else)]

veterinary medicine, the branch of medicine that deals with the causes, prevention, and medical or surgical treatment of diseases and injuries in animals, especially in domestic animals.

vet·i·ver (vet′ə vər), *n.* **1.** the fibrous aromatic roots of an East Indian grass grown in the tropics and the southern United States. They are made into mats, screens, etc., and yield vetiver oil; cuscus. **2.** the plant itself. [< French *vétiver* < Tamil *veṭṭivēru* (literally) root dug up < *vēr* root]

vetiver oil, a fragrant oil derived from vetiver, used in making perfumes, soaps, etc.

ve·to (vē′tō), *n., pl.* **-toes,** *adj., v.,* **-toed, -to·ing.** —*n.* **1.** the right or power of a president, governor, etc., to reject bills passed by a lawmaking body: *The President has the power of veto over most bills passed in Congress.* **2.** the right or power of one branch or part of a government to forbid or prevent an action of another branch or part. **3.** the right or power of any one member of a group or council to inhibit or prevent some action proposed by that body, especially in the United Nations Security Council: *a categorical demand for a veto-ridden three-man administrative control council* (Manchester Guardian). **4.** the use of any such rights: *The governor's veto kept the bill from becoming a law.* **5.** a statement of the reasons for disapproval of a bill passed by the legislature. **6.** the power or right to prevent action through prohibition. **7.** a refusal of consent; prohibition: *Our plan met with three vetoes—from father, mother, and teacher.*
—*adj.* having to do with a veto: *veto power.*
—*v.t.* **1.** to reject (a legislative measure) by a veto: *The President has vetoed two bills during this session of Congress.* **2.** to inhibit or prevent some action proposed by a group or council. **3.** to refuse to consent to.
[< Latin *vetō* I forbid, first person singular present of *vetāre* (used by Roman tribunes of the people in opposing senatorial or executive measures)] —**ve′to·er,** *n.*

vet·tu·ra (vet tü′rä), *n., pl.* **-re** (-rā). a kind of four-wheeled carriage used in Italy. [< Italian *vettura* < Latin *vectūra* carriage < *vehere* carry]

vet·tu·ri·no (vet′tü rē′nō), *n., pl.* **-ni** (-nē). in Italy: **1.** a person who lets out or drives a vettura. **2.** a vettura. [< Italian *vetturino* < *vettura;* see VETTURA]

vex (veks), *v.t.* **1.** to anger by trifles; annoy; provoke: *The child's rude remarks vexed his father.* **2.** to harass (a person, etc.) by aggression or interference with peace or quiet: *With such compelling cause to grieve As vexes the household peace* (Tennyson). **3.** to worry; distress deeply; trouble: *Uncertainty as to the justice of his decision vexed the judge.* **4.** to disturb by causing movement or commotion; agitate: *The island was much vexed by storms.* **5.** to discuss or debate at excessive length. **6.** *Poetic.* to subject to or affect with pain or suffering: *to vex the slave with torture.* —*v.i.* to feel annoyed, unhappy, or distressed: *It is vexing to have to wait a long time for anyone.* [< Middle French *vexer,* learned borrowing from Latin *vexāre*]

vex·a·tion (vek sā′shən), *n.* **1.** a vexing; being vexed: *His face showed his vexation.* **2.** a thing that vexes: *Rain on Saturday was a vexation to the children.* —**Syn. 1.** irritation, exasperation, annoyance, chagrin.

vex·a·tious (vek sā′shəs), *adj.* **1.** vexing; annoying: *a vexatious interruption of an interesting conversation.* **2.** *Law.* (of legal actions) brought with insufficient grounds for the purpose of causing trouble to the defendant. —**vex·a′tious·ly,** *adv.* —**vex·a′tious·ness,** *n.*

vexed (vekst), *adj.* **1.** annoyed; irritated; distressed. **2.** kept in a disturbed or unquiet state; troubled; harassed: *The situation of little magazines is so bound up with vexed questions of cultural economics and with wider questions about writing in modern societies that little can be said about it* (Peter Levi). **3.** subjected to physical force or strain; tossed about; agitated: *the vexed waters of the lake.*

vex·ed·ly (vek′sid lē), *adv.* with vexation; with a sense of annoyance or vexation.

vex·ed·ness (vek′sid nis), *n.* vexation; annoyance.

vex·il (vek′səl), *n.* vexillum.

vex·il·la (vek sil′ə), *n.* the plural of **vexillum.**

vex·il·lar (vek′sə lər), *adj.* **1.** (in ancient Rome) of or having to do with an ensign or standard. **2.** *Botany, Zoology.* of or having to do with the vexillum.

vex·il·lar·y (vek′sə ler′ē), *n., pl.* **-lar·ies,** *adj.* —*n.* in ancient Rome: **a.** one of the oldest class of army veterans serving under a special standard. **b.** a standardbearer. —*adj.* **1.** *Biology.* of or having to do with a vexillum. **2.** of or having to do with an ensign or standard. [< Latin *vexillārius,* noun use of adjective *vexillum* a standard; see VEXILLUM]

vexillary estivation, *Botany.* a mode of estivation in which the exterior petal, as in the case of the vexillum, is largest and encloses and folds over the other petals.

vex·il·late (vek′sə lāt, -lit), *adj. Biology.* having a vexillum or vexilla.

vex·il·lum (vek sil′əm), *n., pl.* **-la. 1.** a square flag or banner carried by ancient Roman troops. **2.** a body of troops grouped under such a flag or banner. **3.** *Botany.* the large upper external petal of a papilionaceous flower. **4.** *Zoology.* the web or vane of a feather. [< Latin *vexillum,* perhaps related to *vehere* to convey, or to *vēla* sail, covering]

vex·ing (vek′sing), *adj.* that vexes; annoying. —**vex′ing·ly,** *adv.*

vext (vekst), *adj.* vexed.

Vexillum (def. 1)

v.f., 1. video frequency. **2.** voice frequency.

VFO (no periods), variable frequency oscillator.

V force, a British airborne patrol for defense and warning against nuclear attack: *The V force ... at its maximum was believed to have numbered about 180 aircraft* (London Times).

VFR (no periods), visual flight rules.

V.F.W. or **VFW** (no periods), Veterans of Foreign Wars (an association of veterans of the U.S. Armed Forces who have taken part in wars in foreign countries).

v.g., for example (Latin, *verbi gratia*).

V.G., Vicar-General.

V-girl (vē′gėrl′), *n. U.S. Slang.* a girl or woman who follows or consorts with servicemen in wartime; a wartime camp follower.

VHF (no periods), **V.H.F.,** or **vhf** (no periods), very high frequency (of or having to do with the electromagnetic spectrum between 30 and 300 megacycles, especially with reference to radio and television transmission and reception).

v.i., **1.** intransitive verb. **2.** see below (Latin, *vide infra*).

Vi (no period), virginium (chemical element).

V.I., Virgin Islands.

vi·a (vī′ə, vē′-), *prep.* by way of; by a route that passes through or over: *He is going from New York to California via the Panama Canal.* [< Latin *viā*, ablative of *via* way]

vi·a·bil·i·ty (vī′ə bil′ə tē), *n.* **1.** the ability to keep alive; the quality or state of being viable: *Many in Seoul ... asked whether it should not be accepted that economic viability without unification was impossible* (Manchester Guardian). **2.** *Biology.* the ability to live in certain conditions of environment, as climatic or geographical.

vi·a·ble (vī′ə bəl), *adj.* **1.** able to keep alive: *viable people, a viable mutation.* **2.** fit to live in; livable: *a viable place. Only controlled disarmament can make a viable world in the nuclear age* (Stuart Chase). **3.** full of life; vigorous; active: *I hope that we can maintain a viable economy here* (John F. Kennedy). **4.** (of a fetus or newborn infant) sufficiently developed to maintain life outside the uterus. **5.** *Botany.* capable of living and growing, as a spore or seed. [< French *viable* < *vie* life < Latin *vīta*]

vi·a cru·cis (vī′ə krü′sis), *Latin.* **1.** a way marked by suffering and torment like that of Jesus: *the via crucis of a war orphan.* **2.** (literally) the way of the cross.

vi·a dol·o·ro·sa (vī′ə dol′ə rō′sə), *Latin.* **1.** a road or course of suffering and torment; via crucis. **2.** (literally) the sorrowful way. [< *Via Dolorosa*, the road in Jerusalem taken by Jesus from the hall of judgment to Calvary]

vi·a·duct (vī′ə dukt), *n.* **1. a.** a bridge consisting of a series of narrow arches of masonry or reinforced concrete supported by high piers, for carrying a road or railroad over a valley, a part of a city, a river, etc. **b.** a similar structure of steel with short spans supported by steel or concrete towers. **2.** any bridge over a road, railroad, canal, etc. [< Latin *via* road + English *-duct*, as in *aqueduct*]

vi·a·graph (vī′ə graf, -gräf), *n.* an instrument that indicates the resistance due to grades, inequalities of surface, etc., that a roadway presents to a wheeled vehicle running over it. [< Latin *via* road + English *-graph*]

vi·al (vī′əl), *n., v.,* **-aled, -al·ing** or (*especially British*) **-alled, -al·ling.** —*n.* **1.** a small glass or plastic bottle for holding medicines or liquids; bottle; phial. **2.** a store or accumulation (of wrath, indignation, etc.) poured out upon an offender, victim, or other object (originally in allusion to the seven vials full of the wrath of God mentioned in Revelations 15:7 and 16:1-17): *For one so patient and good, he had a very large vial of indignation, and on occasion poured it out right heartily over all injustice* (W.G. Blaikie). —*v.t.* to put, keep, or store in a vial. [Middle English *viole, vial*, variant of *fiol* phial]

vi·a me·di·a (vī′ə mē′dē ə), *Latin.* a middle way; intermediate course (especially applied to the Anglican church as standing halfway between the Roman Catholic and Protestant beliefs).

vi·and (vī′ənd), *n.* an article or kind of food. **viands,** articles of choice food: *When I demanded of my friend what viands he preferred, He quoth: "A large cold bottle, and a small hot bird"* (Eugene Field).
[< Anglo-French *viaunde*, Old French *viande* < Vulgar Latin *vīvanda*, for Late Latin *vīvenda* things for living < Latin, to be lived, neuter plural gerundive of *vīvere* to live]

vi·at·ic (vī at′ik), *adj.* viatical. [< Latin *viāticus* of a journey < *via* way]

vi·at·i·cal (vī at′ə kəl), *adj.* of or having to do with a road or way; relating to a journey. —*n.* **viaticals,** articles used or carried along in traveling, especially military baggage: *His back would have been bent ... under the weight of armour and viaticals which Titus carried with him easily and far* (Walter Savage Landor).

vi·at·i·cum (vī at′ə kəm), *n., pl.* **-ca** (-kə), **-cums. 1.** Holy Communion given to or received by one who is dying or in danger of death. **2.** supplies or money for a journey. **3.** (in ancient Rome) supplies and transportation or money given to a public official traveling on state business. [< Latin *viāticum*, noun use of neuter adjective, of a journey < *via* road, journey. Doublet of VOYAGE.]

vi·a·tor (vī ā′tər), *n., pl.* **vi·a·tor·es** (vī′ə-tôr′ēz, -tōr′-). **1.** a traveler; wayfarer. **2.** (in ancient Rome) a servant of certain magistrates, one of whose duties was to deliver summonses. [< Latin *viātor, -ōris* < *via* way]

vibes (vībz), *n.pl. U.S. Slang.* a vibraphone or vibraharp: *Playing the vibes, he joins with guitar and bass for some stimulating reflections on such tunes as Cabin in the Sky, That Old Black Magic [etc.]* (Time).

vi·brac·u·la (vī brak′yə lə), *n.* the plural of **vibraculum.**

vi·brac·u·lar (vī brak′yə lər), *adj.* **1.** of, having to do with, or caused by vibracula. **2.** having vibracula.

vi·brac·u·loid (vī brak′yə loid), *adj.* resembling a vibraculum or vibracula.

vi·brac·u·lum (vī brak′yə ləm), *n., pl.* **-la.** *Zoology.* one of the long, slender, whiplike, movable appendages or organs of certain bryozoans. [< New Latin *vibraculum* < Latin *vibrāre* to shake, oscillate]

vi·bra·harp (vī′brə härp′), *n.* a vibraphone.

vi·bra·harp·ist (vī′brə här′pist), *n.* a vibraphonist.

vi·brance (vī′brəns), *n.* vibrancy: *Rich, glowing shades give vibrance to evening dresses of delicate fabrics* (New York Times).

vi·bran·cy (vī′brən sē), *n.* the quality or condition of being vibrant: *Athens is vibrant; the merit of his book is that it communicates this sense of vibrancy* (New York Times).

vi·brant (vī′brənt), *adj.* **1.** (of sound) characterized by or exhibiting vibration; resounding; resonant. **2. a.** moving or quivering rapidly; vibrating: *a vibrant tongue, a vibrant string.* **b.** vibrating or thrilling something (with): *The stock exchange was vibrant with speculation.* **3.** *Obsolete.* **a.** agitated with anger or emotion. **b.** moving or acting with rapidity or energy. **4.** *Phonetics.* voiced.
—*n. Phonetics.* a vibrant sound.
[< Latin *vibrāns, -antis*, present participle of *vibrāre* to vibrate, shake] —**vi′brant·ly,** *adv.*

vi·bra·phone (vī′brə fōn), *n.* a musical instrument similar to the xylophone, consisting of metal bars and electrically operated resonators that produce rich, vibrant tones: *A recently formed group made up of vibraphone, piano, bass, and drums provides on its first release ... a refreshing contrast* (New Yorker). [< *vibra*(te) + *-phone*]

vi·bra·phon·ist (vī′brə fō′nist), *n.* a person who plays a vibraphone: *Gibbs ... is an astonishingly energetic vibraphonist who drives both his imagination and arms so hard in the course of every number that you begin to fear for his health* (New Yorker).

vi·brate (vī′brāt), *v.,* **-brat·ed, -brat·ing.** —*v.i.* **1. a.** to move rapidly to and fro: *A snake's tongue vibrates. A piano string vibrates and makes a sound when a key is struck.* **b.** *Physics.* to swing to and fro or otherwise move in an alternating or reciprocating motion by disturbing the equilibrium of the particles in an elastic body. **c.** (of a pendulum, etc.) to swing to and fro; oscillate. **2.** to move or oscillate between extreme conditions, opinions, etc.; fluctuate; vacillate. **3.** to thrill: *Their hearts vibrated to the speaker's stirring appeal.* **4. a.** (of sound) to continue to be heard; strike; sound; resound: *The clanging vibrated in his ears.* **b.** to circulate, move, pass, or pierce by or as by vibration (about, through, to): *The mournful sound of the tolling bell vibrated through the air.* —*v.t.* **1.** to cause to move to and fro or up and down, especially with a quick motion; set in vibration: *Virginian rattlesnakes ... swiftly vibrating and shaking their tails* (John Evelyn). **2.** to measure by moving to and fro: *A pendulum vibrates seconds.* **3. a.** to send out, give forth, or emit (light, sound, etc.) by or as by vibration. **b.** *Obsolete.* to launch or hurl (a thunderbolt, sentence, etc.). [< Latin *vibrāre* (with English *-ate*[1]) to shake] —**Syn.** *v.i.* **1. a.** quiver, shake, tremble, throb.

vi·bra·tile (vī′brə təl, -tīl), *adj.* **1.** that can vibrate or be vibrated. **2.** having a vibratory motion. **3.** having to do with, marked, or characterized by vibration.

vi·bra·til·i·ty (vī′brə til′ə tē), *n.* the property or state of being vibratile; disposition to vibration or oscillation.

vi·bra·tion (vī brā′shən), *n.* **1. a.** a rapid or, sometimes, continuous movement to and fro or up and down; quivering or swaying motion; vibrating: *The buses shake the house so much that we feel the vibration.* **b.** an instance of this; quiver; tremor: *The vibration of the ground during an earthquake is terrifying. The vibrations of deathless music* (Edgar Lee Masters). **2. a.** the act of moving or swinging to and fro, especially of a pendulum or other suspended body; oscillation. **b.** a single swing or oscillation. **3.** *Physics.* **a.** the rapid alternating or reciprocating motion back and forth, or up and down, produced in the particles of an elastic body or medium by the disturbance of equilibrium. When the reciprocating movement is comparatively slow, as that of a pendulum, the term *oscillation* is commonly used, while the term *vibration* is generally confined to a motion with rapid reciprocations or revolutions. **b.** a single movement of this kind. **4.** a vacillating or varying of conduct or opinion; change or swinging around: *a great vibration of opinion* (George Bancroft).

vi·bra·tion·al (vī brā′shə nəl), *adj.* of, having to do with, or of the nature of vibration: *The lower the musical tone, the smaller is the number of vibrational cycles a second* (Simeon Potter). —**vi·bra′tion·al·ly,** *adv.*

vi·bra·tion·less (vī brā′shən lis), *adj.* free from vibration.

vi·bra·tion-proof (vī brā′shən prüf′), *adj.* that will not vibrate: *Vibration-proof buildings near the jet runways will soon be required.*

vi·bra·ti·un·cle (vī brā′shē ung′kəl), *n.* a slight vibration: *We may gain new respect for the speculations of the English physician-philosopher David Hartley, who 200 years ago suggested that ideas were represented in the brain as vibrations and vibratiuncles* (Scientific American). [a diminutive form of *vibration*]

vi·bra·tive (vī′brə tiv), *adj.* vibrating; vibratory.

vi·bra·to (vē brä′tō), *n., pl.* **-tos,** *adv. Music.* —*n.* a vibrating or pulsating effect produced in the human voice or on stringed and wind instruments by a wavering of pitch, for shading or expressive purposes: *Betty Bennett's voice, a young, clear one with an agreeable vibrato, floats along prettily above some cool but frequently overintellectual jazz arrangements* (New Yorker). —*adv.* with much vibration of tone. [< Italian *vibrato* < *vibrare* vibrate < Latin *vibrāre*]

vi·bra·tor (vī′brā tər), *n.* **1.** a thing that vibrates. **2.** any of various appliances, instruments, or parts that have or cause a vibratory motion or action: **a.** a hammer, as in an electric bell, that vibrates. **b.** one of the vibrating reeds of an organ. **3.** an electrical device used to massage a part of the body: *Electric vibrators are used on the scalp.* **4.** *Electricity.* **a.** an apparatus for setting a given component in vibration by means of continual impulses. **b.** a device for causing oscillations.

vi·bra·to·ry (vī′brə tôr′ē, -tōr′-), *adj.* **1. a.** vibrating or easily vibrated: *a vibratory set of strings.* **b.** capable of vibration: *a tuning fork is vibratory.* **2.** of or having to do with vibration: *vibratory motion.* **3.** causing or producing vibration: *a vibratory current of electricity.* **4.** of the nature of, characterized by, or consisting of vibration: *Periodic oscillation is vibratory.*

vib·ri·o (vib′rē ō), *n., pl.* **-ri·os.** *Bacteriology.* any of a group of short, curved bacteria, often shaped like a comma, spiral, or S, and characterized by lively motion, as the species that causes Asiatic cholera. [< New Latin *Vibrio* the genus name < Latin *vibrāre* to vibrate]

vib·ri·oid (vib′rē oid), *adj.* resembling a vibrio.

vibrioid body, *Botany.* any of various cylindrical bodies present in the outer layers of the cytoplasm of certain algae and fungi.

vib·ri·o·sis (vib′rē ō′sis), *n.* a disease of cattle and sheep caused by a species of vibrio and characterized by abortion or infertility. [< *vibrio* + *-osis*]

vi·bris·sa (vī bris′ə), *n., pl.* **-bris·sae** (-bris′ē). **1.** *Anatomy.* a hair growing in a nostril. **2.** *Zoology.* one of the long, bristlelike, tactile organs growing upon the upper lip and elsewhere on the head of most mammals; a whisker, as of a mouse. **3.** *Zoology.* one of the special set of long, slender, bristlelike feathers that grow in a series along each side of the rictus (gape of the mouth) of many birds, as flycatchers and goatsuckers. The vibrissae entangle the legs and wings of insects, and thus diminish or prevent their struggling when caught. [< Late Latin *vibrissae,* plural < Latin *vibrāre* to vibrate]

vi·bro·graph (vī′brə graf, -gräf), *n.* an instrument for recording vibrations: *Vibrographs installed in the rooms of the temples provided the criteria for the mode of excavation used* (New Scientist). [< Latin *vibrāre* vibrate + English *-graph*]

vi·bro·scope (vī′brə skōp), *n.* an instrument for observing or for registering vibrations. [< Latin *vibrāre* to vibrate + English *-scope*]

vi·bur·num (vī bėr′nəm), *n.* **1.** any of an extensive group of shrubs or small trees of the honeysuckle family, natives of the northern hemisphere and of the Andes, having showy clusters of white or pinkish flowers, as the snowball, withe rod, and dockmackie. **2.** the dried bark of certain species, used in medicine. [< Latin *vīburnum*]

Viburnum (def. 1)

vic·ar (vik′ər), *n.* **1.** in the Church of England: **a.** the minister of a parish, who receives a salary from the legal holder of the tithes. **b.** a person acting as parish priest in place of the actual rector. **2.** in the Protestant Episcopal Church: **a.** a clergyman in charge of a chapel subordinate to a parish church. **b.** a clergyman acting for a bishop, in a church where the bishop is rector or in a mission. **3.** in the Roman Catholic Church: **a.** a clergyman who represents the Pope or a bishop. **b.** the Pope, as the earthly representative of God or Christ. **4.** a person acting, or appointed to act, in place of another, especially in administrative functions; representative; vicegerent. [< Anglo-French *vikere, vicare,* Old French *vicaire,* learned borrowing from Latin *vicārius* (originally) substituted < *vicis* change, alteration. Doublet of VICARIOUS.]

Vi·car·a (vī kar′ə), *n. Trademark.* a woollike synthetic fiber made from zein, a protein abstracted from corn: *Vicara . . . is used in blends with wool and synthetics to produce knit and woven fabrics having the soft, lofty feeling of cashmere* (William D. Appel). [< *Vi*(rginia) *-Car*(olin)*a* chemical company that produces this fiber]

vic·ar·age (vik′ər ij), *n.* **1.** the residence or household of a vicar: *She goes to every service at the church, but is not a frequenter of the vicarage* (J.W.R. Scott). **2.** the position, office, or duties of a vicar. **3.** the salary paid to a vicar.

vicar apostolic, in the Roman Catholic Church: **a.** a missionary or titular bishop stationed either in a country where no episcopal see has yet been established, or in one where the succession of bishops has been interrupted. **b.** (formerly) a bishop, archbishop, or other ecclesiastic with delegated authority from the Pope.

vic·ar·ate (vik′ə rāt, -ər it), *n.* a parish or district under the jurisdiction of a vicar; vicariate.

vicar choral, an assistant to the canons or prebendaries of the Church of England in the parts of public worship performed in the chancel or choir, especially in connection with the music.

vic·ar·ess (vik′ər is), *n.* **1.** the Roman Catholic sister ranking immediately beneath the abbess or mother superior in a convent: *In 1931 she was elected vicaress (second in command), and in 1935 she spent a year traveling as Mother Mary Joseph's deputy* (Time). **2. a.** the wife of a Protestant Episcopal vicar. **b.** a woman vicar in the Protestant Episcopal Church.

vicar fo·rane (fə rān′), (in the Roman Catholic Church) an ecclesiastic dignitary or parish priest appointed by a bishop to exercise a limited jurisdiction in a particular town or district of his diocese. [*forane* < Late Latin *forāneus* living outside. Compare FOREIGN.]

vic·ar-gen·er·al (vik′ər jen′ər əl, -jen′rəl), *n., pl.* **vic·ars-gen·er·al. 1.** (in the Roman Catholic Church) a deputy of a bishop or an archbishop assisting him in the administration of a diocese. **2.** (in the Church of England) an ecclesiastical officer, usually a layman, serving as deputy or assistant to a bishop or to the Archbishop of Canterbury or York in legal or jurisdictional matters. **3.** the title given to Thomas Cromwell by Henry VIII in 1535 as his representative in ecclesiastical affairs.

vi·car·i·al (vī kãr′ē əl, vi-), *adj.* **1.** of or belonging to a vicar or vicars. **2.** holding the office of a vicar. **3.** delegated, as duties or authority; vicarious.

vi·car·i·ate (vī kãr′ē it, -āt; vi-), *n.* **1. a.** the office or authority of a vicar. **b.** a district in the charge of a vicar. **2. a.** a political office held by a person as deputy for another. **b.** the exercise of delegated authority by a person or governing body. **c.** a district under the rule of a deputy governor.

vi·car·i·ous (vī kãr′ē əs, vi-), *adj.* **1.** done or suffered for others: *vicarious work, vicarious punishment.* **2.** felt by sharing in the experience of another: *The invalid received vicarious pleasure from reading travel stories.* **3.** taking the place of another; doing the work of another: *a vicarious agent.* **4.** delegated: *vicarious authority.* **5.** based upon the substitution of one person for another: *this vicarious structure of society, based upon what others do for us.* **6.** *Physiology.* denoting the performance by or through one organ of functions normally discharged by another; substitutive. [< Latin *vicārius* (with English *-ous*) substituted < *vicis* a turn, change, substitution. Doublet of VICAR.] —**vi·car′i·ous·ly,** *adv.* —**vi·car′i·ous·ness,** *n.*

vicarious menstruation, bleeding from some part other than the uterus at the time of and instead of menstruation.

vic·ar·ly (vik′ər lē), *adj.* having to do with, appropriate to, or resembling a vicar, especially in dress.

Vicar of Bray, a person who changes his principles or opinions to suit the time or circumstances. [< a *vicar of Bray* in the 1500's, in Berkshire, England, who is said to have held his office in this way]

Vicar of Christ, (in the Roman Catholic Church) the Pope, as standing in the place of and acting for Christ.

vic·ar·ship (vik′ər ship), *n.* the office or position of a vicar.

vice[1] (vīs), *n.* **1.** an evil, immoral, or wicked habit or tendency: *Lying and cruelty are vices.* **2.** evil; wickedness: *There is never an instant's truce between virtue and vice* (Thoreau). **3.** a moral fault or defect; a flaw in character or conduct: *So for a good old-gentlemanly vice, I think I must take up with avarice* (Byron). *Ferocity and insolence were not among the vices of the national character* (Macaulay). **4.** a mechanical defect in action or procedure; an imperfection in the construction, arrangement, or constitution of a thing. **5.** a physical defect or blemish; an imperfection or weakness in some part of the system. **6.** (of horses) any of several bad habits or tricks, as bolting or shying. **7.** Also, **Vice.** (formerly) a buffoon, often named for some vice, who supplied the comic relief in English morality plays. [< Old French *vice,* learned borrowing from Latin *vitium*] —**Syn. 2.** sin, iniquity, depravity, corruption.

vice[2] (vīs), *n., v.t.,* **viced, vic·ing.** *Especially British.* vise.

vi·ce[3] (vī′sē), *prep.* instead of; in the place of; in succession to. [< Latin *vice,* adverb; properly ablative of *vicis* a turn, change]

vice-, *prefix.* one who acts in place of another; substitute; deputy; subordinate, as in *viceroy, vice-president, vice-chairman, vice-admiral, vice-chancellor.* [< Late Latin *vice-* < Latin *vice* vice[3]]

vice-ad·mi·ral (vīs′ad′mər əl), *n.* a naval officer ranking next below an admiral and next above a rear admiral. *Abbr.:* V.Adm.

vice-ad·mi·ral·ty (vīs′ad′mər əl tē), *n., pl.* **-ties.** the rank or position of a vice-admiral.

vice-chair·man (vīs′chãr′mən), *n., pl.* **-men.** a person who substitutes for the regular chairman, or acts as his assistant: *In the absence of the chairman, the vice-chairman presided over the meeting.*

vice-chan·cel·lor (vīs′chan′sə lər, -chän′-), *n.* **1.** a person who substitutes for the regular chancellor or acts as his assistant. **2.** an officer of a university, acting for the chancellor, and in fact the chief administrative officer. **3.** *Law.* a judge in a court of equity who assists the chancellor (presiding judge).

vice-chan·cel·lor·ship (vīs′chan′sə lər-ship, -chän′-), *n.* **1.** the office or dignity of a vice-chancellor. **2.** the term of office of a vice-chancellor.

vice-con·sul (vīs′kon′səl), *n.* a person next in rank below a consul. He acts as his assistant or substitute or, in more remote areas, his agent. *Abbr.:* V.C.

vice-con·su·lar (vīs′kon′sə lər), *adj.* of or having to do with a vice-consul.

vice-con·su·late (vīs′kon′sə lit), *n.* vice-consulship.

vice-con·sul·ship (vīs′kon′səl ship), *n.* **1.** the office or duties of a vice-consul. **2.** the term of office of a vice-consul.

vice·ge·ral (vīs′jir′əl), *adj.* of or having to do with a vicegerent.

vice·ge·ren·cy (vīs′jir′ən sē), *n., pl.* **-cies. 1.** the position or administration of vicegerent. **2.** a district or province ruled by a vicegerent.

vice·ge·rent (vīs′jir′ənt), *n.* **1.** a person appointed by a king or other ruler to act in his place or exercise his powers, authority, or administrative duties: *He was trusted by the sultan as the faithful vicegerent of his power* (Edward Gibbon). **2.** a person who takes the place of another in the discharge of some office or duty; deputy.
—*adj.* **1.** taking the place or performing the functions of another. **2.** characterized by delegated power: *Under his great Vicegerent reign abide . . . For ever happy* (Milton).
[< Medieval Latin *vicegerens, -entis* < Latin *vice* instead (of) + *gerere* to manage]

vice·less (vīs′lis), *adj.* free from vice.

vice·like (vīs′līk), *adj. Especially British.* viselike: *Peak hour control of America's traffic flow has been developed to a fine art, mainly by a vicelike grip on all waiting vehicles* (London Times).

vic·e·nar·y (vis′ə ner′ē), *adj.* **1.** having to do with or consisting of twenty. **2.** *Mathematics.* having 20 for the base: *a vicenary scale.* [< Latin *vīcēnārius* of twenty < *vīcēnī* twenty each < *vīgintī* twenty]

vi·cen·ni·al (vī sen′ē əl, -sen′yəl), *adj.* **1.** of or for twenty years. **2.** occurring once in twenty years. [< Latin *vīcennium* twenty-year period (< stem of *vīciēs* twenty times + *annus* year) + English *-al*[1]]

vice-pre·mier (vīs′pri mir′, -prē′mē ər), *n.* a deputy or assistant premier; an official ranking immediately below a premier: *This would be another promotion for Muñoz Grandes, who was named vice-premier in a Cabinet change in July 1962* (Bruce B. Solnick).

Vice Pres., Vice-President.

vice-pres·i·den·cy (vīs′prez′ə dən sē, -prez′dən-), *n.* the position of vice-president.

vice-pres·i·dent (vīs′prez′ə dənt, -prez′dənt), *n.* an officer next in rank to the president, who takes the president's place when necessary. The Vice-President of the United States is elected at the same time as the President, serves as president of the Senate but without a vote except in cases of ties, may participate in cabinet meetings if invited by the President, and becomes President in the event of the death, removal, resignation, or disability of the President. *Abbr.:* V.P.

vice-pres·i·den·tial (vīs′prez ə den′shəl), *adj.* of or having to do with the vice-president.

vice·re·gal (vīs′rē′gəl), *adj.* of or having to do with a viceroy. —**vice′re′gal·ly,** *adv.*

vice-re·gen·cy (vīs′rē′jən sē), *n., pl.* **-cies. 1.** the office or duties of a vice-regent. **2.** the term of office of a vice-regent.

vice-re·gent (vīs′rē′jənt), *n.* a person who takes the place of the regular regent whenever necessary; deputy regent. —*adj.* of, having to do with, or occupying the position of a vice-regent.

vice·roy (vīs′roi), *n.* **1.** a person ruling a country, colony, or province as the deputy of the sovereign. 2. an American butterfly, whose coloration and markings closely resemble those of the monarch butterfly, and whose larvae feed on willow, poplar, and other trees. [< French *vice-roi* < *vice* vice[3] + *roi* king < Latin *rēx, rēgis*]

vice·roy·al·ty (vīs′roi′əl tē), *n., pl.* **-ties.** 1. the office, rank, or authority of a viceroy. 2. a country, colony, or province administered by a viceroy. 3. the period during which a particular viceroy holds office.

vice·roy·ship (vīs′roi ship), *n.* the dignity, office, or jurisdiction of a viceroy; viceroyalty.

vice squad, *U.S.* a police squad responsible for enforcing laws against gambling and other vices: *In Detroit, a vice squad broke up a dice game, smashed dice tables and chairs, carted the players off to jail* (Time).

vi·ce ver·sa (vī′sē vėr′sə, vīs), the other way round; conversely; *John blamed Harry, and vice versa (Harry blamed John).* [< Latin *vice versa* < *vice* vice[3] + *vertere* to turn]

Vich·y (vish′ē), *n.* Vichy water.

Vich·y·ite (vish′ē īt), *n.* a supporter of the government of unoccupied France from July, 1940 to August, 1944, and its policy of collaboration with the Nazis. [< *Vichy*, the capital of unoccupied France + *-ite*[1]]

Vi·chys·sois (vē shē swȧ′), *adj.* 1. of or having to do with the city of Vichy in central France. 2. of or supporting the Vichyite government: *Later still as Nuncio in Paris, he defended the accused Vichyssois bishops* (London Times).
—*n.* 1. a native or inhabitant of the city of Vichy. 2. a Vichyite.
[< French *vichyssois* of *Vichy*]

vi·chys·soise (vish′ē swäz′), *n.* a creamy potato-and-leek soup, sprinkled with chives, and served cold: *Vichyssoise is unquestionably a good soup and a great help in hot weather* (New Yorker). [< French *vichyssoise*, feminine, ultimately < *Vichy*, a city in France, near where the originator of the soup was born]

Vi·chys·soise (vē shē swȧz′), *n. French.* the feminine of **Vichyssois.**

Vichy water, 1. a natural mineral water from springs at Vichy, France, containing sodium bicarbonate and other salts, used in the treatment of digestive disturbances, gout, etc. 2. a natural or artificial water of similar composition.

vic·i·nage (vis′ə nij), *n.* 1. a. surrounding district; neighborhood; vicinity: *to know well the people in his own vicinage.* b. the people living in a certain district or neighborhood: *and to his thought the whole vicinage was haunted by her* (George Eliot). 2. a being or living close to another or others; nearness; proximity. [< Old French *vicenage, voisinage* < *voisin* < Latin *vīcīnus*, see VICINITY]

vic·i·nal (vis′ə nəl), *adj.* 1. neighboring; adjacent; near. 2. local. 3. of or like a vicinal plane. [< Latin *vīcīnālis* < *vīcīnus;* see VICINITY]

vicinal plane, *Mineralogy.* a subordinate plane in a crystal whose position varies little from that of the fundamental plane which it replaces.

vicinal way or **road,** a local road, as distinguished from a highway; crossroad.

vi·cin·i·ty (və sin′ə tē), *n., pl.* **-ties.** 1. the region or area about, near, or adjoining a place; neighborhood; surrounding district: *He knew many people in New York and its vicinity.* 2. nearness in place; being close: *The vicinity of the apartment to his office was an advantage.*
in the vicinity of, in the neighborhood of; near or close to: *a park in the vicinity of town, a boat costing in the vicinity of $1000.*
[< Latin *vīcīnitās* < *vīcīnus* neighbor, neighboring < *vicus* quarter, village, habitation] —**Syn.** 2. propinquity, proximity.

vi·cious (vish′əs), *adj.* 1. evil; wicked: *vicious and weak conduct, a vicious criminal, a dictator's vicious love of power.* 2. having bad habits or a bad disposition; savage: *a vicious horse, the vicious temper of the old man.* 3. spiteful; malicious: *I won't listen to such vicious gossip.* 4. *Informal.* unpleasantly severe: *a vicious headache.* 5. not correct; having faults: *This argument contains vicious reasoning. Oliver's Latin was vicious and scanty* (John Morley). 6. *Logic.* faulty, in the manner of a vicious circle. 7. *Obsolete.* foul; impure; noxious. 8. *Obsolete.* (of a part or function of the body) diseased; irregular. [< Anglo-French *vicious*, Old French *vicieux*, learned borrowing from Late Latin *viciōsus*, for Latin *vitiōsus* < *vitium* fault, vice[1]] —**vi′cious·ly,** *adv.* —**vi′cious·ness,** *n.*

vicious circle, 1. two or more undesirable things, each of which keeps causing the other. 2. *Logic.* a. false reasoning that uses one statement to prove a second statement when the first statement really depends upon the second for proof. b. an inconclusive form of definition, in which two or more undefined terms or their equivalents are used to define each other. 3. *Pathology.* an abnormal process in which one disease or condition causes a second disease that then aggravates the first.

vi·cis·si·tude (və sis′ə tüd, -tyüd), *n.* 1. a change in circumstances or fortune: *The vicissitudes of life may suddenly make a rich man very poor.* 2. a change; variation; mutation: *the whirlpool of political vicissitude* (Hawthorne). 3. regular change: *the vicissitudes of day and night.* [< Latin *vicissitūdō, -inis* < *vicissim* changeably < *vicis* a turn, change]

vi·cis·si·tu·di·nar·y (və sis′ə tü′də ner′ē, -tyü′-), *adj.* marked by alternation; coming alternately or by turns.

vi·cis·si·tu·di·nous (və sis′i tü′də nəs, -tyü′-), *adj.* subject to or experiencing changes of fortune or circumstances.

Vick·ers test (vik′ərz), a method of determining the hardness of metals by indenting them with a diamond pyramid under a specified load and measuring the size of the indentation. It is especially useful for thin samples. [< the *Vickers* Works, a British industrial firm]

vi·comte (vē kôNt′), *n. French.* viscount.

vi·com·tesse (vē kôN tes′), *n. French.* viscountess.

vi·con·ti·el (vī kon′tē əl), *adj. Law.* (in English history) of or having to do with a sheriff or a viscount. [< Anglo-French *vicontiel* < *viconte* viscount]

vic·tim (vik′təm), *n.* 1. a. a person or animal sacrificed, injured, or destroyed: *victims of war, victims of an accident.* b. a person who suffers some hardship or loss: *a victim of poverty.* c. a person who dies or suffers, etc., as a result of voluntarily undertaking some enterprise or pursuit: *a victim of overwork.* 2. a person badly treated or taken advantage of; dupe: *the victim of a swindler.* 3. a person or animal killed and offered as a sacrifice to a god. [< Latin *victima*]

vic·tim·ise (vik′tə mīz), *v.t.,* **-ised, -is·ing.** *Especially British.* victimize: *These safeguards should ensure that the owners are not victimised* (Economist).

vic·tim·iz·a·ble (vik′tə mī′zə bəl), *adj.* that can be victimized.

vic·tim·i·za·tion (vik′tə mə zā′shən), *n.* a victimizing or being victimized: *The descriptions of rituals disclose that the supposedly idyllic South Seas were a scene of rampant cannibalism, tribal wars, human sacrifices, and victimization of children* (Scientific American).

vic·tim·ize (vik′tə mīz), *v.t.,* **-ized, -iz·ing.** 1. to make a victim of; cause to suffer. 2. to cheat; swindle; defraud. 3. to put to death as or like a sacrificial victim; slaughter.

vic·tim·iz·er (vik′tə mī′zər), *n.* a person who victimizes another or others.

vic·tor (vik′tər), *n.* a winner; conqueror: *They see nothing wrong in the rule that to the victors belong the spoils of the enemy* (William Marcy). —*adj.* triumphant; victorious: *Despite thy victor sword . . . thou art a traitor* (Shakespeare). [< Latin *victor, -ōris* < *vincere* to conquer]

Vic·tor (vik′tər), *n. U.S.* a code name for the letter *v*, used in transmitting radio messages.

Victor Charlie, *U.S. Military Slang.* Vietcong: *Said one marine rifleman recently, "I ain't seen one of them Victor Charlies since I been here"* (Time). [< *Victor Charlie*, the code name for *V.C.*, abbreviation of *Vietcong*]

vic·to·ri·a (vik tôr′ē ə, -tōr′-), *n.* 1. a low, four-wheeled carriage with a folding top, a seat for two passengers, and a raised seat in front for the driver, popular in the 1800's. 2. an open automobile with a folding top covering the rear seat only. 3. a South American water lily with huge, strong, circular leaves often six feet or more in diameter, and a solitary, rose-white, nocturnal flower usually 12 to 14 inches in diameter. [< French *victoria* < *Victoria*, 1819-1901, Queen of England]

Victoria (def. 1)

Victoria Cross, a bronze Maltese cross awarded to British soldiers and sailors as a decoration for remarkable valor during battle.

Victoria Day, Empire Day, the anniversary of the birthday of Queen Victoria, May 24.

Vic·to·ri·an (vik tôr′ē ən, -tōr′-), *adj.* 1. of or having to do with the reign or time of Queen Victoria of England (1837-1901). 2. possessing characteristics considered typical of Victorians, as prudishness, bigotry, and conventionality.
—*n.* 1. a person, especially an author, who lived during the reign of Queen Victoria. 2. an article of furniture, piece of clothing, etc., from or identified with the time of Queen Victoria.

Victorian Sofa (def. 2)

Vic·to·ri·a·na (vik tôr′ē ä′nə, -an′ə, -ā′nə; -tōr′-), *n.pl.* furniture, clothing, books, facts, etc., belonging to the Victorian period: *There are visions of interiors crammed with Victoriana, of walls hung with holy pictures and framed diplomas* (New Yorker).

Victorian age, the period during the reign of Queen Victoria of England, from 1837 to 1901.

Vic·to·ri·an·ism (vik tôr′ē ə niz′əm, -tōr′-), *n.* 1. the ideas, beliefs, morals, way of living, etc., common during the reign of Queen Victoria. 2. a novel, piece of furniture, building, etc., characteristic of the Victorian age.

Vic·to·ri·an·ly (vik tôr′ē ən lē, -tōr′-), *adv.* in a Victorian manner: *The tone and manner of this song were Victorianly simple* (Chambers's Journal).

vic·to·ri·ous (vik tôr′ē əs, -tōr′-), *adj.* 1. having won a victory; conquering: *a victorious army.* 2. of or having to do with victory; belonging to or producing victory: *a victorious war.* —**vic·to′ri·ous·ly,** *adv.* —**vic·to′ri·ous·ness,** *n.*

vic·to·ry (vik′tər ē, vik′trē), *n., pl.* **-ries.** 1. the advantage or superiority gained in defeating the enemy or an opponent in battle; triumph gained by force of arms. 2. the defeat of an enemy in combat, battle, or war. 3. success in any contest, struggle, or enterprise; supremacy, superiority, or triumph in any effort: *The game ended in a victory for our school. Health alone is victory* (Thomas Carlyle). [< Latin *victōria* < *victor, -ōris* victor]
—**Syn.** 1, 2, 3. **Victory, conquest, triumph** mean success in a contest or struggle. **Victory** applies to success in any kind of contest or fight: *We celebrated our victory.* **Conquest** emphasizes complete success and absolute control of the defeated: *Some day we may complete the conquest of disease.* **Triumph** applies to a glorious victory or conquest: *The Nineteenth Amendment was a triumph for the suffragettes.* —**Ant.** 1, 2, 3. defeat, failure.

victory garden, (in World War II) a vegetable garden cultivated to help in the wartime effort to produce more food.

Victory girl, *U.S. Slang.* V-girl.

Victory Medal, a bronze decoration awarded at the end of World War I and World War II to all men and women who served in the U.S. Armed Forces during either war.

Victory note, a note of the Victory Liberty Loan issue, put forth by the U.S. Government in May, 1919, after the cessation of fighting in World War I, to provide funds for meeting obligations connected with the war.

victory ribbon, a service ribbon worn in place of the Victory Medal.

Victory Ship, a cargo ship similar to a Liberty Ship, built after World War II.

vic·tress (vik′tris), *n.* a female victor or conqueror.

vic·trix (vik′triks), *n.* victress.

vic·tro·la (vik trō′lə), *n.* 1. any phonograph, especially one having a motor whose spring is wound up with a crank. 2. **Victrola,** *Trademark.* a kind of phonograph. [American English < the *Victor* Talking Machine Company]

vict·ual (vit′əl), *n., v.,* **-ualed, -ual·ing** or (*especially British*) **-ualled, -ual·ling.**
—*n.* **victuals,** *Informal or Dialect.* food or provisions, especially for human beings: *There was . . . decking of the hall in the best hangings . . . ; cooking of victuals, broaching of casks* (Charles Kingsley).
—*v.i.* **1.** to take on or obtain a supply of food: *The ship will victual before sailing.* **2.** to eat or feed: *sheep victualing on new grass.*
—*v.t.* to supply (a ship, castle, troops, etc.) with food, especially with enough to last for some time: *The captain victualed his ship for the voyage.*
[spelling alteration (influenced by Latin) of Middle English *vitaylle* < Old French *vitaille* < Latin *victūalia,* neuter plural of *victūalis* of food < *victus, -ūs* food, sustenance < *vīvere* to live]

vict·ual·age (vit′ə lij), *n.* victuals.

vict·ual·er (vit′ə lər), *n.* **1. a.** a person who sells food and drink. **b.** *Especially British.* a tavern keeper or innkeeper. **2.** a person who supplies food or provisions to a ship, an army, etc. **3.** a ship that carries provisions for other ships or for troops.

vict·ual·ler (vit′ə lər), *n. Especially British.* victualer.

vict·ual·less (vit′əl lis), *adj.* lacking food.

vi·cu·gna (vi kün′yə), *n.* vicuña.

vi·cu·ña (vi kün′yə, -kyü′nə), *n.* **1.** a wild, ruminant mammal of South America, related to and resembling a llama, having soft, delicate wool. **2.** a soft cloth made from this wool, or from some substitute, used for coats, etc. [< Spanish *vicuña* < the Quechua (Peru) name]

Vicuña (def. 1) (2¾ ft. high at the shoulder)

vid., see (Latin, *vide*).

vi·dame (vē däm′), *n.* **1.** (in French feudal use) the deputy or representative of a bishop in temporal affairs, holding a fief from him. **2.** a French minor title of nobility. [< Middle French *vidame* < Old French *visdame* < Medieval Latin *vicedominus* < Latin *vice* vice[3] + *dominus* lord, master]

Vi·dar (vē′där), *n. Norse Mythology.* a strong, silent god of the Aesir, son of Odin and the giantess Grid, and the guardian of the forest or of peace.

vi·de (vī′dē), *v. Latin.* see; refer to; consult (a word indicating reference to something stated elsewhere): *For the past year, the French Communist Party and press (vide the recent affair of Picasso's posthumous portrait of Stalin) have repeatedly got themselves into hot water* (New Yorker).

vi·de an·te (vī′dē an′tē), *Latin.* see before this.

vi·de in·fra (vī′dē in′frə), *Latin.* see below.

vi·de·li·cet (və del′ə set), *adv.* that is to say; namely. *Abbr.:* viz. [< Latin *vidēlicet,* for *vidēre licet* it is permissible to see]
➔ See **viz.** for usage note.

vid·e·o (vid′ē ō), *adj.* of or used in the transmission or reception of images in television. —*n.* television. [< Latin *videō* I see, first person singular present of *vidēre* to see]

vid·e·o·gen·ic (vid′ē ə jen′ik), *adj.* televising very well, especially reproducing colors in correspondingly natural blacks, whites, and tones of gray without undue shadow or brightness: *a videogenic face.*

video recorder, a device for recording sounds and images on videotape.

vid·e·o·tape (vid′ē ō tāp′), *n., v.,* **-taped, -tap·ing.** —*n.* a magnetic tape with tracks for recording and reproducing both sound and image for television: *Thanks to something called videotape, you can see the running of the race twice, and spot a number of things you missed the first time* (New Yorker).
—*v.t.* to record on videotape.

videotape recorder, video recorder: *Videotape recorders can be adjusted to turn on TV sets and record favorite programs while people are away from home* (Time).

vi·de post (vī′dē pōst), *Latin.* see after.

vi·de su·pra (vī′dē sü′prə), *Latin.* see above.

vi·dette (vi det′), *n.* vedette.

vi·de ut su·pra (vī′dē ut sü′prə), *Latin.* see as (given) above.

vid·i·con (vid′ə kon), *n.* a small pickup tube for a television camera: *The key of the camera is a new pickup tube, called a vidicon, which is only one inch in diameter and six inches long* (Science News Letter). [< Latin *vidēre* to see + English *icon*]

vie (vī), *v.,* **vied, vy·ing.** —*v.i.* to strive for superiority; contend in rivalry; compete: *candidates vying for office, brothers vying with each other.* —*v.t.* **1.** *Archaic.* to try to outdo in competition or rivalry; strive or contend; bandy (with): *to vie retorts with an opponent in debate.* **2.** *Obsolete.* to hazard, stake, or bet (a sum, etc.) on a hand of cards. [short for Middle French *envier* increase the stake, Old French, challenge, invite < Latin *invītāre* invite, provoke. Doublet of INVITE.]

vie de bo·hème (vē′ də bô em′), *French.* Bohemian life; the unconventional life of artists, writers, etc., especially in Paris: *Diderot followed his own advice and lived the . . . vie de bohème, made up of much talk, not enough food and more than enough love* (Time).

vielle (vyel), *n.* **1.** one of the large, early forms of the medieval viol: *A series of performances with solo singer, vielles, recorders, lute, drums, in the now increasingly familiar manner of the musical explorers into older music* (Harper's). **2.** a hurdy-gurdy. [< French *vielle,* Old French *viele;* origin uncertain]

Vi·en·nese (vē′ə nēz′, -nēs′), *adj., n., pl.* **-nese.** —*adj.* of or having to do with Vienna, the capital of Austria, or its people.
—*n.* **1.** a native or inhabitant of Vienna. **2.** a dialect of German spoken in Vienna.

vier·kleur (fēr′klœr′), *n.* the flag of the old Transvaal Republic in South Africa: *A green, red, white, and blue flag flashed in the warm, early autumn sky above the Union of South Africa last week. It was the vierkleur . . . banner of the old Transvaal Republic* (Newsweek). [< Afrikaans, Dutch *vierkleur* four-color < Dutch *vier* four + *kleur* color]

vi et ar·mis (vī′ et är′mis), *Latin.* by force of arms; by sheer force.

Vi·et·cong (vē et′kông′, vē′et-; vē et′kong′, vē′et-), *n.,* or **Viet Cong, 1.** the Communist guerrilla force in South Vietnam. **2.** a member of this force: *American interviewers describe the average Vietcong's life as "monkish"* (New York Times). —*adj.* of or having to do with the Vietcong: *The Vietcong village was leveled by napalm* (Time).

Vi·et·minh (vē et′min′, vē′et min′), *n.,* or **Viet Minh,** the Communist party in Indochina, in power in North Vietnam.

Vi·et·nam·ese or **Vi·et·Nam·ese** (vē-et′nä mēz′, -mēs′), *adj., n., pl.* **-ese.** —*adj.* of or having to do with Vietnam, a country in southeastern Asia divided since 1954 into North Vietnam and South Vietnam.
—*n.* **1.** a native or inhabitant of Vietnam. **2.** the Austro-Asiatic language spoken in Vietnam; Annamese.

Vi·et·nam·i·za·tion (vē et′nə mə zā′-shən), *n.* the act or process of Vietnamizing.

Vi·et·nam·ize (vē et′nə mīz), *v.t.,* **-ized, -iz·ing.** to put under Vietnamese control: *General Thieu's major internal task will be to "Vietnamize" the pacification program* (New York Times).

Vi·et·nik (vē et′nik), *n. U.S. Slang.* an opponent of the American policy of fighting the Vietcong in South Vietnam. [< *Viet-*(nam) + *-nik*]

vieux jeu (vyœ zhœ′), *French.* **1.** an old game. **2.** an old-fashioned thing; something out-of-date. **3.** old-fashioned; out-of-date. *The festival was going to be largely vieux jeu by Western standards* (Harper's).

view (vyü), *n.* **1.** the act of seeing; sight: *It was our first view of the ocean.* **2.** the power of seeing; range of sight or vision: *A ship came into view.* **3.** a thing seen; scene: *The view from our house is beautiful.* **4.** a drawing, painting, print, photograph, or other picture of some scene: *Various views of the mountains hung on the walls.* **5.** visual appearance or aspect: *Of stateliest view* (Milton). **6.** a mental picture or impression; idea: *This book will give you a general view of the war.* **7.** a way of looking at or considering a matter or question; opinion: *What are your views on the subject?* **8.** the aspect or light in which something is considered or regarded: *Children take a different view of school from that of their teachers.* **9.** an aim; intention; purpose: *It is my view to leave tomorrow.* **10.** a prospect; expectation; outlook: *with no view of success.* **11.** a general account of something; survey: *The title is: "A View of Modern Art."*
in view, a. in sight: *He had no other job in view.* **b.** under consideration or attention: *I'll keep your advice in view.* **c.** as a purpose or intention: *Keep probability in view* (John Gay). **d.** as a hope or expectation: *Then, too, he had his uncle's bequest in view.*
in view of, a. considering; because of: *In view of the readiness she showed to second my search, all was, or appeared to be, forgiven* (Thomas Hope). **b.** in prospect or anticipation of: *Musters were being taken through England in view of wars with Scotland and France* (Richard Simpson).
on view, open for people to see; to be seen: *He shall be on view in the drawing room before dinner* (Mary E. Braddon).
take a dim view of, to look upon or regard with disapproval, doubt, pessimism, or the like: *President Eisenhower and his assistants have taken a dim view of the old American custom of having beauty queens pictured with the President* (Tuscaloosa News).
with a view to, a. with the aim or object of attaining; with the hope of effecting or accomplishing: *The tendency is more and more to promote individual effort with a view to individual comfort* (Arthur Helps). **b.** with regard to: *War may be considered with a view to its causes and its conduct* (William Paley). **c.** in view of: *With a view to his approaching nuptials, Lord Castleton presented him with a handsome service of plate* (Eleanor Sleath).
—*v.t.* **1.** to see; look at: *They viewed the scene with pleasure.* **2.** to consider; regard: *The plan of reducing school hours was not viewed favorably the the teachers.*
[< Anglo-French *vewe* view, Old French *veüe,* noun use of feminine past participle of *veoir* to see < Latin *vidēre*]
—**Syn.** *n.* **1.** look, survey, inspection, scrutiny. **3. View, scene** mean something seen. **View** applies to something actually seen through the eyes, and applies to what is presented to the sight, or within the range of vision of someone looking from a certain point or position: *That new building spoils the view from our windows.* **Scene** applies to something that can be seen, especially a landscape or setting that is spread out before the eyes: *We have a fine view of the mountain scene.* **6.** notion, conception. **7.** See **opinion.** *-v.t.* **1.** behold, witness, survey, examine, scan.

view·a·bil·i·ty (vyü′ə bil′ə tē), *n.* the quality of being viewable: *[The television show] had won virtually every TV award and maintained a rare reputation for high production standards and general viewability* (Newsweek).

view·a·ble (vyü′ə bəl), *adj.* **1.** worth viewing; pleasant to view: *Limited but decidedly viewable television was being produced in Britain during the last pre-war years* (New York Times). **2.** exposed to view; visible: *Viewable ant colonies, as such, aren't particularly new* (Wall Street Journal).

view·er (vyü′ər), *n.* **1.** a person who views, especially one who views television: *Many viewers, I have no doubt, will learn much from these programmes about the nerve-racking business of being interviewed by top people* (Punch). **2.** a person appointed to examine or inspect something, especially by a law court. **3.** an overseer, manager, or superintendent of a coal mine. **4.** *Photography.* a device that magnifies and sometimes illuminates slides placed in it for viewing.

view·find·er (vyü′fīn′dər), *n.,* or **view finder,** any device attached to or built in a camera for determining how much of a given scene is being photographed or televised: *I looked into the viewfinder, to take another shot as the helicopter began to move away, but to my amazement I saw it fall over and crash on to its side* (London Times).

view halloo, hallo, or **halloa,** the shout given by a huntsman on seeing a fox break cover.

view·i·ness (vyü′ē nis), *n.* the character or state of being viewy.

view·ing (vyü′ing), *n.* the act of a viewer, especially of a television viewer: *Americans take their viewing so seriously that more than one-fourth have their set repaired or replaced within four hours* (Time).

view·less (vyü′lis), *adj.* **1.** that cannot be seen; invisible. **2.** lacking a view or prospect. **3.** without views or opinions. —**view′less·ly,** *adv.*

view·point (vyü′point′), *n.* **1.** a place from which one looks at something. **2.** an attitude of mind: *A heavy rain that is good from the* *viewpoint of farmers may be bad from the viewpoint of tourists.*

view window, picture window: *She had chosen it entirely because the principal room had a view window that went up to the ceiling and let in enough light to make it suitable for a studio* (New Yorker).

view·y (vyü′ē), *adj.* **1.** inclined to be impractical or visionary: *a viewy freshman, a viewy theory.* **2.** *Slang.* attractive in appearance; showy.

vi·ga (vē′gə), *n. Southwestern U.S.* a beam that supports the roof in Indian and Spanish types of houses. [< Spanish *viga* beam, rafter]

vi·gent (vī′jənt), *adj.* flourishing; prosperous: *Durham College . . . after several changes of fortune is now vigent as Trinity College* (J. Wall). [< Latin *vigens, -entis,* present participle of *vigēre* to thrive]

vi·ges·i·mal (vī jes′ə məl), *adj.* **1.** twentieth. **2.** in or by twenties. [< Latin *vīgēsimus,* variant of *vīcēnsimus* twentieth < *vīcēnī* twenty each < *vīgintī* twenty]

vi·gi·a (vi jē′ə), *n.* an indication given on a hydrographic chart of the presence of a rock, shoal, or the like, dangerous to navigation. [< Spanish *vigía* shoal; a lookout < Latin *vigilia;* see VIGIL]

vig·il (vij′əl), *n.* **1.** a staying awake for some purpose; a watching; watch: *All night the mother kept vigil over the sick child.* **2.** wakefulness or a period of wakefulness due to inability to sleep: *Worn out by the labours and vigils of many months* (Macaulay). **3. a.** the watch kept and observed with prayer on the eve of a festival or holy day. **b.** the eve, or the day and night, before a solemn festival or holy day, especially when observed as a fast.

vigils, the devotions, prayers, or services said or sung on the night before a festival: *I have seen the sublime Cathedral of Amiens on the night of Allhallows, when the vigils . . . were sung there* (Kenelm E. Digby).

[< Old French *vigile,* learned borrowing from Latin *vigilia* < *vigil, -ilis* watchful, awake, related to *vigēre* be lively, in full possession of one's powers]

vig·i·lance (vij′ə ləns), *n.* **1.** watchfulness; alertness; caution: *Constant vigilance is necessary in order to avoid accidents in driving. The cat watched the mousehole with vigilance.* **2.** *Pathology.* abnormal wakefulness; sleeplessness; insomnia.

vigilance committee, *U.S.* **1.** a self-appointed and unauthorized committee of citizens to maintain order and punish criminals in a community where law enforcement is imperfectly or insufficiently organized. **2.** (formerly) a self-appointed organization of Southern white citizens whose aim was to intimidate, suppress, and terrorize Negroes, abolitionists, and carpetbaggers.

vig·i·lant (vij′ə lənt), *adj.* keeping steadily on the alert; attentively or closely observant; watchful; cautious: *a vigilant guard around the President, a vigilant supervision of the government.* [< Latin *vigilāns, -antis* watching, present participle of *vigilāre* keep watch < *vigil* watchful; see VIGIL] —**vig′i·lant·ly,** *adv.* —**vig′i·lant·ness,** *n.* —**Syn.** wary, sharp. See **watchful.** —**Ant.** oblivious, careless.

vig·i·lan·te (vij′ə lan′tē), *n. U.S.* a member of a vigilance committee. [American English < Spanish *vigilante* (literally) watchman < Latin *vigilāns;* see VIGILANT]

vig·i·lan·tism (vij′ə lan′tiz əm), *n.* the policies or actions of a vigilante or vigilance committee: *Langdon Street is identified . . . with anti-intellectual vigilantism* (Harper's).

vig·ils (vij′əlz), *n.pl.* See under **vigil,** *n.*

vi·gin·ten·ni·al (vī′jin ten′ē əl), *adj.* occurring once in twenty years: [*The planets'*] *vigintennial conjunction is due a few months hence* (Glasgow Herald). [< Latin *vīgintī* twenty + English *-ennial,* as in *biennial*]

vi·gne·ron (vē nyə rôN′), *n.* a cultivator of grapevines; winegrower: *Moreau . . . told me about the wonderful year of 1893, when conditions had been so favorable that the vignerons were able to start picking grapes on August 16th* (New Yorker). [< French *vigneron* < *vigne* vine]

vi·gnette (vin yet′), *n., v.,* **-gnet·ted, -gnet·ting.** —*n.* **1.** a decorative, usually small, design on a page of a book, especially on or just before the title page, or at the beginning or end of a chapter. **2.** a literary sketch; short verbal description: *"Dinner at Eight" in its original state is an episodic work, really a series of vignettes of the guests at the party and their relationship to each other* (New York Times). **3. a.** an engraving, drawing, photograph, or the like, that shades off gradually at the edge. **b.** any picture or view of small, pleasing, and delicate proportion. **4.** *Obsolete.* the decorative ornamentation of vine leaves, branches, and tendrils, as in architecture.

—*v.t.* **1.** to make a vignette of. **2.** *Photography.* to finish (a photograph or portrait) in the manner of a vignette. [< French *vignette* < Old French (diminutive) < *vigne* vine < Latin *vīnea* < *vīnum* wine]

vi·gnet·ter (vin yet′ər), *n.* **1.** a device for producing photographic vignettes. **2.** vignettist.

vi·gnet·tist (vin yet′ist), *n.* an artist or engraver who produces vignettes.

vig·or (vig′ər), *n.* **1. a.** active physical strength or force; flourishing physical condition: *A brief rest restored the traveler's vigor.* **b.** the time or condition of greatest activity or strength, especially in the life of a man: *in the full vigor of youth.* **2.** mental activity, energy, or power; moral strength or force: *the vigor of a personality. The school board argued with vigor that the new school should have a library.* **3.** a powerful or active force of conditions, qualities, or agencies; intensity of effect, especially in artistic or literary works: *A succinct style lends vigor to writing.* **4. a.** strong or energetic action, especially in administration or government. **b.** the use or exercise of power and action by a ruler or government official. **5.** legal or binding force; validity: *a law in full vigor.* Also, *especially British,* **vigour.** [< Anglo-French *vigour,* learned borrowing from Latin *vigor, -ōris* < *vigēre* be lively, thrive]

vig·or·ish (vig′ər ish), *n. U.S. Slang.* **1.** the percentage of money from bets kept by a bookmaker as his commission or profit: *Despite the small vigorish, bookmakers find baseball their No. 1 sport* (Time). **2.** the interest collected by a loan shark.

vi·go·ro·so (vē′gō rō′sō), *adj. Music.* vigorous; with energy. [< Italian *vigoroso* < *vigore* vigor (< Latin *vigor;* see VIGOR) + *-oso* -ose[1]]

vig·or·ous (vig′ər əs), *adj.* **1.** full of vigor; strong and active in body and mind; full of strength or active force: *He keeps himself vigorous by taking exercise. At forty-five he was so vigorous that he made his way to Scotland on foot* (John R. Green). **2.** characterized by, done with, or acting with vigor or energy: *to wage a vigorous war against disease.* **3.** powerful; forcible: *an able, vigorous and well-informed statesman* (Edmund Burke). *His vigorous understanding and his stout English heart* (Macaulay). —**vig′or·ous·ly,** *adv.* —**vig′or·ous·ness,** *n.*

—**Syn. 1. Vigorous, strenuous** mean having or showing active strength or energy. **Vigorous** emphasizes being full of healthy physical or mental energy or power and displaying active strength or force: *The old man is still vigorous and lively.* **Strenuous** emphasizes having a constant driving force and continuous energetic activity: *A diving champion leads a strenuous life.* —**Ant. 1.** lethargic.

vig·our (vig′ər), *n. Especially British.* vigor.

Vi·ha·ra (və hä′rə), *n.* a Buddhist temple or monastery.

Vi·king or **vi·king** (vī′king), *n.* one of the daring Scandinavian pirates who raided the coastal towns and river ports of Europe from the 700's to the 900's A.D., often establishing settlements there. [< Old Icelandic *víkingr*]

vil., village.

vi·la·yet (vē′lä yet′), *n.* one of the provinces or main governmental divisions of Turkey. Also, **eyalet.** [< Turkish *vilâyet* < Arabic *wilāyat* < *wālī* governor]

vile (vīl), *adj.,* **vil·er, vil·est. 1.** very bad: *vile weather, a vile absurdity.* **2.** foul; disgusting; obnoxious: *a vile smell.* **3.** evil; low; immoral: *vile language, a vile criminal.* **4.** poor; mean; lowly: *The king's son stooped to the vile tasks of the kitchen.* **5.** of little worth or account; trifling: *the vile weeds in the field.* [< Anglo-French, Old French *vile* < Latin *vīlis* cheap; base, common] —**vile′ly,** *adv.* —**vile′ness,** *n.* —**Syn. 3.** See **base.**

vil·i·fi·ca·tion (vil′ə fə kā′shən), *n.* a vilifying or being vilified: *She defends her lovers from the vilification of the chroniclers* (Atlantic).

vil·i·fi·er (vil′ə fī′ər), *n.* a person who vilifies or defames.

vil·i·fy (vil′ə fī), *v.t.,* **-fied, -fy·ing. 1.** to speak evil of; revile; slander: *Dissatisfied men are apt to vilify whatever government is in power.* **2.** *Obsolete.* **a.** to lower in worth or value. **b.** to make morally vile; degrade. **c.** to dirty or defile. **3.** *Obsolete.* to regard as worthless; despise. [< Late Latin *vīlificāre* < Latin *vīlis* vile + *facere* to make] —**Syn. 1.** disparage, defame.

vil·i·pend (vil′ə pend), *v.t.* **1.** to regard as having little value or consequence; treat contemptuously: *A youth . . . vilipends the conversation and advice of his seniors* (Scott). **2.** to speak with contempt; abuse; vilify: *to vilipend a rival.* [< Latin *vilipendere* < *vīlis* vile, cheap + *pendere* to consider; (literally) weigh] —**vil′i·pend′er,** *n.*

vill (vil), *n.* **1.** a territorial unit under the European feudal system, corresponding to the modern township. **2.** *Poetic.* a village. [< Anglo-French *vill,* Old French *ville* country house, village < Latin *vīlla*]

vil·la (vil′ə), *n.* **1. a.** a house in the country, suburbs, or at the seashore, usually large and elegant: *Magnificent villas are found throughout Italy.* **b.** (originally) a country estate, including the land, residence, barns, and other farm buildings. **2.** any house, usually in the suburbs. —*adj.* of, having to do with, or like a villa: *villa style.* [< Italian *villa* < Latin *vīlla,* perhaps related to *vicus* village]

Villa Rotunda (def. 1a)
Vicenza, Italy

vil·la·dom (vil′ə dəm), *n.* **1.** suburban villas or their residents collectively. **2.** a smug, narrow-minded, and moderately prosperous suburban society.

Vil·la·fran·chi·an (vil′ə fran′chē ən), *n.* the early part of the Pleistocene: [*His*] *estimated date of 1.6 million years for the Pleistocene was the Pleistocene as then defined, and not the Pleistocene including the whole of the Villafranchian* (New Scientist). —*adj.* of the early Pleistocene: *Villafranchian fauna.* [< *Villefranche,* a village in southeastern France; form influenced by Italian name *Villafranca*]

vil·lage (vil′ij), *n.* **1. a.** a group of houses in a suburban or country area, usually smaller than a town, and often comprising a small municipality with limited corporate powers. **b.** any group of people living together in separate, and usually rude, dwellings: *an Indian village.* **2.** the people of a village; villagers: *The whole village turned out to watch the parade.* **3.** a group or cluster of prairie dog burrows, often extending over a large area and having several thousand inhabitants. —*adj.* of, having to do with, characteristic of, or living in a village; rural; rustic: *village schools.* [< Old French *village* < Latin *villāticum,* noun use of neuter adjective, having to do with a villa < *vīlla* villa; see VILLA] —**vil′lage·like′,** *adj.*

village community, a primitive economic and political unit, consisting of a group of families living close together and owning the surrounding land more or less in common, as formerly existed in early England, Russia, Germany, India, etc., and out of which many historians believe the modern political state evolved.

vil·lage·less (vil′ij lis), *adj.* having no village.

vil·lag·er (vil′ə jər), *n.* a person who lives in a village.

vil·lag·ey or **vil·lag·y** (vil′ə jē), *adj.* characteristic of or somewhat like a village: *"I love this neighborhood," she says. "It's so informal and villagey"* (New York Times). *The East End is very villagy* (London Times).

vil·lain (vil′ən), *n.* **1.** a very wicked person; scoundrel; knave: *The villain stole the money and cast the blame on his friend.* **2.** a playful name for a mischievous person. **3. a.** a character in a play, novel, etc., whose evil motives or actions form an important element in the plot. **b.** an actor who regularly plays parts of this nature. **4.** villein. [< Anglo-French, Old French *villain, vilein* < Medieval Latin *villanus* farmhand <

Latin *vīlla* country house; see VILLA] —**Syn. 1.** miscreant, reprobate, malefactor.

vil·lain·age (vil′ə nij), *n.* villeinage.

vil·lain·ess (vil′ə nis), *n.* a woman villain.

vil·lain·ize (vil′ə nīz), *v.*, **-ized, -iz·ing.** —*v.t.* **1.** to make villainous; debase or degrade: *Those writings which villainize mankind have a pernicious tendency towards propagating and protecting villainy* (Edmund Law). **2.** to treat or revile as villainous or as a villain: *Our "best writers" villainize computers, automation, and the rest, while our publicists respond by concealing the new technology behind humanized images* (New York Times). —*v.i.* to play the villain; act as a villain.

vil·lain·ous (vil′ə nəs), *adj.* **1.** very wicked; depraved: *a villainous crew of pirates.* **2.** (of actions) deserving condemnation; marked by depravity; immoral: *a villainous act.* **3.** characteristic of a villain; offensive; profane: *a villainous, low oath* (Robert Louis Stevenson). **4.** extremely bad; vile: *villainous weather.* —**vil′lain·ous·ly,** *adv.* —**vil′lain·ous·ness,** *n.*

vil·lain·y (vil′ə nē), *n., pl.* **-lain·ies. 1.** great wickedness: *There was no manifest villainy about this woman* (New Yorker). **2.** a very wicked act; crime. **3.** *Obsolete.* **a.** villeinage. **b.** a base or morally degraded condition. —**Syn. 1.** baseness, rascality, infamy.

vil·lan·age (vil′ə nij), *n.* villeinage.

vil·la·nel·la (vil′ə nel′ə), *n., pl.* **-nel·las, -nel·le** (-nel′ā). **1. a.** an unaccompanied Italian part song of a light and rustic nature, forerunner of the madrigal. **b.** a light, less contrapuntal madrigal. **2.** a brisk, gay air, or the old rustic dance accompanying it. [< Italian *villanella;* see VILLANELLE]

vil·la·nelle (vil′ə nel′), *n.* a fixed form of pastoral or lyric poetry normally consisting of 19 lines with two rhymes, written in five three-line stanzas (tercets) and a final quatrain: *A dainty thing's the villanelle, Sly, musical, a jewel in rhyme* (William E. Henley). [< Middle French *villanelle* < Italian *villanella* rustic < *villano* peasant, rustic < Medieval Latin *villanus;* see VILLAIN]

Vil·la·no·van (vil′ə nō′vən), *adj.* of or having to do with the early Iron Age in Italy, dating from about 1000 B.C.: . . . *an eighth-century B.C. Villanovan . . . handle in the form of a stylized bull with a smaller one on its back* (London Times). [< *Villanova,* a town in Italy, where remains of the age were found]

vil·lat·ic (vi lat′ik), *adj.* of or having to do with a villa or farm; rural; rustic: *tame, villatic fowl* (Milton). [< Latin *vīllāticus* < *vīlla* country house, village]

-ville, *combining form. U.S. Slang.* in a state of; being in or from: *He's Despairville, see, . . . and he's fed up with humanity* (S.J. Perelman). *I just finished it* [*a book*] *and all I can say is like War and Peaceville* (Bruce Jay Friedman). [< *-ville,* place name suffix, as in *Nashville, Louisville*]

vil·lein (vil′ən), *n.* one of a class of half-free peasants in the European feudal system in the Middle Ages; villain. A villein was under the control of his lord, but in his relations with other men had the rights of a freeman. [Middle English variant of *villain*]

vil·lein·age or **vil·len·age** (vil′ə nij), *n.* **1.** the fact or state of being a villein. **2.** the conditions under which a villein held his land. Also, **villainage, villanage.** [< Anglo-French, Old French *villenage* < *vilein* (see VILLAIN) + *-age* -age]

vil·li (vil′ī), *n. pl. of* **vil·lus. 1.** tiny, hairlike parts growing out of a membrane, especially those projecting from the mucous membrane of the small intestine that aid in absorbing certain substances. **2.** *Botany.* the long, straight, soft hairs that cover the fruit, flowers, and other parts of certain plants. [< Latin *villi,* plural of *villus* tuft of hair, related to *vellere* to pluck]

vil·li·form (vil′ə fôrm), *adj.* having the form of villi; so shaped, numerous, slender, and closely set as to resemble the plush or pile of velvet, as the teeth of certain fishes.

vil·li·no (və lē′nō), *n., pl.* **-ni** (-nē). a small country house or villa, usually with a garden. [< Italian *villino* (diminutive) < *villa;* see VILLA]

vil·lose (vil′ōs), *adj.* villous.

vil·los·i·ty (vi los′ə tē), *n., pl.* **-ties. 1.** villous condition. **2.** a villous formation, surface, or coating. **3.** a number of villi together. **4.** a villus.

vil·lous (vil′əs), *adj.* **1.** like villi. **2.** having villi; covered with villi, especially covered with long, soft hairs, as parts of certain plants.
[< Latin *villōsus* shaggy < *villus;* see VILLI]
—**vil′lous·ly,** *adv.*

vil·lus (vil′əs), *n.* the singular of **villi.**

vim (vim), *n.* force; energy; vigor: *to be full of vim.* [American English, apparently < Latin *vim,* accusative of *vīs* force]

vi·ma·na (vi mä′nə), *n.* (in India) a pyramidal tower, built in stories, surmounting the shrine of a temple. [< Sanskrit *vimana*]

vi·men (vī′mən), *n., pl.* **vim·i·na** (vim′ə nə). *Botany.* a long, flexible shoot of a plant; twig. [< Latin *vīmen, -inis* twig, osier]

vim·ful (vim′fəl), *adj.* full of vim or vigor: *Valladolid . . . retains the vimful life of a capital* (Glasgow Herald).

vim·i·nal (vim′ə nəl), *adj.* **1.** of a vimen. **2.** producing vimina.

Vim·i·nal (vim′ə nəl), *n.* one of the seven hills on which the city of Rome was built.

vi·min·e·ous (vi min′ē əs), *adj.* **1.** *Botany.* producing long, flexible shoots or twigs. **2.** made of pliable twigs or wickerwork. [< Latin *vīmineus* (with English *-ous*) < *vīmen, -inis* twig, osier]

v. imp., impersonal verb.

vi·na[1] (vē′nä), *n.* a four- or five-stringed Hindu musical instrument of ancient origin, consisting of a long, fretted, bamboo finger board, and having a gourd at each end for resonance. [< Sanskrit *vīṇā*]

vi·na[2] (vī′nə), *n.* plural of **vinum.**

vi·na·ceous (vī nā′shəs), *adj.* **1.** belonging to wine or grapes. **2.** red, like wine; wine-colored. [< Latin *vīnāceus* (with English *-ous*) < *vīnum* wine]

vin·ai·grette (vin′ə gret′), *n.* **1.** a small ornamental bottle or box usually containing a sponge charged with smelling salts, etc. Also, **vinegarette. 2.** vinaigrette sauce. —*adj.* served with vinaigrette sauce: *Hofmann had also stirred up . . . pickled whale flippers, and walrus flippers vinaigrette* (New Yorker). [< French *vinaigrette* < Old French *vinaigre;* see VINEGAR]

French Vinaigrette with double cover (def. 1)

vinaigrette sauce, a sauce made of vinegar, oil, herbs, etc., used on cold meats or vegetables.

vi·nal[1] (vī′nəl), *adj.* of, produced by, or originating in wine: *vinal spirits, vinal energy.* [< Latin *vīnālis* < *vīnum* wine]

vi·nal[2] (vī′nəl), *n.* any of a group of synthetic fibers with high resistance to fungi, mildew, etc., used for fishing nets, bathing suits, rainwear, etc. Vinals are long-chain polymers composed of measured units of vinyl alcohol and acetal. [< *vin*(yl) *al*(cohol)]

vi·nasse (vi nas′), *n.* the dregs remaining after distilling liquor or pressing wine. [< French *vinasse,* probably < Provençal *vinassa* < Latin *vīnācea* grapeskin; (originally) adjective, feminine of *vīnāceus;* see VINACEOUS]

Vin·a·ya (vin′ə yə), *n.* (in Hinayana Buddhism) the body of monastic rules of discipline. [< Sanskrit *Vinaya*]

vin blanc (vaN blän′), *French.* white wine.

vin·ca (ving′kə), *n.* the periwinkle plant. [< New Latin *Vinca,* the genus name < Latin (*per*)*vinca* periwinkle]

Vin·cen·tian (vin sen′shən), *adj.* of or having to do with the French priest Saint Vincent de Paul (1576-1660) or with certain religious associations of which he was the founder or patron: *Vincentian Fathers, a Vincentian missionary.*
—*n.* a member of an order of Roman Catholic missionary priests founded by St. Vincent de Paul.

Vin·cent's angina (vin′sənts), an inflammation of the mucous membranes of the throat and mouth, characterized by the formation of ulcers and a false membrane at the back of the throat and tonsils; trench mouth; Vincent's stomatitis. [< Jean *Vincent,* 1862-1950, a French physician, who described it]

Vincent's infection, trench mouth.

Vincent's stomatitis, trench mouth.

vin·ci·bil·i·ty (vin′sə bil′ə tē), *n.* the state or character of being vincible; capability of being conquered.

vin·ci·ble (vin′sə bəl), *adj.* easily overcome, defeated, or vanquished; conquerable: *a vincible army, a vincible argument.* [< Latin *vincibilis* < *vincere* to conquer] —**vin′ci·ble·ness,** *n.*

vin·cit om·ni·a ve·ri·tas (vin′sit om′nē ə ver′ə tas), *Latin.* truth conquers all things.

vin·cu·lum (ving′kyə ləm), *n., pl.* **-la** (-lə). **1.** a bond of union; tie: *the vinculum linking cause and effect.* **2.** *Mathematics.* a straight line or brace drawn over several terms to show that they are to be considered together, as in $c\ \overline{a+b}$, meaning ca + cb. [< Latin *vinculum* bond < *vincīre* to bind]

vin·cu·lum ma·tri·mo·ni·i (ving′kyə ləm mat′rə mō′nē ī), *Latin.* the bond of matrimony.

vin d'hon·neur (vaN′ dô nœr′), **1.** wine drunk on a special occasion in honor of a visitor, especially a local wine that is saved for such an occasion. **2.** the ceremony at which this is offered. **3. a.** a cocktail party: *After the ceremony General Gruenther and his staff gave a vin d'honneur for the German representatives* (London Times). **b.** a cocktail. [< French *vin d'honneur* wine of honor]

vin·di·ca·ble (vin′də kə bəl), *adj.* that can be vindicated; justifiable.

vin·di·cate (vin′də kāt), *v.t.*, **-cat·ed, -cat·ing. 1.** to clear from suspicion, dishonor, or hint or charge of wrongdoing: *The verdict of "not guilty" vindicated him.* **2.** to defend successfully against opposition; uphold; justify: *The heir vindicated his claim to the fortune.* **3.** (in Roman and civil law) to claim for oneself as one's rightful property; recover possession of. **4.** *Obsolete.* to avenge, punish, or retaliate. **5.** *Obsolete.* to make or set free; deliver or rescue (from). [< Latin *vindicāre* (with English *-ate*[1]) to set free; avenge, claim, probably < *vim,* accusative of *vīs* force + *dīcere* to say] —**Syn. 1.** exculpate.

vin·di·ca·tion (vin′də kā′shən), *n.* a vindicating or being vindicated; defense; justification.

vin·dic·a·tive (vin dik′ə tiv, vin′də kā′-), *adj.* **1.** tending to vindicate; justifying. **2.** *Obsolete.* vindictive. [< Medieval Latin *vindicativus* < Latin *vindicāre;* see VINDICATE]

vin·di·ca·tor (vin′də kā′tər), *n.* a person who vindicates; one who justifies, maintains, or defends.

vin·di·ca·to·ry (vin′də kə tôr′ē, -tōr′-), *adj.* **1.** serving to vindicate or justify; defensive. **2.** avenging; punitive; retaliatory.

vin·dic·tive (vin dik′tiv), *adj.* **1.** feeling a strong tendency toward revenge; bearing a grudge: *He is so vindictive that he never forgives anybody.* **2.** showing a strong tendency toward revenge: *Vindictive acts rarely do much good.* [< Latin *vindicta* revenge (< *vindicāre* vindicate) + English *-ive*] —**vin·dic′tive·ly,** *adv.* —**vin·dic′tive·ness,** *n.*
—**Syn. 1, 2.** revengeful, spiteful.

vin du pa·ys (vaN′ dY pā ē′), *French.* **1.** locally produced wine: *Most rosés are vin du pays and should be drunk where they grow and when they're young* (Atlantic). **2.** (literally) wine of the country.

vine (vīn), *n.* **1.** any plant with a long, slender stem that grows along the ground, or that climbs by attaching itself to a wall, tree, or other support. **2.** the stem of any trailing or climbing plant. **3.** a grapevine. **wither on the vine,** to end prematurely or fruitlessly; abort: *An enterprise that does not attract customers soon withers on the vine* (William Henry Chamberlin).
[< Old French *vine* < Latin *vīnea* vine, vineyard < *vīnum* wine. Related to WINE.]
—**vine′like,** *adj.*

vine borer, the larva of any of certain beetles and moths, that bores into the wood or root of vines and is often very destructive.

vine-clad (vīn′klad′), *adj.* clad or covered with vines.

vined (vīnd), *adj.* **1.** having leaves like those of a vine; ornamented with vine leaves: . . . *wreathed and vined and figured columns* (Henry Wotton). **2.** separated from the pod or vine: *Most vegetables, including vined peas, are air-dried* (London Times).

vine·dress·er (vīn′dres′ər), *n.* a person who prunes, trains, and cultivates vines, especially grapevines.

vin·e·gar (vin′ə gər), *n.* **1.** a sour liquid produced by the fermentation of cider, wine, beer, ale, malt, etc., consisting largely of dilute, impure acetic acid. Vinegar is used in flavoring and preserving food. **2.** a preparation made by macerating a drug in dilute acetic acid and filtering. **3.** speech or temper of a sour or acid character: *several little sprinklings of wordy vinegar* (Dickens). —*v.t.* to treat with vinegar; put vinegar in or on.
[< Old French *vinaigre,* or *vinagre* < *vin* wine (< Latin *vīnum*) + *aigre,* and *egre* sour < Latin *ācer, ācris*] —**vin′e·gar·like′,** *adj.*

vinegar eel or **worm,** a minute nematode worm found commonly in vinegar, sour paste, etc.

vin·e·gar·ette (vin′ə gə ret′), *n.* vinaigrette. [alteration (influenced by *vinegar*) of *vinaigrette*]

vinegar fly, one of a family of very small, dipterous insects that are attracted by fermentation and develop in pickles, jam, etc.

vin·e·gar·ish (vin′ə gər ish), *adj.* somewhat like vinegar; sourish: [*The*] *Bishop of London . . . had some vinegarish afterthoughts about the meeting of the World Council of Churches last year* (Newsweek).

vin·e·gar·oon (vin′ə gə rün′), *n.* a large whip scorpion of the southwest United States, mistakenly believed to be poisonous, and, when alarmed, having an odor like that of vinegar. [American English, alteration of American Spanish *vinagrón* < Spanish *vinagre* vinegar]

vin·e·gar·y (vin′ə gər ē, -grē), *adj.* of or like vinegar; sour.

vine·less (vīn′lis), *adj.* having no vines.

vine·let (vīn′lit), *n.* a young vine.

vin·er (vī′nər), *n.* a machine for harvesting and shelling peas: *a mobile viner.*

vin·er·y (vī′nər ē), *n., pl.* **-er·ies. 1. a.** a hothouse for the cultivation of grapevines; grapery. **b.** *Obsolete.* a vineyard. **2.** vines collectively.

vine·yard (vin′yərd), *n.* **1.** a place planted with grapevines. **2.** a field or sphere of activity, especially religious work.

vine·yard·ing (vin′yər ding), *n.* the cultivation of vineyards.

vine·yard·ist (vin′yər dist), *n.* a person who engages in growing vines.

vingt-et-un (vaN′tā œN′), *n.* twenty-one, a gambling game at cards, the object of which is to get cards whose pips add up to as near twenty-one as possible without exceeding that number. [< French *vingt-et-un* (literally) twenty-one]

vi·nic (vī′nik), *adj.* of, obtained, or derived from wine or alcohol. [< Latin *vīnum* wine + English *-ic*]

vin·i·cul·tur·al (vin′ə kul′chər əl), *adj.* of or having to do with viniculture. —**vin′i·cul′tur·al·ly,** *adv.*

vin·i·cul·ture (vin′ə kul′chər), *n.* the cultivation of grapes for the production of wine. [< Latin *vīnum* wine + *cultūra* culture]

vin·i·cul·tur·ist (vin′ə kul′chər ist), *n.* a person who cultivates grapes for the production of wine.

vi·nif·er·ous (vī nif′ər əs), *adj.* yielding or producing wine. [< Latin *vīnum* wine + English *-ferous*]

vin·i·fi·ca·tion (vin′ə fə kā′shən), *n.* the process of making wine; conversion of the juice of grapes or the like into wine by fermentation. [< Latin *vīnum* wine + English *-fic* + *-ation*]

vin·i·fi·ca·tor (vin′ə fə kā′tər), *n.* an apparatus for collecting alcoholic vapor that rises from fermenting grape juice in making wine.

vi·no (vē′nō), *n.* **1.** wine: *The Colonel had two bottles of vino pressed into his arms from the jubilant men* (Harper's). **2.** an alcoholic liquor consisting of the fermented leaves and sap of the coconut and the talipot palm, drunk in the Philippines, Guam, and western Mexico. [< Spanish and Italian *vino* wine]

vi·nol·o·gy (vi nol′ə jē, vī-), *n.* the study of wines; oenology. [< Latin *vīnum* wine + English *-logy*]

vi·nom·e·ter (vi nom′ə tər, vī-), *n.* an instrument for measuring the alcoholic strength or the purity of wine. [< Latin *vīnum* wine + English *-meter*]

vin or·di·naire (vaN ôr dē ner′), a low-priced wine (usually red) ordinarily served at meals in France and elsewhere. [< French *vin ordinaire* (literally) ordinary wine]

vi·nos·i·ty (vī nos′ə tē), *n.* **1.** the quality or condition of being vinous. **2.** fondness for, or addiction to, wine. [< Latin *vīnōsitās* wine flavor < *vīnōsus* full of wine, addicted to wine < *vīnum* wine]

vi·nous (vī′nəs), *adj.* **1.** of, like, or having to do with wine. **2.** caused by drinking wine. **3.** addicted to wine. **4.** red, like wine; having a wine-colored tinge. [< Latin *vīnōsus* < *vīnum* wine] —**vi′nous·ly,** *adv.*

vin ro·sé (vaN rō zā′), *French.* rosy wine; rosé.

vin rouge (vaN rüzh′), *French.* red wine.

vint[1] (vint), *v.t.* to make (vintage wine): *I wouldn't give a straw for the best wine that was ever vinted after it had lain here a couple of years* (Anthony Trollope). [back formation < *vintner* or *vintage*]

vint[2] (vint), *n.* a Russian card game resembling auction bridge. [< Russian *vint*]

vin·ta (vēn′tä), *n.* (in the Philippines) a small sailing boat with outriggers, used especially by the Moros. [< Visayan *binta*]

vin·tage (vin′tij), *n., adj., v.,* **-taged, -tag·ing.** —*n.* **1.** a year's crop of grapes. **2.** the wine from a certain crop of grapes: *The finest vintages cost more than others.* **3.** the year in which a particular wine, especially one of outstanding quality, was produced. **4.** the gathering of grapes for making wine. **5.** the season of gathering grapes and making wine. **6.** the crop or output of anything at some particular time: *Her old hat was of the vintage of 1940.* **7.** age, especially old age: *Hamlin's staging respects the play's vintage* (Howard Taubman).
—*adj.* **1.** of outstanding quality; choice: *vintage wines or clarets.* **2.** of antique or classic style or excellence: *a vintage thoroughbred, a vintage Rolls-Royce engine.* **3.** out-of-date; old-fashioned: *a vintage streetcar.*
—*v.t.* to make (wine) from gathered grapes; vint: *. . . Marne, where the true sparkling champagne is vintaged* (Pall Mall Gazette).
[< Anglo-French *vintage,* alteration of Old French *vendange* < Latin *vīndēmia* < *vīnum* wine + *dēmere* take off < *dē-* away + *emere* to take]

vin·tag·er (vin′tə jər), *n.* a person who gathers grapes for making wine; laborer at the vintage.

vintage year, 1. a year in which a particular outstanding wine was produced. **2.** a year distinguished for some particular accomplishment.

vint·ner (vint′nər), *n.* a dealer in wine; wine merchant: *When Prohibition came, the vintners either ground out tons of grape juice or sadly closed down their presses and let their plump grapes wrinkle up into raisins* (Time). [alteration of Middle English *vinter* < Anglo-French *vineter* < Medieval Latin *vinetarius* < Latin *vīnum* wine]

vi·num (vī′nəm), *n., pl.* **-na** (nə). *Pharmacology.* wine, as an ingredient in prescriptions or other medicinal substances. [< Latin *vīnum*]

vin·y (vī′nē), *adj.* **1.** of, like, or having to do with vines. **2.** abounding in or covered with vines; bearing or producing vines.

vi·nyl (vī′nəl), *Chemistry.* —*n.* a univalent radical regarded as an ethylene derivative. *Formula:* CH_2:CH- —*adj.* of, denoting, or containing this radical. [< Latin *vīnum* wine + English *-yl*]

vinyl acetate, a colorless liquid readily polymerized by heat, oxygen, light, etc., to form polyvinyl acetate and other resins. *Formula:* $C_4H_6O_2$

vi·nyl·a·cet·y·lene (vī′nəl ə set′ə lēn, -lin), *n.* a colorless liquid, the dimer of acetylene, used as an intermediate in manufacturing neoprene. *Formula:* C_4H_4

vinyl alcohol, an ethylene derivative, an alcohol, which polymerizes to form polyvinyl alcohol (the only form in which it is known). *Formula:* C_2H_4O

vinyl chloride, a colorless, inflammable gas or liquid used in the manufacture of plastics, as a refrigerant, and in organic synthesis. *Formula:* C_2H_3Cl

vi·nyl·i·dene (vī nil′ə dēn), *n.* a bivalent radical, regarded as an ethylene derivative. *Formula:* CH_2:C– —*adj.* of, denoting, or containing this radical.

vinylidene chloride, a compound, an ethylene derivative, readily polymerized to form polyvinylidene chloride. *Formula:* $C_2H_2Cl_2$

vinylidene fluoride, a colorless gas used in making synthetic rubber. *Formula:* $C_2H_2F_2$

vinylidene resin, any of a group of thermoplastic, synthetic resins produced by polymerizing a compound, such as vinylidene chloride, that contains the radical vinylidene; polyvinylidene resin.

Vi·nyl·ite (vī′nə līt), *n. Trademark.* any of a group of thermoplastic, synthetic resins used in making adhesives, moldings, phonograph records, etc.

vinyl polymer, any of a group of compounds formed by the polymerization of compounds that contain the radical vinyl.

vinyl resin, any of a group of thermoplastic, synthetic resins produced by polymerizing a compound, such as vinyl acetate, that contains the radical vinyl; polyvinyl resin. Vinyl resins are much used for adhesives, moldings, and surface coatings.

vin·yon (vin′yon), *n.* a synthetic fiber similar to nylon, produced from soft coal and brine, and used in industrial fabrics and elastic garments.

vi·ol (vī′əl), *n.* a family of old stringed musical instruments played with a bow, distinguished from the violin by its deeper ribs, flat back, sloping shoulders, number of strings (usually six), and originally fretted neck. In general use until the 1700's, only the double bass, bass, tenor, and treble viol now have counterparts in the violin family as contrabass, cello, viola, and violin. [< Old French *viole,* and *vielle* < Medieval Latin *vitula.* Perhaps related to FIDDLE. Doublet of VIOLA[1].]

vi·o·la[1] (vē ō′lə, vī-), *n.* **1.** a musical instrument of the violin family, somewhat like a violin, but larger, with four strings tuned a fifth below the violin, and held like that instrument while being played; a tenor or alto violin. **2.** a string-toned organ stop, usually of 8-foot pitch, sometimes 4-foot or 16-foot pitch, and similar to the gamba; viola d'orchestre. [< Italian *viola* < Medieval Latin *vitula.* Doublet of VIOL.]

vi·o·la[2] (vī′ə lə, vī ō′-), *n.* **1.** any of a group of low, herbaceous plants, including the violets and pansies, that bear single white, yellow, purple, or variegated flowers, especially any of several hybrid garden plants distinguished from the pansy by a more delicate and uniform coloring of the flowers. **2.** a small, perennial, garden pansy. [< New Latin *Viola* the genus name < Latin *viola* violet]

vi·o·la·bil·i·ty (vī′ə lə bil′ə tē), *n.* capability of being violated.

vi·o·la·ble (vī′ə lə bəl), *adj.* that can be violated or broken: . . . *an abiding conviction that this country is not really violable* (Bulletin of Atomic Scientists). [< Latin *violābilis* < *violāre;* see VIOLATE] —**vi′o·la·ble·ness,** *n.*

vi·o·la·bly (vī′ə lə blē), *adv.* in a violable manner.

vi·o·la·ceous (vī′ə lā′shəs), *adj.* **1.** belonging to a family of dicotyledonous herbs and shrubs or small trees typified by the violet. **2.** of a violet color; purplish-blue. [< Latin *violāceus* (with English *-ous*) violet-colored < *viola* viola, violet]

vi·o·la da brac·cio (vē ō′lə dä brät′chō), an old stringed instrument of the viol family, held like a violin, and corresponding to the modern viola. [< Italian *viola da braccio* (literally) viol for the arm]

vi·o·la da gam·ba (vē ō′lə dä gäm′bä), **1.** an old stringed instrument of the viol family, held between the legs, and corresponding to the modern cello; a bass viol. **2.** a string-toned open organ stop, usually of 8-foot pitch, and sometimes 16-foot or 4-foot pitch. [< Italian *viola da gamba* (literally) viol for the leg; (see VIOLA[1]); *gamba* < Late Latin, leg]

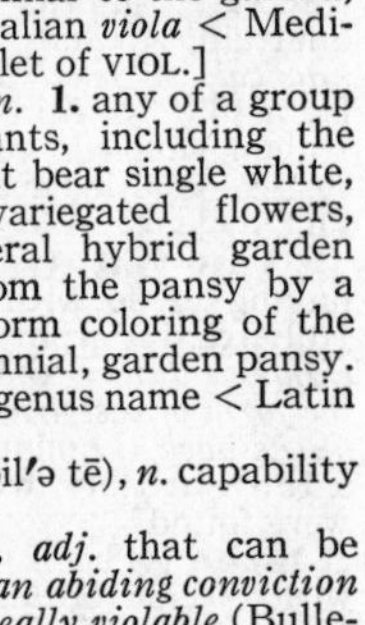

Viola da gamba (def. 1)

vi·o·la d'a·mo·re (vē ō′lə dä mō′rā), **1.** a viol with seven sympathetic strings of metal, in addition to seven gut strings on the finger board, with a sweet delicate tone. **2.** a string-toned open organ stop of 8-foot or 16-foot pitch. [< Italian *viola d'amore* (literally) viol of love]

vi·o·la d'or·ches·tre (vē ō′lə dôr kes′tre), viola (an organ stop).

vi·o·late (vī′ə lāt), *v.t.*, **-lat·ed, -lat·ing. 1. a.** to break (a law, rule, agreement, promise, etc.); act contrary to; fail to perform: *He violated the law and was arrested by the police.* **b.** to trespass on; infringe on: *to violate the right of free speech.* **2.** to treat with disrespect or contempt: *The soldiers violated the church by using it as a stable.* **3.** to break in upon; disturb: *to violate someone's privacy. The sound of guns violated the usual calm of Sunday morning.* **4.** to use force against (a woman or girl); rape. **5.** *Obsolete.* to assail or abuse (a person). [< Latin *violāre* (with English *-ate*[1]), probably < *vīs* violence, strength] —**Syn. 2.** dishonor.

vi·o·la·tion (vī′ə lā′shən), *n.* **1.** the use of force; violence. **2.** a breaking (of a law, rule, agreement, promise, etc.). **3.** the treatment (of something sacred) with contempt. **4.** an interruption or disturbance (of sleep, privacy, etc.). **5.** ravishment; rape. [< Latin *violātiō, -ōnis* < *violāre;* see VIOLATE] —**Syn. 2.** infringement, infraction, breach.

vi·o·la·tive (vī′ə lā′tiv), *adj.* tending to violate; causing or involving violation.

vi·o·la·tor (vī′ə lā′tər), *n.* a person who violates.

vi·o·lence (vī′ə ləns), *n.* **1.** rough force in action: *He slammed the door with violence.* **2.** rough or harmful action or treatment: *the violence of war, to rule with violence.* **3.** *Law.* **a.** the illegal or unjust use of physical force to injure or damage persons or property. **b.** intimidation by threatening such use of force. **c.** an instance of using such force or intimidation. **4. a.** strength of action, feeling, etc. **b.** violent, passionate, or immoderate conduct or language; fury; passion. **5.** the improper treatment or use of a word; distortion of meaning or application. **6.** rape. [< Anglo-French, Old French *violence*, learned borrowing from Latin *violentia* impetuosity, vehemence < *violēns, -entis;* see VIOLENT]

vi·o·lent (vī′ə lənt), *adj.* **1.** acting or done with strong, rough force: *a violent blow, violent exercise, a violent storm.* **2.** caused by strong, rough force: *a violent death.* **3.** very great; severe; extreme: *a violent poison, a violent headache.* **4.** showing or caused by very strong feeling, action, etc.: *violent language, a violent rage.* **5.** that tends to distort meaning. [< Latin *violentus*, for earlier *violēns, -entis* < *vīs* force. Compare VIOLATE.] —**vi′o·lent·ly,** *adv.* —**Syn. 1.** fierce, furious. **4.** vehement.

vi·o·les·cent (vī′ə les′ənt), *adj.* tinged with violet. [< *viol*(a)[2] + *-escent*]

vi·o·let (vī′ə lit), *n.* **1.** any of various low, stemless or leafy-stemmed plants, with single purple, blue, yellow, or white flowers. **2.** the flower of any of these plants. It is the State flower of Illinois, New Jersey, Rhode Island, and Wisconsin. **3.** any of several similar but unrelated plants or their flowers (used with a qualifying word): *the dogtooth violet.* **4.** a bluish purple like that of certain violets, lying at the end of the color spectrum and having a wave length shorter than about 4,000 angstroms. Violet is red and blue mixed. —*adj.* bluish-purple. [< Old French *violette* (diminutive) < *viole* viola, violet < Latin *viola*] —**vi′o·let·like′,** *adj.*

Woolly Blue Violet (def. 1—2 to 6 in. high)

vi·o·let-green swallow (vī′ə lit grēn′), a swallow of western North America with greenish back, wings, and crown and pure white underparts.

violet rays, 1. the shortest rays of the spectrum that can be seen, having wave lengths of about 3,850 angstroms. **2.** (incorrectly) ultraviolet rays.

violet shift, *Astronomy.* a shift of the light of stars, nebulae, etc., toward the violet end of the spectrum.

violet wood, kingwood.

vi·o·lin (vī′ə lin′), *n.* **1.** a musical instrument with four strings played with a bow. It has the highest pitch of the stringed instruments. **2.** a person who plays the violin, especially in an orchestra. [< Italian *violino* (diminutive) < *viola* viola[1]]

Violin (def. 1)

vi·o·lin·ist (vī′ə lin′ist), *n.* a person who plays the violin.

vi·o·lin·is·tic (vī′ə lə nis′tik), *adj.* **1.** of or characteristic of a violinist: *violinistic mannerisms.* **2.** belonging to or characteristic of a violin: *The point of the music, in the main, is violinistic cleverness in a pleasing vein* (Atlantic). —**vi′o·lin·is′ti·cal·ly,** *adv.*

vi·ol·ist (vī′ə list; vē ō′list), *n.* a person who plays the viol.

vi·o·lon·cel·list (vī′ə lən chel′ist, vē′-), *n.* cellist.

vi·o·lon·cel·lo (vī′ə lən chel′ō, vē′-), *n., pl.* **-los.** a stringed musical instrument like a violin, but very much larger; cello. [< Italian *violoncello* (diminutive) < *violone;* see VIOLONE]

vi·o·lo·ne (vē′ə lō′nā), *n.* **1.** the double-bass, or contrabass of the viol family. **2.** a string-toned open labial organ stop of 16-foot pitch, played by the pedals. [< Italian *violone* (originally, augmentative) < *viola* viola[1], viol]

vi·o·my·cin (vī′ō mī′sin), *n.* a purple crystalline antibiotic derived from a soil microorganism and related to streptomycin, used in the treatment of tuberculosis. *Formula:* $C_{18}H_{31-33}N_9O_8$ [< *vio*(let) + *-mycin*, as in *streptomycin*]

vi·os·ter·ol (vī os′tə rōl, -rol), *n.* a preparation containing vitamin D as found in fish-liver oil or an edible vegetable oil, obtained by irradiating ergosterol, and used as a medicine to prevent or cure rickets. [< (ultra)*vio*(let) + (ergo)*sterol*]

VIP (no periods) or **V.I.P.,** *Informal.* very important person: *Almost any time a Washington VIP needs medical attention, one of the two big military hospitals is likely to be picked for his care* (Time).

vi·per (vī′pər), *n.* **1.** any of a group of venomous Old World snakes, as the adder of Great Britain and other parts of Europe, and the Gaboon viper of Africa. **2.** any of a group of venomous snakes of the New World, and parts of the Old World, having perforated fangs and a pit between the eye and nostril, including the rattlesnakes, water moccasins, copperheads, fer-de-lances, and bushmasters; pit viper. **3.** any of certain other poisonous or supposedly poisonous snakes. **4.** a spiteful, treacherous person: *Most loan sharks are vipers of the poor.* —*adj.* extremely bitter; spiteful; venomous: *the viper talk of old maids.* [< Latin *vīpera* < *vīvus* alive + *parere* bring forth, bear] —**vi′per·like′,** *adj.*

vi·per·fish (vī′pər fish′), *n., pl.* **-fish·es** or (*collectively*) **-fish.** a small, elongate deep-sea fish with very long, sharp teeth and photophores along the sides.

vi·per·ine (vī′pər in, -pə rīn), *adj.* of, having to do with, or resembling a viper; viperous.

vi·per·ish (vī′pər ish), *adj.* viperlike; viperous: *the quick and viperish tongue of a spiteful old lady.*

vi·per·ous (vī′pər əs), *adj.* **1.** of or having to do with a viper or vipers. **2.** like a viper. **3.** spiteful; treacherous: *the viperous tongue of an old gossip.* —**vi′per·ous·ly,** *adv.* —**vi′per·ous·ness,** *n.*

viper's bu·gloss (byü′glos, -glôs), the blueweed.

vi·ra·go (və rā′gō), *n., pl.* **-goes** or **-gos. 1.** a violent, bad-tempered, or scolding woman; termagant. **2.** a manlike, vigorous, and heroic woman; amazon. [< Latin *virāgo* a manlike (or warrior) woman < *vir* man] —**Syn. 1.** vixen, shrew.

vi·ral (vī′rəl), *adj.* **1.** of or having to do with a virus. **2.** characterized by a virus. **3.** caused by a virus: . . . *an important therapeutic reagent against viral infections* (New Scientist).

viral hepatitis, a contagious viral disease with inflammation of the liver, and usually jaundice; infectious hepatitis.

vi·re·lai (vēr le′), *n. French.* virelay.

vir·e·lay (vir′ə lā), *n.* **1.** an old French form of short lyric poem with two rhymes to a stanza, the first two lines forming a refrain, repeated at intervals. **2.** any of several similar forms, especially one consisting of longer and shorter lines, the lines of each kind rhyming together in a stanza, and the rhyme of the short lines repeated in the long lines of the following stanza. [< Old French *virelai*, alteration (probably influenced by Old French *lai* lay, lyric) of *vireli* a refrain]

vi·re·mi·a (vī rē′mē ə), *n.* an infection of the blood stream caused by a virus: *Finally the virus is absorbed through lymph vessels into the blood, thus producing viremia* (Science News Letter). [< *vir*(us) + *-emia*]

vir·e·o (vir′ē ō), *n., pl.* **-e·os.** any of a group of small, olive-green, insect-eating songbirds, including the North American black-capped vireo, red-eyed vireo, yellow-throated vireo, white-eyed vireo, blue-headed vireo, and warbling vireo; greenlet. [American English < Latin *vireō, -ōnis* a kind of bird; perhaps, the greenfinch < *virēre* be green]

Red-eyed Vireo (about 6 in. long)

vir·e·o·nine (vir′ē ə nīn, -nin), *adj.* of, having to do with, resembling, or related to a vireo.

vi·res (vī′rēz), *n. Latin.* the plural of **vis.**

vi·res·cence (vī res′əns), *n.* **1.** a turning or becoming green; greenness. **2.** *Botany.* the abnormal assumption of a green color by organs, as petals, normally white or colored other than green.

vi·res·cent (vī res′ənt), *adj.* turning green; tending to a green color; greenish. [< Latin *virēscēns, -entis,* present participle of *virēscere* turn green < *virēre* be green]

vir·ga (vėr′gə), *n. Meteorology.* streamers of rain or snow falling from a cloud, but dissipated before they reach the ground. [< Latin *virga* a twig, streak (in the heavens); colored stripe. Doublet of VERGE[1].]

vir·gate[1] (vėr′git, -gāt), *adj.* **1.** long, slender, and straight; rodlike. **2.** *Botany.* producing a large number of small twigs. [< Latin *virgātus* of a twig, streak < *virga* twig]

vir·gate[2] (vėr′git, -gāt), *n.* an old English unit of measure for land, usually ¼ of a hide or about 30 acres. [< Medieval Latin *virgata* (*terra*) a measure of land, feminine of Latin *virgātus* (see VIRGATE[1]); translation of Old English *gierd-land* (literally) yard-land]

Vir·gil·i·an (vėr jil′ē ən), *adj.* of, having to do with, or suggestive of Virgil, the Roman poet, or his poetry. Also, **Vergilian.**

vir·gin (vėr′jən), *n.* **1.** a woman, especially a young one, who has not had sexual intercourse. **2.** an unmarried woman, especially a young woman or girl. **3.** Also, **Virgin.** a picture or image of the Virgin Mary. **4.** an unmarried woman, distinguished by piety or steadfastness in religion, especially one vowed to lifelong chastity. **5.** a man, especially a young one, who has not had sexual intercourse. **6.** a female animal that has not copulated. **7.** *Zoology.* a female insect producing fertile eggs by parthenogenesis. —*adj.* **1.** being a virgin or virgins; chaste. **2.** composed or consisting of virgins. **3.** of, having to do with, suitable for, or characteristic of a virgin: *virgin modesty.* **4.** pure; spotless: *virgin snow.* **5.** not yet used: *virgin soil, a virgin forest.* **6.** free or clear of something. **7.** found pure or uncombined in nature; native: *virgin gold.* **8. a.** used for the first time, as a sword. **b.** being the first attempt; initial. **9.** (of metal) obtained directly from the ore or as a first product from smelting. **10.** (of olive oil, etc.) obtained from the first pressing, without the application of heat. **11.** *Zoology.* reproducing by parthenogenesis. [< Old French *virgine*, learned borrowing from Latin *virgō, -inis*]

Vir·gin (vėr′jən), *n.* **1.** the Virgin Mary. **2.** a constellation and the sixth sign of the zodiac; Virgo. [< *virgin*]

vir·gin·al[1] (vėr′jə nəl), *adj.* **1.** of or suitable for a virgin; maidenly. **2.** fresh; pure; unsullied; untouched. **3.** *Zoology.* parthenogenetic. [< Latin *virginālis* < *virgō, -inis* virgin, maiden] —**vir′gin·al·ly,** *adv.*

vir·gin·al[2] (vėr′jə nəl), *n.* **1.** a small kind of harpsichord or spinet set in a rectangular box or case without legs, common in England in the 1500's and 1600's. **2.** any harpsichord or spinet. [apparently < *virginal*[1]]

Virginal[2] (def. 1)

vir·gin·al·ist (vėr′jə nə list), *n.* a person who plays the virginal.

virgin birth, 1. the doctrine that Jesus was the Son of God and was miraculously conceived and born to the Virgin Mary. 2. *Zoology.* birth to a virgin; parthenogenesis.
vir·gin·hood (vėr′jən hu̇d), *n.* virginity.
Vir·gin·ia (vər jin′yə), *n. Roman Legend.* a maiden slain by her father to preserve her from the lust of one of the decemvirs.
Virginia bluebell, Virginia cowslip.
Virginia cowslip, a smooth perennial herb of the borage family, native to the eastern United States, with clusters of shell-shaped, blue flowers.
Virginia creeper, an American climbing plant of the grape family, having leaves with five leaflets, distinguishing it from poison ivy which has three leaflets, and inedible bluish-black berries; woodbine; American ivy.
Virginia deer, white-tailed deer.
Virginia fence or **Virginia rail fence,** a fence made of rails laid zigzag; snake fence.
Vir·gin·ian (vər jin′yən), *adj.* 1. of, belonging, or relating to Virginia, a State in the eastern United States. 2. of or having to do with an Algonkian language formerly spoken by Indians in eastern Virginia, North Carolina, and Maryland. —*n.* a native or inhabitant of Virginia.
Virginia opossum, the common opossum of the eastern United States.
Virginia rail, a small reddish-brown rail with a long, slender bill. It lives in the fresh-water marshes of central and eastern North America.
Virginia reel, an American country-dance in which the partners form two lines facing each other and perform a number of figures, usually comprising three distinct parts, the second of which is like the European reel; reel.
Virginia snakeroot, a birthwort of eastern North America, whose rhizome is used as a stimulant or tonic.
Virginia trumpet flower, the trumpet creeper.
vir·gin·i·bus pu·er·is·que (vər jin′ə bəs pū′ə ris′kwē), *Latin.* for maidens and boys.
Vir·gi·nis (vėr′ji nis), *n.* the genitive of **Virgo** (the constellation).
vir·gin·i·ty (vər jin′ə tē), *n.* 1. a. the state or condition of a virgin; maidenhood. b. a condition that presumes a state of chastity; spinsterhood. 2. the state of being virgin; purity; freshness.
vir·gin·i·um (vər jin′ē əm), *n.* the name formerly given to a rare metallic chemical element of atomic number 87, now known as francium. The claim of this discovery is now generally rejected by chemists. *Symbol:* Vi (no period). [American English < New Latin *virginium* < the state of *Virginia* + *-ium,* a suffix meaning "element"]
Virgin Mary, Mary, the mother of Jesus and the wife of Joseph.
Virgin Queen, Queen Elizabeth I (1533-1603) of England.
vir·gin's-bow·er (vėr′jənz bou′ər), *n.* any of various climbing species of clematis, bearing clusters of small white flowers, as a common American and a European species.
virgin wool, wool that has not been previously processed.
Vir·go (vėr′gō), *n., genitive* (*def. 1*) **Vir·gi·nis.** 1. a constellation on the celestial equator between Leo and Libra, containing the bright white star Spica; the Virgin. 2. the sixth sign of the zodiac, which the sun enters August 23; Virgin. [< Latin *Virgō* (literally) maiden]
vir·gu·late (vėr′gyə lit, -lāt), *adj.* shaped like a small rod.
vir·gule (vėr′gyül), *n.* a thin, sloping or upright line (/ or |) used between two words to indicate that the meaning of either word pertains, as in *and/or,* or as part of an abbreviation, as in *c/o.* [< Latin *virgula* punctuation mark, twig; (diminutive) < *virga* rod, virga]
vi·ri·cid·al (vī′rə sī′dəl), *adj.* destructive to virus: *a viricidal compound.* Also, **virucidal.**
vi·ri·cide (vī′rə sīd), *n.* a substance that destroys virus. Also, **virucide.**
vir·id (vir′id), *adj.* green; verdant: *The virid brilliance of the grass in the locust grove* (New Yorker). [< Latin *viridis* green]
vir·i·des·cence (vir′ə des′əns), *n.* a being viridescent.
vir·i·des·cent (vir′ə des′ənt), *adj.* somewhat green; greenish. [< Late Latin *viridēscēns, -entis,* present participle of *viridēscere* turn green < Latin *viridāre* < *viridis* green < *virēre* be green]
vi·rid·i·an (və rid′ē ən), *n.* a clear bluish-green coloring matter, a hydrated chromic oxide. [< Latin *viridis* green + English *-an*]
vi·rid·i·ty (və rid′ə tē), *n.* 1. the quality or state of being green; greenness; verdancy. 2. innocence; inexperience. [< Latin *viriditās* < *viridis* green < *virēre* be green]
vir·i·do·gris·e·in (vir′ə dō gris′ə in), *n.* a crystalline antibiotic derived from a species of streptomyces, used against gram-positive bacteria and certain fungi. *Formula:* $C_{44}H_{62}N_8O_{10}$
vir·ile (vir′əl), *adj.* 1. manly; masculine. 2. full of manly strength or masculine vigor. 3. having to do with or capable of procreation. 4. vigorous; forceful. [< Latin *virīlis* < *vir* man]
vir·il·ism (vir′ə liz əm), *n.* an abnormal condition in any female, in which certain male secondary sex characteristics appear, as abnormally heavy facial hair or a large Adam's apple.
vi·ril·i·ty (və ril′ə tē), *n., pl.* **-ties.** 1. manly strength; masculine vigor. 2. power of procreation; manhood. 3. vigor; forcefulness.
vir·il·i·za·tion (vir′ə lə zā′shən), *n.* the acquiring of secondary male characteristics: *They suspected the high blood pressure and the virilization were caused by adrenal gland disorder* (Science News Letter).
vir·il·ize (vir′ə līz), *v.t., v.i.,* **-ized, -iz·ing.** to cause to acquire secondary male characteristics.
vir·i·lo·cal (vir′ə lō′kəl), *adj. Anthropology.* having the focus in the home of the husband's family; patrilocal. [< Latin *vir* man + *locus* place + English *-al*[1]]
vi·roid (vī′roid), *n.* an ultramicroscopic form theoretically existing in living organisms that is capable of either becoming a virus or giving rise to viruses by mutation. —*adj.* of a viroid: *a viroid mutant, a viroid ancestor.* 2. viral: *a viroid disease.*
vir·o·la (vir′ə lə), *n.* a South American tree related to the nutmeg, having a hard, reddish-brown wood. [< New Latin *Virola* the genus name]
vi·ro·log·ic (vī′rə loj′ik), *adj.* virological.
vi·ro·log·i·cal (vī′rə loj′ə kəl), *adj.* of or having to do with virology: *The most practical results so far of virological research are vaccines* (Time).
vi·rol·o·gist (vī rol′ə jist), *n.* a person skilled in virology: *Top virologists, fresh from successes against polio and other viral diseases, are focusing their powerful electron microscopes on suspected cancer viruses* (Wall Street Journal).
vi·rol·o·gy (vī rol′ə jē), *n.* the scientific study of viruses and virus diseases: *Virology is one of the dark continents of medical science, and yet its subject matter includes some of the most destructive and crippling diseases known to man* (Scientific American).
vi·rol·y·sin (vī rol′ə sin), *n.* an enzyme produced in a healthy cell by a virus, and responsible for the spread of the virus to other cells: *Virolysin . . . causes an explosion of the cell wall thus spreading the infection* (Science News Letter).
vi·ro·sis (vī rō′sis), *n., pl.* **-ses** (-sēz). any disease caused by a virus.
v. irr., irregular verb.
vir·tu (vėr tü′, vėr′tü), *n.* 1. excellence or merit in an object of art because of its workmanship, rarity, antiquity, or the like. 2. objects of art; choice curios. 3. a taste for objects of art or curios; a knowledge of, or interest in, the fine arts. Also, **vertu.** [< Italian *virtù* excellence < Latin *virtus* Doublet of VIRTUE.]
vir·tu·al (vėr′chu̇ əl), *adj.* 1. being something in effect, though not so in name; actual; real: *The battle was won with so great a loss of soldiers that it was a virtual defeat. He is the virtual president, though his title is secretary.* 2. *Optics.* a. having to do with an image formed when the rays from each point of the object diverge as if from a point beyond the reflecting or refracting surface. Such images cannot be placed on a screen. b. having to do with a focus of like nature. 3. having inherent qualities or virtues which exert a powerful influence on other objects. [< Medieval Latin *virtualis* < Latin *virtus;* see VIRTUE]
vir·tu·al·i·ty (vėr′chu̇ al′ə tē), *n.* the state or quality of being virtual.
vir·tu·al·ly (vėr′chu̇ ə lē), *adv.* in effect, though not in name; actually; really: *The factory worker, virtually imprisoned and broken in will by submission to his machines, . . . envies the worker at a trade* (Edmund Wilson).
vir·tue (vėr′chü), *n.* 1. moral excellence; goodness. 2. a particular moral excellence, as the four cardinal virtues (justice, prudence, fortitude, and temperance) or the three theological or Christian virtues (faith, hope, and charity). 3. chastity; purity. 4. a good quality: *He praised the virtues of the car.* 5. the power to produce effects; potency; efficacy: *There is little virtue in that medicine.* 6. *Obsolete.* manliness.
by or **in virtue of,** relying on; because of; on account of: *The king then assumed the power in virtue of his prerogative* (Daniel Webster).
make a virtue of necessity, to do willingly what must be done anyway: *Making a virtue of necessity, I put the best face I could upon it, and went about the work she set me upon* (William Hughes).
virtues, the seventh of the nine orders of angels in medieval theology: *Troops of powers, virtues, cherubims, . . . are chanting praises to their heavenly king* (Francis Quarles).
[Middle English *vertu,* and *virtu* < Anglo-French, Old French *vertu* < Latin *virtus* moral strength; manliness; virile force < *vir* man. Doublet of VIRTU.]
—**Syn.** 1. uprightness, integrity. See **goodness.** 4. merit.
vir·tue·less (vėr′chü lis), *adj.* devoid of virtue; without excellence or merit; bad.
vir·tues (vėr′chüz), *n.pl.* See under **virtue.**
vir·tu·ose (vėr′chu̇ ōs′), *adj.* having the characteristics of a virtuoso; of or having to do with virtuosos.
vir·tu·os·ic (vėr′chu̇ os′ik, -ō′sik), *adj.* showing the artistic qualities and skills of a virtuoso: *a virtuosic performance.*
vir·tu·os·i·ty (vėr′chu̇ os′ə tē), *n., pl.* **-ties.** 1. the character or skill of a virtuoso. 2. a. interest or taste in the fine arts, especially of a trifling, dilettante nature. b. excessive attention to technique, or to the production of special effects, especially in music. 3. lovers of the fine arts.
vir·tu·o·so (vėr′chu̇ ō′sō), *n., pl.* **-sos, -si** (-sē), *adj.* —*n.* 1. a person skilled in the methods of an art, especially in playing a musical instrument. 2. a person who has a cultivated appreciation of artistic excellence; connoisseur. 3. a student or collector of objects of art, curios, antiquities, etc. 4. *Obsolete.* a person who pursues special investigations or has a general interest in the arts or sciences; learned person; scientist or scholar.
—*adj.* virtuosic: *virtuoso singing. The play is built around Sir Alec's virtuoso performance as Dylan* (Maclean's).
[< Italian *virtuoso* learned person; of exceptional worth < Late Latin *virtuōsus;* see VIRTUOUS]
vir·tu·o·so·ship (vir′chu̇ ō′sō ship), *n.* the occupation or pursuits of a virtuoso.
vir·tu·ous (vėr′chu̇ əs), *adj.* 1. good; moral; righteous: *virtuous conduct, a virtuous life.* 2. chaste; pure. 3. *Archaic.* having inherent, natural virtue or power, often of a magic or supernatural nature; endowed with potent medicinal powers beneficial in healing. [< Anglo-French, Old French *vertuous,* learned borrowing from Late Latin *virtuōsus* < *virtus, -ūs* virtue] —**vir′tu·ous·ly,** *adv.* —**vir′tu·ous·ness,** *n.* —**Syn.** 1. upright, worthy.
vir·tu·te et ar·mis (vər tü′tē et är′mis, vər tyü′tē), *Latin.* by valor and arms. This is the motto of Mississippi.
vi·ru·cid·al (vī′rə sī′dəl), *adj.* viricidal.
vi·ru·cide (vī′rə sīd), *n.* viricide.
vir·u·lence (vir′yə ləns, vir′ə-), *n.* 1. the quality of being very poisonous or harmful. 2. intense bitterness or spite; violent hostility.
vir·u·len·cy (vir′yə lən sē, vir′ə-), *n.* virulence.
vir·u·lent (vir′yə lənt, vir′ə-), *adj.* 1. very poisonous or harmful; deadly: *a virulent poison.* 2. (of diseases) characterized by a rapid and severe malignant or infectious condition. 3. (of a microorganism) able to cause a disease by breaking down the protective mechanisms of the host. 4. intensely bitter or spiteful; violently hostile: *virulent*

wrath or abuse. Enemies as virulent as ever (Gouverneur Morris). [< Latin *vīrulentus* < *vīrus* poison; see VIRUS] —**vir′u·lent·ly,** *adv.* —**Syn. 1.** noxious. **4.** acrimonious.

vi·rus (vī′rəs), *n.* **1.** any of a group of disease-producing agents composed of protein and nucleic acid. Viruses are smaller than ordinary bacteria and are dependent upon living tissue for their reproduction and growth. Viruses are filterable and cause such diseases in man as rabies, polio, chicken pox, and the common cold. **2.** vaccine virus. **3.** the poison produced in a person or animal suffering from an infectious disease. **4.** the venom emitted by a poisonous animal. **5.** anything that poisons the mind or morals; corrupting influence: *the virus of bigotry.* [< Latin *vīrus* poison; sap of plants; any slimy liquid] —**vi′rus·like′,** *adj.*

virus disease, any disease caused by a virus, such as tobacco mosaic or influenza.

virus hepatitis, infectious hepatitis.

virus pneumonia, a type of mild but protracted pneumonia caused by a virus: *It may take seven days to several months for a person to recover from virus pneumonia* (Mark D. Altschule).

virus X, an infection or disease of uncertain nature, sometimes resembling influenza.

vis (vis), *n., pl.* **vi·res.** *Latin.* force; power.

Vis., 1. Viscount. **2.** Viscountess.

vi·sa (vē′zə), *n., v.,* **-saed, -sa·ing.** —*n.* an official signature or endorsement upon a passport, showing that it has been examined and approved and that the bearer may enter the country or pass through it. —*v.t.* to examine and sign (a passport or other document). Also, **visé.** [< French *visa,* learned borrowing from Latin (*carta*) *vīsa* (paper) that has been verified, that is, seen; feminine of *vīsus,* past participle of *vidēre* to see]

vis·age (viz′ij), *n.* **1.** the face: *She parted her shaggy locks from her visage* (Charlotte Brontë). *A visage . . . looking no fresher than an apple that has stood the winter* (George Eliot). *His grizzled beard . . . obscured a visage of despair* (Scott). **2.** an appearance or aspect: *to recall the visage of autumn.* [< Old French *visage* < *vis* face, appearance < Latin *vīsus, -ūs* a look < *vidēre* to see] —**Syn. 1.** See **face.**

vis·aged (viz′ijd), *adj.* having a visage: *visaged in sorrow* (Horace Bushnell).

-visaged, *combining form.* having a —— visage: *Grim-visaged = having a grim visage.*

vis-à-vis (vē′zə vē′), *adv., adj.* face to face; opposite: *We sat vis-à-vis. The usual position in modern dancing is vis-à-vis.*

—*prep.* face to face with; opposite to; in relation to: *The President is responsible vis-à-vis Congress for his cabinet.*

—*n.* **1.** a person or thing that is opposite: *New York is the center of commerce as its vis-à-vis, Washington, is of government.* **2.** a light carriage for two persons sitting face to face. **3.** an S-shaped seat built so that two people can sit on it facing each other; tête-à-tête.

[< French *vis-à-vis* (literally) face to face; *vis* < Old French; see VISAGE]

Vi·sa·yan (vi sä′yən), *n.* **1.** a member of a large native race in the Philippines. **2.** the Malay language of this race. Also, **Bisayan.**

Visc., 1. Viscount. **2.** Viscountess.

vis·ca·cha (vis kä′chə), *n.* either of two large burrowing rodents of South America, related to the chinchillas. Also, **vizcacha.** [< Spanish *viscacha* < Quechua (Peru) *huiscacha*]

vis·cer·a (vis′ər ə), *n. pl. of* **vis·cus. 1.** the soft internal organs of the cavities of the body, especially of the abdominal cavity. The heart, stomach, liver, intestines, kidneys, etc., are viscera. **2.** the intestines. [< Latin *vīscera,* neuter plural of *vīscus*]

vis·cer·al (vis′ər əl), *adj.* **1.** of, having to do with, or in the region of the viscera. **2.** (of a disease) affecting the viscera. **3.** consisting of or of the nature of viscera. **4.** touching deeply; affecting inward feelings; irrational; emotional: *The issue of Federal finance seems to stir up such visceral reactions that reasonable discussion . . . has become increasingly difficult* (Wall Street Journal). **5.** crude; blunt: *a visceral description of prison life.* —**vis′cer·al·ly,** *adv.*

vis·cer·o·gen·ic (vis′ər ə jen′ik), *adj.* originating in the viscera or in visceral processes: *viscerogenic hunger, viscerogenic needs.*

vis·cer·o·pto·sis (vis′ər ə tō′sis), *n.* a slipping down of the abdominal viscera. [< *viscera* + *ptosis*]

vis·cer·o·ton·ic (vis′ər ə ton′ik), *n.* an endomorph: *The viscerotonic is a sociable type who loves food, comfort, parties, and people, falls in love easily and makes a good salesman or public relations man* (Maclean's). —*adj.* endomorphic. [< *viscera* + *ton*(us) + *-ic*]

vis·cid (vis′id), *adj.* **1.** thick and sticky like heavy syrup or glue; glutinous; adhesive; sticky; viscous. **2.** *Botany.* covered with a sticky secretion, as leaves. [< Late Latin *viscidus* < Latin *viscum* birdlime] —**vis′cid·ly,** *adv.* —**vis′cid·ness,** *n.* —**Syn. 1.** mucilaginous.

vis·cid·i·ty (vi sid′ə tē), *n.* **1.** the quality of being viscid or sticky; viscidness. **2.** a viscid substance or collection of substances.

vis·co·e·las·tic (vis′kō i las′tik), *adj.* having the properties of viscosity and elasticity.

vis·co·e·las·tic·i·ty (vis′kō i las′tis′ə tē, -ē′las-), *n.* the quality or condition of being viscoelastic.

vis·coid (vis′koid), *adj.* of a viscid or viscous nature. [< *visc*(ous) + *-oid*]

vis·coi·dal (vis koi′dəl), *adj.* viscoid.

vis·com·e·ter (vis kom′ə tər), *n.* viscosimeter.

vis·co·met·ric (vis′kō met′rik), *adj.* viscosimetric.

vis·com·e·try (vis kom′ə trē), *n.* viscosimetry.

vis·cose[1] (vis′kōs), *n.* a plastic material prepared by the treatment of cellulose with caustic soda and carbon disulfide. Viscose is used in manufacturing rayon, in making a product resembling celluloid, for sizing, and for other purposes. —*adj.* having to do with or made from viscose. [< Latin *viscum* birdlime + English *-ose*[2] (because it is a syruplike material)]

vis·cose[2] (vis′kōs), *adj. Obsolete.* viscous; viscid. [< Late Latin *viscōsus.* Compare VISCOUS.]

vis·co·sim·e·ter (vis′kō sim′ə tər), *n.* an instrument for measuring the viscosity of liquids. [< *viscosi*(ty) + *-meter*]

vis·co·si·met·ric (vis′kō sə met′rik), *adj.* of or having to do with a viscosimeter.

vis·co·sim·e·try (vis′kō sim′ə trē), *n.* the measurement of the viscosity of liquids.

vis·cos·i·ty (vis kos′ə tē), *n., pl.* **-ties. 1.** the quality, fact, or degree of being viscous. **2.** *Physics.* **a.** the resistance of a fluid to the motion of its molecules among themselves. **b.** the ability of a solid or semisolid to change its shape gradually under stress.

vis·count (vī′kount), *n.* **1.** an English nobleman, usually the eldest son of an earl, holding the title of viscount during his father's lifetime, ranking next below an earl or count and above a baron. **2.** a person administering a district as the deputy or representative of an earl, especially a sheriff or high sheriff in England. **3.** (on the Continent) the son or younger brother of a count. [< Anglo-French *viscount* < Medieval Latin *vicecomes, -itis* < *vice-* vice- + Latin *cōmes, -itis* companion. Compare COUNT[2].]

vis·count·cy (vī′kount sē), *n., pl.* **-cies.** the title, rank, or dignity of a viscount.

vis·count·ess (vī′koun tis), *n.* **1.** the wife or widow of a viscount. **2.** a woman holding in her own right a rank equivalent to that of a viscount.

vis·count·ship (vī′kount ship), *n.* viscountcy.

vis·count·y (vī′koun tē), *n., pl.* **-count·ies. 1.** viscountcy. **2.** the office or jurisdiction of a viscount, or the territory under his rule.

vis·cous (vis′kəs), *adj.* **1.** (of a liquid) thick like syrup or glue; sticky; viscid. **2.** *Physics.* having or characterized by the property of viscosity. [< Late Latin *viscōsus* < *viscum* birdlime] —**vis′cous·ly,** *adv.* —**vis′cous·ness,** *n.*

Visct., 1. Viscount. **2.** Viscountess.

vis·cus (vis′kəs), *n.* the singular of **viscera.**

vise (vīs), *n., v.,* **vised, vis·ing.** —*n.* a tool having two jaws opened and closed by a screw, used to hold an object firmly while work is being done on it. —*v.t.* to hold, press, or squeeze with or as if with a vise: *He usually has a cigar butt vised in his teeth* (Time). Also, *especially British,* **vice.** [Middle English *vyse* any apparatus driven by screws; screw-shaped < Old French *vis* screw < Vulgar Latin *vītium* < Latin *vītis* tendril of a vine] —**vise′like′,** *adj.*

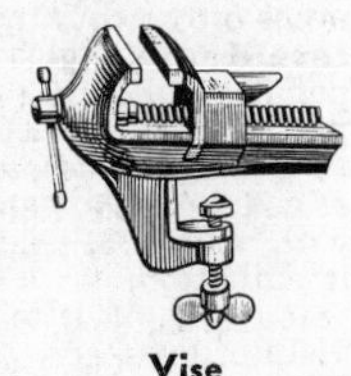
Vise

vi·sé (vē′zā), *n., v.t.,* **-séed, -sé·ing.** visa. [< French *visé,* past participle of *viser* < *visa;* see VISA]

Vish·nu (vish′nü), *n.* (in Hindu religion) the name of one of the three chief deities (Brahma, the creator, Vishnu, the preserver, and Siva, the destroyer), identified by his worshipers with the supreme deity and regarded as the preserver of the world. Of Vishnu's ten appearances on earth in human form (avatars), nine have already occurred. The most important reincarnations, Krishna and Rama, are specially honored. [< Sanskrit *viṣṇu,* probably < root *vis-* to make, do]

vis·i·bil·i·ty (viz′ə bil′ə tē), *n., pl.* **-ties. 1.** the condition or quality of being visible; capability of being seen. **2. a.** the relative clearness of the atmosphere or ability to see with reference to the distance at which things can be clearly seen under the conditions existing at a particular time. **b.** the greatest distance at which objects can be seen, especially with the naked eye or, sometimes, radar; range of vision. **3.** a visible thing or object: *Men are visibilities; ghosts are not.* **4.** the ratio of the luminous flux of a specified wave length to the radiation that produces it.

vis·i·ble (viz′ə bəl), *adj.* **1. a.** that can be seen: *The shore was barely visible through the fog.* **b.** that can be converted, often from one of various forms of energy, into electrical energy in order to be made visible: *heart beats made visible with an electrocardiograph.* **2.** that can be seen under certain particular conditions: *The eclipse of the moon was visible at midnight.* **3.** perceptible; readily evident; apparent: *a tramp having no visible means of support.*

—*n.* **1.** something seen; visible thing. **2.** *Genetics.* a mutation easily seen by examination: *We know how many of the genetical effects are . . . dominant visibles which affect the offspring, or recessive visibles which affect later generations of irradiated flies* (C. Auerbach).

[< Latin *vīsibilis* < *vidēre* to see] —**vis′i·ble·ness,** *n.*

—**Syn.** *adj.* **1. a.** distinct. **3.** manifest.

visible light, light consisting of electromagnetic waves that can be seen, as contrasted with ultraviolet and infrared waves that are invisible: *Visible light occupies less than one octave of the spectrum of electromagnetic waves* (W. C. Vaughan).

visible spectrum, a series of colors merging through continuous hues into each other from red to violet. See **spectroscope** for picture.

visible speech, a system of phonetic notation invented by Alexander Melville Bell, 1819-1905, as an aid for teaching the deaf to speak, consisting of conventionalized diagrams of the organs of speech in position to utter various sounds.

vis·i·bly (viz′ə blē), *adv.* so as to be visible; plainly; evidently.

Vis·i·goth (viz′ə goth), *n.* a member of the western division of the Goths. The Goths plundered Rome in 410 A.D., and formed a monarchy in France and northern Spain about 418 A.D. [< Late Latin *Visigothī* < Germanic; taken as "western Goths". Compare OSTROGOTHS.]

Vis·i·goth·ic (viz′ə goth′ik), *adj.* of or having to do with the Visigoths.

vis·ile (viz′əl, vizh′-), *n. Psychology.* a person in whose mind visual images are predominant, or especially distinct; visualizer. [< Latin *vīsus, -ūs* sight; see VISUAL]

vi·sion (vizh′ən), *n.* **1.** the power of seeing; sense of sight: *The old man wears glasses because his vision is poor.* **2.** the act or fact of seeing; sight. **3.** the power of perceiving something not actually present to the eye, whether by supernatural insight, imagination, or by clear thinking: *a prophet of great vision.* **4.** something seen in the imagination, in a dream, in one's thoughts, or the like: *The beggar had visions of great wealth.* **5.** a phantom. **6.** a very beautiful person, scene, etc.

—*v.t., v.i.* **1.** to see in, or as if in, a vision. **2.** to show in a vision.

[< Anglo-French *visiun,* Old French *vision,*

…ed borrowing from Latin *vīsiō, -ōnis* … *vidēre* to see]

—**Syn.** *n.* **1.** eyesight. **3.** discernment. **4.** fantasy.

vi·sion·al (vizh′ə nəl), *adj.* **1.** connected or concerned with, relating to, or based upon, a vision or visions: *a visional theory explaining the phenomenon of hallucinations.* **2.** of the nature of, part of, or seen or occurring in, a vision; visionary; unreal. —**vi′sion·al·ly,** *adv.*

vi·sion·ar·i·ness (vizh′ə ner′ē nis), *n.* the character of being visionary.

vi·sion·ar·y (vizh′ə ner′ē), *adj., n., pl.* **-ar·ies.** —*adj.* **1.** not practical; dreamy: *Ruth is a visionary girl; she spends her time daydreaming.* **2.** of or belonging to a vision; seen in a vision; imaginary: *The visionary scene faded and John awoke. The danger was not entirely visionary.* **3.** having visions; able to have visions.
—*n.* **1.** a person who has visions of unknown or future things. **2.** a person who has unpractical or fantastic ideas or schemes.
—**Syn.** *adj.* **1.** fanciful. —**Ant.** *adj.* **1.** practical.

vi·sion·less (vizh′ən lis), *adj.* **1.** without vision; blind. **2.** having no vision of unseen things; lacking higher insight or inspiration: *They must, by definition, be alienated by the nationalistic and restrictive policies to which the Labour Party is becoming committed increasingly under its present visionless leadership* (Manchester Guardian Weekly).

vis·it (viz′it), *v.t.* **1.** to go to see; come to see: *to visit a city, church, or museum.* **2.** to go or come to see, to inspect, or to examine officially or as a professional duty: *A doctor visits his patients. The inspector visited the factory.* **3.** to make a call on or stay with for social or other reasons; be a guest of: *to visit one's aunt, to visit the sick.* **4.** to come upon; afflict: *Job was visited by many troubles.* **5.** to send upon; inflict: *to visit one's anger on someone.* **6.** to punish; avenge: *So the sins of my mother should be visited upon me* (Shakespeare). —*v.i.* **1.** to pay a call; make a stay; be a guest: *to visit in the country.* **2.** *U.S. Informal.* to talk or chat. **3.** to inflict punishment or take vengeance.
—*n.* **1.** a going or coming to a place for sightseeing, pleasure, etc. **2.** a going or coming to a person or place for the purpose of inspection, examination, or treatment: *a visit to the dentist.* **3.** a stay as a guest: *to make, pay, or return a visit.* **4.** *U.S. Informal.* an informal talk; chat. **5.** *Maritime Law.* the act of a naval officer boarding a vessel belonging to a neutral state to ascertain its nationality and cargo.
[< Latin *vīsitāre* come to inspect (frequentative) < *vīsere* look at well (intensive) < *vidēre* to see]

vis·it·a·ble (viz′ə tə bəl), *adj.* **1.** that can be visited; suitable for or deserving of a visit: *The tropics are visitable only during the winter.* **2.** subject to official visits or inspections by authorities, etc.

vis·it·ant (viz′ə tənt), *n.* **1.** a visitor; guest. **2.** a migratory bird temporarily frequenting a particular locality. —*adj.* paying a visit or visits; visiting.

vis·it·a·tion (viz′ə tā′shən), *n.* **1.** the act of visiting. **2.** the act of visiting for the purpose of making an official inspection or examination: *A nation at war has the right of visitation of neutral ships; that is, the right to inspect their cargoes.* **3.** a visiting by God or a supernatural power in order to encourage, comfort, or aid, to test or try, or to afflict with sickness or other trouble as a punishment for wrongdoing. **4.** a severe affliction, blow, or trial, regarded as an instance of divine dispensation. **5.** the falling upon a people, country, etc., of some violent or destructive agency or force: *the visitation of the plague.* **6.** *Zoology.* the appearance of animals or birds at a place in unusual numbers or at an unusual time. —**Syn.** **1.** visit, call.

Vis·it·a·tion (viz′ə tā′shən), *n.* **1.** (in the Bible) the visit paid by the Virgin Mary to Elizabeth. Luke 1:39-56. **2.** a church festival commemorating this, celebrated on July 2. [< *visitation*]

vis·it·a·tion·al (viz′ə tā′shə nəl), *adj.* of or having to do with a visitation.

vis·it·a·to·ri·al (viz′ə tə tôr′ē əl, -tōr′-), *adj.* **1.** having to do with, involving, or implying official visitation. **2.** having or exercising the power or authority of visitation.

vis·it·ing card (viz′ə ting), **1.** a small card bearing a person's name, to be left or presented on paying a visit; calling card. **2.** a card issued to a visitor at some institution, military base, etc., allowing him entry.

visiting fireman, *U.S. Slang.* **1.** a visiting dignitary or official accorded special treatment, as by being given a reception, guided tour, etc.: *The U.S. Information Service still had to round up 70 more cars from embassy and military sources for the rest of the visiting firemen* (Wall Street Journal). **2.** a vacationer, tourist, etc., supposed to be a liberal spender: *our local sightseeing guides, whose very livelihood depends on distinguishing at first glance a visiting fireman from a . . . resident* (Newsweek). **3.** any member of a visiting group: *Tuesday, the squad plays a team of visiting firemen* (New Yorker).

visiting professor, a professor on a leave of absence or in retirement who is invited by a college or university to deliver a special course of lectures.

visiting teacher, a schoolteacher trained in social work who comes to the homes of pupils who do not or cannot attend school regularly with the aim of instructing them and improving the social conditions in which they live.

vis·i·tor (viz′ə tər), *n.* **1.** a person who visits or is visiting; guest. **2.** an animal or bird that frequents certain areas at regular seasons.
—**Syn. 1. Visitor, guest** mean someone who comes to stay somewhere or with someone. **Visitor,** the general word, applies to anyone, regardless of the length of his stay or his reason for coming: *Visitors from the East arrived last night.* **Guest** emphasizes the idea of being entertained, and applies especially to someone invited to come or stay: *He usually entertains his guests at the club.*

vis·i·to·ri·al (viz′ə tôr′ē əl, -tōr′-), *adj.* **1.** visitatorial. **2.** capable of or having to do with visiting.

vis·i·tress (viz′ə tris), *n.* **1.** a female visitor. **2.** a woman who makes charitable visits to the poor.

vis ma·jor (vis mā′jər), **1.** *Latin.* a superior or overpowering force. **2.** *Law.* a superior force that cannot be resisted, sometimes releasing one from the obligation to fulfill a contract. [< Latin *vīs major* (literally) greater force]

vi·sor (vī′zər), *n.* **1.** the movable front part of a helmet, lowered to cover the face, or the upper section of this part, the lower being the ventail. See **armet** for picture. **2.** the projecting brim of a cap, to protect the eyes from the sun. **3.** an outward appearance that hides something different under it; mask; disguise: *to conceal hatred under a visor of friendliness.*
—*v.t.* to cover up with or as if with a visor; protect: *Franny, looking at him, now had a hand visored over her eyes* (J.D. Salinger). Also, **vizor.**
[Middle English *viser* < Anglo-French *viser,* Old French *visiere* < *vis* face; see VISAGE]

vi·sored (vī′zərd), *adj.* furnished or covered with a visor.

vi·sor·less (vī′zər lis), *adj.* having no visor.

Vis·queen (vis′kwēn), *n. Trademark.* a flexible polyethylene film used especially to protect walls and floors, etc., against moisture during the construction of a building.

vis·ta (vis′tə), *n.* **1.** a view seen through a narrow passage or opening: *The opening between the two rows of trees afforded a vista of the lake.* **2.** such an opening or passage itself: *a shady vista of elms.* **3.** a mental view: *Education should open up new vistas.* **4.** an extended view of a long period of time or series of events, experiences, etc.: *the dim vista of centuries.* [< Italian *vista* a view, noun use of feminine past participle of *vedere* to see < Latin *vidēre*]

VISTA (no periods), Volunteers in Service to America (an antipoverty agency of the U.S. Government, established in 1964 to send volunteers to work and help in depressed areas of the country).

vista dome, a glass dome enclosing the upper level of a railroad observation car and providing a view of the scenery.

vis·taed (vis′təd), *adj.* **1.** placed or arranged so as to make a vista or avenue. **2.** provided with vistas. **3.** seen as if in prospect by the imagination.

vis·ta·less (vis′tə lis), *adj.* lacking any vista or prospect.

Vis·ta·Vi·sion (vis′tə vizh′ən), *n. Trademark.* a motion-picture medium using picture frames 2½ times larger than the standard frame and a camera that runs the film horizontally instead of vertically, giving sharp, clear images on a flat, wide screen.

vis·u·al (vizh′ů əl), *adj.* **1.** of, having to do with, concerned with, or relating to sight or vision: *visual acuteness of the retina.* **2.** (of organs) having the function of producing vision: *visual rods.* **3.** performed or produced by means of vision: *a visual test.* **4.** that can be seen; perceptible; visible: *visual colors.* **5.** of vision and light in relation to each other; optical: *the visual focus of a lens.* **6.** of the nature of a mental vision; produced or occurring as a picture in the mind: *to form a visual image of the author's description.*
—*n.* a visualist.
visuals, a film or part of a film without a sound track: *The program consists of a live lecture with visuals plus film clips* (Harper's).
[< Late Latin *vīsuālis* < Latin *vīsus, -ūs* sight, a look < *vidēre* to see]

visual acuity, distinctness of vision; the ability of the eye to perceive and distinguish an image.

visual aid, any device or means for aiding or furthering the learning process through the sense of sight, such as charts, diagrams, motion pictures, and filmstrips.

visual binary, a binary or double star that can be seen as two stars with a telescope and sometimes with the unaided eye.

visual education, the use of visual aids in teaching.

visual flight, *Aeronautics.* a flight in which the pilot navigates on the basis of observed bodies of land or water; contact flight.

vis·u·al·ise (vizh′ů ə līz), *v.t., v.i.,* **-ised, -is·ing.** *Especially British.* visualize.

vis·u·al·ist (vizh′ů ə list), *n.* a person who thinks, remembers, imagines, etc., chiefly in terms of sight.

vis·u·al·iz·a·ble (vizh′ů ə lī′zə bəl), *adj.* that can be visualized: *The electron microscope, in which beams of electrons are focused sharply enough to take photographs of objects less than a millionth of an inch across . . . made many virus particles visualizable* (Time).

vis·u·al·i·za·tion (vizh′ů ə lə zā′shən), *n.* **1.** a visualizing or being visualized. **2.** a thing visualized.

vis·u·al·ize (vizh′ů ə līz), *v.,* **-ized, -iz·ing.** —*v.t.* **1.** to form a mental picture of: *to visualize a friend's face when he is away.* **2.** to make visible. —*v.i.* to form a mental picture of something invisible, absent, or abstract.

vis·u·al·iz·er (vizh′ů ə lī′zər), *n.* **1.** a person who visualizes or has the ability to form mental images of invisible things, abstractions, etc. **2.** *Psychology.* a person whose mental images are mainly visual.

vis·u·al·ly (vizh′ů ə lē), *adv.* in a visual manner or respect; by sight.

visual purple or **red,** *Biochemistry.* a purplish-red protein present in the rods of the retina of the eye, that, in the presence of light, is bleached to form a yellow pigment (visual yellow); rhodopsin. Visual purple, in turn, decomposes to form colorless substances and vitamin A. Visual purple is considered an important factor in vision, especially night vision.

vis·u·als (vizh′ů əlz), *n.pl.* See under **visual,** *n.*

visual yellow, retinene.

vis vi·va (vis vī′və), **1.** *Latin.* a living or active force. **2.** the energy of motion or of a moving thing; kinetic energy.

vi·ta (vī′tə), *n.* **1.** *Latin.* life. **2.** a biography. [< Latin *vīta* life, related to *vīvere* to live]

vi·ta·ceous (vī tā′shəs), *adj.* belonging to the grape family. [< New Latin *Vitaceae* the family name (< Latin *vītis* vine, tendril) + English *-ous*]

vi·ta·glass (vī′tə glas′, -gläs′), *n.* **1.** a glass that allows the passage of a large part of the ultraviolet rays of the sunlight. **2.** **Vitaglass,** a trademark for this glass.

vi·tal (vī′təl), *adj.* **1.** of, having to do with, accompanying, or characteristic of life; exhibited by living things: *vital processes, vital energy.* **2.** necessary to life: *Eating is a vital function. The heart is a vital organ.* **3.** very necessary; very important; essential: *a vital question. An adequate army is vital to the defense of a nation. Drainage of the swamp was considered vital to the welfare of the community.* **4.** causing death, failure, or ruin: *a vital wound, a vital blow to an industry.* **5.** *Poetic.* having life; living; animate. **6.** full

of life and spirit; lively. **7.** being that immaterial force that is present in living things and by which they are animated and maintained: *vital spark.*
—*n.* **vitals, a.** the parts or organs essential to life, including the brain, heart, lungs, and stomach: *A slight wound; though it pierced his body, it . . . missed the vitals* (John Fletcher). **b.** the essential parts or features of anything; essentials: *If the vitals were preserved, I should not differ for the rest* (Thomas Burton).
[< Latin *vītālis* < *vīta* life, related to *vīvere* to live] —**vi′tal·ly,** *adv.* —**vi′tal·ness,** *n.*
—**Syn.** *adj.* **3.** fundamental. **4.** mortal. **6.** vigorous.

vital force or **principle,** the animating force in animals and plants; the principle upon which the phenomena of life were supposed to depend.

vi·tal·ise (vī′tə līz), *v.t.,* **-ised, -is·ing.** *Especially British.* vitalize.

vi·tal·ism (vī′tə liz əm), *n.* the doctrine that the behavior of a living organism is, at least in part, due to a vital principle that cannot possibly be explained by physics and chemistry.

vi·tal·ist (vī′tə list), *n.* an adherent of the doctrine of vitalism.

vi·tal·is·tic (vī′tə lis′tik), *adj.* of or like vitalism or vitalists: *Until recently, investigation of the central cerebral processes has been confined to the experimental psychologist who, all too frequently in the last resort, seeks the aid of vitalistic postulates* (George M. Wyburn).

vi·tal·i·ty (vī tal′ə tē), *n., pl.* **-ties. 1.** vital force; power to live: *Her vitality was lessened by illness.* **2.** something having vital force. **3.** the power to endure or be active: *the vitality of Shakespeare's sonnets.* **4.** strength or vigor of mind or body.

vi·tal·i·za·tion (vī′tə lə zā′shən), *n.* **1.** the act or process of vitalizing. **2.** the state of being vitalized.

vi·tal·ize (vī′tə līz), *v.t.,* **-ized, -iz·ing. 1.** to give life to. **2.** to put vitality or vigor into. **3.** to present (a literary or artistic idea) in a lifelike manner.

vi·tal·iz·er (vī′tə lī′zər), *n.* a person or thing that vitalizes.

Vi·tal·li·um (vī tal′ē əm), *n. Trademark.* an alloy consisting essentially of cobalt and chromium, used especially in bone surgery.

vi·tals (vī′təlz), *n. pl.* See under **vital,** *n.*

vital statistics, statistics that give facts about births, deaths, marriages, divorces, etc.

vi·ta·mer (vī′tə mər), *n.* any substance in the diet of an animal that can produce the same effect a vitamin does. Vitamers vary from species to species. [< *vita*(min) + (iso)*mer*]

vi·tam im·pen·de·re ve·ro (vī′tam impen′də rē vir′ō), *Latin.* to devote (one's) life to truth.

vi·ta·min or **vi·ta·mine** (vī′tə min), *n.* any of a group of complex organic compounds, found especially in milk, butter, raw fruits and vegetables, brewers' yeast, wheat, and cod-liver oil. Lack of vitamins in food causes such diseases as rickets and scurvy, as well as general poor health. —*adj.* of or having to do with vitamins. [< Latin *vīta* life + English *amine* (because it was originally thought to be an amine derivative)]

vitamin A, a fat-soluble alcohol, a vitamin present in milk, butter, fish-liver oils, egg yolk, leafy green vegetables, etc., and also synthesized in the body. Vitamin A is essential to growth, increases the resistance of the body to infection, keeps epithelial tissue normal, and prevents night blindness. It exists in two known forms, A_1 (*Formula:* $C_{20}H_{30}O$) and A_2 (*Formula:* $C_{20}H_{28}O$).

vitamin B_1, thiamine.

vitamin B_2, riboflavin; vitamin G.

vitamin B_6, pyridoxine.

vitamin B_{12}, a vitamin found especially in liver, milk, and eggs, that is active against pernicious anemia. *Formula:* $C_{63}H_{90}N_{14}O_{14}PCo$

vitamin B complex, a group of water-soluble vitamins including thiamine (vitamin B_1), riboflavin (vitamin B_2), nicotinic acid, pyridoxine (vitamin B_6), pantothenic acid, inositol, para-aminobenzoic acid, biotin (vitamin H), choline, and folic acid, which are found in high concentration in yeast and liver, and are essential in the diet.

vitamin B_T, a vitamin found chiefly in meat, liver, and milk, essential to the growth of the meal worm and certain insects but not to higher animals or man; carnitine. *Formula:* $C_7H_{15}NO_3$

vitamin C, a crystalline acid, a vitamin present in citrus fruits, tomatoes, green vegetables, etc., that aids in preventing scurvy; ascorbic acid; cevitamic acid. *Formula:* $C_6H_8O_6$

vitamin D, a fat-soluble vitamin present in fish-liver oils, milk, egg yolk, etc., and produced by irradiating ergosterol and other sterols. Vitamin D prevents rickets and is necessary for the growth and health of bones and teeth. It exists in many related forms, including D_2 (calciferol), D_3, and D_4

vitamin E, a pale-yellow liquid, a vitamin present in wheat germ, oil, milk, lettuce and other plant leaves, etc., that is necessary for some reproductive processes and aids in preventing abortions. *Formula:* $C_{29}H_{50}O_2$

vitamin G, riboflavin.

vitamin H, the former name of biotin.

vi·ta·min·ic (vī′tə min′ik), *adj.* of, having to do with, or containing vitamins.

vi·ta·min·ise (vī′tə mə nīz), *v.t.,* **-ised, -is·ing.** *Especially British.* vitaminize.

vi·ta·min·i·za·tion (vī′tə mə nə zā′shən), *n.* **1.** the act or process of vitaminizing. **2.** the state of being vitaminized.

vi·ta·min·ize (vī′tə mə nīz), *v.t.,* **-ized, -iz·ing.** to furnish with vitamins: *Many stores specialize in "health foods," which are supposed to be mineralized and vitaminized and to have special nutritional virtues* (Consumer Reports Buying Guide).

vitamin K, a vitamin present in green leafy vegetables, alfalfa, putrefied fish meal, egg yolk, tomatoes, etc., that promotes clotting of the blood and prevents hemorrhaging. It exists in many related forms.

vitamin L, a vitamin found in beef liver (vitamin L_1) and yeast (vitamin L_2) that promotes normal lactation.

vitamin P, a water-soluble crystalline substance present in citrus fruits and paprika, that promotes capillary resistance to hemorrhaging; citrin.

Vi·ta·phone (vī′tə fōn), *n. Trademark.* a device for recording and reproducing speech, music, etc., to supplement moving pictures. [< Latin *vīta* life + English *-phone*]

vi·ta·scope (vī′tə skōp), *n.* a machine for projecting motion pictures on a screen. [American English < Latin *vīta* life + English *-scope*]

vi·ta·scop·ic (vī′tə skop′ik), *adj.* of or having to do with a vitascope.

vi·ta·tive·ness (vī′tə tiv nis), *n.* (in phrenology) love of life. [< Latin *vīta* life + English *-ive* + *-ness*]

vit·el·lar·i·um (vit′ə lãr′ē əm), *n., pl.* **-i·ums, -i·a** (-ē ə). (in certain invertebrates, especially worms) the gland of the ovary which secretes the vitellus of the egg. [< Latin *vitellus* egg yolk + *ārium* a place for]

vi·tel·lin (vi tel′ən, vī-), *n.* a protein contained in the yolk of eggs. [< Latin *vitellus* egg yolk; (literally) little calf (diminutive) < *vitulus* calf + English *-in*]

vi·tel·line (vi tel′in, vī-), *adj.* **1.** of or having to do with the yolk of an egg. **2.** deep-yellow with a tinge of red; colored like the yolk of an egg. —*n.* an egg yolk. [< Medieval Latin *vitellinus* < Latin *vitellus;* see VITELLIN]

vitelline membrane, the transparent membrane enclosing an egg yolk.

vi·tel·lus (vi tel′əs, vī-), *n.* the yolk of an egg. [< Latin *vitellus* egg yolk; (literally) little calf]

vi·ti·ate (vish′ē āt), *v.t.,* **-at·ed, -at·ing. 1.** to impair the quality of; spoil; pollute: *vitiated air, an abridgment that vitiated the original text.* **2. a.** to destroy the legal force or authority of; invalidate: *The contract was vitiated because one person signed under compulsion.* **b.** to make (an argument, etc.) unconvincing or doubtful: *Uncontrolled experiment vitiated my theory.* [< Latin *vitiāre* (with English *-ate*[1]) < *vitium* fault, vice]

vi·ti·a·tion (vish′ē ā′shən), *n.* **1.** the act of vitiating. **2.** the fact or state of being vitiated.

vi·ti·a·tor (vish′ē ā′tər), *n.* a person or thing that vitiates.

vi·tic·o·lous (vī tik′ə ləs), *adj. Biology.* growing or living upon the grapevine, as certain fungi and insects. [< Latin *vītis* vine + *colere* to inhabit + English *-ous*]

vit·i·cul·tur·al (vit′ə kul′chər əl, vī′tə-), *adj.* of or having to do with viticulture.

vit·i·cul·ture (vit′ə kul′chər, vī′tə-), *n.* **1.** the cultivation of grapes. **2.** the science of grape cultivation. [< Latin *vītis* vine + English *culture*]

vit·i·cul·tur·er (vit′ə kul′chər ər, vī′tə-), *n.* viticulturist.

vit·i·cul·tur·ist (vit′ə kul′chər ist, vī′tə-), *n.* a person whose business is viticulture; grape grower.

vit·i·li·go (vit′ə lī′gō), *n.* a skin disease characterized by the lessening or loss of pigment, in which smooth, whitish patches of various shapes and sizes appear, especially on the parts of the body exposed to the sun. [< Latin *vitilīgō, -inis,* related to *vitium* fault, vice]

Vi·ton (vī′ton), *n. Trademark.* a synthetic rubber resistant to the corrosive effects of acids, alkalis, fuels, and hydrocarbon solvents at very high temperatures.

vit·rain (vit′rān), *n.* a narrow glossy band in bituminous coal, composed chiefly of the decayed cell walls of tree trunks and limbs. [< Latin *vitrum* glass + English *-ain,* as in *fusain*]

vit·re·os·i·ty (vit′rē os′ə tē), *n.* the state or quality of being vitreous.

vit·re·ous (vit′rē əs), *adj.* **1.** like glass; resembling glass in brittleness, composition, luster, etc.; glassy: *vitreous china.* **2.** having to do with glass: *earthenware with a vitreous coating.* **3.** made from glass: *vitreous tableware.* **4.** having to do with the vitreous humor.
—*n.* the vitreous humor: *The cornea, lens, and vitreous are all ocular tissues in which blood vessels do not normally exist* (New Scientist).
[< Latin *vitreus* (with English *-ous*) of glass, glassy < *vitrum* glass] —**vit′re·ous·ly,** *adv.* —**vit′re·ous·ness,** *n.*

vitreous electricity, electricity produced by rubbing glass with silk; positive electricity.

vitreous humor, the transparent, jellylike substance that fills the eyeball in back of the lens: *The vitreous humor helps hold the retina, or visual sense cells, in place* (Science News Letter). See **eye** for diagram.

vi·tres·cence (vi tres′əns), *n.* the state of becoming glassy, or of growing to resemble glass.

vi·tres·cent (vi tres′ənt), *adj.* tending to become glass; that can be turned into glass; glassy. [< Latin *vitrum* glass + English *-escent*]

vi·tres·ci·ble (vi trəs′ə bəl), *adj.* that can be vitrified; vitrifiable.

vit·ric (vit′rik), *adj.* of the nature of or having to do with glass or any glasslike material. [< Latin *vitrum* glass + English *-ic*]

vit·ri·fac·tion (vit′rə fak′shən), *n.* vitrification.

vit·ri·fac·ture (vit′rə fak′chər), *n.* the manufacture of glass. [< Latin *vitrum* glass + English (manu)*facture*]

vit·ri·fi·a·bil·i·ty (vit′rə fī′ə bil′ə tē), *n.* the property of being vitrifiable.

vit·ri·fi·a·ble (vit′rə fī′ə bəl), *adj.* that can be vitrified or changed into glass: *Flint and alkalis are vitrifiable.*

vit·ri·fi·ca·tion (vit′rə fə kā′shən), *n.* **1.** the process of making or becoming glass or a glasslike substance. **2.** something vitrified.

vit·ri·form (vit′rə fôrm), *adj.* having the structure or appearance of glass; vitreous; glasslike. [< Latin *vitrum* glass + English *-form*]

vit·ri·fy (vit′rə fī), *v.,* **-fied, -fy·ing.** —*v.t.* to change into glass or something like glass, especially by fusion due to heat. —*v.i.* to become changed into glass or something like glass. [< Middle French *vitrifier* < *vitre* glass, learned borrowing from Latin *vitrum* + Middle French *-fier* to make < Latin *facere*]

vit·rine (vit′rin), *n.* a glass case or cabinet for displaying articles; showcase: *some remarkable inkwells for gentlemen's desks, the likes of which are not often seen outside a museum vitrine* (New Yorker). [< French *vitrine* < *vitre* glass, learned borrowing from Latin *vitrum*]

vit·ri·ol (vit′rē əl), *n., v.,* **-oled, -ol·ing** or (*especially British*) **-olled, -ol·ling.** —*n.* **1.** *Chemistry.* any of various native or artificial crystalline sulfates of metals, characterized by a glassy appearance, as of copper (blue vitriol), iron (green vitriol or copperas), or zinc (white vitriol). **2.** sulfuric acid; oil of vitriol. Vitriol burns deeply and leaves very bad scars. **3.** intense or bitter

feeling; very sharp speech or severe criticism.
—*v.t.* **1.** *Metallurgy.* to subject to the action of dilute sulfuric acid; pickle. **2.** to injure (a person) by means of vitriol.
[< Medieval Latin *vitriolum* < Latin *vitrum* glass (because of the glassy appearance of the sulfate)]
—**Syn.** *n.* **3.** acerbity, mordancy.

vit·ri·o·late (vit′rē ə lāt), *v.t.*, **-lat·ed, -lat·ing.** to change into a vitriol: *to vitriolate iron sulfide.*

vit·ri·ol·ic (vit′rē ol′ik), *adj.* **1.** of or containing vitriol. **2.** derived from or like vitriol. **3.** bitterly severe; sharp; scathing: *vitriolic criticism.* —**vit′ri·ol′i·cal·ly,** *adv.* —**Syn. 3.** caustic.

vit·ri·ol·i·za·tion (vit′rē ə lə zā′shən), *n.* the act or process of changing into a vitriol or a sulfate.

vit·ri·ol·ize (vit′rē ə līz), *v.t.*, **-ized, -iz·ing.** **1.** to convert into or treat with vitriol. **2.** to injure (a person) by means of vitriol, as by throwing it in one's face; vitriol.

Vi·tru·vi·an (vi trü′vē ən), *adj.* of, having to do with, or in the style of Vitruvius, a Roman architect and writer who lived in the first century B.C.

vit·ta (vit′ə), *n., pl.* **vit·tae** (vit′ē). **1.** a headband or fillet, especially as used by the ancient Greeks and Romans as a decoration of sacred things or persons. **2.** *Botany.* one of a number of elongated, club-shaped canals or tubes for oil, occurring in the fruit of most plants of the parsley family. **3.** *Zoology, Botany.* a band or stripe of color. [< Latin *vitta* fillet (for the head); chaplet]

Greek Vitta (def. 1—about 470 B.C.)

vit·tate (vit′āt), *adj.* **1.** provided with or having a vitta or vittae. **2.** *Zoology, Botany.* striped longitudinally.

vit·u·line (vich′ə līn, -lin), *adj.* belonging to, having to do with, or resembling a calf or veal. [< Latin *vitulīnus* of a calf < *vitulus* calf]

vi·tu·per·ate (vī tü′pə rāt, -tyü′-), *v.t., v.i.*, **-at·ed, -at·ing.** to find fault with in abusive words; revile. [< Latin *vituperāre* (with English *-ate*[1]) < *vitium* fault, vice + *parāre* to prepare, make] —**Syn.** abuse.

vi·tu·per·a·tion (vī tü′pə rā′shən, -tyü′-), *n.* **1.** bitter abuse in words; very severe scolding. **2.** vituperative or abusive language. —**Syn. 1.** objurgation, castigation.

vi·tu·per·a·tive (vī tü′pə rā′tiv, -tyü′-), *adj.* abusive; reviling: *The Bevanite weekly, Tribune, lost no time in launching a vituperative attack on former Chancellor of the Exchequer Hugh Gaitskell* (Newsweek). —**vi·tu′per·a′tive·ly,** *adv.* —**Syn.** opprobrious.

vi·tu·per·a·tor (vī tü′pə rā′tər, -tyü′-), *n.* a person who vituperates; reviler.

vi·va (vē′və), *interj.* (long) live (the person or thing named). —*n.* a shout of applause or good will. [< Italian *viva* may he live < *vivere* to live < Latin *vīvere.* Related to VIVAT, VIVE.]

vi·va·ce (vē vä′chā), *Music.* —*adj.* lively; brisk. —*adv.* in a lively manner. [< Italian *vivace* < Latin *vīvāx, -ācis.* Doublet of VIVACIOUS.]

vi·va·cious (vī vā′shəs, vi-), *adj.* **1.** lively; sprightly; animated; gay: *a vivacious disposition or manner.* **2.** *Obsolete.* remaining alive for a long time; long-lived. [< Latin *vīvāx, -ācis* (with English *-ous*) lively, long-lived < *vīvere* to live. Doublet of VIVACE.] —**vi·va′cious·ly,** *adv.* —**vi·va′cious·ness,** *n.* —**Syn. 1.** jaunty, breezy.

vi·vac·i·ty (vī vas′ə tē, vi-), *n., pl.* **-ties. 1.** liveliness; sprightliness; animation; gaiety. **2.** a vivacious or lively act, expression, scene, etc. [< Latin *vīvācitās* < *vīvāx;* see VIVACIOUS]

vi·van·dière (vē väɴ dyer′), *n.* a woman who formerly accompanied French regiments or Continental armies, selling food and liquor to the troops; sutler. [< Middle French *vivandière* < Medieval Latin *vivenda* victuals, supplies; (literally) noun use of neuter plural gerundive of Latin *vīvere* to live. Compare VIAND.]

vi·var·i·um (vī vãr′ē əm), *n., pl.* **-i·ums, -i·a** (-ē ə). a place or enclosure specially adapted or prepared for keeping living animals or plants in, or under circumstances simulating, their natural state, either as objects of interest or for the purpose of scientific study. [< Latin *vīvārium* fish pond, enclosure for live game < *vīvere* to live + *-ārium* a place for]

vi·vat (vī′vat), *interj., n.* a shout of acclamation wishing long life, as to a ruler or a popular favorite. [< French *vivat* may he live < Latin *vīvat* < *vīvere* to live]

vi·va vo·ce (vī′və vō′sē), by word of mouth; orally; oral: *Shall we vote viva voce or by ballot?* [< Late Latin *vīvā vōce* (literally) by living voice; ablative of Latin *vīva vōx* oral statement]

vi·vax malaria (vī′vaks), a common, persistent form of malaria in which the attacks occur about every 48 hours and may recur after months or years of inactivity. [< New Latin *vivax* the species name of the mosquito that transmits the disease]

vive (vēv), *interj.* (long) live (the person or thing named): "*Vive la république*" *means* "*Long live the republic.*" [< French *vive,* imperative of *vivre* to live < Latin *vīvere*]

vive la ba·ga·telle (vēv′ lä bȧ gȧ tel′), *French.* (long) live frivolity!

vive le roi (vēv′ lə rwȧ′), (long) live the king! [< French *vive le roi*]

vi·ver·rine (vī ver′īn, -in; vi-), *adj.* of or having to do with the civet cat or any related mammal, as the mongoose and the genet. —*n.* any animal of the same family as the civet cat. [< New Latin *viverrinus* < Latin *vīverra* ferret]

vi·vers (vē′vərz), *n.pl. Scottish.* food; provisions; eatables. [< Middle French *vivres,* plural of *vivre* food; noun use of infinitive, live < Latin *vīvere*]

vives (vīvz), *n.* inflammation and hard swelling of the submaxillary glands of a horse. [< Old French *vives* < Medieval Latin *vivae,* plural < Arabic *ad-dība*]

vi·ve va·le·que (vī′vē və lē′kwē), *Latin.* live and be well or strong.

Vi·vi·an or **Vi·vi·en** (viv′ē ən), *n.* an enchantress, known as the Lady of the Lake, who was hostile to King Arthur and imprisoned Merlin by one of his own magic spells.

viv·i·an·ite (viv′ē ə nīt), *n.* a phosphate of iron, usually occurring in crystals of blue and green color. *Formula:* $Fe_3(PO_4)_2 8H_2O$ [< J.G. *Vivian,* an English mineralogist of the 1900's + *-ite*[1]]

viv·id (viv′id), *adj.* **1.** full of life; vigorous, active, or energetic; spirited or lively: *a vivid personality.* **2.** (of feelings, etc.) lively; strong; intense: *vivid interest, vivid indignation.* **3.** occurring or proceeding with great vigor or activity. **4.** brilliant; strikingly bright (used technically of a color of high saturation): *a vivid red, vivid coloring. Dandelions are a vivid yellow.* **5.** that can form clear and striking ideas or concepts; active: *a vivid imagination or fancy.* **6.** presenting subjects or ideas in a clear and striking manner: *a vivid description or report, a vivid picture.* **7.** clearly, distinctly, or strongly felt, perceived, or perceptible: *a vivid impression, a vivid sensation, a vivid memory.* [< Latin *vividus* < *vīvus* alive] —**viv′id·ly,** *adv.* —**viv′id·ness,** *n.* —**Syn. 1.** animated. **7.** keen.

viv·i·fi·ca·tion (viv′ə fə kā′shən), *n.* **1.** the act of vivifying. **2.** the state of being vivified.

viv·i·fi·er (viv′ə fī′ər), *n.* a person or thing that gives life.

viv·i·fy (viv′ə fī), *v.*, **-fied, -fy·ing.** —*v.t.* **1.** to give life or vigor to; quicken; animate: *to vivify the desert by irrigation.* **2.** to make more vivid, brilliant, or striking; enliven: *to vivify an idea with wit.* —*v.i.* to acquire life; become alive. [< Latin *vīvificāre* < *vīvus* alive + *facere* to make]

viv·i·par·i·ty (viv′ə par′ə tē), *n.* the quality of being viviparous.

vi·vip·a·rous (vī vip′ər əs), *adj.* **1.** bringing forth live young, rather than eggs, as most mammals and some other animals do: *Dogs, cats, cows, and human beings are viviparous animals.* **2.** *Botany.* **a.** reproducing from seeds or bulbs that germinate while still attached to the parent plant. **b.** proliferous. [< Latin *vīviparus* (with English *-ous*) < *vīvus* alive + *parere* give birth to, bear] —**vi·vip′a·rous·ly,** *adv.* —**vi·vip′a·rous·ness,** *n.*

viv·i·sect (viv′ə sekt, viv′ə sekt′), *v.t.* to dissect (an animal) while living; perform vivisection upon. —*v.i.* to practice vivisection. [back formation < *vivisection*]

viv·i·sec·tion (viv′ə sek′shən), *n.* **1.** the act of cutting or dissecting some part of a living organism. **2.** the act or practice of dissecting or otherwise experimenting upon living animals, usually anesthetized, as a means of studying physiology and pathology. [< Latin *vīvus* alive + English *section*]

viv·i·sec·tion·al (viv′ə sek′shə nəl), *adj.* of or having to do with vivisection.

viv·i·sec·tion·ist (viv′ə sek′shə nist), *n.* **1.** a person who practices vivisection; vivisector. **2.** a person who favors or defends the scientific practice of vivisection.

viv·i·sec·tor (viv′ə sek′tər), *n.* a person who practices vivisection.

vix·en (vik′sən), *n.* **1.** a female fox. **2.** a bad-tempered or quarrelsome woman; shrew. [unrecorded Old English *fyxen,* feminine of *fox* fox] —**vix′en·ly,** *adj., adv.* —**Syn. 2.** termagant.

vix·en·ish (vik′sə nish), *adj.* ill-tempered; scolding.

Vi·yel·la (vī yel′ə), *n. Trademark.* a soft, lightweight cloth that is a blend of cotton and wool: *Soft tailored casual jackets of Viyella* (New Yorker).

viz., namely (Latin, *videlicet*).
➔ **Viz.** is used mainly in formal or technical writing, and is usually read "namely."

viz·ard (viz′ərd), *n.* **1.** a visor. **2.** a mask to conceal the face. **3.** an outward appearance or show; disguise. [alteration of earlier *vizer* visor]

viz·ard·ed (viz′ər did), *adj.* disguised with or wearing a mask.

viz·ca·cha (vis kä′chə), *n.* viscacha, a rodent of South America: *His companions are vizcachas, strange little animals that seem something like prairie dogs, with a pack rat's habit of carrying off objects* (Saturday Review).

vi·zier or **vi·zir** (vi zir′), *n.* a high government official in Moslem countries, especially in the former Turkish empire; minister of state. [< Turkish *vezir* < Arabic *wazīr* (originally) porter; one who bears the burden of office; a viceroy < *wazara* he carried]

vi·zier·ate or **vi·zir·ate** (vi zir′āt), *n.* the office, state, or authority of a vizier.

vi·zier·i·al or **vi·zir·i·al** (vi zir′ē əl), *adj.* of, having to do with, or issued by a vizier.

vi·zier·ship or **vi·zir·ship** (vi zir′ship), *n.* the office or authority of a vizier.

vi·zor (vī′zər), *n., v.t.* visor.

vi·zored (vī′zərd), *adj.* visored.

vi·zor·less (vī′zər lis), *adj.* visorless.

Vizs·la (vēs′lə), *n.* a short-haired, Hungarian hunting dog with a deep rust- or gold-colored coat, and docked tail. [< *Vizsla,* a village in Hungary]

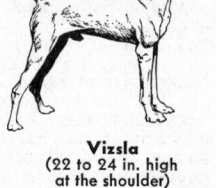

Vizsla (22 to 24 in. high at the shoulder)

V-J Day (vē′jā′), the date of the Allied victory over Japan in World War II, either August 14, 1945 (the surrender of Japan) or September 2, 1945 (the signing of the formal surrender on the U.S.S. Missouri).

VL (no periods), Vulgar Latin.

Vlach (vlak), *n., adj.* Walachian.

vlaie (vlī, flī; vlā, flā), *n. U.S.* vlei (def. 2).

vlei or **vley** (vlī, flī; vlā, flā), *n.* **1.** (in South Africa) a small lake; a large pool of water: *I came full in view of the vley or pool of water beside which I had been directed to encamp* (R.G. Cumming). **2.** *U.S.* Also, **vlaie, vly.** a swamp or marsh; a pond or creek: *Have you reason to believe that an attempt was made to fire the Owl Vlaie?* (Harper's). [< Afrikaans *vlei* < Dutch *vallei.* Related to VALLEY.]

VLF (no periods), very low frequency (of or having to do with the electromagnetic spectrum below 30 kilocycles per second, especially in radio transmission and reception).

vly (vlī, flī), *n. U.S.* vlei (def. 2).

V-Mail (vē′māl′), *n.* a service using microfilm in transmitting letters to and from members of the U.S. Armed Forces overseas during World War II. [< *V*(ictory)]

V.M.D., Doctor of Veterinary Medicine (Latin, *Veterinariae Medicinae Doctor*).

v.n., neuter verb.

V-neck (vē′nek′), *n.* the neck of a sweater, dress, shirt, etc., in the shape of a V.

V-necked (vē′nekt′), *adj.* having a V-neck: *The overblouse is of navy silk twill, and it's V-necked* (New Yorker).

VOA (no periods), Voice of America.

vo-ag (vō′ag′), *n. U.S. Informal.* **1.** vocational agriculture. **2.** a teacher or advocate of vocational agriculture.

voc., vocative.

vocab., vocabulary.

vo·ca·ble (vō′kə bəl), *n.* a word, especially as heard or seen without consideration of its meaning. —*adj.* that can be uttered. [< Latin *vocābulum* < *vocāre* to call]

vo·cab·u·lar·y (vō kab′yə ler′ē), *n., pl.* **-lar·ies. 1.** the stock of words used by a person, class of people, profession, etc.: *Reading will increase your vocabulary.* **2.** a collection or list of words, usually in alphabetical order, with their meanings, especially such a list at the back of a foreign-language text or grammar; glossary. **3.** all the words of a language. **4.** the characteristic expressions of a quality, feeling, etc.: *the vocabulary of prejudice.* [< Medieval Latin *vocabularius* < Latin *vocābulum*; see VOCABLE]

vocabulary entry, 1. a word, term, or item entered in a vocabulary. **2.** (in dictionaries) any word or phrase in alphabetical order and defined, or any related word listed for identification under the word from which it is derived.

vo·cal (vō′kəl), *adj.* **1.** of, by, for, with, or having to do with the voice: *vocal organs, vocal power, vocal talents, a vocal message, vocal music.* **2.** having a voice; giving forth sound: *Men are vocal beings. The gorge was vocal with the roar of the cataract.* **3.** aroused to speech; inclined to talk freely: *He became vocal with indignation.* **4.** *Phonetics.* **a.** of, having to do with, or like a vowel; vocalic. **b.** voiced. —*n.* a vocal sound. All vowels are vocals. [< Latin *vōcālis* < *vōx, vōcis* voice. Doublet of VOWEL.]
—**Syn.** *adj.* **3.** articulate.

vocal cords, two pairs or bands of mucous membranes in the throat, projecting into the cavity of the larynx. The lower pair (inferior or true vocal cords) can be pulled tight and the passage of breath between them then causes them to vibrate, which produces the sound of voice. The upper pair (superior or false vocal cords) do not directly aid in producing voice.
➤ The variant **vocal chords** is also used, especially in Great Britain. Since either term is likely to give a mistaken notion of the structure it designates, some phoneticians prefer *vocal lips* or *vocal folds.*

vo·cal·ic (vō kal′ik), *adj.* **1.** of, having to do with, or like a vowel. **2.** having many vowel sounds.

vo·cal·ise[1] (vō′kə līz), *v.t., v.i.,* **-ised, -is·ing.** *Especially British.* vocalize.

vo·ca·lise[2] (vō′kə lēz′), *n.* a musical composition for a singer, usually without words, designed either as an exercise or for public performance. [< French *vocalise*]

vo·cal·ism (vō′kə liz əm), *n.* **1. a.** the art of using the voice or vocal organs in speaking. **b.** the act, art, or techniques of singing. **2.** *Phonetics.* **a.** the vowel system of a dialect, language, or group of languages. **b.** the variation or range that vowels have in a certain context. **c.** a vocal sound or articulation.

vo·cal·ist (vō′kə list), *n.* a singer.

vo·cal·i·ty (vō kal′ə tē), *n.* the quality of being vocal.

vo·cal·i·za·tion (vō′kə lə zā′shən), *n.* **1.** the act of vocalizing. **2.** the fact of being vocalized.

vo·cal·ize (vō′kə līz), *v.,* **-ized, -iz·ing.** —*v.t.* **1.** to form into voice; utter or sing: *to vocalize old camp songs.* **2.** to make vocal or articulate: *The speaker vocalized the feeling of the entire group.* **3.** *Phonetics.* **a.** to use as a vowel: *to vocalize the n-sound in button.* **b.** to pronounce as a vowel: *Some speakers of English vocalize the "r" in four.* **c.** to voice. **4.** to insert vowels or vowel symbols in (an Arabic, Hebrew, etc., text). —*v.i.* **1. a.** to use the voice; speak; sing; hum. **b.** to sing with one vowel sound for many notes. **2.** *Phonetics.* **a.** (of sounds) to become vocalized. **b.** to vocalize speech sounds.

vo·cal·iz·er (vō′kə lī′zər), *n.* a person who vocalizes.

vo·cal·ly (vō′kə lē), *adv.* **1.** in a vocal manner; with the voice; out loud: *The child vocally demanded a toy.* **2.** verbally; orally. **3.** in song; by means of singing: *Here is a moving musical work that cannot be carried as a piece of theatre by its music alone, either vocally or orchestrally* (Wall Street Journal). **4.** having to do with vowels or vowel sounds.

vo·ca·tion (vō kā′shən), *n.* **1. a.** an occupation, business, profession, or trade: *Teaching is her vocation.* **b.** the persons who are engaged in the same business or profession: *a new law affecting the entire vocation.* **2. a.** an inner or divine call to perform a specific function or fill a certain position, especially of a spiritual nature, as devoting one's life to the ministry. **b.** a divine call to a state of union or salvation with God or Christ. [< Latin *vocātiō, -ōnis* (literally) a calling < *vocāre* to call] —**Syn. 1. a.** métier.
➤ **Vocation, avocation.** *Vocation* applies to one's regular occupation, the way he earns his living. *Avocation* applies to a kind of work one does in his spare time, a hobby: *Bookkeeping is his vocation and photography is his avocation.*

vo·ca·tion·al (vō kā′shə nəl, -kāsh′nəl), *adj.* **1.** of or having to do with some occupation or trade. **2.** of or having to do with studies or training for some occupation or trade: *Vocational agriculture is taught to students who plan to become farmers.*

vocational education, any program of education designed to train a person for a particular occupation, business, profession, or trade.

vocational guidance, professional advice given in schools, specialized agencies, etc., on the basis of tests and interviews, to help a person choose the occupation for which he is best suited.

vo·ca·tion·al·ism (vō kā′shə nə liz′əm, -kāsh′nə-), *n.* belief in, or emphasis on, vocational education, especially in schools and colleges: *Vocationalism . . . demands of education only that it prepare students for a job immediately after graduation* (Newsweek).

vo·ca·tion·al·ize (vō kā′shə nə līz, -kāsh′nə-), *v.t.,* **-ized, -iz·ing.** to design or adjust to vocational ends; make vocational: *Our science faculties have yielded to the pressures of industrial demand for their product and to student demand for good jobs and high salaries, and have vocationalized their instruction* (Bulletin of Atomic Scientists).

vo·ca·tion·al·ly (vō kā′shə nə lē, -kāsh′nə-), *adv.* in regard to vocation.

vocational nurse, practical nurse.

vocational school, a school that trains boys and girls for special trades, such as printing, stenography, or mechanics.

voc·a·tive (vok′ə tiv), *adj.* **1.** *Grammar.* showing the person or thing spoken to. **2.** of, having to do with, or characteristic of calling or addressing.
—*n.* **1.** the vocative case. **2.** a word in that case: *Domine, "O, Lord" is the vocative of the Latin dominus. Abbr.:* voc. **3.** an appeal or call for help.
[< Latin *vocātīvus* < *vocāre* to call] —**voc′a·tive·ly,** *adv.*

vo·ces (vō′sēz), *n. Latin.* the plural of **vox.**

vo·cif·er·ance (vō sif′ər əns), *n.* a noisy or clamorous shouting.

vo·cif·er·ant (vō sif′ər ənt), *adj.* shouting; crying; vociferating. —*n.* a noisy person; one who vociferates. [< Latin *vōciferāns, -antis,* present participle of *vōciferārī;* see VOCIFERATE]

vo·cif·er·ate (vō sif′ə rāt), *v.t., v.i.,* **-at·ed, -at·ing.** to cry out loudly or noisily; shout. [< Latin *vōciferārī* (with English *-ate*[1]) < *vōx, vōcis* voice + *ferre* to bear] —**Syn.** clamor, scream.

vo·cif·er·a·tion (vō sif′ə rā′shən), *n.* a vociferating; noisy oratory; clamor. —**Syn.** outcry.

vo·cif·er·a·tor (vō sif′ə rā′tər), *n.* a person or thing that vociferates; clamorous or noisy shouter.

vo·cif·er·ous (vō sif′ər əs, -sif′rəs), *adj.* **1.** loud and noisy; shouting; clamoring: *The incensed crowd became more vociferous.* **2.** of the nature of, characterized, or accompanied by, loud speech or heated assertions: *vociferous hatred.* [< Latin *vōciferārī* (see VOCIFERATE) + English *-ous*] —**vo·cif′er·ous·ly,** *adv.* —**vo·cif′er·ous·ness,** *n.* —**Syn. 1.** clamorous, thundering.

vo·cod·er (vō′kō′dər), *n.* an electronic device that breaks down and transmits a message in garbled elements consisting of buzzes and hisses of different pitch, frequency, and strength to a receiving apparatus that reconstructs the original message. [< *vo*(ice) + *coder*]

VODER (no periods), voice operation demonstrator.

vod·ka (vod′kə), *n.* an alcoholic liquor, distilled from rye, barley, wheat, potatoes, or other substances. [< Russian *vodka* (diminutive) < *voda* water]

voe (vō), *n.* (in the Shetland and Orkney Islands) a narrow inlet of the sea: *Over headland, ness and voe—The Coastwise Lights of England watch the ships of England go!* (Rudyard Kipling). [< Scandinavian (compare Icelandic *vāgr* bay)]

vo-ed (vō′ed′), *n. U.S. Informal.* vocational education: *Vo-ed, as teachers call it, is dismally inadequate to meet the demands upon it* (Time).

voet·gang·er (fůt′gäng′ər), *n. Afrikaans.* an immature, wingless locust of South Africa, highly destructive to crops.

voet·sak (fůt′sak), *interj. Afrikaans.* be off; begone.

vogue (vōg), *n.* **1.** the fashion: *Hoop skirts were in vogue many years ago.* **2.** popularity; acceptance: *That song had a great vogue at one time.* [< Anglo-French *vogue* success, course; (literally) a rowing < Old French *voguer* to row < Italian *vogare*] —**Syn. 1.** mode. **2.** favor, approval.

vo·gueish (vō′gish), *adj.* voguish. —**vo′gueish·ly,** *adv.*

vogue word, a word currently in vogue: *In recent years "camp" . . . has been expropriated from the critic's vocabulary to become a vogue word* (Nathan Cohen). *"Planning" has now clearly become a vogue word for people of all political persuasions* (London Daily Telegraph).

vo·guey (vō′gē), *adj. Informal.* in vogue or popular for the time being: *Color-pale, tasteful, and a bit voguey . . . paintings at the Hugo Gallery* (New York Times).

vo·guish (vō′gish), *adj.* in vogue or popular for the time being; fashionable: *Current trends suggest . . . that even Mister (and indeed Miss) may ultimately be abandoned, for the voguish style of address now is simply by name: John Brown or Jane Brown straight* (Manchester Guardian Weekly). —**vo′guish·ly,** *adv.*

Vo·gul (vō′gůl), *n.* a Finno-Ugric language of western Siberia.

voice (vois), *n., v.,* **voiced, voic·ing.** —*n.* **1.** a sound or sounds made through the mouth, especially by people in speaking, singing, shouting, etc. **2. a.** the sounds naturally made by a single person in speech or other utterance, often regarded as characteristic of the person and distinguishing him from others: *to recognize someone's voice.* **b.** such sounds considered with regard to character, quality, tone, or expression: *a low, gentle, loud, or angry voice.* **3.** the power to make sounds through the mouth: *to lose or regain one's voice.* **4.** *Music.* **a.** a musical sound made by the vocal cords and resonated by several head and throat cavities; the tones made in singing. **b.** ability as a singer: *to have a voice or no voice.* **c.** a singer: *a choir of fifty voices.* **d.** a part of a piece of music for one kind of singer or instrument. **5.** *Phonetics.* the sound produced when air from the lungs passes through the nearly closed glottis and causes vibration of the vocal cords, as in the vowels and in consonants like *l, v,* and *n.* **6.** anything like speech or song: *the voice of the wind, the voice of the bells.* **7.** anything likened to speech that conveys impressions to the mind or senses: *the voice of one's conscience, the voice of duty.* **8.** expression: *They gave voice to their joy.* **9.** an expressed opinion, choice, wish, etc.: *His voice was for compromise.* **10.** the right to express an opinion or choice: *We have no voice in the matter.* **11.** the means or agency by which something is expressed, represented, or revealed: *Poetry is the voice of imagination* (H. Reed). **12.** *Grammar.* a form of the verb that shows whether the subject is active or passive. **13.** *Obsolete.* **a.** general or common talk; rumor. **b.** reputation; fame.

in voice, in condition to sing or speak well: *You know very well . . . that I am not in voice [for singing] to-day* (Oliver Goldsmith).

lift up (or **raise**) **one's voice, a.** to cry out loudly: *And it came to pass, when the angel of the Lord spake these words unto all the children of Israel, that the people lifted up their*

voice, and wept (Judges 2:4). **b.** to protest; complain: *But London did not raise its voice against the crimes* (London Times).
with one voice, unanimously: *All the members demanded with one voice who it was who was charged with the crime* (M. Pattison).
—*v.t.* **1.** to speak or utter (a word, etc.): *to voice a cry.* **2.** to express: *They voiced their approval of the plan.* **3.** *Phonetics.* to utter with a sound made by vibration of the vocal cords: *"Z" and "V" are voiced; "s" and "f" are not.* **4.** *Music.* **a.** to regulate the tone of (an organ, etc.). **b.** to write the parts of for one kind of singer or instrument.
[< Old French *vois,* and *voiz* < Latin *vōx, vōcis*] —**voic′er,** *n.*
➔ **Voice** (*n.* def. 12). When the subject of a verb is the doer of the action or is in the condition named by its verb, the verb is said to be in the active voice: *The congregation sang "Abide with Me." They will go swimming. Our side had won. Jimmy's father gave him a car. We rested an hour.* When the subject of a verb receives the action, the verb is in the passive voice: *"Abide with Me" was sung by the congregation. Jimmy was given a car by his father. The pit was dug fully eight feet deep. They were caught.*

voice box, the box-shaped cavity in the throat containing the vocal cords; larynx.

voice coil, (in a sound system) a coil of thin wire wound about a cylinder in the loudspeaker cone. Electrical impulses passing through the wire make it vibrate, causing the cone to vibrate and produce sound.

voiced (voist), *adj.* **1.** spoken or expressed: *voiced criticism.* **2.** *Phonetics.* pronounced with vibration of the vocal cords, as any vowel or such consonants as *b, v, l;* sonant.

-voiced, *combining form.* having a —— voice: *Low-voiced = having a low voice.*

voice·ful (vois′fəl), *adj.* **1. a.** having a voice or the power to speak. **b.** having the power to produce or make loud sounds: *the voiceful sea.* **2.** involving much speech or argument; vocal: *voiceful criticism.*

voice·less (vois′lis), *adj.* **1.** having no voice; lacking the power of speech; dumb; silent. **2.** not expressed or uttered; unspoken: *voiceless indignation.* **3.** lacking any voice or singing ability. **4.** having no voice or vote, as in the control of something. **5.** *Phonetics.* spoken without vibration of the vocal cords, as the English consonants *p, t,* and *k;* surd. —**voice′less·ly,** *adv.* —**voice′less·ness,** *n.*

Voice of America, an international broadcasting service of the United States government, used to give overseas listeners a picture of American life, culture, and aims.

voice operation demonstrator, a keyboard device that imitates the sounds of human speech.

voice-o·ver (vois′ō′vər), *n.* narration of a film, separately recorded to be used as a sound track: *The only dialogue is an announcer's voice-over* (Time).

voice part, *Music.* one of the parts or melodies for a voice or instrument in a harmonic or contrapuntal composition.

voice pipe, a speaking tube: *He spoke brusquely into the wheelhouse voice pipe* (Maclean's).

voice·print (vois′print′), *n.* a spectrographic record of the sound patterns formed by a person's voice: *Voiceprints, just as fingerprints, appear to be unique and almost unchangeable* [and] *may eventually take their place with fingerprints as a positive means of identification* (New York Times).

voice vote, a vote on a motion, bill, etc., taken by saying "aye" or "yes" or by saying "nay" or "no" when called upon: *Passage came on a voice vote with a scattering of "ayes" and with no "nay" heard* (Wall Street Journal).

voic·ing (voi′sing), *n.* **1.** the act of a person or thing that voices. **2.** the regulating or obtaining of the correct quality of tone, especially of an organ.

void (void), *adj.* **1.** *Law.* **a.** without legal force or effect; not binding in law: *A contract made by a person under legal age is void.* **b.** that can be declared to have no legal force; voidable. **2.** without effect; useless. **3.** empty; vacant: *a void space.* **4.** having no incumbent or holder, as an office.
void of, devoid of; without; lacking: *His words were void of sense.*
—*v.t.* **1.** *Law.* to make of no legal force or effect. **2.** to empty out (contents); evacuate (excrement); discharge. **3.** *Archaic.* **a.** to empty or clear (a room, place, receptacle, etc.) of something. **b.** to free or rid of something. **4.** *Obsolete.* to leave (a place).
—*n.* **1.** an empty space: *The death of his dog left an aching void in Bob's heart.* **2.** a space, gap, or opening, as that left in a wall for a window or another wall. **3.** emptiness; vacancy. **4.** the state of holding no cards of a suit in a hand, as in bridge, pinochle, etc.
[< Old French *voide,* feminine of *voit* < Vulgar Latin *vocitus* < *vocuus,* for Latin *vacuus* empty] —**void′er,** *n.* —**void′ly,** *adv.* —**void′ness,** *n.* —**Syn.** *adj.* **1.** invalid, null. –*v.t.* **1.** invalidate, nullify.

void·a·ble (voi′də bəl), *adj.* **1.** *Law.* that can be made or declared void; that can be either voided or confirmed: *a contract voidable after twelve months.* **2.** that can be cancelled or given up. —**void′a·ble·ness,** *n.*

void·ance (voi′dəns), *n.* **1.** the act or process of emptying out the contents of something. **2.** the act of making legally void; invalidation; annulment. **3. a.** removal from a benefice. **b.** a vacancy, especially of an ecclesiastical office.

void·ed (voi′did), *adj.* **1.** having a part cut out, leaving a void or vacant space. **2.** made void or empty. **3.** *Heraldry.* having a part cut out to make the field visible with only the edge remaining.

voi·là (vwä lä′), *interj. French.* see there; behold.

voi·là tout (vwä lä tü′), *French.* that's all.

voile (voil), *n.* a very thin cloth of silk, wool, cotton, etc., with an open weave, used for dresses. [< French *voile* < Old French *veile* (originally) veil < Vulgar Latin *vēla,* feminine < Latin, neuter plural of *vēlum* covering. Doublet of VEIL, VELUM.]

voir dire (vwär dir′), *Law.* **1.** an oath administered in a preliminary examination to a proposed witness or juror by which he swears to answer truthfully questions regarding his competence. **2.** such a preliminary examination. [< Old French *voir* truth (< Latin *vēra,* adverbial use of neuter plural of *verus*), and *dire* to say < Latin *dīcere*]

voi·ture (vwä tʏr′), *n., pl.* **voi·tures** (vwä-tʏr′). a carriage or conveyance; vehicle. [< French *voiture* < Latin *vectūra* act of transporting < *vehere* carry]

voi·tu·rette (vwä tʏ ret′), *n., pl.* **voi·tu·rettes** (vwä tʏ ret′). a small motor vehicle. [< French *voiturette* (diminutive) < *voiture* voiture]

voi·vode (voi′vōd), *n.* in Slavic countries: **1.** the title of various rulers and governing or administrative officials in southeastern Europe, as (formerly) the princes of Wallachia and Moldavia. **2.** the leader of an army. Also, **vaivode.** [< Rumanian *voivod* < Bulgarian *vojvoda* < Slavic *voi* warriors + *voditi* to lead]

voix cé·leste (vwä sā lest′), **1.** a soft-toned organ stop of 8-foot pitch having two sets of pipes, one tuned slightly sharper, thus producing a tremulous, wavering tone. **2.** a soft flute stop like a dulciana. [< French *voix céleste* (literally) heavenly voice < Latin *vōx, vōcis* voice, and *caelestis* heavenly < *caelum* heaven]

vol (vol), *n. Heraldry.* two wings expanded and joined at the base. [< French *vol* flight < *voler* to fly < Latin *volāre*]

vol., **1.** volcano. **2.** volume.

Vo·lans (vō′lanz), *n., genitive* **Vo·lan·tis.** a southern constellation near Argo. [< Latin *Volāns, -antis* (literally) flying, present participle of *volāre* to fly]

vo·lant (vō′lənt), *adj.* **1.** flying; able to fly: *volant birds.* **2.** (of animals, especially birds, in coats of arms) represented as flying. **3.** nimble; quick: *the volant fingers of the pianist.* [probably < Middle French *volant,* present participle of *voler* to fly < Latin *volāre* to fly. Doublet of VOLANTE.]

Volant Bird
(def. 2)

vo·lan·te (vō län′tā), *adj. Music.* moving lightly and rapidly; flying. [< Italian *volante* (literally) flying, present participle of *volare* to fly < Latin *volāre.* Doublet of VOLANT.]

Vo·lan·tis (vō lan′tis), *n.* the genitive of **Volans.**

Vo·la·pük or **Vo·la·puk** (vō′lə pʏk), *n.* an artificial language for international use, based chiefly on English, Latin, German, and other European tongues, invented about 1879 by Johann Martin Schleyer, a German priest. [< Volapük *Volapük* < *vol,* reduction of English *world* + *pük,* reduction of English *speak,* or German *Sprache* language]

Vo·la·pük·er or **Vo·la·puk·er** (vō′lə-pʏ′kər), *n.* Volapükist.

Vo·la·pük·ist or **Vo·la·puk·ist** (vō′lə-pʏ′kist), *n.* **1.** a person who is skilled in Volapük. **2.** an advocate of the adoption of Volapük as a universal language.

vo·lar[1] (vō′lər), *adj.* of or having to do with the palm of the hand or the sole of the foot; palmar. [< Latin *vola* hollow of the palm or sole + English *-ar*]

vo·lar[2] (vō′lər), *adj.* used in flying. [< Latin *volāre* to fly + English *-ar*]

vol·a·tile (vol′ə təl), *adj.* **1.** evaporating rapidly at ordinary temperatures; changing into vapor easily: *Gasoline is volatile.* **2.** changing rapidly from one mood or interest to another; fickle; frivolous: *Flighty people often have volatile dispositions.* **3.** readily vanishing or disappearing; transient: *volatile dreams.* **4.** that can fly; flying; volant.
—*n.* **1.** a volatile matter or substance. **2.** a winged creature, such as a bird or a butterfly: *As to the volatiles of this country, there are turkeys . . . parrots, woodquists . . .* (John Davies).
[< Latin *volātilis* flying < *volāre* to fly]
—**vol′a·tile·ness,** *n.*
—**Syn.** *adj.* **2.** capricious, mercurial.

volatile oil, an oil that vaporizes quickly.

volatile salt, **1.** sal volatile. **2.** a solution containing it.

vol·a·til·ise (vol′ə tə līz), *v.i., v.t.,* **-ised, -is·ing.** *Especially British.* volatilize.

vol·a·til·i·ty (vol′ə til′ə tē), *n.* volatile quality or condition.

vol·a·til·iz·a·ble (vol′ə tə lī′zə bəl), *adj.* that can be volatilized.

vol·a·til·i·za·tion (vol′ə tə lə zā′shən), *n.* **1.** the act or process of making volatile. **2.** the state of being volatilized.

vol·a·til·ize (vol′ə tə līz), *v.,* **-ized, -iz·ing.** —*v.i.* to change into vapor; evaporate. —*v.t.* to make volatile; cause to evaporate or disperse in vapor.

vol·a·til·iz·er (vol′ə tə lī′zər), *n.* an apparatus for volatilizing.

vo·la·tion (vō lā′shən), *n.* the act of flying; faculty or power of flight, especially of birds.

vo·la·tion·al (vō lā′shə nəl), *adj.* of or having to do with volation or the faculty of flight.

vol-au-vent (vô′lō väɴ′), *n.* a kind of pie having a shell of very light puff paste filled with a preparation of meat, fish, etc., in a sauce. [< French *vol-au-vent* (literally) flight in the wind]

vol·can·ic (vol kan′ik), *adj.* **1.** of or caused by a volcano; having to do with volcanoes: *a volcanic eruption.* **2.** discharged from, or produced or ejected by, a volcano or volcanoes; consisting of materials produced by igneous action. **3.** characterized by the presence of volcanoes: *volcanic country.* **4.** like a volcano; liable to break out violently: *a volcanic temper.* —**vol·can′i·cal·ly,** *adv.*

volcanic ash, finely pulverized lava thrown out of a volcano in eruption: *The Romans used a mixture of volcanic ash and slaked lime to build the Colosseum and the Pantheon* (Science News Letter).

volcanic bomb, a piece of molten lava, often very large and hollow, thrown out of a volcano in eruption.

volcanic cone, a hill around the rim of a volcano, consisting chiefly of matter thrown out during eruptions.

volcanic dust, very fine particles of lava thrown out of a volcano, sometimes carried very high and to great distances by the wind.

volcanic glass, a natural glass produced by the very rapid cooling of lava; obsidian.

vol·can·ic·i·ty (vol′kə nis′ə tē), *n.* volcanic state or quality; volcanic activity; volcanism.

volcanic neck, a mass of hardened volcanic rock, or magma, that has been thrust upward into a volcanic cone by subterranean pressure and may remain upright after erosion has stripped away the surrounding material.

volcanic rock, rock formed by volcanic action; lava.

volcanic tuff, compressed volcanic ash.

vol·can·ism (vol′kə niz əm), *n.* the phenomena connected with volcanoes and volcanic activity: *Some of the chains of crater pits must have their origin in a type of* *volcanism, perhaps in lava flows of matter liquefied by the impact* (Atlantic).

vol·can·ist (vol′kə nist), *n.* a person who studies or is expert on volcanoes.

vol·can·i·za·tion (vol′kə nə zā′shən), *n.* the process of undergoing, or the state of having undergone, change by volcanic heat or action.

vol·can·ize (vol′kə nīz), *v.t.*, **-ized, -iz·ing.** to subject to or modify by volcanic action or heat.

vol·ca·no (vol kā′nō), *n., pl.* **-noes** or **-nos.** **1.** an opening or openings in the surface of the earth at the top of and sometimes on the sides of a cone-shaped hill or mountain, connected to the interior of the earth by a funnel or crater through which steam, gases, ashes, rocks, and sometimes streams of molten material are expelled in periods of activity. **2.** a cone-shaped hill or mountain around this opening, built up of material thus expelled. **3. a.** a violent feeling or suppressed passion: *a volcano of hatred.* **b.** a state of instability in which people, causes, etc., are likely to burst out violently at some time: *the social volcano below modern society.* [< Italian *volcano* < Latin *Vulcānus*, or *Volcānus* Vulcan]

vol·can·o·log·i·cal (vol′kə nə loj′ə kəl), *adj.* of or having to do with volcanology. Also, **vulcanological.**

vol·can·ol·o·gist (vol′kə nol′ə jist), *n.* a person who studies or is skilled in the science of volcanoes and volcanic phenomena: *The earth remains quiescent but the volcanologist is aware of a deep stirring* (New York Times). Also, **vulcanologist.**

vol·can·ol·o·gy (vol′kə nol′ə jē), *n.* the science or scientific study of volcanoes and volcanic phenomena. Also, **vulcanology.**

vole[1] (vōl), *n.* a rodent belonging to the same family as rats and mice, usually of heavier build and having short limbs and tail, as the redback vole and the meadow mouse. [abstracted < earlier *volemouse* < Norwegian *voll* field + English *mouse*]

American Vole[1] (about 5 in. long)

vole[2] (vōl), *n.* (in cards) a slam. [< French *vole,* apparently < *voler* to fly < Latin *volāre*]

vol·er·y (vol′ər ē), *n., pl.* **-er·ies. 1.** an aviary. **2.** the birds kept in an aviary. [< French *volière* (< *voler* fly) + English *-ery*]

vol·i·tant (vol′ə tənt), *adj.* **1.** constantly moving about; flitting; flying. **2.** characterized by flitting or flying to and fro. [< Latin *volitāns, -antis,* present participle of *volitāre* (frequentative) < *volāre* to fly]

vol·i·ta·tion (vol′ə tā′shən), *n.* the act or power of flight; flying: *Pigeons in circular volitation, soaring gray, flapping white and then gray again, wheeled across the limpid, pale sky* (New Yorker). [< Medieval Latin *volitatio, -onis* < Latin *volitāre;* see VOLITANT]

vol·i·ta·tion·al (vol′ə tā′shə nəl), *adj.* of or having to do with volitation or flight.

vo·li·tient (vō lish′ənt), *adj.* exercising the will; willing. [< *voliti*(on) + *-ent*]

vo·li·tion (vō lish′ən), *n.* **1.** the act of willing: *The man left of his own volition.* **2.** the power or faculty of willing: *The use of drugs has weakened his volition.* **3.** will power. [< Medieval Latin *volitio, -onis* < Latin *vol-,* stem of *velle* to wish] —**Syn. 1.** choice, preference, decision.

vo·li·tion·al (vō lish′ə nəl), *adj.* of or having to do with volition or the act of willing.

vo·li·tion·al·ly (vō lish′ə nə lē), *adv.* by the will; in accordance with the will.

vo·li·tion·ar·y (vō lish′ə ner′ē), *adj.* volitional.

vol·i·tive (vol′ə tiv), *adj.* **1.** of or having to do with volition or the will. **2.** *Grammar.* expressing a wish or desire: *a volitive subjunctive.*

Volks·deut·scher (fôlks′doi′chər), *n., pl.* **-sche** (-chə). *German.* a German by birth or descent who is a citizen of another country: *Last week Bonn announced that Yugoslavia this year would return to Germany 15 German nationals and 150 Volksdeutsche now held in Tito's detention camps* (Time).

Volks·kam·mer (fôlks′kä′mər), *n. German.* the People's Chamber, one of two legislative bodies in East Germany, consisting of over 400 voting members elected by universal suffrage.

Volks·lied (fôlks′lēt′), *n., pl.* **Volks·lie·der** (fôlks′lē′dər). *German.* a folk song.

Volks·po·li·zei (fôlks′pô li tsī′), *n. German.* the People's Police, the police force in East Germany: *Truckloads of Red Army troops and squad cars crowded with Volkspolizei stood by* (Time).

Volks·raad (fôlks′rät′), *n. Afrikaans.* a legislative assembly or a house of parliament in South Africa: *It was therefore decreed by a resolution of the Volksraad that no additional natives should be allowed to take up their residence in the Colony* (C. Barter).

Volks·schu·le (fôlks′shü′lə), *n., pl.* **-len** (-lən). *German.* an elementary school: *At age six a child starts his schooling by attending a Volksschule, which provides a general education up to age fifteen* (New Scientist).

vol·ley (vol′ē), *n., pl.* **-leys,** *v.,* **-leyed, -ley·ing.** —*n.* **1.** the discharge of a number of guns at once. **2.** *Mining.* the simultaneous explosion of two or more blasts in the rock. **3.** a shower of stones, bullets, arrows, etc. **4.** a rapid outpouring or burst of words, oaths, shouts, cheers, etc. **5.** in tennis: **a.** the hitting or return of a ball before it touches the ground. **b.** the flight of a ball in play before it has touched the ground. **6.** (in soccer) a kick given the ball before it bounces on the ground. **7.** (in cricket) a ball bowled so that it strikes the wicket before bouncing.

—*v.t.* **1.** to discharge in a volley, or as if in a volley. **2.** (in tennis) to hit or return (a ball in play) before it touches the ground. **3.** (in soccer) to give (the ball) a kick before it bounces on the ground. **4.** (in cricket) to bowl (a ball) that reaches the wicket before bouncing. —*v.i.* **1.** to be discharged in a volley, or as if in a volley: *Cannon volleyed on all sides.* **2.** to sound together or continuously, as firearms, or in a way suggesting firearms. **3.** to make a volley in tennis, soccer, or cricket.

[< Middle French *volée* flight < *voler* to fly < Latin *volāre*]

vol·ley·ball (vol′ē bôl′), *n.* **1.** a game played with a large ball and a high net. The ball must be kept in the air by hitting it with the hands back and forth over the net without letting it touch the ground. **2.** the ball used in this game.

vol·ley·er (vol′ē ər), *n.* a person who volleys, especially in tennis: *The backcourt or base line game is practically hopeless against a volleyer of any real skill* (New Yorker).

vo·lost (vō′lost), *n.* **1.** a rural soviet (local governmental assembly in the Soviet Union). **2.** (formerly) a small administrative division in Russia. [< Russian *volost′* < Old Russian *volostĭ* territory, rule, related to *volodĕti* to rule]

vol·plane (vol′plān′), *v.,* **-planed, -plan·ing,** *n.* —*v.i.* to glide downward in an airplane without using the motor. —*n.* the act of doing this. [earlier, a controlled dive < French *vol plané* gliding flight; *vol* < *voler* to fly < Latin *volāre; plané,* past participle of *planer* to glide < *plan* level, plane < Latin *plānus*]

vol·plan·ist (vol′plā′nist), *n.* a person who volplanes.

vols., volumes.

Vol·sci (vol′sī), *n.pl.* an ancient, warlike people of eastern Latium, in southwestern Italy, subdued by the Romans in the 300's B.C. [< Latin *Volscī,* plural of *Volscus*]

Vol·scian (vol′shən), *adj.* of, having to do with, or belonging to the Volsci. —*n.* the Italian dialect spoken by the Volsci, related to Umbrian.

Vol·scians (vol′shənz), *n.pl.* the Volsci.

Vol·stead·ism (vol′sted iz əm), *n.* the policy of prohibiting the production or sale of alcoholic liquor; prohibition. [< Andrew J. *Volstead,* 1860–1947, a member of the U.S. House of Representatives, who sponsored the bill + *ism*]

Vol·sung (vol′sủng), *n., pl.* **-sungs.** *Scandinavian Mythology.* **1.** a powerful king, one of the heroes of the Volsunga Saga. **2.** any of a race of heroic warriors who were his descendants. [< Old Icelandic *Völsung*]

Vol·sun·ga Saga (vol′sủng gə), an Icelandic prose legend of the Volsungs and Nibelungs, the equivalent of the German *Nibelungenlied,* the chief hero being Sigurd, son of Volsung. [< Old Icelandic *Völsunga saga* saga of the Volsungs]

volt[1] (vōlt), *n.* the unit of electromotive force or potential difference. One volt causes a current of one ampere to flow through a conductor whose resistance is one ohm. *Abbr.:* v. [< Alessandro *Volta,* 1745-1827, an Italian physicist, who devised the voltaic pile]

volt[2] (vōlt), *n.* **1.** in the manège: **a.** a circular movement executed by a horse. **b.** a gait or maneuver made by a horse going sidewise round a center, with the head turned outward. **2.** (in fencing) a quick step or leap to escape a thrust. [(originally) verb < French *volter* < *volte* a turning < Italian *volta;* see VOLTA]

vol·ta (vol′tə; *Italian* vôl′tä), *n., pl.* **-te** (-tā). **1.** *Music.* a turn; a time. *Una volta* means once; *due volte* means twice. *Prima volta,* first time, marks the first ending of a movement to be repeated, and *seconda volta,* second time, marks the second time for the same movement. **2.** a dance of the 1500's. [< Italian *volta,* noun use of feminine past participle of *volvere* to turn, roll < Latin]

volt·age (vōl′tij), *n.* electromotive force or potential difference expressed in volts: *A current of high voltage is used in transmitting electric power long distances. Abbr.:* v.

voltage divider, *Electricity.* a resistor with two terminals between which the current flows. A portion of the total voltage may be obtained by connecting at any point between the terminals.

vol·ta·ic (vol tā′ik), *adj.* **1.** of, having to do with, or caused by electricity produced by chemical action; galvanic. **2.** producing an electrical current by chemical action. **3.** Also, **Voltaic.** of, relating to, or discovered by Count Alessandro Volta, an Italian physicist. [< Alessandro *Volta* (see VOLT[1]) + *-ic*]

voltaic battery, 1. an electric battery composed of one or more voltaic cells. **2.** a voltaic cell.

voltaic cell, an electric cell; container having two plates, each of a different metal, immersed in some solution or paste that will produce an electric current by reacting with one of the plates.

voltaic couple, (in a voltaic cell) the pair of (commonly) metallic substances that act as the source of the electric current when placed in the electrolyte.

voltaic electricity, electricity produced by a voltaic cell; electric current.

voltaic pile, a galvanic pile.

Vol·tair·e·an or **Vol·tair·i·an** (vol tãr′ē ən), *adj.* of or in the style of the French satirical and philosophical writer François Marie Arouet de Voltaire (1694–1778): *He wrote . . . that . . . Voltairean fairy tale "Le Petit Prince," now the most popular book in France* (Sunday Times).

—*n.* an admirer or imitator of Voltaire or his works.

vol·ta·ism (vol′tə iz əm), *n.* **1.** the branch of electrical science that deals with the production of an electric current by the chemical action of a liquid on metals. **2.** electricity thus produced. [< Alessandro *Volta* (see VOLT[1]) + *-ism*]

vol·tam·e·ter (vol tam′ə tər), *n.* a device for the measuring of electricity passing through a conductor by the amount of electrolytic decomposition it produces, or for measuring the strength of a current by the amount of such decomposition in a given time. [< *volta*(ic) + *-meter*]

vol·ta·met·ric (vol′tə met′rik), *adj.* having to do with or involving the use of a voltameter: *voltametric measurement.*

volt·am·me·ter (vōlt′am′mē′tər), *n.* **1.** an instrument that can measure either volts or amperes. **2.** a wattmeter. [< *volt*[1] + *ammeter*]

volt-am·pere (vōlt′am′pir), *n.* a unit of measurement equivalent to the product of one volt and one ampere. For alternating currents it is a measure of apparent power; for direct currents it is a measure of power and equals one watt. *Abbr.:* va (no periods).

Vol·ta's pile (vol′təz), galvanic pile. [< Alessandro *Volta;* see VOLT[1]]

vol·te-face (vôl′tə fās′, volt fās′), *n.* an about-face; reversal of judgment, belief, or policy: *Whatever the real explanation for the Chinese volte-face, it is unlikely that it will reverse the most significant result of the attack upon India* (London Times). [< French *volte-face* < Italian *volta faccia* < *volta* a turn (see VOLTA) + *faccia* face < Latin *faciēs*]

vol·ti (vôl′tē), *imperative. Music.* turn; turn over (the page), more usually seen as *V.S.* (*volti subito*), turn over swiftly! [< Italian *volti,* imperative of *voltare* turn < Latin *voltāre,* or *volvitāre,* for Latin *volūtāre* < *volvere* to roll, turn]

volt·me·ter (vōlt′mē′tər), *n.* an instrument for measuring electromotive force or potential difference between two points of a circuit in volts. [< *volt*[1] + *-meter*]

vol·u·bil·i·ty (vol′yə bil′ə tē), *n.* **1.** a readiness to talk much; the habit of talking much; garrulousness. **2.** a great flow of words. **3.** the ability to revolve, roll, or turn round on an axis or center. —**Syn. 1.** loquacity, talkativeness. **2.** fluency.

vol·u·ble (vol′yə bəl), *adj.* **1.** tending to talk much; fond of talking: *a voluble speaker.* **2.** having a smooth, rapid flow of words: *a voluble oration.* **3.** *Botany.* twining; twisting. [earlier, moving easily < Latin *volūbilis* (originally) rolling < *volvere* to roll] —**vol′u·ble·ness,** *n.* —**Syn. 2.** See **fluent.**

vol·u·bly (vol′yə blē), *adv.* in a voluble or fluent manner.

vol·u·crar·y (vol′yə krer′ē), *n., pl.* **-crar·ies.** a treatise on birds, of a kind written in the Middle Ages. [< Latin *volucris* bird + English *-ary*]

vol·u·crine (vol′yə krin, -krīn), *adj.* of or having to do with birds. [< Latin *volucris* bird + English *-ine*[1]]

vol·ume (vol′yəm), *n.* **1.** a collection of printed or written sheets bound together to form a book; book; tome: *We own a library of 500 volumes.* **2.** one of a number of books forming part of a set or series: *volume one of an encyclopedia.* **3.** a roll of parchment, papyrus, etc., containing written matter (the ancient form of a book); scroll. **4.** something comparable to a book, especially something that can be studied in the way that one studies a book. **5.** space occupied, as measured in three dimensions; bulk, size, or dimensions expressed in cubic units: *The storeroom has a volume of 800 cubic feet.* **6.** a quantity or mass, especially a large one, of something: *Volumes of smoke poured from the chimney.* **7.** the amount or quantity of something: *the volume of business at a store for a particular period.* **8.** the amount of sound; fullness of tone: *A pipe organ gives much more volume than a violin or flute.* *Abbr.:* vol.

speak volumes, to express much; be full of meaning: *A pause ensued, during which the eyes of Zastrozzi and Matilda spoke volumes to each guilty soul* (Shelley).

—*adj.* of or having to do with large amounts; in large amounts; bulk: *volume mailing. Sylvania Electric Products, Inc., promises to begin volume production ... of 21-inch screen models in April* (Wall Street Journal).

[< Old French *volume,* learned borrowing from Latin *volūmen, -inis* book; roll of parchment, scroll < *volvere* to roll]

—**Syn.** *n.* **7.** See **size.**

➔ See **book** for usage note.

vol·umed (vol′yəmd), *adj.* **1.** made into or filling a volume or volumes of a specified size, number, etc.: *The shelf contains the complete volumed works of Jefferson.* **2.** formed into a rolling, rounded, or dense mass: *volumed smoke.*

vo·lu·men (və lü′mən), *n., pl.* **-mi·na** (-mə nə). a roll or scroll, as of parchment or similar material. [< Latin *volūmen;* see VOLUME]

vo·lu·me·ter (və lü′mə tər), *n.* **1.** any of various instruments used to measure the volume of a gas or liquid directly or of a solid by displacement. **2.** a kind of hydrometer. [< *volu*(me) + *-meter*]

vol·u·met·ric (vol′yə met′rik), *adj.* of or having to do with measurement by volume. —**vol′u·met′ri·cal·ly,** *adv.*

vol·u·met·ri·cal (vol′yə met′rə kəl), *adj.* volumetric.

volumetric analysis, 1. quantitative chemical analysis in which the analyst determines the volume of a solution having a precisely known concentration, that is required to complete a specified chemical reaction. **2.** the measurement of the volume of gases, as by an eudiometer.

vo·lu·me·try (və lü′mə trē), *n.* the measurement of volume; the use of volumeters.

vo·lu·mi·nal (və lü′mə nəl), *adj.* having to do with volume or cubic magnitude.

vo·lu·mi·nos·i·ty (və lü′mə nos′ə tē), *n.* the quality or state of being voluminous; copiousness.

vo·lu·mi·nous (və lü′mə nəs), *adj.* **1.** forming a large book or many books: *the voluminous works of Sir Walter Scott.* **2.** writing so much as to fill a large book or several books: *a voluminous author or correspondent.* **3.** enough to fill a book or books: *voluminous documents, voluminous legislation.* **4.** of great size or volume; very bulky; large: *A voluminous cloak covered him from head to foot.* **5.** *Obsolete.* full of or containing many coils, convolutions, or windings. [< Latin *voluminōsus* with many coils < Latin *volūmen, -inis;* see VOLUME] —**vo·lu′mi·nous·ly,** *adv.* —**vo·lu′mi·nous·ness,** *n.*

vol·un·tar·i·ly (vol′ən ter′ə lē, vol′ən-tãr′-), *adv.* of one's own free will; without force or compulsion. —**Syn.** willingly.

vol·un·tar·i·ness (vol′ən ter′ē nis), *n.* the quality or state of being voluntary: *They assumed that socialism would bring ... a new attitude toward work, which would become a matter of joy and voluntariness* (Wall Street Journal).

vol·un·ta·rism (vol′ən tə riz′əm), *n. Philosophy.* a theory or doctrine that regards the will (rather than the intellect) as the fundamental principle or dominant factor in the individual or in the universe. [< *voluntar*(y) + *-ism*]

vol·un·ta·rist (vol′ən tər ist), *n.* an adherent of voluntarism or the voluntary principle in philosophy.

vol·un·ta·ris·tic (vol′ən tə ris′tik), *adj.* of or like voluntarism or voluntarists.

vol·un·tar·y (vol′ən ter′ē), *adj., n., pl.* **-tar·ies.** —*adj.* **1.** done, made, given, undertaken, entered into, etc., of one's own free will; not forced or compelled: *a voluntary contribution, to go into voluntary exile.* **2.** maintained or supported entirely by voluntary gifts: *a voluntary church or school.* **3.** acting of one's own free will or choice: *Voluntary workers built a road to the boys' camp.* **4.** able to act of one's own free will: *People are voluntary agents.* **5.** *Law.* **a.** done, given, or proceeding from the free or unconstrained will of a person: *a voluntary affidavit.* **b.** acting or done without obligation or without receiving a valuable consideration: *a voluntary partition of land.* **c.** deliberately intended; done on purpose, not by accident: *voluntary manslaughter.* **6.** *Physiology.* controlled by the will: *Talking is voluntary, breathing is only partly so.*

—*n.* **1.** a volunteer. **2.** anything done, made, given, etc., of one's own free will. **3. a.** a piece of music, often improvised, played as a prelude. **b.** an organ solo played before, during, or after a church service.

[< Latin *voluntārius* < *voluntās* will < *vol-,* stem of *velle* to wish. Related to VOLUNTEER.]

—**Syn.** *adj.* **1. Voluntary, spontaneous** mean done, made, given, etc., without being forced or compelled. **Voluntary** emphasizes that it is done of one's own free will or conscious choice: *The state is supported by taxes, the church by voluntary contributions.* **Spontaneous** emphasizes that it is done from natural impulse, without thought or conscious intention: *The laughter at his jokes is never forced, but always spontaneous.*

vol·un·tar·y·ism (vol′ən ter′ē iz əm), *n.* **1.** the principle or system under which churches, schools, etc., are supported by voluntary contributions or assistance, rather than by the state. **2.** the principle or method of voluntary service: *military voluntaryism.* [< *voluntary* + *-ism*]

vol·un·tar·y·ist (vol′ən ter′ē ist), *n.* a person who believes in or advocates voluntaryism, especially in religion.

voluntary minority, a national, religious, or racial group that chooses to remain a minority by preserving the traditions and customs of their forbears without assimilating with the majority.

voluntary muscle, striated muscle.

vol·un·teer (vol′ən tir′), *n.* **1.** a person who enters military or other service, or offers his services in any capacity, of his own free will. **2.** *Law.* **a.** a person who acts of his own free will in a transaction. **b.** a person who receives property by a conveyance made without a valuable consideration. **3.** a plant which grows from self-sown seed.

—*v.i.* **1.** to offer one's services of one's own free will: *to volunteer for an expedition. As soon as war was declared, many men volunteered.* **2.** to offer of one's own free will: *He volunteered to do the job.* —*v.t.* **1.** to offer (one's services or oneself) for some special purpose or enterprise. **2.** to offer to do, undertake, give, or show (something) without being asked: *to volunteer a job or song.* **3.** to tell or say voluntarily: *She volunteered the information.*

—*adj.* **1.** of or made up of volunteers: *a volunteer fire company, a volunteer corps.* **2.** serving as a volunteer: *That man is a volunteer fireman in this town.* **3.** voluntary. **4.** (of vegetation) growing from self-sown seed.

[earlier *voluntier* < French *volontaire* (originally) adjective < Latin *voluntārius.* Related to VOLUNTARY.]

Volunteers of America, an organization for religious reform and charity, similar to the Salvation Army, founded in 1896 by Ballington Booth, son of William Booth, the founder of the Salvation Army.

Volunteer State, a nickname of Tennessee.

vo·lup·tu·ar·y (və lup′chü er′ē), *n., pl.* **-ar·ies,** *adj.* —*n.* a person who cares much for luxurious or sensuous pleasures. —*adj.* of or having to do with luxurious or sensuous pleasures: *He leads a voluptuary life.* [< Latin *voluptuārius,* earlier *voluptārius* < *voluptās* pleasure; see VOLUPTUOUS]

vo·lup·tu·ous (və lup′chü əs), *adj.* **1.** caring much for the pleasures of the senses. **2.** giving pleasure to the senses: *voluptuous music.* **3.** suggestive of sensuous pleasure by fullness and beauty of form: *voluptuous loveliness.* [< Latin *voluptuōsus* < *voluptās* pleasure < *volupe* agreeable] —**vo·lup′tu·ous·ly,** *adv.* —**vo·lup′tu·ous·ness,** *n.*

vo·lute (və lüt′), *n.* **1.** a spiral or twisted thing or form. **2.** *Architecture.* a spiral or scroll-like ornament, especially the ones on Ionic, Corinthian, and Composite capitals. **3.** *Zoology.* **a.** a turn or whorl of a spiral shell. **b.** any of a group of gastropods that have a spiral shell.

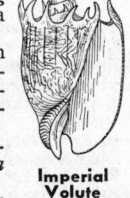

Volutes (def. 2) on Ionic capital

—*adj.* **1.** rolled up; spiral. **2.** of machinery: **a.** forming a spiral curve or curves: *a volute spring, a volute casing of a centrifugal pump.* **b.** moving in a rotary, and usually also a lateral, way.

[< French *volute* < Italian *voluta* < Latin *volūta,* (originally) feminine past participle of *volvere* to roll. Related to VOLTA.]

vo·lut·ed (və lü′tid), *adj.* having a coil, whorl, or volute: *a voluted shell.*

Imperial Volute Shell (def. 3b)

volute spring, a metal spring resembling a volute, commonly one consisting of a flat bar or ribbon coiled in a conical helix so as to be compressible in the direction of the axis about which it is coiled.

vol·u·tin (vol′yə tin), *n.* a granular substance in the cells of bacteria and yeast, that stains with basic dyes. [< New Latin *volutans* the species name of the bacteria in which it was found + English *-in*]

vo·lu·tion (və lü′shən), *n.* **1.** a rolling or winding; twist; convolution; spiral turn; whorl. **2.** a set of whorls, as of a spiral shell. [< Latin *volūtus,* past participle of *volvere* roll + English *-ion*]

vol·va (vol′və), *n. Botany.* the membranous covering that completely encloses many fungi, especially mushrooms, in the early stage of growth. [< Latin *volva,* variant of *vulva;* see VULVA]

vol·vent (vol′vənt), *n.* one of a series of pear-shaped cells on the tentacles of a hydra. The volvents release short, thick threads to capture small swimming animals by coiling about them. [< Latin *volvens, -entis,* present participle of *volvere* roll (because of its coiled structure)]

vol·vox (vol′voks), *n.* any of a group of fresh-water, green algae existing as spherical colonies of thousands of differentiated cells, and provided with cilia that enable them to roll over in the water. [< New Latin *Volvox* the genus name < Latin *volvere* to roll]

vol·vu·lus (vol′vyə ləs), *n. Medicine.* a twisting of the bowel so as to cause intestinal obstruction. [< New Latin *volvulus* (in Latin, small womb of an animal < *volvere* to roll, turn]

vo·mer (vō′mər), *n.* **1.** (in most vertebrates) a bone of the skull in or near the nose. **2.** (in man) a bone forming a large part of the nasal septum (partition between the nostrils) and having the shape of a plowshare. [< Latin *vōmer, -eris* plowshare]

vo·mer·ine (vō′mər in, vom′ər-), *adj.* of or having to do with the vomer.

vom·i·ca (vom′ə kə), *n. Medicine.* **1.** an ulcerous cavity or abscess, usually in the lungs. **2.** the pus in such a cavity or abscess. [< Latin *vomica* boil, ulcer < *vomere* to eject, vomit]

vom·it (vom′it), *v.i.* **1.** to throw up what has been eaten. **2.** to come out with force or violence. —*v.t.* **1.** to bring up and eject through the mouth (swallowed food or drink). **2.** to throw out with force; throw up: *The chimneys vomited forth smoke.* **3.** to cause (a person) to vomit.
—*n.* **1.** the act of vomiting. **2.** the substance thrown up from the stomach by vomiting. **3.** an emetic. **4.** a disease marked by copious vomiting.
[< Latin *vomitus,* past participle of *vomere* spew forth, eject] —**vom′it·er,** *n.*

vom·it·ing gas (vom′ə ting), a gas that causes vomiting, coughing, and sneezing, used chiefly in breaking up riots; chloropicrin.

vom·i·tive (vom′ə tiv), *adj., n.* emetic.

vom·i·to (vom′ə tō), *n.,* or **vomito negro,** black vomit, especially the black vomit of yellow fever. [< Spanish *vómito* (*negro*) (black) vomit < Latin *vomitus*]

vom·i·to·ri·um (vom′ə tôr′ē əm, -tōr′-), *n., pl.* **-to·ri·a** (-tôr′ē ə, -tōr′-). a passage providing entrance and exit in a theater, stadium, or other public place; vomitory: *the great vomitoria . . . designed to handle the crowds in Pennsylvania Station* (Lewis Mumford). [< Latin *vomitōria,* plural < *vomere* spew forth, eject]

vom·i·to·ry (vom′ə tôr′ē, -tōr′-), *adj., n., pl.* **-ries.** —*adj.* **1.** causing vomiting. **2.** of or having to do with vomiting.
—*n.* **1.** an emetic. **2.** an opening through which something is discharged. **3.** a passage by which spectators enter or leave, as in an ancient Roman theater.
[< Latin *vomitōrius* < *vomitus;* see VOMIT]

vom·i·tous (vom′ə təs), *adj.* inclined to vomit; nauseated; queasy: *The boat was a terrible ordeal, windy and smelling of oil. She felt chilled and vomitous* (New Yorker).

vom·i·tu·ri·tion (vom′ə chu̇ rish′ən), *n. Medicine.* ineffectual efforts to vomit, especially vomiting without bringing up any matter. [< Medieval Latin *vomituritio, -onis,* ultimately < Latin *vomere* to vomit]

vom·i·tus (vom′ə təs), *n.* vomited matter; vomit: *They should take the child and a sample of the poison (the vomitus will serve in a pinch) to the hospital right away* (Time). [< Latin *vomitus;* see VOMIT]

von (fôn; *English* von), *prep. German.* from; of.
➔ **von** is used in German personal names (originally before names of places or estates, and later before family names) as an indication of nobility or rank.

V-one (vē′wun′), *n.* V-1.

Von Gier·ke's disease (gir′kəz), a metabolic condition in which excess glycogen causes an abnormal enlargement of the liver, kidneys, or other organ; glycogenosis. [< Edgar *von Gierke,* 1877-1945, a German pathologist]

Von Jaksch's anemia (yäk′shiz), a disease affecting young children, characterized by anemia and a swelling of the spleen. [< Rudolf *von Jaksch,* 1855-1947, a German physician]

voo·doo (vü′dü), *n., pl.* **-doos,** *adj., v.,* **-dooed, -doo·ing.** —*n.* **1.** a body of beliefs and practices, including sorcery, magic, and conjuration. Voodoo came from Africa; belief in it still prevails among some Negroes of the West Indies and southern United States. **2.** a person who practices such magic. **3.** a charm or fetish used in the practice of voodoo.
—*adj.* of, having to do with, used in, or practicing voodoo.
—*v.t.* to affect by voodoo sorcery, magic, or conjuration. Also, **voudou.**
[American English < Creole (Haiti) *voodoo* < Ewe *vodũ* divinity]

voo·doo·ism (vü′dü iz əm), *n.* voodoo rites and practices; belief in or practice of voodoo as a superstition or form of sorcery.

voo·doo·ist (vü′dü ist), *n.* a believer in voodoo; practicer of voodoo.

voo·doo·is·tic (vü′dü is′tik), *adj.* of or having to do with voodooism.

voor·lop·er (fōr′lō′pər), *n. Afrikaans.* the native boy who guides the foremost pair of a team of oxen: *One of the drivers . . . called to his voorloper to turn the cattle loose to graze* (Percy Fitzpatrick).

voor·trek·ker (fōr′trek′ər), *n. Afrikaans.* a pioneer, especially one of the Dutch who emigrated from the Cape of Good Hope region into the lands north of the Orange River about 1835-40: *The Voortrekkers, as the emigrants were called, pushed into the veldt, fighting off and driving out native tribes* (New Yorker).

Vo·po (fō′pō), *n.* **1.** Volkspolizei; the East German People's Police. **2.** a member of Volkspolizei: *At the sector boundary I was stopped by a couple of Vopos* (New Yorker).

VOR (no periods), very high frequency omnidirectional range, a kind of radio range giving bearings in all directions from its transmitter: *VOR is able to utilize all the air space by sending out signals in every direction* (New York Times). [< *v*(ery high frequency) *o*(mnidirectional) *r*(ange)]

vo·ra·cious (və rā′shəs), *adj.* **1.** eating much; greedy in eating; ravenous: *voracious sharks.* **2.** very eager; unable to be satisfied, as an appetite, desire, or pursuit. [< Latin *vorāx, -ācis* greedy (with English *-ous*) < *vorāre* to devour] —**vo·ra′cious·ly,** *adv.* —**vo·ra′cious·ness,** *n.* —**Syn. 1.** gluttonous. **2.** insatiable.

vo·rac·i·ty (və ras′ə tē), *n.* a being voracious. [< Latin *vorācitās* < *vorāx;* see VORACIOUS]

Vor·la·ge (fōr′lä′gə), *n.* a position in skiing in which the skier leans forward by bending at the ankles, without raising the heels from the skis. [< German *Vorlage* < *vor* before + *Lage* position]

vor·spiel (fōr′shpēl′), *n.* a prelude or overture. [< German *Vorspiel* < *vor* before + *Spiel* a play, a playing]

vor·tex (vôr′teks), *n., pl.* **-tex·es** or **-ti·ces. 1.** a swirling mass of water that sucks in everything near it; whirlpool. **2.** a violent whirl of air; cyclone; whirlwind. **3.** a whirl or whirling mass of fire, flame, atoms, fluid, or vapor. **4.** a whirl of activity or other situation from which it is hard to escape: *The two nations were unwillingly drawn into the vortex of war.* **5.** (in old theories, especially that of Descartes) a supposed rotatory movement of cosmic matter round a center or axis, regarded as accounting for the origin or phenomena of the terrestrial and other systems. [< Latin *vortex, -icis,* variant of *vertex;* see VERTEX]

vor·ti·cal (vor′tə kəl), *adj.* **1.** (of motion) like that of a vortex; rotating; eddying; whirling. **2.** moving in a vortex; whirling round: *vortical currents.* —*n.* a vortical motion. —**vor′ti·cal·ly,** *adv.*

vor·ti·cel·la (vôr′tə sel′ə), *n., pl.* **-cel·lae** (-sel′ē). a protozoan that has a ciliated, bell-shaped body on a slender contractile stalk, often found attached to a plant or other object under water. [< New Latin *Vorticella* the typical genus (diminutive) < Latin *vortex* vortex]

vor·ti·ces (vôr′tə sēz), *n.* vortexes; a plural of **vortex.**

vor·ti·cism (vôr′tə siz əm), *n.* a movement in modern art and literature started in England about 1914 and chiefly supported by the poet Ezra Pound and the painter Wyndham Lewis. It emphasized that a work of art should have a point of central meaning obtained by reducing content to its simplest details, as in cubism. [< Latin *vortex, -icis* vortex + English *-ism*]

vor·ti·cist (vôr′tə sist), *n.* a follower or exponent of vorticism: *The reviled . . . Cubists, Futurists, Expressionists, Vorticists of today may be the honoured masters of tomorrow* (Observer). —*adj.* exhibiting or following the principles of vorticism: *A block away, at 105 Mulberry, a chicken and a . . . rabbit have been painted, and a vorticist woman has been chalked* (New Yorker).

vor·tic·i·ty (vôr tis′ə tē), *n.* the condition of a fluid with respect to its vortical motion: *The National Weather Analysis Center . . . provides the daily reports on winds, temperatures and vorticity as well as forecasts of Northern Hemisphere weather* (Science News Letter).

vor·ti·cose (vôr′tə kōs), *adj.* vortical. [< Latin *vorticōsus* < *vortex, -icis* vortex] —**vor′ti·cose′ly,** *adv.*

vor·tig·i·nous (vôr tij′ə nəs), *adj.* **1.** (of motion) vortical. **2.** moving in a vortex; rushing in whirls or eddies. [< Latin *vortīgō, -inis,* variant of *vertīgō* (see VERTIGO) + English *-ous*]

Vor·tum·nus (vôr tum′nəs), *n.* Vertumnus.

vot·a·ble (vō′tə bəl), *adj.* that can be voted for, against, on, etc.

vo·ta·ress (vō′tər is), *n.* a woman votary.

vo·ta·rist (vō′tər ist), *n.* votary.

vo·ta·ry (vō′tər ē), *n., pl.* **-ries,** *adj.* —*n.* **1.** a person bound by vows to a religious life; a monk or nun. **2.** a person who is devoted to a particular religion or to some form of religious worship. **3.** a person who is devoted to a particular pursuit, occupation, study, etc.; devotee: *a votary of golf.* **4.** a devoted admirer or adherent to some person, cause, institution, etc.
—*adj. Obsolete.* **1.** consecrated by a vow. **2.** of the nature of a vow.
[< Latin *vōtum* vow, noun use of neuter past participle of *vovēre* to vow + English *-ary*]
—**Syn.** *n.* **4.** partisan.

vote (vōt), *n., v.,* **vot·ed, vot·ing.** —*n.* **1.** a formal expression of a wish or choice on a proposal, motion, candidate for office, or other matter under discussion, indicated by ballot, holding up the hand, standing up, voice (viva voce), or otherwise: *The person receiving the most votes is elected.* **2.** the right to give such an expression of opinion or choice: *Not everybody has a vote.* **3.** ticket; ballot: *More than a million votes were cast.* **4.** votes considered together: *a light vote, the labor vote.* **5.** what is expressed or granted by a majority of voters: *a vote of confidence. The vote for foreign aid was $50,000,000.* **6.** a voter. **7.** *Obsolete.* **a.** a vow. **b.** a prayer. **c.** an ardent wish or desire.
—*v.i.* to give or cast a vote: *He voted for the Democrats.* —*v.t.* **1.** to elect, enact, establish, ratify, etc., by vote: *to vote a bill through Congress, vote a man to the Senate.* **2.** to pass, determine, or grant by vote: *Money for a new school was voted by the board.* **3.** to support by one's vote: *to vote the Republican ticket.* **4.** to declare, especially by general consent: *They voted the play a success.* **5.** *Informal.* to propose; suggest: *I vote that we leave now.*
vote down, to defeat by voting against: *His proposals were invariably voted down* (Edmund Wilson).
vote in, to elect: *The mayor was voted in by a large majority.*
[< Latin *vōtum* vow, desire. Doublet of vow.]

vote-get·ter (vōt′get′ər), *n. Informal.* a person who is successful in getting votes; a popular candidate: *He is a good senator and might make a good President, but unless he is able to prove himself an irresistible vote-getter he is unlikely to be given the chance to be one* (Manchester Guardian).

vote·less (vōt′lis), *adj.* having no vote; not entitled to vote: *So there arose a demand for someone who could speak officially for Alaska, a voteless delegate, such as every other territory had had from its beginnings* (Atlantic).

vote of confidence, 1. a vote given by the majority of members in a parliament to the government or its chief representative, especially in a period of crisis, to indicate support of its policies: *The Government is asking for a vote of confidence* (London Times). **2.** any expression of approval or support: *British and French officialdom, in a rare vote of confidence in U.S. diplomatic skill, admiringly agreed that Washington had handled Mikoyan adroitly* (Time).

vot·er (vō′tər), *n.* **1.** a person who votes. **2.** a person who has the right to vote.

vot·ing machine (vō′ting), a mechanical device for registering and counting votes: *voting machines have replaced the ballot box.*

voting paper, a paper on which a vote is recorded, especially as used in British parliamentary elections.

voting trust, 1. a method of restraining trade in which a board of trustees controls the affairs of a group of companies by obtaining the right to vote the stocks in each concern. **2.** a method of centralizing control of a company, in which all or a majority of the stockholders relinquish their voting power to a board of trustees for a limited period of time.

vo·tive (vō′tiv), *adj.* **1.** promised by a vow; done, given, etc., because of a vow: *votive offerings to the gods, a knight on his votive quest, to light a votive candle.* **2.** made up or expressive of a vow, desire, or wish: *a votive prayer.* **3.** (in the Roman Catholic Church) done or performed with special intention and not corresponding strictly to the established liturgical order. [< Latin *votīvus* < *vōtum* a vow] —**vo′tive·ly,** *adv.* —**vo′tive·ness,** *n.*

vo·tress (vō′tris), *n.* votaress.

Vo·ty·ak (vō′tē ak, -tyäk), *n.* a Finno-Ugric language, one of the four principal languages of the Permian group.

vouch (vouch), *v.i.* **1.** to be responsible; give a guarantee (for): *I can vouch for the truth of the story. The principal vouched for Bill's honesty.* **2.** to give evidence or assurance of a fact (for): *The success of the attack vouches for the general's ability.* —*v.t.* **1.** to guarantee (a statement, etc.) to be true or accurate; confirm; bear witness to; attest. **2.** to support or uphold with evidence; back with proof. **3.** to support or substantiate (a claim, title, etc.) by vouchers. **4.** to cite, quote, or appeal to (authority, example, a passage in a book, etc.) in support or justification of a view, statement, course, etc. **5.** *Law.* to call into court to give warranty of title. **6.** to sponsor or recommend (a person or thing); support; back. **7.** *Archaic.* to call to witness.
—*n. Obsolete.* an assertion, declaration, or attestation of truth or fact.
[Middle English *vouchen* < Anglo-French *voucher,* Old French *vochier* < Latin *vocāre* call]

vouch·er[1] (vou′chər), *n.* **1.** a person or thing that vouches for something. **2.** written evidence of the payment of money; receipt: *Canceled checks returned from one's bank are vouchers.*

vouch·er[2] (vou′chər), *n.* in early English law: **a.** a person summoned into court to give warranty of a title. **b.** the act of summoning a person into court to give warranty of title.
[< Anglo-French *voucher* a summoning, noun use of infinitive; see VOUCH]

vouch·safe (vouch sāf′), *v.,* **-safed, -saf·ing.** —*v.t.* **1.** to be willing to grant or give; deign (to do or give): *The proud man vouchsafed no reply when we spoke to him.* **2.** *Obsolete.* to guarantee as safe; secure; assure. —*v.i.* to permit; grant; condescend; stoop. [< Middle English phrase *vouchen (it) safe* to guarantee it as safe]

vouch·safe·ment (vouch sāf′mənt), *n.* **1.** the act of vouchsafing. **2.** something vouchsafed.

vou·dou (vü′dü), *n., adj., v.* voodoo.

vouge (vüzh), *n.* a type of weapon carried by foot soldiers in the Middle Ages, having an ax blade with a spear point at the top. [< French *vouge* < Old French *vooulge,* or *veouge,* earlier *vedoge* < Late Latin (Gaul) *vidubium,* probably < Celtic (compare Middle Irish *fidbæ* sickle)]

vous·soir (vü swär′), *n.* one of the wedge-shaped pieces or sections that form part of an arch or a vault. [< French *voussoir* < Old French *vausoir* < Vulgar Latin *volsōrium* < Latin *volvere* to roll]

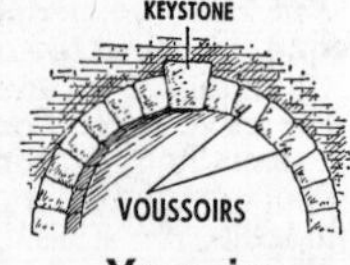

Voussoirs

vow (vou), *n.* **1.** a promise made to God: *a nun's vows.* **2.** a solemn promise: *a vow of secrecy, a marriage vow.* **3.** a solemn declaration or affirmation; asseveration.
take vows, to become a member of a religious order.
—*v.t.* **1.** to make a vow to do, give, get, etc.: *to vow that one will be loyal, to vow not to disclose a secret, to vow revenge.* **2.** to dedicate, consecrate, or devote to some person or service: *to vow oneself to a life of service to God.* **3.** to declare earnestly or emphatically: *I vowed never to leave home again.* —*v.i.* to make a vow.
[< Anglo-French, Old French *vou* < Latin *vōtum,* noun use of past participle of *vovēre* to vow. Doublet of VOTE.] —**vow′er,** *n.*

vow·el (vou′əl), *n., adj., v.,* **-eled, -el·ing** or (*especially British*) **-elled, -el·ling.** —*n.* **1.** *Phonetics.* a speech sound in the production of which the breath stream flows out through an unobstructed passage with no audible friction, with the vocal cords generally but not necessarily vibrating. The various vowel sounds are produced by modification of the shape of the oral chamber by movements of the tongue and lips. **2.** a letter representing such a sound, as English *a, e, i, o, u* and sometimes *y,* as in *bicycle.*
—*adj.* of or having to do with a vowel: *the vowel quality of "y" in "yet."*
—*v.t.* **1.** to supply with vowels or vowel points: *... with pauses, cadence, and well-vowelled words* (John Dryden). **2.** *Slang.* to pay (a creditor) with an I.O.U.: *Do not talk to me, I am voweled by the Count, and cursedly out of humour* (Sir Richard Steele). —*v.i.* to utter or pronounce vowels: *Sir Maurice, vowelling imperially as the Sheldonian ...* (Sunday Times).
[< Old French *vouel* < Latin (*littera*) *vōcālis* sounding (letter) < *vōx, vōcis* voice. Doublet of VOCAL.] —**vow′el·like′,** *adj.*

vow·el·i·za·tion (vou′ə lə zā′shən), *n.* **1.** the act of vowelizing. **2.** the state of being vowelized.

vow·el·ize (vou′ə līz), *v.t.,* **-ized, -iz·ing. 1.** to insert vowel symbols or points in: *to vowelize a Hebrew text.* **2.** to pronounce like a vowel. **3.** to modify by a vowel sound.

vow·el·less (vou′əl lis), *adj.* having no vowel or vowels.

vowel point, (in Hebrew, Arabic, and certain other Eastern writing systems) any of certain marks placed above or below consonants, or attached to them, to indicate vowels.

vox (voks), *n., pl.* **vo·ces.** *Latin.* voice; sound; word; expression.

vox an·gel·i·ca (voks an jel′ə kə), voix celeste. [< Latin *vōx* voice + *angelica,* feminine, angelic]

vox bar·ba·ra (voks bär′bər ə), a barbarous or outlandish word or phrase (commonly used of those terms in botany, zoology, etc., that are ostensibly New Latin, but which are neither Latin nor Greek, nor of classic derivation and formation, although they may be Latin and Greek hybrids). [< Latin *vōx* voice + *barbara,* feminine, (originally) non-Greek or Roman]

vox et prae·te·re·a ni·hil (voks′ et prē ter′ē ə nī′hil), *Latin.* a voice and nothing more; only sound.

vox hu·ma·na (voks hyü mā′nə), an organ reed stop of 8-foot, or occasionally 16-foot, pitch whose tones are intended to imitate those of the human voice. [< Latin *vōx* voice + *hūmāna,* feminine, human]

vox po·pu·li (voks pop′yu̇ lī), *Latin.* the voice or opinion of the people. *Abbr.:* vox pop.

voy·age (voi′ij), *n., v.,* **-aged, -ag·ing.** —*n.* **1. a.** a journey by water; cruise: *to make or take a voyage.* **b.** such a journey in which return is made to the starting point. **2.** a journey or flight through the air or through space: *an airplane voyage, the earth's voyage around the sun.* **3.** (formerly) a journey by either land or sea. **4.** a written account of a voyage; a book describing a voyage (often used in the plural in book titles). **5.** the course of life (or some part of it), or the fate of persons after death: *the voyage of matrimony.* **6.** *Obsolete.* an enterprise or undertaking.
—*v.i.* to make or take a voyage or voyages; go by sea or air: *Columbus voyaged across the ocean in 1492.*
—*v.t.* to cross or travel over; traverse: *Freighters voyage all the seas of the world.*
[< Old French *veiage,* and *voyage* < Latin *viāticum* provision for travel; (originally) of or for a journey. Doublet of VIATICUM.]
—**Syn.** *n.* **1. a.** See **trip.**

voy·age·a·ble (voi′ə jə bəl), *adj.* that can be voyaged over; navigable.

voy·ag·er (voi′ə jər), *n.* a person who makes a voyage; traveler.

vo·ya·geur (vwä′yä zhœr′; *French* vwȧ yȧ-zhœr′), *n., pl.* **-geurs** (-zhœrz′; *French* -zhœr′). a French Canadian or half-breed accustomed to travel on foot or by canoe through unsettled regions and, at one time, generally employed to act as a line of communication for, and carry goods to and from, fur company trading posts. [American English < Canadian French *voyageur* (in Middle French, a traveler) < *voyager* to travel < Old French *voyage,* see VOYAGE]

vo·yeur (vwä′yœr′), *n.* a person who attains sexual gratification by observing others in the nude or watching their sexual acts. [< French *voyeur* < *voir* to see < Latin *vidēre*]

vo·yeur·ism (vwä yœr′iz əm), *n.* the practices of a voyeur.

vo·yeur·is·tic (vwä′yə ris′tik), *adj.* of or having to do with voyeurs or voyeurism: *a voyeuristic tendency.*

V.P. or **VP** (no periods), Vice-President.

V-par·ti·cle (vē′pär′tə kəl), *n.* a name originally given to nuclear particles that produced V-shaped tracks when passing through a cloud chamber, now identified as hyperons or heavy mesons.

VRA (no periods), Vocational Rehabilitation Administration.

vrai·sem·blance (vre sän bläns′), *n.* appearance of truth; likelihood; verisimilitude. [< French *vraisemblance* < *vrai* true + *semblance* appearance]

V.Rev., Very Reverend.

vrouw (vrou; *South African* frou), *n.* **1.** a woman; wife; lady. **2.** Mrs. [< Dutch *vrouw*]

vs., 1. versus. **2.** verse.

v.s., see above (Latin, *vide supra*).

V.S., 1. Veterinary Surgeon. **2.** *Music.* turn over swiftly (Italian, *volti subito*).

V-shaped (vē′shāpt′), *adj.* **1.** shaped like the letter V: *Most of the modern jet airliners have V-shaped wings.* **2.** like the letter V in cross section.

V-sign (vē′sīn′), *n.* a sign indicating victory, especially in wartime, made by spreading out two fingers in the form of a V.

VSTOL (no periods), vertical and short take-off and landing (aircraft)

v.t., transitive verb.

Vt., Vermont.

VT fuse, proximity fuse. [< *v*(ariable) *t*(ime) fuse]

VTO (no periods), vertical take-off.

VTOL (no periods), vertical take-off and landing.

V.T.R. or **VTR** (no periods), videotape recorder.

V-two (vē′tü′), *n.* V-2.

vug, vugg, or **vugh** (vug, vu̇g), *n. Mining.* a cavity; a hollow in a rock or lode, often completely lined with quartz. [< Cornish *vooga,* or *fuogo* cavern]

vug·gy or **vugh·y** (vug′ē, vu̇g′-), *adj. Mining.* full of cavities.

Vul., Vulgate.

Vul·can (vul′kən), *n.* the Roman god of fire and metalworking, the husband of Venus. The Romans identified him with the Greek god Hephaestus.

vul·ca·ni·an (vul kā′nē ən), *adj.* **1.** volcanic. **2.** having to do with metalworking. **3.** *Especially British.* Plutonic.

Vul·ca·ni·an (vul kā′nē ən), *adj.* having to do with, characteristic of, or made by Vulcan.

vul·can·ic·i·ty (vul′kə nis′ə tē), *n.* volcanicity.

vul·can·ism (vul′kə niz əm), *n.* volcanic phenomena; volcanism.

vul·can·ite (vul′kə nīt), *n.* a hard rubber obtained by treating India rubber with a large amount of sulfur and heating it. Vulcanite is used for combs, for shoe soles, for buttons, in electric insulation, and in many other ways. —*adj.* made of this substance.

vul·can·iz·a·ble (vul′kə nī′zə bəl), *adj.* that can be vulcanized.

vul·can·i·zate (vul′kə nə zāt), *n.* a vulcanized material: *Rubber vulcanizates have remarkable strength* (Scientific American).

vul·can·i·za·tion (vul′kə nə zā′shən), *n.* the act or process of vulcanizing.

vul·can·ize (vul′kə nīz), *v.,* **-ized, -iz·ing.** —*v.t.* **1.** to treat (rubber) with sulfur or a sulfur compound and subject it to heat in order to make it more elastic and durable, or with a large amount of sulfur and intense heat in order to harden it, as in the preparation of vulcanite. **2.** to repair (a rubber tire, etc.) by using heat and chemicals to fuse the patch. **3.** to treat (rubber) with sulfur or a sulfur compound, but without subjecting it to heat. **4.** to treat (a substance) by an analogous process, as for hardening. —*v.i.* to undergo the process of vulcanizing: *a tire vulcanized with a new tread.*

Vul·can·ized Fiber (vul′kə nīzd), *Trademark.* a tough, hard substance formed by compressing paper that has been treated with acids or zinc chloride.

vul·can·iz·er (vul′kə nī′zər), *n.* **1.** a person who vulcanizes. **2.** an apparatus that vulcanizes, especially that used in vulcanizing rubber.

vul·can·o·log·i·cal (vul′kə nə loj′ə kəl), *adj.* volcanological.

vul·can·ol·o·gist (vul′kə nol′ə jist), *n.* volcanologist.

vul·can·ol·o·gy (vul′kə nol′ə jē), *n.* volcanology.

vulg., 1. vulgar. **2.** vulgarly.

Vulg., Vulgate.

vul·gar (vul′gər), *adj.* **1.** showing a lack of good breeding, manners, taste, etc.; not refined; coarse; low: *vulgar manners or language, a vulgar display.* **2.** of, belonging to, or comprising the common people: *the vulgar mass, to be held in vulgar contempt.* **3.** current or prevalent among the multitude or general public; popular; general: *vulgar prejudices or superstitions.* **4.** (of language or speech) commonly or customarily used by the people of a country; ordinary; vernacular. **5.** common; ordinary.
—*n. Obsolete.* the vernacular.
the vulgar, the common people: *Nor was this the suspicion of the vulgar alone; it seems to have been shared by the clergy* (Henry Hart Milman).
[< Latin *vulgāris* < *vulgus* the common people, multitude] **—vul′gar·ly,** *adv.* **—vul′gar·ness,** *n.*
—**Syn.** *adj.* **1.** inelegant. See **coarse. 2.** plebeian, lowbrow, ignoble. —**Ant.** *adj.* **1.** cultured, polite.

vulgar fraction, a common fraction.

vul·gar·i·an (vul gãr′ē ən), *n.* **1.** a vulgar person. **2.** a rich person who lacks good breeding, manners, taste, etc.

vul·gar·ise (vul′gə rīz), *v.t.,* **-ised, -is·ing.** *Especially British.* vulgarize.

vul·gar·ism (vul′gə riz əm), *n.* **1.** a word, phrase, or expression used only in ignorant or coarse speech. In "I disremember his name," *disremember* is a vulgarism. **2.** vulgar character or action; vulgarity. **3.** a vulgar expression.

vul·gar·i·ty (vul gar′ə tē), *n., pl.* **-ties. 1.** a lack of refinement; lack of good breeding, manners, taste, etc.; coarseness. **2.** an action, habit, speech, etc., showing vulgarity: *Talking loudly on a train and chewing gum at a dance are vulgarities.*

vul·gar·i·za·tion (vul′gər ə zā′shən), *n.* **1.** the act of making usual or common. **2.** the act or process of making coarse or unrefined.

vul·gar·ize (vul′gə rīz), *v.t.,* **-ized, -iz·ing. 1.** to make vulgar or common; degrade or debase: *Signs and advertisements often vulgarize the countryside.* **2.** to make common or popular.

vul·gar·iz·er (vul′gə rī′zər), *n.* a person who vulgarizes or makes popular.

Vulgar Latin, the popular form of Latin, the main source of French, Spanish, Italian, and Portuguese.

Vul·gate (vul′gāt), *n.* the Latin version of the Bible used in the Roman Catholic Church as the authoritative text. It is primarily a translation from the Hebrew, Greek, and Aramaic texts made by Saint Jerome (at the end of the 300's and beginning of the 400's A.D.) but with subsequent revisions. A thorough modern revision by the Benedictine Order, authorized by Pope Pius X in 1908, is expected to replace the standard Sistine edition of 1592-1593 now in use. *Abbr.:* Vulg.
—*adj.* of or having to do with the Vulgate: *a Vulgate translation.*
[< Late Latin *vulgāta* (*ēditiō*) popular (edition); feminine past participle of *vulgāre* make public < *vulgus* the common people]

vul·gate (vul′gāt), *n.* the ordinary text of a work or author.
the vulgate, a. common or colloquial speech: *"Here's a pretty mess," returned the pompous gentleman, descending to the vulgate* (J.E. Cooke). **b.** substandard speech: *the vulgate of the backwoods country.*
—*adj.* **1.** ordinary or substandard in language. **2.** having to do with the common or usual version of a literary work. [< *Vulgate*]

vul·gus[1] (vul′gəs), *n., pl.* **-gus·es.** the common people; the crowd. [< Latin *vulgus*]

vul·gus[2] (vul′gəs), *n., pl.* **-gus·es.** *British.* (in some public schools) a short set of Latin verses on a given subject to be memorized or written. [probably an alteration of *vulgars,* plural of *vulgar*]

vul·ner·a·bil·i·ty (vul′nər ə bil′ə tē), *n.* vulnerable quality or condition; a being open to attack or injury: *General Charles A. Lindbergh pointed to the vulnerability of air bases as a weak spot in our atomic deterrent potential* (Wall Street Journal).

vul·ner·a·ble (vul′nər ə bəl), *adj.* **1.** that can be wounded or injured; open to attack: *Achilles was vulnerable only in his heel.* **2.** sensitive to criticism, temptations, or influences: *Most people are vulnerable to ridicule.* **3.** (in contract bridge) having won one game towards a rubber and thus in the position where penalties and premiums are increased. [< Late Latin *vulnerābilis* wounding < Latin *vulnerāre* to wound < *vulnus, -eris* wound]

vul·ner·a·bly (vul′nər ə blē), *adv.* in a vulnerable manner.

vul·ne·rant om·nes, ul·ti·ma ne·cat (vul′nə rant om′nēz, ul′tə mə nē′kat), *Latin.* all (hours) wound, the final (one) kills (sometimes inscribed on clocks).

vul·ner·ar·y (vul′nə rer′ē), *adj., n., pl.* **-ar·ies.** —*adj.* used for or useful in healing wounds; curative: *a vulnerary root.* —*n.* a vulnerary plant or remedy: *The Indians taught the New England settlers about many vulneraries.*

Vul·pec·u·la (vul pek′yə lə), *n., genitive* **Vul·pec·u·lae.** a small northern constellation lying between Hercules and Pegasus; Little Fox. [< Latin *Vulpecula* (diminutive) < *vulpēs, -is* fox]

Vul·pec·u·lae (vul pek′yə lē), *n.* the genitive of **Vulpecula.**

vul·pec·u·lar (vul pek′yə lər), *adj.* of or having to do with a fox, especially a young fox; vulpine.

vul·pi·cid·al (vul′pə sī′dəl), *adj.* committing or taking part in, connected with, or of the nature of vulpicide.

vul·pi·cide[1] (vul′pə sīd), *n.* (in England) a person who kills a fox otherwise than by hunting with hounds. [< Latin *vulpēs, -is* fox + English *-cide*[1]]

vul·pi·cide[2] (vul′pə sīd), *n.* (in England) the act of killing a fox otherwise than by hunting with hounds. [< Latin *vulpēs, -is* + English *-cide*[2]]

vul·pine (vul′pīn, -pin), *adj.* of or like a fox; cunning; sly. [< Latin *vulpīnus* < *vulpēs, -is* fox]

vul·pi·nite (vul′pə nīt), *n. Mineralogy.* a granular variety of anhydrite. [< *Vulpino,* Italy, where it is found + *-ite*[1]]

vul·ture (vul′chər), *n.* **1.** any of certain large birds of prey related to the eagles, falcons, and hawks, having keen sight, weak talons, and a usually featherless head and neck, and feeding almost entirely on the flesh of dead animals. Vultures comprise two families, one of the Old World, that includes the griffon vulture, and the other of the New World, that includes the condor, the turkey buzzard or turkey vulture, and the black vulture. **2.** some person or thing that preys upon another; a greedy, ruthless person: *the vultures of graft and dishonesty.* [< Latin *vultur, -uris*] **—vul′ture·like′,** *adj.*

North American Turkey Vulture (def. 1) (about 2½ ft. long)

vul·tur·ine (vul′chə rīn, -chər in), *adj.* of or having to do with vultures; resembling or characteristic of a vulture. [< Latin *vulturīnus* < *vultur, -uris* vulture]

vul·tur·ous (vul′chər əs), *adj.* characteristic of or resembling a vulture.

vul·va (vul′və), *n., pl.* **-vae** (-vē), **-vas.** the external genitals of the female. [< Latin *vulva* womb; wrapper < *volvere* to roll, turn]

vul·val (vul′vəl), *adj.* of or having to do with the vulva.

vul·var (vul′vər), *adj.* vulval.

vul·vi·form (vul′və fôrm), *adj.* **1.** *Zoology.* shaped like the vulva of the human female. **2.** *Botany.* shaped like a cleft with projecting edges.

vul·vi·tis (vul vī′tis), *n.* inflammation of the vulva.

vum (vum), *v.i.,* **vummed, vum·ming.** *U.S. Dialect.* to vow; swear: *I vum, it makes a man come all over uneasy* (New Yorker).

vv., 1. verses. **2.** violins.

v.v., vice versa.

Vy·cor (vī′kôr), *n. Trademark.* a nonporous glass composed of 96 per cent silica, very resistant to heat and chemicals, used for laboratory and industrial apparatus, cooking and baking dishes, etc.

vy·gie (vī′jē), *n.* any of a large group of dicotyledonous, fleshy plants of the carpetweed family, found especially in South Africa, having white, yellow, or rose-colored flowers with unconnected petals. [< Afrikaans *vygie*]

vy·ing (vī′ing), *v.* the present participle of **vie:** *boys vying with each other for a position on the baseball team.*
—*adj.* that vies; competing; emulating. **—vy′ing·ly,** *adv.*

Medieval Scribes

Roman 100's A.D.

Greek 600's B.C.

Phoenician 1000's B.C.

Egyptian 3000's B.C.

Ww Ww *Ww* *Ww*

W, w (dub′əl yü), *n., pl.* **W's** or **Ws, w's** or **ws.** **1.** the 23rd letter of the English alphabet. **2.** a speech sound representing this letter. **3.** the 23rd in a series or, more usually, the 22nd (either *I* or *J* being omitted).

w (no period), watt.

w., an abbreviation for the following:
1. wanting.
2. warden.
3. watt or watts.
4. week or weeks.
5. weight.
6. a. west. **b.** western.
7. a. wide. **b.** width.
8. wife.
9. with.
10. won.
11. *Physics.* work.

W (no period), **1.** watt or watts. **2.** west. **3.** *Chemistry.* tungsten (German, *Wolfram*).

W., an abbreviation for the following:
1. Wales.
2. warden.
3. Washington.
4. Wednesday.
5. weight.
6. Welsh.
7. a. west. **b.** western. **c.** Western (postal district, London).
8. width.
9. *Physics.* work.

wa' (wô, wä), *n. Scottish.* wall.

W.A., 1. West Africa. **2.** Western Australia.

Wa (wä), *n., pl.* **Wa** or **Was. 1.** a member of an aboriginal tribe of the Mon-Khmer linguistic family living in the jungles of northeastern Burma, chiefly in hill villages that can be entered only by tunnels: *The Wa believe that a village's supply of human skulls must be replenished each year to ensure good crops* (Time). **2.** the language of this people.

WAA (no periods), War Assets Administration.

WAAC or **Waac** (wak), *n.* a member of the WAAC.

WAAC (no periods) or **W.A.A.C., 1.** *U.S.* Women's Army Auxiliary Corps (the former name of the Women's Army Corps or WAC). **2.** *British.* Women's Army Auxiliary Corps (a former name of the Women's Royal Army Corps or WRAC).

WAAF or **Waaf** (waf), *n.* a member of the WAAF.

WAAF (no periods) or **W.A.A.F.,** *British.* Women's Auxiliary Air Force (the former name of the Women's Royal Air Force or WRAF).

wab (wab, wäb), *n. Scottish.* web.

wab·ble[1] (wob′əl), *v.i., v.t.,* **-bled, -bling,** *n.* wobble.

wab·ble[2] (wob′əl), *n.* warble[2].

wab·bler (wob′lər), *n.* wobbler.

wab·bling (wob′ling), *adj.* wobbling. —**wab′bling·ly,** *adv.*

wab·bly (wob′lē), *adj.,* **-bli·er, -bli·est.** wobbly[1].

WAC or **Wac** (wak), *n.* a member of the WAC; woman in the U.S. Army, not a nurse.

WAC (no periods), *U.S.* Women's Army Corps.

wack (wak), *n. Slang.* an eccentric or crazy person: *Dear old wack, would you like to walk through the streets of the city tomorrow giving away money?* (Punch). [probably back formation < *wacky*]

wack·e (wak′ə), *n.* **1.** a rock similar to sandstone, resulting from the decomposition of rocks in place. **2.** a soft basaltic rock formed by a similar process. [< German *Wacke* pebbles and gravel in river beds < Middle High German, large stone < Old High German *waggo,* and *wacko* pebble]

wack·i·ly (wak′ə lē), *adv. Slang.* in a wacky manner: *. . . three wackily soulful devotees of adjustment and personal relationships* (Time).

wack·i·ness (wak′ē nis), *n. Slang.* wacky quality or condition: *A pleasant enough, light . . . farce that brings an American touch of wackiness to a French-style exercise in sin* (Time).

wack·y (wak′ē), *adj.,* **wack·i·er, wack·i·est.** *Slang.* unconventional; eccentric; crazy. Also, **whacky.** [American English, perhaps < *whack* to beat; a blow + *-y*[1]. Compare PUNCH-DRUNK, SLAP-HAPPY.]

wad[1] (wod), *n., v.,* **wad·ded, wad·ding.** —*n.* **1.** a small, soft mass: *He plugged his ears with wads of cotton.* **2.** a tight roll; compact bundle or mass: *a wad of bills, a wad of crumpled paper, a wad of chewing gum.* **3.** a round plug of leather, felt, cardboard, jute, or the like, used to hold the powder and shot in place in a gun or cartridge. **4.** *Ceramics.* a small lump of fine clay used to cover inferior material, especially a strip doubled over the edge of a dish. **5.** *Slang.* personal wealth; riches: *He made his wad in oil.* **6.** *British Dialect.* a bundle of hay or straw, especially a small one.

wads, *Slang.* very much or many; a lot: *He will find them well padded by wads of extracts from second-hand authorities* (Saturday Review).

—*v.t.* **1.** to make into a wad; press into a wad. **2.** to line (a garment) with stuffing or padding, as for warmth, softness, etc,; pad; quilt. **3.** to pad for fullness; fill out with padding; stuff. **4. a.** to place a wad in (a gun barrel). **b.** to hold (powder and shot) in place with a wad. **5.** to fill (an opening) with a wad; stop up. —*v.i.* **1.** to become pressed into a wad. **2.** to be formed into a wad easily; hold or stick together well.

[origin uncertain. Compare Swedish *vadd,* Dutch *watte,* Medieval Latin *wadda.*]

wad[2] (wod), *n.* an impure, earthy ore of manganese. [origin unknown]

wad[3] (wäd, wəd), *v. Scottish.* would[1]. [earlier *waude* < *walde,* dialectal variant of Old English *wolde* would]

wad[4] (wod), *n. Scottish.* **1.** a pledge. **2.** a hostage.

in wad of, as security for (a payment, etc.): *jewels held in wad of a sum owed.*

to or **in wad,** as a pledge or hostage: *to lay to wad one's land or valuables.*

[variant of obsolete *wed* a pledge, Old English *wedd.* Related to WED, verb.]

wad[5] (wod), *v.t., v.i.,* **wad·ded, wad·ding.** *Scottish.* to wed.

wad·a·ble (wā′də bəl), *adj.* that can be waded.

wad·der (wod′ər), *n.* **1.** a person or thing that wads. **2.** *Obsolete.* an implement for wadding a gun.

wad·ding (wod′ing), *n.* **1.** a soft material for padding, stuffing, packing, etc., especially carded cotton in sheets. **2.** any material for making wads for guns or cartridges. **3.** wad.

wad·dle (wod′əl), *v.,* **-dled, -dling,** *n.* —*v.i.* to walk with short steps and an awkward, swaying motion, as a duck does. —*n.* **1.** the act of waddling. **2.** an awkward, swaying gait. [< *wade* to proceed + *-le*]

wad·dler (wod′lər), *n.* a person or animal that waddles.

wad·dling·ly (wod′ling lē), *adv.* with a waddling gait.

wad·dy[1] (wod′ē), *n., pl.* **-dies,** *v.,* **-died, -dy·ing.** —*n.* **1.** a heavy war club used by the Australian aborigines. **2.** (in Australia) a walking stick. —*v.t.* to strike, injure, or kill with a waddy. [probably native alteration of English *wood*[1], in sense "club"]

wad·dy[2] (wod′ē), *n., pl.* **-dies.** *U.S.* a temporary ranch hand, hired to punch cattle.

wade (wād), *v.,* **wad·ed, wad·ing,** *n.* —*v.i.* **1.** to walk through water, snow, sand, mud, or anything that hinders free motion: *to wade through slush, to wade in muck, to wade across a brook.* **2.** to come or force one's way as if by wading: *To wade through slaughter to a throne* (Thomas Gray). **3.** to make one's way with difficulty: *to wade through a badly written letter.* **4.** *Obsolete.* to make one's way; proceed; go. —*v.t.* to cross or pass through by wading; ford: *to wade a stream.*

wade in, *Informal.* to thrust or throw oneself into the middle or thick of something and fight, work, etc., with vigor: *to wade in and straighten out a dispute.*

wade into, *Informal.* **a.** to begin to work vigorously on: *to wade into a job and finish it quickly.* **b.** to make a vigorous attack on: *to wade into an opponent and knock him out.*

—*n.* **1.** the act of wading: *to go for a wade, a long wade to the other side.* **2.** a shallow place in a stream; ford.

[Old English *wadan* to proceed, go forward]

wade-in (wād′in′), *n. U.S.* the presence of Negroes at public beaches and swimming pools restricted to whites as a protest against racial segregation.

wad·er (wā′dər), *n.* **1.** a person who wades. **2.** a long-legged bird that wades about in shallow water searching for food: *Cranes, herons, storks, plovers, snipes, and sandpipers are waders.*

waders, high, waterproof boots, used for wading: *Short mackintosh coats to reach the waders will be required* (Walter M. Gallichan).

wa·di (wä′dē), *n., pl.* **-dis** or **-dies.** in Arabia, North Africa, etc.: **1.** a valley or ravine through which a stream flows during the rainy season. **2.** the stream or torrent running through such a ravine. **3.** an oasis: *Later I hid in a nearby wadi, collected food and water and, when night fell, I found myself outside Tobruk on the way to Egypt* (Herbert Hendrick). Also, **wady.** [< Arabic *wādī*]

wad·ing (wā′ding), *adj.* that wades: *a wading bird.*

wading pool, a small, shallow pool for children to wade in.

wad·mal, wad·maal, wad·mol, or **wad·moll** (wod′məl), *n.* a coarse woolen fabric formerly worn by country people in Northern Europe. [< Scandinavian (compare Old Icelandic *vathmāl,* probably ultimately < *vāth* cloth) Related to WEED[2].]

wad·na (wäd′nə), *v. Scottish.* would not. [< *wad*[3] + *na*]

wads (wodz), *n.pl.* See under **wad**[1], *n.*

wad·set (wod′set′), *n., v.,* **-set·ted, -set·ting.** *Scottish Law.* —*n.* **1.** a mortgage. **2.** a pledge.

—*v.t.* **1.** to mortgage. **2.** to place in pawn; pledge.

[variant of Middle English *wedsetten* to set in pledge < *wed* pledge, wad[4] + *setten* to set. Compare Old English *wedd sellan* to deposit a security.]

wad·set·ter (wod′set′ər), *n. Scottish.* a person who holds a wadset; mortgagee.

wa·dy (wä′dē), *n., pl.* **-dies.** wadi.

wae (wā), *n. Obsolete.* woe.

w.a.e., when actually employed.

wae·suck (wā′suk), *interj. Scottish.* woe is me! alas! (expressing grief or pity). [< *wae* + variant of *sake*[1]]

wae·sucks (wā′suks), *interj.* waesuck.

waf (waf, wäf), *adj., n. Scottish.* waff[2].

WAF or **Waf** (waf), *n.* a member of the WAF.

WAF (no periods), *U.S.* Women's Air Force.

Wafd (woft), *n.,* or **Wafd Party,** the (Egyptian) Nationalist party. [< Arabic *wafd* delegation, deputation]

Wafd·ist (wof′tist), *n.* a member of the Wafd. —*adj.* of or having to do with the Wafd or Wafdists: *By 1951 Wafdist foreign policy had simplified itself into an almost unqualified denial of all the arguments on which British policy in the Middle East was based* (Annual Register of World Events).

wa·fer (wā′fər), *n.* **1.** a very thin cake or biscuit, sometimes flavored or sweetened. **2.** the thin, round piece of unleavened bread used in celebrating Holy Communion or the Eucharist: *a consecrated wafer bearing the outline of a cross on its upper surface.* **3.** a thin piece of candy, chocolate, medicine, etc. **4.** a piece of wax, gelatin, sticky paper, dried paste, etc., used as a seal or fastening. **5.** a disk of thin paper, adhesive at the edges, or of some soluble substance, such as was formerly often used alone or as one of a pair to enclose a dose of a powder or other medicine for swallowing.

—*v.t.* to seal or attach with a wafer or wafers: *to wafer a letter, to wafer a note to a window.*

[< Anglo-French *wafre* < Germanic (compare earlier Flemish *wāfer*). Compare GOF-

 PRONUNCIATION KEY: hat, āge, cãre, fär; let, ēqual, tėrm; it, īce; hot, ōpen, ôrder; oil, out; cup, pu̇t, rüle;

FER, WAFFLE[1].] —**wa′fer·like′**, *adj.* —**Syn.** *n.* **2.** Host.

wa·fer-thin (wā′fər thin′), *adj.* very thin; wafery: *The Democrats hold a majority in the lower house, the Republicans a wafer-thin majority in the State Senate* (Wall Street Journal).

wa·fer·y (wā′fər ē), *adj.* like a wafer; very thin.

waff[1] (waf, wäf), *Scottish.* —*n.* **1.** a waving movement; wave. **2. a.** a puff (of wind); gust. **b.** a whiff (of perfume). **3.** a slight attack (of illness); touch. **4.** a passing view; glimpse. **5.** an apparition; wraith.
put out or **set forth a waff,** to wave something as a signal: *When you are about half a mile from shore, as it were passing by the house, . . . set forth a waff* (Earl Cromarty).
—*v.t.* **1. a.** (of the wind) to cause (something) to move to and fro. **b.** (of a bird) to move (the wings) in flight. **2.** to direct a current of air against; fan. —*v.i.* **1.** to wave to and fro; flutter in the wind. **2.** to produce a current of air by waving something to and fro.
[variant of *wave* to move, as with a fanning gesture, or with the wind]

waff[2] (waf, wäf), *Scottish.* —*adj.* **1.** of no account; worthless (used of a person or condition of life). **2. a.** (of an animal) wandering; stray. **b.** (of a person) solitary.
—*n.* a waffie. Also, **waf.** [variant of *waif*]

Waf·fen S.S. (vä′fən), *German.* an elite corps of troops in the Wehrmacht. [< German *Waffen S(chutz)-S(taffel)* (literally) weapons defense-staff]

waff·ie (waf′ē, wäf′ē), *n. Scottish.* a wandering, homeless person; vagabond. [< *waff*[2] + *-ie*]

waf·fle[1] (wof′əl), *n.* a batter cake cooked until brown and crisp between the two halves of a waffle iron, usually eaten while hot with butter, syrup, etc.: *to have waffles for breakfast.* —*adj.* wafflelike: *That university's new art museum . . . with its diagonal staircase . . . and waffle ceilings was hailed as a breakthrough in highly articulated construction* (Time). [American English < Dutch *wafel,* Middle Dutch *wāfel.* Compare WAFER.]

waf·fle[2] (wof′əl), *v.,* **-fled, -fling,** *n. British Slang.* —*v.i.* to talk incessantly or foolishly; prattle; engage in doubletalk: *It might be thought that a council of naturalists would be proof against any tendency to waffle* (Punch).
—*n.* foolish talk; nonsense; double-talk.
[< dialectal *waff* to yelp, bark + *-le*]

waffle iron, a utensil in which waffles are cooked, consisting of two hinged griddles having projections on the inside which form the alternating ridges and indentations characteristic of a waffle.

waf·fle·like (wof′əl līk′), *adj.* ridged or indented like a waffle or waffle iron; honeycombed: *Its wafflelike tread is designed to grip slick surfaces tenaciously* (Science News Letter).

waffle weave, a texture and appearance woven into a fabric, resembling small squares like those in a waffle. —**waf′fle-weave′,** *adj.*

waf·fly (wof′lē), *adj. British Slang.* foolish; nonsensical: *Too many people . . . accused Mr. Grimond of going in for "vague and waffly talk"* (Manchester Guardian). [< *waffle*[2] + *-y*[1]]

WAFS (no periods), Women's Auxiliary Ferrying Squadron.

waft[1] (waft, wäft), *v.t.* **1.** to carry over water or through air: *The waves wafted the boat to shore.* **2.** to transport or transfer very quickly or as if by magic: *to be wafted by plane from New York to London, to be wafted by sleep into the land of dreams.* —*v.i.* **1.** to float. **2.** (of a breeze) to blow gently; stir.
—*n.* **1.** the act of wafting. **2.** anything wafted, as a murmur, scent, etc. **3.** a breath or puff of air, wind, etc. **4.** a waving movement; wave: *And the lonely sea bird crosses With one waft of the wing* (Tennyson).
[apparently back formation < obsolete *wafter* a convoy ship < Dutch, Low German *wachter* a guard; (literally) watcher]

waft[2] (waft, wäft), *n. Nautical.* **1.** a flag hoisted or intended to be hoisted as a signal; signal flag. **2.** the act of signaling by such a flag or flags.
—*v.t. Obsolete.* **1.** to signal by a wave of the hand; direct, call, etc., by waving. **2.** to avert (one's eyes).
[probably alteration of *waff*[1]]

waft[3] (waft, wäft), *n. Scottish.* weft.

waft·age (waf′tij, wäf′-), *n.* **1.** the act of wafting. **2.** a means of wafting.

waft·er (waf′tər, wäf′-), *n.* **1.** a person or thing that wafts. **2.** a revolving fan or disk in a type of blower. [< *waft*[1] + *-er*[1]]

waf·ture (waf′chər, wäf′-), *n.* **1.** a waving. **2. a.** the act of wafting. **b.** a thing wafted. [< *waft*[1] and *waft*[2] + *-ure*]

wag[1] (wag), *v.,* **wagged, wag·ging,** *n.* —*v.i.* **1.** to move to and fro, up and down, or from side to side: *a slowly wagging tail, an indignantly wagging finger.* **2.** to be busy in or inclined to chatter, gossip, etc.: *a woman with a wagging tongue.* **3.** to sway as one moves or walks; waddle or totter. **4.** *Especially British Informal.* to go away; depart.
—*v.t.* to cause to wag: *The dog wagged its tail. Her high-borne turban'd head she wags and rolls her darkling eye* (Walt Whitman).
—*n.* a wagging motion: *a wag of the tail, head, etc.*
[Middle English *waggen* < root of Old English *wagian* move backwards and forwards]

wag[2] (wag), *n., v.,* **wagged, wag·ging.** —*n.* a person habitually given to joking, clowning, etc.; jocular fellow; wit; joker. —*v.i. Especially British Slang.* to play truant: *to wag from school.*
[probably reduction of obsolete *waghalter* rogue, gallows bird < *wag*[1] + *halter*[1]] —**Syn.** *n.* jester.

wage (wāj), *n., v.,* **waged, wag·ing.** —*n.* **1. a.** an amount paid for work: . . . *to get a day's wage for a day's work* (W.G. Clark). **b.** something given in return; recompense; reward: *The gods give thee fair wage and dues of death* (Algernon Charles Swinburne). **2.** *Obsolete.* a pledge; gage; bet.
wages, a. an amount paid for work: *Thus we have private individuals whose wages are equal to the wages of seven or eight thousand other individuals* (Thomas Carlyle). **b.** reward; recompense: *All Friends shall taste the wages of their virtue* (Shakespeare).
[< Old North French *wage,* Old French *gage* < Germanic (compare Gothic *ga-wadjon, wadi* pledge). Compare WAD[4], WED. Doublet of GAGE[1].]
—*v.t.* **1.** to carry on: *Doctors wage war against disease.* **2.** *British Dialect.* to hire. **3.** *Obsolete.* to pledge; gage; bet. —*v.i. Obsolete.* to struggle; fight.
[< Old North French *wager* < *wage;* see the noun]
—**Syn.** *n.* **1. a.** salary, pay, remuneration, stipend, compensation. **b.** return. *-v.t.* **1.** prosecute.
➔ See **salary** for usage note.

wage earner, 1. a person who works for wages. **2.** a person who receives remuneration for work of any kind; one who is employed: *a family in which both husband and wife are wage earners.*

wage freeze, a fixing of wages and salaries, as by government decree: *In that situation, a wage freeze, whether voluntary or imposed by the Government, deals with a symptom of inflation rather than with inflation itself* (Wall Street Journal).

wage hike, an increase in wages; raise: *It was touched off by the government's offer of a 15 per cent wage hike in response to demands for more pay* (Wall Street Journal).

wage·less (wāj′lis), *adj.* that does not earn or receive wages: *the wageless efforts of the missionary.* —**wage′less·ness,** *n.*

Wa·ge·ni·a (wä gē′nē ə), *n.pl.* a tribe of fishermen in the Congo, who catch fish by lowering large wooden baskets or nets into the river.

wage packet, *British.* a pay envelope: *As yet it had not affected him where it hurts most —in his wage packet* (Manchester Guardian).

wage pattern, a specific wage scale regarded as a model or guide in determining the general wage scale of an industry, region, etc.: *The contracts under discussion set the warehouse wage pattern throughout Northern California* (Wall Street Journal).

wage-price (wāj′prīs′), *adj.* of or having to do with the relation of wages to prices: *So the wage-price spiral works not only vertically from wages to prices but horizontally from wages to other wages* (Atlantic).

wa·ger (wā′jər), *n.* **1.** something staked on an uncertain event: *to double one's wager, to lose a wager.* **2.** the act or fact of betting; bet: *to make a wager with a friend, the wager of $10 on a horse, etc.* **3.** a subject of betting. **4.** a solemn undertaking; pledge. **5.** *Obsolete.* a promising, especially to act, accept an outcome, etc.
—*v.t., v.i.* **1.** to bet; gamble: *to wager more than one can afford to lose, to wager on a horse, etc.* **2.** to offer to prove one's sureness, trust, etc., by or as if by wagering: *I'd wager my life on him. I'll wager that you never hear from him again.*
[< Anglo-French *wageure* < Old North French *wager* to wage < *wage;* see WAGE, noun] —**wa′ger·er,** *n.*

wage rate, the rate of pay assigned to a worker for a certain job or time spent in working; wage scale: *A number of wage agreements made in the last few months indicate that average wage rates are likely to rise by about 6 per cent* (Manchester Guardian).

wager of battle, (in feudal law) a challenge by a defendant to decide his guilt or innocence by single combat.

wag·es (wā′jiz), *n.pl.* See under **wage,** *n.*

wage scale, 1. the schedule of the various rates of pay for similar or related jobs, as in a particular industry. **2.** the range of the wages paid by an employer.

wage slave, a worker whose labor and dependence on wages is regarded as a form of slavery: *These newfangled Labour people tried to persuade them that they were downtrodden wage slaves being exploited by cynical capitalists* (Punch).

wage slavery, the condition or fact of being a wage slave: *Brash young newsmen . . . dream of breaking the ball and chain of wage slavery, starting their own magazine* (Manchester Guardian).

wages of management, the amount paid for directing the work of others, especially when considered as an item of cost to a business or industry and when distinguished both from ordinary wages and from the money earned by capital.

wage·work·er (wāj′wėr′kər), *n.* a person who works for wages, especially as distinguished from a professional, clerical, or other salaried worker.

wage·work·ing (wāj′wėr′king), *n.* work done for wages.
—*adj.* doing work for wages.

wag·ger·y (wag′ər ē), *n., pl.* **-ger·ies. 1.** the act or habit of joking, playing pranks, clowning, etc.; drollery; jocularity. **2.** a joke: *they indulged in a hundred sports, jocularities, waggeries* (Thackeray). [< *wag*[2] + *-ery*]

wag·gish (wag′ish), *adj.* **1.** fond of making jokes. **2. a.** of or characteristic of a wag: *a waggish look.* **b.** done or made in a spirit of waggery or mischievous fun; prankish. —**wag′gish·ly,** *adv.* —**wag′gish·ness,** *n.*
—**Syn. 1.** jocular.

wag·gle (wag′əl), *v.,* **-gled, -gling,** *n.* —*v.t., v.i.* to move quickly and repeatedly from side to side; wag. —*n.* a waggling motion. [< *wag*[1] + *-le.* Compare WIGGLE.]

wag·gling·ly (wag′ling lē), *adv.* with a waggle.

wag·gly (wag′lē), *adj.* waggling; unsteady.

wag·gon (wag′ən), *n. Especially British.* wagon.

Wag·gon·er (wag′ə nər), *n.* Wagoner.

wag·gon·ette (wag′ə net′), *n. Especially British.* wagonette.

wag·gon-head·ed (wag′ən hed′id), *adj. Especially British.* wagon-headed.

Wag·ner·esque (väg′nə resk′), *adj.* like the style of Richard Wagner.

Wag·ne·ri·an (väg nir′ē ən), *adj.* of or having to do with Richard Wagner, German musical composer, or his music, theories, or musical style.
—*n.* an admirer of Richard Wagner's style or theory of music.

Wag·ner·ism (väg′nə riz əm), *n.* **1.** Richard Wagner's theory and practice in the composition of music dramas, placing great stress upon the dramatic effect as well as the musical content, especially in the orchestra, thus departing from the earlier approach of the Italian opera, which consisted of arias, ensembles, etc., and stressed primarily the vocal parts. **2.** the influence of Wagner's music and theories.

Wag·ner·ist (väg′nər ist), *n.* **1.** an adherent of Richard Wagner's musical methods. **2.** an admirer of his works.

Wag·ner·ite (väg′nə rīt), *n.* a Wagnerian: *Though I am not by any means a starry-eyed Wagnerite, I found it rather interesting to expose myself again to this mammoth agglomeration of preposterous drama and inspired music* (New Yorker).

wag·on (wag′ən), *n.* **1.** a four-wheeled vehicle, the body of which is typically either a flat bed with removable boards at the sides or a boxlike enclosure with or without a top, intended to be drawn (usually) by a team of horses, mules, etc., used especially for heavy burdens, as of farm produce or timber, or (formerly) of military equipment or supplies. **2.** a somewhat similar vehicle but with canvas sides and top, used especially for the transport of persons and their possessions; covered wagon. **3.** *U.S.* any of various relatively light, four-wheeled vehicles used especially for carrying loads: *a milk wagon.* **4.** any of various other four-wheeled vehicles, such as a baby carriage or a child's cart. **5.** *British.* a railroad freight car: *a goods wagon, a coal wagon.* **6.** *U.S. Slang.* a battleship; battle wagon. **7. a.** *U.S. Slang.* an automobile: *to get some extra life out of the old wagon* (Wall Street Journal). **b.** *Informal.* a station wagon. **8.** *Obsolete.* a chariot.

Milk Wagon (def. 1) (late 1800's)

hitch one's wagon to a star, to have high hopes and ambitions; aim high: *He hitched his wagon to a star and worked hard to achieve success.*

off the wagon, *Informal.* back to drinking alcoholic liquor: *After the birth of his daughter, he had a night on the town and off the wagon to celebrate* (Canadian Saturday Night).

on the wagon, *Informal.* not drinking any alcoholic liquor; in or into a state of temperance: *"Roberta felt bad about her drinking. She wanted to stay on the wagon—we call it 'going on the wagon' when somebody stops drinking," Mrs. Moon said seriously* (New Yorker).

the wagon, *U.S. Informal.* a police patrol wagon; paddy wagon: *They waited for the wagon to haul the lawbreakers off to jail.*

—*v.t. U.S.* to carry in wagons; transport by wagon. Also, *especially British,* **waggon.**

[< Dutch *wagen.* Related to WAIN.]

Wag·on (wag′ən), *n.* the Big Dipper; Charles's Wain. [< *wagon*]

wag·on·age (wag′ə nij), *n.* **1.** conveyance or transport by wagon. **2.** the money paid for this. **3.** a group of wagons traveling together; wagon train.

wagon boss, a person in charge of a wagon train: *Alderman Griffin will need the qualities of a wagon boss in Apache country* (London Times).

wagon box, the part of a wagon that holds the passengers or freight.

wag·on·er (wag′ə nər), *n.* **1.** a person who drives a wagon, especially for a livelihood. **2.** *Obsolete.* (especially in mythology) the driver of a chariot.

Wag·on·er (wag′ə nər), *n.* **1.** the constellation Auriga. **2.** the Big Dipper; Charles's Wain. [< *wagoner*]

wag·on·ette (wag′ə net′), *n.* a four-wheeled carriage, open or with a removable top, with a seat in front running crosswise and two lengthwise seats facing each other.

wag·on-head·ed (wag′ən hed′id), *adj. Architecture.* having a cylindrical ceiling, roof, or vault.

wag·on·less (wag′ən lis), *adj.* without a wagon or wagons.

wa·gon-lit (vä gôN′lē′), *n.* (in Europe) a railroad sleeping car. [< French *wagon-lit* < *wagon* railway coach (< English *wagon*) + *lit* bed < Latin *lectus*]

wag·on·load (wag′ən lōd′), *n.* **1.** the amount a wagon carries: *There in the yard sat a wagonload of hay.* **2.** *British.* a carload: *This map shows some of the many towns to which British Railways Express Freight Services can give next-day delivery for wagonload traffic* (Economist).

wagon train, 1. a group of wagons traveling together, especially one carrying a company of settlers: *Wagon trains of hope-driven immigrants streamed onto the Prairie in search of their Canaan.* **2.** a convoy of wagons carrying military supplies; military supply train.

wag·some (wag′səm), *adj.* waggish.

wag·tail (wag′tāl′), *n.* **1.** any of a family of various small, mainly Old World birds that have a slender body with a long tail that it habitually moves up and down, as a species of Great Britain or either of the pipits of North America. **2.** *U.S.* **a.** one of the water thrushes. **b.** the ovenbird.

Pied Wagtail (def. 1) (7 in. long)

Wa·ha·bee (wä hä′bē), *n., pl.* **-bees.** Wahabi.

Wa·ha·bi (wä hä′bē), *n., pl.* **-bis.** a member of a very strict Moslem sect, now dominant in Saudi Arabia, which adheres rigidly to the Koran as a guide, rejects all other writings except those of Mohammed's companions, denounces the worship of, or prayers to, the saints, and bars elaborate ritual, dress, or decoration. [< Arabic *Wahhābī* < ʽAbdul-*Wahhāb,* 1691-1787, a Moslem reformer]

Wa·ha·bi·ism (wä hä′bē iz əm), *n.* the doctrines, principles, or practices of the Wahabis.

Wa·ha·bism (wä hä′biz əm), *n.* Wahabiism.

Wa·ha·bit (wä hä′bit), *n.* Wahabi.

Wa·ha·bite (wä hä′bīt), *n.* Wahabi.

Wah·ha·bi (wä hä′bē), *n., pl.* **-bis.** Wahabi.

wa·hi·ne (wä hē′nā), *n. Hawaiian.* a woman; female; wife: *a muumuu-clad wahine.*

wa·hoo[1] (wä′hü, wä hü′), *n., pl.* **-hoos.** a North American shrub or small tree of the staff-tree family, that has a purple fruit and scarlet seeds; burning bush. [American English < Siouan (Dakota) *wanhu* arrowwood]

wa·hoo[2] (wä′hü, wä hü′), *n., pl.* **-hoos.** any of several North American trees: **a.** a small species of elm. **b.** a species of linden. **c.** the cascara. [American English < Muskhogean *ûhawhu* the cork elm]

wa·hoo[3] (wä′hü, wä hü′), *n., pl.* **-hoos.** a marine game fish of warm waters related to the mackerel, with a long, narrow body and pointed snout. [American English; origin unknown]

wa·hoo[4] (wä′hü, wä hü′), *interj., n., pl.* **-hoos.** *U.S.* —*interj.* an exclamation or shout used to express unrestrained pleasure or to attract attention. —*n.* a call or shout of "wahoo."

wai·a·ta (wī′ə tə), *n., pl.* **-ta** or **-tas.** (in New Zealand) a native song: *In common with other waiata, "E Pa To Hau" uses as a formal principle the varied repetition of a basic melody* (Mervyn McLean). [< Maori *waiata* (literally) song]

waif (wāf), *n.* **1.** a person without home or friends, especially a homeless or neglected child. **2.** anything without an owner; stray thing, animal, etc. **3.** *Nautical.* waft. **4.** *Obsolete.* (in English law) goods stolen and abandoned by a thief in his flight.

—*adj. Scottish.* **1.** stray; wandering; homeless. **2.** current (applied to a report or saying).

[< Anglo-French *waif,* probably < Scandinavian (compare Old Icelandic *veif* something waving, flapping, *veifa* to wave). Related to WAIVE[1].] —**waif′like′,** *adj.*

—**Syn.** *n.* **1.** foundling. **2.** estray.

wail (wāl), *v.i.* **1.** to cry long and loud because of grief or pain. **2.** to lament; mourn. **3.** to make a mournful or shrill sound: *The wind wailed around the old house. The sirens were wailing for a total blackout* (Graham Greene). **4.** to cry out piteously (for): *a child wailing for its mother.* —*v.t.* **1.** to grieve for or because of; bewail. **2.** to utter (a wailing cry, bad news, etc.).

—*n.* **1. a.** a long cry of grief or pain. **b.** a sound like such a cry. **2.** any prolonged, bitter complaining; whine. **3.** the act of wailing: *Wail shook Earl Walter's house; His true wife shed no tear* (Elizabeth Barrett Browning).

[< Scandinavian (compare Old Icelandic *vǣla* < *vǣ* woe). Related to WOE.] —**wail′er,** *n.*

wail·ful (wāl′fəl), *adj.* **1. a.** expressive of grievous pain or sorrow. **b.** resembling a wail; plaintive. **c.** producing plaintive sounds: *the wailful wind.* **2.** full of lamentation; sorrowful. —**wail′ful·ly,** *adv.*

wail·ing·ly (wā′ling lē), *adv.* **1.** in a wailing manner. **2.** with a wail or wails.

wail·ing wall (wā′ling), a place where one seeks or finds solace in times of sorrow or unhappiness: *She retired to her dressing table, which has served as a wailing wall for all the years of our marriage* (John Cheever). [< the *Wailing Wall,* a relic of the western wall of the Temple, in Jerusalem, at which Jews gather to pray and especially to lament the destruction of the Temple by the Romans in A.D. 70]

wail·some (wāl′səm), *adj.* **1.** wailing; wailful. **2.** *Obsolete.* that is to be bewailed.

wain (wān), *n. Archaic or Poetic.* a wagon. [Old English *wægen.* Related to WAGON.]

Wain (wān), *n.* **the,** Charles's Wain (the Big Dipper).

wain·rope (wān′rōp′), *n. Archaic.* **1.** a rope used as a trace for drawing a wain (wagon). **2.** a rope used for securing a load on a wain (wagon).

wain·scot (wān′skət, -skot), *n., v.,* **-scot·ed, -scot·ing** or (*especially British*) **-scot·ted, -scot·ting.** —*n.* **1.** a lining of wood, usually in panels, on the walls of a room. **2.** the lower part of the wall of a room when it is decorated differently from the upper part; dado. **3. a.** straight-grained white oak of very good quality, such as was originally imported into England from Russia, Germany, and Holland, used especially for paneling rooms. **b.** a board or piece of this.

—*v.t.* to line (the walls of a room), especially with wood: *a room wainscoted in pine.*

[perhaps < Middle Dutch or Middle Flemish *waghenscote* < *waghen* wagon + *scote* partition]

wain·scot·ing (wān′skə ting, -skot ing), *n.* **1.** wainscot. **2.** material used for wainscots.

wain·scot·ting (wān′skə ting, -skot ing), *n. Especially British.* wainscoting.

wain·wright (wān′rīt′), *n.* a wagonmaker. [< *wain* + *wright*]

wair (wãr), *v.t. Scottish.* ware[3].

waist (wāst), *n.* **1.** the part of the human body between the ribs and the hips. **2.** waistline. **3.** the part of a garment that covers this: *to lengthen a coat in the waist.* **4. a.** a garment or part of a garment covering the body from the neck or shoulders to the waistline; shirtwaist; blouse; bodice. **b.** (formerly) a child's undergarment to which a petticoat or underpants were buttoned. **5.** a narrow place; constricted or narrowest part or section: *the waist of a violin, to cross the waist of a peninsula.* **6.** the part of a ship amidships, as that between the forecastle and the quarterdeck of a sailing vessel, or between the forward and stern superstructure of an oil tanker. **7.** the middle section of an airplane's fuselage, especially that of a bomber. **8.** the slender part of the abdomen of various insects, as wasps, ants, and some flies. [Middle English *wast,* perhaps unrecorded Old English *wæst.* Related to WAX[2] grow]

waist·band (wāst′band′), *n.* a band around the waist: *the waistband of a skirt.* —**Syn.** belt.

waist·cloth (wāst′klôth′, -kloth′), *n.* loincloth.

waist·coat (wāst′kōt′, wes′kət), *n.* **1.** *Especially British.* a man's vest. **2.** an elaborate garment, with or without sleeves, formerly worn by men, so as to show under the doublet.

waist·coat·ed (wāst′kō′tid, wes′kə-), *adj.* provided with a waistcoat.

waist·coat·ing (wāst′kō′ting, wes′kə-), *n.* material for making waistcoats.

waist-deep (wāst′dēp′), *adj., adv.* **1.** of a depth sufficient to reach or cover a person's waist: *They decided to strike out down the slope through the waist-deep snow* (Time). **2.** deeply immersed: *The French literary marketplace was waist-deep in a porridge of ideological dialectics and metaphysical jargon* (Atlantic).

-waisted, *combining form.* having a —— waist: *Long-waisted = having a long waist.*

waist·er (wās′tər), *n. Archaic.* a very unskilled or old and feeble sailor, such as could be employed on a sailing vessel only at simple and menial jobs amidships.

waist·ing (wās′ting), *n.* material for making waists or waistcoats.

waist·less (wāst′lis), *adj.* having no waist or waistline: *a waistless velvet tunic.*

waist·line (wāst′līn′), *n.* **1.** an imaginary line around the body at the smallest part of the waist: *an expanding waistline.* **2.** the place of smallest width in a woman's dress between the arms and the knees. **3.** the line where the waist and skirt of a dress join.

wait (wāt), *v.i.* **1. a.** to stay or be inactive until someone comes or something happens: *Let's wait in the shade. He waited patiently just outside the door.* **b.** to defer or suspend speech, action, etc.; hold up going on (for):

Please be quiet and wait for me to finish. Time and tide wait for no man. **2.** to look forward; be expecting or ready: *The children wait impatiently for vacation.* **3.** to be left undone; be put off: *That problem will have to wait until I solve this one.* **4.** to act as a servant; change plates, pass food, etc., at table. *—v.t.* **1.** to wait for; await: *to wait one's chance, opportunity, turn, or time. Go wait me in the gallery* (Beaumont and Fletcher). **2.** *U.S. Informal.* to delay or put off: *I'll be late; don't wait dinner for me.* **3.** *Obsolete.* to accompany or attend as an escort; escort. **4.** *Obsolete.* to be a consequence of; wait on or upon; follow.

wait on or **upon, a.** to be a servant to; fetch and carry for: *to wait on a sick child.* **b.** to give one's attention to and seek to fill the needs of (a customer): *Will you wait on me, please?* **c.** to serve as a waiter or waitress: *to wait on three tables at once.* **d.** to call on (a superior) to pay a respectful visit: *A deputation had waited upon Lords Salisbury, Redesdale, and Roxburghe* (Manchester Examiner). **e.** to go with; result from: *And live a coward in thine own esteem, Letting I dare not, wait upon I would ...* (Shakespeare). **f.** (of a hawk) to soar in circles over the head of the falconer, waiting for the game to be flushed: *Cressida is sooner or later going to have to wait on—be released for hunting* (New Yorker).

wait out, a. to wait until the end of: *He and his wife started to wait out the war in a modest flat in Montmartre* (New Yorker). **b.** *Baseball.* to refrain from swinging at the pitches of, in the hope of getting a base on balls: *to wait out a pitcher.*

wait up, *Informal.* to stay out of bed (until the arrival of): *Did you wait up long? I'll wait up for him until midnight.*

—n. **1.** the act or time of waiting: *a long wait between trains, a three-hour wait for dinner.* **2.** (in the theater) the time of an audience's waiting between acts, or of an actor's waiting between appearances on stage. **3.** *Obsolete.* member of any of certain bands of musicians maintained by certain towns and cities. **4.** *Obsolete.* a watchman or sentry; sentinel.

lie in wait, to stay hidden ready to attack: *Huge piles of bones and tusks mark their camps beside the Don and other rivers in southern Russia, where they lay in wait for game migrating from winter to summer pastures* (New Scientist).

waits, a group of singers and musicians who go about the streets singing and playing at Christmas time: *The sound of the waits ... breaks upon mid-watches of a winter night* (Washington Irving).

[< Old French *waitier,* (originally) to watch < Germanic (compare Frankish *wahtôn,* Old High German *wahtēn*). Related to WATCH.]

—**Syn.** *v.i.* **1. a.** tarry, linger, remain, abide.

➤ **wait, await.** *Await* is now the more usual in the transitive sense, and *wait* the more usual in the intransitive: *We are eagerly awaiting your arrival. We can wait here until he comes.*

wait-a-bit (wāt′ə bit′), *n.* any of various plants and shrubs that have thorns or hooked and clinging appendages, as the greenbrier or various South African plants. [translation of Afrikaans *wag-n'-bietjie* < Dutch *wacht-een-beetje*]

wait-and-see (wāt′ən sē′), *adj.* waiting until matters develop further or take a turn; watchful: *Congress, meanwhile, was adopting a wait-and-see attitude* (Newsweek).

wait·er (wā′tər), *n.* **1.** a person who waits. **2.** a man who waits on table in a hotel or restaurant. **3.** a tray for carrying dishes. **4.** *Obsolete.* a watchman. —**Syn. 2.** garçon. **3.** salver.

wait·ing (wā′ting), *adj.* **1.** that waits. **2.** used to wait in. *—n.* the time that one waits.

in waiting, a. in attendance on a king, queen, prince, princess, etc.: *Lady Pembroke is in waiting at Windsor* (R. Gale). **b.** (in the British Army and Navy) next due or listed for some duty, privileges, etc.: *to be in waiting for overseas tour of duty.* —**wait′ing·ly,** *adv.*

waiting game, the tactic or strategy of not attempting to secure an advantage immediately, with a view to more effective action at a later stage: *Mr. Smith has ... to justify a "waiting game" to his more impetuous followers* (London Times).

waiting list, a list of persons waiting for appointments, selection for any purpose, or the next chance of obtaining something: *Few holiday bookings for trains and coaches are being cancelled, and these are quickly filled from long waiting lists* (London Times).

waiting maid, a woman servant, especially one in personal attendance on a lady.

waiting man, a man servant or attendant.

waiting room, a room set apart for people to wait in, as in a railroad station or at a doctor's or dentist's office.

waiting woman, a woman servant or attendant.

wait-list (wāt′list′), *v.t.* to enter on a waiting list: *There are now three people wait-listed for every occupancy* (Time).

wait·ress (wā′tris), *n.* a woman who waits on table in a dining room or restaurant. *—v.i.* to be a waitress: *Waitressing in coffee bars can be interesting, but the work is hard* (Cape Times).

waive[1] (wāv), *v.t.,* **waived, waiv·ing. 1.** to give up (a privilege, right, claim, etc.); do without; relinquish: *He ... is glad to waive the distinctions of rank* (Washington Irving). **2.** to refrain from pressing (an objection, argument, etc.). **3.** *Law.* to decline to avail oneself of (an advantage); refuse to accept some provision in one's favor: *The lawyer waived the privilege of cross-examining the witness.* **4.** to refrain from applying (a rule or law). **5.** to put aside; defer: *I waive discussion of this today* (John Ruskin). [earlier, disclaim ownership; withdraw legal protection from < Anglo-French *weyver* to abandon < Scandinavian (compare Old Icelandic *veifa* to wave). Related to WAIF.] —**Syn. 1.** surrender, forgo, abandon.

waive[2] (wāv), *v.t., v.i.,* **waived, waiv·ing.** *Obsolete.* to wave.

waiv·er (wā′vər), *n. Law.* **1.** a giving up of a right or claim. **2.** a written statement of this: *For $100, the injured man signed a waiver of all claims against the railroad.* **3.** a condition in professional baseball and other sports in which the contract of a player to be released by a team is offered to the other clubs in the league at a fixed price. Only if the other teams decline the player may his contract be taken up by a team of another league. *Supposedly, a player, put up for waiver, carries a $10,000 price tag* (New York Times). [< Anglo-French *weyver,* noun use of infinitive; see WAIVE[1]] —**Syn. 1.** relinquishment, renunciation.

waiver of immunity, a giving up of a witness's legal right to immunity from self-incrimination in a criminal case. Public officials under investigation are requested to give such a waiver.

wai·wode (wā′wōd), *n.* voivode.

wa·ka (wä′kə), *n., pl.* **-ka** or **-kas.** a Japanese poem of 31 syllables; tanka. [< Japanese *waka*]

Wa·kam·ba (wä käm′bä), *n.* a member of a native tribe of Kenya, Africa.

wa·kan (wä kän′), *adj., n.* wakanda.

wa·kan·da (wä kän′dä), *adj.* possessing supernatural power; sacred. *—n.* a person or thing possessing supernatural power. [American English < Siouan (Dakota) *wakanda* to reckon as holy < *wakan* a spirit; something sacred]

Wa·kash·an (wä kash′ən), *adj.* of or having to do with an American Indian linguistic stock of the northwest United States and British Columbia, including Nootka. *—n.* this linguistic stock.

wake[1] (wāk), *v.,* **waked** or **woke, waked** or (*Archaic and Dialect*) **wok·en, wak·ing,** *n.* *—v.i.* **1.** to stop sleeping; become awake; awaken: *to wake up early in the morning, to wake at seven every morning.* **2. a.** to become alive or active: *Bears wake up in the spring after a winter of hibernation.* **b.** to be roused from mental inactivity; become alert (to). **c.** to be restored to life; come back from the dead, or from a condition like that of death. **3.** to be or remain awake; not be asleep. **4.** *Archaic.* to be or remain active; not be passive or dormant. **5.** *Especially British and Irish Dialect.* to keep a watch or vigil, especially over a corpse. **6.** *Obsolete.* to carouse or revel late into the night. *—v.t.* **1.** to cause to stop sleeping: *The noise of the traffic always wakes him. Wake him up early.* **2. a.** to make alive or active: *He needs some interest to wake him up.* **b.** to restore to life; resurrect from the grave: *to wake the dead.* **3.** to keep watch over (a dead body) until burial; hold a wake over. **4.** *Poetic.* to break (a silence); disturb.

—n. **1.** a watching. **2.** an all-night watch beside a corpse before its burial (now used chiefly among the Irish). **3.** chiefly in England and Scotland: **a.** an annual festival commemorating the completion and consecration of a church. **b.** (in Lancashire, Yorkshire, etc.) an industrial worker's annual holiday. **c.** *Obsolete.* any merrymaking; festival; fête. **4.** *Obsolete.* any ceremonial watch or solemn vigil. **5.** *Obsolete.* the state of being awake.

[Old English *wacian* to become awake, and *wacan* to awake, arise] —**wake′like′,** *adj.*

—**Syn.** *v.i., v.t.* **1.** awake, waken, rouse, arouse.

➤ In the eastern part of the United States, for which evidence is available, *woke* appears to be by far the more common form of the past tense in spoken use and to be spreading at the expense of *waked.*

wake[2] (wāk), *n.* **1.** the track left on the water's surface by a moving ship. **2.** the track left by any moving thing. **3.** the air currents left by an airplane, missile, or other body in flight: *In the wake, masses of air coil themselves up into vortices or eddies* (O. G. Sutton).

in the wake of, following; behind; after: *disease coming in the wake of disaster, a dog following in the wake of its master.*

[probably < Middle Dutch *wak,* perhaps < Scandinavian (compare Norwegian *vok* a hole or channel in the ice)]

wake day, *Obsolete.* the day of a religious vigil; festival.

wake·ful (wāk′fəl), *adj.* **1.** not able to sleep; restless. **2.** without sleep. **3.** watchful. **4.** *Obsolete.* that rouses from sleep; awakening. —**wake′ful·ly,** *adv.* —**wake′ful·ness,** *n.* —**Syn. 3.** alert, vigilant.

wake·less (wāk′lis), *adj.* without waking; unbroken; undisturbed.

wak·en (wā′kən), *v.i., v.t.* to wake. [Old English *wæcnan,* or *wæcnian*] —**wak′en·er,** *n.*

wak·en·ing (wā′kə ning), *n.* the act of a person or thing that wakens; awakening.

wak·er (wā′kər), *n.* a person who wakes.

wake·rife (wāk′rīf), *adj. Scottish.* wakeful; vigilant. [< *wake*[1] a waking, wakefulness + *rife*] —**wake′rife·ness,** *n.*

wake-rob·in (wāk′rob′ən), *n.* **1.** (in the United States) any of a group of plants with purple, pink, yellow, or white flowers and a disagreeable odor; trillium. **2.** in England: **a.** the cuckoopint. **b.** any of several other arums, or plants closely related to the arums, as the jack-in-the-pulpit. **c.** *Dialect.* a purple European orchid.

wake-up[1] (wāk′up′), *n. U.S. Dialect.* the flicker (bird). [apparently imitative]

wake-up[2] (wāk′up′), *n. Australian Slang.* a person who is alert and not easily fooled; a wide-awake person.

wak·ing·ly (wā′king lē), *adv.* in a waking manner.

wa·ki·za·shi (wä kē′zä shē′), *n., pl.* **-shi.** a short sword worn by Japanese samurai with the cutting edge uppermost: *The sword ... was a wakizashi ... worn by samurai until 1876, when the government forbade people to carry them* (Time). [< Japanese *wakizashi*]

Wal., 1. Walachian. **2.** Walloon.

Walach., Walachian.

Wa·la·chi·an (wo lā′kē ən), *adj.* of or having to do with Walachia, a region in southern Romania, its people, or their language. *—n.* **1.** a native or inhabitant of Walachia. **2.** the language of the Walachians, a dialect of Romanian. Also, **Vlach, Wallachian.**

Wal·den·ses (wol den′sēz), *n.pl.* a Christian sect that arose about 1170 in southern France and in the 1500's joined the Reformation movement. [< Medieval Latin *Waldenses,* plural < *Waldensis,* Latinized name of Peter *Waldo,* a merchant at Lyons, France in the 1100's, who founded the sect. Compare VAUDOIS.]

Wal·den·si·an (wol den′sē ən, -shən), *adj.* of or having to do with the Waldenses. *—n.* a member of the Waldenses.

wald·grave (wôld′grāv), *n.* **1.** (in medieval Germany) an officer having jurisdiction over a royal forest. **2.** any of various former hereditary German noblemen, especially in the area of the lower Rhine, whose title derived from one of these officers. [< German *Waldgraf* < *Wald* woods + *Graf* count; perhaps spelling influenced by *margrave*]

Wal·dorf salad (wôl′dôrf), a salad made of diced apples, celery, nuts (usually walnuts), and mayonnaise. [American English < the old *Waldorf*-Astoria Hotel, in New York City]

wale[1] (wāl), *n., v.,* **waled, wal·ing.** —*n.* **1. a.** a ridge in the weave of cloth, especially corduroy. **b.** the texture of a cloth. **2.** a ridge or streak raised on the skin by a stick or whip; welt; weal. **3.** a ridge woven horizontally into a basket to strengthen it.
wales, a continuous line of thick outside planking on the sides of a wooden ship, as buffers or for reinforcement: *Such a point-blank [shot] would have torn off a streak of our wales* (James Fenimore Cooper).
—*v.t.* **1.** to raise a welt or welts on (the skin). **2.** to weave with ridges. **3.** to brace, strengthen, or protect with wales.
[Old English *walu* mark of a lash, weal; raised line of earth or stone. Compare CHANNEL[2], GUNWALE.]
—**Syn.** *n.* **2.** wheal.

wale[2] (wāl), *n., v.,* **waled, wal·ing.** *Scottish.* —*n.* **1. a.** a choice. **b.** the scope for choice; plurality of things to choose from. **2.** what is chosen or selected as the best; the choicest individual, kind, specimen, etc. —*v.t.* to choose; pick out. [< Scandinavian (compare Old Icelandic *val*)]

Wal·er (wā′lər), *n.* a horse imported from Australia, especially into India and from New South Wales. During the 1800's, many of the horses used by the British military, as mounts for cavalry, infantry officers, etc., were Walers. [< New South *Wale*(s) + *-er*[2]]

Wal·hal·la (wol hal′ə), *n.* Valhalla.

wa·li (wä′lē), *n.* the governor of an Arab province. [< Arabic *wālī*]

walk (wôk), *v.i.* **1.** to go on foot. In walking, a person always has one foot on the ground: *to learn to walk at the age of two, walk slowly backwards, walk to church.* **2.** to roam: *The ghost will walk tonight.* **3.** to go slowly: *Please walk, do not run, to the nearest exit.* **4.** (of things) to move or shake in a manner suggestive of walking. **5.** to stroll for pleasure, exercise, etc.; take a walk or walks. **6.** to conduct oneself in a particular manner; behave; live: *to walk as a man among men. Walk humbly with thy God* (Micah 6:8). **7.** (in baseball) to go to first base after the pitcher has thrown four balls. **8.** (in basketball) to take two or more steps with the ball without bouncing or dribbling it, and thus forfeit possession of it. **9.** *Obsolete.* **a.** to be in motion; move. **b.** (of the tongue, etc.) to move briskly; wag.
—*v.t.* **1.** to go over, on, or through: *to walk the empty rooms of a house. The captain walked the deck.* **2.** to make, put, drive, etc., by walking: *to walk off a headache.* **3.** to cause to walk: *The rider walked his horse.* **4.** to accompany or escort in walking; conduct on foot: *to walk a guest to the door.* **5.** to help or force (a person) to walk: *Mr. Bucket has to take Jo by the arm . . . and walk him on before him* (Dickens). **6.** to traverse on foot in order to measure, examine, etc.; pace off or over: *to walk the back line of a piece of property.* **7.** to move (a heavy object) in a manner suggestive of walking: *He walked his big trunk along the corridor.* **8.** (of a pitcher, in baseball) to give (a batter) a base on balls. **9.** (in basketball) to retain (the ball) for two steps or more without dribbling it.
walk (all) over, to act without regard for; trample on; override: *Are you going to let that old . . . banker walk all over you?* (S.E. White).
walk around, to bypass; circumvent: *The production code has largely dissolved, partly because some producers have walked around it and partly because the movies . . . have had to find new themes* (Maclean's).
walk away from, a. to outdistance easily in a contest or race: *Beaten by a banjo! . . . If it had not been for the banjo I should have walked away from her* (Rhoda Broughton). **b.** to go through or emerge from without damage or injury: *to walk away from an accident.*
walk away with, to gain possession of (something) by means of art, charm, or talent; steal: *Cesare Siepi as Mephistopheles walked away with the show* (Leonard Marcus).
walk off with, a. to take; get; win: *to walk off easily with first prize.* **b.** to steal: *She walked off with an expensive wrist watch.*
walk out, a. to go on strike: *If denied what they consider a fair hearing, labour unionists resort to strikes. They lay down their tools and walk out* (Emory S. Bogardus). **b.** to leave a room or a meeting suddenly: *The dissenting delegate walked out in protest.* **c.** *Informal.* to go out with a person of the opposite sex; keep company; court: *To him, the business of walking out with a girl was miracle enough in itself* (New Yorker).
walk out on, *Informal.* to desert: *She walked out on him on account of his laziness.*
walk up, (in hunting) to start (game birds) by beating up the ground with pointers or setters: *The coveys were far too wild at the end of October to be walked up* (Geoffrey Household).
—*n.* **1. a.** the act of walking, especially walking for pleasure or exercise: *a walk in the country.* **b.** the pace of walking: *to slow down to a walk.* **2.** a distance to walk: *It is a long walk from here.* **3.** a manner of going on foot; gait: *We knew the man was a sailor from his rolling walk.* **4.** a place for walking: **a.** a path: *a long walk of aged elms* (Joseph Addison). *There are many pretty walks in the park.* **b.** a sidewalk. **c.** an ambulatory: *The great cloister . . . has a walk of intersecting arches round its four sides* (Hawthorne). **d.** a ropewalk. **5.** a way of living: *A doctor and a street cleaner are in different walks of life.* **6.** (in baseball) a permitting a batter to reach first base on balls. **7.** a race in which contestants must use a walking pace. **8. a.** a pen or other enclosed place; tract: *a poultry walk.* **b.** a pasture or meadow, fenced or unfenced: *a sheep walk.* **9.** *Especially British.* a plantation of coffee, banana, or other trees, growing in straight rows with wide spaces between them. **10.** *Especially British.* **a.** the round or circuit of a tradesman, official, postman, etc. **b.** the district traversed or served by such a person. **11.** *British.* a division of forest land under the charge of a forester, ranger, or keeper: *a forest divided into five walks.* **12.** *Obsolete.* a haunt; resort.
take a walk, to get out or depart; withdraw: *Backers . . . warn wavering Republican leaders that conservatives will take a walk if the Senator fails to win the GOP race* (Wall Street Journal).
win in a walk, *Informal.* to win without much effort: *If there had been an election, he would have won in a walk* (Time).
[Old English *wealcan* to toss]
—**Syn.** *v.i.* **1. Walk, stride, plod** mean to go on foot at a pace slower than a run. **Walk** is the general word: *He walked downstairs.* **Stride** means to walk with long steps, as in haste, annoyance, or self-importance, or with healthy energy: *He strode along briskly.* **Plod** means to walk heavily, slowly, and with effort: *The old horse plodded up the road.* -*n.* **1. a.** stroll, hike, tramp, promenade.

walk·a·bil·i·ty (wôk′ə bil′ə tē), *n.* the quality or condition of being walkable; ability to stand walking: *He [Mr. Abrams] also advocated the appointment of a Commissioner of Pedestrians to protect what he called the city's "walkability" and to urge more planning for pedestrians* (New York Times).

walk·a·ble (wôk′ə bəl), *adj.* **1.** that can be walked on: *A coastal steamer weighed anchor up through walkable ice floes* (New York Times). **2.** suitable for walking: *walkable clothes.* **3.** that may be walked: *Eleven miles is a very walkable distance* (Robert Southey).

walk·a·bout (wôk′ə bout′), *n.* (in Australia) a brief period of wandering in the bush.

walk·a·thon (wôk′ə thon), *n. U.S. and Canada.* a walking marathon: *Degenerate forms, like the bunion derbies of the twenties and the walkathons, spawned by the dance marathons of the thirties, have had their vogues* (New Yorker). [< *walk* + *-athon,* as in *marathon*]

walk·a·way (wôk′ə wā′), *n. Informal.* an easy victory. —**Syn.** walkover.

walk·down (wôk′doun′), *n. U.S. Informal.* the slow approach of the hero and villain from opposite sides of a street just before the showdown, as in western movies.

walk·er (wô′kər), *n.* **1.** a person who walks. **2.** a lightweight framework of legs and supporting bars for a crippled person to support himself while walking. **3.** a framework on casters with a seat to support babies learning to walk.
walkers, a. walking shorts. **b.** walking shoes.

walk·ie-look·ie (wô′kē lu̇k′ē), *n.* a creepie-peepie: *When it worked, the walkie-lookie (a new NBC hand camera which was promptly dubbed a creepie-peepie) did for the visual audience what the roving candid microphone had done for radio listeners* (Life).

walk·ie-talk·ie (wô′kē tô′kē), *n., pl.* **-talk·ies.** a small, portable receiving and transmitting radio set, deriving power from a battery and carried strapped on the back, originally used by the U.S. Army in World War II: *So violent were the winds that the men could not speak with each other, though with a walkie-talkie they were able to communicate with the base camp 9,000 feet below* (Scientific American). Also, **walky-talky.**

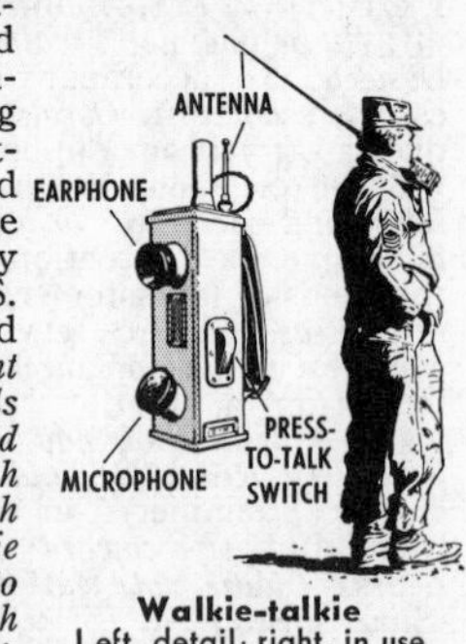

Walkie-talkie
Left, detail; right, in use

walk-in (wôk′in′), *n. Informal.* **1.** an easy or certain victory; sure thing; shoo-in: *Many Republicans say, privately, that next year's contest will be no walk-in for the Senator* (New York Times). **2.** a person who joins of his own accord; volunteer: *The Marine Corps reports a similar spurt in walk-ins* (Wall Street Journal). **3.** a walk-in apartment.
—*adj.* **1.** large enough to walk into: *a walk-in pantry, a bedroom with walk-in closets.* **2.** that can be entered directly from the street: *a walk-in studio apartment.* **3.** that can be walked into without a previous appointment or arrangement: *a walk-in clinic.*

walk·ing (wô′king), *adj.* **1.** used mainly for walking: *walking shoes.* **2.** that is pulled by a horse, mule, etc., or a team, and has no seat for the driver, who walks behind: *a walking plow.* **3.** that oscillates back and forth or up and down at its ends: *a walking beam.* **4.** that moves or is able to be moved with a motion resembling walking: *a walking crane.* **5.** in human form; living: *a walking dictionary, library, etc.*
—*n.* **1. a.** the act of walking. **b.** the manner or style in which a person walks. **2.** the condition of a path or road for walking on: *easy walking, icy walking.*

walking bass (bās), a short series of notes persistently played in the bass, each note of which is usually followed by the note an octave higher, as used in playing boogie-woogie.

walking beam, the beam (lever) of a steam engine.

walking delegate, a union official charged with traveling about on union business, as to represent the union in negotiations or to inspect working conditions.

walking fern, a fern whose fronds taper into a slender prolongation that frequently roots at the tip.

walking horse, Tennessee walking horse.

walking leaf, 1. any of certain insects that have a leaflike appearance when at rest. **2.** the walking fern.

walk·ing-on (wô′king on′, -ôn′), *adj. British.* of a walk-on: *a walking-on part.*

walking papers, *Informal.* a dismissal.

walking shorts, shorts worn for leisure, walking, etc., similar to Bermuda shorts.

walking staff, a staff or long stick which a person carries for support or aid in walking.

walking stick, 1. *Especially British.* a stick used in walking; cane. **2.** any of a group of mostly wingless insects related to the grasshoppers, having a body like a stick or twig; stick insect.

walk-on (wôk′on′, -ôn′), *n.* **1.** a part in a play, movie, etc., in which the performer merely comes on and goes off the stage with little or no speaking. **2.** a performer having such a part: *I started as a walk-on, and later played principal roles and became stage manager* (New Yorker). —*adj.* of a walk-on: *a walk-on part.*

walk·out (wôk′out′), *n.* **1.** a strike of workers: *Striking employees . . . will go back to* *work tomorrow, fifty-seven days after their walkout* (New York Times). **2.** a sudden departure, as from a room or meeting: *France staged the walkout September 30 to protest an Assembly decision to debate nationalist claims in French Algeria* (Wall Street Journal).

walk·o·ver (wôk′ō′vər), *n. Informal.* **1.** an easy victory; walkaway. **2.** a race in which the winner is predetermined either because only one horse starts and can thus walk the course to win or because all starters belong to one owner.

walk shorts, walking shorts.

walk-through (wôk′thrü′), *n.* **1.** in the theater: **a.** a rehearsal at which lines are read and accompanied by actions, such as walking, sitting, etc. **b.** an initial or perfunctory rehearsal. **c.** a walk-on part. **2.** (in television) a rehearsal without cameras, usually for the purpose of checking the cues.

walk-up (wôk′up′), *U.S.* —*n.* **1.** an apartment house or building having no elevator. **2.** a room or apartment in such a building: *a third-floor walk-up.* **3.** (in horse racing) a start in which the jockeys ride the horses as close as possible to the starting line before the signal to race.
—*adj.* of or in an apartment building having no elevator: *a walk-up apartment.*

walk·way (wôk′wā′), *n.* **1.** a structure for walking: *an overhead steel walkway.* **2.** a path; walk: *Built in mellow brickwork they are set well away from the road with private walkways and landscaped areas front and rear* (Sunday Times).

Wal·kyr (wol′kir, vol′-), *n.* a Valkyr.

Wal·kyr·ie (wol kir′ē, vol-), *n.* Valkyrie. [probably < *Valkyrie;* influenced by German *Walküre*]

walk·y-talk·y (wô′kē tô′kē), *n., pl.* **-talk·ies.** walkie-talkie.

wall (wôl), *n.* **1. a.** the side of a room or building between the floor, foundation, etc., and the ceiling, roof, etc.: *a brick outer wall, to paper a bedroom wall.* **b.** the side part of any hollow thing: *the wall of a chimney, the human chest, etc.* **c.** the inside surface of any hollow thing: *to repair the walls of a furnace, boiler, or kiln.* **2.** a structure of stone, brick, or other material, built up to enclose, divide, support, or protect: *a prison wall, a garden surrounded by a stone wall, the high wall of a dike.* **3.** a defensive rampart: *to dig in behind a wall of earth.* **4.** anything like a wall in appearance, use, etc.: *a wall of flame, a wall of ignorance.*

drive or **push to the wall,** to drive to the last extremity: *Being . . . driven to the wall, Addington complied* (L. Harcourt).

drive up the wall, to annoy extremely; exasperate: *[The] five-year-old had been acting up . . . and driving her father up the wall* (Maclean's).

go over the wall, *Slang.* to escape from prison: *He knew it was an unwritten law that an escape extinguished such a debt, and so he decided to go over the wall* (London Times).

go to the wall, a. to give way; be defeated: *Sam and Mayford are both desperately in love with her, and one must go to the wall* (Henry Kingsley). **b.** to give way or precedence (to something else): *Where political interests interfered family arrangements went to the wall* (Justin McCarthy). **c.** to fail in business: *In Berlin a newspaper would very soon go to the wall if it did not present its subscribers with light entertainment* (Nineteenth Century).

hang by the wall, to hang up neglected; remain unused: *All the enrolled penalties Which have, like unscour'd armour, hung by the wall* (Shakespeare).

the Wall, a wall of concrete and barbed wire, 26 miles long, built by East Germany in 1961 to divide East and West Berlin: *Thousands of grinning, gift-laden West Berliners swarmed through the Wall for their first reunions with eastern sector relatives since August 1961* (Time).

up against a (blank, stone, etc.) **wall,** facing an obstacle that cannot be overcome; at a dead end: *His campaign against irresponsible bait advertisements . . . had come up against a stone wall* (London Times).

walls, a series or system of defensive ramparts; encircling fortifications: *to raze the walls of a medieval city.*

—*v.t.* **1.** to enclose, divide, protect, or fill with a wall, or as if with a wall or walls: *to wall in a house, to wall a garden, to wall off a house from the road, to wall out the noise of the city.* **2.** to shut within or as if within walls: *an invalid walled up for years in the hospital.*
—*adj.* **1.** of or having to do with a wall or walls. **2.** planted along and growing up a wall or walls.
[Old English *weall* rampart < Latin *vallum*]
—**wall′er,** *n.* —**wall′-like′,** *adj.* —**Syn.** *n.* **2.** partition.

Wall., Wallace (U.S. Supreme Court Reports).

wal·la (wol′ə), *n.* wallah.

wal·la·ba (wol′ə bə), *n.* a tropical tree of South America, with a hard, heavy, deep-red, resinous wood. [< Arawakan *wallaba*]

wal·la·by (wol′ə bē), *n., pl.* **-bies** or (*collectively*) **-by.** any of various small kangaroos. Some wallabies are no larger than rabbits. [< native Australian *wolabā,* or *wallibah*]

Red Wallaby
(including tail, about 6 ft. long)

Wal·lace's Line (wol′ə siz, wôl′-), an imaginary line in the southwestern Pacific that divides the animal life of the Australian region from that of the Asiatic or Oriental region. [< Alfred Russel *Wallace,* 1823-1913, a British naturalist and explorer]

Wal·la·chi·an (wo lā′kē ən), *adj., n.* Walachian.

wal·lah (wol′ə), *n. British Informal, originally Anglo-Indian.* **1.** a person; chap; fellow. **2.** a person or (sometimes) animal who does or is associated with some (specified) work, thing, etc. *Examples:* kitchen wallah = one who works in the kitchen; jungle wallah = one who dwells in the jungle. Also, **walla.** [< Anglo-Indian *-wālā,* as in *Dilliwālā* person of Delhi < Hindi *-vālā* of or having to do with, perhaps < Sanskrit *bāla* boy]

wal·la·roo (wol′ə rü′), *n.* a large kangaroo that has thick gray fur. [< native Australian *wolarū*]

wall·board (wôl′bôrd′, -bōrd′), *n.* any of various building materials, as plasterboard or fiberboard, made artificially, especially by pressing into large, flat sheets, and used instead of wood or plaster to make or cover inside walls.

wall creeper, a small Old World bird related to the nuthatch, that has bright plumage and that frequents rocky walls and slopes of alpine regions hunting for insects.

walled (wôld), *adj.* having walls: *a walled city, high-walled.*

wal·let (wol′it, wôl′-), *n.* **1.** a small, flat leather case for carrying paper money, cards, etc., in one's pocket; folding pocketbook. **2.** a bag for carrying food and small articles for personal use when on a journey. **3.** *Obsolete.* something (in or on an animal's body) that hangs out and down; protuberant and pendulous growth. [Middle English *walet* pilgrim's scrip, knapsack; origin uncertain]

wal·let·ful (wol′it fu̇l, wôl′-), *n., pl.* **-fuls.** as much as a wallet contains; purseful.

wall·eye (wôl′ī′), *n.* **1.** an eye having a whitish iris, so that it has little or no color. **2. a.** a turning of one or both eyes away from the nose, a form of strabismus. **b.** an eye having such a condition, so as to show a large amount of white. **3.** a large, staring eye. **4. a.** an eye having a white opacity in the cornea (leucoma). **b.** leucoma (of the cornea). **5.** the condition of being walleyed. **6.** any of various fishes with large, staring eyes, especially the walleyed pike, the walleyed surf fish, the alewife or walleyed herring, or the walleyed pollack. [back formation < *walleyed*]

wall·eyed (wôl′īd′), *adj.* **1.** having eyes with a whitish iris or a white opacity in the cornea (leucoma), so as to show little or no color. **2.** having one or both eyes turned away from the nose, so as to show an excessive amount of white. **3.** *U.S.* having large, prominent eyes, as a fish. **4.** *Obsolete.* having glaring eyes (indicative of rage or jealousy). [< Scandinavian (compare Old Icelandic *vagl-eygr* < *vagl* speck in the eye + *eygr* having eyes of a certain kind < *auga* eye)]

walleyed herring, alewife.

walleyed pike or **perch,** an edible American fresh-water fish, a pike perch, with large, prominent eyes (in the southern United States also called *blowfish*).

walleyed pollack, a black North American pollack of the Pacific Coast with large, prominent eyes.

walleyed surf fish, a black marine fish of the California coast with large, prominent eyes.

wall fern, the common polypody.

wall·flow·er (wôl′flou′ər), *n.* **1.** *Informal.* a person, especially a girl or woman, who sits by the wall at a dance instead of dancing. **2. a.** any of a group of plants of the mustard family, especially a perennial plant much cultivated for its sweet-smelling (usually) yellow, orange, or red flowers, and also found growing wild on walls, cliffs, etc., especially in Europe. **b.** any of various plants of a related group. **3.** a desert shrub of the pea family of Australia.

Wallflower
(def. 2a—10 to 15 in. high)

wall fruit, fruit from trees or other plants trained to grow against a wall, as for protection or warmth.

wall·hang·ing (wôl′hang′ing), *n.* a tapestry used as a hanging on walls: *It is surprising that Italy, where magnificent silk wallhangings originated, should purchase a twentieth-century imitation from this country* (London Times).

wal·lie (wol′ē), *n. Scottish.* valet. [< obsolete *wall*(ett) valet + *-ie*]

wal·lies (wā′lēz), *n.pl.* See under **wally,** *n.*

wall·ing (wô′ling), *n.* **1.** the making of walls; a furnishing or fortifying with a wall. **2.** walls collectively; material for walls: *some of the best examples of drystone walling I have seen for a long time* (Manchester Guardian).

wall-less (wôl′lis), *adj.* having no wall.

Wal·lo·ni·an (wo lō′nē ən), *n.* the dialect of the Walloons; Walloon. —*adj.* Walloon.

Wal·loon (wo lün′), *n.* **1.** one of a group of people inhabiting chiefly the southern and southeastern parts of Belgium and adjacent regions in France. **2.** their language, the French dialect of Belgium. —*adj.* of or having to do with the Walloons or their language. [< French *Wallon* < Medieval Latin *Wallo, -onis* < Germanic (compare Old English *wealh* foreigner, Celt). Related to WELSH.]

wal·lop[1] (wol′əp), *v.t. Informal.* **1.** to beat soundly; thrash. **2.** to hit very hard; strike with a vigorous blow. **3.** to defeat thoroughly, as in a game. —*v.i.* **1.** *Informal and Dialect.* to move clumsily or noisily; flounder; plunge. **2.** *Especially Scottish.* to dangle, flap, or wobble. **3.** *Obsolete.* to gallop.
—*n.* **1.** *Informal.* a very hard blow. **2.** *Informal.* the power to hit very hard blows. **3.** *Informal and Dialect.* a heavy, clumsy, noisy movement of the body; a floundering; a lurching. **4.** *Obsolete.* a gallop.

go (down) wallop, *Informal and Dialect.* to fall noisily: *The horse tripped and the rider went down wallop.*
[< Old North French *waloper,* Old French *galoper* to gallop, related to *galop* a gallop. Doublet of GALLOP.] —**Syn.** *v.t.* **1.** flog.

wal·lop[2] (wol′əp), *v.i.* to boil violently and with a noisy bubbling. —*n. Obsolete.* the noisy bubbling of rapidly boiling water. [perhaps special use of *wallop*[1]*;* perhaps imitative of the noise. Compare POT-WALLOPER.]

wal·lop·er (wol′ə pər), *n. Dialect.* anything strikingly large or big; whopper.

wal·lop·ing (wol′ə ping), *Informal.* —*n.* **1.** a sound beating or thrashing. **2.** a thorough defeat. —*adj.* big; powerful; strong; whopping.

wall oven, an oven built into a wall, as in a kitchen, bakery, etc.: *Kitchen equipment includes a . . . built-in wall oven, dishwasher and a range* (New York Times).

wal·low (wol′ō), *v.i.* **1.** to roll about; flounder: *The pigs wallowed in the mud. The boat wallowed helplessly in the stormy sea.* **2.** to live contentedly in filth, wickedness, etc., like a beast; live or continue self-indulgently or luxuriously, as in some form of pleasure, manner of life, etc.: *to wallow*

in wealth, wallow in sentimentality. **3.** to billow up or surge out; gush (from): *dense black smoke wallowing from the chimneys.*
—*n.* **1. a.** the act of wallowing: *a wallow in the mud.* **b.** the state or condition of wallowing: *to sink into a hopeless wallow of despair.* **2. a.** a muddy or dusty place where an animal wallows: *a hog wallow, a buffalo wallow.* **b.** a depression or hollow in such a place, caused by wallowing.
[Old English *wealwian* roll] —**wal′low·er,** *n.*

wall-paint·ing (wôl′pān′ting), *n.* **1.** the painting of the surface of a wall, or similar surfaces, with ornamental designs and figures, as seen in fresco and tempera. **2.** a picture or design so painted.

wall·pa·per (wôl′pā′pər), *n.* paper, usually sold by the roll or in strips, commonly with printed decorative patterns in color, for pasting on and covering inside walls. —*v.t., v.i.* to put wallpaper on (a wall) or on the walls of (a room, house, etc.).

wall pellitory, a low, bushy European variety of pellitory that grows upon or at the foot of old walls.

wall pennywort, the navelwort.

wall plate, 1. a timber (plate) placed horizontally in or along a wall, under the ends of girders, joists, rafters, etc., to distribute pressure. **2.** a metal plate fastened to a wall, etc., as a support or place of attachment for machinery, a bracket, etc.

wall rock, *Mining.* the rock forming the walls of a vein.

wall rocket, a yellow-flowered European plant of the mustard family, naturalized in North America.

wall rue, a small fern, a variety of spleenwort, that grows on walls and cliffs.

walls (wôlz), *n.pl.* See under **wall,** *n.*

Walls·end (wôlz′end′), *n. British.* coal of a specified quality in lumps too large to pass the screen of 5/8-inch mesh. [< *Wallsend,* a town in Northumberland, England, where a certain grade of coal was mined]

wall-sid·ed (wôl′sī′did), *adj. Nautical.* (of a ship or vessel) having sides nearly perpendicular.

Wall Street, 1. a street in downtown New York City, the chief financial center of the United States. **2.** the money market or financiers of the United States.

Wall Street·er (strē′tər), a person who works on Wall Street or in the financial district around it: *Fraunces Tavern, at Broad and Pearl Streets ... a restaurant much favored by Wall Streeters with a sense of history* (New Yorker).

wall tent, a tent with perpendicular sides, usually rising two or three feet from the ground.

wall-to-wall (wôl′tə wôl′), *adj.* covering the entire floor between opposite walls in both directions: *wall-to-wall carpeting.*

wal·ly (wā′lē), *adj., n., pl.* **-lies.** *Scottish.* —*adj.* **1.** handsome; fine. **2.** large; ample. —*n.* a toy or trinket; gewgaw. Also, **waly. wallies,** finery: *bonny wallies.*
[perhaps < *wale*² a choice + *-y*¹]

wal·ly·drag (wā′lē drag, wol′ē-), *n. Scottish.* **1. a.** a weak or runty person or animal. **b.** the youngest (and often feeblest) of a family, brood, etc. **2.** a worthless, slovenly person, especially a woman.

wal·ly·drai·gle (wā′lē drā′gəl, wol′ē-), *n. Scottish.* wallydrag. [origin unknown]

wal·nut (wôl′nut, -nət), *n.* **1.** a large, round, edible nut with a plain division between its two halves and a ridged surface. **2.** any of the trees that it grows on, especially the English or Persian walnut and the black walnut, much grown in north temperate regions for their nuts, their valuable timber, and as shade trees. **3.** the wood of any of these trees. **4.** any of several trees, or their fruits, that resemble the walnut. **5.** *U.S. Dialect.* the shagbark (hickory) or its nut. **6.** the brown color of polished black walnut. [Old English *wealhhnutu* < *wealh* foreign; Welsh (< Celtic tribal name *Volcae*) + *hnutu* nut. Compare WELSH.]

English Walnut

walnut family, a group of dicotyledonous, resinous trees and shrubs, found in north temperate regions. The family includes the walnut, hickory, and pecan.

Wal·po·li·an (wôl′pō′lē ən, wol′-), *adj.* **1.** of or like the English author and letter writer Horace Walpole, 1717-1797, or his writings. **2.** of or like the English statesman and financier Sir Robert Walpole, 1676-1745, or his political views: *"Masterly Inactivity," that almost Walpolian phrase, is widely seen as an apt description of American foreign policy as many would wish it to be* (Sunday Times). —*n.* a follower or admirer of Horace Walpole or Sir Robert Walpole.

Wal·pur·gis·nacht (väl pu̇r′gis näHt′), *n. German.* Walpurgis night.

Wal·pur·gis night (väl pu̇r′gis), the night of April 30, the feast of Saint Walpurgis, when, according to German legend, witches were supposed to hold revels with the Devil on a peak of the Harz Mountains. [translation of German *Walpurgisnacht*]

wal·rus (wôl′rəs, wol′-), *n., pl.* **-rus·es** or (*collectively for 1*) **-rus,** *adj.* —*n.* **1.** either of two large sea mammals of Arctic regions, related to and resembling the seals, but having the two upper canine teeth forming tusks up to three feet long: *Walruses are valuable for their hides, ivory tusks, and blubber oil.* **2.** *Slang.* a very fat, clumsy person or animal.
—*adj.* **1.** of or having to do with a walrus or walruses: *walrus hide, a walrus hunter.* **2.** like a walrus: *a walrus face.*
[< Dutch *walrus,* or *walros* < *wal(visch)* whale + *ros* horse]

Pacific Walrus (def. 1) (about 10 ft. long)

walrus mustache, a man's mustache that is very long and curves downward at the ends, so as to resemble somewhat the tusks of the male walrus.

Wal·ter Mitty (wôl′tər), Mitty.

wal·ty (wôl′tē), *adj.* (of a ship) unsteady; crank. [< obsolete *walt* unsteady, Old English *-wealt,* as in *unwealt* steady + *-y*¹]

waltz (wôlts), *n.* **1.** a smooth, even, gliding ballroom dance in triple time, in which a complete turn is made to each measure (originally, rapidly and always in the same direction; now usually at a moderate pace and with changes of direction). **2.** the music for it, with the same triple time and rhythm. —*v.i., v.t.* **1.** to dance a waltz or as in a waltz. **2.** to move nimbly or quickly.
—*adj.* of, having to do with, or characteristic of the waltz as a dance, piece of music, or rhythm.
[< German *Walzer* < *walzen* to roll] —**waltz′er,** *n.* —**waltz′like′,** *adj.*

waltz-length (wôlts′length′), *adj.* midway to the calf in length: *Waltz-length gowns are meeting better acceptance than longer ones* (New York Times).

waltz·time (wôlts′tīm′), *n.* triple time; three-quarter time.

waltz·y (wôl′tsē), *adj.,* **waltz·i·er, waltz·i·est.** like a waltz; suggesting a waltz in quality, tempo, etc.: *The phrases are natural, even obviously waltzy at times* (London Times).

wal·y¹ (wā′lē, wô′-), *interj. Scottish.* an exclamation of sorrow. [probably < Old English *wā lā.* Compare WELLAWAY, WOE.]

wal·y² (wā′lē, wol′ē), *adj., n., pl.* **wal·ies.** *Scottish.* wally.

wam·ble (wom′əl, wam′-), *v.,* **-bled, -bling,** *n. Dialect.* —*v.i.* **1. a.** to feel nausea. **b.** (of the stomach or its contents) to be felt to roll about (in nausea). **2.** to turn and twist the body about; roll or wriggle (about, over, through). **3.** to move unsteadily; stagger; totter; reel.
—*n.* **1.** a feeling of nausea. **2. a.** an unsteady movement (of a person or thing). **b.** a rolling or staggering gait.
[Middle English *wamelen;* origin uncertain. Compare Danish *vamle* be nauseated, Norwegian *vamla* to stagger.]

wam·bling·ly (wom′ling lē, wam′-), *adv. Dialect.* **1.** with unsteadiness or twisting. **2.** with a nauseating effect.

wam·bly (wom′lē, wam′-), *adj. Dialect.* **1.** affected with nausea. **2.** causing nausea. **3.** shaky; tottering; unsteady.

wame (wām), *n. Scottish.* **1.** the belly; abdomen. **2.** the womb; uterus. [variant of *womb*]

wame·fou or **wame·fu′** (wām′fü), *n. Scottish.* a bellyful. [< *wame* + *-fou,* contraction of *-ful*]

wame·ful (wām′fu̇l, -fül), *n., pl.* **-fuls.** wamefou.

wam·mus (wom′əs), *n.* wamus.

Wam·pa·no·ag (wom′pə nō′ag), *n.* a member of an Indian tribe of southeastern Massachusetts at the time of the Pilgrims.

wam·pee (wom pē′), *n.* **1.** the fruit of an Asiatic tree of the rue family, resembling the grape in size and taste, and growing in clusters. **2.** the tree. [< Chinese *hwang-pī* < *hwang* yellow + *pī* skin]

wamp·ish (wom′pish, wam′-), *v.i., v.t. Scottish.* to wave or toss to and fro. [perhaps imitative]

wam·pum (wom′pəm, wôm′-), *n.* **1.** beads made from shells, formerly used by American Indians as money and ornament. **2.** *Slang.* money. [American English, short for *wampumpeag*]

wam·pum·peag (wom′pəm pēg, wôm′-), *n.* **1.** wampum made of white shells (less valuable than that made of black shells). **2.** any wampum. [American English < Algonkian (probably Narragansett) *waⁿpaⁿpiak* string of white shell beads]

wam·pus (wom′pəs), *n.* wamus.

wa·mus (wôm′əs, wom′-), *n. U.S.* **1.** a type of cardigan (sweater). **2.** an outer jacket of coarse, durable fabric. [American English < Dutch *wammeis,* earlier *wambuis* < Old North French *wambeis,* or *wambois* leather doublet]

wan¹ (won), *adj.,* **wan·ner, wan·nest,** *v.,* **wanned, wan·ning.** —*adj.* **1.** lacking natural or normal color; pale: *Her face looked wan after her long illness.* **2.** looking worn or tired; faint; weak: *The sick boy gave the doctor a wan smile.* **3.** partially obscured; dim: *a wan moon behind scudding clouds, the wan sunlight of winter, etc.* **4.** lacking light or luster; dark-hued; dusky; gloomy (now especially in conventional application in poetry to the sea, waves, etc.). **5.** *Obsolete.* sad; dismal.
—*v.i.* to grow wan: *His round cheek wans in the candlelight* (Walter de la Mare).
[Old English *wann* dark (in hue); lacking luster; leaden, pale gray] —**wan′ly,** *adv.* —**wan′ness,** *n.*
—**Syn.** *adj.* **1.** See **pale.**

wan² (won), *v. Archaic or Scottish.* won, a past tense of **win.**

wan·chanc·y (won chan′sē, -chän′-), *adj. Scottish.* **1.** unlucky; dangerous. **2.** eerie; uncanny. [< obsolete *wanchance* misfortune < Old English *wan-* lacking + *chance* fortune]

wand (wond), *n.* **1.** a slender stick or rod: *The magician waved his wand.* **2.** *British.* a rod or staff borne as a sign of office, especially a tall, slender rod of white wood, sometimes of ebony or silver, carried erect by an officer of the royal household, a court of justice, etc., on occasions of ceremony. **3.** *U.S.* (in archery) a slat, six feet long and two inches wide, set up as a mark for shooting, 100 yards away for men, 60 for women. **4.** *Scottish.* a slender, pliant stick cut from a stem or branch of a shrub or young tree. **5.** *Archaic.* a young shoot; slender stem of a shrub or tree; slender branch or twig. **6.** *Obsolete.* a scepter. [< Scandinavian (compare Old Icelandic *vöndr*). Probably related to WEND, WIND².] —**wand′like′,** *adj.*

wan·der (won′dər), *v.i.* **1.** to move here and there without any special purpose: *to wander around a city, through the fields, or in the woods.* **2.** to follow an erratic or irregular course; meander: *a driver who wanders all over the road.* **3.** to go from the right way; stray: *The dog wandered off and got lost. Don't let your attention wander.* **4.** to be delirious; be incoherent: *His mind wandered when he had a very high fever.* **5.** to fall into wickedness; be morally misled or corrupted.
—*v.t.* to go aimlessly on, over, in, or through; roam: *to wander the city streets.*
—*n.* a wandering; stroll.
[Old English *wandrian.* Related to WEND, WIND².] —**wan′der·er,** *n.*
—**Syn.** *v.i.* **1,3. Wander, stray** mean to go from place to place more or less aimlessly or without a settled course. **Wander** emphasizes moving about without a definite course or destination: *We wandered through the stores, hoping to get ideas for Christmas presents.* **Stray** emphasizes going beyond the usual or proper limits or away from the regular path or course, and often suggests getting lost: *Two of the children strayed from the picnic grounds.*

wan·der·ing (won′dər ing), *adj.* that moves from place to place; nomadic; roving: *wandering tribes, wandering herds of antelope.*

—*n.* the act of a person or thing that wanders: *Migration was at first characterized by aimless wandering, as in the case of primitive tribes moving up and down valleys in search of food for themselves and their flocks* (Emory S. Bogardus). —**wan'der·ing·ly,** *adv.*

wandering albatross, a large albatross, white with black wings, frequenting southern seas. It has the largest wingspread of any living bird.

Wandering Jew, (in medieval legend) a Jew who insulted Christ and was condemned to wander on earth till Christ's second coming.

wandering Jew, one of two trailing plants of the spiderwort family that grow and spread rapidly: **a.** a variety native to eastern South America with white flowers. **b.** a variety native to Mexico with white and purplish flowers. [< *Wandering Jew*]

wandering kidney, a floating kidney.

Wan·der·jahr (vän'dər yär'), *n., pl.* **-jahre** (-yä'rə). a year of travel, especially one taken before settling down to work. [< German *Wanderjahr* < *wandern* wander + *Jahr* year]

wan·der·lust (won'dər lust'), *n.* a strong desire to wander: *His wanderlust led him all over the world.* [< German *Wanderlust* < *wandern* wander + *Lust* desire, longing]

wan·der·oo (won'də rü'), *n.* **1.** the langur monkey. **2.** (incorrectly) an Indian macaque monkey. [< Singhalese *wanderu,* probably < Sanskrit *vānara,* or *vanara* monkey < *vana* forest]

wan·der·year (won'dər yir'), *n.* Wanderjahr. [translation of German *Wanderjahr*]

wan·dle (wän'dəl), *adj. Scottish.* **1.** (of a thing) flexible; supple. **2.** (of a person) lithe, agile, or nimble. [apparently < *wand* in a Scottish sense of "supple rod"]

wane (wān), *v.,* **waned, wan·ing,** *n.* —*v.i.* **1.** (of the visible part of the moon) to become smaller gradually after the full moon; diminish. **2.** to decline in power, influence, importance, etc.: *Many great empires have waned.* **3.** to decline in strength, intensity, etc.: *Their early enthusiasm was waning. The light of day wanes in the evening.* **4.** (of a period of time) to draw to its close: *Summer wanes as autumn approaches.*

—*n.* **1.** the act or fact of waning. **2.** the amount by which a plank or log falls short of a correctly squared shape.

in or **on the wane,** growing less; waning: *While overt anti-Catholicism had been on the wane for some years, there were, and still are, many people, including politicians, who benefit from religious divisions* (Manchester Guardian Weekly).

[Old English *wanian*]

—**Syn.** *v.i.* **2.** ebb. **3.** abate. *-n* **1.** decrease, lessening.

wane·y (wā'nē), *adj.* wany.

wan·gan (wong'gən), *n.* wanigan.

wan·gle[1] (wang'gəl), *v.,* **-gled, -gling.** *Informal.* —*v.t.* **1.** to manage to get by schemes, tricks, persuasion, etc.: *to wangle an interview with the president.* **2.** to change (an account, report, etc.) dishonestly for one's advantage. —*v.i.* **1.** to make one's way through difficulties. **2.** to obtain something by wangling; use irregular means to accomplish a purpose. [perhaps alteration of *waggle*] —**Syn.** *v.t.* **2.** falsify, fake, counterfeit.

wan·gle[2] (wang'gəl), *v.,* **-gled, -gling.** *British Dialect.* —*v.i.* to be unsteady; shake; totter; walk unsteadily. —*v.t.* to wiggle; jiggle. [perhaps alteration of *waggle;* influenced by *wankle*]

wan·gler[1] (wang'glər), *n.* a person who gets things by wangling.

wan·gler[2] (wang'glər), *n. British Dialect.* a person who wangles, or walks unsteadily.

wan·i·gan (won'ə gən), *n.* **1.** (in lumbering regions) a place or receptacle for small supplies, miscellaneous stores, etc. **2.** a kind of boat used by loggers for carrying supplies, tools, etc., and as a houseboat. [American English < Algonkian (Abnaki) *wanigan* trap, a receptacle for stray objects]

wan·ing (wā'ning), *adj.* **1.** (of the moon) becoming smaller gradually after the full moon. **2.** decreasing or declining in importance, power, influence, etc. **3.** declining in strength, intensity, etc.

—*n.* **1.** (of the moon) the periodic decrease in apparent size. **2.** a decrease or decline in importance, power, influence, etc.

wan·ion (won'yən), *n. Archaic.*

with a (wild) wanion, with a vengeance: *Come away, or I'll fetch thee with a wanion* (Shakespeare).

[alteration of Middle English *waniand,* present participle of *wanien,* Old English *wanian* wane, probably in phrase "in the waning moon," that is "in an unlucky hour"]

wan·kle (wang'kəl), *adj. British Dialect and Scottish.* **1.** unsteady; shaky; tottering. **2.** uncertain; precarious. [Middle English *wankel,* Old English *wancol*]

wan·nish (won'ish), *adj.* somewhat wan.

wan·rest·ful (won rest'fəl), *adj. Scottish.* restless. [Old English *wan-* lacking + *restful*]

want (wont, wônt), *v.t.* **1.** to feel that one needs or would like to have; wish for: *to want food, want to sleep, etc.* **2.** to be without; lack: *It sounds fine, but wants sense. The fund for a new church wants only a few hundred dollars of the sum needed.* **3.** to need; require: *Your hands want washing. Plants want water.* —*v.i.* **1.** to need food, clothing, and shelter; be very poor: *Waste not, want not.* **2.** to be lacking.

want for, to be in need of; suffer a shortage of; lack: *to want for nothing. He never wants for money.*

want in, *Slang.* to desire to enter or have a share in something: *That big advertiser liked the show, too, and wanted in* (New York Times).

want out, *Slang.* to desire to leave or take no part in something: *Despite his high standing with the boss, Gordon decided several months ago that he wanted out* (Time).

want to, *Informal.* ought to: *You want to eat a balanced diet.*

[< Scandinavian (compare Old Icelandic *vanta* < *vant*); see the noun]

—*n.* **1.** something desired or needed: *the selfish wants of a spoiled child. Food and water are primary wants of human life.* **2.** a lack: *a complete want of common sense. The plant died from want of water.* **3.** a need: *to supply a long-felt want.* **4.** a lack of food, clothing, or shelter; great poverty: *The old soldier is now in want.*

for want of, because of the lack or absence of: *We sold the store for want of customers. I have deferred doing so, for want of opportunity* (Dickens).

[< Scandinavian (compare Old Icelandic *vant,* neuter of *vanr,* adjective, lacking)]

—**Syn.** *v.t.* **1.** desire, crave. See **lack.** *-n.* **2.** dearth, deficiency, scarcity, insufficiency. **3.** requirement, necessity. **4.** destitution, privation, indigence, straits. See **poverty.**

—**Ant.** *n.* **2.** abundance, plenty.

➔ **a.** The use of **want** followed by a noun clause with or without *that* is nonstandard: *I want (that) John should come home.* So too is the use of **want for** followed by an infinitive phrase: *I want for John to come home.* **b.** The omission of the infinitive in locutions like *The cat wants out* or *I want off at the next corner* is common in the popular speech of many regions of the United States. This construction has often been ascribed to the influence of Pennsylvania German, but it appears to be largely of Scotch-Irish origin.

wan't (wont, wônt), *U.S. Dialect.* wasn't.
➔ See usage note under **wasn't.**

want ad, *Informal.* a small notice, usually on a special page or pages of a newspaper, stating that an employee, an apartment, etc., is wanted; classified ad.

want·age (won'tij, wôn'-), *n.* deficiency; shortage.

want·er (won'tər, wôn'-), *n.* **1.** a person who wants. **2.** *Scottish and British Dialect.* a person who wants a wife or a husband.

want·ing (won'ting, wôn'-), *adj.* **1.** lacking; missing: *A dollar of the price is still wanting. One volume of the set is wanting.* **2.** not coming up to a standard or need: *The vegetables were weighed and found wanting.* **3.** *British Dialect.* mentally defective; weak-minded.

—*prep.* without; less; minus; lacking: *a year wanting three days, a man wanting one leg.* —**Syn.** *adj.* **2.** deficient.

want·less (wont'lis, wônt'-), *adj.* having no want; abundant; fruitful.

want·less·ness (wont'lis nis, wônt'-), *n.* the state or condition of having no lack or want: *What are the economic consequences of this wantlessness?* (Bulletin of Atomic Scientists).

wan·ton (won'tən), *adj.* **1.** reckless; heartless: *That bad boy hurts animals from wanton cruelty.* **2.** without reason or excuse: *a wanton attack, wanton mischief.* **3. a.** not moral; not chaste: *a wanton woman.* **b.** lewd; lascivious: *And dancing round him, with wanton looks and bare arms* (Edward G. Bulwer-Lytton). **4.** *Poetic.* frolicsome; playful: *Who for thy table feeds the wanton fawn* (Alexander Pope). **5.** capricious and unrestrained in movement; undisciplined: *When wanton gales along the valleys play* (William Collins). **6.** profuse in growth; luxuriant; rank: *On the wanton rushes lay you down* (Shakespeare). **7.** unrestrained in expression: *a wanton mood. How does your tongue grow wanton in her praise* (Joseph Addison). **8.** *Obsolete.* luxurious; lavish.

—*n.* a wanton person, especially a woman.

—*v.i.* **1.** to act in a wanton manner: *The wind wantoned with the leaves.* **2.** to behave as a wanton. **3.** (of plants) to grow in profusion; run riot. —*v.t.* to waste foolishly; squander; dissipate: *With this money the King shall wanton away his time in pleasures* (Samuel Pepys).

[Middle English *wantowen* < Old English *wan-* not, lacking + *togen* brought up, past participle of *tēon* to bring] —**wan'ton·er,** *n.* —**wan'ton·ly,** *adv.* —**wan'ton·ness,** *n.*

—**Syn.** *adj.* **2.** unjustified. **3. a.** dissolute, licentious. **7.** extravagant.

want·wit (wont'wit', wônt'-), *n. Informal.* a person who lacks wit or sense; simpleton: *Only a wantwit . . . can fail to get some notion of [Samuel] Johnson's character in his definition of a dedication as "a servile address to a patron"* (Time).

wan·y (wā'nē), *adj.* **1.** having a natural curve or bevel: *a plank with a wany edge.* **2.** (of lumber) poor because of curved or beveled edges. Also, **waney.**

wap[1] (wop, wap), *v.,* **wapped, wap·ping,** *n. Dialect.* —*v.t.* to throw quickly or with violence (down, to the ground, etc.). —*v.i.* to knock (upon); strike (through).

—*n.* **1.** a blow, knock, or thump. **2.** *Scottish.* a sudden storm (of snow). **3.** *Scottish.* a fight; quarrel.

[apparently imitative. Compare WHOP.]

wap[2] (wop, wap), *v.,* **wapped, wap·ping,** *n. Obsolete.* —*v.t.* to wrap. —*n.* a turn of a string wrapped around something. [origin unknown]

wap·en·shaw or **wap·in·schaw** (wop'ən-shô, wap'-), *n. Scottish.* wappenschawing.

wap·en·take (wop'ən tāk, wap'-), *n.* (formerly, in certain northern and midland counties in England) a division of the county corresponding to the hundred of other counties. [Old English *wǣpentæc,* apparently (originally) the local assembly < Scandinavian (compare Old Icelandic *vāpnatak* (literally) taking of weapons)]

wap·i·ti (wop'ə tē), *n., pl.* **-tis** or (*collectively*) **-ti.** a large, reddish deer of western North America, with long, slender antlers; the American elk. [American English < Algonkian (Shawnee) *wapetee*]

wap·pen·schaw or **wap·pen·shaw** (wop'ən shô, wap'-), *n. Scottish.* wappenschawing.

wap·pen·schaw·ing or **wap·pen·shaw·ing** (wop'ən shô'ing, wap'-), *n.* (in Scottish history) a periodical muster or review of the men under arms in a particular district. [< Scottish *wapin* weapon + *schawing* showing]

wap·per-jawed (wop'ər jôd'), *adj. Informal.* having a crooked or undershot jaw. [American English, perhaps < obsolete *wapper* to waver]

war[1] (wôr), *n., v.,* **warred, war·ring,** *adj.* —*n.* **1. a.** a fight carried on by armed force between nations or parts of a nation: *to repudiate war as a means of settling international disputes, to prepare for war.* **b.** an instance or particular period of this: *a veteran of two wars, to remember the dead on both sides in the last war.* **2.** a fight; strife; conflict: *a trade war. Doctors carry on war against disease.* **3. a.** the occupation or art of fighting with weapons; military science: *Soldiers are trained for war.* **b.** the division of a government responsible for the armed forces, military planning, budgets, etc.: *to appoint a new secretary of war.* **4.** *Archaic.* a battle.

at war, engaged in war: *The United States was at war with Great Britain in 1812. Teetotalers and moderate drinkers will probably be at war on this point . . . as long as the world lasts* (Graphic).

go to war, a. to enter into a state of war; begin hostilities: *The aim of the nation in going to war is exactly the same as that of an individual in entering a court; it wants its rights, or what it alleges to be its rights*

(James Mozley). **b.** to go as a soldier, sailor, etc., in a war: *The minstrel boy to the war is gone* (Thomas Moore).
make war, to engage in war; fight a war: *Aristotle maintained the general right of making war upon barbarians* (William Paley).
—*v.i.* **1.** to make war; fight: *brother warring against brother, to war with an aggressor.* **2.** to carry on any struggle actively; contend; battle: *to war against all things mean or petty.*
—*adj.* **1.** of or having to do with war. **2.** used in war. **3.** caused by war.
[< Old North French *werre,* Old French *guerre* < Germanic (compare Old High German *werra*)]
—**Syn.** *n.* **1. a.** warfare, hostilities.

war[2] (wär), *adj., adv. Scottish.* worse. Also, **waur.** [< Scandinavian (compare Old Icelandic *verri,* adjective, and *verr,* adverb). Related to WORSE.]

war[3] (wär), *v.t., v.i. Dialect.* ware[2].

war[4] (wär), *n. Obsolete.* ware[1].

war baby, 1. a child born in wartime; child of a soldier: *about 1965, when the greatest number of so-called war babies, born in the nineteen-forties, will be of college age* (New Yorker). **2.** *Informal.* **a.** an industry that is stimulated by war or threat of war. **b.** a stock or security of such an industry: *The war babies—copper, chemical, oil, rubber and steel issues—attracted most investor interest* (New York Times).

war·ble[1] (wôr′bəl), *v.,* **-bled, -bling,** *n.* —*v.t.* **1.** to sing with melodious runs, trills, quavers, or turns. **2.** to express in or as if in song; sing. —*v.i.* **1.** to utter a song, musical notes, etc.: *Birds warbled in the trees.* **2.** *Poetic.* to make a sound like that of a bird warbling: *The brook warbled over its rocky bed.* **3.** *U.S.* to yodel.
—*n.* **1.** a warbling or being warbled. **2.** any sound like warbling, as a melody with quavers, etc.; trill.
[< Old North French *werbler* < *werble* a flourish, melody < Germanic (compare Old High German *wirbel* a whirl)]
—**Syn.** *v.i.* **2.** purl, ripple.

war·ble[2] (wôr′bəl), *n.* **1.** a small, hard tumor, caused by the pressure of the saddle on a horse's back. **2.** a small tumor or swelling on the back of cattle, deer, etc., produced by the larva of the warble fly. **3.** a warble fly, especially in its larval form. Also, **wabble.** [origin uncertain. Compare obsolete Swedish *varbulde* boil.]

war·bled (wôr′bəld), *adj.* affected with or injured by warbles.

warble fly, any of certain flies whose larvae burrow under the skin of cattle, deer, and other animals, forming warbles.

war·bler (wôr′blər), *n.* **1.** a person, bird, etc., that warbles; songster. **2.** any of a family of small, usually bright-colored songbirds, the wood warblers, including the redstart, water thrush, chat, yellow warbler, myrtle warbler, ovenbird, etc. **3.** any of various small, plain-colored songbirds of the Old World, as the blackcap and whitethroat.

Olive Warbler (def. 2) (5 in. long)

war·bling vireo (wôr′bling), a small, plain-colored vireo that lives in high woodlands of North America and has a melodious warble.

war bond, *U.S.* a government bond issued in World War II.

war bonnet, an American Indian headdress of skin set with feathers and often a long trailing piece with feathers: *Indians . . . with the long red streamers of their war bonnets reaching nearly to the ground* (John C. Frémont).

War Bonnet

war-born (wôr′bôrn′), *adj.* produced or developed during war; resulting from a war: *The war-born alliance grew to greatness out of sheer necessity and through the personal relationships of Roosevelt and Churchill* (Atlantic).

war bride, the bride of a soldier or sailor in wartime.

war-built (wôr′bilt′), *adj.* built during a war; developed for a war: *After the war, Canada's economy used its war-built industry to take off like a three-stage rocket* (Time).

war chest, a fund of money put aside to pay for the costs of some struggle, especially a political campaign: *In the current campaign businessmen are actively at work in a traditional role for them in politics—raising money for party war chests* (Wall Street Journal).

war cloud, 1. a cloud of dust and smoke rising from a battlefield. **2.** something that threatens war: *Markets fall into a well-known pattern when war clouds gather* (Economist).

war club, a heavy club used as a weapon.

war college, a school for teaching advanced military techniques to officers.

war correspondent, a person employed by a newspaper, magazine, or radio station to send news from overseas about a war, especially first-hand accounts of the fighting: *Stephen Crane was another great writer to gain fame as a war correspondent* (Gordon Sabine).

war·craft (wôr′kraft′, -kräft′), *n., pl.* **-craft. 1.** any ship or aircraft used in war: *Among other Red warcraft observed in the Baltic Sea this month were: one 42,000-ton Soviet battleship* (Newsweek). *Still other jet and propellered warcraft provided close air support* (New York Times). **2.** the science or art of war; cunning and skill in warfare.

war crime, a violation of the rules of warfare, especially any inhuman act against civilians, political prisoners, etc., in time of war.

war criminal, a person convicted of committing a war crime: *Berlin's ancient Spandau Fortress today serves as a prison for Germany's most notorious war criminals* (Newsweek).

war cry, 1. a word or phrase shouted in fighting; battle cry. **2.** a party cry in any contest.

ward (wôrd), *n.* **1. a.** a section or division, often a long room, of a hospital, accommodating several or many patients: *a children's ward, a charity ward.* **b.** a single large room or group of rooms, cells, etc., formerly comprising a section of a prison, especially in Great Britain. **2. a.** an administrative or electoral district of a city or town, especially one represented by an alderman. **b.** (in northern England and Scotland) an administrative division of certain counties; wapentake; hundred. **c.** the people in any of these. **3.** a small administrative district within the Mormon Church. It is part of a stake. **4. a.** a person, especially a child or lunatic, who is legally under the control and protection of a guardian or of a court. **b.** the status of such a person; legal guardianship. **c.** any guardianship; custody. **5.** guard: *The soldiers kept watch and ward over the castle.* **6. a.** (in fencing) any defensive movement or posture; parry. **b.** *Archaic.* any defensive movement, attitude, or position. **7. a.** any of the slots or notches in a key that fit (slide past) corresponding projections inside the lock. **b.** such a projection or ridge. **8.** in feudal law: **a.** a lord's guardianship of the infant heir of a deceased tenant, including the control and use of the heir's lands until he came of age. **b.** land given to the (Scottish) crown in payment for exemption from military service. **9.** any of certain fortified parts of a castle, especially: **a.** an open area within or between the walls. **b.** *Obsolete.* a guarded entrance. **c.** *Obsolete.* the part of a fortress entrusted to a particular officer and his men. **10.** *Obsolete.* **a.** a company, group, or detachment of watchmen. **b.** any watchman; sentinel; guard. **c.** a garrison. **11.** *Obsolete.* **a.** any of the three parts (van, middle, rear) of an army on the march. **b.** a separate part of an army led by a subordinate commander. [Old English *weard* a guarding, guard. Compare WARE[2].]
—*v.t.* **1.** to put into a ward, especially of a hospital. **2.** *Archaic.* to keep watch over.
—*v.i. Archaic.* to parry blows; stand on the defensive.

ward off, to keep away; turn aside: *The telephone is his lifeline; through it he tries to ward off insanity and to forestall his collapse* (New Yorker).
[Old English *weardian* to guard. Related to GUARD.]

-ward, *suffix.* tending or leading to ——; in the —— direction; toward, as in *backward, heavenward, homeward, onward, seaward.* See also **-wards.**
[Old English *-weard,* adjective and adverb suffix]
➔ When pairs like *downward-downwards, eastward-eastwards* exist, both are used as adverbs (or, in the case of *toward-towards,* as a preposition), but only the forms without *-s* occur as adjectives: *He fell forward(s); a forward movement.* The adjectival form is the one usually employed as a noun: *looking to the westward.*

war dance, a dance of primitive tribes before going to war or to celebrate a victory.

ward boss, *U.S.* the political leader of a ward: *Jauntily, Nikita Khrushchev moved among his hard-drinking guests, smiling and shaking hands like a ward boss* (Time).

ward·ed (wôr′did), *adj.* (of a key or lock) constructed with wards.

ward·en[1] (wôr′dən), *n.* **1.** the official in charge of a prison; head keeper. **2.** an official of a county, state, etc., whose duty is to enforce laws relating to hunting, fishing, etc.; game warden. **3.** an air-raid warden. **4.** a person in charge of a place or its contents; custodian; keeper. **5.** a churchwarden. **6.** in England: **a.** the superintendent of a port, market, etc. **b.** an officer holding any of certain positions of trust, now usually honorary or ceremonial, under the Crown: *Warden of the Cinque Ports.* **c.** any of the trustees of certain schools, hospitals, guilds, etc. **d.** (as a title) the head of certain colleges; principal; master. **7.** *Historical.* the chief official in a town or area. **8.** *Obsolete.* anyone who guards; protector; defender; guardian; custodian. **9. a.** (in Connecticut) the head of a borough. **b.** (in Canada) the head of a county council. **c.** (in Australia) a magistrate who is the chief government officer in a gold field. **10.** a gatekeeper. [< Old North French *wardein,* Anglo-French *guardein.* Doublet of GUARDIAN.] —**Syn. 4.** watchman.

ward·en[2] or **Ward·en** (wôr′dən), *n. Especially British.* a variety of winter cooking pear. [Middle English *wardon,* probably < unrecorded Anglo-French < *warder* to keep, Old French *garder.* Compare GUARD.]

ward·en·ry (wôr′dən rē), *n., pl.* **-ries.** the office or position of warden.

ward·en·ship (wôr′dən ship), *n.* the office of a warden.

ward·er[1] (wôr′dər), *n.* **1.** a guard; watchman. **2.** *Especially British.* a warden; jailor. [< Anglo-French *wardere,* and *wardour,* Old North French *warder,* Old French *guarder.* Compare GUARD.] —**Syn. 1.** sentinel.

ward·er[2] (wôr′dər), *n.* **1.** (in early use) a staff or wand. **2.** (later) the baton or truncheon carried as a symbol of office, command, or authority, especially as used to give the signal for the commencement or cessation of hostilities in a battle or tournament. [origin uncertain]

ward·er·ship (wôr′dər ship), *n.* **1.** the office or position of warder. **2.** the carrying out of the duties of a warder.

ward heeler, *U.S. and Canada.* a follower of a political boss, who distributes literature, asks for votes, etc.: *Back-benchers find it harder than ministers do to see the evil of patronage, and ward heelers find it hardest of all* (Maclean's).

War·di·an case (wôr′dē ən), a close-fitting case with glass sides and top for growing and transporting small ferns and other plants. [< Nathaniel B. *Ward,* 1791-1868, the English botanist who invented it + *-ian*]

ward·less (wôrd′lis), *adj.* that cannot be warded off or avoided.

ward·mote (wôrd′mōt), *n. British.* a meeting of the citizens of a ward, especially a meeting of the liverymen of a ward under the presidency of the alderman to discuss local affairs. [< *ward* + *mote,* as in *gemote*]

ward·ress (wôr′dris), *n.* a female warder in a prison.

ward·robe (wôrd′rōb′), *n.* **1. a.** a stock of clothes: *She is shopping for her spring wardrobe.* **b.** a stock of anything: *More and more it makes sense to analyze a family's needs and provide a wardrobe of cars to meet them* (Wall Street Journal). **2.** a room, closet, or piece of furniture for holding clothes. **3. a.** the

 PRONUNCIATION KEY: hat, āge, cãre, fär; let, ēqual, tėrm; it, īce; hot, ōpen, ôrder; oil, out; cup, pu̇t, rüle;

department of a royal or noble household charged with the care of the wearing apparel. **b.** the building in which the officers of this department conduct their business. [< Old North French *warderobe*, Old French *garderobe* < *guarder* to guard + *robe* gown, robe. Compare GUARD, ROBE.] —**Syn. 1. a.** apparel, clothing.

wardrobe case, a suitcase in which suits, dresses, etc., are carried on hangers to avoid wrinkling.

wardrobe mistress, a woman in charge of the professional wardrobe of an actress or of a theatrical company.

wardrobe trunk, a trunk designed to stand on end when opened, usually with hangers and drawers for clothes.

ward·room (wôrd′rüm′, -rům′), *n.* **1.** the living and eating quarters for all the commissioned officers on a warship except the commanding officer. **2.** these officers as a group.

-wards, *suffix.* in the direction of, as in *backwards, forwards, upwards.* [Old English *-weardes*, adverbial suffix]
➤ See **-ward** for usage note.

ward·ship (wôrd′ship), *n.* **1. a.** guardianship over a minor or ward; guardianship; custody. **b.** (in feudal law) the guardianship and custody of a minor with all profits accruing during his minority. **c.** any guardianship; custody. **2.** the state or condition of being a ward, or under a legal or feudal guardianship.

ward sister, *British.* a nurse in charge of a hospital ward.

ware[1] (wãr), *n.* **1.** a kind of manufactured thing or article for sale; goods (now chiefly in compounds): *silverware and tinware.* **2.** what anyone produces by his own effort and offers for sale: *the ware of a sculptor, short stories and other literary wares.* **3. a.** pottery or other ceramic objects: *porcelain ware. Delft is a blue-and-white ware.* **b.** such objects in a raw or unfinished state: *The ware must be thoroughly dry before firing.*
wares, manufactured things; articles for sale: *The peddler sold his wares cheap.*
[Old English *waru*]

ware[2] (wãr), *adj., v.,* **wared, war·ing.** *Archaic.* —*adj.* **1.** aware. **2.** watchful; vigilant. **3.** prudent; sagacious; cunning. [Old English *wær* alert, wise]
—*v.t., v.i.* to look out (for); beware (of).
[partly Old English *warian* give heed; partly Old North French *warer* to guard; protect. Related to WARN.]

ware[3] (wãr), *v.t.,* **wared, war·ing.** *Scottish.* **1.** to spend; lay out (money or goods in, on, upon). **2.** to squander or dissipate (time, energy, emotion, etc.); waste. [< Scandinavian (compare Old Icelandic *verja* lay out or invest money; originally, to clothe). Related to WEAR[1].]

ware·house (*n.* wãr′hous′; *v.* wãr′houz′, -hous′), *n., v.,* **-housed, -hous·ing.** —*n.* **1.** a place where goods are kept, especially in large quantities; storehouse. **2.** *Especially British.* **a.** a store where goods are sold wholesale. **b.** a large retail establishment.
—*v.t.* **1.** to put or deposit in a warehouse, as for storage. **2.** to place in a bonded warehouse, or in government or customhouse custody, to be kept until duties are paid.
—**Syn.** *n.* **1.** depot, depository, entrepôt.

ware·house·man (wãr′hous′mən), *n., pl.* **-men. 1.** a person who receives and stores the goods of others for pay, without assuming ownership, as the owner of a warehouse. **2.** a person who works in a warehouse.

ware·hous·er (wãr′hou′zər), *n.* a warehouseman.

warehouse receipt, a receipt given to the owner of goods stored in a warehouse, serving as an assignable instrument, often negotiable, for transferring title of the goods to another (the assignee).

ware·hous·ing (wãr′hou′zing), *n.* **1. a.** the depositing of goods, etc., in a warehouse: *The building, containing 6,000 square feet of space, will be used for manufacturing, warehousing, and distribution* (New York Times). **b.** the money paid for the service of a warehouse. **2.** a financial transaction in which a short-term lender, such as a commercial bank, extends credit on long-term investments, such as mortgages, to individuals or institutions, until the borrower is able to get a long-term lender, such as a savings bank or insurance company, to take over the loan.

ware·room (wãr′rüm′, -rům′), *n.* a room in which goods are shown and offered for sale.

wares (wãrz), *n.pl.* See under **ware**[1].

war·fare (wôr′fãr′), *n.* **1.** war; fighting. **2.** any struggle or contest. [Middle English *werefare* < *werre* war, conflict + *fare* a going, Old English *faru* journey]

war·far·in (wôr′fər in), *n.* a highly potent drug used as an anticoagulant for humans, and as a rat poison. *Formula:* $C_{19}H_{16}O_4$ [< *W*(isconsin) *A*(lumni) *R*(esearch) *F*(oundation) + *-arin*, as in *coumarin*]

war footing, the condition or state of being engaged in or prepared, mobilized, and equipped for war.

war game, a training exercise that imitates war. It may be an exercise on a map or maneuvers with actual troops, weapons, and equipment.

war·hawk (wôr′hôk′), *n. U.S.* a person who is eager for war.

war·head (wôr′hed′), *n.* the forward or nose part of a torpedo, ballistic missile, etc., that contains the explosive, and by the attaching of which the weapon is made ready (armed) for use: *A missile carrying an atomic warhead can speed 6,000 miles in 25 minutes, giving little opportunity for advance warning* (Leo A. Hoegh).

war horse, 1. a horse used in war; charger. **2.** *Informal.* **a.** a person who has taken part in many wars, campaigns, battles, etc.; veteran solider, sailor, etc. **b.** a veteran actor, politician, or other public figure. **c.** any well-known, standard, and somewhat trite work of art, activity, etc.: . . . *two old war horses—the grammar school play and the social studies project* (New York Times).

war·i·ly (wãr′ə lē), *adv.* cautiously; carefully: *He hesitated warily before going into politics* (Time). —**Syn.** gingerly, heedfully.

war·i·ness (wãr′ē nis), *n.* caution; care: *He looked at her with the hopeful wariness of a puppy who isn't sure whether he has done wrong* (John Strange). —**Syn.** vigilance, watchfulness.

war·i·son (war′ə sən), *n.* a war cry; battle cry. Also, **warrison.** [mistaken by Sir Walter Scott from Old English *warison* gift; wealth, treasure < Old North French, Old French *garison.* Doublet of GARRISON.]

wark[1] (wärk), *Dialect.* —*n.* a pain; ache. —*v.i.* to ache; suffer pain. [Old English *wærc*]

wark[2] (wärk), *n., adj., v.i., v.t. Dialect.* work.

War Labor Board, a board of twelve men, established in 1942 to mediate labor disputes in industries involved in war production.

war·less (wôr′lis), *adj.* free or exempt from war; not engaging in war: *There is in many places a willingness to face war again, if that be necessary, rather than see the new hopes lost to warless conquest* (Wall Street Journal).

war·like (wôr′līk′), *adj.* **1.** fit for war; ready for war; fond of war: *warlike tribes.* **2.** courageous in war; valiant. **3.** threatening war: *a warlike speech.* **4.** of or having to do with war. —**war′like′ness,** *n.* —**Syn. 3.** belligerent, hostile. **4.** martial. See **military.**

war·lock (wôr′lok), *n.* **1.** a wizard. **2.** a magician; conjurer. [Old English *wǣrloga* devil, traitor; (literally) oath-breaker < *wǣr* covenant + *-loga* one who denies, related to *lēogan* to lie, dissemble] —**Syn. 2.** sorcerer.

war lord or **war·lord** (wôr′lôrd′), *n.* **1.** a military commander or commander in chief, especially one who has sovereign authority in a particular country, region, etc., whether conferred under law or usurped by force. **2.** the military head of a province in China during the period 1916-1923; tuchun: *The Nationalist forces swept northward from their base at Canton, brushing out of the way the mercenary armies of old-fashioned war lords who tried to oppose them* (Wall Street Journal).

war·lord·ism (wôr′lôr′diz əm), *n.* the principles and practices of a war lord: *The United States Embassy has hailed the ouster of General Thi as "a step toward political stability" and "a defeat for warlordism"* (New York Times).

warm (wôrm), *adj.* **1.** more hot than cold; having heat; giving forth heat: *a warm fire. She sat in the warm sunshine.* **2. a.** having a feeling of heat: *to be warm from running.* **b.** producing such a feeling: *warm work.* **3.** that makes or keeps warm: *a warm coat.* **4.** subject to or characterized by the prevalence of a comparatively high temperature, or of moderate heat: *a warm climate, warm countries.* **5.** having the degree of heat natural to living beings, as the blood and body. **6.** (of colors) suggesting heat, as red, orange, or yellow. **7. a.** having or showing affection, enthusiasm, or zeal: *a warm heart, warm regard, warm thanks, a warm welcome.* **b.** amorous or passionate. **8. a.** easily excited: *a warm temper.* **b.** showing irritation or anger: *warm language.* **9.** exciting; lively: *a warm debate or dispute.* **10.** fresh and strong: *a warm scent.* **11.** *Informal.* near what one is searching for, as in games. **12.** *Informal.* uncomfortable, unpleasant, or disagreeable: *to make things warm for a person.* **13.** *Informal.* well-to-do; wealthy; rich.
—*adv.* so as to be warm; warmly.
—*v.t.* **1.** to make warm, as by heating, exercise, clothing, etc.; heat: *to warm a room.* **2.** to make cheered, interested, friendly, or sympathetic: *Her happiness warms my heart.* **3.** to make excited, enthusiastic, eager, or zealous: *He is warmed by his success.* —*v.i.* **1.** to become warm. **2.** to become cheered, interested, friendly, or sympathetic: *The speaker warmed to his subject.*
warm over, *Informal.* to rehash: *The Mirror got the Bishop of Woolwich to warm over his controversial views* (Time).
warm up, a. to heat or cook again: *She requests to have that little bit of sweetbread that was left, warmed up for the supper* (Dickens). **b.** to become cheered, interested, friendly, etc.; acquire zest: *She warmed up on the subject* (Harper's). **c.** to practice or exercise for a few minutes before entering a game, contest, etc.: *Actors could warm up before the curtain by, for instance, improvising the faculty party that takes place before Albee's "Virginia Woolf?" begins* (Manchester Guardian Weekly).
—*n. Informal.* the act or process of warming; heating.
[Old English *wearm*] —**warm′er,** *n.* —**warm′ly,** *adv.* —**warm′ness,** *n.*
—**Syn.** *adj.* **7. a.** cordial, hearty, fervent, enthusiastic. **8. a.** fiery, peppery.

war·mak·er (wôr′mā′kər), *n.* a warmonger: *The purpose of his crusade in Europe was to rid the world of warmakers and turn it over to the peacemakers* (Newsweek).

war·mak·ing (wôr′mā′king), *adj.* of or for making or waging war: *Our nation has enough power in its strategic retaliatory forces to bring near annihilation to the warmaking capacities of any country* (Newsweek).

warm-blood·ed (wôrm′blud′id), *adj.* **1.** having warm blood and a body temperature somewhere from 98 to 112 degrees: *Cats and birds are warm-blooded; snakes and turtles are cold-blooded.* **2.** with much feeling; eager; ardent. —**Syn. 2.** fervent, passionate.

warmed-o·ver (wôrmd′ō′vər), *adj.* **1.** warmed again, as food that has become cold; reheated. **2.** not fresh or new; old; stale: *American televiewers are in for the largest helping of warmed-over fare in TV history this summer* (Newsweek).

war memorial, a monument in memory of a battle or those killed in battle: . . . *the marble war memorial, that the best local stonemason builds in the market place—set round with the green of living grass and with benches for widows* (Wolfgang Borchert).

warm front, *Meteorology.* the advancing edge of a warm air mass as it passes over and displaces a cooler one.

warm-heart·ed (wôrm′här′tid), *adj.* kind; sympathetic; friendly: *He was, by the account of such intimates as Secretary of State Frank B. Kellogg, "a warm-hearted, charming gentleman"* (Newsweek). —**warm′-heart′edly,** *adv.* —**warm′-heart′ed·ness,** *n.* —**Syn.** kindly, tender.

warm·ing pan (wôr′ming), a covered pan with a long handle for holding hot coals, formerly used to warm beds.

warm·ing-up (wôr′ming up′), *n.* a making or becoming warm or warmer; increase of warmth: *a warming-up of the weather.*

warm·ish (wôr′mish), *adj.* rather warm. —**warm′ish·ly,** *adv.* —**warm′ish·ness,** *n.* —**Syn.** lukewarm, tepid.

war·mon·ger (wôr′mung′gər, -mong′-), *n.* a person who is strongly in favor of war or attempts to bring about war: *On May Days past . . . the chunky rulers of Russia had* *hurled the condemnations at the U.S. warmongers and bellicosely pointed to their own armed strength in the square below and in the skies above* (Time).

war·mon·ger·ing (wôr′mung′gər ing, -mong′-), *n.* the acts or practices of a warmonger: *As the tension increased and Americans became more concerned about the war in Europe, the isolationists became extremely worried, and some of them accused Roosevelt of warmongering* (Gerald Johnson). —*adj.* of or having to do with a warmonger or warmongers.

war·mouth (wôr′mouth′), *n.* a large-mouthed, voracious, fresh-water sunfish of the eastern and southern United States.

warmth (wôrmth), *n.* **1.** a being warm: *the warmth of the open fire.* **2.** warm or friendly feeling: *to greet a person with warmth.* **3.** liveliness of feelings or emotions; fervor: *He spoke with warmth of the natural beauty of the country.* **4.** (in painting) a glowing effect, as produced by the use of reds and yellows. —**Syn. 3.** zeal, ardor.

warm-up (wôrm′up′), *n.* **1.** the practice or exercise taken for a few minutes before entering a game, contest, etc.: *My fingers felt cold, so I played some Bach, which is a very good warm-up* (New Yorker). **2.** a period of running required for a machine to reach normal working condition before use: *Transistor radios require no warm-up. Four planemakers . . . have spent $2,742,000 on equipment to muffle the sound of jet warm-ups* (Newsweek). **3.** a preliminary trial or session before the main contest, exhibition, or undertaking: *two wonderful pre-session warm-ups . . . while the studio engineers were adjusting their equipment* (Saturday Review). *The observations planned this year . . . at observatories all over the world will be a warm-up for the even closer approach two years from now* (Science News Letter).
—*adj.* for or as a warm-up; preliminary: *a warm-up run, a warm-up game before the season.*

warn (wôrn), *v.t.* **1.** to give notice to in advance; put on guard (against danger, evil, harm, etc.): *The clouds warned us that a storm was coming.* **2.** to give notice to; inform: *The whistle warned us that the ship was about to sail.* **3.** to give notice to go, stay, etc.: *to warn off trespassers, to warn a child to remain in the house.* **4.** to remind (of); counsel (against); admonish: *to warn a man of his duty, warn a driver against speeding.* —*v.i.* to give a warning or warnings; sound an alarm. [Old English *wearnian.* Related to WARE².] —**warn′er,** *n.*
—**Syn.** *v.t.* **1. Warn, caution** mean to give notice of possible or coming danger, harm, risk, unpleasantness, etc. **Warn** implies giving clear and firm notice, especially of an imminent or serious danger: *Her mother warned her not to speak to strangers.* **Caution** implies giving notice of a possible danger and advice about avoiding it: *Citrus growers are cautioned to protect the fruit from frost.* **2.** apprise, notify.

war neurosis, shell shock.

warn·ing (wôr′ning), *n.* something that warns; notice given in advance. —*adj.* that warns. —**warn′ing·ly,** *adv.* —**Syn.** *n.* admonition, advice.

warning net, any system or network of communications set up to give warning of aggressive enemy movements, such as those of enemy aircraft.

war nose, 1. the nose of a shell, which contains the detonator for the bursting charge. **2.** a warhead.

warn't (wornt, wôrnt), *U.S. Dialect.* wasn't.

war of liberation, (in Communist parlance) warfare, especially guerrilla warfare, conducted against a government that is pro-Western, neocolonialist, imperialist, etc.: *A Communist takeover in South Vietnam would be followed by similar "wars of liberation" in other countries* (New York Times).

war of nerves, a conflict in which tension is built up by intimidation, propaganda, or obstructive or delaying tactics rather than by use or threat of violence: *Both sides are digging in for a war of nerves with each determined to wait out the other to get the price it wants* (Wall Street Journal).

warp (wôrp), *v.t.* **1.** to bend, curve, or twist (an object) out of shape; permanently distort the shape of, as by shrinking, heating, etc. **2.** to mislead; pervert: *Prejudice warps our judgment.* **3. a.** to pervert the meaning of (a statement); misrepresent. **b.** to distort (a meaning, purpose, etc.); misinterpret. **4.** to move (a ship, etc.) by taking up on ropes fastened to something else. **5.** to bend or twist (a wing, airfoil, etc.) at the end or ends: *The aviator warped a wing tip to regain balance.* **6.** to arrange (threads or yarn) so as to form a warp. **7.** to improve the quality of (land) by flooding with a deposit of alluvial soil. —*v.i.* **1.** to become bent, curved, or twisted out of shape, by contraction or expansion, or both: *A steel girder may warp in a fire. The floor has warped so that it is not level.* **2.** to be turned from the normal or proper course; be distorted, twisted, confused, perverted, etc.: *There is our commission From which we would not have you warp* (Shakespeare). **3. a.** (of a ship) to be moved by warping. **b.** (of the crew) to move a ship thus. **4.** *Obsolete.* to leave one's proper route; swerve; stray (from). [Old English *weorpan* to throw, hit with a missile; twist]
—*n.* **1.** the threads or yarn running lengthwise in a fabric. The warp is crossed by the woof. See **weave** for picture. **2.** the act of warping (wood, metal, etc.) or state of being twisted; bend; twist; distortion. **3.** a distortion of judgment; mental twist; bias. **4. a.** a rope fixed at one end and pulled upon to move a ship. **b.** (in trawl fishing) a rope attached to a net. **c.** (in whaling) a harpoon line attached to the main line. **5. a.** alluvial sediment; silt. **b.** a rich bed or layer of this, made by artificial flooding.
[Old English *wearp* < *werp-*, root of *weorpan* to throw, warp] —**warp′er,** *n.*

warp·age (wôr′pij), *n.* **1.** a warping or being warped: *Lumber will be glued together in laminations for less warpage* (Science News Letter). **2.** a charge for warping or hauling ships entering certain harbors.

war paint, 1. (among North American Indians) paint put on the face or body before going to war. **2.** *Slang.* **a.** best clothes and finery; full dress; ornaments. **b.** lipstick, rouge, powder, etc., worn by women; make-up.

war·path (wôr′path′, -päth′), *n.* (among North American Indians) the way taken by a fighting expedition.
on the warpath, a. at or ready for war: *It is a safe prophecy that the Cretans will again be on the warpath* (London Daily News). **b.** looking for a fight; angry: *A tremendous rapping at my door announced that Bobby was again on the warpath* (Mrs. J.H. Riddell).

warp beam, the roller or other apparatus in a loom around which the warp is wound.

warp-knit·ted (wôrp′nit′id), *adj.* (of fabrics) made by warp knitting.

warp knitting, knitting by machine using many threads of yarn in the direction of the length.

war·plane (wôr′plān′), *n.* an aircraft designed or used for fighting rather than pleasure or commerce.

warp-print·ed (wôrp′prin′tid), *adj.* (of textiles) woven after a roller print design has been applied to the warp yarns only, using a filling yarn that is a solid color for unusual effects: *A lovely short evening dress in . . . warp-printed satin was lightly swathed over the shoulders with pink and mauve velvet* (London Times).

warp-proof (wôrp′prüf′), *adj.* protected against warping: *The door, which has extruded aluminum frames, is said to be weather-resistant, shatterproof, and warp-proof* (Science News Letter).

War Production Board, an agency of the U.S. government, established in 1942 and abolished in 1945, that controlled procurement and production of war materials. *Abbr.:* WPB (no periods).

warp sizing, the application of a sizing solution to the warp yarns of a fabric before weaving, to increase strength and smoothness and add weight to the finished fabric.

war·rant (wôr′ənt, wor′-), *n.* **1.** that which gives a right; authority: *an action without warrant in custom, tradition, or law.* **2.** a good and sufficient reason; promise; guarantee: *to have warrant for hopes, to suspect a friend without warrant.* **3.** *Law.* a writ or order giving authority to do something: *a warrant to search a house, a warrant for the payment of money.* **4. a.** a document certifying something, especially to a purchaser; written guarantee. **b.** any guarantee; certification; promise. **5.** the official certificate of appointment issued to a noncommissioned officer in the army or navy. **6.** a written document authorizing one person to pay or deliver, and another to receive, a sum of money: *a warrant on a municipal treasury.* **7.** *Especially British.* a receipt given to a person who has deposited goods in a warehouse, by assignment of which the title to the goods is transferred; warehouse receipt. **8.** a person who answers for a fact; authoritative witness. **9.** *Obsolete.* a person or thing that serves as guaranty; security.
—*v.t.* **1.** to authorize: *The law warrants his arrest.* **2.** to justify: *Nothing can warrant such rudeness.* **3.** to give one's word for; guarantee; promise: *The storekeeper warranted the quality of the coffee.* **4.** to attest the truth or authenticity of; authenticate. **5. a.** to guarantee to (the purchaser of goods) the security of the title to the goods; guarantee to indemnify for loss. **b.** to guarantee (a title) or guarantee the title to (a person) of granted property. **6.** *Informal.* to assert as probable to the point of certainty; declare positively: *I'll warrant he won't try that again.*
[< Old North French *warant,* Old French *guarant;* see WARRANTY]
—**Syn.** *n.* **1.** sanction, authorization. —*v.t.* **1.** sanction. **3.** assure. **6.** affirm, attest.

war·rant·a·bil·i·ty (wôr′ən tə bil′ə tē, wor′-), *n.* the quality of being warrantable.

war·rant·a·ble (wôr′ən tə bəl, wor′-), *adj.* **1.** that can be warranted; justifiable; defensible. **2.** old enough to be hunted, as deer. —**war′rant·a·ble·ness,** *n.*

war·rant·a·bly (wôr′ən tə blē, wor′-), *adv.* in a warrantable manner; justifiably; defensibly.

war·ran·tee (wôr′ən tē′, wor′-), *n. Law.* a person to whom a warranty is made.

war·rant·er (wôr′ən tər, wor′-), *n.* a person who warrants.

war·rant·less (wôr′ənt lis, wor′-), *adj.* without warrant; unauthorized; unjustifiable: *warrantless invasion of privacy.*

warrant officer, 1. an army or navy officer who has received a certificate of appointment, but not a commission, ranking between commissioned officers and enlisted men. **2.** (in the United States Navy) any of various subordinate officers, as a boatswain, carpenter, gunner, pay clerk, or torpedoman. **3.** an officer of similar rank in the armed forces of certain other countries. *Abbr.:* WO (no periods).

war·ran·tor (wôr′ən tər, wor′-; wôr′ən tôr′, wor′-), *n. Law.* a person who makes a warranty; guarantor.

war·ran·ty (wôr′ən tē, wor′-), *n., pl.* **-ties. 1.** warrant; authority; justification. **2.** *Law.* **a.** a promise or pledge that something is what it is claimed to be; guarantee: *a warranty against defects in goods.* **b.** a covenant annexed to a deed to land in which the seller guarantees that the title is good. In feudal law, the warranty given by a grantor of a freehold estate obliged him to give the grantee lands of equal value if the latter were evicted. **c.** (in an insurance contract) a promise or pledge made by the insured, breach of which invalidates the policy. **d.** a warrant, writ, etc. **3.** *Obsolete except Dialect.* an assurance; promise. [< Old North French *warantie,* Anglo-French *guarantie* < *warantir* to warrant < *warant,* Old French *guarant* warrant < Germanic (compare Middle Low German *warend,* and *warent,* present participle of *waren* to assure, protect). Doublet of GUARANTY.] —**Syn. 1.** authorization.

warranty deed, a deed that contains a warranty that the title is good.

war·ren (wôr′ən, wor′-), *n.* **1.** a piece of ground filled with burrows, where rabbits live or are raised. **2.** a crowded district or building. **3.** *English Law.* **a.** a piece of land enclosed and preserved for breeding game. **b.** a right to keep or hunt beasts and fowl of warren (hares, partridge, woodcock, etc.). [< Anglo-French, Old North French *warenne,* probably < Germanic (compare the root *war-*, as in English *ward, ware²*)]

war·ren·er (wôr′ə nər, wor′-), *n.* **1.** a person who owns or rents a rabbit warren. **2.** the keeper of a warren, especially: **a.** a servant who has the charge of a rabbit warren. **b.** an officer employed to watch over the game in a park or preserve.

Warren hoe, a hoe with a triangular-shaped blade. [perhaps < a proper name]

war·ring (wôr′ing), *n.* the act of waging war; fighting. —*adj.* at war; antagonistic; hostile; conflicting: *warring opinions.*

war·ri·or (wôr′ē ər, wor′-), *n.* a fighting man; soldier. —*adj.* belonging to or characteristic of a warrior; martial. [< Old North French *werreieor* < *werreier* wage war < *werre;* see WAR[1]] —**war′ri·or·like′,** *adj.*

war risk insurance, term insurance issued by the U.S. government for members of the Armed Forces.

war·ri·son (war′ə sən), *n.* warison.

war room, a room used at a military headquarters for briefings, film showings, map displays, etc., dealing with conditions at one or more theaters of operation.

war·saw (wôr′sô), *n.* a large grouper of the southeastern coast of the United States. [American English; alteration of Spanish *guasa*]

Warsaw Pact, the Eastern European Mutual Assistance Treaty, a military alliance of Albania, Bulgaria, Czechoslovakia, the German Democratic Republic, Hungary, Poland, Romania, and the Soviet Union, signed in Warsaw in May, 1955.

Warsaw Powers, the nations that signed the Warsaw Pact.

war·ship (wôr′ship′), *n.* any ship armed and manned for war. —**Syn.** battleship.

war·sle (wär′səl), *v.,* **-sled, -sling,** *n. Scottish.* —*v.i.* **1.** to wrestle; struggle. **2.** to move with effort; flounder. —*v.t.* to wrestle with (an adversary).
—*n.* **1.** a wrestling bout. **2.** any struggle; tussle.
[alteration of Middle English *wrastlen;* see WRESTLE]

war·sler (wärs′lər), *n. Scottish.* wrestler.

war·stle (wär′səl), *v.i., v.t.,* **-stled, -stling,** *n. Scottish.* warsle. —**war′stler,** *n.*

war surplus, equipment, materials, clothing, etc., no longer required by the military services, and usually disposed of by direct sale or auction: [*He*] *sank the rest of his capital into building a . . . factory on his island and buying war surplus navy boats, gear and harpoons* (Time).

wart (wôrt), *n.* **1.** a small, hard, dry, abnormal outgrowth on the skin, now believed to be caused by a virus. **2.** *Botany.* a rounded, glandular protuberance or excrescence on the surface of a plant. [Old English *wearte*] —**wart′like′,** *adj.*

war tax, a tax to provide money for a war.

wart·ed (wôr′tid), *adj.* having a wart or warts; verrucose.

wart hog, a wild hog of Africa that has two large tusks and large wartlike growths on each side of the face.

Wart Hog (about 30 in. high at the shoulder)

war·time (wôr′tīm′), *n.* a time of war. —*adj.* taking place during or characteristic of a time of war: *What the senators want is expert opinion as to whether . . . production and missile development should be placed on a wartime footing at once* (Newsweek).

war time, *British.* double summer time.

war-torn (wôr′tôrn′, -tōrn′), *adj.* disrupted, damaged, or destroyed by war: *The American people . . . endorsed the government's economic aid and technical assistance to underdeveloped and war-torn countries of the postwar world* (Bulletin of Atomic Scientists).

wart·y (wôr′tē), *adj.,* **wart·i·er, wart·i·est. 1.** having warts. **2.** covered with lumps like warts. **3.** of or like a wart.

warve (wôrv), *n.* wharve.

war vessel, warship.

war-wea·ri·ness (wôr′wir′ē nis), *n.* war-weary condition or feeling: *The people of South Vietnam have been at war for 25 years and war-weariness is deep in their bones* (New York Times).

war-wea·ry (wôr′wir′ē), *adj.* wearied of war and its hardships: *Some observers here think this might be acceptable to the war-weary rebels now as a basis for a cease-fire* (Wall Street Journal).

war whoop, 1. a war cry of American Indians. **2.** any war cry; shout of battle.

war·y (wãr′ē), *adj.,* **war·i·er, war·i·est. 1.** on one's guard against danger, deception, etc.: *a wary fox.* **2.** cautious; careful: *He gave wary answers to all of the stranger's questions.*
wary of, cautious about; careful about: *to be wary of driving in heavy traffic.*
—**Syn. 1.** alert, vigilant, watchful, guarded. **2.** circumspect, prudent. See **careful.**

was (woz, wuz; *unstressed* wəz), *v.* the 1st and 3rd person singular, past indicative of **be:** *I was late. Was he late, too?* [Old English *wæs*]

➔ **Was** in the second person singular (*you was*), formerly common in standard English, is no longer in good use. See **were** for another usage note.

wa·sa·bi (wä sä′bē), *n.* **1.** a plant of the mustard family, cultivated in Japan for its roots, which taste like horseradish. **2.** the grated root of this plant, served with raw fish in a Japanese meal. [< Japanese *wasabi*]

wash (wosh, wôsh), *v.t.* **1.** to clean with water or other liquid: *to wash a floor, wash one's hands, wash clothes, wash dishes.* **2.** to remove (dirt, stains, paint, etc.) by or as by the action of water or other liquid: *to wash a spot out.* **3.** to make clean: *washed from sin.* **4.** to make wet; moisten thoroughly with water or other liquid: *The flowers are washed with dew.* **5.** to flow over or past (the shore, coast, etc.); beat upon (walls, cliffs, etc.); lave: *a beach washed by waves.* **6.** to carry (by a liquid): *Wood is often washed ashore by the waves.* **7.** to wear (by water or any liquid): *The cliffs are being washed away by the waves. Rain washed channels in the ground.* **8.** to pass (a gas or gaseous mixture) through or over a liquid in order to remove impurities or to dissolve out some component. **9.** to cover with color mixed with water or a watery liquid: *The house was washed white.* **10.** to cover with a film of metal deposited from a solution: *to wash copper with silver.* **11.** *Mining.* **a.** to sift (earth, ore, etc.) by the action of water to separate valuable material, especially gold, from waste. **b.** to separate (gold, etc.) in this way. **12.** *Informal.* to dismiss or reject from a school, course of study, etc., as not qualified or able to be qualified.
—*v.i.* **1.** to wash clothes: *to wash once a week. She washes for a living.* **2.** to wash oneself: *He washed before eating dinner.* **3.** to undergo washing without damage: *This material washes well.* **4.** *Informal.* to stand being put to the proof: *Patriotism that won't wash. That argument won't wash.* **5.** to be carried along or away by water or other liquid: *Cargo washed ashore. The topsoil washed away.* **6.** to flow or beat with a lapping sound: *The waves washed upon the rock. The flood waters washed against the house.*
wash down, a. to wash from top to bottom or from end to end: *to wash down the walls of a kitchen.* **b.** to swallow liquid along with or after (solid food) to help in swallowing or digestion: *After his dinner, he washed it all down with a cup of good hot tea.*
wash out, a. to cleanse or rinse the interior of: *to wash out one's mouth. It is requisite that it* [*the bottle*] *be washed out after every experiment, the last two or three rinsings being made with distilled water* (Michael Faraday). **b.** to rinse so as to remove soap or other substance from the fabric: *After soaping the dyed cloth she washed it out.* **c.** to lose color, body, or vigor: *Candidates should wear light blue or gray shirts because white washes out on the screen* (Time). **d.** to carry or be carried away by water: *The rain washed out part of the pavement. The road washed out during the storm.* **e.** *Informal.* to fail and be released from a school, course of study, etc.; flunk out: *He was absent so often that he finally washed out of school.*
wash up, a. to wash one's hands and face, as before eating: *When they finished eating lunch, the children went to wash up.* **b.** *British.* to wash the dishes: *His supper over, . . . Ernana . . . retired into the kitchen to wash up* (R. Bagot). **c.** to be done for; be done with; finish: *Everybody thought he was all washed up as an actor; then he made his big comeback.*
—*n.* **1.** the act or process of washing: *to give a dog a wash.* **2.** the state of being washed. **3.** a quantity of clothes or other articles washed or to be washed: *a week's wash.* **4.** a liquid for a special use: *a hair wash, a mouth wash.* **5. a.** (in water-color painting) a broad, thin layer of color laid on by a continuous movement of the brush, sometimes partly painted over with other colors while it is still damp. **b.** a thin coat of water color or distemper spread over a wall or similar surface; a preparation used for this purpose: *Pictures and fragments have . . . been inset flush with the wall, which is covered with a honey-coloured wash* (Observer). **6.** a thin coat of metal. **7.** waste liquid matter; liquid garbage. **8.** washy or weak liquid food. **9.** the fermented wort from which the spirit is extracted in distilling. **10.** the motion, rush, or sound of water: *to hear the wash of the sea.* **11.** wear or attrition caused by the action of water. **12. a.** the rough or broken water left behind a moving ship. **b.** a disturbance in air made by an airplane or any of its parts: *prop wash.* **13.** a tract of land sometimes overflowed with water and sometimes left dry; tract of shallow water; fen, marsh, or bog. **14.** a shallow pool or stream formed by the overflow of a river. **15.** *Western U.S.* the dry bed of an intermittent stream. **16.** material carried by moving water and then deposited as sediment; alluvial deposit. **17.** earth, ore, etc., from which gold or the like can be washed. **18.** the action of rain and flowing water in wearing away or removing soil: *Even after a light rainfall a heavy wash of soil-laden water flows from the high ground into the wadis* (Scientific American).
come out in the wash, to be discovered in the end: *It all comes out in the wash, to mock the riddled corpses round Bapaume* (Sunday Times).
—*adj.* that can be washed without damage: *a wash dress.*
[Old English *wascan,* or *wæscan*]
—**Syn.** *v.t.* **1.** cleanse, rinse. *-v.i.* **2.** bathe.

Wash., Washington.

wash·a·bil·i·ty (wosh′ə bil′ə tē, wôsh′-), *n.* the quality of being washable.

wash·a·ble (wosh′ə bəl, wôsh′-), *adj.* that can be washed without damage.

wash-and-wear (wosh′ən wãr′, wôsh′-), *adj.* specially treated to require little or no ironing after washing and drying: *Clothing manufacturers said the new wash-and-wear fabrics were merely a gimmick when it came to tailored clothes* (New York Times).

wash·ball (wosh′bôl′, wôsh′-), *n.* a ball of soap, sometimes perfumed or medicated, used for washing the hands and face, and for shaving.

wash·ba·sin (wosh′bā′sən, wôsh′-), *n.* a basin for holding water to wash one's face and hands.

wash·board (wosh′bôrd′, -bōrd′; wôsh′-), *n.* **1.** *U.S.* a board having ridges on it, used for rubbing the dirt out of clothes. **2.** a baseboard or skirting board. **3. a.** a thin board extending upward from the gunwale of a boat as a guard against spray. **b.** a similar guard on the sill of a port.
—*adj.* full of ridges or ruts: *a washboard road.*

wash·boil·er (wosh′boi′lər, wôsh′-), *n.* a large metal receptacle with a removable cover, for boiling clothes, table linen, etc.

wash bottle, a glass flask having a stopper that is perforated by tubes, arranged so that by blowing in one tube the water or other liquid in the flask may be forced out in a small stream through another tube: *Wash bottles are used in laboratories, for washing precipitates on filters.*

wash·bowl (wosh′bōl′, wôsh′-), *n.* a bowl to hold water to wash one's hands and face.

wash·cloth (wosh′klôth′, -kloth′; wôsh′-), *n.* a small cloth for washing oneself. —**Syn.** washrag.

wash·day (wosh′dā′, wôsh′-), *n.* a day when clothes are washed.

wash-down (wosh′doun′, wôsh′-), *n.* a washing from top to bottom or from end to end.

wash drawing, 1. a representation of an object produced by laying in the shades in washes, with merely the outlines and chief details in line. **2.** the method of producing such representations.

washed-out (wosht′out′, wôsht′-), *adj.* **1.** lacking color; faded. **2.** *Informal.* lacking life, spirit, etc. **3.** damaged by flood; eroded.

washed-up (wosht′up′, wôsht′-), *adj. Informal.* **1. a.** done with; through, especially after having failed. **b.** done for; finished. **2.** fatigued.

wash·er (wosh′ər, wôsh′-), *n.* **1.** a person who washes. **2.** a machine that washes. **3.** a flat ring of metal, rubber, leather, etc., with a hole in the middle, used with bolts or nuts, or to make joints tight, as in a water faucet. **4.** a device for washing gases; scrubber.

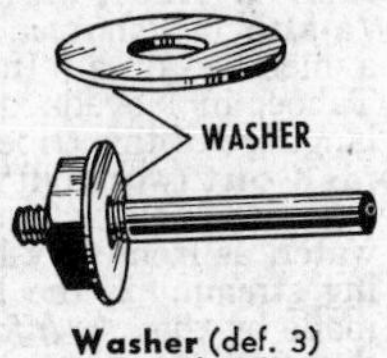

Washer (def. 3) Top, detail; bottom, in use

wash·er-dry·er (wosh′ər drī′ər,

wôsh′-), *n.* a machine that washes clothes and then dries them.

wash·er·man (wosh′ər mən, wôsh′-), *n., pl.* **-men.** a man whose work is washing clothes.

wash·er-up (wosh′ər up′, wôsh′-), *n. British.* a person who washes dishes; dishwasher.

wash·er·wom·an (wosh′ər wu̇m′ən, wôsh′-), *n., pl.* **-wom·en.** a woman whose work is washing clothes. —**Syn.** laundress.

wash·er·y (wosh′ər ē, wôsh′-), *n., pl.* **-er·ies.** a place where something is washed: *A pipe to take the coal from pit top to washery has been installed* (London Times).

wash-fast·ness (wosh′fast′nis, wôsh′-; -fäst′-), *n.* the quality of not fading when washed: *finishes which increase wrinkle resistance and wash-fastness of dyes* (Wall Street Journal).

wash goods, washable fabrics.

wash-hand basin (wosh′hand′, wôsh′-), *British.* a washbasin.

wash·house (wosh′hous′, wôsh′-), *n.* **1.** an outbuilding or room for washing clothes: *At one end of the cottage there was a further addition, a washhouse, also separate from the interior* (London Times). **2.** a public building for washing clothes: *I looked about me at my own children, playing happily though hungrily on the cobbles by the communal washhouse* (Punch).

wash·ing (wosh′ing, wôsh′-), *n.* **1.** a cleaning with water: *to give a car, one's hands, or clothes, a good washing.* **2.** the act of washing as part of an industrial process: *the washing of coal or ore.* **3.** a washing away of material; erosion by action of water: *to build a wall to prevent washing of soil from a bank.* **4. a.** a batch of clothes washed or to be washed at one time: *to do two washings before lunch.* **b.** laundry: *to send out one's washing.* **5.** a thin coat, as of a metal applied by electrolysis. **6.** Sometimes, **washings.** liquid that has been used to wash something. **7.** *Mining.* **a.** Sometimes, **washings.** metal, as gold dust, obtained by washing soil, ore, etc. **b.** places containing soil, ore, etc., from which metal is obtained by washing. **8.** *Finance.* a manipulating of a security by means of a wash sale.
—*adj.* **1.** for washing. **2.** that washes.

washing bear, the raccoon (so called from its habit of putting its food into water before eating it).

washing bottle, a wash bottle.

washing machine, a machine that washes clothes, sheets, towels, etc.

washing soda, crystallized sodium carbonate, used in washing; sal soda.

Wash·ing·to·ni·an (wosh′ing tō′nē ən, wôsh′-), *n.* a native or inhabitant of Washington, D.C., or the State of Washington. —*adj.* of or having to do with Washington, D.C., or the State of Washington.

Wash·ing·to·ni·a·na (wosh′ing tō′nē ä′nə, -an′ə, -ā′nə; wôsh′-), *n.pl.* a collection of objects, documents, books, facts, etc., about or belonging to George Washington.

Wash·ing·ton palm (wosh′ing tən, wôsh′-), one of two fan palms growing in southern California and neighboring areas.

Washington pie, *U.S.* a layer cake with a jam, cream, or other filling.

Washington's Birthday, February 22, the date of George Washington's birth, celebrated as a holiday in the United States.

Washington thorn, a species of hawthorn native to the southern United States, with white flowers and scarlet fruit.

wash·ing-up (wosh′ing up′, wôsh′-), *n. British.* the act of washing dishes.

washing-up bowl, *British.* a dishpan.

washing-up machine, *British.* a dishwasher: *Labour-saving kitchen, including washing-up machine* (Sunday Times).

wash leather, chamois or the like, used for gloves.

wash 'n' wear, wash-and-wear.

Wa·sho (wä′shō), *n., pl.* **-sho** or **-shos. 1.** a member of an Indian tribe near Lake Tahoe, in Nevada and California. **2.** the language of this tribe.

wash·out (wosh′out′, wôsh′-), *n.* **1.** a washing away of earth, gravel, a roadbed, etc., by water, as from very heavy rains or a flooding stream. **2.** the hole, cavity, or break made by this. **3.** *Informal.* a person who is dismissed or rejected from a school, course of study, etc., as not qualified or able to be qualified; person who washes out. **4.** *Slang.* a failure; disappointment: *The party was a complete washout.*

wash·pot (wosh′pot′, wôsh′-), *n.* **1.** a vessel used for washing, especially one's hands. **2.** a vessel containing melted tin, into which iron plates are plunged to be converted into tin plate.

wash·rack (wosh′rak′, wôsh′-), *n.* a section of a service station, hangar, etc., equipped for the quick washing of vehicles.

wash·rag (wosh′rag′, wôsh′-), *n.* a washcloth.

wash·room (wosh′rüm′, -ru̇m′; wôsh′-), *n. U.S.* **1.** a room where toilet facilities are provided; lavatory. **2.** *Obsolete.* a laundry.

wash sale, *Finance.* a fictitious buying and selling of a security, now prohibited by law, as by two brokers at the same time for a single customer, to give an appearance of market activity and encourage outside participation in helping to raise or lower the price.

wash·stand (wosh′stand′, wôsh′-), *n.* **1.** a bowl with pipes and faucets for running water to wash one's hands and face. **2.** a stand for holding a basin, pitcher, etc., for washing.

wash·trough (wosh′trôf′, -trof′; wôsh′-), *n.* **1.** a trough used for washing the hands and face. **2.** a trough in which ore is washed; buddle.

wash·tub (wosh′tub′, wôsh′-), *n.* a tub used to wash or soak clothes in.

wash-up (wosh′up′, wôsh′-), *n.* the act or process of washing oneself: *One of the principal issues before and after the . . . settlement was the amount of time allotted employes for rest and wash-up* (Wall Street Journal).

wash·wom·an (wosh′wu̇m′ən, wôsh′-), *n., pl.* **-wom·en.** washerwoman.

wash·y (wosh′ē, wôsh′ē), *adj.,* **wash·i·er, wash·i·est. 1.** too much diluted; weak; watery: *washy coloring, washy poetry, washy sentiment.* **2.** lacking strength and stamina; feeble: *a washy style of writing or lecturing.* **3.** (of a horse or cow) liable to sweat or scour after slight exertion. **4.** *Obsolete.* **a.** having too much moisture; water-logged. **b.** (of wind or weather) bringing moisture or rain.

was·n't (woz′ənt, wuz′-), was not.

➔ The form *wan't* (wont, wônt) for *wasn't* is particularly common in New England and in the coastal areas of the South Atlantic States. It occurs both in folk speech and in the usage of cultivated, but old-fashioned, speakers.

wasp (wosp, wôsp), *n.* any of various insects that have a slender body and a powerful sting. They belong to a group of insects, including the ants and the bees, that have four membranous wings, and usually feed on other insects, spiders, etc. The social wasps, including the yellow jackets and hornets, build paper nests. Solitary wasps, including the sand wasp and the mud wasp, build mud nests or tunnel into the ground, trees, etc. See also **nest** for picture. [Old English *wæps, wæsp.* Related to WEAVE.]

Ichneumon Wasp (Line shows actual length.)

WASP[1] or **Wasp**[1] (wosp, wôsp), *n.* a member of the WASP (Women's Air Force Service Pilots).

WASP[2] or **Wasp**[2] (wosp, wôsp), *n., adj.* White Anglo-Saxon Protestant (used in an unfriendly way).

WASP (no periods), *U.S.* Women's Air Force Service Pilots (an organization formed in the early part of World War II, and dissolved in 1944).

wasp·ish (wos′pish, wôs′-), *adj.* **1.** like a wasp; like that of a wasp. **2. a.** bad-tempered; irritable: *a waspish person.* **b.** marked or characterized by virulence or petulance; spiteful: *a waspish remark.* —**wasp′ish·ly,** *adv.* —**wasp′ish·ness,** *n.* —**Syn. 2. a.** irascible, snappish, fractious.

wasp·like (wosp′līk′, wôsp′-), *adj.* resembling a wasp in structure, form, movement, etc.; vespiform.

wasp waist, a very slender waist.

wasp-waist·ed (wosp′wās′tid, wôsp′-), *adj.* having a very slender waist.

wasp·y (wos′pē, wôs′-), *adj.,* **wasp·i·er, wasp·i·est.** wasplike; waspish.

was·sail (wos′əl, was′-), *n.* **1.** a drinking party; revel with drinking of healths. **2.** spiced ale or other liquor drunk at a wassail. **3.** a salutation meaning "Your health!" The reply is "Drink hail!" **4.** *Obsolete.* a carol or song sung by wassailers. —*v.i.* to take part in a wassail; revel. —*v.t.* to drink to the health of; toast. —*interj.* your health! [Middle English *wassail* < Scandinavian (compare Old Icelandic *ves heill* be healthy!)]

was·sail·er (wos′əl ər, was′-), *n.* **1.** a reveler. **2.** a drinker of toasts.

Wasser·mann test, or **Was·ser·mann** (wä′sər mən), *n.* a test for syphilis, made on a sample of blood or spinal fluid. [< August von *Wassermann,* 1866-1925, a German bacteriologist]

wast[1] (wost), *v. Archaic or Poetic.* the 2nd person singular, past tense of **be,** used only with *thou.* "Thou wast" means "you were."

wast[2] (wast, wäst), *n., adj., adv. Scottish.* west.

wast·age (wās′tij), *n.* **1.** loss or diminution by use, wear, decay, leakage, etc.; waste. **2.** the amount wasted; quantity lost.

waste (wāst), *v.,* **wast·ed, wast·ing,** *n., adj.* —*v.t.* **1.** to make poor use of; spend uselessly; fail to get value from: *Don't waste time or money.* **2.** to wear down little by little; destroy or lose gradually: *The sick man was wasted by disease. To . . . waste huge stones with little water drops* (Shakespeare). **3.** to damage greatly; destroy: *The soldiers wasted the enemy's fields.* —*v.i.* **1.** to be consumed or spent uselessly, extravagantly, or without adequate return. **2.** to be used up or worn away gradually. **3.** (of time) to pass away; be spent.
—*n.* **1.** a poor use; useless spending; failure to get the most out of something: *a waste of money, goods, time, or effort, a waste of a man's ability.* **2.** a wearing down little by little; gradual destruction or loss: *Both waste and repair are constantly going on in our bodies.* **3.** destruction or devastation caused by war, floods, fires, etc. **4.** *Law.* an injury to an estate caused by an act or neglect on the part of a tenant. **5.** bare or wild land; desert; wilderness. **6.** a vast, dreary, desolate, or empty expanse or tract, as of water or snow-covered land. **7.** a piece of land uncultivated or unused, producing little or no herbage or wood. **8.** useless or worthless material; stuff to be thrown away: *Garbage or sewage is waste.* **9.** cotton or wool threads in bunches, used for cleaning machinery, or wiping off oil, grease, etc. **10.** *Physical Geography.* material derived by mechanical and chemical erosion from the land, carried by streams to the sea.
go to waste, to be wasted: *There is not a particle of vapour in the universe that goes to waste* (H. Hunter).
—*adj.* **1.** not cultivated; that is a desert or wilderness; bare; wild. **2.** in a state of desolation or ruin. **3.** left over; not used: *waste energy.* **4.** thrown away as worthless or useless: *waste products.* **5.** carrying off or holding refuse: *a waste drain.* **6.** unused by or unusable to, and therefore excreted by, an animal or human body.
lay waste, to damage greatly; devastate: *War laid waste his native land once more* (Thomas Campbell).
[< Old North French *waster,* Old French *guaster* < Latin *vāstāre* lay waste < *vāstus* vast, waste. Compare DEVASTATE.]
—**Syn.** *v.t.* **1.** squander, dissipate. **2.** diminish. *-n.* **8.** trash, rubbish, refuse. *-adj.* **1.** desolate, uninhabited. **2.** devastated. **4.** rejected.

waste·bas·ket (wāst′bas′kit, -bäs′-), *n.* a basket or other container for wastepaper or other small or light items of dry trash.

waste·ful (wāst′fəl), *adj.* using or spending too much: *to be wasteful of water.* —**waste′ful·ly,** *adv.* —**waste′ful·ness,** *n.* —**Syn.** extravagant, prodigal, improvident.

waste·land (wāst′land′, -lənd), *n.* **1.** land in its natural, uncultivated state: *The now barren wasteland covered with ice and snow 200 feet to two miles deep* (Science News Letter). **2.** an area despoiled or ruined by poor management or other excess: *a sprawling mass of expressways, cloverleaves, bridges, viaducts, airports, garages, operating in an urban wasteland* (Lewis Mumford).

waste·lot (wāst′lot′), *n. Canadian.* a vacant lot in a city, especially one neglected and left to run to weeds: *Untidy streets and wastelots . . . do their best to make us feel that life is drab and disheartening* (Maclean's).

waste·ness (wāst′nis), *n.* the state of lying waste or being barren; desolation.

 PRONUNCIATION KEY: hat, āge, cãre, fär; let, ēqual, tėrm; it, īce; hot, ōpen, ôrder; oil, out; cup, pu̇t, rüle;

waste·pa·per (wāst′pā′pər), *n.* paper thrown away or to be thrown away as useless or worthless. —*adj.* of or for wastepaper: *a wastepaper basket.*
waste pipe, a pipe for carrying off waste water, etc., from any plumbing fixture except toilets.
wast·er (wās′tər), *n.* a person or thing that wastes; squanderer; spendthrift. —**Syn.** prodigal.
wast·ing (wās′ting), *adj.* **1.** laying waste; devastating. **2.** gradually destructive to the body: *a wasting disease.* —*n.* gradual decay of life or organic tissue; gradual loss of strength and vitality: *The disease . . . a progressive wasting of the muscles which causes helplessness* (Newsweek).
wasting asset, *Accounting.* any asset that progressively decreases in value through depletion or exhaustion, such as a mine, oil well, stand of timber, or other natural resource.
wast·rel (wās′trəl), *n.* **1.** an idle, worthless person; good-for-nothing. **2.** a waster; spendthrift. **3.** something useless, inferior, or imperfect. [< *waster* + *-el,* a diminutive suffix]
wast·ry, wast·rie, or **wast·er·y** (wās′trē), *n. Scottish.* reckless extravagance, especially in living.
wat[1] (wät, wot), *n. Scottish.* wet.
wat[2] (wät, wot), *v.t., v.i. Scottish.* to know; wot.
wat[3] (wät), *n.* a Siamese Buddhist temple: *Gaze at Bombay's ghats, wonder at wats in Bangkok* (New Yorker). [< Thai *wat*]
watch (woch, wôch), *v.t.* **1.** to look at; observe with care or interest: *to watch people passing by, watch a play, watch an operation.* **2.** to keep in mental view; stay informed about: *to watch a person's career, watch the stockmarket.* **3.** to look or wait for with care and attention: *The police watched the prisoner.* **4.** to keep guard over; tend: *a shepherd watching his flock. The dog was supposed to watch the little boy.* —*v.i.* **1.** to look attentively or carefully: *Medical students watched while the doctor performed the operation.* **2.** to look or wait (for) with care and attention; be very careful: *The boy watched for a chance to cross the street.* **3.** to keep guard: *He watched throughout the night.* **4.** to stay awake for some purpose: *The nurse watches with the sick.* **5.** to remain awake for devotional purposes; keep vigil.
watch out, *Informal.* to look out; be on one's guard: *The ways of God are strange. You have to watch out for any chances that He gives you* (New Yorker).
watch over, to guard or supervise; protect or preserve from danger, harm, error, etc.: *The eye of the rulers is required always to watch over the young* (Benjamin Jowett).
—*n.* **1.** a careful looking; attitude of attention: *Be on the watch for automobiles when you cross the street.* **2.** a protecting; guarding: *A man keeps watch over the bank at night.* **3.** a staying awake for some purpose. **4. a.** a person or persons kept to guard and protect: *The man's cry aroused the night watch, who came running to his aid.* **b.** a period of time for guarding: *a watch in the night.* **c.** *Archaic.* the duty or post of a guard or watchman: *to stand upon one's watch.* **5.** *Nautical.* **a.** one of the periods of duty of one part (commonly one half) of a ship's crew, usually lasting four hours. **b.** the part of a crew on duty at the same time. **6.** one of the periods into which the night was regularly divided in ancient times: three, and later four, among the Hebrews, four or five among the Greeks, four among the Romans. **7.** a spring-driven device for telling time, small enough to be carried in a pocket or worn on the wrist. **8.** any device for indicating the passage of time, as a ship's chronometer or a candle marked into sections, each of which requires a certain amount of time to burn.
—*adj.* of or for a watch (timepiece).
[Old English *wæccan*]
—**Syn.** *v.t.* **1.** view. **4.** protect. *-n.* **1.** vigilance. **2.** surveillance. **4. a.** watchman. **7.** timepiece.
watch·a·ble (woch′ə bəl, wôch′-), *adj.* pleasant to watch; viewable.
watch and ward, the old custom of watching by day and night in towns and cities, as in medieval times.
keep watch and ward, to keep constant vigilance by night and day.
watch·band (woch′band′, wôch′-), *n.* a band of leather, metal, cloth, etc., to fasten a watch on the wrist.
watch cap, a snugly fitting cap of knitted blue wool worn by sailors on watch in cold weather, originally especially as part of their uniform by enlisted men in the U.S. Navy.
watch·case (woch′kās′, wôch′-), *n.* the outer covering for the works of a watch, usually exclusive of the glass face.
watch chain, a chain attached to a watch and fastened to one's clothing or worn, especially by women, around the neck.
watch·dog (woch′dôg′, -dog′; wôch′-), *n., adj., v.* **-dogged, -dog·ging.** —*n.* **1.** a dog kept to guard property. **2.** a watchful guardian.
—*adj.* having to do with or characteristic of a watchdog: *The City Council authorized Mayor Wagner to appoint a watchdog committee to see that the taxicab fleets did not retain the increase for themselves* (New York Times).
—*v.t. Informal.* to guard vigilantly; watch carefully.
watch·er (woch′ər, wôch′-), *n.* a person who watches. —**Syn.** observer.
watch·es of the night (woch′iz, wôch′-), the nighttime.
watch·et (woch′it, wôch′-), *Archaic.* —*n.* **1.** a light blue. **2.** a light-blue fabric. —*adj.* light-blue. [< Old French *wachet;* origin uncertain]
watch fire, a fire kept burning during the night, especially for the use of a sentinel, party, or person on watch.
watch fob, a fob chain.
watch·ful (woch′fəl, wôch′-), *adj.* **1.** watching carefully; on the lookout; wide-awake: *to be watchful against errors.* **2.** *Archaic.* **a.** wakeful; sleepless. **b.** (of time) passed in wakefulness. —**watch′ful·ly,** *adv.* —**watch′ful·ness,** *n.*
—**Syn. 1. Watchful, vigilant, alert** mean wide-awake and attentive or on the lookout. **Watchful** means paying close attention or keeping careful guard: *He is watchful of his health.* **Vigilant** means being especially and necessarily watchful: *Because the enemy was so close, they kept a particularly vigilant watch.* **Alert** means being wide-awake and ready for whatever may happen: *The alert driver avoided an accident.*
watch glass, 1. a watch crystal. **2.** a thin, concave piece of glass used as a receptacle for small objects under close examination.
watch guard, a chain, cord, or ribbon for securing a watch when worn on the person.
watch hand, any of the hands of a watch; the hour hand, minute hand, or second hand.
watch·ing brief (woch′ing, wôch′-), **1.** a brief instructing a lawyer to observe proceedings on one's behalf. **2.** a watchful attitude; surveillance: *No less important is the utilisation section which regards itself as holding a watching brief for timber growers and traders by following developments in research* (New Scientist).
watch·keep·er (woch′kē′pər, wôch′-), *n.* **1.** a person who keeps watch. **2.** a person who serves as a member of a watch on board ship; an officer in charge of a watch.
watch·keep·ing (woch′kē′ping, wôch′-), *n.* the work or duty of a watchkeeper.
watch·mak·er (woch′mā′kər, wôch′-), *n.* a person who makes and repairs watches.
watch·mak·ing (woch′mā′king, wôch′-), *n.* the business of making and repairing watches.
watch·man (woch′mən, wôch′-), *n., pl.* **-men.** a man employed to guard or watch over property, a building, etc., especially while it is otherwise unoccupied, not in use, etc., as during the night.
watch meeting, a church service held at night, especially on the last night of the year until midnight.
watch night, 1. New Year's Eve, among the Methodists and certain other denominations, a time for religious services until the arrival of the new year. **2.** a watch meeting.
watch pocket, a small pocket for holding a watch.
watch·tow·er (woch′tou′ər, wôch′-), *n.* a tower or other high structure from which a watch is kept for enemies, fires, ships, etc.; lookout station.
watch·word (woch′wėrd′, wôch′-), *n.* **1.** a secret word or short phrase that allows a person to pass a guard; password. **2.** a word or short phrase used as embodying the guiding principle or rule of action of a party or individual; motto; slogan: *"Forward" is our watchword. His watchword is honor, his pay is renown* (Scott).
wa·ter (wôt′ər, wot′-), *n.* **1.** the liquid that constitutes rain, oceans, rivers, lakes, and ponds. Perfectly pure water is a transparent, colorless (except as seen in large quantities, when it has a blue tint), tasteless, scentless compound of hydrogen (11.188 per cent by weight) and oxygen (88.812 per cent). It freezes at 32 degrees Fahrenheit or 0 degrees centigrade, boils at 212 degrees Fahrenheit or 100 degrees centigrade, and has its maximum density at 39 degrees Fahrenheit or 4 degrees centigrade, one cubic centimeter weighing one gram. *Formula:* H_2O **2.** any of various watery substances or secretions occurring in or discharged from the human body, especially: **a.** tears: *a . . . rap on the nose . . . which brought the water into his eyes* (Dickens). **b.** saliva: *the thought of . . . oysters brought the water to his mouth* (W. S. Gilbert). **c.** urine: *to void water.* **d.** any of various other bodily liquids, as perspiration or serum. **3. a.** any liquid preparation that suggests water: *lavender water, barley water.* **b.** *Pharmacology.* a saturated solution in water of some volatile or aromatic substance: *ammonia water.* **4. a.** a body of water; sea, lake, river, etc.: *to cross the water on a ferry.* **b.** an underground flow, pool, etc., of water: *to strike water at 267 feet.* **5. a.** the water of a river, lake, etc., with reference to its relative depth or height: *to reach low water in August, to sail at high water.* **b.** the depth of water, or of a body of water, with regard to suitability for navigation: *to sail in shallow water, to require 22 feet of water when loaded.* **6.** the surface of a body of water: *to swim under the water.* **7.** the degree of clearness and brilliance of a precious stone: *A diamond of the first water is a very clear and brilliant one.* **8.** a wavy marking on silk, mohair, metal, etc. **9.** *Finance.* **a.** additional shares or securities issued without a corresponding increase of capital or assets. **b.** an inflationary quality; excess: *It has been suggested that there may be some water in current steel backlogs, meaning that many users may have placed orders some time ago hoping to beat the obviously forthcoming steel price increase* (New York Times). **10.** a water color.
above water, a. above the surface of the water; not submerged; afloat: *Our Carpenter . . . was lost for want of having fastened on somewhat that might have kept him above water* (J. Davies). **b.** out of trouble or difficulty: *A number of struggling men, who have managed to keep above water during the bad seasons, must now go under* (Field, Farm, Garden).
back water. See under **back**[1], *v.*
by water, on a ship or boat: *to ship by water.*
hold water, to stand the test; be true, dependable, effective, etc.: *I think these documents will hold water* (G. Allen). *"Brothers," said he, "the demand of Loggerhead will not hold water"* (Tobias Smollett).
in deep water, in trouble, difficulty, or distress: *Once he had been very nearly in deep water because Mrs. Proudie had taken it in dudgeon that a certain young rector, who had been left a widower, had a very pretty governess for his children* (Anthony Trollope).
like water, very freely: *to spend money like water.*
like water off a duck's back, without having any effect: *It had all passed off like water off a duck's back* (L.B. Walford).
make water, (of a boat, ship, etc.) to take in water through leaks or over the side: *Almost simultaneously a similar SOS was received from the stricken Dutch vessel. It said: "Dutch vessel making water, require immediate assistance"* (New York Times).
of the first water, of the highest degree: *That boy is a scamp of the first water.*
pour, throw, or **dash cold water on,** to discourage: *Congressmen . . . have poured cold water on that plan* (Wall Street Journal).
take (the) water, a. (of an animal, bird, or person) to go swimming: *I heard a splash and saw a deer take the water 300 yards or so above me* (Scribner's Monthly). **b.** (of a ship) to be launched: *The cruiser Kent . . . took the water without a hitch* (Scotsman).

c. to embark; take ship: *For see, the Queen's barge lies at the stairs, as if her Majesty were about to take water* (Scott). **d.** *Western U.S.* to leave abruptly; run away: *The fellow, who was really a coward, though nearly twice as big as myself, took water at once* (L. Roberts).

take (the) waters, to drink mineral water at a health resort, usually in a scheduled course of treatment: *He went to Hot Springs last winter to take the waters.*

tread water, a. to keep oneself from sinking by moving the feet up and down: *Barely managing to breathe, he treaded water until the lifeguard pulled him out.* **b.** to be in a state of uncertainty; be unsettled: *The channel-tunnel discussions had acted as a negative influence, and . . . British Railways had largely been treading water while awaiting the decision* (London Times).

water over the dam, something that is finished and cannot be changed or remedied: *Mr. Ferrers did not like talking about the past. "That's all water over the dam"* (New Yorker).

waters, a. flowing water: *the broad waters of the Mississippi.* **b.** water moving in waves; the sea; the high seas: *And hear the mighty waters rolling evermore* (Wordsworth). **c.** flood water; floods: *The waters are out in Lincolnshire* (Dickens). **d.** spring water; mineral water: *to drink the waters.* **e.** the amniotic fluid: *The amnion, which encloses the amniotic fluid, is often called the bag of waters.*

—*v.t.* **1.** to sprinkle or wet with water: *to water the streets, to water grass.* **2. a.** to supply with drinking water: *to water cattle.* **b.** to supply water to (an army, ship, engine, etc.); fill the tanks, reservoirs, etc., of: *He seized the town . . . and watered his ship . . . at the enemy's wells* (Charles Kingsley). **3. a.** to supply (land, crops, etc.) with water by means of a watering can, hose, etc., or by irrigation. **b.** to be the source of water supply for (a region, district, etc.): *New England is well watered by rivers and brooks.* **4.** to weaken by adding water: *It is against the law to sell watered milk.* **5.** to produce a wavy marking on (silk, etc.) by sprinkling it with water and passing it through a calender. **6.** *Finance.* to increase (stock, etc.) by issue of additional shares or securities without a corresponding addition in capital or assets. —*v.i.* **1. a.** to fill with water; flow with tears: *Her eyes watered.* **b.** (of the mouth) to secrete abundant saliva, usually in anticipation of food. **2.** to drink water; get drinking water. **3.** (of a ship) to take in a supply of fresh water on board: *The Utrecht . . . watered, and proceeded on her voyage* (Frederick Marryat).

water down, a. to reduce in strength by diluting with water: *to water down whiskey.* **b.** to weaken the force or strength of by addition or alteration: *An amendment to almost the same effect—though somewhat watered down in wording—was promptly offered* (Newsweek). **c.** to reduce in quality or value: *How can the needs of the slow learner be met more adequately without stultifying and watering down the intellectual performance of brighter pupils?* (Atlantic).

—*adj.* **1.** of, connected with, or designed for the holding, storing, conveying, or distributing of water: *a water jug, a water pipe, a water system.* **2.** done or used in or on water: *water sports.* **3.** prepared with water; diluted with water; mixed with water: *water paint.* **4.** at or near the edge of a body of water: *water frontage.* **5.** associated with the water; having rule over water: *a water spirit, a water god.* **6.** growing in or near water; having water as its habitat: *water plants, water insects.* **7.** worked, driven, or powered by water.

[Old English *wæter*] —**wa′ter·er,** *n.*

wa·ter·age (wôt′ər ij, wot′-), *n.* **1.** conveyance by ship, boat, etc.; transport by water. **2.** the charge or payment for this.

water arum, a plant of the arum family growing in moist woods and marshes, with greenish-yellow flowers that bloom in early spring and red berries.

water back, a tanklike receptacle or reservoir for heating water, built into the back of a wood or coal stove.

water bag, 1. a bag of skin or leather used for holding or carrying water, especially in Oriental countries. **2.** the reticulum of an animal. **3.** the membranous sac filled with amniotic fluid; bag of waters. **4.** a hot-water bottle.

water bailiff, *British.* an official responsible for the enforcement of bylaws relating to fishing waters: *Water bailiffs always interpret the taking of fish as an infringement of the rights they are employed to protect* (London Times).

water ballet, a rhythmic, synchronized dance performed by swimmers in the water.

wa·ter-based (wôt′ər bāst′, wot′-), *adj.* using water as the base, thinner, or emulsifying agent: *water-based paint.*

water bath, 1. a bath composed of water, rather than vapor, etc. **2.** *Chemistry.* a device for heating or cooling something by means of a surrounding medium of water.

water bear, a tardigrade animal.

Water Bearer, Aquarius (a northern constellation).

wat·er-bear·ing (wôt′ər bãr′ing, wot′-), *adj.* **1.** (of a stratum) through which water percolates; holding water: *Because of substantial water-bearing fissures, considerable difficulties have been experienced since the start of mining operations* (London Times). **2.** (of a country) producing water; not arid.

water beetle, any of the aquatic beetles having the legs broad and fringed so as to be well adapted for swimming, as the diving beetle and whirligig beetle.

water bird, any bird that swims or wades in water; aquatic bird.

water biscuit, a cracker made of flour, shortening, and water.

wa·ter·blink (wôt′ər blingk′, wot′-), *n.* a spot of dull or dark color in the sky, due to reflection from open water beneath, seen in arctic regions.

water blister, a blister containing a clear, watery fluid derived from serum.

water bloom, a discoloration on a pond, lake, or other slow-moving body of water, produced by a sudden accumulation of algae or other microscopic plants or animals.

water boa, the anaconda of South America.

water boatman, any of a family of water bugs with long, oarlike hind legs that enable them to move through the water at great speed.

water boiler, an atomic reactor that uses a uranyl salt in heavy water as its fuel and coolant to produce steam for electric power.

water bomb, a paper bag or other container filled with water, usually dropped by hand on a target below: *They received only a pelting by water bombs apparently thrown by irate office workers* (New York Times).

wa·ter-borne (wôt′ər bôrn′, -bōrn′; wot′-), *adj.* **1.** supported by water, especially so as to be clear of the ground or bottom upon which it has rested; floating; afloat. **2.** conveyed by a ship, boat, or the like; transported by water.

water bottle, a bottle, bag, etc., for holding water.

wa·ter-bound (wôt′ər bound′, wot′-), *adj.* **1.** shut in by water or floods: *While water-bound, it [a foraging party] was attacked by guerrillas* (New York Tribune). **2.** (of macadamized roads) solidified by rolling and watering: *Oiled gravel roads are a natural development of the water-bound macadam variety* (New Scientist).

water boy, a boy who supplies or distributes water to a group, such as soldiers, laborers, etc.: *He [Mr. Madigan] started as a water boy before World War I, toting water to thirsty construction workers* (New York Times).

wa·ter·brain (wôt′ər brān′, wot′-), *n.* gid, a disease of sheep.

water brash, pyrosis. [< *water* + *brash*[1] rash]

wa·ter·buck (wôt′ər buk′, wot′-), *n., pl.* **-bucks** or (*collectively*) **-buck. 1.** either of two African antelopes that frequent rivers and marshes. **2.** any of several other antelopes of similar habits. [< Afrikaans *waterbok* < Dutch]

Waterbuck (def. 1) (3 ft. high at the shoulder)

water buffalo, a wild ox, native to India and now widely used in southern Asia and the Philippines as a draft animal, etc.; water ox. See **buffalo** for picture.

water bug, 1. any of certain hemipterous insects that live in, on, or near the water, especially any of several large bugs with flattened bodies, grasping front legs, and a poisonous bite. **2.** the croton bug (a kind of small cockroach).

wa·ter·bus (wôt′ər bus′, wot′-), *n., pl.* **-bus·es** or **-bus·ses.** a motorboat used to carry passengers along a certain route on a canal or waterway: *Part of the gondoliers' woe stems from the motorized water-bus* (San Francisco Chronicle).

wa·ter-butt (wôt′ər but′, wot′-), *n.* a large open cask set up on end to receive and store rain water.

water cabbage, water lettuce.

water carrier, 1. a person or thing that transports passengers, goods, etc., by water, instead of by land, railway, or air. **2.** a man or animal that carries water, especially, in Oriental countries, a native who supplies an establishment or a number of troops with water. **3.** a tank or other vessel for carrying water: *It is, therefore, necessary for fire brigades to have water carriers available* (Manchester Guardian Weekly). **4.** an open channel for water, as in an irrigated meadow. **5.** a rain cloud.

Water Carrier, Aquarius (a northern constellation).

water chestnut or **caltrop, 1.** any of a group of aquatic plants, whose nutlike fruit contains a single, large, edible seed, especially a species native to Eurasia that has become a troublesome weed in parts of the United States. **2.** the fruit.

water chinquapin, 1. a North American water plant, a variety of nelumbo, that bears yellow flowers and edible, nutlike seeds. **2.** its seed.

wa·ter·chute (wôt′ər shüt′, wot′-), *n.* **1.** a gutter or channel for the overflow of water. **2.** an artificial cascade for the amusement or exercise of sliding down the rapids in a boat or by swimming. Also, **water-shoot.**

wa·ter-clear (wôt′ər klir′, wot′-), *adj.* as clear as water; very clear: *Not from her did the young ones get those water-clear eyes* (Katherine Anne Porter).

water clock, an instrument, as a clepsydra, for measuring time by the flow of water.

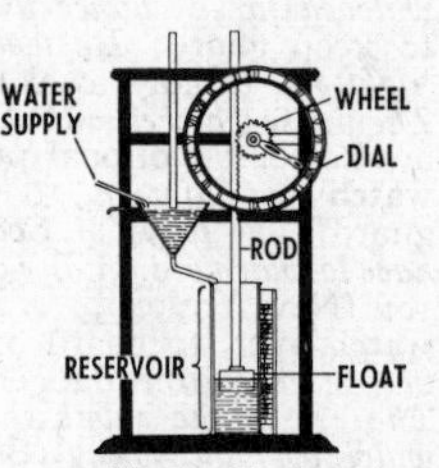

Water Clock
Water is piped through funnel into reservoir. As the water level is raised in reservoir, a float, and cogged wheel to which float is attached, rise. Cogs in rod and cogs in wheel mesh, moving the hand around the dial.

water closet, 1. a toilet flushed by water. **2. a.** a small room or enclosure containing such a toilet. **b.** a room containing such a toilet and also a hand basin, shower or tub, etc.; bathroom. **3.** any enclosed place for urination or defecation; privy; latrine. *Abbr.:* w.c.

water color, 1. a pigment for which water and not oil is used as a solvent. **2.** the art or method of painting or drawing with these pigments, done largely with washes (which may range from transparent to opaque) on paper. Opaque water color (gouache) is sometimes used with transparent in the same painting. **3.** a picture painted with water colors.

wa·ter-col·or (wôt′ər kul′ər, wot′-), *adj.* having to do with, used for, or made with water colors.

wa·ter-col·or·ist (wôt′ər kul′ər ist, wot′-), *n.* an artist who paints in water colors.

water conversion, the conversion of sea water into fresh water.

wa·ter-cool (wôt′ər kül′, wot′-), *v.t.* to reduce the heat produced by combustion, friction, etc., by causing water to pass through a chamber or casing (water jacket) surrounding all or part of the mechanism of (an engine, motor, machine gun, etc.).

water cooler, any device for cooling water, or for cooling something by means of water: *Another executive foresees the day when machines will be able to do everything in the office except sit on the boss' lap and hang around the water cooler* (New York Times).

wa·ter·course (wôt′ər kôrs′, -kōrs; wot′-), *n.* **1.** a stream of water; river; brook. **2.** the channel or bed of a stream of water: *dried-up watercourses.* **3.** an artificial channel for the conveyance of water, as an irrigation ditch.

wa·ter·craft (wôt′ər kraft′, -kräft′; wot′-), *n.* **1.** activity or skill in water sports, such as boating, swimming, etc. **2. a.** a ship or boat. **b.** ships and boats collectively.
water crake, 1. spotted crake. **2.** water ouzel.
water crane, a swinging pipe or other apparatus for supplying water from an elevated tank, as to locomotive tenders or watering carts.
water cress, 1. a hardy perennial of the mustard family, found in the wild state in and near springs and small running streams, and also cultivated for its pungent leaves that are used for salad and as a garnish. **2.** its leaves. —**wa′ter-cress′,** *adj.*

Water Cress (def. 1)
(2 to 3 ft. high)

water culture, hydroponics.
water cure, 1. treatment of disease by the use of water; hydropathy. **2.** *Slang.* the forcing of water down a person's throat in such a quantity as to cause severe physical pain, through distention of the stomach, used as a means of torture.
water cycle, a cycle whereby water evaporates from oceans, lakes, etc., to form clouds that move over land areas and fall as rain, the run-off largely flowing back to oceans, lakes, etc.
water deer, a small deer without antlers, that frequents river banks in China and Korea. It resembles the musk deer.
water diviner, a person who searches for water with a divining rod; dowser.
water dog, 1. a dog that is trained or bred for swimming, especially one trained to retrieve game from the water. **2.** *Informal.* a man thoroughly at home either on or in the water: **a.** a sailor, especially an experienced one; sea dog. **b.** a good swimmer. **3.** *U.S.* the mud puppy (a kind of salamander).
wa·ter·drop (wôt′ər drop′, wot′-), *n.* **1.** a drop of water: *The waterdrops shoot from the salad basket and fall like stars to the dreary wooden floor* (New Yorker). **2.** a tear; teardrop: *Let not women's weapons, waterdrops, stain my man's cheeks* (Shakespeare).
wa·tered (wôt′ərd, wot′-), *adj.* having a wavy, lustrous pattern or marking, as that produced on a silk fabric by moisture and pressure, or that formed naturally or artificially on the surface of certain steels.
wa·tered-down (wôt′ərd doun′, wot′-), *adj.* **1.** diluted with water: *We half slept through the bread and butter with jam, and flat, icy, watered-down milk, totally unrelated to milk straight from a cow* (New Yorker). **2.** weakened in character or force by alteration or addition: *The measure is a watered-down version of the bill the Senate had approved* (Wall Street Journal).
watered stock, 1. *U.S.* cattle given little water while being driven to market, and then given all the water they can drink to increase their weight before weighing in. **2.** shares or securities that have been increased without a corresponding increase in capital or assets.
wa·ter·fall (wôt′ər fôl′, wot′-), *n.* **1.** a fall of water from a high place; cascade; cataract. **2. a.** a chignon. **b.** a wave of hair falling down the neck below the chignon or net.
wa·ter·fern (wôt′ər fėrn′, wot′-), *n.* any of a group of ferns, growing in boggy places and wet woods, that form tufts of large bipinnate fronds.
wa·ter·find·er (wôt′ər fīn′dər, wot′-), *n.* a dowser.
water flea, a cladoceran, especially a freshwater kind that swims with a jerky movement; daphnia.
wa·ter·flood (wôt′ər flud′, wot′-), *v.t.* to subject (an oil field or oil well) to waterflooding. —*n.* a waterflooding operation: *Tax dollars wanted to develop a secondary recovery oil project located between two major oil companies' successful waterfloods* (Wall Street Journal).
wa·ter·flood·ing (wôt′ər flud′ing, wot′-), *n.* the underground pumping of water into an oil field or oil well to force residual oil to the surface or toward producing wells.
wa·ter·flow (wôt′ər flō′, wot′-), *n.* **1.** the flow or current of water: *A push of a button restores waterflow through the sink faucet* (Science News Letter). **2.** the amount of water flowing per unit of time: *The work concludes with articles on . . . meters for measuring waterflow* (Westminster Review).
wa·ter·fly (wôt′ər flī′, wot′-), *n., pl.* **-flies. 1.** any fly that frequents water or the waterside. **2.** the stone fly, an insect whose nymphs are aquatic.
Wa·ter·ford glass (wôt′ər fərd, wot′-), fine glass or glassware of a smoky color, made in Waterford, Ireland, from 1783 to 1851, and again since 1951.
wa·ter·fowl (wôt′ər foul′, wot′-), *n., pl.* **-fowls** or (*collectively*) **-fowl.** a water bird, especially a swimming one.
wa·ter·front (wôt′ər frunt′, wot′-), *n.* **1.** the part of a city beside a river, lake, or harbor. **2.** land at the water's edge. —*adj.* of or having to do with the waterfront, especially with its harbor activities: *A prime reason for waterfront turbulence is the lack of understanding between the dock worker and his employer* (New York Times).
water gage, water gauge.
water gap, a gap in a mountain ridge through which a stream flows. —**Syn.** flume.
water garden, 1. a garden with a running brook at its center. **2.** a garden for aquatic plants.
water gas, a poisonous gas consisting largely of carbon monoxide and hydrogen, made by passing steam over very hot coal or coke. It is used for lighting when carbureted, and sometimes for fuel. —**wa′ter-gas′,** *adj.*
water gate, 1. a gate or gateway through which water passes. **2.** a gate that controls the flow of water; sluice or floodgate. **3.** a gate (of a town, a castle, etc.) opening on water.
water gauge, 1. any of various apparatuses for measuring quantity of water, as in a tank, boiler, etc., or flow of water, as from or into a reservoir. **2.** the part of such an apparatus by which the datum of measurement at a given moment is recorded, as a calibrated glass tube in which the level of water indicates the level inside a tank, boiler, etc.
wa·ter-girt (wôt′ər gėrt′, wot′-), *adj.* surrounded by water: *On May 23 a sleek gray Swedish cruiser sailed from its anchorage in the shadow of the palace in water-girt Stockholm* (Newsweek).
water glass, or **wa·ter·glass** (wôt′ər-glas′, -gläs′; wot′-), *n.* **1. a.** a glass to hold water; tumbler. **b.** *Obsolete.* a glass finger bowl. **2.** an aqueous jellylike, or powdery compound of sodium, silicon, and oxygen that solidifies when exposed to the air, used especially in soaps, in preserving eggs and wood, in cement manufacture, and in fireproofing wood, cloth, and paper: *Water glass is [also] used in the purification of fats and oils, in refining petroleum and in the manufacture of silica gel* (World Book Encyclopedia). **3.** a water clock; clepsydra. **4.** an instrument for making observations beneath the surface of water, consisting of a bucketlike or boxlike frame with a glass bottom. **5.** a water gauge.
water grass, 1. any of various grasses and grasslike plants growing in water. **2.** *British Dialect.* water cress.
wa·ter·guard (wôt′ər gärd′, wot′-), *n.* **1.** a body of men employed by a custom house to watch ships in order to prevent smuggling or other violations of law. **2.** a member of such a body.
water gum, 1. (in the United States) a tupelo. **2.** (in Australia) any of several trees of the myrtle family, growing in moist places.
water gun, water pistol.
water hammer, 1. the concussion of water in a pipe when its flow is suddenly stopped, or when live steam is admitted. **2.** the sound of this, typically a sharp thump or series of thumps.
wa·ter-ham·mer (wôt′ər ham′ər, wot′-), *v.i.* (of a pipe, system of pipes, etc.) to give off a sharp thump or series of thumps, from concussion of water or live steam.
water hazard, a stream, pond, or ditch filled with water on a golf course, intended as an obstacle: *If a golfer's ball goes into one of these water hazards, . . . he must add an extra stroke to his score as a penalty* (World Book Encyclopedia).
water haze, a light-gray haze composed of small drops of water mixed with smoke or dust.
water hemlock, any of a group of poisonous bog herbs of the parsley family, of north temperate regions that have finely divided leaves and white flowers, as the spotted cowbane.
water hen, 1. the moor hen. **2.** the coot of America.
water hole, a hole in the ground where water collects; small pond; pool.
water hyacinth, a floating or rooting aquatic plant with violet or blue flowers and ovate leaves with inflated, bladderlike petioles, native to tropical South America, and cultivated elsewhere. When introduced into inland waters of Florida and Louisiana, it became a troublesome weed, seriously impeding navigation.
water ice, 1. *Especially British.* a frozen mixture of fruit juice, sugar, and water; sherbet. **2.** solid ice formed by the direct freezing of water, and not by the compacting of snow.
wa·ter-inch (wôt′ər inch′, wot′-), *n. Obsolete.* a unit equal to the quantity of water flowing in a given period, as one minute or 24 hours, through a circular opening one inch in diameter.
wa·ter·i·ness (wôt′ər ē nis, wot′-), *n.* the state of being watery; watery quality or nature.
wa·ter·ing (wôt′ər ing, wot′-), *n.* the act of a person or thing that waters.
—*adj.* **1.** (of eyes) discharging watery fluid; running. **2.** (of the mouth) secreting saliva profusely in anticipation of appetizing food. **3.** irrigating.
watering can, a can with a spout for sprinkling water on plants, etc.
watering cart, a cart designed to carry water for watering plants or the streets.
watering hole, 1. water hole. **2.** *U.S. Informal.* a resort where there is bathing, boating, etc.; watering place. **3.** *U.S. Slang.* **a.** a popular or stylish night club, restaurant, etc. **b.** any popular or stylish public place or establishment: *a watering hole for artists, politicians, etc.*
watering place, 1. *Especially British.* **a.** a resort with springs containing mineral water. **b.** a resort where there is bathing, boating, etc. **2.** a place where water may be obtained.
watering pot, *British.* watering can.
watering trough, 1. a trough in which water is provided for domestic animals. **2.** a long, shallow trough parallel to the rails, from which water is scooped by steam locomotives in passing.
wa·ter·ish (wôt′ər ish, wot′-), *adj.* watery. —**wa′ter·ish·ly,** *adv.* —**wa′ter·ish·ness,** *n.*
water jacket, a casing with water in it, put around something to keep it cool or at a certain temperature.
wa·ter-jack·et (wôt′ər jak′it, wot′-), *v.t.* to enclose in or fit with a water jacket.
wa·ter-jet (wôt′ər jet′, wot′-), *adj.* operated by a stream of water sent out with force from a small opening: *a water-jet loom.*
water jump, an obstacle consisting of or including a body of water across which horses must jump in a steeplechase.
wa·ter·leaf (wôt′ər lēf′, wot′-), *n., pl.* **-leaves.** any of a group of North American herbs with clusters of white or purplish flowers.
waterleaf family, a group of dicotyledonous herbs having characteristics similar to those of the borage family and commonly cultivated as ornamentals. The family includes the waterleaf, baby blue-eyes, and tarbush.
wa·ter·less (wôt′ər lis, wot′-), *adj.* using or containing little or no water: *waterless cooking. We know that the moon is an airless, waterless world* (Atlantic).
water lettuce, a common floating plant of the tropics with a rosette of rounded and downy leaves: *Water lettuce . . . spends its life afloat, supported by spongy, air-filled tissue on the bottom surface of its leaves* (Scientific American).
water level, 1. a. the surface level of a stream, lake, or other body of water. **b.** the surface level of a body of static water, as in a tank, boiler, or cistern. **2.** the plane below which the rock or soil is saturated with water; water table. **3.** *Nautical.* water line. **4.** an instrument for showing the level of fluid, in which water is used instead of alcohol.

water lily, **1.** any of a group of water plants having flat, floating leaves and showy, fragrant, white, pink, yellow, or blue flowers. A common North American variety has fragrant, white or pink flowers; pond lily; water nymph. **2.** any other plant of the water-lily family. **3.** any showy-flowered aquatic plant. **4.** the flower of any of these plants.

Common American Water Lily (def. 1) (flower, 3 to 4 in. across)

wa·ter-lil·y family (wôt′ər lil′ē, wot′-), a widely distributed group of dicotyledonous water plants that are herbs and are characterized by large floating leaves and showy flowers, as the water lily, fanwort, lotus, and spatterdock.

water line, or **wa·ter·line** (wôt′ər līn′, wot′-), *n.* **1.** the line where the surface of the water touches the side of a ship or boat. **2.** any of several lines marked on the hull of a ship to show the depth to which it sinks when unloaded, partly loaded, or fully loaded.

wa·ter-log (wôt′ər lôg′, -log′; wot′-), *v.t., v.i.,* **-logged, -log·ging.** to cause to be or to become water-logged.

wa·ter-logged (wôt′ər lôgd′, -logd′; wot′-), *adj.* **1.** so full of water that it will barely float. **2.** thoroughly soaked with water. **3.** bogged down.

Wa·ter·loo (wôt′ər lü, wot′-; wôt′ər lü′, wot′-), *n.* any decisive or crushing defeat. [< *Waterloo,* a town in Belgium, scene of Napoleon's final defeat in 1815]

water main, a large pipe for carrying water, especially one by which water is supplied, through smaller pipes, to many buildings or to various parts of a large building.

wa·ter·man (wôt′ər mən, wot′-), *n., pl.* **-men. 1.** a man who works on a boat or among boats; boatman. **2.** an oarsman.

wa·ter·man·ship (wôt′ər mən ship, wot′-), *n.* the art of a waterman; skill in rowing or managing boats.

water marigold, an aquatic composite herb of North America, having yellow flower heads and submerged, finely dissected leaves.

wa·ter·mark (wôt′ər märk′, wot′-), *n.* **1.** a mark showing how high water has risen or how low it has fallen. **2. a.** a distinguishing mark or device impressed in the substance of a sheet of paper during manufacture, usually barely noticeable except when the sheet is held against the light. **b.** the metal design from which the impression is made, usually an ornamental figure of wire, fastened on the mold or dandy roll, pressure of which makes the paper thinner and more translucent at that point.
—*v.t.* **1.** to put a watermark in: *Some letter paper is watermarked.* **2.** to impress (a design or device) as a watermark.

water meadow, a meadow kept fertile by the overflow of adjoining streams from time to time: *He also looks after the cattle and sheep in the water meadows* (Manchester Guardian).

wa·ter·mel·on (wôt′ər mel′ən, wot′-), *n.* **1.** the large, roundish or oblong fruit of a slender, trailing vine of the gourd family, having an edible, red, pink, or yellow pulp with much sweet, watery juice, and a hard, green rind. **2.** the vine bearing this fruit.

water meter, an apparatus for measuring and recording the amount of water drawn from a water main, public water system, etc., by a particular user or group of users.

water milfoil, any of a group of perennial water plants, having very finely divided submerged leaves.

water mill, a mill, especially a grist mill, whose machinery is run by water power.

water mite, water spider.

water moccasin, **1.** a poisonous snake, a pit viper like the rattlesnake, that lives in swamps and along streams in the southern United States; cottonmouth. **2.** any of various similar but harmless snakes.

water mold, a fungus that lives in water or wet soil, feeding on decaying plants and animals, and sometimes parasitic on aquatic animals.

water motor, any form of prime mover, or motor, that is operated by the kinetic energy, pressure, or weight of water, especially a small turbine or waterwheel fitted to a pipe supplying water, as for driving sewing machines or other light machinery.

water mouse, an Australian murine rodent.

water nymph, **1.** *Greek and Roman Mythology.* a nymph or goddess living in or associated with some body of water, as a Naiad, Nereid, or Oceanid. **2.** any of a group of water plants; a water lily.

water oak, **1.** an oak found especially along streams and in swamps in the southeastern United States. **2.** any of several other American oaks.

water of crystallization, water that is present in chemical combination in certain crystalline substances. When the water is removed by heating, the crystals break up into a powder.

water of hydration, water that is present in chemical combination with some substance to form a hydrate: water of crystallization.

water on the brain, hydrocephalus.

water on the knee, a painful swelling of the knee, caused by inflammation, infection, or injury of the cartilages or membranes of the knee joint; hydroarthrosis of the knee.

water ouzel, any of a group of small water birds that are related to the thrushes, and swim and dive in deep water for food; dipper; ouzel; water crake.

water ox, water buffalo.

water parsnip, any of a group of herbs of the parsley family that grow chiefly in watery places.

water parting, a watershed or divide.

water pepper, **1.** the smartweed. **2.** any of certain closely related plants.

water pig, a large aquatic rodent of South America; capybara.

water pimpernel, **1.** brookweed. **2.** the common pimpernel.

water pipe, **1.** a pipe through which water is conducted. **2.** a hookah, narghile, or kalian.

water pipit, a variety of pipit of northern regions of both hemispheres.

water pistol, a toy pistol that shoots water taken in by suction.

wa·ter·plane (wôt′ər plān′, wot′-), *n.* an airplane adapted for alighting on, ascending from, and traveling on the water; seaplane.

water plantain, any of a group of water plants, especially a species common in shallow water in north temperate regions, whose leaves suggest those of the plantain.

water polo, a game played by two teams of seven swimmers who try to throw or push an inflated ball into the opponent's goal.

wa·ter·pot (wôt′ər pot′, wot′-), *n.* **1.** a vessel, usually of earthenware, for holding water. **2.** watering can.

water power, **1.** the power from flowing or falling water. It can be used to drive machinery and make electricity. **2.** a fall or flow of water that can supply power. **3.** the right or privilege of a mill to make use of this.

water pox, chicken pox.

wa·ter·proof (wôt′ər prüf′, wot′-), *adj.* that will not let water through; resistant to water.
—*n.* **1.** a waterproof material. **2.** *Especially British.* a waterproof coat; raincoat.
—*v.t.* to make waterproof.

wa·ter·proof·er (wôt′ər prü′fər, wot′-), *n.* **1.** a person who makes something waterproof. **2.** a waterproof material: *Invisible silicone waterproofers are extremely useful for porous brick or stone walls exposed to heavy driving rain* (London Times).

wa·ter·proof·ing (wôt′ər prü′fing, wot′-), *n.* **1.** the act or process of making waterproof. **2.** a substance, as rubber, oil, etc., used to make something waterproof.

water pump, **1.** a pump for raising water: [*He*] *stopped in the store to order a valve for the old water pump at his summer cottage* (Wall Street Journal). **2.** any of various devices for circulating water through the cooling system of an automobile, etc.

water purslane, any of several marsh plants resembling the purslane, as two species of the evening-primrose family.

water quenching, the dipping or immersion of hot steel into water to harden it by rapid cooling.

water rail, a gray and brownish rail with a long, mostly red bill, found in marshes of the Old World north of the tropics.

water rat, **1.** any of various water rodents, especially a large vole of Great Britain. **2.** muskrat. **3.** (in Australia) a water mouse. **4.** *Slang.* a person who is or poses as a sailor, longshoreman, etc., but who lives by petty thievery, smuggling, etc., rather than honest work.

wa·ter-re·pel·len·cy (wôt′ər ri pel′ən sē, wot′-), *n.* the quality of repelling water or moisture: *Water-repellency is a handicap in garments that lie close to the skin* (Wall Street Journal).

wa·ter-re·pel·lent (wôt′ər ri pel′ənt, wot′-), *adj.* impervious to water or moisture: *The duck hunter's jacket has been copied in moss-green, water-repellent cotton poplin* (New Yorker). —*n.* a chemical agent that makes something water-repellent.

wa·ter-re·sist·ance (wôt′ər ri zis′təns, wot′-), *n.* the quality of resisting the penetration of water: *There is an expanding consumption in channels where its properties of water-resistance and electrical insulation can be conveniently employed* (New Scientist).

wa·ter-re·sist·ant (wôt′ər ri zis′tənt, wot′-), *adj.* resisting the penetration of water: *His company's laboratories have turned out a tough, flexible, water-resistant film similar to cellophane* (Wall Street Journal).

water right, a riparian right.

water sapphire, a variety of iolite. [translation of French *saphir d'eau*]

wa·ter·scape (wôt′ər skāp, wot′-), *n.* scenery consisting of water, or a picture of this.

water scorpion, any of a family of large, aquatic, hemipterous insects that have a long, anal breathing tube.

water screw, a ship's propeller.

wa·ter·shed (wôt′ər shed′, wot′-), *n.* **1.** the ridge between the regions drained by two different river systems. **2.** the region drained by one river system. **3.** a critical or decisive point; turning point: *The two short papers . . . mark a watershed in the intellectual history of mankind* (Science). [< *water* + *shed*², in the Scottish sense of "portion of land." Compare German *Wasserscheide.*]

water shield, **1.** a plant of the water lily family having shield-shaped, floating leaves covered with a viscid, jellylike substance and small, dull-purple flowers. **2.** any of a group of allied plants, especially the fanwort.

wa·ter-shoot (wôt′ər shüt′, wot′-), *n.* water-chute.

water shrew, either of two amphibious shrews of North America, with the hind feet fringed with hair for swimming and running across the water.

wa·ter-sick (wôt′ər sik′, wot′-), *adj.* (of land) unworkable and unproductive because of too much irrigation.

wa·ter·side (wôt′ər sīd′, wot′-), *n.* land along the sea, a lake, a river, etc. —*adj.* **1.** of, on, or at the waterside: *waterside flowers, waterside property.* **2.** that works near the waterside or on the waterfront.

wa·ter·sid·er (wôt′ər sī′dər), *n. British.* a dockside laborer.

water ski, one of a pair of wooden skis used for gliding over water while being towed at the end of a rope by a boat.

wa·ter-ski (wôt′ər skē′, wot′-), *v.i.,* **-skied, -ski·ing.** to glide over the water on water skis: *Bronzed girls in Bikinis water-skied on the Mediterranean* (Newsweek).

water skier, a person who is using water skis.

wa·ter-ski·ing (wôt′ər skē′ing, wot′-), *n.* the sport of skiing with water skis.

wa·ter·skin (wôt′ər skin′, wot′-), *n.* a vessel or bag of skin used for the storage or transportation of water.

water snail, **1.** any of a group of gastropods that live in or frequent water. **2.** the Archimedean screw.

water snake, **1.** any of a group of nonpoisonous colubrine snakes that live in or frequent water. **2.** any of several other snakes that live in or frequent water.

wa·ter-soak (wôt′ər sōk′, wot′-), *v.t.* to soak thoroughly with water.

water softener, **1.** a chemical added to hard water to remove dissolved mineral matter. **2.** a device containing such a chemical attached to a water line to soften water coming from it.

wa·ter-soft·en·ing (wôt′ər sôf′ə ning, wot′-; -sof′-), *n.* the process of converting hard water to soft by chemical means.

wa·ter-sol·u·bil·i·ty (wôt′ər sol′yə bil′ə tē, wot′-), *n.* the quality of dissolving easily in water.

wa·ter-sol·u·ble (wôt′ər sol′yə bəl, wot′-), *adj.* that will dissolve in water: *water-soluble vitamin P.*

water spaniel, any of certain breeds of spaniels having a curly coat, often trained to swim out for wild ducks, geese, etc., that have been shot down by hunters. See **Irish water spaniel** for picture.

water speedwell, a common speedwell growing in wet places.

water spider, any of various aquatic spiders, as a European fresh-water spider that makes a baglike nest opening downward beneath the surface of the water, so that it may be filled with air brought down in bubbles on the spider's body.

wa·ter·splash (wôt′ər splash′, wot′-), *n.* a shallow stream or ford crossing a road.

wa·ter·spout (wôt′ər spout′, wot′-), *n.* **1.** a pipe that takes away or spouts water. **2.** *Meteorology.* a rotating column or inverted cone of mist, spray, and water, produced by the action of a whirlwind over the ocean or a large lake. **3.** *Obsolete.* a sudden, very heavy fall of rain; cloudburst.

Waterspout (def. 2)

water sprite, a sprite, nymph, spirit, etc., supposed to live in water, as a Naiad, Nereid, or kelpie.

water starwort, any of a group of slender, tiny-flowered herbs growing either in water or damp soil.

water strider, any of a family of long-legged bugs that walk on the surface of water and feed on other insects.

wa·ter-struck (wôt′ər struk′, wot′-), *adj.* (of bricks) that have been dipped in water after leaving the mold and before firing.

water supply, **1.** water for the use of a community or particular area. **2.** the process of collecting and piping water for a community or particular area.

water system, **1. a.** reservoirs, wells, pipes, etc., together with the persons responsible for them, by which water is provided to a city, etc.; physical plant and personnel of a water supply. **b.** water supply. **2.** a river with all its tributary streams.

water table, **1.** the level below which the ground is saturated with water. See **well**[2] for diagram. **2.** *Architecture.* a projecting course, molding, etc., sloping on top, to throw off rainfall.

water thrush, **1.** any of a group of American warblers, usually found close to a running stream and resembling small thrushes, as the Louisiana water thrush and the northern water thrush. **2.** a European water ouzel.

wa·ter·tight (wôt′ər tīt′, wot′-), *adj.* **1.** so tight that no water can get in or out: *Ships are often divided into watertight compartments.* **2.** leaving no opening for misunderstanding, criticism, etc.; perfect: *a watertight argument.* —**wa′ter-tight′ness,** *n.*

water tower, **1.** a very tall structure for the storage of water, as a standpipe, or that by which a tank cistern, etc., is supported, by means of which water may be supplied to a building, community, etc., at a constant pressure. **2.** a fire-extinguishing apparatus used to throw water on the upper parts of tall buildings.

wa·ter-tube boiler (wôt′ər tüb′, -tyüb′; wot′-), a steam boiler in which the water circulates through tubes exposed to fire and the gases of combustion.

water turkey, a large, blackish bird with a long tail and snakelike neck, found in swampy areas of the southern United States and south through tropical America; snakebird; anhinga.

water vapor, water in a gaseous state, especially when diffused, as in the air, and below the temperature of boiling, as contrasted with steam.

wa·ter-vas·cu·lar (wôt′ər vas′kyə lər, wot′-), *adj.* of or having to do with the circulation of water in the vessels of certain animals, especially the echinoderms.

water wagon, *U.S.* a truck or cart fitted with a large tank for carrying water. **on the water wagon,** *Informal.* not drinking alcoholic liquor; in or into a state of temperance: *Spain took the pledge and got on the water wagon* (Wall Street Journal).

wa·ter·ward (wôt′ər wərd, wot′-), *adv.* toward the water: *The thoughts of the five million boatowners throughout our land turn waterward* (Saturday Review).

water wave, **1.** a wave set into wet hair with combs and dried with heat. **2.** a wave of water.

wa·ter-wave (wôt′ər wāv′, wot′-), *v.t.*, **-waved, -wav·ing.** to arrange (hair) in a water wave.

wa·ter·way (wôt′ər wā′, wot′-), *n.* **1.** a river, canal, or other body of water that ships can go on. **2.** a channel for water. **3.** a hollowed plank along either side of a ship's deck for draining off water through the scuppers.

wa·ter·weed (wôt′ər wēd′, wot′-), *n.*, or **water weed,** **1.** any aquatic plant with inconspicuous flowers. **2.** any of a group of American herbs of the frogbit family, found in quiet fresh water.

water wheel, **1.** a wheel designed to drive machinery, as that of a mill, pump, etc., turned with water. See pictures of **undershot** and **overshot.** **2.** a wheel for raising water, especially for irrigation purposes, by means of buckets or boxes fitted on its circumference.

wa·ter-white (wôt′ər hwīt′, wot′-), *adj.* colorless and transparent, as water or glass. —**wa′ter-white′ness,** *n.*

water wings, two waterproof bags filled with air and put under a person's arms to hold him afloat while he is learning to swim.

water witch, **1.** waterfinder; dowser. **2.** grebe.

water witching, dowsing.

Water Wonderland, a nickname for Michigan.

wa·ter·work (wôt′ər wėrk′, wot′-), *n. Obsolete.* **1.** a pageant exhibited on the water. **2.** waterworks.

wa·ter·works (wôt′ər wėrks′, wot′-), *n.pl. or sing.* **1.** Also, **water works** (*often sing. in use*). **a.** a system of pipes, reservoirs, water towers, pumps, etc., for supplying a city or town with water. **b.** a building containing engines and pumps for pumping water; pumping station. **2.** *Slang.* a flow of tears, especially a sudden and violent flow. **3.** *Obsolete.* an ornamental fountain or cascade.

wa·ter·worn (wôt′ər wôrn′, -wōrn′; wot′-), *adj.* worn or smoothed by the action of water: *waterworn shingle rattling under the pounding surf.*

wa·ter·y (wôt′ər ē, wot′-), *adj.* **1.** of water; connected with water. **2.** full of water; wet: *watery soil.* **3.** containing too much water: *watery soup.* **4.** like water: *a watery discharge.* **5. a.** pale or thin in color: *a watery blue.* **b.** insipid; ineffectual; vapid: *a watery but harmless story.* **6.** tearful: *watery eyes.* **7. a.** indicating rain: *a watery sky.* **b.** having much rain; rainy: *a watery summer.* **8.** in or under water: *A drowned person or a sunken ship goes to a watery grave.*

watt (wot), *n. Physics.* a unit of activity or power (used chiefly with reference to electricity) corresponding to 10^7 ergs of work per second, to one joule per second, to the rate of work represented by a current of one ampere under the pressure of one volt, or to 1/746 horsepower. *Abbr.:* w (no period).
[< James *Watt,* 1736-1819, a Scottish engineer, who pioneered in the development of the steam engine]

watt·age (wot′ij), *n.* **1.** power expressed in watts. **2.** the power, in watts, necessary for the operation of an electrical appliance, motor, etc.

Wat·teau (wä tō′; *French* vȧ tō′), *adj.* designating things associated with Antoine Watteau, a French painter, or his paintings, as style of dress and coloring.

Watteau back, an arrangement of the back of a dress with a broad pleat falling from the neck to the end of the skirt without being gathered in at the waist.

Watteau Back (1731)

watt-hour (wot′our′), *n.* a unit of electrical energy or work, equal to one watt maintained for one hour. *Abbr.:* w.-hr.

watt-hr., watt-hour.

wat·tle (wot′əl), *n., v.,* **-tled, -tling,** *adj.* —*n.* **1.** Also, **wattles.** *Especially British.* **a.** sticks interwoven with twigs or branches; framework of wicker: *a hut built of wattle.* **b.** a framework of poles or rods for a thatched roof. **2. a.** a fleshy, wrinkled fold of skin, usually bright-red, hanging down from the throat on the males of domestic fowls and certain other birds. **b.** a fleshy appendage below the throat of certain reptiles, as the iguana. **c.** the barbel of a fish. **3.** (chiefly in Australia) any of various acacias used to make wattles and in tanning. **4.** *British Dialect.* **a.** any stick, wand, rod, twig, etc. **b.** a sheep hurdle made of wattle. **5.** *Slang.* a loose fold of skin hanging under a person's chin.
—*v.t.* **1.** to make (a fence, wall, roof, hut, etc.) of wattle. **2.** to twist or weave together (twigs, branches, etc.). **3.** to bind together with interwoven twigs, branches, etc.
—*adj.* made or built of wattle.
[Old English *watol*]

Wattle (def. 2a) of a turkey

wattle and daub or **dab,** *Especially British.* a building material consisting of wattle plastered with clay.

wat·tle·bird (wot′əl bėrd′), *n.* any of certain Australian honey eaters that have wattles.

wat·tled (wot′əld), *adj.* **1.** having wattles. **2.** formed by interwoven twigs; interlaced.

watt·less (wot′lis), *adj. Electricity.* without watts or power (applied to an alternating current that differs in phase by 90 degrees from the electromotive force, or to an electromotive force that differs in phase by 90 degrees from the current).

watt·me·ter (wot′mē′tər), *n.* an instrument for measuring electric power in watts; voltammeter.

watt-sec·ond (wot′sek′ənd), *n.* a unit of electrical energy or work, equal to one watt maintained for one second.

Wa·tu·si or **Wa·tus·si** (wä tü′sē), *n., pl.* **-si** or **-sis.** a member of a people of central Africa, originally from Ethiopia, many of the men of which are over seven feet tall. Also, **Tusi, Tussi, Tutsi, Watutsi.**

wa·tu·si (wä tü′sē), *n., v.,* **-sied, -si·ing.** —*n.* a dance in two-beat rhythm, marked by vigorous, jerky movements of the arms, head, etc. —*v.i.* to dance the watusi. [< *Watusi*]

Wa·tut·si (wä tüt′sē), *n., pl.* **-si** or **-sis.** Watusi.

waucht or **waught** (wäHt, wôHt), *Scottish.* —*n.* a copious draft. —*v.t., v.i.* to drink at a gulp or in large drafts; drain (a goblet). [perhaps variant of *quaff.* Compare QUAICH.]

waugh (wôf), *adj. Scottish.* **1.** tasteless; insipid. **2.** unpleasant to the smell or taste. **3.** faint; weak. [Old English *wealg* insipid. Compare dialectal *wallow* tasteless.]

wauk[1] (wôk, wäk), *v.i., v.t. Scottish.* to walk.

wauk[2] (wôk, wäk), *v.i., v.t. Scottish.* to wake.

wauk·rife (wôk′rīf, wäk′-), *adj. Scottish.* wakerife.

waul (wôl), *v.i.* to wail, especially loudly and harshly. —*n.* a howling cry; wail.

waulk (wôk), *v.t.* to shrink and thicken (woolen cloth) by soaking, heating, pounding, and rubbing. [apparently related to WALK]

waur (wôr, wär), *adj., adv. Scottish.* war (worse).

wave (wāv), *n., v.,* **waved, wav·ing.** —*n.* **1.** a moving ridge or swell of water. **2.** any movement like this. **3.** *Poetic.* a body of water; the sea. **4.** a swell, surge, or rush; increase of some emotion, influence, condition, etc.; outburst: *a wave of enthusiasm, waves of immigrants or invaders.* **5.** a curve or series of curves: *waves in a girl's hair.* **6.** a permanent wave. **7.** a wavy line of color or texture, as on a watered fabric. **8.** a waving, especially of something, as a signal. **9.** *Physics.* a movement of particles to and fro; vibration. In a longitudinal wave, the motion of the particles is parallel to the direction in which the wave travels; in a transverse wave, it is perpendicular to the direction in which the wave travels. **10.** *Meteorology.* a change of atmospheric pressure or temperature moving in a particular direction; heat wave or cold wave.

—*v.i.* **1.** to move as waves do; move up and down or back and forth; sway: *The tall grass waved in the breeze.* **2.** to be moved back and forth or up and down regularly, especially as a signal: *The lady's handkerchief waved in token of encouragement and triumph* (Edward G. Bulwer-Lytton). **3.** to have a wavelike or curving form: *Her hair waves naturally.* —*v.t.* **1.** to cause (something) to sway or move back and forth or up and down: *The wind waved the flag.* **2.** to signal or direct by waving: *She waved him away.* **3.** to shake in the air; brandish: *He waved the stick at them.* **4. a.** to give a wavelike form or pattern to: *to wave hair.* **b.** to give a wavelike appearance or texture to, as silk; water.
[Old English *wafian*]
—**Syn.** *n.* **1. Wave, breaker, ripple** mean a moving ridge on the surface of water. **Wave** is the general term: *The raft rose and fell on the waves.* **Breaker** applies to a heavy ocean wave that breaks into foam as it nears the shore or strikes rocks: *Our favorite sport is riding the breakers in.* **Ripple** applies to a tiny wave, such as one caused by the ruffling of a smooth surface by a breeze: *There is scarcely a ripple on the lake tonight.* -*v.i.* **1.** rock, fluctuate, undulate.

WAVE or **Wave** (wāv), *n.* a member of the WAVES.

wave·band (wāv′band′), *n.* a series of wave lengths of electromagnetic waves that fall between two given limits: *The honeyed tones of the announcers fill every waveband on local wireless sets* (London Times).

waved (wāvd), *adj.* **1.** having a wave or waves. **2.** having a wavy or undulating form or outline; marked with wavy lines; watered, as silk.

wave form, 1. the form assumed by a wave. **2.** *Electricity.* the shape of the curve obtained by plotting the instantaneous values of an alternating current against time.

wave front, *Physics.* the continuous line or surface including all the points in space reached by a wave or vibration at the same instant in traveling through a medium.

wave function, (in quantum mechanics) a mathematical function describing the propagation of waves by an elementary particle.

wave guide, *Electronics.* a piece of hollow metal tubing, commonly rectangular or circular in cross section, or a dielectric cylinder, used to propagate ultrahigh-frequency electromagnetic waves.

wave length, or **wave·length** (wāv′-lengkth′, -length′), *n. Physics.* the distance between any particle of a medium through which waves are passing and the next particle that is in the same phase with it.

wave·less (wāv′lis), *adj.* free from waves; undisturbed; still.

wave·let (wāv′lit), *n.* a little wave.

wave·like (wāv′līk′), *adj.* resembling a wave; undulating: . . . *the wavelike deflection of the trade winds, advancing on a broad front* (Scientific American).

wa·vell·ite (wā′və līt), *n. Mineralogy.* hydrous phosphate of aluminum, found in globular aggregates with a radiating structure. *Formula:* $Al_3(OH)_3(PO_4)_2.5H_2O$ [< William *Wavell,* died 1829, an English physician, who discovered it + *-ite*[1]]

wave-me·chan·i·cal (wāv′mə kan′ə kəl), *adj.* of or having to do with wave mechanics: *In the newer wave-mechanical picture of the atom the orbits are replaced by probability distribution of electrons* (W.D. Corner).

wave mechanics, *Physics.* a theory ascribing characteristics of waves to matter and attempting to interpret physical phenomena on this basis.

wave·me·ter (wāv′mē′tər), *n. Electricity.* an instrument used to measure the wave length of electromagnetic waves.

wave motion, 1. motion like that of waves in water, alternately concave and convex. **2.** the forward undulating or vibrational motion of waves by which disturbance of equilibrium is transmitted.

wave number, (in a series of regularly fluctuating waves) the number of waves in one centimeter's length along the line of advance.

wave offering, (in the Bible) an offering that was moved (waved) from left to right or vice versa by the priest when presented, and became the portion of the priests and their families. Exodus 29:27.

wav·er[1] (wā′vər), *n.* a person or thing that waves.

wa·ver[2] (wā′vər), *v.i.* **1. a.** to be undecided; hesitate: *Her choice wavered between the blue dress and the green one.* **b.** (of resolution, courage, purpose, etc.) to be undermined by doubt. **2.** to move to and fro; flutter. **3.** to vary in intensity; flicker: *a wavering light.* **4.** to grow fainter, then louder, or change pitch up and down fairly quickly; quaver, tremble, or pulsate. **5.** to become unsteady; begin to give way: *The battle line wavered and broke.* **6.** *Obsolete.* to wander about; rove. —*n.* a wavering. [perhaps < *wave,* verb + *-er*[6]. Compare Old English *wæfre* unsteady.] —**wa′ver·er,** *n.* —**wa′ver·ing·ly,** *adv.* —**Syn.** *v.i.* **1. a,b.** See **hesitate.**

Wa·ver·ley (wā′vər lē), *n.* **1.** the first of a famous series of novels by Sir Walter Scott. **2.** a pen name of Sir Walter Scott.

wa·ver·y (wā′vər ē), *adj.* wavering; unsteady; fluttering; tremulous: *high, wavery tenors.*

WAVES or **Waves** (wāvz), *n.pl.* Women's Reserve, United States Naval Reserve. [< *W*(omen) *A*(ccepted for) *V*(olunteer) *E*(mergency) *S*(ervice)]

wave set, a preparation used before setting the hair to give it waves or make it stay curly.

wave theory, *Physics.* undulatory theory.

wave train, *Physics.* a group of waves sent out at successive intervals along the same path from a vibrating body.

wave trap, a device for eliminating an undesired radio signal by absorbing it in an extra circuit that can be tuned to the wave length of the signal.

wa·vey (wā′vē), *n., pl.* **-veys.** *Canadian.* the snow goose. Also, **wavy.** [< Cree *wehwew* goose]

wav·i·ly (wā′və lē), *adv.* in a wavy manner, form, or direction.

wav·i·ness (wā′vē nis), *n.* the state or quality of being wavy or undulating.

wav·y[1] (wā′vē), *adj.,* **wav·i·er, wav·i·est. 1.** having waves; having many waves: *wavy hair, a wavy line.* **2. a.** moving to and fro or up and down with a wavelike motion. **b.** (of movements) taking place in undulating curves; sinuous. **3.** (of ground or the surface of the country) rising and falling gently in a succession of rounded heights and hollows. **4.** *Botany.* **a.** undulating, as a margin. **b.** having an undulating margin, as a leaf.

wa·vy[2] (wā′vē), *n., pl.* **-vies.** wavey.

wawl (wôl), *v.i., n.* waul.

wax[1] (waks), *n.* **1. a.** a yellowish substance made by bees for constructing their honeycombs. Wax is hard when cold, but can be easily shaped when warm. **b.** a similar substance made by various kinds of scale insects. **2.** a substance like this, as ozocerite or paraffin: *sealing wax. Most of the wax used for candles, for keeping air from jelly, etc., is really paraffin.* **3.** a thing or person easily manipulated: *The poor fellow is wax in her hands.* **4.** earwax; cerumen. **5.** a polishing compound for floors, furniture, etc.; floor wax. **6.** *Botany.* a waxlike secretion of certain plants. **7.** *Slang.* a phonograph record: *The Dukes of Dixieland, familiar here only as performers on wax, tape, and the air, can now be seen by the naked eye* (New Yorker).
—*v.t.* **1.** to treat with wax; rub, stiffen, polish, etc., with wax or something like wax: *to wax leather, a mustache, a floor.* **2.** *Slang.* to make a phonograph recording of: *Artur Schnabel waxed the Beethoven piano sonatas* (New York Times).
—*adj.* of wax; waxen.
[Old English *weax*] —**wax′er,** *n.* —**wax′-like′,** *adj.*

wax[2] (waks), *v.i.,* **waxed, waxed** or (*Poetic*) **wax·en, wax·ing. 1.** to grow bigger or greater; increase: *The moon waxes till it becomes full, and then wanes.* **2.** to become: *to wax impatient. The party waxed merry.* [Old English *weaxan*]

wax[3] (waks), *n. Especially British Informal.* a fit of rage; angry condition: *to be in a wax.* [perhaps < phrase "to wax angry" < *wax*[2]]

wax bean, a yellow string bean with a waxy appearance.

wax·ber·ry (waks′ber′ē), *n., pl.* **-ries. 1. a.** the wax myrtle. **b.** the bayberry. **c.** the snowberry. **2.** the fruit of any of these.

wax·bill (waks′bil′), *n.* **1.** any of a group of small birds allied to the weaverbirds, with a white, pink, or red bill having a waxy appearance. **2.** the Java sparrow, a common cage bird.

waxed end (wakst), a thread having its end stiffened with shoemakers' wax, and often pointed with a bristle, for passing through holes made with an awl, used in sewing shoes.

wax·en (wak′sən), *adj.* **1.** of wax; made of wax: *For now my love is thaw'd; Which, like a waxen image 'gainst a fire Bears no impression of the thing it was* (Shakespeare). **2.** like wax; smooth, soft, and pale: *waxen skin.* **3.** covered or filled with wax. [< *wax*[1] + *-en*[2]]

wax gourd, 1. the tallow gourd. **2.** its fruit.

wax·i·ness (wak′sē nis), *n.* a waxy quality or character; waxy appearance.

wax·ing (wak′sing), *n.* **1.** the coating of thread with wax before sewing. **2.** a method of blacking, dressing, and polishing leather, to give it a finish. **3.** the process of stopping out colors in batik.

waxing moon, the moon between the new moon and full moon.

wax insect, any of various species of scale insects that secrete or produce wax, as the Chinese scale insect.

wax·jack (waks′jak′), *n.* a device for melting sealing wax that was used in the 1700's, consisting of a length of wick wound around a spindle, with the part for burning fed through a small hole.

wax·light (waks′līt′), *n.* a candle, taper, or nightlight made of wax.

wax moth, a moth whose larvae prey on the honeycomb; bee moth.

wax myrtle, 1. an evergreen shrub or tree of the eastern United States, related to the sweet gale, whose clusters of small berries are coated with wax that is used for candles; candleberry; waxberry. **2.** any of certain related plants, as the bayberry.

wax palm, 1. an Andean pinnate-leaved palm. Its stem and leaves are the source of a resinous wax. **2.** a Brazilian palmate-leaved palm whose young leaves are coated with wax; carnauba.

wax paper, paper coated with paraffin or other waxlike substance, used for moisture-proof wrappings.

wax·plant (waks′plant′, -plänt′), *n.* any of a group of tropical Asiatic and Australian plants of the milkweed family that have shiny leaves and waxy flowers.

wax tree, any of various trees yielding wax, as a sumac of Japan, or the wax myrtle.

wax·weed (waks′wēd′), *n.* a small, purple-flowered, American plant of the loosestrife family that has a viscid down on the foliage.

wax·wing (waks′wing′), *n.* any of several small, crested, perching birds that have smooth, brown plumage and red markings (resembling bits of red sealing wax) on the tips of the wings, as the cedar waxwing or cedarbird, and the Bohemian waxwing; chatterer.

Cedar Waxwing
(7 in. long)

wax·work (waks′wėrk′), *n.* a figure or figures made of wax. **waxworks, a.** an exhibition of figures made of wax, especially of figures representing celebrated or notorious characters. **b.** the place of such an exhibition.

wax·work·er (waks′wėr′kər), *n.* **1.** a person who works in wax; a maker of waxwork. **2.** a bee that produces wax.

wax worm, the larva of the wax moth.

wax·y (wak′sē), *adj.,* **wax·i·er, wax·i·est. 1.** like wax. **2.** made of wax; containing wax; waxen. **3.** abounding in or covered with wax; waxed. **4.** *Medicine.* characterized by or affected with the formation and deposit of an insoluble protein in tissues and organs.

way (wā), *n.* **1.** manner; style; fashion; mode: *a new way of cooking, a new way of treating a disease.* **2.** a point; feature; respect; detail: *The plan is bad in several ways.* **3.** Often, **ways.** habit; custom: *Don't mind his teasing; it's just his way.* **4.** a method; means: *Doctors are using new ways of preventing disease.* **5.** a course of life, action, or experience: *the way of the ungodly.* **6.** one's wish; will: *A spoiled child wants his own way all the time.* **7.** range of experience or notice: *The best idea that ever came my way.* **8.** *Informal.* **a.** a kind of work or business; an occupation; calling: *in the steel way.* **b.** condition; state: *That sick man is in a bad way.* **9.** a road; path; street; course: *He lives just across the way. The hunter found a way through the forest.* **10. a.** space for passing or going ahead. **b.** freedom of action;

scope; opportunity: *to find one's way clear to leave earlier than usual.* **11.** *Law.* a right of way. **12.** motion along a course: *The guide led the way.* **13.** movement forward; forward motion: *The ship slowly gathered way.* **14. a.** distance: *The sun is a long way off.* **b.** *Informal.* district; area; region: *He lives out our way.* **15.** direction: *Look this way. Which way are you going?* **16.** the direction of the weave in fabric. **17.** parallel sills forming a track for the slides of the uprights of a planing machine, the carriage of a lathe, etc.

all the way, without reservation; completely: *The hotel's lobby was plastered with posters calling for the I.L.A. to go "all the way" with Mr. Gleason* (New York Times).

by the way, a. in passing; incidentally: *By the way, have you read the book we are discussing?* **b.** on the road; during a journey: *We stopped by the way to eat.*

by way of, a. by the route of; through; via: *He went to India by way of Japan.* **b.** for the purpose of; to serve as: *a summary given by way of introduction.* **c.** *Especially British.* making a profession of or having a reputation for (being or doing something): *He is by way of being a clever cartoonist.*

come or **fall one's way,** to happen to one: *That was a wonderful experience; I didn't expect it to fall my way.*

every which way, *Informal.* in all directions; in disorder: *children with hair and clothes every which way. Wires led every which way from the truck to the Mansion* (New Yorker).

find one's way, a. to make one's way by observation, search, or inquiry: *He finally found his way home.* **b.** to come to a place by natural course or by force of circumstances: *The river finds its way to the sea. The picture found its way to the auction room.*

give way, a. to make way; retreat; yield: *to give way to superior forces. We have adhered to quality and not given way to the cry for the production of construction* (London Times). **b.** to break down or fail, as health, strength, or one's voice: *His heart finally gave way and he died.* **c.** to abandon oneself to emotion: *to give way to despair.* **d.** *Finance.* to drop in value: *The dollar keeps giving way.*

go out of the way, to make a special effort: *The government still seems to be going out of its way to court unpopularity about money for the universities* (New Scientist).

have a way with, to be persuasive or successful with: *He had a way with and an eye for the ladies* (Time).

in a way, to some extent: *He is handsome in a way. In a way it's better you came late.*

in the way, as an obstacle, hindrance, annoyance, etc.: *He is cast as an irritating gadfly, standing in the way of Lloyd George's efforts to win a peace that would give Germany its just due* (Saturday Review).

in the way of, a. in a favorable position for doing or getting: *He put me in the way of a good investment.* **b.** in the matter or business of; as regards: *We have a small stock in the way of hats.*

know one's way around, to be completely familiar with: *The Home Office men really know their way around a roulette table* (Manchester Guardian Weekly).

look the other way, to turn aside so as not to see; pretend unawareness: *What the statistics did not show was the thousands of times the police simply looked the other way* (Time).

lose one's way, not to know any longer where one is: *She lost her way in the streets of London.*

make one's way, a. to go: *It was in despair of reaching Italy that the young scholar [Erasmus] made his way to Oxford* (John Green). **b.** to get ahead; succeed: *He made his way rapidly in the world of finance.*

make way, a. to give space for passing or going ahead; make room: *If a young man sees his mother-in-law coming along the path, he must retreat into the bush and make way for her* (Gouldsbury and Sheane). **b.** to move forward: *We lost our maintopmast, so that after the storm was over we could not make any way* (M. Bishop).

once in a way, occasionally: *Now I like this kind of thing once in a way* (Anthony Trollope).

out of the way, a. so as not to be an obstacle, hindrance, etc.: *We moved the fallen tree out of the way.* **b.** far from where most people live or go: *Leslies don't mix with the county; and Rood lies very much out of the way* (Edward G. Bulwer-Lytton). **c.** out of reach; not in danger: *While the fight was going on, he tried to keep out of the way.* **d.** to death: *to put an animal out of the way.* **e.** unusual; remarkable: *Her abilities are not out of the way.* **f.** off the right path; improper; wrong: *Did you ever know me to do anything out of the way?* (William Dean Howells).

pave the way, to make ready; prepare: *Parents can do much in advance to pave the way for a smooth transition from home to camp for a child* (New York Times).

pick one's way, to move with great care and caution over treacherous ground, a difficult situation, etc.: *One has to crawl through narrow passages . . . pick his way down sharp descents* (Scientific American).

rub the right way, to please; pacify: *It is impossible to rub him the right way when he is in such a state.*

rub the wrong way, to annoy; irritate: *They rub everybody the wrong way because of their clear implication that . . . doctors are incompetent* (Bulletin of Atomic Scientists).

see one's way, to be willing or able: *He did not see his way clear to allow their names to remain upon the register* (Law Times).

stroke the wrong way, a. to stroke (an animal) in a direction contrary to that in which the fur naturally lies: *The kitten doesn't mind being stroked the wrong way.* **b.** to ruffle or irritate (a person), as by going counter to his wishes: *Somebody's been stroking him the wrong way* (Anthony Trollope).

take one's way, to set out; go: *She took her way sadly and slowly down the pier* (Joseph Ashby-Sterry).

under way, going on; in motion; in progress: *. . . their obstinate failure to recognize, even after it was well under way, the rise and domination of Prussia* (Edmund Wilson).

ways, timbers on which a ship is built and launched: *to slide a ship down the launching ways.*

—adv. Informal. at or to a (great) distance; far: *The cloud of smoke stretched way out to the pier.*

[Old English *weg*]

—**Syn.** *n.* **1, 4. Way, method, manner** mean mode or means. **Way** is the general word, sometimes suggesting a personal or special mode of doing or saying something: *The way she spoke hurt me.* **Method** applies to an orderly way, suggesting a special system of doing something or a definite arrangement of steps to follow: *Follow her method of cooking.* **Manner** applies to a characteristic or particular method or way: *He rides in the western manner.* **9.** route, highway, avenue, lane. **13.** progress, advance.

➔ **way, ways.** *Way,* meaning distance (def. 14a), is standard; *ways* is nonstandard: *a long way* (not *ways*) *off.*

➔ The nautical phrase **under way** (*The ship is under way*) is sometimes written *under weigh* from the mistaken notion that it refers to the weighing of the anchor.

wa·yang (wä′yäng), *n.* a stylized Indonesian puppet play based on legend and performed to music, and sometimes with live actors. [< Javanese *wayang*]

way·bill (wā′bil′), *n.* a list of goods with a statement of where they are to go and how they are to get there.

way·fare (wā′fãr′), *v.i.*, **-fared, -far·ing.** to journey or travel, especially on foot. [back formation < *wayfaring*]

way·far·er (wā′fãr′ər), *n.* a traveler.

way·far·ing (wā′fãr′ing), *adj., n.* traveling; journeying. [Middle English *wayfaringe,* Old English *wayfarende* < *weg* way + *farende,* present participle of *faran* to fare]

wayfaring tree, 1. a European shrub or small tree of the honeysuckle family with dense cymes of small, white flowers, common along roadsides. **2.** the hobblebush, a related species of North America.

way·go·ing (wā′gō′ing), *n. Scottish.* a going away or leaving; departure. *—adj.* **1.** *Scottish.* departing; outgoing. **2.** *Law, especially British.* having to do with or designating a crop that will not ripen until after a tenant has left, but in which he has the sole or a partial ownership interest.

way·laid (wā′lād′, wā′lād′), *v.* the past tense and past participle of **waylay.**

Way·land (wā′lənd), *n.,* or **Wayland the Smith,** a marvelously skilled smith, normally invisible but able to become visible under certain circumstances, so called in English folklore, but encountered as a standard figure in all early Germanic folklore.

way·lay (wā′lā′, wā′lā′), *v.t.*, **-laid, -lay·ing.** **1.** to lie in wait for; attack on the way: *Robin Hood waylaid travelers and robbed them.* **2.** to stop (a person) on his way. [< *way* + *lay*[1]; probably patterned on Middle Low German *wegelagen* < *wegelage* an ambush] —**way′lay′er,** *n.*

way·leave (wā′lēv′), *n. Law.* **1.** permission to make or use a way across private land. **2.** payment for such permission.

way·mark (wā′märk′), *n.* a mark or sign set up along a way; guidepost; milestone.

way-off (wā′ôf′, -of′), *adj.* distant: *The way-off sound of children's voices* (New Yorker).

way of life, the habits of an individual, family, or community with respect to food, habitation, manners, morals, etc.

way of the cross, 1. the way or course followed by Christ in going to Calvary to be crucified. **2.** a way or course marked by stations of the cross in commemoration of Christ's course. **3.** the devotion of the stations of the cross.

way-out (wā′out′), *adj. Slang.* far-out: *a way-out book or play.*

way point, *U.S.* a stopping place on a route or during a journey.

ways (wāz), *n.pl.* See under **way,** *n.*

-ways, a suffix forming adverbs showing direction or position as in *edgeways, sideways,* or adverbs showing manner, as in *anyways, noways.* [< *way* + *-s*[3]]

ways and means, 1. (in legislation) ways of raising revenue for current governmental expenditures. **2.** methods and resources that are at a person's disposal for effecting some object.

way·side (wā′sīd′), *n.* the edge of a road or path.

go by the wayside, to be put or left aside: *Several records went by the wayside during the session just ending, with Oct. 31 the banner day* (New York Times).

—adj. of or having to do with the wayside; situated on, lying near, occurring, growing, or living by the wayside.

way station, *U.S.* a station between main stations on a railroad, bus line, etc.

way-stop (wā′stop′), *n.* a stop between main stations in the course of a journey.

way train, local train.

way·ward (wā′wərd), *adj.* **1.** turning from the right way; disobedient; willful. **2.** irregular; unsteady; erratic. **3.** *Obsolete.* untoward. —**way′ward·ly,** *adv.* —**way′ward·ness,** *n.* —**Syn. 1.** perverse, stubborn.

way·ward·en (wā′wôr′dən), *n. Especially British.* a person elected to supervise highways, usually as a member of an official board.

way·wi·ser (wā′wī′zər), *n.* an instrument for measuring and indicating a distance traveled by road: *During the time that they were made and used waywisers were also known as hodometers, odometers, and perambulators* (London Times). [partial translation of German *Wegweiser* < *Weg* way + *Weiser* one that shows]

way·worn (wā′wôrn′, -wōrn′), *adj.* wearied or worn by traveling.

wayz·goose (wāz′güs′), *n., pl.* **-goos·es.** *British.* an annual festivity held in summer by the employees of a printing establishment, consisting of a dinner and usually an excursion into the country. [origin unknown]

wa·zir (wä zir′), *n.* vizier.

w.b., 1. warehouse book. **2.** water ballast. **3.** westbound.

W.B., waybill.

WBA (no periods) or **W.B.A.,** World Boxing Association.

w.c., 1. water closet. **2.** without charge.

W.C., 1. water closet. **2.** Western-Central (a postal district in London).

WCC (no periods), World Council of Churches.

W.C.T.U. or **WCTU** (no periods), Woman's Christian Temperance Union.

W.D. or **WD** (no periods), War Department.

we (wē; *unstressed* wi), *pron., pl. nom.; poss.,* **our** or **ours;** *obj.,* **us.** the 1st person nominative plural of **I. 1.** the speaker plus the person or persons addressed or spoken about. An author, an editor, a king, or a judge sometimes uses *we* to mean *I.* **2.** people in general, including the speaker. [Old English *wē*]

➔ **We** is frequently used as an indefinite

pronoun in expressions like *we find, we sometimes feel,* to avoid passive and impersonal constructions.

WEA (no periods) or **W.E.A.,** Workers' Educational Association (of Great Britain).

weak (wēk), *adj.* **1.** that can easily be broken, crushed, overcome, torn, etc.; not strong: *a weak chair, weak foundation, weak wrapping, weak defenses.* **2. a.** lacking bodily strength or health: *A weak old man totters as he walks.* **b.** not functioning well; somewhat impaired: *weak eyes, weak hearing.* **3.** lacking power, authority, force, etc.: *a weak government, a weak law.* **4.** lacking mental power: *a weak mind.* **5.** lacking moral strength or firmness: *a weak character.* **6.** lacking or poor in amount, volume, loudness, taste, intensity, etc.: *a weak voice, weak arguments, a weak current of electricity.* **7. a.** containing relatively little of the active ingredient or ingredients; not concentrated; diluted: *a weak solution of boric acid.* **b.** of less than the normal or desired strength: *weak coffee.* **8.** lacking or poor in something specified: *a composition weak in spelling.* **9.** (of a faith, conviction, etc.) not strongly or consistently held; not whole-hearted. **10. a.** damaged or defective; likely to give way or break: *a weak link in a chain.* **b.** inadequate for the purpose; likely to lose, fail, etc.: *a weak candidate.* **11.** (of flour, wheat, etc.) containing little gluten. **12.** *Commerce.* of prices on an exchange, etc.: **a.** having a downward tendency; not firm. **b.** characterized by a fluctuating or downward tendency: *a weak market. Industrials continue to be weak.* **13.** *Prosody.* weakly stressed (especially of a word at the end of a line of poetry). **14.** *Photography.* (of a negative) with the light and dark not strongly contrasted; thin. **15.** *Phonetics.* **a.** (of a sound or syllable) not stressed. **b.** (of an accent or stress) not strong; light. **16.** in Germanic languages: **a.** (of verbs) inflected by additions of consonants to the stem, not by vowel change; regular. English weak verbs form the past tense and past participle by adding *-ed, -d,* or *-t. Example: want-wanted* (weak); *sing-sang-sung* (strong). **b.** (of nouns and adjectives) inflected with a majority of endings with *-n,* as German *alten* in *zum alten Hunde.* [Middle English *weke* < Scandinavian (compare Old Icelandic *veikr*)]

—**Syn. 1, 2. Weak, feeble, decrepit** mean lacking or inferior in strength, energy, or power. **Weak** is the general word describing people or things not strong enough to act with force or vigor or to undergo pressure, strain, or attack, without risk of breaking, bending, collapsing, etc.: *She has weak ankles.* **Feeble** implies pitiable weakness, loss of strength from sickness or age or, describing things, faintness or ineffectiveness: *He is too feeble to feed himself.* **Decrepit** means worn out or broken down by age or long-continued use: *They have only one decrepit bed.* **5.** irresolute.

weak·en (wē′kən), *v.t.* to make weak or weaker. —*v.i.* **1.** to grow or become weak or weaker. **2.** to take a less firm attitude; give way. —**weak′en·er,** *n.*

—**Syn.** *v.t.* **Weaken, undermine, debilitate** mean to cause to lose strength, energy, or power. **Weaken** is the general word applying to loss or lowering of energy or strength from any cause or by any means: *Poor organization weakened his argument.* **Undermine** means to weaken someone or something gradually by working secretly or treacherously: *Bad companions undermined his mother's influence.* **Debilitate** means to make (a person's constitution, mind, etc.) weak or feeble by damaging and taking away vitality or strength: *He was debilitated by disease.*

weak·er sex, (wē′kər), women.

weaker vessel, (in the Bible) woman. I Peter 3:7.

weak·fish (wēk′fish′), *n., pl.* **-fish·es** or (*collectively*) **-fish.** any of certain spiny-finned marine food fishes with a tender mouth, especially a species found along the Atlantic coast of the United States. [American English < obsolete Dutch *weekvisch* soft fish]

Weakfish (about 2 ft. long)

weak·ish (wē′kish), *adj.* somewhat weak. —**weak′ish·ly,** *adv.* —**weak′ish·ness,** *n.*

weak-kneed (wēk′nēd′), *adj.* **1.** having week knees. **2.** yielding easily to opposition, intimidation, etc.

weak·li·ness (wēk′lē nis), *n.* weakly quality.

weak·ling (wēk′ling), *n.* a weak person or animal. —*adj.* weak; feeble.

weak·ly (wēk′lē), *adv., adj.,* **-li·er, -li·est.** —*adv.* in a weak manner. —*adj.* weak; feeble; sickly.

weak-mind·ed (wēk′mīn′did), *adj.* **1.** having or showing little intelligence; feeble-minded. **2.** lacking firmness of mind. —**weak′-mind′ed·ness,** *n.*

weak·ness (wēk′nis), *n.* **1.** a being weak; lack of power, force, or vigor. **2.** a weak point; slight fault. **3. a.** a liking that one is a little ashamed of; fondness. **b.** something for which one has such a fondness.

weak side, 1. the side of a person's character at which he is most easily influenced or affected. **2.** the side of a football formation away from which players have shifted.

weak sister, *U.S. Slang.* one that is helpless or cannot be depended upon, especially in time of stress; weakling.

weak-willed (wēk′wild′), *adj.* weak-minded; indecisive: *The Indian intruders were . . . so feeble and weak-willed as to recoil from action even before Chinese troops could come on the scene* (Manchester Guardian Weekly).

weal[1] (wēl), *n.* **1.** *Archaic.* well-being; prosperity; happiness: *Good citizens act for the public weal.* **2.** *Obsolete.* a state or community. **3.** *Obsolete.* wealth; riches (often in *world, world's* or *worldly weal*). [Old English *wela* wealth; welfare] —**Syn. 1.** welfare.

weal[2] (wēl), *n.* a streak or ridge raised on the skin by a stick or whip; welt; wale; wheal. [variant of *wale*[1]]

weald (wēld), *n. Poetic.* open country. [Old English *weald* woods, forest. Related to WOLD[1].]

Weald·en (wēl′dən), *adj.* of or having to do with a series of deposits of the Lower Cretaceous in England. [< (the) *Weald,* an area in England + *-en*[2]]

wealth (welth), *n.* **1. a.** much money or property; riches. **b.** the state of having wealth; great material prosperity; affluence. **2.** *Economics.* **a.** all things that have money value. **b.** (more strictly) all material things that are capable of or adaptable to satisfying human wants, and are or can be made subject to ownership, whether private or public. **c.** all such material things, and qualities or attributes of man, as health, intelligence, etc., that increase his ability to produce. **3.** a large quantity; abundance: *a wealth of hair, a wealth of words.* **4.** *Obsolete.* well-being; weal. [< *weal*[1], or *well*[1]; perhaps patterned on *health* and *heal*] —**Syn. 1.** prosperity, fortune. **3.** profusion.

wealth·i·ly (wel′thə lē), *adv.* in a wealthy manner; in the midst of wealth; richly.

wealth·i·ness (wel′thē nis), *n.* the state of being wealthy; wealth.

wealth·y (wel′thē), *adj.,* **wealth·i·er, wealth·i·est,** *n.* —*adj.* **1.** having wealth; rich: *a very wealthy man, a wealthy country.* **2.** abundant; copious: *a wealthy supply of wit, a verse wealthy in satirical allusions.*

—*n.* **the wealthy,** persons having wealth; rich people: *to curry favor with the wealthy.* —**Syn.** *adj.* **1.** See **rich.**

Wealth·y (wel′thē), *n., pl.* **Wealth·ies.** a bright-red, American variety of apple, ripening in autumn. [< *wealthy,* in the sense of "thriving"]

wean[1] (wēn), *v.t.* **1.** to accustom (a child or young animal) to food other than its mother's milk. **2.** to accustom (a person) to do without something; cause to turn away: *Tom was sent away to school to wean him from bad companions.* [Old English *gewenian,* and *āwenian* accustom (to do without)] —**wean′er,** *n.*

wean[2] (wēn, wē′ən), *n. Scottish.* a very young child; baby. [contraction of earlier *wee ane* wee one]

wean·ling (wēn′ling), *n.* a child or animal that has only recently been weaned. —*adj.* recently weaned.

weap·on (wep′ən), *n.* **1. a.** any instrument, device, or other material object used in fighting: *Swords, spears, arrows, clubs, guns, and shields are weapons.* **b.** anything viewed as similar to this in purpose or nature; a means of attack or defense: *to use drugs as a weapon against disease, to use truth as a weapon of freedom.* **2.** any organ of a plant or animal used for fighting or for protection, as claws, horns, teeth, and stings. [Old English *wǣpen*]

weap·oned (wep′ənd), *adj.* armed with weapons.

weap·on·eer (wep′ə nir′), *n.* **1.** a person who develops or produces weapons. **2.** a person who activates a nuclear weapon.

weap·on·eer·ing (wep′ə nir′ing), *n.* the design or production of weapons: *Contemporary weaponeering is essentially a process of miniaturization; of packing more devastation into a smaller and more portable warhead* (Bulletin of Atomic Scientists).

weap·on-grade (wep′ən grād′), *adj.* (of fissionable materials) surpassing the minimum standards set for materials to be used in nuclear weapons: *weapon-grade plutonium.*

weap·on·less (wep′ən lis), *adj.* having no weapon; unarmed.

weap·on·ry (wep′ən rē), *n.* **1.** the developing and producing of weapons: *He pointed out that anything—the knowledge that two and two makes four—may play a part in atomic weaponry* (Harper's). **2.** weapons collectively: *What the U.S. now needs to back up its broadened array of weaponry . . . is a more subtle set of concepts in diplomacy* (Time).

weapons carrier, a military vehicle for transporting weapons not part of its own equipment.

weap·ons-grade (wep′ənz grād′), *adj.* weapon-grade.

weap·on·shaw (wep′ən shô), *n. Scottish.* wappenschawing.

weap·on·shaw·ing (wep′ən shô′ing), *n. Scottish.* wappenschawing.

weap·on·show·ing (wep′ən shō′ing), *n. Scottish.* wappenschawing.

weapons system, a missile, bomber, submarine, or other device required to carry a bomb or warhead to its target: *America's first successful long-range pilotless bomber . . . is a major weapons system conceived and developed in peace-time* (Time).

wear[1] (wãr), *v.,* **wore, worn, wear·ing,** *n.* —*v.t.* **1.** to have on the body: *We wear clothes.* **2.** to use or affect in one's costume or adornment, especially habitually: *to wear green, wear a beard, wear one's hair in a pony tail.* **3.** to have; show: *to wear a big smile. The gloomy old house wore an air of sadness.* **4.** to have as a quality or attribute; bear: *to wear one's honors modestly.* **5.** (of a ship) to fly (a flag or colors). **6.** to cause loss or damage to by using: *These shoes are badly worn.* **7.** to make by rubbing, scraping, washing away, etc.: *to wear a dress to rags, to wear a path across the grass. Walking wore a hole in my shoe.* **8.** to tire; weary: *Age, the common fate of all, has worn thy frame* (William Cullen Bryant). **9.** to spend or pass: *to wear away the night in song.* **10.** to bring (a person) gradually (into a habit or disposition).

—*v.i.* **1.** to suffer loss or damage from being used: *His coat has worn to shreds.* **2. a.** to last long; give good service: *This coat has worn well.* **b.** to stand the test of experience, familiarity, criticism, etc.: *a friendship that did not wear.* **3.** to go gradually; grow or become in time: *His patience began to wear thin during the long wait. It became hotter as the day wore on.* **4.** *Obsolete.* to be in fashion; be worn.

wear down, a. to weary; tire: *Worn down by . . . loneliness, finally smashed by grief, the scholar's mind revolves all these things in a confusion which indicates the onset of death* (New Yorker). **b.** to overcome by persistent effort: *The young Quaker strove to wear down malice by his patient and forgiving mood* (William Hepworth Dixon). **c.** to reduce or erode by use, friction, etc.: *Its [Argentina's] once proud leadership in Latin America is being slowly worn down by the quicker rate of growth of other countries* (Manchester Guardian Weekly).

wear off, to become less gradually; diminish: *The novelty soon wore off.*

wear out, a. to wear until no longer fit for use: *The child needs new shoes; he has worn out his present pair.* **b.** to use up: *He did not strike a blow till all the powers of diplomacy had been thoroughly worn out between himself and his rival* (Edward A. Freeman). **c.** to tire out; weary: *All that thinking about so many things can wear you out* (Harper's). **d.** to exhaust, destroy, or abolish by gradual loss or the lapse of time: *He stayed too late and wore out his welcome. Let me wither and*

 PRONUNCIATION KEY: hat, āge, cãre, fär; let, ēqual, tėrm; it, īce; hot, ōpen, ôrder; oil, out; cup, pu̇t, rüle;

wear out mine age in a ... prison (John Donne).

—*n.* **1.** the act of wearing or the fact of being worn: *clothes for summer wear.* **2.** things worn or to be worn; clothing: *The store sells children's wear.* **3.** gradual loss or damage caused by use: *The rug shows wear.* **4.** lasting quality; good service: *There is still much wear in these shoes.*

[Old English *werian*] —**wear′er,** *n.*

➤ In nonstandard English *wore* is extensively used as the past participle, as well as the past tense.

wear[2] (wãr), *v.,* **wore, worn, wear·ing,** *n.* —*v.t.* to turn (a ship) to sail with the wind at the stern in changing to the other tack, instead of turning the bow into the wind as in tacking. —*v.i.* (of a ship) to turn or be turned to sail with the wind at the stern in changing to the other tack.

—*n.* the act or process of wearing or turning a ship. [apparently alteration of *veer*[1]]

wear·a·bil·i·ty (wãr′ə bil′ə tē), *n.* the quality or condition of being wearable; ability to stand wear: *Synthetic fabrics have attained new heights of fashion success, while working miracles of wearability* (New York Times).

wear·a·ble (wãr′ə bəl), *adj.* **1.** that can be worn; suitable for being worn. **2.** able to stand wear; lasting.

—*n.* **wearables,** something wearable; an article of apparel: *He ... moved off with Mrs. Dutton's wearables and deposited the trunk containing them safely in the boat* (Scott).

—**wear′a·ble·ness,** *n.*

wear and tear, loss or damage caused by use.

wea·ri·ful (wir′ē fəl), *adj.* causing weariness; wearisome. —**wea′ri·ful·ly,** *adv.* —**wea′ri·ful·ness,** *n.*

wea·ri·less (wir′ē lis), *adj.* that does not weary or become weary. —**wea′ri·less·ly,** *adv.*

wea·ri·ly (wir′ə lē), *adv.* in a weary manner.

wea·ri·ness (wir′ē nis), *n.* weary condition or feeling. —**Syn.** fatigue, exhaustion.

wear·ing (wãr′ing), *adj.* **1.** exhausting; tiring: *a very wearing trip, conversation, person, etc.* **2.** of or for wear; intended to be worn. —**wear′ing·ly,** *adv.*

wearing apparel, clothes.

wear·ish (wãr′ish, wir′-), *adj. Dialect.* **1.** tasteless; insipid; unsalted. **2. a.** sickly; feeble. **b.** wizened; shriveled. Also, **wersh.** [origin uncertain. Compare Dutch *wars* disgusted, averse.]

wea·ri·some (wir′ē səm), *adj.* wearying; tiring; tiresome. —**wea′ri·some·ly,** *adv.* —**wea′ri·some·ness,** *n.*

wear-out (wãr′out′), *n.* damage caused by use: *Stretch fabrics ease wear-out at the elbows, knees, and seat* (Time).

wear-re·sist·ant (wãr′ri zis′tənt), *adj.* resistant to wearing or being worn out: *The wear-resistant iron liners are integrally cast with the aluminum housing* (New Scientist).

wea·ry (wir′ē), *adj.,* **-ri·er, -ri·est,** *v.,* **-ried, -ry·ing.** —*adj.* **1.** tired: *weary feet, a weary brain.* **2.** causing tiredness; tiring: *a weary wait.* **3.** having one's patience, tolerance, or liking exhausted: *to be weary of excuses.*

—*v.t.* to make weary; fatigue; tire. —*v.i.* **1.** to become weary. **2.** to long (for): *She is wearying for home.*

[Old English *wērig*] —**wea′ry·ing·ly,** *adv.*

—**Syn.** *adj.* **1.** fatigued, exhausted, fagged. See **tired.**

Weary Willie or **Willy,** *British Slang.* a person of little strength or energy: *Mr. Mikardo ... said that Opposition members were a bunch of Weary Willies* (London Times).

wea·sand (wē′zənd), *n. Archaic.* **1.** the windpipe. **2.** the throat. [Old English *wāsend*]

wea·sel[1] (wē′zəl), *n.* any of several small, carnivorous mammals related to the mink and skunk, with a long, slender body and short legs, that feed on rats, birds, eggs, etc., as the least weasel and short-tailed weasel. The weasel is brown and white, except in northern regions where it turns white in winter and is called an ermine. —*v.t. Informal.* to deprive (a word or phrase) of its force or meaning; take away (the meaning) from a word or phrase. —*v.i. Informal.* to get out of a difficult place or situation; use tricky actions or words; hedge. [Old English *weosule, wesle*]

Weasel[1] (not including tail, 6 to 8 in. long)

wea·sel[2] (wē′zəl), *n.* a military vehicle with a roofless, boxlike body that runs on treads for travel in snow, mud, sand, etc. [< *weasel*[1]]

wea·sel·ing (wē′zə ling), *Informal.* —*n.* the use of tricky actions or words; equivocation: *precampaign weaseling.* —*adj.* tricky; equivocating; evasive.

wea·sel·ly (wē′zə lē), *adj.* like a weasel; tricky; evasive.

weasel word, *U.S. Informal.* a word that takes away the force or meaning of a sentence, phrase, etc.; an ambiguous word or one used ambiguously: *"Standardization" is one of the subtlest, trickiest weasel words ever coined* (Atlantic).

wea·sel-word·ed (wē′zəl wėr′did), *adj. Informal.* worded in an evasive way: *mutual defense, a weasel-worded device for committing further follies by a more palatable name* (Wall Street Journal).

wea·son (wē′zən), *n. Archaic.* weasand.

weath·er (weᴛʜ′ər), *n.* **1.** the condition of the atmosphere with respect to temperature, humidity, violence or gentleness of winds, presence or absence of precipitation, clearness or cloudiness, etc.: *to forecast clear weather for two days in most of New England.* **2. a.** windy, rainy, or stormy weather; the elements: *to protect a building against damage by the weather.* **b.** the level of the atmosphere characterized by this: *to fly above the weather.*

under the weather, *Informal.* sick; ailing: *They had been very well as a general thing, although now and then they might have been under the weather for a day or two* (Frank R. Stockton).

—*v.t.* **1.** to go or come through safely: *to weather a storm, weather an economic depression.* **2.** to expose (anything) to the weather; wear by sun, rain, frost, etc.; discolor thus: *Wood turns gray if weathered for a long time.* **3.** *Nautical.* to sail to the windward of; pass safely around: *The ship weathered the cape.* **4.** *Architecture.* to build (a roof, top of a wall, etc.) on a slant so as to shed water. —*v.i.* **1.** to become discolored or worn by air, rain, sun, frost, etc. **2.** (of a material) to resist exposure to the weather; endure; last.

weather in, a. to ground (an aircraft) because of bad weather: *Most of the planes were weathered in during the storm.* **b.** to close (an airport or airfield) because of bad weather: *Santa Fe's airport was weathered in for several hours during the day* (New York Times).

weather out, a. to shut out of a place because of bad weather: *So far as that other difficulty—the one about cargo vessels being weathered out of some bases for nine months—it strikes us that may have been something of a blessing* (Wall Street Journal). **b.** to cancel or curtail because of bad weather: *the usual air show was weathered out* (Time).

—*adj.* toward the wind; of the side exposed to the wind; windward from: *It was very cold on the weather side of the ship.*

[Old English *weder*]

weather balloon, a balloon (often unmanned) in which instruments are carried for recording meteorological data of the upper air, used especially in weather forecasting.

weather beam, *Nautical.* the side of a ship toward the wind; weatherboard.

weath·er-beat·en (weᴛʜ′ər bē′tən), *adj.* worn or hardened by the wind, rain, and other forces of the weather.

weath·er·board (weᴛʜ′ər bôrd′, -bōrd′), *n.* **1.** *British.* thin board, thicker along one edge than along the other; clapboard. **2.** *Nautical.* the side of a ship or boat toward the wind. —*v.t., v.i. British.* to cover or protect with weatherboards.

weath·er·board·ing (weᴛʜ′ər bôr′ding, -bōr′-), *n. British.* **1.** a covering or surface consisting of weatherboards, as on a wall or roof. **2.** weatherboards collectively.

weath·er-bound (weᴛʜ′ər bound′), *adj.* delayed by bad weather.

weather breeder, a fine, clear day, popularly supposed to betoken a coming storm.

Weather Bureau, a division of the U. S. Department of Commerce that records and forecasts the weather.

weath·er-burned (weᴛʜ′ər bėrnd′), *adj.* burned, scorched, or browned by the sun, wind, or other forces of the weather.

weath·er·cast (weᴛʜ′ər kast′, -käst′), *n.* a report on the weather which is broadcast on radio or television.

weath·er·cast·er (weᴛʜ′ər kas′tər, -käs′-), *n.* a person who gives weather reports on radio or television.

weather cloth, *Nautical.* a covering of canvas or tarpaulin used to protect boats or to shelter persons from wind and spray.

weath·er·coat (weᴛʜ′ər kōt′), *n. Especially British.* a coat that protects against wet or cold weather; stormcoat.

weath·er·cock (weᴛʜ′ər kok′), *n.* **1.** a device to show which way the wind is blowing, especially one in the shape of a rooster; weather vane. **2.** a person or thing that is changeable or inconstant, especially one who veers easily to conform to the prescribed attitudes, popular beliefs, etc., of the moment.

Weathercock (def. 1)

—*v.i.* to veer or vary like a weathercock: *It is easy enough to make a stable hovercraft which is capable of "weathercocking" quickly into the wind* (New Scientist).

—*v.t.* to provide with a weathercock; to serve as a weathercock for: *Elaborately adorned gables, ... scrolled, and weathercocked* (Harper's).

weath·er·con·di·tion (weᴛʜ′ər kən dish′ən), *v.t.* to prepare or protect against all kinds of weather: *to weathercondition a cabin.*

weath·ered (weᴛʜ′ərd), *adj.* **1.** worn, stained, or seasoned by the weather. **2.** (of rocks) altered by the weather or other atmospheric influence. **3.** *Architecture.* made sloping, so as to shed water: *a weathered sill.*

weather eye, 1. a device used for measuring and reporting meteorological conditions: *This coast-to-coast system of radar weather eyes [is] linked by teletype with a central computer* (Wall Street Journal). **2.** a weather satellite. **3.** a careful and alert watch: *While Hollywood keeps a weather eye on church groups, it has never been in trouble with the Protestant National Council of Churches, which traditionally avoids anything that smacks of censorship* (Time).

weather gauge, *Nautical.* the position of a vessel, especially a sailing vessel, when it is windward of another, and thus able to make more advantageous use of the wind relative to the other in maneuvering.

have or **keep the weather gauge of, a.** to be to windward of: *The rest ... entered as far as the place permitted and their own necessities, to keep the weather gauge of the enemy* (Sir Walter Raleigh). **b.** to get the better of: *He has got the weather gauge of them, and for us to run down to them would be to run ourselves into the lion's mouth* (John M. Wilson).

weather girl, *U.S.* a woman weathercaster.

weath·er·glass (weᴛʜ′ər glas′, -gläs′), *n.* an instrument designed to show the state of the atmosphere, as a barometer, a baroscope, or a hygroscope.

weath·er·ing (weᴛʜ′ər ing), *n.* the destructive or discoloring action of air, water, frost, etc., especially on rock.

weath·er·li·ness (weᴛʜ′ər lē nis), *n.* (of ships and boats) weatherly character or qualities.

weath·er·ly (weᴛʜ′ər lē), *adj.* (of a sailing vessel) that can sail close to the wind; making very little leeway when close-hauled.

weath·er·man (weᴛʜ′ər man′), *n., pl.* **-men.** *Informal.* a man who forecasts the weather, now especially a meteorologist or other person who is employed particularly to do so.

weather map, a map or chart showing conditions of temperature, barometric pressure, precipitation, direction and velocity of winds, etc., over a wide area for a given time or period.

weather mark, *Nautical.* a mark used in boat racing to indicate the direction from which the wind is blowing.

weath·er·most (weᴛʜ′ər mōst), *adj.* furthest to windward. [< *weather* + *-most*]

weath·er·om·e·ter (weᴛʜ′ə rom′ə tər), *n.* an instrument used to determine the ability of a paint to withstand exposure to all kinds of weather.

weath·er·proof (weᴛʜ′ər prüf′), *adj.* protected against rain, snow, or wind; able to stand exposure to all kinds of weather. —*v.t.* to make weatherproof. —*n. Especially British.* a raincoat.
weather satellite, an artificial earth satellite that measures and reports meteorological conditions, especially as an aid in forecasting.
weather ship, any of a group of ships stationed at points in the North Atlantic for weather observation and reporting, maintained by the United States and other members of the International Civil Aviation Organization.
weather side, 1. *Nautical.* the side of a ship facing windward. **2.** the side of a building, tree, etc., that is most exposed to injury from weather: *During winter storms they [the goats] found shelter in the numerous caves that rain, wind, and the Adriatic had gouged out of the weather side* (Atlantic).
weather stain, a stain or discoloration left or produced by the weather: . . . *the grey old towers of the ruin . . . bearing the rusty weather stains of ages* (Scott).
weather-stained (weᴛʜ′ər stānd′), *adj.* bearing weather stains.
weather station, a station where weather conditions are observed, recorded, or forecast.
weather strip, a narrow strip of cloth, metal, etc., to fill or cover the space between a door or window and the casing, so as to keep out rain, snow, and wind.
weath·er-strip (weᴛʜ′ər strip′), *v.t.,* **-stripped, -strip·ping.** to fit or seal with weather strips.
weather stripping, 1. a weather strip. **2.** material for weather strips.
weather tide, a tide running to windward, or in the direction opposite to that in which the wind is blowing.
weath·er·tight (weᴛʜ′ər tīt′), *adj.* so tight that it can stand exposure to all kinds of weather; weatherproof: *weathertight windows, a weathertight building.*
weather vane, a weathercock; vane.
weath·er·vi·sion (weᴛʜ′ər vizh′ən), *n.* the communication of weather information to aircraft pilots by a system of radar and television.
weath·er-wise (weᴛʜ′ər wīz), *adv.* with reference to weather.
weath·er-wise (weᴛʜ′ər wīz′), *adj.* **1.** skillful in forecasting the changes of the weather. **2.** skillful in forecasting changes in anything, as the mood of the populace or political climate.
weath·er·worn (weᴛʜ′ər wôrn′, -wōrn′), *adj.* weather-beaten.
weath·er·y (weᴛʜ′ər ē), *adj.,* **-er·i·er, -er·i·est.** changing like the weather; fitful: . . . *the weathery dalliance of gnats* (Richard D. Blackmore).
weave (wēv), *v.,* **wove** or (*Rare*) **weaved, wo·ven** or **wove, weav·ing,** *n.* —*v.t.* **1.** to form (threads or strips) into a thing or fabric: *to weave yarn into a blanket, straw into hats, reeds into baskets.* **2.** to make (something) out of threads or strips: *to weave a rug or a fabric.* **3.** to combine into a whole: *The author wove three plots together into one story.* **4.** to make by combining parts: *The author wove a story from three plots.* **5.** (of a spider) to spin (its web). **6.** to make with care, by or as if by weaving: *to weave a web of lies, a pattern of love, etc.* **7.** to twist and turn in making (one's way): *to weave one's way home.* —*v.i.* **1.** to work with a loom. **2.** to undergo weaving; become interlaced. **3.** to progress by or as if by twisting and turning; move with a rocking or swaying motion: *a car weaving in and out of traffic.* —*n.* a method or pattern of weaving: *Homespun is a cloth of coarse weave.*
[Old English *wefan*] —**weav′ing·ly,** *adv.*
➔ As past participle, **wove** is chiefly used in certain technical terms like *wire-wove* and *wove paper.*

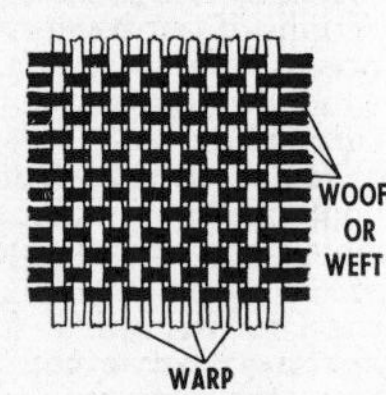

Weaving

weav·er (wē′vər), *n.* **1.** a person who weaves. **2.** a person whose work is weaving. **3.** a weaverbird.
weav·er·bird (wē′vər bėrd′), *n.* any of a family of birds similar to finches, mostly of Asia, Africa, and Australia, that build elaborately woven nests. The whidah, English sparrow, and republican grosbeak are weaverbirds.
weaver's hitch or **knot,** a sheet bend.
wea·zen (wē′zən), *v.i., v.t., adj.* wizen.
web (web), *n., v.,* **webbed, web·bing.** —*n.* **1.** something woven, especially the fabric of delicate, silken threads spun by a spider or some insect larvae; cobweb. **2.** a whole piece of cloth made at one time. **3.** anything like a web: *His story was a web of lies.* **4.** anything flimsy or fanciful. **5. a.** a membrane or skin joining the toes of ducks, geese, and other swimming birds. **b.** a malformation of skin somewhat resembling this, between human fingers or toes. **c.** *Anatomy.* connective tissue. **6. a.** the series of barbs on each side of the shaft of a bird's feathers; the vane or vexillum. **b.** the two series of barbs of a feather, collectively. **7.** a thin metal sheet, especially between heavier or projecting parts. **8. a.** the vertical plate (or its equivalent) that connects the upper and lower lateral plates in a beam or girder. **b.** one of these lateral plates or flanges. **9.** *Papermaking.* **a.** an endless belt of wire cloth working on rollers and carrying the pulp. **b.** the sheet of pulp on this belt, in process of being made into paper. **c.** a large roll of paper made in this way, as that used in a rotary press for printing newspapers. **10.** *Architecture.* the masonry between the ribs of a ribbed vault. **11.** *Machinery.* the arm of a crank, connecting the shaft and crank pin. **12.** webbing. **13.** *Obsolete.* a kind of cataract, or similar growth on the eye.
—*v.t.* **1.** to envelop or trap in a web. **2.** to join by or as if by a web; twine; interlock. [Old English *webb*] —**web′like′,** *adj.*

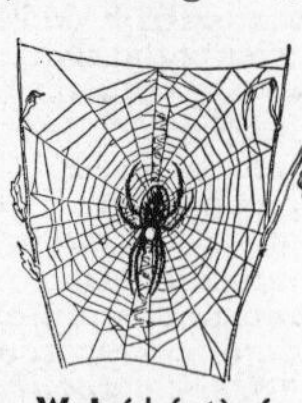
Web (def. 1) of orange-and-black garden spider

webbed (webd), *adj.* **1.** formed like a web or with a web. **2.** having the toes joined by a web, as the feet of certain birds.

Webbed Foot (def. 2) of a duck

web·bing (web′ing), *n.* **1.** cloth woven into strong, wide strips, used in upholstery and for belts. **2.** the plain foundation fabric left for protection at the edge of some rugs, etc. **3.** the skin joining the toes, as in a duck's feet.
we·ber (vā′bər, wē′-), *n. Electricity.* **1.** a unit of magnetic flux, equivalent to 10^8 maxwells. **2.** formerly: **a.** a coulomb. **b.** an ampere. **c.** a maxwell. [< Wilhelm E. *Weber,* 1804-1891, a German physicist]
We·bern·esque (vā′bər nesk′), *adj.* having to do with or characteristic of the Austrian composer Anton von Webern, 1883-1945, or his work: . . . *Webernesque tonal delicacies* (Sunday Times).
web-fed (web′fed′), *adj.* (of a printing press) having the paper fed from a continuous roll instead of in single sheets.
web-fin·gered (web′fing′gərd), *adj.* having the fingers united for a considerable part of their length by a fold of skin.
web·foot (web′fu̇t′), *n., pl.* **-feet. 1.** a foot in which the toes are joined by a web. **2.** an animal having webbed feet.
web-foot·ed (web′fu̇t′id), *adj.* having the toes joined by a web.
web·less (web′lis), *adj.* not furnished with a web.
web press, a rotary printing press in which the paper is fed from a roll.
web·ster (web′stər), *n. Obsolete.* a weaver.
web-toed (web′tōd′), *adj.* web-footed.
web-winged (web′wingd′), *adj.* (of bats) having wings consisting of a large web or membrane supported and extended by the fore limbs and four elongated digits.
web·work (web′wėrk′), *n.* **1.** the structural part or web of a textile pattern. **2.** network: . . . *the webwork of the city's highways* (Time).
web·worm (web′wėrm′), *n.* any of certain more or less gregarious caterpillars that spin large webs.
Wechs·ler-Belle·vue Scale (weks′lər bel′vyü), *Psychology.* a series of tests for adults or children, to determine intelligence and mental age. [< David *Wechsler,* born 1896, an American psychologist, who devised it at *Bellevue* Psychiatric Hospital, New York City]
wecht (weʜt), *n. Scottish.* weight.
wed (wed), *v.,* **wed·ded, wed·ded** or **wed, wed·ding.** —*v.t.* **1. a.** to marry. **b.** to unite in marriage; conduct the marriage ceremony for (a man and woman). **c.** to give (a woman) in marriage. **2.** to unite or join very closely, as in marriage. **3.** to be obstinately attached to (an opinion, one's own will, a habit, a faction, etc.) —*v.i.* to enter into marriage; become married; contract matrimony (with). [Old English *weddian* < *wedd* a pledge. Compare WAD[4], WADSET.]
we'd (wēd; *unstressed* wid), **1.** we had. **2.** we should; we would.
Wed., Wednesday.
wed·ded (wed′id), *adj.* **1.** joined in wedlock; married. **2.** of or having to do with marriage or married persons; connubial: *wedded bliss.* **3.** united. **4.** devoted.
Wed·dell seal (wed′əl), a large, common hair seal of the antarctic regions. It lives mostly in the water and below the ice in winter. [< James *Weddell,* 1787-1834, an English navigator, who commanded antarctic sealing ships]
wed·ding (wed′ing), *n.* **1.** the marriage ceremony with its attendant festivities. **2.** an anniversary of this: *A golden wedding is the fiftieth anniversary of a marriage.* **3.** a close union or association; joining; combination; merger: *A chemical wedding between the element boron and organic substances promised industry a new family of compounds* (Science News Letter). [Old English *weddung* < *weddian* to wed] —**Syn. 1.** See **marriage.**
wedding cake, a large, rich cake, usually arranged in tiers, covered with icing and decorated with sugar ornaments, cut and distributed to the guests at a wedding reception.
wedding ring, a ring of platinum, gold, etc., placed on the third finger of the left hand of the bride. In a double-ring ceremony, the bride places a ring on the bridegroom's finger.
we·deln (vā′dəln), *n.* the act or technique of skiing with fast, swiveling turns to the right and left while skis are kept parallel and close together. —*v.i.* to ski in this manner: *The tests cover . . . the first snow-plow turn to how to hold a pole to wedeln in deep powder* (Newsweek). [< German *wedeln* (literally) to wag < *Wedel* whisk, tail]
wedge (wej), *n., v.,* **wedged, wedg·ing.** —*n.* **1.** a piece of wood, metal, etc., thick at one end and tapering to a thin edge at the other, used in splitting, separating, etc. It is one of the simple machines. **2. a.** something shaped like a wedge: *a wedge of cheese, pie, or rock.* **b.** a cuneiform stroke or character of this shape. **3.** something used like a wedge: *to drive a wedge of suspicion between friends, to drive a wedge of tanks through the enemy line.* **4.** *Meteorology.* a long, narrow area of high pressure between two cyclonic systems. **5.** a golf club used for high, short shots, lofting the ball out of traps, heavy grass, etc.: *[She] clinched the match with a 100-foot wedge shot* (New York Times).

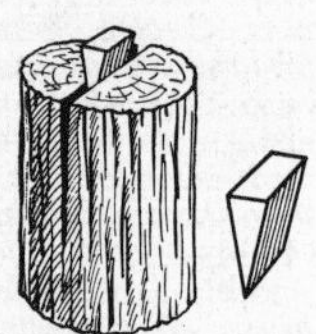
Wedge (def. 1) Left, splitting a log; right, detail

—*v.t.* **1.** to split or separate with or as with a wedge or wedges. **2.** to fasten or tighten with a wedge or wedges. **3.** to thrust or pack in tightly; squeeze: *to wedge passengers into a subway train. He wedged himself through the narrow window.* **4.** *Ceramics.* to expel air bubbles from (clay) by cutting it into lumps or wedges and beating it. —*v.i.* **1.** to force a way, opening, etc.: *to wedge through a crowd.* **2.** to become stuck, caught, etc.: *Two fat men wedged in a doorway.*
[Old English *wecg*] —**wedge′like′,** *adj.*
wedge·bill (wej′bil′), *n.* any of a group of South American hummingbirds with a thick bill that abruptly tapers to a point at the end.
wedg·er (wej′ər), *n.* a workman who cuts clay into lumps or wedges and beats it to expel air bubbles.
wedge-shaped (wej′shāpt′), *adj.* shaped like a wedge; cuneate.
wedge-tailed eagle (wej′tāld′), a large, black eagle of Australia with tail feathers that taper to the shape of a wedge.

wedg·ie (wej′ē), *n.* a woman's shoe resembling a clog, with a thick, wedgelike piece forming a sole, all of which touches the ground, without the customary arched instep.
Wedg·wood (wej′wu̇d), *n.* one of various kinds of English pottery, especially with a blue or black glaze and a design of white-colored Greek and Roman models in relief. See **vase** for picture. *—adj.* of or having to do with the type of pottery originated by Josiah Wedgwood. [< Josiah *Wedgwood,* 1730-1795, an English potter who developed a kind of pottery and design]
Wedgwood blue, a shade of medium blue characteristic of Wedgwood ware.
wedg·y (wej′ē), *adj.* **1.** formed or adapted to use as a wedge. **2.** fitted for prying into or among.
wed·lock (wed′lok), *n.* **1.** married life; marriage: *to be united in wedlock.* **2.** *Obsolete.* the marriage ceremony; wedding. [Old English *wedlāc* marriage vow < *wedd* a pledge + *-lāc,* a noun suffix]
Wednes·day (wenz′dē, -dā), *n.* the fourth day of the calendar week, between Tuesday and Thursday. *Abbr.:* Wed., W. [Old English *Wōdnesdæg* Woden's day < *Wōden* Woden; translation of Late Latin *Mercurii diēs* day of Mercury]
wee (wē), *adj.,* **we·er, we·est,** *n.* *—adj.* very small; tiny. *—n.* a little; bit; mite. [Middle English *we,* variant of *wei* < Old English *wǣge* weight]
weed[1] (wēd), *n.* **1.** a useless or troublesome plant, either growing wild or in cultivated ground to the exclusion or injury of the desired crop, or to the detriment of the beauty of the place. **2. a.** a useless animal, especially a horse unfit for racing or breeding. **b.** any very weak or malformed thing. **3.** *Informal.* **a.** a cigarette or cigar. **b.** tobacco. **c.** marijuana. **4.** *Archaic.* profusely growing wild plants; luxuriant underbrush.
—v.t. to take weeds out of: *to weed one's garden.* *—v.i.* **1.** to take out weeds or the like. **2.** to clear anything of harmful or useless elements, persons, etc.
weed out, a. to free from what is useless or worthless: *Mother weeded out the old letters she wanted to save and threw away the rest of the stuff in the trunk.* **b.** to remove as useless or worthless: *But de Gaulle weeded out suspect commanders, arresting some, retiring others and transferring still others to inactive European posts* (New York Times).
[Old English *wēod*] **—weed′like′,** *adj.*
weed[2] (wēd), *n.* **1.** a black cloth band, worn on the arm or (sometimes) the hat of a man, as a token of mourning. **2.** *Obsolete.* costume: *monastic weeds.* **3.** *Archaic.* any garment.
weeds, mourning garments: *widow's weeds.*
[Old English *wǣd,* or *wǣde* garment. Compare WADMAL.]
weed·ed (wē′did), *adj.* **1.** from which the weeds have been removed: *a freshly weeded garden.* **2.** overgrown with weeds.
weed·er (wē′dər), *n.* **1.** a person who weeds. **2.** a tool or machine for digging up weeds.
weed-grown (wēd′grōn′), *adj.* overgrown with weeds; covered with weeds: *They stood in the weed-grown parade ground . . .* (Time).
weed·i·cide (wē′də sīd), *n.* a weedkiller.
weed·i·ly (wē′də lē), *adv.* in a weedy manner or way.
weed·i·ness (wē′dē nis), *n.* weedy character or state: *the weediness of the lawn.*
weed·kill·er (wēd′kil′ər), *n.* a chemical for killing weeds: *Poison ivy plants can now be eradicated successfully by spraying with a weedkiller* (New York Times).
weed·kill·ing (wēd′kil′ing), *n.* the act or process of killing weeds: *Weeds . . . could easily get life insurance were it not for the modern technique of chemical weedkilling* (R.N. Higinbotham). *—adj.* of or for killing weeds: *weedkilling operations.*
weed·less (wēd′lis), *adj.* free from weeds.
weeds (wēdz), *n.pl.* See under **weed**[2].
weed·y (wē′dē), *adj.,* **weed·i·er, weed·i·est. 1.** full of weeds: *a weedy garden.* **2.** of the nature of or like a weed or weeds. **3. a.** thin and lanky; gangling. **b.** weak and underdeveloped; scrawny.
wee hours, the early morning hours: *Beginning in the wee hours next Sunday, air coach passengers will be boarding the same swift DC-7's* (Wall Street Journal).
week (wēk), *n.* **1.** seven days, one after another. **2.** a period of seven days as designated by the calendar, beginning on Sunday and ending on Saturday. **3.** the working days of this period, usually beginning on Monday and ending on Friday: *the banking week. A school week is five days. Abbr.:* wk.
Monday (or **Tuesday,** etc.) **week,** the Monday (or Tuesday, etc.) one week from this Monday: *Let us say Thursday week, dear—This is Saturday, so it is quite enough notice to give* (J.S. Winter).
this day week, one week from today: *Can you make it convenient to be there this day week?* (D.C. Murray).
week in, week out, week after week: *She sat on her rocking chair sewing, week in, week out.*
[Middle English *weke,* Old English *wice,* probably (originally) turn, a turning]
week·day (wēk′dā′), *n.* any day except Sunday or (now often) Saturday. *—adj.* of or on a weekday.
week·end or **week-end** (wēk′end′), *n.,* or **week end, 1.** Saturday and Sunday as a time for recreation, visiting, etc. **2.** a house party occurring over a weekend, as at a college or university.
—adj. of or on a weekend.
—v.i. to spend a weekend: *to weekend with friends in the country.*
week·end·er (wēk′en′dər), *n.* a person who spends a weekend away from home: *Boating takes vacationists and weekenders off crowded highways* (New York Times).
week·long (wēk′lông′, -long′), *adj.* continuing for a week; of a week's duration: *Concurrently, a weeklong series of meetings . . . will be held in various auditoriums and meeting places* (New York Herald Tribune).
week·ly (wēk′lē), *adj., adv., n., pl.* **-lies.**
—adj. **1.** done, happening, or appearing once a week or each week: *a weekly letter home.* **2.** lasting for a week. **3.** of or having to do with the working week or weekdays: *His weekly wage is $75.*
—adv. **1.** once each week; every week. **2.** by the week; on the basis of weeks.
—n. a newspaper or magazine published once a week.
weekly bill, bills of mortality.
week of Sundays, *Informal.* a period long enough to include seven Sundays; an indefinitely long time.
weel (wēl), *adv., adj. Scottish.* well[1].
ween (wēn), *v.t., v.i. Archaic.* to think; suppose; believe; expect. [Old English *wēnan*]
wee·nie (wē′nē), *n. U.S. Informal.* a wiener; frankfurter.
ween·y (wē′nē), *adj.,* **ween·i·er, ween·i·est.** *Informal.* very small; little; tiny: *They sound like . . . teachers who have grown a weeny bit tired of their energetic, articulate, expressive little charges* (New Yorker). [< *wee* + *-ny,* as in *teeny, tiny*]
weep[1] (wēp), *v.,* **wept, weep·ing,** *n.* *—v.i.* **1.** to shed tears; cry: *to weep in silent anguish, with rage, or for joy.* **2.** to show sorrow or grief: *In some good cause . . . To perish, wept for, honour'd, known* (Tennyson). **3.** to shed water or moisture in drops; exude drops of water, as the stem of a plant, soil, a sore, etc. *—v.t.* **1.** to shed tears for; mourn: *No poet wept him* (William Cowper). **2.** to let fall in drops; shed: *She wept bitter tears.* **3.** to spend in crying: *to weep one's life away.* **4.** to shed (moisture or water) in drops; exude (a liquid, etc.): *And trees weep amber on the banks of Po* (Alexander Pope).
—n. an oozing of moisture; sweating; exudation.
the weeps, *Informal.* a period or fit of weeping; cry (used especially in reference to women): *to have the weeps, to get over the weeps.*
[Old English *wēpan*]
—Syn. *v.i.* **1.** sob. *—v.t.* **1.** bewail.
weep[2] (wēp), *n.* a lapwing. [imitative of its cry]
weep·er (wē′pər), *n.* **1.** a person who weeps. **2.** a person hired to weep at funerals; professional mourner. **3.** the capuchin monkey of South America.
weepers, a conventional badge of mourning: *Our merry mourners clap bits of muslin on their sleeves, and these are called weepers* (Oliver Goldsmith).
weep hole, an opening through which water drips, as in a wall of a building, to let out accumulated moisture: *Even the building itself leaks; it has weep holes in the spandrels* (New Yorker).
weep·i·ly (wē′pə lē), *adv.* in a weepy manner.
weep·i·ness (wē′pē nis), *n.* the state or condition of being weepy.
weep·ing (wē′ping), *adj.* **1.** that weeps. **2.** having branches that arch over and hang down drooping: *a weeping willow.* **3.** (of climate, weather, skies, etc.) dripping; rainy. **—weep′ing·ly,** *adv.*
weeping birch, a variety of the white birch of northern Europe and the northern United States having drooping branches.
weeping cherry, any of various flowering cherry trees with drooping branches, native to Japan.
weeping sinew, *Informal.* a gathering of fluid in the synovial sheath of a tendon; ganglion.
weeping willow, a large willow tree, a native of eastern Asia, widely cultivated in Europe and America for ornament, distinguished by its very long and slender hanging branches. See **willow**[1] for picture.
weeps (wēps), *n.pl.* See under **weep,** *n.*
weep·y (wē′pē), *adj.,* **weep·i·er, weep·i·est. 1.** *Informal.* inclined to weep; tearful: *the bold dragoon sang . . . with such pathos . . . that his audience felt almost weepy* (George Du Maurier). **2.** *British Dialect.* exuding moisture; oozy; moist: *An old marlpit full of black water, where weepy, hairy moss hangs around the stumps of the willows and alders* (Rudyard Kipling).
wee·ver (wē′vər), *n.* any of a group of small, edible marine fishes found along the coasts of Europe, Africa, and Chile, that have eyes directed upward and sharp poisonous spines. [probably < Old North French *wivre,* Old French *guivre* (originally) serpent, dragon (because of its venomous spines); see WIVERN]
wee·vil (wē′vəl), *n.* **1.** any of a family of small beetles that have elongated snouts and are injurious to crops, the larvae feeding inside of nuts, fruits, and grain, as the seed weevil and rice weevil, or in the stems or roots of plants, as the sweet potato weevil. See also pictures of **nut weevil** and **boll weevil. 2.** any of certain small insects that damage stored grain. [Middle English *wevel* < Old English *wifel*]

White Pine Weevil (def. 1)
(Line shows length.)

wee·vil·y or **wee·vil·ly** (wē′və lē), *adj.* infested with weevils.
weft (weft), *n.* **1.** the threads running from side to side across a fabric; woof. See **weave** for picture. **2.** something woven or spun, as a web. [Old English *weft,* or *wefta* < *wefan* to weave]
Wehr·macht (vār′mäHt′), *n.* the armed forces of (Nazi) Germany. [< German *Wehrmacht* < *Wehr* defense; weapon + *Macht* power; might]
wei·ge·la (wī jē′lə, -gē′-), *n.* any of a group of Asiatic shrubs of the honeysuckle family, species of which are often grown for their funnel-shaped white, red, or pink flowers. [< New Latin *Weigela* the genus name < Christian E. *Weigel,* 1748-1831, a German physician]
weigh[1] (wā), *v.t.* **1.** to find the weight of; measure the heaviness of by means of scales: *to weigh oneself, to weigh a bag of sugar.* **2.** to measure by weight: *The grocer weighed out five pounds of apples.* **3.** to bend by weight; burden: *The boughs of the apple tree are weighed down with fruit.* **4. a.** to hold in the hand or hands in order to estimate or compare the weight of. **b.** to balance or fondle (an object or objects) as if doing this; hold and move gently up and down or tip from side to side: *to weigh one's hat in one's hands while waiting for someone to take it.* **5. a.** to balance in the mind; consider carefully: *He weighed his words before speaking.* **b.** to estimate in comparison: *weigh our sorrow with our comfort* (Shakespeare). **6.** to lift up (a ship's anchor) from the bottom before sailing; hoist (anchor). **7.** *Obsolete.* to regard highly; esteem; value.
—v.i. **1.** to have as a measure by weight (the apparent direct object of the verb being actually adverbial in function): *to weigh 140 pounds. He weighs more than I do.* **2.** to have importance or influence; carry weight: *The amount of his salary does not weigh with Mr. Black at all, because he is very rich.* **3.** to lie as a burden or worry; bear down: *Don't let that little mistake weigh upon your mind.* **4.** to lift anchor.
weigh in, *Sports.* **a.** to verify the weight of (a jockey) before or after a horse race:

The Clerk of the Scales . . . shall in all cases weigh in the riders of the horses, and report to the stewards any jockey not presenting himself to be weighed in (Encyclopedia of Sports). **b.** to determine the weight of (a boxer) before a fight, in accordance with restrictions on exceeding the limit for his class: *The contender was weighed in by members of the commissioner's staff.* **c.** to be weighed in in this way: *Both boxers weighed in this afternoon* (Daily Express). *He was six feet four and weighed in at 135* (O. Henry).

weigh in with, *Informal.* to introduce or produce (something that is additional or extra): *[He] weighed in with some genially barbed compliments and a Latin quotation* (Punch).

weigh on or **upon,** to be a burden to: *The London atmosphere weighs on me* (Jane Welsh Carlyle). *The silence began to weigh upon her* (J.L. Allen).

weigh out, a. to verify the weight of (a jockey) before or after a horse race: *The stakeholder shall not allow a jockey to be weighed out for any horse until such horse's stake [shall] have been paid* (Encyclopedia of Sports). **b.** to be weighed out in this way: *The rider of Musjid . . . is said to have weighed in and weighed out with a whip weighing 7 or 9 lbs. and to have exchanged it for a lighter whip before and after the race* (J. Rice).

[Old English *wegan* weigh, lift, heft; bear] —**weigh′er,** *n.*

—**Syn.** *v.t.* **5. a.** See **consider.**

weigh[2] (wā), *n.*

under weigh, under way: *She got under weigh with very little fuss, and came so near us as to throw a letter on board* (Richard H. Dana).

[spelling variant of *way;* influenced by *aweigh*]

➔ See **way** for a usage note.

weigh·a·bil·i·ty (wā′ə bil′ə tē), *n.* the capability of being weighed.

weigh·a·ble (wā′ə bəl), *adj.* that can be weighed. —**weigh′a·ble·ness,** *n.*

weigh·a·bly (wā′ə blē), *adv.* so as to be weighed.

weigh·bridge (wā′brij′), *n.* a weighing machine with a platform on which cattle, loaded carts, etc., are weighed.

weigh-in (wā′in′), *n.* **1.** *Sports.* a weighing in, as in horse racing, boxing, etc.: *I got to the Stadium in plenty of time for the weigh-in* (New Yorker). **2.** a checking of the baggage weight of a passenger before he boards a commercial airplane. **3.** a weighing: *For junior: Weekly weigh-ins, and full-scale check-ups every twelve weeks* (Maclean's).

weigh·ing machine (wā′ing), any of various machines for weighing.

weigh·man (wā′mən), *n., pl.* **-men.** a man whose work is weighing things: *In 1904, Phil slugged a Keystone weighman who was shorting him at the scales* (Time).

weigh·mas·ter (wā′mas′tər, -mäs′-), *n.* **1.** an official in charge of public scales. **2.** a person in charge of weighing any product, as coal at a mine or produce at a cannery.

weight (wāt), *n.* **1.** how heavy a thing is; amount a thing weighs: *to find the weight of a feather or a rock. That man's weight is 175 pounds.* **2.** *Physics.* **a.** the quality that makes all things tend toward the center of the earth; heaviness; ponderability. **b.** the quantity of a portion of matter as measured by the amount of its downward force due to gravitation, varying with latitude and elevation above sea level. Weight is generally considered as the product of the mass and the acceleration due to gravity. **3. a.** system of standard units used for expressing weight: *avoirdupois weight, troy weight.* **b.** a unit of such a system. **c.** a piece of metal or other substance, having a specific weight, used on a balance or scale for weighing things: *a pound weight.* **4.** a quantity that has a certain weight: *a half-ounce weight of gold dust, a ten-ton weight of coal.* **5.** any of various heavy or massive objects: **a.** an object by which another or others may be pulled down, held down, flattened, etc.: *to tie a weight on a fishing line, place a weight on a pile of letters.* **b.** an object that balances by its weight; counterpoise: *a sash weight.* **c.** an object that is raised by winding and affords power by its descent: *a clock with two weights.* **6.** downward thrust; load; burden: *The pillars support the weight of the roof.* **7.** the burden of care, responsibility, etc.; mental load: *the weight of high office. That's a great weight off my mind.* **8.** influence; importance; value: *a man of weight in his community, evidence of little weight.* **9.** preponderant portion: *the weight of public opinion.* **10.** the relative heaviness of an article of clothing appropriate to the season's weather: *summer weight.* **11.** *Statistics.* **a.** a number assigned to an item in a statistical compilation, as in a cost-of-living index, to make its effect in the compilation reflect its importance. **b.** the frequency of an item in a statistical compilation. **12.** *Sports.* a metal ball thrown, pushed, or lifted in contests of strength. **13.** (in archery) the force, expressed in pounds, needed to pull a bow a given distance, as the length of an arrow. **14.** (in horse racing) the total load that a horse must carry, according to its handicap for age, sex, type of race, etc., including the jockey, the saddle, and any weights added to make up the total: *The Experimental Free Handicap . . . will be contested by horses carrying the weights already assigned by the handicapper* (New York Times). **15.** force; strength; impetus: *The sailing instructions give the length of the course as 60 sea miles. If there is enough weight in the wind it could be a fast race* (London Times). *Abbr.:* wt.

by weight, measured by weighing: *The proportions of acid and water were equal by weight* (A.T. Thomson).

carry weight, to be of importance; count: *What he says carries much weight with me.*

pull one's weight, to do one's part or share: *In boating phraseology, he "pulled his weight" . . .; he was not a mere passenger* (London Daily News).

throw one's weight around or **about,** *Informal.* to make too much use of one's rank or position; assert one's importance improperly or excessively: *The varsity star became unpopular after he began to throw his weight around.*

—*v.t.* **1.** to load down; burden: *a heavily weighted truck, a man weighted by care.* **2.** to add weight to; put weight on: *The elevator is weighted too heavily.* **3.** to load (fabric, thread, etc.) with mineral to make it seem of better quality: *weighted silk.* **4.** *Statistics.* to give a weight to: *a weighted average.* **5.** *Skiing.* to direct all or most of the downward thrust onto: *to weight the left ski.*

[Middle English *weighte,* alteration (by analogy with *weigh*) of *wighte,* Old English *gewiht* < *wegan* weigh]

weight density, the weight of a substance per unit volume.

weight-for-age (wāt′fər āj′), *n.* (in horse racing) the weight assigned to a horse based on age, without regard to other considerations.

weight·i·ly (wā′tə lē), *adv.* in a weighty manner; heavily; ponderously; momentously; forcibly.

weight·i·ness (wā′tē nis), *n.* the quality or state of being weighty: *The weightiness of the problems the President faces causes men to age considerably while holding that high and lonely office.*

weight·less (wāt′lis), *adj.* **1.** of little or no weight: *The reflection of the night glow . . . lit the cherry trees . . . and made their branches look as if they were smothered in weightless snow* (New Yorker). **2.** having or seeming to have little or no gravitational pull: *Space men still aren't sure how long a human being can endure a weightless condition* (Wall Street Journal).

weight·less·ly (wāt′lis lē), *adv.* in a weightless manner: *How will . . . [man] react, work, and sleep while floating weightlessly through outer space?* (Times of India).

weight·less·ness (wāt′lis nis), *n.* weightless quality or condition; especially, the feeling or experience of the apparent absence of gravitational force: *Probably because of weightlessness, the animal's heart took three times longer to regain its normal rhythm than in acceleration experiments in the laboratory* (Scientific American).

weight lifter, a person who lifts weights as a body-building exercise or in sports competition: *Weight lifters and other athletes are prime candidates for back trouble* (Harper's).

weight lifting, the lifting of barbells, dumbbells, etc., as a body-building exercise or in sports competition: *Eight or ten years ago, as a result of a program of weight lifting, he put an inch on his biceps in two weeks* (New Yorker).

weight throw, a sport in which a heavy metal ball at the end of a flexible cable is thrown competitively for distance: *In winning the weight throw Thomson gave a remarkable exhibition of consistency* (New York Times).

weight thrower, a person who competes in the weight throw: *Spring-legged sprinters, brawny weight throwers and durable distance runners gathered . . . for the . . . championships* (Time).

weight·y (wā′tē), *adj.,* **weight·i·er, weight·i·est. 1.** heavy. **2.** burdensome: *weighty cares of state.* **3.** important; influential: *a weighty speaker.* **4.** convincing: *weighty arguments.* —**Syn. 1.** ponderous. See **heavy. 2.** onerous. **3.** momentous. —**Ant. 1.** light. **3.** trivial, unimportant.

Weil's disease (vīlz, wīlz), an infectious disease characterized by jaundice and fever; leptospirosis. [< Adolph *Weil,* 1848-1916, a German physician, who described it]

Wei·ma·ra·ner (vī′mə rä′nər), *n.* any of a breed of medium-sized gray dogs with a docked tail, bred in Germany as a hunting dog. [< German *Weimaraner* < *Weimar,* a city in Germany where the breed was developed]

Weimaraner (23 to 27 in. high at the shoulder)

weir (wir), *n.* **1.** a dam erected across a river to stop and raise the water, as for conveying a stream to a mill. **2.** a fence of stakes or broken branches put in a stream or channel to catch fish. **3.** an obstruction erected across a channel or stream to divert the water through a special opening in order to measure the quantity flowing. [Old English *wer*]

weird (wird), *adj.* **1.** unearthly; mysterious: *They were awakened by a weird shriek.* **2.** *Informal.* odd; fantastic; queer: *a rather weird pattern, answer, or person.* **3.** *Archaic or Scottish.* having to do with fate or destiny. —*n. Archaic or Scottish.* **1. a.** the power or agency by which events are predetermined; fate; destiny. **b.** magical power; enchantment. **2.** a witch, wizard, or soothsayer. **3. a.** what is fated to happen to a particular person, etc.; one's appointed lot or fortune. **b.** an evil fate inflicted by supernatural power, especially by way of retribution. **4.** what is destined or fated to happen; predetermined events collectively. **5. a.** a prophecy. **b.** a supernatural or marvelous occurrence or tale. **c.** *Obsolete.* an omen.

[Old English *wyrd* fate] —**weird′ly,** *adv.* —**weird′ness,** *n.*

—**Syn.** *adj.* **1. Weird, eerie, uncanny** mean mysteriously or frighteningly strange. **Weird** describes something that seems not of this world or due to something above or beyond nature: *All night weird cries came from the jungle.* **Eerie** suggests the frightening effect of something weird or ghostly or vaguely and evilly mysterious: *They told tales of eerie lights hovering over the bog.* **Uncanny** suggests a strangeness that is disturbing because it is unnatural: *I had an uncanny feeling that eyes were peering from the darkness.*

weird·ie (wir′dē), *n. Slang.* a person or thing regarded as weird, odd, or eccentric: *It is milk and coffee that . . . nourish the Teddy-boy and the Chelsea weirdie* (Punch).

weird·o (wir′dō), *n. Slang.* a weirdie: *The weirdo in this melodrama [is] a young man who kidnaps a girl* (New York Times).

Weirds (wirdz), *n.pl.* the Fates. [Old English *wyrd* fate; in plural, the Fates]

weird sisters or **Weird Sisters, 1.** the Fates. **2.** the witches in *Macbeth.*

Weis·mann·ism (vīs′män iz əm), *n. Biology.* the theory of evolution and heredity propounded by August Weismann, a German biologist, especially his theory that germ plasm is the material basis of heredity and that acquired characters are not transmissible.

weiss beer (wīs; *German* vīs), a very pale, highly effervescent beer, usually prepared from wheat. [half translation of German *Weissbier* (literally) white beer]

we·jack (wē′jak), *n.* a fisher, the weasellike mammal. [American English; see WOODCHUCK]

 PRONUNCIATION KEY: hat, āge, cãre, fär; let, ēqual, tėrm; it, īce; hot, ōpen, ôrder; oil, out; cup, pu̇t, rüle;

we·ka (wā′kä, wē′kə), *n.* any of certain flightless birds of New Zealand. Wekas are rails about the size of a chicken, with short legs and brown plumage. [< Maori *weka;* probably imitative]

welch (welch, welsh), *v.i.* welsh. —**welch′er,** *n.*

Welch (welch, welsh), *adj., n.* Welsh.

Welch·man (welch′mən, welsh′-), *n., pl.* **-men.** Welshman.

wel·come (wel′kəm), *v.,* **-comed, -com·ing,** *n., adj., interj.* —*v.t.* **1.** to greet (a person) with pleasure on his arrival; give a friendly reception to. **2.** to receive gladly: *to welcome suggestions or contributions.*
—*n.* **1.** the act of welcoming or being welcomed; kind reception: *a friend always sure of a welcome.* **2.** a word or phrase expressing this; kindly greeting: *to voice a warm welcome.*
wear out one's welcome, to visit a person too often or for too long a time: *We decided not to visit them every Sunday lest we wear out our welcome.*
—*adj.* **1.** gladly received: *a welcome letter.* **2.** gladly or freely permitted: *You are welcome to use the phone.* **3.** free to enjoy courtesies, etc., without obligation (used as a conventional response to *thanks*): *You are quite welcome.*
—*interj.* a word of kindly greeting: *Welcome home!*
[alteration (perhaps influenced by *well*[1]) of Old English *wilcuma* (originally) desired guest < *willa* pleasure, desire + *cuma* a comer < *cuman* to come] —**wel′come·ly,** *adv.* —**wel′come·ness,** *n.*
➔ As a reply to "Thank you," **you're welcome** is usual in the United States and certain parts of northern England, while the southern and western English reply is normally another "Thank you."

welcome mat, 1. a doormat, especially one with the word "Welcome" on it: *One day she opened her front door, and there, lying across the welcome mat, was a man, sound asleep or dead drunk* (New Yorker). **2.** *Informal.* a hearty welcome or reception: *Throughout all of Tidewater Virginia the welcome mat is out for industry seeking new locations* (Wall Street Journal).

wel·com·er (wel′kə mər), *n.* a person or thing that welcomes or greets.

welcome wagon, *U.S.* an organization that officially greets new residents to a town, city, county, or state, by extending to them free souvenirs, samples of merchandise and other items of local promotion.

weld[1] (weld), *v.t.* **1.** to join or combine (pieces of metal, plastic, etc.) by heating either by a flame torch or an electric current and hammering or pressing together while soft, or by melting a similar metal or plastic into the joint: *He welded the broken rod.* **2.** to unite closely; join intimately or inseparably: *to weld nations into an alliance. . . . welding words into the crude mass from the new speech round him* (Browning).
—*v.i.* to be welded or be capable of being welded: *Some metals weld better than other metals.* —*n.* **1.** a welded joint or fitting. **2.** a welding. [alteration of *well*[2], in sense of "to boil"] —**weld′er,** *n.* —**weld′less,** *adj.*

weld[2] (weld), *n.* **1.** a European mignonette, from which a yellow dye is obtained; dyer's-weed; yellowweed. **2.** the dye. Also, **woald, wold, would.** [Middle English *welde,* and *wald,* probably unrecorded Old English *wealde.* Apparently related to WEALD, WOLD[1].]

weld·a·bil·i·ty (wel′də bil′ə tē), *n.* the quality or property of being weldable: *Columbium in stainless steel improved the alloy's weldability* (Science News Letter).

weld·a·ble (wel′də bəl), *adj.* that can be welded.

weld·ing (wel′ding), *n.* the process of joining with a weld.

welding rod, a metal rod melted into the joint of a weld to bond two pieces of metal.

welding torch, a torch using gas as the source of heat for welding.

weld·ment (weld′mənt), *n.* an assembly of parts welded together: *Rohr pioneered the manufacture of stainless steel honeycomb structures and high-strength weldments* (Wall Street Journal).

wel·fare (wel′fãr′), *n.* **1.** the state or condition of doing or being well; health, happiness, and prosperity. **2.** welfare work. **3.** public financial assistance given to poor people for living expenses; relief: *Mrs. Perry had been receiving forty dollars a month in welfare for herself and her four children* (New Yorker).
on welfare, receiving public financial assistance for living expenses; on relief: *The services and the programs of the city are to help the poor, whether they are actually on welfare or whether they are trying to support a family on the wages earned* (Atlantic).
[< earlier phrase *wel fare* < *wel* well + *fare* go]

welfare fund, a fund to provide benefits for workers, set up by a union from its own dues, or by an employer under terms of the Taft-Hartley Act.

welfare state, a state whose government provides for the welfare of its citizens through social security, unemployment insurance, free medical treatment, etc.

welfare stater, welfare statist.

welfare statism, 1. the condition of being a welfare state. **2.** the principles and practices of a welfare state.

welfare statist, a supporter of the principles and practices of a welfare state. —**wel′fare-stat′ist,** *adj.*

welfare work, work done to improve the conditions of people who need help, carried on by government, private organizations, or individuals.

welfare worker, a person who does welfare work.

wel·far·ism (wel′fãr iz əm), *n.* the principles, practices, or condition of a welfare state: *He was marching ideologically in the spirit of the great wave of welfarism that inundated this state* (Newsweek). *The upset was also a rebuke by farmers and ranchers — who paid welfarism's costs — to the citified beneficiaries* (Time).

wel·i (wel′ē), *n.* in Moslem countries: **1.** a saint or holy man. **2.** a tomb or shrine of a saint, commonly a domed structure. [< Arabic *walī,* or *welī* friend (of God), saint]

wel·kin (wel′kən), *n. Archaic.* the sky. [Middle English *welken,* variant of *wolken,* Old English *wolcen* cloud]

well[1] (wel), *adv.,* **bet·ter, best,** *adj., interj.* —*adv.* **1.** in a satisfactory, favorable, or advantageous manner; all right: *The job was well done. Is everything going well at school?* **2. a.** to a satisfactory or adequate degree; sufficiently; enough: *to be well fed.* **b.** thoroughly; fully: *a roast well done. Shake well before using.* **3.** to a considerable degree; considerably; much: *The fair brought in well over a hundred dollars.* **4.** in detail; intimately: *He knows the subject well.* **5.** fairly; reasonably: *I couldn't very well refuse to lend him the book.*
as well, a. also; besides: *Marx had to fight the French Blanquists as well, on somewhat similar grounds* (Edmund Wilson). **b.** equally: *He thought he might as well strive to promote his own needs* (J.E.T. Rogers).
as well as, a. in addition to; besides: *It permits telling others who the actors are, as well as letting actors know a world beyond themselves* (Saturday Review). **b.** as much as: *Thus the Government may understandably regard the US build-up as a source of provocation as well as protection* (Manchester Guardian Weekly).
be or **get well away,** *British.* to have made a good start or good progress: *From the drop [kick] Andrew got well away but Henry pulled him up* (Glasgow Herald).
—*adj.* **1.** satisfactory; good; right: *All's well. It is well you came along.* **2.** in good health: *Is he well enough to travel?* **3.** desirable; advisable: *It is always well to start a bit early.*
—*interj.* an expression used to show mild surprise, agreement, etc., or merely to fill in: *Well! Well! here's Jack. Well, I'm not sure.*
[Old English *wel*]
—**Syn.** *adj.* **2.** hale, sound, hearty.
➔ **a.** Compound adjectives whose first element is **well** are normally hyphenated when used attributively and written as separate words in other uses: *a well-written book. The book was well written.* But those whose second element is a noun plus *-ed* (*well-intentioned*) and a few others, like *well-read,* are hyphenated in all positions. *Wellborn* is exceptional in being written solid. **b. Well** is both adverb (*He plays well*) and adjective (*He looks well*). *To feel good* and *to feel well* are both standard English, the first implying a sense of satisfaction or elation, the second the absence of illness.
➔ See **good** for a usage note.

well[2] (wel), *n.* **1.** a hole dug or shaft bored in the ground to get water, oil, gas, etc. **2.** the source of anything; spring; fountainhead; fount: *a well of everlasting love.* **3.** something like a well in shape or use: *the well of a fountain pen.* **4.** a shaft or opening for stairs or elevators, extending vertically through the floors of a building. **5.** a compartment around a ship's pumps making them accessible for inspection and maintenance, and protecting them from damage. **6.** a storage compartment for fish in the hold of a fishing boat, kept filled with water to keep the catch alive. **7.** (in English law courts) the space where the solicitors sit, directly in front of the judge or judges. **8.** the part of a meeting hall where the speaker's rostrum is: *as he spoke from the well of the House* (Time). **9.** a hollow part in a wing or fuselage of an aircraft into which a wheel of the landing gear is moved when the plane is airborne. **10.** *Archaic.* **a.** a spring (of water). **b.** a pool fed by a spring.
[Old English *welle, wielle* < stem of *weallan,* to boil]
—*v.i.* **1.** to spring; rise: *Tears welled up in her eyes.* **2.** to surge, gush, or billow: *Smoke welled out of the front window.* —*v.t.* to send gushing up or pouring forth: *a spring welling up cool water.*
[Old English *wellan,* or *wiellan* (causative) < *weallan* to boil]

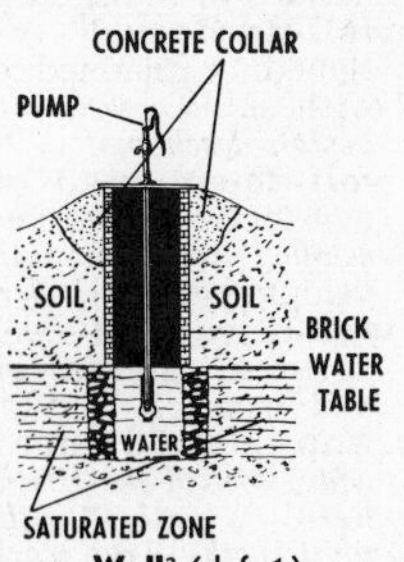

Well[2] **(def. 1)**

we'll (wēl; *unstressed* wil), we will; we shall.

well-act·ed (wel′ak′tid), *adj.* **1.** skillfully performed on the stage. **2.** cleverly feigned or simulated.

well·a·day (wel′ə dā′), *interj. Archaic.* wellaway; alas! [alteration of *wellaway;* influenced by *lackaday*]

well-ad·ver·tised (wel′ad′vər tīzd), *adj.* given much advertising or publicity: *A well-advertised brand recently cut its price . . . and doubled sales* (Newsweek).

well-ad·vised (wel′ad vīzd′), *adj.* **1.** prudent; careful; doing the wise or proper thing: *The author was no doubt well-advised to send his work abroad* (Atlantic). **2.** based on wise counsel or careful consideration: *well-advised plans, a well-advised silence.*

well-ap·point·ed (wel′ə poin′tid), *adj.* having good furnishings or equipment.

well·a·way (wel′ə wā′), *interj. Archaic.* alas! [Old English *wei lā wei,* alteration of *wā lā wā* (literally) woe, lo! woe]

well-bal·anced (wel′bal′ənst), *adj.* **1.** rightly balanced, adjusted, or regulated. **2.** sensible; sane.

well-be·haved (wel′bi hāvd′), *adj.* showing good manners or conduct.

well-be·ing (wel′bē′ing), *n.* health and happiness; welfare.

well-be·lov·ed (wel′bi luv′id, -luvd′), *adj.* dearly beloved.

well·born (wel′bôrn′), *adj.* belonging to a good family; of good lineage.

well-bred (wel′bred′), *adj.* **1.** well brought up; having or showing good manners; courteous. **2.** (of animals) of good breed or stock.

well-built (wel′bilt′), *adj.* **1.** put together well; solid; sturdy: *The well-designed motels are badly built or else the well-built ones are badly designed* (Harper's). **2.** *Informal.* having a muscular, shapely, or coordinated build: *a well-built athlete, a well-built dancer.*

well car, a railroad flatcar with a depressed center section and additional wheels, for carrying heavy shipment.

well-cho·sen (wel′chō′zən), *adj.* carefully selected (used especially of words).

well-con·nect·ed (wel′kə nek′tid), *adj.* **1.** thought out well; planned carefully: *a well-connected paragraph.* **2.** of good family and connections.

well-con·tent (wel′kən tent′), *adj.* highly pleased or satisfied.

well-cut (wel′kut′), *adj.* tailored in the proper style or fashion.

well deck, an open space on the main deck of a ship, lying at a lower level between the forecastle and poop.

well-de·fined (wel′di fīnd′), *adj.* clearly defined or indicated; distinct.

well-de·signed (wel′di zīnd′), *adj.* designed or planned competently; arranged with skill: *a well-designed building, a well-designed scheme.*

well-de·vel·oped (wel′di vel′əpt), *adj.* **1.** developed or worked out well: *a well-developed system or plan.* **2.** showing good development: *a well-developed physique.*

well-di·rect·ed (wel′də rek′tid, -dī-), *adj.* **1.** aimed, guided, or addressed with skill and care. **2.** conducted, led, or coached with skill and care: *The well-directed rioters who stormed the British embassy in Baghdad were . . . symbols of the confusion and the turmoil in the Arab world* (Economist).

well-dis·ci·plined (wel′dis′ə plind), *adj.* **1.** carefully trained; conditioned or ordered well: *a well-disciplined body or mind.* **2.** having controls; following an established order and methods: *a relic of the past, when archaeology was a rich man's hobby rather than a well-disciplined subject* (New Scientist).

well-dis·posed (wel′dis pōzd′), *adj.* **1.** rightly or properly disposed. **2.** well-meaning. **3.** favorably or kindly disposed.

well-do·er (wel′dü′ər), *n.* a person whose deeds are good.

well-do·ing (wel′dü′ing), *n.* a doing right; good conduct or action. —*adj.* acting well; doing what is right and satisfactory.

well-done (wel′dun′), *adj.* **1.** performed well; skillfully done or executed: *a well-done job, a well-done translation.* **2.** (of meat) thoroughly cooked: *a well-done steak.*

well-dressed (wel′drest′), *adj.* **1.** fashionably dressed; in good taste. **2.** properly prepared, cultivated, trimmed, cooked, etc.

well-dress·ing (wel′dres′ing), *n.* a traditional custom in the rural areas of England of decorating the wells at Whitsuntide.

well-es·tab·lished (wel′ə stab′lisht), *adj.* firmly established in being or acceptance: *a well-established belief, family, or business.*

well-fa·vored (wel′fā′vərd), *adj.* of pleasing appearance; good-looking.

well-fa·voured (wel′fā′vərd), *adj. Especially British.* well-favored.

well-fed (wel′fed′), *adj.* showing the result of good feeding; fat; plump.

well-fixed (wel′fikst′), *adj. Informal.* well-to-do.

well-formed (wel′fôrmd′), *adj.* rightly or finely formed; shapely.

well-found (wel′found′), *adj.* well-supplied or equipped.

well-found·ed (wel′foun′did), *adj.* rightly or justly founded: *a well-founded faith in schools.*

well-groomed (wel′grümd′), *adj.* well cared for; neat and trim.

well-ground·ed (wel′groun′did), *adj.* **1.** based on good grounds; well-founded. **2.** thoroughly instructed in the fundamental principles of a subject: *to be well-grounded in mathematics.*

well-grown (wel′grōn′), *adj.* well-advanced in growth.

well-han·dled (wel′han′dəld), *adj.* accomplished or managed with skill and dexterity: *a well-handled campaign.*

well·head (wel′hed′), *n.* **1.** a spring of water. **2.** the chief source or fountainhead of anything.

well-heeled (wel′hēld′), *adj. U.S. Informal.* **1.** dressed well and giving the impression of having enough money to maintain oneself: *They are all well-heeled and live universally beyond their means* (Phyllis McGinley). **2.** prosperous: *A group of well-heeled oilmen are in the process of acquiring 5,000 acres of choice land between Dallas and Fort Worth for $10 million* (Time).

well·hole (wel′hōl′), *n.* **1.** the hole or shaft of a well. **2.** a well or shaft in a building, as for stairs or elevators. **3.** an enclosed space within which a balancing weight rises and falls.

well-in·formed (wel′in fôrmd′), *adj.* **1.** having reliable or full information on a subject. **2.** having information on a wide variety of subjects.

Wel·ling·ton boot, or **Wel·ling·ton** (wel′ing tən), *n.* **1.** a high boot covering the knee in front and cut away behind. **2.** a somewhat shorter boot worn under the trousers. [< the first Duke of *Wellington,* 1769-1852, a British general, victor over Napoleon at Waterloo]

Wel·ing·to·ni·a or **wel·ing·to·ni·a** (wel′ing tō′nē ə), *n.* the big tree, a large California evergreen tree; giant sequoia: *dwarfing neighboring houses and smaller blocks, making even Wellingtonias look like bushes* (Sunday Times). [< New Latin *Wellingtonia* the genus name < the first Duke of *Wellington*]

Wel·ling·to·ni·an (wel′ing tō′nē ən), *adj.* of, having to do with, or characteristic of the first Duke of Wellington: *There is a Wellingtonian vigor in his way of stating a case* (Nation).

well-in·ten·tioned (wel′in ten′shənd), *adj.* having or showing good intentions; well-meaning: *politicians who were clever and well-intentioned* (Baron Charnwood). *The climate in which English scientists went about their work was crammed full of confidence, socially well-intentioned, and, in a serious working sense, international* (C.P. Snow).

well-judged (wel′jujd′), *adj.* done with or resulting from good judgment; judicious: *Mr. Rattigan has had a remarkably well-judged shot at all this* (Manchester Guardian).

well-kept (wel′kept′), *adj.* **1.** well cared for; carefully tended: *a well-kept house or garden.* **2.** faithfully observed or guarded: *Undoubtedly all efforts will be made to preserve this deep and well-kept secret* (New York Times).

well-knit (wel′nit′), *adj.* **1.** firmly joined or put together; closely linked or connected: *I found it an extremely well-knit and occasionally exciting work* (New Yorker). **2.** strong and compact of build; well-developed; well-built: *As he approached, his well-knit figure was a picture of confidence.*

well-known (wel′nōn′), *adj.* **1.** clearly or fully known. **2.** familiar. **3.** generally or widely known.

well log, the log kept as a record of a well logging project.

well logging, the making of exploratory test borings in an underground mineral formation, and maintaining a record or log of what is found.

well-made (wel′mād′), *adj.* **1.** (of a thing) skillfully made; sturdily constructed: *a well-made old desk.* **2.** (of a person or animal) well-proportioned.

well-man·nered (wel′man′ərd), *adj.* having or showing good manners; polite; courteous.

well-marked (wel′märkt′), *adj.* clearly marked or distinguished; distinct.

well-matched (wel′macht′), *adj.* **1.** that fit or go well together; harmonious: *They are a well-matched couple.* **2.** of equal ability, strength, etc.: *It was like the sixth or seventh round in a long championship fight between two well-matched heavyweights* (Time).

well-mean·ing (wel′mē′ning), *adj.* **1.** having good intentions. **2.** proceeding from good intentions.

well-meant (wel′ment′), *adj.* done or proceeding from good intentions: *a cold return for a well-meant kindness* (Scott). *They are well-meant proposals and they may succeed* (Manchester Guardian).

well·ness (wel′nis), *n.* the state of being well.

well-nigh (wel′nī′), *adv.* very nearly; all but entirely; almost.

well-off (wel′ôf′, -of′), *adj.*, or **well off, 1.** in a good condition or position; favorably circumstanced. **2.** fairly rich.

well-oiled (wel′oild′), *adj.* in good running condition; smooth; frictionless: *The President heads a well-oiled, relatively trouble-free Administration* (Time).

well-or·dered (wel′ôr′dərd), *adj.* ordered or arranged well; well-regulated.

well-paid (wel′pād′), *adj.* liberally rewarded or compensated: *When some comedian or wit told Queen Victoria jokes, they weren't supplied to him by six well-paid gag writers, but just occurred to him* (Newsweek).

well-pay·ing (wel′pā′ing), *adj.* giving a good salary or return: *It is appreciably below the . . . average for such a well-paying industry* (Wall Street Journal).

well-placed (wel′plāst′), *adj.* **1.** directed or aimed well: *One well-placed missile . . . would destroy most of the tanks, trucks . . . and other equipment* (Time). **2.** holding a good social or official position: *That's from a well-placed Eastern European diplomat here* (Newsweek). **3.** set in a good place or position; rightly or fitly placed; handy: *That would not explain the absence of shower curtains in hotels, the absence of well-placed shaving mirrors in hotel bathrooms* (Harper's).

well point, a hollow pipe or tube that is set in the ground to pump out ground water which could cause flooding during construction.

well-pre·served (wel′pri zėrvd′), *adj.* showing few signs of age.

well-pro·por·tioned (wel′prə pôr′shənd, -pōr′-), *adj.* having good or correct proportions; having a pleasing shape.

well-read (wel′red′), *adj.* having read much; knowing a great deal about books and literature.

well-reg·u·lat·ed (wel′reg′yə lā′tid), *adj.* **1.** regulated well; kept in due order; well-ordered: *a well-regulated household, mind, or life. Social virtues not to be disregarded in any well-regulated community* (Harriet Beecher Stowe). **2.** being what a person or thing should be: *He was to return as any respectable, well-regulated prodigal ought to return—abject, broken-hearted, asking forgiveness* (Samuel Butler).

well-round·ed (wel′roun′did), *adj.* **1.** having a properly rounded shape; well filled out: *But she grew up well-rounded, just the same, and at 15 . . . she got a small part in a movie* (Newsweek). **2.** complete in all parts or respects: *The boy or girl who goes to work in . . . adolescence is prevented from completing a well-rounded education* (Emory S. Bogardus).

well shrimp, a fresh-water crustacean found in wells.

Wells·i·an (wel′zē ən), *adj.* of, having to do with, or characteristic of the writings of H.G. Wells, 1866-1946, English author, especially his anticipation of future conditions.

wells·ite (wel′zīt), *n.* a mineral, a colorless to white, hydrous silicate of aluminum, barium, calcium, and potassium, occurring in crystals. [< Horace L. *Wells,* 1855-1924, an American chemist + *-ite*[1]]

well-spo·ken (wel′spō′kən), *adj.* **1.** speaking well, fittingly, or pleasingly; polite in speech. **2.** spoken well.

well·spring (wel′spring′), *n.* **1.** the source of a stream; fountainhead. **2.** a source, especially the source of a supply that never fails.

well-suit·ed (wel′sü′tid), *adj.* suitable; convenient.

well sweep, a tapering or weighted pole swung on a pivot and having a bucket hung on the smaller or lighter end, used for drawing water from a well.

well-tem·pered (wel′tem′pərd), *adj.* **1.** *Music.* (of keyboard instruments) adjusted to the equal temperament. **2.** having a good temper; controlled; mild: *and also see Mr. Dunn's well-tempered disquietude about a society that seems to be planning its own obsolescence* (New Yorker). **3.** *Metallurgy.* brought to the right degree of hardness and elasticity.

well-thought-of (wel′thôt′ov′, -uv′), *adj.* highly respected; esteemed.

well-thumbed (wel′thumd′), *adj.* bearing marks of frequent handling: *They pore over . . . well-thumbed pages as if touring their favorite market place* (Time).

well-timed (wel′tīmd′), *adj.* timely: *a well-timed sermon.*

well-to-do (wel′tə dü′), *adj.* having enough money to live well; prosperous: *A well-to-do widow bought the big corner house.*
—*n.* **the well-to-do,** well-to-do persons: *No government is interested in putting up low-rent housing for the well-to-do* (Wall Street Journal).
—**well′-to-do′ness,** *n.*

well-trav·eled (wel′trav′əld), *adj.* **1.** that has traveled far; experienced in travel: *Any alert, well-traveled American will be aware that men . . . pay almost as much attention to their dress as women do* (Newsweek). **2.** much traveled; carrying much traffic: *Payments vary according to routes, running low on well-traveled airways, and higher in the hinterlands* (Wall Street Journal).

well-turned (wel′tėrnd′), *adj.* **1.** turned or shaped well, as with rounded or curving form: *a well-turned ankle.* **2.** gracefully or happily expressed: *a well-turned compliment. A few well-turned paragraphs . . . in the Bishop's most approved style* (John L. Motley).

well-turned-out (wel′tėrnd′out′), *adj.* dressed well; stylish: *But a man otherwise well-turned-out, who stretches his arms on the dinnertable . . . is bound to feel a passing unease* (Punch).

well-wish (wel′wish′), *n.* a good wish: *Harry Truman, like Lyndon Johnson after him, had the well-wishes of everybody* (Vermont Royster).

well-wish·er (wel′wish′ər), *n.* a person who wishes well to a person, cause, etc.: *The well-wishers came around to congratulate the winning candidate.*

well-wish·ing (wel′wish′ing), *adj.* that wishes well to others; benevolent. —*n.* **1.** the act of wishing well to another. **2.** an expression of good wishes.

well-worn (wel′wôrn′, -wōrn′), *adj.* **1.** much worn by use: *a well-worn pair of shoes.* **2.** used too much; trite; stale; hackneyed: *Ray bored the neighbors with his well-worn jokes.*

Wels·bach burner (welz′bak, -bäk; *German* vels′bäH), a gas burner like a Bunsen burner, having an incombustible mantle which becomes incandescent and emits a brilliant light. [< K. Auer von *Welsbach,* 1858-1929, an Austrian chemist, who invented it]

Welsbach mantle, the gas mantle of a Welsbach burner, consisting of thorium oxide with a trace of cerium oxide around the flame.

welsh (welsh, welch), *Slang.* —*v.t.* to cheat by failing to pay a bet. —*v.i.* to evade the fulfillment of an obligation. Also, **welch.**
welsh on, to fail to keep an agreement with: *to welsh on a business deal.*
[origin uncertain] —**welsh′er,** *n.*

Welsh (welsh, welch), *adj.* of or having to do with Wales, its people, or their Celtic language.
—*n.* **1.** the inhabitants or natives of Wales, collectively. **2.** their Celtic language. **3.** any of a certain breed of dairy cattle. Also, **Welch.**
[Old English *Welisc* < *Wealh* a Briton, foreigner < *Volcae,* the name of a Celtic tribe. Compare WALLOON, WALNUT.]

Welsh Black, one of a breed of black, long-horned cattle raised for its high-quality beef.

Welsh corgi or **Corgi,** either of two breeds of Welsh working dogs having a long body, short legs, and a foxlike head. The Cardigan breed has rounded ears and a long tail, and the Pembroke breed has pricked ears and a short tail. [< Welsh *corgi* < *cor* dwarf + *ci* dog]

Pembroke Welsh Corgi (10 to 12 in. high at the shoulder)

Welsh·man (welsh′mən, welch′-), *n., pl.* **-men.** a native of Wales.

Welsh·ness (welsh′nis, welch′-), *n.* Welsh character or quality.

Welsh rabbit or **rarebit,** a dish of cheese melted with some liquid (often beer or ale), egg, etc., and poured over toast or crackers. It is served piping hot.
➔ **Welsh rabbit,** the original form, is a humorous coinage like *Cape Cod turkey* for codfish. The variant *Welsh rarebit* is the result of folk etymology.

Welsh springer spaniel, any of a breed of red-and-white hunting dogs similar to the English springer spaniel, used for retrieving game on land or in water.

Welsh terrier, any of a breed of black-and-tan, wiry-haired terriers, thought to be originally from Wales.

Welsh Terrier (14 to 15 in. high at the shoulder)

welt (welt), *n.* **1.** a strip of leather placed between and sewn to the edge of the uppers and the sole of a shoe or boot. **2.** a narrow strip of material or cord fastened on the edge or at a seam of a garment or upholstery, for trimming or strengthening. **3.** a seam similar to a flat fell seam, used in tailoring. **4.** (in leatherworking, blacksmithing, etc.) any of various ribs, flanges, or seams in which one edge is lapped back for strength. **5. a.** a streak or ridge made on the skin by a stick or whip; wale; wheal; weal. **b.** a heavy blow.
—*v.t.* **1.** to put a welt or welts on. **2.** *Informal.* to beat severely.
[Middle English *welte,* or *walte.* Perhaps related to WALE[1].]

Welt·an·schau·ung (velt′än′shou′ůng), *n.* a scheme or concept of human history, especially one by which a particular individual or group seeks to understand or explain things as they are, and possibly or probably may be, in order to be guided in forming a policy or program. [< German *Weltanschauung* (literally) world view < *Welt* world + *Anschauung* view, perception]

Welt·an·sicht (velt′än′ziHt), *n.* a special concept or particular interpretation of reality. [< German *Weltansicht* (literally) world view < *Welt* world + *Ansicht* view]

wel·ter[1] (wel′tər), *v.i.* **1.** to roll or toss about; wallow. **2.** to lie soaked; be drenched. **3.** to be sunk or deeply involved (in). **4.** (of waves, the water, or sea) to surge.
—*n.* **1.** a rolling and tossing. **2.** a surging or confused mass. **3.** confusion; commotion.
[< Middle Dutch, or Middle Low German *welteren*]

wel·ter[2] (wel′tər), *adj. Racing.* of or having to do with a race in which horses carry welterweights. —*n. Informal.* a welterweight. [< *welt* to thrash or whip + *-er*[1]]

wel·ter·weight (wel′tər wāt′), *n.* **1.** a professional boxer weighing between 135 and 147 pounds. **2.** a professional wrestler weighing between 147 and 160 pounds. **3.** a weight of 28 pounds sometimes carried by a horse as a handicap in addition to that added for age.

Welt·po·li·tik (velt′pô li tēk′), *n.* world politics; international politics. [< German *Weltpolitik* < *Welt* world + *Politik* politics]

Welt·schmerz (velt′shmerts′), *n.* sorrow or pain caused by pondering the troubles of the world; pessimistic melancholy. [< German *Weltschmerz* (literally) world sorrow < *Welt* world + *Schmerz* sorrow]

wen[1] (wen), *n.* a harmless tumor of the skin, especially on the scalp. [Old English *wenn*]

wen[2] (wen), *n.* the name of the Old English runic letter ᚹ (= w) and of the manuscript form of this (Ƿƿ) in Old and early Middle English. [Old English *wen,* variant of *wyn* (literally) joy]

wench (wench), *n.* **1.** a girl or young woman. **2. a.** a servant girl: *a kitchen wench.* **b.** any girl considered as belonging to the class of workers, peasants, etc.: *a buxom country wench.* **3.** *Archaic.* a wanton woman.
—*v.i.* to seek out and consort with wenches.
[short for Middle English *wenchel* child, Old English *wencel,* probably related to *wancol* unsteady, weak. Compare WANKLE.]
—**wench′er,** *n.*

wend (wend), *v.,* **wend·ed** or (*Archaic*) **went, wend·ing.** —*v.t.* to direct (one's way): *We wended our way home.* —*v.i.* to go; travel. [Old English *wendan*]

Wend (wend), *n.* one of a Slavic people living in Lusatia in central Germany; Sorb. [< German *Wende.* Compare Medieval Latin *Venedi.*]

Wend·ic (wen′dik), *adj.* Wendish.

wen·di·go (wen′di gō), *n., pl.* **-gos** *for 1,* **-go** or **-goes** *for 2.* **1.** (in Algonkian mythology) an evil spirit of a cannibalistic nature. **2.** *Canadian.* a hybrid trout; splake. [< Algonkian (Ojibwa) *weendigo* cannibal]

Wend·ish (wen′dish), *adj.* of or having to do with the Wends or their language; Sorbian. —*n.* the language of the Wends.

wen·nish (wen′ish), *adj.* **1.** having the character or appearance of a wen. **2.** affected with wens. [< *wen*[1] + *-ish*]

wen·ny (wen′ē), *adj.* wennish.

Wens·ley·dale (wenz′lē dāl′), *n.* a variety of white cheese with blue veins. [< *Wensleydale,* a district of Yorkshire, England, where the cheese is made]

went (went), *v.* the past tense of **go:** *I went home.* [(originally) past tense of *wend*]
➔ In nonstandard English **went** is also used as the past participle: *I could have went yesterday.*

wen·tle·trap (wen′təl trap′), *n.* any of a group or family of marine gastropods that have an elongated, white, spiral shell. [< Dutch *wenteltrap* winding staircase; spiral shell]

wept (wept), *v.* the past tense and past participle of **weep**[1]: *She wept for hours.*

wer (wėr, wer), *n.* wergild.

were (wėr; *unstressed* wər), *v.* **1.** the plural and 2nd person singular past indicative of **be:** *The officers were obeyed by the soldiers.* **2.** the past subjunctive of **be:** *If I were rich, I would travel.*
as it were, in some way; so to speak: *She has thought fit, as it were, to mock herself* (Sir Richard Steele).
[Old English *wǣron*]
➔ **a.** Subjunctive **were** is used in clauses stating conditions contrary to fact or not capable of being met (*If I were young again . . .*) and conditions which are hypothetical but possible (*If he were to be chosen unanimously . . .*). Sometimes the conjunction is omitted and the subject and verb are inverted: *Were I young again . . . .* **b. Were** is also used in noun clauses after *wish: I wish I were there.*
➔ See **was** for another usage note.

we're (wir), we are.

were·gild (wir′gild′, wer′-), *n.* wergild.

weren't (wėrnt), were not.

were·wolf (wir′wůlf′, wėr′-), *n., pl.* **-wolves** (-wůlvz′). (in folklore) a person who has been changed into a wolf or is capable of changing himself at times into a wolf, while retaining human intelligence. [Old English *werewulf,* probably < *wer* man + *wulf* wolf]

wer·gild (wėr′gild′, wer′-), *n.* (in early English and Germanic law) the price set upon a man according to his rank, paid to his relatives in cases of homicide and certain other crimes, to free the offender from further obligation or punishment. [Old English *wergeld,* or *weregild* (literally) man-compensation]

wer·ner·ite (wėr′nə rīt), *n.* any of a group of minerals, silicates of aluminum, calcium, and sodium; scapolite. [< Abraham G. *Werner,* 1750-1817, a German mineralogist + *-ite*[1]]

wersh (wersh), *adj. Scottish.* wearish.

wert (wėrt; *unstressed* wərt), *v. Archaic.* second person singular past indicative and subjunctive of **be.** "Thou wert" means "you were."

Wer·the·ri·an or **Wer·te·ri·an** (ver tir′ē ən), *adj.* of or characteristic of Werther, the fictional character in Goethe's romance *The Sorrows of Werther;* morbidly sentimental: *An ancient lovelorn swain . . . full of imaginary sorrows and Wertherian grief* (Anthony Trollope).

Wer·ther·ism (ver′tə riz əm), *n.* Wertherian character or quality; morbid sentimentality.

wer·wolf (wėr′wůlf′, wer′-), *n., pl.* **-wolves** (-wůlvz′). werewolf.

wes·kit (wes′kit), *n. Informal.* a waistcoat; vest: *The Prime Minister wore a weskit that was not in startling colors but was less than sober raiment* (Harper's).

Wes·ley·an (wes′lē ən; *especially British* wez′lē ən), *n.* **1.** a follower of John Wesley, 1703-1791, English clergyman who founded the Methodist Church. **2.** a Methodist.
—*adj.* **1.** of or having to do with John Wesley or his teaching. **2.** of or having to do with the Methodist Church.

Wes·ley·an·ism (wes′lē ə niz′əm; *especially British* wez′lē ə niz′əm), *n.* the system of doctrines and church polity of the Wesleyan Methodists.

west (west), *n.* **1.** the direction of the sunset; point of the compass midway between north and south. *Abbr.:* W. or W (no period). **2.** the part of any country, region, or area toward the west.
—*adj.* **1.** toward the west: *a west window.* **2.** from the west: *a west wind.* **3.** in the west: *west New York.* **4.** in the western part; western. **5.** in or toward the part of a church furthest from the altar.
—*adv.* **1.** toward the west; westward: *to go west.* **2.** in the west: *The wind was blowing west.*
[Old English *west,* adverb, to the west, and *westan* from the west]
➔ A **west** or **westerly** wind carries a ship *east* or on an *easterly* course.

West (def. 1) on a compass

West (west), *n.* **1.** the western part of the United States. **2.** the countries in Europe and the Americas, as contrasted with those in Asia, especially southwestern Asia; the Western Hemisphere and Europe; the Occident. **3.** the non-Communist countries of Europe and America as a group, usually also including Australia, New Zealand, India, Japan, etc.: *The problems dividing East and West should be discussed peacefully and soberly* (Manchester Guardian). **4.** the Western Roman Empire. **5.** one of the four players or positions in bridge.

West Atlantic, of or having to do with a branch of the Niger-Congo linguistic group spoken in West Africa, including Fulani and Wolof.

west·bound (west′bound′), *adj.* bound westward; going west.

west by north, the point of the compass or the direction, one point or 11 degrees 15 minutes to the north of west.

west by south, the point of the compass or the direction, one point or 11 degrees 15 minutes to the south of west.

West End, a fashionable part of a city or town.

west·er (wes′tər), *v.i.* **1.** to move westward in its course; draw near the west. **2.** to shift to the west.

west·er·ing (wes′tər ing), *adj.* **1.** that declines from the meridian toward the west (used chiefly of the sun when it is nearing the western horizon). **2. a.** that moves in a westward direction. **b.** (of the wind) that shifts to the west.

west·er·li·ness (wes′tər lē nis), *n.* a westerly situation.

west·er·ly (wes′tər lē), *adj., adv., n., pl.* **-lies.** *—adj., adv.* **1.** toward the west. **2.** from the west.
—*n.* a wind that blows from the west.
westerlies, the prevailing westerly winds found in certain latitudes: *Between the westerlies and the trades are the horse latitudes* (Scientific American).
➔ See **west** for a usage note.

west·ern (wes′tərn), *adj.* **1.** toward the west; in the west. **2.** from the west. **3.** of or belonging to the west; found or produced in the west.
—*n.* **1.** *Informal.* a story or motion picture dealing with life in the West, especially cowboy life. **2.** a westerner or Westerner.
[Old English *westerne*]

West·ern (wes′tərn), *adj.* **1.** of or in the West part of the United States. **2.** of or in the countries of Europe and America, especially as contrasted with those of Asia. **3.** of or in North and South America. **4.** of or having to do with the non-Communist West: *In international affairs the conference supported neither the Western nor the Communist bloc* (Listener). **5.** of or having to do with the Western Church. [< *western*]

western catalpa, a catalpa of the western United States, with light, soft, but durable wood, often cultivated as an ornamental tree and for its showy, white flowers; Shawneewood.

Western Church, 1. the part of the Catholic Church that acknowledges the Pope as its spiritual leader and follows the Latin Rite; Roman Catholic Church. **2.** the Christian churches of Europe and America, as a group; western Christendom.

Western civilization, European and American civilization.

western diamondback rattlesnake, a large rattlesnake found from Arkansas and Texas to California and nearby Mexico.

Western Empire, the Western Roman Empire.

West·ern·er (wes′tər nər), *n.* **1.** a person born or living in the western part of the United States. **2.** a person who lives in the non-Communist West: *The French probably are happier than any other Westerners that the Soviet Union is willing to discuss a European settlement* (New York Times). [American English < *western* + *-er*[1]]

west·ern·er (wes′tər nər), *n.* **1.** a person born or living in the western part of any country. **2.** a person belonging to a people or country of Europe or America; Occidental. [< *Westerner*]

Western European Union, a defensive alliance organized in 1954-1955 among Great Britain, France, Italy, West Germany, and the Benelux nations to act upon armaments and also cultural and economic affairs: *If "history is but the unrolled scroll of prophecy," then the Western European Union will prove to be the father of the United States of Europe* (New York Times). *Abbr.:* W.E.U.

western grebe, a large black and white grebe of western North America.

Western Hemisphere, the half of the world that includes North and South America.

western hemlock, a large hemlock of the Pacific Northwest, used for lumber and pulp.

west·ern·ise (wes′tər nīz), *v.t.,* **-ised, -is·ing.** *Especially British.* westernize.

west·ern·ism (wes′tər niz əm), *n.* **1.** Also, **Westernism.** methods, customs, or traits peculiar to Western nations: *To outward appearance, Japan's gloss of Westernism has deepened since the end of the Allied Occupation* (New York Times). **2.** a word, idiom, custom, or manner peculiar to people or life in the western United States.

west·ern·i·za·tion or **West·ern·i·za·tion** (wes′tər nə zā′shən), *n.* the act or process of making western or Western in habits, customs, or character: *A certain amount of Westernization has been taking place in Soviet politics* (New Yorker).

west·ern·ize or **West·ern·ize** (wes′tər-nīz), *v.t.,* **-ized, -iz·ing.** to make western or Western in character, ideas, ways, etc.: *Leningrad is as near to being Westernized as any Russian city can be without jukeboxes* (Punch). —**west′ern·iz′er** or **West′ern·iz′er,** *n.*

west·ern·most (wes′tərn mōst), *adj.* farthest west; most westerly.

Western Ocean, (in classical times) the Atlantic Ocean, which was to the west of the world then known.

Western omelet, an omelet filled with ham, onions, green peppers, etc.

western paper birch, a variety of paper birch growing in western North America, eastern Canada, and New England.

western red cedar, an evergreen of the northwestern United States and western Canada, valued for its wood. It is a kind of arbor vitae.

western roll, a style of high jumping in which the body is parallel to the crossbar at the height of the jump.

Western Roman Empire, the western part of the Roman Empire after its division in 395 A.D.; Western Empire. The Western Roman Empire ended with the capture of Rome by the Vandals in 455.

Western saddle, a saddle with a high, curved pommel, to tie the end of a lariat to when roping cattle, so that the horse can pull against the steer.

western sandpiper, a small sandpiper that nests in Alaska and winters along the coasts of the United States south to northern South America.

Western sandwich, a sandwich filled with a mixture of fried eggs, diced ham, onions, and green peppers.

western tanager, a tanager of western North America, the male of which has a yellow body, red face, and black back, tail, and wings; Louisiana tanager.

western union, a predecessor of the Western European Union which did not include Italy or West Germany.

western X disease, a virus disease of peach and cherry trees, carried by a leaf hopper.

western yellow pine, the ponderosa pine.

West German, 1. of or having to do with West Germany. **2.** a native or inhabitant of West Germany.

West Germanic, the division of Germanic consisting of English, Frisian, Dutch, and German.

West Highland white terrier, a small, white terrier of a breed originating in Scotland.

West Highland White Terrier (10 to 11 in. high at the shoulder)

West Indian, 1. of or having to do with the West Indies, a group of islands in the Atlantic Ocean between Florida and South America. **2.** a native or inhabitant of the West Indies.

West Indian corkwood, balsa, a light, strong, porous wood.

west·ing (wes′ting), *n.* the distance westward covered by a ship on any westerly course; movement to the west.

west·lin (west′lin), *adj. Scottish.* western; westerly. [variant of earlier *westland,* adjective]

west·lins (west′linz), *adv. Scottish.* westward. [< *west* + *-lins,* variant of Old English *-ling,* an adverbial suffix]

Westm., Westminster.

west·mark (west′märk; *German.* vest′-märk′), *n.* the Deutsche mark of West Germany. [< German *Westmark* < *West* west + *Mark* mark[2]]

West·min·ster (west′min′stər), *n. British Informal.* Parliament, or the British government: *The danger facing Westminster is that once released from the current tensions of a spring election, it will relapse into somnolence* (Sunday Times). [< *Westminster,* the part of London that contains the Houses of Parliament]

Westminster Assembly, an assembly, mostly of divines, summoned by the Long Parliament, held at Westminster, London, from 1643 to 1649, that drew up the confession of faith, catechisms, etc., that remain the orthodox statements of Presbyterianism.

west-north·west (west′nôrth′west′), *n.* the point of the compass or the direction midway between west and northwest, two points or 22 degrees 30 minutes to the north of west. —*adj., adv.* of, from, or toward the west-northwest.

West·pha·li·an (west fā′lē ən), *adj.* of or having to do with Westphalia, a western province of Prussia (formerly a duchy, later, with larger territory, a Napoleonic kingdom). —*n.* a native or inhabitant of Westphalia.

West Pointer, a student or graduate of the U.S. Military Academy at West Point, N.Y.: *In three years of Korean fighting, 118 West Pointers were killed in action, or died of wounds or injuries* (Newsweek).

West Saxon, 1. a member of the division of the Saxons in England south of the Thames and westward from Surrey and Sussex. **2.** the dialect of Old English used by the West Saxons. **3.** of, having to do with, or characteristic of the West Saxons or their speech.

west-south·west (west′south′west′), *n.* the point of the compass or the direction midway between west and southwest, two points or 22 degrees 30 minutes to the south of west. —*adj., adv.* of, from, or toward the west-southwest.

Wes·tral·ian (wes trāl′yən), *adj.* of or having to do with Western Australia or its people. —*n.* a native or inhabitant of Western Australia.

West Virginian, 1. a native or inhabitant of West Virginia, an Eastern State of the United States. **2.** of or having to do with West Virginia.

West·wall (west′wôl′; *German* vest′väl′), *n.* the Siegfried Line. [< German *Westwall* < *west* West + *Wall* wall]

west·ward (west′wərd), *adv.* toward the west; in a westerly direction: *to sail westward.* —*adj.* toward, facing, or at the west; westerly; west: *the westward slope of the hill.* —*n.* the direction or part which lies to the west; west. —**west′ward·ly,** *adj., adv.*

west·wards (west′wərdz), *adv.* westward.

wet (wet), *adj.,* **wet·ter, wet·test,** *v.,* **wet** or **wet·ted, wet·ting,** *n.* —*adj.* **1.** covered, soaked, or sprinkled with water or other liquid: *wet hands, a wet sponge.* **2.** not yet dry: *wet paint, wet ink.* **3.** rainy; drizzly; showery: *wet weather, a wet day.* **4.** watery; liquid: *Her eyes were wet with tears.* **5.** using, or performed by the use or presence of, water or other fluid, as chemical analysis. **6.** preserved in syrup; bottled in a liquid. **7.** *U.S. Informal.* having or favoring laws that permit making and selling of alcoholic drinks.
all wet, *Slang.* completely wrong or mistaken: *The lull gave Johnson a chance to show such critics . . . that they were all wet in arguing that a halt in the bombing might open the way to negotiations* (Time).
wet behind the ears. See under **ear**[1].
—*v.t.* **1.** to make wet, moist, or damp. **2.** to pass urine in or on: *A child wets the bed, and no attempted medication has helped* (Saturday Review). —*v.i.* **1.** to become wet, moist, or damp. **2.** to pass urine.
—*n.* **1.** water or other liquid; moisture. **2.** wetness; rain. **3.** *U.S. Informal.* a person who favors laws that permit making and selling of alcoholic drinks.
[Middle English *wett,* past participle of *weten* to wet, Old English *wǣtt,* for *wǣted,* past participle of *wǣtan* to make wet]
—**wet′ly,** *adv.* —**wet′ness,** *n.*
—**Syn.** *adj.* **1.** moist, damp. *–v.t., v.i.* **1. Wet, drench, soak** mean to make or become very moist. **Wet** is the general word: *Wet the material well before applying soap.* **Drench** means to wet thoroughly, as by a pouring rain: *We were drenched by a sudden downpour.* **Soak** means to wet thoroughly by putting or being in a liquid for some time: *Soak the stained spot in milk.*

wet·back (wet′bak′), *n. U.S. Informal.* a Mexican who enters the United States illegally, especially by swimming or wading across the Rio Grande. [American English < *wet* + *back*[1]]

wet bargain, a bargain agreed upon by the parties drinking together.

wet basin, a dock at which a new ship is fitted out after launching.

wet blanket, a person or thing that has a discouraging or depressing effect. —**Syn.** killjoy.

wet-blan·ket (wet′blang′kit), *v.t.* to throw a damper on; discourage; depress: *His gravity at birthday parties, surprise parties, didn't wet-blanket them* (J.D. Salinger).

wet brain, an abnormal accumulation of watery fluid in the brain tissues, associated with acute alcoholism.

wet bulb, the one of the two thermometers of a psychrometer whose bulb is kept moistened during the period when humidity determinations are being made.

wet-bulb thermometer (wet′bulb′), **1.** a wet bulb. **2.** a psychrometer.

wet cell, *Electricity.* a cell having a free-flowing electrolyte.

wet-clean (wet′klēn′), *v.t.* to clean (clothes, etc.) with water: *Customers send their suits back to London and . . . have them wet-cleaned and pressed by hand* (Time).

wet dock, a dock or basin at a seaport furnished with gates, used where the withdrawal of the tide would otherwise leave a ship resting on the bottom, as in parts of England, to keep ships floating as at high tide, while loading, unloading, etc.

wet fly, an artificial fishing fly that is designed to sink below the surface of the water when cast.

wet gas, natural gas containing heavy hydrocarbons such as propane, butane, and pentane, that must be refined for use as gasoline.

weth·er (weᴛʜ′ər), *n.* a castrated ram. [Old English *wether*]

wet·land (wet′land′), *n.* a swamp, marsh, or bog.

wet monsoon, a monsoon during the summer that blows landward from the ocean, bringing rain.

wet nurse, a woman employed to suckle the infant of another.

wet-nurse (wet′nėrs′), *v.t.,* **-nursed, -nurs·ing. 1.** to act as wet nurse to. **2.** to treat with special care; coddle; pamper: *We plan to wet-nurse the most promising little men to the point where they are good customers for First National's conventional banking operations* (Wall Street Journal).

wet pack, a blanket, etc., wet and wrung out and put on the body for medical purposes.

wet plate, *Photography.* a glass plate coated with wet sensitized collodion, formerly (and still occasionally) used, like the modern dry plate, for making pictures in a camera, etc., so called because it must remain wet during the processes of sensitization, exposure, and development.

wet rot, decay in wood or timber caused by excessive moisture: *Wet rot is the destructive agent at work more or less on all telegraph poles* (Preece and Sivewright).

wet steam, steam in which water particles are held in suspension.

wet strength, the ability to hold together and not tear or break to pieces when wet, as of paper: *The product's wet strength is achieved through use of . . . melamine resin, a chemical compound that binds paper fibers together much the way cement binds bricks* (Wall Street Journal).

wet suit, a skin-tight rubber suit worn by skin divers, surfers, etc.: *In wintertime he will don a . . . wet suit and go right on surfing* (Peter Bart).

wet·ta·bil·i·ty (wet′ə bil′ə tē), *n.* wettable quality, property, or extent: *the wettability of a fabric.*

wet·ta·ble (wet′ə bəl), *adj.* that can be wetted: *A wettable powder, the chemical is mixed with water and sprayed onto plants* (Science News Letter).

wet·ter (wet′ər), *n.* a person or thing that wets, as a workman who dampens paper to be used in printing.

wet·ting (wet′ing), *n.* **1.** the act of a person or thing that wets; sprinkling, dabbling, or drenching with water (especially rain) or the like. **2.** something used to make a thing wet.

wetting agent, a substance capable of reducing surface tension so that a liquid will spread more easily on a surface.

wet·ting-out agent (wet′ing out′), a wetting agent.

wet·tish (wet′ish), *adj.* somewhat wet. —**Syn.** damp, moist.

wet water, water to which a detergent has been added to increase its penetrating quality, used in fighting fires.

wet way, *Chemistry.* the method of analysis in which the reactions are produced mostly in solutions and by the use of liquid reagents.

W.E.U. or **WEU** (no periods), Western European Union: *The commission is made up of one member from each of the W.E.U. countries* (London Times).

we've (wēv; *unstressed* wiv), we have.

wey (wā), *n.* a British unit of weight or measure, varying widely according to commodity and locality. [Old English *wǣge.* Compare WEIGH[1].]

w.f. or **wf** (no periods), *Printing.* wrong font.

WFTU (no periods) or **W.F.T.U.,** World Federation of Trade Unions.

w.g., wire gauge.

W. Ger., West Germanic.

wh., watt-hour.

whack (hwak), *n.* **1.** *Informal.* **a.** a sharp, resounding blow. **b.** the sound of this. **2.** *Slang.* a portion, share, or allowance, especially a full share. **3.** wack.

have or **take a whack at,** *U.S. Slang.* to make an attempt or attack upon: *Perhaps one should . . . take a whack at reducing this appalling catalogue of ignorance* (New York Times).

in whack, *Slang.* in line; in proper order or condition: *Their members . . . work toward a solution of the bedevilling problem of keeping prices and incomes in whack* (New Yorker).

out of whack, *Slang.* **a.** not in proper condition; disordered: *Their stomachs are out of whack* (Sinclair Lewis). **b.** out of proper condition; into disorder: *The space man's sense of balance would be thrown out of whack* (New Yorker).

—*v.t., v.i.* **1.** to strike with a sharp, resounding blow. **2.** to beat or win in a contest. **3.** *Slang.* to reduce; knock off: *Filling stations have whacked as much as a dime off their regular prices* (Wall Street Journal).

whack out, *Slang.* to perform or produce vigorously: *. . . a woman pianist at a concert grand, whacking out Bach as only the gentler sex can* (Manchester Guardian Weekly). *He has a second contract for six mysteries a year and somehow whacks out a short story every Monday, rain or shine* (Maclean's).

whack up, *Slang.* **a.** to share; divide: *to whack up the loot.* **b.** to increase: *The thinner rural areas will be forced to whack up the tax rates steeply for the distinctly unamused householders left therein* (New Yorker).

[imitative. Compare THWACK.] —**whack′er,** *n.*

whacked (hwakt), *adj. British Slang.* tired out; exhausted: *Let's sit the next one out—I'm whacked* (Punch).

whack·i·ness (hwak′ē nis), *n.* wackiness.

whack·ing (hwak′ing), *adj. Informal.* large; forcible.

whack·y (hwak′ē), *adj.,* **whack·i·er, whack·i·est.** wacky.

whale[1] (hwāl), *n., pl.* **whales** or (*collectively*) **whale,** *v.,* **whaled, whal·ing.** —*n.* **1.** a mammal shaped like a huge fish and living in the sea. Men get oil and whalebone from whales. **2.** *Informal.* something very big, great, impressive, etc.

Bowhead Whale[1] (def. 1) (to 60 ft. long)

a whale of, a very excellent, large, etc.: *a whale of a party. One of Mr. Taylor's daughters got married recently and the guests . . . had a whale of a time* (Manchester Guardian Weekly).

—*v.i.* to hunt and catch whales.

[Old English *hwæl*]

whale[2] (hwāl), *v.t.,* **whaled, whal·ing.** *Informal.* **1.** to whip severely; beat; flog; thrash: *I caught Stockings trying to open the gate again, and I whaled him with a rope, and then tied the gate up* (Atlantic). **2.** to hit hard. [apparently variant of *wale*[1], verb]

whale·back (hwāl′bak′), *n.* **1.** a type of freighter with a rounded upper deck shaped like a whale's back, used especially on the Great Lakes. **2.** any mass having the shape of the back of a whale.

whale·bird (hwāl′bėrd′), *n.* any of various birds which inhabit the places where whales are found, or which feed on their oil or offal.

whale·boat (hwāl′bōt′), *n.* a long, narrow rowboat, with a pointed bow and stern, formerly much used in whaling, now used as a lifeboat.

whale·bone (hwāl′bōn′), *n.* **1.** an elastic, horny substance growing in place of teeth in the upper jaw of certain whales and forming a series of thin, parallel plates; baleen. **2.** a thin strip of this used for stiffening corsets, dresses, etc.

whalebone whale, any of a group of whales that yield whalebone, as the right whale, finback, gray whale, and humpback.

whale fishing, the work or industry of taking whales; whaling.

whale·man (hwāl′mən), *n., pl.* **-men. 1.** a man engaged in whaling: *a well-to-do, retired whaleman* (Herman Melville). **2.** a vessel engaged in whaling: *In most American whalemen the mast-heads are manned almost simultaneously with the vessel's leaving her port* (Herman Melville).

whale·meat (hwāl′mēt′), *n.* the flesh of the whale, used for food.

whale oil, oil obtained from the blubber of whales.

whal·er (hwā′lər), *n.* **1.** a person who hunts whales. **2.** a ship used for hunting and catching whales. **3.** a whaleboat.

whaler shark, any of various large, maneating sharks found off the coast of Australia.

whal·er·y (hwā′lər ē), *n., pl.* **-er·ies. 1.** the industry of whaling or whale fishing. **2.** an establishment for canning whalemeat.

whale shark, a very large, spotted, harmless shark of warm seas, often more than 50 feet long.

whal·ing[1] (hwā′ling), *n.* the hunting and killing of whales.

whal·ing[2] (hwā′ling), *n. Informal.* a sound whipping, thrashing, or beating.

whal·ing[3] (hwā′ling), *adj. Informal.* extraordinary or uncommonly big of its kind; whopping.

whaling ship, a ship used for hunting whales; whaler.

whaling station, a place where whale blubber is boiled to make oil, either on a factory ship or on shore.

wham (hwam), *n., interj., v.,* **whammed, wham·ming.** *Informal.* —*n., interj.* an exclamation or sound as of one thing striking hard against another: *Then, wham into the station* (New York Times). —*v.t., v.i.* to hit with a hard, striking sound: *Other photographers, crowded out onto the deck, whammed their fists against the glass wall to catch her attention* (Time). [imitative]

wham·my (hwam′ē), *n., pl.* **-mies.** *Slang.* the power or invocation of magic; a jinx; hex: *The witch doctor, a thoroughly wrong sort, has put the whammy on him* (Atlantic).

whan (hwän), *n., pl.* **whan.** hwan; a former unit of money in South Korea.

whang[1] (hwang), *Informal.* —*n.* a resounding blow or bang. —*v.t., v.i.* to strike with a blow or bang. [imitative]

whang[2] (hwang), *v.i. Scottish.* to throw, drive, pull, etc., with force or with violent impact. [partly < *whang*[1]; partly < *whang*[3], verb, in earlier sense of "to lash with a thong"]

whang[3] (hwang), *n. Scottish.* a large or thick slice, especially of cheese, bread, etc. —*v.i.* to cut in large slices. [variant of Scottish *thwang* thong]

whang·doo·dle (hwang′dü′dəl), *n. Slang.* an imaginary animal whose nature and features are purposely left undefined.

whang·ee (hwang ē′), *n.* **1.** a Chinese plant allied to the bamboo. **2.** a cane made from it. [probably < Chinese *hwang* hard bamboo]

whap (hwop, wop), *v.t., v.i.,* **whapped, whap·ping,** *n.* whop.

whap·per (hwop′ər), *n.* whopper.

wharf (hwôrf), *n., pl.* **wharves** or **wharfs,** *v.* —*n.* **1.** a platform built on the shore or out from the shore beside which ships can load and unload; dock; pier. See **berth** for picture. **2.** any structure to which a vessel

may tie in docking. **3.** *Obsolete.* the bank of a river.
—*v.t.* **1.** to furnish (a harbor, etc.) with a wharf or wharves. **2.** to bring, place, or store (cargo, etc.) on a wharf. **3.** to direct or steer (a ship) to a wharf. —*v.i.* to tie up to a wharf; dock.
[Old English *hwearf* shore, (where ships could tie up), related to *hweorfan* to turn]

wharf·age (hwôr′fij), *n.* **1.** the use of a wharf for mooring a vessel, storing and handling goods, etc. **2.** the fee or charge made for this. **3.** wharves: *There are miles of wharfage in New York City.*

wharf·ie (hwôr′fē), *n. Australian.* a dock-worker.

wharf·in·ger (hwôr′fin jər), *n.* a person who owns or has charge of a wharf. [alteration of earlier *wharfager* < *wharfage.* Compare PASSENGER.]

wharf rat, 1. the common brown rat when living in or about a wharf. **2.** *Informal.* a man or boy, without regular or ostensible occupation, who loafs about wharves.

wharf·side (hwôrf′sīd′), *n.* the area on or at the side of a wharf: *Why must young scholars still trudge . . . along a long dreary cobbled wharfside?* (Manchester Guardian).
—*adj.* on or at the side of a wharf: *Once, while on a lovely Greek island, we dined at a wharfside cafe* (Atlantic).

Whar·ton's jelly (hwôr′tənz), mucoid connective tissue which constitutes most of the bulk of the umbilical cord. [< Thomas *Wharton,* 1614-1673, an English anatomist]

wharve (hwôrv), *n.* **1.** a small flywheel fixed on the spindle of a spinning wheel to maintain or regulate the speed. **2.** a small pulley in a spinning machine for driving the spindle; whorl. [variant of earlier *wherve,* Old English *hweorfa* whorl of a spindle, related to *hweorfan* to whirl]

wharves (hwôrvz), *n.* a plural of **wharf.**

what (hwot, hwut; *unstressed* hwət), *pron., pl.* **what,** *adj., adv., n., interj., conj.* —*pron.* **1.** (as an interrogative pronoun) a word used in asking about people or things: *What is your name? What is the matter?* **2.** *British Informal.* a word used as a (more or less) interrogative expletive, usually at the end of a sentence: *She is a clever girl, what?* **3.** as a relative pronoun: **a.** that which: *I know what you mean.* **b.** whatever; anything that: *Do what you please.*

and what not, and all kinds of other things: *Clara collected buttons, beads, bangles, and what not.*

give one what for, *Informal.* to give one something to cry, suffer, or be miserable for; punish; castigate: *The teacher gave the unruly boys what for.*

what for, why: *I can't imagine what she bought that silly hat for.*

what have you, *Informal.* anything else like this; and so on: *Wintertime there are no bears, no cars—but herds, coveys, schools and what have you of elk, bison and deer* (New York Times).

what if, what would happen if: *What if she told her husband how much her new dress really cost?*

what's what, *Informal.* the true state of affairs: *to know what's what.*

what's with, *Informal.* what is the matter with: *Miss Flinch had already slammed the door. . . . "What's with Miss Flinch?" I asked Louisa* (Harper's).

what then? what happens (or would happen) in that case? what of that? *If the diagnosis is not correct, what then?*

what with, in consequence of; considering: *They expect their partygoing to be somewhat curtailed what with the fair and the baby* (New York Times).
—*adj.* **1.** (as an interrogative adjective) a word used in asking questions about persons or things: *What time is it?* **2.** as a relative adjective: **a.** that which; those which: *Put back what money is left.* **b.** whatever; any that: *Take what supplies you will need.* **3.** (a word used to show surprise, doubt, anger, liking, etc., or to add emphasis) how great; how remarkable: *What a pity that Andy missed you!*
—*adv.* **1.** how much; how: *What does it matter? What do we, as a nation, care about books?* (John Ruskin). **2.** *Obsolete.* **a.** in what way or respect: *But alas, what can I help you?* (Miles Coverdale). **b.** for what cause or reason; why: *What sit we then projecting Peace and War?* (Milton). **3.** partly: *What with the wind and what with the rain, our walk was spoiled.* **4.** (a word used to show surprise, doubt, anger, liking, etc., or to add emphasis) how very: *What happy times we had together at the seashore last summer!*
—*n.* the essence or substance of a thing in question: *In the relations between governments the how is generally at least as important as the what* (Atlantic).
—*interj.* a word used to show surprise, doubt, anger, liking, etc., or to add emphasis: *What! Is that young whipper-snapper late again?*
—*conj. Dialect.* to the extent that; as much as; so far as: *to help one's friends what one can.*

but what. See under **but**[1], *conj.*
[Old English *hwæt*]

what·cha·ma·call·it (hwot′chə mə kôl′it, hwut′-), *n. Informal.* what-do-you-call-it: *Nobody's going to buy a plastic whatchamacallit for $500* (New York Times).

what-do-you-call-it (hwot′də yə kôl′it, hwut′-), *n. Informal.* something whose name one forgets, does not know, or thinks not worth mentioning; thingumbob: *She forgot the word "orange" and kept telling me she was out of what-do-you-call-its* (Atlantic).

what·e'er (hwot ãr′, hwət-), *pron., adj. Poetic.* whatever.

what·ev·er (hwot ev′ər, hwət-), *pron.* **1.** anything that: *Do whatever you like.* **2.** no matter what: *Whatever happens, he is safe.* **3.** *Informal.* what in the world: *Whatever do you mean?*
—*adj.* **1.** any that: *Ask whatever girls you like to the party.* **2.** no matter what: *Whatever excuse he makes will not be believed.* **3.** at all: *Any person whatever can tell you the way to the old mill.*

what-is-it (hwot iz′it, hwət-), *n. Informal.* any curious, rare, or nameless object or contraption: *Others saw the what-is-it flying with others in a diamond-shaped formation* (New York Times).

what·not (hwot′not′, hwut′-), *n.* **1.** a stand with several shelves for books, ornaments, etc. **2.** a thing or person that may be variously named or described; nondescript.

what's (hwots, hwuts), **1.** what is: *What's the latest news?* **2.** what has: *What's been going on here lately?*

what·sis (hwot′sis, hwut′-), *n. Informal.* what-is-it: . . . *a charming little whatsis that looks like an India-print lampshade and is really a travelling hat stand* (New Yorker).

what·sit (hwot′sit, hwut′-), *n. Informal.* what-is-it.

what·so (hwot′sō, hwut′-), *pron., adj. Archaic.* whatever: *Whatso thou wilt do with us, Our end shall not be piteous* (William Morris).

what·so·e'er (hwot′sō ãr′, hwut′-), *pron., adj. Poetic.* whatsoever; whatever.

what·so·ev·er (hwot′sō ev′ər, hwut′-), *pron., adj.* whatever: *Whatsoever is troubling him? The mayor got no support whatsoever for his program to build a new city hall.*

whaup (hwäp, hwôp), *n. Scottish.* the curlew. [probably imitative. Compare Old English *hwilpe* curlew.]

wheal[1] (hwēl), *n.* **1.** a flat, usually circular, hard elevation of the skin, accompanied by burning and itching. **2.** a ridge on the skin made by a blow, as of a whip; welt; weal. [variant of *weal*[2]]

wheal[2] (hwēl), *n. Obsolete.* a pimple or pustule. [Middle English *whele,* probably < Old English *hwelian* to suppurate. Compare WHELK[2].]

wheat (hwēt), *n.* **1.** the grain or seed of a widely distributed cereal grass, used to make flour, which is the chief breadstuff in temperate countries. **2.** the plant, closely related to barley and rye, which bears grains or seeds in dense, four-sided spikes that sometimes have awns (bearded wheat), and sometimes do not (beardless or bald wheat). Certain varieties are planted in the spring (spring or summer wheat), others in the fall, maturing the next spring or summer (winter wheat). [Old English *hwǣte*]

Wheat (def. 2)

Wheat., Wheaton (designating the U.S. Supreme Court Reports written by Henry Wheaton, 1785-1848, an American lawyer and diplomat).

wheat belt, a region in which wheat is the leading crop.

wheat bulb fly, a European fly whose larva infests the stems of wheat.

wheat·cake (hwēt′kāk′), *n.* a pancake, especially if made of wheat flour; griddlecake; flapjack.

wheat·ear (hwēt′ir′), *n.* a small bird related to the thrushes and stonechat, brown with a black-and-white tail, that frequents open ground in the northern parts of North America, Europe, and Asia; fallow chat.

wheat·en (hwē′tən), *adj.* **1.** made of the grain or flour of wheat, as bread made of the whole grain as distinct from white bread. **2.** of or belonging to wheat as a plant.

wheat germ, a tiny, golden particle in the wheat kernel, obtained before milling. It is rich in vitamins and is used as a cereal or food supplement.

wheat·grass (hwēt′gras′, -gräs′), *n.* any of several wild, weedlike grasses, especially couch grass.

wheat·land (hwēt′land′), *n.* land on which wheat is grown or which is suitable for growing wheat: *Grain from both the Canadian and the American wheatlands will be able to compete more successfully on world markets* (Atlantic).

wheat·less (hwēt′lis), *adj.* without wheat; characterized by refraining from the use of wheat: *wheatless days.*

wheat rust, any of various fungi that attack the roots of wheat plants, and produce reddish rust marks on the stems and leaves.

Wheat·stone bridge (hwēt′stōn, -stən), an apparatus for measuring electrical resistance. It consists essentially of two arms of known resistance and an adjustable resistor, connected in circuit with the unknown resistor. [< Sir Charles *Wheatstone,* 1802-1875, a British physicist, who brought the invention to notice]

Wheatstone's bridge, Wheatstone bridge.

wheat·worm (hwēt′wėrm′), *n.* a small nematode worm that causes a disease in wheat.

whee·dle (hwē′dəl), *v.,* **-dled, -dling.** —*v.t.* **1.** to persuade by flattery, smooth words, caresses, etc.; coax: *The children wheedled their mother into letting them go to the picnic.* **2.** to get by wheedling: *They finally wheedled the secret out of him.* —*v.i.* to use soft, flattering words. [origin uncertain. Compare Old English *wǣdlian* to beg; be poor < *wǣdl* poverty.] —**whee′dler,** *n.* —**whee′dling·ly,** *adv.* —**Syn.** *v.t.* **1.** cajole, blandish.

wheel (hwēl), *n.* **1.** a round frame turning on a pin or shaft in the center and having various uses, as moving vehicles and transmitting motion or power. **2. a.** any instrument, machine, apparatus, or other object shaped or moving like a wheel, or the essential feature of which is a wheel: *a spinning wheel, a potter's wheel.* **b.** a circular frame, often having handles around the rim, that turns the rudder to steer a ship. **c.** a steering wheel. **d.** *Informal.* a bicycle or (occasionally) a tricycle. **e.** (formerly) a contrivance shaped like a wheel on which a person was stretched for torture or punishment while his limbs were broken by an iron bar: *Her niceness shines through her charmingly florid prose and it's evident in her clear disapproval of such practices as breaking slaves on the wheel merely because they'd tried to blow up Government House* (Harry Bruce). **3.** something like a wheel in form or movement, as a firework that revolves on an axis while burning; a circle or circular object; disk. **4.** any force thought of as moving or propelling: *the wheels of the government, the wheel of life, fate, etc.* **5.** wheel of fortune. **6.** a circling or circular motion or movement; rotation (not necessarily completely around); revolution. **7.** a military or naval movement by which troops or ships in line change direction while maintaining a straight line. **8.** a song's refrain. **9.** *U.S. Slang.* a person who manages affairs, personnel, etc., as in a business; executive: *We have more trouble from company wheels trying to save a buck than we do with the little fellows* (Wall Street Journal). **10.** a round frame of natural cheese in the form in which it is cured: *The 175 lb. wheels of Emmenthal—are the largest and heaviest cheeses in the world* (Punch).

at the wheel, a. at the steering wheel: *You're at the wheel of a car that's sized for six-footers* (Newsweek). **b.** in control: *His father's death left him at the wheel of the firm.*

wheels, a. machinery; system: *the wheels of industry, of government, of justice, etc.* **b.**

U.S. Slang. an automobile: *Guess what Sister Luci Baines was doing for wheels back in Washington ... a new 350-h.p. Corvette* (Time).

wheels within wheels, complicated circumstances, motives, influences, etc.: *There are wheels within wheels ... in the social world of Paris* (H.S. Merriman).

—v.i. **1.** to turn or revolve about an axis or center, as a wheel does; rotate. **2.** *British, Military.* to turn to the right or left while in line. **3.** to turn: *He wheeled around suddenly.* **4.** to change or reverse one's opinion, attitude, or course of action. **5.** to move or perform in a curved or circular direction; circle: *gulls wheeling about.* **6. a.** to go along on or as if on wheels; proceed smoothly. **b.** *Informal.* to ride a bicycle or tricycle. *—v.t.* **1.** to turn (something) on or as on a wheel or wheels; cause to revolve or rotate. **2.** to cause (something) to move or perform in a curved or circular direction. **3.** to move on wheels: *The workman was wheeling a load of bricks on a wheelbarrow.* **4.** to furnish with a wheel or wheels. **5.** *U.S.* to transmit (power or electricity): *The power company agreed to wheel electricity from the dam to the Co-ops* (Wall Street Journal).

wheel and deal, *U.S. Slang.* to do business or trade freely and rapidly, with little restraint: *Unhampered by debates in press or Parliament, [it] can wheel and deal as it pleases, buying up surpluses here, dumping there* (Newsweek).

[Old English *hwēol, hweogl*]

wheel and axle, a device consisting, in its typical form, of a cylindrical axle on which a wheel is fastened, used to lift weights by winding a rope onto the axle as the wheel is turned (one of the simple machines).

Wheel and Axle

wheel animalcule or **animal,** a rotifer.

wheel barometer, a barometer in which a float at the surface of the column of mercury is connected to the hand that indicates changes on the face of the instrument; weatherglass.

wheel·bar·row (hwēl′bar′ō), *n.* a frame with a wheel at one end and two handles at the other, used for carrying loads. *—v.t.* to convey in a wheelbarrow.

Wheelbarrow

wheel·base (hwēl′bās′), *n.* the distance measured in inches between the centers of the front and rear axles of an automobile, truck, etc.

wheel bug, a large hemipterous bug of the southern United States, that has a semicircular crest on the thorax and preys on other insects.

wheel chair, a chair mounted on wheels. It is used especially by invalids and can be propelled by the person sitting in it.

wheeled (hwēld), *adj.* having a wheel or wheels: *Tubeless tires will one day be used on practically all wheeled vehicles, establishing new standards of tire safety and service* (Wall Street Journal).

wheel·er (hwē′lər), *n.* **1.** a person or thing that wheels. **2.** a thing, as a vehicle or a boat, that has a wheel or wheels: *a four-wheeler, side-wheeler.* **3.** a wheel horse.

wheel·er-deal·er (hwē′lər dē′lər), *n. U.S. Slang.* a person who wheels and deals; schemer; shrewd person: *In Texas, where such a man is admiringly known as a wheeler-dealer, [he] is the biggest wheeler-dealer of them all* (Time).

wheel horse, 1. the horse, or either of the team of horses, nearest to the wheels. **2.** *Informal.* a person who works hard, long, and effectively. **—Syn. 2.** workhorse.

wheel·house (hwēl′hous′), *n.* a small, enclosed place on a ship to shelter the steering wheel and those who steer the ship; pilot house.

wheel·ing (hwē′ling), *n.* **1.** the act of a person or thing that wheels. **2.** the condition of a roadbed with reference to passing over it on wheels.

wheel·less (hwēl′lis), *adj.* **1.** without a wheel or wheels; having no wheels. **2.** not adapted to wheeled vehicles.

wheel lock, an old gunlock of the firelock type, in which sparks were produced by a small steel wheel wound on a spring so that it revolved against a piece of iron pyrites when released. It was superseded by the flintlock.

wheel·man (hwēl′mən), *n., pl.* **-men. 1.** a man who steers a ship; helmsman. **2.** a man who attends to a wheel in some piece of mechanism. **3.** *Informal.* a male cyclist.

wheel of fortune, 1. the revolving device that fortune is fabled to turn, emblematic of the vicissitudes of life. **2.** a revolving wheel, used as a device for gambling in roulette. **3.** a lottery wheel.

wheels (hwēlz), *n.pl.* See under **wheel,** *n.*

wheels·man (hwēlz′mən), *n., pl.* **-men.** wheelman.

wheel·spin (hwēl′spin′), *n.* the spinning of the wheel of a vehicle without traction: *A heavy foot on the accelerator produces violent wheelspin on wet roads, and sometimes, in the dry* (London Times).

wheel static, static in an automobile radio produced by the rotation of the wheels.

wheel window, an ornamental circular window with radiating tracery or mullions more or less resembling the spokes of a wheel.

wheel·work (hwēl′wėrk′), *n.* a combination of wheels, especially gearwheels, as in a watch or other mechanism.

wheel·wright (hwēl′rīt′), *n.* a man whose work is making or repairing wheels, carriages, and wagons. [< *wheel* + *wright*]

wheen (hwēn), *n. Scottish.* a fair number: *a wheen of toys on the floor.* [earlier Scottish *quheyn,* Old English *hwēne* somewhat; (originally) instrumental case of *hwōn* a few]

wheep (hwēp), *n., v.i., v.t. Scottish.* wheeple. [imitative. Compare WHAUP.]

whee·ple (hwē′pəl), *n., v.,* **-pled, -pling.** *Scottish.* *—n.* the whistle or cry of a curlew or plover. *—v.i., v.t.* to cry as a curlew or plover; whistle. [imitative]

wheeze (hwēz), *v.,* **wheezed, wheez·ing,** *n.* *—v.i.* **1.** to breathe with difficulty and a whistling sound. **2.** to make a sound like this: *The old engine wheezed, but it didn't stop.* *—v.t.* to utter with a sound of wheezing. *—n.* **1.** a wheezing: *an asthmatic wheeze, the wheeze of an old engine, etc.* **2.** *Slang.* a funny saying or story, especially one made familiar by constant repetition; old or familiar joke, trick, etc.

[probably < Scandinavian (compare Old Icelandic *hwǣsa* to hiss). Compare Old English *hwōsan* to cough.] **—wheez′er,** *n.* **—wheez′ing·ly,** *adv.*

wheez·i·ly (hwē′zə lē), *adv.* in a wheezing manner; as if with difficulty of breathing.

wheez·i·ness (hwē′zē nis), *n.* the quality or condition of being wheezy.

wheez·y (hwē′zē), *adj.,* **wheez·i·er, wheez·i·est. 1.** wheezing: *The old dog was fat and wheezy.* **2.** *Slang.* old and familiar; trite: *[His] interpretation of the Charlotte Brontë novel is a rather wheezy business* (New Yorker).

wheft (hweft), *n. Nautical.* waft².

whelk¹ (hwelk), *n.* any of a group of marine mollusks that have a spiral shell, especially a kind commonly used for food in Europe. [alteration of Middle English *welke,* or *wilke,* Old English *weoloc,* or *wioloc*]

Whelk¹ Shell

whelk² (hwelk), *n.* a pimple; pustule. [Old English *hwylca* < *hwelian* to suppurate. Compare WHEAL².]

whelm (hwelm), *v.t.* **1.** to overwhelm. **2.** to submerge. [Middle English *whelmen* turn with the concave side down, probably fusion of Old English *-hwielfan* and *helmian* to cover] **—Syn. 1.** overpower. **2.** immerse.

whelp (hwelp), *n.* **1.** a puppy or cub; young dog or animal of prey, as a young wolf, lion, tiger, bear, etc. **2.** a good-for-nothing boy or young man. **3.** *Machinery.* **a.** one of the longitudinal projections on the barrel of a capstan or the drum of a windlass. **b.** one of the teeth of a sprocket wheel.

—v.i., v.t. to give birth to (whelps).

[Old English *hwelp*]

—Syn. *n.* **2.** scamp.

when (hwen; *unstressed* hwən), *adv.* at what time: *When does school close? When did I say such a thing?*

say when, *Informal.* to call a halt to something; stop: *George P. Elliott never seems to know when to say when* (New York Times).

—conj. **1.** at or during the time that: *His father died when he was a child. Rise when your name is called.* **2.** at any time that: *He is impatient when he is kept waiting.* **3.** at which time: *We were just leaving, when it began to snow.* **4.** at or on which (preceded by *time, day,* etc.): *at the time when I wrote the story.* **5.** in the, or any, case or circumstances in which: *Most confident, when palpably most wrong* (William Cowper). **6.** although: *We have only three books when we need five.* **7.** considering that; inasmuch as; since: *How can I help you when I don't know how to do the problems myself?*

—pron. what time; which time: *Since when have they had a car?*

—n. the time or occasion: *the when and where of an event.*

[Old English *hwenne, hwaenne*]

when·as (hwen az′, hwən-), *conj. Archaic.* when; while; whereas.

whence (hwens), *adv.* **1.** from what place; from where: *Whence do you come?* **2.** from what source or cause; from what: *Whence has he so much wisdom?* **3.** from which: *Let him return to the country whence he came.*

from whence, whence (a pleonasm): *From whence have we derived that spiritual profit?* (Dickens).

—conj. from what place, source, cause, etc.: *He told whence he came.*

[Middle English *whennes* < Old English *hwanone* whence + adverbial genitive *-s*]

whence·so·ev·er (hwens′sō ev′ər), *conj., adv.* from whatever place, source, or cause.

when·e'er (hwen ãr′, hwən-), *conj., adv. Poetic.* whenever.

when·ev·er (hwen ev′ər, hwən-), *conj., adv.* at whatever time; at any time that; when.

when-is·sued (hwen′ish′üd), *adj.* (of stocks and securities) at such time as it is issued, referring to the trading that is permitted between the time a security is authorized and its actual issuance. If issuance does not take place, all prior trading in the security becomes invalid. *Over-the-counter trading, on a when-issued basis, began in New York as soon as the S.E.C. clearance was announced* (Wall Street Journal).

when·so·ev·er (hwen′sō ev′ər), *conj., adv.* at whatever time; whenever.

where (hwãr), *adv.* **1.** in what place; at what place: *Where is he?* **2.** to what place: *Where are you going?* **3.** from what place: *Where did you get that story?* **4.** in which; at which: *the house where he was born.* **5.** to which: *the place where he is going.* **6.** in or at which place: *I don't know where he is.* **7.** in what way; in what respect: *Where is the harm in trying?*

where away? *Nautical* (of an object, ship, etc., seen by the lookout) what is the bearing? what direction? *"Sail ho!" shouted the lookout from the masthead. "Where away?" asked the officer on the deck.*

—n. **1.** in what place: *Where does he come from?* **2.** a place; scene.

—conj. **1.** in the place in which; at the place at which: *The book is where you left it.* **2.** in any place in which; at any place at which: *Use the salve where the pain is felt.* **3.** any place to which: *I will go where you go.* **4.** in or at which place: *They came to the town, where they stayed for the night.* **5.** in the case, circumstances, respect, etc., in which: *Some people worry where it does no good.*

[Old English *hwǣr*]

where·a·bout (hwãr′ə bout′), *adv., conj., n.* whereabouts.

where·a·bouts (hwãr′ə bouts′), *adv., conj.* **1.** near what place; where: *Whereabouts can I find a doctor? We did not know whereabouts we were.* **2.** *Obsolete.* **a.** about or around which. **b.** concerning or in regard to which (used interrogatively or relatively).

—n. the place where a person or thing is: *Do you know his whereabouts? I've forgotten the whereabouts of his present home.*

where·as (hwãr az′), *conj., n., pl.* **-as·es.** *—conj.* **1.** on the contrary; but; while: *Some children like school, whereas others do not.* **2.** considering that; since (now only introducing a preamble or recital in a legal or other formal document): *"Whereas the people* *of the colonies have been grieved and burdened with taxes. . . .*" —*n.* a statement introduced by "whereas," especially the preamble of a formal document or something likened to this.

where·at (hwãr at′), *adv., conj.* at what; at which.

where·by (hwãr bī′), *adv., conj.* **1.** by what; by which: *There is no other way whereby he can be saved.* **2. a.** by, beside, or near what; in what direction. **b.** by what means; how. **c.** *Obsolete.* for what reason; why.

wher·e'er (hwãr ãr′), *conj., adv. Poetic.* wherever.

where·fore (hwãr′fôr, -fōr), *adv.* **1.** for what reason? why? **2.** for which reason; therefore; so.
—*conj.* for what reason; why.
—*n.* a reason; cause: *Can you understand the why and wherefore of his behavior?*
[Middle English *hwarfore* < *hwar* where + *fore* for, preposition]

where·from (hwãr from′, -frum′), *adv.* whence.

where·in (hwãr in′), *adv., conj.* in what; in which; how.

where·in·so·ev·er (hwãr in′sō ev′ər), *conj.* in whatsoever place, thing, respect, etc.

where·in·to (hwãr in′tü, hwãr′in tü′), *adv., conj.* into what; into which.

where·ness (hwãr′nis), *n.* the state or property of having place or local relation; ubication.

where·of (hwãr ov′, -uv′), *adv., conj.* of what; of which; of whom: *Does he realize whereof he speaks?*

where·on (hwãr on′, -ôn′), *adv., conj.* on which; on what.

where·so (hwãr sō′), *conj. Archaic.* wherever: *I will go with thee Whereso thou willest* (William Morris).

where·so·e'er (hwãr′sō ãr′), *conj., adv. Poetic.* wheresoever; wherever.

where·so·ev·er (hwãr′sō ev′ər), *conj., adv.* wherever.

where·through (hwãr thrü′), *adv., conj.* through which.

where·to (hwãr tü′), *adv., conj.* **1.** to what; to which; where: *He went to that place whereto he had been sent.* **2.** for what purpose; why: *Whereto do you lay up riches?*

where·un·der (hwãr un′dər), *adv.* under which: *The Vietnamese have suggested the desirability of a change in Saigon whereunder the chief representative of France should be a civilian rather than a military commander* (New York Times).

where·un·to (hwãr un′tü, hwãr′un tü′), *adv., conj. Archaic.* whereto.

where·up·on (hwãr′ə pon′, -pôn′), *adv., conj.* **1.** upon what; upon which. **2.** at which; after which.

wher·ev·er (hwãr ev′ər), *conj., adv.* **1.** to whatever place; in whatever place; where: *Wherever are you going?* (*adv.*) *Sit wherever you like.* (*conj.*) *He will be happy wherever he lives.* (*conj.*) **2.** in any case, condition, or circumstances in which.

where·with (hwãr wiᴛʜ′, -with′), *adv., conj.* with what; with which.

where·with·al (*n.* hwãr′wiᴛʜ ôl; *adv., conj.* hwãr′wiᴛʜ ôl′), *n.* means, supplies, or money needed: *Has she the wherewithal to pay for the trip?* —*adv., conj. Archaic.* with what; with which: *Wherewithal shall we be fed?*

wher·ry (hwer′ē), *n., pl.* **-ries,** *v.,* **-ried, -ry·ing.** —*n.* **1.** a light, shallow rowboat for carrying passengers and goods on rivers, especially in England. **2.** a light, one-man rowboat used for racing. **3.** *British.* any of several types of larger boats, varying in different localities, as a barge, a fishing boat, a sailboat, etc., used on rivers.
—*v.t.* to carry in or as in a wherry.
[origin unknown]

whet (hwet), *v.,* **whet·ted, whet·ting,** *n.* —*v.t.* **1.** to sharpen by rubbing; hone: *to whet a knife.* **2.** to make keen or eager; stimulate: *The smell of the food whetted my appetite.*
—*n.* **1.** the act of whetting; sharpening. **2.** something that whets. **3.** an appetizer. **4.** *Dialect.* **a.** the interval between two sharpenings of a scythe, etc., during which the tool is used for cutting. **b.** any occasion of work, action, etc.; turn.
[Old English *hwettan*]
—**Syn.** *v.t.* **2.** kindle, quicken.

wheth·er (hweᴛʜ′ər), *conj.* **1.** expressing a choice or alternative: *He does not know whether to work or play. His neighbors might well doubt whether it were more dangerous to be at war or at peace with him* (Macaulay). **2.** if: *He asked whether he should finish the work.* **3.** either: *He was not sent a ticket, whether by accident or design.* **4.** *Obsolete.* introducing a direct question expressing doubt between alternatives.
—*pron. Archaic.* which of two; whichever of the two (used both as an interrogative and as a relative): *Whether would ye? gold of field?* (Tennyson).
[Middle English *whether* < Old English *hwether, hwæther*]
➤ See **if** for usage note.

whet·stone (hwet′stōn′), *n.* a stone for sharpening knives or tools, especially a shaped stone for giving a very fine edge after grinding.

whet·ter (hwet′ər), *n.* **1.** a sharpener of an instrument. **2.** a person or thing that sharpens, stimulates, or incites the intellect, desires, appetite, etc.

whew (hwyü), *interj., n.* an exclamation of surprise, dismay, etc. [imitative]

whey (hwā), *n.* the watery part of milk that separates from the curd when milk sours and becomes coagulated, or when cheese is made. [Old English *hwǣg*]

whey·ey (hwā′ē), *adj.* of, like, or containing whey.

whey·face (hwā′fās′), *n.* **1.** a person having a pale face. **2.** a pale face; pallid visage.

whey·faced (hwā′fāst′), *adj.* having a white or pale face; pallid: *The book begins in epilogue with . . . wheyfaced Edward Enger lying gravely ill on a bed in his mansion after a coronary attack* (Time).

whey·ish (hwā′ish), *adj.* wheyey.

which (hwich), *pron.* **1.** (as an interrogative pronoun) a word used in asking questions about persons or things: *Which seems the best plan? Which is your car?* **2.** as a relative pronoun: **a.** a word used in connecting a group of words with some word in the sentence, the one or ones indicated by the antecedent: *Read the book which you have.* **b.** the one that; any that: *Here are three boxes. Choose which you like best.* **3.** a thing that: *and, which is worse, you were late.*
which is which, which is one and which is the other: *The Jones twins look so alike that it is impossible to tell which is which.*
—*adj.* **1.** (as an interrogative adjective) a word used in asking questions about persons or things: *Which cities did you visit? Which boy won the prize?* **2.** (as a relative adjective) a word used in connecting a group of words with some word in the sentence: **a.** referring to something just mentioned: *It rain'd all night and all day . . . during which time the ship broke in pieces* (Daniel Defoe). **b.** referring to the one or ones specified: *Choose which books you like best.*
[Old English *hwilc, hwelc*]
➤ **which.** As a relative pronoun *which* refers to things and to groups of people regarded impersonally: *They returned for his ax which they had forgotten. The legislature which passed the act deserves most of the credit.*
➤ See **this** and **that** for usage notes.

which·a·way (hwich′ə wā′), *adv. U.S. Dialect.* in which direction; where: *I can't go after her, not knowing whichaway she is* (New Yorker).

which·ev·er (hwich ev′ər), *pron., adj.* **1.** any one that; any that: *Take whichever you want. Buy whichever hat you like.* **2.** no matter which: *Whichever side wins, I shall be satisfied. You will find deer crossings whichever road you take.*

which·so (hwich sō′), *pron. Archaic.* whichever.

which·so·ev·er (hwich′sō ev′ər), *pron., adj.* whichever.

whick·er (hwik′ər, wik′-), *v.i.* (of a horse) to whinny. —*n.* a whinny: *The little boy was frightened by Dobbin's whicker.* [probably imitative. Compare NICKER².]
➤ In the Eastern States, for which evidence is available, **whicker** is found in southeastern and northeastern New England and is the favored term from the Chesapeake Bay south along the coast, including most of the Carolinas.

whid (hwid), *v.i.,* **whid·ded, whid·ding.** *Scottish.* to move nimbly without noise. [earlier, blast of wind, perhaps < Scandinavian (compare Old Icelandic *hvitha* a squall)]

whid·ah (hwid′ə), *n.* any of certain African weaverbirds, the male of which grows long tail feathers during the breeding season; widow bird. The female lays its eggs in other birds' nests. Also, **whydah.** [alteration of *widow bird;* influenced by *Whidah* (now *Ouidah*), a town in Dahomey]

Male Whidah (including tail, 20½ in. long)

whidah bird or **finch,** whidah.

whiff (hwif), *n.* **1.** a slight gust; puff; breath: *A whiff of fresh air cleared his head. Not a whiff of life left in either of the bodies* (Thomas Hardy). **2.** a blow; puff. **3.** a slight smell; puff of air having an odor: *a whiff of garlic.* **4.** a puff of tobacco smoke. **5.** a slight outburst. **6.** *Informal.* **a.** a swing at a ball without hitting it, as in baseball, golf, etc. **b.** (in baseball) a strikeout.
—*v.i.* **1.** to blow or move with or as with a whiff or puff. **2.** to exhale or inhale whiffs or puffs, as when smoking tobacco. **3.** *Informal.* (in baseball) to be struck out: *He got only three hits in 21 tries and tied an all-time Series record by whiffing eight times* (Newsweek). —*v.t.* **1.** to drive or carry by or as by a whiff or puff; waft. **2.** to exhale (tobacco smoke) in whiffs or puffs. **3.** to smoke (a pipe, cigarette, etc.). **4.** *Informal.* (in baseball) to strike out: *His peak strike-out effort was against Boston . . . when he whiffed thirteen Red Sox* (New York Times).
[imitative; perhaps partly Middle English *wheffe* vapor, whiff, variant of *waff*¹]
—**whiff′er,** *n.*
—**Syn.** *n.* **5.** flurry.

whif·fet (hwif′it), *n.* **1.** *Informal.* an insignificant person or thing. **2.** a small dog. [American English, probably variant of *whippet;* perhaps influenced by *whiff*]
—**Syn. 1.** whipper-snapper.

whif·fle (hwif′əl), *v.,* **-fled, -fling,** *n.* —*v.i.* **1.** to blow in puffs or gusts. **2. a.** (of the wind, a ship, etc.) to veer or shift (about). **b.** to back and fill; vacillate. **3.** to blow lightly; scatter. —*v.t.* to blow or drive with or as with a puff of air.
—*n.* **1.** something light or insignificant; a trifle. **2.** a slight blast of air.
[apparently < *whiff* + *-le*]

whif·fler¹ (hwif′lər), *n.* **1.** a person who whiffles, or shifts about in thought, opinion, intention, etc. **2.** a trifler. [< *whiffl(e)* + *-er*¹]

whif·fler² (hwif′lər), *n. Historical.* one of a body of attendants armed with a javelin, battle-ax, sword, or staff, and wearing a chain, employed to keep the way clear for a procession or at some public spectacle. [< obsolete *wifle* javelin, ax + *-er*²]

whif·fler·y (hwif′lər ē), *n., pl.* **-fler·ies.** the characteristics or habits of a whiffler; trifling; levity.

whif·fle·tree (hwif′əl trē′), *n.* the swinging bar of a carriage or wagon, to which the traces of a harness are fastened; singletree. Also, **whippletree.** [American English, variant of *whippletree,* apparently < *whip* in sense of "move quickly to and fro" + *tree* a staff, wooden bar. Compare WHIFFET.]

Whig (hwig), *n.* **1.** a member of a former political party in Great Britain that favored reforms and progress. The Whig Party became the Liberal Party. **2.** an American colonist who favored the Revolution against England. **3.** a member of a political party in the United States that was formed about 1834 in opposition to the Democratic Party.
—*adj.* composed of Whigs; having to do with Whigs; like Whigs.
[short for *whiggamore*]

whig·ga·more (hwig′ə môr, -mōr), *n.* **1.** any of the people of western Scotland who marched on Edinburgh in 1648, in opposition to the engagement entered into with Charles I of England against the followers of Oliver Cromwell. **2.** a Scotch Presbyterian. [earlier *whiggamaire,* perhaps < dialectal *whig* to urge forward, drive briskly + *mare*¹ (because many rode on horses to Edinburgh)]

Whig·ger·y (hwig′ər ē), *n.* the principles or practices of Whigs: *When Gladstone first* *took his seat in the House of Commons (1833), the Victorian era was moving in, pushing back into history the last remnants of irreverent, aristocratic Whiggery, pushing forward the businessman* (Time).

Whig·gish (hwig′ish), *adj.* **1.** of, having to do with, or characteristic of Whigs; inclined to Whiggism. **2.** like Whigs. —**Whig′gish·ly,** *adv.* —**Whig′gish·ness,** *n.*

Whig·gism (hwig′iz əm), *n.* the principles or practices of Whigs; Whiggery.

whig·ma·lee·rie or **whig·ma·lee·ry** (hwig′mə lir′ē), *n., pl.* **-ries.** *Scottish.* **1.** a fantastic notion; whim; crotchet. **2.** a fanciful ornament, contrivance, etc.

while (hwīl), *n., conj., v.,* **whiled, whil·ing.** —*n.* **1.** a space of time; time: *He kept us waiting a long while. The postman came a while ago.* **2.** *Archaic.* a particular time at which something occurs or is done; occasion. **3.** *Obsolete.* the time spent (and hence also the effort or labor expended) in doing something.
between whiles, at times; at intervals: *A sort of . . . dashing (as it were) of waves, and between whiles, a noise like that of thunder* (George Berkeley).
once in a while, now and then: *We see him once in a while.*
the while, during the time; in the meantime: *Top athletes will do their eight months of compulsory military training in these platoons and enjoy major mollycoddling the while* (Sports Illustrated).
worth (one's) while, worth (one's) time, attention, or effort: *In one word, Madam, make it worth my while* (Frances Brooke).
—*conj.* **1.** during the time that; in the time that; in the same time that: *While I was speaking he said nothing. Summer is pleasant while it lasts.* **2.** in contrast with the fact that; although: *While I like the color of the hat, I do not like its shape. Walnut is a hard wood, while pine is soft.* **3.** *Dialect.* until.
—*v.t.* to pass or spend in some easy, pleasant manner: *The children while away many afternoons on the beach.*
[Old English *hwīl,* noun]
—**Syn.** *v.t.* **While, beguile** mean to pass time pleasantly. **While,** followed by *away,* suggests spending a period of free time in as pleasant a way as possible under the circumstances: *He whiled away the hours on the train by talking to other passengers.* **Beguile** suggests charming away the tediousness of the time by doing something interesting: *A good book helped him to beguile the long hours of the journey.*
➤ **While,** as a subordinate conjunction, is used chiefly to introduce adverbial clauses of time: *They waited on the bank while he swam to the raft.* It is also used, rather weakly, in the sense of "although" or "but": *While the doctor did all he could, he couldn't save her.* *While* is occasionally used for *and: The second number was an acrobatic exhibition, while the third was a lady trapeze artist.*

whiles (hwīlz), *Archaic.* —*adv.* **1.** sometimes. **2.** in the meantime. —*conj.* while. [Old English *-hwīles* < *hwīl* while, noun + adverbial genitive *-s*]

whilk (hwilk), *pron., adj. Obsolete.* which.

whil·ly-wha or **whil·ly-whaw** (hwil′ē-hwô), *Scottish.* —*v.t., v.i.* to cajole, or use cajolery; wheedle. —*n.* **1.** a cajoling speech. **2.** a cajoler. [origin unknown]

whi·lom (hwī′ləm), *Archaic.* —*adj.* former: *a whilom friend.* —*adv.* formerly; once. [Old English *hwīlum* at times; dative plural of *hwīl* while, noun]

whilst (hwīlst), *conj. Especially British.* while. [< *whiles;* the *-t* is a later addition. Compare AMIDST, AMONGST.]

whim (hwim), *n., v.,* **whimmed, whim·ming.** —*n.* **1.** a sudden fancy or notion; freakish or capricious idea or desire: *Her whim for gardening won't last long.* **2.** *Mining.* a kind of capstan used especially for raising ore or water from mines. It has one or more radiating arms to which a horse or horses, etc., may be yoked and by which it may be turned.
—*v.i.* to desire as a sudden fancy or notion: *piecework which could be used, ignored, changed, rewritten, or combined with the work of other writers as the producer willed or whimmed* (Harper's).
[perhaps < Scandinavian (compare Old Icelandic *hvim* unsteady look, *hvima* roll the eyes). Compare WHIMWHAM.]
—**Syn.** *n.* **1.** whimsy.

whim·brel (hwim′brəl), *n.* a curlew of arctic regions; hudsonian curlew. [probably < *whimp,* or *whimper* (because of its cry)]

whim·my (hwim′ē), *adj.,* **-mi·er, -mi·est. 1.** full of whims; whimsical. **2.** of or like a whim.

whim·per (hwim′pər), *v.i.* **1.** to cry with low, broken, mournful sounds: *The sick child whimpered.* **2.** to make a low, mournful sound. **3.** to complain in a weak way; whine: *to whimper for mercy.* —*v.t.* to say with a whimper.
—*n.* a whimpering cry or sound.
[probably imitative. Compare German *wimmern.*] —**whim′per·er,** *n.* —**whim′per·ing·ly,** *adv.*

whim·sey (hwim′zē), *n., pl.* **-seys.** whimsy.

whim·si·cal (hwim′zə kəl), *adj.* **1.** having many odd notions or fancies; fanciful; odd: *However absurd the story may sound when thus reduced, Garnett is much too fine an artist to be whimsical* (Newsweek). **2.** full of, subject to, or characterized by a whim or whims. [< *whims*(y) + *-ic* + *-al*[1]] —**whim′si·cal·ly,** *adv.* —**whim′si·cal·ness,** *n.* —**Syn. 1.** capricious, notional.

whim·si·cal·i·ty (hwim′zə kal′ə tē), *n., pl.* **-ties. 1.** whimsical character or quality. **2.** a whimsical notion, speech, act, etc. —**Syn. 1.** oddity, singularity. **2.** whimsy.

whim·sy (hwim′zē), *n., pl.* **-sies,** *adj.* —*n.* **1.** an odd or fanciful notion. **2.** odd or fanciful humor; quaintness: *His books are full of whimsy.* **3.** something showing this. **4.** a whim.
—*adj.* whimsical: *It's Disney and a bit whimsy but children should find the animals fun* (Observer).
[earlier, a whim, dizziness; probably < *whim*]
—**Syn. 1.** vagary, caprice. **2.** drollery.

whim·wham (hwim′hwam′), *n. Archaic or Dialect.* **1.** any odd or fanciful object or thing; gimcrack; trifle. **2.** a fanciful notion; an odd fancy. [varied reduplication of *whim*]

whin[1] (hwin), *n.* a low, prickly shrub with yellow flowers, common on waste lands in Europe; furze. [perhaps < Scandinavian (compare Icelandic *hvingras* bent grass, Norwegian *hvine*)]

whin[2] (hwin), *n.* whinstone. [origin uncertain]

whin·chat (hwin′chat′), *n.* a small, tan, European songbird, closely allied to the stonechat; furze-chat. [< *whin*[1] + *chat*[1] a bird]

whine (hwīn), *v.,* **whined, whin·ing,** *n.* —*v.i.* **1.** to make a low, complaining cry or sound: *The dog whined to go out with us.* **2.** to complain in a peevish, childish way: *Some people are always whining about trifles.* —*v.t.* to utter in a whining tone.
—*n.* **1.** a low, complaining cry or sound. **2.** a peevish, childish complaint.
[Old English *hwīnan* to whiz (like an arrow)] —**whin′er,** *n.*

whing·ding (hwing′ding′), *n., adj.* wingding.

whinge (hwinj), *v.i.* **whinged, whing·ing.** *British.* to whine: *A baby whinges in a tasselled pram* (Punch).

whing·er (hwing′ər), *n. Obsolete.* a whinyard. [spelling for variant pronunciation of *whinyard*]

whin·ing·ly (hwī′ning lē), *adv.* in a whining manner.

whin·ny[1] (hwin′ē), *n., pl.* **-nies,** *v.,* **-nied, -ny·ing.** —*n.* the prolonged, rather soft or gentle, quavering sound that a horse makes. —*v.i.* to utter a whinny or whinnies, or any sound thought of as resembling this. —*v.t.* to express by whinnying. [probably related to WHINE]
➤ In the eastern part of the United States, for which evidence is available, **whinny** is the favored term from Pennsylvania north. See also **whicker.**

whin·ny[2] (hwin′ē), *adj.* abounding in whin or furze. [< *whin*[1] + *-y*[1]]

whin·stone (hwin′stōn′), *n.* any of various hard, fine-grained, dark-colored rocks, such as basalt, diabase, or dolerite.

whin·y (hwī′nē), *adj.,* **whin·i·er, whin·i·est.** characterized by whining; disposed to whine; fretful: *Milney was in a whiny mood early in December when the time came again to select his courses for the next semester* (Harper's).

whin·yard (hwin′yərd), *n. Obsolete.* a short sword. [Middle English *whineard;* origin uncertain]

whip (hwip), *v.,* **whipped** or **whipt, whip·ping,** *n.* —*v.t.* **1.** to move, put, or pull quickly and suddenly: *He whipped off his coat and whipped out his knife.* **2.** to strike; lash: *He whipped the horse.* **3.** to strike as if whipping: *the rain whipping the pavement* (Thackeray). **4.** to bring, get, make, or produce by or as by whipping: *to whip the nonsense out of someone.* **5.** to incite; rouse; revive: *to whip up some enthusiasm.* **6.** to criticize or reprove with cutting severity. **7.** *Informal.* to defeat; vanquish; beat. **8.** to summon (in, up) to attend, as the members of a political party in a legislative body, for united action. **9.** to beat (cream, eggs, etc.) to a froth. **10.** to fish upon: *to whip a stream.* **11. a.** to wind (a rope, stick, etc.) closely with thread or string. **b.** to wind (cord, twine, or thread) in this way around something. **12. a.** to sew with stitches passing over and over an edge; overcast. **b.** to overcast the rolled edge of (a fabric) and draw it into gathers. **13.** to hoist or haul with a rope and pulley.
—*v.i.* **1.** to move suddenly and nimbly; start, go, etc., quickly; whisk; dart: *He whipped round the corner and disappeared.* **2.** to beat, flap, or thrash about as the lash of a whip does; swish. **3.** to fish by casting with a motion like that of using a whip.
whip in, (in hunting) to keep from scattering, as hounds: *to whip in the foxhounds.*
—*n.* **1.** an instrument to whip with, usually either a flexible switch or a stick with a lash at the end: *It is cruel to use a whip to punish a child.* **2.** a blow or stroke with or as with a whip. **3.** a whipping or lashing motion. **4. a.** a person who uses a driving whip; driver of horses; coachman. **b.** the person who manages the hounds of a hunting pack. **5. a.** a member of a political party who controls and directs the other members in a lawmaking body, as by seeing that they attend meetings in which important votes will be taken, and finding out how the vote is likely to go; party whip. **b.** *British.* a call made on members of a political party in a legislature to attend a given session or remain in attendance for it. **6.** a dessert made by beating cream, eggs, etc., into a froth and adding fruit or a flavoring: *prune whip.* **7.** something that moves briskly, as each of the vanes of a windmill. **8.** a simple kind of tackle or pulley, consisting of a single block with a rope through it, used for hoisting. **9.** any of various mechanical parts that move as a whip does. **10.** a vibrating spring for closing an electric circuit. **11.** a ride in an amusement park on a chain of cars changing direction sharply: *Features of particular interest to children will be pony rides, a ferris wheel, merry-go-round, the whip* (New York Times).
[Middle English *whippen,* probably < Middle Dutch and Middle Low German *wippen* to swing, move up and down, oscillate]
—**Syn.** *v.t.* **2.** scourge, flog, thrash, switch. —*n.* **1.** scourge, switch.

whip·cord (hwip′kôrd′), *n.* **1.** a close-woven, strong worsted cloth with diagonal ridges on it, used for suits, etc. **2.** a thin, tough, tightly twisted cord, sometimes used for or braided into the lashes of whips. **3.** a kind of catgut.

whip·crack (hwip′krak′), *n.* **1.** the crack of a whip. **2.** anything resembling or suggesting this: *The words [need] more whipcrack of sharp, modern speech rhythms* (Sunday Times).

whip graft, *Horticulture.* a graft made by cutting the scion and stock in a sloping direction so as to fit each other, and by inserting a tongue on the scion into a slit in the stock; tongue graft.

whip-graft (hwip′graft′, -gräft′), *v.t. Horticulture.* to graft by cutting the scion and stock in a sloping direction and by inserting a tongue on the scion into a slit in the stock.

whip grafting or **graftage,** the act or method of making a whip graft.

whip hand, 1. the hand (normally, the right hand) that holds the whip in driving. **2.** a position of control; advantage: *A clever person frequently gets the whip hand over others.* —**Syn. 2.** mastery.

whip·lash (hwip′lash′), *n.* **1.** the lash of a whip. **2.** anything considered as similar to this: *the whiplash of fear.* **3.** an injury to the neck caused by a sudden jolt that snaps

the head backward and then forward, as to a driver whose car is struck with force from behind.
—*v.t.* to beat or lash with or as if with a whiplash; treat harshly; punish: *For consumers, whiplashed the past couple of years by inflationary forces, the prospect of a price comedown . . . is welcome news* (Wall Street Journal).

whip·like (hwip′līk′), *adj.* shaped like a whip; long and slender; flexible: *Some bacteria . . . are equipped with whiplike appendages called flagella* (Scientific American).

whip·per (hwip′ər), *n.* a person or thing that whips.

whip·per-in (hwip′ər in′), *n., pl.* **whippers-in.** **1.** a huntsman's assistant who keeps the hounds from straying by driving them back with the whip into the main body of the pack. **2.** *Historical.* a (party) whip.

whip·per-snap·per or **whip·per·snap·per** (hwip′ər snap′ər), *n.* a young or insignificant person who thinks he is smart or important: *Don't pay any attention to that little whipper-snapper.* [apparently < *whip* + *-er*[1] + *snapper* a cracker of whips]

whip·pet (hwip′it), *n.* **1.** any of a breed of small, swift racing dogs that looks somewhat like a small greyhound. **2.** Also, **whippet tank.** a small, relatively fast, lightly armored tank developed and used in World War I. **3.** *Obsolete.* a nimble, diminutive person. [< *whip* + *-et*]

Whippet (def. 1) (18 to 22 in. high at the shoulder)

whip·ping (hwip′ing), *n.* **1. a.** a striking with or as if with a whip; flogging. **b.** a defeat; beating: *The favored team got a good whipping from the underdogs.* **2. a.** the act of overlaying or binding with cord, twine, or the like, wound closely round and round. **b.** an arrangement of cord, twine, or the like, wound about a thing: *We fastened the broken rod with a whipping of wire.* **3.** a beating to a froth or thickness: *Whipping is fast and easy when the cream is cold.* **4.** the bending or springing motion of something held rigidly at one end: *the whipping of an antenna in a strong wind.* **5.** an overcasting in sewing. —**Syn. 1. a.** flagellation.

whipping boy, 1. a person or thing that is the target of unmerited indignation or punishment; scapegoat. **2.** (formerly) a boy educated together with a young prince or royal personage, and flogged in his stead when the prince committed a fault that was considered to deserve flogging.

whipping cream, heavy cream: *Whipping cream is higher in fat content than either light cream or half-and-half* (New York Times).

whipping post, a post to which lawbreakers are tied to be whipped.

whip·ple·tree (hwip′əl trē), *n.* whiffletree.

whip·poor·will (hwip′ər wil′, hwip′ər wil), *n.* a North American goatsucker whose call sounds somewhat like its name. It is active at night or twilight. [American English; imitative]

Whippoorwill (9 to 10 in. long)

whip·py (hwip′ē), *adj.,* **-pi·er, -pi·est. 1.** bending like a whip; flexible; springy: *With prestressed concrete we can make a whippy fishpole or a bouncy diving board* (Scientific American). **2.** *Informal.* pert; snappy; saucy: *The girl—long, thin, and whippy—was instantly a-grin* (New Yorker).

whip-round (hwip′round′), *n. British.* a request for or a collection of contributions: *Thanks to a whip-round, the paupers are assured of ample supplies of beef, plum pudding, porter and snuff* (Punch). *Let's have a quick whip-round, four or five ideas apiece, and we'll call it an afternoon* (Manchester Guardian).

whip·saw (hwip′sô′), *n.* a long, narrow saw with its ends held in a frame, used especially for curved work.
—*v.t.* **1.** to cut with a whipsaw. **2. a.** to win at one turn or play (two bets from the same player), as in faro. **b.** to beat (a player) two ways at once. **3.** *U.S. Informal.* **a.** to defeat or cause to fail in two opposite ways at the same time: *Instances of selling in the decline before the election with the intention of buying back later were whipsawed* (Wall Street Journal). **b.** to have or take the advantage of, as by playing one against the other: *A major problem for dozens of U.S. industries: they must either stand together or risk being whipsawed by unions* (Time). —*v.i.* **1.** to bend back and forth; whip: *The next morning the 5-inch steel cable, worn by constant whipsawing, snapped* (Newsweek). **2.** to play one person, company, etc., against another: *Whipsawing is striking one company at a time, while permitting others to operate and thus adding to the pressure on the closed company* (Wall Street Journal).
—*adj.* of or characteristic of whipsawing: *When some industry strategists feared the union might adopt whipsaw tactics steel companies talked of setting up a mutual aid program to help individual concerns closed by a strike* (Wall Street Journal).

whip scorpion, any of a family of arachnids similar to the scorpions but having a slender, whiplike process on the abdomen and no sting.

whip-shaped (hwip′shāpt′), *adj.* shaped like the lash of a whip; long and slender; flagelliform.

whip snake, any of various snakes whose long, slender form somewhat resembles a whip.

whip·stall (hwip′stôl′), *n.* Also, **whip stall.** a stall in which the nose of an airplane falls suddenly downward, often just after the plane has slipped backward and downward along the angle of a sharp climb. —*v.i.* to go into a whipstall. —*v.t.* to cause (an airplane) to whipstall.

whip·ster (hwip′stər), *n. Archaic.* a whipper-snapper: *every puny whipster* (Shakespeare). [< *whip* + *-ster*]

whip·stitch (hwip′stich′), *v.t.* to sew with stitches passing over and over an edge; whip. —*n.* stitch made in whipstitching.

whip·stock (hwip′stok′), *n.* **1.** the handle of a whip. **2.** a wedge-shaped tool used with the thick end down to deflect a drill from obstructions, etc., in oil-well drilling. —*v.t., v.i.* to drill with a whipstock.

whipt (hwipt), *v.* whipped; a past tense and past participle of **whip.**

whip-tailed lizard (hwip′tāld′), any of various lizards having a long, slender tail like a whiplash, with species widely distributed in North, Central, and South America.

whip·worm (hwip′wėrm′), *n.* a nematode worm, often parasitic in the intestines of human beings, that has a stout posterior and slender anterior part, like a whipstock with a lash.

whir (hwėr), *n., v.,* **whirred, whir·ring.** —*n.* **1.** a buzzing noise: *the whir of a small machine.* **2.** *Obsolete.* **a.** violent or rapid movement; rush; hurry. **b.** commotion of mind or feeling; mental or nervous shock: *The news of her mother's illness put Alice in a whir.*
—*v.i.* to move quickly with a whir: *The motor whirs.* —*v.t.* to carry or hurry along; move or stir with a whir: *A lasting storm, whirring me from my friends* (Shakespeare). Also, **whirr.**
[probably imitative. Compare Danish *hvirre* whirl.]

whirl (hwėrl), *v.i.* **1.** to move in a circle or in a curving course; circle; circulate. **2.** to turn or swing round and round; spin; gyrate: *The leaves whirled in the wind.* **3.** to turn around or aside quickly; wheel. **4.** to move, go, travel, be carried, etc., swiftly on or as if on wheels. **5.** to feel dizzy or confused; reel: *The strong medicine made Martha whirl.*
—*v.t.* **1.** to cause to move in a circle or the like, or to rotate or revolve rapidly. **2.** to move or carry swiftly: *We were whirled away in an airplane. The last red leaf is whirl'd away* (Tennyson). **3.** *Obsolete.* to hurl; fling.
—*n.* **1.** a whirling motion or movement. **2.** something that whirls or the part at which this takes place; eddy; vortex. **3.** a rapid round of happenings, parties, etc.: *the endless whirl of the holiday season.* **4.** a dizzy or confused condition of mind or feeling.
give (something) **a whirl,** *Informal.* to try, test, or experiment with (something): *The Society decided to toss communism out the window and give capitalism a whirl* (Wall Street Journal).
[probably < Scandinavian (compare Old Icelandic *hvirfla,* related to *hverfa* to turn)]
—**whirl′er,** *n.*
—**Syn.** *n.* **4.** vertigo.

whirl·a·bout (hwėrl′ə bout′), *n.* **1.** the act of whirling about. **2.** something that whirls about, or is in a whirl. —*adj.* characterized by whirling about.

whirl·a·way (hwėrl′ə wā′), *n.* a rapid, whirling or spiraling movement or course: *In the labor-hungry whirlaway of U.S. production, job discrimination has begun to melt* (Time). —*adj.* moving or developing rapidly as if in a whirl: *Two years ago the first installment . . . was a whirlaway bestseller* (Time).

whirl·blast (hwėrl′blast′, -bläst′), *n.* a whirlwind.

whirl·ey·bird (hwėr′lē bėrd′), *n. Informal.* whirlybird; a helicopter.

whirl·i·gig (hwėr′lē gig), *n.* **1. a.** any of various toys that are whirled, twirled, or spun around. **b.** *Obsolete.* a top. **2.** a merry-go-round. **3. a.** something that is continually whirling, or in constant movement or activity of any kind. **b.** a circling movement, or condition figured as such. **4.** a whirligig beetle. **5.** *Obsolete.* a fantastic notion; whim; crotchet. [< obsolete *whirly-,* combining form of *whirl* + *gig*[1] something that whirls]

whirligig beetle, any of a family of gregarious beetles that circle about on the surface of water.

Whirligig Beetle (actual size)

whirl·ing dervish (hwėr′ling), dancing dervish.

whirl·pool (hwėrl′pül′), *n.* **1.** a place in or part of a river or the sea where the water whirls round and round rapidly and violently; eddy or vortex. **2.** anything like a whirlpool.

whirl·wind (hwėrl′wind′), *n.* **1.** a current of air whirling violently round and round; whirling windstorm. **2.** anything like a whirlwind.
reap the whirlwind, to suffer disastrous consequences, especially as a result of recklessness or folly (in allusion to Hosea 8:7): *Now the B.B.C. appear to be reaping the whirlwind of their decision to ban . . . the film* (London Times).
—*adj. Informal.* marked by great speed; fast; hasty: *a whirlwind tour. [He] married her after a whirlwind courtship* (Maclean's).
[< *whirl* + *wind*[1]; probably influenced by Scandinavian (compare Old Icelandic *hvirfilvindr*)]
—**Syn.** *n.* **1.** cyclone, tornado.

whirl·y (hwėr′lē), *adj.,* **whirl·i·er, whirl·i·est.** that can whirl; whirling: *There are some dresses of red and white checked gingham with whirly skirts* (New Yorker).

whirl·y·bird (hwėr′lē bėrd′), *n. Informal.* a helicopter.

whirr (hwėr), *n., v.i., v.t.* whir.

whir·ry (hwėr′ē), *v.t., v.i.,* **-ried, -ry·ing.** *Scottish.* to hurry. [probably < *whir* + *-y,* as in *hurry*]

whish (hwish), *n.* a soft, rushing sound, as that of something moving rapidly through the air or over the surface of water; whiz; swish. —*v.i.* to make such a sound. [imitative]

whisht (hwisht, wisht; *Scottish* hwusht), *Scottish.* —*interj.* an exclamation enjoining silence; hush!
—*n.* **1.** a whisper. **2.** (with negative) not a whisper; not the least utterance.
—*adj.* silent; quiet; still; hushed.
—*v.i.* to be silent; keep silence. —*v.t.* to put to silence; silence; hush.
[variant of *whist*[2], interjection]

whisk[1] (hwisk), *v.t.* **1.** to sweep or brush (dust, crumbs, etc.) from a surface: *She whisked the crumbs from the table.* **2.** to move (something) quickly: *She whisked the letter out of sight.* —*v.i.* to move quickly: *The mouse whisked into its hole at the sight of the cat.*
—*n.* **1.** a light stroke of a whisk broom, etc.; a quick sweep: *a whisk of her broom.* **2.** a light, quick movement; a brief, rapid sweeping motion.
[< Scandinavian (compare Danish *viske* wipe, Swedish *viska* sweep off)]

whisk[2] (hwisk), *v.t. Especially British.* to

beat or whip (cream, eggs, etc.) to a froth, especially with a whisk. [< Scandinavian (compare Swedish *viska* to sponge, sweep off)]
—*n.* **1.** a wire beater for eggs, cream, etc. **2.** a small bundle of twigs, hair, straw, feathers, etc., fixed on a handle, used for brushing or dusting. **3.** a whisk broom.
[earlier, a bristle < Scandinavian (compare Norwegian *viske*, Swedish *viska* a besom, swab). Related to WHISK[1].]

whisk broom, a small broom for brushing clothes, etc.

whisk·er (hwis′kər), *n.* **1.** a single hair of a man's beard. **2.** one of the long, stiff hairs or bristles growing near the mouth of certain animals, as a cat, rat, or bird; vibrissa. **3.** Also, **whisker boom.** *Nautical.* either of two wooden or iron spars extending laterally, one on each side of the bowsprit, to spread the guys of the jib or flying jib boom. **4.** *Dialect.* something that whisks or is used for whisking. **5.** a microscopic crystal filament on the surface of a metal or other crystalline solid. **6.** a very small amount or degree: . . . *missed the edge of the bat by a whisker* (Manchester Guardian).
whiskers, the hair growing on a man's face, especially that on his cheeks: *His whiskers . . . squared off in a line which met the large stiff collar below at an angle of forty-five* (Besant and Rice).
[< *whisk*[2] + *-er*[1]]

whisk·ered (hwis′kərd), *adj.* **1.** having whiskers: *a grave whiskered young man* (Arnold Bennett). **2.** in the form of whiskers: *whiskered hair.*

whisk·er·less (hwis′kər lis), *adj.* lacking whiskers.

whisk·ers (hwis′kərz), *n.pl.* See under **whisker.**

whisk·er·y (hwis′kər ē), *adj.* **1.** having whiskers: *a ruddy, whiskery Englishman dressed in shorts* (Harper's). **2.** suggestive of whiskers and age; very old: *a whiskery saying or superstition.*

whis·key (hwis′kē), *n., pl.* **-keys,** *adj.* —*n.* **1.** a strong alcoholic liquor made from various grains, in the United States chiefly corn or rye, in Scotland, Ireland, and Britain often malted barley, consisting usually of from two fifths to one half alcohol by volume. **2.** a drink of whiskey. —*adj.* of, having to do with, composed of, or like whiskey. [short for obsolete *whiskybae*, variant of *usquebaugh* < Gaelic *uisge beatha* (literally) water of life. Compare AQUA VITAE, USQUEBAUGH.]
➔ **Whiskey, whisky.** The preferred spelling in the United States is *whiskey*. Outside of the United States, except in Ireland, the preferred form is *whisky*. Scotch made in the United States, however, is spelled *whisky* in imitation of the Scots' spelling.

Whis·key (hwis′kē), *n. U.S.* a code name for the letter *w*, used in transmitting radio messages.

whiskey and soda, a drink made with whiskey and carbonated water, served with or without ice; highball.

whiskey sour, a cocktail made with whiskey, lemon juice, and sugar shaken with ice, strained, and usually served with a slice of orange and a cherry.

whis·ky (hwis′kē), *n., pl.* **-kies,** *adj.* whiskey.

whis·ky-jack (hwis′kē jak′), *n.* a jay, chiefly of northern North America, with plain grayish feathers; Canada jay. [American English; alteration of earlier *whisky-john* < Algonkian (Cree) *wiskatjân*]

whisp (hwisp), *n., v.t., v.i.* wisp.

whis·per (hwis′pər), *v.i.* **1. a.** to speak very softly and low. **b.** to talk in this way, especially in another's ear, for the sake of secrecy or privacy. **2.** to talk quietly or secretly (usually implying hostility, malice, conspiracy, gossip, etc.). **3.** to make a soft, rustling sound: *The wind whispered in the pines.* —*v.t.* **1.** to speak in a whisper or low voice. **2.** to tell secretly or privately: *It is whispered that Mr. Smith's business is failing.* **3.** to utter without vibration of the vocal cords.
—*n.* **1. a.** the utterance of words in a low, soft voice; a speaking under one's breath: *to converse in whispers.* **b.** *Phonetics.* the sound produced by the outgoing breath stream when the glottis is closed almost as much as for voice, but the vocal cords are tightened so that they do not vibrate, used in pronouncing the voiced sounds when whispering, the voiceless sounds being produced as in normal speech. **2.** a whispered word, phrase, remark, or speech. **3.** something told secretly or privately: *the whispers of one's conscience.* **4.** a soft, rustling sound.
[Old English *hwisprian*] —**whis′per·er,** *n.*

whis·per·ing (hwis′pər ing), *n.* the act of a person or thing that whispers. —*adj.* **1.** that whispers; speaking in a whisper. **2.** making a soft, rustling sound. —**whis′per·ing·ly,** *adv.*

whispering campaign, a campaign of spreading rumors, insinuations, etc., to discredit a person or group, as by whispered communication: *A whispering campaign started against electing any party member to the council* (Atlantic).

whispering gallery, 1. a gallery, as that in St. Paul's Cathedral, London, so shaped that a whisper uttered at a certain point can be heard (by reflection and concentration of the sound) at a distant point, beyond the range of ordinary hearing. **2.** any chamber or hollow place, as a cave, having the same acoustic property.

whis·per·ous (hwis′pər əs), *adj.* full of or characterized by whispers; resembling a whisper.

whis·per·y (hwis′pər ē), *adj.* whisperous: *He leaned closer to catch the soft, whispery words his uncle spoke* (Harper's).

whisp·y (hwis′pē), *adj.,* **whisp·i·er, whisp·i·est.** *wispy.*

whist[1] (hwist), *n.* a card game somewhat like bridge for two pairs of players. Auction and contract bridge developed from it. [alteration of earlier *whisk*, perhaps < *whisk*[1] (because the players whisked in the tricks), probably influenced by *whist*[2] (because of the silence required for the game)]

whist[2] (hwist), *Archaic or Dialect.* —*interj.* hush! silence! —*adj.* hushed; silent. —*adv.* silently; quietly. —*n.* silence.
hold one's whist, to keep silence: *'Tis your brother that's . . . askin' you to hold your whist* (Michael MacDonagh).

whis·tle (hwis′əl), *v.,* **-tled, -tling,** *n.* —*v.i.* **1.** to make a clear, shrill sound: *The policeman whistled for the automobile to stop. A blackbird whistles.* **2.** to blow a whistle: *Locomotives whistle at crossings.* **3.** to move or rush with a shrill sound: *The wind whistled around the house.* —*v.t.* **1.** to produce or utter by whistling: *to whistle a tune.* **2.** to call, direct, or signal by or as by a whistle. **3.** to send or drive with a whistling or whizzing sound.
whistle for, *Informal.* to go without; fail to get: *Without him [the Mayor] the city might still have been whistling for its fair and for its railway* (Manchester Guardian Weekly).
whistle in the dark, to try to be courageous or hopeful in a fearful or trying situation: *[He] said he was not whistling in the dark or crying alarms, but declared he had tremendous confidence that business is basically strong* (Wall Street Journal).
—*n.* **1.** an instrument for making whistling sounds. **2.** the sound made by whistling: *the whistle of the wind.* **3.** the act of whistling or blowing a whistle. **4.** a call; summons. **5.** a whistling or whizzing sound, as of wind blowing through trees or a missile flying through the air. **6.** a simple flute with one end plugged.
(as) clean as a whistle, a. neatly; without impediment or trouble; easily: *As the last seconds flitted painfully by, . . . up went little McCalliog, a fleck of the head, and the ball was home clean as a whistle* (London Times). **b.** completely and entirely clean; without fault or error: *The match, though tough, was as clean as a whistle and the injuries were just bad luck* (Michael Green).
blow the whistle on, *Informal.* **a.** *Sports.* to penalize: *The referee blew the whistle on his tactics under the boards.* **b.** to declare illegal or dishonest: *Senator John Williams, who first blew the whistle on Baker and who was sitting in on the hearings although not a member of the committee, was unwilling to let it go at that* (Time).
wet one's whistle, *Informal.* to take a drink: *Let's . . . wet our whistles, and so sing away all sad thoughts* (Izaak Walton).
[Old English *hwistlian*]

whis·tle·a·ble (hwis′ə lə bəl, hwis′lə-), *adj.* that can be or is suitable for whistling; tuneful: *whistleable tunes.*

whis·tler (hwis′lər), *n.* **1.** a person or thing that whistles. **2.** a large North American marmot resembling a woodchuck. **3.** any of certain birds whose wings make a hissing sound when in flight, such as the goldeneye and widgeon. **4.** a horse suffering from a defect of the respiratory system similar to the condition called "roaring." **5.** *Physics.* a radio signal with a whistling sound rapidly decreasing in frequency and then usually rising again. It originates in a flash of lightning that may be thousands of miles away.

Whis·tle·ri·an (hwis lir′ē ən), *adj.* of or having to do with James MacNeill Whistler, 1834-1903, an American painter and etcher, or his style of painting.

whistle stop, *U.S. Informal.* **1.** a small, little-known town along a railroad line at which a train stops only when signaled. **2.** a stop at such a town or station for a brief appearance or speech, as in a political campaign tour: *When the campaign train stops in a city or town the general steps out on the rear platform, delivers his speech or, if it is truly a whistle stop, simply waves and grins* (Life).

whis·tle-stop (hwis′əl stop′), *adj., v.,* **-stopped, -stop·ping.** *U.S. Informal.* —*adj.* of, having to do with, or at a whistle stop: *whistle-stop speeches. The President plans a whistle-stop tour to the West Coast for early October* (New York Times). —*v.i.* to make brief appearances or speeches at small towns or stations along a railroad, as in a political campaign tour: *Then I had a wonderful day whistle-stopping through the Central Valley of California* (New York Times). —*v.t.* to make whistle stops across or through: *In a sort of swan song to the Democratic Party as its leader, he offered to whistle-stop the country for his successor* (Birmingham News).

whis·tle-stop·per (hwis′əl stop′ər), *n. U.S. Informal.* **1.** a political candidate or speaker who makes whistle stops: *The chancellor is no whistle-stopper. He speaks in public halls or outdoor meetings but not from the train's rear end* (Wall Street Journal). **2.** a whistle-stop campaign or trip: *It is the second whistle-stopper of the campaign for the president* (Birmingham News).

whis·tling (hwis′ling), *n.* **1.** the act of a person or thing that whistles. **2.** a defect of the respiratory system in which a horse breathes hard with a shrill sound.
—*adj.* **1.** producing a whistle or whistling. **2.** characterized by whistling. **3.** sounding like a whistle. [Old English *hwistlung* < *hwistlian* to whistle] —**whis′tling·ly,** *adv.*

whistling buoy, a type of buoy that produces a whistling noise.

whistling swan, a wild swan of Siberia and North America, that has white plumage and a small, yellow spot next to the eye, at the base of the bill.

whit (hwit), *n.* a very small bit; particle; jot: *not to care a whit. The sick man is not a whit better.* [apparently variant of *wight*[1]]
—**Syn.** mite, tittle.

Whit (hwit), *adj. British.* Whitsun.

white (hwit), *adj.,* **whit·er, whit·est,** *n., v.,* **whit·ed, whit·ing.** —*adj.* **1.** having the color of snow or salt; reflecting light without absorbing any of the rays composing it. **2.** approaching this color: *white bread.* **3.** silvery; gray: *white hair, a white beard.* **4.** snowy: *a white winter.* **5.** of a light or pale color: *white meat.* **6.** (of wines) light-colored; ranging in color from pale yellow to amber. **7.** transparent and colorless: *white glass.* **8.** (of silverware) chased or roughened so as to retain a light-gray color and lustrous appearance; not burnished. **9.** made or consisting of silver. **10.** not written or printed upon; blank: *a white space.* **11. a.** having a light-colored skin; of or having to do with the Caucasian race. **b.** controlled by or including only members of this race. **12.** *Informal.* honorable; trustworthy; fair. **13.** *Especially Poetic.* light; fair; blond. **14.** pale: *She turned white with fear.* **15.** wearing white clothing: *a white friar.* **16.** ultraconservative; reactionary; royalist. **17.** spotless; pure; innocent. **18.** good; beneficent: *white magic.* **19.** propitious; favorable; auspicious. **20.** being at white heat.
bleed white. See under **bleed,** *v.*
—*n.* **1.** the color of snow or salt. It is the color of a surface that is nonselective in reflecting polychromatic light uniformly throughout the spectrum. The incident light when mixed in proper proportion is also said to be *white,* as is the reflected light. **2. a.** the quality of being white; white coloration or appearance; whiteness. **b.** whiteness as a symbol of purity, goodness,

and truth. **3.** a white coloring matter or pigment. **4.** whiteness or fairness of skin or complexion. **5.** a white person; a person of the Caucasian race. **6.** something, or a part of something, that is white or light-colored: **a.** the translucent, viscous fluid surrounding the yolk of an egg; albumen. **b.** the white part of the eyeball; sclera. **c.** white wine. **d.** Also, **whites.** *Printing.* any unprinted space. **7.** Also, **whites.** white clothing: *attired in white, a sailor wearing his whites.* **8.** white cloth. **9.** an ultraconservative; reactionary; royalist. **10.** Often, **White.** an animal, especially a swine, of a species, breed, or variety white in color. **11.** *Archery.* **a.** one of the bands or rings of a target, usually the outside ring (formerly painted white). **b.** a shot that hits this ring. **c.** *Archaic.* a white target. **12. a.** the light-colored pieces used in chess, checkers, backgammon, etc. **b.** the player moving these pieces. Traditionally white moves first in chess and has the burden of winning or drawing chess problems.

whites, a. the finest grade of white flour: *At a meeting of the London Flour Millers' Association ... the following prices were fixed ... whites, 31s.* (London Daily News). **b.** leucorrhea: *Among novices there is some difficulty in distinguishing the discharge of whites from that of blennorrhoea* (John M. Good).

—*v.t.* **1.** *Printing.* to space out (type, etc.). **2.** to make white; whiten, whitewash, or bleach.

[Old English *hwīt*] —**white′ness,** *n.*

—**Syn.** *adj.* **2.** milky, chalky. **14.** pallid, ashy.

white admiral, a butterfly with a dark green upper surface and white bands across its wings.

white agate, a white variety of chalcedony.

White Alice, a microwave communications system that links the stations of the DEW line with military installations and centers of population in Alaska.

white alkali, 1. a whitish crust formed on some alkaline soils by a mixture of salts. **2.** soda ash that has been refined or purified.

white ant, a pale-white insect; termite. White ants eat wood and are very destructive to buildings.

white arsenic, arsenic trioxide, a white, poisonous compound.

white ash, a tall variety of ash of eastern North America; American ash.

white backlash, a hostile reaction on the part of whites to Negro demands for racial equality: *The removal of* Little Black Sambo *from the schools provoked some local white backlash* (Canadian Forum).

white·bait (hwīt′bāt′), *n., pl.* **-bait. 1.** a young herring or sprat an inch or two long, used whole as food. **2.** any of certain similar fishes used as food.

white·bark pine (hwīt′bärk′), a low pine of the mountains of western North America with brown or creamy-white scales on the bark, and a fragrant resin, from which is obtained an ingredient often used in making perfumes. Its large, sweet seeds were eaten by the Indians.

white bass, a fresh-water food fish of the central United States, silvery in color with blackish lines along the sides and yellow underneath.

white·beam (hwīt′bēm′), *n.* a small European tree, with large leaves dark green on top and silvery white and silky on the underside, and a mealy fruit of a reddish color.

white bear, a polar bear.

white·beard (hwīt′bird′), *n.* a very old man.

white belt, the lowest order in judo.

white birch, 1. a common European birch that has a whitish bark. **2.** the paper birch of North America. See **birch** for picture.

white blood cell, a colorless nucleated blood cell; leucocyte.

white blood corpuscle, a leucocyte.

white book, a book of official government reports bound in white.

White·boy (hwīt′boi′), *n.* a member of an illegal agrarian association formed in Ireland about 1761. [because the members wore white frocks over their other clothes at their nightly meetings and in their raids]

white-breast·ed nuthatch (hwīt′bres′tid), a common nuthatch of North America with black crown and white underparts.

white bryony, a European species of bryony.

white canon, a Premonstratensian canon, so called from the white habit.

white·cap (hwīt′kap′), *n.* **1.** a wave with a foaming white crest. **2.** a person wearing or entitled to wear a white cap.

White·cap (hwīt′kap′), *n. U.S.* a member of a self-appointed and unauthorized secret committee of citizens in the late 1800's that tried to punish persons whom it considered harmful to the community.

white cast iron, a silvery-white, hard, and brittle cast iron made by chilling heated cast iron.

white cedar, 1. a coniferous evergreen tree of the cypress family, much like a cypress, with pale-green or silvery needles, growing in swamps in the eastern United States. **2.** its soft wood. **3.** a common North American species of arbor vitae, grown in many varieties for ornament.

white cell, a leucocyte.

white-cheeked goose (hwīt′chēkt′), a dark-colored variety of Canada goose of the northern Pacific Coast of North America.

White Citizens Council, *U.S.* any of various groups of white people organized in the South in the 1950's and 1960's to oppose racial integration and preserve States' rights.

white clover, a kind of clover with white flowers, common in fields and lawns.

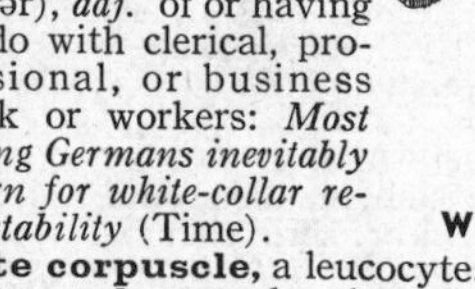

White Clover

white coal, water used as a source of power.

white-col·lar (hwīt′kol′ər), *adj.* of or having to do with clerical, professional, or business work or workers: *Most young Germans inevitably yearn for white-collar respectability* (Time).

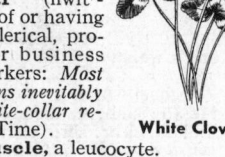

white corpuscle, a leucocyte.

white crab, a sand crab; sprite.

white-crowned pigeon (hwīt′kround′), a wild pigeon of the West Indies and the southern tip of Florida, having slate-colored plumage with a white crown.

white-crowned sparrow, a North American sparrow with a gray breast and black-and-white striped crown.

white damp, carbon monoxide.

white diarrhea, pullorum disease in chickens.

whit·ed sepulcher (hwī′tid), (in the Bible) a hypocrite. Matthew 23:27.

white dwarf, *Astronomy.* a white star of low luminosity, small size, and very great density.

white elephant, 1. anything that is expensive and troublesome to keep and take care of. **2.** a whitish or pale-gray Indian elephant, considered holy in several Asiatic countries, as Thailand (Siam) and Burma.

white elm, a tall elm of eastern North America, commonly planted as a shade tree; American elm.

white-eye (hwīt′ī′), *n.* **1.** any of various birds whose eyes have white or colorless irises. **2.** any of various small songbirds of tropical regions of the Old World, having a ring of white feathers around the eye.

white-eyed vireo (hwīt′īd′), a vireo of the eastern United States having white eyes ringed with yellow.

white·face (hwīt′fās′), *n.* **1. a.** makeup used to whiten the faces of clowns, mimes, etc.: *A sad-eyed clown in whiteface trails behind a circus troupe* (Time). **b.** a clown, mime, etc., in whiteface. **2.** a white-faced animal, as a Hereford. —*adj.* of, having to do with, or in whiteface.

white-faced (hwīt′fāst′), *adj.* **1.** pale; pallid: *a group of tired, undernourished, white-faced children.* **2.** having a large patch of white or whitish hair between the muzzle and the top of the head: *a white-faced pony.*

white-faced glossy ibis, an ibis with glossy-purple plumage and white feathers about the base of the bill in summer, found in the western United States south to Argentina.

white-faced hornet, a common American hornet, black with white face and markings.

white feather, 1. a symbol of cowardice (in allusion to the fact that a white feather in a gamecock's tail is a mark of inferior breeding). **2.** a coward.

show the white feather, to act like a coward: *No one will defend him who shows the white feather* (Scott).

white·fish (hwīt′fish′), *n., pl.* **-fish·es** or (*collectively*) **-fish. 1.** any of a group of American fresh-water food fishes with white or silvery sides, related to the salmons and trouts, found throughout the Great Lakes region. **2.** any of certain other white or silver fishes, as the whiting, the menhaden, and the young bluefish. **3.** the beluga whale.

Common Whitefish (def. 1) (to 24 in. long)

white flag, a plain white flag used as a sign of truce or surrender.

white flax, a plant, gold-of-pleasure.

white fly, any of a group of flies with a long body and wings that are covered by a waxy, white dust. White flies attack many plants and citrus trees.

white-foot·ed mouse (hwīt′fu̇t′id), any of a group of small North American mice with large ears and snow-white feet and underparts; vesper mouse; deer mouse.

white fox, 1. the arctic fox in its winter phase. **2.** its fur, used for, on, or in women's coats, jackets, etc.

white friar or **White Friar,** a Carmelite.

white·front (hwīt′frunt′), *n.* the white-fronted goose.

white-front·ed goose (hwīt′frun′tid), a grayish-brown goose with white on the front of the face, nesting in arctic regions of both hemispheres.

white frost, the white, feathery crystals of ice formed when water vapor in the air condenses at a temperature below freezing; hoarfrost; rime.

white fuel, water used as a source of power.

white gasoline, unleaded gasoline.

white gerfalcon, the gerfalcon during its white phase.

white gold, any of several alloys consisting essentially of gold and nickel or platinum, with some copper and zinc. White gold looks much like platinum and is used for jewelry.

white goods, 1. sheets, pillow cases, towels, napkins, tablecloths, etc.: *In New York, a major store has moved white goods "especially fast," it reports, thanks to August sale promotions* (Wall Street Journal). **2.** heavy household appliances such as stoves, refrigerators, and washing machines, often coated with white enamel.

white gourd, 1. the tallow gourd. **2.** its fruit.

white gum, 1. any eucalyptus with a white or light-colored bark. **2.** the sweet gum.

white-haired (hwīt′hãrd′), *adj.* having white or grayish-white hair, especially from age: *a white-haired gaffer with twinkling blue eyes and an air of secret wisdom* (New Yorker).

white-haired boy, *Informal.* a favorite; fair-haired boy: *At the moment Christopher Fry is the white-haired boy of the London theatre* (New York Times).

white hake, a marine fish related to the hake.

White·hall (hwīt′hôl′), *n.* the British government or its policies. [< *Whitehall,* a London street adjacent to the Houses of Parliament, site of many government offices]

white-head·ed (hwīt′hed′id), *adj.* **1.** (of an animal) having the head (wholly or partly) white; having white hair, plumage, etc., on the head. **2.** of a person: **a.** white-haired, especially from age. **b.** having very light or fair hair; flaxen-haired.

white-headed boy, *Irish Informal.* a fair-haired boy; favorite.

white heart, 1. a small, delicate, perennial plant with flattened, heart-shaped flowers, growing in shady woods in the eastern United States and Canada; Dutchman's-breeches. **2.** a disease of lettuce, caused by a virus.

white heat, 1. extremely great heat, at which metals and some other bodies give off a dazzling white light. **2.** a state of extremely great activity, excitement, or feeling.

white hellebore, a European variety of false hellebore whose roots have medicinal properties.

white heron, **1.** the great white heron. **2.** the egret.

white hope, *Slang.* a person expected to be a success: *the young American writer who, in the far off days of the middle nineteen-fifties, was regarded as the white hope of the medium* (Observer).

white horse, a white-topped wave; whitecap.

white-hot (hwīt′hot′), *adj.* **1.** white with heat; extremely hot. **2.** very enthusiastic; excited; violent. **3.** that gives rise to excitement, enthusiasm, violence, etc.: *The dues issue was a white-hot thing four years ago* (Wall Street Journal).

White House, the office, authority, opinion, etc., of the President of the United States.

white hunter, a white man employed to guide a safari: *If there were breakdowns, white hunters would stand ready to rescue the cars' occupants, but he expected no danger from the beasts* (London Times).

white ibis, a white ibis with black wing tips and red face and legs, found from the southern United States south to northern South America.

white iron, tin.

white iron pyrites, marcasite.

white lead, **1.** a heavy, white, poisonous, powdery compound, basic lead carbonate, used in making paint and in putty; ceruse. *Formula:* $2PbCO_3.Pb(OH)_2$ **2.** the putty or paste prepared by grinding this substance with oil (white lead in oil). **3.** Also, **white lead ore.** cerussite.

white leather, leather treated with salt and alum to retain its natural light color.

white lie, a lie about some small matter; polite or harmless lie.

white light, **1.** the light which comes directly from the sun, and which has not been decomposed, as by refraction. **2.** any light producing the same color or color sensation as direct sunlight.

white lightning, *U.S. Slang.* unaged, illegally distilled corn whiskey; moonshine.

white line, **1.** a white (or yellow) strip painted on a road or street, for the guidance of drivers of vehicles. **2.** the flaky white layer in the wall of a horse's hoof.

white-lipped peccary (hwīt′lipt′), a large peccary with white markings on the face, living from Mexico south to Paraguay.

white list, *U.S.* a list of members of diplomatic households who are entitled to diplomatic immunity from the jurisdiction of federal, state, or local courts.

white-liv·ered (hwīt′liv′ərd), *adj.* **1.** cowardly. **2.** pale; unhealthy looking. —**Syn. 1.** lily-livered. **2.** wan.

white lupine, an Old World lupine with white flowers, much used in Europe as fodder.

white·ly (hwīt′lē), *adv.* so as to be or appear white; with a white color or aspect.

white mahogany, the wood of the primavera.

white-maned (hwīt′mānd′), *adj.* having a heavy shock of white hair: *An elderly, white-maned member dozes peacefully in an over-sized leather chair* (Wall Street Journal).

white mangrove, a tree or shrub of western Africa and tropical America as far north as Florida, with greenish-white flowers and a reddish gark rich in tannin.

white man's burden, the assumed duty of members of the Caucasian race to care for, educate, and govern the underdeveloped countries and uncivilized peoples of the world, especially of Asia and Africa.

➔ The phrase **White Man's Burden,** coined by Rudyard Kipling in his *From Sea to Sea* (1899), was felt by many supporters of imperialism to justify their cause by reconciling it with Christian duty.

white marlin, a small marlin of Atlantic waters with a conspicuous lateral line.

white matter, whitish nerve tissue, especially in the brain and spinal cord, that consists chiefly of nerve fibers with myelin sheaths (thick, white, fatty sheaths).

white meat, **1.** any light-colored meat, such as veal or breast of chicken or turkey. **2.** *Dialect.* dairy products.

white metal, **1.** any of several light-colored or white alloys, as Babbitt metal. **2.** any of several other alloys containing a large percentage of lead or tin.

white mouse, an albino strain of the common house mouse, bred for medical and biological research and sometimes for a pet.

white mouth, a contagious disease of infants and children characterized by small, white patches in the mouth and throat and on the tongue, usually associated with malnutrition; thrush.

white mulberry, a mulberry native to China whose leaves are used for feeding silkworms.

white mule, *U.S. Slang.* raw, illegally distilled liquor; moonshine: *South Africa's version of white mule is a raw, locally distilled brandy which scalds its way down the throats of South Africans of all shades and colors* (Time).

white muscle disease, a serious disease which affects lambs and calves by wasting of muscle tissue; stiff lamb disease.

white mustard, a variety of mustard plant cultivated for its seeds, which are used for seasoning, and for its edible leaves.

whit·en (hwī′tən), *v.t.* to make white: *Sunshine helps to whiten clothes.* —*v.i.* to become white: *Nellie whitened as she tore open the telegram.* —**whit′en·er,** *n.*

—**Syn.** *v.t.* **Whiten, bleach** mean to make white or nearly white. **Whiten,** the more general word, particularly suggests applying or rubbing some substance on the outside of the thing: *The dentist used a powder to whiten my teeth.* **Bleach** means to make white or lighter in color or colorless by exposing to sunlight and air or by using chemicals: *You can bleach those handkerchiefs by leaving them out on the clothesline for several days.*

whit·en·ing (hwīt′ə ning), *n.* **1. a.** a making white; bleaching, whitewashing, tinning, etc. **b.** the fact or process of becoming white. **2.** whiting.

white noise, the sound heard when the entire range of audible frequencies is produced at once, as in the operation of a jet engine.

white oak, **1.** a large oak of eastern and central North America which has a light-gray or whitish, ridged bark and is highly valued for its hard, tough, durable wood. **2.** an oak of British and other European forests; durmast. **3.** any of various other oaks, as the robur, a common species in Great Britain, or the roble, a shade tree of California and Mexico. **4.** the wood of any of these trees.

white-on-white (hwīt′on hwīt′, -ôn-), *n.* **1.** a white cloth with a figured design in an off-white woven into it, used for shirts, blouses, etc. **2.** a shirt made of this cloth: *He ordered three white-on-whites and two of plain broadcloth.*

white·out (hwīt′out′), *n.* **1.** a condition in arctic and antarctic regions in which the sky, the horizon, and the ground become a solid mass of dazzling reflected light obliterating all shadows and distinctions: *A whiteout can be more devastating than a blizzard, for the snow on the ground merges with a solid white overcast of clouds, with no visible point of junction* (John Brooks). **2.** a temporary loss of vision resulting from this: *Travelers in Arctic snow on an overcast day, in fog, or under an unbroken sky may suffer not a blackout but a whiteout* (Science News Letter).

white paper, **1. a.** paper of a white color. **b.** blank paper, not written or printed upon. **2.** an official report, especially one from the British government dealing with less important matters than a blue book.

white pelican, a large white pelican of western North America with black flight feathers.

white pepper, a seasoning, less pungent than black pepper, made from the dried, fully ripened berries of a tropical climbing shrub, by removing the outer layer of the same berries used in preparing black pepper.

white perch, a small, silvery food fish of the eastern United States, found in both fresh and marine waters.

white phosphorus, the common form of phosphorus, in which it appears yellow and luminous in the dark.

white pigweed, a coarse weed of the goosefoot family with narrow, notched leaves; lambsquarter.

white pine, **1.** a tall pine tree of eastern North America, valued for its soft, light wood. Its green cone and tassel are the state emblem of Maine. See **pine cone** for picture. **2.** the wood itself, much used for building. **3.** any of various similar pines.

white-pine weevil (hwīt′pīn′), a kind of weevil whose larvae feed on the new stems of the white pine and some other coniferous trees.

white plague, tuberculosis, especially of the lungs.

white poplar, **1.** a large, spreading poplar, a native of Europe and Asia, whose deeply indented, roundish leaves have a silvery-white down on the under surface; abele. **2. a.** the tulip tree. **b.** its soft wood; tulipwood.

white potato, a very common variety of potato with a whitish inside; Irish potato.

white primary, *U.S.* a primary election held in some Southern states, in which only white persons are permitted to vote.

white quebracho, a South American tree of the dogbane family whose bark is used for tanning, and in medicine as a respiratory stimulant.

white race, the Caucasian race.

white rat, **1.** an albino variety of the brown or Norway rat, used in laboratory experiments. **2.** any albino rat.

white room, clean room: *These tools are useful also to white room operations ... and biological work* (Science News Letter).

white rose, the emblem of the house of York.

white rot, **1.** any of several small herbaceous plants, such as the pennywort. **2.** any of various fungous plant diseases characterized by numerous white or grayish spots on the affected parts.

white-rumped sandpiper (hwīt′rumpt′), a small sandpiper that nests in arctic America and winters in southern South America. It reveals a conspicuous white rump when in flight.

White Russian, **1.** a Russian living in the western part of the Soviet Union, north of the Ukraine. **2.** a Russian who recognizes the former czarist government of Russia as the legal government of that country; Russian monarchist.

white rust, **1.** a fungous disease of plants characterized by the eruption of white spores on the affected parts. **2.** the fungus causing this.

whites (hwīts), *n.pl.* See under **white,** *n.*

white sale, a sale of white goods: *Merchants reported that January White Sales business was good* (New York Times).

white sandalwood, a variety of sandalwood cultivated in India, having a hard, fragrant wood used for construction and in making medicines, perfumes, and cosmetics.

white sapphire, a colorless variety of corundum or sapphire.

white sauce, a sauce made of milk, butter, and flour cooked together until thick and smooth, frequently with seasoning added.

white shark, the great white shark.

white sheep, the Dall's sheep, a wild sheep of Alaska and northwestern Canada that is white in the northern part of its range.

white sidewall, an automobile tire with a white rim on the outer casing.

white slave, **1.** a woman forced to be a prostitute. **2.** a white person held as a slave. —**white′-slave′,** *adj.*

white slaver, a person whose business is white slavery.

white slavery, **1.** the condition of a white slave or slaves. **2.** the practice or business of a white slaver; traffic in white slaves.

white-slav·ing (hwīt′slā′ving), *n.* white slavery.

white·smith (hwīt′smith′), *n.* **1.** a worker in tin (white iron); tinsmith. **2.** a person who finishes or polishes iron articles.

white snakeroot, a North American herb of the composite family, a variety of eupatorium with clusters of white flowers.

white spruce, a small spruce of northern North America with light-gray bark and unpleasant-smelling foilage.

white squall, a squall of wind without clouds.

white·ster (hwīt′stər), *n. Obsolete.* a bleacher, as of linen.

white stork, the common European stork, also occurring in Africa and Asia, having white feathers with black on the wings.

white supremacist, a believer in or supporter of white supremacy: *You cannot deal honestly with the question of race without infuriating the white supremacists in the South or the Negro liberals in the North* (Listener).

white-su·prem·a·cist (hwīt′sə prem′ə sist), *adj.* of or having to do with white supremacy or white supremacists: *I have never known him to say one word that could by any possible stretch of the imagination be interpreted as even faintly white-supremacist in attitude* (William S. White).

white supremacy, the belief that the white race is superior to and should have supremacy over all others, especially the Negro race: *Already the idea of white supremacy has a certain fustiness about it, which before long could make it a merely curious anachronism* (New Yorker).

white·tail (hwīt′tāl′), *n.* white-tailed deer.

white-tailed deer (hwīt′tāld′), the common deer of eastern North America, white on the underside of the tail, known also in its summer coat as a red deer; Virginia deer. See **deer** for picture.

white-tailed kite, a falconlike hawk with white tail and underparts, a variety of kite found from California and Texas south to Chile.

white-tailed sea eagle, an eagle of northern Europe with a white tail, closely related to the bald eagle.

white-thatched (hwīt′thacht′), *adj.* having white hair: *The committeemen wound up by blaming everything on the white-thatched, mild-mannered coach* (Time).

white·thorn (hwīt′thôrn′), *n.* the English hawthorn.

white·throat (hwīt′thrōt′), *n.* **1.** any of certain European warblers, brown with a whitish throat and belly. **2.** the white-throated sparrow.

white-throat·ed (hwīt′thrō′tid), *adj.* having a white throat.

white-throated sparrow, a large sparrow of eastern North America, brown with a white patch on the throat; peabody bird; whitethroat.

white-throated swift, a black and white swift (bird) found from British Columbia south through the western United States to Guatemala.

white tie, 1. a white bow tie, such as is worn by a man in formal evening clothes. **2.** *Informal.* formal evening clothes for a man: *decreeing that all male guests appear in white tie* (New Yorker).

white trash, 1. poor whites, as a group (used in an unfriendly way). **2.** a descendant or the descendants of poor whites, regardless of means (used in an unfriendly way).

white turnip, a kind of turnip.

white vitriol, a white or colorless, crystalline substance used as an antiseptic, and for dyeing calico, preserving wood, etc.; zinc sulfate. *Formula:* $ZnSO_4.7H_2O$

white·wall (hwīt′wôl′), *n.* a white sidewall tire: *Then he'll probably kick the tires—first the front and then the back, only most of the time he'll kick the whitewalls* (Newsweek).

white·ware (hwīt′wãr′), *n.* articles made of white pottery, earthenware, porcelain, etc., such as plumbing fixtures, dinnerware, electrical insulators, etc.

white·wash (hwīt′wosh′, -wôsh′), *n.* **1.** a liquid mixture of lime and water or of whiting, size, and water, used as an inexpensive substitute for paint in whitening walls, woodwork, etc. **2.** a covering up of faults or mistakes. **3.** anything that covers up faults or mistakes. **4.** *Informal.* a defeat in a game without a score for the loser; shut-out. **5.** *Obsolete.* a cosmetic formerly used to make the skin fair.

—*v.t.* **1.** to whiten with whitewash. **2.** to cover up the faults or mistakes of. **3.** *Informal.* to defeat without a score for the loser: *The faltering world champions meekly submitted to a 6-0 whitewashing . . . at the Polo Grounds last night* (New York Times).

—**white′wash′er,** *n.*

white water, water with breakers or foam, as in shallows or rapids on the sea or a river.

white wax, *British.* paraffin.

white·weed (hwīt′wēd′), *n.* the common or oxeye daisy.

white whale, a beluga.

white·wing (hwīt′wing′), *n. Informal.* a person employed to clean the streets, remove rubbish, etc., especially an employee of a municipal department of sanitation (from the white uniforms now or formerly worn).

white-winged crossbill (hwīt′wingd′), a rose-colored crossbill of northern regions of both hemispheres, with white bars on the wings.

white-winged dove, a large dove of southern and western North America, with a white patch on each wing.

white-winged scoter, a blackish, North American sea duck with a large white patch on the rear edge of each wing.

white·wood (hwīt′wu̇d′), *n.* **1.** any of various trees with white or light-colored wood, as the North American tulip tree and the North American linden or basswood. **2.** the wood of any of these trees. **3.** the cottonwood.

white wreath aster, the heath aster, a white-flowered aster of eastern United States; fall flower.

Whit·ey (hwī′tē), *n., pl.* **-ties.** a white man (used in an unfriendly way).

whith·er (hwiᴛʜ′ər), *adv., conj.* to what place; to which place; where. [Old English *hwider,* alteration of *hwæder;* apparently influenced by *hider* hither]

whith·er·so·ev·er (hwiᴛʜ′ər sō ev′ər), *adv., conj.* to whatever place; wherever.

whith·er·ward (hwiᴛʜ′ər wərd), *adv. Archaic.* **1. a.** toward or to what place; in what direction; whither. **b.** toward what. **2. a.** whithersoever. **b.** toward which.

whith·er·wards (hwiᴛʜ′ər wərdz), *adv.* whitherward.

whit·ing[1] (hwī′ting), *n., pl.* **-ings** or (*collectively*) **-ing. 1.** a European food fish related to the cod. **2.** the silver hake. **3.** any of certain sciaenoid fishes, as an edible variety of the entire Atlantic Coast of the United States. [probably < Middle Dutch *wijting.* Compare Old English *hwītling* a kind of fish.]

whit·ing[2] (hwī′ting), *n.* a preparation of finely powdered chalk, used in making putty, whitewash, and silver polish. [apparently < *whit*(e) + *-ing*[1]. Compare Old English *hwīting,* implied in *hwīting-melu* whiting meal.]

whit·ish (hwī′tish), *adj.* somewhat white; of a color inclining to or approaching white. —**whit′ish·ness,** *n.*

whit·leath·er (hwit′leᴛʜ′ər), *n.* white leather. [Middle English *whitlether* < *whit* white + *lether* leather]

whit·low (hwit′lō), *n.* an abscess on a finger or toe, usually near a nail; a felon or agnail. [alteration of Middle English *whitflaw,* probably < *whit* white, Old English *hwīt* + *flawe,* related to *flake* a layer, covering]

Whit·man·esque (hwit′mə nesk′), *adj.* of, having to do with, or suggestive of Walt Whitman, an American poet, 1819-1892, or his style of poetry: *The pretentiousness derives . . . from a kind of Whitmanesque grandiosity that runs through the book* (New Yorker).

Whit·mon·day (hwit′mun′dē, -dā), *n.* the Monday after Whitsunday, a bank holiday in England.

Whit·sun (hwit′sən), *adj.* of, having to do with, or occurring at Whitsunday or Whitsuntide. —*n.* Whitsuntide. [Middle English *whitsone,* misdivision of *whitsondei* Whitsunday, Old English *Hwīta Sunnandæg;* see WHITSUNDAY]

Whit·sun·day (hwit′sun′dē, -dā; hwit′sən dā), *n.,* or **Whitsun Day,** the seventh Sunday after Easter; Pentecost. [Old English *Hwīta Sunnandæg* < *hwīt* white + *Sunnandæg* Sunday (probably because of the custom of wearing white baptismal robes on this day)]

Whit·sun·tide (hwit′sən tīd′), *n.,* or **Whitsun Tide,** the week beginning with Whitsunday, especially the first three days.

whit·ter (hwit′ər, wit′-), *n. Scottish.* a draft of liquor; drink. [compare obsolete *whittle* to ply with drink]

whit·tle (hwit′əl), *v.,* **-tled, -tling,** *n.* —*v.t.* **1.** to cut shavings or chips from (wood, etc.) with a knife. **2.** to shape (an object) in this way; carve. **3.** to cut down or reduce gradually; trim: *to whittle costs. Production schedules can be whittled* (Wall Street Journal). —*v.i.* to cut shavings from a stick, etc, with a knife, as in making something or for idle amusement.

whittle down or **away,** to cut down little by little: *to whittle down expenses. These proposals were gradually whittled away during the talks until they ended as a general proposal to set up a Defence and Security Council to control the existing forces* (Manchester Guardian Weekly).

[< noun]

—*n. Scottish.* a large knife.

[Middle English *whittel* a knife, variant of *thwittle,* ultimately < Old English *thwītan* to cut] —**whit′tler,** *n.*

whit·tling (hwit′ling), *n.* the act of a person or thing that whittles.

whittlings, chips or slivers cut off in whittling; shavings: *Litter of shavings and whittlings strewed the floor* (William Dean Howells).

whit·y (hwī′tē), *adj.* whitish.

whiz or **whizz** (hwiz), *n., v.,* **whizzed, whizzing.** —*n.* **1. a.** a humming or hissing sound. **b.** a swift movement producing such a sound. **2.** *Slang.* **a.** a very clever person; expert. **b.** something skillful or appealing: *I did a whiz of a pantomime* (Atlantic).

—*v.i.* **1.** to make a humming or hissing sound. **2.** to move or rush swiftly with or as with the sound of a whiz: *An arrow whizzed past his head.* —*v.t.* to cause to whiz; hurl, shoot, or send swiftly with or as with a whiz.

[imitative]

whiz-bang or **whizz-bang** (hwiz′bang′), *n.* **1.** a shell fired in a flat trajectory at high velocity from a rifled piece of artillery of relatively small caliber, so that the sound of its explosion is heard almost simultaneously with the whizzing sound of its passage through the air. **2.** a firework that makes a short, whizzing or buzzing sound and then explodes, intended to imitate the characteristic sound of such a shell. —*adj. Informal.* excellent; first-rate: *Brown is a whiz-bang campaigner with a wide personal following* (Time).

whiz kid, *U.S. Slang.* **1.** a child prodigy: *a musical whiz kid.* **2.** a superior pupil. **3.** a young man of outstanding intelligence and skill; whiz: *an accounting whiz kid. Fuzzy-cheeked whiz kids with computers telling battle-scarred dogfaces how to fight and win wars* (Wall Street Journal).

whiz·zer (hwiz′ər), *n.* **1.** a person or thing that whizzes. **2.** a machine for drying various articles or materials by the centrifugal force of rapid revolution.

who (hü; *unstressed relative* ü), *pron., poss.* **whose,** *obj.* **whom. 1.** (as an interrogative pronoun) a word used in asking a question about a person or persons: *Who is your friend? Who told you? Who is coming? Who is the Lord that I should obey him?* (Exodus 5:2). **2.** as a relative pronoun: **a.** a word used in connecting a group of following words with some previous words in the sentence; the person or persons indicated by the antecedent: *The girl who spoke is my sister. We saw several friends who were waiting for tickets.* **b.** the person who; any person who; one that; whoever: *Who is not for us is against us.*

as who should or **would say,** as if saying; as if one should say; as much as to say: *Sid beamed at Kips, as who should say, "You don't meet a character like this every dinnertime"* (H.G. Wells).

who's who, a. which person is which; who each person is: *In such large and noisy parties as this, I can never tell who's who.* **b.** which people are important: *As a society columnist it's her business to know who's who.* **c.** a collection or gathering of important people: *The reviewing stand became a who's who of city and state politicians* (New York Times). **d.** a reference book containing short biographies of important people: *a who's who of the theater. Crockford's Clerical Directory . . . an ecclesiastical Who's Who* (Newsweek).

[Old English *hwā*]

➔ **Who** refers to people, to personified objects (a ship, a country), and occasionally to animals: *They have three dogs who always give us a big welcome.*

➔ See **that** for another usage note.

WHO (no periods) or **W.H.O.,** World Health Organization (an agency acting within the United Nations).

whoa (hwō, wō), *interj.* stop! (used especially to horses). [variant of obsolete *who,* interjection, variant of *ho*]

who'd (hüd), **1.** who had: *I'm the one who'd seen him last.* **2.** who would: *Who'd have thought he could do such a thing!*

who·dun·it (hü dun′it), *n. Slang.* a story, motion picture, etc., dealing with crime, especially murder, and its detection. [spelling alteration of "who done it"]

who·ev·er (hü ev′ər), *pron.* **1.** any person that; who: *Whoever wants the book may have it.* **2.** no matter who: *Whoever else goes hungry, he won't.* **3.** *Informal.* (as an interrogative pronoun implying perplexity or surprise) who: *Whoever could have done such a dreadful thing?*

➔ **a.** In standard, written English **whoever** and **whomever** are used as subject and object respectively. In informal, spoken English, *whoever,* like *who,* frequently serves as either subject or object. **b.** In *They gave tickets to whoever requested them,* the whole clause *whoever requested them* is the object of *to* and *whoever* is the subject of *requested.* In sentences of this type, *whomever* is sometimes substituted because of the mistaken notion that it is required by the preceding preposition.

whole (hōl), *adj.* **1.** comprising the full quantity, amount, extent, number, etc.; entire: *to tell the whole story, to work the whole day, to give a matter one's whole attention, to eat a whole melon. The whole state was hit by the hurricane.* **2.** having all its parts or elements; complete; full: *He gave her a whole set of dishes.* **3.** in one piece; undivided: *to swallow a piece of meat whole.* **4.** *Mathematics.* not fractional; integral: *a whole number.* **5.** being fully or entirely such: *a whole brother or sister* (a son or daughter of both parents). **6.** not injured, broken, or defective: *to get out of a fight with a whole skin.* **7. a.** well; healthy. **b.** *Archaic.* restored to good health, as from disease, an injury, or a wound; well again. **c.** *Obsolete.* (of a wound) healed.

—*n.* **1.** all of a thing; the total: *Four quarters make a whole.* **2.** something complete in itself; a system: *the complex whole of civilization.*

as a whole, as one complete thing; altogether: *The public must be represented when the wage bargains are struck because the nation as a whole is an interested third party* (Manchester Guardian Weekly).

on or **upon the whole, a.** in general; for the most part: *But on the whole the people of Coronation Street don't bother about the outside world* (Maclean's). **b.** as the upshot of the matter; in sum: *Upon the whole he was unanimously sentenced to die* (Oliver Goldsmith).

[spelling variant of Middle English *hole,* Old English *hāl.* Doublet of HALE[1]. Related to HEAL, HOLY.] —**whole′ness,** *n.*

—**Syn.** *adj.* **1. Whole, total** mean consisting of and including all the parts or elements. **Whole** emphasizes that no element or part is left out or taken away: *The whole class was invited to the party.* **Total** emphasized that every element or part is counted or taken in: *His total income is less this year than last.* **2.** perfect, intact. **6.** unimpaired, uninjured, unbroken. **7. a.** hale, sound. *-n.* **1.** entirety, aggregate, sum. —**Ant.** *n.* **1.** portion, part.

whole blood, natural blood with none of the essential components removed: *A seaweed compound mixed with water can substitute for whole blood in transfusions, two Japanese surgeons have reported* (Science News Letter).

whole gale, a gale.

whole-heart·ed (hōl′här′tid), *adj.* earnest; sincere; hearty; cordial: *a whole-hearted friend, whole-hearted support.* [American English < *whole;* perhaps patterned on *half-hearted*] —**whole′-heart′ed·ly,** *adv.* —**whole′-heart′ed·ness,** *n.*

whole-hog (hōl′hog′, -hôg′), *adj. Slang.* that goes the whole hog; thoroughgoing; unlimited: *Anything less than whole-hog public ownership would seem like backsliding* (New Yorker).

whole-hog·ger (hōl′hog′ər, -hôg′-), *n. Slang.* a person who goes the whole hog; one who does something thoroughly: *Temperamentally a whole-hogger, de Foucauld plunged into Trappist monasteries* (Manchester Guardian Weekly).

whole-hoofed (hōl′hu̇ft′, -hüft′), *adj.* having the hoof undivided or not cloven, as the horse; solidungulate.

whole·ly (hō′lē, hōl′lē), *adv.* wholly: *He was wholely dedicated to his work, and his patients of all ages regarded him as a very real friend* (London Times).

whole-meal (hōl′mēl′), *adj.* **1.** made of the entire wheat grain kernels: *whole-meal flour.* **2.** made of whole-meal flour.

whole milk, milk from which none of the natural constituents have been separated.

whole note, a note indicating a tone to be given as much time as four quarter notes; the longest duration of sound commonly encountered in music today; semibreve. It is the standard unit of time measurement in modern music notation.

whole number, a number denoting one or more whole things or units; integer. 1, 2, 3, 15, 106 are whole numbers; 1/2, 3/4, and 7/8 are fractions; 1-3/8, 2-1/2, and 12-2/3 are mixed numbers.

whole rest, *Music.* a rest as long as a whole note.

whole·sale (hōl′sāl′), *n., adj., adv., v.,* **-saled, -sal·ing.** —*n.* the sale of goods in large quantities at a time, usually to retailers rather than to consumers directly: *He buys at wholesale and sells at retail.*

by wholesale, a. in large quantities: *a commodity sold by wholesale.* **b.** in a large way and indiscriminately: *They despise a valuable book, and . . . throw contempt upon it by wholesale* (Isaac Watts).

—*adj.* **1.** in large lots or quantities: *The wholesale price of this coat is $22; the retail price is $30.* **2.** selling in large quantities: *a wholesale merchant, a wholesale house.* **3.** broad and general; extensive and indiscriminate: *Avoid wholesale condemnation.*

—*adv.* in large quantities or lots; at or by wholesale: *to buy something wholesale.*

—*v.t.* to sell (goods, etc.) in large quantities: *New car dealers are using their good trade-ins instead of wholesaling them* (Wall Street Journal).

—*v.i.* to be sold in large quantities. —**whole′-sal′er,** *n.*

—**Syn.** *adj.* **3.** sweeping, unlimited.

wholesale price index, *U.S.* a list of prices paid for a representative number of goods in various cities during a given month compared with average prices paid in a recent base period. It is compiled by the Bureau of Labor Statistics.

whole snipe, (in Europe) the common variety of snipe.

whole·some (hōl′səm), *adj.* **1.** good for the health; healthful: *Milk is a wholesome food.* **2.** suggesting good health; healthy-looking: *a wholesome face.* **3.** good for the mind or morals; beneficial: *Read wholesome books.* **4.** free from disease or taint: *Ere the wholesome flesh decay* (A.E. Housman). [spelling variant of Middle English *holsum* < *hol* whole + *-sum* -some[1]] —**whole′some·ly,** *adv.* —**whole′some·ness,** *n.* —**Syn. 2.** See **healthy.**

whole-souled (hōl′sōld′), *adj.* whole-hearted: *She has adopted America and its ways in the whole-souled fashion in which she does everything* (Harper's).

whole step, *Music.* an interval consisting of two semitones or half steps, and equal to one sixth of an octave, such as D to E, or E to F♯; major second.

whole-time (hōl′tīm′), *adj. British.* for all of the usual or required time; full-time: . . . *those who wanted to take social work as their whole-time employment* (Times of India).

whole tone, *Music.* a whole step.

whole-tone scale (hōl′tōn′), *Music.* a scale proceeding in whole steps, dividing the octave in six equal parts, used in the first decade of the 1900's.

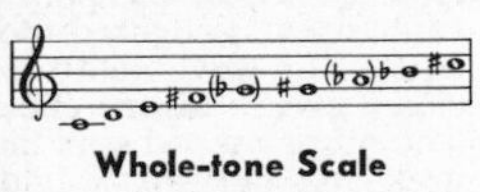

Whole-tone Scale

whole-wheat (hōl′hwēt′), *adj.* **1.** made of the entire wheat kernel: *whole-wheat flour.* **2.** made from whole-wheat flour: *whole-wheat bread.*

whole-word method (hōl′wėrd′), word method.

who·lism (hō′liz əm), *n.* holism.

who·lis·tic (hō lis′tik), *adj.* holistic.

who'll (hül), who will; who shall.

whol·ly (hō′lē, hōl′lē), *adv.* **1.** to the whole amount or extent; completely; entirely; altogether; totally: *to be wholly finished.* **2.** as a whole; in its entirety; in full: *A man who can see truth at all, sees it wholly, and neither desires nor dares to mutilate it* (John Ruskin). **3.** exclusively; solely: *A creature wholly given to brawls and wine* (Tennyson). —**Syn. 1.** utterly. **3.** only.

whom (hüm), *pron.* the objective case of **who.** [Old English *hwām,* dative of *hwā* who, and *hwæt* what]

whom·ev·er (hüm′ev′ər), *pron.* **1.** whom; any person whom. **2.** no matter whom.

➔ See **whoever** for usage note.

whomp (hwomp), *Informal.* —*n.* a loud outburst of sound: *For four nights . . . the heart of Warsaw echoed to the whomp and hiss of exploding tear-gas bombs* (Time).

—*v.i.* to hit or fall with such a sound; thump: *The Sunday edition of the New York Times . . . whomped to the floor outside my apartment door* (New Scientist). —*v.t.* **1.** to beat or knock down with such a sound: *jailed and systematically whomped by the local police* (New York Times). **2.** to defeat; drub: *The whomping the Republicans and we conservatives took in this past election hurts* (Wall Street Journal).

whom·so·ev·er (hüm′sō ev′ər), *pron.* any person whom.

whoop (hüp, hwüp), *n.* **1.** a loud cry or shout: *The man gave a whoop of rage.* **2.** such a cry or shout used by North American Indians as a signal or war cry (war whoop). **3.** the loud, gasping noise of a person with whooping cough after a fit of coughing. **4.** the cry of an owl, crane, etc.; hoot. **5.** *Informal.* a bit; scarcely anything: *not worth a whoop. Who could possibly believe it or care two whoops?* (Atlantic).

a whoop and a holler, *U.S. Informal.* **a.** a comparatively short distance: *Eudora Welty's characters have till now been found no farther than a whoop and a holler from Jackson, Natchez, or Vicksburg, Miss.* (New York Times). **b.** a great to-do; hullabaloo: *The Republicans make a great whoop and a holler about the honesty of federal employees* (Harry S. Truman).

—*v.i.* **1.** to shout or call loudly. **2.** to make the loud, gasping noise characteristic of whooping cough. **3.** to hoot, as an owl or crane.

—*v.t.* **1.** to utter with a whoop; express by whooping. **2.** to call, urge, drive, etc., with or as if with shouts or whoops: *to whoop dogs on. The Senate whooped it through and sent it to the House* (Time).

whoop it up, *Slang.* **a.** to revel; make merry; celebrate: *No one was happy except him, his wife, and two brothers, whooping it up in a Milwaukee hotel* (Manchester Guardian). **b.** to act or work in a rousing way; support vigorously: *One of the most persistent clichés about democracy is that the thoughtless masses, being given their head, would run headlong to disaster by whooping it up for . . . spending by the government while howling down the taxes* (Wall Street Journal).

—*interj.* a cry or shout to attract attention or to express excitement, encouragement, etc. Also, **hoop.**

[variant of *hoop*[2] (influenced by *who*) < Old French *houper* to cry out; probably ultimately imitative]

whoop-de-do (hüp′dē dü′, hwüp′-, hwu̇p′-), *n. U.S. Slang.* noisy commotion or excitement; hullabaloo: *Despite all the whoop-de-do in the public press about it no one knows the real extent of juvenile delinquency* (Harper's).

whoop·ee (hü′pē, wu̇p′ē, hwü′pē, hwu̇p′ē), *interj.* an exclamation expressing unrestrained pleasure, joy, etc., or the intent to have a hilariously good time. —*n.* **1.** a cry of "whoopee." **2.** noisy commotion or revelry; hilarity.

make whoopee, to rejoice noisily or hilariously; have a good time: *When he received a raise in pay, he spent the weekend making whoopee.*

[< *whoop*]

whoop·er (hü′pər, hwü′-), *n.* **1.** a person or animal that whoops. **2.** a whooper swan. **3.** a whooping crane.

whooper swan, an Old World swan that has a whooping call: *There, in the still water, was a pair of whooper swans, the first of the winter* (Manchester Guardian Weekly).

whoop·ing cough (hü′ping, hu̇p′-), an infectious bacterial disease usually of children, characterized by inflammation of the air passages, with convulsive fits of coughing that end with a loud, gasping sound (whoop); pertussis.

whooping crane, a large white, very rare crane of North America with a red face and black wing tips, noted for its loud, trumpet-like call: *Whooping cranes once ranged widely in the United States, but now there are less than 50 alive* (World Book Encyclopedia).

whoop-up (hüp′up′, hwüp′-, hwu̇p′-), *n. U.S. Informal.* noisy commotion, excitement, or revelry: *Many were no doubt getting over the Saturday-night whoop-up, which in my time used to absorb most of the week's spending money* (New Yorker).

whoosh (hwu̇sh), *n.* a dull, soft, hissing sound like that of something rushing through the air: *The . . . autos are away from the starting line, some with a whoosh, others at a more leisurely pace* (Wall Street Journal).

—*v.i.* to make, or move with, such a sound: *When the time comes that people whoosh across vast reaches of the Earth in rocket carriages* (Saturday Review). —*v.t.* to carry, move, etc., with such a sound: *Boeing's 707 . . . can whoosh 80 first-class*

passengers across the Atlantic at 550 miles per hour (Wall Street Journal).
—*interj.* a sound made to describe a rushing through the air with a soft, hissing noise: *"At first it was a real little thing," he said, "then it caught in some of the blowing sawdust and—whoosh—up it went"* (New York Times).

whoo·zit (hü′zit), *n. Slang.* what-do-you-call-it: *He spends the next few days racing around to conferences with a company sales manager or district whoozit* (New Yorker).

whop (hwop, wop), *v.*, **whopped, whop·ping,** *n.* —*v.t.* **1.** *Informal.* to strike with heavy blows; beat soundly; flog; belabor. **2.** *Dialect.* to throw, take, or put violently and suddenly.
—*v.i. U.S. Informal.* to flop: *to whop down in a chair.*
—*n. Informal.* an act of whopping; heavy blow, bump, etc.: *a sudden whop on the head.* Also, **whap, wop.**
[dialectal variant of *wap*[1]]

whop·per (hwop′ər), *n. Informal.* **1.** something uncommonly large of its kind. **2.** a big lie. Also, **whapper.**
[< *whop* in sense of "to beat, overcome" + *-er*[1]]

whop·ping (hwop′ing), *adj. Informal.* very large of its kind; huge: *a whopping lie.* Also, **whapping.**

whore (hôr, hōr), *n.*, *v.*, **whored, whor·ing.** —*n.* **1.** a prostitute. **2.** an unchaste woman.
—*v.i.* **1. a.** to have sexual intercourse with a whore or whores. **b.** (of a woman) to be or act as a whore. **2.** (in the Bible) to commit an act of idolatry; be guilty of unfaithfulness to the true God. Exodus 34:15. —*v.t. Obsolete.* to debauch (a woman).
[spelling variant of Middle English *hore,* Old English *hōre,* perhaps < Scandinavian (compare Old Icelandic *hōra*)]

whore·dom (hôr′dəm, hōr′-), *n. Archaic.* **1.** the act of a whore. **2.** fornication. **3.** (in the Bible) unfaithfulness to the true God; idolatry.

whore·house (hôr′hous′, hōr′-), *n.* a brothel.

whore·mas·ter (hôr′mas′tər, -mäs′-; hōr′-), *n.* whoremonger.

whore·mon·ger (hôr′mung′gər, -mong′-; hōr′-), *n.* **1.** a lecher. **2.** a pander.

whore·mon·ging (hôr′mung′ging, -mong′-; hōr′-), *n.* fornication.

whore·son (hôr′sən, hōr′-), *adj.*, *n. Archaic.* bastard. [Middle English *hores son,* or *hore son* whore's son]

whor·ish (hôr′ish, hōr′-), *adj. Obsolete.* lewd; unchaste. —**whor′ish·ly,** *adv.* —**whor′ish·ness,** *n.*

whorl (hwėrl, hwôrl), *n.* **1.** *Botany.* a set of leaves or flowers round the stem of a plant; a verticil. **2.** each of the turns of a spiral shell. **3. a.** a convolution, coil, curl, or wreath, especially of something whirling, or suggesting a whirling movement. **b.** a type of fingerprint in which the ridges in the center make a turn through at least one complete circle. **c.** one of the spiral curves in the cochlea of the ear. **4.** wharve. **5.** (in ancient hand spinning) a bowl of stone or baked clay in which a spindle was set to allow it to spin freely. [Middle English *whorle,* and *whorlwyl* flywheel or pulley on a spindle, apparently variants of *whirl.* Compare earlier Dutch *worvel,* and *wervel.*]

Whorls
Top, (def. 1); bottom, (def. 2)

whorled (hwėrld, hwôrld), *adj.* **1.** having a whorl or whorls. **2.** arranged in a whorl: *whorled petals.*

whort (hwėrt), *n.* **1.** the whortleberry. **2.** its fruit. [dialectal variant of obsolete *hurt.* Compare HURTLEBERRY.]

whor·tle (hwėr′təl), *n.* whort.

whor·tle·ber·ry (hwėr′təl ber′ē), *n.*, *pl.* **-ries. 1.** a small, edible, black berry much like the blueberry, the fruit of any of several European and Siberian shrubs of the heath family; bilberry. **2.** the shrub that it grows on. **3.** a huckleberry. [dialectal variant of *hurtleberry*]

who's (hüz), **1.** who is: *Who's at the door?* **2.** who has: *Who's been using my pen?*

whose (hüz), *pron.* **1.** the possessive case of **who** and of **which:** *a dog whose bark is loud. Whose fault is this? Hand me that book whose cover is frayed. A hamlet, inhabited by fishermen, whose humanity he had occasion to remember* (Oliver Goldsmith). **2.** (historically) the possessive case of **what.**
[Middle English *whos, hwas,* Old English *hwæs,* genitive of *hwā* who; influenced in Middle English by nominative *wha*]
➔ The use of **whose** as a relative referring to a nonpersonal antecedent (*generators whose combined capacity . . .*), frequently condemned by prescriptive grammarians, has been thoroughly established for centuries, in both literary and general English. The equivalent construction, *of which,* often produces a stiff and clumsy sentence.

whose·so·ev·er (hüz′sō ev′ər), *pron. Archaic.* of any person whatsoever; whose.

who·so (hü′sō), *pron. Archaic.* whoever.

who·so·ev·er (hü′sō ev′ər), *pron.* anybody who; whoever.

w.-hr or **whr.,** watt-hour.

whup (hwup), *v.t.*, **whupped, whup·ping.** *Dialect or Informal.* to beat soundly; whip; wallop: *The Bundawallop Workers were our deadliest rivals, a mean bunch who whupped us consistently* (Punch). [probably alteration of *whip*]

why (hwī), *adv.*, *n.*, *pl.* **whys,** *interj.* —*adv.* **1.** for what cause, reason, or purpose; wherefore: *Why did you do it? I don't know why I did it.* **2.** for which; because of which: *That is the reason why he failed.* **3.** the reason for which: *That is why he raised the question.*
—*n.* the cause; reason; purpose: *She tried to find out the whys and wherefores of his strange behavior.*
—*interj.* an expression of surprise, doubt, hesitancy, etc., or just to fill in: *Why, yes, I will go with you if you wish.*
[Old English *hwȳ,* instrumental case of *hwā* who, and *hwæt* what]

whyd·ah (hwid′ə), *n.* whidah.

why·ev·er (hwī ev′ər), *adv.* for whatever reason; why: *Laughter in your Church? Whyever not!* (London Times).

w.i., when issued.

W.I., 1. West Indian. **2.** West Indies.

wib·bly-wob·bly (wib′lē wob′lē), *adj.* wobbly: *The gait of a motor car was ungainly because of the wibbly-wobbly nature of a rear wheel* (Motor-Car Journal).

Wich·i·ta (wich′ə tô), *n.*, *pl.* **-ta** or **-tas. 1.** a member of a tribe of Plains Indians formerly found in Kansas and now chiefly in Oklahoma. **2.** the Caddoan language of this tribe.

wick[1] (wik), *n.* the part of an oil lamp or candle that is lighted, now usually loosely twisted or woven cotton, immersed or enclosed except at one end in the oil or wax. The oil or melted wax is drawn up by the wick and burned. [Middle English *wicke, weke* < Old English *wice, wēoce*]

wick[2] (wik), *n.* (in the game of curling) a narrow opening in the course left between the stones of previous players. [< obsolete *wick,* verb, to drive a stone through the opening between two guards]

wick·ed (wik′id), *adj.* **1.** bad; evil; sinful: *a wicked man, wicked deeds, wicked words, a wicked heart.* **2.** unpleasant; severe: *a wicked task, a wicked smell, a wicked blow, a wicked storm.* **3.** playfully sly; mischievous: *a wicked smile.* **4.** (of an animal) savage; vicious: *The wicked mongrel fought for his life.*
—*n.* **the wicked,** wicked persons: *There must the wicked cease from their tyranny* (Miles Coverdale).
[Middle English *wicked,* earlier *wicke* wicked, perhaps related to Old English *wīcan* yield, give way, fall down] —**wick′ed·ly,** *adv.*
—**Syn.** *adj.* **1.** ungodly, corrupt, depraved, vile, infamous, immoral. See **bad.**

wick·ed·ness (wik′id nis), *n.* **1.** the quality of being wicked; sinfulness. **2.** a wicked thing or act. —**Syn. 1.** wrongdoing, turpitude. **2.** vice.

wick·er (wik′ər), *n.* **1.** a slender, easily bent branch or twig, usually of willow, especially as used for making baskets, chairs, etc.; osier; withe. **2.** twigs or branches woven together, used in making baskets and furniture. **3.** a basket, chair, etc., made of wicker. —*adj.* **1.** made of wicker. **2.** covered with wicker. [< Scandinavian (compare dialectal Swedish *vikker* branch of willow)]

wick·er·work (wik′ər wėrk′), *n.* **1.** twigs or branches woven together; wicker. **2.** objects made of wicker.

wick·et (wik′it), *n.* **1.** a small door or gate: *The big door has a wicket in it.* **2.** a small window or opening, usually having a grate or grill over it: *Buy your tickets at this wicket.* **3.** a small gate or valve for emptying the chamber of a canal lock, or in the chute of a water wheel for regulating the passage of water. **4.** (in croquet) a wire arch stuck in the ground for the ball to be knocked through; hoop. **5.** in cricket: **a.** either of the two sets of sticks at either end of the playing pitch at which the ball is bowled, each consisting of three uprights (stumps) across which two small sticks (bails) are laid in grooves. The bowler's object is to strike the stumps, the batsman's to prevent the ball from hitting them. **b.** the pitch or ground between and near the wickets, especially with reference to its condition for bowling: *a fast wicket.* **c.** the turn of a batsman. **d.** the period during which two men bat together. **e.** an incomplete (or unopened) inning for any batsman. **6.** an entrance turnstile. [< Anglo-French *wiket,* perhaps ultimately < Scandinavian (compare Old Icelandic *vīkja* a move, turn)]

Wickets
Left, (def. 4); right, (def. 5a)

wick·et·keep·er (wik′it kē′pər), *n.* (in cricket) the fielder who stands behind the wicket.

wick·ing (wik′ing), *n.* material for wicks.

wick·i·up (wik′ē up′), *n.* **1.** an American Indian hut made of brushwood or covered with mats, formerly used by nomadic tribes in the West and Southwest. **2.** *U.S.* any small hut or shanty. Also, **wikiup.** [American English < Algonkian (Sauk, or Fox) *wickīyapi* lodge, dwelling]

wic·o·py (wik′ə pē), *n.*, *pl.* **-pies. 1.** leatherwood. **2.** any of several willow herbs. **3.** basswood (linden). [American English < Algonkian (compare Massachusetts *wik'pi* stringy bark of basswood)]

wid·der·shins (wid′ər shinz), *adv. Scottish.* withershins.

wid·dy[1] or **wid·die** (wid′ē), *n.*, *pl.* **-dies.** *Scottish.* **1.** a band or rope, especially one made of intertwined osiers or the like. **2.** a rope for hanging (used, like *gallows,* in various expressions alluding to hanging). [variant of earlier *withy* < *with*(e) + *-y*[1]]

wid·dy[2] (wid′ē), *n.*, *pl.* **-dies.** *Dialect.* a widow. [variant of *widow*]

wide (wīd), *adj.*, **wid·er, wid·est,** *adv.*, *n.* —*adj.* **1.** filling more space from side to side than the usual thing of the same sort; not narrow; broad: *a wide street, a wide hall.* **2.** extending a certain distance from side to side: *a door three feet wide.* **3.** filling much space from side to side; extensive; vast; great: *the wide world or ocean.* **4.** full; ample; roomy: *wide shoes.* **5.** of great range; extensive; comprehensive: *wide experience, wide knowledge, wide reading.* **6.** far or fully open; distended: *to stare with wide eyes.* **7.** extending far between limits: *a wide difference or distinction, wide fluctuations.* **8.** far apart in nature, character, views, etc. **9.** far from a named point, object, target, etc.; too far or too much to one side: *a shot wide of the target, a pitch wide of the plate.* **10.** *Phonetics.* uttered with the tongue relatively relaxed, as the vowel in *bid* or *bed;* lax. **11.** (of a stock quotation, etc.) having a big difference between the buying and selling prices. **12.** (of livestock feed) containing a proportionately small amount of protein.
—*adv.* **1.** to a great or relatively great extent from side to side: *opinions that are wide apart.* **2.** over an extensive space or region: *to travel far and wide.* **3.** to the full extent; fully: *Open your mouth wide.* **4.** aside; astray: *His arrow went wide.*
wide of, far from: *Fort Cumberland lying . . . wide of all other forts* (George Washington).
—*n.* **1.** a wide space or expanse. **2.** (in cricket) a ball bowled wide of the wicket, counting as a run for the batsman's side. **3.** *Phonetics.* a wide vowel.
[Old English *wīd*] —**wide′ness,** *n.*
—**Syn.** *adj.* **1, 3. Wide, broad** mean far or large across. **Wide** emphasizes the distance from one side to the other; **broad** empha-

sizes the expanse between the two sides: *A wide ocean separates America from Europe. Ships sail on the broad ocean.* —**Ant.** *adj.* **1, 3.** narrow.

wide-an·gle (wīd′ang′gəl), *adj.* requiring the use of or made with a wide-angle lens: *a wide-angle shot.*

wide-angle lens, a lens of short focus, the field of which extends through a wide angle, used especially for photographing at short range.

wide-a·wake (wīd′ə wāk′), *adj.* **1.** with the eyes wide open; fully awake. **2.** alert; keen; knowing.
—*n.* **1.** the sooty tern (a sea bird). **2.** Also, **wide-awake hat.** a soft felt hat with a broad brim and a low crown.
—**Syn.** *adj.* **2.** sharp, acute.

wide·band (wīd′band′), *adj. Electronics.* covering, transmitting, or receiving over a wide range of frequencies: *a wideband antenna, wideband magnetic tape.*

wide boy, *British Slang.* a young man of unscrupulous morals and manners; delinquent: *These young men rarely work and . . . by their insulting behaviour, by creating nuisance or by causing wilful damage . . . they build themselves a reputation for being wide boys whom nobody can control* (London Times).

wide-brimmed (wīd′brimd′), *adj.* having a wide brim: *a group of Pennsylvania Dutch in their black beards and wide-brimmed hats* (Horace Sutton).

wide-eyed (wīd′īd′), *adj.* **1.** with the eyes wide open. **2.** simple; artless; innocent: *Readers of fiction in popular magazines think of the wide-eyed blonde as dumb* (Newsweek). **3.** greatly surprised; astonished: *Many orthodox Moslem traditionalists just stared wide-eyed, stunned, and aghast at the appearance in public of Her Royal Highness . . . unveiled and unashamed* (Time).

wide-field (wīd′fēld′), *adj.* encompassing a wide field of view or perspective: *Most satellite observers will also want a good low-power, wide-field telescope* (Scientific American).

wide·ly (wīd′lē), *adv.* to a wide extent: *a widely distributed plant, a man who is widely known to be widely read, widely opened eyes, two widely different accounts of a quarrel.*
—**Syn.** extensively.

wid·en (wī′dən), *v.t., v.i.* to make or become wide or wider. —**wid′en·er,** *n.*

wide-o·pen (wīd′ō′pən), *adj.* **1.** opened as much as possible; fully open. **2.** lax in the enforcement of laws, especially those having to do with the sale of liquor, with gambling, and with prostitution: *a wide-open city.*

wide-range (wīd′rānj′), *adj.* having a broad extent of use or application: *a wide-range antibiotic claimed to fight more diseases than penicillin* (Wall Street Journal). *It could be made of thin metal foil and act as a wide-range television reflector or micro-wave relay station* (Science News Letter).

wide-rang·ing (wīd′rān′jing), *adj.* taking in a wide field; extending far; far-reaching: *a wide-ranging fishing fleet, wide-ranging conclusions, wide-ranging interests. It is undeniable that the Council has influenced American policy with wide-ranging effects upon the average citizen* (Harper's).

wid·er·shins (wid′ər shinz), *adv. Scottish.* withershins.

wide-scale (wīd′skāl′), *adj.* wide in area, extent, or degree; widespread: *Security in the long run requires that there be a universal reduction and control of the methods of wide-scale destruction* (Bulletin of Atomic Scientists). *In countries using wide-scale vaccination, the disease is already on the decline* (Time). *There has been no wide-scale general testing . . . that would offer conclusive proof* (Atlantic).

wide screen, a screen for showing motion pictures that has greater width than height and is curved to give the illusion of realism: *Such processes as Cinemascope, Cinerama, and Vistavision require a wide screen.* —**wide′-screen′,** *adj.*

wide-spec·trum (wīd′spek′trəm), *adj.* broad-spectrum.

wide·spread (wīd′spred′), *adj.* **1.** spread widely: *widespread wings.* **2.** spread over a wide space: *a widespread flood.* **3.** occurring in many places or among many persons far apart: *a widespread belief.* —**Syn. 1.** outspread

wide·spread·ing (wīd′spred′ing), *adj.* widespread.

wide-wale (wīd′wāl′), *adj.* (of cloth) having wide ridges or wales: *wide-wale corduroy.*

widg·eon (wij′ən), *n., pl.* **-eons** or (*collectively for 1*) **-eon. 1.** any of several kinds of fresh-water wild ducks, slightly larger than a teal, as a species of Europe and northern Asia, and the baldpate, a common American species. **2.** *Obsolete.* a simpleton; ninny (applied to a person in allusion to the supposed stupidity of the bird). Also, **wigeon.** [origin unknown]

American Widgeon (def. 1) (baldpate 19½ in. long)

widg·et (wij′it), *n. U.S. Slang.* a gadget.

wid·ish (wī′dish), *adj.* somewhat wide: *The skirt is navy, and a series of widish tucks sweeps around it* (New Yorker).

wid·ow (wid′ō), *n.* **1.** a woman whose husband is dead and who has not married again. **2.** (in card games) a hand, or group of cards, not dealt to any player but capable of being used by a player who bids for it. **3.** *Printing.* a word or group of words constituting less than a full line at the head of a column or page, generally considered to be typographically undesirable and therefore often required either to be filled out to the full width of the column or page or moved back to the bottom of the preceding column or page.
—*v.t.* **1.** to make a widow or (rarely) widower of. **2.** to deprive (of a valuable or highly prized possession, whether person, thing, or quality). **3.** *Obsolete.* **a.** to survive as a widow; become the widow of. **b.** to endow with a widow's right.
—*adj.* that is a widow; widowed.
[Old English *widewe,* or *widuwe*]
—**Syn.** *n.* **1.** relict.

widow bewitched, *Informal.* a grass widow.

widow bird, the whidah. [translation of New Latin *Vidua* the genus name < Latin *vidua* widow (because of its black plumage). Compare WHIDAH.]

wid·ow·er (wid′ō ər), *n.* a man whose wife is dead and who has not married again.

wid·ow·hood (wid′ō hu̇d), *n.* the condition or time of being a widow or widower.

widow's cruse, an inexhaustible supply (in allusion to II Kings 4:1-7, I Kings 17:8-16): *a widow's cruse of money and goods.*

widow's mite, a small amount of money given cheerfully by a poor person (in allusion to Mark 12:42).

widow's peak, hair that grows or has the appearance of growing low and to a point on the forehead, traditionally supposed to presage early widowhood.

widow's walk, *U.S.* a balcony, on or near the roof of a house along a seacoast, giving a good view of the ocean. New England seafaring men used to build widow's walks on their houses to give their wives a place from which to watch for returning ships.

widow's weeds, the mourning clothes of a widow: *Huey Long . . . persuaded "Miss Hattie" to put aside her bright clothes for more poignant widow's weeds* (Time).

width (width, witth), *n.* **1. a.** how wide a thing is; distance across; breadth: *a plank 15 inches in width.* **b.** extent of opening; distance apart of the two parts of something, as a pair of compasses. **2. a.** a piece of a certain width. **b.** (in sewing) a piece extending the full breadth of the material: *curtains taking two widths of organdy.* **3.** extension or breadth in general; quality of wideness: *great width of mind, vision, etc.* [< *wid*(e) + *-th,* as in *breadth*]

width·way (width′wā′, witth′-), *adv.* widthwise.

width·ways (width′wāz′, witth′-), *adv.* widthwise.

width-wise (width′wīz′, witth′-), *adv.* in the direction of the width; transversely.

Wie·gen·lied (vē′gən lēt′), *n., pl.* **-lie·der** (-lē′dər). *German.* a cradle song; lullaby.

wield (wēld), *v.t.* **1. a.** to hold and use: *A soldier wields the sword.* **b.** to exercise (power, authority, or influence); control; manage: *The people wield the power in a democracy.* **c.** to use after the fashion of a tool or weapon for the performance of something: *to wield the pen.* **2.** *Obsolete.* to govern; command. [Middle English *welden,* Old English *weldan*] —**wield′er,** *n.*

wield·a·ble (wēl′də bəl), *adj.* that can be wielded.

wield·y (wēl′dē), *adj.,* **wield·i·er, wield·i·est.** easily controlled or handled; manageable. [< *wield* + *-y*[1]; later, taken as back formation < *unwieldy*]

wie·ner (wē′nər), *n. U.S.* a frankfurter. [American English, probably short for *wienerwurst*]
➔ In popular usage, as on the signs in butchers' windows, the spelling *weiner* is not uncommon.

wiener roast, an informal, usually outdoor, party at which wieners are roasted.

Wie·ner schnitzel (vē′nər), schnitzel.

wie·ner·wurst (wē′nər wėrst′), *n. U.S.* a frankfurter. [American English < German *Wiener Würstchen* Viennese sausages]

wie·nie (wē′nē), *n. U.S. Informal.* a wiener; frankfurter.

wife (wīf), *n., pl.* **wives. 1.** a married woman. **2.** *Archaic or Dialect.* a woman.
take to wife, to marry: *James had . . . taken to wife the princess Mary of Modena* (Macaulay).
[Old English *wīf* woman, wife]

wife·dom (wīf′dəm), *n.* wifehood.

wife·hood (wīf′hu̇d), *n.* the condition of being a wife.

wife·less (wīf′lis), *adj.* without a wife; unmarried. —**wife′less·ness,** *n.*

wife·li·ness (wīf′lē nis), *n.* wifely character or quality.

wife·ly (wīf′lē), *adj.,* **-li·er, -li·est.** of, having to do with, characteristic of, or suitable for a wife.

wif·ie (wī′fē), *n.* wife (endearing or familiar usage).

wig (wig), *n., v.,* **wigged, wig·ging.** —*n.* an artificial covering of hair for the head: *The bald man wore a wig.*
wigs on the green, *Slang.* a sharp altercation; quarrel: *Neither Mr. Cousins nor Mr. Gaitskell would go to the scaffold, but there would be wigs on the green* (Annual Register of World Events).
—*v.t.* **1.** to supply with, or cover with, a wig or wigs. **2.** *Slang or Informal.* to rebuke; scold.
[short for *periwig*]
—**Syn.** *n.* peruke.

wig·an (wig′ən), *n.* a stout calico resembling canvas, used for stiffening parts of garments. [< *Wigan,* a city in Lancashire, England, where it was made originally]

wig·eon (wij′ən), *n.* widgeon.

wigged (wigd), *adj.* wearing a wig.

wig·ger·y (wig′ər ē), *n., pl.* **-ger·ies. 1. a.** wigs or false hair collectively. **b.** a wig. **2.** the practice of wearing a wig. **3.** empty formality; red tape: *some wisdom amid . . . mountains of wiggeries and folly* (Thomas Carlyle).

wig·ging (wig′ing), *n. Slang or Informal.* a rebuke; reprimand; scolding: *a well-deserved wigging.* [< *wig,* in slang sense of "a scolding" + *-ing*[1]]

wig·gle (wig′əl), *v.,* **-gled, -gling,** *n.* —*v.i.* to move with short, quick movements from side to side; wriggle: *The restless child wiggled in his chair.* —*v.t.* to move, especially to push or pull, with short, quick movements from side to side: *to wiggle a trunk across the floor.*
—*n.* **1.** a wiggling movement. **2.** fish or shellfish served in a white sauce with peas: *shrimp wiggle.*
[perhaps < Dutch, or Flemish *wiggelen* (frequentative) < *wiegen* to rock]
—**Syn.** *v.i.* squirm, twist.

wig·gler (wig′lər), *n.* **1.** a person or thing that wiggles. **2.** the larva of a mosquito. **3.** (in fishing) a lure used in casting that zigzags across the water when drawn in.

wig·gly (wig′lē), *adj.* **1.** wiggling. **2.** wavy: *editorials . . . printed in bold type surrounded by a wiggly border* (Sinclair Lewis).

wig·gy (wig′ē), *adj.,* **wig·gi·er, wig·gi·est. 1.** wearing a wig; wigged. **2.** extremely grave or formal. **3.** *Slang.* very stylish; classy: *. . . wearing a wiggy brown duffel coat, no hat, no gloves* (New Yorker).

wight[1] (wīt), *n.* **1.** *Archaic.* a human being; person. **2.** *Obsolete.* any living being; creature. [Old English *wiht* any living creature. Compare WHIT.]

wight[2] (wīt), *adj. Archaic.* **1.** strong and courageous; valiant. **2. a.** exercising strength; robust; stalwart. **b.** powerful in effect; violent. **3.** moving briskly or rapidly;

nimble; swift. [Middle English *wihte* < Scandinavian (compare Old Icelandic *vīgt* in self-defense; neuter of *vīgr* of fighting age]

wig·let (wig′lit), *n.* a small hair-piece.

wig·mak·er (wig′mā′kər), *n.* a person who makes or sells wigs.

wig·wag (wig′wag′), *v.*, **-wagged, -wag·ging,** *n.* —*v.t., v.i.* **1.** to move to and fro; wag. **2.** to signal by waving or holding in various positions flags, the arms, lights, etc., according to a code.
—*n.* **1.** the act or system of signaling in this manner. **2.** the message signaled. [probably varied reduplication of *wag*[1]; perhaps influenced by *wiggle*] —**wig′wag′ger,** *n.*

Wigwagging (def. 1)

wig·wam (wig′wom, -wôm), *n.* **1. a.** any hut of poles covered with bark, mats, or skins, made by North American Indians, as the tepee. **b.** a hut used especially by the Algonkian Indians of the region of the Great Lakes and eastward, made of bark, mats, or skins laid over a dome-shaped frame of poles. **2.** *U.S. Obsolete.* a large structure used for political conventions. [American English < Algonkian (compare Abnaki *wigwâm* a dwelling)]

Wigwam (def. 1a)

Wig·wam (wig′wom, -wôm), *n.* Tammany Hall.

wik·i·up (wik′ē up′), *n.* wickiup.

wi·ki·wi·ki (wē′kē wē′kē), *adv. Hawaiian.* quickly.

Wil·bur·ite (wil′bə rīt), *n.* one of a seceding body of American Quakers, founded by John Wilbur, opposed to evangelicalism.

wil·co (wil′kō), *interj.* (in radio transmission) will comply.

wild (wīld), *adj.* **1.** living or growing in the forests or fields; not tamed; not cultivated: *The tiger is a wild animal. The daisy is a wild flower.* **2.** produced or yielded naturally, without the aid of man; uncultivated: *wild honey, wild cherries.* **3.** with no people living in it; waste; desolate; desert: *a wild field, wild hills.* **4. a.** not civilized; savage: *wild tribes.* **b.** fierce; ferocious; destructive: *a wild bull.* **5.** not in proper control or order: *wild hair.* **6. a.** not checked; not restrained: *a wild rush for the ball. The children wild in the streets* (Dickens). **b.** resisting control or restraint; unruly or insubordinate; wayward or self-willed: *He has turned out very wild* (Jane Austen). **c.** dissolute; dissipated: licentious: *wild living, to live a wild life. The wildest of libertines* (Macaulay). **7.** violent: *a wild storm, wild winds.* **8.** boisterous: *wild laughter, wild shouts, wild boys.* **9.** violently excited; frantic: *wild with rage or joy.* **10.** *Informal.* very eager: *wild to go home.* **11. a.** out of one's wits; distracted; mad: *driven almost wild with pain.* **b.** showing distraction or madness: *wild eyes.* **12. a.** rash; crazy: *wild schemes.* **b.** absurdly improbable; fantastic: *wild stories of riches.* **13.** unconventional, barbaric, or fanciful: *a wild tune or song.* **14.** strange or fantastic in appearance: *a wild shape in the mist* (Elizabeth Barrett Browning). **15.** far from the mark: *a wild shot, a wild pitch.* **16.** (of a card) of arbitrary denomination or suit.
run wild, a. to live in or revert to an undomesticated or natural state: *Of all countries . . . where the horse runs wild, Arabia produces the most beautiful breed* (Oliver Goldsmith). **b.** to take one's own way in defiance of obligation or authority; be unruly: *The boy had run wild since his young mother's death* (Longman's Magazine).
wild and woolly, *U.S.* rough and uncivilized like the American West during frontier times; rough-and-tumble: *Clarke is a wild and woolly county, where bobcats roam the streets of its largest community* (Clarke County Democrat).
—*n.* an uncultivated or desolate region or tract; waste; desert.
wilds, wild country: *Huge Forests . . . and sandy perilous wilds* (Milton).
—*adv.* in a wild manner; to a wild degree. [Old English *wilde* in the natural state; uncultivated or undomesticated] —**wild′ly,** *adv.* —**wild′ness,** *n.*
—**Syn.** *adj.* **1.** undomesticated. **3.** uninhabited. **4. a.** barbarous. **10.** enthusiastic, excited. **12. a.** reckless. —**Ant.** *adj.* **1.** tame.

wild allspice, spicebush.

wild boar, a wild hog of Europe, southern Asia, and northern Africa, generally considered as the ancestor of the domestic hog. See **boar** for picture.

wild brier, 1. dog rose. **2.** sweetbrier. **3.** any other uncultivated brier.

wild canary, 1. the goldfinch. **2.** the yellow warbler.

wild carrot, a common weed of the parsley family, a native of Europe, Asia, and Africa, having a thin, woody, acrid root and clusters (umbels) of lacy, white flowers; Queen Anne's lace. It is the origin of the cultivated carrot.

wild·cat (wīld′kat′), *n., adj., v.,* **-cat·ted, -cat·ting.** —*n.* **1.** a lynx or other wild animal like a cat, but larger, as the bobcat of North America, related cats of Europe and North Africa, or any of various servals, ocelots, and margays. **2.** a fierce fighter. **3.** a risky or unsafe business undertaking. **4.** a well drilled for oil or gas in a region where none has been found before. **5.** *U.S. Informal.* a locomotive and its tender operating without other cars.
—*adj.* **1.** not safe; wild; reckless: *a wildcat company, wildcat stocks.* **2.** of or denoting an illicit business or enterprise or its products. **3.** running without control or without a schedule: *a wildcat engine.* **4.** not authorized by proper union officials; precipitated by small groups or local unions: *a wildcat strike.*
—*v.t., v.i.* to drill wells in regions not known to contain oil or gas. —**wild′cat′ter,** *n.*

wildcat bank, *U.S.* a bank that issued notes although it possessed little or no capital, before the passage of the National Bank Act of 1863.

wild celery, eelgrass, a fresh-water plant growing in shallow ponds.

wild chervil, a variety of chervil that grows as a weed in parts of North America.

wil·de·beest (wil′də bēst′), *n.* the gnu, an African antelope. [< Afrikaans *wildebeest* wild beast]

wil·der (wil′dər), *Poetic or Archaic.* —*v.t.* to bewilder. —*v.i.* to lose one's way; be perplexed. [apparently < *wilderness,* on analogy of *wander.* Compare Middle Dutch *verwilderen.*]

wil·der·ment (wil′dər mənt), *n. Poetic or Archaic.* bewilderment; confusion.

wil·der·ness (wil′dər nis), *n.* **1. a.** a wild place; region with no people living in it. **b.** a waste or desolate region of any kind, as of the open sea, arctic regions, etc. **2.** a bewildering mass or collection: *a wilderness of streets.* **3.** *Obsolete.* uncultivated condition; wildness. [Middle English *wildernesse* < *wilderne* wild (< Old English *wildēoren* like wild beasts < *wilde* wild + *dēor* animal) + *-ness* -ness] —**Syn.** See desert[1].

wilderness area, *U.S.* an area of virgin land 100,000 acres or more in extent, set apart by law as a national park.

wild-eyed (wīld′īd′), *adj.* **1.** having wild eyes; staring wildly or angrily. **2.** senseless; irrational: *wild-eyed bigots, wild-eyed notions.*

wild fig, caprifig.

wild·fire (wīld′fīr′), *n.* **1.** any highly inflammable substance hard to put out, such as Greek fire, formerly used in warfare. **2.** sheet lightning without audible thunder; heat lightning. **3.** the will-o'-the-wisp; ignis fatuus. **4.** any of various inflammatory, eruptive diseases, especially of sheep. **5.** a bacterial wilt of tobacco plants. **6.** *Obsolete.* erysipelas or a similar inflammatory, eruptive disease. **7.** *Obsolete.* furious or destructive fire; conflagration.
like wildfire, with immense rapidity and effect; very swiftly: *We can't keep up with the demand . . .. Sales are growing like wildfire* (Wall Street Journal).

wild flax, 1. gold-of-pleasure. **2.** toadflax or butter-and-eggs.

wild flower, or **wild·flow·er** (wīld′flou′ər), *n.* **1.** any flowering plant that grows in the woods, fields, etc.; uncultivated plant. **2.** the flower of such a plant.

wild fowl, 1. birds ordinarily hunted, such as wild ducks or geese, partridges, quail, and pheasants. **2.** any such bird.

wild-fowl·er (wīld′fou′lər), *n.* a hunter of wild fowl: *Wild-fowlers will find much to interest them in the display of duck decoys, which is believed to be one of the finest in existence* (New York Times).

wild-fowl·ing (wīld′fou′ling), *n.* the hunting of wild fowl for sport: *Wild-fowling used to be one of the few sports left in Britain which were still done the hard way* (Atlantic).

wild ginger, an aromatic herb of the birthwort family with heart-shaped leaves, common in moist areas of temperate North America.

wild goose, any undomesticated goose, such as the graylag of Great Britain or the Canada goose of North America.

wild-goose chase (wīld′güs′), **1.** a useless search or attempt; foolish or hopeless quest. **2.** an erratic course taken or led by one person (or thing) and followed (or that may be followed) by another.

wild honeysuckle, 1. any of several uncultivated varieties of honeysuckle. **2.** the pinxter flower.

wild horse, 1. an untamed horse. **2.** a domestic horse run wild, or a wild descendant of such a horse.

Wild Hunt, (in European folklore) a nighttime ride of phantom hunters through the wilderness or across the sky.

Wild Huntsman, (in European folklore) the phantom leader of the Wild Hunt, probably originally Odin.

wild hyacinth, 1. a plant, a camass, of eastern North America, bearing white or blue flowers. **2.** the bluebell or wood hyacinth.

wild indigo, any of a group of American perennial plants of the pea family, especially a yellow-flowered species whose root is used as a purgative; false indigo.

wild·ing (wīl′ding), *n.* **1.** a plant that is wild or grows without cultivation. **2. a.** a wild crab-apple tree. **b.** its fruit. **3.** a plant once cultivated but now growing wild; escape. **4.** any person or thing that deviates from or refuses to conform with the multitude or norm of its type.
—*adj.* growing wild; wild.

wild·ish (wīl′dish), *adj.* somewhat wild.

wild lettuce, any uncultivated species of lettuce growing as a weed, especially a prickly-stemmed European species with yellow flower heads.

wild·life (wīld′līf′), *n.* animals and plants in the natural state, especially as they exist in national parks or other lands in the public domain, under government programs of conservation: *Widespread use of DDT in strong concentrations endangers human beings as well as wildlife* (Science News Letter).
—*adj.* of or for wildlife: *wildlife conservation.*

wild·ling (wīld′ling), *n.* a wild plant or animal.

wild madder, 1. madder. **2.** either of two bedstraws.

wild mandrake, May apple.

wild mustard, charlock.

wild oats, 1. Also, **wild oat.** any of a group of grasses growing as weeds in meadows, etc., especially a tall grass resembling the cultivated oat. **2.** youthful dissipation.
sow one's wild oats, to indulge in youthful dissipation before settling down in life: *A young man must sow his wild oats and reform* (Frederick W. Robertson).

wild olive, 1. any of various trees resembling the olive or bearing similar fruit. **2.** the wild variety of the cultivated olive, having more or less thorny branches and small, worthless fruit; oleaster.

wild pansy, the common pansy, occurring as a weed in grain fields, etc., with small flowers compounded of purple, yellow, and white; heartsease; Johnny-jump-up; love-in-idleness.

wild parsley, any of several weeds of the parsley family, with foliage like that of the parsley.

wild parsnip, a weed of the parsley family, found in Europe and America, from which the cultivated parsnip originated.

wild peach, any of a group of American trees or shrubs of the rose family, especially the cherry laurel.

wild pink, a catchfly or campion of eastern United States, with notched petals and white or pink flowers.

wild rice, a North American aquatic grass, whose grain is used for food.

wild rose, any of various roses that grow wild, as the sweetbrier and dog rose.

wild rubber, rubber from trees growing wild, especially from a Brazilian species.
wild rye, any of a group of grasses that resemble rye.
wilds (wīldz), *n.pl.* See under **wild,** *n.*
wild sage, the red sage.
wild service tree, service tree.
wild silk, tussah silk.
wild spinach, any of several plants occasionally used as a spinach substitute.
wild strawberry, **1.** any of various wild varieties of strawberry, from which the cultivated forms have been developed. **2.** their reddish, edible fruit.
wild thyme, a creeping evergreen of the mint family.
wild turkey, a turkey of the woodlands of eastern and southern United States and Mexico. It closely resembles the common domestic turkey that was developed from it.
wild vanilla, a perennial composite herb of the southeastern United States, whose leaves smell like vanilla.
wild West or **Wild West,** the western United States during pioneer days.
wild·wood (wīld′wu̇d′), *n.* trees growing in their natural state; forest.
wild yam, any of several yams growing wild.
wile (wīl), *n., v.,* **wiled, wil·ing.** *—n.* **1.** a trick to deceive; a cunning way; ruse; stratagem. **2.** subtle trickery; slyness; craftiness. *—v.t.* to coax; lure; entice: *The sunshine wiled me from work.*
wile away, to while away; pass easily or pleasantly: *I was reading a book tonight, to wile the time away* (Dickens).
[Middle English *wil* wile, trick. Ultimately related to GUILE.]
wil·ful (wil′fəl), *adj.* willful. **—wil′ful·ness,** *n.*
wil·ful·ly (wil′fə lē), *adv.* willfully.
wil·ga (wil′gə), *n.* an Australian tree of the rue family, yielding a hard, aromatic wood. [< a native Australian name]
wi·li·ly (wī′lə lē), *adv.* in a wily manner; craftily; cunningly.
wi·li·ness (wī′lē nis), *n.* wily quality; craftiness; slyness.
will[1] (wil; *unstressed* wəl), *v., pres. indic. sing., 1st and 3rd pers.* **will,** *2nd* **will** or (*Archaic*) **wilt,** *3rd* **will,** *pl.* **will;** *past tense sing. 1st and 3rd pers.* **would,** *2nd* **would** or (*Archaic*) **wouldst,** *pl.* **would;** *pp.* (*Obsolete*) **would** or **wold** (wōld); *imperative and infinitive* lacking.
—auxiliary v. (with infinitive without *to*): **1.** am going to; is going to; are going to: *He will come tomorrow.* **2.** am willing to; is willing to; are willing to: *I will admit that I am wrong. People will read what is well written.* **3.** be able to; can; may: *This pail will hold four gallons. One hour will be enough time to finish the work.* **4.** must: *You will do it at once!* **5.** do often or usually: *She will read for hours at a time.* *—v.t., v.i.* to wish, desire, want, or be willing: *to do as one wills.* [Old English *willan*]
➔ **shall, will.** The usage of *shall* and *will* is not uniform in English, differing mainly in formal English (where the rules of prescriptive grammarians are followed more or less consistently) and in informal English (where these rules are virtually ignored).
1. *Formal usage.* **a.** *Simple future. Shall* is used in the first person, *will* in the second and third:
First person: *I shall ask, we shall ask.*
Second person: *you will ask, you will ask.*
Third person: *he, she will ask, they will ask.*
In questions, *shall* is used in the first person, *will* in the third, and *shall* in the second, provided the expected answer contains *shall: Shall you go?* Expected answer: *I shall* (not *will*) go.
b. *Determination or obligation.* In declarative sentences, the use of *shall* and *will* is the reverse of that noted above:
First person: *I will ask, we will ask.*
Second person: *you shall ask, you shall ask.*
Third person: *he, she shall ask, they shall ask.*
2. *Informal usage.* **a.** *Simple future.* In writing as well as in speech, the prevailing use in the United States, and in many other parts of the English-speaking world, is *will* in all persons: *I will ask, you will ask, he will ask, etc.* In questions, *shall* is usual in the first person, and *will* in the *second* and *third,* but practice is not consistent: *Shall I go? Will you go? What will he do with it?* In the negative, *won't,* rather than *shan't,* is usual: *Won't I look funny in that? What won't he think of next?* In contractions, *'ll* is used for *shall* and *will* (*I'll, you'll, he'll*). *Won't* is used for *will not* and *shan't* for *shall not.*
b. *Determination or obligation.* In spoken English, determination is expressed by stressing *shall* (or *will*). In written English, there is a growing tendency to express it by using *shall* in all persons: *I, you, he, she, we, you, they shall ask.*
will[2] (wil), *n., v.,* **willed, will·ing.** *—n.* **1.** the power of the mind to decide and do; deliberate control over thought and action: *A good leader must have a strong will. The will of man is by his reason swayed* (Shakespeare). **2.** the act of choosing to do something, sometimes including also all deliberation that precedes making the choice; volition: *He strove to speak, but no voice answered his will* (George P.R. James). **3.** purpose; determination: *a will to live, win, or succeed.* **4.** an order, command, or decree: *My will is law* (Tennyson). **5.** what is chosen to be done; (one's or its) pleasure: *Leaving misrule and violence to work their will among men* (John Ruskin). **6.** wish; desire: *Thy will be done* (Lord's Prayer). *This boundless will to please* (A. E. Housman). **7.** feeling toward another: *good will or ill will.* **8.** *Law.* **a.** a legal statement of a person's wishes about what shall be done with his property after he is dead. **b.** the written document containing such a statement. **c.** (formerly) a statement of a person's wishes regarding the disposal of his real property after his death, his personal property being disposed of by testament. **9.** *Obsolete.* carnal desire; lust.
against one's will, unwillingly; in opposition to one's own inclination or to another's wish: *to force a child to eat against his will. He that complies against his will is of his own opinion still* (Samuel Butler).
at will, whenever or wherever one wishes: *. . . to allow a President, in case of disability, to delegate whatever powers he thinks necessary to the Vice-President, and to terminate this voluntary delegation of power at will* (Newsweek).
do the will of, to obey: *to do the will of one's parents.*
with a will, with energy and determination: *He cleaned out the attic with a will.*
[Old English *will, willa*]
—v.t. **1.** to decide by using the power of the mind; use the will: *She willed to keep awake.* **2.** to determine; decide: *Fate has willed it otherwise.* **3.** to influence or try to influence by deliberate control over thought and action, as by hypnotism: *She willed the person in front of her to turn around.* **4.** to give or dispose of by a will or testament: *to will a house to someone.* **5.** *Rare.* to wish; desire. **6.** *Archaic.* to request or entreat; command or decree. *—v.i.* to exercise the will.
[Old English *willian* < *will,* noun] **—will′er,** *n.*
—**Syn.** *n.* **3.** resolution, decision. **6.** inclination, preference, choice. *—v.t.* **2.** purpose, intend. **4.** bequeath.
will·a·ble (wil′ə bəl), *adj.* that can be willed.
wi·la·ya (wi lä′yə), *n.* a military district or zone in northern Africa. [< Arabic *wilāya* < *waliya* administer]
will contest, *Law.* litigation over the existence or validity of a will.
-willed, *combining form.* having a ____ will: *Strong-willed = having a strong will.*
wil·lem·ite (wil′ə mīt), *n.* a mineral, a silicate of zinc, found in masses or hexagonal prisms of various colors from light greenish-yellow to red and black. It is a minor zinc ore. *Formula:* Zn_2SiO_4 [< German *Willemit* < *Willem I* William I, 1772-1843, king of the Netherlands + *-it* -ite[1]]
wil·let (wil′it), *n.* a large, grayish North American wading bird, related to the snipes and sandpipers, that reveals a striking black and white pattern on the wings when in flight. [American English; imitative of its call]

Willet
(about 16 in. long)

will·ful (wil′fəl), *adj.* **1.** wanting or taking one's own way; stubborn. **2.** done on purpose; intended: *a willful murder, willful waste.* Also, **wilful.** [< *will*[2] + *-ful*] **—will′ful·ness,** *n.* —**Syn.** **1.** obstinate, headstrong, perverse. **2.** deliberate, intentional.
will·ful·ly (wil′fə lē), *adv.* **1.** by choice; voluntarily. **2.** by design; intentionally. **3.** selfishly; perversely; obstinately; stubbornly. Also, **wilfully.**
wil·lies (wil′ēz), *n.pl. U.S. Informal.* a spell of nervousness: *Bert gives me the willies the way he's always lookin' for trouble* (Jack London). [origin unknown]
will·ing (wil′ing), *adj.* **1.** ready; consenting: *He is willing to wait.* **2.** cheerfully ready: *willing obedience, a willing worker.* **3.** **a.** exercising or capable of exercising the will; volitional. **b.** conveying impulses of the will. **—will′ing·ly,** *adv.* **—will′ing·ness,** *n.*
—**Syn.** **1.** disposed, inclined.
wil·li·waw (wil′ē wô), *n.* **1.** *Especially Nautical.* a violent blast of wind descending from the mountainsides into a body of water, as one into the fiords of Tierra del Fuego or into the Strait of Magellan. **2.** any agitated state of affairs; storm; tempest; squall: *The President in press conference tried to head off a williwaw by insisting that Glennan's move was only part of a "study" in which the President himself would make the final ruling* (Time). [origin unknown]
will·less (wil′lis), *adj.* **1.** lacking will or will power. **2.** involuntary.
will-o'-the-wisp (wil′ə ᴛʜə wisp′), *n.* **1.** a moving light appearing at night over marshy places, caused by combustion of marsh gas; ignis fatuus. **2.** a thing (rarely a person) that deludes or misleads by luring on: *Through what extraordinary labyrinths this Love, this will-o'-the-wisp, guides his votaries* (Scott). [earlier *Will with the wisp,* apparently < *Will,* short for *William,* a proper name]
wil·low[1] (wil′ō), *n.* **1.** any of a group of trees and shrubs, widely distributed in temperate and cold regions, with tough, slender branches and long, narrow leaves, as the weeping willow. The branches of most willows bend easily and are used to make furniture. **2.** the wood of any of these trees. **3.** a cricket bat (made of willow wood).

Weeping Willow[1]
(def. 1)
(30 to 40 ft. tall)

wear the willow, to be lovelorn: *You are quite wrong . . . in supposing that I have any call . . . to wear the willow* (Richard Blackmore).
—adj. of or having to do with willow; made of the wood of the willow.
[Middle English *wilwe,* variant of *wilghe,* Old English *welig*]
wil·low[2] (wil′ō), *n.* a revolving cylindrical machine with spikes inside, used for opening and cleaning wool, cotton, etc. *—v.t.* to put (wool, cotton, etc.) through a willow. [variant of *willy*]
wil·low·er (wil′ō ər), *n.* **1.** a person or thing that willows. **2.** willow. [< *willow*[2] + *-er*[1]]
willow family, a group of dicotyledonous shrubs and trees, bearing small flowers in aments or catkins. The family includes the willows and poplars.
willow herb, **1.** a plant of the evening-primrose family that grows in moist places, and has long, narrow, willowlike leaves and long clusters (racemes) of purple flowers; rosebay. **2.** any other plant of the same group. **3.** the purple loosestrife.
willow oak, an oak found in the eastern United States, having narrow, entire leaves resembling those of the willow.
willow pattern, a pattern of domestic crockery in blue, originally designed by Thomas Turner in the late 1700's, having willow trees as a prominent feature.
willow ptarmigan, a ptarmigan of arctic regions with brown body, white wings, and black tail. In winter the brown plumage becomes white.
willow warbler, a small woodland bird of Europe and the British Isles, about five inches long, greenish above, whitish below. It is related to the chiffchaff.
willow ware, crockery ware of a willow pattern.
willow wren, the willow warbler.
wil·low·y (wil′ō ē), *adj.* **1.** like a willow; slender; supple; graceful. **2.** having many willows. —**Syn.** **1.** lithe, lissome.
will·pow·er (wil′pou′ər), *n.* strength of will; firmness: *Queen Elizabeth II keeps her trim figure with lots of walking and willpower* (New York Times).

wil·ly (wil′ē), *n., pl.* **-lies,** *v.,* **-lied, -ly·ing.** —*n.* willow². —*v.t.* to willow. [Middle English *wile,* Old English *wilige* < *welig* willow¹]

will·yard (wil′yərd), *adj. Scottish.* **1.** wild; shy. **2.** self-willed; obstinate. **3.** bewildered.

will·yart (wil′yərt), *adj.* willyard.

wil·ly-nil·ly (wil′ē nil′ē), *adv.* **1.** willingly or not; with or against one's wishes. **2.** in a disordered manner; helter-skelter: *Books were piled willy-nilly in the attic.*
—*adj.* **1.** undecided; vacillating. **2.** that is such, or that takes place, whether one wishes or not: *a willy-nilly spinster; a willy-nilly current of sensations* (Tennyson).
[< early phrase *will I (he, ye), nill I (he, ye); nill* not will, Old English *nyllan* < *ne* not + *willan* will]

wil·ly-wil·ly (wil′ē wil′ē), *n., pl.* **-lies.** (in Australia) a violent windstorm or rainstorm. [perhaps < a native name]

Wilms's tumor (vilm′ziz), a painless tumor in the kidneys of very young children. It can be removed by X-ray treatment or by surgery. [< Max *Wilms,* 1867-1918, a German surgeon, who described it]

Wilms' tumor (vilmz), Wilms's tumor.

Wil·son chamber (wil′sən), a type of cloud chamber.

Wil·so·ni·an (wil sō′nē ən), *adj.* of or having to do with Woodrow Wilson, 1856-1924, or his policies or principles: *Hoover's book is essentially a documentation, a blueprint of the Wilsonian ordeal* (Time).

Wil·so·ni·an·ism (wil sō′nē ə niz′əm), *n.* the political doctrines or practices of Woodrow Wilson.

Wil·son's disease (wil′sənz), a hereditary, degenerative disease in which a deficiency of ceruloplasmin causes copper to accumulate in the liver, brain, and other tissues. [< Samuel A.K. *Wilson,* 1878-1936, an English neurologist]

Wilson's petrel, a petrel of the Antarctic and the Atlantic Ocean, black with a patch of white on the rump. [< Alexander *Wilson,* 1766-1813, American ornithologist]

Wilson's phalarope, a phalarope that nests in central North America and winters in South America.

Wilson's plover, a brown and white plover of the southeastern United States with a black band across the breast.

Wilson's snipe, the American snipe. See **snipe** for picture.

Wilson's thrush, the veery.

Wilson's warbler, a small yellow and olive-green, black-capped warbler of North America.

wilt¹ (wilt), *v.i.* **1.** to become limp and drooping; wither. **2.** to lose strength, vigor, assurance, etc. —*v.t.* to cause to wilt. [variant of obsolete *welt,* alteration of *welk* to wither. Compare Middle Dutch *welken.*]

wilt² (wilt), *v. Archaic.* second person singular present of **will**¹. "Thou wilt" means "you will."

wilt³ (wilt), *n.* **1.** Also, **wilt disease. a.** *Botany.* any of various fungous or bacterial plant diseases, characterized by the withering and drying out of the parts of the plant above the soil, and generally caused by interference with the passage of water through the plant. **b.** an infectious disease of various caterpillars, which causes their bodies to liquefy. **2.** the act of wilting. [special use of *wilt*¹]

Wil·ton (wil′tən), *n.,* or **Wilton carpet** or **rug,** a kind of carpet or rug resembling Brussels carpet in weave but having the loops cut so as to produce a velvety surface. [< *Wilton,* a town in Wiltshire, England, where such carpets were made]

Wilt·shire (wilt′shir, -shər), *n.* **1.** any of an English breed of pure white sheep having long, spiraling horns. **2.** Wiltshire cheese. [< *Wiltshire,* a county in England]

Wiltshire cheese, a cheddar cheese.

wil·y (wī′lē), *adj.,* **wil·i·er, wil·i·est.** using subtle tricks to deceive; crafty; cunning; sly: *a wily thief, wily schemes. The wily fox got away. The wily subtleties and reflexes of man's thoughts* (Milton). [< *wil(e)* + *-y*¹]
—**Syn.** artful, subtle, designing, insidious.

wim·ble (wim′bəl), *n., v.,* **-bled, -bling.** —*n.* a tool for boring: **a.** a gimlet. **b.** an auger or brace. **c.** an instrument for boring in soft ground, or for extracting rubbish from a bore hole in mining. —*v.t. Dialect.* to pierce with or as with a wimble; make (a hole) with a wimble. [perhaps < Anglo-French *wimbel,* Old French *guimbel* < Middle Low German *wemel.* Compare GIMLET¹.]

wim·ple (wim′pəl), *n., v.,* **-pled, -pling.** —*n.* **1.** a cloth for the head arranged in folds about the head, cheeks, chin, and neck, worn by nuns and formerly by other women. **2.** *Archaic or Dialect.* **a.** a fold or wrinkle. **b.** a turn, winding, or twist. **c.** a ripple or rippling in a stream. **3.** *Scottish.* a crafty turn or twist; wile.
—*v.t.* **1. a.** to cover or muffle with a wimple. **b.** to veil. **2.** *Archaic or Dialect.* to cause to ripple. **3.** *Archaic.* to lay in folds, as a veil. —*v.i.* **1.** to ripple. **2.** *Archaic.* to lie in folds, as a veil. **3.** *Archaic or Dialect.* to move shiftily or unsteadily. [Old English *wimpel*]

Wimple (def. 1)

Wims·hurst machine (wimz′hėrst), an apparatus for generating electricity by electrostatic action. [< James *Wimshurst,* 1832-1903, English engineer, who devised it]

win¹ (win), *v.,* **won** or (*Archaic*) **wan** (won), **won, win·ning,** *n.* —*v.t.* **1.** to get victory or success in: *He won the race.* **2.** to get by or as by effort; gain: *to win fame, win a prize.* **3.** to get the love of; persuade to marry. **4. a.** to achieve or progress by or as by struggle, through ability, etc.: *to win one's way, win one's point in a dispute.* **b.** to get to; reach, often by effort; arrive at: *to win the summit of a mountain.* **5. a.** to gain the favor of: *The speaker soon won his audience.* **b.** to gain the affection or love of, often gradually and increasingly: *to win new friends.* **c.** to prevail upon; influence; persuade; induce: *She could not win him, however, to any conversation* (Jane Austen). **6.** *Especially British.* **a.** to get or extract (coal, ore, etc.) by mining. **b.** to sink a shaft or make an excavation so as to reach (a vein, seam, etc.) and prepare it for working. **7.** *Metallurgy.* to obtain (metal, etc.) from ore. —*v.i.* to get victory or success: *The tortoise won in the end. The army won through to the Mediterranean ports.*
win out, a. to be victorious: *to win out over an opponent.* **b.** to succeed; prevail: *As long as a fellow's got some good horse sense . . . he can win out in the law business* (A.D. McFaul).
win over, to prevail upon; persuade: *The President had won over his audience again* (London Times).
—*n. Informal.* **1.** the act or fact of winning; success; victory. **2.** Often, **wins.** gains; winnings.
[Middle English *winnen,* probably fusion of Old English *winnan* struggle (for); work (at), and *gewinnan* to win]
—**Syn.** *v.t.* **2.** secure, obtain, earn, attain.

win² (win), *v.t.,* **winned, winned, win,** or **won, win·ning.** *Scottish.* **1.** to dry (hay, seed, turf, wood, etc.). **2.** to winnow. [perhaps < *win*¹; influenced by *wind*³]

win³ (win), *n. Scottish.* wind.

wince¹ (wins), *v.,* **winced, winc·ing,** *n.* —*v.i.* to draw back suddenly; flinch slightly: *The boy winced at the sight of the dentist's drill.* —*n.* the act of wincing. [< unrecorded Anglo-French *wencir,* Old French *guencir,* and *guenchir* < Germanic (compare Old High German *winkan* move sidewards, sway)] —**Syn.** *v.i.* shrink, recoil.

wince² (wins), *n.* a reel or roller placed over the division between two vats of dye in such a way that a fabric spread upon it may be lowered into either vat. [variant of *winch*¹]

wince pits, the vats over which a wince is placed.

winch¹ (winch), *n.* **1.** a hoisting or hauling machine consisting essentially of a horizontal drum around which a rope passes and a crank by which it is turned. **2.** the cranked handle by means of which the axis of a revolving machine is turned. **3.** wince². **4.** a fishing reel. —*v.t.* to hoist, haul, etc., with a winch. [Middle English *wynch,* Old English *wince*] —**winch′er,** *n.*

Winch¹ (def. 1)

winch² (winch), *v.i., n. Dialect.* wince; flinch.

Win·ches·ter (win′ches′tər, -chə stər), *n.,* or **Winchester rifle,** a kind of breechloading repeating rifle, having a tubular magazine under the barrel and a bolt operated by a lever, invented and first made about 1866. See **magazine** for picture. [< Oliver F. *Winchester,* 1810-1880, an American manufacturer, who produced them]

Winchester bushel, a unit of dry measure equivalent to 2150.4 cubic inches. [< *Winchester,* a city in southern England where the standard was originally deposited]

winch·man (winch′mən), *n., pl.* **-men.** a man who operates a winch.

winc·ing (win′sing), *adj.* that winces; flinching; recoiling. —**winc′ing·ly,** *adv.*

wind¹ (*n.* wind, *Archaic and Poetic* wind; *v.* wind), *n., v.,* **wind·ed, wind·ing.** —*n.* **1.** air in motion. Winds are classified according to velocity by the U.S. Weather Bureau, as *light air, breeze, gale, storm,* and *hurricane.* **2.** a strong wind; gale: *Blow, blow, thou winter wind! Thou art not so unkind As man's ingratitude* (Shakespeare). **3.** the direction or point of the compass from which the wind blows, especially one of the four cardinal points of the compass (the four winds). **4.** a current of air filled with some smell: *The deer caught wind of the hunter and ran off.* **5.** a current of air considered as driving a person or thing along, as conveying information, as striking upon a person or thing, or the like: *What wind blows you here? It's an ill wind that blows nobody good.* **6.** air as used for sounding a musical instrument. **7.** a wind instrument or the player on such an instrument. **8.** a blast of air artificially produced, as by bellows, a fan, a rapidly moving body, etc.: *the wind of a bullet.* **9.** gas in the stomach or bowels. **10. a.** the power of breathing; breath: *A runner needs good wind.* **b.** *Boxing Slang.* the pit of the stomach, where a blow checks the action of the diaphragm and takes away the breath. **11. a.** empty, useless talk. **b.** vanity; conceit.
before the wind, in the direction toward which the wind is blowing: *We got before the wind to the Cape of Good Hope* (William Phillip).
between wind and water, a. near the water line of a ship: *They . . . had received a shot between wind and water, and the ship leaked very much* (William R. Chetwood). **b.** in a dangerous or vulnerable place: *The cynicism of his own reflection struck him between wind and water* (John Galsworthy).
by the wind, pointing as nearly as possible toward the direction from which the wind blows: *Having struck our sails, we did nothing but lie by the wind* (Thomas Washington).
down (the) wind, in the direction that the wind is blowing: *Down the wind she swims, and sails away* (William Cowper).
get or **have wind of,** to find out about; get a hint of: *Because the police had wind of their plans for a park battle, the gangs met halfway between their homes and the park* (Harper's).
haul on or **to the wind,** to sail closer to the direction of the wind: *The Spanish fleet . . . hauled to the wind on the larboard tack* (Horatio Nelson).
in the eye or **teeth of the wind,** directly against the wind: *to sail in the eye of the wind.*
in the wind, happening or about to happen; impending: *There is nothing in the wind to justify fears that the "bad old days" are coming back* (Manchester Guardian Weekly).
into the wind, pointing toward the direction from which the wind is blowing: *You are tempted to turn into the wind and land* (Blackwood's Magazine).
off the wind, with the wind blowing from behind: *The Enterprise was again steered more off the wind* (Frederick Marryat).
on the or **a wind,** as nearly as possible in the direction from which the wind is blowing: *Clippers are fastest on the wind* (Richard Henry Dana).
raise the wind, *Informal.* **a.** to raise money for a purpose: *Somebody, somehow will raise the wind that is needed—at least $80 millions all told* (Manchester Guardian Weekly). **b.** to make a disturbance: *to raise the wind after being insulted.*
run or **sail close to the wind, a.** *Nautical.* sail with the ship pointed as nearly as possible in the direction from which the

wind is blowing: *The only hope in the storm was to run close to the wind.* **b.** to just barely follow rules or laws: *In court he sailed so close to the wind as to risk disbarment.* **c.** to manage with close calculation or the utmost economy: *He realized that ... he was sailing rather close to the wind financially* (Theodore Dreiser).

take or **knock the wind out of one's sails,** to take away one's advantage, argument, etc., suddenly or unexpectedly: *Whether he can knock the wind out of the bubbling McKinley's sails remains to be seen* (London Times).

the way the wind blows or **is blowing,** the tendency, turn, or condition of affairs: *Another interesting index of the way the wind is blowing was afforded ... by the publication of three articles in Paris-Match which openly attack the Gaullist policy of lavish aid to foreign countries* (Atlantic).

to the wind, to the point from which the wind blows: *Gascoigne went to the helm, [and] brought the boat up to the wind* (Frederick Marryat).

up (the) wind, with the wind blowing from in front: *Passing over the earths, he came away directly with his head up wind* (Sporting Magazine).

winds, wind instruments, especially those in an orchestra, considered collectively: *The second movement begins with a slow fugue by the winds.*

—*v.t.* **1.** to expose to wind or air; air. **2.** to follow (an animal, person, or thing) by scent; smell. **3.** to put out of breath; cause difficulty in breathing: *The fat man was winded by the climb up the steep hill.* **4.** to let recover breath: *They stopped in order to wind their horses.*

[Old English *wind*]

—**Syn.** *n.* **1. Wind, breeze** mean air in motion. **Wind** is the general word: *The wind is from the north.* **Breeze,** except as a technical term (meteorology), means a light, gentle wind, especially one that is cool or refreshing: *We nearly always have a breeze at night.* **2.** blast.

wind[2] (wīnd), *v.,* **wound** or (*Rare*) **wind•ed, wind•ing,** *n.* —*v.i.* **1.** to move this way and that; move in a crooked way; change direction; turn: *a bicycle winding through the crowded streets. A brook winds through the woods.* **2.** to proceed in a roundabout or indirect manner: *I winded and winded ... till ... out comes the truth* (Maria Edgeworth). **3.** to twist or turn around something; twine: *The vine winds round a pole.* **4.** to be warped or twisted: *That board will wind.* **5.** (of a horse) to move with a winding gait. **6.** to be wound: *This clock winds easily.*

—*v.t.* **1.** to fold, wrap, or place (about something): *to wind a scarf around one's neck. The mother wound her arms about the child.* **2.** to cover (with something put, wrapped, or folded around): *The man's arm is wound with bandages.* **3.** to roll into a ball or on a spool: *Grandma was winding yarn. Thread comes wound on spools.* **4.** to make (some machine) go by turning some part of it: *to wind a clock.* **5.** to haul or hoist by turning a winch, windlass, or the like. **6.** to tighten the strings, pegs, etc., of (a musical instrument); tune. **7.** to make (one's or its way) in a curved, crooked, or zigzagging course: *We wound our way through the crooked streets.* **8.** to bend or turn at will; exercise complete control over. **9.** to insinuate (oneself in or into); worm: *to wind oneself into a position of importance.*

wind off, to unwind: *Would you wind off some string for me? The thread winds off easily.*

wind up, a. *Informal.* to end; settle; conclude: *He wound up their conference at Blackpool on Saturday* (Manchester Guardian Weekly). **b.** (in baseball) to swing the ball in the hand before pitching it: *The pitcher is winding up.* **c.** to roll or coil; wind completely: *When the weight is down on the grandfather clock we have to wind it up* (Listener). **d.** to put into a state of tension, great strain, intensity of feeling, etc.; excite: *Chicago exhibitors are all wound up about polypropylene* (New York Times). **e.** *Informal.* to come to a place or a circumstance: *to wind up exhausted. Emotionally unstable young people do wind up in the village* (Canadian Saturday Night).

—*n.* a bend; turn; twist.

[Old English *windan*]

—**Syn.** *v.i.* **1.** curve, crook, twist, bend.

wind[3] (wīnd, wind), *v.t.,* **wind•ed** or **wound, wind•ing. 1.** to sound by forcing the breath through; blow: *The hunter winds his horn.* **2.** to blow (a blast, call, or note), as on a horn. [special use of *wind*[1]]

wind•age (win′dij), *n.* **1.** the power of the wind to turn a missile from its course. **2.** the distance that a missile is turned from its course by the wind. **3.** a change in aim to compensate for windage, accomplished on a rifle by a slight lateral adjustment of the rear sight. **4.** atmospheric disturbance produced by the passage of a bullet, shell, or other missile. **5.** the part of a ship's surface affected by the action of wind. **6.** the slight difference between the diameter of a bullet, shell, etc., and of the bore of a gun of the same caliber, a necessary characteristic of certain smoothbore guns and rifled guns firing spherical shot.

wind•bag (wind′bag′), *n.* **1.** a bag full of wind. **2.** *Slang.* a person who talks a great deal but does not say much. **3.** the chest or body considered as a receptacle of breath (a humorous use). **4.** *Obsolete.* the bellows of an organ.

wind bell (wind), a bell or bell-like percussion instrument made of metal, glass, ceramic, or wood, freely suspended so as to be sounded by the wind.

wind-blown (wind′blōn′), *adj.* **1.** blown along or about by the wind. **2.** with the hair cut short and brushed forward. **3.** (of trees) slanted or twisted in growth as a result of the prevailing winds.

wind-borne (wind′bôrn′, -bōrn′), *adj.* carried by the wind, as seed and pollen.

wind•box (wind′boks′), *n.* an airtight box which receives air under pressure from a bellows or similar source, and from which the air passes into a furnace, organ pipes, or similar apparatus.

wind•break (wind′brāk′), *n.* *Especially U.S.* something, especially a fence, row of trees, or shrubs, used to break the force of the wind, or serving as a protection against it.

wind•break•er (wind′brā′kər), *n.* *U.S.* **1.** a short sports jacket of wool, leather, etc., having a tight-fitting band at the waist and cuffs, used for outdoor wear. **2. Windbreaker.** a trademark for this jacket.

wind-bro•ken (wind′brō′kən), *adj.* (of horses) unable to breathe properly because of damage to the respiratory organs, and therefore unable to sustain hard work or move at a quick pace.

wind burn (wind), **1.** a roughening or reddening of the skin caused by prolonged exposure to the wind. **2.** any injury to leaves or bark caused by the wind.

wind-burned (wind′bėrnd′), *adj.* having a wind burn: *a wind-burned face, a wind-burned farmer.*

wind•cheat•er (wind′chē′tər), *n.* *Especially British.* a windbreaker: *a ginger-haired boy dressed in corduroy shorts and windcheater* (Punch).

wind•chest (wind′chest′), *n.* a windbox.

wind chill, the combined cooling effect on the human body of air temperature and wind speed.

wind cone (wind), wind sock.

wind direction (wind), the direction from which the wind is blowing, as indicated by a weathercock.

wind•ed (win′did), *adj.* **1.** out of breath; breathless. **2.** exposed to wind or air, especially spoiled or tainted by exposure to air.

-winded, *combining form.* being ____ of wind, or breath: *Short-winded = being short of wind, or breath.*

wind•er[1] (wīn′dər), *n.* **1.** a person or thing that winds. **2.** an apparatus for winding thread, etc. **3.** an operative employed in winding wool, etc. **4.** a key for winding a jack, clock, or other mechanism. **5.** *Obsolete.* a twining plant.

winders, winding steps in a staircase: *The best staircases are those without winders* (John C. Loudon).

wind•er[2] (wīn′dər, win′dər *for 1,* win′dər *for 2*), *n.* **1.** a person who winds (blows) a wind instrument: *Winder of the horn, When snouted wild boars ... Anger our Huntsmen* (Keats). **2.** *Informal.* something that takes one's breath away, as a blow, a run, a climb, etc.

wind erosion (wind), the removal of topsoil by dust storms.

wind•fall (wind′fôl′), *n.* **1.** fruit blown down from a tree by the wind. **2.** an unexpected piece of good luck: *We would urge great caution in any shifting and refunding of our bonding structure which might result in a windfall of profits to bondholders* (New York Times). —**Syn. 2.** godsend.

wind•flaw (wind′flô′), *n.* a sudden gust (of wind); flaw. [< *wind*[1] + *flaw*[2]]

wind•flow•er (wind′flou′ər), *n.* **1.** any anemone. **2.** rue anemone. [translation of Latin *anemōnē* < Greek *anemṓnē*]

wind•gall (wind′gôl′), *n.* a soft tumor or swelling of the synovial bursa at the fetlock joint of a horse, once thought to contain air.

wind•galled (wind′gôld′), *adj.* having windgalls.

wind gap (wind), a depression in a mountain ridge not deep enough to give passage to a watercourse.

wind gauge (wind), anemometer.

wind harp (wind), Aeolian harp.

wind•hov•er (wind′huv′ər), *n.* *Dialect.* the kestrel. [< *wind*[1] + *hover* (because it hovers in the air with its head to the wind)]

wind•i•ly (win′də lē), *adv.* in a windy manner.

wind•i•ness (win′dē nis), *n.* the state of being windy.

wind•ing (wīn′ding), *n.* **1.** the act of a person or thing that winds. **2.** a bend; turn. **3.** something that is wound or coiled. **4.** a faulty gait of a horse in which one leg tends to curve around another. **5.** *Electricity.* **a.** a continuous coil of wire forming a conductor in a generator, motor, etc. **b.** the manner in which the wire is coiled: *a series winding.*

—*adj.* bending; turning.

—**wind′ing•ly,** *adv.*

winding frame, a machine that winds yarn.

winding sheet, a cloth in which a dead person is wrapped for burial; shroud.

wind instrument (wind), a musical instrument sounded by means of wind, particularly one sounded by the breath of the player. Trumpets, trombones, and French horns are brass winds. Clarinets, flutes, bassoons, and oboes are wood winds.

wind•jam•mer (wind′jam′ər), *n.* **1.** *Informal.* **a.** a sailing ship, especially a square-rigged ship. **b.** a member of its crew. **2.** *U.S. Slang.* a loquacious person; windbag. [American English < *wind*[1] + *jam*[1] + *-er*[1] (because sailors on steamships derided its capabilities)]

wind•lass (wind′ləs), *n.* a machine for pulling or lifting things, consisting of a horizontal roller or beam, resting on supports, around which a rope or chain is wound; winch. —*v.t., v.i.* to hoist or haul with a windlass. [perhaps fusion of obsolete *windas* windlass < Anglo-French < Scandinavian (compare Old Icelandic *windāss* < *vinda* wind, turn + *āss* pole), and obsolete *windle* winding apparatus < Middle English *winden* wind, turn]

win•dle (win′dəl), *v.i.,* **-dled, -dling.** *Dialect.* **1.** to move circularly or sinuously; meander; wind. **2.** to wind thread, etc.

wind•less (wind′lis), *adj.* **1.** free from wind; calm. **2.** out of breath. —**wind′less•ness,** *n.*

win•dle•strae (win′dəl strā′), *n.* *Scottish.* windlestraw.

win•dle•straw (win′dəl strô′), *n.* *Scottish.* **1.** a dry, thin, withered stalk of grass. **2.** a person or thing of trifling worth or a flimsy nature. [Old English *windelstrēaw* dry grass stalk, type of grass, perhaps < *windel* a basket + *strēaw* straw]

wind meter (wind), an anemometer.

wind•mill (wind′mil′), *n.* **1. a.** a mill or machine operated by the wind acting upon a wheel of oblique vanes or sails set around a horizontal shaft, usually mounted on a tall tower and used for pumping water, grinding grain, etc. **b.** the wheel on which the wind acts to drive such a mill. **2.** any of various objects that resemble a windmill in appearance or method of working, as certain toys. **3.** a small turbine on an airplane, exposed to and driven by the force of the air, used to

Windmill (def. 1a)

operate various auxiliary mechanisms. **4.** *Informal.* a helicopter.

tilt at or **fight windmills,** to expend one's energy in futile attacks on what cannot be overcome (in allusion to the story of Don Quixote tilting at windmills under the delusion that they were giants): *The whimsy [a play] will be about a gentle knight tilting at the windmills of government* (Wall Street Journal).

—v.i. **1.** to move one's arms or legs in a manner suggesting a windmill. **2.** (of a propeller) to rotate by the force of air acting upon it, without power from the engine: *With the engine dead, the prop was windmilling loosely in the air* (Time). *—v.t.* **1.** to move in a manner suggestive of a windmill: *Some of the jumpers windmilled their arms awkwardly in trying to keep their balance* (Time). **2.** to cause to rotate by force of air, without engine power: *to windmill a propeller.*

wind motor (wind), any prime mover or motor using the force of the wind directly, including the ordinary windmills and apparatus of other construction.

wind of change, an irresistible movement toward political or economic change; social turmoil or upheaval: . . . *the wind of change now sweeping through Africa* (Wall Street Journal).

win·dow (win′dō), *n.* **1.** an opening in the wall or roof of a building, boat, car, etc., to let in light or air, usually enclosed by a frame that holds a movable sash or sashes fitted with panes of glass: *a good view from the window. But, soft! what light through yonder window breaks?* (Shakespeare). **2.** such an opening with the frame, sashes, and panes of glass. **3.** the sashes and panes that fit such an opening: *to open the window.* **4.** a windowpane: *to break a window.* **5. a.** an opening like a window in shape or function, such as the transparent part of some envelopes through which the address is seen. **b.** anything suggesting a window: *The window of my heart, mine eye* (Shakespeare). **6.** *Aeronautics.* the conjunction of time and planetary position in a condition that permits successful space flight: *The Soviet and American vehicles flew to Venus close together because both were fired during one of the periodic windows for such shots* (New York Times). **7.** Also, **Window.** strips of metal foil dropped from airplanes to interfere with enemy radar indicators by reflecting the radar beams.

—v.t. to furnish with windows or openings likened to windows. [< Scandinavian (compare Old Icelandic *vindauga* < *vindr* wind, gust + *auga* eye)]

window box, 1. a box for growing plants, especially ornamental plants, placed (usually) just outside and at the base of a window. **2.** one of the vertical shafts or boxes at each side of the frame of a double-hung window, that houses the cords and weights that counterbalance a sliding sash.

window display, the display of goods for sale in the window of a store to advertise its products and attract passers-by.

win·dow-dress (win′dō dres′), *v.t., v.i.,* **-dressed** or **-drest, -dress·ing.** to engage in, make use of, or subject to window dressing.

window dresser, a person employed to arrange in the windows of a store attractive displays of goods for sale.

window dressing, 1. the dressing of a window with goods attractively displayed. **2.** a display made in such a manner as to give a falsely favorable impression of the facts, as the arrangement of a balance sheet so as to suggest that the business concerned is more prosperous than it is: *Although lacking the best-in-show competition that the officers of the club consider "window dressing," other dog show features are included* (New York Times).

-windowed, *combining form.* having a ___ window or windows: *Many-windowed = having many windows.*

window envelope, an envelope with an opening or transparent part in the front through which the address can be seen.

win·dow·less (win′dō lis), *adj.* without windows: *a windowless wall.*

win·dow·pane (win′dō pān′), *n.* a piece of glass in or for a window; pane.

window sash, a frame for the glass in a window.

window seat, a bench built into the wall of a room, under a window.

window shade, 1. a. a sheet of opaque material wound or intended to be wound on a roller, by which, when it is unwound, a window is covered. **b.** the roller together with such a sheet, fastened or intended to be fastened at the top of the frame of a window. **2.** any adjustable inside covering for a window.

win·dow-shop (win′dō shop′), *v.i.,* **-shopped, -shop·ping.** to look at articles in store windows without going in to buy anything

window shopper, a person who looks at articles in the windows of shops, instead of going in to do actual shopping.

window sill, a piece of wood or stone across the bottom of a window.

win·dow·y (win′dō ē), *adj.* full of windows or openings.

wind·pipe (wind′pīp′), *n.* the passage by which air is carried from the throat to the lungs, in man situated in front of the esophagus; trachea. See **epiglottis** for picture.

wind-pol·li·nat·ed (wind′pol′ə nā′tid), *adj.* fertilized by pollen carried by the wind; anemophilous.

wind-pol·li·na·tion (wind′pol′ə nā′shən), *n.* fertilization by pollen carried by the wind.

wind·proof (wind′prüf′), *adj.* resistant to wind; that will not let wind through: *Windproof clothing, as any hiker or climber will know, has a close weave and is expensive* (New Scientist).

wind·puff (wind′puf′), *n.* windgall.

wind pump, a pump operated by a windmill.

wind rose (wind), *Meteorology.* a diagram indicating the relative frequency, force, etc., of the winds from various directions at some given place.

wind·row (wind′rō′), *n.* **1.** a row of hay raked together to dry before being made into cocks or heaps. **2.** any similar row, as of sheaves of grain, made for the purpose of drying, or a row of dry leaves, dust, etc., swept together by the wind or the like. **3.** a deep furrow for planting, especially one in which cut sugar-cane stalks are put and covered with earth.

—v.t. to arrange in a windrow or windrows; bring together in long rows.

[< *wind*[1] + *row*[1] (because it was set up to be dried by the wind)]

wind·row·er (wind′rō′ər), *n.* a person or thing that windrows, especially an attachment to a mowing machine.

winds (windz), *n.pl.* See under **wind**[1], *n.*

wind scale, a system of numbers or words used to record the speed of the wind.

wind·screen (wind′skrēn′), *n. British.* windshield.

wind shake, 1. a flaw or crack in timber supposed to be due to a strain caused by the force of the wind. **2.** such flaws or cracks collectively.

wind-shak·en (wind′shā′kən), *adj.* **1.** (of timber) affected by wind shake. **2.** shaken or agitated by the wind.

wind·shield (wind′shēld′), *n.* a sheet of glass above the dashboard of an automobile, Diesel locomotive, etc., by which the driver is enabled to see the road, track, etc., ahead without being exposed to the rush of air caused by the forward movement of the vehicle. [American English]

windshield wiper, a metal strip with a rubber insert attached to a rod that usually swings in an arc across the outside of a windshield to wipe away moisture.

wind sock or **sleeve** (wind), a cone-shaped sleeve mounted on a pole or the like, showing the direction of the wind; wind cone.

Wind·sor (win′zər), *n.* the name of the British royal family since 1917.

Windsor chair, a kind of comfortable wooden chair, with a spindle back and slanting legs, much used in England and the American colonies in the 1700's. [< *Windsor* (officially *New Windsor*), a city in Berkshire, England, where it was first made]

Windsor Writing-arm Chair

Windsor knot, the knot of a Windsor tie.

Windsor tie, a wide necktie of soft silk, tied in a loose, double or triangular bow.

wind sprint, any short spell of running, rowing, swimming, etc., performed at top speed to develop breathing power and stamina: *At 11:30, the squad heads for the swimming pool for a series of wind sprints or a 1,500-yard trial to build up endurance* (Time).

wind·storm (wind′stôrm′), *n.* a storm with much wind but little or no rain.

wind-suck·er (wind′suk′ər), *n.* a horse given to crib-biting and wind sucking; crib-biter.

wind sucking (wind), a drawing in and swallowing of air, as in a horse that cribbites. **—wind′-suck′ing,** *adj.*

wind·swept or **wind-swept** (wind′swept′), *adj.* exposed to the full force of the wind: *a windswept hillside.*

wind tee (wind), *Aviation.* a weather vane in the form of a T, on or near a landing field.

wind tunnel (wind), a tunnel for testing the aerodynamic efficiency of aircraft, missiles, etc., with air forced through at high speeds.

wind-up (wīnd′up′), *n.* **1.** a winding up; end; close; conclusion; finish. **2.** (in baseball) the movements of the arm made by a pitcher just before pitching the ball.

—adj. **1.** that must be wound up in order to work: *a wind-up toy, a wind-up motor.* **2.** being the last; closing: *a wind-up game.*

wind vane (wind), weathercock.

wind·ward (wind′wərd; *Nautical* win′dərd), *adv.* toward the wind.

—adj. **1.** on the side toward the wind; facing into the wind. **2.** in the direction from which the wind is blowing; moving against the wind.

—n. **1.** the side toward the wind. **2.** the direction from which the wind is blowing.

cast an anchor to windward. See under **anchor**[1], *n.*

get to windward of, to gain an advantage over: *If I happen to have got to windward of the young woman, why, so much the better for me* (H. Rider Haggard).

keep to windward of, to keep out of the reach of: *He had developed the skill of keeping to windward of his creditors.*

wind·way (wind′wā′), *n.* **1.** a ventilating passage in a mine; airway. **2.** the access of the wind to a sailing vessel so as to give her freedom of passage. **3.** *Music.* flue.

wind·y (win′dē), *adj.,* **wind·i·er, wind·i·est.** **1.** having much wind: *a windy day, windy weather, the windy seas.* **2.** exposed to or blown upon or through by the wind: *a windy street; as he paces the windy deck* (Lowell). **3.** of or consisting of wind: *March, departed with his windy rage* (William Basse). **4.** like the wind in quality of sound, swiftness, etc.: *her windy sighs* (Shakespeare). **5.** causing gas in the stomach or intestines; flatulent. **6.** made of wind; empty: *windy talk, a windy political speech.* **7.** talking a great deal; voluble; loquacious. **8.** *Scottish.* boastful. [Old English *windig* < *wind* wind[1], gust]

wine (wīn), *n., v.,* **wined, win·ing.** *—n.* **1.** the juice of grapes after it has fermented and contains alcohol, widely used as a beverage and also used in religious rites. Red wines are made by allowing the juice of dark-colored grapes to remain in contact with the skins while fermenting; white wines are made from light-colored grapes or from dark-colored grapes whose skins have been removed. Wines are also classified as sweet or dry, and still or sparkling. **2.** the fermented juice of other fruits or plants, especially when used as a beverage: *currant wine, dandelion wine.* **3.** intoxication from drinking wine. **4.** something that exhilarates or intoxicates like wine. **5.** *British.* a party, especially of undergraduates, for drinking wine. **6.** the color of red wine. **7.** *Pharmacology.* a solution of a medicinal substance in wine; vinum.

new wine in old bottles, something new that is too strong to be held back by old forms (in allusion to Matthew 9:17): *The younger generation sees itself as new wine in old bottles.*

—v.t. to entertain with wine: *to wine and dine someone.*

—v.i. to drink wine.

[Old English *wīn,* ultimately < Latin *vīnum.* Related to VINE.]

wine·bib·ber (wīn′bib′ər), *n.* a person who drinks much wine. [< *wine* + *bibber*]

wine·bib·bing (wīn′bib′ing), *n.* the habit of drinking wine to excess. *—adj.* drinking much wine.

wine card, *Especially British.* wine list.

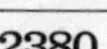

wine cellar, 1. a cellar where wine is stored. 2. the wine stored there.

wine color, purplish red.

wine-col·ored (wīn′kul′ərd), *adj.* of a dark purplish-red color.

wine-fat (wīn′fat′), *n. Archaic.* a vat or vessel in which grapes were trodden in making wine. [< *wine* + *fat*[2]]

wine gallon, a former British unit of liquid measure for wine, equal to the standard U.S. gallon; 231 cu. in.

wine·glass (wīn′glas′, -gläs′), *n.* any of various glasses for drinking wine, ranging in capacity from about two to about six fluid ounces and varying in shape for different types of wine.

wine·glass·ful (wīn′glas′fu̇l, -gläs′-), *n., pl.* **-fuls.** about two fluid ounces (the amount held by a wineglass of the type normally used for sherry, port, and other fortified wines).

wine·grow·er (wīn′grō′ər), *n.* a person who raises grapes and makes wine.

wine·grow·ing (wīn′grō′ing), *n.* the cultivation of grapes to make wine.

wine·house (wīn′hous′), *n.* **1.** a tavern where wine is drunk. **2.** a firm of wine merchants.

wine·less (wīn′lis), *adj.* without wine.

wine list, a list of the wines that may be obtained at a restaurant.

wine·mak·er (wīn′mā′kər), *n.* a winegrower.

wine measure, an old British system of measure for wine.

wine palm, any of various palms from whose sap wine is made.

wine press, 1. a machine for pressing the juice from grapes. **2.** a vat in which grapes are trodden in the process of making wine.

win·er·y (wī′nər ē), *n., pl.* **-er·ies.** a place where wine is made. [American English < *win*(e) + *-ery*]

Wine·sap or **wine·sap** (wīn′sap), *n.* a red, winter variety of apple, much cultivated in the United States.

wine·shop (wīn′shop′), *n.* a winehouse.

wine·skin (wīn′skin′), *n.* a container made of the nearly complete skin of a goat, hog, etc., used especially in some countries of southern Europe and Asia for holding wine.

wine·tast·er (wīn′tās′tər), *n.* a person who judges the quality of wine by tasting it: *A winetaster, savoring a fine wine, can sometimes guess from its bouquet not only the type of wine but also the vineyard from which it came and the year in which the grapes were grown* (Science News Letter).

wine·y (wī′nē), *adj.,* **win·i·er, win·i·est.** winy.

wing (wing), *n.* **1. a.** the part of a bird by which it flies. In a few birds the wings are functionless (emu, kiwi), or used only to assist in swimming or walking (penguin) or running (ostrich). **b.** the part of a bat by which it flies. **c.** the part of an insect by which it flies, or a similar part of various flightless insects. **d.** any similar structure, as the parachute of a flying squirrel or one of the enlarged fins of a flying fish. **2.** the wing of a bird or domesticated fowl used as food. **3.** a winglike organ attributed to supernatural beings (angels, demons, etc.) and to fabulous creatures (dragons, griffins, etc.). **4. a.** an arm of a human or a foreleg of a quadruped (used in a humorous way). **b.** *Slang.* the throwing or pitching arm of a baseball player. **5.** a figure or representation of a wing. **6.** a means of flight, travel, or passage. **7.** the act or manner of flying; winged flight. **8.** something (inanimate or abstract) considered as flying or as carrying one swiftly along: *on the wings of time.* **9.** anything like a wing in shape or use, such as one of the major lifting and supporting surfaces of an airplane, one of the vanes of a windmill, or the feather of an arrow. **10.** a subordinate part of a building projecting on one side of the main or central part. **11.** either of the longer sides of an outwork, by which it is joined to the main fortification. **12.** *Theater.* **a.** Often, **wings.** one of the spaces at either side of the stage, between the side scenes, out of sight of the audience. **b.** any of the side scenes on the stage. **13.** a lateral or outlying portion of a region. **14.** a sidepiece projecting frontwards at the top of the back of an armchair. **15.** either part of a double door, screen, or the like, which may be folded or otherwise moved back. **16.** *Anatomy.* the ala of the nose. **17.** *Botany.* **a.** a leafy or membranous expansion or thin extension, as of a samara. **b.** one of the two lateral petals of a papilionaceous flower; ala. **18.** *British.* a mudguard or fender over the wheel of a motor vehicle, carriage, etc. **19.** the part of the plowshare of a moldboard plow that extends sideways and cuts the bottom of the furrow. **20. a.** the part of a military or naval unit formed to the left or right of the main force when ready for battle. **b.** *U.S.* a tactical unit of the Air Force, usually composed of two or more groups, and smaller than a command. **21.** a part of an organization holding certain views; faction: *The radicals of a political party are called the left wing.* **22.** in American football and some other team games: **a.** one of the positions, or a player in such a position, on the right (right wing) or left (left wing) of the center, when facing the opponents' goal. **b.** such a position or player on the forward line.

Airplane Wing (def. 9)
Cutaway showing construction of wing for lightweight plane

clip one's wings, to curtail one's power: *His enemies . . . had combined to clip his wings, and he had been removed from the key Ministry of the Interior to a more innocuous post* (Atlantic).

in the wings, just beyond public view; behind the scenes: *There are four announced Democratic candidates—and several others . . . lurking in the wings* (New York Times).

on (the) wing, a. flying: *The bird that flutters least is longest on the wing* (William Cowper). **b.** moving; active; busy: *I have been, since I saw you in town, pretty much on the wing, at Hampton, Twickenham, and elsewhere* (Thomas Gray). **c.** going away: *He's wild, and soon on wing, if watchful eyes come near* (John Dryden).

take wing, a. to fly away: *And now, from the trees, from the earth all around them, the locusts were taking wing* (New Yorker). **b.** to depart: *I found a fellow who was in the same regiment with him, and knew this Mrs. Glasher before she took wing* (George Eliot).

under the wing of, under the protection or sponsorship of: *There liv'd Miss Cicely . . . under the wing of an old maiden aunt* (Samuel Foote).

wings, insignia awarded by the U.S. Air Force to men who have qualified as pilots, navigators, etc.: *In their third and final year cadets . . . are awarded their wings* (Observer).

—*v.t.* **1.** to fly: *The bird wings its way south.* **2.** to fly through, upon, or across. **3. a.** to supply with wings. **b.** to furnish with side parts or projections, as a building, etc. **4.** to make able to fly; give speed to; hasten: *Terror winged his steps as the bear drew near.* **5.** to convey by or as by means of wings. **6.** to let fly; send flying. **7.** to wound in the wing or arm. **8.** *Informal.* to disable (an airplane) by a shot. **9.** to brush with a bird's wing. **10.** *Theatrical Slang.* to play (a part) with little preparation, by studying it in the wings or being prompted from the wings. —*v.i.* to take flight with or as if with wings.

[Middle English *wenge* < Scandinavian (compare Old Icelandic *vængr*)] —**wing′-like′,** *adj.*

wing and wing, with two sails extended on opposite sides by booms, as a schooner or other fore-and-aft-rigged vessel sailing before the wind.

wing back, (in American football) an offensive back whose position is beyond and behind an end.

wing back formation, (in American football) an offensive formation in which the position of a back or the backs is a little beyond and behind either or both ends.

wing·beat (wing′bēt′), *n.* the stroke or sweep of the wings in flying: *With easy and deliberate wingbeats, with that strange flick on the upstroke so characteristic of cranes, the whooper appears to be moving slowly* (Maclean's).

wing bow (bō), the feathers of a distinctive coloring at the bend of a bird's wing.

wing case or **cover,** either of the hardened front wings of certain insects; elytron.

wing chair, a comfortable upholstered chair with sidepieces extending forward from the back.

wing collar, a stand-up collar with the corners folded down, worn especially in men's formal dress.

wing commander, 1. the commander of a wing. **2.** a commissioned officer in the Royal Air Force or Royal Canadian Air Force, equivalent to a lieutenant colonel in the United States Air Force.

wing coverts, the feathers concealing the bases of the flight feathers of a bird's wing.

wing·ding (wing′ding′), *U.S. Slang.* —*n.* **1.** a party or celebration, especially a lavish or noisy one. **2.** something extraordinary; a humdinger: *a wingding of a fight.* **3.** a thing; device; gadget.

—*adj.* festive, especially lavish or boisterous: *The big wingding Christmas parties for employees are definitely decreasing* (Wall Street Journal). Also, **whingding.**

winged (wingd; *especially poetic* wing′id), *adj.* **1.** having wings, as a bird and a bat. **2.** having a part or parts resembling or analogous to a wing. **3.** swift; rapid. **4.** lofty; elevated; sublime. **5.** wounded or disabled in the wing or arm. **6.** *Obsolete.* crowded with flying birds.

wing·er (wing′ər), *n. Especially British.* (in sports) a wing.

wing·fish (wing′fish′), *n., pl.* **-fish·es** or (*collectively*) **-fish.** a flying fish, especially a flying gurnard.

wing-foot·ed (wing′fu̇t′id), *adj.* having or seeming to have wings on the feet; swiftly moving.

wing·less (wing′lis), *adj.* **1.** having no wings. **2.** having rudimentary wings, as the ostrich and kiwi.

wing·let (wing′lit), *n.* **1.** a little wing. **2.** an alula.

wing loading or **load,** the gross weight of a fully loaded airplane divided by the total square feet or other units of square measure of the wings and other supporting surfaces, not including the stabilizer, elevators, etc.

wing·man (wing′man′, -mən), *n., pl.* **-men. 1. a.** a pilot who flies at the side and to the rear of an element leader, usually in a two-plane or three-plane formation. **b.** the airplane flown in this position. **2.** (in sports) a wing.

wing over, a lateral turning movement of an airplane.

wing rail, (on a railroad track) an additional rail at a switch, laid so as to prevent the wheels from leaving the track.

wing root, the base of an airplane's wing, where it joins and is faired into the fuselage.

wings (wingz), *n.pl.* See under **wing,** *n.*

wing shell, 1. a stromb (so called from the winglike lip of the aperture). **2.** any of a family of various bivalves, characterized by winglike expansions of the hinge margin.

wing shooting, the practice of shooting birds that are in flight.

wing·span (wing′span′), *n.,* or **wing span,** the wingspread of an airplane, including ailerons projecting beyond the wing tips.

wing spar, the spar of a wing, as contrasted with that of any other airfoil.

wing·spread (wing′spred′), *n.* **1.** the distance between the tips of the wings of a bird, bat, insect, etc., when they are spread. **2.** the distance between the tips of the wings of an airplane.

wing tank, a fuel tank in the wing of an airplane, or an auxiliary one attached to a wing.

wing tip, 1. the outer end of a wing, as of a bird, insect, airplane, etc. **2.** an ornamental tip on a shoe which is carried back along the sides. **3.** a shoe with such a tip.

wing-wea·ry (wing′wir′ē), *adj.* fatigued by prolonged flying.

wink[1] (wingk), *v.i.* **1. a.** to close the eyes and open them again quickly. **b.** (of the eyes or eyelids) to close and open again quickly. **2.** to close one eye and open it again quickly as a hint or signal. **3.** to twinkle: *The stars winked.* —*v.t.* **1.** to close (the eyes or an eye) for a moment. **2.** to move by winking: *to wink back tears.* **3.** to give (a signal) or express (a message) by a winking of the eye, a flashlight, etc.

wink at, to pretend not to notice: *Critics say the commission isn't doing much for the law when it finds a practice illegal and then announces it may wink at the violation* (Wall Street Journal).

—*n.* **1.** the act of winking. **2.** a hint or signal given by winking: *a knowing wink.* **3.** a very short time: *He'll be here in a wink. I didn't sleep a wink.* **4.** a twinkle.

forty winks. See under **forty winks.**

[Old English *wincian*]

wink[2] (wingk), *n.* one of the small colored disks used in the game of tiddlywinks: *Winks (the ones you flick) must be either seven-eighths or five-eighths of an inch in diameter* (London Times). [< (tiddly)-*wink*(s)]

wink·er (wing′kər), *n.* **1.** a person or thing that winks. **2.** *Informal.* **a.** an eyelash. **b.** an eye. **3.** a blinder or blinker for a horse's eye. **winkers, a.** *Slang.* the eyes: *As soon as my winkers are opened I am always blessed with one of your epistles* (Mary Delany). **b.** blinkers: *He weareth a pair of winkers over his eyes like a mill horse* (William Fulke). **c.** *Rare.* spectacles: *to look through a pair of winkers.*

win·kle[1] (wing′kəl), *n.* a periwinkle or any of certain other relatively large marine snails used for food. [short for *periwinkle*[2]]

win·kle[2] (wing′kəl), *v.t.*, **-kled, -kling.** *Especially British.* to dig (out); force; wrest: *... to winkle out the hard core of Omani rebels from their last stronghold* (Manchester Guardian). [probably partly < *winkle*[1] and partly < German *winkel* corner]

win·kle·pick·er (wing′kəl pik′ər), *n. British Slang.* a shoe with a sharply pointed toe: *Winklepickers, it seems, are doing much damage to the feet of Britain's young people* (Listener). [< *winkle*[1] + *picker*[1]]

win·less (win′lis), *adj.* without a win or victory; having lost every encounter thus far: *a winless season.*

win·na·ble (win′ə bəl), *adj.* capable of being won: *He ... is convinced that the war is not militarily winnable* (Time).

Win·ne·ba·go (win′ə bā′gō), *n., pl.* **-gos** or **-goes.** a member of an American Indian tribe speaking a Siouan language and living mostly in eastern Wisconsin.

win·ner (win′ər), *n.* one that wins. —**Syn.** victor.

winner's circle, a small enclosure at a race track where the winning horse and jockey are given the award.

win·ner-take-all (win′ər tāk′ôl′), *adj.* in which the winner receives all the prizes, points, etc., and the other contestants nothing: *a winner-take-all contest.*

Win·nie (win′ē), *n.* an award presented annually in the United States for outstanding achievements in fashion design: *The American Fashion Critics' "Winnie" went to dress designer Donald Brooks, of Townley* (Berta Mohr). (< *winn*(er) + *-ie*]

win·ning (win′ing), *adj.* **1.** that wins: *a winning team, a winning tactic.* **2.** having more victories than defeats. **3.** charming; attractive: *a winning smile.*
—*n.* **1.** the act of a person or thing that wins. **2.** the process of obtaining metal from ore. **3.** *Especially British.* **a.** a shaft or pit which is being sunk to win (open) a bed of coal. **b.** a portion of a coal field or mine ready for working.
winnings, what is won; money won: *One loss may be of more consequence to him, than all his former winnings* (John Dryden).
—**win′ning·ly,** *adv.* —**win′ning·ness,** *n.*

win·ning·est (win′ing ist), *adj. Informal.* winning or having won the most.

winning gallery, (in court tennis) the opening on the back wall on the hazard side, farthest from the dedans or spectators' gallery, one of three winning openings.

winning opening, (in court tennis) any of the three openings in the back walls of the court into which a ball is hit to score a point; the dedans, winning gallery, or grille.

winning post, a post marking the finish line on a race track.

win·nings (win′ingz), *n.pl.* See under **winning,** *n.*

Win·ni·peg couch (win′ə peg), a kind of couch having no arms or back and opening out into a double bed. [< *Winnipeg,* Canada]

Win·ni·peg·ger (win′ə peg′ər), *n.* a native or inhabitant of Winnipeg, Canada.

win·nock (win′ək), *n. Scottish.* a window. [variant of *window;* perhaps influenced by Gaelic *uinneag*]

win·now (win′ō), *v.t.* **1.** to blow off the chaff from (grain); drive or blow away (chaff). **2.** to sort out; separate; sift: *to winnow the facts from a wordy report, to winnow the truth from falsehood.* **3.** to blow on or away, as the wind does in removing chaff from grain; scatter or disperse. **4.** to fan (with wings); flap (wings). **5.** to follow (a course) with flapping wings. —*v.i.* **1.** to blow chaff from grain. **2.** to move with flapping wings; flutter.
—*n.* **1.** a contrivance for winnowing grain. **2.** the act of winnowing or a motion resembling it.
[Old English *windwian* < *wind* wind[1], gust]
—**win′now·er,** *n.*

wi·no (wī′nō), *n., pl.* **-nos.** *U.S. Slang.* an alcoholic addicted to wine.

win·some (win′səm), *adj.* **1.** charming; attractive; pleasing. **2.** *Dialect.* cheerful; joyous; gay. [Old English *wynsum* agreeable, pleasant < *wynn* joy + *-sum* -some[1]]
—**win′some·ly,** *adv.* —**win′some·ness,** *n.*

wint (wint), *v. Scottish.* wound; the past tense of **wind**[2].

win·ter (win′tər), *n.* **1.** the coldest of the four seasons; time of the year between fall and spring. In northern latitudes winter is reckoned astronomically as beginning about December 22 (the winter solstice) and ending about March 21 (the vernal equinox), and popularly as comprising the months of December, January, and February or (in British use) November, December, and January. In southern latitudes winter corresponds in calendar time to the northern summer. *His uncle and he would go toiling up the mountain side, sometimes striding over rutted, clay-caked, and frost-hardened roads, sometimes beating their way downhill ... smashing their way through the dry and brittle undergrowth of barren Winter* (Thomas Wolfe). **2.** a year as denoted by this season: *a man of eighty winters.* **3.** the last period of life: *Father Mapple was in the hardy winter of a healthy old age* (Herman Melville). **4.** a period of decline, dreariness, or adversity: *It was the best of times, it was the worst of times ... it was the spring of hope, it was the winter of despair* (Dickens).
—*adj.* **1.** of, having to do with, or characteristic of winter: *winter weather, winter winds. The winter moon, brightening the skirts of a long cloud* (Tennyson). **2.** adapted to or used, existing, active, or performed in winter: *winter clothing, winter sports.* **3.** (of fruit and vegetables) that keep well during the winter: *winter apples.* **4.** (of crops) that are sown in the fall and harvested in the spring: *winter wheat.*
—*v.i.* to pass or spend the winter: *to winter in the south.* —*v.t.* to keep, feed, or manage during winter: *We wintered our cattle in the warm valley.*
[Old English *winter*] —**win′ter·er,** *n.*

winter aconite, any of a group of small Old World herbs of the crowfoot family, whose bright-yellow flowers appear very early in the spring.

winter apple, 1. an apple that does not ripen till winter. **2.** an apple that keeps well in winter.

win·ter·ber·ry (win′tər ber′ē), *n., pl.* **-ries.** any of various North American hollies with berries, usually scarlet, that persist through the winter.

win·ter·bloom (win′tər blüm′), *n.* the witch hazel.

win·ter·bourne (win′tər bôrn′, -bōrn′, -bûrn′), *n.* an intermittent stream that flows only in winter or at long intervals, found especially in certain chalk and limestone regions of England. [< *winter* + *bourne*[1]]

winter cress, any of a group of plants of the mustard family, especially a common European weed naturalized in North America and sometimes used in salads.

win·ter·feed (win′tər fēd′), *v.,* **-fed, -feeding,** *n.* —*v.t.* to feed or maintain (animals, etc.) during winter. —*n.* food supplied to animals during winter.

winter flounder, a flounder of the coast of the eastern United States with the eyes on the right side of the head.

win·ter·green (win′tər grēn′), *n.* **1.** a small, creeping, evergreen plant of North America of the heath family, with small, white, drooping flowers, edible, bright-red berries, and aromatic leaves, from which a heavy volatile oil (oil of wintergreen or wintergreen oil) is made. The wintergreen is also called *checkerberry, spiceberry, teaberry,* and (incorrectly) *partridgeberry.* **2.** this oil, used in medicine and as a flavoring for candy. **3.** its flavor, or something flavored with it. **4.** any other plant of the same group. **5.** any of a group of evergreen herbs, especially a woodland plant with roundish, drooping, white flowers; shinleaf. **6.** any of various low plants of an allied group; pipsissewa.

Wintergreen (def. 1)

wintergreen oil, oil of wintergreen.

winter gull, kittiwake, a sea gull of the North Atlantic and Arctic oceans.

win·ter-har·dy (win′tər här′dē), *adj.* able to withstand the effects of cold weather: *Plant breeders often search other countries for alfalfa plants that are winter-hardy* (C. H. Hanson).

win·ter·ize (win′tə rīz), *v.t.,* **-ized, -iz·ing. 1.** to make (a mechanism, especially a vehicle or its engine) ready for operation or use during the winter, as by putting antifreeze in the radiator and replacing a relatively heavy engine lubricant with a relatively light one. **2.** to prepare (anything) for winter use or occupation: *to winterize a house.*

win·ter·kill (win′tər kil′), *U.S.* —*v.t., v.i.* to kill by or die from exposure to cold weather: *The rosebushes were winterkilled.* —*n.* death of a plant or animal due to exposure to cold weather.

win·ter·less (win′tər lis), *adj.* having no winter; without wintry weather.

win·ter·ly (win′tər lē), *adj.* **1.** of, belonging to, or occurring in winter. **2.** like winter or that of winter; cold and cheerless; wintry.

winter melon, a variety of melon that keeps through part of the winter.

winter solstice, 1. (for the Northern Hemisphere) the time when the sun is farthest south from the equator, December 21 or 22. **2.** the point on the ecliptic farthest south of the celestial equator, which the sun reaches at this time. It was formerly in the constellation Cancer, but is now in Sagittarius. *Off the tip of the Archer's bow is the place of the winter solstice, where the sun is found about December 21* (Hubert J. Bernhard).

win·ter·tide (win′tər tīd′), *n. Poetic* or *Archaic.* wintertime. [Old English *wintertīd* < *winter* winter + *tīd* tide, time]

win·ter·time (win′tər tīm′), *n.* the season of winter; winter.

winter wheat, wheat planted in the autumn and ripening in the following spring or summer.

winter wren, a small, short-tailed wren of northern parts of the Northern Hemisphere.

win·ter·y (win′tər ē, -trē), *adj.,* **-ter·i·er, -ter·i·est.** wintry.

win·tle (win′təl), *v.,* **-tled, -tling,** *n. Scottish.* —*v.i.* **1.** to roll or swing from side to side. **2.** to tumble, capsize, or be upset. —*n.* a rolling or staggering movement. [< earlier Flemish *windtelen* < *winden* to wind]

win·tri·ly (win′trə lē), *adv.* in a wintry manner.

win·tri·ness (win′trē nis), *n.* wintry quality.

win·try (win′trē), *adj.,* **-tri·er, -tri·est. 1.** of or having the quality of winter; of such a kind as occurs in winter; characteristic of winter: *a wintry sky.* **2. a.** devoid of fervor or affection; cold; chilling: *a wintry smile.* **b.** destitute of warmth or brightness; dismal; dreary; cheerless: *a wintry gathering.* **3. a.** aged. **b.** (of hair) white with age; snowy. —**Syn. 1.** hibernal.

win·y (wī′nē), *adj.,* **win·i·er, win·i·est.** tasting, smelling, or looking like wine.

winze[1] (winz), *n. Scottish.* an imprecation; curse. [origin uncertain. Compare earlier Flemish *wensch.*]

winze[2] (winz), *n. Mining.* a shaft or an inclined passage connecting one level with another, but not rising to the surface. [earlier *winds,* perhaps < *wind*[2]]

wipe (wīp), *v.,* **wiped, wip·ing,** *n.* —*v.t.* **1.** to rub (something) with cloth, paper, etc., in order to clean or dry: *to wipe a table, wipe one's hands.* **2.** to take (away, off, or out) in this way: *Wipe away your tears. She wiped off dust.* **3.** to remove: *The rain wiped away the footprints.* **4.** to rub or draw (something) over a surface, as for cleaning or drying. **5.** to apply (a soft substance) by rubbing it on with a cloth, pad, etc.: *to wipe ointment on a burn.* **6. a.** to form or seal (a joint in lead pipe) by spreading solder with a leather or cloth pad. **b.** to apply (solder) in this way.

wipe out, a. to remove by death; annihilate: *A vast slag heap slipped down a mountain to wipe out a school full of children* (Manchester Guardian Weekly). **b.** to do away with; abolish: *Automation . . . is wiping out about 40,000 unskilled jobs a week* (Saturday Review).
—*n.* **1.** the act of wiping clean or dry. **2.** *Informal.* a slashing or sweeping blow; swipe. **3.** *Informal or Dialect.* a cutting remark; jeer; gibe. **4.** *Slang.* a handkerchief. **5.** *Machinery.* a cam or other wiper.
[Old English *wīpian*]

wip·er (wī′pər), *n.* **1.** a person who wipes, especially a member of the crew of a ship who is employed in the engine room to clean and polish machinery, fittings, etc. **2. a.** a cloth or appliance used for wiping. **b.** *Slang.* a handkerchief. **3.** *Electricity.* a moving piece that makes contact with the terminals of a device, as a rheostat. **4.** (in machinery) a projecting piece fixed on a rotating or oscillating part, and periodically communicating movement by a rubbing action to some other part; a cam, eccentric, or tappet, especially one serving to lift a hammer, stamper, valve rod, etc., that in the intervals falls by its own weight.

wire (wīr), *n., adj., v.,* **wired, wir·ing.** —*n.* **1.** metal drawn out into a slender, flexible form that varies from a thin rod to a fine thread. **2. a.** such metal as a material, as for fences. **b.** a fence made of barbed wire. **3.** a piece, length, or line of such metal used for various purposes, as a cross hair of an optical instrument. **4.** a long piece of metal drawn out into a thread for electrical transmission, as in electric lighting, telephones, and telegraphs. **5.** telegraph: *to send a message by wire.* **6.** *Informal.* a telegram. **7.** wire netting. **8.** Often, **wires. a.** a metal bar of a cage. **b.** *Music.* a metallic string of an instrument. **9.** the finish line of a racecourse. **10.** a metal snare for hares or rabbits. **11.** a long, wiry, hairlike growth of the plumage of various birds.
down to the wire, to the very last minute; to the end: *The World Series pursued its peculiar pattern down to the wire today* (New York Times).
pull wires, *Informal.* to use secret influence to accomplish one's purpose: *to pull wires on behalf of a political candidate.*
under the wire, just before it is too late: *The Trumbull Terrace, a building for refreshments, came in just under the wire and was ready for the first festival goers* (New York Times).
—*adj.* made of or consisting of wire: *wire netting.*
—*v.t.* **1.** to furnish with a wire or wires: *to wire a house for electricity.* **2.** to fasten with a wire or wires: *He wired the two pieces together.* **3.** to fence (in) with wire. **4.** to stiffen with wire; place on a wire. **5.** to catch or trap in a wire snare. **6.** *Informal.* to telegraph: *to wire a birthday greeting.* **7.** (in croquet) to hit (a ball) so that it rests behind an arch and thus blocks another ball. —*v.i.* *Informal.* to send a message by telegraph.
[Old English *wīr*] —**wire′like′,** *adj.* —**wir′er,** *n.*

wire·bar (wīr′bär′), *n.* a bar of copper or other refined metal, cast into a suitable form for drawing into wire.

wire brush, a brush with metal bristles, for cleaning surfaces of rust, paint, etc.

wire cloth, a fabric woven from wire, used for strainers. —**wire′-cloth′,** *adj.*

wire coat, a coat of rough, wiry hair, as of some dogs.

wire cutter, a tool for cutting wire.

wire·danc·er (wīr′dan′sər, -dän′-), *n.* a person who dances or performs acrobatic stunts on a taut wire high above the ground.

wire·danc·ing (wīr′dan′sing, -dän′-), *n.* the performance or work of a wiredancer.

wire·draw (wīr′drô′), *v.t.,* **-drew, -drawn, -draw·ing. 1.** to draw out (metal) into wire. **2.** to draw out (a material thing) to an elongated form; stretch; elongate. **3. a.** to protract excessively; spin out. **b.** to draw out to an extreme tenuity; attenuate. —**wire′draw′er,** *n.*

wire·draw·ing (wīr′drô′ing), *n.* **1.** the art of drawing metal into wire. **2.** the act of drawing out an argument or a discussion to prolixity.

wire·drawn (wīr′drôn′), *adj.* **1.** drawn out into a wire. **2.** treated with too much hair-splitting and refinement. —*v.* the past participle of **wiredraw.**

wire edge, a thin, wirelike bur or thread of metal often formed at the edge of a cutting tool during the process of sharpening.

wire entanglement, an arrangement or system of barbed wire set up to impede enemy troops.

wire gauge, a device for measuring the diameter of wire, the thickness of metal sheets, etc., usually a disk with notches of different sizes cut in its edge.

wire gauze, a fabric of very fine wire.

wire glass, glass in which wire is embedded to strengthen it.

wire grass, any of various grasses having wiry stems or leaves, especially a slender Old World meadow grass, naturalized in North America, and the yard grass.

wire·hair (wīr′hãr′), *n.* a fox terrier with a rough, wiry coat.

wire-haired (wīr′hãrd′), *adj.* having short, coarse, stiff, wiry hair.

wire-haired pointing griffon, a medium-sized hunting dog with a rough, stiff coat, used to point and retrieve game.

wire-haired terrier, wirehair.

wire house, a brokerage firm that communicates with its branch offices by private telephone or telegraph.

wire·less (wīr′lis), *adj.* **1.** having no wire; operated without wire or wires: *wireless telegraphy.* **2.** *Especially British.* radio.
—*n.* *Especially British.* **1.** radio. **2.** a message sent by radio; radiogram.
—*v.t., v.i.* *Especially British.* to send or transmit by radio.

wireless telegraphy or **telegraph,** a system of telegraphy in which no conducting wire is used between the transmitting and receiving stations, the signals or messages being transmitted through space by means of electromagnetic waves.

wireless telephone, a radiotelephone.

wireless telephony, a system of telephony in which there are no conducting wires, the messages being transmitted by means of radio.

wire·man (wīr′mən), *n., pl.* **-men. 1.** a man who puts electric wires in place and maintains them, as for a telegraph, telephone, electric lighting, or electric power system; lineman. **2.** *Obsolete.* a man who makes or works in wire.

wire nail, a small, thin nail made from iron or steel wire, with a small head produced by compression of the end.

wire netting, a fabric of woven wire, used for screens for windows and doors.

Wire·pho·to (wīr′fō′tō), *n., pl.* **-tos.** *Trademark.* a photograph transmitted by wirephoto.

wire·pho·to (wīr′fō′tō), *n., pl.* **-tos,** *v.,* **-toed, -to·ing.** —*n.* a method for transmitting photographs by reproducing a facsimile through electric signals. —*v.t.* to transmit by wirephoto. [< *Wirephoto*]

wire·pull (wīr′pu̇l′), *v.t., v.i.* *Informal.* to promote by wirepulling.

wire·pull·er (wīr′pu̇l′ər), *n.* *Informal.* a person who uses secret influence to accomplish his purposes. —**Syn.** manipulator.

wire·pull·ing (wīr′pu̇l′ing), *n.* **1.** *Informal.* the use of secret influence to accomplish a purpose. **2.** *Obsolete.* manipulation of the strings or wires by which a marionette or marionettes are caused to move.

wire recorder, a device for recording sound on a fine steel wire, the sound impulses from the microphone being magnetically impressed on the wire by an electromagnet. The sounds are reproduced as the magnetized wire moves past a receiver.

wire recording, a reproduction of voices, music, etc., made on a wire recorder.

wire rope, rope or cable made of twisted strands of wire.

wire service, a news agency that gathers foreign and domestic news and photographs and distributes them to member newspapers and radio stations, as the Associated Press (AP) and United Press International (UPI) in the United States.

wire·smith (wīr′smith′), *n.* a person who makes metal into wire.

wire·spun (wīr′spun′), *adj.* wiredrawn.

wire·tap (wīr′tap′), *n., v.,* **-tapped, -tap·ping,** *adj.* —*n.* Also, **wire tap. 1.** an instance of wiretapping: *to be guilty of a wiretap.* **2.** the information obtained or recorded by wiretapping: *a conviction based on a wiretap.*
—*v.t.* **1.** to make a secret connection with (a telephone or telegraph system) for listening to or recording messages. **2.** to record or obtain by means of a wiretap: *to wiretap a conversation.*
—*adj.* of or having to do with wiretapping or a wiretap: *wiretap evidence, a wiretap law. William J. Keating said yesterday that a wiretap center illegally operated by two detectives had been discovered last year by special agents of the New York Telephone Company* (New York Times).

wire·tap·per (wīr′tap′ər), *n.,* or **wire tapper,** a person who practices wiretapping or who makes a wiretap.

wire·tap·ping (wīr′tap′ing), *n.,* or **wire tapping,** the making of a secret connection with telephone or telegraph wires to listen to or record the messages sent over them, forbidden by law in many countries and states, except as specifically authorized by a qualified authority. —*adj.* of or having to do with wiretapping: *a wiretapping system, wiretapping equipment. He faces trial on wiretapping charges in New York* (Wall Street Journal). *The two biggest wiretapping agencies in the U.S. are the FBI . . . and the New York City Police Department* (Time).

wire-walk·er (wīr′wô′kər), *n.* an acrobat who walks and performs feats on a wire rope: *The circus acts are the usual flat performances of elephants, horses, dogs, . . . and wire-walkers* (New York Times).

wire-walk·ing (wīr′wô′king), *n.* the act of walking or performing on a wire rope.

wire·work (wīr′wėrk′), *n.* **1.** the making of wire. **2.** work done in or made with wire.

wireworks, an establishment where wire is made or where wire goods are manufactured.

wire·work·er (wīr′wėr′kər), *n.* **1.** a wiresmith. **2.** *Informal.* a wirepuller.

wire·worm (wīr′wėrm′), *n.* **1.** the slender, hard-bodied larva of an elaterid or click beetle. Wireworms feed on the roots of plants and do much damage to crops. **2.** a millepede. **3.** a stomach worm.

wire-wove (wīr′wōv′), *adj.* **1.** designating a fine grade of smooth paper, made on a mold of wire gauze, used especially for letter paper. **2.** made of woven wire.

wir·i·ly (wīr′ə lē), *adv.* in a wiry manner.

wir·i·ness (wīr′ē nis), *n.* the state or character of being wiry.

wir·ing (wīr′ing), *n.* **1.** a system of wires for conducting and distributing an electric current, as in a switchboard or in a building. **2.** the act of a person who wires.
—*adj.* **1.** that wires: *a wiring crew.* **2.** of, having to do with, or required for wiring: *a wiring plan, wiring equipment.*

wir·ra (wir′ə), *interj.* *Irish.* an exclamation of sorrow or lament. [< Irish *a Mhuire* (literally) O Mary]

wir·y (wīr′ē), *adj.,* **wir·i·er, wir·i·est. 1.** like wire: *wiry hair, a wiry coat of fur, wiry grass.* **2.** lean, strong, and tough: *a man with a wiry build.* **3.** made of wire. **4. a.** (of sound) produced by or as by the plucking or vibration of a wire. **b.** (of a voice) thin and metallic.

wis (wis), *v.t.* *Archaic.* to know (used only in *I wis*).
[< *iwis* (erroneously understood as *I wis*) < Old English *gewiss* certain, sure]

Wis. or **Wisc.,** Wisconsin.

Wis·con·sin·ite (wis kon′sə nīt), *n.* a native or inhabitant of Wisconsin.

Wisd., Wisdom of Solomon (Book of the Old Testament Apocrypha).

wis·dom (wiz′dəm), *n.* **1.** knowledge and good judgment based on experience; being wise. **2.** scholarly knowledge: *Moses was learned in all the wisdom of the Egyptians* (Acts 7:22). **3.** *Archaic.* wise conduct; wise words.
[Old English *wīsdōm* < *wīs* wise, smart + *-dōm* -dom]
—**Syn. 1.** sagacity, sapience. **2.** learning, erudition. **3.** prudence, discretion.

Wis·dom (wiz′dəm), *n.* **1.** a form of literature common to the ancient Egyptians, Syrians, Mesopotamians, etc., consisting chiefly of wise sayings, and exemplified by the Old Testament books of Proverbs, Job, and Ecclesiastes. **2.** Wisdom of Solomon.

Wisdom of Jesus, Son of Si·rach (sī′rak), Ecclesiasticus.

Wisdom of Solomon, a philosophical book of the Old Testament Apocrypha, traditionally attributed to Solomon, included in the canon of the Roman Catholic Bible. *Abbr.:* Wisd.

wisdom tooth, the back tooth on either

side of both the upper and lower jaw, usually appearing between the ages of 17 and 25.

wise[1] (wīz), *adj.*, **wis·er, wis·est,** *v.*, **wised, wis·ing.** —*adj.* **1.** having or showing knowledge and good judgment: *a wise judge, wise advice, wise plans.* **2.** learned; erudite; well-informed. **3.** having knowledge or information: *We are none the wiser for his explanation.* **4.** *Archaic.* having knowledge of occult or supernatural things.

get wise, *Slang.* to find out; understand; realize: *By the time they got wise they'd be paying off* (Harper's).

wise to, *Slang.* aware of; informed about: *to put someone wise to something.*

—*v.t., v.i.* **wise up,** *Slang.* **a.** to inform or enlighten (a person): *You won't wise him up that I threw a spanner into the machinery?* (P.G. Wodehouse). **b.** to become enlightened; gain awareness or understanding: *I wish you'd wise up about these things.*

[Old English *wīs*] —**wise′ly,** *adv.* —**wise′ness,** *n.*

—**Syn.** *adj.* **1. Wise, sage** mean having or showing knowledge and good judgment. **Wise** implies having knowledge and understanding of people and of what is true and right in life and conduct, and showing sound judgment in applying such knowledge: *His wise father knows how to handle him.* **Sage** suggests deep and mature wisdom based on wide knowledge, experience, and profound thought: *The old professor gave us sage advice we have never forgotten.* —**Ant.** *adj.* **1.** foolish.

wise[2] (wīz), *n.* way; manner; fashion; mode; style (now seldom used as an independent word except in such phrases as *in any wise, in no wise, on this wise*). [Old English *wīse.* Related to GUISE.]

wise[3] (wīz), *v.t.*, **wised, wis·ing.** *Scottish.* **1.** to guide; direct. **2.** to induce or entice (away, from). [Old English *wīsian.* Related to WISE[1].]

-wise, *suffix.* **1.** in a ___ manner, as in *anywise, likewise.*
2. in a ___ing manner, as in *slantwise.*
3. in the characteristic way of a ___; like a ___. *Clockwise* means in the way the hands of a clock go.
4. in the ___ respect or case, as in *leastwise, otherwise.*
5. in the direction of ___, as in *lengthwise.*
6. special meanings, as in *sidewise.*
[< *wise*[2]]

➔ In popular jargon, and that of certain professions, **-wise** is often suffixed to polysyllabic nouns to form words for the occasion: *We have made a number of changes curriculumwise.*

wise·a·cre (wīz′ā′kər), *n.* **1.** a person who thinks that he knows everything. **2.** a learned person; sage (usually contemptuous or ironical, with implication of pedantry, impracticality, etc.).
[half translation of Middle Dutch *wijssegger* soothsayer. Compare Middle High German *wīssager.*]

wise·crack (wīz′krak′), *U.S. Slang.* —*n.* a snappy comeback; smart remark. —*v.i.* to make wisecracks: *An attendant directed me up a flight of stairs to an antechamber of the court, where I was soon joined by . . . a half dozen defiant-looking youths, wisecracking to keep up their courage* (Maclean's). —**wise′crack′er,** *n.*

wise guy, *U.S. Slang.* a person who is brashly or impudently bold in asserting himself, his views, etc., especially one who pretends to know more than he really does.

wise·ling (wīz′ling′), *n.* a pretender to wisdom; wiseacre: *This may well put to the blush those wiselings that show themselves fools in so speaking* (John Donne).

wis·en·heim·er (wī′zən hī′mər), *n. U.S. Slang.* a wise guy: *Scent of Mystery has been tagged by the Hollywood wisenheimers as "the first movie that ever smelled on purpose"* (Time).

wi·sent (wē′zənt), *n.* an aurochs. [< German *Wisent* < Old High German *wisunt.* Compare BISON]

wish (wish), *v.t.* **1.** to have a desire for; be glad to have, get, do, or realize; want: *to wish help, to wish money. I wish that it would snow tomorrow. Do you wish to speak to me?* **2.** to feel or express a desire for (a person or thing to be as specified): *to wish oneself at home, wish a speech were finished.* **3. a.** to desire (something) for someone; have a hope for: *to wish someone joy, good luck, etc. I don't wish him any harm.* **b.** to express a hope for: *to wish someone good night. I wish you a happy new year.* **4.** to request, entreat, or command (a thing or action, or a person to do something): *Do you wish me to send him in now?* —*v.i.* **1.** to have, feel, or express a desire; long (for): *to wish for more money or a new house.* **2.** to desire or hope for something, especially something good, for another: *to wish well to a friend.*

wish on, *Informal.* to pass on to; foist on: *They wished the hardest job on him. Professor Henry's efforts to dissociate himself from the museum that Congress had wished on him did not meet with . . . success* (New Yorker).

—*n.* **1.** a turning of the mind toward the doing, having, getting, etc., of something; desire or longing: *He had no wish to be king.* **2. a.** an expression of a wish: *She sends you best wishes for a happy new year.* **b.** a request; entreaty: *to grant his slightest wish.* **3.** a thing wished for: *to get one's wish.*

[Old English *wӯscan.* Related to WEEN[1].] —**wish′er,** *n.*

—**Syn.** *v.t.* **1. Wish, desire** mean to long for something. **Wish** is the least emphatic word, sometimes suggesting only that one would like to have, do, or get a certain thing, sometimes suggesting a longing that can never be satisfied: *I wish I could have my hair cut tomorrow.* **Desire,** sometimes used as a formal substitute for *wish* or, especially, *want,* suggests wishing strongly for something and usually being willing or determined to work or struggle to get it: *He finally received the position he desired.*

wish·a (wish′ə), *interj. Irish.* an exclamation of surprise, regret, etc.: *But no sooner would the excursion be over than she would sigh, "Wisha, it would have been far better for me to have gone to the chapel and said my rosary"* (Atlantic).

wish·bone (wish′bōn′), *n.* the forked bone in the front of the breastbone in poultry and other birds; furcula. [< *wish* + *bone*[1] (because of the custom of breaking it between two persons, one, usually the one with the longer end, getting his wish). Compare MERRYTHOUGHT.]

wish·ful (wish′fəl), *adj.* having or expressing a wish desiring; desirous: *Wishful thinking is a disasterous substitute for hard work.* —**wish′ful·ly,** *adv.* —**wish′ful·ness,** *n.*

wish fulfillment, *Psychoanalysis.* indirect fulfillment of a frustrated wish, as through a daydream: *Every time that we fully understand a dream it proves to be a wish fulfillment* (Sigmund Freud).

wishful thinker, a person who engages in wishful thinking.

wishful thinking, a believing something to be true that one wishes or wants to be true: *It is wishful thinking to assume that the Soviet Union . . . will approach the negotiating table with the serious intention of reaching . . . enforceable agreements on our many differences* (Chester Bowles).

wish·ing cap (wish′ing), a fabulous cap supposed to ensure fulfillment of any wish made by one wearing it.

wish-wash (wish′wosh′, -wôsh′), *n.* a wishy-washy thing.

wish·y-wash·y (wish′ē wosh′ē, -wôsh′-), *adj.* **1.** thin and weak; insipid; watery. **2.** lacking in substantial qualities; feeble; inferior: *a wishy-washy attitude.*
[varied reduplication of *washy* thin, watery]

wisp (wisp), *n.* **1.** a small bundle; small bunch: *a wisp of hay.* **2.** a small tuft, lock, or portion of anything; shred; fragment: *a wisp of hair, a wisp of smoke.* **3.** a little thing: *a wisp of a girl.* **4.** a twisted bundle of hay, straw, etc., or a twist of paper, especially when burned as a torch or used as kindling. **5.** a will-o'-the-wisp; ignis fatuus. **6.** a whisk broom.
—*v.t.* to twist into or as a wisp.
—*v.i.* to move or drift as a wisp of smoke, vapor, etc.
[origin uncertain. Compare Frisian *wisp.*] —**wisp′like′,** *adj.*

wisp·ish (wis′pish), *adj.* of the nature of or resembling a wisp; somewhat wispy: *As they went higher and higher, she looked out at the very white, wispish clouds* (New Yorker).

wisp·y (wis′pē), *adj.*, **wisp·i·er, wisp·i·est.** like a wisp; thin; slight: *A number of them are decorated with wispy feathers trailing down one cheek or over the forehead* (New Yorker).

wist (wist), *v. Archaic.* the past tense and past participle of **wit**[2].

wis·tar·i·a (wis târ′ē ə), *n.* wisteria.

wis·te·ri·a (wis tir′ē ə), *n.* any of a group of climbing shrubs of the pea family, with large, drooping spikes (racemes) of showy, purple, blue, or white flowers, especially the Chinese wisteria and the Japanese wisteria, species often grown to cover verandas and walls. [American English < New Latin *Wistaria* the genus name < Caspar *Wistar,* 1761-1818, an American anatomist]

Chinese Wisteria

➔ Although **wistaria** accords better with the name *Wistar,* **wisteria** is both the earlier and the more common form.

wist·ful (wist′fəl), *adj.* **1.** longing; yearning: *to look with wistful eyes at what one wants and cannot have.* **2.** pensive; melancholy. **3.** *Obsolete.* closely attentive; intent. [< obsolete *wist,* back formation < *wistly* intently + *-ful;* origin uncertain] —**wist′ful·ly,** *adv.* —**wist′ful·ness,** *n.* —**Syn. 1.** wishful. **2.** musing, meditative.

wit[1] (wit), *n.* **1.** the power to perceive quickly and express cleverly ideas that are unusual, striking, and amusing: *Brevity is the soul of wit* (Shakespeare). **2.** a person with such power. **3.** a person noted for his brilliant or sparkling sayings, clever repartee, or the like. **4.** understanding; mind; sense: *People with quick wits learn easily. The child was out of his wits with fright.*

at one's wit's end, not knowing what to do or say; utterly perplexed: *What shall we do? is the doleful cry of men at their wits' end* (John Flavel).

have or **keep one's wits about one,** to be alert: *Have all your wits about you, . . . you are nursing a viper in your bosom* (Benjamin H. Malkin).

live by one's wits, to get one's living by clever or crafty devices rather than by any settled occupation: *Living by his wits—which means by the abuse of every faculty that, worthily employed, raises man above the beasts* (Dickens).

[Old English *witt.* Ultimately related to WIT[2].]

—**Syn. 1. Wit, humor** mean the power to see and express what is amusing or causes laughter. **Wit** means a mental sharpness and quickness in perceiving what is striking, unusual, inconsistent, or out of keeping and in expressing it in cleverly surprising and amusing sayings: *Bernard Shaw was famous for his wit.* **Humor** means a power to see and show with warm sympathy and kindness the things in life and human nature that are funny or absurdly out of keeping: *Her sense of humor eased her trouble.* **4.** intelligence.

wit[2] (wit), *v.t., v.i., pres. 1st pers.* **wot,** *2nd pers.* **wost** (wost), *3rd pers.* **wot,** *pl.* **wit;** *pt. and pp.* **wist;** *pres. p.* **wit·ting.** *Archaic.* to know.

to wit, that is to say; namely: *To my son I leave all I own —to wit: my house, what is in it, and the land on which it stands.*
[Old English *witan*]

wit·an (wit′ən), *n.pl.* in Anglo-Saxon times: **1.** the members of the national council (witenagemot). **2.** the council itself. [modern revival of Old English *witan,* plural of *wita* council or (literally) one who knows < *witan* wit, know]

witch (wich), *n.* **1.** a female magician; sorceress, especially (in later use) a woman supposed to be under the influence of spirits and to have magic power: *I have heard of one old witch changing herself into a pigeon* (John Rhys). **2.** an ugly old woman; hag. **3.** *Informal.* a charming or fascinating girl or woman. **4.** *Dialect.* a male practitioner of magic; magician; sorcerer; wizard. —*v.t.* **1. a.** to use the power of a witch on; put a spell upon. **b.** to bring, draw, put, or change by witchcraft. **2.** to charm; fascinate; bewitch. [Old Englich *wicce*] —**Syn.** *n.* **2.** crone. **3.** charmer. *-v.t.* **2.** enthrall, captivate.

witch-broom (wich′brüm′, -bru̇m′), *n.,* or **witch broom,** witches'-broom.

witch·craft (wich′kraft′, -kräft′), *n.* **1.** what a witch does or can do; magic power or influence: *There are few superstitions which have been so universal as a belief in witchcraft* (Henry T. Buckle). **2.** bewitching or fascinating attraction or charm.

witchcrafts, magic arts: *All these witchcrafts ceased after the coming of Christ* (Fynes Moryson). —**Syn. 1.** sorcery.

witch doctor, a medicine man, especially among African tribes.
witch-elm (wich′elm′), *n.* wych-elm.
witch·er·y (wich′ər ē, wich′rē), *n., pl.* **-er·ies. 1.** witchcraft; magic. **2.** charm; fascination.
witch·es′-be·som (wich′iz bē′zəm), *n.* witches′-broom.
witch·es′-broom (wich′iz brüm′, -brům′), *n.* **1.** an abnormal growth on trees and shrubs, especially conifers, consisting of a dense mass of small, thin branches, caused chiefly by various fungi; hexenbesen. **2.** a similar growth on the potato, caused by a virus.
witches′ or **Witches′ Sabbath,** a midnight meeting of demons, sorcerers, and witches, supposed in medieval times to have been held annually as a festival; Sabbat.
witch·et·ty (wich′ə tē), *n. Australian.* the larva of some species of longicorn beetles, eaten as food by the aborigines.
witch grass, 1. a North American panic grass having a brushlike panicle. **2.** couch grass. [American English, probably variant of *quitch grass*]
witch hazel, 1. a shrub or small tree of eastern North America that has straight-veined, wavy-margined leaves and bears yellow flowers in the fall or winter after the leaves have fallen. **2.** a lotion for cooling and soothing inflammations, bruises, sprains, etc., made by steeping the bark and leaves of this shrub in alcohol. **3.** any other plant of the same genus. Also, **wych-hazel.** [earlier *wyche hasill,* apparently < Old English *wice* wych-elm; taken as *witch,* noun]

Japanese Witch Hazel (def. 1)

witch hunt, or **witch-hunt** (wich′hunt′), *n. Informal.* a persecuting or defaming (a person) to gain political advantage: *He denounced the investigation as a "witch hunt" and invoked his constitutional right not to testify against himself* (Wall Street Journal).
witch-hunt·er (wich′hun′tər), *n. Informal.* a person who conducts a witch hunt.
witch-hunt·ing (wich′hun′ting), *Informal.* —*n.* a witch hunt. —*adj.* of or having to do with a witch hunt.
witch·ing (wich′ing), *adj.* magical; enchanting. —*n.* **1.** witchcraft. **2.** enchantment; fascination. —**witch′ing·ly,** *adv.*
witch·like (wich′līk′), *adj.* having the nature of or resembling a witch: *Her eyes weren't witchlike, not black and beady and evil but large and milky blue and kind* (New Yorker).
witch·man (wich′mən), *n., pl.* **-men.** a witch doctor.
witch moth, any of certain large, dark, noctuid moths.
witch·weed (wich′wēd′), *n., pl.* **-weeds** or (*collectively*) **-weed.** a small weed of Africa and the United States belonging to the figwort family. It lives as a parasite on roots of corn and other grains.
wite (wīt), *n., v.,* **wit·ed, wit·ing.** *Scottish.* —*n.* **1.** blame; reproach. **2.** blameworthiness; fault. —*v.t.* to blame. [Old English *wītan* to blame]
wit·e·na·ge·mot or **wit·e·na·ge·mote** (wit′ə nə gə mōt′), *n.* the royal council of the Anglo-Saxons; assembly of the witan. [modern revival of Old English *witena gemōt* (literally) assembly of wise men < *witena,* genitive plural of *wita* councilor (see WITAN) + *gemōt* meeting]
with (wiTH, with), *prep.* **1.** in the company, society, or presence of: *to sit with a friend. Come with me.* **2.** accompanied by; including; and: *two men with their servants, tea with sugar and lemon.* **3.** among; into: *They will mix with the crowd.* **4.** having, wearing, carrying, etc.: *a book with a red cover, a man with a beard, a telegram with bad news.* **5.** in spite of; notwithstanding: *With all his weight he was not a strong man.* **6.** in the keeping or service of: *to leave a package with a friend. Leave the dog with me.* **7.** receiving; having; being allowed: *I went with his permission.* **8.** association or connection in thought, action, or condition: *one day with another.* **9.** accompaniment as a circumstance or attendance as a result: *a suggestion received with silence, to interrupt with a laugh.* **10.** as an addition to; added to: *Do you want sugar with your tea?* **11.** on the side of; for: *to vote or side with someone. They are with us in our plans.* **12.** at the same time as: *With this battle the war ended.* **13.** in the same direction as: *to sail with the tide.* **14.** in proportion to: *An army's power increases with its size.* **15.** in the course, process, or duration of: *to mellow with age.* **16.** from: *I hate to part with my favorite things.* **17.** against: *The English fought with the Germans.* **18.** in the region, sphere, experience, opinion, or view of: *It is summer with us while it is winter with the Australians.* **19.** by means of; by using: *to work with a machine, cut meat with a knife.* **20.** using; showing: *Work with care.* **21.** as a result of; because of; on account of: *green with age, eyes dim with tears.* **22.** by adding, furnishing, filling, etc., a material to something: *a ring set with diamonds.*
with it, *Slang.* informed; up-to-date; hip: *Mr. Gillard, a bachelor, is one of the new school of BBC heads—frank, approachable, and in every way "with it"* (Manchester Guardian Weekly). *Faced with a work of modern art,* [*he*] *isn't "with it"* (Harper's).
with that. See under **that,** *pron.*
[Old English *with* against]
—**Syn. 19. With, by, through** are used to connect to a sentence a word naming the agent that has performed an action or the means or instrument used to perform it. **With** is used to connect the word naming the instrument: *Write the letter with a pen.* **By** is used to connect the word naming the agent when it has not been named in the subject of the sentence, and sometimes to name the means: *The meat was taken by the dog. I travel by airplane.* **Through** is used to connect the word naming the means or the reason: *They ran through fear. We found out through him.*
with-, *prefix.* **1.** away; back, as in *withdraw, withhold.*
2. against; opposing, as in *withstand.*
3. along with; alongside; toward, as in *withal, without, within.*
[Old English *with-,* related to *with* with]
with·al (wiTH ôl′, with-), *Archaic.* —*adv.* **1.** with it all; as well; besides; also; moreover; likewise: *The lady is rich and fair and wise withal.* **2.** at the same time; in spite of all; notwithstanding; nevertheless. **3.** therewith: *Having spoiled the gods Of honours, crown withal thy mortal men* (Elizabeth Barrett Browning).
—*prep.* with: *Such eyes and ears as Nature had been pleased to endow me withal* (Lowell). [Middle English *with alle* < *with* + *all*]
with·draw (wiTH drô′, with-), *v.,* **-drew, -drawn, -draw·ing.** —*v.t.* **1.** to draw back; draw away: *He quickly withdrew his hand from the hot stove.* **2.** to take back; remove: *Worn-out money is withdrawn from use by the government. He withdrew his savings from the bank.* —*v.i.* **1.** to draw back; draw away. **2.** to go away: *She withdrew from the room.* **3.** to demand the withdrawal of a statement, motion, proposal, etc. [< *with-* away + *draw*] —**Syn.** *v.t.* **2.** recall, retract. —*v.i.* **2.** leave. See **depart.** —**Ant.** *v.t.* **2.** deposit.
with·draw·a·ble (wiTH drô′ə bəl, with-), *adj.* that can be withdrawn.
with·draw·al (wiTH drô′əl, with-), *n.* **1.** a withdrawing or being withdrawn. **2.** a depriving or being deprived of the use of narcotic drugs: *Sudden withdrawal is the only procedure recognized and sanctioned by the Narcotics Bureau* (Wall Street Journal). —**Syn. 1.** retreat.
withdrawal symptom, any of various symptoms, such as profuse sweating, nausea, etc., induced in a person addicted to a drug when he is deprived of that drug: *If morphine is withheld, gross homeostatic imbalances occur that cause the distressing effects known as withdrawal symptoms* (Scientific American).
with·draw·ing room (wiTH drô′ing, with-), *Archaic or Historical.* a drawing room.
with·draw·ment (wiTH drô′mənt, with-), *n.* withdrawal.
with·drawn (wiTH drôn′, with-), *v.* the past participle of **withdraw.** —*adj.* retiring; reserved: *Overly sensitive persons are frequently withdrawn.*
with·drawn·ness (wiTH drôn′nis, with-), *n.* withdrawn or retired character.
with·drew (wiTH drü′, with-), *v.* the past tense of **withdraw.**
withe (wiTH, with, wīTH), *n., v.,* **withed, with·ing.** —*n.* **1.** a tough, flexible twig or branch, especially of willow, used for binding or tying, and sometimes for plaiting; withy. **2.** a flexible handle of a tool, to prevent or lessen jarring of the wrist.
—*v.t. Dialect.* **1. a.** to bind with a withe or withes. **b.** *U.S.* to take (deer) with a noose made of withes. **2.** to twist like a withe. [Old English *withthe*]
with·er (wiTH′ər), *v.i., v.t.* **1.** to lose or cause to lose freshness, vigor, etc.; dry up; shrivel: *The grass withered in the hot sun. Age had withered the old lady's face.* **2.** to feel or cause to feel ashamed or confused: *to wither at the thought of a public rebuke, to be withered by a scornful look.* [variant of Middle English *wydderen,* probably variant of *wederen* to weather. Compare WEATHER, verb.]
with·er·ing·ly (wiTH′ər ing lē), *adv.* in a manner tending to wither.
with·er·ite (wiTH′ə rīt), *n.* native barium carbonate, a rare white, gray, or yellowish mineral. *Formula:* $BaCO_3$ [< William *Withering,* 1741-1799, an English physician, who first described and analyzed it + *-ite*[1]]
withe rod, either of two North American shrubs of the honeysuckle family, varieties of viburnum, with tough, osierlike shoots and white or yellowish flowers.
with·ers (wiTH′ərz), *n.pl.* the highest part of a horse's or other animal's back, behind the neck.
wring one's withers, to subject one to emotional stress, pain, etc.; cause anguish; distress: *He wrings our withers in this, but perhaps he lacks the ability to awe us with the agonies of the soul* (Punch).
[apparently reduction of obsolete *widersome,* perhaps < Old English *wither* opposite, back]
with·er·shins (wiTH′ər shinz), *adv. Scottish.* **1.** in a direction contrary to the apparent course of the sun (considered as unlucky or causing disaster). **2.** *Obsolete.* in a direction opposite to the usual; in the wrong way. Also, **widdershins, widershins.** [earlier *widdershins* < Middle Low German *weddersinnes,* Middle High German *widersinnes* < *wider* against, opposed + *-sind* way, direction + *-es* -s[2]]
with·held (with held′, wiTH-), *v.* the past tense and past participle of **withhold.**
with·hold (with hōld′, wiTH-), *v.,* **-held, -hold·ing.** —*v.t.* **1.** to refrain from giving or granting: *There was no school play because the principal withheld his consent.* **2.** to hold back; keep back: *to withhold one's men from attacking.* —*v.i.* to refrain (from): *to withhold from spreading the news.* [< *with-* back, away + *hold*[1]] —**with·hold′er,** *n.* —**Syn.** *v.t.* **2.** See **keep.**
with·hold·ing tax (with hōl′ding, wiTH-), a tax deducted from a salary, wage, or other income at the time of payment by the person who pays it, on behalf of the government.
with·hold·ment (with hōld′mənt, wiTH-), *n.* the act of withholding.
with·in (wiTH in′, with-), *prep.* **1.** inside the limits of; not beyond: *The task was within the man's power. He guessed my weight within five pounds.* **2.** in or into the inner part of; inside of: *By the X ray, doctors can see within the body.* **3.** in the (inner) being, soul, or mind of: *And fire and ice within me fight* (A.E. Housman).
—*adv.* **1.** in or into the inner part; inside: *The house had been painted within and without. The curtains were white without and green within.* **2.** in the inner being; in the being, soul, or mind; inwardly: *to keep one's grief within.*
[Old English *withinnan* < *with* with, against + *innan,* adverb, inside]
with·in·doors (wiTH in′dôrz′, -dōrz′; with-), *adv. Archaic.* indoors.
with·in-named (wiTH in′nāmd′, with-), *adj.* specified by name within this or that document, clause, or other piece of writing.
with-it (wiTH′it′, with′-), *adj. Slang.* up-to-date and appreciative of the latest trends, fashions, etc.; hip; in: *Etams, who set out to get with-it trendy clothes as quickly as possible on to the backs of the girls* (Scotsman).
with·out (wiTH out′, with-), *prep.* **1.** with no; not having; free from; lacking: *A cat walks without noise. I drink tea without sugar.* **2.** so as to omit, avoid, or neglect: *She walked past without noticing us.* **3.** outside of; beyond: *Soldiers are camped within and without the city walls.*
—*adv.* **1.** on the outside; outside: *The house is clean within and without.* **2.** outside of the

inner being; with regard to external actions or circumstances; in relation to others: *at ease without and at peace within* (James Martineau).
—*conj. Dialect.* unless: *I will not come without you invite me.*
[Old English *withūtan* < *with* with, against + *ūtan,* adverb, outside]
➔ **a. Without** as a conjunction meaning "unless" (*He could not move without the Congress sent him supplies*), formerly common in both general and literary English, is now confined to nonstandard use.
b. For *without hardly* (or *scarcely*), see **hardly.**

with·out·doors (wiTH out′dôrz′, -dōrz′; with-), *adv. Obsolete.* outdoors.

with·stand (with stand′, wiTH-), *v.,* **-stood, -stand·ing.** —*v.t.* to stand against; hold out against; bear up under; oppose, especially successfully: *Soldiers have to withstand hardships. These shoes will withstand much hard wear.* —*v.i.* to offer resistance or opposition. [Old English *withstandan* < *with-* against + *standan* to stand] —**Syn.** *v.t., v.i.* resist, endure. See **oppose.**

with·stood (with stu̇d′, wiTH′-), *v.* the past tense and past participle of **withstand.**

with·y (wiTH′ē, with′-), *n., pl.* **with·ies,** *adj.* —*n.* **1.** a willow or osier; withe. **2.** a band or halter made of withes. —*adj.* resembling a withe in flexibility. [Old English *wīthig* < *withthe* withe + *-ig* -y[1]]

wit·less (wit′lis), *adj.* **1.** lacking sense; stupid; foolish: *a witless person, remark, etc.* **2.** not knowing; unaware: *to be witless of danger.* —**wit′less·ly,** *adv.* —**wit′less·ness,** *n.* —**Syn. 1.** brainless.

wit·ling (wit′ling), *n.* a person who fancies himself to be clever at repartee; would-be wit. [< *wit*[1] + *-ling*]

wit·loof (wit′lōf), *n.* endive. [< Dutch *witloof* (literally) white leaf]

wit·ness (wit′nis), *n.* **1.** a person who saw something happen; spectator; eyewitness. **2.** a person or thing that furnishes evidence or proof of the thing or fact mentioned: *Their tattered clothes were a witness of their poverty.* **3.** a person who swears to tell the truth in a court of law. **4.** a person selected to be present at some transaction in order to be able to testify that it occurred, especially one who signs a document to certify that he saw it executed. **5.** evidence; testimony.
bear witness, to be evidence; give evidence; testify: *The man's fingerprints bore witness to his guilt.*
—*v.t.* **1.** to see; perceive: *He witnessed the accident.* **2.** to be the scene or setting of (a fact or event): *the years that witnessed the Industrial Revolution.* **3.** to testify to; give evidence of: *Her whole manner witnessed her surprise.* **4.** to furnish evidence or proof of; betoken. **5.** to sign (a document) as a witness: *The two servants witnessed Mr. Smith's will.* —*v.i.* to give evidence; bear witness; testify (to, against).
[Old English *witnes* (originally) knowledge < *wit* wit, cleverness] —**wit′ness·er,** *n.*

Wit·ness (wit′nis), *n.* a member of Jehovah's Witnesses.

witness box, a rectangular enclosure in a British court occupied by a witness while giving evidence.

witness chair, a chair for a witness, especially on a witness stand.

witness stand, a place where a witness stands or sits to give evidence in a law court.

-witted, *combining form.* having a ____ wit or wits: *Quick-witted = having a quick wit.*

wit·ti·cism (wit′ə siz əm), *n.* a witty remark. —**Syn.** quip, mot.

wit·ti·ly (wit′ə lē), *adv.* in a witty manner; with wit.

wit·ti·ness (wit′ē nis), *n.* the character of being witty; quality of being ingenious or clever.

wit·ting (wit′ing), *adj.* done or acting consciously, and so with responsibility; not unwitting; intentional: *a witting aggressor, aggression, etc.* —*n. Dialect.* **1.** tidings; news. **2.** notice; warning.

wit·ting·ly (wit′ing lē), *adv.* knowingly; intentionally. —**Syn.** purposely, designedly.

wit·tol (wit′əl), *n. Archaic.* a man who is aware of and complaisant about the infidelity of his wife; contented cuckold. [Middle English *wetewold,* apparently < *weten* to wit, know + *-wold,* as in *cokewold* cuckold]

wit·ty (wit′ē), *adj.,* **-ti·er, -ti·est. 1.** full of wit; clever and amusing: *a witty person, a witty remark.* **2.** *Dialect.* **a.** intelligent; clever. **b.** skillful; expert. [Old English *wittig* wise, clever < *witt* reasoning + *-ig* -y[1]] —**Syn. 1.** facetious, droll.

wit·wall (wit′wôl), *n.* the green woodpecker. [< earlier German *Wittewal,* related to Middle Low German *wedewale.* Related to WOODWALL.]

wive (wīv), *v.,* **wived, wiv·ing.** —*v.i.* to take a wife; get married; marry (with). —*v.t.* **1.** to take as a wife. **2.** *Archaic.* to furnish with a wife. [Old English *wīfian*]

wi·vern (wī′vərn), *n. Heraldry.* a two-legged, winged dragon with a long, barbed tail. Also, **wyvern.** [earlier *wiver,* special use of Middle English *wyver,* and *guivre* serpent, viper < Old North French *wivre,* Old French *guivre* < Latin *vīpera*]

Wivern

wives (wīvz), *n.* the plural of **wife.**

wiz (wiz), *n. Informal.* wizard: *He thinks he's such a wiz at cars, but he couldn't locate that squeak* (Sinclair Lewis).

wiz·ard (wiz′ərd), *n.* **1.** a man supposed to have magic power. **2.** *Informal.* a very clever person; expert: *to be a wizard at math.* **3.** *Obsolete.* a wise man; sage (often contemptuous).
—*adj.* **1.** magic. **2.** *British Slang.* very good, excellent, etc.: *a wizard time.*
[Middle English *wysard* < *wise* wise, smart + *-ard,* a noun suffix]

wiz·ard·ly (wiz′ərd lē), *adj.* of or like a wizard.

wiz·ard·ry (wiz′ər drē), *n.* magic skill; magic. —**Syn.** sorcery, witchcraft.

wiz·en (wiz′ən, wē′zən), *v.i.* to dry up; shrivel; wither. —*v.t.* to cause to wither or shrivel. —*adj.* wizened. Also, **weazen.** [Old English *wisnian* dry up, shrivel]

wiz·ened (wiz′ənd, wē′zənd), *adj.* dried up; withered; shriveled: *a wizened apple, a wizened face.* —**Syn.** shrunken, wrinkled.

wiz·en-faced (wiz′ən fāst′, wē′zən-), *adj.* having a thin, shriveled face.

wk., **1.** week. **2.** work.

wks., **1.** weeks. **2.** works.

w.l., **1.** water line. **2.** wave length.

WLB (no periods), War Labor Board.

w. long. or **W. long.,** west longitude.

Wm., William.

W.M., worshipful master (in Freemasonry).

WMC (no periods), War Manpower Commission.

wmk., watermark.

WMO (no periods) or **W.M.O.,** World Meteorological Organization.

WNW (no periods) or **W.N.W.,** between west and northwest; west-northwest.

wo (wō), *n., interj.* woe.

W.O. or **WO** (no periods), **1.** War Office. **2.** warrant officer.

woad (wōd), *n.* **1.** a European plant of the mustard family, formerly extensively cultivated for the blue dye furnished by its leaves; dyer's-weed; pastel. **2.** the dye. [Old English *wād*]

woad·ed (wō′did), *adj.* dyed or colored blue with woad.

woad·wax·en (wōd′wak′sən), *n.* an Old World yellow-flowered shrub of the pea family; dyeweed; dyer's-broom. Its flowers were formerly used as the source of a yellow dye. Also, **woodwaxen.** [alteration (influenced by *woad*) of *woodwaxen* < Old English *wuduweaxen,* oblique case of *wuduweaxe* < *wudu* wood, tree + *-weaxe,* related to *weaxan* to wax, grow]

woald (wōld), *n.* weld[2].

wob·ble (wob′əl), *v.,* **-bled, -bling,** *n.* —*v.i.* **1.** to move unsteadily from side to side. **2.** to shake or quiver, as jelly, one's voice, etc.; tremble; quaver. **3.** to be uncertain, unsteady, or inconstant; waver. —*v.t. Informal.* to cause to wobble.
—*n.* the act of wobbling. Also, **wabble.**
[perhaps < Low German *wabbeln*]

wobble pump, a hand pump in an airplane by which fuel may be transferred from an auxiliary tank to a main tank, or to the engine, or for use when the power pump fails.

wob·bler (wob′lər), *n.* **1.** a person or thing that wobbles. **2.** a person or animal that walks unsteadily. **3.** a person who wavers in his opinions. Also, **wabbler.**

wob·bli·ness (wob′lē nis), *n.* the state of being wobbly: *We feel the wobbliness of a bear on roller skates* (Atlantic).

wob·bling (wob′ling), *adj.* that wobbles. Also, **wabbling.** —**wob′bling·ly,** *adv.*

wob·bly[1] (wob′lē), *adj.,* **-bli·er, -bli·est.** unsteady; shaky; wavering. Also, **wabbly.**

wob·bly[2] or **Wob·bly** (wob′lē), *n., pl.* **-blies.** *U.S. Slang.* a member or adherent of the Industrial Workers of the World (a federation of industrial unions active in the United States between about 1905 and 1918). [American English; origin unknown]

wo·be·gone (wō′bi gôn′, -gon′), *adj.* woebegone.

WOC (no periods) or **W.O.C.,** *U.S.* **1.** without compensation (said of a businessman working without pay as an expert for the federal government while drawing a salary from his firm). **2.** such a businessman.

Wo·den or **Wo·dan** (wō′dən), *n.* the most important Anglo-Saxon god, corresponding to Odin in Norse mythology. [modern revival of Old English *Wōden.* Compare ODIN, WEDNESDAY.]

wodge (woj), *n. British.* a lumpy, protuberant object: . . . *A wodge in his left breast pocket* (Chambers's Journal). [perhaps alteration of *wedge*]

woe (wō), *n.* great grief, trouble, or distress: *Sickness and poverty are common woes. For never was a story of more woe Than this of Juliet and her Romeo* (Shakespeare).
—*interj.* an exclamation of grief, trouble, or distress; alas! Also, **wo.**
woe worth, *Archaic.* a curse upon; cursed be: *Woe worth the day, while, time, etc.*
[Old English *wā* interjection]
—**Syn.** *n.* sorrow.

woe·be·gone (wō′bi gôn′, -gon′), *adj.* **1.** looking sad, sorrowful, or wretched. **2.** *Obsolete.* beset with woe or woes. Also, **wobegone.** [< Middle English *wo bigon,* in phrase *me is wo begon* woe has beset me < *wo* woe + *begon* beset] —**woe′be·gone′ness,** *n.*

woe·ful (wō′fəl), *adj.* **1.** full of woe; sad; sorrowful; wretched. **2.** pitiful. **3.** of wretched quality. —**woe′ful·ly,** *adv.* —**woe′ful·ness,** *n.* —**Syn. 1.** mournful, distressed, miserable.

woe·some (wō′səm), *adj.* woeful.

wo·ful (wō′fəl), *adj.* woeful. —**wo′ful·ly,** *adv.* —**wo′ful·ness,** *n.*

wog[1] (wog), *n. British Slang.* a native of one of the former British colonies, especially in the Middle East (used in an unfriendly way). [origin uncertain]

wog[2] (wog), *n. Australian.* any germ, small insect, or grub. [origin uncertain]

woi·wode (woi′wōd), *n.* voivode.

W.O. (jg.), warrant officer (junior grade).

woke (wōk), *v.* waked; a past tense and a past participle of **wake**[1].
➔ See **wake**[1] for a usage note.

wo·ken (wō′kən), *v. Archaic and Dialect.* waked; a past participle of **wake**[1].

wold[1] (wōld), *n.* **1.** high, rolling country, bare of woods. **2.** *Obsolete.* wooded upland. [Old English *wald* (originally) wooded country, a wood. Related to WEALD.]

wold[2] (wōld), *n.* weld[2].

wold[3] (wōld), *v. Obsolete.* a past participle of **will**[1].

wolf (wu̇lf), *n., pl.* **wolves,** *v.* —*n.* **1.** any of several wild carnivorous mammals, somewhat like a dog and belonging to the same family. See **timber wolf** for picture. **2.** the fur of any of these animals. **3.** any animal in some way resembling a wolf, as the thylacine (Tasmanian wolf) or the hyena. **4.** any of certain beetle or moth larvae that infest granaries. **5.** a cruel, greedy person. **6.** *Slang.* a man who flirts with or tries to entice women; philanderer. **7.** *Music.* **a.** the harsh, dissonant sound heard in some chords on the organ and other keyboard instruments when tuned by a system of unequal temperament. **b.** a chord or interval characterized by such a sound. **c.** a harsh sound due to faulty vibration in certain tones, the result of a defect in the instrument.
cry wolf, to give a false alarm: *The men . . . who have been veering ever closer to Moscow as the price of Soviet Military and economic aid, have a habit of crying wolf* (Wall Street Journal).
keep the wolf from the door, to ward off or keep safe from hunger or starvation: *Business began to flag, and the most I could do was to keep the wolf from the door* (Peter Drake).
throw to the wolves, to abandon to a hostile enemy: *Canada will not be saved by throwing Rhodesia to the wolves* (Maclean's).

 PRONUNCIATION KEY: hat, āge, cãre, fär; let, ēqual, tėrm; it, īce; hot, ōpen, ôrder; oil, out; cup, pu̇t, rüle;

wolf in sheep's clothing, a hypocrite: *This tender lamb has been allowed to wander out . . . while a wolf in sheep's clothing was invited into the* [*community*] (Anthony Trollope).
—*v.t.* to eat like a wolf; devour greedily or ravenously.
[Old English *wulf*] —**wolf'like',** *adj.*

Wolf (wu̇lf), *n.* the southern constellation Lupus.

wolf·ber·ry (wu̇lf'ber'ē), *n., pl.* **-ries.** a North American shrub of the honeysuckle family, allied to the snowberry, sometimes grown for its ornamental white berries.

wolf child, a child believed to have been raised by wolves or other animals: *Those who want to emphasize the importance of environment can quote as their extreme case wolf children* (Punch).

wolf cub, a member of the junior organization of Boy Scouts in Great Britain, corresponding to an American cub scout.

wolf dog, **1.** any of various large dogs formerly kept for hunting wolves. **2.** a hybrid of a dog and a wolf.

wolf eel, the wolf fish of California.

wolf·er (wu̇l'fər), *n.* a hunter of wolves; wolver.

Wolff·i·an (wu̇l'fē ən, vôl'-), *adj.* having to do with or first noted by Kaspar Friedrich Wolff, 1733-1794, a German anatomist, physiologist, and embryologist.

Wolffian body, mesonephros.

wolf fish, **1.** any of certain large, voracious marine fishes having numerous sharp teeth and edible flesh, related to the blennies. **2.** lancet fish.

wolf·hound (wu̇lf'hound'), *n.* any of various breeds of large dogs formerly kept for hunting wolves and other animals, as the Irish wolfhound, the tallest (about 30 inches at the shoulder) of all dogs, somewhat similar to a greyhound in build but with a rough coat, and the borzoi or Russian wolfhound, a smaller dog with a silky coat. See **Irish wolfhound** and **borzoi** for pictures.

wolf·ish (wu̇l'fish), *adj.* **1.** like a wolf; greedy; savage: *a wolfish-looking dog, a wolfish cruelty, a wolfish appetite.* **2.** of or having to do with a wolf or wolves. —**wolf'ish·ly,** *adv.* —**wolf'ish·ness,** *n.* —**Syn. 1.** rapacious.

wolf·kin (wu̇lf'kin), *n.* a young wolf.

wolf·ling (wu̇lf'ling), *n.* a wolfkin.

wolf pack, **1.** a pack of wolves. **2.** (in World War II) a body of submarines acting in concert against enemy shipping, especially a body of German submarines using tactics such as are traditionally ascribed to wolves, as of harrying pursuit or mass assault at night.

wolf·ram (wu̇l'frəm), *n.* **1.** a metallic chemical element used in making steel and for electric lamp filaments; tungsten. It has stable and radioactive isotopes. *Symbol:* W (no period). **2.** wolframite. [< German *Wolfram*, perhaps < *Wolf* wolf + *Rahm* cream, foam (in Middle High German, filth, soot) (because it was originally thought to be of inferior quality)]

wolf·ram·ite (wu̇l'frə mīt), *n. Mineralogy.* a native, black or brownish tungstate of iron and manganese, an ore of tungsten. [< German *Wolframit* < *Wolfram* + *-it* -ite[1]]

wolf·ra·mi·um (wu̇l frā'mē əm), *n.* tungsten. [< New Latin *wolframium* < *wolfram* wolfram + *-ium*, a suffix meaning "element"]

wolf's·bane or **wolfs·bane** (wu̇lfs'bān'), *n.* any of several varieties of aconite, especially a European variety with yellowish flowers, sometimes called monkshood.

wolf·skin (wu̇lf'skin'), *n.* the skin or pelt of a wolf.

wolf spider, any of various large spiders with keen eyesight and strong legs and jaws, that stalk, rather than lie in wait for, their prey.

wolf whistle, *Slang.* a whistle consisting of a high and a low note, made by a male in appreciation of an attractive female: *This is one of the recognized meeting places of the sexes in Birmingham, and wolf whistles have become an everyday sound* (London Times).

wol·las·ton·ite (wu̇l'ə stə nīt), *n. Mineralogy.* a native silicate of calcium, occurring as crystals or in massive form. *Formula:* $CaSiO_3$ [< William H. *Wollaston*, 1766-1828, a British physicist and chemist + *-ite*]

Wo·lof (wō'lof), *n.* **1.** a member of a native tribe of Senegal and Gambia. **2.** the West Atlantic language of this tribe.

wolv·er (wu̇l'vər), *n.* a person who hunts wolves; wolfer.

wol·ver·ine or **wol·ver·ene** (wu̇l'və rēn', wu̇l'və rēn), *n.* **1.** a clumsy, heavily built carnivorous mammal of northern North America, Europe, and Asia, related to the weasel and badger; carcajou. It is noted for its strength, ferocity, and stealth, and is called the glutton in Europe. **2.** its fur. [earlier *wolvering*, perhaps < obsolete *wolver* a wolfish animal < *wolf*]

Wolverine (def. 1) (about 2½ ft. long)

Wol·ver·ine (wu̇l'və rēn', wu̇l'və rēn), *n.* a nickname for a native or inhabitant of Michigan.

Wolverine State, a nickname for Michigan.

wolves (wu̇lvz), *n.* the plural of **wolf.**

wolv·ish (wu̇l'vish), *adj. Obsolete.* wolfish.

wom·an (wu̇m'ən), *n., pl.* **wom·en. 1.** the adult human female. **2.** women as a group; the average woman: *When lovely woman stoops to folly* (Oliver Goldsmith). **3.** woman's nature; womanliness. **4.** a female servant or attendant. **5.** a wife. **6.** a mistress; paramour.
—*adj.* **1.** of or characteristic of a woman or women; feminine. **2.** female (used especially with designations of occupation or profession, and in the plural with a plural noun): *a woman lawyer, women lawyers.*
—*v.t.* **1.** to call (a person) "woman," especially derogatorily or jocularly. **2.** *Obsolete.* **a.** to cause to act like a woman. **b.** to unite to or accompany by a woman.
[Middle English *womman*, earlier *wummon*, Old English *wimman*, alteration of *wīfman* < *wīf* woman + *man* human being]
—**Syn.** *n.* **1.** See **female.**
➤ See **man** for usage note.

wom·an-hat·er (wu̇m'ən hā'tər), *n.* a person who hates or dislikes women.

wom·an·hood (wu̇m'ən hu̇d), *n.* **1.** the condition or time of being a woman. **2.** the character or qualities of a woman. **3.** women as a group; womankind: *Joan of Arc was an honor to womanhood.*

wom·an·ish (wu̇m'ə nish), *adj.* **1. a.** characteristic of a woman or women; womanly; feminine. **b.** (of a girl) like a grown woman. **2.** like a woman; womanlike; effeminate (now chiefly derogatory). —**wom'an·ish·ly,** *adv.* —**wom'an·ish·ness,** *n.*

wom·an·i·ty (wu̇ man'ə tē), *n.* the normal disposition or character of womankind: *What will it profit a woman to gain an Oxford degree and lose her womanity* (London Daily Telegraph). [*woman* + *-ity*, patterned on *humanity*]

wom·an·ize (wu̇m'ə nīz), *v.,* **-ized, -iz·ing.** —*v.t.* to make effeminate or weak; emasculate. —*v.i. Informal.* to consort illicitly with women: *We womanized, we cheated, and we stole* (Edmund Wilson).

wom·an·iz·er (wu̇m'ə nī'zər), *n. Informal.* a man who pursues or consorts illicitly with women.

wom·an·kind (wum'ən kīnd'), *n.* the female sex; women.

wom·an·less (wu̇m'ən lis), *adj.* without a woman or women.

wom·an·like (wu̇m'ən līk'), *adj.* **1.** like a woman; womanly. **2.** (in derogatory use) womanish; effeminate.

wom·an·li·ness (wu̇m'ən lē nis), *n.* the character of being womanly.

wom·an·ly (wu̇m'ən lē), *adj.,* **-li·er, -li·est. 1.** like a woman. **2.** as a woman should be. **3.** suitable for a woman.

woman of the world, a woman who knows people and customs, and is tolerant of both.

wom·an·pow·er (wu̇m'ən pou'ər), *n.* power supplied by the physical work of women.

woman's rights, social, political, and legal rights for women, equal to those of men.

woman suffrage, **1.** the political right of women to vote. **2.** women's votes. —**wom'an-suf'frage,** *adj.*

wom·an-suf·fra·gist (wu̇m'ən suf'rə jist), *n.* a person who favors the right of women to vote.

womb (wüm), *n.* **1.** the organ in mammals that holds, protects, and (usually) nourishes the young till birth; uterus. **2.** a place containing or producing anything: *to emerge from the womb of time.* **3.** a hollow space or cavity, or something conceived as such, as the depth of night. **4.** *Obsolete.* the belly. [Old English *wamb*] —**womb'like',** *adj.*

wom·bat (wom'bat), *n.* any of a family of Australian burrowing mammals that have a thick, heavy body, short legs, and a general resemblance to a small bear (in Australia also called badger). A female wombat has a pouch for carrying her young. [< native Australian name]

Wombat (2 to 3 ft. long)

womb·y (wü'mē), *adj.* having a womblike cavity; hollow.

wom·en (wim'ən), *n.* the plural of **woman.**

wom·en·folk (wim'ən fōk'), *n.pl.* women.

wom·en·folks (wim'ən fōks'), *n.pl. Informal or Dialect.* womenfolk.

wom·er·a, wom·er·ah, or **wom·mer·ah** (wom'ər ə), *n.* a device used to throw spears by aborigines of Australia. Also, **woomera.** [< native Australian name]

won[1] (wun), *v.* a past tense and the past participle of **win.**

won[2] (wun, wu̇n, wōn), *v.i. Scottish.* to dwell; live (in a place or with someone). [Old English *wunian* dwell, be accustomed]

won[3] (won), *n., pl.* **won. 1.** the unit of money of North Korea. **2.** the unit of money of South Korea, used until 1953 and reestablished in place of the hwan in 1962, worth about ⅘ of a cent. [< Korean *won*]

won·der (wun'dər), *n.* **1.** a strange and surprising thing or event: *He saw the wonders of the city. It is a wonder that he turned down the offer.* **2.** a miracle: *to work wonders.* **3.** the feeling caused by what is strange and surprising: *The baby looked with wonder at the Christmas tree.*
do wonders, to do wonderful things; achieve or produce extraordinary results: *Inspired by your Ladyship . . . my steward has really done wonders* (Benjamin Disraeli).
for a wonder, as a strange and surprising thing: *For a wonder he was not seasick* (Charles Reade).
no wonder, a. no marvel or prodigy: *The lecturer is no wonder.* **b.** nothing surprising; not surprising: *It is no wonder that he resigned. No wonder he resigned. He resigned, and no wonder.*
—*v.i.* **1.** to feel wonder: *We wonder at the splendor of the stars.* **2.** to feel some doubt or curiosity; wish to know or learn; speculate: *to wonder about his sudden departure.* —*v.t.* **1.** to feel wonder at: *I didn't wonder that he won the prize.* **2.** to be curious about; think about; wish to know: *I wonder what happened.*
[Old English *wundor*] —**won'der·er,** *n.*
—**Syn.** *n.* **3.** amazement. -*v.i.* **2.** ponder.

wonder boy, a young man who is outstanding in his profession or field: *Dylan Thomas, the wild Welsh wonder boy, was the greatest lyric poet produced in this century* (Time).

wonder child, Wunderkind: *By reason of his marvellous piano playing, he was looked upon as a wonder child* (Catholic Magazine).

wonder drug, a drug with high, often spectacular success in treating diseases, especially an antibiotic; miracle drug.

won·der·ful (wun'dər fəl), *adj.* **1.** causing wonder; marvelous; remarkable: *The explorer had wonderful adventures.* **2.** surprisingly large, fine, excellent, etc. [Old English *wunderfull* (literally) full of wonder] —**won'der·ful·ly,** *adv.* —**won'der·ful·ness,** *n.*
—**Syn. 1. Wonderful, marvelous** mean causing wonder. **Wonderful** describes something so new and unfamiliar, out of the ordinary, beyond expectation, or imperfectly understood that it excites a feeling of surprise, admiration, puzzled interest, or, sometimes, astonishment: *The boys from New York saw some wonderful sights on their first trip across the continent.* **Marvelous** describes something so extraordinary, surprising, or astonishing that it seems hardly believable: *The machine that can translate from foreign languages is a marvelous scientific invention.*

won·der·ing (wun'dər ing), *adj.* that wonders. —**won'der·ing·ly,** *adv.*

won·der·land (wun'dər land'), *n.* a country, realm, or domain full of wonders.

won·der·less (wun'dər lis), *adj.* destitute of wonder: *. . . stood sick and wonderless at the same old clutter of bones and lies* (Atlantic).

won·der·ment (wun′dər mənt), *n.* **1.** wonder; surprise. **2.** an object of or a matter for wonder; wonderful thing.
wonder metal, a lightweight metal, such as titanium or zirconium, capable of withstanding great pressure, strain, and heat.
won·der·strick·en (wun′dər strik′ən), *adj.* overcome or very much affected by wonder, amazement, etc.
won·der·struck (wun′dər struk′), *adj.* wonder-stricken.
won·der·work (wun′dər wėrk′), *n.* **1.** a marvelous or miraculous act, achievement, etc. **2.** a wonderful work or structure. [Old English *wundorweorc* < *wundor* wonder + *weorc* work]
won·der·work·er (wun′dər wėr′kər), *n.* a person who performs wonders or surprising things.
won·der·work·ing (wun′dər wėr′king), *adj.* doing wonders or surprising things.
won·drous (wun′drəs), *adj.* wonderful. —*adv.* wonderfully. [alteration of Middle English *wonders* wondrous; genitive of *wonder* wonder] —**won′drous·ly,** *adv.* —**won′drous·ness,** *n.*
won·ky (wong′kē), *adj.,* **-ki·er, -ki·est.** *British Slang.* in poor condition, working order, etc.; likely to break down, collapse, etc.; unsound. [perhaps related to WANKLE]
won·na (wun′nə), *Scottish.* will not. [alteration of earlier *willna* < *will*[1] + *na*]
wont (wōnt, wunt), *adj., n., v.,* **wont, wonted** or **wont, wont·ing.** —*adj.* accustomed: *He was wont to read the paper at breakfast.*
—*n.* custom; habit: *He rose early, as was his wont.*
—*v.t. Archaic.* to make (a person, etc.) used (to); accustom. —*v.i. Archaic.* to be accustomed (to do something).
[Middle English *wuned* (originally) past participle of Old English *wunian* dwell, be accustomed. Related to WON[2].]
➤ Since **wont** has become relatively rare in spoken use, various spelling pronunciations have arisen, of which (wōnt) is the most common. The inherited pronunciation is (wunt).
won't (wōnt, wunt), will not. [contraction of Middle English *woll not* will not]
➤ In the eastern United States, for which evidence is available, (wunt) is the prevailing pronunciation in New England, most of New York, and northern Pennsylvania; (wōnt) predominates in and around New York City and Charleston.
wont·ed (wun′tid, wōn′-), *adj.* **1.** accustomed; customary; usual. **2.** *U.S.* made familiar with one's environment. —**wont′ed·ly,** *adv.* —**wont′ed·ness,** *n.* —**Syn. 1.** habitual.
won ton (won′ ton′), a thin soup containing dumplings made of noodle dough wrapped around meat. [< Chinese *wan t'an*]
woo (wü), *v.t.* **1.** to make love to; seek to marry. **2.** to seek to win; try to get: *to woo fame.* **3.** to try to persuade; urge. —*v.i.* **1.** to make love; court. **2.** to make solicitation or entreaty; sue (for). [Old English *wōgian*]
wood[1] (wůd), *n.* **1.** Often, **woods.** a large number of growing trees. **2.** the hard, compact, fibrous substance of which the stem of a tree, shrub, or other plant and its branches consist, lying between the bark outside and the pith within; xylem. **3.** trees cut into boards, planks, etc., for use; lumber or timber: *The carpenter brought wood to build a garage.* **4.** firewood. **5.** a thing made of wood. **6.** a cask; barrel; keg: *Wine drawn from the wood.* **7.** *Printing.* woodcuts collectively or a woodcut. **8.** *Music.* one of the wood winds. **9.** any of several golf clubs having a wooden head.
knock (on) wood, a. to hit a wooden object in the belief that this will prevent evil or misfortune: *"Right now," Egan said, doing so, "I'm knocking on wood"* (New York Times). **b.** to hope that misfortune will not happen or recur: *Only accident I've ever been damaged in. Knock wood* (New Yorker).
not to see the wood for the trees, to lose the view of the whole in the multitude of details: *Garrick . . . bears no very distinct figure. One hardly sees the wood for the trees* (Walter Pater).
out of the woods or (*British*) **wood,** out of danger or difficulty: *When a patient reaches this stage [of convalescence], he is out of the woods* (Owen Wister).
saw wood, *Informal.* **a.** to attend to one's own affairs: *Read what happened to Hannibal at Capua while the defeated Romans were busy sawing wood* (New York Evening Post). **b.** to sleep heavily: *When he is sawing wood, he really snores.*
touch wood, to knock wood: *We haven't had too many people killed, touch wood* (New York Times).
woods, the wood winds collectively of an orchestra or band: *The conductor signaled the strings to join the brasses and woods.*
—*adj.* **1.** made or consisting of wood; wooden. **2.** used to store or convey wood: *a wood box.* **3.** dwelling or growing in woods: *wood moss.*
—*v.t.* **1.** to plant with trees. **2.** to supply with wood, especially firewood. —*v.i.* Also, **wood up,** to get or take in a supply of wood for fuel: *We went on down the river, . . . stopping . . . occasionally to wood up* (Cecil Roberts).
[Old English *wudu,* earlier *widu*]
➤ **Woods** (def. 1), though plural in form, is usually singular (or collective) in meaning and is used both as a singular (*a woods*) and as a plural (*the woods are*).
wood[2] (wüd, wōd, wůd), *adj. Obsolete or Dialect.* **1.** mad; demented. **2.** furious; enraged. Also, **wud.** [Old English *wōd*]
wood acid, wood vinegar.
wood alcohol, methyl alcohol.
wood anemone, any of various anemones growing wild in woods. The common wood anemone has a white flower in the spring.
wood ant, 1. a large ant which lives in the woods. **2.** a white ant; termite.
wood betony, 1. betony. **2.** an herb, a lousewort, of the figwort family, growing in eastern North America, and bearing spikes of yellow or reddish flowers.
wood·bin (wůd′bin′), *n.* a bin or box for firewood.
wood·bind (wůd′bīnd′), *n.* woodbine.
wood·bine (wůd′bīn′), *n.* **1.** the common European honeysuckle, a climbing shrub with pale-yellow, fragrant flowers. **2.** any of certain other honeysuckles. **3.** the Virginia creeper. [Old English *wudubinde* any climbing plant < *wudu* wood + *binde* wreath. Compare BINE. Related to BIND.]
wood block, 1. a block of wood. **2.** a woodcut. —**wood′-block′,** *adj.*
➤ See **woodcut** for usage note.
wood·bor·er (wůd′bôr′ər, -bōr′-), *n.* an insect, crustacean, or mollusk that bores in wood: *The huge volumes of logs introduced into seawater provided ideal conditions for the breeding and growth of woodborers* (New Scientist).
wood·carv·er (wůd′kär′vər), *n.* a person who carves wood or makes woodcarvings.
wood·carv·ing (wůd′kär′ving), *n.* **1.** some object, as a figure, carved from wood. **2.** the art or process of making woodcarvings.
wood·chat (wůd′chat′), *n.* **1.** a European shrike. **2.** any of certain Asiatic birds related to the thrush. [< *wood*[1] + *chat*[1] a bird]
wood·chop·per (wůd′chop′ər), *n.* a person who chops wood, especially one who chops down trees; lumberjack.
wood·chuck (wůd′chuk′), *n.* a North American marmot; ground hog. Woodchucks grow fat in summer and sleep in their holes in the ground all winter. [American English, alteration (influenced by *wood*[1]) of *wejack* < Algonkian (Cree) *otchek,* or (Ojibwa) *otchig,* the name of the fisher, that is, the marten, transferred to the ground hog]

Woodchuck
(not including tail, 1¼ to 1½ ft. long)

wood coal, 1. lignite. **2.** *Archaic.* charcoal.
wood·cock (wůd′kok′), *n., pl.* **-cocks** or (*collectively*) **-cock. 1.** a small Old World game bird related to the snipe, with short legs and a long, sensitive bill used to probe the ground for worms. **2.** a similar and related bird of eastern North America. **3.** *Archaic.* a fool; simpleton (in allusion to the ease with which the woodcock is taken in a snare or net). [Old English *wuducoc* < *wudu* wood + *cocc* cock]

American Woodcock
(def. 2—including bill, about 1 ft. long)

wood·craft (wůd′kraft′, -kräft′), *n.* **1.** knowledge about how to get food and shelter in the woods; skill in hunting, trapping, finding one's way, etc. **2.** skill in working with wood.
wood·crafts·man (wůd′krafts′mən, -kräfts′-), *n., pl.* **-men.** a person skilled in woodcraft.
wood·cut (wůd′kut′), *n.* **1.** an engraved block of wood to print from. **2.** a print made from such a block.
➤ **Woodcut** in its broadest sense includes both *wood block* and *wood engraving.* In both, printing is by the relief method. In terms of black-and-white prints, the *wood-block* method produces black lines and masses against a white background, *wood engraving* the reverse. The strict technical distinction lies in the tools and the kind of block employed: in *wood block* knives and gouges are used on wood sawed with the grain; in *wood engraving* burins and sometimes punches are used on wood sawed across the grain.
wood·cut·ter (wůd′kut′ər), *n.* a man who cuts down trees or chops wood.
wood·cut·ting (wůd′kut′ing), *n.* **1.** the act or work of cutting down trees for wood. **2.** wood engraving.
—*adj.* **1.** having to do with or used in woodcutting: *Foresters naturally expect their woodcutting saws to become blunter* (New Scientist). **2.** of or having to do with the making of woodcuts.
wood duck, a North American duck with a large crest, short neck, and long tail, that builds its nest in hollow trees in the woods and frequents ponds and streams. The male is richly colored with green, blue, and purple upper feathers, and red, yellow, and white underparts.
wood·ed (wůd′id), *adj.* **1.** covered with trees: *The park is well wooded.* **2.** full of woods or forests: *a heavily wooded region.*
wood·en (wůd′ən), *adj.* **1.** made of wood. **2.** stiff; awkward: *a wooden manner.* **3.** dull; stupid. —**wood′en·ly,** *adv.* —**wood′en·ness,** *n.*
wood engraver, a person skilled in wood engraving.
wood engraving, 1. the art or process of making woodcuts. **2.** a woodcut.
➤ See **woodcut** for usage note.
wood·en·head (wůd′ən hed′), *n.* a stupid person; blockhead.
wood·en·head·ed (wůd′ən hed′id), *adj.* dull; stupid. —**wood′en-head′ed·ness,** *n.*
wooden horse, 1. *Greek Legend.* a huge, hollow horse made of wood and filled with Greek soldiers, used, according to Virgil's *Aeneid,* as a ruse by the Greeks during the Trojan War; Trojan horse. After the Trojans took it into their city, the Greeks stole out during the night and let their army into Troy. **2.** any of various wooden frames or supports, especially one having four legs, as a sawhorse.
wooden Indian, 1. a figure of an American Indian carved from a block of wood and brightly painted, often holding a tomahawk in one hand and cigars in the other, formerly often placed in front of a tobacco store as a means of identification and advertisement. **2.** *Informal.* a silent and impassive person.
wooden nickel, *U.S. Slang.* a worthless or fraudulent thing; wooden nutmeg: *You can't change the political system from above, because it produces leaders that are always trying to sell you wooden nickels* (New York Times).

Wooden Indian
(def. 1)

wooden nutmeg, 1. an imitation nutmeg made of wood, an alleged article of manufacture in Connecticut for export. **2.** something fraudulent.
wooden spoon, 1. a spoon made of wood, especially one presented at a college or university to the lowest of those taking honors. **2.** the lowest position in any list or set.
wooden tongue, actinomycosis affecting the tongues of cattle, hogs, and sheep.
wooden walls, ships or shipping as a defensive force: *The old wooden walls of Britain,*

as the Fleet was called a century or so ago (London Times).

wood·en·ware (wu̇d′ən wãr′), *n.* containers, etc., made of or carved from wood: *Tubs and rolling pins are woodenware.*

wood flour, very fine sawdust, especially that made from pine wood for use as a surgical dressing, in plastics, and in dynamite.

wood frog, a common brown frog of damp woodlands of northern and eastern North America, with a black spot on each side of the face.

wood grouse, any of various grouse inhabiting woods, as the spruce grouse.

wood hen, weka.

wood hoopoe, any of a group of African birds; irrisor.

wood·house (wu̇d′hous′), *n.* a house or shed in which wood is stored; woodshed.

wood hyacinth, an Old World plant, a squill, having drooping, usually blue, flowers. It is also called bluebell, (in Scotland) harebell, and wild hyacinth.

wood ibis, a large white wading bird with a naked head and black and white wings, that inhabits tropical and subtropical America; jabiru. See **ibis** for picture.

wood·i·ness (wu̇d′ē nis), *n.* the quality or state of being woody.

wood·land (*n.* wu̇d′land′, -lənd; *adj.* wu̇d′lənd), *n.* land covered with trees. —*adj.* of or in the woods; having to do with woods.

Wood·land (wu̇d′lənd), *adj.* of or having to do with a stage of North American Indian culture dating from 500 B.C., characterized by large burial mounds, core tools and grooved axes, and simple pottery: *He traced the derivation of some of the ceramic styles in this region to Woodland cultures of North America* (New York Times).

woodland caribou, a large caribou of wooded areas of southern Canada.

wood·land·er (wu̇d′lən dər), *n.* a person who lives in the woods.

wood·lark (wu̇d′lärk′), *n.* a European lark.

wood·less (wu̇d′lis), *adj.* without wood, timber, or woods; treeless.

wood lice, the plural of **wood louse.**

wood lily, orangecup lily.

wood lot, or **wood·lot** (wu̇d′lot′), *n. Especially U.S.* a plot of land on which trees are grown and cut.

wood louse, **1.** any of several small, terrestrial, isopod crustaceans that have flat, oval bodies and live in decaying wood, damp soil, etc. **2.** any of certain small insects, as termites, book lice, and mites, that live in the woodwork of houses.

wood·man (wu̇d′mən), *n., pl.* **-men. 1.** a man who cuts down trees for timber or fuel. **2.** a person who takes care of trees; forester. **3.** *Obsolete.* a person who lives in the woods. **4.** *Obsolete.* person who hunts game in a wood or forest. —**Syn. 1.** woodcutter.

wood·man·craft (wu̇d′mən kraft′, -kräft′), *n.* the business or skill of a woodman.

wood mice, the plural of **wood mouse.**

wood mouse, a deer mouse or other mouse that habitually lives in the woods.

wood note, or **wood-note** (wu̇d′nōt′), *n.* a musical sound made by a bird or animal of the forest.

wood nymph, **1.** a nymph that lives in the woods; dryad or hamadryad. **2.** a moth that destroys grapevines. **3.** any of certain tropical American hummingbirds. **4.** satyr.

wood opal, wood that has become petrified in the form of opal.

wood·peck·er (wu̇d′pek′ər), *n.* any of a group of birds of almost world-wide distribution having a sharp, chisel-like bill for drilling in trees, a long, sharp tongue for spearing insects, strong feet adapted for climbing tree trunks, and stiff tail feathers which serve as props, as the red-headed woodpecker, black and white with a red head, the downy woodpecker, having a black back with white markings, the similar but larger hairy woodpecker, the three-toed woodpecker, having ladderlike markings on its back, and the ivory-billed woodpecker, having a large crest.

Red-headed Woodpecker (9¾ in. long)

wood pewee, a small flycatcher of eastern North America with a plaintive call suggesting its name; pewee.

wood pigeon, **1. a.** a European pigeon with two whitish patches on the neck; ringdove. **b.** any of several related pigeons. **2.** a wild pigeon of western North America.

wood·pile (wu̇d′pīl′), *n.* a pile of wood, especially wood for fuel.

wood pitch, the dark residue yielded by wood tar on further distillation.

wood·print (wu̇d′print′), *n.* a print from an engraved or carved wood block; woodcut.

wood pulp, wood made into pulp by mechanical or chemical disintegration of wood fiber, used for making paper.

wood pussy, or **wood·puss·y** (wu̇d′pu̇s′ē), *n., pl.* **wood pussies** or **wood·puss·ies.** *U.S. Informal.* a skunk.

wood rabbit, the cottontail.

wood rat, pack rat.

wood ray, *Botany.* medullary ray.

wood rosin, rosin obtained from the stumps of pine trees by extraction and distillation.

wood·ruff (wu̇d′ruf), *n.* any of a group of low-growing Old World herbs of the madder family, with clusters of small white, pink, or bluish flowers and whorls of sweet-scented leaves. [Old English *wudurofe* < *wudu* wood + *-rofe,* meaning unknown]

woods (wu̇dz), *n.pl.* See under **wood**[1], *n.*

wood screw, a screw used in wood.

wood·shed (wu̇d′shed′), *n., v.,* **-shed·ded, -shed·ding.** —*n.* a shed for storing wood. —*v.i. Jazz Slang.* to practice or rehearse playing a piece of music, a musical instrument, etc.

wood·si·a (wu̇d′zē ə), *n.* any of a group of delicate ferns growing in rocky places in temperate and cold regions. [< New Latin *Woodsia* the genus name < Joseph *Woods,* 1776-1864, a British botanist]

wood·side (wu̇d′sīd′), *n.* the side or border of woods or a forest: *a lonely spot by a woodside* (George R. Gissing).

woods·man (wu̇dz′mən), *n., pl.* **-men. 1.** a man used to life in the woods and skilled in hunting, fishing, trapping, etc. **2.** a man whose work is cutting down trees; lumberman.

woods·man·ship (wu̇dz′mən ship), *n.* the condition or the skill of a woodsman; woodcraft.

Wood's metal, a fusible metal, an alloy of bismuth, lead, tin, and cadmium with a melting point between 60 and 75 degrees centigrade, used for electric fuses and plugs, in automatic fire alarms and sprinkler systems, etc. [< Bertram *Wood,* born 1889, an American metals engineer]

wood sorrel, **1.** any of a group of ornamental plants, especially a low woodland plant having small, white flowers streaked with purple; oxalis. **2.** sheep sorrel.

wood spirit, **1.** a spirit or imaginary being, fabled to dwell in or haunt woods. **2.** methyl alcohol.

wood stork, wood ibis.

wood sugar, the dextrorotatory form of xylose.

woods·y (wu̇d′zē), *adj.,* **woods·i·er, woods·i·est.** of, having to do with, or characteristic or suggestive of the woods; sylvan. [American English < *woods* + *-y*[1]]

wood tar, a dark-brown, poisonous, sticky substance produced by the distillation of wood, and containing resins, turpentine, etc. It yields pyroligneous acid, creosote and oils, and a dark residue (wood pitch) on further distillation. Wood tar is used as a preservative, disinfectant, etc.

wood thrush, **1.** a thrush with a white, spotted breast, common in the thickets and woods of eastern North America, noted for its sweet song; bellbird. **2.** (locally in England and Scotland) the missel thrush.

wood tick, **1.** any of a family of ticks (acarids) found frequently in woods. **2.** a deathwatch (insect).

wood turner, a person skilled in wood turning.

wood turning, the making of pieces of wood into various shapes by using a lathe.

wood-turn·ing (wu̇d′tėr′ning), *adj.* of or having to do with wood turning.

wood vinegar, a crude acetic acid; pyroligneous acid; wood acid.

wood·wall (wu̇d′wôl), *n. British Dialect.* the green woodpecker. Also, **witwall.** [< Middle Low German *wedewale* < *wede* wood + *wale,* meaning unknown. Related to WITWALL.]

wood warbler, any of a family of small American birds; warbler.

wood·ward (wu̇d′wərd), *n.* (formerly, in England) a forestkeeper or forester: *The woodward . . . could claim every tree that the wind blew down* (John R. Green).

wood·ware (wu̇d′wãr′), *n.* articles made of wood.

wood wasp, **1.** any of various wasps that burrow in wood, as species of a family, the female of which excavates a cell in decayed wood as a place to deposit her eggs. **2.** any insect of a family, the larvae of which burrow in the wood of trees.

wood·wax (wu̇d′waks′), *n. Obsolete.* woodwaxen (woadwaxen).

wood·wax·en (wu̇d′wak′sən), *n.* woadwaxen.

wood wind (wind), any one of the wood winds of an orchestra.

wood-wind (wu̇d′wind′), *adj.* of or having to do with wooden wind instruments.

wood winds, the wooden wind instruments of an orchestra, such as the clarinet, flute, bassoon, and oboe.

wood wool, fine shavings made from pine wood, used as a surgical dressing, in plaster, and as an insulating material: *The roof construction has been changed to slabs of wood wool in place of boarding* (Science).

wood·work (wu̇d′wėrk′), *n.* things made of wood; wooden parts inside of a house, such as doors, stairs, moldings, and the like.

wood·work·er (wu̇d′wėr′kər), *n.* a person who makes things of wood; worker in wood. —**Syn.** carpenter.

wood·work·ing (wu̇d′wėr′king), *n., adj.* making or shaping things of wood.

wood·worm (wu̇d′wėrm′), *n.* any worm or larva that is bred in wood or bores in wood.

wood·y[1] (wu̇d′ē), *adj.,* **wood·i·er, wood·i·est. 1. a.** of the nature of or consisting of wood; ligneous. **b.** (of a plant) of which wood is a constituent part; forming wood. **2.** like wood; tough and stringy: *Turnips become woody when they are old.* **3.** having many trees; covered with trees: *a woody hillside.* **4. a.** of, having to do with, or situated in a wood. **b.** *Obsolete.* belonging to, inhabiting, or growing in woods or woodland; sylvan.

wood·y[2] (wu̇d′ē, wü′dē), *n., pl.* **wood·ies.** *Scottish.* widdy (rope). [variant of *widdy*[1]]

wood·yard (wu̇d′yärd′), *n.* a yard or enclosure in which wood is chopped, sawed, or stored, especially for use as fuel.

woody nightshade, bittersweet.

woo·er (wü′ər), *n.* a person or animal that woos; suitor.

woof[1] (wüf), *n.* **1.** the threads or yarn running from side to side across a loom, or those in a woven fabric which cross the warp; filling; weft. See **weave** for picture. **2.** fabric; cloth; texture. [earlier *wofe,* alteration (influenced by *wove*) of Middle English *ōf,* Old English *ōwef* < *ō-,* a prefix + *wefan* to weave. Compare WEFT.]

woof[2] (wüf), *n.* the sound of a dog barking. —*v.i.* to make such a sound. [imitative]

woof·er (wu̇f′ər), *n.* a loudspeaker that reproduces or is designed especially to reproduce sound below the treble register. [apparently < *woof*[2] + *-er*[1]. Compare TWEETER.]

woo·ing·ly (wü′ing lē), *adv.* in the manner of wooing; invitingly.

wool (wu̇l), *n.* **1.** the fine, soft, curly hair forming the fleece or fleecy coat of the sheep and some other animals, as the goat and alpaca, characterized by its property of felting due to the overlapping of minute surface scales. Sheep's wool is next to cotton in importance as a material for clothing. **2. a.** clothing or material made of wool: *to wear wool in cold weather.* **b.** yarn made of wool, used for knitting, embroidery, etc.; worsted. **3.** any of various fine, fibrous substances, naturally or artificially produced, used in place of wool. **4.** a yarn or material resembling wool, made from cellulose. **5.** something like wool: *steel wool.* **6.** a downy substance found on certain plants, or the furry hair of some insects, as the caterpillar. **7.** short, thick, curly hair. **8.** wool sponge.

pull the wool over one's eyes, *Informal.* to deceive or trick one: *I don't propose he shall pull the wool over my eyes* (William Dean Howells).

—*adj.* **1.** made of wool; woolen. **2.** of or having to do with the manufacture, storage, transportation, or sale of wool or woolen goods.

[Old English *wull*]

wool clip, the quantity of raw wool produced annually; total amount of wool sheared in a year.

wool·comb·er (wu̇l′kō′mər), *n.* a person or thing that combs or cards wool.
wooled (wu̇ld), *adj.* covered with wool; with the wool still on; unshorn: *a wooled lamb, wooled sheepskins.*
-wooled, *combining form.* having ____ wool: *Fine-wooled = having fine wool.*
wool·en (wu̇l′ən), *adj.* **1.** made of wool. **2.** of or having to do with wool or cloth made of wool. —*n.* yarn or fabric made of wool.
woolens, cloth or clothing made of wool: *The exportation of Irish woolens to the colonies and to foreign countries was prohibited* (George Bancroft).
wool fat or **grease,** the fatty coating on sheep's wool; lanolin.
wool·fell (wu̇l′fel′), *n.* a sheepskin with the fleece on it. [Middle English *wolle felle* < *wolle* wool + *felle* fell, skin]
wool·gath·er·er (wu̇l′gaᴛʜ′ər ər), *n.* a daydreaming or absent-minded person.
wool·gath·er·ing (wu̇l′gaᴛʜ′ər ing, -gaᴛʜ′-ring), *n.* **1.** an absorption in daydreaming; absent-mindedness. **2.** the gathering up of fragments of wool torn from sheep by bushes, etc. —*adj.* inattentive; absent-minded.
wool·grow·er (wu̇l′grō′ər), *n.* a person who raises sheep for their wool.
wool·grow·ing (wu̇l′grō′ing), *adj.* producing sheep and wool. —*n.* the raising of sheep for their wool.
wool·hat (wu̇l′hat′), *U.S. Informal.* —*n.* a Southern farmer or back-country rustic: *The businessmen like him; so do the Republicans and the downstate woolhats* (Harper's). —*adj.* of the Southern back-country region: *a woolhat politician.*
wool·i·ness (wu̇l′ē nis), *n.* woolliness.
woolled (wu̇ld), *adj. Especially British.* wooled.
wool·len (wu̇l′ən), *adj., n. Especially British.* woolen.
wool·li·ness (wu̇l′ē nis), *n.* the quality or state of being woolly.
wool·ly (wu̇l′ē), *adj.,* **-li·er, -li·est,** *n., pl.* **-lies.** —*adj.* **1.** consisting of wool; fleecy: *the woolly coat of a sheep.* **2.** of the nature, texture, or appearance of wool; like wool: *woolly hair, woolly clouds.* **3.** covered with wool or something like it: *woolly sheep.* **4.** not definite; confused and hazy; muddled; unclear: *The report . . . is woolly in such a way that almost anything can be read into it, or out of it* (Manchester Guardian). *He considered the Act a very badly drafted one with very woolly thinking* (London Times). **5.** *U.S. Informal.* rough and uncivilized like the Western part of the United States in frontier times (used especially in *wild and woolly*).
—*n.* **1.** *Western U.S.* a sheep. **2.** *Informal.* an article of clothing made from wool. Also, **wooly.**
woollies, *Informal.* woolen underwear: *I can still feel the thrill of exchanging my prickly woollies for soft cool cotton* (Maclean's).
—**Syn.** *adj.* **4.** vague, fuzzy, indistinct.
woolly bear, the hair-covered larva of a tiger moth. [because of its appearance]
wool·ly-head·ed (wu̇l′ē hed′id), *adj.* **1.** stupid; muddle-headed. **2.** having woolly hair on the head.
woolly mammoth, a large, extinct elephant formerly native to Europe and northern Asia, remains of which have been found in Siberia. See **mammoth** for picture.
wool maggot, the larva of the blowfly.
wool·man (wu̇l′mən), *n., pl.* **-men.** a dealer in wool; wool merchant: *The woolmen expect this trend to grow stronger even in the face of competition from synthetic fibers* (London Times).
wool·pack (wu̇l′pak′), *n.* **1.** a large cloth bag for carrying wool. **2.** a bundle or bale of wool weighing 240 pounds. **3.** a round, fleecy, cumulus cloud.
wool·sack (wu̇l′sak′), *n.* **1.** a bag of wool. **2. a.** the cushion, a large cloth-covered bag of wool, on which the Lord Chancellor sits in the British House of Lords. **b.** the office of Lord Chancellor.
wool·shed (wu̇l′shed′), *n.* a building or enclosure where sheep are sheared and their wool processed and stored: *Streams of sheep being driven towards the . . . big woolshed on a New Zealand high country sheep station* (London Times).
wool·skin (wu̇l′skin′), *n.* a sheepskin with the fleece on it.
wool·sort·er (wu̇l′sôr′tər), *n.* a person who sorts wool, especially one skilled in dividing wool into lots according to length, fineness of fiber, etc.
woolsorters' disease, a form of anthrax attacking man and caused by the inhalation of dust contaminated with spores of a bacterium; pulmonary anthrax.
wool sponge, any of certain tough, flexible sponges, important commercially.
wool stapler, a merchant who buys wool from the producer, grades it, and sells it to the manufacturer.
wool top, fleece from the sheep's back, cleaned and combed into strands, but not yet spun into yarn.
wool wax, wool fat.
wool·work (wu̇l′wėrk′), *n.* needlework done with wool, as on canvas.
wool·y (wu̇l′ē), *adj.,* **wool·i·er, wool·i·est,** *n., pl.* **wool·ies.** woolly.
woo·mer·a (wü′mər ə), *n.* womera.
woo·ra·li (wü rä′lē), *n.* curare; oorali.
woo·ra·ri (wü rä′rē), *n.* curare.
wooz·i·ly (wü′zə lē, wu̇z′ə-), *adv.* in a woozy manner: *I sat up woozily and felt the back of my head, wet and pulpy, like a bruised avocado* (Punch).
wooz·y (wü′zē, wu̇z′ē), *adj.,* **wooz·i·er, wooz·i·est.** *Informal.* **1.** somewhat dizzy or weak: *to be just over an illness and still a little woozy. "Motion sickness"—the woozy feeling suffered by some troops while riding* (Baltimore Sun). **2.** muddled; confused: *a mind woozy from fatigue.* **3.** slightly drunk; tipsy. [probably a variant of *oozy*[2] muddy]
wop (wop), *v.,* **wopped, wop·ping,** *n.* whop.
wops (wops), *n. Dialect.* a wasp or hornet. [Old English *waps.* Compare WASP.]
wor·ble (wôr′bəl), *n.* the larva of a botfly, that infests squirrels. [variant of *warble*[2]]
Worces·ter china or **porcelain** (wu̇s′tər), a kind of china originating in Worcester, England.
Worces·ter·shire (wu̇s′tər shir, -shər), *n.,* or **Worcestershire sauce,** a highly seasoned sauce containing soy, vinegar, etc., originally made in Worcester, England.
Worcs (no period), Worcestershire.
word (wėrd), *n.* **1.** a sound or a group of sounds that has meaning and is an independent unit of speech; vocable: *We speak words when we talk. A free form which is not a phrase is a word. A word, then, is a free form which does not consist entirely of . . . lesser free forms; in brief, a word is a minimum free form* (Leonard Bloomfield). **2.** the writing, or printing, that stands for a word. *Bat, bet, bit,* and *but* are words: *This page is filled with words. Proper words in proper places make the true definition of style* (Jonathan Swift). **3.** a short talk: *May I have a word with you?* **4.** speech: *honest in word and deed.* **5.** a brief expression: *The teacher gave us a word of advice.* **6.** a command; order: *His word was law.* **7.** a signal; watchword; password: *The word for tonight is "the King."* **8.** a promise: *The boy kept his word.* **9.** news; tidings; information: *No word has come from the battle front.* **10.** a saying; proverb; maxim. **11.** *Electronics.* any set of symbols or characters stored and transferred by computer circuits as a unit of meaning.
be as good as one's word, to keep one's promise: *To be as good as my word, I bade Will to get me a rod* (Samuel Pepys).
beyond words, incapable of being expressed; indescribable; unutterable: *grief beyond words. Her kindness is beyond words.*
by word of mouth, by spoken words; orally: *He would rather tell him of this by word of mouth than by letter* (D.C. Murray).
eat one's words, to take back what one has said; retract: *The pretence that prices need not go up would . . . compel some Ministers to eat their words once it became clear that prices had in fact moved* (Manchester Guardian Weekly).
from the word go, *Slang.* from the very beginning: *The whole thing prospered from the word go* (Maclean's).
in a word, briefly: *Man, in a word, is dependent on that which lies outside himself* (Brooke F. Westcott).
in so many words, literally; in precisely that number of words; in those very words: *The Lord Mayor had threatened in so many words to pull down the old London Bridge* (Dickens).
man of his word. See under **man,** *n.*
mince words, to avoid coming to the point, telling the truth, or taking a stand by using ambiguous or evasive words: *The teacher did not mince words in telling the students of their poor homework.*
my word! an expression of surprise: *My word! . . . that's something like a mob* (Rolf Boldrewood).
not breathe a word, not to tell anything; keep something silent or confidential: *Promise not to breathe a word of this to anyone.*
on or **upon my word,** an expression of surprise: *Upon my word, I think the truth is the hardest missile one can be pelted with* (George Eliot).
put words into one's mouth, to change the meaning of or add to what someone is saying: *Mr. Stewart was saying they no longer wanted a defence agreement . . . . "You mustn't put words into my mouth," Mr. Stewart retorted* (Manchester Guardian Weekly).
take one at one's word, to take one's words seriously and act accordingly: *He started out with a confession that he knew nothing about it, and, confessing so much, I take it that the Senate will take him at his word* (New Yorker).
take one's word (for it), to believe one: *Take my word for it, there is nothing in it* (Sir Richard Steele).
take the words out of one's mouth, to anticipate what another was about to say: *That's just what I had in mind; you took the words out of my mouth.*
the last word. See under **last word.**
the Word, a. the Bible; the Scriptures or a part of them: *Read us a chapter out of the Bible. I am very low in my mind, and at such times I like to hear the Word* (Henry Kingsley). **b.** the message of the gospel: *to spread the Word.* **c.** the Logos; the Son of God as a manifestation of God to mankind; the second person of the Trinity: *In the beginning was the Word, and the Word was with God, and the Word was God* (John 1:1).
word for word, in the exact words: *to repeat something word for word.*
words, a. angry talk; quarrel; dispute: *sharp words, to have words with a person.* **b.** the text of a song as distinguished from the notes; lyrics: *To the selfsame tune and words . . .* (Shakespeare).
—*v.t.* to put into or express in words; phrase: *Word your ideas clearly.*
[Old English *word*]
—**Syn.** *n.* **3.** conversation. **4.** utterance. **6.** bidding, behest. **8.** pledge. **9.** report.
word·age (wėr′dij), *n.* words collectively; verbiage.
word-blind (wėrd′blīnd′), *adj.* suffering from word blindness.
word blindness, loss of the ability to read; alexia.
word·book (wėrd′bu̇k′), *n.* **1.** a list of words, usually with explanations, etc.; dictionary. **2.** the libretto of an opera or other musical work. —**Syn. 1.** lexicon.
word class, *Linguistics.* **1.** a class of words grouped together on the basis of the distribution of these words in sentences. **2.** such a class of words in Indo-European; part of speech.
word element, a combining form, prefix, suffix, or other element that by addition to a word modifies the word's meaning or use.
word-for-word (wėrd′fər wėrd′), *adj.* verbatim.
word·i·ly (wėr′də lē), *adv.* in a wordy manner; verbosely.
word·i·ness (wėr′dē nis), *n.* the quality of being wordy; verbosity.
word·ing (wėr′ding), *n.* a way of saying a thing; choice and use of words; phrasing: *Careful wording is needed for clearness.* —**Syn.** See **diction.**
word·less (wėrd′lis), *adj.* **1.** without words; silent; speechless. **2.** not put into words; unexpressed. —**word′less·ly,** *adv.* —**word′less·ness,** *n.*
word-mag·ic (wėrd′maj′ik), *n.* the use of a word or name in the belief that its utterance will magically alter, influence, or dispel the thing mentioned or named.
word·man (wėrd′man′), *n., pl.* **-men.** a man who deals with or has a command of words; a master of language: *Behind the derivations given in the dictionaries are stories that beguile wordmen and laymen alike* (Saturday Review).
word method, a way of teaching reading by learning words before teaching the letters.

word·mon·ger (wėrd′mung′gər, -mong′-), *n.* a person who deals in words, especially in pedantic or empty words: *The wordmongers who could clothe one shivering thought in a hundred thousand garments* (John Motley).

word·mon·ger·ing (wėrd′mung′gər ing, -mong′-), *n.* the act of dealing with words as a wordmonger does: *Too much time spent in mere wordmongering and lingual dissection* (Henry N. Hudson).

Word of God, the Word.

word of honor, a solemn promise.

word-of-mouth (wėrd′əv mouth′), *adj.* communicated by spoken words; oral. —*n.* word-of-mouth communication: *Chartercraft owners also rely on travel agents, word-of-mouth and advertising ... to drum up business* (Wall Street Journal).

word order, the arrangement of words in a sentence, phrase, etc. In English, the usual word order for statements is subject plus predicate, as in *John hit the ball. The ball hit John.* Other word orders (*Away ran John, Him the Almighty hurled ..., Sweet are the uses of adversity*) are chiefly rhetorical and poetic. In English, with its relative absence of inflections, word order is the chief grammatical device for indicating the function of words and their relation to each other.

➤ **word order.** The order of words and of other locutions in a sentence is a fundamental part of English grammar and in addition contributes to some effects of style, especially emphasis. The work done in many languages by inflections (endings) is in English performed largely by function words (prepositions, auxiliary verbs, and so on) and by the word order. Since we pick up the standard word order as we learn to talk, it offers little difficulty. We use naturally the subject-verb-object order of clauses and sentences, we put adjectives before their nouns and relative clauses after their nouns, and in general put modifiers near the words modified. Three instances in which word order is variable are: **1.** *Position changed for emphasis.* As a rule an element taken out of its usual position receives increased emphasis, as when the object is put before both subject and verb: Object first: *That book I read when I was sixteen.* (Instead of: *I read that book when I was sixteen.*) Predicate adjective first: *Lucky are the ones who register early.* (Instead of: *The ones who register early are lucky.*) **2.** *Interrupted constructions.* When a word or words interrupt a construction, the effect is usually unhappy unless the interrupting word deserves special emphasis: Between subject and verb: *Newspaper headlines in these trying and confused times are continually intensifying the fears of the American people.* (More natural: *In these trying and confused times newspaper headlines are ...*) Between verb and adverb: *He played quietly, efficiently on.* (More natural: *He played on, quietly, efficiently.*) **3.** *Misleading word order.* English usually has a modifier close to the word modified and care must be taken that modifiers separated from their main words are not misleading. Misleading: *Her uncle, King Leopold, was even unable to influence her. This success in villages will probably be duplicated in the cities as time goes on at an accelerated rate. Until recently the chains have been able to get special prices on the goods they buy from producers with little opposition.* Improved: *Even her uncle, King Leopold, was unable to influence her. As time goes on, this success in villages will probably be duplicated at an accelerated rate in cities. Until recently the chains have been able to get with little opposition special prices on the goods they buy from manufacturers.*

word painting, the art of describing or portraying in words; graphic, vivid, or colorful description.

word-per·fect (wėrd′pėr′fikt), *adj.* letter-perfect: *He went to the rostrum without notes of any kind, yet his exposition was word-perfect, logical and lucid* (London Times).

word picture, a picture presented in words; graphic or vivid description.

word·play (wėrd′plā′), *n.* a play of or upon words; repartee.

words (wėrdz), *n.pl.* See under **word,** *n.*

word-sign (wėrd′sīn′), *n.* any symbol or character that stands for a word. Word-signs in English are + for plus, $ for dollar, and F for Fahrenheit.

word·smith (wėrd′smith′), *n.* a person who deals with or has a command of words; a master of language.

word square, a set of words of the same number of letters to be arranged in a square so as to read the same horizontally and vertically.

P	A	S	T	E
A	C	T	O	R
S	T	O	M	A
T	O	M	B	S
E	R	A	S	E

Word Square

Words·wor·thi·an (wėrdz′wėr′thē ən, wėrdz′wėr′-), *adj.* of, having to do with, or characteristic of the English poet William Wordsworth, 1770-1850, or his works. —*n.* an admirer of Wordsworth.

word·y (wėr′dē), *adj.,* **word·i·er, word·i·est.** **1.** using too many words; verbose. **2.** consisting of or expressed in words; verbal (now used chiefly in *wordy war*).

—**Syn. 1. Wordy, verbose** mean using more words than are necessary. **Wordy** emphasizes the lack of succinctness apparent when many words are used to say something that could be expressed just as effectively in a few. **Verbose** emphasizes the obscurity and turgid effect produced by using too many long, high-sounding words and long, roundabout sentences that do not express meaning clearly or simply. —**Ant. 1.** terse, concise.

wore (wôr, wōr), *v.* the past tense of **wear**[1] and **wear**[2].

➤ See **wear**[1] for usage note.

work (wėrk), *n., adj., v.,* **worked** or **wrought, work·ing.** —*n.* **1.** physical or mental effort in doing or making something: *to stop work at five. Some people like hard work.* **2.** something to do; occupation; employment: *He went to work at sixteen.* **3.** something made or done; result of effort: *a work of art, works of Dickens.* **4.** a particular task, job, or undertaking: *to plan one's work for the day.* **5.** that on which effort is put: *The dressmaker took her work out on the porch.* **6.** *Physics.* **a.** the transference of energy from one body or system to another, causing motion of the body acted upon in the direction of the force producing it and against resistance. **b.** a measure of this; the product of the force and the distance that the point of application of the force moves, commonly expressed in ergs, kilogram-meters, or foot-pounds. *Abbr.:* w. **7.** the action, activity, or operation (of a person or thing), especially of a particular kind and with reference to result: *The medicine and suggestion have done their work.* **8.** embroidery; needlework. **9.** a fortification. **10.** material at any stage of manufacture or processing, as in a machine tool. **11.** a froth produced by fermentation during the process of making vinegar. *Abbr.:* wk. **12.** *Obsolete.* workmanship.

at work, working; operating: *Officials were insisting until a few days ago that the deflationary forces already at work in the economy ... would be sufficient* (Manchester Guardian Weekly).

make short work of, to do or get rid of quickly: *He watched enthusiastic samplers making short work of the cake* (New York Times).

out of work, having no job; unemployed: ... *the panic of '73, when there were a hundred and eighty thousand men out of work in New York State* (Edmund Wilson).

[Old English *weorc*]

—*adj.* of, for, having to do with, or used in work: *a work routine.*

—*v.i.* **1.** to do work; labor: *Most people must work for a living.* **2.** to be employed: *He works at an airplane factory.* **3.** to act; operate, especially effectively: *The radio will not work. The plan worked.* **4.** to behave (in a specified way) while being kneaded, pressed, shaped, etc.: *clay that works easily.* **5.** to ferment: *Yeast makes beer work.* **6.** to become (up, round, loose, etc.): *The window catch has worked loose.* **7.** to go slowly or with effort: *The ship worked to windward.* **8.** to go in a particular direction in some operation: *to work from left to right, work toward the back.* **9.** to move as if with effort: *Her face worked as she tried to keep back the tears.* **10.** to seethe, rage, or toss, as a stormy sea. **11.** (of a ship) to strain so that the fastenings become slack. **12.** *Machinery.* to move irregularly or unsteadily so as to become out of gear.

—*v.t.* **1.** to form; shape: *He worked an essay into an article.* **2.** to make by needlework; sew, knit, embroider, etc.: *to work a pair of socks, work embroidery.* **3.** to bring about; cause; do: *to work a change. The plan worked harm.* **4.** to put effort on: *He worked his farm with success.* **5.** to get or obtain (ore, coal, etc.) from a mine, etc.; get ore, coal, etc., from (a mine, quarry, etc.). **6. a.** to treat or handle in making; knead; mix: *to work butter, work dough to mix it.* **b.** to stretch, twist, or pull, to achieve a certain result: *to work rope to soften it.* **7.** to solve: *Work all the problems on the page.* **8.** to cause to do work: *He works his men long hours.* **9.** to carry on operations in (districts, etc.): *The salesman worked the Eastern States.* **10.** to put into operation; use; manage: *puppets worked with wires, to work a scheme, to work a ship away from the rocks.* **11.** to make, get, do, or bring about by effort: *He worked his way through college.* **12.** to influence; persuade: *to work men to one's will.* **13.** to move; stir; excite: *Don't work yourself into a temper.* **14.** *Slang.* to use tricks on to get something: *to work a friend for a job.* **15.** to cause (beer, etc.) to ferment.

work in, to put in; insert: *A ... tale in which several particulars ... are worked in with a lofty contempt for chronology* (Edward A. Freeman).

work off, to get rid of, especially by continuous action or effort: *to work off a debt.*

work on or **upon, a.** to affect or influence: *The medicine finally worked on him.* **b.** to try to persuade or influence: *He had many minds to work upon and to win over to his cause* (Edward A. Freeman).

work out, a. to plan; develop: *And they ... worked out with some precision the mechanics of a planned society* (Edmund Wilson). **b.** to solve; find out: *This ought to be worked out on paper like a problem in mathematics* (Graham Greene). **c.** to use up: *As soon as one tunnel was worked out, the miners dug another.* **d.** to exercise; practice: *I saw Barber work out in the gymnasium* (London Daily Express). **e.** to accomplish: *O lift your natures up: ... work out your freedom* (Tennyson). **f.** to proceed to a result; conclude: *It is ... impossible to tell ... how the situation in Ireland will work out* (Spectator). **g.** to make its way out, especially from being embedded or enclosed: *The splinter worked out from his finger.*

work out at, to amount to (so much): *The permutations ... for each of these functions work out at the alarming figure of 49 million* (Manchester Guardian Weekly).

work over, a. to do again or anew; repeat: *The old story was worked over for television.* **b.** *U.S. Slang.* to beat up; rough up: *One of my buddies got into an argument with a couple of German sharpies in a restaurant ... They waited outside and worked him over good* (Newsweek).

work up, a. to ascend; advance: *The Torridge is in full flood, and plenty of salmon are working up to spawn* (London Daily Telegraph). *He was merely working up to a peroration* (Rudyard Kipling). **b.** to make into something or prepare for use by labor: *The raw and prepared material [silk] ... is worked up in various ways* (Edmund Burke). **c.** to plan; develop: *Mártov had worked up a plan for persuading the German government to let them return through Germany* (Edmund Wilson). **d.** to stir up; arouse; excite: *It is never difficult for him to work himself up into a frenzy* (Manchester Guardian Weekly).

[Old English *wyrcean,* verb]

—**Syn.** *n.* **1. Work, labor, toil** mean effort or exertion turned to making or doing something. **Work** is the general word, applying to physical or mental effort or to the activity of a force or machine: *Keeping house is not easy work. This lathe does the work of three of the older type.* **Labor** applies to hard physical or mental work: *That student's understanding of his subjects shows the amount of labor he puts into his homework.* **Toil,** a word with some literary flavor, applies to long and wearying labor: *The farmer's toil was rewarded with good crops.* **3.** product, achievement, feat, deed. —*v.i.* **1.** toil, drudge, strive. **3.** perform. —*v.t.* **1.** fashion, mold. **3.** accomplish, effect. **10.** execute.

work·a·bil·i·ty (wėr′kə bil′ə tē), *n.* the quality of being workable; practicability; feasibleness.

work·a·ble (wėr′kə bəl), *adj.* that can be worked or used. —**work′a·ble·ness,** *n.* —**Syn.** practicable, feasible.
work·a·bly (wėr′kə blē), *adv.* in a workable manner; so as to be workable.
work·a·day (wėr′kə dā′), *adj.* of or characteristic of working days; practical; commonplace; ordinary: *workaday clothes.* —**Syn.** everyday.
work·bag (wėrk′bag′), *n.* a bag to hold the things that a person works with, especially a bag for sewing materials.
work·bas·ket (wėrk′bas′kit, -bäs′-), *n.* a basket to hold the things that a person works with, especially sewing materials.
work·bench (wėrk′bench′), *n.* a table at which a mechanic, carpenter, or other artisan works, especially a sturdy, benchlike table specially designed for and fitted with certain accessories required to do a certain kind of work.
work·boat (wėrk′bōt′), *n.* a boat used for work, as a fishing boat, etc.: . . . *workboats to carry out the steady stream of supplies needed by a drilling crew* (Listener).
work·book (wėrk′bu̇k′), *n.* **1.** a book containing outlines for the study of some subject. **2.** a book in which a student does parts of his written work, as answering questions and solving problems, and which also usually contains some instructional material. **3.** a book containing rules for doing certain work. **4.** a book for notes of work planned or work done.
work·box (wėrk′boks′), *n.* a box to hold the materials and tools a person works with.
work camp, 1. a summer camp for teenagers with a program of activities such as farming, building, arts and crafts, etc. **2.** a prison camp where inmates do farm work, build roads, etc. **3.** a camp where work is provided for unemployed youth.
work·day (wėrk′dā′), *n.* **1.** a day for work; usual working day, especially a weekday, not Sunday or a holiday. **2.** the part of a day during which work is done: *to put in a long workday.* —*adj.* workaday.
worked (wėrkt), *adj.* ornamented with needlework, engraving, or the like; shaped, fashioned, or dressed for use or ornament.
work·er (wėr′kər), *n.* **1.** a person or thing that works. **2.** the neuter or undeveloped female of certain social insects, as ants, bees, and wasps, that supplies food and performs other services for the community. **3.** (in communist or socialistic use) a person, other than a soldier or sailor, who works for a living. **4.** *Printing.* an electrotype plate used for printing. —**Syn. 1.** laborer, toiler, artisan, craftsman.
work·er-priest (wėr′kər prēst′), *n.* (in France and some other European countries) a Roman Catholic priest who spends part of his time working in a factory, etc., and living as an ordinary worker.
work·fel·low (wėrk′fel′ō), *n.* a person engaged in the same work with another.
work·folk (wėrk′fōk′), *n.pl.* working people, especially farm laborers.
work·folks (wėrk′fōks′), *n.pl.* workfolk.
work force, 1. a. the number of workers employed in an area, industry, plant, etc. **b.** the number potentially available for such employment. **2.** the group of workers in a specific plant or activity.
work function, the energy required to release an electron as it passes through the surface of a metal: *The minimum energy required, called the work function, can be supplied by heat, light or bombarding particles, usually other electrons or positive ions* (Scientific American).
work·horse (wėrk′hôrs′), *n.,* or **work horse, 1.** a horse used for labor, and not for showing, racing, or hunting. **2.** a very hard worker, especially one able to do many jobs or work long hours: *The bulldozer, workhorse of World War II, soon will get its biggest peacetime working orders from Dwight D. Eisenhower* (New York Times). —*adj.* of, having to do with, or like a workhorse: *The freighter is the workhorse vessel whose deep holds and cluttered decks carry American-produced autos, machine tools, foodstuffs, and other cargoes all over the globe* (Wall Street Journal). *Many U.S. technicians believe that the Russians have probably long since frozen their basic rocket design upon one model, and it now functions with workhorse reliability* (Time).

work·house (wėrk′hous′), *n.* **1.** *U.S.* a place where petty criminals are kept and made to work. **2.** *British.* **a.** (originally) a house established for the provision of work for the unemployed poor of a parish. **b.** (later) a house where very poor people are lodged and set to work. **3.** *Obsolete.* a place of regular work; workshop.
work·ing (wėr′king), *n.* **1.** the performance of work or labor: *laws to prevent working on Sunday.* **2. a.** the manufacture, production, or preparation of something, often of something requiring skill. **b.** the manner or style in which something is made; workmanship. **3.** the act of performing work on something; management of a machine, ship, mine, etc. **4.** the putting into operation or carrying on, as of a scheme, system, or law. **5.** operation; action: *We bend to that, the working of the heart* (Shakespeare). **6.** the process of solving a mathematical problem. **7.** a restless or agitated movement, as of the face or mouth, due to emotion. **8.** gradual movement or progress, especially against resistance. **9.** the act or process of fermenting, as of liquor.
workings, a. operation; action: *the workings of the mind. Do you understand the workings of this machine?* **b.** the parts of a mine, quarry, tunnel, etc., where work is being or has been done: *A warning system . . . for use at a colliery where methane was extracted from boreholes near the workings and piped to the surface* (Science News).
—*adj.* **1.** that works: *the working population.* **2.** of, for, or used in working: *working hours, working clothes.* **3.** used to operate with or by: *working expenses, a working majority.* **4. a.** performing its function; that goes: *a working model of a train.* **b.** that can be arranged or accomplished; workable: *a working agreement, a working arrangement.* **5.** providing a basis for further work: *a working hypothesis.* **6.** moving convulsively, as the features from emotion. **7.** (of liquor, etc.) fermenting.
working assets, invested capital that is more or less available for use if needed.
working capital, 1. the amount of capital necessary to run a business. **2.** the amount by which current assets exceed current liabilities. **3.** *Finance.* the capital of a business placed in liquid assets, as distinguished from buildings or other fixed assets.
working class, the lower and middle income groups of people who work for others.
work·ing-class (wėr′king klas′, -kläs′), *adj.* of, belonging to, or characteristic of the working class.
working cylinder, (in an internal-combustion engine) a cylinder in which the gas or vapor explodes.
working day, workday.
work·ing-day (wėr′king dā′), *adj.* workaday.
working drawing, a drawing, as of the whole or a part of a structure or machine, made to scale and in such detail with regard to dimensions, etc., as to form a guide for the workmen in the construction of the object represented.
work·ing·girl (wėr′king gėrl′), *n.* **1.** a girl who works. **2.** a girl who works with her hands or with machines.
work·ing·man (wėr′king man′), *n., pl.* **-men. 1.** a man who works. **2.** a man who works with his hands or with machines.
working papers, documents, as a certificate of age, that permit a child to leave school and go to work.
work·ings (wėr′kingz), *n.pl.* See under **working,** *n.*
working stroke, (in engines) the stroke of the piston during which the working fluid performs its useful work, that is, drives the piston outward.
working substance, the substance, such as a working fluid, that operates an engine or other prime mover.
working week, workweek.
work·ing·wom·an (wėr′king wu̇m′ən), *n., pl.* **-wom·en. 1.** a woman who works. **2.** a woman who works with her hands or with machines.
work·less (wėrk′lis), *adj.* out of work; unemployed.
work·load (wėrk′lōd′), *n.* the amount of work carried by or assigned to a worker or position: *Mr. Eisenhower's heart attack . . . increased the workload of the Vice President's office* (Wall Street Journal).
work·man (wėrk′mən), *n., pl.* **-men. 1.** a worker. **2.** a man who works with his hands or with machines.

work·man·like (wėrk′mən līk′), *adj.* skillful; well-done: *a neat, workmanlike job.* —*adv.* skillfully.
work·man·ly (wėrk′mən lē), *adj., adv.* workmanlike.
work·man·ship (wėrk′mən ship), *n.* **1.** the art or skill of a worker or his work. **2.** the quality or manner of work; craftsmanship. **3.** the work done. —**Syn. 3.** performance, achievement.
work·men's compensation (wėrk′mənz), the compensation which, as specified by law, an employer must pay to a worker who is injured or contracts a disease as a result of his employment.
work of art, a product of any of the arts, as a painting, statue, or literary or musical work; anything done or made with great skill; work of an artist.
work of supererogation, (in the Roman Catholic Church) a good work above and beyond what is prescribed for man by God, by which typically the lives of saints are characterized, but of which any human being is capable.
work·out (wėrk′out′), *n. Informal.* **1.** exercise; practice. **2.** a trial; test. —**Syn. 2.** tryout.
work·peo·ple (wėrk′pē′pəl), *n.pl. Especially British.* people who work, especially those who work with their hands or with machines.
work·piece (wėrk′pēs), *n.* a piece of metal or other material that is being worked on in a manufacturing process.
work·place (wėrk′plās′), *n.* a place where one does his work; workshop.
work·room (wėrk′rüm′, -ru̇m′), *n.* a room where work is done.
works (wėrks), *n.pl.* **1.** a place for doing some kind of work; factory. **2.** the moving parts of a machine or device: *the works of a watch.* **3.** buildings, bridges, docks, etc. **4.** acts that are done to obey or accord with the law of God; moral actions, especially in contrast to *faith* or *grace* in the doctrine of justification.
give (one) the works, *U.S. Slang.* **a.** to attack, criticize, or beat soundly; punish severely: *Anti-immigration members of Congress are set "to give President Eisenhower the works" in his attempt to liberalize the Refugee Relief Act* (New York Times). **b.** to kill: *They gave Caesar the works in the Capitol* (Punch).
in the works, *Informal.* in the planning stage; upcoming: *The usual struggle over public housing and slum clearance legislation is in the works* (Newsweek).
shoot the works, *U.S. Slang.* to go to the limit; go all-out in something; use, spend, etc., completely: *She suddenly decides to shoot the works with the little fortune he left behind* (New Yorker).
the works, *U.S. Slang.* everything: *Ray produced the works . . . needed to prepare heroin for injection* (New Yorker).
works council, *British.* a group of factory workers or other employees that consults with the employer on problems involving working conditions, wages, etc.
work·shop (wėrk′shop′), *n.* **1.** a shop or building where work is done. **2.** a course of study, discussion, or work for a group of people in a particular field or sphere of activity, with special stress on the learning of new techniques and developments: . . . *intensive journalism workshops* (New York Times).
Works Projects Administration, WPA.
work-shy (wėrk′shī′), *adj.* not willing to work; idle: *He argues very logically against the view that immigrants are work-shy parasites* (Manchester Guardian Weekly).
work song, a song sung by a gang of workers in rhythm with the motions made during their work.
work stoppage, a stopping of work within a company, plant, or industry, as due to a strike, layoff, etc.
work study, *British.* time and motion study.
work·ta·ble (wėrk′tā′bəl), *n.* a table to work at.
work to rule, *British.* **1.** a form of slowdown used by labor to force concessions from management in which work is slowed down by the deliberate, punctilious observance of every working rule and regulation. **2.** to slow down work by the punctilious observance of working rules.
work-up (wėrk′up′), *n. Printing.* the imprint of a quadrat, lead, or other piece that has worked up out of position so as to be unintentionally inked and printed.
work·week (wėrk′wēk′), *n.* the part of the

week in which work is done, usually Monday through Friday.

work·wom·an (wėrk′wům′ən), *n., pl.* **-wom·en.** **1.** a woman worker. **2.** a woman who works with her hands or with machines.

world (wėrld), *n.* **1.** the earth: *Ships can sail around the world.* **2.** all of certain parts, people, or things of the earth: **a.** a particular division of the earth: *The New World is North America and South America. The Old World is Europe, Asia, and Africa.* **b.** a group or system of things or beings having common characteristics or considered as forming a complex whole: *Fashionable people belong to the world of fashion. Ants are part of the insect world.* **c.** any sphere, realm, or domain, as of action, thought, or interest: *the world of ideas. With no aspirations beyond the little world in which she moved* (Benjamin Disraeli). **3.** all things; everything; the universe; cosmos. **4.** a star; planet, especially when considered as inhabited: *The War of the Worlds* (H. G. Wells). **5.** all people; the human race; the public: *The whole world knows it. You know that these two parties still divide the world — Of those that want, and those that have* (Tennyson). **6.** the things of this life and the people devoted to them: *Monks and nuns live apart from the world.* **7.** any time, condition, or place of life: *Heaven is in the world to come.* **8.** a great deal; very much; large amount: *The vacation did her a world of good.*

all the world and his wife, everybody, male and female, especially everybody of any social pretensions: *Aunt Charlotte knows all the world and his wife* (Mrs. Humphry Ward).

bring into the world, to give birth to: *I was brought into the world on the 28th February* (Samuel Bamford).

come into the world, to be born: *He died . . . six months before I came into the world* (Dickens).

for all the world, a. for any reason, no matter how great: *I am sure I would not do such a thing for all the world* (Jane Austen). **b.** in every respect; exactly: *He . . . swung about his arms, for all the world as if he were going through the sword exercise* (Thomas Hardy).

in the world, a. anywhere: *He was . . . the most retiring man in the world* (Dickens). **b.** at all; ever: *How in the world did you persuade the captain?* (Adeline D.T. Whitney).

out of this world, *Informal.* of which there is nothing like; great; wonderful; distinctive: *The cuisine is both American and Continental and is out of this world* (Time).

the world, the flesh, and the devil, the world with its interests, the flesh with its appetites, and the devil with his evil promptings, as the great sources of temptation and sin for mankind: *From all the deceits of the world, the flesh, and the devil, Good Lord, deliver us* (Book of Common Prayer).

world without end, eternally; forever: *Jesus Christ our Lord, to whom, with thee and the Holy Ghost, be all honor and glory, world without end. Amen* (Book of Common Prayer).

[Old English *worold,* earlier *weorold* literally, age of man]

—**Syn. 1.** See **earth.**

World Bank, the International Bank for Reconstruction and Development, an organization founded in 1944 to provide loans and other banking services to member nations, especially to help them build up or develop their economies.

world-beat·er (wėrld′bē′tər), *n. Especially U.S. Informal.* a champion: *The aging Dodgers may not be the world-beaters of other summers* (Time).

World Calendar, a proposed twelve-month calendar that would not change from year to year. Its year is divided into four equal quarters, each quarter having three months of 31, 30, and 30 days respectively, totaling 91 days or exactly 13 weeks. Every year and every quarter thus begins on the first day of the week (Sunday) and ends on the seventh day (Saturday). An extra day between Saturday and Sunday is added at the end of the year and still another every leap year at the end of June. *The World Calendar . . . achieves the regular flow of seasons, days and years* (Elizabeth Achelis).

World Court, a court made up of representatives of various nations, established as the Permanent Court of International Justice in 1920 under the covenant of the League of Nations to settle disputes between nations, and continued as the International Court of Justice under the United Nations.

world-famed (wėrld′fāmd′), *adj.* world-famous.

world-fa·mous (wėrld′fā′məs), *adj.* famous the world over: *a world-famous writer.*

world federalism, a movement that advocates world government by a federation of all the nations of the world.

world federalist, an advocate of world federalism.

world·ful (wėrld′fəl), *n., pl.* **-fuls.** enough to fill the world: *To choose from a worldful of events is a difficult, exciting and sometimes painful business* (Time).

world government, a proposed government that would govern and serve everybody in the world, taking the place of individual governments: *World government . . . is probably accepted by most thinking people today as a necessity at some time in the not too distant future* (Bulletin of Atomic Scientists).

world island, (in geopolitics) the land mass that constitutes Asia, Africa, and Europe.

world·li·ness (wėrld′lē nis), *n.* worldly ideas, ways, or conduct.

world·ling (wėrld′ling), *n.* a person who cares much for the interests and pleasures of this world. [< *world* + *-ling*]

world·ly (wėrld′lē), *adj.,* **-li·er, -li·est,** *adv.* —*adj.* **1.** of, having to do with, or belonging to this world; not of heaven: *worldly wealth, worldly knowledge, worldly ambition.* **2. a.** caring much for the interests and pleasures of this world. **b.** caring too much for such interests and pleasures. **3.** worldly-wise.
—*adv.* in a worldly manner; with a worldly intent or disposition.
—**Syn.** *adj.* **1.** mundane. See **earthly.**
—**Ant.** *adj.* **1, 2.** spiritual.

world·ly-mind·ed (wėrld′lē mīn′did), *adj.* having or showing a worldly mind; caring much for the interests and pleasures of this world. —**world′ly-mind′ed·ly,** *adv.* —**world′ly-mind′ed·ness,** *n.*

world·ly-wise (wėrld′lē wīz′), *adj.* wise about or experienced in the ways and affairs of this world. —**world′ly-wise′ness,** *n.* —**Syn.** sophisticated, urbane.

world power, an independent nation or other sovereign body having such military or other power as to be able to act decisively in or to exert a decisive influence on the course of world affairs: *The United States and Russia are two of the chief world powers in this part of the twentieth century.*

world-re·nowned (wėrld′ri nound′), *adj.* world-famous.

world or **world's series,** a series of baseball games played each fall between the winners of the two major-league championships, to decide the professional championship of the United States. The first team to win four games wins the series.

world's fair, an international exposition, with exhibits from various countries.

world-shak·er (wėrld′shā′kər), *n.* a world-shaking person or event: *Goya is one of the great world-shakers* (London Times).

world-shak·ing (wėrld′shā′king), *adj.* of world-wide importance or effect; earth-shaking: *a world-shaking debate.*

world soul or **spirit,** the animating principle that informs the physical world.

world-view (wėrld′vyü′), *n.* view of life; Weltanschauung. [translation of German *Weltanschauung*]

World War, 1. Usually, **World War I.** a war in Europe, Asia, and elsewhere, from July 28, 1914 to November 11, 1918; First World War; Great War. The United States, Great Britain, France, Russia, and their allies were on one side; Germany, Austria-Hungary, and their allies were on the other side. **2.** Usually, **World War II.** a war in Europe, Asia, and elsewhere, from September 1, 1939 to August 14, 1945, beginning as a war between Great Britain, France, and Poland on one side and Germany on the other, ultimately involving most of the world; Second World War. The chief conflict was between Great Britain, the United States, and the Soviet Union on one side and Germany, Italy, and Japan on the other. *Abbr.:* WW (no periods).

world-wea·ri·ness (wėrld′wir′ē nis), *n.* the state or condition of being tired of living.

world-wea·ry (wėrld′wir′ē), *adj.* weary of this world; tired of living.

world-wide (wėrld′wīd′), *adj.* spread throughout the world; extending over or involving the entire earth or its peoples: *the world-wide threat of atomic radiation.* —**world′-wide′ly,** *adv.*

world-wise (wėrld′wīz′), *adj.* worldly-wise.

worm (wėrm), *n.* **1.** any of the small, slender, elongated invertebrates, (usually) having soft, bilaterally symmetrical bodies and lacking legs, comprising the earthworms, flatworms, roundworms, etc. **2.** (in popular usage) any of numerous small, slender, crawling or creeping animals, usually without legs, and having an elongated, soft body, as a maggot, grub, or caterpillar, various crustaceans or mollusks (the shipworm), and the adult of some insects (the glowworm). **3.** something like a worm in shape or movement, especially: **a.** the thread of a screw. **b.** a short, continuously threaded shaft or screw, the thread of which gears with the teeth of a toothed wheel. **c.** an Archimedean screw or a device using the same principle. **d.** (in a still) a long, spiral or coiled tube in which the vapor is condensed. **4.** a person who deserves contempt, scorn, or pity. **5.** something that slowly eats away, or the pain or destruction it causes: *The worm of conscience still begnaw thy soul!* (Shakespeare). **6.** the lytta, as of a dog. **7.** *Anatomy.* the median lobe of the cerebellum; vermiform process.

worms, a disease characterized by the presence of parasitic worms in the body, especially in the intestines; helminthiasis: *A dose of santonin often produces results which will seem to justify a diagnosis of worms* (Patrick Manson).

—*v.i.* **1.** to look for or catch worms. **2.** to move like a worm; crawl or creep slowly, silently, or stealthily: *soldiers worming through the grass toward the enemy lines.* **3. a.** to make one's way insidiously (into): *Already some of these riffraff are worming into it [a club]* (Booth Tarkington). **b.** to wriggle (out of trouble, etc.). —*v.t.* **1.** to make (one's way, etc.) by creeping or crawling slowly, silently, or stealthily: *The soldier wormed his way toward the enemy's lines.* **2.** to work or get by persistent and secret means: *John tried to worm the secret out of me. He wormed himself into our confidence.* **3.** to remove worms from (a living organism); treat (an animal) for internal parasites. **4.** to remove a rod of cartilage (the lytta or worm) from the tongue of (a dog, etc.). **5.** *Nautical.* to wind yarn, small rope, etc., spirally around (a rope or cable) so as to fill up the grooves between the strands and make the surface smooth for parceling or serving.

[Old English *wurm,* variant of *wyrm*] —**worm′er,** *n.*

worm-eat·en (wėrm′ē′tən), *adj.* **1.** eaten into by worms: *worm-eaten timbers.* **2.** worn-out; worthless; out-of-date.

worm-eat·ing warbler (wėrm′ē′ting), a dull-colored warbler of eastern North America with black stripes on its crown.

wormed (wėrmd), *adj.* damaged by worms; worm-eaten.

worm fence, snake fence.

worm gear, 1. worm wheel. **2.** a worm wheel and an endless screw together. By a worm gear the rotary motion of one shaft can be transmitted to another.

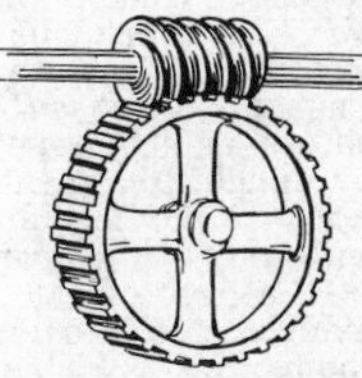

Worm Gear (def. 2)

worm·hole (wėrm′hōl′), *n.* a hole made by a burrowing worm, larva, insect, etc.: *an apple filled with wormholes.*

worm·holed (wėrm′hōld′), *adj.* having wormholes.

worm·i·ness (wėr′mē nis), *n.* the state or condition of being wormy.

worm·like (wėrm′līk′), *adj.* resembling a worm in structure, form, movement, etc.; vermiform.

worm lizard, the amphisbaena: *The worm lizards are either limbless or vestigially limbed* (New Yorker).

worm·root wėrm′rüt′, -růt′), *n.* the pinkroot.

worms (wėrmz), *n.pl.* See under **worm,** *n.*

worm·seed (wėrm′sēd′), *n.* **1.** the dried flower heads of any of various plants of the composite family, especially the Levant wormseed, used as a vermifuge. **2.** the seeds of various goosefoots, used similarly. **3.** one of these plants.

worm's-eye (wėrmz′ī′), *adj.* seen from below or very closely; narrow; detailed: *a worm's-eye view of city life.*

worm shell, 1. the shell of any of a family of gastropod mollusks, in the young animal regularly conic and spiral, but later having whorls separate, and often crooked or contorted, with a wormlike appearance. **2.** the animal itself.

worm wheel, a wheel with teeth that fit a revolving screw. —**worm′-wheel′,** *adj.*

worm·wood (wėrm′wu̇d′), *n.* **1.** a somewhat woody, perennial, bitter herb, a native of Europe, whose leaves and tops were formerly used in medicine as a tonic and vermifuge, and are now used for making absinthe and some brands of vermouth. **2.** any composite plant of the same genus, as santonica, moxa, and tarragon; artemisia. Wormwoods of the western United States are usually called sagebrush. **3.** something bitter or extremely unpleasant. [alteration (influenced by *worm* + *wood*[1]) of earlier *wermod,* Old English *wermōd.* Compare VERMOUTH.]

Wormwood Leaf (def. 1)

worm·y (wėr′mē), *adj.,* **worm·i·er, worm·i·est. 1.** having worms, especially infested with worms; containing many worms. **2.** damaged by worms; worm-eaten. **3.** resembling a worm; wormlike. **4.** of or having to do with worms.

worn (wôrn, wōrn), *v.* the past participle of **wear**[1] and **wear**[2]. —*adj.* **1.** damaged by long or hard wear or use: *a worn suit, worn rugs.* **2.** tired and drawn; wearied: *a worn face.* —**Syn.** *adj.* **1.** threadbare.

worn-out (wôrn′out′, wōrn′-), *adj.* **1.** used until no longer fit for use. **2.** physically exhausted; completely fatigued.

wor·ried (wėr′id), *adj.* troubled; distressed: *He is also a worried man, worried that Britain may not succeed in adapting her institutions successfully to modern pressures* (St. Louis Dispatch).

wor·ried·ly (wėr′id lē), *adv.* in a manner showing worry; with worry.

wor·ri·er (wėr′ē ər), *n.* a person or thing that worries.

wor·ri·less (wėr′ē lis), *adj.* free from worry.

wor·ri·ment (wėr′ē mənt), *n. Informal.* **1.** worrying. **2.** worry; anxiety.

wor·ri·some (wėr′ē səm), *adj.* **1.** causing worry. **2.** inclined to worry. —**wor′ri·some·ly,** *adv.* —**Syn. 1.** troublesome. **2.** apprehensive.

wor·rit (wėr′it), *v.t., v.i., n. Dialect.* worry. [alteration of *worry*]

wor·ry (wėr′ē), *v.,* **-ried, -ry·ing,** *n., pl.* **-ries.** —*v.t.* **1.** to cause to feel anxious or troubled: *The problem worried him. Increasing anxieties about money have worried her* (George Eliot). **2.** to annoy; bother: *Don't worry me with so many questions.* **3.** to seize and shake with the teeth; bite at; snap at: *A cat will worry a mouse.* **4.** to harass, as if by repeated biting, etc.; harry by rough treatment or repeated attacks. —*v.i.* **1.** to feel anxious or uneasy: *She will worry if we are late.* **2.** to pull or tear at an object with the teeth; shake, mangle, or bite an animal, object, etc., with the teeth.

worry along or **through,** to manage somehow: *She must . . . try to worry along without him* (William Dean Howells).

—*n.* **1.** an anxious, troubled, or uneasy state of mind; care: *Worry kept her awake.* **2.** a cause of trouble or care: *A mother of sick children has many worries.* **3.** the act of seizing and shaking an animal, etc. [Middle English *worien,* Old English *wyrgan* to strangle]

—**Syn.** *v.t.* **1. Worry, annoy, harass** mean to disturb or distress someone. **Worry** means to cause great uneasiness, care, or anxiety: *The change in his disposition and habits worries me.* **Annoy** means to irritate or vex by constant interference, repeated interruption, etc.: *The new girl annoys her fellow workers by interrupting their work to ask foolish questions.* **Harass** means to annoy deeply and unceasingly: *He is harassed by business troubles and a nagging wife.*

wor·ry·wart (wėr′ē wôrt′), *n. U.S. Slang.* a person who worries too much.

worse (wėrs), *adj., comparative of* **bad. 1.** more harmful, painful, regrettable, unpleasant, unfavorable, etc.: *The accident could have been worse.* **2.** more unattractive, unsuitable, faulty, incorrect, ill-advised, etc.: *His pen was poor and his writing even worse.* **3.** less good; more evil: *Bill is a bad boy, but his brother is worse.* **4.** of lower quality or value; inferior: *The soil is worse in the valley.* **5.** less well; more ill: *The patient is worse today.* **6.** less fortunate or well off.

—*adv.* in a more severe or evil manner or degree: *It is raining worse than ever.*

—*n.* that which is worse: *Loss of his property was bad enough, but worse followed.*

[Old English *wyrsa*]

wors·en (wėr′sən), *v.t.* to make worse. —*v.i.* to become worse.

wors·er (wėr′sər), *adj., adv.* worse.

➔ **Worser** was a common variant of *worse* in the 1500's and 1600's but is now a nonstandard usage except as a literary survival (especially in phrases like *the worser part, sort,* or *half*).

wor·set (wėr′sit), *n., adj. Scottish.* worsted.

wor·ship (wėr′ship), *n., v.,* **-shiped, -ship·ing** or (*especially British*) **-shipped, -ship·ping.** —*n.* **1.** great honor and respect: *the worship of God, hero worship.* **2.** ceremonies or services, often formally prescribed, in honor of God: *a place of worship, public worship.* **3.** great love and admiration; adoration. **4.** an object of worship. **5.** *Especially British.* a title used in addressing certain magistrates and various others of high rank or position: *"Yes, your worship," he said to the judge.* **6.** *Archaic.* **a.** honorable character; honor; distinction; renown. **b.** honorable or high rank or standing; importance; dignity. —*v.t.* **1.** to pay great honor and respect to: *People go to church to worship God.* **2.** to consider extremely precious; hold very dear; adore: *A miser worships money. I worshiped the very ground she walked on* (Dickens). —*v.i.* **1.** to perform or take part in any act, rite, or service of religious worship. **2.** to feel extreme adoration or devotion for a person or thing.

[Old English *worthscip,* variant of *weorthscipe* < *weorth* worth + *-scipe* -ship] —**wor′ship·er,** *especially British* **wor′ship·per,** *n.*

—**Syn.** *n.* **1.** reverence. *-v.t.* **1.** revere, venerate.

wor·ship·ful (wėr′ship fəl), *adj.* **1.** worshiping: *the worshipful eyes of a dog watching its master.* **2.** honorable. **3.** deserving or capable of being worshiped. —**wor′ship·ful·ly,** *adv.* —**wor′ship·ful·ness,** *n.*

worst (wėrst), *adj., superlative of* **bad. 1.** least well; most ill: *This is the worst cold I ever had.* **2.** least good; most evil: *He is the worst boy in school.* **3.** of the lowest quality or value; least good, valuable, desirable, or successful: *the worst diet imaginable, the worst sheep of the herd, the worst room in the hotel.*

—*adv.* to an extreme degree of badness or evil: *This child acts worst when his parents have guests.*

—*n.* that which is worst: *The mean boy kept the best of the fruit for himself and gave the worst to his friends.*

at (**the**) **worst,** under the least favorable circumstances: *I thought . . . that if a man played long enough he was sure to win . . . or, at the worst, not to come off a loser* (Dickens).

give one the worst of it, to defeat one: *He fought well, but in the end was given the worst of it.*

if worst comes to (**the**) **worst,** if the very worst thing happens: *Even if worst comes to worst, I've got enough to live on for six months* (Theodore Dreiser).

—*v.t.* to beat; defeat: *The hero worsted his enemies.*

[Old English *wyrresta* < *wyrsa* worse + *-sta,* a superlative suffix]

wor·sted (wu̇s′tid), *n.* **1.** a firmly twisted thread or yarn made of long-stapled wool. **2.** a cloth made from such thread or yarn. **3.** a fine, soft woolen yarn for knitting, crocheting, and needlework.

—*adj.* made of worsted.

[< *Worsted* (now *Worstead*), a town in England, where it was originally made]

➔ The (r) was lost from **worsted,** as from *Worcester,* in Early Modern English, but the letter representing it was retained in the spelling. A spelling pronunciation (wûr′stid) is sometimes heard.

wort[1] (wėrt), *n.* **1.** the liquid made from malt which later becomes beer, ale, or other liquor when fermented. **2.** any of various similar infusions. [Old English *wyrt*]

wort[2] (wėrt), *n.* a plant, herb, or vegetable, used for food or medicine (now used chiefly in combinations in various plant names, as in *liverwort, figwort*). [Middle English *wort,* earlier *wurt,* Old English *wyrt*]

worth[1] (wėrth), *adj.* **1.** good or important enough for; deserving of: *The book is worth reading. New York is a city worth visiting.* **2.** equal in value to: *a book worth $5.00.* **3.** having possessions, property, or income that amounts to: *That man is worth millions.*

—*n.* **1.** merit; usefulness; importance: *We should read books of real worth.* **2.** value: *the worth of a house. Jane got her money's worth out of that coat.* **3.** a quantity of something of specified value: *to get a dollar's worth of gasoline.* **4.** excellence of character; personal merit. **5.** *Archaic.* property; wealth.

[Old English *weorth*]

—**Syn.** *n.* **1, 2.** See **merit.**

worth[2] (wėrth), *v.i. Archaic.* to come to be; come about; happen. [Old English *weorthan* become, come about; (originally) to turn]

wor·thi·ly (wėr′ᴛʜə lē), *adv.* **1.** in a manner that is worthy; honorably: *He fought worthily but he was no match for the champion.* **2.** rightly; suitably; fittingly. **3.** deservedly; justly.

wor·thi·ness (wėr′ᴛʜē nis), *n.* the quality or condition of being worthy; merit; excellence: *I am awaken'd to see more worthiness in you, than ever I saw in any lady in the land* (Samuel Richardson).

worth·less (wėrth′lis), *adj.* without worth; good-for-nothing; useless. —**worth′less·ly,** *adv.* —**worth′less·ness,** *n.* —**Syn.** valueless, trashy.

worth-while or **worth·while** (wėrth′-hwīl′), *adj.* worth time, attention, or effort; having real merit. —**worth′-while′ness, worth′while′ness,** *n.* —**Syn.** valuable, useful.

➔ **Worth-while** or **worthwhile** is the form used before a noun: *a worthwhile undertaking.* As predicate complement it is written as two words: *It's hardly worth while.*

wor·thy (wėr′ᴛʜē), *adj.,* **-thi·er, -thi·est,** *n., pl.* **-thies.** —*adj.* **1.** having worth or merit: *a worthy opponent.* **2.** deserving; meriting: *She helps the worthy poor.* **3.** *Obsolete.* deserved or merited by default or wrongdoing; condign.

worthy of, a. deserving: *His courage was worthy of high praise.* **b.** having enough worth for: *Your sentiments and conduct are worthy of the noble house you descend from* (Scott).

—*n.* a person of great merit; admirable person.

wost (wost), *v. Archaic.* 2nd person singular of **wit**[2]. "Thou wost" means "you know."

wot (wot), *v. Archaic.* 1st and 3rd person singular of **wit**[2]. "I wot" means "I know." "He wot" means "He knows." [Old English *wāt*]

Wo·tan (wō′tən), *n.* the most important Old High German god, identified with the Norse god Odin. [< Old High German *Wotan.* Related to ODIN, WODEN.]

would[1] (wu̇d; *unstressed* wəd), *v.* **1.** the past tense of **will**[1]. **2.** special uses: **a.** to express future time: *He said that he would soon go.* **b.** to express action done again and again in the past time: *The children would play for hours on the beach.* **c.** to express a wish or desire: *Would I were dead!* **d.** to make a statement or question less direct or blunt: *Would that be fair? Would you help us, please?* **e.** to express conditions: *If he would only try, he could do it.* [Old English *wolde,* past tense of *willan* to will]

➔ **a.** The frequent misspelling **would of** for *would have* arises out of the fact that *have* and *of,* when completely unstressed, are pronounced identically. **b. Would rather** is used to express a strong preference: *I would rather stay home than dance with him.*

would[2] (wōld), *n.* weld[2].

would-be (wu̇d′bē′), *adj.* **1.** wishing or pretending to be: *a would-be actor.* **2.** intended to be: *a would-be work of art.* —*n.* a person who wishes or pretends to be something: *The theatrical would-be hoped to get a starring role.*

would·n't (wůd′ənt), would not.

wouldst (wůdst), *v. Archaic and Poetic.* 2nd person singular past tense of **will**[1]. "Thou wouldst" means "you would."

Woulfe's apparatus (wůlfs), a series of Woulfe's bottles with connecting tubes. [< Peter *Woulfe,* about 1727-1803, an English chemist]

Woulfe's bottle, a bottle or jar with two or three necks, used in washing gases, saturating liquids with gases, etc.

wound[1] (wünd; *Archaic and Poetic* wound), *n.* **1.** a hurt or injury to a person or animal in which the skin or a membrane is broken, or the tissue separated, caused by cutting, stabbing, shooting, etc., and not the result of disease. **2.** a similar injury due to external violence, in any part of a tree or plant. **3.** any hurt or injury to feelings, reputation, etc.: *The loss of his job was a wound to his pride.*
—*v.t.* **1.** to inflict a wound or wounds upon; injure; damage. **2.** to injure in feelings, reputation, etc.: *His unkind words wounded her.* —*v.i.* to inflict a wound or wounds; do harm or injury (physically or mentally).
[Old English *wund*]
—**Syn.** *n.* **1.** laceration.

wound[2] (wound), *v.* a past tense and a past participle of **wind**[2] and **wind**[3].

wound·ed (wün′did), *adj.* **1.** suffering from a wound or wounds: *Kay near him groaning like a wounded bull* (Tennyson). **2.** deeply pained or grieved: *The quiet of my wounded conscience* (Shakespeare). —**wound′ed·ly,** *adv.*

wound·less (wünd′lis; *Archaic and Poetic* wound′lis), *adj.* without wounds.

wove[1] (wōv), *v.* a past tense and a past participle of **weave.**
➔ See **weave** for usage note.

wove[2] (wōv), *n.* wove paper.

wo·ven (wō′vən), *v.* a past participle of **weave.**

wove paper, a paper made on a mold of closely woven wire and having a plain surface or one finely marked by the mold.

wow[1] (wou), *n.* **1.** a bark or similar short, explosive sound. **2.** a wail. **3.** a fluctuation in the pitch of sounds coming from a phonograph or tape recorder, caused by a slight irregularity in the speed of the turntable or tape drive mechanism.
—*v.i.* to utter such a sound or sounds.
—*interj.* an exclamation of surprise, joy, dismay, etc.
[imitative]

wow[2] (wou), *U.S. Slang.* —*n.* an unqualified success; hit. —*v.t.* to overwhelm, as with delight or amazement: *He wanted to wow his classmates by the thoroughness of his research* (New York Times). [American English, noun and verb use of *wow*[1], interjection]

wow·ser (wou′zər), *n.* (in Australia) a person who is rigidly moral or proper, especially one who concerns himself with and seeks to suppress whatever he disapproves of, however minor or petty; bigoted and puritanical person. [origin uncertain]

W.P., worthy patriarch (in Freemasonry).

WPA (no periods), Works Projects Administration (an agency of the U.S. Government established in 1935 as the *Works Progress Administration,* and abolished in 1942, to provide jobs especially in public works).

WPB (no periods), War Production Board.

wpm (no periods) or **w.p.m.,** words per minute: *A very fast typist can do 80 wpm.*

WRAC (no periods) or **W.R.A.C.,** *British.* Women's Royal Army Corps.

wrack[1] (rak), *n.* **1.** ruin; destruction. **2. a.** seaweed cast ashore by the waves or growing on the tidal seashore. **b.** any of several species of brown algae. **3. a.** *Archaic.* what remains afloat when a vessel is wrecked; wreckage. **b.** *Dialect.* a wrecked vessel.
—*v.t. Archaic or Dialect.* to wreck. —*v.i. Archaic or Dialect.* to undergo wrecking or ruin.
[probably < earlier Flemish *wrack* < Middle Low German *wrak* wreck < *wraken* shoot out, eject. Compare RACK[2], WREAK.]

wrack[2] (rak), *n.* rack (broken clouds). [spelling variant of *rack*[4]]

Wraf or **WRAF** (raf, räf), *n. British.* a member of the WRAF.

WRAF (no periods) or **W.R.A.F.,** *British.* Women's Royal Air Force.

wraith (rāth), *n.* **1.** the ghost of a person seen before or soon after his death. **2.** a specter; ghost. [perhaps < Old English *wrāth* wroth, in sense of "angry person or spirit"] —**wraith′like′,** *adj.* —**Syn. 2.** apparition.

wran·gle (rang′gəl), *v.,* **-gled, -gling,** *n.* —*v.i.* **1.** to dispute noisily; quarrel angrily: *The children wrangled about who should sit in front.* **2.** (formerly) to dispute or discuss publicly, as at a university for or against a thesis.
—*v.t.* **1.** to argue. **2.** *Western U.S.* to herd or tend (horses, etc.) on the range. —*n.* a noisy dispute; angry quarrel.
[perhaps < Low German *wrangeln.* Related to WRING.]
—**Syn.** *v.i.* **1.** squabble, brawl.

wran·gler (rang′glər), *n.* **1.** a person who wrangles. **2.** *Western U.S.* a herder in charge of horses. **3.** *British.* (at Cambridge University) a person winning high honors in mathematics as the result of the final examination (tripos).

wrap (rap), *v.,* **wrapped** or **wrapt, wrap·ping,** *n.* —*v.t.* **1.** to cover, enclose, or envelop (a person or part of the body) by winding or folding something around: *She wrapped herself in a shawl. She wrapped the child in a blanket.* **2.** to cover (an object or objects) in or with a covering of paper, etc., and tie up or fasten: *to wrap a book in tissue paper.* **3.** to wind, fold, or arrange (a garment, covering, etc., about, around, or round a person, object, etc.): *to wrap one's arms about someone, wrap paper around a book.* **4.** to cover; envelop; hide: *The mountain peak is wrapped in clouds. She sat wrapped in thought. The crime is wrapped in mystery.* **5.** to involve or infold (in a soothing state or condition): *The house is wrapped in slumbers* (Dickens). **6.** to roll or fold up. —*v.i.* **1.** to wrap oneself in a garment, etc. **2.** to twine or circle around or about something.

wrapped up in, a. devoted to; thinking mainly of: *wrapped up in one's work.* **b.** involved in; associated with: *I put mine [happiness] under your guardianship also, for mine is wrapped up in yours* (George P.R. James).

wrap up, a. to put on warmer or protective clothing: *He had to be wrapped up against the cold and further fortified by a cup of black coffee* (Annie F. Hector). **b.** *Informal.* to make assured in ending; clinch: *They wrapped up the game with three runs in the ninth.*
—*n.* **1.** a loose garment used or designed for folding about the person, such as a scarf, shawl, or the like. **2.** Often, **wraps.** an outer garment for outdoor wear, as a cloak or furs. **3.** a blanket.

under wraps, secret or concealed: *For reasons of security the new bomber design was kept under wraps.*

wraps, a cloak of secrecy or concealment: *Since the first major application of the new fuels probably will be military — as propellants for rockets or guided missiles — most of the research is shrouded in secrecy. But it's hard to keep the wraps completely over such developments* (Wall Street Journal).
[Middle English *wrappen.* Compare earlier Middle English *biwrabled* bewrapped.]

wrap-a·round or **wrap·a·round** (rap′ə round′), *adj.* **1.** worn by drawing, folding, or shaping around: *a wrap-around skirt, blouse, or coat.* **2.** curving around and along part of the sides: *a wrap-around windshield.* —*n.* a wrap-around garment.

wrap·page (rap′ij), *n.* **1.** the act of wrapping. **2.** that in which something is wrapped.

wrap·per (rap′ər), *n.* **1.** a person who wraps: *a parcel wrapper.* **2.** a thing in which something is wrapped; covering; cover. **3.** a woman's long, loose outer garment to wear in the house. **4.** the leaf or leaves rolled around smaller leaves or pieces to form the outside layer of tobacco in a cigar.

wrap·ping (rap′ing), *n.* or **wrap·pings** (rap′ingz), *n.pl.* paper, cloth, etc., in which something is wrapped: *wrappings for Christmas gifts.* —*adj.* used for wrapping: *wrapping paper.*

wraps (raps), *n.pl.* See under **wrap,** *n.*

wrapt (rapt), *v.* wrapped; a past tense and a past participle of **wrap.**

wrap-up (rap′up′), *n. Informal.* the final item or summary of a news report.

wrasse (ras), *n.* any of a family of spiny-finned fishes of warm seas, especially a genus having thick, fleshy lips, powerful teeth, and usually a brilliant coloration. [perhaps < Cornish *gwrach*]

wrath (rath, räth; *especially British* rôth), *n.* **1.** very great anger; rage. **2.** anger displayed in action (often in *wrath of God* or *day of wrath*): *The wrath of the stupid has laid waste the world quite as often as has the craft of the bright* (Time). —*adj.* wrathful.
[Old English *wrǣththu*]
—**Syn.** *n.* **1.** ire, fury, indignation, resentment. See **anger.**

wrath·ful (rath′fəl, räth′-; *especially British* rôth′fəl), *adj.* feeling or showing wrath. —**wrath′ful·ly,** *adv.* —**wrath′ful·ness,** *n.*
—**Syn.** irate, furious, raging, incensed.

wrath·i·ly (rath′ə lē, räth′-; *especially British* rô′thə lē), *adv.* with wrath or great anger; angrily.

wrath·y (rath′ē, räth′-; *especially British* rô′thē), *adj.,* **wrath·i·er, wrath·i·est.** wrathful.

wreak (rēk), *v.t.* **1.** to give expression to; work off (feelings, desires, etc.): *The cruel boy wreaked his bad temper on his dog.* **2.** to inflict (vengeance, punishment, etc.): *. . . the ravages wrought by French privateers* (New Statesman). **3.** *Archaic.* to avenge.
[Old English *wrecan.* Related to WRACK[1], WRECK.] —**wreak′er,** *n.*

wreath (rēth), *n., pl.* **wreaths** (rēᴛʜz). **1.** a ring of flowers or leaves twisted together. **2.** something suggesting a wreath: *a wreath of smoke.* [Old English *wrǣth,* related to *wrīthan* to writhe] —**Syn. 1.** garland. **2.** curl.

Wreath (rēth), *n.* the southern constellation Corona Australis.

wreathe (rēᴛʜ), *v.,* **wreathed, wreathed** or (*Archaic*) **wreath·en, wreath·ing.** —*v.t.* **1.** to make into a wreath; twist. **2.** to decorate or adorn with wreaths; garland. **3.** to make a ring around; encircle: *Mist wreathed the hills.* **4.** to unite, form, or make by twining together; entwine; intertwine: *An eagle and a serpent wreathed in fight* (Shelley). **5.** to envelop: *a face wreathed in smiles.* —*v.i.* **1.** to twist, coil, bend, or curve. **2.** to move in rings: *The smoke wreathed upward.* [partly < Middle English *wrethen,* alteration of *writhen* writhe; influenced by *wreath*]
—**wreath′er,** *n.*

wreck (rek), *n.* **1.** partial or total destruction of a ship, building, train, automobile, or airplane. **2.** destruction or serious injury: *The war caused the wreck of many fortunes.* **3.** what is left of anything that has been destroyed or much injured: *The wrecks of six ships were cast upon the shore.* **4.** a person who has lost his health or money: *a wreck of his former self, a nervous wreck.* **5.** *Law.* goods or cargo cast up by the sea from a disabled or foundered vessel.
—*v.t.* **1.** to cause or bring about the wreck of; destroy; ruin: *Robbers wrecked the mail train.* **2.** to cause to lose health or money. **3.** to involve (a person) in a wreck. —*v.i.* **1.** to be wrecked; suffer serious injury. **2.** to act as wrecker.
[perhaps < Anglo-French *wrec* < Scandinavian (compare Old Icelandic *rek*). Related to RACK[4], WREAK.]

wreck·age (rek′ij), *n.* **1.** what is left of a thing that has been wrecked: *The shore was covered with the wreckage of a ship.* **2.** a wrecking or being wrecked.

wreck·er (rek′ər), *n.* **1.** a person or thing that causes wrecks. **2.** a person whose work or business is tearing down buildings. **3.** a person who causes shipwrecks by showing false lights or signals on shore so as to plunder the wrecks. **4.** a person, car, train, or machine that removes wrecks. **5.** a person or ship that recovers wrecked or disabled ships or their cargoes.

wrecker's ball, a large steel ball attached to a crane, used for demolition: *The wrecker's ball will soon shatter the French Renaissance structure to clear the site for a 40-story office building* (New York Times).

wreck·ful (rek′fəl), *adj. Archaic.* causing or involving wreck, ruin, or destruction.

wreck·ing (rek′ing), *n.* **1.** the act or business of a wrecker. **2.** the act or business of salvaging a wreck or wrecks.
—*adj.* **1.** used for or having to do with salvaging a wreck or wrecks: *He [the motorman] was freed early yesterday after 300 rescue workers used blowtorches, sledge hammers, and wrecking bars* (New York Times). **2.** engaged in salvaging a wreck or wrecks: *a wrecking company.*

wrecking ball, wrecker's ball.

wrecking car, a car provided with means and appliances for clearing wreckage, etc., from railroad tracks.

wren (ren), *n.* **1.** any of a family of small brown or grayish songbirds with slender bills and short tails, as the house wren and the Carolina wren of North America. Wrens often build their nests near houses. **2.** any of certain similar birds. [Old English *wrenna*] —**wren′like′,** *adj.*

House Wren (def. 1) (including tail, about 5 in. long)

Wren or **WREN** (ren), *n. British Informal.* a member of the Women's Royal Naval Service (W.R.N.S.), made part of the regular navy in 1949. [spelling for pronunciation of *W.R.N.(S.)*]

wrench (rench), —*n.* **1.** a violent twist or twisting pull: *The knob broke off when he gave it a sudden wrench.* **2.** an injury caused by twisting. **3.** grief; pain: *It was a wrench to leave the old home.* **4.** distortion of the proper or original meaning, interpretation, etc. **5.** a tool for turning nuts, bolts, etc. [< verb]

Pipe Wrench (def. 5)

v.t. **1.** to twist or pull violently: *The policeman wrenched the gun out of the man's hand.* **2.** to injure by twisting: *He wrenched his back in falling from the horse.* **3.** to distress or pain greatly; rack. **4.** to twist the meaning of.

—*v.i.* to pull or tug (at something) with a twist or turn.

[Old English *wrencan* to twist]

—**Syn.** *v.t.* **1.** wring, wrest. **2.** strain, sprain.

wren-tit (ren′tit′), *n.* a small, brownish bird somewhat resembling the wrens and the titmice, found in Oregon, California, and Baja California.

wrest (rest), *v.t.* **1.** to twist, pull, or tear away with force; wrench away: *The nurse bravely wrested the knife from the insane patient.* **2.** to take by force: *The usurper wrested the authority from the king.* **3.** to obtain by extortion, persistence, or persuasion; wring: *to wrest a secret from someone.* **4.** to twist or turn (a writing, passage, word, etc.) from the proper meaning, use, etc.

—*n.* **1.** a wresting; a violent twist; wrench. **2.** a key, wrench, or other implement for tuning certain stringed musical instruments, as a harp, piano, or zither, by turning the pegs (wrest pins) around which the ends of the strings are coiled.

[Old English *wrǣstan.* Related to WRIST, WRITHE.] —**wrest′er,** *n.*

wres·tle (res′əl), *v.*, **-tled, -tling,** *n.* —*v.t.* **1. a.** to try to throw or force (an opponent) to the ground. **b.** to engage in (a wrestling match). **2.** to contend with as if in wrestling.

—*v.i.* **1.** to be a contestant in a wrestling match; grapple with an opponent and seek to throw him to the ground. **2.** to struggle: *We wrestle with problems, temptations, and difficulties.*

—*n.* **1.** a wrestling match. **2.** a struggle. [Middle English *wrestlen, wrastlen,* unrecorded Old English *wrǣstlian* (frequentative) < *wrǣstan;* see WREST]

wres·tler (res′lər), *n.* **1.** a person who wrestles. **2.** *Western U.S.* a person who throws cattle for the purpose of branding.

wres·tling (res′ling), *n.* a sport or contest in which each of two opponents tries to throw or force the other to the ground. The rules for wrestling do not allow using the fists or certain holds on the body.

wrest pin, a peg or pin around which the ends of the strings are coiled in a stringed musical instrument.

wretch (rech), *n.* **1.** a very unfortunate or unhappy person. **2.** a very bad person. [Old English *wrecca* exile] —**Syn. 2.** scoundrel, villain, rogue.

wretch·ed (rech′id), *adj.* **1.** very unfortunate or unhappy. **2.** very unsatisfactory; miserable: *a wretched hut.* **3.** very bad: *a wretched traitor.* —**wretch′ed·ly,** *adv.* —**wretch′ed·ness,** *n.*

—**Syn. 1. Wretched, miserable** mean very unhappy or deeply disturbed. **Wretched** suggests a state of unhappiness and extreme lowness of spirits marked by discouragement and hopelessness, caused by sorrow, sickness, worry, etc.: *He was wretched when he failed the examination again.* **Miserable** suggests a state of severe suffering or distress of mind, caused especially by conditions or circumstances such as poverty, humiliation, or misfortune: *After the loss of their savings and their home they felt too miserable to see their old friends.* **2.** pitiful, shabby. **3.** despicable, base, mean.

wrick (rik), *v.t., n.* strain; sprain. [apparently < Middle English *wricken* to twist]

wried (rīd), *v.* the past tense and past participle of **wry.**

wri·er (rī′ər), *adj.* the comparative of **wry.**

wri·est (rī′ist), *adj.* the superlative of **wry.**

wrig (rig), *v.i., v.t.,* **wrigged, wrig·ging.** *Obsolete or British Dialect.* to wriggle. [variant of *wrick*]

wrig·gle (rig′əl), *v.*, **-gled, -gling,** *n.* —*v.i.* **1.** to twist and turn; squirm; wiggle: *Children wriggle when they are restless.* **2.** to move by twisting and turning: *A snake wriggled across the road.* **3.** to make one's way by shifts and tricks: *Some people can wriggle out of any difficulty.* —*v.t.* **1.** to cause to wriggle. **2.** to make (one's way) by sinuous motion.

—*n.* **a** wriggling.

[probably < Dutch *wriggelen* (frequentative) < *wrikken* to move to and fro, wriggle, loosen. Related to WRY.]

wrig·gler (rig′lər), *n.* **1.** a person who wriggles. **2.** the larva of a mosquito: *Wrigglers ... change their old skins for new ones several times, becoming larger at each molt, until they are about three-eighths of an inch long in most species* (Science News Letter).

wrig·gly (rig′lē), *adj.*, **-gli·er, -gli·est.** twisting and turning.

wright (rīt), *n.* (now usually in combinations) a maker of something. A wheelwright makes wheels. A playwright makes plays for the theater.

[Old English *wryhta,* variant of *wyrhta* < *weorc* work]

wring (ring), *v.*, **wrung** or (*Rare*) **wringed, wring·ing,** *n.* —*v.t.* **1.** to twist with force; squeeze hard: *to wring clothes.* **2.** to force by twisting or squeezing: *The laundress wrings water from the wet clothes.* **3.** to twist violently, especially out of place or relation; wrench: *to wring a chicken's head off.* **4.** to get by force, effort, or persuasion: *The old beggar could wring money from anyone with his sad story.* **5.** to cause distress, pain, pity, etc., in: *Their poverty wrung his heart.* **6.** to clasp; press: *He wrung his old friend's hand.*

—*v.i.* to twist about in or as if in struggle or anguish; writhe.

wring out, a. to twist so as to force out water: *to wring out a towel.* **b.** to force out by or as if by twisting; squeeze out: *to wring out water, tears, blood, etc.* **c.** to draw out by force or pressure; extract: *to wring out a confession.*

—*n.* a twist or squeeze.

[Old English *wringan.* Related to WRANGLE.]

wring·er (ring′ər), *n.* **1.** a machine for squeezing water out of clothes. **2.** a person who wrings clothes or the like after washing. **3.** a person or thing that wrings.

put through the wringer, *Informal.* to put through an ordeal; subject to severe stresses: *Students asking for loans are really put through the wringer* (Wall Street Journal).

wring·ing-wet (ring′ing wet′), *adj.* so wet that water may be wrung out.

wrin·kle[1] (ring′kəl), *n.*, *v.*, **-kled, -kling.** —*n.* a ridge; fold: *An old man's face has wrinkles. I must press out the wrinkles in this dress.*

—*v.t.* to make a wrinkle or wrinkles in: *He wrinkled his forehead.* —*v.i.* **1.** to have wrinkles; acquire wrinkles: *These sleeves wrinkle.* **2.** (of persons, the face, etc.) to assume or undergo marking with wrinkles, creases, or lines. **3.** to contract (into smiles, etc.) by puckering.

[perhaps back formation < Middle English *wrynkled* winding, Old English *gewrinclod* winding (of a ditch)]

—**Syn.** *v.t.* crease, crinkle.

wrin·kle[2] (ring′kəl), *n. Informal.* **1.** a useful hint or idea; clever trick. **2.** a special or unusual technique, approach, device, etc.; novelty: *The newest wrinkle in the $2.5 billion cosmetics business is a lotion that camouflages ... creases* (Time). [perhaps special use of *wrinkle*[1]]

wrin·kly (ring′klē), *adj.*, **-kli·er, -kli·est.** wrinkled.

—**Syn.** creased, puckered.

wrist (rist), *n.* **1.** the joint that connects the hand with the arm. **2.** a corresponding joint or part of the forelimb of an animal. **3.** the bones of this part; carpus. **4.** the part of a glove, mitten, or garment covering the wrist. **5.** wrist pin.

[Old English *wrist.* Related to WREST, WRITHE.]

wrist·band (rist′band′), *n.* the band of a sleeve fitting around the wrist.

wrist-drop (rist′drop′), *n.*, or **wrist drop,** a disorder characterized by the inability to extend the hand and fingers, usually caused by a paralysis of the extensor muscles of the hand.

wrist·er (ris′tər), *n. U.S. Dialect.* a wristlet.

wrist·let (rist′lit), *n.* **1.** a band worn around the wrist to keep it warm or for ornament. **2.** a bracelet. **3.** a handcuff.

wrist·lock (rist′lok′), *n.* a hold in wrestling in which one contestant grasps the wrist of the other and twists it so as to force his body in some desired direction.

Double Wristlock

wrist pin, a stud or pin projecting from the side of a crank, wheel, or the like, and forming a means of attachment to a connecting rod.

wrist watch, a small watch worn on a strap around the wrist.

wrist·work (rist′wėrk′), *n.* flexure of the wrist, as in batting: *Shifting to an entirely new grip, which makes nonsense of all that preliminary wristwork, he speeds away* (Punch).

writ[1] (rit), *n.* **1.** something written; piece of writing: *The Bible is Holy Writ.* **2. a.** a formal written order, usually under seal, issued by a court in the name of the government, sovereign, or other competent authority, directing a person to do or not to do something: *The lawyer got a writ from the judge to release the man wrongly held in jail.* **b.** (in early English law) any of certain documents issued under seal in the form of a letter, in the king's name. [Old English *writ,* related to *wrītan* to write]

writ[2] (rit), *v. Archaic.* a past tense and a past participle of **write.**

writ·a·tive (rī′tə tiv), *adj.* disposed or inclined to write; given to writing: *Increase in years makes men more talkative, but less writative* (Alexander Pope).

write (rīt), *v.*, **wrote** or (*Archaic*) **writ, written** or (*Archaic*) **writ, writ·ing.** —*v.t.* **1. a.** to make (letters, words, etc.) on paper, parchment, or the like, with a pencil, pen, crayon, chalk, etc.; inscribe. **b.** to carve, engrave, or incise (letters, words, symbols, etc.) on a hard or plastic surface. **2.** to put down the letters, words, etc., of: *Write your name and address.* **3.** to give in writing; record: *She writes all that happens. She wrote that she was feeling better.* **4.** to write a letter to: *I wrote my friend to come.* **5.** to make (books, stories, articles, poems, letters, etc.) by using written letters, words, etc.; compose: *to write a sonnet.* **6. a.** to draw up or draft (a document); put into proper written form: *to write one's last will.* **b.** to fill in (a form) with writing: *to write a check.* **7.** to spell (a word, name, etc.) in a certain way in writing: *Many words written alike are pronounced differently.* **8.** to cover or fill with writing; produce in writing: *to write three pages, write three copies.* **9.** to impress marks indicating; show plainly: *Honesty is written on his face.*

—*v.i.* **1.** to make letters, words, symbols, etc., with pen, pencil, chalk, etc., or on a hard or plastic surface with a sharp instrument: *He learned to write.* **2.** to produce (a specified kind of) writing: *a pen that writes poorly, to write legibly or illegibly.* **3.** to write a letter: *He writes to her every week.* **4.** to be an author or writer: *to write for the stage, write about the stage. But you cannot*

teach a man to write or to edit; if he has latent abilities in these areas, you can develop them; you cannot inject them as so much vaccine (Harper's). **5.** to work as a clerk, amanuensis, journalist, etc.
write down, a. to put into writing: *I will ... write down all they say to me* (Sir Richard Steele). **b.** to reduce the value of (an item) in an accounting record: *The properties produced so little that they were written down on Javelin's books to $1* (Wall Street Journal).
write in, a. to insert (a fact, statement, etc.) in a piece of writing: *The teacher wrote in corrections between the sentences on the paper.* **b.** to send (a message) to a headquarters, etc., in writing: *The customers ... were not slow about writing in their suggestions* (Publishers' Weekly). **c.** to cast a vote for an unlisted candidate by writing his name on a ballot: *to write in the candidate of one's choice, to write in a vote in a primary.*
write off, a. to cancel: *The company wrote off the loss as a bad debt* (Law Times). **b.** to note the deduction of for depreciation: *During the early life of a piece of equipment, the company bookkeeper could write off each year more of its value, and subtract that sum from taxable income* (Wall Street Journal). **c.** to give up; treat as if nonexistent: *The new blow ... came at a time when his own ... colleagues have, in effect, written him off and are looking for a way to dump him* (Wall Street Journal).
write out, a. to put into writing: *Write out a check. We wrote out a contract.* **b.** to write in full, especially from a rough draft: *He wrote out his speech and memorized it.* **c.** to exhaust one's resources or stock of ideas by excessive writing: *The author had ... written himself out* (Scott).
write up, a. to write a description or account of, especially a full or detailed account: *After interviewing the sentry ... they departed to write up the tragedy* (Julian Hawthorne). **b.** to bring up to date in writing: *He ... writes up the journal neglected for a week or two* (Longfellow). **c.** to bring to public notice by writing, especially by praising in writing: *to write up a candidate.* **d.** *Accounting.* to put a higher value on: *It ... is the policy of the bank to ... "write up" such securities should they appreciate* (Sunday Times).
[Old English *wrītan* (originally) to scratch]
➤ **Wrote** as the past participle, found in the standard language in Early Modern English, is still widespread in the nonstandard dialects.

write-down (rīt′doun′), *n.* a reduction in the amount of an account, capital, assets, etc., as in an accounting record: *Everybody got scared that prices would be cut, and started using up their stocks to avoid big inventory write-downs* (Wall Street Journal).

write-in (rīt′in′), *adj.* of or having to do with a candidate who is not listed but who is voted for by having his name written in on a ballot: *a write-in candidate, a write-in vote.* —*n.* a write-in candidate or vote: *There were no other candidates, no places for write-ins, nothing to mark* (Time).

write-off (rīt′ôf′, -of′), *n.* a cancellation; amount written off or canceled, especially as a bad debt, a tax-deductible expense, etc.: *His profits were helped along through an accelerated write-off of his equipment for tax purposes* (Harper's). *The write-offs of $3,837,000 were for unabsorbed overhead in operating* (Wall Street Journal).

writ·er (rī′tər), *n.* **1.** a person who writes or is able to write: *Was he the writer of that letter?* **2.** a person whose profession or business is writing; author: *... Mr. Fuller goes on to discuss a variety of authors whom he believes pass Emerson's test of a writer ("Talent alone cannot make a writer. There must be a man behind the book")* (Wall Street Journal). **3.** (in Scots law) an attorney; lawyer.

writer's cramp, palsy, or **spasm,** an occupational nervous disorder and cramp characterized by pain and spasm of the muscles of the hand and fingers.

write-up (rīt′up′), *n.* **1.** *Informal.* a written description or account: *to give a short write-up in the paper.* **2.** *Accounting.* a writing up (of an asset).

writhe (rīᴛʜ), *v.*, **writhed, writhed** or (*Obsolete except Poetic*) **writh·en, writh·ing,** *n.* —*v.i.* **1.** to twist and turn; twist: *The snake writhed along the branch. The wounded man writhed in agony.* **2.** to suffer mentally; be very uncomfortable.
—*v.t.* to twist or coil (something); bend by twisting.
—*n.* a writhing movement of the body, countenance, etc.; contortion.
[Old English *wrīthan.* Related to WREST, WRIST.]

writh·en (riᴛʜ′ən), *adj. Rare.* twisted; contorted. —*v. Poetic.* writhed; a past participle of **writhe.**

writh·er (rī′ᴛʜər), *n.* a person who writhes or twists.

writ·ing (rī′ting), *n.* **1.** the act of making letters, words, etc., with pen, pencil, etc.: *For the period since the invention of writing (around 4000 B.C.) there are records on clay, stone, metal, and paper giving precise dates for many events and clues to the relative dates of other events* (Frank Hole). **2.** a written form: *an agreement in writing. Put your ideas in writing.* **3.** something written (or typewritten), as a letter, document, or inscription. **4. a.** a book, story, article, poem, or other literary composition: *the writings of Dickens.* **b.** the profession or business of a person who writes. **5.** handwriting; penmanship; chirography: *to recognize someone's writing.*
commit to writing, to write down: *No one knows who first committed Homer's epics to writing.*
—*adj.* **1.** that writes. **2.** used to write with or on.

writing desk, 1. a desk or piece of furniture for use in writing, commonly with drawers, pigeonholes, etc., for holding materials, papers, or the like. See **Hepplewhite** for picture. **2.** a portable case for holding materials for writing, and affording when opened a surface to rest the paper on in writing.

writing paper, paper of a suitable kind and size for writing on: *The bulletin announcing the birth of the new Prince was written by hand on a sheet of red-crested palace writing paper in a gilded frame* (Manchester Guardian Weekly).

writ of assistance, a search warrant issued without naming the place to be searched, used by British customs officials before the American Revolution.

writ of execution, *Law.* a writ ordering a sheriff or other judicial officer to execute a judgment.

writ of extent, *Law.* a writ to recover debts due the crown.

writ of prohibition, *Law.* a writ from a higher court forbidding a lower court to proceed with a suit.

writ of right, 1. (in early English law) either of two writs issued in cases concerning freehold property brought before manorial courts by feudal tenants. **2.** *U.S.* a similar writ in common law for restoring real property to its rightful owner.

writ·ten (rit′ən), *v.* a past participle of **write.** —*adj.* **1.** that is written; committed to writing: *Written English in our present alphabet is hardly fifteen hundred years old* (John S. Kenyon). **2.** (of laws) formulated in documents, codes, or printed works.

W.R.N.S., *British.* Women's Royal Naval Service.

wrnt., warrant.

wrong (rông, rong), *adj.* **1.** not right; bad; unjust; unlawful: *It is wrong to tell lies.* **2. a.** not conforming to facts or truth; incorrect: *He gave the wrong answer.* **b.** judging, acting, believing, etc., contrary to the facts; mistaken; in error: *I admit that I was wrong.* **3.** unsuitable; improper: *to get on the wrong bus, the wrong clothes for the occasion.* **4.** in a bad state or condition; out of order; amiss: *Something is wrong with the car.* **5.** not meant to be seen; less or least important: *Cloth often has a wrong side and a right side.*
—*adv.* in a wrong manner; in the wrong direction; astray: *Tintoret ... may lead you wrong if you don't understand him* (Ruskin).
go wrong, a. to turn out badly: *Everything went wrong today.* **b.** to stop being good and become bad: *Thus men go wrong ...; Bend the straight rule to their own crooked will* (William Cowper).
—*n.* **1.** what is wrong; wrong thing or things: *Two wrongs do not make a right.* **2.** injustice; injury: *You do an honest man a wrong to call him a liar or a thief.* **3.** *Law.* a violation of law; an infringement on the rights of another resulting in damage or injury to him, especially a tort.
in the wrong, wrong: *I quarrelled with her last night. I was quite in the wrong* (Henry Kingsley).
—*v.t.* **1.** to do wrong to; treat unjustly; injure: *He forgave those who had wronged him.* **2.** to discredit or dishonor unjustly by statement, opinion, etc.; impute evil to undeservedly. **3.** to cheat or defraud (a person of something).
[Old English *wrang,* apparently < Scandinavian (compare Old Icelandic *rangr* crooked)] —**wrong′er,** *n.* —**wrong′ly,** *adv.* —**wrong′ness,** *n.*
—**Syn.** *adj.* **1.** wicked, reprehensible. **2. a.** inaccurate, erroneous, faulty. **3.** inappropriate, unfit. -*n.* **1.** evil, sin, misdemeanor. -*v.t.* **1.** harm, maltreat, abuse, oppress.

wrong·do·er (rông′dü′ər, rong′-), *n.* a person who does wrong.

wrong·do·ing (rông′dü′ing, rong′-), *n.* a doing wrong; evil; wrong: *The ruling indicated the Government could escape liability for the payment if it's found wrongdoing was connected with the power contract* (Wall Street Journal).

wrong font or **fount,** *Printing.* a correction used on proofs, to designate a character of the wrong size, style, etc. *Abbr.:* w.f.

wrong·ful (rông′fəl, rong′-), *adj.* **1.** wrong. **2. a.** that is contrary to law, statute, or established rule; unlawful; illegal. **b.** (of persons) that is such without legitimacy or right; having no legal right or claim. —**wrong′ful·ly,** *adv.* —**wrong′ful·ness,** *n.*

wrong-head·ed or **wrong·head·ed** (rông′hed′id, rong′-), *adj.* **1.** wrong in judgment or opinion. **2.** stubborn even when wrong. —**wrong′-head′ed·ly** or **wrong′-head′ed·ly,** *adv.* —**wrong′-head′edness** or **wrong′head′ed·ness,** *n.*

wrote (rōt), *v.* a past tense of **write.**
➤ See **write** for usage note.

wroth (rôth, roth), *adj.* very angry; wrathful: *As usual, the columnist for Lord Rothermere's London Evening News was wroth* (Time). [Old English *wrāth.* Related to WRATH.]

wroth·y (rôth′ē, roth′-), *adj.*, **wroth·i·er, wroth·i·est.** wrathful; angry: *I am writing letters, wrothy letters* (New Yorker).

wrought (rôt), *v.* worked; a past tense and a past participle of **work.**
—*adj.* **1.** made; fashioned; formed: *The gate was wrought with great skill.* **2.** formed with care; not rough or crude. **3.** manufactured or treated; not in a raw state. **4.** (of metals or metalwork) formed by hammering.

wrought iron, a commercial form of iron containing some slag (one to two per cent), as distinguished from ingot iron and soft steel, and very little carbon (less than 0.3 per cent), commonly produced from pig iron by puddling; malleable iron. It is tough and malleable and soft enough to be forged and welded easily, but does not break as readily as cast iron. —**wrought′-i′ron,** *adj.*

wrought-i·ron casting (rôt′ī′ərn), **1.** the operation of casting with mitis metal. **2.** a casting of mitis metal.

wrought-up (rôt′up′), *adj.* stirred up; excited.

wrung (rung), *v.* a past tense and past participle of **wring.**

wry (rī), *adj.*, **wri·er, wri·est,** *v.*, **wried, wry·ing.** —*adj.* **1.** turned to one side; twisted: *to make a wry face, a wry smile.* **2. a.** (of words, thoughts, etc.) contrary to that which is right, fitting, or just; wrong. **b.** perverted; distorted. [< verb]
—*v.i.* to writhe. —*v.t.* **1.** to twist or turn (the body, neck, etc.) around or about; contort. **2.** to twist out of shape, form, or relationship; contort.
[Old English *wrīgian* to turn; move, go]
—**wry′ly,** *adv.* —**wry′ness,** *n.*

wry·neck (rī′nek′), *n.* **1.** a twisted neck caused by unequal contraction of the muscles; torticollis. **2.** a bird related to the woodpeckers, that habitually twists its neck and head in a peculiar way. **3.** *Informal.* a person who has wryneck (torticollis).

wry-necked (rī′nekt′), *adj.* having wryneck (torticollis): *The wry-necked verger, his dues paid in the past to pain, has a speech that queries the physically agonized part of Christ's passion* (New Statesman).

WSB (no periods), Wage Stabilization Board.

WSW (no periods) or **W.S.W.,** between west and southwest.

wt., weight.

wud (wůd), *adj. Scottish.* wood (demented).

wul·fen·ite (wůl′fə nīt), *n. Mineralogy.*

a molybdate of lead, found in brilliant crystals. *Formula:* $PbMoO_4$ [< German *Wulfenit* < Franz X. von *Wulfen*, 1728-1805, an Austrian scientist + *-it* -ite[1]]

Wun·der·kind (vůn′dər kint′, wun′-), *n., pl.* **-kin·der** (-kin′dər). a remarkably brilliant child; young prodigy: *Maazel ... is that rare specimen among musicians, a Wunderkind who not only grew up but matured* (Atlantic). [< German *Wunderkind* (literally) wonder child]

wur·ley (wėr′lē), *n., pl.* **-leys.** (in South Australia) a hut of the aborigines; native hut. [< native Australian name]

Würm (vůrm, wėrm; *German* vʏrm), *n. Geology.* the fourth glaciation of the Pleistocene period in Europe: *Dr. Oakley believes that ... the beginning of the Würm glaciation can therefore be pushed up by hundreds of thousands of years* (Sunday Times). [< *Würm,* a lake in Germany]

wurst (wėrst, wůrst), *n.* a sausage: *... such an assortment of bolognas, salamis, and head cheeses that my plate looked like an explosion in a wurst factory* (Saturday Review). [< Germany *Wurst*]

wurtz·ite (wėrt′sīt), *n.* a native sulfide of zinc. *Formula:* ZnS

wuth·er (wuᴛʜ′ər), *Scottish.* —*v.i.* **1.** to blow with a roaring sound, as the wind; bluster. **2.** to rush noisily; whiz.
—*n.* a wuthering sound or movement: *the "wuther" of wind amongst trees* (Charlotte Brontë).
[variant of Scottish *whither,* verb < Scandinavian (compare Norwegian *kvidra* to go with quick movements, related to *hvitha* squall of wind)]

wuth·er·ing (wuᴛʜ′ər ing), *Scottish.* —*adj.* **1.** that wuthers: *Hatless, his hair a little ruffled in the wuthering northern air, Mr. Macmillan today stepped out of the Westminster doldrums and into active politics* (Manchester Guardian Weekly). **2.** (of a place) characterized by a wuthering sound or sounds: *Wuthering Heights* (Emily Brontë). —*v.* the present participle of **wuther.**

W.Va., West Virginia.

W.V.S. or **WVS** (no periods), *British.* Women's Voluntary Service.

WW (no periods) or **W.W.,** World War.

Wy., Wyoming.

Wy·an·dot (wī′ən dot), *n.* **1.** an American Iroquoian Indian of the Huron tribe or confederacy that once lived in the Middle Western United States. **2.** the Iroquoian language of the Wyandots.

Wy·an·dotte (wī′ən dot), *n.* any of an American breed of medium-sized, hardy domestic fowls, kept for the production of meat and eggs. [< *Wyandot* (because the tribe bred them)]

wych-elm (wich′elm′), *n.* **1.** an elm tree found especially in northern and western Europe, having broader leaves and more spreading branches than the English elm. **2.** its wood. Also, **witch-elm.** [< Old English *wice* wych-elm + *elm* elm]

wych-ha·zel (wich′hā′zəl), *n.* **1.** witch hazel. **2.** wych-elm.

Wyc·liff·ite or **Wyc·lif·ite** (wik′li fīt), *n.* a person who adhered to or propagated the religious tenets or doctrines of John Wycliffe, the English religious reformer and translator of the Bible.
—*adj.* **1.** of or having to do with John Wycliffe or his followers. **2.** (of a person) that is a follower of John Wycliffe.

wyd·ah (wid′ə), *n.* whidah.

wye (wī), *n.* **1.** the letter Y. **2.** *Electricity.* a type of three-phase circuit arrangement. Three conductors are connected to three terminals in the form of the letter Y.

wye level, a surveying level with the telescope mounted on Y-shaped forks in which it can be rotated.

Wye Level

Wyke·ham·ist (wik′ə mist), *n.* a student or alumnus of Winchester College in England, founded by William of Wykeham (1324-1404), Bishop of Winchester and Chancellor of England, as a preparatory school for New College at Oxford, also founded by him: *Wykehamists will ... dwell instead on the memorable game with Eton, which admittedly, Winchester lost, but in a blaze of glory* (London Times).

wyle (wīl), *v.t.,* **wyled, wyl·ing.** wile.

wy·lie·coat (wī′lē kōt′, wil′ē-, wul′ē-), *n. Scottish.* **1.** an underwaistcoat, in earlier use especially one worn under a doublet. **2.** a petticoat. [origin uncertain]

wynd (wīnd), *n. Scottish.* an alley between houses; narrow lane or street: *It was up a wynd off a side street in St. Bride's that Jessie had her lodging* (Robert Louis Stevenson). [apparently variant of *wind*[2], noun]

Wyo., Wyoming.

Wy·o·ming·ite (wī ō′ming īt), *n.* a native or inhabitant of Wyoming, a Western State of the United States.

wyte (wīt), *n., v.t.,* **wyt·ed, wyt·ing.** *Scottish.* wite (blame).

wythe (wīᴛʜ, with, wiᴛʜ), *n., v.,* **wythed, wyth·ing.** withe.

wy·vern (wī′vərn), *n.* wivern.

X

Roman
100's A.D.

Greek
600's B.C.

Phoenician
1000's B.C.

Semitic
1500's B.C.

Egyptian
3000's B.C.

Xx Xx *Xx* *Xx*

X or **x**[1] (eks), *n., pl.* **X's** or **Xs, x's** or **xs. 1.** the 24th letter of the English alphabet. **2.** any sound represented by this letter. **3.** used as a symbol for: **a.** the 24th, or more usually the 23rd, of a series (either *I* or *J* being omitted). **b.** an unknown quantity, (especially in algebraic equations, along with *y* and *z*. **c.** (the multiplication sign) times; by: *3×6=18; a box 14×20 inches.* **d.** abscissa. **4.** a term often used to designate a person, thing, agency, factor, or the like that has not yet been named or whose true name is unknown or withheld: *virus X, Mr. X.* **5.** a thing shaped like an X. **6.** the Roman numeral for 10. **7.** *Informal.* a ten-dollar bill.

x[2] (eks), *v.t.,* **x-ed** or **x'd, x-ing** or **x'ing. 1.** to cross out with or as if with an x or x's: *She x-ed out the last word and continued* (New Yorker). **2.** to indicate or mark with an x: *He x-ed his answers in the little boxes on the test sheet.*

X (no period), **1.** xenon (chemical element). **2.** a symbol for motion pictures to which only adults are admitted.

X (no period), **1.** Christ. **2.** Christian. [< the Greek letter *X* chi, which begins the word *Christós* Christ]

xanth-, *combining form.* the form of **xantho-** before vowels, as in *xanthoma.*

xan·thate (zan′thāt), *n. Chemistry.* a salt or esther of xanthic acid: *Xanthates are produced from wheat flour or corn starch. They're added to wood pulp. The resulting paper is eight times stronger than other types made from wood pulp alone* (Wall Street Journal).

xan·the·in (zan′thē in), *n.* the yellow water-soluble coloring matter of flowers. [< French *xanthéine* < Greek *xanthós* yellow + French *-ine* -ine[2]]

xan·thic (zan′thik), *adj.* **1.** yellow (applied especially in botany to a series of colors in flowers passing from yellow through orange to red). **2.** of or having to do with xanthin or xanthine.

xanthic acid, any of a group of unstable acids having the general formula ROCSSH, especially a colorless, oily liquid, $C_3H_6OS_2$, with a strong odor.

xan·thin (zan′thin), *n.* **1.** the yellow non-water-soluble coloring matter of flowers. **2.** a yellow coloring matter obtained from madder. **3.** xanthine.
[< German *Xanthin* < Greek *xanthós* yellow + German *-in* -in]

xan·thine (zan′thēn, -thin), *n.* a crystalline, nitrogenous substance, present in the urine, blood, liver, and muscle tissue, and also in various plants. *Formula:* $C_5H_4O_2N_4$

xanthine oxidase, an oxidizing enzyme that converts xanthine into uric acid.

Xan·thip·pe (zan tip′ē), *n.* a scolding woman; shrew. Also, **Xantippe.** [< *Xanthippe,* who lived in the 400's B.C., the wife of Socrates]
—**Syn.** termagant, virago.

xan·thism (zan′thiz əm), *n.* a condition, as of the skin, marked by an abnormal amount of yellow pigment: *All examples of albinism (whitening), melanism (darkening), xanthism (yellowing), or erythrism (reddening) are throwing light on genetic divergence as well as colour changes of a noncongenital kind* (New Scientist).

xantho-, *combining form.* yellow: *Xanthophyll = a yellow pigment.* Also, **xanth-** before vowels. [< Greek *xanthós* yellow]

xan·tho·chro·ic (zan′thə krō′ik), *adj.* xanthochroid.

xan·tho·chroid (zan′thə kroid), *Ethnology.* —*adj.* having yellow hair and pale complexion. —*n.* a xanthochroid person. [< New Latin *xanthochroi* (coined by Thomas Huxley) < Greek *xanthós* yellow + *ōchrós* pale]

xan·tho·ma (zan thō′mə), *n.* a disease of the skin with yellowish patches: *An increased incidence of atherosclerosis has been observed in diseases . . . such as xanthoma* (Science News Letter).

xan·tho·ma·to·sis (zan thō′mə tō′sis), *n.* a disease with soft, yellowish, tumorlike patches on the body, caused by an unbalanced cholesterol metabolism.

xan·thom·a·tous (zan thom′ə təs), *adj.* of or having to do with xanthoma.

xan·tho·my·cin (zan′thə mī′sin), *n.* an antibiotic obtained from streptomyces.

xan·tho·phore (zan′thə fôr, -fōr), *n.* a chromatophore containing a yellow pigment: *Unlike melanophores, the cells that carry the yellow pigment (xanthophores) do not increase or decrease in number in response to outside stimulation* (Scientific American).

xan·tho·phyll or **xan·tho·phyl** (zan′thə fil), *n.* **1.** a yellow pigment related to carotene, present in autumn leaves, and thought to be a product of the decomposition of chlorophyll; lutein. *Formula:* $C_{40}H_{56}O_2$ **2.** any of various related yellow pigments. [< French *xanthophylle* < Greek *xanthós* yellow + *phýllon* leaf]

xan·tho·pro·te·ic (zan′thō prō tē′ik), *adj.* having to do with xanthoprotein.

xanthoproteic acid, an acid that does not crystallize, resulting from the decomposition of albuminoids by nitric acid.

xan·tho·pro·tein (zan′thō prō′tēn), *n.* the yellow substance formed by the action of hot nitric acid on protein.

xan·thop·ter·in (zan thop′tər in), *n.* a yellow pigment found in the wings of butterflies. *Formula:* $C_6H_5N_5O_2$ [< *xantho-* + Greek *pterón* wing + English *-in*]

xan·thous (zan′thəs), *adj.* **1.** of or having to do with peoples having yellowish, reddish, or light-brown hair. **2.** of or having to do with peoples having a yellowish skin, as the Mongolians: *It is true that the Greek and Roman writers do describe the various barbarous tribes of Europe . . . representing some to be of the fair, or as it has been styled, xanthous complexion; others of the dark, or melanic* (T. Price). **3.** yellow. [< Greek *xanthós* yellow (with English *-ous*)]

xanth·u·ren·ic acid (zan′thů ren′ik), a yellowish, crystalline acid in the urine of those deficient in pyridoxine, and with an unbalanced metabolism of tryptophan. *Formula:* $C_{10}H_7NO_4$

Xan·tip·pe (zan tip′e), *n.* Xanthippe: *For the time being the worst of Xantippes must turn into an angel of amiability if she gives a ball* (William Habington).

x-ax·is (eks′ak′sis), *n.* the horizontal axis in a system of rectangular coordinates, as on a chart or graph.

X.C. or **x.c.,** *Finance.* ex coupon.

X chromosome, *Biology.* one of the chromosomes that determine sex. An egg containing two X chromosomes, one from each parent, develops into a female.

x-cp., *Finance.* ex coupon.

X.D., x.d., or **x-div.,** *Finance.* ex-dividend.

X-dis·ease (eks′də zēz′), *n.* **1.** hyperkeratosis: *The reduction or entire elimination of X-disease . . . in cattle may be possible on many farms if cattle are kept away from tractors, combines, bulldozers, and other farm machinery where they might consume grease or oil* (Science News Letter). **2.** a virus disease of peach trees with yellow and red patches on the leaves, and withered fruit.

Xe (no period), xenon (chemical element).

xe·bec (zē′bek), *n.* a small, three-masted vessel of the Mediterranean: *The sails of the xebec are in general similar to those of the polacre, but the hull is extremely different* (William Falconer). See **lateen sail** for picture. [< French *chébec* < Italian *sciabecco* < Arabic *shabbāk*]

xe·ni·a (zē′nē ə), *n. Botany.* the action of pollen on the seed showing in the same generation the characteristics which result from pollination.
[< New Latin *xenia* < Greek *xeníā* being a guest < *xénos* guest]

xe·ni·al (zē′nē əl), *adj.* having to do with hospitality, especially in ancient Greece. [< Greek *xeníā* (see XENIA) + English *-al*[1]]

xeno-, *combining form.* **1.** stranger: *Xenophobia = fear of strangers.*
2. foreign, strange, as in *xenolith, xenomorphic.*
[< Greek *xénos* guest]

xen·o·do·chei·on (zen′ə dō kī′on), *n., pl.* **-chei·a** (-kī′ə). a xenodochium.

xen·o·do·chi·um (zen′ə dō kī′əm), *n., pl.* **-chi·a** (-kī′ə). (especially in the Middle Ages and ancient times) an inn; hotel: *I once spent eighteen hours in a suite in the Mark Hopkins Hotel and never saw the rest of this fabled Frisco xenodochium, for I snoozed out my entire stay* (Maclean's). [< Late Latin *xenodochīum* < Greek *xenodocheîon* < *xénos* guest, stranger + *déchesthai* to receive]

xe·nog·a·mous (zə nog′ə məs), *adj. Botany.* of or produced by cross-fertilization.

xe·nog·a·my (zə nog′ə mē), *n. Botany.* cross-fertilization.

xen·o·gen·e·sis (zen′ə jen′ə sis), *n. Biology.* **1.** heterogenesis. **2.** the supposed production of offspring wholly and permanently unlike the parent. **3.** spontaneous generation.

xen·o·ge·net·ic (zen′ə jə net′ik), *adj. Biology.* of the nature or having to do with xenogenesis.

xen·o·gen·ic (zen′ə jen′ik), *adj.* xenogenetic.

xe·nog·e·ny (zə noj′ə nē), *n.* xenogenesis.

xen·o·lith (zen′ə lith), *n.* a fragment of older rock embedded in an igneous mass: *A "xenolith" is simply a "stranger"—one not belonging to the rock system of the district* (T. Hannan).

xen·o·ma·ni·a (zen′ə mā′nē ə), *n.* a fondness for what is foreign: *a command of pure English, unadulterated by xenomania* (George Saintsbury).

xen·o·mor·phic (zen′ə môr′fik), *adj.* of rock having a form different from the normal form because of pressure. [< *xeno-* + Greek *morphḗ* form, shape + English *-ic*] —**xen′o·mor′phi·cal·ly,** *adv.*

xe·non (zē′non, zen′on), *n.* a heavy, colorless, not readily active gaseous element, present in very small quantities in the air and used in filling flash bulbs, radio tubes, etc. Xenon is obtained from liquid air and it forms compounds with fluorine and oxygen. *There was the moment of crisis at the start of the first Hanford reactor when the chain reaction threatened to die off because of the unexpectedly high neutron-capture cross section of an isotope of xenon* (Bulletin of Atomic Scientists). *Symbol:* Xe; *at.wt.:* (C^{12}) 131.3 or (O^{16}) 131.3; *at.no.:* 54. [< Greek *xénon,* neuter of *xénos,* adjective, strange]

xen·o·phile (zen′ə fīl), *n.* a person who is friendly toward foreign persons or things.

xen·o·phil·i·a (zen′ə fil′ē ə), *n.* friendship toward foreign persons or things: *American intellectuals themselves have debated the question with every shade of reaction from ferocious chauvinism to ferocious dissent, though more commonly with intermediate tinges of embarrassment, self-hate, xenophilia, and double-mindedness* (Manchester Guardian Weekly).

xen·o·phobe (zen′ə fōb), *n.* a person who fears or hates foreign persons or things: *The vision of the melting pot, with its ideal of inclusiveness, has often been severely challenged by bigots and xenophobes of various stripe* (Atlantic).

xen·o·pho·bi·a (zen′ə fō′bē ə), *n.* a hatred or fear of foreign persons or things: *The darkest cloud over the cultural landscape is that of steadily increasing xenophobia* (Atlantic).

xen·o·pho·bic (zen′ə fō′bik), *adj.* of or having to do with xenophobia: *A xenophobic view is taken in the Yemen of all foreigners* (Sunday Times). —**xen′o·pho′bi·cal·ly,** *adv.*

xen·o·time (zen′ə tīm), *n.* a yellowish-brown, natural phosphate of yttrium. It resembles zircon in form but is not as hard. *Formula:* YPO_4 [< *xeno-* + Greek *tīmḗ* honor]

xer-, *combining form.* the form of **xero-** before vowels, as in *xeric.*

xer·arch (zir′ärk), *adj. Ecology.* originating in dry habitats: *a xerarch plant succession.* [< *xer-* + Greek *archḗ* beginning]

xe·ric (zir′ik), *adj. Botany.* lacking moisture: *varieties of xeric wheat.*

xero-, *combining form.* dry: *Xeroderma = (a disease characterized by) dry skin. Xeroph-*

ilous = *adapted to a dry climate.* Also, **xer-** before vowels. [< Greek *xērós* dry]

xe·ro·der·ma (zir′ə dėr′mə), *n.* a disease characterized by dryness and discoloration of the skin. [< *xero-* + Greek *dérma* skin]

xe·ro·graph·ic (zir′ə graf′ik), *adj.* of or having to do with xerography: *In the xerographic process the characters are optically projected onto the charged surface of a rotating selenium-coated drum* (Hugo Gernsback).

xe·rog·ra·phy (zi rog′rə fē), *n.* **1.** a printing process that uses electrically charged particles to make a positive photographic contact print. Paper is placed on a metal plate sprayed with electrons before exposure, and dusted with black powder and the image is transferred to the paper by heat. Xerography is used for printing such material as engineering drawings and ruled forms, and for making quick copies of office records and correspondence: *Other items that are speeded up by xerography are the budgets for circulation to directors, the minutes of board meetings and many other internal documents* (London Times). **2. Xerography,** a trademark for this process.

xe·ro·ma (zi rō′mə), *n.* xerophthalmia.

xe·ro·morph (zir′ə môrf), *n.* a plant adapted to salt-water marshes or highly alkaline soils. [< *xero-* + Greek *morphḗ* form]

xe·roph·a·gy (zi rof′ə jē), *n., pl.* **-gies.** the practice of living on dry food, especially a form of abstinence in which only bread, herbs, salt, and water are consumed: *As for xerophagies, says Tertullian, they charge them with being a novel title for a pretended duty* (Frederic W. Farrar). [< Late Latin *xērophagia* < Greek *xērophagíā* < *xērós* dry + *phageîn* eat]

xe·roph·i·lous (zi rof′ə ləs), *adj.* adapted to a dry climate. [< *xero-* + Greek *phílos* (with English *-ous*) loving]

xe·roph·i·ly (zi rof′ə lē), *n.* the condition or character of being xerophilous.

xe·roph·thal·mi·a (zir′of thal′mē ə), *n.* an abnormal condition of mucous membrane of the eyeball, characterized by dryness and thickness, and often accompanied by night blindness or day blindness: *Malaria and yaws have been practically eliminated in central Java, but one now finds disquieting evidence of clinical malnutrition . . . and xerophthalmia, the blindness of Vitamin A deficiency* (New Scientist). [< Greek *xērophthalmíā* < *xērós* dry + *ophthalmíā* eye disease < *ophthalmós* eye]

xe·ro·phyte (zir′ə fīt), *n. Botany.* a plant that loses very little water and can grow in deserts or very dry ground: *Cactuses, sagebrush, century plants, etc., are xerophytes.*

xe·ro·phyt·ic (zir′ə fit′ik), *adj. Botany.* of or having to do with a xerophyte: *This is at all times less frequented than the main beach, and here grow many xerophytic plants, and curlew and other wading birds here alight, where mud and sand mingle* (Manchester Guardian).

xe·ro·phyt·i·cal·ly (zir′ə fit′ə klē), *adv.* in the manner of a xerophyte.

xe·ro·phyt·ism (zir′ə fī tiz′əm), *n.* the quality or condition of being adapted to live in a very dry climate.

xe·ro·ra·di·o·graph (zir′ō rā′dē ə graf, -gräf), *n.* a picture made by xeroradiography.

xe·ro·ra·di·og·ra·phy (zir′ō rā′dē og′rə fē), *n.* a process of X-ray photography that uses an electrically charged metal plate instead of film: *A picture taken by xeroradiography can be developed in 15 seconds, without recourse to darkroom or wet chemicals* (New Scientist).

xe·ro·sis (zi rō′sis), *n. Medicine.* abnormal dryness, as of the skin or the eyeball. [< New Latin *xerosis* < Greek *xḗrōsis* a drying up < *xērós* dry + *-ōsis* -osis]

xe·rot·ic (zi rot′ik), *adj. Medicine.* **1.** characterized by dryness; of the nature of xerosis. **2.** having to do with xerosis.

Xe·rox (zir′oks), *n. Trademark.* **1.** a xerographic process for making copies of written, typewritten, or drawn materials: *Microfilm takes weeks and is costly. Positive photostat takes time. What about Xerox?* (Harper's). **2.** a copying machine using this process.

xe·rox (zir′oks), *v.t., v.i.* to make copies by the Xerox process or machine: *We xeroxed thirty . . . sample essays to be graded by all the teachers* (New Yorker).

Xho·sa (ksō′sə), *n.* Xosa: *The three and a half million Xhosas who are about to have their own state (in which fewer than one and a half million of them can scratch a living) may be getting something in return for stateless status in white South Africa* (London Times).

xi (sī, zī, ksē), *n.* the 14th letter of the Greek alphabet (Ξ ξ), corresponding to English X, x. [< Greek *xí*]

X.i. or **x-i.,** *Finance.* ex interest.

XI (no periods), **1.** the Roman numeral for 11. **2.** *British Informal.* a team of eleven players, as in cricket: *The first XI, beaten by seven wickets* (Punch).

x-int., *Finance.* ex interest.

-xion, *suffix. British.* a variant of **-tion,** as in *connexion.*

xi particle, a hyperon, either neutral or negative, present in cosmic rays and existing very briefly during a high-energy nuclear collision in a large atomic reactor: *If a nucleon is struck so violently that it loses two K-mesons, it changes into a xi-particle, which thus differs from the original nucleon by two units of hypercharge* (Victor F. Weisskopf).

xiph·i·oid (zif′ē oid), *adj.* **1.** resembling the swordfish. **2.** belonging to the same family as the swordfish. [< Latin *xiphias* swordfish (< Greek *xiphías* < *xíphos* sword)]

xiph·i·ster·nal (zif′ə stėr′nəl), *adj.* xiphoid.

xiphisternal cartilage, the cartilaginous lower end of the sternum; xiphisternum.

xiph·i·ster·num (zif′ə stėr′nəm), *n., pl.* **-na** (-nə). the posterior or lower part of the sternum of mammals (in man usually called *xiphoid cartilage*). [< New Latin *xiphisternum* < Greek *xíphos* sword + Latin *sternum* sternum]

xiph·oid (zif′oid), *Anatomy.* —*adj.* **1.** shaped like or resembling a sword; ensiform. **2.** of or having to do with the xiphisternum or xiphisternal cartilage. —*n.* the xiphisternal or xiphoid cartilage. [< New Latin *xiphoides* < Greek *xiphoeidḗs* < *xíphos* sword + *eîdos* form]

xi·phoi·dal (zə foi′dəl), *adj.* xiphoid.

xiphoid cartilage, the cartilaginous lower end of the sternum in man.

xiph·o·phyl·lous (zif′ə fil′əs), *adj. Botany.* having sword-shaped or ensiform leaves. [< Greek *xíphos* sword + *phýllon* leaf]

xiph·o·su·ran (zif′ə su̇r′ən), *adj.* of or belonging to an order of arthropods comprising the king crabs. —*n.* a xiphosuran arthropod; king crab. [< New Latin *Xiphosura* the order name (< Greek *xíphos* sword + *ourā́* tail) + English *-an*]

X-ir·ra·di·ate (eks′i rā′dē āt), *v.t.,* **-at·ed, -at·ing.** to subject to the action of X rays: *When the male gametes [of guinea pigs and mice] are heavily x-irradiated in post-spermatogonial stages the offspring show high incidences of dominant defects* (Bulletin of Atomic Scientists).

X-ir·ra·di·a·tion (eks′i rā′dē ā′shən), *n.* a subjection to X rays, as in the treatment of disease: *Recent research . . . has shown that X-irradiation has a damaging effect on the fatty acids* (Science News Letter).

xi zero, a xi particle: *The newly discovered particle is the xi zero, or neutral cascade hyperon, one of the "strange" fleeting fragments of matter found only in cosmic rays and in beams produced by the most powerful atom smashers* (Science News Letter).

X.L. or **XL** (no periods), extra large.

X·mas (kris′məs), *n.* Christmas. [< *X* Christ + (Christ)*mas*]

Xn., Christian.

Xnty., Christianity.

Xo·sa (ksō′sə), *n.* **1.** a member of a group of Bantu tribes living mainly in the Transkei, east of the Cape Province: *The Xosas came first. . . . They killed or chased away the Bushmen — all invaders did that — but the Xosas especially mixed freely with the Hottentots and borrowed much of their clicking speech* (Eric Walker). **2.** any of the languages of these tribes: *The Xosa speaking peoples are, for the most part, inhabitants of rural areas* (S. B. van der Westhuizen). Also, **Xhosa.**

XP (kī′rō′, kē′-), the first two letters (*chi* and *rho*) of the Greek word ΧΡΙΣΤΟΣ (Christos, Christ), used in early times as an abbreviation alone or in combination.

X particle, meson.

X-ra·di·a·tion (eks′rā dē ā′shən), *n.* **1.** X rays: *Ultraviolet light from an atom electrically excited in a discharge tube might have the same frequency as low-voltage X-radiation* (Edgar N. Grisewood). **2.** examination, treatment, etc., with X rays: *A special technique has been developed of very soft X-radiation to improve delicate photographic contrasts* (London Times).

X-ray (eks′rā′), *n. U.S.* a code name for the letter *x*, used in transmitting radio messages.

X ray, 1. a ray with an extremely short wave length formed when cathode rays impinge upon a solid body (such as the wall of a vacuum tube), that can penetrate opaque substances; a Roentgen ray. X rays are used to locate breaks in bones, bullets lodged in the body, etc., and to diagnose and treat certain diseases. **2.** a picture made by means of X rays. [half-translation of obsolete German *X-Strahlen* plural < *X*, in sense of "unknown" + *Strahl* ray, beam]

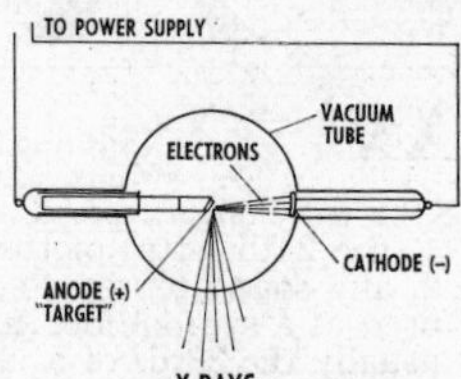

X Ray (def. 1)
High voltage is applied to two electrodes enclosed in vacuum tube, creating a flow of electrons from the cathode (–) toward the anode (+). When high-speed electrons strike the metal target or anode, it gives off X rays.

➤ **X ray** is usually written with a capital *X*. It is not hyphenated as a noun, but it is as a verb or adjective: *to X-ray the chest, an X-ray examination.*

X-ray (eks′rā′), *v.t.* **1.** to examine, photograph, or treat with X rays. **2.** to subject to very close scrutiny; examine minutely: *The Republicans X-rayed the charge for legitimate political dynamite, and the Democrats prayed that it would pass* (Manchester Guardian Weekly). —*v.i.* to use X rays: *If . . . a doctor suspects tuberculosis, he may X-ray* (Time).
—*adj.* **1.** of or having to do with X rays. **2.** by X rays: *an X-ray examination of one's teeth.*

X-ray astronomy, 1. the study of X-ray stars: *X-ray astronomy . . . can be carried out only from rockets and satellites sent above the atmosphere, since the atmosphere screens out the radiation* (New York Times). **2.** the branch of astronomy dealing with this study.

X-ray crystallography, the study of the arrangement of atoms and molecules in crystals and chemical substances by X rays.

X-ray diffraction, the diffusion of X rays on contact with matter, with changes in radiation intensity as a result of differences in atomic structure within the matter. It is an important method of studying atomic structure and is used in X-ray crystallography. *the techniques of X-ray diffraction, which have contributed so much to the understanding of the inner structure of metals and alloys* (F.A. Fox).

X-ray microscope, a microscope using X rays for studying the internal structure of metals, plastics, etc., and the interiors of minute organisms. It is capable of magnifying up to 1,500 diameters.

X-ray photograph, a photograph made by means of X rays.

X-ray spectrometer, a spectrometer using X rays by which the chemical constituents of a substance are separated into their characteristic spectral lines for identification and determination of their concentration.

X-ray spectrometry, the use of an X-ray spectrometer; chemical analysis by means of an X-ray spectrometer.

X-ray star, any of a group of stellar bodies that emit X rays, first observed in 1962.

X-ray therapy, therapy, as in treating cancer, in which X rays are used.

X-ray tube, a vacuum tube for generating X rays. See **X ray** for picture.

X-rts., *Finance.* ex rights.

Xt., Christ.

Xtian., Christian.

Xty., Christianity.

XV (no periods), **1.** the Roman numeral for 15. **2.** *British Informal.* a team consisting of fifteen players, as in Rugby.

xyl-, *combining form.* the form of **xylo-** before vowels, as in *xylan, xylene.*

xy·lan (zī′lan), *n. Chemistry.* a yellow, gelatinous compound, a pentosan, found in woody tissue. It yields xylose when hydrolyzed. *One disadvantage of hardwoods over soft is that hardwood contains a higher percentage of xylan, a gummy substance that must be removed* (Science News Letter).

xy·la·ry ray (zī′lər ē), *Botany.* medullary ray.

xy•lem (zī′lem), *n. Botany.* the tissue in a plant or tree that conveys upward the water and dissolved minerals absorbed by the roots and provides support; the wood, as a tissue of the plant body. It is the harder portion of a vascular bundle, and consists usually of tracheids, tracheae or vessels, wood fibers, parenchyma, etc. [< German *Xylem* < Greek *xýlon* wood + German *-em*, as in *Phloem* phloem]

xy•lene (zī′lēn), *n.* one of three isomeric, colorless, liquid hydrocarbons of the benzene series, present in coal and wood tar, naphtha, etc. Commercial xylene is a mixture of all three, and is used in making dyes, as a raw material for polyester fibers, etc.; xylol. *Formula:* C_8H_{10}

xy•lic (zī′lik, zil′ik), *adj. Chemistry.* of or having to do with any of several isomeric acids which are derivatives of xylene.

xylic acid, one of a group of six isomeric acids which are carboxyl derivatives of xylene. *Formula:* $C_9H_{10}O_2$

xy•li•din (zī′lə din, zil′ə-), *n.* xylidine.

xy•li•dine (zī′lə dēn, -din; zil′ə-), *n.* one of a group of six isomeric compounds which are amino derivatives of xylene, homologous with aniline. Commercial xylidine is an oily liquid composed of a mixture of five of these substances, and is used in making dyes. *Formula:* $C_8H_{10}N$
[< *xyl*(ene) + *-id* + *-ine*[2]]

xylo-, *combining form.* wood; woody: *Xylograph = a woodcut.* Also, **xyl-** before vowels. [< Greek *xýlon* wood]

Xy•lo•cain (zī′lə kān), *n. Trademark.* a yellowish-white, crystalline chemical compound used in the form of a hydrochloride as a local anesthetic. *Formula:* $C_{14}H_{22}N_2O$

xy•lo•carp (zī′lə kärp), *n. Botany.* a hard and woody fruit. [< *xylo-* + Greek *karpós* fruit]

xy•lo•car•pous (zī′lə kär′pəs), *adj. Botany.* having fruit which becomes hard and woody.

xy•lo•gen (zī′lə jən), *n. Botany.* **1.** wood or xylem in a formative state. **2.** lignin.

xy•lo•graph (zī′lə graf, -gräf), *n.* a woodcut.

xy•log•ra•pher (zī log′rə fər), *n.* an engraver on wood, especially one of the earliest wood engravers, as of the 1400's.

xy•lo•graph•ic (zī′lə graf′ik), *adj.* **1.** of or having to do with xylography: *The woodcuts, if . . . coarse from a xylographic point of view, are admirably characteristic* (Athenaeum). **2.** cut in or on wood: *The xylographic picture is a good specimen of popular art* (Nation).

xy•lo•graph•i•cal (zī′lə graf′ə kəl), *adj.* xylographic.

xy•log•ra•phy (zī log′rə fē), *n.* the art of engraving on wood, or of making prints from such engravings: *The forthcoming edition of the New Testament, illustrated with all the powers of modern xylography* (Saturday Review). [< French *xylographie* < Greek *xýlon* wood + French *-graphie* -graphy]

xy•loid (zī′loid), *adj.* **1.** of or having to do with wood. **2.** like wood; ligneous. [< Greek *xyloeidḗs* < *xýlon* wood + *eîdos* form]

xy•lol (zī′lōl, -lol), *n.* xylene: *Xylol is the best solvent of Canada balsam for such hermetical sealing* (British Journal of Photography).

xy•lol•o•gy (zī lol′ə jē), *n.* the study of the structure of wood.

xy•lo•nite (zī′lə nīt), *n.* celluloid: *Paper knives, hairpin boxes, and various other small articles . . . made in xylonite look remarkably well when carved* (Eleanor Rowe).

xy•lo•phage (zī′lə fāj), *n.* an insect, mollusk, or crustacean that eats or destroys wood. [< *xylophagous*]

xy•loph•a•gous (zī lof′ə gəs), *adj.* **1.** feeding on wood, as some insect larvae. **2.** boring into or destroying wood, as some mollusks and crustaceans. [< New Latin *xylophagus* (with English *-ous*) < Greek *xýlon* wood + *phageîn* to eat]

xy•lo•phone (zī′lə fōn, zil′ə-), *n.* a musical percussion instrument, consisting of a graduated series of flat wooden bars, played by striking with small wooden hammers. [< *xylo-* + *-phone*]

Xylophone

xy•lo•phon•ist (zī′lə fō′nist, zil′ə-; zī lof′ə-, zi-), *n.* one who plays on a xylophone.

xy•lo•rim•ba (zī′lə rim′bə, zil′ə-), *n.* a lightweight marimba resembling a xylophone.

xy•lose (zī′lōs), *n.* a crystalline, pentose sugar obtained from the decomposition of xylan in straw, corn cobs, etc., by the action of warm, dilute sulfuric acid. *Formula:* $C_5H_{10}O_5$

xy•lot•o•mist (zī lot′ə mist), *n.* a person skilled in xylotomy.

xy•lot•o•mous (zī lot′ə məs), *adj.* able to bore into or cut wood, as some insects.

xy•lot•o•my (zī lot′ə mē), *n.* the preparation of sections of wood, especially with a microtome, for examination with a microscope. [< *xylo-* + Greek *-tomía* a cutting]

xy•lyl (zī′ləl), *n. Chemistry.* a univalent radical, part of xylene. *Formula:* C_8H_9-

xy•lyl•ene (zī′lə lēn), *n. Chemistry.* a bivalent radical part of xylene. *Formula:* -C_8H_8-

xyst (zist), *n.* **1.** (among the ancient Greeks) a portico in a gymnasium where athletes exercised in winter. **2.** (among the ancient Romans) a walk in a garden, between rows of trees. [< Latin *xystus* < Greek *xystós* polished (floor) < *xýein* to smooth]

xys•tus (zis′təs), *n.* xyst.

Y

Roman 100's A.D.

Greek 600's B.C.

Phoenician 1000's B.C.

Egyptian 3000's B.C.

Yy Yy *Yy* *Yy*

Y[1] or **y** (wī), *n., pl.* **Y's** or **Ys, y's** or **ys. 1.** the 25th letter of the English alphabet. **2.** any sound represented by this letter. **3.** the 25th, or more usually the 24th, of a series (either *I* or *J* being omitted). **4.** used as a symbol for: an unknown quantity, especially in algebraic equations. **5.** a thing shaped like a Y.

Y. or **Y**[2] (wī), *n. Informal.* Y.M.C.A. or Y.W.C.A.; Y.M.H.A or Y.W.H.A.

-y[1], *suffix.* **1.** full of, composed of, containing, or having the qualities of ——, as in *airy, cloudy, dewy, icy, watery.*
2. somewhat, as in *chilly, salty, yellowy.*
3. inclined to, as in *chatty, fidgety.*
4. resembling or suggesting, as in *sloppy, sugary, tinny, willowy.*
5. In certain words, chiefly adjectives, such as *paly, steepy, stilly,* the addition of *-y* does not change the meaning.
[Old English *-ig*]

-y[2], *suffix.* **1.** small, as in *dolly.*
2. used to show kind feeling or intimacy, as in *aunty, daddy.* [Middle English *-y*]

-y[3], *suffix.* **1.** state or quality, as in *jealousy, victory.* **2.** activity as in *delivery, entreaty.* [Middle English *-ye, -ie* < Old French *-ie* < Latin *-ia* < Greek *-ia*]

y., **1.** yard or yards. **2.** year or years.

Y (no period), **1.** yen (Japanese unit of currency. **2.** yttrium (chemical element).

yab·ber (yab′ər), *Especially in Australia:* —*n.* speech; language. —*v.i., v.t.* to talk. [apparently < native Australian *yabba* < a root *ya-* to speak]

yab·bie (yab′ē), *n.* a small fresh-water crawfish of the Australian bush: *There are . . . yabbies . . . roasted on fire-heated stones for breakfast* (Punch). [< a native Australian name]

yacht (yot), *n.* a boat for pleasure trips or racing: *Anchored in the harbor among other luxury craft is the Prince's 360-ton yacht* (Newsweek). —*v.i.* to sail or race on a yacht. [< earlier Dutch *jaght* < *jaghtship* pursuit ship] —**yacht′er,** *n.*

yacht chair, a folding armchair with a canvas back and seat.

yacht·ing (yot′ing), *n.* **1.** the art of sailing a yacht. **2.** pastime of sailing on a yacht. —*adj.* **1.** of yachting or yachts. **2.** interested in yachting.

yachts·man (yots′mən), *n., pl.* **-men.** a person who owns or sails a yacht.

yachts·man·ship (yots′mən ship), *n.* skill or ability in handling a yacht.

yachts·wom·an (yots′wu̇m′ən), *n., pl.* **-wom·en.** a woman who owns or sails a yacht.

yack (yak), *Slang.* —*v.i.* to talk endlessly and foolishly; chatter: *We'll be in your hair all the time, yacking and quarrelling and everything* (New Yorker). —*n.* endless, foolish talk: *Local stations are either full of yack or turn out gloom by the square yard* (Cape Times). Also, **yak.** [imitative]

yack·e·ty-yak (yak′ə tē yak′), *v.i.,* **-yakked, yak·king,** *n.* yack: *He banned all syndicated columnists, snorting that they print "the yackety-yak that fills the room after the fourth dry martini"* (Time).

yaff (yaf, yäf), *Scottish.* —*v.i.* to bark; yelp. —*n.* a bark or yelp. [imitative]

yaf·fle (yaf′əl), *n. Dialect.* the green woodpecker. [imitative of its cry]

ya·ger (yā′gər), *n.* jaeger.

Ya·gi (yä′gē), *adj.* of, having to do with, or designating a powerful type of directional radio antenna or array that is like a dipole but with four conducting rods in a plane parallel to the ground. [< Hidetsugu *Yagi,* a Japanese engineer who invented it]

yah (yä), *interj.* an exclamation of derision, disgust, defiance, or impatience. [imitative]

Ya·hoo (yä′hü, yä hü′), *n.* (in Jonathan Swift's *Gulliver's Travels*) a brute in human shape who works for a race of intelligent horses.

ya·hoo (yä′hü, yä hü′), *n.* a rough, coarse, or uncouth person: *She launches into a philippic against the yahoos who desecrate picnic sites* (New Yorker). [< *Yahoo*]

ya·hoo·ism (yä′hü iz əm, yä hü′-), *n.* a style or quality characteristic or suggestive of a yahoo: *One must go back to McCarthy days to find a rival to this hearing for sheer yahooism* (Harper's).

Yahr·zeit (yär′tsīt′), *n. Judaism.* the yearly anniversary of the death of a parent or close relative, observed by saying kaddish and by the lighting of a memorial candle. [< Yiddish *yortsayt* (literally) a year's time]

Yah·veh or **Yah·ve** (yä′vā), *n.* Yahweh.

Yah·vism (yä′viz əm), *n.* Yahwism.

Yah·vist (yä′vist), *n.* Yahwist.

Yah·vis·tic (yä vis′tik), *adj.* Yahwistic.

Yah·weh or **Yah·we** (yä′wā), *n.* **1.** God (a transliteration of one of the Hebrew names used in the Old Testament, often rendered as *Jehovah*). **2.** the ancient god of the Hebrew tribes. Also, **Jahve, Jahveh.** [< Hebrew *Yahweh*]

Yah·wism (yä′wiz əm), *n.* **1.** the ancient religion of the Hebrews. **2.** the use of *Yahweh* as God's name. Also, **Jahvism.**

Yah·wist (yä′wist), *n.* the writer or writers of certain portions of the Old Testament, forming a separate source of the Hexateuch, characterized by the use of the name *Yahweh* for God. —*adj.* **1.** Yahwistic. **2.** of or having to do with Yahwism: *The primitive Yahwist faith of Israel . . . preached an afterlife* (Time). Also, **Jahvist, Jehovist.**

Yah·wis·tic (yä wis′tik), *adj.* **1.** of or by the Yahwist. **2.** using *Yahweh* as the name of God. Also, **Jahvistic, Jahwistic, Jehovistic.**

yak[1] (yak), *n.* a long-haired ox of the high plateaus of Tibet and central Asia, now largely domesticated and valued for its milk and hair, and as a beast of burden. [<Tibetan *gyak*]

Domestic Yak[1]
(5½ to 6 ft. high at the shoulder)

yak[2] (yak), *v.i.,* **yakked, yak·king,** *n.* yack: *They all yak their pretty heads off* (Cape Times).

yak lace, heavy lace made from yak hair.

Ya·kut (yä küt′), *n., pl.* **-kuts. 1.** a member of a Turkic people living in eastern Siberia. **2.** the Turkic language of this people.

yale (yāl), *n.* a fabulous beast with horns and tusks, resembling the two-horned rhinoceros: *The yale has the tail of an elephant and the jowls of a boar* (New York Times). [< Latin *ealē*]

yam (yam), *n.* **1.** the starchy, tuberous root of various vines, widely cultivated for food in tropical and subtropical countries, where it takes the place of the potato. **2.** any of these vines. **3.** *Southern U.S.* the sweet potato. **4.** *Scottish.* the potato. [< Spanish *ñame,* ultimately < Senegalese *nyami* eat]

Ya·ma·to (yä′mä tō), *n.* **1.** one of the legendary ancestors of the Japanese people, who migrated from the mainland in ancient times. **2.** the Japanese people. —*adj.* of the Japanese, especially the legendary Japanese.

ya·men (yä′mən), *n.* **1.** the official residence of a high Chinese official before 1912. **2.** the headquarters of any department of the civil service in China. Also, **yamun.** [< Manchu *yamun* official residence, courthouse]

ya·mil·ke (yä′məl kə), *n.* yarmulka.

yam·mer (yam′ər), —*v.i.* **1.** to lament. **2.** to whine; whimper. **3.** to howl; yell: *These inflationary actions illustrate the Administration's policy: yammer against inflation, but actually let it ride* (Time). —*v.t.* to say in a querulous tone.
—*n.* a yammering.
[alteration (perhaps influenced by Middle Dutch *jammeren*) of Middle English *yomeren,* Old English *geōmrian* to lament < *geōmor* sorrowful]

ya·mun (yä′mən), *n.* yamen.

yang (yang), *n.* the beneficial element in Chinese dualistic philosophy, representing the male qualities of goodness, light, and the earth: *We have spent many a pleasant moment in the past, browsing among the packaged shark fins . . . and contemplating the yang and the yin of things* (New Yorker). [< Chinese (Peking) *yang*]

yank (yangk), *Informal.* —*v.t., v.i.* to pull with a sudden motion; jerk: *where a lifting foresail-foot is yanking at the sheet* (John Masefield). —*n.* a sudden pull; jerk; tug. [origin uncertain]

Yank (yangk), *n., adj. Slang.* Yankee: *With all the publicity there has been, many authorities, Latin as well as Yank, also worry that expectations may be built too high* (Wall Street Journal).

Yan·kee (yang′kē), *n.* **1.** *Especially U.S.* **a.** a native of New England. **b.** a native of any of the Northern States. **2.** *Southern U.S.* a Northerner (often used in an unfriendly way). **3.** a native or inhabitant of the United States. **4.** *U.S.* a code name for the letter *y,* used in transmitting radio messages. —*adj.* of or having to do with Yankees: *Yankee shrewdness.*
[American English, perhaps ultimately < Dutch *Jan Kees,* dialectal variant of *Jan Kaas* (literally) John Cheese, a nickname for Dutch and English settlers; the *-s* was taken in English as a plural ending]

Yan·kee·dom (yang′kē dəm), *n.* **1.** Yankees collectively. **2.** the region inhabited by Yankees.

Yankee Doodle, an American song, probably of English origin and taken over by the American soldiers in the Revolutionary War.

Yan·kee·fied (yang′kē fīd), *adj.* made or become like a Yankee; characteristic of a Yankee: *Japan is . . . Yankeefied in more ways than one* (New York Voice).

Yan·kee·ism (yang′kē iz əm), *n.* **1.** Yankee character or characteristics. **2.** a Yankee peculiarity, as of speech. Saying *guess* for *think* is a Yankeeism.

Yan·kee·land (yang′kē land′), *n.* **1.** New England: *Gift shop operators in Yankeeland bought cautiously at the fall giftware show here* [*Boston*] (Wall Street Journal). **2.** the United States: *The Dominion populace of 16 million is less than one-tenth of Yankeeland's 169 million* (Wall Street Journal). **3.** the northern part of the United States: *Don't you realize that these hillbillies are bringing the precious "Southern way of life" to unenlightened Yankeeland?* (Time).

yan·ki (yäng′kē), *n., adj.* yanqui.

yan·ni·gan (yan′ə gən), *n. Baseball Slang.* a player not on the regular or starting team.

yan·qui or **Yan·qui** (yäng′kē), *n., adj.* (in Spanish America) Yankee: *This could be built up into the standard charge of "yanqui imperialism"* (Newsweek).

Ya·o[1] (yä′ō), *n., pl.* **Ya·o** or **Ya·os. 1.** a member of a people living chiefly in southwestern China, but also found in the mountains of northern Burma, Thailand, Laos, and Vietnam. **2.** the language of this people.

Ya·o[2] (yä′ō), *n., pl.* **Ya·o** or **Ya·os. 1.** a member of a Bantu people of eastern Africa, living on the southeastern shores of Lake Nyasa. **2.** the language of this people.

yap (yap), *n., v.,* **yapped, yap·ping.** —*n.* **1.** a snappish bark; yelp. **2.** *Slang.* snappish, noisy, or foolish talk. **3.** *Slang.* a peevish or noisy person. **4.** *Slang.* the mouth: *Those prissy college boys . . .* [*are*] *scared speechless every time McAlmon opens his yap* (Atlantic).
—*v.i.* **1.** to bark snappishly; yelp. **2.** *Slang.* to talk snappishly, noisily, or foolishly. **3.** *Slang.* to chatter or talk idly: *They're always yapping about life* (Philip Gibbs). [imitative]

Yap·ese (ya pēz′, -pēs′), *n., pl.* **-ese,** *adj.* —*n.* a native or inhabitant of Yap, an island in the Pacific. —*adj.* of or having to do with the island of Yap or its people.

ya·pok or **ya·pock** (yə pok′), *n.* a South and Central American water opossum, hav-

 PRONUNCIATION KEY: hat, āge, cãre, fär; let, ēqual, tėrm; it, īce; hot, ōpen, ôrder; oil, out; cup, pu̇t, rüle;

ing webbed toes. [< French *yapok* < *Oyabok*, a river in French Guiana]

yapp (yap), *n.* a style of bookbinding in limp leather with overlapping edges or flaps. —*adj.* of or having to do with this. [< *Yapp*, the name of a London bookseller]

yap·py (yap′ē), *adj.*, **-pi·er, -pi·est.** inclined to yap or yelp; yapping: *a yappy dog.*

ya·qo·na (yä kō′nä), *n.* a traditional or ceremonial drink of the Fiji Islands, prepared from the dried roots of the kava. [< Fijian]

Ya·qui (yä′kē), *n., pl.* **-qui** or **-quis,** *adj.* —*n.* a member of a tribe of American Indians of Uto-Aztecan language.
—*adj.* of this tribe of Indians.

Yar·bor·ough or **yar·bor·ough** (yär′bėr′ō; *especially British* yär′bər ə), *n.* a hand at whist or bridge with no card higher than a nine. [supposedly < an Earl of *Yarborough* who used to bet 1,000 to 1 against its occurrence]

yard[1] (yärd), *n.* **1.** a piece of ground near or around a house, barn, school, etc. **2.** a piece of enclosed ground for some special purpose: *a chicken yard.* **3.** a space with tracks where railroad cars are stored, shifted around, etc. **4.** *U.S. and Canada.* an area in which moose and deer gather for feeding during the winter.
—*v.t.* to put into or enclose in a yard.
[Old English *geard* an enclosure]
—**Syn.** *n.* **2.** court, enclosure.

yard[2] (yärd), *n.* **1.** a unit of linear measure, equal to 36 inches or 3 feet, and equivalent to .9144 meter. *Abbr.:* yd., y. **2.** *Nautical.* a long, slender beam or pole fastened across a mast, used to support a sail. [Old English *gerd*, or *gierd* rod]

Yards[2] **(def. 2)**

yard·age[1] (yär′dij), *n.* **1.** the service, use, or hire of a railroad yard or enclosure, as for storing freight or cattle. **2.** the charge for such use.

yard·age[2] (yär′dij), *n.* **1.** length in yards: *A high point of Nevers' college career was the 1925 Rose Bowl game against Notre Dame, in which he rolled up more yardage (134) than Notre Dame's famous Four Horsemen together* (Newsweek). **2.** an amount measured in yards: *Textile executives contend the actual yardage of goods being sold, while not as good as they'd like, is "not bad"* (Wall Street Journal).

yard·arm (yärd′ärm′), *n. Nautical.* either end of a yard which supports a square sail.

yard·bird (yärd′bėrd′), *n. Slang.* **1.** an army recruit: *The hero is a bemused, irreverent yardbird who gets himself and his officers into every kind of Army-life trouble* (Newsweek). **2.** a member of any of the armed forces, restricted to camp or given menial duties for breaking regulations.

yard goods, cloth cut to measure and sold by the yard: *There was no doubt that he had made a mistake in judgment in the autumn when he had ordered the yard goods for his spring line* (New Yorker).

yard grass, dog's-tail.

yard·land (yärd′land′), *n.* an area of land held by a tenant in villeinage in early English manors, varying in different counties from 15 to 40 acres.

yard·man[1] (yärd′mən), *n., pl.* **-men. 1.** a man who has charge of, or works in, a yard, as a railroad yard. **2.** a gardener.

yard·man[2] (yärd′mən), *n., pl.* **-men.** a sailor working on the yards of a ship.

yard·mas·ter (yärd′mas′tər, -mäs′-), *n.* the man in charge of a railroad yard.

yard·stick (yärd′stik′), *n.* **1.** a measuring stick one yard long; 36-inch ruler. **2.** any standard of judgment or comparison: *The food chains . . . have shown a declining trend in those two critical yardsticks for at least five years* (Advertising Age). —**Syn. 2.** criterion, gauge.

yard·wand (yärd′wond′), *n. Especially British.* a yardstick.

yare (yär), *adj.* **1.** ready; prepared. **2.** ready for use. **3.** alert; nimble; active; brisk; quick. **4.** (of a ship) easily steered or managed. [Old English *gearu*] —**yare′ly,** *adv.*

yarl (yärl), *n.* jarl.

Yar·mouth bloater (yär′məth), *British.* a herring that has been smoked but not salted. [< *Yarmouth*, a fishing town on the coast of Norfolk, in England]

yar·mul·ka or **yar·mul·ke** (yär′məl kə), *n.* a skullcap worn by Jewish men and boys, especially for prayer and ceremonial occasions. [< Yiddish < Polish *yarmulka* a kind of hat or cap]

yarn (yärn), *n.* **1.** any spun thread especially prepared for weaving or knitting. **2.** *Informal.* a story; tale: *The old sailor made up his yarns as he told them.* —*v.i. Informal.* to tell stories: *Thomas was yarning and clowning* (Time). [Old English *gearn* spun fiber]

yarn-dyed (yärn′dīd′), *adj.* made from yarn that was dyed before weaving.

yar·o·vize (yär′ə vīz), *v.t.,* **-vized, -viz·ing.** jarovize (vernalize).

yar·row (yar′ō), *n.* **1.** a common European composite herb, naturalized in North America, having finely divided leaves and close, flat clusters of white or pink flowers; milfoil. **2.** any other plant of the same genus. [Old English *gearwe*]

yash·mak or **yash·mac** (yäsh mäk′, yash′mak), *n.* a double veil concealing the part of the face below the eyes, worn by Moslem women in public: *Brown eyes, each pair expressionless as the last, peer from behind multi-coloured yashmaks* (Punch). [< Arabic *yashmaq*]

yat·a·ghan or **yat·a·gan** (yat′ə gan), *n.* a type of sword having no guard between the hilt and the blade, but usually a large pommel on the end, used by Moslems. Also, **ataghan.** [< Turkish *yatağan*]

Yataghan

yat·ter (yat′ər), *v.i.* to chatter. —*n.* chatter: *The yatter over Prohibition died with Repeal* (Time).

yaud (yôd, yäd), *n. Scottish.* **1.** an old mare. **2.** a worn-out horse. [< Scandinavian (compare Old Icelandic *jalda* mare). Compare JADE[2].]

yaul (yôl), *n.* yawl[2].

yauld (yôd, yäd, yäld), *adj. Scottish.* **1.** active; sprightly. **2.** strong; vigorous.

yaup (yôp, yäp), *v.i., n. Dialect or Informal.* yawp. —**yaup′er,** *n.*

yau·pon (yô′pon), *n.* a holly, of the southern United States, whose leaves have been used as a substitute for tea. Also, **yopon.** [American English < Siouan (Catawba) *yopún* (diminutive) < *yop* tree, shrub]

yau·ti·a (you tē′ä), *n.* a tropical plant of the West Indies and South America whose starchy root is used for food; taro; dasheen. [< American Spanish *yautía* < a native word]

yaw (yô), *v.i.* **1.** to turn from a straight course; go unsteadily. **2.** (of an aircraft) to turn from a straight course about its vertical axis. —*v.t.* to cause (a ship, aircraft, or missile) to yaw.
—*n.* **1.** a movement from a straight course. **2.** the amount of this.
[origin uncertain]
—**Syn.** *n.* **1.** deviation.

yawl[1] (yôl), *n.* **1.** a type of boat rigged like a sloop, with a large mast forward and a short mast near the stern, usually aft of the rudder post. **2.** a ship's boat rowed with four or six oars. [apparently < Dutch *jol*]

Yawl[1] **(def. 1)**

yawl[2] (yôl), *v.i., v.t., n. Dialect.* yowl; howl. [probably ultimately imitative. Compare Low German *jaulen.*]

yaw·me·ter (yô′mē′tər), *n.* an instrument for measuring the yaw of an aircraft.

yawn (yôn), *v.i.* **1.** to open the mouth wide because one is sleepy, tired, or bored: *The reader must not yawn, or yield to tickles in the throat, or tire of the tale in the middle* (London Times). **2.** to open wide: *A wide gorge yawned in front of us.*
—*v.t.* **1.** to utter with a yawn: *to yawn a reply.* **2.** to make or produce by opening wide.
—*n.* **1.** a yawning. **2.** something that yawns.
[variant of Middle English *yonen*, Old English *geonian, ginian*] —**yawn′er,** *n.*

yawn·ful (yôn′fəl), *adj.* causing one to yawn; tiresome; tedious: *He writes at yawnful length about . . . distortions of his positions as carried in the press, and at even greater length about what those positions really were* (Time). —**yawn′ful·ly,** *adv.*

yawn·ing (yô′ning), *adj.* **1.** characterized by or producing yawns; yawny; yawnful: *The account of the character of Mr. Legge is the most yawning pamphlet I ever read* (John Wilkes). **2.** opening or open wide: . . . *a lofty pass . . . surrounded by yawning precipices* (James Gilmour). —**yawn′ing·ly,** *adv.*

yawn·y (yô′nē), *adj.,* **yawn·i·er, yawn·i·est.** characterized by a yawn or yawns; inclined to yawning: *There were those first few unbelievable steps when you are nervously tired and yawny and must learn . . . the easy rhythm* (Harper's).

yawp (yôp, yäp), *Dialect or Informal.* —*v i.* **1.** to utter a loud, harsh cry. **2.** to speak foolishly. **3.** to gape.
—*n.* a loud, harsh cry: *The prevailing interest does not come from Ornette's yawps and squeals* (Saturday Review). Also, **yaup.**
[probably imitative] —**yawp′er,** *n.*

yaws (yôz), *n.pl.* a contagious tropical disease resembling syphilis but nonvenereal, characterized by raspberrylike skin lesions on the face, hands, feet, etc., and caused by a spirochete; frambesia: *Yaws is known the world over as a painful, crippling, and highly contagious disease that covers the body with sores and eventually eats away the outer flesh* (Time). [probably < Carib *yaya*, the native name for the disease]

y-ax·is (wī′ak′sis), *n.* the vertical axis in a system of rectangular coordinates, as on a chart or graph.

Yaz·i·di (yä′zə dē), *n., pl.* **-di** or **-dis.** Yezidi.

Yaz·oo (ya′zü), *n., pl.* **-oo** or **-oos.** a member of an American Indian tribe that formerly lived along the Yazoo River in Mississippi.

Yb (no period), ytterbium (chemical element).

Y.C., Yacht Club.

Y chromosome, *Biology.* one of the chromosomes that determine sex and related to maleness. An egg containing a Y chromosome develops into a male.

y·clad or **y-clad** (i klad′), *v. Archaic.* clad; clothed; a past participle of **clothe.** [Middle English *ycladde* < Old English *ge-*, past participial prefix + *clathod* clad]

y·clept or **y·cleped** (i klept′), *adj. Archaic.* called; named; styled. [Middle English *ycleped*, or *yclipted* < Old English *geclipod* named, past participle of *geclipian*, or *gecleopian* to speak, call]

yd., yard or yards.

yds., yards.

ye[1] (yē; *unstressed* yi), *pron. pl. Archaic.* you: *If ye are thirsty, drink.* [Old English *gē*]
➔ Originally **ye** was the subject, **you** the object form. In Late Middle English *you* began to be used as subject and in the Early Modern period the two forms were extensively confused. Before 1700 *you* had become regular for both cases.
➔ See **thou** for another usage note.

ye[2] (ᴛʜē; *popularly* yē), *definite article.* old way of writing the definite article "the."
➔ In Old and Middle English **the** was commonly written as *þe*. The early printers, who ordinarily did not have this consonant symbol (called "thorn") in their fonts, substituted *y* for it, but this was never intended to be read with the value of *y*.

yea (yā), *adv.* **1.** yes (used in affirmation or assent). **2.** indeed; truly (used to introduce a sentence or clause). **3.** *Archaic.* not only that, but also; moreover.
—*n.* an affirmative answer, vote, or voter.
[Old English *gēa*, or *gē*]

yeah (yeə), *adv. U.S. Informal.* yes: *"Yeah, that's right," said Buster* (New Yorker).

yean (yēn), *v.t., v.i.* (of a sheep or goat) to bring forth (young). [unrecorded Old English *geēanian.* Compare Old English *ēanian* to yean, *geēan* pregnant.]

yean·ling (yēn′ling), *n.* the young of a sheep or goat; lamb or kid. —*adj.* very young or newborn.

year (yir), *n.* **1.** 12 months or 365 days (366 days every fourth year); January 1 to December 31. **2.** 12 months reckoned from any point: *A fiscal year is a period of 12 months at the end of which the accounts of a government, business, or the like, are balanced.*

3. the part of a year spent in a certain activity: *A school year is 8 to 12 months.* 4. the period of the earth's revolution around the sun: *The solar or astronomical year is 365 days, 5 hours, 48 minutes, 46 seconds.* 5. the time it takes for the sun to make an apparent journey from a given star back to it again: *The sidereal year is 20 minutes, 23 seconds longer than the solar year.* 6. 12 lunar months, about 354 days long (lunar year). 7. the time in which any planet completes its revolution around the sun. 8. a class or grade of a school, college, etc.: *He is in his sophomore year. Abbr.:* yr.
a year and a day, *Law.* a period constituting a term for certain purposes, in order to insure that a full year is completed: *They shall lose the rights to the estate if they do not claim it within a year and a day of the death of the testator.*
stricken in years, advanced in years; old: *A man well stricken in years* (Anthony Trollope).
year by year, with each succeeding year; as years go by: *Be it your fortune, year by year, the same resource to prove* (William Cowper).
year in, (and) year out, always; continuously: *You see other girls having splendid times, while you grind, grind, year in and year out* (Louisa May Alcott).
years, a. age (of a person): . . . *young in years, but in sage counsel old* (Milton). *You may change your opinion, if you live to my years* (Henry Fielding). **b.** age; period; times: *years of prosperity.* **c.** a very long time: *I haven't seen him in years.* **d.** *Archaic.* old age: *a man of (or in) years.*
[Old English *gēar*]

year·a·round (yir′ə round′), *adj.* year-round.

year·book (yir′bůk′), *n.* **1.** a book or a report published every year. **2.** a classbook.

year-by-year (yir′bī yir′), *adv., adj.* from one year to another; with each succeeding year.

year-end (yir′end′), *n.* **1.** the end of the year. **2.** *Informal.* a stock dividend given at the end of the year. —*adj.* the end of the year.

year·ling (yir′ling, yėr′-), *n.* **1.** an animal one year old: *Rustlers work in late fall and winter to pick up yearlings missed by the branding iron at roundup* (Newsweek). **2.** (in horse racing) a horse in the second calendar year since it was foaled. **3.** *U.S.* a cadet in the second year at a military academy. —*adj.* one year old: *a yearling colt.*

year·long (yir′lông′, -long′), *adj.* **1.** lasting for a year. **2.** lasting for years.

year·ly (yir′lē), *adj.* **1.** once a year; in every year: *a yearly trip to Europe.* **2.** lasting a year: *the yearly revolution of the earth around the sun.* **3.** for a year: *He is paid a yearly salary of $5,000.*
—*adv.* once a year; in every year; annually.

yearn (yėrn), *v.i.* **1.** to feel a strong desire or longing; desire earnestly: *He yearns for home.* **2.** to feel pity; have tender feelings: *Her heart yearned for the starving children.* [Old English *geornan,* or *giernan*] —**Syn. 1.** hanker, pine. **2.** mourn, commiserate.

yearn·ful (yėrn′fəl), *adj.* **1.** full of yearning. **2.** sorrowful. —**yearn′ful·ly,** *adv.*

yearn·ing (yėr′ning), *n.* **1.** earnest or strong desire; longing. **2.** the state of being moved with compassion. —*adj.* that yearns. —**yearn′ing·ly,** *adv.*

year-round (yir′round′), *adj., adv.* throughout the year: *year-round residents.*

year-round·er (yir′roun′dər), *n. Informal.* a person who lives in a place all year long.

years (yirz), *n.pl.* See under **year.**

year-to-year (yir′tə yir′), *adj.* occurring or done from year to year.

yea·say (yā′sā′), *v.t., v.i.* to say yea (to); assent; agree; vote in the affirmative. —**yea′say′er,** *n.*

yeast (yēst), *n.* **1.** the substance used in raising bread, making beer, etc. Yeast consists of very small single-celled plants (ascomycetous fungi) that grow quickly in a liquid containing sugar. **2.** a yeast plant. **3.** a yeast cake. **4.** an influence, element, etc., that acts as a leaven. **5.** foam or froth. **6.** fermentation; agitation.
—*v.i.* to ferment; be covered with froth.
[Old English *gist*] —**yeast′like′,** *adj.*
—**Syn.** *n.* **5.** spume.

yeast bread, bread baked with yeast.

yeast cake, flour or meal mixed with yeast and pressed into a small cake.

yeast·i·ness (yēs′tē nis), *n.* the quality or state of being yeasty.

yeast plant, any of a group of minute, one-celled, ascomycetous fungi, which produce alcoholic fermentation in saccharine fluids.

yeast·y (yēs′tē), *adj.,* **yeast·i·er, yeast·i·est. 1.** of, containing, or resembling yeast. **2.** frothy or foamy: *yeasty waves.* **3.** light or trifling; frivolous: *Miller writes what is probably the yeastiest scandal column printed anywhere* (Time).

Yeats·i·an (yā′tsē ən), *adj.* of or having to do with the Irish poet and playwright William Butler Yeats, 1865-1939, or his writings: *Yeatsian lyricism.*

yegg (yeg), *n. U.S. Slang.* **1.** a burglar who robs safes; safecracker. **2.** any burglar. [American English; origin uncertain]

yegg·man (yeg′mən), *n., pl.* **-men.** yegg.

yeld (yeld), *adj. Scottish.* **1.** (of an animal) not able to bear young. **2.** (of cattle) not yielding milk; dry. Also, **yell.** [Old English *gelde;* perhaps related to GELD[1]]

yelk (yelk), *n. Archaic.* yolk[1].

yell[1] (yel), *v.i., v.t.* to cry out with a strong, loud sound: *to yell abuse.* —*n.* **1.** a strong, loud outcry. **2.** *U.S.* a special shout or cheer, used by a school or college. [Old English *gellan,* or *giellan*] —**yell′er,** *n.*

yell[2] (yel), *adj. Scottish.* yeld.

yel·low (yel′ō), *n.* **1.** the color of gold, butter, or ripe lemons. **2.** a yellow pigment, dye, fabric, etc. **3.** the yolk of an egg.
—*adj.* **1.** having a yellow color. **2. a.** having a yellowish skin, as the Mongolians. **b.** of the Mongolian race. **3.** *Informal.* cowardly. **4.** sensational: *yellow journalism.*
—*v.t., v.i.* to turn yellow: *Paper yellows with age.*
[Old English *geolu*] —**yel′low·ly,** *adv.* —**yel′low·ness,** *n.*

yellow arsenic, orpiment.

yellow asphodel, an asphodel native to the Mediterranean regions, with yellow, fragrant, flowers.

yellow avens, herb bennet.

yel·low-back (yel′ō bak′), *n. Informal.* **1.** shilling shocker. **2.** *U.S.* a currency note printed on the back in a yellowish color.

yel·low-bel·lied (yel′ō bel′ēd), *adj.* **1.** having a yellow belly or underside. **2.** *Slang.* cowardly; craven.

yellow-bellied flycatcher, a small flycatcher of eastern North America with yellowish underparts.

yellow-bellied sapsucker, a North American woodpecker with a yellowish underside and a red forehead. See **sapsucker** for picture.

yel·low-bel·ly (yel′ō bel′ē), *n., pl.* **-lies.** *Slang.* a coward: *Some of them called me a traitor and a yellow-belly—things like that* (Harper's).

yellow bile, choler.

yel·low-billed cuckoo (yel′ō bild′), a North American cuckoo having a partly yellow bill: *In the mountains of Colombia such winter visitors from North America as the yellow-billed cuckoo . . . have been observed ranging freely* (Scientific American).

yellow birch, a North American birch yielding a strong, light-brown wood: *When valuable yellow birch forests are cut in central Ontario the ensuing forest isn't yellow birch any more; it's a hardwood forest of maple, and usually a pretty poor one* (Maclean's).

yel·low·bird (yel′ō bėrd′), *n.* **1.** the American goldfinch. **2.** the North American yellow warbler. **3.** any of certain other yellow birds such as an oriole of Europe.

yellow body, corpus luteum.

yel·low-breast·ed chat (yel′ō bres′tid), a large North American warbler with an olive-green back and yellow breast.

yellow buckeye, a large horse chestnut tree with yellow flowers of the Ohio Valley and Appalachian Mountains.

yellow cake, a yellow powder obtained by processing uranium ore.

yellow clover, a hop clover with yellow flowers.

yel·low-cov·ered (yel′ō kuv′ərd), *adj.* **1.** covered with yellow. **2.** cheap; trashy.

yel·low-crowned night heron (yel′ō-kround′), a gray heron with a black and white head, chiefly of swamps of the southern United States and south to Brazil.

yellow daisy, 1. the black-eyed Susan. **2.** any daisy or daisylike flower with yellow rays, as anthemis.

yellow dog, *U.S. Slang.* **1.** a worker who does not join or assist a labor union. **2.** a despicable or worthless person.

yel·low-dog contract (yel′ō dôg′, -dog′), *U.S.* an agreement between employer and employee that the worker will not join or assist a labor union. The Norris-La Guardia Act of 1932 made such contracts illegal.

yellow dwarf, a virus disease of onion, barley, and soybean plants, which turns leaves yellow and stunts the plants.

yellow enzyme, a flavoprotein.

yellow fat, a condition caused by a deficiency of vitamin E in domestic animals.

yellow fever, an acute, often fatal, viral disease of the tropics, characterized by chills, high fever, jaundice, etc. It is transmitted by the bite of the mosquito.

yel·low·fin (yel′ō fin′), *n.* a tunny of the Atlantic and Pacific oceans.

yellow gold, an orange-yellow alloy of gold containing about nine parts gold to one part copper, used in jewelry.

yel·low-green algae (yel′ō grēn′), green algae.

yellow gum, a eucalyptus.

yel·low·ham·mer (yel′ō ham′ər), *n.* **1.** a European bunting, having the head, throat, and under parts bright yellow. **2.** *U.S.* the yellow-shafted flicker. [alteration of earlier *yelambre,* probably < Old English *geolu* yellow + Middle English *amore, omer,* or *emer* a kind of bird]

yel·low-head·ed blackbird (yel′ō hed′-id), a blackbird of western North America, the male of which has a yellow head and breast.

yel·low·ish (yel′ō ish), *adj.* somewhat yellow.

yellow jack, 1. yellow fever. **2.** a yellow flag used as a signal of quarantine. **3.** a carangoid fish of the West Indies and Florida.

yellow jacket, a social wasp having bright-yellow markings.

yellow jasmine or **jessamine,** a twining shrub of the southern United States having fragrant, yellow flowers; gelsemium. It is the floral emblem of South Carolina.

yellow lead ore, wulfenite.

yel·low·legs (yel′ō legz′), *n.* either of two American shore birds with yellow legs, having a gray back marked with white and a white breast streaked with gray.

yellow light, a signal cautioning traffic to slow down, usually preceding a red light.

yellow loosestrife, a common loosestrife bearing clusters (racemes) of yellow flowers.

yellow metal, 1. gold. **2.** a yellowish alloy containing copper (about 60 per cent) and zinc (about 40 per cent).

yellow pages, *U.S.* a telephone directory or a section of it, printed on pages of a yellow color, in which the names are classified according to types of business, services, professions, etc.: *I opened the yellow pages and picked out the first restaurant listed —A La Fourchette, on West Forty-sixth street* (New Yorker).

yellow perch, a North American perch. See **perch**[2] for picture.

yellow peril, the alleged danger to the rest of the world, especially to Europe and America, from the growth and activities of Japan or China.

yellow pine, 1. any of various American pines with yellow or yellowish wood. **2.** the wood of any of these trees. **3.** tulip tree.

yellow poplar, tulip tree.

yellow press, that portion of the press that practices yellow journalism.

yellow race, the Mongolian race.

yellow rail, a small, rare, yellowish rail of North America.

yel·lows (yel′ōz), *n.pl.* (*often singular in use*). **1.** *Botany.* any of various unrelated diseases of plants in which the foliage turns yellow and growth is checked, as in peaches and cabbages. **2.** jaundice, especially of horses and cattle. **3.** *Obsolete.* jealousy.

yellow sapphire, topaz.

yel·low-shaft·ed flicker (yel′ō shaf′tid; -shäf′-), the flicker, a woodpecker of North America with yellow shafts in its wing and tail feathers; yellowhammer.

yellow sponge, horse sponge.

yellow spot, a yellowish depression on the retina, the region of most distinct vision.

yellow streak, 1. cowardice. **2.** an indication of cowardice.

yel·low·tail (yel′ō tāl′), *n., pl.* **-tails** or (*collectively*) **-tail. 1.** any of a group of fishes, especially a game fish, of the California coast. **2.** a snapper of the Atlantic Coast of tropical America. **3.** any of certain fishes having a yellow tail, as the menhaden. **4.** a large South African mackerel.

yel·low-tailed (yel′ō tāld′), *adj.* having the tail more or less yellow.

yel·low·throat (yel′ō thrōt′), *n.* any of certain North American warblers, especially the Maryland yellowthroat.

yel·low-throat·ed vireo (yel′ō thrō′tid), a North American vireo.

yellow-throated warbler, an American warbler with gray back, white belly, and yellow throat.

yellow warbler, a small, greenish-yellow American warbler having fine reddish streaks on the chest; golden warbler; yellowbird.

yellow water lily, any of a group of yellow-flowered aquatic plants.

yel·low·weed (yel′ō wēd′), *n.* **1.** the European ragwort. **2.** the sneezeweed. **3.** *U.S. Dialect.* any of several coarse goldenrods. **4.** *British Dialect.* weld.

yel·low·wood (yel′ō wůd′), *n.* **1.** a tree of the pea family, bearing showy, white flowers; gopherwood. It is found in the southern United States. **2.** its hard, yellow wood, which yields a clear yellow dye. **3.** any of several other trees yielding yellow wood or a yellow extract or dye, as the Osage orange. **4.** the wood of any of these trees.

yel·low·y (yel′ō ē), *adj.* yellowish.

yelp (yelp), *n.* a sharp, shrill bark or cry characteristic of foxes, dogs, etc., especially small or excited dogs. [< verb]
—*v.i.* to utter a yelp or yelps. —*v.t.* to utter with a yelp. [Old English *gelpan,* or *gielpan* to boast] —**yelp′er,** *n.*

Yem·e·ni (yem′ə nē), *n., pl.* **-ni** or **-nis,** *adj.* Yemenite.

Yem·en·ite (yem′ə nīt), *n.* a native or inhabitant of Yemen, a country in southwestern Arabia. —*adj.* of or having to do with Yemen or its people.

yen[1] (yen), *n., pl.* **yen. 1.** the basic Japanese monetary unit, worth about ¼ of a cent. **2.** a former Japanese gold or silver coin. [< Japanese *yen* < Chinese *yüan* (literally) round object. Doublet of YUAN.]

yen[2] (yen), *n., v.,* **yenned, yen·ning.** *Informal.* —*n.* a sharp or intense desire or hunger; urgent fancy: *a sudden yen to leave. She had a yen for something sweet.* —*v.i.* to have a yen; desire. [American English, perhaps < dialectal pronunciation of *yearn*]
—**Syn.** *n.* yearning.

yeo·man (yō′mən), *n., pl.* **-men. 1.** *U.S. Navy.* a petty officer who does clerical and secretarial work. **2.** *Historical.* **a.** a servant or attendant in a royal or noble household, usually of superior grade, ranking between a sergeant and a groom, or a squire and a page. **b.** an assistant to an official: *the sheriff's yeoman.* **3.** *British.* a yeoman of the guard. **4.** in England (chiefly historically): **a.** a man owning a small amount of land and ranking as a commoner; freeholder. **b.** a man who farms his own land, especially a man of respectable standing. **5.** *British.* a member of the yeomanry. [Middle English *yoman,* and *yeman;* origin uncertain. Compare Frisian *gāman* villager.]

yeo·man·ette (yō′mə net′), *n.* (formerly) a woman yeoman in the U.S. Naval Reserve.

yeo·man·ly (yō′mən lē), *adj.* **1.** having to do with a yeoman. **2.** characteristic of a yeoman; sturdy; honest. **3.** befitting a yeoman. **4.** having the rank of a yeoman.
—*adv.* like a yeoman; bravely.
—**Syn.** *adj.* **2.** dependable, trustworthy.

yeoman of the guard, a member of the bodyguard of the English sovereign, first appointed in 1485 by Henry VII and consisting of 100 men who still wear the uniform of the 1400's and whose duties are now purely ceremonial; beefeater.

yeo·man·ry (yō′mən rē), *n.* **1.** a body of yeomen. **2.** a British volunteer cavalry force organized for internal defense, incorporated in 1907 into the British Territorial Army.

yeoman's or **yeoman service,** good, efficient, or useful service, such as is rendered by a conscientious, unassuming servant or assistant; faithful support or assistance.

yeo·wom·an (yō′wům′ən), *n., pl.* **-wom·en.** a woman yeoman in the United States Navy.

yep (yep), *adv. U.S. Informal.* yes: *The only ethical thing to do was to return my salary . . .. Yep, the whole estimated $200,000 salary* (Time).

-yer, *suffix.* the form of **-ier** after *w* or a vowel, as in *lawyer.*

yer·ba maté (yėr′bə), a South American tea; maté [< Spanish *yerba maté*]

yerk (yėrk), *Dialect.* —*n.* **1.** a kick. **2.** a jerk. **3.** a sharp blow
—*v.i.* **1.** to draw stitches tight. **2.** (of a whip) to crack. **3.** to kick. **4.** to spring. **5.** to engage eagerly in some proceeding. —*v.t.* **1.** to bind. **2.** to flog. **3.** to jerk.

Yer·u·shal·mi (yer′ů shäl′mē), *n.* the Palestinian version of the Talmud. [< Hebrew *Yərūshālāyim* Jerusalem]

yes (yes), *adv., n., pl.* **yes·es,** *v.,* **yessed, yes·sing.** —*adv.* **1.** a word used to express agreement, consent, or affirmation: *Will you go? Yes.* **2.** and what is more; in addition to that: *The boy learned to endure—yes, even to enjoy—the hardships of a sailor's life.*
—*n.* an answer that agrees, consents, or affirms.
—*v.i., v.t.* to say yes; approve of.
[Old English *gīse,* and *gēse* < *gēa, gīe* so, yea + *sī* be it]
—**Syn.** *n.* assent, affirmation, concurrence.
➔ **Yes** and **no,** as adverbs, may modify a sentence (*Yes, you're right*) or may have the value of a coordinate clause (*No; but you should have told me*) or may stand as complete sentences (*"Do you really intend to go with him?" "Yes."*).

ye'se (yēs), *Scottish.* ye (you) shall.

Ye·shi·va (yə shē′və), *n., pl.* **Ye·shi·vas, Ye·shi·voth** (ye′shē vōt′). **1.** a school for Jewish higher education, especially for students preparing for the rabbinate. **2.** a Jewish parochial school in which religious and secular academic subjects are taught. [< Hebrew *yeshībah* (literally) sitting]

yes-man (yes′man′), *n., pl.* **-men.** *Informal.* a person who habitually agrees with those of higher rank, greater authority, etc., than himself, especially one who does so obsequiously and in order to curry favor: *You do not get good science as soon as you have reduced the scientists to yes-men* (Bulletin of Atomic Scientists).

yes·ter (yes′tər), *adj. Archaic or Poetic.* of or belonging to yesterday. —*adv. Obsolete.* yesterday. [abstracted from *yesterday*]

yester-, *combining form.* **1.** the ___ of the day before the present day: *Yestereve = yesterday evening.*
2. last; previous: *Yesteryear = last year.*
[< *yester*]

yes·ter·day (yes′tər dē, -dā), *n.* **1.** the day before today. **2.** the recent past; period not very long past: *We are often amused by fashions of yesterday.*
—*adv.* **1.** on the day before today. **2.** a short time ago; only lately; recently.
—*adj. Obsolete.* belonging to yesterday or the immediate past; very recent.
[Old English *geostran dæg* < *geostra* of yesterday, probably (literally) the next day + *dæg* day]

yes·ter·eve (yes′tər ēv′), *n., adv. Archaic or Poetic.* yesterday evening.

yes·ter·eve·ning (yes′tər ēv′ning), *n., adv. Archaic or Poetic.* yesterday evening.

yes·ter·morn (yes′tər môrn′), *n., adv. Archaic or Poetic.* yesterday morning.

yes·ter·morn·ing (yes′tər môr′ning), *n., adv. Archaic or Poetic.* yesterday morning.

yes·ter·night (yes′tər nīt′), *n., adv. Archaic or Poetic.* last night; the night before today: *I did yesternight dream a dreadful dream* (S.M. Ponniah).

yes·ter·noon (yes′tər nün′), *adv., n. Archaic or Poetic.* yesterday noon.

yes·ter·week (yes′tər wēk′), *adv., n. Archaic or Poetic.* last week.

yes·ter·year (yes′tər yir′), *n., adv. Archaic or Poetic.* last year; the year before this.

yes·treen (yes′trēn′), *n., adv. Scottish or Poetic.* yesterday evening. [contraction of Scottish *yistrewin* < *yistir* yester + *ewin* evening]

yet (yet), *adv.* **1.** up to the present time; hitherto; thus far: *The work is not yet finished. The most important event that had yet occurred* (Henry T. Buckle). **2.** at the present time; so soon as this; now: *Don't go yet. It is not yet dark.* **3.** up to and at the present time; even now; still: *She is talking yet.* **4.** at some time in the future; before all is over or done; eventually; ultimately: *The thief will be caught yet. We may go there yet.* **5.** in addition or continuation; also; again: *Yet once more I forbid you to go.* **6.** as much as; even; moreover: *She would not answer your letter nor yet mine.* **7.** still; even; even more (used to strengthen comparatives): *He spoke yet more harshly.* **8.** in spite of that; nevertheless; notwithstanding: *He was poor, yet honest. The story was strange, yet true.*
as yet, up to now: *There were . . . extensions of this practice as yet but little noticed* (John P. Mahaffy).
—*conj.* nevertheless; however: *The work is good, yet it could be better.*
[Old English *gēt,* or *gīet*]
—**Syn.** *conj.* although.
➔ **Yet** is chiefly used as an adverb: *The books haven't come yet.* In rather formal English it is also used as a coordinating conjunction, equivalent to *but: His speech was almost unintelligible, yet for some unknown reason I enjoyed it.*

Ye·ti (ye′tē), *n., pl.* **-ti.** the Abominable Snowman: *For 60 years there have been stories about the Yeti, the hairy wild men who live in the eternal snows of the Himalayas* (Sunday Times). [< a Tibetan word]

yeuk or **yewk** (yük), *v.i., n. Scottish.* itch. [alteration of Middle English *yike,* Old English *gicce* itch]

yeuk·y or **yewk·y** (yü′kē), *adj. Scottish.* itchy.

yew (yü), *n.* **1.** any of a group of evergreen coniferous trees, especially the English yew of Europe and Asia, having heavy, elastic wood and dense, dark-green foliage. **2.** the wood of any of these trees, especially as the material of bows. **3.** an archer's bow made of this. [Old English *īw,* and *ēow*]

Japanese Yew Branch (def. 1) with berries

yé-yé (ye′ye′), *adj. Slang.* of or having to do with a style of teen-age dress, such as above-the-knee skirts and ankle-high boots, associated with discothèques, rock'n'roll dancing, etc.: *yé-yé fashions, yé-yé girls.* [< French Slang *yé-yé* < English *yeah, yeah,* refrain used by rock'n'roll singing groups]

Yez·i·di (yez′ə dē), *n., pl.* **-di** or **-dis.** a member of a religious sect in Kurdistan, Armenia, and the Caucasus, who believes in a Supreme God, but reveres the Devil as well: *He calls attention to the 70,000 devil worshippers still on earth, the heretical Moslem sect of Yezidi* (Newsweek). Also, **Yazidi.**

Y·gerne (i gern′), *n.* Igraine.

Ygg·dra·sil or **Yg·dra·sil** (ig′drə sil), *n. Norse Mythology.* the ash tree whose branches and roots bind together earth, heaven, and hell. [< Old Icelandic (*askr*) *yggdrasils,* or *yggdrasill* (ash tree) of Yggdrasil < *yggr* a name of Odin, meaning "terrible, frightful"]

YHWH (no periods) or **YHVH** (no periods), the Tetragrammaton.

Yid·dish (yid′ish), *n.* a language which developed from a dialect of Middle High German but contains many Hebrew and Slavic words and is written in Hebrew characters. Yiddish is spoken mainly by Jews of Russia and central Europe. —*adj.* having to do with this language. [< Yiddish *yidish* (*daytsh*) Jewish (German) < Middle High German *jüdisch* (*diutsch*)]

Yid·dish·ism (yid′i shiz əm), *n.* **1.** devotion to the Yiddish language, literature, etc. **2.** a Yiddish word, phrase, or meaning: *Among Gentiles, it is becoming quite in to pepper one's talk with a Yiddishism or two* (*"what chutzpah!"*) (Time).

Yid·dish·ist (yid′i shist), *n.* a person who is devoted to the Yiddish language, literature, etc.

yield (yēld), *v.t.* **1. a.** to produce; bear: *Land yields crops; mines yield ores.* **b.** to give in return; bring in: *an investment which yielded a large profit.* **c.** to fill a need; furnish; afford: *The narrow valley . . . yielded fresh pasturage* (Washington Irving). **2.** to give; grant: *to yield a point in an argument. Mary's mother yielded her consent to the plan.* **3.** to give up to: *to yield oneself up to the mercy of the enemy.* **4.** *Archaic.* to pay; reward; remunerate. —*v.i.* **1.** to bear produce; be productive. **2.** to give up; surrender: *The enemy yielded to our soldiers. The night has yielded to the morn* (Scott). **3.** to give way: *The door yielded to his push. Theory should yield to fact* (Henry T. Buckle). **4.** to give place: *We yield to nobody in love of freedom.*
—*n.* something yielded; amount produced; product: *This year's yield from the silver mine was very large.*
[Old English *geldan* or *gieldan* to pay]
—**yield′er,** *n.*
—**Syn.** *v.t.* **1. a.** furnish, supply. *-v.i.* **2. Yield, submit** mean give up to someone or something. **Yield** suggests giving way before, or giving up to, a stronger force and, usually, ceasing to fight against it: *The obstinate man will not yield in an argument even*

when he is proved wrong. **Submit** suggests giving up all resistance and giving in to the power, will, or authority of another: *Finally, he submitted to the unjust treatment.* *-n.* harvest. See **crop.**

yield·a·ble (yēl′də bəl), *adj.* **1.** that can be yielded. **2.** *Obsolete.* inclined to yield; compliant.

yield·ing (yēl′ding), *adj.* **1.** not resisting; submissive; compliant. **2.** not stiff or rigid; easily bent, twisted, shaped, etc. **—yield′ing·ly,** *adv.* **—Syn. 2.** flexible.

yill (yil), *n. Scottish.* ale. [variant of *ale*]

yin[1] (yin), *n.* the negative or destructive element in traditional Chinese dualistic philosophy, representing the female qualities of evil, darkness, and the sky, in constant struggle with its opposing force (yang): *Light gives way to darkness, reason to feeling, yang to yin, the head to the heart* (Esquire). [< Chinese (Peking) *yin*]

yin[2] (yin), *n. Scottish.* one.

yip (yip), *v.,* **yipped, yip·ping,** *n.* *—v.i.* (especially of dogs) to bark briskly; yelp. *—n.* a sharp barking sound. [American English; imitative]

yip·pee (yip′ē), *interj.* a shout of joy: *The boss left this morning for Rotterdam. Marvellous. Field clear. Long lunch. Home. Yippee!* (London Times).

Yip·pie or **yip·pie** (yip′ē), *n.* a member of the Youth International Party, an organization of politically active hippies.

yird (yėrd), *n. Scottish.* earth. [variant of *earth*]

yirr (yėr), *n., v.i. Scottish.* snarl or growl. [imitative]

Yiz·kor (yiz′kər, yis′-), *n.* the Jewish memorial service for the dead, held in the synagogue on Yom Kippur, on the eighth day of Sukkoth, on the eighth day of Passover, and on the second day of Shabuoth. [< Hebrew *yizkōr* (literally) remember]

-yl, *combining form. Chemistry.* a radical composed of two or more elements (with one usually designated by the base word) acting like a simple element and forming the foundation of a series of compounds, as in *acetyl, carbonyl, salicyl.* [< French *-yle* < Greek *hȳ́lē* wood; stuff, matter]

y·lang-y·lang (ē′läng ē′läng), *n.* **1.** a tree of the Philippines, Java, etc., having fragrant, drooping, greenish-yellow flowers. **2.** a fragrant oil or perfume obtained from its flowers. Also, **ilang-ilang.** [< Tagalog *ílang-ílang*]

y·lem (ī′ləm), *n.* a chaotic, dense, very hot mass of matter, the supposed original substance of the universe, believed to have consisted only of protons, neutrons, and electrons. [Middle English *ylem,* ultimately < Greek *hȳ́lē* substance, matter]

Y-lev·el (wī′lev′əl), *n.* a form of surveyor's level in which the telescope rests on two forked supports called Y's.

Y.M., *Informal.* Young Men's Christian Association.

Y.M.C.A. or **YMCA** (no periods), Young Men's Christian Association (an organization for promoting the spiritual, intellectual, physical, and social well-being of young men, founded in London in 1844 by George Williams, 1821-1905).

Y.M.Cath.A., Young Men's Catholic Association.

Y.M.H.A. or **YMHA** (no periods), Young Men's Hebrew Association (an organization for the moral, mental, physical, and social improvement of Jewish young men, founded in Baltimore in 1854).

Y·mir (ē′mir), *n. Norse Mythology.* a giant, formed from blocks of ice and sparks of fire, from whose body the gods made the universe. [< Old Icelandic *Ymir* (literally) noisemaker. Compare Old Icelandic *ymja* make a noise.]

yob (yob), *n. British Slang.* a coarse young man; boor. [reverse spelling of *boy*]

yoc·co (yok′ō), *n.* **1.** a South American and African shrub, the bark of which is rich in caffeine, used to make a stimulating, nonintoxicating drink. **2.** the drink made from this shrub: *Yocco, an African jungle drink, cuts hunger and fatigue* (Science News Letter). [< a native word]

yock (yok), *U.S. Slang.* *—n.* a deep, hearty laugh: *Her laugh is one of those welcome, old-fashioned yocks* (Newsweek). *—v.i., v.t.* to laugh or cause to laugh heartily: *Phil Napoleon's minions are yocking it up here* (New Yorker). Also, **yuk.** [perhaps imitative]

yod (yōd, yu̇d), *n.* the tenth letter of the Hebrew alphabet. [< Hebrew *yōdh*]

yo·del (yō′dəl), *v.,* **-deled, -del·ing** or (*especially British*) **-delled, -del·ling,** *n.* *—v.t., v.i.* to sing (a melody) with abrupt changes from the ordinary voice to a forced shrill voice or falsetto, and back again, typical for songs of mountaineers of Switzerland and Tirol. *—n.* an act or sound of yodeling. [< German *jodeln* < *jo,* the name of a syllable used in the singing] **—yo′del·er,** *especially British* **yo′del·ler,** *n.*

yo·dle (yō′dəl), *v.t., v.i.,* **-dled, -dling,** *n.* yodel. **—yo′dler,** *n.*

yo·ga or **Yo·ga** (yō′gə), *n.* **1.** (in Hindu religious philosophy) a system of ascetic practice, abstract meditation, and mental concentration, used as a method of attaining union with the supreme spirit. **2.** a system of exercises or rigid physical positions for achieving serenity and well-being. [< Hindustani *yoga* < Sanskrit, union]

yogh (yōH), *n.* a letter (ȝ) of the Middle English alphabet, used to represent both a velar and a palatal fricative. [Middle English *yogh,* Old English *ēoh*]

yo·ghourt or **yo·ghurt** (yō′gərt), *n.* yogurt.

yo·gi (yō′gē), *n., pl.* **-gis.** a person who practices or follows yoga. [< Hindustani *yogī* < Sanskrit *yogin* (nominative *yogī*) < *yoga* yoga]

yo·gic (yō′gik), *adj.* of or having to do with yogis or yoga: *yogic exercises.*

yo·gin (yō′gin), *n.* yogi.

yo·gism (yō′giz əm), *n.* the doctrine or practice of the yogis.

yo·gurt (yō′gėrt), *n.* a thickened, slightly fermented, semisolid or liquid food made from milk acted upon by bacteria, originally made in Turkey and other Oriental countries, now prepared commercially and widely sold in the United States and elsewhere. Also, **yoghourt, yoghurt, yohourt.** [< Turkish *yoğurt*]

yo-heave-ho (yō′hēv′hō′), *interj.* an exclamation used by sailors in pulling or lifting together, as when hauling at a rope or a capstan, or heaving an anchor up.

yo·him·bé (yō him′bā), *n.* a tropical African tree of the madder family, the bark of which is used to make yohimbine. [< a West African native word]

yo·him·be·ho·a (yō him′bā hō′ə), *n.* yohimbé.

yo·him·bine (yō him′bēn, -bin), *n.* an alkaloid derived from the bark of the yohimbé tree, used as an aphrodisiac and as a stimulant in treating difficult breathing associated with certain heart conditions. *Formula:* $C_{21}H_{26}N_2O_3$

yo-ho (yō hō′), *interj., n., v.,* **-hoed, -ho·ing.** *—interj.* a call or shout used especially by sailors to attract attention, accompany effort, etc. *—n.* a call or shout of "yo-ho." *—v.i.* to shout "yo-ho": *the men . . . yo-hoing at their work* (Robert Louis Stevenson).

yoh·ourt (yō′u̇rt), *n.* yogurt.

yoicks (yoiks), *interj. Especially British.* a cry used to urge on the hounds in fox hunting. [perhaps alteration of earlier *hoicks,* also *hoik,* variant of *hike*]

yoke (yōk), *n., v.,* **yoked, yok·ing.** *—n.* **1.** a wooden frame to fasten two oxen or other draft animals together for drawing a plow or vehicle, usually consisting of a crosspiece fitted with hoops (oxbow) which are placed around the animals' necks. **2.** a pair of animals that are or may be coupled by a yoke (after a numeral the plural is usually *yoke*): *two yoke of oxen. The plow was driven by a yoke of oxen.* **3.** any frame connecting two other parts, as a frame fitted to the neck and shoulders of a person for carrying a pair of pails, baskets, etc.: *The man carried two buckets on a yoke.* **4.** a part of a garment fitting the neck and shoulders closely. **5.** a top piece to a skirt, fitting the hips. **6.** a clamp which holds two parts firmly in place; double clamp. **7.** a modified crosshead used instead of a connecting rod between the piston and crankshaft in certain small engines. **8.** a crossbar at the top of the rudder of a boat, and having two lines or ropes attached for steering. **9.** a crossbar connecting the tongue of a wagon, carriage, etc., to the collars of two horses, mules, etc. **10.** among the ancient Romans and others: **a.** a contrivance similar to a yoke for oxen, etc., placed on the neck of a captive. **b.** a symbol of this consisting of two upright spears with a third placed across them, under which captives were forced to walk. **11.** something that joins or unites; bond; tie. **12.** something that holds people in slavery or submission: *Throw off your yoke and be free.* **13.** rule; dominion. **14.** a steering column in certain aircraft, consisting of a wheel or the like mounted at the upper end of a lever, for controlling the aircraft in flight.

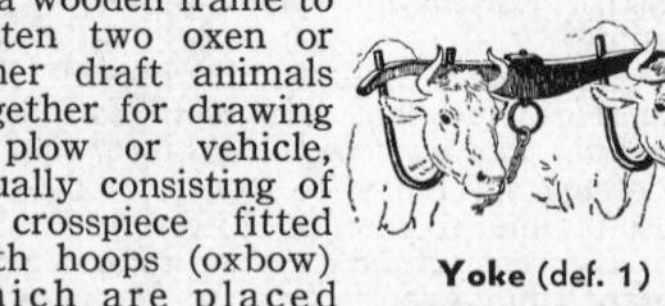

Yoke (def. 1)

—v.t. **1.** to put a yoke on; fasten with a yoke. **2.** to harness or fasten a work animal to. **3.** to join; unite: *to be yoked in marriage.* [Old English *geoc*]

yoke·fel·low (yōk′fel′ō), *n.* **1.** a person joined or united with another in a task; fellow worker; partner. **2.** a person joined in marriage to another; husband or wife; spouse. **—Syn. 1.** colleague. **2.** consort.

yo·kel (yō′kəl), *n.* a crude or boorish country fellow; bumpkin; rustic: *We don't want television cameras showing some yokel in the legislature reading a newspaper and smoking a cigar with his feet on a desk* (Wall Street Journal). [origin uncertain. Compare German *Jokel* a disparaging name for a farmer; (diminutive) < *Jakob* Jacob.]

yo·kel·ish (yō′kə lish), *adj.* characteristic of a yokel: *The Civil War had such a strangely civilian look—the shoddy, ill-matched uniforms; the pathetic, yokelish aspect of the fighting men* (New Yorker).

yo·kel·ry (yō′kəl rē), *n.* yokels as a group: *It seems a pity to waste so much elegant wit on so sluggish and easy a mark as the local yokelry* (Canadian Saturday Night).

yoke·mate (yōk′māt′), *n.* yokefellow.

Yo·kuts (yō′kuts), *n.* a North American Indian linguistic family comprising a number of small tribes in California.

yol·dring (yol′dring, yōl′-; -drin), *n. Scottish.* the yellowhammer of Europe. [variant of obsolete *yowlring,* reduction of *yowlow* yellow + *ring*[1]]

yolk[1] (yōk, yōlk), *n.* **1.** the yellow internal part of an egg of a bird or reptile, surrounded by the albumen or white, and serving as nourishment for the young before it is hatched; yellow. **2.** the corresponding part in any animal ovum (egg cell), which serves for the nutrition of the embryo (deutoplasm, or parablast), together with the protoplasmic substances from which the embryo is developed (archiblast). [Old English *geolca, geoloca* < *geolu* yellow]

yolk[2] (yōk, yōlk), *n.* the fat in sheep's wool secreted by the skin; suint. [earlier *yoak,* unrecorded Old English *eowoca,* implied in *eowocig* yolky; spelling influenced by *yolk*[1]]

yolked (yōkt), *adj.* containing a yolk or yolks: *a double-yolked egg.*

yolk sac, a membranous sac filled with yolk, attached to and providing food for the embryo. In cephalopods and lower vertebrates, it is the only source of food for the embryo, for these animals do not develop a placenta.

yolk·y (yō′kē, yōl′kē), *adj.,* **yolk·i·er, yolk·i·est. 1.** resembling yolk. **2.** consisting of yolk. **3.** *British Dialect.* greasy or sticky, as unwashed wool.

Yom Kip·pur (yom kip′ər), the Day of Atonement, the most solemn day in the Jewish calendar, observed with complete fasting for 24 hours. It falls on the tenth day of Tishri, the first month of the Jewish year (corresponding to September-October). [< Hebrew *yōm kippūr* day of atonement]

yon (yon), *adj., adv. Archaic.* yonder. *—pron. Obsolete.* that or those (usually denoting a visible object or objects pointed out, at a distance but within view). [Old English *geon,* adjective, that (over there)]

yond (yond), *adj., adv. Archaic.* yonder. [Old English *geondan,* preposition, adverb, throughout, yonder]

yon·der (yon′dər), *adv.* within sight, but not near; over there: *Look yonder.* *—adj.* **1.** situated over there; being within sight, but not near: *He lives in yonder cottage.* **2.** farther; more distant; other: *There is snow on the yonder side of the mountains.* [Middle English *yonder.* Related to YON, YOND.]

yoo-hoo (yü′hü′), *interj., v.,* **-hooed, -hoo·ing.** *—interj.* a call or shout used to attract someone's attention: *"Yoo-hoo," I shouted, as though I were calling someone at least two hundred feet away from me* (New Yorker). —*v.i.* to shout yoo-hoo: *She yoo-hooed from her window to the deliveryman.*

yop·on (yop′ən), *n.* yaupon.

yore (yôr, yōr), *adv.* long ago; years ago. [Old English *gēara,* adverb; (originally) genitive plural of *gēar* year]

york (yôrk), *v.t.* in cricket: **a.** to bowl (a batsman) out: *Soon Watson was yorked* (London Times). **b.** to strike (the wicket) with a yorker. [back formation < *yorker*]

York (yôrk), *n.* the English royal house, a branch of the Plantagenets, descended from Richard, Duke of York, which reigned from 1461 to 1485. Its emblem was a white rose. The three kings of this house were Edward IV, Edward V, and Richard III.

york·er (yôr′kər), *n.* (in cricket) a bowled ball that strikes the ground just barely in front of the bat. [probably < *York* + *-er*[2] (perhaps because the county had championship teams)]

York·ist (yôr′kist), in English history: —*n.* a supporter or member of the house of York, especially in opposition to the Lancastrians in the Wars of the Roses. —*adj.* **1.** of or having to do with the royal house of York. **2.** of or having to do with the party that fought against the Lancastrians.

York Rite, one of the two branches of advanced Freemasonry.

Yorks (no period), Yorkshire.

York·shire·man (yôrk′shir mən, -shər), *n., pl.* **-men.** a native or resident of Yorkshire, England.

York·shire pudding (yôrk′shir, -shər), a batter cake made of milk, flour, egg, and salt, baked in the drippings of, and served as an accompaniment to, roast beef. [< *Yorkshire,* a county in England]

Yorkshire terrier, any of an English breed of small, shaggy dogs with a steel-blue coat, weighing 4 to 8 pounds.

Yorkshire Terrier (8 to 9 in. high at the shoulder)

yorsh (yôrsh), *n. Russian.* a drink that is a mixture of vodka and beer.

Yo·ru·ba (yō′rü-bä), *n., pl.* **-bas** or **-ba. 1.** a member of a large linguistic group of coastal West Africa. **2.** the Sudanic language of this group.

Yo·ru·ban (yō′rů bən), *adj.* of or having to do with the Yoruba people or language.

you (yü; *unstressed* yů, yə), *pron. pl. or sing., poss.* **your** or **yours,** *obj.* **you. 1.** the person or persons spoken to: *Are you ready? Then you may go.* **2.** one; anybody: *You push this button to turn on the light.* [Old English *ēow,* dative and accusative of *gē* ye[1]]

➔ **You** is used as an indefinite pronoun in informal English: *It's a good book, if you like detective stories.* In formal English *one* is more usual.

➔ **you all.** In Southern American *you all,* contracted to *y'all,* is frequently used as the plural of *you,* as in some other regions *yous* or *youse* is used. It is also used when addressing one person regarded as one of a group, usually a family, but rarely, if ever, in addressing one person alone.

you'd (yüd; *unstressed* yůd, yəd), **1.** you had. **2.** you would.

you'll (yül; *unstressed* yůl, yəl), **1.** you will. **2.** you shall.

young (yung), *adj.,* **young·er** (yung′ger), **young·est** (yung′gist), *n.* —*adj.* **1.** in the early part of life or growth; not old; youthful: *A puppy is a young dog.* **2.** having the appearance, freshness, vigor, or other qualities of young persons or youth: *She looks young for her age.* **3.** of, having to do with, or belonging to youth; early: *In his young days he was very hot-tempered.* **4.** not as old as another; junior (used especially to distinguish the younger of two persons in the same family having the same name or title): *Young Mr. Jones worked for his father.* **5.** being in its early stage; lately begun, formed, introduced, brought into use, etc.; recent; new: *a young firm, a young country. The night was still young when they left the party.* **6.** representing or favoring new and usually progressive or radical policies, tendencies, or the like. **7.** without much experience or practice; green; raw. **8.** *Physical Geography.* youthful. —*n.* young animals, collectively; offspring: *a lioness and her young.*

the young, young people, collectively: *I have always lived with people older than myself, . . . though it is very nice to be with the young* (Annie F. Hector).

with young, pregnant: *Goats grow fat when they are with young* (Edward Topsell).

[Old English *geong*] —**young′ness,** *n.*

—**Syn.** *adj.* **1.** immature, undeveloped. **3. Young, youthful, juvenile** mean of or having to do with persons between childhood and adulthood. **Young** is the general term: *They are too young to marry.* **Youthful** emphasizes having the qualities of a young person, especially the more appealing ones such as freshness, vitality, and optimism: *With youthful earnestness, the boys debated the problems of the world.* **Juvenile** emphasizes immaturity: *He was rebuked for his juvenile behavior.* —**Ant.** *adj.* **1.** old.

young·ber·ry (yung′ber′ē), *n., pl.* **-ries.** the large, sweet, purplish-black fruit of a trailing bramble, developed from a cross between a hybrid similar to the loganberry and a dewberry, grown largely in the southwestern United States. [< B.M. *Young,* an American horticulturist.

young blood, 1. young people. **2.** youthful vigor, energy, enthusiasm, etc.

Young·er Edda (yung′gər), a collection of old Norse legends, poems, and rules for writing poetry, written in the first half of the 1200's.

young-eyed (yung′īd′), *adj.* **1.** having the outlook of one who is young; not cynical through age or experience. **2.** having the bright or lively eyes of a young person.

young·ish (yung′ish), *adj.* somewhat young.

young·ling (yung′ling), *n.* **1.** a young person, animal, or plant. **2.** *Obsolete.* a novice; beginner. —*adj.* young; youthful. [Old English *geongling* < *geong* young + *-ling*]

young man, 1. a man who is young or in early manhood. **2.** a lover; fiancé.

Young Men's Christian Association, Y.M.C.A.

Young Men's Hebrew Association, Y.M.H.A.

young·ster (yung′stər), *n.* **1.** a young person, especially: **a.** a person who is no longer an infant but not yet at the age of puberty; child: *a toy certain to please any youngster.* **b.** a person who is not yet an adult; one who is, or is viewed as being, still a youth: *an army largely made up of youngsters.* **2.** anything regarded as being young or new: *Alberta is one of the youngsters of the Canadian family —it has been a province only since 1905* (Newsweek). **3.** a young animal. **4.** *U.S.* a midshipman in the second year at the United States Naval Academy. **5.** *British.* a midshipman in grade less than four years.

Young Turks, 1. a reformist body of relatively young army officers, government functionaries, intellectuals, etc., that originated in Turkey in the 1800's. **2.** the political group that grew out of this, active just before and during World War I, by which in large part Kemal Ataturk was enabled to seize the reins of power in Turkey. **3.** any group considered as resembling these, especially in impatience with the existing regime, methods, etc.: *I've heard some of the Young Turks on your editorial staff talk that way* (Esquire).

Young Women's Christian Association, Y.W.C.A.

Young Women's Hebrew Association, Y.W.H.A.

youn·ker (yung′kər), *n.* **1.** *Archaic.* a young fellow; youngster. **2.** *Obsolete.* a young nobleman or gentleman. [< Middle Dutch *jonckher,* or *jonchere* < *jonc* young + *hēre* lord, master]

your (yůr; *unstressed* yər), *adj. Possessive form of* **you. 1.** of or belonging to you: *Wash your hands.* **2.** having to do with you: *We enjoyed your visit.* **3.** that you know; well-known; that you speak of; that is spoken of: *your real lover of music, your modern girl.* **4.** part of a title: *Your Lordship, Your Highness, Your Honor, Mayor Jones. Abbr.:* yr. [Old English *ēower,* genitive of *gē* ye[1]]

you're (yůr; *unstressed* yər), you are.

yourn (yůrn), *pron. Substandard or Dialect.* yours.

yours (yůrz), *pron. sing. and pl., possessive case of* **you. 1.** the one or ones belonging to or having to do with you: *I like ours better than yours.* **2.** at your service: *I remain yours to command.*

of yours, belonging to or having to do with you: *Is he a friend of yours?*

your·self (yůr self′, yər-), *pron., pl.* **-selves. 1.** the emphatic form of **you:** *You yourself know the story is not true.* **2.** the reflexive form of **you:** *You will hurt yourself.* **3.** your real self: *You aren't yourself today.*

yours truly, 1. a phrase used at the end of a letter, before the signature. **2.** *Informal.* I; me: *Yours truly, sir, has an eye for a . . . fine horse* (Wilkie Collins).

yous or **youse** (yüz), *pron. Substandard or Dialect.* you (usually used in addressing two or more people).

youth (yüth), *n., pl.* **youths** (yüths, yüᴛʜz) or (*collectively*) **youth. 1.** the fact or quality of being young; youngness: *He has the vigor of youth. If I had youth and strength* (Edmund Burke). **2.** the appearance, freshness or vigor, rashness, or other quality characteristic of the young: *She keeps her youth well.* **3.** the time when one is young; early part of life. **4.** the time between childhood and adulthood; period between puberty and maturity; adolescence. **5.** the first or early stage of anything; early period of growth or development: *during the youth of this country.* **6.** a young man between boyhood and adulthood. **7.** any young person or persons (used without article): *Almost everything that is great has been done by youth* (Benjamin Disraeli). **8.** (*plural in use*) young people, collectively: *Now all the youth of England are on fire* (Shakespeare). [Old English *geoguth*] —**Syn. 4.** teens. **6.** lad, stripling.

youth-and-old-age (yüth′ən ōld′āj′), *n.* the zinnia plant.

youth·en (yü′thən), *v.t.* to make youthful; impart a youthful appearance to: *No dress youthens a girl so much as white* (Evening Star). —*v.i.* to become youthful; acquire youthful qualities: *You will always be forty to strangers perhaps: and youthen as you get to know them* (C.H. Sorley).

youth·ful (yüth′fəl), *adj.* **1.** young: *a youthful person.* **2.** of youth; suitable for young people: *youthful enthusiasm.* **3.** having the looks or qualities of youth; fresh and vigorous. **4.** early; new. **5.** *Physical Geography.* having eroded or been eroded for a relatively short time. —**youth′ful·ness,** *n.* —**Syn. 1.** immature. See **young.**

youth·ful·ly (yüth′fə lē), *adv.* in a youthful manner: *Your attire . . . not youthfully wanton* (Samuel Richardson).

youth hostel, a supervised lodging place for young people on bicycle trips, hikes, etc.; hostel.

you've (yüv; *unstressed* yův, yəv), you have.

yow[1] (you), *interj.* **1.** an exclamation of vague meaning. **2.** an imitation of the yelp or bark of a dog, or the meow of a cat.

yow[2] (yō, you), *n. Obsolete.* ewe.

yowl (youl), *n.* a long, distressful, or dismal cry; howl. —*v.i., v.t.* to howl. [Middle English *yowlen;* imitative]

yowl·er (you′lər), *n.* a person or thing that yowls: *There are not many good girl singers these days, although there are plenty of echo chamber yowlers* (Time).

yo·yo (yō′yō), *n., pl.* **-yos,** *v.,* **-yoed -yo·ing.** —*n.* **1.** a small disk-shaped toy, which is spun out and reeled in by an attached string. **2. Yo-yo,** a trademark for this toy. **3.** *Aerospace.* a wide-swinging orbit around the earth by an artificial satellite. —*v.i.* **1.** to go back and forth, as if attached to a string. **2.** to waver in mind or opinion, especially from one point of view to the other: *There is plenty of room for debate on this point, because the Supreme Court has yoyoed on the issue of the right to travel* (New York Times). [American English; origin uncertain]

y·per·ite (ē′pə rīt), *n.* mustard gas. [< French *ypérite* < *Ypres,* a town in Belgium, near where it was used in World War I + *-ite* -ite[1]]

Y potential, *Electricity.* the difference between the potential at a terminal and that at the neutral point in an armature activated by a three-phase alternating current.

Y.P.S.C.E., Young People's Society of Christian Endeavor.

Y·quem (ē kem′), *n.* a kind of sauterne, considered by many to be the finest of all sauternes. [< French (*Château*) *Yquem* (originally) place where it is made]

yr., **1.** year or years. **2.** younger. **3.** your.

yrs., **1.** years. **2.** yours.

Y·seult (i sült′), *n.* Iseult.

Yt (no period), yttrium (chemical element).

Y.T., Yukon Territory.

Y-track (wī′trak′), *n.* a short track laid at right angles to a line of railroad, with which it is connected by two curved branches resembling the branches of the letter Y, used instead of a turntable for reversing engines or cars.

yt·ter·bi·a (i tėr′bē ə), *n.* a heavy, white powder, an oxide of ytterbium, which forms colorless salts. *Formula:* Yb_2O_3 [< New Latin *ytterbia* < *ytterbium;* see YTTERBIUM]

yt·ter·bid (i tėr′bid), *adj.* **1.** of ytterbium. **2.** containing ytterbium.

yt·ter·bic (i tėr′bik), *adj.* containing ytterbium.

yt·ter·bite (i tėr′bīt), *n. Mineralogy.* gadolinite.

yt·ter·bi·um (i tėr′bē əm), *n.* a rare-earth metallic chemical element whose compounds resemble those of yttrium; neoytterbium. It occurs with yttrium in gadolinite and various other minerals. *Symbol:* Yb; *at.wt.:* (C^{12}) 173.04 or (O^{16}) 173.04; *at. no.:* 70; *valence:* 3. [< New Latin *ytterbium* < *Ytterby,* a town in Sweden, where it was first discovered. Compare ERBIUM, TERBIUM.]

ytterbium metals, *Chemistry.* yttrium metals.

yt·tri·a (it′rē ə), *n.* a heavy, white powder, an oxide of yttrium, obtained from gadolinite and other rare minerals. *Formula:* Y_2O_3 [< New Latin *yttria,* alteration (influenced by Swedish *ytterjord*) of *Ytterby;* see YTTERBIUM]

yt·tric (it′rik), *adj.* **1.** of yttrium. **2.** containing yttrium.

yt·trif·er·ous (i trif′ər əs), *adj.* containing or yielding yttrium.

yt·tri·um (it′rē əm), *n.* a metallic chemical element resembling and associated with the rare earths, occurring in combination in gadolinite and various other minerals. Yttrium compounds are used in making incandescent gas mantles. *Symbol:* Y or Yt; *at.wt.:* (C^{12}) 88.905 or (O^{16}) 88.92; *at.no.:* 39; *valence:* 3. [< New Latin *yttrium* < *yttria* yttria]

yttrium metals, a group of metals that include yttrium and the rare-earth metals dysprosium, erbium, holmium, lutecium, thulium, and ytterbium.

yu·an (yü än′), *n., pl.* **-an.** the basic Chinese monetary unit, established in 1914 as a silver coin containing 23.4934 grams of pure silver. [< Chinese *yüan* circle, round thing. Doublet of YEN[1].]

Yu·an (yü än′), *n.* the national assembly of Nationalist China (the Republic of China on Taiwan). Also, **Yuen.**

yuan dollar, yuan.

Yuc., Yucatan.

yu·ca (yü′kə), *n.* a cassava.

Yu·ca·tec·an (yü′kə tek′ən), *adj.* of or having to do with Yucatan, a peninsula of southeastern Mexico. —*n.* a native or inhabitant of Yucatan.

yuc·ca (yuk′ə), *n.* **1.** any of a group of plants of the agave family, native to the warmer parts of North America, and extensively cultivated for ornament, characterized by a woody stem with a crown of usually rigid, narrow, pointed leaves and an upright cluster of white, bell-shaped flowers, as Adam's-needle and Spanish bayonet. **2.** the flower of one of these plants. It is the floral emblem of New Mexico. [< New Latin *Yucca* the genus name < Spanish *yuca;* origin uncertain]

Yucca (def. 1) (Adam's-needle) (8 to 10 ft. tall)

Yu·en (yü en′), *n.* Yuan.

Yu·ga (yu̇′gə), *n.* (in Hindu cosmology) any of the four ages in the duration of the world, the four ages comprising 4,320,000 years and constituting a great Yuga. [< Sanskrit *yuga* an age; (originally) a yoke]

Yu·go·slav (yü′gō släv′, -slav′), *n.* a native or inhabitant of Yugoslavia. —*adj.* of or having to do with Yugoslavia or its people. Also, **Jugoslav, Jugo-Slav.**

Yu·go·sla·vi·an (yü′gō slä′vē ən, -slav′ē-), *adj., n.* Yugoslav.

Yu·go·slav·ic (yü′gō slä′vik, -slav′ik), *adj.* Yugoslav.

yuk (yuk), *n., v.,* **yukked, yuk·king.** *U.S. Slang.* —*n.* a deep, hearty laugh. —*v.i., v.t.* to laugh or cause to laugh heartily. Also, **yock.**

yu·ka·ta (yü kä′tä), *n., pl.* **-ta.** *Japanese.* a man's lightweight kimono: *They wear Western clothes to work, slip into cool yukata at home* (Time).

yu·kin (yü kin′), *n.* a Chinese four-stringed musical instrument with a large circular body and a short neck. [< Chinese *yukin*]

Yu·kon·er (yü′kon ər), *n.* a native or inhabitant of the Yukon Territory.

Yukon Standard Time (yü′kon), the standard time in the Yukon Territory and part of southern Alaska, one hour behind Pacific Standard Time.

Yule or **yule** (yül), *n.* **1.** Christmas. **2.** the Christmas season. [Old English *geōl* < Scandinavian (compare Old Icelandic *jōl*)] —**Syn. 1.** Noël. **2.** Yuletide.

Yule log, block, or **clog,** a large log burned in the fireplace at Christmas.

Yule·tide or **yule·tide** (yül′tīd′), *n.* the season of Christmas; Christmastide.

Yule·time or **yule·time** (yül′tīm′), *n.* Yuletide; Christmastide.

Yu·ma (yü′mə), *n., pl.* **-ma** or **-mas. 1.** a member of an Indian tribe formerly of southwestern Arizona and now living chiefly in California. **2.** the Yuman language of this tribe.

Yu·man (yü′mən), *adj.* of or having to do with an American linguistic group of the southwestern United States and Mexico. —*n.* this linguistic group.

yum·my (yum′ē), *adj.,* **-mi·er, -mi·est,** *n., pl.* **-mies.** *Slang.* —*adj.* very pleasing to the senses; delicious; delightful: *Take your pick of yummy pecans, butterflies, filled rings.* (Maclean's). —*n.* something delicious or delightful. [< *yum*(-yum) + *-y*[1]]

yum-yum (yum′yum′), *interj.* an expression of pleasure or delight, especially with reference to food. [imitative]

yurt (yu̇rt), *n.* a portable, tentlike dwelling made of a framework of branches covered with felt, used by nomadic Mongols in central Asia. [< Russian *jurta* < Turkic]

Y.W., *Informal.* Young Women's Christian Association.

Y.W.C.A. or **YWCA** (no periods), Young Women's Christian Association (an organization for promoting the spiritual, physical, and social welfare of young women, which originated in England in 1855 simultaneously in two different bodies, united in 1877).

Y.W.H.A. or **YWHA** (no periods), Young Women's Hebrew Association (an organization of Jewish young women, especially the women's branch of the Y.M.H.A.).

y·wis (i wis′), *adv. Archaic.* certainly; indeed. [variant of *iwis*]

Z

Roman 100's A.D.

Greek 600's B.C.

Phoenician 1000's B.C.

Semitic 1500's B.C.

Egyptian 3000's B.C.

Zz Zz

Z or **z** (zē), *n.*, *pl.* **Z's** or **Zs, z's** or **zs.** **1.** the 26th and last letter of the English alphabet. **2.** any sound represented by this letter. **3.** used as a symbol for: **a.** the 26th, or more usually the 25th, of a series (either *I* or *J* being omitted). **b.** an unknown quantity, especially in algebraic equations. **4.** a thing shaped like a Z.

z., zone.

Z (no period), **1.** atomic number. **2.** zenith. **3.** zenith distance.

Z., zone.

za·ba·glio·ne (zä'bäl yō'nā), *n.* a sweet mixture of sugar, egg yolks, and wine cooked slightly, served hot or cold as a dessert, or as a sauce on puddings, fruits, etc. [alteration of Italian *zabaione*]

za·ba·io·ne or **za·ba·jo·ne** (zā'bä yō'nē), *n.* zabaglione: *Zabaione ... is one of the best known Italian sweets, yet it is rarely correctly prepared* (London Times).

Zab·u·lon (zab'yə lən), *n.* (in the Douay Bible) Zebulun.

za·ca·tón (sä'kä tōn', zak'ə-), *n.* any of several coarse grasses of the dry regions of the southwestern United States; sacaton. [< Spanish *zacatón* < *zacate*, or *sacate* grass, hay < Nahuatl *zacatl*]

Zac·che·us or **Zac·chae·us** (za kē'əs), *n.* (in the Bible) a tax collector so short he had to climb a tree, because of the crowd, to see Jesus, and who later entertained Him at dinner. Luke 19:1-10.

Zach·a·ri·ah (zak'ə rī'ə), *n.* in the Bible: **1.** a king of Israel. II Kings 15:8-11. **2.** Zacharias.

Zach·a·ri·as (zak'ə rī'əs), *n.* in the Bible: **1.** a Jewish priest, slain "between the temple and the altar." Matthew 23:35. **2.** the father of John the Baptist. Luke 1:5. **3.** in the Douay Bible: **a.** Zechariah. **b.** Zachariah.

Zach·a·ry (zak'ər ē), *n.* **1.** Zachariah. **2.** Zacharias.

zad·dik (tsä'dik), *n.*, *pl.* **zad·dik·kim** (tsä-dē'kim). a holy man among the Jews; righteous or saintly man, especially a leader of the Hasidim.
[< Hebrew *ṣaddiq*]

zaf·fer, zaf·far, or **zaf·fir** (zaf'ər), *n.* an impure oxide of cobalt, obtained by roasting cobalt ore, used as a blue coloring matter (cobalt blue) for pottery, glass, etc. [< Italian *zaffera*]

zag (zag), *n.*, *v.*, **zagged, zag·ging.** *Informal.* —*n.* a part, movement, or direction at an angle to that of a zig in a zigzag. —*v.i.* to move on the second turn of a zigzag: *When an American Communist functionary has nightmares, he dreams that he zigged when the party line zagged* (Newsweek).

zai·bat·su (zī bät'sü), *n.pl. or sing.* the leading families of Japan, who control and direct most of the country's industries, banks, etc. [< Japanese *zaibatsu* < *zai* property + *batsu* clan, family]

Zai·di (zī'dē), *n.*, *pl.* **-di** or **-dis.** a member of a Shiitic sect of northern Yemen. [< *Zaid* or *Zayd*, the founder of this sect]

Za·ire (zä'ir), *n.* the monetary unit of the Congo (Kinshasa), worth about $2.00.

za·kus·ka (zä küs'kə), *n.*, *pl.* **-ki** (-kē). *Russian.* an hors d'oeuvre; appetizer.

Zam·bi·an (zam'bē ən), *adj.* of or having to do with Zambia (the former Northern Rhodesia), its people, or their language. —*n.* a native or inhabitant of Zambia.

zam·bo (zam'bō), *n.* sambo.

zam·bra (zam'brə), *n.* a Spanish or Moorish dance. [< Spanish *zambra*]

za·mi·a (zā'mē ə), *n.* any of a group of tropical and subtropical American cycads, having a short, thick trunk, a crown of palmlike leaves, and oblong cones. [< New Latin *Zamia* the genus name < *zamiae*, plural, apparently misreading of Latin *azāniae* pine nuts < Greek *azánein* to dry up]

za·min·dar (zə mēn'där'), *n.* in India:. **1.** (formerly) a native landlord who held land for which he paid tax directly to the British government. **2.** (under Mogul rule) a collector of revenue, required to pay a fixed sum on the tract or district assigned to him. Also, **zemindar.** [< Hindustani *zamīndār* < Persian *zamīn* land + *-dār*, an agent suffix]

za·min·da·ri (zə mēn'dä'rē), *n.* **1.** the status or jurisdiction of a zamindar. **2.** the territory of a zamindar. **3.** the system of landholding and revenue collection under zamindars. Also, **zemindary.** [< Hindustani *zamīndārī* < *zamīndār*; see ZAMINDAR]

zan·der (zan'dər), *n.* a European perch valued as a food fish. [< German *Zander*, probably < Slavic]

za·ni·ly (zā'nə lē), *adv.* in a zany manner.

za·ni·ness (zā'nē nis), *n.* zany quality or behavior: *Ginsberg, for all his carefully cultivated (and natural) zaniness, is a writer far above Kerouac in my estimation* (John Ciardi).

zan·thox·y·lum (zan thok'sə ləm), *n.* the bark of various shrubs or small trees of the madder family, used medicinally. [alteration of New Latin *Xanthoxylum* the genus name < Greek *xanthós* yellow + *xýlon* wood]

za·ny (zā'nē), *n.*, *pl.* **-nies,** *adj.*, **-ni·er, -ni·est.** —*n.* **1.** a fool; simpleton. **2.** *Archaic or Historical.* an assistant or attendant to a clown, acrobat, etc., who imitates his master in a ludicrously awkward way. —*adj.* that is, or is characteristic of, a zany; clownish; foolish; idiotic: *Mann deliriously festooned himself with pith helmets, monocles, drooping mustaches, sou'westers—a new and zanier assortment every show* (Maclean's). [< French *zani* < Italian (Venetian) *Zanni*, variant of *Giovanni* John]

za·ny·ish (zā'nē ish), *adj.* like a zany; foolish.

za·ny·ism (zā'nē iz əm), *n.* fantastic folly; buffoonery.

Zan·zi·ba·ri (zan'zi bä'rē), *adj.* of or having to do with Zanzibar, a British island and protectorate in southeastern Africa, or its people. —*n.* a native or inhabitant of Zanzibar.

zap (zap), *interj.*, *v.*, **zapped, zap·ping.** *Slang.* —*interj.* **1.** the sound of a sudden slap, blow, blast, etc. **2.** an exclamation of surprise, dismay, etc.: *"Zap!" he thought. "Wrong vaccine"* (Time).
—*v.t.* **1.** to hit with a hard blow. **2.** to kill: *With its pistol grip and nubby barrel, the instrument looks like the handy ray gun with which Buck Rogers and Wilma used to zap Killer Kane* (Time). **3.** to beat; defeat: *Maybe truce negotiations won't be possible until the Viet Cong are zapped* (Punch). —*v.i.* to move very fast; zip; zoom: *... curious low cars blatting and zapping before us* (Atlantic).

za·pa·te·a·do (thä pä'tä ä'ᴛʜō, sä-), *n.* *Spanish.* a dance of flamenco origin, in which the rhythm is marked chiefly by tapping with the feet, usually danced by men.

za·po·te (zə pō'tē; *Spanish* thä pō'tā, sä-), *n.* sapota.

Za·po·tec (sä'pō tek), *n.*, *pl.* **-tec** or **-tecs.** **1.** a member of an Indian people of southern Mexico whose culture shows both Mayan and Toltec influences: *The Maya, the Zapotecs, ... and the Aztecs evidently developed urban communities on a major scale* (Scientific American). **2.** the Zapotecan language of this people: *Born in poverty in a hill village, and speaking no language but Zapotec in his childhood, he [Juarez] became the poor man's champion* (Observer).

Za·po·tec·an (sä'pō tek'ən), *n.* **1.** a group of related Indian languages of southern Mexico and Guatemala. **2.** any of various peoples speaking Zapotecan. —*adj.* of or having to do with the Zapotecans or their languages: *In the nearby dead cities of Mitla and Monte Alban the spirit of ... Zapotecan civilizations pervades the carefully preserved halls and palaces* (Maclean's).

zap·ti·ah or **zap·ti·eh** (zup tē'ə), *n.* (in Turkey) policeman. [earlier *zaptié* < Turkish *zaptiye* < Arabic *ḍabṭ* administration]

Zar·a·thus·tri·an (zar'ə thüs'trē ən), *adj.*, *n.* Zoroastrian.

za·ra·tite (zär'ə tīt), *n.* a hydrous carbonate of nickel, of a green color, found as an incrustation and in stalactites. [< Spanish *zaratita*; origin uncertain]

zar·a·zue·la (zär'ə zwā'lə), *n.* zarzuela.

za·re·ba or **za·ree·ba** (zə rē'bə), *n.* in the Sudan and adjacent parts of Africa: **1.** a fence or enclosure, usually constructed of thorn bushes, for defense against the attacks of enemies or wild beasts. **2.** a camp protected by such a fence. [< Arabic *zarība* cattle pen, lair < *zaraba* he enclosed or penned up (cattle)]

zarf (zärf), *n.* a cup-shaped metal holder for a hot coffee cup without a handle, used in the Levant. Also, **zurf.** [< Arabic *ẓarf* vessel]

zar·zue·la (thär thwā'lä, sär swā'-), *n.* a short drama with incidental music, similar to an operetta or musical comedy. Also, **zarazuela.** [< Spanish *zarzuela* < the Palace of La *Zarzuela*, near Madrid, where festive dramas were presented]

zas·tru·ga (zäs trü'gə), *n.*, *pl.* **-gi** (-gē). (in Siberia and elsewhere) one of a series of wavelike ridges formed in snow by the action of the wind, and running in the direction of the wind. Also, **sastruga.** [< Russian *zastruga* groove]

zax (zaks), *n.* a type of ax for shaping roofing slates, having a pointed peen for making nail holes: *Chicago's A to Z Rental ... rents everything for the home from axes to zaxes* (Time). [variant of *sax*[1]]

za·yin (zä'yin, zī'ən), *n.* the seventh letter of the Hebrew alphabet. [< Hebrew *zayin*]

za·zen (zä'zen'), *n.* (in Zen Buddhism) omphaloskepsis. [< Japanese *zazen*]

Z-bar (zē'bär'), *n.* a steel bar used in constructing steel columns for buildings, etc., consisting essentially of a web with two flanges at right angles to it, and having the cross section somewhat resembling the letter Z.

zeal (zēl), *n.* intense ardor in the pursuit of some end; passionate eagerness in favor of a person or cause; earnest enthusiasm (for something or someone) as displayed in action: *A good citizen feels zeal for his country's welfare.* [< Latin *zēlus* < Greek *zêlos*] —**Syn.** fervor.

zeal·ot (zel'ət), *n.* a person who shows too much zeal; immoderate partisan; fanatical enthusiast: *A band of zealots ... is pushing his candidacy hard* (Wall Street Journal). [< Latin *zēlōtēs* < Greek *zēlōtḗs* < *zēloûn* be zealous < *zêlos* zeal] —**Syn.** bigot.

Zeal·ot (zel'ət), *n.* a member of a strict, militant Jewish sect which fiercely resisted the Romans in Palestine until Jerusalem was destroyed in 70 A.D.

zeal·ot·ry (zel'ə trē), *n.*, *pl.* **-ries.** **1.** action or feeling characteristic of a zealot; fanaticism. **2.** an instance of this.

zeal·ous (zel'əs), *adj.* full of or incited by zeal; characterized by passionate ardor; intensely earnest; actively enthusiastic: *The children made zealous efforts to clean up the house for the party.* [< Medieval Latin *zelosus* < Latin *zēlus* zeal] —**zeal'ous·ly,** *adv.* —**zeal'ous·ness,** *n.*
—**Syn.** ardent, fervent. —**Ant.** apathetic, indifferent.

ze·bec or **ze·beck** (zē'bek), *n.* xebec.

Zeb·e·dee (zeb'ə dē), *n.* (in the Bible) the father of the Apostles James and John. Matthew 4:21.

ze·bra (zē'brə), *n.*, *pl.* **-bras** or (*collectively*) **-bra.** any of certain wild, swift, hoofed mammals of southern and eastern Africa, related to the horses and asses but striped with dark bands on white, especially the Burchell's zebra or dauw. [< Portuguese *zebra*, perhaps < the native Congo name]

Zebra (4 to 5 ft. high at the shoulder)

zebra butterfly, a tropical American butterfly having black wings barred with yellow.

zebra crossing, *British.* a crosswalk painted black with white stripes, giving pedestrians right of way in crossing streets.

zebra fish, a percoid fish with dark stripes found in Australian waters.

ze·brass (zē'bras'), *n.* the offspring of a male zebra and female ass.

zebra swallowtail, a large North American swallowtail butterfly with black wings banded with brilliant yellow.

ze·bra·wood (zē′brə wu̇d′), *n.* **1.** the hard, striped wood of a large tree of tropical America, used especially for cabinetwork. **2.** this tree. **3.** any of several similar woods or the trees or shrubs yielding them.

ze·brine (zē′brīn, -brin), *adj.* **1.** having to do with a zebra. **2.** resembling a zebra.

ze·broid (zē′broid), *adj.* resembling the zebra. —*n.* a zebroid animal; a cross between the zebra and the ass, or the zebra and the horse.

ze·bru·la (zē′bru̇ lə, zeb′ru̇-), *n.* the offspring of a male zebra and a female horse. [< *zebr*(a) + Latin (*m*)*ūla*, feminine of *mūlus* mule]

ze·brule (zē′brül), *n.* zebrula.

ze·bu (zē′byü), *n., pl.* **-bus** or (*collectively*) **-bu.** a domesticated ox of Asia and East Africa, with a large, fatty hump over the shoulders, and a large dewlap. [< French *zébu*]

Zebu (6 ft. high at the shoulder)

Zeb·u·lun (zeb′yə lən), *n.* **1.** (in the Bible) the tenth son of Jacob, by Leah. Genesis 30:19,20. **2.** the tribe of Israel that claimed descent from him.

zec·chin (zek′in), *n.* a sequin, a former gold coin of Venice and Turkey: *If you don't choose to submit to be cheated by them out of a ducat here and a zecchin there, you will be cheated by them out of your picture* (John Ruskin). Also, **zechin.** [< Italian *zecchino.* Doublet of SEQUIN.]

zec·chi·no (tsek kē′nō), *n., pl.* **-ni** (-nē). *Italian.* sequin, a former gold coin of Venice.

Zech., Zechariah (book of the Old Testament).

Zech·a·ri·ah (zek′ə rī′ə), *n.* **1.** a Hebrew prophet of the 500's B.C. **2.** a prophetic book of the Old Testament attributed to him, *Abbr.:* Zech.

zech·in (zek′in), *n.* zecchin; a sequin.

zed (zed), *n. Especially British.* a name for the letter *Z, z.* [< Middle French *zède,* learned borrowing from Late Latin *zēta* < Greek *zêta.* Doublet of ZETA.]

Zed·e·ki·ah (zed′ə kī′ə), *n.* (in Biblical history) the last king of Judah, whose reign ended with the Exile (500's B.C.). II Kings 24:17-20.

zed·o·ar·y (zed′ō er′ē), *n.* **1.** the aromatic tuberous root of one of two East Indian plants of the ginger family, used as a drug. **2.** either of these plants. [< Medieval Latin *zedoaria,* or *zedoarium* < Arabic *zedwār*]

zee (zē), *n. Especially U.S.* a name for the letter *Z, z.*

Zee·man effect (zā′män), *Physics.* the separation of lines of the spectrum that occurs in light emanating from a source in a magnetic field. [< Pieter *Zeeman,* 1865-1943, a Dutch physicist]

Zef·ran (zef′ran), *n. Trademark.* a fabric of acrylic fiber used for clothing.

ze·in (zē′in), *n. Biochemistry.* a protein contained in corn, used in plastics, coatings, adhesives, etc. [< earlier *zea* (< New Latin *Zea* the maize genus < Latin *zēa* spelt < Greek *zeiá*) + *-in*]

Zeiss planetarium (zīs; *German* tsīs), an apparatus showing the movements of the sun, moon, planets, and stars by projecting lights on the inside of a dome shaped like a hemisphere; planetarium. [< Carl *Zeiss* Optical Works in Jena, Germany, which produced the original planetarium]

Zeiss projector, Zeiss planetarium.

Zeit·geist (tsīt′gīst′), *n.* the characteristic thought or feeling of a period of time; spirit of the age: *Arthur Panter was not the sort of person who drifts along with the Zeitgeist* (New Yorker). [< German *Zeitgeist* (literally) spirit of the time < *Zeit-*time + *Geist* spirit]

Ze·lan (zē′lan), *n. Trademark.* a chemical finish applied to fabrics to make them water- and stain-repellent.

ze·min·dar (zə mēn′där′), *n.* zamindar.

ze·min·da·ry (zə mēn′dä′rē), *n., pl.* **-ries.** zamindari.

zem·stvo (zem′stvō), *n., pl.* **-stvos.** (in Russia before the Revolution) a local elective assembly having authority over certain affairs of a district. [< Russian *zemstvo* (originally) rural population, rural officials < *zem′*, variant of *zemlya* land]

Zen (zen), *n.* Zen Buddhism: *As we are not all able to study our Zen under a master, perhaps the next best thing is to make use of words in relation to paintings by a Zen master* (Manchester Guardian Weekly). [< Japanese *zen* religious meditation]

ze·na·na (ze nä′nə), *n.* the part of a house set aside for the women in a Moslem home in Pakistan, India, and certain other parts of Asia. [< Hindustani *zenana* < Persian *zanāna* < *zan* woman]

Zen Buddhism, a mystical form of the Mahayana Buddhism of Japan, that emphasizes solitary meditation and study to achieve a sense of self-control that leads to selflessness and identification with the spiritual world: *Hipsters go to Zen Buddhism, to extract from it whatever confirms them in their present convictions* (Harper's).

Zen Buddhist, a believer in Zen Buddhism.

Zend (zend), *n.* **1.** the commentary usually accompanying the Zoroastrian Avesta. **2.** the language of the Avesta; Avestan. [< French *zend* < Pahlavi *Zend*]

Zend-A·ves·ta (zend′ə ves′tə), *n.* the sacred writings of Zoroastrianism, consisting of the Avesta and the Zend. [alteration (influenced by Persian *zandawastā*) of Pahlavi *Avistāk va Zend* (literally) Avesta with Zend]

ze·nith (zē′nith), *n.* **1. a.** the point in the heavens directly overhead: *To an observer at the North Pole, the North Star would be about at his zenith.* **b.** the point of highest altitude of a heavenly body, etc., relative to a particular observer or place. **2.** highest point or state; culmination; climax; acme: *At the zenith of its power, Rome ruled all of civilized Europe.* [< Old French, or Medieval Latin *cenith* < Arabic *samt* (*ar-rās*) the way (over the head)] —**Syn. 2.** top, apex, summit.

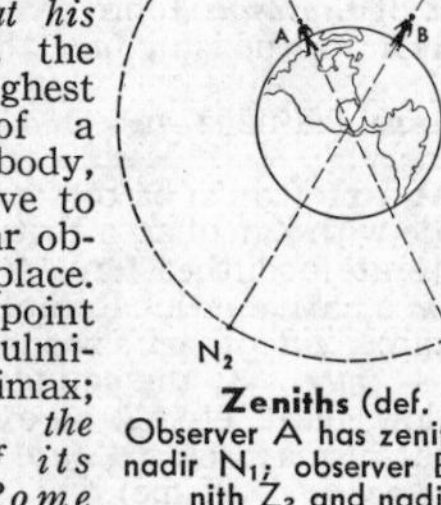

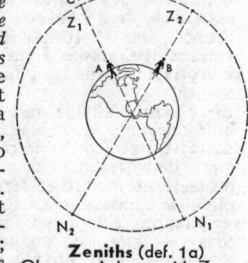

Zeniths (def. 1a)
Observer A has zenith Z_1 and nadir N_1; observer B has zenith Z_2 and nadir N_2.

ze·nith·al (zē′nə thəl), *adj.* **1.** of or having to do with the zenith. **2.** occurring at the zenith.

zenithal projection, a map projection in which all points have their true compass direction from the center of the map; azimuthal equidistant projection.

zenith distance, the distance of a heavenly body from the zenith of a particular observer or place, the complement of its altitude, measured in degrees along the vertical circle passing through the zenith and the body: *At the North Pole, the zenith distance of the North Star is about 0 degrees.*

zenith telescope, a telescope for measuring the difference of zenith distances of pairs of stars north and south of the zenith: *A zenith telescope . . . is a telescope provided with a plumb line to ensure that it is vertical* (Listener).

Zen·nist (zen′ist), *n.* a Zen Buddhist.

ze·o·lite (zē′ə līt), *n.* any of a large group of minerals consisting of hydrous silicates of aluminum with alkali metals, commonly found in the cavities of igneous rocks. [< Swedish *zeolit* < Greek *zeîn* to boil + Swedish *-lit* -lite (because it boils or swells under the blowpipe)]

ze·o·lit·ic (zē′ə lit′ik), *adj.* **1.** having to do with zeolite. **2.** consisting of zeolite. **3.** resembling zeolite.

ze·ol·i·tize (zē ol′ə tīz), *v.t.* **-tized, -tiz·ing.** to change into a zeolite: *An unusual cave in zeolitized dolerite was found in Tasmania* (Gordon Warwick).

Zeph., Zephaniah (book of the Old Testament).

Zeph·a·ni·ah (zef′ə nī′ə), *n.* **1.** a Hebrew prophet of the 600's B.C. **2.** a prophetic book of the Old Testament attributed to him, placed among the minor prophets. *Abbr.:* Zeph.

Zeph·i·ran Chloride (zef′ə ran), *Trademark.* a mixture of alkyl-dimethyl-benzyl-ammonium chlorides, used as an antiseptic on skin and mucous membranes.

Zeph·yr (zef′ər), *n.* the west wind personified; Zephyrus. [< Latin *zephyrus* < Greek *zéphyros*]

zeph·yr (zef′ər), *n.* **1.** a soft, gentle wind; mild breeze: *The flowers, the zephyrs, and the warblers of spring, returning after a tedious absence* (Washington Irving). **2.** the west wind. **3.** a light, soft yarn or worsted. **4.** a very light garment, as a light shawl, light shirt, etc. [< *Zephyr*]

zephyr cloth, a light kind of cassimere used for women's garments.

zephyr lily, a low-growing plant of the amaryllis family found in warm regions of the Western Hemisphere and often cultivated for its white, rose, or yellow flowers; fairy lily.

Zeph·y·rus (zef′ər əs), *n. Greek Mythology.* the west wind personified, considered to be the mildest and gentlest of sylvan deities: *With voice Mild, as when Zephyrus on Flora breathes* (Milton).

zephyr yarn or **worsted,** a very light yarn or worsted, used for knitting, etc.

Zep·pe·lin or **zep·pe·lin** (zep′ə lən, zep′-lən; *German* tsep′ə lēn′), *n.* a large, cigar-shaped, dirigible balloon having a rigid frame of light metal within which are separate gas compartments. The engines and freight or passenger compartments are contained in or slung from its bottom part. [< German *Zeppelin* < Count Ferdinand von *Zeppelin,* 1838-1917, who invented it]

Zeppelin moored

ze·ro (zir′ō), *n., pl.* **-ros** or **-roes,** *adj., v.,* **-roed, -ro·ing.** —*n.* **1.** the figure or symbol 0; cipher: *Add two zeros to 5 and get 500.* **2. a.** the point marked with a zero on the scale of a thermometer, etc. **b.** the temperature corresponding to zero on the scale of a thermometer. **3.** the complete absence of quantity; nothing; none at all. **4.** the lowest point or degree. **5.** the correct sight setting of a rifle for elevation and windage at a given range.

—*adj.* **1.** of or at zero: *the zero point of a thermometer, zero weather.* **2.** none at all; not any: *a zero result.* **3.** *Meteorology, Aeronautics.* **a.** denoting a ceiling not more than 50 feet high. **b.** denoting visibility of not more than 165 feet in a horizontal direction.

—*v.t.* to adjust (an instrument or device) to zero point or line or to any given point from which readings will then be measured.

zero in, to adjust the sights of (a rifle) for a given range so a bullet will strike the center of the target: *He zeroed in his .22 caliber rifle at 50 yards.*

zero in on, a. to get the range of by adjusting the sights of a firearm, etc.: *After settling in the prone position, Allen began zeroing in on a chuck at an estimated range of 400 yards* (New York Times). **b.** to direct with precision toward a target, etc.: *Like a plane zeroed in on target, the streamliner roared through a red signal* (Newsweek). **c.** to locate as a target; find the range of: *A new sound must repeat itself many times in a hinting rhythm before one can zero in on it and find out what went wrong* (Atlantic).

[< Italian *zero* < Arabic *ṣifr* empty. Doublet of CIPHER.]

—**Syn.** *n.* **3.** nullity, nil. **4.** nadir.

Ze·ro (zir′ō), *n., pl.* **-ros** or **-roes.** a Japanese fighter plane of World War II. [< Mitsubishi (the Japanese manufacturer), type *0,* the official designation]

zero g, zero gravity: *It appears from Russian flights that one week of "zero g" . . . required for a lunar round trip poses no insuperable dangers* (Wall Street Journal).

zero gravity, the absence of gravity; weightlessness: *There is also such a thing as a zero gravity and when in that state the pilot just floats in the air with no weight whatsoever* (Atlantic).

zero grazing, *British.* zero pasture.

zero hour, 1. the precise point in time at which an attack or some phase of an attack is scheduled to begin; H-hour. **2.** any point in time viewed as similar to this; crucial moment. **3.** midnight: *Zero hour . . . is the moment of beginning of the day, so that a new day is forever on its journey around the earth* (Bernhard, Bennett, and Rice).

zero magnitude, *Astronomy.* a measure of brilliance of certain stars, being 2½ times as bright as first magnitude.

zero pasture, a technique of feeding green forage to livestock in a barn or feed lot rather than allowing them to graze: *Using a technique called soilage, or zero pasture, they cut the grass in the pasture twice a day, chop it up, and carry it to the cows* (Atlantic).

zero point energy, *Physics.* the kinetic energy remaining in a substance at the temperature of absolute zero.

ze·roth (zi′rōth), *adj.* of or at zero; being zero: *$x^0 = x$ to the zeroth power.*

ze·ro-ze·ro (zir′ō zir′ō), *adj. Meteorology, Aeronautics.* denoting conditions of severely limited visibility in both the horizontal and vertical directions: *zero-zero weather.*

zest (zest), *n.* **1.** keen enjoyment; relish; gusto: *a youthful zest for life. The hungry man ate with zest.* **2.** a pleasant or exciting quality, flavor, etc.: *to give zest to food by the use of herbs. Wit gives zest to conversation.* —*v.t.* to give a zest to; impart a piquant quality to. [< French *zeste* orange or lemon peel] —**Syn.** *n.* **2.** piquancy, tang.

zest·ful (zest′fəl), *adj.* full of zest; characterized by keen relish or hearty enjoyment: *A zestful sort of place in which to spend a fortnight* (Fraser's Magazine). —**zest′ful·ly,** *adv.* —**zest′ful·ness,** *n.* —**Syn.** exhilarating.

zest·y (zes′tē), *adj.* having much zest; full of zest; zestful: *Guests can shell their own [crustaceans] and dip them into a zesty mayonnaise* (New Yorker).

ze·ta (zā′tə, zē′-), *n.* the sixth letter (Z, ζ, corresponding to English Z, z) of the Greek alphabet. [< Greek *zêta,* name of the letter *z.* Doublet of ZED.]

ze·tet·ic (zə tet′ik), *adj.* **1.** having to do with inquiry or investigation. **2.** proceeding by inquiry or investigation. [< New Latin *zeteticus* < Greek *zētētikós* < *zēteîn* to seek, inquire]

Ze·thus (zē′thəs), *n. Greek Mythology.* the twin brother of Amphion.

zeug·ma (züg′mə), *n. Grammar.* the use of a word to relate to two or more words in a sentence, when properly applying in sense to only one of them. [< Greek *zeûgma* (literally) a yoking < *zeugnýnai* to yoke, related to *zygón* a yoke]

zeug·mat·ic (züg mat′ik), *adj. Grammar.* **1.** having to do with zeugma. **2.** of the nature of zeugma.

Zeus (züs), *n.* the chief god of the ancient Greeks, the ruler of gods and men, son of Cronus and Rhea, and husband of Hera, identified with the Roman god Jupiter. He was the god of the sky and weather.

Zhda·nov·ism (zhdä′nə viz əm), *n.* a policy to purge Soviet literature of Western influence, especially during Stalin's regime. [< Andrei *Zhdanov,* 1888-1948, a Soviet official who implemented this policy + *-ism*]

zho (zhō), *n.* dzo.

zib·el·ine or **zib·el·line** (zib′ə līn, -lin), *n.* **1.** sable (the fur). **2.** a woolen fabric with a slightly furry surface, used for dresses, coats, etc. —*adj.* of or having to do with sable or the sable. [< Middle French *zebeline* or *zibeline* < Italian *zibellino,* ultimately < Slavic (compare Russian *sobol′* sable)]

zib·et or **zib·eth** (zib′it), *n.* a civet cat of India and the Malay Peninsula. [< Medieval Latin *zibethum* civet < Arabic *zabād.* Doublet of CIVET.]

zig (zig), *n., v.,* **zigged, zig·ging.** *Informal.* —*n.* the first movement or turn of a zigzag: *The foreign parties slavishly followed every zig and zag of Kremlin maneuvering* (Wall Street Journal). —*v.i.* to make the first movement or turn of a zigzag: *In the pursuit of this policy they zig and zag, change strategy and tactics, advance and retreat* (New York Times). [< *zig*(zag)]

zig·gu·rat (zig′ů rat), *n.* a pyramidal tower having stages or stories each successively smaller than that below it, so as to leave a terrace all around, a characteristic temple form in ancient Assyrian and Babylonian architecture. Also, **zikkurat, zikurat.** [< Akkadian *ziqquratu* temple tower; pinnacle, peak < *zaqāru* be high]

zig·zag (zig′zag′), *adj., adv., v.,* **-zagged, -zag·ging,** *n.* —*adj.* having a series of short, sharp turns from one side to another; characterized by such turns: *to go in a zigzag direction.* See **indented** for picture.
—*adv.* with short, sharp turns from one side to another: *The path ran zigzag up the hill.*
—*v.i.* to go or move in, or have, a zigzag course or direction: *Lightning zigzagged across the sky.* —*v.t.* to give a zigzag form to.
—*n.* **1.** a zigzag line or course. **2.** one of the short, sharp turns of a zigzag.
[(originally) noun < French *zigzag* < German *Zickzack,* perhaps varied reduplication of *Zacke* tooth, prong]
—**Syn.** *adj.* jagged, serrated, notched.

zigzag stitch, a stitch made with a sewing machine in a zigzag pattern, for joining two edges in places where a straight-line stitch is difficult or awkward.

zik·ku·rat or **zik·u·rat** (zik′ů rat), *n.* ziggurat.

zil·lah (zil′ə), *n.* (formerly, in British India) an administrative division of a province. [< Hindustani *ḍilah* district; part; side < Arabic *ḍil′* part; rib]

zil·lion (zil′yən), *Slang.* —*n.* any very large but indefinite number. —*adj.* of such a number; very many; innumerable: *The locus of Smith's boyhood was Mount Vernon, N.Y., but it could have been a zillion other places* (Newsweek). [< *z* (last letter) + *-illion,* as in *million*]

Zil·pah (zil′pə), *n.* (in the Bible) Leah's maid, mother of Gad and Asher. Genesis 30:9-13.

zim·ba·lon (zim′bə lon), *n.* a cymbalom: *Old Hungarian specialties, such as goulash and the zimbalon, are served up in a manner that is all quite folksy* (New Yorker).

zinc (zingk), *n., v.,* **zincked** or **zinced** (zingkt), **zinck·ing** or **zinc·ing** (zing′king). —*n.* **1.** a hard, bluish-white, metallic chemical element, brittle at ordinary temperatures, but malleable and ductile between 110 degrees and 210 degrees centigrade (230-410 degrees Fahrenheit). It is little affected by air and moisture at ordinary temperatures, but at high temperatures it burns in air with a bright blue-green flame. Zinc is obtained from various ores, especially the sulfide (sphalerite), the carbonate and silicate (calamine, smithsonite), and the red oxide (zincite). It is used for coating or galvanizing iron, for roofing, in alloys such as brass, in electric batteries, in paint, etc. *Symbol:* Zn; *at.wt.:* (C^{12}) 65.37 or (O^{16}) 65.38; *at.no.:* 30; *valence:* 2. **2.** a piece of zinc used in a voltaic cell.
—*v.t.* to coat or cover with zinc or a zinc compound.
[< German *Zink,* related to *Zinken* prong, point (perhaps because of the form which zinc assumes in blast furnaces)]

zinc·ate (zing′kāt), *n.* a salt of zinc hydroxide, such as $Zn(OH)_2$, when it acts as a feeble acid.

zinc bacitracin, the antibiotic bacitracin with 7 per cent zinc, used in medicine as flavoring, and as a silage preservative, etc.

zinc blende, *Mineralogy.* sphalerite.

zinc chloride, a water-soluble crystal or crystalline powder, used in galvanization, electroplating, and as a wood preservative, disinfectant, etc. *Formula:* $ZnCl_2$

zinc dust, a gray powder, usually containing zinc oxide, used as a reducing agent, a bleach, in rust-resistant paints, etc.

zinc·ic (zing′kik), *adj.* **1.** having to do with zinc. **2.** consisting of zinc. **3.** containing zinc. **4.** resembling zinc.

zinc·if·er·ous (zing kif′ər əs, zin sif′-), *adj.* **1.** containing zinc. **2.** producing zinc.

zinc·i·fi·ca·tion (zing′kə fə kā′shən), *n.* **1.** the process of coating or impregnating an object with zinc: *Argentiferous zinc may settle in the cavities during zincification* (Manuel Eissler). **2.** the state resulting from such a process.

zinc·i·fy (zing′kə fī), *v.t.,* **-fied, -fy·ing.** to coat or impregnate with zinc; zinc.

zinc·ite (zing′kīt), *n. Mineralogy.* native zinc oxide, of a deep-red or orange-yellow color, also called red oxide of zinc or red zinc ore. *Formula:* ZnO. Also, **zinkite.**

zinck·en·ite (zing′kə nīt), *n.* zinkenite.

zinck·ic (zing′kik), *adj.* zincic.

zinck·if·er·ous (zing kif′ər əs), *adj.* zinciferous.

zinck·y (zing′kē), *adj.* **1.** having to do with zinc. **2.** containing zinc. **3.** resembling zinc.

zin·co·graph (zing′kə graf, -gräf), *n.* **1.** the plate used in zincography. **2.** a design or impression produced by zincography.

zin·cog·ra·pher (zing kog′rə fər), *n.* a person who makes zincographic plates.

zin·co·graph·ic (zing′kə graf′ik), *adj.* having to do with zincography.

zin·co·graph·i·cal (zing′kə graf′ə kəl), *adj.* zincographic.

zin·cog·ra·phy (zing kog′rə fē), *n.* the art or process of etching or engraving designs on zinc, as on a zinc plate from which illustrations, etc., are to be printed.

zinc ointment, a preparation containing 20 per cent zinc oxide, used in treating skin disorders.

zin·co·type (zing′kə tīp), *n.* zincograph.

zinc·ous (zing′kəs), *adj. Chemistry.* **1.** of zinc; zincic. **2.** *Obsolete.* electropositive.

zinc oxide, an insoluble white powder, used in making pigments, rubber, glass, cosmetics, ointments, etc. *Formula:* ZnO

zinc phosphide, an insoluble, dark-gray powder, used chiefly as a rat poison: *Until a few years ago, only acute or quick-acting poisons such as zinc phosphide or arsenic were used in baits for the control of the house mouse* (New Scientist). *Formula:* Zn_3P_2

zinc sulfate, white vitriol.

zinc sulfide, a yellowish or white powder occurring naturally as sphalerite. Zinc sulfide is used as a pigment and as a phosphor in television screens and on watch faces. *Formula:* ZnS

zinc white, zinc oxide used as a white pigment in paints.

zinc·y (zing′kē), *adj.* zincky.

zin·fan·del (zin′fən del), *n.* **1.** a variety of wine grape native to and much grown in California, once believed (erroneously) to be a variety of European grape. **2.** a wine made from this grape. [American English; origin uncertain]

zing (zing), *n.* **1.** a sharp humming sound: *Her cool presence silenced the customary zing and swish of hurled hardware* (Punch). **2.** *Slang.* spirit; vitality; liveliness; zest: *The week's TV dramas were thin, talky, and without dramatic zing* (Time).
—*interj. Slang.* a sound used to express enthusiasm, spirit, or the like.
—*v.i.* to make a sharp humming sound, especially in going rapidly: *A bullet zinged past the ear of the Japanese consul from Manila* (New Yorker). —*v.t. Slang.* to bring forth with spirit or zest: *Whammy, we zing in a couple of great production numbers* (S.J. Perelman).
[imitative]

zin·ga·ra (tsěng′gä rä), *n., pl.* **-re** (-rā). *Italian.* a Gypsy girl or woman.

zin·ga·ro (tsěng′gä rō), *n., pl.* **-ri** (-rē). *Italian.* a Gypsy boy or man: *I am a zingaro, a Bohemian, an Egyptian, or whatever the Europeans . . . may choose to call our people* (Scott).

zing·el (tsing′əl), *n. German.* a small fish of the perch family, found in the Danube.

zin·gi·ber·a·ceous (zin′jə bə rā′shəs), *adj.* belonging to the ginger family. Also, **zinziberaceous.** [< New Latin *Zingiberaceae* the order name (< Latin *zingiberi* ginger) + English *-ous*]

zing·y (zing′ē), *adj.,* **zing·i·er, zing·i·est.** *Slang.* full of vitality; lively; zesty: *A soupçon of wisdom, a lot of wit are laced into Jean Kerr's zingy comedy* (Time).

Zin·jan·thro·pus (zin′jan thrō′pəs), *n.* a primitive man whose remains were discovered in Tanganyika in 1959. He was nicknamed "the Nutcracker Man" because of his huge teeth: *Leakey . . . has abandoned his earlier opinion that Zinjanthropus, a manlike creature whose bones he found in Africa in 1959, was on the line of evolution to man* (Scientific American). [< New Latin *Zinjanthropus* the genus name < *zinj* East Africa + Greek *ánthrōpos* man]

zin·ke (zing′kə), *n.* a small cornet of wood or horn with finger holes and a cupped mouthpiece, formerly common in Europe. [< German *Zinke*]

zin·ken·ite (zing′kə nīt), *n. Mineralogy.* a steel-gray sulfide of antimony and lead. *Formula:* $Pb_6Sb_{14}S_{27}$ Also, **zinckenite.** [< German *Zinkenit* < J.K.L. *Zinken,* director of the Anhalt mines + *-it* -ite[1]]

zink·ite (zing′kīt), *n.* zincite.

zink·y (zing′kē), *adj.* zincky.

zin·ni·a (zin′ē ə), *n.* any of a group of composite herbs, natives of Mexico and the southwestern United States. Various kinds of zinnia are often grown for their showy flowers of many colors. [< New Latin *Zinnia* the genus name < Johann G. *Zinn,* 1727-1759, a German botanist]

Cactus-flowered Zinnia

zin·zi·ber·a·ceous (zin′zə bə rā′shəs), *adj.* zingiberaceous.

Zi·on (zī′ən), *n.* **1.** a hill in Jerusalem on which the royal palace and the Temple were built. **2.** the Israelites, whose national religious life centered on Mount Zion. **3.** Heaven (as the final home of those who are virtuous and truly devout). **4.** the ancient Hebrew nation or the Christian church of God. Also, **Sion.** [Old English *Sion* < Late Latin *siōn* < Greek *Seiōn* < Hebrew *ṣiyyon* hill]

Zi·on·ism (zī′ə niz əm), *n.* a movement that originated in the late 1800's, having as its primary goal the resettlement of Jews in Palestine, and which now seeks to help Israel as a Jewish national state.

Zi·on·ist (zī′ə nist), *n.* an advocate or adherent of Zionism. —*adj.* of or having to do with Zionists or Zionism.

Zi·on·is·tic (zī′ə nis′tik), *adj.* **1.** of or having to do with Zionism. **2.** like Zionism; resembling Zionism.

Zi·on·ite (zī′ə nīt), *n.* a Zionist.

Zi·on·ward (zī′ən wərd), *adv.* toward Zion.

zip (zip), *n., v.,* **zipped, zip·ping.** —*n.* **1.** a sudden, brief hissing sound, as of a flying bullet. **2.** *Informal.* energy or vim: *Satisfied with what's inside the can, the National Brewing Company is attempting to add a little zip to the outside* (New York Times). **3.** *British.* a zipper.
—*v.i.* **1.** to make a sudden, brief hissing sound. **2.** *Informal.* to proceed with energy; move briskly. —*v.t.* to fasten or close with a zipper. [imitative]

ZIP (no periods), Zone Improvement Plan, a plan set up by the United States Post Office Department to facilitate delivery of mail, in which each delivery area has its own identifying number.

Zi·pan·go (zi pang′gō), *n.* Cipango.

Zi·pan·gu (zi pang′gü), *n.* Cipango, Marco Polo's name for Japan.

Zip code (zip), ZIP: *We have been trying to come to terms with the Post Office's . . . system, called, with somewhat unnerving cajolery, the Zip Code* (New Yorker).

zip fastener, *British.* zipper.

zip gun, a crude gun made of metal tubing and a wooden handle. Rubber bands or a spring fire the cartridge.

zip-in lining (zip′in′), a removable lining that fits into a topcoat, raincoat, etc., by means of a zipper.

zip·per (zip′ər), *n.* **1.** a fastener consisting of two flexible parts interlocked or separated by an attached sliding device which is pulled along between them, used in place of buttons, laces, etc., on clothing, etc.; slide fastener. **2. Zipper,** a trademark for this fastening. **3. Zipper,** a trademark for an overshoe or a boot with a zipper.
—*v.i., v.t.* to close or fasten with a zipper: *He was wearing a slate-blue flying suit zippered up to his chest* (New Yorker).
[American English < *zip* + *-er*[1]] —**zip′per·less,** *adj.*

zipper bag, a bag that opens or closes by means of a zipper.

zip·pered (zip′ərd), *adj.* furnished with a zipper: *a zippered closure.*

zipper fleet, *U.S.* ships taken out of active service and held in reserve; mothball fleet.

zip·py (zip′ē), *adj.,* **-pi·er, -pi·est.** *Informal.* full of energy; lively; gay.

zirc·al·loy (zėrk′al′oi, zėr′kə loi′), *n.* an alloy of zirconium and some other metal or metals.

zir·con (zėr′kon), *n.* a common mineral, a silicate of zirconium, occurring in tetragonal crystals, variously colored, red, yellow, brown, green, etc. Transparent zircon is used as a gem. The reddish-orange variety is sometimes called hyacinth in jewelry. The colorless, yellowish, or smoky zircon of Ceylon is there called jargon. *Formula:* $ZrSiO_4$ [probably < French *zircon,* ultimately < Arabic *zarqūn* < Persian *zargūn* (literally) golden < *zar* gold. Doublet of JARGON[2].]

zir·con·ate (zėr′kə nāt), *n.* a salt of zirconium hydroxide when it acts as an acid.

zir·co·ni·a (zėr kō′nē ə), *n.* a dioxide of zirconium, usually obtained as a white, amorphous powder by heating zirconium to redness in contact with air. It is noted for its infusibility and its luminosity when heated, and is therefore used in making incandescent gas mantles, refractory utensils, etc. *Formula:* ZrO_2 [< New Latin *zirconia* < *zircon* zircon]

zir·con·ic (zėr kon′ik), *adj.* **1.** of or having to do with zirconia or zirconium. **2.** containing zirconia or zirconium.

zir·co·ni·um (zėr kō′nē əm), *n.* a metallic chemical element having both acidic and basic properties, commonly obtained from zircon as a black powder or as a grayish, crystalline substance. It is used in alloys for wires, filaments, etc., in making steel, etc. *Symbol:* Zr; *at.wt.:* (C^{12}) 91.22 or (O^{16}) 91.22; *at.no.:* 40; *valence:* 4, 3, 2. [< New Latin *zirconium* < *zirconia* zirconia]

zirconium hydroxide, a white powder used in making pigments and dyes. *Formula:* $Zr(OH)_4$

zir·co·nyl (zėr′kə nəl), *n.* a bivalent radical, ZrO-.

zith·er (zith′ər, ziᴛʜ′-), *n.* a musical instrument having from 30 to 40 strings stretched over a shallow sounding box, played in a horizontal position with a plectrum and the fingers. [< German *Zither* < Latin *cithara.* Doublet of CITHARA, GUITAR.]

Zither

zith·er·ist (zith′ər ist), *n.* a person who plays the zither.

zith·ern (zith′ərn), *n.* **1.** cithern. **2.** zither.

zit·tern (zit′ərn), *n.* zithern.

zi·zith (tsē tsēt′, tsi′tsis), *n.pl.* **1.** the fringe of twisted threads, especially knotted threads at the four corners, on the shorter ends of the Jewish prayer shawl (tallith). Numbers 15:37-41. **2.** the corded strings of a kind of scapular worn as an undergarment by Orthodox Jews. [< Hebrew *ṣiṣith*]

zizz (ziz), *British Informal.* —*n.* **1.** a humming sound; buzz. **2.** a snooze: . . . *Rip Van Winkle, the U.S. champion, who managed to leap twenty years in a single prodigious zizz* (Punch). —*v.i.* to make a humming or buzzing sound: *A seriously frustrated bumblebee soon ceases to be an object of amusement. Her anxiety and distress communicated itself to me as she zizzed and boomed about* (H.F. Ellis). [imitative]

zl., zloty.

zlo·ty (zlô′tē), *n., pl.* **-tys** or (*collectively*) **-ty.** the basic Polish gold monetary unit and nickel coin, worth about 25 cents. [< Polish *zloty* (literally) golden < *zloto* gold]

Zn (no period), zinc (chemical element).

zo (zō), *n., pl.* **zos.** zobo.

zo-, *combining form.* the form of **zoo-** before vowels, as in *zooid.*

zo·a (zō′ə), *n.* the plural of **zoon.**

Z.O.A. or **ZOA** (no periods), Zionist Organization of America.

zo·ar·i·um (zō ãr′ē əm), *n., pl.* **-ar·i·a** (-ãr′ē ə). *Zoology.* the colony or aggregate of individuals of a compound animal. [< New Latin *zoarium* < *zoon* animal < Greek *zôion*]

zo·bo (zō′bō), *n., pl.* **-bos.** a domesticated animal of eastern Asia that is a cross between a yak and a zebu. Also, **zo, zomo.** [< a native name]

zo·di·ac (zō′dē ak), *n.* **1.** an imaginary belt of the heavens, extending about 8 degrees on both sides of the ecliptic (the apparent yearly path of the sun) and including the apparent paths of the major planets and the moon. The zodiac is divided into 12 equal parts, called *signs,* named after 12 constellations, each constellation now (because of the precession of the equinoxes) being in the sign named for the following constellation. **2.** a diagram representing the zodiac, used in astrology. **3.** a recurrent series, round, or course. **4.** compass; range. **5.** a set of twelve. **6.** a girdle. [< Old French *zodiaque,* learned borrowing from Latin *zōdiacus* < Greek *zōidiakòs* (*kýklos*) (circle) of the figures < *zōidion* zodiacal sign; (originally) sculptured figure of an animal; (diminutive) < *zôion* animal]

Zodiac (def. 2)

zo·di·a·cal (zō dī′ə kəl), *adj.* **1.** of or having to do with the zodiac. **2.** situated in the zodiac.

zodiacal light, an area of nebulous light in the sky, seen near the ecliptic at certain seasons of the year, either in the west after sunset or in the east before sunrise, and supposed to be the glow from a cloud of meteoric matter revolving around the sun.

zo·e mou, sas a·ga·po (zō′ē mü säs ä′gä-pō′), *Greek.* my life, I love thee.

zo·e·trope (zō′ə trōp), *n.* an optical instrument consisting of a cylinder open at the top, with a series of slits in the circumference, and a series of figures representing successive positions of a moving object arranged along the inner surface, which when viewed through the slits while the cylinder is in rapid rotation produce the impression of actual movement of the object. Also, **zootrope.**
[< Greek *zōē̂* life + *-tropos* a turning < *trépein* to turn]

zo·e·trop·ic (zō′ə trop′ik), *adj.* **1.** of or like a zoetrope. **2.** adapted to the zoetrope. **3.** shown by the zoetrope.

Zo·har (zō′här), *n.* the fundamental work of Jewish cabalism, a collection of mystical interpretations of the Bible written in Aramaic. Its author is unknown: *It was a world that honored learning by letting the women labor and their scholar-husbands pore over books: Scripture and commentary, Zohar and cabala* (New York Times). [< Hebrew *zōhār* (literally) brightness]

zo·ic (zō′ik), *n.* of or having to do with living beings or animals; characterized by animal life. [< Greek *zōikós* < *zôion* animal]

Zo·i·lus (zō′ə ləs), *n.* a spiteful or malignant critic. [< *Zoilus,* a Greek grammarian of the 300's B.C., who was a severe critic of Homer]

zois·ite (zoi′sīt), *n.* a mineral, a silicate of aluminum and calcium, sometimes containing iron instead of aluminum. *Formula:* $HCa_2Al_3Si_3O_{13}$ [< German *Zoisit* < Baron von *Zois,* 1747-1819, the discoverer + *-ite*[1]]

Zo·la·esque (zō′lə esk′), *adj.* of or having to do with Émile Zola or Zolaism: *Somewhat Zolaesque in its fashion of realism and distinctly Jamesian in narrative method . . .* (London Times).

Zo·la·ism (zō′lə iz əm), *n.* the characteristic qualities of the works of the French novelist Émile Zola, 1840-1902, noted for his unreserved realism or naturalism: *Set the maiden fancies wallowing in the troughs of Zolaism* (Tennyson).

Zoll·ver·ein (tsôl′fer īn′), *n.* **1.** a union of various German states from 1834 to 1871 to promote free trade among themselves and uniform conditions of trade with other nations, the formation and existence of which was an important step in the unification of Germany. **2.** any similar union of states or countries; customs union. [< German *Zollverein* (literally) toll union < *Zoll* toll + *Verein* union]

zom·bi (zom′bē), *n., pl.* **-bis. 1.** a corpse supposedly brought back to life by a supernatural power. **2.** the python god in certain West African voodoo cults. **3.** the snake god of voodoo, derived from this. **4.** a supernatural power or force by which the dead may be endowed with a capacity for mute, trancelike action somewhat resembling life, alleged to be possessed by certain practitioners of West Indian voodoo. **5.** an alcoholic drink of several kinds of rum, fruit juice, sugar, and brandy, served very cold and in a tall glass. **6.** *Slang.* a very stupid, lethargic person. [American English < Creole *zôbi* < West African (compare Kongo *zumbi* fetish)]

zom·bie (zom′bē), *n.* zombi.

zom·bi·ism (zom′bē iz əm), *n.* the state or character of being a zombi.

zo·mo (zō′mō), *n., pl.* **-mos.** zobo.

zon·al (zō′nəl), *adj.* **1.** of a zone; having to do with zones. **2.** characterized by or arranged in zones, circles, or rings; divided into zones. **3.** of the nature of or forming a zone. **4.** marked with zones or circular bands of color, as certain varieties of geranium having leaves so marked. —**zon'al·ly,** *adv.*

zo·na pel·lu·ci·da (zō'nə pe lü'sə də), *Embryology.* a thick, tough, transparent membrane surrounding the yolk of a developed mammalian ovum.
[< New Latin *zona pellucida* (literally) pellucid zone]

zon·a·ry (zō'nər ē), *adj.* **1.** occurring in a zone or zones. **2.** having the form of a zone or girdle.

zon·ate (zō'nāt), *adj.* **1.** marked with zones, rings, or bands of color; zoned. **2.** *Botany.* arranged in one row.

zon·at·ed (zō'nā tid), *adj.* zonate.

zo·na·tion (zō nā'shən), *n.* distribution in zones or regions of definite character: *Light penetration limits the distribution of plants, resulting in a zonation of the seaweeds: the green algae live in the uppermost, well-lighted zones; the brown algae in the intermediate zone; and the red algae at greatest depths* (Clarence J. Hylander).

zon·da (zon'də; *Spanish* sôn'dä), *n.* a wind of the foehn type in the Argentine pampas.
[< American Spanish *zonda,* perhaps < a native word]

zone (zōn), *n., v.,* **zoned, zon·ing.** —*n.* **1.** any of the five great divisions of the earth's surface, bounded by lines parallel to the equator, and distinguished by differences of climate (the Torrid Zone, the two Temperate Zones, and the two Frigid Zones). **2.** a definite region or area distinguished from adjacent regions by some special quality or condition: *the Canal Zone. A war zone is a district where fighting is going on.* **3.** a region or area characterized by certain forms of animal or vegetable life which are in turn determined by certain environmental conditions. **4.** an area or district in a town or city that is restricted by law to homes or businesses, or to other specific purposes. **5.** in the United States postal system: **a.** one of the sections into which a large city is divided, each of which is assigned a number to be used on addresses in order to expedite mail delivery. **b.** an area to all points within which the same rate of postage prevails for parcel-post shipments from a particular place. **6.** an area, commonly circular, to all points within which a uniform rate prevails for transportation, telephone service, or some other service from a particular place. **7.** the aggregate of railroad stations situated within a specific circumference around a particular shipping center. **8.** *Geology.* a horizon. **9.** *Mathematics.* a part of the surface of a sphere contained between two parallel planes. **10.** *Poetic.* a girdle; belt. **11.** an encircling or enclosing line, band, or ring, sometimes differing in color, texture, etc., from the surrounding medium.
—*v.t.* **1.** to divide into zones, especially to divide (a town or city) into areas which are restricted to homes, businesses, etc. **2.** to surround with a belt or girdle. **3.** to surround like a belt or girdle; encircle. **4.** to mark with rings or bands of color. —*v.i.* to be formed or divided into zones.
[< Latin *zōna* < Greek *zōnē* (originally) girdle < *zōnnýnai* to gird]

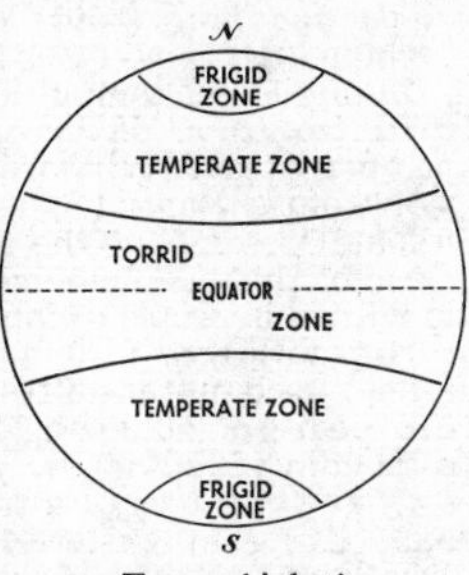

Zones (def. 1)

zoned (zōnd), *adj.* **1.** marked with or having zones. **2.** divided into zones.

zone defense, a defensive technique in which a team's defensive area is divided into zones, with each player assigned to a zone, used especially in basketball.

zone electrophoresis, electrophoresis conducted in a porous, solid, or semisolid medium, such as filter paper, a sheet of starch, etc., whereby the components of a liquid can be separated ionically into various zones of the medium.

zone·less (zōn'lis), *adj.* **1.** not marked with or divided into zones. **2.** not confined by or wearing a zone or girdle: *The ruling goddess with the zoneless waist* (Cowper).

zone melting, a technique for purifying metal based on the fact that molten metal absorbs impurities more readily than solid metal.

Zon·i·an (zō'nē ən), *n.* an American citizen who is a native or inhabitant of the Panama Canal Zone: *Many Zonians . . . regard the Zone as something sacred* (Time).

zon·ing (zō'ning), *n.* the building restrictions in an area of a city or town.

zonked (zongkt), *adj. Slang.* intoxicated; drunk. [origin unknown]

zon·ule (zō'nyül), *n.* a little zone or band, as of tissue, ligament, etc., in an organism.
[< New Latin *zonula* (diminutive) < Latin *zōna;* see ZONE]

zoo (zü), *n.* a place where wild animals are kept and shown; zoological garden. [short for *zoological (garden)*]

zoo-, *combining form.* a living being; animal or animals: *Zoochemistry = animal chemistry. Zoology = the science of animals.* Also, **zo-** before vowels. [< Greek *zôion* animal]

zoochem., zoochemistry.

zo·o·chem·i·cal (zō'ə kem'ə kəl), *adj.* of or having to do with zoochemistry.

zo·o·chem·is·try (zō'ə kem'ə strē), *n.* the chemistry of the components of animal bodies; animal chemistry.

zo·o·dy·nam·ic (zō'ə dī nam'ik), *adj.* of or having to do with zoodynamics.

zo·o·dy·nam·ics (zō'ə dī nam'iks), *n.* the branch of biology that deals with the vital force of animals; animal physiology.

zoo·ful (zü'fu̇l), *n., pl.* **-fuls.** as much or as many as a zoo will hold.

zo·og·a·my (zō og'ə mē), *n.* the coupling, mating, or pairing of animals of opposite sexes for the purpose of reproduction; sexual reproduction of animals.

zo·og·e·ny (zō oj'ə nē), *n.* the origin and development of animals.

zoogeog., zoogeography.

zo·o·ge·og·ra·pher (zō'ə jē og'rə fər), *n.* a person who studies the geographical distribution of animals, or is an expert in zoogeography.

zo·o·ge·o·graph·ic (zō'ə jē'ə graf'ik), *adj.* of or having to do with zoogeography; faunistic; chorological.

zo·o·ge·o·graph·i·cal (zō'ə jē'ə graf'ə kəl), *adj.* zoogeographic.

zo·o·ge·o·graph·i·cal·ly (zō'ə jē'ə graf'ə klē), *adv.* in relation to zoogeography.

zo·o·ge·og·ra·phy (zō'ə jē og'rə fē), *n.* **1.** the study of the geographical distribution of animals. **2.** the study of the causes and effects of such distribution and of the relationships between certain areas and the groups of animals inhabiting them.

zo·o·ge·ol·o·gy (zō'ə jē ol'ə jē), *n.* that branch of geology which deals with fossil animal remains; paleozoology.

zo·o·gloe·a (zō'ə glē'ə), *n.* a jellylike cluster of bacteria swollen by the absorption of water. [< New Latin *zoogloea* < Greek *zôion* animal + *gloiós* gelatinous substance]

zo·og·ra·pher (zō og'rə fər), *n.* a person who describes or depicts animals; a descriptive zoologist.

zo·o·graph·ic (zō'ə graf'ik), *adj.* having to do with zoography.

zo·o·graph·i·cal (zō'ə graf'ə kəl), *adj.* zoographic.

zo·o·graph·i·cal·ly (zō'ə graf'ə klē), *adv.* in relation to zoography.

zo·og·ra·phy (zō og'rə fē), *n.* the branch of zoology dealing with the description of animals and animal habits; descriptive zoology.

zo·oid (zō'oid), *n.* **1.** *Biology.* a free-moving cell or other organism resembling an animal, although it is actually not one, as a spermatozoan or antherozooid. **2.** *Zoology.* **a.** an independent organism produced by another asexually, as by budding or fission. **b.** any individual which comes between the sexually produced organisms in the alternation of generations, as various free-swimming medusae. **c.** each of the distinct individuals which make up a colonial or compound animal organism.
—*adj.* resembling or having the character of an animal.
[< *zo-* + *-oid.* Compare Late Greek *zōioeidês* like an animal.]

zo·oi·dal (zō oi'dəl), *adj.* zooid.

zoo·keep·er (zü'kē'pər), *n.* a person who owns or works in a zoo.

zool., **1.** zoological. **2.** zoology.

zo·ol·a·ter (zō ol'ə tər), *n.* a person who worships animals or practices zoolatry.

zo·ol·a·trous (zō ol'ə trəs), *adj.* **1.** worshiping animals; practicing zoolatry. **2.** of or relating to zoolatry.

zo·ol·a·try (zō ol'ə trē), *n.* the worship of animals. [< *zoo-* + Greek *latreíā* worship]

zo·o·lite (zō'ə līt), *n.* a fossil animal.

zo·o·lith (zō'ə lith), *n.* zoolite.

zo·o·log·ic (zō'ə loj'ik), *adj.* zoological.

zo·o·log·i·cal (zō'ə loj'ə kəl), *adj.* **1.** having to do with animals or animal life. **2.** of, having to do with, or concerned with zoology. —**zo'o·log'i·cal·ly,** *adv.*

zoological garden, zoo.

zo·ol·o·gist (zō ol'ə jist), *n.* a person skilled or trained in zoology: *Zoologists are interested for the most part in the instinctive activities of animals drawn from the lower end of the evolutionary scale, since in them the mechanisms underlying behavior seem particularly accessible* (M.E. Bitterman).

zo·ol·o·gy (zō ol'ə jē), *n., pl.* **-gies. 1.** the science that deals with animals and animal life, including their structure, physiology, classification, etc., comprising one of the two main branches (zoology and botany) of biology. *Abbr.:* zool. **2.** a treatise on zoology. **3.** the animals inhabiting a certain area.
[< New Latin *zoologia* < New Greek *zōiologiā* (originally) science of pharmaceuticals derived from animals < Greek *zôion* animal + *-logia* -logy]

zoom (züm), *v.i.* **1.** to move suddenly upward. **2.** to fly suddenly upward in a nearly vertical ascent at great speed, in or as in an airplane. **3.** to make a continuous, low-pitched humming or buzzing sound. **4.** to travel or move with a humming or buzzing sound. **5.** to move rapidly from one focus to another, as with a zoom lens: *With this lens, the camera operator can focus on a single object only a few feet from the eye of the camera, and also zoom out to focus automatically on a faraway object* (World Book Encyclopedia).
—*v.t.* to cause to move suddenly upward, especially to fly (an airplane) suddenly upward.
—*n.* an act of zooming; sudden upward flight. [imitative]

Zoom·ar lens (zü'mär), *Trademark.* a special zoom lens for television.

zo·o·met·ric (zō'ə met'rik), *adj.* of or having to do with zoometry.

zo·om·e·try (zō om'ə trē), *n.* the measurement of the dimensions and proportions of the bodies of animals.

zoom·ing (zü'ming), *adj.* rapidly rising; soaring: *Such periods were likely to be followed by other periods of zooming prices* (Atlantic).

zoom lens, a type of motion-picture camera lens which can be adjusted from wide-angle shots down to telephoto close-ups.

zo·o·morph (zō'ə môrf), *n.* a representation of an animal, as in primitive art; a zoomorphic image or design. [< *zoo-* + Greek *morphḗ* form, shape]

zo·o·mor·phic (zō'ə môr'fik), *adj.* **1.** representing or using animal forms: *zoomorphic ornament.* **2.** ascribing animal form or attributes to beings or things not animal; representing a deity in the form of an animal. **3.** characterized by or involving such ascription or representation.

zo·o·mor·phism (zō'ə môr'fiz əm), *n.* the attribution of animal form or nature to a deity or superhuman being.

zo·on (zō'on), *n., pl.* **zo·a.** *Zoology.* **1.** a completely developed individual that makes up a colonial or compound animal organism. **2.** an animal which is the total product of an impregnated ovum. [< New Latin *zoon* < Greek *zôion* animal]

zo·on·al (zō'ə nəl), *adj.* **1.** having to do with a zoon. **2.** of the nature of a zoon.

zo·on·o·my (zō on'ə mē), *n.* the science treating of the causes and relations of the phenomena of living animals. [< New Latin *zoonomia* < Greek *zôion* animal + *nómos* law]

zo·o·nose (zō'ə nōs), *n.* zoonosis.

zo·o·no·sis (zō'ə nō'sis), *n., pl.* **-ses** (-sēz). a disease or infection in animals that can be transmitted to man, such as tuberculosis, rabies, parrot fever, etc.

zo·o·not·ic (zō'ə not'ik), *adj.* of or having to do with a zoonosis: *Veterinarians in the United States employed a variety of control methods as well as drugs and vaccines to achieve significant progress in the eradication of a wide range of zoonotic diseases* (D.W. Bruner).

zo·o·par·a·site (zō'ə par'ə sīt), *n.* a parasitic animal.

zo·o·par·a·sit·ic (zō′ə par ə sit′ik), *adj.* of or having to do with zooparasites: *a zooparasitic disease.*

zo·o·pa·thol·o·gy (zō′ə pə thol′ə jē), *n.* the science treating of the diseases of animals; veterinary pathology.

zo·oph·a·gous (zō of′ə gəs), *adj.* feeding on animals; carnivorous. [< *zoo-* + Greek *phageîn* to eat + English *-ous*]

zo·o·phile (zō′ə fīl), *n.* **1.** a zoophilous plant. **2.** the seed of such a plant. **3.** a person who is extremely or excessively fond of animals. [< *zoo-* + *-phile*]

zo·o·phil·ic (zō′ə fil′ik), *adj.* of or having to do with a zoophile: *In England, presumably owing to the prevalence of zoophilic organizations such as the R.S.P.C.A., such practices are illegalised* (Alec Parker).

zo·oph·i·list (zō of′ə list), *n.* a zoophile.

zo·oph·i·lous (zō of′ə ləs), *adj.* **1.** *Botany.* (of plants) adapted for being pollinated by animals. **2.** that is extremely or excessively fond of animals.

zo·o·pho·bi·a (zō′ə fō′bē ə), *n.* a morbid or superstitious fear of animals. [< *zoo-* + *-phobia*]

zo·o·phor·ic (zō′ə fôr′ik, -for′-), *adj.* bearing a figure of a man or an animal, or more than one such figure: *a zoophoric column.*

zo·o·phys·ics (zō′ə fiz′iks), *n.* the study of the physical structure of animals; comparative anatomy as a branch of zoology.

zo·o·phys·i·ol·o·gy (zō′ə fiz′ē ol′ə jē), *n.* animal physiology.

zo·o·phyte (zō′ə fīt), *n.* any of various invertebrate animals, being usually fixed and often having a branched or radiating structure, thus resembling plants or flowers, as crinoids, sea anemones, corals, hydroids, sponges, etc. [< New Latin *zoophyton* < Greek *zōióphyton* a plant with animal qualities < *zôion* animal + *phytón* plant]

zo·o·phyt·ic (zō′ə fit′ik), *adj.* **1.** of the nature of a zoophyte. **2.** of or having to do with zoophytes; phytozoic.

zo·o·phyt·i·cal (zō′ə fit′ə kəl), *adj.* zoophytic.

zo·o·phy·tol·o·gy (zō′ə fī tol′ə jē), *n.* the science that treats of zoophytes.

zo·o·plank·ton (zō′ə plangk′tən), *n.* the part of the plankton of any body of water that is of animal origin: *The phytoplankton serves as food for tiny sea animals known as zooplankton, which in turn are eaten by fish, birds and other sea-going animals* (Science News Letter). [< *zoo-* + *plankton*]

zo·o·plank·ton·ic (zō′ə plangk′ton′ik), *adj.* of or having to do with zooplankton: *zooplanktonic crops.*

zo·o·plas·tic (zō′ə plas′tik), *adj.* of or having to do with zooplasty.

zo·o·plas·ty (zō′ə plas′tē), *n., pl.* **-ties.** plastic surgery in which living tissue is transplanted from a lower animal to the human body.

zo·o·psy·chol·o·gy (zō′ə sī kol′ə jē), *n.* the psychology of animals other than man; animal psychology.

zo·o·sperm (zō′ə spėrm), *n.* **1.** spermatozoon. **2.** zoospore.

zo·o·sper·mat·ic (zō′ə spėr mat′ik), *adj.* spermatozoic.

zo·o·spo·ran·gi·al (zō′ə spə ran′jē əl), *adj.* having to do with a zoosporangium.

zo·o·spo·ran·gi·um (zō′ə spə ran′jē əm), *n., pl.* **-gi·a** (-jē ə). *Botany.* a receptacle or sporangium in which zoospores are produced.

zo·o·spore (zō′ə spôr, -spōr), *n.* **1.** *Botany.* an asexual spore that can move about by means of cilia or flagella, produced by some algae and fungi. **2.** *Zoology.* any of the minute, freely moving, flagellate or amoeboid organisms released by the sporocyst of various protozoans.

zo·o·spor·ic (zō′ə spôr′ik, -spor′-), *adj.* **1.** of the nature of a zoospore. **2.** having to do with zoospores.

zo·o·spo·rif·er·ous (zō′ə spə rif′ər əs), *adj. Botany.* bearing or producing zoospores.

zo·os·po·rous (zō os′pər əs; zō′ə spôr′-, -spōr′-), *adj.* **1.** producing zoospores. **2.** of the nature of zoospores. **3.** effected by zoospores.

zo·o·tech·nic (zō′ə tek′nik), *adj.* of or having to do with zootechny.

zo·o·tech·nics (zō′ə tek′niks), *n.* zootechny.

zo·o·tech·ny (zō′ə tek′nē), *n.* the keeping and breeding of animals in domestication. [< *zoo-* + Greek *téchnē* art, science]

zo·o·the·ism (zō′ə thē iz′əm), *n.* the attribution of deity to an animal; the worship of animals or animal forms.

zo·o·the·ist (zō′ə thē ist), *n.* a person who worships animals or animal forms.

zo·o·the·is·tic (zō′ə thē is′tik), *adj.* of or having to do with zootheism; relating to the worship of animals; zoolatrous.

zo·o·tom·ic (zō′ə tom′ik), *adj.* zootomical.

zo·o·tom·i·cal (zō′ə tom′ə kəl), *adj.* of or having to do with zootomy. —**zo′o·tom′i·cal·ly,** *adv.*

zo·ot·o·mist (zō ot′ə mist), *n.* a person who dissects the bodies of animals; an expert in zootomy; a comparative anatomist.

zo·ot·o·my (zō ot′ə mē), *n.* the anatomy of animals. [< *zoo-* + (ana)*tomy*]

zo·o·trope (zō′ə trōp), *n.* zoetrope.

zoot suit (züt), *Slang.* a man's suit with a long, tight-fitting jacket having exaggerated, padded shoulders, and baggy trousers extending above the waist, tapering down to tight cuffs at the ankles. [American English; origin uncertain]

zoot-suit·ed (züt′sü′tid), *adj. Slang.* wearing a zoot suit or zoot suits.

zoot-suit·er (züt′sü′tər), *n. Slang.* **1.** a man wearing a zoot suit. **2.** a person who tries to dress fashionably, especially in cheap clothes.

Zo·phi·el (zō′fē əl), *n.* (in Christian tradition) one of the archangels.

zop·po (tsop′ō), *adj., adv. Music.* with syncopation. [< Italian *zoppo* (literally) limping]

zo·ri (zō′rē), *n., pl.* **-ri.** flat sandals, usually of rubber or woven straw. [< Japanese *zori*]

zor·il (zôr′əl, zor′-), *n.* a skunklike, carnivorous, South African mammal related to the weasel. [< French *zorille* < Spanish *zorrilla,* feminine, and *zorillo,* masculine (diminutives) < *zorra,* and *zorro* fox]

zo·ril·la (zə ril′ə), *n.* zoril.

Zo·ro·as·tri·an (zôr′ō as′trē ən, zōr′-), *adj.* of or having to do with Zoroaster, a Persian religious teacher who lived about 1000 B.C., or Zoroastrianism, the religion founded by him. —*n.* one of the followers of Zoroastrianism, now represented by the Ghebers and the Parsees. Also, **Zarathustrian.**

Zo·ro·as·tri·an·ism (zôr′ō as′trē ə niz′əm, zōr′-), *n.* the dualistic religious system, expounded in the Avesta, prevalent in Persia until the Moslem conquest in the 600's, teaching of the lasting struggle between good and evil as typified in the personified powers called Ahura Mazda (Ormuzd), the creator of good and the ultimate victor, and Ahriman, the creator of evil. The symbolizing of good as light has led to the incorrect identification of Zoroastrians as fire worshipers.

Zo·ro·as·trism (zôr′ō as′triz əm, zōr′-), *n.* Zoroastrianism.

zos·ter (zos′tər), *n.* **1.** shingles (herpes zoster). **2.** a belt or girdle worn in ancient Greece, especially by men. [< Latin *zoster* shingles, a girdle < Greek *zōstḗr* girdle < *zōnnýnai* to gird. Compare ZONE.]

Zou·ave (zü äv′, zwäv), *n.* formerly: **1.** a member of any of certain light infantry regiments in the French army, especially in North Africa, noted for their bravery and dash and distinguished by brilliant Oriental uniforms and a peculiar type of drill. The Zouaves were originally recruited from the Kabyle and other Algerian tribes, later were chiefly French. **2.** a soldier of any unit patterned on these in style of uniform, especially a member of certain volunteer regiments in the Union Army during the Civil War. [< French *Zouave* < *Zouaoua* the tribe < Kabyle *Zwawa*]

Zouave jacket, a short jacket ending at or above the waist and open in front.

zounds (zoundz), *interj. Archaic.* a mild oath, or an exclamation of surprise, anger, etc. [reduction of obsolete *God's wounds,* an oath]

zow·ie (zou′ē), *interj.* an exclamation of wonder, surprise, delight, etc.: *He snapped a cheroot in two. "Zowie!" he said* (Punch).

zox·a·zo·la·mine (zok′sə zō′lə mēn), *n.* a drug used to relax the muscles, in treating certain forms of palsy, arthritis, and gout. *Formula:* $C_7H_5ClN_2O$

zo·ys·i·a (zō is′ē ə), *n.* a type of hardy lawn grass, for use in warm, dry climates: *Zoysias . . . have tolerance to the hottest weather* (New York Times). [< New Latin *Zoysia* the genus name]

Zr (no period), zirconium (chemical element).

zu·brow·ka (zü′brev kə), *n.* a yellow-colored vodka flavored with a sweet grass or herb: *Zubrowka is . . . greatly admired in Poland, Czechoslovakia, and the Soviet Union* (New York Times). [< Polish *żubrowka*]

zuc·chet·to (zü ket′ō; *Italian* tsük ket′tō), *n., pl.* **-tos** (*Italian* **-ti** -tē). the small, round skullcap worn by Roman Catholic ecclesiastics. A priest wears black, a bishop violet, a cardinal red, and the Pope white. [alteration of Italian *zucchetta* cap; small gourd (diminutive) < *zucca* gourd; head]

zuc·chi·ni (zü kē′nē), *n., pl.* **-ni** or **-nis. 1.** any of several varieties of a summer squash, the fruit of which has smooth, dark-green skin, sometimes striped or flecked with light green, turning yellow when mature, and tender white flesh, more or less cylindrical in shape and produced on a bushy, large-leaved plant. **2.** the fruit itself, used as a vegetable. [American English < Italian *zucchino* (diminutive) < *zucca* squash, gourd]

Zug·zwang (tsük′tsfäng′), *n. Chess.* a situation in which a player is compelled to move against his will: *Black is in virtual Zugzwang . . . owing to the immobility of his knight and king* (New York Times). [< German *Zugzwang* < *Zug* a drawing, pulling + *Zwang* force, compulsion]

Zu·lu[1] (zü′lü), *n., pl.* **-lus** or **-lu,** *adj.* —*n.* **1.** a member of a large, warlike South African people of the Bantu linguistic family, chiefly in Natal, resembling the Kaffirs. **2.** the language of this people. —*adj.* of or having to do with this people or language.

Zu·lu[2] (zü′lü), *n. U.S.* a code name for the letter *z,* used in transmitting radio messages.

Zum·pan·go (zum pang′gō), *n.* Cipango.

Zu·ñi (zün′yē, zü′nē), *n., pl.* **-ñis** or **-ñi,** *adj.* —*n.* **1.** a member of a tribe of Pueblo Indians living in western New Mexico. **2.** their language, which constitutes an independent linguistic family. —*adj.* of or having to do with this tribe or language.

Zu·ñi·an (zün′yē ən, zü′nē-), *adj., n.* Zuñi.

zurf (zėrf), *n.* zarf.

zwie·back (tswē′bäk′, swē′-, zwē′-), *n.* a kind of bread or rusk which, after baking, is cut into slices and toasted brown and crisp in an oven. [American English < German *Zwieback* biscuit, rusk < *zwie-* twice + *backen* to bake, loan translation of Italian *biscotto.* Compare BISCUIT.]

Zwing·li·an (zwing′glē ən, tsving′lē-), *adj.* of or having to do with Ulrich Zwingli, 1484-1531, a Swiss Protestant reformer, or his doctrines. —*n.* a follower of Ulrich Zwingli.

Zwing·li·an·ism (zwing′glē ə niz′əm, tsving′lē-), *n.* the doctrinal system of Ulrich Zwingli, Lutheran in essence but differing principally in denying the real presence of Christ in the Eucharist, which he maintained was a commemoration of the sacrifice of Christ rather than a renewal of it.

Zwing·li·an·ist (zwing′glē ə nist, tsving′lē-), *n., adj.* Zwinglian.

zwit·ter·i·on (tsvit′ər ī′ən, swit′-), *n. Physics.* an ion which has both a positive and a negative charge, on opposite sides, as in certain protein molecules. [< German *Zwitterion* < *Zwitter* hybrid (< *zwie-* two, double) + *Ion* ion]

zwit·ter·i·on·ic (tsvit′ər ī on′ik, swit′-), *adj.* of or having to do with a zwitterion.

zyg-, *combining form.* the form of **zygo-** before vowels, as in *zygapophysis.*

zyg·ap·o·phys·e·al or **zyg·ap·o·phys·i·al** (zig′ap ə fiz′ē əl), *adj.* of or having to do with a zygapophysis; articular, as a vertebral process.

zyg·a·poph·y·sis (zig′ə pof′ə sis, zī′gə-), *n., pl.* **-ses** (-sēz). *Anatomy.* one of the lateral processes upon the neural arch of a vertebra which interlock each vertebra with the one above and below. Each vertebra normally has four, two anterior and two posterior. [< *zyg-* + *apophysis*]

zygo-, *combining form.* **1.** yoke; yoked or paired. *Zygodactyl = having the toes in pairs.* **2.** reproduction by zygosis, as in *zygospore.* Also, **zyg-** before vowels. [< Greek *zygón* yoke]

zy·go·dac·tyl (zī′gə dak′təl, zig′ə-), *adj.* having the toes arranged in pairs, with two before and two behind, as the feet of a climbing bird, or the bird itself. —*n.* a zygodactyl bird, as a parrot. [< New Latin *Zygodactyles* the order name < Greek *zygón* yoke + *dáktylos* finger, toe]

zy·go·ma (zī gō′mə, zi-), *n., pl.* **-ma·ta** (-mə tə). *Anatomy.* **1.** the bony arch below the socket of the eye in vertebrates, formed by the zygomatic bone (cheekbone) and the zygomatic process of the temporal bone; zygomatic arch. **2.** the zygomatic process. **3.** the zygomatic bone. [< New Latin *zygoma* < Greek *zýgōma, -atos* < *zygón* yoke]

zy·go·mat·ic (zī′gə mat′ik, zig′ə-), *adj.* **1.** of or having to do with the zygoma. **2.** constituting the zygoma. —*n.* the zygomatic bone.

zygomatic arch, *Anatomy.* zygoma.

zygomatic bone, *Anatomy.* the three-sided bone forming the lower boundary of the socket of the eye; cheekbone; malar bone; jugal bone; zygoma.

zygomatic process, *Anatomy.* a process of the temporal bone which articulates with the zygomatic bone to form the zygoma.

zy·go·mor·phic (zī′gə môr′fik, zig′ə-), *adj. Botany.* (of a flower) divisible vertically into similar halves in only one way, as the sweet pea. [< *zygo-* + Greek *morphḗ* form + English *-ic*]

zy·go·mor·phism (zī′gə môr′fiz əm, zig′ə-), *n.* the character of being zygomorphic.

zy·go·mor·phous (zī′gə môr′fəs, zig′ə-), *adj.* zygomorphic.

zy·go·phyl·la·ceous (zī′gə fə lā′shəs, zig′ə-), *adj.* belonging to a family of dicotyledonous herbs, shrubs, and trees typified by the bean caper, and including the creosote bush and lignum vitae. [< New Latin *Zygophyllaceae* the family name (< *Zygophyllum* the typical genus < Greek *zygón* yoke + *phýllon* leaf) + English *-ous*]

zy·go·phyte (zī′gə fīt, zig′ə-), *n. Botany.* a plant in which reproduction consists of the fusion of two similar gametes (zygospores). [< *zygo-* + *-phyte*]

zy·go·sis (zī gō′sis, zi-), *n. Biology.* conjugation. [< New Latin *zygosis* < Greek *zýgōsis* a balancing < *zygoûn* to yoke < *zygón* a yoke]

zy·go·spore (zī′gə spôr, -spōr; zig′ə-), *n. Botany.* a spore arising from the fusion of two similar reproductive cells (gametes), as in various algae and fungi. [< German *Zygospor* < Greek *zygón* a yoke + German *Spor* spore]

zy·gote (zī′gōt, zig′ōt), *n. Biology.* **1.** any cell formed by the fusion of two reproductive cells (gametes): *A fertilized egg is a zygote.* See **conjugation** for picture. **2.** the individual which develops from this cell. [< Greek *zygōtós* yoked < *zygoûn* to yoke < *zygón* a yoke]

zy·got·ic (zī got′ik, zi-), *adj.* **1.** of a zygote or zygosis. **2.** of the nature of a zygote or zygosis.

zym-, *combining form.* the form of **zymo-** before vowels, as in *zymoid.*

zy·mase (zī′mās), *n.* an enzyme complex in yeast which, in the absence of oxygen, changes sugar into alcohol and carbon dioxide or into lactic acid, or, in the presence of oxygen, changes sugar into carbon dioxide and water. [< French *zymase* < Greek *zýmē* leaven + French *-ase* -ase]

zyme (zīm), *n.* **1.** the substance or principle causing a zymotic disease. **2.** a substance causing fermentation; ferment. [< Greek *zýmē* leaven]

zy·min (zī′min), *n.* **1.** a ferment; zyme. **2.** a pancreatic extract, used to aid digestion. [< *zym-* + *-in*]

zymo-, *combining form.* fermentation: *Zymometer = an instrument that measures fermentation.* Also, **zym-** before vowels. [< Greek *zýmē* leaven]

zy·mo·gen (zī′mə jən), *n.* **1.** *Biochemistry.* a substance formed in an organism, from which, by some internal change, an enzyme is produced. **2.** *Biology.* any of several enzyme-producing bacterial organisms. [< German *Zymogen* < *zymo-* zymo- + *-gen* -gen]

zy·mo·gene (zī′mə jēn), *n.* zymogen.

zy·mo·gen·e·sis (zī′mə jen′ə sis), *n. Biochemistry.* the conversion of a zymogen into an enzyme. [< *zymo-* + *genesis*]

zy·mo·gen·ic (zī′mə jen′ik), *adj.* **1.** of or relating to a zymogen. **2.** causing fermentation. [< *zymo-* + *-gen* + *-ic*]

zymogenic organism, any microorganism, as yeast, causing fermentative processes.

zy·moid (zī′moid), *adj.* resembling a zyme or ferment. [< *zym-* + *-oid*]

zy·mo·log·ic (zī′mə loj′ik), *adj.* of or having to do with zymology.

zy·mo·log·i·cal (zī′mə loj′ə kəl), *adj.* zymologic.

zy·mol·o·gist (zī mol′ə jist), *n.* an expert in zymology.

zy·mol·o·gy (zī mol′ə jē), *n.* the study of fermentation and of ferments and their action. [< *zymo-* + *-logy*]

zy·mol·y·sis (zī mol′ə sis), *n.* **1.** the action of enzymes, as in digestion and fermentation. **2.** fermentation or other changes produced by the action of enzymes. [< *zymo-* + Greek *lýsis* a loosening]

zy·mo·lyt·ic (zī′mə lit′ik), *adj.* zymotic.

zy·mom·e·ter (zī mom′ə tər), *n.* an instrument for measuring the degree of fermentation of a fermenting liquid. [< *zymo-* + *-meter*]

zy·mo·san (zī′mə san), *n.* a drug, derived from the cell walls of yeast, used to raise the level of properdin in the blood, to guard against or promote immunity to infection, disease, etc.

zy·mo·sis (zī mō′sis), *n.* **1.** an infectious disease caused by a fungus. **2.** an abnormal process considered analogous to fermentation, by which a zymotic disease was formerly supposed to be produced. **3.** fermentation. [< New Latin *zymosis* < Greek *zýmōsis* fermentation < *zȳmoûn* to leaven; ferment < *zýmē* leaven]

zy·mot·ic (zī mot′ik), *adj.* **1.** of or having to do with fermentation. **2.** causing fermentation. **3.** caused by fermentation. **4.** denoting or having to do with any infectious disease due to a fungus, originally regarded as being caused by a process analogous to fermentation.

—*n.* a zymotic disease.

[< Greek *zȳmōtikós* causing fermentation < *zȳmoûn;* see ZYMOSIS] —**zy·mot′i·cal·ly,** *adv.*

zymotic disease, any of various infectious and contagious diseases, as smallpox, typhoid fever, etc., which were formerly regarded as due to the presence in the system of a morbific principle acting in a manner analogous to the process of fermentation.

zy·mur·gy (zī′mėr jē), *n.* the branch of chemistry dealing with the processes of fermentation, as in brewing, the making of wine or yeast, etc. [< Greek *zýmē* leaven + *-ourgos* making < *érgon* work. Compare Greek *zȳmourgós* a maker of leaven.]

Zyr·i·an (zir′ē ən), *n.* **1.** a member of a Finno-Ugric people living in northeastern Russia. **2.** the Finno-Ugric language or dialect of this people. Also, **Syrian.**

Complete Pronunciation Key

The pronunciation of each word is shown just following the word, in this way: **ab·bre·vi·ate** (ə brē′ vē āt). The symbols within parentheses are pronounced as in the words in the key below.

Diacritical marks appear above some of the vowel symbols listed below. Here are their names, and the vowels with which they appear:

circumflex (sėr′kəm fleks)—the mark over the ô, as in order.

dieresis (dī er′ ə sis)—two dots over the ä, as in father, or the ü, as in rule.

macron (mā′kron)—the long mark over the ā, as in age; the ē, as in equal; the ī, as in ice; and the ō, as in open.

single dot—over the ė in the ėr, as in term, and over the u̇, as in full.

tilde (til′də)—the curved mark over the ã, as in care.

These diacritics have arbitrary values and do not necessarily correspond to their values elsewhere.

The stress mark ′ is placed after a syllable with primary or strong accent, as in the pronunciation of *abbreviate*, the example above. The stress mark ′ after a syllable shows a secondary or lighter accent, as in **ab·bre·vi·a·tion** (ə brē′vē a′shən).

Some words, taken from foreign languages, are spoken with sounds that otherwise do not occur in English. Symbols for these sounds are given at the end of the table below as "Foreign Sounds."

a	hat, cap	j	jam, enjoy	u	cup, butter
ā	age, face	k	kind, seek	u̇	full, put
ã	care, air	l	land, coal	ü	rule, move
ä	father, far	m	me, am		
		n	no, in	v	very, save
b	bad, rob	ng	long, bring	w	will, woman
ch	child, much			y	young, yet
d	did, red	o	hot, rock	z	zero, breeze
		ō	open, go	zh	measure, seizure
e	let, best	ô	order, all		
ē	equal, see	oi	oil, voice	ə	represents:
ėr	term, learn	ou	house, out		a in about
					e in taken
f	fat, if	p	paper, cup		i in pencil
g	go, bag	r	run, try		o in lemon
h	he, how	s	say, yes		u in circus
		sh	she, rush		
		t	tell, it		
i	it, pin	th	thin, both		
ī	ice, five	ŦH	then, smooth		

Foreign Sounds

Y	as in French *du*. Pronounce ē with the lips rounded as for English ü in *rule*.
œ	as in French *peu*. Pronounce ā with the lips rounded as for ō.
N	as in French *bon*. The N is not pronounced, but shows that the vowel before it is nasal.
H	as in German *ach*. Pronounce k without closing the breath passage.
à	as in French *ami*. The quality of this vowel is midway between the a of *hat* and the ä of *far*, but closer to the former.

Etymology Key

The origin of a word is its etymology. This dictionary includes etymologies under main entries. The etymologies are placed at the end of the definition of the entry. Etymologies are enclosed in square brackets.

ba·zoo·ka . . . [American English <name of a trombome-like instrument invented and named by comedian Bob Burns]

Two symbols are used in describing etymologies: < means "derived from; taken from."

ca·jole . . . [< French *cajoler*] . . . .

+ means "and."

clyp·e·i·form . . . [< Latin *clypeus* round shield + English *–form*]